JOEL WHITBURN'S
TOP POP
ALBUMS

1955-1992

COMPILED EXCLUSIVELY FROM **Billboard**®

Compiled from *Billboard's* pop album charts, 1955-1992

Record Research Inc.
P.O. Box 200
Menomonee Falls, Wisconsin 53052-0200
U.S.A.

ISBN 0-89820-093-8

Record Research Inc.
P.O. Box 200
Menomonee Falls, Wisconsin 53052-0200
U.S.A.

Dedicated to
the resplendent 12" vinyl albums.
Never has the long-play record
had a more vivid display.

****

The author extends a special note of thanks to:

Joyce Riehl — my sister and a devoted researcher. Joyce spent five years of her life entering album cut after album cut after album cut. Nearing the end of her project, her research was cut short by a near-fatal aneurysm. My satisfaction in the completion of the album project is minute in comparison to my joy at the steady recovery of my middle sister.

Ruth Whitburn — my mother and a meticulous scholar. She did the original research on the first edition of the **Top Pop Albums** back in 1971. For this third edition, she documented, week by week, every position from every chart for all of the albums within this book. This was not an easy task considering the multiple charts of the early years. Mom handled this monumental task with ease and without complaint.

Jerry Osborne and Rocky Kruegel — these record pricing experts assisted in putting together Record Research's first-ever album price guide.

The staff of Record Research — the following employees explored the full meaning of "proofing" and turned this book inside-out, upside-down and thoroughly dissected and reconstructed every album in this book: Bill Hathaway, Kim Whitburn, Kim Gaarder, Troy Kluess, Jeanne Olynick, Paul Haney, Joyce Riehl and Ruth Whitburn. Brent Olynick, Joanne Wagner, Brian Niese, Nestor Vidotto, Fran Whitburn and Oscar Vidotto did not let this mammoth group effort get in the way of the daily business activities of Record Research and made sure that this research arrived at your doorstep.

Finally, I am ever grateful to *Billboard* magazine for the nearly 2,000 pop album charts which they published accurately and faithfully week by week, providing years of informative entertainment.

CONTENTS

A chronological listing, by peak date, of every pop album chart-topper.

AUTHOR'S NOTE

Combine 40 years of record collecting, five solid years of data entry mixed, with continual proofing and editing, and an industrious staff, and you have Record Research's most ambitious project yet — **Top Pop Albums 1955-1992**.

I had the idea for a book containing every album track about a dozen years ago. I was preparing the second edition of the **Top Pop Albums** and thought it would be fantastic to give a thorough account of each album by listing all of the cuts. Although the albums were there, the time and the manpower required to tackle this exhaustive task were not available.

Time brought growth in staff and computer capacity, and my idea became five full years of painstaking research — more time and effort than ever invested in any other Record Research book project. And now, our unabridged investigation is printed within these pages.

The most remarkable feature of this book is, in fact, the listing of each music track of every charted album. This is the first book that lists on which charted album(s) a particular song appeared, regardless if that album has long been unavailable. The complete track listings of major pop artists such as Bob Dylan, Eric Clapton, Elton John, Elvis Presley, Billy Joel, Barbra Streisand, The Beach Boys, etc. document nearly all of their recorded output.

The track listings illuminate each charted artist's musical legacy. Here are the many celebrated cuts which never hit a *Billboard* singles chart (most were never released as singles) — the rock classics of Led Zeppelin, Pink Floyd, Rush, Black Sabbath, Deep Purple, Frank Zappa and other consummate album heroes — the individual cuts that make up the concept albums of Emerson, Lake & Palmer, Yes, Jethro Tull, Traffic and King Crimson — the many offerings of the prolific MOR favorites Mantovani and Ray Conniff — the songs written for or featured on soundtrack and original cast albums — and so much more.

The blockbuster addition of the track listings overshadows several other advancements within **Top Pop Albums**. New and greatly expanded artist biographies provide a brief yet detailed background on all but a smattering of artists. This book also acts as a complete album price guide with pricing assistance provided by top record price expert Jerry Osborne. Visual aides include photos of the Top 100 artists of our new Top 500 album artists ranking; and, a special photo section displays the all-time Top 100 albums.

Read on and you will find that the third edition of **Top Pop Albums** is more than a revision. It is a whole new dimension in record reference books. I'm sure you will find, as we have at our office, this is an indispensable tool in album research.

JOEL WHITBURN

WHAT'S NEW IN THIS EDITION?

This third edition of the **Top Pop Albums** is a revision in the fullest sense of the word. Not only is this a compendium of our research of the *Billboard* pop album charts, it offers a wealth of information beyond that. Here's a glimpse at the new offerings. (More detailed explanations of the Tracks Index, the Complete Price Guide, and the Album and Artist Rankings appear on the following pages.)

NEW ALPHABETIZATION SYSTEM

We found it was necessary to reorganize our alphabetization system as it became increasingly difficult to place initialized, hyphenated, abbreviated names, like D-Mob and L.L. Cool J, within our previous order.

Our new streamlined, easier-to-use alphabetization system is similar to those used within dictionaries. All names of groups and last names of individual artists are shown in bold, uppercase letters. And, for quick identification, the last names of solo artists are shown first.

Look at all uppercase letters collectively, ignoring spacing and punctuation (ex.: SHANA precedes SHA NA NA). If a group's name is exactly the same as a solo artist's last name, then the group's name is shown first (ex: RUSH precedes RUSH, Jennifer). If the first word of a group's name is the same as the last name of the solo artist, then the group will follow the solo artist (ex.: PRATT, Andy precedes PRATT & McCLAIN). If a group's name begins with "The," and the following part of the group's name is the same as another artist's last name, then the latter will be listed first (ex.: WINANS, BeBe & CeCe precedes WINANS, The).

TRACKS INDEX

All music tracks from all of an artist's charted albums are listed in alphabetical order in one comprehensive index for each artist. Now, you can quickly find on which charted album(s) a track appeared. Or, discover all the tracks listed on an album. See page 12 for Tracks Index. This will prove to be an indispensable tool for finding out on which album you can find an artist's particular song.

NEW AND IMPROVED BIOGRAPHIES

The second edition of the Top Pop Albums book contained abbreviated artist biographies. This edition hosts a ton of biographical research with hundreds of new, comprehensive artist biographies, along with thousands of previous artists' biographies newly updated and vastly expanded.

COMPLETE PRICE GUIDE

Listed for every album in this book is the average dealer asking price for a near-mint copy of the album. Assistance in assigning each of these prices was largely provided by Jerry Osborne, a top record pricing expert, and Rocky Kruegel, a leading record dealer.

TOP 500 ALBUM ARTISTS RANKING

An artist's overall ranking in the Top 500 Artists of the pop album charts from 1955 through 1992 is designated by the number listed to the left of the artist name. A look at The Ventures' entry immediately tells you that they rank 24th out of the Top 500 pop album artists of the rock era.

SPOTLIGHT ON HIGHEST-CHARTED ALBUMS

A glance is all it takes to find the highest-charting album of an artist with 10 or more charted albums. Their highest-charted album is boxed out in a thin frame.

MULTI-PLATINUM STATUS

The superscript number to the right of the triangle platinum symbol indicates how many million-selling certifications the album received according to the Recording Industry of America Association (RIAA).

SPECIAL CHRISTMAS CHARTS

If a pop-charted album concurrently charted on *Billboard's* Special Christmas charts, the album's title trivia lists the peak position(s) followed by the year(s) it made the special Christmas charts.

TOP 100 ARTISTS PHOTOS

Features 1-3/4" square, black-and-white photos of the Top 100 artists that lead the Top 500 Artists Ranking.

TOP 100 ALBUMS PHOTOS

Features 1-5/8" square, black-and-white photos of the original covers of the all-time Top 100 albums, ranked by overall chart performance.

RESEARCHING THE *BILLBOARD* POP ALBUM CHARTS

Please keep the following items in mind for a full understanding of this research.

Billboard began publishing a Top 5 pop albums chart in 1945.* Since then, the chart evolved with various names, growing in size. Today, *Billboard's* pop albums chart numbers 200 positions and is known as *The Billboard 200*.

The pop album chart research of this book begins with *Billboard* magazine's first pop album chart of 1955 (January 8), since 1955 is widely recognized as the debut year of the rock era. Every album that hit the pop album charts from 1955 through the last chart of 1992 (December 26) appears in this book. The research cutoff date for albums that were on the last chart of 1992 is February 6, 1993; weeks charted and peak positions are current through that chart.

To make this book a complete digest of all of *Billboard's* popular album charts of the rock era, we also consulted two pop album charts not outlined in the Synopsis Of The *Billboard* Pop Album Charts (page 11). The *Most Played by Jockeys* chart, published from July 14, 1956 to December 8, 1958, was a top 15 chart. The *Pop Albums Coming Up Strong* chart, published from July 14, 1956 through August 26, 1957, served the purpose of a "Bubbling Under The Top Lps" chart.

We checked the *Most Played by Jockeys* and *Pop Albums Coming Up Strong* charts only for albums which made these charts but did not make the *Billboard* pop album charts. To the 47 albums that only charted on the *Most Played by Jockeys* chart, we added 10 points (or positions) to their peak position. To the 39 albums that only charted on the *Coming Up Strong* charts, we added 15 points (or positions) to their peak position.

From 1959 to 1961, *Billboard* ran concurrent Mono and Stereo charts. For the characteristics and method of researching those charts, see the Synopsis Of The Billboard Album Charts.

From 1976 through 1991, *Billboard* did not publish an issue on the final week of the year. The last published chart of the year was considered "frozen" and all chart positions of that final issue remained the same for the unpublished week. This frozen chart data is included in our tabulations. In 1992, *Billboard* tabulated and made available through *Billboard's* computerized information network, BIN, a December 26, 1992 chart that did not appear in their magazine. The weeks and positions of this chart were not frozen. The research of the December 26, 1992 chart is included in this book.

Billboard's compilation of the pop album chart has always been based on album sales. For over 30 years, *Billboard* tallied the pop album charts from rankings of best-selling records as reported by a representative sampling of stores nationwide. On May 25, 1991, *Billboard* ushered in a new era in sales charts compilation. *Billboard* now bases the pop album chart on actual units sold data as collected by point-of-sale scanning machines which read the album's UPC bar code. The music research firm SoundScan Inc. provides *Billboard* with the actual sales of all albums from a continually revised representative sampling of stores. It is likely that the pop album chart of the last few years, *The Billboard 200*, is the most accurate ever.

*Our chart research of the pop albums that charted from 1945 through 1954 will appear in a future Record Research publication.

SYNOPSIS OF THE *BILLBOARD* POP ALBUM CHARTS
1955-1992

DATE	POSITIONS	CHART TITLE
1/8/55	15	**BEST SELLING POPULAR ALBUMS** (a biweekly chart with the exception of a seven-week gap and several three-week gaps)
3/24/56	10-15-20-30	**BEST SELLING POPULAR ALBUMS** (published weekly with size varying from a top 10 to a top 30)
6/2/56	15	**BEST SELLING POP ALBUMS**
9/2/57	25	**BEST SELLING POP LPs**
5/25/59	50	**BEST SELLING MONOPHONIC LPs**
5/25/59	30	**BEST SELLING STEREOPHONIC LPs** (separate Stereo and Mono charts published through 8/10/63)
1/4/60	40	**MONO ACTION CHARTS** (mono albums charted 39 weeks or less)
1/4/60	30	**STEREO ACTION CHARTS** (stereo albums charted 19 weeks or less; changed to 29 weeks or less on 5/30/60)
1/4/60	25	**ESSENTIAL INVENTORY -- MONO** (mono albums charted 40 weeks or more)
1/4/60	20	**ESSENTIAL INVENTORY -- STEREO** (stereo albums charted 20 weeks or more; changed to 30 weeks or more on 5/30/60)
1/9/61	25	**ACTION ALBUMS -- MONOPHONIC** (mono albums charted nine weeks or less)
1/9/61	15	**ACTION ALBUMS -- STEREOPHONIC** (stereo albums charted nine weeks or less)
1/9/61	—	Approximately 200 albums listed by category (no positions) and shown as essential inventory
4/3/61	150	**TOP LPs -- MONAURAL**
4/3/61	50	**TOP LPs -- STEREO**
8/17/63	150	**TOP LPs** (one chart)
4/1/67	175	**TOP LPs**
5/13/67	200	**TOP LPs**
11/25/67	200	**TOP LPs** (three pages)
2/15/69	200	**TOP LPs** (two pages with A-Z artist listing)
2/19/72	200	**TOP LPs & TAPES**
10/20/84	200	**TOP 200 ALBUMS**
1/5/85	200	**TOP POP ALBUMS**
9/7/91	200	**THE BILLBOARD 200 TOP ALBUMS**
3/14/92	200	**THE BILLBOARD 200**

An album appearing on both the Mono and Stereo charts in the same week is tabulated as one weekly appearance. The album's highest position is determined by the chart (Mono or Stereo) on which the album reached its highest position.

The Essential Inventory charts list albums which have already been charted for months on the Mono and Stereo charts; therefore, we researched the Essential Inventory charts for weeks charted only and did not count peak positions reached on this chart.

TRACKS INDEX

FORMAT

Below each artist's chronological listing of charted albums is an alphabetical title index of all of the tracks on those albums.

A slightly different format appears for Soundtracks and Various Artists. See those sections for an explanation.

The number(s) in parentheses listed to the immediate right of the track title refers to the sequential album count of the album on which the track appears.

If the artist had only one charted album, no numbers are listed next to the tracks.

HOT 100 HITS

All tracks that charted on *Billboard's Hot 100* chart (and *Billboard's* multiple pre-*Hot 100* pop singles charts from 1955-58) are highlighted in bold type with their peak position listed to the right in bold, italics type. If a song hit the charts as a B-side and never achieved its own highest position, then "flip" is listed to the right in bold, italics type. An arrow (↑) is shown next to the *Hot 100* position of tracks which were still going up the *Hot 100* as of the 2/6/93 cutoff date.

If the spelling on the *Hot 100* single differs from the spelling listed on the album, we show the title's spelling as it appears on the single (and thus, as it appears in our **Top Pop Singles** book).

If the same version of a song hit the pop singles charts more than once, only the highest position is shown.

If the *Hot 100* version of a song did not appear on any of the artist's charted albums but a different (live, studio or remix) version did, that title is not highlighted and the *Hot 100* position is not shown. (Also see the rules for DIFFERENT VERSIONS below.)

VINYL ALBUMS VS. COMPACT DISCS

Tracks were taken from the vinyl releases of albums that charted prior to 1990.

For albums that charted from 1990 through 1992, the listed tracks refer to the album's release on compact disc.

Whenever possible, title trivia notes indicate if bonus tracks were available on compact disc and/or cassette. The CD bonus tracks of albums that charted since 1990 appear in the index; they do not appear in the index for albums that charted prior to 1990.

Non-music tracks are listed if they are separately titled on the album (as are some monologues on comedy albums or speeches on spoken word albums) and are, in most cases, longer than one minute.

WHICH TRACKS ARE NOT LISTED

Generally, album content not listed are short segments (usually less-than-a-minute long comprised of talking, sound effects, etc.) and untitled tracks not listed on either the album's label or jacket cover.

Not shown within the Artist Section are short segments which are titled or feature within their titles: "Intro," "Introduction," "Introductions," "Opening," "Prelude," "Narration," "Reprise," "Overture," "Epilogue," "Finale" or "Ending"; however, these do appear within the Original Cast and Soundtrack Sections.

DIFFERENT VERSIONS

In most cases, different versions of a song (live, studio, acoustic, a capella or instrumental, etc.) are grouped together under one title. The album symbols listed across from the album titles, such as [L] for a live album, and notes in the album title trivia are good indications as to which version appears on a particular album.

The exception to this rule is if more than one version of a song hit the *Hot 100* chart, then the versions are separated and specified (live, instrumental, remix, etc.) and their peak positions are listed. For example, the two *Hot 100* versions of "Lola" by The Kinks are shown as: **Lola** (11,13,14,25) *9*

Lola [live] (24, 29) *81*

SPELLING

If a track's spelling on the album label and album jacket conflict, the spelling on the label is usually shown unless the label spelling is proven incorrect.

ALPHABETIZATION

If either of the articles "A," "An," or "The" is the first word of a title, it is not shown. However, if the title is made up of only one other word, then it is shown. (Example: "Wanderer, The").

Tracks that begin with "Theme From," "Love Theme From," etc. are alphabetized under the subsequent part of the title. (Example: "Romeo & Juliet, Love Theme From").

PARTS

"Part" is not shown within the tracks index if there is only one "Part" of a song that appeared on any of an artist's charted albums.

If more than one "Part" of a song appeared on an album, then the "Parts" are grouped together as one title with an indication of how many "Parts" there are.

If more than one "Part" of a song appeared on other albums, then those "Parts" are treated as separate titles.

"Part" is also shown if it is within the proper title of a *Hot 100* hit.

In most cases, if only one "Part" of a song with several "Parts" made the *Hot 100* chart and all of the "Parts" appear on only one album, then they are grouped together, the title is highlighted and the peak position of the pop hit is shown with this grouping.

MEDLEYS

If a medley has a name (example: Bomber Medley) and the songs within the medley do not appear as separate tracks on any of the artist's albums, then the name of the medley appears as the track title. If a medley does not have a specific name and the songs are simply separated by slashes, then each of the songs are listed individually within the tracks index and "(medley)" appears after each title.

If a song within a medley also appears as an individual track on an album(s), then that title is not shown with a medley designation. For example, Paul McCartney's *Jet* appears as an individual track on four albums and as part of a medley on a live album, so it is listed as follows: **Jet** (5,8,10,18,20) *7*

The songs of a medley are not separated within the tracks title index if the medley is a *Hot 100* hit, such as the 5th Dimension's "Aquarius/Let The Sunshine In," in which the two songs are listed as one title.

DUOS

For duo or trio albums in which each of the participating artists contributed solo tracks to the album, the solo tracks will appear in the performing artist's tracks index. For example, Harry Belafonte and Miriam Makeba's album, *An Evening With Belafonte/ Makeba*, is listed under both artists; however, their solo tracks are only listed under the artist who sang them.

In rare instances, tracks are performed on an album by a person or group that does not have a charted solo album. Those cuts are listed under the album title and do not appear in the tracks index. For example, on the album *The Beatles with Tony Sheridan and Their Guests*, a group named The Titans perform six solo songs; those titles are noted under the album title and are not shown in the Beatles' track index.

THE RECORD PRICING

This is the first edition of the **Top Pop Albums** book to feature prices. The dollar amounts listed in the price column are estimates of the dealer-asking prices for near-mint commercial copies. Please keep in mind that this book is not intended to be an all-purpose album price guide but a novice's tool to album pricing. To fully explore all possible values of an album, consult several of the fine record price guides available at your local bookstore.

The compilation of the prices involved Jerry Osborne, Joel Whitburn and Rocky Kruegel. Jerry Osborne, a record pricing authority and the author of the extensive **Rockin' Records** series, submitted his prices for each of the albums. Joel Whitburn and the ever-traveling record dealer Rocky Kruegel then reviewed each of these prices and offered their estimates. The printed prices are the averages of all three appraisals. Their estimations were based on averages from sources around the country and the album's chart action. Albums that charted very low on the chart are generally worth more than a million-selling hit album. Chances are few were pressed; and, with the passage of time, these low-charting albums become quite scarce.

These prices apply only to near-mint vinyl albums or compact discs. A near-mint album is almost perfect. It is of extremely high grade and contains only a few tiny blemishes. Only careful scrutiny will reveal the minimal flaws of a near-mint album.

For albums that charted from 1955 through 1989, the album pricing corresponds to the vinyl album configuration. From 1990 on, the pricing refers to the compact disc configuration. And, as is true with current releases, the price of a compact disc album is several dollars higher than the price of a vinyl album or a cassette album. For this reason, you will notice that the average price of a more recent single album is $8 and the average price of a recent single compact disc is $12. (Note: "not released on vinyl" appears in title trivia only for albums charted prior to 1990)

From approximately 1958 through 1968, most albums were issued concurrently in both mono and stereo. When format is not specified by the manuafacturer's prefix and/or number, the price reflects a low average of mono and stereo copies. In most cases, there is little or no difference between the two. Keep in mind that for some late '50s and early '60s albums, the stereo pressing is considerably rarer and thus more valuable than the mono. Conversely, several late '60s albums can be much more valuable in mono than in stereo.

Early limited pressings or variations from the original commercial release, such as promotional copies, mistakes or differentiations on the label, colored vinyl, etc. can vastly increase or, in very rare cases, decrease the price of the record. One of the most notable cases is *"Yesterday"...And Today* by The Beatles. The jacket cover of the album's first issue featured The Beatles dressed in butcher smocks with toy doll parts and raw meat scattered around them. Subsequently referred to as the "butcher cover," Capitol recalled the record and replaced the controversial cover with a less incendiary photo of the The Beatles gathered around a trunk. The price listed in this book is for the widely distributed "trunk" cover as this is the more common of the two.

Aside from this and a few other oddities, the price listed is for first pressings. These prices do not apply to promotional copies which can be priced anywhere from slightly to significantly higher than the commercial releases.

Record prices vary from dealer to dealer. It is not unusual for prices of the same record of identical grade to fluctuate widely. Always remember that an album's true value is dependent on the demand for it and its availability.

USER'S GUIDE

The Artist Section lists by artist name, alphabetically, every album that charted on *Billboard* magazine's pop album charts from January 8, 1955 through December 26, 1992. (See page 11 for a chart synopsis.) Each artist's charted hits are listed in chronological order and are sequentially numbered. At the bottom of each artist's album listing is a comprehensive index of all musical tracks from their charted albums. (See Tracks Index on page 16 for further explanation.)

EXPLANATION OF COLUMNAR HEADINGS

DEBUT DATE: Date first charted

PEAK POS: Highest charted position (highlighted in bold type)

WKS CHR: Total weeks charted

GOLD: RIAA-certified gold or platinum record

$: Average dealer price of near-mint commercial copy of album

LABEL & NUMBER: Original record label and number

EXPLANATION OF SYMBOLS

★★30★★ Number to the left of an artist name denotes an artist's ranking among the Top 500 Album Artists of All Time

[1] Superior number to the right of the No. 1 or No. 2 peak position is the total weeks the album held that position

+ Beside debut date indicates that album peaked in the year after it first charted

↑ Beside the peak position and/or weeks charted indicates that the album was still on the charts as of the February 6, 1993 research cutoff date

● RIAA-certified gold album (500,000 units sold)

▲ RIAA-certified platinum album (1,000,000 units sold)

The Recording Industry Association of America (RIAA) began certifying gold albums in 1958, platinum albums in 1976 and multi-platinum albums in 1984. Some record labels have never requested RIAA certification for albums which would have qualified for these awards.

The superscript number to the right of the platinum triangle indicates if an album was awarded multi-platinum status (ex.: ▲[3] indicates an album was certified triple platinum).

For artists that charted ten or more albums, their hightest-charting album is blocked out in a thin-lined box. This does not necessarily mean that it is their best-selling album. For example, Pink Floyd's *Dark Side Of The Moon* spent over 14 years on the charts and has, so far, received 14 platinum designations yet it spent only one week at the top of the charts; whereas, the blocked-out album *The Wall* was #1 for 15 weeks. Ties are broken based on peak weeks and weeks charted.

LETTER(S) IN BRACKETS AFTER TITLES

C - Comedy

E - Early Recordings

EP - 7" Extended Play Album

F - Foreign Language

G - Greatest Hits

I - Instrumental Recording

K - Compilation

L - Live Recording

M - Mini Album (10" or 12" EP, lower-priced CD)

N - Novelty

OC - Original Cast

R - Reissue or re-release of a previously charted or previously recorded album

S - Film Soundtrack

T - Talk/Spoken Word Recording

TV - Television Show Soundtrack

X - Christmas (If an album also charted on *Billboard's* special Christmas charts, its title trivia lists the highest position reached and year it made the Christmas albums chart. For example:

Christmas charts: 5/'67, 10/'68

indicates that an album hit position five on the Christmas chart in 1967 and position 10 on that chart in 1968.)

TRACKS INDEX

Below each artist's chronological listing of charted albums is an alphabetical title index of all of the tracks on those albums. The number(s) in parentheses listed to the immediate right of the title refers to the sequential album count of the album on which the track appears. All tracks that charted on *Billboard's Hot 100* chart (and *Billboard's* multiple pre-*Hot 100* pop singles charts from 1955-58) are highlighted in bold type with their peak position listed to the right in bold, italics type.

↑ Beside the *Hot 100* position of tracks which were still going up the *Hot 100* as of the February 6, 1993 research cutoff date

See Tracks Index on page 12 for further guidelines.

ALBUMS BY ARTIST

Lists, alphabetically by artist name, every album that charted on *Billboard's* pop albums chart from January 8, 1955 through December 26, 1992. Each artist listing includes an alphabetical index of all tracks to appear on each of their albums.

DEBUT DATE	PEAK POS	WKS CHR	GOLD	ARTIST — Album Title	$	Label & Number

A

★★322★★ ABBA

Pop quartet formed in Stockholm, Sweden in 1970, using their first initials as an acronym. Consisted of Anni-Frid "Frida" Lyngstad and Agnetha Faltskog (vocals), Bjorn Ulvaeus (guitar) and Benny Andersson (keyboards). Benny and Bjorn recorded together in 1966. Bjorn and Agnetha married in 1971, divorced in 1979. Benny and Frida married in 1978, divorced in 1981. Disbanded in the early 1980s. Bjorn and Benny co-wrote the *Chess* musical with Tim Rice.

DEBUT DATE	PEAK POS	WKS CHR	GOLD	#	Album Title	$	Label & Number
8/17/74	145	8		1	Waterloo	$15	Atlantic 18101
11/15/75	174	3		2	Abba	$15	Atlantic 18146
9/18/76	48	61	▲	3	Greatest Hits .....[G]	$12	Atlantic 18189
1/22/77	20	50	●	4	Arrival	$12	Atlantic 18207
2/18/78	14	41	▲	5	The Album	$12	Atlantic 19164
7/7/79	19	27	●	6	Voulez-Vous	$12	Atlantic 16000
					translation of French title: Will You		
12/22/79+	46	14	●	7	Greatest Hits, Vol. 2 .....[G]	$12	Atlantic 16009
12/13/80+	17	38	●	8	Super Trouper	$12	Atlantic 16023
1/9/82	29	17		9	The Visitors	$12	Atlantic 19332
12/18/82+	62	18		10	The Singles (The First Ten Years) .....[G]	$15	Atlantic 80036 [2]

Andante, Andante (8)
Angeleyes (6,7) *64*
Another Town, Another Train (3)
Arrival (4)
As Good As New (6)
Bang-A-Boomerang (2,3)
Chiquitita (6,7,10) *29*
Dance (While The Music Still Goes On) (1,3)
Dancing Queen (4,7,10) *1*
Day Before You Came (10)
Does Your Mother Know (6,7,10) *19*
Dum Dum Diddle (4)
Eagle (5,7)
Fernando (3,10) *13*

Gimme! Gimme! Gimme! (A Man After Midnight) (7,10)
Gonna Sing You My Lovesong (1)
Happy New Year (8)
Hasta Manana (1)
He Is Your Brother (3)
Head Over Heels (9)
Hey, Hey Helen (2)
Hole In Your Soul (5)
Honey, Honey (1,3) *27*
I Do, I Do, I Do, I Do, I Do (2,3,10) *15*
I Have A Dream (6,10)
I Let The Music Speak (9)
I Wonder (Departure) (5,7)
I'm A Marionette (5)

I've Been Waiting For You (2)
If It Wasn't For The Nights (6)
Intermezzo No 1 (2)
King Has Lost His Crown (6)
King Kong Song (1)
Kisses Of Fire (6)
Knowing Me, Knowing You (4,7,10) *14*
Lay All Your Love On Me (8)
Like An Angel Passing Through My Room (9)
Lovers (Live A Little Longer) (6)
Mamma Mia (2,3,10) *32*
Man In The Middle (2)
Me And I (8)

Money, Money, Money (4,7,10) *56*
Move On (5)
My Love, My Life (4)
My Mama Said (7)
Name Of The Game (5,7,10) *12*
Nina Pretty Ballerina (3)
On And On And On (8) *90*
One Man, One Woman (5)
One Of Us (9,10)
Our Last Summer (8)
People Need Love (3)
Piper, The (8)
Ring Ring (1,3,10)
Rock Me (2,7)
SOS (2,3,10) *15*

Sitting In The Palmtree (1)
Slipping Through My Fingers (9)
So Long (2,3,10)
Soldiers (9)
Summer Night City (7,10)
Super Trouper (8,10) *45*
Suzy-Hang-Around (1)
Take A Chance On Me (5,7,10) *3*
Thank You For The Music (5,7)
That's Me (4)
Tiger (1)
Tropical Loveland (2)
Two For The Price Of One (9)
Under Attack (10)

Visitors, The (9) *63*
Voulez-Vous (6,10) *80*
Watch Out (1)
Waterloo (1,3,10) *6*
Way Old Friends Do (8)
What About Livingstone (1)
When All Is Said And Done (9) *27*
When I Kissed The Teacher (4)
Why Did It Have To Be Me (4)
Winner Takes It All (8,10) *8*

ABBOTT, Gregory

Soul singer/songwriter from New York. At age eight, member of St. Patrick's Cathedral Choir. Psychology major at Boston University and Stanford; taught English at Berkeley.

DEBUT DATE	PEAK POS	WKS CHR	GOLD	#	Album Title	$	Label & Number
11/1/86+	22	36	●	1	Shake You Down	$8	Columbia 40437
6/4/88	132	9		2	I'll Prove It To You	$8	Columbia 44087

Back To Stay (2)
Crazy Over You (1)
I Got The Feelin'(It's Over) (1) *56*

I'll Find A Way (1)
I'll Prove It To You (2)
I'll Be Your Hero (1)
Let Me Be Your Hero (1)

Magic (1)
Prisoner Of Love (2)
Rhyme And Reason (1)

Runaway (2)
Say You Will (1)
Shake You Down (1) *1*

She's An Entertainer (2)
Take Me Back (2)
Two Of A Kind (2)

Unfinished Business (2)
Wait Until Tomorrow (1)
You're My Angel (1)

ABC

Electro-pop group from Sheffield, England. Formed as Vice Versa with Stephen Singleton and Mark White. Lead singer Martin Fry joined in 1980, group renamed ABC. Singleton left group in 1985.

DEBUT DATE	PEAK POS	WKS CHR	GOLD	#	Album Title	$	Label & Number
9/25/82+	24	39		1	the Lexicon of Love	$8	Mercury 4059
12/17/83+	69	14		2	Beauty Stab	$8	Mercury 814661
10/5/85	30	41		3	how to be a...Zillionaire!	$8	Mercury 824904
8/22/87	48	25		4	Alphabet City	$8	Mercury 832391

A To Z (3)
All Of My Heart (1)
Ark-Angel (4)
Avenue A (4)
Avenue Z (4)
Bad Blood (4)
Be Near Me (3) *9*
Beauty Stab (2)
Between You & Me (3)

Bite The Hand (2)
By Default By Design (2)
Date Stamp (1)
Fear Of The World (3)
15 Storey Halo (3)
4 Ever 2 Gether (1)
Hey Citizen (2)
(How To Be A) Millionaire (3) *20*

If I Ever Thought You'd Be Lonely (2)
Jealous Lover (4)
King Money (2)
King Without A Crown (4)
Look Of Love (Part One) (1) *18*
Look Of Love (Part Four) (1)

Love's A Dangerous Language (2)
Many Happy Returns (1)
Night You Murdered Love (4)
Ocean Blue (4)
One Day (4)
Poison Arrow (1) *25*
Power Of Persuasion (2)

Rage And Then Regret (4)
S.O.S. (2)
Show Me (1)
So Hip It Hurts (3)
Tears Are Not Enough (1)
That Was Then But This Is Now (2) *89*
Think Again (4)

Tower Of London (3)
United Kingdom (1)
Unzip (2)
Valentine's Day (1)
Vanity Kills (3) *91*
When Smokey Sings (4) *5*

ABDUL, Paula

Los Angeles singer/choreographer. Born on 6/19/62 of Brazilian and French Canadian parentage. While still a teen, was the choreographer and member of the Los Angeles Lakers cheerleaders. Choreographed Janet Jackson's *Control* videos and *The Tracey Ullman Show*. Married actor Emilio Estevez on 4/29/92.

DEBUT DATE	PEAK POS	WKS CHR	GOLD	#	Album Title	$	Label & Number
7/23/88+	1[10]	175	▲[7]	1	Forever Your Girl	$8	Virgin 90943
5/26/90	7	35	▲	2	Shut Up And Dance (The Dance Mixes) .....[K]	$12	Virgin 91362
					remixes of Paula's hits		
6/1/91	1[2]	70	▲[3]	3	Spellbound	$12	Virgin 91611

Alright Tonight (3)
Blowing Kisses In The Wind (3) *6*
Cold Hearted (1,2) *1*

Forever Your Girl (1,2) *1*
I Need You (1)
(It's Just) The Way That You Love Me (1,2) *3*

Knocked Out (1,2) *41*
My Foolish Heart (3)
Next To You (1)
1990 Medley Mix (2)

One Or The Other (1,2)
Opposites Attract (1,2) *1*
Promise Of A New Day (3) *1*
Rock House (3)

Rush, Rush (3) *1*
Spellbound (3)
State Of Attraction (1)
Straight Up (1,2) *1*

To You (3)
U (3)
Vibeology (3) *16*
Will You Marry Me? (3) *19*

ABOVE THE LAW

Rap outfit led by Cold 187um.

DEBUT DATE	PEAK POS	WKS CHR	GOLD	#	Album Title	$	Label & Number
4/14/90	75	16		1	Livin' Like Hustlers	$12	Ruthless 46041
8/3/91	120	4		2	Vocally Pimpin' .....[M]	$6	Ruthless 47934

DEBUT DATE	PEAK POS	WKS CHR	GOLD	ARTIST — Album Title	$	Label & Number

ABOVE THE LAW — Cont'd

Another Execution (1)
B.M.L. (Commercial) (2)
Ballin' (1)
Dose Of The Mega Flex (2)
Flow On (Move Me No Mountain) (2)
4 The Funk Of It [includes 3 versions] (1)
Freedom Of Speech (1)
Just Kickin' Lyrics (1)
Last Song (1)
Livin' Like Hustlers (1,2)
Menace To Society (1)
Murder Rap (1)
Playin' Your Game (2)
Playlude (2)
Untouchable (1)
Wicked (2)

ABRAMS, Colonel

R&B singer/songwriter. Born in Detroit, raised in New York City. Worked with the band 94 East, when Prince was their guitarist. Colonel Abrams is his real name.

DEBUT DATE	PEAK POS	WKS CHR	GOLD	ARTIST — Album Title	$	Label & Number
4/19/86	75	11		Colonel Abrams	$8	MCA 5682

I'm Not Gonna Let You
Margaux
Never Change
Over And Over
Picture Me In Love With You
Speculation
Table For Two
Trapped
Truth, The

ACCEPT

German heavy-metal quintet led by vocalist Udo Dirkschneider and guitarist Wolf Hoffman. Featured various personnel. Dirkschneider left in 1987; replaced by Colorado-born David Reece.

DEBUT DATE	PEAK POS	WKS CHR	GOLD	ARTIST — Album Title	$	Label & Number
2/4/84	74	26	●	1 Balls To The Wall	$8	Portrait 39241
3/30/85	94	14		2 Metal Heart...	$8	Portrait 39974
5/17/86	114	9		3 Russian Roulette	$8	Portrait 40354
6/24/89	139	9		4 Eat The Heat	$8	Epic 44368

Aiming High (3)
Another Second To Be (3)
Balls To The Wall (1)
Bound To Fail (2)
Chain Reaction (4)
D-Train (4)
Dogs On Leads (2)
Fight It Back (1)
Generation Clash (4)
Guardian Of The Night (1)
Head Over Heels (1)
Heaven Is Hell (3)
Hellhammer (4)
It's Hard To Find A Way (3)
Living For Tonite (4)
London Leatherboys (1)
Losers And Winners (1)
Losing More Than You've Ever Had (1)
Love Child (1)
Love Sensation (4)
Man Enough To Cry (3)
Metal Heart (2)
Midnight Mover (2)
Mistreated (4)
Monsterman (3)
Prisoner (4)
Russian Roulette (3)
Screaming For A Love-Bite (2)
Stand 4 What U R (4)
Stand Tight (3)
T.V.War (2)
Teach Us To Survive (2)
Too High To Get It Right (2)
Turn Me On (1)
Turn The Wheel (4)
Up To The Limit (2)
Walking In The Shadow (3)
Winterdreams (1)
Wrong Is Right (2)
X-T-C (4)

★★106★★ AC/DC

Hard-rock band formed in Sydney, Australia in 1974. Consisted of brothers Angus and Malcolm Young (guitars), Ron Belford "Bon" Scott (lead singer), Phil Rudd (drums) and Mark Evans (bass). Cliff Williams replaced Evans in 1977. Bon Scott died on 2/19/80 (age 33) from alcohol abuse and was replaced by Brian Johnson. Simon Wright replaced Rudd in 1985. Wright joined Dio in 1989, replaced by Chris Slade of The Firm. Angus and Malcolm are the younger brothers of George Young of The Easybeats.

DEBUT DATE	PEAK POS	WKS CHR	GOLD	ARTIST — Album Title	$	Label & Number
8/13/77	154	11	▲	1 Let There Be Rock	$12	Atco 151
6/24/78	133	17	▲	2 Powerage	$10	Atlantic 19180
12/23/78+	113	14	▲	3 If You Want Blood You've Got It..................[L]	$10	Atlantic 19212
8/25/79	17	83	▲4	4 Highway To Hell	$10	Atlantic 19244
8/23/80	4	131	▲10	5 Back In Black	$10	Atlantic 16018
				Brian Johnson replaces Bon Scott as lead singer		
4/18/81	3	55	▲3	6 Dirty Deeds Done Dirt Cheap....................[E-R]	$10	Atlantic 16033
7/18/81+	146	19	▲	7 High Voltage..[E-R]	$10	Atco 142
				above 2 albums recorded in 1976		
12/12/81	1³	30	▲2	8 For Those About To Rock We Salute You	$10	Atlantic 11111
9/10/83	15	23	●	9 Flick Of The Switch	$10	Atlantic 80100
11/17/84	76	14	●	10 '74 Jailbreak ....[E-M]	$10	Atlantic 80178
				Australian releases from 1975-76		
7/20/85	32	30	●	11 Fly On The Wall	$10	Atlantic 81263
6/21/86	33	42	▲2	12 Who Made Who ....[S-K]	$10	Atlantic 81650
				soundtrack from the film Maximum Overdrive		
3/5/88	12	24	▲	13 Blow Up Your Video	$10	Atlantic 81828
10/6/90	2¹	77	▲3	14 The Razors Edge	$12	Atco 91413
11/14/92	15	13↑▲		15 Live ....[L]	$12	Atco 92215
				14 tracks from Live (Special Collector's Edition)		
11/14/92	34	13↑		16 Live (Special Collector's Edition)...............[L]	$22	Atco 92212 [2]
				recorded during their 1990-91 world tour		

Ain't No Fun (Waiting Round To Be A Millionaire) (6)
Are You Ready (14,16)
Baby, Please Don't Go (10)
Back In Black (5,15,16) 37
Back In Business (11)
Bad Boy Boogie (1,3)
Badlands (9)
Beating Around The Bush (4)
Bedlam In Belgium (9)
Big Balls (6)
Bonny (16)
Brain Shake (9)
Breaking The Rules (8)
C.O.D. (9)
Can I Sit Next To You Girl (7)
Chase The Ace (12)
D.T. (12)
Danger (11)
Deep In The Hole (9)
Dirty Deeds Done Dirt Cheap (6,15,16)
Dog Eat Dog (1)
Down Payment Blues (2)
Evil Walks (8)
Fire Your Guns (14,16)
First Blood (11)
Flick Of The Switch (9)
Fly On The Wall (11)
For Those About To Rock (We Salute You) (8,12,15,16)
Get It Hot (4)
Gimme A Bullet (2)
Girls Got Rhythm (4)
Given The Dog A Bone (5)
Go Down (4)
Go Zone (13)
Gone Shootin' (2)
Goodbye and Good Riddance To Bad Luck (14)
Got You By The Balls (14)
Guns For Hire (9) 84
Have A Drink On Me (5)
Heatseeker (13,15,16)
Hell Ain't A Bad Place To Be (1,3)
Hell Or High Water (11)
Hells Bells (5,12,15,16)
High Voltage (3,7,16)
If You Dare (14)
If You Want Blood (You've Got It) (4)
Inject The Venom (8)
It's A Long Way To The Top (If You Wanna Rock 'N' Roll) (7)
Jack, The (3,7,15,16)
Jailbreak (10,16)
Kicked In The Teeth (2)
Kissin' Dynamite (13)
Landslide (9)
Let Me Put My Love Into You (5)
Let There Be Rock (1,3,16)
Let's Get It Up (8) 44
Lets Get It Made (14)
Little Lover (7)
Live Wire (7)
Live At First Feel (6)
Love At First Feel (6)
Love Hungry Man (4)
Meanstreak (13)
Mistress For Christmas (14)
Moneytalks (14,15,16) 23
Nervous Shakedown (9)
Nick Of Time (13)
Night Of The Long Knives (8)
Night Prowler (4)
Overdose (1)
Playing With Girls (11)
Problem Child (1,3,6)
Put The Finger On You (8)
Razors Edge (14,16)
Ride On (6,12)
Riff Raff (2,3)
Rising Power (9)
Rock And Roll Ain't Noise Pollution (5)
Rock 'N' Roll Damnation (2,3)
Rock 'N' Roll Singer (7)
Rock Your Heart Out (14)
Rocker (3,6)
Ruff Stuff (13)
Send For The Man (11)
Shake A Leg (5)
Shake Your Foundations (11,12)
She's Got Balls (7)
Shoot To Thrill (5,15,16)
Shot Down In Flames (4)
Shot Of Love (14)
Show Business (10)
Sin City (2,16)
Sink The Pink (11,12)
Snowballed (8)
Some Sin For Nuthin' (13)
Soul Stripper (10)
Spellbound (8)
Squealer (6)
Stand Up (11)
T.N.T. (7,15,16)
That's The Way I Wanna Rock 'N Roll (13,16)
There's Gonna Be Some Rockin' (6)
This House Is On Fire (9)
This Means War (13)
Thunderstruck (14,15,16)
Touch Too Much (4)
Two's Up (13)
Up To My Neck In You (2)
Walk All Over You (4)
What Do You Do For Money Honey (5)
What's Next To The Moon (2)
Who Made Who (12,15,16)
Whole Lotta Rosie (1,3,15,16)
You Ain't Got A Hold On Me (10)
You Shook Me All Night Long (5,12,15,16) 35

ACE

Pub-rock quintet from Sheffield, England led by vocalist Paul Carrack. Disbanded in 1977. Carrack joined Squeeze in 1981, then Mike + The Mechanics in 1985.

DEBUT DATE	PEAK POS	WKS CHR	GOLD	ARTIST — Album Title	$	Label & Number
3/15/75	11	22		1 Five-A-Side (an Ace album)	$10	Anchor 2001
12/27/75+	153	6		2 Time For Another	$10	Anchor 2013
2/12/77	170	2		3 No Strings	$10	Anchor 2020

DEBUT DATE	PEAK POS	WKS CHR	GOLD	ARTIST — Album Title	$	Label & Number

ACE — Cont'd

Ain't Gonna Stand For This No More (2)	Gleaming In The Gloom (3)	Know How It Feels (1)	**Rock & Roll Runaway** (1) **71**	So Sorry Baby (1)	Why Did You Leave Me (3)	
C'est La Vie (3)	**How Long** (1) **3**	Let's Hang On (3)	Rock And Roll Singer (3)	This Is What You Find (2)	You Can't Lose (2)	
Crazy World (3)	I Think It's Gonna Last (2)	Message To You (2)	Sail On My Brother (2)	Time Ain't Long (1)	You're All That I Need (3)	
Does It Hurt You (2)	I'm A Man (2)	Movin' (3)	Satellite (1)	Tongue Tied (2)	
Found Out The Hard Way (3)	I'm Not Takin' It Out On You (3)	No Future In Your Eyes (2)	Sniffin' About (1)	24 Hours (1)	
		Real Feeling (1)		Why? (1)	

ACE SPECTRUM
New York City R&B group: Henry "Red" Zant, Aubrey "Troy" Johnson, Elliot Isaac and Rudy Gay.

8/23/75	138	7		Low Rent Rendezvous..........................	$10	Atlantic 18143

Beautiful Love	I Just Want To Spend The	Keep Holding On	Third Rate Romance (Low	Trust Me	You Ain't No Match For Me
Do You Remember Yesterday	Night With You	Laughter In The Rain	Rent Rendezvous)	Without You	

ACKLES, David
Pop singer born on 2/20/37 in Rock Island, Illinois. Moved to California as a child and began film/stage career.

8/12/72	167	10		American Gothic..........................	$10	Elektra 75032

produced by Bernie Taupin (songwriting partner of Elton John)

American Gothic	Ballad Of The Ship Of State	Family Band	Midnight Carousel	Oh, California!	Waiting For The Moving Van
Another Friday Night	Blues For Billy Whitecloud	Love's Enough	Montana Song	One Night Stand	

ACKLIN, Barbara
R&B singer/songwriter born on 2/28/44 in Chicago. Cousin to Monk Higgins, who produced her first sessions for Special Agent in 1966 (as Barbara Allen). Backup vocalist at Chess Records in the mid-1960s. Married Eugene Record of The Chi-Lites.

10/5/68	146	5		Love Makes A Woman..........................	$15	Brunswick 754137

Be By My Side	I've Got You Baby	**Love Makes A Woman 15**	Please Sunrise, Please	What The World Needs Now	Yes I See The Love (I Missed)
Come And See Me Baby	Look Of Love	Old Matchmaker	To Sir, With Love	Is Love	Your Sweet Loving

ADAM & THE ANTS — see ANT, Adam

ADAMS, Andy — see EGG CREAM

★★491★★ ADAMS, Bryan
Rock singer/songwriter/guitarist based in Vancouver, Canada. Born on 11/5/59 in Kingston, Ontario. Lead singer of Sweeney Todd in 1976. Teamed with Jim Vallance in 1977 in songwriting partnership. Cameo appearance in the film *Pink Cadillac*.

1/30/82	118	13		1 You Want It, You Got It..........................	$8	A&M 4864
2/19/83	8	89	▲	2 Cuts Like A Knife..........................	$8	A&M 4919
11/24/84+	1²	83	▲⁵	3 Reckless..........................	$8	A&M 5013
4/18/87	7	33	▲	4 Into The Fire..........................	$8	A&M 3907
10/12/91	6	70↑▲³		5 Waking Up The Neighbours..........................	$12	A&M 5367

Ain't Gonna Cry (3)	Don't Drop That Bomb On	Home Again (4)	Last Chance (1)	Only The Strong Survive (4)	**There Will Never Be**
All I Want Is You (5)	Me (5)	House Arrest (6)	Let Him Know (2)	Rebel (4)	**Another Tonight** (5) **31**
Another Day (4)	Don't Leave Me Lonely (2)	I'm Ready (2)	**Lonely Nights** (1) **84**	Remembrance Day (4)	**This Time** (2) **24**
Best Was Yet To Come (2)	Don't Look Now (1)	If You Wanna Leave Me (Can	Long Gone (3)	Run To You (3) **6**	Thought I'd Died And
Can't Stop This Thing We	**(Everything I Do) I Do It**	I Come Too?) (5)	Native Son (4)	She's Only Happy When	Gone To Heaven (5) **13**
Started (5) **2**	**For You** (5) **1**	Into The Fire (4)	No One Makes It Right (1)	She's Dancin' (3)	Tonight (1)
Coming Home (1)	Fits Ya Good (1)	Is Your Mama Gonna Miss	Not Guilty (5)	Somebody (3) **11**	Touch The Hand (5)
Cuts Like A Knife (2) **15**	**Hearts On Fire** (4) **26**	Ya? (5)	One Good Reason (1)	**Straight From The Heart**	Vanishing (5)
Depend On Me (5)	**Heat Of The Night** (4) **6**	**It's Only Love** (3) **15**	One Night Love Affair	(2) **10**	**Victim Of Love** (4) **32**
Do I Have To Say The	**Heaven** (3) **1**	Jealousy (1)	(3) **13**	**Summer Of '69** (3) **5**	What's It Gonna Be (2)
Words? (5) **11**	Hey Honey - I'm Packin' You	Kids Wanna Rock (3)	Only One (2)	Take Me Back (2)	You Want It, You Got It (1)
	In! (1)				

ADAMS, Oleta
Native of Yakima, Washington. Discovered by Tears For Fears in Kansas City; backing singer on their *Seeds Of Love* LP and tour.

9/1/90+	20	44	●	Circle Of One..........................	$12	Fontana 846346

Circle Of One	Everything Must Change	I've Got A Right	Rhythm Of Life	You've Got To Give Me Room
Don't Look Too Closely	**Get Here 5**	I've Got To Sing My Song	Will We Ever Learn	

ADC BAND
R&B eight-man, one-woman band led by Kaiya Matthews and Michael Judkins.

12/16/78+	139	9		Long Stroke..........................	$10	Cotillion 5210

Baby Love	Fire Up	Long Stroke	More & More Disco	Reggae Disco	That's Life
Cause I Love You	Just Another Song				

ADDEO, Leo, & His Orchestra
Brooklyn-born Addeo's orchestra features two ukulele players and three guitarists (including Al Caiola and Billy Mure).

1/9/61	143	13		Hawaii In Hi-Fi.......................... [I]	$12	RCA Camden 510

Aloha Oe	Hindustan	I Get The Blues When It	My Little Grass Shack (In	On Miami Shore	Yaaka Hula Hickey Dula
Blue Hawaii	Hula Blues	Rains	Kealakekua, Hawaii)	Sweet Leilani	
Drifting And Dreaming					

★★496★★ ADDERLEY, "Cannonball", Quintet
Born Julian Edwin Adderley on 9/15/28 in Tampa. Nickname derived from "cannibal" — in tribute to his love of eating. Alto saxophonist/leader of jazz combo featuring brother Nat Adderley (cornet) and Joe Zawinul (piano; left in 1971 to form Weather Report; replaced by George Duke). First recorded for EmArcy in 1955. With the Miles Davis band in the late 1950s. Died of a stroke on 8/8/75 in Gary, Indiana.

5/5/62	30	21		1 Nancy Wilson/Cannonball Adderley..........................	$20	Capitol 1657
				NANCY WILSON/CANNONBALL ADDERLEY		
3/30/63	11	25		2 Jazz Workshop Revisited.......................... [I-L]	$20	Riverside 444
				CANNONBALL ADDERLEY Sextet		
2/25/67	13	27		3 Mercy, Mercy, Mercy!.......................... [I-L]	$15	Capitol 2663
6/10/67	148	12		4 Why Am I Treated So Bad!.......................... [I-L]	$15	Capitol 2617
12/9/67	186	2		5 74 Miles Away - Walk Tall.......................... [I-L]	$15	Capitol 2822

21

DEBUT DATE	PEAK POS	WKS CHR	GOLD	ARTIST — Album Title	$	Label & Number

ADDERLEY, "Cannonball", Quintet — Cont'd

DEBUT DATE	PEAK POS	WKS CHR		ARTIST — Album Title	$	Label & Number
3/14/70	136	22		6 Country Preacher .... [I-L]	$10	Capitol 404
				introduction by Rev. Jesse Jackson		
9/26/70	194	2		7 Experience in E, Tensity, Dialogues .... [I]	$10	Capitol 484
3/6/71	169	2		8 The Price You Got To Pay To Be Free .... [L]	$10	Capitol 636 [2]
2/26/72	167	3		9 The Black Messiah * .... [L]	$10	Capitol 846 [2]
7/1/72	74	20		10 Soul Zodiac *	$10	Capitol 11025 [2]
				featuring the Nat Adderley Sextet; narration by Rick Holmes		
9/29/73	179	5		11 Inside Straight .... [I-L]	$10	Fantasy 9435
9/20/75	121	8		12 Phenix * .... [I]	$12	Fantasy 79004 [2]

*"CANNONBALL" ADDRELEY

Afro-Spanish Omelet (6)
Alto Sex (8)
Aquarius (10)
Aries (10)
Black Messiah (9)
Bridges (8)
Cancer (10)
Capricorn (10)
Chocolate Nuisance (9)
Circumference (9)
Country Preacher (6,12) *86*
Devastatement (8)
Dialogues For Jazz Quintet And Orchestra (7)
Directions (8)
Do Do Do (What Now Is Next) (5)
Dr. Honouris Cousa (9)

Domination (12)
Down In Black Bottom (8)
End, The (11)
Episode From The Music Came (9)
Experience In E (7)
Exquisition (8)
Eye Of The Cosmos (9)
Five Of A Kind (11)
Fun (3)
Games (3)
Gemini (10)
Get Up Off Your Knees (8)
Hamba Nami (12)
Happy Talk (1)
Heritage (9)
High Fly (12)
Hippodelphia (3)

Hummin' (6)
I Can't Get Started (1)
I Remember Bird (5)
I'm On My Way (4)
Inner Journey (11)
Inquisition (8)
Inside Straight (11)
Jessica's Birthday (2)
Jive Samba (2,12) *66*
Leo (10)
Libra (10)
Little Benny Hen (9)
Lonesome Stranger (8)
Marney (2)
Masquerade Is Over (1)
Mellow Buno (2)

Mercy, Mercy, Mercy (3,12) *11*
Mini Mama (4)
Never Say Yes (1)
Never Will I Marry (1)
Oh Babe (5,6)
Old Country (1)
One For Newk (4)
One Man's Dream (1)
1-2-3-Go-o-o-ol (8)
Other Side (4)
Out And In (8)
Painted Desert (8)
Pisces (10)
Pra Dizer Adeus (To Say Goodbye) (8)
Pretty Paul (9)

Price You Got To Pay To Be Free (8)
Primitivo (2)
Rumplestiltskin (8)
Sack O'Woe (3,12)
Sagittarius (10)
Saudade (11)
Save Your Love For Me (1)
Scene, The (4,6,8,9)
Scorpio (10)
Second Son (11)
74 Miles Away (5,12)
Sidewalks Of New York (12)
Sleepin' Bee (1)
Snakin' The Grass (11)
Some Time Ago (8)
Soul Virgo (8)
Stars Fell On Alabama (12)
Steam Drill (9)

Sticks (3)
Taurus (10)
Teaneck (1)
Tensity (7)
This Here (12)
Together (8)
Unit 7 (1)
Untitled (9)
Virgo (10)
Walk Tall (5,6,12)
Why? (Am I Treated So Bad) (4) *73*
Wild-Cat Pee (8)
Work Song (12)
Yvette (4)
Zanek (11)

ADDRISI BROTHERS, The

Pop singing/songwriting duo: Dick and Don Addrisi. Don died of cancer on 11/13/84 (age 45).

DEBUT DATE	PEAK POS	WKS CHR		ARTIST — Album Title	$	Label & Number
4/8/72	137	3		1 We've Got To Get It On Again	$10	Columbia 31296
7/2/77	118	14		2 Addrisi Brothers	$10	Buddah 5694

Baby, Love Is A Two-Way Street (2)
Baguio (2)
Does She Do It Like She Dances (2) *74*

Emergency (2)
I Can Feel You (1)
Love Is On The Line (1)
Monkey See, Monkey Do (2)

Never My Love (1,2) *80*
One Last Time (1)
She's Just Laughing At Me (1)
Twogether (1)

Slow Dancin' Don't Turn Me On (2) *20*
Spoiled Like A Baby (2)

We've Got To Get It On Again (1) *25*
When I Wanted You (1)
Windy Wakefield (1)

Words And Music (1)
You Make It All Worthwhile (1)

ADE, King Sunny, & his African Beats

Nigerian known for his native 'JuJu Music'.

DEBUT DATE	PEAK POS	WKS CHR		ARTIST — Album Title	$	Label & Number
4/9/83	111	29		1 JuJu Music .... [F]	$8	Mango 9712
8/20/83	91	10		2 Synchro System .... [F]	$8	Mango 9737

E Saiye Re (2)
E Wele (2)
Eje Nlo Gba Ara Mi (1)

Ja Funmi (1)
Ma Jaiye Oni (1)
Maajo (2)

Mo Beru Agba (1)
Mo Ti Mo (2)
Penkele (1)

Samba/E Falabe Lewe (1)
Sunny Ti De Ariya (1)
Synchro Feelings - Ilako (2)

Synchro System (2)
365 Is My Number/The Message (1)

Tolongo (2)

ADVENTURES, The

Pop group from Belfast, Ireland featuring lead singer Terry Sharpe.

DEBUT DATE	PEAK POS	WKS CHR		ARTIST — Album Title	$	Label & Number
4/16/88	144	9		The Sea Of Love	$8	Elektra 60772

Broken Land *95*
Drowning In The Sea Of Love

Heaven Knows Which Way
Hold Me Now

One Step From Heaven
Sound Of Summer

Trip To Bountiful (When The Rain Comes Down)

When Your Heart Was Young

You Don't Have To Cry Anymore

★★108★★ AEROSMITH

Hard-rock band formed in Sunapee, New Hampshire in 1970. Consisted of Steven Tyler (lead singer; b: Steven Tallarico), Joe Perry and Brad Whitford (guitars), Tom Hamilton (bass) and Joey Kramer (drums). Perry left for own Joe Perry Project in 1979; replaced by Jimmy Crespo. Whitford left in 1981; replaced by Rick Dufay. Original band reunited in April 1984.

DEBUT DATE	PEAK POS	WKS CHR	GOLD	ARTIST — Album Title	$	Label & Number
10/13/73+	21	59	▲²	1 Aerosmith	$25	Columbia 32005
4/6/74+	74	86	▲²	2 Get Your Wings	$10	Columbia 32847
4/26/75	11	128	▲⁵	3 Toys In The Attic	$10	Columbia 33479
5/29/76	3	53	▲³	4 Rocks	$10	Columbia 34165
12/24/77+	11	20	▲	5 Draw The Line	$10	Columbia 34856
11/11/78+	13	22	▲	6 Live! Bootleg .... [L]	$12	Columbia 35564 [2]
12/1/79+	14	19	●	7 Night In The Ruts	$10	Columbia 36050
11/29/80	53	40	▲⁶	8 Aerosmith's Greatest Hits .... [G]	$10	Columbia 36865
9/25/82	32	19	●	9 Rock In A Hard Place	$10	Columbia 38061
11/30/85	36	28		10 Done With Mirrors	$8	Geffen 24091
4/26/86	84	12	●	11 Classics Live! .... [L]	$8	Columbia 40329
9/19/87	11	67	▲³	12 Permanent Vacation	$8	Geffen 24162
12/10/88+	133	11		13 Gems .... [K]	$8	Columbia 44487
9/30/89	5	110	▲⁴	14 Pump	$8	Geffen 24254
12/7/91+	45	9	●	15 Pandora's Box .... [K]	$42	Columbia 46209 [3]
				band's recordings with Columbia from 1972-82; includes booklet		

Adam's Apple (3,13,15)
All Your Love (15)
Angel (12) *3*
Back In The Saddle (4,6,8,15) *38*
Big Ten Inch Record (3,15)
Bitch's Brew (9)
Bolivian Ragamuffin (9)

Bone To Bone (Coney Island White Fish Boy) (7,15)
Bright Light Fright (5)
Cheese Cake (7,15)
Chip Away The Stone (6,13,15) *77*
Chiquita (7)
Combination (4)

Come Together (6,8,15) *23*
Critical Mass (5,13,15)
Cry Me A River (9)
Don't Get Mad, Get Even (14)
Downtown Charlie (15)
Draw The Line (5,8,15) *42*
Dream On (1,6,8,11,15) *6*

Dude (Looks Like A Lady) (12) *14*
F.I.N.E. (14)
Get It Up (5)
Get The Lead Out (4)
Girl Keeps Coming Apart (12)
Gypsy Boots (9)
Hand That Feeds (5)

Hangman Jury (12)
Heart's Done Time (12)
Helter Skelter (15)
Home Tonight (4) *71*
Hop, The (1)
I Ain't Got You (6)
I Live In Connecticut (15)
I Wanna Know Why (5,15)

I'm Down (12)
Jailbait (9,13,15)
Janie's Got A Gun (14) *4*
Jig Is Up (5)
Joanie's Butterfly (9)
Kings And Queens (5,8,11,15) *70*
Krawhitham (15)

DEBUT DATE	PEAK POS	WKS CHR	GOLD	ARTIST — Album Title	$	Label & Number

AEROSMITH — Cont'd

Last Child (4,6,8,15) *21* — Mia (7) — Other Side (14) *22* — Rock In A Hard Place (Cheshire Cat) (9) — Sight For Sore Eyes (5,6) — Train Kept A Rollin' (2,6,11,13,15)
Let It Slide (15) — Milk Cow Blues (5,15) — Pandora's Box (2,15) — Round And Round (3,13,15) — Simoriah (12) — Uncle Salty (3)
Let The Music Do The Talking (10) — Monkey On My Back (14) — Permanent Vacation (12) — S.O.S. (Too Bad) (2,6) — Somebody (1) — Voodoo Medicine Man (14)
Lick And A Promise (4,13,15) — Mother Popcorn (6) — Prelude To Joanie (9) — Same Old Song And Dance (2,8,15) — Soul Saver (15) — Walk This Way (3,6,8,15) *10*
Lightning Strikes (9) — Movie, The (12) — Push Comes To Shove (9) — Seasons Of Wither (2,15) — South Station Blues (15) — Walkin' The Dog (1,15)
Lord Of The Thighs (2,6,11,13,15) — Movin' Out (1,15) — **Rag Doll** (12) *17* — Shame On You (10) — Spaced (2) — What It Takes (14) *9*
Love In An Elevator (14) *5* — My Fist Your Face (10) — Rats In The Cellar (4,13,15) — Sharpshooter (15) — St. John (12) — When I Needed You (15)
Magic Touch (12) — My Girl (14) — Rattlesnake Shake (15) — She's On Fire (15) — **Sweet Emotion** (3,6,8,11,15) *36* — Woman Of The World (2)
Major Barbra (11,15) — No More No More (3,15) — Reason A Dog (10) — Shela (10) — Think About It (7) — Write Me A Letter (1,15)
Make It (1,15) — No Surprize (7,13,15) — Reefer Head Woman (7,11) — Shit House Shuffle (15) — Three Mile Smile (7,11,15) — You See Me Crying (3,15)
Mama Kin (1,6,11,13,15) — Nobody's Fault (4,13,15) — **Remember (Walking In The Sand)** (7,8) *67* — Sick As A Dog (4,6) — Toys In The Attic (3,6,15) — Young Lust (14)
— On The Road Again (15) —
— One Way Street (1,15) — Riff & Roll (15) —

AFRIQUE
Thirteen-member, R&B-jazz session band featuring David T. Walker (guitar) and Chuck Rainey (bass).

6/16/73	152	8		Soul Makossa .... [I]	$10	Mainstream 394

Dueling Guitars — Hot Doggin' — House Of Rising Funk — Let Me Do My Thing — Slow Motion
Get It — Hot Mud — Kissing My Love — Sleepwalk — Soul Makossa 47

AFTER 7
Indianapolis R&B vocal trio: Keith Mitchell with brothers Kevon and Melvin Edmonds. Keith is the cousin of L.A. Reid. Kevon and Melvin are the brothers of Babyface.

10/14/89+	35	72 ▲		1 After 7	$8	Virgin 91061
9/12/92	76	21↑		2 Takin' My Time	$12	Virgin 86349

All About Love (2) — Don't Cha' Think (1) — **Kickin' It** (2) *45* — My Only Woman (1) — Sayonara (1)
Baby I'm For Real (2) *55* — G.S.T. (2) — Love By Day, Love By Night (2) — No Better Love (2) — Takin' My Time (2)
Can He Love U Like This (2) — He Said, She Said (2) — Love's Been So Nice (1) — One Night (1) — Truly Something Special (2)
Can't Stop (1) *6* — **Heat Of The Moment** (1) *19* — **Ready Or Not** (1) *7*

AFTER THE FIRE
English rock band led by guitarist Andy Piercy.

3/12/83	25	20		ATF	$8	Epic 38282

Carry Me Home — **Der Kommissar** *5* — Love Will Always Make You Cry — 1980-F — Sailing Ship — Starflight
Dancing In The Shadows *85* — Frozen Rivers — One Rule For You — Sometimes
— Laser Love —

A-HA
Pop trio formed in Oslo, Norway: Morten Harket (vocals), Pal Waaktaar (guitar) and Mags Furuholem (keyboards).

7/20/85	15	47 ●		1 Hunting High And Low	$8	Warner 25300
11/1/86	74	20		2 Scoundrel Days	$8	Warner 25501
6/4/88	148	6		3 Stay On These Roads	$8	Warner 25733

And You Tell Me (1) — Hunting High And Low (1) — Living Daylights (3) — Scoundrel Days (2) — **Take On Me** (1) *1* — We're Looking For The Whales (2)
Blood That Moves The Body (3) — Hurry Home (3) — Love Is Reason (1) — Soft Rains Of April (2) — There's Never A Forever Thing (3) — Weight Of The Wind (3)
Blue Sky (1) — I Dream Myself Alive (1) — Manhattan Skyline (2) — Stay On These Roads (3) — This Alone Is Love (3) — You Are The One (3)
Cry Wolf (2) *50* — I've Been Losing You (2) — Maybe Maybe (2) — **Sun Always Shines On T.V.** (1) *20* — Touchy! (3) — You'll End Up Crying (3)
Here I Stand And Face The Rain (1) — Living A Boy's Adventure Tale (1) — October (2) — Out Of Blue Comes Green (3) — Swing Of Things (2) — Train Of Thought (1)

AIR FORCE — see BAKER, Ginger

★★453★★ **AIR SUPPLY**
Melbourne, Australia soft vocal duo: Russell Hitchcock (born on 6/15/49 in Melbourne) and Graham Russell (born on 6/1/50 in Nottingham, England). Disbanded in 1988. Both recorded solo. Reunited in 1991.

5/17/80	22	104 ▲²		1 Lost In Love	$8	Arista 4268
6/13/81	10	60 ▲		2 The One That You Love	$8	Arista 9551
6/19/82	25	38 ▲		3 Now And Forever	$8	Arista 9587
8/20/83	7	51 ▲⁴		4 Greatest Hits .... [G]	$8	Arista 8024
6/29/85	26	21 ●		5 Air Supply	$8	Arista 8283
9/6/86	84	9		6 Hearts In Motion	$8	Arista 8426

After All (5) — **Every Woman In The World** (1,4) *5* — I Can't Let Go (5) — Keeping The Love Alive (2) — One More Chance (5) — Taking The Chance (3)
All Out Of Love (1,4) *2* — Great Pioneer (5) — I Wanna Hold You Tonight (5) — **Lonely Is The Night** (6) *76* — One Step Closer (3) — This Heart Belongs To Me (2)
American Hymn (1) — Having You Near Me (4) — I Want To Give It All (2) — **Lost In Love** (1,4) *3* — **One That You Love** (2,4) *1* — Time For Love (6)
Black And Blue (5) — Heart & Soul (4) — I'd Die For You (6) — Make It Right (5) — **Power Of Love (You Are My Lady)** (5) *68* — Tonite (5)
Chances (1,4) — **Here I Am (Just When I Thought I Was Over You)** (2,4) *5* — I'll Never Get Enough Of You (2) — **Making Love Out Of Nothing At All** (4) *2* — Put Love In Your Life (6) — **Two Less Lonely People In The World** (3) *38*
Come What May (3) — Hope Springs Eternal (6) — It's Got Your Love (2) — My Best Friend (1) — Sandy (5) — What Kind Of Girl (3)
Don't Be Afraid (3) — I Can't Get Excited (1) — It's Not Too Late (6) — My Heart's With You (6) — She Never Heard Me Call (3) — When The Time Is Right (5)
Don't Turn Me Away (2) — Just Another Woman (1) — Never Fade Away (5) — Stars In Your Eyes (6) — You're Only In Love (5)
Even The Nights Are Better (3,4) *5* — **Just As I Am** (3) *19* — Now And Forever (3) — Sunset (5) — **Young Love** (3) *38*
— Old Habits Die Hard (1) — **Sweet Dreams** (2,4) *5*

AIRTO — see DEODATO

AKKERMAN, Jan
Dutch guitarist formerly with Focus. Born on 12/24/46 in Amsterdam.

10/13/73	192	4		1 Profile .... [I]	$12	Sire 7407
3/2/74	195	2		2 Tabernakel .... [I]	$10	Atco 7032
4/8/78	198	2		3 Jan Akkerman .... [I]	$8	Atlantic 19159

Andante Sostenuto (1) — Coranto For Mrs. Murcott By Francis Pilkington (2) — Etude (1) — Galliard By Anthonie Holborne (2) — Javeh (2) — Pavane (3)
Angel Watch (3) — Crackers (3) — Fantasy By Laurencini Of Rome (2) — Galliard By John Dowland (2) — Kemps Jig (1) — Skydancer (3)
Blue Boy (1) — Earl Of Derby, His Galliard By John Dowland (2) — Farmers Dance (medley) (1) — Gate To Europe (3) — Lammy (2) — Stick (1)
Britannia By John Dowland (2) — Floatin' (3) — House Of The King (2) — Maybe Just A Dream (1) — Streetwalker (3)
— Fresh Air (2) — Minstrel (medley) (1) —
— Pavan By Thomas Morley (2) —

DEBUT DATE	PEAK POS	WKS CHR	GOLD	ARTIST — Album Title	$	Label & Number

★★115★★ ALABAMA

Country quartet from Fort Payne, Alabama: Randy Owen (vocals, guitar), Jeff Cook (keyboards, fiddle), Teddy Gentry (bass, vocals) and Mark Herndon (drums, vocals). Randy, Jeff and Teddy are cousins.

DEBUT DATE	PEAK POS	WKS CHR	GOLD	ARTIST — Album Title	$	Label & Number
7/19/80	71	21	▲²	1 My Home's In Alabama	$8	RCA 3644
3/28/81	16	161	▲⁴	2 Feels So Right	$8	RCA 3930
3/13/82	14	114	▲⁴	3 Mountain Music	$8	RCA 4229
3/26/83	10	70	▲³	4 The Closer You Get...	$8	RCA 4663
2/11/84	21	62	▲³	5 Roll On	$8	RCA 4939
2/23/85	28	40	▲²	6 40 Hour Week	$8	RCA 5339
11/23/85	75	9	▲	7 Christmas ... [X]	$8	RCA 7014
				Christmas charts: 1/'85, 16/'87, 8/'88, 18/'89, 20/'90, 15/'91, 30/'92		
3/1/86	24	38	▲³	8 Greatest Hits [G]	$8	RCA 7170
10/25/86	42	30	▲	9 The Touch	$8	RCA 5649
10/17/87	55	28	●	10 Just Us	$8	RCA 6495
6/25/88	76	19	●	11 Alabama Live [L]	$8	RCA 6825
2/18/89	62	21	●	12 Southern Star	$8	RCA 8587
6/16/90	57	41	●	13 Pass It On Down	$12	RCA 2108
				CD includes 3 bonus tracks		
10/26/91	72	31	●	14 Greatest Hits II [G]	$12	RCA 61040
8/29/92	46	24↑●		15 American Pride	$12	RCA 66044

Alabama Sky (4)
American Pride (15)
As Right Now (6)
Barefootin' (12)
Between The Two Of Them (15)
Borderline, The (12)
Born Country (14)
Boy, The (5)
Burn Georgia Burn (2)
Can't Forget About You (4)
Can't Keep A Good Man Down (6,11)
Can't You See (11)
Candle In The Window (7)
Carolina Mountain Dewe (6)
Changes Comin' On (3)
Christmas In Dixie (7)
Christmas Memories (7)
Close Enough To Perfect (3) **65**
Closer You Get (4,14) **38**
Country Side Of Life (5)
Cruisin' (9)
Dixie Boy (4)
Dixieland Delight (4,14)
Down Home (13)
Down On Longboat Key (6)

Down On The River (12)
End Of The Lyin' (5)
Face To Face (10)
Fallin' Again (10,14)
Fans, The (8)
Fantasy (2)
Fire On Fire (13)
Fireworks (6,11)
Food On The Table (5)
Forever's As Far As I'll Go (13)
40 Hour Week (For A Livin') (6,8)
Get It While It's Hot (1)
Getting Over You (1)
Gonna Have A Party (3,11)
Goodbye (Kelly's Song) (13)
Green River (3)
Gulf Of Mexico (13)
Hanging Up My Travelin' Shoes (1)
Happy Holidays (7)
Hats Off (14)
Here We Are (13)
High Cotton (12,14)
Hollywood (1)
Homecoming Christmas (7)

Homesick Fever (15)
Hometown Honeymoon (15)
I Ain't Got No Business Doin' Business Today (13)
I Can't Stop (10)
I Saw The Time (10)
I Taught Her Everything She Knows (9)
I Wanna Come Over (1)
I Want To Know You Before We Make Love (5)
(I Wish It Could Always Be) '55 (10)
I'm In A Hurry (And Don't Know Why) (15)
I'm Not That Way Anymore (5)
I'm Stoned (2)
If I Could Just See You Now (10)
If I Had You (12)
If It Ain't Dixie (It Won't Do) (6)
If You're Gonna Play In Texas (You Gotta Have a Fiddle In The Band) (5)
Is This How Love Begins (9)

It's All Comin' Back To Me Now (9)
Joseph And Mary's Boy (7)
Jukebox In My Mind (13)
Keep On Dreamin' (1)
Lady Down On Love (4,11,14) **76**
Let's Hear It For The Girl (9)
Louisiana Moon (6)
Love In The First Degree (2,8,11) **15**
Lovin' Man (4)
Lovin' You Is Killin' Me (3)
Moonlight Lounge (13)
Mountain Music (3,8)
My Home's In Alabama (1,8)
Never Be One (3)
Old Flame (2,8)
Old Man (10)
"Ole" Baugh Road (12)
Once Upon A Lifetime (15)
Pass It On Down (13)
Pictures And Memories (15)
Pony Express (9)
Red River (4,11)
Richard Petty Fans (15)
Ride The Train (2)

Roll On (Eighteen Wheeler) (5,14)
Santa Claus (I Still Believe In You) (7)
See The Embers, Feel The Flame (2)
She And I (8)
She Can (12)
She Put The Sad In All His Songs (4)
(She Won't Have A Thing To Do With) Nobody But Me (6)
Some Other Place, Some Other Time (1)
Sometimes Out Of Touch (15)
Song Of The South (12,14)
Southern Star (12)
Starting Tonight (13)
Take Me Down (3,11,14) **18**
Tar Top (10)
Tennessee Christmas (7)
Tennessee River (1,8,11)
Then Again (14)
(There's A) Fire In The Night (5)
There's No Way (6,11)

Thistlehair The Christmas Bear (7)
Tonight Is Christmas (7)
Touch Me When We're Dancing (9)
True, True Housewife (9)
Until It Happens To You (13)
Vacation (9)
Very Special Love (4)
What In The Name Of Love (4)
When We Make Love (5,11) **72**
Why Lady Why (1,8)
Woman Back Home (2)
Words At Twenty Paces (3)
You Can't Take The Country Out Of Him (4)
You Turn Me On (3)
You're My Explanation For Living (10)
"You've Got" The Touch (9)

ALARM, The

Welsh rock quartet: Mike Peters (lead singer), Dave Sharp, Eddie MacDonald and Nigel Twist. Formed in 1977 by Peters and Twist as the Toilets. MacDonald and Sharp joined in 1978, and group renamed Seventeen (after a Sex Pistols' song). Renamed The Alarm in 1982.

DEBUT DATE	PEAK POS	WKS CHR	GOLD	ARTIST — Album Title	$	Label & Number
7/30/83+	126	37		1 The Alarm [M]	$8	I.R.S. 70504
3/10/84	50	22		2 Declaration	$8	I.R.S. 70608
11/9/85+	39	36		3 Strength	$8	I.R.S. 5666
11/7/87	77	30		4 Eye Of The Hurricane	$8	I.R.S. 42061
10/29/88	167	5		5 Electric Folklore Live [L]	$8	I.R.S. 39108
				recorded in Boston on 4/26/88		
10/14/89	75	23		6 Change.	$8	I.R.S. 82018
12/15/90	177	3		7 Standards [G]	$12	I.R.S. 13056
				CD includes 2 bonus tracks		
5/18/91	161	1		8 Raw	$12	I.R.S. 13087

Absolute Reality (3,7)
Across The Border (1)
Blaze Of Glory (2,5,7)
Change II (6)
Dawn Chorus (3)
Day The Ravens Left The Tower (3)
Deceiver, The (2)
Declaration (2)
Deeside (3)
Devolution Workin' Man Blues (6,7)
Eye Of The Hurricane (4)
Father To Son (3)

For Freedom (Live) (1)
God Save Somebody (8)
Hallowed Ground (4)
Happy Christmas (War Is Over) (7)
Hardland (8)
Hell Or High Water (8)
Howling Wind (2)
Knife Edge (3)
Lead Me Through The Darkness (8)
Let The River Run Its Course (8)
Lie Of The Land (1)

Love Don't Come Easy (6)
Marching On (1,2,7)
Moments In Time (8)
New South Wales (4)
Newtown Jericho (4)
No Frontiers (6)
One Step Closer To Home (4)
Only Love Can Set Me Free (4)
Only The Thunder (3)
Permanence In Change (4,5)
Presence Of Love (4) **77**
Prison Without Prison Bars (6)

Rain In The Summertime (4,5,7) **71**
Raw (8)
Rescue Me (4,5)
Rivers To Cross (6)
Road, The (7)
Rock, The (7)
Rockin' In The Free World (8)
Save Your Crying (8)
Scarlet (6)
Shelter (4)
Shout To The Devil (2)
Sixty Eight Guns (2,7)

Sold Me Down The River (6,7) **50**
Spirit Of '76 (3,5,7)
Stand, The (1,7)
Stand (Prophecy) (2)
Strength (3,5,7) **61**
Tell Me (2)
Third Light (2)
Unsafe Building (7)
Walk Forever By My Side (3)
We Are The Light (2)
Where A Town Once Stood (6)

Where Were You Hiding When The Storm Broke? (2,7)
Wind Blows Away My Words (8)
Wonderful World (8)

ALBERT, Morris

Brazilian singer/songwriter born Morris Albert Kaisermann.

DEBUT DATE	PEAK POS	WKS CHR	GOLD	ARTIST — Album Title	$	Label & Number
9/6/75	37	31		1 Feelings	$8	RCA 1018
6/12/76	135	7		2 Morris Albert	$8	RCA 1496

Back To The Rock (2)
Boombamakaoo (medley) (1)
Christine (1)

Come To My Life (1)
Down To Mexico (medley) (2)

Everybody Loves Somebody (2)
Falling Tears (1)

Father (2)
Feelings (1) **6**
Gipsy (1)

Gonna Love You More (1)
Gotta Go Home (1)
La Puerta (medley) (2)

Land Of Love (2)
Memories (2)
Run Away (2)

DEBUT DATE	PEAK POS	WKS CHR	G O L D	ARTIST — Album Title	$	Label & Number

ALBERT, Morris — Cont'd

Same Things (2)	Summer In Paris (2)	This World Today Is A Mess	Ways Of Fire (medley) (1)	Where Is The Love Of The	Woman (1)
She's My Girl (2)	**Sweet Loving Man** (1) 93	(1)		World (1)	

ALBRIGHT, Gerald
Prominent R&B session musician (saxophone/bass). Born and raised in Los Angeles. Attended Locke High School with Patrice Rushen and Ndugu.

2/27/88	**181**	5		Just Between Us	$8	Atlantic 81813

Come Back To Me	King Boulevard	So Amazing	Trying To Find A Way	You're My #1
Just Between Us	New Girl On The Block	Softly At Sunrise	You Don't Even Know	

AL B. SURE!
R&B singer born Al Brown in Boston and raised in Mt. Vernon, New York.

5/14/88	**20**	54	▲	1 In Effect Mode	$8	Warner 25662
11/3/90	**20**	19	●	2 Private Times...And The Whole 9!	$12	Warner 26005
10/10/92	**41**	11		3 Sexy Versus	$12	Warner 26973

Channel J (2)	I'll Never Hurt You Again (1)	Natalie (3)	Ooh This Jazz Is So (2)	See The Lady (3)	Turn You Out (3)
Die For You (3)	If I'm Not Your Lover (1)	Naturally Mine (1)	Oooh This Love Is So (1)	Shades Of Grey (2)	U & I (3)
Had Enuf? (2)	Just A Taste Of Lovin' (1)	**Nite And Day** (1) 7	Papes In The End (3)	So Special (3)	You Excite Me (2)
Hotel California [includes 2	Just For The Moment (2)	No Matter What You Do (2)	Playing Games (3)	Sure! Thang (2)	
versions] (2)	Kick In The Head (3)	**Off On Your Own (Girl)**	Private Times (2)	Thanks 4 A Great Time Last	
I Don't Wanna Cry (3)	**Killing Me Softly** (1) 80	(1) 45	Rescue Me (1)	Nite (3)	
I Want To Know (2)	**Missunderstanding** (2) 42	Ooh 4 You Girl (3)	**Right Now** (3) 47	Touch You (2)	

ALCATRAZZ
Hard-rock quintet — Graham Bonnet, lead singer (member of Rainbow, the Michael Schenker Group and Impellitteri).

1/7/84	**128**	18		1 No Parole From Rock 'N' Roll	$20	Rocshire 22016
6/9/84	**133**	10		2 Live Sentence ....[L]	$20	Rocshire 22020
				recorded on 1/28/84 in Tokyo		
4/20/85	**145**	16		3 Disturbing The Peace	$20	Capitol 12385

All Night Long (2)	Desert Diamond (3)	Incubus (1)	Mercy (3)	Sons And Lovers (3)	Too Young To Die, Too
Big Foot (1)	Evil Eye (2)	Island In The Sun (1,2)	Night Games (2)	Starcarr Lane (1)	Drunk To Live (1,2)
Breaking The Heart Of The	General Hospital (1)	Jet To Jet (1)	Painted Lover (3)	Stripper (3)	Will You Be Home Tonight (3)
City (3)	God Blessed Video (3)	Kree Nakoorie (1,2)	Since You've Been Gone (2)	Suffer Me (1)	Wire And Wood (3)
Coming Bach (2)	Hiroshima Mon Amour (1,2)	Lighter Shade Of Green (3)	Skyfire (3)		

ALDRICH, Ronnie, And His Two Pianos
British pianist/arranger.

10/23/61+	**20**	33		1 Melody And Percussion For Two Pianos......................[I]	$10	London P. 4 44007
10/6/62	**36**	4		2 Ronnie Aldrich and his Two Pianos................................[I]	$10	London P. 4 44018
5/22/71	**169**	6		3 Love Story ....[I]	$8	London P. 4 22 [2]
				with the London Festival Orchestra		

Air On The 'G' String (3)	Clair De Lune (2,3)	I Think I Love You (3)	Mr Bojangles (3)	Ruby (1)	Unforgettable (1)
Amazing Grace (3)	El Condor Pasa (3)	I'm Always Chasing	My One And Only Love (1)	Secret Love (1)	Vocalise (3)
April In Portugal (1)	Full Moon And Empty Arms	Rainbows (2)	My Sweet Lord (3)	Serenade (3)	What Is Life (3)
April Love (1)	(2)	It's Impossible (3)	Nocturne (3)	Story Of A Starry Night (2)	Woodstock (3)
Autumn Leaves (1)	Gipsy, The (1)	Liebestraum (2)	None But The Lonely Heart	Story Of Three Loves (2)	Young-At-Heart (1)
Barcarolle (3)	Golden Earrings (1)	Love Story, Theme From (3)	(3)	Stranger In Paradise (2)	
Baubles, Bangles And Beads	Goodbye Again, Theme	Meditation (3)	Rachmaninoff's Piano	Till The End Of Time (3)	
(2)	From (2)	Misty (1)	Concert No. 2, Theme	To Each His Own (3)	
Candida (3)	(I Never Promised You A)	Mozart's Piano Concerto No.	From (3)	Togetherness (3)	
	Rose Garden (3)	21, Theme From (3)	Reverie (3)	Tonight We Love (2)	

ALIAS
Rock quintet formed in Los Angeles by former Sheriff bandmates Freddy Curci (vocals) and Steve DeMarchi (guitar), and Roger Fisher (ex-guitarist of Heart).

| 10/6/90+ | **114** | 28 | | Alias.. | $12 | EMI 93908 |

After All The Love Is Gone	Heroes	One More Chance	Standing In The Darkness	What To Do
Haunted Heart	**More Than Words Can Say 2**	Power, The	True Emotion	
		Say What I Wanna Say	**Waiting For Love 13**	

ALICE IN CHAINS
Male hard-rock band from Seattle: Layne Staley (vocals), Jerry Cantrell, Michael Starr and Sean Kinney.

| 4/27/91 | **42** | 58 | ● | 1 Face Lift .... | $12 | Columbia 46075 |
| 10/17/92 | **6** | 17↑ ▲ | | 2 Dirt .... | $12 | Columbia 52475 |

Angry Chair (2)	Down In A Hole (2)	I Know Somethin (Bout You)	Love, Hate, Love (1)	Real Thing (1)	Sunshine (1)
Bleed The Freak (1)	God Smack (2)	(1)	Man In The Box (1)	Rooster (2)	Them Bones (2)
Confusion (1)	Hate To Feel (2)	It Ain't Like That (1)	Put You Down (1)	Sea Of Sorrow (1)	We Die Young (1)
Dam That River (2)	I Can't Remember (1)	Junkhead (2)	Rain When I Die (2)	Sickman (2)	Would? (2)
Dirt (2)					

ALISHA
Dance teen singer from Brooklyn, New York.

| 6/23/90 | **166** | 4 | | Bounce Back .... | $12 | MCA 6378 |

(Ain't No) Better Love	Don't Let Our Love Go	I Need Forever	Love Will Talk	Wrong Number
Bounce Back 54	Everything You Do	Kiss Me Quick	Rescue Me	You've Really Gotten To Me

ALIVE AND KICKING
New York City-based, five-man, one-woman, pop-rock group led by singers Pepe Cardona and Sandy Toder. Member Bruce Sudano later married Donna Summer and was a member of Brooklyn Dreams.

| 10/17/70 | **129** | 3 | | Alive 'N Kickin'.. | $18 | Roulette 42052 |
| | | | | produced by Tommy James | | |

Hitter Man	Junction Creek	Kentucky Fire	Mother Carey's Chicken	**Tighter, Tighter 7**
Jordan	**Just Let It Come 69**	Mississippi Mud	Sunday Morning	

ALLAN, Davie, And The Arrows
Davie began as a session guitarist for Mike Curb in Los Angeles.

10/15/66+	**17**	71		**1** The Wild Angels ....[S]	**$20**	Tower 5043

includes "Lonely In The Chapel" & "Midnight Rider" by The Hands Of Time

4/22/67	**94**	18		**2** The Wild Angels, Vol. II ....[S-I]	**$20**	Tower 5056
8/19/67	**165**	2		**3** Devil's Angels ....[S-I]	**$20**	Tower 5074

Arriba (2)
Blue's Theme (1,2) **37**
Bongo Party (1)
Chase, The (1)
Cody's Theme (3)
Cycle Party (2)
Dark Alley (2)
Devil's Angels (3) **97**
Devil's Rumble (3)
Devils Carnival (3)
Funky (3)
Ghost Story (3)
Hell Rider (3)
Hole In The Wall (3)
Last Ride (2)
Lonely Rider (1)
Losers Burial (2)
Losers Lament (3)
Make-Believe Love (3)
Makin' Love Is Fun (2)
Rockin' Angel (1)
Unknown Rider (1)
Wild Angels, Theme From The (1) **99**
Wild Angels Ballad (Dirge) (1)
Wild Angels Chase (2)
Wild Orgy (2)

ALLEN, Dayton
Comedian on TV's *The Steve Allen Show*. Voice of *Deputy Dawg* TV cartoon and Phineas T. Bluster of TV's *Howdy Doody*.

12/19/60	**35**	1		Why Not!...[C]	**$15**	Grand Award 424

Botanist
Congressman "Dudley"
Criminologist
General Zugsmith
Hello Sickies
International T.V.
Mailman
Safari
Salvador Dooley
Squaw Valley Olympics
Surgeon

ALLEN, Deborah
Born Deborah Lynn Thurmond on 9/30/53 in Memphis. Country singer/songwriter.

12/3/83+	**67**	20		Cheat The Night ....[M]	**$8**	RCA 8514

Baby I Lied 26
Cheat The Night
Fool's Paradise
I Hurt For You
I've Been Wrong Before
What's The Matter With Me

ALLEN, Donna
Soul singer born in Key West and raised in Tampa. Former cheerleader for the Tampa Bay Buccaneers.

4/4/87	**133**	13		Perfect Timing	**$8**	21 Records 90548

Another Affair
Bad Love
Bit By Bit
Daydreams
Perfect Timing
Satisfied
Serious 21
Sweet Somebody
Wild Nights

ALLEN, Peter
Born Peter Allen Woolnough on 2/10/44 in Tenterfield, Australia. Died on 6/18/92 of AIDS. Cabaret-style performer/songwriter. Married to Liza Minnelli from 1967-73. Oscar-winning, co-writer of "Arthur's Theme."

4/21/79	**171**	3		**1** I Could Have Been A Sailor	**$8**	A&M 4739
11/29/80+	**123**	20		**2** Bi-Coastal..	**$8**	A&M 4825
3/12/83	**170**	6		**3** Not The Boy Next Door	**$8**	Arista 9613

Angels With Dirty Faces (1)
Bi-Coastal (2)
Don't Cry Out Loud (1)
Don't Leave Me Now (1)
Don't Wish Too Hard (1)
Easy On The Weekend (3)
Fade To Black (3)
Fly Away (2) 55
Hit In The Heart (2)
I Could Have Been A Sailor (1)
I Could Really Show You Around (2)
I Don't Go Shopping (2)
I'd Rather Leave While I'm In Love (1)
If You Were Wondering (1)
Just Another Make Out Song (1)
Not The Boy Next Door (3)
Once Before I Go (3)
One Step Over The Borderline (2)
Paris At 21 (1)
Pass This Time (2)
Simon (2)
Somebody's Angel (2)
Somebody's Got Your Love (3)
Two Boys (1)
We've Come To An Understanding (1)
When This Love Affair Is Over (2)
You And Me (We Wanted It All) (3)
You Haven't Heard The Last Of Me (3)
You'll Always Get Your Way (3)

ALLEN, Steve
Born on 12/26/21 in New York City. Comedian/actor/songwriter/author. In 1954, became the first host of TV's *Tonight Show*. Played title role in 1956 film *The Benny Goodman Story*. Hosted own variety and talk shows, 1956-80. Married to actress Jayne Meadows.

5/14/55	**7**	10		**1** Music For Tonight ....[I]	**$20**	Coral 57004
3/16/63	**65**	11		**2** Funny Fone-Calls...[C]	**$20**	Dot 3472

from Steve's TV show

4/27/63	**41**	22		**3** Gravy Waltz And 11 Current Hits!...............................[I]	**$20**	Dot 3515

Arthur Goldstein's Mother (2)
Boss Guitar (3)
Call To Eddie, Sr. (2)
Call To Seattle (2)
Calling The Auto Club (2)
Candlelight (1)
Cast Your Fate To The Wind (3)
For Sale: Espresso Machine & Birds Wanted (2)
For The Very First Time (1)
Gravy Waltz (3) 64
I Fall In Love Too Easily (1)
I'm Glad There Is You (In This World Of Ordinary People) (1)
Imagination (1)
Isn't It Romantic? (1)
It Can't Be Wrong (1)
Lawrence Of Arabia, Theme From (3)
Long Ago (And Far Away) (1)
Love For Sale (3)
Man With A Horn (1)
Preacherman (3)
Rebel-Rouser (3)
Rinky Dink (3)
Rose And The Butterfly (3)
Share The Ride (2)
Singer Wanted (2)
Stay Just A Little While (1)
Tonight (1)
Wanted: Girl To Share Apartment (2)
Where Are You? (1)
Whistle Bait (3)
Yakety Sax (3)
Your Theme (3)

ALLEN, Woody
Born Allen Stewart Konigsberg on 12/1/35 in New York City. Oscar-winning screen director/writer/actor. *Annie Hall*, *Manhattan* and *Hannah And Her Sisters* are among his many films.

8/15/64	**63**	11		Woody Allen ....[C]	**$25**	Colpix 518

no track titles listed on this album

ALLMAN, Duane
Born Howard Duane Allman on 11/20/46. The Allman Brothers Band guitarist. Died on 10/29/71 in a motorcycle mishap near his hometown of Macon, Georgia.

12/9/72+	**28**	26	●	**1** An Anthology ....[K]	**$10**	Capricorn 0108 [2]
8/31/74	**49**	16		**2** An Anthology, Vol. II...[K]	**$10**	Capricorn 0139 [2]

above 2 albums feature Duane's session work

B.B. King Medley (1)
Been Gone Too Long (2)
Born To Be Wild (2)
Come On In My Kitchen (2)
Dimples (2)
Dirty Old Man (2)
Don't Keep Me Wondering (1)
Don't Tell Me Your Troubles (2)
Done Somebody Wrong (2)
Down Along The Cove (1)
Dreams (1)
Games People Play (2)
Goin' Down Slow (1)
Goin' Up The Country (2)
Goin Upstairs (2)
Happily Married Man (2)
Hey, Jude (2)
It Ain't Fair (2)
Layla (1)
Leave My Blues At Home (1)
Little Martha (1)
Livin' On The Open Road (1)
Loan Me A Dime (1)
Matchbox (2)
Mean Old World (1)
Midnight Rider (2)
No Money Down (2)
Please Be With Me (1)
Push Push (2)
Road Of Love (1)
Rollin' Stone (1)
Shake For Me (1)
Standback (1)
Statesboro Blues (1)
Stuff You Gotta Watch (2)
Waiting For A Train (2)
Walk On Gilded Splinters (2)
Weight, The (1,2)
You Reap What You Sow (2)

ALLMAN, Duane & Gregg

5/13/72	**129**	8		**1** Duane & Gregg Allman ....[E]	**$25**	Bold 301

recorded in 1968

11/3/73	**171**	8		**2** Early Allman ....[E]	**$12**	Dial 6005

ALLMAN JOYS
recorded in 1966

ALLEN WOODY

Rock'n'roll bassist with a 'southern boogie' flavour

AS A NATIVE of Tennessee, Douglas Allen Woody began playing bass guitar at the age of 14, influenced by the uniquely American style which mixes rock and blues with a honky-tonk barrel-house flavour and is popularly known as "southern boogie".

His early inspirations were Lynyrd Skynyrd and the Allman Brothers Band, the two most significant groups working in this style, and he was later to forge close connections with both. After paying his dues in various bar bands, in the 1980s he joined the Artimus Pyle Band, led by the former drummer with Lynyrd Skynyrd.

Then in 1989 he was invited to join the Allman Brothers when the band reformed after a seven-year hiatus. Woody took the place of Berry Oakley, the original bassist, who had died in a motorcycle accident in 1972, a year after the band's leader Duane Allman had died under similar circumstances. To complete the connection, Lynyrd Skynyrd's best known song, Free Bird, had been dedicated to Duane Allman.

Woody stayed with the Allmans for seven years, making the albums Seven Turns, Shades of Two Worlds, Where It All Begins and Second Set, as well as a live recording. He also appeared with the band at President Clinton's inauguration in January 1993.

But in 1997 he left with guitarist Warren Hayes to form the trio Gov't Mule, another band in the southern boogie tradition. Their debut album Dose appeared in 1998 and Life Before Insanity, their third album, appeared earlier this year. He remained good friends with the Allman Brothers Band and jammed with them on stage at a festival in Lake Harmony, Pennsylvania three weeks before his death. He last played with Gov't Mule in Croton-on-Hudson, New York on August 19 and was due to tour with the group.

He was found dead, sitting in a chair in his room by a chambermaid at a hotel in Queens, New York. He is survived by his wife and a three-year-old daughter.

Allen Woody, rock musician, was born in Nashville. He died on August 26 aged 44.

obituaries@the-times.co.uk

93½	39½	Lilleshall	63	+ ½	...	7.8
102½	57½	Lookers	79½	...	8.3	10.5
157½	84½	Lumination	100½	...	3.5	1.3
452	345	Menzies (John)	452	+ 1	3.9	14.1
6½	0¾	Middlesex	3	...	...	27.1
28½	20½	Midstates	23½	...	...	...
194½	75½	Northamber	116½	...	4.7	11.9
194½	96	Pendragon	150	...	8.8	14.5
140½	77½	Perry Gp	101½	...	9.7	8.3
538½	278	Premier Farnell	537½	...	1.7	33.3
102½	37½	Quicks Group	65½	...	12.2	7.7
80	50	REA	50	...	8.0	...
8¼	0¾	Reece	1¾	...	...	...
4	1	Ronson	1¼	...	...	32.9
46	4	Ross Gp	6¾	+ 1	...	...
90½	37½	Ryland	50½	...	10.5	7.1
23½	8½	SEP Indl	11	...	...	...
238	92½	Sanderson Bram	173½	...	4.3	5.2
245	98	Sytner	129½	+ 1	6.3	5.1
120	82½	Time Products	109	...	7.3	8.8
88½	24½	Toad	44½	...	...	11.9
690	416	UMECO	682½	...	1.5	22.2
145	130	Unidare	145	...	10.2	7.2
27¾	12	United Oseas Gp	26½	+ 1¾	...	...
354½	204	Vardy (Reg)†	343½	+ 1	3.2	8.1
567½	212½	WF Elect	557½	...	3.5	27.5
102½	62½	Young (H)	64½	...	7.9	6.3

DIVERSIFIED INDUSTRIALS

862¾	603¾	Broken Hill	760¼	− 11½	2.6	...
16¼	9¾	Brierley Inv	12½	+ ¼	7.1	11.1
545	224	**Brit Amer Tob†**	446	− 3½	6.0	15.8
232½	169½	Cosalt	212½	− 1	7.0	6.7
460	203	Gallaher	372	− 8	6.0	10.1
1215¼	541½	Hutch Whamp	973½	+ 20¾	1.5	74.4
770	364	**Imperial Tob**	623	− 23	4.6	10.5
342¼	194¼	Jardine Math	342¼	+ 6¾	5.0	13.3
49	13½	Lonrho Africa	22½	...	...	...
78½	47½	Staveley	59½	− ½	...	4.6
479	262¾	Swire Pacific	462½	− 9½	1.8	17.2
77½	27½	Widney	39½	...	6.3	...

HEALTHCARE

34	12½	AdvancedMedical	18½	...	...	...
520	301½	Alnce UniChem	509½	− ½	2.3	18.3
1172½	357½	Axis-Shield	792½	− 2½	...	...
647	435	Bespak†	560	...	3.0	12.3
635	143	Biocomps Intl	430	+ 15	...	...
264½	210	Care UK	255	...	0.7	21.8
61¼	24½	Celsis	31¼	...	...	11.8
637½	308½	Community H	530	...	2.8	14.6
251½	140	Ferraris Group	249½	− ½	1.8	17.2
415	169½	Gyrus	369	+ 1	...	...
153½	132½	Health Clinic	152½	− 1	...	...
337½	232½	Huntlgh Tec	299½	+ 7	1.3	13.5
148	75½	Intercare Gp	141½	...	3.4	10.3
540	355	Isotron	465	...	1.7	18.1
18½	4¼	Maisha	9¼	+ ½	...	...
169½	25	Medisys	134½	+ 13½	...	...
686	379	Nestor Hlth	497½	+ 17½	1.2	41.0
750	340	**Nycomed Amsh**	621	+ 6	1.0	32.4
798	522	SSL Intl	788½	+ 12½	1.5	46.2
179½	136½	Shiloh	142½	...	3.1	...
399½	160½	Smith & Neph	283½	− 3	2.0	17.9
57	11½	Theratase	30½	...	...	10.4
363	151	Whatman	245	...	1.5	36.7

HOUSEHOLD GDS & TEXT

146	100½	Airsprung	106	+ 1½	7.5	7.2
117½	57½	Albion	67½	...	10.1	11.7
180½	132½	Alexandra	134	...	6.0	13.2
108½	42½	BLP Group	53½	...	3.3	...
115½	40½	Baird (Wm)	68	...	7.7	10.7
93½	55½	Black Arrow	82½	...	6.3	...
374½	251½	Black (Peter)	345	...	2.6	12.6
158½	96½	British Mohair	158½	+ 5	5.7	...
42	22½	Chapelthorpe	27	...	9.6	8.1
62½	37½	Coats Viyella	50¾	...	5.9	...
97½	29	Cornwell Prkr 5p	37	...	12.2	...
36½	7½	Creighton	9½	...	...	...
11	1¾	Dailywin	4¼	...	...	...

128½	69	Hend TR Pac	106¾	− 1	0.2	...
544½	200½	Hend Tech	541	+ 8½	...	...
715½	247½	Herald	585	− 2½	0.1	...
114½	94½	High Income T	105½	...	7.6	...
312½	172½	I&S UK Smllr	274½	+ ½	1.4	64.2
228	175¼	Inv Cap†	227½	...	2.7	34.0
367	52	Int Biotech	312½	− 11½	...	...
83½	57¾	INVESCO Asia	78	− ½	0.8	...
342½	163½	INVESCO Eng Int	280¾	+ ¼	0.7	53.2
175¼	125½	INVESCO IncGth	173¾	− ¼	2.2	36.8
250	111½	INVESCO Jap Dis	148	+ 1	...	...
70	42¾	INVESCO Tokyo	50	...	...	...
166½	127½	Jupiter Ex Inc†	162	+ 1	7.4	23.9
65	28½	Jupiter Ex IncWt	65	...	...	...
185	155	Jupiter Intl Grn†	182	+ 2½	2.4	...
1315	885	Jupiter Prima	1065	...	0.7	...
437¼	254	Korea Euro	357¼	− 2¼	0.2	...
1207	940	Law Debenture†	1207	+ 2	2.8	31.3
334	180	LeggMsn Euro U	252½	...	2.4	58.8
158	107	LeggMsn Util†	157	+ 1½	5.4	25.8
96½	76½	LeggMsn Utl Inc†	92½	...	9.2	15.2
140	125½	Life Off Opp	139	...	...	...
219½	138½	Lloyds Sm Cap	219½	+ 2	...	...
18½	8½	Lloyds Sm Div	10¼	...	...	2.1
227½	150	Lloyds Sm Pkg	227½	+ 3	2.1	...
217½	170	Lon St Lawrence	212½	...	3.7	25.1
434½	328½	Lowland	417½	...	3.2	30.1
95½	58¼	M&G Inc Geared	83½	...	7.8	...
75½	49½	M&G Inc Inv Tst Cp	74½	...	...	...
19¾	9	M&G Inc Inv Tst Inc	10¼	...	...	1.6
180	145	M&G Inc Package	173	...	3.8	...
94	87¾	M&G Inc Zero Div	94	...	...	...
75¾	43½	M&G Rec Cap	75¾	+ ¾	...	...
84½	56	M&G Rec Geared	84¼	+ ¾	6.4	...
21¼	10¾	M&G Rec Inc	13	...	...	2.8
215¼	177½	M&G Rec Pacge	215	+ ½	2.5	...
133¼	124½	M&G Rec Zero Div	132¾	...	...	...
100½	81½	M Cur En Inc Ord D	85½	+ ¼	9.2	...
112½	99¾	M Cur En Inc Z D	111½	+ ¼	...	...
337	193½	M Currie Euro†	318½	+ 1	0.3	...
159½	112	M Currie Japan†	138	...	0.2	...
193¾	126¾	M Currie Pac	166	...	0.5	...
106½	79¼	M Currie Portfolio	104½	...	1.4	56.3
391½	322½	Majedie	385½	...	1.9	46.3
428	294	Merchants	391	− 1½	4.1	21.8
161½	105½	Merc Asst Allctr	134½	+ 1	...	...

12 month High	Low	Stock	Price £
SHORTS (under 5 years)			
103.16	100.51	Treas 8% 2000	100.51
100.31	99.95	Treas Fltg 2001	100.05
106.15	101.84	Treas 10% 2001	101.84
106.76	102.81	Conv 9½% 2001	102.81
107.49	103.29	Conv 9¾% 2001	103.29
102.48	100.05	Treas 7% 2001	100.99
109.65	105.87	Conv 10% 2002	105.87
102.95	100.82	Treas 7% 2002	101.57
108.97	105.63	Conv 9½% 2002	105.63
108.79	105.74	Exch 9% 2002	105.88
112.36	108.78	Conv 9¾% 2003	108.86
110.25	106.71	Treas 9¾% 2002	106.71
102.58	99.86	Treas 6½% 2003	101.59
107.03	104.13	Treas 8% 2003	105.06
114.29	110.57	Treas 10% 2003	110.91
107.34	100.00	Treas 13¾% 2000-03	100.00
108.47	102.92	Treas 11½% 2001-04	102.92
116.39	112.33	Treas 10% 2004	113.12
97.69	94.53	Treas 5% 2004	97.17
93.27	89.41	Fund 3½% 1999-04	92.76
116.47	112.17	Conv 9½% 2004	113.30
104.63	101.32	Treas 6¾% 2004	103.58
MEDIUMS (5 to 15 years)			
114.46	110.08	Treas 8½% 2005	112.25
117.36	113.23	Conv 9½% 2005	114.70
123.44	118.78	Exch 10½% 2005	120.19
124.07	118.77	Treas 12½% 2003-05	118.77
111.42	106.40	Treas 7½% 2006	109.38
112.20	107.25	Treas 7¾% 2006	110.19
105.48	102.84	Treas 8% 2002-06	103.44
124.42	118.84	Conv 9¾% 2006	121.10
117.51	112.34	Treas 11¾% 2003-07	112.34
118.56	112.94	Treas 8½% 2007	115.93
111.94	106.17	Treas 7¼% 2007	109.63
130.68	124.57	Treas 13½% 2004-08	124.57

DEBUT DATE	PEAK POS	WKS CHR	G O L D	ARTIST — Album Title	$	Label & Number

ALLMAN, Duane & Gregg — Cont'd

Back Down Home With You (1) • Come Down And Get Me (1) • Gotta Get Away (2) • Melissa (1) • Northern Boundry (2) • Stalling For Time (2)
Bell Bottom Britches (2) • Doctor Fone Bone (2) • I'll Change For You (1) • Morning Dew (1) • Oh John (2) • Street Singer (2)
Changing Of The Guard (2) • Forest For The Trees (2) • In The Morning When I'm Real (1) • Nobody Knows You When You're Down And Out (1) • Old Man River (2) • Well I Know Too Well (1)
God Rest His Soul (1) • Spoonful (2) • You'll Learn Someday (2)

ALLMAN, Gregg

Keyboardist/vocalist born on 12/8/47 in Nashville and raised in Daytona Beach, Florida. In 1965, Greg and brother Duane formed the Allman Joys which evolved into the Allman Brothers Band by 1969. Married to Cher from 1975-77. Acted in the film *Rush*.

DEBUT DATE	PEAK POS	WKS CHR	G	Album	$	Label & Number
11/24/73+	13	39	●	1 Laid Back	$10	Capricorn 0116
11/16/74	50	12		2 The Gregg Allman Tour ....[L]	$10	Capricorn 0141 [2]

with orchestra, and guest "Cowboy"

THE GREGG ALLMAN BAND:

6/11/77	42	12		3 Playin' Up A Storm	$10	Capricorn 0181
3/7/87	30	28	●	4 I'm No Angel	$8	Epic 40531
8/6/88	117	11		5 Just Before The Bullets Fly	$8	Epic 44033

All My Friends (1) • Come And Go Blues (3) • Evidence Of Love (4) • Let This Be A Lesson To Ya' (3) • One More Try (3) • Thorn And A Wild Rose (5)
Anything Goes (4) • Cryin' Shame (3) • Faces Without Names (4) • Matthew's Arrival (3) • Please Call Home (1) • Time Will Take Us (2)
Are You Lonely For Me Baby (2) • Demons (5) • Fear Of Falling (5) • Midnight Rider (1) 19 • Queen Of Hearts (1,2) • Turn On Your Love Light (2)
Before The Bullets Fly (5) • Don't Mess Up A Good Thing (1,2) • Feel So Bad (2) • I'm No Angel (4) 49 • Multi-Colored Lady (1) • Slip Away (5) • Where Can You Go? (2)
Brightest Smile In Town (3) • Don't Want You No More (4) • Island (5) • Night Games (5) • Stand Back (2) • Will The Circle Be Unbroken (1,2)
Bring It On Back (3) • Double Cross (2) • It Ain't No Use (3) • Ocean Awash The Gunwale (5) • Sweet Feelin' (3) • Yours For The Asking (4)
Can't Get Over You (5) • Dreams (2) • It's Not My Cross To Bear (4) • These Days (1)
Can't Keep Running (4) • Every Hungry Woman (5) • Lead Me On (4) • Oncoming Traffic (2) • Things That Might Have Been (4)

★★125★★ ALLMAN BROTHERS BAND, The

Southern-rock band formed in Macon, Georgia in 1969. Consisted of brothers Duane (lead guitar) and Gregg Allman (keyboards), Dickey Betts (guitar), Berry Oakley (bass), and the drum duo of Butch Trucks and Jai Johnny Johanson (pronounced: Jay Johnny Johnson). Duane and Gregg known earlier as the Allman Joys and Hour Glass. Duane was the top session guitarist at Muscle Shoals studio; he was killed in a motorcycle crash on 10/29/71 (age 24). Oakley died in another cycle accident on 11/11/72 (age 24); he was replaced by Lamar Williams. Chuck Leavell (keyboards) added in 1972. Group split up in 1976. Gregg formed the Gregg Allman Band. Betts formed Great Southern. Leavell, Williams and Johanson formed the fusion-rock band Sea Level. Allman and Betts reunited with a new Allman Brothers' lineup in 1978. Disbanded in 1981. Allman, Betts, Trucks and Johanson regrouped with Warren Haynes (guitar), Allen Woody (bass) and Johnny Neel (keyboards) in 1989. Neel left in 1990.

1/24/70	188	5		1 The Allman Brothers Band	$20	Atco 308
10/24/70	38	22		2 Idlewild South	$20	Atco 342
7/24/71	13	47	▲	3 At Fillmore East ....[L]	$20	Capricorn 802 [2]
3/18/72	4	48	●	4 Eat A Peach ....[L]	$12	Capricorn 0102 [2]
				includes Duane's last 3 studio recordings		
3/10/73	25	55	●	5 Beginnings ....[R]	$20	Atco 805 [2]
				reissue of albums #1 and 2 above		
8/25/73	1⁵	56	●	6 Brothers And Sisters	$12	Capricorn 0111
9/13/75	5	14	●	7 Win, Lose Or Draw	$12	Capricorn 0156
12/13/75+	43	14		8 The Road Goes On Forever, A Collection Of Their Greatest Recordings ....[G]	$15	Capricorn 0164 [2]
12/4/76	75	10		9 Wipe The Windows-Check The Oil-Dollar Gas ....[L]	$15	Capricorn 0177 [2]
				live recordings from 1972-75		
3/17/79	9	24	●	10 Enlightened Rouges	$12	Capricorn 0218
8/23/80	27	13		11 Reach For The Sky	$8	Arista 9535
8/22/81	44	12		12 Brothers Of The Road	$8	Arista 9564
11/21/81	189	3	●	13 The Best Of The Allman Brothers Band ....[G]	$8	Polydor 6339
7/15/89	103	11	●	14 Dreams ....[K]	$40	Polydor 839417 [6]
				55 remastered songs and never-released tracks, recorded from 1966-1988; includes selections by The Allman Joys, Duane Allman, Gregg Allman and Dickey Betts; features a 36-page booklet		
7/21/90	53	16		15 Seven Turns	$12	Epic 46144
7/20/91	85	17		16 Shades Of Two Worlds	$12	Epic 47877
6/27/92	80	8		17 An Evening With The Allman Brothers Band	$12	Epic 48998

Ain't No Good To Cry (14) • Desert Blues (16) • Good Time Feeling (14) • Just Ain't Easy (10,14) • Mountain Jam (4) • She Has Funny Cars (14)
Ain't Wastin' Time No More (4,8,9,14) **77** • Dimples (14) • Heat Is On (12) • Just Another Love Song (7) • Mystery Woman (11) • Shine It On (15)
Angeline (11,14) **58** • Don't Keep Me Wonderin' (2,5) • Hell & High Water (11) • Keep On Keepin' On (11) • Nancy (14) • So Long (11)
BB King Medley (14) • Don't Want You No More (1,5,9,14) • High Falls (7) • Kind Of Bird (16) • Need Your Love So Bad (10) • Soul Serenade (medley) (14)
Bad Rain (16) • Hoochie Coochie Man (2,5,8,14) • Leave My Blues At Home (2,5) • Never Knew How Much (I Needed You) (12) • Southbound (6,9,13,14,17)
Black Hearted Woman (1,5,8) • Done Somebody Wrong (3) • Hot'Lanta (3,8) • Leavin' (12) • **Nevertheless** (7) **67** • Spoonful (14)
Blind Love (10) • Down In Texas (14) • I Beg Of You (12) • Les Brers In A Minor (4) • Nobody Knows (16,17) • Stand Back (4,8,13)
Blue Sky (4,8,13,14,17) • Dreams (1,5,8,13,14,17) • I Got A Right To Be Wrong (11) • Let Me Ride (15) • One More Ride (14) • Statesboro Blues (3,8,13,14)
Bougainvillea (14) • Drunken Hearted Boy (14) • I'm Gonna Move To The Outskirts Of Town (14) • Little Martha (4,8,13,14) • **One Way Out** (4,8,14) **86** • Stormy Monday (3,8)
Brothers Of The Road (12) • Duane's Tune (14) • **Louisiana Lou And Three Card Monty John** (7) **78** • Loaded Dice (14) • Pegasus (10) • **Straight From The Heart** (12) **39**
Can You Fool (14) • End Of The Line (16,17) • Long Time Gone (14) • Please Call Home (2,5) • Sweet Mama (7)
Can't Lose What You Never Had (7,9,14) • Every Hungry Woman (1,5) • I'm No Angel (14) • Low Down Dirty Mean (15) • Pony Boy (6) • Things You Used To Do (12,14)
Can't Take It With You (10,14) • Famous Last Words (11) • In Memory Of Elizabeth Reed (2,3,9,14) • Maybe We Can Go Back To Yesterday (12) • **Ramblin' Man** (6,8,9,13,14) **2** • Trouble No More (1,4,5,14)
Cast Off All My Fears (14) • From The Madness Of The West (11) • It Ain't Over Yet (15) • **Melissa** (4,8,13,14,17) **86** • **Revival (Love Is Everywhere)** (2,5,14,17) **92** • True Gravity (15)
Come And Go Blues (6,9,14) • Gambler's Roll (15) • It's Not My Cross To Bear (1,5,9,14) • Midnight Blues (17) • Sail Away (10) • Try It One More Time (10)
Come On In My Kitchen (16) • Get On With Your Life (16,17) • Jelly Jelly (6) • Midnight Man (16) • Seven Turns (15) • Two Rights (12)
Crazy Love (10,13,14) **29** • God Rest His Soul (14) • **Jessica** (6,8,9,13,14) **65** • Midnight Rider (2,5,8,13,14) • Shapes Of Things (14) • Wasted Words (6,8,9,14)
Crossroads (14) • Goin' Down Slow (14) • Judgement, The (12) • Morning Dew (14) • Whipping Post (1,3,5,8,14)
Demons (14) • Good Clean Fun (15) • Win, Lose Or Draw (7,13)
You Don't Love Me (3,14)

ALMEIDA, Laurindo, and The Bossa Nova All Stars
Born on 9/2/17 in Sao Paulo, Brazil. Guitarist/bandleader. To U.S. in 1947. Member of Stan Kenton's orchestra until 1950.

| 12/8/62+ | 9 | 27 | | Viva Bossa Nova! ....[I] | $15 | Capitol 1759 |

Desafinado Lollipops And Roses Moon River Naked City Theme Petite Fleur Route 66 Theme
Lazy River Maria Mr. Lucky One Note Samba Ramblin' Rose Teach Me Tonight

ALMOND, Marc
Half of the Soft Cell duo. Singer/songwriter born on 7/9/57 in Southport, England.

| 1/28/89 | 144 | 11 | | The Stars We Are .... | $8 | Capitol 91042 |

Bitter Sweet Sensualist, The Somethings Gotten Hold Of **Tears Run Rings 67** Your Kisses Burn
Only The Moment She Took My Soul In My Heart These My Dreams Are Yours
Istanbul Stars We Are Very Last Pearl

★★22★★ ALPERT, Herb
Herb was born on 3/31/35 in Los Angeles. Producer/composer/trumpeter/bandleader. Played trumpet since age eight. A&R for Keen Records. Produced first Jan & Dean session. Wrote "Wonderful World" hit for Sam Cooke. Formed A&M Records with Jerry Moss in 1962. Used studio musicians until early 1965, then formed own band.

HERB ALPERT & THE TIJUANA BRASS:

12/29/62+	24	157	●	1 The Lonely Bull ....[I]	$12	A&M 101
1/16/65+	6	163	●	2 South Of The Border * ....[I]	$12	A&M 108
5/15/65	1⁸	185	●	3 Whipped Cream & Other Delights * ....[I]	$12	A&M 110
10/16/65+	1⁶	164	●	4 Going Places ....[I]	$12	A&M 112
1/15/66	17	56	●	5 Herb Alpert's Tijuana Brass, Volume 2 * ....[I]	$12	A&M 103

Herb's second album, recorded in 1963

*HERB ALPERT'S TIJUANA BRASS

5/14/66	1⁹	129	●	6 What Now My Love ....[I]	$8	A&M 4114
12/10/66	2⁶	85	●	7 S.R.O. ....[I]	$8	A&M 4119
6/3/67	1¹	53	●	8 Sounds Like ....[I]	$8	A&M 4124
12/23/67+	4	49	●	9 Herb Alpert's Ninth ....[I]	$8	A&M 4134
5/11/68	1²	54	●	10 The Beat Of The Brass ....[I]	$8	A&M 4146
7/5/69	28	26	●	11 Warm ....[I]	$8	A&M 4190
11/22/69+	30	20		12 The Brass Are Comin' ....[I]	$8	A&M 4228
3/21/70	43	32	●	13 Greatest Hits ....[G-I]	$8	A&M 4245
7/24/71	111	10		14 Summertime ....[I]	$8	A&M 4314
6/17/72	135	9		15 Solid Brass ....[K-I]	$8	A&M 4341
12/8/73	196	4		16 Foursider ....[K-I]	$8	A&M 3521 [2]

HERB ALPERT & THE T.J.B.:

6/1/74	66	11		17 You Smile-The Song Begins ....[I]	$8	A&M 3620
4/26/75	88	10		18 Coney Island ....[I]	$8	A&M 4521
2/11/78	65	19		19 Herb Alpert/Hugh Masekela ....[I]	$8	Horizon 728

HERB ALPERT/HUGH MASEKELA

HERB ALPERT:

10/13/79	6	39	▲	20 Rise ....[I]	$8	A&M 4790
7/26/80	28	12		21 Beyond ....[I]	$8	A&M 3717
8/22/81	61	10		22 Magic Man ....[I]	$8	A&M 3728
5/29/82	100	26		23 Fandango ....[I]	$8	A&M 3731
9/24/83	120	8		24 Blow Your Own Horn ....[I]	$8	A&M 4949
8/25/84	75	10		25 Bullish ....[I]	$8	A&M 5022

HERB ALPERT/TIJUANA BRASS

| 8/24/85 | 151 | 10 | | 26 Wild Romance .... | $8 | A&M 5082 |
| 4/25/87 | 18 | 31 | ● | 27 Keep Your Eye On Me .... | $8 | A&M 5125 |

Acapulco (15)
Acapulco 1922 (1)
Adios, Mi Corazon (2)
African Flame (26)
African Summer (19)
All My Loving (2)
Alone Again (Naturally) (17)
Always Have A Dream (Pour Le Coeur, A Mon Pere) (25)
A-Me-Ri-Ca (5,13)
And The Angels Sing (4)
Angel (23)
Angelina (20)
Angelito (2)
Anna (12)
Aranjuez (Mon Amour) (20)
Aria (23)
Banda, A (9,15) **35**
Bean Bag (7)
Beautiful Friend (10)
Behind The Rain (20)
Belz Mein Shtetele Belz (My Home Town) (10)
Besame Mucho (22)
Beyond (21) **50**
Bittersweet Samba (3)
Blow Your Own Horn (24)
Blue Sunday (7)
Bo-Bo (8)
Brasilia (6)

Brass Are Comin' (The Little Train Of Calpira) (12)
Bud (9)
Bullish (25) **90**
Butterball (3)
Cabaret (10,16) **72**
California Blues (23)
Cantina Blue (6)
Carmen (9) **51**
Carmine (18)
Casino Royale (8,15,16) **27**
Cat Man Do (27)
Catch A Falling Star (14)
Catch Me (26)
Catfish (18)
Charmer, The (8)
Cinco De Mayo (4)
Coco Loco (La Guajira) (23)
Coney Island (18)
Continental, The (11,21)
Country Lake (12)
Cowboys And Indians (9)
Crave, The (18)
Crawfish (1)
Crea Mi Amor (5)
Dancing In The Light (26)
Darlin' (14)
Desafinado (1)
Diamonds (27) **5**
Dida (17)

Don't Go Breaking My Heart (7)
"8" Ball (26)
El Garbanzo (3)
El Lobo (The Wolf) (1)
El Presidente (2)
Factory, The (21)
Fandango (23)
Fantasy Island (22)
Felicia (4)
Five Minutes More (6)
Flea Bag (9)
For Carlos (7)
Fox Hunt (17) **84**
Freckles (18)
Freight Train Joe (7)
Garden Party (24) **81**
Gently (Suavemente) (24)
Girl From Ipanema (2,16)
Girl Talk (11)
Good Morning, Mr. Sunshine (7)
Gotta Lotta Livin' To Do (8)
Great Manolete (La Virgen De La Macarena) (5)
Green Leaves Of Summer (5)
Green Peppers (3)
Happening, The (9) **32**
Happy Hanna (19)

Hello, Dolly (2,16)
Hot Shot (27)
Hurt So Bad (14)
I Belong (18)
I Can't Go On Living Baby Without You (17)
I Get It From You (22)
I Have Dreamed (18)
I Might Frighten Her Away (17)
I Will Wait For You (7)
I'll Be Back (12)
I'll Be There For You (19)
I'm An Old Cowhand (From The Rio Grande) (12)
I'm Getting Sentimental Over You (4,13)
I've Grown Accustomed to Her Face (2)
If I Were A Rich Man (6,16)
If You Could Read My Mind (14)
In A Little Spanish Town (8)
Interlude (For Erica) (21)
It Was A Very Good Year (6)
It's All For You (26)
Jerusalem (14,15) **74**
Kamali (21)
Keep It Goin' (21)

Keep Your Eye On Me (27) **46**
Lady Godiva (8)
Lady Love (26)
Ladyfingers (3)
Last Tango In Paris (16,17) **77**
Latin Lady (24)
Latin Medley (23)
Legend Of The One-Eyed Sailor (17)
Lemon Tree (3)
Let It Be Me (4)
Life Is My Song (25)
Limbo Rock (1)
Lobo (19)
Lollipops And Roses (3)
Lonely Bull (1,13,16) **6**
Love Is (20)
Love Nest (9)
Love Potion #9 (3,13)
Love So Fine (9)
Love Without Words (25)
Mae (4)
Magic Man (22) **79**
Magic Trumpet (6)
Make A Wish (25)
Making Love In The Rain (27) **35**
Maltese Medley (12,15)

Mame (7,16) **19**
Manhattan Melody (22)
Maniac (25)
Marching Thru Madrid (5) **96**
Margarita (23)
Marjorine (11)
Martha My Dear (14)
Memories Of Madrid (6)
Mexican Corn (5)
Mexican Road Race (7)
Mexican Shuffle (2,13) **85**
Mexico (1)
Mickey (C'Est Ainsi Que Les Choses Arrivent) (18)
Midnight Tango (24)
Milord (5)
Miss Frenchy Brown (8)
Moments (12)
Monday, Monday (10)
Montezuma's Revenge (14)
Moon River (12,16)
Moonza (19)
More (5,16)
More And More Amor (4)
My Heart Belongs To Daddy (9)
Never On Sunday (1,13)
Nicest Things Happen (14)
1980 (20)

ALPERT, Herb — Cont'd

No Time For Time (26)
Numero Cinco (2)
Ob-La-Di, Ob-La-Da (11)
Oriental Eyes (24)
Our Day Will Come (7)
Our Song (27)
Panama (10)
Paradise Cove (24)
Passion Play (25)
Peanuts (3)
Pillow (27)
Plucky (6)
Pretty World (11)
Promises, Promises (17)
Push And Pull (23)
Quiereme Tal Como Soy (Love Me The Way I Am) (23)

Quiet Tear (Lagrima Quieta) (1)
Ratatouille (Rata Too Ee) (Coisa No. 1) (18)
Reach For The Stars (21)
Red Hot (21,24) **77**
Ring Bell (19)
Rise (20) **1**
Robbers And Cops (12)
Robin, The (10)
Rocket To The Moon (8)
Rotation (20) **30**
Route 101 (23) **37**
Salud, Amor Y Dinero (2)
Sandbox (11)
Save The Sunlight (17)
Sea Is My Soil (11)
Secret Garden (22)
Senor Mouse (18)

Shades Of Blue (8)
Shadow Of Your Smile (6,16)
She Touched Me (10)
Skokiaan (19)
Slick (10,15)
So What's New? (6,15)
Song For Herb (17)
South Of The Border (2,13)
Spanish Harlem (5)
Spanish Flea (4,13) **27**
Stranger On The Shore (27)
Street Life (20)
Strike Up The Band (14)
Struttin' On Five (25)
Struttin' With Maria (1)
Sugarloaf (23)
Summertime (14,15)
Sundown (24)
Sunny (12,16)

Surfin' Senorita (5)
Sweet Georgia Brown (18)
Swinger From Seville (5)
Talk To The Animals (10)
Tangerine (3)
Taste Of Honey (3,13,16) **7**
Thanks For The Memory (10)
That's The Way Of The World (21)
3rd Man Theme (4) **47**
This Guy's In Love With You (10,15,16) **1**
This Masquerade (18)
This One's For Me (22)
Tijuana Sauerkraut (1)
Tijuana Taxi (4,13,16) **38**
To Wait For Love (11) **51**
Town Without Pity (8)
Traffic Jam (9)

Treasure Of San Miguel (8)
Trolley Song (9)
True Confessions (24)
Up Cherry Street (2,17)
Vento Bravo (18)
Wade In The Water (8,15) **37**
Walk, Don't Run (4)
Walk In The Black Forest (4)
Wall Street Rag (7)
Warm (11,16)
What Now My Love (6,15,16) **24**
Whipped Cream (3,13,16) **68**
Wild Romance (26)
Winds Of Barcelona (5)
With A Little Help From My Friends (9,16)

Without Her (11,15,16) **63**
Work Song (7,15) **18**
You Are My Life (12)
You Are The One (26)
You Smile-The Song Begins (17,22)
Zazueira (11) **78**
Zorba The Greek (4,13,16) **11**

ALPHAVILLE

Pop male trio formed in Berlin in 1983: Marian Gold (vocals), Bernhard Lloyd and Frank Mertens. Ricky Echolette replaced Mertens in 1989.

DEBUT DATE	PEAK POS	WKS CHR	GOLD	ARTIST — Album Title	$	Label & Number
12/22/84+	**180**	15		**1** Forever Young	$8	Atlantic 80186
8/30/86	**174**	6		**2** Afternoons In Utopia	$8	Atlantic 81667

Afternoons In Utopia (2)
Big In Japan (1) **66**
Carol Masters (2)
Dance With Me (2)

Fallen Angel (1)
Fantastic Dream (2)
Forever Young (1) **65**
IAO (1)

In The Mood (1)
Jerusalem (2)
Jet Set (1)
Lady Bright (2)

Lassie Come Home (2)
Lies (1)
Red Rose (2)
Sensations (2)

Sounds Like A Melody (1)
Summer In Berlin (1)
To Germany With Love (1)
20th Century (2)

Universal Daddy (2)
Victory Of Love (1)
Voyager, The (2)

ALVIN, Dave

Born in Los Angeles in 1955. Songwriter/lead guitarist with The Blasters, The Knitters, and X. Brother of Blasters' lead singer, Phil Alvin.

DEBUT DATE	PEAK POS	WKS CHR	GOLD	ARTIST — Album Title	$	Label & Number
9/26/87	**116**	13		Romeo's Escape	$8	Epic 40921

features Al Kooper, David Hidalgo (Los Lobos) & The Allnighters

Border Radio
Brother On The Line

Every Night About This Time
Far Away

Fourth Of July
I Wish It Was Saturday Night

Jubilee Train
Long White Cadillac

New Tattoo
Romeo's Escape

You Got Me

AMAZING RHYTHM ACES, The

Memphis country-rock group: Russell Smith (lead vocals, guitar), Barry "Byrd" Burton (guitar, dobro), Billy Earhart III (keyboards), Jeff Davis (bass) and Butch McDade (drums). Disbanded in 1980.

DEBUT DATE	PEAK POS	WKS CHR	GOLD	ARTIST — Album Title	$	Label & Number
10/18/75	**120**	8		**1** Stacked Deck	$10	ABC 913
6/5/76	**157**	7		**2** Too Stuffed To Jump	$10	ABC 940
4/16/77	**114**	11		**3** Toucan Do It Too	$10	ABC 1005
4/15/78	**116**	9		**4** Burning The Ballroom Down	$10	ABC 1063
2/17/79	**144**	7		**5** The Amazing Rhythm Aces	$10	ABC 1123
				re-released on Columbia 36083		
10/4/80	**175**	3		**6** How The Hell Do You Spell Rythum?	$8	Warner 3476

All That I Had Left (With You) (4)
Amazing Grace (Used To Be Her Favorite Song) (1) **72**
Anything You Want (1)
Ashes Of Love (4)
Beautiful Lie (1)
Big Ole Brew (6)
Burning The Ballroom Down (4)
Dancing The Night Away (4)
Della's Long Brown Hair (4)
"Ella B" (1)

Emma-Jean (1)
End Is Not In Sight (The Cowboy Tune) (2) **42**
Everybody's Talked Too Much (3)
Farther On Down The Road (6)
Fool For The Woman (2)
Geneva's Lullaby (3)
Give Me Flowers While I'm Living (6)
Hit The Nail On The Head (3)
Homestead In My Heart (5)
I Got the Feeling (6)

I Musta Died And Gone To Texas (6)
I Pity The Mother And The Father (When The Kids Move Away) (1)
I'll Be Gone (2)
I'm Setting You Free (3)
If I Just Knew What To Say (2)
If You Gotta Make A Fool Of Somebody (3)
Jackass Gets His Oats (4)
Just Between You And Me And The Wall, You're A Fool (3)

King Of The Cowboys (1)
Last Letter Home (3)
Life's Railway To Heaven (1)
Lipstick Traces (On A Cigarette) (2)
Little Italy Rag (2)
Living In A World Unknown (3)
Living On Borrowed Time (6)
Lonely One (3)
Love And Happiness (5)
My Tears Still Flow (1)
Never Been Hurt (3)

Never Been To The Islands (Howard & Hugh's Blues) (3)
Object Of My Affection (6)
Out Of Control (1)
Out Of The Snow (2)
Pretty Words (5)
Red To Blue (When Dreams Come True) (4)
Rodrigo, Rita And Elaine (1)
Same Ole' Me (2)
Say You Lied (5)
Spirit Walk (4)
These Dreams Of Losing You (2)

Third Rate Romance (1) **14**
Two Can Do It Too (3)
Typical American Boy (2)
What Kind Of Love Is This? (6)
Whispering In The Night (5)
Who Will The Next Fool Be (1)
Who's Crying Now (3)
Why Can't I Be Satisfied (1)
Wild Night (6)
You Left The Water Running (6)

AMBOY DUKES, The

Detroit rock group led by Ted Nugent. After group split in 1975, Nugent embarked on prolific solo career before forming Damn Yankees in 1989.

DEBUT DATE	PEAK POS	WKS CHR	GOLD	ARTIST — Album Title	$	Label & Number
2/10/68	**183**	4		**1** The Amboy Dukes	$30	Mainstream 6104
6/15/68	**74**	23		**2** Journey To The Center Of The Mind	$30	Mainstream 6112
3/21/70	**191**	2		**3** Marriage On The Rocks/Rock Bottom	$15	Polydor 4012
3/6/71	**129**	5		**4** Survival Of The Fittest/Live [L]	$12	Polydor 4035

TED NUGENT AND THE AMBOY DUKES

Baby Please Don't Go (1)
Brain Games Of Yesteryear (3)
Breast-Fed 'Gator (Bait) (3)
Children Of The Woods (3)
Colors (1)
Death Is Life (2)
Dr. Slingshot (2)

Down On Phillps Escalator (1)
Flight Of The Byrd (2)
Get Yer Guns (3)
Gimme Love (1)
I Feel Fine (1)
I'll Prove I'm Right (2)

Inexhaustible Quest For The Cosmic Cabbage Part 1 & 2 (3)
It's Not True (1)
Ivory Castles (2)
Journey To The Center Of The Mind (2) **16**
Let's Go Get Stoned (1)

Lovely Lady (1)
Marriage Parts 1-3 (3)
Missionary Mary (2)
Mississippi Murderer (2)
Mr. Jones' Hanging Party (4)
Night Time (1)
Non-Conformist Wilderbeast Man (3)

Papa's Will (4)
Prodigal Man (4)
Psalms Of Aftermath (1)
Rattle My Snake (4)
Saint Phillps Friend (2)
Scottish Tea (2)
Slidin' On (1)
Surrender To Your Kings (2)

Survival Of The Fittest (4)
Today's Lesson (Ladies & Gentlemen) (3)
Why Is A Carrot More Orange Than An Orange (2)
Young Love (1)

AMBROSIA

Los Angeles-based pop group. Lead singers David Pack and Joe Puerta with Burleigh Drummond and Christopher North (left in 1977).

DEBUT DATE	PEAK POS	WKS CHR	GOLD	ARTIST — Album Title	$	Label & Number
5/3/75	**22**	33		**1** Ambrosia	$10	20th Century 434
9/18/76	**79**	17		**2** Somewhere I've Never Travelled	$10	20th Century 510
8/12/78	**19**	29		**3** Life Beyond L.A.	$8	Warner 3135
4/19/80	**25**	33		**4** One Eighty	$8	Warner 3368

DEBUT DATE	PEAK POS	WKS CHR	G O L D	ARTIST — Album Title	$	Label & Number
5/29/82	115	7	5	Road Island	$8	Warner 3638

And (2)	Danse With Me George (2)	**Holdin' On To Yesterday**	Life Beyond L.A. (3)	Rock N' A Hard Place (4)	**You're The Only Woman**
Angola (3)	Drink Of Water (1)	(1) **17**	Livin' On My Own (4)	Runnin' Away (2)	**(You & I)** (4) **13**
Apothecary (3)	Endings (5)	**How Can You Love Me**	Lover Arrive (1)	Shape I'm In (4)	
Art Beware (3)	Feelin' Alive Again (5)	(5) **86**	Make Us All Aware (1)	Somewhere I've Never	
Biggest Part Of Me (4) **3**	Fool Like Me (5)	**How Much I Feel** (3) **3**	Mama Frog (1)	Travelled (2)	
Brunt, The (2)	For Openers (Welcome	I Wanna Know (2)	**Nice, Nice, Very Nice** (1) **63**	Still Not Satisfied (5)	
Can't Let A Woman (2)	Home) (5)	Ice Age (5)	No Big Deal (3)	Time Waits For No One (1)	
Cowboy Star (2)	Harvey (2)	If Heaven Could Find Me (3)	Not As You Were (3)	We Need You Too (2)	
Cryin' In The Rain (4)	Heart To Heart (3)	Kamikaze (4)	Ready (4)	World Leave Me Alone (1)	
Dancin' By Myself (3)		Kid No More (5)	Ready For Camarillo (3)		

AMECHE, Don, & Frances Langford

Don (b: 5/31/08 in Kenosha, Wisconsin) and Frances (b: 4/4/13 in Lakeland, Florida) both began their film careers in 1935.

DEBUT DATE	PEAK POS	WKS CHR	G O L D	ARTIST — Album Title	$	Label & Number
4/7/62	76	12	1	The Bickersons .... [C]	$15	Columbia 1692
11/3/62	109	6	2	The Bickersons Fight Back .... [C]	$20	Columbia 1883

comedy skits written and created by Philip Rapp

Bickersons At Sea (1)	Breakfast With John And	Later That Same Evening (1)	Round I-IV (2)	Wedding Anniversary (1)
	Blanche (1)			

★★166★★ AMERICA

Trio formed in London in 1969. Consisted of Americans Dan Peek and Gerry Beckley, with Englishman Dewey Bunnell. All played guitars. Met at U.S. Air Force base. Members of Daze in 1970. Moved to the U.S. in February 1972. Won the 1972 Best New Artist Grammy Award. Peek left in 1976 and became a popular Contemporary Christian artist.

DEBUT DATE	PEAK POS	WKS CHR	G O L D	ARTIST — Album Title	$	Label & Number
2/19/72	1⁵	40	▲	1 America	$15	Warner 2576
12/2/72+	9	32	●	2 Homecoming	$10	Warner 2655
11/17/73	28	18		3 Hat Trick	$10	Warner 2728
7/13/74	3	53	●	4 Holiday	$10	Warner 2808
4/5/75	4	44	●	5 Hearts	$10	Warner 2852
11/22/75	3	63	▲⁴	6 History/America's Greatest Hits .... [G]	$10	Warner 2894
5/1/76	11	22	●	7 Hideaway	$10	Warner 2932
3/12/77	21	14		8 Harbor	$10	Warner 3017
12/17/77+	129	7		9 America/Live .... [L]	$10	Warner 3136

recorded at the Greek Theatre, Los Angeles

7/7/79	110	6		10 Silent Letter	$8	Capitol 11950
9/6/80	142	6		11 Alibi	$8	Capitol 12098
8/28/82	41	28		12 View From The Ground	$8	Capitol 12209
7/2/83	81	14		13 Your Move	$8	Capitol 12277
11/10/84	185	3		14 Perspective	$8	Capitol 12370

All Around (10)	**Don't Cross The River**	Horse With No Name	Molten Love (3)	Riverside (1)	Three Roses (1)
All My Life (10)	(2,6) **35**	(1,6,9) **1**	Monster (8)	Sandman (1,6)	Till The Sun Comes Up
All Night (10)	Don't Let It Get You Down (7)	Hurricane (8)	Moon Song (2)	Sarah (8)	Again (2)
Amber Cascades (7,9) **75**	Don't Let Me Be Lonely (13)	I Do Believe In You (11)	**Muskrat Love** (3,6,9) **67**	Saturn Nights (2)	**Tin Man** (4,6,9) **4**
And Forever (10)	Don't You Cry (8)	I Don't Believe In Miracles	My Dear (13)	Seasons (5)	To Each His Own (2,9)
Another Try (4,9)	Donkey Jaw (1)	(11)	My Kinda Woman (13)	See How The Love Goes (14)	**Today's The Day** (7) **23**
Are You There (8)	Down To The Water (8)	**I Need You** (1,6,9) **9**	Never Be Lonely (12)	Sergeant Darkness (8,9)	Tomorrow (5)
Baby It's Up To You (4)	Even The Score (13)	In The Country (4)	Never Found The Time (1)	She's A Liar (9)	Tonight Is For Dreamers (13)
Bell Tree (5)	Fallin' Off The World (14)	Inspector Mills (12)	1960 (10)	She's A Runaway (13)	Unconditional Love (14)
Border, The (13) **33**	5th Avenue (14)	It's Life (3)	No Fortune (10)	She's Beside You (7)	Valentine (14)
California Revisited (2)	Foolin' (10)	(It's Like You) Never Left At	Old Man Took (4,9)	She's Gone (8)	**Ventura Highway** (2,6,9) **8**
(Can't Fall Asleep To A)	Glad To See You (4)	All (14)	Old Virginia (5)	She's Gonna Let You Down	Watership Down (7)
Lullaby (14)	God Of The Sun (8)	Jet Boy Blue (7)	One In A Million (11)	(3)	We Got All Night (14)
Can't You See (7)	Goodbye (5)	Jody (12)	One Morning (10)	**Sister Golden Hair** (5,6,9) **1**	What Does It Matter (4)
Cast The Spirit (13)	Green Monkey (3)	Lady With A Bluebird (14)	Only Game In Town (10)	Slow Down (8)	Who Loves You (7)
Catch That Train (11)	Half A Man (5)	Letter (7)	**Only In Your Heart** (2,6) **62**	Someday Woman (13)	Willow Tree Lullaby (3)
Children (1)	Hangover (11)	**Lonely People** (4,6) **5**	People In The Valley (5)	Sometimes Lovers (12)	Wind Wave (3)
Cinderella (14)	Hat Trick (3)	Love On The Vine (12)	Pigeon Song (1)	Special Girl (14)	**Woman Tonight** (5,6) **44**
Clarice (1)	Head & Heart (2)	Love's Worn Out Again (13)	Political Poachers (8)	Stereo (11)	You (4)
Coastline (11)	Here (1)	Lovely Night (7)	Rainbow Song (3)	Story Of A Teenager (5)	**You Can Do Magic** (12) **8**
Company (5,9)	Hideaway Part I & II (7)	Mad Dog (4)	Rainy Day (1)	Submarine Ladies (3)	You Could've Been The One
Cornwall Blank (2)	High In The City (10)	Midnight (5)	Right Back To Me (11)	Survival (1)	(11)
Daisy Jane (5,6,9) **20**	Hollywood (4,9)	Might Be Your Love (11)	**Right Before Your Eyes**	Tall Treasures (10)	You Girl (12)
Desperate Love (12)	Honey (3)	Miniature (4)	(12) **45**	These Brown Eyes (8)	Your Move (13)

AMERICAN ANGEL

Hard-rock quintet from New Jersey: Rocco "Fury" Furiero (vocals), Petey D., Danny Monchek, Steve Evetts and Eric Nilla.

DEBUT DATE	PEAK POS	WKS CHR	G O L D	ARTIST — Album Title	$	Label & Number
3/24/90	164	9		American Angel	$12	Grudge 4518

After The Laughter	Bring The World Back	How Can I Miss You	It Don't Come Easy	Lonely Brown
Back To You	Grand Theft Ecstasy	I Wanna Be A Millionaire	Lessons	Teenage Runaway

AMERICAN BREED, The

Interracial rock quartet from Cicero, Illinois led by Gary Loizzo. Drummer Andre Fischer was later a member of Rufus and husband of Natalie Cole.

DEBUT DATE	PEAK POS	WKS CHR	G O L D	ARTIST — Album Title	$	Label & Number
2/24/68	99	10		Bend Me, Shape Me	$20	Acta 38003

Before And After	Bird	Don't Make Me Leave You	I've Been Tryin'	No Easy Way Down	Sometime In The Morning
Bend Me, Shape Me 5	Don't It Make You Cry	**Green Light 39**	Mindrocker	Something You've Got	

AMERICAN DREAM

Rock quartet led by guitarist Nick Jameson and vocalist Nicky Idelicato. Jameson went on to produce several albums as a member of Foghat.

DEBUT DATE	PEAK POS	WKS CHR	G O L D	ARTIST — Album Title	$	Label & Number
2/28/70	194	2		The American Dream	$20	Ampex 10101

produced by Todd Rundgren

Big Brother	Credemphels	Future's Folly	I Ain't Searchin'	My Babe	Raspberries
Cadillac	Frankford El	Good News	I Am You	Other Side	Storm

AMERICAN FLYER

Folk-rock quartet: Craig Fuller (Pure Prairie League), Eric Kaz (Blues Magoos), Steve Katz (Blood, Sweat & Tears) and Doug Yule (Velvet Underground).

DEBUT DATE	PEAK POS	WKS CHR	GOLD	ARTIST — Album Title	$	Label & Number
9/4/76	87	10		1 American Flyer	$10	United Art. 650
7/2/77	171	5		2 Spirit Of A Woman	$10	United Art. 720

Back In '57 (1)
Call Me, Tell Me (1)
Dear Carmen (2)
Drive Away (1)
End Of A Love Song (1)
Flyer (2)
Gamblin Man (2)
Good Years (2)
I'm Blowin' Away (2)
Keep On Tryin' (2)
Lady Blue Eyes (1)
Let Me Down Easy (1) 80
Light Of Your Love (1)
Love Has No Pride (1)
M (1)
My Love Comes Alive (2)
Queen Of All My Days (1)
Spirit Of A Woman (2)
Such A Beautiful Feeling (1)
Victoria (2)
Woman In Your Heart (1)

★★370★★ AMES, Ed

One of The Ames Brothers. Born Ed Urick on 7/9/27 in Malden, Massachusetts. Played the Indian "Mingo" on the *Daniel Boone* TV series.

DEBUT DATE	PEAK POS	WKS CHR	GOLD	ARTIST — Album Title	$	Label & Number
11/5/66	90	7		1 More I Cannot Wish You	$8	RCA 3636
3/4/67	4	81	●	2 My Cup Runneth Over	$8	RCA 3774
7/8/67	77	38		3 Time, Time	$8	RCA 3834
12/16/67+	24	25		4 When The Snow Is On The Roses	$8	RCA 3913
2/24/68	13	50	●	5 Who Will Answer? And Other Songs Of Our Time	$8	RCA 3961
8/10/68	135	14		6 Apologize	$8	RCA 4028
12/21/68	186	6		7 The Hits Of Broadway And Hollywood	$8	RCA 4079
3/8/69	114	14		8 A Time For Living, A Time For Hope	$8	RCA 4128
7/5/69	157	6		9 The Windmills Of Your Mind	$8	RCA 4172
10/18/69	119	16		10 The Best Of Ed Ames [G]	$8	RCA 4184
1/3/70	172	6		11 Love Of The Common People	$8	RCA 4249
7/11/70	194	2		12 Sing Away The World	$8	RCA 4381
2/20/71	199	1		13 The Songs Of Bacharach And David	$8	RCA 4453

tunes of the hit songwriting team of Burt Bacharach and Hal David

Adios Amor (Goodbye My Love) (12)
After All The Loves Of My Life (6)
Alfie (13)
Au Revoir (2)
Ballad Of The Sad Young Men (1)
Blowin' In The Wind (5)
Bon Soir Dame (2,10)
Born Free (6)
Bound For Glory (El Camino Real) (11)
Bridge Over Troubled Water (12)
Cabaret (3)
Can't Take My Eyes Off You (5)
Canticle ..see: Scarborough Fair
Cast Your Fate To The Wind (1)
Changing, Changing (8,10)
Cherish (5)
Climb Ev'ry Mountain (1)
Color Of Snow (6,10)
Deserted Carousel (1)
Do You Know The Way To San Jose (13)
Don't Blame Me (2)
Early In The Morning (12)
Edelweiss (2)
Elvira (6)
Feelings (9)
Funny Girl (7)
Games People Play (11)
Happy Heart (9)
Here With You (3)
Honey (6)
Honey, What's The Matter? (9)
How Are Things In Glocca Morra (7)
How Does A Man Become A Puppet (13)
I Believe (8)
I Can't Give You Anything But Love (7)
I Just Can't Help Believin' (9)
I Say A Little Prayer (13)
I Still See Elisa (1)
I Wanna Be Free (7)
I'll Get By (As Long As I Have You) (4)
I'll Never Fall In Love Again (12)
I'll Stay Lonely (9)
If I Can Dream (8)
If I Can Help Somebody (8)
If I Ever Get To Saginaw Again (9)
If I Had A Hammer (The Hammer Song) (8)
If She Walked Into My Life (1)
Impossible Dream (The Quest) (1,10)
In The Arms Of Love (2)
It's Today (1)
Just A Drop Of Rain (8)
Kiss Her Now (7,10)
Leave Them A Flower (11)
Let Me So Love (4)
Let's Get Together (11)
Lift Ev'ry Voice And Sing (1)
Little Green Apples (11)
Look Of Love (7,13)
Love Is Blue (6)
Love Of The Common People (11)
Love That Lasts Forever (3)
Make It Easy On Yourself (13)
Mary In The Morning (4)
Massachusetts (5)
Melinda (2)
Michelle (3)
Monday, Monday (5)
More (4)
More I Cannot Wish You (1)
My Cup Runneth Over (2,10) **8**
My Love Is Gone From Me (4)
Nikki (4,13)
On A Clear Day (You Can See Forever) (7)
One Little Girl At A Time (3)
Other Man's Grass Is Always Greener (5)
Our Love Is A Living Thing (2)
Pale Venetian Blind (5)
Peaceful Waters (8)
Pretend (3)
Proud Mary (9)
Put A Little Love In Your Heart (11)
Raindrops Keep Fallin' On My Head (12,13)
Rose Of Washington Square (1)
Scarborough Fair/Canticle (6)
Seasons Of Love (4)
Shadow Of Your Smile (7)
Sing Away The World (12)
(Sittin' On) The Dock Of The Bay (9)
Six Words (8)
Somethin' Stupid (3)
Somewhere (8)
Somewhere, My Love (7)
Son Of A Travelin' Man (9) **92**
Sound Of Silence (8)
Strangers (4)
Sunny (6)
Sunrise, Sunset (3)
There's A Kind Of Hush (All Over The World) (5)
There's A Time For Everything (2)
There's No Business Like Show Business (7)
(They Long To Be) Close To You (13)
Thing Called Love (11)
Thirty Days Hath September (6)
This Guy's In Love With You (11)
Three Good Reasons (12)
Time, Time (3,10) **61**
Timeless Love (4)
To Say Goodbye To Anne (9)
Today Is The First Day Of The Rest Of Our Lives (11)
Traces (9)
Travelin' Band (6)
Trolley Song (1)
True Love (2)
Try To Remember (10) **73**
Two Different Worlds (12)
Two For The Road (4)
Until It's Time For You To Go (12)
Walking Happy (7)
Watch What Happens (2)
What A Wonderful World (8)
What Are You Doing The Rest Of Your Life (12)
What The World Needs Now Is Love (3,13)
When The Snow Is On The Roses (4,10) **98**
Who Will Answer? (5,10) **19**
Who Will Buy? (7)
Windmills Of Your Mind (9)
Wish Me A Rainbow (3)
Without A Song (1)
Wives And Lovers (13)
Yesterday (5)

AMES, Nancy

Spanish/English vocalist born in Washington, D.C. Her grandfather was once president of Panama.

DEBUT DATE	PEAK POS	WKS CHR	GOLD	ARTIST — Album Title	$	Label & Number
9/26/64	133	4		1 This Is The Girl That Is [F]	$12	Liberty 7369
10/29/66	133	8		2 Latin Pulse [F]	$8	Epic 26189

above 2 sung in Spanish

Anna (1)
Ayer (Yesterday) (2)
Besame Mucho (1)
Carcara (1)
Choucoune (1)
Dimelo (Call Me) (2)
El Dia Que Me Quieras (2)
El Gallito Kikiriki (1)
El Tambor De La Alegria (1)
Eso Beso (That Kiss!) (2)
Fay-O (1)
Guantanamera (1)
Guarare (1)
La Sombra De Tu Sonrisa (The Shadow Of Your Smile) (2)
La Ultima Noche (1)
Malaguena Salerosa (1)
Michel (2)
Noche De Ronda (1) 1-2-3 (2)
Perdoname Mi Vida (2)
Un Gusto A Miel (A Taste Of Honey) (2)
Yours (Quiereme Mucho) (1)

AMES BROTHERS, The

Pop vocal group from Malden, Massachusetts formed in 1947. Family name Urick. Consisted of Ed (b: 7/9/27), Gene (b: 2/13/25), Joe (b: 5/3/24) and Vic (b: 5/20/26; d: 1/23/78). Own TV series in 1955. Ed recorded solo and acted on Broadway and TV.

DEBUT DATE	PEAK POS	WKS CHR	GOLD	ARTIST — Album Title	$	Label & Number
12/2/57	16	4		There'll Always Be A Christmas [X]	$25	RCA 1541

C-h-r-i-s-t-m-a-s
Christmas Song (Chestnuts Roasting On An Open Fire)
Deck The Halls
Go Tell It On The Mountain
Good King Wenceslas
Jingle Bells
Night Before Christmas Song
O Holy Night! (Cantique De Noel)
Santa Claus Is Comin' To Town
Silver Bells
There'll Always Be A Christmas
What Child Is This (Greensleeves)

AMG

Male rapper.

DEBUT DATE	PEAK POS	WKS CHR	GOLD	ARTIST — Album Title	$	Label & Number
12/21/91+	63	32		Bitch Betta Have My Money	$12	Select 21642

Backseat Queenz
Bitch Betta Have My Money
D. Control
Givva Dogga Bone
I Wanna Be Yo Ho
Jiggable Pie
La Queeda
Lick 'Em Low Lover
Mai Sista Izza Bitch
My Ho, My Kids
Nu Exasize
Once A Dawg (Janine 2)
P-Funk
Sylk's Cellular
Tha Booty Up
Trunk O' Funk
Vertical Interlude
Vertical Joyride
When She Calls
Word 2 Tha D
Yo Momma Told Me...

DEBUT DATE	PEAK POS	WKS CHR	GOLD	ARTIST — Album Title	$	Label & Number

AMMONS, Gene
Born Eugene Ammons on 4/14/25 in Chicago. Son of boogie-woogie pianist Albert Ammons. Nicknamed "Jug." Tenor sax player with the Billy Eckstine Band, 1944-47, and Woody Herman in 1949. Formed own group in 1950. Had the first release on the Chess label. Died in 1974 (age 49).

DEBUT DATE	PEAK POS	WKS CHR	GOLD	ARTIST — Album Title	$	Label & Number
12/22/62+	53	17		1 Bad! Bossa Nova ....[I]	$20	Prestige 7257
6/6/70	174	2		2 The Boss Is Back! ....[I]	$12	Prestige 7739

Anna (1) — Cae' Cae' (1) — Here's That Rainy Day (2) — Jungle Boss (2) — Moito Mato Grosso (1) — Tastin' The Jug (2)
Ca'Purange (1) — Feeling Good (2) — I Wonder (2) — Madame Queen (2) — Pagan Love Song (1) — Yellow Bird (1)

AMOS, Tori
Native of North Carolina. At age five, won a scholarship for piano to Baltimore's Peabody Conservatory.

4/4/92	54	35↑●		Little Earthquakes	$12	Atlantic 82358

China — Girl — Leather — Me And A Gun — Precious Things — Tear In Your Hand
Crucify — Happy Phantom — Little Earthquakes — Mother — Silent All These Years — Winter

ANA
Female singer signed, at the age of 10, to Parc Records. Native of Cuba. Moved to Orlando, Florida in 1979. Thirteen years old in 1987. Discovered by Maurice Starr (producer of New Kids On The Block).

6/23/90	191	2		Body Language	$12	Parc 45355

Angel Of Love — Everytime We Say Goodbye — **Got To Tell Me** — Miracles — So Outrageous — What Could I Do
Body Language — Friendly — Something 66 — Over And Over — Three Steps Closer

ANDA, Geza
Classical pianist born in Budapest, Hungary. Moved to Switzerland in 1942.

6/29/68	115	17		Mozart: Piano Concertos Nos. 17 & 21 ....[I]	$12	DG 138783

contains the theme from the film *Elvira Madigan*

Mozart: Concerto For Piano — Mozart: Concerto For Piano
And Orchestra No. 17 In G — And Orchestra No. 21 In C
Major, K. 453 — Major, K. 467

ANDERSEN, Eric
Folk singer/songwriter. Born on 2/14/43 in Pittsburgh, Pennsylvania. Part of the Greenwich Village folk scene of the early '60s.

7/15/72	169	11		1 Blue River....................	$10	Columbia 31062
4/19/75	113	9		2 Be True To You	$8	Arista 4033

Be True To You (2) — Can't Get You Out Of My — Is It Really Love At All (1) — More Often Than Not (1) — Sheila (1) — Wind And Sand (1)
Blue River (1) — Life (2) — Liza, Light The Candle (2) — Ol '55 (2) — Time Run Like A Freight — Woman, She Was Gentle (2)
Blues Keep Fallin' Like The — Faithful (1) — Love Is Just A Game (2) — Pearl's Goodtime Blues (1) — Train (2)
Rain (2) — Florentine (1) — Moonchild River Song (2) — Round The Bend (1) — Wildcrow Blues (2)

ANDERSON, Bill
Born James William Anderson III on 11/1/37 in Columbia, South Carolina. Country singer/songwriter/actor. Hosted Nashville Network's TV game show *Fandango*. Member of the *Grand Ole Opry* since 1961. Known as "Whispering Bill."

7/6/63	36	17		Still....................	$20	Decca 74427

Down Came The Rain — Happiness — Little Band Of Gold — Reverend Mr. Black
From A Jack To A King — I Wish It Was Mine — Molly — **Still 8**
Get A Little Dirt On Your — It's Been So Long Darling — Restless — Take These Chains From My
Hands — Heart

ANDERSON, Carl
R&B singer/actor. Born on 2/27/45 in Lynchburg, Virginia. Played "Judas" in the original Broadway cast and film version of the rock opera *Jesus Christ Superstar*. Appeared in the film *The Color Purple* and the 1990 TV series *Cop Rock*. Sang theme song of the *Santa Barbara* soap opera.

8/23/86	87	12		Carl Anderson....................	$8	Epic 40410

Buttercup — Can't Stop This Feeling — **Friends And Lovers 2** — Mr. V.J. — You Are My Shining Star
C'Est La Vie — First Time On A Ferris Wheel — Just A Little Love — Woman In Love

ANDERSON, Ernestine
Jazz singer. Born on 11/11/28 in Houston. Formerly with Eddie Heywood and Lionel Hampton.

10/20/58	15	6		Hot Cargo!	$20	Mercury 20354

Autumn In New York — Experiment — Little Girl Blue — My Man — Wrap Your Troubles In
Day Dream — Ill Wind (You're Blowin' Me — Love For Sale — Song Is Ended — Dreams (And Dream Your
Did I Remember — No Good) — Mad About The Boy — That Old Feeling — Troubles Away)

ANDERSON, John
Honky-tonk country singer. Born on 12/13/54 in Apopka, Florida.

4/9/83	58	12	●	1 Wild & Blue	$8	Warner 23721
10/29/83	163	5		2 All The People Are Talkin'	$8	Warner 23912
2/29/92	35	50↑▲		3 Seminole Wind....................	$12	BNA 61029

All The People Are Talkin' (2) — Haunted House (2) — Last Night I Laid Your — Look What Followed Me — She Never Looked That — Things Ain't Been The Same
Black Sheep (2) — Hillbilly Hollywood (3) — Memory To Rest (3) — Home (2) — Good When She Was Mine — Around The Farm (2)
Blue Lights And Bubbles (2) — Honky Tonk Hearts (1) — Let Go Of The Stone (3) — Occasional Eagle (2) — (1) — Waltz You Saved For Me (1)
Call On Me (2) — Honky Tonk Saturday Night — Let Somebody Else Drive (2) — Old Mexico (2) — Steamy Windows (2) — When It Comes To You (3)
Cold Day In Hell (3) — (1) — Long Black Veil (1) — Price Of A Thin Silver Dime — Straight Tequila Night (3) — Who Got Our Love (1)
Disappearing Farmer (1) — If A Broken Heart Could Kill — Look Away (3) — (1) — **Swingin' (1) 43** — Wild And Blue (1)
Goin' Down Hill (1) — (1) — Seminole Wind (3)

ANDERSON, John W. — see KASANDRA

ANDERSON, Jon
Lead singer of Yes. Born on 10/25/44 in Lancashire, England. Also recorded in Jon & Vangelis.

7/24/76	47	13		1 Olias Of Sunhillow....................	$8	Atlantic 18180
12/6/80+	143	11		2 Song Of Seven	$8	Atlantic 16021
7/3/82	176	5		3 Animation	$8	Atlantic 19355
12/28/85+	166	5		4 3 Ships .... [X]	$8	Elektra 60469

All Gods Children (3) — Animation (3) — Dance Of Ranyart Olias (To — Day Of Days (4) — Ding Dong Merrily On High — Don't Forget (Nostalgia) (2)
All In A Matter Of Time (3) — Boundaries (3) — Build The Moorglade) (1) — Days (2) — (4) — Easier Said Than Done (4)

ANDERSON, Jon — Cont'd

Everybody Loves You (2)	Holly And The Ivy (4)	Moon Ra Chords Song Of
Flight Of The Moorglade (1)	How It Hits You (4)	Search (1)
For You For Me (2)	Jingle Bells (4)	Much Better Reason (3)
Forest Of Fire (4)	Meeting (Garden Of Geda)	Ocean Song (1)
Hear It (2)	Sound Out The Galleon (1)	Oh Holy Night (4)
Heart Of The Matter (2)		Olympia (3)

Pressure Point (3) — Qoquaq En Transic Naon Transic To (1) — Save All Your Love (4) — Solid Space (1) — Some Are Born (2) — Song Of Seven (2) — Surrender (3) — Take Your Time (2) — Three Ships (4) — To The Runner (1) — 2,000 Years (4) — Unlearning (The Dividing Line) (3) — Where Were You? (4)

ANDERSON, Laurie
Avant-garde performance artist born in 1947 in Chicago. From 1973-75, taught Art History and Egyptian Architecture at City College of New York. Composed the score to the film *Swimming To Cambodia*.

DEBUT DATE	PEAK POS	WKS CHR	GOLD	ARTIST — Album Title	$	Label & Number
5/29/82	124	12		1 Big Science	$8	Warner 3674
3/17/84	60	19		2 Mister Heartbreak	$8	Warner 25077
1/26/85	192	5		3 United States Live [L]	$40	Warner 25192 [5]
				recorded at the Brooklyn Academy of Music in February 1983; contains 77 musical works on the theme of America		
4/26/86	145	12		4 Home Of The Brave [S]	$8	Warner 25400
11/18/89	171	12		5 Strange Angels	$8	Warner 25900

Babydoll (5)	Difficult Listening Hour (3)	Hiawatha (5)	Looking For You (3)
Bagpipe Solo (3)	Dr. Miller (3)	Hothead (La Langue	Mach 20 (3)
Beautiful Red Dress (5)	Dog Show (3)	D'Amour) (3)	Mailman's Nightmare (3)
Beginning French (3)	Dream Before (5)	I Dreamed I Had To Take A	Monkey's Paw (5)
Big Science (1,3)	English (3)	Test (3)	My Eyes (5)
Big Top (3)	Example #22 (1,3)	If You Can't Talk About It,	Neon Duet (5)
Blue Lagoon (2,3)	Excellent Birds (2)	Point To It (3)	New Jersey Turnpike (3)
Born, Never Asked (1,3)	False Documents (3)	It Tango (1,3)	New York Social Life (3)
Cartoon Song (3)	Finnish Farmers (3)	It Was Up In The Mountains	O Superman (For Massenet)
Cello Solo (3)	Fireworks (3)	(3)	(1,3)
City Song (3)	For A Large And Changing	Kokoku (2)	Odd Objects (3)
Classified (3)	Room (3)	Language Is A Virus From	Over The River (3)
Closed Circuits (3)	Four, Three, Two, One (3)	Outer Space (3,4)	Pictures Of It (3)
Coolsville (3)	Frames For The Pictures (3)	Language Of The Future (3)	Private Property (3)
Credit Racket (4)	From The Air (1,3)	Langue D'Amour (3)	Radar (4)
Curious Phenomenon (3)	Going Somewhere? (3)	Late Show (4)	Ramon (5)
Dance Of Electricity (3)	Gravity's Angel (2)	Let X=X (1,3)	Red Map (3)
Day The Devil (5)	Healing Horn (3)	Lighting Out For The	Reverb (3)
Democratic Way (3)	Hey Ah (3)	Territories (3)	Rising Sun (3)

Running Dogs (3) — Sax Duet (3) — Sax Solo (3) — Say Hello (3) — Sharkey's Day (3) — Sharkey's Night (2,4) — Small Voice (3) — Smoke Rings (4) — So Happy Birthday (3) — Song For Two Jims (3) — Steven Weed (3) — Stiff Neck (3) — Strange Angels (5) — Stranger, The (3) — Strike (3) — Sweaters (1,3) — Talk Normal (4) — Talkshow (3) — Telephone Song (3)

Three Songs For Paper, Film And Video (3) — Three Walking Songs (3) — Time And A Half (3) — Violin Solo (3) — Violin Walk (3) — Visitors, The (3) — Voices On Tape (3) — Walk The Dog (3) — Walking And Falling (1,3) — We've Got Four Big Clocks (And They're All Ticking) (3) — White Lily (4) — Yankee See (3)

ANDERSON, Lynn
Born on 9/26/47 in Grand Forks, North Dakota; raised in Sacramento. Country singer; daughter of country singer Liz Anderson. An accomplished equestrian, she was the California Horse Show Queen in 1966.

DEBUT DATE	PEAK POS	WKS CHR	GOLD	ARTIST — Album Title	$	Label & Number
4/12/69	197	2		1 With Love, From Lynn	$12	Chart 1013
5/3/69	180	3		2 The Best Of Lynn Anderson [G]	$12	Chart 1009
1/9/71	19	33	▲	3 Rose Garden	$8	Columbia 30411
7/24/71	99	14		4 You're My Man	$8	Columbia 30793
10/30/71	174	4		5 The World Of Lynn Anderson [E-R]	$8	Columbia 30902 [2]
				reissue of Lynn's first 2 Columbia albums from 1970		
12/4/71	132	5		6 How Can I Unlove You	$8	Columbia 30925
4/8/72	114	9		7 Cry	$8	Columbia 31316
9/9/72	160	7		8 Listen To A Country Song	$8	Columbia 31647
11/11/72	129	14		9 Lynn Anderson's Greatest Hits [G]	$8	Columbia 31641
8/11/73	179	3		10 Top Of The World	$8	Columbia 32429

Alabam' (5)	Fickle Fortune (10)	I Still Belong to You (3)	Lonely Women Make Good
All Day Sucker (5,6)	Flattery Will Get You	I Wish I Was A Little Boy	Lovers (10)
All You Add Is Love (1)	Everywhere (1)	Again (3)	Million Shades Of Blue (1)
Another Lonely Night (3)	Flower Of Love (1)	I Won't Mention It Again (7)	Never Ending Song Of Love
Ask Any Woman (1)	Flying Machine (4)	I'd Run A Mile To You (5)	(7)
Auctioneer (1)	Fool Me (8)	I'm Gonna Write A Song (4,9)	Night The Lights Went Out
Be Quiet Mind (1)	For The Good Times (3)	I'm Still Loving You (10)	In Georgia (10)
Bedtime Story (7)	Good (5)	I've Been Everywhere (2)	No Another Time (2)
Beggars Can't Be Choosers	Heavenly Sunshine (5)	If I Can't Be Your Woman (8)	No Love At All (5,9)
(2)	Hello Darlin' (5)	If I Kiss You (Will You Go	Nobody Wins (10)
Big Girls Don't Cry (2)	Help Me Make It Through	Away) (2)	Nothing Between Us (3,9)
Cotton Jenny (7)	The Night (4)	It Don't Do No Good To Be A	Only Baby That'll Walk The
Country Girl (5)	Here I Go Again (3)	Good Girl (8)	Line (1)
Cry (7,9) 71	Honey Come Back (5)	It's Only Make Believe (3)	Our House Is Not A Home
Cry, Cry Again (4)	How Can I Unlove You	Joy To The World (4)	(For It's Never Been Loved
Danny's Song (10)	(6,9) 63	Just Keep It Up (8)	In) (1)
Don't Leave The Leaving Up	Husband Hunting (5)	Kids Say The Darndest	Promises, Promises (2)
To Me (5)	I Can Spot A Cheater (4)	Things (10)	Proud Mary (4)
Don't Say Things You Don't	I Don't Want To Play House	Killing Me Softly With His	Put Your Hand In The Hand
Mean (6,9)	(3)	Song (10)	(4)
Easy Lovin' (6)	I Live To Love You (2)	Kiss Away (7)	Reason To Believe (8)
Everybody's Reaching Out	I Might As Well Be Here	Knock Three Times (4)	Ride, Ride, Ride (2)
For Someone (8)	Alone (4)	Listen To A Country Song	**Rose Garden** (3,9) 3
Fancy (5)		(8,9)	Simple Words (6)

Sing About Love (10) — Sing Me A Sad Song (2) — Snowbird (3) — Someday Soon (5) — Stand By Your Man (1) — Stay There Til I Get There (5,9) — Strangers (2) — Sunday Morning Coming Down (3) — Take Me Home, Country Roads (6) — Take Me To Your World (8) — That's What Loving You Has Meant To Me (6,8,9) — There Oughta Be A Law (2) — There's A Party Goin' On (8) — There's Never Been Anyone Like You (6) — Thing Called Love (10) — Time's Just Right (5) — Tomorrow Never Comes (5) — Tonight My Baby's Coming Home (7)

Too Many Dollars, Not Enough Sense (1) — Too Much Of You (2) — **Top Of The World** (10) 74 — True Love's A Blessing (3) — Wave By Bye To The Man (1) — We Can Make It (7) — We've Got To Get It On Again (7) — What's Made Milwaukee Famous (6) — When You Hurt Me More Than I Love You (5) — When You Say Love (7) — Wife You Save May Be Your Own (1) — Woman Lives For Love (5) — Words (5) — You're Everything (8) — **You're My Man** (4,9) 63 — You've Got A Friend (6) — Your Sweet Love Lifted Me (3)

ANDERSON, Michael
Los Angeles-based rock singer/songwriter born and raised in Grand Rapids, Michigan.

DEBUT DATE	PEAK POS	WKS CHR	GOLD	ARTIST — Album Title	$	Label & Number
8/13/88	194	2		Sound Alarm	$8	A&M 5203

I Know That You Can Stand	Little Bit O' Love	Sanctuary	Sound Alarm	Time To Go Home
I Need You	Memphis Radio	Shine A Light	Soweto Soul	Until You Loved Me

ANDERSON, BRUFORD, WAKEMAN, HOWE — see YES

DEBUT DATE	PEAK POS	WKS CHR	GOLD	ARTIST — Album Title	$	Label & Number

ANDREWS, Julie
Born Julia Welles on 10/1/35 in Walton-on-Thames, England. Noted Broadway and film actress. Starred in the acclaimed Broadway productions of *My Fair Lady* and *Camelot*. Won 1964's Best Actress Oscar for *Mary Poppins*. Won an Emmy for her TV show *The Julie Andrews Hour*.

DEBUT	PEAK	WKS		ARTIST — Album	$	Label
9/1/62	85	9		Julie And Carol at Carnegie Hall ....[L]	$20	Columbia 2240

JULIE ANDREWS & CAROL BURNETT
a musical concert performed on 6/11/62

From Russia: The Nausiev Ballet	From Switzerland: The Pratt Family	From Texas: Big "D" History Of Musical Comedy	Meantime No Mozart Tonight

Oh Dear What Can The Matter Be · You're So London

ANDREWS SISTERS, The
Patty, Maxene and LaVerne emerged from Minneapolis to become the most popular female vocal group of the entire pre-1955 era. LaVerne died on 5/8/67 (age 52). The trio appeared in many '40s movies. Also see Bing Crosby.

DEBUT	PEAK	WKS		ARTIST — Album	$	Label
10/6/73	126	9	1	The Best Of The Andrews Sisters ....[G]	$10	MCA 4024 [2]
10/13/73	167	7	2	Boogie Woogie Bugle Girls ....[K]	$8	Paramount 6075
7/13/74	137	3	3	Over Here! ....[OC]	$8	Columbia 32961

from the Broadway musical featuring Patty and Maxene; includes the following tracks by members of the cast: "Beat Begins (Overture)," "Don't Shoot The Hooey To Me, Louie," "Dream Drummin'/Soft Music," "Hey Yvette/The Grass Grows Green," "My Dream For Tomorrow," "Since You're Not Around" and "Wait For Me, Marlena"

| 7/20/74 | 198 | 1 | 4 | In The Mood ....[K] | $8 | Paramount 1023 [2] |

Beat Me Daddy, Eight To The Bar (1,2,4)	Charlie's Place (3)	Hawaiian Wedding Song (4)	Nobody's Darling' But Mine (4)	Rhumboogie (1,2,4)	Three Little Fishes (Itty Bitty Poo) (2,4)
Beer Barrel Polka (1,4)	Ciribiribin (4)	Hold Tight (Sea Food) (1,2)	Oh Johnny, Oh Johnny, Oh! (1,2)	Rum And Coca-Cola (1,2)	Ti-Pi-Tin (1)
Bei Mir Bist Du Schoen (1,2,4)	Cool Water (4)	I Can Dream, Can't I? (1,4)	Oh! Ma-Ma! (The Butcher Boy) (1,4)	Sabre Dance (4)	Tico-Tico (1)
Big Beat (3)	Daddy (2)	I Wanna Be Loved (1,4)	Old Piano Roll Blues (2,4)	Say "Si Si" (1,4)	Wartime Wedding (3)
Blue Hawaii (4)	Dixie (4)	I'll Be With You In Apple Blossom Time (1,4)	Over Here! (3)	Sonny Boy (1)	We Got It! (3)
Boogie Woogie Bugle Boy (1,2,4)	Don't Sit Under The Apple Tree (With Anyone Else But Me) (1,2)	In The Mood (2,4)	Pennsylvania Polka (1,2,4)	South American Way (1)	Well All Right (1)
Buy A Victory Bond (3)	Down In The Valley (4)	Joseph! Joseph! (1)	Pistol Packin' Mama (2,4)	Strip Polka (4)	Where Did The Good Times Go? (3)
	Good Time Girl (3)	Near You (4)		Tennessee Waltz (4)	Yes, My Darling Daughter (1)
		No Goodbyes (3)		There Will Never Be Another You (1)	

ANGEL
East Coast heavy-metal quintet featuring Frank DiMino (vocals), Punky Meadows (guitar) and Gregg Giuffria (keyboards; member of Giuffria and House Of Lords).

DEBUT	PEAK	WKS		ARTIST — Album	$	Label
12/20/75+	156	6	1	Angel	$15	Casablanca 7021
6/19/76	155	10	2	Helluva Band	$8	Casablanca 7028
3/5/77	76	12	3	On Earth As It Is In Heaven	$8	Casablanca 7043
2/4/78	55	13	4	White Hot	$8	Casablanca 7085
3/3/79	159	5	5	Sinful	$8	Casablanca 7127
2/23/80	149	4	6	Live Without A Net ....[L]	$20	Casablanca 7203 [2]

Ain't Gonna Eat Out My Heart Anymore (4) **44**	Cast The First Stone (3)	Fortune, The (2)	Just A Dream (3)	Over And Over (4,6)	20th Century Foxes (6)
All The Young Dudes (6)	Chicken Soup (2)	Got Love If You Want It (4,6)	Just Can't Take It (5)	Pressure Point (2)	Under Suspicion (4)
Angel (Theme) (1,2)	Dr. Ice (2)	Hold Me, Squeeze Me (4,6)	L.A. Lady (5)	Rock & Rollers (1,6)	Waited A Long Time (5)
Anyway You Want It (2,6)	Don't Leave Me Lonely (4,6)	I Ain't Gonna Eat Out My Heart Anymore (4)	Long Time (1)	She's A Mover (3)	White Lightning (3,6)
Bad Time (5)	Don't Take Your Love (5)	I'll Bring The Whole World To Your Door (5)	Lovers Live On (5)	Stick Like Glue (4)	Wild And Hot (5,6)
Big Boy (Let's Do It Again) (3)	Feelin' Right (2,6)	I'll Never Fall In Love Again (5)	Mariner (1)	Sunday Morning (1)	Winter Song (4)
Broken Dreams (1)	Feelings (2)	On & On (1)	Mirrors (2)	Telephone Exchange (3,6)	You Can't Buy Love (5)
Can You Feel It (3,6)	Flying With Broken Wings (Without You) (4)	On The Rocks (3,6)		**That Magic Touch** (3) **77**	You Could Lose Me (4)
				Tower (1,6)	You're Not Fooling Me (3)

ANGEL CITY
Australian hard-rock quintet led by vocalist Doc Neeson, formed in 1976. Changed name to Angels in 1989.

DEBUT	PEAK	WKS		ARTIST — Album	$	Label
5/10/80	152	7	1	Face To Face	$8	Epic 36344
11/8/80	133	6	2	Darkroom	$8	Epic 36543
3/20/82	174	5	3	Night Attack	$8	Epic 37702

After The Rain (1)	Comin' Down (1)	Living On The Outside (3)	No Exit (1)	Shadow Boxer (1)	Wasted Sleepless Nights (medley) (2)
Am I Ever Gonna See Your Face Again (1)	Darkroom (medley) (2)	Long Night (3)	No Secrets (1)	Storm The Bastille (3)	
Back On You (3)	Devil's Gate (2)	Marseilles (1)	Nothin To Win (3)	Straightjacket (1)	
Can't Shake It (1)	Face The Day (2)	Moment, The (2)	Out Of The Blue (1)	Take A Long Line (1)	
City Out Of Control (3)	Fashion & Fame (3)	Night Attack (3)	Poor Baby (2)	Talk About You (3)	
	Ivory Stairs (2)	Night Comes Early (2)	Runnin Wild (3)	Waiting For The World (1)	

ANGELS, The
Female pop trio from Orange, New Jersey. Formed as the Starlets with sisters Phyllis "Jiggs" & Barbara Allbut, and Linda Jansen (lead singer; replaced by Peggy Santiglia in 1962. Disbanded in 1967.

DEBUT	PEAK	WKS		ARTIST — Album	$	Label
9/28/63	33	14		My Boyfriend's Back	$50	Smash 67039

Guy With The Black Eye	He's So Fine	**My Boyfriend's Back 1**	Someday My Prince Will Come	Thank You And Goodnight 84	Why Don't The Boy Leave Me Alone
Has Anybody Seen My Boyfriend	Hurdy-Gurdy Man	Night Has A Thousand Eyes		'Til 14	World Without Love
	Love Me Now				

ANIMAL LOGIC
Drummer Stewart Copeland, bassist Stanley Clarke and singer/songwriter Deborah Holland. Copeland was a member of The Police. Clarke was with Return To Forever.

DEBUT	PEAK	WKS		ARTIST — Album	$	Label
12/9/89+	106	21		Animal Logic	$8	I.R.S. 82020

As Soon As The Sun Goes Down	Firing Up The Sunset Gun	I'm Sorry Baby (I Want You In My Life)	I'm Through With Love	Someone To Come Home To	Winds Of Santa Ana
Elijah	I Still Feel For You		Someday We'll Understand	There's A Spy (In The House Of Love)	

★★193★★   ANIMALS, The
Rock group formed in Newcastle, England in 1958 as the Alan Price Combo. Consisted of Eric Burdon (vocals), Alan Price (keyboards), Bryan "Chas" Chandler (bass), Hilton Valentine (guitar) and John Steel (drums). Price left in May 1965, replaced by Dave Rowberry. Steel left in 1966, replaced by Barry Jenkins. Group disbanded in July 1968. After a period with War, Burdon and the other originals reunited in 1983.

DEBUT	PEAK	WKS		ARTIST — Album	$	Label
9/5/64	7	27	1	The Animals	$20	MGM 4264
3/20/65	99	9	2	The Animals On Tour	$20	MGM 4281
9/18/65	57	25	3	Animal Tracks	$20	MGM 4305

DEBUT DATE	PEAK POS	WKS CHR	GOLD	ARTIST — Album Title	$	Label & Number
				ANIMALS, The — Cont'd		
2/12/66+	6	113	● 4	The Best Of The Animals ....[G]	$20	MGM 4324
8/20/66	20	30	5	Animalization	$20	MGM 4384
12/3/66+	33	22	6	Animalism	$20	MGM 4414
				ERIC BURDON & THE ANIMALS:		
3/25/67	121	13	7	Eric Is Here	$20	MGM 4433
6/10/67	71	24	8	The Best Of Eric Burdon And The Animals, Vol. II........[G]	$20	MGM 4454
9/23/67	42	20	9	Winds Of Change	$20	MGM 4484
4/6/68	79	29	10	The Twain Shall Meet	$20	MGM 4537
8/24/68	152	8	11	Every One Of Us	$20	MGM 4553
1/11/69	123	10	12	Love Is	$20	MGM 4591 [2]
3/15/69	153	6	13	The Greatest Hits Of Eric Burdon And The Animals.........[G]	$20	MGM 4602
				THE ANIMALS:		
8/25/73	188	2	14	Best Of The Animals ....[G]	$10	Abkco 4226
8/27/77	70	11	15	Before We Were So Rudely Interrupted.....................	$8	United Art. 790
9/10/83	66	10	16	Ark	$8	I.R.S. 70037
9/15/84	193	4	17	Rip It To Shreds - the Animals greatest hits live!.........[L]	$8	I.R.S. 70043

Ain't Got You (2)
All Is One (10)
All Night Long (6)
Anything (9,13) *80*
Around And Around (1,14)
As The Crow Flies (3)
As The Years Go Passing By (12)
Baby Let Me Take You Home (1,14)
Being There (16)
Biggest Bundle Of Them All (7)
Black Plague (9)
Blue Feeling (6)
Boom Boom (2,4,14,17) *43*
Bright Lights, Big City (2)
Bring It On Home To Me (3,4,14,17) *32*
Brother Bill (The Last Clean Shirt) (15)
Bury My Body (3,14)
Cheating (5,8)
Closer To The Truth (10)
Club A-GoGo (3)
Colored Rain (12)
Crystal Nights (16)

Dimples (2,14)
Don't Bring Me Down (5,8,17) *12*
Don't Let Me Be Misunderstood (3,4,14,17) *15*
Fire On The Sun (15)
For Miss Caulker (3)
Gemini - The Madman (12)
Gin House Blues (5)
Girl Can't Help It (1)
Girl Named Sandoz (8)
Going Down Slow (6)
Gonna Send You Back To Walker (Gonna Send You Back To Georgia) (1,4,14) *57*
Good Times (9)
Gotta Get Back To You (16)
Hallelujah, I Love Her So (2)
Hard Times (16)
Help Me Girl (7,8) *29*
Hey Gyp (6,8)
Hit The Road, Jack (6)
Hotel Hell (9)

House Of The Rising Sun (1,4,14,17) *1*
How You've Changed (2)
I Believe To My Soul (2)
I Can't Believe It (3)
I Put A Spell On You (5)
I Think It's Gonna Rain Today (7)
I'm An Animal (12)
I'm Crying (2,4,14,17) *19*
I'm Dying, Or Am I? (12)
I'm In Love Again (1,4,14)
I'm Mad (1,4)
I've Been Around (1)
Immigrant Lad (11)
In The Night (7)
Inside-Looking Out (5,8) *34*
It's All Meat (9)
It's All Over Now, Baby Blue (15)
It's Been A Long Time Comin' (7)
It's My Life (4,14,17) *23*
It's Not Easy (7)
It's Too Late (17)
Just A Little Bit (15)

Just Can't Get Enough (16)
Just The Thought (10)
Let The Good Times Roll (2)
Lonely Avenue (15)
Loose Change (16)
Losin' Control (7)
Louisiana Blues (6)
Love Is For All Time (16)
Lucille (6)
Mama Told Me Not To Come (7)
Man - Woman (9)
Many Rivers To Cross (15)
Maudie (5)
Melt Down (16)
Memphis, Tennessee (1)
Mess Around (2)
Monterey (10,13) *15*
My Favorite Enemy (9)
New York 1963-America 1968 (11)
Night, The (16) *48*
No Self Pity (10)
O Lucky Man! (17)
One Monkey Don't Stop No Show (5)

Orange And Red Beams (10)
Other Side Of This Life (6,8)
Outcast (6)
Paint It Black (9)
Please Send Me Someone To Love (15)
Poem By The Sea (9)
Prisoner Of The Light (16)
Right Time (1)
River Deep, Mountain High (12,13)
Riverside County (15)
Roberta (3,4)
Rock Me Baby (6)
San Franciscan Nights (9,13) *9*
See See Rider (5,8) *10*
Serenade To A Sweet Lady (11)
Shake (6)
She Said Yeah (2)
She'll Return It (5,8)
Sky Pilot (Part One) (10,13) *14*
Smoke Stack Lightning (6)

St. James Infirmary (11)
Story Of Bo Diddley (3,14)
Sweet Little Sixteen (5)
Take It Easy Baby (3)
Talkin' 'Bout You (1,14)
That Ain't Where It's At (7,8)
That's All I Am To You (6)
This Side Of Goodbye (7)
To Love Somebody (12,13)
True Love (Comes Only Once In A Lifetime) (7)
Trying To Get To You (16)
Uppers And Downers (11)
Wait Till Next Year (7)
We Gotta Get Out Of This Place (3,4,14,17) *13*
We Love You Lil (10)
What Am I Living For (5)
When I Was Young (8) *15*
White Houses (11,13) *67*
Winds Of Change (9,13)
Worried Life Blues (5)
Year Of The Guru (11,13)
Yes I Am Experienced (9)
You're On My Mind (5,8)

ANIMOTION

Techno-pop quintet led by Astrid Plane and Bill Wadhams. Four of five members replaced in 1988, including Plane and Wadhams. New vocalists: Paul Engemann (formerly of Device) and actress/dancer Cynthia Rhodes (appeared in the films *Staying Alive* and *Dirty Dancing*; married Richard Marx on 1/8/89). Plane married group's founding bassist, Charles Ottavio, on 10/13/90.

2/23/85	28	30	1	Animotion	$8	Mercury 822580
3/15/86	71	14	2	Strange Behavior	$8	Casablanca 826691
3/25/89	110	17	3	Animotion	$8	Polydor 837314

Anxiety (2)
Best Mistake (3)
Calling It Love (3) *53*
Do Like I Do (3)
Essence, The (2)

Everything's Leading To You (1)
Fun Fun Fun (1)
Ground Zero (1)
Holding You (1)

House Of Love (3)
I Engineer (2) *76*
I Want You (2) *84*
Let Him Go (1) *39*
Message Of Love (3)

Obsession (1) *6*
One Step Ahead (2)
Open Door (1)
Out Of Control (2)
Room To Move (3) *9*

Run To Me (1)
Send It Over (3)
Staring Down The Demons (2)
Stealing Time (2)

Stranded (2)
Strange Behavior (2)
Tremble (1)
Turn Around (1)
Way Into Your Heart (3)

★★205★★ ANKA, Paul

Born on 7/30/41 in Ottawa, Canada. Performer since age 12. Father financed first recording, "I Confess," on RPM 472 in 1956. Wrote "My Way" for Frank Sinatra, "She's A Lady" for Tom Jones. Also wrote theme for TV's *Tonight Show*. Own variety show in 1973. Longtime popular entertainer in Las Vegas.

7/4/60	4	140	1	Paul Anka Sings His Big 15 ....[G]	$40	ABC-Para. 323
12/5/60+	23	27	2	Anka At The Copa ....[L]	$35	ABC-Para. 353
9/25/61	72	12	3	Paul Anka Sings His Big 15, Vol. 2 ....[G]	$30	ABC-Para. 390
4/14/62	61	12	4	Young, Alive And In Love!	$25	RCA 2502
9/15/62	137	2	5	Let's Sit This One Out	$25	RCA 2575
7/6/63	65	33	6	Paul Anka's 21 Golden Hits ....[G]	$25	RCA 2691
				newly recorded versions of ABC-Paramount hits		
3/15/69	101	11	7	Goodnight My Love	$25	RCA 4142
12/27/69+	194	2	8	Life Goes On	$25	RCA 4250
1/15/72	188	4	9	Paul Anka	$8	Buddah 5093
6/3/72	192	4	10	Jubilation	$8	Buddah 5114
8/31/74	9	28	● 11	**Anka**	$8	United Art. 314
12/14/74+	125	9	12	Paul Anka Gold ....[G]	$12	Sire 3704 [2]
				original ABC-Paramount recordings		
4/5/75	36	29	13	Feelings	$8	United Art. 367
12/13/75+	22	25	● 14	Times Of Your Life ....[K]	$8	United Art. 569
				9 of 10 cuts from previous 2 United Artists albums		
10/23/76+	85	15	15	The Painter	$8	United Art. 653
6/18/77	195	3	16	The Music Man	$8	United Art. 746

DEBUT DATE	PEAK POS	WKS CHR	GOLD	ARTIST — Album Title	$	Label & Number

ANKA, Paul — Cont'd

11/25/78	179	7		17 Listen To Your Heart	$10	RCA 2892
5/9/81	171	6		18 Both Sides Of Love	$8	RCA 3926
8/13/83	156	8		19 Walk A Fine Line	$8	Columbia 38442

Adam And Eve (1,6,12) *90*
Aldous (15)
(All Of A Sudden) My Heart
Sings (1,2,12) *15*
Anchors Aweigh (2)
Anytime (I'll Be There)
(13,14) *33*
Aren't You Glad You're You?
(4)
Bring The Wine (11,14)
Brought Up In New York
(Brought Down In L.A.) (17)
Can't Get You Out Of My
Mind (8)
Cinderella (6,12) *70*
Closing Doors (15)
Crazy Love (1,6,12) *15*
Daddy's Home (7)
Dance On Little Girl
(3,6,12) *10*
Dannon (19)
Darlin', Darlin' (19)
Diana (1,2,6,12) *1*
Do I Love You (9,15) *53*
Do What You Gotta Do (8)
Don't Ever Leave Me (1,6,12)
Don't Ever Say Goodbye (17)
Don't Gamble With Love
(1,6,12)
Double Life (10)
Down By The Riverside (2)
Eleanor Rigby (8)
Embraceable You (5)
Everybody Ought To Be In
Love (16) *75*
Everything's Been Changed
(9)
Falling In Love With Love (4)
Find My Way (8)
For Once In My Life (7)
Forgive And Forget (7)

Gimme the Word (19)
Girl, You Turn Me On (13)
Golden Boy (19)
Goodnight My Love (7) *27*
Happier (15) *60*
Happy (8) *86*
Hello Young Lovers
(2,12) *23*
Hold Me 'Til The Mornin'
Comes (19) *40*
House Upon A Hill (9)
How Can Anything Be
Beautiful (After You) (11)
(I Believe) There's Nothing
Stronger Than Our Love
(13,14) *15*
I Can't Give You Anything
But Love (2)
I Don't Like To Sleep
Alone (13,14) *8*
I Gave A Little And Lost A
Lot (11)
I Love Life (4)
I Love You (4)
I Love You, Baby
(1,6,12) *97*
I Love You In The Same
Old Way (1,14) *40*
I Miss You So (1,12) *33*
I Only Have Eyes For You (5)
I Wanna Be Loved (5)
I Was There (8)
I'd Even Let You Go (18)
I'd Have To Share (3)
I'll Help You (15)
I'll See You In My Dreams (5)
I'm A Do-It-Yourself Type
Song Man (medley) (2)
I'm By Myself Again (17)

I'm Glad There Is There (In
This World Of Ordinary
People) (5)
I'm Still Waiting Here For
You (6)
I've Been Waiting For You
All Of My Life (18) *48*
I've Gotta Be Me (7)
If I Had My Life To Live Over
(16)
In The Still Of The Night
(7) *64*
It Doesn't Matter Any More
(6,11)
It Had To Be You (5)
It's Sad To See The Old
Hometown Again (13)
It's Time To Cry (1,2,12) *4*
Jealous Lady (16)
Jubilation (10) *65*
Just Young (3,12) *80*
Kathum (10)
Keeping One Foot In The
Door (8)
Kissin' On The Phone
(12) *35*
Lady Lay Down (18)
Late Last Night (3)
Les Filles De Paris (9)
Let Me Be The One (10)
Let Me Get To Know You
(11,14) *80*
Let The Bells Keep
Ringing (3,12) *16*
Let's Fall In Love (5)
Let's Sit This One Out (5)
Let's Start It Over (17)
Life Goes On (8)
Life Is Just A Bowl Of
Cherries (4)
Life Song (10)

Listen To Your Heart (17)
Living Isn't Living (15)
Lonely Boy (1,2,6,12) *1*
Longest Day (6)
Look What You've Done (18)
Love Is (10)
Love Is A Lonely Song (11)
Love Land (6)
Love Me Lady (17)
Love Your Spell Is
Everywhere (4)
Mexican Night (16)
Midnight (1,12) *69*
Music Man (16)
My Best Friend's Wife
(16) *80*
My Home Town (2,3,6,12) *8*
My Little Girl's Become A
Big Girl Now (16)
My Way (9)
Nearness Of You (5)
Never Gonna Fall In Love
Again (Like I Fell In Love
With You) (15)
Next Year (7)
No Way Out (19)
One For My Baby (And One
More For The Road) (2)
One Man Woman/One
Woman Man (11,14) *7*
Out Of My Mind In Love (13)
Painter, The (15)
Papa (11,14)
Pickin' Up The Pieces (7)
Pretty Good (10)
Puppy Love (1,6,12) *2*
Put Your Head On My
Shoulder (1,2,6,12) *2*
Roses Ain't Red (18)
Second Chance (19)
Second Thoughts (16)

She's A Lady (9)
Silhouettes (7)
Sing Sing Sing (medley) (2)
Slowdown (16)
Some Kind Of Friend (10)
Something About You (11)
Something Good Is Coming
(10)
Something Happened
(3,12) *41*
Something Has Changed Me
(3)
Starmaker (17)
Starting All Over Again (17)
Story Of My Love (3,12) *16*
Summer's Gone (3,6,12) *11*
Swanee (2)
Take Me In Your Arms (19)
Teach Me Tonight (5)
Tell It Like It Is (8)
Tell Me That You Love Me (3)
That's Love (1)
That's What Living's About
(9)
There Is Something I'd Like
To Say To You (9)
Think I'm In Love Again (18)
Think It Over Baby (2)
This Is Love (17) *35*
This Is The First Time (19)
This Life Of Mine (4)
Time To Cry (6)
Times Of Your Life (14) *7*
Today I Became A Fool (13)
Tonight (9)
Tonight My Love, Tonight
(3,6,12) *13*
Waiting For You (12)
Wake Up (13,14)
Walk A Fine Line (19)
Walk Away (13)

Water Runs Deep (13)
We Love Each Other (18)
We Made It Happen (9)
What's Forever For (18)
When I Stop Loving You
(That'll Be The Day) (3)
Why Don't We Sleep On It
Tonight (18)
Wildflower (15)
Yesterday My Life (9)
You And Me Today (10)
You And The Night And The
Music (5)
You Are My Destiny
(1,2,6,12) *7*
**(You Bring Out) The Best In
Me** (15)
You Go To My Head (5)
You Made Me Feel So Young
(4)
You Send Me (7)
You Spoiled Me (17)
(You're) Having My Baby
(11,14) *1*
You're Just In Love (4)
You're Still A Part Of Me (18)
Young, Alive, And In Love (4)
Young And Foolish (4)
Younger Than Springtime (4)
Your Love (3,12)

ANNETTE
Born Annette Funicello on 10/22/42 in Utica, New York. Became a Mouseketeer in 1955. Acted in several
teen films in the early 1960s. Co-starred with Frankie Avalon in the 1987 film *Back To The Beach*.
Revealed that she had suffered from multiple sclerosis in mid-1992.

3/21/60	21	21		1 Annette Sings Anka	$60	Buena Vista 3302
9/26/60	38	3		2 Hawaiiannette	$50	Buena Vista 3303
10/19/63	39	13		3 Annette's Beach Party [S]	$50	Buena Vista 3316

half of the songs are from the film *Beach Party*

Aloha Oe (2)
And So It's Goodbye (1)
Battle Of San Onofre (3)
Beach Party (3)
Blue Hawaii (2)
Blue Muu Muu (2)

California Sun (3)
Don't Stop Now (3)
(Every Night Is) Date Night
In Hawaii (2,3)
Hawaiiannette (2)
Hey, Mama (1)

Holiday In Hawaii (2)
Hukilau Song (2)
I Love You (1)
I Love You Baby (1)
It's Really Love (1)
Like A Baby (1)

Lonely Girl (1)
Luau Cha Cha Cha (2)
My Little Grass Shack (In
Kealakekua, Hawaii) (2)
Now Is The Hour (2)
Pineapple Princess (2,3) *11*

Promise Me Anything (3)
Secret Surfin' Spot (3)
Song Of The Islands (Na Lei
O'Hawaii) (2,3)
Surfin' Luau (3)
Swingin' Surfin' (3)

Talk To Me Baby (1) *92*
Teddy (1)
Tell Me That You Love Me (1)
Train Of Love (1) *36*
Treat Him Nicely (3)
Waiting For You (1)

ANN-MARGRET — see GARY, John, and HIRT, Al

ANOTHER BAD CREATION
Pre-teen R&B/rap vocal quintet managed and produced by Michael Bivins of Bell Biv DeVoe. Made up of
Atlanta natives: Chris Sellers, Dave Shelton, Romell Chapman, with brothers Marliss & Demetrius Pugh.

| 3/9/91 | 7 | 52 | ▲ | coolin' at the PLAYGROUND ya' know! | $12 | Motown 6318 |

A.B.C.
Iesha *9*

Jealous Girl
Little Soldiers

Mental (So Pay Attention)
Interlude

My World
Parents

Playground *10*
Spydermann

That's My Girl

ANT, Adam
Born Stuart Goddard on 11/3/54 in London. Formed romantic-punk group Adam & The Ants in 1976. Ant headed
new lineup in 1980. Original members Matthew Ashman and Dave Barbarossa founded Bow Wow Wow. Ant went
solo in 1982. Appeared in the films *World Gone Wild* and *Slam Dance*, and the TV show *The Equalizer*.

ADAM & THE ANTS:

| 2/28/81 | 44 | 35 | | 1 Kings Of The Wild Frontier | $8 | Epic 37033 |
| 12/12/81+ | 94 | 21 | | 2 Prince Charming | $8 | Epic 37615 |

ADAM ANT:

12/11/82+	16	16	●	3 Friend Or Foe	$8	Epic 38370
12/10/83	65	26		4 Strip	$8	Epic 39108
10/19/85	131	7		5 Vive Le Rock	$8	Epic 40159
3/3/90	57	20		6 Manners & Physique	$12	MCA 6315

Amazon (4)
Anger Inc. (6)
Ant Rap (2)
Antmusic (1)
Ants Invasion (1)
Apollo 9 [includes 2 versions]
(5)

Baby, Let Me Scream At You
(4)
Bright Lights Black Leather
(6)
Cajun Twisters (3)
Can't Set Rules About Love
(6)

Crackpot History And The
Right To Lie (3)
Desperate But Not Serious
(3) *66*
Dog Eat Dog (1)
Don't Be Square (Be There)
(1)
Feed Me To The Lions (1)

5 Guns West (2)
Friend Or Foe (3)
Goody Two Shoes (3) *12*
Hell's Eight Acres (5)
Hello, I Love You (3)
Here Comes The Grump (3)
Human Beings (1)
If You Keep On (6)

Jolly Roger (1)
Killer In The Home (1)
Kings Of The Wild Frontier
(1)
Libertine (4)
Los Rancheros (1)
Made Of Money (3)
Magnificent Five (1)

Man Called Marco (3)
Manners & Physique (6)
Mile High (2)
Miss Thing (5)
Mohair Lockeroom Pin-Up
Boys (5)
Montreal (4)
Mowhok (2)

36

DEBUT DATE	PEAK POS	WKS CHR	GOLD	ARTIST — Album Title	$	Label & Number

ANT, Adam — Cont'd

Navel To Neck (4)
No Zap (5)
P.O.E. (5)
Physical (You're So) (1)
Picasso Visita El Planeta De Los Simios (2)

Piccadilly (6)
Place In The Country (3)
Playboy (4)
Press Darlings (1)
Prince Charming (2)
Puss 'N Boots (4)

Razor Keen (5)
Rip Down (5)
Rough Stuff (6)
Scorpio Rising (5)
Scorpios (2)

S.E.X. (2)
Something Girls (3)
Spanish Games (4)
Stand And Deliver (2)
Strip (4) *42*
That Voodoo (2)

Try This For Sighs (3)
U.S.S.A. (6)
Vanity (4)
Vive Le Rock (5)
Young Dumb And Full Of It (6)

Room At The Top (6) *17*

ANTHONY, Ray

Big band leader/trumpeter. Born Raymond Antonini on 1/20/22 in Bentleyville, Pennsylvania and raised in Cleveland. Joined Al Donahue in 1939, then with Glenn Miller and Jimmy Dorsey from 1940-42. Led U.S. Army band. Own band in 1946. Own TV series in the '50s. Appeared in the film *Daddy Long Legs* with Fred Astaire in 1955. Wrote "Bunny Hop." Married for a time to actress Mamie Van Doren.

DEBUT DATE	PEAK POS	WKS CHR	GOLD	ARTIST — Album Title	$	Label & Number
3/19/55	10	6		1 Golden Horn ...... [I]	$12	Capitol 563
6/23/56	15	1		2 Dream Dancing ...... [I]	$12	Capitol 723
10/28/57	11	21		3 Young Ideas ...... [I]	$12	Capitol 866
5/19/58	12	10		4 The Dream Girl ...... [I]	$12	Capitol 969
7/21/62	14	19		5 Worried Mind ...... [I]	$12	Capitol 1752

Amor (1)
Bewitched (4)
Birth Of The Blues (1)
Born To Lose (5)
Brave Bulls (1)
Button Up Your Overcoat (3)
Careless Love (5)
Coquette (3)
Darn That Dream (4)
Dream Dancing (2)
Dream Girl (4)
Embraceable You (2)
Golden Horn (1)

Half As Much (8)
Holiday For Strings (1)
I Can't Stop Loving You (5)
I Didn't Know What Time It Was (4)
I Don't Know Why (I Just Do) (2)
I Fell In Love (4)
I Love You (3)
I Only Have Eyes For You (2)
I'll Never Smile Again (2)
It Ain't Necessarily So (1)

It Makes No Difference Now (5)
It's The Talk Of The Town (4)
Jeepers Creepers (1)
Just One Of Those Things (3)
Laura (2)
Lonely Night In Paris (3)
Moonglow (3)
Moonlight In Vermont (2)
My Foolish Heart (4)
My Private Melody (4)
Nearness Of You (4)

Nice Work If You Can Get It (3)
Out Of Nowhere (2)
Pretend (4)
Release Me (5)
September Song (2)
Skylark (1)
Stars Fell On Alabama (2)
Street Of Dreams (2)
Taking A Chance On Love (1)
Tango La Polma (1)
That Old Feeling (3)

This Love Of Mine (2)
Too Late To Worry - Too Late To Cry (5)
Trumpet Sorrento (1)
Trumpeter's Lullaby (1)
Walking The Floor Over You (5)
Weary Blues From Waitin' (5)
When I Fall In Love (4)
Why Do I Love You? (3)
Worried Mind (5) *74*

Wrap Your Troubles In Dreams (And Dream Your Troubles Away) (3)
You Nearly Lose Your Mind (5)
You Turned The Tables On Me (3)
You'll Never Know (4)
Young Ideas (3)
Your Cheatin' Heart (5)

ANTHRAX

New York hard-rock quintet: Joey Belladonna (vocals), Dan Spitz (guitar), Scott Ian (guitar), Frank Bello (bass) and Charlie Benante (drums). Greg D'Angelo of White Lion was an early member. Band appeared on TV's *Married...With Children* in 1992. Belladonna left in early 1992.

DEBUT DATE	PEAK POS	WKS CHR	GOLD	ARTIST — Album Title	$	Label & Number
12/21/85+	113	18		1 Spreading The Disease	$8	Island 90480
4/11/87	62	36	●	2 Among The Living	$8	Megaforce 90584
12/19/87+	53	40	●	3 I'm The Man	$8	Island 90685
				includes 3 live tracks recorded on 7/11/87 in Dallas		
10/8/88	30	36	●	4 State Of Euphoria	$8	Island 91004
9/8/90	24	31	●	5 Persistence Of Time	$12	Island 846480
7/13/91	27	25	●	6 Attack Of The Killer B's ...... [K]	$12	Megaforce 848804
				unreleased material and B-sides recorded over the past 3 1/2 years		

A.D.I. (medley) (2)
Aftershock (1)
A.I.R. (1)
Among The Living (2)
Antisocial (4)
Armed And Dangerous (1)
Be All, End All (4)
Belly Of The Beast (5,6)
Blood (5)

Bring The Noise (6)
Caught In A Mosh (2,3)
Chromatic Death (6)
Discharge (5)
Efilnikufesin (N.F.L.) (2)
Enemy, The (1)
Got The Time (5)
Gridlock (5)
Gung-Ho (1)

H8 Red (5)
Horror Of It All (medley) (2)
I Am The Law (2,3)
I'm The Man [includes 3 versions] (3)
I'm The Man '91 (6)
Imitation Of Life (2)
In My World (5)
Indians (2)

Intro To Reality (5)
Keep It In The Family (5,6)
Lone Justice (1)
Madhouse (1)
Make Me Laugh (4)
Medusa (1)
Milk (Ode To Billy) (6)
Misery Loves Company (4)
N.F.B. (Dallabnikufesin) (6)

Now It's Dark (4)
One Man Stands (5)
One World (2)
Out Of Sight, Out Of Mind (4)
Parasite (6)
Pipeline (6)
Protest And Survive (6)
S.S.C. (medley) (1)

Sabbath Bloody Sabbath (3)
Schism (4)
Sects (6)
Skeleton In The Closet (2)
Stand Or Fall (medley) (1)
Startin' Up A Posse (6)
13 (4)
Time (5)
Who Cares Wins (4)

ANVIL

Canadian heavy-metal quartet led by vocalist Lips.

DEBUT DATE	PEAK POS	WKS CHR	GOLD	ARTIST — Album Title	$	Label & Number
7/18/87	191	2		Strength Of Steel	$8	Enigma 73267

Bumble Beast
Concrete Jungle
Cut Loose

I Dreamed It Was The End Of The World
Kiss Of Death

Mad Dog
9-2-5
Paper General

Straight Between The Eyes
Strength Of Steel
Wild Eyes

AORTA

Rock quartet: Bobby Jones, Jim Donlinger, Jim Nyeholt and Billy Herman.

DEBUT DATE	PEAK POS	WKS CHR	GOLD	ARTIST — Album Title	$	Label & Number
4/12/69	167	8		Aorta	$15	Columbia 9785

Catalyptic
Heart Attack

Magic Bed
Main Vein I-IV

Ode To Missy Mztsfpklk
Sleep Tight

Sprinkle Road To Cork Street
Strange

Thoughts And Feelings (medley)

Thousand Thoughts
What's In My Mind's Eye

APOLLONIA 6

Female R&B trio formed by Prince. Led by Patty "Apollonia" Kotero (co-star of film *Purple Rain* and castmember of TV's *Falcon Crest*, 1985-86). With former Vanity 6 members Brenda Bennett and Susan Moonsie.

DEBUT DATE	PEAK POS	WKS CHR	GOLD	ARTIST — Album Title	$	Label & Number
10/27/84	62	17		Apollonia 6	$8	Warner 25108

Blue Limousine
Happy Birthday, Mr. Christian

In A Spanish Villa
Million Miles (I Love You)

Ooo She She Wa Wa
Sex Shooter *85*

Some Kind Of Lover

APOLLO 100

English studio band featuring keyboardist Tom Parker.

DEBUT DATE	PEAK POS	WKS CHR	GOLD	ARTIST — Album Title	$	Label & Number
2/19/72	47	16		Joy ...... [I]	$8	Mega 1010

Air For The G String
Classical Wind

Evil Midnight (Danse Macabre)
Exercise In A Minor

Jazz Pizzicato
Joy *6*
Libido

Mad Mountain King (Hall Of The Mountain King)

Mendelssohn's 4th (Second Movement) *94*

Reach For The Sky
Tamara

APPALOOSA

Boston folk-rock quartet led by Al Kooper.

DEBUT DATE	PEAK POS	WKS CHR	GOLD	ARTIST — Album Title	$	Label & Number
8/16/69	178	4		Appaloosa	$12	Columbia 9819

Bi-Weekly
Feathers

Georgia Street
Glossolalia

Now That I Want You
Pascal's Paradox

Rivers Run To The Sea
Rosalie

Thoughts Of Polly
Tulu Rogers

Yesterday's Roads

DEBUT DATE	PEAK POS	WKS CHR	G O L D	ARTIST — Album Title	$	Label & Number

APPICE, Carmine — see BECK, Jeff

APRIL WINE
Rock quintet from Montreal: Myles Goodwyn (lead singer, guitar), Brian Greenway (guitar), Steve Lang (bass), Gary Moffet (guitar) and Jerry Mercer (drums). Lang, Moffet and Mercer replaced by Daniel Barbe (keyboards), Jean Pellerin (bass) and Marty Simon (drums) in 1985.

DEBUT	PEAK	WKS		TITLE	$	LABEL
4/21/79	114	11		1 First Glance	$8	Capitol 11852
11/10/79	64	40	●	2 Harder...Faster	$8	Capitol 12013
1/31/81	26	34	▲	3 The Nature Of The Beast	$8	Capitol 12125
7/10/82	37	20		4 Power Play	$8	Capitol 12218
3/17/84	62	12		5 Animal Grace	$8	Capitol 12311
10/5/85	174	4		6 Walking Through Fire	$8	Capitol 12433

Ain't Got Your Love (4) / All It Will Ever Be (6) / All Over Town (3) / Anejo (6) / Anything You Want, You Got It (4) / Babes In Arms (2) / Bad Boys (3) / Before The Dawn (2) / Beg For Your Love (6) / Better Do It Well (2) / Big City Girls (3) / Blood Money (4) / Caught In The Crossfire (3) / Comin' Right Down On Top Of Me (1) / Crash And Burn (3) / Doin' It Right (4) / **Enough Is Enough** (4) **50** / Future Tense (3) / Get Ready For Love (1) / Gimme That Thing Called Love (5) / Hard Rock Kid (5) / Hold On (6) / Hot On The Wheels Of Love (1) / **I Like To Rock** (2) **86** / I'm Alive (1) / If You See Kay (4) / **Just Between You And Me** (3) **21** / Ladies Man (2) / Last Time I'll Ever Sing The Blues (1) / Let Yourself Go (1) / Love Has Remembered Me (6) / Money Talks (5) / One More Time (3) / Open Soul Surgery (6) / Right Down To It (1) / Rock Myself To Sleep (6) / Rock N' Roll Is A Vicious Game (1) / Rock Tonite (5) / **Roller** (1) **34** / Runners In The Night (4) / Say Hello (2) / **Sign Of The Gypsy Queen** (3) **57** / Silver Dollar (1) / Sons Of The Pioneers (5) / Tell Me Why (4) / Tellin' Me Lies (3) / **This Could Be The Right One** (5) **58** / Tonite (2) / Too Hot To Handle (5) / 21st Century Schizoid Man (2) / Wait Any More (6) / Waiting On A Miracle (4) / Wanna Rock (3) / Wanted Dead Or Alive (6) / What If We Fall In Love (4) / Without Your Love (5) / You Don't Have To Act That Way (6)

AQUARIAN DREAM
Disco group formed by Norman Connors, featuring singer Connie Harvey.

10/9/76	154	6		Norman Connors presents Aquarian Dream	$10	Buddah 5672

East 6th Street / Guitar Talk / I'll Always Love You "T" / Let Me Be The One / Look Ahead / Once Again / Phoenix / Treat Me Like The One You Love

AQUARIANS
Vladimir Vassilieff, piano.

11/1/69	192	2		Jungle Grass [I]	$12	United Art. 73053

Adela / Aquarians, The / Batakum / Bayu-Bayu / Excuses, Excuses / Head, The / Jungle Grass / Mucho Soul / Saja / What Do You Mean, What Do I Mean?

ARABIAN PRINCE
Rapper from Compton, California. Founding member of N.W.A. Recorded solo in 1988. Member of Bobby Jimmy & The Critters.

12/16/89	193	3		Brother Arab	$8	Orpheus 175614

Get On Up / Gettin' Down / It's A Dope Thang / It's Time To Bone / Let The Good Times Roll (Nickel Bag) / Never Caught Slippin' / Now You Have To Understand / She's Got A Big Posse / Situation Critical / Sound Check

ARBORS, The
Pop vocal group formed at the University of Michigan in Ann Arbor by two pairs of brothers: Edward and Fred Farran, and Scott and Tom Herrick.

2/11/67	144	2		A Symphony For Susan	$15	Date 3003

Day In The Life Of A Fool (Manha De Carnaval) / Dreamer Girl / Just Let It Happen / Love Is The Light / Mas Que Nada (Pow Pow Pow) / My Foolish Heart / Open A New Window / So Nice (Summer Samba) / **Symphony For Susan 51** / When I Fall In Love / You Are The Girl

ARCADIA
English group featuring Duran Duran's Simon LeBon, Nick Rhodes and Roger Taylor.

12/21/85+	23	17	▲	So Red The Rose	$8	Capitol 12428

El Diablo / **Election Day 6** / Flame, The / **Goodbye Is Forever 33** / Keep Me In The Dark / Lady Ice / Missing / Promise, The / Rose Arcana

ARC ANGELS
Texas-bred quartet led by vocalists/guitarists Charlie Sexton and Doyle Bramhall II, with Tommy Shannon (bass) and Chris Layton (drums), both formerly of Stevie Ray Vaughan's Double Trouble. Bramhall's father was a drummer with Stevie Ray and Jimmie Vaughan. Arc is an acronym for Austin Rehearsal Complex.

5/16/92	127	22		Arc Angels	$12	DGC 24465

Always Believed In You / Carry Me On / Famous Jane / Good Time / Living In A Dream / Paradise Cafe / See What Tomorrow Brings / Sent By Angels / Shape I'm In / Spanish Moon / Sweet Nadine / Too Many Ways To Fall

ARCHIES, The
Studio group created by Don Kirshner; based on the Saturday morning cartoon television series. Lead vocalist Ron Dante (b: Carmine Granito on 8/22/45 in Staten Island, New York) was also the ghost voice of The Cuff Links. All tunes written and produced by Jeff Barry who was half of a prolific hit-writing partnership with his then-wife Ellie Greenwich.

11/2/68+	88	21		1 The Archies	$20	Calendar 101
9/6/69	66	36		2 Everything's Archie	$20	Calendar 103
1/3/70	125	10		3 Jingle Jangle	$20	Kirshner 105
9/12/70	137	6		4 Sunshine	$20	Kirshner 107
11/28/70	114	12		5 The Archies Greatest Hits [G]	$20	Kirshner 109

Archie's Party (3) / Archie's Theme (Everything's Archie) (1) / **Bang-Shang-A-Lang** (1,5) **22** / Bicycles, Roller Skates And You (2) / Boys And Girls (1) / Catchin' Up On Fun (1) / Circle Of Blue (2) / Comes The Sun (4) / Dance (4) / Don't Touch My Guitar (4) / Everything's Alright (3,5) / **Feelin' So Good (S.k.o.o.b.y-D.o.o)** (2,5) **53** / Get On The Line (3,5) / Hide And Seek (1) / Hot Dog (2) / I'm In Love (1) / Inside Out - Upside Down (2) / It's The Summertime (4) / **Jingle Jangle** (3,5) **10** / Justine (3) / Kissin' (2) / La Dee Doo Down Down (1) / Look Before You Leap (3) / Love And Rock 'N Roll Music (4) / Love Light (2) / Melody Hill (2) / Mr. Factory (4) / Nursery Rhyme (3) / One Big Family (4) / Over And Over (4,5) / Ride, Ride, Ride (1) / Rock & Roll Music (2) / Senorita Rita (3) / Seventeen Ain't Young (1,5) / She's Putting Me Thru Changes (2) / Suddenly Susan (4) / **Sugar, Sugar** (2,5) **1** / Sugar And Spice (3,5) / Summer Prayer For Peace (4) / **Sunshine** (4,5) **57** / Time For Love (1) / Truck Driver (1) / Waldo P. Emerson Jones (4,5) / Who's Gonna Love Me (4) / **Who's Your Baby?** (5) **40** / Whoopee Tie Ai A (3) / You Know I Love You (3) / You Little Angel, You (2) / You Make Me Wanna Dance (1)

DEBUT DATE	PEAK POS	WKS CHR	GOLD	ARTIST — Album Title	$	Label & Number

AREA CODE 615
The 615 area code is in Tennessee. Session group which includes Charlie McCoy and Norbert Putnam.

10/18/69	191	4		Area Code 615 .... [I]	$10	Polydor 4002

Classical Gas	Hey Jude	Just Like A Woman	Nashville 9 - New York 1	Why Ask Why?
Crazy Arms (medley)	I've Been Loving You Too	Lady Madonna	Ruby	
Get Back (medley)	Long (To Stop Now)	Lil' Maggie	Southern Comfort	

ARENA BRASS
Robert Mersey, conductor of Tijuana Brass imitators.

1/5/63	130	5		The Lonely Bull .... [I]	$12	Epic 26039

Amor	Desafinado	La Bamba	La Virgen De La Macarena	Mexico	Spanish Lace
Comancheros, The	Eso Beso (That Kiss!)	La Paloma (The Dove)	Lonely Bull	Spanish Harlem	Tequila

ARGENT
British rock quartet. Consisted of ex-Zombies member Rod Argent (vocals, keyboards), Jim Rodford (bass; Argent's cousin), Robert Henrit (drums) and Russ Ballard (guitar; later a successful songwriter/producer). Rodford and Henrit were later members of The Kinks.

7/1/72	23	23		1 All Together Now	$15	Epic 31556
4/7/73	90	11		2 In Deep	$15	Epic 32195
5/4/74	149	6		3 Nexus	$15	Epic 32573
1/11/75	151	4		4 Encore-Live In Concert .... [L]	$20	Epic 33079 [2]
3/29/75	171	3		5 Circus	$15	Epic 33422

Be Glad (2)	Clown (5)	Highwire (5)	It's Only Money Part 1 & 2 (2,4)	Love (3)	Shine On Sunshine (5)
Be My Lover, Be My Friend (1)	Coming Of Kohoutek (3,4)	**Hold Your Head Up** (1,4) **5**	Jester, The (5)	Man For All Reasons (3)	Thunder And Lightning (3,4)
Candles On The River (2)	God Gave Rock And Roll To You (2,4)	I Am The Dance Of Ages (1,4)	Keep On Rollin' (1,4)	Music From The Spheres (3,4)	Time Of The Season (4)
Christmas For The Free (2)	Gonna Meet My Maker (3)	I Don't Believe In Miracles (4)	Keeper Of The Flame (3)	Once Around The Sun (3)	Tragedy (1)
Circus (5)	He's A Dynamo (1)	Infinite Wanderer (3)	Losing Hold (2)	Pure Love Medley (1)	Trapeze (5)
				Ring, The (5)	

ARMADA ORCHESTRA, The
Thirty-seven members of The London Symphony Orchestra.

1/17/76	196	2		The Armada Orchestra .... [I]	$6	Scepter 5123

Band Of Gold	Do Me Right	Feel The Need In Me	Same Old Song	You Want It You Got It
Cochise	Drifter, The	Hustle, The	Tell Me What You Want	

ARMAGEDDON
Rock quartet formed by vocalist Keith Relf (The Yardbirds, Renaissance; electrocuted on 5/14/76 [age 33]). Included Martin Pugh (guitar), Louis Cennamo (bass) and Bobby Caldwell (drums; Johnny Winter, Rick Derringer, Captain Beyond).

6/7/75	151	6		Armageddon	$15	A&M 4513

Basking In The White Of The Midnight Sun Medley	Buzzard Last Stand Before	Paths And Planes And Future Gains	Silver Tightrope

★★321★★ ARMATRADING, Joan
Born on 12/9/50 in St. Kitts, West Indies. Vocalist/pianist/guitarist/composer. To Birmingham, England in 1958. First recorded for Cube in 1971.

10/9/76+	67	27		1 Joan Armatrading	$10	A&M 4588
10/22/77	52	21		2 Show Some Emotion	$10	A&M 4663
11/11/78	125	12		3 To The Limit	$10	A&M 4732
12/8/79+	136	18		4 How Cruel .... [M]	$10	A&M 3302
6/7/80	28	23		5 Me Myself I	$10	A&M 4809
10/17/81+	88	32		6 Walk Under Ladders	$10	A&M 4876
4/30/83	32	22		7 The Key	$10	A&M 4912
1/21/84	113	10		8 Track Record .... [G]	$10	A&M 4987
3/30/85	73	19		9 Secret Secrets	$10	A&M 5040
7/5/86	68	16		10 Sleight Of Hand	$8	A&M 5130
8/20/88	100	13		11 The Shouting Stage	$8	A&M 5211
6/30/90	161	10		12 Heart And Flowers	$12	A&M 5298

All A Woman Needs (11)	Eating The Bear (6)	(I Love It When You) Call Me Names (7,8)	Love And Affection (1,8)	Reach Out (10)	Tall In The Saddle (1)
All The Way From America (5)	Everybody Gotta Know (7)	I Love My Baby (7)	Love By You (9)	Romancers (6)	Tell Tale (7)
Always (3)	Feeling In My Heart (For You) (5)	I Need You (5)	Ma-Me-O-Beach (5)	Rosie (4,8)	Temptation (9)
Am I Blue For You (3)	Figure Of Speech (10)	I Really Must Be Going (4)	Mama Mercy (2)	Russian Roulette (10)	Thinking Man (9)
Angel Man (10)	Foolish Pride (7)	I Wanna Hold You (6)	Me Myself I (5,8)	Save Me (1)	Turn Out The Light (5)
At The Hop (6)	Free (12)	I'm Lucky (6,8)	More Than One Kind Of Love (12)	Secret Secrets (9)	Warm Love (2)
Baby I (3)	Friends (5)	Is It Tomorrow Yet (5)	Moves (9)	Shouting Stage (11)	Watch Your Step (11)
Bad Habits (7)	Friends Not Lovers (9)	Jesse (9)	Never Is Too Late (2)	Show Some Emotion (2,8)	Water With The Wine (1)
Barefoot And Pregnant (3)	Fustration (8)	Join The Boys (1)	No Love (6)	Simon (5)	Weakness In Me (6,8)
Bottom To The Top (3)	Game Of Love (7)	Key, The (7)	One More Chance (10)	Somebody Who Loves You (1)	What Do Boys Dream (7)
Can't Let Go (12)	Get In The Sun (2)	Killing Time (10)	One Night (9)	Someone's In The Background (12)	What Do You Want (10)
Dark Truths (11)	Good Times (12)	Kind Words (And A Real Good Heart) (10)	Only One (6)	Something In The Air Tonight (12)	When I Get It Right (6,8)
Dealer, The (7)	He Wants Her (4)	Kissin' And A Huggin' (2)	Opportunity (2)	Straight Talk (11)	When You Kisses Me (5)
Devil I Know (11)	Hearts And Flowers (12)	Laurel And The Rose (10)	Peace In Mind (2)	Strange (9)	Willow (2,8)
Did I Make You Up (11)	Heaven (8)	Let It Last (3)	People (1)	Stronger Love (11)	Wishing (3)
Don Juan (10)	Help Yourself (1)	Like Fire (1)	Persona Grata (9)	Taking My Baby Up Town (3)	Woncha Come On Home (2)
Down To Zero (1,8)	How Cruel (4)	Living For You (11)	Power Of Dreams (12)	Talking To The Wall (9)	Words (11)
Drop The Pilot (7,8) **78**	I Can't Lie To Myself (6)		Promise Land (12)		You Rope You Tie Me (3)
					Your Letter (3)

ARMORED SAINT
Los Angeles-based rock quintet: John Bush (lead vocals), Gonzo, Joey Vera and Dave Pritchard.

12/22/84+	138	16		1 March Of The Saint	$8	Chrysalis 41476
12/7/85+	108	19		2 Delirious Nomad	$8	Chrysalis 41516
9/26/87	114	12		3 Raising Fear	$8	Chrysalis 41601

ARMORED SAINT — Cont'd

Aftermath (2)
Book Of Blood (3)
Can U Deliver (1)
Chemical Euphoria (3)
Conqueror (2)
Envy (1)
False Alarm (1)

For The Sake (2)
Frozen Will (medley) (3)
Glory Hunter (1)
Human Vulture (3)
In The Hole (2)
Isolation (3)

Laugh, The (2)
Legacy (medley) (3)
Long Before I Die (2)
Mad House (1)
March Of The Saint (1)
Mutiny On The World (1)

Nervous Man (2)
Out On A Limb (3)
Over The Edge (2)
Raising Fear (3)
Released (2)
Saturday Night Special (3)

Seducer (1)
Stricken By Fate (1)
Take A Turn (1)
Terror (3)
Underdogs (3)
You're Never Alone (2)

ARMSTRONG, Louis

Born Daniel Louis Armstrong in New Orleans on 8/4/01 (not 7/4/1900, as Armstrong claimed). Nickname: "Satchmo." Joined the legendary band of Joe "King" Oliver in Chicago in 1922. By 1929, had become the most widely known black musician in the world. Influenced dozens of singers and trumpet players, both black and white. Numerous appearances on radio, TV and in films. Won Lifetime Achievement Grammy in 1972. Died on 7/6/71 in New York. Inducted into the Rock and Roll Hall of Fame in 1990 as a forefather of rock music.

10/1/55	10	2		1 Satch Plays Fats	$40	Columbia 708
				LOUIS ARMSTRONG and his All-Stars — a tribute to Fats Waller		
12/15/56	12	2		2 Ella And Louis	$50	Verve 4003
				ELLA FITZGERALD and LOUIS ARMSTRONG — backing by the Oscar Peterson Trio, plus Buddy Rich		
5/16/64	1[6]	74	●	3 Hello, Dolly!	$15	Kapp 3364

Ain't Misbehavin' (1)
All That Meat And No Potatoes (1)
April In Paris (2)
Be My Life's Companion (1)
Blue Turning Grey Over You (1)
Blueberry Hill (3)

Can't We Be Friends (2)
Cheek To Cheek (2)
Foggy Day (2)
Hello, Dolly! (3) 1
Hey, Look Me Over (3)
Honeysuckle Rose (1)
I Still Get Jealous (3) 45

I'm Crazy 'Bout My Baby (1)
And My Baby's Crazy 'Bout Me (1)
I've Got A Feeling I'm Falling (1)
Isn't This A Lovely Day (2)
It's Been A Long, Long Time (3)

Jeepers Creepers (3)
Keepin' Out Of Mischief Now (1)
Kiss To Build A Dream On (3)
Lot Of Livin' To Do (3)
Moon River (2)
Moonlight In Vermont (2)

Nearness Of You (2)
Someday (3)
Squeeze Me (1)
Stars Fell On Alabama (2)
Tenderly (2)
They Can't Take That Away From Me (2)
Under A Blanket Of Blue (2)

(What Did I Do To Be So) Black And Blue (1)
You Are Woman, I Am Man (3)

★★190★★ ARNOLD, Eddy

Born Richard Edward Arnold on 5/15/18 near Henderson, Tennessee. Ranked as the #1 artist in *Joel Whitburn's Top Country Singles 1944-1988* book. Became popular on Nashville's *Grand Ole Opry* as a singer with Pee Wee King (1940-43). Nicknamed "The Tennessee Plowboy" on all RCA recordings through 1954. Elected to the Country Music Hall of Fame in 1966. CMA award: Entertainer of the Year - 1967.

10/26/63	131	5		1 Cattle Call	$20	RCA 2578
10/16/65+	7	58	●	2 My World	$15	RCA 3466
3/26/66	26	28		3 I Want To Go With You	$15	RCA 3507
7/30/66	46	22		4 The Last Word In Lonesome	$15	RCA 3622
12/24/66+	36	30		5 Somebody Like Me	$15	RCA 3715
3/18/67	57	24		6 Lonely Again	$15	RCA 3753
5/6/67	34	57	●	7 The Best Of Eddy Arnold .... [G]	$15	RCA 3565
10/7/67	34	36		8 Turn The World Around	$15	RCA 3869
2/24/68	122	21		9 The Everlovin' World Of Eddy Arnold	$15	RCA 3931
6/15/68	56	32		10 The Romantic World Of Eddy Arnold	$15	RCA 4009
11/9/68	70	13		11 Walkin' In Love Land	$15	RCA 4089
3/8/69	77	13		12 Songs Of The Young World	$15	RCA 4110
7/5/69	167	5		13 The Glory Of Love	$15	RCA 4179
11/1/69	116	8		14 The Warmth Of Eddy	$15	RCA 4231
5/2/70	191	3		15 Love & Guitars	$12	RCA 4304
5/30/70	146	2		16 The Best Of Eddy Arnold, Volume II .... [G]	$12	RCA 4320
3/13/71	141	4		17 Portrait Of My Woman	$12	RCA 4471

After Losing You (3)
After The Laughter (Comes The Tears) (4)
All I Have To Do Is Dream (11)
All The Time (9,16)
Am I That Easy To Forget (10)
Anything That's Part Of You (17)
Anytime (7)
Apples, Raisins And Roses (11)
As Long As I Love (13)
As Usual (2)
At Sunset (5)
Baby (6)
Baby I Will (17)
Baby That's Living (9)
Band Of Gold (14)
Bear With Me A Little Longer (6)
Boquet Of Roses (7)
But For Love (13)
By The Time I Get To Phoenix (10)
Can't Take My Eyes Off You (10)
Carry Me Back To The Lone Prairie (1)
Castle Made Of Walls (9)
Cattle Call (1,7) 42
Come By Me Nice And Slow (5)

Come Live With Me And Be My Love (3)
Cool Water (1)
Cowboy's Dream (1)
Cowpoke (1)
Cycles (14)
Days Gone By (2)
Dear Heart (9)
Did It Rain (6)
Don't Forget I Still Love You (3)
Don't Keep Me Lonely Too Long (8)
Don't Laugh At My Love (5)
Don't Touch Me (4)
Ev'ry Step Of The Way (5)
Evergreen (10)
Faithfully (13)
Forty Shades Of Green (1)
From This Minute On (10)
Gentle On My Mind (10)
Glory Of Love (13)
Good Woman's Love (3)
Good-bye Sunshine (3)
He's Got You (6)
Heaven Below (13)
Heaven Everyday (17)
Here Comes Heaven (9) 91
Here Comes My Baby (4)
Honey (10)
How Is She (9)
I Get Baby On My Mind (12)
I Guess I'll Never Understand (8)

I Just Can't Help Believin' (15)
I Love How You Love Me (12)
I Love You Drops (5)
I Really Don't Want To Know (7,17)
I Really Go For You (10)
I Started A Joke (14)
I Want To Go With You (3,7) 36
I Was Born To Love You (17)
I'll Always Be In Love With You (3)
I'll Give You Three Guesses (15)
I'll Hold You In My Heart (7)
I'll Love You More (8)
I'll Never Smile Again (11)
I'm In Love With You (12)
I'm Letting You Go (2)
I'm Walking Behind You (2)
If You Were Mine, Mary (2)
In The Misty Moonlight (9)
It Ain't No Big Thing (17)
It Comes And Goes (2)
It's Only Love (5)
It's Over (10,16) 74
It's Such A Pretty World Today (8,16)
(Jim) I Wore A Tie Today (1)
Just A Bend In The Road (13)
Just A Little Lovin' (Will Go A Long Way) (7)

Just Across The Mountain (11)
Just Enough To Start Me Dreamin (15)
Last Word In Lonesome Is Me (4,7) 40
Lay Some Happiness On Me (5)
Leanin' On The Old Top Rail (1)
Leaving On A Jet Plane (15)
Little Girls And Little Boys (11)
Little Green Apples (12)
Lonely Again (6,16) 87
Long, Long Friendship (4)
Love Finds A Way (8)
Love Me Like That (3)
Love On My Mind (17)
Make The World Go Away (2,7) 6
Man's Kind Of Woman (15)
Mary Claire Melvina Rebecca Jane (2)
Mary In The Morning (15)
Mary Who (6)
Meet Me At The Altar (6)
Millions Of Roses (4)
Misty Blue (4,16) 57
My Dream (11)
My Home Town Sweetheart (4)
My Way (14)

No Matter Whose Baby You Are (10)
Nobody's Darling But Mine (6)
Nothing But Time (9)
Oh So Far From Home (6)
Ole Faithful (1)
Olive Tree (11)
One Kiss For Old Times' Sake (3)
Other Side Of Lonely (4)
Pardon Me (3)
Please Don't Go (13)
Portrait Of My Woman (17)
Release Me (And Let Me Love Again) (8,16)
San Francisco Is A Lonely Town (14)
Secret Love (9)
Shadows Of Her Mind (15)
She's Everywhere (17)
Sierra Sue (1)
Since You've Been Loving Me (12)
Somebody Like Me (5,16) 5
Somebody Loves You (3)
Song For Shara (9)
Song Of Long Ago (13)
Soul Deep (15)
Streets Of Laredo (1)
Suddenly My Thoughts Are All Of You (12)
Summer Wind (11)

Sunny (9)
Sunshine Belongs To Me (12)
Sweet Bird Of Youth (13)
Sweet Marilyn (12)
Take A Little Time (12)
Taking Chances (2)
Tender Is Her Name (12)
Tennessee Stud (16) 48
That's A Lie (4)
That's All I Want From You (6)
That's All That's Left Of My Baby (8)
That's How Much I Love You (7)
Then I'll Be Over You (14)
Then She's A Lover (13)
Then You Can Tell Me Goodbye (11,16) 84
There You Go (9)
There's Always Me (5)
There's This About You (8)
They Don't Make Love Like They Used To (12) 99
Thing Called Sadness (4)
Tip Of My Fingers (5,16) 43
To Sleep With You (14)
(Today) I Started Loving You Again (15)
Too Many Rivers (2)
Town And Country (13)
Tumbling Tumbleweeds (1)
Turn Around, Look At Me (11)

ARNOLD, Eddy — Cont'd

Turn The World Around (8,16) **66**	What A Wonderful World (10)	When The Wind Blows (In Chicago) (15)	Why (4)	You Don't Need Me Anymore (14)	You Still Got A Hold On Me (2)
Until It's Time For You To Go (11)	What Have I Done For Her Lately (14)	When There's A Fire In Your Heart (8)	Wichita Lineman (12)	You Fool (14)	You'd Better Stop Tellin' Lies (About Me) (3)
Wait For Sunday (17)	What Now My Love (10)	When Your World Stops Turning (6)	With Pen In Hand (15)	You Gave Me A Mountain (13,16)	
Walk With Me (8)	**What's He Doing In My World** (2,7) **60**	Where The Mountains Meet The Sky (1)	World I Used To Know (9)	You Made Up For Everything (5)	
Walkin' In Love Land (11)	Wheel Of Hurt (6)		Yesterday, When I Was Young (14)		
Wayward Wind (1)			You Don't Know Me (7)		

ARPEGGIO
Black disco quartet.

2/10/79	75	16		Let The Music Play	$8	Polydor 6180

| Let The Music Play Medley | **Love And Desire (Part I)** 70 | Runaway | Spellbound |

ARRESTED DEVELOPMENT
Coed rap outfit from Georgia led by Milwaukee-born Todd "Speech" Thomas. Includes his cousin Aerlee Taree (pronounced Early Ta-Ree), Tim "Headliner" Barnwell, Montsho Eshe, Rasa Don and Baba Oje.

4/18/92	13	43↑ ▲²		3 Years 5 Months & 2 Days In The Life Of	$12	Chrysalis 21929

title refers to the length of time between group's formation and the signing of its recording contract

Blues Happy	Eve Of Reality	Mama's Always On Stage	Natural	**Tennessee** 6
Children Play With Earth	Fishin' 4 Religion	Man's Final Frontier	**People Everyday** 8	U
Dawn Of The Dreads	Give A Man A Fish	**Mr. Wendal** 10↑	Raining Revolution	Washed Away

ARRINGTON, Steve
R&B vocalist/drummer from Dayton, Ohio. Ex-member of Slave.

3/12/83	101	17		1 Steve Arrington's Hall Of Fame: I	$8	Atlantic 80049
2/25/84	141	9		2 Positive Power	$8	Atlantic 80127

above 2: **STEVE ARRINGTON'S Hall Of Fame**

5/18/85	185	5		3 Dancin' In The Key Of Life	$8	Atlantic 81245

Beddie-Biey (1)	15 Rounds (2)	Money On It (2)	Stand With Me (3)	Weak At The Knees (1)	Young And Ready (2)
Brown Baby Boy (3)	Gasoline (3)	Nobody Can Be You (1)	Strange (Soft & Hard) (1)	What Do You Want From Me (2)	
Dancin' In The Key Of Life (3) 68	Hump To The Bump (2)	Positive Power (2)	Sugar Momma Baby (2)	Willie Mae (3)	
Feel So Real (3)	Last Nite/Nite Before (1)	She Just Don't Know (3)	Turn Up Love (3)	You Meet My Approval (1)	
	Mellow As A Cello (2)	Speak With Your Body (1)	Way Out (1)		

ARROWS, The — see ALLAN, Davie

ART IN AMERICA
Family trio: Chris, Dan and Shishonee Flynn.

3/26/83	176	3		Art In America	$8	Pavillion 38517

| Art In America | If I Could Fly | Loot | Too Shy To Say | Won't It Be Strange |
| Brett & Hibby | Line, The | Sinatra Serenade | Undercover Lover | |

ARTISTS UNITED AGAINST APARTHEID
Benefit group of 49 superstar artists formed to protest the South African apartheid government; proceeds went to political prisoners in South Africa. Organized by Little Steven and Arthur Baker. Featuring Pat Benatar, Bono (U2), Jackson Browne, Jimmy Cliff, Bob Dylan, Peter Gabriel, Bonnie Raitt, Lou Reed, Bruce Springsteen and many others.

11/23/85	31	18		Sun City	$8	Manhattan 53019

| Let Me See Your I.D. | No More Apartheid | Revolutionary Situation | Silver And Gold | Struggle Continues | **Sun City** [2 versions] 38 |

ART OF NOISE, The
British techno-pop trio: Anne Dudley (keyboards), J.J. Jeczalik (keyboards, programmer) and Gary Langan (engineer). All three were part of Trevor Horn's production team in the early 1980s. Worked with ABC, Frankie Goes To Hollywood and others. Disbanded in mid-1990.

7/14/84	85	13		1 (Who's Afraid Of?) The Art Of Noise!	$8	Island 90179
5/3/86	53	30		2 In Visible Silence	$8	Chrysalis 41528
10/17/87	134	9		3 In-No-Sense? Nonsense!	$8	Chrysalis 41570
12/17/88+	83	14		4 The Best Of The Art Of Noise [G]	$8	China 837367

Backbeat (2)	Crusoe (3)	Galleons Of Stone (3)	Moments In Love (3)	**Peter Gunn** (2,4) 50	Something Always Happens (4)
Beat Box (Diversion One) (1,4)	Day At The Races (3)	How Rapid? (3)	Nothing Was Going To Stop Them Then, Anyway (3)	Ransom On The Sand (3)	Time For Fear (Who's Afraid) (1)
Beatback (2)	Debut (3)	How To Kill (1)	Ode To Don Jose (3)	Realization (1)	Who's Afraid (Of The Art Of Noise) (1)
Camilla (2)	Dragnet (3)	Instruments Of Darkness (2)	One Earth (3)	Roller 1 (3)	
Chameleon's Dish (2)	Dragnet '88 (4)	**Kiss** (4) 31	Opus 4 (2,4)	Roundabout 727 (3)	
Close (To The Edit) (1,4)	E.F.L. (3)	Legacy (4)	Opus For Four (3)	Slip Of A Tongue (2)	
Counterpoint (3)	Eye Of A Needle (2)	Legs (2)	**Paranoimia** (2,4) 34	Snapshot (1)	
	Fin Du Temps (3)	Momento (1)			

A's, The
Philadelphia-area rock quintet — Richard Bush, lead vocals.

7/11/81	146	7		A Woman's Got The Power	$8	Arista 9554

| Electricity | How Do You Live | Insomnia | Little Mistakes | When The Rebel Comes Home | Woman's Got The Power |
| Heart Of America | I Pretend She's You | Johnny Silent | | | Working Man |

ASH, Daniel
British guitarist/singer/songwriter. Founding member of Bauhaus and Love And Rockets.

3/9/91	109	10		Coming Down	$12	Begr. B. 3014

| Blue Angel | Candy Darling | Coming Down | Day Tripper | Not So Fast | This Love |
| Blue Moon | Closer To You | Coming Down Fast | Me And My Shadow | Sweet Little Liar | Walk This Way |

★★304★★ ASHFORD & SIMPSON
Husband-and-wife R&B vocal/songwriting duo: Nickolas Ashford (b: 5/4/42, Fairfield, South Carolina) and Valerie Simpson (b: 8/26/46, New York City). Team wrote for Chuck Jackson and Maxine Brown. Joined staff at Motown and wrote and produced for many of the label's top stars. Valerie recorded solo in 1972. They married in 1974. Valerie's brother, Ray Simpson, was the lead singer of Village People.

11/10/73+	156	13		1 Gimme Something Real	$8	Warner 2739
7/20/74	195	4		2 I Wanna Be Selfish	$8	Warner 2789

DEBUT DATE	PEAK POS	WKS CHR	GOLD	ARTIST — Album Title	$	Label & Number

ASHFORD & SIMPSON — Cont'd

DEBUT DATE	PEAK POS	WKS CHR	GOLD	#	Album Title	$	Label & Number
5/8/76	189	4		3	Come As You Are	$8	Warner 2858
2/5/77	180	3		4	So So Satisfied	$8	Warner 2992
10/15/77	52	46	●	5	Send It	$8	Warner 3088
9/9/78	20	28	●	6	Is It Still Good To Ya	$8	Warner 3219
9/1/79	23	23	●	7	Stay Free	$8	Warner 3357
8/23/80	38	12		8	A Musical Affair	$8	Warner 3458
10/17/81	125	6		9	Performance [L]	$10	Warner 3524 [2]
					3 of 4 sides recorded live		
5/29/82	45	20		10	Street Opera	$8	Capitol 12207
9/17/83	84	12		11	High-Rise	$8	Capitol 12282
11/10/84+	29	36		12	Solid	$8	Capitol 12366
9/6/86	74	18		13	Real Love	$8	Capitol 12469
3/18/89	135	8		14	Love Or Physical	$8	Capitol 46946

Ain't It A Shame (6)
Ain't No Mountain High Enough (medley) (9)
Ain't Nothin' But A Maybe (2)
Ain't Nothing Like The Real Thing (medley) (9)
Ain't That Good Enough (1)
Ain't That Somethin' (2)
As Long As It Holds You (6)
Babies (12)
Believe In Me (3)
Bend Me (1)
Boss, The (medley) (9)
Bourgie Bourgie (5,9)
By Way Of Love's Express (5)
Can You Make It Brother (1)
Caretaker (3)
Cherish Forever More (12)
Closest To Love (12)
Clouds (medley) (9)
Come On, Pretty Baby (9)
Comes With The Package (14)

Cookies And Cake (14)
Couldn't Get Enough (4)
Count Your Blessings (13) *84*
Crazy (7)
Dance Forever (7)
Debt Is Settled (6)
Destiny (4)
Don't Cost You Nothing (5,9) *79*
Don't Fight It (2)
Everybody's Got To Give It Up (2)
Experience (Love Had No Face) (11)
Finally Got To Me (7)
Flashback (6)
Follow Your Heart (7)
Found A Cure (7,9) *36*
Get Out Your Handkerchief (8)
Get Up And Do Something (6)

Gimme Something Real (1,9)
Happy Endings (8)
Have You Ever Tried It (1)
High-Rise (11)
Honey I Love You (12)
How Does It Fit (13)
I Ain't Asking For Your Love (8)
I Had A Love (2)
I Need Your Light (1,9)
I Waited Too Long (5)
I Wanna Be Selfish (2)
(I'd Know You) Anywhere (1) *88*
I'll Be There For You (14)
I'll Take The Whole World On (10)
I'm Determined (1)
I'm Not That Tough (11)
If You're Lying (4)
In Your Arms (14)
Is It Still Good To Ya (6,9)
It Came To Me (3)

It Seems To Hang On (6,9)
It Shows In The Eyes (9)
It'll Come, It'll Come, It'll Come (3)
It's A Rush (11)
It's Much Deeper (11)
It's The Long Run (9)
It's You (4)
Jungle, The (12)
Landlord (medley) (9)
Let Love Use Me (5)
Love Don't Make It Right (8,9)
Love It Away (10)
Love Or Physical (14)
Main Line (2)
Make It To The Sky (9)
Make It Work Again (10)
Maybe I Can Find It (4)
Mighty Mighty Love (10)
My Kinda Pick Me Up (11)
Nobody Knows (7,9)
Nobody Walks In L.A. (13)

One More Try (3)
Outta The World (12)
Over And Over (4)
Over To Where You Are (2)
Real Love (13)
Relations (13)
Rushing To (8)
Sell The House (3)
Send It (5)
Side Effect (11)
So So Satisfied (4)
Solid (12) *12*
Somebody Told A Lie (3)
Something To You (14)
Spoiled (2)
Stay Free (7)
Still Such A Thing (11)
Street Corner (10) *56*
Take All The Time You Need (2)
Tell It All (3)
10th Round (13)
Til We Get It Right (14)

Time (1)
Times Will Be Good Again (10)
Timing (14)
Tonight We Escape (We Make Love) (12)
Too Bad (5)
Top Of The Stairs (5)
Tried, Tested And Found True (4)
Way Ahead (13)
We'll Meet Again (8)
What Becomes Of Love (13)
Who Will They Look To (10)
Working Man (10)
You Always Could (6)
You Never Left Me Alone (8)
You're All I Need (medley) (9)

ASHTON, GARDNER & DYKE

British pop trio: Tony Ashton, Kim Gardner and Roy Dyke. Keyboardist Ashton and drummer Dyke later joined Medicine Head.

DEBUT DATE	PEAK POS	WKS CHR	#	Album Title	$	Label & Number
8/7/71	185	6		Resurrection Shuffle	$10	Capitol 563

Don't Want No War No More
Hymn To Everyone

I'm Your Spiritual Breadman
Let It Roll

Mister Freako
Momma's Getting Married

Oh Lord
Paper Head, Paper Mind

Resurrection Shuffle *40*
Sweet Patti O'Hara Smith

ASIA

British rock supergroup: guitarist Steve Howe (Yes), drummer Carl Palmer (Emerson, Lake & Palmer, Atomic Rooster), keyboardist Geoff Downes (Buggles, Yes) and vocalist/bassist John Wetton (King Crimson, Uriah Heep, U.K.). Howe replaced by Mandy Meyer (Krokus) in 1985. Meyer replaced in 1990 by Oakland, California native Pat Thrall (Automatic Man, Pat Travers Band).

DEBUT DATE	PEAK POS	WKS CHR	GOLD	#	Album Title	$	Label & Number
4/3/82	1⁹	64	▲³	1	Asia	$8	Geffen 2008
8/27/83	6	25	▲	2	Alpha	$8	Geffen 4008
12/7/85	67	17		3	Astra	$8	Geffen 24072
9/1/90	114	10		4	Then & Now [G]	$12	Geffen 24298
					side a: greatest hits; side b: new tracks		

After The War (3)
Am I In Love? (4)
Countdown To Zero (3)
Cutting It Fine (1)
Days Like These (4) *64*
Don't Cry (2,4) *10*

Eye To Eye (2)
Go (3) *46*
Hard On Me (3)
Heat Goes On (2)
Heat Of The Moment (1,4) *4*
Here Comes The Feeling (1)

Last To Know (2)
Love Now Till Eternity (3)
Midnight Sun (2)
My Own Time (I'll Do What I Want) (2)
Never In A Million Years (2)

One Step Closer (1)
Only Time Will Tell (1,4) *17*
Open Your Eyes (2)
Prayin' 4 A Miracle (3)
Rock And Roll Dream (3)

Smile Has Left Your Eyes (2,4) *34*
Sole Survivor (1)
Summer (Can't Last Too Long) (4)
Suspicion (3)

Time Again (1)
Too Late (3)
True Colors (2)
Voice Of America (3,4)
Wildest Dreams (1,4)
Wishing (3)
Without You (1)

ASLEEP AT THE WHEEL

Austin-based western swing band formed in Paw Paw, West Virginia by Ray Benson (vocals, guitar).

DEBUT DATE	PEAK POS	WKS CHR	#	Album Title	$	Label & Number
9/20/75	136	8	1	Texas Gold	$12	Capitol 11441
9/18/76	179	3	2	Wheelin' And Dealin'	$12	Capitol 11546
4/16/77	162	4	3	The Wheel	$12	Capitol 11620
9/6/80	191	2	4	Framed	$8	MCA 5131

Am I High? (3)
Blues For Dixie (2)
Bump Bounce Boogie (1)
Cajun Stripper (2)
Cool As A Breeze (4)
Dollar Short & A Day Late (3)
Don't Get Caught Out In The Rain (4)
Fat Boy Rag (1)

Fiddle Funk - Corn Fusion (4)
I Can't Handle It Now (3)
I Wonder (3)
If I Can't Love You (2)
Let Me Go Home Whiskey (1)
Let's Face Up (3)
Letter That Johnny Walker Read (1)

Lonely Avenue Revisited (4)
Lost Mind (2)
Midnight In Memphis (3)
Miles And Miles Of Texas (4)
Musical Talk (4)
My Baby Thinks She's A Train (3)
Nothin' Takes The Place Of You (1)

Ragtime Annie (3)
Red Stick (3)
Roll 'Em Floyd (1)
Route 66 (2)
Runnin' After Fools (1)
Shout Wa Hey (2)
Slow Dancing (4)
Somebody Stole His Body (3)
They Raided The Joint (2)

Tonight The Bartender Is On Wheel, The (3)
The Wrong Side Of The Bar (1)
Trouble In Mind (1)
Trouble With Lovin' Today (2)
Up, Up, Up (4)
We've Gone As Far As We Can Go (2)
Whatever It Takes (4)

When Love Goes Wrong (3)
Where No One Stands Alone (1)
You Wanna Give Me A Lift (4)

★★320★★ ASSOCIATION, The

Group formed in Los Angeles in 1965. Consisted of Terry Kirkman (plays 23 wind, reed and percussion instruments), Gary "Jules" Alexander (guitar), Brian Cole (bass), Jim Yester (guitar), Ted Bluechel, Jr. (drums) and Russ Giguere (percussion). Larry Ramos, Jr. joined in early 1968. Richard Thompson (keyboards) replaced Giguere in 1970. Cole on 8/2/72 of a heroin overdose. Thompson replaced by Rick Ulsky in 1974. Regrouped with original surviving members on 9/26/80.

DEBUT DATE	PEAK POS	WKS CHR	GOLD	#	Album Title	$	Label & Number
8/20/66	5	59	●	1	And Then...Along Comes The Association	$15	Valiant 5002
1/7/67	34	15		2	Renaissance	$15	Valiant 5004

DEBUT DATE	PEAK POS	WKS CHR	GOLD	ARTIST — Album Title	$	Label & Number

ASSOCIATION, The — Cont'd

DEBUT DATE	PEAK POS	WKS CHR	GOLD	ARTIST — Album Title	$	Label & Number
7/22/67	**8**	68	●	3 Insight Out	$10	Warner 1696
5/4/68	**23**	26		4 Birthday	$10	Warner 1733
12/28/68+	**4**	75	▲²	5 Greatest Hits ....[G]	$10	Warner 1767
5/10/69	**99**	18		6 Goodbye, Columbus ....[S]	$10	Warner 1786

includes 6 instrumentals by Charles Fox: "Dartmouth? Dartmouth!!," "How Will I Know You?," "Love Has A Way," "A Moment To Share," "Ron's Reverie Medley" and "A Time For Love"

DEBUT DATE	PEAK POS	WKS CHR	GOLD	ARTIST — Album Title	$	Label & Number
10/4/69	**32**	17		7 The Association	$10	Warner 1800
7/18/70	**79**	12		8 The Association "Live" ....[L]	$12	Warner 1868 [2]
8/14/71	**158**	4		9 Stop Your Motor	$10	Warner 1927
5/20/72	**194**	5		10 Waterbeds In Trinidad!	$10	Columbia 31348

All Is Mine (2)
Along Comes Mary (1,5,8) 7
Along The Way (9)
Angeline (2)
Another Time, Another Place (2)
Are You Ready (7,8)
Babe, I'm Gonna Leave You (8)
Barefoot Gentleman (4)
Birthday Morning (4)
Blistered (1,8)
Boy On The Mountain (7)
Bring Yourself Home (9)
Broccoli (7)
Bus Song (4)
Changes (1)

Cherish (1,5,8) 1
Come On In (4)
Come The Fall (10)
Come To Me (2)
Darling Be Home Soon (10)
Don't Blame It On Me (1)
Dream Girl (Dressing Room) (8)
Dubuque Blues (7,8)
Enter The Young (1,5,8)
Everything That Touches You (4,5) 10
First Sound (9)
Funny Kind Of Song (9)
Goodbye Columbus (6,8) 80
Goodbye Forever (7,8)
Happiness (3)

Hear In Here (4)
I Am Up For Europe (7)
I'll Be Your Man (1,8)
I'm The One (2)
Indian Wells Woman (10)
It's Gotta Be Real (6,9)
Just About The Same (8)
Kicking The Gong Around (10)
Last Flower (8)
Let's Get Together (8)
Like Always (4,5)
Little Road And A Stone To Roll (3)
Look At Me, Look At You (7)
Looking Glass (8)
Love Affair (7)

Memories Of You (2)
Message Of Our Love (1)
Midnight Wind (10)
Nest, The (7)
Never My Love (3,5,8) 2
No Fair At All (2,5) 51
On A Quiet Night (3)
One Too Many Mornings (8)
P.F. Sloan (9)
Pandora's Golden Heebie Jeebies (2) 35
Please Don't Go (Round The Bend) (10)
Rainbows Bent (10)
Remember (1,8)
Reputation (8)
Requiem For The Masses (3,5,8) 100

Rose Petals, Incense And A Kitten (4)
Round Again (1)
Seven Man Band (8)
Seven Virgins (9)
Silent Song Thru The Land (10)
Silver Morning (9)
Snow Queen (10)
So Kind To Me (Brenda's Theme) (6)
Sometime (3)
Songs In The Wind (2)
Standing Still (1)
That's Racin' (9)
Time For Livin' (4,5) 39

Time It Is Today (4,5,8)
Toymaker (4)
Travelers Guide (Spanish Flyer) (9)
Under Branches (7)
Wantin' Ain't Gettin' (3)
Wasn't It A Bit Like Now (3,8)
We Love Us (3,5)
What Were The Words (7,8)
When Love Comes To Me (3)
Windy (3,5,8) 1
Yes, I Will (7)
You Hear Me Call Your Name (2)
You May Think (2)
Your Own Love (1)

ASTLEY, Jon

Noted rock producer (The Who, Eric Clapton and Corey Hart). Born in Manchester, England.

DEBUT DATE	PEAK POS	WKS CHR	GOLD	ARTIST — Album Title	$	Label & Number
8/1/87	**135**	10		Everyone Loves The Pilot (Except The Crew)	$8	Atlantic 81740

Animal, The
Better Never Than Late

Disclaimer
Emperor, The

I Want To Dance
Jane's Getting Serious 77

Jumping In The Deep End
Lipservice

Suffering Fools
Target Practise

ASTLEY, Rick

Pop singer/guitarist born on 2/6/66 in Warrington and raised in Manchester, England.

DEBUT DATE	PEAK POS	WKS CHR	GOLD	ARTIST — Album Title	$	Label & Number
1/23/88	**10**	60	▲²	1 Whenever You Need Somebody	$8	RCA 6822
1/28/89	**19**	23	●	2 Hold Me In Your Arms	$8	RCA 8589
3/30/91	**31**	18		3 Free..	$12	RCA 3004

Ain't Too Proud To Beg (2) 89
Be With You (3)
Behind The Smile (3)
Bottom Line (3)
Cry For Help (3) 7
Dial My Number (2)

Don't Say Goodbye (1)
Giving Up On Love (2) 38
Hold Me In Your Arms (2)
I Don't Want To Be Your Lover (2)
I Don't Want To Lose Her (2)
I'll Never Let You Down (2)

In The Name Of Love (3)
Is This Really Love? (3)
It Would Take A Strong Strong Man (1) 10
Love Has Gone (1)
Move Right Out (3) 81

Never Gonna Give You Up (1) 1
Never Knew Love (3)
No More Looking For Love (1)
Really Got A Problem (3)
She Wants To Dance With Me (2) 6

Slipping Away (1)
Take Me To Your Heart (2)
This Must Be Heaven (3)
Till Then (Time Stands Still) (2)
Together Forever (1) 1
When I Fall In Love (1)

Whenever You Need Somebody (1)
Wonderful You (3)
You Move Me (1)

ASTRONAUTS, The

Boulder, Colorado surf-rock quintet. Guitarists Bob Demmon, Dennis Lindsey, Rich Fifield and Storm Patterson, with drummer Jim Gallagher.

DEBUT DATE	PEAK POS	WKS CHR	GOLD	ARTIST — Album Title	$	Label & Number
8/3/63	**61**	14		1 Surfin' With The Astronauts	$30	RCA 2760
2/8/64	**100**	9		2 Everything Is A-OK! ....[L]	$25	RCA 2782
3/28/64	**123**	5		3 Competition Coupe	$35	RCA 2858

Baby Let's Play House (1)
Baja (1) 94
Banzai Pipeline (1)
Batman (1)
Big Boss Man (2)
Bo Diddley (1)

Chevy Scarfer (3)
Competition Coupe (3)
Devil Driver (3)
Devil Driver's Theme (3)
Dream Lover (2)
El Aguila (The Eagle) (3)

'55 Bird (3)
4:56 Stingray (3)
Happy Ho-Daddy (3)
Hearse, The (3)
I Need You (2)
If I Had A Hammer (2)

It's So Easy (2)
Kuk (1)
Let's Go Trippin' (1)
Little Ford Ragtop (3)
Misirlou (1)
Money (2)

Movin' (1)
Our Car Club (3)
Pipeline (1)
Shortnin' Bread (2)
650 Scrambler (3)
Stormy Monday Blues (2)

Surfer's Stomp (1)
Surfin' U.S.A. (1)
Susie-Q (1)
What'd I Say (2)
Wine, Wine, Wine (2)

ASWAD

British reggae band formed in 1976: Brinsley Forde (vocals), Angus "Drummie" Zeb (drums) and Courtney Hemmings (keyboards) who was replaced by Tony Gad in 1979. Aswad means "black" in Arabic.

DEBUT DATE	PEAK POS	WKS CHR	GOLD	ARTIST — Album Title	$	Label & Number
8/13/88	**173**	7		Distant Thunder..	$8	Mango 9810

Bittersweet
Don't Turn Around

Feelings
Give A Little Love

I Can't Get Over You
International Melody

Justice
Message, The

Set Them Free
Smokey Blues

Tradition

ASYLUM CHOIR — see RUSSELL, Leon

ATKINS, Chet

★★198★★

Born on 6/20/24 in Luttrell, Tennessee. Revered guitarist, began recording for RCA in 1947. Moved to Nashville in 1950 and became prolific studio musician/producer. RCA's A&R manager in Nashville from 1960-68; RCA vice president from 1968-82. Entered the Country Music Hall of Fame in 1973 as the youngest inductee (age 49).

DEBUT DATE	PEAK POS	WKS CHR	GOLD	ARTIST — Album Title	$	Label & Number
6/16/58	**21**	4		1 Chet Atkins At Home ....[I]	$20	RCA 1544
2/22/60	**16**	12		2 Teensville ....[I]	$15	RCA 2161
2/13/61	**7**	24		3 Chet Atkins' Workshop ....[I]	$15	RCA 2232
7/10/61	**119**	10		4 The Most Popular Guitar ....[I]	$15	RCA 2346
3/17/62	**31**	24		5 Down Home ....[I]	$15	RCA 2450
10/13/62	**33**	9		6 Caribbean Guitar ....[I]	$15	RCA 2549
3/23/63	**135**	5		7 Our Man In Nashville ....[I]	$15	RCA 2616
9/21/63	**93**	6		8 Teen Scene ....[I]	$15	RCA 2719
2/29/64	**64**	8		9 Guitar Country ....[I]	$15	RCA 2783

DEBUT DATE	PEAK POS	WKS CHR	GOLD	ARTIST — Album Title	$	Label & Number
				ATKINS, Chet — Cont'd		
4/9/66	112	13	10	Chet Atkins Picks On The Beatles................[I]	$15	RCA 3531
6/18/66	62	23	11	The "Pops" Goes Country * ....[I]	$15	RCA 2870
12/17/66+	140	4	12	From Nashville With Love ....[I]	$15	RCA 3647
5/6/67	148	9	13	It's A Guitar World.......................[I]	$15	RCA 3728
1/20/68	189	2	14	Class Guitar ....[I]	$15	RCA 3885
3/30/68	184	3	15	Solo Flights ....[I]	$15	RCA 3922
10/11/69	160	4	16	Chet Picks On The Pops * ....[I]	$15	RCA 3104
				*CHET ATKINS/BOSTON POPS/ARTHUR FIEDLER		
12/13/69+	150	7	17	Solid Gold '69 ....[I]	$12	RCA 4244
4/25/70	139	5	18	Yestergroovin'..........................[I]	$12	RCA 4331
5/29/76	172	5	19	Chester & Lester........................[I]	$10	RCA 1167
				CHET ATKINS & LES PAUL		
4/27/85	145	13	20	Stay Tuned...........................[I]	$8	Columbia 39591
				featuring an all-star lineup of guitarists: George Benson, Larry Carlton, Earl Klugh, Mark Knopfler and Steve Lukather.		
11/3/90	127	25	21	Neck And Neck	$12	Columbia 45307
				CHET ATKINS/MARK KNOPFLER		
				vocals are included on only half of the tracks		

Acutely Cute (14)
Adios Amigo (11)
After The Tears (12)
Al-Di-La (12)
Alabama Jubilee (11)
Alexander's Ragtime Band (7)
Alley Cat (8)
Always On Saturday (7)
And I Love Her (10)
April In Portugal (1)
Aquarius (17)
Autumn Leaves (15)
Avalon (19)
Ave Maria (14)
Ay-Ay-Ay (1)
Back Home Again In Indiana (8)
Banana Boat Song (6)
Bandit, The (6)
Battle Of New Orleans (medley) (16)
Birth Of The Blues (19)
Black Orpheus, Theme From ..see: Manha De Carnaval
Blackbird (17)
Blue Steel Blues (5)
Bonita (7)
Boo Boo Stick Beat (2) 49
Boot And The Stone (20)
Both Sides Now (17)
Bring Me Sunshine (18)
By The Time I Get To Phoenix (16)
Bye Bye Birdie (8)
Can't Buy Me Love (10)
Cancion Triste (Sad Song) (14)
Canticle ..see: Scarborough Fair
Caravan (19)
Cast Your Fate to The Wind (13)
Cheek To Cheek (15)
Cherokee (18)
Chet's Tune (15)
Choro Da Saudade (15)
Cindy, Oh Cindy (15)
Cold, Cold Heart (11)

Come September, Theme From (6)
Come Softly To Me (2)
Come To The Mardi Gras (6)
Copper Kettle (9)
Cosmic Square Dance (20)
Country Champagne (18)
Country Gentleman (11)
Cricket Ballet (20)
Czardas (1)
Deed I Do (19)
Delilah (16)
Django's Castle (Manoir De Mes Reves) (2)
Dobro (9)
Down Home (7)
Drina (12)
Drive-In (15)
Drown In My Own Tears (7)
East Of The Sun (West Of The Moon) (4)
El Humahuaqueno (Carnavalito) (14)
Enchanted Sea (6)
English Leather (12)
Et Maintenant (What Now My Love) (13)
Faded Love (11)
Folsom Prison Blues (17)
For No One (13)
Freight Train (9)
From Nashville With Love (12)
Galveston (16)
Georgy Girl (15)
Girl Friend Of The Whirling Dervish (5)
Give The World A Smile (5)
Goin' Home (4)
Gone (9)
Gonna Get Along Without You Now (15)
Goodnight Irene (7)
Goofus (3)
Gotta Travel On (18)
Guitar Country (9)
Hard Day's Night (10)
Hey Jude (17)
Hi-Lili, Hi-Lo (4)

Hot Mocking Bird (3)
Hot Toddy (2)
House In New Orleans (7)
How High The Moon (18)
I Ain't Gonna Work Tomorrow (5)
I Feel Fine (10)
I Feel Pretty (14)
I Got A Woman (8)
I Love How You Love Me (8)
I Love Paris (12)
I Will (8)
I'll Cry Instead (10)
I'll Fly Away (11)
I'll Follow The Sun (10)
I'll Never Fall In Love Again (17)
I'll See You In My Dreams (21)
I'm A Pilgrim (5)
I'm Thinking Tonight Of My Blue Eyes (11)
If I Fell (10)
If I Should Lose You (20)
In A Little Spanish Town ('Twas On A Night Like This) (2)
In The Chapel In The Moonlight (1)
In The Pines (medley) (11)
Inka Dinka Doo (18)
Intermezzo (4)
It Ain't Necessarily So (4)
It Had To Be You (19)
It's Been A Long, Long Time (19)
January In Bombay (13)
Jean (17)
John Henry (medley) (11)
Jungle Dream (6)
Jungle Drums (1)
Just One Time (21)
Kentucky (9)
La Fiesta (12)
Lagrima (medley) (14)
Lambeth Walk (3)
Lara's Theme (13)
Last Waltz (16)
Liberty (18)

Listen To The Mockingbird (medley) (11)
Little Bit Of Blues (9)
Little Bitty Tear (7)
Little Evil (8)
Little Feet (5)
Little Music Box (La Alborada) (14)
Lover Come Back to Me (19)
Lullaby Of Birdland (3)
Malaguenas (medley) (14)
Manha De Carnaval (14)
Marie (1)
Martha (1)
Mayan Dance (6)
Melissa (7)
Mercy, Mercy, Mercy (15)
Michelle (7)
Monte Carlo Melody (4)
Montego Bay (6)
Moon Over Miami (6)
Moonglow/Picnic (19)
Morenita Do Brazil (14)
Moulin Rouge (Where Is Your Heart), Song From (12)
Mouse In The House (20)
Music To Watch Girls By (3)
My Dear Little Sweetheart (4)
My Prayer (4)
My Way (17)
'Na Voce, 'Na Chitarra E'o Poco 'E Luna (13)
Nagasaki (1)
Never On Sunday (5)
Next Time I'm In Town (21)
Night Train (2)
Nine Pound Hammer (9)
Ode To Billy Joe (16)
Oh, Lonesome Me (2)
Old Double Shuffle (7)
On Top Of Old Smoky (medley) (11)
One Mint Julep (2) 82
Orange Blossom Special (11)
Out Of Nowhere (19)
Pickin' Nashville (13)
Picnic ..see: Moonglow
Please Stay Tuned (20)

Poor Boy Blues (21)
Que Sera, Sera ..see: Whatever Will Be, Will Be
Quiet Eyes (20)
Ranjana (13)
Rock-A-Bye Bay (4)
Rocky Top (18)
Romance (12)
Romeo And Juliet, Love Theme From (17)
Rumpus (8)
Salty Dog Rag (5)
Say "Si Si" (1)
Scarborough Fair/Canticle (16)
Scare Crow (7)
Scherzino Mexicano (14)
Sempre (13)
She Loves You (10)
She's A Woman (10)
Sleep (3)
Sleep Walk (2)
So Soft, Your Goodbye (21)
So What's New (17)
Some Leather And Lace (20)
Someday Sweetheart (19)
Something Tender (12)
Son Of A Preacher Man (1)
Soul Journey (12)
Spanish Harlem (7,16)
Star-Time (1)
Stay As Sweet As You Are (4)
Steel Guitar Rag (5)
Steeplechase Lane (18)
Stranger On The Shore (12)
Streamlined Cannon Ball (7)
Sugarfoot Rag (9,16)
Summer Place, Theme From A (3)
Sunrise (20)
Susie-Q (8)
Sweet Dreams (21)
Sweetie Baby (8)
Tahitian Skies (21)
Take A Message To Mary (2)
Tammy (3)
Tap Room (20)
Taste Of Honey (13)

Tears (21)
Teen Scene (8)
Teensville (2) 73
Temptation (6)
Tennessee Pride (18)
Tennessee Waltz (11)
Testament Of Amelia (14)
There'll Be Some Changes Made (21)
Things We Said Today (10)
This Guy's In Love With You (16)
Three Little Words (15)
Till There Was You (2)
To Be In Love (14)
Trambone (5)
Tuxedo Junction (5)
Vanessa (1)
Vaya Con Dios (9)
Walk Right In (8)
(What Now My Love) ..see: Et Maintenant
What'd I Say (13)
Whatever Will Be, Will Be (Que Sera, Sera) (3)
When Day Is Done (4)
When You Wish Upon A Star (1)
(Where Is Your Heart) ..see: Moulin Rouge, Song From
White Silver Sands (2)
Wild Orchids (4)
Wildwood Flower (medley) (11)
Wimoweh (16)
Windy And Warm (5,11)
Winter Walkin' (3)
Yakety Axe (21)
Yankee Doodle Dixie (1)
Yellow Bird (6,14)
Yes Ma'am (9)
Yesterday (1)
Yestergroovin' (18)
You're Just In Love (1)

ATLANTA
Nine-man country band from Atlanta.

5/26/84	140	7		Pictures	$8	MCA 5463

Atlanta Burned Again Last Night
Blue Side Of The Grey

Dixie Dreaming
Long Cool Woman In A Black Dress

(Nothing Left Between Us) But Alabama

Pictures
Sweet Country Music

Sweet Was Our Rose
Wishful Drinkin'

You Are The Wine

ATLANTA DISCO BAND, The
Disco studio group from Atlanta.

1/17/76	172	9		Bad Luck ....[I]	$8	Ariola Am. 50004

Bad Luck 94
Buckhead

Do What You Feel
I Am Trying

It's Love
Let It Ride

My Soul Is Satisfied
Ole Goat

★★371★★ ATLANTA RHYTHM SECTION
Group formed of musicians from Studio One, Doraville, Georgia in 1971. Consisted of Rodney Justo (vocals), Barry Bailey and J.R. Cobb (guitars), Paul Goddard (bass), Dean Daughtry (keyboards) and Robert Nix (drums). Cobb, Daughtry and band manager Buddy Buie had been with the Classics IV, others had been with Roy Orbison. Justo left after first album, replaced by Ronnie Hammond.

9/14/74	74	12	1	Third Annual Pipe Dream..........................	$8	Polydor 6027
9/6/75	113	9	2	Dog Days	$8	Polydor 6041

DEBUT DATE	PEAK POS	WKS CHR	G O L D	ARTIST — Album Title	$	Label & Number

ATLANTA RHYTHM SECTION — Cont'd

DEBUT DATE	PEAK POS	WKS CHR	GOLD	ARTIST — Album Title	$	Label & Number
6/5/76	146	15		3 Red Tape..	$8	Polydor 6060
1/15/77	11	39	●	4 A Rock And Roll Alternative.................................	$8	Polydor 6080
4/9/77	154	4		5 Atlanta Rhythm Section ....[E-R]	$10	MCA 4114 [2]
				reissue of their first 2 Decca albums *Atlanta Rhythm Section* and *Back Up Against The Wall* from 1972 and 1973		
4/1/78	7	40	▲	6 Champagne Jam	$8	Polydor 6134
6/23/79	26	21	●	7 Underdog..	$8	Polydor 6200
11/10/79	51	12		8 Are You Ready!.................................[L]	$10	Polydor 6236 [2]
8/16/80	65	11		9 The Boys From Doraville	$8	Polydor 6285
9/19/81	70	16		10 Quinella..	$8	Columbia 37550

Alien (10) *29*
All In Your Mind (5)
All Night Rain (2)
Angel (What In The World's Come Over Us) (1,8) *79*
Another Man's Woman (3,5,8)
Baby No Lie (5)
Back Up Against The Wall (5,8)
Ballad Of Lois Malone (6)
Beautiful Dreamers (3)
Bless My Soul (2)
Blues In Maude's Flat (1)
Boogie Smoogie (2)
Born Ready (7)
Can't Stand It No More (5)

Champagne Jam (6,8) *43*
Close The Door (1)
Cocaine Charlie (9)
Cold Turkey,Tenn. (5)
Conversation (5,8)
Crazy (2)
Cuban Crisis (2)
Days Of Our Lives (5)
Do It Or Die (7) *19*
Dog Days (2) *64*
Don't Miss The Message (4)
Doraville (1,8) *35*
Earnestine (5)
Everybody Gotta Go (4)
Evileen (6)
Forty Days And Forty Nights (5)
Free Spirit (3) *85*

Georgia Rhythm (4,8) *68*
Get Your Head Out Of Your Heart (1)
Going To Shangri-La (10)
Great Escape (6)
Help Yourself (1)
Higher (10)
Hitch Hikers' Hero (4)
Homesick (10)
I Ain't Much (9)
I Hate The Blues (medley) (7)
I'm Not Gonna Let It Bother Me Tonight (6,8) *14*
Imaginary Lover (6,8) *7*
Indigo Passion (7)
It Just Ain't Your Moon (2)
It Must Be Love (5)

It's Only Music (7)
Jesus Hearted People (1)
Join The Race (1)
Jukin (3) *82*
Large Time (6,8)
Let's Go Get Stoned (medley) (7)
Livin' Lovin' Wreck (5)
Long Tall Sally (8)
Love Me Just A Little (Sometime) (5)
Make Me Believe It (5)
Mixed Emotions (3)
My Song (7)
Neon Nites (4) *42*
Next Year's Rock & Roll (9)
Normal Love (6)
Oh What A Feeling (3)

One More Problem (5)
Outlaw Music (10)
Outside Woman Blues (4)
Pedestal (9)
Police! Police! (3)
Pretty Girl (10)
Putting My Faith In Love (9)
Quinella (10)
Redneck (9)
Rough At The Edges (9)
Shanghied (3)
Silent Treatment (2)
Silver Eagle (9)
Sky High (4,8)
So In To You (4,8) *7*
Southern Exposure (10)
Spooky (7) *17*
Strictly R & R (9)

Superman (5)
Tara's Theme (8)
Try My Love (9)
War Is Over (1)
What You Gonna Do About It (5)
While Time Is Left (7)
Who You Gonna Run To (1)
Will I Live On (5)
Wrong (5)
You're So Strong (10)
Yours And Mine (5)

★★404★★ ATLANTIC STARR

Soul band formed in 1976 in White Plains, New York by brothers Wayne, David and Jonathan Lewis. Wayne and David on vocals with Sharon Bryant. In 1984, reduced to a quintet; Barbara Weathers replaced Bryant. Porscha Martin replaced Weathers in 1989. Rachel Oliver replaced Martin in 1991.

DEBUT DATE	PEAK POS	WKS CHR	GOLD	ARTIST — Album Title	$	Label & Number
8/26/78	67	13		1 Atlantic Starr	$8	A&M 4711
6/2/79	142	7		2 Straight To The Point	$8	A&M 4764
3/14/81	47	30		3 Radiant	$8	A&M 4833
3/27/82	18	29		4 Brilliance	$8	A&M 4883
11/19/83+	91	28		5 Yours Forever	$8	A&M 4948
5/25/85+	17	68	●	6 As The Band Turns	$8	A&M 5019
4/25/87	18	31	●	7 All In The Name Of Love	$8	Warner 25560
5/20/89	125	6		8 We're Movin' Up	$8	Warner 25849
2/8/92	134	14		9 Love Crazy	$12	Reprise 26545

All In The Name Of Love (7)
Always (7) *1*
Am I Dreaming (3)
Being In Love With You Is So Much Fun (1)
Bring It Back Home Again (4)
Bullseye (7)
Circles (4) *38*
Come Lover (9)
Cool, Calm, Collected (6)
Does It Matter (3)
Don't Abuse My Love (1)
Don't Start The Fire (8)
Don't Take Me For Granted (7)
Fallin' In Love With You (2)

Females (7)
Freak-A-Ristic (6) *90*
Friends (8)
Gimme Your Luvin' (1)
Girl, Your Love's So Fine (9)
Hold On (9)
I Can't Wait (8,9)
I Want Your Love (5)
(I'll Never Miss) The Love I Never Had (1)
I'm In Love With You (8)
If You Knew What's Good For You (9)
If Your Heart Isn't In It (6) *57*
In The Heat Of Passion (6)

Interlude (7)
Island Dream (5)
Keep It Comin' (1)
Kissin' Power (2)
Let The Spirit Move Ya (2)
Let The Sun In (7)
Let's Get Closer (4)
(Let's) Rock 'N' Roll (2)
Let's Start It Over (6)
Lookin' For Love Again (9)
Losin' You (2)
Love Crazy (9) *75*
Love Me Down (4)
Love Moves (4)
Masterpiece (9) *3*
More, More, More (5)

More Time For Me (5)
My First Love (8)
My Mistake (7)
My Special Lover (9)
My Sugar (8)
My Turn Now (3)
Mystery Girl (3)
One Love (6)
One Lover At A Time (7) *58*
Perfect Love (4)
Second To None (8)
Secret Lovers (6) *3*
Send For Me (9)
Sexy Dancer (4)
Silver Shadow (6)
Stand Up (1)

Straight To The Point (2)
Thank You (6)
Thankful (7)
Think About That (3)
Touch A Four Leaf Clover (5) *87*
Tryin' (5)
Unconditional Love (4)
Under Pressure (3)
Under Your Spell (8)
Visions (1)
We Got It Together (1)
We're Movin' Up (8)
What 'Cha Feel Inside (2)
When Love Calls (3)

Where There's Smoke There's Fire (1)
Who Could Love You Better? (5)
With Your Love I Come Alive (1)
You Belong With Me (7)
You Deserve The Best (8)
You Hit The Spot (9)
You're The One (4)
Your Love Finally Ran Out (4)
Yours Forever (5)

ATOMIC ROOSTER

British rock quartet. Fluctuating lineup included keyboardist Vincent Crane and drummer Carl Palmer (Emerson, Lake & Palmer; Asia). Both Crane and Palmer were members of The Crazy World of Arthur Brown.

DEBUT DATE	PEAK POS	WKS CHR	GOLD	ARTIST — Album Title	$	Label & Number
7/3/71	90	15		1 Death Walks Behind You	$14	Elektra 74094
12/11/71+	167	9		2 In Hearing Of Atomic Rooster......................	$14	Elektra 74109
10/7/72	149	8		3 Made In England	$10	Elektra 75039

All In Satan's Name (3)
Black Snake (2)
Break The Ice (2)
Breakthrough (2)
Breathless (3)

Close Your Eyes (3)
Death Walks Behind You (1)
Decision/Indecision (2)
Devil's Answer (2)

Don't Know What Went Wrong (3)
Gershatzer (1)
Head In The Sky (2)
I Can't Take No More (1)

Little Bit Of Inner Air (3)
Never To Lose (3)
Nobody Else (1)
People You Can't Trust (3)
Price, The (2)

Rock, The (2)
Seven Streets (1)
Sleeping For Years (1)
Space Cowboy (3)
Spoonful Of Bromide Helps The Pulse Rate Go Down (2)

Stand By Me (1)
Time Take My Life (3)
Tomorrow Night (1)
Vug (1)

AUDIENCE

British rock group led by singer/guitarist Howard Werth.

DEBUT DATE	PEAK POS	WKS CHR	GOLD	ARTIST — Album Title	$	Label & Number
6/24/72	175	5		Lunch	$10	Elektra 75026

Ain't The Man You Need (5)
Barracuda Dan

Buy Me An Island
Hula Girl

In Accord
Party Games

Seven Sore Bruises
Stand By The Door

Thunder And Lightning
Trombone Gulch

AUDIO TWO

Brooklyn rap duo of brothers: Milk Dee (DJ) and Gizmo (rapper). Their father, Nat Robinson, formed the First Priority record company.

DEBUT DATE	PEAK POS	WKS CHR	GOLD	ARTIST — Album Title	$	Label & Number
6/25/88	185	4		What More Can I Say?	$8	First Pri. 90907

Giz Starts Buggin'
Hickeys Around My Neck

I Don't Care
I Like Cherries

Make It Funky
Put It 2 Music

Questions, The
Top Billin' [includes 2 versions]

What More Can I Say?
When The 2 Is On The Mic

DEBUT DATE	PEAK POS	WKS CHR	GOLD	ARTIST — Album Title	$	Label & Number

AUGER, Brian

Jazz-rock keyboardist. Born on 7/18/39 in Bihar, India and raised in London. Voted best new jazz artist by *Melody Maker* in 1964 — the same year that he switched to R&B and formed band with future Mahavishnu Orchestra members John McLaughlin (guitar) and Rick Laird (bass). In 1965, formed Trinity with Rick Brown (bass) and Micky Waller (drums). Added vocalists Long John Baldry, Rod Stewart and ex-model Julie Driscoll, and changed name to Steampacket. By mid-1966, group dissolved and Auger reorganized Trinity with Driscoll, Dave Ambrose (bass), Clive Thacker (drums) and Gary Boyle (guitar). Disbanded in mid-1970. Everchanging personnel of Oblivion Express included future AWB members Robbie McIntosh and Steve Ferrone, and Alex Ligertwood, later of Santana.

JULIE DRISCOLL/BRIAN AUGER & THE TRINITY:

DEBUT DATE	PEAK POS	WKS CHR	GOLD	ARTIST — Album Title	$	Label & Number
5/10/69	194	2		1 Jools & Brian	$12	Capitol 136
6/14/69	41	16		2 Streetnoise	$15	Atco 701 [2]

BRIAN AUGER & THE TRINITY:

8/1/70	184	3		3 Befour	$8	RCA 4372

BRIAN AUGER'S OBLIVION EXPRESS:

6/3/72	170	7		4 Second Wind	$8	RCA 4703
8/4/73	64	31		5 Closer To It!	$8	RCA 0140
4/6/74	45	20		6 Straight Ahead	$8	RCA 0454
12/7/74+	51	13		7 Live Oblivion, Vol. 1 [L]	$8	RCA 0645
10/11/75	115	8		8 Reinforcements	$8	RCA 1210
3/13/76	169	4		9 Live Oblivion, Vol. 2 [L]	$10	RCA 1230 [2]
2/19/77	127	5		10 Happiness Heartaches	$8	Warner 2981
4/23/77	151	3		11 The Best Of Brian Auger [G]	$8	RCA 2249

Adagio Per Archi E Organo (3)
All Blues (2)
Back Street Bible Class (10)
Beginning Again (6,7)
Big Yin (8)
Brain Damage (8)
Bumpin' On Sunset (6,7)
Change (6)
Compared To What (5,9)
Czechoslovakia (2)
Don't Do It No More (1)
Don't Look Away (4,7)
Ellis Island (2)
Finally Found You Out (2)
Flesh Failures (Let The Sunshine In) (2)
Fool Killer (1)
Foolish Girl (8,11)
Freedom Jazz Dance (4,9,11)
Future Pilot (8)
Gimme A Funky Break (10)
Got To Be Born Again (10)
Green Onions (1)
Happiness Heartaches (10)
Happiness Is Just Around The Bend (5,9,11)
I Didn't Want To Have To Do It (1)
I Got Life (2)
I Know You (1)
I Know You Love Me Not (1)
I Wanna Take You Higher (3)
If You Should Ever Leave Me (1)
In Search Of The Sun (2)
Indian Rope Man (2)
Inner City Blues (5,9,11)
Just You Just Me (3,4)
Kiko (1)
Let's Do It Tonight (1)
Light My Fire (2)
Light On The Path (5)
Listen Here (3,11) *100*
Looking In The Eye Of The World (2)
Maiden Voyage (3,9)
Never Gonna Come Down (10)
No Time To Live (3)
Oh, Baby Won't You Come Back Home To Croydon, Where Everybody Beedle An' Bo's (1)
Paging Mr. McCoy (10)
Pavane (3)
Plum (8)
Save The Country (2)
Second Wind (4,9)
Somebody Help Us (4)
Something Out Of Nothing (8)
Spice Island (10)
Straight Ahead (6,9,11)
Take Me To The Water (2)
Thoughts From Afar (8)
Tiger (1)
Tropic Of Capricorn (2)
Truth (4,7)
Vauxhall To Lambeth Bridge (2)
Voices Of Other Times (5)
When I Was A Young Girl (2)
Whenever You're Ready (5,9)
Word About Color (2)
You'll Stay In My Heart (6)

AURRA

Ohio soul band: ex-Slave members Steve Washington and Tom Lockett, Jr. (saxophones) with Philip Fields (keyboards) and vocalists Starleana Young and Curt Jones. Young and Jones later formed the duo Deja.

DEBUT DATE	PEAK POS	WKS CHR	GOLD	ARTIST — Album Title	$	Label & Number
6/13/81	103	13		1 Send Your Love	$8	Salsoul 8538
2/27/82	38	15		2 A Little Love	$8	Salsoul 8551

Are You Single (1)
Checking You Out (2)
Forever (1)
In My Arms (2)
It's You (2)
Keep Doin' It (1)
Kingston Lady (1)
Little Love (2)
Living Too Fast (1)
Make Up Your Mind (2) *71*
Nasty Disposition (1)
Party Time (1)
Patience (2)
Send Your Love (1)
Still Free (2)
Thinking Of You (2)

AUSTIN, Patti

Born on 8/10/48 in New York City. R&B backing vocalist in New York. Goddaughter of Quincy Jones. Made Harlem's Apollo Theatre debut at age four. In the 1988 film *Tucker*.

DEBUT DATE	PEAK POS	WKS CHR	GOLD	ARTIST — Album Title	$	Label & Number
12/3/77+	116	13		1 Havana Candy	$8	CTI 5006
10/3/81+	36	44		2 Every Home Should Have One	$8	Qwest 3591
3/31/84	87	18		3 Patti Austin	$8	Qwest 23974
11/9/85	182	4		4 Gettin' Away With Murder	$8	Qwest 25276
4/14/90	93	17		5 Love Is Gonna Getcha	$12	GRP 9603

All Behind Us Now (3)
Any Way You Can (3)
Anything Can Happen Here (4)
Baby, Come To Me (2) *1*
Believe The Children (5)
Big Bad World (4)
Change Your Attitude (3)
Do You Love Me? (2)
Every Home Should Have One (2) *62*
Fine Fine Fella (Got To Have You) (3)
First Time Love (5)
Genie, The (2)
Gettin' Away With Murder (4)
Girl Who Used To Be Me (5)
Golden Oldies (1)
Good In Love (5)
Havana Candy (1)
Heat Of Heat (3) *55*
Honey For The Bees (4)
Hot! In The Flames Of Love (3)
I Just Want To Know (1)
I Need Somebody (1)
I've Got My Heart Set On You (3)
If I Believed (4)
In My Dream (5)
In My Life (5)
Island, The (2)
It's Gonna Be Special (3) *82*
Little Baby (1)
Lost In The Stars (5)
Love Is Gonna Getcha (5)
Love Me To Death (2)
Oh No, Margarita (2)
Only A Breath Away (4)
Ooh-Whee (The Carnival) (5)
Rhythm Of The Street (3)
Shoot The Moon (3)
Starstruck (3)
Stop, Look, Listen (3)
Summer Is The Coldest Time Of Year (4)
Symphony Of Love (2)
Talkin' 'Bout My Baby (4)
That's Enough For Me (5)
Through The Test Of Time (5)
Too Soon To Know (5)
Wait For Me (5)
Way I Feel (2)
We're In Love (5)

AUTOGRAPH

Los Angeles-based rock quintet led by vocalist Steve Plunkett.

DEBUT DATE	PEAK POS	WKS CHR	GOLD	ARTIST — Album Title	$	Label & Number
1/5/85	29	29	●	1 Sign In Please	$8	RCA 8040
11/16/85	92	15		2 That's The Stuff	$8	RCA 7009
4/11/87	108	15		3 Loud And Clear	$8	RCA 5796

All I'm Gonna Take (1)
Bad Boy (3)
Blondes In Black Cars (3)
Built For Speed (2)
Changing Hands (3)
Cloud 10 (1)
Crazy World (2)
Dance All Night (3)
Deep End (1)
Down 'N Dirty (3)
Everytime I Dream (3)
Friday (1)
Hammerhead (2)
In The Night (1)
Just Got Back From Heaven (3)
Loud And Clear (3)
More Than A Million Times (3)
My Girlfriend's Boyfriend Isn't Me (1)
Night Teen & Non Stop (1)
Paint This Town (1)
Send Her To Me (1)
She Never Looked That Good For Me (3)
She's A Tease (3)
Six String Fever (2)
Take No Prisoners (2)
That's The Stuff (2)
Thrill Of Love (1)
Turn Up The Radio (1) *29*
When The Sun Goes Down (3)
You'll Get Over It (2)

AUTOMATIC MAN

Rock group formed in San Francisco by drummer Michael Shrieve in 1975 after leaving Santana. Included guitarist Pat Thrall who joined Asia in 1990. Shrieve left after first album (later charted with Sammy Hagar; replaced by Glenn Symmonds).

DEBUT DATE	PEAK POS	WKS CHR	GOLD	ARTIST — Album Title	$	Label & Number
10/2/76	120	7		1 Automatic Man	$8	Island 9397
10/8/77	109	8		2 Visitors	$8	Island 9429

DEBUT DATE	PEAK POS	WKS CHR	GOLD	ARTIST — Album Title	$	Label & Number

AUTOMATIC MAN — Cont'd

Atlantis Rising Fanfare (1)	Comin' Through (1)	Here I Am Now (2)	My Pearl (1) 97	So You Wanna Be (2)	Y - 2 - Me (2)
Atlantis Rising Theme	Daughter Of Neptune (2)	I.T.D. Interstellar Tracking	Newspapers (1)	There's A Way (1)	
Turning Of The Axis (1)	Geni-Geni (1)	Devices (1)	One And One (1)	Visitors (2)	
Automatic Man (1)	Give It To Me (2)	Live Wire (2)	Right Back Down (1)	What's Done (2)	

AVALON, Frankie

Born Francis Avallone on 9/18/39 in Philadelphia. Teen idol managed by Bob Marcucci. Worked in bands in Atlantic City, New Jersey in 1953. Radio and TV with Paul Whiteman, mid-1950s. Singer/trumpet player with Rocco & His Saints in 1957 which included Bobby Rydell. Co-starred in many films with Annette. Appeared in films *Disc Jockey Jamboree* (1957), *Guns Of The Timberland* (1960) and *Back To The Beach* (1987).

12/28/59+	9	14		1 Swingin' On A Rainbow	$50	Chancellor 5004
10/23/61+	59	20		2 A Whole Lotta Frankie ....[G]	$30	Chancellor 5018

All Of Everything (2) 70	Don't Let Love Pass Me By	I'll Wait For You (2) 15	Step In The Right Direction	Togetherness (2) 26	What's The Reason (I'm Not
Birds Of A Feather (1)	(2) 85	Just Ask Your Heart (2) 7	(1)	Trouble With Me Is You (1)	Pleasin' You) (1)
Bobby Sox To Stockings	Don't Throw Away All	Perfect Love (2) 47	Swingin' On A Rainbow	Try A Little Tenderness (1)	Where Are You (2) 32
(2) 8	Those Teardrops (2) 22	Sandy (1)	(1) 39	Tuxedo Junction (2) 82	Why (2) 1
Call Me Anytime (2)	Ginger Bread (2) 9	Secret Love (1)	Talk, Talk, Talk (1,2)	Two Fools (2) 54	You're Just Too Much (1)
Dede Dinah (2) 7	I Do Adore Her (1)	She's Funny That Way (1)	Them There Eyes (1)	Venus (2) 1	

★★313★★ AVERAGE WHITE BAND

Vocal/instrumental group formed in Scotland in 1972. Consisted of Alan Gorrie (vocals, bass; Forever More), Hamish Stuart (vocals, guitar), Onnie McIntyre (vocal, guitar), Malcolm Duncan (saxophone), Roger Ball (keyboards, saxophone) and Robbie McIntosh (drums). McIntosh died of drug poisoning on 9/23/74, replaced by Steve Ferrone. McIntosh and Ferrone were members of Brian Auger's Oblivion Express.

9/21/74+	1¹	43	●	1 AWB	$10	Atlantic 7308
4/5/75	39	13		2 Put It Where You Want It ....[E-R]	$10	MCA 475
				reissue of 1973 album *Show Your Hand*		
6/28/75	4	24	●	3 Cut The Cake	$10	Atlantic 18140
7/17/76	9	32	▲	4 Soul Searching	$10	Atlantic 18179
1/22/77	28	18	●	5 Person To Person ....[L]	$12	Atlantic 1002 [2]
7/23/77	33	21		6 Benny And Us	$8	Atlantic 19105
				AVERAGE WHITE BAND & BEN E. KING		
4/1/78	28	17	●	7 Warmer Communications	$8	Atlantic 19162
4/7/79	32	15		8 Feel No Fret	$8	Atlantic 19207
5/31/80	116	12		9 Shine	$8	Arista 9523
9/20/80	182	2		10 Volume VIII ....[G]	$8	Atlantic 19266
				side 2 contains their greatest hits		

Ace Of Hearts (8)	Goin' Home (4)	Imagine (6)	Nothing You Can Do (1)	She's A Dream (7)	Walk On By (8) 92
Atlantic Avenue (8)	Got The Love (1)	Into The Night (9)	One Look Over My Shoulder	Shine (9)	Warmer Communications (7)
Back In '67 (2)	Groovin' The Night Away (4)	It's A Mystery (3)	(Is This Really Goodbye?)	Show Your Hand (2)	What Is Soul (6)
Big City Lights (9)	Growing Pains (10)	Just Wanna Love You	(7)	Someday We'll All Be Free (6)	Whatcha' Gonna Do For Me
Catch Me (Before I Have To	Help Is On The Way (9)	Tonight (1)	Our Time Has Come (9)	Soul Searching (4)	(9)
Testify) (9)	High Flyin' Woman (3)	Keepin' It To Myself (1,6)	Person To Person (1,5,10)	Star In The Ghetto (6)	When They Bring Down The
Cloudy (3,5)	How Can You Go Home (2)	Kiss Me (10)	Pick Up The Pieces	Stop The Rain (8)	Curtain (9)
Cut The Cake (3,5,10) 10	How Sweet Can You Get (9)	Let's Go 'Round Again	(1,5,10) 1	Sunny Days (Make Me	When Will You Be Mine (8)
Daddy's All Gone (7)	I Heard It Through The	(9) 53	Please Don't Fall In Love (8)	Think Of You) (4)	Why (3)
Digging Deeper (4)	Grapevine (5)	Love Gives, Love Takes	Price Of The Dream (7)	Sweet & Sour (7)	Work To Do (1)
Everybody's Darling (4)	I Just Can't Give You Up (1)	Away (10)	Queen Of My Soul (4,10) 40	T.L.C. (2,5)	Would You Stay (4)
Feel No Fret (8)	I'm The One (4,5)	Love Of Your Own (4,10)	Reach Out (2)	There's Always Someone	You Got It (1)
Fire Burning (8)	If I Ever Lose This Heaven	Love Won't Get In the Way	Same Feeling, Different	Waiting (1)	Your Love Is A Miracle (7)
Fool For You Anyway (6)	(3,5) 39	(10)	Song (7)	This World Has Music (2)	
For You, For Love (9)	If Love Only Lasts For One	Love Your Life (4,5)	School Boy Crush (3,5) 33	Too Late To Cry (8)	
Get It Up For Love (6)	Night (9)	Message, The (6)		Twilight Zone (2)	

AXE

Florida-based rock band led by vocalist Edgar Riley and guitarist Bobby Barth.

6/26/82	81	20		1 Offering	$8	Atco 148
9/10/83	156	6		2 Nemesis	$8	Atco 90099

All Through The Night (1)	Girls, Girls, Girls (2)	I Think You'll Remember	Keep Playing That Rock 'N'	Now Or Never (1) 64	Silent Soldiers (1)
Burn The City Down (1)	Heat In The Street (2)	Tonight (2) 94	Roll (2)	Rock 'N' Roll Party In The	Steal Another Fantasy (1)
Eagle Flies Alone (2)	Holdin' On (1)	Jennifer (1)	Let The Music Come Back (2)	Streets (1)	Video Inspiration (1)
Foolin' Your Mama Again (2)	I Got The Fire (1)		Masquerade (2)	She's Had The Power (2)	Young Hearts (2)

AXTON, Hoyt

Born on 3/25/38 in Duncan, Oklahoma. Son of songwriter Mae Axton ("Heartbreak Hotel"). Appeared in the movies *The Black Stallion* and *Gremlins*. Wrote hits "Greenback Dollar" for The Kingston Trio, "The Pusher" for Steppenwolf, and "Joy To The World" for Three Dog Night.

4/12/75	188	2		1 Southbound	$8	A&M 4510
4/10/76	171	4		2 Fearless	$8	A&M 4571

Beyond These Walls (2)	Flash Of Fire (2)	Idol Of The Band (2)	Lion In The Winter (1)	Paid In Advance (2)	Southbound (1)
Blind Fiddler (1)	Greensleeves (1)	In A Young Girls Mind (1)	Nashville (1)	Penny Whistle Song (2)	Speed Trap (Out Of State
Devil, The (2)	Gypsy Moth (2)	Jealous Man (2)	No No Song (1)	Pride Of Man (1)	Cars) (1)
Evangelina (2)	I Love To Sing (1)	Lay, Lady, Lay (1)	Old Greyhound (2)	Roll Your Own (1)	Stone And A Feather (2)
				Sometimes It's Easy (1)	Whiskey (1)

★★375★★ AYERS, Roy

Born on 9/10/40 in Los Angeles. R&B-jazz vibraphone player/keyboardist/vocalist. At age five, was given a pair of mallets by famed vibraphonist Lionel Hampton. With Herbie Mann from 1966-70. In 1970, formed Ubiquity whose guest players included drummer Billy Cobham, flutist Herbert Laws, guitarist George Benson, trombonist Wayne Henderson (The Crusaders) and vocalist Dee Dee Bridgewater.

ROY AYERS UBIQUITY:

10/5/74	156	4		1 Change Up The Groove	$8	Polydor 6032
2/21/76	90	18		2 Mystic Voyage	$8	Polydor 6057
8/14/76	51	17		3 Everybody Loves The Sunshine	$8	Polydor 6070
1/15/77	74	12		4 Vibrations	$8	Polydor 6091

DEBUT DATE	PEAK POS	WKS CHR	GOLD	ARTIST — Album Title	$	Label & Number

AYERS, Roy — Cont'd

DEBUT DATE	PEAK POS	WKS CHR	GOLD	ARTIST — Album Title	$	Label & Number
7/2/77	72	25		5 Lifeline	$8	Polydor 6108

ROY AYERS:

3/11/78	33	13		6 Let's Do It	$8	Polydor 6126
8/19/78	48	15		7 You Send Me	$8	Polydor 6159
5/26/79	67	15		8 Fever	$8	Polydor 6204
12/15/79+	82	18		9 No Stranger To Love	$8	Polydor 6246
11/1/80	157	3		10 Love Fantasy	$8	Polydor 6301
8/15/81	197	2		11 Africa, Center Of The World	$8	Polydor 6327
3/20/82	160	7		12 Feeling Good	$8	Polydor 6348

Africa, Center Of The World (11)
And Don't You Say No (7)
Baby Bubba (10)
Baby I Need Your Love (4)
Baby You Give Me A Feeling (4)
Believe In Yourself (10)
Betcha Gonna (10)
Better Days (4)
Black Five (2)
Boogie Back (The Disco King) (2)
Brother Green (The Disco King) (2)
Can't You See Me? (7)
Change Up The Groove (1)
Cincinnati Growl (5)
Come Out And Play (4)
Destination Motherland (11)
Domelo (Give It To Me) (4)

Don't Hide Your Love (9)
Don't Let Our Love Slip Away (9)
Don't Stop The Feeling (9)
Don't You Worry 'Bout A Thing (1)
Everybody Loves The Sunshine (3)
Everytime I See You (7)
Evolution (2)
Feel Like Makin' Love (1)
Feeling Good (12)
Fever (8)
Fikisha (1)
Fire Up The Funk (12)
Freaky Deaky (6)
Fruit (5)
Funky Motion (2)
Get On Up, Get On Down (7)
Golden Rod (3)

Gotta Find A Lover (5)
Hey Uh-What You Say Come On (3)
Higher (4)
I Still Love You (5)
I Wanna Feel It (I Wanna Dance) (8)
I Wanna Touch You Baby (7)
I'll Just Keep Trying (11)
If You Love Me (8)
Is It Too Late To Try? (8)
It Ain't Your Sign It's Your Mind (3,7)
Keep On Walking (3)
Kiss (6)
Knock, Knock (12)
Land Of Fruit & Honey (11)
Leo (8)
Let's Do It (6)
Let's Stay Together (12)

Life Is Just A Moment (2)
Lifeline (5)
Lonesome Cowboy (3)
Love Fantasy (10)
Love Will Bring Us Back Together (8)
Mash, Theme From (1)
Melody Maker (6)
Memory, The (4)
Mo Mise Si E (I Love You) (11)
Moving, Grooving (4)
Mystic Voyage (2)
No Stranger To Love (medley) (9)
One Sweet Love To Remember (4)
Ooh (12)
Our Time Is Coming (12)
People And The World (3)

Rhythm (7)
River Niger (11)
Rock Your Roll (10)
Running Away (5)
Sanctified Feeling (5)
Searching (4)
Sensitize (1)
Shack Up, Pack Up, It's Up (When I'm Gone) (9)
"Sigh" (Feel The Vibration) (10)
Simple And Sweet (8)
Slyde (9)
Spirit Of Doo Do (2)
Stairway To The Stars (12)
Stranded In The Jungle (5)
Sweet Tears (6)
Take All The Time You Need (2)

Take Me Out To The Ball Game (8)
There's A Master Plan (11)
Third Eye (3,11)
This Side Of Sunshine (5)
Together (5)
Tongue Power (3)
Turn Me Loose (12)
Vibrations (4)
Want You (medley) (9)
Wee Bit (2)
What You Won't Do For Love (9)
When Is Real, Real? (1,6)
You And Me My Love (3)
You Came Into My Life (9)
You Send Me (7)

AZTECA
Seventeen-member band led by Coke Escovedo (timbales) and his brother Pete (vocals; father of Sheila E.). Members included guitarist Neal Schon (later of Journey, Bad English) and drummer Lenny White.

| 1/13/73 | 151 | 9 | | Azteca .... | $10 | Columbia 31776 |

Ah! Ah!
Ain't Got No Special Woman

Azteca
Can't Take The Funk Out Of Me

Empty Prophet
La Piedra Del Sol

Love Not Then
Mamita Linda

Non Pacem
Peace Everybody

AZTEC CAMERA
Rock group formed in Glasgow, Scotland in 1980 by Roddey Frame (at the age of 16).

9/10/83	129	10		1 High Land, Hard Rain	$8	Sire 23899
10/13/84	175	6		2 Knife	$8	Sire 25183
4/13/85	181	3		3 Aztec Camera ....[M-L]	$8	Sire 25285
				10" album; 4 of 5 cuts recorded live at the Dominion Theatre, London on 10/16/84		
12/19/87	193	3		4 Love	$8	Sire 25646

All I Need Is Everything (2)
Back Door To Heaven (2)
Back On Board (1)
Backwards And Forwards (2,3)
Birth Of The True (2,3)

Boy Wonders (1)
Bugle Sounds Again (1,3)
Deep & Wide & Tall (4)
Down The Dip (1)
Everybody Is A Number One (4)

Head Is Happy (Heart's Insane) (2)
How Men Are (4)
Jump (3)
Just Like The USA (2)
Killermont Street (4)

Knife (2)
Lost Outside The Tunnel (1)
Mattress Of Wire (3)
More Than A Law (4)
Oblivious (1)
One And One (4)

Paradise (4)
Pillar To Post (1)
Release (1)
Somewhere In My Heart (4)
Still On Fire (2)
Walk Out To Winter (1)

We Could Send Letters (1)
Working In A Goldmine (4)

AZTEC TWO-STEP
Pop/rock duo: Rex Fowler and Neal Shulman.

| 12/25/76+ | 181 | 4 | | Two's Company .... | $8 | RCA 1497 |

Conversation In A Car
Finding Somebody New

Give It Away
Isn't It Sweet To Think So

Loving Game
Pajama Party

Penthouse
So We Danced

Where'd Our Loving Go
Whiskey Man

You've Got A Way

B

BABE RUTH
English rock quintet — Janita "Jenny" Haan, lead singer.

8/11/73	178	6		1 First Base	$14	Harvest 11151
2/22/75	75	7		2 Babe Ruth	$8	Harvest 11367
10/25/75	169	6		3 Stealin' Home	$8	Harvest 11451

Black Dog (1)
Can You Feel It (3)
Caught At The Plate (3)
Dancer (2)
Duchess Of Orleans (2)

Elusive (3)
Fascination (3)
Fistful Of Dollars (2)
It'll Happen In Time (3)
Jack O'Lantern (2)

Joker (1)
King Kong (1)
Mexican, The (1)
Private Number (2)
Runaways, The (1)

Sad But Rich (2)
Say No More (3)
Somebody's Nobody (2)
Tomorrow (Joining Of The Day) (3)

Turquoise (2)
2000 Sunsets (3)
We People Who Are Darker Than Blue (2)
Wells Fargo (1)

Winner Takes All (3)

BABYFACE
R&B vocalist/instrumentalist Kenneth Edmonds, formerly with Manchild and The Deele. Brother of Kevon and Melvin Edmonds of After 7. Prolific writing/production duo with L.A. Reid of The Deele.

| 8/5/89+ | 14 | 61 | ▲² | Tender Lover .... | $8 | Solar 45288 |

Can't Stop My Heart
Given A Chance

It's No Crime 7
Let's Be Romantic

My Kinda Girl 30
Soon As I Get Home

Sunshine
Tender Lover 14

Where Will You Go
Whip Appeal 6

DEBUT DATE	PEAK POS	WKS CHR	GOLD	ARTIST — Album Title	$	Label & Number

BABYLON A.D.
Hard-rock band. Lead singer Derek with Danny DeLaRosa, Ron Freschi, James Pacheco and Robb Reid.

12/2/89+	**88**	28		Babylon A.D.	$8	Arista 8580

Back In Babylon   Caught Up In The Crossfire   Hammer Swings Down   Maryanne   Shot O' Love
Bang Go The Bells   Desperate   Kid Goes Wild   Sally Danced   Sweet Temptation

BABYS, The
British rock group: John Waite (vocals), Walt Stocker, Mike Corby and Tony Brock. By 1980, keyboardist Jonathan Cain (later of Journey) had replaced Corby and bassist Ricky Phillips joined group. In 1989, Waite formed Bad English with Phillips and Cain.

3/5/77	**133**	13		1 The Babys	$8	Chrysalis 1129
10/8/77	**34**	26		2 Broken Heart	$8	Chrysalis 1150
1/27/79	**22**	25		3 Head First	$8	Chrysalis 1195
1/19/80	**42**	22		4 Union Jacks	$8	Chrysalis 1267
11/15/80	**71**	15		5 On The Edge	$8	Chrysalis 1305
11/7/81	**138**	7		6 Anthology ....[G]	$8	Chrysalis 1351

And If You Could See Me Fly (2)   **Every Time I Think Of You** (3,6) **13**   **If You've Got The Time** (1,6) **88**   **Midnight Rendezvous** (4,6) **72**   Rock 'N' Roll Is (Alive And Well) (5)   **Turn And Walk Away** (5,6) **42**
Anytime (4)   Give Me Your Love (2,6)   In Your Eyes (4)   Money (6)   Rodeo (1)   Turn Around In Tokyo (4)
Back On My Feet Again (4,6) **33**   Golden Mile (2)   **Isn't It Time** (2,6) **13**   Over And Over (1)   Run To Mexico (3)   Union Jack (4)
Broken Heart (2)   Gonna Be Somebody (5)   Jesus, Are You There? (4)   Piece Of The Action (2)   She's My Girl (5)   White Lightning (3)
California (3)   **Head First** (3,6) **77**   Laura (1)   Please Don't Leave Me Here (3)   **Silver Dreams** (2) **53**   Wild Man (1)
Darker Side Of Town (5)   I Believe In Love (1)   Looking For Love (1)   Postcard (5)   Sweet 17 (5,6)   Wrong Or Right (2)
Downtown (5)   I Love How You Love Me (1)   Love Don't Prove I'm Right (3)   Read My Stars (5)   Too Far Gone (5)   You (Got It) (3)
Dying Man (1)   I Was One (1)   Love Is Just A Mystery (4)   Read My Stars (5)   True Love True Confession (4)
   I'm Falling (2)   Love Won't Wait (5)   Rescue Me (2)

BACHARACH, Burt
Born on 5/12/28 in Kansas City. Conductor/arranger/composer. With lyricist Hal David wrote "Close To You," "What's New Pussycat" and most of Dionne Warwick's hits. Formerly married to actress Angie Dickinson. Now married to songwriter Carole Bayer Sager.

10/28/67+	**96**	65	●	1 Reach Out	$8	A&M 4131
6/28/69	**51**	87	●	2 Make It Easy On Yourself	$8	A&M 4188
6/19/71	**18**	24	●	3 Burt Bacharach	$8	A&M 3501
1/5/74	**181**	6		4 Living Together	$8	A&M 3527
12/14/74	**173**	5		5 Burt Bacharach's Greatest Hits ....[G]	$8	A&M 3661

Alfie (1,5)   Bond Street (1)   I Say A Little Prayer (1,5)   Lost Horizon (4)   Promises, Promises (2)   This Guy's In Love With You (2,5)
All Kinds Of People (3)   Do You Know The Way To San Jose (2)   **I'll Never Fall In Love Again** (2,5) **93**   Make It Easy On Yourself (2,5)   Raindrops Keep Fallin' On My Head (5)   Walk The Way You Talk (4)
And The People Were With Her (3)   Freefall (3)   Knowing When To Leave (2)   Message To Michael (1)   Reach Out For Me (1,5)   Wanting Things (2)
Any Day Now (2)   Hasbrook Heights (3)   Lisa (2)   Mexican Divorce (3)   Reflections (4)   What The World Needs Now Is Love (1,5)
April Fools (3)   House Is Not A Home (1)   Living Together, Growing Together (4)   Monterey Peninsula (3)   She's Gone Away (2)   Whoever You Are I Love You (2)
Are You There (With Another Girl) (1)   I Come To You (4)   Long Ago Tomorrow (4)   Nikki (2)   Something Big (4)   Windows Of The World (1)
Balance Of Nature (3)   I Might Frighten Her Away (4)   Look Of Love (1,5)   One Less Bell To Answer (3)   (They Long To Be) Close To You (3,5)   Wives & Lovers (3,5)
   Pacific Coast Highway (2)

BACHELORS, The
Pop vocal trio from Dublin, Ireland: brothers Declan and Con Cluskey, with John Stokes. Formed as a harmonica instrumental trio known as the Harmonichords.

6/20/64	**70**	16		1 Presenting: The Bachelors	$15	London 353
11/7/64	**142**	3		2 Back Again	$15	London 393
4/3/65	**136**	4		3 No Arms Can Ever Hold You	$15	London 418
9/4/65	**89**	6		4 Marie	$15	London 435

Always (4)   He's Got The Whole World In His Hands (2)   I'm Yours (3)   Maybe (2,4)   Pennies From Heaven (3)   Whispering Grass (1)
Charmaine (1)   If (1)   Melody Of Love (2)   Put Your Arms Around Me, Honey (2)   Whistle Down The Wind (3)
Danny Boy (4)   **I Believe** (1,4) **33**   If I Should Fall In Love Again (3)   Mistakes (3)   Ramona (2)   With All My Heart (3)
Diane (1) **10**   I Do Adore Her (3)   Light A Candle In The Chapel (4)   Moments To Remember (1)   Saints, The (3)   With These Hands (1,2)
Down Among The Sheltering Palms (4)   **I Wouldn't Trade You For The World** (2) **69**   Little White Cloud That Cried (2)   Moonlight And Roses (2)   Sittin' In The Sun (4)   You'll Never Walk Alone (1)
Dream (1)   I'll Be With You In Apple Blossom Time (4)   **No Arms Can Ever Hold You** (3) **27**   Skip To My Lou (3)   You're Next (4)
Far Away Places (4)   I'm Getting Sentimental Over You (3)   Love To Last A Lifetime (4)   Old Bill (1)   Ten Pretty Girls (2)
Far Far Away (3)   **Marie** (4) **15**   Only You (1)   Pagan Love Song (2)   Till Then My Love (4)   Whispering (1)

★★319★★ BACHMAN-TURNER OVERDRIVE
Hard-rock group formed in Vancouver, Canada in 1972. Brothers Randy (vocals, guitar), Tim (guitar) and Robbie Bachman (drums), with C. Fred Turner (vocals, bass). Originally known as Brave Belt. Randy had been in The Guess Who and recorded solo. Tim left in 1973, replaced by Blair Thornton. Randy left in 1977. Randy and Tim regrouped with C.F. Turner in 1984.

8/18/73+	**70**	68	●	1 Bachman-Turner Overdrive	$10	Mercury 673
1/19/74	**4**	75	●	2 Bachman-Turner Overdrive II	$10	Mercury 696
8/31/74	**1**[1]	50	●	3 Not Fragile	$10	Mercury 1004
3/8/75	**180**	3		4 Bachman-Turner-Bachman As Brave Belt...........[R]	$10	Reprise 2210
				reissue of 1972 LP Brave Belt II		
5/31/75	**5**	22	●	5 Four Wheel Drive	$10	Mercury 1027
1/3/76	**23**	21	●	6 Head On	$10	Mercury 1067
8/14/76	**19**	15	●	7 Best Of B.T.O. (So Far) ....[G]	$10	Mercury 1101
3/19/77	**70**	9		8 Freeways	$10	Mercury 3700
3/18/78	**130**	4		9 Street Action	$10	Mercury 3713
4/7/79	**165**	4		10 Rock N' Roll Nights	$10	Mercury 3748
				above 2: **BTO**		
9/29/84	**191**	2		11 Bachman Turner Overdrive	$8	Compleat 1010

Amelia Earhart (10)   Another Way Out (4)   Away From Home (6)   Blown (3)   Blue Moanin' (3)   Can We All Come Together (8)
Another Fool (11)   Average Man (6)   Be A Good Man (4)   **Blue Collar** (1,7) **68**

BACHMAN-TURNER OVERDRIVE — Cont'd

Can You Feel It (4)
City's Still Growin' (11)
Don't Get Yourself In Trouble (1)
Don't Let The Blues Get You Down (5)
Down And Out Man (1)
Down, Down (8)
Down The Road (9)
Dunrobin's Gone (4)
Easy Groove (8)
End Of The Line (10)
Find Out About Love (6)
Flat Broke Love (5)
For Love (9)
For The Weekend (11)

Four Wheel Drive (5)
Free Wheelin' (3) *flip*
Freeways (8)
Gimme Your Money Please (1,7) **70**
Give It Time (2)
Givin' It All Away (3)
Goodbye, Soul Shy (4)
Heartaches (10) **60**
Heaven Tonight (10)
Here She Comes Again (10)
Hey You (5,7) **21**
Hold Back the Water (1)
I Don't Have To Hide (2)
I'm In Love (9)
It's Over (6)

Jamaica (10)
Just For You (8)
Just Look At Me Now (11)
Let It Ride (2,7) **23**
Life Still Goes On (I'm Lonely) (8)
Little Gandy Dancer (1)
Long Time For A Little While (9)
Long Way 'Round (4)
Lookin' Out For #1 (6,7) **65**
Lost In A Fantasy (11)
Lowland Fling (4)
Madison Avenue (9)
My Sugaree (1)
My Wheels Won't Turn (8)

Never Comin' Home (4)
Not Fragile (3)
Put It In A Song (4)
Quick Change Artist (5)
Rock And Roll Hell (10)
Rock And Roll Nights (10)
Rock Is My Life, And This Is My Song (3)
Roll On Down The Highway (3,7) **14**
Second Hand (3)
Service With A Smile (11)
She's A Devil (5)
She's Keepin' Time (5)
Shotgun Rider (8)
Sledgehammer (3)

Stay Alive (6)
Stayed Awake All Night (1)
Stonegates (2)
Street Action (9)
Summer Soldier (4)
Take It Like A Man (6,7) **33**
Takes A Lot Of People (9)
Takin' Care Of Business (2,7) **12**
Thank You For The Feelin' (1)
Toledo (11)
Too Far Away (4)
Tramp (2)
Wastin' Time (10)
Waterloo Country (4)

Welcome Home (2)
Wild Spirit (6)
Woncha Take Me For A While (6)
World Is Waiting For A Love Song (9)
You Ain't Seen Nothing Yet (3,7) **1**
You're Gonna Miss Me (9)

BACK STREET CRAWLER

British rock group led by Paul Kossoff (guitarist of Free; died on 3/19/76 of drug-induced heart failure).

11/15/75	111	10		1 The Band Plays On	$10	Atco 125
8/14/76	140	5		2 2nd Street	$10	Atco 138
9/10/77	85	13		3 Crawler	$8	Epic 34900

CRAWLER

All The Girls Are Crazy (1)
Band Plays On (1)
Blue Soul (2)
Hoo Doo Woman (1)
It's A Long Way Down To The Top (1)

Jason Blue (1)
Just For You (2)
Leaves In The Wind (2)
Never Loved A Woman (3)
New York.

New York (1)
On Your Life (2)
One Too Many Lovers (3)
Pastime Dreamer (3)
Raging River (2)

Rock & Roll Junkie (1)
Selfish Lover (2)
Sold On Down The Line (1)
Some Kind Of Happy (2)
Stealing My Way (1)

Stone Cold Sober (3)
Stop Doing What You're Doing (2)
Survivor (1)
Sweet, Sweet Beauty (2)

Train Song (1)
Without You Babe (3)
You And Me (3)
You Are My Saviour (3)
You Got Money (3)

★★217★★ BAD COMPANY

British rock band: Paul Rodgers (vocals), Mick Ralphs (guitar), Simon Kirke (drums) and Boz Burrell (bass). Rodgers and Kirke from Free; Ralphs from Mott The Hoople; and Burrell from King Crimson. Rodgers, who left group in late 1982, was a member of the supergroup The Firm (1984-86) and The Law (since 1991). In 1986, vocalist Brian Howe joined Kirke and Ralphs in group. Bassist Paul Cullen and guitarist Geoffrey Whitehorn joined in 1990. Rick Wills (bass; Foreigner) joined in late 1992.

7/27/74	1¹	64	▲⁴	1 Bad Company	$8	Swan Song 8410
4/19/75	3	33	▲³	2 Straight Shooter	$8	Swan Song 8413
2/14/76	5	28	▲	3 Run With The Pack	$8	Swan Song 8415
3/26/77	15	24	●	4 Burnin' Sky	$8	Swan Song 8500
3/31/79	3	37	▲²	5 Desolation Angels	$8	Swan Song 8506
9/4/82	26	18	●	6 Rough Diamonds	$8	Swan Song 90001
1/18/86	137	14	▲²	7 10 From 6 .... [G]	$8	Atlantic 81625
				10 songs taken from their 6 charted albums		
10/25/86	106	9		8 Fame And Fortune	$8	Atlantic 81684
9/17/88	58	40	●	9 Dangerous Age	$8	Atlantic 81884
6/30/90	35	75	▲	10 Holy Water	$12	Atco 91371
10/10/92	40	18↑		11 Here Comes Trouble	$12	Atco 91759

Anna (2)
Bad Company (1,7)
Bad Man (9)
Ballad Of The Band (6)
Both Feet In The Water (11)
Boys Cry Tough (4)
Brokenhearted (11)
Burnin' Sky (4) **78**
Burning Up (8)
Call On Me (2)
Can't Get Enough (1,7) **5**
Crazy Circles (5)
Cross Country Boy (8)
Dangerous Age (9)
Dead Of The Night (10)
Deal With The Preacher (2)
Dirty Boy (9)
Do Right By Your Woman (3)
Don't Let Me Down (1)

Downhill Ryder (6)
Early In The Morning (5)
Electricland (6,7) **74**
Everything I Need (4)
Evil Wind (5)
Fade Away (3)
Fame And Fortune (8)
Fearless (10)
Feel Like Makin' Love (2,7) **10**
Gone, Gone, Gone (5) **56**
Good Lovin' Gone Bad (2) **36**
Heartbeat (4)
Here Comes Trouble (11)
Hold On My Heart (8)
Hold To My Heart (11)
Holy Water (10) **89**
Honey Child (3) **59**

How About That (11) **38**
I Can't Live Without You (10)
I Don't Care (10)
If I'm Sleeping (8)
If You Needed Somebody (10) **16**
Kickdown (6)
Lay Your Love On Me (10)
Leaving You (4)
Like Water (4)
Little Angel (11)
Live For The Music (3,7)
Lonely For Your Love (5)
Long Walk (8)
Love (4)
Love Me Somebody (3)
Man Needs Woman (4)
Master Of Ceremony (4)
Morning Sun (4)

Movin' On (1,7) **19**
My Only One (11)
Never Too Late (10)
No Smoke Without A Fire (4)
Nuthin' On The TV (6)
Oh, Atlanta (5)
Old Mexico (6)
100 Miles (10)
One Night (9)
Painted Face (6)
Passing Time (4)
Peace Of Mind (4)
Racetrack (6)
Ready For Love (1,7)
Rhythm Machine (5)
Rock 'N' Roll Fantasy (5,7) **13**
Rock Of America (9)
Rock Steady (1)

Run With The Pack (3,7)
Seagull (1)
Shake It Up (9) **82**
She Brings Me Love (5)
Shooting Star (2,7)
Silver, Blue & Gold (3)
Simple Man (3)
Something About You (9)
Stranger Stranger (10)
Stranger Than Fiction (11)
Sweet Lil' Sister (3)
Take The Time (5)
Take This Town (11)
Tell It Like It Is (8)
That Girl (8)
This Could Be The One (11) **87**
This Love (8) **85**
Too Bad (4)

Untie The Knot (6)
Valerie (8)
Walk Through Fire (10) **28**
Way I Choose (1)
Way That It Goes (9)
Weep No More (8)
What About You (11)
When We Made Love (8)
Wild Fire Woman (2)
With You In A Heartbeat (10)
Young Blood (3) **20**

BAD ENGLISH

Rock supergroup: John Waite (vocals), Ricky Phillips (bass), Jonathan Cain (keyboards), Neal Schon (guitar) and Deen Castronovo (drums). Waite, Phillips and Cain were members of The Babys. Cain and Schon (ex-Santana) were members of Journey. Schon and Castronovo with Harline in 1992.

| 7/15/89 | 21 | 52 | ▲ | 1 Bad English .... | $8 | Epic 45083 |
| 9/14/91 | 72 | 8 | | 2 Backlash .... | $12 | Epic 46935 |

Best Of What I Got (1)
Dancing Off The Edge Of The World (2)
Don't Walk Away (1)
Forget Me Not (1) **45**

Ghost In Your Heart (1)
Heaven Is A 4 Letter Word (1) **66**
Lay Down (1)
Life At The Top (2)

Make Love Last (2)
Possession (1) **21**
Pray For Rain (2)
Price Of Love (1) **5**
Ready When You Are (1)

Rebel Say A Prayer (2)
Restless Ones (1)
Rockin' Horse (1)
Savage Blue (2)
So This Is Eden (2)

Straight To Your Heart (2) **42**
Time Alone With You (2)
Time Stood Still (2)
Tough Times Don't Last (1)

When I See You Smile (1) **1**

BADFINGER

Welsh rock quartet originally known as The Iveys. Leader Pete Ham (b: 4/27/47) committed suicide on 4/23/75. Group disbanded from 1975-78. Bassist Tom Evans committed suicide on 11/23/83 (age 36). Keyboardist Tony Kaye (Yes, Badger) was a member from 1978 until group disbanded in 1982.

3/28/70	55	17		1 Magic Christian Music	$25	Apple 3364
				also see soundtrack *Magic Christian*		
11/28/70	28	15		2 No Dice	$35	Apple 3367

DEBUT DATE	PEAK POS	WKS CHR	GOLD	ARTIST — Album Title	$	Label & Number
				BADFINGER — Cont'd		
12/25/71+	**31**	32		3 Straight Up	$80	Apple 3387
				produced by Todd Rundgren and George Harrison		
12/15/73+	**122**	8		4 Ass	$15	Apple 3411
3/9/74	**161**	5		5 Badfinger	$15	Warner 2762
11/9/74	**148**	6		6 Wish You Were Here	$25	Warner 2827
3/24/79	**125**	8		7 Airwaves	$12	Elektra 175
3/28/81	**155**	6		8 Say No More	$8	Radio 16030

Airwaves (7)
Andy Norris (5)
Apple Of My Eye (4)
Baby Blue (3) *14*
Beautiful And Blue (1)
Because I Love You (8)
Believe Me (2)
Better Days (2)
Blind Owl (4)
Blodwyn (2)
Carry On Till Tomorrow (1) *7*
Come Down Hard (7)
Come One (8)
Constitution (4)
Cowboy (4)

Crimson Ship (1)
Crocadillo (8)
Day After Day (3) *4*
Dear Angie (1)
Dennis (6)
Dreamer, The (7)
Fisherman (1)
Flying (3)
Get Away (4)
Give It Up (5)
Got To Get Out Of Here (6)
Hold On (8) *56*
I Can Love You (4)
I Can't Take It (4)
I Don't Mind (2)
I Got You (8)

I Miss You (5)
I'd Die Babe (3)
I'm In Love (1)
Icicles (6)
In The Meantime (medley) (6)
Island (5)
It Had To Be (2)
It's Over (3)
Just A Chance (6)
King Of The Load (1) (6)
Knocking Down Our Home (1)
Know One Knows (6)
Lonely You (5)
Look Out California (7)
Lost Inside Your Love (7)

Love Is Easy (5)
Love Is Gonna Come At Last (7) *69*
Love Me Do (2)
Love Time (6)
Matted Spam (5)
Maybe Tomorrow (1) *67*
Meanwhile Back At The Ranch (medley) (6)
Midnight Caller (2)
Midnight Sun (1)
Money (3)
My Heart Goes Out (5)
Name Of The Game (1)
No Matter What (2) *8*
No More (8)

Passin' Time (8)
Perfection (3)
Rock N' Roll Contract (8)
Rock Of All Ages (1)
Sail Away (7)
Shine On (1)
Should I Smoke (medley) (6)
Some Other Time (medley) (6)
Sometimes (3)
Song For A Lost Friend (5)
Suitcase (3)
Sweet Tuesday Morning (3)
Sympathy (7)
Take It All (3)
Three Time Loser (8)

Timeless (4)
Too Hung Up On You (8)
Walk In The Rain (1)
Watford John (2)
We're For The Dark (2)
When I Say (4)
Where Do We Go From Here? (5)
Why Don't We Talk? (3)
Winner, The (4,7)
Without You (2)
Your So Fine (6)

BADGER

British rock quartet led by Tony Kaye (former keyboardist with Yes and later with Badfinger).

8/11/73	**167**	8		One Live Badger .... [L]	$10	Atco 7022

Fountain
On The Way Home
Preacher, The
River
Wheel Of Fortune
Wind Of Change

BADLANDS

Hard-rock quartet: Ray Gillen (vocals) Jake E. Lee (former guitarist with Ozzy Osbourne), Greg Chaisson and Eric Singer (former member of Black Sabbath). Singer replaced by Jeff Martin in 1990.

6/10/89	**57**	26		1 Badlands	$8	Atlantic 81966
6/29/91	**140**	3		2 Voodoo Highway	$12	Atlantic 82251

Dancing On The Edge (1)
Devil's Stomp (1)
Dreams In The Dark (1)
Fire And Rain (1)

Hard Driver (1)
Heaven's Train (2)
High Wire (1)
In A Dream (2)

Jade's Song (1)
Joe's Blues (2)
Last Time (2)
Love Don't Mean A Thing (2)

Rumblin' Train (1)
Seasons (1)
Shine On (2)
Show Me The Way (2)

Silver Horses (2)
Soul Stealer (2)
Streets Cry Freedom (1)
3 Day Funk (2)

Voodoo Highway (2)
Whiskey Dust (2)
Winter's Call (1)

BAERWALD, David

Half of the David & David duo. Born in 1960 in Oxford, Ohio.

7/7/90	**149**	19		Bedtime Stories	$12	A&M 5289

All For You
Best Inside You
Colette
Dance
Good Times
Hello Mary
In The Morning
Liberty Lies
Sirens In The City
Stranger
Walk Through Fire
Young Anymore

★★53★★ BAEZ, Joan

Preeminent folk song stylist. Born Joan Chandos Baez in Staten Island, New York on 1/9/41 to a Mexican father and British mother. Became a political activist while attending Boston University in the late 1950s. Made her professional debut in July 1959 at the first Newport Folk Festival. Orientation changed from traditional to popular folk songs in the early '60s. Influential in fostering career of Bob Dylan. Founded the Institute for the Study of Nonviolence in Carmel Valley, California in 1965. Married to Stanford University student leader David Harris from 1968-71. Appeared in Bob Dylan's Rolling Thunder Revue in 1975 and his 1978 film *Renaldo And Clara*. Joan's sister Mimi Farina was in a folk song-writing/singing duo with her husband, the late Richard Farina.

11/27/61+	**13**	125	●	1 Joan Baez, Vol. 2	$20	Vanguard 2097
3/3/62	**15**	140	●	2 Joan Baez	$25	Vanguard 2077
				Joan's first album, recorded in 1960		
10/27/62	**10**	114	●	3 **Joan Baez In Concert** .... [L]	$20	Vanguard 2122
11/23/63	**45**	18		4 The Best Of Joan Baez .... [E]	$15	Squire 33001
				first recordings from 1959 with Bill Wood and Ted Alevizos		
12/7/63+	**7**	36		5 **Joan Baez In Concert, Part 2** .... [L]	$20	Vanguard 2123
11/21/64	**12**	66		6 Joan Baez/5	$20	Vanguard 79160
10/23/65	**10**	27		7 **Farewell, Angelina**	$20	Vanguard 79200
9/2/67	**38**	20		8 Joan	$20	Vanguard 79240
8/10/68	**84**	25		9 Baptism	$20	Vanguard 79275
1/25/69	**30**	20	●	10 Any Day Now	$20	Vanguard 79306 [2]
				songs of Bob Dylan		
6/7/69	**36**	14		11 David's Album	$8	Vanguard 79308
				dedicated to her husband, David Harris, imprisoned for draft resistance		
3/21/70	**80**	14		12 One Day At A Time	$8	Vanguard 79310
11/21/70	**73**	11		13 The First 10 Years .... [K]	$10	Vanguard 6560 [2]
9/18/71	**11**	23	●	14 Blessed Are	$10	Vanguard 6570 [2]
1/1/72	**164**	5		15 Carry It On .... [S]	$8	Vanguard 79313
				film features Joan and husband David		
5/27/72	**48**	24		16 Come From The Shadows	$8	A&M 4339
12/16/72+	**188**	7		17 The Joan Baez Ballad Book .... [K]	$10	Vanguard 41/42 [2]
				selections from first 5 Vanguard LPs		
5/19/73	**138**	9		18 Where Are You Now, My Son?	$8	A&M 4390
				side 2 has actual war sounds recorded in Vietnam		
7/7/73	**163**	8		19 Hits/Greatest & Others .... [G]	$8	Vanguard 79332
5/17/75	**11**	46	●	20 Diamonds & Rust	$8	A&M 4527
2/7/76	**34**	17		21 From Every Stage .... [L]	$10	A&M 3704 [2]
11/6/76	**62**	17		22 Gulf Winds	$8	A&M 4603

BAEZ, Joan — Cont'd

6/25/77	54	14		23 Blowin' Away	$8	Portrait 34697
12/17/77+	121	8		24 The Best Of Joan C. Baez .... [G]	$8	A&M 4668
8/4/79	113	7		25 Honest Lullaby	$8	Portrait 35766

(Ain't Gonna Let Nobody) Turn Me Around (21)
All In Green Went My Love Riding (9)
All My Trials (2,17)
All The Pretty Little Horses (9)
Alter Boy And The Thief (23)
Amazing Grace (3)
Angeline (14)
Annabel Lee (8)
Astrapsen (The Sun Is Risen) (4)
Ate Amanha (3)
Babe, I'm Gonna Leave You (3)
Ballad Of Sacco & Vanzetti (21)
Banks Of The Ohio (1,4)
Barbara Allen (1,17)
Battle Hymn Of The Republic (5)
Be Not Too Hard (8)
Before The Deluge (25)
Best Of Friends (18)
Birmingham Sunday (6)
Black Is The Color Of My True Love's Hair (3,4,17)
Blessed Are... (14,19,21)
Blowin' In The Wind (21)
Blue Sky (20) **57**
Boots Of Spanish Leather (10)
Boulder To Birmingham (21)
Brand New Tennessee Waltz (14,19)
Careless Love (4)
Carry It On (12,13,15)
Caruso (22)
Casida Of The Lament (9)
Cherry Tree Carol (1)
Childhood III (9)
Children And All That Jazz (20,24)
Children Of Darkness (8)
Colours (7,9)
Copper Kettle (3)
Cry Me A River (23)
Daddy, You Been On My Mind (7)
Danger Waters (3)
Dangling Conversation (8,19)
Danny Boy (medley) (20)
David's Song (12)
Dear Landlord (10)
Death Of Queen Jane (6)

Diamonds And Rust (20,21,24) **35**
Dida (20)
Do Right Woman, Do Right Man (15)
Don't Think Twice, It's All Right (5,13)
Don't Weep After Me (4)
Donna Donna (2)
Drifter's Escape (10)
East Virginia (2,17)
El Preso Numero Nueve (The Ninth Prisoner) (2)
Eleanor Rigby (8,19)
Engine 143 (1)
Epitaph For A Poet (9)
Evil (9)
Fare Thee Well ..see: Ten Thousand Miles
Farewell Angelina (7,13)
Fennario (5,17)
Fifteen Months (14)
For All We Know (25)
For Sasha (25)
Forever Young (21,24)
Fountain Of Sorrow (20)
Free At Last (25)
From Portrait Of The Artist As A Young Man (9)
Gabriel And Me (14)
Gacela Of The Dark Death (9)
Geordie (3,13)
Ghetto (12,13)
Glad Bluebird Of Happiness (11)
Go Way From My Window (6,17)
Gospel Ship (3)
Gracias A La Vida (Here's To Life) (24)
Green, Green Grass Of Home (11,13)
Greenwood Side (8)
Gulf Winds (22)
Hard Rain's A-Gonna Fall (7,13)
Heartfelt Line Or Two (23)
Heaven Help Us All (14,19)
Hello In There (20)
Help Me Make It Through The Night (14,19)
Henry Martin (2,17)
Hickory Wind (11,15)
Hitchhikers' Song (14)
Honest Lullaby (25)

House Carpenter (3,17)
House Of The Rising Sun (2,17)
Hush Little Baby (5)
I Dream Of Jeannie (medley) (20)
I Dreamed I Saw St. Augustine (10)
I Pity The Poor Immigrant (10,19)
I Saw The Vision Of Armies (9)
I Shall Be Released (10,15,21)
I Still Miss Someone (6)
I'm Blowin' Away (23)
Idols And Heroes (15)
If I Knew (11,13)
If I Were A Carpenter (8,13)
Imagine (16,24)
In Forty Days (15)
In Guernica (9)
In The Quiet Morning (16) **69**
It Ain't Me, Babe (6)
It's All Over Now, Baby Blue (7)
Jackaroe (5,17)
Jesse (20)
Joe Hill (12,15,21)
John Henry (4)
John Riley (2,13,17)
Jolie Blonde (12)
Just A Closer Walk With Thee (11)
Kingdom Of Childhood (22)
Kitty (4)
Kumbaya (3)
La Colombe - The Dove (8)
Lady Came From Baltimore (8)
Lady Mary (3)
Last, Lonely And Wretched (14)
Last Thing On My Mind (15)
Less Than The Song (18)
Let It Be (14,19) **49**
Let Your Love Flow (25)
Life Is Sacred (15)
Light A Light (25)
Lily Of The West (1,17)
Lily, Rosemary And The Jack Of Hearts (21)
Lincoln Freed Me (The Slave) (14)
Little Moses (2)

London (9,13)
Lonesome Road (1)
Long Black Veil (5,12)
Love Is Just A Four-Letter Word (10,13,15,19,21) **86**
Love Minus Zero/No Limit (10)
Love Song To A Stranger (16,21,24)
Lowlands (4)
Luba The Baroness (23)
Magic Wood (9)
Manha De Carnaval (5,13)
Many A Mile To Freedom (23)
Marie Flore (medley) (14)
Mary Call (18)
Mary Hamilton (2,13,17)
Matty Groves (3,17)
Michael (25)
Milanese Waltz (medley) (14)
Minister Of War (9)
Miracles (23)
My Home's Across The Blue Ridge Mountains (11)
Myths (16)
Natalia (21)
Never Dreamed You'd Leave In Summer (20,24)
Night They Drove Old Dixie Down (14,19,21,24) **3**
No Expectations (12,13)
No Man Is An Iland (9)
No Woman, No Cry (25)
North (8)
North Country Blues (10)
'Nu Bello Cardillo (5)
O Brother! (22)
O'Cangaceiro (6)
Of The Dark Past (9)
Oh, Happy Day (15,21)
Oh, Little Child (9)
Oh! What A Beautiful City (4)
Old Blue (1,17)
Old Welsh Song (9,13)
Once I Had A Sweetheart (5,17)
Once I Knew A Pretty Girl (1)
One Day At A Time (12)
One Too Many Mornings (4)
Only Heaven Knows (Ah, The Sad Wind Blows) (18)
Outside The Nashville City Limits (14)
Pal Of Mine (1)

Parable Of The Old Man And The Young (9)
Partisan, The (16)
Pauvre Ruteboeuf (9)
Plaisir D'Amour (1)
Please Come To Boston (21,24)
Poems From The Japanese (9)
Poor Wayfaring Stranger (11)
Portland Town (5)
Pretty Boy Floyd (3)
Prison Trilogy (Billy Rose) (16,24)
Put Your Hand In The Land (14)
Queen Of Hearts (5,17)
Railroad Boy (1,17)
Rainbow Road (16)
Rake And Rambling Boy (2)
Ranger's Command (7)
Restless Farewell (10)
Rider, Pass By (18)
River In The Pines (7)
Rock Salt And Nails (11)
Sad-Eyed Lady Of The Lowlands (10)
Sagt Mir Wo Die Blumen Sind (7)
Saigon Bride (8)
Sail Away Ladies (4)
Sailing (3)
Salt Of The Earth (14)
San Francisco Mabel Joy (14)
Satisfied Mind (7)
Seabirds (22)
Seven Bridges Road (12)
Silkie (1)
Silver Dagger (2,13,17)
Simple Twist Of Fate (20,24)
So Soon In The Morning (4)
So We'll Go No More A Roving (6)
Song At The End Of The Movie (25)
Song In The Blood (9)
Song Of Bangladesh (16)
Stephanie's Song (7)
Stewball (6,21)
Still Waters At Night (22)
Stranger In My Place (16)
Suzanne (15,21)
Sweet Sir Galahad (12,13)
Sweeter For Me (22,24)

Swing Low, Sweet Chariot (21)
Take Me Back To The Sweet Sunny South (12)
Te Ador (5,13)
Tears Of Rage (10)
Ten Thousand Miles (2,17)
There But For Fortune (6,13,19) **50**
33rd Of August (14)
Three Fishers (5)
Three Horses (14)
Time Is Passing Us By (22)
Time Rag (23)
To Bobby (16)
Tramp On The Street (11)
Travellin' Shoes (4)
Trees They Do Grow High (1,17)
Tumbleweed (16)
Turquoise (8,13)
Unquiet Grave (6)
Villa-Lobos: Bachianas Brasilerias No. 5 - Aria (6)
Wagoner's Lad (1,17)
Walie Walie (3)
Walkin' Down The Line (10)
Walls Of Redwing (10)
We Shall Overcome (5,15) **90**
Weary Mothers (People's Union 1) (16)
What Have They Done To The Rain (3)
What You Gonna Call Your Pretty Little Baby (4)
When Time Is Stolen (14)
When You Hear Them Cuckoos Hollerin' (6)
Where Are You Now, My Son? (18)
Who Mudered The Minutes (9)
Wild Mountain Thyme (7)
Wildwood Flower (2)
Will The Circle Be Unbroken (11,13)
Windrose (18)
Winds Of The Old Days (20)
With God On Our Side (5,13)
Yellow Coat (23)
You Ain't Goin' Nowhere (10,13)
Young Gypsy (18)

BAILEY, Philip

Born on 5/8/51 in Denver. R&B percussionist/co-lead vocalist with Earth, Wind & Fire since 1971.

9/10/83	71	14		1 Continuation	$8	Columbia 38725
11/10/84+	22	35		2 Chinese Wall	$8	Columbia 39542
5/24/86	84	11		3 Inside Out	$8	Columbia 40209

Back It Up (3)
Because Of You (3)
Children Of The Ghetto (2)
Day Will Come (3)
Desire (1)
Don't Leave Me Baby (3)

Easy Lover (2) **2**
Echo My Heart (3)
For Every Heart That's Been Broken (2)
Go (2)

Good Guy's Supposed To Get The Girls (1)
I Go Crazy (2)
I Know (1)
I'm Hurtin' For Your Love (1)
It's Our Time (1)

Long Distance Love (3)
Photogenic Memory (2)
Show You The Way To Love (2)
Special Effect (3)
State Of The Heart (3)

Take This With You (3)
Time Is A Woman (2)
Trapped (1)
Vaya (Go With Love) (1)
Walking On The Chinese Wall (2) **46**

Welcome To The Club (3)
Woman (2)
Your Boyfriend's Back (1)

BAILEY, Razzy

Born Rasie Michael Bailey on 2/14/39 in Five Points, Alabama. Country singer/songwriter. Big break came when Dickey Lee recorded Razzy's "9,999,999 Tears."

| 6/20/81 | 183 | 2 | | 1 Makin' Friends | $8 | RCA 4026 |
| 2/27/82 | 176 | 4 | | 2 Feelin' Right | $8 | RCA 4228 |

Anywhere There's A Jukebox (1)
Bad News Look (2)
Best Kept Secret In Town (1)
Blaze Of Glory (2)

Blind Faith And The Naked Truth (1)
Everytime You Cross My Mind (You Break My Heart) (2)
Friends (1)

I Loved 'Em All (2)
I've Had My Limit (Of Two-Timing Women) (2)
Late Night Honky Tonk Country Song (1)
Midnight Hauler (1)

Night Life (2)
Old No Homer (1)
Scratch My Back (And Whisper In My Ear) (1)
She Left Love All Over Me (2)

Sittin' Here Wishing (I Was Someplace Else) (2)
Spending My Nights With You (1)
Too Far Gone And Much Too Close To You (1)

Travelin' Time (2)
Your Momma And Daddy Sure Did Something Right (2)

BAIO, Scott

Cast member of TV's Happy Days, Joanie Loves Chachi and Charles In Charge. Born on 9/22/60 in New York City.

| 9/4/82 | 181 | 4 | | Scott Baio | $8 | RCA 8025 |

Half The World
How Do You Talk To Girls

Looking For The Right Girl
Midnight Confessions

Runnin' Out Of Reasons To Go

Wanted For Love
What Am I Supposed To Do

What Was In That Kiss
When You Find Someone Who Loves You

Woman, I Love Only You

BAJA MARIMBA BAND
Nine-man band led by marimbaist Julius Wechter (member of Herb Alpert's Tijuana Brass).

4/25/64	**88**	12	**1**	Baja Marimba Band .... [I]	**$8**	A&M 104
4/24/65	**123**	3	**2**	Baja Marimba Band Rides Again .... [I]	**$8**	A&M 109
1/8/66	**102**	16	**3**	For Animals Only .... [I]	**$8**	A&M 113
11/19/66+	**54**	43	**4**	Watch Out! .... [I]	**$8**	A&M 4118
5/27/67	**77**	44	**5**	Heads Up! .... [I]	**$8**	A&M 4123

JULIUS WECHTER AND THE BAJA MARIMBA BAND:

1/20/68	**168**	9	**6**	Fowl Play .... [I]	**$8**	A&M 4136
8/31/68	**171**	8	**7**	Do You Know The Way To San Jose? .... [I]	**$8**	A&M 4150
3/8/69	**117**	10	**8**	Those Were The Days .... [I]	**$8**	A&M 4167
10/18/69	**176**	3	**9**	Fresh Air.. [I]	**$8**	A&M 4200
4/4/70	**180**	6	**10**	Greatest Hits ....[G-I]	**$8**	A&M 4248

Acapulco 1922 (1,10) · **Along Comes Mary** (6,10) *96* · Back To Cuernavaca (1) · Baja Humbug (6) · Baja Nights (1) · Baja Nova (5) · Ballad Of Bonnie And Clyde (7) · Big Red (8) · Born Free (5) · Brasilia (2,10) · By The Time I Get To Phoenix (7) · Cabeza Arriba! (Heads Up!) (5) · Cast Your Fate To The Wind (4) · Charade (1) · Cielito Lindo (9)

Comin' In The Back Door (1,10) *41* · Cry Of The Wild Goose (5) · Dear Heart (2) · December's Child (1) · Do You Know The Way To San Jose (7) · Domingo (5) · Dream A Little Dream Of Me (8) · El Gazelle (3) · Eleanor Rigby (9) · Elenore (8) · Elephant Soul (9) · Fiddler On The Roof (6) · Flyin' High (8) · For Animals Only (3) · For Bud (7) · Fowl Play (6,10) · Fresh Air (9) · Gay Ranchero (4)

Georgy Girl (5,10) *98* · **Ghost Riders In The Sky** (4,10) *52* · Gnu Bossa Nova (3) · Goin' Out The Side Door (2) · Guacamole (2) · Happening To Me (8) · Hecho En Mexico (2) · Here (9) · Here, There And Everywhere (8) · How Much Is That Doggie In The Window (3) · I Don't Want To Walk Without You (9) · I Say A Little Prayer (7) · I'll Marimba You (9) · In A Vera Cruz Vein (5) · Juarez (2) · Knowing When To Leave (8) · La Cucaracha (3)

Las Mananitas (3) · Last Of The Red Hot Llamas (3) · Les Bicyclettes De Belsize (8) · Look Of Love (6,10) · Madagascar (4) · Majorca (2) · Maria Elena (1,10) · Maria's First Rose (1) · Moonglow/Picnic Theme (1) · More (2) · More I See You (4) · Odd One (5) · Partridge In A Pear Tree (Twelve Days Of Christmas) (3) · Pedro's Porch, Part II (1) · Peru '68 (3) · Portuguese Washerwoman (4) · Puff (The Magic Dragon) (3)

Red Roses For A Blue Lady (2) · Rhode Island Red (6) · Sabor A Mi (Be True To Me) (4) · Samba De Orfeu (1) · Samba Nuevo (9) · San Fernando (7) · She's Leaving Home (6) · Somewhere My Love (4,10) · Sounds Of Silence (6) · Spanish Eyes (5,10) · Spanish Moss (4) · Spanish Rose (2) · Summer Samba (6) · Sunday Mornin' (7) · Sunrise, Sunset (7) · Swan Waltz (4) · Telephone Song (4) · Temptation (5)

(There's) Always Something There To Remind Me (8) · There's Gotta Be Something Better Than This (7) · They Call The Wind Maria (5) · Those Were The Days (8) · Tomorrow Will Be Better (4) · Up Cherry Street (1) · Walk On By (2) · Winchester Cathedral (5) · Windmills Of Your Mind (9) · Windy (6) · Woody Woodpecker Song (2) · Yellow Bird (3) · Yellow Days (6) · Yes Sir, That's My Baby (7) · Yours (4,10)

BAKER, Anita
Soul singer born on 1/26/58 in Toledo, Ohio and raised in Detroit. Female lead singer of Chapter 8 from 1976-84.

10/29/83	**139**	11	**1**	The Songstress	**$8**	Beverly G. 10002
4/19/86+	**11**	157	▲⁴ **2**	Rapture	**$8**	Elektra 60444
11/5/88	**1⁴**	42	▲³ **3**	Giving You The Best That I Got	**$8**	Elektra 60827
7/21/90	**5**	40	▲ **4**	Compositions	**$12**	Elektra 60922

Angel (1) · Been So Long (2) · **Caught Up In The Rapture** (2) *37* · Do You Believe Me (1) · Fairy Tales (4)

Feel The Need (1) · **Giving You The Best That I Got** (3) *3* · Good Enough (3) · Good Love (3) · **Just Because** (3) *14* · Lead Me Into Love (3)

Lonely (4) · Love You To The Letter (4) · More Than You Know (4) · Mystery (2) · No More Tears (1) · **No One In The World** (2) *44* · No One To Blame (1)

Perfect Love Affair (4) · Priceless (3) · Rules (3) · **Same Ole Love (365 Days A Year)** (2) *44* · Sometimes (1) · **Soul Inspiration** (4) *72*

Squeeze Me (1) · **Sweet Love** (2) *8* · **Talk To Me** (4) *44* · Watch Your Step (2) · Whatever It Takes (4) · Will You Be Mine (1) · You Belong To Me (3)

You Bring Me Joy (2) · You're The Best Thing Yet (1)

BAKER, Chet — see MARIACHI BRASS

BAKER, George, Selection
Baker is Johannes Bouwens (b: 12/9/44). Pop vocalist/guitarist/keyboardist of Dutch group.

7/4/70	**107**	6	**1**	Little Green Bag	**$15**	Colossus 1002
1/31/76	**153**	7	**2**	Paloma Blanca	**$12**	Warner 2905

African Dream (2) · As Long As The Sun Will Shine (2) · **Dear Ann** (1) *93* · Fisherman, The (2)

Fly (1) · Funny Girl (1) · Goodbye (1) · Have Another Drink (1) · I Wanna Love You (1)

I'll Be Your Baby Tonight (1) · Impressions (1) · Israel (1) · **Little Green Bag** (1) *21* · Morning Sky (1)

Paloma Blanca (2) *26* · Prisoner, The (1) · Road Of Peace (1) · Seagull (1)

Send Me The Pillow You Dream On (2) · Song For You (2) · Superstar (1)

Take Me Home (2) · Winter Time (1)

BAKER('S), Ginger, Air Force
Drummer for Cream and Blind Faith. Born Peter Baker on 8/19/39 in Lewisham, England. Got start as replacement for Charlie Watts (who left to join The Rolling Stones) in Alexis Korner's Blues Incorporated in 1962. Then with the Graham Bond Organization. Air Force featured Steve Winwood, Denny Laine (member of Moody Blues and Wings) and Rick Grech (Family, Traffic, Blind Faith).

5/23/70	**33**	15		Ginger Baker's Air Force .... [L]	**$15**	Atco 703 [2]
				recorded live at London's Royal Albert Hall		

Aiko Biaye · Da Da Man · Do What You Like · Doin' It · Don't Care · Early In The Morning · **Man Of Constant Sorrow** *85* · Toad

BAKER GURVITZ ARMY
British rock trio: drummer Ginger Baker with brothers Paul and Adrian Gurvitz (guitar).

2/15/75	**140**	7	**1**	The Baker Gurvitz Army	**$10**	Janus 7015
11/15/75	**165**	5	**2**	Elysian Encounter	**$10**	Atco 123

Artist, The (2) · Dreamer, The (2) · 4 Phil (1)

Gambler, The (2) · Help Me (1) · Hustler, The (2)

I Wanna Live Again (1) · Inside Of Me (1) · Key, The (2)

Love Is (1) · Mad Jack (1) · Memory Lane (1)

People (2) · Remember (2) · Since Beginning (1)

Time (2)

BALAAM & THE ANGEL
British rock band: brothers Mark (vocals), Jim (guitar) and Des (drums) Morris. Discovered by The Cult's lead singer Ian Astbury. Trio expanded to a quartet in 1989 with the addition of Ian McKean (guitar).

4/30/88	**174**	3		Live Free Or Die	**$8**	Virgin 90869

Big City Fun Time Girl · I Love The Things You Do To Me · I Won't Be Afraid · I'll Show You Something Special · It Goes On · Live Free Or Die · Long Time Loving You · On The Run · Running Out Of Time · Would I Die For You

BALANCE
New York City-based rock trio led by Illinois native Peppy Castro (founder of the Blues Magoos).

8/29/81	133	12		Balance	$8	Portrait 37357

American Dream
Breaking Away 22
Falling In Love 58
Fly Through The Night
Haunting
Hot Summer Nights
I'm Through Loving You
It's So Strange
(Looking For The) Magic
No Getting Around My Love

BALDRY, Long John
Influential blues rocker from England. Born on 1/12/41. Formed Steampacket with Rod Stewart, and Bluesology with Elton John.

7/3/71	83	18		1 It Ain't Easy	$10	Warner 1921
5/6/72	180	6		2 Everything Stops For Tea	$10	Warner 2614

above 2 produced by Rod Stewart and Elton John

Armit's Trousers (2)
Black Girl (1)
Come Back Again (2)
Don't Try To Lay No Boogie-Woogie On The King Of Rock And Roll (1) 73
Everything Stops For Tea (2)
Flying (1)
Hambone (2)
I'm Ready (1)
Iko Iko (2)
It Ain't Easy (1)
Jubilee Cloud (2)
Let's Burn Down The Cornfield (1)
Lord Remember Me (2)
Morning, Morning (1)
Mother Ain't Dead (2)
Mr. Rubin (1)
Rock Me When He's Gone (1)
Seventh Son (2)
Wild Mountain Thyme (2)
You Can't Judge A Book By The Cover (2)

BALIN, Marty
Born on 1/30/43 in Cincinnati. Co-founder of Jefferson Airplane/Jefferson Starship/KBC.

6/6/81	35	23		1 Balin	$8	EMI America 17054
3/12/83	156	6		2 Lucky	$8	EMI America 17088

All We Really Need (2)
Atlanta Lady (Something About Your Love) (1) 27
Born To Be A Winner (2)
Do It For Love (2)
Elvis And Marilyn (1)
Heart Of Stone (2)
Hearts (1) 8
I Do Believe In You (1)
Just Like That (2)
Lydia! (1)
Music Is The Light (1)
Palm Of Your Hand (2)
Spotlight (1)
Tell Me More (1)
What Do People Like (1)
What Love Is (2) 63
When Love Comes (2)
Will You Forever (2)
You Left Your Mark On Me (1)

BALL, Kenny And His Jazzmen
Born on 5/22/30 in Ilford, England. Leader of English Dixieland jazz band formed in 1958.

3/17/62	13	32		Midnight In Moscow ....[I]	$20	Kapp 1276

American Patrol
Big Noise From Winnetka
Dark Eyes
High Society
Midnight In Moscow 2
My Mother's Eyes
Puttin' On The Ritz
Savoy Blues
Tin Roof Blues
Yes She Do, No She Don't
(I'm Satisfied With My Girl)
You Must Have Been A Beautiful Baby

BALLARD, Russ
Born on 10/31/47 in Waltham Cross, England. Pop-rock singer/songwriter/producer. Guitarist of Argent, 1969-74. Wrote "Come And Get Your Love," "Since You've Been Gone," and more.

8/16/80	187	2		1 Barnet Dogs	$8	Epic 36186
6/9/84	147	13		2 Russ Ballard	$8	EMI America 17108
8/3/85	166	4		3 The Fire Still Burns	$8	EMI America 17162

Ain't No Turning Back (1)
Bad Boy (1)
Beware (1)
Day To Day (2)
Dream On (3)
Feels Like The Real Thing (1)
Fire Still Burns (3)
Hey Bernadette (3)
I Can't Hear You No More (2)
In The Night (2)
It's Too Late (3)
Last Time (2)
Omen, The (3)
On The Rebound (1) 58
Once A Rebel (3)
Playing With Fire (2)
Rene Didn't Do It (1)
Riding With The Angels (1)
Searching (3)
She Said "Yeah" (1)
Time (3)
Two Silhouettes (2)
Voices (2)
Woman Like You (2)
Your Time Is Gonna Come (3)

BALLIN' JACK
Interracial jazz-rock sextet.

1/2/71	180	8		Ballin' Jack	$10	Columbia 30344

Ballin' The Jack
Carnival
Festival
Found A Child
Hold On
Never Let 'Em Say
Only A Tear
Street People
Super Highway 93
Telephone

BALTIMORA
Baltimora is pop singer Jimmy McShane; born in Londonderry, Northern Ireland.

1/18/86	49	17		Living In The Background	$8	Manhattan 53026

originally released on Manhattan 53020 with different cover and 2 less tracks

Chinese Restaurant
Jukebox Boy
Living In The Background 87
Pull The Wires
Running For Your Love
Tarzan Boy 13
Up With Baltimora
Woody Boogie

BALTIMORE and OHIO MARCHING BAND, The

1/20/68	177	3		Lapland ....[I]	$12	Jubilee 8008

B&O Marching Band Song
Bach Minuet
Childrens' Marching Song
Col. Bogey March
Do Re Mi
Girl Watchers Theme
Happy Wanderer
Kazoo Special
Lapland 94
Seventy-Six Trombones
St. Louie Street March
Whistle While You Work (medley)
Yellow Rose Of Texas (medley)

BANANARAMA
Female pop-rock trio from London: Sarah Dallin, Keren Woodward and Siobhan Fahey. Group name is combination of the children's show *The Banana Splits* and the Roxy Music song "Pyjamarama." Fahey married Dave Stewart (Eurythmics) on 8/1/87; left group in early 1988, replaced by Jacqui O'Sullivan (who left in mid-1991). Fahey later formed duo Shakespear's Sister.

4/16/83	63	19		1 Deep Sea Skiving	$8	London 810102
6/2/84	30	36		2 Bananarama	$8	London 820036

reissued (#820165) October 1984 with new song "Wild Life"

8/16/86	15	28	●	3 True Confessions	$8	London 828013
9/26/87	44	26		4 Wow!	$8	London 828061
12/3/88	151	9		5 Greatest Hits Collection ....[G]	$8	London 828127

Bad For Me (4)
Boy Trouble (1)
Cheers Then (1)
Come Back With My Heart (4)
Cruel Summer (2,5) 9
Cut Above The Rest (3)
Dance With A Stranger (3)
Do Not Disturb (3)
Doctor Love (1)
Dream Baby (1)
He Was Really Sayin' Somethin' (1,5)
Hey Young London (1)
Hooked On Love (3)
Hot Line To Heaven (2)
I Can't Help It (4,5) 47
I Heard A Rumour (4,5) 4
I Want You Back (4,5)
King Of The Jungle (2)
Love In The First Degree (4,5) 48
Love, Truth & Honesty (5) 89
More Than Physical (3) 73
Na Na Hey Hey Kiss Him Goodbye (1,5)
Nathan Jones (4,5)
Once In A Lifetime (4,5)
Perfect World (3)
Promised Land (3)
Ready Or Not (3)
Robert DeNiro's Waiting (2,5) 95
Rough Justice (2)
Shy Boy (Don't It Make You Feel Good) (1,5) 83
Some Girls (4)
State I'm In (2)
Strike It Rich (4)
Through A Childs Eyes (2)
Trick Of The Night (3) 76
True Confessions (3)
Venus (3,5) 1
What A Shambles (1)
Wild Life (2) 70
Wish You Were Here (1)
Young At Heart (1)

DEBUT DATE	PEAK POS	WKS CHR	GOLD	ARTIST — Album Title	$	Label & Number

★★154★★ BAND, The

Rock group formed in Woodstock, New York in 1967: Robbie Robertson (guitar), Levon Helm (drums), Rick Danko (bass), Richard Manuel and Garth Hudson (keyboards). All from Canada (except Helm from Arkansas) and all were with Ronnie Hawkins' Hawks. Disbanded on Thanksgiving Day in 1976. Manuel committed suicide on 3/4/86 (age 42).

DEBUT DATE	PEAK POS	WKS CHR	GOLD	#	Album Title	$	Label & Number
8/10/68	30	40		1	Music From Big Pink	$20	Capitol 2955
					Big Pink: The Band's communal home in West Saugerties, New York		
10/18/69+	9	49	▲	2	The Band	$15	Capitol 132
9/5/70	5	22	●	3	Stage Fright	$12	Capitol 425
10/16/71	21	14		4	Cahoots	$12	Capitol 651
9/9/72	6	28	●	5	Rock Of Ages [L]	$15	Capitol 11045 [2]
11/17/73+	28	20		6	Moondog Matinee	$12	Capitol 11214
2/9/74	1⁴	21		7	Planet Waves	$15	Asylum 1003
					BOB DYLAN With The Band		
7/13/74	3	19		8	Before The Flood [L]	$15	Asylum 201 [2]
					BOB DYLAN/THE BAND		
7/26/75	7	14		9	The Basement Tapes [E]	$15	Columbia 33682 [2]
					BOB DYLAN AND THE BAND recorded in 1967 at Big Pink		
12/13/75+	26	19		10	Northern Lights-Southern Cross	$12	Capitol 11440
9/4/76	51	14		11	The Best Of The Band [G]	$12	Capitol 11553
3/26/77	64	10		12	Islands	$12	Capitol 11602
4/29/78	16	20		13	The Last Waltz [S-L]	$20	Warner 3146 [3]
					farewell concert at the San Francisco Winterland with guests Bob Dylan, Eric Clapton, Neil Diamond, Ringo Starr & others		

Acadian Driftwood (10)
Across The Great Divide (2,5)
Ain't Got No Home (6) **73**
Ain't No More Cane (9)
Ain't That A Lot Of Love (12)
All Along The Watchtower (8)
All La Glory (3)
Apple Suckling Tree (9)
Baby Let Me Follow You Down (13)
Ballad Of A Thin Man (8)
Bessie Smith (9)
Blowin' In The Wind (8)
Caledonia Mission (1,5)
Caravan (13)
Change Is Gonna Come (6)
Chest Fever (1,5)
Christmas Must Be Tonight (12)
Clothes Line Saga (9)
Coyote (13)
Crash On The Levee (Down In The Flood) (9)
Daniel And The Sacred Harp (3)
Dirge (7)
Don't Do It (5,11) **34**
Don't Think Twice, It's All Right (8)
Don't Ya Tell Henry (9)

Down South In New Orleans (13)
Dry Your Eyes (13)
Endless Highway (13)
Evangeline (13)
Forbidden Fruit (10)
Forever Young (7,13)
4% Pantomime (4)
Further On Up The Road (13)
Genetic Method (5)
Georgia On My Mind (12)
Get Up Jake (5)
Goin' To Acapulco (9)
Going Going Gone (7)
Great Pretender (6)
Hazel (7)
Helpless (13)
Highway 61 Revisited (8)
Hobo Jungle (10)
Holy Cow (6)
I Don't Believe You (She Acts Like We Never Have Met) (13)
(I Don't Want To) Hang Up My Rock And Roll Shoes (5)
I Shall Be Released (1,8,13)
I'm Ready (6)
In A Station (1)
Islands (12)

It Makes No Difference (10,11,13)
It's Alright, Ma (I'm Only Bleeding) (8)
Jawbone (2)
Jemima Surrender (4)
Jupiter Hollow (10)
Just Another Whistle Stop (3)
Just Like A Woman (8)
Katie's Been Gone (9)
King Harvest (Has Surely Come) (2,5)
Knockin' Lost John (12)
Knockin' On Heaven's Door (8)
Last Of The Blacksmiths (4)
Last Waltz, Theme From [includes 2 versions] (13)
Last Waltz Refrain (13)
Lay Lady Lay (8)
Let The Night Fall (12)
Life Is A Carnival (4,5,11,13) **72**
Like A Rolling Stone (8)
Livin' In A Dream (12)
Lo And Behold! (9)
Lonesome Suzie (1)
Long Black Veil (1)
Long Distance Operator (9)

Look Out Cleveland (2)
Mannish Boy (13)
Million Dollar Bash (9)
Moon Struck One (4)
Most Likely You Go Your Way (And I'll Go Mine) (8) **66**
Mystery Train (6,13)
Never Say Goodbye (7)
Night They Drove Old Dixie Down (2,5,8,11,13)
Nothing Was Delivered (9)
Odds And Ends (9)
On A Night Like This (7) **44**
Open The Door, Homer (9)
Ophelia (10,11,13) **62**
Orange Juice Blues (Blues For Breakfast) (9)
Out Of The Blue (13)
Please, Mrs. Henry (9)
Promised Land (6)
Rag Mama Rag (2,5) **57**
Rags And Bones (10)
Rainy Day Women #12 & 35 (8)
Right As Rain (12)
Ring Your Bell (10)
River Hymn (9)
Rockin' Chair (2)
Ruben Remus (9)

Rumor, The (3)
Saga Of Pepote Rouge (12)
Saved (6)
Shape I'm In (3,5,8,11,13)
Share Your Love (6)
Shoot Out In Chinatown (4)
Sleeping (3)
Smoke Signal (4)
Something There Is About You (7)
Stage Fright (3,5,8,11,13)
Strawberry Wine (3)
Street Walker (2)
Such A Night (13)
Tears Of Rage (1,9,11)
Thinkin' Out Loud (4)
Third Man Theme (6)
This Wheel's On Fire (1,5,9)
Time To Kill (3) **77**
Tiny Montgomery (9)
To Kingdom Come (1)
Too Much Of Nothing (9)
Tough Mama (7)
Tura Lura Lural (That's An Irish Lullaby) (13)
Twilight (11)
Unfaithful Servant (2,5)
Up On Cripple Creek (2,8,11,13) **25**
Volcano (4)

W.S. Walcott Medicine Show (3,5)
We Can Talk (1)
Wedding Song (7)
Weight, The (1,5,8,11,13) **63**
Well, The (3)
When I Paint My Masterpiece (4)
When You Awake (2,8)
Where Do We Go From Here? (4)
Whispering Pines (2)
Who Do You Love (13)
Yazoo Street Scandal (9)
Yea! Heavy And A Bottle Of Bread (9)
You Ain't Goin' Nowhere (9)
You Angel You (7)

BAND OF THE BLACK WATCH, The

Scottish military unit.

DEBUT DATE	PEAK POS	WKS CHR		Album Title	$	Label & Number
3/20/76	164	4		Scotch On The Rocks [I]	$8	Private St. 2007

Birmingham Brass Band
Bump, The

Caribbean Honeymoon
Highland Safari

Hoots Mon!
Lass Of Fyve

Let's Go To Jersey
Pipers Waltz

Purple Heather
Scotch On The Rocks 75

Sons Of The Thistle
Y Viva Espana

BANDY, Moe, & Joe Stampley

Country duo. Mississippi native Bandy had own TV show in the early '70s. Louisianan Stampley was the lead singer of The Uniques in the late '60s.

DEBUT DATE	PEAK POS	WKS CHR		Album Title	$	Label & Number
4/11/81	170	4		Hey Joe!/Hey Moe!	$8	Columbia 37003

Country Boys
Drinkin', Dancin'

Drunk Front
Get Off My Case

Girl Don't Ever Get Lonely
Hey Joe (Hey Moe)

Honky Tonk Queen
I'd Rather Be A-Pickin'

Let's Hear It For The Workin' Man

Two Beers Away

BANG

Rock trio from Florida — Frank Ferrara, lead singer.

DEBUT DATE	PEAK POS	WKS CHR		Album Title	$	Label & Number
4/8/72	164	10		Bang	$15	Capitol 11015

Come With Me
Future Shock

Last Will & Testament
Lions, Christians

Our Home
Queen, The

Questions 90
Redman

B ANGIE B

Angela Boyd, singer/dancer/songwriter with M.C. Hammer's posse. Native of Morton, Mississippi.

DEBUT DATE	PEAK POS	WKS CHR		Album Title	$	Label & Number
5/4/91	133	6		B Angie B	$12	Bust It 95236

I Am Angie B
I Don't Want To Lose Your Love 54

I'm So Sorry
Men Get Lonely

My Prayer To You
Pump It Up

So Much Love
Sweet Thang

This Is A Jam For You
Woman's Perspective

BANGLES

Female pop-rock quartet formed in Los Angeles in January 1981. Consisted of sisters Vicki (lead guitar) and Debbi Peterson (drums), Michael Steele (bass) and Susanna Hoffs (guitar). Originally named The Bangs. Steele was previously in The Runaways. Disbanded in October 1989.

DEBUT DATE	PEAK POS	WKS CHR		#	Album Title	$	Label & Number
8/4/84	80	30		1	All Over The Place	$8	Columbia 39220

DEBUT DATE	PEAK POS	WKS CHR	GOLD	ARTIST — Album Title	$	Label & Number

BANGLES, The — Cont'd

DEBUT DATE	PEAK POS	WKS CHR	GOLD	Album Title	$	Label & Number
2/1/86+	2[2]	82	▲[2]	2 **Different Light**	$8	Columbia 40039
11/5/88+	15	42	▲	3 **Everything**	$8	Columbia 44056
5/26/90	97	9		4 Greatest Hits .... [G]	$12	Columbia 46125

All About You (1)
Angels Don't Fall In Love (2)
Be With You (3,4) *30*
Bell Jar (3)
Complicated Girl (3)
Crash And Burn (3)
Dover Beach (1)
Eternal Flame (3,4) *1*
Everything I Wanted (4)

Following (2,4)
Glitter Years (3)
Going Down To Liverpool (1,4)
Hazy Shade Of Winter (4) *2*
He's Got A Secret (1)
Hero Takes A Fall (1,4)
I'll Set You Free (3,4)

If She Knew What She Wants (2,4) *29*
In A Different Light (2)
In Your Room (3,4) *5*
James (1)
Let It Go (2)
Live (1)
Make A Play For Her Now (3)

Manic Monday (2,4) *2*
More Than Meets The Eye (1)
Not Like You (2)
Restless (1)
Return Post (2)
September Gurls (2)
Silent Treatment (1)
Some Dreams Come True (3)

Something To Believe In (3)
Standing In The Hallway (2)
Tell Me (1)
Waiting For You (3)
Walk Like An Egyptian (2,4) *1*
Walking Down Your Street (2,4) *11*

Watching The Sky (3)
Where Were You When I Needed You (4)

BANGOR FLYING CIRCUS
David Wolinski (vocals), Alan de Carlo and Michael Tegza.

| 12/27/69 | 190 | 2 | | Bangor Flying Circus .... | $15 | Dunhill 50069 |

Change In Our Lives
Come On People

Concerto For Clouds
In The Woods

Mama Don't You Know (That Your Daughter's Acting Mighty Strange)

Norwegian Wood (This Bird Has Flown)

Ode To Sadness
Someday I'll Find

Violent Man

BANG TANGO
Los Angeles-based, heavy-metal quintet led by vocalist Joe LeSte.

| 7/1/89 | 58 | 39 | | 1 Psycho Cafe .... | $8 | Mechanic 6300 |
| 6/15/91 | 113 | 3 | | 2 Dancin' On Coals .... | $12 | Mechanic 10196 |

Attack Of Life (1)
Big Line (2)
Breaking Up A Heart Of Stone (1)

Cactus Juice (2)
Dancin' On Coals (2)
Do What You're Told (1)
Don't Stop Now (1)

Dressed Up Vamp (2)
Emotions In Gear (2)
I'm In Love (2)
Just For You (1)

Last Kiss (2)
Love Injection (1)
Midnight Struck (2)
My Saltine (2)

Shotgun Man (1)
Someone Like You (1)
Soul To Soul (2)
Sweet Little Razor (1)

Untied And True (2)
Wrap My Wings (1)

BANKS, Peter
Former member of Yes and Flash. Born on 4/8/47 in England.

| 9/8/73 | 152 | 8 | | Two Sides Of Peter Banks .... | $12 | Sovereign 11217 |

featuring Phil Collins, Steve Hackett and Jan Akkerman

Battles
Beyond The Loneliest Sea

Get Out Of My Fridge
Knights Medley

Last Eclipse
Stop That!

Vision Of The King
White Horse Vale Medley

BANKS, Tony
Keyboardist with Genesis. Born on 3/27/51 in East Heathly, Sussex, England.

| 12/15/79+ | 171 | 5 | | A Curious Feeling .... | $8 | Charisma 2207 |

After The Lie
Curious Feeling

For A While
Forever Morning

From The Undertow
In The Dark

Lie, The
Lucky Me

Somebody Else's Dream
Waters Of Lethe

You

BARBER, Frank, Orch.
Big band led by British arranger/conductor Frank Barber.

| 6/5/82 | 94 | 16 | | Hooked On Big Bands .... [I] | $8 | Victory 702 |

discofied medleys of 6 big bands

Artie Shaw Medley

Benny Goodman Medley

Dorsey Brothers Medley

Duke Ellington Medley

Glenn Miller Medley *61*

Louis Armstrong Medley

BARBIERI, Gato
Jazz tenor saxophone player. Born Leandro Barbieri on 11/28/33 in Rosario, Argentina. Toured Europe with Jim Hall, Lalo Schifrin and Ted Curson in the '60s. With jazz trumpeter Don Cherry in the late '60s.

5/5/73	166	7		1 Last Tango in Paris .... [S-I]	$8	United Art. 045
10/26/74	160	3		2 Chapter Three - Viva Emiliano Zapata .... [I]	$8	Impulse! 9279
				Zapata: revolutionary leader in Mexico (killed in 1919)		
10/2/76+	75	32		3 Caliente! .... [I]	$8	A&M 4597
10/29/77	66	20		4 Ruby, Ruby .... [I]	$8	A&M 4655
7/29/78	96	7		5 Tropico .... [I]	$8	A&M 4710
8/11/79	116	9		6 Euphoria .... [I]	$8	A&M 4774

Adios (3,4)
Behind The Rain (3)
Blue Angel (4)
Bolero (5)
Carnavalito (6)
Cuando Vuelva A Tu Lado (What A Difference A Day Makes) (2)
Don't Cry Rochelle (3)
El Sublime (2)

Europa (Earth's Cry Heaven's Smile) (3)
Evil Eyes (5)
Fake Ophelia (1)
Fiesta (3)
Fireflies (3)
Firepower, Theme From (6)
Girl In Black (Para Mi Negra) (1)
Gods And Astronauts (6)

Goodbye (Un Largo Adios) (1)
I Want You (3)
It's Over (1)
Jeanne (1)
La Podrida (2)
Last Tango In Paris [includes 3 versions] (1)
Latin Lady (5)
Latin Reaction (4)
Lions Also Cry (6)

Lluvia Azul (2)
Los Desperados (3)
Midnight Tango (4)
Milonga Triste (2)
Ngiculela - Es Una Historia -I Am Singing (4)
Nostalgia (4)
Odara (5)
Picture In The Rain (1)

Poinciana (Song Of The Tree) (5)
Return (La Vuelta) (1)
Ruby (4)
Secret Fiesta (6)
She Is Michelle (5)
Sophia (6)
Speak Low (6)
Sunride (4)
Viva Emiliano Zapata (2)

Where Is The Love (5)
Why Did She Choose You (1)

BARBOUR, Keith
Pop singer/songwriter; formerly with The New Christy Minstrels. Married to TV actress Deidre Hall (*Our House* and *Days of Our Lives*) from 1971-78.

| 11/1/69 | 163 | 4 | | Echo Park .... | $15 | Epic 26485 |

All Of Your Loving
Baby Lit A Candle

Echo Park *40*
Here I Am Losing You

Here I Find
Home

If Only I Could Touch You
Reaching High

Today
Wind Is The Color Of Lace

You Try Not To Show

BARCLAY JAMES HARVEST
British art-rock quartet: John Lees, Les Holroyd, Woolley Wolstenholme and Mel Pritchard.

| 2/19/77 | 174 | 3 | | Octoberon .... | $10 | MCA 2234 |

Believe In Me
May Day

Polk Street Rag

Ra

Rock 'N' Roll Star

Suicide?

World Goes On

DEBUT DATE	PEAK POS	WKS CHR	GOLD	ARTIST — Album Title	$	Label & Number

BARDENS, Pete

British rock keyboardist. In Hamilton King's Blues Messengers with Mick Fleetwood in the early '60s. Formed the Lunars with Fleetwood and Peter Green. Lunars evolved into Shotgun Express in 1966, co-fronted by Rod Stewart. After band split, joined Them. Formed Camel in 1972. Much session work (late '70s).

DEBUT DATE	PEAK POS	WKS CHR	GOLD	Album	$	Label & Number
10/17/87	148	5		Seen One Earth ....[I]	$8	Capitol 12555

Home Thoughts In Dreams   Man Alive   Many Happy Returns   Seascape   Seen One Earth   Stargate, The

BARDEUX

Los Angeles female dance duo: Stacy "Acacia" Smith and Jazz (replaced by Melanie Taylor in 1989).

4/30/88	104	12	1	Bold As Love	$8	Enigma 73312
0/14/89	133	7	2	Shangri-La	$8	Enigma 73522

eeding Heart (1)   **I Love To Bass** (2) *68*   Now I've Got Your Number (2)   Sex Machine (1)   **When We Kiss** (1) *36*
Caution (1)   Just Say The Word (1)   Now Or Never (2)   Shangri-La (2)   You Can Rock My Body (2)
Dancing In The Wind (1)   **Magic Carpet Ride** (1) *81*   Now Or Never (2)   Three Time Lover (1)   You're My Only Kind Of
Hardline (2)   Nervous (2)   One Last Kiss (2)   Thumbs Up (2)   Lover (1)
Hold Me, Hold Me (1)

BARE, Bobby

Born Robert Joseph Bare on 4/7/35 in Ironton, Ohio. Prominent country singer/songwriter/guitarist. Drafted by the Army in 1958; left a demo tape of "The All American Boy" with Fraternity Records. The song was released erroneously as by Bill Parsons. Wrote songs for the film *Teenage Millionaire* and acted in the film *A Distant Trumpet* in 1964. Own TV series in the mid-1980s.

10/26/63	119	3	1	"Detroit City" And Other Hits..............	$20	RCA 2776
2/1/64	133	5	2	500 Miles Away From Home	$20	RCA 2835

Abilene (2)   **Detroit City** (1) *16*   Gotta Travel On (2)   I'd Fight The World (1)   Lorena (1)   What Kind Of Bird Is That (2)
All American Boy (1) *2*   **500 Miles Away From**   Homestead On The Farm (2)   Is It Wrong (For Loving You)   Lynchin' Party (2)   Worried Man Blues (2)
Book Of Love (1)   **Home** (2) *10*   I Don't Believe I'll Fall In   (1)   Noah's Ark (2)
Brooklyn Bridge (1)   God's Were Angry With Me   Love Today (1)   Jeannie's Last Kiss (2)   Sailor Man (2)
Dear Wastebasket (1)   (1)   I Wonder Where You Are   Let Me Tell You About Mary   **Shame On Me** (1) *23*
   Tonight (2)   (2)   She Called Me Baby (1)

★★269★★   BAR-KAYS

R&B vocal/instrumental combo: Jimmy King (guitar), Ronnie Caldwell (organ), James Alexander (bass), Carl Cunningham (drums), Phalon Jones (saxophone) and Ben Cauley (trumpet). Formed by Al Jackson, drummer with Booker T & The MG's. The plane crash that killed Otis Redding (12/10/67) also claimed the lives of all the Bar-Kays except Alexander (not on the plane) and Cauley (survived the crash). Alexander re-formed the band. Appeared in the film *Wattstax*; much session work at Stax. Lineup since 1987: Larry Dodson (vocals), Harvey Henderson (tenor sax) and Winston Stewart (keyboards). Alexander's son Phalon began solo career in 1990.

2/27/71	90	12		1 Black Rock	$12	Volt 6011
11/13/76+	69	22		2 Too Hot To Stop	$8	Mercury 1099
12/10/77+	47	23	●	3 Flying High On Your Love	$8	Mercury 1181
11/11/78+	72	15		4 Money Talks	$8	Stax 4106
12/23/78+	86	17		5 Light Of Life	$8	Mercury 3732
11/10/79	35	24	●	6 Injoy	$8	Mercury 3781
12/13/80+	57	16		7 As One	$8	Mercury 3844
11/14/81+	55	29	●	8 Nightcruising	$8	Mercury 4028
11/20/82	51	29		9 Propositions	$8	Mercury 4065
4/21/84	52	22		10 Dangerous	$8	Mercury 818478
9/21/85	115	9		11 Banging The Wall	$8	Mercury 824727
11/7/87	110	14		12 Contagious	$8	Mercury 830305

Angel Eyes (5)   Dance Your Body, Desara   Holy Ghost *[includes 2*   Money Talks (4)   Shut The Funk Up (3)   Whatever It Is (3)
Anticipation (9)   (11)   *versions]* (4)   Monster (4)   Six O'Clock News Report (1)   Whitehouseorgy (2)
Are You Being Real (5)   Dangerous (10)   How Sweet It Would Be (1)   Montego Bay (1)   Something In The Air (12)   Woman Of The Night (3)
As One (7)   Deliver Us (7)   I Can't Believe You're   More And More (6)   Spellbound (2)   Work It Out (7)
Attitudes (3)   Dirty Dancer (10)   Leaving Me (9)   **Move Your Boogie Body**   Standing On The Outside (3)   You Can't Run Away (3)
Baby I Love You (1)   Do It (Let Me See You   I Lean On You/You Lean On   (6) *57*   Summer Of Our Love (2)   You Don't Know Like I Know
Backseat Driver (8)   Shake) (9)   Me (5)   Nightcruising (8)   Take The Time To Love   (1)
Bang, Bang (Stick 'Em Up)   Don't Hang Up (12)   I'll Dance (5)   Open Your Heart (7)   Somebody (7)   You Made A Change In My
(2)   Feelin' Alright (4)   I've Been Trying (1)   Paper Doll (11)   This Could Be The Night (12)   Life (9)
Banging The Walls (11)   Feels Like I'm Falling In   Let's Have Some Fun (3)   Piece Of Your Peace (1)   Time Out (12)   You're So Sexy (2)
Bodyfever (7)   Love (8)   Loose Talk (10)   Propositions (9)   **Too Hot To Stop (Pt. 1)**   You've Been (6)
Boogie Body Land (7)   Flying High On Your Love (3)   Love Don't Wait (11)   Running In And Out Of My   (2) *74*   Your Place Or Mine (11)
(Busted) (9)   Freak City U.S.A. (12)   Love's What It's All About (5)   Life (6)   Touch (12)
Can't Keep My Hands Off   **Freakshow On The Dance**   Lovers Should Never Fall In   Say It Through Love (7)   Touch Tone (8)
You (3)   **Floor** (10) *73*   Love (10)   Sex Driver (11)   Traffic Jammer (8)
Certified True (12)   Freaky Behavior (8)   Loving You Is My   Sexomatic (10)   Tripping Out (9)
Contagious (12)   Get Up 'N Do It (5)   Occupation (6)   **Shake Your Rump To The**   Unforgettable Dream (8)
Cozy (2)   Gina (11)   Make Believe Lover (10)   **Funk** (2) *23*   Up In Here (6)
Dance, Party, Etc. (10)   Girl I'm On Your Side (6)   Many Mistakes (12)   She Talks To Me With Her   We're The Happiest People
Dance To The Music (1)   Give It Up (5)   Mean Mistreater (4)   Body (6)   In The World (5)
   Hit And Run (8)   Missiles On Target (11)   Shine (5)

BARNES, Jimmy

Born in Glasgow, Scotland; moved to Australia at age 5. Lead singer of Australian group Cold Chisel.

3/8/86	109	16	1	Jimmy Barnes	$8	Geffen 24089
6/11/88	104	15	2	Freight Train Heart	$8	Geffen 24146

American Heartbeat (1)   I Wanna Get Started With   Last Frontier (2)   Ride The Night Away (1)   Waitin' For The Heartache (2)
Boys Cry Out For War (1)   You (2)   Lessons In Love (1)   Seven Days (2)   Walk On (2)
Daylight (1)   I'd Die To Be With You   No Second Prize (1)   Thick Skinned (1)   Without Your Love (1)
Do Or Die (2)   Tonight (1)   Paradise (1)   **Too Much Ain't Enough**   **Working Class Man** (1) *74*
Driving Wheels (2)   I'm Still On Your Side (2)   Promise Me You'll Call (1)   Love (2) *91*

BARNSTORM — see WALSH, Joe

DEBUT DATE	PEAK POS	WKS CHR	GOLD	ARTIST — Album Title	$	Label & Number

BARRABAS
Rock sextet led by Jo Tejada.

| 8/23/75 | 149 | 7 | | Heart Of The City .... | $8 | Atco 118 |

Along The Shore / Checkmate / Family Size / Four Season Woman / Make It Easy / Mellow Blow / Take A Wild Ride / Thank You Love

BARRETT, Syd
Original lead guitarist of Pink Floyd. Born Roger Barrett on 1/6/46 in Cambridge, England.

| 8/17/74 | 163 | 4 | | The Madcap Laughs/Barrett .... | $25 | Harvest 11314 [2] |

Baby Lemonade / Dark Globe / Dominoes / Effervescing Elephant (medley) / Feel / Gigolo Aunt / Golden Hair / Here I Go / I Never Lied To You (medley) / If It's In You / It Is Obvious / Late Night / Long Gone / Love Song / Love You / Maisie / No Good Trying / No Man's Land / Octopus / Rats / She Took A Long Cold Look / Terrapin / Waving My Arms In The Air (medley) / Wined And Dined / Wolfpack (medley)

BARRY, Claudja
Disco singer from Jamaica. Raised in Toronto. Appeared in the musicals *Hair* and *Catch My Soul.*

| 2/25/78 | 131 | 10 | | 1 Claudja .... | $8 | Salsoul 5525 |
| 6/2/79 | 101 | 10 | | 2 Boogie Woogie Dancin' Shoes .... | $8 | Chrysalis 1232 |

Boogie Tonight (2) / **Boogie Woogie Dancin' Shoes (2) 56** / Cold Fire (2) / **Dancin' Fever (1) 72** / Every Beat Of My Heart (1) / Forget About You (1) / Give It Up (2) / Heavy Makes You Happy (2) / Johnny, Johnny Please / Come Home (1) / Love Machine (1) / Nobody But You (2) / Open The Door (1) / Sexy Talkin' Lover (1) / Take It Easy (1) / Take Me In Your Arms (1) / Way You Are Dancing (2) / When Life Was Just A Game (1)

BARRY, Len
Born Leonard Borisoff on 12/6/42 in Philadelphia. In The Dovells from 1957-63.

| 11/20/65 | 90 | 13 | | 1-2-3 .... | $20 | Decca 74720 |

At The Hop '65 / Bullseye / Don't Throw Your Love Away / Happiness (Is A Girl Like Mine) / I.O.U. / **Like A Baby 27** / **Lip Sync (To The Tongue Twisters) 84** / 1-2-3 2 / Treat Her Right / Will You Love Me Tomorrow / Would I Love You? / You Baby

BARTON, Lou Ann
Singer from Austin, Texas. Member of the blues trio Triple Threat that included Stevie Ray Vaughan and W.C. Clark.

| 4/24/82 | 133 | 9 | | Old Enough .... | $10 | Asylum 60032 |
| | | | | produced by Glenn Frey | | |

Brand New Lover / Doodle Song / Every Night Of The Week / Finger Poppin' Time / I'm Right Enough / It Ain't Right / It's Raining / Maybe / Stop These Teardrops / Sudden Stop

BASIA
Britain-based, female pop-jazz singer/composer Basia Trzetrzelewska (pronounced: Basha Tshet-shel-ev-ska). Raised in Jaworzno, Poland. Former vocalist of the group Matt Bianco.

| 2/20/88 | 36 | 77 | ▲ | 1 Time And Tide .... | $8 | Epic 40767 |
| 3/3/90 | 20 | 38 | ▲ | 2 London Warsaw New York .... | $12 | Epic 45472 |

Astrud (2) / Baby You're Mine (2) / Best Friends (2) / Brave New Hope (2) / Copernicus (2) / **Cruising For Bruising (2) 29** / Freeze Thaw (1) / From Now On (1) / How Dare You (1) / Miles Away (1) / **New Day For You (1) 53** / Not An Angel (2) / Ordinary People (2) / Prime Time TV (1) / Promises (1) / Reward (2) / Run For Cover (1) / Take Him Back, Rachel (2) / **Time And Tide (1) 26** / Until You Come Back To Me (2)

BASIC BLACK
R&B four-man band: Darryl (Dee) Adams (vocals), Walter Scott, Lloyd Turner and Kelvin Bradshaw.

| 11/17/90 | 178 | 1 | | Basic Black .... | $12 | Motown 6307 |

Baby Can We Talk / Don't Make Me Fall In Love / Give Your Love To Me / It's A Man's Thang / Nothing But A Party / Now Or Never / She's Mine / Special Kind Of Fool / Stupid / What Ever It Takes

★★444★★ BASIE, Count
Born William Basie on 8/21/04 in Red Bank, New Jersey. Died on 4/26/84 of pancreatic cancer. World-renowned jazz, big-band leader/pianist/organist. Learned music and piano from mother, organ from Fats Waller. First recorded with own band in 1937 for Decca. Appeared in many films and toured into the '70s. Won the Grammy's Trustees Award in 1981.

2/2/63	5	42		1 Sinatra-Basie	$15	Reprise 1008
				FRANK SINATRA/COUNT BASIE		
7/20/63	19	27		2 This Time By Basie! Hits of the 50's And 60's ....[I]	$12	Reprise 6070
9/7/63	123	5		3 Li'l Ol' Groovemaker...Basie! ....[I]	$12	Verve 8549
10/19/63	69	20		4 Ella And Basie	$20	Verve 4061
				ELLA FITZGERALD/COUNT BASIE		
2/22/64	150	1		5 More Hits Of The 50's And 60's ....[I]	$12	Verve 8563
8/22/64	13	31		6 It Might As Well Be Swing	$15	Reprise 1012
				FRANK SINATRA/COUNT BASIE		
3/27/65	141	4		7 Our Shining Hour	$15	Verve 8605
				SAMMY DAVIS, JR. & COUNT BASIE		
3/26/66	107	13		8 Arthur Prysock/Count Basie	$15	Verve 8646
				ARTHUR PRYSOCK/COUNT BASIE		
12/10/66	143	2		9 Broadway Basie's...Way ....[I]	$12	Command 905
4/6/68	145	6		10 The Board Of Directors	$10	Dot 25838
				COUNT BASIE & THE MILLS BROTHERS		
6/1/68	195	3		11 Manufacturers of Soul	$15	Brunswick 754134
				JACKIE WILSON/COUNT BASIE		

Ain't Misbehavin' (4) / Ain't No Use (8) / All Of Me (5) / Apartment, Theme From The (2) / April In Paris (7,10) / Baubles, Bangles And Beads (9) / Belly Roll (3) / Best Is Yet To Come (6) / Bill Basie Won't You Please Come Home (7) / Blues For Mr. Charlie (7) / Boody Rumble (3) / **Chain Gang (1) 84** / Come Fly With Me (5) / Come Home (8) / Come Rain Or Come Shine (8) / Count 'Em (3) / December (10) / 'Deed I Do (4) / Don't Go To Strangers (8) / Down - Down - Down (10) / Dream A Little Dream Of Me (4) / Dum Dum (3) / Even When You Cry (11) / Everything's Coming Up Roses (9) / Fly Me To The Moon (2,6) / **For Your Precious Love (11) 49** / From This Moment On (9) / Funky Broadway (11) / Girl From Ipanema (7) / Gone Again (8) / Good Life (6) / Hello, Dolly! (6) / Hello Young Lovers (9) / Here's That Rainy Day (9) / Hey, Jealous Lover (5) / Honeysuckle Rose (4) / I Believe In You (6) / **I Can't Stop Loving You (2,6) 77** / I Could Have Told You (8) / I Could Write A Book (8) / I Dig Rock And Roll Music (10) / I Left My Heart In San Francisco (2)

DEBUT DATE	PEAK POS	WKS CHR	GOLD	ARTIST — Album Title	$	Label & Number

BASIE, Count — Cont'd

I May Be Wrong But I Think You're Wonderful (10)
I Never Loved A Woman (The Way I Love You) (11)
I Only Have Eyes For You (1)
I Thought About You (5)
I Wanna Be Around (6)
I Want To Be Happy (10)
I Was Made To Love Her (11)
I Wish You Love (6)
I Won't Dance (1)
I Worry 'Bout You (8)
I'll Never Smile Again (5)
I'm Beginning To See The Light (4)

I'm Gonna Sit Right Down And Write Myself A Letter (1,8)
I'm Lost (8)
In The Midnight Hour (11)
In The Wee Small Hours Of The Morning (5)
Into Each Life Some Rain Must Fall (4)
It's All Right With Me (9)
Just In Time (9)
Kansas City Wrinkles (3)
Keepin' Out Of Mischief Now (7)
Lazy River (10)
Learnin' The Blues (1)
Let Me Dream (9)

Li'l Ol' Groovemaker...Basie (3)
Looking At The World Thru Rose Colored Glasses (1)
Lot Of Livin' To Do (9)
(Love Is) The Tender Trap (1)
Lullabye For Jolie (3)
Mame (9)
Moon River (2)
More (Theme from Mondo Cane) (6)
My Girl (1)
My Kind Of Girl (1)
My Last Affair (4)
My Shining Hour (7)
Nasty Magnus (3)
New York City Blues (7)

Nice 'N' Easy (2)
Nice Work If You Can Get It (1)
Ode To Billy Joe (11)
On A Clear Day (You Can See Forever) (9)
On The Road To Mandalay (5)
On The Street Where You Live (9)
On The Sunny Side Of The Street (4)
One Mint Julep (2)
Only The Lonely (5)
Pennies From Heaven (1)
People (9)
Please Be Kind (1)

Pleasingly Plump (3)
Release Me (10)
Respect (1)
Satin Doll (4)
Saturday Night (Is The Loneliest Night Of The Week) (5)
Second Time Around (5)
She's A Woman (7)
Shiny Stockings (4)
South Of The Border (Down Mexico Way) (5)
Swingin' Shepherd Blues (2)
Tea For Two (4)
Teach Me Tonight (7)
Them There Eyes (4)

This Could Be The Start Of Something Big (2)
This Love Of Mine (5)
Tiny Bubbles (10)
Uptight (Everything's Alright) (11)
Walk, Don't Run (2)
What Kind Of Fool Am I? (2)
What Will I Tell My Heart (8)
Why Try To Change Me Now (7)
Wives And Lovers (6)
Work Song (7)
You're Nobody Till Somebody Loves You (7)

BASIL, Toni
Los Angeles-based choreographer/actress/video director. Born in 1950. Worked on TV shows *Shindig* and *Hullabaloo*. Choreographed the film *American Graffiti*. Appeared in the film *Easy Rider* and others.

| 10/23/82 | 22 | 30 ● | | Word Of Mouth | $8 | Chrysalis 1410 |

Be Stiff
Little Red Book

Mickey *1*
Nobody

Rock On
Shoppin' From A To Z 77

Space Girls
Thief On The Loose

Time After Time
You Gotta Problem

BASS, Fontella
Born on 7/3/40 in St. Louis. Soul vocalist/pianist/organist. Mother was a member of Clara Ward Gospel Troupe. Sang in church choirs; with Oliver Sain Band, St. Louis; with Little Milton blues show to 1964. Married to trumpet player Lester Bowie.

| 2/26/66 | 93 | 8 | | The 'New' Look | $15 | Checker 2997 |

Come And Get These Memories
Gee Whiz

How Glad I Am
I Know
I'm A Woman

Impossible
Oh No, Not My Baby
Our Day Will Come
Soul Of The Man

Rescue Me 4
Since I Fell For You

You've Lost That Lovin' Feelin'

BASS BOY
Male solo artist from Florida. Mixer/scratcher of bass-heavy samples. Discovered by Techmaster P.E.B.

| 6/6/92 | 160 | 12 | | I Got The Bass | $12 | Newtown 2209 |

Bass Boy Crazy
Bass Me Up

Bass Wave
Big 10"

Blinded By The Bass
Funkin' Bass

I Got The Bass
Mo' Better Bass

Non-Stop Bass
Rebel Bass

BASSEY, Shirley
Born on 1/8/37 in Cardiff, Wales. Soul songstress. Began professional career at age 16 as a member of touring show *Memories Of Al Jolson*. Became a popular club attraction in America in 1961.

4/24/65	85	9	1	Shirley Bassey Belts The Best!	$12	United Art. 6419
10/17/70	105	13	2	Shirley Bassey Is Really "Something"	$12	United Art. 6765
6/12/71	123	24	3	Something Else	$12	United Art. 6797
3/18/72	94	13	4	I Capricorn	$12	United Art. 5565
11/25/72	171	8	5	And I Love You So	$12	United Art. 5643
5/26/73	60	19	6	Never, Never, Never	$8	United Art. 055
9/22/73	136	8	7	Live At Carnegie Hall [L]	$10	United Art. 111 [2]
				featuring Woody Herman's band		
9/21/74	142	6	8	Nobody Does It Like Me	$8	United Art. 214
11/29/75	186	3	9	Good, Bad But Beautiful	$8	United Art. 542
10/9/76	149	8	10	Love, Life And Feelings	$8	United Art. 605

All In Love Is Fair (9)
All That Love Went To Waste (8)
Alone Again (Naturally) (10)
And I Love You So (5,7)
Baby I'm-A Want You (6)
Ballad Of The Sad Young Men (5)
Big Spender (7)
Bless The Beasts And Children (5)
Born To Lose (10)
Breakfast In Bed (3)
Bridge Over Troubled Water (3)
Davy (8)
Day By Day (5,7)
Diamonds Are Forever (7) *57*
Easy To Be Hard (2)
Emotion (9)
Everything That Touches You (10)
Everything's Coming Up Roses (1)

Excuse Me (3)
Feel Like Makin' Love (9)
Feelings (10)
First Time Ever I Saw Your Face (7)
For All We Know (4,7)
Going, Going, Gone (6)
Goldfinger (1,7) *8*
Good, Bad But Beautiful (9)
Greatest Performance Of My Life (4)
He Loves Me (1)
Hungry Years (10)
I Believe In You (1)
I, Capricorn (4,7)
I Could Have Danced All Night (1)
I Don't Know How To Love Him (5)
I Who Have Nothing (7)
I Won't Last A Day Without You (6)
I'd Do It All Again (5)

I'd Like To Hate Myself In The Morning (And Raise A Little Hell Tonight) (3,7)
I'll Be Your Audience (9)
I'm Not Anyone (8)
I'm Nothing Without You (8)
I've Never Been A Woman Before (4)
If Ever I Would Leave You (1)
If I Never Sing Another Song (10)
If We Only Have Love (5)
Isn't It A Shame (10)
It's Impossible (Somos Novios) (3)
Jesse (9)
Jezahel (5)
Johnny One Note (7)
Killing Me Softly With His Song (6)
Leave A Little Room (8)
Let Me Sing And I'm Happy (7)
Life Goes On (2)

Light My Fire (2)
Living (9)
Look Of Love (4)
Losing My Mind (4)
Lost And Lonely (4)
Lot Of Livin' To Do (1)
Love (4)
Love Story, Theme From (3)
Lovely Way To Spend An Evening (7)
Make The World A Little Younger (4)
Midnight Blue (10)
Morning In Your Eyes (8)
My Way (2)
Natali (10)
Never, Never, Never (6,7) *48*
No Regrets (6)
Nobody Does It Like Me (8)
Old-Fashioned Way (6)
Once In A Lifetime (1)
One Less Bell To Answer (4)
Other Side Of Me (9)

Party's Over (7)
People (1)
Pieces Of Dreams (3)
Run On And On And On (9)
Sea And Sand (2)
Send In The Clowns (9)
Sing (9)
Someday (5)
Somehow (6)
Someone Who Cares (6)
Something (2,7) *55*
Something Wonderful (1)
Somewhere (1)
Spinning Wheel (2)
Sweetest Sounds (1)
There's No Such Thing As Love (6)
This Is My Life (La Vita) (7)
Till Love Touches Your Life (3)
Together (6)
Trouble With Hello Is Goodbye (8)
Until It's Time For You To Go (3)

Way A Woman Loves (4)
Way I Want To Touch You (10)
Way Of Love (5)
Way We Were (9)
What About Today? (2)
What Are You Doing The Rest Of Your Life? (2)
What I Did For Love (10)
What's Done Is Done (3)
When You Smile (8)
Where Am I Going (4,7)
(Where Do I Begin) ..see: Love Story, Theme From
Where Is Love (4)
Without You (5)
Yesterday I Heard The Rain (2)
Yesterday When I Was Young (Hier Encore) (2)
You And I (2,7)
You Are The Sunshine Of My Life (8)
You've Made Me So Very Happy (10)

BATDORF & RODNEY
John Batdorf and Mark Rodney. John formed the group Silver in 1976.

| 10/28/72 | 185 | 7 | 1 | Batdorf & Rodney | $10 | Asylum 5056 |
| 7/12/75 | 140 | 10 | 2 | Life Is You | $8 | Arista 4041 |

Ain't It Like Home (2)
All I Need (1)
Another Part Of Me (2)
Between The Ages (1)

By Today (1)
Caught In The Rain (2)
Grab At A Straw (2)
Happy Town (1)

Home Again (1)
Is It Love (2)
Let Me Live The Life (1)
Life Is You (2)

Long Way From Heaven (2)
Oh, Can You Tell Me (1)
Poor Man's Dream (1)
She Made Me Smile (2)

To A Gentler Time (2)
Under Five (1)
You Are A Song (2) *87*

DEBUT DATE	PEAK POS	WKS CHR	GOLD	ARTIST — Album Title	$	Label & Number

BATON ROUGE
Male hard-rock quintet formed by Louisiana natives Kelly Keeling (vocals) and Lance Bulen (lead guitar).

6/2/90	**160**	12		Shake Your Soul	**$12**	Atlantic 82073

Baby's So Cool	Doctor	It's About Time	Midge, The	There Was A Time (The	Walks Like A Woman
Bad Time Comin' Down	Hot Blood Movin'	Melenie	Spread Like Fire	Storm)	Young Hearts
Big Trouble					

BATTLE, Kathleen
Star of the New York Metropolitan Opera.

5/4/91	**186**	2		Spirituals In Concert ....[L]	**$12**	Deutsche G. 429790

KATHLEEN BATTLE & JESSYE NORMAN (highly acclaimed operatic soprano from Augusta, Georgia); chorus and orchestra conducted by James Levine; recorded live at Carnegie Hall on 3/18/90

Gospel Train	In That Great Getting Up	Lordy, Won't You Help Me	Over My Head (medley) [solo:	Swing Low, Sweet Chariot
Great Day	Morning	(medley)	Kathleen]	(medley) [solo: Kathleen]
He's Got The Whole World In	Lil' David (medley) [solo:	My God Is So High [solo:	Ride Up In The Chariot	Talk About A Child [solo:
His Hand	Kathleen]	Kathleen]	(medley) [solo: Kathleen]	Kathleen]
I Believe I'll Go Back Home	Lord, How Come Me Here	Oh, Glory [solo: Kathleen]	Scandalize My Name	There Is A Balm In Gilead
(medley)	[solo: Kathleen]	Oh, What A Beautiful City		

BAUHAUS
British post-punk quartet: Peter Murphy (keyboards), Daniel Ash (guitar), Kevin Haskins (drums) and David J (bass). Previously known as Bauhaus 1919, the name of a German art school. Disbanded in 1983. Murphy went solo. The latter three formed Love & Rockets.

8/12/89	**169**	6		Swing The Heartache - The BBC Sessions ....[K]	**$10**	Begr. B. 9804 [2]

tracks recorded for broadcast on Britain's national radio, BBC, in 5 sessions between 1980 and 1983

Departure	In Fear Of Fear	Party Of The First Part	Silent Hedges	Swing The Heartache	Third Uncle
Double Dare	In The Flat Field	Poison Pen	Spy In The Cab	Telegram Sam	Three Shadows (Part 2)
God In An Alcove	Night Time	She's In Parties	St. Vitus Dance	Terror Couple Kill Colonel	Ziggy Stardust

BAXTER, Les
Born on 3/14/22 in Mexia, Texas. Orchestra leader/arranger. Began as a conductor on radio shows in the 1930s. Member of Mel Torme's vocal group, the Mel-Tones. Musical arranger for Capitol Records (Nat King Cole, Margaret Whiting and others) in the 1950s. Composed over 100 film scores.

1/28/56	**6**	2		1 Tamboo! ....[I]	**$15**	Capitol 655

LES BAXTER/His Chorus and Orchestra

3/16/57	**21**	2		2 Skins! ....[I]	**$15**	Capitol 774

Afro-Deesia (2)	Conversation (2)	Maracaibo (2)	Pantan (1)	Shoutin' Drums (2)	Wotuka (1)
Batumba (1)	Cuchibamba (2)	Mood Tattooed (2)	Poppin' Panderos (2)	Simba (1)	Zambezi (1)
Brazilian Bash (2)	Gringo (2)	Mozambique (1)	Reverbasia (2)	Talkin' Drums (2)	
Bustin' The Bongos (2)	Havana (2)	Oasis Of Dakhla (1)	Rio (1)	Tehran (1)	

BAY CITY ROLLERS
Rock group formed in 1967 in Edinburgh, Scotland as the Saxons. Original members: brothers Alan and Derek Longmuir, Les McKeoun (lead singer), Eric Faulkner and Stuart "Woody" Wood.

9/27/75+	**20**	35	●	1 Bay City Rollers	**$8**	Arista 4049
3/20/76	**31**	16	●	2 Rock N' Roll Love Letter..	**$8**	Arista 4071
9/18/76	**26**	25	●	3 Dedication	**$8**	Arista 4093
7/23/77	**23**	11	●	4 It's A Game	**$8**	Arista 7004
12/3/77+	**77**	11	●	5 Greatest Hits ....[G]	**$8**	Arista 4158
10/14/78	**129**	4		6 Strangers In The Wind..	**$8**	Arista 4194

All Of The World Is Falling	Don't Let The Music Die (4)	Inside A Broken Dream (4)	Love Power (4)	Rock N' Roller (3)	When I Say I Love You (The
In Love (6)	Don't Stop The Music (2,5)	It's A Game (4)	Marlina (1)	**Saturday Night** (1,5) *1*	Pie) (6)
Another Rainy Day In New	Don't Worry Baby (3)	Keep On Dancing (1)	Maybe I'm A Fool To Love	Shang-A-Lang (1)	Where Will I Be Now (6)
York City (6)	Eagles Fly (2)	La Belle Jeane (2)	You (2,5)	Shanghai'd In Love (2)	Wouldn't You Like It (2)
Are You Cuckoo (3)	Every Tear I Cry (6)	Let's Go (A Huggin' And A	My Lisa (3)	Shoorah Shoorah For	Write A Letter (3)
Back On The Street (6)	Give A Little Love (1)	Kissin' In The Moonlight)	My Teenage Heart (1)	Hollywood (6)	**Yesterday's Hero** (3,5) *54*
Be My Baby (1)	I Only Wanna Dance With	(1)	Rebel Rebel (4)	Strangers In The Wind (6)	**You Made Me Believe In**
Bye Bye Baby (1)	You (2)	Let's Pretend (3)	Remember (Sha La La La) (1)	Summer Love Sensation (1)	**Magic** (4,5) *10*
Dance Dance Dance (4)	**I Only Want To Be With**	Love Brought Me Such A	**Rock And Roll Love Letter**	Sweet Virginia (4)	You're A Woman (3)
Dedication (3,5) *60*	**You** (3,5) *12*	Magical Thing (6)	(2,5) *28*	Too Young To Rock & Roll (2)	
Disco Kid (2)	If You Were My Woman (6)	Love Fever (4)	**Rock And Roll Love Letter**	**Way I Feel Tonight** (4,5) *24*	

B.B.&Q. BAND — see BROOKLYN, BRONX & QUEENS BAND

★★12★★ BEACH BOYS, The
Group formed in Hawthorne, California in 1961. Consisted of brothers Brian (keyboards, bass), Carl (guitar), and Dennis Wilson (drums); their cousin Mike Love (lead vocals, saxophone), and Al Jardine (guitar). Known in high school as Kenny & The Cadets, Carl & The Passions, then The Pendletones. First recorded for X/Candix in 1961. Jardine replaced by David Marks from March 1962 to March 1963. Brian quit touring with group in December 1964, replaced briefly by Glen Campbell until Bruce Johnston (of Bruce & Terry) joined permanently in April 1965. Johnston and Campbell also recorded in the studio band Sagittarius in 1967. Brian continued to write for and produce group, returned to stage in 1983. Daryl Dragon (of Captain & Tennille) was a keyboardist in their stage band. Dennis Wilson drowned on 12/28/83 (age 39). Lineup of Carl, Brian, Mike, Alan and Bruce continues to perform today. Carnie and Wendy Wilson, daughters of Brian Wilson, are members of Wilson Phillips. Group was inducted into the Rock and Roll Hall of Fame in 1988.

11/24/62+	**32**	37		1 Surfin' Safari	**$30**	Capitol 1808
5/4/63	**2²**	78	●	2 Surfin' U.S.A.	**$25**	Capitol 1890
10/12/63	**7**	56	●	3 Surfer Girl	**$25**	Capitol 1981
11/9/63+	**4**	46	▲	4 Little Deuce Coupe	**$25**	Capitol 1998
4/11/64	**13**	38	●	5 Shut Down, Volume 2	**$15**	Capitol 2027
				Volume 1 listed in Miscellaneous section: Cars		
8/1/64	**4**	49	●	6 All Summer Long	**$15**	Capitol 2110
11/7/64	**1⁴**	62	●	7 Beach Boys Concert ....[L]	**$10**	Capitol 2198
3/27/65	**4**	50	●	8 The Beach Boys Today!	**$15**	Capitol 2269

DEBUT DATE	PEAK POS	WKS CHR	GOLD	ARTIST — Album Title	$	Label & Number
				BEACH BOYS, The — Cont'd		
7/24/65	**2**[1]	33	● 9	**Summer Days (And Summer Nights!!)**	$30	Capitol 2354
11/27/65+	**6**	24	10	**Beach Boys' Party!**	$30	Capitol 2398
5/28/66	**10**	39	11	**Pet Sounds**	$15	Capitol 2458
7/23/66	**8**	78	▲² 12	**Best Of The Beach Boys** ....[G]	$12	Capitol 2545
8/12/67	**50**	22	▲² 13	Best Of The Beach Boys, Vol. 2 ....[G]	$12	Capitol 2706
9/30/67	**41**	21	14	Smiley Smile	$15	Brother 9001
12/30/67+	**24**	15	15	Wild Honey	$12	Capitol 2859
7/6/68	**126**	10	16	Friends	$12	Capitol 2895
9/7/68	**153**	6	17	Best Of The Beach Boys, Vol. 3 ....[G]	$35	Capitol 2945
3/1/69	**68**	11	18	20/20	$20	Capitol 133
8/16/69	**136**	6	19	Close-Up ....[R]	$35	Capitol 253 [2]
				reissue of *Surfin' U.S.A./All Summer Long* LPs		
9/26/70	**151**	4	20	Sunflower	$10	Brother 6382
9/11/71	**29**	17	21	Surf's Up	$20	Brother 6453
6/3/72	**50**	20	22	Pet Sounds/Carl And The Passions - So Tough ....[R]	$15	Brother 2083 [2]
				reissue of *Pet Sounds* plus new Carl And The Passions LP		
1/27/73	**36**	30	23	Holland	$10	Brother 2118
12/8/73+	**25**	24	● 24	The Beach Boys In Concert ....[L]	$12	Brother 6484 [2]
7/20/74	**1**[1]	155	● 25	**Endless Summer** ....[K]	$20	Capitol 11307 [2]
8/3/74	**50**	11	26	Wild Honey & 20/20 ....[R]	$12	Brother 2166 [2]
11/9/74	**125**	6	27	Friends & Smiley Smile ....[R]	$12	Brother 2167 [2]
5/3/75	**8**	43	● 28	**Spirit Of America** ....[K]	$15	Capitol 11384 [2]
7/19/75	**25**	23	29	Good Vibrations-Best Of The Beach Boys ....[G]	$12	Brother 2223
7/17/76	**8**	27	● 30	**15 Big Ones**	$12	Brother 2251
				15: age of band and number of tracks		
12/11/76+	**75**	10	31	Beach Boys '69 (The Beach Boys Live In London) ....[L]	$12	Capitol 11584
4/30/77	**53**	7	32	Love You	$10	Brother 2258
10/21/78	**151**	4	33	M.I.U. Album	$10	Brother 2268
				MIU: Maharishi International University		
4/7/79	**100**	13	34	L.A. (Light Album)	$8	Caribou 35752
4/12/80	**75**	6	35	Keepin' The Summer Alive	$8	Caribou 36283
12/26/81+	**156**	8	36	Ten Years Of Harmony (1970-1980) ....[K]	$10	Caribou 37445 [2]
7/3/82	**180**	6	37	Sunshine Dream ....[K]	$10	Capitol 12220 [2]
6/29/85	**52**	14	38	The Beach Boys	$8	Caribou 39946
7/26/86	**96**	12	● 39	Made In U.S.A. ....[G]	$10	Capitol 12396 [2]
				released in celebration of their 25th anniversary		
9/16/89	**46**	22	● 40	Still Cruisin'	$8	Capitol 92639
				6 of 10 tracks were featured in films from the 1980s		
6/16/90	**162**	5	41	Pet Sounds ....[R]	$12	Capitol 48421
				re-released on CD with 3 bonus tracks		

Add Some Music To Your Day (20,29,36) **64**
Airplane (32)
All I Wanna Do (20)
All I Want To Do (18,26,37)
All Summer Long (6,19,25)
All This Is That (22)
Alley Oop (10)
Amusement Parks U.S.A. (9)
And Your Dream Comes True (9)
Angel Come Home (34)
Anna Lee, The Healer (16,27)
Aren't You Glad (15,26,31,37)
At My Window (20)
Baby Blue (34)
Back Home (30)
Ballad Of Ole' Betsy (4)
Barbara Ann (10,13,28,31,39) **2**
Be Here In The Mornin' (16,27,37)
Be Still (16,27)
Be True To Your School (4,25,39) **6**
Be With Me (18,26)
Beach Boys Medley (37) **12**
Beaks Of Eagles (medley) (23)
Belles Of Paris (33)
Big Sur (medley) (23)
Blueberry Hill (30)
Bluebirds Over The Mountain (18,26,31,37) **61**
Boogie Woogie (3)
Break Away (28) **63**
Busy Doin' Nothin' (16,27)
Cabinessence (18,26)
California (medley) (23,36)
California Calling (38)
California Dreamin' (39) **57**

California Girls (9,13,24,25,31,39,40) **3**
California Saga (On My Way To Sunny Californ-i-a) (medley) (23,36) **84**
Car Crazy Cutie (4)
Carl's Big Chance (6)
Caroline, No (11,22,24,29,37,39,41) **32**
"Cassius" Love Vs "Sonny" Wilson (5)
Casual Look (30)
Catch A Wave (3,12,25)
Chapel Of Love (30)
Cherry, Cherry Coupe (4)
Chug-A-Lug (1)
Come Go With Me (33,36,39) **18**
Cool, Cool Water (20,36)
Cotton Fields (18,26,37)
Country Air (15,26)
County Fair (1)
Crack At Your Love (38)
Cuckoo Clock (1)
Cuddle Up (22)
Custom Machine (4,28)
Dance, Dance, Dance (8,17,28,39) **8**
Darlin' (15,17,24,26,29,31,36,37) **19**
Day In The Life Of A Tree (21)
Deirdre (20,36)
Denny's Drums (5)
Devoted To You (10)
Diamond Head (16,27)
Ding Dang (32)
Disney Girls (1957) (21,36)
Do It Again (18,26,29,31,37,39) **20**
Do You Remember? (6,19,28)

Do You Wanna Dance? (8,28) **12**
Don't Back Down (6,19,28)
Don't Go Near The Water (21,36)
Don't Hurt My Little Sister (8)
Don't Talk (Put Your Head On My Shoulder) (11,22,41)
Don't Worry Baby (5,13,24,25,39) **24**
Drive-In (6,19,28)
Endless Harmony (35)
Everyone's In Love With You (30)
Fall Breaks And Back To Winter (14,27)
Farmer's Daughter (2,19)
Feel Flows (21,36)
Finders Keepers (2,19)
Forever (20)
409 (1,4,13,17,28,39) **76**
Friends (16,27,29,37) **47**
Frosty The Snowman (17)
Full Sail (34)
Fun, Fun, Fun (5,7,12,24,25,39) **5**
Funky Pretty (23,24)
Getcha Back (38,39) **26**
Gettin' Hungry (14,27)
Girl Don't Tell Me (9,17,25)
Girl From New York City (9)
Girls On The Beach (6,19,25)
God Only Knows (11,22,29,31,37,39,41) **39**
Goin' On (35,36) **83**
Goin' South (11,22,41)
Good Time (32)
Good Timin' (34,36) **40**
Good To My Baby (8,28)

Good Vibrations (14,17,24,27,29,31,37,39) **1**
Got To Know The Woman (20)
Graduation Day (7,28)
Had To Phone Ya (30)
Hang On To Your Ego (41)
Hawaii (3,7,28)
He Come Down (22)
Heads You Win - Tails I Lose (1)
Help Me, Rhonda (8,9,13,24,25,39) **1**
Here Comes The Night (15,26,34) **44**
Here She Comes (22)
Here Today (11,22,37,41)
Heroes And Villains (14,17,24,27,29,37,39) **12**
Hey Little Tomboy (33)
Hold On Dear Brother (22)
Honkin' Down The Highway (32)
Honky Tonk (2,19)
How She Boogalooed It (15,26,37)
Hully Gully (10)
Hushabye (6,28)
I Can Hear Music (18,26,37) **24**
I Do Love You (38)
I Get Around (6,7,10,13,19,25,39,40) **1**
I Just Wasn't Made For These Times (11,22,41)
I Know There's An Answer (11,22,41)
I Should Have Known Better (10)
I Wanna Pick You Up (32)
I Was Made To Love Her (15,26)

I Went To Sleep (18,26)
I'd Love Just Once To See You (15,26)
I'll Bet He's Nice (32)
I'm Bugged At My Ol' Man (9)
I'm So Lonely (38)
I'm So Young (8)
I'm Waiting For The Day (11,22,37,41)
In My Car (40)
In My Room (3,7,12,25) **23**
In The Back Of My Mind (8)
In The Parkin' Lot (5)
In The Still Of The Night (30)
Island Girl (40)
It's A Beautiful Day (36)
It's About Time (20)
It's Gettin' Late (38) **82**
It's Just A Matter Of Time (38)
It's O.K. (30,36) **29**
Johnny B. Goode (7)
Johnny Carson (32)
Just Once In My Life (30)
Keep An Eye On Summer (5,37)
Keepin' The Summer Alive (35)
Kiss Me, Baby (8,12)
Kokomo (40) **1**
Kona Coast (33)
Lady Lynda (34,36)
Lana (34)
Leaving This Town (23,24)
Let Him Run Wild (9,13,25)
Let The Wind Blow (15,24,26)
Let Us Go On This Way (32)
Let's Go Away For Awhile (11,22,41)
Let's Go Trippin' (2,7)
Let's Put Our Hearts Together (32)

Little Bird (16,27)
Little Deuce Coupe (3,4,7,10,12,25) **15**
Little Girl I Once Knew (17,28) **20**
Little Girl (You're My Miss America) (1)
Little Honda (6,12,19,28) **65**
Little Old Lady From Pasadena (7)
Little Pad (14,27)
Little Saint Nick (13)
Lonely Sea (2,19)
Long Promised Road (21,36) **89**
Long, Tall Texan (7,13)
Lookin' At Tomorrow (A Welfare Song) (21)
Louie, Louie (5,13)
Love Is A Woman (32)
Love Surrounds Me (34)
Make It Big (40)
Make It Good (22)
Mama Says (15,26)
Marcella (22,24,36)
Match Point Of Our Love (33)
Maybe I Don't Know (38)
Meant For You (16,27)
Misirlou (32)
Mona (32)
Monster Mash (7)
Moon Dawg (1)
Mountain Of Love (10)
My Diane (33)
Nearest Faraway Place (18,26)
Never Learn Not To Love (18,26)
Night Was So Young (32)
No-Go Showboat (4)
Noble Surfer (2,19)

DEBUT DATE	PEAK POS	WKS CHR	GOLD	ARTIST — Album Title	$	Label & Number

BEACH BOYS, The — Cont'd

Oh Darlin' (35)
Only With You (23)
Our Car Club (3,4)
Our Prayer (18,26)
Our Sweet Love (20)
Palisades Park (30)
Papa-Oom-Mow-Mow (7,10)
Passing By (16,27)
Passing Friend (38)
Peggy Sue (33) *59*
Pet Sounds (11,22,41)
Pitter Patter (33)
Please Let Me Wonder (8,13,28) *52*
Pom, Pom Play Girl (5)
River Song (36)
Rock And Roll Music (30,36,39) *5*
Rock 'N' Roll To The Rescue (39) *68*
Rocking Surfer (3)
Roller Skating Child (32,36)
Sail On Sailor (23,24,29,36) *49*

Salt Lake City (9,28)
San Miguel (36)
Santa Ana Winds (35)
School Day (Ring! Ring! Goes The Bell) (35,36)
Sea Cruise (36)
She Believes In Love Again (38)
She Knows Me Too Well (8,17)
She's Goin' Bald (14,27)
She's Got Rhythm (33,36)
Shift, The (1)
Shortenin' Bread (34)
Shut Down (2,4,5,19,25) *23*
Slip On Through (20)
Sloop John B (11,22,24,29,31,37,39,41) *3*
Solar System (32)
Some Of Your Love (35)
Somewhere Near Japan (40)
South Bay Surfer (3)
Spirit Of America (4,28)

Steamboat (23)
Still Cruisin' (40) *93*
Stoked (2,19)
Student Demonstration Time (21)
Sumahama (34)
Summer Means New Love (9)
Summertime Blues (1)
Sunshine (35)
Surf Jam (2,19)
Surf's Up (21,29,36)
Surfer Girl (3,12,24,25,36,39) *7*
Surfer Moon (3)
Surfer's Rule (3)
Surfin (1,17) *75*
Surfin' Safari (1,13,25,39) *14*
Surfin' U.S.A. (2,12,19,24,25,39) *3*
Susie Cincinnati (30)
Sweet Sunday Kinda Love (33)
T M Song (30)

Take A Load Off Your Feet (21)
Talk To Me (30)
Tears In The Morning (20)
Tell Me Why (10,28)
Ten Little Indians (1) *49*
That Same Song (30)
That's Not Me (11,22,41)
Their Hearts Were Full Of Spring (31)
Then I Kissed Her (9,37)
There's No Other (Like My Baby) (10,37)
Thing Or Two (15,26)
This Car Of Mine (5,28)
This Whole World (20,36)
'Til I Die (21,36)
Time To Get Alone (18,26)
Times They Are A-Changin' (10)
Trader, The (23,24,36)
Transcendental Meditation (16,27)
Trombone Dixie (41)

Vegetables (14,27,37)
Wake The World (16,27,31)
Wanderer, The (7)
Warmth Of The Sun (5,12,25)
We Got Love (24)
We'll Run Away (6,19)
Wendy (6,12,19,25) *44*
When A Man Needs A Woman (16,27)
When Girls Get Together (35) (9,12,25)
When I Grow Up (To Be A Man) (8,13,28,39) *9*
Where I Belong (38)
Whistle In (14,27)
Why Do Fools Fall In Love (5,28)
Wild Honey (15,26,37) *31*
Wind Chimes (14,27)
Winds Of Change (33)
Wipeout (40) *12*
With Me Tonight (14,27)
Wonderful (14,27)

Wontcha Come Out Tonight (33,36)
Wouldn't It Be Nice (11,22,24,29,31,37,39,40,41) *8*
You Need A Mess Of Help To Stand Alone (22)
You Still Believe In Me (11,22,24,41)
You're So Good To Me (16,27)
You've Got To Hide Your Love Away (10)
Young Man Is Gone (4,28)
Your Summer Dream (3)

BEACON STREET UNION
Boston rock quintet — John Lincoln Wright, lead singer.

DEBUT DATE	PEAK POS	WKS CHR	GOLD	ARTIST — Album Title	$	Label & Number
3/9/68	75	16		1 The Eyes Of The Beacon Street Union	$20	MGM 4517
9/14/68	173	10		2 The Clown Died In Marvin Gardens	$20	MGM 4568

Angus Of Aberdeen (2)
Baby Please Don't Go (2)
Beautiful Delilah (1)
Blue Avenue (1)

Blue Suede Shoes (2)
Clown Died In Marvin Gardens (2)
Clown's Overture (1)

Four Hundred And Five (1)
Green Destroys The Gold (1)
King Of The Jungle (2)
May I Light Your Cigarette (2)

My Love Is (1)
Mystic Mourning (1)
Not Very August Afternoon (2)

Now I Taste The Tears (2)
Prophet, The (1)
Sadie Said No (1)

South End Incident (I'm Afraid) (1)
Speed Kills (1)
Sportin' Life (1)

BEAR, Edward — see EDWARD

BEARS, The
Pop quartet founded by prolific sessionman/vocalist Adrian Belew. Includes: Rob Fetters, Bob Nyswonger and Chris Arduser.

DEBUT DATE	PEAK POS	WKS CHR	GOLD	ARTIST — Album Title	$	Label & Number
4/30/88	159	5		Rise And Shine	$8	I.R.S. 42139

Aches And Pains
Best Laid Plans
Complicated Potatoes

Girl With Clouds
Highway 2
Holy Mack

Little Blue River
Nobody's Fool
Not Worlds Apart

Old Fat Cadillac
Rabbit Manor
Robobo's Beef

Save Me
You Can Buy Friends

BEAST
Denver rock septet — David Raines, lead singer.

DEBUT DATE	PEAK POS	WKS CHR	GOLD	ARTIST — Album Title	$	Label & Number
9/13/69	195	2		Beast	$10	Cotillion 9012

Alley Sam (I Feel A Change)
Cannabis Sativa L
Dear Ruth

Ev'ry Man Hears Different Music
Floating (Down By The River)

Goin' Downtown
Listen
Love Like

On My Way
Prelude For Today
Spaceman

(Strange Places Like) Santo Domingo
Treat Her Right

When We Rise
Wow Wow

BEASTIE BOYS
New York white rap trio formed in 1981, consisting of King Ad-Rock (Adam Horovitz, son of playwright Israel Horovitz), MCA (Adam Yauch) and Mike D (Michael Diamond). Horovitz starred in the film *Lost Angels* in 1988. Their DJ, Dr. Dre, became host of *Yo! MTV Raps.*

DEBUT DATE	PEAK POS	WKS CHR	GOLD	ARTIST — Album Title	$	Label & Number
11/29/86+	1[7]	68	▲[4]	1 Licensed To Ill	$8	Def Jam 40238
8/12/89	14	15	●	2 Paul's Boutique	$8	Capitol 91743
5/9/92	10	35↑ ●		3 Check Your Head	$12	Capitol 98938

Ask For Janice (2)
B-Boy Bouillabaisse Medley (2)
Brass Monkey (1) *48*
Car Thief (2)
Egg Man (2)
Finger Lickin' Good (3)
5-Piece Chicken Dinner (2)
Funky Boss (3)

Girls (1)
Gratitude (3)
Groove Holmes (3)
Hey Ladies (2) *36*
High Plains Drifter (2)
Hold It Now, Hit It (1)
In 3's (3)
Jimmy James (3)
Johnny Ryall (2)

Lighten Up (3)
Live At P.J.'s (3)
Looking Down The Barrel Of A Gun (2)
Maestro, The (3)
Mark On The Bus (3)
Namaste (3)
New Style (1)
No Sleep Till Brooklyn (1)

POW (3)
Pass The Mic (3)
Paul Revere (1)
Posse In Effect (1)
Professor Booty (3)
Rhymin & Stealin (1)
Shadrach (1)
Shake Your Rump (2)
She's Crafty (1)

Slow And Low (1)
Slow Ride (1)
So What'cha Want (3) *93*
Something's Got To Give (3)
Sounds Of Science (2)
Stand Together (3)
3-Minute Rule (2)
Time For Livin' (3)
Time To Get Ill (1)

To All The Girls (2)
What Comes Around (2)
(You Gotta) Fight For Your Right (To Party!) (1) *7*

BEAT FARMERS, The
Southern California rock quartet: Joey Harris (lead vocals, guitar), Jerry Raney, Country Dick Montana, and Rolle Love.

DEBUT DATE	PEAK POS	WKS CHR	GOLD	ARTIST — Album Title	$	Label & Number
6/8/85	186	3		1 Tales of the New West	$8	Rhino 853
7/12/86	135	9		2 Van Go	$8	MCA/Curb 5759
9/5/87	131	8		3 The Pursuit Of Happiness	$8	MCA/Curb 5993

Big Big Man (3)
Big River (3)
Big Ugly Wheels (2)
Bigger Fool Than Me (2)
Bigger Stones (1)
Blue Chevrolet (2)

Buy Me A Car (2)
California Kid (1)
Dark Light (3)
Deceiver (2)
Elephant Day Parade (3)
God Is Here Tonight (3)

Goldmine (1)
Gun Sale At The Church (2)
Happy Boy (1)
Hollywood Hills (1)
I Want You, Too (2)
Key To The World (3)

Lonesome Hound (1)
Lost Weekend (1)
Make It Last (3)
Never Going Back (1)
Powderfinger (2)
Reason To Believe (1)

Ridin' (3)
Riverside (2)
Road To Ruin (2)
Rosie (3)
Selfish Heart (1)
Seven Year Blues (2)

Showbiz (2)
Texas (3)
There She Goes Again (1)
Where Do They Go (1)

★★3★★ BEATLES, The

The world's #1 rock group was formed in Liverpool, England in the late 1950s. Known in early forms as The Quarrymen, Johnny & the Moondogs, The Rainbows, and the Silver Beatles. Named The Beatles in 1960. Originally consisted of John Lennon, Paul McCartney, George Harrison (guitars), Stu Sutcliffe (bass) and Pete Best (drums). Sutcliffe left in April 1961 (died on 4/10/62 of a brain hemorrhage); McCartney moved to bass. Best replaced by Ringo Starr in August 1962. Group managed by Brian Epstein (died on 8/27/67 of sleeping-pill overdose) and produced by George Martin. First U.S. tour in February 1964. Won the 1964 Best New Artist Grammy Award. Group starred in films *A Hard Day's Night* (1964), *Help* (1965), *Magical Mystery Tour* (1967) and *Let It Be* (1970); contributed soundtrack to the animated film *Yellow Submarine* (1968). Own Apple label in 1968. McCartney publicly anounced group's dissolution on 4/10/70. Won the Grammy's Trustees Award in 1972. Lennon was shot to death on 12/8/80. Inducted into the Rock and Roll Hall of Fame in 1988.

DEBUT DATE	PEAK POS	WKS CHR	GOLD	#	ARTIST — Album Title	$	Label & Number
2/1/64	1[11]	71	▲[5]	1	Meet The Beatles!	$40	Capitol 2047
2/8/64	2[9]	49		2	Introducing...The Beatles	$750	Vee-Jay 1062
					1st U.S. album; released July 1963		
2/15/64	68	14		3	The Beatles with Tony Sheridan and Their Guests ...[E]	$100	MGM 4215
					features 6 cuts by Tony & The Beatles (shown in tracks index) and also these 6 cuts by The Titans: "Darktown Strutters' Ball," "Flying Beat," "Happy New Year Beat," "Johnson Rag," "Rye Beat" and "Summertime Beat"		
4/4/64	104	6		4	Jolly What! The Beatles & Frank Ifield ...[K]	$250	Vee-Jay 1085
					includes 8 cuts by Frank Ifield: "Anytime," "I Listen To My Heart," "I Remember You," "I'm Smiling Now," "Lovesick Blues," "Nobody's Darling," "Unchained Melody" and "The Wayward Wind"; a repackaged version showing a portrait of The Beatles on the cover was released briefly in late 1964 and is valued at $1500-$2000 for a stereo copy		
4/25/64	1[5]	55	●	5	The Beatles' Second Album	$30	Capitol 2080
6/6/64	20	13		6	The American Tour With Ed Rudy ...[T]	$45	RadioPulsebeat 2
					interviews with The Beatles		
7/18/64	1[14]	51		7	A Hard Day's Night ...[S]	$50	United Art. 6366
					includes 4 instrumentals by George Martin: "And I Love Her," "Hard Day's Night," "I Should Have Known Better" and "Ringo's Theme (This Boy)"		
8/8/64	2[9]	41	▲	8	Something New	$35	Capitol 2108
					includes 5 tunes from *A Hard Day's Night* album		
10/10/64	142	3		9	The Beatles vs. The Four Seasons ...[R]	$500	Vee-Jay 30 [2]
					Introducing The Beatles & Golden Hits Of The 4 Seasons LPs		
10/31/64	63	11		10	Songs, Pictures And Stories Of The Fabulous Beatles ...[R]	$150	Vee-Jay 1092
					2nd reissue of *Introducing The Beatles*		
12/12/64+	7	17	●	11	The Beatles' Story ...[T]	$50	Capitol 2222 [2]
					narrative featuring bits of their hits		
1/2/65	1[9]	71	▲[2]	12	Beatles '65	$40	Capitol 2228
4/24/65	43	35	●	13	The Early Beatles ...[E]	$40	Capitol 2309
					reissue by Capitol of Vee-Jay recordings		
6/26/65	1[6]	41	●	14	Beatles VI	$40	Capitol 2358
8/28/65	1[9]	44	●	15	Help! ...[S]	$40	Capitol 2386
					includes 5 instrumentals by Ken Thorne: "The Bitter End," "Another Hard Day's Night," "The Chase," "From Me To You Fantasy" and "In The Tyrol"		
12/25/65+	1[6]	59	▲[4]	16	Rubber Soul	$30	Capitol 2442
7/9/66	1[5]	31	●	17	"Yesterday"...And Today ...[G]	$50	Capitol 2553
					originally featured the "butcher cover" (proper name of photo on cover is "Somnambulant Adventure") which is valued at $2000-$5000 for a mono copy and $5000-$10,000 for stereo; LP quickly withdrawn after its release and a new photo was pasted over the controversial original cover		
9/3/66	1[6]	77	▲[3]	18	Revolver	$30	Capitol 2576
6/24/67	1[15]	175	▲[8]	19	Sgt. Pepper's Lonely Hearts Club Band	$35	Capitol 2653
					1967 Grammy winner: Album of the Year; also see soundtrack of the same name		
12/23/67+	1[8]	91	▲[5]	20	Magical Mystery Tour ...[S-G]	$35	Capitol 2835
					6 tunes from the film and 5 singles hits		
12/14/68	1[9]	155	▲[7]	21	The Beatles [White Album]	$30	Apple 101 [2]
					simply titled *The Beatles*, however, because of stark cover, commonly referred to as *The White Album*		
2/8/69	2[2]	25	▲	22	Yellow Submarine ...[S]	$20	Apple 153
					side 1: The Beatles; side 2: instrumentals by George Martin: "March Of The Meanies," "Pepperland," "Pepperland Laid Waste," "Sea Of Time/Sea Of Holes," "Sea Of Monsters" and "Yellow Submarine In Pepperland"		
10/18/69	1[11]	129	▲[9]	23	Abbey Road	$20	Apple 383
					Abbey Road is the London studio where group recorded 191 songs		
3/21/70	2[4]	33	▲[3]	24	Hey Jude ...[G]	$20	Apple 385
5/16/70	117	7		25	The Beatles featuring Tony Sheridan - In The Beginning (Circa 1960) ...[E]	$20	Polydor 4504
5/30/70	1[4]	59	●	26	Let It Be ...[S]	$15	Apple 34001
					film features The Beatles during recording sessions		
4/14/73	3	164	▲[5]	27	The Beatles/1962-1966 ...[G]	$20	Apple 3403 [2]
4/14/73	1[1]	169	▲[5]	28	The Beatles/1967-1970 ...[G]	$20	Apple 3404 [2]
6/26/76	2[2]	30	▲	29	Rock 'N' Roll Music ...[K]	$20	Capitol 11537 [2]
5/21/77	2[2]	17	▲	30	The Beatles At The Hollywood Bowl ...[E-L]	$10	Capitol 11638
					concert recordings of 8/23/64 and 8/30/65		
7/2/77	111	7		31	The Beatles Live! at the Star-Club in Hamburg, Germany; 1962 ...[E-L]	$12	Lingasong 7001 [2]
11/12/77	24	31	●	32	Love Songs ...[K]	$12	Capitol 11711 [2]
4/12/80	21	15		33	Rarities ...[K]	$10	Capitol 12060
4/10/82	19	12	●	34	Reel Music ...[K]	$10	Capitol 12199
					tunes from The Beatles' 5 films		

DEBUT DATE	PEAK POS	WKS CHR	GOLD	ARTIST — Album Title	$	Label & Number
				BEATLES, The — Cont'd		
11/13/82+	**50**	28 ▲	35	20 Greatest Hits .... [G]	**$10**	Capitol 12245
				The Beatles' 20 #1 singles		
4/2/88	**149**	6	36	Past Masters - Volume One .... [K]	**$10**	Capitol 90043
4/2/88	**121**	7	37	Past Masters - Volume Two .... [K]	**$10**	Capitol 90044
				above 2: A and B-sides of singles and special EP tracks; available only on CD; volumes later combined and released as *Past Masters* on a double LP and double cassette (Capitol 91135)		

Across The Universe (26,28,33,37)
Act Naturally (17) 47
Ain't Nothing Shakin' (Like The Leaves On A Tree) (31)
Ain't She Sweet (25) 19
All I've Got To Do (1)
All My Loving (1,27,30) 45
All Together Now (22)
All You Need Is Love (20,22,28,34,35) 1
And I Love Her (7,8,27,32,33,34) 12
And Your Bird Can Sing (17)
Anna (2,9,10,13)
Another Girl (15)
Any Time At All (8,29)
Ask Me Why (4,9,10,13)
Baby It's You (2,9,10,13)
Baby You're A Rich Man (20) 34
Baby's In Black (12)
Back In The U.S.S.R. (21,28,29)
Bad Boy (14,29,36)
Ballad Of John And Yoko (24,28,37) 8
Be-Bop-A-Lula (31)
Beatle Medley (11)
Because (23)
Being For The Benefit Of Mr. Kite (19)
Besame Mucho (31)
Birthday (21,29)
Blackbird (21)
Blue Jay Way (20)
Boys (2,9,10,13,29,30)
Can't Buy Me Love (7,24,27,30,34,35) 1
Carry That Weight (23)
Chains (2,9,10,13)
Come Together (23,28,35) 1
Continuing Story Of Bungalow Bill (21)
Cry Baby Cry (21)
Cry For A Shadow (3,25)
Day In The Life (19,28)
Day Tripper (17,27,37) 5
Dear Prudence (21)
Devil In Her Heart (5)
Dig It (26)
Dizzy Miss Lizzie (14,29,30)
Do You Want To Know A Secret (2,9,10,13) 2
Dr. Robert (17)
Don't Bother Me (1)
Don't Let Me Down (24,28,37) 35

Don't Pass Me By (21,33)
Drive My Car (17,27,29)
Eight Days A Week (14,27,35) 1
Eleanor Rigby (18,27) 11
End, The (23)
Every Little Thing (14,32)
Everybody's Got Something To Hide Except Me And My Monkey (21)
Everybody's Trying To Be My Baby (12,29,31) 68
hit "Hot 100" as part of "4-By The Beatles"
Falling In Love Again (31)
Fixing A Hole (19)
Flying (20)
Fool On The Hill (20,28)
For No One (18,32)
For You Blue (26) *flip*
From Me To You (4,27,36) 41
Get Back (26,28,29,34,35,37) 1
Getting Better (19)
Girl (16,27,32)
Glass Onion (21)
Golden Slumbers (23)
Good Day Sunshine (18)
Good Morning Good Morning (19)
Good Night (21)
Got To Get You Into My Life (18,29) 7
Hallelujah I Love Her So (31)
Happiness Is A Warm Gun (21)
Hard Day's Night (7,27,30,34,35) 1
Hello Goodbye (20,28,35) 1
Help! (15,27,30,33,34,35) 1
Helter Skelter (21,29,33)
Her Majesty (23)
Here Comes The Sun (23,28)
Here, There And Everywhere (18,32)
Hey Bulldog (22,29)
Hey Hey Hey Hey (medley) (31)
Hey Jude (24,28,35,37) 1
Hippy Hippy Shake (31)
Hold Me Tight (1)
Honey Don't (12) 68
hit "Hot 100" as part of "4-By The Beatles"
Honey Pie (21)
I Am The Walrus (20,28,33,34) 56

I Call Your Name (5,29,36)
I Dig A Pony (26)
I Don't Want To Spoil The Party (14) 39
I Feel Fine (12,27,35,36) 1
I Need You (15,32)
I Remember You (31)
I Saw Her Standing There (1,2,9,10,29) 14
I Should Have Known Better (7,24,34) 53
I Wanna Be Your Man (1,29)
I Want To Hold Your Hand (1,27,35,36) 1
I Want To You (18)
I Want You (She's So Heavy) (23)
I Will (21,32)
I'll Be Back (12,32)
I'll Cry Instead (7,8) 25
I'll Follow The Sun (12,32)
I'll Get You (5,36)
I'm A Loser (12) 68
hit "Hot 100" as part of "4-By The Beatles"
I'm Down (29,36)
I'm Gonna Sit Right Down And Cry Over You (31)
I'm Happy Just To Dance With You (7,8) 95
I'm Looking Through You (16)
I'm Only Sleeping (17,33)
I'm So Tired (21)
I've Got A Feeling (26)
I've Seen A Face (16)
If I Fell (7,8,32) 53
If I Needed Someone (17)
In My Life (16,27,32)
Inner Light (33,37) 96
It Won't Be Long (1)
It's All Too Much (22)
It's Only Love (16,32)
Julia (21)
Kansas City (14,29,31)
Komm, Gib Mir Deine Hand (I Want To Hold Your Hand) (8,36)
Lady Madonna (24,28,37) 4
Lend Me Your Comb (31)
Let It Be (26,28,34,35,37) 1
Let's Dance (31)
Little Child (1)
Little Queenie (31)
Long And Winding Road (26,28,34,35) 1
Long, Long, Long (21)

Long Tall Sally (5,29,30,31,36)
Love Me Do (2,13,27,33,35,36) 1
Love You To (18)
Lovely Rita (19)
Lucy In The Sky With Diamonds (19,28)
Maggie Mae (26)
Magical Mystery Tour (20,28,34)
Martha My Dear (21)
Matchbox (8,29,31,36) 17
Maxwell's Silver Hammer (23)
Mean Mr. Mustard (23)
Michelle (16,27,32)
Misery (2,9,10,33)
Money (That's What I Want) (5,29)
Mother Nature's Son (21)
Mr. Moonlight (12,31) 68
hit "Hot 100" as part of "4-By The Beatles"
My Baby (My Bonnie Lies Over The Ocean) (3,25) 26
Night Before (15,29)
No Reply (12)
Nobody's Child (25)
Norwegian Wood (This Bird Has Flown) (16,27,32)
Not A Second Time (1)
Nowhere Man (17,27) 3
Ob-La-Di, Ob-La-Da (21,28) 49
Octopus's Garden (23,28)
Oh! Darling (23)
Old Brown Shoe (24,28,37)
One After 909 (26)
Only A Northern Song (22)
P.S. I Love You (2,13,32) 10
Paperback Writer (24,27,35,37) 1
Penny Lane (20,28,33,35) 1
Piggies (21)
Please Mister Postman (5) 92
hit "Hot 100" as part of "Four By The Beatles"
Please Please Me (4,9,10,13,27) 3
Polythene Pam (23)
Rain (24,37) 23
Red Sails In The Sunset (31)

Revolution (21,24,28,29,37) 12
Revolution 9 (21)
Ringo's Theme ..see: This Boy
Rock And Roll Music (12,29)
Rocky Raccoon (21)
Roll Over Beethoven (5,29,30,31) 68
Ruby Baby (25)
Run For Your Life (16)
Saints (When The Saints Go Marching In) (3,25)
Savoy Truffle (21)
Sexy Sadie (21)
Sgt. Pepper's Lonely Hearts Club Band (19,28) 71
hit "Hot 100" as a medley with "With A Little Help From My Friends"
She Came In Through The Bathroom Window (23)
She Loves You (5,27,30,35,36) 1
She Said She Said (18)
She's A Woman (12,30,36) 4
She's Leaving Home (19,32)
Sheila (31)
Shimmy Shake (31)
Sie Liebt Dich (She Loves You) (33,36) 97
Slow Down (8,29,36) 25
Something (23,28,32) 3
Strawberry Fields Forever (20,28) 8
Sun King (23)
Swanee River (3)
Sweet Georgia Brown (25)
Sweet Little Sixteen (31)
Take Out Some Insurance On Me, Baby (25)
Talkin 'Bout You (31)
Taste Of Honey (2,9,10,13,31)
Taxman (18,29)
Tell Me What You See (14,32)
Tell Me Why (7,8)
Thank You Girl (4,5,36) 35
There's A Place (2,9,10,33,37)
Things We Said Today (8,30)
Think For Yourself (16)
This Boy (37)
hit "Hot 100" as part of "Four By The Beatles"
Ticket To Ride (15,27,30,34,35) 1

Till There Was You (1,31)
To Know Her Is To Love Her (31)
Tomorrow Never Knows (18)
Twist And Shout (2,9,10,13,29,30) 2
Two Of Us (26)
Wait (16)
We Can Work It Out (17,27,35,37) 1
What Goes On (17) 81
What You're Doing (14)
What'd I Say (25)
When I Get Home (8)
When I'm Sixty-Four (19)
Where Have You Been All My Life (31)
While My Guitar Gently Weeps (21,28)
Why (3,25) 88
Why Don't We Do It In The Road? (21)
Wild Honey Pie (21)
With A Little Help From My Friends (19,28) 71
hit "Hot 100" as a medley with "Sgt. Pepper's Lonely Hearts Club Band"
Within You Without You (19)
Word, The (16)
Words Of Love (14,32)
Ya Ya (31)
Yellow Submarine (18,22,27,34) 2
Yer Blues (21)
Yes It Is (14,32,36) 46
Yesterday (17,27,32,35) 1
You Are My Sunshine (3)
You Can't Do That (5,29) 48
You Know My Name (Look Up My Number) (33,37)
You Like Me Too Much (14)
You Never Give Me Your Money (23)
You Really Got A Hold On Me (5)
You Won't See Me (16)
You're Going To Lose That Girl (15,32)
You've Got To Hide Your Love Away (15,27,32,34)
hit POS 12 on "Hot 100" as part of "Beatles' Movie Medley"
Your Feets Too Big (31)
Your Mother Should Know (20)

BEATS INTERNATIONAL
British ensemble led by DJ Norman Cook (b: 1963 in London). Includes singers Lester Noel and Lindy Layton, keyboardist Andy Boucher and percussionist Luke Cresswell. Cook was bassist of The Housemartins.

DEBUT DATE	PEAK POS	WKS CHR		ALBUM	$	Label & Number
5/19/90	**162**	6		Let Them Eat Bingo	**$12**	Elektra 60921
				CD includes a bonus track		

Babies Makin' Babies
Before I Grow Too Old
Blame It On The Bassline
Burundi Blues
Dance To The Drummer's Beat
Dub Be Good To Me 76
For Spacious Lies *[includes 2 versions]*
Ragged Trousered Percussionists
Tribute To King Tubby
Whole World's Down On Me
Won't Talk About It 76

BEAU BRUMMELS, The
Rock group formed in 1964 in San Francisco. Led by Sal Valentino (b: Sal Spaminato on 9/8/42, San Francisco; vocals) and Ron Elliott (b: 10/21/43, Haddsburg, California; guitar):

DEBUT DATE	PEAK POS	WKS CHR		ALBUM	$	Label & Number
5/8/65	**24**	21	1	Introducing The Beau Brummels	**$35**	Autumn 103
9/30/67	**197**	2	2	Triangle	**$20**	Warner 1692
7/5/75	**180**	3	3	The Beau Brummels	**$20**	Warner 2842

Ain't That Loving You Baby (1)
And I've Seen Her (2)
Are You Happy? (2)
Down To The Bottom (3)
First In Line (3)
Gate Of Hearts (3)
Goldrush (3)
I Want More Loving (1)
I Would Be Happy (1)
It Won't Get Better (1)
Just Wait And See (1)
Keeper Of Time (2)
Laugh, Laugh (1) 15
Lonely Side (3)
Magic Hollow (2)
Nine Pound Hammer (2)
Not Too Long Ago (1)
Oh Lonesome Me (1)
Old Kentucky Home (2)
Only Dreaming Now (2)
Painter Of Women (2)
Singing Cowboy (3)
Stick Like Glue (1)
Still In Love With You Baby (1)
Tennessee Walker (3)
That's, If You Want Me To (1)
They'll Make You Cry (1)
Today By Day (3)
Triangle (2)
Wolf (3)
Wolf Of Velvet Fortune (2)
You Tell Me Why (3) 38

BEAUVOIR, Jean
New York bassist/producer/singer of Haitian descent. At age 14, worked with Gary U.S. Bonds' touring band. The Plasmatics' bassist at age 17. Later with Little Steven & the Disciples Of Soul.

DEBUT DATE	PEAK POS	WKS CHR		ALBUM	$	Label & Number
6/28/86	**93**	15		Drums Along The Mohawk	**$8**	Columbia 40403

DEBUT DATE	PEAK POS	WKS CHR	GOLD	ARTIST — Album Title	$	Label & Number

BEAUVOIR, Jean — Cont'd

Drive You Home	If I Was Me	Never Went Down	Rockin In The Street	Sorry I Missed Your	This Is Our House
Feel The Heat 73	Missing The Young Days	Nina	Same Song Plays On And On	Wedding Day	

BE-BOP DELUXE

English techno-rock quartet: Bill Nelson (vocals), Andy Clark, Charles Tumahai and Simon Fox.

2/7/76	96	17		1 Sunburst Finish	$8	Harvest 11478
10/16/76	88	8		2 Modern Music	$8	Harvest 11575
8/20/77	65	15		3 Live! In The Air Age ....[L]	$10	Harvest 11666 [2]
3/11/78	95	9		4 Drastic Plastic	$8	Harvest 11750

Adventures In A Yorkshire	Dance Of The Uncle Sam	Gold At The End Of The	Lost In The Neon World (2)	Panic In The World (4)	Superenigmatix (Lethal
Landscape (3)	Humanoids (2)	Rainbow (2)	Love In Flames (4)	Piece Of Mine (3)	Appliances For The Home
Beauty Secrets (1)	Dancing In The Moonlight	Heavenly Homes (1)	Maid In Heaven (3)	Possession (4)	With Everything) (4)
Bird Charmer's Destiny (2)	(All Alone) (2)	Honeymoon On Mars (2)	Make The Music Magic (2)	Shine (3)	Surreal Estate (4)
Blazing Apostles (1,3)	Dangerous Stranger (4)	Islands Of The Dead (4)	Mill Street Junction (3)	Ships In The Night (1,3)	Twilight Capers (4)
Bring Back The Spark (2)	Down On Terminal Street (2)	Japan (4)	Modern Music (2)	Sister Seagull (3)	
Crying To The Sky (1)	Electrical Language (4)	Kiss Of Light (2)	New Mysteries (4)	Sleep That Burns (1)	
Crystal Gazing (1)	Fair Exchange (1,3)	Life In The Air Age (1,3)	New Precision (4)		
	Forbidden Lovers (2)	Like An Old Blues (1)	Orphans Of Babylon (2)		

★★240★★ BECK, Jeff

Veteran guitarist. Born on 6/24/44 in Surrey, England. With The Yardbirds from 1964-66. Rod Stewart and Ron Wood were members of the Jeff Beck Group from 1967-69. Member of supergroup The Honeydrippers.

8/24/68	15	33		1 Truth	$14	Epic 26413
7/12/69	15	21		2 Beck-Ola *	$14	Epic 26478
				above 2 with Rod Stewart (vocals)		
11/6/71	46	16		3 Rough And Ready *	$10	Epic 30973
5/13/72	19	26	●	4 Jeff Beck Group *	$10	Epic 31331
				*JEFF BECK GROUP		
4/7/73	12	27	●	5 Jeff Beck, Tim Bogert, Carmine Appice	$10	Epic 32140
				BECK, BOGERT, APPICE		
				Bogert (bass) and Appice (drums) were both formerly with Cactus and Vanilla Fudge; Appice was later with Blue Murder and KGB		
4/12/75	4	25	▲	6 Blow By Blow ....[I]	$10	Epic 33409
6/26/76	16	25	▲	7 Wired ....[I]	$10	Epic 33849
4/2/77	23	15		8 Jeff Beck with The Jan Hammer Group Live ...[I-L]	$10	Epic 34433
7/12/80	21	20		9 There And Back ....[I]	$10	Epic 35684
7/20/85	39	18		10 Flash	$10	Epic 39483
10/21/89	49	18		11 Jeff Beck's Guitar Shop	$10	Epic 44313
				JEFF BECK WITH TERRY BOZZIO & TONY HYMAS		
				Bozzio was the drummer of Missing Persons; Hymas was the keyboardist with the Jack Bruce Band		

Air Blower (6)	Earth In Search Of A Sun	Got The Feeling (3)	Let Me Love You (1)	Savoy (11)	Tonight I'll Be Staying Here
All Shook Up (2)	(medley) (8)	Greensleeves (1)	Livin' Alone (5)	Scatterbrain (6,8)	With You (4)
Ambitious (4)	Earth (Still Our Only Home)	Guitar Shop (11)	Lose Myself With You (5)	Shapes Of Things (1)	Too Much To Lose (9)
Beck's Bolero (1)	(8)	Hangman's Knee (2)	Love Is Green (7)	She's A Woman (6,8)	Train Train (medley) (3)
Behind The Veil (11)	Ecstasy (10)	Head For Backstage Pass (7)	Max's Tune (3)	Short Business (3)	Two Rivers (11)
Big Block (11)	El Becko (9)	Highways (4)	Morning Dew (1)	Situation (3)	Where Were You (11)
Black Cat Moan (5)	Escape (10)	I Ain't Superstitious (1)	New Ways (medley) (3)	Sling Shot (11)	Why Should I Care (5)
Blue Wind (7,8)	Final Peace (9)	I Can't Give Back The Love I	Night After Night (10)	Sophie (3)	You Know, We Know (10)
Blues De Luxe (1)	Freeway Jam (6,8)	Feel For You (4)	Oh To Love You (5)	Space Boogie (9)	You Know What I Mean (6)
Cause We've Ended As	Full Moon Boogie (8)	I Got To Have A Song (4)	Ol' Man River (1)	Spanish Boots (2)	You Never Know (9)
Lovers (6)	Get Workin' (10)	I'm So Proud (5)	**People Get Ready** (10) 48	Stand On It (11)	You Shook Me (1)
Come Dancing (7)	Gets Us All In The End (10)	I've Been Used (3)	Play With Me (7)	Star Cycle (9)	
Constipated Duck (6)	Girl From Mill Valley (2)	Ice Cream Cakes (4)	Plynth (Water Down The	Stop, Look And Listen (10)	
Darkness (medley) (8)	Glad All Over (4)	Jailhouse Rock (2)	Drain) (2)	Sugar Cane (4)	
Day In The House (11)	Going Down (4)	Jody (3)	Pump, The (9)	Superstition (3)	
Definitely Maybe (4)	Golden Road (9)	Lady (5)	Rice Pudding (2)	Sweet Sweet Surrender (5)	
Diamond Dust (6)	Goodbye Pork Pie Hat (7)	Led Boots (7)	Rock My Plimsoul (1)	Thelonius (6)	

BECK, Joe

Jazz-funk guitarist. Born on 7/29/45 in Philadelphia. Performed with Miles Davis, Duke Ellington, Buddy Rich, Stan Getz, Paul Desmond and Steely Dan. Also see Esther Phillips.

| 6/28/75 | 140 | 5 | | Beck ....[I] | $10 | Kudu 21 |

Brothers And Others	Cactus	Cafe Black Rose	Red Eye	Star Fire	Texas Ann

★★27★★ BEE GEES

Trio of brothers from Manchester, England: Barry (b: 9/1/47) and twins Robin and Maurice Gibb (b: 12/22/49). First performed December 1955. To Australia in 1958, performed as the Gibbs, later as BG's, finally the Bee Gees. First recorded for Leedon/Festival in 1963. Returned to England in February 1967, with guitarist Vince Melouney and drummer Colin Peterson. Toured Europe and the U.S. in 1968. Melouney left in December 1968; Robin left for solo career in 1969. When Peterson left in August 1969, Barry and Maurice went solo. After eight months, the brothers reunited. Composed soundtracks of *Saturday Night Fever* and *Staying Alive*. Acted in film *Sgt. Pepper's Lonely Hearts Club Band*. Youngest brother Andy Gibb was a successful solo singer (d: 3/10/88).

8/26/67	7	52		1 **Bee Gees' 1st**	$20	Atco 223
2/10/68	12	22		2 Horizontal	$20	Atco 233
8/31/68	17	27		3 Idea	$15	Atco 253
12/7/68+	99	12		4 Rare Precious & Beautiful ....[E]	$15	Atco 264
				early Australian recordings (1963-1966)		
2/22/69	20	25		5 Odessa	$20	Atco 702 [2]
7/26/69	9	49	●	6 **Best Of Bee Gees** ....[G]	$15	Atco 292
3/28/70	100	8		7 Rare Precious & Beautiful, Volume 2 ......[E]	$15	Atco 321
				more Australian recordings (1963-1966)		
5/9/70	94	8		8 Cucumber Castle	$15	Atco 327
1/30/71	32	14		9 2 Years On	$15	Atco 353

65

DEBUT DATE	PEAK POS	WKS CHR	GOLD	ARTIST — Album Title	$	Label & Number
				BEE GEES — Cont'd		
9/25/71	**34**	14	10	Trafalgar	$15	Atco 7003
11/11/72	**35**	14	11	To Whom It May Concern	$15	Atco 7012
2/3/73	**69**	13	12	Life In A Tin Can	$10	RSO 870
8/4/73	**98**	16	13	Best Of Bee Gees, Vol. 2 .... [G]	$10	RSO 875
				Atco hits (1969-1972)		
6/15/74	**178**	5	14	Mr. Natural	$10	RSO 4800
6/21/75+	**14**	75	● 15	Main Course	$10	RSO 4807
10/2/76	**8**	63	▲ 16	**Children Of The World**	$10	RSO 3003
11/13/76+	**50**	33	● 17	Bee Gees Gold, Volume One...................... [G]	$10	RSO 3006
				Atco hits (1967-1972)		
6/4/77	**8**	90	▲ 18	Here At Last...Bee Gees...Live ....[L]	$12	RSO 3901 [2]
11/26/77+	**1**²⁴	120	▲¹¹ 19	**Saturday Night Fever** ....[S]	$10	RSO 4001 [2]

1978 Grammy winner: Album of the Year; the #1-selling soundtrack album of all time (25 million); includes "Boogie Shoes" by KC & The Sunshine Band, "Calypso Breakdown" by Ralph McDonald, "Disco Inferno" by The Trammps, "A Fifth Of Beethoven" by Walter Murphy, "If I Can't Have You" by Yvonne Elliman, "K-Jee" by MFSB, "Open Sesame" by Kool & The Gang, "More Than A Woman" by Tavares and "Manhattan Skyline," "Night On Disco Mountain" & "Salsation" by David Shire.

DEBUT DATE	PEAK POS	WKS CHR	GOLD	ARTIST — Album Title	$	Label & Number
2/17/79	**1**⁶	55	▲ 20	**Spirits Having Flown**	$10	RSO 3041
11/17/79+	**1**¹	32	▲ 21	**Bee Gees Greatest**............................... [G]	$12	RSO 4200 [2]
				RSO hits only		
11/21/81	**41**	12	22	Living Eyes	$10	RSO 3098
7/16/83	**6**	27	▲ 23	Staying Alive ....[S]	$10	RSO 813269

side 1: Bee Gees; side 2: includes "Far From Over" & "Moody Girl" by Frank Stallone, "Finding Out The Hard Way" by Cynthia Rhodes, "I'm Never Gonna Give You Up" by Frank Stallone & Cynthia Rhodes and "Look Out For Number One" & "(We Dance) So Close To The Fire" by Tommy Faragher.

DEBUT DATE	PEAK POS	WKS CHR	GOLD	ARTIST — Album Title	$	Label & Number
10/17/87	**96**	9	24	E-S-P	$8	Warner 25541
8/19/89	**68**	13	25	One	$8	Warner 25887

Alive (11,13) **34**
All Of My Life (7)
All This Making Love (15)
Alone Again (9)
And The Sun Will Shine (2,13)
Angela (24)
Baby As You Turn Away (15)
Back Home (9)
Backtafunk (24)
Bad Bad Dreams (11)
Be Who You Are (22)
Big Chance (4)
Birdie Told Me (2)
Black Diamond (5)
Bodyguard (25)
Boogie Child (16,18) **12**
Born A Man (7)
Breakout (23)
British Opera (5)
Bury Me Down By The River (8)
Can't Keep A Good Man Down (16,18)
Chance Of Love (8)
Change Is Made (2)
Charade (14)
Cherry Red (7)
Children Of The World (16,21)
Claustrophobia (5)
Close Another Door (1)
Come Home Johnny Bride (12)
Come On Over (15,18)
Could It Be (7)
Country Lanes (15)
Craise Finton Kirk Royal Academy Of Arts (1)
Crazy For Your Love (24)
Cryin' Every Day (22)
Cucumber Castle (1)
Day Time Girl (2)
Dearest (10)
Dogs (14)
Don't Fall In Love With Me (22)

Don't Forget To Remember (8,13) **73**
Don't Say Goodbye (7)
Don't Wanna Live Inside Myself (10,13) **53**
Down The Road (14,18)
Down To Earth (3)
E-S-P (24)
Earnest Of Being George (2)
Edge Of The Universe (15,18) **26**
Edison (5)
Every Christian Lion Hearted Man Will Show You (1,6)
Every Second, Every Minute (9)
Everyday I Have To Cry (7)
Fanny (Be Tender With My Love) (15,21) **12**
1st Mistake I Made (9)
First Of May (5,6) **37**
Flesh And Blood (25)
Follow The Wind (7)
Give A Hand, Take A Hand (14)
Give Your Best (5)
Giving Up The Ghost (24)
Glass House (4)
Greatest Man In The World (10)
Had A Lot Of Love Last Night (14)
Harry Braff (2)
He's A Liar (22) **30**
Heavy Breathing (14)
Holiday (1,6,17,18) **16**
Horizontal (2)
House Of Shame (25)
How Can You Mend A Broken Heart (10,13,17,18) **1**
How Deep Is Your Love (19,21) **1**
How Many Birds (4)
I.O.I.O. (8,13) **94**
I Can Bring Love (11)

I Can't Let You Go (14)
I Can't See Nobody (1,6,17,18)
I Close My Eyes (1)
I Do Adore Her (1)
I Don't Know Why I Bother Myself (4)
I Don't Wanna Be The One (12)
I Have Decided To Join The Air Force (3)
I Held A Party (11)
I Laugh In Your Face (5)
I Lay Down And Die (8)
I Love You Too Much (23)
I Started A Joke (3,6,17,18) **6**
I Still Love You (22)
I Was A Lover, A Leader Of Men (7)
I Was The Child (8)
I'm Satisfied (20)
I'm Weeping (9)
I've Gotta Get A Message To You (3,6,17,18) **8**
Idea (3)
If I Can't Have You (21)
If Only I Had My Mind On Something Else (8) **91**
In My Own Time (1)
In The Summer Of His Years (3)
Indian Gin And Whisky Dry (3)
Israel (10)
It's Just The Way (10)
It's My Neighborhood (25)
Jingle Jangle (4)
Jive Talkin' (15,18,19,21) **1**
Kilburn Towers (3)
Kitty Can (3)
Lamplight (5)
Lemons Never Forget (2)
Let There Be Love (3,13)
Life Goes On (23)

(Lights Went Out In) **Massachusetts** (2,6,17,18) **11**
Lion In Winter (10)
Live Or Die (Hold Me Like A Child) (24)
Living In Chicago (12)
Living Together (20)
Lonely Days (9,13,17,18) **3**
Longest Night (3)
Lord, The (8)
Lost In Your Love (14)
Love Me (16,21)
Love So Right (16,18,21) **3**
Love You Inside Out (20,21) **1**
Lovers (16)
Man For All Seasons (9,13)
Marley Purt Drive (3)
Massachusetts ..see: (Lights Went Out In)
Melody Fair (5,13)
Method To My Madness (12)
Monday's Rain (4)
More Than A Woman (19,21)
Morning Of My Life (In The Morning) (13)
Mr. Natural (14) **93**
My Life Has Been A Song (23) **49**
My Thing (8)
My World (13,17) **16**
Never Been Alone (11)
Never Say Never Again (5)
New York Mining Disaster 1941 (Have You Seen My Wife, Mr. Jones) (1,6,17,18) **14**
Night Fever (19,21) **1**
Nights On Broadway (15,18,21) **7**
Nothing Could Be Good (22)
Odessa (City On The Black Sea) (3)
One (25) **7**
One Minute Woman (1)

Ordinary Lives (25)
(Our Love) Don't Throw It All Away (21)
Overnight (24)
Paper Mache, Cabbages & Kings (11)
Paradise (22)
Playdown (4)
Please Don't Turn Out The Lights (11)
Please Read Me (1)
Portrait Of Louise (9)
Reaching Out (24)
Really And Sincerely (2)
Red Chair, Fade Away (1)
Remembering (9)
Rest Your Love On Me (21)
Road To Alaska (11)
Run To Me (11,13,17,18) **16**
Saved By The Bell (13)
Saw A New Morning (12) **94**
Sea Of Smiling Faces (11)
Search, Find (20)
Second Hand People (4)
Seven Seas Symphony (5)
Sincere Relation (9)
Soldiers (22)
Somebody Stop The Music (10)
Someone Belonging To Someone (23) **49**
Songbird (15)
Sound Of Love (5)
South Dakota Morning (12)
Spicks And Specks (4,6)
Spirits (Having Flown) (20,21)
Stayin' Alive (19,21,23) **1**
Stop (Think Again) (20)
Subway (16)
Suddenly (5)
Swan Song (3)
Sweet Song Of Summer (11)
Sweetheart (8)
Take Hold Of That Star (7)
Tears (25)
Tell Me Why (9)
Then You Left Me (8)

This Is Your Life (24)
Three Kisses Of Love (7)
Throw A Penny (14)
Tint Of Blue (4)
To Be Or Not To Be (7)
To Love Somebody (1,6,17,18) **17**
Tokyo Nights (25)
Too Much Heaven (20,21) **1**
Trafalgar (10)
Tragedy (20,21) **1**
Travels Of Jamie McPheeters, Theme From The (7)
Turn Of The Century (11)
Turning Tide (8)
2 Years On (9)
Until (20)
Voices (14)
Walking Back To Waterloo (10)
Way It Was (16)
We Lost The Road (11)
When Do I (10)
When The Swallows Fly (3)
Where Are You (4)
While I Play (12)
Whisper Whisper (5)
Wildflower (25)
Will You Ever Let Me (25)
Wind Of Change (15,18,21)
Wish You Were Here (25)
With All Nations (International Anthem) (5)
With The Sun In My Eyes (2)
Woman In You (23) **24**
Words (6,17,18) **15**
World (2,6,18)
Wouldn't I Be Someone (13)
You Know It's For You (11)
You Should Be Dancing (16,18,19,21) **1**
You Stepped Into My Life (16,21)
You Win Again (24) **75**
You'll Never See My Face Again (5)

★★**34**★★ **BELAFONTE, Harry**

Born Harold George Belafonte, Jr. on 3/1/27 in Harlem to a Jamaican mother and a West Indian father. Actor in American Negro Theater, Drama Workshop, mid-1940s. Started career as a "straight pop" singer. Recorded for Jubilee Records in 1949, shortly afterward began specializing in folk music. Rode the crest of the calypso craze to worldwide stardom. Starred in eight films from 1953-74. Replaced Danny Kaye in 1987 as UNICEF goodwill ambassador. Father of actress Shari Belafonte.

DEBUT DATE	PEAK POS	WKS CHR	GOLD	ARTIST — Album Title	$	Label & Number
1/28/56	**3**	6	1	"Mark Twain" And Other Folk Favorites	$25	RCA 1022
2/25/56	**1**⁶	62	● 2	Belafonte	$25	RCA 1150
6/16/56	**1**³¹	99	● 3	Calypso	$25	RCA 1248

DEBUT DATE	PEAK POS	WKS CHR	G O L D	ARTIST — Album Title	$	Label & Number
				BELAFONTE, Harry — Cont'd		
3/30/57	**2**²	20	●	4 **An Evening With Belafonte**	**$25**	RCA 1402
9/16/57	**3**	16		5 **Belafonte Sings Of The Caribbean**	**$25**	RCA 1505
10/20/58	**16**	15		6 **Belafonte Sings The Blues**	**$25**	RCA 1006
5/25/59	**18**	11		7 Love Is A Gentle Thing	**$25**	RCA 1927
6/22/59	**13**	22		8 Porgy & Bess	**$25**	RCA 1507
				LENA HORNE/HARRY BELAFONTE		
11/9/59+	**3**	168	●	9 **Belafonte At Carnegie Hall** ....[L]	**$25**	RCA 6006 [2]
3/21/60	**34**	1		10 My Lord What A Mornin'	**$20**	RCA 2022
				spirituals		
12/26/60+	**3**	39	●	11 **Belafonte Returns To Carnegie Hall** ....[L]	**$20**	RCA 6007 [2]
				includes "I've Been Driving On Bald Mountain/Water Boy" by Odetta, "The Click Song" by Miriam Makeba, "Ballad Of Sigmund Freud," "I Do Adore Her" & "Vaichazkem (Vayiven Uziaho)" by the Chad Mitchell Trio		
8/28/61	**3**	67	●	12 **Jump Up Calypso**	**$20**	RCA 2388
5/12/62	**8**	24		13 **The Midnight Special**	**$30**	RCA 2449
10/20/62	**25**	22		14 The Many Moods Of Belafonte	**$20**	RCA 2574
12/22/62	**125**	2		15 To Wish You A Merry Christmas ....[X]	**$20**	RCA 2626
				Christmas charts: 34/'64, 58/'66, 47/'67		
6/22/63	**30**	26		16 Streets I Have Walked	**$20**	RCA 2695
4/18/64	**17**	20		17 Belafonte At The Greek Theatre ....[L]	**$20**	RCA 6009 [2]
10/17/64	**103**	7		18 Ballads, Blues And Boasters	**$20**	RCA 2953
7/10/65	**85**	11		19 An Evening With Belafonte/Makeba	**$15**	RCA 3420
				HARRY BELAFONTE/MIRIAM MAKEBA		
4/9/66	**124**	8		20 An Evening With Belafonte/Mouskouri	**$15**	RCA 3415
				HARRY BELAFONTE/NANA MOUSKOURI		
7/16/66	**82**	10		21 In My Quiet Room	**$15**	RCA 3571
4/29/67	**172**	2		22 Calypso In Brass	**$15**	RCA 3658
7/29/67	**199**	3		23 Belafonte On Campus	**$15**	RCA 3779
1/10/70	**192**	3		24 Homeward Bound..................................	**$15**	RCA 4255

All My Trials (7,9)
Amen (16)
Ananias (18)
Angelina (12)
Angelique-O (5)
Baby Boy (12)
Back Of The Bus (18)
Bally Mena (12)
Bamotsweri (14)
Banana Boat (Day-O) (3,9) **5**
Be My Woman, Gal (medley) (17)
Bella Rosa (7)
Bess, Oh Where's My Bess (8)
Bess, You Is My Woman (8)
Betty An' Dupree (14)
Big Boat Up The River (18)
Black Betty (18)
Blue Willow Moan (18)
Boot Dance (17)
Borning Day (16)
Boy (18)
Brown Skin Girl (3)
Buked And Scorned (10)
Chickens (11)
Christmas Is Coming (15)
Cocoanut Woman (5,22) **25**
Come Away Melinda (16)
Come Back Liza (3,9)
Come O My Love (4)
Contemporary Dance (17)
Cordelia Brown (5)
Cotton Fields (6,9)
Crawdad Song (13)
Cruel War (7)
Cu Cu Ru Cu Cu Paloma (4,9)
Danny Boy (4,9)
Dark As A Dungeon (14)
Darlin' Cora (9)
Day-O ..see: Banana Boat
Deck The Halls (medley) (15)
Delia (1,23)
Delia's Gone (7)
Did You Hear About Jerry (13)
Didn't It Rain [Belafonte Folk Singers] (11)
Dog Song (Your Dog) (23)

Dolly Dawn (3)
Dolphin, The (24)
Don't Ever Love Me (5) **90**
Don't Talk Now (24)
Drummer And The Cook (1,4)
Eden Was Like This (4)
Erev Shel Shoshanim (Night Of Roses) (16)
Ezekiel (10)
Far Side Of The Hill (23)
Fare Thee Well (6)
Fifteen (7)
First Noel (medley) (15)
First Time Ever I Saw Your Face (23)
Fool For You (6)
Four Strong Winds (18)
Fox, The (1)
Gifts They Gave (15)
Girls In Their Summer Dresses (14)
Give Us Our Land [solo: Harry] (19)
Gloria (12)
Glory Manger (17)
Go Down Emanuel Road (12)
Go Way From My Window (7)
God Bless' The Child (6)
God Rest Ye Merry, Gentlemen (medley) (15)
Goin' Down Jordan (12)
Gone Are My Children [solo: Harry] (19)
Gotta Travel On (13)
Green Grow The Lilacs (7)
Haiti Cherie (5)
Hallelujah I Love Her So (6)
Hands I Love (23)
Hava Nageela (4,9)
Hayoshevet Baganim (17)
Hene Ma Tov (11)
Hoedown Blues (17)
Hold On To Me Babe (23)
Hole In The Bucket (11)
Homeward Bound (24)
Honey Wind Blows (21)
Hosanna (3)
Hush, Hush [solo: Harry] (19)

I Do Adore Her (3,12)
I Heard The Bells On Christmas Day (15)
I Know Where I'm Going (11)
I Never Will Marry (7)
I Wants To Stay Here (8)
I'm Goin' Away (7)
I'm Just A Country Boy (21) flip
I'm On My Way To Saturday (14)
If I Were A Carpenter (24)
If You Are Thirsty (20)
In My Father's House (17)
In That Great Gettin' Up Mornin' (2)
In The Evenin' Mama (6)
In The Small Boat [solo: Harry] (20)
Irene (20)
Island In The Sun (3) **30**
It Ain't Necessarily So (8)
Jack-Ass Song (3)
Jamaica Farewell (3,9) **14**
Jehovah The Lord Will Provide (15)
John Henry (1,9)
John The Revelator (18)
Joy To The World (medley) (15)
Joys Of Christmas (medley) (15)
Judy Drownded (5,22)
Jump And Bray Medley (22)
Jump Down, Spin Around (2,11)
Jump In The Line (12,22)
Kalenda Rock (1)
Kingston Market (12)
La Bamba (11)
Land Of The Sea And Sun (12)
Last Thing On My Mind (23)
Last Time I Saw Her (24)
Lead Man Holler (5)
Little Bird (3)
Little Lyric Of Great Importance (11)
'Long About Now (14,21)

Look Over Yonder (medley) (17)
Lord Randall (1)
Losing Hand (6)
Love, Love Alone (5)
Lucy's Door (19)
Lullaby [solo: Harry] (19)
Lyla, Lyla (14)
Makes A Long Time Man Feel Bad (13)
Mama Look At Bubu (9,22) **11**
Man Piaba (1,9)
Man Smart (Woman Smarter) (3,9,22)
Mangwene Mpulele (16)
March Down To Jordan (10)
Marching Saints ..see: When The Saints Go Marching In
Mark Twain (1)
Mary Ann (6)
Mary, Mary (15)
Mary's Boy Child (4,15) **12**
Matilda (2,9)
Memphis Tennessee (13)
Merci Bon Dieu (4,9)
Merry Minuet (17)
Michael Row The Boat Ashore (13)
Midnight Special (13)
Mo Mary (1)
Monkey (12)
Muleskinner (13)
My Angel (19)
My Lord What A Mornin' (10)
My Love Is A Dewdrop (18)
My Man's Gone Now (8)
My Moon [solo: Harry] (20)
My Old Paint (1)
Naughty Little Flea (22)
Next Big River (1)
Noah (2)
O Come, All Ye Faithful (medley) (15)
O Little Town Of Bethlehem (medley) (15)
Oh Freedom (10)
Oh, I Got Plenty Of Nothin' (8)
Oh Let Me Fly (10)

Old King Cole (11)
On Top Of Old Smokey (13)
Once Was (4)
One For My Baby (6)
One More Dance (11)
Our Time For Loving (21)
Ox Drivers [Belafonte Folk Singers] (11)
Pastures Of Plenty (18)
Pig (17)
Portrait Of A Sunday Afternoon (21)
Quiet Room (21)
Raindrops (21)
Red Rosy Bush [Belafonte Folk Singers] (11)
Reincarnation (21)
Roll On, Buddy (23)
Sad Heart (24)
Sail Away Ladies (23)
Sailor Man (17)
Sakura (16)
Scarlet Ribbons (For Her Hair) (2)
Scratch, Scratch (5)
Shake That Little Foot (17)
Shenandoah (4,9)
Show Me The Way, My Brother [solo: Harry] (19)
Silent Night (15)
Sinner's Prayer (6)
Sit Down (24)
Small One (7)
Softly (24)
Soldier, Soldier (1)
Son Of Mary (15)
Star In The East (15)
Star O (3)
Stars Shinin' (By 'N By) (10)
Steal Away (10)
Street Calls Medley (9)
Summertime (8)
Summertime Love (14,21)
Suzanne (24)
Suzanne (Every Night When The Sun Goes Down) (2,11)
Sweetheart From Venezuela (12,22)
Swing Low (10)
Sylvie (2,9)

Take My Mother Home (2,9)
There's A Boat That's Leavin' Soon For New York (8)
These Are The Times (12)
This Land Is Your Land (16)
This Wicked Race (16)
Those Three Are On My Mind (23)
Times Are Gettin' Hard (7)
Tol' My Captain (1)
Tomorrow Is A Long Time (24)
Tone The Bell Easy (18)
Tongue Tie Baby (14,22)
Train Song (19)
Troubles (2)
Try To Remember (14,17,21)
Tunga (16)
Turn Around (7)
Twelve Days Of Christmas (15)
Unchained Melody (2)
Wake Up Jacob (10)
Walkin' On The Green Grass (7)
Walking On The Moon [solo: Harry] (20)
Waltzing Matilda (16)
Waly, Waly (23)
Waterboy (2)
Way That I Feel (6)
We Wish You A Merry Christmas (medley) (15)
Were You There When They Crucified My Lord (10)
When The Saints Go Marching In (4,9)
Where The Little Jesus Sleeps (15)
Who's Gonna Be Your Man (14)
Why 'N' Why (17)
Wide Sea [solo: Harry] (20)
Will His Love Be Like His Rum (3)
Windin' Road (17)
Woman Is A Sometime Thing (8)
Zombie Jamboree (14,17,22)

BELEW, Adrian
Prolific rock guitarist from Kentucky. Discovered by Frank Zappa. Sideman with Talking Heads, David Bowie, Tom Tom Club, Laurie Anderson, Paul Simon and others. Member of King Crimson from 1981-84. Member of The Bears from 1985-88.

7/24/82	**82**	9		1 Lone Rhino	**$10**	Island 9751
10/1/83	**146**	7		2 Twang Bar King......................................	**$10**	Island 90108

67

DEBUT DATE	PEAK POS	WKS CHR	GOLD	ARTIST — Album Title	$	Label & Number
7/22/89	**114**	11	3	Mr. Music Head	$8	Atlantic 81959
6/2/90	**118**	11	4	Young Lions	$12	Atlantic 82099

guest vocals by David Bowie

Adidas In Heat (1)	Coconuts (3)	I Am What I Am (4)	Men In Helicopters (4)	Paint The Road (2)	Small World (4)
Animal Grace (1)	Final Rhino (1)	I Wonder (2)	Momur, The (1)	Peaceable Kingdom (3)	Stop It (1)
Another Time (2)	Fish Head (2)	I'm Down (2)	Motor Bungalow (3)	Phone Call From The Moon	Swingline (1)
Bad Days (3)	Gunman (4)	Ideal Woman (2)	Naive Guitar (1)	(4)	Twang Bar King (2)
Ballet For A Blue Whale (2)	Heartbeat (4)	Life Without A Cage (1)	1967 (3)	Pretty Pink Rose (4)	Young Lions (4)
Big Electric Cat (1)	Hot Sun (1)	Lone Rhinoceros (1)	Not Alone Anymore (4)	Rail Song (2)	
Bird In A Box (3)	Hot Zoo (3)	Looking For A U.F.O. (4)	**Oh Daddy** (3) **58**	Sexy Rhino (2)	
Bumpity Bump (3)	House Of Cards (3)	Man In The Moon (1)	One Of Those Days (3)	She Is Not Dead (2)	

BELL, Archie, & The Drells

Archie was born on 9/1/44 in Henderson, Texas. Lead singer of the Drells, R&B vocal group from Leo Smith Junior High School in Houston. First recorded for Ovid in 1967. Recorded "Tighten Up" with group consisting of Bell, Huey "Billy" Butler, Joe Cross and James Wise. Bell was in U.S. Army at time of hit. Later recordings consisted of Bell, Wise, Lee Bell and Willie Parnell. Still active in "beach music" scene.

DEBUT DATE	PEAK POS	WKS CHR	GOLD	ARTIST — Album Title	$	Label & Number
5/25/68	**142**	8	1	Tighten Up	$15	Atlantic 8181
8/16/69	**163**	3	2	There's Gonna Be A Showdown	$15	Atlantic 8226
1/10/76	**95**	20	3	Dance Your Troubles Away	$10	TSOP 33844

Dance Your Troubles Away (3)	Go For What You Know (2)	**I Love My Baby** (2) **94**	Knock On Wood (1)	Soldier's Prayer, 1967 (1)	When You Left Heartache
Do The Hand Jive (2)	Green Power (2)	I Love You (But You Don't	Let's Go Disco (3)	Soul City Walk (3)	Began (1)
Girl You're Too Young	Here I Go Again (2)	Even Know It) (3)	Let's Groove (3)	**There's Gonna Be A**	You're Mine (1)
(2) **59**	Houston Texas (2)	I Won't Leave You Honey,	Mama Didn't Teach Me That	**Showdown** (2) **21**	
Give Me Time (1)	I Could Dance All Night (3)	Never (3)	Way (2)	Thousand Wonders (1)	
Giving Up Dancing (2)	I Don't Wanna Be A Playboy	In The Midnight Hour (1)	**My Balloon's Going Up**	**Tighten Up** (1) **1**	
	(1)	Just A Little Closer (2)	(2) **87**	Tighten Up (Part 2) (1)	

BELL, Maggie

Born on 1/12/45 in Glasgow, Scotland. Lead singer of Stone The Crows.

DEBUT DATE	PEAK POS	WKS CHR	GOLD	ARTIST — Album Title	$	Label & Number
4/20/74	**122**	13	1	Queen Of The Night	$10	Atlantic 7293
4/5/75	**130**	8	2	Suicide Sal	$10	Swan Song 8412

After Midnight (1) **97**	Comin' On Strong (2)	I Was In Chains (2)	Oh My My (1)	Suicide Sal (1)	Wishing Well (1)
As The Years Go Passing By	Hold On (2)	If You Don't Know (2)	Other Side (1)	Trade Winds (1)	Woman Left Lonely (1)
(1)	I Saw Him Standing There	In My Life (2)	Queen Of The Night (1)	We Had It All (1)	Yesterday's Music (1)
Caddo Queen (1)	(2)	It's Been So Long (2)	Souvenirs (1)	What You Got (2)	

BELL, Vincent

Veteran studio guitarist. Born Vincent Gambella. Formerly with the East Coast vocal group The Gallahads.

DEBUT DATE	PEAK POS	WKS CHR	GOLD	ARTIST — Album Title	$	Label & Number
6/20/70	**75**	8		Airport Love Theme ....[I]	$12	Decca 75212

Airport Love Theme (Gwen	Darling Lili	Farewell, Farewell	Marilyn's Theme	Romeo & Juliet, Love Theme	Shadow Of Your Smile
And Vern) **31**	Everybody's Talkin'	Loss Of Love	Nikki	From ..see: Time For Us	Time For Us
Damned, Theme From The					

BELL, William

Born William Yarborough on 7/16/39 in Memphis. R&B singer. Own Peachtree and Wilbe labels. With Rufus Thomas band in 1953. In U.S. Army from 1962-66.

DEBUT DATE	PEAK POS	WKS CHR	GOLD	ARTIST — Album Title	$	Label & Number
4/2/77	**63**	12		Coming Back For More	$10	Mercury 1146

Coming Back For More	I Wake Up Cryin'	Malnutrition	You Don't Miss Your Water	
I Absotively, Posolutely Love	If Sex Was All We Had	Relax	You've Really Got A Hold On	
You	Just Another Way To Feel	**Tryin' To Love Two 10**	Me	

BELLAMY BROTHERS

Country duo from Darby, Florida: brothers Howard (b: 2/2/46; guitar) and David Bellamy (b: 9/16/50; guitar, keyboards). Made their professional debut in 1958. David wrote "Spiders And Snakes" hit for Jim Stafford. Moved to Los Angeles in 1973.

DEBUT DATE	PEAK POS	WKS CHR	GOLD	ARTIST — Album Title	$	Label & Number
5/15/76	**69**	12	●	Bellamy Brothers	$10	Warner 2941

Hell Cat 70	I'm The Only Sane Man Left	Let Fantasy Live	Nothin' Heavy	**Satin Sheets 73**	
Highway 2-18 (Hang On To	Alive	**Let Your Love Flow 1**	Rainy, Windy, Sunshine		
Your Dreams)	Inside Of My Guitar	Livin' In The West	(Roadeo Road)		

BELL & JAMES

R&B duo of Leroy Bell and Casey James. Began as songwriting team for Bell's uncle, producer Thom Bell.

DEBUT DATE	PEAK POS	WKS CHR	GOLD	ARTIST — Album Title	$	Label & Number
2/3/79	**31**	19		1 Bell & James	$8	A&M 4728
11/3/79	**125**	4		2 Only Make Believe	$8	A&M 4784

Ask Billie (They Tell Me) (1)	Fare Thee Well (2)	Laughing In The Face Of	Only Make Believe (2)	Three Way Love Affair (1)
(Babe) You Don't Love Me	I Love The Music (1)	Love (2)	Say It's Gonna Last Forever	You Never Know What
Like You Should (2)	I Need You (Beside Me) (1)	**Livin' It Up (Friday Night)**	(2)	You've Got (1)
Don't Let The Man Get You	Just Can't Get Enough (Of	(1) **15**	Shakedown (2)	
(1)	Your Love) (1)	Nobody Knows It (2)	Stay (2)	

BELL BIV DeVOE

Trio of New Edition members: Ricky Bell, Michael Bivins and Ronnie DeVoe. Bivins produced Another Bad Creation, Boyz II Men and M.C. Brains, formed own record label, Biv 10, and assembled East Coast Family.

DEBUT DATE	PEAK POS	WKS CHR	GOLD	ARTIST — Album Title	$	Label & Number
4/7/90	**5**	77	▲3	1 Poison	$12	MCA 6387
9/14/91	**27**	27	●	2 WBBD - Bootcity! The Remix Album	$12	MCA 10345

Ain't Nut'in Changed! (1,2)	**Do Me!** (1,2) **3**	Let Me Know Something?!	Ronnie, Bobby, Ricky, Mike,	She's Dope! (2)	
B.B.D. (I Thought It Was	Dope! (1)	(1,2)	Ralph And Johnny (Word	**When Will I See You Smile**	
Me)? (1,2) 26	I Do Need You (1,2)	**Poison** (1,2) **3**	To The Mutha!) (1,2)	**Again?** (1,2) **63**	

BELLE, Regina

Soul vocalist raised in Englewood, New Jersey. Featured female vocalist with The Manhattans, 1986-87.

DEBUT DATE	PEAK POS	WKS CHR	GOLD	ARTIST — Album Title	$	Label & Number
7/11/87	**85**	15		1 All By Myself	$8	Columbia 40537
9/16/89	**63**	44	●	2 Stay With Me	$8	Columbia 44367

BELLE, Regina — Cont'd

After The Love Has Lost Its Shine (1)
Baby Come To Me (2) **60**
Dream Lover (2)
Good Lovin' (2)

Gotta Give It Up (1)
How Could You Do It To Me (1)
Intimate Relations (1)
It Doesn't Hurt Anymore (2)

(It's Gonna Take) All Our Love (2)
Make It Like It Was (2) **43**
Please Be Mine (1)

Save The Children (medley) (2)
Show Me The Way (1) **68**
So Many Tears (1)

Someday We'll All Be Free (medley) (2)
Take Your Love Away (1)
This Is Love (2)

What Goes Around (2)
When Will You Be Mine (2)
You Got The Love (1)

BELLE STARS, The

English female band formed as The Bodysnatchers in 1981. Changed name to The Belle Stars in 1983. Features Jennie McKeown (vocals) and Sarah-Jane Owen (guitar).

5/28/83	191	2		The Belle Stars	$8	Warner 23866

Baby I'm Yours
Burning
Ci Ya Ya

Clapping Song
Harlem Shuffle

Iko Iko
new version charted at POS 14 on "Hot 100" in 1989

Indian Summer
Mockingbird
Needle In A Haystack

Reason, The
Sign Of The Times 75
Snake, The

BELLS, The

Canadian pop quintet — lead singers Jacki Ralph and Cliff Edwards.

5/1/71	90	14		Fly, Little White Dove, Fly	$12	Polydor 4510

Fly Little White Dove Fly 95

I Can Make It With You
I'm Gonna Get Out

Maxwell's Silver Hammer
Moody Manitoba Morning

Proud Mary
Rain

Sing A Song Of Freedom
Stay Awhile 7

Yesterday Will Never Come Again

BELMONTS, The

Angelo D'Aleo, Fred Milano and Carlo Mastrangelo. Sang with Dion from 1957-60. Named after Belmont Avenue in the Bronx. Frank Lyndon replaced Mastrangelo in May 1962.

10/27/62	113	7		The Belmonts' Carnival Of Hits [G]	$100	Sabina 5001

Come On Little Angel 28
Don't Get Around Much Anymore 57

Have You Heard
Hombre
How About Me

I Confess
I Don't Know How To Cry
I Need Some One 75

Searching For A New Love
Tell Me Why 18
That American Dance

This Love Of Mine

BELOVED, The

British alternative pop duo of Jon Marsh (vocals, keyboards) and Steve Waddington (guitars). Waddington left in 1991, replaced by Jon's wife Helena.

4/14/90	154	9		Happiness	$12	Atlantic 82047

Don't You Worry
Found

Hello
I Love You More

Scarlet Beautiful
Sun Rising

Time After Time
Up, Up And Away

Wake Up Soon
Your Love Takes Me Higher

★★202★★ BENATAR, Pat

Born Patricia Andrzejewski in Lindenhurst, Long Island, New York in 1952. Rock singer. Married her producer/guitarist Neil Giraldo on 2/20/82. Acted in the film *Union City* and the 1989 ABC afterschool TV special *Torn Between Two Fathers*.

10/20/79+	12	122	▲	1 In The Heat Of The Night	$8	Chrysalis 1236
8/23/80+	2⁵	93	▲⁴	2 Crimes Of Passion	$8	Chrysalis 1275
7/25/81	1¹	54	▲²	3 Precious Time	$8	Chrysalis 1346
11/20/82+	4	46	▲	4 Get Nervous	$8	Chrysalis 1396
10/15/83	13	34	▲	5 Live From Earth [L]	$8	Chrysalis 41444
				2 of the 10 songs are new studio tracks		
11/24/84	14	22	▲	6 Tropico	$8	Chrysalis 41471
12/14/85	26	20		7 Seven The Hard Way	$8	Chrysalis 41507
7/23/88	28	29	●	8 Wide Awake In Dreamland	$8	Chrysalis 41628
11/25/89	67	20	●	9 Best Shots [G]	$8	Chrysalis 21715
				CD includes 3 bonus tracks		
4/27/91	37	22		10 True Love	$12	Chrysalis 21805
				CD includes bonus track		

All Fired Up (8,9) **19**
Anxiety (Get Nervous) (4)
Art Of Letting Go (7)
Big Life (10)
Bloodshot Eyes (10)
Cerebral Man (8)
Cool Zero (8)
Crazy World Like This (6)
Diamond Field (6)
Don't Happen No More (10)
Don't Let It Show (1)
Don't Walk Away (8)
Evening (10)
Evil Genius (3)
Fight It Out (4)
Fire And Ice (3,5,9) **17**
Good Life (10)

Hard To Believe (3)
Heartbreaker (1,5,9) **23**
Hell Is For Children (2,5,9)
Helter Skelter (3)
Hit Me With Your Best Shot (2,5,9) **9**
I Feel Lucky (10)
I Get Evil (10)
I Need A Lover (1)
I Want Out (4,5)
I'll Do It (4)
I'm Gonna Follow You (2)
I've Got Papers On You (10)
If You Think You Know How To Love Me (1)
In The Heat Of The Night (1)
Invincible (7,9) **10**

It's A Tuff Life (3)
Just Like Me (3)
Le Bel Age (7) **54**
Let's Stay Together (8)
Lift 'Em On Up (8)
Lipstick Lies (5)
Little Paradise (2)
Little Too Late (4) **20**
Looking For A Stranger (4,5) **39**
Love In The Ice Age (6)
Love Is A Battlefield (5,9) **5**
My Clone Sleeps Alone (1)
Never Wanna Leave You (2)
No You Don't (1)
One Love (8,9)
Ooh Ooh Song (6) **36**

Out-A-Touch (2)
Outlaw Blues (6)
Painted Desert (6)
Payin' The Cost To Be The Boss (10)
Please Come Home For Christmas (10)
Precious Time (3)
Prisoner Of Love (2)
Promises In The Dark (3,5,9) **38**
Rated X (1)
Red Vision (7)
Run Between The Raindrops (7)
7 Rooms Of Gloom (7)
Sex As A Weapon (7) **28**

Shadows Of The Night (4,9) **13**
Silent Partner (4)
So Long (10)
So Sincere (1)
Suburban King (6)
Suffer The Little Children (8)
Take It Anyway You Want It (3)
Takin' It Back (6)
Tell It To Her (4)
Temporary Heroes (6)
Too Long A Soldier (8)
Treat Me Right (2) **18**
True Love (10)
Victim, The (4)

Walking In The Underground (7)
We Belong (6,9) **5**
We Live For Love (1,5,9) **27**
Wide Awake In Dreamland (8)
Wuthering Heights (2)
You Better Run (2) **42**

BENITEZ, Jellybean — see JELLYBEAN

★★97★★ BENNETT, Tony

Born Anthony Dominick Benedetto on 8/13/25 in Queens, New York. One of the top jazz vocalists of the past 40 years. Worked local clubs while in high school, sang in U.S. Army bands. Breakthrough with Bob Hope in 1949 who suggested that he change his then-stage name, Joe Bari, to Tony Bennett. Audition record of "Boulevard Of Broken Dreams" earned a Columbia contract in 1950. Appeared in the film *The Oscar*.

2/23/57	14	9		1 Tony	$25	Columbia 938
7/7/62	5	149	●	2 I Left My Heart In San Francisco	$12	Columbia 8669
10/13/62	37	19		3 Tony Bennett At Carnegie Hall [L]	$12	Columbia 23 [2]
4/6/63+	5	44		4 I Wanna Be Around	$12	Columbia 8800
8/24/63	24	30		5 This Is All I Ask	$12	Columbia 8856
2/22/64	20	24		6 The Many Moods Of Tony	$12	Columbia 8941
5/23/64	79	12		7 When Lights Are Low	$12	Columbia 8975
12/19/64+	42	19		8 Who Can I Turn To	$12	Columbia 9085

DEBUT DATE	PEAK POS	WKS CHR	G O L D	ARTIST — Album Title	$	Label & Number
				BENNETT, Tony — Cont'd		
5/22/65	**47**	22	**9**	If I Ruled The World - Songs For The Jet Set	**$12**	Columbia 9143
8/21/65	**20**	42	● **10**	Tony's Greatest Hits, Volume III................................ [G]	**$12**	Columbia 9173
3/12/66	**18**	29	**11**	The Movie Song Album................................	**$12**	Columbia 9272
10/8/66+	**68**	18	**12**	A Time For Love	**$12**	Columbia 9360
5/13/67	**178**	6	**13**	Tony Makes It Happen!................................	**$12**	Columbia 9453
1/13/68	**164**	7	**14**	For Once In My Life	**$12**	Columbia 9573
5/10/69	**174**	8	**15**	Tony Bennett's Greatest Hits, Volume IV .... [G]	**$12**	Columbia 9814
9/6/69	**137**	5	**16**	I've Gotta Be Me	**$12**	Columbia 9882
2/28/70	**144**	11	**17**	Tony Sings The Great Hits Of Today!	**$12**	Columbia 9980
11/14/70	**193**	2	**18**	Tony Bennett's "Something"	**$12**	Columbia 30280
3/6/71	**67**	13	**19**	Love Story	**$12**	Columbia 30558
11/20/71	**195**	2	**20**	Get Happy with the London Philharmonic Orchestra ....[L]	**$12**	Columbia 30953
2/19/72	**182**	4	**21**	Summer Of '42	**$12**	Columbia 31219
7/1/72	**167**	14	**22**	With Love	**$12**	Columbia 31460
10/21/72	**175**	7	**23**	Tony Bennett's All-Time Greatest Hits .... [G]	**$12**	Columbia 31494 [2]
				hits from 1951-72		
12/9/72	**196**	6	**24**	The Good Things In Life................................	**$10**	MGM/Verve 5088
6/21/86	**160**	8	**25**	The Art Of Excellence	**$10**	Columbia 40344
10/3/92	**102**	19↑	**26**	Perfectly Frank	**$12**	Columbia 52965

Tony sings the "torch and saloon songs" of Frank Sinatra; backed by the Ralph Sharon Trio: Sharon (piano), Paul Langosch (bass) and Joe LaBarbera (drums)

Ain't Misbehavin' (7)
Alfie (16)
All My Tomorrows (9)
All The Things You Are (3)
Always (1,3)
Angel Eyes (26)
Anything Goes (3)
April In Paris (3)
Autumn In Rome (5)
Autumn Leaves (8)
Baby Don't You Quit Now (16)
Baby, Dream Your Dream (14)
Beautiful Friendship (13)
Because Of You (3,23)
Best Is Yet To Come (2,10)
Best Thing To Be Is A Person (8)
Between The Devil And The Deep Blue Sea (8)
Blue Velvet (3)
Blues For Breakfast (24)
Boulevard Of Broken Dreams (1,23)
Brightest Smile In Town (8)
Broadway (medley) (14)
Call Me Irresponsible (26)
Can't Get Out Of This Mood (13)
Candy Kisses (2)
Caravan (6)
City Of The Angels (25)
Climb Ev'ry Mountain (3) **74**
Coco (4)
Coffee Break (21)
Come Saturday Morning (18)
Country Girl (13,19,20)
Crazy Rhythm (medley) (14)
Cute (24)
Day In, Day Out (26)
Day You Leave Me (25)
Days Of Love (14)
Days Of Wine And Roses (11)
De Glory Road (3)
Don't Get Around Much Anymore (13)
Don't Wait Too Long (6) **54**
Don't Worry 'Bout Me (26)
Dream (22)
East Of The Sun (West Of The Moon) (26)
Easy Come, Easy Go (22)
Eleanor Rigby (17)
Emily (11)
End Of A Love Affair (24)
Everybody Has The Blues (25)
Everybody's Talkin' (18)
Firefly (3,23) **20**

Fly Me To The Moon (In Other Words) (9,15) **84**
Foggy Day (26)
For Once In My Life (14,15,20,23) **91**
Forget The Woman (25)
Gentle Rain (11,15,19)
Georgia Rose (12,15) **89**
Get Happy (20)
Girl Talk (11)
Good Life (4,10) **18**
Good Things In Life (24)
Got Her Off My Hands (But Can't Get Her Off My Mind) (5)
Got The Gate On The Golden Gate (8)
Harlem Butterfly (22)
Have I Told You Lately? (2)
Here (17)
Here, There And Everywhere (17)
Here's That Rainy Day (22,26)
How About You (3)
How Do You Keep The Music Playing? (25)
How Do You Say Auf Wiedersehen (14)
How Insensitive (9,15)
I Can't Give You Anything But Love (1)
I Do Not Know A Day I Did Not Love You (19)
I Don't Know Why (I Just Do) (13)
I Fall In Love Too Easily (26)
(I Got A Woman Crazy For Me) She's Funny That Way (13)
I Got Lost In Her Arms (25)
I Left My Heart In San Francisco (2,3,10,20,23) **19**
I Let A Song Go Out Of My Heart (13)
I See Your Face Before Me (26)
I Thought About You (26)
I Walk A Little Faster (8)
I Wanna Be Around (4,10,20,23) **4**
I Wanna Be In Love Again (26)
I Want To Be Happy (19,20)
I Will Live My Life For You (4) **85**
I Wished On The Moon (26)
I'll Be Around (6)
I'll Be Seeing You (1,26)
I'll Begin Again (19,20)

I'll Only Miss Her When I Think Of Her (12)
I'm Always Chasing Rainbows (2)
I'm Glad There Is You (26)
I'm Just A Lucky So And So (1,3)
I'm Losing My Mind (21)
I've Got Just About Everything (7)
I've Got The World On A String (26)
I've Got Your Number (4)
I've Gotta Be Me (16)
I've Never Seen (8)
If I Ruled The World (9,10,20) **34**
If You Were Mine (4)
In The Wee Small Hours (12)
Indian Summer (26)
Individual Thing (19)
Invitation (24)
Irena (21)
Is That All There Is? (17)
It Amazes Me (3)
It Could Happen To You (7)
It Had To Be You (1,7)
It Was Me (4,21)
It Was You (7)
It's A Sin To Tell A Lie (7) **99**
Judy (7)
Just In Time (3,23) **46**
Keep Smiling At Trouble (Trouble's A Bubble) (5,14)
Kid's A Dreamer (The Kid From Fool's Paradise) (6)
Lady Is A Tramp (26)
Lady's In Love With You (13)
Last Night When We Were Young (26)
Lazy Afternoon (3)
Lazy Day (22)
Let There Be Love (20)
Let's Face The Music And Dance (4)
Limehouse Blues (6)
Listen, Little Girl (8)
Little Boy (6) **52**
Little Green Apples (17)
Live For Life (17)
London By Night (24)
Lonely Place (16)
Long About Now (5)
Long And Winding Road (18)
Look Of Love (17)
Lost In The Stars (1,3)
Love (2)
Love For Sale (2)
Love Is Here To Stay (3)

Love Look Away (3,23)
Love Scene (9)
Love Story, Love Theme From ..see: (Where Do I Begin)
Love Walked In (1)
Lullaby Of Broadway (3,14)
MacArthur Park (17)
Make It Easy On Yourself (18)
Marry Young (2)
(Maybe September) ..see: Oscar, Song From The
Maybe This Time (22,23)
Midnight Sun (24)
Mimi (24)
Moment Of Truth (5,10)
Moments Like This (25)
More And More (21)
My Cherie Amour (17)
My Favorite Things (15)
My Funny Valentine (12)
My Heart Tells Me (3)
My Inamorata (21)
Nancy (26)
Never Too Late (11)
Night And Day (26)
Nightingale Sang In Berkeley Square (26)
Nobody Else But Me (7)
O Sole Mio (24)
Oh Lady Be Good (24)
Oh! You Crazy Moon (7)
Ol' Man River (3)
Old Devil Moon (13,20)
On A Clear Day (You Can See Forever) (18)
On Green Dolphin Street (7)
On The Other Side Of The Tracks (5)
On The Sunny Side Of The Street (13,20)
Once Upon A Summertime (4)
Once Upon A Time (2,10)
One For My Baby (And One More For The Road) (26) **49**
One For My Baby (And One More For The Road) (3) **49**
Oscar, Song From The (11)
Out Of This World (14)
Over The Sun (16)
Passing Strangers (24)
Pawnbroker, The (11)
People (15)
Play It Again, Sam (16)
Put On A Happy Face (4)
Quiet Nights Of Quiet Stars (Corcovado) (4,10)
Rags To Riches (3,23)

Remind Me (22)
Right To Love (9)
Riviera, The (22)
Rules Of The Road (2,7)
Samba De Orfeu (11)
Sandpiper (The Shadow Of Your Smile), Love Theme From The (11,15,23) **95**
Sandy's Smile (5)
Second Time Around (11)
(Shadow Of Your Smile) ..see: Sandpiper
Shining Sea (12,21)
Sing You Sinners (3,23)
Sleepy Time Gal (12)
Smile (2,11,23) **73**
So Long, Big Time! (6)
Solitude (3)
Someone To Light Up My Life (Se Todos Fossem Iguals A Voce) (24)
Someone To Love (4)
Something (17,18,23)
Something In Your Smile (14)
Sometimes I'm Happy (3,14)
Somewhere Along The Line (21)
Song Of The Jet (Samba Do Aviao) (9)
Soon It's Gonna Rain (6,19)
Speak Low (18)
Spring In Manhattan (6) **92**
Stranger In Paradise (3,23)
Street Of Dreams (18)
Summer Of '42 (The Summer Knows), Theme From (21)
Sunrise, Sunset (17)
Sweet Lorraine (9)
Take The Moment (9)
Taking A Chance On Love (1,2)
Taste Of Honey (6,10,19) **94**
Tea For Two (19,20)
Tender Is The Night (2)
That Night (16)
Then Was Then And Now Is Now (9)
There Will Never Be Another You (20)
There's A Lull In My Life (8)
These Foolish Things (Remind Me Of You) (1)
They All Laughed (7)
They Can't Take That Away From Me (14,19)
This Is All I Ask (5,10,23) **70**
Till (21)
Time After Time (26)

Time For Love (12,15,23)
Touch The Earth (12)
Trapped In The Web Of Love (12)
Tricks (5)
True Blue Lou (5) **99**
Twilight World (22)
Two By Two (9)
Until I Met You (4)
Valley Of The Dolls, Theme From (16)
Very Thought Of You (12)
Walkabout (21)
Waltz For Debby (8)
Watch What Happens (9,15)
Wave (18,20)
Way That I Feel (5)
What A Wonderful World (18)
What Are You Afraid Of? (25)
What Good Does It Do (3)
What Makes It Happen (13)
What The World Needs Now Is Love (16,20)
When I Look In Your Eyes (18)
When Joanna Loved Me (6,10,19) **94**
When Lights Are Low (7)
When Love Was All We Had (25)
(When We're Together Again) Think How It's Gonna Be (18)
(Where Do I Begin) Love Story (19,20,23)
Who Can I Turn To (When Nobody Needs Me) (8,10,23) **33**
Whoever You Are, I Love You (16)
Why Do People Fall In Love (25)
Without A Song (1)
Wrap Your Troubles In Dreams (And Dream Your Troubles Away) (8)
Yellow Days (18)
Yesterday I Heard The Rain (Esta Tarde Vi Llover) (15)
Yesterdays (12)
You Can Depend On Me (1)
You Go To My Head (26)
You've Changed (6)
Young And Foolish (5)

DEBUT DATE	PEAK POS	WKS CHR	GOLD	ARTIST — Album Title	$	Label & Number

BENNO, Marc
Born on 7/1/47 in Dallas. Rock guitarist/songwriter/singer. Formed partnership, Asylum Choir, with Leon Russell in 1968. Songwriter for Rita Coolidge and session work for The Doors.

12/4/71+	**70**	20		1 Asylum Choir II ....[E]	$15	Shelter 8910
				LEON RUSSSELL & MARC BENNO recorded April 1969		
9/23/72	**171**	8		2 Ambush	$10	A&M 4364

Ballad For A Soldier (1)　Hall Street Jive (2)　Lady In Waiting (1)　Share (2)　Sweet Home Chicago (1)
Donut Man (2)　Hello, Little Friend (1)　Learn To Boogie (1)　Southern Woman (2)　Tryin' To Stay 'Live (1)
Down On The Base (1)　Here To Stay Blues (2)　Poor Boy (2)　Straight Brother (1)　When You Wish Upon A Fag (1)
Either Way It Happens (2)　Jive Fade Jive (2)　Salty Candy (1)　Sunshine Feelin (2)

BENOIT, David
Contemporary jazz keyboardist from Hermosa Beach, California.

6/4/88	**129**	14		1 Every Step Of The Way .... [I]	$8	GRP 1047
5/13/89	**101**	14		2 Urban Daydreams .... [I]	$8	GRP 9587
				all tracks are instrumental except for vocal by Jennifer Warnes		
11/11/89	**187**	3		3 Waiting For Spring .... [I]	$8	GRP 9595
10/27/90	**161**	4		4 Inner Motion.. [I]	$12	GRP 9621

After The Snow Falls (3)　El Camino Real (4)　Key To You (1)　ReBach (1)　Snow Dancing (2)
Along Love's Highway (4)　Every Corner Of The World (4)　Last Request (4)　Remembering What You Said (1)　Some Other Sunset (3)
Cabin Fever (3)　Every Step Of The Way (1)　Looking Back (2)　Safari (1)　South East Quarter (4)
Cast Your Fate To The Wind (3)　Funkallero (3)　M.W.A. (Musicians With Attitude) (4)　Sailing Through The City (2)　Turn Out The Stars (3)
Cat On A Windowsill (3)　Houston (4)　My Romance (1)　Sao Paulo (1)　Urban Daydreams (2)
Cloud Break (2)　I Just Can't Stop Loving You (1)　No Worries (1)　Seattle Morning (2)　Waiting For Spring (2)
Coconut Roads (4)　I Remember Bill Evans (3)　Once Running Free (1)　Shibuya Station (1)　When The Winter's Gone (Song For A Stranger) (2)
Deep Light (4)　　Painted Desert (1)　6-String Poet (4)　Wild Kids (4)

★★**109**★★ **BENSON, George**
Born on 3/22/43 in Pittsburgh. R&B-jazz guitarist. Played guitar from age eight. Played in Brother Jack McDuff's trio in 1963. House musician at CTI Records to early '70s. Influenced by Wes Montgomery. Member of Fuse One.

8/23/69	**145**	3		1 Tell It Like It Is .... [I]	$12	A&M 3020
12/28/74+	**78**	19		2 Bad Benson .... [I]	$10	CTI 6045
4/17/76	**1**[2]	78	▲[3]	3 Breezin'..	$10	Warner 2919
6/26/76	**51**	16		4 Good King Bad .... [I]	$10	CTI 6062
7/24/76	**125**	8		5 The Other Side Of Abbey Road ....[E]	$10	A&M 3028
				version of Beatles' *Abbey Road* album; recorded 1969		
10/30/76	**100**	8		6 Benson & Farrell .... [I]	$10	CTI 6069
				GEORGE BENSON & JOE FARRELL (jazz flutist)		
1/29/77	**122**	8		7 George Benson In Concert-Carnegie Hall .... [I-L]	$10	CTI 6072
				recorded January 1975; with guest: Hubert Laws		
2/12/77	**9**	35	▲	8 In Flight	$10	Warner 2983
2/11/78	**5**	38	▲	9 Weekend In L.A. .... [L]	$12	Warner 3139 [2]
3/17/79	**7**	26	●	10 Livin' Inside Your Love	$10	Warner 3277 [2]
8/9/80	**3**	38	▲	11 Give Me The Night	$8	Warner 3453
11/21/81+	**14**	26	●	12 The George Benson Collection ....[G]	$10	Warner 3577 [2]
6/18/83	**27**	35	●	13 In Your Eyes	$8	Warner 23744
1/26/85	**45**	32	●	14 20/20	$8	Warner 25178
9/20/86	**77**	24		15 While The City Sleeps..	$8	Warner 25475
7/11/87	**59**	31	●	16 Collaboration... [I]	$8	Warner 25580
				GEORGE BENSON/EARL KLUGH		
9/24/88	**76**	10		17 Twice The Love	$8	Warner 25705
8/5/89	**140**	6		18 Tenderly	$8	Warner 25907

Affirmation (3)
Are You Happy? (1)
At The Mambo Inn (18)
Because (medley) (5)
Before You Go (10)
Being With You (13)
Beyond The Ozone (6)
Beyond The Sea (La Mer) (14)
Brazilian Stomp (16)
Breezin' (3,12) **63**
California P.M. (9)
Camel Hump (6)
Cast Your Fate To The Wind (4,12)
Change Is Gonna Come (10)
Changing World (7)
Collaboration (16)
Come Together (medley) (5)
Did You Hear Thunder (15)
Dinorah, Dinorah (11)
Dontcha Hear Me Callin' To Ya (1)
Down Here On The Ground (9)
Dreamin' (16)
Em (4)
End, The (5)
Everybody Does It (17)
Everything Must Change (8)
Feel Like Making Love (13)

Flute Song (6)
Full Compass (2)
Give Me The Night (11,12) **4**
Golden Slumbers (5)
Gone (7)
Gonna Love You More (8) **71**
Good Habit (17)
Greatest Love Of All (9,12) **24**
Here Comes The Sun (5,12)
Here, There And Everywhere (12)
Hey Girl (10)
Hold Me (14)
I Could Write A Book (18)
I Just Wanna Hang Around You (14)
I Want You (She's So Heavy) (5)
In Search Of A Dream (13)
In Your Eyes (13)
Inside Love (So Personal) (13) **43**
It's All In The Game (9)
Jackie, All (1)
Jama Joe (1)
Jamaica (1)
Kisses In The Moonlight (15)
Lady (3)

Lady Blue (9)
Lady Love Me (One More Time) (13) **30**
Land Of 1000 Dances (1)
Last Train To Clarksville (12)
Late At Night (13)
Let's Do It Again (17)
Livin' Inside Your Love (10,12)
Living On Borrowed Love (17)
Love All The Hurt Away (12) **46**
Love Ballad (10,12) **18**
Love Dance (11)
Love Is A Hurtin' Thing (10)
Love Is Here Tonight (15)
Love X Love (11) **61**
Love Will Come Again (13)
Midnight Love Affair (11)
Mimosa (13)
Moody's Mood (11,12)
Mt. Airy Road (16)
My Cherie Amour (5)
My Latin Brother (2)
My Woman's Good To Me (1)
Nassau Day (10)
Nature Boy (6)
Never Give Up On A Good Thing (12) **52**
Never Too Far To Fall (13)

New Day (14)
No One Emotion (14)
No Sooner Said Than Done (2)
Nothing's Gonna Change My Love For You (14)
Octane (7)
Octopus's Garden (medley) (5)
Ode To A Kudu (9)
Off Broadway (11)
Oh! Darling (5)
Old Devil Moon (6)
On Broadway (9,12) **7**
One Rock Don't Make No Boulder (4)
Out In The Cold Again (1)
Please Don't Walk Away (14)
Prelude To Fall (10)
Rolling Home (6)
Secrets In The Night (15)
Shell Of A Man (4)
Shiver (13)
Siberian Workout (4)
Since You're Gone (16)
Six To Four (3)
So This Is Love? (3)
Something (medley) (5)
Soul Limbo (1)
Soulful Strut (10)

Stand Up (14)
Star Of A Story (X) (11)
Stardust (18)
Starting All Over (17)
Stella By Starlight (18)
Stephanie (7)
Summer Wishes, Winter Dreams (2)
Summertime (7)
Take Five (2,7)
Teaser (15)
Tell It Like It Is (1)
Tender Love (17)
Tenderly (18)
Theme From Good King Bad (4)
This Is All I Ask (18)
This Masquerade (3,12) **10**
Too Many Times (15)
Turn Out The Lamplight (11)
Turn Your Love Around (12) **5**
20/20 (14) **48**
Twice The Love (17)
Unchained Melody (10)
Until You Believe (17)
Use Me (13)
Valdez In The Country (8)
Water Brother (1)
We All Remember Wes (9)

We As Love (9)
We Got The Love (12)
Weekend In L.A. (9)
Welcome Into My World (10)
What's On Your Mind (11)
While The City Sleeps (15)
White Rabbit (12)
Wind And I (8)
Windsong (9)
World Is A Ghetto (8)
You Are The Love Of My Life (14)
You Don't Know What Love Is (18)
You Never Give Me Your Money (5)
You're Never Too Far From Me (10)
You're Still My Baby (17)

BENTON, Brook

R&B singer/songwriter. Born Benjamin Franklin Peay on 9/19/31 in Camden, South Carolina; died on 4/9/88 of complications from spinal meningitis. In The Camden Jubilee Singers. To New York in 1948, joined Bill Langford's Langfordaires. With Jerusalem Stars in 1951. First recorded under own name for Okeh in 1953. Wrote "Looking Back," "A Lover's Question," "The Stroll," "It's Just A Matter Of Time" and "Endlessly."

DEBUT DATE	PEAK POS	WKS CHR		ARTIST — Album Title	$	Label & Number
6/5/61	82	20		1 Golden Hits [G]	$30	Mercury 60607
9/25/61	70	13		2 The Boll Weevil Song And 11 Other Great Hits	$30	Mercury 60641
2/17/62	77	7		3 If You Believe	$30	Mercury 60619
				spirituals		
10/27/62	40	15		4 Singing The Blues - Lie To Me	$30	Mercury 60740
4/13/63	82	6		5 Golden Hits, Volume 2 [G]	$30	Mercury 60774
10/28/67	156	4		6 Laura (What's He Got That I Ain't Got)	$12	Reprise 6268
7/19/69	189	2		7 Do Your Own Thing	$10	Cotillion 9002
2/21/70	27	23		8 Brook Benton Today	$10	Cotillion 9018
8/22/70	199	2		9 Home Style	$10	Cotillion 9028

Are You Sincere (9)
Aspen Colorado (9)
Baby (8)
Boll Weevil Song (2,5) **2**
Born Under A Bad Sign (9)
Break Out (7)
Can't Take My Eyes Off You (8)
Careless Love (2)
Chains Of Love (4)
Child Of The Engineer (2)
Deep River (3)
Desertion (8)
Destination Heartbreak (7)
Do Your Own Thing (7) *99*
Don't It Make You Want To Go Home (7) *45*
Don't Think Twice It's All Right (9)
Endlessly (1) *12*
Fools Rush In (Where Angels Fear To Tread) (5) *24*

For Lee Ann (9)
Four Thousand Years Ago (2)
Frankie And Johnny (2,5) *20*
Glory Of Love (6)
Go Tell It On The Mountain (3)
Going Home (3)
Got You On My Mind (4)
He'll Understand And Say Well Done (3)
Here We Go Again (6)
Hiding Behind The Shadow Of A Dream (7)
Hit Record (5) *45*
Hither And Thither And Yon (1) *58*
Honey Babe (2)
Hotel Happiness (5) *3*
How Many Times (1)
Hurtin' Inside (1) *78*
I Got What I Wanted (4) *28*

I Just Don't Know What To Do With Myself (7)
I Left My Heart In San Francisco (medley) (6)
I've Gotta Be Me (8)
Intoxicated Rat (2)
It's All In The Game (9)
It's Just A House Without You (5) *45*
It's Just A Matter Of Time (1) *3*
It's My Lazy Day (2)
Johnny-O (2)
Just A Closer Walk With Thee (3)
Key To The Highway (2)
Kiddio (1) *7*
Laura (Tell Me What He's Got That I Ain't Got) (6) *78*
Let Me Fix It (9)
Lie To Me (4,5) *13*

Life Has Its Little Ups And Downs (8)
Lingering On (6)
Little Bit Of Soap (8)
Looking Back (4)
Lost Penny (3) *77*
Man Without Love (7)
My Last Dollar (9)
My True Confession (4) *22*
My Way (8) *72*
Nothing Can Take The Place Of You (7) *74*
Ode To Billie Joe (6)
Oh Lord, Why Lord (7)
Only Believe (3)
Pledging My Love (4)
Rainy Night In Georgia (8) *4*
Remember Me (3)
Revenge (5) *15*
Same One (1) *16*

San Francisco (Be Sure To Wear Some Flowers In Your Hair) (medley) (6)
Send For Me (4)
Set Me Free (7)
Shadrack (3,5) *19*
She Knows What To Do For Me (7)
So Close (1) *38*
So Many Ways (1) *6*
Steal Away (3)
Stick-To-It-ivity (6)
Still Waters Run Deep (5) *89*
Take Good Care Of Her (4)
Thank You Pretty Baby (1) *16*
(There Was A) Tall Oak Tree (6)
Think Twice (5) *11*
This Is Worth Fighting For (6)
Ties That Bind (1) *37*

Tomorrow Night (4)
Touch 'Em With Love (7)
Valley Of Tears (4)
Walk On The Wild Side (5) *43*
We're Gonna Make It (9)
Where Do I Go From Here? (8)
Whoever Finds This I Love You (9)
Will You Love Me Tomorrow (4)
Willie And Laura Mae Jones (9)
With All Of My Heart (1) *82*
With Pen In Hand (7)
Worried Man (2)
You're The Reason I'm Living (6)

BERG, Gertrude

Molly Goldberg of radio and TV shows; died in 1966 (age 67).

| 7/17/65 | 131 | 12 | | How To Be A Jewish Mother [C] | $15 | Amy 8007 |

announcer: David Ross; writer: Dan Greenburg

Basic Techniques Of Jewish Motherhood
Glossary Of Terms: Final Word

How To Be A Jewish Grandmother
Jewish Mother's Guide To Education

Jewish Mother's Guide To Entertaining
Jewish Mother's Guide To Food Distribution

Jewish Mother's Guide To Relaxation
Jewish Mother's Guide To Sex And Marriage

Jewish Mother's Guide To Thrift

BERGEN, Polly

Born on 7/4/30 in Knoxville, Tennessee. Real name: Nellie Burgin. Singer/actress in movies and TV.

| 6/10/57 | 10 | 5 | | 1 **Bergen Sings Morgan** | $20 | Columbia 994 |

Polly portrayed 1920s "torch singer" Helen Morgan in a TV film

| 11/4/57 | 20 | 1 | | 2 The Party's Over | $20 | Columbia 1031 |

Bill (medley) (1)
Body And Soul (1)
But Not For Me (2)
Can't Help Lovin' That Man (1)
Don't Ever Leave Me! (1)
Ev'ry Time We Say Goodbye (2)

(Here Am I) Broken Hearted (1)
I Guess I'll Have To Change My Plan (2)
I'm Thru With Love (2)
(I've Got) Sand In My Shoes (1)
It Never Entered My Mind (2)

Little Things You Used To Do (1)
Make The Man Love Me (2)
Mean To Me (1)
More Than You Know (1)
My Melancholy Baby (2)
Party's Over (2)

Something To Remember You By (1)
What Wouldn't I Do For That Man! (1)
(When Your Heart's On Fire) Smoke Gets In Your Eyes (2)

Where's The Boy I Saved For A Rainy Day? (2)
Why Was I Born? (medley) (1)
You Don't Know What Love Is (2)
You'll Never Know (2)

BERLIN

Los Angeles electro-pop group. Went from a sextet to a trio in 1985 featuring Terri Nunn (vocals), John Crawford (bass) and Rob Brill (drums). Nunn, who as a teen acted on *Lou Grant* and several other TV shows, left band in 1987.

2/19/83	30	34	●	1 Pleasure Victim	$8	Geffen 2036
3/31/84	28	30	●	2 Love Life	$8	Geffen 4025
11/8/86	61	20		3 Count Three And Pray	$8	Geffen 24121

Beg, Steal Or Borrow (2)
Dancing In Berlin (2)
Fall (2)
For All Tomorrow's Lies (2)
Heartstrings (3)
Hideaway (3)

In My Dreams (2)
Like Flames (3) *82*
Masquerade (1) *82*
Metro, The (1) *58*
No More Words (2) *23*
Now It's My Turn (2) *74*

Pictures Of You (2)
Pink And Velvet (3)
Pleasure Victim (1)
Sex (I'm A...) (1) *62*
Sex Me, Talk Me (3)
Take My Breath Away (3) *1*

Tell Me Why (1)
Torture (1)
Touch (2)
Trash (3)
When Love Goes To War (1)
When We Make Love (2)

Will I Ever Understand You (3)
World Of Smiles (1)
You Don't Know (3)

★★466★★ BERMAN, Shelley

Born on 2/3/26 in Chicago. Popular nightclub comedian/actor. Made TV debut on the *Jack Paar Show*. In films *The Best Man*, *The Wheeler Dealer* and *Divorce American Style*.

4/27/59	2⁵	134		1 **Inside Shelley Berman** [C]	$20	Verve 15003
11/30/59	6	77		2 **Outside Shelley Berman** [C]	$20	Verve 15007
7/25/60	4	52		3 **The Edge Of Shelley Berman** [C]	$20	Verve 15013
11/6/61+	25	19		4 A Personal Appearance [C]	$20	Verve 15027

no track titles listed for above 4 albums

| 9/26/64 | 88 | 8 | | 5 The Sex Life Of The Primate (and other Bits of Gossip) [C] | $20 | Verve 15043 |

with Jerry Stiller, Anne Meara and Lovelady Powell

DEBUT DATE	PEAK POS	WKS CHR	GOLD	ARTIST — Album Title	$	Label & Number

BERMAN, Shelley — Cont'd

Associated Wives Of America (5)	Cleans And Dirtys (5)	Drugstore Problem (5)	More Cleans And Dirtys (5)	Spermatozoa Plus The Roe
Beginning Is A Clean, The End Is A Dirty (5)	Cleans And Dirtys Rise Again (5)	Expurgated...., An (5)	My Friends The Gorillas (5)	Make The Little Fishes Grow (5)
	Divorce New York Style (5)	"It Was The Lark" Or Goodnight Already (5)	Ooby Dooby Ooby Doo (5)	
			Sex Is Un-American (5)	

BERNARDI, Herschel

Born on 10/20/23 in New York City. Portrayed Tevye in Broadway's *Fiddler On The Roof*. Died on 5/9/86.

11/12/66+	138	5		Fiddler On The Roof..	$20	Columbia 6610

Anatevka	If I Were A Rich Man	Miracle Of Miracles	Sunrise, Sunset	Tradition
Fiddler On The Roof	Matchmaker, Matchmaker	Sabbath Prayer	To Life	When Messiah Comes

BERNSTEIN, Leonard

Born on 8/25/18 in Lawrence, Massachusetts. Died on 10/14/90 of emphysema-related heart attack. Conductor/pianist/composer. First classical international superstar from U.S. Conductor of numerous major orchestras worldwide, including the New York Philharmonic (1958-69) and the Vienna Philharmonic. Composed music for *West Side Story*, the film *On The Waterfront* and others. Won Lifetime Achievement Grammy in 1985. Married Chilean actress Felicia Montealegre Cohn in 1951. Retired only five days before his death.

12/12/60+	13	15		1	Bernstein Plays Brubeck Plays Bernstein .... [I]	$25	Columbia 8257

side 1: New York Philharmonic with the Dave Brubeck Quartet conducted by Leonard Bernstein; side 2: Dave Brubeck Quartet

12/25/71+	53	20		2	Mass (from the Liturgy of the Roman Mass)...............	$8	Columbia 31008 [2]

created for the opening of the John F. Kennedy Center for the Performing Arts

5/25/85	70	20		3	West Side Story...	$10	DG 415253 [2]

studio production featuring opera stars Kiri Te Kanawa, Jose Carreras, Tatiana Troyanos, Kurt Ollmann and Marilyn Horne; originally composed by Bernstein in 1956; the soundtrack version held the #1 spot longer than any album in history — 54 weeks

Agnus Dei (2)	Credo (2)	Epistle: "The Word of the Lord" (2)	Gospel-Sermon: "God Said" (2)	Meditation #1, 2 & 3 (2)	Something's Coming (3)
America (3)	Dance At The Gym (3)	First Introit (Rondo) (2)	I Feel Pretty (3)	Offertory (2)	Taunting Scene (3)
Balcony Scene (3)	Devotions Before Mass (2)	Fraction: "Things Get Broken" (2)	I Have A Love (3)	One Hand, One Heart (3)	Tonight (3)
Ballet Sequence (3)	Dialogues For Jazz Combo And Orchestra (Movements 1-4) (1)	Gee, Officer Krupke (3)	Jet Song (3)	Pax: Communion (2)	
Boy Like That (3)		Gloria (2)	Lord's Prayer (2)	Rumble, The (3)	
Confession (2)			Maria (3)	Sanctus (2)	
Cool (3)				Second Introit (2)	

BERRY, Chuck

Born Charles Edward Anderson Berry on 10/18/26 in San Jose, California. Grew up in St. Louis. Muddy Waters introduced Chuck to Leonard Chess (Chess Records) in Chicago. First recording, "Maybellene," was an instant success. Appeared in the film *Rock, Rock, Rock* in 1956, and several others. Won Lifetime Achievement Grammy in 1984. Inducted into the Rock and Roll Hall of Fame in 1986. Film documentary/concert tribute to Chuck, *Hail! Hail! Rock 'N' Roll*, released in 1987. Acclaimed as one of rock and roll's most influential artists.

8/24/63	29	17		1	Chuck Berry On Stage .... [L]	$50	Chess 1480
6/6/64	34	21		2	Chuck Berry's Greatest Hits .... [G]	$40	Chess 1485
12/12/64+	124	7		3	St. Louis To Liverpool	$40	Chess 1488
5/20/67	191	3		4	Chuck Berry's Golden Decade .... [G]	$20	Chess 1514 [2]
6/10/72	8	47	●	5	**The London Chuck Berry Sessions** .... [L]	$15	Chess 60020

side 1: studio; side 2: live

10/21/72	72	17		6	Chuck Berry's Golden Decade .... [R]	$15	Chess 1514 [2]

new cover features a pink radio

11/4/72	185	7		7	St. Louie To Frisco To Memphis .... [L]	$20	Mercury 6501 [2]

record 1: live at the Fillmore with the Steve Miller Band

2/24/73	110	8		8	Chuck Berry's Golden Decade, Vol. 2 .... [G]	$15	Chess 60023 [2]
9/8/73	175	6		9	Chuck Berry/Bio	$15	Chess 50043

All Aboard (1)	Everyday I Have The Blues (7)	It Don't Take But A Few Minutes (8)	Maybellene (1,2,4,6) 5	Rock & Roll Music (2,4,6) 8	Thirty Days (2,4,6)
Almost Grown (4,6) *32*	Feelin' It (7)	It Hurts Me Too (7)	Mean Old World (5)	Rockin' At The Fillmore (7)	Together We Will Always Be (8)
Anthony Boy (4,6) *60*	Fillmore Blues (7)	It's Too Dark In There (7)	Memphis (1,2,4,6)	Rockin' At The Philharmonic (8)	Too Much Monkey Business (2,4,6)
Back In The U.S.A. (4,6) *37*	Flying Home (7)	Jaguar & The Thunderbird (1,8)	Merry Christmas Baby (3,8) 71	Rocking On The Railroad (1)	**Too Pooped To Pop** ("Casey") (4,6) *42*
Back To Memphis (7)	Go Bobby Soxer (3)	Joe Joe Gun (8) *83*	Misery (7)	Roll Over Beethoven (2,4,6) 29	Trick Or Treat (1)
Betty Jean (8)	Go Go Go (1,8)	Johnny B. Goode (2,4,5,6,7) 8	My Ding-A-Ling (5) 1	'Round And 'Round (4,6)	Wee Baby Blues (7)
Bio (9)	Got It And Gone (9)	La Juanda (Espanola) (8)	My Heart Will Always Belong To You (7)	Run Rudolph Run (8) 69	Wee Wee Hours (4,6)
Brenda Lee (3)	Guitar Boogie (8)	Let It Rock (8) 64	My Tambourine (7)	School Day (2,4,6) 3	Woodpecker (9)
Brown Eyed Handsome Man (1,2,4,6)	Havana Moon (4,6)	Let's Boogie (5)	Nadine (Is It You?) (2,4,6) 23	So Long (7)	You Can't Catch Me (4,6)
Bye Bye Johnny (4,6)	Hello Little Girl, Goodbye (9)	Little Fox (7)	Night Beat (3)	Soul Rockin' (7)	**You Never Can Tell** (3,8) *14*
C.C. Rider (7)	I Can't Believe (7)	Little Marie (3) 54	No Money Down (8)	Still Got The Blues (1)	You Two (3)
Carol (8) *18*	I Do Really Love You (7)	Little Queenie (8) 80	**No Particular Place To Go** (3,4,6) *10*	Surfin' USA (1)	
Check Me Out (7)	I Just Want To Make Love To You (1)	Liverpool Drive (3)	Oh Baby Doll (2,4,6) 57	Surfing Steel (1)	
Come On (8)	I Love You (5)	London Berry Blues (5)	Our Little Rendezvous (3)	**Sweet Little Rock And Roll** (4,6) *42*	
Deep Feeling (4,6)	I Will Not Let You Go (5)	Louis to Frisco (7)	Promised Land (3,8) *41*	**Sweet Little Sixteen** (2,4,6) *2*	
Don't You Lie To Me (8)	I'm Talking About You (8)	Ma Dear, Ma Dear (7)	Rain Eyes (9)	Talkin' About My Buddy (9)	
Down The Road Apiece (8)	I'm Your Hoochie Coochie Man (7)	Mad Lad (8)	**Reelin' & Rockin'** (4,5,6) *27*	Things I Used To Do (3)	
Driftin' Aimlessly (9)		Man And The Donkey (1)			
Driftin' Blues (7,8)					

BETH, Karen

Folk-rock vocalist.

9/6/69	171	6			The Joys Of Life	$15	Decca 75148

April Rain	I Know That You Know	It's All Over Now	Nothing Lasts	Song To A Shepherd	White Dakota Hill
Come December	In The Morning	Joys Of Life	Something To Believe In	Tomorrow's A New Day	

BETTS, Dickey

Born on 12/12/43 near Sarasota, Florida. Lead guitarist of The Allman Brothers Band. Wrote "Ramblin' Man" and "Jessica." In the late 1970s, formed Great Southern.

8/31/74	19	16		1	Highway Call..	$10	Capricorn 0123

RICHARD BETTS
side 1: vocals; side 2: instrumentals

DEBUT DATE	PEAK POS	WKS CHR	GOLD	ARTIST — Album Title	$	Label & Number
4/30/77	**31**	12		2 Dickey Betts & Great Southern	$10	Arista 4123
4/29/78	**157**	5		3 Atlanta's Burning Down	$10	Arista 4168
				above 2: **DICKEY BETTS & GREAT SOUTHERN**		
11/12/88	**187**	4		4 Pattern Disruptive	$8	Epic 44289
				THE DICKEY BETTS BAND		

Atlanta's Burning Down (3)   Dealin' With The Devil (3)   Highway Call (1)   Mr. Blues Man (3)   Shady Streets (3)   You Can Have Her (I Don't
Back On The Road Again (3)   Duane's Tune (4)   Kissimmee Kid (1)   Nothing You Can Do (2)   Stone Cold Heart (4)   Want Her) (3)
Blues Ain't Nothin' (4)   Far Cry (4)   Leavin' Me Again (3)   Out To Get Me (2)   Sweet Virginia (2)
Bougainvillea (2)   Good Time Feeling (3)   Let Nature Sing (1)   Rain (1)   Time To Roll (4)
C'est La Vie (4)   Hand Picked (1)   Long Time Gone (1)   Rock Bottom (4)   Under The Guns Of Love (4)
California Blues (2)   Heartbreak Line (4)   Loverman (4)   Run Gypsy Run (2)   Way Love Goes (2)

★★351★★   B-52'S, The

Formed in 1977 in Athens, Georgia as a new wave dance band: Cindy Wilson (guitar, vocals) and her brother Ricky Wilson (guitar; died of AIDS on 10/12/85), Kate Pierson (organ, vocals), Fred Schneider (keyboards, vocals) and Keith Strickland (drums; moved to guitar after Ricky's death). B-52 is slang for the bouffant hairstyle worn by Kate and Cindy. Cindy left in 1991, replaced on tour by Julee Cruise.

DEBUT DATE	PEAK POS	WKS CHR	GOLD	ARTIST — Album Title	$	Label & Number
8/11/79+	**59**	74	▲	1 The B-52's	$8	Warner 3355
9/20/80	**18**	27	●	2 Wild Planet	$8	Warner 3471
8/8/81	**55**	11		3 Party Mix! .... [K-M]	$8	Warner 3596
				6-cut party remix of *Wild Planet* LP		
2/20/82	**35**	18		4 Mesopotamia .... [M]	$8	Warner 3641
5/21/83	**29**	26		5 Whammy!	$8	Warner 23819
10/4/86	**85**	15		6 Bouncing Off The Satellites	$8	Warner 25504
7/22/89+	**4**	65	▲^{2}	7 **Cosmic Thing**	$8	Reprise 25854
2/23/91	**184**	3		8 Party Mix!/Mesopotamia .... [R]	$12	Reprise 26401
				albums #3 and 4 above released together on 1 CD; *Mesopotamia* remixed in summer of 1990		
7/11/92	**16**	15	●	9 Good Stuff	$12	Reprise 26943

Ain't It A Shame (6)   **Deadbeat Club** (7) *30*   Girl From Ipanema Goes To   **Love Shack** (7) *3*   **Rock Lobster** (1) *56*   Throw That Beat In The
Bad Influence (9)   Deep Sleep (4,8)   Greenland (6)   Loveland (4,8)   Runnin' Around (2)   Garbage Can (4,8)
Big Bird (5)   Detour Thru Your Mind (6)   Give Me Back My Man (2,3,8)   Mesopotamia (4,8)   She Brakes For Rainbows (6)   Topaz (7)
Breezin' (9)   Devil In My Car (2)   **Good Stuff** (9) *28*   Nip It In The Bud (4,8)   6060-842 (1)   Trism (5)
Bushfire (7)   Dirty Back Road (2)   Hero Worship (1)   Nude Beach, Theme For A (6)   Song For A Future   Vision Of A Kiss (9)
Butterbean (5)   Don't Worry (5)   Hot Pants Explosion (9)   Party Out Of Bounds (2,3,8)   Generation (5)   Whammy Kiss (5)
Cake (4,8)   Downtown (1)   Housework (4)   Planet Claire (1)   Strobe Light (2)   Wig (5)
Channel Z (7)   Dreamland (9)   Is That You Mo-Dean? (9)   **Private Idaho** (2,3,8) *74*   Summer Of Love (6)   Work That Skirt (5)
Communicate (6)   Dry County (7)   Juicy Jungle (6)   Queen For A Day (5)   Tell It Like It T-I-Is (9)   World's Green Laughter (9)
Cosmic Thing (7)   53 Miles West Of Venus (3)   Junebug (3)   Quiche Lorraine (2)   There's A Moon In The Sky
Dance This Mess Around   52 Girls (1,3,8)   Lava (1,3,8)   Revolution Earth (9)   (Called The Moon) (1)
(1,3,8)   Follow Your Bliss (7)   **Legal Tender** (5) *81*   **Roam** (7) *3*

BICKERSONS, The — see AMECHE, Don

BIDDU ORCHESTRA

Biddu is an Indian-born songwriter/producer. To England, worked as a baker.

DEBUT DATE	PEAK POS	WKS CHR	GOLD	ARTIST — Album Title	$	Label & Number
2/21/76	**170**	3		Biddu Orchestra .... [I]	$8	Epic 33903

Aranjuez Mon Amour   Couldn't We Be Friends   **I Could Have Danced All**   Northern Dancer   You Don't Stand A Chance
Black Magic Man   Exodus (Main Theme)   **Night** *72*   **Summer Of '42** *57*   (If You Don't Dance)
Blue Eyed Soul   Hot Ice   **Jump For Joy** *flip*

BIG AUDIO DYNAMITE

British band formed by guitarist/vocalist Mick Jones (co-founder of The Clash; not to be confused with Mick Jones of Foreigner). Included Don Letts (keyboards), Greg Roberts (drums), Dan Donovan (keyboards; married to Eighth Wonder's Patsy Kensit, 1989-91) and Leo "E-Zee Kill" Williams (bass). Group disbanded in 1989. Jones formed Big Audio Dynamite II in 1990 with Gary Stonadge (bass), Chris Kavanagh (drums) and Nick Hawkins (guitar).

DEBUT DATE	PEAK POS	WKS CHR	GOLD	ARTIST — Album Title	$	Label & Number
11/23/85+	**103**	35		1 This is Big Audio Dynamite	$8	Columbia 40220
11/1/86	**119**	23		2 No. 10, Upping St.	$8	Columbia 40445
				co-produced by Joe Strummer of The Clash		
8/13/88	**102**	12		3 Tighten Up Vol. '88	$8	Columbia 44074
9/23/89	**85**	13		4 Megatop Phoenix	$8	Columbia 45212
8/24/91	**76**	37		5 The Globe	$12	Columbia 46147
				BIG AUDIO DYNAMITE II		

All Mink & No Manners (4)   Champagne (3)   Green Grass (5)   Kool-Aid (5)   **Rush** (5) *32*   2000 Shoes (3)
Applecart (3)   Contact (4)   Green Lady (4)   Limbo The Law (2)   Sambadrome (2)   Union, Jack (4)
Around The Girl In 80 Ways   Dial A Hitman (2)   Hip, Neck & Thigh (3)   London Bridge (4)   Sightsee M.C! (2)   V. Thirteen (2)
(4)   Dragon Town (4)   Hollywood Boulevard (2)   Medicine Show (1)   Sony (1)   When The Time Comes (5)
Baby, Don't Apologise (4)   E=MC^2 (1)   House Arrest (4)   Mick's A Hippie Burning (4)   Stalag 123 (4)
Bad (1)   End (4)   I Don't Know (5)   Mr. Walker Said (3)   Start (4)
Battle Of All Saints Road (3)   Esquerita (3)   In My Dreams (5)   Other 99 (3)   Stone Thames (1)
Beyond The Pale (2)   Everybody Needs A Holiday   Innocent Child (5)   Party, A (1)   Sudden Impact! (1)
Bottom Line (1)   (4)   Is Yours Working Yet? (4)   Rewind (4)   Tea Party (5)
C'mon Every Beatbox (2)   Funny Names (3)   James Brown (1)   Rock Non Stop (All Night   Ticket (2)
Can't Wait (5)   **Globe, The** (5) *72*   Just Play Music! (3)   Long) (3)   Tighten Up Vol. '88 (3)

BIG BROTHER AND THE HOLDING COMPANY

Rock group formed in San Francisco in 1965. Janis Joplin joined as lead singer in 1966. Other members: Peter Albin (bass), James Gurley (guitar), Sam Andrew (guitar) and David Getz (drums). Sensation at the Monterey Pop Festival in 1967. Disbanded in 1972.

DEBUT DATE	PEAK POS	WKS CHR	GOLD	ARTIST — Album Title	$	Label & Number
9/2/67	**60**	30		1 Big Brother & The Holding Company *	$25	Mainstream 6099
8/31/68	**1**^{8}	66	●	2 **Cheap Thrills** *	$20	Columbia 9700
11/28/70	**134**	6		3 Be A Brother	$20	Columbia 30222
5/15/71	**185**	4		4 Big Brother & The Holding Company * .... [R]	$20	Columbia 30631
				reissue + 2 more cuts of album #1 above;		
				*Janis Joplin, lead singer		
9/4/71	**157**	3		5 How Hard It Is	$20	Columbia 30738

BIG BROTHER & THE HOLDING COMPANY — Cont'd

All Is Loneliness (1,4)
Ball And Chain (2)
Be A Brother (3)
Black Widow Spider (5)
Blindman (1,4)
Buried Alive In The Blues (5)
Bye, Bye Baby (1,4)
Call On Me (1,4)

Caterpillar (1,4)
Combination Of The Two (2)
Coo Coo (4) **84**
Down On Me (1,4) **43**
Easy Rider (1,4)
Funkie Jim (3)
Heartache People (3)
Home On the Strange (3)

House On Fire (5)
How Hard It Is (5)
I Need A Man To Love (2)
I'll Change Your Flat Tire, Merle (3)
Intruder (2)
Joseph's Coat (3)
Keep On (3)

Last Band On Side One (5)
Last Time (4)
Light Is Faster Than Sound (1,4)
Maul (5)
Mr. Natural (3)
Nu Boogaloo Jam (5)
Oh, Sweet Mary (2)

Piece Of My Heart (2) **12**
Promise Her Anything But Give Her Arpeggio (5)
Shine On (5)
Someday (3)
Summertime (2)
Sunshine Baby (3)
Turtle Blues (2)

Women Is Losers (1,4)
You've Been Talkin' 'Bout Me, Baby (5)

BIG COUNTRY

Rock quartet formed in Dunfermline, Scotland: Stuart Adamson (vocals, guitar), Bruce Watson (guitar), Tony Butler (bass) and Mark Brzezicki (drums).

9/24/83	18	42	●	1 The Crossing	$8	Mercury 812870
5/5/84	65	12		2 Wonderland [M]	$8	Mercury 818835
11/24/84	70	17		3 Steeltown	$8	Mercury 822831
7/19/86	59	17		4 The Seer	$8	Mercury 826844
10/29/88	160	6		5 Peace in Our Time	$8	Reprise 25787

All Fall Together (2)
Angle Park (2)
Broken Heart (Thirteen Valleys) (5)
Chance (1)
Close Action (1)
Come Back To Me (3)
Crossing, The (2)

East Of Eden (3)
Elledon (4)
Everything I Need (5)
Fields Of Fire (1) **52**
Flame Of The West (3)
From Here To Eternity (3)
Girl With Grey Eyes (3)
Great Divide (3)

Harvest Home (1)
Hold The Heart (4)
I Could Be Happy Here (5)
I Walk The Hill (4)
In A Big Country (1) **17**
In This Place (5)
Inwards (1)
Just A Shadow (3)

King Of Emotion (5)
Look Away (4)
Lost Patrol (1)
One Great Thing (4)
1000 Stars (1)
Peace In Our Time (5)
Porrohman (1)
Rain Dance (3)

Red Fox (4)
Remembrance Day (4)
River Of Hope (5)
Sailor, The (4)
Seer, The (4)
Steeltown (3)
Storm, The (1)
Tall Ships Go (3)

Teacher, The (4)
Thousand Yard Stare (5)
Time For Leaving (5)
Where The Rose Is Sown (4)
Wonderland (2) **86**

BIG PIG

Six-man, one-woman Australian rock band founded by drummer Oleh Witer.

3/26/88	93	17		Bonk	$8	A&M 5185

Big Hotel
Boy Wonder
Breakaway 60

Charlie
Devil's Song
Fine Thing

Hungry Town
I Can't Break Away ..see: Breakaway

Iron Lung
Money God
Nation

Tin Drum

BILK, Mr. Acker

Clarinetist/composer. Born Bernard Stanley Bilk on 1/28/29 in Somerset, England.

5/5/62	3	29	●	1 Stranger On The Shore [I]	$10	Atco 129
9/1/62	48	9		2 Above The Stars & Other Romantic Fancies [I]	$10	Atco 144

Above The Stars (2) **59**
Acker's Lacquer (2)
And The Angels Sing (2)
Babette (2)
Brahms' Lullaby (1)

Carolina Moon (1)
Cielito Lindo (1)
Deep Purple (1)
Della (2)
Greensleeves (1)

I Can't Get Started (1)
Is This The Blues? (1)
Limelight (2) **92**
Londonderry Air (2)
Lonely (2)

Mean To Me (1)
Moonlight Becomes You (2)
Nobody Knows The Trouble (1)
Sentimental Journey (1)

Skye Boat Song (2)
Soft Sands (2)
Stranger On The Shore (1) **1**
Take My Lips (1)

When You Smile (2)

BILLION DOLLAR BABIES

Alice Cooper's backup band.

6/11/77	198	2		Battle Axe	$15	Polydor 6100

Battle Axe (medley)
Dance With Me

Ego Mania
I Miss You

Love Is Rather Blind
Rock Me Slowly

Rock N' Roll Radio
Shine Your Love

Sudden Death (medley)
Too Young

Wasn't I The One
Winner

BILLY & THE BEATERS — see VERA, Billy

BILLY SATELLITE

Rock quartet from Oakland, California, led by Monty Byrom (vocals).

9/1/84	139	6		Billy Satellite	$8	Capitol 12340

Bye Bye Baby
Do Ya

I Wanna Go Back 78
Last Call

Lonely Boy
Rockin' Down The Highway

Satisfy Me 64
Standin' With The Kings

Trouble
Turning Point

BIONIC BOOGIE

A Gregg Diamond disco production.

1/28/78	88	16		Bionic Boogie	$8	Polydor 6123

Big West
Boogie Boo

Dance Little Dreamer

Don't Lose That Number (Mumbo Jumbo)

Feel Like Dancing
Risky Changes

Stop The Music
We Must Believe In Magic

BIRKIN, Jane, & Serge Gainsbourg

Popular British/French duo on records and in films. Actress Birkin was born on 12/12/46. Singer/songwriter Lucien "Serge" Gainsbourg died on 3/2/91 (age 62) of cardiac complications.

3/7/70	196	2		Je T'Aime (Beautiful Love) [F]	$10	Fontana 67610

18-39
Elisa
Jane B

Je T'Aime...Moi Non Plus 58
L'Anamour (The Lover)

Le Canari Est Sur Le Balcon (The Canary Is On The Balcony)

Les Sucettes (The Little Sweets)
Manon

Orang Outan (Orangutan)
69 Annee Erotique (69 The Erotic Year)

Sous Le Soleil Exactement (Underneath The Sun Exactly)

BISHOP, Elvin

Born on 10/21/42 in Tulsa, Oklahoma. Lead guitarist with The Paul Butterfield Blues Band (1965-68).

7/27/74	100	17		1 Let It Flow	$10	Capricorn 0134
5/10/75	46	17		2 Juke Joint Jump	$10	Capricorn 0151
1/24/76	18	34		3 Struttin' My Stuff	$10	Capricorn 0165
11/20/76	70	12		4 Hometown Boy Makes Good!	$10	Capricorn 0176
8/27/77	38	12		5 Live! Raisin' Hell [L]	$12	Capricorn 0185 [2]

Arkansas Line (2)
Bourbon Street (1)
Bring It On Home To Me (medley) (5)
Calling All Cows (2,5)
Can't Go Back (1)
Change Is Gonna Come (medley) (5)
Crawlin' Kingsnake (2)

D.C. Strut (4)
Do Nobody Wrong (2)
Fishin' (1)
Fooled Around And Fell In Love (3,5) **3**
Give It Up (4,5)
Grab All The Fun (5)
Graveyard Blues (4)
Ground Hog (1)

Have A Good Time (3)
Hey, Good Lookin' (1)
Hey, Hey, Hey, Hey (3,5)
Hold On (2)
Holler And Shout (3)
Honey Babe (1)
I Can't Hold Myself In Line (1)
I Love The Life I Lead (3)

Joy (3,5)
Juke Joint Jump (2,5)
Keep It Cool (4)
Let It Flow (1)
Let The Good Times Roll (medley) (5)
Little Brown Bird (5)
My Girl (3)
Once In A Lifetime (4)

Raisin' Hell (5)
Rock My Soul (5)
Rollin' Home (2)
Sidelines (4)
Slick Titty Boom (3)
Spend Some Time (4) **93**
Stealin' Watermelons (1,5)
Struttin' My Stuff (3,5) **68**

Sunshine Special (1)
Sure Feels Good (2,5) **83**
Travelin' Shoes (1,5) **61**
Twist & Shout (4)
Wide River (3)
Yes Sir (4,5)

DEBUT DATE	PEAK POS	WKS CHR	GOLD	ARTIST — Album Title	$	Label & Number

BISHOP, Stephen
Pop-rock singer/songwriter born in 1951 in San Diego. Wrote movie theme for *The China Syndrome*. Cameo role as the "Charming Guy With Guitar" in *National Lampoon's Animal House*. Also see soundtrack *Tootsie*.

| 1/8/77 | 34 | 32 | | 1 Careless | $10 | ABC 954 |
| 9/16/78 | 35 | 19 ● | | 2 Bish | $10 | ABC 1082 |

Bish's Hideaway (2)
Careless (1)
Every Minute (1)
Everybody Needs Love (2) 32

Fool At Heart (2)
I've Never Known A Nite Like This (2)
If I Only Had A Brain (2)
Little Italy (1)

Looking For The Right One (2)
Losing Myself In You (2)
Madge (1)
Never Letting Go (1)

On And On (1) 11
One More Night (1)
Only The Heart Within You (2)
Recognized (2)

Rock And Roll Slave (1)
Same Old Tears On A New Background (1)
Save It For A Rainy Day (1) 22

Sinking In An Ocean Of Tears (1)
Vagabond From Heaven (1)
What Love Can Do (2)
When I Was In Love (2)

BIZ MARKIE
Rapper born in Harlem on 4/8/64. Real name: Marcel Hall.

3/19/88	90	18		1 Goin' Off	$8	Cold Chill. 25675
10/28/89	66	30 ●		2 The Biz Never Sleeps	$8	Cold Chill. 26003
				THE DIABOLICAL BIZ MARKIE		
9/14/91	113	2		3 I Need A Haircut	$12	Cold Chill. 26648

Albee Square Mall (1)
Alone Again (3)
Biz Dance (Part One) (1)
Biz In Harmony (3)
Biz Is Goin' Off (1)
Buck Wild (3)
Busy Doing Nuthin' (3)
Check It Out (2)

Cool V's Tribute To Scratching (1)
Dedication (2)
Dragon, The (2)
I Hear Music (2)
I Told You (3)
Just A Friend (2) 9
Kung Fu (3)

Let Go My Eggo (3)
Make The Music With Your Mouth Biz (1)
Me Versus Me (2)
Mudd Foot (3)
My Man Rich (2)
Nobody Beats The Biz (1)
On And On (3)

Pickin' Boogers (1)
Return Of The Biz Dance (1)
Road Block (3)
Romeo And Juliet (3)
She's Not Just Another Woman (Monique) (2)
Spring Again (2)
T.S.R. (Toilet Stool Rap) (3)

Take It From The Top (3)
Thing Named Kim (2)
Things Get A Little Easier (2)
This Is Something For The Radio (1)
To My Boys (3)
Vapors (1)

What Comes Around Goes Around (3)

BJOERLING, Jussi
Operatic tenor. Born on 2/5/11 in Stora Tuna, Sweden. Died on 9/9/60. Regular performer at all great opera centers throughout his professional life.

| 4/17/61 | 142 | 1 | | The Beloved Bjoerling, Volume One [E] | $20 | Capitol 7239 |
| | | | | opera arias 1936-48 | | |

Bizet: Carmen-La Fleur Que Tu M'Avais Jetee (Flower Song)
Cilea: L'Arlesiana-E La Solita Storia

Donizetti: L'Elisir D'Amore-Una Furtiva Lagrima
Leoncavallo: I Pagliacci-Vesti La Giubba

Mascagni: Cavalleria Rusticana-O Lola, Bianca Come Fior (Siciliana)
Massenet: Manon-Instant Charmant...(Act 1 & 2)

Meyerbeer: L'Africana-Mi Batte Il Cor...O Paradiso
Ponchielli: La Gioconda-Cielo E Mar
Puccini: La Boheme-Che Gelida Manina

Puccini: Manon Lescaut-Donna Non Vidi Mai!
Puccini: Turandot-Nessun Dorma

Verdi: Rigoletto-Questa O Quella

BLACK('S), Bill, Combo
Bill was born on 9/17/26 in Memphis; died of a brain tumor on 10/21/65. Bass guitarist. Session work in Memphis; backed Elvis Presley (with Scotty Moore, guitar; D.J. Fontana, drums) on most of his early records. Formed own band in 1959. Labeled as "The Untouchable Sound."

11/14/60	23	28		1 Solid And Raunchy [I]	$25	Hi 12003
1/20/62	35	19		2 Let's Twist Her [I]	$20	Hi 12006
7/11/64	143	4		3 Plays Tunes By Chuck Berry [I]	$15	Hi 32017
11/28/64	139	3		4 Bill Black's Combo Goes Big Band [I]	$15	Hi 32020
8/19/67	195	2		5 Bill Black's Greatest Hits [G-I]	$15	Hi 32032
9/13/69	168	4		6 Solid And Raunchy The 3rd [I]	$15	Hi 32052

Blue Tango (5) 16
Blueberry Hill (1)
Bo Diddley (1)
Brown Eyed Handsome Man (3)
Cab Driver (6)
Canadian Sunset (4)
Carol (3)
Cherry Pink (1)
Coco Brown (6)
Come See About Me (6)
Corrina, Corrina (2)

Creepin' Around (6)
Do It – Rat Now (5) 51
Don't Be Cruel (1,5) 11
Groovin' Easy (6)
Hearts Of Stone (5) 20
Hold It Down (6)
Honky Tonk (1)
Huckle-Buck (Twist) (2)
I Almost Lost My Mind (1)
If I Had A Hammer (6)
In The Mood (4)
Java (1)

Johnny B. Goode (2,3)
Josephine (5) 18
Leap Frog (4)
Leavin' Town (6)
Little Queenie (3) 73
Love Is Here And Now You're Gone (6)
Mabellene (3)
Mack The Knife (1)
Memphis Tennessee (3)
Mona Lisa (1)
My Girl Josephine (2)

Nadine (3)
Near You (4)
Night Train (5)
O (Oh!) (4)
Ole Buttermilk Sky (5) 25
Raunchy (1)
Reelin' And Rockin' (3)
Roll Over Beethoven (3)
Rollin' (5)
Royal Blue (5)
Royal Twist (2)
School Days (3)

Sentimental Journey (4)
Singin' The Blues (1)
Slippin' & Slidin' (Twist) (2)
Smokie – Part 2 (5) 17
Smokie Part II (Twist) (2)
So Rare (4)
Son Of Hickory Holler's Tramp (4)
Stranger On The Shore (4)
Sweet Little Sixteen (3)
T.D.'s Boogie Woogie (4)
Tequila (1) 91

Thirty Days (3)
Tuxedo Junction (4)
Twist-Her (2) 26
Twist With Me Baby (2)
Twisteroo (2)
Two O'Clock Jump (4)
Watch Your Step (6)
White Silver Sands (5) 9
Willie (5)
Yogi (5)
Yogi (Twist) (2)
You Win Again (1)

BLACK, Clint
Country singer from Houston. Former construction worker. Signed to RCA in December 1987. Married actress Lisa Hartman (TV's *Knot's Landing*, *Tabitha*) on 10/20/91.

6/10/89+	31	143 ▲²		1 Killin' Time	$8	RCA 9668
11/24/90	18	80 ▲²		2 Put Yourself In My Shoes	$12	RCA 2372
8/1/92	8	28↑▲		3 The Hard Way	$12	RCA 66003

Better Man (1)
Burn One Down (3)
Buying Time (3)
Good Old Days (3)
Goodnight-Loving (2)
Gulf Of Mexico (2)

Hard Way (3)
Heart Like Mine (2)
Killin' Time (1)
Live And Learn (1)
Loving Blind (2)
Muddy Water (2)

Nobody's Home (1)
Nothing's News (1)
Old Man (2)
One More Payment (2)
Put Yourself In My Shoes (2)
Something To Cry About (3)

Straight From The Factory (1)
There Never Was A Train (3)
This Nightlife (2)
Wake Up Yesterday (3)
Walkin' Away (1)

We Tell Ourselves (3)
When My Ship Comes In (3)
Where Are You Now (2)
Winding Down (1)
Woman Has Her Way (3)

You're Gonna Leave Me Again (1)

BLACK, Stanley, and his Orchestra
Born on 6/14/13 in London. Pianist/arranger/composer. Conducted BBC Dance Orchestra for nine years, beginning in 1944. Wrote many film scores.

2/10/62	30	8		1 Exotic Percussion [I]	$10	London P. 4 44004
8/18/62	33	10		2 Spain [I]	$10	London P. 4 44016
8/10/63	50	4		3 Film Spectacular [I]	$10	London P. 4 44025
6/12/65	148	3		4 Music Of A People [I]	$10	London P. 4 44060
				above 2 with the London Festival Orchestra		

Adieu Tristesse (1)
And The Angels Sing (4)
Around The World (3)
Ay-Ay-Ay (2)

Babalu (1)
Baia (1)
Big Country (3)
Breakfast At Tiffany's (3)

Bulerias (1)
By The Waters Of Minnetonka (1)
Caravan (1)

Carmen Fantasy (2)
Eili Eili (4)
Estrellita (2)
Exodus (3)

Flamingo (1)
Granada (2)
Hatikvah (4)
Hava Nagila (medley) (4)

Hebrew Melody (4)
Henry V (3)
Hymn To The Sun (1)
Joseph! Joseph! (4)

DEBUT DATE	PEAK POS	WKS CHR	GOLD	ARTIST — Album Title	$	Label & Number

BLACK, Stanley, and his Orchestra — Cont'd

Jungle Drums (1)	Macarenas (2)	Moon Of Manakoora (1)	Ritual Fire Dance (2)	Shema (medley) (4)	Valencia (2)
Letter To My Mother (4)	Malaguena (2)	Old Devil Moon (1)	Samson And Delilah (3)	Temptation (1)	West Side Story (3)
Longest Day (3)	Misirlou (1)	Raisins And Almonds (4)	Sevillanas (2)	Tzena Tzena Tzena (4)	Yes, My Darling Daughter (4)

BLACK BOX

Male Italian dance trio of producer Daniele Davoli and musicians Mirko Limoni and Valerio Semplici. Videos feature French model Katrin Quinol as lead singer; however, Martha Wash (Weather Girls) is the uncredited lead vocalist on all but one cut of *Dreamland* LP.

8/11/90	56	61 ●	Dreamland..	$12	RCA 2221

Dreamland	Fantasy	Hold On	**I Don't Know Anybody**	Open Your Eyes	**Strike It Up 8**
Everybody Everybody 8	Ghost Box		**Else 23**	Ride On Time	

BLACKBYRDS, The

Soul group founded in 1973 by Donald Byrd while teaching at Howard University in Washington, D.C.

6/22/74	96	23		1 The Blackbyrds..	$15	Fantasy 9444
12/7/74+	30	39		2 Flying Start...	$15	Fantasy 9472
7/5/75	150	6		3 Cornbread, Earl and Me .... [S]	$15	Fantasy 9483
11/22/75+	16	40	●	4 City Life	$15	Fantasy 9490
11/27/76+	34	24	●	5 Unfinished Business..	$15	Fantasy 9518
10/8/77	43	30	●	6 Action	$12	Fantasy 9535
1/6/79	159	7		7 Night Grooves.. [K]	$12	Fantasy 9570
1/17/81	133	11		8 Better Days	$12	Fantasy 9602

All I Ask (4)	Do It Girl (8)	Hash And Eggs (4)	Mother/Son Bedroom Talk (3)	Soft And Easy (6,7)	What's On Your Mind (8)
April Showers (2)	Do You Wanna Dance? (8)	Heavy Town (3)		Something Special (6)	Wilford's Gone (3)
At The Carnival (3)	Don't Know What To Say (8)	Hot Day Today (1)	Mother/Son Talk (3)	Soulful Source (4)	Without Your Love (8)
Baby, The (2)	Dreaming About You (6)	I Need You (2)	Mother/Son Theme (3)	Spaced Out (2)	You've Got That Something (5)
Better Days (8)	Enter In (5)	In Life (5)	Mysterious Vibes (6)	Street Games (2)	
Blackbyrds' Theme (2)	**Flyin' High** (4) **70**	Lady (5)	One-Eye Two-Step (3)	Summer Love (1)	
Candy Store Dilemma (3)	Funky Junkie (1)	Life Styles (1)	One-Gun Salute (3)	Supernatural Feeling (6,7)	
City Life (4)	Future Children, Future Hopes (2)	Lonelies For Your Love (8)	Party Land (5)	Thankful 'Bout Yourself (4)	
Cornbread (3)		Lookin' Ahead (6)	Reggins (1)	**Time Is Movin'** (5) **95**	
Courtroom Emotions (3)	Gut Level (1,7)	Love Don't Strike Twice (8)	Riot (3)	Unfinished Business (5)	
Dancin' Dancin' (8)	Gym Fight (3)	Love Is Love (2)	**Rock Creek Park** (4,7) **93**	**Walking In Rhythm** (2,7) **6**	
Do It, Fluid (1,7) **69**	**Happy Music** (4,7) **19**	Love So Fine (4)	Runaway, The (1)	What We Have Is Right (8)	

BLACK CROWES, The

Hard-rock quintet from Atlanta led by brothers Chris (vocals) and Rich (guitar) Robinson. Includes Jeff Cease, Steve Gorman and Johnny Colt. Cease left in late 1991, replaced by Marc Ford (ex-Burning Tree).

3/24/90+	4	151 ↑ ▲3	1 Shake Your Money Maker	$12	Def Amer. 24278
			LP title is an Elmore James' blues song
5/30/92	1¹	37 ↑ ▲	2 The Southern Harmony And Musical Companion	$12	Def Amer. 26976
			title derived from a famous book of hymns

Bad Luck Blue Eyes Goodbye (2)	**Hard To Handle** (1) **26**	No Speak No Slave (2)	Sister Luck (1)	Struttin' Blues (1)	Twice As Hard (1)
Black Moon Creeping (2)	Hotel Illness (2)	**Remedy** (2) **48**	Sometimes Salvation (2)	Thick N' Thin (1)	
Could I've Been So Blind (1)	**Jealous Again** (1) **75**	Seeing Things (2)	Stare It Cold (1)	**Thorn In My Pride** (2) **80**	
	My Morning Song (2)	**She Talks To Angels** (1) **30**	Sting Me (2)	Time Will Tell (2)	

BLACKFOOT

Rock band from Jacksonville, Florida. Rick "Rattlesnake" Medlocke (lead singer) was a second drummer for Lynyrd Skynyrd. Bassist Greg Walker was also with Lynyrd Skynyrd.

5/12/79	42	41 ▲	1 Strikes	$8	Atco 112
6/21/80	50	20	2 Tomcattin'	$8	Atco 101
7/25/81	48	12	3 Marauder	$8	Atco 107
6/11/83	82	13	4 Siogo	$8	Atco 90080
10/27/84	176	5	5 Vertical Smiles	$8	Atco 90218

Baby Blue (1)	**Fly Away** (3) **42**	I Got A Line On You (1)	Payin' For It (3)	Searchin' (3)	We're Goin' Down (4)
Crossfire (4)	Fox Chase (2)	In For The Kill (5)	Rattlesnake Rock 'N' Roller (3)	Send Me An Angel (4)	White Man's Land (4)
Diary Of A Workingman (3)	Get It On (5)	In The Night (2)		Spendin' Cabbage (2)	Wishing Well (1)
Dream On (2)	Gimme, Gimme, Gimme (3)	Left Turn On A Red Light (4)	Reckless Abandoner (2)	Street Fighter (2)	Young Girl (5)
Drivin' Fool (4)	Goin' In Circles (4)	Legend Never Dies (5)	Ride With You (5)	Summer Days (5)	
Dry County (3)	Good Morning (3)	Livin' In The Limelight (5)	Road Fever (1)	Teenage Idol (4)	
Every Man Should Know (Queenie) (1)	Heart's Grown Cold (4)	Morning Dew (5)	Run And Hide (1)	Too Hard To Handle (3)	
	Heartbeat And Heels (5)	On The Run (2)	Run For Cover (4)	**Train, Train** (1) **38**	
Fire Of The Dragon (3)	**Highway Song** (1) **26**	Pay My Dues (1)	Sail Away (4)	Warped (2)	

BLACK IVORY

New York City trio formed as the Mellow Sounds: lead singer LeRoy Burgess III, Stuart Bascombe and Russell Patterson. Discovered by Patrick Adams, leader of the Sparks. Burgess was later in The Aleems.

| 4/22/72 | 158 | 9 | 1 Don't Turn Around.. | $10 | Today 1005 |
| 1/20/73 | 188 | 9 | 2 Baby, Won't You Change Your Mind .... | $10 | Today 1008 |

Baby, Won't You Change Your Mind (2)	Got To Be There (1)	Just Leave Me Some (2)	Push Come To Shove (1)	Time Is Love (2)	
	I Keep Asking You Questions (1)	No Ifs Ands Or Buts (2)	She Said That She's Leaving (1)	Time To Say Goodbye (2)	
Don't Turn Around (1)		One Way Ticket To Loveland (2)		Wishful Thinking (2)	
Find The One Who Loves You (1)	I'll Find A Way (1)	Our Future (1)	Spinning Around (2)	You And I (1)	
	If I Could Be A Mirror (1)		Surrender (1)		

BLACKJACK

New York City-based rock quartet led by singer Michael Bolton who began solo career in 1983.

| 7/21/79 | 127 | 7 | Blackjack... | $8 | Polydor 6215 |

Countin' On You	For You	Heart Of Stone	**Love Me Tonight 62**	Southern Ballad (If This Means Losing You)	Without Your Love
Fallin'	Heart Of Mine	I'm Aware Of Your Love	Night Has Me Calling For You		

BLACKMORE, Ritchie — see RAINBOW

BLACK 'N BLUE

Los Angeles-based, hard-rock quintet from Portland, Oregon: Jaime St. James (vocals), Tommy Thayer, Woop, Patrick Young and Pete Holmes.

DEBUT DATE	PEAK POS	WKS CHR	GOLD	ARTIST — Album Title	$	Label & Number
9/15/84	116	11		1 Black 'N Blue	$8	Geffen 24041
10/25/86	110	20		2 Nasty Nasty	$8	Geffen 24111
4/23/88	133	9		3 In Heat	$8	Geffen 24180

Action (1)
Autoblast (1)
Best In The West (2)
Chains Around Heaven (1)
Do What You Wanna Do (2)
Does She Or Doesn't She (2)
Get Wise To The Rise (3)
Gimme Your Love (3)
Great Guns Of Fire (3)
Heat It Up! Burn It Out! (3)
Hold On To 18 (1)
I Want It All (I Want It Now) (2)
I'll Be There For You (2)
I'm The King (1)
Kiss Of Death (2)
Live It Up (3)
Nasty Nasty (2)
One For The Money (1)
Rock On (3)
Rules (2)
School Of Hard Knocks (1)
Show Me The Night (1)
Sight For Sore Eyes (3)
Snake, The (3)
Stranger (3)
Strong Will Rock (1)
Suspicious (3)
12 O'Clock High (2)
Wicked Bitch (1)

BLACK OAK ARKANSAS

Southern-rock sextet led by Jim "Dandy" Mangrum (b: 3/30/48; vocals). Extensive touring group, named after their hometown. Original members included bassist Pat Daugherty and guitarists Stan Knight, Rick Reynolds and Harvey Jett. Milwaukee vocalist Ruby Starr appeared on many of group's recordings and tours. By 1975, drummer Tommy Aldrich added and Jim Henderson replaced Jett. Various members since 1976.

DEBUT DATE	PEAK POS	WKS CHR	GOLD	ARTIST — Album Title	$	Label & Number
8/28/71	127	12	●	1 Black Oak Arkansas	$15	Atco 354
2/12/72	103	10		2 Keep The Faith	$15	Atco 381
7/8/72	93	19		3 If An Angel Came To See You, Would You Make Her Feel At Home?	$15	Atco 7008
3/17/73	90	16	●	4 Raunch 'N' Roll/Live	[L] $15	Atco 7019
11/24/73+	52	22	●	5 High On The Hog	$15	Atco 7035
7/27/74	56	12		6 Street Party	$12	Atco 101
5/31/75	145	8		7 Ain't Life Grand	$12	Atco 111
10/18/75+	99	17		8 X-Rated	$12	MCA 2155
2/28/76	194	2		9 Live! Mutha	[L] $12	Atco 128
6/12/76	173	7		10 Balls Of Fire	$12	MCA 2199

Ace In The Hole (8)
All My Troubles (10)
Back Door Man (7)
Back To The Land (5)
Big One's Still Coming (2)
Brink Of Creation (6)
Bump 'N Grind (8)
Cryin' Shame (7,9)
Dancing In The Streets (6)
Diggin' For Gold (7)
Dixie (6)
Don't Confuse What You Don't Know (2)
Everybody Wants To See Heaven "Nobody Wants To Die" (6)
Fancy Nancy (7,9)
Feet On Earth, Head In Sky (2)
Fertile Woman (3)
Fever In My Mind (2,9)
Fightin' Cock (8)
Fistful Of Love (10)
Flesh Needs Flesh (8)
Full Moon Ride (3)
Gettin' Kinda Cocky (4)
Gigolo (4)
Goin' Home (6)
Good Good Woman (6)
Good Stuff (7)
Gravel Roads (3)
Great Balls Of Fire (10)
Happy Hooker (5)
Hey Ya'll (6,9)
High Flyer (8)
High 'N' Dry (5)
Highway Pirate (8)
Hills Of Arkansas (1)
Hot And Nasty (1,4,9)
Hot Rod (4)
I Can Feel Forever (10)
I Could Love You (1)
I'm A Man (6)
Jail Bait (8)
Jim Dandy (5,9) 25
Just To Fall In Love (10)
Keep On (7)
Keep The Faith (2)
Leather Angel (10)
Let Life Be Good To You (7)
Lord Have Mercy On My Soul (1,9)
Love Can Be Found (7)
Mad Man (5)
Make That Scene (4)
Memories At The Window (1)
Moonshine Sonata (5)
Movin' (5)
Mutants Of The Monster (3,4)
Our Eyes Ere On You (3)
Our Minds Eye (3)
Ramblin' Gamblin' Man (10)
Rebel (3)
Red Hot Lovin' (5)
Revolutionary All American Boys (2)
Rock 'N' Roll (10)
Short Life Line (2)
Singing The Blues (1)
Son Of A Gun (6)
Spring Vacation (3)
Sting Me (6)
Storm Of Passion (10)
Strong Enough To Be Gentle (8) 89
Sure Been Workin' Hard (6)
Swimmin' In Quicksand (5)
Taxman (7)
To Make Us What We Are (3)
Too Hot To Stop (8)
Uncle Lijiah (1)
Up (4)
We Help Each Other (3)
We Live On Day To Day (2)
When Electricity Came To Arkansas (1,4)
White-Headed Woman (2)
Why Shouldn't I Smile (5)
Wild Men From The Mountains (8)

BLACK PEARL

West Coast rock group led by Bernie "B.B." Fieldings.

DEBUT DATE	PEAK POS	WKS CHR	GOLD	ARTIST — Album Title	$	Label & Number
5/3/69	130	5		1 Black Pearl	$15	Atlantic 8220
10/17/70	189	2		2 Black Pearl-Live!	[L] $18	Prophesy 1001

Bent Over (1)
Climbing Up The Walls (1)
Cold Sweat (2)
Crazy Chicken (1)
Endless Journey (1)
Forget It (1)
Hermit Freak Show (2)
I Get The Blues Most Every Night (2)
Mr. Soul Satisfaction (1)
People Get Ready (2)
Reach Up (1)
Thinkin' 'Bout The Good Times (1)
Uptown (2)
White Devil (1)

★★123★★ BLACK SABBATH

Heavy-metal group formed as blues band Earth in Birmingham, England in 1968. Changed name to Black Sabbath in late 1969. Original lineup included: John "Ozzy" Osbourne (vocals), Tony Iommi (guitar), William Ward (drums) and Terry "Geezer" Butler (bass). Osbourne formed the Blizzard of Ozz in 1979, replaced by Ronnie James Dio (Rainbow). Ward left for a year in 1981, replaced by Vinnie Appice. Ian Gillan (Deep Purple) replaced Dio in 1983. Fluctuating lineup since 1986. Iommi was the only original member in lineups that included vocalists Glenn Hughes (1986; ex-Deep Purple) and Tony Martin (since 1987); bassists Dave Spitz (1986-87), Bob Daisley (1987), Laurence Cottle (1989) and Neil Murray (since 1990); drummers Eric Singer (1986-87), Bev Bevan (1987; Move, ELO) and Cozy Powell (since 1989; ELP), and keyboardist Geoff Nicholls (1983-89). In 1991, reunion of Iommi, Butler, Appice and Dio.

DEBUT DATE	PEAK POS	WKS CHR	GOLD	ARTIST — Album Title	$	Label & Number
8/29/70	23	65	▲	1 Black Sabbath	$12	Warner 1871
2/20/71	12	70	▲³	2 Paranoid	$12	Warner 1887
9/4/71	8	43	▲	3 **Master Of Reality**	$12	Warner 2562
10/21/72	13	31	▲	4 Black Sabbath, Vol. 4	$12	Warner 2602
1/26/74	11	32	▲	5 Sabbath Bloody Sabbath	$12	Warner 2695
8/23/75	28	14		6 Sabotage	$12	Warner 2822
2/28/76	48	10	▲	7 We Sold Our Soul For Rock 'N' Roll	[K] $15	Warner 2923 [2]
10/30/76	51	12		8 Technical Ecstasy	$12	Warner 2969
10/28/78	69	14		9 Never Say Die!	$8	Warner 3186
6/14/80	28	24	▲	10 Heaven And Hell	$8	Warner 3372
11/28/81	29	18	●	11 Mob Rules	$8	Warner 3605
2/5/83	37	12		12 Live Evil	[L] $10	Warner 23742 [2]
10/22/83	39	16		13 Born Again	$8	Warner 23978
2/15/86	78	11		14 Seventh Star	$8	Warner 25337
				BLACK SABBATH Featuring Tony Iommi		
12/26/87+	168	6		15 The Eternal Idol	$8	Warner 25548
5/13/89	115	8		16 Headless Cross	$8	I.R.S. 82002
7/18/92	44	8		17 Dehumanizer	$12	Reprise 26965

BLACK SABBATH — Cont'd

After All (The Dead) (17)
After Forever (3)
Air Dance (9)
All Moving Parts (Stand Still) (8)
Am I Going Insane (Radio) (6,7)
Ancient Warrior (15)
Angry Heart (14)
Back Street Kids (8)
Bassically (1)
Behind The Wall Of Sleep (1)
Bit Of Finger (1)
Black Moon (16)
Black Sabbath (1,7,12)
Born Again (13)
Born To Lose (15)
Breakout (9)
Buried Alive (17)
Call Of The Wild (16)
Changes (4,7)
Children Of The Grave (3,7,12)
Children Of The Sea (10,12)
Computer God (17)

Cornucopia (4)
Country Girl (11)
Danger Zone (14)
Dark, The (13)
Devil And Daughter (16)
Die Young (10)
Digital Bitch (13)
Dirty Women (8)
Disturbing The Priest (13)
Don't Start (Too Late) (6)
E5150 (11,12)
Electric Funeral (2)
Embryo (3)
Eternal Idol (15)
Every Day Comes And Goes (medley) (2)
FX (4)
Fairies Wear Boots (2,7)
Falling Off The Edge Of The World (11)
Fluff (5,12)
Gates Of Hell (16)
Glory Ride (15)
Gypsy (8)
Hand Of Doom (2)

Hard Life To Love (15)
Hard Road (9)
Headless Cross (16)
Heart Like A Wheel (14)
Heaven And Hell (10,12)
Hole In The Sky (6)
Hot Line (13)
I (17)
In For The Kill (14)
In Memory... (14)
Into The Void (3)
Iron Man (2,7,12) **52**
It's Alright (8)
Jack The Stripper (medley) (2)
Johnny Blade (9)
Junior's Eyes (9)
Keep It Warm (13)
Kill In The Spirit World (16)
Killing Yourself To Live (5)
Lady Evil (10)
Laguna Sunrise (4,7)
Letters From Earth (17)
Lonely Is The Word (10)
Looking For Today (5)

Lord Of This World (3)
Lost Forever (15)
Luke's Wall (medley) (2)
Master Of Insanity (17)
Megalomania (6)
Mob Rules (11,12)
N.I.B. (1,7,12)
National Acrobat (5)
Neon Knights (10,12)
Never Say Die (9)
Nightmare (15)
Nightwing (16)
No Stranger To Love (14)
Orchid (3)
Over And Over (11)
Over To You (9)
Paranoid (2,7,12) **61**
Planet Caravan (2)
Rat Salad (2)
Rock 'N' Roll Doctor (8)
Sabbath, Bloody Sabbath (5,7)
Sabbra Cadabra (5)
Scarlet Pimpernel (15)
Seventh Star (14)

She's Gone (8)
Shining, The (15)
Shock Wave (9)
Sign Of The Southern Cross (11,12)
Sins Of The Father (17)
Sleeping Village (1)
Slipping Away (11)
Snowblind (4,7)
Solitude (3)
Sphinx (The Guardian) (14)
Spiral Architect (5)
St. Vitus' Dance (4)
Stonehenge (13)
Supernaut (4)
Supertzar (6)
Sweet Leaf (3,7)
Swinging The Chain (9)
Symptom Of The Universe (6)
TV Crimes (17)
Thrill Of It All (6)
Time Machine [includes 2 versions] (17)
Tomorrow's Dream (4,7)
Too Late (17)

Trashed (13)
Turn To Stone (14)
Turn Up The Night (11)
Under The Sun (medley) (4)
Voodoo (11,12)
Walk Away (10)
War Pigs (2,7,12)
Warning (1,7)
Wasp (1)
Wheels Of Confusion (4)
When Death Calls (16)
Who Are You? (5)
Wicked World (1)
Wishing Well (10)
Wizard, The (1,7)
Writ, The (6)
You Won't Change Me (8)
Zero The Hero (13)

BLACK SHEEP

Bronx rap duo of Andre "Dres" Titus and William "Mista Lawnge" (pronounced: long) McLean.

11/9/91+	30	41	●	A Wolf In Sheep's Clothing	$12	Mercury 848368

CD includes 2 bonus tracks

Are You Mad?
Black With N.V. (No Vision)
Blunted 10
Butt In The Meantime

Choice Is Yours [includes 2 versions] **57**
Flavor Of The Month
For Doz That Slept

Gimme The Finga
Go To Hail
Have U.N.E. Pull
Hoes We Knows

L.A.S.M.
La Menage
Pass The 40
Similak Child

Strobelite Honey 80
To Whom It May Concern
Try Counting Sheep
U Mean I'm Not

Yes

BLACK UHURU

Jamaican reggae vocal group formed in the mid-1970s by Don Carlos, Duckie Simpson and Garth Dennis. Carlos and Dennis left in 1977, Michael Rose and female vocalist Puma Jones joined. Rose and Jones left in 1985, Delroy "Junior" Reid and Janet "Olafunke" Reid were added. Carlos, Simpson and Dennis reunited in 1987. Uhuru means freedom in Swahili.

7/24/82	146	7		1 Chill Out	$8	Island 9752
3/10/90	121	11		2 Now	$12	Mesa 79021

Army Band (2)
Chill Out (1)
Darkness (1)
Emotional Slaughter (1)

Eye Market (1)
Fleety Foot (1)
Freedom Fighter (1)
Heathen (2)

Hey Joe (2)
Imposter (2)
Mondays (1)
Moya (Queen Of I Jungle) (1)

Peace And Love (2)
Reggae Rock (2)
Right Stuff (1)
Take Heed (2)

Thinking About You (2)
Wicked Act (1)
Word Sound (2)

BLADES, Ruben

Popular Latin singer/actor. Born on 7/16/48 in Panama City, Panama. Acted in *The Milagro Beanfield War, Crazy From The Heart* and other films.

5/7/88	156	6		Nothing But The Truth	$8	Elektra 60754

his first all-English album

Calm Before The Storm
Chameleons

Hit, The
Hopes On Hold

I Can't Say
In Salvador

Letter, The
Letters To The Vatican

Miranda Syndrome
Ollie's Doo-Wop

Shamed Into Love

BLANCHARD, Jack, & Misty Morgan

Husband-and-wife country duo. Both born in Buffalo. Jack (b: 5/8/42) plays saxophone and keyboards. Misty (b: 5/23/45) plays keyboards. Met and married while working in Florida.

7/4/70	185	5		Birds Of A Feather	$12	Wayside 001

Bethlehem Steel
Big Black Bird (Spirit Of My Love)

Changin' Times
Chapel Hill
Clock Of St. James

Dum Song
Humphrey The Camel 78
Poor Jody

Tennessee Bird Walk 23
With Pen In Hand
Yellow Bellied Sapsucker

You've Got Your Troubles (I've Got Mine)

BLAND, Bobby

Born Robert Calvin Bland on 1/27/30 in Rosemark, Tennessee. Nicknamed "Blue." Sang in gospel group The Miniatures in Memphis, late '40s. Member of the Beale Streeters which included Johnny Ace, B.B. King, Rosco Gordon, Earl Forest and Willie Nix in 1949. Driver and valet for B.B. King; appeared in the Johnny Ace Revue, early '50s. First recorded in 1952 for the Modern label. Toured with B.B. King into the '80s.

9/1/62	53	7		1 Here's The Man!!!	$40	Duke 75
7/13/63	11	26		2 Call On Me/That's The Way Love Is	$40	Duke 77
8/1/64	119	8		3 Ain't Nothing You Can Do	$35	Duke 78
11/3/73+	136	19		4 His California Album	$10	Dunhill 50163
				BOBBY BLUE BLAND		
8/3/74	172	7		5 Dreamer	$10	Dunhill 50169
10/26/74+	43	20	●	6 Together For The First Time...Live [L]	$12	Dunhill 50190 [2]
				B.B. KING & BOBBY BLAND		
9/13/75	154	5		7 Get On Down With Bobby Bland	$8	ABC 895
7/17/76	73	14		8 Together Again...Live [L]	$10	ABC/Impulse 9317
				BOBBY BLAND & B.B. KING		
5/14/77	185	4		9 Reflections In Blue	$8	ABC 1018
7/1/78	185	3		10 Come Fly With Me	$8	ABC 1075
10/27/79	187	2		11 I Feel Good, I Feel Fine	$8	MCA 3157

After It's Too Late (3)
Ain't Something (10)
Ain't It A Good Thing (2)
Ain't No Love In The Heart Of The City (5) **91**

Ain't Nothing You Can Do (3) **20**
Ain't That Loving You (1) **86**
Black Night (3,6) **99**
Blind Man (3) **78**

Blues In The Night (1)
Bobby's Blues (2)
Call On Me (2) 22
Care For Me (2)
Chains Of Love (medley) (6)
Cherry Red (medley) (6)

Cold Day In Hell (5)
Come Fly With Me (10)
Cry, Lover, Cry (2)
Don't Answer The Door (6)
Don't Cry No More (6) **71**
Dreamer (5)

Driftin' Blues (6) 96
Driving Wheel (medley) (6)
End Of The Road (5)
Everyday (I Have The Blues) (8)
Feel So Bad (8)

Feeling Is Gone (2) **91**
Five Long Years (9)
Friday The 13th Child (4)
Goin' Down Slow (4,6) **69**
Gonna Get Me An Old Woman (medley) (6)

DEBUT DATE	PEAK POS	WKS CHR	GOLD	ARTIST — Album Title	$	Label & Number

BLAND, Bobby — Cont'd

Good To Be Back Home (medley) (6)
Help Me Through The Day (4)
Honky Tonk (2)
I Ain't Gonna Be The First To Cry (5,8)
I Can't Take No Mo' (11)
I Feel Good, I Feel Fine (11)
I Got The Same Old Blues (9)
I Hate You (7)
I Intend To Take Your Place (9)
I Like To Live The Love (6)
I Take It On Home (7)
I Wouldn't Treat A Dog (The Way You Treated Me) *88*
I'll Be Your Fool Once More (9)
I'll Take Care Of You (6) *89*

I'm Gonna Cry (3)
I'm Just Your Man (10)
I'm Sorry (6) *97*
I've Got To Use My Imagination (4)
If Fingerprints Showed Up On Skin (7)
If I Hadn't Called You Back (3)
If I Weren't A Gambler (9)
(If Loving You Is Wrong) I Don't Want To Be Right (4)
If You Could Read My Mind (3)
In His Eyes (11)
It Ain't The Real Thing (9)
It's All Over (9)
It's My Own Fault (6)
It's Not The Spotlight (4)
Jelly Jelly Jelly (1)

Lady Lonely (10)
Let The Good Times Roll (8)
Little Mama (11)
Loneliness Hurts (3)
Love To See You Smile (10)
Lovin' On Borrowed Time (5)
Mean Old World (medley) (8)
Mother-In-Law Blues (medley) (8)
Night Games (10)
No Sweeter Girl (9)
Presenting Dynamic Bobby Bland 36-22-36 (11)
Queen For A Day (2)
Reconsider (3)
Red Sails In The Sunset (11)
Right Place At The Right Time (4)
Rock Me Baby (medley) (6)

Share Your Love With Me (2) *42*
Sittin' On A Poor Man's Throne (9)
Someone To Belong To (11)
Someone To Give My Love To (7)
Soon As The Weather Breaks (11)
Soul Of A Man (9)
Steal Away (3)
Stormy Monday Blues (1,8) *43*
Strange Things Happen (medley) (8)
That's The Way Love Is (2,6) *33*
This Bitter Earth (10)
This Time I'm Gone For Good (4) *42*

3 O'Clock Blues (6)
Thrill Is Gone (medley) (8)
Tit For Tat (11)
To Be Friends (10)
Today (3)
Today I Started Loving You Again (7)
Too Far Gone (7)
Turn On Your Love Light (1) *28*
Twenty-Four Hour Blues (5)
Twistin' Up The Road (1)
Up And Down World (4)
When You Put Me Down (3)
Where Baby Went (4)
Who Will The Next Fool Be (1) *76*
Who's Foolin' Who (5)
Why I Sing The Blues (6)
Wishing Well (2)

Worried Life Blues (medley) (6)
Yolanda (5)
You Can Count On Me (10)
You're Gonna Love Yourself (In The Morning) (7)
You're The One (That I Adore) (1)
You're Worth It All (1)
You've Always Got The Blues (7)
You've Never Been This Far Before (7)
Your Friends (1)

BLASTERS, The
Los Angeles rockabilly group led by brothers Phil (lead singer, guitar) and Dave (lead guitar) Alvin. Dave was also a member of The Knitters.

DEBUT DATE	PEAK POS	WKS CHR	GOLD	ARTIST — Album Title	$	Label & Number
1/9/82	36	30		1 The Blasters	$10	Slash 3680
10/30/82	117	8		2 Over There-Live At The Venue, London ...[M-L]	$10	Slash 23735
5/14/83	95	8		3 Non Fiction	$10	Slash 23818
3/23/85	86	19		4 Hard Line	$8	Slash 25093

American Music (1)
Barefoot Rock (3)
Boomtown (3)
Border Radio (1)
Bus Station (3)
Colored Lights (4)
Common Man (4)

Dark Night (4)
Fool's Paradise (3)
Go, Go, Go (2)
Help You Dream (4)
Hey, Girl (4)
High School Confidential (2)
Highway 61 (1)

Hollywood Bed (1)
I Don't Want To (4)
I Love You So (1)
I'm Shakin' (1)
It Must Be Love (3)
Jubilee Train (3)
Just Another Sunday (4)

Keep A Knockin' (2)
Leaving (3)
Little Honey (4)
Long White Cadillac (3)
Marie Marie (1)
Never No More Blues (1)
No Other Girl (1)

One More Dance (3)
Red Rose (3)
Rock And Roll Will Stand (4)
Rock Boppin' Baby (2)
Roll 'Em Pete (2)
Samson And Delilah (4)
So Long Baby Goodbye (1)

Stop The Clock (1)
Tag Along (3)
This Is It (1)
Trouble Bound (4)

BLESSING, Adam — see DAMNATION OF

BLIGE, Mary J.
Born in Atlanta and raised in Yonkers, New York. Twenty-one years old in 1992.

DEBUT DATE	PEAK POS	WKS CHR	GOLD	ARTIST — Album Title	$	Label & Number
8/15/92	6	26↑▲		**What's The 411?**	$12	Uptown 10681

Changes I've Been Going Through
I Don't Want To Do Anything

Intro Talk
Leave A Message

Love No Limit
My Love

Real Love 7
Reminisce 57

Slow Down
Sweet Thing

What's The 411?
You Remind Me 29

BLIND FAITH
Short-lived British rock supergroup: Eric Clapton (The Yardbirds, John Mayall's Bluesbreakers, Cream), Steve Winwood (Spencer Davis Group, Traffic, Ginger Baker's Air Force), Ginger Baker (Cream, Air Force) and Rick Grech (Family, Traffic, Air Force). Formed and disbanded in 1969. Also see Eric Clapton's History Of Eric Clapton and Crossroads albums.

DEBUT DATE	PEAK POS	WKS CHR	GOLD	ARTIST — Album Title	$	Label & Number
8/16/69	1²	37	●	1 **Blind Faith**	$20	Atco 304
2/26/77	126	8		2 Blind Faith ...[R]	$8	RSO 3016
				new cover features a naked young girl		

Can't Find My Way Home (1,2)

Do What You Like (1,2)

Had To Cry Today (1,2)

Presence Of The Lord (1,2)

Sea Of Joy (1,2)

Well All Right (1,2)

BLODWYN PIG
British rock quartet led by Mick Abrahams of Jethro Tull.

DEBUT DATE	PEAK POS	WKS CHR	GOLD	ARTIST — Album Title	$	Label & Number
12/13/69+	149	5		1 Ahead Rings Out	$12	A&M 4210
6/27/70	96	5		2 Getting To This	$12	A&M 4243

Ain't Ya Coming Home? (1)
Backwash (1)
Change Song (1)

Dear Jill (1)
Drive Me (2)
It's Only Love (1)

Long Bomb Blues (2)
Meanie Mornay (2)
Modern Alchemist (1)

San Francisco Sketches
Medley (2)
See My Way (1)

Send Your Son To Die (2)
Squirreling Must Go On (2)
Summer Day (1)
Toys (2)

Variations On Nainos (2)
Walk On The Water (1)
Worry (2)

★★461★★ BLONDIE
New York City techno-pop sextet formed in 1975. Consisted of Debbie Harry (lead singer), Chris Stein, Frank Infante, Jimmy Destri, Gary Valentine and Clem Burke. Harry had been in the folk-rock group Wind In The Willows. She did solo work from 1980; appeared in several films. Group disbanded in 1983.

DEBUT DATE	PEAK POS	WKS CHR	GOLD	ARTIST — Album Title	$	Label & Number
2/25/78	72	17		1 Plastic Letters	$8	Chrysalis 1166
9/23/78+	6	103	▲	2 **Parallel Lines**	$8	Chrysalis 1192
10/20/79	17	51	▲	3 Eat To The Beat	$8	Chrysalis 1225
12/13/80+	7	34	▲	4 Autoamerican	$8	Chrysalis 1290
10/31/81	30	23	●	5 The Best Of Blondie ...[G]	$8	Chrysalis 1337
6/19/82	33	12		6 The Hunter	$8	Chrysalis 1384

Accidents Never Happen (3)
Angels On The Balcony (4)
Atomic (3,5) *39*
Beast, The (6)
Bermuda Triangle Blues (Flight 45) (1)
Call Me (5) *1*
(Can I) Find The Right Words (To Say) (6)
Cautious Lip (1)
Contact In Red Square (1)
Danceway (6)
Denis (1)

Detroit 442 (1)
Die Young Stay Pretty (3)
Do The Dark (4)
Dragonfly (6)
Dreaming (3,5) *27*
Eat To The Beat (3)
11:59 (2)
English Boys (6)
Europa (4)
Faces (4)
Fade Away And Radiate (2)
Fan Mail (1)
Follow Me (4)

For Your Eyes Only (6)
Go Through It (4)
Hanging On The Telephone (2,5)
Hardest Part (3) *84*
Heart Of Glass (2,5) *1*
Here's Looking At You (4)
Hunter Gets Captured By The Game (6)
I Didn't Have The Nerve To Say No (1)
I Know But I Don't Know (2)

(I'm Always Touched By Your) Presence, Dear (1,5)
I'm Gonna Love You Too (2)
I'm On E (1)
In The Flesh (5)
Island Of Lost Souls (6) *37*
Just Go Away (2)
Kidnapper (1)
Little Caesar (6)
Live It Up (4)
Living In The Real World (3)
Love At The Pier (1)
No Imagination (1)

One Way Or Another (2,5) *24*
Orchid Club (6)
Picture This (2)
Pretty Baby (2)
Rapture (4,5) *1*
Rip Her To Shreds (1)
Shayla (3)
Slow Motion (3)
Sound-A-Sleep (3)
Sunday Girl (2,5)
T-Birds (4)
Tide Is High (4,5) *1*

Union City Blue (3)
Victor (3)
Walk Like Me (4)
War Child (6)
Will Anything Happen? (2)
Youth Nabbed As Sniper (1)

DEBUT DATE	PEAK POS	WKS CHR	GOLD	ARTIST — Album Title	$	Label & Number

BLOODROCK

Rock group from Fort Worth, Texas — Jim Rutledge, lead vocals. Rutledge headed own production company in the 1970s; produced Meri Wilson's top 20 pop single "Telephone Man."

DEBUT DATE	PEAK POS	WKS CHR	GOLD		$	Label & Number
4/25/70	160	5		1 Bloodrock	$15	Capitol 435
11/7/70+	21	37	●	2 Bloodrock 2	$15	Capitol 491
4/10/71	27	23		3 Bloodrock 3	$15	Capitol 765
11/6/71	88	7		4 Bloodrock U.S.A.	$15	Capitol 645
6/3/72	67	22		5 Bloodrock Live ....[L]	$15	Capitol 11038 [2]
9/30/72	104	14		6 Bloodrock Passage	$15	Capitol 11109

Abracadaver (4)
America, America (3)
American Burn (4)
Breach Of Lease (3,5)
Castle Of Thoughts (1,5)
Certain Kind (3)
Cheater (2,5)
Children's Heritage (2)
Crazy 'Bout You Babe (4)
D.O.A. (2,5) 36
Days And Nights (6)
Dier Not A Lover (2)
Don't Eat The Children (4)
Double Cross (1)
Fallin' (2)
Fancy Space Odyssey (2)
Fantastic Piece Of Architecture (1)
Fantasy (6)
Fatback (3)
Gimme Your Head (1)
Gotta Find A Way (1,5)
Hangman's Dance (4)
Help Is On The Way (6)
It's A Sad World (4)
Jessica (3,5)
Juice (6)
Kool-Aid-Kids (3,5)
Life Blood (6)
Lost Fame (6)
Lucky In The Morning (2,5)
Magic Man (4)
Melvin Laid An Egg (1)
Power, The (6)
Promises (4)
Rock & Roll Candy Man (4)
Sable And Pearl (2)
Scottsman (6)
Song For A Brother (3)
Thank You Daniel Ellsberg (6)
Timepiece (1)
Whiskey Vengeance (3)
Wicked Truth (1)
You Gotta Roll (3,5)

BLOODSTONE

Soul group from Kansas City, Missouri. Formed in 1962 as the Sinceres. Consisted of Charles McCormick, Willis Draffen, Charles Love, Henry Williams and Roger Durham (d: 1973).

DEBUT DATE	PEAK POS	WKS CHR	GOLD		$	Label & Number
4/14/73	30	36		1 Natural High	$10	London 620
1/5/74	110	22		2 Unreal	$10	London 634
8/10/74	141	8		3 I Need Time	$10	London 647
2/22/75	147	6		4 Riddle Of The Sphinx	$10	London 645
7/17/82	95	11		5 We Go A Long Way Back	$8	T-Neck 38115

Closer Together (3)
Damn That Rock 'N' Roll Medley (1)
Everybody Needs Love (2)
For The First Time Medley (4)
Funkin' Around (5)
Funky Park (3)
Get Up (Or Get Out) (5)
Go On And Cry (5)
How Does It Feel (5)
I Believe You Now (3)
I Just Learned To Walk (4)
I Need Time (3)
I Need Your Love (1)
Keep Our Own Thing Together (2)
Let Me Ride (2)
Little Linda (3)
Loving You Is Just A Pastime (3)
Moulded Oldies Medley (2)
My Kind Of Woman (5)
My Little Lady (4) 57
My Love Grows Stronger (5)
Natural High (1) 10
Never Let You Go (1) 43
Nite Time Fun (5)
Nobody But You (4)
Out Of My Life (3)
Outside Woman (2) 34
Peter's Jones (1)
Ran It In The Ground (1)
Save Me Medley (4)
Sign For Me Dad (4)
Something (2)
Something's Missing (4)
Tell It To My Face (1)
That's Not How It Goes (3) 83
That's The Way We Make Our Music (1)
This World Is Funky (4)
Time For Reflection (4)
Traffic Cop (Dance) (2)
Unreal (2)
Wasted Time (4)
We Did It (3)
We Go A Long Way Back (5)
What Did You Do To Me? Part 1 & 2 (2)
Who Has The Last Laugh Now (1)
You Know We've Learned (1)
Young Times Old Times (4)

★★250★★ BLOOD, SWEAT & TEARS

Pop-jazz group formed by Al Kooper (The Royal Teens, The Blues Project) in 1968. Nucleus consisted of Kooper (keyboards), Steve Katz (guitar; The Blues Project), Bobby Colomby (drums) and Jim Fielder (bass). Kooper replaced by lead singer David Clayton-Thomas in 1969. Clayton-Thomas replaced by Jerry Fisher in 1972. Katz left in 1973. Clayton-Thomas rejoined in 1974. Colomby later worked as a television music reporter and an executive with Epic, Capitol, EMI and CBS.

DEBUT DATE	PEAK POS	WKS CHR	GOLD		$	Label & Number
4/13/68	47	55	●	1 Child Is Father To The Man	$20	Columbia 9619
2/1/69	1[7]	109	▲[3]	2 Blood, Sweat & Tears	$12	Columbia 9720
				1969 Grammy winner: Album of the Year		
7/18/70	1[2]	41	●	3 Blood, Sweat & Tears 3	$12	Columbia 30090
7/10/71	10	23	●	4 B, S & T; 4	$12	Columbia 30590
3/11/72	19	27	▲	5 Blood, Sweat & Tears Greatest Hits ....[G]	$12	Columbia 31170
11/4/72	32	17		6 New Blood	$12	Columbia 31780
8/25/73	72	12		7 No Sweat	$12	Columbia 32180
9/7/74	149	6		8 Mirror Image	$12	Columbia 32929
5/31/75	47	13		9 New City	$12	Columbia 33484
7/31/76	165	3		10 More Than Ever	$12	Columbia 34233

Almost Sorry (7)
Alone (6)
And When I Die (2,5) 2
Applause (9)
Are You Satisfied (8)
Back Up Against The Wall (7)
Battle, The (3)
Blues - Part II (2)
Cowboys And Indians (4)
Django (An Excerpt) (7)
Down In The Flood (6)
Empty Pages (7)
Fire And Rain (3)
For My Lady (4)
40,000 Headman (3)
Go Down Gamblin' (4,5) 32
God Bless The Child (2,5)
Got To Get You Into My Life (9) 62
He's A Runner (3)
Heavy Blue (10)
Hi-De-Ho (3,5) 14
High On A Mountain (4)
Hip Pickles (7)
Hold On To Me (8)
Hollywood (10)
House In The Country (1)
I Can't Move No Mountains (6)
I Can't Quit Her (1,5)
I Love You More Than Ever (10)
I Love You More Than You'll Ever Know (1,5)
I Was A Witness To A War (9)
Inner Crisis (7)
John The Baptist (Holy John) (4)
Just One Smile (1)
Katy Bell (10)
Life (9)
Lisa, Listen To Me (4,5) 73
Lonesome Suzie (1)
Look To My Heart [includes 2 versions] (4)
Look Up To The Sky (8)
Love Looks Good On You (You're Candy Sweet) (8)
Lucretia Mac Evil (3,5) 29
Lucretia's Reprise (3)
Maiden Voyage (6)
Mama Gets High (4)
Mary Miles (7)
Meagan's Gypsy Eyes (1)
Mirror Image (8)
Modern Adventures Of Plato, Diogenes And Freud (1)
More And More (2)
Morning Glory (6)
My Days Are Numbered (1)
My Old Lady (7)
Naked Man (3)
No Show (9)
One Room Country Shack (9)
Over The Hill (6)
Redemption (4)
Ride Captain Ride (9)
Roller Coaster (7)
Rosemary (7)
Save Our Ship (7)
Saved By The Grace Of Your Love (10)
She's Coming Home (8)
Smiling Phases (4)
Snow Queen (6)
So Long Dixie (6) 44
So Much Love (1)
Somethin' Comin' On (3)
Somethin' Goin' On (1)
Sometimes In Winter (2,5)
Song For John (7)
Spinning Wheel (2,5) 2
Sweet Sadie The Savior (10)
Sympathy For The Devil (medley) (3)
Symphony For The Devil (medley) (3)
Take Me In Your Arms (Rock Me A Little While) (4)
Takin' It Home (9)
Tell Me That I'm Wrong (8) 83
They (1)
Thinking Of You (8)
Touch Me (6)
Valentine's Day (4)
Variations On A Theme By Erik Satie (1st And 2nd Movements) (2)
Velvet (3)
Without Her (1)
Yesterday's Music (9)
You're The One (10)
You've Made Me So Very Happy (2,5) 2

BLOOM, Bobby

Pop singer/songwriter, much session work in the '60s. Died from an accidental shooting on 2/28/74.

DEBUT DATE	PEAK POS	WKS CHR	GOLD		$	Label & Number
11/28/70	126	3		The Bobby Bloom Album	$12	L&R 1035

Brighten Your Flame
Careful Not To Break The Spell
Fanta
Give 'Em A Hand
Heavy Makes You Happy
Heidi
Little On The Heavy Side
Montego Bay 8
Oh I Wish You Knew
This Thing I've Gotten Into
Try A Little Harder

BLOOMFIELD, Mike

Born on 7/28/44 in Chicago; died on 2/15/81 of a drug overdose. Blues guitarist. With The Paul Butterfield Blues Band and Electric Flag. Later joined KGB.

DEBUT DATE	PEAK POS	WKS CHR	GOLD		$	Label & Number
8/31/68	12	37	●	1 Super Session	$15	Columbia 9701
				MIKE BLOOMFIELD/AL KOOPER/STEVE STILLS		

DEBUT DATE	PEAK POS	WKS CHR	GOLD	ARTIST — Album Title	$	Label & Number
2/8/69	18	20	2	The Live Adventures Of Mike Bloomfield And Al Kooper ....[L] **MIKE BLOOMFIELD & AL KOOPER**	$15	Columbia 6 [2]
10/11/69	127	5	3	It's Not Killing Me... **MICHAEL BLOOMFIELD**	$12	Columbia 9883
6/16/73	105	12	4	Triumvirate .... **MIKE BLOOMFIELD/JOHN PAUL HAMMOND/DR. JOHN**	$10	Columbia 32172

Albert's Shuffle (1) / Baby Let Me Kiss You (4) / Cha-Dooky-Doo (4) / Dear Mr. Fantasy (2) / Don't Think About It, Baby (3) / Don't Throw Your Love On Me So Strong (2) / Far Too Many Nights (3) / 59th Street Bridge Song (Feelin' Groovy) (2) / For Anyone You Meet (3) / Good Old Guy (3) / Goofers (3) / Green Onions (2) / Ground Hog Blues (4) / Harvey's Tune (1) / Her Holy Modal Highness (2) / His Holy Modal Majesty (1) / I Wonder Who (2) / I Yi Yi (4) / If You See My Baby (3) / It Hurts Me Too (4) / It Takes A Lot To Laugh, It Takes A Lot To Cry (1) / It's Not Killing Me (3) / Just To Be With You (4) / Last Night (4) / Man's Temptation (1) / Mary Ann (4) / Michael's Lament (3) / Next Time You See Me (3) / No More Lonely Nights (2) / Ones I Loved Are Gone (3) / Pretty Thing (4) / Really (1) / Refugee (2) / Rock Me Baby (4) / Season Of The Witch (1) / Sho Bout To Drive Me Wild (4) / Sonny Boy Williamson (2) / Stop (1) / That's All Right (2) / Together 'Til The End Of Time (2) / Weight, The (2) / Why Must My Baby (3) / You Don't Love Me (1)

BLOW, Kurtis
Born Kurt Walker on 8/9/59 in New York City. Began as a disco DJ.

DEBUT DATE	PEAK POS	WKS CHR	GOLD	ARTIST — Album Title	$	Label & Number
10/18/80	71	10	1	Kurtis Blow	$8	Mercury 3854
7/18/81	137	5	2	Deuce	$8	Mercury 4020
10/9/82	167	5	3	Tough ....[M]	$8	Mercury 505
10/13/84+	83	37	4	Ego Trip	$8	Mercury 822420
11/2/85	153	15	5	America	$8	Mercury 826141
12/13/86	196	2	6	Kingdom Blow..	$8	Mercury 830215

AJ Is Cool (5) / AJ Meets Davy DMX (5) / AJ Scratch (4) / All I Want In This World (Is To Find That Girl) (1) / America [includes 2 versions] (5) / Baby, You've Got To Go (3) / **Basketball** (4) *71* / Boogie Blues (3) / **Breaks, The (Part 1)** (1) *87* / Bronx, The (6) / Daydreamin' (3) / Deuce, The (2) / Do The Do (2) / Don't Cha Feel Like Making Love (1) / Ego Trip (4) / 8 Million Stories (4) / Fallin' Back In Love Again (4) / Getaway (2) / Hard Times (1) / Hello Baby (5) / I Can't Take It No More (4) / I'm Chillin' (6) / If I Ruled The World (5) / It's Gettin' Hot (2) / Juice (3) / Kingdom Blow (6) / MC Lullaby (6) / Magilla Gorilla (6) / Rappin' Blow (Part 2) (1) / Reasons For Wanting You (6) / Respect To The King (5) / Rockin' (2) / Starlife (4) / Street Rock (6) / Summertime Groove (5) / Sunshine (6) / Super Sperm (5) / Take It To The Bridge (4) / Takin' Care Of Business (1) / Throughout Your Years (1) / Tough (3) / Under Fire (4) / Unity Party Jam (6) / Way Out West (1)

BLOWFLY
Blowfly is Clarence Reid. Born on 2/14/45 in Cochran, Georgia. Soul singer/composer/arranger/producer. With Miami vocal group, the Delmiros, early 1960s.

DEBUT DATE	PEAK POS	WKS CHR	GOLD	ARTIST — Album Title	$	Label & Number
5/24/80	82	20		Blowfly's Party [X-Rated]	$8	Weird World 2034

Blowfly's Rapp / Can I Come In Your Mouth / Nobody's Butt But Yours, Babe / Panty Lines / Prick Ryder / Rapp Dirty / Show Me A Man Who Don't Like To Fuck / Who Did I Eat Last Night?

BLOW MONKEYS, The
British quartet led by Dr. Robert (Robert Howard). Includes: Mick Anker, Neville Henry and Tony Kiley.

DEBUT DATE	PEAK POS	WKS CHR	GOLD	ARTIST — Album Title	$	Label & Number
6/21/86	35	18	1	Animal Magic	$8	RCA 8065
4/25/87	134	8	2	She Was Only A Grocer's Daughter	$8	RCA 6246

Aeroplane City Lovesong (1) / Animal Magic (1) / Beautiful Child (2) / Burn The Rich (1) / Cash (2) / Checking Out (2) / Day After You (2) / **Digging Your Scene** (1) *14* / Don't Be Scared Of Me (1) / Don't Give It Up (2) / Forbidden Fruit (1) / Heaven Is A Place I'm Moving To (1) / How Long Can A Bad Thing Last (2) / I Backed A Winner (In You) (1) / I Nearly Died Laughing (1) / It Doesn't Have To Be This Way (2) / Man At The End Of His Tether (2) / Out With Her (2) / Rise Above (2) / Some Kind Of Wonderful (2) / Sweet Murder (1) / Wicked Ways (1)

BLUE CHEER
San Francisco hard-rock group led by Dickie Peterson (vocals, bass).

DEBUT DATE	PEAK POS	WKS CHR	GOLD	ARTIST — Album Title	$	Label & Number
3/9/68	11	27	1	Vincebus Eruptum...	$30	Philips 264
9/28/68	90	16	2	Outsideinside...	$30	Philips 278
5/3/69	84	14	3	New! Improved! Blue Cheer	$30	Philips 305
11/7/70	188	5	4	The Original Human Being	$30	Philips 347

Aces 'N' Eights (3) / As Long As I Live (3) / Babaji (Twilight Raga) (4) / Babylon (2) / Black Sun (2) / Come And Get It (2) / Doctor Please (1) / Feathers From Your Tree (2) / Fruit & Iceburgs (3) / Good Times Are So Hard To Find (4) / Gypsy Ball (2) / Honey Butter Lover (3) / Hunter, The (2) / (I Can't Get No) Satisfaction (2) / Babyfinger (2) / I Want My Baby Back (3) / It Takes A Lot To Laugh, It Takes A Train To Cry (3) / **Just A Little Bit** (2) *92* / Love Of A Woman (4) / Magnolia Caboose Babyfinger (2) / Make Me Laugh (4) / Man On The Run (4) / Out Of Focus (4) / Parchment Farm (1) / Peace Of Mind (3) / Pilot (4) / Preacher (4) / Rest At Ease (4) / Rock Me Baby (1) / Sandwich (4) / Second Time Around (1) / **Summertime Blues** (1) *14* / Sun Cycle (2) / Tears By My Bed (4) / West Coast Child Of Sunshine (3) / When It All Gets Old (3)

BLUE MAGIC
Soul vocal group from Philadelphia. Consisted of Theodore Mills (lead vocals), Vernon Sawyer, Wendell Sawyer, Keith Beaton and Richard Pratt.

DEBUT DATE	PEAK POS	WKS CHR	GOLD	ARTIST — Album Title	$	Label & Number
3/16/74	45	34	1	Blue Magic	$10	Atco 7038
12/28/74+	71	13	2	The Magic Of The Blue	$10	Atco 103
10/4/75	50	12	3	Thirteen Blue Magic Lane	$10	Atco 120
9/25/76	170		4	Mystic Dragons	$10	Atco 140

Answer To My Prayer (1) / Born On Halloween (3) / Chasing Rainbows (3) / Freak-N-Stein (4) / Haunted (By Your Love) (3) / I Like You (3) / It's Something About Love (4) / Just Don't Want To Be Lonely (1) / Let Me Be The One (2) / Loneliest House On The Block (4) / Look Me Up (1) / Looking For A Friend (2) / Love Has Found Its Way To Me (2) / Magic Of The Blue (3) / Making Love To A Memory (4) / Maybe Just Maybe (We Can Fall In Love Again) (2) / Mother Funk (4) / Never Get Over You (2) / Rock N Roll Revival (4) / See The Bedroom (4) / Spark Of Love (4) / Spell (1) / Stop And Get A Hold Of Yourself (3) / **Stop To Start** (1) *74* / Stringin' Me Along (2) / Summer Snow (4) / Talking To Myself (2) / Tear It Down (1) / **Three Ring Circus** (2) *36* / To Get Love (You Must Give Love) (4) / We're On The Right Track (3) / Welcome To The Club (1) / What's Come Over Me (1,3) / When Ya Coming Home (3) / You Won't Have To Tell Me Goodbye (2)

BLUE MERCEDES
Pop duo formed in London in 1984: singer David Titlow and keyboardist Duncan Millar.

DEBUT DATE	PEAK POS	WKS CHR	GOLD	ARTIST — Album Title	$	Label & Number
5/14/88	165	5		rich and famous	$8	MCA 42143

Crunchy Love Affaire / Heaven On Earth / I Hate New York / **I Want To Be Your Property** *66* / Love Is The Gun / Run For Your Love / See Want Must Have / Treehouse / Welcome To Lovesville / Your Secret Is Safe With Me

DEBUT DATE	PEAK POS	WKS CHR	GOLD	ARTIST — Album Title	$	Label & Number

BLUE MURDER
British rock trio: guitarist/vocalist John Sykes (Thin Lizzy, Whitesnake), bassist Tony Franklin (The Firm) and drummer Carmine Appice (Vanilla Fudge, Cactus, Rod Stewart and KGB).

| 5/13/89 | **69** | 21 | | Blue Murder .... | **$8** | Geffen 24212 |

Billy
Black-Hearted Woman

Blue Murder
Jelly Roll

Out Of Love
Ptolemy

Riot
Sex Child

Valley Of The Kings

BLUE NILE, The
Scottish melodic pop trio: Paul Buchanan, Robert Bell and Paul Moore. Met at Glasgow University.

| 2/24/90 | **108** | 14 | | Hats .... | **$12** | A&M 5284 |

Downtown Lights
From A Late Night Train

Headlights On The Parade
Let's Go Out Tonight

Over The Hillside
Saturday Night

Seven A.M.

★★234★★ BLUE OYSTER CULT
Hard-rock quintet formed in Long Island, New York in 1970: Donald "Buck Dharma" Roeser (guitar), Eric Bloom (vocal), Allen Lanier (keyboards), and brothers Joe (bass) and Albert Bouchard (drums). Earlier incarnations of band known as Soft White Underbelly, then the Stalk Forrest Group. Drummers Rick Downey and Jimmy Wilcox replaced Albert Bouchard from 1982 until his return to group in 1988. Tommy Zvoncheck filled in for Allen Lanier for a year in 1986. All original members back together since 1988. Bloom is the cousin of New York's shock radio DJ Howard Stern.

5/20/72	**172**	8		1 Blue Oyster Cult	**$10**	Columbia 31063
3/17/73	**122**	13		2 Tyranny And Mutation	**$10**	Columbia 32017
4/27/74	**53**	14	●	3 Secret Treaties	**$10**	Columbia 32858
3/15/75	**22**	13	●	4 On Your Feet Or On Your Knees .... [L]	**$12**	Columbia 33371 [2]
6/19/76	**29**	35	▲	5 Agents Of Fortune	**$8**	Columbia 34164
11/12/77	**43**	14	●	6 Spectres	**$8**	Columbia 35019
9/30/78	**44**	12	▲	7 Some Enchanted Evening .... [L]	**$8**	Columbia 35563
7/7/79	**44**	17		8 Mirrors	**$8**	Columbia 36009
7/12/80	**34**	16		9 Cultosaurus Erectus	**$8**	Columbia 36550
7/11/81	**24**	31	●	10 Fire Of Unknown Origin	**$8**	Columbia 37389
5/15/82	**29**	19		11 Extraterrestrial Live .... [L]	**$10**	Columbia 37946 [2]
11/26/83+	**93**	16		12 The Revolution By Night...............................	**$8**	Columbia 38947
2/22/86	**63**	14		13 Club Ninja..	**$8**	Columbia 39979
8/20/88	**122**	8		14 Imaginos	**$8**	Columbia 40618

After Dark (10)
Are You ..see: R. U.
Astronomy (3,7,14)
Baby Ice Dog (2)
Beat 'Em Up (13)
Before The Kiss, A Redcap (1,4)
Black Blade (9,11)
Blue Oyster Cult (1)
Born To Be Wild (4)
Buck's Boogie (4)
Burnin' For You (10,11) *40*
Cagey Cretins (3)
Career Of Evil (3)
Celestial The Queen (6)
Cities The Flame With Rock And Roll (1,4,11)
Dancin' In The Ruins (13)
Deadline (9)
Death Valley Nights (6)
Debbie Denise (5)
Del Rio's Song (14)
Divine Wind (9)

Dr. Music (8,11)
Dominance And Submission (3,11)
(Don't Fear) The Reaper (5,7,11) *12*
Don't Turn Your Back (10)
Dragon Lady (12)
E.T.I. (Extra Terrestrial Intelligence) (5,7,11)
Eyes On Fire (9)
Fallen Angel (9)
Feel The Thunder (12)
Fire Of Unknown Origin (10)
Fireworks (6)
Flaming Telepaths (3)
Godzilla (6,7,11)
Goin' Through The Motions (6)
Golden Age Of Leather (6)
Great Sun Jester (8)
Harvester Of Eyes (3,4)
Heavy Metal: The Black And Silver (10)

Hot Rails To Hell (2,4,11)
Hungry Boys (9)
I Ain't Got You (4)
I Am The One You Warned Me Of (14)
I Am The Storm (8)
I Love The Night (6)
I'm On The Lamb But I Ain't No Sheep (1)
Imaginos (14)
In The Presence Of Another World (14)
In Thee (8) *74*
Joan Crawford (10,11)
Kick Out The Jams (7)
Les Invisibles (14)
Let Go (12)
Light Years Of Love (12)
Lips In The Hills (9)
Lonely Teardrops (8)
ME 262 (3,4)
Madness To The Method (13)
Magna Of Illusion (14)

Make Rock Not War (13)
Marshall Plan (9)
Mirrors (8)
Mistress Of The Salmon Salt (Quicklime Girl) (2)
Monsters (9)
Moon Crazy (8)
Morning Final (5)
Nosferatu (6)
O.D.'d On Life Itself (2)
Perfect Water (13)
R. U. Ready 2 Rock (6,7)
Red & The Black (2,4,11)
Redeemed (1)
Revenge Of Vera Gemini (5)
Roadhouse Blues (11)
Screams (1)
Searchin' For Celine (6)
7 Screaming Diz-Busters (2,4)
Shadow Of California (12)
Shadow Warrior (13)

She's As Beautiful As A Foot (1)
Shooting Shark (12) *83*
Siege And Investiture Of Baron Von Frankenstein's Castle At Weisseria (14)
Sinful Love (5)
Sole Survivor (10)
Spy In The House Of The Night (13)
Stairway To The Stars (1)
Subhuman (3,4)
Take Me Away (12)
Tattoo Vampire (5)
Teen Archer (2)
Tenderloin (5)
Then Came The Last Days Of May (1,4)
This Ain't The Summer Of Love (5)
Transmaniacon (1)
True Confessions (5)
Unknown Tongue (9)

Veins (12)
Vengeance (The Pact) (10)
Veteran Of The Psychic Wars (10,11)
Vigil, The (8)
We Gotta Get Out Of This Place (7)
When The War Comes (13)
White Flags (13)
Wings Wetted Down (2)
Workshop Of The Telescopes (1)
You're Not The One (I Was Looking For) (8)

BLUE RIDGE RANGERS, The — see FOGERTY, John

BLUES BROTHERS
Joliet "Jake" (John Belushi; b: 1/24/49, Wheaton, Illinois; d: 3/5/82) and Elwood Blues (Dan Aykroyd; b: 7/1/52, Ottawa, Ontario); originally created for TV's *Saturday Night Live*.

| 12/23/78+ | **1**[1] | 29 | ▲[2] | 1 **Briefcase Full Of Blues** .... | **$12** | Atlantic 19217 |
| 6/28/80 | **13** | 19 | ● | 2 The Blues Brothers .... [S] | **$10** | Atlantic 16017 |

with Aretha Franklin, James Brown and Ray Charles

| 12/27/80+ | **49** | 12 | | 3 Made In America .... [L] | **$10** | Atlantic 16025 |
| 1/9/82 | **143** | 3 | | 4 Best Of The Blues Brothers .... [G] | **$10** | Atlantic 19331 |

"B" Movie Box Car Blues (1,4)
Do You Love Me (medley) (3)
Everybody Needs Somebody To Love (3)
Expressway To Your Heart (4)
Flip, Flop And Fly (1,4)

From The Bottom (3)
Funky Broadway (medley) (3)
Gimme Some Lovin' (2,4) *18*
Going Back To Miami (3,4)
Green Onions (1)
Groove Me (1)
Guilty (3)

Hey Bartender (1)
I Ain't Got You (3)
I Can't Turn You Loose (1)
I Don't Know (1,4)
(I Got Every Thing I Need) Almost (1)
Jailhouse Rock (2)
Messin' With The Kid (1)

Minnie The Moocher (2)
Mother Popcorn (You Got To Have A Mother For Me) (medley) (3)
Old Landmark (2)
Perry Mason Theme (3)
Peter Gunn Theme (2)
Rawhide, Theme From (2)

Riot In Cell Block Number Nine (3)
Rubber Biscuit (1,4) *37*
Shake Your Tailfeather (2)
She Caught The Katy (2,4)
Shot Gun Blues (1)
Soul Finger (medley) (3)
Soul Man (1,4) *14*

Sweet Home Chicago (2)
Think (2)
Who's Making Love (3) *39*

BLUES IMAGE
Tampa, Florida rock quintet led by Mike Pinera, a featured guitarist with Iron Butterfly in 1970.

| 8/16/69 | **112** | 9 | | 1 Blues Image .... | **$15** | Atco 300 |
| 4/25/70 | **147** | 13 | | 2 Open .... | **$15** | Atco 317 |

Clean Love (2)
Consuelate (2)
(Do You Have) Somethin' To Say (1)
Fugue U (2)

In Front Behind You (1)
La Bamba (2)
Lay Your Sweet Love On Me (1)
Lazy Day Blues (1)

Leaving My Troubles Behind (1)
Love Is The Answer (2)
Outside Was Night (1)
Parchman Farm (2)

Pay My Dues (2)
Reality Does Not Inspire (1)
Ride Captain Ride (2) *4*
Running The Water (2)
Take Me (2)

Take Me To The Sunrise (1)
Wrath Of Daisey (2)
Yesterday Could Be Today (1)

BLUES MAGOOS

Bronx, New York psychedelic rock quintet led by singer/guitarist Peppy Castro (real name: Emil Thielhelm). Originally known as the Bloos Magoos. Castro later became lead singer of Balance.

12/3/66+	**21**	32	1	Psychedelic Lollipop	**$15**	Mercury 61096
4/22/67	**74**	16	2	Electric Comic Book..	**$25**	Mercury 61104

Albert Common Is Dead (2)	I'll Go Crazy (1)	Love Seems Doomed (1)	Rush Hour (2)	Take My Love (2)	Tobacco Road (1)
Baby, I Want You (2)	Let's Get Together (2)	**One By One** (1) 71	She's Coming Home (1)	**That's All Folks** (2)	**(We Ain't Got) Nothin' Yet**
Gloria (2)	Life Is Just A Cher	**Pipe Dream** (2) 60	Sometimes I Think About (1)	**There's A Chance We Can**	(1) **5**
Gotta Get Away (1)	O'Bowlies (2)	Queen Of My Nights (1)	Summer Is The Man (2)	**Make It** (2) 81	Worried Life Blues (1)

BLUES PROJECT, The

New York City blues band formed by Danny Kalb (guitar) and Roy Blumenfeld (drums). Vocalist Tommy Flanders left group after first LP. Guitarist Steve Katz and organist Al Kooper took over vocals. Katz and Kooper left to form Blood, Sweat & Tears in 1968.

5/21/66	**77**	21	1	Live At the Cafe Au Go Go.................................[L]	**$15**	Verve F. 3000
12/17/66+	**52**	36	2	Projections...[L]	**$20**	Verve Folk. 3008
10/7/67	**71**	11	3	The Blues Project Live At Town Hall ....[L]	**$15**	Verve F. 3025
8/9/69	**199**	2	4	Best Of The Blues Project ....[G]	**$15**	Verve F. 3077

Alberta (1)	Flute Thing (2,3,4)	I Want To Be Your Driver	**No Time Like The Right**	Violets Of Dawn (1,4)	Who Do You Love (1)
Back Door Man (1)	Fly Away (2)	(1)	**Time** (3,4) 96	Wake Me, Shake Me (2,3,4)	You Can't Catch Me (2)
Caress Me Baby (2)	Goin' Down Louisiana (1)	Jelly Jelly Blues (1)	Spoonful (1)	Way My Baby Walks (1)	You Go, And I'll Go With
Catch The Wind (1)	I Can't Keep From Crying	Love Will Endure (3)	Steve's Song (2,4)	Where There's Smoke,	You (1)
Cheryl's Going Home (2,4)	(2,3,4)	Mean Old Southern (3)	Two Trains Running (2)	There's Fire (3)	

BLUE SWEDE

Swedish pop sextet — Bjorn Skifs, lead singer.

4/6/74	**80**	17		Hooked On A Feeling...	**$10**	EMI 11286

Destiny	**Hooked On A Feeling** 1	Never My Love 7	**Silly Milly** 71	(There's) Always Something	Working In The Coal Mine
Gotta Have Your Love	Lonely Sunday Afternoon	Pinewood Rally	Something's Burning	There To Remind Me	

BLUES TRAVELER

Blues-rock band: John Popper (vocals), Chan Kinchla, Bobby Sheehan and Brendan Hill.

3/2/91	**136**	12	1	Blues Traveler..	**$12**	A&M 5308
9/21/91	**125**	5	2	Travelers & Thieves...	**$12**	A&M 5373

All In The Groove (2)	But Anyway (1)	Gotta Get Mean (1)	Mulling It Over (1)	Slow Change (1)	Sweet Talking Hippie (1)
Alone (1)	Crystal Flame (1)	I Have My Moments (2)	100 Years (1)	Support Your Local Emperor	Tiding, The (2)
Bagheera (2)	Dropping Some NYC (1)	Ivory Tusk (2)	Onslaught (2)	(2)	Warmer Days (1)
Best Part (2)	Gina (1)	Mountain Cry (1)	Optimistic Thought (2)	Sweet Pain (2)	What's For Breakfast (2)

BOBBY & THE MIDNITES

Rock quintet led by Bob Weir (Grateful Dead).

11/21/81	**158**	7	1	Bobby & The Midnites..	**$8**	Arista 9568
8/25/84	**166**	4	2	Where the Beat Meets the Street.............................	**$8**	Columbia 39276

Ain't That Peculiar (2)	Far Away (1)	(I Want To) Fly Away (1)	Lifeguard (2)	She's Gonna Win Your	Where The Beat Meets The
Book Of Rules (1)	Festival (1)	(I Want To Live In) America	Lifeline (2)	Heart (2)	Street (2)
Carry Me (1)	Gloria Monday (2)	(2)	Me, Without You (1)	Thunder & Lightning (2)	
Falling (2)	Haze (1)	Josephine (1)	Rock In The 80's (2)	Too Many Losers (1)	

BOBBY JIMMY & THE CRITTERS

Los Angeles comic rap group. Bobby Jimmy is standup comedian Russ Parr. He also worked as a DJ at KDAY-AM in Los Angeles. The Critters included the Arabian Prince.

11/29/86	**200**	1		Roaches: The Beginning..................................... [N]	**$8**	Macola 0933

Bag Bobby Jimmy Jam	Bring It On Home	New York Rapper	Rush It
Big Butt	Gotta Party	Roaches	We Like Ugly Women

BOBO, Willie

Latin-jazz percussionist. Born William Correa on 2/28/34 in New York City of Puerto Rican heritage; died on 9/15/83. Tutored by Mongo Santamaria in 1948. Joined Tito Puente's band in 1954. Also played with Carl Tjader.

2/26/66	**137**	8		Spanish Grease.. [I]	**$15**	Verve 8631

Blind, Man, Blind Man	Blues In The Closet	Haitian Lady	It's Not Unusual [includes 2	Nessa	Shot Gun (medley)
(medley)	Elation	Hurt So Bad	versions]	Our Day Will Come	Spanish Grease

BoDEANS

Rock group from Waukesha, Wisconsin fronted by guitarists/vocalists Sammy Llanas and Kurt Neumann, with Bob Griffin and Guy Hoffman. In 1989, Hoffman left and Michael Ramos and Danny Gayol joined.

6/7/86	**115**	19	1	Love & Hope & Sex & Dreams	**$8**	Slash 25403
10/10/87	**86**	20	2	Outside Looking In..	**$8**	Slash 25629
				produced by Jerry Harrison (Talking Heads)		
7/22/89	**94**	13	3	home.	**$8**	Slash 25876
4/20/91	**105**	5	4	Black And White	**$12**	Slash 26487

Angels (1)	Do I Do (4)	Forever Young (The Wild	Lookin' For Me Somewhere	Red River (3)	Take It Tomorrow (2)
Any Given Day (4)	Don't Be Lonely (2)	Ones) (2)	(1)	Rickshaw Riding (1)	That's All (1)
Bad For You (4)	Dreams (2)	Going Home (4)	Misery (1)	Say About Love (2)	True Devotion (4)
Ballad Of Jenny Rae (2)	Fadeaway (2)	Good Things (4)	Naked (2)	Say You Will (1)	Ultimately (4)
Beaujolais (3)	Far Far Away From My	Good Work (3)	No One (3)	She's A Runaway (1)	What It Feels Like (2)
Beautiful Rain (3)	Heart (2)	Hand In Hand (3)	Only Love (2)	Someday (3)	When The Love Is Good (4)
Black, White And Blood Red	Fire In The Hole (3)	Hell Of A Chance (4)	Paradise (4)	Still The Night (1)	Worlds Away (1)
(4)	Forever On My Mind (4)	Long Hard Day (4)	Pick Up The Pieces (2)	Strangest Kind (1)	You Don't Get Much (3)
Brand New (3)					

BODY COUNT

Speed-metal band formed by rapper Ice-T (vocals) and Ernie-C (guitar), with D-Roc (guitar), Mooseman (bass) and Beatmaster V (drums). All are alumni of Crenshaw High School in South Central Los Angeles.

4/18/92	**26**	20	●	Body Count	**$12**	Sire 26878

national controversy over album due to lyrics of the track "Cop Killer" — releases of album from August on replaced "Cop Killer" with "Freedom Of Speech"

BODY COUNT — Cont'd

Body Count	Bowels Of The Devil	Evil Dick	Momma's Gotta Die Tonight	Voodoo
Body Count Anthem	C Note	Freedom Of Speech	There Goes The	Winner Loses
Body Count's In The House	Cop Killer	KKK Bitch	Neighborhood	

BOFILL, Angela
Born in West Bronx, New York in 1954 to a French-Cuban father and Puerto Rican mother. Studied voice at Hartford Conservatory and at Manhattan School Of Music. Performed with Dizzy Gillespie and Cannonball Adderley. Featured vocalist for the Dance Theater of Harlem at age 22.

DEBUT	PEAK	WKS		ALBUM	$	LABEL
2/17/79	47	26		1 Angie	$10	GRP 5000
11/3/79+	34	33		2 Angel of the Night	$10	GRP 5501
11/21/81	61	22		3 Something About You	$8	Arista 9576
2/12/83	40	32		4 Too Tough	$8	Arista 9616
11/26/83+	81	21		5 Teaser	$8	Arista 8198

Accept Me (I'm Not A Girl Anymore) (4)	Crazy For Him (5)	Love You Too Much (4)	Rainbow Inside My Heart (4)	Three Blind Mice (3)	You Could Come Take Me Home (4)
Ain't Nothing Like The Real Thing (4)	Feelin's Love (2)	Nothin' But A Teaser (5)	Rough Times (1)	Time To Say Goodbye (3)	You Should Know By Now (3)
Angel Of The Night (2)	Gotta Make It Up To You (5)	On And On (3)	Share Your Love (1)	Tonight I Give In (4)	You're A Special Part Of Me (5)
Baby, I Need Your Love (1)	Holdin' Out For Love (3)	Only Love (3)	Something About You (3)	Too Tough (4)	
Break It To Me Gently (3)	I Can See It In Your Eyes (4)	Only Thing I Would Wish For (1)	Song For A Rainy Day (4)	Tropical Love (3)	
Call Of The Wild (5)	I Do Love You (3)	Penetration (4)	Special Delivery (5)	Under The Moon And Over The Sky (1)	
Children Of The World United (1)	I Try (2)	People Make The World Go 'Round (2)	Still A Thrill (5)	Voyage, The (2)	
	I'm On Your Side (5)	Rainbow Child (Little Pas) (4)	Stop Look Listen (3)	What I Wouldn't Do (For The Love Of You) (2)	
	Is This A Dream (4)		Summer Days (1)		
	Love To Last (2)		This Time I'll Be Sweeter (1)		

BOGERT, Tim — see BECK, Jeff

BOGGUSS, Suzy
Country singer. Born on 12/30/56 in Aledo, Illinois.

2/1/92	83	53	●	1 Aces	$12	Capitol 95847
10/31/92	116	15↑		2 Voices In The Wind	$12	Liberty 98585

Aces (1)	Eat At Joe's (1)	Let Goodbye Hurt (1)	Music On The Wind (1)	Save Yourself (1)
Cold Day In July (2)	Heartache (2)	Letting Go (1,2)	Other Side Of The Hill (2)	Someday Soon (1)
Don't Wanna (2)	How Come You Go To Her (2)	Love Goes Without Saying (2)	Outbound Plane (1)	Still Hold On (1)
Drive South (2)	In The Day (2)	Lovin' A Hurricane (2)	Part Of Me (1)	Yellow River Road (1)

BOHANNON, Hamilton
Born on 3/7/42 in Newnan, Georgia. Stevie Wonder's drummer from 1965-67.

8/12/78	58	19		Summertime Groove	$10	Mercury 3728

I Wonder Why	Let's Start The Dance	Listen To The Children Play	Me And The Gang	Street Dance	Summertime Groove

BOHN, Rudi, and his Band
German conductor of polkas.

10/16/61	38	9		Percussive Oompah .... [I]	$12	London P. 4 44009

Accordion Joe	Good-Bye	In Munchen Steht Ein	Mack The Knife-March	Too Fat Polka
Auf Wiederseh'n Sweetheart	Happy Wanderer	Hofbrauhaus	O Du Lieber Augustin	Trink, Trink, Bruderlein,
Beer Barrel Polka		Liechtensteiner Polka	Pennsylvania Polka	Trink

BOLIN, Tommy
Guitarist with Zephyr, James Gang and Deep Purple. Born in Sioux City, Iowa in 1951. Died of a drug overdose on 12/4/76.

12/20/75+	96	14		1 Teaser	$10	Nemperor 436
10/2/76	98	8		2 Private Eyes	$10	Columbia 34329

Bustin' Out For Rosey (2)	Hello, Again (2)	People, People (1)	Someday Will Bring Our	Wild Dogs (1)
Dreamer (1)	Homeward Strut (1)	Post Toastee (2)	Love Home (2)	You Told Me That You Loved
Grind, The (1)	Lotus (1)	Savannah Woman (1)	Sweet Burgundy (2)	Me (2)
Gypsy Soul (2)	Marching Powder (1)	Shake The Devil (2)	Teaser (1)	

★★449★★ BOLTON, Michael
Born Michael Bolotin on 2/26/54 in New Haven, Connecticut. Lead singer of Blackjack in the late '70s. Began recording as Michael Bolton in 1983.

5/7/83	89	13	●	1 Michael Bolton	$8	Columbia 38537
10/10/87+	46	41	▲	2 The Hunger	$8	Columbia 40473
7/22/89+	3	186↑▲⁴		3 Soul Provider	$8	Columbia 45012
5/11/91	1¹	92↑▲⁶		4 Time, Love & Tenderness	$12	Columbia 46771
10/17/92	1¹	17↑▲³		5 Timeless (The Classics)	$12	Columbia 52783

Back In My Arms Again (1)	**Georgia On My Mind** (3) 36	It's Only My Heart (3)	She Did The Same Thing (1)	**Time, Love And**
Bring It On Home To Me (5)	Gina (2)	Knock On Wood (5)	Since I Fell For You (5)	**Tenderness** (4) 7
Can't Hold On, Can't Let Go (1)	Hold On, I'm Comin' (5)	Love Cuts Deep (3)	**(Sittin' On) The Dock Of**	To Love Somebody (5)
Carrie (1)	Hometown Hero (1)	**Love Is A Wonderful Thing**	**The Bay** (2) 11	Walt On Love (2) 79
Drift Away (5)	Hot Love (2)	(4) 4	**Soul Provider** (3) 17	Walk Away (2)
Fighting For My Life (1)	**How Am I Supposed To**	**Missing You Now** (4) 12	Stand Up For Love (3)	We're Not Makin' Love
Fools Game (1) 82	**Live Without You** (3) 1	New Love (4)	Steel Bars (4)	Anymore (4)
Forever Isn't Long Enough (4)	**How Can We Be Lovers**	Now That I Found You (4)	Take A Look At My Face (2)	**When A Man Loves A**
From Now On (3)	(3) 3	Paradise (1)	**That's What Love Is All**	**Woman** (1) 1
	Hunger, The (2)	Reach Out I'll Be There (5)	**About** (2) 19	**When I'm Back On My**
	I Almost Believed You (1)	Save Me (4)		**Feet Again** (3) 7
				White Christmas (5)
				Yesterday (5)
				You Send Me (5)
				You Wouldn't Know Love (3)
				You're All That I Need (2)

BOND, Angelo
R&B singer from Detroit.

8/2/75	179	2		Bondage	$10	ABC 889

Eve	He Gained The World (But	I Love You For What You Are	Man Can't Serve Two	Reach For The Moon (Poor	What's Bad About Feeling
Goodbye My Love	Lost His Soul)	I Never Sang For My Baby	Masters	People)	Good 64662

BOND, Johnny
Born Cyrus Whitfield Bond on 6/1/15 in Enville, Oklahoma; died of a heart attack on 6/12/78. Country singer/songwriter/actor/author; worked on radio from age 19. Appeared with Jimmy Wakely in 1937 and joined Gene Autry's Melody Ranch in 1940. Appeared in over 50 movies.

5/29/65	142	3		Ten Little Bottles .... [N]	$15	Starday 333

DEBUT DATE	PEAK POS	WKS CHR	G O L D	ARTIST — Album Title	$	Label & Number

BOND, Johnny — Cont'd

Barrel House Bessie	Judge Roy Bean's Court	New Year's Day (Tall Tale)	Sick, Sober, And Sorry	Three Sheets In The Wind
Dang Hangover (Tall Tale)	(Tall Tale)	Sadie Was A Lady	**10 Little Bottles** *(includes 2 versions) 43*	Winter Blizzard (Tall Tale)

BONDS, Gary U.S.
Born Gary Anderson on 6/6/39 in Jacksonville, Florida. To Norfolk, Virginia in the mid-1950s. Signed to Legrand by Frank Guida. Wrote "Friend Don't Take Her," hit for Johnny Paycheck in 1972.

8/7/61	**6**	28		1 Dance 'til Quarter To Three	$60	Legrand 3001
				U.S. BONDS		
5/2/81	**27**	20		2 Dedication	$8	EMI America 17051
6/26/82	**52**	17		3 On The Line	$8	EMI America 17068

above 2 produced by Bruce Springsteen and Steve Van Zant

All I Need (3)	Dedication (2)	I Know Why Dreamers Cry	Love's On The Line (3)	Please Forgive Me (1)	That's All Right (1)
Angelyne (3)	Don't Go To Strangers (1)	(1)	Minnie The Moocher (3)	Pretender, The (2)	**This Little Girl** (2) *11*
Bring Her Back (3)	From A Buick 6 (2)	It's Only Love (2)	**New Orleans** (1) *6*	**Quarter To Three** (1) *1*	Trip To The Moon (1)
Cecilia (1)	Hold On (To What You Got)	**Jole Blon** (2) *65*	Not Me (1)	Rendezvous (3)	Turn The Music Down (3)
Club Soul City (3)	(3)	Just Like A Child (2)	One Million Tears (1)	**School Is Out** (1) *5*	Way Back When (2)
Daddy's Come Home (2)		Last Time (2)	**Out Of Work** (3) *21*	Soul Deep (3)	Your Love (2)

BONEY M
Vocal group created in Germany by producer/composer Frank Farian. Farian sang solo on first recording in 1975, group formed later. Consisted of Marcia Barrett, Maizie Williams, Liz Mitchell and Bobby Farrell. All were from the West Indies. Farian created the Far Corporation in 1986 and Milli Vanilli in 1988.

| 9/2/78 | **134** | 10 | | Nightflight To Venus .... | $8 | Sire 6062 |

Brown Girl In The Ring	Heart Of Gold	Never Change Lovers In The	Nightflight To Venus	Rasputin'	Voodoo Night
He Was A Steppenwolf	King Of The Road	Middle Of The Night	Painter Man	**Rivers Of Babylon** *30*	

BONHAM
British hard-rock quartet led by drummer Jason Bonham, the son of Led Zeppelin's drummer, the late John Bonham. Includes Daniel MacMaster (vocals), Ian Hatton (guitar) and John Smithson (keyboards, bass).

| 10/7/89 | **38** | 29 | ● | The Disregard Of Timekeeping .... | $8 | WTG 45009 |

Bringing Me Down	Disregard Of Timekeeping	Dreams	Holding On Forever	Playing To Win	**Wait For You** *55*
Cross Me And See	Don't Walk Away	Guilty	Just Another Day	Room For Us All	

★★287★★ BON JOVI
Hard-rock quintet formed in Sayreville, New Jersey: Jon Bon Jovi (b: 3/2/62; actual spelling: Bongiovi), lead vocals), Richie Sambora (b: 7/11/59; guitar), Dave Bryan (b: 2/7/62; keyboards), Alec John Such (b: 11/14/56; bass) and Tico Torres (b: 10/7/53; drums).

2/25/84	**43**	86		1 Bon Jovi	$8	Mercury 814982
5/18/85	**37**	104	▲	2 7800 Fahrenheit	$8	Mercury 824509
				title refers to the temperature of an exploding volcano		
9/13/86	**1**[8]	94	▲[9]	3 Slippery When Wet	$8	Mercury 830264
10/8/88	**1**[4]	76	▲[5]	4 New Jersey	$8	Mercury 836345
8/25/90	**3**	41	▲[2]	5 Blaze Of Glory/Young Guns II ....[S]	$12	Mercury 846473
				JON BON JOVI		
				songs from and songs inspired by the film Young Guns II		
11/21/92	**5**	12↑▲		6 Keep The Faith	$12	Jambco 514045

Always Run To You (2)	Come Back (1)	I'll Sleep When I'm Dead (6)	Love For Sale (4)	Secret Dreams (4)	**You Give Love A Bad Name**
Bad Medicine (4) *1*	Dry County (6)	Love Lies (1)	**She Don't Know Me** (1) *48*	(3) *1*
Bang A Drum (5)	Dyin' Ain't Much Of A Livin'	**In And Out Of Love** (2) *69*	**Miracle** (5) *12*	Shot Through The Heart (1)	You Really Got Me Now (5)
Bed Of Roses (6) *40↑*	(5)	In These Arms (6)	Never Say Die (3)	Silent Night (3)	
Billy Get Your Guns (5)	Fear (6)	Justice In The Barrel (5)	Never Say Goodbye (3)	Social Disease (3)	
Blame It On The Love Of	Get Ready (1)	**Keep The Faith** (6) *29*	99 In The Shade (3)	Stick To Your Guns (4)	
Rock & Roll (6)	Guano City (5)	King Of The Mountain (2)	**Only Lonely** (2) *54*	To The Fire (2)	
Blaze Of Glory (5) *1*	Hardest Part Is The Night (2)	**Lay Your Hands On Me**	Price Of Love (2)	Tokyo Road (2)	
Blood Money (5)	Homebound Train (4)	(4) *7*	Raise Your Hands (3)	**Wanted Dead Or Alive** (3) *7*	
Blood On Blood (4)	I Believe (6)	Let It Rock (3)	Ride Cowboy Ride (4)	Wild In The Streets (3)	
Born To Be My Baby (4) *3*	I Want You (6)	Little Bit Of Soul (6)	Roulette (3)	Wild Is The Wind (4)	
Breakout (1)	I'd Die For You (3)	**Livin' On A Prayer** (3) *1*	**Runaway** (1) *39*	Without Love (3)	
Burning For Love (1)	I'll Be There For You (4) *1*	Living In Sin (4) *9*	Santa Fe (5)	Woman In Love (6)	

BONOFF, Karla
Pop singer/songwriter/pianist. Born on 12/27/52 in Los Angeles.

10/1/77	**52**	40	●	1 Karla Bonoff	$8	Columbia 34672
9/29/79	**31**	26		2 Restless Nights	$8	Columbia 35799
4/3/82	**49**	35		3 Wild Heart Of The Young	$8	Columbia 37444

Baby Don't Go (2) *69*	Flying High (1)	If He's Ever Near (1)	Lose Again (1)	**Please Be The One** (3) *63*	Trouble Again (1)
Dream (3)	Gonna Be Mine (3)	Isn't It Always Love (1)	Loving You (3)	Restless Nights (2)	Water Is Wide (2)
Even If (2)	Home (1)	It Just Takes One (3)	Never Stop Her Heart (2)	Rose In The Garden (1)	When You Walk In The
Faces In The Wind (1)	**I Can't Hold On** (1) *76*	Just Walk Away (1)	Only A Fool (2)	Someone To Lay Down	Room (2)
Falling Star (1)	I Don't Want To Miss You (3)	Letter, The (2)	**Personally** (3) *19*	Beside Me (1)	Wild Heart Of The Young (3)

BONZO DOG BAND
British satirical band. Member Neil Innes was later with The Rutles. Group appeared in the 1967 Beatles film *Magical Mystery Tour*.

| 6/10/72 | **199** | 2 | | Let's Make Up And Be Friendly .... | $12 | United Art. 5584 |

Bad Blood	Fresh Wound	Rawlinson End	Slush	Strain, The	Waiting For The Wardrobe
Don't Get Me Wrong	King Of Scurf	Rusty (Champion Thrust)	Straight From My Heart	Turkeys	

BOOGIE BOYS, The
Harlem-based rap group: William (Boogie Knight) Stroman, Joe (Romeo J.D.) Malloy and Rudy (Lil' Rahiem) Sherrif (left group in 1988).

8/31/85	**53**	17		1 City Life	$8	Capitol 12409
8/9/86	**124**	9		2 Survival Of The Freshest	$8	Capitol 12488
3/19/88	**117**	11		3 Romeo Knight	$8	Capitol 46917

BOOGIE BOYS, The — Cont'd

Always On My Mind (3) • Dealin' With Life (2) • Home Girl (3) • Party Asteroid (1) • Romeo Knight (3) • Starvin' Marvin (2)
Body (3) • Do Or Die (1) • I'm A Lover (3) • Peep It (3) • Run It (2) • This Is Us (3)
Break Dancer (1) • Fly Girl (1) • I'm Comin' (3) • Pit Bull (3) • Runnin' From Your Love (1) • You Ain't Fresh (1)
City Life (1) • Friend Or Foe (2) • Kick It (3) • Pussi Cat (3) • Shake And Break (1)
Colorblind World (2) • Girl Talk (2) • Love List (3) • Rise Up (3) • Share My World (2)

BOOGIE DOWN PRODUCTIONS

Brooklyn-based rap outfit led by Blastmaster KRS One (Kris Parker). Co-founder/DJ Scott "La Rock" Sterling fatally shot on 8/25/87 (age 24) in a scuffle in the Bronx. Rapper Derrick "D-Nice" Jones later recorded solo. Parker is the brother-in-law of female rapper Harmony.

4/30/88	75	23	●	1 By All Means Necessary	$8	Jive 1097
7/22/89	36	17	●	2 Ghetto Music: The Blueprint Of Hip Hop	$8	Jive 1187
8/25/90	32	16	●	3 Edutainment	$12	Jive 1358
				CD includes 3 bonus tracks		
4/6/91	115	7		4 Live Hardcore Worldwide .... [L]	$12	Jive 1425
				recorded live in New York, Paris and London		
3/14/92	42	9		5 Sex And Violence	$12	Jive 41470

Beef (3) • Eye Opener (4) • Lick A Shot (4) • Questions And Answers (5) • Super Hoe (4) • Ya Strugglin' (3)
Blackman In Effect (3) • Ghetto Music (2) • Like A Throttle (4) • Racist, The (3) • T'cha - T'cha (3) • You Must Learn (2)
Blueprint, The (2) • Gimme Dat, (Woy) (2) • Love's Gonna Get'cha • Real Holy Place (5) • 13 And Good (5)
Bo! Bo! Bo! (2,4) • Hip Hop Rules (2) • (Material Love) (2) • Reggae Medley (4) • 30 Cops Or More (3)
Breath Control (2,4) • Homeless, The (3) • My Philosophy (1,4) • Ruff Ruff (5) • Up To Date (4)
Breath Control II (3) • House Nigga's (3,4) • Necessary (1) • Say Gal (5) • We In There (5)
Bridge Is Over (3) • How Not To Get Jerked (5) • Nervous (1) • Self Destruction (4) • Who Are The Pimps? (5)
Build And Destroy (5) • I'm Still #1 (1,4) • 100 Guns (3) • 7 Dee Jays (3) • Who Protects Us From You?
Come To The Teacher (4) • Illegal Business (1) • Original Lyrics (4) • Sex And Violence (5) • (2)
Criminal Minded (4) • Jack Of Spades (2,4) • Original Way (5) • South Bronx (4) • Why Is That? (2,4)
Drug Dealer (5) • Jah Rulez (2) • Part Time Suckers (1) • Stop The Violence (1,4) • World Peace (2)
Duck Down (5) • Jimmy (1,4) • Poetry (4) • Style You Haven't Done Yet • Ya Know The Rules (3,4)
Edutainment (3) • Kenny Parker Show (3) • Poisonous Products (5) • (2) • Ya Slippin' (1)

BOOKER, Bob, & George Foster — see COMEDY section

BOOKER, Chuckii

R&B multi-instrumentalist from Los Angeles. Session keyboard work with Vanessa Williams, Gerald Albright and Troop. Godson of Barry White.

7/22/89	116	10		CHUCKii	$8	Atlantic 81947

(Don't U Know) I Love U • Hotel Happiness (1) • Oh Lover • That's My Honey • Turned Away 42
Heavenly Father • Let Me Love U • Res Q Me • Touch

BOOKER T. & PRISCILLA

Booker T. Jones and wife Priscilla (sister of Rita Coolidge).

8/14/71	106	6		1 Booker T. & Priscilla	$10	A&M 3504 [2]
7/22/72	190	4		2 Home Grown	$10	A&M 4351

Born Under A Bad Sign (2) • Don't Think Twice, It's All • He (1) • Mississippi Voodoo (1) • Sequence, The (2) • Water Brothers (1)
California Girl (1) • Right (2) • Indian Song (1) • Muddy Road (2) • She (1) • Wedding Song (1)
Color Your Mama (2) • Earth Children (1) • Maggie's Farm (2) • Ole Man Trouble (1) • Sister Babe (1) • Who Killed Cock Robin? (2)
Cool Black Dream (1) • For Priscilla (1) • Medley From The Jones • Save Us From Ourselves (2) • Sun Don't Shine (1) • Why (1)
Delta Song (1) • Funny Honey (1) • Ranch (1) • Sea Gull (1) • Sweet Child You're Not
 • • • • Alone (1)

★★397★★ BOOKER T. & THE MG'S

Band formed by sessionmen from Stax Records, Memphis, in 1962. Consisted of Booker T. Jones (b: 11/12/44, Memphis), keyboards; Steve Cropper (b: 10/21/42, Ozark Mountains, Missouri.), guitar; Donald "Duck" Dunn (b: 11/24/41, Memphis), bass; and Al Jackson, Jr. (b: 11/27/34, Memphis; murdered on 10/1/75), drums. MG stands for Memphis Group. Jones was in a band with classmate Maurice White of Earth, Wind & Fire. Cropper and Dunn had been in the Mar-Keys. Much session work, recordings included horns by Andrew Love, Wayne Jackson and Joe Arnold, plus Isaac Hayes, piano. Group disbanded in 1968, and reorganized for a short time in 1973. Cropper and Dunn joined the Blues Brothers. Jones received music degree from Indiana University; married Priscilla Coolidge (sister of Rita); and did production work for Rita Coolidge, Earl Klugh, Bill Withers and Willie Nelson (his *Stardust* album.)

11/10/62+	33	17		1 Green Onions .... [I]	$35	Stax 701
6/24/67	35	29		2 Hip Hug-Her .... [I]	$25	Stax 717
8/26/67	98	4		3 Back To Back .... [I-L]	$15	Stax 720
				THE MAR-KEYS/BOOKER T. & THE MG's includes "Grab This Thing," "Last Night" and "Philly Dog" by The Mar-Keys		
5/18/68	176	4		4 Doin' Our Thing .... [I]	$25	Stax 724
10/19/68	127	9		5 Soul Limbo .... [I]	$15	Stax 2001
11/23/68	167	11		6 The Best Of Booker T. & The MG's .... [G-I]	$12	Atlantic 8202
2/8/69	98	27		7 Uptight .... [S]	$15	Stax 2006
6/14/69	53	18		8 The Booker T. Set .... [I]	$15	Stax 2009
5/2/70	107	15		9 McLemore Avenue .... [I]	$15	Stax 2027
				version of Beatles' *Abbey Road* album; McLemore is the street outside the Stax studios		
11/14/70	132	8		10 Booker T. & The M.G.'s Greatest Hits .... [G-I]	$15	Stax 2033
2/13/71	43	38		11 Melting Pot .... [I]	$15	Stax 2035

Back Home (11) • Born Under A Bad Sign (5) • Doin' Our Thing (4) • Gimme Some Lovin' (solo: • I Can Dig It (4) • Let's Go Get Stoned (4)
Be Young, Be Foolish, Be • Can't Be Still (6) • Double Or Nothing (2) • Booker T. & The MG's] (3) • I Can't Sit Down (1) • Light My Fire (8)
Happy (5) • Carnaby St. (2) • Down At Ralph's Joint (7) • Golden Slumbers (medley) (9) • I Got A Woman (1) • Lonely Avenue (1)
Beat Goes On (4) • Carry That Weight (medley) • Eleanor Rigby (5,10) • Green Onions (1,3,6) **3** • I Want You (medley) (9) • Love Child (8)
Because (medley) (9) • (9) • End, The (medley) (9) • Groovin' (2,6) **21** • I've Never Found A Girl (9) • Mean Mr. Mustard (medley)
Behave Yourself (1) • Chicken Pox (11) • Exodus Song (4) • Hang 'Em High (5,10) **9** • It's Your Thing (8) • (9)
Blue On Green (4) • Children, Don't Get Weary • Expressway (To Your Heart) • Heads Or Tails (5,10) • Johnny, I Love You (7,10) • Meditation (10)
Blues In The Gutter (7) • (7) • (4) • Here Comes The Sun • Kinda Easy Like (1) • Melting Pot (11) **45**
Booker Loo (solo: Booker T. • Cleveland Now (7) • Foxy Lady (8) • (medley) (9) • L.A. Jazz Song (11) • Michelle (8)
 & The MG's] (3) • Come Together (medley) (9) • Fuquawi (11) • Hi Ride (11) • La La Means I Love You (5) • Mo-Onions (1,6) **97**
Booker's Notion (2) • Comin' Home Baby (1) • Get Ready (2) • Hip Hug-Her (2,3,6,10) **37** • Lady Madonna (8) • More (2)
Boot-Leg (6) **58** • Deadwood Dick (7) • • Horse, The (8) • • Mrs. Robinson (8,10) **37**

BOOKER T. & THE MG'S — Cont'd

Never My Love (4)
Ode To Billie Joe (4)
One Who Really Loves You (1)
Outrage [solo: Booker T. & The MG's] (3)
Over Easy (5,10)
Pigmy (2)
Polythene Pam (medley) (9)

Red Beans And Rice (3,6)
Rinky-Dink (1)
Run Tank Run (7)
She Came In Through The Bathroom Window (medley) (9)
She's So Heavy (medley) (9)
Sing A Simple Song (8)

Slim Jenkin's Place (2,6) **70**
Something (9,10) **76**
Soul Dressing (6) **95**
Soul-Limbo (5,10) **17**
Soul Sanction (2)
Stranger On The Shore (1)
Summertime (6)
Sun King (medley) (9)

Sunny (2)
Sunny Monday (11)
(Sweet, Sweet, Baby) Since You've Been Gone (5)
Tank's Lament (7)
This Guy's In Love With You (8)
Tic-Tac-Toe (3,6)
Time Is Tight (7,10) **6**

Twist And Shout (1)
We've Got Johnny Wells (7)
Willow Weep For Me (5)
Woman, A Lover, A Friend (1)
You Don't Love Me (4)
You Keep Me Hanging On (4)
You Never Give Me Your Money (medley) (9)

You're All I Need To Get By (8)

BOOK OF LOVE
Dance-pop quartet from New York and Philadelpha: Susan Ottaviano (lead vocals), Ted Ottaviano (despite same last name, Susan and Ted are not related), Lauren Roselli and Jade Lee.

7/23/88	156	10		1 Lullaby	$8	Sire 25700
2/23/91	174	4		2 Candy Carol	$12	Sire 26389

Alice Everyday (2)
Butterfly (2)
Candy Carol (2)
Champagne Wishes (1)

Counting The Rosaries (2)
Flower Parade (2)
Lullaby (2)
Melt My Heart (1)

Miss Melancholy (2)
Orange Flip (2)
Oranges And Lemons (1)

Pretty Boys And Pretty Girls (1) **90**
Quiver (2)
Sea Of Tranquility (1)

Sunny Day (2)
Tubular Bells (1)
Turn The World (2)
Wall Song (2)

Witchcraft (1)
With A Little Love (1)
You Look Through Me (1)

BOOM, Taka
Former member of The Undisputed Truth and Glass Family. Real name: Yvonne Stevens. Sister of Chaka Khan and Mark Stevens (of the Jamaica Boys).

6/9/79	171	4		Taka Boom	$8	Ariola 50041

Anything You Want
Cloud Dancer

Dance Baby Dance
Dance Like You Do At Home

Night Dancin' 74
Red Hot

Troubled Waters
You're My Everything

BOOMTOWN RATS, The
Post-punk sextet formed in Dun Laoghaire, Ireland in 1975. Leader Bob Geldof organized Band Aid.

3/3/79	112	13		1 A Tonic For The Troops	$8	Columbia 35750
12/1/79+	103	16		2 The Fine Art Of Surfacing	$8	Columbia 36248
2/21/81	116	8		3 Mondo Bongo	$8	Columbia 37062
5/25/85	188	4		4 In The Long Grass	$8	Columbia 39335

Another Piece Of Red (3)
Another Sad Story (4)
Banana Republic (3)
Blind Date (1)
Diamond Smiles (2)
Don't Believe What You Read (1)
Don't Talk To Me (3)
Drag Me Down (4)

Elephants Graveyard (3)
Go Man Go (3)
Hard Times (4)
Having My Picture Taken (2)
Hold Of Me (4)
Hurt Hurts (3)
I Don't Like Mondays (2) 73
(I Never Loved) Eva Braun (1)
Icicle In The Sun (3)

Joey's On The Street Again (1)
Keep It Up (2)
Like Clockwork (1)
Living In An Island (1)
Lucky (4)
Mary Of The 4th Form (1)
Me And Howard Hughes (1)
Mood Mambo (3)

Nice 'N' Neat (2)
Nothing Happened Today (2)
Over Again (4)
Please Don't Go (3)
Rain (4)
Rat Trap (1)
She's So Modern (1)
Sleep (Fingers' Lullaby) (2)

Someone's Looking At You (2)
Straight Up (3)
This Is My Room (3)
Tonight (4)
Under Their Thumb...Is Under My Thumb (3)
Up All Night (3)
Up Or Down (4)

When The Night Comes (2)
Wind Chill Factor (Minus Zero) (2)

BOONE, Daniel
English singer/songwriter. Real name: Peter Lee Stirling.

10/7/72	142	9		Beautiful Sunday	$10	Mercury 649

Annabelle 86
Beautiful Sunday 15

Crying
Darling Honey

Funny Little Things
Home Again

In Love Again
In Ohio

Sleepy Head
Sunshine Lover

Sweet Joanna
Taste The Wine

BOONE, Debby
Born on 9/22/56 in Hackensack, New Jersey. Third daughter of Pat and Shirley Boone and granddaughter of Red Foley. Worked with the Boone Family from 1969, sang with sisters in the Boones' gospel quartet. Went solo in 1977. Winner of three Grammys including Best New Artist of 1977. Popular Contemporary Christian artist. Married Gabriel Ferrer, the son of Rosemary Clooney and Jose Ferrer, in 1982.

10/29/77	6	37	▲	1 **You Light Up My Life**	$10	Warner 3118
8/12/78	147	5		2 Midstream	$10	Warner 3130

Another Goodbye (2)
Baby, I'm Yours (1) flip
California (2) 50
Come Share My Love (2)
Don't You Want Me Anymore (1)

End Of The World (2)
From Me To You (1)
God Knows (2) 74
Hasta Manana (1)
Hey Everybody (1)

I'd Rather Leave While I'm In Love (2)
If Ever I See You Again (2)
It Was Such A Good Day (2)
It's Just A Matter Of Time (1)
Micol's Theme (1)

Oh, No, Not My Baby (2)
Rock And Roll Song (1)
What Becomes Of My World (2)
When I Look At You (My Love) (1)

When It's Over (2)
When The Lovelight Starts Shining Through His Eyes (1)
When You're Loved (2)
You Light Up My Life (1) 1

Your Love Broke Through (1)

BOONE, Pat
★★**143**★★
Born Charles Eugene Boone on 6/1/34 in Jacksonville, Florida. To Tennessee in 1936. Direct descendant of Daniel Boone. Married country singer Red Foley's daughter, Shirley, on 11/7/53. Won on *Ted Mack's Amateur Hour* and *Arthur Godfrey's Talent Scouts* in 1954. First recorded for Republic Records in 1954. Graduated from New York's Columbia University in 1958. Hosted own TV show, *The Pat Boone-Chevy Showroom*, 1957-60. Appeared in 15 films. Toured with wife and daughters Cherry, Linda, Debby and Laura in the mid-1960s. Recording artist Nick Todd is his younger brother. Pat's trademark: white buck shoes.

10/27/56	14	4		1 Howdy!	$20	Dot 3030
6/24/57	13	7		2 A Closer Walk with Thee ... [EP]	$20	Dot 1056
				7" EP (four sacred songs)		
7/8/57	19	3		3 "Pat"	$20	Dot 3050
9/2/57	5	5		4 **Four By Pat** ... [EP]	$20	Dot 1057
				7" EP (four songs)		
10/7/57	20	2		5 Pat Boone	$20	Dot 3012
				Pat's first album		
10/21/57	3	36	●	6 **Pat's Great Hits** ... [G]	$20	Dot 3071
12/23/57+	12	13		7 April Love ... [S]	$20	Dot 9000
				includes 8 instrumentals by Lionel Newman: "Main Title," "First Meeting," "Tugfire," "Tugfire's Escape," "Sulky Race," "Lovers' Quarrel," "Tugfire's Illness" and "Finale"		
12/23/57	21	4		8 Hymns We Love	$20	Dot 3068
7/28/58	2[1]	32		9 **Star Dust**	$20	Dot 3118
11/24/58	13	2		10 Yes Indeed!	$20	Dot 3121
7/13/59	17	11		11 Tenderly	$20	Dot 3180

DEBUT DATE	PEAK POS	WKS CHR	GOLD	ARTIST — Album Title	$	Label & Number
				BOONE, Pat — Cont'd		
5/23/60	**26**	3		12 Moonglow	$15	Dot 3270
7/17/61	**29**	30		13 Moody River	$15	Dot 3384
1/6/62	**39**	2		14 White Christmas ....[X]	$15	Dot 3222
9/15/62	**66**	13		15 Pat Boone's Golden Hits ....[G]	$15	Dot 3455
12/29/62	**116**	1		16 White Christmas ....[X-R]	$15	Dot 3222

Christmas charts: 50/'66

Adeste Fideles (14)
Again (12)
Ain't Nobody Here But Us Chickens (3)
Ain't That A Shame (5) *1*
Alabam (15) *47*
All I Do Is Dream Of You (1)
American Beauty Rose (10)
Anastasia (6) *37*
Angel On My Shoulder (13)
Anniversary Song (9)
April Love (7) *1*
At My Front Door (Crazy Little Mama) (5) *7*
Autumn Leaves (9)
Because Of You (1)
Beg Your Pardon (1)
Begin The Beguine (1)
Bentonville Fair (7)
Bernardine (6) *14*
Beyond The Sunset (8) *71*
Big Cold Wind (15) *19*
Blue Moon (13)
Blueberry Hill (9)
Cathedral In The Pines (4)
Chains Of Love (6) *10*
Chattanooga Shoe Shine Boy (1)
Clover In The Meadow (7)
Cold, Cold Heart (9)
Corinna, Corinna (13)
Dear John (15) *44*
Deep Purple (9)
Do It Yourself (7)

Don't Forbid Me (6) *1*
Don't Worry 'Bout Me (10)
Ebb Tide (9)
Ev'ry Little Thing (1)
Fascination (11)
First Noel (14)
Five, Ten, Fifteen Hours (3)
Flip, Flop And Fly (3)
For A Penny (15) *23*
Forgive Me (1)
Friendly Persuasion (Thee I Love) (6) *5*
Gee Whittakers! (5) *19*
Georgia On My Mind (13)
Girl Of My Dreams (12)
Give Me A Gentle Girl (7)
God Rest Ye Merry, Gentlemen (14)
Gone Fishin' (10)
Great Pretender (13)
Hands Across The Table (12)
Harbor Lights (1)
Hark! The Herald Angels Sing (14)
Have Thine Own Way, Lord (8)
He'll Understand (And Say "Well Done") (8)
Heartaches (9)
Here Comes Santa Claus (14)
Honey Hush (3)
How Soon (11)
Hummin' The Blues (1)

I Almost Lost My Mind (6) *1*
I'll Be Home (5) *4*
I'll Be Home For Christmas (14)
I'll Build A Stairway To Paradise (1)
I'll Walk Alone (9)
I'm In Love Again (3)
I'm In Love With You (6) *57*
I'm In The Mood For Love (11)
I'm Waiting Just For You (6) *27*
I've Heard That Song Before (10)
I've Told Ev'ry Little Star (13)
Imagination (12)
In The Garden (8)
It Came Upon A Midnight Clear (14)
It Is No Secret (8)
It's A Pity To Say Goodnight (10)
It's A Sin To Tell A Lie (12)
Jingle Bells (14)
Johnny Will (15) *35*
Joy To The World (14)
Just A Closer Walk With Thee (2)
Lazy River (10)
Little White Lies (9)
Lonesome Road (10)
Louella (4)

Love Letters In The Sand (6) *1*
Love Makes The World Go 'Round (13)
Maybe You'll Be There (11)
Money Honey (3)
Moody River (13) *1*
Moonglow (12)
More Than You Know (11)
My Baby Just Cares For Me (10)
My God Is Real (Yes, God Is Real) (8)
Nearness Of You (11)
No Other Arms (No Arms Can Ever Hold You) (5) *26*
Now I Know (5)
Now The Day Is Over (8)
O Holy Night (14)
O Little Town Of Bethlehem (14)
Old Rugged Cross (8)
Peace In The Valley (2)
Please Send Me Someone To Love (3)
Pledging My Love (3)
Remember You're Mine (6) *6*
Rich In Love (5)
Robins And Roses (10)
Rock Around The Clock (3)
San Antonio Rose (12)
Santa Claus Is Comin' To Town (14)

Secret Love (11)
September Song (9)
Shake A Hand (3)
Shot Gun Boogie (3)
Silent Night (14)
Silver Bells (14)
Sleep (13)
Softly And Tenderly (8)
Solitude (9)
Speedy Gonzales (15) *6*
St. Louis Blues (9)
Star Dust (9)
Steal Away (2)
Sunday (1)
Sweet Georgia Brown (10)
Sweet Hour Of Prayer (8)
Sweet Sue (10)
Take The Time (5)
Technique (4)
Tenderly (11)
Tennessee Saturday Night (5)
That Lucky Old Sun (1)
There's A Gold Mine In The Sky (6) *14*
There's A Moon Out Tonight (13)
They Can't Take That Away From Me (10)
Thousand Years (13)
To Each His Own (9)
Tomorrow Night (3)
Tra-La-La (5)
True Love (11)
Tutti' Frutti (5) *12*

Twixt Twelve And Twenty (15) *17*
Two Hearts (5) *16*
Unchained Melody (12)
Very Thought Of You (12)
Walking The Floor Over You (15) *44*
Wang Dang Taffy-Apple Tango (15) *62*
We Love But Once (12)
(Welcome) New Lovers (15) *18*
Whispering Hope (8)
White Christmas (14)
Who's Sorry Now (12)
Why Baby Why (6) *5*
Why Don't You Believe Me (11)
Will The Circle Be Unbroken (8)
Will You Love Me Tomorrow (13)
With The Wind And The Rain In Your Hair (15) *21*
With You (1)
Without My Love (4)
Words (15) *94*
Would You Like To Take A Walk (1)
Yes Indeed (10)
Yield Not To Temptation (8)
You Always Hurt The One You Love (12)
You Belong To Me (11)

BOOTSY'S RUBBER BAND

Bootsy was born William Collins on 10/26/51 in Cincinnati. Member of James Brown's JB's from 1969-71. Became bassist of Funkadelic/Parliament in 1972. Featured guitarist with Deee-Lite.

5/1/76	**59**	27		1 Stretchin' Out In Bootsy's Rubber Band	$8	Warner 2920
2/5/77	**16**	23	●	2 Ahh...The Name Is Bootsy, Baby!	$8	Warner 2972
2/25/78	**16**	24	●	3 Bootsy? Player Of The Year	$8	Warner 3093
7/21/79	**52**	9		4 This Boot Is Made For Fonk-n	$8	Warner 3295
12/6/80	**70**	9		5 Ultra Wave	$8	Warner 3433
				BOOTSY		
5/29/82	**120**	8		6 The One Giveth, The Count Taketh Away	$8	Warner 3667

WILLIAM "BOOTSY" COLLINS

Ahh...The Name Is Bootsy, Baby (2)
Another Point Of View (1)
As In (I Love You) (3)
Bootsy Get Live (4)
Bootsy? (What's The Name Of This Town) (3)
Bootzilla (2)
Can't Stay Away (2)
Chug-A-Lug (The Bunn Patrol) (4)

Countracula (This One's For You) (6)
Excon (Of Love) (6)
F-Encounter (5)
Fat Cat (5)
Funky Funktioneer (6)
Hollywood Squares (3)
I'd Rather Be With You (1)
Is That My Song? (5)
It's A Musical (5)
Jam Fan (Hot) (4)

Landshark (Just When You Thought It Was Safe) (6)
Love Vibes (1)
May The Force Be With You (3)
Mug Push (5)
Munchies For Your Love (2)
Music To Smile By (6)
#1 Funkateer (6)
Oh Boy Gorl (4)
Physical Love (1)

Pinocchio Theory (2)
Play On Playboy (2)
Preview Side Too (2)
Psychoticbumpschool (1)
Roto-Rooter (3)
Rubber Duckie (2)
Sacred Flower (5)
Shejam (Almost Bootsy Show) (4)
Shine-O-Myte (Rag Popping) (6)

So Nice You Name Him Twice (6)
Sound Crack (5)
Stretchin' Out (In A Rubber Band) (1)
Take A Lickin' And Keep On Kickin' (6)
Under The Influence Of A Groove (4)
Vanish In Our Sleep (1)
Very Yes (3)

We Want Bootsy (2)
What's A Telephone Bill? (2)
What's W-R-O-N-G Radio (6)

BOO-YAA T.R.I.B.E.

Los Angeles-based rap group: Ted, Donald, David, Danny, Paul and Roscoe Devoux — six brothers of Samoan heritage between the ages of 20-27. Appeared as breakdancers in Michael Jackson's Disney film *Captain EO*, and TV's *Fame* and *The A-Team*. Boo-Yaa is slang for the sound of a shotgun blast.

4/28/90	**117**	15		New Funky Nation	$12	4th & B'way 4017

Don't Mess
New Funky Nation

Once Upon A Drive By
Pickin' Up Metal

Psyko Funk
R.A.I.D.

Rated R
Riot Pump

Six Bad Brothas
T.R.I.B.E.

Walk The Line

BORDEN, Lizzy — see LIZZY

BOSTON

Rock group from Boston, spearheaded by Tom Scholz (guitars and keyboards) and Brad Delp (lead vocals). Originally a quintet, group also included Barry Goudreau (guitar), Fran Sheehan (bass) and Sib Hashian (drums). Goudreau formed Orion The Hunter in 1990. After a long absence from the charts, Boston returned in 1986 as a duo: Scholz and Delp. Delp and Goudreau spearheaded RTZ in 1991.

9/25/76	**3**	132	▲11	1 **Boston**	$15	Epic 34188
9/2/78	**1**[2]	45	▲6	2 **Don't Look Back**	$8	Epic 35050
10/18/86	**1**[4]	50	▲4	3 **Third Stage**	$8	MCA 6188

Amanda (3) *1*
Can'tcha Say (You Believe In Me)/Still In Love (3) *20*
Cool The Engines (3)
Don't Be Afraid (2)

Don't Look Back (2) *4*
Feelin' Satisfied (2) *46*
Hitch A Ride (1)
Hollyann (3)
I Think I Like It (3)

It's Easy (2)
Journey, The (2)
Launch Medley (3)
Let Me Take You Home Tonight (1)

Long Time (1) *22*
Man I'll Never Be (2) *31*
More Than A Feeling (1) *5*
My Destination (3)
New World (3)

Party (2)
Peace Of Mind (1) *38*
Rock & Roll Band (1)
Smokin' (1)
Something About You (1)

To Be A Man (3)
Used To Bad News (2)
We're Ready (3) *9*

DEBUT DATE	PEAK POS	WKS CHR	GOLD	ARTIST — Album Title	$	Label & Number

★★223★★ BOSTON POPS ORCHESTRA

Conductor Arthur Fiedler was born in Boston on 12/17/1894; died on 7/10/79. Fiedler joined the Boston Pops Orchestra around 1915 as a viola player. Began his long reign as conductor in 1930, where he remained until his death. John Williams succeeded Fiedler as conductor in 1980.

BOSTON POPS/ARTHUR FIEDLER:

DEBUT DATE	PEAK POS	WKS CHR		ARTIST — Album Title	$	Label & Number
2/2/59	9	16	1	Offenbach: Gaite Parisienne; Khachaturian: Gayne Ballet Suite ....[I]	$20	RCA 2267
7/14/62	29	14	2	Pops Roundup ....[I]	$20	RCA 2595
3/9/63	36	6	3	Our Man In Boston ....[I]	$20	RCA 2599
4/6/63	5	23	4	"Jalousie" And Other Favorites In The Latin Flavor ....[I]	$20	RCA 2661
6/22/63	29	14	5	Star Dust ....[I]	$20	RCA 2670
10/19/63	116	4	6	Concert In The Park ....[I]	$20	RCA 2677
9/26/64	18	31	7	"Pops" Goes The Trumpet ....[I]	$15	RCA 2729

AL HIRT/BOSTON POPS/ARTHUR FIEDLER

11/21/64+	53	14	8	Peter And The Commissar ....[C]	$20	RCA 2773

ALLAN SHERMAN/BOSTON POPS/ARTHUR FIEDLER

10/23/65	86	16	9	Nero Goes "Pops" ....[I]	$15	RCA 2821

PETER NERO/ARTHUR FIEDLER/BOSTON POPS

5/14/66	145	3	10	The Duke At Tanglewood ....[I-L]	$15	RCA 2857

DUKE ELLINGTON/BOSTON POPS/ARTHUR FIEDLER

6/18/66	62	23	11	The "Pops" Goes Country ....[I]	$15	RCA 2870

CHET ATKINS/BOSTON POPS/ARTHUR FIEDLER

10/26/68	157	7	12	Up Up And Away ....[I]	$10	RCA 3041
4/5/69	192	2	13	Glenn Miller's Biggest Hits ....[I]	$10	RCA 3064
10/11/69	160	4	14	Chet Picks On The Pops...........................[I]	$15	RCA 3104

CHET ATKINS/BOSTON POPS/ARTHUR FIEDLER

1/9/71	190	2	15	Fabulous Broadway ....[I]	$8	Polydor 5003
12/4/71	174	5	16	Arthur Fiedler "Superstar" ....[I]	$8	Polydor 5008
2/26/72	196	3	17	The Music Of Paul Simon ....[I]	$8	Polydor 5018
9/8/79	147	6	18	Saturday Night Fiedler...........................[I]	$8	Midsong Int. 011

BOSTON POPS/JOHN WILLIAMS:

12/20/80+	181	6	19	Pops In Space ....[I]	$8	Philips 9500 921
5/17/86	155	8	20	Swing, Swing, Swing ....[I]	$8	Philips 412626

Adios Amigo (11)
Alabama Jubilee (11)
American Patrol (13)
"And Now A Word From Our Sponsor" Medley (3)
Apartment, Theme From The (3)
Bachmania (18)
Battle Of New Orleans (medley) (14)
Begin The Beguine (20)
Benjamin: Jamaican Rhumba (4)
Bidin' My Time (9)
Blue Moon (5)
Borel-Clerc: La Sorella-March (4)
Bridge Over Troubled Water (16,17)
Bugler's Holiday (3,7)
By The Time I Get To Phoenix (14)
Cabaret (12)
Canticle ..see: Scarborough Fair
Caravan (10)
Carnival Of Venice (7)
Cecilia (17)
Chattanooga Choo Choo (13)
Clair De Lune (Moonlight) (5)
Close Encounters Of The Third Kind Suite (19)
Codina: Zacatecas-March (4)
Cold, Cold Heart (11)
Company Medley (15)
Cool Water (2)
Country Gentleman (11)
Dangling Conversation (17)

Deep Purple (5)
Delilah (14)
Do Nothin' Til You Hear From Me (10)
Elli, Elli (7)
El Condor Pasa (17)
Embraceable You (9)
Empire Strikes Back Medley (19)
End Of A Symphony (8)
Exodus, Theme From (3)
Faded Love (11)
Fiddler On The Roof Medley (15)
59th Street Bridge Song (Feelin' Groovy) (17)
Gade: Jalousie (4)
Galveston (14)
Gentle On My Mind (14)
Georgy Girl (12)
Glow Worm (5)
Gomez: Il Guarany-Overture (4)
Gounod: Funeral March Of A Marionette (4)
Guarnieri: Brazilian Dance (4)
Guys And Dolls Medley (3)
Hair Medley (15)
Hazy Shade Of Winter (17)
Hey, Look Me Over (3)
Home On The Range (4)
Homeward Bound (17)
I Got It Bad And That Ain't Good (10)
I Got Rhythm (9)
I Let A Song Go Out Of My Heart (10)

I Think I Love You (16)
I'll Fly Away (11)
I'm Beginning To See The Light (10)
I'm Thinking Tonight Of My Blue Eyes (11)
In The Mood (13,20)
In The Pines (medley) (11)
Java (7)
Jesus Christ Superstar (16)
John Henry (medley) (11)
Khachaturian: Gayne Ballet Suite - Medley (1)
La Virgen De La Macarena (7)
Lara's Theme (12)
Last Roundup (14)
Last Waltz (14)
Let It Be (16)
Listen To The Mockingbird (medley) (11)
Liszt: Grand Galop Chromatique, Op. 12 (6)
Little Brown Jug (13)
Lost Chord (7)
Love Is Blue (12)
Love Is Here To Stay (9)
Love Me Tonight (16)
Love Scene (19)
Love Story, Theme From (16)
Lover's Concerto (12)
Mack The Knife (3)
Mah-Na Mah-Na (16)
Man And A Woman (12)
Man I Love (9)
Man Of La Mancha Medley (15)
March Of The Charioteers (3)

Marquina: Espana Cani (4)
Mass. net: Le Cid (4)
Michelle (12)
Mooch, The (10)
Mood Indigo (10)
Moonlight Cocktail (13)
Moonlight Serenade (13,20)
Mozart: Piano Concerto No. 21: Andante (12)
Mrs. Robinson (17)
Never On Sunday (3)
Night Was Made For Love (5)
O Bury Me Not On The Lone Prairie (2)
Ode To Billy Joe (14)
Offenbach: Gaite Parisienne (1)
Old Friends (17)
On Top Of Old Smoky (medley) (11)
Opus One (20)
Orange Blossom Special (11)
Pavanne (7)
Peter And The Commissar (8)
Pops Hoe-Down (2)
Pops Roundup (2)
Press: Wedding Dance (Freilachs) (6)
Proud Mary (16)
Red River Valley (2)
Reverie (5)
Rhapsody In Blue (9)
Riders In The Sky (2)
Satin Doll (10,20)
Saturday Night Fever Medley (18)
Scarborough Fair/Canticle (14,17)

Schonherr: Austrian Peasant Dances, Op. 14 (6)
Schuman: Chester (6)
Sing, Sing, Sing (20)
Sinigaglia: Danze Piemontesi Op. 31, No. 1 (4)
Sleepy Lagoon (14)
Smoke Gets In Your Eyes (3)
Snowfall (20)
Solitude (10)
Song Fest Medley (6)
Song Of India (20)
Song Of The Volga Boatmen (13)
Sophisticated Lady (10)
Song Of Silence (17)
Spanish Harlem (14)
St. Louis Blues March (13)
Stairway To The Stars (5)
Star Dust (5)
Star Wars Medley (19)
Stompin' At The Savoy (20)
String Of Pearls (13,20)
Sugarfoot Rag (medley) (14)
Sunrise Serenade (13,20)
Superman Medley (19)
Swing, Swing, Swing (20)
Tennessee Waltz (11)
They Can't Take That Away From Me (9)
This Guy's In Love With You (14)
Timon Of Athens March (10)
Tonight (5)
Toy Trumpet (7)
Trumpet Concerto (7)
Trumpeter's Lullaby (7)
Tumbling Tumbleweeds (2)

Tuxedo Junction (13,20)
Up, Up And Away (12)
Valerius: Prayer Of Thanksgiving (6)
Valley Of The Dolls, Theme From (12)
Variations On "How Dry I Am" (8)
Victor Herbert Favorites Medley (6)
Wagon Wheels (2)
What Have They Done To My Song, Ma (16)
When You Wish Upon A Star (5)
White: Mosquito Dance (6)
Whoopie-Ti-Yi-Yo (Git Along Little Dogies) (2)
Wildwood Flower (medley) (11)
Wimoweh (14)
Windy And Warm (11)
Wunderbar (5)
Yellow Rose Of Texas (2)
Yesterday (12)
You And The Night And The Music (5)

BOSTON SYMPHONY Orchestra

5/11/63	17	8	1	Ravel: Bolero/Pavan For A Dead Princess/La Valse ....[I]	$15	RCA 2664

Charles Munch, conductor

5/18/63	41	4	2	Mahler: Symphony No. 1 ....[I]	$15	RCA 2642

Erich Leinsdorf, conductor

3/28/64	82	12	3	Mozart: Requiem Mass	$15	RCA 7030 [2]

a Requiem Mass conducted by Erich Leinsdorf in memory of President Kennedy - celebrated by Richard Cardinal Cushing, the Archbishop of Boston, on 1/19/64 at Boston's Cathedral of the Holy Cross

DEBUT DATE	PEAK POS	WKS CHR	GOLD	ARTIST — Album Title	$	Label & Number

BOSTON SYMPHONY Orchestra — Cont'd

Mahler: Symphony No. 1 In D First Movement: Langsam Schleppend Wie Ein Naturlaut (2)	Mahler: Symphony No. 1 In D Second Movement: Kräftig Bewegt Doch Nicht Zu Schnell (2)	Mahler: Symphony No. 1 In D Third Movement: Feierlich Und Gemessen, Ohne Zu Schleppen (2) Mahler: Symphony No. 1 In D Fourth Movement: Stürmisch Bewegt (2)	Mozart: Requiem Mass, K.626: Agnus Dei; Lux Aeterna (3) Mozart: Requiem Mass, K.626: Domine Jesu; Hostias; Santus; Benedictus (3)	Mozart: Requiem Mass, K.626: Requiem; Kyrie; Dies Irae (3) Mozart: Requiem Mass, K.626: Tuba Mirum; Rex Tremendae; Recordare; Confutatis; Lacrim (3)	Ravel: Bolero (1) Ravel: La Valse (1) Ravel: Pavan For A Dead Princess (1)

BOURGEOIS TAGG
West Coast rock quintet formed in 1984 and led by Brent Bourgeois and Larry Tagg.

DEBUT DATE	PEAK POS	WKS CHR	GOLD	ARTIST — Album Title	$	Label & Number
5/31/86	139	7		1 Bourgeois Tagg..	$8	Island 90496
10/24/87	84	21		2 YoYo	$8	Island 90638

Best Of All Possible Worlds (2)	Coma (2)	15 Minutes In The Sun (2)	Move Up (1)	Pencil & Paper (2)	Waiting For The Worm To Turn (2)
Body Count (1)	Cry Like A Baby (2)	Heart Of Darkness (1)	**Mutual Surrender (What A**	Perfect Life (1)	What's Wrong With This
Changed (1)	Dying To Be Free (1)	**I Don't Mind At All** (2) 38	**Wonderful World)** (1) 62	Stress (2)	Picture (2)
	Electric Train (1)	Let The War Begin (1)	Out Of My Mind (1)		

★★35★★ BOWIE, David
Born David Robert Jones on 1/8/47 in London. First recorded as David Jones & the King Bees, Lower Third, and Manish Boys in 1963. Brought highly theatrical values to rock through work with Lindsay Kemp Mime Troupe. Periods of reclusiveness heightened his appeal. Films *The Man Who Fell To Earth* (1976), *Labyrinth*, *Absolute Beginners* (1986) and others. In Broadway play *The Elephant Man* (1980). Married to Angie Barnet, the subject of The Rolling Stones' song "Angie," from 1970-80. Formed the group Tin Machine in 1988. Married Somalian actress/supermodel Iman on 4/24/92.

DEBUT DATE	PEAK POS	WKS CHR	GOLD	ARTIST — Album Title	$	Label & Number
4/15/72+	93	16		1 Hunky Dory	$12	RCA 4623
6/17/72+	75	72	●	2 The Rise And Fall Of Ziggy Stardust And The Spiders From Mars	$12	RCA 4702
11/18/72+	16	36		3 Space Oddity .... [E-R]	$12	RCA 4813
				first released on Mercury 61246 in 1968		
11/18/72+	105	23		4 The Man Who Sold The World .... [E-R]	$12	RCA 4816
				first released on Mercury 61325 in 1970		
3/17/73	144	9		5 Images 1966-1967 .... [E]	$20	London 628/9 [2]
				first recordings in London on Pye and Decca labels		
5/12/73	17	22	●	6 Aladdin Sane	$12	RCA 4852
11/10/73	23	21		7 Bowie Pin Ups	$12	RCA 0291
				David's versions of his favorite pop hits from '64-'67; supermodel Twiggy appears on the cover		
6/15/74	5	25	●	8 Diamond Dogs	$15	RCA 0576
				original cover, which is worth $2000+, features Bowie as a dog with his genitals visible — controversial and quickly withdrawn		
10/26/74	8	21	●	9 David Live .... [L]	$12	RCA 0771 [2]
				recorded at the Tower Theatre, Philadelphia		
3/22/75	9	51	●	10 Young Americans	$12	RCA 0998
2/7/76	3	32	●	11 Station To Station	$12	RCA 1327
6/19/76	10	39	▲	12 Changesonebowie .... [G]	$12	RCA 1732
1/29/77	11	19		13 Low	$12	RCA 2030
11/12/77	35	19		14 "Heroes"	$12	RCA 2522
5/6/78	136	8		15 David Bowie narrates Prokofiev's "Peter and The Wolf"	$12	RCA 2743
				DAVID BOWIE/EUGENE ORMANDY & THE PHILADELPHIA ORCHESTRA		
10/21/78	44	13		16 Stage .... [L]	$10	RCA 2913 [2]
6/16/79	20	15		17 Lodger...	$8	RCA 3254
10/4/80	12	27		18 Scary Monsters	$8	RCA 3647
12/12/81+	68	18		19 Changestwobowie .... [G]	$8	RCA 4202
4/3/82	135	7		20 Christiane F. .... [S]	$8	RCA 4239
				soundtrack features 9 of David's songs		
4/30/83	4	68	▲	21 Let's Dance	$8	EMI America 17093
8/27/83	99	9		22 Golden Years .... [G]	$8	RCA 4792
11/12/83	89	15		23 Ziggy Stardust/The Motion Picture .... [S-L]	$10	RCA 4862 [2]
				documentary of David's final tour as his character Ziggy		
4/21/84	147	6		24 Fame and Fashion (David Bowie's All Time Greatest Hits) .... [G]	$8	RCA 4919
10/20/84	11	24	▲	25 Tonight	$8	EMI America 17138
7/19/86	68	8		26 Labyrinth .... [S]	$8	EMI America 17206
				includes 6 instrumentals by Trevor Jones: "Into The Labyrinth," "Sarah," "Hallucination," "Goblin Battle," "Thirteen O'Clock" and "Home At Last"		
5/23/87	34	26	●	27 Never Let Me Down	$8	EMI America 17267
				features Peter Frampton (lead guitar)		
10/14/89	97	16		28 Sound + Vision .... [K]	$12	Rykodisc 0120 [6]
				David's material recorded from 1969-80		
4/7/90	39	27	▲	29 Changesbowie .... [G]	$12	Rykodisc 20171
				David's greatest hits from 1969-90		
7/7/90	93	9		30 The Rise And Fall Of Ziggy Stardust And The Spiders From Mars .... [R]	$12	Rykodisc 10134
				CD includes 5 bonus tracks not featured on original album		

Across The Universe (10)	Anyway, Anyhow, Anywhere (7,28)	Beauty And The Beast (14,16)	Britten: Young Person's Guide To The Orchestra, Op. 34 (15)	Chilly Down (26)	Did You Ever Have A Dream (5)
African Night Flight (17)	Art Decade (13,16)	Because You're Young (18)		**China Girl** (21,29) 10	**Dodo** (medley) (28)
After All (4)	As The World Falls Down (26)	Bewlay Brothers (1,28)	Can You Hear Me (10)	Come And Buy My Toys (5)	Don't Bring Me Down (7,28)
After Today (28)		Big Brother (8,9,28)	Candidate (8)	Cracked Actor (6,9,23,28)	Don't Look Down (25)
Aladdin Sane (1913-1938-197?) (6,9,19)	Ashes To Ashes (18,19,22,24,28,29)	Black Country Rock (4,28)	**Cat People (Putting Out Fire)** (21) 67	Criminal World (21)	Drive-In Saturday (6,28)
All The Madmen (4)	Bang Bang (27)	Blackout (14,16)		Cygnet Committee (3)	Eight Line Poem (medley) (1)
All The Young Dudes (9,23)	Be My Wife (13,28)	**Blue Jean** (25,29) 8	Changes	D. J. (17,19,24)	'87 And Cry (27)
Always Crashing In The Same Car (13)	Beat Of Your Drum (27)	Boys Keep Swinging (17,20,28)	(1,9,12,23,24,28,29) 41	Dancing With The Big Boys (25)	Everything's All Right (7)
Andy Warhol (medley) (1)		Breaking Glass (13,16,28)	Chant Of The Ever Circling Skeletal Family (8)	**Day-In Day-Out** (27) 21	**Fame** (10,12,16,24) 1
				Diamond Dogs (8,9,12,29)	Fame '90 (29)

91

DEBUT DATE	PEAK POS	WKS CHR	G O L D	ARTIST — Album Title	$	Label & Number

BOWIE, David — Cont'd

Fantastic Voyage (17)
Fascination (10,28)
Fashion (18,19,22,24,29) **70**
Fill Your Heart (medley) (1)
Five Years (2,16,30)
Friday On My Mind (7)
Future Legend (8)
Glass Spider (27)
God Knows I'm Good (3)
God Only Knows (25)
Golden Years (11,12,22,24,29) **10**
Gospel According To Tony Day (5)
Hang On To Yourself (2,16,23,30)
Helden (20,28)
Here Comes The Night (7)
Heroes (14,16,20,24,29)
I Can't Explain (7,22)
I Keep Forgetting (25)
I Wish You Would (7)
In The Heat Of The Morning (5)
It Ain't Easy (2,30)
It's Hard To Be A Saint In The City (28)
It's No Game (Part 1 & 2) (18)
Janine (3)
Jean Genie (6,9,12,29) **71**

Joe The Lion (14,22,28)
John, I'm Only Dancing (12,28,29,30)
John I'm Only Dancing (Again) 1975 (19)
Join The Gang (5)
Karma Man (5)
Kingdom Come (18,28)
Knock On Wood (9)
Kooks (1)
Lady Grinning Soul (6)
Lady Stardust (2,30)
Laughing Gnome (5)
Let Me Sleep Beside You (5)
Let's Dance (21,29) **1**
Let's Spend The Night Together (6,23)
Letter To Hermione (3)
Life On Mars? (1)
Little Bombadier (5)
London Boys (5)
London Bye Ta-Ta (28)
Look Back In Anger (17,20,22,28)
Love You Till Tuesday (5)
Loving The Alien (25)
Magic Dance (26)
Maid Of Bond Street (5)
Man Who Sold The World (4,28)

Memory Of A Free Festival (3)
Modern Love (21,29) **14**
Moonage Daydream (2,9,23,28,30)
Moss Garden (14)
Move On (17)
My Death (23)
Neighborhood Threat (25)
Neukoln (14)
Never Let Me Down (27) **27**
New Career In A New Town (13)
New York's In Love (27)
1984 (8,9,19,24,28)
Occasional Dream (3)
Oh! You Pretty Things (1,19,23)
On Broadway (medley) (19)
Panic In Detroit (6,28)
Please Mr. Gravedigger (5)
Prettiest Star (6,28)
Prokofiev: Peter And The Wolf, Op. 67 (15)
Queen Bitch (1)
Quicksand (1)
Rebel Rebel (8,9,12,28,29) **64**
Red Money (17)
Red Sails (17,22,28)

Repetition (17)
Ricochet (21)
Right (10)
Rock 'N' Roll Suicide (2,9,23,28,30)
Rock 'N' Roll With Me (8,9)
Rosalyn (7)
Round And Round (28)
Rubber Band (5)
Running Gun Blues (4)
Saviour Machine (4)
Scary Monsters (And Super Creeps) (18,22)
Scream Like A Baby (18)
Secret Life Of Arabia (14)
See Emily Play (7)
Sell Me A Coat (5)
Sense Of Doubt (14,16,20)
Shake It (21)
Shapes Of Things (7)
She Shook Me Cold (4)
She's Got My Medals (5)
Shining Star (Makin' My Love) (27)
Silly Boy Blue (5)
Somebody Up There Likes Me (10)
Song For Bob Dylan (1)
Sons Of The Silent Age (14,28)

Sorrow (7,28)
Soul Love (2,16,30)
Sound And Vision (13,19,28) **69**
Space Oddity (3,12,23,24,28,29) **15**
Speed Of Life (13,16,28)
Star (2,16,30)
Starman (2,19,24,30) **65**
Station To Station (11,16,20,28)
Stay (11,20)
Subterraneans (13)
Suffragette City (2,9,12,23,28,29,30)
Superman, The (4)
Sweet Head (30)
Sweet Thing (8,9)
There Is A Happy Land (5)
Time (6,23)
Time Will Crawl (27)
Too Dizzy (27)
Tumble And Twirl (25)
Uncle Arthur (5)
Underground (26)
Unwashed And Somewhat Slightly Dazed (3)

Up The Hill Backwards (18,28)
V-2 Schneider (14,20)
Velvet Goldmine (30)
Warszawa (13,16,20,28)
Watch That Man (6,9,23,28)
We Are Hungry Men (5)
We Are The Dead (8)
Weeping Wall (13)
What In The World (13,16)
When I Live My Dream (5)
Where Have All The Good Times Gone! (24)
White Light/White Heat (23,28)
Width Of A Circle (4,9,23)
Wild Eyed Boy From Freecloud (3,23,28)
Wild Is The Wind (11,19,22,28)
Win (10)
Within You (26)
Word On A Wing (11)
Yassassin (17)
Zeroes (27)
Ziggy Stardust (2,12,16,23,28,29,30)

TVC 15 (11,16,20,24,28) **64**
Teenage Wildlife (18)
Tonight (25) **53**
Without You (21) **73**
Young Americans (10,12,24,28,29) **28**

BOW WOW WOW

Assembled in London by Malcolm McLaren (former Sex Pistols manager). Consisted of Annabella Lwin (Myant Myant Aye, b: 10/31/65 in Burma) and three members of the original Adam & The Ants.

DEBUT DATE	PEAK POS	WKS CHR	GOLD	ARTIST — Album Title	$	Label & Number
11/21/81	192	2		1 See Jungle! See Jungle! Go Join Your Gang Yeah! City All Over, Go Ape Crazy	$8	RCA 4147
5/15/82	67	22		2 The Last Of The Mohicans ....[M]	$8	RCA 4314
9/18/82	123	9		3 I Want Candy	$8	RCA 4375
				cuts from first 2 albums above + 2 new songs		
3/26/83	82	13		4 When The Going Gets Tough, The Tough Get Going	$8	RCA 4570

Aphrodisiac (4)
Baby, Oh No (3)
Chihuahua (1)
Cowboy (2,3)
Do You Wanna Hold Me? (4) **77**

El Boss Dicho (3)
Elimination Dancing (1)
Go Wild In The Country (1,3)
Golly! Golly! Go Buddy! (1)
Hello, Hello Daddy (I'll Sacrifice) (1)

I Want Candy (2,3) **62**
(I'm A) T.V. Savage (1,3)
I'm Not A Know It All (1)
Jungle Boy (1)
King Kong (1,3)
Lonesome Tonight (4)

Louis Quatorze (2,3)
Love Me (4)
Love, Peace And Harmony (4)
Man Mountain (4)
Mario (Your Own Way To Paradise) (4)

Mickey, Put It Down (4)
Mile High Club (2,3)
Orang-outang (1)
Quiver (Arrows In My) (4)
Rikki Dee (1)
Roustabout (4)

Sinner! Sinner! Sinner! (Prince Of Darkness) (1)
Tommy Tucker (4)
What's The Time (Hey Buddy) (4)
Why Are Babies So Wise? (1)

BOX OF FROGS

British quartet: John Fiddler (vocals), Chris Dreja (guitar), Paul Samwell-Smith (bass) and Jim McCarty (drums). The latter three were members of The Yardbirds. McCarty also with Renaissance and Illusion.

DEBUT DATE	PEAK POS	WKS CHR	GOLD	ARTIST — Album Title	$	Label & Number
7/7/84	45	20		1 Box Of Frogs	$8	Epic 39327
6/14/86	177	3		2 Strange Land	$8	Epic 39923

Another Wasted Day (1)
Asylum (2)
Average (2)
Back Where I Started (1)

Edge, The (1)
Get It While You Can (2)
Hanging From The Wreckage (2)

Harder (1)
Heart Full Of Soul (1)
House On Fire (2)
Into The Dark (1)

Just A Boy Again (1)
Love Inside You (1)
Poor Boy (1)
Strange Land (2)

Trouble (2)
Two Steps Ahead (1)
You Mix Me Up (2)

BOX TOPS, The

Pop-rock group formed in Memphis in 1966. Included Alex Chilton (b: 12/28/50; lead singer, guitar, bass, harmonica), Bill Cunningham (keyboards) and Gary Talley (guitar, bass). Reorganized after first hit to include Tom Boggs (drums) and Rick Allen (organ). Disbanded in 1970. Chilton later formed the power pop band Big Star. Cunningham is the brother of B.B. Cunningham of The Hombres.

DEBUT DATE	PEAK POS	WKS CHR	GOLD	ARTIST — Album Title	$	Label & Number
11/18/67+	87	15		1 The Letter/Neon Rainbow	$15	Bell 6011
4/27/68	59	19		2 Cry Like A Baby	$15	Bell 6017
12/7/68+	45	26		3 The Box Tops Super Hits ....[G]	$15	Bell 6025
9/6/69	77	11		4 Dimensions	$15	Bell 6032

Ain't No Way (4)
Break My Mind (1,3)
Choo Choo Train (3) **26**
Cry Like A Baby (2,3) **2**
Deep In Kentucky (4)
Every Time (2)
Everything I Am (1)

Fields Of Clover (2)
Gonna Find Somebody (1)
Good Morning Dear (2)
Happy Song (4)
Happy Times (1)
I Met Her In Church (3) **37**
I Must Be The Devil (4)

I Pray For Rain (1)
I Shall Be Released (4) **67**
I'll Hold Out My Hand (4)
I'm The One For You (2)
I'm Your Puppet (1,3)
Letter, The (1,3) **1**
Lost (2)

Midnight Angel (4)
Neon Rainbow (1,3) **24**
People Make The World (1)
Rock Me Baby (4)
727 (2)
She Knows How (1)

She Shot A Hole In My Soul (3)
Soul Deep (4) **18**
Sweet Cream Ladies, Forward March (4) **28**
Together (4)

Trains & Boats & Planes (1,3)
Trouble With Sam (2)
Weeping Analeah (2)
Whiter Shade Of Pale (1,3)
You Keep Me Hanging On (2,3)

BOYCE, Tommy, & Bobby Hart

Top songwriting duo/production team. Writers of "Pretty Little Angel Eyes," "Come A Little Bit Closer," much of The Monkees material and others. Toured and recorded with The Monkees' Davy Jones and Mickey Dolenz in 1975. Boyce was born on 9/29/44 in Charlottesville, Virginia. Phoenix native Hart was born in 1944.

DEBUT DATE	PEAK POS	WKS CHR	GOLD	ARTIST — Album Title	$	Label & Number
9/9/67	200	1		1 Test Patterns	$15	A&M 4126
4/20/68	109	5		2 I Wonder What She's Doing Tonite?	$15	A&M 4143

Abe's Tune (1)
Countess, The (2)
For Baby (1)
Girl, I'm Out To Get You (1)

Goodbye Baby (I Don't Want To See You Cry) (2) **53**
I Should Be Going Home (1)

I Wanna Be Free (2)
I Wonder What She's Doing Tonite (2) **8**
I'm Digging You, Digging Me (2)

In The Night (1)
Leaving Again (2)
Life Medley (1)
Love Every Day (2)
My Little Chickadee (1)

Out & About (1) **39**
Population (2)
Pretty Flower (2)
Shadows (1)

Sometimes She's A Little Girl (1)
Teardrop City (2)
Two For The Price Of One (2)

DEBUT DATE	PEAK POS	WKS CHR	GOLD	ARTIST — Album Title	$	Label & Number

BOYER, Charles
French romantic actor. Born on 8/28/1899; died on 8/26/78.

| 1/8/66 | 148 | 2 | | Where Does Love Go .... spoken versions of love songs | $20 | Valiant 5001 |

All The Things You Are — Gigi — I Believe — Once Upon A Time — Venice Blue — When The World Was Young
Autumn Leaves — Hello, Young Lovers — La Vie En Rose — Softly, As I Leave You — What Now My Love — Where Does Love Go

BOY GEORGE
Born George O'Dowd on 6/14/61 in Bexleyheath, England. Former lead singer of Culture Club. Previously known as Lieutenant Lush, a backing singer with Bow Wow Wow.

| 8/1/87 | 145 | 5 | | 1 Sold.. | $8 | Virgin 90617 |
| 3/25/89 | 126 | 11 | | 2 High Hat.. | $8 | Virgin 91022 |

Don't Cry (2) — Girl With Combination Skin (2) — Just Ain't Enough (1) — Next Time (1) — To Be Reborn (1) — Whisper (2)
Don't Take My Mind On A Trip (2) — I Asked For Love (1) — Keep Me In Mind (1) — Sold (1) — We've Got The Right (1) — You Are My Heroin (2)
Everything I Own (1) — I'm Not Sleeping Anymore (2) — Kipsy (2) — Something Strange Called Love (2) — Where Are You Now? (1) — You Found Another Guy (2)
Freedom (1) — Little Ghost (1) — Whether They Like It Or Not (2)

BOYLAN, Terence
Brother of record producer John Boylan.

| 11/5/77 | 181 | 3 | | Terence Boylan .... | $8 | Asylum 1091 |

Don't Hang Up Those Dancing Shoes — Hey Papa — Shake It — Sundown Of Fools — War Was Over
Rain King — Shame — Trains — Where Are You Hiding?

BOY MEETS GIRL
Seattle songwriting/recording duo: Shannon Rubicam and George Merrill. Wrote Whitney Houston's hits "How Will I Know" and "I Wanna Dance With Somebody." Married in 1988.

| 5/4/85 | 76 | 11 | | 1 Boy meets Girl.. | $8 | A&M 5046 |
| 10/22/88+ | 50 | 26 | | 2 Reel Life... | $8 | RCA 8414 |

Be My Baby (1) — From Now On (1) — Is Anybody Out There In Love (2) — Oh Girl (1) 39 — Restless Dreamer (2) — Stormy Love (2)
Bring Down The Moon (2) 49 — I Wish You Were Here (1) — Kissing, Falling, Flying (1) — One Sweet Dream (2) — Someone's Got To Send Out Love (2) — Touch, The (1)
Don't Tell Me We Have Nothing (1) — If You Run (2) — No Apologies (2) — Pieces (1) — Stay Forever (2) — Waiting For A Star To Fall (2) 5
— In Your Eyes (1) — Premonitions (1)

BOYS, The
Quartet of brothers, ages 9-14 in 1988, from Northridge, California: Khiry (lead), Hakeem, Tajh and Bilal Samad. All are members of performing gymnastic troupes.

11/26/88+	33	36	▲	1 Messages From The Boys	$8	Motown 6260
10/27/90	108	7	●	2 The Boys..	$12	Motown 6302
5/30/92	191	1		3 The Saga Continues...	$12	Motown 6336

Applejuice (3) — Doin' It With The B (3) — Happiness (3) — Little Romance (1) — Smpte (2) — Tonite (3)
Be My Girl (1) — Freak Of The Week (3) — Happy (1) — Love Gram (1) — Strings 'N Things (2) — You Got Me Cryin' (3)
Be Yo Man (3) — Funny (2) — I Had A Dream (2) — Lucky Charm (1) — Sunshine (1)
Bush, The (2) — Funny '92 (3) — I'm Yours (3) — My Love (2) — Thanx 4 The Funk (2)
Crazy (2) 29 — Got To Be There (1) — Just For The Fun Of It (1) — Personality (1) — Thing Called Love (2)
Dial My Heart (1) 13 — Hak's House Of Pleasure (3) — Let's Dance (1) — Saga Continues... (3) — Thought You Knew (3)

BOYS CLUB
Duo formed in Minneapolis: vocalists Joe Pasquale and Gene Hunt (real name: Eugene Wolfgramm, formerly with his family group, The Jets).

| 11/26/88+ | 93 | 16 | | Boys Club .... | $8 | MCA 42242 |

At It Again — I Remember Holding You 8 — Naked Truth — Tell Me — Victim Of The Heart
Danglin' On A String — Loneliest Heart — Step By Step — Time Starts Now — When You're Letting Go

BOYS DON'T CRY
British quintet — Nick Richards, lead singer.

| 6/21/86 | 55 | 19 | | Boys Don't Cry .... | $8 | Profile 1219 |

Cities On Fire — I Wanna Be A Cowboy 12 — Lipstick — Take My Love And Run — Turn Over (I Like It Better That Way) — 22nd Century Boy
Hearts Bin Broken — Josephine — Ships In The Night

BOYZ II MEN
R&B vocal quartet formed in 1988 at Philadelphia's High School of Creative and Performing Arts: Wanya Morris (age 17 in 1991), Michael McCary, Shawn Stockman and Nathan Morris. Discovered by Michael Bivins (New Edition, Bell Biv DeVoe).

| 6/1/91 | 3 | 89↑▲5 | | Cooleyhighharmony.. | $12 | Motown 6320 |

It's So Hard To Say Goodbye To Yesterday 2 — Little Things — Motownphilly 3 — Sympin — Uhh Ahh 16 — Your Love
— Lonely Heart — Please Don't Go 49 — This Is My Heart — Under Pressure

BRAGG, Billy
Post-punk, protest singer/songwriter. Born in Barking, England on 12/20/57.

| 11/5/88 | 198 | 1 | | Workers Playtime.. | $8 | Elektra 60824 |

Life With The Lions — Must I Paint You A Picture — Price I Pay — She's Got A New Spell — Tender Comrade — Waiting For The Great Leap Forwards
Little Time Bomb — Only One — Rotting On Remand — Short Answer — Valentine's Day Is Over

BRAINSTORM
Seven-man, two-woman, soul-disco band from Detroit.

| 3/26/77 | 145 | 16 | | Stormin'... | $8 | Tabu 2048 |

Easy Thangs — Lovin' Is Really My Game — This Must Be Heaven — Wake Up And Be Somebody 86 — We Know A Place
Hangin' On — Stormin' — Waiting For Someone

BRAMLETT, Bonnie
Half of Delaney & Bonnie. Born Bonnie Lynn O'Farrell on 11/8/44 in Acton, Illinois. Backing vocalist for Fontella Bass and Albert King. First white member of The Ikettes. Married to Delaney Bramlett from 1967-72. Their daughter Bekka is the lead vocalist of The Zoo. Acting since 1987; as Bonnie Sheridan, in film The Doors and castmember of TV's Roseanne since 1990.

| 2/22/75 | 168 | 5 | | It's Time... | $10 | Capricorn 0148 |

DEBUT DATE	PEAK POS	WKS CHR	GOLD	ARTIST — Album Title	$	Label & Number

BRAMLETT, Bonnie — Cont'd

Atlanta, Georgia
Cover Me
Cowboys And Indians

Higher & Higher
It's Time

Oncoming Traffic
Since I Met You Baby

Where You Come From
Your Kind Of Kindness

(Your Love Has Brought Me
From A) Mighty Long Way

BRAM TCHAIKOVSKY — see TCHAIKOVSKY, Bram

BRAND NEW HEAVIES, The
London funk band: Andrew Levy, Simon Bartholomew, Lascelles Gordon, Jan Kincaid and Jim Wellman. Female vocals by N'Dea Davenport.

| 8/22/92 | 139 | 3 | | Heavy Rhyme Experience: Vol. 1 .... | $12 | Delicious 92178 |

featuring vocals by: Main Source, Gang Starr, Grand Puba, Masta Ace, Jamalski, Ed O. G., Black Sheep, Kool G. Rap, Tiger and The Pharcyde.

Bonafied Funk
Death Threat

Do Whatta I Gotta Do
It's Gettin Hectic

Jump N' Move
Soul Flower

State Of Yo
Wake Me When I'm Dead

Whatgabouthat
Who Makes The Loot?

BRAND NUBIAN
Rap outfit from New Rochelle, New York: "Grand Puba" Maxwell, Lord Jamar, and cousins Derek X & DJ Alamo. Grand Puba went solo by 1992.

| 2/23/91 | 130 | 28 | | One For All .... | $12 | Elektra 60946 |

CD includes bonus track

All For One
Brand Nubian
Concerto In X Minor
Dance To My Ministry

Dedication
Drop The Bomb
Feels So Good

Grand Puba, Positive And
L.G.
Ragtime

Slow Down
Step To The Rear
To The Right

Try To Do Me
Wake Up [includes 2 versions]

Who Can Get Busy Like This Man...

BRANDOS, The
New York-based quartet: Dave Kincaid (vocals), Larry Mason, Ernie Mendillo and Ed Rupprecht.

| 9/26/87 | 108 | 19 | | Honor Among Thieves .... | $8 | Relativity 8192 |

Come Home
Gettysburg

Hard Luck Runner
Honor Among Thieves

In My Dreams
Matter Of Survival

Nothing To Fear
Strychnine

Walking On The Water

BRAND X
British jazz-fusion group — Phil Collins (Genesis), drummer.

11/13/76	191	3		1 Unorthodox Behaviour .... [I]	$8	Passport 98019
5/21/77	125	8		2 Moroccan Roll .... [I]	$8	Passport 98022
11/3/79	165	6		3 Product .... [I]	$8	Passport 9840

Algon (Where An Ordinary
Cup Of Drinking Chocolate
Costs £8,000,000,000) (3)
...And So To F... (3)
April (3)
Born Ugly (1)

Collapsar (2)
Dance Of The Illegal Aliens (3)
Disco Suicide (2)
Don't Make Waves (3)
Euthanasia Waltz (1)

Hate Zone (2)
Macrocosm (2)
Malaga Virgen (2)
...Maybe I'll Lend You Mine After All (2)
Not Good Enough-See Me! (3)

Nuclear Burn (1)
Orbits (2)
Rhesus Perplexus (3)
Running On Three (1)
Smacks Of Euphoric Hysteria (1)

Soho (3)
Sun In The Night (2)
Touch Wood (1)
Unorthodox Behaviour (1)
Wal To Wal (3)

Why Should I Lend You Mine (When You've Broken Yours Off Already) (2)

BRANIGAN, Laura
Born on 7/3/57 in Brewster, New York. Former backing vocalist with Leonard Cohen. Acted in the TV show CHiPS and in the 1984 film Mugsy's Girl.

9/25/82	34	36	●	1 Branigan	$8	Atlantic 19289
4/9/83	29	37	●	2 Branigan 2	$8	Atlantic 80052
4/28/84	23	45	●	3 Self Control	$8	Atlantic 80147
8/10/85	71	15		4 Hold Me	$8	Atlantic 81265
8/1/87	87	28		5 Touch	$8	Atlantic 81747
4/28/90	133	6		6 Laura Branigan	$12	Atlantic 82086

All Night With Me (1) 69
Angels Calling (5)
Bad Attitude (6)
Best Was Yet To Come (6)
Breaking Out (3)
Close Enough (2)
Cry Wolf (5)
Deep In The Dark (2)
Don't Show Your Love (2)
Down Like A Rock (1)
Find Me (2)
Foolish Lullaby (4)

Forever Young (3)
Gloria (1) 2
Heart (3)
Hold Me (4) 82
How Am I Supposed To Live Without You (2) 12
I Found Someone (4) 90
I Wish We Could Be Alone (1)
I'm Not The Only One (2)
If You Loved Me (1)
Let Me In (6)
Living A Lie (1)

Lovin' You Baby (1)
Lucky (2)
Lucky One (3) 20
Mama (2)
Maybe I Love You (1)
Maybe Tonight (4)
Meaning Of The Word (5)
Moonlight On Water (6) 59
Name Game (5)
Never In A Million Years (6)
No Promise, No Guarantee (6)

Over Love (5)
Please Stay, Go Away (1)
Power Of Love (5) 26
Reverse Psychology (6)
Sanctuary (4)
Satisfaction (3)
Self Control (3) 4
Shadow Of Love (5)
Shattered Glass (5) 48
Silent Partners (3)
Smoke Screen (6)
Solitaire (2) 7

Spanish Eddie (4) 40
Spirit Of Love (5)
Squeeze Box (2)
Take Me (3)
Tenderness (4)
Ti Amo (3) 55
Touch (5)
Turn The Beat Around (6)
Unison (6)
Whatever I Do (5)
When I'm With You (4)

When The Heat Hits The Streets (4)
Will You Still Love Me Tomorrow (3)
With Every Beat Of My Heart (3)

BRANNEN, John
Rock singer from South Carolina.

| 3/12/88 | 156 | 14 | | Mystery Street .... | $8 | Apache 71650 |

Desolation Angel
Dreaming Girl

Drifter, The
Mystery Street

Paradise Highway
Primitive Emotion

Running With The Storm
Searching For Satisfaction

Shadows In The Night
Twilight Is Over

Wild One

BRASS CONSTRUCTION
Nine-man, multi-ethnic disco ensemble. Formed in Brooklyn in 1968 as Dynamic Soul by Guyana-born vocalist Randy Muller. Randy also produced the band Skyy.

2/7/76	10	35	▲	1 Brass Construction	$8	United Art. 545
11/20/76	26	22	●	2 Brass Construction II	$8	United Art. 677
11/19/77	66	14	●	3 Brass Construction III	$8	United Art. 775
11/18/78	174	4		4 Brass Construction IV	$8	United Art. 916
12/15/79+	89	20		5 Brass Construction 5	$8	United Art. 977
9/20/80	121	5		6 Brass Construction 6	$8	United Art. 1060
5/22/82	114	8		7 Attitudes	$8	Liberty 51121
6/11/83	176	6		8 Conversations	$8	Capitol 12268

Attitude (7)
Blame It On Me (Introspection) (2)
Breakdown (8)
Can You See The Light (7)

Celebrate (1)
Changin' (1)
Dance (1)
Do That Thang (7)
Do Ya (6)

Don't Try To Change Me (6)
E.T.C. (7)
Easy (8)
Forever Love (7)
Funtimes (7)

Get It Together (3)
Get To The Point (Summation) (2)
Get Up (4)
Get Up To Get Down (5)

Ha Cha Cha (Funktion) (2) 51
Happy People (3)
Help Yourself (4)
Hotdog (7)

How Do You Do (What You Do To Me) (6)
I Do Love You (8)
I Want Some Action (5)
I'm Not Gonna Stop (6)

DEBUT DATE	PEAK POS	WKS CHR	GOLD	ARTIST — Album Title	$	Label & Number

BRASS CONSTRUCTION — Cont'd

It's A Shame (8)
It's Alright (5)
Love (1)
L-O-V-E-U (3)
Message (Inspiration) (2)
Movin' (1) *14*

Music Makes You Feel Like
 Dancing (5)
Night Chaser (4)
No Communication (8)
Now Is Tomorrow
 (Anticipation) (2)
One To One (4)

Peekin' (1)
Perceptions (What's The
 Right Direction) (4)
Physical Attraction (8)
Pick Yourself Up (4)
Right Place (5)
Sambo (Progression) (2)

Screwed (Conditions) (2)
Shakit (5)
Starting Tomorrow (4)
Sweet As Sugar (1)
Talkin' (1)
Top Of The World (3)
Wake Up (3)

Walkin' The Line (8)
Watch Out (5)
We (3)
We Are Brass (6)
We Can Do It (6)
We Can Work It Out (8)

What's On Your Mind
 (Expression) (2)
Working Harder Every Day
 (6)
Yesterday (3)

BRASS RING, The

New York studio band headed by Phil Bodner (producer/arranger; sax, clarinet).

DEBUT DATE	PEAK POS	WKS CHR	GOLD	ARTIST — Album Title	$	Label & Number
6/25/66	109	8		1 Love Theme From The Flight Of The Phoenix [I]	$10	Dunhill 50008
4/15/67	157	3		2 Sunday Night At The Movies [I]	$10	Dunhill 50015
6/24/67	193	2		3 The Dis-Advantages Of You [I]	$10	Dunhill 50017

Al Di La (2)
Amen (2)
(And We Were Lovers) ..see:
 Sand Pebbles, Theme
 From The
Baby The Rain Must Fall (2)
Born Free (3)
California Dreamin' (3)

Colonel Bogey March (2)
Dating Game (3)
Day In The Life Of A Fool (2)
Dis-Advantages Of You
 (3) *36*
Hud, Theme From (2)
I Will Wait For You (3)
Lara's Theme (1)

Laura (1)
Lightening Bug (3)
Long Ships (2)
Look For A Star (2)
Love Is A Many Splendored
 Thing (1)
Man & A Woman (2)
Moment To Moment (1)

Moon River (1)
Moonglow & Theme From
 Picnic (2)
Music To Watch Girls By (3)
My Foolish Heart (1)
Pakistan (3)
Phoenix Love Theme (1) *32*
Sambe De Orfeo (2)

Sand Pebbles, Theme From
 The (3)
Secret Love (1)
Shadow Of Your Smile (1)
Somewhere, My Love ..see:
 Lara's Theme
Summer Place, Theme From
 A (1)

Tara's Theme (1)
True Love (2)
Unchained Melody (1)
Very Precious Love (2)
Wait For Me (3)

BRAUN, Bob

Born Robert Earl Brown on 4/20/29 in Ludlow, Kentucky. Hosted TV show in Cincinnati.

DEBUT DATE	PEAK POS	WKS CHR	GOLD	ARTIST — Album Title	$	Label & Number
10/27/62	99	6		Till Death Do Us Part	$15	Decca 74339

Because Of You
How Deep Is The Ocean
 (How High Is The Sky)

Is It Right Or Wrong?
Just In Time
Nearness Of You

Our Anniversary Of Love
That Certain Something (We
 Call Love)

Till Death Do Us Part *26*
Wasn't The Summer Short
When I Fall In Love

Why I Love You
You'll Never Know

BRAVE BELT — see BACHMAN-TURNER OVERDRIVE

★★328★★ **BREAD**

Formed in Los Angeles in 1969. Consisted of leader David Gates (vocals, guitar, keyboards), James Griffin (guitar), Robb Royer (guitar) and Jim Gordon (drums). Originally called Pleasure Faire. Griffin and Royer co-wrote award-winning "For All We Know" with Fred Karlin in 1969. Mike Botts replaced Gordon after first album. Royer replaced by Larry Knechtel (top sessionman, member of Duane Eddy's Rebels) in 1971. Disbanded in 1973, reunited briefly in 1976. All songs written and produced by David Gates.

DEBUT DATE	PEAK POS	WKS CHR	GOLD	ARTIST — Album Title	$	Label & Number
10/18/69	127	9		1 Bread	$12	Elektra 74044
8/8/70	12	32	●	2 On The Waters	$12	Elektra 74076
3/27/71	21	25	●	3 Manna	$12	Elektra 74086
2/5/72	3	56	●	4 Baby I'm-A Want You	$20	Elektra 75015
11/18/72	18	29	●	5 Guitar Man	$12	Elektra 75047
3/31/73	2[1]	119	●	6 The Best Of Bread [G]	$12	Elektra 75056
6/1/74	32	18	●	7 The Best Of Bread, Volume Two [G]	$10	Elektra 1005
1/15/77	26	16	●	8 Lost Without Your Love	$10	Elektra 1094

Any Way You Want Me (1)
Aubrey (5,7) *15*
Baby I'm-A Want You
 (4,6) *3*
Be Kind To Me (3)
Been Too Long On The Road
 (2,7)
Belonging (8)
Blue Satin Pillow (2)
Call On Me (2)
Change Of Heart (8)
Chosen One (3)
Come Again (3)
Coming Apart (2)

Could I (1)
Daughter (4,7)
Diary (4,6) *15*
Didn't Even Know Her Name
 (5)
Dismal Day (1)
Don't Shut Me Out (1)
Don't Tell Me No (5)
Down On My Knees (4,6)
Dream Lady (4,7)
Easy Love (2)
Everything I Own (4,6) *5*
Family Doctor (1)
Fancy Dancer (5,7)

Fly Away (8)
Friends And Lovers (1,7)
Games Of Magic (4)
Guitar Man (5,7) *11*
He's A Good Lad (3,7)
Hold Tight (8)
Hooked On You (8) *60*
I Am That I Am (2)
I Don't Love You (4)
I Say Again (3)
I Want You With Me (2)
If (3,6) *4*
In The Afterglow (4)

It Don't Matter To Me
 (1,6) *10*
Just Like Yesterday (4,7)
Last Time (1)
Lay Your Money Down (8)
Let Me Go (5)
Let Your Love Go (3,6) *28*
Live In Your Love (3)
London Bridge (1,7)
Look At Me (1)
Look What You've Done (2,6)
Lost Without Your Love
 (8) *9*
Make It By Yourself (5)

Make It With You (2,6) *1*
Mother Freedom (4,6) *37*
Move Over (1)
Nobody Like You (4)
Other Side Of Life (2)
Our Lady Of Sorrow (8)
Picture In Your Mind (5)
She Was My Lady (3)
She's The Only One (8)
Sweet Surrender (5,7) *15*
Take Comfort (3)
Tecolote (3)
This Isn't What The
 Governmeant (4)

Today's The First Day (8)
Too Much Love (3,6)
Truckin' (3,6)
Welcome To The Music (5)
What A Change (3)
Why Do You Keep Me
 Waiting (2)
You Can't Measure The Cost
 (1)
Yours For Life (5,7)

BREAKFAST CLUB

New York-based quartet. Madonna was with the group for a short time in the early '80s. Member Steve Bray co-produced Madonna's *True Blue* album.

DEBUT DATE	PEAK POS	WKS CHR	GOLD	ARTIST — Album Title	$	Label & Number
3/28/87	43	30		Breakfast Club	$8	MCA 5821

Always Be Like This
Expressway To Your Heart

Kiss And Tell *48*
Never Be The Same

Rico Mambo
Right On Track *7*

Specialty
Standout

Tongue Tied

BREAKWATER

Eight-man group from Philadelphia, formed in 1971 as Black Magic: Kae Williams (lead vocals), Lincoln "Love" Gilmore, James "Gee" Jones, Vince Garnell, Gene Robinson Jr., Greg Scott, Steve Green, and John "Dutch" Braddock.

DEBUT DATE	PEAK POS	WKS CHR	GOLD	ARTIST — Album Title	$	Label & Number
4/21/79	173	5		1 Breakwater	$8	Arista 4208
6/7/80	141	5		2 Splashdown	$8	Arista 4264

Do It Till The Fluid Gets Hot
 (1)
Feel Your Way (1)
Free Yourself (1)

Let Love In (2)
Love Of My Life (2)
No Limit (1)
One In My Dreams (2)

Release The Beast (2)
Say You Love Me Girl (2)
Splashdown Time (2)

That's Not What We Came
 Here For (1)
Time (2)
Unnecessary Business (1)

Work It Out (1)
You (2)
You Know I Love You (1)

BREATHE

Band from suburban London: David Glasper (vocals), Ian "Spike" Spice, Marcus Lillington and Michael Delahunty (who left in 1988).

DEBUT DATE	PEAK POS	WKS CHR	GOLD	ARTIST — Album Title	$	Label & Number
6/4/88	34	51	●	1 All That Jazz	$8	A&M 5163
9/22/90	116	20		2 Peace Of Mind	$12	A&M 5320

All That Jazz (1)
All This I Should Have
 Known (1)
Any Trick (1)

Does She Love That Man?
 (2) *34*
Don't Tell Me Lies (1) *10*
Got To Get By (2)
Hands To Heaven (1) *2*

How Can I Fall? (1) *3*
I Hear You're Doing Fine (2)
Jonah (1)
Liberties Of Love (1)
Mississippi Water (2)

Monday Morning Blues (1)
Perfect Love (2)
Say A Prayer *[includes 2
 versions]* (2) *21*
Say Hello (1)

Where Angels Fear (2)
Will The Circle Be
 Unbroken (2)
Without Your Love (2)
Woman (2)

Won't You Come Back? (1)

DEBUT DATE	PEAK POS	WKS CHR	GOLD	ARTIST — Album Title	$	Label & Number

BRECKER BROTHERS, The

Formed in New York City by sessionmen/Philadelphia-born brothers Randy (b: 11/27/45; trumpet) and Michael Brecker (b: 3/29/49; reeds). The brothers began recording together in their group Dreams.

DEBUT	PEAK	WKS	GOLD	Album	$	Label
6/7/75	102	13		1 The Brecker Brothers ....[I]	$8	Arista 4037
2/28/76	82	16		2 Back To Back	$8	Arista 4061
5/7/77	135	6		3 Don't Stop The Music ....[I]	$8	Arista 4122
6/20/81	176	3		4 Straphangin' ....[I]	$8	Arista 9550

As Long As I've Got Your Love (3)
Bathsheba (4)
Creature Of Many Faces (1)
D.B.B. (1)
Dig A Little Deeper (2)
Don't Stop The Music (3)
Finger Lickin' Good (3)
Funky Sea, Funky Dew (3)
Grease Piece (2)
I Love Wastin' Time With You (2)
If You Wanna Boogie...Forget It (2)
Jacknife (4)
Keep It Steady (Brecker Bump) (2)
Levitate (1)
Lovely Lady (2)
Night Flight (4)
Not Ethiopia (4)
Oh My Stars (1)
Petals (3)
Rocks (1)
Slick Stuff (2)
Sneakin' Up Behind You (1) **58**
Some Skunk Funk (1)
Sponge (1)
Spreadeagle (4)
Squids (3)
Straphangin' (4)
Tabula Rasa (3)
Threesome (4)
Twilight (1)
What Can A Miracle Do (2)
Why Can't I Be There (4)

BREMERS, Beverly

Chicago-born actress/singer.

DEBUT	PEAK	WKS	GOLD	Album	$	Label
9/16/72	124	8		I'll Make You Music	$10	Scepter 5102

All That's Left Is The Music
At My Place
Baby I Don't Know You
Colors Of Love
Don't Say You Don't Remember 15
Get Smart Girl
Guy Like You
I Made A Man Out Of You
Jimmy
I'll Make You Music 63
May The Road Rise To Meet You
Poor Side Of Town
We're Free 40

BRENDA & THE TABULATIONS

R&B group from Philadelphia, formed in 1966, with Brenda Payton, Jerry Jones, Eddie Jackson and Maurice Coates. Bernard Murphy was added in 1969. Reorganized in 1970 with vocalists Brenda Payton, Pat Mercer and Deborah Martin. Payton died on 6/14/92.

DEBUT	PEAK	WKS	GOLD	Album	$	Label
7/1/67	191	4		Dry Your Eyes	$30	Dionn 2000

Dry Your Eyes 20
Forever
God Only Knows
Hey Boy
Just Once In A Lifetime 97
Oh Lord What Are You Doing To Me
Stay Together Young Lovers 66
Summertime
Walk On By
Wash, The
Where Did Our Love Go
Who's Lovin' You 66

BRENNAN, Walter

Beloved character actor born on 7/25/1894 in Swampscott, Massachusetts. Died on 9/21/74. First film role in 1924. Three-time Oscar winner. Played Grandpa on *The Real McCoys* TV series.

DEBUT	PEAK	WKS	GOLD	Album	$	Label
6/23/62	54	10		Old Rivers	$20	Liberty 3233

Boll Weevil
Conversation With A Mule
Farmer And The Lord
Happy Birthday Old Folk
It Takes A Heap Of Living (To Make A House A Home)
Old Kelly Place
Old Rivers 5
Old Rivers' Trunk
Pickin' Time
Steal Away

BREWER & SHIPLEY

Folk-rock duo formed in Los Angeles: Mike Brewer (b: 1944 in Oklahoma City) and Tom Shipley (b: 1942 in Mineral Ridge, Ohio).

DEBUT	PEAK	WKS	GOLD	Album	$	Label
3/6/71	34	26		1 Tarkio	$10	Kama Sutra 2024
12/25/71+	164	8		2 Shake Off The Demon	$10	Kama Sutra 2039
1/27/73	174	7		3 Rural Space	$10	Kama Sutra 2058
5/11/74	185	5		4 ST-11261	$10	Capitol 11261

album title refers to the label prefix and number

Back To The Farm (2)
Ballad Of A Country Dog (4)
Black Sky (3)
Blue Highway (3)
Bound To Fall (4)
Can't Go Home (1)
Crested Butte (3)
Don't Want To Die In Georgia (1)
Eco-Catastrophe Blues (4)
Fair Play (4)
Fifty States Of Freedom (1)
Fly, Fly, Fly (This Seat Is Occupado) (1)
Got To Get Off The Island (3)
Have A Good Life (3)
How Are You (4)
It Did Me In (4)
Keeper Of The Keys (4)
Light, The (1)
Look Up, Look Out (4)
Merciful Love (2)
Message From The Mission (Hold On) (1)
Natural Child (2)
Oh Mommy (1)
Oh So Long (4)
One By One (2)
One Toke Over The Line (1) **10**
Platte River, Song From (1)
Rock Me On The Water (2)
Ruby On The Morning (1)
Seems Like A Long Time (1)
Shake Off The Demon (2) **3**
Shine So Strong (4)
Sleeping On The Way (3)
Sweet Love (2)
Tarkio Road (1) **55**
When Everybody Comes Home (2)
When The Truth Finally Comes (3)
Where Do We Go From Here (3)
Working On The Well (2)
Yankee Lady (3)

BRICK

Disco-jazz group formed in Atlanta in 1972. Consisted of Jimmy Brown (vocals), Ray Ransom, Donald Nevins, Reggie Hargis and Eddie Irons. Session work in the early 1970s.

DEBUT	PEAK	WKS	GOLD	Album	$	Label
11/13/76+	19	24		1 Good High	$8	Bang 408
9/10/77	15	32		2 Brick	$8	Bang 409
5/19/79	100	8		3 Stoneheart	$8	Bang 35969
7/12/80	179	5		4 Waiting On You	$8	Bang 36262
9/5/81	89	10		5 Summer Heat	$8	Bang 37471

Ain't Gonna' Hurt Nobody (2) **92**
All The Way (4)
Babe (5)
Brick City (1)
By The Moonlight (3)
Can't Wait (1)
Dancin' Man (3)
Dazz (1) **3**
Don't Ever Lose Your Love (4)
Dusic (2) **18**
Free (4)
Fun (2)
Get Fired Up (4)
Get Started (4)
Good High (1)
Good Morning Sunshine (2)
Happening, The (5)
Happy (2)
Hello (2)
Here We Come (1)
Honey Chile (2)
I Want You To Know (That I'm In Love With You) (5)
Let Me Make You Happy (4)
Life Is What You Make It (3)
Living From The Mind (1)
Magic Woman (2)
Music Matic (1)
Push, Push (4)
Raise Your Hands (3)
Right Back (Where I Started From) (5)
Sea Side Vibes (5)
Sister Twister (1)
Southern Sunset (1)
Spread Love (4)
Stoneheart (3)
Summer Heat (5)
Sure Feels Good (3)
Sweat (Till You Get Wet) (5)
Sweet Lips (4)
That's What It's All About (1)
To Me (3)
Waiting On You (4)
We Don't Wanna' Sit Down (We Wanna' Git Down) (2)
We'll Love (3)
Wide Open (5)

BRICKELL, Edie, & New Bohemians

Vocalist Brickell (pronounced: BREE-kell) joined the Dallas-based band in 1985. Varying personnel since then. Brickell was born in Oak Cliff, Texas; her father, Eddie, is a pro bowler. Bohemians' lineup: Brad Houser, Kenny Withrow and John Bush. Joining the band by 1990 were Wes Burt-Martin and Matt Chamberlain. Married Paul Simon in June 1992.

DEBUT	PEAK	WKS	GOLD	Album	$	Label
9/24/88+	4	54 ▲		1 **Shooting Rubberbands At The Stars**	$8	Geffen 24192
11/17/90	32	18		2 Ghost Of A Dog	$12	Geffen 24304

Air Of December (1)
Beat The Time (1)
Black & Blue (2)
Carmelito (2)
Circle (1) **48**
Forgiven (2)
Ghost Of A Dog (2)
He Said (2)
Keep Coming Back (1)
Little Miss S. (1)
Love Like We Do (1)
Mama Help Me (2)
Me By The Sea (2)
Nothing (1)
Now (1)
Oak Cliff Bra (2)
She (1)
Strings Of Love (2)
Stwisted (2)
10,000 Angels (2)
This Eye (2)
Times Like This (2)
What I Am (1) **7**
Wheel, The (1)
Woyaho (2)

BRIDES OF FUNKENSTEIN, The
Offshoot group of George Clinton's Parliament/Funkadelic corporation. Included Lynn Mabry, Dawn Silva, Ron Banks and Larry Demps.

DEBUT DATE	PEAK POS	WKS CHR	GOLD	Album	$	Label & Number
11/4/78	70	13		1 Funk Or Walk	$8	Atlantic 19201
2/16/80	93	7		2 Never Buy Texas From A Cowboy	$8	Atlantic 19261

Amorous (1)
Birdie (1)
Didn't Mean To Fall In Love (2)

Disco To Go (1)
I'm Holding You Responsible (2)

Just Like You (1)
Mother May I? (2)
Nappy (1)

Never Buy Texas From A Cowboy (2)
Party Up In Here (2)

Smoke Signals (2)
War Ship Touchante (1)
When You're Gone (1)

BRIDGES, Alicia
Atlanta-based disco singer/songwriter; originally from Lawndale, North Carolina.

DEBUT DATE	PEAK POS	WKS CHR	GOLD	Album	$	Label & Number
9/30/78+	33	32		Alicia Bridges	$8	Polydor 6158

Body Heat 86
Break Away

Broken Woman
City Rhythm

Diamond In The Rough
High Altitudes

I Love The Nightlife (Disco 'Round) 5

In The Name Of Love
Self Applause

We Are One

BRIDGEWATER, Dee Dee
Born on 5/27/50 in Memphis; raised in Flint, Michigan. Jazz singer. Sang professionally since age 16. Toured the U.S.S.R. with Illinois Jazz Band. With Thad Jones-Mel Lewis Big Band in 1970. In the Broadway show *The Wiz*, as Glinda The Good Witch, in 1975.

DEBUT DATE	PEAK POS	WKS CHR	GOLD	Album	$	Label & Number
5/6/78	170	7		1 Just Family.................................	$8	Elektra 119
5/26/79	182	4		2 Bad For Me	$8	Elektra 188

Back Of Your Mind (2)
Bad For Me (2)
Children Are The Spirit (Of The World) (1)

Don't Say It (If You Don't Mean It) (2)
For The Girls (2)
Is This What Feeling Gets? (2)

It's The Fallin In Love (2)
Just Family (1)
Love Won't Let Me Go (2)
Maybe Today (1)
Melody Maker (1)

Night Moves (1)
Open Up Your Eyes (1)
Sorry Seems To Be The Hardest Word (1)
Streetsinger (2)

Sweet Rain (1)
Tequila Mockingbird (2)
Thank The Day (1)

BRILEY, Martin
British session musician/songwriter. Moved to New York City in 1977.

DEBUT DATE	PEAK POS	WKS CHR	GOLD	Album	$	Label & Number
5/7/83	55	22		1 One Night With A Stranger	$8	Mercury 810332
2/9/85	85	10		2 Dangerous Moments	$8	Mercury 822423

Alone At Last (2)
Before The Party Ends (2)
Dangerous Moments (2)
Dirty Windows (2)
Dumb Love (1)

Ghosts (2)
I Wonder What She Thinks Of Me (1)
If This Is What It Means (2)

It Shouldn't Have To Hurt That Much (2)
Just A Mile Away (1)
Maybe I've Waited Too Long (1)

One Night With A Stranger (1)
Put Your Hands On The Screen (1)

Rainy Day In New York City (1)
Salt In My Tears (1) 36
School For Dogs (2)

She's So Flexible (1)
Think Of Me (2)
Underwater (2)

BRILL, Marty, & Larry Foster — see COMEDY section

BRINKLEY, David — HUNTLEY, Chet

BRISTOL, Johnny
Soul vocalist/composer/producer from Morgantown, North Carolina. Teamed with Jackie Beaver, recorded as Johnny & Jackie for Tri-Phi, 1961. Teamed with Harvey Fuqua as Motown producers until 1973.

DEBUT DATE	PEAK POS	WKS CHR	GOLD	Album	$	Label & Number
8/31/74	82	17		1 Hang On In There Baby.....................	$10	MGM 4959
12/11/76+	154	11		2 Bristol's Creme	$8	Atlantic 18197

Baby's So Much Fun To Dream About (2)
Do It To My Mind (2) 43
Hang On In There Baby (1) 8

Have Yourself A Good Time Thinkin' 'Bout The Good Times... (2)
I Got Cha Number (1)
I Love Talkin' 'Bout Baby (2)

I Sho Like Groovin' With Ya (2)
It Don't Hurt No More (1)
Love Me For A Reason (1)
Love To Have A Chance To Taste The Wine (2)

Memories Don't Leave Like People Do (1)
Reachin' Out For Your Love (1)
She Came Into My Life (1)
Take Care Of You For Me (1)

Woman, Woman (1)
You And I (1) 48
You Turned Me On To Love (2)

BRITISH LIONS
Birmingham, England rock quintet formed by Mott The Hoople alumnus: Pete "Overend" Watts, Morgan Fisher and Dale "Buffin" Griffin. Vocals by John Fiddler.

DEBUT DATE	PEAK POS	WKS CHR	GOLD	Album	$	Label & Number
4/29/78	83	15		British Lions	$8	RSO 3032

Big Drift Away
Booster

Break This Fool
Eat The Rich

Fork Talking Man
International Heroes

My Life's In Your Hands
One More Chance To Run

Wild In The Streets 87

BRITNY FOX
Heavy-metal quartet from Philadelphia: "Dizzy" Dean Davidson (vocals), Michael Kelly Smith, Billy Childs and Johnny Dee. Smith was an original member of Cinderella. Dee was a member of Waysted.

DEBUT DATE	PEAK POS	WKS CHR	GOLD	Album	$	Label & Number
7/23/88	39	37	●	1 Britny Fox	$8	Columbia 44140
11/25/89	79	23		2 Boys In Heat	$8	Columbia 45300

Angel In My Heart (2)
Don't Hide (1)
Dream On (2)
Fun In Texas (1)

Girlschool (1)
Gudbuy T Jane (1)
Hair Of The Dog (2)
Hold On (1)

In America (1)
In Motion (2)
Kick 'N' Fight (1)
Left Me Stray (2)

Livin' On A Dream (2)
Long Way From Home (2)
Long Way To Love (1) 100
Longroad (2)

Plenty Of Love (2)
Rock Revolution (1)
Save The Weak (1)
She's So Lonely (2)

Shine On (2)
Standing In The Shadows (2)
Stevie (2)

BRITTEN, Benjamin
British conductor; died on 12/4/76 (age 63).

DEBUT DATE	PEAK POS	WKS CHR	GOLD	Album	$	Label & Number
9/7/63	68	8		Britten: War Requiem	$15	London 4255 [2]

with The London Symphony Orchestra

Britten: War Requiem, Op. 66 (Requiem Aeternam/Dies Irae)

Britten: War Requiem, Op. 66 (Offertorium)

Britten: War Requiem, Op. 66 (Sanctus/Agnus Dei)

Britten: War Requiem, Op. 66 (Libera Me)

BROMBERG, David
New York folk session guitarist. Born in September 1945 in Philadelphia. Backed Jerry Jeff Walker, Bob Dylan, Doug Kershaw, Tom Paxton and others.

DEBUT DATE	PEAK POS	WKS CHR	GOLD	Album	$	Label & Number
3/25/72	194	2		1 David Bromberg	$10	Columbia 31104
2/23/74	167	5		2 Wanted Dead Or Alive	$10	Columbia 32717
7/12/75	173	3		3 Midnight On The Water	$10	Columbia 33397
10/9/76	104	11		4 How Late'll Ya Play 'Til? ....[L]	$12	Fantasy 79007 [2]
				record 1: studio; record 2: live		
11/19/77	132	9		5 Reckless Abandon	$10	Fantasy 9540

97

DEBUT DATE	PEAK POS	WKS CHR	GOLD	ARTIST — Album Title	$	Label & Number

BROMBERG, David — Cont'd

| 6/17/78 | 130 | 9 | | 6 Bandit In A Bathing Suit | $10 | Fantasy 9555 |
| 2/24/79 | 152 | 4 | | 7 My Own House | $10 | Fantasy 9572 |

Baby Breeze (5)
Bandit In A Bathing Suit (6)
Battle Of Bull Run Medley (5)
Beware Brother Beware (5)
Black And Tan (7)
Blackberry Blossom (medley) (6)
Bluebird (4)
Boggy Road To Milledgeville (Arkansas Traveler) (1)
Bullfrog Blues (4)
Child's Song (5)
Chubby Thighs (4)
Chump Man Blues (7)
Church Bell Blues (medley) (2)
Cocaine Blues (7)

Come On In My Kitchen (4)
Dallas Rag (medley) (4)
Danger Man (2)
Danger Man II (4)
Dark Hollow (3)
Dehlia (1)
Dixie Hoedown (medley) (6)
Don't Let Your Deal Go Down Medley (7)
Don't Put That Thing On Me (3)
Dyin' Crapshooter's Blues (4)
Early This Morning (7)
Fiddle Tunes (medley) (4)
Georgia On My Mind (7)
Get Up And Go (medley) (4)
Holdup, The (1,2)

I Like To Sleep Late In The Morning (3)
I Want To Go Home (5)
Idol With A Golden Head (4)
If I Get Lucky (3)
If You Don't Want Me Baby (6)
Joke's On Me (3)
June Apple (medley) (6)
Kaatskill Serenade (4)
Kansas City (2)
Kitchen Girl (7)
Last Song For Shelby Jean (1)
Lonesome Dave's Lovesick Blues #3 (1)

Love Please Come Home (medley) (6)
Lower Left Hand Corner Of The Night (7)
Main Street Moan (2)
Maple Leaf Rag (medley) (4)
Midnight On The Water Medley (3)
Mississippi Blues (1)
Mr. Blue (3)
Mrs. Delion's Lament (5)
My Own Home Medley (7)
New Lee Highway Blues (2)
Nobody's (3)
Nobody's Fault But Mine (5)
Northeast Texas Women (6)
Peanut Man (6)

Pine Tree Woman (1)
Queen Ellen (6)
Sally Goodin' Medley (5)
Sammy's Song (1)
Send Me To The 'Lectric Chair (2)
Sheebeg And Sheemore (7)
Sloppy Drunk (4)
Someone Else's Blues (2)
Spanish Johnny (7)
Statesboro Blues (medley) (2)
Stealin' (5)
Such A Night (4)
Suffer To Sing The Blues (1)
Summer Wages (4)
Sweet Home Chicago (4)
Sweet Sweet Sadness (6)

To Know Her Is To Love Her (7)
Travelling Man (6)
Ugly Hour (6)
Wallflower (1)
What A Town (5)
(What A) Wonderful World (3)
Whoopee Ti Yi Yo (4)
Will Not Be Your Fool (4)
Yankee's Revenge Medley (3)
Young Westley (4)

BRONSKI BEAT

British techno-pop trio: Jimmy Somerville (vocals), Steve Bronski and Larry Steinbachek (synthesizers). Somerville formed the Communards in 1986.

| 1/19/85 | 36 | 25 | | 1 The Age Of Consent | $8 | MCA 5538 |
| 8/2/86 | 147 | 6 | | 2 Truthdare Doubledare | $8 | MCA 5751 |

C'Mon! C'Mon! (2)
Do It (2)
Dr. John (2)
Heatwave (1)

Hit That Perfect Beat (2)
I Feel Love (medley) (1)
In My Dreams (2)
It Ain't Necessarily So (1)

Johnny Remember Me (medley) (1)
Junk (1)
Love And Money (1)

Need A Man Blues (1)
No More War (1)
Punishment For Love (2)
Screaming (1)

Smalltown Boy (1) 48
This Heart (2)
Truthdare Doubledare (2)
We Know How It Feels (2)

Why? (1)

BROOD, Herman

Leader of rock band from the Netherlands. Born on 11/5/46 in Zwolle, Holland.

| 5/26/79 | 122 | 19 | | Herman Brood & His Wild Romance | $10 | Ariola 50059 |

Back (In Yr Love)
Champagne (& Wine)
Doin' It

Dope Sucks
Doreen
Get Lost

Hit
Hot Talk
Never Enough

Pain
Prisoners
R & Roll Junkie

Saturdaynight 35
Skid Row

BROOKLYN BRIDGE

Long Island, New York outfit led by vocalist Johnny Maestro (of The Crests). The Del-Satins, a vocal quartet led by Maestro, and The Rhythm Method, a seven-piece band, united as Brooklyn Bridge in 1967.

3/29/69	54	30		1 Brooklyn Bridge	$20	Buddah 5034
10/11/69	145	8		2 The Second Brooklyn Bridge	$20	Buddah 5042
10/18/69	169	4		3 Live At Yankee Stadium [L]	$12	T-Neck 3004

side A: Isley Brothers; side B: Edwin Hawkins Singers; side C: Brooklyn Bridge; side D: "Don't Change Your Love" by The Five Stairsteps, "Somebody's Been Messin'" by Judy White and "Love Is What You Make It" by Sweet Cherries

Also Sprach Zarathustra ..see: Space Odessey
Amen (medley) (3)
Blessed Is The Rain (1) 45
Caroline (2)
Echo Park (2)
Free As The Wind (1)

Glad She's A Woman (1)
I'm So Proud (medley) (3)
I've Been Lonely Too Long (1)
In The End (2)
Inside Out (Upside Down) (2)
It's All Right (medley) (3)
Keep On Pushin' (medley) (3)

Look At Me (2)
Minstral Sunday (2)
People Get Ready (medley) (3)
Piece Of My Heart (1)
Requiem (1)
Space Odessey-2001 (Thus Spake Zarathustra) (1)

Talkin' About My Baby (medley) (3)
12:29 Is Taking My Baby Away (2)
Welcome Me Love (1) 48
Which Way To Nowhere (1)
Without Her (Father Paul) (1)

Worst That Could Happen (1) 3
You Must Believe Me (medley) (3)
You'll Never Walk Alone (2) 51

Your Husband - My Wife (2) 46
Your Kite, My Kite (1)

BROOKLYN, BRONX & QUEENS BAND (B.B.&Q. Band)

R&B quintet led by vocalist Lucious Isiah Floyd.

| 8/29/81 | 109 | 9 | | The Brooklyn, Bronx & Queens Band | $8 | Capitol 12155 |

Don't Say Goodbye
I'll Cut You Loose

Lovin's What We Should Do
Mistakes

On The Beat
Starlette

Time For Love

BROOKLYN DREAMS

New York trio: Joe "Bean" Esposito, Eddie Hokenson and Bruce Sudano (Donna Summer's husband). Sudano was a member of Alive & Kicking.

| 3/24/79 | 151 | 7 | | Sleepless Nights | $8 | Casablanca 7135 |

Coming Up The Hard Way
Fashion For Me
First Love

Heaven Knows 4
Long Distance
Make It Last 69

Send Me A Dream (medley)
Sleepless Nights (medley)
Street Man

That's Not The Way That Your Mama Taught You To Be

Touching In The Dark

★★254★★ BROOKS, Garth

Born on 2/7/62 in Tulsa and raised in Yukon, Oklahoma. Attended Oklahoma State on a track scholarship (javelin). His mother, Colleen Carroll, signed with Capitol in 1954 and was a regular on Red Foley's *Ozark Jubilee* TV show. Brooks' immense popularity contributed to a resurgence of Country music in the '90s.

5/12/90+	13	144↑▲4		1 Garth Brooks	$12	Capitol 90897
9/22/90+	3	125↑▲9		2 No Fences	$12	Capitol 93866
9/28/91	1 18	72↑▲9		3 Ropin' The Wind	$12	Capitol 96330
9/12/92	2 1	22↑▲2		4 Beyond The Season [X]	$12	Liberty 98742

Christmas charts: 1/'92

| 10/10/92 | 1 7 | 18↑▲5 | | 5 The Chase | $12 | Liberty 98743 |

Against The Grain (3)
Alabama Clay (1)
Burning Bridges (3)
Cold Shoulder (1)
Cowboy Bill (1)
Dance, The (1)
Dixie Chicken (5)
Every Now And Then (5)

Everytime That It Rains (1)
Face To Face (5)
Friendly Beasts (4)
Friends In Low Places (1)
Gift, The (4)
Go Tell It On The Mountain (4)

God Rest Ye Merry Gentlemen (4)
I Know One (1)
I've Got A Good Thing Going (1)
If Tomorrow Never Comes (1)
In Lonesome Dove (3)
Learning To Live Again (5)

Mary's Dream (4)
Mr. Blue (2)
Mr. Right (5)
Much Too Young (To Feel This Damn Old) (1)
New Way To Fly (2)
Night Rider's Lament (5)

Nobody Gets Off In This Town (1)
Not Counting You (1)
Old Man's Back In Town (4)
Papa Loved Mama (3)
River, The (3)
Rodeo (3)
Same Old Story (2)

Santa Looked A Lot Like Daddy (4)
Shameless (3)
Silent Night (4)
Somewhere Other Than The Night (5)
That Summer (5)
Thunder Rolls (2)

DEBUT DATE	PEAK POS	WKS CHR	GOLD	ARTIST — Album Title	$	Label & Number

BROOKS, Garth — Cont'd

Two Of A Kind, Workin' On A Full House (2)
Unanswered Prayers (2)
Unto You This Night (4)
Victim Of The Game (2)
Walking After Midnight (5)
We Bury The Hatchet (3)
We Shall Be Free (5)
What Child Is This (4)
What She's Doing Now (3)
White Christmas (4)
Wild Horses (2)
Wolves (2)

BROOKS, Mel — see REINER, Carl

BROOKS & DUNN
Country veterans Kix Brooks (born in Louisiana) and Ronnie Dunn (born in Coleman, Texas).

| 9/7/91+ | 10 | 61↑▲² | | Brand New Man | $12 | Arista 18658 |

Boot Scootin' Boogie 50
Brand New Man

Cheating On The Blues
Cool Drink Of Water
I'm No Good
I've Got A Lot To Learn
Lost And Found
My Next Broken Heart
Neon Moon
Still In Love With You

BROS
British pop trio: Matt and Luke Goss (twin brothers, b: 9/29/68) and Craig Logan (b: 4/22/69). Group's name rhymes with "cross." Logan left in early 1988.

| 7/23/88 | 171 | 5 | | Push | $8 | Epic 44285 |

Cat Among The Pigeons
Drop The Boy
I Owe You Nothing
I Quit
It's A Jungle Out There
Liar
Love To Hate You
Shocked
Ten Out Of Ten
When Will I Be Famous? 83

BROTHERHOOD OF MAN, The
British studio group featuring Tony Burrows, Johnny Goddison and Sunny (female singer). Burrows was lead singer of Edison Lighthouse, First Class, The Pipkins and White Plains.

| 8/8/70 | 168 | 8 | | United We Stand | $10 | Deram 18046 |

For Old Times Sake
For The Rest Of Our Lives
Little Bit Of Heaven
Living In The Land Of Love
Love Is A Good Foundation
Love One Another
Say A Prayer
Sing In The Sunshine
Too Many Heartaches
United We Stand 13
Where Are You Going To My Love 61

★★374★★ BROTHERS FOUR, The
Folk-pop quartet: Dick Foley, Bob Flick, John Paine and Mike Kirkland. Formed while Phi Gamma Delta fraternity brothers at the University of Washington.

4/18/60	11	19		1 The Brothers Four	$15	Columbia 1402
2/13/61	4	35		2 B.M.O.C. (Best Music On/Off Campus)	$15	Columbia 1578
12/18/61	71	14		3 The Brothers Four Song Book	$15	Columbia 1697
10/6/62	102	4		4 The Brothers Four: In Person [L]	$15	Columbia 1828
5/4/63	81	12		5 Cross-Country Concert [L]	$15	Columbia 1946
10/12/63	56	20		6 The Big Folk Hits	$15	Columbia 8833
10/31/64	134	4		7 More Big Folk Hits	$15	Columbia 9013
5/1/65	118	5		8 The Honey Wind Blows	$15	Columbia 9105
11/13/65+	76	15		9 Try To Remember	$15	Columbia 9179
7/30/66	97	7		10 A Beatles' Songbook (The Brothers Four sing Lennon/McCartney)	$15	Columbia 9302

Across The Sea (4)
All My Loving (10)
And I Love Her (10)
Angelique-O (1)
Banana Boat Song (7)
Banua (1)
Battle Of New Orleans (7)
Beast (Song Of The Punch Press Operator) (5)
Beautiful Brown Eyes (2)
Boa Constrictor (5)
Born Free (9)
Brady, Brady, Brady (5)
Brandy Wine Blues (5)
Brother Where Are You (7)
Cleano (8)
Come For To Carry Me Home (3)
Come Kiss Me Love (9)
Come To My Bedside, My Darlin' (7)
Damsel's Lament (I Never Will Marry) (1)
Darlin' Sportin' Jenny (4)
Darlin', Won't You Wait (1)
Darling Corey (6)
Don't Let The Rain Come Down (Crooked Little Man) (7)
Don't Think Twice, It's All Right (7)
Drillers' Song (8)
East Virginia (1)
Eddystone Light (1)
El Paso (6)
Feed The Birds (8)
First Battalion (4)
500 Miles (6)
Frogg (3) 32
Gimme That Wine (9)
Girl (10)
Goodnight, Irene (3)
Green Leaves Of Summer (2) 65
Greenfields (1,4) 2
Hard Travelin' (1)
Help! (10)
Honey Wind Blows (8)
House Of The Rising Sun (8)
I Am A Roving Gambler (2,4)
I Remember When I Loved Her (9)
I'll Follow The Sun (10)
I'm Just A Country Boy (7)
If I Fell (10)
If I Had A Hammer (6)
Island In The Sun (10)
Jamaica Farewell (6)
John B. Sails (6)
Just A Little Rain (Low Down You Big Thunderhead) (5)
Lady Greensleeves (3)
Lazy Harry's (8)
Little Play Soldiers (8)
Malaika (5)
Michael Row The Boat Ashore (6)
Michelle (10)
Midnight Special (4)
Moulin Rouge (Where Is Your Heart), Song From The (9)
Mr. Tambourine Man (8)
Muleskinner (3)
My Little John Henry (Got A Mighty Know) (2)
Nancy O. (4)
New "Frankie And Johnnie" Song (5)
Nobody Knows (3)
Norwegian Wood (This Bird Has Flown) (10)
Nowhere Man (10)
Old Settler's Song (2)
Ole Smokey (3)
Poverty Hill (8)
Pretty Girl Is Like A Little Bird (2)
Puff (The Magic Dragon) (7)
Riders In The Sky (2)
Rock Island Line (3,4)
Run, Come, See Jerusalem (4)
Sakura (9)
Sama Kama Wacky Brown (1)
San Francisco Bay Blues (7)
Scarlet Ribbons (For Her Hair) (2)
Silver Threads And Golden Needles (6)
Since My Canary Died (5)
Sloth (9)
Somewhere (8)
Song Of The Ox Driver (5)
St. James Infirmary (2)
Summer Days Alone (3)
Summertime (4)
Superman (1)
Sweet Rosyanne (2)
Symphonic Variation (The Violins Play Along) (5)
Tarrytown (3)
Tavern Song (3)
Thinking Man, John Henry (4)
Tie Me Kangaroo Down, Sport (6)
Try To Remember (9) 91
Turn Around (8)
25 Minutes To Go (5)
Variation On An Old English Theme (4)
Viva La Compagnie (3)
Walk Right In (6)
Waves Roll On (8)
We Can Work It Out (10)
We Shall Overcome (7)
Well, Well, Well (2)
What Now My Love (9)
When Everything Was Green (9)
When The Sun Goes Down (2)
Where Have All The Flowers Gone (7)
Whoa, Back, Buck! (4)
Wild Colonial Boy (9)
Winken, Blinken And Nod (5)
Wish I Was In Bowling Green (5)
With You Fair Maid (2)
Wolverton Mountain (6)
Yellow Bird (1)
Yesterday (10)
Zulu Warrior (1)

★★460★★ BROTHERS JOHNSON, The
Los Angeles R&B-funk duo of brothers George (b: 5/17/53) and Louis Johnson (b: 4/13/55). Own band, the Johnson Three + 1, with brother Tommy and cousin Alex Weir. With Billy Preston's band to 1975. Also see Quincy Jones.

3/6/76	9	49	▲	1 Look Out For #1	$8	A&M 4567
5/21/77	13	31	▲	2 Right On Time	$8	A&M 4644
8/12/78	7	24	▲	3 Blam!!	$8	A&M 4714
3/8/80	5	30	▲	4 Light Up The Night	$8	A&M 3716
7/18/81	48	13		5 Winners	$8	A&M 3724
1/22/83	138	5		6 Blast! (The Latest And The Greatest) [G]	$8	A&M 4927

side 1: new tracks; side 2: greatest hits

| 8/4/84 | 91 | 11 | | 7 Out Of Control | $8 | A&M 4965 |

Ain't We Funkin' Now (3,6)
All About The Heaven (4)
Blam!! (3)
Brother Man (2)
Caught Up (5)
Celebrations (4)
Closer To The One That You Love (4)
Come Together (1)
Dancin' And Prancin' (1)
Dancin' Free (5)
Daydreamer Dream (5)
Dazed (7)
Devil, The (1)
Do It For Love (5)
Do You (7)
Free And Single (1)
Free Yourself, Be Yourself (4)
Funk It (Funkadelala) (6)
Get The Funk Out Ma Face (1,6) **30**
Great Awaking (6)
Hot Mama (5)
I Came Here To Party (4)
I Want You (5)
I'll Be Good To You (1,6) **3**
I'm Giving You All Of My Love (6)
In The Way (5)
It's All Over Now (7)
It's You Girl (3)
Land Of Ladies (2)
Let's Try Love Again (7)
Light Up The Night (4)
Love Is (2)
Lovers Forever (7)
Mista' Cool (3)
Never Leave You Lonely (2)
Out Of Control (7)
"Q" (1)
Real Thing (5,6) **67**

99

BROTHERS JOHNSON, The — Cont'd

Ride-O-Rocket (3)	Smilin' On Ya (4)	Streetwave (4)	Thunder Thumbs And	You Make Me Wanna Wiggle
Right On Time (2)	So Won't You Stay (3)	Sunlight (5)	Lightnin' Licks (1)	(4)
Runnin' For Your Lovin' (2)	**Stomp!** (4,6) **7**	Teaser (5)	Tokyo (7)	
Save Me (7)	Strawberry Letter 23 (2,6) **5** This Had To Be (4)	Tomorrow (4)	

Treasure (4) **73**
Welcome To The Club (6)
You Keep Me Coming Back (7)

BROWN, Arthur, The Crazy World Of

Born Arthur Wilton on 6/24/44 in Whitby, England. Theatrical rock singer. Band included drummer Carl Palmer, later of Atomic Rooster, Emerson, Lake & Palmer and Asia.

9/7/68	7	24		The Crazy World Of Arthur Brown	$15	Track 8198

Child Of My Kingdom	Confusion (medley)	Fire Poem	I've Got Money	Rest Cure	Time (medley)
Come And Buy	**Fire 2**	I Put A Spell On You	Nightmare	Spontaneous Apple Creation	

BROWN, Bobby

Born on 2/5/69 in Boston. Former member of the teen R&B-pop group New Edition. Had a bit part in the film *Ghostbusters II*. Married Whitney Houston on 7/18/92.

12/13/86+	88	17		1 King Of Stage	$8	MCA 5827
7/23/88+	1[6]	97	▲[6]	2 **Don't Be Cruel**	$8	MCA 42185
12/2/89+	9	33	▲	3 **Dance!...Ya Know It!** .... [K]	$8	MCA 6342
				previously unreleased, remixed versions of Bobby's hits		
9/12/92	2[1]	22↑ ▲		4 **Bobby**	$12	MCA 10417

All Day All Night (2)	Girl Next Door (1,3)	King Of Stage (1)	**Rock Wit'cha** (2,3) **7**	That's The Way Love Is (4)
Baby, I Wanna Tell You	**Girlfriend** (1) **57**	Love Obsession (1)	**Roni** (2,3) **3**	Til The End Of Time (4)
Something (1,3)	**Good Enough** (4) **7**	Lovin' You Down (4)	Seventeen (1,3)	Two Can Play That Game (4)
College Girl (4)	**Humpin' Around** (4) **3**	**My Prerogative** (2,3) **1**	Something In Common (4)	You Ain't Been Loved Right
Don't Be Cruel (2,3) **8**	I Really Love You Girl (2)	On Our Own (3)	Spending Time (1)	(1)
Every Little Step (2,3) **3**	I'll Be Good To You (2)	One More Night (4)	Storm Away (4)	Your Tender Romance (1)
Get Away (4) **25↑**	I'm Your Friend (4)	Pretty Little Girl (4)	Take It Slow (2)	

BROWN, Chuck, & The Soul Searchers

Washington, D.C.-based, nine-member R&B group.

2/17/79	31	14	●	Bustin' Loose	$8	Source 3076

Berro E Sombaro	Could It Be Love	I Gotcha Now	Never Gonna Give You Up
Bustin' Loose Part 1 34	Game Seven	If It Ain't Funky	

BROWN, Danny Joe

Lead singer of Molly Hatchet. Born in 1951 in Jacksonville, Florida.

7/4/81	120	7		Danny Joe Brown And The Danny Joe Brown Band	$8	Epic 37385

Alamo, The	Edge Of Sundown	Hear My Song	Nobody Walks On Me	Sundance
Beggar Man	Gambler's Dream	Hit The Road	Run For Your Life	Two Days Home

★★13★★ BROWN, James

Born on 5/3/28 in Macon, Georgia. Raised in Augusta. Formed own vocal group, the Famous Flames. Cut a demo record of own composition "Please Please Please" in November 1955 at radio station WIBB in Macon. Signed to King/Federal Records in January 1956 and re-recorded the song. Cameo appearances in films *The Blues Brothers* and *Rocky IV*. One of the originators of "Soul" music, variously billed on Polydor hits as "Soul I," "The Creator," "The Godfather Of Soul," "The Hit Man" and "Minister Of New New Super Heavy Funk." His backing group, The JB's, featured various personnel, including Nat Kendrick, Bootsy Collins, Maceo Parker and Fred Wesley. Inducted into the Rock and Roll Hall of Fame in 1986. On 12/15/88, received a six-year prison sentence after leading police on an interstate car chase; released from prison on 2/27/91. Ranked as the #1 artist in *Joel Whitburn's Top R&B Singles 1942-1988* book.

6/29/63	2[2]	66		1 Live At The Apollo .... [L]	$60	King 826
				recorded at the Apollo Theater, New York City, 10/24/62		
9/28/63	73	17		2 Prisoner Of Love	$50	King 851
2/29/64	10	22		3 **Pure Dynamite! Live At The Royal** .... [L]	$50	King 883
				recorded at the Royal Theater, Baltimore, Maryland		
5/9/64	61	18		4 Showtime .... [L]	$20	Smash 67054
4/10/65	124	10		5 Grits & Soul .... [I]	$20	Smash 67057
9/11/65+	26	27		6 Papa's Got A Brand New Bag	$30	King 938
11/20/65+	42	19		7 James Brown Plays James Brown - Today & Yesterday .... [I]	$20	Smash 67072
1/22/66	36	17		8 I Got You (I Feel Good)	$30	King 946
4/16/66	101	11		9 James Brown Plays New Breed .... [I]	$20	Smash 67080
9/10/66	90	9		10 It's A Man's Man's Man's World	$30	King 985
12/3/66	135	3		11 Handful Of Soul .... [I]	$20	Smash 67084
4/8/67	88	14		12 Raw Soul	$20	King 1016
6/10/67	41	17		13 Live At The Garden .... [L]	$20	King 1018
7/15/67	164	5		14 James Brown Plays The Real Thing .... [I]	$15	Smash 67093
9/16/67	35	17		15 Cold Sweat	$20	King 1020
3/23/68	17	14		16 I Can't Stand Myself (When You Touch Me)	$15	King 1030
5/18/68	135	14		17 I Got The Feelin'	$15	King 1031
8/24/68	150	5		18 James Brown Plays Nothing But Soul .... [I]	$15	King 1034
9/7/68	32	39		19 Live At The Apollo, Volume II .... [L]	$15	King 1022 [2]
4/12/69	53	22		20 Say It Loud-I'm Black And I'm Proud	$15	King 1047
5/31/69	99	14		21 Gettin' Down To It	$15	King 1051
8/23/69	40	22		22 James Brown plays & directs The Popcorn .... [I]	$15	King 1055
9/6/69	26	24		23 It's A Mother	$15	King 1063
2/14/70	43	12		24 Ain't It Funky .... [I]	$15	King 1092
5/16/70	125	10		25 Soul On Top	$15	King 1100
				with the Louie Bellson Orchestra		
7/4/70	121	6		26 It's A New Day So Let A Man Come In	$15	King 1095
9/12/70	29	31		27 Sex Machine .... [L]	$15	King 1115 [2]
1/30/71	61	15		28 Super Bad .... [L]	$15	King 1127

DEBUT DATE	PEAK POS	WKS CHR	GOLD	ARTIST — Album Title	$	Label & Number

DEBUT DATE	PEAK POS	WKS CHR	GOLD	ARTIST — Album Title	$	Label & Number
				BROWN, James — Cont'd		
5/1/71	137	4		29 Sho Is Funky Down Here .... [I]	$15	King 1110
9/4/71	22	18		30 Hot Pants	$10	Polydor 4054
12/25/71+	39	21		31 Revolution Of The Mind - Live At The Apollo, Volume III .... [L]	$10	Polydor 3003 [2]
6/17/72	83	16		32 James Brown Soul Classics .... [G]	$10	Polydor 5401
7/8/72	60	21		33 There It Is	$10	Polydor 5028
12/9/72+	68	17		34 Get On The Good Foot	$10	Polydor 3004 [2]
3/3/73	31	21		35 Black Caesar .... [S]	$10	Polydor 6014
7/28/73	92	11		36 Slaughter's Big Rip-Off .... [S]	$10	Polydor 6015
1/5/74	34	36	●	37 The Payback	$10	Polydor 3007 [2]
7/27/74	35	19		38 Hell	$10	Polydor 9001 [2]
1/25/75	56	10		39 Reality	$10	Polydor 6039
5/24/75	103	8		40 Sex Machine Today	$10	Polydor 6042
10/4/75	193	2		41 Everybody's Doin' The Hustle & Dead On The Double Bump	$10	Polydor 6054
8/14/76	147	8		42 Get Up Offa That Thing	$10	Polydor 6071
1/15/77	126	10		43 Bodyheat	$10	Polydor 6093
5/6/78	121	22		44 Jam/1980's	$10	Polydor 6140
8/11/79	152	6		45 The Original Disco Man	$10	Polydor 6212
8/16/80	170	5		46 James Brown...Live/Hot On The One .... [L]	$10	Polydor 6290 [2]
				recorded in Tokyo, Japan		
11/22/80	163	3		47 Live And Lowdown At The Apollo, Vol. 1 .... [R]	$8	Solid Smoke 8006
				reissue of album #1 above		
10/18/86	156	6		48 Gravity	$8	Scotti Br. 40380
6/18/88	96	14		49 I'm Real	$8	Scotti Br. 44241
				all music and background vocals performed by Full Force		

After You Done It (24)
After You're Through (5)
Again (2)
Ain't It A Groove (34)
Ain't It Funky Now (Parts 1 and 2) (24) 24
Ain't Nobody Here But Us Chickens (4)
Ain't That A Groove (10,13) 42
All About My Girl (9)
All For One (39)
All The Way (21)
And I Do Just What I Want (6)
Any Day Now (23)
Baby, Baby, Baby, Baby (16)
Baby, You're Right (6) 49
Back Stabbin' (15)
Bells, The (10) 68
Bernadette (14)
Bewildered (1,2,10,27,31,47) 40
Big Strong (36)
Blind Man Can See It (35)
Blues & Pants (30)
Blues For My Baby (4)
Bob Scoward (29)
Bodyheat (43,46) 88
Boss, The (35)
Bring It Up (12,13,19) 29
Brother Rap (27,36)
Buddy-E (18)
By The Time I Get To Phoenix (28)
Caledonia (4) 95
Calm & Cool (41)
Can Mind (29)
(Can You) Feel It (Part 1) (2)
Can't Git Enough (49)
Can't Stand It (30)
(also see: I Can't Stand It)
Can't Take It With You (42)
Chase, The (22,35)
Check Your Body (39)
Chicago (21)
Chicken, The (22)
Cold Sweat (15,19,21,24,32,34) 7
Coldblooded (38) flip
Come Over Here (10)
Come Rain Or Come Shine (15)
Cross Firing (6)
"D" Thing (14)
Dancin' Little Thing (8)
Dead On It (40)
Deep In It (40)
Devil's Hideaway (5)
Dirty Harri (34,35)
Doin' The Limbo (6)
Doing The Best I Can (37)

Don't Be A Drop Out (12) 50
Don't Cry Baby (4)
Don't Fence Me In (39)
Don't Mind (29)
Don't Tell A Lie About Me And I Won't Tell The Truth On You (38)
Don't Tell It (43)
Down And Out In New York City (35) 50
Escape-ism (30,31) 35
Every Beat Of My Heart (7) 99
Every Day I Have The Blues (25)
Evil (4)
Eyesight (44)
Fat Soul (18)
Fat Wood (Parts 1 and 2) (24)
Fever (15)
For Once In My Life (25)
For You My Love (4)
Forever Suffering (37)
Funky Broadway (14)
Funky President (People It's Bad) (35) 44
Funky Side Of Town (34)
Funky Soul #1 (16)
Further On Up The Road (39)
Georgia On My Mind (26)
Get It Together (16) 40
Get Loose (11)
Get On The Good Foot (34,46) 18
Get Up, Get Into It, Get Involved (31)
Get Up I Feel Like Being Like A Sex Machine (27,31,32) 15
(also see: Sex Machine)
Get Up Off Of Me (40)
Get Up Off That Thing (42,46) 45
Gittin' A Little Hipper (18)
Give It Up Or Turnit A Loose (24,26,27,31,32) 15
Giving Out Of Juice (28)
Go On Now (18)
Godfather Runnin' The Joint (49)
Goliath (48)
Gonna Have A Funky Good Time (46)
Good, Good Loving (3,8)
Good Rockin' Tonight (15)
Goodbye My Love (20) 31
Gravity (48) 93
Grits (5)
Happy For The Poor (36)
Have Mercy Baby (6) 92
Headache (5)
Hell (38)

Here I Go (17)
Hip Bag '67 (13)
Hold It (7)
Hold On, I'm Comin' (11)
Home Again (42)
Hooks (9)
Hot Mix (11)
Hot Pants (She Got To Use What She Got To Get What She Wants) (30,31) 15
How Do You Stop (48)
How Long Can I Keep It Up (36)
How Long Darling (2)
Hustle!!! (Dead On It) (41)
I Can't Help It (I Just Do-Do-Do) (8)
I Can't Stand It (medley) (31)
(also see: Can't Stand It)
I Can't Stand It "76" (38)
I Can't Stand Myself (When You Touch Me) (16,27) 28
I Don't Mind (1,10,47) 47
I Don't Want Nobody To Give Me Nothing (27)
I Feel Good (40)
I Found Someone (1,47)
I Got A Bag Of My Own (34) 44
I Got The Feelin' (17,23,27,31,46) 6
I Got You (I Feel Good) (8,13,19,32) 3
I Guess I'll Have To Cry, Cry, Cry (20) 55
I Love You (20)
(I Love You) For Sentimental Reasons (21)
I Love You, Yes I Do (1,10,47)
I Loves You Porgy (15)
I Need Help (I Can't Do It Alone) (33)
I Need Your Key (To Turn Me On) (25)
I Never Loved A Man The Way I Love You (14)
I Never, Never, Never Will Forget (44)
I Refuse To Lose (42)
I Stay In The Chapel Every Night (Just Won't Do Right) (6)
I Want To Be Around (15,19)
I Want You So Bad (1,47)
I'll Go Crazy (1,47)
I'll Lose My Mind (20)
I'll Never Let You Go (3)
I'm A Greedy Man (Part 1 And 2) (33) 35
I'm Broken Hearted (39)

I'm Not Demanding (Part 1) (26)
I'm Real (49)
I'm Satisfied (43)
I'm Shook (23)
I've Got Money (8)
If I Ruled The World (17,23,26,27)
In The Middle (22)
In The Wee Wee Hours (Of The Nite) (10)
Infatuation (5)
Is It Yes Or Is It No? (10)
It Had To Be You (21)
It May Be The Last Time (13,19)
It Won't Be Me (17)
It's A Man's Man's Man's World (10,19,25,26,27,32,46) 8
It's A New Day (Part 1 And 2) (26) 57
It's A New Day So Let A Man Come In And Do The Popcorn (31)
It's Magic (25)
It's Too Funky In Here (45,46)
It's Your Money$ (49)
Jabo (9)
Jam (4)
Jam 1980 (46)
James Brown's Boo-Ga-Loo (9)
Jimmy Mack (14)
Just Enough Room For Storage (29)
Just Plain Funk (17)
Just You Me, Darling (10)
Kansas City (15,19,41) 55
Keep Keepin' (49)
King, The (11)
King Heroin (33) 40
King Slaughter (36)
Kiss In 77 (43)
Let A Man Come In And Do The Popcorn (Part 1) (26) 21
Let A Man Come In And Do The Popcorn (Part 2) (26) 40
Let It Be Me (28)
Let The Boogie Do The Rest (45)
Let Them Talk (20)
Let Yourself Go (12,13,19) 46
Let's Get Personal (48)
Let's Go Get Stoned (11)
Licking Stick - Licking Stick (20,27) 14
Like A Baby (3)
Like It Is, Like It Was (35)
Payback, The (37) 26

Peewee's Groove In "D" (14)
People Get Up And Drive Your Funky Soul (36)
Please Don't Go (1,47)
Please, Please (34)
Please, Please, Please (1,3,13,19,27,38,46,47) 95
Popcorn, The (22) 30
Popcorn With A Feeling (23)
Prisoner Of Love (2,13,19) 18
Problems (40)
Public Enemy #1 (Part 1 And 2) (33)
Reality (39) 80
Really, Really, Really (36)
Recitation By Hank Ballard (34)
Release The Pressure (medley) (42)
Repeat The Beat (Faith) (48)
Return To Me (48)
Say It Loud - I'm Black And I'm Proud (20) 10
Sayin' It And Doin' It (38)
Scratch, The (17)
September Song (25)
Sex Machine Part I And Part II (40,46) 61
(also see: Get Up I Feel Like Being Like A Sex Machine)
Sexy, Sexy, Sexy (36) 50
Shades Of Brown (20)
She Looks All Types A'Good (49)
Shhhhhh (For A Little While) (17)
Sho Is Funky Down Here (29)
Shoot Your Shot (37)
Shout And Shimmy (3)
Sidewinder (7)
Signed, Sealed, And Delivered (2,3) 77
634-5789 (11)
Slaughter Theme (36)
Slow Walk (9)
So Long (2)
Somebody Changed The Lock On My Door (4)
Sometime (28,38)
Song For My Father (7)
Soul Of J.B. (16)
Soul Power (31,32) 29
Soul Pride (Part 1) (22)
Soul Pride (Part 1 & 2) (22)
Soul With Different Notes (18)
Spank, The (44)
Spinning Wheel (27) 90
Sportin' Life (35)
Stagger Lee (15)
Star Generation (45)

DEBUT DATE	PEAK POS	WKS CHR	GOLD	ARTIST — Album Title	$	Label & Number

BROWN, James — Cont'd

Static (Part 1 And 2) (49)
Still (45)
Stone Fox (12,17)
Stoned To The Bone (37) **58**
Stormy Monday (38)
Straight Ahead (36)
Strangers In The Night (21)
Suds (8)
Sudsy (22)
Sumpin' Else (9)
Sunny (21)
Super Bad (28,31,32) **13**
Superbad, Superslick (41)
Sweet Lorraine (4)
Take Some-Leave Some (37)
Talking Loud And Saying Nothing (33) **27**
Tell Me That You Love Me (12)

Tempted (5)
That's Life (19,21)
That's My Desire (25)
Things That I Used To Do (4) **99**
Then You Can Tell Me Goodbye (20)
There (5)
There It Is (Part 1 And 2) (33) **43**
There Was A Time (16,19,21,27) **36**
These Foolish Things (3,38)
Thing In "G" (2)
Think (1,8,19,47) **33**
This Feeling (42)
This Old Heart (6) **79**
Three Hearts In A Tangle (8) **93**
Till Then (12)

Time After Time (16,21)
Time Is Running Out Fast (37)
Time To Get Busy (49)
To My Brother (36)
Top Of The Stack (23)
Transmograpfication (36)
Tribute (49)
Try Me (1,2,13,19,31,46,47) **48**
Try Me [instrumental] (7) **63**
Tryin' To Get Over (36)
Turn Me Loose, I'm Dr. Feelgood (48)
Turn On The Heat And Build Some Fire (41)
Twist, The (39)
Uncle (21)
Use Your Mother (24)
Vonshelia (9)

Waiting In Vain (2)
Wake Up And Give Yourself A Chance To Live (43)
Wee Wee (5)
What Do You Like (14)
What Kind Of Fool Am I (25)
What The World Needs Now Is Love (43)
When A Man Loves A Woman (11)
When The Saints Go Marching In (38)
White Lightning (I Mean Moonshine) (35)
Who Am I (33)
Who Can I Turn To (39)
Who's Afraid Of Virginia Woolf? (5)
Whole World Needs Liberation (34)

Why Am I Treated So Bad (22)
Why Did You Take Your Love Away From Me (16)
Why Do You Do Me (1,47)
Why Does Everything Happen To Me (1,47)
Willow Weep For Me (21)
Woman (43)
Women Are Something Else (45)
World (Part 1 And Part 2) (26) **37**
You And Me (49)
You Don't Have To Go (6)
You Mother You (29)
You Took My Heart (42)
You're Nobody Till Somebody Loves You (4)
You're Still Out Of Sight (23)

You've Got The Power (1,8,17,47) **86**
You've Got To Change Your Mind (16)
Your Cheating Heart (25)
Your Love (41)
Your Love Was Good For Me (34)
Yours And Mine (12)

BROWN, Jim Ed
Born on 4/1/34 in Sparkman, Arkansas. Leader of The Browns. Had over 50 hits on the country charts. Hosted Nashville Network's TV talent show *You Can Be A Star!*. Member of *Grand Ole Opry* since 1963.

| 2/6/71 | 81 | 9 | | Morning .... | $10 | RCA 4461 |

Ain't Life Sweet
Dime At A Time

Every Mile Of The Way
Good Brother John

How To Lose A Good Woman
Laying Here Lying In Bed

Morning 47
Rainy Jane

Sunday Morning We'll Be Singing

Wake Me Up In Oklahoma

BROWN, Julie
Singer/actress. Appeared in the film *Earth Girls Are Easy*. Hosted own MTV show, *Just Say Julie*, broadcast from 1986-92 (known as "West Coast" Julie Brown, not to be confused with MTV's VJ "Downtown" Julie Brown).

| 2/2/85 | 168 | 7 | | Goddess In Progress .... [M-N] | $8 | Rhino 610 |

'Cause I'm A Blonde
Earth Girls Are Easy

Homecoming Queen's Got A Gun

I Like 'Em Big And Stupid

Will I Make It Through The Eighties?

BROWN, Les, and His Band of Renown
Big band leader/clarinetist. Born on 3/14/12 in Reinerton, Pennsylvania. Worked as an arranger for Jimmy Dorsey, Larry Clinton and others before own band's success. In the 1950s, Brown's band was featured on Steve Allen's TV show. Worked on Bob Hope's programs and overseas tours for over two decades.

| 2/19/55 | 15 | 2 | | Concert At The Palladium .... [I-L] | $25 | Coral CX-1 [2] |

recorded at the Hollywood Palladium, September 1953

Baby, I Need You
Back In Your Own Backyard
Begin The Beguine
Brown's Little Jug
Caravan
Cherokee (Indian Love Song)

Crazy Legs
Flying Home
From This Moment On
Happy Holligan
I Let A Song Go Out Of My Heart

I Would Do Anything For You
Invitation
Jersey Bounce
Laura
Leap Frog
Midnight Sun

Montoona Clipper
One O'Clock Jump
Rain
Sentimental Journey
Speak Low (When You Speak, Love)

Strange
Street Of Dreams
You're The Cream In My Coffee

BROWN, Maxine
R&B singer. Born in Kingstree, South Carolina. With gospel groups Manhattans and Royaltones in New York City in the late 1950s.

| 11/29/69 | 195 | 2 | | We'll Cry Together .... | $15 | Common. 6001 |

Darling, Be Home Soon
Didn't You Know (You'd Have To Cry Sometime)

I Can't Get Along Without You

Johnny's Coming Home
Piece Of My Heart

Reason To Believe
See And Don't See

We'll Cry Together 73
You're The Reason I'm Living

BROWN, Odell, & The Organ-Izers
Jazz quartet formed in Nashville in 1961.

| 9/9/67 | 173 | 4 | | Mellow Yellow .... [I] | $15 | Cadet 788 |

Ain't That A Groove
Baby, You Just Don't Know

Mas Que Nada
Mellow Yellow

Que Son Uno
Quiet Village

Tommy's Thing

BROWN, Peter
Soul vocalist/keyboardist/producer. Born on 7/11/53 in Blue Island, Illinois.

| 1/14/78 | 11 | 44 | | A Fantasy Love Affair .... | $8 | Drive 104 |

Dance With Me 8
Do Ya Wanna Get Funky With Me 18

Fantasy Love Affair
For Your Love

It's True What They Say About Love

Singer's Become A Dancer Without Love

You Should Do It 54

BROWN, Shirley
Soul vocalist. Born on 1/6/47 in West Memphis, Arkansas and raised in East St. Louis.

| 1/25/75 | 98 | 11 | | Woman To Woman .... | $10 | Truth 4206 |

Between You And Me
I Can't Give You Up

I Need You Tonight
I've Got To Go On Without You

It Ain't No Fun 94
Long As You Love Me

Passion
So Glad To Have You

Stay With Me Baby
Woman To Woman 22

BROWNE, Duncan

| 5/19/79 | 174 | 5 | | The Wild Places .... | $8 | Sire 6065 |

Camino Real (Part 1, 2 & 3)
Crash, The

Kisarazu
Planet Earth

Roman Vecu
Samurai

Wild Places

BROWNE, Jackson
★★261★★
Born on 10/9/48 in Heidelberg, Germany. Rock singer/guitarist/pianist/composer. To Los Angeles in 1951. With Tim Buckley and Nico in 1967 in New York City. Returned to Los Angeles, concentrated on songwriting. His songs were recorded by Linda Ronstadt, Tom Rush, Joe Cocker, The Byrds, Johnny Rivers, Bonnie Raitt, and many others. Worked with the Eagles. Produced Warren Zevon's first album. Wife Phyllis committed suicide on 3/25/76. Activist against nuclear power.

| 3/18/72 | 53 | 23 | ● | 1 Jackson Browne .... | $12 | Asylum 5051 |
| 11/10/73 | 43 | 38 | ▲ | 2 For Everyman .... | $10 | Asylum 5067 |

DEBUT DATE	PEAK POS	WKS CHR	GOLD	ARTIST — Album Title	$	Label & Number

BROWNE, Jackson — Cont'd

DEBUT DATE	PEAK POS	WKS CHR	GOLD	ARTIST — Album Title	$	Label & Number
10/12/74	14	29	▲	3 Late For The Sky	$10	Asylum 1017
11/20/76	5	35	▲	4 **The Pretender**	$10	Asylum 1079
1/7/78	3	65	▲	5 **Running On Empty**	$10	Asylum 113
7/19/80	1[1]	38	▲	6 **Hold Out**	$8	Asylum 511
8/20/83	8	33	●	7 **Lawyers In Love**	$8	Asylum 60268
3/22/86	23	31	●	8 **Lives In The Balance**	$8	Asylum 60457
6/24/89	45	16		9 World In Motion	$8	Elektra 60830

Anything Can Happen (9)
Before The Deluge (3)
Black And White (8)
Boulevard (6) *19*
Call It A Loan (6)
Candy (8)
Chasing You Into The Light (9)
Child In These Hills (1)
Cocaine (5)
Colors Of The Sun (2)
Cut It Away (7)
Daddy's Tune (4)
Disco Apocalypse (6)
Doctor My Eyes (1) *8*
Downtown (7)

Enough Of The Night (9)
Farther On (3)
For A Dancer (3)
For A Rocker (7) *45*
For America (8) *30*
For Everyman (2)
Fountain Of Sorrow (3)
From Silver Lake (1)
Fuse, The (4)
Here Come Those Tears Again (4) *23*
Hold On Hold Out (6)
Hold Out (6)
How Long (9)
I Am A Patriot (9)
I Thought I Was A Child (2)

In The Shape Of A Heart (8) *70*
Jamaica Say You Will (1)
Knock On Any Door (7)
Late For The Sky (3)
Late Show (3)
Lawless Avenues (8)
Lawyers In Love (7) *13*
Lights And Virtues (9)
Linda Paloma (4)
Lives In The Balance (8)
Load-Out, The (5) *flip*
Looking Into You (1)
Love Needs A Heart (5)
My Opening Farewell (1)
My Personal Revenge (9)

Nothing But Time (5)
Of Missing Persons (6)
On The Day (7)
Only Child (4)
Our Lady Of The Well (4)
Ready Or Not (2)
Redneck Friend (2) *85*
Road, The (5)
Road And The Sky (3)
Rock Me On The Water (1) *48*
Rosie (5)
Running On Empty (5) *11*
Say It Isn't True (7)
Shaky Town (5)

Sing My Songs To Me (2)
Sleep's Dark And Silent Gate (4)
Soldier Of Plenty (8)
Something Fine (1)
Song For Adam (1)
Stay (5) *20*
Take It Easy (2)
Tender Is The Night (7) *25*
That Girl Could Sing (6) *22*
These Days (2)
Till I Go Down (8)
Times You've Come (1)
Under The Falling Sky (1)
Walking Slow (3)

When The Stone Begins To Turn (9)
Word Justice (9)
World In Motion (9)
You Love The Thunder (5)
Your Bright Baby Blues (4)

BROWNE, Tom
Jazz-funk trumpeter. First played classical music at the High School of Music and Art in New York City. With Weldon Ervine in 1975, Sonny Fortune and Fatback Band in 1976. Member of Fuse One.

DEBUT DATE	PEAK POS	WKS CHR	GOLD	ARTIST — Album Title	$	Label & Number
8/11/79	147	6		1 Browne Sugar .... [I]	$8	GRP 5003
7/26/80	18	26	●	2 Love Approach	$8	GRP 5008
2/21/81	37	19		3 Magic	$8	GRP 5503
12/12/81+	97	14		4 Yours Truly	$8	GRP 5507
12/3/83+	147	12		5 Rockin' Radio .... [I]	$8	Arista 8107

Angeline (5)
Antoinette Like (1)
Bebopafunkadiscolypso (medley) (4)
Brighter Tomorrow (5)
Brother, Brother (1)
Bye Gones (4)
Can't Give It Away (4)
Charisma (4)

Closer I Get To You (1)
Come For The Ride (4)
Crusin' (5)
Dreams Of Lovin' You (2)
Feel Like Making Love (5)
Forever More (2)
Fungi Mama (medley) (4)
Funkin' For Jamaica (N.Y.) (2)

God Bless The Child (3)
Her Silent Smile (2)
Herbal Scent (1)
I Know (3)
I Never Was A Cowboy (1)
Lazy Bird (4)
Let's Dance (3)
Magic (3)
Making Plans (3)

Martha (2)
Message (Pride And Pity) (4)
Midnight Interlude (3)
Moon Rise (2)
Mr. Business (5)
My Latin Sky (4)
Naima (4)
Never My Love (5)
Night Wind (3)

Nocturne (2)
Promises For Spring (1)
Rockin' Radio (5)
Thigh's High (Grip Your Hips And Move) (3)
Throw Down (1)
Turn It Up (Come On Y'all) (5)
Weak In The Knees (2)

What's Going On (1)

BROWNSVILLE STATION
Rock trio from Ann Arbor, Michigan: Cub Koda (guitar), Michael Lutz (vocals) and Henry Weck (drums). Koda writes a column for the record collector's magazine *Goldmine*.

DEBUT DATE	PEAK POS	WKS CHR	GOLD	ARTIST — Album Title	$	Label & Number
10/7/72	191	5		1 A Night On The Town	$10	Big Tree 2010
9/15/73+	98	19		2 Yeah!	$10	Big Tree 2102
6/15/74	170	8		3 School Punks	$10	Big Tree 89500

All Night Long (2)
Barefootin' (2)
Country Flavor (1)
Fast Phyllis (3)
Go Out And Get Her (2)
Hey Little Girl (3)
I Get So Excited (3)
I Got It Bad For You (3)

I Got Time (1)
I'm A King Bee (medley) (3)
I'm The Leader Of The Gang (3) *48*
I've Got Love If You Want It (medley) (3)
Jonah's Here To Stay (1)
Kings Of The Party (3) *31*

Leavin' Here (1)
Let Your Yeah Be Yeah (2) *57*
Lightnin' Bar Blues (2)
Love, Love, Love (2)
Lovin' Lady Lee (1)
Mad For Me (1)

Mama Don't Allow No Parkin' (3)
Man Who Wanted More (Saints Rock & Roll) (1)
Meet Me On The Fourth Floor (3)
Mister Robert (1)
Ostrich (4)

Question Of Temperature (2)
Rock With The Music (1)
Smokin' In The Boy's Room (2) *3*
Sweet Jane (2)
Take It Or Leave It (2)
Wanted (Dead Or Alive) (1)

★★129★★ **BRUBECK, Dave, Quartet**
Born David Warren on 12/6/20 in Concord, California. Leader of jazz quartet consisting of Brubeck (piano), Paul Desmond (alto sax), Joe Morello (drums) and Eugene Wright (bass). One of America's all-time most popular jazz groups on college campuses.

DEBUT DATE	PEAK POS	WKS CHR	GOLD	ARTIST — Album Title	$	Label & Number
2/5/55	8	6		1 **Dave Brubeck At Storyville: 1954** .... [I-L]	$65	Columbia 590
3/19/55	5	22		2 **Brubeck Time** .... [I]	$50	Columbia 622
11/12/55	7	3		3 **Jazz: Red Hot And Cool** .... [I-L]	$50	Columbia 699
7/8/57	18	1		4 Jazz Impressions of the U.S.A. .... [I]	$40	Columbia 984
9/30/57	24	1		5 Jazz Goes To Junior College .... [I-L]	$30	Columbia 1034
11/28/60+	2[1]	164	●	6 **Time Out Featuring "Take Five"** .... [I]	$25	Columbia 8192
12/12/60+	13	15		7 Bernstein Plays Brubeck Plays Bernstein ... [I] side 1: New York Philharmonic with the Dave Brubeck Quartet conducted by Leonard Bernstein; side 2: Dave Brubeck Quartet	$25	Columbia 8257
12/25/61+	8	46		8 **Time Further Out** .... [I]	$25	Columbia 8490
6/16/62	24	21		9 Countdown - Time In Outer Space .... [I]	$25	Columbia 8575
3/16/63	14	15		10 Bossa Nova U.S.A. .... [I]	$25	Columbia 8798
7/27/63	37	4		11 The Dave Brubeck Quartet At Carnegie Hall ... [I-L]	$25	Columbia 826 [2]
12/21/63	137	3		12 Brandenburg Gate: Revisited .... [I] with Orchestra	$25	Columbia 8763
4/18/64	81	9		13 Time Changes .... [I]	$20	Columbia 8927
2/27/65	142	4		14 Jazz Impressions Of New York .... [I]	$20	Columbia 9075
10/9/65	122	3		15 Angel Eyes .... [I]	$20	Columbia 9148
3/26/66	133	5		16 My Favorite Things .... [I]	$20	Columbia 9237
7/30/66	104	4		17 Dave Brubeck's Greatest Hits .... [G-I]	$20	Columbia 9284
1/10/76	167	5		18 1975: The Duets .... [I] **DAVE BRUBECK & PAUL DESMOND**	$10	Horizon 703

BRUBECK, Dave, Quartet — Cont'd

Alice In Wonderland (18)
Angel Eyes (15)
Audrey (2)
Autumn In Washington Square (14)
Back Bay Blues (1)
Back To Earth (9)
Balcony Rock (18)
Blue Dove (18)
Blue Rondo A La Turk (6,11,17)
Blue Shadows In The Street (8)
Bluette (8)
Bossa Nova U.S.A. (10,11,17) *69*
Brandenburg Gate Medley (12)
Broadway Bossa Nova (14)
Broadway Romance (14)
Brother, Can You Spare A Dime (5)
Bru's Blues (5)
Bru's Boogie Woogie (8)
Cable Car (13)
Camptown Races (17)

Cantiga Nova Swing (10)
Castilian Blues (9)
Castilian Drums (9,11)
Charles Matthew Hallelujah (8)
Circus On Parade (16)
Coracao Sensivel (Tender Heart) (7)
Countdown (9)
Curtain Time (4)
Danse Duet (9)
Dialogues For Jazz Combo And Orchestra (Movements 1-4) (7)
Don't Worry 'Bout Me (1)
Duke, The (3,17)
Elementals (13)
Eleven Four (9,11)
Everybody's Jumpin' (6)
Everything Happens To Me (15)
Far More Blue (8)
Far More Drums (8)
Fare Thee Well, Annabelle (3)
Fast Life (9)
Fine Romance (2)

For All We Know (11)
G Flat Theme (12)
Gone With The Wind (1)
Here Lies Love (1)
History Of A Boy Scout (4)
Home At Last (4)
I Feel Pretty (7)
I'm Afraid The Masquerade Is Over (5)
I'm In A Dancing Mood (17)
Iberia (13)
In Your Own Sweet Way (12,17)
Indiana (3)
Irmao Amigo (Brother Friend) (10)
It's A Raggy Waltz (8,11,17)
Jeepers Creepers (2)
June, Theme For (10)
Kathy's Waltz (6,12)
Keepin' Out Of Mischief Now (2)
King For A Day (11)
Koto Song (18)
Lamento (10)

Let's Get Away From It All (15)
Little Girl Blue (3,16)
Little Man With A Candy Cigar (15)
Lonely Mr. Broadway (14)
Love Walked In (3)
Lover (3)
Maori Blues (8)
Marla (7)
Most Beautiful Girl In The World (16)
Mr. Broadway, Theme From (14)
Mr. Broadway, Theme From (17)
My Favorite Things (16)
My Romance (16)
Night We Called It A Day (15)
Ode To A Cowboy (4)
On The Alamo (1)
One Moment Worth Years (5)
Over And Over Again (16)
Pennies From Heaven (2,11)
Pick Up Sticks (6)
Plain Song (4)

Quiet Girl (7)
Shim Wha (13)
Sixth Sense (14)
Someday My Prince Will Come (9)
Something To Sing About (14)
Sometimes I'm Happy (3)
Somewhere (7)
Sounds Of The Loop (4)
Southern Scene (Briar Bush) (11)
Spring In Central Park (14)
St. Louis Blues (5,11)
Stardust (18)
Stompin' For Mili (2)
Strange Meadow Lark (6)
Summer On The Sound (14)
Summer Song (4,12,18)
Take Five (6,11,17) *25*
There'll Be No Tomorrow (10)
These Foolish Things (5,18)
This Can't Be Love (10,16)
Three To Get Ready (6,11)
Three's A Crowd (9)
Tonight (7)

Trolley Song (10,17)
Unisphere (13)
Unsquare Dance (8,17) *74*
Upstage Rumba (14)
Vento Fresco (Cool Wind) (10)
Violets For Your Furs (15)
Waltz Limp (9)
When You're Smiling (The Whole World Smiles With You) (1)
Why Can't I? (16)
Why Do I Love You (2)
Why Phillis (3)
Will You Still Be Mine? (15)
Winter Ballad (14)
World's Fair (13)
Yonder For Two (4)
You Go To My Head (18)

BRUCE, Jack

Born on 5/14/43 in Lanarkshire, Scotland. Bass player of Cream. Started career with Alexis Korner's Blues Inc. Prior to Cream was with the Graham Bond Organization, John Mayall's Bluesbreakers and Manfred Mann. Also see West, Bruce & Laing.

DEBUT DATE	PEAK POS	WKS CHR	GOLD	ARTIST — Album Title	$	Label & Number
10/25/69	55	11		1 Songs For A Tailor	$12	Atco 306
12/7/74	160	3		2 Out Of The Storm	$8	RSO 4805
5/7/77	153	5		3 How's Tricks	$8	RSO 3021
				JACK BRUCE BAND		
12/13/80	182	2		4 I've Always Wanted To Do This	$8	Epic 36827
				JACK BRUCE & FRIENDS		
				friends: Clem Clempson (Humble Pie), Billy Cobham & David Sancious		
1/30/82	109	6		5 Truce	$8	Chrysalis 1352
				JACK BRUCE/ROBIN TROWER		

Baby Jane (3)
Bird Alone (4)
Boston Ball Game, 1967 (1)
Clearout, The (1)
Dancing On Air (1)
Facelift 318 (4)
Fall In Love (5)
Fat Gut (5)
Golden Days (2)
Gone Too Far (5)

Gonna Shut You Down (5)
He The Richmond (1)
Hit And Run (4)
How's Tricks? (3)
Imaginary Western, Theme For An (1)
In This Way (4)
Into The Storm (2)
Johnny B '77 (3)
Keep It Down (2)

Keep On Wondering (2)
Last Train To The Stars (5)
Little Boy Lost (5)
Livin' Without Ja (4)
Lost Inside A Song (3)
Madhouse (3)
Mickey The Fiddler (4)
Ministry Of Bag (1)
Never Tell Your Mother She's Out Of Tune (1)

One (2)
Out To Lunch (4)
Outsiders (3)
Pieces Of Mind (3)
Rope Ladder To The Moon (1)
Running Back (4)
Running Through Our Hands (2)
Shadows Touching (5)
Something To Live For (3)

Take Good Care Of Yourself (5)
Thin Ice (5)
Tickets To Water Falls (1)
Times (3)
Timeslip (2)
To Isengard (1)
Waiting For The Call (3)
Weird Of Hermiston (1)
Wind And The Sea (4)

Without A Word (3)

BRUCE, Lenny

Satirical comedian. Born Leonard Alfred Schneider in 1925 in Long Island, New York. Died of a heroin overdose on 8/3/66 (age 41). Dustin Hoffman portrayed Bruce in the 1974 autobiographical film. Also see soundtrack *Lenny*.

DEBUT DATE	PEAK POS	WKS CHR	GOLD	ARTIST — Album Title	$	Label & Number
3/15/75	178	2		1 Lenny Bruce/Carnegie Hall .... [C]	$15	United Art. 9800 [3]
				the complete show; recorded on 2/4/61		
4/5/75	191	2		2 The Real Lenny Bruce .... [E-C]	$10	Fantasy 79003 [2]
				recorded 1958-1959		

Airlines, The (1)
Burlesque House (1)
Christ And Moses (1)
Clap, The (1)
Comic At The Palladium (2)
Dear Abby (1)
Djinni In The Candy Store (2)
Dykes And Faggots (1)
Enchanting Transylvania (2)

End, The (1)
Equality (1)
Fat Boy (2)
Father Flotski's Triumph (Unexpurgated) (2)
Flag And Communism (1)
Girl Singing (1)
Homosexuality (1)

How To Relax Your Colored Friends At Parties (2)
Internal Revenue (1)
Joke, The (1)
Judge Saperstein Decision (1)
Kennedy Acceptance Speech (1)
Kidnap, The (1)

Ku Klux Klan (1)
Las Vegas Tits And Ass (1)
Lima, Ohio (1)
Miracle On 57th Street (1)
My Werewolf Mama (2)
Nightclubs (1)
Non Skeddo Flies Again (2)
On Contemporaries (1)
On Humor (1)

Operation, The (1)
Pills (1)
Point Of View (1)
Religions, Inc. (1)
Shelley Berman (1)
Sound, The (1,2)
Tarzan (1)
Thank You Masked Man (2)
What's It Mean (1)

White Collar Drunk (2)

BRUFORD, Bill

Percussionist with Yes, King Crimson, Genesis and Anderson, Bruford, Wakeman, Howe. Born on 5/17/49 in Sevenoaks, Kent, England.

DEBUT DATE	PEAK POS	WKS CHR	GOLD	ARTIST — Album Title	$	Label & Number
7/7/79	123	5		1 One Of A Kind .... [I]	$8	Polydor 6205
3/29/80	191	2		2 Gradually Going Tornado	$8	Polydor 6261

Abingdon Chasp (1)
Age Of Information (2)
Fainting In Coils (1)

Five G (1)
Forever Until Sunday (1)
Gothic 17 (2)

Hell's Bells (1)
Joe Frazier (1)
Land's End (2)

One Of A Kind - Part One & Two (1)
Palewell Park (2)

Plans For J.D. (2)
Q. E. D. (2)
Sahara Of Snow - Part One & Two (1)

Sliding Floor (2)
Travels With Myself-And Someone Else (1)

BRYANT, Anita

Born on 3/25/40 in Barnsdale, Oklahoma. As Miss Oklahoma, she was 2nd runner-up to Miss America in 1958.

DEBUT DATE	PEAK POS	WKS CHR	GOLD	ARTIST — Album Title	$	Label & Number
9/15/62	145	2		1 In A Velvet Mood	$12	Columbia 8685
1/21/67	146	4		2 Mine Eyes Have Seen The Glory	$12	Columbia 9373

All The Way (1)
America (2)
America The Beautiful (2)
Battle Hymn Of The Republic (2)
Cry Me A River (1)

God Bless America (2)
House I Live In (That's America To Me) (2)
In God We Trust (2)
Love Is A Many-Splendored Thing (1)

Love Letters In The Sand (1)
Misty (1)
Moon River (1)
Moulin Rouge (Where Is Your Heart), Song From (1)
My Prayer (1)

Never On Sunday (1)
Onward, Christian Soldiers (2)
Power And The Glory (2)
Star-Spangled Banner (2)
Tammy (1)

This Is My Country (2)
This Is Worth Fighting For (2)
Tonight (1)
Volare (Nel Blu Dipinto Di Blu) (1)

DEBUT DATE	PEAK POS	WKS CHR	GOLD	ARTIST — Album Title	$	Label & Number

BRYANT, Ray
Born Raphael Bryant on 12/24/31 in Philadelphia. R&B-jazz pianist/bandleader. Uncle of jazz guitarist Kevin Eubanks.

DEBUT DATE	PEAK POS	WKS CHR	GOLD	ARTIST — Album Title	$	Label & Number
6/25/66	111	12		1 Gotta Travel On .... [I]	$15	Cadet 767
5/13/67	193	3		2 Slow Freight .... [I]	$15	Cadet 781

Ah, The Apple Tree (When The World Was Young) (2)
All Things Are Possible (1)
Amen (2)
Bag's Groove (1)
Erewhon (1)
Fox Stalker (2)
Gotta Travel On (1)
If You Go Away (2)
It Was A Very Good Year (1)
Little Soul Sister (1)
Midnight Stalkin' (1)
Monkey Business (1)
Return Of The Prodigal Son (2)
Satin Doll (2)
Slow Freight (2)
Smack Dab In The Middle (1)

BRYANT, Sharon
Lead singer of Atlantic Starr from 1976-84. Native of White Plains, New York. Married Rick Gallwey (former percussionist with the group Change) in 1984.

DEBUT DATE	PEAK POS	WKS CHR	GOLD	ARTIST — Album Title	$	Label & Number
9/9/89	139	13		Here I Am	$8	Wing 837313

Body Talk
Falling
Foolish Heart *90*
Here I Am
In The Nite Time
Let Go *34*
No More Lonely Nights
Old Friend

★★233★★ BRYSON, Peabo
Born Robert Peabo Bryson on 4/13/51 in Greenville, South Carolina. R&B singer with Al Freeman & The Upsetters in 1965, with Moses Dillard & The Tex-Town Display from 1968-73. First solo recording for Bang in 1970. Married Juanita Leonard, former wife of boxer Sugar Ray Leonard, in 1992.

DEBUT DATE	PEAK POS	WKS CHR	GOLD	ARTIST — Album Title	$	Label & Number
3/11/78	49	29	●	1 Reaching For The Sky	$8	Capitol 11729
12/9/78+	35	26	●	2 Crosswinds	$8	Capitol 11875
12/15/79+	44	19		3 We're The Best Of Friends	$10	Capitol 12019
				NATALIE COLE/PEABO BRYSON		
5/3/80	79	16		4 Paradise	$8	Capitol 12063
12/20/80+	52	19		5 Live & More .... [L]	$10	Atlantic 7004 [2]
				ROBERTA FLACK & PEABO BRYSON		
2/28/81	82	11		6 Turn The Hands Of Time	$8	Capitol 12138
11/28/81+	40	24		7 I Am Love	$8	Capitol 12179
12/4/82+	55	21		8 Don't Play With Fire	$8	Capitol 12241
8/13/83	25	42	●	9 Born To Love	$8	Capitol 12284
				PEABO BRYSON/ROBERTA FLACK		
6/16/84	44	26		10 Straight From The Heart	$8	Elektra 60362
7/14/84	168	10		11 The Peabo Bryson Collection .... [G]	$8	Capitol 12348
				side 2: 4 duets with Roberta Flack and 1 with Natalie Cole		
7/6/85	102	13		12 Take No Prisoners	$8	Elektra 60427
2/13/88	157	6		13 Positive	$8	Elektra 60753
7/13/91	88	19		14 Can You Stop The Rain	$12	Columbia 46823

Another Love Song (6)
Back Together Again (5)
Blame It On Me (9)
Born To Love (9)
Can We Find Love Again (9)
Can You Stop The Rain (14) *52*
Closer Than Close (14)
Come On Over Tonight (13)
Comin' Alive (9)
Crosswinds (2)
Don't Make Me Wait Too Long (5)
Don't Play With Fire (8)
Don't Touch Me (2)
Dwellers Of The City (6)
Falling For You (12)
Feel Like Makin' Love (5)
Feel The Fire (1,5,11)
Fool Already Knows (1)
Fool Such As I (6)
Friction (6)
Get Ready To Cry (7)
Gimme Some Time (3)
Give Me Your Love (8)
Go For It (8)
God Don't Like Ugly (5)
Have A Good Time (1)
Heaven Above Me (9,11)
Hold On To The World (1)
Hurt (13)
I Am Love (7)
I Believe In You (4,5)
I Can't Imagine (14)
I Get Nervous (10)
I Just Came Here To Dance (9,11)
I Just Had To Fall (14)
I Love The Way You Love (4)
I Wanna Be With You (14)
I Want To Be Where You Are (3)
I Want To Know (13)
I Wish You Love (14)
I'm In Love (12)
I'm So Into You (2,11)
I've Been Down (6)
If Ever You're In My Arms Again (10) *10*
If It's Really Love (14)
If Only For One Night (5)
Impossible (7)
Irresistible (Never Run Away From Love) (5)
Killing Me Softly With His Song (5)
Learning The Ways Of Love (10)
Let Me Be The One You Need (8)
Let The Feeling Flow (7,11) *42*
Let's Apologize (12)
Let's Fall In Love (medley) (3)
Life Is A Child (4)
Lost In The Night (14)
Love Always Finds A Way (12)
Love From Your Heart (1)
Love Has No Shame (4)
Love In Every Season (4,5)
Love Is A Waiting Game (5)
Love Is On The Rise (7)
Love Is Watching You (2)
Love Means Forever (10)
Love Walked Out On Me (1)
Love Will Find You (3)
Make The World Stand Still (5)
Man On A String (6)
Maybe (9)
Minute By Minute (4)
More Than Everything (5)
Move Your Body (7)
My Life (6)
Only Heaven Can Wait (For Love) (5)
Piece Of My Heart (6)
Point Of View (2)
Positive (13)
Reaching For The Sky (1,5,11)
Real Deal (10)
Remember When (So Much In Love) (8)
She's A Woman (2)
She's Over Me (12)
Shower You With Love (14)
Slow Dancin' (10) *82*
Smile (2)
Soul Provider (14)
Split Decision (7)
Spread Your Wings (2)
Still Water (13)
Straight From The Heart (10)
Take No Prisoners (In The Game Of Love) (12) *78*
There's No Getting Over You (La Theme De Sharon) (10)
There's No Guarantee (7)
There's Nothin' Out There (12)
This Love Affair (3)
This Time Around (13)
Tonight (13)
Tonight, I Celebrate My Love (9,11) *16*
Turn It On (8)
Turn The Hands Of Time (6)
We Don't Have To Talk (About Love) (8,11)
We're The Best Of Friends (3)
What You Won't Do For Love (3,11)
When We Need It Bad (13)
When Will I Learn (4,5)
When You Talk To Me (12)
Why Don't You Make Up Your Mind (6)
Without You (13) *89*
Words (8)
You (7)
You Are My Heaven (medley) (5)
You Don't Have To Beg (14)
You Haven't Learned About Love (1)
You Send Me (medley) (3)
You're Looking Like Love To Me (9,11) *58*
Your Lonely Heart (3)

B.T. EXPRESS
Brooklyn, New York R&B-disco outfit earlier known as Brooklyn Trucking Express. Keyboardist Michael Jones, who joined group at age 15, later recorded solo as techno-funk musician Kashif.

DEBUT DATE	PEAK POS	WKS CHR	GOLD	ARTIST — Album Title	$	Label & Number
11/23/74+	5	31	●	1 Do It ('Til You're Satisfied)	$10	Roadshow 5117
8/2/75	19	19		2 Non-Stop	$10	Roadshow 41001
5/29/76	43	12		3 Energy To Burn	$8	Columbia 34178
5/28/77	111	5		4 Function at the Junction	$8	Columbia 34702
2/25/78	67	11		5 Shout!	$8	Columbia 35078
5/31/80	164	4		6 B.T. Express 1980	$8	Columbia 36333

Better Late Than Never (6)
Can't Stop Groovin' Now, Wanna Do It Some More (3) *52*
Close To You (2) *82*
Closer (6)
Depend On Yourself (3)
Devil's Workshop (2)
Discotizer (2)
Do It ('Til You're Satisfied) (1) *2*
Do You Like It (1)
Does It Feel Good (6)
Door To My Mind (4)
Energy Level (3)
Energy To Burn (3)
Everything Good To You (Ain't Always Good For You) (1)
Expose Yourself (4)
Eyes (4)
Funk Theory (6)
Funky Music (4)
Give It What You Got (2) *40*
Give Up The Funk (Let's Dance) (4)
Happiness (2)
Have Some Fun (6)
Heart Of Fire (6)
Herbs (3)
How Big Can You Dream (4)
I Want You With Me (5)
If It Don't Turn You On (You Oughta' Leave It Alone) (1)
It's In Your Blood (5)
Look At The People (5)
Make Your Body Move (3)
Mental Telepathy (1)
Now That We Found Love (3)
Once You Get It (1)
Peace Pipe (2) *31*
Put It In (In The Pocket) (5)
Ride On B. T. (3)
Scratch My Itch (4)
Shake It Off (5)
Shout It Out (5)
Star Gazer (4)
Still Good-Still Like It (2)
Sunshine (4)
Takin' Off (5)
That's What I Want For You Baby (1)
This House Is Smokin' (1)
Time Tunnel (3)
We Got It Together (4)
What You Do In The Dark (5)
Whatcha Think About That? (2)
You Got It-I Want It (2)
You Got Something (5)

DEBUT DATE	PEAK POS	WKS CHR	G O L D	ARTIST — Album Title	$	Label & Number

BUBBLE PUPPY, The
Psychedelic rock band from Houston. Later recorded as Demian.

5/17/69	176	6		A Gathering Of Promises	$75	Int'l. Artists 10

Beginning   Gathering Of Promises   Hurry Sundown   It's Safe To Say   Road To St. Stephens
Elizabeth   **Hot Smoke & Sassafrass 14**   I've Got To Reach You   Lonely   Todd's Tune

BUCHANAN, Roy
Prolific rock/blues guitarist. Born on 9/23/39 in Ozark, Arkansas; raised in Pixley, California. At 15, toured with Dale Hawkins for three years; then joined Ronnie Hawkins' band, The Hawks. East Coast session work until solo career in 1972. Hanged self in Fairfax, Virginia jail, on 8/14/88, after arrested for public drunkenness.

9/9/72	107	12	1	Roy Buchanan	$12	Polydor 5033
3/10/73	86	13	2	Second Album ....[I]	$12	Polydor 5046
2/23/74	152	10	3	That's What I Am Here For	$12	Polydor 6020
12/28/74+	160	6	4	In The Beginning	$12	Polydor 6035
5/15/76	148	7	5	A Street Called Straight	$10	Atlantic 18170
6/18/77	105	8	6	Loading Zone ....[I]	$10	Atlantic 18219
5/20/78	119	7	7	You're Not Alone ....[I]	$10	Atlantic 19170
1/24/81	193	2	8	My Babe	$8	Waterhouse 12
8/3/85	161	13	9	When A Guitar Plays The Blues	$8	Alligator 4741
6/28/86	153	8	10	Dancing On The Edge	$8	Alligator 4747

Adventures Of Brer Rabbit And Tar Baby (6) | Down By The River (7) | I Still Think About Ida Mae (5) | My Baby Says She's Gonna Leave Me (3) | Running Out (5) | When A Guitar Plays The Blues (9)
After Hours (2) | Drowning On Dry Land (10) | I Won't Tell You No Lies (2) | My Friend Jeff (5) | Secret Love (8) | Whiplash (10)
Baby, Baby, Baby (10) | 1841 Shuffle (2) | I'm A Ram (4) | My Sonata (8) | She Can't Say No (4) | Why Don't You Want Me? (4)
Beer Drinking Woman (10) | Filthy Teddy (2) | If Six Was Nine (5) | Nephesh (8) | She Once Lived Here (2) | You Can't Judge A Book By The Cover (10)
Blues For Gary (8) | Five String Blues (2) | In The Beginning (4) | Nickel And A Nail (9) | Short Fuse (9) | You Gotta Let Me Know (8)
CC Ryder (4) | Fly...Night Bird (7) | It Should've Been Me (8) | Okay (5) | Sneaking Godzilla Through The Alley (9) | You're Killing My Love (4)
Cajun (1) | Good God Have Mercy (5) | John's Blues (1) | Opening...Miles From Earth (7) | Supernova (7) | You're Not Alone (7)
Caruso (5) | Green Onions (6) | Judy (6) | Petal To The Metal (10) | Sweet Dreams (1) | Your Love (6)
Chicago Smokeshop (9) | Guitar Cadenza (5) | Jungle Gym (4) | Pete's Blue (1) | Thank You Lord (2) |
Chokin' Kind (10) | Haunted House (1) | Keep What You Got (5) | Peter Gunn (10) | That's What I Am Here For (3) |
Circle, The (6) | Hawaiian Punch (9) | Lack Of Funds (8) | Please Don't Turn Me Away (3) | Treat Her Right (2) |
Country Boy (9) | Heat Of The Battle (6) | Man On The Floor (5) | Ramon's Blues (6) | Tribute To Elmore James (2) |
Country Preacher (4) | Hey, Good Lookin' (1) | Matthew (10) | Rescue Me (4) | Turn To Stone (7) |
Cream Of The Crop (10) | Hey Joe (3) | Messiah Will Come Again (1,5) | Rodney's Song (3) | Voices (3) |
Dizzy Miss Lizzy (8) | Hidden (6) | Mrs. Pressure (5) | Roy's Bluz (3) | Wayfaring Pilgrim (4) |
Dr. Rock & Roll (8) | Home Is Where I Lost Her (3) | My Babe (8) | | |
Done Your Daddy Dirty (6) | I Am A Lonesome Fugitive (1) | | | |

BUCHANAN & GOODMAN — see GOODMAN, Dickie

BUCKINGHAM, Lindsey
Born on 10/3/47 in Palo Alto, California. Rock guitarist/vocalist/songwriter. In group Fritz from 1967-71; with Stevie Nicks (Fritz lead singer) formed duo, Buckingham Nicks, in early '70s. Both joined Fleetwood Mac in 1975. Lindsey left Fleetwood Mac in 1987. His grandfather founded Keystone Coffee; his father founded Alta Coffee. Lindsey's brother Gregg won a silver medal in swimming in the 1968 Olympics.

11/7/81	32	24	1	Law And Order	$8	Asylum 561
9/1/84	45	16	2	Go Insane	$8	Elektra 60363
7/4/92	128	9	3	Out Of The Cradle	$12	Reprise 26182

All My Sorrows (3) | **Go Insane** (2) **23** | Love From Here, Love From There (1) | September Song (1) | That's How We Do It In L.A. (1) | You Do Or You Don't (3)
Bang The Drum (2) | I Must Go (2) | Loving Cup (2) | Shadow Of The West (1) | This Is The Time (3) |
Bwana (1) | I Want You (2) | Mary Lee Jones (1) | Slow Dancing (2) | This Nearly Was Mine (3) |
Countdown (3) | I'll Tell You Now (1) | Play In The Rain (2) | Soul Drifter (3) | **Trouble** (1) **9** |
D.W. Suite (3) | It Was I (1) | Satisfied Mind (1) | Street Of Dreams (3) | Turn It On (3) |
Doing What I Can (3) | Johnny Stew (1) | Say We'll Meet Again (3) | Surrender The Rain (3) | Wrong (3) |
Don't Look Down (3) | | | | |

BUCKINGHAMS, The
Chicago rock quintet: Dennis Tufano (lead singer), Carl Giammarese, Nick Fortune, Jon Paulos and Dennis Miccoli. Martin Grebb replaced Miccoli in 1967. Paulos died of a drug overdose on 3/26/80 (age 32). Tufano and Giammarese recorded as a duo in 1973.

3/25/67	109	8	1	Kind Of A Drag	$30	U.S.A. 107
6/10/67	58	23	2	Time & Charges	$20	Columbia 9469
2/10/68	53	16	3	Portraits	$20	Columbia 9598
9/21/68	161	5	4	In One Ear And Gone Tomorrow	$20	Columbia 9703
5/24/69	73	12	5	The Buckinghams' Greatest Hits ....[G]	$20	Columbia 9812

And Our Love (2,5) | **Don't You Care** (2,5) **6** | I've Been Wrong (1) | **Mercy, Mercy, Mercy** (2,5) **5** | Sweets For My Sweet (1) | You Make Me Feel So Good (1)
Any Place In Here (3) | Foreign Policy (2,5) | Inside Looking Out (3) | Our Wrong To Be Right (4) | This Nearly Was Mine (4) |
Are You There (With Another Girl) (4) | Have You Noticed You're Alive (3) | Just Because I've Fallen Down (3) | Pitied Be The Dragon Hunter (2) | Till The Sun Doesn't Shine (4) |
Back In Love Again (4,5) **57** | **Hey Baby (They're Playing Our Song)** (3,5) **12** | **Kind Of A Drag** (1,5) **1** | Remember (2) | Time Of My Life (4) |
Beginners Love (1) | | **Laudy Miss Claudy** (5) **41** | Say We'll Meet Again (4) | Virginia Wolf (1) |
Big Business Advisor (3) | I Call Your Name (1) | Love Ain't Enough (1) | Simplicity (4) | We Just Know (3) |
C'mon Home (3) | I Know I Think (4) | Mail, The (3) | Song Of The Breeze (4) | What Is Love (4) |
Can I Get A Witness (3) | I Love All Of The Girls (3) | Makin' Up & Breakin' Up (1) | Summertime (4) | Why Don't You Love Me (2,5) |
Can't Find The Words (4) | I'll Be Back (2) | Married Life (2) | **Susan** (3,5) **11** | You Are Gone (2) |
Don't Want To Cry (1) | I'll Go Crazy (1,5) | | | |

BUCKLEY, Tim
Singer/songwriter from Orange County, California. Born on 2/14/47 in Washington, D.C. Died of a heroin/morphine overdose on 6/29/75.

11/4/67	171	5	1	Goodbye And Hello	$20	Elektra 7318
4/19/69	81	12	2	Happy Sad	$20	Elektra 74045
2/7/70	192	2	3	Blue Afternoon	$20	Straight 1060

DEBUT DATE	PEAK POS	WKS CHR	GOLD	ARTIST — Album Title	$	Label & Number

BUCKLEY, Tim — Cont'd

Blue Melody (3)	Goodbye And Hello (1)	I Never Asked To Be Your	Morning Glory (1)	River, The (3)
Buzzin' Fly (2)	Gypsy Woman (2)	Mountain (1)	No Man Can Find The War	Sing A Song For You (2)
Cafe (3)	Hallucinations (2)	Knight-Errant (1)	(1)	So Lonely (3)
Carnival Song (1)	Happy Time (3)	Love From Room 109 At The	Once I Was (1)	Strange Feelin' (2)
Chase The Blues Away (3)	I Must Have Been Blind (3)	Islander (On Pacific Coast	Phantasmagoria In Two (1)	Train, The (3)
Dream Letter (2)		Highway) (2)	Pleasant Street (1)	

BUCKNER & GARCIA
Atlanta-based duo: Jerry Buckner and Gary Garcia. Recorded as Willis "The Guard" & Vigorish in 1980.

DEBUT DATE	PEAK POS	WKS CHR	GOLD	ARTIST — Album Title	$	Label & Number
3/13/82	24	16	●	Pac-Man Fever ....[N]	$8	Columbia 37941

album inspired by popular video games

Defender, The	Froggy's Lament	Hyperspace	Ode To A Centipede
Do The Donkey Kong	Goin' Berzerk	Mousetrap	**Pac-Man Fever 9**

BUCKWHEAT
American pop quartet led by Timmy Harrison (vocals) and Michael Smotherman (keyboards).

DEBUT DATE	PEAK POS	WKS CHR	GOLD	ARTIST — Album Title	$	Label & Number
4/1/72	179	6		Movin' On	$10	London 609

Crazy Songs And Looney	Does Anybody Care	Gunfighter, The	Movin' On (Part I & II)	Song For Billy
Tunes	Good Book	I'm Goin' Home	**Simple Song Of**	
		Indian Song	**Freedom 84**	

BUCKWHEAT ZYDECO
Louisiana-based zydeco outfit formed and fronted by Stanley "Buckwheat" Dural, Jr. Includes members of the Ils Sont Partis Band and the Dirty Dozen Brass Band. Zydeco is a mix of blues, country, rock, Cajun waltzes and two-step.

DEBUT DATE	PEAK POS	WKS CHR	GOLD	ARTIST — Album Title	$	Label & Number
11/14/87	172	5		1 On A Night Like This	$8	Island 90622
9/17/88	104	7		2 Taking It Home..	$8	Island 90968
7/7/90	140	11		3 Where There's Smoke There's Fire	$12	Island 842925

features Steve Berlin (Los Lobos) on baritone sax; produced by David Hidalgo (Los Lobos)

Be Good Or Be Gone (3)	Hey, Good Lookin' (3)	Maybe I Will (3)	Taking It Home (2)	Why Does Love Got To Be So
Beast Of Burden (3)	Hot Tamale Baby (1)	On A Night Like This (1)	These Things You Do (2)	Sad (2)
Buck's Hot Rod (3)	In And Out Of My Life (2)	Ooh Wow (2)	Time Is Tight (1)	Zydeco Honky Tonk (1)
Buckwheat's Special (1)	It's Getting Late (3)	People's Choice (1)	We're Having A Party (3)	
Creole Country Part 1 & 2 (2)	Ma 'Tit Fille (1)	Pour Tout Quelque'un (3)	What You Gonna Do? (3)	
Down Dallas Alley (2)	Make A Change (2)	Route 66 (3)	Where There's Smoke	
Drivin' Old Grey (2)	Marie Marie (1)	Space Zydeco (1)	There's Fire (3)	

BUD AND TRAVIS
Balladeers Bud Dashiel and Travis Edmonson. Formed duo in San Francisco, 1958. Bud died on 6/2/89.

DEBUT DATE	PEAK POS	WKS CHR	GOLD	ARTIST — Album Title	$	Label & Number
11/9/63	126	4		1 Bud & Travis...In Concert ....[L]	$15	Liberty 11001 [2]

recorded 3/24/60 at Santa Monica's Civic Auditorium

DEBUT DATE	PEAK POS	WKS CHR	GOLD	ARTIST — Album Title	$	Label & Number
3/28/64	129	6		2 Perspective on Bud & Travis	$15	Liberty 7341

Abilene (2)	Come To The Dance (Vamos	Guess I'll Go Home (1)	Maria Cristina (2)	Sabras Que Te Quiero (2)
Ay! Jalisco (2)	Al Baile) (1)	I Never Will Marry (2)	Merry Minuet (Rioting In	Sloop John B (1)
Ay, Maria (2)	Delia's Gone (1)	Johnny, I Hardly Knew Ye'	Africa) (1)	So Long, Stay Well (1)
Bonsoir Dame (1)	Everybody Loves Saturday	(1)	Mexican Wedding Dance (La	Take Off Your Old Coat (2)
Carmen Carmella (1)	Night (1)	La Vaquilla Colorada (2)	Bamba) (1)	They Call The Wind Maria (1)
Cloudy Summer Afternoon	Fiesta In Guadalajara (2)	Long Time Back (2)	Myra (1)	Tomorrow Is A Long Time (2)
(1)	Goin' To California (2)	Malaguena Salerosa (1)	Raspberries, Strawberries (1)	Two Brothers (2)

BUFFALO SPRINGFIELD, The
Superstar group formed in Los Angeles in 1966: Stephen Stills, Neil Young, Richie Furay, Dewey Martin and Bruce Palmer (replaced by Jim Messina after first two albums). Disbanded in 1968. Stills and Young formed Crosby, Stills, Nash & Young. Furray and Messina formed Poco.

DEBUT DATE	PEAK POS	WKS CHR	GOLD	ARTIST — Album Title	$	Label & Number
3/25/67	80	16		1 Buffalo Springfield	$25	Atco 200
11/18/67+	44	14		2 Buffalo Springfield Again	$25	Atco 226
8/17/68	42	19		3 Last Time Around	$25	Atco 256
3/1/69	42	24	▲	4 Retrospective/The Best Of Buffalo Springfield.............[G]	$25	Atco 283
12/8/73	104	13		5 Buffalo Springfield ....[K]	$20	Atco 806 [2]

Bluebird (2,4,5) 58	**Expecting To Fly (2,4,5) 98**	Hot Dusty Roads (1)	Nowadays Clancy Can't	**Rock 'N' Roll Woman**
Broken Arrow (2,4,5)	Flying On The Ground Is	Hour Of Not Quite Rain (3,5)	Even Sing (1,4,5) 44	(2,4,5) 44
Burned (1,5)	Wrong (1)	Hung Upside Down (2,5)	**On The Way Home**	Sad Memory (2)
Carefree Country Day (3)	**For What It's Worth (Stop,**	I Am A Child (3,4,5)	(3,4,5) 82	Sit Down I Think I Love You
Child's Claim To Fame (2,5)	**Hey What's That Sound)**	It's So Hard To Wait (3)	Out Of My Mind (1,5)	(1,4,5)
Do I Have To Come Right	**(1,4,5) 7**	Kind Woman (3,4,5)	Pay The Price (1,5)	Special Care (3,5)
Out And Say It (1)	Four Days Gone (3,5)	Leave (1)	Pretty Girl Why (3,5)	Uno Mundo (3,5)
Everybody's Wrong (1)	Go And Say Goodbye (1,4,5)	Merry-Go-Round (3)	Questions (3,5)	
Everydays (2)	Good Time Boy (2)	Mr. Soul (2,4,5)		

★★121★★ BUFFETT, Jimmy
Born on 12/25/46 in Mobile, Alabama. Has BS degree in history and journalism from the University of Southern Mississippi. After working in New Orleans, moved to Nashville in 1969. Settled in Key West in 1971. Owns a store called Margaritaville and has his own line of tropical clothing.

DEBUT DATE	PEAK POS	WKS CHR	GOLD	ARTIST — Album Title	$	Label & Number
3/2/74	176	13		1 Living and Dying in 3/4 Time................................	$12	Dunhill 50132
2/8/75	25	27		2 A1A	$12	Dunhill 50183
				A1A: beach access road off U.S. 1 in Florida		
2/14/76	65	14		3 Havana Daydreamin'	$10	ABC 914
2/12/77	12	42	▲	4 Changes In Latitudes, Changes In Attitudes	$10	ABC 990
4/8/78	10	29	▲	5 Son Of A Son Of A Sailor..	$10	ABC 1046
11/11/78	72	18	●	6 You Had To Be There ....[L]	$12	ABC 1008 [2]
9/15/79	14	28	●	7 Volcano	$10	MCA 5102
2/21/81	30	18		8 Coconut Telegraph	$8	MCA 5169
1/23/82	31	15		9 Somewhere Over China..	$8	MCA 5285
10/8/83	59	24		10 One Particular Harbour	$8	MCA 5447
9/29/84	87	14		11 Riddles In The Sand	$8	MCA 5512

DEBUT DATE	PEAK POS	WKS CHR	GOLD	ARTIST — Album Title	$	Label & Number
				BUFFETT, Jimmy — Cont'd		
7/6/85	**53**	20		12 Last Mango In Paris	$8	MCA 5600
11/16/85	**100**	24	▲²	13 Songs You Know By Heart - Jimmy Buffett's Greatest Hit(s) .... [G]	$8	MCA 5633
6/28/86	**66**	16		14 Floridays	$8	MCA 5730
7/9/88	**46**	14		15 Hot Water	$8	MCA 42093
7/15/89	**57**	13		16 Off To See The Lizard	$8	MCA 6314
11/17/90	**68**	15	●	17 Feeding Frenzy ....[L]	$12	MCA 10022
				recorded in Atlanta and Cincinnati		
6/6/92	**68**	19	▲	18 Boats Beaches Bars & Ballads	$48	Margarit. 10613 [4]

African Friend (5,18)
Baby's Gone Shoppin' (15)
Ballad Of Spider John (1,18)
Banana Republics (4)
Beyond The End (12)
Big Rig (3)
Bigger Than The Both Of Us (11)
Biloxi (4,18)
Boat Drinks (7,13,18)
Boomerang Love (16)
Brahma Fear (1)
Brand New Country Star (1)
Bring Back The Magic (15)
Brown Eyed Girl (10,18)
Burn That Bridge (11)
California Promises (10,18)
Captain And The Kid (3,6,18)
Carnival World (16)
Changes In Latitudes,
Changes In Attitudes
(4,6,13,18) 37
Changing Channels (16,18)
Chanson Pour Les Petits Enfants (7)
Cheeseburger In Paradise
(5,13,17,18) 32
Christmas In The Caribbean (18)
City, The (17)
Cliches (3)
Coast Of Marseilles (5,18)
Coconut Telegraph (8,18)
Come Monday
(1,6,13,17,18) 30
Come To The Moon (11)
Cowboy In The Jungle (5)
Creola (14)

Cuban Crime Of Passion (18)
Dallas (2)
Defying Gravity (3,18)
Desperation Samba (Halloween In Tijuana) (12,18)
Distantly In Love (10,18)
Dixie Diner (6)
Domino College (18)
Door Number Three (2)
Dreamsicle (7)
Elvis Imitators (18)
Everlasting Moon (18)
Everybody's On The Run (12)
Fins (7,13,17,18) 35
First Look (14,18)
Floridays (14)
Fool Button (5)
Frank And Lola (12,18)
God's Own Drunk (1,6)
Good Fight (8)
Grapefruit-Juicy Fruit (6,13,18)
Gravity Storm (16)
Great Filling Station Holdup (18)
Great Heart (15)
Growing Older But Not Up (8)
Gypsies In The Palace (12,17)
Havana Daydreamin' (3,6,18)
He Went To Paris (6,13,18)
Homemade Music (15)
Honey Do (10,17)
I Have Found Me A Home (18)
I Heard I Was In Town (9,18)

I Love The Now (14)
I Used To Have Money One Time (10)
I Wish Lunch Could Last Forever (16)
If I Could Just Get It On Paper (9)
If It All Falls Down (14)
If The Phone Doesn't Ring, It's Me (12,18)
In The Shelter (4)
Incommunicado (8,18)
Island (8,18)
It's Midnight And I'm Not Famous Yet (9)
It's My Job (8) 57
Jamaica Farewell (17)
Jolly Mon Sing (12,17,18)
Kick It In Second Wind (3,18)
King Of Somewhere Hot (15)
Knees Of My Heart (11,18)
L'Air De La Louisiane (15)
La Vie Dansante (11)
Lady I Can't Explain (7)
Landfall (4,6)
Last Line (5)
Last Mango In Paris (12,17)
Life Is Just A Tire Swing (7)
Lip Service (9)
Little Miss Magic (8,18)
Livin' It Up (10)
Livingston Saturday Night (5,18) 52
Livingston's Gone To Texas (1)
Love And Luck (18)
Love In Decline (11)

Love Song (From A Different Point Of View) (17)
Lovely Cruise (4,18)
Makin' Music For Money (2)
Manana (5,18) 84
Margaritaville (4,6,13,17,18) 8
Meet Me In Memphis (14)
Mermaid In The Night (16)
Middle Of The Night (18)
Migration (2)
Miss You So Badly (4,6)
Money Back Guarantee (18)
Morris' Nightmare (6)
My Barracuda (15)
My Head Hurts, My Feet Stink And I Don't Love Jesus (3)
Nautical Wheelers (2,18)
No Plane On Sunday (14)
Nobody Speaks To The Captain No More (14)
Off To See The Lizard (18)
On A Slow Boat To China (9,18)
One Particular Harbour (10,17,18)
Pascagoula Run (16,18)
Pencil Thin Mustache (1,6,13,18)
Perfect Partner (12)
Perrier Blues (6)
Pirate Looks At Forty (2,4,6,13,17,18)
Please Bypass This Heart (12)
Pre-You (15,18)
Presents To Send You (2)

Prince Of Tides (15)
Ragtop Day (11,18)
Ringling, Ringling (1)
Saxophones (1)
Sendin' The Old Man Home (7,18)
She's Going Out Of My Mind (11)
Smart Woman (In A Real Short Skirt) (15)
Something So Feminine About A Mandolin (3)
Son Of A Son Of A Sailor (5,6,13,18)
Stars Fell On Alabama (8,18)
Stars On The Water (10,18)
Steamer (9,18)
Stories We Could Tell (2)
Stranded On A Sandbar (7)
Strange Bird (16)
Survive (7,18) 77
Take Another Road (16)
Take It Back (18)
Tampico Trauma (4,6,18)
That's My Story And I'm Stickin' To It (16)
That's What Living Is To Me (15)
They Don't Dance Like Carmen No More (18)
This Hotel Room (3)
Tin Cup Chalice (2,18)
Today's Message (17)
Treat Her Like A Lady (7,18)
Trying To Reason With Hurricane Season (2,18)
Twelve Volt Man (10,18)

Volcano (7,13,17,18) 66
We Are The People Our Parents Warned Us About (10)
Weather Is Here, Wish You Were Beautiful (8,18)
West Nashville Grand Ballroom Gown (1)
When Salome Plays The Drum (9,18)
When The Coast Is Clear (14,18)
When The Wild Life Betrays Me (11)
Where's The Party (9)
Who's The Blonde Stranger? (11,18)
Why Don't We Get Drunk And Screw (6,13,18)
Why The Things We Do (16)
Why You Wanna Hurt My Heart (10)
Wino And I Know (1,18)
Woman Goin' Crazy On Caroline Street (3)
Wonder Why We Ever Go Home (4,6)
You'll Never Work In Dis Bidness Again (14,17)

BUGGLES, The

English rock duo: Geoff Downes and Trevor Horn. Both joined the group Yes in 1980. Downes joined Asia in 1981. Horn became a prolific producer. Their hit single, "Video Killed The Radio Star," was the premier video on MTV's first show on 8/1/81.

3/27/82	**161**	5		Adventures In Modern Recording	$8	Carrere 37926

Adventures In Modern Recording
Beatnik
I Am A Camera
Inner City
Lenny
On T.V.
Rainbow Warrior
Vermillion Sands

BUGNON, Alex

Born in Montreux, Switzerland. Former keyboardist for Keith Sweat, Freddie Jackson and New Edition. Nephew of jazz trumpeter Donald Byrd.

4/1/89	**127**	11		1 Love Season	$8	Orpheus 75602
5/26/90	**131**	7		2 Head Over Heels ....[I]	$12	Orpheus 75615

Any Love (2)
Around 12:15 AM (1)
Can't Get Over You (2)
Dance Of The Ghosts (2)
Earth Interlude (2)
Elis (2)
Falling For You (1)
Going Out (1)
Head Over Heels (2)
Human Epilogue (2)
Love Season (1)
Noire Noire (2)
Missing You (2)
No Other Love (2)
Piano In The Dark (1)
Time Is Running Out (2)
Winnie (2)
Yearning For Your Love (1)

BULGARIAN STATE FEMALE VOCAL CHOIR

Twenty-six-member female choir, conducted by Dora Hriztova. Established in 1951 in Bulgaria by Philip Koutev, choir's vocal sound is a combination of Bulgarian folk and Western classical music.

12/17/88+	**165**	10		Le Mystere des Voix Bulgares .... [F-K]	$8	None./Exp. 79165

translation of Bulgarian title: The Mystery of Bulgarian Voices; compiled over a 20-year period, tracks feature various conductors and choir members

Brei Yvane (Dancing Song)
Erghen Diado (Song Of Schopsko)
Kalimankou Denkou (The Evening Gathering)
Messetschinko Lio Greilivko (Love Song From The Mountains)
Mir Stanke Le (Harvest Song from Thrace)
Pilentze Pee (Pilentze Sings)
Polegnala E Pschenitza (Harvest Song from Thrace)
Polegnala E Todora (Love Song)
Pritouritze Planinata (Song From The Thracian Plain)
Sableyalo Mi Agontze (The Bleating Lamb)
Schopska Pesen (Diaphonic Chant)
Strati Na Angelaki
Doumasche (Haiduk Song)
Svatba (The Wedding)

BULLDOG

Rock quintet led by former Rascals Gene Cornish and Dino Danelli. Also see Fotomaker.

11/18/72+	**176**	11		Bulldog	$15	Decca 75370

Don't Blame It On Me
Good Times Are Comin'
Have A Nice Day
I'm A Madman
Juicin' With Lucy
No 44
Parting People Should Be Good Friends
Rockin' Robin
Too Much Monkey Business
You Underlined My Life

BULLETBOYS

Los Angeles hard-rock quartet: Marq Torien (vocals), Mick Sweda, Lonnie Vencent and Jimmy D'Anda.

10/29/88+	**34**	47	●	1 BulletBoys	$8	Warner 25782
3/30/91	**69**	8		2 Freakshow	$12	Warner 26168

DEBUT DATE	PEAK POS	WKS CHR	GOLD	ARTIST — Album Title	$	Label & Number

BULLETBOYS — Cont'd

Badlands (1)	For The Love Of Money	Hang On St. Christopher (2)	Huge (2)	Ripping Me (2)	THC Groove (2)
Crank Me Up (1)	(1) 78	Hard As A Rock (1)	Kissin' Kitty (1)	Say Your Prayers (2)	Talk To Your Daughter (2)
Do Me Raw (2)	Freakshow (2)	Hell On My Heels (1)	O Me O My (2)	Shoot The Preacher Down (1)	Thrill That Kills (2)
F#9 (1)	Goodgirl (2)	Hell Yeah! (2)	Owed To Joe (1)	**Smooth Up** (1) **71**	

BUONO, Victor
Heavy-set character actor; died on 1/1/82 (age 43).

9/18/71	66	17		Heavy! .... [C]	$8	Dore 325

Bless Me Doctor	I Am	Lard Lib	Skinny Poems For Fat Lovers	We're The Most	You Don't Have To Be Fat To
Fat Man's Prayer	I'm Fat	New Gig	Someday When I'm Skinny	Word To The Wide	Hate Rome

BURDON, Eric
Eric was born on 5/11/41 in Newcastle-On-Tyne, England. Lead singer of The Animals.

ERIC BURDON AND WAR:

5/16/70	18	27	1	Eric Burdon Declares "War"	$12	MGM 4663
12/26/70+	82	9	2	The Black-Man's Burdon	$15	MGM 4710 [2]

THE ERIC BURDON BAND:

12/21/74+	51	16	3	Sun Secrets	$10	Capitol 11359
8/9/75	171	5	4	Stop	$10	Capitol 11426

WAR featuring ERIC BURDON:

12/25/76+	140	5	5	Love Is All Around .... [E]	$10	ABC 988

recorded 1969-70

All I Do (4)	Day In The Life (5)	I'm Lookin' Up (4)	Mr. Charlie (1)	Real Me (3)	Tobacco Road (1,5)
Bare Back Ride (2)	Dedication (1)	It's My Life (3)	Nights In White Satin I & II	Ring Of Fire (3)	War (medley) (3)
Be Mine (4)	Don't Let Me Be	Jimbo (1)	(2)	Roll On Kirk (1)	Way It Should Be (4)
Beautiful New Born Child (2)	Misunderstood (medley) (3)	Laurel & Hardy (2)	Nina's School (medley) (3)	**Spill The Wine** (1) 3	When I Was Young (medley)
Bird & The Squirrel (2)	Funky Fever (4)	Letter From The County	Nuts, Seeds & Life (2)	Spirit (2)	(3)
Birth (1)	Gotta Get It On (4)	Farm (3)	Out Of Nowhere (2)	Stop (4)	You're No Stranger (1)
Black Bird (2)	Gun (2)	Love Is All Around (5)	P.C. 3 (2)	Sun Secrets (3)	
Black On Black In Black (2)	Home Cookin' (2)	Magic Mountain (5)	Paint It Black (2,5)	Sun/Moon (2)	
City Boy (4)	Home Dream (5)	Man, The (4)	Pretty Colors (2)	**They Can't Take Away Our**	
Danish Pastry (1)	I Have A Dream (1)	Mother Earth (1)	Rainbow (4)	**Music** (2) 50	

BURKE, Solomon
Soul singer. Born in 1936 in Philadelphia. Preached and broadcast from own church, "Solomon's Temple," in Philadelphia from 1945-55 as the "Wonder Boy Preacher." Church was founded for him by his grandmother. First recorded for Apollo in 1954. Left music to attend mortuary school, returned in 1960.

7/31/65	141	3	1	The Best Of Solomon Burke .... [G]	$30	Atlantic 8109
7/5/69	140	4	2	Proud Mary	$20	Bell 6033

Cry To Me (1) 44	Got To Get You Off My	I Can't Stop (2)	I'm Hanging Up My Heart	Please Send Me Someone To	These Arms Of Mine (2)
Don't Wait Too Long (2)	**Mind** (1) 22	I Really Don't Want To	For You (1) 85	Love (2)	**Tonight's The Night** (1) 28
Down In The Valley (1) 71	Home In Your Heart (1)	Know (1) 93	If You Need Me (1) 37	Price, The (1) 57	Uptight Good Woman (2)
Everybody Needs	How Big A Fool (Can A Fool	I'll Be Doggone (2)	**Just Out Of Reach (Of My**	Proud Mary (2) 45	What Am I Living For (2)
Somebody To Love (1) 58	Be) (2)		**Two Open Arms)** (1) 24	That Lucky Old Sun (2)	Words (1)

BURNETT, Carol
Comedic actress. Born on 4/26/33 in San Antonio. Star of own variety TV show from 1967-78 and 1991. Married to TV producer Joe Hamilton; their daughter is actress Carrie Hamilton.

9/1/62	85	9	1	Julie And Carol at Carnegie Hall .... [L]	$20	Columbia 2240

JULIE ANDREWS & CAROL BURNETT
a musical concert performed on 6/11/62

1/29/72	199	2	2	Carol Burnett featuring If I Could Write A Song	$10	Columbia 31048

For All We Know (2)	From Texas: Big "D" (1)	It's Too Late (2)	Rainy Days And Monday (2)	Those Were The Days (2)	You're So London (1)
From Russia: The Nausiev	Guess Who (medley) (2)	Meantime (1)	Rose Garden (2)	Try To Remember (2)	
Ballet (1)	History Of Musical Comedy	No Mozart Tonight (1)	Saturday Morning	Turn Around, Look At Me	
From Switzerland: The Pratt	(1)	Oh Dear What Can The	Confusion (2)	(medley) (2)	
Family (1)	If I Could Write A Song (1)	Matter Be (1)	Sunrise, Sunset (2)	Who's Sorry Now (2)	

BURNETT, T-Bone
Born John Henry Burnett in St. Louis in 1948. Moved to Fort Worth, Texas in the early '50s. With Bob Dylan's Rolling Thunder Revue, 1975-76. Formed the Alpha Band in 1977. Production work for Los Lobos, Elvis Costello and others. Married singer Sam (Leslie) Phillips.

10/1/83	188	5		Proof Through The Night	$8	Warner 23921

After All These Years	Fatally Beautiful	Hula Hoop	Pressure	Sixties, The	When The Night Falls
Baby Fall Down	Hefner And Disney	Murder Weapon	Shut It Tight	Stunned	

BURNETTE, Rocky
Born on 6/12/53 in Memphis. Son of Johnny Burnette, nephew of Dorsey Burnette and cousin of Billy Burnette (of Fleetwood Mac).

6/21/80	53	14		The Son Of Rock And Roll..	$8	EMI America 17033

Angel In Chambray	Baby Tonight	Clowns From Outer Space	Roll Like A Wheel	Woman In Love	
Anywhere Your Body Goes	Boogie Man	Fallin' In Love (Bein' Friends)	**Tired Of Toein' The Line** 8	You're So Easy To Love	

BURNING SENSATIONS
Rock sextet led by former Motels guitarist Tim McGovern.

7/30/83	175	4		Burning Sensations .... [M]	$8	Capitol 15009

Belly Of The Whale	Carnivals Of Souls	Check Your Mail	Jokenge		

BURNS, George
Born Nathan Birnbaum on 1/20/1896 in New York City. Starred with wife Gracie Allen in vaudeville, radio, films and TV until her death in 1964. Won the 1975 Best Supporting Actor Oscar for *The Sunshine Boys*. Holds record for longest span between pop charted singles (47 years).

2/9/80	93	10		I Wish I Was Eighteen Again..	$8	Mercury 5025

Arizona Whiz	**I Wish I Was Eighteen**	Old Bones	One Of The Mysteries Of Life		
Baby Song	**Again** 49	Old Dogs, Children And	Only Way To Go		
Forgive Her A Little (And	Nickels And Dimes	Watermelon Wine	Real Good Cigar		
Love Her A Lot)					

DEBUT DATE	PEAK POS	WKS CHR	G O L D	ARTIST — Album Title	$	Label & Number

BURRELL, Kenny
Jazz guitarist from Detroit. Veteran sessionman with Blue Note and Prestige. Featured guitarist on albums by Jimmy Smith and Kai Winding.

DEBUT DATE	PEAK POS	WKS CHR	GOLD	ARTIST — Album Title	$	Label & Number
11/30/63	108	4		1 Blue Bash!.....................[I]	$25	Verve 8553
				KENNY BURRELL/JIMMY SMITH		
12/17/66	146	2		2 The Tender Gender.....................[I]	$15	Cadet 772
8/31/68	191	2		3 Blues-The Common Ground.....................[I]	$15	Verve 8746

Angel Eyes (3) • Blue Bash (1) • Blues For Del (1) • Burning Spear (3) • Common Ground (3) • Easy Living (1) • Every Day (I Have The Blues) (3) • Everydays (3) • Fever (1) • Girl Talk (2) • Hot Bossa (2) • I'm Confessin' (2) • If Someone Had Told Me (2) • Isabella (2) • Kenny's Sound (1) • La Petite Mambo (2) • Mother-In-Law (2) • People (2) • Preacher, The (3) • Sausalito Nights (3) • See See Rider (3) • Soft Winds (1) • Soulful Brothers (3) • Suzy (2) • Tender Gender (2) • Travelin' (1) • Were You There (3) • Wonder Why (3)

BURTNICK, Glen
Pop singer/guitarist from New Jersey. Worked with Marshall Crenshaw & Cyndi Lauper. Joined Styx in 1990.

| 10/24/87 | 147 | 6 | | Heroes & Zeros | $8 | A&M 5166 |

Abalene • Day Your Ship Gets Thru • **Follow You 65** • Heard It On The Radio • Here Comes Sally • Love Goes On • Scattered • Spinning My Wheels • Stupid Boys (Suckers For Love) • Walls Came Down

BURTON, Jenny
Born on 11/18/57 in New York City. Former lead singer of C-Bank, the R&B studio band of John Robie.

| 3/24/84 | 181 | 4 | | In Black And White.....................| $8 | Atlantic 80122 |

All The Time (medley) • Players • **Remember What You Like 81** • Rock Steady • Small Rewards • Time (medley) • Vena Cava • You'll Never Come Again

BUS BOYS, The
Los Angeles-based sextet. Appeared in the film *48 HRS.*

| 11/29/80+ | 85 | 15 | | 1 Minimum Wage Rock & Roll | $8 | Arista 4280 |
| 8/21/82 | 139 | 7 | | 2 American Worker | $8 | Arista 9569 |

American Workers (2) • Anggie (1) • D-Day (1) • Did You See Me? (1) • Dr. Doctor (2) • Falling In Love (2) • Heart And Soul (2) • I Believe (2) • I Get Lost (2) • Johnny Soul'd Out (1) • KKK (1) • Last Forever (2) • Minimum Wage (1) • New Shoes (2) • Opportunity (2) • Respect (1) • Soul Surfing U.S.A. (2) • Tell The Coach (1) • There Goes The Neighborhood (1) • We Stand United (1) • Yellow Lights (2)

BUSH, Kate
Born on 7/30/58 in Bexley, Kent, England. Discovered by Dave Gilmour of Pink Floyd. Signed to EMI at age 16.

11/13/82	157	11		1 The Dreaming	$10	EMI America 17084
7/9/83	148	6		2 Kate Bush.....................[M]	$10	EMI America 19004
10/26/85	30	27		3 Hounds Of Love	$10	EMI America 17171
12/20/86+	76	27		4 The Whole Story.....................[G]	$10	EMI America 17242
11/4/89	43	26		5 The Sensual World	$8	Columbia 44164

All The Love (1) • And Dream Of Sheep (3) • Army Dreamers (4) • Baboshka (2,4) • Between A Man And A Woman (5) • Big Sky (3) • Breathing (4) • Cloudbusting (3,4) • Deeper Understanding (5) • Dreaming, The (1,4) • Experiment IV (4) • Fog, The (5) • Get Out Of My House (1) • Heads We're Dancing (5) • Hello Earth (3) • Houdini (1) • Hounds Of Love (3,4) • James And The Cold Gun (2) • Jig Of Life (3) • Leave It Open (1) • Love And Anger (5) • **Man With The Child In His Eyes** (4) **85** • Morning Fog (3) • Mother Stands For Comfort (3) • Never Be Mine (5) • Night Of The Swallow (1) • Pull Out The Pin (1) • Reaching Out (5) • Rocket's Tail (5) • **Running Up That Hill** (3,4) **30** • Sat In Your Lap (1,2,4) • Sensual World (5) • Suspended In Gaffa (1,2) • There Goes A Tenner (1) • This Woman's Work (5) • Un Baisser D'Enfant (The Infant Kiss) (4) • Under Ice (3) • Waking The Witch (3) • Watching You Without Me (3) • Wow (4) • Wuthering Heights (4)

BUSHKIN, Joe
Born on 11/7/16 in New York City. Pianist/composer.

| 5/26/56 | 14 | 1 | | Midnight Rhapsody.....................[I] | $20 | Capitol 711 |

Above All, You • As Time Goes By • Come Rain Or Come Shine • Embraceable You • I Can't Get Started • I Cover The Waterfront • It's The Talk Of The Town • Laura • Manhattan • September Song • Song Is You • Stormy Weather

BUSHWICK BILL
Richard Shaw, member of Houston-based rap group The Geto Boys. Born in Jamaica. Lost his right eye in a shooting on 5/10/91.

| 10/17/92 | 32 | 9 | | Little Big Man | $12 | Rap-A-Lot 57189 |

Call Me Crazy • Chuckwick • Copper To Cash • Dollars And Sense • Don't Come To Big • Ever So Clear • Letter From KKK • Little Big Man • Skitso • Stop Lying • Take Em' Off

BUTCHER, Jon, Axis
Black rock guitarist/vocalist Butcher is from Boston. Went solo from Axis in 1987.

3/26/83	91	13		1 Jon Butcher Axis	$8	Polydor 810059
3/31/84	160	6		2 Stare At The Sun	$8	Polydor 817493
10/12/85	66	17		3 Along The Axis	$8	Capitol 12425
				JON BUTCHER:		
4/4/87	77	27		4 Wishes	$8	Capitol 12542
2/18/89	121	8		5 Pictures From The Front	$8	Capitol 90238

Along The Axis (3) • Angel Dressed In Blue (4) • Beating Drum (5) • Between The Lines (3) • Breakout (2) • Call To Arms (2) • Can't Be The Only Fool (1) • Can't Tell The Dancer From The Dance (2) • Carrie (3) • Churinga (5) • Come And Get It (5) • Division Street (5) • Don't Say Goodnight (2) • Dreams Fade Away (2) • Electricity (3) • Eros Arriving (2) • Fairlight (1) • Goodbye Saving Grace (4) • Holy War (4) • I'm Only Dreaming (5) • I've Got Money (3) • It's Only Words (1) • Life Takes A Life (4) • Little Bit Of Magic (4) • Live Or Die (5) • Living For Tomorrow (4) • Long Way Home (4) • Might As Well Be Free (5) • Mission, The (5) • New Man (1) • 99 (May Be All You Need) (4) • Ocean In Motion (1) • Only The Fox (3) • Partners In Crime (4) • Prisoners Of The Silver Chain (4) • Ritual, The (3) • Send Me Somebody (5) • Send One, Care Of (1) • Sentinel (1) • Show Me Some Emotion (4) • **Sounds Of Your Voice** (3) **94** • Stay Low (2) • Stop (3) • That's How Strong My Love Is (3) • 2 Hearts Running (3) • Victims (2) • Waiting For A Miracle (5) • Walk Like This (1) • Walk On The Moon (2) • We Will Be As One (1) • Wind It Up (2) • Wishes (4)

DEBUT DATE	PEAK POS	WKS CHR	GOLD	ARTIST — Album Title	$	Label & Number

BUTLER, Carl
Country singer. Born on 6/2/27 in Knoxville, Tennessee. Died on 9/4/92. His wife, Pearl, who sang harmony, died in 1989.

4/27/63	104	9		Don't Let Me Cross Over	$15	Columbia 2002

Don't Let Me Cross Over *88*   Grief In My Heart   I Know What It Means To Be   I Know Why I Cry   I'll Cry Again Tomorrow   Wonder Drug
For The First Time   Honky Tonkitis   Lonesome   I Know You Don't Love Me   I'm A Prisoner Of Love
    I Like To Pretend   River Of Tears

★★409★★   BUTLER, Jerry
Born on 12/8/39 in Sunflower, Mississippi. Older brother of soul singer Billy Butler. Sang in the Northern Jubilee Gospel Singers, with Curtis Mayfield. Later with the Quails. In 1957, Butler and Mayfield joined the Roosters with Sam Gooden and brothers Arthur and Richard Brooks. Changed name to The Impressions in 1957. Left for solo career in autumn of 1958. Dubbed "The Ice Man."

10/3/64	102	11	1	Delicious Together	$35	Vee-Jay 1099

BETTY EVERETT & JERRY BUTLER

1/20/68	154	7	2	Mr. Dream Merchant	$15	Mercury 61146
3/16/68	178	2	3	Jerry Butler's Golden Hits Live .... [L]	$15	Mercury 61151
7/27/68	195	2	4	The Soul Goes On	$15	Mercury 61171
1/4/69	29	47	5	The Ice Man Cometh	$15	Mercury 61198
10/4/69	41	23	6	Ice On Ice	$15	Mercury 61234
6/27/70	167	5	7	The Best Of Jerry Butler .... [G]	$12	Mercury 61281
7/11/70	172	4	8	You & Me	$12	Mercury 61269
2/6/71	186	4	9	Jerry Butler Sings Assorted Sounds	$12	Mercury 61320
3/27/71	143	5	10	Gene & Jerry - One & One	$12	Mercury 61330

GENE CHANDLER & JERRY BUTLER

10/2/71+	123	22	11	The Sagittarius Movement	$12	Mercury 61347
6/17/72	92	24	12	The Spice Of Life	$12	Mercury 7502 [2]
2/5/77	199	2	13	The Vintage Years .... [G]	$12	Sire 3717 [2]

featuring 13 hits by Jerry Butler, 13 by The Impressions (see The Impressions for cuts), and 2 by Curtis Mayfield: "Freddie's Dead" and "Superfly"

3/12/77	146	11	14	Suite For The Single Girl	$8	Motown 878
6/18/77	53	12	15	Thelma & Jerry	$8	Motown 887

THELMA HOUSTON & JERRY BUTLER

1/13/79	160	4	16	Nothing Says I Love You Like I Love You	$8	Phil. Int. 35510

Ain't That Good News (4) Ain't That Loving You Baby (1) **Ain't Understanding Mellow** (11) *21* Alfie (2) All Kinds Of People (12) Amen (3) And You've Got Me (15) **Are You Happy** (5) *39* Are You Lonely Tonight (16) Baby I'm A Want You (12) Be Yourself (10) Been A Long Time (6) Beside You (2) Brand New Me (6,7) Built My World Around You (9) Can't Forget About You, Baby (5) Cause I Love You So (3) Chain Gang (4) Chalk It Up (14) Change Is Gonna Come (4) Close To You Love (6) Do You Finally Need A Friend (9) **Don't Let Love Hang You Up** (6) *44* Don't Rip Me Off (12) Dream Music (medley) (14) Dream World (16) Everybody Is Waiting (10) Fever (1) **Find Another Girl** (13) *27*

For Your Precious Love (3,7) *11* Get On The Case (12) Girl In His Mind (11) Give Up A Taste (10) **Giving Up On Love** (13) *56* Go Away-Find Yourself (5) Going Back To My Baby's Love (9) Goodnight My Love (4) **Got To See If I Can't Get Mommy (To Come Back Home)** (6,7) *62* Guess Who (4) He Will Break Your Heart (3,13) *7* **Hey, Western Union Man** (5,7,13) *16* How Can I Get In Touch With You (5) **How Did We Lose It Baby** (9) *85* How Does It Feel (9) I Can't Stand It (1) I Come To You (2) **I Could Write A Book** (8) *46* **I Dig You Baby** (3,7) *60* I Forgot To Remember (6) I Found That I Was Wrong (10) I Love You Through Windows (15) I Need You (12) **I Only Have Eyes For You** (12) *85* I Stand Accused (3)

I Stop By Heaven (5) **I Wanna Do It To You** (14) *51* **I'm A Telling You** (13) *25* I'm Glad To Be Back (14) (I'm Just Thinking About) Cooling Out (16) I've Been Loving You Too Long (4) If I Could Remember (Not Ever Having You) (12) **If It's Real What I Feel** (9) *69* If You Leave Me Now (medley) (15) It's A Lifetime Thing (15) It's All Right (1) Joy Inside My Tears (15) Just Be True (1) Just Because I Really Love You (5) **Let It Be Me** (1,3) *5* Let Me Be (11) Let The Good Times Roll (1) Let's Get Together (15) Let's Go Get Out Of Town (14) Let's Make Love (16) Life's Unfortunate Sons (8) Loneliness (7) **Lost** (2,5,7) *62* Love Is Strange (1) Love So Right (medley) (15) Mail Call Time (10) **Make It Easy On Yourself** (3,13) *62* Real Good Man (8)

Masquerade Is Over (medley) (12) Mighty Good People (16) **Moody Woman** (6,7,13) *24* **Moon River** (3,13) *11* Mr. Dee Jay (I Got A Heartache) (2) **Mr. Dream Merchant** (2,7,13) *38* Ms. Fine (14) Music In Her Dreams (medley) (14) **Need To Belong** (13) *31* **Never Give You Up** (4,5,7,13) *20* No Money Down (8) (Nobody Ever Loved Anybody) The Way I Love You (2) Nothing Says I Love You Like I Love You (16) One Hand Washes The Other (10) 100 Lbs. Of Clay (2) **One Night Affair** (12) *52* One Woman Man (8) Only Pretty Girls (14) Only The Beginning (15) **Only The Strong Survive** (5,7,13) *4* Ordinary Joe (8) Our Day Will Come (1) (Play The Game Of) Let's Pretend (15) Prayer, A (12)

Respect (4) Sad Eyes (16) Said A Mother Said A Father (11) Sail Away (11) Sho' Is Groovin' (10) Simple Country Girl (11) Since I Don't Have You (13) Since I Fell For You (medley) (12) Since I Lost You Lady (6) Sittin' On The Dock Of The Bay (4) So Far Away (12) Something (8) Special Memory (9) Stop Steppin' On My Dreams (12) (Strange) I Still Love You (5) Strong Enough To Take It (9) Suite For The Single Girl (14) Sweet Love I've Found (5) Tammy Jones (8) Ten And Two (Take This Woman Off The Corner) (10) That's The Way It Was (That's The Way It Is) (12) These Arms Of Mine (4) **(They Long To Be) Close To You** (12) *91* To Make A Big Man Cry (2) True Love Don't Come Easy (11) **Walk Easy My Son** (11) *93*

Walking Around In Teardrops (6) Way You Do The Things You Do (1) What A Pleasant Surprise (14) What Is It (9) What's So Good About It (You're My Baby) (12) **What's The Use Of Breaking Up** (6,7,13) *20* When A Woman Loves A Man (When A Man Loves A Woman) (2) When You're Alone (6) Why Are You Leaving Me (9) Windy City Soul (11) Winter Of A Loving Heart (8) World Keeps Changing (10) Yes, My Goodness, Yes (4) Yesterday (2) You And Me (8) You Can't Always Tell (12) You Gotta Believe In Me (14) **You Just Can't Win (By Making The Same Mistake)** (10) *94* You Send Me (4)

BUTLER, Jonathan
Born in Capetown, South Africa. Soul guitarist/singer/songwriter. Migrated to London, 1984 (at age 21).

5/24/86	101	16		1	Introducing Jonathan Butler	$8	Jive 8408
5/30/87	50	33	●	2	Jonathan Butler	$10	Jive 1032 [2]
11/5/88	113	22		3	More Than Friends	$8	Jive 1136

Afrika (1) All Over You (2) Baby Please Don't Take It (I Need Your Love) (1) Barenese (2) Breaking Away (3) Calm Before The Storm (1) Crossroads Revisited (1)

Gentle Love (1) Give A Little More Lovin' (2) Going Home (2) Haunted By Your Love (1) High Tide (2) Holding On (2) I Miss Your Love Tonight (2)

It's So Hard To Let You Go (3) **Lies** (2) *27* Love Songs, Candlelight And You (2) Loving You (2) More Than Friends (3) One More Dance (2)

Overflowing (2) Reunion (2) Rumours (1) Sarah Sarah (3) Say We'll Be Together (2) Sekona (3) 7th Avenue South (3) She's A Teaser (3)

She's Hot (Burning Up) (3) Song For Jon (3) Sunset (2) Take Good Care Of Me (2) Take Me Home (3) There's One Born Every Minute (I'm A Sucker For You) (3)

Thinking Of You (1) True Love Never Fails (3)

BUTTERFIELD, Billy — see CONNIFF, Ray

DEBUT DATE	PEAK POS	WKS CHR	G O L D	ARTIST — Album Title	$	Label & Number
	★★497★★			**BUTTERFIELD, Paul**		

White blues vocalist/harmonica player. Born on 12/17/42 in Chicago. Died on 5/4/87. Formed interracial blues band in Chicago in 1965. His University of Chicago classmate Elvin Bishop was guitarist with group through 1968. Mike Bloomfield was the slide guitarist from 1965-66. Various members including saxophonist David Sanborn worked on and off with Butterfield from 1967-72.

DEBUT DATE	PEAK POS	WKS CHR	GOLD	ARTIST — Album Title	$	Label & Number
12/4/65+	123	9		1 The Paul Butterfield Blues Band	$20	Elektra 7294
				THE BUTTERFIELD BLUES BAND:		
10/8/66+	65	29		2 East-West	$20	Elektra 7315
1/13/68	52	16		3 The Resurrection Of Pigboy Crabshaw	$20	Elektra 74015
				Pigboy Crabshaw is Elvin Bishop's nickname		
8/24/68	79	17		4 In My Own Dream	$20	Elektra 74025
11/1/69	102	10		5 Keep On Moving	$20	Elektra 74053
1/16/71	72	12		6 The Butterfield Blues Band/Live	[L] $15	Elektra 2001 [2]
9/4/71	124	6		7 Sometimes I Just Feel Like Smilin'	$15	Elektra 75013
5/20/72	136	6		8 Golden Butter/The Best Of The Paul Butterfield Blues Band	[G] $15	Elektra 2005 [2]
				PAUL BUTTERFIELD'S BETTER DAYS:		
2/3/73	145	13		9 Better Days	$10	Bearsville 2119
11/3/73	156	8		10 It All Comes Back	$10	Bearsville 2170

All In A Day (5)
All These Blues (2)
Baby Please Don't Go (9)
Blind Leading The Blind (7,8)
Blues With A Feeling (1)
Born In Chicago (1,8)
Born Under A Bad Sign (3,6)
Boxer, The (6)
Broke My Baby's Heart (9)
Buddy's Advice (5)
Buried Alive In The Blues (9)
Done A Lot Of Wrong Things (9)
Double Trouble (3)
Driftin' And Driftin' (3,6,8)
Drivin' Wheel (3)
Droppin' Out (3)

Drowned In My Own Tears (7)
Drunk Again (4)
East West (2,8)
Everything Going To Be Alright (6)
Except You (5)
Get Out Of My Life, Woman (2,8)
Get Together Again (6)
Get Yourself Together (4)
Highway 28 (9)
I Got A Mind To Give Up Living (2)
I Got My Mojo Working (1)
I Want To Be With You (6)
If You Live (10)

In My Own Dream (4,8)
It All Comes Back (10)
It's Getting Harder To Survive (10)
Just To Be With You (4)
Keep On Moving (5)
Last Hope's Gone (4,8)
Last Night (1)
Little Piece Of Dying (7)
Look Over Yonders Wall (1,8)
Losing Hand (5)
Louisiana Flood (10)
Love Disease (5,6)
Love March (5,8)
Mary, Mary (2,8)
Mellow Down Easy (1,8)
Mine To Love (4)

Morning Blues (4)
Morning Sunrise (5)
Mystery Train (1,8)
Never Say No (2)
New Walkin Blues (9)
Night Child (7)
No Amount Of Loving (5,6)
Nobody's Fault But Mine (1,8)
One More Heartache (3,8)
One More Mile (8)
1000 Ways (7)
Our Love Is Drifting (1,8)
Pity The Fool (3)
Play On (7)
Please Send Me Somone To Love (9)

Poor Boy (10)
Pretty Woman (7)
Rule The Road (9)
Run Out Of Time (3)
Screamin' (1)
Shake Your Money-Maker (1,8)
Small Town Talk (10)
So Far So Good (5,6)
Song For Lee (7)
Spoonful (8)
Take Your Pleasure Where You Find It (10)
Thank You Mr. Poobah (1)
Tollin' Bells (3)
Too Many Drivers (10)
Trainman (7)

Two Trains Running (2)
Walkin' Blues (2,8)
Walking By Myself (5)
Where Did My Baby Go (5)
Win Or Lose (10)
Work Song (2)

BUZZCOCKS

Pop-punk quartet from Manchester, England led by Peter Shelley (vocals).

DEBUT DATE	PEAK POS	WKS CHR	GOLD	ARTIST — Album Title	$	Label & Number
2/23/80	163	6		A Different Kind Of Tension	$8	I.R.S. 009

Different Kind Of Tension
Hollow Inside

I Believe
I Don't Know What To Do With My Life

Mad Mad Judy
Money
Paradise

Radio Nine
Raison D'Etre
Sitting Round At Home

You Know You Can't Help It
You Say You Don't Love Me

BY ALL MEANS

Los Angeles-based R&B trio: James Varner (vocals, piano), Lynn Roderick (vocals, actress) and composer Billy Sheppard (guitar). Varner and Roderick were members of Bill Withers' band.

DEBUT DATE	PEAK POS	WKS CHR	GOLD	ARTIST — Album Title	$	Label & Number
1/20/90	160	11		Beyond A Dream	$12	Island 91319

Do You Remember
Early Fall

I Know You Well
I Think I Fell In Love

I'd Rather Be Lonely
Let's Get It On

More You Give, The More You Get
Point Of View
Stay With Me Tonight

Tender Love

BYRD, Charlie

Born on 9/16/25 in Chuckatuch, Virginia. Jazz and classical guitar virtuoso. Studied under classical master guitarist Segovia. With Woody Herman in 1959. Own tour of Latin America in 1961.

DEBUT DATE	PEAK POS	WKS CHR	GOLD	ARTIST — Album Title	$	Label & Number
9/15/62+	1[1]	70		1 **Jazz Samba**	[I] $25	Verve 8432
				STAN GETZ/CHARLIE BYRD		
3/23/63	128	5		2 Bossa Nova Pelos Passaros	[I] $20	Riverside 9436
				translation of Pelos Passaros: By The Birds		
6/28/69	197	4		3 Aquarius	[I] $15	Columbia 9841
9/6/69	129	4		4 Let Go	[I-L] $15	Columbia 9869
				THE CHARLIE BYRD QUARTET		

Aquarius/Let The Sunshine In (3)
Baia (1)
Bim Bom (2)
Bird Of Paradise (4)
Blues 13 (4)
Coisa Mais Linda (A Most Beautiful Thing) (2)
Desafinado (1,2) **15**
E Luxo So (1)

Ela Me Deixou (She Has Gone) (2)
Esperando O Sol (4)
Galveston (3)
Happy Heart (3)
Here's That Rainy Day (4)
Ho-Ba-La-La (2)
How Long Has This Been Going On (4)
Julia (3)

Let Go (Canto de Ossanha) (4)
Let The Sunshine In ...see: Aquarius
Lonely Princess (4)
Meditation (Meditacao) (2) **66**
Mood Indigo (medley) (4)
My Way (3)
O Barquinho (Little Boat) (2)

O Passaro (The Bird) (2)
O Pato (1)
Promises, Promises (4)
Samba De Uma Nota So (1)
Samba Dees Days (1)
Samba Triste (1,2)
Satin Doll (medley) (4)
This Guy's In Love With You (4)
Time Of The Season (3)

Traces (3)
Un Abraco Do Bonfa (A Salute To Bonfa) (2)
Voce E Eu (You And I) (2)
Way It Used To Be (3)
Where's The Playground Susie? (3)
While My Guitar Gently Weeps (3)

You've Made Me So Very Happy (3)
Yvone (2)

DEBUT DATE	PEAK POS	WKS CHR	GOLD	ARTIST — Album Title	$	Label & Number
	★★480★★			**BYRD, Donald**		

R&B-jazz trumpeter/flugelhorn player. Born on 12/9/32 in Detroit. With Air Force bands, 1951-53, and George Wallington in 1955. With Art Blakey Jazz Messengers in the mid-1950s. Own bands from the '60s. Founded The Blackbyrds in 1973 while teaching jazz at Howard University in Washington, D.C.

DEBUT DATE	PEAK POS	WKS CHR	GOLD	ARTIST — Album Title	$	Label & Number
7/11/64	110	8		1 A New Perspective	[I] $20	Blue Note 84124
				with Herbie Hancock (piano) and Kenny Burrell (guitar)		
4/28/73	36	34		2 Black Byrd	$15	Blue Note 047
3/30/74	33	28		3 Street Lady	$15	Blue Note 140
3/29/75	42	19		4 Stepping Into Tomorrow	[I] $15	Blue Note 368
11/15/75+	49	29		5 Places And Spaces	$15	Blue Note 549
12/18/76+	167	4		6 Donald Byrd's Best	[G] $15	Blue Note 700
2/12/77	60	14		7 Caricatures	$15	Blue Note 633
11/18/78	191	4		8 Thank You...For F.U.M.L. (Funking Up My Life)	$8	Elektra 144

112

DEBUT DATE	PEAK POS	WKS CHR	G O L D	ARTIST — Album Title	$	Label & Number
10/3/81	**93**	10	9	Love Byrd .... with Isaac Hayes and 125th Street, N.Y.C.	$8	Elektra 531

Beast Of Burden (1)
Black Byrd (2,6) **88**
Black Disciple (1)
Butterfly (9)
Caricatures (4)
Change (Makes You Want To Hustle) (5,6)
Chant (1)
Close Your Eyes And Look Within (8)
Cristo Redentor (1,8)
Dance Band (7)

Dancing In The Street (7)
Design A Nation (4)
Dominoes (5)
Elijah (1)
Falling (9)
Flight Time (2,6)
Have You Heard The News? (8)
I Feel Like Loving You Today (9)
I Love The Girl (4)
I Love Your Love (9)

I'll Always Love You (9)
In Love With Love (8)
Just My Imagination (5)
Lansana's Priestess (3,6)
Love For Sale (9)
Love Has Come Around (9)
Love's So Far Away (2)
Loving You (8)
Makin' It (4)
Miss Kane (3)
Mr. Thomas (2)
Night Whistler (5)

Onward 'Til Morning (7)
Places And Spaces (5)
Return Of The King (7)
Rock And Roll Again (4,6)
Science Funktion (7)
Sister Love (3)
Sky High (2,6)
Slop Jar Blues (2)
Stepping Into Tomorrow (4,6)
Street Lady (3,6)
Sunning In Your Loveshine (8)

Tell Me (7)
Thank You For Funking Up My Life (8)
Think Twice (4)
We're Together (4)
Where Are We Going? (2)
Wild Life (7)
Wind Parade (5)
Witch Hunt (3)
Woman Of The World (3)
You And Music (5)
You Are The World (4)

Your Love Is My Ecstasy (8)

★★**170**★★   **BYRDS, The**
Folk-rock group formed in Los Angeles in 1964. Consisted of James "Roger" McGuinn, (12-string guitar), David Crosby (guitar), Gene Clark (percussion), Chris Hillman (bass) and Mike Clarke (drums). McGuinn, who changed his name to Roger in 1968, had been with Bobby Darin and The Chad Mitchell Trio. Clark had been with The New Christy Minstrels. All except Clarke had folk music background. First recorded as the Beefeaters for Elektra in 1964. Also recorded as the Jet Set. Professional debut in March 1965. Clark left after "Eight Miles High." Crosby left in late 1967 to form Crosby, Stills & Nash. Re-formed in 1968 with McGuinn, Hillman, Kevin Kelly (drums) and Gram Parsons (guitar). Hillman and Parsons left that same year to form the Flying Burrito Brothers. McGuinn again re-formed with Clarence White (guitar), John York (bass) and Gene Parsons (drums). Reunions with original members in 1973 and 1979. Gram Parsons died on 9/19/73 (age 26) of a heroin overdose. McGuinn, Clark and Hillman later recorded as a trio. In 1986, Hillman formed popular country group, The Desert Rose Band. McGuinn, Crosby and Hillman reunited on stage on 2/24/90 for a Roy Orbison tribute. Clark died on 5/24/91 (age 46) of natural causes. Group inducted into the Rock and Roll Hall of Fame in 1991.

DEBUT DATE	PEAK POS	WKS CHR	G O L D	ARTIST — Album Title	$	Label & Number
6/26/65	**6**	38	1	**Mr. Tambourine Man**	$20	Columbia 9172
1/1/66	**17**	40	2	Turn! Turn! Turn!	$20	Columbia 9254
8/27/66	**24**	28	3	Fifth Dimension	$20	Columbia 9349
3/18/67	**24**	24	4	Younger Than Yesterday	$20	Columbia 9442
9/2/67	**6**	29	▲ 5	**The Byrds' Greatest Hits** ....[G]	$20	Columbia 9516
2/3/68	**47**	19	6	The Notorious Byrd Brothers	$20	Columbia 9575
8/31/68	**77**	10	7	Sweetheart Of The Rodeo	$20	Columbia 9670
3/15/69	**153**	7	8	Dr. Byrds & Mr. Hyde	$20	Columbia 9755
9/6/69	**84**	12	9	Preflyte ....[E] recorded in 1964	$20	Together 1001
12/13/69+	**36**	17	10	Ballad Of Easy Rider	$20	Columbia 9942
10/17/70	**40**	21	11	The Byrds (Untitled)...[L] record 1: live; record 2: studio	$10	Columbia 30127 [2]
7/24/71	**46**	10	12	Byrdmaniax	$10	Columbia 30640
12/25/71+	**152**	7	13	Farther Along	$10	Columbia 31050
12/16/72+	**114**	13	14	The Best Of The Byrds (Greatest Hits, Volume II) ....[G]	$10	Columbia 31795
3/24/73	**20**	17	15	Byrds .... reunion of original 5 Byrds	$8	Asylum 5058
9/8/73	**183**	3	16	Preflyte ....[R] new cover features a futuristic drawing of the band	$10	Columbia 32183
11/10/90	**151**	4	17	The Byrds ....[K] 84 tracks recorded from 1965-71, plus 2 tracks recorded at the Roy Orbison Tribute on 2/24/90 and 4 new compositions recorded in 1990 by reunited lineup of David Crosby, Chris Hillman and Roger McGuinn; includes a 55-page booklet	$41	Columbia 46773 [4]

Absolute Happiness (12)
Airport Song (9,16)
All I Really Want To Do (1,5,17) **40**
All The Things (11)
America's Great National Pastime (13,14)
Antique Sandy (13)
Armstrong, Aldrin And Collins (10)
Artificial Energy (6)
B. J. Blues (medley) (8)
B.B. Class Road (13)
Baby, What Do You Want Me To Do (medley) (8)
Bad Night At The Whiskey (8,17)
Ballad Of Easy Rider (10,14,17) **65**
Bells Of Rhymney (1,5,17)
Black Mountain Rag (Soldier's Joy) (17)
Blue Canadian Rockies (7)
Born To Rock 'N Roll (15)
Borrowing Time (15)
Boston (9,16)
Bristol Steam Convention Blues (17)
Bugler (13,17)
C.T.A. - 102 (4)
Candy (15)
Captain Soul (3)
Change Is Now (6)
Changing Heart (15)
Chestnut Mare (11,14,17)
Child Of The Universe (8)

Chimes Of Freedom (1,5,17)
Christian Life (7,17)
Citizen Kane (12,14)
Cowgirl In The Sand (15)
Day Walk (Never Before) (17)
Deportee (Plane Wreck At Los Gatos) (10,17)
Dolphins' Smile (6,17)
Don't Doubt Yourself, Babe (1)
Draft Morning (6,17)
Drug Store Truck Drivin' Man (8,14,17)
Eight Miles High (3,5,11,17) **14**
Everybody's Been Burned (4,17)
Farther Along (13,17)
Fido (10)
5 D (Fifth Dimension) (3,5,17) **44**
For Free (15)
For Me Again (9,16)
From A Distance (17)
Full Circle (15)
Get Down Your Line (13)
Get To You (6)
Girl With No Name (4,17)
Glory, Glory (12,17)
Goin' Back (6,17) **89**
Green Apple Quick Step (12,17)
Gunga Din (10)
Have You Seen Her Face (4,17) **74**

He Was A Friend Of Mine (2,14,17)
Here Without You (1,9,16)
Hey Joe (Where You Gonna Go) (3,17)
Hickory Wind (7,17)
Hungry Planet (11)
I Am A Pilgrim (7,17)
I Come And Stand At Every Door (3)
I Knew I'd Want You (1,9,16)
I Know My Rider (17)
I See You (3,17)
I Trust (12,17)
I Wanna Grow Up To Be A Politician (12,14,17)
I'll Feel A Whole Lot Better (1,5,17)
If You're Gone (2)
It Happens Each Day (17)
It's All Over Now, Baby Blue (10,17)
It's No Use (1)
Jack Tarr The Sailor (10)
Jamaica Say You Will (12)
Jesus Is Just Alright (10,14,17) **97**
John Riley (3,17)
Just A Season (11,17)
Just Like A Woman (17)
Kathleen's Song (12,17)
King Apathy III (8)
Lady Friend (17) **82**
Laughing (15)

Lay Down Your Weary Tune (2,17)
Lay Lady Lay (17)
Lazy Days (17)
Lazy Waters (13,17)
Life In Prison (7)
Long Live The King (15)
Love That Never Dies (17)
Lover Of The Bayou (11,17)
Mae Jean Goes to Hollywood (17)
Mind Gardens (4)
Mr. Spaceman (3,5,11,17) **36**
Mr. Tambourine Man (1,5,9,11,16,17) **1**
My Back Pages (4,5,8,17) **30**
My Destiny (17)
Nashville West (8,11,17)
Natural Harmony (6)
It Won't Be Wrong (2,17) **63**
Nothing Was Delivered (7,17)
Oh! Susannah (2)
Oil In My Lamp (10,17)
Old Blue (8,17)
Old John Robertson (6,17)
One Hundred Years From Now (7,17)
Pale Blue (13)
Paths Of Victory (17)
Positively 4th Street (11,17)
Precious Kate (13)
Pretty Boy Floyd (7,17)
Pretty Polly (17)
Psychodrama City (17)
Reason Why (9,16)
Renaissance Fair (4,17)

Reputation (17)
Roll Over Beethoven (17)
Satisfied Mind (2)
(See The Sky) About To Rain (15)
Set You Free This Time (2) **79**
She Don't Care About Time (17)
She Has A Way (9,16,17)
So Fine (13)
So You Want To Be A Rock 'N' Roll Star (4,5,11,17) **29**
Space Odyssey (6)
Spanish Harlem Incident (1,17)
Stanley's Song (17)
Sweet Mary (15)
Take A Whiff (On Me) (11)
There Must Be Someone (10)
Things Will Be Better (15)
This Wheel's On Fire (8,17)
Thoughts And Words (4)
Tiffany Queen (13,14,17)
Time Between (4,17)
Times They Are A-Changin' (2,17)
Triad (17)
Tribal Gathering (6)
Truck Stop Girl (11,17)
Tulsa County (10,17)
Tunnel Of Love (12)
Turn! Turn! Turn! (To Everything There Is A Season) (2,5,17) **1**

2-4-2 Fox Trot (The Lear Jet Song) (3)
Wait And See (2)
Wasn't Born To Follow (6,14,17)
We'll Meet Again (11)
Well Come Back Home (11)
What's Happening?!?! (3)
White's Lightning (17)
Why (4,17)
Wild Mountain Thyme (3)
Willin' (17)
World Turns All Around Her (2,17)
Yesterday's Train (11)
You Ain't Going Nowhere (7,14,17) **74**
You All Look Alike (11)
You Don't Miss Your Water (7,17)
You Movin' (9,16)
You Showed Me (9,16)
You Won't Have To Cry (1,9,16)
You're Still On My Mind (7)
Your Gentle Way Of Loving Me (8)

DEBUT DATE	PEAK POS	WKS CHR	GOLD	ARTIST — Album Title	$	Label & Number

BYRNE, David
Lead singer of the Talking Heads. Born on 5/14/52 in Dumbarton, Scotland. Composed scores for various films and plays, among them *The Last Emperor*, *The Catherine Wheel*, and *Music for The Knee Plays*. Album producer of the B-52's *Mesopotamia* and *Waiting* by Fun Boy Three. Formed own world music record label, Luaka Bop. Also see Concept Albums (*Brazil Classics*).

DEBUT DATE	PEAK POS	WKS CHR		ARTIST — Album Title	$	Label & Number
3/21/81	44	13		1 My Life In The Bush Of Ghosts ....[I]	$8	Sire 6093
				BRIAN ENO-DAVID BYRNE		
12/19/81+	104	12		2 The Catherine Wheel ....[OC]	$8	Sire 3645
6/1/85	141	6		3 Music for The Knee Plays....................................	$8	ECM 25022
				from an offbeat theatrical project created with Robert Wilson from Wilson's epic opera *The CIVIL WarS*		
10/21/89	71	18		4 Rei Momo	$8	Luaka Bop 25990
				Brazilian-flavored tunes written by Byrne, backed by a Brazilian ensemble		
3/21/92	125	6		5 Uh-Oh	$12	Sire 26799
				3 tracks feature Nona Hendryx on backing vocals		

Admiral Perry (3)
America Is Waiting (1)
Big Blue Plymouth (Eyes Wide Open) (2)
Big Business (2)
Call Of The Wild (4)
Carnival Eyes (4)
Carrier, The (1)
Cloud Chamber (2)
Come With Us (1)
Cowboy Mambo (Hey Lookit Me Now) (5)

Dirty Old Town (4)
Don't Want To Be Part Of Your World (4)
Dream Police (4)
Eggs In A Briar Patch (4)
(Gift Of Sound) Where The Sun Never Goes Down (3)
Girls On My Mind (5)
Hanging Upside Down (5)
Help Me Somebody (1)
His Wife Refused (2)
I Bid You Goodnight (3)

I Know Sometimes A Man Is Wrong (4)
I've Tried (3)
In The Future (3)
In The Upper Room (3)
Independence Day (4)
Jezebel Spirit (1)
Jungle Book (3)
Lie To Me (4)
Light Bath (2)
Make Believe Mambo (4)

Marching Through The Wilderness (4)
Mea Culpa (1)
Million Miles Away (5)
Monkey Man (5)
Moonlight In Glory (1)
Mountain Of Needles (1)
My Big Hands (Fall Through The Cracks) (2)
Now I'm Your Mom (5)
Poison (2)
Qu'Ran (1)

Red House (2)
Regiment (1)
Rose Tattoo (4)
Secret Life (1)
She's Mad (5)
Social Studies (3)
Somebody (5)
Something Ain't Right (5)
Sound Of Business (3)
Theadora Is Dozing (3)
Tiny Town (5)

Tree (Today Is An Important Occasion) (3)
Twistin' In The Wind (5)
Two Soldiers (2)
Walk In The Dark (5)
What A Day That Was (2)
Winter (3)
Women Vs. Men (4)

BYRON, D.L.
Male singer/songwriter/guitarist.

DEBUT DATE	PEAK POS	WKS CHR		ARTIST — Album Title	$	Label & Number
2/16/80	133	10		This Day And Age	$8	Arista 4258

Am I Falling In Love Again
Backstage Girl

Big Boys
Get With It

Listen To The Heartbeat
Lorryanne

Love In Motion

No Romance, No Weekend, No Love

Today
21st Century Man

C

CACTUS
U.S. rock group formed by bassist Tim Bogert (Vanilla Fudge) and drummer Carmine Appice (Vanilla Fudge, Rod Stewart's band, KGB, Blue Murder), with guitarist Jim McCarty (not to be confused with same-named Yardbirds drummer) and vocalist Rusty Day. The latter two left in 1972, replaced by guitarist Werner Fritzschings, vocalist Peter French and keyboardist Duane Hitchings. Bogert and Appice left in late 1972 and Hitchings formed New Cactus Band with Roland Robinson (bass), Mike Pinera (Iron Butterfly, Blues Image, Ramatam; guitar, vocals) and Jerry Norris (drums).

DEBUT DATE	PEAK POS	WKS CHR		ARTIST — Album Title	$	Label & Number
7/25/70	54	18		1 Cactus	$20	Atco 340
3/20/71	88	13		2 One Way...Or Another..	$20	Atco 356
11/27/71	155	10		3 Restrictions	$20	Atco 377
10/28/72	162	5		4 'Ot 'N' Sweaty ....[L]	$20	Atco 7011
				side 1 recorded live at the Mar Y Sol Festival in Puerto Rico		
5/12/73	183	6		5 Son Of Cactus	$15	Atco 7017
				NEW CACTUS BAND		

Alaska (3)
Bad Mother Boogie (4)
Bad Stuff (4)
Bag Drag (3)
Bedroom Mazurka (4)
Big Mama Boogie - Parts I & II (3)
Blue Gypsy Woman (5)

Bringing Me Down (4)
Bro. Bill (1)
Daddy Ain't Gone (5)
Evil (3)
Feel So Bad (2)
Feel So Good (1)
Guiltless Glider (3)
Hold On To My Love (5)

Hometown Bust (2)
Hook Line And Sinker (5)
I Can't Wait (5)
It's Getting Better (5)
It's Just A Feelin' (5)
Lady (Spend My Life With You) (5)
Let Me Swim (1)

Long Tall Sally (2)
Man Is A Boy (5)
Mean Night In Cleveland (3)
My Lady From South Of Detroit (1)
No Need To Worry (1)
Oleo (5)
One Way...Or Another (2)

Our Lil Rock-N-Roll Thing (4)
Parchman Farm (1)
Ragtime Suzy (5)
Rock N' Roll Children (2)
Rockout, Whatever You Feel Like (2)
Senseless Rebel (5)

Song For Aries (2)
Sweet Sixteen (3)
Swim (4)
Telling You (4)
Token Chokin' (3)
Underneath The Arches (4)
You Can't Judge A Book By The Cover (1)

CACTUS WORLD NEWS
Irish quartet — E. McEvey, lead singer.

DEBUT DATE	PEAK POS	WKS CHR		ARTIST — Album Title	$	Label & Number
8/9/86	179	5		Urban Beaches	$8	MCA 5747

Bridge, The
Church Of The Cold

In A Whirlpool
Jigsaw Street

Maybe This Time
Pilots Of Beka

Promise, The
State Of Emergency

Worlds Apart
Years Later

CAFFERTY, John, And The Beaver Brown Band
Rock sextet from Narragansett, Rhode Island. Band, led by singer/guitarist Cafferty, includes Bob Cotoia, Gary Gramolini, Kenny Jo Silva, Pat Lupo and Michael Antunes.

DEBUT DATE	PEAK POS	WKS CHR	GOLD	ARTIST — Album Title	$	Label & Number
10/15/83+	9	62	▲²	1 Eddie And The Cruisers ....[S]	$8	Scotti Br. 38929
6/8/85	40	32		2 Tough All Over	$8	Scotti Br. 39405
8/26/89	121	6		3 Eddie And The Cruisers II ....[S]	$8	Scotti Br. 45297

Betty Lou's Got A New Pair Of Shoes (1)
Boardwalk Angel (1)
C-I-T-Y (2) *18*
Dixieland (2)
Down On My Knees (1)

Emotional Storm (3)
Garden Of Eden (3)
Hang Up My Rock And Roll Shoes (1)
Just A Matter Of Time (3) (Keep My Love) Alive (3)
Maryla (3)

More Than Just One Of The Boys (2)
NYC Song (3)
On The Dark Side (1) *7*
Open Road (3)
Pride & Passion (3) *66*
Runaround Sue (1)

Runnin' Thru The Fire (3)
Season In Hell (Fire Suite) (1)
Small Town Girl (2) *64*
Some Like It Hot (3)
Strangers In Paradise (2)
Tender Years (1) *31*
Tex-Mex (Crystal Blue) (2)

Those Oldies But Goodies (Remind Me Of You) (1)
Tough All Over (2) *22*
Voice Of America's Sons (2) *62*
Where The Action Is (2)
Wild Summer Nights (1)

DEBUT DATE	PEAK POS	WKS CHR	GOLD	ARTIST — Album Title	$	Label & Number

CAIN, Tane
Former wife of Jonathan Cain (of The Babys, Journey and Bad English). Daughter of actor Doug McClure. First name pronounced: tawnee. Born and raised in Hawaii.

| 9/11/82 | 121 | 10 | | Tane Cain .... | $8 | RCA 4381 |

Almost Any Night   Danger Zone   Hurtin' Kind   Suspicious Eyes   Vertigo
Crazy Eyes   **Holdin' On 37**   My Time To Fly   Temptation

CALDERA
Group consisting of Jorge Stranz, Eduardo del Barrio (vocals), Steve Tavaglione, Michael Azevedo, Carlos Vega and Dean Cortez.

| 10/1/77 | 159 | 4 | | Sky Islands .... [I] | $10 | Capitol 11658 |

Ancient Source   Indigo Fire   Pegasus   Seraphim (Angels)   Triste
Carnavalito   It Used To Be   Pescador (Fisherman)   Sky Islands

CALDWELL, Bobby
Born on 8/15/51 in New York City. Raised in Florida. Multi-instrumentalist/songwriter. Percussionist with Johnny Winter, Rick Derringer, Captain Beyond and Armageddon. Wrote tracks for *New Mickey Mouse Club* TV show, commercials, and Peter Cetera and Amy Grant's "The Next Time I Fall."

11/18/78+	21	31	1	Bobby Caldwell	$8	Clouds 8804
3/29/80	113	15	2	Cat In The Hat	$8	Clouds 8810
4/17/82	133	13	3	Carry On	$8	Polydor 6347

All Of My Love (3) 77   **Coming Down From Love**   It's Over (2)   Mother Of Creation (2)   Take Me Back To Then (1)   Wrong Or Right (2)
Can't Say Goodbye (1)   (2) 42   Jamaica (3)   My Flame (1)   To Know What You've Got (2)   You Belong To Me (3)
Carry On (3)   Down For The Third Time (1)   Kalimba Song (1)   Open Your Eyes (2)   **What You Won't Do For**   You Promised Me (2)
Catwalk (3)   I Don't Want To Lose Your   Love Won't Wait (1)   Special To Me (1)   **Love** (1) 9   Words (3)
Come To Me (1)   Love (2)   Loving You (3)   Sunny Hills (3)

CALE, J.J.
Born Jean Jacques Cale on 12/5/38 in Oklahoma City. Rock singer/songwriter/guitarist. Wrote Eric Clapton's "After Midnight" and "Cocaine." In high school bands with Leon Russell. Worked with Phil Spector and Delaney & Bonnie. Session work with Art Garfunkel, Bob Seger and Neil Young.

1/22/72	51	32	1	Naturally	$15	Shelter 8098
12/30/72+	92	11	2	Really	$15	Shelter 8912
6/15/74	128	11	3	Okie	$12	Shelter 2107
9/25/76	84	18	4	Troubadour	$12	Shelter 52002
9/8/79	136	9	5	5	$12	Shelter 3163
2/28/81	110	7	6	Shades	$8	MCA 5158
4/3/82	149	8	7	Grasshopper	$8	Mercury 4038
3/17/90	131	10	8	Travel-Log	$12	Silvertone 1306

After Midnight (1) 42   Deep Dark Dungeon (6)   Hold On (4)   Let's Go To Tahiti (5)   Playing In The Street (2)   Travelin' Light (4)
Anyway The Wind Blows (3)   Devil In Disguise (7)   Hold On Baby (8)   **Lies** (2) 42   Precious Memories (3)   What Do You Expect (6)
Boilin' Pot (5)   Disadvantage (8)   Humdinger (3)   Lou-Easy-Ann (5)   Ride Me High (4)   Who's Talking (8)
Bringing It Back (1)   Dr. Jive (7)   I Got The Same Old Blues (3)   Louisiana Women (2)   Ridin' Home (2)   Wish I Had Not Said That (6)
Cajun Moon (3)   Does Your Mama Like To   I'd Like To Love You Baby (3)   Love Has Been Gone (6)   Right Down Here (2)   Woman I Love (1)
Call Me The Breeze (1)   Reggae (7)   I'll Be There (If You Ever   Magnolia (1)   River Boat Song (8)   Woman That Got Away (4)
Call The Doctor (1)   Don't Cry Sister (5)   Want Me) (3)   Mama Don't (6)   River Runs Deep (1)   You Got Me On So Bad (4)
Can't Live Here (7)   Don't Go To Strangers (1)   I'll Kiss The World Goodbye (1)   Mississippi River (7)   Rock And Roll Records (3)   You Got Something (4)
Carry On (6)   Don't Wait (7)   I'll Make Love To You   Mo Jo (2)   Runaround (6)   You Keep Me Hangin' On (7)
Change Your Mind (8)   Downtown L.A. (7)   Anytime (5)   Mona (5)   Sensitive Kind (5)
Changes (2)   Drifters Wife (7)   I'm A Gypsy Man (4)   New Orleans (8)   Shanghai'd (8)
Cherry (4)   End Of The Line (8)   If You Leave Her (6)   No Time (8)   Soulin' (2)
City Girls (7)   Everlovin' Woman (3)   If You're Ever In Oklahoma   Nobody But You (7)   Starbound (3)
Cloudy Day (6)   Everything Will Be Alright (2)   (2)   Nowhere To Run (1)   Super Blue (4)
Clyde (1)   Fate Of A Fool (5)   Katy Kool Lady (5)   Okie (3)   That Kind Of Thing (8)
Cocaine (4)   Friday (5)   Lady Luck (8)   Old Man And Me (3)   Thing Going On (7)
Crazy Mama (1) 22   Going Down (2)   Lean On Me (8)   One Step Ahead Of The   Thirteen Days (5)
Crying (3)   Grasshopper (7)   Let Me Do It To You (4)   Blues (7)   Tijuana (8)
Crying Eyes (1)   **Hey Baby** (4) 96   Pack My Jack (6)   Too Much For Me (5)

CALE, John
Co-founded the Velvet Underground with Lou Reed in 1964. Born on 12/4/40 in Garnant, South Wales. Production work for Iggy Pop, Patti Smith, Jennifer Warnes, Nico, Squeeze and Jonathan Richman.

| 4/11/81 | 154 | 5 | 1 | Honi Soit (o nee swa) .... | $8 | A&M 4849 |
| 5/12/90 | 103 | 8 | 2 | Songs For Drella .... | $12 | Sire 26140 |

LOU REED/JOHN CALE
fictitious account of the life of the late artist Andy Warhol

Dead Or Alive (1)   Hello It's Me (2)   It Wasn't Me (2)   Russian Roulette (1)   Strange Times In   Wilson Joliet (1)
Dream, A (2)   Honi Soit (La Premiere   Magic & Lies (1)   Slip Away (A Warning) (2)   Casablanca (1)   Work (2)
Faces And Names (2)   Lecon De Francais) (1)   Nobody But You (2)   Smalltown (2)   Streets Of Laredo (1)
Fighter Pilot (1)   I Believe (2)   Open House (2)   Starlight (2)   Style It Takes (1)
Forever Changed (2)   Images (2)   Riverbank (2)   Trouble With Classicists (2)

CALIFORNIA RAISINS, The
Studio group produced by Ross Vanelli (producer of Earth, Wind & Fire and Howard Hewett; brother of Gino Vannelli). Features R&B vocalist/drummer Buddy Miles and vocalist Alfie Silas. Based on the Claymation characters of a California Raisin Growers' television advertisement.

| 12/5/87+ | 60 | 36 | ▲ 1 | The California Raisins Sing The Hit Songs .... | $8 | Priority 9706 |
| 10/8/88 | 140 | 15 | 2 | Sweet, Delicious, & Marvelous .... | $8 | Priority 9755 |

above 2 feature cover versions of classic Pop/R&B tunes

Dancing In The Street (2)   Lean On Me (1)   (Sittin' On) The Dock Of The   Sweet, Delicious &   When A Man Loves A
Heartbreak Hotel (1)   Mony, Mony (1)   Bay (2)   Marvelous (California   Woman (1)
I Got You (I Feel Good) (2)   My Girl (2)   Stand By Me (1)   Raisins Theme Song) (2)   You Can't Hurry Love (1)
I Heard It Through The   Never Can Say Goodbye (2)   Stop! In The Name Of Love   Tracks Of My Tears (2)   You Don't Have To Wait (2)
Grapevine (1,2) 84   Respect (1)   (2)   What Does It Take (To Win
La Bamba (1)   Your Love) (2)

DEBUT DATE	PEAK POS	WKS CHR	GOLD	ARTIST — Album Title	$	Label & Number

CALL, The
California-based rock quartet — Michael Been (vocals), Tom Ferrier, Greg Freeman and Scott Musick. Keyboardist Jim Goodwin replaced bassist Freeman in 1984.

3/26/83	84	15		1 Modern Romans	$8	Mercury 810307
3/8/86	82	30		2 Reconciled	$8	Elektra 60440
7/4/87	123	13		3 Into The Woods...	$8	Elektra 60739
7/1/89	64	22		4 Let The Day Begin	$8	MCA 6303

All About You (1) | Expecting (3) | Jealousy (4) | Surrender (4) | **Walls Came Down** (1) **74**
Back From The Front (1) | Face To Face (1) | **Let The Day Begin** (4) **51** | Time Of Your Life (1) | Watch (4)
Blood Red (America) (2) | For Love (4) | Memory (3) | Too Many Tears (3) | When (4)
Closer (4) | I Don't Wanna (3) | Modern Romans (1) | Tore The Old Place Down (2) | With Or Without Reason (2)
Day Or Night (3) | I Still Believe (Great Design) | Morning, The (2) | Turn A Blind Eye (4) | Woods, The (3)
Destination (1) | (2) | Oklahoma (2) | Uncovered (4) | You Run (4)
Even Now (2) | In The River (3) | Same Ol' Story (4) | Violent Times (1) |
Everywhere I Go (2) | It Could Have Been Me (3) | Sanctuary (2) | Walk Walk (3) |

CALLAS, Maria
Renown operatic soprano. Born on 12/4/23 in New York. Died in Paris in 1977. Accepted by the Athens Conservatoire at age 13. Enjoyed a long international career after her professional debut at age 16.

2/27/65	87	8		Bizet: Carmen	$15	Angel 3650 [3]

includes the complete opera

CALLOWAY
R&B duo of brothers Reggie and Cino-Vincent Calloway from Cincinnati. Both founded Midnight Star.

3/31/90	80	14		All The Way	$12	Solar 75310

All The Way 63 | Holiday | I Want You | Sir Lancelot | You Are My Everything
Freaks Compete | **I Wanna Be Rich 2** | Love Circles | Sugar Free | You Can Count On Me

CAMARATA — see SOUNDTRACK: Parent Trap!

CAMBRIDGE, Godfrey
Comedian; died on 11/29/76 (age 43). Starred in the 1970 film *Watermelon Man*.

7/11/64	42	13		1 Ready Or Not...Here's Godfrey Cambridge .... [C]	$15	Epic 13101
4/3/65	142	9		2 Them Cotton Pickin' Days Is Over .... [C]	$15	Epic 13102

Airplanes - Next Time Take | I'm A Bad Luck Drunk (2) | Is That The Way He Really | Method Acting (1) | Movies (1)
The Train (2) | Irresistible Me (Women | Looks? (2) | Middle Income Frustrations | New Hobbies - Sky Diving (2)
Arthur Uncle (1) | Around The World) (1) | Las Vegas And Other | (1) | Rent-A-Negro Plan (1)
Block Busting (1) | Is Black Muslim Really A | Goodies (2) | Misinterpretation - Cary | Theater In The Sky (2)
Gadfly Overseas (2) | Textile? (2) | Manual Of Arms And Other | Grant Is The White |
I Love Barry (1) | | Put-Ons (2) | Godfrey Cambridge (1) |

CAMEL
British rock band led by keyboardist Peter Bardens (Them). Includes Doug Ferguson (bass), Andy Ward (drums) and Andy Latimer (guitar).

11/30/74	149	13		1 Mirage..	$10	Janus 7009
7/19/75	162	5		2 The Snow Goose....................................[I]	$10	Janus 7016
5/22/76	118	13		3 Moonmadness...	$10	Janus 7024
11/12/77	136	5		4 Rain Dances..	$10	Janus 7035
2/10/79	134	10		5 Breathless...	$8	Arista 4206

Air Born (3) | Elke (4) | Great Marsh (2) | One Of These Days I'll Get | Sanctuary (medley) (2) | Supertwister (1)
Another Night (3) | Encounter (medley) (1) | Highways Of The Sun (4) | An Early Night (4) | Skylines (4) | Tell Me (4)
Aristillus (3) | Epitaph (medley) (2) | La Princesse Perdue (2) | Preparation (2) | Sleeper, The (5) | Unevensong (4)
Breathless (5) | First Light (4) | Lady Fantasy (medley) (1) | Procession (medley) (1) | Smiles For You (medley) (1) | White Rider (medley) (1)
Chord Changes (3) | Flight Of The Snow Goose (2) | Lunar Sea (3) | Rain Dances (4) | Snow Goose (2) | Wing And A Prayer (5)
Down On The Farm (3) | Freefall (1) | Metrognome (4) | Rainbow's End (5) | Song Within A Song (3) | You Make Me Smile (5)
Dunkirk (2) | Friendship (medley) (2) | Migration (medley) (2) | Rhavader (2) | Spirit Of The Water (3) |
Earthrise (1) | Fritha (medley) (2) | Nimrodel (medley) (1) | Rhavader Alone (medley) (2) | Starlight Ride (3) |
Echoes (5) | Fritha Alone (medley) (2) | | Rhavader Goes To Town (2) | Summer Lightning (5) |

★★189★★ CAMEO
New York City soul-funk group, formed in 1974 as The New York City Players by Larry "Mr. B" Blackmon (drums) and Gregory "Straps" Johnson (keyboards). Vocals by Wayne Cooper and Tomi "Tee" Jenkins. By 1985, group pared down to a trio of Blackmon, Jenkins and Nathan Leftenant.

8/20/77	116	15		1 Cardiac Arrest...	$10	Choc. City 2003
2/18/78	58	23		2 We All Know Who We Are..............................	$10	Choc. City 2004
11/4/78	83	15		3 Ugly Ego	$10	Choc. City 2006
7/28/79	46	21	●	4 Secret Omen	$10	Choc. City 2008
5/24/80	25	26	●	5 Cameosis	$8	Choc. City 2011
12/6/80+	44	17	●	6 Feel Me	$8	Choc. City 2016
6/20/81	44	13	●	7 Knights Of The Sound Table	$8	Choc. City 2019
4/10/82	23	24	●	8 Alligator Woman	$8	Choc. City 2021
5/7/83	53	12		9 Style	$8	Atl. Art. 811072
3/17/84	27	24	●	10 She's Strange	$8	Atl. Art. 814984
7/13/85	58	27	●	11 Single Life	$8	Atl. Art. 824546
9/27/86	8	54	▲	12 **Word Up!**	$8	Atl. Art. 830265
11/12/88	56	19		13 Machismo	$8	Atl. Art. 836002
7/14/90	84	8		14 Real Men...Wear Black	$12	Atl. Art. 846297

Alligator Woman (8) | Be Yourself (8) | DKWIG (13) | Flirt (8) | Good Times (1) | I Like The World (13)
Am I Bad Enough (14) | Better Days (6) | Don't Be Lonely (12) | For You (8) | Groove With You (10) | I Never Knew (7)
Anything You Wanna Do (3) | C On The Funk (2) | Don't Be So Cool (7) | Freaky Dancin' (7) | Hangin' Downtown (10) | I Owe It All To You (8)
Aphrodisiac (9) | Cameo's Dance (3) | Energy (4) | Friend To Me (3) | Heaven Only Knows (9) | I Want It Now (14)
Attack Me With Your Love | Cameosis (5) | Enjoy Your Life (8) | Funk Funk (1) | Honey (13) | I Want You (3)
(11) | Can't Help Falling In Love (9) | Fast, Fierce & Funny (12) | Get Paid (14) | I Care For You (5) | I'll Always Stay (7)
Attitude (14) | **Candy** (12) **21** | Feel Me (6) | Give Love A Chance (3) | I Just Want To Be (4) | I'll Be With You (3)
Back And Forth (12) **50** | Close Quarters (14) | Find My Way (1,4) | Good-Bye, A (11) | I Like It (7) | I'll Never Look For Love (11)

DEBUT DATE	PEAK POS	WKS CHR	GOLD	ARTIST — Album Title	$	Label & Number

CAMEO — Cont'd

I've Got Your Image (11) · In The Night (13) · Inflation (2) · Insane (3) · Is This The Way (6) · It's Over (2) · It's Serious (2) · Just A Broken Heart (14) · Keep It Hot (6) · Knights By Nights (7) · Let's Not Talk Slot (9) · Leve Toll (10) · Little Boys - Dangerous Toys (11) · Love You Anyway (10) · Macho (4) · Me (14) · Nan-Yea (14) · New York (4) · On The One (5) · Please You (5) · Post Mortem (1) · Pretty Girls (13) · Promiscuous (13) · Rigor Mortis (1) · Rock, The (4) · Roller Skates (6) · Secrets Of Time (8) · Shake Your Pants (5) · She's Mine (12) · **She's Strange** (10) 47 · Single Life (11) · Skin I'm In (13) · Slow Movin' (9) · Smile (1) · Soul Army (8) · Soul Tightened (1) · Sound Table (7) · Sparkle (4) · Stand Up (2) · Stay By My Side (1) · Still Feels Good (1) · Style (9) · Talkin' Out The Side Of Your Neck (10) · This Life Is Not For Me (9) · Throw It Down (6) · Time, Fire & Space (14) · Tribute To Bob Marley (10) · Two Of Us (3) · Ugly Ego (3) · Urban Warrior (11) · Use It Or Lose It (7) · We All Know Who We Are (2) · We're Goin' Out Tonight (5) · Why Have I Lost You (2,5) · **Word Up** (12) 6 · You Can Have The World (12) · **You Make Me Work** (13) 85 · You're A Winner (9) · Your Love Takes Me Out (6)

CAMERON, Rafael
Native of Guyana.

DEBUT DATE	PEAK POS	WKS CHR	GOLD	ARTIST — Album Title	$	Label & Number
8/2/80	67	18		1 Cameron	$8	Salsoul 8535
7/18/81	101	12		2 Cameron's In Love	$8	Salsoul 8542

All That's Good To Me (2) · Boogie's Gonna Get Ya' (2) · Can't Live Without Ya' (1) · Daisy (2) · Feelin' (1) · Funkdown (2) · Funtown U.S.A. (2) · Get It Off (1) · I'd Go Crazy (2) · In Love (2) · Let's Get Married (2) · Magic Of You (1) · Number One (1) · Together (1)

CAMOUFLAGE
German dance trio founded in 1981: Marcus Meyn, Heiko Maile and Oliver Kreyssig (left band in 1990).

DEBUT DATE	PEAK POS	WKS CHR	GOLD	ARTIST — Album Title	$	Label & Number
1/14/89	100	14		Voices & Images	$8	Atlantic 81886

From Ay To Bee · **Great Commandment** 59 · Helpless Helpless · I Once Had A Dream · Music For Ballerinas · Neighbours · Strangers Thoughts · That Smiling Face · Where Has The Childhood Gone · Winner Takes Nothing

★★58★★ CAMPBELL, Glen
Born on 4/22/36 in Billstown, Arkansas. Vocalist/guitarist/composer. With his uncle Dick Bills' band, 1954-58. To Los Angeles; recorded with The Champs in 1960. Became prolific studio musician; with The Beach Boys in 1965 and Sagittarius in 1967. Own TV show *The Glen Campbell Goodtime Hour*, 1968-72. In films *True Grit*, *Norwood* and *Strange Homecoming*; voice in animated film *Rock-A-Doodle*. Also see the Folkswingers.

DEBUT DATE	PEAK POS	WKS CHR	GOLD	ARTIST — Album Title	$	Label & Number
12/2/67+	5	75	▲	1 Gentle On My Mind	$15	Capitol 2809
12/30/67+	15	80	▲	2 By The Time I Get To Phoenix	$15	Capitol 2851
				1968 Grammy winner: Album of the Year		
4/6/68	26	51	●	3 Hey, Little One	$15	Capitol 2878
6/22/68	24	33		4 A New Place In The Sun	$15	Capitol 2907
10/12/68	11	47	●	5 Bobbie Gentry & Glen Campbell	$15	Capitol 2928
				BOBBIE GENTRY & GLEN CAMPBELL		
11/16/68	1⁵	46	▲²	6 Wichita Lineman	$15	Capitol 103
4/12/69	2¹	42	▲	7 Galveston	$15	Capitol 210
9/20/69	13	29	●	8 Glen Campbell - "Live" [L]	$15	Capitol 0268 [2]
2/7/70	12	28	●	9 Try A Little Kindness	$12	Capitol 389
5/23/70	38	19		10 Oh Happy Day	$12	Capitol 443
				inspirational songs		
6/27/70	90	13		11 Norwood [S]	$12	Capitol 475
				includes 6 instrumentals by Al DeLory: "Country Girl," "Brass Ensemble Of Ralph, Texas," "Hot Wheels," "Fring Thing," "Chicken Out (Joann's Theme)" and "Different Kind Of Rock"		
10/3/70	27	21		12 The Glen Campbell Goodtime Album	$12	Capitol 493
4/17/71	39	27	▲	13 Glen Campbell's Greatest Hits [G]	$12	Capitol 752
8/7/71	87	9		14 The Last Time I Saw Her	$12	Capitol 733
12/11/71+	128	8		15 Anne Murray/Glen Campbell	$12	Capitol 869
				ANNE MURRAY/GLEN CAMPBELL		
11/25/72+	148	13		16 Glen Travis Campbell	$10	Capitol 11117
6/9/73	154	6		17 I Knew Jesus (Before He Was a Star)	$10	Capitol 11185
11/16/74	166	5		18 Reunion (the songs of Jimmy Webb)	$10	Capitol 11336
8/9/75	17	30	●	19 Rhinestone Cowboy	$10	Capitol 11430
5/1/76	63	9		20 Bloodline	$10	Capitol 11516
11/27/76	116	6		21 The Best Of Glen Campbell [G]	$10	Capitol 11577
3/19/77	22	22	●	22 Southern Nights	$10	Capitol 11601
1/7/78	171			23 Live At The Royal Festival Hall [L]	$12	Capitol 11707 [2]
				with the Royal Philharmonic Orchestra		
12/16/78	164	5		24 Basic	$10	Capitol 11722
2/28/81	178	3		25 It's The World Gone Crazy	$8	Capitol 12124

About The Ocean (18) · Adoration (18) · All My Tomorrows (16) · All The Way (9) · Amazing Grace (17,23) · And The World Keeps Spinning (9) · Angels In The Sky (10) · Ann (6) · Any Which Way You Can (25) · As Far As I'm Concerned (12) · Baby Don't Be Givin' Me Up (20) · Back In The Race (2) · Bad Seed (2) · Bloodline (20) · Both Sides, Now (9) · Bottom Line (20) · Bowling Green (1) · Break My Mind (3) · Bridge Over Troubled Water (12) · Bring Back The Love (15) · Burning Bridges (13) · **By The Time I Get To Phoenix** (2,8,13,21,23) 26 (also see: I Say A Little Prayer) · California (24) · **Can You Fool** (24) 38 · Canadian Sunset (15) · Canticle ..see: Scarborough Fair · Catch The Wind (1) · Christiaan No (20) · Classical Gas (23) · Cold December (In Your Heart) (2) · Comeback (19) · Count On Me (19) · **Country Boy (You Got Your Feet In L.A.)** (19,21) 11 · Country Girl (9) · Cryin' (1) · Daddy Sang Bass (10) · Daisy A Day (25) · Didn't We (8) · **Don't Pull Your Love/Then You Can Tell Me Goodbye** (20) 27 · Down Home (11) · **Dream Baby (How Long Must I Dream)** (4) · Dream Sweet Dreams About Me (12) · **Dreams Of The Everyday Housewife** (6,8,13,23) 32 · Early Morning Song (22) · Ease Your Pain (15) · Elusive Butterfly (3) · Every Time I Itch I Wind Up Scratchin' You (7) · **Everything A Man Could Ever Need** (11) 52 · Everytime I Sing A Love Song (20) · Fate Of Man (6) · Folk Singer (7) · For Cryin' Out Loud (22) · For My Woman's Love (9) · For Once In My Life (8) · Freeborn Man (4) · Funny Kind Of Monday (12) · **Galveston** (7,13,21,23) 4 · **Gentle On My Mind** (1,5,8,13,21) 39 · Give Me Back That Old Familiar Feeling (17) · God Only Knows (22,23) · Good Ole Mountain Dew (8) · Good Vibrations (medley) (23) · Gotta Have Tenderness (7) · Gotta Travel On (8) · Grafhaldh Me Thu (24) · Guide Me (22) · Have I Stayed Away Too Long? (4) · He (10) · He Ain't Heavy, He's My Brother (14) · He's Got The Whole World In His Hands (10) · Heart To Heart Talk (5) · Help Me Make It Through The Night (14) · Help Me, Rhonda (medley) (23) · Here We Go Again (14) · **Hey Little One** (2,3) 54 · Home Again (9) · Homeward Bound (2) · **Honey Come Back** (9,13) 19 · **Houston (I'm Comin' To See You)** (21) 68 · How High Did We Go (22) · I Believe (10) · I Don't Believe You (She Acts Like We Never Have Met) (3) · **I Don't Want To Know Your Name** (25) 65 · I Got Love For You Ruby (20) · I Have No One To Love Me Anymore (4) · I Keep It Hid (18) · **I Knew Jesus (Before He Was A Star)** (17,21) 45

CAMPBELL, Glen — Cont'd

I Miss You Tonight (19)
I Say A Little Prayer/By The Time I Get To Phoenix (15) *81*
(also see: By The Time I Get To Phoenix)
I See Love (24)
I Take It On Home (17)
I Wanna Live (3,13) *36*
I Want To Be With You Always (17)
I Will Never Pass This Way Again (16) *61*
I'd Build A Bridge (19)
I'll Be Lucky Someday (2)
I'll Paint You A Song (11)
(I'm Getting) Used To The Crying (22)
I'm Gonna Love You (24)
If Not For You (17)
If This Is Love (7)
If You Could Read My Mind (14)
If You Go Away (6,8,23)
Impossible Dream (The Quest) (3,8)
In Cars (25)
It's A Sin (18)
It's Only Make Believe (12,21) *10*
(It's Only Your) Imagination (5)
It's Over (1,3,8)

It's The World's Gone Crazy (Cotillion) (25)
It's Your World (25)
Just Another Man (1)
Just Another Piece Of Paper (12)
Just For What I Am (16)
Just This One Time (18)
Last Letter (4)
Last Thing On My Mind (16)
Last Time I Saw Her (14,21) *61*
Lay Me Down (Roll Me Out To Sea) (20)
Legend Of Bonnie And Clyde (4)
Less Of Me (5)
Let It Be Me (5) *36*
Let Me Be The One (15)
(Let Me Be Your) Teddy Bear (medley) (23)
Let's All Sing A Song About It (24)
Little Green Apples (5)
Lord's Prayer (8)
Love Is A Lonesome River (2)
Love Is Not A Game (9)
Love Me As Though There Were No Tomorrow (1)
Love Story (You & Me) (15)
Love Takes You Higher (24)
Loving You (medley) (23)

Mac Arthur Park (12,23)
Marie (11,19)
Mary In The Morning (1)
Moon's A Harsh Mistress (18,21)
More (medley) (8)
Mornin' Glory (5) *74*
My Baby's Gone (2)
My Cricket (16)
My Ecstasy (15)
My Elusive Dreams (5)
My Girl (19)
My Way (17)
Never Tell You No Lies (24)
Norwood (Me And My Guitar) (11)
Nothing Quite Like Love (25)
Ocean In His Eyes (18)
Oh Happy Day (10) *40*
Oh What A Woman (7)
Ol' Norwood's Comin' Home (11)
On This Road (17)
Once More With Feeling (9)
One Last Time (16) *78*
One Pair Of Hands (10)
Pave Your Way Into Tomorrow (12)
Pencils For Sale (19)
People Get Ready (10)
Place In The Sun (4)
Reason To Believe (6)
Repo Man (11)

Rhinestone Cowboy (19,21,23) *1*
Roll Me Easy (18)
Rollin' (25)
Rose Garden (14)
Running Scared (16)
San Francisco Is A Lonely Town (20)
Scarborough Fair (5)
See You On Sunday (20)
She Called Me Baby (4)
She Thinks I Still Care (16)
She Understands Me (14)
Shoulder To Shoulder (25)
(Sittin' On) The Dock Of The Bay (6,8)
Sold American (17)
Soliloquy (23)
Someday Soon (17)
Someone Above (10)
Someone To Give My Love To (16)
Somewhere (medley) (8)
Southern Nights (22,23) *1*
Stars (medley) (23)
Straight Life (6)
Stranger In The Mirror (24)
Streets Of London (23)
Sunday Mornin' (5)
Sunflower (22,23) *39*
Sunny Day Girl (4)
Surfer Girl (medley) (23)
Surfin' U.S.A. (medley) (23)

Sweet Fantasy (16)
Take Me Back (3)
Take My Hand For A While (7)
Terrible Tangled Web (5)
That's All That Matters (3)
That's Not Home (6)
That's When The Music Takes Me (23)
This Is Sarah's Song (22,23)
Time (7)
Today (7)
Today Is Mine (14)
Tomorrow Never Comes (2)
Try A Little Kindness (9,13,21,23) *23*
Turn Around And Look At Me (3)
Turn It Around In Your Mind (12)
Twelfth Of Never (4)
United We Stand (1)
Until It's Time For You To Go (7)
Visions Of Sugarplums (4)
Walk Right In (8)
We All Pull The Load (15)
We're Over (19)
(When I Feel Like) I Got No Love In Me (24)
Where Do I Begin (14)
Where Do You Go (9)

Where's The Playground Susie (7,8,13) *26*
White Lightning (8)
Why Don't We Just Sleep On It Tonight (25)
Wichita Lineman (6,13,21,23) *3*
William Tell Overture (23)
Wishing Now (18)
Within My Memory (4)
Without Her (1)
Woman, Woman (3)
Words (6)
World I Used To Know (1)
Yakety Sax (8)
You All Come (Y'All Come) (8)
You Better Sit Down Kids (6)
You Might As Well Smile (18)
You'll Never Walk Alone (10)
You're Easy To Love (15)
You're My World (1)
You're The One (17)
You're Young And You'll Forget (2)
(You've Got To) Sing It Nice And Loud For Me Sonny (24)

CAMPBELL, Tevin

Texas native born in 1978. Won role in 1988 for the TV show *Wally & The Valentines*. Discovered by Quincy Jones. Appeared in the film *Graffiti Bridge*.

12/7/91+	38	44 ●		T.E.V.I.N.	$12	Qwest 26291

Alone With You *72*
Confused
Goodbye *85*

Just Ask Me To *88*
Lil' Brother

Look What We'd Have (If You Were Mine)
One Song

Perfect World
Round And Round *12*
She's All That

Strawberry Letter 23 *53*
Tell Me What You Want Me To Do *6*

CAMPER VAN BEETHOVEN

Rock quintet from Santa Cruz, California: Victor Krummenacher, David Lowery (vocals), Greg Lisher, Chris Pedersen and Jonathan Segel (left in 1989). Female violinist Morgan Fichter, from Ohio, joined in 1989. Lowery later formed Cracker.

6/18/88	124	17	1	Our Beloved Revolutionary Sweetheart	$8	Virgin 90918
10/7/89	141	13	2	Key Lime Pie	$8	Virgin 91289

All Her Favorite Fruit (2)
Borderline (2)
Change Your Mind (1)
Come On Darkness (2)
Devil Song (1)

Eye Of Fatima (Pt. 1 & 2) (1)
Flowers (2)
Fool, The (1)
Humid Press Of Days (2)

(I Was Born In A) Laundromat (2)
Jack Ruby (2)
June (2)
Life Is Grand (1)

Light From A Cake (2)
My Path Belated (1)
Never Go Back (1)
O Death (1)
One Of These Days (1)

Pictures Of Matchstick Men (2)
She Divines Water (1)
Sweethearts (2)
Tania (1)

Turquoise Jewelry (1)
Waka (1)
When I Win The Lottery (2)

C & C MUSIC FACTORY

Dance outfit led by producers/songwriters David Cole (keyboards, Tennessee native) and Robert Clivilles (percussion, New York native). Featured vocalists include Freedom Williams and Deborah Cooper (Fatback, Change). Martha Wash (Two Tons O' Fun, The Weather Girls) is the actual vocalist of "Gonna Make You Sweat," lip-synched in video by Liberian-born Zelma Davis.

1/12/91	2[7]	85 ▲³	1	Gonna Make You Sweat	$12	Columbia 47093
2/29/92	87	9	2	Greatest Remixes Vol. I .... [K]	$12	Columbia 48840

CLIVILLES + COLE
13 updated versions of their previously released remixes of own recordings and hits by Seduction, Lisa Lisa & Cult Jam and others

Bang That Beat (1)
Because Of You (2)
Clouds (2)
Deeper Love (2) *44*
Do It Properly (2)

Don't Take Your Love Away (2)
Givin' It To You (1)
Gonna Make You Sweat (Everybody Dance Now) (1,2) *1*

Groove Of Love (What's This Word Called Love?) (1)
Here We Go (1,2) *3*
Just A Touch Of Love (1) *50*
Let The Beat Hit 'Em (2)

Let's Get Funkee (1)
Live Happy (1)
Mind Your Business (2)
Notice Me (1)
Oooh Baby (1)

Pride (In The Name Of Love) (2) *54*
Things That Make You Go Hmmmm... (1,2) *4*
True Love (2)
Two To Make It Right (2)

You Take My Breath Away (2)

CANDLEMASS

Heavy-metal Swedish rock group led by bassist Leif Edlin with Messiah Marcolin (vocals), Lars Johansson, Mats Bjorkman and Jan Lindh.

1/21/89	174	6		Ancient Dreams	$8	Metal Blade 73340

Ancient Dreams
Bearer Of Pain

Bell Of Acheron
Cry From The Crypt

Darkness In Paradise
Epistle No. 81

Incarnation Of Evil
Mirror Mirror

CANDYMAN

Rapper from Los Angeles born on 6/25/68. Backing rapper/dancer with Tone Loc.

10/27/90+	40	36 ●		Ain't No Shame In My Game	$12	Epic 46947

Ain't No Shame In My Game(show)
Candyman

Don't Leave Home Without It
5 Verses Of Def
Keep On Watcha Doin'

Knockin' Boots *9*
Mack Is Back
Melt In Your Mouth *69*

Nightgown *91*
Playin' On Me
Today's Topic

Who Shakes The Best

CANDYMEN, The

Roy Orbison's former backup band — Rodney Justo (vocals). Pianist Dean Daughtry, drummer Bob Nix and Justo later joined the Atlanta Rhythm Section.

11/11/67	195	4		The Candymen	$20	ABC 616

DEBUT DATE	PEAK POS	WKS CHR	GOLD	ARTIST — Album Title	$	Label & Number

CANDYMEN, The — Cont'd

Deep In The Night
Even The Grass Has Died
Georgia Pines *81*

Happier Than Them
Hope
Lonely Eyes

Movies In My Mind
Roses Won't Grow In My Garden

See Saw
Stone Blues Man
Stormy Monday Blues

★★367★★ **CANNED HEAT**

Blues-rock band formed in Los Angeles in 1966. Consisted of Bob "The Bear" Hite (vocals, harmonica), Alan "Blind Owl" Wilson (guitar, harmonica, vocals), Henry Vestine (guitar), Larry Taylor (bass) and Frank Cook (drums). Cook replaced by Fito de la Parra in 1968. Vestine replaced by Harvey Mandel in 1969. Wilson died of a drug overdose on 9/3/70 (age 27). Hite died of a drug-related heart attack on 4/6/81 (age 36).

DEBUT DATE	PEAK POS	WKS CHR	GOLD	ARTIST — Album Title	$	Label & Number
8/12/67	76	23		1 Canned Heat	$20	Liberty 7526
2/24/68	16	52		2 Boogie With Canned Heat	$20	Liberty 7541
12/7/68+	18	17		3 Living The Blues .... [L]	$20	Liberty 27200 [2]
				the second LP is live		
8/9/69	37	15		4 Hallelujah	$15	Liberty 7618
12/6/69+	86	19		5 Canned Heat Cook Book (The Best Of Canned Heat) ...... [G]	$15	Liberty 11000
1/17/70	173	5		6 Vintage-Canned Heat .... [E]	$12	Janus 3009
9/12/70	59	19		7 Future Blues	$12	Liberty 11002
2/27/71	73	16		8 Hooker 'N Heat	$15	Liberty 35002 [2]

CANNED HEAT & JOHN LEE HOOKER

DEBUT DATE	PEAK POS	WKS CHR	GOLD	ARTIST — Album Title	$	Label & Number
7/17/71	133	9		9 Canned Heat Concert (Recorded Live in Europe) .... [L]	$12	United Art. 5509
10/30/71	182	2		10 Living The Blues .... [L-R]	$15	United Art. 9955 [2]
				new cover features a drawing of an open mouth		
3/4/72	87	12		11 Historical Figures And Ancient Heads	$12	United Art. 5557

Almonia Blues (8)
Amphetamine Annie (2,5)
Back Out On The Road (medley) (9)
Big Fat (4)
Big Road Blues (1,6)
Boogie Chillen No. 2 (8)
Boogie Music (3,5,10)
Bottle Up And Go (8)
Bring It On Home (9)
Bullfrog Blues (1,5)
Burning Hell (8)
Can't Hold On Much Longer (6)
Canned Heat (4)
Catfish Blues (8)
Change My Ways (4)
Cherokee Dance (11)

Dimples (6)
Do Not Enter (4)
Down In The Gutter, But Free (4)
Drifter (8)
Dust My Broom (1)
Evil Is Going On (1)
Evil Woman (2)
Feelin' Is Gone (8)
Fried Hockey Boogie (2,5)
Future Blues (7)
Get Off My Back (4)
Goin' Down Slow (1)
Going Up The Country (3,5,10) *11*
Goodbye For Now (8)
Got My Mojo Working (6)
Help Me (1)

Hill's Stomp (11)
Huautla (4)
I Don't Care What You Tell Me (11)
I Got My Eyes On You (8)
I'm Her Man (8)
Just You And Me (8)
Let's Make It (8)
Let's Work Together (7,9) *26*
London Blues (7,9)
Long Way From L.A. (11)
Louise (6)
Marie Laveau (2)
Meet Me In The Bottom (8)
Messin' With The Hook (8)
My Crime (2)
My Mistake (3,10)

My Time Ain't Long (7)
On The Road Again (2,5,9) *16*
One Kind Favor (3,10)
Owl Song (2)
Parthenogenesis Medley (3,10)
Peavine (8)
Pony Blues (3,10)
Pretty Thing (6)
Pulling Hair Blues (9)
Refried Boogie (Part I & II) (3,10)
Rich Woman (2)
Road Song (1)
Rockin' With The King (11) *88*
Rollin' And Tumblin' (1,5,6)

Same All Over (4,5)
Sandy's Blues (3,10)
Scat (7)
Send Me Your Pillow (8)
Shake It And Break It (7)
Sic 'Em Pigs (4,5)
Sittin' Here Thinkin' (8)
Sneakin' Around (11)
So Sad (The World's In A Tangle) (7)
Spoonful (6)
Story Of My Life (1)
Straight Ahead (6)
Sugar Bee (7)
That's All Right (11)
That's All Right Mama (7,9)
Time Was (4,5) *67*
Turpentine Moan (2)

Utah (11)
Walking By Myself (3,10)
Whiskey And Wimmen' (8)
Whiskey Headed Woman No. 2 (8)
World In A Jug (2)
World Today (8)
You Talk Too Much (8)

CANNIBAL and THE HEADHUNTERS

Four Mexican-American youths based in Los Angeles; led by Frankie "Cannibal" Garcia.

DEBUT DATE	PEAK POS	WKS CHR	GOLD	ARTIST — Album Title	$	Label & Number
5/8/65	141	4		Land Of 1000 Dances	$45	Rampart 3302

Boy From New York City
Devil In Disguise

Don't Let Her Go
Fat Man

Get Your Baby
Here Comes Love

Land Of 1000 Dances *30*
My Girl

Out Of Sight
Searchin'

Shotgun
Strange World

CANNON, Ace

Born on 5/5/34 in Grenada, Mississippi. Saxophonist since age 10. Worked with Bill Black's Combo.

DEBUT DATE	PEAK POS	WKS CHR	GOLD	ARTIST — Album Title	$	Label & Number
5/19/62	44	17		"Tuff"-Sax .... [I]	$15	Hi 32007

Basin Street Blues
Blues In My Heart

Blues (Stay Away From Me) *36*
Cannonball

Careless Love
I've Got A Woman

Kansas City
Lonesome Road

St. Louis Blues
Trouble In Mind

Tuff *17*
Wabash Blues

CANNON, Freddy

Born Frederick Picariello on 12/4/39 in Lynn, Massachusetts. Local work with own band, Freddy Karmon & The Hurricanes. Nickname "Boom Boom" came from big bass drum-sound on his records. Band arrangements by Frank Slay on all Swan recordings.

DEBUT DATE	PEAK POS	WKS CHR	GOLD	ARTIST — Album Title	$	Label & Number
9/1/62	101	5		Freddy Cannon At Palisades Park	$75	Swan 507

Buzz Buzz A-Diddle-It *51*
For Me And My Gal *71*
Forever True

Itsy Bitsy Teenie Weenie Yellow Polkadot Bikini
June, July, August

Meet Me In St. Louis
Merry-Go-Round Broke Down

Palisades Park *3*
Splish Splash
Summer's Comin'

Teen Queen Of The Week *92*
Transistor Sister *35*

CANO, Eddie

Latin-jazz pianist/bandleader. Played with Latin bandleader Miguilito Valdez in the late 1940s. Died of a heart attack in Los Angeles on 1/30/88 (age 60).

DEBUT DATE	PEAK POS	WKS CHR	GOLD	ARTIST — Album Title	$	Label & Number
9/1/62	31	12		Eddie Cano At P.J.'s .... [I]	$12	Reprise 6030

Cal's Pals
Cotton Candy

First One
Hello Young Lovers

Laura
Maha

Oye Corazon
P.J.'s

Panchita
Taste Of Honey

Trolley Song
Watusi Walk

CANTRELL, Lana

Showbiz star from Australia.

DEBUT DATE	PEAK POS	WKS CHR	GOLD	ARTIST — Album Title	$	Label & Number
11/16/68	166	2		Lana!	$12	RCA 4026

Baby, Now That I've Found You

Can't Take My Eyes Off Of You
Fool On The Hill

For Me (Arrastao)
Gentle On My Mind
Honey

How Can I Be Sure
Mine (Is A Quiet Love)

Music Played (Was Ich Dir Sagen Will)

Sound Of Silence
Workin' On A Groovy Thing

CAPALDI, Jim

Born on 8/24/44 in Evesham, England. Drummer with Traffic, 1967-74.

DEBUT DATE	PEAK POS	WKS CHR	GOLD	ARTIST — Album Title	$	Label & Number
3/4/72	82	11		1 Oh How We Danced	$10	Island 9314
9/7/74	191	3		2 Whale Meat Again	$10	Island 9254
2/14/76	193	4		3 Short Cut Draw Blood	$10	Island 9336
5/21/83	91	12		4 Fierce Heart	$8	Atlantic 80059
12/17/88+	183	8		5 Some Come Running	$8	Island 91024

CAPALDI, Jim — Cont'd

Anniversary Song (1)
Back At My Place (4)
Bad Breaks (4)
Big Thirst (1)
Boy With A Problem (3)
Dancing On The Highway (5)
Don't Be A Hero (1)

Don't Let Them Control You (4)
Eve (1) *91*
Gifts Of Unknown Things (4)
Goodbye Love (3)
How Much Can A Man Really Take (1)
I'll Always Be Your Fool (4)

I've Got So Much Lovin' (2)
It's All Right (2) *55*
It's All Up To You (3)
Johnny Too Bad (3)
Keep On Trying (3)
Last Day Of Dawn (1)
Living On A Marble (3)
Living On The Edge (4) *75*

Love Hurts (3) *97*
Love Is All You Can Try (1)
Love Used To Be A Friend Of Mine (5)
Low Rider (2)
My Brother (2)
Oh Lord, Why Lord (5)
Open Your Heart (1)

Runaway (4)
Seagull (3)
Short Cut Draw Blood (3)
Some Come Running (5)
Something So Strong (5)
Summer Is Fading (2)
Take Me Home (5)
That's Love (4) *28*

Tonight You're Mine (4)
Voices In The Night (5)
Whale Meat Again (2)
Yellow Sun (2)
You Are The One (5)

CAPITOLS, The
R&B vocal trio from Detroit. Consisted of lead singer Sam George (murdered on 3/17/82 [age 39]), "Donald Norman" Storball and "Richard Mitchell" McDougall.

7/23/66	95	12		Dance The Cool Jerk	$30	Atco 190

Cool Jerk *7*
Dog & Cat
Good Lovin'

Hello Stranger
I Got My Mojo Working
In The Midnight Hour

Kick, The
Love Makes The World Go Round

My Girl
Please Please Please
Tired Running From You

Zig Zaggin'

★★478★★ CAPTAIN & TENNILLE
Daryl "The Captain" Dragon (b: 8/27/42, Los Angeles) and his wife, Toni Tennille (b: 5/8/43, Montgomery, Alabama). Dragon is the son of noted conductor Carmen Dragon. Keyboardist with The Beach Boys, nicknamed the "Captain" by Mike Love. Duo had own TV show on ABC from 1976-77.

6/14/75	2[1]	104	●	1 Love Will Keep Us Together	$10	A&M 3405
3/20/76	9	61	▲	2 Song Of Joy	$10	A&M 4570
4/23/77	18	15	●	3 Come In From The Rain	$10	A&M 4700
12/10/77+	55	12	●	4 Captain & Tennille's Greatest Hits .... [G]	$10	A&M 4667
7/22/78	131	30		5 Dream	$10	A&M 4707
11/17/79+	23	24	●	6 Make Your Move	$8	Casablanca 7188

Baby You Still Got It (6)
Back To The Island (5)
Broddy Bounce (1)
Butterscotch Castle (2)
Can't Stop Dancin' (3,4) *13*
Circles (3,4)
Come In From The Rain (3,4) *61*
Cuddle Up (1)
"D" Keyboard Blues (5)
Deep In The Dark (6)
Disney Girls (1,4)
Dixie Hummingbird (5)

Do That To Me One More Time (6) *1*
Don't Be Scared (3)
Dream (5)
Easy Evil (3)
Feel Like A Man (1)
Gentle Stranger (1)
God Only Knows (1)
Going Bananas (2)
Good Enough (5)
Good Songs (1)
Happier Than The Morning Sun (3)

Happy Together (A Fantasy) (6) *53*
Honey Come Love Me (1)
How Can You Be So Cold (6)
I Write The Songs (1,4)
I'm On My Way (5) *74*
If There Were Time (5)
Ka-Ding-Dong (3)
Ladybug (3)
Let Mama Know (3)
Lonely Night (Angel Face) (2,4) *3*

Love Is Spreading Over The World (5)
Love Me Like A Baby (5)
Love On A Shoestring (6) *55*
Love Will Keep Us Together (1,4) *1*
Mind Your Love (2)
Muskrat Love (2,4) *4*
Never Make A Move Too Soon (6)
1954 Boogie Blues (2)
No Love In The Morning (6)

Sad Eyes (3)
Shop Around (2,4) *4*
Smile For Me One More Time (2)
Song Of Joy (2)
Thank You, Baby (5)
Way I Want To Touch You (1,4) *4*
We Never Really Say Goodbye (3,4)
Wedding Song (There Is Love) (2,4)

You Need A Woman Tonight (5) *40*
You Never Done It Like That (5) *10*

CAPTAIN BEEFHEART
Born Don Van Vliet on 1/15/41 in Glendale, California. Multi-octave rock singer. Collaborations with high school friend Frank Zappa. Backed by various personnel. Beefheart retired from music in 1986 to become a professional painter.

2/19/72	131	9		1 The Spotlight Kid	$15	Reprise 2050

CAPTAIN BEEFHEART & THE MAGIC BAND:

12/23/72+	191	7		2 Clear Spot	$20	Reprise 2115
4/27/74	192	4		3 Unconditionally Guaranteed	$10	Mercury 709
11/1/75	66	8		4 Bongo Fury .... [L]	$10	DiscReet 2234

FRANK ZAPPA/CAPTAIN BEEFHEART/THE MOTHERS

Advance Romance (4)
Alice In Blunderland (1)
Big Eyed Beans From Venus (2)
Blabber 'N Smoke (1)
Carolina Hard-Core Ecstasy (4)
Circumstances (2)
Clear Spot (2)
Click Clack (1)

Crazy Little Thing (2)
Cucamonga (4)
Debra Kadabra (4)
Full Moon, Hot Sun (3)
Glider (1)
Golden Birdies (1)
Grow Fins (1)
Happy Love Song (3)
Her Eyes Are A Blue Million Miles (2)

I Got Love On My Mind (3)
I'm Gonna Booglarize You Baby (1)
Lazy Music (3)
Long Neck Bottles (2)
Low Yo Yo Stuff (2)
Magic Be (3)
Man With The Woman Head (4)
Muffin Man (4)

My Head Is My Only House Unless It Rains (2)
New Electric Ride (3)
Nowadays A Woman's Gotta Hit A Man (2)
Peaches (3)
Poofter's Froth Wyoming Plans Ahead (4)
Sam With The Showing Scalp Flat Top (4)

Spotlight Kid (1)
Sugar Bowl (3)
Sun Zoom Spark (2)
There Ain't No Santa Claus On The Evenin' Stage (1)
This Is The Day (3)
Too Much Time (2)
200 Years Old (4)
Upon The My-O-My (3)
When It Blows Its Stacks (1)

White Jam (1)

CAPTAIN BEYOND
Rock group formed by vocalist Rod Evans (Deep Purple), percussionist Bobby Caldwell (Johnny Winter, Rick Derringer, Armageddon), guitarist Rhino and bassist Lee Dorman (Iron Butterfly). Various personnel after first album. Evans left after second album; replaced by Willy Daffern.

8/19/72	134	12		1 Captain Beyond	$30	Capricorn 0105
9/1/73	90	10		2 Sufficiently Breathless	$12	Capricorn 0115
6/11/77	181	2		3 Dawn Explosion	$10	Warner 3047

Armworth (2)
As The Moon Speaks (To The Waves Of The Sea) (1)
Astral Lady (1)
Breath Of Fire - Part 1 & 2 (3)

Bright Blue Tango (2)
Dancing Madly Backwards (On A Sea Of Air) (1)
Distant Sun (2)
Do Or Die (3)
Drifting In Space (2)

Everything's A Circle (2)
Evil Men (2)
Fantasy (3)
Frozen Over (1)
I Can't Feel Nothin' (Part I & II) (1)

Icarus (3)
If You Please (3)
Mesmerization Eclipse (1)
Midnight Memories (3)
Myopic Void (1)
Oblivion (medley) (3)

Raging River Of Fear (1)
Space (medley) (3)
Starglow Energy (2)
Sufficiently Breathless (2)
Sweet Dreams (3)

Thousand Days Of Yesterdays (Time Since Come And Gone) (1)
Voyages Of Past Travellers (2)

CAPTAIN SKY
Born Daryl L. Cameron on 7/10/57 in Chicago. Attended Chicago Conservatory of Music.

1/27/79	157	12		The Adventures Of Captain Sky	$8	AVI 6042

Can't Stop Now
Now That I Have You

Saturday Night Move-Ease
Super Sperm

Wonder Worm

CARA, Irene
Vocalist/actress/dancer/pianist. Born on 3/18/59 in New York City. Professional debut at age seven. Won Obie Award for *The Me Nobody Knows* in 1970. Much TV work, including *Electric Company* and *Roots 2*; in films *Fame, D.C. Cab* and *The Cotton Club*.

1/30/82	76	17		1 Anyone Can See	$8	Network 60003
12/10/83+	77	37		2 What A Feelin'	$8	Geffen 4021

DEBUT DATE	PEAK POS	WKS CHR	GOLD	ARTIST — Album Title	$	Label & Number

CARA, Irene — Cont'd

Anyone Can See (1) *42*
Breakdance (2) *8*
Cue Me Up (2)
Don't Throw Your Love Away (1)

Dream (Hold On To Your Dream) (2) *37*
Flashdance...What A Feeling (2) *1*
Keep On (2)

My Baby (He's Something Else) (1)
Reach Out I'll Be There (1)
Receiving (1)
Romance '83 (2)

Slow Down (1)
Thunder In My Heart (1)
True Love (1)
Whad'Ya Want (1)
Why (1)

Why Me? (2) *13*
You Hurt Me Once (1)
You Took My Life Away (2)
You Were Made For Me (2) *78*

CARAVAN
Rock quintet based in Canterbury, England — Pye Hastings, vocals, guitar.

| 8/23/75 | 124 | 10 | | Cunning Stunts... | $8 | BTM 5000 |

Dabsong Conshirtoe Medley
Fear And Loathing In Tollington Park Rag

Lover
No Back Stage Pass

Show Of Our Lives
Stuck In A Hole

Welcome The Day

CARAVELLES, The
English pop duo: Andrea Simpson and Lois Wilkinson.

| 2/15/64 | 127 | 4 | | You Don't Have To Be A Baby To Cry................................. | $30 | Smash 67044 |

Don't Blow Your Cool
Don't Sing Love Songs
Forever

Gonna Get Along Without You Now
Half As Much

Have You Ever Been Lonely (Have You Ever Been Blue) *94*

I Really Don't Want To Know
I Was Wrong
Last One To Know

My How The Time Goes By
Tonight You Belong To Me

You Don't Have To Be A Baby To Cry *3*

CAREY, Mariah
Born on 3/27/70 of Irish and Black/Venezuelan parentage. Her mother is Patricia Carey, former singer with the New York City Opera. Mariah sang backup for Brenda K. Starr. Won the 1990 Best New Artist Grammy Award.

6/30/90+	1[11]	113	▲[6]	1 Mariah Carey...	$12	Columbia 45202
				CD jacket shows only 10 of the 11 tracks on the CD — "Love Takes Time" is excluded		
10/5/91	4	54	▲[3]	2 Emotions...	$12	Columbia 47980
6/20/92	3	34↑[1]		3 MTV Unplugged EP ....[L-M]	$6	Columbia 52758
				recorded on 3/16/92 for the MTV program *Unplugged*		

All In Your Mind (1)
Alone In Love (1)
And You Don't Remember (2)
Can't Let Go (2,3) *2*

Emotions (2,3) *1*
I Don't Wanna Cry (1) *1*
I'll Be There (3) *1*
If It's Over (2,3)

Love Takes Time (1) *1*
Make It Happen (2,3) *5*
Prisoner (1)
Someday (1,3) *1*
There's Got To Be A Way (1)

Sent From Up Above (1)
So Blessed (2)
Till The End Of Time (2)
To Be Around You (2)
Vanishing (1)
Vision Of Love (1,3) *1*

Wind, The (2)
You Need Me (1)
You're So Cold (2)

CAREY, Tony
Born on 10/16/53. Native of Fresno, California. Ex-keyboardist with Rainbow and lead singer of Planet P. Project. Settled in Germany in 1978.

| 4/2/83 | 167 | 9 | | 1 Tony Carey [I Won't Be Home Tonight]............................ | $8 | Rocshire 0001 |
| 3/31/84 | 60 | 24 | | 2 Some Tough City... | $8 | MCA 5464 |

Carry My Love (1)
Eddie Goes Underground (2)
Fine Fine Day (2) *22*
First Day Of Summer (2) *33*
Hungry (2)

I Can Stop The World (2)
I Don't Care (1)
I Won't Be Home Tonight (1) *79*

I'll Tell The World About Her (1)
Lonely Life (2)
Natalia (1)

Reach Out (2)
Running Away From The Thought Of You (1)
She Can Bring Me Love (2)
Sing Along (1)

Some Tough City (2)
Something For Nothing (1)
Tinseltown (2)
Vigilante (1)

West Coast Summer Nights (1) *64*

CARGILL, Henson
Born on 2/5/41 in Oklahoma City. Country singer.

| 3/23/68 | 179 | 2 | | Skip A Rope... | $10 | Monument 18094 |

Black Jack County Chain
By The Time I Get To Phoenix

Distant Drums
Four Long Seasons
Green Green Grass Of Home

It's Over
Just As Much As Ever
Little Girls And Little Boys

Saginaw, Michigan
Skip A Rope *25*
Very Well Traveled Man

★★421★★ CARLIN, George
Comedian/actor. Born on 5/12/37 in New York City. In films *Bill & Ted's Excellent Adventure*, *Outrageous Fortune, Car Wash* and *Americathon*. Replaced Ringo Starr as Mr. Conductor on PBS-TV's *Shining Time Station* in 1991.

2/19/72	13	35	●	1 FM & AM ....[C]	$8	Little David 7214
10/14/72	22	35	●	2 Class Clown ....[C]	$8	Little David 1004
11/10/73	35	21	●	3 Occupation: Foole ....[C]	$8	Little David 1005
12/7/74+	19	17	●	4 Toledo Window Box ....[C]	$8	Little David 3003
11/8/75+	34	15		5 An Evening With Wally Londo Featuring Bill Slaszo.............[C]	$8	Little David 1008
5/21/77	90	9		6 On The Road ....[C]	$8	Little David 1075
1/6/79	112	8		7 Indecent Exposure (some of the best of George Carlin)..........[G-C]	$8	Little David 1076
12/19/81+	145	13		8 A Place For My Stuff! ....[C]	$8	Atlantic 19326
8/4/84	136	11		9 Carlin on Campus ....[C]	$8	Eardrum 1001

Abortion (8)
Asshole, Jackoff, Scumbag (8)
Baseball - Football (5,9)
Birth Control (1)
Black Consciousness (3)
Bodily Functions (5,7)
Breakfast Wine And Who's Boss (9)
Cars And Driving (9)
Childhood Cliches (3)
Class Clown (2)
Confessional, The (2,7)
Cute Little Farts (3,7)
Death And Dying (6)
Divorce Game (1)
Drugs (1)
Ed Sullivan Self Taught (1)

11 O'Clock News (1)
Few More Farts (4)
Filthy Words (3,7)
First Leftfielders (9)
Flesh Colored Band-Aids (5)
For Names' Sake (9)
Fourth Leftfielders (9)
Fussy Eater (Part 1 & 2) (8)
Gay Lib (4)
God (1)
Good Sports (5)
Goofy Shit (4)
Grass Swept The Neighborhood (3)
Hair Piece (3)
Hallway Groups (3)
Have A Nice Day (8)
Head Lines (6)

Heavy Mysteries (9)
High On The Plane (5)
How's Your Dog? (6)
I Used To Be Irish Catholic (2)
Ice Box Man (8)
Incomplete List Of Impolite Words (9)
Interview With Jesus (8)
Join The Book Club (8)
Kids Are Too Small (6)
Let's Make A Deal (1)
Mental Hot Foots (4)
Metric System (4)
Moment Of Silence (9)
Muhammad Ali - America The Beautiful (2)
New News (3)

New York Voices (3)
Nursery Rhymes (4)
Occupation: Foole (3)
On The Road (6)
Parents' Cliches And Children's Secret Answers (6)
Place For My Stuff (8)
Prayer, The (9)
Radio Dial (9)
Raisin Rhetoric (3)
Religious Lift (5)
Rice Krispies (9)
Rules, Rules, Rules! (6)
Second Leftfielders (9)
Seven Words You Can Never Say On Television (2,7)
Sex In Commercials (1,7)

Shoot (1)
Snot, The Original Rubber Cement (4)
Some Werds (4)
Son Of Wino (1)
Special Dispensation - Heaven, Hell, Purgatory And Limbo (2)
Supermarkets (6)
Teenage Masturbation (5,7)
Third Leftfielders (9)
Toledo Window Box (4)
Unrelated Things (5)
Urinals Are 50 Percent Universal (4,7)
Values (How Much Is That Dog Crap In The Window) (2)

Wasted Time - Sharing A Swallow (2)
Water Sez (4)
Welcome To My Job (3)
White Harlem (3)
Words We Leave Behind (6)
Wurds (5)
Y'Ever (5)

CARLISLE, Belinda
Born on 8/17/58 in Hollywood. Lead singer of the Go-Go's, 1978-84. Married to Morgan Mason, son of late actor James Mason.

| 6/7/86 | 13 | 34 | ● | 1 Belinda .... | $8 | I.R.S. 5741 |

DEBUT DATE	PEAK POS	WKS CHR	GOLD	ARTIST — Album Title	$	Label & Number

CARLISLE, Belinda — Cont'd

| 10/24/87+ | 13 | 51 ▲ | | **2** Heaven On Earth | $8 | MCA 42080 |
| 10/21/89 | 37 | 25 ● | | **3** Runaway Horses | $8 | MCA 6339 |

Band Of Gold (1)	**Heaven Is A Place On**	I Never Wanted A Rich Man	Runaway Horses (3)	Valentine (3)
Circle In The Sand (2) 7	**Earth** (2) 1	(1)	Shades Of Michaelangelo (3)	Vision Of You (3)
Deep Deep Ocean (3)	**I Feel Free** (2) 88	La Luna (3)	Shot In The Dark (1)	We Can Change (2)
Fool For Love (2)	**I Feel The Magic** (1) 82	**Leave A Light On** (3) 11	Should I Let You In? (3)	(We Want) The Same Thing
From The Heart (1)	**I Get Weak** (2) 2	Love Never Dies... (2)	Since You've Gone (1)	(3)
Gotta Get To You (1)	I Need A Disguise (1)	**Mad About You** (1) 3	Stuff And Nonsense (1)	Whatever It Takes (3)
		Nobody Owns Me (2)	**Summer Rain** (3) 30	World Without You (2)

CARLOS, Walter
Born in 1939 in Pawtucket, Rhode Island. Classical musician who performs on the Moog Synthesizer. Had a sex change and known as Wendy Carlos by 1992.

1/18/69	10	56 ●		**1** Switched-On Bach	[I] $10	Columbia 7194
1/3/70	199	2		**2** The Well-Tempered Synthesizer	[I] $10	Columbia 7286
7/8/72	146	9		**3** Walter Carlos' Clockwork Orange	[I] $10	Columbia 31480
				features music from the film's soundtrack		
7/8/72	168	7		**4** Sonic Seasonings	[I] $10	Columbia 31234 [2]

Bach: Air On A G String (1)	Bach: Prelude And Fugue	Bach: Two-Part Invention In	Clockwork Orange, Title	Rossini: William Tell	Summer (4)
Bach: Brandenburg	No. 7 In E-Flat Major (1)	F Major (1)	Music From A (3)	Overture, Abridged (3)	Timesteps (3)
Concerto No. 4 In G Major,	Bach: Prelude And Fugue	Beethoven: Ninth	Country Lane (3)	Scarlatti: Sonata In D Major,	Winter (4)
BWV 1049 (2)	No. 2 In C Minor (1)	Symphony: Fourth	Fall (4)	L. 164 (2)	
Bach: Brandenburg	Bach: Sinfonia To Cantata	Movement, Abridged (3)	Handel: Water Music (3)	Scarlatti: Sonata In D Major,	
Concerto No. 3 In G Major	No. 29 (1)	Beethoven: Ninth	Monteverdi: Domine Ad	L. 465 (2)	
(1)	Bach: Two-Part Invention In	Symphony: Second	Adjuvandum (2)	Scarlatti: Sonata In E Major,	
Bach: Chorale Prelude	B-Flat Major (1)	Movement (Scherzo) (3)	Monteverdi: Orfeo Suite (2)	L. 430 (2)	
"Wachet Auf" (1)	Bach: Two-Part Invention In	Clockwork Orange, Theme	Rossini: La Gazza Ladra	Scarlatti: Sonata In G Major,	
Bach: Jesu, Joy Of Man's	D Minor (1)	From A (3)	(The Thieving Magpie),	L. 209 (2)	
Desiring (1)			Abridged (3)	Spring (4)	

CARLTON, Carl
Soul singer. Born in 1952 in Detroit. Singing since age nine. First recorded for Lando Records in 1964.

1/18/75	132	7		**1** Everlasting Love	$10	ABC 857
8/8/81	34	19		**2** Carl Carlton	$8	20th Century 628
10/23/82	133	7		**3** The Bad C.C.	$8	RCA 4425

Baby, I Need Your Loving (3)	Fighting In The Name Of	I Wanna Be Your Main	Lonely Teardrops (1)	**She's A Bad Mama Jama**	This Feeling's Rated X-Tra
Dance With You (3)	Love (2)	Squeeze (1)	Morning, Noon And	**(She's Built, She's**	(2)
Don't You Wanna Make Love	Fooled Myself Again (3)	I've Got That Boogie Fever (2)	Nighttime (1)	**Stacked)** (2) 22	Under The Boardwalk (3)
(2)	Groovin' (3)	Just One Kiss (1)	Our Day Will Come (1)	Signed, Sealed And	
Everlasting Love (1) 6	Hurt So Bad (1)	La La Song (1)	Sexy Lady (2)	Delivered (1)	
Everyone Can Be A Star (3)	I Think It's Gonna Be Alright	Let Me Love You 'Til The		Smokin' Room (1) 91	
	(2)	Morning Comes (2)		Swing That Sexy Thang (3)	

CARLTON, Larry
Born on 3/2/48 in Torrance, California. Top session guitarist. Member of The Crusaders, 1972-77. Fully recovered from a near-fatal gunshot wound suffered in a robbery attack in 1988. Married to Contemporary Christian artist Michelle Pillar.

8/26/78	174	10		**1** Larry Carlton	[I] $8	Warner 3221
9/6/80	138	8		**2** Strikes Twice	[I] $8	Warner 3380
1/30/82	99	16		**3** Sleepwalk	[I] $8	Warner 3635
6/18/83	126	11		**4** Friends	[I] $8	Warner 23834
6/28/86	141	11		**5** Alone/But Never Alone	[I] $8	MCA 5689
8/1/87	180	6		**6** Discovery	[I] $8	MCA 42003
6/10/89	126	8		**7** On Solid Ground	[I] $8	MCA 6237
6/30/90	156	5		**8** Collection	[K] $12	GRP 9611
				features Al Jarreau (skat), B.B. King (guitar), Michael McDonald (keyboards) and others		

Ain't Nothin' For A	Discovery (6)	In My Blood (2)	Minute By Minute (6,8)	Rio Samba (1)	Strikes Twice (2)
Heartache (2)	Don't Give It Up (1)	(It Was) Only Yesterday (1)	Mulberry Street (2)	Room 335 (1)	10:00 P.M. (3,8)
All In Good Time (7)	For Heaven's Sake (8)	Josie (2)	My Home Away From Home	Sea Space (7)	Tequila (4,8)
Alone/But Never Alone (5)	For Love Alone (2)	Knock On Wood (6)	(6)	**Sleepwalk** (3,8) 74	Those Eyes (6)
Blues Bird (3)	Frenchman's Flat (3)	L.A., N.Y. (4)	Nite Crawler (1,8)	Small Town Girl (8)	Upper Kern (3)
Blues For T.J. (4,8)	Friends (4)	Last Nite (3)	On Solid Ground (7)	Smiles And Smiles To Go	Waffer, The (7)
Breaking Ground (4)	Hello Tomorrow (4,8)	Layla (7)	Perfect Peace (7)	(5,8)	Whatever Happens (5)
Bubble Shuffle (7,8)	Her Favorite Song (6)	Lord's Prayer (5)	Philosopher, The (7)	Song For Katie (3)	Where Did You Come From
Carrying You (5)	High Steppin' (5,8)	Magician, The (2)	Place For Skipper (6)	Song In The 5th Grade (4)	(1)
Chapter II (7)	Honey Samba (7)	March Of The Jazz Angels (6)	Point It Up (1)	South Town (4)	You Gotta Get It While You
Cruisin' (4)	I Apologize (1)	Midnight Parade (2)	Pure Delight (5)	Springville (4)	Can (1)

CARMEN, Eric
Born on 8/11/49 in Cleveland. Classical training at Cleveland Institute of Music from early years to mid-teens. Lead singer of the Raspberries from 1970-74.

11/15/75+	21	51 ●		**1** Eric Carmen	$8	Arista 4057
9/10/77	45	13		**2** Boats Against The Current	$8	Arista 4124
10/28/78	137	12		**3** Change Of Heart	$8	Arista 4184
6/28/80	160	5		**4** Tonight You're Mine	$8	Arista 9513
2/9/85	128	10		**5** Eric Carmen	$8	Geffen 24042
6/11/88	59	20		**6** The Best Of Eric Carmen	[G] $8	Arista 8547

All By Myself (1,6) 2	**Boats Against The Current**	Everything (1)	Hey Deanie (3,6)	**I'm Through With Love**	Lost In The Shuffle (4)
All For Love (4)	(2,6) 88	Foolin' Myself (4)	**Hungry Eyes** (6) 4	(5) 87	
American As Apple Pie (5)	**Change Of Heart** (3,6) 19	Great Expectations (5)	I Think I Found Myself (2)	Inside Story (6)	
Baby, I Need Your Lovin'	Come Back To My Love (5)	Haven't We Come A Long	**I Wanna Hear It From**	It Hurts Too Much (4,6) 75	
(3) 62	Desperate Fools (3)	Way (3)	**Your Lips** (5) 35	Last Night (1)	
	End Of The World (3)	Heaven Can Wait (3)		Living Without Your Love (5)	

DEBUT DATE	PEAK POS	WKS CHR	GOLD	ARTIST — Album Title	$	Label & Number

CARMEN, Eric — Cont'd

Love Is All That Matters (2)	**Never Gonna Fall In Love**	On Broadway (1)	Sleep With Me (4)	Take It Or Leave It (2)	You Need Some Lovin' (4)	
Marathon Man (2)	**Again** (1,6) *11*	Runaway (2)	Someday (3)	That's Rock & Roll (1,6)	You Took Me All The Way (5)	
Maybe My Baby (5)	No Hard Feelings (1,6)	**She Did It** (2,6) *23*	Spotlight (5)	Tonight You're Mine (4)	
My Girl (1)	Nowhere To Hide (1)	She Remembered (5)	**Sunrise** (1) *34*	Way We Used To Be (5)	

CARN, Jean

Born Sarah Jean Perkins in Columbus, Georgia. Attended Morris Brown College in Atlanta. Worked with Doug Carn Band, recorded for Black Jazz in 1969. Backup singer for Earth, Wind & Fire and Duke Ellington.

2/19/77	122	10		1 Jean Carn	$8	Phil. Int. 34394
8/15/81	176	3		2 Sweet And Wonderful	$8	TSOP 36775
9/6/86	162	6		3 Closer Than Close	$8	Omni 90492

JEAN CARNE

Anything For Money (3)	Don't Say No (To Love) (2)	Free Love (1)	Love Don't Love Nobody (2)	No Laughing Matter (1)	Where Did You Ever Go (1)
Bet Your Lucky Star (2)	Don't You Know Love When	I Just Thought Of A Way (2)	Love (Makes Me Do Foolish	Sexy Eyes (3)	You Are All I Need (1)
Break Up To Make Up (3)	You See It (1)	I'm In Love Once Again (1)	Things) (2)	Sweet And Wonderful (2)	You Got A Problem (1)
Candy Love (3)	Everything Must Change (3)	If You Wanna Go Back (1)	Lucky Charm (3)	Time Waits For No One (1)	
Closer Than Close (3)	Flame Of Love (3)	It Must Be Love (3)	Mystic Stranger (2)	We Got Some Catchin' Up To Do (2)	

CARNES, Kim

Vocalist/pianist/composer. Born on 7/20/45 in Los Angeles. Member of The New Christy Minstrels with husband/co-writer Dave Ellingson and Kenny Rogers, late 1960s. Wrote for and performed in commercials.

7/5/80	57	17		1 Romance Dance	$8	EMI America 17030
5/2/81	1⁴	52 ▲		2 **Mistaken Identity**	$8	EMI America 17052
9/25/82	49	22		3 Voyeur	$8	EMI America 17078
11/19/83	97	16		4 Cafe Racers	$8	EMI America 17106
6/29/85	48	14		5 Barking at Airplanes	$8	EMI America 17159
6/14/86	116	7		6 Light House	$8	EMI America 17198

Abadabadango (5) *67*	**Crazy In The Night**	He Makes The Sun Rise	Merc Man (3)	Swept Me Off My Feet (The	**You Make My Heart Beat**
Along With The Radio (6)	**(Barking At Airplanes)**	(Orpheus) (5)	Met You At The Wrong Time	Part Of The Fool) (1)	**Faster (And That's All**
And Still Be Loving You (1)	(5) *15*	Hit And Run (2)	Of My Life (4)	Take It On The Chin (3)	**That Matters)** (4) *54*
Arrangement, The (3)	**Cry Like A Baby** (1) *44*	Miss You Tonite (2)	Take Me Apart (1)	You Say You Love Me (But I
Begging For Favors	Dancin' At The Lighthouse	I Pretend (4) *74*	**Mistaken Identity** (2) *60*	That's Where The Trouble	Know You Don't) (6)
(Learning How Things	(6)	I'd Lie To You For Your Love	More Love (1) *10*	Lies (6)	Young Love (4)
Work) (5)	**Divided Hearts** (6) *79*	(6)	My Old Pals (3)	Thrill Of The Grill (3)	
Bette Davis Eyes (2) *1*	**Does It Make You**	I'll Be Here Where The Heart	Oliver (Voice On The Radio)	Touch And Go (5)	
Black And White (6)	**Remember** (3) *36*	Is (4)	(5)	Undertow (3)	
Bon Voyage (5)	Don't Call It Love (2)	In The Chill Of The Night (1)	One Kiss (5)	Universal Song (4)	
Break The Rules Tonight	Don't Pick Up The Phone	**Invisible Hands** (4) *40*	Only Lonely Love (6)	**Voyeur** (3) *29*	
(Out Of School) (2)	(Pick Up The Phone) (5)	Kick In The Heart (4)	Piece Of The Sky (6)	When I'm Away From You (2)	
Breakin' Away From Sanity	**Draw Of The Cards** (2) *28*	Looker (3)	Rough Edges (5)	Where Is Your Heart (1)	
(3)	Hangin' On By A Thread (A	Love Me Like You Never Did	Say You Don't Know Me (3)	Will You Remember Me (1)	
Changin' (1)	Sad Affair Of The Heart) (4)	Before (6)	Still Hold On (2)		

CARNIVAL, The

Pop vocal quartet from Los Angeles.

12/6/69	191	2		The Carnival	$12	World Pac. 21894

Canto De Carnival	Laia Ladaia	Son Of A Preacher Man	Turn, Turn, Turn (To	Walk On By
Famous Myth	Love So Fine	Sweets For My Sweet	Everything There Is A	Word, The
Hope	Reach Out For Me	Take Me For A Little While	Season)	

CARPENTER, Mary-Chapin

Born in Princeton, New Jersey in 1958. Moved to Washington, D.C. in 1974. Graduated from Brown University. Pursued folk music before she became a top country vocalist.

12/9/89+	183	10		1 State Of The Heart	$8	Columbia 44228
11/3/90+	70	52 ●		2 Shooting Straight In The Dark	$12	Columbia 46077
7/18/92	31	30↑▲		3 Come On Come On	$12	Columbia 48881

Bug, The (3)	Down In Mary's Land (1)	How Do I (1)	Moon And St. Christopher (2)	Quittin' Time (1)	This Shirt (1)
Can't Take Love For Granted	Going Out Tonight (2)	I Am A Town (3)	More Things Change (2)	Read My Lips (1)	Too Tired (1)
(2)	Goodbye Again (1)	I Feel Lucky (3)	Never Had It So Good (1)	Rhythm Of The Blues (3)	Walking Through Fire (3)
Come On Come On (3)	Halley Came To Jackson (2)	I Take My Chances (3)	Not Too Much To Ask (3)	Right Now (2)	What You Didn't Say (2)
Down At The Twist And	Hard Way (3)	It Don't Bring You (1)	Only A Dream (3)	Slow Country Dance (1)	When She's Gone (2)
Shout (2)	He Thinks He'll Keep Her (3)	Middle Ground (2)	Passionate Kisses (3)	Something Of A Dreamer (1)	You Win Again (2)

★★167★★ CARPENTERS

Richard Carpenter (b: 10/15/46) and sister Karen (b: 3/2/50; d: 2/4/83 of heart failure due to anorexia nervosa). From New Haven, Connecticut. Richard played piano from age nine. To Downey, California in 1963. Karen played drums in group with Richard and bass player Wes Jacobs in 1965. The trio recorded for RCA in 1966. After a period with the band Spectrum, the Carpenters recorded as a duo for A&M in 1969. Won the 1970 Best New Artist Grammy Award. Hosts of the TV variety show *Make Your Own Kind Of Music* in 1971. 1988 TV movie *The Karen Carpenter Story* was based on Karen's life.

9/19/70	2¹	87 ●		1 **Close To You**	$12	A&M 4271
3/6/71	150	16		2 Ticket To Ride	$12	A&M 4205
				Carpenters' first album		
6/5/71	2²	59 ●		3 **Carpenters**	$12	A&M 3502
7/8/72	4	41 ●		4 **A Song For You**	$12	A&M 3511
6/2/73	2¹	41 ●		5 **Now & Then**	$12	A&M 3519
				side 2: medley of '60s hits with D.J. Tony Peluso		
12/1/73+	1¹	49 ▲⁴		6 **The Singles 1969-1973** [G]	$12	A&M 3601
6/28/75	13	18 ●		7 Horizon	$12	A&M 4530
7/10/76	33	16 ●		8 A Kind Of Hush	$12	A&M 4581
10/22/77	49	18		9 Passage	$12	A&M 4703
12/9/78+	145	7 ●		10 Christmas Portrait [X]	$12	A&M 4726
				also released on A&M 3210; Christmas charts: 5/83, 2/84, 7/85, 7/87, 7/88, 8/89		
7/4/81	52	15		11 Made In America	$12	A&M 3723

DEBUT DATE	PEAK POS	WKS CHR	GOLD	ARTIST — Album Title	$	Label & Number

CARPENTERS — Cont'd

DEBUT DATE	PEAK POS	WKS CHR	GOLD	#	ARTIST — Album Title	$	Label & Number
11/19/83+	46	19		12	Voice Of The Heart	$12	A&M 4954
1/5/85	190	1		13	An Old-Fashioned Christmas .... [X]	$12	A&M 3270
					Christmas charts: 29/'87, 29/'88, 25/'90		
5/25/85	144	8		14	Yesterday Once More .... [G]	$15	A&M 6601 [2]
12/22/90+	159	3	●	15	Christmas Portrait - The Special Edition .... [X-R]	$12	A&M 5171

expanded edition of #10 above with new sequencing plus some substituted songs; first released as a double cassette (A&M 5171); later released on CD (A&M 5173); Christmas charts: 8/'90, 5/'91, 10/'92

All I Can Do (2)
All Of My Life (2)
All You Get From Love Is A Love Song (9,14) 35
Angels We Have Heard On High (medley) (13,15)
Another Song (1)
At The End Of A Song (12)
Aurora (7)
Ave Maria (10,15)
Away In A Manger (medley) (10)
Baby It's You (1)
Because We Are In Love (The Wedding Song) (11,14)
Beechwood 4-5789 (11) 74
Bless The Beasts And Children (4,14) 67
Boat To Sail (8)
Breaking Up Is Hard To Do (8)
Calling Occupants Of Interplanetary Craft (9,14) 32
Can't Smile Without You (8)
Carol Of The Bells (10,15)
Christ Is Born (10,15)
Christmas Song (Chestnuts Roasting On An Open Fire) (10,15)
Christmas Waltz (10,15)
Crescent Noon (1)
Crystal Lullaby (4)
Da Doo Ron Ron (When He Walked Me Home) (medley) (5)
Deadman's Curve (medley) (5)
Deck The Hall (medley) (10)
Desperado (7)

Do You Hear What I Hear? (13)
Do You Know The Way To San Jose (medley) (3)
Don't Be Afraid (2)
Don't Cry For Me Argentina (medley) (9)
Druscilla Penny (3)
End Of The World (medley) (5)
Eve (2)
Eventide (7)
First Noel (medley) (13,15)
First Snowfall (medley) (10)
Flat Baroque (4)
For All We Know (3,6,14) 3
Frosty The Snowman (medley) (13,15)
Fun, Fun, Fun (medley) (5)
Gesu Bambino (medley) (13,15)
Get Together (2)
God Rest Ye Merry Gentlemen (medley) (10)
Good King Wenceslas (medley) (13,15)
Goodbye To Love (4,6,14) 7
Goofus (8) 56
Happy (7)
Happy Holiday (medley) (13,15)
Have Yourself A Merry Little Christmas (10,15)
He Came Here For Me (13)
Heather (5)
Help (1)
Here Comes Santa Claus (medley) (13,15)
Home For The Holidays (13,15)

Hurting Each Other (4,6,14) 2
I Believe You (11) 68
I Can Dream Can't I (7)
I Can't Make Music (5)
I Have You (8)
I Heard The Bells On Christmas Day (13)
I Just Fall In Love Again (9)
I Kept On Loving You (1)
I Need To Be In Love (8,14) 25
I Saw Mommy Kissing Santa Claus (medley) (13,15)
I Saw Three Ships (medley) (10)
I Won't Last A Day Without You (4,14) 11
I'll Be Home For Christmas (10,15)
I'll Never Fall In Love Again (1,3)
(I'm Caught Between) Goodbye And I Love You (7)
In Dulce Jubilo (medley) (13,15)
It Came Upon A Midnight Clear (13,15)
It's Christmas Time (10,15)
It's Going To Take Some Time (4,6,14) 12
Jambalaya (On The Bayou) (5)
Jingle Bells (10)
Johnny Angel (medley) (5)
Knowing When To Leave (medley) (3)
Let It Snow (medley) (10)
Let Me Be The One (3)
Little Altar Boy (13,15)
Little Jesus (medley) (13,15)

Look To Your Dreams (12)
Love Is Surrender (1)
Love Me For What I Am (7)
Make Believe It's Your First Time (12,14)
Make It Easy On Yourself (medley) (3)
Man Smart, Woman Smarter (9)
March Of The Toys (medley) (13,15)
Maybe It's You (1)
Merry Christmas Darling (10,15)
Mr. Guder (1)
My Favorite Things (13)
Night Has A Thousand Eyes (medley) (5)
Now (12)
Nowadays Clancy Can't Even Sing (2)
"Nutcracker" Medley (13,15)
O Come All Ye Faithful (Adeste Fideles) (medley) (10)
O Come, O Come Immanuel (10)
O Holy Night (13,15)
O Little Town Of Bethlehem (medley) (13,15)
Old-Fashioned Christmas (13,15)
On The Balcony Of The Casa Rosada (medley) (9)
One Fine Day (medley) (5)
One Love (3)
One More Time (3)
Only Yesterday (7,14) 4
Ordinary Fool (12)
Our Day Will Come (medley) (5)

Piano Picker (4)
(Place To) Hideaway (3)
Please Mr. Postman (7,14) 1
Prime Time Love (12)
Rainy Days and Mondays (3,6,14) 2
Reason To Believe (1)
Road Ode (4)
Rudolph The Red-Nosed Reindeer (medley) (13,15)
Sailing On The Tide (12)
Sandy (8)
Santa Claus Is Comin' To Town (10,13,15)
Saturday (4)
Silent Night (10,15)
Silver Bells (medley) (10,15)
Sing (5,6,14) 3
Sleep Well, Little Children (medley) (10)
Sleigh Ride (10,15)
Solitaire (7) 17
Somebody's Been Lyin' (11)
Someday (2)
Sometimes (3)
Song For You (4)
Strength Of A Woman (11)
Superstar (3,6,14) 2
Sweet, Sweet Smile (9,14) 44
There's A Kind Of Hush (All Over The World) (8,14) 12
(There's) Always Something There To Remind Me (medley) (3)
(They Long To Be) Close To You (1,6,14) 1
This Masquerade (5,14)
Those Good Old Dreams (11,14) 63

Ticket To Ride (2,6,14) 54
Top Of The World (4,6,14) 1
Touch Me When We're Dancing (11,14) 16
Turn Away (2)
Two Lives (12)
Two Sides (9)
Walk On By (medley) (3)
(Want You) Back In My Life Again (11,14) 72
We've Only Just Begun (1,6,14) 2
What Are You Doing New Year's Eve? (13)
What Child Is This (medley) (10)
What's The Use (2)
When It's Gone (It's Just Gone) (1)
When You've Got What It Takes (1)
White Christmas (medley) (10,15)
Winter Wonderland (medley) (10,15)
Yesterday Once More (5,6,14) 2
You (8)
You're Enough (12)
Your Baby Doesn't Love You Anymore (12)
Your Wonderful Parade (2)

★★380★★ **CARR, Vikki**

Born Florencia Martinez Cardona on 7/19/41 in El Paso, Texas. Regular on TV's *Ray Anthony Show*, 1962.

DEBUT DATE	PEAK POS	WKS CHR	#	ARTIST — Album Title	$	Label & Number
7/18/64	114	4	1	Discovery!	$15	Liberty 7354
10/21/67+	12	47	2	It Must Be Him	$15	Liberty 7533
3/23/68	63	16	3	Vikki!	$15	Liberty 7548
3/29/69	29	34	4	For Once In My Life .... [L]	$15	Liberty 7604
5/9/70	111	8	5	Nashville by Carr	$15	Liberty 11001
7/10/71	60	14	6	Vikki Carr's Love Story	$10	Columbia 30662
1/8/72	118	4	7	Superstar	$10	Columbia 31040
6/24/72	146	12	8	The First Time Ever (I Saw Your Face)	$10	Columbia 31453
9/9/72	106	25	9	En Espanol .... [F]	$10	Columbia 31470
6/23/73	142	7	10	Ms. America	$10	Columbia 32251
11/24/73	172	7	11	Live At The Greek Theatre .... [L]	$10	Columbia 32656 [2]
9/28/74	155	5	12	One Hell Of A Woman	$10	Columbia 32860

Adoro (9)
After Today (medley) (4)
After You've Gone (medley) (4)
Afternoon Of A Faun (11)
Ahora Que Soy Libre (9)
Ain't No Mountain High Enough (6)
Ain't No Way To Treat A Lady (12)
Alfie (2)
Amanece (9)
Baby Don't Walk Out On Me (10)
Bit Of Love (2)
Bluesette (1)
Brian's Song (The Hands Of Time) (8)
By The Time I Get To Phoenix (3)
Cabaret (8)
Can't Take My Eyes Off You (2,4,11)

Carnival (Manha De Carnaval) (4)
Come Rain Or Come Shine (medley) (4)
Crazy Love (7)
Crying Time (medley) (5)
Daddy's Dream (11)
Danny's Song (10)
Days (4)
Don't Talk To Me (1)
El Triste (9)
Everybody's Talkin' (5)
Everything I Touch Turns To Tears (3)
First Time Ever (I Saw Your Face) (8)
For All We Know (6)
For Once In My Life (3,4)
Forget You (2)
Garland Medley (11)
Go (Vois) (3)
Godfather (Speak Softly Love), Love Theme From The (8)

Grande, Grande, Grande (9)
Gypsies, Tramps And Thieves (8)
Happy Together (4)
Have You Heard The News (11)
Haven't Got Time For The Pain (12)
Help Me Make It Through The Night (8)
Her Little Heart Went To Loveland (2)
Historia De Amor (Love Story) (9)
Hold My Hand (12)
How Can You Mend A Broken Heart? (7)
How Insensitive (Insensatez) (1)
Hurt (6)
I Believe In The Sunshine (11)
I Can't Give Back The Love I Feel For You (7)

I Can't Stop Loving You (11)
I Cry Alone (1)
I Keep It Hid (6)
I Wonder Who's Kissing Her Now (11)
I Would Be Your Friend (10)
I'd Do It All Again (7)
I'll Be Home (6) 96
I'll Have To Say I Love You In A Song (12)
I'm Gonna Love You (7)
I've Never Been A Woman Before (6)
If I Were Your Woman (6)
If You Could Read My Mind (6)
It Must Be Him (2,4,11) 3
Killing Me Softly With His Song (10)
La Nave Del Olvido (9)
(Last Night) I Didn't Get To Sleep At All (8)
Last Song (10)
Lazy Day (3)

Lean On Me (11)
Leave A Little Room (11)
Lesson, The (3) 34
Let Me Be The One (12)
Living On A Prayer, A Hope And A Hand-Me-Down (5)
Look Again (2)
Love Song (11)
Loving Him Was Easier (Than Anything I'll Ever Do Again) (7)
Make It Rain (5)
Million Years Or So (2)
Ms. America (10)
Need To Be (12)
Never My Love (3)
Never Will I Marry (1)
Night They Drove Old Dixie Down (7)
No Sun Today (3)
One Hell Of A Woman (12)

One Less Bell To Answer (6)
One More Mountain (2)
Other Man's Grass Is Always Greener (4)
Overcrowded Dreams (11)
Pero Te Extrano (9)
Poor Butterfly (medley) (1)
Portrait (7)
Put Your Arms Around Me (1)
Raindrops Keep Fallin' On My Head (5)
Real Me (3)
Rescue Me (10)
Se Acabo (9)
Should I Follow (5)
Singing My Song (5)
Six Weeks Every Summer (Christmas Every Other Year) (6)
Sleeping Between Two People (12)
So Far Away (7)
So In Love (1)

124

DEBUT DATE	PEAK POS	WKS CHR	GOLD	ARTIST — Album Title	$	Label & Number

CARR, Vikki — Cont'd

So Much In Love With You (2)	Spanish Medley (11)	Surrey With The Fringe On Top (1)	Tip Of My Fingers (5)	What Are You Afraid Of? (1)	Yesterday, When I Was Young (Heir Encore) (5)
Soap Opera (11)	Stay (medley) (11)	That's The Way We Fall In Love (12)	Today I Started Loving You Again (medley) (5)	Where Are You (1)	You Are (5)
Some Of These Days (medley) (4)	Summer Of '42 (The Summer Knows), Theme From (8)	There I Go (Se Pe Te C' E' Soltanto Qull' Uomo) (3)	Tomorrow Is My Friend (5)	(Where Do I Begin) Love Story (6)	You Are The Sunshine Of My Life (11)
Somebody Loves You (10)	Sunday Mornin' Comin' Down (1)	This Girl Is Gonna Cry (10)	Tunesmith (2)	Wind Me Up (12)	
Somos Novios (It's Impossible) (9)	Sunshine On My Shoulders (12)	This Girl's In Love With You (medley) (4)	Until It's Time For You To Go (5)	With Pen In Hand (4,11) 35	
Song For You (11)	Superstar (7)	This Is The House That Jack Built (3)	Watch What Happens (3)	Without You (8)	
Song Sung Blue (8)			Way Of Love (8)	Y Volvere (9)	
Spanish Harlem (7)			We Didn't Know The Time Of Day (10)	Yesterday I Heard The Rain (Esta Tarde Vi Llover) (4)	

CARRACK, Paul
Born on 4/22/51 in Sheffield, England. Lead singer of Ace (1973-76), Squeeze (1981) and Mike + The Mechanics (since 1985). Keyboardist with Roxy Music (1978-80).

9/11/82	78	14		1 Suburban Voodoo	$8	Epic 38161
11/21/87+	67	31		2 One Good Reason	$8	Chrysalis 41578
11/11/89	120	18		3 Groove Approved	$8	Chrysalis 21709

After The Love Is Gone (3)	Call Me Tonight (1)	Don't Shed A Tear (2) 9	I Found Love (1)	Little Unkind (1)	Out Of Touch (1)
Always Better With You (1)	Collrane (2)	Double It Up (2)	I Live By The Groove (3) 31	Love Can Break Your Heart (3)	So Right, So Wrong (1)
Bad News (At The Best Of Times) (3)	Dedicated (3)	Fire With Fire (2)	I Need You (1) 37	Loveless (3)	Tip Of My Tongue (3)
Battlefield (3)	(Do I Figure) In Your Life (2)	From Now On (1)	I'm In Love (1)	One Good Reason (2) 28	What A Way To Go (1)
Button Off My Shirt (2) 91	Don't Give My Heart A Break (1)	Give Me A Chance (2)	I'm On Your Tail (1)	Only My Heart Can Tell (3)	When You Walk In The Room (2) 90
		Here I Am (1)	Lesson In Love (1)		

CARRADINE, Keith
Born on 8/8/49 in San Mateo, California. Leading actor in dozens of films including *Pretty Baby*, *Nashville*, *The Long Riders* and others. Son of actor John Carradine; half-brother of David Carradine.

| 6/26/76 | 61 | 17 | | I'm Easy | $10 | Asylum 1066 |

Been Gone So Long	Honey Won't You Let Me Be Your Friend	I Will Never Forget Your Face	I'm Easy 17	Raining In The City	Spellbound
High Sierra		I'll Be There	It's Been So Long	Soul Is Strong	

CARRERAS, Jose
Operatic tenor. Born in Barcelona, Spain in 1946. Began performing opera as a child. Battled leukemia in 1991.

| 10/6/90+ | 35 | 90 | ▲ | CARRERAS DOMINGO PAVAROTTI in concert | [L] $12 | London 430433 |

CARRERAS DOMINGO PAVAROTTI
concert on 7/7/90 of opera tenors: Jose Carreras, Placido Domingo, Luciano Pavarotti with orchestra conducted by Zubin Mehta at the Baths of Caracalla in Rome

Amapola (medley)	Cilea: L'Arlesiana - Il Lamento De Federico	La Vie En Rose (medley)	'O Paese D' 'O Sole (medley)	Tonight (medley)
Caminito (medley)		Lara: Granada	'O Sole Mio ..see: Di Capua	Wien, Wien, Nur Du Allein (medley)
Cardillo: Core 'Ngrato	Di Capua: 'O Sole Mio	Maria (medley)	Ochi Tchorniye (medley)	
Cielito Lindo (medley)	Giordano: Andrea Chenier - L'Improviso	Mattinata (medley)	Puccini: Turandot - Nessun Dorma	
		Memory (medley)		

CARRINGTON, Terri Lyne
Twenty-three-year-old female jazz drummer from Medford, Massachusetts. Member of the house band on TV's *The Arsenio Hall Show* until June 1989.

| 4/29/89 | 169 | 7 | | Real Life Story | [I] $8 | Forecast 837697 |

3 of 9 tracks feature vocals

Blackbird	Message True	Obstacle Illusion	Real Life Story	Skeptic Alert
Human Revolution	More Than Woman	Pleasant Dreams	Shh	

CARROLL, David, And His Orchestra
Born Nook Schrier on 10/15/13 in Chicago. Arranger/conductor since 1951 for many top Mercury artists.

| 6/1/59 | 21 | 6 | | 1 Let's Dance | $15 | Mercury 60001 |
| 1/11/60 | 6 | 30 | | 2 Let's Dance Again | $15 | Mercury 60152 |

Adios (2)	Dancing Tambourine (1)	Glow-Worm, The (1)	My Sin (1)	Soft Shoe Song (The Dance My Darling Used To Do) (2)	Would You Like To Take A Walk (2)
Armen's Theme (1)	Dixie Dawn Patrol (1)	Hey Chick! (2)	Play A Simple Melody (2)	Swamp Fire (2)	Yearning (1)
Bouncing Ball (2)	Doodlin' Drummer (2)	Irene (2)	Pretty Baby (2)	Trouble With Harry (1)	
Cha-Cha-Panecas (2)	Euphrates (2)	Let's Dance (1)	Puerto Rican Pedlar (1)		
Cuddle Up A Little Closer (1)	Gliss To Remember (1)	Let's Dance Again (2)	Side Saddle (2)		

CARROLL, Jim, Band
Jim was born in New York City in 1950. Poet/rock singer.

| 11/15/80+ | 73 | 23 | | 1 Catholic Boy | $8 | Atco 132 |
| 5/22/82 | 156 | 7 | | 2 Dry Dreams | $8 | Atco 145 |

Barricades (1)	Day And Night (1)	It's Too Late (1)	Nothing Is True (1)	Them (2)
Catholic Boy (1)	Dry Dreams (2)	Jealous Twin (2)	People Who Died (1)	Three Sisters (1)
City Drops Into The Night (1)	Evangeline (2)	Jody (2)	Rooms (2)	Wicked Gravity (1)
Crow (1)	I Want The Angel (1)	Lorraine (2)	Still Life (2)	Work Not Play (2)

★★311★★ CARS, The
Rock group formed in Boston in 1976. Consisted of Ric Ocasek (lead vocals, guitar), Elliot Easton (guitar), Greg Hawkes (keyboards), Benjamin Orr (bass, vocals) and David Robinson (drums; formerly with the Modern Lovers). Ocasek, Orr and Hawkes had been in trio in the early 1970s. Group named by Robinson, got A Lot At the Rat Club in Boston. All songs written by Ocasek. Disbanded in 1988.

7/1/78+	18	139	▲	1 The Cars	$8	Elektra 135
6/30/79	3	62	▲	2 Candy-O	$8	Elektra 507
9/6/80	5	28	▲	3 Panorama	$8	Elektra 514
11/28/81	9	41	▲	4 Shake It Up	$8	Elektra 567
4/7/84	3	69	▲³	5 Heartbeat City	$8	Elektra 60296
11/23/85	12	39	▲	6 The Cars Greatest Hits	[G] $8	Elektra 60464
9/12/87	26	23	●	7 Door To Door	$8	Elektra 60747

All Mixed Up (1)	Cruiser (4)	Door To Door (7)	Dream Away (4)	Getting Through (3)	Got A Lot On My Head (2)
Bye Bye Love (1)	Dangerous Type (2)	Double Life (2)	Drive (5,6) 3	Gimme Some Slack (3)	Heartbeat City (5)
Candy-O (2)	Don't Cha Stop (1)	Double Trouble (7)	Everything You Say (7)	Go Away (7)	Hello Again (5) 20
Coming Up You (7) 74	Don't Tell Me No (3)	Down Boys (3)	Fine Line (7)	Good Times Roll (1,6) 41	I Refuse (5)

DEBUT DATE	PEAK POS	WKS CHR	G O L D	ARTIST — Album Title	$	Label & Number

CARS, The — Cont'd

I'm In Touch With Your World (1)	Looking For Love (5)	Nightspots (2)	**Strap Me In** (7) *85*	**Why Can't I Have You** (5) *33*	You're All I've Got Tonight (1)
I'm Not The One (4,6) *32*	Lust For Kicks (2)	Panorama (3)	Ta Ta Wayo Wayo (7)	Wound Up On You (7)	
It's All I Can Do (2) *41*	**Magic** (5,6) *12*	Running To You (3)	Think It Over (4)	**You Are The Girl** (7) *17*	
It's Not The Night (5)	Maybe Baby (4)	**Shake It Up** (4,6) *4*	This Could Be Love (4)	You Can't Hold On Too Long (2)	
Just What I Needed (1,6) *27*	Misfit Kid (3)	Shoo Be Doo (2)	**Tonight She Comes** (6) *7*		
Leave Or Stay (7)	Moving In Stereo (1)	Since I Held You (2)	**Touch And Go** (3,6) *37*	**You Might Think** (5,6) *7*	
Let's Go (2,6) *14*	**My Best Friend's Girl** (1,6) *35*	**Since You're Gone** (4,6) *41*	Up And Down (3)	You Wear Those Eyes (3)	
		Stranger (5)	Victim Of Love (4)		

CARTER, Betty — see CHARLES, Ray

CARTER, Carlene
Born on 9/26/55. Daughter of country singers June Carter and Carl Smith. Worked with the Carter Family from the late '60s into the early '70s. Married for a time to Nick Lowe.

10/4/80	139	6		Musical Shapes	$8	Warner 3465

Appalachian Eyes	Bandit Of Love	Foggy Mountain Top	Madness	That Very First Kiss	Too Bad About Sandy
Baby Ride Easy	Cry	I'm So Cool	Ring Of Fire	To Drunk (Too Remember)	Too Proud

CARTER, Clarence
Born in 1936 in Montgomery, Alabama. R&B vocalist/guitarist. Blind since age one; self-taught on guitar at age 11. Teamed with vocalist/pianist Calvin Scott as Clarence & Calvin, recorded for Fairlane in the early 1960s. Carter went solo in 1966. Married for a time to Candi Staton.

12/7/68	200	2		1 This Is Clarence Carter...	$25	Atlantic 8192
4/5/69	169	4		2 The Dynamic Clarence Carter	$20	Atlantic 8199
8/16/69	138	3		3 Testifyin'	$20	Atlantic 8238
9/26/70	44	12		4 Patches	$15	Atlantic 8267
5/22/71	103	10		5 The Best Of Clarence Carter...[G]	$15	Atlantic 8282
2/28/81	189	2		6 Let's Burn	$8	Venture 1005

Another Night (6)	**I Can't Leave Your Love Alone** (4,5) *42*	Just Searching (6)	Say Man (4)	Think About It (2)	Your Love Lifted Me (4)
Back Door Santa (3)	I Can't See Myself (1)	Let It Be (4)	Scratch My Back (6)	**Thread The Needle** (1) *98*	
Bad News (3)	I Smell A Rat (3,5)	Let Me Comfort You (2)	Set Me Free (1)	Till I Can't Take It Anymore (4)	
C.C. Blues (4)	I'd Rather Go Blind (2)	Let's Burn (6)	She Ain't Gonna Do Right (1)	**Too Weak To Fight** (2,5) *13*	
Changes (4)	I'm Just A Prisoner (Of Your Good Lovin') (4)	Light My Fire (2)	She's Out To Get Me (6)	Weekend Love (2)	
Do What You Gotta Do (1)	I'm Qualified (1)	Look What I Got (2)	**Slip Away** (1,5) *6*	Willie And Laura Mae Jones (4)	
Doin' Our Thing (3,5) *46*	I'm So Tired (6)	**Looking For A Fox** (1) *62*	Slippin' Around (1)	Wind It Up (1)	
Feeling Is Right (3,5) *65*	If I Stay (6)	Love Building (6)	**Snatching It Back** (3,5) *31*	You Can't Miss What You Can't Measure (3,5)	
Funky Fever (1,5) *88*	Instant Reaction (3)	Making Love (At The Dark End Of The Street) (3,5)	Soul Deep (3)	You've Been A Long Time Comin' (2)	
Getting The Bills (But No Merchandise) (4)	**It's All In Your Mind** (4) *51*	Part Time Love (2)	Steal Away (2)		
Harper Valley P.T.A. (2)	Jimmy's Disco (6)	**Patches** (4,5) *4*	**Take It Off Him And Put It On Me** (5) *94*		
I Can't Do Without You (3)		Road Of Love (2)	That Old Time Feeling (2)		

CARTER, Mel
Soul singer/TV actor. Born on 4/22/39 in Cincinnati. Sang on local radio from age four; with Lionel Hampton on stage show at age nine. Named Top Gospel Tenor in 1957. Recorded in late '50s for Tri-State, Arwin, then Mercury. Acted on TV's *Quincy, Sanford And Son, Marcus Welby, MD* and *Magnum P.I.*

9/18/65	62	12		1 Hold Me, Thrill Me, Kiss Me	$20	Imperial 12289
10/1/66	81	11		2 Easy Listening	$20	Imperial 12319

Alfie (2)	**Hold Me, Thrill Me, Kiss Me** (1) *8*	I'll Never Be Free (1)	Richest Man Alive (1)	**Take Good Care Of Her** (2) *78*	You Don't Have To Say You Love Me (2)
Can I Trust You? (2)	I Am (1)	Impossible Dream (The Quest) (2)	Somewhere, My Love (2)	Tar And Cement (2)	**You You You** (2) *49*
Detour (1)	I Just Can't Imagine (1)	Love Letters (2)	Strangers In The Night (2)	Wanted (1)	You're Gonna Hear From Me (2)
Funny World (1)	I Need You Now (1)	More I See You (2)	Sweet Little Girl (1)	What's On Your Mind (1)	
High Noon (1)					

CARTER, Ron
Jazz bassist. Born on 5/4/37 in Ferndale, Michigan. In early 1960s, worked with Cannonball Adderley. Member of Miles Davis' band from 1963-68. Worked with Stanley Turrentine, Hubert Laws and others.

3/12/77	193	1		1 Pastels..[I]	$10	Milestone 9073
10/21/78	178	3		2 A Song For You ....[I]	$10	Milestone 9086

Ballad (1)	Good Time (2)	One Bass Rag (1)	Quiet Place (2)	Song For You (2)	Woolaphant (1)
El Ojo De Dios (2)	N.O. Blues (2)	Pastels (1)	Someday My Prince Will Come (2)	12 + 12 (1)	

CARTER, Valerie
Session vocalist. Sang backup for Eddie Money, Randy Newman and James Taylor.

4/2/77	182	5		Just A Stone's Throw Away	$10	Columbia 34155

Back To Blue Some More	Face Of Appalachia	Ooh Child	Ringing Doorbells In The Rain	So, So Happy	Stone's Throw Away
City Lights	Heartache			Stone's Throw Away	
Cowboy Angel					

CARTWRIGHT, Lionel
Ohio-born country singer/actor raised in West Virginia. Starred on The Nashville Network's TV series *I-40 Paradise* and *Pickin' At The Paradise*; also a songwriter/musical director for both shows.

10/5/91	170	2		Chasin' The Sun	$12	MCA 10307

Family Tree	I'm Your Man	Smack Dab In The Middle Of Love	Susannah	Waitin' For The Sun To Shine	What Kind Of Fool
Great Expectations	Leap Of Faith		30 Nothin'		When You Cross That Line

CASCADES, The
Pop group from San Diego consisting of John Gummoe (lead vocals), Eddie Snyder, David Stevens, David Wilson and David Zabo.

4/20/63	111	10		Rhythm Of The Rain	$50	Valiant 405

Angel On My Shoulder	I Wanna Be Your Lover	Let Me Be	My First Day Alone	**Rhythm Of The Rain** *3*	There's A Reason
Dreamin'	**Last Leaf** *60*	Lucky Guy	Punch And Judy	**Shy Girl** *91*	Was I Dreamin'?

★★73★★ CASH, Johnny

Born on 2/26/32 in Kingsland, Arkansas. To Dyess, Arkansas at age three. Brother Roy led the Dixie Rhythm Ramblers band in late 1940s. In U.S. Air Force, 1950-54. Formed trio with Luther Perkins (guitar) and Marshall Grant (bass) in 1955. First recorded for Sun in 1955. On *Louisiana Hayride* and *Grand Ole Opry* in 1957. Own TV show for ABC from 1969-71. Worked with June Carter from 1961, married her in March 1968. Elected to the Country Music Hall of Fame in 1980. Won Grammy's Living Legends Award in 1990. Daughter Rosanne Cash and stepdaughter Carlene Carter currently enjoying successful singing careers. According to Joel Whitburn's *Top Country Singles* book, Johnny ranks within the top three artists of the country charts. Acted in the 1993 TV series *Dr. Quinn, Medicine Woman* and other TV movies. Also see *Highwayman* in Concept Albums.

DEBUT DATE	PEAK POS	WKS CHR	GOLD	#	ARTIST — Album Title	$	Label & Number
12/8/58	19	11		1	The Fabulous Johnny Cash	$25	Columbia 1253
3/16/63	80	15		2	Blood, Sweat & Tears	$20	Columbia 8730
7/27/63	26	68	●	3	Ring Of Fire (The Best Of Johnny Cash) [K]	$20	Columbia 8853
7/25/64	53	17	●	4	I Walk The Line	$20	Columbia 8990
					includes 6 newly recorded Sun label hits		
11/7/64	47	13		5	Bitter Tears (Ballads of The American Indian)	$20	Columbia 9048
3/20/65	49	13		6	Orange Blossom Special	$20	Columbia 9109
7/9/66	88	9		7	Everybody Loves A Nut [N]	$20	Columbia 9292
7/22/67+	82	71	▲²	8	Johnny Cash's Greatest Hits, Volume 1 [G]	$20	Columbia 9478
10/7/67	194	3		9	Carryin' On with Johnny Cash & June Carter	$20	Columbia 9528
					JOHNNY CASH & JUNE CARTER		
6/15/68	13	122	▲²	10	Johnny Cash At Folsom Prison [L]	$20	Columbia 9639
2/15/69	54	20		11	The Holy Land	$12	Columbia 9726
					gospel music with narrative		
7/5/69	1⁴	70	▲²	12	**Johnny Cash At San Quentin** [L]	$12	Columbia 9827
9/27/69	95	13		13	Original Golden Hits, Volume I [K]	$12	Sun 100
9/27/69	98	8		14	Original Golden Hits, Volume II [K]	$12	Sun 101
10/11/69	186	2		15	Johnny Cash [K]	$12	Harmony 11342
					reissue of earlier Columbia recordings		
11/29/69	164	6		16	Get Rhythm [K]	$12	Sun 105
12/27/69+	181	4		17	Showtime [K]	$12	Sun 106
12/27/69	197	2		18	Story Songs Of The Trains And Rivers [K]	$12	Sun 104
2/14/70	6	30	●	19	**Hello, I'm Johnny Cash**	$10	Columbia 9943
5/16/70	186	3		20	The Singing Story Teller [K]	$10	Sun 115
					all Sun albums were recorded from 1955-58		
6/6/70	54	34	●	21	The World Of Johnny Cash [K]	$12	Columbia 29 [2]
11/14/70	44	18		22	The Johnny Cash Show [L]	$12	Columbia 30100
					recorded at the Grand Ole Opry		
12/12/70	176	6		23	I Walk The Line [S]	$12	Columbia 30397
					the film is based on the novel *An Exile*		
6/26/71	56	12		24	Man In Black	$12	Columbia 30550
10/23/71	94	8	●	25	The Johnny Cash Collection (His Greatest Hits, Volume II) [G]	$12	Columbia 30887
4/29/72	112	9		26	A Thing Called Love	$12	Columbia 31332
9/16/72	176	7		27	Johnny Cash: America (A 200-Year Salute In Story And Song)	$12	Columbia 31645
2/24/73	188	4		28	Any Old Wind That Blows	$12	Columbia 32091
7/17/76	185	2		29	One Piece At A Time	$12	Columbia 34193

Accidentally On Purpose (21)
All Of God's Children Ain't Free (6)
Amazing Grace (medley) (23)
Amen (6)
Another Man Done Gone (2)
Any Old Wind That Blows (28)
Apache Tears (5)
Arkansas Lovin' Man (26)
As Long As The Grass Shall Grow (5)
At Calvary (11)
At The Wailing Wall (11)
Austin Prison (7)
Bad News (4,15)
Ballad Of A Teenage Queen (14,17) *14*
Ballad Of Annie Palmer (28)
Ballad Of Ira Hayes (5,8)
Battle Of New Orleans (27)
Beautiful Words (11)
Begin West Movement (27)
Belshazah (16)
Best Friend (28)
Big Battle (3,27)
Big Foot (27)
Big River (4,14,17,18,25) *flip*
Blistered (19,25) *50*
Blue Train (18)
Boa Constrictor (7)
Bonanza! (3) *94*
Boy Named Sue (12,25) *2*
Bug That Tried To Crawl Around The World (7)
Busted (2,21)
Casey Jones (2,21)
'Cause I Love You (19,23)

Chain Gang (2)
Church Of The Holy Sepulchre (11)
Cocaine Blues (10)
Come Along And Ride This Train Medley I & II (22)
Come In Stranger (14,17,20) *66*
Come Take A Trip In My Airship (7)
Come To The Wailing Wall (11)
Committed To Parkview (29)
Country Boy (16)
Country Trash (28)
Cry, Cry, Cry (13,17)
Cup Of Coffee (7)
Custer (5)
Daddy (26)
Daddy Sang Bass (11,25) *42*
Danny Boy (6)
Dark As The Dungeon (10)
Darling Companion (12)
Daughter Of A Railroad Man (29)
Dear Mrs. (24)
Della's Gone (19)
Devil To Pay (19)
Dirty Old Egg-Sucking Dog (7,10)
Doin' My Time (16)
Don't Make Me Go (13)
Don't Take Your Guns To Town (1,8) *32*
Don't Think Twice, It's All Right (6,15)
Down The Street To 301 (18) *85*
Drums (5)

Everybody Loves A Nut (7) *96*
Face Of Despair (23)
Fast Boat To Sydney (9)
Five Feet High And Rising (8) *76*
Flesh And Blood [includes 2 versions] (23) *54*
Flushed From The Bathroom Of Your Heart (10)
Folsom Prison Blues (4,10,12,13,17,25) *32*
Forty Shades Of Green (9)
Fourth Man (11)
Frankie's Man, Johnny (1,15,21,25) *57*
Get Rhythm (13,16) *60*
Gettysburg Address (27)
Give My Love To Rose (4,10,14,20)
Go On Blues (29)
God Is Not Dead (11)
Good Earth (28)
Goodbye, Little Darlin' Goodbye (4,20)
Green, Green Grass Of Home (10)
Greystone Chapel (10)
Guess Things Happen That Way (14,17,25) *11*
He Turned The Water Into Wine (11)
Here Was A Man (22)
Hey Good Lookin' (20)
Hey Porter (4,13,17,25)
Home Of The Blues (13) *88*
Hungry (23)
I Can't Help It (20)

I Could Never Be Ashamed Of You (20)
I Couldn't Keep From Crying (20)
I Feel Better All Over (21)
I Forgot More Than You'll Ever Know (21)
I Got A Woman (20)
I Got Stripes (10)
I Heard That Lonesome Whistle (18)
I Just Thought You'd Like To Know (14) *85*
I Love You Because (20)
I Promise You (26)
I Still Miss Someone (1,3,4,10,15,21)
I Talk To Jesus Every Day (24)
I Walk The Line (4,8,12,13,17,23) *17*
I Want To Go Home (21)
I'd Rather Die Young (1)
I'd Still Be There (3)
I'm Gonna Try To Be That Way (22)
I'm So Lonesome I Could Cry (21)
I've Got A Thing About Trains (19)
If I Had A Hammer (28)
If I Were A Carpenter (19,25) *36*
If Not For Love (24)
In A Young Girl's Mind (29)
In Bethlehem (11)
In Garden Of Gethsemane (11)
In The Jailhouse Now (21)

In Them Old Cottonfields Back Home (21)
It Ain't Me, Babe (6,8,9) *58*
Jackson (8,9,10)
Jesus Was A Carpenter (19)
Joe Bean (7)
Just About Time (14)
Kate (26) *75*
Kentucky Straight (28)
Land Of Israel (11)
Legend Of John Henry's Hammer (2,21)
Let There Be Country (29)
Life Goes On (18)
Like A Young Colt (27)
Long Black Veil (6,10,15)
Long-Legged Guitar Pickin' Man (9,25)
Look For Me (24)
Lorena (15,27)
Love Has Lost Again (29)
Loving Gift (28)
Luther's Boogie (14,16)
Mama, You Been On My Mind (22)
Man In Black (24) *58*
Mean Eyed Cat (16)
Melva's Wine (26)
Michigan City Howdy Do (29)
Miracle Man (26)
Mississippi Sand (26)
Mister Garfield (27)
Mother's Love (11)
Mountain Lady (29)
My Shoes Keep Walking Back To You (21)
My Wife June At Sea Of Galilee (11)
Nazarene (11)

Ned Kelly (24)
New Mexico (16)
Next In Line (13,20) *99*
Nine Pound Hammer (2,15)
No, No, No (9)
Oh Lonesome Me (16) *93*
Oh, What A Good Thing We Had (9)
On The Via Dolorosa (11)
On Wheels And Wings (27)
One More Ride (1,21)
One On The Right Is On The Left (7,8) *46*
One Piece At A Time (29) *29*
Oney (28)
Opening The West (27)
Orange Blossom Special (6,8,10) *80*
Orphan Of The Road (24)
Our Guide Jacob At Mount Tabor (11)
Pack Up Your Sorrows (9)
Papa Was A Good Man (26)
Paul Revere (27)
Pickin' Time (1,21)
Please Don't Play Red River Valley (7)
Port Of Lonely Hearts (18)
Preacher Said, "Jesus Said" (24)
Proud Land (27)
Reaching For The Stars (27)
Rebel - Johnny Yuma (3,8)
Remember The Alamo (3,27)
Ring Of Fire (3,8) *17*
Road To Kaintuck (27)
Rock Island Line (17,18) *93*
Roughneck (2)

DEBUT DATE	PEAK POS	WKS CHR	GOLD	ARTIST — Album Title	$	Label & Number

CASH, Johnny — Cont'd

Route #1, Box 144 (19)
Run Softly, Blue River (1)
San Quentin (12)
See Ruby Fall (19) **75**
Send A Picture Of Mother (10)
Shantytown (9)
Shepherd Of My Heart (1)
Sing A Traveling Song (19)
Sing It Pretty, Sue (21)
Singin' In Viet Nam Talkin' Blues (24)
Singing Star's Queen (7)
So Doggone Lonesome (13)
Sold Out Of Flagpoles (29)
Southwestward (27)

Southwind (19)
Standing On The Promises (medley) (23)
Starkville City Jail (12)
Still In Town (4)
Streets Of Laredo (15)
Sugartime (16)
Sunday Morning Coming Down (22,25) **46**
Supper-Time (1,21)
Take Me Home (7)
Talking Leaves (5)
Tear Stained Letter (26)
Tell Him I'm Gone (2)
Ten Commandments (11)

Tennessee Flat-Top Box (3) **84**
Thanks A Lot (14)
That's All Over (1)
That's Enough (1)
There You Go (13,17)
(There'll Be) Peace In The Valley (For Me) (3,12)
These Are My People (27)
These Hands (22)
Thing Called Love (26)
This Is Nazareth (11)
This Side Of The Law (23)
This Town (23)
To Beat The Devil (19)

To The Shining Mountains (27)
Too Little, Too Late (28)
Town Of Cana (11)
Train Of Love (13,18)
Troubadour, The (1)
Troublesome Waters (4)
25 Minutes To Go (10)
Two Timin' Woman (16)
Understand Your Man (4,8) **35**
Vanishing Race (5)
Waiting For A Train (2,21)
Wall, The (6,10)
Wanted Man (12)

Ways Of A Woman In Love (14,20) **24**
Welcome Back Jesus (28)
Were You There (When They Crucified My Lord) (3)
West, The (27)
What Do I Care (3) **52**
What'd I Say (9)
When It's Springtime In Alaska (It's Forty Below) (6)
When Papa Played The Dobro (15,21)
White Girl (5)
Wide Open Road (18)
Wildwood Flower (6)

World's Gonna Fall On You (23)
Wreck Of The Old 97 (4,12,17,18)
Wrinkled, Crinkled, Wadded Dollar Bill (19)
You Wild Colorado (6)
You Win Again (16)
You'll Be All Right (9)
You're The Nearest Thing To Heaven (14,20) *flip*
You've Got A New Light Shining In Your Eyes (24)

CASH, Rosanne
Born on 5/24/55 in Memphis. Daughter of Johnny Cash and Vivian Liberto. Raised by her mother in California, then moved to Nashville after high school graduation. Worked in the Johnny Cash Road Show. Married Rodney Crowell in 1979 and divorced in April 1992.

DEBUT DATE	PEAK POS	WKS CHR	GOLD	#	ARTIST — Album Title	$	Label & Number
3/28/81	26	32	●	1	Seven Year Ache	$8	Columbia 36965
7/10/82	76	12		2	Somewhere In The Stars	$8	Columbia 37570
6/22/85	101	21		3	Rhythm & Romance	$8	Columbia 39463
8/15/87+	138	20		4	King's Record Shop	$8	Columbia 40777
					produced by Rosanne's husband, Rodney Crowell		
4/1/89	152	7		5	Hits 1979-1989 [G]	$8	Columbia 45054
11/17/90	175	4		6	Interiors	$12	Columbia 46079

Ain't No Money (2)
Black And White (5)
Blue Moon With Heartache (1,5)
Closing Time (3)
Dance With The Tiger (6)
Down On Love (3)
Green, Yellow And Red (4)
Halfway House (3)
Hold On (3,5)
Hometown Blues (1)
I Can't Resist (1)

I Don't Have To Crawl (4)
I Don't Know Why You Don't Want Me (3,5)
I Don't Want To Spoil The Party (5)
I Look For Love (2)
I Want A Cure (6)
I Wonder (2,5)
If You Change Your Mind (1)
It Hasn't Happened Yet (2)
Land Of Nightmares (6)
Looking For A Corner (2)

Mirror Image (6)
My Baby Thinks He's A Train (1,5)
My Old Man (3)
Never Alone (3)
Never Be You (3,5)
Never Gonna Hurt (3)
No Memories Hangin' Around (5)
Oh Yes I Can (2)
On The Inside (6)
On The Surface (6)

Only Human (1)
Paralyzed (3)
Pink Bedroom (3)
Rainin' (1)
Real Me (4)
Real Woman (6)
Rosie Strike Back (4)
Runaway Train (4)
Second To No One (3)
Seven Year Ache (1,5) **22**
Somewhere In The Stars (2)
Somewhere Sometime (4)

Tennessee Flat Top Box (4,5)
That's How I Got To Memphis (2)
Third Rate Romance (2)
This World (6)
Way We Make A Broken Heart (4,5)
What Kinda Girl? (1)
What We Really Want (6)
Where Will The Words Come From? (1)

Why Don't You Quit Leaving Me Alone (4)
You Don't Have Very Far To Go (1)

CA$HFLOW
Atlanta funk-rap quartet — Kary Hubbert, lead singer.

DEBUT DATE	PEAK POS	WKS CHR	GOLD	#	ARTIST — Album Title	$	Label & Number
5/3/86	144	11			Ca$hflow	$8	Atl. Art. 826028

Can't Let Love Pass Us By
I Need Your Love

It's Just A Dream
Mine All Mine

Party Freak
Reach Out

Spending Money

CASHMAN & WEST
Duo of pop record producers/songwriters/singers Dennis "Terry Cashman" Minogue (b: 7/5/41) and Thomas "Tommy West" Picardo, Jr. (b: 8/17/42).

DEBUT DATE	PEAK POS	WKS CHR	GOLD	#	ARTIST — Album Title	$	Label & Number
10/14/72	168	8		1	A Song Or Two	$10	Dunhill 50126
8/11/73	192	2		2	Moondog Serenade	$10	Dunhill 50141

AM-FM Blues (2)
American City Suite (1) **27**
Because You're Free (1)
Follow The Man With The Music (2)

Girls Next Door (2)
I Belong To You (1)
If You Were A Rainbow (1)
Is It Raining In New York City (2)

It Ain't Easy (1)
King Of Rock 'N Roll (1)
Let Your Feelings Go (2)
Mixed Emotions (2)
Only A Woman Like You (1)

Six-Man Song Band (1)
Somebody Stole The Sun (2)
Songman (1) **59**
Time-Traveler (2)
We Let Love Slip Away (1)

Will You Be My Lady (2)

CASINOS, The
Nine-man pop group from Cincinnati formed by Gene Hughes (lead singer).

DEBUT DATE	PEAK POS	WKS CHR	GOLD	#	ARTIST — Album Title	$	Label & Number
5/13/67	187	4			Then You Can Tell Me Goodbye	$30	Fraternity 1019

Certain Girl
Gee Whiz
Gina

Hold On I'm Coming
I Still Love You
Magic Circle

Maybe
Rag Doll
Talk To Me

Then You Can Tell Me Goodbye 6
To Be Loved

What Kind Of Fool Am I

CASSIDY, David
Son of actor Jack Cassidy and actress Evelyn Ward. Born on 4/12/50 in New York City. Played Keith Partridge, the lead singer of TV's *The Partridge Family*. Married for a time to actress Kay Lenz.

DEBUT DATE	PEAK POS	WKS CHR	GOLD	#	ARTIST — Album Title	$	Label & Number
2/12/72	15	23	●	1	Cherish	$12	Bell 6070
11/11/72	41	17		2	Rock Me Baby	$12	Bell 1109
11/3/90	136	11		3	David Cassidy	$12	Enigma 73554

All Because Of You (1)
Being Together (1)
Blind Hope (1)
Boulevard Of Broken Dreams (3)
Cherish (1) **9**
Could It Be Forever (1) **37**
Go Now (2)

Hi-Heel Sneakers (3)
How Can I Be Sure (2) **25**
I Am A Clown (1)
I Just Wanna Make You Happy (1)
I Lost My Chance (1)
Labor Of Love (3)
Livin' Without You (3)

Lonely Too Long (2)
Lyin' To Myself (3) **27**
Message To The World (3)
My First Night Alone Without You (1)
(Oh No) No Way (1)
Prisoner (3)
Ricky's Tune (1)

Rock Me Baby (2) **38**
Soft As A Summer Shower (2)
Some Kind Of A Summer (2)
Song For A Rainy Day (2)
Song Of Love (2)
Stranger In Your Heart (3)
Two Time Loser (2)

Warm My Soul (2)
We Could Never Be Friends ('Cause We've Been Lovers Too Long) (1)
Where Is The Morning (1)
You Remember Me (3)

CASSIDY, Shaun
Born on 9/27/59 in Los Angeles. Son of actor Jack Cassidy and actress Shirley Jones. Played Joe Hardy on TV's *The Hardy Boys*. Shaun and David Cassidy are half-brothers. Cast member of the TV soap *General Hospital* in 1987.

DEBUT DATE	PEAK POS	WKS CHR	GOLD	#	ARTIST — Album Title	$	Label & Number
6/25/77	3	57	▲	1	Shaun Cassidy	$10	Warner 3067
11/26/77+	6	37	▲	2	Born Late	$10	Warner 3126
8/19/78	33	13	▲	3	Under Wraps	$10	Warner 3222

CASSIDY, Shaun — Cont'd

Amblin' (1)
Audrey (2)
Baby, Baby, Baby (2)
Be My Baby (1)
Carolina's Comin' Home (2)
Da Doo Ron Ron (1) *1*

Do You Believe In Magic (2) *31*
Girl Like You (2)
Hard Love (3)
Hey Deanie (2) *7*
Hey There Lonely Girl (1)
Holiday (1)

I Wanna Be With You (1)
It's Like Heaven (3)
It's Too Late (1)
It's Up To You (2)
Lie To Me (3)
Midnight Sun (3)
Morning Girl (1)

One More Night Of Your Love (3)
Our Night (3) *80*
Right Before Your Skies (3)
She's Right (3)
Strange Sensation (2)

Take Good Care Of My Baby (1)
Taxi Dancer (3)
Teen Dream (2)
That's Rock 'N' Roll (1) *3*
Walk Away (3)

CASTOR, Jimmy, Bunch

R&B singer/saxophonist/composer/arranger. Born on 6/2/43 in New York City. Formed the Jimmy Castor Bunch in 1972, with Gerry Thomas (keyboards), Doug Gibson (bass), Harry Jensen (guitar), Lenny Fridie, Jr. (congas) and Bobby Manigault (drums).

4/22/72	27	23		1 It's Just Begun	$12	RCA 4640
9/23/72	192	4		2 Phase Two	$12	RCA 4783
3/1/75	74	17		3 Butt Of Course	$10	Atlantic 18124
9/25/76	132	9		4 E-Man Groovin'	$10	Atlantic 18186

Bad (1)
Bertha Butt Boogie-Part 1 (3) *16*
Creation (1)
Daniel (3)
Dracula Pt. I & II (4)
E-Man Boogie (3)
E-Man Groovin' (4)

Everything Is Beautiful To Me (4)
Fanfare (2)
First Time Ever I Saw Your Face (2)
Hallucinations (3)
I Don't Want To Lose You (4)
I Love A Mellow Groove (4)

I Promise To Remember (1)
It's Just Begun (1)
L.T.D. (Life, Truth & Death) (1)
Let's Party Now (3)
Luther The Anthropoid (Ape Man) (2)
My Brightest Day (1)

One Precious Word (3)
Paradise (2)
Party Life (2)
Potential (3)
Psyche (1)
Say Leroy (The Creature From The Black Lagoon Is Your Father) (2)

Space Age (4)
Super Love (4)
Tribute To Jimi Medley (2)
Troglodyte (Cave Man) (1) *6*
When? (2)
You Better Be Good (Or The Devil Gon' Getcha) (1)

You Make Me Feel Brand New (3)

CATE BROS.

Pop duo of twins Ernie (vocals, piano) and Earl Cate (guitar), born on 12/26/42 in Fayetteville, Arkansas.

2/7/76	158	9		1 Cate Bros.	$8	Asylum 1050
10/30/76	182	2		2 In One Eye And Out The Other	$8	Asylum 1080

Always Waiting (1)
Can't Change My Heart (1) *91*
Can't Stop (2)
Easy Way Out (1)

Give It All To You (2)
I Don't Want Nobody (Standing Over Me) (1)
I Just Wanna Sing (1)

In One Eye And Out The Other (2)
Lady Luck (1)
Let's Just Let It Be (2)
Livin' On Dreams (1)

Music Making Machine (2)
Standin' On A Mountain Top (1)
Start All Over Again (2)
Stuck In Chicago (2)

Time For Us (1)
Travelin' Man (2)
Union Man (1) *24*
When Love Comes (1)
Where Can We Go (2)

CAT MOTHER and the ALL NIGHT NEWS BOYS

New York rock quintet produced by Jimi Hendrix.

7/5/69	55	15		The Street Giveth...And The Street Taketh Away	$20	Polydor 4001

Bad News
Boston Burglar

Bramble Bush
Can You Dance To It?

Charlie's Waltz
Good Old Rock 'N Roll *21*
How I Spent My Summer

Marie
Probably Won't

Track In "A" (Nebraska Nights)

CAUSE & EFFECT

Northern California-based duo: Sean Rowley (keyboards) and British-born Robert Rowe (vocals, guitar). Joined on tour by drummer Evan Parandes, then Richard Shepherd. Rowley died of asthma-related cardiac arrest on 11/12/92 (age 23).

4/4/92	141	11		Another Minute	$12	SRC 11019

Another Minute *75*
Beginning Of The End

Echoing Green
Farewell To Arms

New World
Nothing Comes To Mind

Something New
What Do You See

You Think You Know Her *[includes 2 versions]* *38*

C.C.S.

British jazz-rock band featuring blues guitarist Alexis Korner (d: 1984). Name stands for Collective Consciousness Society. Korner's Blues Inc., pioneer blues-rock band of the early 1960s, featured future Rolling Stones members and other rock notables.

4/3/71	197	2		Whole Lotta Love	$15	RAK 30559

Boom Boom
Dos Cantos

(I Can't Get No) Satisfaction
Living In The Past

Lookin' For Fun
Sunrise

Wade In The Water
Waiting Song

Walking
Whole Lotta Love *58*

CELI BEE & THE BUZZY BUNCH

Puerto Rican disco band led by female vocalist Celinas.

7/23/77	169	5		Celi Bee & The Buzzy Bunch	$8	APA 77001

Closer, Closer

Hurt Me, Hurt Me

It's Sad

One Love

Smile

Superman *41*

CENTRAL LINE

London-based R&B group consisting of Linton Beckles (vocals, percussion), Henry Defoe (guitar), Lipson Francis (keyboards) and Camelle Hinds (bass).

1/9/82	145	9		Central Line	$8	Mercury 4033

Breaking Point
Don't Tell Me

Goodbye
I Need Your Love

Shake It Up

That's No Way To Treat My Love

Walking Into Sunshine *84*

CERRONE

Composer/producer/drummer. Born Jean-Marc Cerrone in France in 1952. Also see Kongas.

2/26/77	153	10		1 Love In C Minor	$8	Cotillion 9913
8/6/77	162	5		2 Cerrone's Paradise	$8	Cotillion 9917
1/21/78	129	8		3 Cerrone 3 - Supernature	$8	Cotillion 5202
11/18/78+	118	13		4 Cerrone IV - The Golden Touch	$8	Cotillion 5208

Black Is Black (1)
Cerrone's Paradise (2)
Give Me Love (3)

In The Smoke (3)
Je Suis Music (4)
Look For Love (4)

Love In 'C' Minor - Pt. I (1) *36*
Love Is Here (3)

Love Is The Answer (3)
Midnite Lady (1)
Music Of Life (4)

Rocket In The Pocket (4)
Supernature (3) *70*
Sweet Drums (3)

Take Me (2)
Time For Love (2)

CETERA, Peter

Born on 9/13/44 in Chicago. Lead singer/bass guitarist of Chicago for their first 17 albums.

1/23/82	143	10		1 Peter Cetera	$8	Full Moon 3624
7/12/86	23	43	●	2 Solitude/Solitaire	$8	Warner 25474
8/20/88	58	17		3 One More Story	$8	Full Moon 25704
8/8/92	163	9		4 World Falling Down	$12	Warner 26894

CETERA, Peter — Cont'd

Best Of Times (3) 59
Big Mistake (2) 61
Body Language (There In The Dark) (3)
Daddy's Girl (2)
Dip Your Wings (4)
Even A Fool Can See (4)
Evil Eye (1)

Feels Like Heaven (4) 72↑
Glory Of Love (2) 1
Have You Ever Been In Love (4)
Heaven Help This Lonely Man (3)
Holding Out (3)
Holy Moly (1)

How Many Times (1)
I Can Feel It (1)
Ivy Covered Walls (1)
Karate Kid Part II, Theme From The ...see: Glory Of Love
Last Place God Made (4)
Livin' In The Limelight (1)

Man In Me (4)
Mona Mona (1)
Next Time I Fall (2) 1
Not Afraid To Cry (1)
On The Line (1)
One Good Woman (3) 4
One More Story (3)
Only Love Knows Why (2)

Peace Of Mind (3)
Practical Man (1)
Queen Of The Masquerade Ball (2)
Restless Heart (4) 35
Save Me (3)
Scheherazade (3)
Solitude/Solitaire (2)

They Don't Make 'Em Like They Used To (2)
Wake Up To Love (2)
Where There's No Tomorrow (4)
Wild Ways (4)
World Falling Down (4)
You Never Listen To Me (3)

CHACKSFIELD, Frank, And His Orchestra

Frank was born on 5/9/14 in Sussex, England.

DEBUT DATE	PEAK POS	WKS CHR		ARTIST — Album Title	$	Label & Number
1/9/61	36	14	1	Ebb Tide	$15	Richmond 30078
11/28/64	120	9	2	The New Ebb Tide	$12	London P. 4 44053

Among My Souvenirs (1)
Autumn Leaves (1)
Boulevard Of Broken Dreams (1)

Deep Purple (2)
Deep River (2)
Ebb Tide (1,2)
How Deep Is The Ocean (2)

I Only Have Eyes For You (1)
Limelight (1)
Love By Starlight (1)
Moon River (2)

Moonlight On The Ganges (2)
Red Sails In The Sunset (1)
Sea, The (2)
Sea Mist (2)

Shenandoah (2)
Sleepy Lagoon (2)
Smoke Gets In Your Eyes (1)
Stranger On The Shore (1)

Victory At Sea (2)

CHAD & JEREMY

Folk-rock duo formed in the early 1960s: Chad Stuart (b: 12/10/43, England) and Jeremy Clyde (b: 3/22/44, England). Broke up in 1967. Re-formed briefly in 1982.

DEBUT DATE	PEAK POS	WKS CHR		ARTIST — Album Title	$	Label & Number
9/26/64+	22	39	1	Yesterday's Gone	$25	World Art. 2002
3/27/65	69	14	2	Chad & Jeremy Sing For You	$25	World Art. 2005
6/26/65	37	18	3	Before And After	$20	Columbia 9174
11/6/65	77	11	4	I Don't Want To Lose You Baby	$20	Columbia 9198
4/23/66	49	23	5	The Best Of Chad & Jeremy	[G] $15	Capitol 2470
8/20/66	144	4	6	More Chad & Jeremy	$15	Capitol 2546
				above 2 albums feature World Artists' recordings		
9/24/66	61	14	7	Distant Shores	$20	Columbia 9364
11/11/67	186	5	8	Of Cabbages And Kings	$20	Columbia 9471

Ain't It Nice (7)
Baby Don't Go (4)
Before And After (3) 17
Busman's Holiday (8)
Can I See You (8)
Can't Get Used To Losing You (3)
Dirty Old Town (1,6)
Distant Shores (7) 30
Don't Make Me Do It (7)
Don't Think Twice, It's All Right (4)
Donna, Donna (2,6)
Early Mornin' Rain (7)

Everyone's Gone To The Moon (7)
Evil-Hearted Me (3)
Family Way (8)
Fare Thee Well (I Must Be Gone) (3)
For Lovin' Me (3)
Four Strong Winds (2,6)
From A Window (2,5) 97
Funny How Love Can Be (4)
Gentle Cold Of Dawn (8)
Girl From Ipanema (2,6)
Girl Who Sang The Blues (3)
Homeward Bound (7)

I Don't Wanna Lose You Baby (4) 35
I Have Dreamed (4) 91
I Won't Cry (7)
I'll Get Around To It When And If I Can (8)
I'm In Love Again (3)
If I Loved You (5) 23
If She Was Mine (1)
If You've Got A Heart (2,5)
It Was A Very Good Year (6)
Lemon Tree (6)
Like I Love You Today (1,5)

Little Does She Know (3)
Morning (7)
Mr. Tambourine Man (4)
My Coloring Book (2,6)
My How The Time Goes By (2,5)
No Other Baby (2)
No Tears For Johnnie (1,6)
Now And Forever (1,8)
Only For The Young (1)
Only Those In Love (2,5)
Progress Suite - Movements 1 Thru 5 (8)
Rest In Peace (8)

Say It Isn't True (3)
September In The Rain (1,6)
Should I (4)
Sleep Little Boy (2)
Summer Song (1,5) 7
Tell Me Baby (3)
There But For Fortune (4)
These Things You Don't Forget (4)
Too Soon My Love (1,5)
Truth Often Hurts The Heart (1,6)
Way You Look Tonight (7)

What Do You Want With Me (2,3,5) 51
When Your Love Has Gone (7)
Why Should I Care (3)
Willow Weep For Me (1,5) 15
Woman In You (4)
Yesterday's Gone (1,5) 21
You Are She (7) 87
You Know What (2)

CHAIRMEN OF THE BOARD

Soul vocal group formed in Detroit in 1969. Consisted of General Norman Johnson, Danny Woods, Harrison Kennedy and Eddie Curtis. First recorded for Invictus in 1969. Johnson was leader of The Showmen from 1961-67; wrote "Patches," hit for Clarence Carter. Johnson went solo in 1976.

DEBUT DATE	PEAK POS	WKS CHR		ARTIST — Album Title	$	Label & Number
5/2/70	133	10	1	Give Me Just A Little More Time	$15	Invictus 7300
11/28/70+	117	16	2	In Session	$15	Invictus 7304
5/6/72	178	3	3	Bittersweet	$15	Invictus 9801

All We Need Is Understanding (2)
Bittersweet (3)
Bless You (1)
Bravo, Horray (1)
Bridge Over Troubled Water (2)

Chairman Of The Board (2) 42
Children Of Today (2)
Come Together (1)
Didn't We (1)
Elmo James (3)
Everything's Tuesday (2) 38

Feelin' Alright? (1)
Give Me Just A Little More Time (1) 3
Hanging On To A Memory (2)
I Can't Find Myself (2)
I'll Come Crawling (1)
I'm A Sign Of Changing Times (3)

I'm On My Way To A Better Place (3)
It Was Almost Something (2)
Men Are Getting Scarce (3)
My Way (1)
Patches (1,2)
Pay To The Piper (2) 13
Saginaw County Line (3)

Since The Days Of Pigtails (And Fairy Tales) (1)
So Glad You're Mine (3)
Tricked & Trapped (1)
Twelfth Of Never (2)
Weary Traveler (3)
When Will She Tell Me She Needs Me (2)

Working On A Building Of Love (3)
(You've Got Me) Dangling On A String (1) 38

CHAKACHAS, The

Band led by the fictional Gaston Boogaerts. Actually was a sextet of Belgian studio musicians. Bario, a New York Latino group, posed as The Chakachas on tour.

DEBUT DATE	PEAK POS	WKS CHR		ARTIST — Album Title	$	Label & Number
4/8/72	117	11		Jungle Fever	[F] $10	Polydor 5504

Ay Mulata
Cha Ka Cha

Chica Chica Bau Bau
El Canyon Rojo

El Rico Son
Eso Es El Amor

Harlem Nocturne
Jungle Fever 8

Latin Can Can
Un Rayo Del Sol

Yo Soy Cubano

CHAKIRIS, George

Born on 9/16/34 in Norwood, Ohio. Portrayed Bernardo (leader of the Sharks gang) in the film West Side Story.

DEBUT DATE	PEAK POS	WKS CHR		ARTIST — Album Title	$	Label & Number
9/1/62	28	16	1	George Chakiris	$15	Capitol 1750
2/2/63	45	17	2	Memories Are Made Of These	$15	Capitol 1813

All I Need Is The Girl (1)
Autumn Leaves (2)
By Myself (1)
Fever (2)
Hallelujah, I Love Her So (2)
I Believe In You (1)

I Left My Heart In San Francisco (1)
I'm Falling In Love With Someone (1)
Ill Wind (1)
Lollipops And Roses (2)

Lot Of Livin' To Do (1)
Maria (1)
Memories Are Made Of This (2)
Moon River (2)
Mr. Lucky (1)

Naked City Theme (Somewhere In The Night) (2)
Once Upon A Time (1)
One Girl (1)
Second Time Around (2)

Taste Of Honey (2)
Tonight (1)
Two For The Seesaw (A Second Chance), Song From (2)
Witchcraft (2)

You Stepped Out Of A Dream (1)

CHAMBERLAIN, Richard

Born on 3/31/35 in Los Angeles. Leading film, theater and TV actor. Played lead role in TV's Dr. Kildare, 1961-66.

DEBUT DATE	PEAK POS	WKS CHR		ARTIST — Album Title	$	Label & Number
2/2/63	5	36		Richard Chamberlain Sings	$20	MGM 4088

All I Do Is Dream Of You
All I Have To Do Is Dream 14

Dr. Kildare (Three Stars Will Shine Tonight), Theme From 10
Hi-Lili, Hi-Lo 64

I Hadn't Anyone Till You
I Will Love You 65
I'll Be Around

It's A Lonesome Old Town (When You're Not Around)
Love Me Tender 21
Quiet Kind Of Love

True Love 98

DEBUT DATE	PEAK POS	WKS CHR	GOLD	ARTIST — Album Title	$	Label & Number

CHAMBERS BROTHERS, The
Four Mississippi-born brothers: George (bass), Willie (guitar), Lester (harmonica) and Joe Chambers (guitar). Formed as a gospel group in Los Angeles in 1954. Drummer Brian Keenan added in 1965.

DEBUT DATE	PEAK POS	WKS CHR	GOLD	ARTIST — Album Title	$	Label & Number
2/17/68	4	58	●	1 The Time Has Come..............................	$15	Columbia 9522
10/12/68	16	21		2 A New Time-A New Day..........................	$15	Columbia 9671
12/27/69+	58	33		3 Love, Peace And Happiness..................[L]	$20	Columbia 20 [2]
				record 2: live at Bill Graham's Fillmore East		
12/5/70	193	2		4 The Chambers Brothers Greatest Hits..........[E]	$15	Vault 135 [2]
				reissue of 1965-1966 recordings		
2/27/71	145	7		5 New Generation	$15	Columbia 30032
12/4/71+	166	7		6 The Chambers Brothers' Greatest Hits.........[G]	$15	Columbia 30871

All Strung Out Over You (1,6)
Are You Ready (5,6)
Baby Please Don't Go (4)
Bang Bang (3)
Blues, Get Off My Shoulder (4)
Call Me (4)
Do Your Thing (2)
Don't Lose Your Cool (4)
Everybody Needs Somebody (3)
Funky (5,6)
Girls, We Love You (4)
Going To The Mill (5)
Guess Who (2)
Have A Little Faith (3)
High Heel Sneakers (4)
Hooka Tooka (4)
House Of The Rising Sun (4)
I Can't Stand It (1)
I Can't Turn You Loose (2,3,6) **37**
I Got It (medley) (4)
I Wish It Would Rain (2)
If You Want Me To (3)
In The Midnight Hour (1,6)
It Rained The Day You Left (4)
It's Groovin' Time (4)
Johnny B. Goode (4)
Just A Closer Walk With Thee (4)
Let's Do It (Do It Together) (3,6)
Love Is All I Have (2)
Love! Love! Love! (medley) (3)
Love, Peace And Happiness (3,6) **96**
New Generation (5)
New Time - A New Day (2)
No, No, No, Don't Say Good-By (2)
People Get Ready (1,3,4,6)
Please Don't Leave Me (1)
Pollution (5)
Practice What You Preach (5)
Pretty Girls Everywhere (4)
Reflections (5)
Rock Me Mama (2)
Romeo And Juliet (1)
Satisfy You (2)
Seventeen (4)
Shout! - Part 1 (medley) (4) **83**
So Fine (4)
So Tired (1)
There She Goes (4)
Time Has Come Today (1,6) **11**
To Love Somebody (3)
Travel On My Way (4)
Undecided (3,4)
Uptown (1)
Wade In The Water (3)
Wake Up (3) **92**
What The World Needs Now Is Love (1)
When The Evening Comes (5)
Where Have All The Flowers Gone (2)
You Got The Power - To Turn Me On (2)
You're So Fine (3)
You've Got Me Running (4)
Young Girl (5)

CHAMPAIGN
Interracial sextet from Champaign, Illinois — Pauli Carman and Rena Jones, lead singers. Reduced to a duo of Pauli Carman and Rena Day.

DEBUT DATE	PEAK POS	WKS CHR	GOLD	ARTIST — Album Title	$	Label & Number
3/21/81	53	20		1 How 'Bout Us	$8	Columbia 37008
4/2/83	64	24		2 Modern Heart	$8	Columbia 38284
11/10/84	184	3		3 Woman in Flames...............................	$8	Columbia 39365

Be Mine Tonight (3)
Can You Find The Time? (1)
Capture The Moon (3)
Cool Running (2)
Dancin' Together Again (1)
Get It Again (2)
How 'Bout Us (1) **12**
I'm On Fire (1)
If One More Morning (1)
International Feel (2)
Intimate Strangers (3)
Keep It Up (2)
Let Your Body Rock (2)
Lighten Up (1)
Love Games (2)
Mardi Gras (3)
Off And On Love (3)
Party Line (2)
Party People (1)
Prisoner (1)
Spinnin' (1)
This Time (3)
Try Again (2) **23**
Walkin' (2)
Whiplash (1)
Woman In Flames (3)

CHAMPLIN, Bill
Leader of San Francisco's Sons Of Champlin for 13 years. Member of Chicago since 1982.

DEBUT DATE	PEAK POS	WKS CHR	GOLD	ARTIST — Album Title	$	Label & Number
2/6/82	178	4		1 Runaway	$8	Elektra 563

Fool Is All Alone
Gotta Get Back To Love
One Way Ticket
Runaway
Sara *61*
Satisfaction
Stop Knockin' On My Door
Take It Uptown
Tonight Tonight *55*
Without You

CHANDLER, Gene
R&B singer/producer. Born Eugene Dixon on 7/6/37 in Chicago. Formed the Gaytones at Englewood High School in 1955. Joined The Dukays vocal group in 1957. U.S. Army, Germany, 1957-60. Rejoined The Dukays in 1960; they first recorded for Nat in 1961. Group then recorded "Duke Of Earl" for Vee-Jay. Due to contract conflicts with Nat, Dixon left the group, changed his name to Gene Chandler and promoted "Duke Of Earl." Own label, Mr. Chand, 1969-73.

DEBUT DATE	PEAK POS	WKS CHR	GOLD	ARTIST — Album Title	$	Label & Number
3/31/62	69	8		1 The Duke Of Earl	$100	Vee-Jay 1040
1/8/66	124	3		2 Gene Chandler - Live On Stage In '65..........[L]	$25	Constellation 1425
10/31/70	178	9		3 The Gene Chandler Situation	$15	Mercury 61304
3/27/71	143	5		4 Gene & Jerry - One & One	$12	Mercury 61330
				GENE CHANDLER & JERRY BUTLER		
11/25/78+	47	20		5 Get Down	$10	Chi-Sound 578
8/25/79	153	3		6 When You're #1	$8	20th Century 598
6/7/80	87	18		7 Gene Chandler '80	$8	20th Century 605

Ain't No Use (2)
All About The Paper (7)
Am I Blue (3)
Be Yourself (4)
Big Lie (1)
Bless Our Love (2)
Bright Lights And You, Girl (3)
Daddy's Home (1)
Dance Fever (6)
Do It Baby (7)
Do What Comes So Natural (6)
Does She Have A Friend? (7)
Duke Of Earl (1) *1*
Everybody Is Waiting (4)
Festival Of Love (1)
Get It Again (2)
Give Me A Chance (3)
Give Me The Cue (5)
Give Up A Taste (1)
Greatest Love Ever Known (5)
Groovy Situation (3) *12*
Hallelujah, I Love Her So (3)
Hey, Little Angel (3)
I Found That I Was Wrong (4)
I Wake Up Crying (1)
I'll Be There (7)
I'll Follow You (1)
I'll Remember You (6)
I'm The Traveling Kind (5)
If You Can't Be True (2)
It's Your Love I'm After (3)
Just Be True (2)
Kissin' In The Kitchen (1)
Lay Me Gently (7)
Let Me Make Love To You (7)
Lonely Island (1)
Lovequake (5)
Mail Call Time (4)
Monkey Time (2)
Nite Owl (1)
Not The Marrying Kind (3)
One Hand Washes The Other (4)
Please Sunrise (5)
Rainbow '65 (Part I) (2) *69*
Rainbow '80 (7)
Sho' Is Groovin' (4)
Simply Call It Love (3) *75*
So Many Ways (1)
Song Called Soul (2)
Soul Hootenanny (2)
Stand By Me (1)
Stay Here In My Heart (6)
Ten And Two (Take This Woman Off The Corner) (4)
That Funky Disco Rhythm (6)
Tomorrow I May Not Feel The Same (5)
Turn On Your Love Light (1)
Unforgettable (3)
What Now (2,5)
When You're #1 (6) *99*
World Keeps Changing (4)
You Just Can't Win (By Making The Same Mistake) (4) *94*
You've Been So Sweet To Me (7)

CHANGE
European-American studio group formed by Italian producer Jacques Fred Petrus. Led by Paolo Granolio (guitar) and David Romani (bass). Luther Vandross sang on several songs from group's first two albums. Later group, based in New York, included lead vocals by James Robinson and Deborah "Crab" Cooper. One-time band member Rick Gallwey married Sharon Bryant, former lead singer of Atlantic Starr.

DEBUT DATE	PEAK POS	WKS CHR	GOLD	ARTIST — Album Title	$	Label & Number
5/10/80	29	25	●	1 The Glow Of Love	$8	RFC 3438
4/18/81	46	22		2 Miracles	$8	Atlantic 19301
5/15/82	66	9		3 Sharing Your Love	$8	Atlantic 19342
4/2/83	161	7		4 This Is Your Time................................	$8	Atlantic 80053
4/28/84	102	15		5 Change of Heart.................................	$8	Atlantic 80151

CHANGE — Cont'd

Angel (4)	Got To Get Up (4)	Lovely Lady (5)	Say You Love Me Again (5)	True Love (5)
Angel In My Pocket (1)	Hard Times (It's Gonna Be	Lover's Holiday (1) 40	Searching (1)	Very Best In You (3) 84
Change Of Heart (5)	Alright) (3)	Magical Night (4)	Sharing Your Love (3)	Warm (5)
Don't Wait Another Night (4)	Heaven Of My Life (2)	Miracles (2)	Stay 'N Fit (4)	You Are My Melody (5)
End, The (1)	Hold Tight (2) 89	Oh What A Night (3)	Stop For Love (2)	You'll Never Realize (4)
Everything And More (3)	It Burns Me Up (5)	On Top (2)	Take You To Heaven (3)	You're My Girl (3)
Glow Of Love (1)	It's A Girl's Affair (1)	Paradise (2) 80	Tell Me Why (4)	You're My Number 1 (3)
Got My Eyes On You (5)	Keep It On (3)	Promise Your Love (3)	This Is Your Time (4)	Your Move (2)

CHANNEL, Bruce

Born on 11/28/40 in Jacksonville, Texas. Appeared on *Louisiana Hayride* in 1958.

5/19/62	114	5		Hey! Baby (and 11 Other Songs About Your Baby)	$40	Smash 67008

Ain't Got No Home	Baby, You've Got What It	Chantilly Lace	Hey! Baby 1	Since I Met You Baby
Baby, It's You	Takes	Dream Baby	If Only I Had Known	Sorry Baby
	Breakin' Up Is Hard To Do	Dream Girl	Love Me	

CHANSON

Studio disco band. Lead vocals by James Jamerson Jr. and David Williams. Jamerson's father was a prominent Motown bassist.

10/14/78+	41	21		Chanson	$8	Ariola 50039

All The Time You Need	Did You Ever	Don't Hold Back 21	I Can Tell	I Love You More	Why

CHANTAY'S

Teenage surf-rock quintet from Santa Ana, California: Bob Spickard (lead guitar), Brian Carman (rhythm guitar), Rob Marshall (piano), Warren Waters (bass) and Bob Welsh (drums).

5/18/63	26	18		Pipeline	[I]	$40	Dot 25516

Banzai	El Conquistador	Lonesome Road	Pipeline 4	Runaway	Tragic Wind
Blunderbus	Last Night	Night Theme	Riders In The Sky	Sleep Walk	Wayward Nile

★★354★★ CHAPIN, Harry

Folk-rock balladeer. Born on 12/7/42 in New York City. As a child, was a member of the Brooklyn Heights Boys Choir. Documentary filmmaker in the '60s. Signed to Elektra in 1971. Died in an auto accident on 7/16/81.

3/18/72	60	27		1 Heads & Tales	$10	Elektra 75023
10/28/72	160	8		2 Sniper and Other Love Songs	$10	Elektra 75042
12/29/73+	61	23		3 Short Stories	$10	Elektra 75065
9/7/74	4	33	●	4 Verities & Balderdash	$10	Elektra 1012
10/4/75	53	8		5 Portrait Gallery	$10	Elektra 1041
5/1/76	48	19	●	6 Greatest Stories-Live	[L]	$12	Elektra 2009 [2]
10/30/76	87	6		7 On The Road To Kingdom Come	$10	Elektra 1082
9/17/77	58	10		8 Dance Band On The Titanic	$12	Elektra 301 [2]
7/1/78	133	8		9 Living Room Suite	$10	Elektra 142
10/27/79	163	3		10 Legends Of The Lost And Found - New Greatest Stories Live	[L]	$12	Elektra 703 [2]
11/1/80	58	15		11 Sequel	$8	Boardwalk 36872

And The Baby Never Cries (2)	Dirt Gets Under The	If You Want To Feel (9)	One Light In A Dark Valley	Sniper (2)	30,000 Pounds Of Bananas
Any Old Kind Of Day (1)	Fingernails (5)	It Seems You Only Love Me	(An Imitation Spiritual) (8)	Somebody Said (9)	(4,6)
Babysitter (5)	Dogtown (1)	When It Rains (8)	Paint A Picture Of Yourself	Someone Keeps Calling My	Up On The Shelf (11)
Barefoot Boy (2)	Dreams Go By (5,6)	Jenny (9)	(Michael) (8)	Name (5)	Vacancy (4)
Better Place To Be (Parts 1	Empty (1)	Laugh Man (7)	Parade's Still Passing By (7)	Sometime, Somewhere Wife	WOLD (3,6) 36
& 2) (2,6) 86	Everybody's Lonely (1)	Legends Of The Lost And	Poor Damned Fool (9,10)	(1)	We Grew Up A Little Bit (8)
Bluesman (8)	Fall In Love With Him (7)	Found (10)	Pretzel Man (1)	Song For Myself (3)	We Were Three (10)
Bummer (5)	Flowers Are Red (9,10)	Let Time Go Lightly (6)	Remember When The Music	Song Man (3)	What Made America
Burning Herself (2)	Get On With It (10)	Love Is Just Another Word	(11)	Star Tripper (5)	Famous? (4)
Caroline (7)	God Babe, You've Been	(6)	Rock, The (5)	Stop Singing These Sad	Why Do Little Girls (9)
Cat's In The Cradle (4,6) 1	Good For Me (11)	Mail Order Annie (3,10)	Roll Down The River (7)	Songs (5)	Why Should People Stay The
Changes (3)	Greyhound (1)	Manhood (8)	Salt And Pepper (11)	Story Of A Life (11)	Same (8)
Circle (2,6)	Halfway To Heaven (4)	Mayor Of Candor Lied (7)	Same Sad Singer (1)	Stranger With The Melodies	Winter Song (2)
Copper (10)	I Do It For You, Jane (8)	Mercenaries (8)	Sandy (5)	(10)	Woman Child (2)
Corey's Coming (7,10)	I Finally Found It Sandy (11)	Mismatch (8)	Saturday Morning (6)	Sunday Morning Sunshine	You Are The Only Song (10)
Could You Put Your Light	I Miss America (11)	Mr. Tanner (3,6)	Sequel (11) 23	(2) 75	
On, Please (1)	I Wanna Learn A Love	My Old Lady (8)	She Is Always Seventeen (6)	Tangled Up Puppet (5,10)	
Country Dreams (8)	Song (4,6) 44	Northwest 222 (11)	She Sings Songs Without	Taxi (1,6) 24	
Dance Band On The Titanic	I Wonder What Happened To	Odd Job Man (10)	Words (4)	There Only Was One Choice	
(8)	Him (2)	Old College Avenue (3)	Shooting Star (4)	(8)	
Dancin' Boy (9)	I Wonder What Would	Old Folks (10)	Short Stories (3)	There's A Lot Of Lonely	
Day They Closed The	Happen To This World (9)	On The Road To Kingdom	Shortest Story (6)	People Tonight (3)	
Factory Down (10)	If My Mary Were Here (7,10)	Come (7)	Six String Orchestra (4)	They Call Her Easy (3)	

CHAPMAN, Tracy

Boston-based singer/songwriter. Born in Cleveland. Graduated from Tufts University in 1986 with an anthropology degree. Won the 1988 Best New Artist Grammy Award.

4/30/88	1[1]	61	▲[3]	1 Tracy Chapman	$8	Elektra 60774
10/21/89	9	26	▲	2 Crossroads	$8	Elektra 60888
5/16/92	53	11		3 Matters Of The Heart	$12	Elektra 61215

Across The Lines (1)	Behind The Wall (1)	For My Lover (1)	If These Are The Things (3)	She's Got Her Ticket (1)	This Time (2)
All That You Have Is Your	Born To Fight (2)	For You (1)	Love That You Had (3)	Short Supply (3)	Why? (1)
Soul (2)	Bridges (2)	Freedom Now (2)	Material World (2)	So (3)	Woman's Work (3)
Baby Can I Hold You (1) 48	Crossroads (2) 90	Hundred Years (2)	Matters Of The Heart (3)	Subcity (2)	
Bang Bang Bang (3)	Dreaming On A World (3)	I Used To Be A Sailor (3)	Mountains O' Things (1)	Talkin' 'Bout A Revolution	
Be Careful Of My Heart (2)	Fast Car (1) 6	If Not Now... (1)	Open Arms (3)	(1) 75	

CHARLATANS UK, The

Manchester, England-based rock quintet led by vocalist Tim Burgess.

11/10/90+	73	27		1 Some Friendly	$12	Begr. B. 2411
5/2/92	173	2		2 Between 10th & 11th	$12	Begr. B. 61108

DEBUT DATE	PEAK POS	WKS CHR	GOLD	ARTIST — Album Title	$	Label & Number

CHARLATANS UK, The — Cont'd

Believe You Me (1)	Flower (1)	(No One) Not Even The Rain (2)	Opportunity (1)	Sproston Green (1)	Weirdo (2)
Can't Even Be Bothered (2)	I Don't Want To See The Sights (2)	109 pt2 (1)	Page One (2)	Subtitle (2)	White Shirt (1)
Chewing Gum Weekend (2)	Ignition (2)	Only One I Know (1)	Polar Bear (1)	Then (1)	You're Not Very Well (1)
End Of Everything (2)			Sonic (1)	Tremelo Song (2)	

CHARLENE

Pop singer Charlene Duncan (nee: D'Angelo). Born on 6/1/50 in Hollywood.

DEBUT DATE	PEAK POS	WKS CHR	GOLD	ARTIST — Album Title	$	Label & Number
4/10/82	36	20		1 I've Never Been To Me	$8	Motown 6009
11/27/82	162	7		2 Used To Be	$8	Motown 6027

After The Ball (1)	I Need A Man (1)	I've Never Been To Me (1) 3	It Ain't Easy Comin' Down (1) 97	Rainbows (2)	Used To Be (2) 46
Can't We Try (1)	I Want To Go Back There Again (1)	If I Could See Myself (1)	Johnny Doesn't Love Here Anymore (1)	Richie's Song (For Richard Oliver) (2)	You're Home (2)
Heaven Help Us All (2)	I Won't Remember Ever Loving You (1)	If You Take Away The Pain Until The Morning (2)	Last Song (2)	Some Things Never Change (2)	
Hey Mama (1)					
Hungry (1)					

★★20★★ CHARLES, Ray

Born Ray Charles Robinson on 9/23/30 in Albany, Georgia. To Greenville, Florida while still an infant. Partially blind at age five, completely blind at seven (glaucoma). Studied classical piano and clarinet at State School for Deaf and Blind Children, St. Augustine, Florida, 1937-45. With local Florida bands; moved to Seattle in 1948. Formed the McSon Trio (also known as the Maxim Trio and the Maxine Trio) with Gossady McGhee (guitar) and Milton Garred (bass). First recordings were very much in the King Cole Trio style. Formed own band in 1954. The 1950s female vocal group, The Cookies, became his backing group The Raeletts. Inducted into the Rock and Roll Hall of Fame in 1986. Recipient of the Grammy Lifetime Achievement Award in 1987. Popular performer with many TV and film appearances.

DEBUT DATE	PEAK POS	WKS CHR	GOLD	ARTIST — Album Title	$	Label & Number
2/15/60	17	82		1 The Genius Of Ray Charles	$30	Atlantic 1312
7/18/60	13	37		2 Ray Charles In Person ....[L]	$30	Atlantic 8039
				recorded on 5/28/59 at Herndon Stadium, Atlanta		
10/10/60	9	50		3 **The Genius Hits The Road**	$25	ABC-Para. 335
3/6/61	11	31		4 Dedicated To You	$25	ABC-Para. 355
3/27/61	4	48		5 **Genius + Soul = Jazz**	$25	Impulse! 2
				featuring top jazz artists including Count Basie's band		
8/28/61+	20	73		6 What'd I Say ....[K]	$30	Atlantic 8029
8/28/61	49	17		7 The Genius After Hours ....[K-I]	$30	Atlantic 1369
9/4/61	52	15		8 Ray Charles & Betty Carter	$25	ABC-Para. 385
				RAY CHARLES & BETTY CARTER jazz singer Carter (b: 1930 in Flint, Michigan) worked with Miles Davis		
11/13/61+	73	12		9 The Genius Sings The Blues ....[K]	$25	Atlantic 8052
12/18/61+	11	52		10 Do The Twist! ....[K]	$25	Atlantic 8054
4/21/62	1¹⁴	101	●	11 **Modern Sounds In Country And Western Music**	$25	ABC-Para. 410
8/11/62	14	38		12 The Ray Charles Story ....[K]	$35	Atlantic 900 [2]
				all of above Atlantic albums recorded 1952-59		
8/18/62	5	47	●	13 **Ray Charles' Greatest Hits** ....[G]	$25	ABC-Para. 415
11/3/62	2²	67	●	14 **Modern Sounds In Country And Western Music (Volume Two)**	$25	ABC-Para. 435
8/31/63	2²	36		15 **Ingredients In A Recipe For Soul**	$25	ABC-Para. 465
3/21/64	9	23		16 **Sweet & Sour Tears**	$25	ABC-Para. 480
8/29/64	36	16		17 Have A Smile With Me	$25	ABC-Para. 495
2/20/65	80	18		18 Ray Charles Live In Concert ....[L]	$20	ABC-Para. 500
9/11/65	116	7		19 Country & Western Meets Rhythm & Blues	$20	ABC-Para. 520
3/12/66	15	36		20 Crying Time	$20	ABC-Para. 544
9/17/66	52	17		21 Ray's Moods	$12	ABC 550
3/25/67	77	62	●	22 A Man And His Soul ....[G]	$20	ABC 590 [2]
7/8/67	76	34		23 Ray Charles invites you to Listen	$12	ABC/TRC 595
4/13/68	51	24		24 A Portrait Of Ray	$12	ABC/TRC 625
4/5/69	167	11		25 I'm All Yours-Baby!	$12	ABC/TRC 675
7/26/69	172	3		26 Doing His Thing	$12	ABC/TRC 695
7/11/70	155	2		27 My Kind Of Jazz ....[I]	$10	Tangerine 1512
8/22/70	192	4		28 Love Country Style	$10	ABC/TRC 707
5/29/71	52	16		29 Volcanic Action Of My Soul	$10	ABC/TRC 726
11/20/71	152	10		30 A 25th Anniversary in Show Business Salute to Ray Charles ......[G]	$10	ABC 731 [2]
				record 1: Atlantic hits; record 2: ABC hits		
4/29/72	52	22		31 A Message From The People	$10	ABC/TRC 755
11/25/72+	186	8		32 Through The Eyes Of Love	$10	ABC/TRC 765
5/19/73	182	5		33 Ray Charles Live ....[R-L]	$12	Atlantic 503 [2]
				record 1: recorded at The Newport Jazz Festival, 7/5/58; record 2: reissue of album #2 above		
6/28/75	175	3		34 Renaissance	$12	Crossover 9005
12/4/76	138	11		35 Porgy & Bess	$12	RCA 1831 [2]
				RAY CHARLES/CLEO LAINE includes 7 instrumentals by Frank DeVol: "Summertime," "I Got Plenty O'Nuttin'," "Strawberry Woman," "It Ain't Necessarily So," "There's A Boat Dat's Leavin' Soon For New York," "I Loves You, Porgy" and "Oh, Bess, O Where's My Bess"		
11/12/77	78	20		36 True To Life	$10	Atlantic 19142
2/23/85	75	20		37 Friendship	$8	Columbia 39415
				duets with 10 superstar Country artists		

Abraham, Martin, And John (31)	All For You (23)	**Baby, Don't You Cry** (16,18) 39	Birth Of The Blues (5)	Born To Be Blue (15)	By The Light Of The Silvery Moon (21)
After My Laughter Came Tears (16)	All I Ever Need Is You (29)	**Baby It's Cold Outside** (8,22) 91	Blue Hawaii (3)	**Born To Lose** (11,22,30) 41	Bye Bye, Love (11)
Ain't Misbehavin' (7)	All Night Long (19)	Baby Please (26)	Blue Moon Of Kentucky (24)	**Busted** (15,22,30) 4	California, Here I Come (3)
Ain't That Love (12,30)	Alone Together (8)	Basin Street Blues (3)	(Swingova) (19)	**But On The Other Hand Baby** (13) 72	Candy (4)
Alabamy Bound (3)	Am I Blue (1,24)	Be My Love (36)	Blues Waltz (33)		Careless Love (11) 60
Alexander's Ragtime Band (1)	America The Beautiful (31)	Bess, You Is My Woman (35)	Bluesette (27)	Buzzard Song [solo: Ray] (35)	Carry Me Back To Old Virginny (3)
	Angel City (27)		**Booty Butt** (27,30) 36		
	Anonymous Love (36)		Born Loser (21)		

CHARLES, Ray — Cont'd

Charlesville (7)
Chattanooga Choo-Choo (3)
Cherry (4)
Chitlins With Candied Yams (21,22)
Cocktails For Two (8)
Come And Get It (26)
Come Back Baby (12)
Come Rain Or Come Shine (1,12) **83**
Crab Man *[solo: Ray]* (35)
Crazy Old Soldier (37)
Cry (16,22) **58**
Cry Me A River (16)
Crying Time (20,22,30) **6**
Danger Zone (13)
Dawn Ray (7)
Deed I Do (1)
Deep In The Heart Of Texas (3)
Diane (4)
Don't Change On Me (28,30) **36**
Don't Cry Baby (16)
Don't Let Her Know (19)
Don't Let The Sun Catch You Cryin' (1,30) **95**
Don't Set Me Free (18)
Don't Tell Me Your Troubles (14)
Don't You Know (12,30)
Don't You Think I Ought To Know (20)
Doodlin' (12)
Down In The Valley (29)
Drifting Blues (20)
Drown In My Own Tears (2,12,30,33)
Early In The Mornin' (9)
Eleanor Rigby (24,30) **35**
Ev'ry Time We Say Goodbye (8)
Every Saturday Night (31)
Feel So Bad (29,30) **68**
Feelin' Sad (9)
Feudin' And Fightin' (17)
Finders Keepers, Losers Weepers (26)
Fool For You (12,30,33)
For All We Know (8)
For Mama (La Mamma) (34)
Frenesi (2,33)
Friendship (37)
From The Heart (5,22)
Game Number Nine (36)
Gee, Baby Ain't I Good To You (23)
Genius After Hours (7)
Georgia On My Mind (3,13,22,30) **1**
Girl I Used To Know (21)
Gloomy Sunday (36)
Going Down Slow (20)
Golden Boy (27)
Good Morning Dear (28)
Goodbye (medley) (8)
Granny Wasn't Grinning That Day (21)

Guess I'll Hang My Tears Out To Dry (16)
Half As Much (11)
Hallelujah I Love Her So (12,18,30)
Hang Your Head In Shame (14)
Hard Times (No One Knows Better Than I) (9)
Hardhearted Hannah (4) **55**
Heartbreaker (10)
Heaven Help Us All (31)
Heavenly Music (36)
Here Come De Honeyman (35)
Here We Go Again (23) **15**
Hey, Good Lookin' (11)
Hey Mister (31)
Hide Nor Hair (18)
Hit The Road Jack (13,22,30) **1**
Hornful Soul (7)
Hot Rod (33)
How Deep Is The Ocean (How High is The Sky) (23)
How Long Has This Been Going On (36)
I Believe In My Soul (9,30)
I Can Make It Thru The Days (But Oh Those Lonely Nights) (32) **81**
I Can See Clearly Now (36)
I Can't Stop Loving You (11,22,30) **1**
I Chose To Sing The Blues (22) **32**
I Cried For You (16)
I Didn't Know What Time It Was (25)
I Don't Care (19)
I Don't Need No Doctor (22) **72**
I Dream Of You (More Than You Dream I Do) (25)
I Gotta Woman (Part One) (10,12,18,30,33) **79**
I Had The Craziest Dream (25)
I Keep It Hid (28)
I Like To Hear It Sometime (19)
I Love You So Much It Hurts (11)
I May Be Wrong (But I Think You're Wonderful) (29)
I Never See Maggie Alone (17)
I Remember Clifford (27)
I Told You So (26)
I Won't Leave (24)
I Wonder (13)
I Wonder Who (9)
I'll Be Seeing You (23)
I'll Never Stand In Your Way (14)
I'm Gonna Move To The Outskirts Of Town (5,13) **84**
I'm Movin' On (9,10,12) **40**

I'm Ready (26)
I've Got A Tiger By The Tail (Swingova) (19)
I've Got News For You (5,13) **66**
If It Wasn't For Bad Luck (26) **77**
If You Were Mine (28,30) **41**
If You Wouldn't Be My Lady (32)
In A Little Spanish Town (33)
In The Evening (When The Sun Goes Down) (15)
Indian Love Call (25)
It Ain't Easy Being Green (34)
It Ain't Gonna Worry My Mind (37)
It Ain't Necessarily So (35)
It Had To Be You (1)
It Makes No Difference Now (11)
It Should've Been Me (12,30)
It's A Man's World (21)
Jealous Kind (36)
Josephine (4)
Joy Ride (7)
Jumpin' In The Mornin' (6)
Just A Little Lovin' (11)
Just For A Thrill (1,12,30)
Just You, Just Me (8)
Leave My Woman Alone (10)
Let It Be (36)
Let The Good Times Roll (1,12) **78**
Let's Go (5)
Let's Go Get Stoned (20,22,30) **31**
Lift Every Voice And Sing (31)
Light Out Of Darkness (19)
Little Hotel Room (37)
Living For The City (34) **91**
Lonely Avenue (12,30)
Long And Winding Road (34)
Losing Hand (12)
Love Is Here To Stay (25)
Love Walked In (23)
Ma (She's Making Eyes At Me) (17)
Makin' Whoopee (18,22) **46**
Making Believe (14)
Man I Love (7)
Man With The Weird Beard (34)
Margie (4,18)
Marie (4)
Mary Ann (12,30)
Maybe It's Because Of Love (21)
Maybe It's Nothing At All (19)
Memories Of You (25)
Mess Around (12,30)
Midnight (14)
Midnight Hour (9)
Mississippi Mud (3)
Mister C (2)
Moanin' (5)
Moon Over Miami (3)

Moonlight In Vermont (3)
Move It On Over (17)
Mr. Charles Blues (9)
Music, Music, Music (7)
My Bonnie (6,12)
My First Night Alone Without You (32)
My God And I (34)
Nancy (4)
Naughty Lady Of Shady Lane (17)
Never Ending Song Of Love (32)
Never Say Naw (24)
New York's My Home (3)
Next Door To The Blues (19)
(Night Time Is) The Right Time (30) **95**
No Letter Today (14)
No One To Cry To (16) **55**
No Use Crying (20,22)
Nobody Cares (9)
Oh, Bess, Oh Where's My Bess *[solo: Ray]* (35)
Oh Lawd, I'm On My Way *[solo: Ray]* (35)
Oh, Lonesome Me (14)
Oh, What A Beautiful Mornin' (36)
Ol' Man River (15,22)
Ol' Man Time (15)
One Mint Julep (5,13,22,30) **8**
Over The Rainbow (15)
Pas-Se-O-Ne Blues (27)
Peace Of Mind (20)
People (23)
People Will Say We're In Love (8)
Perfect Love (32)
Please Forgive And Forget (19)
Please Say You're Fooling (21) **64**
Rainy Night In Georgia (32)
Ray's Blues (9)
Right Time (2,9,12,33)
Ring Of Fire (28)
Rock And Roll Shoes (37)
Rockhouse (Part 2) (6,12,30) **79**
Roll With My Baby (6)
Rosetta (4)
Ruby (4,13,22,30) **28**
Sail Away (34)
Same Thing That Can Make You Laugh (Can Make You Cry) (26)
See You Then (29)
Seems Like I Gotta Do Wrong (31)
Senor Blues (27)
Sentimental Journey (21)
Seven Spanish Angels (37)
She's Funny That Way (I Got A Woman Crazy For Me) (23)
She's Lonesome Again (21)
Sherry (33)

Show Me The Sunshine (28)
Side By Side (8)
Sidewinder (27)
Smack Dab In The Middle (17) **52**
Some Day Baby (9)
Someday (25)
Someday (You'll Want Me To Want You) (14)
Someone To Watch Over Me (32)
Something (29)
Spirit-Feel, The (2,33)
Stella By Starlight (4)
Sticks And Stones (13) **40**
Stompin' Room Only (5)
Stranger In Town (15)
Strike Up The Band (5)
Summertime (35)
Sun Died (24)
Sun's Gonna Shine Again (12)
Sunshine (34)
Swanee River Rock (Talkin' 'Bout That River) (12,30) **34**
Sweet Georgia Brown (4)
Sweet Memories (28)
Sweet Sixteen Bars (12)
Sweet Young Thing Like You (24) **83**
Swing A Little Taste (18)
Take Me Home, Country Roads (31)
Take These Chains From My Heart (14) **8**
Takes Two To Tango (8,22)
Talkin' 'Bout You (10,12,33)
Tear Fel (16) **50**
Teardrops From My Eyes (16,22)
Teardrops In My Heart (14)
Tears (20)
Tell All The World About You (6,12)
Tell Me How Do You Feel (6,10)
Tell Me You'll Wait For Me (6,10)
Tell The Truth (2,10,33)
That Lucky Old Sun (15) **20**
That Thing Called Love (26)
That's Enough (6)
Them That Got (13) **58**
Then We'll Be Home (34)
There'll Be No Peace Without All Men As One (31)
There's A Boat Dat's Leavin' Soon For New York *[solo: Ray]* (35)
Thing, The (17)
This Here (27)
This Little Girl Of Mine (12)
This Old Heart (Is Gonna Rise Again) (37)
Three Bells (29)
Till I Can't Take It Anymore (28)
Till The End Of Time (25)

Together (8)
Together Again (19) **19**
Two Old Cats Like Us (37)
Two Ton Tessie (17)
Two Years Of Torture (1)
Unchain My Heart (13,22,30) **9**
Understanding (24,30) **46**
Watch It Baby (19)
We Can Make It (26)
We Didn't See A Thing (37)
We Don't See Eye To Eye (20)
We'll Be Together Again (medley) (8)
We're Gonna Make It (34)
What Am I Living For (29) **54**
What-Cha Doing In There (I Wanna Know) (21)
What Have They Done To My Song, Ma (31)
What Kind Of Man Are You (6,12)
What'd I Say (Part I) (2,6,10,12,18,22,30,33) **6**
When I Stop Dreamin' (24)
When Your Lover Has Gone (1)
Where Can I Go? (15)
Who Cares (37)
Who Cares (For Me) (17)
Wichita Lineman (29)
Willow Weep For Me (16)
Woman Is A Sometime Thing *[solo: Ray]* (35)
Worried Mind (11,22)
Yes Indeed! (2,12,30,33)
Yesterday (23,30) **25**
Yesterdays (24)
You And I (8)
You Are My Sunshine (14,22,30) **7**
You Be My Baby (6,10)
You Don't Know Me (11,18) **2**
You Don't Understand (21)
You Leave Me Breathless (32)
You Made Me Love You (I Didn't Wanna Do It) (32)
You Ought To Change Your Ways (26)
You Win Again (11)
You Won't Let Me Go (1)
You'll Never Walk Alone (15)
You're In For A Big Surprise (20)
You're Just About To Lose Your Clown (32) **91**
You've Got A Problem (20)
You've Got Me Crying Again (16)
You've Still Got A Place In My Heart (28)
Your Cheating Heart (14) **29**
Your Love Is So Doggone Good (28)
Yours (25)
Zig Zag (27)

CHARLES, Ray, Singers

Born Charles Raymond Offenberg on 9/13/18 in Chicago. Arranger/conductor for many TV shows including the *Perry Como Show, Glen Campbell Goodtime Hour* and *Sha-Na-Na*. Winner of two Emmys.

DEBUT DATE	PEAK POS	WKS CHR		ARTIST — Album Title	$	Label & Number
4/4/64	**11**	33	**1**	Something Special For Young Lovers	$10	Command 866
9/5/64	**45**	22	**2**	Al-Di-La and other Extra-Special songs for Young Lovers	$10	Command 870
12/5/64+	**88**	20	**3**	Songs For Lonesome Lovers	$10	Command 874
8/21/65	**125**	6	**4**	Songs For Latin Lovers	$10	Command 886

Adios (4)
Al-Di-La (2) **29**
Amo, Amas, Amamus (4)
Bluesette (2)
By Myself (3)
Call Me Irresponsible (2)
Carnival (Manha De Carnaval) (4)
Charade (1)
Dear Heart (3)
Desafinado (Slightly Out Of Tune) (4)

Do You Want To Know A Secret (1)
Dominique (1)
Friendliest Thing (2)
Girl From Ipanema (2)
Hello, Dolly! (1)
I Ain't Gonna Cry No More (3)
I Left My Heart In San Francisco (1)
I Wish You Love (3)
I'll Never Smile Again (3)

Johann Sebastian Bach (2)
Love Me With All Your Heart (Cuando Calienta El Sol) (2) **3**
Maria Elena (4)
More (1)
My Guitar And My Song (Ti Regalo La Luna) (4)
My Love, Forgive Me (Amore, Scusami) (4)
No More Blues (Chega De Saudade) (4)

One More Time (3) **32**
Over The Rainbow (3)
People (3)
Quiet Night (Corcovado) (1)
Real Live Girl (1)
Satin Doll (2)
Smile (3)
Something Extra Special (2)
Song Of The Jet (Samba Do Aviao) (4)
Sweet Little Mountain Bird (1)

There I've Said It Again (1)
This Could Be The Start Of Something (1)
This Is All I Ask (1)
This Is My Prayer (3) **72**
Till The End Of Time (2) **83**
To You (E Lei) (4)
Toy For A Boy (3)
Vaya Con Dios (4)
What Kind Of Fool Am I? (1)
Willow Weep For Me (3)
Yo No Que Te Quiero (4)

You Are Never Far Away From Me (2)
You're Mine (4)

CHARLES, Sonny

R&B vocalist from Fort Wayne, Indiana. Former lead of The Checkmates, Ltd.

DEBUT DATE	PEAK POS	WKS CHR		ARTIST — Album Title	$	Label & Number
12/25/82+	**136**	7		The Sun Still Shines	$8	Highrise 102

DEBUT DATE	PEAK POS	WKS CHR	GOLD	ARTIST — Album Title	$	Label & Number

CHARLES, Sonny — Cont'd

Always On My Mind	One Eyed Jacks	**Put It In A Magazine** *40*	Week-end Father Song
Can't Get Enough	Per-so-nal-ly	Treasure Of Your Pleasure	Whet Your Whistle

CHARLES & EDDIE
Soul vocal duo of Charles Pettigrew (from Philadelphia) and Eddie Chacon (from Oakland, California).

10/31/92	**153**	5		Duophonic	$12	Capitol 97150

Be A Little Easy On Me	House Is Not A Home	Love Is A Beautiful Thing	Unconditional	**Would I Lie To You?** *13*
December 2	Hurt No More	N.Y.C.	Vowel Song	
Father To Son	I Understand	Shine	Where Do We Go From Here?	

CHARLESTON CITY ALL-STARS
Conducted by Enoch Light.

7/8/57	**16**	14		1 The Roaring 20's, Volume 2 .... [I]	$15	Grand Award 340
9/2/57	**17**	2		2 The Roaring 20's, Volume 3 .... [I]	$15	Grand Award 353

Ain't She Sweet (1)	I Can't Give You Anything	Ma, He's Making Eyes At Me	Show Me The Way To Go	Varsity Drag (1)
April Showers (2)	But Love (1)	(2)	Home (1)	When My Baby Smiles At
Baby Face (2)	I Love My Baby, My Baby	Margie (2)	Singin' In The Rain (2)	Me (1)
Bye, Bye Blackbird (2)	Loves Me (2)	Paddlin' Madelin' Home (1)	Sleepy Time Gal (2)	When The Red, Red Robin
Collegiate (1)	I'm Just Wild About Harry (2)	Runnin' Wild (1)	Sugar Blues (1)	Comes Bob, Bob Bobbin'
Five Foot Two (1)	I'm Sitting On Top Of The	Sheik Of Araby (2)	Swinging Down The Lane (1)	Along (2)
	World (2)		That Certain Party (1)	

CHARLIE
British rock quintet led by Terry Thomas (vocals, guitar).

6/4/77	**111**	15		1 No Second Chance	$10	Janus 7032
4/15/78	**75**	14		2 Lines	$10	Janus 7036
9/1/79	**60**	10		3 Fight Dirty	$8	Arista 4239
10/10/81	**99**	11		4 Fifth Flight	$8	Vertigo 2003
7/23/83	**145**	9		5 Charlie	$8	Mirage 90098

California (3)	Heartless (3)	L.A. Dreamer (2)	Out Of Control (2)	Tempted (5)
Can't Wait Til Tomorrow (5)	I Like To Rock And Roll (2)	Life So Cruel (2)	Playing To Win (5)	Thirteen (1)
Don't Count Me Out (3)	**It's Inevitable** (5) *38*	Love Is Alright (1)	Pressure Point (3)	This Time (5)
Don't Look Back (1)	Johnny Hold Back (1)	Lovers (1)	Runaway (3)	Too Late (3)
End Of It All (3)	Just One More Smiling Face	Never Too Late (5)	**She Loves To Be In Love**	Turning To You (1) *96*
Fight Dirty (3)	(3)	No More Heartache (3)	(2) *54*	Watching T.V. (2)
Guitar Hero (1)	Keep Me In Mind (2)	No Second Chance (1)	So Alone (3)	You're Everything I Need (5)
Heartaches Begin (5)	**Killer Cut** (3) *60*	No Strangers In Paradise (5)	Spend My Life With You (5)	

CHARO & The Salsoul Orchestra
Charo is Maria Rosario Pilar Martinez. Singer/actress born on 1/15/51 in Murcia, Spain. Once married to the late Xavier Cugat.

11/26/77+	**100**	15		Cuchi-Cuchi	$8	Salsoul 5519

Borriquito	Dance A Little Bit Closer	Let's Spend The Night	Only You (Can Make My	You're Just The Right Size
Cookie Jar	El Reloj (The Clock)	Together	Empty Life Worthwhile)	
Cuchi-Cuchi		More Of You	Speedy Gonzales	

CHASE
Jazz-rock band organized by trumpeter Bill Chase (formerly with Woody Herman and Stan Kenton). Chase and three other members were killed in a plane crash on 8/9/74.

5/8/71	**22**	26		1 Chase	$10	Epic 30472
4/8/72	**71**	12		2 Ennea	$10	Epic 31097
4/27/74	**155**	10		3 Pure Music	$10	Epic 32572

Aphrodite Part I & II (Venus)	**Get It On** (1) *24*	Invitation To A River Medley	Open Up Wide (1)	Weird Song #1 (3)
(2)	Hades (Pluto) (2)	(1)	Poseidon (Neptune) (2)	Woman Of The Dark (2)
Bochawa (3)	**Handbags And Gladrags**	It Won't Be Long (2)	Run Back To Mama (3)	Zeus (Jupiter) (2)
Boys And Girls Together (1)	(1) *84*	Livin' In Heat (1)	**So Many People** (2) *81*	
Close Up Tight (3)	Hello Groceries (1)	Love Is On The Way (3)	Swanee River (2)	
Cronus (Saturn) (2)	I Can Feel It (2)	Night (2)	Twinkles (3)	

★★221★★   CHEAP TRICK
Rock quartet from Rockford, Illinois founded by Rick Nielsen (guitar) and Tom Petersson (bass), with Bun E. Carlos (real name: Brad Carlson; drums) and Robin Zander (vocals). Discovered by Aerosmith's producer Jack Douglas. Petersson replaced by Jon Brant in 1980; returned in 1988, replacing Brant.

9/24/77	**73**	12	●	1 In Color	$8	Epic 34884
6/10/78	**48**	22	●	2 Heaven Tonight	$8	Epic 35312
2/24/79	**4**	53	▲³	3 Cheap Trick At Budokan .... [L]	$8	Epic 35795
10/6/79	**6**	25	▲	4 Dream Police	$8	Epic 35773
7/5/80	**39**	12		5 Found All The Parts .... [M]	$8	Epic 36453
				10" mini LP; recorded 1976-79		
11/15/80	**24**	15	●	6 All Shook Up	$8	Epic 36498
5/29/82	**39**	27	▲	7 One On One	$8	Epic 38021
9/10/83	**61**	11		8 Next Position Please	$8	Epic 38794
8/17/85	**35**	19		9 Standing On The Edge	$8	Epic 39592
10/18/86	**115**	9		10 The Doctor	$8	Epic 40405
5/7/88	**16**	47	▲	11 Lap Of Luxury	$8	Epic 40922
8/4/90	**48**	17		12 Busted	$12	Epic 46013
10/19/91	**174**	3		13 The Greatest Hits .... [G]	$12	Epic 48681

Ain't That A Shame	Big Eyes (1,3)	Can't Stop It But I'm Gonna	**Don't Be Cruel** (11,13) *4*	Gonna Raise Hell (4)	Hello There (1,3)
(3,13) *35*	Borderline (8)	Try (6)	Downed (1)	Good Girls Go To Heaven	High Priest Of Rhythmic
All We Need Is A Dream (11)	Busted (12)	Clock Strikes Ten (1,3)	**Dream Police** (4,13) *26*	(Bad Girls Go Everywhere)	Noise (6)
All Wound Up (11)	California Man (2)	Come On, Come On (1,3)	**Flame, The** (11,13) *1*	(10)	High Roller (2)
Are You Lonely Tonight (10)	**Can't Stop Fallin' Into**	Cover Girl (9)	Four Letter Word (7)	Goodnight (3)	House Is Rockin' (With
Auf Wiedersehen (2)	**Love** (12,13) *12*	Dancing The Night Away (8)	**Ghost Town** (11) *33*	Had To Make You Mine (12)	Domestic Problems) (4)
Baby Loves To Rock (6)	Can't Hold On (5)	Day Tripper (5)	Go For The Throat (Use Your	Heaven Tonight (2)	How About You (9)
Back 'N Blue (12)		Doctor, The (10)	Own Imagination) (6)	Heaven's Falling (8)	How Are You (2)

DEBUT DATE	PEAK POS	WKS CHR	GOLD	ARTIST — Album Title	$	Label & Number

CHEAP TRICK — Cont'd

I Can't Take It (8,13)
I Can't Understand It (12)
I Don't Love Here Anymore (8)
I Know What I Want (4)
I Love You Honey But I Hate Your Friends (6)
I Want Be Man (7)
I Want You (7)
I Want You To Want Me (1,3,13) **7**
I'll Be With You Tonight (4)
If You Need Me (12)

If You Want My Love (7,13) **45**
Invaders Of The Heart (8)
It's Only Love (10)
It's Up To You (10)
Just Got Back (6)
Kiss Me Red (10)
Let Go (11)
Little Sister (9)
Lookin' Out For Number One (7)
Lookout (3)
Love Comes (9)

Love Comes A-Tumblin' Down (6)
Love's Got A Hold On Me (7)
Magical Mystery Tour (13)
Man-U-Lip-U-Lator (10)
Name Of The Game (10)
Need Your Love (3,4)
Never Had A Lot To Lose (11) **75**
Next Position Please (8)
No Mercy (11)
Oh Caroline (1)
On The Radio (2)
On Top Of The World (2)

One On One (7)
Oo La La La (7)
Rearview Mirror Romance (10)
Rock All Night (9)
Rock 'N' Roll Tonight (12)
Saturday At Midnight (7)
She's Got Motion (9)
She's Tight (7,13) **65**
So Good To See You (1)
Southern Girls (1)
Space (11)
Standing On The Edge (9)
Stiff Competition (2)

Stop This Game (6) **48**
Such A Good Girl (5)
Surrender (2,3,13) **62**
Take Me I'm Yours (5)
Take Me To The Top (10)
Takin' Me Back (2)
This Time Around (9)
3-D (8)
Time Is Runnin' (7)
Tonight It's You (9,13) **44**
Voices (4,13) **32**
Walk Away (12)
Way Of The World (4)
When You Need Someone (12)

Wherever Would I Be (12) **50**
Who D' King (6)
Wild Wild Women (9)
Won't Take No For An Answer (8)
World's Greatest Lover (6)
Writing On The Wall (4)
Wrong Side Of Love (11)
Y.O.Y.O.Y. (8)
You Drive, I'll Steer (12)
You Say Jump (8)
You're All Talk (1)
Younger Girls (8)

★★107★★ CHECKER, Chubby

Born Ernest Evans on 10/3/41 in Philadelphia. Did impersonations of famous singers. First recorded for Parkway in 1959. Dick Clark's then-wife Bobbie suggested that Evans change his name to Chubby Checker due to his resemblance of a teenage Fats Domino. Cover version of Hank Ballard's "The Twist" started worldwide dance craze. On 4/12/64, married Miss World 1962, Dutch-born Catharina Lodders ("Loddy Lo" written for her).

DEBUT DATE	PEAK POS	WKS CHR	GOLD	ARTIST — Album Title	$	Label & Number
10/31/60+	3	86		1 Twist With Chubby Checker	$25	Parkway 7001
5/29/61	110	16		2 It's Pony Time	$25	Parkway 7003
9/25/61+	11	47		3 Let's Twist Again	$25	Parkway 7004
12/4/61+	8	38		4 For Twisters Only	$25	Parkway 7002
12/11/61+	2[6]	67		5 Your Twist Party	[K] $25	Parkway 7007
				features songs from albums #1, 3 & 4		
12/18/61+	7	30		6 Bobby Rydell/Chubby Checker	$25	Cameo 1013
				BOBBY RYDELL/CHUBBY CHECKER		
3/31/62	17	27		7 For Teen Twisters Only	$35	Parkway 7009
4/28/62	54	11		8 Twistin' Round The World	$25	Parkway 7008
6/9/62	29	20		9 Don't Knock The Twist	[S] $40	Parkway 7011
				includes 6 cuts by Chubby, who also stars in the film; also: "Bristol Stomp" & "Do The Continental" by The Dovells; "Bo Diddely" by Carroll Brothers; "Mashed Potato Time" by Dee Dee Sharp; "Smashed Potatoes" (instrumental) and "Salome Twist" by Various Artists		
10/27/62	23	24		10 All The Hits (For Your Dancin' Party)	$25	Parkway 7014
11/17/62	117	4		11 Down To Earth	$25	Cameo 1029
				CHUBBY CHECKER/DEE DEE SHARP		
12/15/62+	11	24		12 Limbo Party	$25	Parkway 7020
12/29/62+	27	23		13 Chubby Checker's Biggest Hits	[G] $25	Parkway 7022
3/30/63	87	17		14 Let's Limbo Some More	$25	Parkway 7027
8/10/63	90	4		15 Beach Party	$25	Parkway 7030
10/12/63	104	4		16 Chubby Checker In Person	[L] $25	Parkway 7026
				labeled as Twist It Up		
12/23/72+	152	10		17 Chubby Checker's Greatest Hits	[G] $10	Abkco 4219 [2]
3/6/82	186	2		18 The Change Has Come	$8	MCA 5291

Alouette (All You Twisters) (8)
At The Hop (4,17)
Baby, Come Back (12)
Ballin' The Jack (3,5)
Banana Boat Limbo Song (12)
Birdland (15,17) **12**
Blueberry Hill (4,5)
Bossa Nova (12)
Bristol Stomp (10)
Burn Up The Night (18)
But Girls! (18)
C.C. Rider Stroll (1)
Charleston, The (2)
Chicken, The (1)
Cindy, Oh Cindy (14)
Class, The (17) **38**
Continental Walk (3)
Dance-A-Long (3)
Dance The Mess Around (13) **24**
Dance With Me, Henry (4)
Dancin' Party (10,13,17) **12**
Dear Lady Twist (7)
Desafinado (Slightly Out Of Tune) (12)
Do The Freddy (17)
Do You Love Me (11)
(Don't Be Afraid,) It's Only Rock And Roll (18)
Don't Knock The Twist (9)
Don't Let Go (16)
Don't You Just Know It (16)
Down To Earth (11)

Fishin' (3)
Fly, The (7,9,13,17) **7**
Girl With The Swingin' Derriere (14)
Good, Good Lovin' (13) **43**
Gravy (For My Mashed Potatoes) (10)
Harder Than Diamond (18)
Hava Nagela (8)
Having A Party (10)
Hello, Baby, Goodbye (11)
Hey, Bobba Needle (17) **23**
Hi-Ho Silver (2,16)
Hold Tight (4)
Hooka Tooka (17) **17**
Hound Dog (4,5)
How Can You Go? (14)
Hucklebuck, The (1,5,13,17) **14**
Hully Gully (2)
Hully Gully Baby (10)
I Almost Lost My Mind (3)
I Could Have Danced All Night (3,5)
I Love To Twist (9)
I Need Your Loving (10)
I Really Don't Want To Know (11)
I'm Walkin' (16)
I've Got Love (That's Hard To Find) (18)
Jamaica Farewell (12)
Jet, The (3)

Jingle Bell Rock (6) **21**
Jingle Bells Imitations (6)
Johnny B. Goode (16)
Kansas City (16)
Killer, The (15)
La Bamba (12)
La La Limbo (12)
La Paloma Twist (9) **72**
Lazy Elsie Molly (17) **40**
Let The Good Times Roll (11)
Let's Dance, Let's Dance, Let's Dance (2)
Let's Limbo Some More (14,17) **20**
Let's Surf Again (15)
Let's Twist (A La Paloma) (8)
Let's Twist Again (3,5,13,16,17) **8**
Let's Twist Again (Der Twist Beginnt) (8)
Limbo Rock (10,12,13,17) **2**
Limbo Side By Side (15)
Loddy Lo (17) **12**
Lose Your Inhibitions Twist (7)
Lotta Limbo (14)
Love Is Like A Twist (7)
Love Is Strange (1,11)
Loving You (11)
Madison, The (1)
Make Love To Me (11)
Mama Look A Boo Boo (14)
Man Smart, Woman Smarter (12)

Manana (Is Soon Enough For Me) (14)
Mary Ann Limbo (12)
Mashed Potato Love (15)
Mashed Potato Time (10)
Mashed Potatoes (2)
Maybelline (16)
Mess Around (2)
Mexican Hat Twist (1,5)
Miserlou (8)
Mister Twister (4,5)
Mother Goose Limbo (14)
My Baby Just Cares For Me (6)
Never On Sunday (8)
Nothin' But The Twist (15)
O Sole Mio (8)
One More Time (11)
Oo-Kook-A-Boo (15)
Ooh Poo Pah Doo Shimmy (1)
Peanut Butter (3)
Peanut Vendor (14)
Peppermint Twist (2)
Play It Fair (11)
Pledging My Love (11)
Pony, The (1)
Pony Express (2)
Pony Time (2,13,17) **1**
Popeye The Hitchhiker (10,13) **10**
Quarter To Three (3)
Ray Charles-ton (3)
Rip It Up (16)

Rock Around The Clock (4,5)
Rock It To Me Rudy (18)
Rockin' Good Way (To Mess Around And Fall In Love) (medley) (18)
Rum And Coca Cola (14)
Run, Chico, Run (14)
Run Around Sue (7)
Run To Me (18)
Running (18) **91**
Shake Rattle And Roll (4,17)
She Said (15)
She's A Hippy (15)
Shimmy, The (2)
Shout (1)
Side By Side (6)
Slop, The (1)
Slow Twistin' (7,9,13,16,17) **3**
Somebody Bad Stole De Wedding Bell (12)
Strand, The (1)
Stroll, The (2)
Surf Party (15) **55**
Swingin' Together (6)
T-82 (18)
Takes Two To Tango (3)
Tea For Two (3)
Teach Me To Twist (6)
Twenty Miles (14) **15**
Twist, The (1,5,13,16,17) **1**
Twist-A-Long (7)
Twist And Shout (10,17)
Twist It Up (15,16,17) **25**

Twist Marie (8)
Twist Mit Mir (Mus I Denn) (8)
Twist Train (4)
Twistin' (9)
Twistin' Bones (7)
Twistin' Matilda (8)
Twistin' Round The World (8)
Twistin' The Blues (7)
Twistin' U.S.A. (1,5) **68**
Under My Thumb (18)
Voodoo (You Remind Me Of The Guy) (14)
Wah-Watusi, The (2,10)
Walkin' My Baby Back Home (6)
We Like Birdland (2,10)
(We're Gone) Surfin' (15)
What Are You Doing New Year's Eve (8)
When The Saints Go Limbo In (12)
Whole Lotta Shakin' Goin' On (4,5,13) **42**
You Came A Long Way From St. Louis (11)
Your Feet's Too Big (4)
Your Hits And Mine Medley (6)
Your Lips And Mine (7)
Your Love (18)

CHECKMATES, LTD., The

Interracial quintet from Fort Wayne, Indiana. Consisted of Sonny Charles (vocals), Bobby Stevens, Harvey Trees, Bill Van Buskirk and Marvin Smith. Discovered by Nancy Wilson. Sonny Charles also recorded solo.

DEBUT DATE	PEAK POS	WKS CHR	GOLD	ARTIST — Album Title	$	Label & Number
10/18/69	178	4		Love Is All We Have To Give	$20	A&M 4183

DEBUT DATE	PEAK POS	WKS CHR	GOLD	ARTIST — Album Title	$	Label & Number

CHECKMATES, LTD., The — Cont'd

Black Pearl *13*   I Keep Forgettin'   Love Is All I Have To   Proud Mary *69*   Spanish Harlem
Hair Anthology Suite Medley   Give *65*

★★372★★ CHEECH & CHONG

Comedians Richard "Cheech" Marin (b: 7/13/46, Watts, California) and Thomas Chong (b: 5/24/38, Edmonton, Alberta, Canada). Starred in movies since 1980. Chong, the father of actress Rae Dawn Chong, was the guitarist of Bobby Taylor's Vancouvers. Cheech is a cast member of TV's *Golden Palace.*

DEBUT DATE	PEAK POS	WKS CHR	GOLD	ARTIST — Album Title	$	Label & Number
9/25/71+	28	64	●	1 Cheech And Chong [C]	$10	Ode 77010
7/1/72	2[1]	111	●	2 Big Bambu [C]	$10	Ode 77014
9/8/73	2[1]	69	●	3 Los Cochinos [C]	$10	Ode 77019
				translation of Spanish title: The Pigs		
10/19/74	5	25	●	4 Cheech & Chong's Wedding Album [C]	$10	Ode 77025
6/26/76	25	13		5 Sleeping Beauty [C]	$10	Ode 77040
12/2/78+	162	7		6 Up In Smoke [C-S]	$8	Warner 3249
				includes 3 instrumentals by Yesca: "Here Come The Mounties To The Rescue," "Lost Due To Incompetence (Theme For A Big Green Van)" and "Strawberry's" plus one cut by War: "Low Rider"		
7/19/80	173	3		7 Let's Make A New Dope Deal [C]	$8	Warner 3391
10/12/85	71	11		8 Get Out Of My Room [C]	$8	MCA 5640

Acapulco Gold Filters (1)   Championship Wrestling (4)   Finkelstein Shit Kid (6)   Other Tapes (4)   Sometimes When You Gotta Go, You Can't (6)   Vietnam (1)
Acupuncture (7)   Cheborneck (3)   1st Gear, 2nd Gear (6)   Pedro And Man At The Drive-Inn (3)   Waiting For Dave (1)
Adventures Of Red & Roy (The Last Round-Up) (5)   China Town (7)   **Framed** (5,6) *41*   Strawberry Revival Festival (3)   Wake Up America (4)
Ajax Lady (6)   Coming Attractions (4)   Get Out Of My Room (8)   Pedro's Request (5)   Warren Beatty (8)
Baby Sitters Featuring Pedro & Man (4)   Continuing Adventures Of Pedro De Pacas And Man (2)   Hey Margaret (4)   Peter Rooter (3)   Streets Of New York Or Los Angeles Or San Francisco Or... (2)   Welcome To Mexico (1)
I Didn't Know Your Name Was Alex (6)   Pope: Live At The Vatican (1)   White World Of Sports (3)
Basketball Jones Featuring Tyrone Shoelaces (3) *15*   Cruisin' With Pedro De Pacas (1)   I'm A (Modern) Man (8)   Queer Wars (7)   Wink Dinkerson (1)
I'm Not Home Right Now (8)   Radio News (8)   Stupid Early Show (8)
Big Sniff (Starring Ralph & Herbie) (5)   Dave (1)   Jimmy (3)   Rainbow Bar & Grill (7)   Sushi Bar (8)
Disco Disco (7)   Juan Coyote (8)   Ralph And Herbie (2)   T.W.A.T. (Tactical Women's Alert Team) (5)
Black Lassie Featuring Johnny Stash (4) *55*   Don't Bug Me (3)   Lard Ass (6)   Rebuttal: Speaker Ashley Roachclip (2)   Television Medley (2)
Dork Radio (7)   Les Morpions (3)   Rock Fight (6)   Testimonial By R. Zimmerman (4)
Blind Melon Chitlin' (1)   Dorm Radio I (8)   Let's Make A New Dope Deal (7)   Sargent Stadanko (3)   Three Little Pigs (6)
Bloat On Featuring The Bloaters (7) *41*   **Earache My Eye Featuring Alice Bowie** (4,6) *9*   Love Is Strange (8)   Searchin' (6)   Trippin' In Court (1)
Moe Money (Rudolph The Red Nosed Reindeer) (7)   17th American Tour (7)   Uncle Pervy (5)
Born In East L.A. (8) *48*   Emergency Ward (1)   **Sister Mary Elephant (Shudd-Up!)** (2) *24*   Up His Nose (3)
Bust, The (2)   Evelyn Woodhead Speed Reading Course (3)   Music Lesson (8)   Sleeping Beauty (5)   Up In Smoke (6)

CHEQUERED PAST

Veteran hard-rock quintet: Michael Des Barres (vocals, Detective), Steve Jones (Sex Pistols), Tony Sales (Utopia, Tin Machine), and Blondie members Clem Burke and Nigel Harrison.

DEBUT DATE	PEAK POS	WKS CHR	GOLD	ARTIST — Album Title	$	Label & Number
9/15/84	151	6		Chequered Past	$8	EMI America 17123

Are You Sure Hank Done It This Way   How Much Is Too Much?   Never In A Million Years   Only The Strong (Will Survive)   Tonight And Every Night   World Gone Wild
Let Me Rock   No Knife   Underworld

★★141★★ CHER

Born Cherilyn LaPierre on 5/20/46 in El Centro, California. Worked as backup singer for Phil Spector. Recorded as "Bonnie Jo Mason" and "Cherilyn" in 1964. Recorded with Sonny Bono as "Caesar & Cleo" in 1963, then as Sonny & Cher from 1965-73. Married to Bono from 1963-74. Married to Gregg Allman from 1975-77. Own TV series with Bono from 1971-77. Member of the group Black Rose in 1980. Acclaimed film actress (won Best Actress Oscar in 1987 for *Moonstruck*).

DEBUT DATE	PEAK POS	WKS CHR	GOLD	ARTIST — Album Title	$	Label & Number
9/18/65	16	24		1 All I Really Want To Do	$25	Imperial 12292
4/23/66	26	19		2 The Sonny Side Of Cher	$20	Imperial 12301
10/1/66	59	16		3 Cher	$20	Imperial 12320
11/18/67+	47	14		4 With Love - Cher	$20	Imperial 12358
11/30/68	195	3		5 Cher's Golden Greats [G]	$20	Imperial 12406
8/16/69	160	3		6 3614 Jackson Highway	$15	Atco 298
				address of the Muscle Shoals Sound Studio		
9/25/71	16	45	●	7 Gypsys, Tramps & Thieves	$15	Kapp 3649
				original pressing simply titled *Cher*		
1/8/72	92	10		8 Cher Superpak [K]	$12	United Art. 88 [2]
7/29/72	43	22		9 Foxy Lady	$15	Kapp 5514
10/7/72	95	9		10 Cher Superpak, Vol. II [K]	$12	United Art. 94 [2]
				Superpaks: Imperial recordings		
4/14/73	140	8		11 Bittersweet White Light	$12	MCA 2101
9/22/73	28	25	●	12 Half-Breed	$12	MCA 2104
6/1/74	69	14		13 Dark Lady	$12	MCA 2113
11/16/74	152	7		14 Greatest Hits [G]	$12	MCA 2127
5/10/75	153	7		15 Stars	$12	Warner 2850
2/24/79	25	21	●	16 Take Me Home	$10	Casablanca 7133
12/5/87+	32	41	▲	17 Cher	$8	Geffen 24164
7/22/89	10	53	▲²	18 Heart Of Stone	$8	Geffen 24239
7/6/91	48	34	●	19 Love Hurts	$12	Geffen 24369

After All (18) *6*   **Behind The Door** (4) *97*   Catch The Wind (3,8)   Dangerous Times (17)   Don't Ever Try To Close A Rose (9)   Fire & Rain (7)
Alfie (3,5,8) *32*   Bell Bottom Blues (15)   Chastity Sun (12)   **Dark Lady** (13,14) *1*   Fires Of Eden (19)
All Because Of You (18)   Bells Of Rhymney (1,8)   Click Song (8)   David's Song (12)   **Don't Hide Your Love** (9,14) *46*   First Time (9)
All I Really Want To Do (1,5,8) *15*   Bigger They Come The Harder They Fall (15)   Come And Stay With Me (8)   Dixie Girl (13)   For What It's Worth (6)
Do Right Woman, Do Right Man (6)   Don't Think Twice, It's All Right (1,10)   Geronimo's Cadillac (5)
Am I Blue (11)   Blowin' In The Wind (1,8)   Come To Your Window (2,10)   Girl Don't Come (1,8)
Apples Don't Fall Far From The Tree (13)   But I Can't Love You More (4)   Could've Been You (19)   Do You Believe In Magic (8)   Down, Down, Down (9)   Girl From Ipanema (2,10)
By Myself (11)   Cruel War (3,10)   Does Anybody Really Fall In Love Anymore? (18)   Dream Baby (1,5)   Git Down (Guitar Groupie) (16)
Bang Bang (My Baby Shot Me Down) (2,5,8,17) *2*   Carnival (10)   Cry Like A Baby (6)   Elusive Butterfly (2,5,8)
Carousel Man (12,14)   Cry Myself To Sleep (1,10)   Emotional Fire (18)

DEBUT DATE	PEAK POS	WKS CHR	GOLD	ARTIST — Album Title	$	Label & Number

CHER — Cont'd

Give Our Love A Fightin' Chance (17)
Go Now (10)
Greatest Song I Ever Heard (12)
Gypsys, Tramps & Thieves (7,14) *1*
Half-Breed (12,14) *1*
Happy Was The Day We Met (16)
Hard Enough Getting Over You (17)
He Ain't Heavy, He's My Brother (7)
He'll Never Know (7)
Heart Of Stone (18) *20*
Hey Joe (4,5,10) *94*
Homeward Bound (3,8)
House Is Not A Home (8)
How Can You Mend A Broken Heart (7)
How Long Has This Been Going On (11)
I Found Someone (17) *10*
I Go To Sleep (3)
I Got It Bad And That Ain't Good (11)
I Hate To Sleep Alone (7)

I Saw A Man And He Danced With His Wife (13,14) *42*
I Threw It All Away (6)
I Walk On Guilded Splinters (6)
I Want You (3,10)
I Wasn't Ready (10)
I Will Wait For You (4,10)
I'll Never Stop Loving You (19)
I'm In The Middle (7)
If I Could Turn Back Time (18) *3*
If I Knew Then (9)
Impossible Dream (The Quest) (10)
It Might As Well Stay Monday (From Now On) (9)
It's Not Unusual (2,10)
It's Too Late To Love Me Now (16)
Jolson Medley (11)
(Just Enough To Keep Me) Hangin' On (6)
Just Like Jesse James (18) *8*
Just This One Time (15)

Just What I've Been Lookin' For (13)
Kiss To Kiss (18)
Lay Baby Lay (6)
Let Me Down Easy (9)
Let This Be A Lesson To You (16)
Like A Rolling Stone (2,10)
Living In A House Divided (9,14) *22*
Long And Winding Road (12)
Look At Me (4)
Love And Understanding (19) *17*
Love Enough (15)
Love Hurts (15,19)
Love On A Rooftop (3)
Magic In The Air (3)
Main Man (17)
Make The Man Love Me (13)
Mama (When My Dollies Have Babies) (4,8)
Man I Love (11)
Man That Got Away (11)
Melody (12,14)
Milord (2,10)
Miss Subway Of 1952 (13)
More Than You Know (11)
Mr. Soul (15)

My Love (12)
My Song (Too Far Gone) (16)
Needles And Pins (1,5,8)
Never Been To Spain (9)
Ol' Man River (2,10)
One Honest Man (3)
One Small Step (19)
Our Day Will Come (2,10)
Pain In My Heart (16)
Perfection (17)
Pied Piper (3)
Please Don't Tell Me (6)
Reason To Believe (8)
Rescue Me (13)
Rock And Roll Doctor (15)
Save The Children (6)
Save Up All Your Tears (19) *37*
Say The Word (16)
See See Rider (1)
She Thinks I Still Care (1,10)
Sing For Your Supper (4,10)
(Sittin' On) The Dock Of The Bay (6)
Skin Deep (17) *79*
Song Called Children (10)
Song For You (9)
Stars (15)
Starting Over (18)

Still In Love With You (18)
Sunny (3,5,8)
Take Me For A Little While (5,10)
Take Me Home (16) *8*
There But For Fortune (4,8)
These Days (15)
This God-Forsaken Day (12)
Time (2,8)
Times They Are A-Changin' (4,10)
Tonight I'll Be Staying Here With You (6)
Touch And Go (7)
Train Of Thought (13,14) *27*
Twelfth Of Never (3,10)
Two People Clinging To A Thread (12)
Until It's Time For You To Go (3,8)
Wasn't It Good (16) *49*
Way Of Love (7,14) *7*
We All Sleep Alone (17) *14*
What'll I Do (13)
When Love Calls Your Name (19)
When Lovers Become Strangers (19)

When You Find Out Where You're Goin' Let Me Know (7)
Where Do You Go (2,5,8) *25*
Who You Gonna Believe (19)
Why Was I Born (11)
Will You Love Me Tomorrow (3,8)
Working Girl (17)
World Without Heroes (19)
You Better Sit Down Kids (4,5,8) *9*
You Don't Have To Say You Love Me (8)
You Don't Have To Say You Love Me (Io Che Non Vivo) (Senza Te) (8)
You Wouldn't Know Love (18)
Young Girl (2,10)

CHERRELLE

Born Cheryl Norton in Los Angeles. Soul vocalist/drummer. Cousin of vocalist Pebbles. Moved to Detroit in 1979. Discovered by Michael Henderson.

| 9/8/84 | 144 | 8 | | 1 Fragile .... | $8 | Tabu 39144 |
| 2/1/86 | 36 | 30 | | 2 High Priority .... | $8 | Tabu 40094 |

above 2 albums accompanied by The Secrets: Jimmy "Jam" Harris, Terry Lewis and Monte Moir (all ex-members of Time)

| 11/19/88 | 106 | 15 | | 3 Affair .... | $8 | Tabu 44148 |

Affair (3)
Artificial Heart (2)
Crazy (For Loving You) (3)
Discreet (3)
Everything I Miss At Home (3)

Fragile...Handle With Care (1)
Happy That You're With Me (3)
High Priority (2)
Home (3)

I Didn't Mean To Turn You On (1) *79*
I Need You Now (1)
I Will Wait For You (1)
Keep It Inside (3)
Like I Will (1)

Looks Aren't Everything (3)
Lucky (3)
My Friend (3)
New Love (2)
Oh No It's U Again (2)
Pick Me Up (3)

Saturday Love (2) *26*
Stay With Me (1)
What More Can I Do For You (3)
When You Look In My Eyes (1)

Where Do I Run To (2)
Who's It Gonna Be (1)
Will You Satisfy? (2)
You Look Good To Me (2)

CHERRY, Don

Born on 1/11/24 in Wichita Falls, Texas. Studied voice after the service in mid-1940s. Vocalist with Jan Garber band in the late '40s. Accomplished professional golfer.

| 9/22/56 | 15 | 7 | | Swingin' For Two .... | $25 | Columbia 893 |

with Ray Conniff & His Orchestra

For You
I Didn't Know About You
I Don't Care If The Sun Don't Shine

I'll String Along With You
I'm Gonna Sit Right Down And Write Myself A Letter

I'm Yours
Love Is Just Around The Corner

My Future Just Passed
Please Be Kind
Sleepy Time Gal

So Rare
When The Sun Comes Out

CHERRY, Neneh

London-based R&B singer. Born on 8/10/64 in Stockholm, of Swedish and West African parentage and raised in New York City. Stepdaughter of jazz trumpeter Don Cherry.

| 6/24/89 | 40 | 35 | | Raw Like Sushi .... | $8 | Virgin 91252 |

Buffalo Stance *3*
Heart *73*

Inna City Mamma
Kisses On The Wind *8*

Love Ghetto
Manchild

Next Generation
Outre Risque Locomotive

Phoney Ladies
So Here I Come

CHESNUTT, Mark

Country singer. Native of Beaumont, Texas. Son of regional Texas star Bob Chesnutt.

| 10/27/90 | 132 | 38 | ● | 1 Too Cold At Home .... | $12 | MCA 10032 |
| 4/18/92 | 68 | 43↑ | ● | 2 Longnecks & Short Stories .... | $12 | MCA 10530 |

Blame It On Texas (1)
Broken Promise Land (1)
Brother Jukebox (1)
Bubba Shot The Jukebox (2)
Danger At My Door (1)

Friends In Low Places (1)
Hey You There In The Mirror (1)
I'll Think Of Something (1)

I'm Not Getting Any Better At Goodbyes (2)
It's Not Over (If I'm Not Over You) (2)
Lucky Man (1)

Old Country (2)
Old Flames Have New Names (2)
Postpone The Pain (2)
Talking To Hank (2)

Too Cold At Home (1)
Too Good A Memory (1)
Uptown Downtown (Misery's All The Same) (2)

Who Will The Next Fool Be (2)
Your Love Is A Miracle (1)

CHI-ALI

Sixteen-year-old male rapper from New York. Real name is Chi Ali. Appeared in the HBO movie *Strapped*.

| 4/18/92 | 189 | 2 | | Fabulous Chi-Ali .... | $12 | Violator 1082 |

Age Ain't Nothin' But A #
Check My Record
Chi-Ali Vs. Vanilla Shake

Fabulous Chi
Funky Lemonade

In My Room
Jump To The Rhythm
Let The Horns Blow

Looped It
Maniac Psycho
Murder Chi Wrote

Roadrunner
Shorty Said Nah
Step Up

CHIC

R&B-disco group formed in New York City by prolific producers Bernard Edwards (bass) and Nile Rodgers (guitar). Vocalists: Norma Jean Wright (replaced by Alfa Anderson) and Luci Martin; drums: Tony Thompson. Wright began solo career in 1978 as Norma Jean. Edwards recorded with the studio group Roundtree in 1978. Rodgers joined The Honeydrippers in 1984. Thompson joined the Power Station in 1985 and Edwards became their producer. Wright along with supporting Chic member Raymond Jones formed State Of Art in 1991. Rodgers and Edwards regrouped as Chic in 1992 with female lead vocalists/South Carolina natives Sylvester Logan Sharp and Jenn Thomas.

12/17/77+	27	40	●	1 Chic	$8	Atlantic 19153
12/2/78	4	48	▲	2 C'est Chic	$8	Atlantic 19209
8/25/79	5	17	▲	3 Risque	$8	Atlantic 16003

DEBUT DATE	PEAK POS	WKS CHR	GOLD	ARTIST — Album Title	$	Label & Number
				CHIC — Cont'd		
12/22/79+	88	9	4	Les Plus Grands Succes De Chic - Chic's Greatest Hits ....[G]	$8	Atlantic 16011
7/26/80	30	15	5	Real People..	$8	Atlantic 16016
12/19/81+	124	9	6	Take It Off	$8	Atlantic 19323
12/4/82	173	6	7	Tongue In Chic	$8	Atlantic 80031

At Last I Am Free (2)
Baby Doll (6)
Burn Hard (6)
Can't Stand To Love You (3)
Chic Cheer (2,4)
Chic (Everybody Say) (7)
Chip Off The Old Block (5) *flip*
City Lights (7)

Dance, Dance, Dance (Yowsah, Yowsah, Yowsah) (1,4) 6
Est-Ce Que C'est Chic (1)
Everybody Dance (1,4) 38
Falling In Love With You (1)
Flash Back (6)
(Funny) Bone (2)
Good Times (3,4) 1

Hangin' (7)
Happy Man (2)
Hey Fool (7)
I Feel Your Love Comin' On (7)
I Got Protection (5)
I Loved You More (5)
I Want Your Love (2,4) 7
Just Out Of Reach (6)

Le Freak (2,4) 1
My Feet Keep Dancing (3,4)
My Forbidden Lover (3) 43
Open Up (5)
Real People (5) 79
Rebels Are We (5) 61
Sao Paulo (1)
Savoir Faire (2)
Sharing Love (7)

So Fine (6)
Sometimes You Win (2)
Stage Fright (6)
Strike Up The Band (1)
Take If Off (6)
Telling Lies (6)
26 (5)
Warm Summer Night (3)
What About Me (3)

When You Love Someone (7)
Will You Cry (When You Hear This Song) (3)
Would You Be My Baby (6)
You Can Get By (1)
You Can't Do It Alone (5)
Your Love Is Cancelled (6)

★★30★★ **CHICAGO**

Jazz-oriented rock group formed in Chicago in 1967. Consisted of Robert Lamm (keyboards), James Pankow (trombone), Lee Loughnane (trumpet), Terry Kath (guitar; d: 1/23/78 [age 31] of accidental self-inflicted gunshot), Walt Parazaider (reeds), Peter Cetera (bass) and Danny Seraphine (drums). Originally called The Big Thing, later Chicago Transit Authority. To Los Angeles in the late '60s. Kath replaced by Donnie Dacus (left in 1979). Bill Champlin (keyboards) joined in 1982. Cetera left in 1985, replaced by Jason Scheff. Seraphine left in 1989, guitarist DaWayne Bailey added.

DEBUT DATE	PEAK POS	WKS CHR	GOLD	ARTIST — Album Title	$	Label & Number
5/17/69	17	171	▲²	1 Chicago Transit Authority	$20	Columbia 8 [2]
2/14/70	4	134	●	2 Chicago II	$20	Columbia 24 [2]
1/30/71	2²	63	▲	3 Chicago III	$20	Columbia 30110 [2]
11/13/71+	3	46	▲	4 Chicago At Carnegie Hall ....[L]	$30	Columbia 30865 [4]
7/29/72	1⁹	51	▲²	5 Chicago V	$20	Columbia 31102
7/14/73	1⁵	73	▲²	6 Chicago VI	$15	Columbia 32400
3/30/74	1¹	69	▲	7 Chicago VII	$15	Columbia 32810 [2]
4/12/75	1²	29	▲	8 Chicago VIII	$15	Columbia 33100
11/29/75	1⁵	72	▲⁵	9 Chicago IX - Chicago's Greatest Hits ....[G]	$15	Columbia 33900
7/4/76	3	44	▲²	10 Chicago X	$15	Columbia 34200
10/1/77	6	20	▲	11 Chicago XI	$15	Columbia 34860
10/21/78	12	29	▲	12 Hot Streets	$15	Columbia 35512
9/1/79	21	10	●	13 Chicago 13	$15	Columbia 36105
8/9/80	71	9		14 Chicago XIV	$10	Columbia 36517
12/12/81	171	5		15 Chicago - Greatest Hits, Volume II ....[G]	$10	Columbia 37682
6/26/82	9	38	▲	16 Chicago 16	$10	Full Moon 23689
6/2/84+	4	72	▲⁴	17 Chicago 17	$10	Full Moon 25060
10/18/86+	35	45	●	18 Chicago 18	$8	Warner 25509
7/9/88+	37	42	▲	19 19	$8	Reprise 25714
12/9/89+	37	25	▲	20 Greatest Hits 1982-1989 ....[G]	$8	Reprise 26080
2/16/91	66	11		21 Twenty 1	$12	Reprise 26391

A.M. Mourning (2)
Ain't It Blue? (8)
Ain't It Time (12)
Aire (7)
Alive Again (12,15) 14
All Is Well (3)
Alma Mater (5)
Aloha Mama (13)
Along Comes A Woman (17,20) 14
American Dream (14)
Another Rainy Day In New York City (10) 32
Anxiety's Moment (2,4)
Anyway You Want (8)
Approaching Storm (3)
At The Sunrise (3)
Baby, What A Big Surprise (11,15) 4
Bad Advice (7)
Ballet For A Girl In Buchannon ..see: Wake Up Sunshine
Beginnings (1,4,9) 7
Birthday Boy (14)
Brand New Love Affair (Part I & II) (8) 61
Byblos (7)
Call On Me (7,9) 6
Canon (13)
Chains (16)
Chasin' The Wind (21) 39
Colour My World (2,4,9) *flip*
Come In From The Night (19)
Critic's Choice (7)
Darlin' Dear (6)
Devil's Sweet (7)
Dialogue (Part I & II) (5,15) 24
Does Anybody Really Know What Time It Is? (1,4,9) 7

Dreamin' Home (3)
Explain It To My Heart (21)
Fallin' Out (3)
Fancy Colours (2,4)
Feelin' Stronger Every Day (6,9) 10
Flight 602 (3,4)
Follow Me (16)
Forever (18)
Free (3,4) 20
Free Country (3)
Free Form Guitar (1)
Gently I'll Wake You (10)
Get Away (medley) (16,20)
Gone Long Gone (12,15) 50
Goodbye (5)
Greatest Love On Earth (12)
Hallan From New York (7)
Hanky Panky (7)
Happy 'Cause I'm Going Home (3,4)
Happy Man (7,15)
Hard Habit To Break (17,20) 3
Hard Risin' Morning Without Breakfast (3)
Hard To Say I'm Sorry (medley) (16,20) 1
Harry Truman (8) 13
Heart In Pieces (19)
Hideaway (8)
Hit By Varese (5)
Hold On (14)
Holdin' On (21)
Hollywood (6)
Hope For Love (10)
Hot Streets (12)
I Believe (18)
I Don't Wanna Live Without Your Love (19,20) 3

I Don't Want Your Money (3,4)
I Stand Up (19)
I'd Rather Be Rich (14)
I'm A Man (1,4) 49
(I've Been) Searchin' So Long (7,9) 9
If It Were You (21)
If She Would Have Been Faithful... (18,20) 17
If You Leave Me Now (10,15) 1
In Terms Of Two (6)
In The Country (2,4)
Inner Struggles Of A Man (1)
It Better End Soon (Movements 1-5) (2,4)
It's Alright (18)
Jenny (6)
Just You 'N' Me (6,9) 4
Liberation (1)
Life Is What It Is (13)
Life Saver (7)
Listen (11)
Little One (11) 44
Little Miss Lovin' (12)
Loneliness Is Just A Word (3)
Long Time No See (8)
Look Away (19,20) 1
Loser With A Broken Heart (13)
Love Me Tomorrow (16,20) 22
Love Was New (12)
Lowdown (3,4) 35
Make Me Smile (2,4,9) 9
Mama Mama (10)
Mama Take (13)
Man To Woman (21)
Man Vs. Man: The End (3)
Manipulation (14)

Memories Of Love (2)
Mississippi Delta City Blues (11)
Mongonucleosis (7)
Morning Blues Again (3)
Mother (3,4)
Motorboat To Mars (3,4)
Movin' In (2)
Must Have Been Crazy (13) 83
Never Been In Love Before (8)
Niagara Falls (18) 91
No Tell Lover (12,15) 14
Nothin's Gonna Stop Us Now (18)
Now More Than Ever (2,4)
Now That You've Gone (5)
Off To Work (3)
Oh, Thank You Great Spirit (3)
Old Days (8,15) 5
Once In A Lifetime (17)
Once Or Twice (10)
Once Upon A Time... (3)
One From The Heart (21)
One More Day (18)
Only Time Can Heal The Wounded (21)
Only You (17)
Over And Over (18)
Overnight Cafe (14)
P.M. Mourning (2)
Paradise Alley (13)
Please Hold On (17)
Poem 58 (1)
Poem For The People (2)
Policeman (11)
Prima Donna (17)
Progress? (3)
Questions 67 And 68 (1,4,15) 24
25 Or 6 To 4 (2,4,9) 4
25 Or 6 To 4 (18) 48
Rediscovery (6)

Remember The Feeling (17)
Reruns (8)
Rescue You (16)
Road, The (2)
Run Away (13)
Runaround (19)
Saturday In The Park (5,9) 3
Scrapbook (10)
Show Me The Way (12)
Sing A Mean Tune Kid (3,4)
Skin Tight (10)
Skinny Boy (7)
So Much To Say, So Much To Give (2,4)
Somebody, Somewhere (21)
Someday (1)
Something In This City Changes People (6)
Song For Richard And His Friends (3)
Song For You (14)
Song Of The Evergreens (7)
Sonny Think Twice (16)
South California Purples (1,4)
State Of The Union (5)
Stay The Night (17,20) 16
Street Player (13)
Take A Chance (17)
Take Me Back To Chicago (11,15) 63
Takin' It On Uptown (11)
This Time (11)
Thunder And Lightning (14) 56
Till The End Of Time (11)
Till We Meet Again (8)
To Be Free (2,4)
Together Again (10)

Upon Arrival (14)
Victorious (19)
Vote For Me (11)
Waiting For You To Decide (16)
Wake Up Sunshine (Ballet For A Girl In Buchannon) (2,4)
We Can Last Forever (19,20) 55
We Can Stop The Hurtin' (17)
West Virginia Fantasies (2,4)
What Can I Say (14)
What Does It Take (21)
What Else Can I Say (3)
What Kind Of Man Would I Be? (19,20) 5
What You're Missing (16) 81
What's This World Comin' To (6)
When All The Laughter Dies In Sorrow (3)
Where Did The Lovin' Go (14)
Where Do We Go From Here (2,4)
While The City Sleeps (5)
Who Do You Love (7)
Will You Still Love Me? (18,20) 3
Window Dreamin' (13)
Wishing You Were Here (7,9) 11
Women Don't Love Me (7)
You Are On My Mind (10) 49
You Come To My Senses (21)
You Get It (13)
You're Not Alone (19,20) 10
You're The Inspiration (17,20) 3

DEBUT DATE	PEAK POS	WKS CHR	GOLD	ARTIST — Album Title	$	Label & Number

CHIEFTAINS, The
Irish folk band led by Paddy Moloney (pipes, whistles). Includes fiddlers Martin Fay and Sean Keane, Derek Bell (keyboards), Kevin Conneff (vocals) and Matt Molloy (flute).

2/28/76	187	4		1 The Chieftains 5 ....[I]	$8	Island 9334
7/23/88	102	13		2 Irish Heartbeat	$8	Mercury 834496

VAN MORRISON & THE CHIEFTAINS
traditional Irish folk songs arranged by Morrison and Moloney

12/14/91+	107	5		3 The Bells Of Dublin ....[X]	$12	RCA 60824

features Elvis Costello, Marianne Faithull, Nanci Griffith, Jackson Browne, Rickie Lee Jones, Burgess Meredith and others; Christmas charts: 14/'91, 25/'93

3/14/92	120	4		4 An Irish Evening-Live At The Grand Opera House, Belfast............[L]	$12	RCA 60916

5 tracks feature vocals by Roger Daltrey and Nanci Griffith; recorded live in 1991

Any Old Iron (medley) (4)
Arrival Of The Wren Boys (3)
Behind Blue Eyes (4)
Bells Of Dublin (medley) (3)
Boar's Head (3)
Brafferton Village (medley) (3)
Breton Carol (3)
Ca Berger (medley) (3)
Carrickfergus (2)
Celtic Ray (2)
Ceol Bhriotanach (Breton Music) (1)
Chieftains Knock On The Door (1)
Christmas Eve (medley) (3)
Damhsa (4)
Dance Duet-Reels (3)
Ding Dong Merrily On High (3)
Dingle Set-Dance (3)
Dochas (medley) (4)
Don Oiche Ud I mBeithil (3)
Farewell, The (3)
Ford Econoline (medley) (4)
Ghe Agus An Gra Geal (The Goose And Bright Love) (1)
God Rest Ye Merry Gentlemen (3)
Humours Of Carolan (1)
I Saw Three Ships A Sailing (3)
I'll Tell Me Ma (2)
Il Est Ne (medley) (3)
Irish Heartbeat (2)
Kerry Slides (1)
King Of Laois (medley) (4)
Lilly Bolero (medley) (4)
Little Love Affairs (4)
Marie's Wedding (2)
Mason's Apron (4)
Miscellany Medley (4)
My Lagan Love (2)
North Americay (4)
O Come All Ye Faithful (3)
O Holy Night (3)
O Murchu's Hornpipe (medley) (4)
O The Holly She Bears A Berry (3)
O'Keefes/Chattering Magpie-Reels (medley) (4)
Once In Royal David's City (3)
Paddy's Jig (medley) (4)
Past Three O'Clock (3)
Rachamid a Bhean Bheag (medley) (4)
Raglan Road (2,4)
Rebel Jesus (3)
Red Is The Rose (4)
Robbers' Glen (1)
Samhradh, Samhradh (Summertime, Summertime) (1)
She Moved Through The Fair (2)
Skyline Jig (3)
Sliabh Geal gCua na Feile (medley) (4)
St. Stephen's Day Murders (3)
Star Of The County Down (2)
Stone, The (4)
Ta Mo Chleamhnas Deanta (2)
Tabhair Dom Do Lamh (Give Me Your Hand) (1)
Three Kerry Polkas (1)
Timpan Reel (1)
Walsh's Hornpipe (medley) (3)
Wandering Minstrel (medley) (4)
Wexford Carol (3)
White Cockade (medley) (4)
Wren In The Furze (3)

CHIFFONS, The
Black female vocal group from the Bronx. Formed while high school classmates; worked as backup singers in 1960. Consisted of Judy Craig, Barbara Lee Jones (d: 5/15/92 [age 48] of heart attack), Patricia Bennett and Sylvia Peterson. Also recorded as The Four Pennies on the Rust label.

5/18/63	97	11		1 He's So Fine	$45	Laurie 2018
8/20/66	149	3		2 Sweet Talkin' Guy	$45	Laurie 2036

ABC - 123 (1)
Down, Down, Down (2)
He's So Fine (1) 1
Just A Boy (2)
Keep The Boy Happy (2)
Lucky Me (1)
March (2)
My Block (1) 67
My Boyfriends' Back (2)
Mystic Voice (1)
Nobody Knows What's Goin' On (In My Mind But Me) (2) 49
Oh My Lover (1)
Open Your Eyes (I Will Be There) (1)
Out Of This World (2) 67
See You In September (1,2)
Sweet Talkin' Guy (2) 10
Thumbs Down (2)
Up On The Bridge (2)
When I Go To Sleep At Night (1)
Why Am I So Shy (1)
Why Do Fools Fall In Love (1)
Will You Still Love Me Tomorrow (1)
Wishing (1)

CHILD, Desmond, and Rouge
Prolific producer/songwriter. Born John Charles Barrett Jr. in Miami on 10/28/53 to a Cuban mother and a Hungarian father. Formed vocal group Rouge with Diane Grasselli, Myriam Valle and Maria Vidal in 1974.

3/24/79	157	6		Desmond Child and Rouge...	$10	Capitol 11908

City In Heat
Fight, The
Givin' In To My Love
Lazy Love
Lovin' Your Love
Main Man
Otti
Our Love Is Insane 51
Westside Pow Wow

CHILD, Jane
Toronto native. Member of the Children's Chorus of the Canadian Opera Company at age 12. Studied piano at the Royal Conservatory of Music.

3/3/90	49	22		Jane Child...	$12	Warner 25858

Biology
DS 21
Don't Let It Get To You
Don't Wanna Fall In Love 2
Hey Mr. Jones
I Got News For You
Welcome To The Real World 49
World Lullaby
You're My Religion Now

CHILDS, Toni
Female vocalist from Orange, California.

6/25/88	63	45		1 Union	$8	A&M 5175
7/13/91	115	13		2 House Of Hope	$12	A&M 5358

Daddy's Song (2)
Dead Are Dancing (2)
Don't Walk Away (1) 72
Dreamer (1)
Heaven's Gate (2)
House Of Hope (2)
Hush (1)
I Want To Walk With You (2)
I've Got To Go Now (2)
Let The Rain Come Down (1)
Next To You (2)
Put This Fire Out (2)
Stop Your Fussin' (1)
Three Days (2)
Tin Drum (1)
Walk And Talk Like Angels (1)
Where's The Light (2)
Where's The Ocean (1)
Zimbabwae (1)

★★486★★ CHI-LITES, The
R&B vocal group from Chicago. Consisted of Eugene Record (lead vocals), Robert "Squirrel" Lester (tenor), Marshall Thompson (baritone) and Creadel "Red" Jones (bass). First recorded as the Hi-Lites on Daran in 1963. Eugene Record (husband of Barbara Acklin) went solo in 1976.

9/13/69	180	3		1 Give It Away	$15	Brunswick 754152
8/21/71	12	32		2 (For God's Sake) Give More Power To The People	$12	Brunswick 754170
4/29/72	5	36		3 A Lonely Man...	$12	Brunswick 754179
10/21/72	55	24		4 The Chi-Lites Greatest Hits.................................[G]	$12	Brunswick 754184
3/24/73	50	13		5 A Letter To Myself	$12	Brunswick 754188
9/15/73	89	14		6 Chi-Lites	$12	Brunswick 754197
7/13/74	181	5		7 Toby	$12	Brunswick 754200
11/29/80	179	6		8 Heavenly Body	$8	Chi-Sound 619
4/10/82	162	9		9 Me And You..	$8	Chi-Sound 635
6/4/83	98	12		10 Bottom's Up	$8	Larc 8103

Ain't Too Much Of Nothin' (3)
All I Wanna Do Is Make Love To You (8)
Are You My Woman? (Tell Me So) (4) 72
Bad Motor Scooter (10)
Being In Love (3)
Bet You'll Never Be Sorry (6)
Bottom's Up (10)
Changing For You (10)
Coldest Days Of My Life (Part 1) (3,4) 47
First Time (Ever I Saw Your Face) (7)
(For God's Sake) Give More Power To The People (2,4) 26
Get Down With Me (9)
Gettin' On Outta Town (9)
Give It Away (1,4) 88
Give Me A Dream (8)
Go Away Dream (6)
Happiness Is Your Middle Name (7)
Have You Seen Her (2,4,8) 3
Heavenly Body (8)
Homely Girl (6) 54
Hot On A Thing (Called Love) (9)
I Forgot To Say I Love You Till I'm Gone (6)
I Found Sunshine (6) 47
I Heard It Through The Grapevine (1)
I Just Wanna Hold You (10)
I Lied (7)
I Like To Live The Love (That I Sing About) (6)
I Like Your Lovin' (Do Like Mine) (4) 72
I Love (10)
I Never Had It So Good (And Felt So Bad) (6)

140

DEBUT DATE	PEAK POS	WKS CHR	GOLD	ARTIST — Album Title	$	Label & Number

CHI-LITES, The — Cont'd

I Want To Pay You Back (For Loving Me) (2,4) **95**
I'm Gonna Make You Love Me (1)
I'm Ready If I Don't Get To Go (4)
Inner City Blues (Make Me Wanna Holler) (3)
Just Two Teenage Kids (Still In Love) (5)
Let Me Be The Man My Daddy Was (1,4) **94**
Letter To Myself (5) **33**

Living In The Footsteps Of Another Man (3,4)
Lonely Man (3,4) **57**
Love Comes In All Sizes (5)
Love Is (3)
Love Shock (8)
Love Uprising (2,4)
Making Love (10)
Man & The Woman (The Boy & The Girl) (3) *flip*
Marriage License (6)
Me And You (9)
My Heart Just Keeps On Breakin' (5) **92**

My Whole World Ended (1)
Never Speak To A Stranger (9)
Oh Girl (3,4,9) *1*
One Man Band (6)
Round & Round (8)
Sally (5)
Someone Else's Arms (5)
Sound Of Lonely (7)
Stoned Out Of My Mind (6) *30*
Strung Out (8)
Super Mad (About You Baby) (8)

Tell Me Where It Hurts (9)
That's How Long (7) *flip*
That's My Baby For You (1)
There Will Never Be Any Peace (Until God Is Seated At The Conference Table) (7) *63*
To Change My Love (1)
Toby (7) *78*
Too Good To Be Forgotten (6)
Too Late To Turn Back Now (5)
Touch Me (10)
Troubles A'Comin' (2)

Try My Side (Of Love) (9)
Twelfth Of Never (1)
24 Hours Of Sadness (1,4)
We Are Neighbors (2,4) *70*
What Do I Wish For (1,2)
We Need Order (5) *61*
Whole Lot Of Good Good Lovin' (9)
Yes I'm Ready (If I Don't Get To Go) (2)
You Got Me Walkin' (2)
You Got To Be The One (7) *83*

You Smiled The Same Old Way (5)
You Take The Cake (10)
You're No Longer Part Of My Heart (1)

CHILLIWACK

Canadian rock group led by Bill Henderson (vocals).

DEBUT DATE	PEAK POS	WKS CHR	GOLD	ARTIST — Album Title	$	Label & Number
3/26/77	142	13		1 Dreams, Dreams, Dreams	$10	Mushroom 5006
8/12/78	191	4		2 Lights From The Valley	$10	Mushroom 5011
10/3/81	78	30		3 Wanna Be A Star	$8	Millennium 7759
11/27/82	112	10		4 Opus X	$8	Millennium 7766

Arms Of Mary (2) **67**
Baby Blue (1)
California Girl (1)
Don't It Make You Feel Good (4)
(Don't Wanna) Live For A Living (3)
Fly At Night (1) **75**

How Can You Hide Your Love? (2)
I Believe (3) *33*
I Wanna Be The One (2)
In Love With A Look (2)
Lean On Me (4)
Living In Stereo (3)
Lookin' For A Place (1)

Midnight (4)
Mr. Rock (3)
My Girl (Gone, Gone, Gone) (3) *22*
Never Be The Same (2)
Night Time (4)
No Love At All (2)
Rain-O (1)

Really Don't Mind (4)
Rockin' Girl (1)
Roll On (1)
Secret Information (4)
She Don't Know (4)
She Keeps On Cryin' (2)
Sign Here (3)
So You Wanna Be A Star (3)

Something Better (1)
Tell It To The Telephone (3)
Tonight (2)
Too Many Enemies (4)
Walk On (3)
(We Don't Have To) Fall In Love (2)
Whatcha Gonna Do (4) *41*

You're Gonna Last (4)

CHIMES, The

Scottish pop-soul trio: Pauline Henry (vocals), Mike Peden (bass) and James Locke (drums).

DEBUT DATE	PEAK POS	WKS CHR	GOLD	ARTIST — Album Title	$	Label & Number
6/2/90	162	6		The Chimes	$12	Columbia 46008

Don't Make Me Wait
Heaven

I Still Haven't Found What I'm Looking For
Love Comes To Mind
Love So Tender

1-2-3 **86**
Stay

Stronger Together
True Love

Underestimate

CHINA CRISIS

Liverpool, England rock quintet led by Garry Daly and Eddie Lundon.

DEBUT DATE	PEAK POS	WKS CHR	GOLD	ARTIST — Album Title	$	Label & Number
6/1/85	171	4		1 Flaunt The Imperfection	$8	Warner 25296

produced by Walter Becker (Steely Dan)

| 3/7/87 | 114 | 12 | | 2 What Price Paradise | $8 | A&M 5148 |

Arizona Sky (2)
Best Kept Secret (2)
Bigger The Punch I'm Feeling (1)
Black Man Ray (1)

Blue Sea (1)
Day's Work For The Dayo's Done (2)
Gift Of Freedom (1)
Hampton Beach (2)

Highest High (1)
It's Everything (2)
June Bride (2)
King In A Catholic Style (1)
Safe As Houses (2)

Strength Of Character (1)
Understudy, The (2)
Wall Of God (1)
We Do The Same (2)

World Spins, I'm Part Of It (1)
Worlds Apart (2)
You Did Cut Me (1)

★★364★★ CHIPMUNKS, The

Characters created by Ross Bagdasarian ("David Seville") who named Alvin, Simon and Theodore after Liberty executives Alvin Bennett, Simon Waronker and Theodore Keep. The Chipmunks starred in own prime-time animated TV show in the early 1960s and a Saturday morning cartoon series in the mid-1980s. Bagdasarian died on 1/16/72 (age 52). His son, Ross Jr., resurrected the act in 1980.

DAVID SEVILLE AND THE CHIPMUNKS:

DEBUT DATE	PEAK POS	WKS CHR	GOLD	ARTIST — Album Title	$	Label & Number
11/30/59+	4	41		1 Let's All Sing With The Chipmunks ...[N]	$25	Liberty 3132
6/20/60	31	5		2 Sing Again With The Chipmunks ...[N]	$25	Liberty 3159

THE CHIPMUNKS With DAVID SEVILLE:

| 12/22/62 | 84 | 2 | | 3 Christmas With The Chipmunks ...[N-X] | $20 | Liberty 3256 |

Christmas charts: 33/'65, 36/'66, 33/'67, 23/'87

| 9/5/64 | 14 | 23 | | 4 The Chipmunks Sing The Beatles Hits ...[N] | $20 | Liberty 7388 |

THE CHIPMUNKS:

8/9/80	34	26	●	5 Chipmunk Punk ...[N]	$8	Excelsior 6008
6/6/81	56	35	●	6 Urban Chipmunk ...[N]	$8	RCA 4027
11/21/81+	72	9	●	7 A Chipmunk Christmas ...[N-X]	$8	RCA 4041

Christmas charts: 10/'83, 8/'84

| 6/5/82 | 109 | 6 | | 8 Chipmunk Rock ...[N] | $8 | RCA 4304 |

ALVIN & THE CHIPMUNKS:

| 10/24/92 | 21 | 16↑● | | 9 Chipmunks In Low Places | $12 | Epic/Chip. 53006 |

with special guests: Billy Ray Cyrus, Aaron Tippin, Tammy Wynette, Charlie Daniels, Alan Jackson and Waylon Jennings

Achy Breaky Heart (9)
All My Loving (4)
Alvin's Harmonica (1) *3*
Alvin's Orchestra (2) *33*
Another Somebody Done Somebody Wrong Song (6)
Bette Davis Eyes (8)
Brothers & Old Boots (9)
Call Me (5)
Can't Buy Me Love (4)
Chipmunk Fun (1)
Chipmunk Song (1,3,7) *1*
Coming 'Round The Mountain (2)
Country Pride (9)
Coward Of The County (6)
Crashcup's Christmas (7)

Crazy Little Thing Called Love (5)
Deck The Halls (7)
Do You Want To Know A Secret (4)
Don't Rock The Jukebox (9)
Down At The Twist And Shout (9)
From Me To You (4)
Frosty The Snowman (3)
Frustrated (5)
Gambler, The (6)
Good Girls Don't (5)
Good Morning Song (1)
Gotta Believe In Pumpkins (9)
Hard Day's Night (4)

Have Yourself A Merry Little Christmas (7)
Heartbreaker (8)
Here Comes Santa Claus (Right Down Santa Claus Lane) (3,7)
Hit Me With Your Best Shot (8)
Hold On Tight (8)
Home On The Range (2)
How Do I Make You (5)
I Ain't No Dang Cartoon (9)
I Feel Lucky (9)
I Love A Rainy Night (6)
I Saw Her Standing There (4)
I Want To Hold Your Hand (4)

I Wish I Had A Horse (2)
If You Love Me (Alouette) (1)
It's Beginning To Look Like Christmas (3,7)
Jessie's Girl (8)
Jingle Bells (3,7)
Leader Of The Pack (8)
Let's Go (5)
Little Dog (1)
Losing You (I Really Wanna Lose You) (8)
Love Me Do (4)
Luckenbach, Texas (Back To The Basics Of Love) (6)
Lunchbox (6)
Made For Each Other (6)

Mammas Don't Let Your Babies Grow Up To Be Cowboys Chipmunks (6)
My Sharona (5)
Old MacDonald Cha Cha Cha (1)
On The Road Again (6)
Outlaws (9)
Over The River And Through The Woods (3)
P.S. I Love You (4)
Please, Please Me (4)
Pop Goes The Weasel (1)
Queen Of Hearts (8)
Ragtime Cowboy Joe (1) *16*
Refugee (2)
Row Your Boat (2)

Rudolph The Red Nosed Reindeer (3) *21*
Santa Claus Is Comin' To Town (3)
She Loves You (4)
Silent Night (7)
Silver Bells (3)
Sing A Goofy Song (2)
Sing Again With The Chipmunks (7)
Sleigh Ride (7)
Spirit Of Christmas (7)
Stand By Your Man (9)
Swanee River (2)
Swing Low Sweet Chariot (8)
Take A Chance On Me (8)

CHIPMUNKS, The — Cont'd

Thank God I'm A Country Boy (6)
There Ain't Nothin' Wrong With The Radio (9)
Three Blind-(Folded) Mice (1)
Twist And Shout (4)
Up On The House-Top (3)
We Wish You A Merry Christmas (3,7)
When Johnny Comes Marching Home (2)
Whip It (8)
Whistle While You Work (1)
White Christmas (3)
Witch Doctor (2)
Working On The Railroad (2)
Yankee Doodle (1)
You May Be Right (5)

CHOCOLATE MILK

R&B group from New Orleans. Consisted of Frank Richard (lead vocals), Amadee Castanell (saxophone), Joe Foxx (trumpet), Robert Dabon (keyboards), Mario Tio (guitar) and Dwight Richards (drums).

DEBUT	PEAK	WKS		ARTIST — Album Title	$	Label
10/25/75	191	3	1	Action Speaks Louder Than Words	$8	RCA 1188
6/24/78	171	5	2	We're All In This Together	$8	RCA 2331
4/14/79	161	6	3	Milky Way	$8	RCA 3081
12/12/81+	162	10	4	Blue Jeans	$8	RCA 3896

Action Speaks Louder Than Words (1) 69
Ain't Nothin' But A Thing (1)
America (2)
Blue Jeans (4)
Chocolate Pleasure (1)
Confusion (1)
Doc (3)
Fertility (2)
Girl Callin' (2)
Grand Theft (2)
Groove City (3)
Help Me Find The Road (2)
Honey Bun (4)
Hurry Down Sunset (3)
I've Been Loving You Too Long (4)
Let's Go All The Way (4)
Like My Lady's Love (4)
Milky Way (3)
My Mind Is Hazy (1)
Out Among The Stars (1)
Over The Rainbow (2)
Paradise (3)
People (1)
Pretty Pimpin' Willie (1)
Running On Empty (4)
Save The Last Dance (3)
Say Won'tcha (3)
That's The Way She Loves (2)
Thinking Of You (2)
Time Machine (1)
Tin Man (1)
Video Queen (4)
We're All In This Together (2)
You're The One (3)

CHRISTIANS, The

Liverpool-based trio formed in 1983: brothers Garry (vocals) and Russell (saxophone) Christian, with multi-instrumentalist Henry Priestman.

3/12/88	158	8		The Christians	$8	Island 90852

...And That's Why
Born Again
Forgotten Town
Hooverville
Ideal World
One In A Million
Sad Songs
Save A Soul In Every Town
When The Fingers Point

CHRISTIE

English rock trio: Jeff Christie, Vic Elms and Mike Blakely (brother of Alan Blakely of The Tremeloes).

12/12/70+	115	10		Yellow River	$12	Epic 30403

Coming Home Tonight
Country Boy
Down The Mississippi Line
Gotta Be Free
I've Got A Feeling
Inside Looking Out
Johnny One Time
New York City
Put Your Money Down
San Bernadino 100
Yellow River 23

CHRISTIE, Lou

Born Lugee Sacco on 2/19/43 in Glen Willard, Pennsylvania. Joined vocal group the Classics; first recorded for Starr in 1960. Started long association with songwriter Twyla Herbert. Recorded as Lugee & The Lions for Robbee in 1961.

8/24/63	124	6		1	Lou Christie	$40	Roulette 25208
3/5/66	103	14		2	Lightnin' Strikes	$18	MGM 4360

All That Glitters Isn't Gold (1)
Baby We Got To Run Away (2)
Cryin' In The Streets (2)
Diary (2)
Goin' Out Of My Head (2)
Gypsy Cried (1) 24
Have I Sinned (1)
How Many Teardrops (1) 46
If I Fell (2)
Jungle (2)
Lightnin' Strikes (2) 1
Love Is Like A Heat Wave (2)
Mr. Tenor Man (1)
Since I Fell For You (2)
Stay (1)
Tears On My Pillow (1)
(There's) Always Something There To Remind Me (2)
To Be Loved (1)
Tonight (I Fell In Love) (1)
Trapeze (2)
Two Faces Have I (1) 6
When You Dance (1)
You And I (Have A Right To Cry) (1)
You've Got Your Troubles (2)

CHRISTOPHER, Gavin

Chicago-born soul singer/composer/producer. His sister is singer Shawn Christopher.

7/5/86	74	15		One Step Closer	$8	Manhattan 53024

Are We Running From Love
Back In Your Arms
Could This Be The Night
In The Heat Of Passion
Love Is Knocking At Your Door
Once You Get Started
One Step Closer To You 22
Sparks Turn Into Fire
That's The Kind Of Guy I Am

CHRISTY, June

Born Shirley Luster on 11/20/25 in Springfield, Illinois. Jazz singer. Achieved national fame with the Stan Kenton band. Orchestra conducted by Pete Rugolo. Died on 6/21/90 of kidney failure.

9/29/56	14	4		1	The Misty Miss Christy	$25	Capitol 725
7/22/57	16	4		2	June - Fair and Warmer!	$25	Capitol 833

Best Thing For You (2)
Better Luck Next Time (2)
Beware My Heart (1)
Day-Dream (1)
Dearly Beloved (1)
For All We Know (1)
I Didn't Know About You (1)
I Know Why (And So Do You) (2)
I Want To Be Happy (2)
I've Never Been In Love Before (2)
Imagination (2)
Irresistible You (2)
It's Always You (2)
Let There Be Love (2)
Lovely Way To Spend An Evening (1)
Maybe You'll Be There (1)
No More (2)
'Round Midnight (1)
Sing Something Simple (1)
That's All (1)
There's No You (1)
This Year's Kisses (1)
When Sunny Gets Blue (2)
Wind, The (1)

CHUBB ROCK

Rapper Richard Simpson. Born on 5/28/68 in Jamaica. Raised in New York City. Cousin of rapper Howie Tee. Acted in the film Private Times.

3/23/91	73	10		1	Treat 'Em Right	$12	Select 9063
6/8/91	71	21		2	The One	$12	Select 21640
9/19/92	127	3		3	I Gotta Get Mine Yo! - Book Of Rhymes	$12	Select 61299

Another Statistic (2)
Arrival, The (3)
Bad Boyz (2)
Big Man (2)
Black Trek IV The Voyage Home (3)
Bring 'Em Home Safely (2)
Cat (2)
Chubbster, The (2)
Don't Drink The Milk (3)
Enjoy Ya Self (2)
Enter The Dragon (3)
Five Deadly Venoms (2)
Funky, The (3)
Hatred, The (3)
I Don't Want To Be Lonely (3)
I Gotta Get Mine Yo (3)
I Need Some Blow (3)
I'm The Man (3)
I'm Too Much (3)
Just The Two Of Us (2)
Keep It Street (1,2)
Lost In The Storm (3)
Message To The B.A.N. (3)
My Brother (3)
Night Scene (2)
One, The (2)
Organizer, The (1,2)
Pop 'Nuff Shit (3)
Regiments Of Steel (1,2)
So Much Things To Say (3)
Some-O-Next Shit (3)
3 Men At Chung King (3)
Treat 'Em Right (1,2) 95
What's The Word (1,2)
Which Way Is Up (3)
Yabadabadoo (3)

CHUNKY A

Chunkston Arthur Hall is actually Arsenio Hall. The Cleveland native (b: 2/12/57) is a comic/actor and host of his own late night talk show Arsenio. Appeared in films Coming To America & Harlem Nights.

12/16/89+	71	13		Large And In Charge	[N] $8	MCA 6354

Dipstick
Dope, The Big Lie
Ho Is Lazy
I Command You To Dance
Large And In Charge
Owwww! 77
Sorry
Stank Breath
Very High Key

DEBUT DATE	PEAK POS	WKS CHR	G O L D	ARTIST — Album Title	$	Label & Number

CHURCH, The
Australian folk-rock quartet: Steve Kilbey (vocals), Peter Koppes, Marty Willson-Piper and Richard Ploog. By 1992, Ploog left and Jay Dee Daugherty joined.

DEBUT DATE	PEAK POS	WKS CHR	GOLD	ARTIST — Album Title	$	Label & Number
6/21/86	146	11		1 Heyday	$8	Warner 25370
3/12/88	41	36	●	2 Starfish	$8	Arista 8521
3/31/90	66	20		3 Gold Afternoon Fix	$12	Arista 8579
				CD includes 2 bonus tracks		
3/28/92	176	2		4 Priest = Aura	$12	Arista 18683

Already Yesterday (1)
Antenna (2)
Aura (4)
Blood Money (2)
Chaos (4)
City (3)
Columbus (1)
Destination (2)
Disappointment (3)
Disenchanted (1)
Disillusionist, The (4)
Dome (4)
Essence (3)
Fading Away (3)
Feel (4)
Film (4)
Grind (3)
Happy Hunting Ground (1)
Hotel Womb (2)
Kings (4)
Laughing (3)
Lost (2)
Lustre (4)
Metropolis (3)
Mistress (4)
Monday Morning (3)
Myrrh (1)
New Season (2)
Night Of Light (1)
North, South, East And West (2)
Old Flame (4)
Paradox (4)
Pharoah (3)
Reptile (4)
Ripple (4)
Roman (1)
Russian Autumn Heart (3)
Spark (2)
Swan Lake (4)
Tantalized (1)
Terra Nova Cain (3)
Transient (3)
Tristesse (1)
Under The Milky Way (2) 24
Witch Hunt (4)
You're Still Beautiful (3)
Youth Worshipper (1)

CINDERELLA
Pennsylvania-based, heavy-metal band consisting of Tom Keifer (vocals, guitar), Jeff LaBar (guitar), Eric Brittingham (bass) and Fred Coury (drums).

DEBUT DATE	PEAK POS	WKS CHR	GOLD	ARTIST — Album Title	$	Label & Number
7/19/86+	3	70	▲³	1 Night Songs	$8	Mercury 830076
7/23/88	10	66	▲²	2 Long Cold Winter	$8	Mercury 834612
12/8/90	19	32	▲	3 Heartbreak Station	$12	Mercury 848018

Back Home Again (1)
Bad Seamstress Blues (medley) (2)
Coming Home (2) 20
Dead Man's Road (3)
Don't Know What You Got (Till It's Gone) (2) 12
Electric Love (3)
Fallin' Apart At The Seams (medley) (2)
Fire And Ice (2)
Gypsy Road (2) 51
Heartbreak Station (3) 44
Hell On Wheels (1)
If You Don't Like It (2)
In From The Outside (1)
Last Mile (2) 36
Long Cold Winter (2)
Love Gone Bad (3)
Love's Got Me Doin' Time (3)
Make Your Own Way (3)
More Things Change (3)
Night Songs (1)
Nobody's Fool (1) 13
Nothin' For Nothin' (1)
Once Around The Ride (3)
One For Rock And Roll (3)
Push, Push (1)
Second Wind (2)
Shake Me (1)
Shelter Me (3) 36
Sick For The Cure (3)
Somebody Save Me (1) 66
Take Me Back (1)
Winds Of Change (3)

CIRCUS OF POWER
Hard-rock quartet formed in 1987: Toronto native Alex Mitchell (vocals) with New Yorkers Ryan Maher, Gary Sunshine and Ricky Mahler. Zowie Ackerman joined in 1989.

DEBUT DATE	PEAK POS	WKS CHR	GOLD	ARTIST — Album Title	$	Label & Number
11/12/88	185	2		Circus Of Power	$8	RCA 8464

Backseat Mama
Call Of The Wild
Crazy
Heart Attack
In The Wind
Letters Home
Machine
Motor
Needles
White Trash Queen

CITY BOY
British rock sextet — Lol Mason, lead singer.

DEBUT DATE	PEAK POS	WKS CHR	GOLD	ARTIST — Album Title	$	Label & Number
8/28/76	177	3		1 City Boy	$10	Mercury 1098
2/12/77	170	4		2 Dinner At The Ritz	$10	Mercury 1121
9/16/78	115	9		3 Book Early	$10	Mercury 3737

Beth (3)
Cigarettes (3)
Dangerous Ground (3)
Deadly Delicious (1)
Dinner At The Ritz (2)
Do What You Do, Do Well (3)
Don't Know Can't Tell (medley) (1)
5.7.0.5. (3) 27
5000 Years (medley) (1)
Goodbye Blue Monday (2)
Goodbye Laurelie (3)
Greatest Story Ever Told (1)
Hap-ki-do Kid (1)
Haymaking Time (1)
Momma's Boy (2)
(Moonlight) Shake My Head And Leave (1)
Moving In Circles (3)
Narcissus (2)
Oddball Dance (1)
Raise Your Glass (To Foolish Me) (3)
State Secrets - A Thriller Medley (2)
Summer In The School Yard (3)
Sunset Boulevard (1)
Surgery Hours (Doctor Doctor) (1)
Violin, The (2)
Walk On The Water (2)
What A Night (3)
World Loves A Dancer (3)

C.J. & CO.
Detroit group assembled by Dennis Coffey. Included Cornelius Brown Jr., Curtis Durden, Joni Tolbert, Connie Durden and Charles Clark.

DEBUT DATE	PEAK POS	WKS CHR	GOLD	ARTIST — Album Title	$	Label & Number
7/9/77	60	23		Devil's Gun	$8	Westbound 6100

Devil's Gun 36
Free To Be Me
Get A Groove In Order To Move
Sure Can't Go To The Moon
We Got Our Own Thing

CLANCY BROTHERS & TOMMY MAKEM
Irish folk quartet. The brothers first began recording in the '50s for Tradition Records. Group founder, Tom Clancy, acted on off-Broadway and in television through the '80s; died of stomach cancer on 11/7/90 (age 67) in Cork, Ireland.

DEBUT DATE	PEAK POS	WKS CHR	GOLD	ARTIST — Album Title	$	Label & Number
11/16/63	60	12		1 In Person At Carnegie Hall	[L] $15	Columbia 1950
5/2/64	91	6		2 The First Hurrah!	$15	Columbia 2165

Au Poc Als Buille (The Mad Goat) (2)
Bonny Charlie (2)
Carrickfergus (2)
Children's Medley (1)
Gallant Forty TWA (2)
Galway Bay (1)
Johnny Todd (2)
Johnson's Motor Car (1)
Jug Of Punch (1)
Juice Of The Barley (1)
Kelly (2)
Leaving Of Liverpool (2)
Legion Of The Rearguard (1)
Mermaid, The (2)
O'Driscoll (The Host Of The Air) (1)
Oro Se Do Bheatha Bhaile (1)
Parting Glass (1)
Patriot Game (1)
Reilly's Daughter (1)
Rocky Road To Dublin (2)
Rosin The Bow (2)
Row, Bullies, Row (2)
West's Awake (2)

CLANNAD
Irish pop quintet: Maire (pronounced Moya) Brennan (lead singer) with brothers Pol & Ciaran (pronounced Keeron) Brennan, and twin uncles Noel & Padraig (pronounced Poric) Duggan. Group name is Gaelic for "family." Singer Enya, the sister of the Brennans, was a member from 1980-82.

DEBUT DATE	PEAK POS	WKS CHR	GOLD	ARTIST — Album Title	$	Label & Number
3/22/86	131	12		1 Macalla	$8	RCA 8063
				Macalla: Gaelic for Echo		
3/5/88	183	5		2 Sirius	$8	RCA 6846

Almost Seems (Too Late To Turn) (1)
Blackstairs (1)
Buachaill On Eirne (1)
Caislean Oir (1)
Closer To Your Heart (1)
In A Lifetime (1)
In Search Of A Heart (2)
Indoor (1)
Journey's End (1)
Live And Learn (2)
Many Roads (2)
Northern Skyline (1)
Second Nature (2)
Sirius (2)
Skellig (2)
Something To Believe In (2)
Stepping Stone (2)
Turning Tide (2)
White Fool (2)
Wild Cry (1)

★★32★★ **CLAPTON, Eric**
Prolific rock-blues guitarist/vocalist. Born on 3/30/45 in Ripley, England. With The Roosters in 1963, The Yardbirds, 1963-65, and John Mayall's Bluesbreakers, 1965-66. Formed Cream with Jack Bruce and Ginger Baker in 1966. Formed Blind Faith in 1968; worked with John Lennon's Plastic Ono Band, and Delaney & Bonnie. Formed Derek and The Dominos in 1970. After two years of reclusion (1971-72), Clapton performed his comeback concert at London's Rainbow Theatre in January 1973. Began actively recording and touring again in 1974. Eric's four-year-old son, Conor, killed on 3/20/91 in a 53-floor fall in New York City. Nicknamed Slowhand in 1964 while with The Yardbirds.

DEBUT DATE	PEAK POS	WKS CHR	GOLD	ARTIST — Album Title	$	Label & Number
7/25/70	13	30		1 Eric Clapton	$15	Atco 329
11/21/70	16	65	●	2 Layla	$15	Atco 704 [2]
				DEREK AND THE DOMINOS (Eric, Duane Allman, and Delaney & Bonnie alumni: Bobby Whitlock, Jim Gordon and Carl Radle [d: 5/30/80])		
4/15/72	**6**	42	●	3 **History Of Eric Clapton**	[K] $20	Atco 803 [2]
				recordings with groups listed in above artist notes		
10/14/72	87	17		4 Eric Clapton At His Best	[K] $12	Polydor 3503 [2]
				recordings from first Atco album + Derek & The Dominos Layla LP		
1/27/73	20	21	●	5 Derek & The Dominos In Concert	[L] $10	RSO 8800 [2]
				DEREK AND THE DOMINOS		
2/17/73	67	11		6 Clapton	[K] $10	Polydor 5526
				more recordings - same as above note		
9/22/73	18	14		7 Eric Clapton's Rainbow Concert	[L] $12	RSO 877
				Clapton's comeback concert at London's Rainbow Theatre with Pete Townshend, Steve Winwood, Ron Wood, Jim Capaldi and Rick Grech		
7/20/74	**1**⁴	25	●	8 **461 Ocean Boulevard**	$12	RSO 4801
				address where recorded in Miami, Florida		
8/10/74	107	10		9 Layla	[R] $12	Polydor 3501 [2]
				DEREK AND THE DOMINOS		
4/12/75	21	14		10 There's One In Every Crowd		$12	RSO 4806
9/6/75	20	13		11 E.C. Was Here	[L] $12	RSO 4809
10/16/76	15	21		12 No Reason To Cry		$12	RSO 3004
2/19/77	183	2		13 Layla	[R] $12	RSO 3801 [2]
				DEREK AND THE DOMINOS		
3/5/77	194	2		14 Eric Clapton	[R] $12	RSO 3008
				reissue of album #1 above		
11/26/77+	**2**⁵	74	▲	15 **Slowhand**	$12	RSO 3030
12/2/78+	**8**	37	▲	16 **Backless**	$12	RSO 3039
5/3/80	**2**⁶	31	●	17 **Just One Night**	[L] $12	RSO 4202 [2]
				recorded live at the Budokan Theatre, Japan		
3/21/81	**7**	21	●	18 **Another Ticket**	$10	RSO 3095
5/22/82	101	14	▲³	19 Time Pieces/The Best Of Eric Clapton	[G] $8	RSO 3099
2/19/83	16	19		20 Money And Cigarettes	$8	Duck 23773
4/6/85	34	28	●	21 Behind the Sun	$8	Duck 25166
12/27/86+	37	34	●	22 August	$8	Duck 25476
5/7/88	34	26	▲²	23 Crossroads	[K] $40	Polydor 835261 [6]
				contains 73 digitally-mastered tracks of Clapton's 25-year career		
11/25/89+	16	51	▲²	24 Journeyman	$8	Duck 26074
10/6/90	157	5		25 The Layla Sessions - 20th Anniversary Edition	[K] $38	Polydor 847083 [3]
				DEREK AND THE DOMINOS remix of album #2 above plus rare and unreleased cuts from the original Layla session tapes		
10/26/91	38	19	●	26 24 Nights	[L] $23	Duck 26420 [2]
				recorded over 24 nights at The Royal Albert Hall, London, 1990-91, with a 4-piece band, 9-piece band, band of blues legends and an orchestra; with guests: Phil Collins, Buddy Guy, Jimmy Vaughn, Joey Spampinato (NRBQ), Katie Kissoon, Robert Cray and others		
2/1/92	24	31	●	27 Rush	[S] $12	Reprise 26794
9/12/92	**2**⁵	22↑	▲³	28 **Unplugged**	[L] $12	Duck 45024
				Eric's 3/12/92 performance on the MTV program Unplugged		

After Midnight (1,4,7,14,17,19,23) **18**
Ain't Going Down (20)
Ain't That Lovin' You (23)
Alberta (3)
All Our Pastimes (12,17)
All Your Love [John Mayall's Bluesbreakers] (23)
Another Ticket (18) **78**
Anyday (2,4,9,13,25)
Anyone For Tennis [Cream] (23) **64**
Anything For Your Love (24)
Baby What's Wrong [Yardbirds] (23)
Bad Boy (1,6,14)
Bad Influence (22)
Bad Love (24,26) **88**
Badge (7,26)
Badge [Cream] (3,23) **60**
Beautiful Thing (12)
Before You Accuse Me (24,28)
Behind The Mask (22)
Behind The Sun (21)
Bell Bottom Blues (2,4,6,9,13,25,26) **78**
Bernard Jenkins (23)

Better Make It Through Today (10,23)
Black Rose (18)
Black Summer Rain (12)
Blow Wind Blow (18)
Blues Power (1,3,4,5,14,17,23) **76**
Boom Boom [Yardbirds] (23)
Bottle Of Red Wine (1,4,5,14)
Breaking Point (24)
Can't Find My Way Home (11)
Can't Find My Way Home [Blind Faith] (23)
Carnival (12)
Catch Me If You Can (18)
Certain Girl [Yardbirds] (23)
Cocaine (15,17,19,23) flip
Cold Turkey (27)
Comin' Home (23) **84**
Core, The (15)
County Jail Blues (12)
Crazy Country Hop (20)
Crosscut Saw (23)
Crossroads [Cream] (3,23) **28**
Don't Blame Me (10)
Don't Know Which Way To Go (27)

Don't Know Why (1,6,14)
Double Trouble (12,17,23)
Drifting Blues (11)
Early In The Morning (16,17)
Easy Now (1,4,14)
Edge Of Darkness (26)
Everybody Oughta Make A Change (20)
Evil (23)
Farther On Up The Road (11,17,23)
Floating Bridge (18)
For Your Love [Yardbirds] (23) **6**
Forever Man (21) **26**
Get Ready (8)
Give Me Strength (8)
Golden Ring (16)
Good Morning Little Schoolgirls [Yardbirds] (23)
Got To Get Better In A Little While (5)
Got To Hurry [Yardbirds] (23)
Hard Times (24,26)
Have You Ever Loved A Woman (2,5,6,9,11,13,25,26)

Have You Ever Loved A Woman [John Mayall's Bluesbreakers] (23)
Heaven Is One Step Away (21)
Hello Old Friend (12,23) **24**
Help Me Up (27)
Hey Hey (28)
Hideaway [John Mayall's Bluesbreakers] (3,23)
High (10)
Hold Me Lord (18)
Hold On (22)
Holy Mother (22)
Honey In Your Hips [Yardbirds] (23)
Hoodoo Man (23)
Hound Dog (24)
Hung Up On Your Love (22)
Hungry (12)
I Ain't Got You [Yardbirds] (3,23)
I Am Yours (2,9,13,25)
I Can't Stand It (18,23) **10**
I Don't Want To Discuss It [Delaney & Bonnie] (3)
I Feel Free [Cream] (23)

I Found A Love (23)
I Looked Away (2,4,9,13,25)
I Shot The Sheriff (8,19,23) **1**
I Want To Know (3)
I Wish You Would [Yardbirds] (23)
I'll Make Love To You Anytime (16)
I've Got A Rock N' Roll Heart (20) **18**
I've Told You For The Last Time (14)
If I Don't Be There By Morning (16,17,23)
Innocent Times (12)
It All Depends (8)
It's In The Way That You Use It (22)
It's Too Late (2,9,13,25)
Jam I-V (25)
Just Like A Prisoner (21)
Keep On Growing (2,4,9,13,25)
Key To The Highway (2,4,9,13,23,25)
Knock On Wood (21)

Knockin' On Heaven's Door (19,23)
Kristen And Jim (27)
Lawdy Mama [Cream] (23)
Lay Down Sally (15,17,19,23) **3**
Layla (2,3,4,9,13,19,23,25) **10**
Layla [live] (28) **12**
Lead Me On (24)
Let It Grow (8,23)
Let It Rain (1,4,5,14,23) **48**
Little Rachel (10)
Little Wing (2,4,7,9,13,25)
Lonely Stranger (28)
Lonely Years (23)
Lonesome And A Long Way From Home (1,4,14)
Lovin' You Lovin' Me (1,6,14)
Mainline Florida (8)
Malted Milk (28)
Man In Love (24)
Man Overboard (20)
May You Never (15)
Mean Old Frisco (15,23)
Mean Old World (23,25)
Miss You (22)
Motherless Children (8,23)

DEBUT DATE	PEAK POS	WKS CHR	GOLD	ARTIST — Album Title	$	Label & Number

CLAPTON, Eric — Cont'd

Never Make You Cry (21)
New Recruit (27)
Next Time You See Her (15)
No Alibis (24)
Nobody Knows You When You're Down And Out (2,6,9,13,25,28)
Old Love (24,26,28)
One More Chance (23)
Only You Know And I Know [Delaney & Bonnie] (3) **20**
Opposites (10)
Peaches And Diesel (15)
Pearly Queen (7)
Please Be With Me (8)
Preludin Fugue (27)
Presence Of The Lord (4,5,7,11)

Presence Of The Lord [Blind Faith] (23)
Pretending (24,26) **55**
Pretty Blue Eyes (10)
Pretty Girl (20)
Promises (16,19,23) **9**
Ramblin' On My Mind (11,17)
Ramblin' On My Mind [John Mayall's Bluesbreakers] (23)
Realization (27)
Rita Mae (18)
Roll It (16)
Roll It Over (5,7,23)
Rollin' & Tumblin' (28)
Run (22)
Run So Far (24)
Running On Faith (24,26,28)
Same Old Blues (21)

San Francisco Bay Blues (28)
Sea Of Joy (4)
Sea Of Joy [Blind Faith] (3)
See What Love Can Do (21) **89**
Setting Me Up (17)
Shape You're In (20,23)
She's Something Special (18)
She's Waiting (21,23)
Sign Language (12,23)
Signe (28)
Singin' The Blues (10)
Sky Is Crying (10,23)
Sleeping In The Ground [Blind Faith] (23)
Slow Down Linda (20)
Slunky (1,4,14)
Snake Lake Blues (23)
Someone Like You (23)
Something's Happening (21)

Spoonful [Cream] (3,23)
Steady Rollin' Man (8)
Steppin' Out [Cream] (23)
Strange Brew [Cream] (23)
Sunshine Of Your Love (26)
Sunshine Of Your Love [Cream] (3,23) **5**
Swing Low Sweet Chariot (10,19)
Take A Chance (22)
Tales Of Brave Ulysses [Cream] (23)
Tangled In Love (21)
Tearing Us Apart (23)
Tears In Heaven (27,28) **2**
Teasin' (3)
Tell Me That You Love Me (16)
Tell The Truth (2,3,5,6,9,13,23,25)

Tender Love (25)
Thorn Tree In The Garden (2,9,13,25)
Told You For The Last Time (1,6)
Too Bad (23)
Tracks And Lines (27)
Tribute To Elmore (3)
Tulsa Time (16,17) **30**
Walk Away (22)
Walk Out In The Rain (16)
Walkin' Blues (28)
Wanna Make Love To You (23)
Watch Out For Lucy (16) **40**
Watch Yourself (26)
We're All The Way (15)
We've Been Told (Jesus Coming Soon) (10)
Whatcha Gonna Do (23)

(When Things Go Wrong) It Hurts Me Too (23,25)
White Room (26)
White Room [Cream] (23) **6**
Why Does Love Got To Be So Sad? (2,4,5,9,13,25)
Will Gaines (27)
Willie And The Hand Jive (8,19) **26**
Wonderful Tonight (15,17,19,23,26) **16**
Worried Life Blues (17,26)
Wrapping Paper [Cream] (23)

★★218★★ CLARK, Dave, Five

Dave formed the rock group in Tottenham, England in 1960. Consisted of Clark (drums), Mike Smith (lead vocals, keyboards), Lenny Davidson (guitar), Dennis Payton (sax) and Rick Huxley (bass). First recorded for Ember/Pye in 1962. On *The Ed Sullivan Show* in March 1964. In the film *Having A Wild Weekend* in 1965. Disbanded in 1973. Clark had been a stuntman in films; formed group to raise money for his soccer team, the Tottenham Hotspurs. Clark wrote the 1986 London stage musical *Time*.

DEBUT DATE	PEAK POS	WKS CHR	GOLD	#	ARTIST — Album Title	$	Label & Number
4/11/64	3	32	●	1	Glad All Over	$25	Epic 26093
6/20/64	5	22		2	The Dave Clark Five Return!	$25	Epic 26104
8/29/64	11	28		3	American Tour	$20	Epic 26117
1/2/65	6	21		4	Coast To Coast	$20	Epic 26128
4/3/65	24	23		5	Weekend In London	$20	Epic 26139
8/14/65	15	21		6	Having A Wild Weekend [S]	$20	Epic 26162
					the Dave Clark Five star in the film		
12/11/65+	32	16		7	I Like It Like That	$20	Epic 26178
2/26/66	9	62	●	8	The Dave Clark Five's Greatest Hits [G]	$20	Epic 26185
6/25/66	77	11		9	Try Too Hard	$20	Epic 26198
10/1/66	127	6		10	Satisfied With You	$20	Epic 26212
12/10/66+	103	7		11	The Dave Clark Five/More Greatest Hits [G]	$20	Epic 26221
3/25/67	119	7		12	5 By 5	$20	Epic 26236
8/12/67	149	3		13	You Got What It Takes	$20	Epic 26312

All Night Long (11)
All Of The Time (1)
Any Time You Want Love (3)
Any Way You Want It (4,8) **14**
At The Scene (11) **18**
Because (3,8) **3**
Bernedette (12)
Bits And Pieces (1,8) **4**
Blue Monday (5)
Blue Suede Shoes (5)
Can I Trust You (8)
Can't You See That She's Mine (2,8) **4**
Catch Us If You Can (6,8) **4**
Chaquita (1)
Come Home (5,11) **14**
Come On Over (3)
Crying Over You (4)
Do You Love Me (1,8) **11**
Do You Love Me? (10)
Doctor Rhythm (13)
Don't Be Taken In (6)
Don't Let Me Down (11)

Don't You Know (4)
Don't You Realize (8)
Doo Dah (1)
Dum-Dee-Dee-Dum (6)
Ever Since You've Been Away (9)
Everybody Knows (I Still Love You) (4,8) **15**
Forever And A Day (2)
Funny (2)
Glad All Over (1,8) **6**
Go On (10)
Good Lovin' (10)
Goodbye My Friends (7)
Having A Wild Weekend (6)
How Can I Tell You (12)
Hurting Inside (5)
I Am On My Own (7)
I Can't Stand It (4)
I Can't Stop Loving You (4)
I Cried Over You (3)
I Know (9)
I Know You (1)
I Like It Like That (7,8) **7**
I Love You No More (2)

I Meant You (11)
I Need Love (7)
I Need You, I Love You (2)
I Never Will (9)
I Really Love You (9)
I Said I Was Sorry (8)
I Still Need You (10)
I Want You Still (3)
I'll Be Yours My Love (7)
I'll Never Know (3)
I'm Thinking (5,11)
I've Got To Have A Reason (13) **44**
If You Come Back (6)
It Don't Feel Good (9)
It'll Only Hurt For A Little While (10)
It's Not True (4)
Let Me Be (13)
Little Bit Of Love (7)
Little Bit Strong (12)
Little Bitty Pretty One (5)
Long Ago (3)
Look Before You Leap (10,11)
Looking In (9)

Lovin' So Good (13)
Maybe It's You (7)
Mighty Good Loving (5)
Move On (3)
New Kind Of Love (6)
Nineteen Days (12) **48**
No Stopping (6)
No Time To Lose (1)
Ol' Sol (3)
On Broadway (2)
On The Move (6)
Over And Over (8) **1**
Pick Up Your Phone (12)
Picture Of You (12)
Play With Me (13)
Please Love Me (7)
Please Tell Me Why (10,11) **28**
Pumping (7)
Reelin' And Rockin' (11) **23**
Remember, It's Me (5)
Rumble (2)
Satisfied With You (10,11) **50**
Say You Want Me (4)

Scared Of Falling In Love (9)
She's A Loving Girl (7)
She's All Mine (1)
Sitting Here Baby (12)
Small Talk (12)
Somebody Find A New Love (9)
Something I've Always Wanted (12)
Sometimes (3)
Stay (1)
Sweet Memories (6)
Tabatha Twitchit (13)
That's How Long Our Love Will Last (7)
Theme Without A Name (2)
Thinking Of You Baby (13)
'Til The Right One Comes Along (5)
Time (1)
To Me (3)
Today (9)
Try Too Hard (9,11) **12**
We'll Be Running (3)
What Is There To Say (5)

When (4)
When I'm Alone (6)
Whenever You're Around (3)
Who Does He Think He Is (3)
You Don't Play Me Around (13)
You Don't Want My Loving (12)
You Got What It Takes (13) **7**
You Know You're Lying (10)
You Never Listen (10)
Your Turn To Cry (5)
Zip-A-Dee-Doo-Dah (2)

CLARK, Dick — see RADIO/TV CELEBRITY COMPILATIONS

CLARK, Gene

Original member of The Byrds. Native of Tipton, Missouri. Died on 5/24/91 (age 46) of natural causes. Also see McGuinn, Clark & Hillman.

DEBUT DATE	PEAK POS	WKS CHR	GOLD	#	ARTIST — Album Title	$	Label & Number
11/2/74	144	5			No Other	$10	Asylum 1016

From A Silver Phial
Lady Of The North

Life's Greatest Fool
No Other

Silver Raven
Some Misunderstanding

Strength Of Strings
True One

★★264★★ CLARK, Petula

Born on 11/15/32 in Epsom, England. Pop singer/actress. On radio at age nine; own show *Pet's Parlour* at age 11. TV series in England in 1950. First U.S. record release for Coral in 1951. Appeared in over 20 British films from 1944-57; revived her film career in the late 1960s, starring in *Finian's Rainbow* and *Goodbye Mr. Chips*.

DEBUT DATE	PEAK POS	WKS CHR	GOLD	#	ARTIST — Album Title	$	Label & Number
2/13/65	21	36		1	Downtown	$20	Warner 1590
5/29/65	42	17		2	I Know A Place	$20	Warner 1598
10/23/65	129	9		3	The World's Greatest International Hits!	$20	Warner 1608
4/9/66	68	12		4	My Love	$20	Warner 1630
9/3/66	43	16		5	I Couldn't Live Without Your Love	$20	Warner 1645
2/18/67	49	27		6	Color My World/Who Am I	$15	Warner 1673

DEBUT DATE	PEAK POS	WKS CHR	GOLD	ARTIST — Album Title	$	Label & Number
				CLARK, Petula — Cont'd		
9/2/67	**27**	27		7 These Are My Songs	$15	Warner 1698
2/17/68	**93**	23		8 The Other Man's Grass Is Always Greener	$15	Warner 1719
9/7/68	**51**	21		9 Petula	$15	Warner 1743
12/28/68+	**57**	17		10 Petula Clark's Greatest Hits, Vol. 1 ...... [G]	$15	Warner 1765
5/17/69	**37**	11		11 Portrait Of Petula	$15	Warner 1789
12/27/69+	**176**	7		12 Just Pet	$15	Warner 1823
8/8/70	**198**	2		13 Memphis	$15	Warner 1862
4/10/71	**178**	3		14 Warm And Tender	$15	Warner 1885

Ad, The (11)
Answer Me My Love (8)
At The Crossroads (8)
Baby It's Me (1)
Ballad Of A Sad Young Man (8)
Bang Bang (5)
Be Good To Me (1)
Beautiful (14)
Beautiful In The Rain (9)
Black Coffee (8)
Boy From Ipanema (3)
Butterfly (12)
Call Me (2,10)
Cat In The Window (The Bird In The Sky) (8) **26**
Cherish (8)
Color My World (6,10) **16**
Come Rain Or Come Shine (5)
Couldn't Sleep (14)
Cry Like A Baby (14)
Crying Through A Sleepless Night (1)
Cuando Calienta El Sol (Love Me With All Your Heart) (2)
Dance With Me (4)
Dancing In The Street (2)
Days (9)
Don't Give Up (9) **37**
Don't Say I Didn't Tell You So (14)

Don't Sleep In The Subway (7) **5**
Downtown (1,10) **1**
Elusive Butterfly (5)
England Swings (6)
Eternally (7)
Every Little Bit Hurts (2)
Everything In The Garden (2)
Fill The World With Love (12)
Foggy Day (2)
Fool On The Hill (12)
For Free (14)
For Love (8)
For Those In Love (12)
Games People Play (11)
Goin' Out Of My Head (2)
Good Life (9)
Goodnight Sweet Dreams (13)
Gotta Tell The World (2)
Groovin' (7)
Groovy Kind Of Love (5)
Happy Heart (11) **62**
Happy Together (12)
Have Another Dream On Me (9)
Have I The Right (3)
Heart (2)
Hello, Dolly! (3)
Here, There & Everywhere (6)
Hey, Jude (12)
Hold On To What You've Got (4)

Homeward Bound (5)
Houses (12)
How Insensitive (7)
How We Gonna Live To Be A Hundred Years Old Together (7)
I Can't Remember Ever Loving You (4)
I Could Have Danced All Night (8)
I Couldn't Live Without Your Love (5,10) **9**
I Just Can't Wait To Hold You (14)
I Know A Place (2,10) **3**
I Wanna See Morning With Him (13)
I Want To Hold Your Hand (3)
I (Who Have Nothing) (3)
I Will Wait For You (7)
I've Got My Eyes On You (14)
If Ever You're Lonely (11)
If I Only Had Time (12)
If I Were A Bell (4)
Imagine (7)
"In" Crowd (2)
In Love (1)
It Don't Matter To Me (13)
Just Say Goodbye (4)
Kiss Me Goodbye (9) **15**
L'ile De France (8)
Las Vegas (6)

Last Waltz (8)
Let It Be Me (11)
Let Me Be The One (14)
Let Me Tell You Baby (1)
Life And Soul Of The Party (4)
Lights Of Night (12)
Loss Of Love (14)
Love Is Here (7)
Love Is The Only Thing (11)
Lover Man (7)
Lovin' Things (11)
Maybe I'm Amazed (14)
Monday, Monday (5)
Morgen (One More Sunrise) (3)
Music (1)
My Funny Valentine (11)
My Love (4,10) **1**
Neon Rainbow (13)
Never On Sunday (3)
No One Better Than You (12) **93**
Nothing's As Good As It Used To Be (13)
Now That You've Gone (1)
On The Path Of Glory (7)
One In A Million (9)
Other Man's Grass Is Always Greener (8) **31**
People Get Ready (13)
Please Don't Go (6)
Rain (5)

Reach Out, I'll Be There (6)
Resist (7)
Right On (13)
Round Every Corner (10) **21**
San Francisco (Be Sure To Wear Some Flowers In Your Hair) (7)
Sign Of The Times (4,10) **11**
Smile (8)
Some (11)
Song Of My Life (14)
Special People (6)
Strangers And Lovers (2)
Strangers In The Night (5)
Sun Shines Out Of Your Shoes (9)
Tell Me (That It's Love) (1)
That Old Time Feeling (13)
That's What Life Is All About (13)
There Goes My Love, There Goes My Life (5)
Things Bright & Beautiful (12)
Thirty-First Of June (4)
This Girl's In Love With You (9)
This Is Goodbye (1)
This Is My Song (7) **3**
Time And Love (14)
Time For Love (4)

Today, Tomorrow (8)
True Love Never Runs Smooth (1)
Two Rivers (5,10)
Volare (Nel Blu, Dipinto Di Blu) (3)
Wasn't It You (5)
We Can Work It Out (4)
We're Falling In Love Again (9)
What Now My Love (3)
What Would I Be (6)
When I Give My Heart (11)
When I Was A Child (11)
When The World Was Round (13)
Where Did We Go Wrong (4)
While The Children Play (6)
Who Am I (6,10) **21**
Why Can't I Cry? (9)
Why Don't They Understand (3)
Winchester Cathedral (6)
Windmills Of Your Mind (11)
You Belong To Me (1)
You Can't Keep Me From Loving You (3)
You'd Better Come Home (10) **22**
You're The One (2,10)
Your Love Is Everywhere (9)

CLARK, Roy
Born on 4/15/33 in Meherrin, Virginia. Superb guitar, banjo and fiddle player. Acted in TV series *The Beverly Hillbillies*, appearing as both Cousin Roy and Roy's mother, Big Mama Halsey. With the TV series *Hee Haw* since the first show in 1969.

DEBUT DATE	PEAK POS	WKS CHR	GOLD	ARTIST — Album Title	$	Label & Number
7/5/69	**50**	20		1 Yesterday, When I Was Young	$12	Dot 25953
1/3/70	**129**	9		2 The Everlovin' Soul Of Roy Clark	$10	Dot 25972
8/29/70	**176**	6		3 I Never Picked Cotton	$10	Dot 25980
4/3/71	**178**	8		4 The Best Of Roy Clark ...... [G]	$10	Dot 25986
8/14/71	**197**	2		5 The Incredible Roy Clark	$10	Dot 25990
7/29/72	**112**	12		6 Roy Clark Country!	$10	Dot 25997
5/5/73	**172**	6		7 Roy Clark/Superpicker ...... [I]	$10	Dot 26008
4/13/74	**186**	3		8 Roy Clark/The Entertainer	$10	Dot 2001

All The Way (2)
April's Fool (1)
As Far As I'm Concerned (5)
Aura Lee (7)
Back In The Race (5)
Carolyn (6)
Chomp 'N' (8)
Darby's Castle (6)
Days Of Sand And Shovels (1)
Do You Believe This Town (4)
Don't Touch Me (5)
Dozen Pairs Of Boots (6)
Drink To Me Only With Thine Eyes (8)
Duelin' Banjos (8)
Family Man (6)
For Once In My Life (2)

For The Good Times (5)
For The Life Of Me (1)
Hangin' On (5)
He'll Have To Go (6)
Honeymoon Feelin' (8)
I Need To Be Needed (2)
I Never Picked Cotton (3,4)
I Really Don't Want To Know (8)
I Remember Loving Someone (5)
I'll Take The Time (6)
Is Anybody Goin' To San Antone (3)
It's All Over (All Over Again) (8)
January, April And Me (3)
Just Another Man (1)

Kiss An Angel Good Morning (6)
Last Letter (2)
Let Me Be There (8)
Lonesome Too Long (3)
Lord, Let It Rain (8)
Love Is Just A State Of Mind (1,4)
Love Story, Theme From (7)
Love's All Around You (8)
Malaguena (4)
Mary Ann Regrets (5)
Me And Bobby McGee (2)
Middle Of The Road (3)
Midnight Cowboy Rides Again (7)
Morningside Of The Mountain (2)

Most Beautiful Girl (8)
My Goal For Today (5)
Never On Sunday (7)
Odds And Ends (Bits And Pieces) (1)
Ode To A Critter (6)
Raggedy Ann (1)
Riders In The Sky (7)
Right Or Left At Oak Street (2,4)
Rocky Top (5)
Roy's Guitar Boogie (7)
Say Amen (4)
September Song (1,4)
She Cried (5)
She Cries For Me (3)
She Makes The Living Worthwhile (8)

She's All I Got (6)
Simple Thing As Love (1,4)
Since December (3)
Snowbird (7)
Somewhere, My Love (7)
Strangers (3)
Sunday Mornin' Comin' Down (3)
Sunday Sunrise (8)
Tara Theme (7)
Thank God And Greyhound (3,4) **90**
That's All That Matters (5)
Then She's A Lover (2,4) **94**
Tips Of My Fingers (1,4)
Today (2)
Today I Started Loving You Again (7)

True Love (2)
Unchained Melody (2)
When A Man Becomes A Man (1)
When The Wind Blows (In Chicago) (4)
Yesterday, When I Was Young (1,4) **19**
You Don't Have Very Far To Go (2)
You Gotta Love People (3)

★★388★★ **CLARKE, Stanley**
Born on 6/30/51 in Philadelphia. R&B-jazz bassist/violinist/cellist. With Chick Corea in Return To Forever in 1973. Much session work, solo debut in 1974. Member of Fuse One in 1982 and Animal Logic in 1989.

DEBUT DATE	PEAK POS	WKS CHR	GOLD	ARTIST — Album Title	$	Label & Number
1/18/75	**59**	16		1 Stanley Clarke ...... [I]	$10	Nemperor 431
11/1/75	**34**	19		2 Journey To Love ...... [I]	$10	Nemperor 433
9/25/76	**34**	22		3 School Days ...... [I]	$10	Nemperor 439
4/29/78	**57**	19		4 Modern Man ...... [I]	$10	Nemperor 35303
7/21/79	**62**	14		5 I Wanna Play For You ...... [I-L]	$12	Nemperor 35680 [2]
				half is live and half is studio		
6/28/80	**95**	11		6 Rocks, Pebbles And Sand	$8	Epic 36506
5/9/81	**33**	23		7 The Clarke/Duke Project *	$8	Epic 36918
8/21/82	**114**	8		8 Let Me Know You	$8	Epic 38086

146

| 11/26/83+ | 146 | 10 | 9 | The Clarke/Duke Project II * .... | $8 | Epic 38934 |

*STANLEY CLARKE/GEORGE DUKE

| 4/28/84 | 149 | 13 | 10 | Time Exposure .... | $8 | Epic 38688 |

All About (5)
All Hell Broke Loose (6)
Are You Ready (For The Future) (10)
Atlanta (9)
Blues for Mingus (5)
Christopher Ivanhoe (3)
Concerto For Jazz (medley) (2)
Dancer, The (3)
Danger Street (6)
Dayride (5)
Desert Song (3)
Every Reason To Smile (9)
Finding My Way (7)
Force Of Love (8)
Future (10)

Future Shock (10)
Good Times (9)
Got To Find My Own Place (4)
Great Danes (9)
He Lives On (Story About The Last Journey Of A Warrior) (4)
Heaven Sent You (10)
Hello Jeff (2)
Heroes (9)
Hot Fun (3,5)
I Just Want To Be Your Brother (8)
I Just Want To Love You (7)
I Know Just How You Feel (10)

I Wanna Play For You (5)
It's What She Didn't Say (4)
Jamaican Boy (5)
Journey To Love (2)
Just A Feeling (5)
Let Me Know You (8)
Life Is Just A Game (3)
Life Suite (Part I, II, III, IV) (1)
Lopsy Lu (5)
Louie Louie (7)
Modern Man (4)
More Hot Fun (4)
My Greatest Hits (5)
Never Judge A Cover By It's Book (7)
New York City (8)

Off The Planet (5)
Play The Bass (8,10)
Power (1)
Put It On The Line (9)
Quiet Afternoon (3,5)
Relaxed Occasion (4)
Rock 'N' Roll Jelly (4,5)
Rock Orchestra (medley) (5)
Rocks, Pebbles And Sand (6)
School Days (3,5)
Secret To My Heart (8)
Serious Occasion (4)
Silly Putty (2)
Slow Dance (4)
Song To John (2)
Spacerunner (10)

Spanish Phases For Strings & Bass (1)
Speedball (10)
Story Of A Man And A Woman Medley (5)
Straight To The Top (8)
Strange Weather (5)
Streets Of Philadelphia (5)
Sweet Baby (7) **19**
Time Exposure (10)
Together Again (5)
Touch And Go (7)
Trip You In Love (9)
Try Me Baby (9)
Underestimation (6)
Vulcan Princess (1)
We Supply (6)

Wild Dog (7)
Winners (7)
Yesterday Princess (1)
You Are The One For Me (8)
You're Gonna Love It (9)
You/Me Together (6)

★★493★★ CLASH, The

Eclectic new wave rock group formed in London in 1976. Consisted of John "Joe Strummer" Mellor (vocals, lyrics), Mick Jones (guitar), Paul Simonon (bass) and Nicky "Topper" Headon (drums). Political activists, they wrote songs protesting racism and oppression. Headon left in May 1983; replaced by Peter Howard. Jones (not to be confused with Mick Jones of Foreigner) left band in 1984 to form Big Audio Dynamite. Strummer disbanded The Clash in early 1986, and appeared in the 1987 film *Straight To Hell.*

2/24/79	128	10		1	Give 'Em Enough Rope	$8	Epic 35543
9/8/79	126	6	●	2	The Clash	$8	Epic 36060
2/9/80	27	33	●	3	London Calling	$10	Epic 36328 [2]
11/22/80	74	16		4	Black Market Clash	$8	Epic 36846
					10" album		
2/7/81	24	20		5	Sandinista!	$15	Epic 37037 [3]
6/12/82+	7	61	▲	6	Combat Rock	$8	Epic 37689
12/7/85+	88	12		7	Cut The Crap	$8	Epic 40017
5/28/88	142	8		8	The Story Of The Clash, Volume I ....[G]	$10	Epic 44035 [2]

All The Young Punks (New Boots And Contracts) (1)
Are You Red..Y (7)
Armagideon Time (4,8)
Atom Tan (6)
Bankrobber (4,8)
Brand New Cadillac (3)
Broadway (5)
Call Up (5)
Capital Radio One (4,8)
Car Jamming (6)
Card Cheat (3)
Career Opportunities (2,5,8)
Charlie Don't Surf (5)
Cheapskate (1)
Cheat (4)
City Of The Dead (4)
Clampdown (3)
Clash City Rockers (2,8)
Complete Control (2,8)
Cool Under Heat (6)
Corner Soul (5)

Crooked Beat (5)
Death Is A Star (6)
Death Or Glory (3)
Dictator (7)
Dirty Punk (7)
Drug-Stabbing Time (1)
English Civil War (1,8)
Equaliser, The (5)
Fingerpoppin' (7)
Four Horsemen (3)
Garageland (2)
Ghetto Defendant (6)
Guns Of Brixton (3,8)
Guns On The Roof (1)
Hate And War (2)
Hateful (3)
Hitsville U.K. (5)
I Fought The Law (2,8)
I'm Not Down (3)
I'm So Bored With The U.S.A. (2)
If Music Could Talk (5)

Inoculated City (6)
Ivan Meets G.I. Joe (5)
Jail Guitar Doors (2)
Janie Jones (2)
Jimmy Jazz (3)
Julie's In The Drug Squad (1)
Junco Partner (5)
Junkie Slip (5)
Justice Tonight (medley) (4)
Kick It Over (medley) (4)
Kingston Advice (5)
Know Your Rights (6)
Koka Kola (3)
Last Gang In Town (1)
Leader, The (5)
Let's Go Crazy (5)
Life Is Wild (5)
Lightning Strikes (Not Once But Twice) (5)
Living In Fame (5)
London Calling (3,8)
London's Burning (2,8)

Look Here (5)
Lose This Skin (5)
Lost In The Supermarket (3,8)
Lover's Rock (3)
Magnificent Seven (5,8)
Mensforth Hill (5)
Midnight Log (5)
Movers And Shakers (5)
North And South (7)
One More Dub (5)
One More Time (5)
Overpowered By Funk (6)
Play To Win (7)
Police And Thieves (2,8)
Police On My Back (5)
Pressure Drop (4)
Prisoner, The (4)
Rebel Waltz (5)
Red Angel Dragnet (6)
Remote Control (1)
Revolution Rock (3)

Right Profile (3)
Rock The Casbah (6,8) **8**
Rudie Can't Fail (3)
Safe European Home (1,8)
Sean Flynn (6)
Shepherds Delight (5)
Should I Stay Or Should I Go? (6,8) **45**
Silicone On Sapphire (5)
Somebody Got Murdered (5,8)
Something About England (5)
Sound Of The Sinners (5)
Spanish Bombs (3,8)
Stay Free (1,8)
Straight To Hell (6,8)
Street Parade (5)
This Is England (7)
This Is Radio Clash (8)
Three Card Trick (6)
Time Is Tight (4)

Tommy Gun (1,8)
Train In Vain (Stand By Me) (3,8) **23**
Up In Heaven (Not Only Here) (5)
Version City (5)
Version Pardner (5)
Washington Bullets (5)
We Are The Clash (7)
What's My Name (2)
White Man In Hammersmith Palais (2,8)
White Riot (2,8)
Wrong 'Em Boyo (3)

CLASSICS IV

Quintet formed in Jacksonville, Florida. Consisted of Dennis Yost (vocals), J.R. Cobb (lead guitar), Wally Eaton (rhythm guitar), Joe Wilson (bass; replaced by Dean Daughtry) and Kim Venable (drums). Cobb, Daughtry and producer Buddy Buie joined the Atlanta Rhythm Section in 1974.

3/9/68	140	7		1	Spooky	$15	Imperial 12371
2/1/69	196	3		2	Mamas And Papas/Soul Train	$15	Imperial 12407
4/26/69	45	20		3	Traces	$15	Imperial 12429
12/6/69+	50	20		4	Dennis Yost & The Classics IV/Golden Greats-Volume I	$15	Imperial 16000

Bed Of Roses (2)
Book A Trip (1)
Bus Stop (1)
By The Time I Get To Phoenix (1)
Change Of Heart (4) **49**
Daydream Believer (1)

Everyday With You Girl (3,4) **19**
Free (3)
Girl From Ipanema (Garota De Ipanema) (2)
Goin' Out Of My Head (1)
It Ain't Necessarily So (2)
Just Between You And Me (1)

Ladies Man (2)
Letter, The (1)
Mama's And Papa's (2)
Mary, Mary Row Your Boat (1,4)
Mr. Blue (3)
Nobody Loves You But Me (3)
Our Day Will Come (3)

Pity The Fool (2)
Poor People (1)
Rainy Day (3)
Sentimental Lady (3)
Something I'll Remember (3,4)
Soul Train (2,4) **90**
Spooky (1,4) **3**

Stormy (2,4) **5**
Strange Changes (2,4)
Sunny (3,4)
Traces (3,4) **2**
Traffic Jam (3)
24 Hours Of Loneliness (2,4)
Waves (2,4)
You Are My Sunshine (1)

CLAY, Andrew Dice

Comedian from Brooklyn. Appeared in the films *Pretty In Pink, Casual Sex, The Adventures of Ford Fairlane* and TV's *Crime Story.*

4/29/89	94	47		1	Dice ....[C]	$8	Def Amer. 24214
4/21/90	39	24		2	The Day The Laughter Died ....[C]	$14	Def Amer. 24287 [2]
5/4/91	81	12		3	Dice Rules ....[C]	$12	Def Amer. 26555
5/2/92	144	4		4	40 Too Long ....[C]	$12	Def Amer. 26854

A+ (2)
Action (3)
Apartment Life (3)
Attitude, The (1)
Automatic Pilot (2)
Backwards (3)

Bad Press (3)
Bait, The (1)
Bambi (3)
Birds (3)
Black Chicks (3)
Brooklyn Bad Boy (3)

Car Ride (Goin' To A Party) (3)
Chicks Aren't Funny (Joey Will) (3)
Christmas Presents (3)
Cigarettes (2)

Concave (2)
Couples In Love (1)
Day At The Beach (3)
Debbie Duz Everything (3)
Dice And Truckdrivers (4)
Dice At The Drive Thru (4)

Dice Buys A Suit (4)
Dice Does It Like Dis (4)
Dice Gets Creative In Bed (4)
Dice Goes To The Mall (3)
Dice Greeting Cards (4)

Dice Has Random Thoughts (4)
Dice Jerks Off (4)
Dice Just Says No Leno (4)
Dice Knows When To Say When (4)

DEBUT DATE	PEAK POS	WKS CHR	GOLD	ARTIST — Album Title	$	Label & Number

CLAY, Andrew Dice — Cont'd

Dice Learns To Mambo (4)
Dice On Bodybuilders (4)
Dice On Complaints (4)
Dice On Disasters (4)
Dice On Lasting Relationships (4)
Dice On Manners (4)
Dice On Nutrition (4)
Dice On Orgasms (4)
Dice On Reading Material (4)
Dice On Redheaded Men (4)
Dice On Redheads (4)
Dice Rewrites History (4)
Dice Stops For Gas (4)
Dice Talks To The Salesmen (4)
Dice The Advocate (4)
Dice Vs. PeeWee (4)
Dice's Checklist (4)

Divider, The (2)
Doctors And Nurses (1)
Dogs & Birds (2)
Don't Move (3)
Double Date (2)
Double Parking (3)
Driveway, The (3)
Fat Orgasms (3)
Female Anatomy (2)
Filthy In Bed (3)
First Blow-Job (3)
First Kiss (2)
Frozen Food (2)
Gift, The (2)
Golden Age Of Television (1)
Grocery Store (3)
Handicaps, Cripples (3)
History Lesson (2)
Hoggin' (1)

Holdy Toidy Chicks (3)
Holiday Season (2)
Hot Mama (2)
Hour Back ... Get It? (2)
How Are Ya? (2,3)
Industrial Size (3)
Japs (3)
Jerkin' Off (2)
Joey (1)
Judy (2)
Kids (2)
Laughter Vs. Comedy (2)
Let Yourself Go (4)
Masturbation (2)
Milk & Shampoo (2)
Moby And The Japs (1)
Mother & Son (2)
Mother Goose (1)

Mothers, Daughters & Sisters (2)
Multiple Sclerosis (2)
News, The (3)
1989 - A Review (3)
1990 (2)
No Guilt (1)
No Pity (1)
Opportunity In America (Al Capone's Safe) (3)
Osmonds, The (2)
People Are Pricks (3)
Personal Delivery Service (2)
Phone Sex (3)
Pizza (2)
Places To Meet Chicks (2)
Rhyme Renditions (2)
Salt & Pepper (3)
Shakin' Hands (3)

Shampoo (1)
Silence Is Golden (2)
Smokin' (1)
Smokin' For Your Health (3)
Something Soft (2)
Speedin' (1)
Subway Travel (3)
Texas (2)
3 Beautiful Dates (3)
Tree, The (2)
True Stories (2)
Turn-On Words (2)
Under 2 Minutes (2)
Urinal, The (3)
Vibrant Beautiful Woman (3)
What A Mess (2)
What Did She Say? (2)
What If The Chick Gets Pregnant... (1)

What'll It Be (2)
When I Was Young (1)
While The Cats Away (2)
Woman's World (2)
Women Comics (2)
Ya Can't Be Nice To Them (3)
Ya Hear? (3)
You May Be Dancing With Me (4)

CLAY, Cassius

Born on 1/18/42 in Louisville, Kentucky. Former world heavyweight boxing champ. Changed name to Muhammad Ali in 1966. Also see soundtrack *The Greatest*.

| 10/12/63 | 61 | 20 | | I Am The Greatest!.. [C] | $35 | Columbia 2093 |

comedy bits and poetry from Clay

Round 1: I Am The Greatest
Round 2: I Am The Double Greatest
Round 3: Do You Have To Ask?
Round 4: "I Have Written A Drama," He Said Playfully
Round 5: Will The Real Sonny Liston Please Fall Down
Round 6: Funny You Should Ask
Round 7: 2138
Round 8: The Knockout

CLAY, Tom

Working as a substitute DJ at KGBS-Los Angeles when he created this recording.

| 8/28/71 | 92 | 5 | | What The World Needs Now Is Love................................. | $12 | MoWest 103 |

Baby I Need Your Loving
Both Sides Now
Bridge Over Troubled Water
For Years?
Mac Arthur Park
This Guy's In Love With You
Victors, The
What The World Needs Now Is Love/Abraham, Martin And John 8
What's Going On
Whatever Happened To Love

CLAYDERMAN, Richard

French pianist — real name: Phillipe Pages.

| 11/24/84 | 160 | 9 | | Amour...[I] | $8 | Columbia 39603 |

Ave Maria
Ballade Pour Adeline
Chariots Of Fire
Harmony
Hello
How Deep Is Your Love
Memory
Only You
Up Where We Belong
Way I Loved You
Way We Were

CLAYTON, Merry

Real name: Mary Clayton. Backup vocalist from Los Angeles. In The Raeletts, Ray Charles' backing group. Formed R&B vocal group, Sisters Love, in 1971. Acted in the 1987 film *Maid To Order*.

| 11/20/71+ | 180 | 11 | | 1 Merry Clayton .... | $10 | Ode 77012 |
| 9/6/75 | 146 | 8 | | 2 Keep Your Eye On The Sparrow .... | $10 | Ode 77030 |

After All This Time (1) 71
Do What You Know (2)
Gets Hard Sometimes (2)
Gold Fever (2)
Grandma's Hands (1)
How'd I Know (2)
If I Lose (2)
Keep Your Eye On The Sparrow (2)
Light On The Hill (1)
Love Me Or Let Me Be Lonely (1)
Loving Grows Up Slow (2)
One More Ride (2)
Rainy Day Women #12 & 35 (2)
Room 205 (2)
Same Old Story (1)
Sho' Nuff (1)
Sink Or Swim (2)
Song For You (1)
Southern Man (1)
Steamroller (1)
Walk On In (1)
Whatever (1)

CLAYTON-THOMAS, David

Born David Thomsett on 9/13/41 in England. Lead singer of Blood, Sweat & Tears.

| 9/27/69 | 159 | 8 | | 1 David Clayton-Thomas! .... [E] | $20 | Decca 75146 |

recordings prior to BS&T days

| 4/15/72 | 184 | 3 | | 2 David Clayton-Thomas .... | $15 | Columbia 31000 |

Boom Boom (1)
Call It Stormy Monday (1)
Caress Me Pretty Music (2)
Don't Let It Bring You Down (2)
Done Somebody Wrong (1)
Dying To Live (2)
Good Lovin' (1)
Howlin' For My Darling (1)
I Got A Woman (1)
Magnificent Sanctuary Band (2)
North Beach Racetrack (2)
Once Burned (1)
Poison Ivy (1)
Say Boss Man (1)
She (2)
Sing A Song (2)
Stealin' In The Name Of The Lord (2)
Tobacco Road (1)
We're All Meat From The Same Bone (2)
Who's Been Talkin' (1)

CLEAR LIGHT

Los Angeles rock band — Cliff DeYoung, lead singer.

| 11/25/67+ | 126 | 13 | | Clear Light .... | $20 | Elektra 74011 |

Ballad Of Freddie & Larry
Black Roses
Child's Smile
How Many Days Have Passed
Mr. Blue
Night Sounds Loud
Sand
Street Singer
They Who Have Nothing
Think Again
With All In Mind

CLEGG, Johnny, & Savuka

Vocalist/guitarist/dancer Clegg with the multi-racial, Zulu-pop South African band Savuka. Clegg, born in Rochdale, U.K., was raised in South Africa. A former college lecturer of social anthropology, Clegg co-founded Juluka, in 1979; disbanded in late 1985. In 1986, formed Savuka (Zulu for "we have arisen") with Dudu Zulu and Derek De Beer (both of Juluka), Steve Mavuso, Solly Letwaba and Keith Hutchinson.

| 9/10/88 | 155 | 7 | | 1 Shadow Man.. | $8 | Capitol 90411 |
| 5/12/90 | 123 | 13 | | 2 Cruel, Crazy, Beautiful World .... | $12 | Capitol 93446 |

African Shadow Man (1)
Bombs Away (2)
Cruel, Crazy, Beautiful World (2)
Dance Across The Centuries (1)
Dela (I Know Why The Dog Howls At The Moon) (2)
Human Rainbow (1)
I Call Your Name (1)
It's An Illusion (2)
Jericho (2)
Joey Don't Do It (1)
Moliva (2)
One (Hu)Man One Vote (2)
Rolling Ocean (2)
Siyayilanda (1)
Take My Heart Away (1)
Talk To The People (1)
Too Early For The Sky (1)
Vezandlebe (2)
Waiting, The (1)
Warsaw 1943 (I Never Betrayed The Revolution) (2)
Woman Be My Country (2)

CLEMONS, Clarence

Saxophonist with Bruce Springsteen's E Street Band. Born on 1/11/42.

| 11/5/83 | 174 | 5 | | 1 Rescue.. | $8 | Columbia 38933 |

with The Red Bank Rockers - John "J.T." Bowen, lead singer

| 11/23/85+ | 62 | 18 | | 2 Hero.. | $8 | Columbia 40010 |

DEBUT DATE	PEAK POS	WKS CHR	G O L D	ARTIST — Album Title	$	Label & Number

CLEMONS, Clarence — Cont'd

Christina (2)	It's Alright With Me Girl (2)	Liberation Fire (Mokshagun)	Money To The Rescue (1)	Sun Ain't Gonna Shine
Cross The Line (2)	Jump Start My Heart (1)	(2)	Resurrection Shuffle (1)	Anymore (2)	Woman's Got The Power (1)
Heartache #99 (1)	Kissin' On U (2)	Man In Love (1)	Rock 'N' Roll DJ (1)	Temptation (2)	**You're A Friend Of Mine**
I Wanna Be Your Hero (2)			Savin' Up (1)		(2) **18**

CLEVELAND ORCHESTRA
Michael Tilson Thomas, conductor.

3/29/75	**152**	4		Carl Orff: Carmina Burana	$10	Columbia 33172
				includes the complete opera (composed in 1936)		

CLIBURN, Van
Born Harvey Cliburn, Jr. on 7/12/34 in Shreveport, Louisiana. Classical pianist.

8/4/58	**1**[7]	125	▲	**1 Tchaikovsky: Piano Concerto No. 1** .... [I]	$30	RCA 2252
				Kiril Kondrashin, conductor		
7/13/59+	**10**	60		**2 Rachmaninoff: Piano Concerto No. 3** ....[I-L]	$20	RCA 2355
				Carnegie Hall performance of 5/19/58		
1/9/61	**134**	13		**3** Schumann: Piano Concerto in A Minor .... [I]	$15	RCA 2455
				Fritz Reiner conducts the Chicago Symphony Orchestra		
2/3/62	**71**	29	●	**4** My Favorite Chopin .... [I]	$12	RCA 2576
3/10/62	**25**	13		**5** Brahms: Piano Concerto No. 2 .... [I]	$12	RCA 2581
				Fritz Reiner conducts the Chicago Symphony Orchestra		

Brahms: Concerto No. 2 In B-Flat, Op. 83 (5)	Chopin: Etude In E, Op. 10, No. 3 (4)	Chopin: Polonaise No. 6 In A-Flat, Op. 53 (4)	Chopin: Waltz No. 7 In C-Sharp Minor, Op. 64, No. 2 (4)	Schumann: Piano Concerto In A Minor, Op. 54 (3)
Chopin: Ballade No. 3 In A-Flat, Op. 47 (4)	Chopin: Fantaisie In F Minor, Op. 49 (4)	Chopin: Scherzo No. 3 In C-Sharp Minor, Op. 39 (4)	Rachmaninoff: Piano Concerto No. 3 In D Minor, Op. 30 (2)	Tchaikovsky: Piano Concerto No. 1, In B-Flat Minor, Op. 23 (1)
Chopin: Etude In A Minor, Op. 25, No. 11 (4)	Chopin: Nocturne No. 17 In B, Op. 62, No. 1 (4)			

CLIFF, Jimmy
Born James Chambers in 1948. Jamaican reggae singer/composer. Starred in films *The Harder They Come* (1975) and *Club Paradise* (1986). Also see *Club Paradise* soundtrack.

3/22/75	**140**	8		**1** The Harder They Come ....[S]	$15	Mango 9202
				includes "Draw Your Brakes" by Scotty, "Rivers Of Babylon" by The Melodians, "Johnny Too Bad" by The Slickers, "Shanty Town" by Desmond Dekker and "Sweet And Dandy" & "Pressure Drop" by The Maytals.		
11/1/75	**195**	2		**2** Follow My Mind	$10	Reprise 2218
8/14/82	**186**	2		**3** Special	$8	Columbia 38099

Dear Mother (2)	If I Follow My Mind (2)	News, The (2)	Roots Radical (3)	Where There Is Love (3)
Going Mad (2)	Keep On Dancing (3)	No Woman, No Cry (2)	Rub-A-Dub Partner (3)	Who Feels It, Knows It (2)
Harder They Come (1)	Look At The Mountains (2)	Originator (3)	Sitting In Limbo (1)	You Can Get It If You Really
Hypocrites (2)	Love Heights (3)	Peace Officer (3)	Special (3)	Want (1)
I'm Gonna Live, I'm Gonna Love (2)	Love Is All (3)	Remake The World (2)	Treat The Youths Right (3)	You're The Only One (2)
	Many Rivers To Cross (1)	Rock Children (3)	Wahjahka Man (2)	

CLIFFORD, Linda
Black vocalist from Brooklyn. Former Miss New York State. With Jericho Jazz Singers; own trio in 1967.

5/20/78	**22**	22		**1** If My Friends Could See Me Now	$15	Curtom 5021
4/7/79	**26**	17		**2** Let Me Be Your Woman	$10	RSO 3902 [2]
12/1/79	**117**	9		**3** Here's My Love	$8	RSO 3067
7/19/80	**180**	4		**4** The Right Combination..	$8	RSO 3084
				LINDA CLIFFORD/CURTIS MAYFIELD		
10/4/80	**160**	6		**5** I'm Yours	$8	RSO 3087

Ain't No Love Lost (4)	Don't Let Me Have Another Bad Dream (2)	I Had A Talk With My Man (5)	If You Let Me (5)	One Of Those Songs (2)	Sweet Melodies (2)
Bailin' Out (3)	Gypsy Lady (1)	I Just Wanna Wanna (3)	It Don't Hurt No More (5)	Please Darling, Don't Say	You Are, You Are (1)
Between You Baby And Me (4)	Here's My Love (3)	I Want To Get Away With You (5)	It's Lovin' Time (Your Baby's Home) (4)	Goodbye (3)	
Bridge Over Troubled Water (2) **41**	Hold Me Close (2)	I'm So Proud (4)	King For A Night (3)	Red Light (5) **41**	
Broadway Gypsy Lady (1)	I Can't Let This Good Thing Get Away (2)	I'm Yours (5)	Let Me Be Your Woman (2)	Repossessed (3)	
Don't Give It Up (2)	I Feel Like Falling In Love Again (1)	**If My Friends Could See Me Now** (1) **54**	Lonely Night (3)	Right Combination (4)	
			Love's Sweet Sensation (4)	Rock You To Your Socks (4)	
			Never Gonna Stop (3)	**Runaway Love** (1) **76**	
				Shoot Your Best Shot (5)	

CLIMAX
Los Angeles-based pop quintet — Sonny Geraci, lead singer (formerly with The Outsiders).

6/24/72	**177**	7		Climax..	$12	Rocky Road 3506

Child Of December	I've Got Everything	It's Coming Today	Merlin	**Precious And Few 3**
Face The Music	If It Feels Good - Do It	**Life And Breath 52**	Picnic In The Rain	Rainbow Rides Are Free

CLIMAX BLUES BAND
Blues-rock band formed in Stafford, England. Nucleus consisted of Colin Cooper (sax, vocals), Peter Haycock (guitar, vocals), Derek Holt (bass) and John Cuffley (drums).

11/28/70	**197**	1		**1** The Climax Chicago Blues Band Plays On	$12	Sire 97023
2/17/73	**150**	10		**2** Rich Man	$12	Sire 7402
12/1/73+	**107**	30		**3** FM/Live .... [L]	$12	Sire 7411 [2]
6/15/74	**37**	29		**4** Sense Of Direction	$12	Sire 7501
9/13/75	**69**	11		**5** Stamp Album	$12	Sire 7507
10/23/76+	**27**	44		**6** Gold Plated	$12	Sire 7523
4/29/78	**71**	11		**7** Shine On	$10	Sire 6056
6/16/79	**170**	6		**8** Real To Reel	$8	Sire 3334
4/25/81	**175**	16		**9** Flying The Flag	$8	Warner 3493

All The Time In The World (2,3)	Berlin Blues (6)	Children Of The Nightime (8)	Crazy 'Bout My Baby (1)	Extra (6)	Goin' To New York (3)
Amerita (medley) (4)	Blackjack And Me (9)	City Ways (1)	Crazy World (8)	Fallen In Love (For The Very Last Time) (8)	Gospel Singer (7)
Before You Reach The Grave (4)	Champagne & Rock 'N Roll (7)	Cobra (5)	Cubano Chant (1)	Fat City (8)	**Gotta Have More Love** (9) **47**
	Chasing Change (6)	**Couldn't Get It Right** (6) **3**	Dance The Night Away (9)	Flight (1,3)	Grinnin' In Your Face (2)
		Country Hat (3)	Devil Knows (5)		

CLIMAX BLUES BAND — Cont'd

Hey Baby, Everything's Gonna Be Alright, Yeh Yeh Yeh (1)
Hold On To Your Heart (9)
Horizontalized (9)
I Am Constant (3,5)
I Love You (9) *12*
If You Wanna' Know (2)
Let's Work Together (3)
Like A Movie (7)
Little Girl (1)
Long Distance Love (8)
Loosen Up (5)
Losin' The Humbles (4)
Lovin' Wheel (8)
Makin' Love (7) *91*
Mesopopmania (3)
Mighty Fire (6)
Milwaukee Truckin' Blues (Chipper's Song) (4)
Mistress Moonshine (7)
Mole On The Dole (2)
Money In Your Pocket (8)
Money Talkin' (9)
Mr. Goodtime (5)
Mum's The Word (1)
Nogales (4)
Nothing But Starlight (8)
One For Me And You (9)
Reaching Out (4)
Rich Man (2)
Right Now (4)
Rollin' Home (6)
Running Out Of Time (5)
Sav'ry Gravy (6)
Sense Of Direction (medley) (4)
Seventh Son (3)
Shake Your Love (2,3)
Shopping Bag People (4)
Sky High (5)
So Good After Midnight (9)
So Many Roads (1,3)
Spirit Returning (5)
Standing By A River (2,3)
Summer Rain (8)
Teardrops (7)
Temptation Rag (medley) (1)
Together And Free (6)
Twenty Past Two (medley) (1)
Using The Power (5)
Whatcha Feel (7)
When Talking Is Too Much Trouble (7)
You Make Me Sick (2,3)

CLIMIE FISHER

U.K.-based pop/rock duo: Simon Climie (vocals) and Rob Fisher (keyboards). Fisher was a member of Naked Eyes. Chrysalis songwriter Climie wrote Pat Benatar's "Invincible" and "I Knew You Were Waiting (For Me)" by Aretha Franklin and George Michael.

5/28/88	**120**	16		Everything..	$8	Capitol 48338

Bite The Hand That Feeds
Break The Silence
I Won't Bleed For You
Keeping The Mystery Alive
Love Changes (Everything) *23*
Never Let A Chance Go By
Precious Moments
Rise To The Occasion
Room To Move
This Is Me

CLINE, Patsy

Born Virginia Patterson Hensley on 9/8/32 in Winchester, Virginia. Killed in a plane crash with Cowboy Copas and Hawkshaw Hawkins on 3/5/63 near Camden, Tennessee. Elected to the Country Music Hall of Fame in 1973. Jessica Lange played Patsy in the 1985 biographical film *Sweet Dreams*.

3/31/62+	**73**	21		1 Patsy Cline Showcase..	$35	Decca 4202
8/31/63	**74**	12		2 The Patsy Cline Story..[G]	$35	Decca 7176 [2]
11/16/85	**29**	18	●	3 Sweet Dreams - The Life And Times Of Patsy Cline.................[S]	$8	MCA 6149
				featuring Patsy's original vocals		
1/4/92	**166**	1		4 The Patsy Cline Collection...[K]	$48	MCA 10421 [4]
				104 cuts from her entire recording career, 1954-63; includes a 68-page booklet		

Always (4)
Anytime (4)
Back In Baby's Arms (2,4)
Bill Bailey, Won't You Please Come Home [includes 2 versions] (4)
Blue Moon Of Kentucky (3,4)
Church, A Courtroom, And Then Goodbye (4)
Come On In (And Make Yourself At Home) [includes 2 versions] (4)
Crazy (1,2,3,4) *9*
Crazy Arms (4)
Crazy Dreams (4)
Does Your Heart Beat For Me (4)
Don't Ever Leave Me Again (4)
Faded Love (4) *96*
Foolin' 'Round (1,2,3,4)
For Rent (4)
Gotta Lot Of Rhythm In My Soul (4)
Half As Much (3,4)
Have You Ever Been Lonely (Have You Ever Been Blue) (1,4)
He Called Me Baby (4)
Heart You Break May Be Your Own (4)
Heartaches (2,4) *73*
Honky Tonk Merry Go Round (4)
How Can I Face Tomorrow (4)
Hungry For Love (4)
I Can See An Angel (4)
I Can't Forget (4)
I Can't Help It (If I'm Still In Love With You) (4)
I Don't Wanta (4)
I Fall To Pieces (1,2,3,4) *12*
I Love You, Honey (4)
I Love You So Much It Hurts (1,2,4)
I'll Sail My Ship Alone (4)
I'm Blue Again (4)
I'm Moving Along (4)
I'm Walking The Dog (4)
I've Loved And Lost Again (4)
If I Could Only Stay Asleep (4)
If I Could See The World (Through The Eyes Of A Child) (4)
Imagine That (2,4) *90*
In Care Of The Blues (4)
It Wasn't God Who Made Honky Tonk Angels (4)
Just A Closer Walk With Thee [includes 2 versions] (4)
Just Out Of Reach (4)
Leavin' On Your Mind (2,4) *83*
Let The Teardrops Fall (4)
Life's Railway To Heaven (4)
Lonely Street (4)
Loose Talk (4)
Love Letters In The Sand (4)
Love, Love, Love Me Honey Do (4)
Lovesick Blues (3,4)
Lovin' In Vain (4)
Never No More (4)
Pick Me Up On Your Way Down (4)
Poor Man's Roses (Or A Rich Man's Gold) (4)
San Antonio Rose (1,2,3,4)
Seven Lonely Days (1,2,3,4)
She's Got You (2,3,4) *14*
Shoes (4)
Side By Side (4)
So Wrong (2,4) *85*
Someday (You'll Want Me To Want You) (4)
South Of The Border (Down Mexico Way) (1,2,4)
Stop, Look And Listen (4)
Strange (2,4) *97*
Stupid Cupid (4)
Sweet Dreams (Of You) (2,3,4) *44*
Tennessee Waltz (4)
That Wonderful Someone (4)
That's How A Heartache Begins (4)
That's My Desire (4)
Then You'll Know (4)
There He Goes (4)
Three Cigarettes In An Ashtray (4)
Today, Tomorrow And Forever (4)
Too Many Secrets (4)
Tra Le La Le Triangle (2,4)
True Love (1,2,4)
Try Again (4)
Turn The Cards Slowly (4)
Walkin' After Midnight (1,2,3,4) *12*
Wayward Wind (1,2,4)
When I Get Thru With You (You'll Love Me Too) (4) *53*
When You Need A Laugh (4)
When Your House Is Not A Home (4)
Who Can I Count On (4) *99*
Why Can't He Be You (2,4)
Yes, I Know Why (4)
Yes, I Understand (4)
You Belong To Me (2,4)
You Made Me Love You (I Didn't Want To Do It) (4)
You Took Him Off My Hands (4)
You Were Only Fooling (While I Was Falling In Love) (4)
You're Stronger Than Me (2,4)
Your Cheatin' Heart (2,3,4)
Your Kinda Love (4)

CLINTON, George

Born on 7/22/40 in Plainfield, Ohio. Lead singer of The Parliaments. Became leader/producer of Funkadelic and Parliament. Headed "A Parliafunkadelicament Thang," a corporation of nearly 40 musicians that recorded as Parliament and Funkadelic plus various offshoot bands: Bootsy's Rubber Band, The Brides Of Funkenstein, Horny Horns, Parlet and the P. Funk All Stars. Appeared in the film *House Party*.

12/18/82+	**40**	33		1 Computer Games...	$8	Capitol 12246
1/7/84	**102**	18		2 You Shouldn't-Nuf Bit Fish...	$8	Capitol 12308
8/10/85	**163**	6		3 Some Of My Best Jokes Are Friends....................................	$8	Capitol 12417
5/24/86	**81**	12		4 R&B Skeletons In The Closet...	$8	Capitol 12481
9/2/89	**192**	4		5 The Cinderella Theory..	$8	Paisley P. 25994

Airbound (5)
Atomic Dog (1)
Banana Boat Song (5)
Bangladesh (3)
Bodyguard (3)
Bullet Proof (3)
Cinderella Theory (5)
Computer Games (1)
Cool Joe (4)
Do Fries Go With That Shake (4)
Double Oh-Oh (3)
Electric Pygmies (4)
Free Alterations (1)
French Kiss (5)
Get Dressed (1)
Hey Good Lookin' (4)
Intense (4)
Last Dance (2)
Loopzilla (medley) (1)
Man's Best Friend (medley) (1)
Mixmaster Suite Medley (4)
Nubian Nut (2)
One Fun At A Time (1)
Pleasures Of Exhaustion (Do It Till I Drop) (3)
Pot Sharing Tots (1)
Quickie (2)
R&B Skeletons (In The Closet) (4)
Serious Slammin' (5)
(She Got It) Goin' On (5)
Silly Millameter (2)
Some Of My Best Jokes Are Friends (3)
Stingy (2)
There I Go Again (5)
Thrashin' (3)
Tweakin' (5)
Why Should I Dog U Out? (5)
You Shouldn't-Nuf Bit Fish (2)

CLIQUE, The

Pop-rock quintet from Texas.

1/17/70	**177**	3		The Clique..	$20	White Whale 7126

Hallelujah!
Holiday
I'll Hold Out My Hand *45*
Judy, Judy, Judy
Little Miss Lucy
My Darkest Hour
Shadow Of Your Love
Soul Mates
Sugar On Sunday *22*
Superman
(There Ain't) No Such Thing As Love

CLIVILLES & COLE — see C & C MUSIC FACTORY

CLOONEY, Rosemary

Born on 5/23/28 in Maysville, Kentucky. One of the most popular singers of the 1950s, Rosemary and sister Betty sang with the Tony Pastor band in the late '40s before her solo career was launched. Rosemary was featured in *White Christmas* and several other '50s movies. After a period of personal difficulties, she re-emerged in the late '70s as a successful jazz and ballad singer. Married for a time to actor Jose Ferrer; their son Gabriel married Debby Boone.

7/22/57	**14**	7		Ring Around The Rosie...	$25	Columbia 1006
				ROSEMARY CLOONEY AND THE HI-LO'S		

DEBUT DATE	PEAK POS	WKS CHR	GOLD	ARTIST — Album Title	$	Label & Number

CLOONEY, Rosemary — Cont'd

Coquette				Everything Happens To Me I Could Write A Book	I'm In The Mood For Love	Moonlight Becomes You	Together
Doncha Go 'Way Mad				How About You I'm Glad There Is You	Love Letters	Solitude	What Is There To Say

CLUB NOUVEAU

Sacramento-based, dance-disco group formed and fronted by Jay King (producer/owner of King Jay Records; produced the Timex Social Club). Early lineup: vocalists Valerie Watson and Samuelle Prater with Denzil Foster and Thomas McElroy. Prater, Foster and McElroy left in 1988, replaced by David Agent and Kevin Irving. Agent left in 1989.

| 12/20/86+ | 6 | 44 | ▲ | 1 Life, Love & Pain... | $8 | Warner 25531 |
| 6/18/88 | 98 | 6 | | 2 Listen To The Message .... | $8 | Warner 25687 |

Better Way (2) For The Love Of Francis (2) Jealousy (1) Listen To The Message (2) Situation #9 (1) **Why You Treat Me So Bad** (1) *39*
Dancin' To Be Free (2) Heavy On My Mind (1) **Lean On Me** (1) *1* Only The Strong Survive (2) What's Going 'Round? (2)
Envious (2) It's A Cold, Cold World! (2) Let Me Go (1) Promises Promises (1) Why Is It That? (2)

COBHAM, Billy

Born on 5/16/44 in Panama; raised in New York City. Jazz-rock drummer. Formerly with Miles Davis and John McLaughlin.

11/17/73+	26	43		1 Spectrum.. [I]	$15	Atlantic 7268
5/4/74	23	21		2 Crosswinds.. [I]	$8	Atlantic 7300
12/21/74+	36	13		3 Total Eclipse .... [I]	$8	Atlantic 18121
6/28/78	74	8		4 Shabazz (Recorded Live In Europe)................... [I-L]	$8	Atlantic 18139
11/15/75	79	7		5 A Funky Thide Of Sings .... [I]	$8	Atlantic 18149
4/10/76	128	8		6 Life & Times .... [I]	$8	Atlantic 18166
10/23/76	99	9		7 "Live"-On Tour In Europe .... [L]	$8	Atlantic 18194

THE BILLY COBHAM/GEORGE DUKE BAND

| 6/3/78 | 172 | 4 | | 8 Inner Conflicts .... [I] | $8 | Atlantic 19174 |
| 10/14/78 | 166 | 6 | | 9 Simplicity Of Expression-Depth Of Thought .... | $8 | Columbia 35457 |

Almustafa The Beloved (7) Frankenstein Goes To The Last Frontier (3) Nickels And Dimes (8) Shabazz (4) Stratus (1)
Anxiety (medley) (1) Disco (7) Le Lis (medley) (1) On A Natural High (6) Siesta (medley) (6) Sweet Wine (7)
Arroyo (8) Funky Kind Of Thing (5) Life & Times (6) Opelousas (9) Snoopy's Search (medley) (1) Taurian Matador (1,4)
Bandits (3) Funky Thide Of Sings (5) Light At The End Of The Panhandler (5) Solarization Medley (3) Tenth Pinn (4)
Bolinas (9) Heather (2) Tunnel (5) Pleasant Pheasant (2) Some Skunk Funk (5) Thinking Of You (5)
Crosswind (2) Hip Pockets (7) Lunarputians (3) Pocket Change (9) Song For A Friend (Part I & To The Women In My Life
Do What Cha Wanna (7) Indigo (9) Moody Modes (5) Quadrant 4 (1) II) (6) (medley) (1)
Early Libra (9) Inner Conflicts (8) Moon Ain't Made Of Green Red Baron (1,4) Sorcery (5) Total Eclipse (3)
Earthlings (6) Ivory Tattoo (7) Cheese (3) Sea Of Tranquility (3) Space Lady (7) 29 (6)
East Bay (6) Juicy (7) Moon Germs (3) Searching For The Right Spanish Moss Medley (2) Wake Up!!!!! That's What
El Barrio (8) La Guernica (9) Muffin Talks Back (8) Door (medley) (1) Spectrum (medley) (1) You Said (medley) (6)

COCHRAN, Wayne

Flamboyant rock singer, with the C.C. Riders.

| 3/30/68 | 167 | 4 | | Wayne Cochran!.. | $25 | Chess 1519 |

Big City Woman Get Ready I'm Your Hoochie Coochie Peak Of Love You Can't Judge A Book By
Boom Boom I'm Leaving It Up To You Man Some-A' Your Sweet Love The Cover
Get Down With It Little Bitty Pretty One When My Baby Cries You Don't Know Like I Know

COCHRANE, Tom/Red Rider

Toronto-based rock singer/songwriter. Born on 5/13/53 in Lynn Lake, Manitoba, Canada. Formed Red Rider in 1980. Nucleus of group includes guitarist Ken Greer and keyboardist John Webster.

RED RIDER:

4/26/80	146	5		1 Don't Fight It	$8	Capitol 12028
9/12/81	65	24		2 As Far As Siam	$8	Capitol 12145
2/5/83	66	16		3 Neruda...	$8	Capitol 12226
				dedicated to exiled Chilean poet Pablo Neruda		
6/23/84	137	8		4 Breaking Curfew	$8	Capitol 12317

TOM COCHRANE AND RED RIDER:

| 8/2/86 | 112 | 12 | | 5 Tom Cochrane and Red Rider............................ | $8 | Capitol 12484 |
| 11/12/88 | 144 | 13 | | 6 Victory Day .... | $8 | RCA 8532 |

TOM COCHRANE:

| 5/9/92 | 46 | 29 | ● | 7 Mad Mad World... | $12 | Capitol 97723 |

All The King's Men (7) Cowboys In Hong Kong (As How's My Little Girl Tonight Napoleon Sheds His Skin (3) Shake Monster (4) **White Hot** (1) *48*
Among The Ruins (I'll Be Far As Siam) (2) (1) No Regrets (7) Ships (2) Winner Take All (3)
Here) (4) Crack The Sky (Breakaway) Human Race (3) Not So Far Away (6) Sights On You (3) Work Out (3)
Ashes To Diamonds (5) (3) Iron In The Soul (1) Ocean Blues (Emotion Blue) Sinking Like A Sunset (7) **Young Thing, Wild Dreams**
Avenue "A" (1) Different Drummer (6) Just The Way It Goes (1) (5) Someone's Watching (4) **(Rock Me)** (4) *71*
Beacon Hill (4) Don't Fight It (1) Lasting Song (5) One More Time (Some Old Sons Beat Down (6)
Big League (6) Don't Let Go Of Me (2) Laughing Man (2) Habits) (5) Thru The Curtain (2)
Bigger Man (7) Emotional Truth (7) **Life Is A Highway** (7) *6* One Way Out (4) Untouchable One (5)
Boy Inside The Man (5) Everything Comes Around (7) Light In The Tunnel (3) Only Game In Town (2) Vacation (In My Mind) (6)
Brave And Crazy (7) Friendly Advice (7) Loading, The (5) Power (Strength In Victory Day (6)
Breaking Curfew (4) Get Back Up (7) Look Out Again (1) Numbers) (3) Walking The Fine Line (3)
Calling America (6) Good Man (Feeling Bad) (6) Love Under Fire (5) River Of Stone (5) **Washed Away** (7) *88*
Can't Turn Back (3) Good News (1) Lunatic Fringe (2) Saved By The Dawn (6) What Have You Got To Do
Caught In The Middle (2) Good Times (6) Mad Mad World (7) Secret Is To Know When To (To Get Off Tonight) (2)
Citizen Cain (5) Hold Tight (4) Make Myself Complete (1) Stop (7) Whipping Boy (4)

COCKBURN, Bruce

Cockburn (pronounced: Co-burn) was born on 5/27/45 in Canada. Pop-rock singer/songwriter.

2/23/80	45	24		1 Dancing In the Dragon's Jaws	$8	Millennium 7747
10/18/80	81	9		2 Humans	$8	Millennium 7752
5/23/81	174	5		3 Bruce Cockburn/Resume	$8	Millennium 7757
8/25/84+	74	31		4 Stealing Fire	$8	Gold Mt. 80012
7/26/86	143	8		5 World Of Wonders	$8	MCA 5772
2/25/89	182	7		6 Big Circumstance..	$8	Gold Castle 71320

151

DEBUT DATE	PEAK POS	WKS CHR	GOLD	ARTIST — Album Title	$	Label & Number

COCKBURN, Bruce — Cont'd

After The Rain (1)
Anything Can Happen (6)
Badlands Flashback (1)
Berlin Tonight (5)
Call It Democracy (5)
Can I Go With You (3)
Coldest Night Of The Year (3)
Creation Dream (1)
Dancing In Paradise (5)
Dialogue With The Devil (3)
Don't Feel Your Touch (6)
Down Here Tonight (5)
Dust And Diesel (4)

Facist Architecture (2)
Gift, The (6)
Gospel Of Bondage (6)
Grim Travelers (2)
Guerilla Betrayed (2)
Hills Of Morning (1)
How I Spent My Fall
  Vacation (2)
If A Tree Falls (6)
**If I Had A Rocket
  Launcher** (4) *88*
Incandescent Blue (1)
Laughter (3)

Lily Of The Midnight Sky (5)
Lord Of The Starfields (3)
Lovers In A Dangerous Time
  (4)
Making Contact (4)
Mama Justs Wants To
  Barrelhouse All Night Long
  (3)
Maybe The Poet (4)
More/Not More (2)
Nicaragua (4)
No Footprints (1)
Northern Lights (1)

Outside A Broken Phone
  Booth With Money In My
  Hand (3)
Pangs Of Love (6)
Peggy's Kitchen Wall (4)
People See Through You (5)
Radium Rain (6)
Rose Above The Sky (2)
Rumours Of Glory (6)
Sahara Gold (4)
Santiago Dawn (5)
See How I Miss You (5)

Shipwrecked At The Stable
  Door (6)
Silver Wheels (3)
Tibetan Side Of Town (6)
To Raise The Morning Star
  (4)
Tokyo (2)
Understanding Nothing (6)
Water Into Wine (3)
What About The Bond (2)
Where The Death Squad
  Lives (6)

**Wondering Where The
  Lions Are** (1) *21*
World Of Wonders (5)
You Get Bigger As You Go (2)

★★155★★ COCKER, Joe
Born John Robert Cocker on 5/20/44 in Sheffield, England. Own skiffle band, the Cavaliers, late 1950s, later reorganized as Vance Arnold & The Avengers. Assembled the Grease Band in the mid-1960s. Performed at Woodstock in 1969. Successful tour with 43-piece revue, Mad Dogs & Englishmen, in 1970. Notable spastic stage antics were based on Ray Charles' movements at the piano.

5/31/69	35	37	●	1 With A Little Help From My Friends	$15	A&M 4182
				with Jimmy Page and Stevie Winwood		
11/22/69+	11	53	●	2 Joe Cocker!	$15	A&M 4224
				with Leon Russell and The Grease Band		
9/5/70	2¹	53	●	3 Mad Dogs & Englishmen .... [S-L]	$12	A&M 6002 [2]
				title refers to Cocker's 1970 concert tour with an entourage of 43 including Leon Russell and Chris Stainton		
12/2/72+	30	21		4 Joe Cocker	$12	A&M 4368
8/24/74	11	36		5 I Can Stand A Little Rain	$12	A&M 3633
8/30/75	42	10		6 Jamaica Say You Will	$12	A&M 4529
5/15/76	70	10		7 Stingray	$12	A&M 4574
12/10/77	114	8		8 Joe Cocker's Greatest Hits .... [G]	$12	A&M 4670
9/16/78	76	13		9 Luxury You Can Afford	$8	Asylum 145
7/10/82	105	23		10 Sheffield Steel	$8	Island 9750
5/19/84	133	9		11 Civilized Man	$8	Capitol 12335
4/12/86	50	18		12 Cocker	$8	Capitol 12394
11/14/87+	89	27		13 Unchain My Heart	$8	Capitol 48285
9/16/89+	52	30		14 One Night Of Sin	$8	Capitol 92861
6/23/90	95	14		15 Joe Cocker Live .... [L]	$12	Capitol 93416
				recorded live on 10/15/89 in Lowell, Massachusetts		
8/1/92	111	10		16 Night Calls	$12	Capitol 97801

A To Z (12)
All Our Tomorrows (13)
Another Mine Gone (14)
Bad Bad Sign (14)
Bird On The Wire (2,3)
Black-Eyed Blues (4,8) *flip*
Blue Medley (3)
Boogie Baby (9)
Born Thru Indifference (7)
Bye Bye Blackbird (1)
Can't Find My Way Home
  (16)
Catfish (7)
Change In Louise (1)
Civilized Man (11)
Come On In (11)
Crazy In Love (11)
Cry Me A River (3,8) *11*
Darling Be Home Soon (2,8)
Dear Landlord (2)
Delta Lady (2,3,8)
Do I Still Figure In Your
  Life? (1)
Do Right Woman (4)
Don't Drink The Water (12)
Don't Forget Me (5)
Don't Let Me Be
  Misunderstood (1)
Don't Let The Sun Go Down
  On Me (16)
Don't You Love Me Anymore
  (12)

Even A Fool Would Let Go
  (11)
Feeling Alright
  (1,3,8,15) *33*
Feels Like Forever (16)
Fever (14)
Five Women (16)
Forgive Me Now (6)
Fun Time (9) *43*
Girl From The North
  Country (3)
Girl Like You (11)
Guilty (5,15)
Heart Of The Matter (12)
Heaven (12)
Hello Little Friend (2)
High Time We Went
  (4,8,15) *22*
Hitchcock Railway (2,15)
Hold On (I Feel Our Love Is
  Changing) (11)
Honky Tonk Women (3)
I Broke Down (7)
I Can Hear The River (16)
I Can Stand A Little Rain (5)
I Can't Say No (9)
I Get Mad (5)
I Heard It Through The
  Grapevine (9)
I Know (You Don't Want Me
  No More) (9)
I Love The Night (11)

I Shall Be Released (1)
I Stand In Wonder (13)
I Think It's Going To Rain
  Today (6,8)
I Will Live For You (14)
I'm Your Man (14)
I've Got To Use My
  Imagination (14)
If I Love You (6)
Inner City Blues (12)
Isolation (13)
**It's A Sin When You Love
  Somebody** (5) *flip*
It's All Over But The
  Shoutin' (16)
Jack-A-Diamonds (6)
Jamaica Say You Will (6)
Jealous Kind (7,8)
Just Like A Woman (1)
Just Like Always (10)
Just To Keep From
  Drowning (14)
Lady Put The Light Out (9)
Lawdy Miss Clawdy (2)
Let's Go Get Stoned (3)
Letter, The (3,8,15) *7*
Letting Go (14)
Living In The Promiseland
  (15)
Living Without Your Love
  (12)

Long Drag Off A Cigarette
  (11)
Look What You've Done (10)
Love Is Alive (16)
Love Is On A Fade (12)
Lucinda (6)
Man In Me (10)
Many Rivers To Cross (10)
Marie (10)
Marjorine (1)
Midnight Rider (4) *27*
Moon Dew (7)
Moon Is A Harsh Mistress (5)
Night Calls (16)
Now That The Magic Has
  Gone (16)
Oh Mama (6)
One, The (13)
One Night Of Sin (14)
Out Of The Rain (16)
Pardon Me Sir (4) *51*
Performance (5)
Please Give Peace A Chance
  (3)
Please No More (16)
Put Out The Light (5) *46*
River's Rising (13)
Ruby Lee (10)
Sandpaper Cadillac (1)
Satisfied (13)
Seven Days (10)

**She Came In Through The
  Bathroom Window**
  (2,3,15) *30*
She Don't Mind (4)
Shelter Me (12,15) *91*
Shocked (10)
Sing Me A Song (10)
So Good So Right (10)
Something (3)
Something To Say (4)
Song For You (7)
Southern Lady (9)
Space Captain (3)
St. James Infirmary Blues (4)
Sticks And Stones (3)
Superstar (3)
Sweet Li'l Woman (10)
Talking Back To The Night
  (10)
Tempted (11)
(That's What I Like) In My
  Woman (4)
That's Your Business Now (2)
There Goes My Baby (11)
Trust In Me (13)
Two Wrongs (13)
Unchain My Heart (13,15)
Up Where We Belong (15)
Wasted Years (9)
Watching The River Flow (9)

**What Are You Doing With
  A Fool Like Me** (15) *96*
What You Did To Me Last
  Night (9)
When A Woman Cries (16)
When The Night Comes
  (14,15) *11*
Where Am I Now (6)
Whiter Shade Of Pale (4)
**With A Little Help From
  My Friends** (1,8,15) *68*
Woman Loves A Man (2)
Woman To Woman (4,8) *56*
Worrier (7)
You Are So Beautiful
  (5,8,15) *5*
You Came Along (7)
You Can Leave Your Hat On
  (12,15)
You Know We're Gonna
  Hurt (14)
You've Got To Hide Your
  Love Away (16)

COCK ROBIN
Los Angeles pop quartet — Peter Kingsbery and Anna LaCazio, vocals.

7/13/85	61	19		1 Cock Robin	$8	Columbia 39582
9/5/87	166	3		2 After Here Through Midland	$8	Columbia 40375

After Here Through Midland
  (2)
Another Story (2)
Because It Keeps On
  Working (1)

Biggest Fool Of All (2)
Born With Teeth (1)
Coward's Courage (2)
El Norte (2)
Every Moment (2)

I'll Send Them Your Way (2)
Just Around The Corner (2)
Just When You're Having
  Fun (1)
Little Innocence (1)

More Than Willing (1)
Once We Might Have Known
  (1)
Precious Dreams (2)
Promise You Made (1)

Thought You Were On My
  Side (1)
When Your Heart Is Weak
  (1) *35*

DEBUT DATE	PEAK POS	WKS CHR	GOLD	ARTIST — Album Title	$	Label & Number

COCTEAU TWINS

Pop trio formed in Grangemouth, Scotland in 1980: guitarist Robin Guthrie, vocalist Elizabeth Fraser and bassist Will Heggie. Simon Raymonde replaced Heggie in 1984. Guthrie and Fraser also recorded in 1984 as This Mortal Coil. Name Cocteau Twins is taken from a Simple Minds song.

10/15/88	**109**	18		**1** Blue Bell Knoll	**$8**	Capitol 90892
10/6/90	**99**	19		**2** Heaven or Las Vegas	**$12**	4 A.D. 93669

Athol-Brose (1)   Ella Megalast Burls Forever (1)   Frou-Frou Foxes In Midsummer Fires (2)   Itchy Glowbo Blow (1)   Spooning Good Singing Gum (1)
Blue Bell Knoll (1)   For Phoebe Still A Baby (1)   Heaven Or Las Vegas (2)   Kissed Out Red Floatboat (1)   Suckling The Mender (1)
Carolyn's Fingers (1)   Fifty-Fifty Clown (2)   I Wear Your Ring (2)   Pitch The Baby (2)   Wolf In The Breast (2)
Cherry-Coloured Funk (2)   Fotzepolitic (2)   Iceblink Luck (2)   Road, River And Rail (2)
Cico Buff (1)

COE, David Allan

Country singer. Born on 9/6/39 in Akron, Ohio. Billed as "The Mysterious Rhinestone Cowboy" until 1978. In film *Take This Job And Shove It* (also wrote the title tune for Johnny Paycheck) and others.

7/9/83	**179**	5		**1** Castles In The Sand	**$8**	Columbia 38535

Castles In The Sand   Don't Be A Stranger   For Lovers Only (Part 1)   I Can't Let You Be A Memory   Ride, The
Cheap Thrills   Fool Inside Of Me   Gotta Serve Somebody   Missin' The Kid   Son Of A Rebel Son

COFFEY, Dennis, And The Detroit Guitar Band

Detroit native Coffey was a session guitarist for The Temptations, The Jackson 5 and others. Coffey later formed C.J. & Co.

11/13/71+	**36**	25		**1** Evolution .... [I]	**$10**	Sussex 7004
3/25/72	**90**	14		**2** Goin' For Myself .... [I]	**$10**	Sussex 7010
1/20/73	**189**	6		**3** Electric Coffey .... [I]	**$10**	Sussex 7021
1/17/76	**147**	7		**4** Finger Lickin Good .... [I]	**$8**	Westbound 212

Big City Funk (1)   **Getting It On** (1) 93   If You Can't Dance To This You Got No Business (2)   Man And Boy (Main Theme) (2)   Son Of Scorpio (3)
Bridge Over Troubled Water (2)   Good Time Rhythm And Blues (1)   Havin' Feet (4)   Midnight Blue (2)   Summer Time Girl (1)
Can You Feel It (2)   Guitar Big Band (3)   Impressions Of (1)   Never Can Say Goodbye (2)   **Taurus** (2) 18
Capricorn's Thing (3)   Honky Tonk (4)   It's Too Late (2)   **Ride, Sally, Ride** (2) *flip*   Toast And Jam (2)
El Tigre (4)   I've Got A Real Good Feeling (4)   Live Wire (4)   Sad Angel (1)   Twins Of Gemini (3)
Fame (4)   Lonely Moon Child (3)   Sagittarian, The (3)   Virgo's Song (3)
Finger Lickin Good (4)   Love And Understanding (3)   **Scorpio** (1) 6   Whole Lot Of Love (1)
Garden Of The Moon (1)   Love Song For Libra (3)   Some Like It Hot (4)   Wild Child (4)   Wild Song (1)

COHEN, Leonard

Songwriter/singer/poet/novelist. Born in Montreal, Canada on 9/21/34. His numerous works include the novels *The Favorite Game* and *Beautiful Losers*, six volumes of poetry, several documentaries, and songs recorded by Judy Collins, Tim Hardin and Jennifer Warnes.

3/2/68	**83**	14	●	**1** Songs Of Leonard Cohen	**$10**	Columbia 9533
4/12/69	**63**	17		**2** Songs From A Room	**$10**	Columbia 9767
5/1/71	**145**	11		**3** Songs Of Love And Hate	**$10**	Columbia 30103
5/26/73	**156**	5		**4** Leonard Cohen: Live Songs .... [L]	**$10**	Columbia 31724

Avalanche (3)   Hey, That's No Way To Say Goodbye (1)   Master Song (1)   Please Don't Pass Me By (A Disgrace) (4)   Stories Of The Street (1)
Bird On The Wire (2,4)   Improvisation (4)   Nancy (4)   Queen Victoria (4)   Story Of Isaac (2)
Bunch Of Lonesome Heros (2)   Joan Of Arc (3)   Old Revolution (2)   Seems So Long Ago, Nancy (2)   Stranger Song (1)
Butcher, The (2)   Lady Midnight (2)   One Of Us Cannot Be Wrong (1)   Suzanne (1)
Diamonds In The Mine (3)   Last Year's Man (3)   Partisan, The (2)   Sing Another Song, Boys (3)   Teachers (1)
Dress Rehearsal Rag (3)   Love Calls You By Your Name (3)   Passing Thru (4)   Sisters Of Mercy (1)   Tonight Will Be Fine (2,4)
Famous Blue Raincoat (3)   So Long, Marianne (1)   Winter Lady (1)   You Know Who I Am (2,4)

COHEN, Myron

Bronx-born comic storyteller; died on 3/10/86 (age 83).

4/2/66	**102**	13		Everybody Gotta Be Someplace .... [C]	**$12**	RCA 3534

Affairs Of The Heart   Flies   Husbands And Wives And Lovers   Life At "The Stage"   Long Coat Tale   Short Stories
Assortment Of Yarns   Foreign Intrigue   Life In The Sun   Parlor Stories   Two Elephant Stories

COHN, Marc

Cleveland-born singer/songwriter. Formed a 14-piece band in New York, the Supreme Court, which was discovered by Carly Simon and played at Caroline Kennedy's wedding. Won the 1991 Best New Artist Grammy Award.

4/27/91+	**38**	63	●	Marc Cohn	**$12**	Atlantic 82178

Dig Down Deep   Miles Away   Saving The Best For Last   Strangers In A Car   29 Ways   **Walking In Memphis 13**
Ghost Train   Perfect Love   **Silver Thunderbird 63**   **True Companion 80**   Walk On Water

COLD BLOOD

Bay-area rock group led by Lydia Pense (vocals). Original members Raul Matute (piano), Rod Ellicott (bass) and Danny Hull (sax) were longtime members of everchanging personnel. Max Haskett (trumpet) and Michael Sasaki (guitar) were also regular members.

12/27/69+	**23**	29		**1** Cold Blood	**$12**	San Francisco 200
1/23/71	**60**	13		**2** Sisyphus	**$12**	San Francisco 205
4/22/72	**133**	11		**3** First Taste Of Sin	**$10**	Reprise 2074
4/28/73	**97**	14		**4** Thriller!	**$10**	Reprise 2130
8/10/74	**126**	8		**5** Lydia	**$8**	Warner 2806
3/13/76	**179**	4		**6** Lydia Pense & Cold Blood	**$8**	ABC 917

LYDIA PENSE & COLD BLOOD

All My Honey (3)   Feel So Bad (4)   I Only Wanted Someone To Hear Me (5)   Just Like Sunshine (5)   Simple Love Life (5)   When My Love Hand Comes Down (5)
Baby I Love You (4)   Feel The Fire (6)   Kissing My Love (4)   Sleeping (4)   You Are The Sunshine Of My Life (4)
Back Here Again (6)   Funky On My Back (2)   I Wish I Knew How It Would Feel To Be Free (1)   Let Me Be The One (6)   Too Many People (2)
Blinded By Love (6)   I Can't Stay (2)   Let Me Down Easy (1)   Under Pressure (5)
Cold Blood Smokin' (6)   I Get Off On You (6)   I'll Be Long Gone (4)   Live Your Dream (4)   Understanding (2)   **You Got Me Hummin** (1) 52
Come Back Into My Life Again (5)   I Got Happiness (6)   I'm A Good Woman (1)   Lo And Behold (3)   Valdez In The Country (3)   You Had To Know (3)
Consideration (5)   I Just Want To Make Love To You (1)   If You Will (1)   My Lady Woman (3)   Visions (3)   You're Free Lovin' Me (5)
Down To The Bone (3)   I Love You More Than You'll Ever Know (6)   Inside Your Soul (3)   No Way Home (3)   Watch Your Step (1)   Your Good Thing (2)
Drink The Wine (6)   It Takes A Lotta Good Lovin' (6)   Ready To Live (5)   We Came Down Here (6)
Shop Talk (2)   When It's Over (5)

153

DEBUT DATE	PEAK POS	WKS CHR	GOLD	ARTIST — Album Title	$	Label & Number

COLD CHISEL
Australian rock quintet — Jimmy Barnes, lead singer.

6/13/81	171	6		East	$8	Elektra 336

Best Kept Lies · Choirgirl · My Baby · Never Before · Standing On The Outside · Tomorrow
Cheap Wine · Khe Sanh · My Turn To Cry · Rising Sun · Star Hotel

COLE, Jude
Native of East Moline, Illinois. Male guitarist/vocalist of Moon Martin's band. Touring guitarist with Billy Thorpe, Del Shannon and Dwight Twilley.

5/5/90	140	12		1 A View from 3rd Street	$12	Reprise 26164
10/17/92	177	3		2 Start The Car	$12	Reprise 26898

Baby, It's Tonight (1) *16* · Get Me Through The Night (1) · **House Full Of Reasons** (1) *69* · Place In The Line (2) · **Tell The Truth** (2) *75↑*
Blame It On Fate (2) · Hallowed Ground (1) · It Comes Around (1) · Prove Me Wrong (1) · This Time It's Us (1)
Compared To Nothing (1) · Heart Of Blues (1) · Just Another Night (2) · Right There Now (2) · **Time For Letting Go** (1) *32*
First Your Money (Then · Open Road (2) · **Start The Car** (2) *71* · Worlds Apart (2)
Your Clothes) (2) · Stranger To Myself (1)

★★171★★ COLE, Natalie
Born on 2/6/50 in Los Angeles. Daughter of Nat "King" Cole. Professional debut at age 11. Married for a time to her producer, Marvin Yancey, Jr. Later married Andre Fischer, former drummer of Rufus and producer for Brenda Russell, Michael Franks and Andrea Crouch, until 1992. Natalie won the 1975 Best New Artist Grammy Award. Hosted own syndicated variety TV show *Big Break* in 1990.

8/30/75	18	56	●	1 Inseparable	$10	Capitol 11429
5/29/76	13	30	●	2 Natalie	$10	Capitol 11517
3/5/77	8	28	▲	3 **Unpredictable**	$10	Capitol 11600
12/10/77+	16	39	▲	4 Thankful	$10	Capitol 11708
7/15/78	31	16	●	5 Natalie...Live! ....[L]	$12	Capitol 11709 [2]
4/7/79	52	15	●	6 I Love You So	$10	Capitol 11928
12/15/79+	44	19		7 We're The Best Of Friends..	$10	Capitol 12019
				NATALIE COLE/PEABO BRYSON		
6/14/80	77	22		8 Don't Look Back	$8	Capitol 12079
9/26/81	132	4		9 Happy Love	$8	Capitol 12165
9/17/83	182	3		10 I'm Ready	$8	Epic 38280
6/29/85	140	9		11 Dangerous	$8	Modern 90270
8/8/87+	42	58		12 Everlasting	$8	Manhattan 53051
5/27/89	59	23		13 Good To Be Back	$8	EMI 48902
6/29/91	1⁵	85↑▲⁵		14 **Unforgettable With Love**	$12	Elektra 61049

Natalie sings her dad's (Nat King Cole) classics from 1944-64

Across The Nation (9) · Gift, The (11) · I'm Ready (10) · Mona Lisa (14) · Smile (14) · Time (Heals All Wounds) (10)
Almost Like Being In Love (14) · Gimme Some Time (7) · I'm The One (12) · More Than The Stars (12) · **Someone That I Used To Love** (8) *21* · Too Much Mister (10)
Annie Mae (4) · Gonna Make You Mine (13) · I'm Your Mirror (10) · **Mr. Melody** (2,5) *49* · Someone's Rockin' My Dreamboat (13) · Too Young (14)
As A Matter Of Fact (13) · Good Morning Heartache (2) · **I've Got Love On My Mind** (3,5) *5* · Nature Boy (1) · Something For Nothing (1) · Touch Me (2)
Autumn Leaves (medley) (14) · Good To Be Back (13) · (I've Seen) Paradise (8) · No Plans For The Future (2) · Something's Got A Hold On Me (5) · **Unforgettable** (14) *14*
Avalon (14) · Hard To Get Along (2) · In My Reality (12) · Nobody's Soldier (11) · Unpredictable Yo (3)
Be Mine Tonight (3) · Heaven Is With You (2) · **Inseparable** (1,5) *32* · Non Dimenticar (14) · **Sophisticated Lady (She's** · Very Thought Of You (14)
Be Thankful (4,5) · Hold On (8) · It's Been You (6) · Not Like Mine (2) · **A Different Lady)** (2,5) *25* · We're The Best Of Friends (7)
Beautiful Dreamer (8) · How Come You Won't Stay · Joey (1) · Nothin' But A Fool (9) · Split Decision (12) · What You Won't Do For Love
Billy The Kid Next Door (1) · Here (1) · Joke Is On You (9) · Nothing Stronger Than Love · Stairway To The Stars (8) · (7)
Can We Get Together Again · I Can't Breakaway (3) · Keep It On The Outside (10) · (4) · Stand By (6) · When A Man Loves A
(2,5) · I Can't Cry (13) · Keep Smiling (4) · Oh, Daddy (6) · Starting Over Again (13) · Woman (9)
Cole-Blooded (8) · I Can't Let Go (9) · Keeping A Light (4) · Only Love (9) · Still In Love (3) · **When I Fall In Love** (12) *95*
Cry Baby (5) · I Can't Say No (1,5) · La Costa (1) · Opposites Attract (11) · Straighten Up And Fly Right · Where's Your Angel? (10)
Danger Up Ahead (8) · I Can't Stay Away (4) · Let's Fall In Love (medley) (7) · Orange Colored Sky (14) · (14) · Who Will Carry On (6)
Dangerous (11) *57* · I Do (13) · **Little Bit Of Heaven** (11) *81* · **Our Love** (4,5) *10* · Tenderly (medley) (14) · Winner, The (6)
Darling, Je Vous Aime · I Live For Your Love · L-O-V-E (14) · Our Love Is Here To Stay (14) · That Sunday That Summer · You (1)
Beaucoup (14) · (12) *13* · Love And Kisses (9) · Paper Moon (14) · (14) · You Send Me (medley) (7)
Don't Get Around Much · I Love Him So Much (1) · Love Is On The Way (11) · **Party Lights** (3,5) *79* · These Eyes (9) · You Were Right Girl (9)
Anymore (14) · I Love You So (6) · Love Will Find You (7) · Peaceful Living (3) · This Can't Be Love (14) · You're So Good (6)
Don't Look Back (8) · I Want To Be Where You Are · Lovers (4) · **Pink Cadillac** (12) *5* · This Heart (3) · Your Car (My Garage) (11)
Don't Mention My Heartache · (7) · Lucy In The Sky With · Que Sera, Sera (3) · This Love Affair (7) · Your Eyes (3)
(13) · I Won't Deny You (10) · Diamonds (5) · Rest Of The Night (13) · This Will Be (1,5) *6* · Your Face Stays In My Mind
Everlasting (12) · I'm Catching Hell (3,5) · Lush Life (14) · Route 66 (14) · Thou Swell (14) · (1)
For Sentimental Reasons · (I'm Coming) Straight From · L-O-V-E · Safe (13) · · Your Lonely Heart (6,7)
(medley) (14) · The Heart (10) · **Miss You Like Crazy** (13) *7* · Secrets (11) · ·
· I'm Getting In To You (8) · · · ·

★★39★★ COLE, Nat "King"
Born Nathaniel Adams Coles on 3/17/17 in Montgomery, Alabama and raised in Chicago. Died of lung cancer on 2/15/65 in Santa Monica, California. Own band, the Royal Dukes, at age 17. First recorded in 1936 in band led by brother Eddie. Toured with "Shuffle Along" musical revue, stranded in Los Angeles. Formed King Cole Trio in 1939: Nat (piano), Oscar Moore (guitar; later joined brother's group, Johnny Moore's Three Blazers) and Wesley Prince (bass); replaced several years later by Johnny Miller. Long series of top-selling records led to his solo career in 1950. In films *St. Louis Blues*, *Cat Ballou*, and many other film and TV appearances. Stopped performing in 1964 due to ill health. His daughter Natalie is a recording star. Won Lifetime Achievement Grammy in 1990.

4/28/56	16	2		1 Ballads Of The Day	$30	Capitol 680
3/9/57	13	2		2 After Midnight...	$30	Capitol 782
				with the King Cole Trio		
4/6/57	1⁸	94	▲	3 **Love Is The Thing**	$25	Capitol 824
9/23/57	18	3		4 This Is Nat "King" Cole	$25	Capitol 870
12/16/57+	18	6		5 Just One Of Those Things	$25	Capitol 903
5/5/58	18	3		6 St. Louis Blues ....[S]	$35	Capitol 993
				Nat portrayed W.C. Handy in the film about Handy's life		
9/22/58	12	5		7 Cole Espanol ....[F]	$25	Capitol 1031
12/1/58	17	2		8 The Very Thought Of You	$25	Capitol 1084

DEBUT DATE	PEAK POS	WKS CHR	GOLD	ARTIST — Album Title	$	Label & Number
				COLE, Nat "King" — Cont'd		
6/22/59	**45**	5		9 To Whom It May Concern	$20	Capitol 1190
4/18/60	**33**	2		10 Tell Me All About Yourself..	$20	Capitol 1331
10/24/60	**4**	23		11 **Wild Is Love**	$20	Capitol 1392
5/15/61	**79**	17		12 The Touch Of Your Lips	$20	Capitol 1574
5/5/62	**27**	16		13 Nat King Cole sings/George Shearing plays	$20	Capitol 1675
9/22/62	**3**	162	▲	14 **Ramblin' Rose**	$20	Capitol 1793
12/29/62+	**24**	36		15 Dear Lonely Hearts	$20	Capitol 1838
5/25/63	**68**	6		16 Where Did Everyone Go?	$20	Capitol 1859
7/6/63	**14**	36		17 Those Lazy-Hazy-Crazy Days Of Summer	$20	Capitol 1932
8/1/64	**18**	45		18 I Don't Want To Be Hurt Anymore	$15	Capitol 2118
9/26/64	**74**	23		19 My Fair Lady	$15	Capitol 2117
2/6/65	**4**	38		20 L-O-V-E	$15	Capitol 2195
3/20/65	**30**	39	▲	21 Unforgettable..[R]	$15	Capitol 357
				reissue of his 1953 10" album		
7/3/65	**77**	9		22 Songs From "Cat Ballou" And Other Motion Pictures ....[K]	$15	Capitol 2340
				features Nat's film hits		
9/4/65	**60**	14		23 Looking Back ....[G]	$15	Capitol 2361
2/19/66	**74**	11		24 Nat King Cole At The Sands ....[L]	$15	Capitol 2434
11/26/66	**145**	3		25 The Great Songs!...[E]	$15	Capitol 2558
				recorded in 1957		
9/14/68	**187**	5	▲	26 The Best Of Nat King Cole ....[G]	$12	Capitol 2944
8/23/69	**197**	3		27 Close-Up ....[R]	$12	Capitol 252 [2]
				reissue of *Ballads Of The Day/Nat King Cole's Top Pops LPs*		
7/13/91	**86**	28	●	28 Collectors Series ....[G]	$12	Capitol 93590
				Nat's hits from 1944-64		

Acercate Mas (Come Closer To Me) (7)
Adelita (7)
Affair To Remember (25)
After The Ball Is Over (17)
Again (23)
(Ah, The Apple Trees) When The World Was Young (16)
Ain't Misbehavin' (3)
All By Myself (15)
All Over The World (15,28) *42*
Alone Too Long (1,27)
Am I Blue? (16)
Angel Eyes (1,27)
Annabelle (4)
Answer Me, My Love (21,26,28)
Are You Disenchanted? (11)
Around The World (25)
Arrivederci, Roma (Goodbye To Rome) (7)
At Last (3)
Azure-Te (13)
Ballad Of Cat Ballou (22)
Ballerina (24) *18*
Beale Street Blues (6,22)
Beautiful Friendship (13)
Because You're Mine (27)
Beggar For The Blues (11)
Best Thing For You (10)
Blame It On My Youth (2)
Blossom Fell (1,27,28) *2*
Blue Gardenia (1,22,27)
Brush Those Tears From Your Eyes (11)
But Beautiful (8)
Cachito (7)
Can't Help It (9)
Caravan (2)
Careless Love (6)
Chantez Les Bas (6)
Cherchez La Femme (8)
Cherie, I Love You (8)
China Gate (22)
Christmas Song (Merry Christmas To You) (28) *65*
Continental, The (24)
Coquette (20)
Cottage For Sale (5)
Crazy She Calls Me (10)
Darling Je Vous Aime Beaucoup (1,27,28) *7*
Dear Lonely Hearts (15,26,28) *42*
Dedicated To You (10)
Don't Forget (17)
Don't Get Around Much Anymore (5)
Don't Go (13)

Don't Let It Go To Your Head (2)
Don't You Remember? (18)
Dreams Can Tell A Lie (4)
El Bodeguero (Grocer's Cha-Cha) (7)
End Of A Love Affair (16)
Faith Can Move Mountains (27)
Farewell To Arms (25)
Fascination (25)
Fly Me To The Moon (In Other Words) (13)
For All We Know (8)
For The Want Of A Kiss (25)
For You (10)
Forgive My Heart (4) *13*
Friendless Blues (6)
Funny (12,24,27)
Get Me To The Church On Time (19)
Get Out And Get Under The Moon (17)
(Get Your Kicks On) Route 66 ..see: Route 66
Girl From Ipanema (20)
Go, If You're Going (18)
Good Times (14)
Goodnight, Irene, Goodnight (14)
Hajji Baba (22)
Happy New Year (25)
Harlem Blues (6)
He Who Hesitates (11)
He'll Have To Go (14)
Hesitating Blues (medley) (6)
How I'd Love To Love You (20)
Hundreds And Thousands Of Girls (11)
Hymn To Him (19)
I Could Have Danced All Night (19)
I Don't Want It That Way (14)
I Don't Want To Be Hurt Anymore (18,26) *22*
I Don't Want To See Tomorrow (18) *34*
I Found A Million Dollar Baby (In A Five And Ten Cent Store) (8)
I Got It Bad And That Ain't Good (13)
I Had The Craziest Dream (25)
I Just Found Out About Love (4)
I Keep Goin' Back To Joe's (16)
I Know That You Know (2)
(I Love You) For Sentimental Reasons (21,28)

I Must Be Dreaming (23) *69*
I Remember You (12)
I Should Care (5)
I Thought About Marie (3)
I Understand (5)
I Wish I Knew (8,25)
I Wish You Love (24)
(I Would Do) Anything For You (10)
I'm All Cried Out (18)
I'm Alone Because I Love You (18)
I'm An Ordinary Man (19)
I'm Gonna Laugh You Right Out Of My Life (4) *57*
I'm Lost (13)
I'm Never Satisfied (27)
I've Grown Accustomed To Her Face (19)
If I Give My Heart To You (27)
If I May (23) *8*
If Love Ain't There (16)
If Love Is Good To Me (1,27)
If You Said No (9)
Illusion (12)
Impossible (8)
In Love Again (11)
In The Cool Of The Day (27)
In The Good Old Summertime (17)
In The Heart Of Jane Doe (9)
Is It Better To Have Loved And Lost (23)
It Happens To Be Me (1,27)
It's A Beautiful Evening (11)
It's A Lonesome Old Town (When You're Not Around) (15)
It's All In The Game (3)
It's Only A Paper Moon (2)
Joe Turner's Blues (6,24)
Just As Much As Ever (17)
Just For The Fun Of It (5)
Just One Of Those Things (5)
Just You, Just Me (2)
Las Mananitas (7)
Laughing On The Outside (Crying On The Inside) (16)
Let There Be Love (13)
Lights Out (12)
Lonely One (2)
Lonesome And Sorry (15)
Looking Back (23) *5*
Lost April (13,21)
L-O-V-E (20,26,28) *81*
Love Is The Thing (3)
Love Me As Though There Were No Tomorrow (4)
Love-Wise (9)
Lovesville (9)

Magnificent Obsession (8)
Make Her Mine (21)
Making Believe You're Here (8)
Maria Elena (7)
Memphis Blues (6)
Midnight Flyer (23) *51*
Miss Otis Regrets (She's Unable To Lunch Today) (24)
Miss You (15)
Mona Lisa (21,26,28)
More (20)
More I See You (8)
Morning Star (6)
My First And Only Lover (15)
My Heart Tells Me (Should I Believe My Heart?) (8)
My Heart's Treasure (9)
My Kind Of Girl (20)
My Kind Of Love (24)
My Life (10)
My Need For You (12)
My One Sin (1) *24*
Nature Boy (28)
Near You (15)
Never Let Me Go (4,22) *79*
Night Of The Quarter Moon (22)
Nightingale Sang In Berkeley Square (12)
No, I Don't Want Her (16)
Noche De Ronda (7)
Non Dimenticar (Don't Forget) (28) *45*
Not So Long Ago (12)
Nothing Ever Changes My Love For You (4) *72*
Oh, How I Miss You Tonight (15)
On A Bicycle Built For Two (17)
On The Sidewalks Of New York (17)
On The Street Where You Live (19)
Once In A While (5)
One Has My Name The Other Has My Heart (14)
Only Forever (12)
Only Yesterday (18)
Our Old Home Team (17)
Paradise (8)
Party's Over (5)
Pick-Up (11)
Pick Yourself Up (13)
Poinciana (12)
Portrait Of Jennie (21)
Pretend (21,28)
Quizas, Quizas, Quizas (Perhaps, Perhaps, Perhaps) (7)

Rain In Spain (19)
Ramblin' Rose (14,26,28) *2*
Red Sails In The Sunset (21)
Return To Paradise (1)
Road To Nowhere (18)
Route 66 (2,26,28)
Ruby And The Pearl (27)
Sand And The Sea (1,27) *23*
Say It Isn't So (16)
Send For Me (23,28) *6*
September Song (13)
Serenata (13)
Show Me (19)
Sing Another Song (And We'll All Go Home) (14)
Skip To My Lou (14)
Smile (1,27)
Someone To Tell It To (16)
Someone You Love (4) *13*
Somewhere Along The Way (27)
Song Is Ended (But The Melody Lingers On) (8)
Song Of Raintree County (22) *flip*
Spring Is Here (16)
St. Louis Blues, Love Theme (medley) (6)
St. Louis Blues (6,22)
Stardust (3) *79*
Stay (6)
Stay As Sweet As You Are (3)
Stay With It (11)
Straighten Up And Fly Right (28)
Sunday, Monday, Or Always (12)
Surrey With The Fringe On Top (24)
Sweet Bird Of Youth (23) *96*
Sweet Lorraine (2,26)
Swiss Retreat (20)
Te Quiero, Dijiste (Magic Is The Moonlight) (7)
Teach Me Tonight (27)
Tell Her In The Morning (11)
Tell Me All About Yourself (10)
Thanks To You (20)
That Sunday, That Summer (17) *12*
That's All (4)
That's All There Is (16)
That's What They Meant (By The Good Old Summertime) (17)
There Is A Tavern In The Town (17)
There's A Gold Mine In The Sky (25)
There's A Lull In My Life (13)

There's Love (20)
These Foolish Things Remind Me Of You (5)
They Can't Make Her Cry (22)
This Is All I Ask (8)
This Is Always (10)
This Morning It Was Summer (9)
Those Lazy-Hazy-Crazy Days Of Summer (17,26,28) *6*
Thou Swell (24)
Thousand Thoughts Of You (9)
Three Little Words (20)
Time And The River (23) *30*
To The Ends Of The Earth (4) *25*
To Whom It May Concern (9)
Too Much (9)
Too Young (21,26,28)
Too Young To Go Steady (4) *21*
Touch Of Your Lips (12)
Tu, Mi Delirio (7)
Twilight On The Trail (14)
Unbelievable (1,27)
Unfair (9)
Unforgettable (21,28) *14*
Until The Real Thing Comes Along (10)
Very Thought Of You (8)
Walkin' My Baby Back Home (27,28)
Was That The Human Thing To Do? (18)
Weaver Of Dreams (27)
When I Fall In Love (3)
When Sunny Gets Blue (3)
When You Walked By (10)
When You're Smiling (14)
When Your Lover Has Gone (5)
Where Can I Go Without You? (3)
Where Did Everyone Go? (16)
Where Or When (24)
Who's Next In Line? (15)
Who's Sorry Now? (5)
Why Should I Cry Over You? (15)
Wild Is Love (11)
With A Little Bit Of Luck (19)
Wolverton Mountain (14)
World In My Arms (23)
World Of No Return (11)
Wouldn't It Be Loverly (19)
Wouldn't You Know (Her Name Is Mary) (11)

DEBUT DATE	PEAK POS	WKS CHR	GOLD	ARTIST — Album Title	$	Label & Number

COLE, Nat "King" — Cont'd

Yearning (Just For You) (15)
Yellow Dog Blues (6)
You Are My Love (10)
You Did It (19)
You Leave Me Breathless (24)
You Tell Me Your Dream (17)
You're Bringing Out The Dreamer In Me (9)
You're Crying On My Shoulder (18)
You're Looking At Me (2)
You're Mine, You! (12)
You're My Everything (18)
You're My Thrill (25)
You've Got The Indian Sign On Me (10)
Your Cheatin' Heart (14)
Your Love (20)

COLEMAN, Durell

Native of Roanoke, Virginia. R&B singer. Moved to Los Angeles in 1983. Was the 1985 winner of TV's *Star Search* (male vocalist category).

| 9/28/85 | 155 | 7 | | Durell Coleman .... | $8 | Island 90293 |

Do You Love Me
I Had A Sure Thing
I Should Have Known Better
One False Move
Run To Me
Somebody Took My Love
Take Me Back To My Love In China
Tender Blue
When A Man Loves A Woman

COLLEGE BOYZ, The

Los Angeles-based male rap quartet: Rom, Squeak, The Q and DJ B-Selector.

| 5/2/92 | 118 | 11 | | Radio Fusion Radio .... | $12 | Virgin 91658 |

College Boyz In The House
Funky Quartet
Hollywood Paradox
How Ta Act
Humpin'
Politics Of A Gangster [includes 2 versions]
Real Man
Rigmarole
Underground Blues
Victim Of The Ghetto 68

COLLINS, Albert

Blues vocalist/guitarist, born on 10/1/32 in Leona, Texas. Cousin of Lightnin' Hopkins. Appeared in the film *Adventures In Babysitting*. Dubbed "The Master of the Telecaster" and "The Iceman."

| 2/12/72 | 196 | 2 | | 1 There's Gotta Be A Change .... | $12 | Tumbleweed 103 |
| 2/15/86 | 124 | 18 | | 2 Showdown! .... | $8 | Alligator 4743 |

ALBERT COLLINS/ROBERT CRAY/JOHNNY COPELAND
Copeland and Collins are veteran blues guitarists, Cray was a newcomer

Albert's Alley (2)
Black Cat Bone (2)
Blackjack (2)
Bring Your Fine Self Home (2)
Dream, The (2)
Fade Away (1)
Frog Jumpin' (1)
Get Your Business Straight (1)
I Got A Mind To Travel (1)
In Love Wit'cha (1)
Lion's Den (2)
Moon Is Full (2)
She's Into Something (2)
Somethin' On My Mind (1)
Stickin' (1)
T-Bone Shuffle (2)
There's Gotta Be A Change (1)
Today Ain't Like Yesterday (1)

COLLINS, "Bootsy" — see BOOTSY

★★151★★ ## COLLINS, Judy

Contemporary folk singer/songwriter. Born on 5/1/39 in Seattle. Began studying classical piano at age five. Moved to Los Angeles, then to Denver at age nine, where her father, Chuck Collins, was a radio personality. Classical debut at 13, playing with the Denver Businessmen's Symphony Orchestra. Discovered folk music at 15. Signed to Elektra in 1961. Her cover versions gave exposure to then-unknown songwriters Leonard Cohen, Joni Mitchell, Randy Newman and Sandy Denny. Stephen Stills wrote "Suite: Judy Blue Eyes" for her. Appeared in the New York Shakespeare Festival's production of *Peer Gynt*. Nominated for a 1974 Academy Award for co-directing *Antonia: A Portrait of the Woman* — a documentary about Judy's former classical mentor and a pioneer female orchestra conductor, Dr. Antonia Brico.

3/28/64	126	10		1 Judy Collins #3	$35	Elektra 7243
10/2/65	69	13		2 Judy Collins' Fifth Album	$20	Elektra 7300
1/7/67	46	34	●	3 In My Life	$15	Elektra 7320
1/6/68	5	75	●	4 Wildflowers	$15	Elektra 74012
12/21/68+	29	33	●	5 Who Knows Where The Time Goes	$15	Elektra 74033
9/20/69	29	29		6 Recollections .... [K]	$15	Elektra 74055
				recordings from 1963-65		
12/5/70+	17	35	●	7 Whales & Nightingales	$12	Elektra 75010
12/4/71+	64	13		8 Living	$12	Elektra 75014
				4 of 10 tracks are live		
5/27/72	37	24	●	9 Colors Of The Day/The Best Of Judy Collins ..... [G]	$12	Elektra 75030
2/10/73	27	20		10 True Stories And Other Dreams	$12	Elektra 75053
4/12/75	17	34	●	11 Judith	$10	Elektra 1032
9/11/76	25	20		12 Bread & Roses	$10	Elektra 1076
8/6/77	42	27		13 So Early In The Spring, The First 15 Years ..... [K]	$12	Elektra 6002 [2]
3/17/79	54	16		14 Hard Times For Lovers	$10	Elektra 171
5/3/80	142	6		15 Running For My Life	$10	Elektra 253
3/13/82	190	5		16 Times Of Our Lives	$10	Elektra 60001

Albatross (4,9)
All Things Are Quite Silent (8)
Almost Free (15)
Amazing Grace (7,9) **15**
Anathea (1,6)
Angel On My Side (16)
Angel, Spread Your Wings (11)
Anyone Know Love You (15)
Ballata Of Francesco Landini (medley) (4)
Bells Of Rhymney (1,6)
Bird On The Wire (5,13)
Bonnie Ship The Diamond (13)
Born To The Breed (11,13)
Both Sides Now (4,9,13) **8**
Bread And Roses (12,13)
Bright Morning Star (13)
Brother, Can You Spare A Dime (11)
Bullgine Run (1)
Carry It On (2,13)
Che (10)
Chelsea Morning (8) **78**
City Of New Orleans (11)
Coal Tattoo (13)
Come Away Melinda (1)
Come Down In Time (12)
Coming Of The Roads (2)
Cook With Honey (10) **32**
Daddy You've Been On My Mind (2,6)
Dealer (Down And Losin') (10)
Deporte (medley) (1)
Desperado (14)
Don't Say Goodbye Love (16)
Dorothy (14)
Dove, The (1)
Dress Rehearsal Rag (3)
Drink A Round To Ireland (16)
Early Morning Rain (2,6)
Easy Times (8)
Everything Must Change (12)
Famous Blue Raincoat (8)
Farewell (1)
Farewell To Tarwathie (7,9,13)
First Boy I Loved (5)
Fishermen Song (10)
Four Strong Winds (8)
Gene's Song (7)
Golden Apples Of The Sun (13)
Grandaddy (16)
Great Expectations (16)
Green Finch And Linnet Bird (15)
Happy End (14)
Hard Lovin' Loser (3) **97**
Hard Times For Lovers (14) **66**
Hello, Horray (5)
Hey Nelly Nelly (1)
Hey, That's No Way To Say Goodbye (4)
Holly Ann (10,13)
Hostage, The (10,13)
Houses (11,13)
I Could Really Show You (7)
I Didn't Know About You (13)
I Remember Sky (14)
I Think It's Going To Rain Today (1)
I'll Be Seeing You (11)
I'll Never Say Goodbye (14)
I've Done Enough Dyin' Today (15)
In My Life (3,9)
In The Heat Of The Summer (2)
In The Hills Of Shiloh (1)
Innisfree (8)
It Isn't Nice (2)
It's Gonna Be One Of Those Nights (14)
Joan Of Arc (8)
Just Like Tom Thumb's Blues (3,8)
King David (12)
La Chanson Des Vieux Amants (The Song Of Old Lovers) (4)
La Colombe (3,13)
Lasso! Di Donna (medley) (4)
Last Thing On My Mind (6)
Liverpool Lullaby (3)
Lord Gregory (2)
Love Hurts (12)
Loving Of The Game (11,13)
Mama Mama (16)
Marat (medley) (3,13)
Marie (14)
Marieke (7,13,15)
Marjorie (12)
Masters Of War (1)
Memory (15)
Michael From Mountains (4)
Moon Is A Harsh Mistress (11)
Mr. Tambourine Man (2,6)
My Father (5,9,13)
Nightingale I & II (7)
Oh Had I A Golden Thread (7)
Open The Door (Song For Judith) (8) **90**
Out Of Control (12)
Pack Up Your Sorrows (2,6)
Patriot Game (7)
Pirate Jenny (3)
Pirate Ships (11)
Plane Wreck At Los Gatos (medley) (1)
Plegaria A Un Labrador (12)
Poor Immigrant (5)
Pretty Polly (5,13)
Pretty Saro (13)
Pretty Women (15)
Priests (4)
Prothalamium (7)
Rainbow Connection (15)
Rest Of Your Life (16)
Running For My Life (15)
Sade (medley) (3,13)
Salt Of The Earth (11)
Secret Gardens (10,13)
Send In The Clowns (11,13) **19**
Settle Down (11)
Simple Gifts (7)
Since You Asked (4,9,13)
Sisters Of Mercy (4)
Sky Fell (4)
So Begins The Task (7)
So Early, Early In The Spring (7)
Someday Soon (5,9) **55**
Song For David (7)
Song For Duke (13)
(Song For Judith) ..see: Open The Door
Song For Martin (10)
Sons Of (7,9)
Spanish Is The Loving Tongue (12)
Special Delivery (12,13)

DEBUT DATE	PEAK POS	WKS CHR	GOLD	ARTIST — Album Title	$	Label & Number

COLLINS, Judy — Cont'd

Starmaker (14)
Story Of Isaac (5)
Sun Son (16)
Sunny Goodge Street (3,9)

Suzanne (3,9)
Take This Longing (12)
Ten O'Clock All Is Well (1)
Thirsty Boots (2)

This Is The Day (15)
Through The Eyes Of Love (14)
Time Passes Slowly (7)

Tomorrow Is A Long Time (2,6)
Turn! Turn! Turn!/To Everything There Is A Season (1,6) **69**

Vietnam Love Song (8)
Wedding Song (15)
Where Or When (14)

Who Knows Where The Time Goes (5,9)
Winter Sky (6)

★★**288**★★ **COLLINS, Phil**

Born on 1/30/51 in London. Stage actor as a young child; played the Artful Dodger in the London production of *Oliver*. With group Flaming Youth in 1969. Joined Genesis as their drummer in 1970, became lead singer in 1975. Also with jazz-rock group Brand X. First solo album in 1981. Starred in the 1988 film *Buster* and appeared in *Hook* (1991).

DEBUT DATE	PEAK POS	WKS CHR	GOLD	ARTIST — Album Title	$	Label & Number
3/14/81	7	164	▲⁴	1 Face Value	$8	Atlantic 16029
11/27/82+	8	141	▲²	2 Hello, I Must Be Going!	$8	Atlantic 80035
3/9/85	1⁷	123	▲⁷	3 No Jacket Required	$8	Atlantic 81240
				1985 Grammy winner: Album of the Year		
12/2/89+	1³	90	▲³	4 ...But Seriously	$8	Atlantic 82050
11/24/90+	11	97	▲	5 Serious Hits...Live! [L]	$12	Atlantic 82157

recorded during his "Serious Tour 1990"; 22-page booklet included

Against All Odds (Take A Look At Me Now) (5)
All Of My Life (4)
Another Day In Paradise (4,5) *1*
Behind The Lines (1)
Colours (4)
Do You Know, Do You Care? (2)
Do You Remember? (4,5) *4*
Doesn't Anybody Stay Together Anymore (3)

Don't Let Him Steal Your Heart Away (2)
Don't Lose My Number (3,5) *4*
Droned (1)
Easy Lover (5)
Father To Son (4)
Find A Way To My Heart (4)
Groovy Kind Of Love (5)
Hand In Hand (1)
Hang In Long Enough (4) *23*

I Cannot Believe It's True (2) *79*
I Don't Care Anymore (2) *39*
I Don't Wanna Know (3)
I Missed Again (1) *19*
I Wish It Would Rain Down (4) *3*
I'm Not Moving (1)
If Leaving Me Is Easy (1)
In The Air Tonight (1,5) *19*
Inside Out (3)

It Don't Matter To Me (2)
Like China (2)
Long Long Way To Go (3)
One More Night (3,5) *1*
Only You Know And I Know (3)
Roof Is Leaking (1)
Separate Lives (5)
Something Happened On The Way To Heaven (4,5) *4*
Sussudio (3,5) *1*

Take Me Home (3,5) *7*
Thats Just The Way It Is (4)
This Must Be Love (1)
Thru These Walls (2)
Thunder And Lightning (1)
Tomorrow Never Knows (1)
Two Hearts (5)
West Side (2)
Who Said I Would (3,5) *73*
Why Can't It Wait 'Til Morning (2)

You Can't Hurry Love (2,5) *10*
You Know What I Mean (1)

COLLINS, Tyler

Female R&B singer born in Harlem and raised in Detroit.

DEBUT DATE	PEAK POS	WKS CHR	GOLD	ARTIST — Album Title	$	Label & Number
5/26/90	85	22		Girls Nite Out	$12	RCA 9642

Beyond A Shadow Of A Doubt

Girls Nite Out *6*
Give And Take

I Only Wanted
Love Talk

Second Chance *53*
Strut

Two In Love
Whatcha Gonna Do

You And Me

COLOR ME BADD

New York City-based dance vocal quartet of 21-year-olds: Bryan Abrams, Sam Watters, Mark Calderon and Kevin Thornton. Formed while in high school in Oklahoma City.

DEBUT DATE	PEAK POS	WKS CHR	GOLD	ARTIST — Album Title	$	Label & Number
8/10/91	3	77	▲³	C.M.B.	$12	Giant 24429

All 4 Love *1*
Color Me Badd

Groove My Mind
Heartbreaker

I Adore Mi Amor *1*
I Wanna Sex You Up *2*

Roll The Dice
Slow Motion *18*

Thinkin' Back *16*
Your Da One I Onena Love

COLOSSEUM

British jazz-rock band formed by members of John Mayall's Bluesbreakers — Jon Hiseman (drums) and Dick Heckstall-Smith (reeds).

DEBUT DATE	PEAK POS	WKS CHR	GOLD	ARTIST — Album Title	$	Label & Number
11/20/71	192	3		Colosseum Live	$12	Warner 1942 [2]

Lost Angeles

Rope Ladder To The Moon

Skelington

Stormy Monday Blues

Tanglewood '63'

Walking In The Park

COLTER, Jessi

Born Miriam Johnson on 5/25/47 in Phoenix. Country singer/songwriter. Married to Duane Eddy from 1962-68. Married Waylon Jennings in October 1969. Also see Concept Albums (*The Outlaws*).

DEBUT DATE	PEAK POS	WKS CHR	GOLD	ARTIST — Album Title	$	Label & Number
5/3/75	50	27		1 I'm Jessi Colter	$8	Capitol 11363
2/7/76	109	8		2 Jessi	$8	Capitol 11477
8/7/76	79	8		3 Diamond In The Rough	$8	Capitol 11543
3/21/81	43	19	●	4 Leather and Lace	$8	RCA 3931

WAYLON & JESSI

Ain't No Way (3)
All My Life, I've Been Your Lady (2)
Come On In (1)
Darlin' It's Yours (2)
Diamond In The Rough (3)
For The First Time (1)
Get Back (4)
Hand That Rocks The Cradle (2)

Here I Am (2)
Hey Jude (3)
I Ain't The One (4)
I Believe You Can (4)
I Hear A Song (1)
I See Your Face (In The Morning's Window) (2)
I Thought I Heard You Calling My Name (3)
I'll Be Alright (4)

I'm Not Lisa (1) *4*
Is There Any Way (You'd Stay Forever) (1)
It's Morning (And I Still Love You) (2)
Love's The Only Chain (1)
Oh Will (Who Made It Rain Last Night) (3)
One Woman Man (2)
Pastels And Harmony (4)

Rainy Seasons (4)
Rounder (2)
Storms Never Last (1,4)
What's Happened To Blue Eyes (1,4) *57*
Who Walks Thru Your Memory (Billy Jo) (1)
Wild Side Of Life (4)
Without You (2)

Woman's Heart (Is A Handy Place To Be) (3)
Would You Leave Now (3)
Would You Walk With Me (To The Lilies) (2)
You Ain't Never Been Loved (Like I'm Gonna Love You) (1) *64*
You Hung The Moon (Didn't You Waylon?) (3)

You Never Can Tell (C'est La Vie) (4)
You're Not My Same Sweet Baby (4)

COLTRANE, Alice

Jazz keyboardist. Born Alice McLeod on 8/27/37 in Detroit. Widow of John Coltrane. Replaced keyboardist McCoy Tyner in her husband's group from 1966 until John's death in 1967.

DEBUT DATE	PEAK POS	WKS CHR	GOLD	ARTIST — Album Title	$	Label & Number
11/13/71	190	2		1 Universal Consciousness [I]	$10	Impulse! 9210
10/12/74	79	8		2 Illuminations [I]	$10	Columbia 32900

TURIYA ALICE COLTRANE/DEVADIP CARLOS SANTANA

Angel Of Air (medley) (2)
Angel Of Sunlight (2)
Angel Of Water (medley) (2)

Ankh Of Amen-Ra (1)
Battle At Armageddon (1)
Bliss: The Eternal Now (2)

Guru Sri Chinmoy (1)
Aphorism (2)
Hare Krishna (1)

Illuminations (2)
Oh Allah (1)
Sita Ram (1)

Universal Consciousness (1)

COLTRANE, Chi

Born on 11/16/48 in Racine, Wisconsin. Female vocalist/pianist. Chi pronounced: shy.

DEBUT DATE	PEAK POS	WKS CHR	GOLD	ARTIST — Album Title	$	Label & Number
9/23/72	148	10		Chi Coltrane	$10	Columbia 31275

Feelin' Good
Go Like Elijah

Goodbye John
I Will Not Dance

It's Really Come To This
Thunder And Lightning *17*

Time To Come In
Tree, The

Turn Me Around
Wheel Of Life

You Were My Friend

COLTRANE, John

Legendary jazz tenor saxophonist. Born on 9/23/26 in Hamlet, North Carolina. Died on 7/17/67 from liver cancer. With Dizzy Gillespie in the early 1950s, Miles Davis in 1955, Thelonious Monk in 1957, then solo. Married Alice Coltrane in 1966.

| 11/18/67 | 194 | 3 | | 1 Expression ....[I] | $20 | Impulse! 9120 |

John's last recording session, February 1967

| 11/13/71 | 186 | 3 | | 2 Sun Ship ....[I] | $15 | Impulse! 9211 |

recorded 8/26/65

Amen (2) Attaining (2) Expression (1) Ogunde (1) To Be (1)
Ascent (2) Dearly Beloved (2) Offering (1) Sun Ship (2)

COLVIN, Shawn

Female folk singer. Born on 1/10/58 in Vermillion, South Dakota. Backing vocalist for Suzanne Vega.

| 12/16/89+ | 111 | 24 | | 1 Steady On .... | $8 | Columbia 45209 |
| 11/14/92 | 142 | 10↑ | | 2 Fat City .... | $12 | Columbia 47122 |

Another Long One (1) Diamond In The Rough (1) Orion In The Sky (2) Shotgun Down The Stranded (1)
Climb On (A Back That's I Don't Know Why (2) Polaroids (2) Avalanche (1) Tenderness On The Block (2)
Strong) (2) Kill The Messenger (2) Ricochet In Time (1) Something To Believe In (1) Tennessee (2)
Cry Like An Angel (1) Monopoly (2) Round Of Blues (2) Steady On (1)
Dead Of The Night (1) Object Of My Affection (2) Set The Prairie On Fire (2) Story, The (1)

COMMAND ALL-STARS — see LIGHT, Enoch

COMMANDER CODY And His Lost Planet Airmen

Group formed while Cody (George Frayne) attended the University of Michigan. To San Francisco in 1968.

11/27/71+	82	33		1 Lost In The Ozone	$12	Paramount 6017
9/9/72	94	13		2 Hot Licks, Cold Steel & Truckers Favorites	$12	Paramount 6031
6/16/73	104	9		3 Country Casanova	$12	Paramount 6054
2/16/74	105	14		4 Live From Deep In The Heart Of Texas ....[L]	$10	Paramount 1017
3/1/75	58	10		5 Commander Cody & His Lost Planet Airmen	$10	Warner 2847
10/11/75	168	6		6 Tales From The Ozone	$10	Warner 2883
7/31/76	170	3		7 We've Got A Live One Here! ....[L]	$12	Warner 2939 [2]
9/3/77	163	5		8 Rock 'N Roll Again	$8	Arista 4125

COMMANDER CODY BAND

Armadillo Stomp (4) Don't Say Nothin' (8) It's Gonna Be One Of Those My Window Faces The Semi-Truck (2,7) Tutti Fruitti (2)
Back To Tennessee (1,7) 18 Wheels (7) Nights (6,7) South (3,7) Seven-Eleven (8) 20 Flight Rock (1)
Beat Me Daddy Eight To Everybody's Doin' It (3) Keep On Lovin' Her (5) Oh Momma Momma (4) Shadow Knows (6) Watch My .38 (2)
The Bar (1) *81* Family Bible (1) Kentucky Hills Of Tennessee One Man's Meat (Is Another Shall We Meet (Beyond The What's The Matter Now? (1)
Big Mammau (7) Four Or Five Times (5) (2) Man's Poison) (3) River) (3) Where Were You (8)
Boogie Man Boogie (5) Git It (4) Lightnin' Bar Blues (6) One Of Those Nights ..see: Sister Sue (3) Widow (8)
Cajun Baby (6) Good Rockin' Tonight (4) Little Sally Walker (4) It's Gonna Be One Of 6 Years On The Road (8) Willin' (5)
California Okie (5) Gypsy Fiddle (6) Looking At The World Those Nights Smoke! Smoke! Smoke! Wine Do Yer Stuff (1)
Connie (6) Hawaii Blues (5) Through A Windshield (2,7) Paid In Advance (6) **(That Cigarette)** (3,7) *94*
Country Casanova (3) Honeysuckle Honey (6) Lost In The Ozone (1,7) Rave On (1) Snooze You Lose (8)
Cravin' Your Love (2) Honky Tonk Music (6) Mama Hated Diesels (2,7) Riot In Cell Block #9 (4,7) Southbound (5)
Crying Time (4) House Of Blue Lights (5) Mean Woman Blues (4) Rip It Up (2) Sunset On The Sage (4)
Daddy's Gonna Treat You I Been To Georgia On A Fast Midnight Man (8) Rock N' Roll Again (8) That's What I Like About
Right (1) Train (6) Midnight Shift (1) Rock That Boogie (3,7) The South (5)
Danny (8) I'm Comin' Home (4) Milkcow Blues (6) Roll Your Own (6) Tina Louise (6)
Devil And Me (5) It Should've Been Me (2,7) Minnie The Moocher (6) San Antonio Rose (7) Too Much Fun (4,7)
Diggy Liggy Lo (2,4) My Home In My Hand (1) Seeds And Stems (Again) Truck Drivin' Man (2)
Don't Let Go (5,7) *56* (1,4,7) Truck Stop Rock (2)

COMMITMENTS, The — see SOUNDTRACKS

★★114★★ COMMODORES

R&B group formed in Tuskegee, Alabama in 1970. Consisted of Lionel Richie (vocals, saxophone), William King (trumpet), Thomas McClary (guitar), Milan Williams (keyboards), Ronald LaPread (bass) and Walter "Clyde" Orange (drums). First recorded for Motown in 1972. In film Thank God It's Friday. Richie began solo work in 1981, left in 1982.

8/24/74	138	9		1 Machine Gun	$10	Motown 798
3/22/75	26	33		2 Caught In The Act	$10	Motown 820
11/8/75	29	32		3 Movin' On	$10	Motown 848
7/10/76	12	39		4 Hot On The Tracks	$10	Motown 867
4/2/77	3	53		5 Commodores	$10	Motown 884
11/12/77	3	28		6 Commodores Live! ....[L]	$12	Motown 894 [2]
5/27/78	3	33	▲	7 Natural High	$10	Motown 902
11/25/78+	23	20		8 Commodores' Greatest Hits ....[G]	$10	Motown 912
8/18/79	3	41		9 Midnight Magic	$10	Motown 926
6/28/80	7	33	▲	10 Heroes	$8	Motown 939
7/11/81	13	40	▲	11 In The Pocket	$8	Motown 955
12/4/82+	37	24		12 All The Great Hits ....[G]	$8	Motown 6028
6/11/83	141	7		13 Commodores Anthology ....[G]	$10	Motown 6044 [2]
10/1/83	103	11		14 Commodores 13	$8	Motown 6054
2/16/85	12	37	●	15 Nightshift	$8	Motown 6124
11/22/86	101	15		16 United	$8	Polydor 831194

All The Way Down (10) Can't Let You Tease Me (4) **Flying High** (7,13) *38* Gonna Blow Your Mind (1) I Wanna Rock You (16) **Lady (You Bring Me Up)**
Animal Instinct (15) *43* Captured (14) Free (3) Got To Be Together (10) I'm In Love (14) (11,12) *8*
Assembly Line (1) Cebu (3) Funky Situation (5) Heaven Knows (5) I'm Ready (2) Land Of The Dreamer (16)
Been Loving You (11) Celebrate (10) Funny Feelings (5,6) **Heroes** (10) *54* **Janet** (15) *87* Lay Back (15)
Better Never Than Forever (2) Come Inside (4,6) Gettin' It (9) High On Sunshine (4,13) Jesus Is Love (10) Let's Apologize (16)
Brick House (5,6,8,12,13) *5* Don't You Be Worried (13) Gimme My Mule (3) Hold On (3) **Just To Be Close To You** Let's Do It Right (16)
Bump, The (1,2) Easy (5,6,8,12,13) *4* Girl, I Think The World I Feel Sanctified (1,6,13) *75* (4,6,8,13) *7* Let's Get Started (4)
(Can I) Get A Witness (3) **Fancy Dancer** (4,6,8,13) *39* About You (4) I Keep Running (15) Keep On Taking Me Higher Lightnin' Up The Night (15)
Can't Dance All Night (16) Fire Girl (7) **Goin' To The Bank** (16) *65* I Like What You Do (7) (11)

DEBUT DATE	PEAK POS	WKS CHR	GOLD	ARTIST — Album Title	$	Label & Number

COMMODORES — Cont'd

Look What You've Done To Me (2)	Ooo, Woman You (14)	Slippery When Wet (2,6,8,13) 19	This Love (11)	Why You Wanna Try Me (11) 66	Young Girls Are My Weakness (1,13)
Lovin' You (9)	Painted Picture (12) 70	Sorry To Say (10)	Three Times A Lady (7,8,12,13) 1	Wide Open (2)	Zoo (The Human Zoo) (1,13)
Lucy (11)	Patch It Up (5)	Squeeze The Fruit (5)	Thumpin' Music (4)	Woman In My Life (15)	Zoom (5,6,13)
Machine Gun (1,8,12,13) 22	Play This Record Twice (15)	Still (9,12,13) 1	Time (3)	Won't You Come Dance With Me (5,6)	
Mary, Mary (3)	Quick Draw (4)	Such A Woman (7)	Too Hot Ta Trot (6,8,13) 24	Wonderland (9,13) 25	
Midnight Magic (9,13)	Rapid Fire (1)	Superman (1)	Touchdown (14)	X-Rated Movie (7)	
Mighty Spirit (10)	Reach High (12)	Sweet Love (3,6,8,13) 5	Turn Off The Lights (14)	You Don't Know That I Know (2)	
Nightshift (15) 3	Sail On (9,12,13) 4	Take It From Me (16)	12:01 A.M. (9)	You're Special (9)	
Nothing Like A Woman (14)	Saturday Night (11)	Talk To Me (16)	United In Love (16)	You're The Only Woman I Need (16)	
Oh No (11,12) 4	Say Yeah (7)	There's A Song In My Heart (1)	Visions (2)		
Old-Fashion Love (10) 20	Serious Love (16)	This Is Your Life (2,8,13)	Wake Up Children (10)		
Only You (14) 54	Sexy Lady (9)		Welcome Home (14)		
	Slip Of The Tongue (15)				

COMMUNARDS

British rock duo consisting of Bronski Beat vocalist Jimmy Somerville and multi-instrumentalist Richard Coles.

12/20/86+	90	16		1 Communards............	$8	MCA/London 5794
2/6/88	93	9		2 Red............	$8	MCA 42106

C Minor (2)	Don't Slip Away (1)	Hold On Tight (1)	Lover Man (Oh, Where Can You Be?) (1)	Never Can Say Goodbye (2) 51	T.M.T. ♥ .T.B.M.G. (2)
Disenchanted (1)	For A Friend (2)	If I Could Tell You (2)	Lovers And Friends (2)	Reprise (1)	Tomorrow (2)
Don't Leave Me This Way (1) 40	Forbidden Love (1)	La Dolarosa (1)	Matter Of Opinion (2)	So Cold The Night (1)	Victims (2)
	Heavens Above (1)				You Are My World (1)

★★85★★ COMO, Perry

Born Pierino Como on 5/18/12 in Canonsburg, Pennsylvania. Owned barbershop in hometown. With Freddy Carlone band in 1933; with Ted Weems, 1936-42. In the films *Something For The Boys, Doll Face, If I'm Lucky* and *Words And Music*, 1944-48. Own *Supper Club* radio series to late 1940s. Television shows (15 minutes) from 1948-55. Host of hourly TV shows from 1955-63. Winner of five Emmys.

10/15/55	7	15		1 So Smooth	$30	RCA 1085
9/2/57	8	10		2 We Get Letters............	$25	RCA 1463
12/16/57	11	9		3 Dream Along With Me	$20	RCA Camden 403
6/23/58	18	2		4 Saturday Night With Mr. C.	$25	RCA 1004
9/1/58	24	2		5 Como's Golden Records ....[G]	$25	RCA 1007
1/5/59	16	7		6 When You Come To The End Of The Day	$25	RCA 1885
11/2/59	17	12		7 Como Swings............	$25	RCA 2010
9/25/61	50	13		8 Sing To Me, Mr. C.	$20	RCA 2390
9/29/62	32	21		9 By Request	$20	RCA 2567
12/8/62	90	6		10 The Best Of Irving Berlin's Songs From "Mr. President"	$20	RCA 2630
				includes "Is He The Only Man In The World" by The Ray Charles Singers; "Secret Service" by Sandy Stewart with The Ray Charles Singers; and "Song For Belly Dancer" & "They Love Me" by Kay Ballard		
9/21/63	59	18		11 The Songs I Love	$20	RCA 2708
5/29/65	47	17		12 The Scene Changes	$15	RCA 3396
6/11/66	86	9		13 Lightly Latin	$15	RCA 3552
10/22/66	81	16		14 Perry Como In Italy	$15	RCA 3608
6/21/69	93	11		15 Seattle	$15	RCA 4183
1/16/71	22	27		16 It's Impossible	$15	RCA 4473
6/26/71	101	9		17 I Think Of You	$15	RCA 4539
5/26/73	34	19	●	18 And I Love You So	$10	RCA 0100
8/17/74	138	10		19 Perry	$10	RCA 0585
12/20/75+	142	9		20 Just Out Of Reach	$10	RCA 0863
				CHRISTMAS ALBUMS:		
12/16/57	8	5	●	21 Merry Christmas Music ....[X]	$20	RCA 1243
12/15/58	9	4		22 Merry Christmas Music ....[X-R]	$20	RCA 1243
				Christmas charts: 17/'63, 15/'64, 53/'65, 63/'66, 16/'67, 16/'68		
1/4/60	22	1	●	23 Season's Greetings ....[X]	$20	RCA 2066
12/31/60	27	1		24 Season's Greetings ....[X-R]	$20	RCA 2066
1/6/62	33	3		25 Season's Greetings ....[X-R]	$20	RCA 2066
12/15/62	74	3		26 Season's Greetings ....[X-R]	$20	RCA 2066
				Christmas charts: 5/'63, 34/'64, 15/'65, 11/'66, 22/'67, 17/'68		

Accentuate The Positive (medley) (4)	Beyond Tomorrow (19)	Coo Coo Roo Coo Coo Paloma (1)	Everybody Is Looking For An Answer (16)	Gringo's Guitar (12)	Hot Diggity (Dog Ziggity Boom) (5) 1
All By Myself (medley) (8)	Birth Of The Blues (4)	Days Of Wine And Roses (11)	Fellow Needs A Girl (medley) (4)	Gypsy In My Soul (medley) (4)	House Is Not A Home (16)
All I Do Is Dream Of You (medley) (8)	Blue Skies (3,8)	Dear Hearts And Gentle People (7)		Hands Of Time (Brian's Song) (19)	How Deep Is The Ocean (medley) (8)
All Through The Night (6)	Breezin' Along With The Breeze (1)	'Deed I Do (2)	First Lady (10)	Happiness Comes, Happiness Goes (15)	How Insensitive (Insensatez) (13)
Almost Like Being In Love (medley) (4)	Brian's Song ..see: Hands Of Time	Deep In Your Heart (15)	First Noel (medley) (23)	Hatchet, A Hammer, A Bucket Of Nails (12)	Hubba-Hubba-Hubba (5)
And I Love You So (18) 29	Bridge Over Troubled Water (17)	Dindi (13)	Fly Me To The Moon (In Other Words) (11)	Hawaiian Wedding Song (11)	I Believe In Music (18)
And Roses And Roses (13)	Buongiorno Teresa (15)	Don't Let The Stars Get In Your Eyes (5)	For All We Know (17)	He's Got The Whole World In His Hands (6)	I Don't Know What He Told You (19)
Anema E Core (14)	Can't Help Falling In Love (9)	Donkey Serenade (7)	For Me And My Gal (1)	Hearts Will Be Hearts (15)	I Gotta Right To Sing The Blues (1)
Angry (2)	Carnival (11)	Dream Along With Me (I'm On My Way To A Star) (3,4) 85	For The Good Times (18)	Here Comes My Baby (12)	I Had The Craziest Dream (2)
Arrivederci Roma (Goodbye To Rome) (14)	Catch A Falling Star (5) 1		Forget Domani (14)	Here, There And Everywhere (20)	I Left My Heart In San Francisco (1)
As Time Goes By (1)	Chincherinchee (3) 59	Dream Baby (How Long Must I Dream) (12) 25	Frosty The Snow Man (21)	Here We Come A-Caroling (medley) (8)	I May Be Wrong (medley) (4)
Aubrey (18)	C-H-R-I-S-T-M-A-S (21)	Dream On Little Dreamer (12) 25	Funny How Time Slips Away (12)	Here's That Rainy Day (medley) (8)	I May Never Pass This Way Again (6)
Baia (13)	Christmas Song (Merry Christmas To You) (21,23)	E Lei (To You) (14)	Gigi (medley) (8)	Home For The Holidays (23)	I Really Don't Want To Know (12)
Beady Eyed Buzzard (15)	Come, Come, Come To The Manger (medley) (23)	El Condor Pasa (16)	Girl Of My Dreams (3)	Honey, Honey (Bless Your Heart) (2,7)	I Think I Love You (16)
Because (5)	Come Rain Or Come Shine (4)	Empty Pockets Filled With Love (10)	Give Myself A Party (12)		I Think Of You (17) 53
Begin The Beguine (7)	Cominciamo Ad Amarci (14)		Glad To Be Home (10)		
Behind Closed Doors (19)			God Rest Ye Merry Gentlemen (21,23)		
Between The Devil And The Deep Blue Sea (4)			Grass Keeps Right On Growin' (20)		

COMO, Perry — Cont'd

I Thought About You (18)
I Wanna Be Around (11)
I Want To Give (18)
I'll Be Home For Christmas (21)
I'll Remember April (9)
I'm Gonna Get Him (10)
I'm Gonna Sit Right Down And Write Myself A Letter (medley) (8)
I've Got A Feeling I'm Falling (3)
I've Got The World On A String (7)
I've Got You Under My Skin (7)
I've Grown Accustomed To Her Face (medley) (8)
If (17)
If I Loved You (3)
In Our Hide-Away (10)
In The Still Of The Night (1)
Is She The Only Girl In The World (10)
It All Seems To Fall Into Line (18)
It Could Happen To You (4)
It Gets Lonely In The White House (1)
It Had To Be You (4)
It Happened In Monterey (1)
It's A Good Day (1)
It's Easy To Remember (2)
It's Impossible (16) *10*
It's The Talk Of The Town (1)
Jingle Bells (21) *74*
Joy To The World! (21)
Just Out Of Reach (20)

Killing Me Softly With Her Song (18)
La Strada, Love Theme From (14)
Let A Smile Be Your Umbrella (On A Rainy Day) (7)
Let It Be Love (20)
Let Me Call You Baby Tonight (20)
Let's Do It Again (20)
Let's Someone In Love (medley) (4)
Linda (1)
Little Man You've Had A Busy Day (medley) (8)
Lollipops And Roses (9)
Love Letters (4)
Love Put A Song In My Heart (20)
Loving Her Was Easier (Than Anything I'll Ever Do Again) (20)
Magic Moments (5) *4*
Make Love To Life (20)
Manha De Carnaval (13)
Maria (9)
May The Good Lord Bless And Keep You (6)
Me And My Shadow (3)
Me And You And A Dog Named Boo (17)
Meditation (Meditacao) (13)
Mi Casa, Su Casa (My House Is Your House) (5) *50*
Mood Indigo (7)
Moon River (9)
Moonglow And Theme From "Picnic" (9)

More Than Likely (9)
More Than You Know (3)
Most Beautiful Girl (19)
My Coloring Book (11)
My Days Of Loving You (17)
My Favorite Things (9)
My Funny Valentine (1)
My Melancholy Baby (3)
My Own Peculiar Way (12)
No Well On Earth (6)
Nobody But You (15)
O Come, All Ye Faithful (Adeste Fideles) (21,23)
O Holy Night (23)
O Little Town Of Bethlehem (medley) (23)
O Marenariello (14)
Oh, How I Miss You Tonight (1)
Oh Marie (14)
Once I Loved (Amor E Paz) (13)
Once Upon A Time (9)
One For My Baby (1)
Only One (6)
Papa Loves Mambo (5)
Pigtails And Freckles (10)
Portrait Of My Love (medley) (8)
Prayer For Peace (6)
Prisoner Of Love (5)
Put Your Hand In The Hand (17)
Quiet Nights Of Quiet Stars (Corcovado) (13)
Raindrops Keep Fallin' On My Head (16)
Red Sails In The Sunset (3)
Route 66 (7)

Rudolph The Red-Nosed Reindeer (21,23)
Santa Claus Is Comin' To Town (21,23)
Santa Lucia (14)
Say It Isn't So (medley) (8)
Scarlet Ribbons (6)
Seattle (15) *38*
Serpico, Love Theme From ..see: Beyond Tomorrow
Shadow Of Your Smile (13)
Silent Night (21,23)
Sing (18)
Sing To Me, Mr. C (medley) (8)
Sleepy Time Gal (2)
Slightly Out Of Tune (Desafinado) (11)
Smile (medley) (8)
Snowbird (16)
So In Love (medley) (8)
Somebody Cares (9)
Somebody Loves Me (2)
Someone Who Cares (17)
Something (16)
Songs I Love (11)
South Of The Border (2)
Souvenir D'Italie (14)
Sposin' (2)
St. Louis Blues (7)
Stand Beside Me (12)
Stay With Me (15)
Still Small Voice (6)
Sunshine Wine (15)
Sweet Adorable You (12)
Sweetest Sounds (9)
Swinging Down The Lane (2)
Temptation (5,19)
Thank Heaven For Little Girls (medley) (8)

That Ain't All (12)
That Christmas Feeling (21)
That's All This Old World Needs (15)
That's What I Like (2)
That's You (Eres Tu) (19)
Then You Can Tell Me Goodbye (2)
They Can't Take That Away From Me (2)
(They Long To Be) Close To You (16)
They Say It's Wonderful (3)
This Is A Great Country (10)
This Is All I Ask (11)
This Nearly Was Mine (medley) (8)
Tie A Yellow Ribbon Round The Ole Oak Tree (18)
Till The End Of Time (5)
To Know You Is To Love You (7)
Together Forever (15)
Toselli's Serenade (Dreams And Memories) (14)
(Traveling Down A Lonely Road) ..see: La Strada, Love Theme From
Turnaround (15)
'Twas The Night Before Christmas (21)
Twelve Days Of Christmas (21)
Twilight On The Trail (medley) (4)
Un Giorno Dopo L'Altro (One Day Is Like Another) (14)
Vaya Con Dios (medley) (4)
Wanted (5)
Way We Were (19)

Way You Look Tonight (medley) (8)
We Three Kings Of Orient Are (medley) (23)
We Wish You A Merry Christmas (medley) (23)
We've Only Just Begun (16)
Weave Me The Sunshine (19)
What Kind Of Fool Am I? (11)
What's New? (9)
When I Fall In Love (4)
When I Lost You (11)
When You Come To The End Of The Day (6)
When You Were Sweet Sixteen (7)
Where Do I Begin (17)
Where Does A Little Tear Come From (12)
Whiffenpoof Song (medley) (4)
White Christmas (21,23)
Whither Thou Goest (6)
Winter Wonderland (21,23)
Without A Song (3)
Yesterday (13)
Yesterday I Heard The Rain (17)
You Alone (Solo Tu) (medley) (8)
You Are Never Far Away (4,8)
You Are The Sunshine Of My Life (19)
You Came A Long Way From St. Louis (7)
You Do Something To Me (1)
You Made Me Love You (medley) (4)
You Were Meant For Me (medley) (8)

COMPANY B

Miami-based, dance trio founded and produced by Foxy leader Ish Ledesma. Consisted of Lori L, Lezlee Livrano and Susan Johnson. The latter two left in 1989, replaced by Ohioans Donna Huntley and Julie Marie.

| 7/18/87 | 143 | 6 | | Company B | $8 | Atlantic 81763 |

Fascinated *21*
Full Circle
I'm Satisfied
Infatuate Me
Jam On Me
Perfect Lover
Signed In Your Book Of Love
Spin Me Around

COMPANY OF WOLVES

East Coast hard-rock quartet: Kyf Brewer (vocals), Steve Conte, John Conte and Frankie Larocka.

| 3/17/90 | 166 | 6 | | Company Of Wolves | $12 | Mercury 842184 |

Call Of The Wild
Can't Love Ya, Can't Leave Ya
Distance, The
Everybody's Baby
Girl
Hangin' By A Thread
Hell's Kitchen
I Don't Wanna Be Loved
Jilted!
My Ship
Romance On The Rocks
St. Jane's Infirmary

COMPTON'S MOST WANTED

Los Angeles rap outfit fronted by M.C. Eiht ("Experienced In Hardcore-Thumpin'"), produced by Unknown and D.J. Slip (duo collectively known as Big Beat Productions).

7/7/90	133	7		1 It's A Compton Thang	$12	Orpheus 75627
8/3/91	92	9		2 Straight Checkn 'Em	$12	Orpheus 47926
10/17/92	66	9		3 Music To Driveby	$12	Orpheus 52984

Another Victim (3)
Can I Kill It? (2)
Compton 4 Life (3)
Compton's Lynchin (2)
Dead Men Tell No Lies (3)
Def Wish (2)
Def Wish II (3)
Driveby Miss Daisy (2)
Duck Sick (1)
Duck Sick II (3)
8 Iz Enough (3)
Final Chapter (3)
Gangsta Shot Out (2)
Give It Up (1)
Growin' Up In The Hood (2)
Hit The Floor (3)
Hood Took Me Under (3)
Hoodrat (3)
I Don't Dance (2)
I Give Up Nuthin (1)
I Gots Ta Get Over (3)
I Mean Biznez (1)
I'm Wit Dat (1)
N 2 Deep (3)
It's A Compton Thang (1)
Jack Mode (3)
Late Night Hype (1)
Mike T's Funky Scratch (2)
Music To Driveby (3)
Niggaz Strugglin (3)
One Time Gaffled Em Up (1)
Raised In Compton (2)
Rhymes Too Funky Pt. 1 (1)
Straight Checkn 'Em (2)
They Still Gafflin (2)
This Is A Gang (1)
This Is Compton (1)
U's A Bitch (3)
Wanted (1)
Who's Xxxxing Who? (3)

CONCRETE BLONDE

Los Angeles alternative rock group formed in 1982 by female lead singer Johnette Napolitano and bassist James Mankey. Originally known as Dream 6, renamed by Michael Stipe of R.E.M. Other members included Harry Rushakoff, Alan Block (1989) and Paul Thompson (1990). By 1992, a trio of Napolitano, Mankey and Rushakoff (drums).

2/21/87	96	16		1 Concrete Blonde	$8	I.R.S. 5835
5/13/89	148	18		2 Free	$8	I.R.S. 82001
6/9/90	49	44	●	3 Bloodletting	$12	I.R.S. 82037
3/28/92	73	15		4 Walking In London	$12	I.R.S. 13137

Beast, The (3)
Beware Of Darkness (1)
Bloodletting (The Vampire Song) (3)
Caroline (3)
Carry Me Away (2)
City Screaming (4)
Cold Part Of Town (1)
Dance Along The Edge (1)
Darkening Of The Light (3)
Days And Days (4)
Ghost Of A Texas Ladies' Man (4)
God Is A Bullet (2)
Happy Birthday (2)
Help Me (2)
I Don't Need A Hero (3)
I Wanna Be Your Friend Again (4)
It's A Man's World (4)
It's Only Money (2)
Joey (3) *19*
Les Coeurs Jumeaux (4)
Little Conversations (3)
Little Sister (1)
...Long Time Ago (4)
Lullabye (3)
Make Me Cry (4)
Over Your Shoulder (1)
Roses Grow (2)
Run Run Run (2)
Scene Of A Perfect Crime (2)
Sky Is A Poisonous Garden (3)
Someday? (4)
Song For Kim (She Said) (1)
Still In Hollywood (1)
Sun (2)
Tomorrow, Wendy (3)
True *[includes 2 versions]* (1)
Walking In London (4)
Why Don't You See Me (4)
Woman To Woman (4)
Your Haunted Head (1)

DEBUT DATE	PEAK POS	WKS CHR	GOLD	ARTIST — Album Title	$	Label & Number

CONEY HATCH
Rock quartet: Carl Dixon (vocals), Steve Shelski (guitar), Andy Curran (bass) and Dave Ketchum (drums).

9/17/83	**186**	2		Outa Hand	$8	Mercury 812869

Don't Say Make Me   First Time For Everything   Music Of The Night   Some Like It Hot   Too Far Gone
Fallen Angel   Love Games   Shake It   To Feel The Feeling Again

CONFEDERATE RAILROAD
Southern rock band: Danny Shirley, Chris McDaniel, Michael Lamb, Wayne Secrest, Gates Nichols and Mark DuFresne. Worked as house band at Miss Kitty's in Marietta, Georgia.

9/19/92	**146**↑	10	↑	Confederate Railroad	$12	Atlantic 82335

Black Label, White Lies   Long Gone   She Never Cried   Time Off For Bad Behavior   When You Leave That Way   You Don't Know What It's
Jesus And Mama   Queen Of Memphis   She Took It Like A Man   Trashy Women   You Can Never Go Back   Like

★★352★★ CON FUNK SHUN
Soul band formed as Project Soul in Vallejo, California in 1968 by high school classmates Mike Cooper (lead vocals, guitar) and Louis McCall (drums). Moved to Memphis in 1972, changed name to Con Funk Shun. Session work for Stax Records. Included Karl Fuller, Paul Harrell, Felton Pilate II, Danny Thomas, Cedric Martin and Peto Escovedo (son of Azteca's Pete Escovedo and brother of Sheila E).

10/15/77	**51**	28	●	1 Secrets	$8	Mercury 1180
7/1/78	**32**	19	●	2 Loveshine	$8	Mercury 3725
6/2/79	**46**	22	●	3 Candy	$8	Mercury 3754
4/12/80	**30**	20	●	4 Spirit Of Love	$8	Mercury 3806
12/13/80+	**51**	19		5 Touch	$8	Mercury 4002
12/12/81+	**82**	13		6 Con Funk Shun 7	$8	Mercury 4030
12/4/82	**115**	29		7 To The Max	$8	Mercury 4067
12/3/83+	**105**	21		8 Fever	$8	Mercury 814447
5/18/85	**62**	26		9 Electric Lady	$8	Mercury 824345
7/19/86	**121**	11		10 Burnin' Love	$8	Mercury 826963

Ain't Nobody, Baby (7)   Curtain Call (4)   Hide And Freak (7)   Lady's Wild (5)   Rock It All Night (9)   **Too Tight** (5) 40
All Up To You (4)   Da Lady (3)   Honey Wild (4)   (Let Me Put) Love On Your   Secrets (1)   Touch (5)
Baby, I'm Hooked (Right   Do Ya (10)   How Long (10)   Mind (3)   **Shake And Dance With Me**   Turn The Music Up (9)
   Into Your Love) (8) 76   Don't Go (I Want You Back)   I Think I Found The Answer   Let's Ride And Slide (7)   (2) 60   Wanna Be There (2)
Bad Lady (6)   (9)   (2)   Love's Train (7)   She's A Star (10)   Welcome Back To Love (5)
Body Lovers (6)   Don't Let Your Love Grow   I'll Get You Back (6)   Loveshine (2)   She's Sweet (10)   When The Feeling's Right (2)
Burnin' Love (10)   Cold (18)   I'll Set You Out O.K. (1)   Lovestruck 1980 (4)   So Easy (2)   Who Has The Time (1)
By Your Side (4)   DooWhaChaWannaDoo (1)   I'm Leaving Baby (9)   Lovin' Fever (8)   Song For You (6)   You Are The One (7)
California 1 (6)   Early Morning Sunshine (4)   If I'm Your Lover (8)   Magic Woman (2)   Spirit Of Love (4)   You Make Me Wanna Love
Can You Feel The Groove   Electric Lady (9)   If You're In Need Of Love (6)   Make It Last (2)   Straight From The Heart (6)   Again (10)
   Tonight (8)   Everlove (7)   Images (3)   Ms. Got The Body (7)   T.H.E. Freak (7)
Can't Go Away (2)   **Ffun** (1) 23   Indian Summer Love (1)   Not Ready (3)   Take It To The Max (7)
Can't Say Goodbye (5)   Fire When Ready (3)   Indiscreet Sweet (8)   Play Widit (10)   Tears In My Eyes (1)
Candy (3)   Give Your Love To Me (5)   It's Time Girl (10)   Pretty Lady (9)   Tell Me What You're Gonna
Chase Me (3)   Got To Be Enough (4)   Jo Jo (10)   Pride And Glory (5)   Do (9)
Circle Of Love (9)   Happy Face (4)   Juicy (4)   Promise You Love (6)   Thinking About You, Baby
ConFunkShunizeYa (1)   Hard Lovin' (8)   Kidnapped! (5)   (8)

CONLEE, John
Country singer. Born on 8/11/46 in Versailles, Kentucky.

6/11/83	**166**	6	●	John Conlee's Greatest Hits ....[G]	$8	MCA 5405

Baby, You're Something   Common Man   I Don't Remember Loving   Miss Emily's Picture
Backside Of Thirty   Friday Night Blues   You   Rose Colored Glasses
Busted   Lady Lay Down   She Can't Say That Anymore

CONLEY, Arthur
Soul singer, born on 1/4/46 in Atlanta. Discovered by Otis Redding in 1965. First recorded for NRC as Arthur & The Corvets.

5/13/67	**93**	13		1 Sweet Soul Music	$20	Atco 215
8/19/67	**193**	2		2 Shake, Rattle & Roll	$20	Atco 220
7/6/68	**185**	2		3 Soul Directions	$20	Atco 243

Baby What You Want Me To   Hand And Glove (2)   I've Been Loving You Too   **People Sure Act Funny**   This Love Of Mine (3)
   Do (2)   Hear Say (3)   Long (To Stop Now) (2)   (3) 58   Where You Lead Me (1)
Burning Fire (3)   I Can't Stop (No, No, No) (1)   Keep On Talking (2)   Put Our Love Together (3)   Who's Foolin' Who (1)
Change Is Gonna Come (2)   I'll Take The Blame (2)   Let Nothing Separate Us (1)   **Shake, Rattle & Roll** (2) 31   Wholesale Love (1)
Funky Street (3) 14   I'm A Lonely Stranger (1)   Love Comes And Goes (3)   **Sweet Soul Music** (1) 2   You Don't Have To See Me (2)
Get Yourself Another Fool (3)   I'm Gonna Forget About You   Love Got Me (2)   Take Me (Just As I Am) (1)   You Really Know How To
Ha! Ha! Ha! (2)   (1)   Otis Sleep On (3)   There's A Place For Us (1)   Hurt A Guy (3)

CONNELLS, The
Quintet from Raleigh, North Carolina: brothers Mike (guitar) and David Connell (bass) with Doug MacMillan (vocals), Peele Wimberley (drums) and George Huntley (guitar, keyboards).

5/6/89	**163**	10		1 Fun & Games	$8	TVT 2550
11/10/90+	**168**	18		2 One Simple Word	$12	TVT 2580

All Sinks In (2)   Hey Wow (1)   Link (2)   Sat Nite (USA) (1)   Stone Cold Yesterday (2)   Uninspired (1)
Another Souvenir (2)   Inside My Head (1)   Motel (1)   Set The Stage (2)   Take A Bow (2)   Upside Down (1)
Fun & Games (1)   Joke, The (2)   One Simple Word (2)   Something To Say (1)   Ten Pins (1)   Waiting My Turn (2)
Get A Gun (2)   Lay Me Down (1)   Sal (1)   Speak To Me (2)   Too Gone (2)   What Do You Want? (2)

★★481★★ CONNICK, Harry Jr.
Jazz-pop pianist/vocalist from New Orleans. Born on 9/11/67. Studied jazz under Ellis Marsalis, the father of Wynton and Branford. Acted in the films *Memphis Belle* and *Little Man Tate*.

8/19/89	**42**	122	▲	1 When Harry Met Sally... ....[S]	$8	Columbia 45319
7/21/90+	**22**	96	▲	2 We Are In Love	$12	Columbia 46146
7/21/90	**94**	11		3 Lofty's Roach Souffle ....[I]	$12	Columbia 46223

     HARRY CONNICK, JR. TRIO
     trio includes Benjamin Wolfe (bass) and Shannon Powell (drums)

DEBUT DATE	PEAK POS	WKS CHR	GOLD	ARTIST — Album Title	$	Label & Number
5/25/91+	133	44	●	4 20 ....[E]	$12	Columbia 44369
				11 classic tunes written by Irving Berlin, Hoagy Carmichael, Duke Ellington, George Gershwin and others; recorded in 1988 when Harry was 20 years old		
10/12/91+	17	52	▲	5 Blue Light, Red Light	$12	Columbia 48685
12/12/92+	19	9↑ ●		6 25	$12	Columbia 53172
				classic tunes written by Hoagy Carmichael, Frederick Lowe & Alan Lerner, Johnny Mercer, John Coltrane, Duke Ellington and others; recorded at age 25		

After You've Gone (6)
Autumn In New York (1)
Avalon (4)
Basin Street Blues (4)
Bayou Maharajah (3)
Blessing And A Curse (5)
Blue Light, Red Light (Someone's There) (5)
Blue Skies (4)
Buried In Blue (2)
But Not For Me (1)
Caravan (6)
Colomby Day (3)
Didn't He Ramble (6)

Do Nothin' Till You Hear From Me (4)
Do You Know What It Means To Miss New Orleans (4)
Don't Get Around Much Anymore (1)
Drifting (4)
Forever, For Now (2)
Harronymous (3)
He Is They Are (5)
Heavenly (2)
Hudson Bommer (3)
I Could Write A Book (1)
I'll Dream Of You Again (2)

I'm An Old Cowhand (From The Rio Grande) (6)
I've Got A Great Idea (2)
If I Could Give You More (5)
If I Only Had A Brain (4)
Imagination (4)
It Had To Be You (1)
It's Alright With Me (2)
It's Time (5)
Jill (5)
Just A Boy (2)
Just Kiss Me (5)
Last Payday (5)
Lazy River (4)
Lazybones (6)

Let's Call The Whole Thing Off (1)
Little Dancing Girl (3)
Lofty's Roach Souffle (3)
Lonely Side (3)
Love Is Here To Stay (1)
Mary Ruth (3)
Moment's Notice (6)
Mr. Spill (3)
Music, Maestro, Please (6)
Muskrat Ramble (6)
Nightingale Sang In Berkeley Square (2)
On The Atchison, Topeka And The Santa Fe (6)

On The Street Where You Live (6)
One Last Pitch (3)
Only 'Cause I Don't Have You (7)
Please Don't Talk About Me When I'm Gone (4)
Recipe For Love (2)
'S Wonderful (4)
She Belongs To Me (5)
Sonny Cried (5)
Stardust (6)
Stars Fell On Alabama (4)
Stompin' At The Savoy (1)
Tangerine (6)

This Time The Dream's On Me (6)
We Are In Love (2)
Where Or When (1)
Winter Wonderland (1)
With Imagination (I'll Get There) (5)
You Didn't Know Me When (5)

★★8★★ **CONNIFF, Ray**
Born on 11/0/16 in Attleboro, Massachusetts. Trombonist/arranger with Bunny Berigan, Bob Crosby, Harry James, Vaughn Monroe and Artie Shaw bands. Long string of hit albums beginning in 1957. Ray's non-instrumental albums feature The Ray Conniff Singers.

DEBUT DATE	PEAK POS	WKS CHR	GOLD	ARTIST — Album Title	$	Label & Number
3/23/57	11	16		1 'S Wonderful! ....[I]	$15	Columbia 925
12/23/57+	10	37	●	2 'S Marvelous ....[I]	$15	Columbia 1074
6/23/58+	9	52		3 'S Awful Nice ....[I]	$15	Columbia 1137
9/29/58	9	50	●	4 Concert In Rhythm ....[I]	$15	Columbia 1163
5/25/59+	10	20		5 Broadway In Rhythm ....[I]	$15	Columbia 1252
6/29/59	29	8		6 Hollywood In Rhythm ....[I]	$15	Columbia 1310
11/23/59+	8	36		7 Conniff Meets Butterfield ....[I]	$20	Columbia 1346
				RAY CONNIFF & BILLY BUTTERFIELD (jazz trumpeter)		
12/28/59+	14	2	●	8 Christmas With Conniff ....[X]	$15	Columbia 1390
2/15/60	8	54		9 It's The Talk Of The Town ....[I]	$15	Columbia 1334
3/7/60	13	33		10 Concert In Rhythm - Volume II ....[I]	$15	Columbia 1415
8/15/60+	6	28		11 Young At Heart ....[I]	$15	Columbia 1489
10/10/60	4	58		12 Say It With Music (A Touch Of Latin)......................[I]	$15	Columbia 1490
12/31/60	15	1		13 Christmas With Conniff..[X-R]	$15	Columbia 1390
2/13/61	4	34	●	14 Memories Are Made Of This ....[I]	$15	Columbia 1574
9/11/61	14	34		15 Somebody Loves Me ....[I]	$15	Columbia 1642
12/18/61+	16	6		16 Christmas With Conniff...[X-R]	$15	Columbia 1390
				Christmas charts: 39/'65, 35/'67, 11/'68, 7/'69		
2/17/62	5	34	●	17 So Much In Love ....[I]	$15	Columbia 1720
5/5/62	6	25		18 'S Continental ....[I]	$15	Columbia 1776
10/6/62	28	16		19 Rhapsody In Rhythm ....[I]	$15	Columbia 1878
12/8/62	32	4	▲	20 We Wish You A Merry Christmas ....[X]	$15	Columbia 1892
				Christmas charts: 7/'63, 10/'64, 13/'65, 20/'66, 12/'67, 18/'68, 5/'72		
3/9/63	20	15		21 The Happy Beat ....[I]	$15	Columbia 8749
9/14/63	85	13		22 Just Kiddin' Around ....[I]	$15	Columbia 8822
				RAY CONNIFF & BILLY BUTTERFIELD		
2/15/64	73	17		23 You Make Me Feel So Young ....[I]	$15	Columbia 8918
5/30/64	50	19		24 Speak To Me Of Love ....[I]	$10	Columbia 8950
10/3/64	23	27		25 Invisible Tears ....[I]	$10	Columbia 9064
4/3/65	141	5		26 Friendly Persuasion ....[I]	$10	Columbia 9010
6/5/65	34	19		27 Music From Mary Poppins, The Sound Of Music, My Fair Lady, & Other Great Movie Themes	$10	Columbia 9166
9/18/65	54	16		28 Love Affair..	$10	Columbia 9152
4/2/66	80	9		29 Happiness Is	$10	Columbia 9261
7/16/66	3	90	▲	30 Somewhere My Love	$10	Columbia 9319
3/18/67	78	10		31 Ray Conniff's World Of Hits ....[I]	$10	Columbia 9300
5/13/67	180	2		32 En Espanol! ....[F]	$10	Columbia 9408
6/3/67	30	46		33 This Is My Song	$10	Columbia 9476
10/28/67+	39	15		34 Hawaiian Album	$10	Columbia 9547
2/17/68	25	41	●	35 It Must Be Him	$10	Columbia 9595
6/1/68	22	39	●	36 Honey	$10	Columbia 9661
10/26/68+	70	22		37 Turn Around Look At Me	$10	Columbia 9712
3/8/69	101	14		38 I Love How You Love Me.......................................	$10	Columbia 9777
7/12/69	158	5		39 Ray Conniff's Greatest Hits ....[G]	$10	Columbia 9839
12/20/69+	103	21		40 Jean	$10	Columbia 9920
4/25/70	47	28		41 Bridge Over Troubled Water	$10	Columbia 1022
9/26/70	177	5		42 Concert In Stereo/Live At The Sahara/Tahoe......................[L]	$10	Columbia 30122 [2]
12/26/70+	120	13		43 We've Only Just Begun	$10	Columbia 30410
3/27/71	98	15		44 Love Story	$10	Columbia 30498
9/11/71	185	5		45 Great Contemporary Instrumental Hits.................[I]	$10	Columbia 30755
2/12/72	138	11		46 I'd Like To Teach The World To Sing	$10	Columbia 31220

DEBUT DATE	PEAK POS	WKS CHR	GOLD	ARTIST — Album Title	$	Label & Number

CONNIFF, Ray — Cont'd

6/3/72	114	14	47	Love Theme From "The Godfather"	$10	Columbia 31473
10/7/72	180	10	48	Alone Again (Naturally)	$10	Columbia 31629
2/10/73	165	10	49	I Can See Clearly Now	$10	Columbia 32090
7/7/73	176	5	50	You Are The Sunshine Of My Life	$10	Columbia 32376
10/13/73	194	4	51	Harmony	$10	Columbia 32553

Abraham, Martin And John (38)
Affair To Remember (23)
African Safari (18)
Alexander's Ragtime Band (22)
All By Myself (29)
All I Have To Do Is Dream (41)
All Or Nothing At All (15)
All The Things You Are (3,7)
Alley Cat (31)
Alone Again (Naturally) (48)
Angel Of The Morning (37)
April In Paris (3)
April Love (24)
Aquarius/Let The Sunshine In (40)
Are You Lonesome Tonight? (25)
Around The World (14)
Arriesgando En Amore ..see: Taking A Chance On Love
As Time Goes By (2)
Autumn Leaves (17)
Baby, I'm A Want You (46)
Bah Bah Conniff Sprach (Zarathustra) (50)
Bali Ha'i (5)
Be My Love (2)
Beautiful Love (19)
Because (48)
Begin The Beguine (1)
Ben (41)
Besame Mucho (12,39,42)
Bewitched (17)
Beyond The Blue Horizon (7)
Beyond The Reef (34)
Beyond The Sea (La Mer) (18,24)
Blue Hawaii (34)
Blue Moon (29)
Blueberry Hill (21)
Born Free (33)
Brand New Key (46)
Brandy (You're A Fine Girl) (48)
Brazil (41)
Bridge Over Troubled Water (41)
But Not For Me (22)
Buttons And Bows (9)
By The Time I Get To Phoenix (36)
Cabaret (33,39)
Can't Take My Eyes Off You (37)
Can't We Be Friends (7)
Candida (43)
Candy Man (48)
Canticle ..see: Scarborough Fair
Caravan (23)
Chances Are (17)
Chanson D'Amour (Song Of Love) (21)
Chao, Chao ..see: Downtown
Charade (30)
Cheek To Cheek (6)
Cherish (46)
Chim Chim Cher-ee (27)
Chloe (28)
Chopin's Nocturne In E-Flat, Improvisation On (10,42)
Christmas Bride (8)
Christmas Song (Merry Christmas To You) (8)
Clair (49)
Climb Ev'ry Mountain (44)
Come Saturday Morning (44)
Conniff's Dance Of The Hours (45)
Continental (You Kiss While You're Dancing) (18)
Count Your Blessings (Instead Of Sheep) (medley) (20)

Cowboy's Work Is Never Done (47)
Creemos En El Amor ..see: Three Coins In The Fountain
Cry (21)
Daddy Don't You Walk So Fast (48)
Dance Of The Sugar-Plum Fairy, Improvisation On (10)
Dancing In The Dark (1,17)
Dancing On The Ceiling (17)
Dancing With Tears In My Eyes (11)
Danke Schoen (31)
Day By Day (48)
Days Of Wine And Roses [includes English & foreign versions] (30,32)
Dear Heart [includes English & foreign versions] (27,32)
Deck The Hall With Boughs Of Holly (medley) (20)
Deep In The Heart Of Texas (9)
Deep Purple (12)
Delilah (45)
Delta Dawn (51)
Dias De Vino Y Rosas ..see: Days Of Wine And Roses
Do You Know The Way To San Jose (37)
Don't Blame Me (24)
Don't Fence Me In (15)
Don't Sleep In The Subway (35)
Downtown [includes English & foreign versions] (30,32)
Dueling Voices (Dueling Banjos) (48)
Early Evening (4)
Early In The Morning (41)
Easy To Love (6)
Ebb Tide (26)
Edelweiss (31)
El Amor Es Algo Maravilloso ..see: Love Is A Many-Splendored Thing
El Condor Pasa (If I Could) (44)
Eso Es Felicidad ..see: Happiness Is
Everybody Knows (43)
Everybody Loves Somebody [includes English & foreign versions] (25,32)
Everybody's Talkin' (41)
Everything Is Beautiful (43)
Far Away Places (25)
Feed The Birds (27)
Fibich Poeme, Improvisation On (10)
First Noel (medley) (20)
First Time Ever (I Saw Your Face) (47)
For All We Know (28,44)
For The Good Times (44)
Frenesí (23)
Say A Little Prayer (36)
Friendly Persuasion (Thee I Love) (26)
Frosty The Snowman (8)
Gentle On My Mind (36)
Georgy Girl (31)
Getting To Know You (medley) (5)
Gigi (21)
Go Away Little Girl (46)
Godfather (Speak Softly Love), Love Theme From The (47)
Goin' Out Of My Head (36)
Golden Earrings (48)
Good, The Bad And The Ugly (37,42)
Goodnight, Sweetheart (28)
Granada (31)
Green Eyes (18)

Green Leaves Of Summer (15)
Greenfields (31)
Greensleeves (What Child Is This) (8)
Grieg's A Minor Piano Concerto, Favorite Themes From (10)
Gypsies, Tramps And Thieves (46)
Hands Across The Table (9)
Happiest Girl In The Whole U.S.A. (48)
Happiness Is [includes English & foreign versions] (29,32,39)
Happy Together (45)
Harbor Lights (11)
Hark! The Herald Angels Sing (medley) (20)
Harmony (51)
Harper Valley P.T.A. (38)
Hawaiian Wedding Song (14)
He's Got The Whole World In His Hands (42)
Heartaches (22)
Hello, Dolly! (31)
Hello Young Lovers (5)
Here Comes Santa Claus (8)
Here Today And Gone Tomorrow (51)
Hey Girl (46)
Hey Jude (38)
Hi-Lili, Hi-Lo [includes English & foreign versions] (28,32)
High Noon (Do Not Forsake Me) (26)
Hold Me Tight (38)
Honey Come Back (41)
Honey (I Miss You) (36,42)
Honeycomb (25)
Horse With No Name (47)
How Can I Tell Her (51)
Hukilau Song (34)
Hurting Each Other (47)
I Am Woman (49)
I Believe In Music (49)
I Can See Clearly Now (49)
I Concentrate On You (19)
I Could Have Danced All Night (medley) (5)
I Cover The Waterfront (3)
I Don't Know How To Love Him (45)
I Don't Want To Set The World On Fire (15)
I Fall In Love Too Easily (17)
I Found A Million Dollar Baby (In A Five And Ten Cent Store) (7)
I Get A Kick Out Of You (1)
I Hear A Rhapsody (2)
I Love How You Love Me (38)
I Love You (2)
I Need You (47)
I Only Have Eyes For You (15)
I See Your Face Before Me (22)
I Understand (26)
I Walk The Line (25)
I Want To Hold Your Hand (45)
I Whistle A Happy Tune (medley) (5)
I Will Wait For You (31)
I Wish I Didn't Love You So (17)
I Wish They Didn't Mean Goodbye (34)
I'd Like To Teach The World To Sing (In Perfect Harmony) (46)
I'd Love You To Want Me (49)
I'll Be Seeing You (11)
I'll Be There (43)

I'll Never Fall In Love Again (40,41)
I'll See You Again (10)
I'll See You In My Dreams (11)
I'll Walk Alone (21)
I'm Always Chasing Rainbows (4,28)
I'm An Old Cow Hand (1)
I'm In The Mood For Love (11)
I've Found Someone Of My Own (40)
I've Got You Under My Skin (12)
I've Grown Accustomed To Her Face (5,27)
I've Told Ev'ry Little Star (2)
If I Could Reach You (49)
If I Knew Then (29)
If I Loved You (11)
If You Could Read My Mind (44)
If You Don't Know Me By Now (49)
Imagination (19)
Imagine (46)
Impossible Dream (35)
In The Cool, Cool, Cool Of The Evening (23)
In The Still Of The Night (2)
Invisible Tears [includes English & foreign versions] (25,32,39) **57**
It Had To Be You (3,15)
It Might As Well Be Spring (6)
It Must Be Him (35)
It Never Rains In Southern California (49)
It Was A Very Good Year (37)
It's Been A Long, Long Time (9)
It's Dark On Observatory Hill (11)
It's Impossible (44)
It's Not For Me To Say (17)
It's So Nice To Have A Man Around The House (42)
It's The Talk Of The Town (9)
It's Too Late (45)
Jamaica Farewell (29)
Jean (40)
Jingle Bells (8)
Jolly Holiday (27)
Jolly Old St. Nicholas (medley) (20)
June In January (3)
June Night (26)
Just Friends (28)
Just Kiddin' Around (22)
Just One Of Those Things (12)
Just Walking In The Rain (20)
Killing Me Softly With His Song (medley) (50)
King Of The Road (30)
Kiss Me Goodbye (36)
Kiss Of Fire (19)
Kisses Sweeter Than Wine (25)
Lady Of Spain (19)
Lagrimas Invisibles ..see: Invisible Tears
Lamp Is Low (4)
Laura (6)
Leaving On A Jet Plane (41)
Let It Be (43)
Let It Snow! Let It Snow! Let It Snow! (medley) (20)
Let's Put Out The Lights (9)
Liebestraum, Improvisation On (10)
Lisbon Antigua (18)
Little Drummer Boy (medley) (20)
Little Green Apples (38)

Live And Let Die (51)
Living In A House Divided (47)
Look Of Love (36)
Louise (22)
Love (Can Make You Happy) (40)
Love Has No Rules (24)
Love Is A Many-Splendored Thing [includes English & foreign versions] (6,28,32)
Love Is Blue (L'Amour Est Bleu) (36)
Love Is Born (Song Of The Trumpet) (7)
Love Is The Sweetest Thing (9)
Love Letters (6)
Love Letters In The Sand (14)
Love Me Tender (14)
Love Me Tonight (40,42)
Love Story, Theme From ..see: (Where Do I Begin)
Love Walked In (19)
Lovely To Look At (3)
Lover, Come Back To Me (24)
Lullaby Of Birdland (3)
Lullaby Of The Leaves (2)
Ma, He's Making Eyes At Me (11)
MacArthur Park (37)
Mack The Knife (21,42)
Make It With You (43)
Malaguena (28)
Mam'selle [includes English & foreign versions] (28,32)
Mame (33,39,42)
Man And A Woman (35)
Man Without Love (Quando M'Innamoro) (40)
Marianne (23)
Melodie D'Amour (29)
Memories Are Made Of This (14,39,42)
Mi Corazon ..see: Dear Heart
Midnight Cowboy (41)
Midnight Lace - Part I (29) **92**
Midsummer In Sweden (31)
Miss You (29)
Moments To Remember (14)
Moon River (31,37)
Moon Song (15)
Moonlight And Roses (19)
Moonlight Serenade (2)
More (31)
Morgen (One More Sunrise) (18)
Morning After (51)
Moscow Nights (31)
Moulin Rouge (Where Is Your Heart), Song From (21)
Mrs. Robinson (37,42)
Music To Watch Girls By (35)
Muskrat Ramble (42)
My Cup Runneth Over (33)
My Favorite Things (27)
My Foolish Heart (14)
My Heart At Thy Sweet Voice, Improvisation On (10)
My Heart Cries For You (9)
My Heart Stood Still (6,17)
My Little Grass Shack In Kealakekua, Hawaii (34)
My Old Flame (19)
My Prayer (21)
My Reverie (4)
My Romance (19)
My Special Angel (38)
My Sweet Lord (44)
Neither One Of Us (Wants To Be The First To Say Goodbye) (50)
Never Can Say Goodbye (45)
Never On Sunday (21)
Night And Day (12)

Night The Lights Went Out In Georgia (50)
No Other Love (14)
None But The Lonely Heart, Improvisation On (10)
O Come, All Ye Faithful (medley) (20)
O Holy Night (medley) (20)
Oh Lonesome Me (25)
Oh, What A Beautiful Mornin' (5,7)
Oklahoma! (5,42)
Old Fashioned Love Song (46)
On The Street Where You Live (5,27,39,42)
On The Trail (4)
One Fine Day (10)
One Paddle Two Paddle (34)
Only You (And You Alone) (14)
Our Waltz (19)
Pacific Sunset (6)
Paradise (3)
Pass Me By (27)
Patricia, It's Patricia (23)
Peaceful (50)
Pearly Shells (34)
Peg O' My Heart (22)
People (37)
People Will Say We're In Love (5)
Playground In My Mind (51)
Please (6)
Poor People Of Paris (18)
Popsy (29)
Power Of Love (40)
Precious And Few (47)
Put Your Arms Around Me, Honey (22)
Put Your Hand In The Hand (45)
Quentin's Theme (40)
Rachmaninoff's Second Piano Concerto, Favorite Theme From (4)
Raindrops Keep Fallin' On My Head (41)
Red Roses For A Blue Lady [includes English & foreign versions] (30,32)
Release Me (35)
Remember (11)
Rhapsody In Blue (4)
Right Thing To Do (50)
Ring Christmas Bells (20)
Rosalie (7,9)
Rosas Rojas Para Una Dama Triste ..see: Red Roses For A Blue Lady
Rose Garden (44)
Rose Room (26)
Rudolph, The Red-Nosed Reindeer (8)
Run To Me (48)
S'Posin' (25)
'S Wonderful (1,39) **73**
Santa Claus Is Comin' To Town (8)
Say Has Anybody Seen My Sweet Gypsy Rose (51)
Say It Isn't So (3)
Say It With Music (12)
Scarborough Fair/Canticle (38)
Schubert's Serenade (4)
Schubert's Serenade, Improvisation On (42)
Second Time Around (28)
Sentimental Journey (1)
September Song (1)
Shadow Of Your Smile (31)
Shadows Of The Night ..see: Quentin's Theme
Shaft, Theme From (47)
Shangri-La (26)
Sheik Of Araby (29)
Silver Bells (8)

CONNIFF, Ray — Cont'd

Sing (50)
Singing The Blues (25)
Sleigh Ride (8)
Slow Poke (24)
Snowbird (43)
So Long, Farewell (30)
So Rare (26)
Softly, As In A Morning Sunrise (12)
Solitude (23)
Some Enchanted Evening (5)
Somebody Loves Me (15)
Someone (41)
Someone To Watch Over Me (2)
Somethin' Stupid (35)
Something (41)
Something To Remember You By (7)
Something's Wrong With Me (49)
Sometimes I'm Happy (1)
Somewhere, My Love (30,39,42) **9**
Song Of Love (26)
Song Sung Blue (48)
Sound Of Music (27)
Sounds Of Silence (36)
South Of The Border (7)
South Rampart Street Parade (42)
Spanish Eyes (36)
Speak Low (1)
Speak To Me Of Love (24)
Spinning Wheel (40)
Spoonful Of Sugar (27)
Stardust (1)
Stella By Starlight (6)
Stompin' At The Savoy (26)

Strange Music (18)
Stranger In Paradise (12)
Strangers In The Night (33)
Summer Breeze (49)
Summer Of '42 (The Summer Knows), Theme From (46)
Summertime (12)
Sunny (38)
Sunrise, Sunset (33)
Supercalifragilisticexpialidocious (27)
Superstar (45)
Surrey With The Fringe On Top (5)
Sweet Caroline (44)
Sweet Leilani (34)
Sweet Sue, Just You (29)
Sweetest Sounds (24)
Swing Little Glow Worm (18)
Take Me In Your Arms (19)
Taking A Chance On Love [includes English & foreign versions] (28,32)
Tammy (14)
Taste Of Honey (45)
Tchaikovsky's Fifth Symphony, Favorite Theme From (4)
Tchaikovsky's Romeo And Juliet, Favorite Love Theme From (4)
Tchaikovsky's Sixth Symphony (Pathetique), Favorite Themes From (10)
Tchaikovsky's Swan Lake Ballet, Favorite Theme From (4)

Tchaikovsky's First Piano Concerto, Favorite Theme From (4)
Tea For Two (42)
Temptation (12)
Thanks For The Memory (6)
That Old Black Magic (1)
That Old Feeling (3)
There Was A Girl (medley) (50)
There's A Kind Of Hush (All Over The World) (35)
These Foolish Things (Remind Me Of You) (11)
They Can't Take That Away From Me (2)
They Long To Be Close To You (43)
They Say It's Wonderful (9)
Third Man Theme (23)
This Guy's In Love With You (37)
This Is My Song (33,39)
This Love Of Mine (22)
'This Nearly Was Mine (24)
Those Were The Days (38,42)
Three Coins In The Fountain [includes English & foreign versions] (14,28,32)
Threepenny Opera, Theme From ..see: Mack The Knife
Thrill Is Gone (15)
Tico-Tico (18)
Tie A Yellow Ribbon Round The Ole Oak Tree (50)
Tie Me Kangaroo Down, Sport (34)

Tiger Rag (Hold That Tiger) (26)
Tijuana Taxi (45)
Time For Us (40)
Time On My Hands (You In My Arms) (7)
Tiny Bubbles (34)
To My Love (19)
To You Sweetheart, Aloha (34)
Todos Aman A Alguien ..see: Everybody Loves Somebody
Too Young (12,48)
Touch Me In The Morning (51)
True Love (17)
Try A Little Tenderness (28)
Try To Remember (31)
Turn Around Look At Me (37)
Twelfth Of Never (50)
Twelve Days Of Christmas (20)
Unchained Melody (14)
Under Paris Skies (24)
Up, Up And Away (35)
Usted ..see: Mam'selle
Valley Of The Dolls, Theme From (36)
Very Thought Of You (3)
Volare (Nel Blu Dipinto Di Blu) (21)
Wagon Wheels (1)
Waitin' For The Evening Train (25)
Warsaw Concerto (10)
Watching Scotty Grow (44)
Way Of Love (47)
Way You Look Tonight (2)

We Three Kings Of Orient Are (medley) (20)
We Wish You A Merry Christmas (medley) (20)
We've Only Just Begun (43)
What A Diff'rence A Day Made (7)
What Have They Done To My Song, Ma? (43)
What Kind Of Fool Am I? (23)
What Now My Love (33)
What The World Needs Now Is Love (35)
Whatever Will Be, Will Be (Que Sera, Sera) (17)
Wheel Of Fortune (21)
When I Grow Too Old To Dream (22)
(When Your Heart's On Fire) Smoke Gets In Your Eyes (3,24,39,42)
(Where Do I Begin) Love Story (44)
Where Is The Love (48)
Where Or When (2)
Whiffenpoof Song (18)
White Christmas (8)
White Cliffs Of Dover (18)
Who's Sorry Now? (24)
Wichita Lineman (38)
Winchester Cathedral (33)
Windmills Of Your Mind (40)
Winter Wonderland (8)
With My Eyes Wide Open, I'm Dreaming (23)
Without You (47)
Wonderful Guy (5)
World Will Smile Again (33)
Wouldn't It Be Lovely (30)

Yellow Rose (21)
Yesterday (35)
Yesterday Once More (51)
Yesterdays (6)
You Are The Sunshine Of My Life (50)
You Do Something To Me (2)
You Make Me Feel So Young (23)
You Must Have Been A Beautiful Baby (7)
You Oughta Be In Pictures (22)
You Stepped Out Of A Dream (29)
You'd Be So Nice To Come Home To (15)
You'll Never Know (11,22)
You'll Never Walk Alone (24)
You're An Old Smoothie (9)
You're The Cream In My Coffee (15)
You've Made Me So Very Happy (43)
Young And Foolish (30)
Young At Heart (11)
Young Love (14,51)
Younger Than Springtime (5)
Yours Is My Heart Alone (10)
Zip-A-Dee-Doo-Dah (9)

CONNORS, Norman

Born on 3/1/48 in Philadelphia. Jazz drummer with Archie Shepp, John Coltrane, Pharoah Sanders and others. Own group on Buddah in 1972. Featured vocalists are Michael Henderson, Jean Carn and Phyllis Hyman. Formed disco group Aquarian Dream.

DEBUT DATE	PEAK POS	WKS CHR	GOLD	ARTIST — Album Title	$	Label & Number
10/11/75	150	5		1 Saturday Night Special	$10	Buddah 5643
7/24/76	39	24	●	2 You Are My Starship	$10	Buddah 5655
4/9/77	94	16		3 Romantic Journey	$10	Buddah 5682
5/27/78	68	17		4 This Is Your Life	$8	Arista 4177
1/13/79	175	5		5 The Best Of Norman Connors & Friends ... [G]	$10	Buddah 5716
7/21/79	137	7		6 Invitation	$8	Arista 4216
9/27/80	145	6		7 Take It To The Limit	$8	Arista 9534
12/5/81	197	2		8 Mr. C	$8	Arista 9575

Akia (1)
Anyway You Want (8)
Be There In The Morning (6)
Beijo Partido (6)
Betcha By Golly Wow (2,5)
Black Cow (7)
Bubbles (2)
Butterfly (4)
Captain Connors (4)
Creator, The (4)
Creator Has A Master Plan (2)

Destination Moon (3)
Dindi (1,5)
Disco Land (6)
Everywhere Inside Of Me (7)
For You Everything (3)
Handle Me Gently (6)
I Don't Need Nobody Else (7)
I Have A Dream (6)
Invitation (6)
Just Imagine (2)
Justify (7)
Keep Goin' It (8)

Kingston (6)
Kwasi (1)
Last Tango In Paris (3)
Listen (4)
Love From The Sun (5)
Love's In Your Corner (8)
Maiden Voyage (1)
Melancholy Fire (7)
Mr. C (8)
Once I've Been There (3,5)
Party Town (8)
Romantic Journey (3,5)

Saturday Night Special (1)
Say You Love Me (4)
She's Gone (8)
Sing A Love Song (8)
Skin Diver (1)
So Much Love (2)
Stay With Me (8)
Stella (4)
Take It To The Limit (7)
Thembi (3)
This Is Your Life (4,5)
Together (6)

Valentine Love (1,5) 97
We Both Need Each Other (2,5)
Wouldn't You Like To See (4,5)
You Are Everything (3)
You Are My Starship (2,5) **27**
You Bring Me Joy (7)
You Make Me Feel Brand New (4)
You've Been On My Mind (7)

Your Love (6)

CONTRABAND

Hard-rock project: Richard Black (Shark Island; vocals), Share Pedersen (Vixen; bass), Bobby Blotzer (Ratt; drums), Tracii Guns (L.A. Guns; guitar) and Michael Schenker (MSG; guitar).

DEBUT DATE	PEAK POS	WKS CHR	GOLD	ARTIST — Album Title	$	Label & Number
6/29/91	187	1		Contraband	$12	Impact 10247

All The Way From Memphis
Bad For Each Other

Good Rockin' Tonight
Hang On To Yourself

If This Is Love
Intimate Outrage

Kiss By Kiss

Loud Guitars, Fast Cars & Wild, Wild Livin'

Stand
Tonight You're Mine

CONTROLLERS, The

R&B group from Fairfield, Alabama, formed in 1965 as the Epics. Became the Soul Controllers in 1970. Consisted of Reginald and Larry McArthur, Lenard Brown and Ricky Lewis. Most songs written by David Camon (keyboards). Later based in Miami.

DEBUT DATE	PEAK POS	WKS CHR	GOLD	ARTIST — Album Title	$	Label & Number
12/17/77+	146	6		In Control	$10	Juana 200,001

Heaven Is Only One Step Away

People Want Music
Reaper, The

Sho Nuff A Blessin
Somebody's Gotta Win

This Train
You Ain't Fooling Me

CONWELL, Tommy, And The Young Rumblers

Philadelphia-based rock guitarist Conwell with Paul Slivka, Jim Hannum, Chris Day and Rob Miller (ex-Hooters). Day left, guitarist Billy Kemp joined by 1990. Conwell's older brother is Philadelphia Eagles' tackle Joe Conwell.

DEBUT DATE	PEAK POS	WKS CHR	GOLD	ARTIST — Album Title	$	Label & Number
9/3/88	103	28		Rumble	$8	Columbia 44186

Everything They Say Is True
Gonna Breakdown
Half A Heart

I Wanna Make You Happy
I'm Not Your Man 74
If We Never Meet Again 48

Love's On Fire
Tell Me What You Want Me To Be

Walkin' On The Water
Workout

DEBUT DATE	PEAK POS	WKS CHR	GOLD	ARTIST — Album Title	$	Label & Number

COODER, Ry

Blues-rock guitarist/stylist/composer. Born on 3/15/47 in Los Angeles. As a teen, collaborated with Jackie DeShannon and Taj Mahal. Scored several films including *The Border*, *The Long Riders* and *Paris, Texas*. Member of Little Village.

DEBUT DATE	PEAK POS	WKS CHR	#	Title	$	Label & Number
2/12/72	113	8	1	Into The Purple Valley	$10	Reprise 2052
6/8/74	167	6	2	Paradise And Lunch..	$10	Reprise 2179
10/23/76	177	5	3	Chicken Skin Music..	$10	Reprise 2254

features The Chicken Skin Revue: Hawaiian steel guitarist Gabby Pahinui, Tex-Mex accordionist Flaco Jimenez and a gospel vocal trio led by Bobby King

9/10/77	158	5	4	Show Time..[L]	$8	Warner 3059
8/11/79	62	15	5	Bop Till You Drop	$8	Warner 3358
1/24/81	43	16	6	Borderline	$8	Warner 3489
6/12/82	105	7	7	The Slide Area	$8	Warner 3651
5/10/86	85	9	8	Crossroads ....[S]	$8	Warner 25399
11/28/87	177	12	9	Get Rhythm	$8	Warner 25639

Across The Borderline (9)
Alimony (4)
All Shook Up (9)
Always Lift Him Up (3)
Billy The Kid (1)
Blue Suede Shoes (7)
Borderline (6)
Bourgeois Blues (3)
Chloe (3)
Cotton Needs Pickin' (8)
Crazy 'Bout An Automobile (Every Woman I Know) (6)
Crossroads (8)
Dark End Of The Street (4)
Denomination Blues (1)
Ditty Wa Ditty (2)
Do Re Mi (medley) (4)
Don't You Mess Up A Good Thing (1)

Down In Hollywood (5)
Down In Mississippi (8)
Down In The Boondocks (6)
F.D.R. In Trinidad (1)
Feelin' Bad Blues (8)
Feelin' Good (medley) (2)
Fool For A Cigarette (medley) (2)
Get Rhythm (9)
Girls From Texas (6)
Go Home, Girl (6)
Going Back To Okinawa (9)
Goodnight Irene (3)
Great Dream From Heaven (1)
Gypsy Woman (7)
He Made A Woman Out Of Me (8)
He'll Have To Go (3)

Hey Porter (1)
How Can A Poor Man Stand Such Times And Live (4)
How Can You Keep Moving (Unless You Migrate Too) (1)
I Can Tell By The Way You Smell (9)
I Can't Win (5)
I Got Mine (3)
I Need A Woman (7)
I Think It's Going To Work Out Fine (5)
I'm Drinking Again (7)
If Walls Could Talk (2)
It's All Over Now (5)
Jesus On The Mainline (2,4)
Johnny Porter (7)
Let's Have A Ball (9)

Little Sister (5)
Look At Granny Run Run (5)
Low-Commotion (9)
Mama, Don't Treat Your Daughter Mean (7)
Married Man's A Fool (2)
Mexican Divorce (2)
Money Honey (1)
Never Make Your Move Too Soon (6)
Nitty Gritty Mississippi (8)
On A Monday (1)
School Is Out (4)
See You In Hell, Blind Boy (8)
634-5789 (6)
Smack Dab In The Middle (3,4)

Somebody's Callin' My Name (8)
Speedo (6)
Stand By Me (3)
Tamp 'Em Up Solid (2)
Tattler (2)
Taxes On The Farmer Feeds Us All (1)
Teardrops Will Fall (1)
That's The Way Love Turned Out For Me (7)
13 Question Method (9)
Trouble, You Can't Fool Me (5)
UFO Has Landed In The Ghetto (7)
Very Thing That Makes You Rich (Makes Me Poor) (5)
Vigilante Man (1)

Viola Lee Blues (8)
Viva Sequin (medley) (4)
Volver, Volver (4)
Walkin' Away Blues (8)
Way We Make A Broken Heart (6)
Which Came First (7)
Why Don't You Try Me (6)
Women Will Rule The World (9)
Yellow Roses (3)

★★314★★ COOKE, Sam

Born on 1/2/31 in Clarksdale, Mississippi and raised in Chicago. Died from a gunshot wound on 12/11/64 in Los Angeles. Son of a Baptist minister. Sang in choir from age six. Joined the gospel group, the Highway Q.C.'s. Lead singer of the Soul Stirrers from 1950-56. First recorded secular songs in 1956 as "Dale Cook" on Specialty. String of hits on Keen label led to contract with RCA. Nephew is singer R.B. Greaves. Shot by female motel manager under mysterious circumstances. Inducted into the Rock and Roll Hall of Fame in 1986. Revered as the definitive soul singer.

3/10/58	16	2	1	Sam Cooke	$50	Keen 2001
6/30/62	72	8	2	Twistin' The Night Away	$35	RCA 2555
10/20/62	22	35	3	The Best Of Sam Cooke ....[G]	$35	RCA 2625
3/23/63	94	9	4	Mr. Soul	$35	RCA 2673
9/14/63	62	19	5	Night Beat	$35	RCA 2709
4/4/64	34	19	6	Ain't That Good News	$30	RCA 2899
10/31/64+	29	55	7	Sam Cooke At The Copa ....[L]	$30	RCA 2970
2/13/65	44	23	8	Shake..	$25	RCA 3367
7/24/65	128	8	9	The Best Of Sam Cooke, Volume 2 ....[G]	$25	RCA 3373
10/30/65	120	7	10	Try A Little Love..	$25	RCA 3435
6/22/85	134	8	11	Live at The Harlem Square Club, 1963 ....[E-L]	$8	RCA 5181

recorded in Miami on 1/12/63

4/5/86	175	8	12	The Man And His Music ....[G]	$10	RCA 7127 [2]

includes his big hits, some B-sides and 3 songs from his early years as lead singer of his gospel group, The Soul Stirrers

Ain't Misbehavin' (1)
Ain't That Good News (6,9,12)
All The Way (4)
Another Saturday Night (6,9,12) 10
Around The World (1)
Baby, Baby, Baby (9) 66
Basin Street Blues (9)
Bells Of St. Mary's (1)
Best Things In Life Are Free (7)
Bill Bailey (7)
Blowin' In The Wind (7)
Bridge Of Tears (10)
Bring It On Home To Me (3,11,12) 13
Camptown Twist (2)
Canadian Sunset (1)
Chain Gang (3,11,12) 2
Chains Of love (4)
Change Is Gonna Come (6,8,9,12) 31
Comes Love (8)
Cousin Of Mine (9) 31
Cry Me A River (4)

Cupid (3,11,12) 17
Danny Boy (1)
Don't Cry On My Shoulder (10)
Driftin' Blues (10)
Everybody Likes To Cha Cha Cha (3,12) 31
Falling In Love (6)
Feel It (11)
Fool's Paradise (1)
Frankie And Johnny (7,9) 14
Get Yourself Another Fool (5)
Good Times (6,12) 11
Gypsy, The (10)
Having A Party (3,11,12) 17
Home (6)
Houseboat (Almost In Your Arms), Love Song From (10)
I Fall In Love Every Day (10)
I Lost Everything (5)
(I Love You) For Sentimental Reasons (3,4,7,11) 17
I Wish You Love (4)

I'll Come Running Back To You (12) 18
I'm In The Mood For Love (8)
I'm Just A Country Boy (8)
If I Had A Hammer (The Hammer Song) (7)
It's All Right (medley) (11)
It's Got The Whole World Shakin' (8) 41
Just For You (12)
Laughin' And Clownin' (5)
Little Girl (4)
Little Red Rooster (5,9) 11
Little Things You Do (10)
Lonesome Road (1)
Lost And Lookin' (5)
Love Will Find A Way (9,12)
Love You Most Of All (8) 26
Mean Old World (5)
Meet Me At Mary's Place (6,8,12)
Moonlight In Vermont (1)
Movin' And A'Groovin' (2)
No Second Time (6)
Nobody Knows The Trouble I've Seen (5)

Nobody Knows You When You're Down And Out (7)
Nothing Can Change This Love (4,11,12) 12
Ol' Man River (1)
Only Sixteen (3,12) 28
Please Don't Drive Me Away (5)
Riddle Song (6)
Rome Wasn't Built In A Day (6,12)
Sad Mood (3,12) 29
Send Me Some Lovin' (4) 13
Shake (8,9,12) 7
Shake Rattle And Roll (5)
Sittin' In The Sun (6)
Smoke Rings (4)
So Long (1)
(Somebody) Ease My Troublin' Mind (8)
Somebody Have Mercy (2,11,12) 70
Somebody's Gonna Miss Me (2)
Soothe Me (2,12)

Sugar Dumpling (2) 32
Summertime (1,3) 81
Tammy (1,10)
Tennessee Waltz (6,7,9) 35
That Lucky Old Sun (1)
That's Heaven To Me (12)
That's It-I Quit-I'm Movin' On (2) 31
That's Where It's At (9,12) 93
These Foolish Things (4)
This Little Light Of Mine (7)
To Each His Own (10)
Touch The Hem Of His Garment (12)
Trouble Blues (5)
Try A Little Love (10)
Try A Little Tenderness (medley) (7)
Twist, The (2)
Twistin' In The Kitchen With Dinah (2)
Twistin' In The Old Town Tonight (2)
Twistin' The Night Away (2,3,7,11,12) 9

When A Boy Falls In Love (10,12) 52
When I Fall In Love (7)
Whole Lotta Woman (2)
Willow Weep For Me (4)
Win Your Love For Me (8,12) 22
Wonderful World (3,12) 12
Yeah Man (8)
You Gotta Move (5)
You Send Me (1,3,7,10,12) 1
You're Always On My Mind (10)
You're Nobody Till Somebody Loves You (8)

★★276★★ COOLIDGE, Rita

Born on 5/1/44 in Nashville. Had own group, R.C. and the Moonpies, at Florida State University. Moved to Los Angeles in the late '60s. Did backup work for Delaney & Bonnie, Leon Russell, Joe Cocker and Eric Clapton. With Kris Kristofferson from 1971, married to him from 1973-80. Known as "The Delta Lady," for whom Leon Russell wrote the song of the same name.

DEBUT DATE	PEAK POS	WKS CHR	GOLD	#	Album Title	$	Label & Number
4/3/71	105	10		1	Rita Coolidge	$8	A&M 4291
12/18/71+	135	8		2	Nice Feelin'	$8	A&M 3130
11/11/72+	46	24		3	The Lady's Not For Sale	$8	A&M 4370
9/22/73	26	33	●	4	Full Moon *	$12	A&M 4403
5/25/74	55	15		5	Fall Into Spring	$8	A&M 3627
12/21/74+	103	12		6	Breakaway *	$10	Monument 33278
12/6/75+	85	10		7	It's Only Love	$8	A&M 4531
4/2/77	6	54	▲	8	Anytime...Anywhere	$8	A&M 4616
6/17/78	32	22	●	9	Love Me Again	$8	A&M 4699
2/3/79	106	9		10	Natural Act *	$10	A&M 4690
					*KRIS KRISTOFFERSON & RITA COOLIDGE		
9/22/79	95	16		11	Satisfied	$8	A&M 4781
2/14/81	107	8		12	Rita Coolidge/Greatest Hits [G]	$8	A&M 4836
9/12/81	160	4		13	Heartbreak Radio	$8	A&M 3727

After The Fact (4)
Ain't That Peculiar (1)
Am I Blue (7,12)
Back In My Baby's Arms (10)
Basic Lady (13)
Better Days (2)
Bird On The Wire (3)
Blue As I Do (10)
Born To Love Me (7)
Born Under A Bad Sign (1,12)
Burden Of Freedom (5)
Bye Bye, Love (9)
Can She Keep You Satisfied (11)
Closer You Get (13)
Cowboys And Indians (5)
Crazy Love (1)
Crime Of Passion (11)
Crippled Crow (6)
Dakota (The Dancing Bear) (6)
Desperados Waiting For The Train (5)
Don't Let Love Pass You By (7)
Donut Man (3)
Everybody Loves A Winner (3)
Family Full Of Soul (2)
Fever (3,12) 76
Fool In Me (11)
Fool That I Am (12) 46
From The Bottle To The Bottom (4)
Good Times (8)
Happy Song (1)
Hard To Be Friends (4)
Heartbreak Radio (13)
Heaven's Dream (6)
Hello Love, Goodbye (9)
Hold An Old Friend's Hand (5)
Hold On (I Feel Our Love Is Changing) (13)
Hoola Hoop (10)
Hungry Years (8)
(I Always Called Them) Mountains (11)
I Believe In You (1)
I Did My Part (13)
I Don't Want To Talk About It (8,12)
I Feel Like Going Home (5)
I Feel The Burden (Being Lifted Off My Shoulders) (8)
I Fought The Law (10)
I Heard The Bluebirds Sing (4)
I Never Had It So Good (4)
I Wanted It All (7)
I'd Rather Be Sorry (6)
I'd Rather Leave While I'm In Love (11,12) 38
I'll Be Here (2)
I'll Be Your Baby Tonight (3)
I'm Down (But I Keep Falling) (4)
I've Got To Have You (6)
If You Were Mine (2)
Inside Of Me (3)
It Just Keeps You Dancing (9)
It's All Over (All Over Again) (4)
It's Only Love (7)
Jealous Kind (9)
Journey Thru The Past (2)
Keep The Candle Burning (7)
Lady's Not For Sale (3)
Late Again (7)
Lay My Burden Down (2)
Let's Go Dancin' (11)
Love Don't Live Here Anymore (10)
Love Has No Pride (5)
Love Me Again (9) 68
Lover Please (6)
Loving Arms (4) 86
Loving You Was Easier (Than Anything I'll Ever Do Again) (10)
Mama Lou (5)
Man And A Woman (13)
Mean To Me (7)
Most Likely You Go Your Way (And I'll Go Mine) (2)
Mud Island (1)
My Crew (3) flip
My Rock And Roll Man (7)
Nice Feelin' (2,12)
Nickel For The Fiddler (5)
Not Everyone Knows (10)
Now Your Baby Is A Lady (5)
Number One (10)
One Fine Day (11) 66
One More Heartache (13)
Only You Know And I Know (2,12)
Pain Of Love (11)
Part Of Your Life (4)
Please Don't Tell Me How The Story Ends (10)
Rain (6)
Second Story Window (1)
Seven Bridges Road (1)
Silver Mantis (10)
Slow Dancer (9)
Slow Down (6)
Song I'd Like To Sing (4) 49
Songbird (9)
Southern Lady (8)
Star (7)
Stranger To Me Now (13)
Sweet Emotion (11)
Sweet Inspiration (9)
Sweet Susannah (6)
Take It Home (4)
Take Time To Love (4)
Tennessee Blues (4)
That Man Is My Weakness (1)
That's What Friends Are For (5)
Things I Might Have Been (6)
Trust It All To Somebody (11)
Walk On In (13)
Way You Do The Things You Do (8,12) 20
We Had It All (5)
We Must Have Been Out Of Our Minds (5)
We're All Alone (8,12) 7
What'cha Gonna Do (6)
Whiskey Whiskey (3)
Who's To Bless And Who's To Blame (8)
Wishin' And Hopin' (13)
Woman Left Lonely (3)
Words (8,12)
You (9) 25
You Touched Me In The Morning (2)
You're Gonna Love Yourself (In The Morning) (10)
You're So Fine (10)
(Your Love Has Lifted Me) Higher And Higher (8,12) 2

★★102★★ COOPER, Alice

Born Vincent Furnier on 2/4/48 in Detroit. Formed rock group in Phoenix in 1965; changed name to Alice Cooper in 1966. To Los Angeles in 1968, then to Detroit in 1969. Known primarily for his bizarre stage antics. Appeared in the films *Prince Of Darkness* and *Wayne's World* among others.

DEBUT DATE	PEAK POS	WKS CHR	GOLD	#	Album Title	$	Label & Number
6/28/69	193	6		1	Pretties For You	$40	Straight 1051
3/20/71	35	38	●	2	Love It To Death	$15	Warner 1883
12/4/71+	21	54	▲	3	Killer	$15	Warner 2567
7/1/72	2³	32	▲	4	School's Out	$30	Warner 2623
3/17/73	1¹	50	▲	5	Billion Dollar Babies	$10	Warner 2685
12/8/73+	10	21	●	6	Muscle Of Love	$10	Warner 2748
8/31/74	8	23	▲	7	Alice Cooper's Greatest Hits [G]	$10	Warner 2803
3/22/75	5	37	▲	8	Welcome To My Nightmare	$10	Atlantic 18130
7/17/76	27	32	●	9	Alice Cooper Goes To Hell	$10	Warner 2896
5/28/77	42	16		10	Lace And Whiskey	$10	Warner 3027
12/17/77+	131	6		11	The Alice Cooper Show [L]	$10	Warner 3138
12/16/78+	60	11		12	From the Inside	$10	Warner 3263
5/24/80	44	17		13	Flush The Fashion	$8	Warner 3436
9/19/81	125	5		14	Special Forces	$8	Warner 3581
10/18/86	59	21		15	Constrictor	$8	MCA 5761
10/24/87	73	15		16	Raise Your Fist And Yell	$8	MCA 42091
8/12/89	20	43	▲	17	Trash	$8	Epic 45137
7/20/91	47	13		18	Hey Stoopid	$12	Epic 46786

Alma Mater (4)
Apple Bush (1)
Aspirin Damage (13)
Awakening, The (8)
B. B. On Mars (1)
Ballad Of Dwight Fry (2)
Be My Lover (3,7) 49
Bed Of Nails (17)
Big Apple Dreamin' (Hippo) (6)
Billion Dollar Babies (5,7,11) 57
Black Juju (2)
Black Widow (8,11)
Blue Turk (4)
Burning Our Bed (18)
Caught In A Dream (2) 94
Changing, Arranging (1)
Chop, Chop, Chop (16)
Clones (We're All) (13) 40
Cold Ethyl (8)
Crawlin' (15)
Crazy Little Child (6)
Damned If You Do (10)
Dance Yourself To Death (13)
Dangerous Tonight (18)
Dead Babies (3)
Department Of Youth (8) 67
Desperado (3,7)
Devil's Food (8,11)
Didn't We Meet (9)
Die For You (18)
Dirty Dreams (17)
Don't Talk Old To Me (14)
Earwigs To Eternity (1)
Eighteen (2,7,11) 21
Elected (5,7) 26
Escape (8)
Feed My Frankenstein (18)
Fields of Regret (1)
For Veronica's Sake (12)
Freedom (16)
From The Inside (12)
Gail (16)
Generation Landslide (5)
Generation Landslide '81 (14)
Give It Up (15)
Give The Kid A Break (9)
Give The Radio Back (16)
Go To Hell (9,11)
Going Home (9)
Grande Finale (4)
Great American Success Story (14)
Grim Facts (13)
Guilty (9)
Gutter Cat Vs. The Jets (4)
Hallowed Be My Name (2)
Halo Of Flies (3)
Hard Hearted Alice (6)
He's Back (The Man Behind The Mask) (15)
Headlines (13)
Hell Is Living Without You (17)
Hello Hurray (5,7) 35
Hey Stoopid (18) 78
House Of Fire (17) 56
How You Gonna See Me Now (12) 12
Hurricane Years (18)
I Love The Dead (5,11)
I Never Cry (9,11) 12
I Never Wrote Those Songs (10)

166

COOPER, Alice — Cont'd

I'm Always Chasing Rainbows (9)	Love's A Loaded Gun (18)	Simple Disobedience (15)	Titanic Overture (1)	Working Up A Sweat (6)
I'm The Coolest (9)	Luney Tune (4)	Sing Low Sweet Cheerio (1)	Today Mueller (1)	World Needs Guts (15)
I'm Your Gun (17)	Man With The Golden Gun (6)	Skeletons In The Closet (14)	Trash (17)	Yeah, Yeah, Yeah (3)
Inmates (We're All Crazy) (12)	Mary Ann (5)	Snakebite (18)	Trick Bag (15)	Years Ago (8)
Is It My Body (2,7,11)	Might As Well Be On Mars (18)	Some Folks (8)	Ubangi Stomp (10)	**You And Me** (10,11) **9**
It's Hot Tonight (10)	Millie And Billie (12)	Spark In The Dark (17)	**Under My Wheels** (3,7,11) **59**	You Drive Me Nervous (3)
Jackknife Johnny (12)	Model Citizen (13)	Step On You (16)	Unfinished Sweet (5)	You Gotta Dance (9)
Killer (3)	Muscle Of Love (6,7)	Steven (8)	Vicious Rumours (14)	You Look Good In Rags (13)
King Of The Silver Screen (10)	My God (10)	Street Fight (4)	Wake Me Gently (9)	You Want It, You Got It (14)
Lace And Whiskey (10)	My Stars (4)	Sun Arise (2)	**Welcome To My Nightmare** (8) **45**	You're A Movie (14)
Leather Boots (13)	Never Been Sold Before (6)	Talk Talk (13)	Who Do You Think We Are (14)	
Levity Ball (1)	No Longer Umpire (1)	Teenage Frankenstein (15)	Why Trust You (17)	
Life And Death Of The Party (15)	(No More) Love At Your Convenience (10)	**Teenage Lament '74** (6,7) **48**	Wind-Up Toy (18)	
Little By Little (18)	**No More Mr. Nice Guy** (5,7) **25**	10 Minutes Before The Worm (1)	Wish I Were Born In Beverly Hills (12)	
Living (1)	Not That Kind Of Love (16)	This Maniac's In Love With You (17)	Wish You Were Here (9,11)	
Lock Me Up (16)	Nuclear Infected (13)	Thrill My Gorilla (15)	Woman Machine (6)	
Long Way To Go (2)	Nurse Rozetta (12)	Time To Kill (16)		
	Only My Heart Talkin' (17) **89**			
	Only Women (8,11) **12**			
	Pain (13)			
	Poison (17) **7**			
	Prettiest Cop On The Block (14)			
	Prince Of Darkness (16)			
	Public Animal #9 (4)			
	Quiet Room (12)			
	Raped And Freezin' (5)			
	Reflected (1)			
	Road Rats (10)			
	Roses On White Lace (13)			
	School's Out (4,7,11) **7**			
	Second Coming (2)			
	Serious (12)			
	Seven & Seven Is (14)			
	Sick Things (5,11)			

COOPER, Michael

R&B singer/guitarist/songwriter/producer born and raised in Vallejo, California. Formed Project Soul while in high school in 1968. Changed group name to Con Funk Shun in 1972. Went solo in 1986.

| 1/16/88 | 98 | 25 | | Love Is Such A Funny Game | $8 | Warner 25653 |

Dinner For Two	Look Before You Leave	No Other Lover	Quickness	You've Got A Friend
Just Thinkin' 'Bout Cha	Love Is Such A Funny Game	Oceans Wide	To Prove My Love	

COOPER, Pat

Born Pasquale Caputo in Brooklyn, New York. Comedian/actor. Discovered by Jackie Gleason.

5/28/66	82	42		1 Our Hero...Pat Cooper	[C]	$12	United Art. 6446
12/17/66+	84	14		2 Spaghetti Sauce & Other Delights	[C]	$12	United Art. 6548
3/22/69	193	2		3 More Saucy Stories From...Pat Cooper	[C]	$12	United Art. 6690

And Then The Sun Goes Down (2)	Honeymoon, The (1)	Mama (3)	My Father And His Friends (1)	Spaghetti Sauce & Other Delights (2)
Draft Time (3)	In My Neighborhood (1)	Mama's Moo-Len-Yanna (The Eggplant Song) (1)	Our Children (3)	When I Was A Kid (1)
Everyone Is Equal (1)	Italian Wedding (1)	Memories (3)	Pepperoni Kid (2)	
Family & Holidays (3)	Little Red Scooter (2)	More You Make, The More You Spend (1)	Poppa's Home-Made Wine (2)	
Honeymoon (3)	Lu Zampogna (The Italian Bagpipe Man) (2)			

COPE, Julian

Born in Wales and raised in Tamworth, England. Former lead singer/songwriter/bassist of British group The Teardrop Explodes.

2/21/87	109	6		1 Julian Cope	[M]	$8	Island 90560
4/4/87	105	12		2 Saint Julian		$8	Island 90571
12/10/88+	155	13		3 My Nation Underground		$8	Island 91025

Charlotte Anne (3)	5 O'Clock World (3)	Non-Alignment Pact (1)	Shot Down (2)	Umpteenth Unnatural Blues (1)
China Doll (3)	Great White Hoax (3)	Planet Ride (2)	Someone Like Me (3)	Vegetation (3)
Crack In The Clouds (3)	I'm Not Losing Sleep (3)	Pulsar (2)	Spacehopper (2)	**World Shut Your Mouth** (1,2) **84**
Easter Everywhere (3)	I've Got Levitation (1)	Saint Julian (2)	Trampolene (2)	
Eve's Volcano (2)	My Nation Underground (3)	Screaming Secrets (2)	Transporting (1)	

COPELAND, Johnny — see COLLINS, Albert

COPELAND, Stewart

Born on 7/16/52. Drummer of The Police. Prior to The Police, worked as Joan Armatrading's road manager. Founded Animal Logic in 1989.

12/17/83+	157	5		1 Rumble Fish	[S-I]	$8	A&M 4983
				composed, performed and produced by Copeland		
9/7/85	148	8		2 The Rhythmatist		$8	A&M 5084

African Dream (2)	Coco (2)	Kemba (2)	Party At Someone Else's Place (2)	Tulsa Tango (1)
Biff Gets Stomped By Rusty James (1)	Don't Box Me In (1)	Koteja (Oh Bolilla) (2)	Personal Midget (medley) (1)	West Tulsa Story (1)
Brazzaville (2)	Father On The Stairs (2)	Liberte (2)	Samburu Sunset (2)	Your Mother Is Not Crazy (1)
Brothers On Wheels (1)	Franco (2)	Motorboy's Fate (1)	Serengeti Long Walk (2)	
Cain's Ballroom (medley) (1)	Gong Rock (2)	Our Mother Is Alive (1)	Tulsa Rags (1)	
	Hostile Bridge To Benny's (1)			

COREA, Chick

Born Anthony Armando Corea on 6/11/42 in Chelsea, Massachusetts. Jazz-rock pianist. Worked with Stan Getz, Blue Mitchell, Sarah Vaughan and Gary Burton before joining the Miles Davis band in 1968. Formed group Return To Forever in 1973.

3/6/76	42	15		1 The Leprechaun	[I]	$10	Polydor 6062
1/15/77	55	12		2 My Spanish Heart	[I]	$12	Polydor 9003 [2]
3/11/78	61	14		3 The Mad Hatter	[I]	$10	Polydor 6130
8/19/78	86	10		4 Friends	[I]	$10	Polydor 6160
3/31/79	100	8		5 An Evening With Herbie Hancock & Chick Corea	[I-L]	$12	Columbia 35663 [2]
				HERBIE HANCOCK & CHICK COREA		
11/24/79	175	2		6 An Evening With Chick Corea & Herbie Hancock	[I-L]	$12	Polydor 6238 [2]
				CHICK COREA & HERBIE HANCOCK		
				above 2 albums recorded during their 1978 concert series		
5/10/80	170	3		7 Tap Step	[I]	$8	Warner 3425
8/1/81	179	4		8 Three Quartets	[I]	$8	Warner 3552

Armando's Rhumba (2)	Day Danse (2)	Flamenco (7)	Hook, The (6)	Liza (5)	My Spanish Heart (2)
Bouquet (6)	Dear Alice (3)	Friends (4)	Humpty Dumpty (3)	Looking At The World (1)	Night Streets (2)
Button Up (5)	El Bozo - Parts I-III (3)	Gardens, The (2)	Imp's Welcome (1)	Love Castle (2)	Nite Sprite (1)
Cappucino (4)	Embrace, The (7)	Grandpa Blues (7)	La Fiesta (5,6)	Mad Hatter Rhapsody (3)	One Step (4)
Children's Song #15 (4)	Falling Alice (3)	Hilltop, The (2)	Lenore (1)	Magic Carpet (7)	Ostinato (6)
Children's Song #5 (4)	February Moment (5)	Homecoming (6)	Leprechaun's Dream (1)	Maiden Voyage (5,6)	Pixiland Rag (1)

COREA, Chick — Cont'd

Quartet No. 1-3 (8)	Samba Song (4)	Slide, The (7)	Spanish Fantasy - Parts I-IV (2)	Trial, The (3)	Waltse For Dave (4)
Reverie (1)	Sicily (4)	Soft And Gentle (1)	Tap Step (7)	Tweedle Dee (3)	Wind Danse (2)
Samba L.A. (7)	Sky Medley (2)	Someday My Prince Will Come (4)		Tweedle Dum (3)	Woods, The (3)

CORNELIUS BROTHERS & SISTER ROSE

Family group from Dania, Florida. Consisted of Edward, Carter and Rose. Billie Jo was added in 1973. All 15 Cornelius children play instruments or sing. Carter currently lives in Florida as Gideon Israel, the leader of a Muslim religious sect.

| 7/29/72 | 29 | 25 | | Cornelius Brothers & Sister Rose .... | $12 | United Art. 5568 |

Don't Ever Be Lonely (A Poor Little Fool Like Me) 23 · Gonna Be Sweet For You · Good Loving Don't Come Easy · **I'm Never Gonna Be Alone Anymore** 37 · I'm So Glad (To Be Loved By You) · Just Ain't No Love (Like A Lady's) · **Let Me Down Easy** 96 · Let's Stay Together · Lift Your Love Higher · **Too Late To Turn Back Now** 2 · **Treat Her Like A Lady** 3

CORPORATION

Rock sextet led by vocalist Daniel Peil and guitarist Gerard Smith.

| 3/1/69 | 197 | 4 | | The Corporation .... | $30 | Capitol 175 |

Drifting · Highway · I Want To Get Out Of My Grave · India · Ring That Bell · Smile

CORTEZ, Dave "Baby"

Born David Cortez Clowney on 8/13/38 in Detroit. Keyboardist/composer. First recorded (as David Clowney) for Ember in 1956.

| 9/29/62 | 107 | 3 | | Rinky Dink ....[I] | $30 | Chess 1473 |

Davy's Shuffle · Gettin' Right · Jammin' Part 1 & 2 · Little Paris Melody (Elle Ne Tourne Pas La Terre) · Lost Love · Mr. Gee · **Rinky Dink** 10 · Skins And Sounds · Wobble Part 1 & 2

CORYELL, Larry

Jazz-rock guitarist. Born on 4/2/43 in Galveston, Texas. Founder of Eleventh House.

| 5/31/69 | 196 | 3 | | Lady Coryell .... | $15 | Vanguard 6509 |

Cleo's Mood · Dream Thing · Herman Wright · Lady Coryell · Love Child Is Coming Home · Stiff Neck · Sunday Telephone · Treats Style · Two Minute Classical · You Don't Know What Love Is

★★66★★ COSBY, Bill

Born on 7/12/38 in Philadelphia. Top comedian who has appeared in nightclubs, on film and on TV. His first seven comedy albums were all million sellers. Played Alexander Scott on TV series *I Spy*. Star of the highly-rated NBC-TV series *The Cosby Show*. Winner of five Emmys and nine Grammys.

DEBUT DATE	PEAK POS	WKS CHR	GOLD	#	ARTIST — Album Title	$	Label & Number
6/27/64+	21	128	▲	1	Bill Cosby Is A Very Funny Fellow, Right! .... [C]	$15	Warner 1518
11/21/64+	32	140	▲	2	I Started Out As A Child ....[C]	$15	Warner 1567
8/28/65+	19	152	●	3	Why Is There Air? ....[C]	$15	Warner 1606
5/28/66	7	106	▲	4	**Wonderfulness** ....[C]	$12	Warner 1634
5/13/67	2[1]	73	●	5	**Revenge** ....[C]	$12	Warner 1691
9/2/67	18	26		6	Bill Cosby Sings/Silver Throat	$12	Warner 1709
2/24/68	74	11		7	Bill Cosby Sings/Hooray For The Salvation Army Band!	$12	Warner 1728
4/6/68	7	46	●	8	**To Russell, My Brother, Whom I Slept With** .... [C]	$12	Warner 1734
10/26/68+	16	25	●	9	200 M.P.H. ....[C]	$12	Warner 1757
2/8/69	37	19		10	It's True! It's True! ....[C]	$12	Warner 1771
7/12/69	62	16		11	8:15 12:15 ....[C]	$12	Tetragra. 5100 [2]
					title: times of shows at Harrah's Lake Tahoe		
9/6/69	51	25	▲	12	The Best Of Bill Cosby ....[G-C]	$12	Warner 1798
10/18/69+	70	24		13	Bill Cosby ....[C]	$8	Uni 73066
3/14/70	80	16		14	More Of The Best Of Bill Cosby ....[G-C]	$10	Warner 1836
9/12/70	165	6		15	"Live" Madison Square Garden Center .... [C]	$8	Uni 73082
3/6/71	72	8		16	When I Was A Kid ....[C]	$8	Uni 73100
12/11/71+	181	7		17	For Adults Only ....[C]	$8	Uni 73112
9/30/72	191	4		18	Inside The Mind of Bill Cosby ....[C]	$8	Uni 73139
6/16/73	187	4		19	Fat Albert ....[C]	$8	MCA 333
					Fat Albert And The Cosby Kids was a Saturday morning cartoon, hosted by Bill, based on his childhood buddies		
6/5/76	100	12		20	Bill Cosby Is Not Himself These Days (Rat Own, Rat Own, Rat Own) ....[N]	$8	Capitol 11530
					Bill raps to an instrumental backing		
12/18/82+	64	14		21	Bill Cosby "Himself" ....[C-S]	$8	Motown 6026
					excerpts of his filmed one-man show in Ontario, Canada		
6/21/86	26	15	●	22	Those Of You With Or Without Children, You'll Understand .... [C]	$8	Geffen 241041

American Gambler (10) · Animal Stories (15) · Ants Are Cool (10) · Apple, The (8,12,14) · Aw Shucks, Hush Your Mouth (6) · Baby (3,12) · Baby, What You Want Me To Do (Peepin' 'N' Hidin') (6) · Baseball (8,13) · Basketball (13) · Be Good To Your Wives (17) · Bedroom Slippers (18) · Ben (20) · Big Boss Man (6) · Bill Cosby Fights Back (17) · Bill Cosby Goes To A Football Game (13)

Bill Takes His Daughters To The Zoo (15) · Bill Visits Ray Charles (15) · Bill's Marriage (15,18) · Bill's Two Daughters (17) · Brain Damage (21) · Bright Lights, Big City (6) · Buck, Buck ..see: Fat Albert · Buck Jones (16) · Burlesque Shows (10) · Chick On The Side (20) · Chicken Heart (4) · Chocolate Cake For Breakfast (21) · Christmas Time (2) · Conflict (8,14) · Cool Covers (5) · Cost Of An Egg (17)

Dentist, The (21) · Difference Between Men And Women (1) · Do It To Me (20) · Dogs (16) · Dogs And Cats (9,14) · Don'cha Know (6) · Driving In San Francisco (3,12) · Ennis And His Two Sisters (15) · Ennis' Toilet (18) · Fat Albert (5,12) · Fat Albert Got A Hernia (19) · Fat Albert Plays Dead (19) · Fat Albert's Car (19) · Fernet Branca (19) · Football (13,18)

Foreign Countries (10) · Frogs (3,14) · "Froofie" The Dog (18) · **Funky North Philly** (7) 91 · Garbage Truck Lady (20) · Genesis (22) · Get Out Of My Life Woman (7) · Giant, The (11) · Go Carts (4) · Grandfather, The (9) · Grandparents, The (21) · Greasy Kid Stuff (1) · Great Quote (22) · Half Man (8) · Handball Game At The "Y" (15) · Helicopters (10)

His First Baby (15) · Hofstra (3,14) · Hold On I'm A Comin' (7) · Hoof And Mouth (1) · **Hooray For The Salvation Army Band** (7) 71 · Hush Hush (6) · (I Can't Get No) Satisfaction (7) · I Got A Woman (6) · I Luv Myself Better Than I Luv Myself (20) · (I'm A) Road Runner (7) · Invention Of Basketball (18) · It's The Women's Fault (10) · Karate (1,14) · Kill The Boy (21) · Kindergarten (3)

Las Vegas-Mirror Over My Bed (17) · **Little Ole Man (Uptight-Everything's Alright)** (6) 4 · Little Tiny Hairs (1) · Lone Ranger (2,12) · Losers, The (8) · Lower Tract (18) · Lumps (4) · Luv Is (20) · Masculinity At Its Finest (17) · Medic (1) · Mojo Workout (6) · Mothers And Fathers (9) · Mr. Ike & The Neighborhood T.V. Set (10) · My Boy Scout Troop (16)

DEBUT DATE	PEAK POS	WKS CHR	GOLD	ARTIST — Album Title	$	Label & Number

COSBY, Bill — Cont'd

My Brother Russell (16,19)
My Dad's Car (19)
My Father (16)
My Hernia (16)
My Pet Rhinoceros (2)
My Wife And Kids (19)
Natural Childbirth (21)
Neanderthal Man (2)
Niagara Falls (4)
9th St. Bridge ..see: Old Weird Harold
Noah: And The Neighbor (1,12)

Noah: Me And You, Lord (1,12)
Noah: Right! (1,12)
Nut In Every Car (1)
Old Weird Harold (5,12)
Oops! (2,14)
Pep Talk (1)
Personal Hygiene (3)
Place In The Sun (6)
Planes (5)
Playground, The (4)
Ralph Jameson (2)
Reach Out I'll Be There (7)
Revenge (5,12)

Rigor Mortis (2)
Same Thing Happens Every Night (21)
Seattle (2)
$75 Car (3)
Sgt. Pepper's Lonely Hearts Club Band (7)
Shift Down (20)
Shoelaces (10)
Shop (3,4,14)
Slow Class (18)
Smoking (5,14)
Snakes And Alligators (16)
Sneakers (2)

Spanish Fly (10)
Special Class (4)
Stop, Look & Listen (7)
Story Of The Chicken (15)
Street Football (2,12)
Sulphur Fumes (18)
Sunny (7)
Superman (1)
Survival (18)
T.V. Football (2)
Tank, The (5)
Tell Me You Love Me (6)
Time Brings About A Change (7)

To Russell, My Brother, Whom I Slept With (8)
Tonsils (4)
Toothache, The (3)
Toss Of The Coin (1,14)
Track And Field - High Jump (13)
Track And Field - Mile Relay (13)
Two Brothers (5)
Two Daughters (5,14)
200 M.P.H. (9)
Ursalena (7)
Wallie, Wallie (17)

Water Bottle (2,12)
Why Beat On Your Wife (17)
Wife, The (9)
Window Of Life (22)
Wives (5)
Yes, Yes, Yes (20) *46*
You're Driving Me Crazy (20)

COSTANDINOS, Alec R., & The Syncophonic Orchestra
Costandinos is a European disco producer who also assembled the studio group Love & Kisses.

3/25/78	92	17		Romeo & Juliet	$8	Casablanca 7086

Shakespeare play set to a disco beat; side 1: Acts I & II; side 2: Acts III & IV

★★156★★ COSTELLO, Elvis
Born Declan McManus in Liverpool, England on 8/25/54. Changed name to Elvis Costello in 1976. Formed backing band The Attractions in 1977. Appeared in the 1987 film *Straight To Hell*. Married Cait O'Riordan, former bassist with The Pogues, on 5/16/86. Leading eclectic rock singer.

12/3/77+	32	36	▲	1 My Aim Is True	$10	Columbia 35037
4/15/78	30	17	●	2 This Year's Model	$20	Columbia 35331
1/27/79	10	25	●	3 Armed Forces	$25	Columbia 35709
3/22/80	11	15		4 Get Happy!!	$10	Columbia 36347
10/11/80	28	14		5 Taking Liberties ....[K]	$8	Columbia 36839
				previously released and unreleased tracks		
2/14/81	28	15		6 Trust	$8	Columbia 37051
11/14/81	50	13		7 Almost Blue	$8	Columbia 37562
7/24/82	30	24		8 Imperial Bedroom	$8	Columbia 38157
8/13/83	24	24		9 Punch The Clock	$8	Columbia 38897
7/7/84	35	21		10 Goodbye Cruel World	$8	Columbia 39429
11/30/85+	116	16	●	11 The Best Of Elvis Costello and the Attractions ....[G]	$8	Columbia 40101
3/22/86	39	18		12 The Costello Show (Featuring Elvis Costello) - King Of America.......	$8	Columbia 40173
10/11/86	84	11		13 Blood & Chocolate	$8	Columbia 40518
2/25/89	32	25	●	14 Spike...	$8	Warner 25848
6/1/91	55	7		15 Mighty Like A Rose	$12	Warner 26575
				2 covers released — jewel box and digipak		

Accidents Will Happen (3,11)
After The Fall (15)
Alison (1,11)
All Grown Up (15)
Almost Blue (8,11)
American Without Tears (12)
.....And In Every Home (8)
(Angels Wanna Wear My) Red Shoes (1)
Any King's Shilling (14)
B Movie (1)
Baby Plays Around (14)
Battered Old Bird (13)
Beat, The (2)
Beaten To The Punch (4)
Beyond Belief (8,11)
Big Boys (3)
Big Light (1)
Big Sister's Clothes (6)
Big Tears (5)
Black And White World (4,5)
Blame It On Cain (1)
Blue Chair (1)
Boy With A Problem (8)
Brilliant Mistake (12)
Broken (15)
Brown To Blue (9)
Busy Bodies (3)
Charm School (9)
Chemistry Class (3)
Chewing Gum (14)
Clean Money (5)
Clowntime Is Over (4,5)
Clubland (6,11)
Color Of The Blues (7)
Comedians, The (10)

Couldn't Call It Unexpected No. 4 (13)
Crawling To The U.S.A. (5)
Crimes Of Paris (13)
Deep Dark Truthful Mirror (14)
Deportees Club (10)
Different Finger (6)
Dr. Luther's Assistant (5)
Don't Let Me Be Misunderstand (12)
Eisenhower Blues (12)
Element Within Her (9)
Everyday I Write The Book (9,11) *36*
Fish 'N' Chip Paper (6)
5ive Gears In Reverse (4)
From A Whisper To A Scream (6)
Georgie And Her Rival (13)
Getting Mighty Crowded (5)
Ghost Train (5)
Girls Talk (3)
Glitter Gulch (12)
God's Comic (14)
Good Year For The Roses (7)
Goon Squad (3)
Great Unknown (10)
Greatest Thing (9)
Green Shirt (3)
Hand In Hand (2)
Harpies Bizarre (15)
High Fidelity (4)
Home Is Anywhere You Hang Your Head (13)
Home Truth (10)

Honey, Are You Straight Or Are You Blind? (13)
Honey Hush (7)
Hoover Factory (5)
How Much I Lied (7)
How To Be Dumb (15)
Human Hands (8)
Human Touch (4)
Hurry Down Doomsday (The Bugs Are Taking Over) (15)
I Can't Stand Up For Falling Down (4,11)
(I Don't Want To Go To) Chelsea (5)
I Hope You're Happy Now (13)
I Stand Accused (4)
I Wanna Be Loved (10,11)
I Want You (13)
I'll Wear It Proudly (12)
I'm Not Angry (1)
I'm Your Toy (Hot Burrito #1) (7)
Imposter, The (4)
Inch By Inch (10)
Indoor Fireworks (12)
Invasion Hit Parade (15)
Invisible Man (3)
Jack Of All Parades (12)
Joe Porterhouse (10)
Just A Memory (5)
Kid About It (8)
King Horse (4)
King Of Thieves (9)
Last Boat Leaving (14)
Less Than Zero (1)

Let Him Dangle (14)
Let Them All Talk (9)
Lip Service (2)
Lipstick Vogue (2)
Little Palaces (12)
Little Savage (8)
Little Triggers (2)
Living In Paradise (2)
Long Honeymoon (8)
Lovable (12)
Love Field (10)
Love For Tender (4)
Love Went Mad (9)
Loved Ones (8)
Lovers Walk (6)
Luxembourg (8)
Man Called Uncle (4)
Man Out Of Time (8)
Miracle Man (1)
Miss Macbeth (14)
Moods For Moderns (3)
Motel Matches (4)
Mouth Almighty (9)
My Funny Valentine (5)
Mystery Dance (1)
New Amsterdam (4)
New Lace Sleeves (6)
Next Time Round (13)
Night Rally (5)
No Action (2)
No Dancing (1)
Oliver's Army (3,11)
Only Flame In Town (10,11) *56*
Opportunity (4)
Other Side Of Summer (15)

Our Little Angel (12)
Pads, Paws And Claws (14)
Party Girl (3)
Pay It Back (1)
Peace In Our Time (10)
Pidgin English (8)
Pills And Soap (9)
Playboy To A Man (15)
Poisoned Rose (12)
Poor Napoleon (13)
Possession (4)
Pretty Words (6)
Pump It Up (2,11)
Radio, Radio (2,11)
Radio Sweetheart (5)
Riot Act (4)
Room With No Number (10)
Satellite (14)
Secondary Modern (4)
Senior Service (3)
Shabby Doll (8)
Shipbuilding (9,11)
Shot With His Own Gun (6)
Sittin' And Thinkin' (7)
Sleep Of The Just (12)
Sneaky Feelings (1)
So Like Candy (15)
Sour Milk-Cow Blues (10)
Stalin Malone (14)
Stranger In The House (5)
Strict Time (6)
Success (7)
Suit Of Lights (12)
Sunday's Best (5)
Sweet Dreams (7)
Sweet Pear (5)

T.K.O. (Boxing Day) (9)
Talking In The Dark (5)
Tears Before Bedtime (8)
Temptation (4)
...This Town... (14)
This Year's Girl (2)
Tiny Steps (5)
Tokyo Storm Warning (13)
Tonight The Bottle Let Me Down (7)
Too Far Gone (7)
Town Cryer (8)
Tramp The Dirt Down (14)
Two Little Hitlers (3)
Uncomplicated (13)
Veronica (14) *19*
Waiting For The End Of The World (1)
Watch Your Step (6,11)
Watching The Detectives (1,11)
Wednesday Week (5)
Welcome To The Working Week (1)
(What's So Funny 'Bout) Peace, Love And Understanding (3,11)
White Knuckles (6)
Why Don't You Love Me (Like You Used To Do) (7)
World And His Wife (9)
Worthless Thing (10)
You Belong To Me (1)
You Little Fool (8)
You'll Never Be A Man (6)

COTTON, James, Band
Former sideman with Muddy Waters' band, notable Chicago blues harp player. Born on 7/1/35 in Tunica, Mississippi. Ran away from home to work with Sonny Boy Williamson.

12/16/67	194	2		1 The James Cotton Blues Band	$15	Verve F. 3023
1/18/75	146	9		2 100% Cotton	$12	Buddah 5620

All Walks Of Life (2)
Blues In My Sleep (1)
Boogie Thing (2)
Burner (2)
Creeper Creeps Again (2)

Don't Start Me Talkin' (1)
Fatuation (2)
Feelin' Good (1)
Fever (1)
Good Time Charlie (1)

How Long Can A Fool Go Wrong? (2)
I Don't Know (2)
I Don't Know Why (2)
Jelly, Jelly (1)
Knock On Wood (1)

Off The Wall (1)
Oh Why (1)
One More Mile (2)
Rockett 88 (2)
Something On Your Mind (1)

Sweet Sixteen (1)
Turn On Your Lovelight (1)

COTTON, Josie
Dallas native. Appeared in the film *Valley Girl*.

| 8/7/82 | **147** | 12 | | Convertible Music.. | $8 | Elektra 60140 |

Another Girl / Bye, Bye Baby / **He Could Be The One** 74 / I Need The Night, Tonight / Johnny, Are You Queer? / No Pictures Of Dad / Rockin' Love / So Close / Systematic Way / Tell Him / Waitin' For Your Love

COUCHOIS
Rock quintet led by Chris, Pat and Mike Couchois. Also see Ratchell.

| 4/21/79 | **170** | 4 | | Couchois.. | $8 | Warner 3289 |

Colonel, The / Cripple / Devil's Triangle / Do It In Darkness / Going To The Races / I Could Never Take Her Away From You / Kalahari Cattle Drive / No Longer Needed / Walkin' The Fence

COUGAR, John — see MELLENCAMP

COUNT FIVE
Psychedelic garage rock quintet of teenagers from San Jose, California — Kenn Ellner, lead singer.

| 12/3/66 | **122** | 6 | | Psychotic Reaction.. | $30 | Double Shot 1001 |

Can't Get Your Lovin' / Double-Decker Bus / Morning After / My Generation / Out In The Street / Peace Of Mind / Pretty Big Mouth / **Psychotic Reaction** 5 / She's Fine / They're Gonna Get You / World, The

COUNTRY JOE AND THE FISH
Country Joe (Joseph McDonald, b: 1/1/42, El Monte, California) and The Fish were San Francisco's leading political rock band of the '60s.

6/10/67	**39**	38		1 Electric Music For The Mind And Body...............................	$20	Vanguard 79244
12/23/67+	**67**	28		2 I-Feel-Like-I'm-Fixin'-To-Die..	$20	Vanguard 79266
7/13/68	**23**	16		3 Together...	$20	Vanguard 79277
6/21/69	**48**	11		4 Here We Are Again..	$20	Vanguard 79299
1/3/70	**74**	9		5 Country Joe & The Fish/Greatest Hits ....[G]	$15	Vanguard 6545
5/2/70	**111**	9		6 C.J. Fish...	$15	Vanguard 6555
8/7/71	**185**	4		7 War, War, War *	$15	Vanguard 79315
10/30/71	**197**	2		8 The Life and Times of Country Joe & The Fish from Haight-Ashbury to Woodstock ....[K]	$15	Vanguard 27/28 [2]
2/19/72	**179**	4		9 Incredible! Live! * ....[L]	$12	Vanguard 79316
11/1/75+	**124**	14		10 Paradise With An Ocean View *	$10	Fantasy 9495

*COUNTRY JOE McDONALD

Away Bounce My Bubbles (3) / Baby Song (6) / Baby, You're Driving Me Crazy (4) / Bass Strings (1,5,8) / **Breakfast For Two** (10) 92 / Bright Suburban Mr. & Mrs. Clean Machine (3) / Call, The (7) / Cetacean (3) / Colors For Susan (2) / Crystal Blues (4,8) / Death Sound (1,8) / Deep Down In Our Hearts (9) / Doctor Of Electricity (4) / Donovan's Reef (4) / Eastern Jam (2) / Entertainment Is My Business (9) / Fish Moan (3) / Flying High (1,8) / For No Reason (4) / Forward (7) / Free Some Day (9) / Grace (1,8) / Hand Of Man (6) / Hang On (6) / Harlem Song (3) / Here I Go Again (4,5) / Hey Bobby (6) / Holy Roller (10) / I-Feel-Like-I'm-Fixin'-To-Die Rag (2,5,8) / I'll Survive (4) / I'm On The Road Again (9) / It's So Nice To Have Love (4) / Janis (2,8) / Jean Desprez (7) / Kiss My Ass (9) / Limit, The (10) / Living In The Future In A Plastic Dome (9) / Lonely On The Road (10) / Lost My Connection (10) / Love (1,8) / Love Machine (6,8) / Magoo (2) / Man From Aphabaska (7) / Mara (6) / March Of The Dead (7) / Maria (4,5) / Marijuana (8) / Masked Marauder (1,5,8) / Mojo Navigator (3) / Munition Maker (7) / My Girl (4) / **Not So Sweet Martha Lorraine** (1,5,8) 95 / Oh, Jamaica (10) / Oh, My, My (9) / Pat's Song (2) / Porpoise Mouth (1,5,8) / Return Of Sweet Lorraine (6) / Rock And Soul Music (3,8) / Rock Coast Blues (2) / Rockin' Round The World (6) / Sad And Lonely Times (1) / Save The Whales! (10) / Section 43 (1) / She's A Bird (6) / Silver And Gold (6) / Sing Sing Sing (6,8) / Streets Of Your Town (3,5) / Super Bird (1,8) / Susan (3) / Sweet Marie (9) / Tear Down The Walls (10) / Thought Dream (2) / Thursday (2) / Tricks (10) / Tricky Dicky (9) / Twins, The (7) / Untitled Protest (3,8) / Walk In Santiago (9) / Waltzing In The Moonlight (3,8) / War Widow (7) / Who Am I (2,5,8) / You Know What I Mean (9) / Young Fellow, My Lad (7)

COUNTS, The
Funk group: Mose Davis (vocals), Demetrus Cates, Raoul Keith Mangrum, Andrew Gibson and Leroy Mannuel.

| 7/1/72 | **193** | 2 | | What's Up Front That-Counts .... | $15 | Westbound 2011 |

Bills / Pack Of Lies / Rhythm Changes / Thinking Single / What's Up Front That-Counts / Why Not Start All Over Again

COURTNEY, David
British singer/songwriter/drummer. Formed a songwriting partnership with Leo Sayer in the mid-1970s.

| 2/21/76 | **194** | 4 | | David Courtney's First Day .... | $10 | United Art. 553 |

Don't Let The Photos Fool You / Don't Look Now / Everybody Needs A Little Loving / If You Wanna Dance / It's All For You / Life Is So They Say / My Mind / Silverbird / Stranded / Take This Mask Away / When Your Life Is Your Own / You Ain't Got Me

COVER GIRLS, The
New York City-based female dance trio: Louise "Angel" Sabater, Caroline Jackson and Sunshine Wright (replaced by Margo Urban in 1989). 1992 lineup: Jackson, Evelyn Escalera and Michelle Valentine.

| 8/15/87+ | **64** | 61 | | 1 Show Me.. | $8 | Fever 4 |
| 10/7/89+ | **108** | 19 | | 2 We Can't Go Wrong.. | $8 | Capitol 91041 |

All That Glitters Isn't Gold (2) 49 / **Because Of You** (1) 27 / Cute (2) / **Inside Outside** (1) 55 / Love Emergency (1) / Love Mission (2) / **My Heart Skips A Beat** (2) 38 / No One In This World (2) / Nothing Could Be Better (2) / Once Upon A Time (2) / One Night Affair (1) / **Promise Me** (1) 40 / **Show Me** (1) 44 / Spring Love (1) 98 / That Boy Of Mine (1,2) / Up On The Roof (2) / **We Can't Go Wrong** (2) 8

COWARD, Noel
Born on 12/16/1899 in Teddington, England; died on 3/26/73. Enormously popular and enduring actor/playwright/personality in England. Knighted by Queen Elizabeth II in 1970.

| 1/28/56 | **14** | 2 | | Noel Coward At Las Vegas ....[L] | $25 | Columbia 5063 |

Alice Is At It Again / Bar On The Piccola Marina / Dance, Little Lady (medley) / I'll Follow My Secret Heart (medley) / I'll See You Again (medley) / If Love Were All (medley) / Let's Do It / Loch Lomond / Mad Dogs And Englishmen / Matelot / Nina / Party's Over Now / Play, Orchestra, Play (medley) / Poor Little Rich Girl (medley) / Room With A View / Someday I'll Find You (medley) / Uncle Harry / World Weary

DEBUT DATE	PEAK POS	WKS CHR	GOLD	ARTIST — Album Title	$	Label & Number

COWBOY JUNKIES
Canadian country-punk quartet: vocalist Margo Timmins with brothers Michael and Peter Timmins, and Alan Anton.

1/28/89	26	29	●	1 The Trinity Session	$8	RCA 8568
3/31/90	47	16		2 The Caution Horses	$12	RCA 2058
2/29/92	76	15		3 Black Eyed Man	$12	RCA 61049

Black Eyed Man (3)
'Cause Cheap Is How I Feel (2)
Cowboy Junkies Lament (3)
Dreaming My Dreams With You (1)
Escape Is So Simple (2)
Horse In The Country (3)
I Don't Get It (1)
I'm So Lonesome I Could Cry (1)
If You Were The Woman And I Was The Man (3)
Last Spike (3)
Mariner's Song (2)
Mining For Gold (1)
Misguided Angel (1)
Murder, Tonight, In The Trailer Park (3)
Oregon Hill (3)
Postcard Blues (1)
Powderfinger (2)
Rock And Bird (2)
Southern Rain (3)
Sun Comes Up, It's Tuesday Morning (2)
Sweet Jane (1)
Thirty Summers (2)
This Street, That Man, This Life (3)
To Live Is To Fly (3)
To Love Is To Bury (1)
Townes' Blues (3)
200 More Miles (1)
Walking After Midnight (1)
Where Are You Tonight? (2)
Winter's Song (3)
Witches (2)
You Will Be Loved Again (2)

COWSILLS, The
Family pop group from Newport, Rhode Island. Consisted of five brothers (Bill, Bob, Paul, Barry and John), with their little sister (Susan) and mother (Barbara, d: 1/31/85 [age 56]). Bob, Paul, John and Susan reunited for touring in 1990.

11/4/67+	31	17		1 The Cowsills	$12	MGM 4498
3/9/68	89	14		2 We Can Fly	$12	MGM 4534
9/7/68	105	12		3 Captain Sad And His Ship Of Fools	$12	MGM 4554
1/18/69	127	9		4 The Best Of The Cowsills [G]	$10	MGM 4597
5/10/69	16	24		5 The Cowsills In Concert [L]	$10	MGM 4619
5/8/71	200	1		6 On My Side	$8	London 587

Act Naturally (5)
Ask The Children (3)
Beautiful Beige (2)
Bridge, The (3)
Can You Love? (4)
Can't Measure The Cost Of A Woman Lost (3)
Captain Sad And His Ship Of Fools (3,4)
Cheatin' On Me (6)
(Come 'Round Here) I'm The One You Need (1)
Contact Mae (6)
Cruel War (5)
Devil With A Blue Dress On (medley) (5)
Dover Mine (6)
Down On The Farm (6)
Dreams Of Linda (1)
Fantasy World Of Harry Faversham (3)
Gettin' Into That Sunny, Sunny Feelin' Again (1)
Good Golly Miss Molly (medley) (5)
Good Ole Rock & Roll Song (6)
Good Vibrations (5)
Gotta Get Away From It All (2,4)
Gray, Sunny Day (2,4)
Hair (5)
Heather Says (6)
Heaven Held (2)
Hello, Hello (5)
How Can I Make You See (5)
If You Can't Have It - Knock It (6)
In Need Of A Friend (2,4) *54*
Indian Lake (3,4) *10*
La Rue Du Sole (1)
Make The Music Flow (3)
Meet Me At The Wishing Well (3)
Mister Flynn (2,4)
Monday, Monday (5)
Mystery Of Life (6)
Newspaper Blanket (3,4)
On My Side (6)
Once There Was A Time (6)
One Man Show (2)
Painting The Day (3)
Paperback Writer (5)
Path Of Love (3,4)
Pennies (1)
Please Mister Postman (5)
Poor Baby (4) *44*
Rain, The Park & Other Things (1,4) *2*
Reach Out (I'll Be There) (5)
River Blue (1)
(Stop, Look) Is Anyone There? (1)
Sunshine Of Your Love (5)
That's My Time Of The Day (1)
There Is A Child (6)
Thinkin' About The Other Side (1)
Time For Remembrance (2,4)
Troubled Roses (1)
Walk Away Renee (5)
We Can Fly (1,4) *21*
What Is Happy? (2)
Who Can Teach A Songbird To Sing (3)
Yesterday's Girl (2)

CRABBY APPLETON
West Coast rock quintet led by Michael Fennelly.

6/27/70	175	6		Crabby Appleton	$10	Elektra 74067

Can't Live My Life
Catherine
Go Back *36*
How Long Will It Take
Hunger For Love
Other Side
Peace By Peace
Some Madness
To All My Friends
Try

CRACK THE SKY
Rock sextet from Steubenville, Ohio led by singer John Palumbo. Founding trio (Palumbo, Rick Witkowski and Joe D'Amico) reunited in 1988 after a 10-year split, joined by keyboardist Vince Depaul.

1/24/76	161	6		1 Crack The Sky	$12	Lifesong 6000
10/30/76	142	5		2 Animal Notes	$12	Lifesong 6005
3/11/78	124	8		3 Safety In Numbers	$12	Lifesong 6015
6/24/89	186	5		4 From The Greenhouse	$8	Grudge 4500
4/7/90	164	10		5 Dog City	$12	Grudge 4520

All The Things We Do (4)
Animal Skins (2)
Apathy (3)
Big Money (4)
Can I Play For You (Ian's Song) (4)
Dog City (5)
Dog Redux (5)
Don't Call Me Brother (5)
Flashlight (3)
From The Greenhouse (4)
Frozen Rain (4)
Give Myself To You (3)
Hold On (1)
I Don't Have A Tie (1)
I'll Be There (5)
Ice (1)
Invaders From Mars (2)
Lighten Up McGraw (3)
Long Nights (3)
Lost Boys (5)
Lost In America (4)
Love Me Like A Terrorist (5)
Maybe I Can Fool Everybody (Tonight) (2)
Mind Baby (1)
Monkeyboy (4)
Mr. President (5)
Night On The Town (With Snow White) (3)
Play On (2)
Quicksand (5)
Rangers At Midnight (3)
Robots For Ronnie (1)
Safety In Numbers (3)
Sea Epic (1)
She's A Dancer (1)
Sleep (1)
Surf City (1)
Under Red Skies (4)
Virgin....No (2)
Waiting For The New World (5)
We Want Mine (2)
Wet Teenager (2)

CRADDOCK, Billy "Crash"
Country-rock singer. Born on 6/16/39 in Greensboro, North Carolina. First recorded for Colonial in 1957. Nickname "Crash" came from his stock car racing hobby.

8/24/74	142	5		Rub It In	$8	ABC 817

Arkansas Red
Farmer's Daughter
Home Is Such A Lonely Place To Go
It's Hard To Love A Hungry, Worried Man
Quarter Til Three
Ruby, Baby *33*
Rub It In *16*
Stop! If You Love Me
Walk When Love Walks
Walk Your Kisses

CRAMER, Floyd
Nashville's top session pianist. Born on 10/27/33 in Samti, Louisiana and raised in Huttig, Arkansas. Played piano from age five. Moved to Nashville in 1955. Toured with Elvis Presley, Johnny Cash, Perry Como and Chet Atkins.

8/14/61	70	16		1 On The Rebound [I]	$15	RCA 2359
5/26/62	113	6		2 Floyd Cramer Gets Organ-ized [I]	$15	RCA 2488
10/13/62	130	2		3 I Remember Hank Williams [I]	$15	RCA 2544
10/23/65+	107	13		4 Class Of '65 [I]	$15	RCA 3405
9/17/66	123	7		5 Class Of '66 [I]	$15	RCA 3650
5/6/67	166	6		6 Here's What's Happening! [I]	$15	RCA 3746
4/25/70	183	3		7 The Big Ones, Volume II [I]	$15	RCA 4312
5/24/80	170	5		8 Dallas [I]	$8	RCA 3613

DEBUT DATE	PEAK POS	WKS CHR	GOLD	ARTIST — Album Title	$	Label & Number

CRAMER, Floyd — Cont'd

Again (2)
All In The Family (Those Were The Days) (8)
Alma Mater (1)
Almost Persuaded (6)
Alone And Forsaken (3)
Band Of Gold (5)
Born Free (6)
Both Sides Now (7)
Cast Your Fate To The Wind (4)
Cherish (6)
Cold, Cold Heart (3)
Corinna, Corinna (1)
Crying (5)
Dallas (8)
Danny Boy (1)
Dear Heart (4)
Downtown (4)
Dreamer, The (2)

Faded Love (1)
First Hurt (2)
First Impression (1)
Good Vibrations (6)
Gospel Theme (2)
He (5)
Hey, Good Lookin' (3)
House Of Gold (3)
I Can Just Imagine (1)
I Can't Help It (3)
I Feel Fine (4)
I Just Don't Know What To Do With Myself (6)
I Saw The Light (3)
I'll Be There (4)
I'll Follow The Sun (4)
I'll Never Fall In Love Again (7)
I'm So Lonesome I Could Cry (3)

Incredible Hulk (8)
Jambalaya (3)
Jordu (2)
Kaw-Liga (3)
King Of The Road (4)
Knot's Landing (8)
Laverne And Shirley (Making It's Come True) (8)
Leaving On A Jet Plane (7)
Let It Be Me (1)
Let's Go (2) **90**
Little House On The Prairie (The Little House) (8)
Louie, Louie (6)
Love Letters (5)
Lovesick Blues (3) **87**
Lullaby Of Birdland (2)
M*A*S*H (8)
Message To Michael (5)

Midnight Cowboy (7)
Monday, Monday (5)
Mr. Lonely (4)
My Blue Heaven (1)
My Funny Valentine (2)
My Way (7)
On The Rebound (1) 4
Paperback Writer (5)
Perdido (2)
Put A Little Love In Your Heart (7)
Rain On The Roof (6)
Raindrops Keep Falling On My Head (7)
Red Roses For A Blue Lady (4)
San Antonio Rose (1) **8**
Sentimental Journey (2)
Softly, As I Leave You (7)
Something (7)

Somewhere (6)
Spanish Flea (5)
Strangers In The Night (5)
String Of Pearls (2)
Sweet Pea (5)
Tammy (1)
Taxi (8)
Try To Remember (4)
Two Of A Kind (1)
Two-Twenty-Two, Theme From (7)
Waltons, The (8)
We Have All The Time In The World (7)
When A Man Loves A Woman (5)
Who Am I (6)
Why Don't You Love Me (3)
Willow Weep For Me (4)
Winchester Cathedral (6)

Wonderland By Night (1)
Work Song (6)
(You Don't Have To) Paint Me A Picture (6)
(You're My) Soul And Inspiration (7)
You've Lost That Lovin' Feelin' (4)
Young And The Restless (Nadia's Theme), Main Theme From (8)
Your Cheatin' Heart (3)

CRANE, Les

TV talkshow host from San Francisco.

| 12/4/71+ | 32 | 11 | | Desiderata | $8 | Warner 2570 |

Les talks, accompanied by a musical background

Beauty - Shining From The Inside Out
Courage - Eyes That See

Desiderata 8
Esperanza - Hope
Friends

Happiness - I Got No Cares
Independence - A Different Drummer

Love - Children Learn What They Live
Nature - Wilderness

Vision

CRAWFORD, Hank

Jazz alto saxophonist. Born on 12/21/34 in Memphis. With Ray Charles' band from 1958-63.

8/8/64	143	2		1 True Blue	[I]	$20	Atlantic 1423
4/17/76	159	7		2 I Hear A Symphony	[I]	$12	Kudu 26
1/29/77	167	3		3 Hank Crawford's Back	[I]	$12	Kudu 33

Baby! This Love I Have (2)
Blues In Bloom (1)
Canadian Sunset (3)
Funky Pigeon (3)
Got You On My Mind (1)
Hang It On The Ceiling (2)

I Can't Stop Loving You (3)
I Hear A Symphony (2)
I'll Move You No Mountain (2)
Love Won't Let Me Wait (2)

Madison (Spirit, The Power) (2)
Mellow Down (1)
Merry Christmas Baby (1)
Midnight Over Memphis (3)
Read 'Em And Weep (1)

Save Your Love For Me (1)
Shake A-Plenty (1)
Shooby (1)
Skunky Green (1)
Stripper, The (2)
Sugar Free (2)

Two Years Of Torture (1)
You'll Never Find Another Love Like Mine (3)

CRAWFORD, Johnny

Born on 3/26/46 in Los Angeles. One of the original Mouseketeers. Played Chuck Connor's son (Mark McCain) in the TV series The Rifleman, 1958-63.

| 9/1/62 | 40 | 10 | | 1 A Young Man's Fancy | | $30 | Del-Fi 1223 |
| 5/25/63 | 126 | 5 | | 2 His Greatest Hits | [G] | $30 | Del-Fi 1229 |

Cindy's Birthday (1,2) **8**
Daydreams (2) **70**
Debbie (1,2)

Donna (2)
I'm Walkin' (2)
In The Wee Small Hours (1)

Little White Cloud (1)
Moon River (1,2)
Mr. Blue (1)

Patti Ann (2) **43**
Proud (2) **29**
Rumors (2) **12**

Sittin' And A Watchin' (1,2)
Something Special (1)
We Belong Together (2)

Young At Heart (1)
Your Nose Is Gonna Grow (1,2) **14**

CRAWFORD, Michael

Theater/film/TV actor. Tony Award-winning lead in 1987 musical Phantom of the Opera. Born on 1/19/42 in Salisbury, Wiltshire, England.

| 7/30/88 | 192 | 2 | | 1 Songs From The Stage And Screen | | $8 | Columbia 44321 |

with the London Symphony Orchestra

| 11/30/91+ | 54 | 31 | ● | 2 Michael Crawford performs Andrew Lloyd Webber | | $12 | Atlantic 82347 |

tunes from The Phantom Of The Opera, Evita, Cats and other Lloyd Webber musicals

All I Ask Of You (2)
And The Money Kept Rolling In (And Out) (2)
Any Dream Will Do (2)
Before The Parade Passes By (1)
Bring Him Home (1)

First Man You Remember (medley) (2)
Gethsemane (2)
If I Loved You (1)
In The Still Of The Night (1)
Love Changes Everything (2)
Memory (1,2)

Music Of The Night (2)
Not A Day Goes By (1)
Nothing Like You've Ever Known (2)
Only You (2)
Other Pleasures (medley) (2)
Phantom Of The Opera (2)

Tell Me On A Sunday (2)
Unexpected Song (1)
West Side Story Medley (1)
What'll I Do (1)
When You Wish Upon A Star (1)

Wishing You Were Somehow Here Again (2)
You Remember (2)
You'll Never Walk Alone (1)

CRAWFORD, Randy

Born Veronica Crawford on 2/18/52 in Macon, Georgia and raised in Cincinnati. Recorded and toured Europe with Crusaders. Most Outstanding Performance award at Tokyo Music Festival in 1980.

5/31/80	180	7		1 Now We May Begin		$8	Warner 3421
5/23/81	71	19		2 Secret Combination		$8	Warner 3541
6/26/82	148	10		3 Windsong		$8	Warner 23687
11/5/83	164	5		4 Nightline		$8	Warner 23976
7/26/86	178	4		5 Abstract Emotions		$8	Warner 25423
11/18/89	159	13		6 Rich And Poor		$8	Warner 26002

Actual Emotional Love (5)
Ain't No Foolin' (4)
All It Takes Is Love (6)
Almaz (5)
Believe That Love Can Change The World (6)
Betcha (5)
Blue Flame (1)
Bottom Line (4)
Can't Stand The Pain (5)
Cigarette In The Rain (6)
Desire (5)
Don't Come Knockin' (3)

Don't Wanna Be Normal (5)
Every Kind Of People (6)
Gettin' Away With Murder (5)
Go On And Live It Up (4)
Happy Feet (4)
He Reminds Me (3)
Higher Than Anyone Can Count (5)
I Don't Feel Much Like Crying (6)
I Don't Want To Lose Him (3)
I Have Ev'rything But You (3)
In Real Life (4)

Knockin' On Heaven's Door (5)
Last Night At Danceland (1)
Letter Full Of Tears (3)
Lift Me Up (4)
Living On The Outside (4)
Look Who's Lonely Now (3)
Love Is (6)
My Heart Is Not As Young As It Used To Be (1)
Nightline (4)
Now We May Begin (1)
One Day I'll Fly Away (1)

One Hello (3)
Overnight (5)
Rainy Night In Georgia (4)
Rich And Poor (6)
Rio De Janeiro Blue (2)
Same Old Story (Same Old Song) (1)
Secret Combination (2)
Separate Lives (6)
Tender Falls The Rain (5)
That's How Heartaches Are Made (2)
This Is The Love (6)

This Night Won't Last Forever (1)
This 'Ole Heart Of Mine (4)
Time For Love (2)
Trade Winds (2)
Two Lives (2)
We Had A Love So Strong (3)
When I Lose My Way (2)
When I'm Gone (3)
When Your Life Was Low (1)
Why (4)
Windsong (3)
World Of Fools (5)

Wrap-U-Up (6)
You Bring The Sun Out (2)
You Might Need Somebody (2)

CRAWLER — see BACK STREET CRAWLER

DEBUT DATE	PEAK POS	WKS CHR	GOLD	ARTIST — Album Title	$	Label & Number

CRAY, Robert, Band

Born on 8/1/53 in Columbus, Georgia. Blues guitarist/vocalist. Played bass with fictional band, Otis Day & The Knights, in the film *Animal House*. Band formed in 1974 as backing tour group for Albert Collins. 1988 lineup: Richard Cousins, Peter Boe and David Olson. 1990 lineup: Cousins, Jimmy Pugh, Kevin Hayes and Tim Kaihatsu.

2/15/86	124	18		1 Showdown!	$8	Alligator 4743

ALBERT COLLINS/ROBERT CRAY/JOHNNY COPELAND

4/5/86	141	21		2 False Accusations	$8	Hightone 8005
12/20/86+	13	49	▲	3 Strong Persuader	$8	Mercury 830568
3/7/87	143	11		4 Bad Influence ....[E]	$8	Hightone 8001
8/27/88	32	32	●	5 Don't Be Afraid Of The Dark	$8	Mercury 834923
10/6/90	51	32		6 Midnight Stroll	$12	Mercury 846652

THE ROBERT CRAY BAND FEATURING THE MEMPHIS HORNS

The Memphis Horns: Wayne Jackson (trumpet) and Andrew Love (sax)

9/26/92	103	7		7 I Was Warned	$12	Mercury 512721

ROBERT CRAY

Across The Line (5)
Acting This Way (5)
Albert's Alley (1)
At Last (5)
Bad Influence (4)
Black Cat Bone (1)
Blackjack (1)
Bouncin' Back (6)
Bring Your Fine Self Home (1)
Change Of Heart, Change Of Mind (S.O.F.T.) (2)
Consequences (6)
Don't Be Afraid Of The Dark (5) 74

Don't Touch Me (4)
Don't You Even Care? (5)
Dream, The (1)
False Accusations (2)
Fantasized (3)
Forecast (Calls For Pain) (6)
Foul Play (3)
Got To Make A Comeback (4)
Gotta Change The Rules (5)
Grinder, The (4)
He Don't Live Here Anymore (7)
Holdin' Court (6)
I Can't Go Home (5)
I Guess I Showed Her (3)

I Was Warned (7)
I Wonder (3)
I'm A Good Man (7)
I've Slipped Her Mind (2)
Just A Loser (7)
Labor Of Love (6)
Last Time (I Get Burned Like This) (2)
Laugh Out Loud (5)
Lion's Den (1)
March On (4)
Midnight Stroll (6)
Moon Is Full (1)
More Than I Can Stand (3)
Move A Mountain (6)

My Problem (6)
New Blood (3)
Night Patrol (5)
No Big Deal (4)
Nothin' But A Woman (3)
On The Road Down (7)
Our Last Time (7)
Payin' For It Now (2)
Phone Booth (4)
Picture Of A Broken Heart (7)
Playin' In The Dirt (2)
Porch Light (2)
Price I Pay (7)
Right Next Door (Because Of Me) (3) 80

She's Gone (2)
She's Into Something (1)
Smoking Gun (3) 22
So Many Women, So Little Time (4)
Sonny (2)
Still Around (3)
T-Bone Shuffle (1)
These Things (6)
Things You Do To Me (6)
Waiting For The Tide To Turn (4)
Walk Around Time (6)
Where Do I Go From Here (4)
Whole Lotta Pride (7)

Won The Battle (7)
Your Secret's Safe With Me (5)

CRAZY HORSE

Neil Young's backup group.

3/27/71	84	11		1 Crazy Horse	$12	Reprise 6438
2/5/72	170	6		2 Loose	$12	Reprise 2059

All Alone Now (2)
All The Little Things (2)
And She Won't Even Blow Smoke In My Direction (2)
Beggars Day (1)

Carolay (1)
Crow Jane Lady (1)
Dance, Dance, Dance (1)
Dirty, Dirty (1)
Downtown (1)

Fair Weather Friend (2)
Going Home (2)
Gone Dead Train (1)
Hit And Run (2)
I Don't Believe It (2)

I Don't Want To Talk About It (1)
I'll Get By (1)
Kind Of Woman (2)

Look At All The Things (1)
Move (2)
Nobody (1)
One Sided Love (2)

One Thing I Love (2)
Try (2)
You Won't Miss Me (2)

CRAZY OTTO

German pianist Fritz Schulz-Reichel. Born on 7/4/12.

4/16/55	1²	20		**Crazy Otto** ....[I]	$20	Decca 8113

Beautiful Ohio
Glad Rag Doll 19

In The Mood
Lights Out

My Melancholy Baby
Paddlin' Madelin' Home

Red Sails In The Sunset
Rose Of Washington Square

S-H-I-N-E
Smiles 21

CREACH, Papa John

Rock fiddler — worked with Jefferson Airplane.

1/1/72	94	14		Papa John Creach	$12	Grunt 1003

Danny Boy
Everytime I Hear Her Name

Human Spring
Janitor Drives A Cadillac

Over The Rainbow

Papa John's Down Home Blues

Plunk A Little Funk
Saint Louis Blues

Soul Fever
String Jet Rock

★★265★★ CREAM

British rock supergroup: Eric Clapton (guitar), Ginger Baker (drums) and Jack Bruce (bass). Baker and Bruce had been in Alexis Korner's Blues Inc. and the Graham Bond Organization. Clapton and Bruce were in John Mayall's Bluesbreakers. After Cream disbanded, Clapton and Baker formed Blind Faith. Cream inducted into the Rock and Roll Hall of Fame in 1993. Also see Eric Clapton's *History Of Eric Clapton* and *Crossroads* albums.

5/13/67+	39	92	●	1 Fresh Cream	$30	Atco 206
12/9/67+	4	77	●	2 **Disraeli Gears**	$30	Atco 232
7/13/68	1⁴	46	●	3 **Wheels Of Fire** ....[L]	$30	Atco 700 [2]

record 1: studio; record 2: Live At The Fillmore

2/15/69	2²	26	●	4 **Goodbye**	$25	Atco 7001
7/19/69	3	44	●	5 **Best Of Cream** ....[G]	$25	Atco 291
5/2/70	15	21		6 Live Cream ....[L]	$25	Atco 328
4/1/72	27	16		7 Live Cream - Volume II ....[L]	$20	Atco 7005
10/28/72	135	10		8 Heavy Cream ....[G]	$12	Polydor 3502 [2]
2/19/77	165	6		9 Disraeli Gears ....[R]	$10	RSO 3010

new cover features a pink bar across top and a slightly different psychedelic montage

2/19/77	197	4		10 Wheels Of Fire ....[R]	$12	RSO 3802 [2]

new cover has a flat gray finish versus the previous foil finish

As You Said (3,8,10)
Badge (4,5,8) **60**
Blue Condition (2,9)
Born Under A Bad Sign (3,5,8,10)
Cat's Squirrel (1,8)
Crossroads (3,5,8,10) **28**
Dance The Night Away (2,9)

Deserted Cities Of The Heart (3,7,8,10)
Doing That Scrapyard Thing (4,8)
Dreaming (1)
Four Until Late (1)
I Feel Free (1,5,8)
I'm So Glad (1,4,8)
Lawdy Mama (5)

Mother's Lament (2,9)
N.S.U. (1,6)
Outside Woman Blues (2,9)
Passing The Time (3,5,8,10)
Politician (3,4,7,8,10)
Pressed Rat And Warthog (3,10)
Rollin' And Tumblin' (1,6,8)
SWLABR (2,5,8,9)
Sweet Wine (1,6)

Sitting On Top Of The World (3,4,8,10)
Sleepy Time Time (1,6)
Spoonful (3,5,8,10)
Steppin' Out (7)
Strange Brew (2,5,8,9)
Sunshine Of Your Love (2,5,7,8,9) **5**
Sweet Wine (1,6)

Take It Back (2,8,9)
Tales Of Brave Ulysses (2,5,7,8,9)
Those Were The Days (3,8,10)
Toad (1,3,10)
Traintime (3,10)
We're Going Wrong (2,9)
What A Bringdown (4,8)

White Room (3,5,7,8,10) **6**
World Of Pain (2,9)

CREATIVE SOURCE

Vocal R&B-dance group from Los Angeles. Consisted of Don Wyatt, Celeste Rhodes, Steve Flanagan, Barbara Berryman and Barbara Lewis. Formed in 1972 by Ron Townson of The 5th Dimension.

1/19/74	152	10		Creative Source	$12	Sussex 8027

DEBUT DATE	PEAK POS	WKS CHR	GOLD	ARTIST — Album Title	$	Label & Number

CREATIVE SOURCE — Cont'd

Let Me In Your Life · Lovesville · Magic Carpet Ride · Oh Love · **Who Is He And What Is He To You** ***69*** · Wild Flower · You Can't Hide Love · You're Too Good To Be True

CREATURES, The

British duo: Siouxsie (vocals) and her husband, Budgie (percussion) — both of Siouxsie & The Banshees.

DEBUT DATE	PEAK POS	WKS CHR	GOLD	ARTIST — Album Title	$	Label & Number
3/3/90	**197**	2		Boomerang	$12	Geffen 24275

Fruitman · Fury Eyes · Killing Time · Manchild · Morrina · Pity · Pluto Drive · Simoom · Solar Choir · Speeding · Standing There · Strolling Wolf · Untiedundone · Venus Sands · Willow · You!

★★135★★ **CREEDENCE CLEARWATER REVIVAL**

Rock group formed while members attended high school at El Cerrito, California. Consisted of John Fogerty (vocals, guitar), brother Tom Fogerty (guitar), Stu Cook (keyboards, bass) and Doug Clifford (drums). First recorded as the Blue Velvets for the Orchestra label in 1959. Recorded as the Golliwogs for Fantasy in 1964. Renamed Creedence Clearwater Revival in 1967. Tom Fogerty left for a solo career in 1971 and group disbanded in October 1972. Tom Fogerty died on 9/6/90 (age 48) of respiratory failure. Group inducted into the Rock and Roll Hall of Fame in 1993.

DEBUT DATE	PEAK POS	WKS CHR	GOLD	ARTIST — Album Title	$	Label & Number
7/20/68	**52**	73	▲	1 Creedence Clearwater Revival	$15	Fantasy 8382
2/8/69	**7**	88	▲2	2 **Bayou Country**	$15	Fantasy 8387
9/13/69	**1**4	88	▲3	3 **Green River**	$15	Fantasy 8393
12/13/69+	**3**	60	▲2	4 **Willy and the Poorboys**	$15	Fantasy 8397
7/25/70	**1**9	69	▲4	5 **Cosmo's Factory**	$12	Fantasy 8402
				Cosmo is New Orleans record producer Cosmo Matassa		
12/26/70+	**5**	42	▲	6 **Pendulum**	$12	Fantasy 8410
4/29/72	**12**	24	●	7 Mardi Gras	$12	Fantasy 9404
12/2/72+	**15**	37	▲	8 Creedence Gold [G]	$10	Fantasy 9418
7/21/73	**61**	18		9 More Creedence Gold [G]	$10	Fantasy 9430
11/24/73	**143**	10		10 Live In Europe [L]	$12	Fantasy CCR-1 [2]
				recorded in September 1971		
3/6/76	**100**	30	▲2	11 Chronicle (The 20 Greatest Hits) [G]	$12	Fantasy CCR-2 [2]
12/20/80+	**62**	20		12 The Concert [L]	$8	Fantasy 4501
				originally titled *The Royal Albert Hall Concert*, the album was actually recorded at the Oakland Coliseum in 1970		

Bad Moon Rising (3,8,10,11,12) ***2*** · Before You Accuse Me (5) · Bootleg (2,9) · Born On The Bayou (2,8,10,12) · Born To Move (6) · Chameleon (6) · **Commotion** (3,10,11,12) ***30*** · Cotton Fields (4) · Cross-Tie Walker (3) · Don't Look Now (It Ain't You Or Me) (4,9,12) · Door To Door (7,10) · **Down On The Corner** (4,8,11,12) ***3*** · Effigy (4) · Feelin' Blue (4) · **Fortunate Son** (4,9,10,11,12) ***14*** · Get Down Woman (1) · Gloomy (1) · Good Golly, Miss Molly (2,9) · Graveyard Train (2) · **Green River** (3,10,11,12) ***2*** · **Have You Ever Seen The Rain** (6,8,11) ***8*** · Hello Mary Lou (7) · **Hey Tonight** (6,9,10,11) ***flip*** · **I Heard It Through The Grapevine** (5,8,11) ***43*** · **I Put A Spell On You** (1,9,11) ***58*** · It Came Out Of The Sky (4,10) · It's Just A Thought (6) · Keep On Chooglin' (2,10,12) · **Lodi** (3,9,10,11) ***52*** · **Long As I Can See The Light** (5,11) ***flip*** · Lookin' For A Reason (7) · **Lookin' Out My Back Door** (5,9,11) ***2*** · Midnight Special (4,8,12) · Molina (6,9) · My Baby Left Me (5) · Need Someone To Hold (7) · Night Is The Right Time (3,12) · Ninety-Nine And A Half (Won't Do) (1) · Ooby Dooby (5) · Pagan Baby (6) · Penthouse Pauper (2) · Poorboy Shuffle (4) · Porterville (1,9) · **Proud Mary** (2,8,10,11,12) ***2*** · Ramble Tamble (5) · Rude Awakening #2 (6) · **Run Through The Jungle** (5,9,11) ***flip*** · Sail Away (7) · Sailor's Lament (6) · Side Of The Road (4) · Sinister Purpose (3) · **Someday Never Comes** (7,11) ***25*** · **Suzie Q. (Part One)** (1,8,10,11) ***11*** · **Sweet Hitch-Hiker** (7,9,10,11) ***6*** · Take It Like A Friend (7) · Tearin' Up The Country (7) · Tombstone Shadow (3,12) · **Travelin' Band** (5,10,11,12) ***2*** · **Up Around The Bend** (5,9,10,11) ***4*** · Walk On The Water (1) · What Are You Gonna Do (7) · **Who'll Stop The Rain** (5,9,11,12) ***flip*** · (Wish I Could) Hideaway (6) · Working Man (1) · Wrote A Song For Everyone (3)

CRENSHAW, Marshall

Rockabilly singer/songwriter/guitarist. Born in Detroit in 1954. Played John Lennon in the road show of *Beatlemania* in 1976. Appeared in film *Peggy Sue Got Married* and portrayed Buddy Holly in the 1987 film *La Bamba*.

DEBUT DATE	PEAK POS	WKS CHR	GOLD	ARTIST — Album Title	$	Label & Number
5/29/82	**50**	27		1 Marshall Crenshaw	$8	Warner 3673
6/18/83	**52**	14		2 Field Day	$8	Warner 23873
10/12/85	**110**	18		3 Downtown	$8	Warner 25319

All I Know Right Now (2) · Blues Is King (3) · Brand New Lover (1) · Cynical Girl (1) · Distance Between (3) · For Her Love (2) · Girls... (1) · Hold It (2) · I'll Do Anything (1) · I'm Sorry (But So Is Brenda Lee) (3) · Lesson Number One (3) · Like A Vague Memory (3) · Little Wild One (No. 5) (3) · Mary Anne (1) · Monday Morning Rock (2) · Not For Me (1) · One Day With You (2) · One More Reason (2) · Our Town (2) · Right Now (3) · Rockin' Around In N.Y.C. (1) · She Can't Dance (1) · Soldier Of Love (1) · **Someday, Someway** (1) ***36*** · Terrifying Love (3) · There She Goes Again (1) · Try (2) · Usual Thing (1) · (We're Gonna) Shake Up Their Minds (3) · What Time Is It? (2) · Whenever You're On My Mind (2) · Yvonne (3)

CRETONES, The

Los Angeles rock quartet led by Mark Goldenberg and Peter Bernstein.

DEBUT DATE	PEAK POS	WKS CHR	GOLD	ARTIST — Album Title	$	Label & Number
3/29/80	**125**	10		Thin Red Line	$8	Planet 5

Cost Of Love · Everybody's Mad At Katherine · Here Comes The Wave · I Can't Wait · Justine · Mad Love · Mrs. Peel · **Real Love** ***79*** · Thin Red Line · Ways Of The Heart

CREWE, Bob, Generation

Born on 11/12/37 in Newark, New Jersey. Wrote many hit songs beginning with "Silhouettes" in 1957. One of the top producers of the 1960s; worked with The 4 Seasons. Head of several labels, publishing and production companies. Assembled The Bob Crewe Generation, an aggregation of studio musicians.

DEBUT DATE	PEAK POS	WKS CHR	GOLD	ARTIST — Album Title	$	Label & Number
2/25/67	**100**	11		Music To Watch Girls By [I]	$12	DynoVoice 9003

Anna · Concrete And Clay · Felicidade, A · Girls On The Rocks · Lazy Girl, Theme For A · Let's Hang On · Lover's Concerto · Man And A Woman, Theme From A · **Music To Watch Girls By** ***15*** · Winchester Cathedral

CRICKETS, The — see HOLLY, Buddy and VEE, Bobby

CRISS, Peter

Drummer of Kiss (1973-81). Born Peter Crisscoula on 12/20/47 in New York City.

DEBUT DATE	PEAK POS	WKS CHR	GOLD	ARTIST — Album Title	$	Label & Number
10/14/78	**43**	20	▲	Peter Criss	$15	Casablanca 7122

DEBUT DATE	PEAK POS	WKS CHR	GOLD	ARTIST — Album Title	$	Label & Number

CRISS, Peter — Cont'd

Don't You Let Me Down	Hooked On Rock And Roll	I'm Gonna Love You	Rock Me Baby	That's The Kind Of Sugar	Tossin' And Turnin'
Easy Thing	I Can't Stop The Rain	Kiss The Girl Goodbye		Papa Likes	You Matter To Me

CRITTERS, The
New Jersey pop quintet led by Don Ciccone, who later joined The 4 Seasons.

| 9/24/66 | **147** | 2 | | **1 Younger Girl** | $30 | **Kapp 3485** |

Best Love You'll Ever Have	Children And Flowers	Everything But Time	Gone For A While	I Wear A Silly Grin	**Mr. Dieingly Sad** 17
Blow My Mind	Come Back On A Rainy Day	Forever Or No More	He'll Make You Cry	It Just Won't Be That Way	**Younger Girl** 42

★★383★★ CROCE, Jim
Born on 1/10/43 in Philadelphia; killed in plane crash on 9/20/73 in Natchitoches, Louisiana. Vocalist/guitarist/composer. Recorded with wife Ingrid for Capitol in 1968. Lead guitarist on his hits, Maury Muehleisen, was killed in the same crash.

7/1/72+	**1**[5]	93	●	**1 You Don't Mess Around With Jim**	$12	**ABC 756**
2/17/73	**7**	84	●	**2 Life And Times**	$12	**ABC 769**
12/15/73+	**2**[2]	53	●	**3 I Got A Name**	$12	**ABC 797**
10/5/74	**2**[2]	46	●	**4 Photographs & Memories/His Greatest Hits**	[G] $10	**ABC 835**
11/1/75+	**87**	18		**5 The Faces I've Been**	[E] $12	**Lifesong 900** [2]
				recordings from 1961-71; side 4 is Jim's storytelling with musical accompaniment		
2/26/77	**170**	3		**6 Time In A Bottle/Jim Croce's Greatest Love Songs**	[K] $10	**Lifesong 6007**

Age (3)	Chinese, The (5)	I'll Have To Say I Love You	One Less Set Of Footsteps	Speedball Tucker (2)	**Workin' At The Car Wash**
Alabama Rain (2,6)	Country Girl (5)	In A Song (3,4,6) 9	(2,4) 37	Stone Walls (5)	**Blues** (3,4) 32
Army, The (5)	Dreamin' Again (2,6)	**It Doesn't Have To Be**	Operator (That's Not The	These Dreams (2,4,6)	**You Don't Mess Around**
Bad, Bad Leroy Brown	Five Short Minutes (3)	**That Way** (2,6) 64	**Way It Feels)** (1,4,6) 17	This Land Is Your Land (5)	**With Jim** (1,4) 8
(2,4) 1	Good Time Man Like Me	King's Song (5)	Photographs And Memories	Thursday (3,6)	
Big Fat Woman (5)	Ain't Got No Business	Long Time Ago (1,6)	(1,4,6)	**Time In A Bottle** (1,4,6) 1	
Box #10 (1)	(Singin' The Blues) (2)	Lover's Cross (3,4,6)	Pig's Song (5)	Tomorrow's Gonna Be A	
Careful Man (2)	Greenback Dollar (5)	Maybe Tomorrow (5)	Railroad Song (5)	Brighter Day (1)	
Carmella...South Philly (5)	Gunga Din (5)	Mississippi Lady (5)	Railroads And Riverboats (5)	Top Hat Bar And Grille (3)	
Cars And Dates, Chrome	Hard Time Losin' Man (1)	New York's Not My Home	Rapid Roy (The Stock Car	Trucks And Ups (5)	
And Clubs (5)	Hard Way Every Time (3)	(1,4)	Boy) (1,4)	Walkin' Back To Georgia (1)	
Chain Gang Medley (5)	Hey Tomorrow (1)	Next Time, This Time (2)	Recently (3)	Way We Used To (5)	
Charlie Green Play That	**I Got A Name** (3,4) 10	Old Man River (5)	Roller Derby Queen (2,4)	Which Way Are You Goin' (5)	
Slide Trombone (5)	I Remember Mary (5)		Salon And Saloon (3,6)		

CROPPER, Steve — see KING, Albert

CROSBY, Bing
One of the most popular entertainers of the 20th century's first 50 years. Harry Lillis Crosby was born on 5/2/01 (or 04) in Tacoma, Washington. He and singing partner Al Rinker were hired in 1926 by Paul Whiteman; with Harry Barris they became the Rhythm Boys and gained an increasing following. The trio split from Whiteman in 1930, and Bing sang briefly with Gus Arnheim's band. It was his early-1931 smash with Arnheim, "I Surrender, Dear," which earned Bing a CBS radio contract and launched an unsurpassed solo career. Over the next three decades the resonant Crosby baritone and breezy persona sold more than 300 million records and was featured in over 50 movies (won Academy Award for *Going My Way*, 1944). Crosby died of a heart attack on 10/14/77 on a golf course near Madrid, Spain. Won the Lifetime Achievement Grammy in 1962. Ranked as the #1 artist in *Joel Whitburn's Pop Memories 1890-1954* book.

3/31/58	**13**	2		**1 Shillelaghs and Shamrocks**	$25	**Decca 8207**
5/30/64	**116**	7		**2 America, I Hear You Singing**	$12	**Reprise 2020**
				FRANK SINATRA/BING CROSBY/FRED WARING		
3/29/69	**162**	8		**3 Hey Jude/Hey Bing!**	$10	**Amos 7001**
12/10/77+	**98**	9		**4 Bing Crosby's Greatest Hits**	[G] $10	**MCA 3031**
				recordings from 1939-47		
				CHRISTMAS ALBUMS:		
12/22/56	**21**	1		**5 A Christmas Sing With Bing Around The World**	[X] $25	**Decca 8419**
				from the CBS Radio Program; features various choirs		
12/2/57	**1**[1]	7	●	**6 Merry Christmas**	[X-R] $15	**Decca 8128**
				first charted in 1945		
12/15/58+	**2**[1]	4		**7 Merry Christmas**	[X-R] $15	**Decca 8128**
12/28/59+	**17**	2		**8 Merry Christmas**	[X-R] $15	**Decca 8128**
12/19/60	**9**	3		**9 Merry Christmas**	[X-R] $15	**Decca 8128**
12/18/61+	**22**	7		**10 Merry Christmas**	[X-R] $15	**Decca 8128**
12/22/62	**46**	2		**11 Merry Christmas**	[X-R] $15	**Decca 8128**
				Christmas charts: 4/'63, 2/'64, 3/'65, 5/'66, 8/'67, 6/'68, 3/'69, 6/'70, 4/'71, 2/'72, 8/'73, 3/'83, 21/'87, 13/'88, 15/'89, 15/'90, 10/'91, 12/92		
12/22/62	**50**	2		**12 I Wish You A Merry Christmas**	[X] $15	**Warner 1484**
				Christmas charts: 40/'65		

Ac-Cent-Tchu-Ate The	First Noel (5)	It Came Upon A Midnight	Livin' On Lovin' (3)	This Is A Great Country	Where The Blue Of The
Positive (4)	Frosty The Snow Man (12)	Clear (medley) (2)	Lonely Street (3)	(medley) [duet: Bing &	Night Meets The Gold Of
Adeste Fideles (Oh, Come,	God Rest Ye Merry	It's All In The Game (3)	MacNamara's Band (1)	Fred] (2)	The Day (1)
All Ye Faithful) (5,6) 45	Gentlemen (5,6)	It's Beginning To Look Like	Mele Kalikimaka (Merry	This Land Is Your Land	Where The River Shannon
Angels We Have Heard On	Good King Wenceslas (5)	Christmas (6)	Christmas) (6)	[duet: Bing & Fred] (2)	Flows (1)
High (Gloria In Excelsis) (5)	Happy Holiday (5)	It's The Same Old Shillelagh	More And More (3)	Those Were The Days (3)	Whiffenpoof Song (4)
Away In A Manger (5)	Hark! The Herald Angels	(3)	O Holy Night (12)	Thou Descendeth From The	While Shepherds Watched
Blue Skies (4)	Sing (5,12)	Jesus, Sweet Saviour	Oh, Little Town Of	Stars (Tucendi De La Stelli)	Their Sheep (medley) (12)
Both Sides Now (3)	Have Yourself A Merry Little	(Jesus, Sauveur Adorable)	Bethlehem (5)	(5)	**White Christmas** (4,5,6) 7
Carol Of The Bells (5)	Christmas (12)	(5)	Pat-A-Pan (medley) (12)	Too-Ra-Loo-Ra-Loo-Ral	Who Threw The Overalls In
Christmas In Killarney (6)	Hey Jude (3)	Jingle Bells (12)	Pistol Packin' Mama (4)	(That's An Irish Lullaby) (4)	Mrs. Murphy's Chowder?
Dear Old Donegal (1)	Holly And The Ivy (medley)	Joy To The World (5)	Rose Of Tralee (1)	Two Shilleglah O'Sullivan (1)	(1)
Deck The Hall (5)	(12)	Just For Tonight (3)	Santa Claus Is Comin' To	We Three Kings Of Orient	Winter Wonderland (12)
Deep In The Heart Of Texas	Home In The Meadow [duet:	Let It Snow! Let It Snow! Let	Town (6)	Are (5)	With My Shillelagh Under
(4)	Bing & Fred] (2)	It Snow! (12)	**Silent Night** (5,6) 54	What Child Is This? (medley)	My Arm (1)
Did Your Mother Come	I Surrender Dear (4)	Let Us Break Bread	**Silver Bells** (6) 78	(12)	You Are My Sunshine (4)
From Ireland? (1)	I Wish You A Merry	Together (2)	St. Patrick's Day Parade (3)	What Christmas Means To	You Never Had It So Good (2)
Don't Fence Me In (4)	Christmas (12)	Little Drummer Boy (12)	Straight Life (3)	Me (5)	
Donovans, The (1)	I'll Be Home For Christmas	Little Green Apples (3)	Swinging On A Star (4)	When Irish Eyes Are Smiling	
Faith Of Our Fathers (6)	(If Only In My Dreams) (6)	Littlest Angel (12)		(1)	

DEBUT DATE	PEAK POS	WKS CHR	GOLD	ARTIST — Album Title	$	Label & Number

CROSBY, David

Born David Van Cortland on 8/14/41 in Los Angeles. Vocalist/guitarist with The Byrds from 1964-68 and later Crosby, Stills & Nash. Frequent troubles with the law due to drug charges. Film cameos in *Backdraft, Hook* and *Thunderheart*; appeared on TV's *Roseanne*.

3/20/71	12	18	●	1 **If I Could Only Remember My Name**	$15	Atlantic 7203
				with West Coast guests Jerry Garcia, Grace Slick and Joni Mitchell		
				DAVID CROSBY/GRAHAM NASH:		
4/22/72	4	26	●	2 **Graham Nash/David Crosby**	$12	Atlantic 7220
10/11/75	6	31	●	3 **Wind On The Water**	$10	ABC 902
7/24/76	26	15	●	4 **Whistling Down The Wire**	$10	ABC 956
11/19/77	52	8		5 **Crosby/Nash - Live** ....[L]	$10	ABC 1042
10/28/78	150	4		6 **The Best Of Crosby/Nash** ....[G]	$10	ABC 1102
2/18/89	104	10		7 **Oh Yes I Can**	$8	A&M 5232
				DAVID CROSBY		

Bittersweet (3,6)
Blacknotes (2)
Broken Bird (4)
Carry Me (3,6) *52*
Chicago (6)
Cowboy Movie (1)
Cowboy Of Dreams (3)
Dancer (4)
Deja Vu (6)
Distances (7)
Drive My Car (7)
Drop Down Mama (7)
Fieldworker (3,5)
Flying Man (7)
Foolish Man (4,5)
Frozen Smiles (2)
Games (2)
Girl To Be On My Mind (7)
Homeward Through The Haze (3)
I Used To Be A King (5)
I'd Swear There Was Somebody Here (1)
Immigration Man (2,5) *36*
In The Wide Ruin (7)
J.B.'s Blues (4)
Lady Of The Harbor (7)
Laughing (1,6)
Leeshore, The (5)
Love Work Out (3,6)
Low Down Payment (3)
Mama Lion (3,5)
Marguerita (4)
Melody (7)
Monkey And The Underdog (7)
Music Is Love (1) *95*
Mutiny (4)
My Country 'Tis Of Thee (7)
Naked In The Rain (7)
Oh Yes I Can (7)
Orleans (3)
Out Of The Darkness (4,6) *89*
Page 43 (2,5)
Simple Man (5)
Song With No Words (Tree With No Leaves) (1)
Southbound Train (2,6) *99*
Spotlight (4)
Strangers Room (2)
Take The Money And Run (3)
Taken At All (4)
Tamalpais High (At About 3) (1)
Time After Time (4)
To The Last Whale Medley (3,6)
Tracks In The Dust (7)
Traction In The Rain (1)
Wall Song (2,6)
What Are Their Names (1)
Where Will I Be? (2)
Whole Cloth (2)
Wild Tales (6)

★★191★★ CROSBY, STILLS & NASH

Trio formed in Laurel Canyon, California in 1968. Consisted of David Crosby (guitar), Stephen Stills (guitar, keyboards, bass) and Graham Nash (guitar). Crosby had been in The Byrds, Stills had been in Buffalo Springfield, and Nash was with The Hollies. Won the 1969 Best New Artist Grammy Award. Neil Young (guitar), formerly with Buffalo Springfield, joined group in 1969, left in 1974. Reunion in 1988.

6/28/69	6	107	●	1 **Crosby, Stills & Nash**	$20	Atlantic 8229
4/4/70	1[1]	97	▲[7]	2 **Deja Vu** *	$15	Atlantic 7200
4/24/71	1[1]	42	▲[4]	3 **4 Way Street** * ....[L]	$15	Atlantic 902 [2]
9/7/74	1[1]	27	▲[6]	4 **So Far** * ....[G]	$10	Atlantic 18100
7/9/77	2[4]	33	▲[4]	5 **CSN**	$10	Atlantic 19104
1/10/81	122	5		6 **Replay** ....[K]	$8	Atlantic 16026
				cuts from C.S.& N. and Stephen Stills albums		
7/17/82	8	41	▲	7 **Daylight Again**	$8	Atlantic 19360
7/2/83	43	12		8 **Allies** ....[L]	$8	Atlantic 80075
12/3/88+	16	22	▲	9 **American Dream** *	$8	Atlantic 81888
				***CROSBY, STILLS, NASH & YOUNG**		
7/14/90	57	11		10 **Live It Up**	$12	Atlantic 82107
1/4/92	109	2	●	11 **CSN** ....[G]	$56	Atlantic 19104 [4]

After The Dolphin (10,11)
Almost Cut My Hair (2,11)
America's Children (medley) (3)
American Dream (9)
Another Sleep Song (11)
Anything At All (5)
Arrows (10)
As I Come Of Age (11)
Barrel Of Pain (8)
Barrel Of Pain (Half-Life) (11)
Bittersweet (11)
Black Queen (11)
Blackbird (8,11)
Carried Away (5)
Carry Me [duet: Crosby/Nash] (11) *52*
Carry On (2,3,6,11)
Cathedral (9)
Change Partners [solo: Stephen Stills] (6,11) *43*
Chicago [solo: Graham Nash] (3,11) *35*
Clear Blue Skies (9)
Cold Rain (5,11)
Compass (9)
Country Girl Medley (2)
Cowboy Of Dreams (11)
Cowgirl In The Sand (11)
Dark Star (5,8,11)
Daylight Again (medley) (7,11)
Dear Mr. Fantasy (11)
Deja Vu (2,4,11)
Delta (7,11)
Don't Let It Bring You Down (3)
Don't Say Goodbye (9)
Drive My Car (11)
Drivin' Thunder (9)
Everybody I Love You (2)
Fair Game (5) *43*
Feel Your Love (9)
50/50 (11)
Find The Cost Of Freedom (3,4,7,11)
First Things First (6)
For What It's Worth (8)
49 Bye-Byes (1,3)
4 + 20 (2,11)
Got It Made (9,11) *69*
(Got To Keep) Open (10)
Guinnevere (1,4,11)
Haven't We Lost Enough? (10,11)
He Played Real Good For Free (8)
Helpless (2,4,11)
Helplessly Hoping (1,4,11)
Homeward Through The Haze (11)
Horses Through A Rainstorm (11)
House Of Broken Dreams (10)
I Give You Give Blind (5,6)
I Used To Be A King (11)
I'd Swear There Was Somebody Here (11)
If Anybody Had A Heart (11)
Immigration Man [duet: Crosby/Nash] (3,4,7,11)
In My Dreams (5,11)
Into The Darkness (7)
It Doesn't Matter [solo: Stephen Stills] (11) *61*
Johnny's Garden (11)
Just A Song Before I Go (5,6,11) *7*
Lady Of The Island (1,11)
Laughing (11)
Lee Shore (3,11)
Live It Up (10)
Long Time Gone (1,3,11)
Love The One You're With [solo: Stephen Stills] (3,6,11) *14*
Man In The Mirror (11)
Marrakesh Express (1,6,11) *28*
Might As Well Have A Good Time (7)
Military Madness [solo: Graham Nash] (11) *73*
Music Is Love [solo: David Crosby] (11) *95*
My Love Is A Gentle Thing (11)
Name Of Love (9)
Night Song (9)
Nighttime For The Generals (9)
Ohio (3,4,11) *14*
Old Times Good Times (11)
On The Way Home (3)
Our House (2,4,11) *30*
Page 43 (11)
Pre-Road Downs (1,3,6)
Prison Song (11)
Questions (11)
Raise A Voice (8)
Right Between The Eyes (9)
Run From Tears (5)
See The Changes (5,11)
Shadow Captain (5,6,8,11)
Shadowland (9)
Simple Man (11)
Since I Met You (7)
So Begins The Task (11)
Soldiers Of Peace (9,11)
Song For Susan (7)
Song With No Words (Tree With No Leaves) (11)
Southbound Train [duet: Crosby/Nash] (11) *99*
Southern Cross (7,11) *18*
Southern Man (3)
Straight Line (10)
Suite: Judy Blue Eyes (1,3,4,11) *21*
Taken At All (11)
Teach Your Children (2,3,4,11) *16*
That Girl (11)
This Old House (9)
Thoroughfare Gap (11)
To The Last Whale Medley (6,11)
Tomboy (10)
Too Much Love To Hide (7) *69*
Tracks In The Dust (11)
Triad (3)
Turn Back The Pages [solo: Stephen Stills] (11) *84*
Turn Your Back On Love (7,8)
Urge For Going (11)
War Games (8) *45*
Wasted On The Way (7,8,11) *9*
We Can Change The World (medley) (11)
Where Will I Be? (11)
Wild Tales (11)
Woodstock (2,4,11) *11*
Wooden Ships (1,4,11)
Word Game (11)
You Are Alive (7)
You Don't Have To Cry (1,11)
Yours And Mine (10,11)

CROSS, Christopher

Born Christopher Geppert on 5/3/51 in San Antonio, Texas. Formed own group with Rob Meurer (keyboards), Andy Salmon (bass) and Tommy Taylor (drums) in 1973. Won the 1980 Best New Artist Grammy Award.

2/16/80	6	116	▲[4]	1 **Christopher Cross**	$8	Warner 3383
				1980 Grammy winner: Album of the Year		
2/19/83	11	31	●	2 **Another Page**	$8	Warner 23757
11/30/85	127	6		3 **Every Turn Of The World**	$8	Warner 25341

All Right (2) *12*
Baby Says No (2)
Charm The Snake (3) *68*
Deal 'Em Again (2)
Don't Say Goodbye (3)
Every Turn Of The World (3)
I Hear You Call (3)
I Really Don't Know Anymore (1)
It's You That Really Matters (3)
Light Is On (1)
Long World (2)
Love Found A Home (3)
Love Is Love (In Any Language) (3)
Minstrel Gigolo (1)
Nature Of The Game (2)
Never Be The Same (1) *15*
No Time For Talk (2) *33*
Open Your Heart (3)
Poor Shirley (1)
Ride Like The Wind (1) *2*
Sailing (1) *1*
Say You'll Be Mine (1) *20*
Spinning (3)
Swing Street (3)
Talking In My Sleep (2)
That Girl (3)
Think Of Laura (2) *9*
What Am I Supposed To Believe (2)
Words Of Wisdom (2)

DEBUT DATE	PEAK POS	WKS CHR	GOLD	ARTIST — Album Title	$	Label & Number

CROSS COUNTRY
Jay Siegel, Mitch and Phil Margo; all formerly with The Tokens.

DEBUT DATE	PEAK POS	WKS CHR	GOLD	ARTIST — Album Title	$	Label & Number
10/13/73	198	2		Cross Country	$12	Atco 7024

Ball Song / Choir Boy / Cross Country / Extended Wings / Fall Song / **In The Midnight Hour** *30* / Just A Thought / Smile Song / Tastes So Good To Me / Things With Wings / Today

CROW
Rock-blues quintet from Minneapolis — Dave Wagner, lead singer. Drummer Denny Craswell was a member of The Castaways.

DEBUT DATE	PEAK POS	WKS CHR	GOLD	ARTIST — Album Title	$	Label & Number
9/13/69+	69	24		1 Crow Music	$12	Amaret 5002
6/6/70	181	4		2 Crow By Crow	$12	Amaret 5006

Annie Fannie (medley) (2) / Busy Day (1) / Colors (2) / **Cottage Cheese** (2) *56* / Da Da Song (1) / Death Down To Your Soul (medley) (2) / **Evil Woman Don't Play Your Games With Me** (1) *19* / Get Yourself A Number (medley) (2) / Gone, Gone, Gone (2) / Gonna Leave A Mark (1) / Heading North (2) / I Stand To Blame (2) / Last Prayer (medley) (2) / Listen To The Bop (1) / Rollin' (1) / Sleepy Woman (1) / Slow Down (2) / Smokey Joe (2) / Thoughts (1) / Time To Make A Turn (1) / White Eyes (1)

CROWBAR — see KING BISCUIT BOY

CROWDED HOUSE
New Zealand/Australian trio founded by former Split Enz members Neil Finn (vocals, guitar, piano) and Paul Hester (drums), with Nick Seymour (bass). Neil's brother, Tim Finn (also of Split Enz) joined the band in 1991.

DEBUT DATE	PEAK POS	WKS CHR	GOLD	ARTIST — Album Title	$	Label & Number
8/30/86+	12	58	▲	1 Crowded House	$8	Capitol 12485
7/23/88	40	19		2 Temple of Low Men	$8	Capitol 48763
7/20/91	83	17		3 Woodface	$12	Capitol 93559

2 covers released — jewel box and digipak

All I Ask (3) / As Sure As I Am (3) / **Better Be Home Soon** (2) *42* / Chocolate Cake (3) / **Don't Dream It's Over** (1) *2* / **Fall At Your Feet** (3) *75* / Fame Is (3) / Four Seasons In One Day (3) / Hole In The River (1) / How Will You Go (3) / I Feel Possessed (2) / I Walk Away (1) / In The Lowlands (2) / Into Temptation (2) / It's Only Natural (3) / Italian Plastic (3) / Kill Eye (3) / Love This Life (2) / Love You 'Till The Day I Die (1) / Mansion In The Slums (2) / Mean To Me (1) / Never Be The Same (2) / Now We're Getting Somewhere (1) / She Goes On (3) / Sister Madly (2) / **Something So Strong** (1) *7* / Tall Trees (3) / That's What I Call Love (1) / There Goes God (1) / Tombstone (1) / Weather With You (3) / When You Come (2) / Whispers And Moans (3) / **World Where You Live** (1) *65*

CROWELL, Rodney
Born on 8/7/50 in Houston. Country singer/songwriter/guitarist. Married Rosanne Cash in 1979 and divorced in April 1992. Wrote the Dirt Band's "American Dream" and many other country hits.

DEBUT DATE	PEAK POS	WKS CHR	GOLD	ARTIST — Album Title	$	Label & Number
4/26/80	155	10		1 But What Will The Neighbors Think	$8	Warner 3407
10/3/81	105	8		2 Rodney Crowell	$8	Warner 3587
8/23/86	177	5		3 Street Language	$8	Columbia 40116
10/6/90	180	2		4 Keys To The Highway	$12	Columbia 45242
6/6/92	155	9		5 Life Is Messy	$12	Columbia 47985

Ain't No Money (1) / All You've Got To Do (2) / Alone But Not Alone (5) / Answer Is Yes (5) / **Ashes By Now** (1) *37* / Ballad Of Fast Eddie (3) / Best I Can (3) / Blues In The Daytime (1) / Don't Let Your Feet Slow You Down (4) / Don't Need No Other Now (2) / Faith Is Mine (4) / Heartbroke (1) / Here Come The 80's (1) / I Guess We've Been Together For Too Long (4) / I Hardly Know How To Be Myself (5) / If Looks Could Kill (4) / It Don't Get Better Than This (5) / It's Not For Me To Judge (5) / It's Only Rock 'N' Roll (1) / Just Wanta Dance (2) / Let Freedom Ring (3) / Let's Make Trouble (5) / Life Is Messy (5) / Looking For You (3) / Lovin' All Night (5) / Many A Long & Lonesome Highway (4) / Maybe Next Time (5) / My Past Is Present (4) / Now That We're Alone (4) / Oh King Richard (3) / Oh, What A Feeling (1) / Old Pipeliner (2) / On A Real Good Night (1) / One About England (1) / Only Two Hearts (2) / Past Like A Mask (3) / Queen Of Hearts (1) / Shame On The Moon (2) / She Ain't Going Nowhere (2) / She Loves The Jerk (3) / Soul Searchin' (4) / Stars On The Water (2) / Stay (Don't Be Cruel) (3) / Tell Me The Truth (4) / Things I Wish I'd Said (4) / 'Till I Gain Control Again (2) / Victim Or A Fool (3) / We Gotta Go On Meeting Like This (4) / What Kind Of Love (5) / When I'm Free Again (3) / When The Blue Hour Comes (3) / You Been On My Mind (4)

CROWN HEIGHTS AFFAIR
R&B-disco group from Bedford-Stuyvesant, New York, formed as the Neu Day Express, and led by vocalist Phil Thomas.

DEBUT DATE	PEAK POS	WKS CHR	GOLD	ARTIST — Album Title	$	Label & Number
10/4/75	121	17		1 Dreaming A Dream	$10	De-Lite 2017
3/29/80	148	12		2 Sure Shot	$8	De-Lite 9517

Dreaming A Dream (1) *43* / **Every Beat Of My Heart** (1) *83* / Feeling Tall (1) / Foxy (1) / I Am Me (1) / I Don't Want To Change You (2) / I See The Light (2) / Na, Na, Hey, Hey (1) / Picture Show (1) / Sure Shot (2) / Tell Me You Love Me (2) / Use Your Body & Soul (2) / You Gave Me Love (2) / You Smiled (1) / You've Been Gone (2)

CRUISE, Julee
Singer/actress. Born in Creston, Iowa. Appeared on the 1990 TV series *Twin Peaks*. Married to Edward Grinnan, an editor for Norman Vincent Peale's magazine *Guidepost*. Joined The B-52's in 1992.

DEBUT DATE	PEAK POS	WKS CHR	GOLD	ARTIST — Album Title	$	Label & Number
6/2/90	74	20		Floating Into The Night	$12	Warner 25859

lyrics and co-production by movie/TV producer/director David Lynch (*Twin Peaks*)

Falling / Floating / I Float Alone / I Remember / Into The Night / Mysteries Of Love / Nightingale, The / Rockin' Back Inside My Heart / Swan, The / World Spins

★★163★★ CRUSADERS, The
Instrumental jazz-oriented group formed in Houston, as the Swingsters, in the early '50s. To California in the early '60s, name changed to Jazz Crusaders. Became The Crusaders in 1971. Included Joe Sample (keyboards), Wilton Felder (reeds), Nesbert "Stix" Hooper (drums) and Wayne Henderson (trombone). Henderson left in 1975. Hooper left in 1983. Sample and Felder reunited with a new lineup in 1991.

THE JAZZ CRUSADERS:

DEBUT DATE	PEAK POS	WKS CHR	GOLD	ARTIST — Album Title	$	Label & Number
1/4/69	184	2		1 Powerhouse [I]	$20	Pacific Jz. 20136
10/17/70+	90	16		2 Old Socks, New Shoes...New Socks, Old Shoes [I]	$12	Chisa 804

CRUSADERS:

DEBUT DATE	PEAK POS	WKS CHR	GOLD	ARTIST — Album Title	$	Label & Number
6/26/71	168	4		3 Pass The Plate [I]	$12	Chisa 807
3/4/72	96	29		4 Crusaders 1 [I]	$12	Blue Th. 6001 [2]
3/10/73	45	29		5 The 2nd Crusade [I]	$12	Blue Th. 7000 [2]
11/24/73	173	14		6 Unsung Heroes [I]	$12	Blue Thumb 6007

DEBUT DATE	PEAK POS	WKS CHR	GOLD		ARTIST — Album Title	$	Label & Number
					CRUSADERS, The — Cont'd		
4/13/74	73	20		7	Scratch .... [I-L]	$10	Blue Thumb 6010
10/26/74	31	23	●	8	Southern Comfort .... [I]	$10	Blue Th. 9002 [2]
8/23/75	26	17		9	Chain Reaction .... [I]	$10	Blue Thumb 6022
5/22/76	38	18		10	Those Southern Knights .... [I]	$10	Blue Thumb 6024
12/18/76+	122	10		11	The Best Of The Crusaders .... [G]	$12	Blue Th. 6027 [2]
6/18/77	41	15		12	Free As The Wind .... [I]	$10	Blue Thumb 6029
7/15/78	34	18	●	13	Images .... [I]	$10	Blue Thumb 6030
6/9/79	18	39	●	14	Street Life .... [I]	$8	MCA 3094
					with guest vocalist Randy Crawford on "Street Life"		
7/12/80	29	16		15	Rhapsody And Blues .... [I]	$8	MCA 5124
					with guest vocalist Bill Withers on "Soul Shadows"		
10/10/81	59	16		16	Standing Tall	$8	MCA 5254
					with guest vocalist Joe Cocker		
7/17/82	144	7		17	Royal Jam .... [L]	$10	MCA 8017 [2]
					with B.B. King & The Royal Philharmonic Orchestra		
4/21/84	79	22		18	Ghetto Blaster	$8	MCA 5429
5/11/91	174	2		19	Healing The Wounds .... [I]	$12	GRP 9638

Ain't Gon' Change A Thang (5)
And Then There Was The Blues (10)
Ballad For Joe (Louis) (8,11)
Bayou Bottoms (13)
Better Not Look Down (17)
Burnin' Up The Carnival (17)
Carnival Of The Night (14)
Cause We've Ended As Lovers (19)
Chain Reaction (9,11)
Cookie Man (1)
Cosmic Reign (13)
Covert Action (13)
Creole (9)
Crossfire (6)
Dead End (18)
Do You Remember When? (5,11)
Don't Let It Get You Down (5,11) 86
Double Bubble (8)
Dream Street (18)
Eleanor Rigby (7)
Elegant Evening (15)
Fairy Tales (13)
Fancy Dance (1)
Feel It (12)
Feeling Funky (10)
Fire Water (1)

Fly With Wings Of Love (17)
Free As The Wind (12)
Freedom Sound (6)
Full Moon (4)
Funny Shuffle (2)
Georgia Cottonfield (4)
Get On The Soul Ship (It's Sailing) (8)
Give It Up (9)
Goin' Down South (3)
Golden Slumbers (2)
Gotta Get It On (5)
Gotta Lotta Shakalada (18)
Greasy Spoon (3,8,11)
Hallucinate (9)
Hard Times (2,6,7,11)
Healing The Wounds (19)
Heavy Up (Don't Get Light With Me) (6)
Hey Jude (1)
Hold On (17)
Honky Tonk Struttin' (15)
Hot's It (9)
Hustler, The (14)
I Felt The Love (9,12)
I Just Can't Leave Your Love Alone (17)
I'm So Glad I'm Standing Here Today (16,17) 97
In The Middle Of The River (6)

It Happens Everyday (12)
It's Just Gotta Be That Way (4)
Jackson! (2)
Jazz! (2)
Journey From Within (5)
Keep That Same Old Feeling (10,11)
Last Call (15,17)
Lay It On The Line (6)
Let's Boogie (8)
Lilies Of The Nile (8)
Listen And You'll See (3)
Little Things Mean A Lot (19)
Longest Night (16)
Look Beyond The Hill (5)
Love And Peace (1)
Love Can't Grow Where The Rain Won't Fall (2)
Love Is Blue (L'Amour Est Bleu) (1)
Luckenbach, Texas (Back To The Basics Of Love) (16)
Maputo (19)
Marcella's Dream (13)
Mellow Out (9)
Mercy, Mercy, Mercy (19)
Merry-Go-Round (13)
Message From The Inner City (5)
Mosadi (Woman) (4)

Mr. Cool (18)
Mud Hole (4)
My Lady (14)
My Mama Told Me So (10)
Mystique Blues (4)
Never Make A Move Too Soon (17)
New Moves (18)
Night Faces (14)
Night Ladies (18)
Night Theme (6)
Nite Crawler (12)
No Place To Hide (5)
Now I Lay Me Down To Sleep (6)
One Day I'll Fly Away (17)
Pass The Plate Medley (3)
Pessimisticism (19)
Promises, Promises (1)
Put It Where You Want It (4,11) 52
Rainbow Visions (9)
Rainy Night In Georgia (3)
Rhapsody And Blues (15)
River Rat (12)
Rodeo Drive (High Steppin') (14)
Running Man (19)
Scratch (7,11) 81
Search For Soul (5)
Serenity (10)

Shade Of Blues (4)
Shake Dance (19)
Snowflake (13)
So Far Away (4,7,11)
Soul Caravan (9,11)
Soul Shadows (15)
Southern Comfort (8)
Spiral (10)
Standing Tall (16)
Sting Ray (5)
Stomp And Buck Dance (8,11)
Street Life (14,17) 36
Sugar Cane (9)
Sunshine In Your Eyes (16)
Super-Stuff (8)
Sweet Gentle Love (15)
Sweet 'N' Sour (12)
Sweet Revival (2)
Take It Or Leave It (5)
Thank You Falettinme Be Mice Elf Agin (2)
That's How I Feel (4,11)
This Old World's Too Funky For Me (16)
Three Children (4)
Thrill Is Gone (17)
'Til The Sun Shines (10)
Time Bomb (8)
Time Has No Ending (2)

Tomorrow Where Are You? (5)
Tough Talk (5)
Treat Me Like Ye Treat Yaself (3)
Unsung Heroes (6)
Upstairs (1)
Way Back Home (2,7,11) 90
Way We Was (12)
Well's Gone Dry (8)
When There's Love Around (8)
Where There's A Will There's A Way (3)
Whispering Pines (8)
Why Do You Laugh At Me? (2)
Young Rabbits--'71-'72 (3)
Zalal'e Mini (Take It Easy) (18)

CRUZADOS

Los Angeles rock group: Tito Larriva (lead singer), Chalo Quintana, Tony Marsico, Steve Hufsteter.

DEBUT DATE	PEAK POS	WKS CHR			ARTIST — Album Title	$	Label & Number
11/2/85	76	18		1	Cruzados	$8	Arista 8383
8/1/87	106	21		2	After Dark	$8	Arista 8439

Bed Of Lies (2)
Blue Sofa (Still A Fool) (2)
Chains Of Freedom (2)
Cryin' Eyes (1)

Flor De Mal (1)
Hanging Out In California (1)
I Want Your World To Turn (2)

Just Like Roses (1)
Last Ride (2)
Motorcycle Girl (1)
1,000 Miles (1)

Rising Sun (1)
Road Of Truth (2)
Seven Summers (1)
Small Town Love (2)

Some Day (1)
Summer's Come, Summer's Gone (2)
Time For Waiting (2)

Wasted Years (1)
Young And On Fire (2)

CRYAN' SHAMES, The

Six-man rock band from Chicago — Thomas Doody, lead singer.

DEBUT DATE	PEAK POS	WKS CHR			ARTIST — Album Title	$	Label & Number
5/13/67	192	4		1	Sugar & Spice	$20	Columbia 9389
1/13/68	156	5		2	A Scratch In The Sky	$20	Columbia 9586
2/15/69	184	9		3	Synthesis	$20	Columbia 9719

Baltimore Oriole (3)
Ben Franklin's Almanac (1)
Carol For Lorelei (2)
Cobblestone Road (2)
Dennis Dupree From Danville (3)
First Train To California (3)

Greenburg, Glickstein, Charles, David Smith & Jones (3)
Heat Wave (1)
Hey Joe (Where You Gonna Go) (1)
I Wanna Meet You (1) 85
I Was Lonely When (2)

If I Needed Someone (1)
In The Cafe (2)
It Could Be We're In Love (2) 85
It's All Right (3)
July (1)
Let's Get Together (3)
Master's Fool (3)

Mr. Unreliable (2)
Painter, The (3)
Sailing Ship (2)
She Don't Care About Time (1)
Sugar And Spice (1) 49
Sunshine Psalm (2)
Sweet Girl Of Mine (3)

Symphony Of The Wind (3)
Town I'd Like To Go Back To (2)
20th Song (3)
Up On The Roof (2) 85
We Could Be Happy (1)
We Gotta Get Out Of This Place (1)

We'll Meet Again (1)
Your Love (3)

CRYSTAL, Billy

Actor/comedian born on 3/14/48 in Long Beach, New York. Cast member of TV's *Soap*, 1977-81, and a regular on *Saturday Night Live*, 1984-85. Star of several films.

DEBUT DATE	PEAK POS	WKS CHR			ARTIST — Album Title	$	Label & Number
9/21/85	65	13			Mahvelous! .... [C]	$8	A&M 5096

Buddy Young, Jr. Face

Fernando's Special Gift
Godammit, You...Bastard

Howard Cosell, Right There!
I Hate When That Happens

"Live" From The Bottom Line
Mind Of Its Own

Now!
Sammy For Africa

Where's Your Messiah Now?
You Look Marvelous 58

CRYSTALS, The

Female vocal group from Brooklyn. Consisted of Barbara Alston, Lala Brooks, Dee Dee Kennibrew, Mary Thomas and Patricia Wright. Discovered by producer Phil Spector.

DEBUT DATE	PEAK POS	WKS CHR			ARTIST — Album Title	$	Label & Number
3/16/63	131	2			He's A Rebel	$200	Philles 4001

Another Country-Another World
Frankenstein Twist

He Hit Me
He's A Rebel 1

He's Sure The Boy I Love 11
I Love You Eddie

No One Ever Tells You
Oh Yeah, Maybe Baby
On Broadway

There's No Other (Like My Baby) 20
Uptown 13

What A Nice Way To Turn Seventeen

DEBUT DATE	PEAK POS	WKS CHR	G O L D	ARTIST — Album Title	$	Label & Number

CUBA, Joe, Sextet
Raunchy Latin-rock combo.

DEBUT DATE	PEAK POS	WKS CHR	GOLD	ARTIST — Album Title	$	Label & Number
9/17/66	119	3		1 We Must Be Doing Something Right! .... [F]	$20	Tico 1133
1/7/67	131	6		2 Wanted Dead Or Alive (Bang! Bang! Push, Push, Push) .... [F]	$20	Tico 1146

Alafla (2)
Arecibo (1)
Asi Soy (2)
"Bang" "Bang" (2) 63

Bochinchosa (1)
Clave Mambo (1)
Cocinando (2)
El Pito (I'll Never Go Back To Georgia) (1)

Incomparable (1)
La Malanga Brava (1)
Lo Bueno Ya Viene (1)
Mujer Divina (Petite) (2)

My Wonderful You (Baby When I'm Down) (1)
Oh Yeah! (2) 62
Pruebalo (1)

Push, Push, Push (2)
Que Son Uno (2)
Si Te Dicen (1)
Sock It To Me (2)

Triste (2)
Y Tu Abuela Donde Esta (1)
Ya No Aguanto Mas (1)

CUFF LINKS, The
Group is actually the overdubbed voices of Ron Dante (The Archies).

DEBUT DATE	PEAK POS	WKS CHR	GOLD	ARTIST — Album Title	$	Label & Number
12/6/69+	138	11		Tracy	$20	Decca 75160

All The Young Women
Early In The Morning
Heather

I Remember
Lay A Little Love On Me

Put A Little Love In Your Heart

Sally Ann (You're Such A Pretty Baby)
Tracy 9

Sweet Caroline (Good Times Never Seemed So Good)

When Julie Comes Around 41
Where Do You Go?

CULT, The
Nucleus of British rock group: Ian Astbury (vocals), Billy Duffy (guitar) and Jamie Stewart (bass; left in 1989). One-time drummer Matt Sorum joined Guns N' Roses in 1990.

DEBUT DATE	PEAK POS	WKS CHR	GOLD	ARTIST — Album Title	$	Label & Number
12/28/85+	87	34	●	1 Love	$8	Sire 25359
4/25/87	38	32	●	2 Electric	$8	Sire 25555
4/29/89	10	33	▲	3 Sonic Temple	$8	Sire 25871
10/12/91	25	12		4 Ceremony	$12	Sire 26673

American Horse (3)
Aphrodisiac Jacket (2)
Automatic Blues (3)
Bad Fun (2)
Bangkok Rain (4)
Big Neon Glitter (1)
Black Angel (1)
Born To Be Wild (2)
Brother Wolf, Sister Moon (1)

Ceremony (4)
Earth Mofo (4)
Edie (Ciao Baby) (3) 93
Electric Ocean (2)
Fire Woman (3) 46
Full Tilt (4)
Heart Of Soul (4)
Hollow Man (3)
If (4)

Indian (4)
King Contrary Man (2)
Lil' Devil (2)
Love (1)
Love Removal Machine (2)
Memphis Hip Shake (2)
New York City (3)
Nirvana (1)
Outlaw (2)

Peace Dog (2)
Phoenix, The (1)
Rain (1)
Revolution (1)
She Sells Sanctuary (1)
Soldier Blue (3)
Soul Asylum (3)
Sun King (3)
Sweet Salvation (4)

Sweet Soul Sister (3)
Wake Up Time For Freedom (3)
White (4)
Wild Flower (2)
Wild Hearted Son (4)
Wonderland (4)

CULTURE CLUB
Formed in London in 1981. Consisted of George "Boy George" O'Dowd (b: 6/14/61; vocals), Roy Hay (guitar, keyboards), Michael Craig (bass) and Jon Moss (drums). Designer Sue Clowes originated distinctive costuming for the group. Won the 1983 Best New Artist Grammy Award. Boy George went solo in 1987.

DEBUT DATE	PEAK POS	WKS CHR	GOLD	ARTIST — Album Title	$	Label & Number
1/8/83	14	88	▲	1 Kissing To Be Clever............................	$8	Epic 38398
11/5/83+	2⁶	59	▲⁴	2 Colour By Numbers	$8	Epic 39107
11/24/84	26	20	▲	3 Waking Up With The House On Fire........	$8	Virgin 39881
4/26/86	32	17		4 From Luxury To Heartache...................	$8	Virgin 40345

Black Money (2)
Boy, Boy, (I'm The Boy) (1)
Changing Every Day (2)
Church Of The Poison Mind (2) 10
Come Clean (4)
Crime Time (3)
Dangerous Man (3)
Dive, The (3)

Do You Really Want To Hurt Me (1) 2
Don't Talk About It (3)
God Thank You Woman (4)
Gusto Blusto (4)
Heaven's Children (4)
Hello Goodbye (3)
I Pray (4)
I'll Tumble 4 Ya (1) 9

I'm Afraid Of Me (1)
It's A Miracle (2) 13
Karma Chameleon (2) 1
Love Twist (1)
Mannequin (3)
Medal Song (4)
Miss Me Blind (2) 5
Mistake No. 3 (3) 33
Mister Man (3)

Move Away (4) 12
Reasons (4)
Sexuality (4)
Stormkeeper (2)
Take Control (1)
That's The Way (I'm Only Trying To Help You) (2)
Time (Clock Of The Heart) (1) 2

Too Bad (4)
Unfortunate Thing (3)
Victims (2)
War Song (3) 17
White Boy (1)
White Boys Can't Control It (1)
Work On Me Baby (4)
You Know I'm Not Crazy (1)

CUMMINGS, Burton
Born on 12/31/47 in Winnipeg, Canada. Lead singer of The Guess Who.

DEBUT DATE	PEAK POS	WKS CHR	GOLD	ARTIST — Album Title	$	Label & Number
11/6/76+	30	20		1 Burton Cummings	$10	Portrait 34261
7/9/77	51	6		2 My Own Way To Rock	$10	Portrait 34698

Burch Magic (1)
Charlemagne (2)
Come On By (2)
Framed (2)

Gotta Find Another Way (2)
I'm Scared (1) 61
Is It Really Right (1)

My Own Way To Rock (2) 74
Never Had A Lady Before (2)
Niki Hokey (1)

Nothing Rhymed (1)
Song For Him (2)
Stand Tall (1) 10

Sugartime Flashback Joys (1)
That's Enough (1)
Timeless Love (2)

Try To Find Another Man (2)
You Ain't Seen Nothin' Yet (1)
Your Back Yard (1)

CURB, Mike, Congregation
Mike was born on 12/24/44 in Savannah, Georgia. Pop music mogul and politician. President of MGM Records, 1969-73. Elected lieutenant governor of California in 1978. Formed own company, Curb Records.

DEBUT DATE	PEAK POS	WKS CHR	GOLD	ARTIST — Album Title	$	Label & Number
7/4/70	105	5		1 Come Together...................................	$8	CoBurt 1002
11/21/70	185	2		2 Sweet Gingerbread Man	$8	CoBurt 1003
3/13/71	117	8		3 Burning Bridges and Other Great Motion Picture Themes	$8	MGM 4761

All For The Love Of Sunshine (1)
Arizona (medley) (1)
Bringing In The Sheaves (2)
Burning Bridges (2,3) 34
Come Together (medley) (1)
Dirty Dingus Magee (3)
Everything Is Beautiful (2)
Games People Play (1)

Give Peace A Chance (medley) (1)
Happy Together (medley) (1)
Hey Jude (medley) (1)
I Was Born In Love With You (3)
It Was A Good Time (Rosy's Theme) (3)
Lead Us On (2)
Let It Be (2,3)

Let's Get Together (medley) (1)
Long And Winding Road (1)
Long Haired Lover From Liverpool (3)
Midnight Special (medley) (1)
My Home Town (2)
No Blade Of Grass (3)
Put A Little Love In Your Heart (1)

Raindrops Keep Fallin' On My Head (1)
Spirit In The Sky (2)
Suspicious Minds (medley) (1)
Sweet Caroline (Good Times Never Seemed So Good) (medley) (1)
Sweet Gingerbread Man (2,3)
Teach Your Children (1)

This Land Is Your Land (2)
Walk A Mile In My Shoes (1)
We'll Sing In The Sunshine (1)
(Where Do I Begin) Love Story (3)
Where Was I When The Parade Went By? (The Major) (3)

You Don't Need A Reason For Love (medley) (1)

★★392★★ CURE, The
British techno-rock group led by Robert Smith (b: 4/21/59; vocals, guitar). Producer and early member Phil Thornalley joined Johnny Hates Jazz as lead singer in 1989. Co-founder/keyboardist Laurence Tolhurst left by 1990.

DEBUT DATE	PEAK POS	WKS CHR	GOLD	ARTIST — Album Title	$	Label & Number
8/13/83	179	8		1 The Walk .... [M]	$8	Sire 23928
2/25/84	181	5		2 Japanese Whispers .... [K]	$8	Sire 25076
				features cuts from mini LP *The Walk* and 2 1983 maxi-singles		
6/23/84	180	4		3 The Top	$8	Sire 25086
10/5/85	59	49	●	4 The Head On The Door	$8	Elektra 60435

DEBUT DATE	PEAK POS	WKS CHR	GOLD	ARTIST — Album Title	$	Label & Number

CURE, The — Cont'd

| 6/14/86 | 48 | 57 ▲ | 5 | Standing On A Beach - The Singles .... [K] | $8 | Elektra 60477 |

a compilation of all their singles (1979-85)

6/20/87	35	52 ▲	6	Kiss Me, Kiss Me, Kiss Me	$10	Elektra 60737 [2]
5/20/89	12	55 ▲	7	Disintegration	$8	Elektra 60855
11/17/90	14	41 ▲	8	Mixed Up .... [G]	$12	Elektra 60978

extended mixes of most of their hits

| 5/9/92 | 2[1] | 26 ▲ | 9 | Wish .... | $12 | Fiction 61309 |

All I Want (6)
Apart (9)
Baby Screams (4)
Bananafishbones (3)
Birdmad Girl (3)
Blood, The (4)
Boys Don't Cry (5)
Catch (6)
Caterpillar, The (3,5,8)
Charlotte Sometimes (5)
Close To Me (4,5,8) 97
Closedown (7)
Cut (9)
Disintegration (7)
Doing The Unstuck (9)

Dream, The (1,2)
Dressing Up (3)
Empty World (3)
End (9)
Fascination Street (7,8) 46
Fight (8)
Forest, A (5,8)
Friday I'm In Love (9) 18
From The Edge Of The Deep Green Sea (9)
Give Me It (3)
Hanging Garden (5)
Hey You!!! (8)
High (9) 42
Hot Hot Hot!!! (6,8) 65

How Beautiful You Are... (6)
Icing Sugar (6)
If Only Tonight We Could Sleep (6)
In Between Days (Without You) (4,5,8) 99
Jumping Someone Else's Train (5)
Just Like Heaven (6) 40
Just One Kiss (1,2)
Killing An Arab (5)
Kiss, The (6)
Kyoto Song (4)
La Ment (1,2)
Let's Go To Bed (1,2,5)

Letter To Elise (9)
Like Cockatoos (6)
Love Cats (2,5)
Love Song (7,8) 2
Lullaby (7,8) 74
Never Enough (8) 72
Night Like This (4)
One More Time (6)
Open (9)
Perfect Girl (6)
Pictures Of You (7,8) 71
Piggy In The Mirror (3)
Plainsong (7)
Prayers For Rain (7)
Primary (5)

Push (4)
Same Deep Water As You (7)
Screw (4)
Shake Dog Shake (3)
Shiver And Shake (6)
Sinking (4)
Six Different Ways (4)
Snakepit, The (6)
Speak My Language (2)
Thousand Hours (6)
To Wish Impossible Things (9)
Top, The (3)
Torture (6)
Trust (9)

Untitled (7)
Upstairs Room (1,2)
Wailing Wall (3)
Walk, The (1,2,5,8)
Wendy Time (9)
Why Can't I Be You? (6) 54

CURIOSITY KILLED THE CAT

Pop quartet formed in London in 1984: Nick Thorpe, Miguel Drummond, Julian Brookhouse and Ben Volpeliere-Pierrot (vocals). Group name taken from a password in an adventure game.

| 8/22/87 | 55 | 29 | | Keep Your Distance .... | $8 | Mercury 832025 |

Curiosity Killed The Cat
Down To Earth

Free
Know What You Know

Mile High
Misfit 42

Ordinary Day
Red Lights

Shallow Memory

CURRY, Tim

British actor/vocalist born in 1947. Starred as Dr. Frank-N-Furter in the cult film *The Rocky Horror Picture Show*. Also in the films *Annie*, *Blue Money* and others.

| 9/8/79 | 53 | 24 | 1 | Fearless .... | $8 | A&M 4773 |
| 8/29/81 | 112 | 8 | 2 | Simplicity .... | $8 | A&M 4830 |

Betty Jean (2)
Charge It (1)
Cold Blue Steel And Sweet Fire (1)

Dancing In The Streets (2)
Hide This Face (1)
I Do The Rock (1) 91
I Put A Spell On You (2)

No Love On The Street (1)
On A Roll (2)
Out Of Pawn (2)
Paradise Garage (1)

Right On The Money (1)
S.O.S. (1)
She's Not There (1)
Simplicity (2)

Something Short Of Paradise (1)
Summer In The City (2)
Take Me I'm Yours (2)

Working On My Tan (2)

CUTTING CREW

British rock group led by singer Nick Van Eede, with Kevin Scott MacMichael (guitar; from Canada), Colin Farley (bass) and Martin Beedle (drums).

| 3/21/87 | 16 | 45 ● | 1 | Broadcast .... | $8 | Virgin 90573 |
| 6/3/89 | 150 | 6 | 2 | The Scattering .... | $8 | Virgin 91239 |

Any Colour (1)
(Between A) Rock And A Hard Place (2) 77
Big Noise (2)
Broadcast, The (1)

Don't Look Back (1)
Everything But My Pride (2)
Fear Of Falling (1)
Feel The Wedge (2)
Handcuffs For Houdini (2)

(I Just) Died In Your Arms (1) 1
I've Been In Love Before (1) 9

It Shouldn't Take Too Long (1)
Last Thing (2)
Life In A Dangerous Time (1)

One For The Mockingbird (1) 38
Reach For The Sky (2)
Sahara (1)

Scattering, The (2)
Tip Of Your Tongue (2)
Year In The Wilderness (2)

CYMANDE

Eight-man, afro-rock band from the West Indies.

| 1/13/73 | 85 | 17 | 1 | Cymande .... | $10 | Janus 3044 |
| 6/30/73 | 180 | 4 | 2 | Second Time Round .... | $10 | Janus 3054 |

Anthracite (2)
Bird (2)
Bra (1)
Crawshay (2)

Dove (1)
For Baby Ooh (2)
Fug (2)
Genevieve (2)

Getting It Back (1)
Listen (1)
Message, The (1) 48
One More (1)

Ras Tafarian Folk Song (1)
Rickshaw (1)
Them And Us (2)
To You (2)

Trevorgus (2)
Willies' Headache (2)
Zion I (1)

CYMARRON

Male pop vocal trio formed in Memphis: Richard Mainegra, Rick Yancey and Sherrill Parks.

| 10/2/71 | 187 | 3 | | Rings .... | $12 | Entrance 30962 |

Across The Kansas Sky
Break My Mind

Good Place To Begin
Hello Love

How Can You Mend A Broken Heart

In Your Mind
Rings 17

Table For Two For One
Tennesse Waltz

True Confession
Valerie 96

CYMONE, Andre

Born Andre Simon Anderson in Minneapolis. Former bass player of Prince's band, The Revolution. Went solo in 1981. Much production work for Jody Watley.

| 10/15/83 | 185 | 4 | 1 | Survivin' In The 80's .... | $8 | Columbia 38902 |
| 9/21/85 | 121 | 8 | 2 | A.C. .... | $8 | Columbia 40037 |

Body Thang (1)
Book Of Love (2)
Dance Electric (2)

Don't Let The Future (Come Down On You) (1)
Lipstick Lover (2)

Lovedog (2)
M.O.T.F. (1)
Make Me Wanna Dance (1)

Neon Pussycat (2)
Pretty Wild Girl (2)
Satisfaction (2)

Stay (1)
Survivin' In The 80's (1)
Sweet Sensuality (2)

Vacation (2)
What Are We Doing Here (1)

CYPRESS HILL

Rap trio based in Los Angeles: Sen "Sen Dog" Reyes (Cuban-born, older brother of Mellow Man Ace), Louis "B-Real" Freeze and Lawrence "Mixmaster Muggs" Muggerud (former member of The 7A3). Band named for Cypress Street in the Southgate section of Los Angeles.

| 1/4/92 | 31 | 58↑▲ | | Cypress Hill .... | $12 | Ruffhouse 47889 |

Born To Get Busy
Break It Up
Funky Cypress Hill Shit
Hand On The Pump

Hole In The Head
How I Could Just Kill A Man 77
Latin Lingo

Light Another
Phuncky Feel One 94
Pigs
Psycobetabuckdown

Real Estate
Something For The Blunted
Stoned Is The Way Of The Walk

Tres Equis
Ultraviolet Dreams

CYRKLE, The
Pop group formed while attending Lafayette College in Easton, Pennsylvania. Signed to Columbia Records and managed by The Beatles' Brian Epstein. Featured vocalists Don Dannemann and Tom Dawes.

| 8/6/66 | 47 | 15 | | 1 Red Rubber Ball | $20 | Columbia 9344 |
| 4/1/67 | 164 | 2 | | 2 Neon | $20 | Columbia 9432 |

Baby, You're Free (1)
Big, Little Woman (1)
Bony Moronie (1)
Cloudy (1)
Cry (1)
Don't Cry, No Fears, No Tears Comin' Your Way (2)

How Can I Leave Her (1)
I Wish You Could Be Here (2) *70*
I'm Happy Just To Dance With You (2)
I'm Not Sure What I Wanna Do (2)

It Doesn't Matter Anymore (2)
Money To Burn (1)
Our Love Affair's In Question (2)
Please Don't Ever Leave Me (2) *59*

Problem Child (2)
Red Rubber Ball (1) *2*
There's A Fire In The Fireplace (1)
Turn-Down Day (1) *16*
Two Rooms (2)
Visit (She Was Here) (2)

Weight Of Your Words (2)
Why Can't You Give Me What I Want (1)

CYRUS, Billy Ray
Country singer from Flatwoods, Kentucky. Born on 8/25/61.

| 6/6/92 | 1 [17] | 36↑▲[6] | | **Some Gave All** | $12 | Mercury 510635 |

Achy Breaky Heart 4
Ain't No Good Goodbye
Could've Been Me 72

I'm So Miserable
Never Thought I'd Fall In Love With You

She's Not Cryin' Anymore
Some Gave All

Someday, Somewhere, Somehow

These Boots Are Made For Walkin'

Wher'm I Gonna Live?

D

D.A.D.
Hard-rock quartet from Copenhagen, Denmark: Jesper Binzer (vocals) and his brother Jacob with Stig Pedersen and Peter Jensen. D.A.D. is abbreviation for Disneyland After Dark.

| 9/30/89 | 116 | 11 | | No Fuel Left For The Pilgrims | $8 | Warner 25999 |

Girl Nation
Ill Will

Jihad
Lords Of The Atlas

Overmuch
Point Of View

Rim Of Hell
Siamese Twin

Sleeping My Day Away
True Believer

Wild Talk
ZCMI

da'KRASH
Funk quintet formed in 1981 in East St. Louis. Discovered by Jesse Johnson (The Time). Featured vocalist Robert Jordan. Group evolved into Kool Skool with new vocalist Dion Craig in 1990.

| 4/16/88 | 184 | 3 | | da'KRASH | $8 | Capitol 48355 |

Dance With Me
Easy Come, Easy Go

Feeling Like This
Temptation Sensation

Trapped In Phases
Tu Madre

Uptown
Wasn't I Good To Ya?

DALE, Dick, and The Del-Tones
Dick was southern California's most influential surf-rock guitarist.

| 1/26/63 | 59 | 17 | | 1 Surfers' Choice | $50 | Deltone 1886 |
| 12/14/63+ | 106 | 11 | | 2 Checkered Flag | $35 | Capitol 2002 |

Big Black Cadillac (2)
Death Of A Gremmie (1)
Fanny Mae (1)
426 - Super Stock (2)

Grudge Run (2)
Ho-Dad Machine (2)
Hot Rod Racer (2)
It Will Grow On You (2)

Let's Go Trippin' (1) *60*
Lovey Dovey (1)
Mag Wheels (2)
Misirlou Twist (1)

Motion (2)
Night Owl (1)
Night Rider (2)
Peppermint Man (1)

Scavenger, The (2) *98*
Shake N' Stomp (1)
Sloop John B. (1)
Surf Beat (1)

Surf Buggy (2)
Surfing Drums (1)
Take If Off (1)
Wedge, The (2)

DALE & GRACE
Pop vocal duo: Dale Houston (of Ferriday, Louisiana) and Grace Broussard (of Prairieville, Louisiana).

| 2/1/64 | 100 | 7 | | I'm Leaving It Up To You | $50 | Montel 100 |

Bye Bye Love
Casual Look

Darling It's Wonderful
Gee Baby

Happy, Happy Birthday Baby
Hey Baby

I'm Leaving It Up To You *1*
Let The Good Times Roll

Love Is Strange
Our Teenage Love

Tip Of My Finger
We Belong Together

DA LENCH MOB
Rap trio: T-Bone, J-Dee and Shorty.

| 10/10/92 | 24 | 18↑● | | Guerillas In Tha Mist | $12 | Street Know. 92206 |

produced by Ice Cube

Ain't Got No Class
All On My Nut Sac
Ankle Blues

Buck Tha Devil
Capital Punishment In America

Freedom Got An A.K.
Guerillas In Tha Mist

Inside Tha Head Of A Black Man
Lenchmob Also In Tha Group

Lord Have Mercy
Lost In Tha System

Who Ya Gonna Shoot Wit That
You & Your Heroes

DALTON, Kathy
Songstress from Memphis.

| 11/16/74 | 190 | 3 | | Boogie Bands & One Night Stands | $10 | DiscReet 2208 |

At The Tropicana
Boogie Bands And One Night Stands 72

Cannibal Forest
Gypsy Dancer
I Need You Tonight

Justine
Light That Shines
Midnight Creeper

Musical Chairs
Pour Your Wine All Over Me
Ride, Ride, Ride

DALTREY, Roger
Born on 3/1/44 in London. Formed band the Detours, which later became The Who. Roger was The Who's lead singer and starred in the films *Tommy, Lisztomania, The Legacy* and *McVicar*.

5/26/73	45	20		1 Daltrey	$12	Track 328
8/9/75	28	23		2 Ride A Rock Horse	$12	MCA 2147
7/9/77	46	19		3 One Of The Boys	$12	MCA 2271
8/16/80	22	15		4 McVicar [S]	$10	Polydor 6284

soundtrack features all members of The Who

3/27/82	185	5		5 Best Bits [G]	$10	MCA 5301
3/17/84	102	9		6 Parting Should Be Painless	$8	Atlantic 80128
10/12/85	42	26		7 Under A Raging Moon	$8	Atlantic 81269

DEBUT DATE	PEAK POS	WKS CHR	GOLD	ARTIST — Album Title	$	Label & Number

DALTREY, Roger — Cont'd

| | | | | | | |

After The Fire (7) *48*
Avenging Annie (3,5) *88*
Bitter And Twisted (4)
Breaking Down Paradise (7)
Come And Get Your Love (2) *68*
Doing It All Again (3)
Don't Talk To Strangers (7)
Don't Wait On The Stairs (6)
Escape Parts 1 & 2 (4)
Fallen Angel (7)
Feeling (2)
Free Me (4,5) *53*

Giddy (3)
Giving It All Away (1,5) *83*
Going Strong (6)
Hard Life (1,5)
Heart-s Right (2)
How Does The Cold Wind Cry (6)
I Was Born To Sing Your Song (2)
Is There Anybody Out There? (6)
It Don't Satisfy Me (7)
Just A Dream Away (4)

Leon (3)
Let Me Down Easy (7) *86*
Looking For You (6)
Martyrs And Madmen (5)
McVicar (4)
Milk Train (2)
Move Better In The Night (7)
My Time Is Gonna Come (4)
Near To Surrender (2)
Oceans Away (2,5)
One Day (6)
One Man Band (1)
One Of The Boys (3)

Parade (3)
Parting Would Be Painless (6)
Pride You Hide (7)
Prisoner, The (3)
Proud (2,5)
Reasons (1)
Rebel (7)
Satin And Lace (3)
Say It Ain't So, Joe (3,5)
Single Man's Dilemma (3)
Somebody Told Me (6)
Story So Far (1)

Thinking (1)
Treachery (5)
Under A Raging Moon (7)
Waiting For A Friend (4)
Walking In My Sleep (6) *62*
Walking The Dog (2)
Way Of The World (1)
When The Music Stops (1)
White City Lights (4)
Without Your Love (4,5) *20*
World Over (2)
Would A Stranger Do? (6)
You And Me (1)

You Are Yourself (1)
You Put Something Better Inside Of Me (5)

DAMIAN, Michael

Born Michael Weir on 4/26/62 in San Diego. Played Danny Romalotti on TV's *The Young & The Restless* since 1981 when discovered by the show's producers while performing on *American Bandstand*.

| 6/17/89 | 61 | 26 | | Where Do We Go From Here...... | $8 | Cypress 0130 |

Cover Of Love *31*
Heartbreak Monday

My Mistake
Photograph

Question Of Time
Rock On *1*

Straight From My Heart
Touch Of Gray

Turn From My Love
Was It Nothing At All *24*

DAMNATION OF ADAM BLESSING

Rock group led by vocalist Adam Blessing and guitarist Jim Quinn.

| 3/28/70 | 181 | 2 | | The Damnation Of Adam Blessing...... | $12 | United Art. 6738 |

Cookbook
Dreams

Hold On
Last Train To Clarksville

Le' Voyage
Lonely

Morning Dew
Strings And Things

You Don't Love Me

DAMN YANKEES

Superstar rock group: guitarist Ted Nugent (Amboy Dukes), bassist/vocalist Jack Blades (Night Ranger), guitarist/vocalist Tommy Shaw (Styx) and drummer Michael Cartellone.

| 3/31/90+ | 13 | 78 ▲ | 1 | Damn Yankees...... | $12 | Warner 26159 |
| 8/29/92 | 22 | 24↑● | 2 | Don't Tread...... | $12 | Warner 45025 |

Bad Reputation (1)
Come Again (1) *50*
Coming Of Age (1) *60*
Damn Yankees (1)

Dirty Dog (2)
Don't Tread On Me (2)
Double Coyote (2)
Fifteen Minutes Of Fame (1)

Firefly (2)
High Enough (1) *3*
Mister Please (2)
Mystified (1)

Piledriver (1)
Rock City (1)
Runaway (1)
Silence Is Broken (2)

Someone To Believe (2)
Tell Me How You Want It (1)
This Side Of Hell (2)
Uprising (2)

Where You Goin' Now (2) *20*

DAMON('S), Liz, Orient Express

Liz is the leader of the three-woman, six-man vocal/instrumental group from Hawaii.

| 3/6/71 | 190 | 2 | | Liz Damon's Orient Express...... | $10 | White Whale 5003 |

Bring Me Sunshine
But For Love

Close To You
Everything Is Beautiful

Let It Be
1900 Yesterday *33*

Something
That Same Old Feeling

You Make Me Feel Like Someone

You're Falling In Love

DAMONE, Vic

Born Vito Farinola on 6/12/28 in Brooklyn. Vic is among the most popular of postwar ballad singers. Appeared in several movies and hosted own TV series (1956-57). Married actress Diahann Carroll on 1/3/87.

10/13/56	14	8	1	That Towering Feeling!......	$25	Columbia 900
3/3/62	64	17	2	Linger Awhile with Vic Damone......	$15	Capitol 1646
10/13/62	57	10	3	The Lively Ones......	$15	Capitol 1748
7/10/65	86	10	4	You Were Only Fooling......	$15	Warner 1602

After The Lights Go Down Low (2)
All The Things You Are (1)
And Roses And Roses (4)
Careless Hands (2)
Change Partners (2)
Charmaine (3)
Cheek To Cheek (1)
Cherokee (3)
Close Your Eyes (2)

Dearly Beloved (3)
Deep Night (2)
Diane (3)
Dream On Little Dreamer (4)
For Mama (La Mamma) (4)
I Want A Little Girl (3)
I'll Never Find Another You (4)
I'm Glad There Is You (4)
I've Been Looking (4)

In The Still Of The Night (2)
It's Not Unusual (4)
Laura (3)
Let's Face The Music And Dance (2)
Let's Fall In Love (1)
Linger Awhile (1)
Little Girl (3)
Lively Ones (3)
Marie (4)

Most Beautiful Girl In The World (3)
Nina Never Knew (3)
One Love (2)
Out Of Nowhere (1)
Please Help Me, I'm Falling (In Love With You) (4)
Ruby (3)
Soft Lights And Sweet Music (2)

Song Is You (1)
Spring Is Here (1)
Stella By Starlight (2)
Stranger In The World (4)
There! I've Said It Again (3)
Thrill Of Loving You (4)
Time On My Hands (You In My Arms) (1)
Touch Of Your Lips (1)
Wait Till You See Her (1)

When Lights Are Low (2)
(When Your Heart's On Fire) Smoke Gets In Your Eyes (1)
Why Don't You Believe Me (4)
You Stepped Out Of A Dream (1)
You Were Only Fooling (While I Was Falling In Love) (4) *30*

DANA, Bill — see JIMENEZ, Jose

DANA, Vic

Born on 8/26/42 in Buffalo, New York. Moved to California as a teen. Adult Contemporary vocalist.

11/16/63+	111	9	1	More......	$15	Dolton 8026
5/16/64	116	5	2	Shangri-La......	$15	Dolton 8028
4/10/65	13	21	3	Red Roses For A Blue Lady......	$15	Dolton 8034

Call Me Irresponsible (2)
Charade (2)
Danke Schoen (1)
Diane (2)
End Of The World (1)
Good News (2)
He Gives Me Love (1)
Hello Dolly! (2)

I Was The One (1)
I Will (1) *47*
I'd Trade All Of My Tomorrows (For Just One Yesterday) (3)
I'll Be Around (3)
I'll Be Seeing You (3)
I'll Get By (3)

I'll See You In My Dreams (3)
I'm In The Mood For Love (3)
It Had To Be You (3)
Love After Midnight (3)
More (1) *42*
More I See You (3)
My Heart Belongs To Only You (2)

My Heart Cries For You (2)
My World (1)
Once In A While (3)
Red Roses For A Blue Lady (3) *10*
Shangri-La (2) *27*
Shelter Of Your Arms (2)
So Much In Love (1)

Softly As I Leave You (3)
Stairway To The Stars (2)
That's Why I'm Sorry (1)
What Good Would It Do (1)
When A Boy Falls In Love (1)
You Were Meant For Me (3)
You're My Everything (3)

You're Nobody 'Till Somebody Loves You (1)

DANE, Dana

Rapper and art alumnus of New York's High School of Music and Art. Rap partner is DJ Clark Kent.

| 9/12/87 | 46 | 32 ● | 1 | Dana Dane With Fame...... | $8 | Profile 1233 |
| 11/10/90 | 150 | 4 | 2 | Dana Dane 4-Ever...... | $12 | Profile 1298 |

Bedie Boo (2)
Cinderfella Dana Dane (1)
Dana Dane 4-Ever (2)
Dana Dane To It (2)

Dana Dane With Fame (1)
Dedication (1)
Dedication 2 (2)
Delancey Street (1)

Johnny The Dipper (3)
Just Here To Have Fun (1)
Keep The Groove (1)
Little Bit Of Dane Tonight (2)

Lonely Man (2)
Love At First Sight (1)
Makes Me Wanna Sing (2)
Nightmares (1)

Something Special (2)
Tales From The Dane Side (2)
This Be The Def Beat (1)

We Wanna Party (1)
What Dirty Minds U Have (2)

DEBUT DATE	PEAK POS	WKS CHR	GOLD	ARTIST — Album Title	$	Label & Number

DANGER DANGER

Hard-rock quintet formed in Queens, New York by Bruno Ravel (bass) and Steve West (drums). Includes Ted Poley (vocals), Andy Timmons (guitar) and Kasey Smith (keyboards).

| 8/19/89 | 88 | 42 | | 1 Danger Danger .... | $8 | Epic 44342 |
| 10/19/91 | 123 | 5 | | 2 Screw It!.............................. | $12 | Epic/Assc. 46977 |

Bang Bang (1) 49 | D.F.N.S. (2) | Find Your Way Back Home (2) | Live It Up (1) | Rock America (1) | Yeah, You Want It! (2)
Beat The Bullet (2) | Don't Blame It On Love (2) | Monkey Business (2) | Saturday Nite (1)
Boys Will Be Boys (1) | Don't Walk Away (1) | Get Your Shit Together (2) | Naughty Naughty (1) | Slipped Her The Big One (2)
Comin' Home (2) | Everybody Wants Some (2) | Horny S.O.B. (1) | One Step From Paradise (1) | Turn It On (1)
Crazy Nites (2) | Feels Like Love (1) | I Still Think About You (1) | Puppet Show (1) | Under The Gun (1)

DANGERFIELD, Rodney

Born Jack Roy on 11/22/21 in Babylon, New York. Comedian and star of the films *Caddyshack*, *Easy Money*, *Back To School* and others. Owner of Dangerfields, a club in New York City.

| 8/2/80 | 48 | 19 | | 1 No Respect .... [C] | $8 | Casablanca 7229 |
| 11/12/83 | 36 | 20 | | 2 Rappin' Rodney .... [C] | $8 | RCA 4869 |

No Respect (1) | **Rappin' Rodney** (2) 83 | Rodney Continues Rappin' (2) | Rodney Rappin' (2) | Son Of No Respect (1)

DANGEROUS TOYS

Texas hard-rock quintet: Jason McMaster (vocals), Scott Dalhover, Mike Watson, Mark Geary and Danny Aaron.

| 6/17/89 | 65 | 36 | | 1 Dangerous Toys .... | $8 | Columbia 45031 |
| 6/22/91 | 67 | 9 | | 2 Hellacious Acres .... | $12 | Columbia 46754 |

Angel N U (2) | Feels Like A Hammer (1) | Here Comes Trouble (1) | Scared (1) | Teas'n, Pleas'n (1)
Bad Guy (2) | Gimme' No Lip (2) | Line 'Em Up (2) | Sport'n A Woody (1) | Ten Boots (Stompin) (1)
Best Of Friends (2) | Gunfighter (2) | On Top (2) | Sticks & Stones (2) | That Dog (1)
Bones In The Gutter (1) | Gypsy (Black-N-Blue) | Outlaw (1) | Sugar, Leather & The Nail (2)
Feel Like Makin' Love (2) | Valentine) (2) | Queen Of The Nile (1) | Take Me Drunk (1)

★★274★★ DANIELS, Charlie, Band

Daniels (b: 10/28/36, Wilmington, North Carolina; vocals, guitar, fiddle) formed band in Nashville in 1971. Included Tom Crain (guitar), Joe "Taz" DiGregorio (keyboards), Charles Hayward (bass) and James W. Marshall (drums). Daniels led the Jaguars from 1958-67. Went solo in 1968 and worked as a session musician in Nashville. Played on Bob Dylan's *Nashville Skyline* hit album. In the film *Urban Cowboy*.

7/28/73	164	9		1 Honey In The Rock *	$15	Kama Sutra 2071
12/28/74+	38	34	▲	2 Fire On The Mountain	$15	Kama Sutra 2603
10/4/75	57	12		3 Nightrider	$15	Kama Sutra 2607
5/15/76	35	18	●	4 Saddle Tramp	$10	Epic 34150
12/4/76	83	10		5 High Lonesome	$10	Epic 34377
11/12/77	105	11		6 Midnight Wind	$10	Epic 34970
5/12/79	5	43	▲²	7 **Million Mile Reflections**	$10	Epic 35751
8/9/80	11	33	▲	8 Full Moon	$8	Epic 36571
4/3/82	26	19	●	9 Windows	$8	Epic 37694
7/23/83	84	12	▲²	10 A Decade Of Hits .... [G]	$8	Epic 38795
11/12/88	181	2		11 Homesick Heroes	$8	Epic 44324
11/25/89+	82	25	●	12 Simple Man	$8	Epic 45316
5/25/91	139	3		13 Renegade *	$12	Epic 46835

*CHARLIE DANIELS

Ain't No Ramblers Anymore (9) | Damn Good Cowboy (3) | Ill Wind (11) | Money (8) | Saddle Tramp (4) | Uneasy Rider '88 (11)
Alligator (11) | Dance Gypsy Dance (8) | In America (8,10) 11 | Nashville Moon (9) | Saturday Night Down South (12) | Universal Hand (9)
Behind Your Eyes (7) | **Devil Went Down To Georgia** (7,10) 3 | Indian Man (6) | New York City, King Size Rosewood Bed (2) | Simple Man (12) | Was It 26 (12)
Big Bad John (11) | Dixie On My Mind (4) | It's My Life (4,12) | No Place To Go (1,2) | Slow Song (5) | We Had It All One Time (9)
Big Man (1) | El Toreador (8) | Jitterbug (7) | No Potion For The Pain (8) | Somebody Loves You (1) | What My Baby Sees In Me (13)
Billy The Kid (5) | Everything Is Kinda' All Right (3) | Lady In Red (9) | Ode To Sweet Smoky (6) | South Sea Song (8) | (What This World Needs Is)
Birmingham Blues (3) | Everytime I See Him (10) | Layla (13) | Oh Atlanta (12) | **South's Gonna Do It** (2,10) 29 | A Few More Rednecks (12)
Black Bayou (6) | Evil (3) | **Legend Of Wooley Swamp** (8,10) 31 | Old Rock 'N Roller (12) | Still In Saigon (9,10) 22 | Why Can't People (1)
Blind Man (7) | Fathers And Sons (13) | Let Freedom Ring (13) | Orange Blossom Special (2) | Stroker's Theme (10) | Wichita Jail (4)
Blowing Along With The Wind (9) | Feeling Free (2) | Let It Roll (10) | Partyin' Gal (9) | Sugar Hill Saturday Night (6) | Willie Jones (3,13)
Blue Star (2) | Franklin Limestone (3) | Little Folks (13) | Passing Lane (7) | Sweet Louisiana (4) | You Can't Pick Cotton (11)
Boogie Woogie Fiddle Country Blues (11) | Funky Junky (1,3) | Lonesome Boy From Dixie (8) | Play Me Some Fiddle (12) | Sweetwater Texas (4)
Boogie Woogie Man (11) | Georgia (2) | **Long Haired Country Boy** (2,10) 56 | Ragin' Cajun (9) | Talk To Me Fiddle (13)
Caballo Diablo (2) | Get Me Back To Dixie (11) | Makes You Want To Go Home (9) | Rainbow Ride (7) | Tennessee (5)
Carolina (5) | Good Ole Boy (6) | Maria Teresa (6) | Redneck Fiddlin' Man (6) | **Texas** (3) 91
Carolina (I Remember You) (8) | Grapes Of Wrath (6) | Midnight Lady (1) | Reflections (7) | Tomorrow's Gonna' Be Another Day (3)
Cowboy Hat In Dallas (11) | Heaven Can Be Anywhere (Twin Pines Theme) (6) | Midnight Train (11) | Renegade (1) | Trudy (2)
Cumberland Mountain Number Nine (4) | High Lonesome (5) | Midnight Wind (6,12) | Revelations (1) | Turned My Head Around (5)
 | Honky Tonk Avenue (11) | Mississippi (7) | Right Now Tennessee Blues (5) | Twang Factor (13)
 | Honky Tonk Life (13) | Mister DJ (12) | Roll Mississippi (5) | **Uneasy Rider** (1,10) 9
 | | | Running With The Crowd (5) |

DANKO, Rick

Bassist of The Band. Born on 12/29/42 in Canada.

| 12/24/77+ | 119 | 8 | | Rick Danko............................ | $8 | Arista 4141 |

Brainwash | New Mexicoe | Shake It | Small Town Talk | Tired Of Waiting
Java Blues | Once Upon A Time | Sip The Wine | Sweet Romance | What A Town

DANNY WILSON

Trio from Dundee, Scotland: brothers Gary (lead vocals, guitar) and Kit Clark (keyboards, percussion), with Ged Grimes (bass). Group takes its name from a mid-1950s Frank Sinatra film. Disbanded in 1990.

| 7/18/87 | 79 | 16 | | Meet Danny Wilson .... | $8 | Virgin 90596 |

Aberdeen | Five Friendly Aliens | I Won't Be Here When You Get Home | **Mary's Prayer** 23 | Spencer-Tracey | You Remain An Angel
Broken China | Girl I Used To Know | | Nothing Ever Goes To Plan | Steamtrains To The Milky Way
Davy | | Lorraine Parade | Ruby's Golden Wedding |

DEBUT DATE	PEAK POS	WKS CHR	GOLD	ARTIST — Album Title	$	Label & Number

DANZIG
Heavy-metal quartet led by singer/songwriter Glenn Danzig. Includes Chuck Biscuits (ex-drummer of Black Flag and The Circle Jerks), John Christ and Eerie Von.

10/8/88	125	9		1 Danzig	$8	Def Amer. 24208
7/14/90	74	13		2 Danzig II - Lucifuge	$12	Def Amer. 24281
8/1/92	24	7		3 Danzig III - How The Gods Kill	$12	Def Amer. 26914

Am I Demon (1)
Anything (3)
Blood And Tears (2)
Bodies (3)
Devil's Plaything (2)
Dirty Black Summer (3)

Do You Wear The Mark (3)
End Of Time (1)
Evil Thing (1)
Girl (2)
Godless (3)
Heart Of The Devil (3)

Her Black Wings (2)
How The Gods Kill (3)
Hunter, The (1)
I'm The One (2)
Killer Wolf (2)
Left Hand Black (3)

Long Way Back From Hell (2)
Mother (1)
Not Of This World (1)
Pain In The World (2)
Possession (1)
777 (2)

She Rides (1)
Sistinas (3)
Snakes Of Christ (2)
Soul On Fire (1)
Tired Of Being Alive (2)
Twist Of Cain (1)

When The Dying Calls (3)

D'ARBY, Terence Trent
England-based, soul-pop singer. Born on 3/15/62 in New York City. Last name originally spelled Darby. Was a member of U.S. Army boxing team.

10/24/87+	4	60	▲²	1 **Introducing The Hardline According To Terence Trent D'Arby** .	$8	Columbia 40964
11/25/89	61	15		2 Terence Trent D'Arby's Neither Fish Nor Flesh	$8	Columbia 45351

...And I Need To Be With
  Someone Tonight (2)
As Yet Untitled (2)
Attracted To You (2)
Billy Don't Fall (2)

Dance Little Sister (Part One) (1) *30*
I Don't Want To Bring Your
  Gods Down (2)
I Have Faith In These
  Desolate Times (2)

I'll Be Alright (2)
I'll Never Turn My Back On
  You (Father's Words) (1)
If You All Get To Heaven (1)
If You Let Me Stay (1) *68*

It Feels So Good To Love
  Someone Like You (2)
Let's Go Forward (1)
Neither Fish Nor Flesh (2)
Rain (1)
Roly Poly (2)

Seven More Days (1)
Sign Your Name (1) *4*
This Side Of Love (2)
To Know Someone Deeply Is
  To Know Someone Softly
  (2)
Who's Lovin' You (1)

Wishing Well (1) *1*
You Will Pay Tomorrow (2)

★★212★★
DARIN, Bobby
Vocalist/pianist/guitarist/drummer. Born Walden Robert Cassotto on 5/14/36 in the Bronx; died of heart failure on 12/20/73 in Los Angeles. First recorded in 1956 with The Jaybirds (Decca). First appeared on TV in March 1956 on *The Tommy Dorsey Show*. Won the 1959 Best New Artist Grammy Award. Married to actress Sandra Dee from 1960-67. Nominated for an Oscar for his performance in the film *Captain Newman, MD* (1963). Formed own record company, Direction. Inducted into the Rock and Roll Hall of Fame in 1990.

10/5/59+	7	52		1 **That's All**	$35	Atco 104
3/7/60	6	50		2 **This Is Darin**	$30	Atco 115
10/17/60	9	38		3 **Darin At The Copa** .... [L]	$30	Atco 122
5/22/61	18	42		4 The Bobby Darin Story .... [G]	$40	Atco 131
9/11/61	92	10		5 Love Swings	$30	Atco 134
1/27/62	48	31		6 Twist With Bobby Darin	$30	Atco 138
5/12/62	96	11		7 Bobby Darin Sings Ray Charles	$30	Atco 140
10/6/62	45	10		8 Things & Other Things	$30	Atco 146
11/7/62	100	6		9 Oh! Look At Me Now	$25	Capitol 1791
3/16/63	43	15		10 You're The Reason I'm Living	$25	Capitol 1866
8/24/63	98	5		11 18 Yellow Roses	$25	Capitol 1942
12/26/64+	107	8		12 From Hello Dolly To Goodbye Charlie	$25	Capitol 2194
7/10/65	132	4		13 Venice Blue	$25	Capitol 2322
2/11/67	142	5		14 If I Were A Carpenter	$25	Atlantic 8135

Ain't That Love (7)
All By Myself (9)
All Nite Long (2)
Alright, O.K., You Win (3)
Always (9)
Amy (14)
Artificial Flowers (4) *20*
Be Honest With Me (10)
Beachcomber (8) *100*
Beyond The Sea (1,4) *6*
Black Coffee (2)
Blue Skies (9)
Bullmoose (6)
By Myself (medley) (3)
Call Me Irresponsible (12)
Can't Get Used To Losing
  You (11)
Caravan (2)
Charade (12)
Clementine (2,3,4) *21*
Come September, Theme
  From (8)
Day Dream (14)
Days Of Wine And Roses (12)
Dear Heart (13)
Don't Dream Of Anybody
  But Me (2)
Don't Make Promises (14)
Down With Love (2)
Dream Lover (3,4) *2*
Drown In My Own Tears (7)

Early In The Morning
  (4,6) *24*
18 Yellow Roses (11) *10*
End Of Never (12)
End Of The World (11)
For Baby (14)
From A Jack To A King (11)
Gal That Got Away (2)
Girl That Stood Beside Me
  (14) *66*
Good Life (13)
Goodbye Charlie (12)
Guys And Dolls (2)
Hallelujah I Love Her So (7)
Have You Got Any Castles,
  Baby (2)
Hello, Dolly! (12) *79*
Here I Am (10)
How About You (5)
I Ain't Sharin' Sharon (6)
I Can't Give You Anything
  But Love (2,3)
I Didn't Know What Time It
  Was (5)
I Got A Woman (3,7)
I Guess I'll Have To Change
  My Plan (5)
I Have Dreamed (5)
(I Heard That) Lonesome
  Whistle (10)
I Wanna Be Around (13)
I Will Follow Her (11)

I'll Be There (8) *79*
I'll Remember April (1)
I'm Beginning To See The
  Light (9)
If I Were A Carpenter (14) *8*
In A World Without You (13)
In Love In Vain (5)
Irresistible You (6) *15*
It Ain't Necessarily So (7)
It Had To Be You (5)
It Keeps Right On A-Hurtin' (11)
Jailer Bring Me Water (8)
Just Friends (5)
Keep A Walkin' (6)
Lazy River (4) *14*
Leave My Woman Alone (7)
Lonesome Road (medley) (3)
Long Ago And Far Away (5)
Look At Me (12)
Look For My True Love (8)
Lost Love (8)
Love For Sale (3)
Mack The Knife (1,3,4) *1*
Mighty Mighty Man (6)
Misty Roses (14)
More (12)
More I See You (5)
Multiplication (6) *30*
My Bonnie (7)
My Buddy (5)
My Gal Sal (2)

Nature Boy (8) *40*
Nightingale Sang In
  Berkeley Square (9)
No Greater Love (5)
Not For Me (11)
Now We're One (8)
Oh Lonesome Me (10)
Oh! Look At Me Now (9)
On Broadway (11)
Once In A Lifetime (12)
Oo-Ee-Train (8)
Our Day Will Come (11)
Party's Over (9)
Pete Kelly's Blues (2)
Plain Jane (4) *38*
Please Help Me, I'm Falling
  (10)
Queen Of The Hop (4,6) *9*
Reason To Believe (14)
Red Balloon (9)
Release Me (10)
Reverend Mr. Black (11)
Rhythm Of The Rain (11)
Right Time (7)
Roses Of Picardy (9)
Ruby Baby (11)
Sally Was A Good Old Girl
  (10)
She Needs Me (1)
Sittin' Here Lovin' You (14)

Skylark (5)
Softly, As I Leave You (13)
Softly As In A Morning
  Sunrise (2)
Some Of These Days (1,3)
Somebody To Love (4,6) *45*
Something To Remember
  You By (5)
Somewhere (11)
Sorrow Tomorrow (8)
Splish Splash (4) *3*
Spring Is Here (5)
Sunday In New York (12)
Swing Low Sweet Chariot
  (medley) (3)
Taste Of Honey (13)
Tell All The World About
  You (7)
Tell Me How Do You Feel (3)
That's All (1,3)
That's Enough (7)
That's The Way Love Is (1)
There Ain't No Sweet Gal
  That's Worth The Salt Of
  My Tears (13)
There's A Rainbow 'Round
  My Shoulder (9)
Things (8) *3*
Through A Long And
  Sleepless Night (1)
Under Your Spell Again (10)

Until It's Time For You To
  Go (14)
Venice Blue (13)
Walk Right In (11)
Was There A Call For Me (1)
What'd I Say (Part 1) (7) *24*
When Your Lover Has Gone
  (medley) (5)
Where Is The One (1)
Where Love Has Gone (12)
Who Can I Count On (10)
Who Can I Turn To? (13)
**Won't You Come Home Bill
  Bailey** (3,4) *19*
You Just Don't Know (13)
You Know How (4)
You Made Me Love You (9)
**You Must Have Been A
  Beautiful Baby** (6) *5*
You'd Be So Nice To Come
  Home To (3)
You'll Never Know (9)
You're Mine (8)
**You're The Reason I'm
  Living** (10) *3*

DARK ANGEL
Heavy-metal quintet: Ron Rinehart (vocals), Jim Durkin, Mike Gonzalez, Gene Hoglan and Eric Meyer.

4/1/89	159	6		Leave Scars	$8	Combat 8264

Cauterization
Death Of Innocence

Immigrant Song
Leave Scars

Never To Rise Again
No One Answers

Older Than Time Itself
Promise Of Agony

Worms

DEBUT DATE	PEAK POS	WKS CHR	GOLD	ARTIST — Album Title	$	Label & Number

DARLING CRUEL
Los Angeles-based rock group led by vocalist Gregory Darling. Includes Danni Bardot (guitar), Erik Gloege (drums), Janis Massey (sax, flute) and Orlando Sims (bass).

9/9/89	160	8		Passion Crimes	$8	Mika 837920

Beautiful One | Legend | No Stranger | Sad Song Jenie | Tales Of Emotion
Everything's Over (Passion Crime) | Love Child | One By One | Star Collector | Weight On My Shoulders

DARRELL, Johnny
Born on 7/23/40 in Hopewell, Alabama. Country singer.

| 9/6/69 | 172 | 3 | | Why You Been Gone So Long .... | $12 | United Art. 6707 |

Ain't That Livin' | I Ain't Buying | Margie's At The Lincoln Park | River Bottom | Woman Without Love | You're Always The One
House On The Hill | Jimmy Jacob | Inn | Why You Been Gone So Long | World I Used To Know
Hungry Eyes

DARREN, James
Born James William Ercolani on 10/3/36 in Philadelphia. Singer/actor, studied acting in New York City. Moved to Hollywood in 1955. In films *Rumble On The Docks, The Brothers Rico, Operation Mad Ball, Gunman's Walk, The Guns Of Navarone, Because They're Young* and *Let No Man Write My Epitaph*. Played Moondoggie, Gidget's boyfriend, in *Gidget, Gidget Goes Hawaiian* and *Gidget Goes To Rome*. In *The Time Tunnel* TV series from 1966-67.

| 9/25/61 | 132 | 3 | | 1 Gidget Goes Hawaiian (James Darren Sings The Movies) .... | $30 | Colpix 418 |
| 5/11/63 | 48 | 18 | | 2 Teen-Age Triangle ....[G] | $40 | Colpix 444 |

JAMES DARREN/SHELLEY FABARES/PAUL PETERSEN
includes 4 cuts by Shelley Fabares (see Fabares) and 4 cuts by Paul Petersen: "Keep Your Love Locked (Deep In Your Heart)," "Little Boy Sad," "Lollipops And Roses" and "She Can't Find Her Keys"

| 6/3/67 | 187 | 3 | | 3 James Darren/All .... | $20 | Warner 1688 |

All (3) *35* | **Gidget** (2) *41* | I Miss You So (3) | P.S. I Love You (1) | Until The Real Thing Comes
Because They're Young (1) | Gidget Goes Hawaiian (1) | Lady (3) | Since I Don't Have You (3) | Along (1)
Born Free (3) | **Goodbye Cruel World** (2) *3* | Man And A Woman (Un | Sunny (3) | Wild About That Girl (1)
Come On My Love (1) | Goodbye My Lady Love (1) | Homme Et Une Femme) (3) | This Is My Song (3) | You Are My Dream (1)
Conscience (2) *11* | Hand In Hand (1) | My Cup Runneth Over (3) | Traveling Down A Lonely | Your Smile (1)
Georgy Girl (3) | **Her Royal Majesty** (2) *6* | Not Mine (1) | Road (1)

DARTELLS, The
Oxnard, California rock band consisting of Doug Phillips (vocals, bass), Dick Burns, Corky Wilkie, Rich Peil, Randy Ray and Gary Peeler.

| 7/6/63 | 95 | 5 | | Hot Pastrami! .... | $30 | Dot 25522 |

Daddy's Home | Dill Pickles | Happy Organ | I Scream, You Scream | One Degree North | Surf Dreams
Dartell Stomp | Fanny Mae | **Hot Pastrami** *11* | Night Train | St. James Infirmary | Swiss Cheese

DAS EFX
Rap duo of Andre "Dray" Weston (b: 9/9/70) and Willie "Skoob" Hines (b: 11/27/70) formed at Virginia State. DAS is an acronym for Dray And Skoob (which is "books" spelled backward).

| 4/25/92 | 16 | 42 ● | | Dead Serious .... | $12 | EastWest 91827 |

Brooklyn To T-Neck | East Coast | Jussummen | Looseys | Straight Out The Sewer
Dum Dums | If Only | Klap Ya Handz | Mic Checka | **They Want EFX** *25*

DASH, Sarah
Born on 8/18/43 in Trenton, New Jersey. Original member of The Blue-Belles and LaBelle.

| 1/20/79 | 182 | 7 | | Sarah Dash .... | $8 | Kirshner 35477 |

Charge It | Do It For Love | I Can't Believe (Someone | Look But Don't Touch | We're Lovers After All
(Come And Take This) | Give Your Man A Helping | Like You Could Really Love | **Sinner Man** *71* | You
 Candy From Your Baby | Hand | Me) | Touch And Go

DAVE & SUGAR
Country singer Dave Rowland with female duo.

| 9/17/77 | 157 | 4 | | 1 That's The Way Love Should Be .... | $10 | RCA 2477 |
| 3/7/81 | 179 | 4 | | 2 Dave & Sugar/Greatest Hits ....[G] | $8 | RCA 3915 |

Baby Take Your Coat Off (2) | Got Leavin' On Her Mind (1) | I'm Knee Deep In Loving You | Livin' At The End Of The | Tear Time (2)
Can't Help But Wonder (2) | Gotta' Quit Lookin' At You | (1,2) | Rainbow (2) | That's The Way Love Should
Don't Throw It All Away (1,2) | Baby (2) | It's A Beautiful Morning | My World Begins And Ends | Be (1)
Door Is Always Open (2) | I Ain't Leavin' Dallas 'Til The | With You (1) | With You (2) | We've Got Everything (1)
Feel Like A Little Love (1) | Fire Goes Out (1) | It's A Heartache (2) | Queen Of The Silver Dollar
Golden Tears (2) | I Love To Be Loved By You (1) | | (2)

DAVID & DAVID
Los Angeles duo: David Baerwald and David Ricketts. Also see David Baerwald.

| 8/16/86 | 39 | 38 | | Boomtown .... | $8 | A&M 5134 |

Ain't So Easy *51* | Being Alone Together | River's Gonna Rise | Swallowed By The Cracks | **Welcome To The**
All Alone In The Big City | Heroes | Rock For The Forgotten | Swimming In The Ocean | **Boomtown** *37*

DAVIDSON, John
Born on 12/13/41 in Pittsburgh. Singer/actor. Hosted own TV talk show, 1980-82. Co-hosted TV's *That's Incredible* and the new *Hollywood Squares*.

10/8/66	19	24		1 The Time Of My Life!	$10	Columbia 9380
4/8/67	125	8		2 My Best To You	$10	Columbia 9448
12/2/67	79	12		3 A Kind Of Hush	$10	Columbia 9534
6/29/68	151	10		4 Goin' Places	$10	Columbia 9654
5/17/69	153	7		5 John Davidson	$8	Columbia 9795
11/22/69	165	5		6 My Cherie Amour	$8	Columbia 9859

Blessed Is The Rain (6) | Can't Take My Eyes Off You | Don't Think Twice, It's All | Friend, Lover, Woman, Wife | Goodnight My Love | How Come You Do Me Like
Blowin' In The Wind (1) | (medley) (4) | Right (3) | (6) | (Pleasant Dreams) (5) | You Do (3)
Both Sides Now (5) | Dakota (4) | 59th Street Bridge Song | Games That Lovers Play (2) | Happiest Guy Alive (4) | I Couldn't Live Without Your
By The Time I Get To | Daydream (1) | (Feelin' Groovy) (3) | Georgy Girl (6) | Happy Heart (6) | Love (2)
Phoenix (4) | Didn't We (5) | Flame (4) | Goin' Out Of My Head | High Heel Sneakers (6) | I Really Don't Want To Know
California Bloodlines (6) | | | (medley) (4) | | (2)

DEBUT DATE	PEAK POS	WKS CHR	G O L D	ARTIST — Album Title	$	Label & Number

DAVIDSON, John — Cont'd

I'll Always Remember (2)
I've Gotta Be Me (5)
If I Gave You (3)
If I Were A Carpenter (3)
Just As Much As Ever (3)
Letter, The (6)
Little Green Apples (5)
Love Is Blue (4)
Mame (2)
Michelle (1)

Minstrel Man (4)
More I See You (1)
My Cherie Amour (6)
My Cup Runneth Over (3)
My Love (1)
My Way (6)
Ob-La-Di Ob-La-Da (5)
Shadow Of Your Smile (1)
Somewhere (2)
Somewhere, My Love (1)

Stormy (5)
Strangers In The Night (1)
Sunny (2)
Suzanne (5)
Taste Of Honey (1)
That's Life (2)
There'll Be Some Changes Made (3)
There's A Kind Of Hush (All Over The World) (3)

Those Were The Days (5)
Time For Us (6)
Today (3)
Try To Remember (2)
Valley Of The Dolls, Theme From (4)
Visions Of Sugarplums (4)
What Is A Woman? (3)
What Now My Love (1)
Who Am I (2)

Windmills Of Your Mind (6)
Woman Helping Man (5)
Woman, Woman (4)
Words (5)
You Don't Have To Say You Love Me (Io Che Non Vivo Senza Te) (1)
You've Made Me So Very Happy (6)

DAVIES, Dave
Lead guitarist of the Kinks. Born on 2/3/47 in Muswell Hill, London.

7/26/80	42	14		1 AFL1-3603	$8	RCA 3603
				title refers to label number		
7/18/81	152	8		2 Glamour	$8	RCA 4036

Body (2)
Doing The Best For You (1)
Eastern Eyes (2)
Glamour (2)

Imaginations Real (1)
In You I Believe (1)
Is This The Only Way? (2)
Move Over (1)

Nothin' More To Lose (1)
Reveal Yourself (2)
Run (1)
See The Beast (1)

7th Channel (2)
Telepathy (2)
Too Serious (2)
Visionary Dreamer (1)

Where Do You Come From (1)
World Is Changing Hands (1)
World Of Our Own (2)

DAVIS, Danny, & The Nashville Brass
Danny's real name: George Nowlan. Born on 4/29/25 in Dorchester, Massachusetts. Trumpet player/leader educated at the New England Conservatory of Music. Played and sang in swing bands including Gene Krupa, Bob Crosby, Freddy Martin, Blue Barron, and Sammy Kaye. Producer for Joy and MGM Records in the late '50s. Production assistant to Chet Atkins in 1965. Formed The Nashville Brass in 1968.

2/15/69	78	24		1 The Nashville Sound ....[I]	$10	RCA 4059
7/12/69	143	6		2 More Nashville Sounds ....[I]	$10	RCA 4176
12/27/69+	141	20		3 Movin' On ....[I]	$10	RCA 4232
5/30/70	102	12		4 You Ain't Heard Nothin' Yet ....[I]	$10	RCA 4334
10/31/70	140	12		5 Down Homers ....[I]	$10	RCA 4424
4/3/71	161	3		6 Somethin' Else ....[I]	$10	RCA 4476
9/18/71	184	4		7 Super Country ....[I]	$10	RCA 4571
11/25/72	193	5		8 Turn On Some Happy! ....[I]	$10	RCA 4803
3/15/80	150	5		9 Danny Davis & Willie Nelson with The Nashville Brass....................	$8	RCA 3549

DANNY DAVIS & WILLIE NELSON
new instrumental backing for earlier recordings by Willie

All I Have To Offer You (Is Me) (3)
Anytime (8)
Are You From Dixie (Cause I'm From Dixie Too) (6)
Are You Lonesome Tonight (4)
Big Daddy (7)
Bloody Merry Morning (9)
Blue Bayou (7)
Bonaparte's Retreat (2)
Brassy Down Home Rag (5)
Cajun Baby (2)
Columbus Stockade Blues (4)
Country Gentleman (2)
December Day (9)
Difficult (6)
Distant Drums (5)
Don't It Make You Wanta Go Home (5)

Down Yonder (5)
Early Morning Rain (8)
Fire Ball Mail (2)
Foggy Mountain Breakdown (6)
Four Walls (5)
Freight Train (2)
Funny How Time Slips Away (9)
Games People Play (8)
Give The World A Smile (6)
Good Hearted Woman (3)
Great Speckled Bird (4)
Green, Green Grass Of Home (6)
Hello Walls (9)
Here Comes My Baby Back Again (1)
Hey, Good Lookin' (3)
Highland Brass (6)
Horny (8)

I Can't Stop Loving You (6)
I Fall To Pieces (1)
I Love You Because (1)
I Saw The Light (1)
I Walk The Line (6)
I Walked Out On Heaven (4)
I'll Fly Away (8)
I'm Movin' On (3)
I'm So Lonesome I Could Cry (7)
I've Got A New Heartache (1)
Is Anybody Goin' To San Antone (7)
Jambalaya (On The Bayou) (1)
Jealous Heart (4)
Joey's Song (8)
Just One Time (7)
Kaw-Liga (2)
Lappland (2)
Lassus Trombone (1)

Let It Be Me (1)
Little Bitty Tear (4)
Local Memory (9)
Lonely Street (2)
Long Gone Lonesome Blues (5)
Maiden's Prayer (1)
May The Circle Be Unbroken (5)
Middle Of The Road (1)
Mountain Dew (1)
Mule Skinner Blues (1)
My Own Peculiar Way (9)
New Spanish Two-Step (5)
Night Life (9)
Norman (7)
Oh Baby Mine (I Get So Lonely) (4)
Oh, Lonesome Me (8)
On The Rebound (1)
Orange Blossom Special (7)

Raindrops Keep Fallin' On My Head (8)
Rainy Day Blues (9)
Release Me (3)
Ring Of Fire (3)
Rose Garden (6)
Ruby, Don't Take Your Love To Town (3)
San Antonio Rose (4)
Singing My Song (9)
Slowly (7)
Snowbird (6)
Steel Guitar Rag (4)
Sweet Dreams (3)
Tennessee Waltz (5)
Turn Your Radio On (9)
Under The Double Eagle (7)
Wabash Cannon Ball (3)
Wait For The Light To Shine (7)

Walking The Floor Over You (9)
Ways To Love A Man (3)
Wildwood Brass (2)
Wings Of A Dove (4)
Wolverton Mountain (3)
Woman (Sensuous Woman) (8)
Yakety Axe (2)
Yesterday, When I Was Young (3)
Yesterday's Wine (9)

DAVIS, Jimmy, & Junction
Rock vocalist Jimmy Davis with Tommy Burroughs, Chuck Reynolds and John Scott.

| 10/31/87 | 122 | 8 | | Kick The Wall .... | $8 | MCA 42015 |

Are We Rockin' Yet?
Catch My Heart

Don't Hold Back The Night
Just A Little Bit

Just Having Touched
Kick The Wall 67

Labor Of Love
Over The Top

Shoe Shine Man
Why The West Was Won

★★411★★   DAVIS, Mac
Born on 1/21/42 in Lubbock, Texas. Vocalist/guitarist/composer. Worked as a regional rep for Vee-Jay and Liberty Records. Wrote "In The Ghetto," "Don't Cry Daddy," hits for Elvis Presley. Host of own musical variety TV series from 1974-76. Appearances in several films, including *North Dallas Forty* in 1979.

12/25/71+	160	17		1 I Believe In Music..	$10	Columbia 30926
9/16/72	11	44	▲	2 Baby Don't Get Hooked On Me	$10	Columbia 31770
4/21/73	120	13		3 Mac Davis	$10	Columbia 32206
5/4/74	13	45	●	4 Stop And Smell The Roses	$10	Columbia 32582
10/19/74	182	4		5 Song Painter ....[E-R]	$10	Columbia 9969
				reissue of Mac's first album		
2/8/75	21	14	●	6 All The Love In The World	$10	Columbia 32927
7/5/75	64	10		7 Burnin' Thing	$10	Columbia 33551
4/10/76	156	9		8 Forever Lovers	$10	Columbia 34105
5/24/80	69	15	●	9 It's Hard To Be Humble	$8	Casablanca 7207
10/18/80	67	9		10 Texas In My Rear View Mirror	$8	Casablanca 7239
1/16/82	174	3		11 Midnight Crazy	$8	Casablanca 7257

Baby Don't Get Hooked On Me (2) *1*
Baby, I Just Ain't The Man For You (8)

Beginning To Feel The Pain (3) *92*
Biff, The Friendly Purple Bear (6)
Birthday Song (4)

Boogie Woogie Mama (6)
Burnin' Thing (7) *53*
Christmas Carol (1)
Closest I Ever Came (5)
Comfortable (11)

Daddy's Little Man (5)
Dammit Girl (11)
Dream Me Home (2) *73*
Emily Suzanne (6)
Every Now And Then (8)

Every Woman (6)
Everybody Loves A Love Song (2) *63*
Everything A Man Could Ever Need (3)

Fall In Love With Your Wife (6)
Feel Like Crying (3)
Float Away (11)
Forever Lovers (8) *76*

DEBUT DATE	PEAK POS	WKS CHR	GOLD	ARTIST — Album Title	$	Label & Number

DAVIS, Mac — Cont'd

Freedom Trail (6)	(Hope You Didn't) Chop No Wood (3)	In The Eyes Of My People (1,10)	Once You Get Used To It (5)	Smiley (6)	**Whoever Finds This, I**
Friend, Lover, Woman, Wife (2)	Hot Texas Night (10)	In The Ghetto (5)	**One Hell Of A Woman** (4) **11**	Soft, Sweet Fire (4)	**Love You** (2,5) **53**
Good Friends And Fireplaces (4)	I Believe In Music (1)	It Was Time (9)	Please Tell Her That I Said	Something's Burning (1,11)	Why Don't We Sleep On It (9)
Good Times We Had (8)	I Feel The Country Callin' Me (7)	**It's Hard To Be Humble** (9) **43**	Hello (8)	Special Place In Heaven (7)	Woman Crying (3)
Gravel On The Ground (9)	I Got The Hots For You (11)	Jimmy Brown Song (7)	Poem For My Little Lady (1)	Spread Your Love On Me (2)	Words Don't Come Easy (2)
Greatest Gift Of All (9)	I Know You're Out There Somewhere (9)	Kiss It And Make It Better (4,11)	Poor Boy Boogie (2)	**Stop And Smell The Roses** (4) **9**	Yesterday And You (1)
Half And Half (Song For Sarah) (2,5)	I Still Love You, Still Love Me (2)	Let's Keep It That Way (9)	Poor Man's Gold (4)	Sunshine (3)	You Are So Lovely (11)
Hello Hollywood (9)	I Wanta Wake Up With You (9)	Little Less Conversation (1)	Put Another Notch In Your Belt (7)	Sweet Dreams And Sarah (7)	You're Gonna Love Yourself (In The Morning) (7)
Hello L.A., Bye Bye Birmingham (5)	I Will Always Love You (9)	Lonesomest Lonesome (2)	Remember When (Beverly's Song) (10)	Sweetest Song (4)	You're Good For Me (5)
Hits Just Keep On Coming (7)	I Won't Want To Own You (8)	Love Lamp (8)	**Rock N' Roll (I Gave You The Best Years Of My Life)** (6) **15**	(Tell Me Your) Fantasies (11)	You're My Bestest Friend (11)
Hollywood Humpty Dumpty (1)	I'll Paint You A Song (3)	Lovin' You, Lovin' Me (3)	Tequila Sheila (9)	**Your Side Of The Bed** (3) **88**
Home (5)	I'm A Survivor (8)	Lucus Was A Redneck (4)	**Texas In My Rear View Mirror** (10) **51**	Two Plus Two (4)
Honeysuckle Magic (7)	I'm Just In Love (8)	Magic Mystery (6)	Rodeo Clown (10)	Uncle Boogar Red And Byrdie Nelle (5)
Hooked On Music (10)	**(If You Add) All The Love In The World** (6) **54**	Me And Fat Boy (10)	Rufus Was A Redneck (7)	Watching Scotty Grow (1)
		Memories (3)	Sad Songs (10)	Way You Look Today (3)
		Midnight Crazy (11)	Sarah Between The Lines (1)	
		Naughty Girl (2)	**Secrets** (10) **76**	

DAVIS, Martha

Lead singer of the Motels. Born on 1/15/51 and raised in Berkeley. To Los Angeles in the early '70s. Overcame battle with cancer in 1987.

11/14/87	**127**	13		Policy	$8	Capitol 48054

Don't Ask Out Loud   Hardest Part Of A Broken   Heaven Outside My Door   Lust   Rebecca   What Money Might Buy
Don't Tell Me The Time 80   Heart   Just Like You   My Promise   Tell It To The Moon

★★179★★ DAVIS, Miles

Innovative jazz trumpeter who influenced the jazz fusion movement. Born on 5/26/26 in Alton, Illinois. Died on 9/28/91 of a stroke and pneumonia. Began career in 1944 with Billy Eckstine's orchestra. With Six Brown Cats group in 1944. With Charlie Parker and Coleman Hawkins. Recorded with Parker on Savoy and Dial from 1945-46. Formed own quintet in 1955. Band members included Herbie Hancock and Wayne Shorter. Received 23 Grammy nominations, won the Lifetime Achievement Grammy in 1990. Married to actress Cicely Tyson from 1981-88.

DEBUT DATE	PEAK POS	WKS CHR	GOLD	#	ARTIST — Album Title	$	Label & Number
10/2/61	**68**	19		1	Miles Davis In Person (Friday & Saturday Nights At The Blackhawk, San Francisco) .... [I-L]	$30	Columbia 8494 [2]
3/24/62	**116**	10		2	Someday My Prince Will Come .... [I]	$25	Columbia 8456
10/6/62	**59**	7		3	Miles Davis At Carnegie Hall .... [I-L]	$20	Columbia 8612
9/14/63	**62**	15		4	Seven Steps To Heaven .... [I]	$20	Columbia 8851
4/11/64	**93**	9		5	Quiet Nights .... [I]	$20	Columbia 8906
9/26/64	**116**	10		6	Miles Davis In Europe .... [I-L]	$20	Columbia 8983
4/24/65	**138**	9		7	My Funny Valentine .... [I-L]	$15	Columbia 9106
9/6/69	**134**	6		8	In A Silent Way .... [I]	$15	Columbia 9875
5/16/70	**35**	29	●	9	Bitches Brew .... [I]	$12	Columbia 26 [2]
12/12/70+	**123**	12		10	Miles Davis At Fillmore .... [I]	$12	Columbia 30038 [2]
4/24/71	**159**	8		11	A Tribute To Jack Johnson .... [I-S]	$12	Columbia 30455
					film is a biography of the world heavyweight boxing champ (1908-1915)		
12/25/71+	**125**	13		12	Live-Evil .... [I]	$12	Columbia 30954 [2]
11/18/72	**156**	11		13	On The Corner .... [I]	$12	Columbia 31906
5/5/73	**152**	8		14	In Concert .... [I-L]	$12	Columbia 32092 [2]
10/13/73	**189**	3		15	Basic Miles - The Classic Performances of Miles Davis .... [E-I]	$12	Columbia 32025
					recordings from 1955-58		
6/8/74	**179**	5		16	Big Fun .... [I]	$10	Columbia 32866 [2]
1/4/75	**141**	8		17	Get Up With It .... [I]	$12	Columbia 33236 [2]
					a Duke Ellington tribute album		
3/13/76	**168**	5		18	Agharta .... [I-L]	$12	Columbia 33967 [2]
					recorded at Osaka Festival Hall, Japan on 2/1/75		
5/7/77	**190**	2		19	Water Babies .... [I-K]	$10	Columbia 34396
					late '60's recordings		
4/11/81	**179**	2		20	Directions .... [I-K]	$10	Columbia 36472 [2]
					unreleased recordings 1960-70		
7/25/81	**53**	18		21	The Man With The Horn .... [I]	$8	Columbia 36790
5/29/82	**159**	7		22	We Want Miles .... [I-L]	$10	Columbia 38005 [2]
5/21/83	**136**	7		23	Star People .... [I]	$8	Columbia 38657
6/30/84	**169**	11		24	Decoy .... [I]	$8	Columbia 38991
6/1/85	**111**	12		25	You're Under Arrest .... [I]	$8	Columbia 40023
10/25/86	**141**	10		26	Tutu .... [I]	$8	Warner 25490
6/17/89	**177**	5		27	Amandla .... [I]	$8	Warner 25873
					title is Zulu for power		
7/25/92	**190**	4		28	Doo-Bop .... [I]	$12	Warner 26938
					his last studio album; includes 2 tracks completed after his death		

Aida (21)	Big Time (27)	Code M.D. (24)	Duke Booty (28)	Go Ahead John (16)	In A Silent Way (medley) (8)
All Blues (7)	Billy Preston (17)	Come Get It (23)	Duran (20)	Great Expectations (16)	Inamorata (12)
All Of You (1,6,7)	Bitches Brew (9)	Corcovado (5)	Fantasy (28)	Hannibal (27)	Interlude (18)
Amandla (27)	Black Satin (13)	Decoy (24)	Fast Track (22)	He Loved Him Madly (17)	It Gets Better (23)
Aos Pes Da Cruz (5)	Blow (28)	Devil May Care (11)	Fat Time (21)	Helen Butte (medley) (6)	It's About That Time
Ascent (20)	Budo (15)	Directions I (20)	Fran-Dance (1,15)	High Speed Chase (28)	(medley) (8)
Autumn Leaves (4)	Bye Bye Blackbird (1)	Don't Lose Your Mind (26)	Freaky Deaky (24)	Honky Tonk (17)	Jack Johnson, Theme From
Baby Won't You Please Come Home (4)	Calypso Frelimo (17)	Doo-Bop Song (28)	Friday Miles (10)	Human Nature (25)	(18)
Back Seat Betty (21,22)	Capricorn (19)	Double Image (medley) (12)	Full Nelson (26)	I Fall In Love Too Easily (4)	Jean Pierre (22,25)
Backyard Ritual (26)	Catembe (27)	Drad-Dog (2)	Fun (20)	I Thought About You (2,7)	Jilli (27)
Basin Street Blues (4)	Chocolate Chip (28)	Dual Mr. Tillman Anthony (19)	Funky Tonk (12)	If I Were A Bell (1)	Jo-Jo (27)
	Cobra (27)		Gemini (medley) (12)	Ife (16)	John McLaughlin (9)

187

DAVIS, Miles — Cont'd

Joshua (4,6)
Katia (25)
KIX (22)
Konda (20)
Lament (medley) (3)
Limbo (20)
Little Church (12)
Little Melonae (15)
Lonely Fire (16)
Love, I've Found You (1)
MD1 (medley) (25)
MD2 (medley) (25)
Maiysha (17,18)
Man With The Horn (21)
Meaning Of The Blues (medley) (3)
Miles Ahead (15)
Miles Davis In Concert (14)

Miles Runs The Voodoo Down (9)
Milestones (6)
Mr. Freedom X (medley) (13)
Mr. Pastorius (27)
Ms. Morrisine (25)
Mtume (17)
My Funny Valentine (7)
My Man's Gone Now (22)
Mystery (28)
Nem Um Talvez (12)
Neo (1)
New Rhumba (medley) (3)
New York Girl (medley) (13)
No Blues (1,3)
Old Folks (2)
Oleo (1,3)
On Green Dolphin Street (15)
On The Corner (medley) (13)

Once Upon A Summertime (5)
One And One (13)
One Phone Call (medley) (25)
Peaceful (medley) (8)
Perfect Way (26)
Pfrancing (2)
Pharaoh's Dance (9)
Portia (26)
Prelude Parts I & II (18)
Rated X (17)
Red China Blues (17)
Right Off (11)
Robot 415 (24)
Round Midnight (15,20)
Sanctuary (9)
Saturday Miles (10)
Selim (12)
Seven Steps To Heaven (4)

Shhh (medley) (8)
Shout (21)
Sivad (12)
So Near, So Far (4,20)
So What (1,3)
Someday My Prince Will Come (2,3)
Something's On Your Mind (medley) (25)
Song #1 (5)
Song #2 (5)
Song Of Our Country (20)
Sonya (28)
Spanish Key (9)
Speak (23)
Splatch (26)
Spring Is Here (3)
Star On Cicely (23)
Star People (23)

Stella By Starlight (7,15)
Street Scenes (medley) (25)
Summer Night (5)
Sweet Pea (19)
Sweet Sue, Just You (15)
Teo (2)
That's Right (24)
That's What Happened (24)
Then There Were None (medley) (25)
Thinkin' One Thing And Doin' Another (medley) (13)
Thursday Miles (10)
Time After Time (25)
Tomaas (26)
Tutu (26)
Two Faced (19)
U 'N' I (23)
Ursula (21)

Vote For Miles (medley) (13)
Wait Till You See Her (5)
Walkin' (1,6)
Water Babies (19)
Water On The Pond (20)
Wednesday Miles (10)
Well You Needn't (1)
What I Say (12)
What It Is (24)
Willie Nelson (20)
Yesternow (11)
You're Under Arrest (25)

DAVIS, Paul

Born on 4/21/48 in Meridian, Mississippi. Singer/songwriter/producer. Appeared as "Peter" on the 1970 concept LP *Jesus Christ Superstar*.

DEBUT DATE	PEAK POS	WKS CHR			$	Label & Number
1/11/75	148	6	1	Ride 'Em Cowboy	$12	Bang 401
1/21/78	82	18	2	Singer Of Songs - Teller Of Tales	$12	Bang 410
4/26/80	173	4	3	Paul Davis	$10	Bang 36094
12/19/81+	52	29	4	Cool Night	$8	Arista 9578

All The Way (3)
Bad Dream (2)
Bronco Rider (1)
Can't Get Back To Alabama (medley) (1)
Cool Night (4) *11*
Cry Just A Little (3) *78*
Darlin' (2) *51*
Do Right (3) *23*
Do You Believe In Love (3)

Editorial (2)
Hallelujah Thank You Jesus (2)
He Sang Our Love Songs (3)
I Don't Want To Be Just Another Love (2)
I Go Crazy (1) *7*
I Never Heard The Song At All (2)

I'm The Only Sinner (In Salt Lake City) (1)
Let Me Know If It's Over (3)
Life Of A Cowboy (medley) (1)
Love Or Let Me Be Lonely (4) *40*
Make Her My Baby (1)
Midnight Woman (1)
Nathan Jones (4)

Never Want To Lose Your Love (2)
One More Time For The Lonely (4)
Oriental Eyes (4)
Ride 'Em Cowboy (1) *23*
Simple Country Life (1)
'65 Love Affair (4) *6*
So True (3)

Somebody's Gettin' To You (4)
Southern Man (1)
Sweet Life (2) *17*
Ten Little Indians (medley) (1)
Thank You Shoes (medley) (1)
Too Slow To Disco (3)
We're Still Together (4)

What You Got To Say About Love (4)
When Everything Else Is Gone (3)
You Came To Me (4)
You're Not Just A Rose (1,2)

★★251★★ DAVIS, Sammy Jr.

Born on 12/8/25 in New York City; died of throat cancer on 5/16/90. Vocalist/dancer/actor. With father and uncle in dance act, the Will Mastin Trio, from the early 1940s. First recorded for Decca in 1954. Lost his left eye and had his nose smashed in an auto accident near San Bernardino, California on 11/19/54; returned to performing in January 1955. Frequent appearances on TV, Broadway and in films.

DEBUT DATE	PEAK POS	WKS CHR			$	Label & Number
5/14/55	1[6]	27	1	Starring Sammy Davis, Jr.	$30	Decca 8118
10/15/55	5	9	2	Just For Lovers	$30	Decca 8170
10/20/62	14	22	3	What Kind Of Fool Am I and Other Show-Stoppers	$20	Reprise 6051
3/16/63	96	6	4	Sammy Davis Jr. At The Cocoanut Grove [L]	$20	Reprise 6063 [2]
5/25/63	73	15	5	As Long As She Needs Me	$20	Reprise 6082
3/14/64	139	3	6	Sammy Davis Jr. Salutes The Stars Of The London Palladium	$20	Reprise 6095
4/4/64	26	18	7	The Shelter Of Your Arms	$20	Reprise 6114
3/27/65	141	4	8	Our Shining Hour	$15	Verve 8605
				SAMMY DAVIS, JR. & COUNT BASIE		
9/4/65	104	4	9	Sammy's Back On Broadway	$15	Reprise 6169
1/11/69	24	25	10	I've Gotta Be Me	$15	Reprise 6324
4/29/72	11	26	11	Sammy Davis Jr. Now	$10	MGM 4832
10/14/72	128	15	12	Portrait Of Sammy Davis, Jr.	$10	MGM 4852

And This Is My Beloved (1)
April In Paris (8)
As Long As She Needs Me (5) *59*
Back In Your Own Back Yard (5)
Ballin' The Jack (6)
Because Of You (1)
Bee-Bom (7)
Begin The Beguine (3)
Big Bad John (medley) (4)
Bill Basie Won't You Please Come Home (8)
Birth Of The Blues (1,4)
Blues For Mr. Charlie (8)
Body And Soul (3)
Bye Bye Blackbird (5)
Can't We Be Friends (3)
Candy Man (11) *1*
Climb Ev'ry Mountain (5)
Come On Strong (7)
Come Rain Or Come Shine (2)
Do I Hear A Waltz? (9)
Easy To Love (1)
Falling In Love Again (4)
Falling In Love With Love (5)
Get Out Of Town (2)
Girl From Ipanema (8)

Give Me The Moonlight, Give Me The Girl (6)
Glad To Be Unhappy (1)
Gonna Build A Mountain (3)
Guys And Dolls (7)
Happy Ending (2)
Have A Little Talk With Myself (11)
Hello, Dolly! (9)
Here Am I - Broken Hearted (6)
Here I'll Stay (10)
Hey There (1)
Hound Dog (medley) (4)
I Am Over 25-But You Can Trust Me (11)
I Do Not Love You (12)
I Married An Angel (7)
I Want To Be Happy (11)
I Want To Be With You (9)
I'll Begin Again (11)
I'm A Brass Band (9)
I'm Glad There Is You (10)
I've Got You Under My Skin (4,10)
I've Gotta Be Me (10) *11*
If I Loved You (7)
If My Friends Could See Me Now (10)

In My Own Lifetime (12)
In The Still Of The Night (4)
It's A Musical World (12)
It's All Right With Me (2)
Jalousie (6)
Jam Session (Sam, By George!) (medley) (4)
John Shaft (11)
Joker, The (9)
Keepin' Out Of Mischief Now (8)
Lazy River (6)
Lonesome Road (1)
Look At That Face (9)
Lost In The Stars (3)
Lot Of Livin' To Do (3)
Love Is All Around (12)
(Love Is) The Tender Trap (5)
MacArthur Park (11)
Make Someone Happy (7)
Man With A Dream (7)
Married Man (9)
Me And My Shadow (4) *64*
Meeting The President (4)
Mr. Bojangles (12)
My Funny Valentine (1)
My Kind Of Girl (9)
My Personal Property (10)
My Romance (3)

My Shining Hour (8)
New York City Blues (8)
Night And Day (medley) (4)
Once In A Lifetime (3,4)
Other Half Of Me (9)
Out Of This World (5)
Over The Rainbow (6)
Party's Over? (7)
People (9)
People Tree (12) *92*
River Stay 'Way From My Door (4)
Rock-A-Bye Your Baby With A Dixie Melody (4)
Room Without Windows (9)
Sammy Looks At Old Movies (4)
September Song (1)
She Believes In Me (11)
She's A Woman (8)
Shelter Of Your Arms (7) *17*
Smile (6)
Some Days Everything Goes Wrong (4)
Somebody (10)
Someone Nice Like You (3)
Something's Coming (3)
Sophisticated Lady (6)
Spoken For (1)

Stan' Up An' Fight (1)
Step Out Of That Dream (5)
Sunrise, Sunset (9)
Sweet Gingerbread Man (12)
Sweet November (10)
Take My Hand (11)
Take The Moment (9)
Teach Me Tonight (8)
Tenderly (2)
Tenement Symphony (6)
That's For Me (7)
There Is Nothing Like A Dame (5)
There Was A Tavern In The Town (7)
These Foolish Things (Remind Me Of You) (2)
This Is My Life (11)
This Was My Love (6)
Thou Swell (3)
Thrill Is Gone (2)
Time To Ride (12)
Tomorrow (12)
Too Close For Comfort (3)
Two For The Seesaw (A Second Chance), Song From (5)
We Kiss In A Shadow (5)
West Side Story Medley (4)

What Kind Of Fool Am I (3,4) *17*
What'd I Say (medley) (4)
When The Wind Was Green (12)
When Your Lover Has Gone (2)
Why Try To Change Me Now (8)
Willoughby Grove (11)
Wonderful Day Like Today (9)
Work Song (8)
You Can Have Her (12)
You Do Something To Me (2)
You're My Girl (2)
You're Nobody Till Somebody Loves You (8)

DAVIS, Skeeter

Country singer. Born Mary Penick on 12/30/31 in Dry Ridge, Kentucky. Recorded with friend Betty Davis as the Davis Sisters, until Betty was killed in a car accident on 8/2/53. Formerly married to TV's *Nashville Now* host, Ralph Emery. Later married Joey Spampinato, the bassist of jazz-rock band NRBQ.

4/13/63	**61**	15		The End Of The World	**$20**	RCA 2699

Don't Let Me Cross Over   (I Want To Go) Where   Keep Your Hands Off My   Mine Is A Lonely Life   Silver Threads And Golden   Something Precious
End Of The World 2   Nobody Knows Me   Baby   My Coloring Book   Needles   Why I'm Walkin'
He Called Me Baby   Longing To Hold You Again   Once Upon A Time

DAVIS, Spencer, Group

R&B-styled rock band formed in Birmingham, England in 1963: Spencer Davis (vocals, rhythm guitar) and Peter York (drums), with brothers Steve (lead vocals, lead guitar, keyboards) and Muff Winwood (bass). Steve left to form Traffic; later became successful solo artist. Muff later became the senior director of A&R at CBS Records, U.K.

3/25/67	**54**	25	1	Gimme Some Lovin'	**$25**	United Art. 6578
7/15/67	**83**	9	2	I'm A Man	**$25**	United Art. 6589
3/30/68	**195**	3	3	Spencer Davis' Greatest Hits .... [G]	**$25**	United Art. 6641

Blues In F (3)   Goodbye Stevie (1)   It Hurts Me So (1)   Nobody Knows You When   Stevie's Blues (2)
Dimples (2)   Hammer Song (1)   **Keep On Running** (1,3) 76   You're Down And Out (1)   **Time Seller** (3) 100
Don't Want You No More (3)   Here Right Now (1)   Look Away (2)   On The Green Light (2,3)   Trampoline (1)
Every Little Bit Hurts (2)   I Can't Get Enough Of It (2)   Midnight Special (1,3)   Searchin' (2,3)   When I Come Home (1)
Georgia On My Mind (3)   I Can't Stand It (2)   Midnight Train (2)   Sittin' And Thinkin' (1)
Gimme Some Lovin' (1,3) 7   **I'm A Man** (2,3) 10   My Babe (2)   **Somebody Help Me** (1,3) 47

DAVIS, Tyrone

Soul singer. Born on 5/4/38 in Greenville, Mississippi and raised in Saginaw, Michigan. To Chicago in 1959. Worked as valet/chauffeur for Freddie King until 1962. Working local clubs when discovered by Harold Burrage. First recorded for Four Brothers in 1965 as Tyrone The Wonder Boy. His younger sister, Jean Davis, was a member of the group Facts Of Life.

3/29/69	**146**	6	1	Can I Change My Mind	**$15**	Dakar 9005
7/11/70	**90**	11	2	Turn Back The Hands Of Time	**$12**	Dakar 9027
7/1/72	**182**	6	3	I Had It All The Time	**$12**	Dakar 76901
8/11/73	**174**	6	4	Without You In My Life	**$12**	Dakar 76904
10/2/76	**89**	9	5	Love And Touch	**$10**	Columbia 34268
4/7/79	**115**	12	6	In The Mood With Tyrone Davis	**$10**	Columbia 35723
1/8/83	**137**	6	7	Tyrone Davis	**$8**	Highrise 103

After All This Time (3)   Have You Ever Wondered   I'm Just Your Man (4)   Let Me Be The One (7)   True Love Is Hard to Find (4)   Woman Needs To Be Loved
Ain't Nothing I Can Do (6)   Why (1)   I'm So Excited (7)   Let The Good Times Roll (7)   **Turn Back The Hands Of**   (1)
All The Love I Need (6)   Honey You Are My Sunshine   If It's Love That You're After   Little Bit Of Lovin' (7)   **Time** (2) 3   Wrapped Up In Your Warm
Are You Serious (7) 57   (4)   (2)   Love Bones (2)   Undying Love (2)   And Tender Love (4)
Beware, Beware (5)   How Could I Forget You (3)   If You Had A Change In   Open The Door To Your   Waiting Was Not In Vain (2)   Wrong Doers (5)
Call On Me (1)   I Can't Wait (6)   Mind (4)   Heart (1)   Was I Just A Fool (3)   You Can't Keep A Good Man
Can I Change My Mind (1) 5   I Don't Think You Heard Me   In The Mood (6)   Overdue (7)   Was It Just A Feeling (3)   Down (1)
Close To You (5)   (6)   Just Because Of You (2)   Put Your Trust In Me (5)   We Were In Love Then (6)   You Know What To Do (6)
Come And Get This Ring (3)   I Got A Sure Thing (4)   Just The One I've Been   She's Lookin' Good (1)   Where Did We Lose (7)   You Wouldn't Believe (3,4)
Fool In Me (7)   **I Had It All The Time**   Looking For (1)   Slip Away (1)   Why Is It So Hard (To Say   You're Too Much (5)
Give It Up (Turn It Loose)   (3,4) 61   Keep On Dancin' (6)   Something You Got (2)   You're Sorry) (5)   You've Got To (Save Me) (7)
(5) 38   I Keep Coming Back (2)   Knock On Wood (1)   **There It Is** (4) 32   **Without You In My Life**   Your Love Keeps Haunting
Givin' Myself To You (5)   **I'll Be Right Here** (2) 53   Let Me Back In (2) 58   This Time (3)   (4) 64   Me (3)

DAVIS, Wild Bill — see HODGES, Johnny

★★350★★ DAWN

Pop vocal trio formed in New York City: Tony Orlando (b: 4/3/44, New York City), Telma Hopkins (b: 10/28/48, Louisville) and Joyce Vincent (b: 12/14/46, Detroit). Orlando had recorded solo from 1961-63; Hopkins and Vincent had been backup singers. Orlando was manager for April-Blackwood Music at the time of their first hit. Own TV show from 1974-76. All of their hits produced by Hank Medress (The Tokens) and Dave Appell. Hopkins appeared on TV's *Bosom Buddies*, *Gimme A Break* and *Family Matters*.

12/19/70+	**35**	23		1	Candida	**$12**	Bell 6052
					DAWN featuring TONY ORLANDO:		
12/18/71	**178**	2		2	Dawn featuring Tony Orlando	**$12**	Bell 6069
3/24/73	**30**	34	●	3	Tuneweaving	**$10**	Bell 1112
10/20/73+	**43**	58	●	4	Dawn's New Ragtime Follies	**$10**	Bell 1130
					TONY ORLANDO & DAWN:		
12/7/74+	**16**	17		5	Prime Time	**$10**	Bell 1317
1/11/75	**165**	5		6	Tony Orlando & Dawn II .... [R]	**$10**	Bell 1322
					reissue of album #2 above		
1/18/75	**170**	4		7	Candida & Knock Three Times .... [R]	**$10**	Bell 1320
					reissue of album #1 above		
4/26/75	**20**	17		8	He Don't Love You (Like I Love You)	**$10**	Elektra 1034
6/28/75	**16**	32	●	9	Greatest Hits .... [G]	**$10**	Arista 4045
11/1/75	**93**	6		10	Skybird	**$10**	Arista 4059
3/20/76	**94**	6		11	To Be With You	**$10**	Elektra 1049

All In The Game (10)   Dance, Rosie, Dance (8)   Get Out From Where We Are   House Of Strangers (8)   If Only (He Would Make   **Look In My Eyes Pretty**
Another Rainy Day In My   Dancing To The Music (10)   (2,6)   I Can't Believe How Much I   Love To Me) (8)   **Woman** (5,9) 11
Life (5)   Daydream (4)   Gimme A Good Old Mammy   Love You (3)   In The Park (2,6)   Love In Your Eyes (1,7)
Atlanta (3)   Did You Ever Think She'd   Song (2)   I Didn't Mean To Love You   Jolie (3,10)   Love The One You're With
Candida (1,7,9) 3   Get Away From You (10)   Good Life (2,6)   So Good, Juanita (2,6)   Kelly Blye (10)   (2,6)
Caress Me Pretty Music (11)   Dreamboat (5)   Grandma's Hands (8)   I Don't Know You Anymore   **Knock Three Times**   Maybe I Should Marry
Carmen (2,6)   Easy Evil (3)   Happy Man (11)   (3)   (1,7,9) 1   Jamie (8)
Carolina In My Mind (1,7)   Fancy Meeting You Here   **He Don't Love You (Like I**   I Get Ideas (2,6)   Lazy Susan (3)   Midnight Love Affair (11)
Come Back Billie Jo (10)   Baby (5)   **Love You)** (8) 1   **I Play And Sing** (2,6) 25   Let's Run Away Girl (1,7)   Missin' That Girl (8)
Country (1,7)   Freedom For The Stallion (3)   Here Comes The Spring (5)   If It Wasn't For You Dear (4)   Little Heads In Bunkbeds (5)   **Mornin' Beautiful** (8) 14
Cupid (11) 22   Home (1,7)   Look At... (1,7)   My Love Has No Pride (5)

DEBUT DATE	PEAK POS	WKS CHR	GOLD	ARTIST — Album Title	$	Label & Number

DAWN — Cont'd

Perhaps The Joy Of Giving (1,7)
Personality (10)
Pick It Up (8)
Raindrops (5)
Rainy Day Man (1,7)
Runaway/Happy Together (3) **79**

Say, Has Anybody Seen My Sweet Gypsy Rose (4,9) **3**
Selfish One (11)
She Can't Hold A Candle To You (5)
Skybird (10) **49**
Steppin' Out (Gonna Boogie Tonight) (4,9) **7**
Straight Ahead (10)

Summer Sand (2,6,9) **33**
Sweet Soft Sounds Of Love (2,6)
Sweet Summer Days Of My Life (4)
Talk To Me (11)
That's The Way A Wallflower Grows (10)

Tie A Yellow Ribbon Round The Ole Oak Tree (3,9) **1**
To Be With You (11)
Tomorrow's Got To Be Sunny (Far Fitna Di Ess Ere Sani) (8)
Ukulele Man (4)
Up On The Roof (1,7)

Watch A Clown Break Down (3)
What Are You Doing Sunday (1,2,6,7,9) **39**
When The Party's Over (11)
When We All Sang Along (3)
Who Did A Number On Me (2,6)
Who's In The Strawberry Patch With Sally (4,9) **27**

You Say The Sweetest Things (4,9)
You're A Lady (3,9) **70**
You're All I Need To Get By (11) **34**
(You're) Growin' On Me (11)

★★415★★ DAY, Doris

Born Doris Kappelhoff on 4/3/22 in Cincinnati. Doris sang briefly with Bob Crosby in 1940 and shortly thereafter became a major star with the Les Brown band ("Sentimental Journey"). Her great solo recording success was soon transcended by Hollywood as Doris became the #1 box office star of the late '50s and early '60s. Star of own popular TV series from 1968-73. Her son, Terry Melcher, was a member of the Rip Chords and Bruce & Terry, and a prolific producer (The Beach Boys).

DEBUT DATE	PEAK POS	WKS CHR	GOLD	ARTIST — Album Title	$	Label & Number
2/5/55	15	2		1 Young At Heart ....[S]	$40	Columbia 6339

10" album; 6 cuts by Doris, 2 by Frank Sinatra: "One For My Baby (And One More For The Road)" and "Someone To Watch Over Me"

6/25/55	1¹⁷	28		2 Love Me Or Leave Me ....[S]	$30	Columbia 710

Doris portrayed singer Ruth Etting in the film

2/9/57	11	6		3 Day By Day............	$30	Columbia 942
5/30/60	26	7		4 Listen To Day............	$25	Columbia DD1
10/2/61	97	8		5 I Have Dreamed............	$25	Columbia 8460
3/14/64	102	8		6 Love Him!............	$25	Columbia 8931

All I Do Is Dream Of You (5)
Anyway The Wind Blows (4) **50**
As Long As He Needs Me (6)
At Sundown (2)
Autumn Leaves (3)
But Beautiful (3)
But Not For Me (3)
Can't Help Falling In Love (6)
Day By Day (3)
Don't Take Your Love From Me (3)
Everybody Loves My Baby (But My Baby Don't Love Nobody But Me) (2)

Funny (6)
Gone With The Wind (3)
Gypsy In My Soul (3)
He's So Married (4)
Heart Full Of Love (4)
Hello, My Lover, Goodbye (3)
Hold Me In Your Arms (1)
I Believe In Dreams (5)
I Enjoy Being A Girl (4)
I Hadn't Anyone Till You (3)
I Have Dreamed (5)
I Remember You (3)
I'll Buy That Dream (5)
I'll Never Stop Loving You (2) **13**

Inspiration (4)
It All Depends On You (2)
Just One Of Those Things (1)
Lollipops And Roses (6)
Losing You (6)
Love Him (6)
Love Me In The Daytime (4) **100**
Love Me Or Leave Me (2)
Mean To Me (2)
More (6)
My Ship (5)
Never Look Back (2)
Night Life (6)
No (4)

(Now And Then There's) A Fool Such As I (6)
Oh What A Beautiful Dream (5)
Oh! What A Lover You'll Be (4)
Periwinkle Blue (5)
Pillow Talk (4)
Possess Me (4)
Ready, Willing And Able (4)
Roly Poly (4)
Sam, The Old Accordion Man (2)
Shaking The Blues Away (2)
Since I Fell For You (6)

Softly, As I Leave You (6)
Someday I'll Find You (5)
Song Is You (3)
Stay On The Right Side, Sister (2)
Ten Cents A Dance (2)
There'll Never Be Another You (3)
Till My Love Comes To Me (1)
Time To Say Goodnight (5)
Tunnel Of Love (4) **43**
We'll Love Again (5)
When I Grow Too Old To Dream (5)

You Made Me Love You (I Didn't Want To Do It) (2)
You My Love (1)
You Stepped Out Of A Dream (5)

DAY, Morris

Leader of Minneapolis funk group The Time (formerly Prince's backing band). Born in Springfield, Illinois and raised in Minneapolis. Acted in the films *Purple Rain*, *The Adventures Of Ford Fairlane* and *Graffiti Bridge*.

DEBUT DATE	PEAK POS	WKS CHR	GOLD	ARTIST — Album Title	$	Label & Number
10/19/85	37	31		1 Color Of Success	$8	Warner 25320
3/12/88	41	15		2 Daydreaming	$8	Warner 25651

Addiction (medley) (1)
Are You Ready (2)
Character, The (1)

Color Of Success (1)
Daydreaming (2)
Don't Wait For Me (1)

Fishnet (2) **23**
Love (medley) (1)
Love Is A Game (2)

Love Sign (1)
Man's Pride (2)
Moonlite (Passionlite) (2)

Oak Tree (1) **65**
Sally (2)
Yo' Luv (2)

DAYE, Cory

Born on 4/25/52 in the Bronx, New York. Lead singer of Dr. Buzzard's Original Savannah Band.

DEBUT DATE	PEAK POS	WKS CHR	GOLD	ARTIST — Album Title	$	Label & Number
10/13/79	171	5		1 Cory And Me	$8	New York I. 3408

Be Bop Betty A/K/A Co Co Ree

Green Light
Keep The Ball Rollin'

Pow Wow **76**
Rainy Day Boy

Rhythm Death
Single Again (medley)

What Time Does The Balloon Go Up (medley)

Wiggle & A Giggle All Night

DAYNE, Taylor

Female pop singer born Leslie Wonderman on 7/3/62 on Long Island, New York.

DEBUT DATE	PEAK POS	WKS CHR	GOLD	ARTIST — Album Title	$	Label & Number
1/30/88	21	69	▲²	1 Tell It To My Heart	$8	Arista 8529
11/18/89+	25	55	▲	2 Can't Fight Fate	$8	Arista 8581

Ain't No Good (2)
Carry Your Heart (1)
Do You Want It Right Now (1)
Don't Rush Me (1) **2**
Heart Of Stone (2) **12**

I Know The Feeling (2)
I'll Always Love You (1) **3**
I'll Be Your Shelter (2) **4**
In The Darkness (1)
Up All Night (2)

Love Will Lead You Back (2) **1**
Prove Your Love (1) **7**
Tell It To My Heart (1) **7**
Where Does That Boy Hang Out (1)

Upon The Journey's End (1)
Wait For Me (2)
Want Ads (1)
You Can't Fight Fate (2)
You Meant The World To Me (1)

With Every Beat Of My Heart (2) **5**

DAZZ BAND

Cleveland ultrafunk band, formerly Kinsman Dazz. "Dazz" means "danceable jazz." Formed by Bobby Harris (vocalist, saxophone) by merging Bell Telefunk and the house band at Cleveland's Kinsman Grill. Included Pierre DeMudd, Sennie "Skip" Martin III, Eric Fearman, Kevin Frederick, Kenny Pettus, Michael Wiley and Isaac Wiley.

DEBUT DATE	PEAK POS	WKS CHR	GOLD	ARTIST — Album Title	$	Label & Number
6/27/81	154	11		1 Let The Music Play	$8	Motown 957
4/3/82	14	34	●	2 Keep It Live	$8	Motown 6004
2/12/83	59	16		3 On The One	$8	Motown 6031
12/17/83+	73	33		4 Joystick	$8	Motown 6084
10/20/84	83	29		5 Jukebox	$8	Motown 6117
8/17/85	98	12		6 Hot Spot	$8	Motown 6149
8/30/86	100	11		7 Wild And Free	$8	Geffen 24110

All I Need (7)
All The Way (6)
Bad Girl (3)
Beat That's Right (7)
Body And Mind (7)
Can We Dance (2)
Cheek To Cheek (3)

Don't Get Caught In The Middle (3)
Don't Stop (1)
Dream Girl (1)
Everyday Love (1)
Freaky Lovin' (1)
Gamble With My Love (2)
Heartbeat (5)

Hooks In Me (7)
Hot Spot (6)
I Believe In You (1)
I'll Keep On Lovin' You (2)
I've Been Waiting (5)
If Only You Were In My Shoes (6)
It's All Right (7)

Joystick (4) **61**
Just Believe In Love (2)
Just Can't Wait 'Till The Night (2)
Keep It Live (On The K.I.L.) (2)
Keep You Comin' Back For More (5)

Knock! Knock! (1)
Laughin' At You (4)
Let It All Blow (5) **84**
Let It Whip (2) **5**
Let Me Love You Until (2)
Let The Music Play (1)
L.O.V.E. M.I.A. (1)
Love Song (3)

Main Attraction (5)
Nice Girls (3)
Now That I Have You (4)
On The One For Fun (3)
Paranoid (6)
Party Right Here (3)
Rock With Me (4)

DEBUT DATE	PEAK POS	WKS CHR	GOLD	ARTIST — Album Title	$	Label & Number

DAZZ BAND — Cont'd

S. C. L. & P. (Style, Class, Looks And Personality) (6)
Satisfying Love (1)
Shake What You Got (2)
She Used To Be My Girl (6)
She's The One (5)
Slow Rap (6)
So Much Love (5)
Something You Said (7)
Stay A While With Me (3)
Straight Out Of School (4)
Sunglasses (7)
Swoop (I'm Yours) (4)
T. Mata (4)
This Time It's Forever (1)
Time Will Heal A Broken Heart (7)
To The Roof (4)
Undercover Lover (5)
Until You (4)
We Have More Than Love (3)
What Will I Do Without You (1)
When You Needed Roses (6)
Wild And Free (7)

dB's, The
Peter Holsapple, Will Rigby, Gene Holder and Jeff Beninato.

11/28/87	171	8		The Sound Of Music	$8	I.R.S. 42055

Any Old Thing
Better Place
Bonneville
Change With The Changing Times
I Lie
Looked At The Sun Too Long
Molly Says
Never Before And Never Again
Never Say When
Think Too Hard
Today Could Be The Day
Working For Somebody Else

DEAD BOYS
New York-based, punk-rock quintet formed in Cleveland in 1976 by vocalist Stiv Bators. In 1982, Bators formed Lords Of The New Church. Bators died on 6/4/90 (age 40) after being hit by a car in Paris.

10/22/77	189	4		Young, Loud And Snotty..................	$20	Sire 6038

Ain't Nothin' To Do
All This And More
Caught With The Meat In Your Mouth
Down In Flames
Hey Little Girl
High Tension Wire
I Need Lunch
Not Anymore
Sonic Reducer
What Love Is

DEAD MILKMEN, The
Rock foursome from Philadelphia. Members use ever-changing pseudonyms. Led by vocalist Rodney Cosloy Amadeus Anonymous.

8/1/87	163	7		1 Bucky Fellini	$8	Enigma 73260
12/24/88+	101	23		2 Beelzebubba	$8	Enigma 73351
6/2/90	164	7		3 Metaphysical Graffiti	$12	Enigma 73564

Anderson, Walkman, Buttholes And How! (3)
Bad Party (2)
Badger Song (1)
Beige Sunshine (3)
Big Sleazy (3)
Big Time Operator (1)
Bleach Boys (2)
Bloody Orgy Of The Atomic Fern, (Theme From) (1)
Born To Love Volcanos (2)
Brat In The Frat (2)
City Of Mud (1)
Do The Brown Nose (3)
Dollar Signs In Her Eyes (3)
Epic Tales Of Adventure (3)
Everybody's Got Nice Stuff But Me (2)
Going To Graceland (3)
Guitar Song (2)
Howard Beware (2)
I Against Osbourne (2)
I Am The Walrus (1)
I Hate You, I Love You (3)
I Tripped Over The Ottoman (3)
I Walk The Thinnest Line (2)
If You Love Somebody, Set Them On Fire (3)
In Praise Of Sha Na Na (3)
Instant Club Hit (You'll Dance To Anything) (1)
Jellyfish Heaven (1)
Life Is Shit (2)
Little Man In My Head (3)
Methodist Coloring Book (3)
My Many Smells (2)
Nitro Burning Funny Cars (1)
Now Everybody's Me (3)
Part 3 (3)
Pit, The (1)
Punk Rock Girl (2)
RC's Mom (2)
Ringo Buys A Rifle (2)
Rocketship (1)
Smokin' Banana Peels (2)
Sri Lanka Sex Hotel (2)
Stuart (2)
Surfin' Cow (1)
Tacoland (1)
Take Me To The Specialist (1)
Watching Scotty Die (1)

DEAD ON
Heavy-metal quintet from Long Island, New York fronted by guitarist Michael Caronia. Includes Mike Raptis (vocals), Tony Frazzitta, John Lindner and Mike Caputo.

2/10/90	159	6		Dead On	$12	SBK 93249

Beat A Dead Horse
Dead On
Different Breed
Escape
Full Moon
Matador's Nightmare
Merry Ship
Salem Girls
Widower, The

DEAD OR ALIVE
Dance outfit formed in Liverpool, England by lead singer Pete Burns (b: 8/5/59). Wayne Hussey (later a member of Sisters Of Mercy and Mission) was an early member.

7/13/85	31	20		1 Youthquake	$8	Epic 40119
12/27/86+	52	25		2 Mad, Bad, and Dangerous To Know	$8	Epic 40572
7/30/88	195	2		3 Rip It Up ....[K]	$8	Epic 44255
				remixes of previous hits		
7/22/89	106	9		4 Nude	$8	Epic 45224

Baby Don't Say Goodbye (4)
Big Daddy Of The Rhythm (1)
Brand New Lover (2,3) *15*
Cake And Eat It (1)
Come Home With Me Baby (4) *69*
Come Inside (2)
D.J. Hit That Button (1)
Get Out Of My House (4)
Give It Back That Love Is Mine (4)
Hooked On Love (2,3)
I Cannot Carry On (4)
I Don't Wanna Be Your Boyfriend (4)
I Wanna Be A Toy (1)
I Want You (3)
I'll Save You All My Kisses (2,3)
In Too Deep (1,3)
It's Been A Long Time (1)
Lover Come Back To Me (1,3) *75*
My Forbidden Lover (4)
My Heart Goes Bang (1,3)
Something In My House (2,3) *85*
Son Of A Gun (2)
Special Star (2)
Stop Kicking My Heart Around (4)
Then There Was You (2)
Turn Around And Count 2 Ten (4)
You Spin Me Round (Like A Record) (1,3) *11*

DEAL, Bill, & The Rhondels
Eight-man, brassy-rock band from New York City.

4/11/70	185	2		The Best Of Bill Deal & The Rhondels ....[G]	$15	Heritage 35006

Are You Ready For This
Harlem Shuffle
Hey Bulldog
I've Been Hurt *35*
I've Got My Needs
May I *39*
Nothing Succeeds Like Success *62*
Swingin' Tight *85*
Touch Me
Tuck's Theme
What Kind Of Fool Do You Think I Am *23*
Words

DEAN, Billy
Born on 4/2/62 in Quincy, Florida. Country singer. Attended college in Decatur, Mississippi on a basketball scholarship.

5/25/91	99	26		1 Young Man	$12	Cap./SBK 94302
7/4/92	88	32↑ ●		2 Billy Dean	$12	Cap./SBK 96728

Billy The Kid (2)
Brotherly Love (1)
Daddy's Will (1)
Gone But Not Forgotten (2)
Hammer Down (2)
How Can I Hold You (1)
I Shoulda Listened (2)
I Won't Let You Walk Away (1)
If There Hadn't Been You (2)
Lowdown Lonely (1)
Only Here For A Little While (1)
Only The Wind (2)
She's Taken (1)
Simple Things (2)
Small Favors (2)
Somewhere In My Broken Heart (1)
Tear The Wall Down (1)
What Have You Got Against Love (1)
You Don't Count The Cost (2)
Young Man (1)

DEAN, Jimmy
Born on 8/10/28 in Plainview, Texas. Country vocalist/pianist/guitarist/composer. With Tennessee Haymakers in Washington, D.C. in 1948. Own Texas Wildcats in 1952. Recorded for Four Star in 1952. Own CBS-TV series, 1957-58; ABC-TV series, 1963-66.

12/4/61+	23	28		1 Big Bad John And Other Fabulous Songs And Tales	$25	Columbia 8535
11/3/62	144	2		2 Portrait Of Jimmy Dean	$25	Columbia 8694

Basin Street Blues (2)
Big Bad John (1) *1*
Darktown Poker Club (2)
Gotta Travel On (1)
Grasshopper Mac Clain (1)
Have You Ever Been Lonely (2)
I Was Just Walkin' Out The Door (2)
I Won't Go Huntin' With You Jake (But I'll Go Chasin' Wimmin') (1)
Kentucky Means Paradise (2)
Little Black Book (2) *29*

DEBUT DATE	PEAK POS	WKS CHR	GOLD	ARTIST — Album Title	$	Label & Number

DEAN, Jimmy — Cont'd

Make The Waterwheel Roll (1)
Night Train To Memphis (1)

Nobody (2)
Oklahoma Bill (1)
Old Pappy's New Banjo (2)

P.T. 109 (2) *8*
Please Pass The Biscuits (2)
Sixteen Tons (1)

Smoke, Smoke, Smoke That Cigarette (1)
Steel Men (2) 41

To A Sleeping Beauty (1) 26
You're Nobody 'Til Somebody Loves You (2)

DEAN, Paul
Founding member/lead guitarist of rock group Loverboy. Born on 2/19/46 in Canada.

| 2/25/89 | 195 | 2 | | Hard Core .... | $8 | Columbia 44462 |

Action
Black Sheep

Dirty Fingers
Doctor

Down To The Bottom
Draw The Line

Politics
Sword And Stone

Under The Gun

DEATH ANGEL
San Francisco heavy-metal band, made up of five cousins, formed in 1982. Members ages ranged from 15 to 20 in 1988. Led by guitarist/vocalist Rob Cavestany.

| 8/6/88 | 143 | 11 | | Frolic Through The Park .... | $8 | Enigma 73332 |

Bored
Cold Gin

Confused
Guilty Of Innocence

Mind Rape
Open Up

Road Mutants
Shores Of Sin

3rd Floor
Why You Do This

DEAUVILLE, Ronnie
Lead singer with the Ray Anthony band, 1950-51. Made a miraculous recovery from tuberculosis.

| 12/9/57 | 13 | 2 | | Smoke Dreams .... | $30 | Era 20002 |

As Children Do
I Concentrate On You
I Had The Craziest Dream
I Kiss Your Hand, Madame

I'll Close My Eyes
It's Easy To Remember
Love Is Here To Stay

Say It Isn't So
Smoke Dreams
So In Love

Soft Lights And Sweet Music (And Smoke Dreams Theme)

Something To Remember You By
Wonderful One

DeBARGE
Family group from Grand Rapids, Michigan. Consisted of lead vocalist El (keyboards), Mark (trumpet, saxophone), James (keyboards), Randy (bass) and Bunny DeBarge (vocals). Brothers Bobby and Tommy were in Switch. James was briefly married to Janet Jackson in 1984.

9/11/82+	24	48	●	1 All This Love	$8	Gordy 6012
10/22/83+	36	40	●	2 In A Special Way	$8	Gordy 6061
3/23/85	19	48	●	3 Rhythm Of The Night...............	$8	Gordy 6123

All This Love (1) 17
Baby, Won't Cha Come Quick (2)
Be My Lady (2)
Can't Stop (1)
Dream, A (2)
Give It Up (3)

Heart Is Not So Smart (3) 75
I Give Up On You (2)
I Like It (1) 31
I'll Never Fall In Love Again (1)
I'm In Love With You (1)

It's Getting Stronger (1)
Life Begins With You (1)
Love Me In A Special Way (2) 45
Need Somebody (2)
Prime Time (1)
Queen Of My Heart (2)

Rhythm Of The Night (3) 3
Share My World (3)
Single Heart (3)
Stay With Me (2)
Stop! Don't Tease Me (1)
Time Will Reveal (2) 18

Walls (Came Tumbling Down) (3)
Who's Holding Donna Now (3) **6**
You Wear It Well (3) *46*

DeBARGE, Bunny
Member of the family group DeBarge.

| 3/14/87 | 172 | 5 | | In Love .... | $8 | Motown 6217 |

Dance All Night
Fine Line

I Still Believe
Let's Spend The Night

Life Saver
Never Let Die

Save The Best For Me
So Good For You

Woman In Love

DeBARGE, Chico
DeBarge sibling, but not a member of the group DeBarge.

| 11/15/86+ | 90 | 30 | | Chico DeBarge .... | $8 | Motown 6214 |

Cross That Line
Desperate

Girl Next Door
I Like My Body

I'll Love You For Now
If It Takes All Night

Talk To Me 21
Who Are You Kidding

You Can Make It Better
You're Much Too Fast

DeBARGE, El
Eldra DeBarge (b: 6/4/61), lead singer of family group DeBarge.

| 6/21/86 | 24 | 11 | ● | El DeBarge .... | $8 | Gordy 6181 |

Don't Say It's Over
I Wanna Hear It From My Heart

Lost Without Her Love
Love Always 43

Private Line
Secrets Of The Night

Someone 70
Thrill Of The Chase

When Love Has Gone Away
Who's Johnny 3

DeBURGH, Chris
British pop-rock singer. Born Christopher John Davidson on 10/15/48 in Argentina of Irish parentage.

4/9/83	43	22		1 The Getaway......................	$8	A&M 4929
6/30/84	69	19		2 Man On The Line	$8	A&M 5002
9/20/86+	25	32	●	3 Into The Light	$8	A&M 5121

All The Love I Have Inside (1)
Ballroom Of Romance (3)
Borderline (1)
Crying And Laughing (1)
Don't Pay The Ferryman (1) 34
Ecstasy Of Flight (I Love The Night) (2)

Fatal Hesitation (3)
Fire On The Water (3)
For Rosanna (3)
Getaway, The (1)
Head And The Heart (2)
I'm Counting On You (1)
Lady In Red (3) 3

Last Night (3)
Leader, The (3)
Liberty (1)
Light A Fire (1)
Living On The Island (1)
Man On The Line (2)
Moonlight And Vodka (2)
Much More Than This (2)

One Word (Straight To The Heart) (3)
Revolution, The (1)
Say Goodbye To It All (3)
Ship To Shore (1) *71*
Sight And Touch (2)
Sound Of A Gun (2)
Spirit Of Man (3)

Taking It To The Top (2)
Transmission Ends (2)
Vision, The (3)
What About Me? (3)
Where Peaceful Waters Flow (1)

DeCARO, Nick
Producer of albums for Mac Davis, Helen Reddy, Samantha Sang and others.

| 4/19/69 | 165 | 5 | | Happy Heart ....[I] | $10 | A&M 4176 |

Amy's Theme
Caroline, No
Happy Heart

Hey Jude
I'll Forget You (Chall-Ha-Dichal)

I'm Gonna Make You Love Me

If I Only Had Time 95

Love Is All
Lullaby From Rosemary's Baby

Ob-La-Di, Ob-La-Da
Quiet Sunday

DEE, Dave; Dozy, Beaky, Mick And Tich
English quintet: David Harmon, Trevor Davies, John Dymond, Michael Wilson and Ian Amey.

| 8/5/67 | 155 | 3 | | Greatest Hits .... [G] | $25 | Fontana 67567 |

Bend It
Hands Off

Here's A Heart
Hideaway

Hold Tight!
I'm On The Up

Save Me
Touch Me, Touch Me

You Know What I Want
You Make It Move

DEBUT DATE	PEAK POS	WKS CHR	GOLD	ARTIST — Album Title	$	Label & Number

DEE, Joey, & the Starliters

Born Joseph DiNicola on 6/11/40 in Passaic, New Jersey. In September 1960, Joey & The Starlighters became the house band at the Peppermint Lounge, New York City. After 1964, group included three members who later formed The Young Rascals, plus guitarist Jimi Hendrix. In films *Hey, Let's Twist* and *Two Tickets To Paris*.

DEBUT DATE	PEAK POS	WKS CHR		Album		$	Label & Number
12/11/61+	2[6]	40		1 Doin' The Twist At The Peppermint Lounge	[L]	$25	Roulette 25166
2/17/62	18	23		2 Hey, Let's Twist!	[S]	$25	Roulette 25168

includes "I Wanna Twist" and "Na Voce, 'Na Chitarra E 'O Poco 'E Luna" by Kay Armen; "It's A Pity To Say Goodnight" and "Mother Goose" by Teddy Randazzo; "Let Me Do My Twist" by Jo-Ann Campbell

| 6/30/62 | 97 | 7 | | 3 Back At The Peppermint Lounge-Twistin' | [L] | $25 | Roulette 25173 |

Blue Twister (2)
C C Rider (3)
Fanny Mae (1)
Have You Ever Had The Blues (3)
Hello Josephine (3)
Hey, Let's Twist (2) *20*
Hold It (1)
Honky Tonk (1)
Joey's Blues (2)
Kansas City (3)
Keelee's Twist (2)
Mashed Potatoes (1)
Money (3)
Peppermint Twist - Part I (1,2) *1*
Peppermint Twist - Part II (1)
Rain Drops (3)
Ram-Bunk-Shush (1)
Roly Poly (2) *74*
Shout (2)
Shout - Part I (1) *6*
Slippin' And Slidin' (3)
Sticks And Stones (1)
Talkin' 'Bout You (3)
Will You Love Me Tomorrow (3)
Ya Ya (1)
You Must Have Been A Beautiful Baby (3)

DEE, Kiki

Born Pauline Matthews on 3/6/47 in Yorkshire, England.

11/16/74	28	18		1 I've Got The Music In Me		$10	Rocket 458
				THE KIKI DEE BAND			
5/14/77	159	5		2 Kiki Dee		$10	Rocket 2257

Bad Day Child (2)
Chicago (2)
Do It Right (1)
First Thing In The Morning, Last Thing At Night (2)
Heart And Soul (1)
How Much Fun (2)
I've Got The Music In Me (1) *12*
In Return (2)
Into Eternity (2)
Keep Right On (2)
Little Frozen One (1)
Night Hours (2)
Out Of My Head (1)
Someone To Me (1)
Standing Room Only (2)
Step By Step (1)
Sweet Creation (2)
Walking (2)
Water (1)
You Need Help (1)

DEE, Lenny

Organist, born in the 1920s in Illinois and raised in Florida. Discovered by Red Foley.

7/9/55	11	6		1 Dee-lightful!	[I]	$15	Decca 8114
6/8/68	196	3		2 Gentle On My Mind	[I]	$12	Decca 74994
3/8/69	199	2		3 Turn Around, Look At Me	[I]	$12	Decca 75073
1/3/70	189	3		4 Spinning Wheel	[I]	$10	Decca 75152

Apologize (3)
Ballin' The Jack (1)
Birth Of The Blues (1)
By The Time I Get To Phoenix (2)
Can't Take My Eyes Off You (2)
Day In The Life Of A Fool (4)
Donkey Serenade (1)
Dream A Little Dream Of Me (3)
Exactly Like You (1)
Folsom Prison Blues (3)
Gentle On My Mind (2)
Glory Of Love (3)
Hang 'Em High (3)
Happy Barefoot Boy (2)
Hurt So Bad (4)
Jean (4)
Last Waltz (2)
Laura (3)
Little Brown Jug (1)
Love Is Blue (2)
Man Without Love (3)
Odd Couple (3)
Odds And Ends (Of A Beautiful Love Affair) (4)
Plantation Boogie (1) *19*
Quentin's Theme (4)
Remember When (We Made These Memories) (2)
Romeo And Juliet, Love Theme From (4)
Rossana Theme (2)
Ruby Don't Take Your Love To Town (4)
September Song (1)
Siboney (1)
Spinning Wheel (4)
Sunny (2)
Sunshine (3)
Sweet Caroline (Good Times Never Seemed So Good) (4)
Sweet Georgia Brown (1)
Sweet Mouth (3)
True Grit (4)
Turn Around, Look At Me (3)
What Now My Love (Et Maintenant) (2)
Where The Rainbow Ends (3)
With Pen In Hand (3)
World Is Waiting For The Sunrise (2)
Yes Sir, That's My Baby (1)
Yesterday, When I Was Young (4)

DEEE-LITE

New York-based dance trio: Super DJ Dmitry Brill (from Kiev, Soviet Union), Jungle DJ Towa "Towa" Tei (from Tokyo, Japan) and vocalist Lady Miss Kier (Kier Kirby from Youngstown, Ohio). Group's name inspired by the tune "It's De-lovely" from the 1936 Cole Porter musical *Red, Hot & Blue*. Brill and Kier are married.

| 9/15/90 | 20 | 41 | ● | 1 World Clique | | $12 | Elektra 60957 |
| 7/11/92 | 67 | 8 | | 2 Infinity Within | | $12 | Elektra 61313 |

Build The Bridge (1)
Come On In, The Dreams Are Fine (2)
Deee-Lite Theme (1)
Deep Ending (1)
E.S.P. (1)
Electric Shock (2)
Fuddy Duddy Judge (2)
Good Beat (1)
Groove Is In The Heart (1) *4*
Heart Be Still (2)
I Had A Dream I Was Falling Through A Hole In The Ozone Layer (2)
I Won't Give Up (2)
I.F.O. (Identified Flying Object) (2)
Love Is Everything (2)
Power Of Love (1) *47*
Pussycat Meow (2)
Rubber Lover (2)
Runaway (2)
Smile On (1)
Thank You Everyday (2)
Try Me On ... I'm Very You (1)
Two Clouds Above Nine (2)
Vote, Baby, Vote (2)
What Is Love? (1)
Who Was That? (1)
World Clique (1)

DEELE, The

R&B funk sextet from Cincinnati, led by Darnell "Dee" Bristol. Included the songwriting/production team of Mark "L.A. Reid" Rooney and Kenneth "Babyface" Edmonds. Reid (cousin of Keith Mitchell of After 7 and son of The Exciters' Herb Rooney and Brenda Reid) married Pebbles in 1989. Former member of Manchild, Edmonds (brother of After 7's Kevon and Melvin Edmonds) began solo career as Babyface in 1989.

2/4/84	78	19		1 Street Beat		$8	Solar 60285
7/6/85	155	8		2 Material Thangz		$8	Solar 60410
2/27/88	54	25	●	3 Eyes Of A Stranger		$8	Solar 72555

Body Talk (1) *77*
Can-U-Dance (3)
Crazy 'Bout 'Cha (1)
Eyes Of A Stranger (3)
Hip Chic (3)
I Surrender (1)
I'll Send You Roses (2)
Just My Luck (3)
Let No One Separate Us (3)
Let's Work Tonight (3)
Material Thangz (2)
Sexy Love (1)
She Wanted (2)
Shoot 'Em Up Movies (3)
So Many Thangz (3)
Stimulate (2)
Street Beat (1)
Suspicious (2)
Sweet Nothingz (2)
Sweet November (2)
Two Occasions (3) *10*
Video Villain (1)
Working (9 To 5) (1)
You're All I've Ever Known (2)

★★117★★ DEEP PURPLE

British pioneer heavy-metal band: Ritchie Blackmore (guitar), Rod Evans (vocals), Jon Lord (keyboards), Ian Paice (drums) and Nicky Simper (bass). Evans and Simper left in 1969, replaced by Ian Gillan (vocals) and Roger Glover (bass). Evans formed Captain Beyond. Gillan and Glover left in late 1973, replaced by David Coverdale (vocals) and Glenn Hughes (bass). Blackmore left in early 1975 to form Rainbow (which Glover later joined); replaced by American Tommy Bolin (ex-James Gang guitarist; d: 12/4/76). Band split in July 1976. Coverdale, Lord and Paice formed Whitesnake. Blackmore, Lord, Paice, Gillan and Glover reunited in 1984. Hughes (joined Black Sabbath. Gillan (who joined Black Sabbath for 1983 *Born Again* album) left in 1989 to form Garth Rockett & The Moonshiners. 1990 lineup featured former Rainbow vocalist Joe Lynn Turner, with Blackmore, Lord, Paice and Glover.

9/7/68	24	23		1 Shades Of Deep Purple		$25	Tetragramm. 102
1/11/69	54	14		2 The Book Of Taliesyn		$25	Tetragramm. 107
7/12/69	162	6		3 Deep Purple		$25	Tetragramm. 119

DEBUT DATE	PEAK POS	WKS CHR	GOLD	ARTIST — Album Title	$	Label & Number
				DEEP PURPLE — Cont'd		
5/16/70	149	8		4 Deep Purple/The Royal Philharmonic Ork. "Concerto For Group And Orchestra" ....[L] concert at the Royal Albert Hall; Malcolm Arnold, conductor	$20	Warner 1860
9/12/70	143	21		5 Deep Purple In Rock	$20	Warner 1877
8/21/71	32	18		6 Fireball	$20	Warner 2564
4/15/72+	7	118	▲²	7 Machine Head	$20	Warner 2607
10/21/72	57	20		8 (Purple Passages) ....[K] highlights from albums #1-3 above	$22	Warner 2644 [2]
1/20/73	15	49	●	9 Who Do We Think We Are!	$20	Warner 2678
4/21/73	6	52	▲	10 Made In Japan ....[L]	$22	Warner 2701 [2]
3/2/74	9	30	●	11 Burn	$15	Warner 2766
12/7/74	20	15	●	12 Stormbringer	$15	Warner 2832
12/6/75+	43	14		13 Come Taste The Band	$15	Warner 2895
11/27/76	148	6		14 Made In Europe ....[L] European concerts of early 1975	$15	Warner 2995
11/1/80	148	4		15 Deepest Purple/The Very Best Of Deep Purple ......[G]	$8	Warner 3486
12/1/84+	17	32	▲	16 Perfect Strangers	$8	Mercury 824003
1/31/87	34	22		17 The House Of Blue Light	$8	Mercury 831318
7/23/88	105	9		18 Nobody's Perfect ....[L]	$10	Mercury 835897 [2]
11/10/90	87	19		19 Slaves And Masters	$12	RCA 2421

"A" 200 (11)
And The Address (1,8)
Anthem (2)
Anyone's Daughter (6)
April (3,8)
Bad Attitude (17,18)
Bird Has Flown (3,8)
Black & White (17)
Black Night (15,18) *66*
Blind (3)
Blistering Hot (5)
Bloodsucker (5)
Breakfast In Bed (19)
Burn (11,14,15)
Call Of The Wild (19)
Chasing Shadows (3,8)
Child In Time (5,10,15,18)
Comin' Home (13)
Concerto For Group And Orchestra (Movements I-III) (4)
Cut Runs Deep (19)

Dead Or Alive (17)
Dealer (13)
Demon's Eye (15)
Drifter (13)
Emmeretta (8)
Exposition (medley) (3)
Faultline (medley) (3)
Fire In The Basement (19)
Fireball (6,15)
Flight Of The Rat (5)
Fools (6)
Fortuneteller (19)
Gettin' Tight (13)
Gypsy, The (12)
Gypsy's Kiss (16)
Happiness (medley) (3)
Hard Lovin' Man (5)
Hard Lovin' Woman (17,18)
Hard Road (2,8)
Help (1)
Hey Joe (1,8)
High Ball Shooter (12)

Highway Star (7,10,15,18)
Hold On (12)
Holy Man (12)
Hungry Daze (16)
Hush (1,8,18) *4*
I Need Love (13)
I'm So Glad (medley) (1)
Into The Fire (5)
Kentucky Woman (2,8) *38*
King Of Dreams (19)
Knocking At Your Back Door (16,18) *61*
Lady Double Dealer (12,14)
Lady Luck (13)
Lalena (3)
Lay Down, Stay Down (11)
Lazy (7,10,18)
Listen, Learn, Read On (2)
Living Wreck (5)
Love Child (13)
Love Conquers All (19)

Love Don't Mean A Thing (12)
Love Help Me (1)
Mad Dog (17)
Mandrake Root (1,8)
Mary Long (9)
Maybe I'm A Leo (7)
Mean Streak (16)
Might Just Take Your Life (11) *91*
Mistreated (11,14)
Mitzi Dupree (17)
Mule, The (6,10)
Never Before (7)
No No No (6)
No One Came (6)
Nobody's Home (16)
One More Rainy Day (1)
Our Lady (9)
Owed To G (medley) (13)
Painter, The (medley) (3)
Perfect Strangers (16,18)

Pictures Of Home (7)
Place In Line (9)
Rat Bat Blue (9)
River Deep-Mountain High (2) *53*
Sail Away (11)
Shield, The (2,8)
Smoke On The Water (7,10,15,18) *4*
Smooth Dancer (9)
Soldier Of Fortune (12)
Space Truckin' (7,10,15,18)
Spanish Archer (17)
Speed King (5,15)
Stormbringer (12,14,15)
Strange Kind Of Woman (6,10,15,18)
Strangeways (17)
Super Trouper (9)
This Time Around (medley) (13)
Too Much Is Not Enough (19)

Truth Hurts (19)
Under The Gun (16)
Unwritten Law (17)
Wasted Sunsets (16)
We Can Work It Out (medley) (2)
What's Goin' On Here (11)
Why Didn't Rosemary? (3,8)
Wicked Ways (19)
Woman From Tokyo (9,15,18) *60*
You Can't Do It Right (With The One You Love) (12)
You Fool No One (11,14)
You Keep On Moving (13)

DEES, Rick
Born Rigdon Osmond Dees III in Memphis in 1950. DJ working at WMPS-Memphis when he conceived idea for "Disco Duck." Currently one of America's top radio DJs. Host of TV's *Solid Gold* (1984) and his own late-night talk show *Into The Night*.

| 3/5/77 | 157 | 5 | | The Original Disco Duck ....[N] | $10 | RSO 3017 |

Bad Shark
Barely White (That'll Get It Baby)

Bionic Feet
Dis-Gorilla (Part 1) *56*

Disco Duck (Part 1) *1*
Disco Duck (Part II)

Doctor Disco
Flick The Bick

He Ate Too Many Jelly Donuts

Peanut Prance

★★293★★ DEF LEPPARD
Hard-rock quintet formed in Sheffield, England in 1977: Joe Elliott (lead singer), Pete Willis and Steve Clark (lead guitars), Rick Savage (bass) and Rick Allen (drums; lost his left arm in an auto accident on New Year's Eve in 1984). Phil Collen replaced Pete Willis in late 1982. Clark died on 1/8/91 (age 30) of alcohol-related respiratory failure. Guitarist Vivian Campbell (Whitesnake, Dio, Riverdogs, Shadow King) joined in April 1992.

5/3/80	51	51	▲	1 On Through The Night	$8	Mercury 3828
8/8/81	38	106	▲²	2 High 'n' Dry	$8	Mercury 4021
2/5/83	2²	116	▲⁸	3 Pyromania	$8	Mercury 810308
6/2/84	72	18		4 High 'n' Dry ....[R] added remixed version of *Bringin' On The Heartbreak* plus *Me And My Wine* (previously unavailable)	$8	Mercury 818836
8/22/87+	1⁶	133	▲¹⁰	5 Hysteria	$8	Mercury 830675
4/18/92	1⁵	43↑	▲³	6 Adrenalize	$12	Mercury 512185

Action! Not Words (3)
Animal (5) *19*
Another Hit And Run (2,4)
Answer To The Master (1)
Armageddon It (5) *3*
Billy's Got A Gun (3)
Bringin' On The Heartbreak (2,4) *61*
Comin' Under Fire (3)
Die Hard The Hunter (3)
Don't Shoot Shotgun (5)
Excitable (5)

Foolin' (3) *28*
Gods Of War (5)
Have You Ever Needed Someone So Bad (6) *12*
Heaven Is (6)
Hello America (1)
High 'N' Dry (Saturday Night) (2,4)
Hysteria (5) *10*
I Wanna Touch U (6)
It Could Be You (1)
It Don't Matter (1)

Lady Strange (2,4)
Let It Go (2,4)
Let's Get Rocked (6) *15*
Love And Affection (5)
Make Love Like A Man (6) *36*
Me & My Wine (4)
Mirror, Mirror (Look Into My Eyes) (2,4)
No No No (2,4)
On Through The Night (2,4)

Personal Property (6)
Photograph (3) *12*
Pour Some Sugar On Me (5) *2*
Rock Brigade (1)
Rock Of Ages (3) *16*
Rock! Rock! (Till You Drop) (3)
Rocket (5) *12*
Rocks Off (1)
Run Riot (5)
Satellite (1)

Sorrow Is A Woman (1)
Stagefright (3)
Stand Up (Kick Love Into Motion) (6) *34*
Switch 625 (2,4)
Tear It Down (6)
Tonight (6)
Too Late For Love (3)
Wasted (1)
When The Walls Came Tumbling Down (6)
White Lightning (6)

Women (5) *80*
You Got Me Runnin' (2,4)

DeFRANCO FAMILY featuring TONY DeFRANCO
Family group from Ontario: Tony (age 13 in 1973), Merlina (16), Nino (17), Marisa (18) and Benny (19).

| 10/13/73 | 109 | 16 | | 1 Heartbeat, It's A Lovebeat .... | $10 | 20th Century 422 |
| 6/29/74 | 163 | 7 | | 2 Save The Last Dance For Me .... | $10 | 20th Century 441 |

194

DEBUT DATE	PEAK POS	WKS CHR	GOLD	ARTIST — Album Title	$	Label & Number

DeFRANCO FAMILY featuring TONY DeFRANCO — Cont'd

Abra-Ca-Dabra (1) 32	Gorilla (1)	I Guess You Already Knew (2)	I'm With You (1)	Maybe It's You (2)	**Save The Last Dance For**
Baby Blue (2)	Heartbeat - It's a Lovebeat (1) 3	I Love Everything You Do (1)	Love Is Bigger Than Baseball (1)	Only One (2)	**Me** (2) 18
Because We Both Are Young (2)	Hold Me (2)	I Wanted To Tell You (1)	Love The Way You Do (2)	Poor Boy (2)	Sweet Sweet Loretta (1)
Come A Little Closer (1)				Same Kind A' Love (1)	Write Me A Letter (2)

DEJA

R&B duo of writer/producer/musician Curt Jones and vocalist Starleana Young. First known as Symphonic Express. Both were members of Slave and Aurra. Mysti Day replaced Young in 1989.

12/5/87+	186	6		Serious	$8	Virgin 90601

Heart Beat	Premonition	Some Things Turn Around	Summer Love	What To Do Now
Life	Serious	Straight To The Point	That's Where You'll Find Me	**You And Me Tonight** 54

DEKKER, Desmond, & The Aces

Born Desmond Dacris on 7/16/41 in Kingston, Jamaica. Reggae's first successful artist.

9/6/69	153	3		Israelites	$25	Uni 73059

For Once In My Life	**Israelites** 9	It Mek	Problems	Tip Of My Finger
Intensified	It Is Not Easy	Nincompoop	Rude Boy Train	Too Much Too Soon

DEL AMITRI

Rock quartet from Glasgow, Scotland led by vocalist Justin Currie and guitarist Iain Harvie. Capitalized the "d" in del Amitri in 1992.

4/7/90	95	19		1 Waking Hours....................................	$12	A&M 5287
9/26/92	178	3		2 Change Everything	$12	A&M 5385

Always The Last To Know (2) 30	Empty (1)	**Kiss This Thing Goodbye** (1) 35	Opposite View (1)	To Last A Lifetime (2)
As Soon As The Tide Comes In (2)	First Rule Of Love (2)	Move Away Jimmy Blue (1)	Sometimes I Just Have To Say Your Name (2)	When I Want You (1)
Be My Downfall (2)	Hatful Of Rain (1)	Nothing Ever Happens (1)	When You Were Young (2)	
Behind The Fool (2)	I Won't Take The Blame (2)	Ones That You Love Lead You Nowhere (2)	Stone Cold Sober (1)	You're Gone (1)
	Just Like A Man (2)		Surface Of The Moon (2)	
			This Side Of The Morning (1)	

DELANEY & BONNIE

Delaney Bramlett (b: 7/1/39, Pontotoc County, Mississippi) and wife Bonnie Lynn Bramlett (b: 11/8/44, Acton, Illinois). Married in 1967. Friends — backing artists included, at various times, Leon Russell, Rita Coolidge, Dave Mason, Eric Clapton, Duane Allman and many others. Friends Bobby Whitlock, Carl Radle and Jim Gordon later became Eric Clapton's Dominos. Delaney & Bonnie dissolved their marriage and group in 1972. Their daughter Bekka is the lead singer of Mick Fleetwood's Zoo. Also see Eric Clapton's *History Of Eric Clapton* album.

7/26/69	175	3		1 Accept No Substitute - The Original Delaney & Bonnie & Friends....	$25	Elektra 74039
4/18/70	29	17		2 Delaney & Bonnie & Friends On Tour with Eric Clapton............[L]	$20	Atco 326
10/10/70	58	10		3 To Bonnie From Delaney	$20	Atco 341
4/3/71	65	23		4 Motel Shot..	$20	Atco 358
4/15/72	133	6		5 D&B Together	$20	Columbia 31377

Alone Together (3)	Gift Of Love (3)	I Know Something Good About You (5)	Mama, He Treats Your Daughter Mean (medley) (3)	Someday (1)	Where The Soul Never Dies (4)
Big Change Comin' (5)	God Knows I Love You (3)	Lay Down My Burden (3)	Miss Ann (3)	**Soul Shake** (3) 43	**Where There's A Will**
Come On In My Kitchen (3,4)	Going Down The Road Feeling Bad (3,4)	Let Me Be Your Man (3)	**Move 'Em Out** (5) 59	Sound Of The City (5)	**There's A Way** (2) 99
Comin' Home (2,5) 84	Good Thing (I'm On Fire) (5)	Little Richard Medley (5)	**Never Ending Song Of Love** (4) 13	Talkin' About Jesus (4)	Will The Circle Be Unbroken (4)
Country Life (5)	Groupie (Superstar) (5)	Living On The Open Road (3)	**Only You Know And I Know** (2,5) 20	That's What My Man Is For (2)	
Dirty Old Man (1)	Hard Luck And Troubles (3)	Lonesome And A Long Way From Home (4)	Poor Elijah - Tribute To Johnson Medley (2)	They Call It Rock & Roll Music (3)	
Do Right Woman (1)	I Can't Take It Much Longer (1)	Long Road Ahead (4)	Rock Of Ages (4)	Things Get Better (2)	
Don't Deceive Me (Please Don't Go) (4)	I Don't Want To Discuss It (1)	Love Me A Little Bit Longer (1)	Sing My Way Home (4)	Wade In The River Jordan (5)	
Faded Love (4)	I Know How It Feels To Be Lonely (3)	Love Of My Man (3)	Soldiers Of The Cross (1)	Well, Well (5)	
Free The People (3) 75				When The Battle Is Over (1)	
Get Ourselves Together (1)					
Ghetto (1)					

DE LA SOUL

Psychedelic-rap trio from Amityville, Long Island, New York: Posdnous (Kelvin Mercer), Trugoy the Dove (David Jolicoeur) and P.A. Pasemaster Mase (Vincent Mason, Jr.).

4/1/89	24	29	●	1 3 Feet High And Rising	$8	Tommy Boy 1019
6/1/91	26	17	●	2 De La Soul Is Dead.......................................	$12	Tommy Boy 1029

Afro Connections At A Hi 5 (In The Eyes Of The Hoodlum) (2)	Description (1)	Keepin' The Faith (2)	Oodles Of O's (2)	Say No Go (1)	WRMS: Dedication To The Bitty (1)
Bitties In The BK Lounge (2)	Do As De La Does (1)	Kicked Out The House (2)	Pass The Plugs (2)	Shwingalokate (2)	WRMS: Cat's In Control (2)
Buddy (With Jungle Brothers and Q-Tip) (1)	Eye Know (1)	Let, Let Me In (2)	Pease Porridge (2)	Take It Off (1)	Who Do U Worship? (2)
Can U Keep A Secret? (1)	Fanatic Of The B Word (2)	Little Bit Of Soap (1)	Plug Tunin' (Last Chance To Comprehend) (1)	Talkin' 'Bout Hey Love (2)	
Change In Speak (1)	Ghetto Thang (1)	Magic Number (1)	Potholes In My Lawn (1)	This Is A Recording 4 Living In A Full Time Era (L.I.F.E.) (1)	
Cool Breeze On The Rocks (1)	I Can Do Anything (Delacratic) (1)	**Me Myself And I** (1) 34	Rap De Rap Show (2)	Transmitting Live From Mars (1)	
D.A.I.S.Y. Age (1)	Jenifa Taught Me (Derwin's Revenge) (1)	Millie Pulled A Pistol On Santa (2)	Ring Ring Ring (Ha Ha Hey) (2)	Tread Water (1)	
De La Orgee (1)	Johnny's Dead AKA Vincent Mason (2)	My Brother's A Basehead (2)	Roller Skating Jam Named "Saturdays" (2)		
		Not Over Till The Fat Lady Plays The Demo (2)			

DELEGATION

Soul-disco trio based in England: Jamaicans Ricky Bailey and Ray Patterson, with Texan Bruce Dunbar.

2/17/79	84	16		The Promise Of Love...............................	$8	Shadybrook 010

Back Door Love	Love Is Like A Fire	**Oh Honey** 45	Someone Oughta Write A Song	Soul Trippin'	You've Been Doing Me Wrong
Let Me Take You To The Sun	Mr. Heartbreak	Promise Of Love		Where Is The Love	

DELFONICS, The

Soul group from Philadelphia. Formed in 1965 as the Four Gents. Consisted of William and Wilbert Hart, Ritchie Daniels and Randy Cain. First recorded for Moon Shot in 1967. Daniels left for the service in 1968, group continued as a trio. Cain was replaced by Major Harris in 1971. Harris went solo in 1974.

6/8/68	100	6		1 La La Means I Love You	$25	Philly Groove 1150
3/8/69	155	6		2 Sound Of Sexy Soul	$20	Philly Groove 1151
11/29/69+	111	19		3 The Delfonics Super Hits..........................[G]	$20	Philly Groove 1152
8/15/70	61	18		4 The Delfonics	$15	Philly Groove 1153

DEBUT DATE	PEAK POS	WKS CHR	G O L D	ARTIST — Album Title	$	Label & Number

DELFONICS, The — Cont'd

6/24/72	123	11		5 Tell Me This Is A Dream	$15	Philly Groove 1154

Ain't That Peculiar (2)
Alfie (1)
Baby I Love You (4)
Baby I Miss You (5)
Break Your Promise
(1,3) 35
Can You Remember (1)
Delfonics' Theme (How
Could You) (4,5)
**Didn't I (Blow Your Mind
This Time)** (4) 10

Down Is Up, Up Is Down (4)
Everytime I See My Baby (2)
Face It Girl, It's Over (2)
Funny Feeling (4) 94
Going Out Of My Head (2)
Hey! Love (5) 52
Hot Dog Baby (2)
Hurt So Bad (1)
I Gave To You (4)
I'm A Man (5)
I'm Sorry (1,3) 42

La - La - Means I Love You
(1,3) 4
Let It Be Me (2,3)
Look Of Love (1)
Looking For A Girl (5)
Losing You (1)
Love You Till I Die (5)
Lover's Concerto (1)
Loving Him (2,3)
My New Love (2,3)
Over And Over (4) 58

Ready Or Not Here I Come
(Can't Hide From Love)
(2,3) 35
Round & Round (5)
Scarborough Fair (2)
Shadow Of Your Smile (1)
Somebody Loves You
(2,3) 72
Tell Me This Is A Dream
(5) 86
Think About Me (4)

Too Late (5)
**Trying To Make A Fool Of
Me** (4) 40
Walk Right Up To The Sun
(5) 81
**When You Get Right Down
To It** (4) 53
With These Hands (2,3)
**You Got Yours And I'll Get
Mine** (3) 40
You're Gone (1,3)

DEL FUEGOS, The

Boston rock quartet: Dan Zanes (guitar, vocals), Tom Lloyd (bass), Warren Zanes (guitar) and Woody
Giessmann (drums). By 1989, Adam Roth and Joe Donnelly replaced Warren Zanes and Giessmann.

10/26/85	132	34		1 Boston, Mass.	$8	Slash 25339
4/18/87	167	6		2 Stand Up	$8	Slash 25540
10/28/89	139	22		3 Smoking In The Fields	$8	RCA 9860

Breakaway (3)
Coupe DeVille (1)
Don't Run Wild (1)
Down In Allen's Mills (3)
Dreams Of You (3)
Fade To Blue (1)
Friends Again (3)

Hand In Hand (1)
He Had A Lot To Drink
Today (2)
Headlights (3)
Hold Us Down (1)
I Can't Take This Place (2)
I Still Want You (1) 87

I'll Sleep With You (Cha Cha
D'Amour) (2)
I'm Inside You (3)
It's Alright (1)
Long Slide (For An Out) (3)
Lost Weekend (3)
Move With Me Sister (3)

Name Names (2)
New Old World (2)
News From Nowhere (2)
Night On The Town (1)
No No Never (3)
Offer, The (3)
Part Of This Earth (3)

Scratching At Your Door (2)
Shame (1)
Sound Of Our Town (1)
Stand By You (3)
Town Called Love (2)
Wear It Like A Cape (2)

★★440★★   DELLS, The

R&B vocal group formed at Thornton Township High School in Harvey, Illinois: Johnny Funches (lead),
Marvin Junior (baritone lead), Verne Allison (tenor), Mickey McGill (baritone) and Chuck Barksdale
(bass). First recorded as the El-Rays for Chess in 1953. Signed with Vee-Jay in 1955. Group remained
intact into the 1980s, with the exception of Funches, who was replaced by Johnny Carter (ex-Flamingos)
in 1960.

5/25/68	29	29		1 There Is	$20	Cadet 804
3/8/69	146	10		2 The Dells Musical Menu/Always Together	$20	Cadet 822
6/14/69	102	22		3 The Dells Greatest Hits .... [G]	$20	Cadet 824
8/23/69	54	24		4 Love Is Blue	$20	Cadet 829
3/14/70	126	12		5 Like It Is, Like It Was	$15	Cadet 837
8/28/71	81	16		6 Freedom Means	$15	Cadet 50004
6/24/72	162	5		7 The Dells Sing Dionne Warwicke's Greatest Hits ...	$15	Cadet 50017
6/23/73	99	9		8 Give Your Baby A Standing Ovation	$12	Cadet 50037
5/4/74	156	6		9 The Dells vs. The Dramatics	$12	Cadet 60027
9/21/74	114	8		10 The Mighty Mighty Dells	$12	Cadet 60030
9/23/78	169	3		11 New Beginnings	$10	ABC 1100
8/30/80	137	12		12 I Touched A Dream	$8	20th Century 618

Agatha Van Thurgood (2)
Ain't No Sunshine (8)
Alfie (7)
All About The Paper (12)
All Your Goodies Are Gone
(11)
Always Together (2,3) 18
Be For Real With Me (10)
Believe Me (2)
Bonified Fool (10)
**Bring Back The Love Of
Yesterday** (10) 87
By The Time I Get To
Phoenix (medley) (4)
Call Me (Right By Your Side
I'll Be) (11)
Change We Go Thru (For
Love) (1,3)
Cherish (11)
Close To You (7)
Close Your Eyes (1)
Closer (8)

Come Out, Come Out (5)
Darling Dear (5)
**Does Anybody Know I'm
Here** (2,3) 38
Drowning For Your Love (11)
Free And Easy (6)
Freedom Means (6)
**Give Your Baby A Standing
Ovation** (8) 34
Glory Of Love (4,8) 92
Good-Bye Mary Ann (2)
Hallways Of My Mind
(2,3) 92
Higher And Higher (1)
Honey (4)
House Is Not A Home (7)
**I Can Sing A Rainbow/
Love Is Blue** (4) 22
I Can't Do Enough (2,3) 98
I Just Don't Know What To
Do With Myself (7)

I Say A Little Prayer (7)
I Touched A Dream (12)
I Wanna Testify (11)
I Want My Momma (2)
**I Wish It Was Me You
Loved** (9) 94
I'll Never Fall In Love Again
(7)
I'm In Love (9)
I'm Not Afraid Of Tomorrow
(5)
If You Go Away (medley) (4)
If You Really Love Your Girl
(Show Her) (10)
It's All Up To You (6) 94
Just A Little Love (12)
Learning To Love You Was
Easy (It's So Hard Trying
To Get Over You) (10)
Little Understanding (4)
Long Lonely Nights (5) 74
Look At Us Now (12)

Love Can Make It Easier (8)
Love Is Missing From Our
Lives (9)
Love Is So Simple (1,3)
Love Story (medley) (6)
**Love We Had (Stays On My
Mind)** (6) 30
Make It With You (6)
Make Sure (You Have
Someone Who Loves You)
(2,3)
Melody Man (6)
My Life Is So Wonderful
(When You're Around) (11)
Nadine (5) flip
Nothing Can Stop Me (10)
O-O, I Love You (1,3) 61
Off Shore (5)
Oh What A Day (5) 43
Oh, What A Night (4) 10
On The Dock Of The Bay
(4) 42

One Less Bell To Answer (6)
One Minute Julep (4)
Open Up My Heart (5) 51
Passionate Breezes (12)
Playin' The Love Game (9)
Please Don't Change Me
Now (1,3)
Raindrops Keep Fallin' On
My Head (7)
Rather Be With Me (6)
Run For Cover (1)
Share (8)
Show Me (1)
Since I Fell For You (5)
Since I've Been In Love (10)
So You Are Love (12)
Soul Strollin' (8)
Stand Up And Show The
World (8)
Stay In My Corner (1,3) 10
Strung Out Over You (9)
Summer Place (4)

Super Woman (11)
Sweeter As The Days Go By
(10)
That Special Someone (10)
There Is (1,3) 20
This Guy's In Love With You
(7)
Trains And Boats And
Planes (7)
Tripped, Slipped, Stumbled
And Fell (11)
Walk On By (7)
Way We Were (10)
Wear It On Our Face
(1,3) 44
When I'm In Your Arms (1)
Whiter Shade Of Pale (4)
Wichita Lineman (medley) (4)
Wives And Lovers (7)
You Don't Care (8)
Your Song (12)

DE LUCIA, Paco — see McLAUGHLIN, John

DEMIAN, Max — see MAX DEMIAN

DENNIS, Cathy

Former lead singer of D-Mob. Born in 1970 in Norwich, England.

12/15/90+	67	40		Move To This	$12	Polydor 847267

C'mon And Get My Love 10
shown only as D-Mob on
single release

Everybody Move 90
Got To Get Your Love
Just Another Dream 9

Move To This
My Beating Heart
Taste My Love

Tell Me
Too Many Walls 8

Touch Me (All Night
Long) 2

DENNY, Martin

Born on 4/10/11 in New York City. Composer/arranger/pianist. Originated the "Exotic Sounds of Martin
Denny" in Hawaii, featuring Julius Wechter (Baja Marimba Band) on vibes and marimba.

5/4/59	1⁵	63		1 Exotica .... [I]	$20	Liberty 7034
				The Exciting Sounds Of MARTIN DENNY		
8/31/59+	8	71		2 Quiet Village .... [I]	$20	Liberty 7122
11/23/59	50	1		3 Exotica-Vol. III .... [I]	$20	Liberty 7116
				above 2: **The Exotic Sounds of MARTIN DENNY**		

DEBUT DATE	PEAK POS	WKS CHR	GOLD	ARTIST — Album Title	$	Label & Number
9/29/62	6	27	4	A Taste Of Honey .... [I]	$15	Liberty 7237
1/16/65	123	7	5	Hawaii Tattoo .... [I]	$15	Liberty 7394

Ah Me Furi (1)
A-me-ri-ca (4)
Analanie (5)
Bamboo Lullaby (3)
Beautiful Kahana (3)
Beyond The Reef (5)
Black Orchid (4)
Busy Port (1)
Caravan (3)
China Nights (Shina No Yoru) (1)

Clair De Lune (4)
Congo Train (3)
Coronation (2)
Exodus (4)
Firecracker (2)
Happy Talk (2)
Harbor Lights (3)
Hawaii Tattoo (5)
Hawaiian War Chant (2)
Hawaiian Wedding Song (5)
Hello Young Lovers (3)

Hong Kong Blues (1)
I'm In A Dancing Mood (4)
Jungle Flower (1)
Jungle River Boat (3)
Laura (2)
Leah (3)
Limehouse Blues (3)
Lotus Land (1)
Love Dance (1)
Mama Iti E Papa E (3)
Manila (3)

Martinique (2) 88
Moon Of Manakoora (3)
My Little Grass Shack In Kealakekua, Hawaii - Cha Cha Cha (2)
Now Is The Hour (Maori Farewell Song) (5)
Pagan Love Song (2)
Paradise Found (2)
Pearly Shells (Pupu O Ewa) (5)

Quiet Village (1,2) 4
Red Sails In The Sunset (5)
Return To Paradise (1)
Ringo Oiwake (3)
Route 66 (4)
Sail Along, Silv'ry Moon (5)
Sake Rock (2)
Similau (1)
Song Of The Islands (Na-Leio Hawaii) (5)
Stone God (1)

Stranger In Paradise (2)
Stranger On The Shore (4)
Sweet Leilani (5)
Sweet Someone (5)
Take Five (4)
Taste Of Honey (4) 50
Tune From Rangoon (2)
Violetta (4)
Waipio (1)
Walk On The Wild Side (4)
Wild One (4)

DENNY, Sandy
Lead singer of Fairport Convention. Born on 1/6/41 in the U.K. Died on 4/21/78 of a brain hemorrhage.

| 7/20/74 | 197 | 2 | | Like An Old Fashioned Waltz .... | $10 | Island 9340 |

At The End Of The Day
Carnival

Dark The Night
Friends

(It Will Have To Do) Until The Real Thing Comes Along
No End
Solo

Like An Old Fashioned Waltz
Whispering Grass (Don't Tell The Trees)

★★48★★ DENVER, John
Born John Henry Deutschendorf on 12/31/43 in Roswell, New Mexico. To Los Angeles in 1964. With the Chad Mitchell Trio from 1965-68. Wrote "Leaving On A Jet Plane." Starred in the 1978 film *Oh, God.* Won an Emmy in 1975 for the TV special *An Evening with John Denver.*

10/25/69	148	3		1 Rhymes & Reasons	$15	RCA 4207
5/2/70	197	2		2 Take Me To Tomorrow	$12	RCA 4278
4/17/71	15	80	●	3 Poems, Prayers & Promises	$12	RCA 4499
12/4/71	75	16	●	4 Aerie	$12	RCA 4607
9/16/72+	4	53	●	5 **Rocky Mountain High**	$12	RCA 4731
6/16/73	16	35	●	6 Farewell Andromeda	$10	RCA 0101
12/8/73+	1³	175	●	7 **John Denver's Greatest Hits** .... [G]	$10	RCA 0374
6/29/74	1¹	96	●	8 **Back Home Again**	$8	RCA 0548
3/8/75	2²	50	●	9 **An Evening With John Denver** .... [L]	$10	RCA 0764 [2]
10/4/75	1²	45	●	10 **Windsong**	$8	RCA 1183
11/8/75	14	11	●	11 Rocky Mountain Christmas .... [X]	$8	RCA 1201
12/20/75+	138	6		12 John Denver Gift Pak .... [X]	$10	RCA 1263 [2]
				consists of albums #10 & 11 in a special Christmas sleeve		
9/4/76	7	30	▲	13 **Spirit**	$8	RCA 1694
12/18/76+	115	5		14 Rocky Mountain Christmas .... [X-R]	$8	RCA 1201
3/5/77	6	18	▲	15 **John Denver's Greatest Hits, Volume 2** .... [G]	$8	RCA 2195
12/3/77+	45	25	▲	16 I Want To Live	$8	RCA 2521
1/27/79	25	15	●	17 John Denver	$8	RCA 3075
11/10/79+	26	12	▲	18 A Christmas Together .... [X]	$8	RCA 3451
				JOHN DENVER & THE MUPPETS		
				Christmas charts: 10/83		
3/1/80	39	17		19 Autograph	$8	RCA 3449
7/4/81	32	30	●	20 Some Days Are Diamonds	$8	RCA 4055
3/20/82	39	33	●	21 Seasons Of The Heart	$8	RCA 4256
10/15/83	61	15		22 It's About Time	$8	RCA 4683
7/6/85	90	19		23 Dreamland Express	$8	RCA 5458
11/10/90	185	6		24 The Flower That Shattered The Stone	$12	Windstar 53334

African Sunrise (23)
Alfie, The Christmas Tree (medley) (18)
All Of My Memories (4)
American Child (19)
Amsterdam (2)
Ancient Rhymes (24)
Angels From Montgomery (6)
Annie's Song (8,9,15) *1*
Anthem - Revelation (4)
Around And Around (3)
Aspenglow (2,11,12)
Autograph (19) *52*
Away In A Manger (11,12)
Baby Just Like You (11,12,18)
Baby, You Look Good To Me Tonight (18)
Back Home Again (8,15) *1*
Ballad Of Richard Nixon (1)
Ballad Of Spiro Agnew (1)
Ballad Of St. Anne's Reel (17)
Berkeley Woman (6,17)
Bet On The Blues (16)
Blow Up Your TV (Spanish Pipe Dream) (4)
Box, The (3)
Boy From The Country (9,20)
Calypso (10,12,15) *2*
Carolina In My Mind (2)
Casey's Last Ride (4)
Catch Another Butterfly (1)

Children Of The Universe (21)
Christmas For Cowboys (11,12) *58*
Christmas Is Coming (Round) (18)
Christmas Song (Chestnuts Roasting On An Open Fire) (11,12)
Christmas Wish (18)
Circus (1)
City Of New Orleans (23)
Claudette (23)
Come And Let Me Look In Your Eyes (13)
Cool An' Green An' Shady (8)
Country Love (20)
Coventry Carol (11,12)
Cowboy And The Lady (20) *66*
Cowboy's Delight (10,12)
Dancing With The Mountains (19) *97*
Darcy Farrow (5)
Daydream (1)
Dearest Esmeralda (16)
Deck The Halls (18)
Don't Close Your Eyes, Tonight (18)
Downhill Stuff (17)
Dreamland Express (23)
Dreams (21)
Druthers (16)
Eagle And The Hawk (4,7,9)

Eagles And Horses (24)
Easy, On Easy Street (20)
Eclipse (8)
Eli's Song (13)
Everyday (4) *81*
Fall (5)
Falling Out Of Love (22)
Farewell Andromeda (Welcome To My Morning) (6,9,15) *89*
Fire And Rain (3)
Flight (The Higher We Fly) (22)
Flower That Shattered The Stone (24)
Fly Away (10,12,15) *13*
Follow Me (2)
For Baby (For Bobbie) (5,7)
Forest Lawn (2)
Friends With You (4) *47*
Garden Song (17)
Gift You Are (24)
Gimme Your Love (23)
Goodbye Again (5,7) *88*
Gospel Changes (3)
Got My Heart Set On You (23)
Grandma's Feather Bed (8,9,15)
Gravel On The Ground (20)
Harder They Fall (23)
Have Yourself A Merry Little Christmas (18)
Heart To Heart (21)

High, Wide And Handsome (24)
Hitchhiker (13)
Hold On Tightly (22)
How Can I Leave You Again (16) *44*
How Mountain Girls Can Love (19)
I Guess He'd Rather Be In Colorado (3)
I Remember Romance (22)
I Want To Live (16) *55*
I Watch You Sleeping (21)
I Wish I Knew How It Would Feel To Be Free (1)
I'd Rather Be A Cowboy (6) *62*
I'm In The Mood To Be Desired (23)
I'm Sorry (10,12,15) *1*
If Ever (23)
In My Heart (19)
In The Grand Way (13)
Isabel (2)
Islands (21)
It Amazes Me (16) *59*
It Makes Me Giggle (13) *60*
It's About Time (22)
It's In Everyone Of Us (medley) (18)
It's Up To You (16)
Jimmy Newman (2)
Johnny B. Goode (17)
Joseph & Joe (17)

Junk (3)
Late Nite Radio (10,12)
Late Winter, Early Spring (When Everybody Goes To Mexico) (5)
Leaving, On A Jet Plane (1,7)
Let It Be (3)
Life Is So Good (17)
Like A Sad Song (13,15) *36*
Little Further North (24)
Little Saint Nick (18)
Looking For Space (10,12,15) *29*
Love Is Everywhere (10,12)
Love Of The Common People (1)
Matthew (8,9)
Molly (2)
Mother Nature's Son (5,9)
Mountain Song (19)
Music Is You (8,9)
My Old Man (1)
My Sweet Lady (3,9,15) *32*
Noel: Christmas Eve, 1913 (18)
Nothing But A Breeze (21)
Oh Holy Night (11,12)
On The Road (8)
On The Wings Of A Dream (22)
Opposite Tables (21)
Paradise (5)
Peace Carol (18)
Pegasus (13)

Perhaps Love (21)
Pickin' The Sun Down (9)
Please, Daddy (6,11,12) *69*
Poems, Prayers And Promises (3,7,9)
Polka Dots And Moonbeams (13)
Postcard From Paris (24)
Prisoners (5)
Raven's Child (24)
Readjustment Blues (4)
Relatively Speaking (21)
Rhymes & Reasons (1,7,9)
Ripplin' Waters (16)
River Of Love (6)
Rocky Mountain High (5,7,9) *9*
Rocky Mountain Suite (Cold Nights In Canada) (13)
Rudolph The Red-Nosed Reindeer (11,12)
San Antonio Rose (13)
San Francisco Mabel Joy (20)
Saturday Night In Toledo, Ohio (9)
Seasons Of The Heart (21) *78*
Shanghai Breezes (21) *31*
She Won't Let Me Fly Away (4)
Shipmates And Cheyenne (10,12)

DEBUT DATE	PEAK POS	WKS CHR	GOLD	ARTIST — Album Title	$	Label & Number

DENVER, John — Cont'd

Silent Night, Holy Night (11,12,18)
Silver Bells (11,12)
Singing Skies And Dancing Waters (16)
60 Second Song For A Bank, With The Phrase "May We Help You Today?" (4)
Sleepin' Alone (20)
Some Days Are Diamonds (Some Days Are Stone) (20) *36*
Somethin' About (22)
Song For The Life (19)
Song Of Wyoming (10,12)

Songs Of... (17)
Southwind (17)
Spirit (10,12)
Spring (5)
Starwood In Aspen (4,7)
Sticky Summer Weather (2)
Stonehaven Sunset (24)
Summer (5,9)
Sunshine On My Shoulders (3,7) *1*
Sweet Melinda (17)
Sweet Misery (6)
Sweet Surrender (8,9) *13*
Take Me Home, Country Roads (3,7,9) *2*

Take Me To Tomorrow (2)
Thank God I'm A Country Boy (8,9,15) *1*
Thanks To You (24)
Thirsty Boots (16)
This Old Guitar (8,9,15)
Thought Of You (22)
Till You Opened My Eyes (20)
To The Wild Country (16)
Today (9)
Today Is The First Day Of The Rest Of My Life (Sugacity) (1)
Tools (4)
Tradewinds (16)

Trail Of Tears (23)
Twelve Days Of Christmas (18)
Two Shots (10,12)
We Don't Live Here No More (6)
We Wish You A Merry Christmas (18)
Whalebones And Crosses (19)
What Child Is This (11,12)
What One Man Can Do (21)
What's On Your Mind (17)
When I'm Sixty-Four (1)

When The River Meets The Sea (18)
Whiskey Basin Blues (6)
Wild Flowers In A Mason Jar (The Farm) (20)
Wild Heart Looking For Home (23)
Wild Montana Skies (22)
Windsong (10,12)
Wings That Fly Us Home (13)
Winter (5)
Wooden Indian (3)
World Game (22)
Wrangle Mountain Song (13,19)

Yellow Cat (1)
(You Dun Stomped) My Heart (1)
You Say That The Battle Is Over (19)
You're So Beautiful (17)
Zachary And Jennifer (6)

★★458★★ DEODATO

Born Eumir De Almeida Deodato on 6/21/42 in Rio de Janeiro, Brazil. Keyboardist/composer/producer/arranger. Kool & The Gang's producer from 1979-82.

DEBUT DATE	PEAK POS	WKS CHR	GOLD	#	Title		$	Label & Number
1/20/73	3	26		1	Prelude	[I]	$10	CTI 6021
8/11/73	19	35		2	Deodato 2	[I]	$10	CTI 6029
3/23/74	114	9		3	In Concert	[I]	$10	CTI 6041
					DEODATO/AIRTO (Airto Moreira - Brazilian percussionist)			
5/4/74	63	16		4	Whirlwinds	[I]	$8	MCA 410
11/16/74	102	9		5	Artistry	[I]	$8	MCA 457
9/6/75	110	9		6	First Cuckoo	[I]	$8	MCA 491
10/9/76	86	11		7	Very Together	[I]	$8	MCA 2219
4/29/78	98	17		8	Warner 3132	[I]	$8	Warner 3132
9/27/80	186	3		9	Night Cruiser	[I]	$8	Warner 3467

Adam's Hotel (6)
Also Sprach Zarathustra (2001) (1) *2*
Amani (7)
Area Code 808 (8)
Ave Maria (4)
Baubles, Bangles And Beads (1)
Black Dog (6)
Black Widow (7)
Branches (O Galho Da Roseira) (3)

Caravan (medley) (6)
Carly & Carole (1)
Chariot Of The Gods (8)
Crabwalk (6)
Do It Again (3,4)
East Side Strut (9)
Farewell To A Friend (7)
First Cuckoo (On Hearing The First Cuckoo In Spring) (6)
Funk Yourself (6)
Groovitation (6)

Havana Strut (4)
I Shot The Sheriff (7)
Jivin' (5)
Juanita (7)
Love Island (7)
Love Magic (9)
Moonlight Serenade (4)
Night Cruiser (9)
Nights In White Satin (2)
Parana (7)
Pavane For A Dead Princess (2,5)

Peter Gunn (7) *84*
Pina Colada (8)
Prelude To Afternoon Of A Faun (1)
Rhapsody In Blue (2) *41*
Rio Sangre (5)
San Juan Sunset (8)
September 13 (1)
Skatin' (9)
Skyscrapers (2)
Spanish Boogie (7)
Speak Low (6)

Spirit Of Summer (1,3)
St. Louis Blues (5)
Star Trek, Theme From (7)
Super Strut (2,5)
Tahiti Hut (8)
Take The A Train (8)
Tropea (3)
Uncle Funk (9)
Univac Loves You (7)
Watusi Strut (medley) (6)
West 42nd Street (9)
Whirlwinds (4)

Whistle Bump (8)

★★425★★ DEPECHE MODE

All-synthesized rock band formed in Basildon, England consisting of David Gahan (vocals), Martin Gore, Vince Clarke and Andy Fletcher. Clarke left in 1982 (formed Yaz, then Erasure), replaced by Alan Wilder. Group name is French for "fast fashion."

DEBUT DATE	PEAK POS	WKS CHR	GOLD	#	Title		$	Label & Number
12/26/81+	192	9		1	Speak & Spell		$8	Sire 3642
12/4/82	177	8		2	A Broken Frame		$8	Sire 23751
7/28/84+	71	30	●	3	People Are People		$8	Sire 25124
1/19/85	51	42		4	Some Great Reward		$8	Sire 25194
12/7/85+	113	18	●	5	Catching Up With Depeche Mode	[G]	$8	Sire 25346
					features 4 tracks never before released in America			
4/26/86	90	26	●	6	Black Celebration		$8	Sire 25429
10/24/87	35	59	▲	7	Music For The Masses		$8	Sire 25614
4/1/89	45	19	●	8	101	[S-L]	$10	Sire 25853 [2]
					recorded live at the Pasadena Rose Bowl on 6/18/88 during the filming for their concert movie *101*			
4/7/90	7	74	▲²	9	Violator		$12	Sire 26081

Any Second Now (Voices) (1)
Big Muff (1)
Black Celebration (6,8)
Blasphemous Rumours (4,5,8)
Blue Dress (9)
Boys Say Go! (1)
But Not Tonight (6)
Clean (9)
Dreaming Of Me (1,5)
Dressed In Black (6)
Enjoy The Silence (9) *8*
Everything Counts (3,8)
Flexible (5)
Fly On The Windscreen (5)

Fly On The Windscreen - Final (6)
Get The Balance Right (3)
Halo (9)
Here Is The House (6)
I Want You Now (7)
If You Want (4)
It Doesn't Matter (4)
It Doesn't Matter Two (6)
It's Called A Heart (5)
Just Can't Get Enough (1,5,8)
Leave In Silence (2,3)
Lie To Me (4)
Little 15 (7)

Love In Itself (3,5)
Master And Servant (4,5,8) *87*
Meaning Of Love (2,5)
Monument (2)
My Secret Garden (2)
Never Let Me Down Again (7,8) *63*
New Dress (6)
New Life (1,5)
Nodisco (1)
Nothing (7)
Nothing To Fear (2)
Now This Is Fun (3)

People Are People (3,4,8) *13*
Personal Jesus (9) *28*
Photograph Of You (2)
Photographic (1)
Pimpf (7,8)
Pipeline (3)
Pleasure Little Treasure (8)
Policy Of Lust (9) *15*
Puppets (1)
Question Of Lust (6)
Question Of Time (6,8)
Route 66/Behind The Wheel (7,8) *61*
Sacred (7)

Satellite (2)
See You (2,5)
Shake The Disease (5,8)
Shouldn't Have Done That (2)
Somebody (4,5,8)
Something To Do (4,8)
Sometimes (6)
Stories Of Old (4)
Strangelove (7,8) *76*
Stripped (6,8)
Sun & The Rainfall (2)
Sweetest Perfection (9)
Things You Said (7,8)
To Have And To Hold (7)

Told You So (3)
Tora! Tora! Tora! (1)
Waiting For The Night (9)
What's Your Name? (1)
Work Hard (3)
World Full Of Nothing (6)
World In My Eyes (9) *52*

DEREK AND THE DOMINOS — see CLAPTON, Eric

DERRINGER, Rick

Born Richard Zehringer on 8/5/47 in Celina, Ohio. Lead singer/guitarist of The McCoys. Performed on and produced sessions for both Edgar and Johnny Winter's bands; also a producer for "Weird Al" Yankovic.

DEBUT DATE	PEAK POS	WKS CHR	GOLD	#	Title		$	Label & Number
12/1/73+	25	31		1	All American Boy		$15	Blue Sky 32481
4/26/75	141	8		2	Spring Fever		$12	Blue Sky 33423
7/31/76	154	9		3	Derringer		$12	Blue Sky 34181
2/19/77	169	3		4	Sweet Evil		$10	Blue Sky 34470
7/16/77	123	10		5	Derringer Live	[L]	$10	Blue Sky 34848

DEBUT DATE	PEAK POS	WKS CHR	G O L D	ARTIST — Album Title	$	Label & Number

DERRINGER, Rick — Cont'd

Airport Giveth (The Airport Taketh Away) (1)
Beyond The Universe (3,5)
Cheap Tequila (1)
Comes A Woman (3)
Don't Ever Say Goodbye (2)
Don't Stop Loving Me (4)

Drivin' Sideways (4)
Envy (3)
Gimme More (2)
Goodbye Again (3)
Hang On Sloopy (2) *94*
He Needs Some Answers (2)
Hold (1)

I Didn't Ask To Be Born (4)
It's Raining (1)
Joy Ride (1)
Jump, Jump, Jump (1)
Keep On Makin' Love (4)
Let Me In (3,5) *86*
Let's Make It (4)

Loosen Up Your Grip (3)
One Eyed Jack (4)
Rock (2)
Rock And Roll, Hoochie Koo (1,5) *23*
Roll With Me (2)
Sailor (3,5)

Sittin' By The Pool (4,5)
Skyscraper Blues (2)
Slide On Over Slinky (1)
Still Alive And Well (2,5)
Sweet Evil (4)
Teenage Love Affair (1,5) *80*

Teenage Queen (1)
Time Warp (1)
Tomorrow (2)
Uncomplicated (1,5)
Walkin' The Dog (2)
You Can Have Me (3)

DeSARIO, Teri
Pop singer/songwriter from Miami.

1/19/80	80	13		Moonlight Madness...........................	$8	Casablanca 7178

Dancin' In The Streets *66*
Fallin'

Goin' Thru The Motions
Heart Of Stone

Hold On
Moonlight Madness

Sell My Soul For You
With Your Love

Yes, I'm Ready *2*
You Got What It Takes

DESERT ROSE BAND, The
Nucleus of country stars: Southern California natives Chris Hillman, John Jorgenson and Herb Pedersen. Hillman was a founding member of The Byrds and the Flying Burrito Brothers.

2/17/90	187	4		Pages Of Life...........................	$12	MCA/Curb 42332

Darkness On The Playground

Desert Rose
Everybody's Hero

God's Plan
In Another Lifetime

Just A Memory
Missing You

Our Baby's Gone
Start All Over Again

Story Of Love
Time Passes Me By

DeSHANNON, Jackie
Born Sharon Myers on 8/21/44 in Hazel, Kentucky. Vocalist/composer. On radio at age six. First recorded (as Sherry Lee Myers) for Glenn in 1959. To Los Angeles in 1960. Attained prominence as a prolific songwriter (over 600 to date). Co-writer of mega-pop hit "Bette Davis Eyes." Toured with The Beatles for 26 concerts in 1964. In the films *Surf Party*, *C'mon Let's Live A Little* and *Hide And Seek*. Married composer/film scorer (*Ghostbusters II*, *Twins*, *Kindergarten Cop*) Randy Edelman.

11/1/69	81	15		1 Put A Little Love In Your Heart	$20	Imperial 12442
7/22/72	196	2		2 Jackie	$15	Atlantic 7231

Always Together (1)
Anna Karina (2)
Brand New Start (2)
Full Time Woman (2)
Heavy Burdens Me Down (2)
I Let Go Completely (1)

I Wanna Roo You (2)
I Won't Try To Put Chains On Your Soul (2)
Keep Me In Mind (1)
Laid Back Days (2)
Live (1)

Love Will Find A Way (1) *40*
Mama's Song (1)
Movin' (1)
Only Love Can Break Your Heart (2)
Paradise (2)

Peaceful In My Soul (2)
Put A Little Love In Your Heart (1) *4*
River Of Love (1)
Vanilla Olay (2) *76*

Would You Like To Learn To Dance (2)
You Are The Real Thing (1)
You Can Come To Me (1)
You Have A Way With Me (1)

DESMOND, Johnny — see MILLER, Glenn

DESMOND, Paul
Jazz alto saxophonist with Dave Brubeck. Born on 11/25/24 in San Francisco; died on 5/30/77.

12/28/63+	129	3		1 Take Ten....................... [I]	$20	RCA 2569
				with Jim Hall (guitar)		
1/10/76	167	5		2 1975: The Duets .... [I]	$10	Horizon 703
				DAVE BRUBECK & PAUL DESMOND		

Alice In Wonderland (2)
Alone Together (1)
Balcony Rock (2)

Black Orpheus, Theme From (1)
Blue Dove (1)

El Prince (1)
Embarcadero (1)
Koto Song (2)

Nancy (1)
One I Love (Belongs To Somebody Else) (1)

Samba De Orfeu (1)
Stardust (2)
Summer Song (2)

Take Ten (1)
These Foolish Things (2)
You Go To My Head (2)

DETECTIVE
Rock group featuring British lead singer Michael Des Barres - actor who was married to Pamela Des Barres (author of *I'm With The Band*) and cast member of TV's *Roseanne*, *WKRP* and *MacGyver*. Des Barres later joined Chequered Past and was the touring lead vocalist for The Power Station.

5/14/77	135	9		1 Detective...........................	$12	Swan Song 8417
1/14/78	103	12		2 It Takes One To Know One...........................	$12	Swan Song 8504

Ain't None Of Your Business (1)
Are You Talkin' To Me? (2)
Betcha Won't Dance (2)

Competition (2)
Deep Down (1)
Detective Man (1)
Dynamite (1)

Fever (2)
Got Enough Love (1)
Grim Reaper (1)
Help Me Up (2)

Nightingale (1)
One More Heartache (1)
Recognition (1)
Something Beautiful (2)

Tear Jerker (2)
Warm Love (2)
Wild Hot Summer Nights (1)

DETROIT
Seven-man Detroit rock group — Mitch Ryder, lead singer.

1/29/72	176	6		Detroit	$12	Paramount 6010

Box Of Old Roses
Drink

I Found A Love
Is It You (Or Is It Me)

It Ain't Easy
Let It Rock

Long Neck Goose
Rock 'N Roll

DETROIT EMERALDS
R&B group formed in Little Rock, Arkansas by the Tilmon brothers: Abrim (d: 1982, heart attack), Ivory, Cleophus and Raymond. In 1970, group reduced to trio of: Abrim, Ivory and friend James Mitchell. The group's backing band, from 1971-73, later recorded as Chapter 8.

6/19/71	151	3		1 Do Me Right...........................	$12	Westbound 2006
2/5/72	78	13		2 You Want It, You Got It...........................	$12	Westbound 2013
4/21/73	181	4		3 I'm In Love With You...........................	$12	Westbound 2018

Admit Your Love Is Gone (1)
And I Love Her (1)
Baby Let Me Take You (In My Arms) (2) *24*
Do Me Right (1) *43*
Feel The Need In Me (2)
Heaven Couldn't Be Like This (medley) (3)
Holding On (1)

I Bet You Get The One You Love (2)
I Can't Save Myself (Doing Without You) (1)
I Think Of You (medley) (3)
I'll Never Sail The Sea Again (2)
I'm In Love With You (medley) (1)

I've Got To Move (2)
If I Lose Your Love (1)
Just Now And Then (1)
Lee (1)
Long Live The King (1)
My Dreams Have Got The Best Of Me (3)
Shake Your Head (3)
So Long (3)

Take My Love (2)
There's A Love For Me Somewhere (2)
Till You Decide To Come Home (2)
Wear This Ring (With Love) (1) *91*
What You Gonna Do About Me (1)

Whatcha Gonna Wear Tomorrow (3)
Without You Baby (medley) (3)
You Can't Take This Love For You, From Me (1)
You Control Me (medley) (3)
You Want It, You Got It (2) *36*

You're Getting A Little Too Smart (3)

DeVAUGHN, William
R&B vocalist/songwriter/guitarist from Washington, D.C. Worked for the federal government. Backed on hits by MFSB.

8/3/74	165	11		Be Thankful For What You Got	$10	Roxbury 100

Be Thankful For What You Got *4*

Blood Is Thicker Than Water *43*

Give The Little Man A Great Big Hand

Kiss And Make Up
Sing A Love Song

Something's Being Done
We Are His Children

You Can Do It

DEBUT DATE	PEAK POS	WKS CHR	GOLD	ARTIST — Album Title	$	Label & Number

DEVICE
Los Angeles-based, pop-rock trio: Paul Engemann (lead singer), Holly Knight (keyboards, bass) and Gene Black (guitar). Engemann joined Animotion in 1988. Prolific songwriter Knight was a member of Spider.

| 7/12/86 | 73 | 16 | | 22B3 .... | $8 | Chrysalis 41526 |

Didn't I Read You Right Fall Apart, Golden Heart | **Hanging On A Heart Attack 35** | I've Got No Room For Your Love / Pieces On The Ground | Sand, Stone, Cobwebs And Dust / Tough And Tender | When Love Is Good / **Who Says 79** / Who's On The Line

★★487★★ DEVO
Robotic rock group formed in Akron, Ohio, consisting of brothers Mark and Bob Mothersbaugh, brothers Jerry and Bob Casale, and Alan Myers. David Kendrick replaced Myers by 1988. Mark and Jerry met while both were art students at Kent State. Devo is short for their theory of "de-evolution" (the regression of mankind).

10/28/78	78	18		1 Q:Are We Not Men? A:We Are Devo!	$8	Warner 3239
6/30/79	73	10		2 Duty Now For The Future	$8	Warner 3337
6/14/80	22	51 ▲		3 Freedom Of Choice	$8	Warner 3435
4/18/81	50	12		4 DEV-O Live ....[M-L]	$8	Warner 3548
10/10/81	23	25		5 New Traditionalists	$8	Warner 3595
11/20/82	47	20		6 Oh, No! It's Devo	$8	Warner 23741
11/3/84	83	6		7 Shout..	$8	Warner 25097
7/2/88	189	3		8 Total Devo	$8	Enigma 73303

Agitated (8) / Are You Experienced? (7) / Baby Doll (8) / Be Stiff (4) / Beautiful World (5) / Big Mess (6) / Blockhead (2) / Blow Up (8) / C'mon (7) / Clockout (2) / Cold War (3) / Come Back Jonee (1) / Day My Baby Gave Me A Surprise (2) / Deep Sleep (6) / Devo Corporate Anthem (2)

Disco Dancer (8) / Don't Be Cruel (8) / Don't Rescue Me (7) / Don't You Know (3) / Enough Said (5) / Explosions (6) / 4th Dimension (7) / Freedom Of Choice (3,4) / Gates Of Steel (3,4) / Girl U Want (3,4) / Going Under (5) / Gut Feeling (medley) (1) / Happy Guy (8) / Here To Go (7) / (I Can't Get No) Satisfaction (1)

I Desire (6) / Id Cry If You Died (8) / It's Not Right (3) / Jerkin' Back 'N' Forth (5) / Jocko Homo (1) / Jurisdiction Of Love (7) / Love Without Anger (8) / Man Turned Inside Out (8) / Mongoloid (1) / Mr. B's Ballroom (3) / Mr. DNA (medley) (2) / Out Of Sync (6) / Patterns (6) / Peek-A-Boo! (6) / Pink Pussycat (2) / Pity You (5)

Plain Truth (8) / Planet Earth (3,4) / Please Please (7) / Praying Hands (1) / Puppet Boy (7) / Race Of Doom (5) / Red Eye (2) / S.I.B. (Swelling Itching Brain) (2) / Satisfied Mind (7) / Secret Agent Man (2) / Shadow, The (8) / Shout (7) / Shrivel-Up (1) / Slap Your Mammy (medley) (1)

Sloppy (I Saw My Baby Gettin') (1) / Smart Patrol (medley) (2) / Snowball (3) / Soft Things (5) / Some Things Never Change (8) / Space Junk (1) / Speed Racer (6) / Strange Pursuit (2) / Super Thing (5) / That's Good (6) / That's Pep! (3) / Through Being Cool (5) / Time Out For Fun (6) / Timing X (2)

Ton O' Luv (3) / Too Much Paranoias (1) / Triumph Of The Will (7) / Uncontrollable Urge (1) / What I Must Do (6) / **Whip It (3,4) 14** / Wiggly World (2)

DeVOL, Frank, And The Rainbow Strings
Frank was born on 9/20/11 in Moundsville, West Virginia. Lead alto saxophonist/arranger with Horace Heidt and Alvino Rey. Composer/conductor/arranger for many top singers, radio and TV shows. Received several Academy Award nominations for film scores; composed the TV theme for My Three Sons.

| 1/6/62 | 102 | 2 | | The Old Sweet Songs Of Christmas ....[X-I] | $15 | Columbia 1543 |

album is made up of all medleys

Adeste Fideles (O, Come All Ye Faithful) / Away In A Manger / Christmas Song (Merry Christmas To You) / Deck The Hall With Boughs Of Holly / First Noel

God Rest Ye Merry, Gentlemen / Good King Wenceslas / Hark! The Herald Angels Sing / Here Comes Santa Claus / It Came Upon The Midnight Clear

It's Beginning To Look Like Christmas / Jingle Bells / Jolly Old St. Nicholas / Joy To The World / March Of The Toys / O Holy Night / O Little Town Of Bethlehem

O Tannenbaum / Ring Christmas Bells / Silent Night, Holy Night / Silver Bells / Skaters' Waltz / Toyland / Twelve Days Of Christmas

We Three Kings Of Orient Are / We Wish You A Merry Christmas / White Christmas / Winter Wonderland

DeVORZON, Barry
Songwriter/producer/arranger based in California. Born on 7/31/34 in New York City. Founded Valiant Records (The Cascades were on this label.) Leader of Barry & The Tamerlanes. Began prolific songwriting career in the mid-1950s.

| 11/6/76+ | 42 | 19 | | 1 Nadia's Theme (The Young And The Restless).................................[I] | $10 | A&M 3412 |

3 cuts by DeVorzon and Perry Botkin, Jr.; others by various artists: "Bellavia" and "Chase The Clouds Away" by Chuck Mangione; "Emmanuel" by Michael Colombier; "Feelings" by Herb Ohta; "My Reverie" by Ira Sullivan; "Rainbow City" by Tim Weisberg; "Zero To Sixty In Five" by Pablo Cruise

| 11/6/76+ | 133 | 12 | | 2 Nadia's Theme (The Young And The Restless).................................[I] | $10 | Arista 4104 |

cuts by DeVorzon only

All By Myself (2) / **Bless The Beasts And Children (1,2) 82**

Dancer, The (2) / Down The Line (1) / I Write The Songs (2)

Jelinda's Theme (2) / Midnight (2)

Nadia's Theme (The Young And The Restless) (1,2) 8 / S.W.A.T., Theme From (2)

Shadows (2)

This Masquerade (2) / Winter Song (2)

DEXYS MIDNIGHT RUNNERS
Kevin Rowland (b: 8/17/53, Wolverhampton, England), leader of eight-piece Birmingham, England band.

| 2/12/83 | 14 | 24 | | Too-Rye-Ay .... | $8 | Mercury 4069 |

Kevin Rowland & DEXYS MIDNIGHT RUNNERS

All In All (This One Last Wild Waltz) / **Celtic Soul Brothers 86**

Come On Eileen 1 / I'll Show You (medley)

Jackie Wilson Said (I'm In Heaven When You Smile)

Let's Make This Precious / Liars A To E

Old / Plan B (medley)

Until I Believe In My Soul

DeYOUNG, Dennis
Lead singer/keyboardist of Styx. Born on 2/18/47 in Chicago.

| 10/6/84 | 29 | 25 | | 1 Desert Moon .... | $8 | A&M 5006 |
| 3/29/86 | 108 | 8 | | 2 Back To The World .... | $8 | A&M 5109 |

Black Wall (2) / Boys Will Be Boys (1) / **Call Me (2) 54**

Dear Darling (I'll Be There) (1) / **Desert Moon (1) 10**

Don't Wait For Heroes (1) 83 / Fire (1)

Gravity (1) / I'll Get Lucky (2) / Person To Person (2)

Please (1) / Southbound Ryan (2) / Suspicious (1)

This Is The Time (2) 93 / Unanswered Prayers (2) / Warning Shot (2)

DFX2
San Diego foursome led by twins Douglas and David Farage.

| 8/20/83 | 143 | 8 | | Emotion ....[M] | $8 | MCA 36000 |

Down To The Bone

Emotion

Maureen

No Dough

Something's Always Happening

200

DEBUT DATE	PEAK POS	WKS CHR	G O L D		ARTIST — Album Title	$	Label & Number
	★★15★★				**DIAMOND, Neil**		
					Born Noah Kaminsky on 1/24/41 in Brooklyn. Vocalist/guitarist/prolific composer. Worked as songplugger/ staff writer in New York City. Wrote for *The Monkees* TV show. First recorded for Duel in 1961. Wrote score for the film *Jonathan Livingston Seagull*. Starred in and composed the music for *The Jazz Singer* in 1980.		
10/29/66	**137**	4		1	The Feel Of Neil Diamond	**$85**	Bang 214
9/16/67	**80**	19		2	Just For You	**$40**	Bang 217
8/3/68+	**100**	40		3	Neil Diamond's Greatest Hits ....[G]	**$30**	Bang 219
5/17/69	**82**	25		4	Brother Love's Travelling Salvation Show	**$35**	Uni 73047
					"Sweet Caroline" available only on reissues		
12/13/69+	**30**	47	●	5	Touching You Touching Me.............................	**$25**	Uni 73071
8/22/70	**10**	56	●	6	**Neil Diamond/Gold** ....[L]	**$25**	Uni 73084
					recorded at the Troubadour in Hollywood		
9/12/70	**52**	25		7	Shilo ....[K]	**$40**	Bang 221
11/21/70	**13**	45	●	8	Tap Root Manuscript	**$25**	Uni 73092
2/27/71	**100**	6		9	Do It! ....[K]	**$30**	Bang 224
11/13/71	**11**	25	●	10	Stones	**$25**	Uni 93106
7/15/72	**5**	41	●	11	Moods	**$25**	Uni 93136
12/9/72+	**5**	78		12	**Hot August Night** ....[L]	**$15**	MCA 8000 [2]
					recorded 8/24/72 at the Greek Theatre, Los Angeles		
1/20/73	**36**	21		13	Double Gold ....[K]	**$35**	Bang 227 [2]
9/1/73	**35**	17	●	14	Rainbow...[K]	**$15**	MCA 2103
					reissue of cuts from Uni albums		
11/3/73	**2**[1]	34	▲[2]	15	**Jonathan Livingston Seagull**............[S]	**$12**	Columbia 32550
6/8/74	**29**	42	●	16	Neil Diamond/His 12 Greatest Hits ....[G]	**$15**	MCA 2106
10/26/74	**3**	27	▲	17	**Serenade**	**$12**	Columbia 32919
7/4/76	**4**	33	▲	18	**Beautiful Noise**	**$12**	Columbia 33965
10/9/76	**102**	5		19	And The Singer Sings His Song...................[K]	**$15**	MCA 2227
					reissue of selections from Uni & MCA albums		
2/26/77	**8**	21	▲	20	**Love At The Greek** ....[L]	**$15**	Columbia 34404 [2]
					recorded August 1976 at the Greek Theatre		
12/3/77+	**6**	24	▲[2]	21	**I'm Glad You're Here With Me Tonight** ...	**$12**	Columbia 34990
12/16/78+	**4**	29	▲[2]	22	**You Don't Bring Me Flowers**	**$12**	Columbia 35625
1/12/80	**10**	20	▲	23	**September Morn**	**$12**	Columbia 36121
11/29/80+	**3**	115	▲[5]	24	**The Jazz Singer** ....[S]	**$10**	Capitol 12120
					film is a remake of Al Jolson's 1927 classic		
11/28/81+	**17**	27	▲	25	**On The Way To The Sky**	**$10**	Columbia 37628
5/29/82	**48**	42	▲[2]	26	**12 Greatest Hits, Vol. II** ....[G]	**$10**	Columbia 38068
10/16/82	**9**	34	▲	27	**Heartlight**	**$10**	Columbia 38359
6/25/83	**171**	7	▲	28	**Classics - The Early Years** ....[G]	**$10**	Columbia 38792
					original greatest hits from his Bang label era		
8/18/84	**35**	25	●	29	**Primitive**	**$10**	Columbia 39199
5/24/86	**20**	23	●	30	**Headed For The Future**	**$8**	Columbia 40368
11/21/87+	**59**	17	●	31	**Hot August Night II** ....[L]	**$10**	Columbia 40990 [2]
1/7/89	**46**	16	●	32	**The Best Years Of Our Lives**	**$8**	Columbia 45025
9/14/91	**44**	32		33	**Lovescape**	**$12**	Columbia 48610
6/6/92	**90**	24	●	34	**The Greatest Hits 1966-1992** ....[G]	**$26**	Columbia 52703 [2]
10/24/92	**8**	15	●	35	**The Christmas Album** ....[X]	**$12**	Columbia 52914
					Christmas charts: 3/'92		

Acapulco (24)
Adon Olom (24)
African Suite (8)
Ain't No Way (5)
All I Really Need Is You (33,34)
Amazed And Confused (24)
America (24,26,31,34) **8**
American Popular Song (22)
And The Grass Won't Pay No Mind (4,12,19)
And The Singer Sings His Song (5,6,19)
Angel (30)
Anthem (15)
As If (21)
Baby Can I Hold You (32)
Back In L.A. (31)
Be (15,20,26,34) **34**
Be Mine Tonight (25) **35**
Beautiful Noise (18,20,26,34)
Best Years Of Our Lives (32)
Boat That I Row (2,3,9,13,28)
Both Sides Now (5,6,14)
Brooklyn On A Saturday Night (29)
Brooklyn Roads (16,19,34) **58**
Brother Love's Travelling Salvation Show (4,6,12,16,20,31,34) **22**
Bumble Boogie (medley) (22)
Canta Libre (11,12)

Captain Sunshine (11,19)
Carmelita's Eyes (32)
Chelsea Morning (10,14)
Cherry, Cherry (1,2,3,6,7,13,28,31,34) **6**
"Cherry Cherry" From Hot August Night (12) **31**
Childsong (8)
Christmas Song (35)
Coldwater Morning (8,19)
Comin' Home (27)
Common Ground (33)
Courtin' Disaster (32)
Cracklin' Rosie (8,12,16,31,34) **1**
Crazy (29)
Crooked Street (9,13)
Crunchy Granola Suite (10,12,34) *flip*
Dance Of The Sabres (medley) (21)
Dancing Bumble Bee (medley) (22)
Dancing In The Street (23)
Dear Father (15,20)
Deep In The Morning (4)
Desiree (21,26,34) **16**
Diamond Girls (22)
Dig In (4)
Do It (1,3,9,13,28) **36**
Don't Think....Feel (18) **43**
Don't Turn Around (33)
Done Too Soon (8,12,16) **65**

Drifter, The (25)
Dry Your Eyes (18)
Everybody's Talkin' (5,14)
Everything's Gonna Be Fine (32)
Fear Of The Marketplace (25)
Fire On The Tracks (29)
First You Have To Say You Love Me (27)
Flight Of The Gull (15)
Fool For You (27)
Forever In Blue Jeans (22,26,31,34) **20**
Fortune Of The Night (33)
Free Life (8,19)
Free Man In Paris (21)
Front Page Story (27) **65**
Gift Of Song (19)
Girl, You'll Be A Woman Soon (2,3,7,12,13,28,34) **10**
Gitchy Goomy (11)
Glory Road (4,20)
God Only Knows (21)
God Rest Ye Merry Gentlemen (35)
Good Lord Loves You (23) **67**
Guitar Heaven (25)
Hanky Panky (1,3)
Happy Christmas (War Is Over) (35)
Hard Times For Lovers (32)

Hark The Herald Angels Sing (35)
He Ain't Heavy...He's My Brother (8,14) **20**
Headed For The Future (30,31,34) **53**
Heartbreak Hotel (34)
Heartlight (27,31,34) **5**
Hello Again (24,26,31,34) **6**
Hey Louise (24)
High Rolling Man (11)
Holly Holy (5,6,12,16,20,31,34) **6**
Home Is A Wounded Heart (18)
Hooked On The Memory Of You (32,33)
Hurricane (27)
Hurtin' You Don't Come Easy (4,19)
Husbands And Wives (10,14)
I Am...I Said (10,12,16,31,34) **4**
I Dreamed A Dream (24)
I Feel You (33)
I Got The Feelin' (Oh No No) (1,3,7,13,28,34) **16**
I Thank The Lord For The Night Time (2,3,6,7,13,28,31,34) **13**
I Think It's Gonna Rain Today (10,14)

I'll Come Running (1,7,9,13)
I'll See You On The Radio (Laura) (30)
I'm A Believer (2,7,9,13,23,28,34) **51**
I'm Alive (27) **35**
I'm Glad You're Here With Me Tonight (21)
I'm Guilty (27)
I've Been This Way Before (17,20) **34**
If I Couldn't See You Again (32)
If I Never Knew Your Name (4,19)
If There Were No Dreams (33)
If You Go Away (10,14)
If You Know What I Mean (18,20,26,34) **11**
In Ensenada (27)
It Should Have Been Me (30)
It's A Trip (Go For The Moon) (29)
Jazz Time (23)
Jerusalem (27)
Jingle Bell Rock (35)
Juliet (4,19)
Jungletime (18)
Kentucky Woman (3,6,7,13,20,28,34) **22**
Kol Nidre (medley) (24)
La Bamba (1)
Lady Magdelene (17)

Lady-Oh (18,20)
Lament In D Minor (medley) (21)
Last Picasso (17,20)
Last Thing On My Mind (10,14) **56**
Let Me Take You In My Arms Again (21)
Let The Little Boy Sing (21)
Little Drummer Boy (35)
Lonely Lady #17 (33)
Lonely Looking Sky (15,20)
Long Gone (4)
Long Hard Climb (32)
Long Way Home (2,9,13) **91**
Longfellow Serenade (17,20,26,34) **5**
Lordy (6)
Lost Among The Stars (27)
Lost In Hollywood (30)
Love Burns (25)
Love Doesn't Live Here Anymore (30)
Love On The Rocks (24,26,31,34) **2**
Love To Love (1,9,13)
Love's Own Song (29)
Madrigal (8)
Mama Don't Know (23)
Man You Need (30)
Me Beside You (30)
Memphis Flyer (22)
Memphis Streets (4)

DEBUT DATE	PEAK POS	WKS CHR	GOLD	ARTIST — Album Title	$	Label & Number

DIAMOND, Neil — Cont'd

Merry-Go-Round (19)	Once In A While (21)	Say Maybe (22) 55	Song Of The Whales (Fanfare) (31)	Sweet Caroline (Good Times Never Seemed So Good) (6,12,16,20,31,34) 4	Yes I Will (17)
Missa (8)	One By One (29)	September Morn' (23,26,31,34) 17	Song Sung Blue (11,12,16,20,31,34) 1	Sweet L.A. Days (33)	Yesterday's Songs (25,26,34) 11
Monday, Monday (1,7,13)	One Hand, One Heart (33)	Shelter Of Your Arms (23)	Songs Of Life (24)	Take Care Of Me (32)	You Baby (24)
Morning Has Broken (35)	Only You (25)	Shilo (2,7,12,13,16,28,34) 24	Soolaimon (African Trilogy II) (8,12,16,31,34) 30	That Kind (23)	You Don't Bring Me Flowers (21,22,26,31,34) 1
Morningside (11,12,34)	Play Me (11,12,16,34) 11	Shot Down (9,13)	Stagger Lee (23)	Theme (11)	You Got To Me (2,3,7,13,28,34) 18
Mothers And Daughters, Fathers And Sons (22)	Porcupine Pie (11,12)	Signs (18)	Stand Up For Love (30)	This Time (32)	You Make It Feel Like Christmas (29,35)
Mountains Of Love (33)	Primitive (29)	Silent Night (35)	Star Flight (27)	Turn Around (29) 62	You'll Forget (2,9,13)
Mr. Bojangles (5,14)	Rainy Day Song (25)	Silver Bells (35)	Stargazer (18,20)	Until It's Time For You To Go (5,14) 53	You're So Sweet Horseflies Keep Hangin' 'Round Your Face (4,12)
My Name Is Yussel (medley) (24)	Red Red Wine (2,3,7,9,12,13,28,34) 62	Skybird (15,20) 75	Stones (10,16,19) 14	Walk Off (medley) (12)	You've Got Your Troubles (22)
My Time With You (29)	Red Rubber Ball (1)	Sleep With Me Tonight (29)	Story Of My Life (30)	Walk On Water (11,19) 17	
New Orleans (1,3,13) 51	Reggae Strut (17)	Smokey Lady (5)	Street Life (18,20)	Way, The (33)	
New York Boy (5)	Remember Me (22)	Soggy Pretzels (12)	Summerlove (24)	We Three Kings Of Orient Are (medley) (35)	
O Come, O Come Emmanuel (medley) (35)	Right By You (25)	Solitary Man (1,2,3,6,7,9,12,13,28,34) 21	Sun Ain't Gonna Shine Anymore (22)	When You Miss Your Love (33)	
O Holy Night (35)	River Runs, Newgrown Plums (14)		Surviving The Life (18,20)	White Christmas (35)	
Odyssey Medley (15)	Rosemary's Wine (17)	Someday Baby (1,9,13)	Suzanne (10,14)	Wish Everything Was Alright (33)	
On The Robert E. Lee (24)	Sanctus (medley) (20)	Someone Who Believes In You (33)			
On The Way To The Sky (25) 27	Santa Claus Is Comin' To Town (35)				
	Save Me (25)				

DIAMOND RIO
Six-man country band — Marty Roe (vocals).

| 6/15/91+ | 83 | 84 | ● | 1 Diamond Rio .... | $12 | Arista 8673 |
| 11/21/92 | 87 | 12↑ | | 2 Close To The Edge .... | $12 | Arista 18656 |

Ballad Of Conley And Billy (The Proof's In The Pickin') (1)	I Was Meant To Be With You (2)	Mama Don't Forget To Pray For Me (1)	Oh Me, Oh My, Sweet Baby (2)	They Don't Make Hearts (Like They Used To) (1)
Calling All Hearts (Come Back Home) (2)	In A Week Or Two (2)	Meet In The Middle (1)	Old Weakness (Coming On Strong) (2)	This Romeo Ain't Got Julie Yet (1)
Close To The Edge (2)	It Does Get Better Than This (2)	Mirror Mirror (1)	Pick Me Up (1)	This State Of Mind (1)
Demons And Angels (2)	It's Gone (1)	Norma Jean Riley (1)	Poultry Promenade (1)	
		Nothing In This World (2)	Sawmill Road (2)	
		Nowhere Bound (1)		

DIBANGO, Manu
Jazz-R&B saxophonist/pianist. Born in 1934 in Cameroon, Africa.

| 6/30/73 | 79 | 13 | | Soul Makossa ....[I] | $10 | Atlantic 7267 |

Dangwa	Lily	Nights In Zeralda	Soul Makossa 35
Hibiscus	New Bell	Oboso	

DICKINSON, Bruce
Lead singer of Iron Maiden. Born Paul Bruce Dickinson on 8/7/58 in Worksop, England. Raised in Sheffield, England.

| 5/26/90 | 100 | 17 | | Tattooed Millionaire .... | $12 | Columbia 46139 |

All The Young Dudes	Dive! Dive! Dive!	Hell On Wheels	No Lies	Tattooed Millionaire
Born In '58	Gypsy Road	Lickin' The Gun	Son Of A Gun	Zulu Lulu

DICTATORS
Bronx, New York rock sextet — Dick Manitoba, lead singer.

| 7/30/77 | 193 | 2 | | Manifest Destiny .... | $10 | Asylum 1109 |

Disease	Heartache	Science Gone Too Far!	Sleepin' With The T.V. On	Young, Fast, Scientific
Exposed	Hey Boys	Search & Destroy	Steppin' Out	

DIDDLEY, Bo
Unique and influential R&B-rock & roll guitarist/vocalist. Born Otha Ellas Bates McDaniel on 12/30/28 in McComb, Mississippi. Adopted as an infant by his mother's cousin, Mrs. Gussie McDaniel. Moved to Chicago at age seven. Began recording in 1955 with the Chess/Checker label. Name "bo diddley" is a one-stringed African guitar. His first record was a two-sided #1 hit on the R&B charts, "Bo Diddley"/"I'm A Man." Inducted into the Rock and Roll Hall of Fame in 1987.

| 11/24/62 | 117 | 4 | | Bo Diddley.. | $60 | Checker 2984 |

Babes In The Woods	Diddling	Mama Don't Allow No Twistin'	Sad Sack	You Can't Judge A Book By The Cover 48
Bo's Bounce	Give Me A Break	Mr. Khrushchev	Who May Your Lover Be	
Bo's Twist	I Can Tell		You All Green	

DIESEL
Rock quartet from Holland featuring singer/guitarist Rob Vunderink.

| 8/8/81 | 68 | 24 | | Watts In A Tank .... | $8 | Regency 19315 |

Alibi	Bite Back	Goin' Back To China	Harness, The	Ready For Love	Sausalito Summernight 25
All Because Of You	Down In The Silvermine	Good Mornin' Day	My Kind Of Woman	Remember The Romans	

DIFFIE, Joe
Country singer from Duncan, Oklahoma.

| 2/8/92 | 132 | 12 | | Regular Joe .... | $12 | Epic 47477 |

Ain't That Bad Enough	Goodnight Sweetheart	Is It Cold In Here	Next Thing Smokin'	Startin' Over Blues
Back To Back Heartaches	I Just Don't Know	Just A Regular Joe	Ships That Don't Come In	You Made Me What I Am

DIFFORD & TILBROOK
Chris Difford (b: 4/11/54) and Glenn Tilbrook (b: 8/31/57) — guitarists/vocalists/songwriters of Squeeze.

| 7/14/84 | 55 | 15 | | Difford & Tilbrook .... | $8 | A&M 4985 |

Action Speaks Faster	Hope Fell Down	Man For All Seasons	Picking Up The Pieces	Wagon Train
Apple Tree	Love's Crashing Waves	On My Mind Tonight	Tears For Attention	You Can't Hurt The Girl

DIGITAL UNDERGROUND
Rap-funk crew based in Northern California. Formed by Gregory E. "Shock-G" Jacobs (keyboards, vocals) and Chopmaster J (samples, percussion). Features vocalists Humpty-Hump and Money-B. Appeared in the film *Nothing But Trouble*.

| 4/14/90 | 24 | 31 | ▲ | 1 Sex Packets .... | $12 | Tommy Boy 1026 |
| 2/2/91 | 29 | 27 | ● | 2 This Is An E.P. Release ....[M] | $6 | Tommy Boy 964 |

2 of the 6 tracks are from the film *Nothing But Trouble*

DEBUT DATE	PEAK POS	WKS CHR	GOLD	ARTIST — Album Title	$	Label & Number
11/2/91	44	27	●	3 Sons Of The P	$12	Tommy Boy 1045

Arguin' On The Funk (2)
D-Flowstrumental (3)
DFLO Shuttle (3)
Danger Zone (1)
Doowutchyalike (1)

Family Of The Underground (3)
Flowin' On The D-Line (3)
Freaks Of The Industry (1)
Good Thing We're Rappin' (3)
Gutfest '89 (1)

Heartbeat Props (3)
Higher Heights Of Spirituality (3)
Humpty Dance (1) *11*
Kiss You Back (3) *40*
New Jazz (One) (1)

No Nose Job (3)
Nuttin' Nis Funky (2)
Packet Man (1,2)
Rhymin' On The Funk (1)
Same Song (2)
Sex Packets (1)

Sons Of The P (3)
Street Scene (1)
Tales Of The Funky (3)
Tie The Knot (2)
Underwater Rimes (1)
Way We Swing (1,2)

DILLARDS, The
Country-rock quintet from the Ozarks in Missouri, formed by brothers Doug and Rodney Dillard. Doug left in 1968 to form the Dillard-Clark Expedition.

| 6/10/72 | 79 | 18 | | Roots And Branches | $8 | Anthem 5901 |

Big Bayou
Billy Jack

Forget Me Not
Get Out On The Road

I've Been Hurt
Last Morning

Man Of Constant Sorrow
One A.M.

Redbone Hound
Sunny Day

DILLMAN BAND, The
Country-rock quintet led by Steve Solmonson and Steve Seamans.

| 4/1/78 | 198 | 2 | | 1 The Daisy Dillman Band | $8 | United Art. 838 |
| 5/16/81 | 145 | 7 | | 2 Lovin' The Night Away | $8 | RCA 3909 |

Border Bound (1)
Breakdown (2)
C.O.D. (2)
Darlin' Companion (1)

Flyin' Solo (1)
Hoedown (1)
It Doesn't Matter Anymore (1)

Just A Lady (1)
Learn To Fly (1)
Love Don't Run (2)

Lovin' The Night Away (2) *45*
Mexican Nights (1)
Roll Like A Stone (2)

She's Just A Stranger (2)
Slow Ride Home (2)
So Much The Smoother (2)

Spending Time, Making Love And Going Crazy (2)
Turn My Head (1)

DI MEOLA, Al
Jazz fusion guitar virtuoso. Born on 7/22/54 in Jersey City, New Jersey. Member of Return To Forever from 1974-76.

3/27/76	129	10		1 Land Of The Midnight Sun	[I] $8	Columbia 34074
5/7/77	58	12	●	2 Elegant Gypsy	[I] $8	Columbia 34461
4/29/78	52	17		3 Casino	[I] $8	Columbia 35277
7/12/80	119	14		4 Splendido Hotel	[I] $10	Columbia 36270 [2]
5/30/81	97	13		5 Friday Night In San Francisco	[I-L] $8	Columbia 37152
				JOHN McLAUGHLIN/AL DI MEOLA/PACO DE LUCIA		
2/6/82	55	13		6 Electric Rendezvous	[I] $8	Columbia 37654
12/25/82+	165	7		7 Tour De Force - "Live"	[I-L] $8	Columbia 38373
8/20/83	171	5		8 Passion, Grace & Fire	[I] $8	Columbia 38645
				JOHN McLAUGHLIN/AL DI MEOLA/PACO DE LUCIA		
10/29/83	128	6		9 Scenario	[I] $8	Columbia 38944
1/23/88	190	1		10 Tirami Su	[I] $8	EMI-Man. 46995
				AL DI MEOLA PROJECT		

Advantage (7)
African Night (9)
Al Di's Dream Theme (4)
Alien Chase On Arabian Desert (4)
Andonea (10)
Arabella (10)
Aspan (8)
Beijing Demons (10)
Bianca's Midnight Lullaby (4)
Black Cat Shuffle (6)
Cachaca (9)
Calliope (9)
Casino (3)
Chasin' The Voodoo (3)

Chiquito (8)
Cruisin' (6,7)
Dark Eye Tango (3)
David (8)
Dinner Music Of The Gods (4)
Egyptian Danza (3,7)
Electric Rendezvous (6)
Elegant Gypsy Suite (2,7)
Fantasia Suite (5)
Fantasia Suite For Two Guitars Medley (3)
Flight Over Rio (2)
Frevo Rasgado (5)
God Bird Change (6)

Guardian Angel (5)
Hypnotic Conviction (9)
I Can Tell (9)
Isfahan (4)
Island Dreamer (9)
Jewel Inside A Dream (6)
Lady Of Rome, Sister Of Brazil (2)
Land Of The Midnight Sun (1)
Maraba (10)
Mata Hari (9)
Mediterranean Sundance (2,5)
Midnight Tango (2)

Nena (7)
Orient Blue Suite (Part I, II, III) (4)
Passion, Grace & Fire (6,8)
Pictures Of The Sea, Love Theme From (1)
Race With Devil On Spanish Highway (2,7)
Rhapsody Of Fire (10)
Rio Ancho (medley) (5)
Ritmo De La Noche (6)
Roller Jubilee (4)
Sarabande From Violin Sonata In B Minor (1)
Scenario (9)

Scoundrel (9)
Senor Mouse (3)
Sequencer (9)
Short Tales Of The Black Forest (1,5)
Sichia (8)
Silent Story In Her Eyes (4)
Smile From A Stranger (10)
Somalia (6)
Song To The Pharoah Kings (10)
Song With A View (10)
Spanish Eyes (4)
Splendido Sundance (4)

Suite - Golden Dawn Medley (1)
Two To Tango (4)
Wizard, The (1)

DINO
Born Dino Esposito on 7/20/63 in Encino, California and raised in Hawaii and Connecticut. Former DJ/music director at KCEP in Las Vegas.

| 3/25/89 | 34 | 48 | ● | 1 24/7 | $8 | 4th & B'way 4011 |
| 9/8/90 | 82 | 21 | | 2 Swingin' | $12 | Island 846481 |

After The Sun Goes Down (2)
Boyfriend-Girlfriend (1)
Can't Get Away From You (2)
Falling For You (2)

Gentle (2) *31*
I Like It (1) *7*
In The City (1)
In The Morning (2)

Never 2 Much Of U (1) *61*
No More Heartbreak (1)
Real Love (1)
Romeo (2) *6*

Summergirls (1) *50*
Sunshine (1) *23*
Swingin' (2)
Tongue Kiss (2)

24/7 (1) *42*
Why Do You Do Me? (2)
Wish On A Star (2)

DINO, DESI & BILLY
Dino (Dean Martin's son, Dean Martin, Jr.), Desi (Lucille Ball and Desi Arnaz's son, Desiderio Arnaz IV) & Billy (a schoolmate from Beverly Hills, William Hinsche). Dino (formerly married to Olympic skater Dorothy Hamill) was killed on 3/21/87 (age 35) when his Air National Guard jet crashed.

| 9/25/65 | 51 | 24 | | 1 I'm A Fool | $20 | Reprise 6176 |
| 2/12/66 | 119 | 6 | | 2 Our Time's Coming | $20 | Reprise 6194 |

Act Naturally (2)
Boo-Hoo-Hoo (I Can Tell) (1)
Chimes Of Freedom (1)
Desi's Drums (2)

Everything I Do Is For You (2)
Fun, Fun, Fun (2)
Get Off Of My Cloud (2)

Hang On Sloopy (2)
(I Can't Get No) Satisfaction (1)
I'm A Fool (1) *17*

It Ain't Me, Babe (1)
Let Me Be (2)
Like A Rolling Stone (1)
Mr. Tambourine Man (1)
Not The Lovin' Kind (1) *25*

Rebel Kind (1)
Seventh Son (1)
She's So Far Out She's In (2)
Shelia (2)
So Many Ways (1)

Turn, Turn, Turn (2)
Yesterday (2)
You've Got To Hide Your Love Away (2)

DINOSAUR JR.
Amherst, Massachusetts male duo: J. Mascis (founder/vocalist) and Murph (drums).

| 3/30/91 | 168 | 6 | | Green Mind | $12 | Sire 26479 |

Blowing It
Flying Cloud
Green Mind

How'd You Pin That One On Me

I Live For That Look
Muck

Puke + Cry
Thumb

Wagon, The
Water

DIO

Ronnie James Dio, former lead singer of hard-rock groups Black Sabbath and Rainbow. Born Ronald Padavona on 7/10/49 in Portsmouth, New Hampshire; raised in Cortland, New York.

DEBUT DATE	PEAK POS	WKS CHR	GOLD	#	ARTIST — Album Title	$	Label & Number
6/25/83	56	38	▲	1	Holy Diver	$8	Warner 23836
7/21/84	23	35	▲	2	The Last In Line	$8	Warner 25100
8/31/85	29	29	●	3	Sacred Heart	$8	Warner 25292
6/28/86	70	16		4	Intermission [M-L]	$8	Warner 25443
					contains 5 live tracks and one studio track		
8/15/87	43	11		5	Dream Evil	$8	Warner 25612
6/2/90	61	13		6	Lock Up The Wolves	$12	Reprise 26212

All The Fools Sailed Away (5)
Another Lie (3)
Between Two Hearts (6)
Born On The Sun (6)
Breathless (2)
Caught In The Middle (1)
Don't Talk To Strangers (1)
Dream Evil (5)
Eat Your Heart Out (2)
Egypt (The Chains Are On) (2)
Evil Eyes (2)
Evil On Queen Street (6)
Faces In The Window (5)
Fallen Angels (3)
Gypsy (1)
Hey Angel (6)
Holy Diver (1)
Hungry For Heaven (3)
I Could Have Been A Dreamer (5)
I Speed At Night (2)
Invisible (1)
Just Another Day (3)
King Of Rock And Roll (3,4)
Last In Line (2)
Like The Beat Of A Heart (3)
Lock Up The Wolves (6)
Long Live Rock 'N' Roll (medley) (4)
Man On The Silver Mountain (medley) (4)
My Eyes (5)
Mystery (2)
Naked In The Rain (5)
Night Music (6)
Night People (5)
One Night In The City (2)
Overlove (5)
Rainbow In The Dark (1,4)
Rock 'N' Roll Children (3,4)
Sacred Heart (3,4)
Shame On The Night (1)
Shoot Shoot (3)
Stand Up And Shout (1)
Straight Through The Heart (1)
Sunset Superman (5)
Time To Burn (4)
Twisted (6)
Walk On Water (6)
When A Woman Cries (5)
Why Are They Watching Me (6)
Wild One (6)

★★468★★ DION

Born Dion DiMucci on 7/18/39 in the Bronx. First recorded as Dion & The Timberlanes on Mohawk in 1957. Formed vocal group, Dion & The Belmonts, in the Bronx in 1958. Consisted of Dion (lead), Angelo D'Aleo (b: 2/3/40; first tenor), Fred Milano (b: 8/22/39; second tenor) and Carlo Mastrangelo (b: 10/5/38; bass). Named for Belmont Avenue in the Bronx. Angelo was in the Navy in 1959 and missed some recording and picture sessions. Dion went solo in 1960. Moved to Miami in 1968. Brief reunion with the Belmonts in 1967 and 1972, periodically since then. Also records contemporary Christian songs. Inducted into the Rock and Roll Hall of Fame in 1989.

DEBUT DATE	PEAK POS	WKS CHR	GOLD	#	ARTIST — Album Title	$	Label & Number
11/27/61	11	51		1	Runaround Sue	$50	Laurie 2009
7/14/62	12	22		2	Lovers Who Wander	$50	Laurie 2012
12/15/62+	29	22		3	Dion Sings His Greatest Hits [G]	$60	Laurie 2013
					2 cuts by Dion; 10 cuts by Dion & The Belmonts		
3/23/63	20	21		4	Ruby Baby	$20	Columbia 8810
6/22/63	115	6		5	Dion Sings To Sandy (and all his other girls) [K]	$40	Laurie 2017
					6 cuts by Dion; 6 cuts by Dion & The Belmonts		
12/21/68+	128	11		6	Dion	$20	Laurie 2047
1/1/72	200	2		7	Sanctuary	$15	Warner 1945
12/2/72	197	4		8	Suite For Late Summer	$15	Warner 2642
2/24/73	144	8		9	Reunion-Live at Madison Square Garden 1972 [L]	$15	Warner 2664
					DION & THE BELMONTS		
3/24/73	194	5		10	Dion's Greatest Hits [G]	$20	Columbia 31942
					Dion(4) and Dion & The Belmonts(6) original Laurie hits		
5/20/89	130	19		11	Yo Frankie	$8	Arista 8549

Abraham, Martin And John (6,7) 4
Almond Joy (7)
Always In The Rain (11)
And The Night Stood Still (11) 75
Brand New Morning (7)
Come Go With Me (2) 48
Didn't You Change? (8)
Dolphins, The (6)
Don't Pity Me (3) 40
Dream Lover (1)
Drip, Drop (9)
Drive All Night (11)
End Of The World (4)
Everybody's Talkin' (medley) (6)
Fever (4)
From Both Sides Now (6) 91
Go Away Little Girl (4)
Gonna Make It Alone (4)
Gotta Get Up (7)
Harmony Sound (7)
He Looks A Lot Like Me (6)
He'll Only Hurt You (4)
I Can't Go On (Rosalie) (4) 42
(I Was) Born To Cry (2)
I Wonder Why (3,9,10) 22
I've Cried Before (5)
I've Got To Get To You (11)
In The Still Of The Night (1,3) 38
It All Fits Together (8)
Jennifer Knew (8)
Just You (5)
Kansas City (1)
King Of The New York Streets (11)
King Without A Queen (2)
Life Is But A Dream (1)
Little Diane (2,5,9) 8
Little Girl (5)
Little Miss Blue (3) 96
Little Star (1,11)
Loneliest Man In The World (4)
Lonely Teenager (3,10) 12
Lonely World (1)
Lost For Sure (2)
Love Came To Me (5) 10
Lover's Prayer (3,10) 73
Lovers Who Wander (2)
Loving You Is Killing Me (11)
Loving You Is Sweeter Than Ever (6)
Majestic, The (1) 36
My Mammy (1)
My Private Joy (5)
No One Knows (3,9,10) 19
Please Be My Friend (medley) (7)
Purple Haze (6) 63
Queen Of The Hop (2,5)
Ruby Baby (4,7,9) 2
Runaround Sue (1,9,10) 1
Runaway Girl (1,5)
Running Close Behind You (8)
Sanctuary (7)
Sandy (2,5) 21
Sea Gull (8)
Serenade (11)
Shout (2)
Sisters Of Mercy (6)
Soft Parade Of Years (8)
Somebody Nobody Wants (1)
Stagger Lee (2)
Sun Fun Song (6)
Sunshine Lady (7)
Take A Little Time (medley) (7)
Take Good Care Of My Baby (1)
Teen Angel (3,5)
Teenager In Love (3,9,10) 5
Tennessee Madonna (8)
That's My Desire (3,9)
To Dream Tomorrow (8)
Tomorrow Is A Long Time (medley) (6)
Tonight, Tonight (2)
Tower Of Love (11)
Traveler In The Rain (8)
Twist, The (2)
Unloved, Unwanted Me (4)
Wanderer, The (1,7,9,10) 2
Wedding Song (4)
When You Wish Upon A Star (3,10) 30
Where Or When (3,9,10) 3
Will Love Ever Come My Way (4)
Willigo (7)
Wonderful Girl (5)
Written On The Subway Wall (medley) (11)
Yo Frankie (She's All Right With Me) (11)
You Better Watch Yourself (Sonny Boy) (6)
You Made Me Love You (I Didn't Want To Do It) (4)
You're Nobody 'Til Somebody Loves You (4)

DION, Celine

Born on 3/30/68 in Charlemagne, Quebec. Popular singer in France and Canada since her teen years.

DEBUT DATE	PEAK POS	WKS CHR	GOLD	#	ARTIST — Album Title	$	Label & Number
1/19/91	74	26		1	Unison	$12	Epic 46893
4/18/92	34	43↑	●	2	Celine Dion	$12	Epic 52473

Beauty And The Beast (2) 9
Did You Give Enough Love (2)
Halfway To Heaven (2)
Have A Heart (1)
I Feel Too Much (1)
I Love You, Goodbye (2)
I'm Loving Every Moment With You (1)
If I Were You (2)
If Love Is Out The Question (1)
(If There Was) Any Other Way (1) 35
If We Could Start Over (1)
If You Asked Me To (2) 4
If You Could See Me Now (2)
Last To Know (1)
Little Bit Of Love (2)
Love By Another Name (1)
Love Can Move Mountains (2) 36↑
Nothing Broken But My Heart (2) 29
Show Some Emotion (2)
Unison (1)
Water From The Moon (2)
Where Does My Heart Beat Now (1) 4
With This Tear (2)

★★242★★ DIRE STRAITS

Rock group formed in London by songwriter/producer Mark Knopfler (lead vocals, lead guitar) and his brother David guitar), with John Illsley (bass) and Pick Withers (drums). David left in mid-1980, replaced by Hal Lindes (left in 1985). Added keyboardist Alan Clark in 1982. Terry Williams replaced drummer Pick Withers in 1983. Guitarist Guy Fletcher added in 1984. Mark and Guy were also members of The Notting Hillbillies in 1990. Dire Straits' 1991 lineup: Knopfler, Illsley, Fletcher and Clark with Chris White (sax), Paul Franklin (pedal steel), Danny Cummings (percussion), Phil Palmer (guitar) and Chris White (drums).

DEBUT DATE	PEAK POS	WKS CHR	GOLD	#	ARTIST — Album Title	$	Label & Number
1/6/79	2¹	41	▲²	1	Dire Straits	$8	Warner 3266
6/30/79	11	19	●	2	Communique	$8	Warner 3330

DEBUT DATE	PEAK POS	WKS CHR	GOLD	ARTIST — Album Title	$	Label & Number
				DIRE STRAITS — Cont'd		
11/15/80	19	31	●	3 Making Movies	$8	Warner 3480
10/16/82	19	32	●	4 Love Over Gold	$8	Warner 23728
3/12/83	53	15		5 Twisting By The Pool ....[M]	$8	Warner 29800
4/21/84	46	18		6 Dire Straits Live - Alchemy ....[L]	$10	Warner 25085 [2]
6/8/85	1[9]	97	▲6	7 **Brothers In Arms**	$8	Warner 25264
11/12/88	62	17	●	8 Money For Nothing..[G]	$8	Warner 25794
9/28/91	12	32	▲	9 On Every Street	$12	Warner 26680

Angel Of Mercy (2)
Badges, Posters, Stickers, T-Shirts (5)
Brothers In Arms (7,8)
Bug, The (9)
Calling Elvis (9)
Communique (2)
Down To The Waterline (1,8)
Expresso Love (3,6)
Fade To Black (9)
Follow Me Home (2)
Going Home (6)
Hand In Hand (3)
Heavy Fuel (9)
How Long (9)
If I Had You (5)
In The Gallery (1)
Industrial Disease (4) 75
Iron Hand (9)
It Never Rains (4)
It's Boys (3)
Lions (1)
Local Hero, Theme From ..see: Going Home
Love Over Gold (4)
Man's Too Strong (7)
Money For Nothing (7,8) 1
My Parties (9)
News (2)
On Every Street (9)
Once Upon A Time In The West (2,6)
One World (7)
Planet Of New Orleans (9)
Portobello Belle (2)
Portobello Belle (live) (8)
Private Investigation (4,6,8)
Ride Across The River (7)
Romeo And Juliet (3,6,8)
Setting Me Up (1)
Single-Handed Sailor (2)
Six Blade Knife (1)
Skateaway (3) 58
So Far Away (7) 19
Solid Rock (3,6)
Southbound Again (1)
Sultans Of Swing (1,6,8) 4
Telegraph Road (4,6)
Ticket To Heaven (6)
Tunnel Of Love (3,6,8)
Twisting By The Pool (5,8)
Two Young Lovers (5,6)
Walk Of Life (7,8) 7
Water Of Love (1)
When It Comes To You (9)
Where Do You Think You're Going? (2,8)
Why Worry (7)
Wild West End (1)
You And Your Friend (9)
Your Latest Trick (7)

DIRKSEN, Senator Everett McKinley

U.S. senator from Illinois, 1950-69. Born in Pekin, Illinois in 1896; died on 9/7/69 (age 73).

DEBUT DATE	PEAK POS	WKS CHR	GOLD	ARTIST — Album Title	$	Label & Number
1/7/67	16	16		1 Gallant Men ....[T]	$15	Capitol 2643
				features patriotic stories and recitations to a musical background		
8/5/67	148	3		2 Man Is Not Alone ....[T]	$15	Capitol 2754
				narration with musical background, conducted by John Cacavas		

Beatitudes, The (2)
Carpenter Came (2)
Gallant Men (1) 29
Gettysburg Address (1)
Greatest Thing In The World (2)
In The Beginning (2)
Man Is Not Alone (2)
Pledge Of Allegiance To The Flag (1)
Prayer Of A Humble Man (2)
Shepherd And His Flock (2)
Star Spangled Banner (1)
Story Of Gettysburg (1)
Story Of The Battle For Independence (1)
Story Of The Flag (1)
Story Of The Mayflower (1)
The Mayflower Compact (1)
Story Of The Statue Of Liberty And The New Colossus (1)
Way Is Swift (1)
Word To Guide The Way (2)
You Are The Captain Of Your Soul (2)

DIRT BAND, The — see NITTY GRITTY DIRT BAND

DIRTY LOOKS

Heavy-metal quartet formed in Pennsylvania. Consists of Danish-born vocalist/guitarist Henrik Ostergaard, bassist Jack Pyers, guitarist Paul Lidel and drummer Gene Barnett.

DEBUT DATE	PEAK POS	WKS CHR	GOLD	ARTIST — Album Title	$	Label & Number
5/21/88	134	14		1 Cool From The Wire	$8	Atlantic 81836
8/19/89	118	11		2 Turn Of The Screw	$8	Atlantic 81992

Always A Loser (2)
C'mon Frenchie (2)
Can't Take My Eyes Off Of You (1)
Cool From The Wire (1)
Get It Right (1)
Get Off (1)
Go Away (2)
Have Some Balls (2)
Hot Flash Jelly Roll (2)
It's A Bitch (1)
It's Not The Way You Rock (1)
L.A. Anna (2)
Love Screams (2)
No Brains Child (1)
Nobody Rides For Free (2)
Oh Ruby (1)
Put A Spell On You (1)
Slammin' To The Big Beat (2)
Take What Ya Get (2)
Tokyo (1)
Turn Of The Screw (Who's Screwing You) (2)
Wastin' My Time (1)

DISCO TEX & THE SEX-O-LETTES

Disco studio group assembled by producer Bob Crewe. Featuring lead voice Sir Monti Rock III (real name: Joseph Montanez, Jr.), owner of a chain of hairdressing salons.

DEBUT DATE	PEAK POS	WKS CHR	GOLD	ARTIST — Album Title	$	Label & Number
5/3/75	36	22		Disco Tex & His Sex-O-Lettes	$10	Chelsea 505

Around The World (medley)
Boogie Flap
Get Dancin' 10
(I See Your) Name Up In Lights
I Wanna Dance Wit' Choo (Doo Dat Dance), Part 1 23
Jam Band 80
Love Is A Killer
Outrageous
Shirley Wood (medley)

DIVINYLS

Vocalist Christina Amphlett and guitarist Mark McEntee formed Australian rock group in 1981. Bassist Rick Grossman joined the Hoodoo Gurus in 1989.

DEBUT DATE	PEAK POS	WKS CHR	GOLD	ARTIST — Album Title	$	Label & Number
12/7/85+	91	18		1 What A Life!	$8	Chrysalis 41511
2/16/91	15	26	●	2 DiVINYLS	$12	Virgin 91397

Bless My Soul (It's Rock-N-Roll) (2)
Bullet (2)
Casual Encounter (1)
Dear Diary (1)
Don't You Go Walking (1)
Follow Through (2)
Good Die Young (1)
Guillotine Day (1)
Heart Telegraph (1)
I Touch Myself (2) 4
I'm On Your Side (2)
If Love Was A Gun (2)
In My Life (1)
Lay Your Body Down (2)
Love School (2)
Make Out Alright (2)
Motion (1)
Need A Lover (2)
Pleasure And Pain (1) 76
Sleeping Beauty (1)

DIXIE CUPS, The

Black female trio from New Orleans: Barbara Ann Hawkins (b: 10/23/43), her sister Rosa Lee Hawkins (b: 9/24/44) and their cousin Joan Marie Johnson. Discovered by singer/producer Joe Jones.

DEBUT DATE	PEAK POS	WKS CHR	GOLD	ARTIST — Album Title	$	Label & Number
8/29/64	112	5		Chapel Of Love	$40	Red Bird 100

Ain't That Nice
All Grown Up
Another Boy Like Mine
Chapel Of Love 1
Gee Baby Gee
Gee The Moon Is Shining Bright
Girls Can Tell
I'm Gonna Get You Yet
Iko Iko 20
People Say 12
Thank You Mama, Thank You Papa

DIXIE DREGS

Instrumental rock quintet led by Steve Morse (guitar, banjo) with Rod Morgenstein (Winger; drums), T Lavitz (keyboards), Allen Sloan (violin) and Dave LaRue (bass).

DEBUT DATE	PEAK POS	WKS CHR	GOLD	ARTIST — Album Title	$	Label & Number
5/27/78	182	4		1 What If ....[I]	$8	Capricorn 0203
5/19/79	111	13		2 Night Of The Living Dregs..............................[I-L]	$8	Capricorn 0216
				side 2 recorded live at the Montreux Jazz Festival		
5/10/80	81	17		3 Dregs of the Earth ....[I]	$8	Arista 9528
				DREGS:		
4/18/81	67	14		4 Unsung Heroes...[I]	$8	Arista 9548
3/27/82	56	15		5 Industry Standard ....[I]	$8	Arista 9588

Assembly Line (5)
Attila The Hun (4)
Bash, The (2)
Bloodsucking Leeches (5)
Broad Street Strut (3)
Chips Ahoy (5)
Conversation Piece (2)
Country House Shuffle (2)
Crank It Up (5)
Cruise Control (4)
Day 444 (4)
Divided We Stand (5)
Gina Lola Breakdown (1)
Go For Baroque (4)
Great Spectacular (3)
Hereafter (3)
I'll Just Pick (4)
I'm Freaking Out (3)
Ice Cakes (4)
Kat Food (4)
Leprechaun Promenade (2)
Little Kids (1)
Long Slow Distance (2)
Night Meets Light (4)

DEBUT DATE	PEAK POS	WKS CHR	G O L D	ARTIST — Album Title	$	Label & Number

DIXIE DREGS — Cont'd

Night Of The Living Dregs (2) Patchwork (2) Ridin' High (5) Rock & Roll Park (4) Twiggs Approved (3) What If (1)
Odyssey (1) Pride O' The Farm (3) Riff Raff (2) Take It Off The Top (1) Up In The Air (5) Where's Dixie? (5)
Old World (3) Punk Sandwich (2) Road Expense (3) Travel Tunes (1) Vitamin Q (5)

DIXON, Don

Rock singer/guitarist/producer from Athens, Georgia. Produced albums for R.E.M., The Smithereens, Guadalcanal Diary, Marshall Crenshaw and Marti Jones (his wife).

3/7/87	162	8		Most Of The Girls Like To Dance But Only Some Of The Boys Like To	$8	Enigma 73239

Andy Ice On The River Renaissance Eyes Talk To Me (You're A) Big Girl Now
Cliche Just Rites Skin Deep Wake Up
Girls L.T.D. Praying Mantis Southside Girl When A Man Loves A Woman

D.J. JAZZY JEFF & THE FRESH PRINCE

Philadelphia rap duo: D.J. Jeff Townes and rapper Will Smith. Smith stars in the TV sitcom *Fresh Prince of Bel Aire.*

4/25/87+	83	38	1	Rock The House	$8	Jive 1026
				re-released in 1988 with the additional cut "Special Announcement"		
4/23/88	4	55	▲²	2 He's The D.J., I'm The Rapper	$10	Jive 1091 [2]
11/18/89	39	20	●	3 And In This Corner...	$8	Jive 1188
7/27/91	12	42	▲	4 Homebase	$12	Jive 1392

Another Special Everything That Glitters **I Think I Can Beat Mike** My Buddy (2) Special Announcement (1) Who Stole The D.J. (4)
Announcement (?) (Ain't Always Gold) (3) **Tyson** (3) *58* **Nightmare On My Street** Summertime (4) *4* You Got It (Donut) (3)
As We Go (2) **Girls Ain't Nothing But** I'm All That (4) (2) *15* Taking It To The Top (1) You Saw My Blinker (4)
Brand New Funk (2) **Trouble** (1) *57* Jazzy's Groove (3) Numero Uno (3) Then She Bit Me (3)
Caught In The Middle (Love Guys Ain't Nothing But Jazzy's In The House (2) **Parents Just Don't** Things That U Do (4)
& Life) (4) Trouble (1) Just One Of Those Days (1) **Understand** (2) *12* This Boy Is Smooth (4)
Charlie Mack-The First Out He's The D.J., I'm The Just Rockin' (1) Pump Up The Bass (2) Time To Chill (2)
The Limo (2) Rapper (2) Let's Get Busy Baby (2) Reverend, The (3) Too Damn Hype (3)
D.J. On The Wheels (2) Here We Go Again (2) Live At Union Square, Rhythm Trax-House Party Touch Of Jazz (1)
Dog Is A Dog (4) Hip Hop Dancer's Theme (2) November 1986 (2) Style (2) Trapped On The Dance
Don't Even Try It (1) Human Video Game (2) Magnificent Jazzy Jeff (3) **Ring My Bell** (4) *20* Floor (4)
Dumb Dancin' (4) Men Of Your Dreams (3) Rock The House (1) Who Stole My Car? (3)

D.J. MAGIC MIKE

Mike Hampton, a native of Orlando, Florida. Executive Vice President of Cheetah Records. Rap producer.

7/21/90	157	18	●	1 Bass Is The Name Of The Game	$12	Cheetah 9403
1/26/91	153	22		2 Back To Haunt You!	$12	Cheetah 9404
				VICIOUS BASE Featuring D.J. MAGIC MIKE!		
11/23/91+	72	23	●	3 Ain't No Doubt About It	$12	Cheetah 9405
7/25/92	149	7		4 Twenty Degrees Below Zero	$12	Cheetah 9412
				above 2: D.J. MAGIC MIKE & M.C. MADNESS		

Abracadabra (3) Class Is In Session (3,4) Give It To 'Em (1) Listen To The Bass Go Boom Night At The Studio (2) Vicious Groove (2)
Afternoon In Orlando (2) Comin On Strong (2) Government, The (2) (4) No Stop To The Madness (2) Wack Rappers (2)
Ain't Finished Yet (1) Dance All Night (3) Hard To Keep A Good Lower The Dynamite (1,4) Orlando's In The House (3) Whats The Name Of The
Ain't No Doubt About It (3,4) Do You Like Bass? (3) Rhyme Down (2) M&M's Gettin' Off (1) Party With Peace In Mind (3) Game (2)
All Wild D.J.'s He Will Tame Drop The Bass (Pt. 2) (1) House Of Magic (1) Madness To The Brink Of Rock The Funky Beat (1) Yo! (1)
(2) Dynamic Duo (3) How The F*?k Do You Insanity (3) Royalty's Arrived (2) You Want Bass (2)
Are You Ready (2) E And The Sea-Gull (3) Figure? (4) Magic And Isaam's Groove Sgt. Fester (3)
Back To Haunt You (2) Exile Via Freestyle (3) I'm Gonna Make It Real (1) Shake Your Booty Baby (3)
Boo-Boo Of Rough J. Rough Feel The Bass Again (1) Funky For U (3) Magic Meets Lace (2) Slow Draggin (3)
(3) Feel The Bass, III (3) It's Automatic [includes 2 Meeting, The (2) Sorry, Wrong Beat (2)
Booty Dub (1) Flight Back To Orlando (2) versions] (2) Moment Of Pleasure (2) Speedy And Poncho (3)
Break, The (2) For The Easy Listeners (1) Just Cruisin (3) Moment Of Silence (2) Suckers Frontin (3)
Buy This Record (2) Get Laid, Get Funked (2) Just Get On Down And Murder In The 1st Degree (3) That's It -- Outro (2)
Cellular Phone #1 (3) Give 'Em An Example How A Rock (1) Nice & Nasty (2) Twenty Degrees Below Zero
Cellular Phone #2 (3) D.J. Works (3) Night After The Rapper (2) (4)

DJ QUIK

Rapper from Compton, California. Twenty years old in 1991.

| 3/2/91 | 29 | 42 | ● | 1 Quik Is The Name .... | $12 | Profile 1402 |
| 8/8/92 | 10 | 14 | ● | 2 Way 2 Fonky .... | $12 | Profile 1430 |

America'z Most Complete 8 Ball (1) Me Wanna Rip Your Girl (2) Quik's Groove (1) Bombudd, Tha (1)
Artist (2) I Got That Feelin' (1) Mo' Pussy (2) Quik'z Groove II (For U 2 Rip **Tonite** (1) *49*
Born And Raised In **Jus Lyke Compton** (2) *62* Niggaz Still Trippin' (2) 2) (2) Way 2 Fonky (2)
Compton (1) Last Word (2) No Bullshit (2) Skanless (1) When You're A Gee (2)
Dedication (1) Let Me Rip Tonite (2) Only Fo' Tha Money (2) Sweet Black Pussy (1)
Deep (1) Loked Out Hood (1) Quik Is The Name (1) Tear It Off (1)

D-MOB

British dance outfit headed by producer Danny D. Lead vocalist Cathy Dennis went solo in late 1990.

| 1/27/90 | 82 | 20 | | A Little Bit Of This, A Little Bit Of That .... | $12 | FFRR 828159 |

All I Do It Is Time To Get Funky Put Your Hands Together That's The Way Of The Trance Dance
C'mon And Get My Love [includes 2 versions] Rhythm From Within **World** *59* We Call It Acieed
[includes 2 versions] 10 It Really Don't Matter

D-NICE

Born Derrick Jones in June 1970. East Coast rapper with Boogie Down Productions.

| 8/11/90 | 75 | 13 | | 1 Call Me D-Nice .... | $12 | Jive 1202 |
| 12/14/91 | 137 | 5 | | 2 To Tha Rescue .... | $12 | Jive 41466 |

And There U Have It (2) Crumbs On The Table (1) Glory (1) No, No, No (2) Time To Flow (1)
And You Don't Stop (1) 808 Is Coming (1) I Send This Out To... (2) Pimp Of The Year (1) To Tha Rescue (2)
Call Me D-Nice (1) Few Dollars More (1) It's All About It (2) Rhymin' Skills (2) 25 Ta Life (2)
Check Yourself (2) Get In Touch With Me (2) It's Over (1) Straight From Tha Bronx (2) Under Some Budda' (1)

DEBUT DATE	PEAK POS	WKS CHR	GOLD	ARTIST — Album Title	$	Label & Number

D.O.A.
Punk-rock quartet from Vancouver, Canada formed in 1987: Joe Keithley (vocals), Brian Goble, Jon Card and Chris Prohom.

| 6/9/90 | 184 | 5 | | Murder. | $12 | Restless 72376 |

Afrikana Security · Banana Land · Concrete Beach · Midnight Special · Suicidal · Warrior Lives Again
Agony And The Ecstasy · Boomtown · Guns, Booze & Sex · No Productivity · Waiting For You - Part 2 · We Know What You Want

D.O.C., The
Pronounced: dock. Twenty-one-year-old Dallas rapper Tray Curry.

| 8/19/89 | 20 | 34 | ● | No One Can Do It Better | $8 | Ruthless 91275 |

Beautiful But Deadly · D.O.C. & The Doctor · It's Funky Enough · Mind Blowin' · Whirlwind Pyramid
Comm. Blues · Formula, The · Lend Me An Ear · No One Can Do It Better
Comm. 2 · Grand Finale · Let The Bass Go · Portrait Of A Master Piece

DOCTOR AND THE MEDICS
Glam-rock sextet from London: The Doctor (vocals), The Anadin Brothers (Wendi and Collette), Richard Searle, Steve Maguire and Vom.

| 9/13/86 | 125 | 8 | | Laughing At The Pieces | $8 | I.R.S. 5797 |

Burn · Kettle On A Long Chain · Miracle Of The Age · No-One Loves You When · Smallness Of The Mustard · **Spirit In The Sky** 69
Come On Call Me · Lucky Lord Jim · Moon Song · You've Got No Shoes · Pot · Watermelon Runaway

DR. BUZZARD'S ORIGINAL "SAVANNAH" BAND
New York City 1930s-styled disco group formed by brothers Stony Browder and August Darnell (real name: Thomas August Darnell Browder), with Cory Daye, lead singer. Darnell left in 1980 to form Kid Creole & The Coconuts.

| 8/21/76+ | 22 | 49 | ● | 1 Dr. Buzzard's Original Savannah Band | $10 | RCA 1504 |
| 2/11/78 | 36 | 9 | | 2 Dr. Buzzard's Original Savannah Band Meets King Penett | $10 | RCA 2402 |

Auf Wiedersehen, Darrio (2) · I'll Always Have A Smile For · March Of The Nignies · Sour And Sweet (medley) (1) · **Whispering/Cherchez La**
Betcha' The Love Bug · You (2) · (medley) (1) · Sunshower (1) · **Femme/Se Si Bon** (1) 27
Bitcha' (medley) (1) · **I'll Play The Fool** (1) 80 · Mister Love (2) · Transistor Madness (medley) · You've Got Something
Future D.J. (medley) (2) · Lemon In The Honey · Nocturnal Interludes (2) · (2) · (medley) (1)
Gigolo And I (2) · (medley) (1) · Organ Grinder's Tale (1) · We Got It Made (1)
Hard Times (1) · · Soraya (medley) (2)

DR. DEMENTO — see VARIOUS - Radio/TV Celebrity Compilations

★★456★★ **DR. HOOK**
Group formed in New Jersey in 1968. Fronted by vocalists/guitarists Ray Sawyer (dubbed "Dr. Hook" because of eye patch; b: 2/1/37) and Dennis Locorriere (b: 6/13/49). Appeared in and performed the music for the film *Who Is Harry Kellerman And Why Is He Saying Those Terrible Things About Me?*.

DR. HOOK AND THE MEDICINE SHOW:

4/29/72	45	23		1 Dr. Hook & The Medicine Show	$15	Columbia 30898
12/2/72+	41	31		2 Sloppy Seconds	$15	Columbia 31622
10/27/73	141	6		3 Belly Up!	$15	Columbia 32270

DR. HOOK:

7/5/75+	141	16		4 Bankrupt	$10	Capitol 11397
5/15/76	62	31		5 A Little Bit More	$10	Capitol 11522
11/18/78+	66	34	●	6 Pleasure & Pain	$10	Capitol 11859
11/24/79+	71	32		7 Sometimes You Win	$10	Capitol 12018
12/6/80	175	8		8 Rising	$10	Casablanca 7251
12/20/80+	142	12		9 Dr. Hook/Greatest Hits	[G]	$8	Capitol 12122
4/3/82	118	7		10 Players In The Dark	$8	Casablanca 7264

Acapulco Goldie (3) · Do Downs (4) · I Can't Say No To Her (10) · Life Ain't Easy (3) 68 · Queen Of The Silver Dollar · Walk Right In (9) 46
Baby Makes Her Blue · Do You Right Tonight (8) · I Can't Touch The Sun (4) · Little Bit More (5,9) 11 · (2) · What About You (5)
Jeans Talk (10) 25 · Doin' It (8) · I Don't Feel Much Like · Love Monster (7) · Radio, The (5) · What Do You Want? (7)
Bad Eye Bill (5) · Dooley Jones (8) · Smilin' (7) · **Loveline** (10) 60 · **Roland The Roadie And** · When Lilly Was Queen (4)
Ballad Of... (3) · Everybody Loves Me (4) · I Don't Want To Be Alone · Makin' It Natural (1) · **Gertrude The Groupie** · When She Cries (1)
Before The Tears (8) · Everybody's Makin' It Big · Tonight (6) · Mama, I'll Sing One Song · (3) 83 · **When You're In Love With**
Better Love Next Time · But Me (4) · I Gave Her Comfort (6) · For You (1) · S.O.S. For Love (8) · **A Beautiful Woman** (6,9) 6
(7,9) 12 · Fire In The Night (10) · I Got Stoned And I Missed It · Marie Lavaux (1) · **Sexy Eyes** (7,9) 5 · Wonderful Soup Stone (3)
Blown Away (8) · Four Years Older Than Me · (4) · Millionaire, The (4) 95 · **Sharing The Night** · Wups (4)
Body Talking (8) · (1) · If I'd Only Come And Gone · Monterey Jack (3) · **Together** (6,9) 6 · **Years From Now** (7,9) 51
Bubblin' Up (4) · Freakin' At The Freaker's · (2) · More Like The Movies (5) · Sing Me A Rainbow (1) · You Ain't Got The Right (3)
Carry Me, Carrie (2) 71 · Ball (2) · If Not You (5) 55 · Mountain Mary (7) · Stayin' Song (2) · You Make My Pants Want
Chained To Your Memory · Get My Rocks Off (2) · In Over My Head (7) · 99 And Me (8) · Storms Never Last (6) · To Get Up And Dance (6)
(10) · **Girls Can Get It** (8) 34 · Judy (1) · Oh! Jesse (7) · Sweetest Of All (6) ·
Clyde (6) · Hearts Like Yours And Mine · Jungle To The Zoo (5) · On The Way To The Bottom · **Sylvia's Mother** (1,9) 5 ·
Come On In (3) · (10) · Kiss It Away (1) · (4) · **That Didn't Hurt Too Bad** ·
Cooky And Lila (4) · Help Me Mama (7) · Knowing She's There (6) · **Only Sixteen** (4,5,9) 6 · (8) 69 ·
Couple More Years (6) · Hey, Lady Godiva (1) · Lady Sundown (1) · Penicillin Penny (3) · Things I Didn't Say (2) ·
Cover Of "Rolling Stone" · Hold Me Like You Never Had · Last Mornin' (2) · Pity The Fool (10) · Turn On (10) ·
(2,9) 6 · Me (4) · Let Me Be Your Lover (4) · Put A Little Bit On Me (3) · Turn On The World (2) ·
Devil's Daughter (10) · I Call That True Love (1) · Levitate (4) · · Up On The Mountain (5) ·

DR. JOHN
Born Malcolm "Mac" Rebennack on 11/21/40 in New Orleans. Pioneer "swamp rock"-styled instrumentalist. With Leonard James & The Nighttrainers and Paul Gayten in 1955. Session work in the mid-1950s. Recorded with Ronnie Baron as "Drits & Dravy." Moved to Los Angeles in the mid-1960s. Character "Dr. John The Night Tripper" is based on the act originated by Lawrence "Prince Lala" Nelson.

| 10/9/71 | 184 | 5 | | 1 Dr. John, The Night Tripper (The Sun, Moon & Herbs) | $15 | Atco 362 |

with Eric Clapton and Mick Jagger

5/13/72	112	11		2 Dr. John's Gumbo	$10	Atco 7006
3/24/73	24	33		3 In The Right Place	$10	Atco 7018
6/16/73	105	12		4 Triumvirate	$10	Columbia 32172

MIKE BLOOMFIELD/JOHN PAUL HAMMOND/DR. JOHN

| 5/4/74 | 105 | 8 | | 5 Desitively Bonnaroo | $10 | Atco 7043 |

DEBUT DATE	PEAK POS	WKS CHR	G O L D	ARTIST — Album Title	$	Label & Number

DR. JOHN — Cont'd

| 5/27/89 | 142 | 11 | 6 | In A Sentimental Mood | $8 | Warner 25889 |

classic jazz-blues hits

Accentuate The Positive (6) · Baby Let Me Kiss You (4) · Big Chief (2) · Black John The Conqueror (1) · Black Night (6) · Blow Wind Blow (2) · Can't Git Enuff (5) · Candy (6) · Cha-Dooky-Doo (4) · Cold Cold Cold (3) · Craney Crow (1) · Desitively Bonnaroo (5) · Don't Let The Sun Catch You Cryin' (6) · **(Everybody Wanna Get Rich) Rite Away** (5) *92* · Familiar Reality (1) · Go Tell The People (5) · Ground Hog Blues (4) · Huey Smith Medley (2) · I Been Hoodood (3) · I Yi Yi (4) · **Iko Iko** (2) *71* · In A Sentimental Mood (6) · It Hurts Me Too (4) · Junko Partner (2) · Just The Same (3) · Just To Be With You (4) · Last Night (4) · Let The Good Times Roll (2) · Let's Make A Better World (5) · Life (3) · Little Liza Jane (2) · Love For Sale (6) · Makin' Whoopee! (6) · Me - You = Loneliness (5) · Mess Around (2) · More Than You Know (6) · Mos' Scocious (5) · My Buddy (6) · Peace Brother Peace (3) · Pots On Flyo (File Gumbo) (medley) (1) · Pretty Thing (4) · Qualified (3) · Quitters Never Win (5) · R U 4 Real (5) · **Right Place Wrong Time** (3) *9* · Rock Me Baby (4) · Same Old Same Old (3) · Sho Bout To Drive Me Wild (4) · Shoo Fly Marches On (3) · Sing Along Song (5) · Somebody Changed The Lock (2) · Stack-A-Lee (3) · Stealin' (5) · Such A Night (3) *42* · Those Lonely Lonely Nights (2) · Tipitina (2) · Traveling Mood (3) · What Comes Around (Goes Around) (5) · Where Ya At Mule (1) · Who I Got To Fall On (If The Pot Get Heavy) (medley) (1) · Zu Zu Mamou (1)

DOCTOR J.R. KOOL & The Other Roxannes

| 7/20/85 | 113 | 13 | | The Complete Story of Roxanne...The Album | $8 | Compleat 671014 |

8 different "Roxanne" songs with rap/vocals by male and female singers

Queen Of Rox (Shante Rox On) · Rap Your Own Roxanne · Real Roxanne · Roxanne, Roxanne · Roxanne's A Man (The Untold Story - Final Chapter) · Roxanne's Doctor - The Real Man · Roxanne's Revenge · Sparky's Turn (Roxanne You're Through)

DOE, John

Born John Nommensen in Decatur, Illinois. Founded the punk band X with then-wife Exene Cervenka. Appeared in the films *Great Balls Of Fire*, *Salvador*, *Slamdance* and others. Took name from the Frank Capra film *Meet John Doe*.

| 6/23/90 | 193 | 3 | | Meet John Doe | $12 | DGC 24291 |

By The Light · Dyin' To Get Home · It's Only Love · Knockin' Around · Let's Be Mad · Matter Of Degrees · My Offering · Real One · Take #52 · Touch Me, Baby · With Someone Like You · Worldwide Brotherhood

DOG, Tim

Bronx rapper — Tim Blair.

| 11/30/91 | 155 | 2 | | Penicillin On Wax | $12 | Ruffhouse 48707 |

Bronx Nigga · Can't Fuck Around · DJ Quick Beat Down · Dog's Gonna Getcha · Fuck Compton · Get Off The Dick · Goin Wild In The Penile · I Ain't Havin It · I Ain't Takin No Shorts · I'll Wax Anybody · Low Down Nigga · Michelle Conversation · NFL Shit · Patriotic Pimp · Phone Conversation W/Reporter · Robin Harris Shit · Secret Fantasies · Step To Me · You Ain't Shit

DOKKEN

Los Angeles-based, hard-rock band: Don Dokken (lead vocals), George Lynch (guitar), Jeff Pilson (bass) and Mick Brown (drums). Disbanded in 1988. Don Dokken assembled new self-named band in 1990 with John Norum (guitar), Billy White (guitar), Peter Baltes (bass) and Mikkey Dee (drums). Lynch and Brown formed Lynch Mob in 1990.

10/15/83	136	13		1 Breaking The Chains	$8	Elektra 60290
10/13/84+	49	74 ▲		2 Tooth And Nail	$8	Elektra 60376
12/21/85+	32	67 ▲		3 Under Lock And Key	$8	Elektra 60458
12/5/87	13	33 ▲		4 Back For The Attack	$8	Elektra 60735
12/3/88	33	17 ●		5 Beast From The East [L]	$10	Elektra 60823 [2]

recorded live in Japan in April 1988

| 9/15/90 | 50 | 11 | | 6 Up From The Ashes | $12 | Geffen 24301 |

DON DOKKEN

Alone Again (2,5) *64* · Breaking The Chains (1,5) · Bullets To Spare (2) · **Burning Like A Flame** (4) *72* · Crash 'N Burn (6) · Cry Of The Gypsy (4) · Don't Close Your Eyes (2) · Don't Lie To Me (3) · Down In Flames (6) · Dream Warriors (4,5) · Felony (1) · Forever (6) · Give It Up (6) · Heartless Heart (2) · Heaven Sent (4,5) · Hunger, The (6) · Hunter, The (3) · I Can't See You (1) · **In My Dreams** (3,5) *77* · In The Middle (1) · Into The Fire (2,5) · It's Not Love (3,5) · Jaded Heart (3) · Just Got Lucky (2,5) · Kiss Of Death (4,5) · Lightnin' Strikes Again (3) · Live To Rock (Rock To Live) (1) · Living A Lie (6) · Lost Behind The Wall (4) · Mirror Mirror (6) · Mr. Scary (4,5) · Night By Night (4) · Nightrider (1) · 1000 Miles Away (6) · Paris Is Burning (1) · Prisoner (4) · Seven Thunders (1) · Sleepless Nights (4,5) · Slippin' Away (3) · So Many Tears (4) · Standing In The Shadows (4,5) · Stay (6) · Stick To Your Guns (1) · Stop Fighting Love (4) · Til The Livin' End (3) · Tooth And Nail (2,5) · Turn On The Action (2,5) · Unchain The Night (3,5) · Walk Away (5) · When Heaven Comes Down (2,5) · When Love Finds A Fool (6) · When Some Nights (6) · Will The Sun Rise (3) · Without Warning (2) · Young Girls (1)

DOLBY, Thomas

Born Thomas Morgan Dolby Robertson of British parentage on 10/14/58 in Cairo, Egypt. Master of computer-generated rock music and self-directed videos. Keyboardist of Bruce Woolley & The Camera Club, and the Lene Lovich band (1979-80). Film *Howard The Duck* featured Dolby's music under moniker Dolby's Cube. Married to actress Kathleen Beller (Kirby Colby of TV's *Dynasty*).

2/5/83	20	31		1 Blinded By Science [M]	$8	Harvest 15007
3/19/83	13	28		2 The Golden Age Of Wireless	$8	Capitol 12271
3/17/84	35	18		3 The Flat Earth	$8	Capitol 12309
5/7/88	70	19		4 Aliens Ate My Buick	$8	EMI-Man. 48075

Ability To Swing (4) · Airhead (4) · Airwaves (1,2) · Budapest By Blimp (4) · Cloudburst At Shingle Street (2) · Commercial Breakup (2) · Dissidents (3) · **Europa And The Pirate Twins** (2) *67* · Flat Earth (3) · Flying North (1,2) · Hot Sauce (4) · **Hyperactive** (3) *62* · I Scare Myself (3) · Key To Her Ferrari (4) · Mulu The Rain Forest (3) · My Brain Is Like A Sieve (4) · One Of Our Submarines (1,2) · Pulp Culture (4) · Radio Silence (2) · Screen Kiss (3) · **She Blinded Me With Science** (1,2) *5* · Weightless (2) · White City (3) · Windpower (1,2)

DOLCE, Joe

Born in 1947 of Italian-American parents in Painesville, Ohio.

| 6/27/81 | 181 | 4 | | Shaddap You Face | $8 | MCA 5211 |

featuring Lyn Van Hecke (vocals)

Ain't Been Missing You · Ain't No U.F.O. Gonna Catch My Diesel · Boat People · How Can Our Love Be Gone · If You Want To Be Happy · Return (Parts 1 & 2) · **Shaddap You Face** *53* · Stick It Out · Walking The Dog

DEBUT DATE	PEAK POS	WKS CHR	GOLD	ARTIST — Album Title	$	Label & Number

DOMINGO, Placido
Born on 1/21/41 in Madrid. One of the world's leading operatic tenors. Emigrated to Mexico in 1950. Debuted at the New York Metropolitan Opera in 1968.

DEBUT DATE	PEAK POS	WKS CHR	GOLD	ARTIST — Album Title	$	Label & Number
11/7/81+	18	27	▲	1 Perhaps Love	$8	CBS 37243
				with John Denver on the title cut		
3/13/82	164	6		2 Domingo-Con Amore	$8	RCA 4265
4/9/83	117	11		3 My Life For A Song	$8	CBS 37799
10/6/90+	35	90	▲	4 CARRERAS DOMINGO PAVAROTTI in concert [L]	$12	London 430433
				CARRERAS DOMINGO PAVAROTTI concert on 7/7/90 of opera tenors: Jose Carreras, Placido Domingo, Luciano Pavarotti with orchestra conducted by Zubin Mehta at the Baths of Caracalla in Rome		
3/2/91	171	6		5 Be My Love...An Album Of Love	$12	EMI/Gini 95468

Aida (Celeste Aida) (2); Amapola (medley) (4); American Hymn (1); Annie's Song (1); Autumn Leaves (3); Be My Love (5); Because You're Mine (5); Besame Mucho (3); Blue Moon (medley) (3); Caminito (medley) (4); Carmen (Flower Song) (2); Cavalleria Rusticana (Brindisi) (4); Cielito Lindo (medley) (4); El Condor Pasa (5); En Aranjuez Con Tu Amor (5); Follow Me (3); Have I The Courage To Say I Love You (Il Coraggio Di Dire Ti Amo) (2); He Couldn't Love You More (1); I Couldn't Live Without You For A Day (3); I Don't Talk To Strangers (3); Il Trovatore (Di Quella Pira) (2); Jealousy Tango (5); L'Elisir D'Amore (Una Furtiva Lagrima) (2); La Boheme (Che Gelida Manina) (2); La Golondrina (5); La Vie En Rose (4,5); Lehar: Das Land Des Lachelns - Dein Ist Mein Ganzes Herz (4); Love Be My Guiding Star (5); Love Story (5); Mamma (5); Man In The Crowd (Un Uomo Tra La Folla) (2); Mattinata (medley) (4); Memory (medley) (4); Meyerbeer: L'Africaine - O Paradis! (4); Moon River (medley) (3); My Life For A Song (3); My Treasure (1); Now While I Still Remember How (1); 'O Paese D' 'O Sole (medley) (4); O Sole Mio (4,5); Ochi Tchornlye (medley) (4); Pagliacci (Vesti La Giubba) (2); **Perhaps Love** (1) 59; Puccini: Tosca - E Lucevan Le Stelle (4); Puccini: Turandot - Nessun Dorma (4); Quireme Mucho (5); Remembering (3); Rigoletto (La Donna E Mobile) (2); Rigoletto (Questa O Quella) (2); Sometimes A Day Goes By (1); Somewhere, My Love (5); Somewhere Over The Rainbow (5); Songs Of Summer (3); Sorozabel: La Tabernera Del Puerto - No Puede Ser (4); Spanish Eyes (5); There Will Be Love (3); Time After Time (1); To Love (1); Tonight (medley) (4); Tosca (E Lucevan Le Stelle) (2); Valencia (5); Wien, Wien, Nur Du Allein (medley) (4); Yesterday (1)

DOMINO, Fats
Born Antoine Domino on 2/26/28 in New Orleans. Classic New Orleans R&B piano-playing vocalist; heavily influenced by Fats Waller and Albert Ammons. Joined the Dave Bartholomew Band, mid-1940s. Signed to Imperial record label in 1949. His first recording "The Fat Man" reportedly was a million seller. Heard on many sessions cut by other R&B artists, including Lloyd Price and Joe Turner. In films *Shake, Rattle And Roll*, *Jamboree*, *The Big Beat* and *The Girl Can't Help It*. Teamed with co-writer Dave Bartholomew on majority of his hits. Lives in New Orleans with wife Rosemary and eight children. Frequently appears in Las Vegas. Inducted into the Rock and Roll Hall of Fame in 1986. Winner of Grammy's Hall of Fame (1987) and Lifetime Achievement (1987) Awards.

DEBUT DATE	PEAK POS	WKS CHR	GOLD	ARTIST — Album Title	$	Label & Number
11/10/56+	18	6		1 Fats Domino - Rock And Rollin'	$90	Imperial 9009
2/23/57	19	2		2 This Is Fats Domino!	$90	Imperial 9028
3/23/57	17	4		3 Rock And Rollin' With Fats Domino	$90	Imperial 9004
				Fats' first album		
7/21/62	113	6		4 Million Sellers By Fats [G]	$40	Imperial 9195
				greatest hits from 1960-62		
10/5/63	130	4		5 Here Comes...Fats Domino	$20	ABC-Para. 455
10/19/68	189	2		6 Fats Is Back	$30	Reprise 6304

Ain't Gonna Do It (4); **Ain't That A Shame** (3) 10; All By Myself (3); Are You Going My Way (1); **Blue Monday** (2) 5; **Blueberry Hill** (2) 2; **Bo Weevil** (3) 35; Bye Baby, Bye Bye (5); Can't Go On Without You (5); Careless Love (1); Don't Blame It On Me (3); Fat Man (3); Fat Man's Hop (2); Fat's Frenzy (1); Forever, Forever (5); Goin' Home (3); Going To The River (3); Goodbye (1); Honest Papas Love Their Mamas Better (2); Honey Chile (2); I Got A Right To Cry (5); I Know (3); I Love Her (1); **I'm In Love Again** (1) 3; I'm Livin' Right (5); I'm Ready (5); **If You Need Me** (1) 98; **Jambalaya (On The Bayou)** (4) 30; Just A Lonely Man (5); La La (2); **Lady Madonna** (6) 100; Land Of 1,000 Dances (5); **Let The Four Winds Blow** (4) 15; Lovely Rita (6); Make Me Belong To You (6); **My Blue Heaven** (3) 19; **My Girl Josephine** (4) 14; My Heart Is Bleeding (4); My Heart Is In Your Hands (1); My Old Friend (6); **My Real Name** (4) 59; **Natural Born Lover** (4) 38; One For The Highway (6); One More Song For You (6); Please Don't Leave Me (3); Poor Me (3); Poor Poor Me (2); **Red Sails In The Sunset** (5) 35; Reeling And Rocking (2); Rose Mary (3); Second Line Jump (1); **Shu Rah** (2) 32; **So-Long** (2) 44; So Swell When You're Well (6); Song For Rosemary (5); Swanee River Hop (1); Tell Me The Truth, Baby (5); **There Goes (My Heart Again)** (5) 59; **Three Nights A Week** (4) 15; Tired Of Crying (3); Troubles Of My Own (2); Trust In Me (2); Wait Till It Happens To You (6); **Walking To New Orleans** (4) 6; **What A Price** (4) 22; **What's The Reason I'm Not Pleasing You** (2) 50; When I'm Walking (Let Me Walk) (5); **When My Dreamboat Comes Home** (1) 14; You Done Me Wrong (2); You Said You Love Me (3); **You Win Again** (4) 22

DONALDSON, Bo, & The Heywoods
Cincinnati septet led by keyboardist Bo Donaldson (b: 6/13/54) and lead vocalist Michael Gibbons.

DEBUT DATE	PEAK POS	WKS CHR	GOLD	ARTIST — Album Title	$	Label & Number
7/6/74	97	16		Bo Donaldson & The Heywoods	$8	ABC 824

Billy, Don't Be A Hero 1; Deeper And Deeper; Don't Ever Look Back; Fool's Way Of Lovin'; Girl Don't Make Me Wait; Goodbye, Goodbye; Goodnight And Good Morning; Hang Your Lamp In The Window; Keep On Believin' In Love; Last Blues Song; **Who Do You Think You Are** 15

DONALDSON, Lou
Born on 11/1/26 in Badin, North Carolina. Jazz alto saxophonist. Leader of small combos in the East.

DEBUT DATE	PEAK POS	WKS CHR	GOLD	ARTIST — Album Title	$	Label & Number
6/15/63	141	2		1 The Natural Soul [I]	$25	Blue Note 84108
10/7/67	141	11		2 Alligator Bogaloo [I]	$20	Blue Note 84263
10/26/68	182	6		3 Midnight Creeper [I]	$20	Blue Note 84280
				above 2 feature George Benson (guitar) and Lonnie Smith (organ)		
4/5/69	153	7		4 Say It Loud! [I]	$20	Blue Note 84299
10/4/69	158	6		5 Hot Dog [I]	$20	Blue Note 84318
7/11/70	190	2		6 Everything I Play Is Funky [I]	$15	Blue Note 84337
9/22/73	176	4		7 Sassy Soul Strut [I]	$15	Blue Note 109
9/28/74	185	3		8 Sweet Lou [I]	$15	Blue Note 259

Alligator Bogaloo (2) 93; Aw Shucks! (2); Bag Of Jewels (3); Bonnie (5); Brother Soul (4); Caravan (3); City, Country, City (7); Dapper Dan (3); Donkey Walk (6); Elizabeth (5); Everything I Do Gonh Be Funky (From Now On) (6); Funky Mama (1); Good Morning Heartache (7); Hamp's Hump (6); Herman's Mambo (8); Hip Trip (8); Hot Dog (5); I Want A Little Girl (4); If You Can't Handle It, Give It To Me (8); Inner Space (7); It's Your Thing (5); Lost Love (8); Love Eyes (8); Love Power (3); Love Walked In (1); Midnight Creeper (3); Minor Bash (6); Nice 'N Greasy (1); One Cylinder (2); Over The Rainbow (6); Peepin' (8); Pillow Talk (7); Rev. Moses (2); Sanford And Son Theme (7); Sassy Soul Strut (7); Say It Loud (4); Snake Bone (4); Sow Belly Blues (1); Spaceman Twist (1); Summertime (4); Thang, The (2); That's All (1); This Is Happiness (7); Turtle Walk (5); West Indian Daddy (6); Who's Making Love (5); You're Welcome, Stop On By (8)

DEBUT DATE	PEAK POS	WKS CHR	GOLD	ARTIST — Album Title	$	Label & Number

DON AND THE GOODTIMES
Pacific Northwest rock quintet led by Li'l Don Gallucci (keyboardist with The Kingsmen).

| 8/5/67 | 109 | 4 | | So Good .... | $20 | Epic 26311 |

And It's So Good   Good Day Sunshine   I Could Never Be   Music Box   Sweet, Sweet, Mama
Gimme Some Lovin'   **I Could Be So Good To**   If You Love Her, Cherish Her   My Color Song   With A Girl Like You
     You 56   And Such

★★137★★ DONOVAN
Born Donovan Phillip Leitch on 2/10/46 near Glasgow, Scotland. Singer/songwriter/guitarist. To London at age 10. Worked Newport Folk Festival in 1965. Wrote score for film *If It's Tuesday This Must Be Belgium*. In films *The Pied Piper Of Hamlin* (1972) and *Brother Sun, Sister Moon* (1973). In retirement from 1974-81. Father of actress Ione Skye (*Say Anything*) and actor Donovan Leitch, Jr.

7/17/65	30	23		1 Catch The Wind	$30	Hickory 123
12/18/65+	85	13		2 Fairytale	$30	Hickory 127
9/24/66	11	29		3 Sunshine Superman	$20	Epic 26217
10/1/66	96	7		4 The Real Donovan .... [K]	$30	Hickory 135
2/18/67	14	21		5 Mellow Yellow	$20	Epic 26239
12/30/67+	60	15		6 Wear Your Love Like Heaven	$20	Epic 26349
1/6/68	19	22	●	7 A Gift From A Flower To A Garden	$20	Epic 171 [2]
				deluxe box set of the albums *Wear Your Love Like Heaven* and *For Little Ones*		
1/13/68	185	3		8 For Little Ones	$20	Epic 26350
4/6/68	177	4		9 Like It Is, Was And Evermore Shall Be .... [K]	$30	Hickory 143
7/27/68	18	31		10 Donovan In Concert ....[L]	$20	Epic 26386
10/19/68	20	20		11 The Hurdy Gurdy Man	$20	Epic 26420
2/22/69	4	56 ▲		12 **Donovan's Greatest Hits** .... [G]	$20	Epic 26439
9/13/69	23	24		13 Barabajagal	$20	Epic 26481
				with The Jeff Beck Group on 2 cuts		
11/8/69	135	7		14 The Best Of Donovan .... [K]	$30	Hickory 149
7/18/70	16	19		15 Open Road	$15	Epic 30125
11/14/70	128	8		16 Donovan P. Leitch .... [K]	$15	Janus 3022 [2]
				compilation of Hickory recordings		
3/31/73	25	20		17 Cosmic Wheels	$12	Epic 32156
2/2/74	174	5		18 Essence To Essence	$12	Epic 32800
12/14/74+	135	6		19 7-Tease	$12	Epic 33245
6/5/76	174	3		20 Slow Down World	$12	Epic 33945

Alamo, The (1,4,16)
Appearances (17)
As I Recall It (11)
Atlantis (13) **7**
Ballad Of Geraldine (2,14)
Ballad Of The Crystal Man (2,4,16)
Belated Forgiveness Plea (2,4,16)
Bert's Blues (3)
Black Widow (20)
Bleak City Woman (5)
Boy For Every Girl (18)
Candy Man (2,14,16)
Car Car (Riding In My Car) (1)
Catch The Wind (1,4,9,12,14,16) **23**
Celeste (3,10)
Celtic Rock (15)
Changes (15)
Children Of The World (20)
Circus Of Sour (2)
Clara Clairvoyant (15)
Colours (2,4,9,12,14,16) **61**
Cosmic Wheels (17)
Cryin' Shame (20)
Curry Land (15)
Cuttin' Out (1)
Dark-Eyed Blue Jean Angel (20)
Dignity Of Man (18)

Divine Daze Of Deathless Delight (18)
Do You Hear Me Now (9)
Donna Donna (1,14)
Earth Sign Man (17)
Enchanted Gypsy (7,8)
Entertaining Of A Shy Girl (11)
Epistle To Dippy (12) **19**
Epistle To Derroll (7,8)
Fat Angel (3,10)
Ferris Wheel (3)
Get Thy Bearings (11)
Goldwatch Blues (1)
Goo Goo Barabajagal (Love Is Hot) (13) **36**
Great Song Of The Sky (19)
Guinevere (3,10)
Hampstead Incident (5)
Happiness Runs (13)
Hey Gyp (4,9,14,16)
Hi It's Been A Long Time (11)
House Of Jansch (5)
How Silly (19)
Hurdy Gurdy Man (11,12) **5**
I Like You (17) **66**
I Love My Shirt (13)
Intergalactic Laxative (17)
Isle Of Islay (7,8,10)
Jennifer Juniper (11,12) **26**
Jersey Thursday (2,14,16)
Joe Bean's Theme (15)
Josie (1,4,9,16)

Keep On Truckin' (1,16)
Lalena (12) **33**
Land Of Doesn't Have To Be (6,7)
Lay Of The Last Tinker (7,8)
Lazy Daze (18)
Legend Of A Girl Child Linda (3)
Liberation Rag (20)
Life Goes On (18)
Life Is A Merry-Go-Round (18)
Little Boy In Corduroy (6,7)
Little Tin Soldier (2,14,16)
Love Of My Life (19)
Love Song (13)
Lullaby Of Spring (7,8,10)
Mad John's Escape (6,7)
Magpie (7,8)
Mandolin Man And His Secret (7,8)
Maria Magenta (17)
Mellow Yellow (5,10,12) **2**
Moon Rok (19)
Mountain, The (20)
Museum (5)
Music Makers (17)
My Love Is True (Love Song) (20)
New Year's Resovolution (15)
Observation, The (5)
Oh Deed I Do (4)
Oh Gosh (6,7)

Only The Blues (17)
Operating Manual For Spaceship Earth (18)
Ordinary Family (19)
Pamela Jo (13)
Pebble And The Man (10)
People Used To (15)
Peregrine (17)
Poke At The Pope (15)
Poor Cow (10)
Preachin' Love (10)
Quest, The (19)
Ramblin' Boy (1,4,16)
Ride-A-Mile (19)
Riki Tiki Tavi (15) **55**
River Song (11)
Rock And Roll Souljer (19)
Roots Of Oak (15)
Rules And Regulations (10)
Sadness (15)
Sailing Homeward (18)
Salt Valentines Angel (18)
Salvation Stomp (19)
Sand And Foam (5)
Season Of Farewell (15)
Season Of The Witch (3,12)
Skip-A-Long Sam (6,7)
Sleep (17)
Slow Down World (20)
Someone's Singing (6,7)
Song For John (15)
Song Of The Naturalist's Wife (7,8)

Starfish-On-The-Toast (7,8)
Summer Day Reflection Song (2,9,16)
Sun (6,7)
Sun Is A Very Magic Fellow (11)
Sunshine Superman (3,12) **1**
Sunny Day (11)
Sunny Goodge Street (2,9,16)
Sunny South Kensington (5)
Superlungs My Supergirl (13)
Tangerine Puppet (1,14)
Tangier (11)
Teas (11)
There Is A Mountain (10,12) **11**
There Is An Ocean (18)
There Was A Time (6,7)
Three King Fishers (3)
Tinker And The Crab (7,8)
To Sing For You (1,16)
To Susan On The West Coast Waiting (13) **35**
To Try For The Sun (2,4,9,16)
Trip, The (3)
Trudi (13)
Turquoise (4,16)
Under The Greenwood Tree (6,7)
Universal Soldier (2,9,14,16) **53**

Voice Of Protest (19)
Voyage Into The Golden Screen (7,8)
War Drags On (4,9,16)
Wear Your Love Like Heaven (6,7,12) **23**
Well Known Has-Been (20)
West Indian Lady (11)
Where Is She (13)
Why Do You Treat Me Like You Do (9,16)
Widow With Shawl (A Portrait) (7,8,10)
Wild Witch Lady (17)
Writer In The Sun (5,10)
Yellow Star (18)
You're Gonna Need Somebody On Your Bond (1)
Young Girl Blues (5,10)
Your Broken Heart (19)

★★112★★ DOOBIE BROTHERS, The
Rock/R&B-styled group formed in San Jose, California in 1970: Pat Simmons (vocals, guitar), Tom Johnston (lead vocals, guitar, keyboards), John Hartman (percussion) and Dave Shogren (bass). First recorded for Warner in 1971. Shogren replaced by Tiran Porter (bass). Mike Hossack (percussion) added in 1972 (later replaced by Keith Knudsen). Jeff "Skunk" Baxter (slide guitar), formerly with Steely Dan, added in 1974. Michael McDonald (lead vocals, keyboards), added in 1975. Johnston left, 1978. Baxter, Hartman replaced by Cornelius Bumpus (keyboards, saxophone), John McFee (guitar) and Chet McCracken (drums) in 1979. Tom Johnston wrote majority of hits from 1972-75; Michael McDonald from 1976-83. Disbanded in 1983. Re-formed in early 1988 with Johnston, Simmons, Hartman, Porter, Hossack, and Bobby LaKind (percussion).

8/26/72	21	119 ▲		1 Toulouse Street	$12	Warner 2634
3/31/73	7	102 ▲²		2 **The Captain And Me**	$12	Warner 2694
3/16/74+	4	62 ▲		3 **What Were Once Vices Are Now Habits**	$10	Warner 2750
5/17/75	4	25 ●		4 **Stampede**	$10	Warner 2835
4/3/76	8	44 ▲		5 **Takin' It To The Streets**	$10	Warner 2899
11/20/76+	5	93 ▲⁶		6 **Best Of The Doobies** .... [G]	$10	Warner 2978
9/10/77	10	21 ●		7 **Livin' On The Fault Line**	$10	Warner 3045

DEBUT DATE	PEAK POS	WKS CHR	G O L D	ARTIST — Album Title	$	Label & Number
				DOOBIE BROTHERS, The — Cont'd		
12/23/78+	1[5]	87	▲[3]	8 **Minute By Minute**	$10	Warner 3193
10/11/80	3	28	▲	9 **One Step Closer**	$8	Warner 3452
11/21/81	39	15	●	10 **Best Of The Doobies, Volume II** ....[G]	$8	Warner 3612
7/23/83	79	9		11 The Doobie Brothers Farewell Tour ....[L]	$10	Warner 23772 [2]
6/10/89	17	20	●	12 **Cycles**	$8	Capitol 90371
5/11/91	82	9		13 Brotherhood	$12	Capitol 94623

Another Park, Another Sunday (3) *32*
Black Water (3,6,11) *1*
Busted Down Around O Connelly Corners (2)
Can't Let It Get Away (11)
Captain And Me (2)
Carry Me Away (5)
China Grove (2,6,11) *15*
Chinatown (7)
Clear As The Driven Snow (2)
Cotton Mouth (1)
Dangerous (1)
Dark Eyed Cajun Woman (2)
Daughters Of The Sea (3)
Dedicate This Heart (9)
Depend'n On You (8,10) *25*
Disciple (1)
Divided Highway (13)
Doctor, The (12) *9*
Don't Start Me To Talkin' (1,11)
Don't Stop To Watch The Wheels (8)

Double Dealin' Four Flusher (4)
Down In The Track (3)
Echoes Of Love (7,10,11) *66*
8th Avenue Shuffle (5)
Evil Woman (3)
Excited (13)
Eyes Of Silver (3) *52*
Flying Cloud (3)
For Someone Special (5)
Here To Love You (8,10) *65*
How Do The Fools Survive? (8)
I Been Workin' On You (4)
I Can Read Your Mind (12)
I Cheat The Hangman (4) *60*
Is Love Enough (3)
It Keeps You Runnin' (5,6) *37*
Jesus Is Just Alright (1,6,11) *35*
Just In Time (9)

Keep This Train A-Rollin' (9) *62*
Larry The Logger Two-Step (7)
Listen To The Music (1,6,11) *11*
Little Darling (I Need You) (7,10) *48*
Livin' On The Fault Line (4)
Long Train Runnin' (2,6,11) *8*
Losin' End (5)
Mamaloi (2)
Minute By Minute (8,10,11) *14*
Music Man (4)
Natural Thing (2)
Neal's Fandango (4)
Need A Lady (7)
Need A Little Taste Of Love (12) *45*
No Stoppin' Us Now (9)
Nothin' But A Heartache (7)
Olana (11)

One By One (9,10)
One Chain (Don't Make No Prison) (12)
One Step Closer (9,10) *24*
Open Your Eyes (8)
Our Love (13)
Precis (4)
Pursuit On 53rd Street (3)
Rainy Day Crossroad Blues (4)
Real Love (9,10) *5*
Rio (5)
Road Angel (3)
Rockin' Down The Highway (1,6)
Rollin' On (13)
Showdown (13)
Slat Key Soquel Rag (4,11)
Slippery St. Paul (11)
Snake Man (1)
Something You Said (13)
Song To See You Through (3)
South Bay Strut (9)

South City Midnight Lady (2,6,11)
South Of The Border (12)
Spirit (3)
Steamer Lane Breakdown (8,11)
Sweet Maxine (4) *40*
Take Me In Your Arms (Rock Me) (4,6) *11*
Take Me To The Highway (12)
Takin' It To The Streets (5,6,11) *13*
Tell Me What You Want (And I'll Give You What You Need) (3)
Texas Lullaby (4)
Thank You Love (9)
There's A Light (7)
This Train I'm On (13)
Time Is Here And Gone (12)
Tonight I'm Coming Through (The Border) (12)

Too High A Price (12)
Toulouse Street (1)
Turn It Loose (5)
Ukiah (2)
Under The Spell (13)
What A Fool Believes (8,10,11) *1*
Wheels Of Fortune (5) *87*
White Sun (1)
Without You (2,6)
Wrong Number (12)
You Belong To Me (7,10,11) *79*
You Just Can't Stop It (3)
You Never Change (8)
You're Made That Way (7)

★★62★★ **DOORS, The**

Rock group formed in Los Angeles in 1965. Consisted of Jim Morrison (b: 12/8/43, Melbourne, Florida; d: 7/3/71, Paris; lead singer), Ray Manzarek (keyboards), Robby Krieger (guitar) and John Densmore (drums). Controversial onstage performances by Morrison caused several arrests and cancellations. Morrison left group on 12/12/70. In film *A Feast Of Friends*. Group disbanded in 1973. 1991 film based on their career, *The Doors*, starred Val Kilmer as Morrison. Group inducted into the Rock and Roll Hall of Fame in 1993.

DEBUT DATE	PEAK POS	WKS CHR	GOLD	ARTIST — Album Title	$	Label & Number
3/25/67	2[2]	121	▲[2]	1 **The Doors**	$20	Elektra 74007
11/4/67	3	63	●	2 **Strange Days**	$20	Elektra 74014
8/10/68	1[4]	41	▲	3 **Waiting For The Sun**	$15	Elektra 74024
8/9/69	6	28	▲	4 **The Soft Parade**	$15	Elektra 75005
3/7/70	4	27	●	5 **Morrison Hotel/Hard Rock Cafe**	$12	Elektra 75007
8/8/70	8	20	●	6 **Absolutely Live** ....[L]	$15	Elektra 9002 [2]
12/19/70+	25	21	▲	7 13 ....[G]	$15	Elektra 74079
5/8/71	9	34	▲[2]	8 **L.A. Woman**	$25	Elektra 75011
11/6/71	31	15		9 Other Voices *	$12	Elektra 75017
2/12/72	55	11	●	10 Weird Scenes Inside The Gold Mine ....[K]	$15	Elektra 6001 [2]
8/5/72	68	15		11 Full Circle *	$12	Elektra 75038
				*trio of Manzarek, Krieger and Densmore		
9/29/73	158	8	▲	12 The Best Of The Doors ....[G]	$15	Elektra 5035
12/16/78+	54	13		13 An American Prayer - Jim Morrison	$8	Elektra 502
				Morrison recites his poems, supported musically by the Doors		
11/1/80	17	99	▲[2]	14 The Doors Greatest Hits ....[G]	$8	Elektra 515
				cassette hit the charts on 3/30/91 (re-released only on cassette)		
11/5/83	23	20	●	15 Alive, She Cried ....[E-L]	$8	Elektra 60269
				recorded 1968-1970		
6/8/85	124	7		16 Classics ....[K]	$8	Elektra 60417
				featuring tracks from 7 Doors' albums		
7/11/87	154	11		17 Live At The Hollywood Bowl ....[M-L]	$8	Elektra 60741
				features 6 previously unreleased performances; recorded at the Hollywood Bowl, Los Angeles on 7/5/68		
8/8/87+	32	43		18 The Best Of The Doors ....[G]	$10	Elektra 60345 [2]
				features 18 digitally-remastered Doors' classics; re-entered the chart on 3/16/91 as CD with bonus track and new peak		
3/23/91	8	20	●	19 **The Doors** ....[S]	$12	Elektra 61047
				includes "Heroin" by Velvet Underground & Nico and an introduction by the Atlanta Symphony Orchestra; CD includes bonus track		
6/8/91	50	13		20 In Concert ....[K-L]	$17	Elektra 61082 [2]
				comprised of live recordings previously released on *Absolutely Live, Alive She Cried* and *Live At The Hollywood Bowl*		

Alabama Song (Whiskey Bar) (1,6,18,20)
American Night (13)
American Prayer (13)
Angels And Sailors (medley) (13)
Awake (13)
Back Door Man (1,6,7,20)
Been Down So Long (8)
Black Polished Chrome (medley) (13)
Blue Sunday (5,10)

Break On Through (To The Other Side) (1,10,14,18,19)
Break On Through, #2 (6,20)
Build Me A Woman (6,20)
Cars Hiss By My Window (8)
Celebration Of The Lizard (6)
Changeling, The (8)
Close To You (6,20)
Crawling King Snake (8)
Crystal Ship (1,7,18,18)
Curses, Invocations (13)
Dawn's Highway (medley) (13)

Dead Cats, Dead Rats (20)
Do It (4)
Down On The Farm (9)
Easy Ride (4)
End, The (1,10,18,19,20)
End Of The Night (1,10)
Five To One (3,6,10,16,18,20)
4 Billion Souls (11)
Get Up And Dance (11)
Ghost Song (13,19)
Gloria (15,20) *71*
Good Rockin' (11)

Hang On To Your Life (9)
Hardwood Floor (11)
Hello, I Love You (3,7,12,14,18) *1*
Hill Dwellers (17,20)
Hitchhiker, The (13)
Horse Latitudes (2,10)
Hyacinth House (8)
I Can't See Your Face In My Mind (2,16)
I Looked At You (1)
I'm Horny, I'm Stoned (9)
In The Eye Of The Sun (9)

Indian Summer (5)
It Slipped My Mind (11)
L'America (8)
Lament (13)
Land Ho! (5,7,16)
Latino Chrome (medley) (13)
Light My Fire (1,7,12,14,15,17,18, 19,20) *1*
Lions In The Street (20)
Little Game (17,20)
Little Red Rooster (15,20)

Love Her Madly (8,10,12,16,18) *11*
Love Hides (6,20)
Love Me Two Times (2,7,12,14,15,18,20) *25*
Love Street (3,10,19)
Maggie M'Gill (5,10)
Moonlight Drive (2,7,12,15,20)
Mosquito, The (11) *85*
Movie, The (13,19)
My Eyes Have Seen You (2,16)

DEBUT DATE	PEAK POS	WKS CHR	GOLD	ARTIST — Album Title	$	Label & Number

DOORS, The — Cont'd

My Wild Love (3)	Petition The Lord With	Soft Parade (4)	To Come Of Age (13)	Wandering Musician (9)	**You Make Me Real**
Names Of The Kingdom (20)	Prayer (20)	Soul Kitchen (1,6,12,20)	**Touch Me** (4,7,12,14,18) 3	Wasp (Texas Radio & The	(5,15,20) **50**
New Born Awakening	Piano Bird (11)	Spanish Caravan	Twentieth Century Fox (1)	Big Beat) (8,10,16)	(You Need Meat) Don't Go
(medley) (13)	**Queen Of The Highway** (5)	(3,10,17,18)	Unhappy Girl (2)	We Could Be So Good	No Further (10)
Not To Touch The Earth	**Riders On The Storm**	Spy, The (5,10)	Universal Mind (6,20)	Together (3)	You're Lost Little Girl (2,7)
(3,14,20)	(8,10,12,14,18,19) **14**	Stoned Immaculate (13,19)	**Unknown Soldier**	When The Music's Over	
Palace Of Exile (20)	**Roadhouse Blues**	Strange Days (2,10,16,18)	(3,7,16,17,18,20) **39**	(2,6,10,18,19,20)	
Peace Frog (5,10,16)	(5,7,13,14,16,18,19,20) *flip*	Summer's Almost Gone (3)	Variety Is The Spice Of Life	Who Do You Love (6,12,20)	
Peking King And The New	**Runnin' Blue** (4,10) **64**	Take It As It Comes (1,10,12)	(9)	Who Scared You (10)	
York Queen (11)	Severed Garden (19)	**Tell All The People** (4) **57**	Verdilac (11)	Wild Child (4,7,16)	
People Are Strange	Shaman's Blues (4,10)	Texas Radio & The Big Beat	Waiting For The Sun	Wintertime Love (3)	
(2,7,12,14,18) **12**	Ship Of Fools (5,10)	(15,20)	(5,16,18)	**Wishful Sinful** (4) **44**	
	Ships W/Sails (9)	**Tightrope Ride** (9) **71**	Wake Up (17,20)	Yes, The River Knows (3)	

DORATI, Antal

Hungarian-born composer/conductor. Principal conductor of BBC Symphony from 1962-66 and of Stockholm Philharmonic from 1966-74; music director of Washington National Symphony from 1970-77; principal conductor of Britain's Royal Philharmonic from 1975-78; music director of Detroit Symphony from 1977-81.

3/16/59	**3**	54	●	1 Tchaikovsky: 1812 Festival Overture/Capriccio Italien ....[I]	$30	Mercury 50054

with the Minneapolis Symphony Orchestra

2/27/61	**20**	16		2 Beethoven: Wellington's Victory/Leonore Overture No. 3/		
				Prometheus Overture ....[I]	$25	Mercury 9000

with the London Symphony Orchestra

Beethoven: Capriccio Italien,	Beethoven: Prometheus	Beethoven: Wellington's	Tchaikovsky: 1812 - Festival	Tchaikovsky: Leonore
Op. 45 (1)	Overture, Opus 43 (2)	Victory (or, "The Battle Of	Overture, Op. 49 (1)	Overture No. 3, Opus 72A
		Victoria") (2)		(2)

DORE, Charlie

British female vocalist.

4/26/80	**145**	7		Where To Now..	$8	Island 9559

Falling	Hula Valley	**Pilot Of The Airwaves 13**	Sleepless	Where To Now
Fear Of Flying	Pickin' Apples	Sad Old World	Sweetheart	Wise Owl

DORO

Doro Pesch, female leader of the German heavy-metal group Warlock. Assembled Warlock with German lineup in 1982. Recruited new American lineup in 1989 and recorded only as Doro.

4/29/89	**154**	11		Force Majeure	$8	Mercury 838016

Angels With Dirty Faces	Cry Wolf	Hellraiser	Mission Of Mercy	Save My Soul	Whiter Shade Of Pale
Beyond The Trees	Hard Times	I Am What I Am	River Of Tears	Under The Gun	World Gone Wild
Bis Aufs Blut					

DORSEY, Jimmy

Esteemed alto sax and clarinet soloist/bandleader. Born on 2/29/04 in Shenandoah, Pennsylvania. Died of cancer on 6/12/57. Recorded with his brother Tommy in the Dorsey Brothers Orchestra, 1928-35 and 1953-56. Also see Tommy Dorsey.

10/7/57	**19**	4		The Fabulous Jimmy Dorsey	$20	Fraternity 1008

8 of 12 cuts were recorded after Jimmy's death

Amapola	**Jay-Dee's Boogie**	Just Swingin'	No One Ever Lost More	Speak Low
Contrasts	**Woogie 77**	Maria Elena	**So Rare 2**	
It's The Dreamer In Me	**June Night 21**	Mombo En Sax	Sophisticated Swing	

DORSEY, Lee

Born Irving Lee Dorsey on 12/24/24 in New Orleans. Moved to Portland, Oregon at age 10. Prizefighter in early '50s as "Kid Chocolate." Major hits produced by Allen Toussaint and Marshall Sehorn. Lee died of emphysema in New Orleans on 12/1/86.

11/12/66	**129**	5		The New Lee Dorsey	$25	Amy 8011

Can You Hear Me	Don't You Ever (Leave Me)	Greatest Love	Mellow Good Time	**Ride Your Pony 28**
Confusion	**Get Out Of My Life,**	**Holy Cow 23**	Mexico	**Working In The Coal**
	Woman 44	Little Dab A Do Ya	Neighbor's Daughter	**Mine 8**

DORSEY, Tommy, Orchestra

Esteemed trombonist and bandleader. Born on 11/19/05 in Mahanoy Plane, Pennsylvania; choked to death on 11/26/56. Tommy and brother Jimmy recorded together as the Dorsey Brothers Orchestra from 1928-35 and 1953-56. Hosted musical variety TV show from 1954-56. Warren Covington fronted band after Tommy's death.

5/19/58	**15**	6		1 The Fabulous Dorseys In Hi-Fi.................................[I]	$20	Columbia 1190

TOMMY DORSEY and his orchestra featuring JIMMY DORSEY

5/25/59	**38**	2		2 Tea For Two Cha Chas.......................................[I]	$20	Decca 8842

band led by Warren Covington

Cha Cha For Gia (2)	I Dream Of You (1)	It Started All Over Again (1)	Por Favor (Please..) (2)	This Love Of Mine (1)	We've Crossed The Widest
Corazon De Melon (2)	I Still Get Jealous - Cha Cha	Judgement Is Coming (1)	Rain (1)	Together 1-2-3 (2)	River (1)
Dardanella - Cha Cha (2)	(2)	Nevada (1)	Rico Vacilon (2)	Trumpet Cha-Cha-Cha (2)	Yesterdays (1)
Dinah - Cha Cha (2)	**I Want To Be Happy Cha**	Patricia (2)	**Tea For Two Cha Cha** (2) 7	Wagon Wheels (1)	
How Far Is It To Jordan (1)	**Cha** (2) **70**	Peace Pipe (1)	This Is What Gabriel Says (1)		

DOUBLE

Swiss pop duo (pronounced: doo-BLAY) of Kurt Maloo and Felix Haug. Both were in jazz trio Ping Pong.

7/26/86	**30**	21		Blue	$8	A&M 5133

Captain Of Her Heart 16	Love Is A Plane	Tomorrow	Woman Of The World
I Know A Place	Rangoon Moon	Urban Nomads	Your Prayer Takes Me Off

DOUBLE EXPOSURE

Soul quartet from Philadelphia, featuring lead singer James Williams.

8/21/76	**129**	11		Ten Percent	$10	Salsoul 5503

Baby I Need Your Loving	Gonna Give My Love Away	My Love Is Free	**Ten Percent 54**
Everyman	Just Can't Say Hello	Pick Me	

DOUCETTE

Jerry Doucette — Canadian rock singer/guitarist.

3/25/78	**159**	8		Mama Let Him Play	$10	Mushroom 5009

DEBUT DATE	PEAK POS	WKS CHR	GOLD	ARTIST — Album Title	$	Label & Number

DOUCETTE — Cont'd

All I Wanna Do   Down The Road   Keep On Running   **Mama Let Him Play 72**   What's Your Excuse?
Back Off   It's Gonna Hurt So Bad   Love Is Gonna Find You   People Say   When She Loves Me

DOUG E. FRESH & THE GET FRESH CREW
Rap trio formed in 1985 by Doug E. Fresh with Barry Bee and Chill Will.

| 6/18/88 | 88 | 13 | | The World's Greatest Entertainer | $8 | Reality 9658 |

Africa (Goin' Back Home)   Cut That Zero   Ev'rybody Got 2 Get Some   Greatest Entertainer   I'm Gettin' Ready   On The Strength
Crazy 'Bout Cars   D.E.F. = Doug E. Fresh   Ev'rybody Loves A Star   Guess? Who?   Keep Risin' To The Top   Plane (So High)

DOUGLAS, Carl
Born in Jamaica, West Indies and raised in California. Studied engineering in the U.S. and in England.

| 12/14/74+ | 37 | 17 | | Kung Fu Fighting And Other Great Love Songs | $12 | 20th Century 464 |

Blue Eyed Soul   **Dance The Kung Fu 48**   I Want To Give You My   **Kung Fu Fighting 1**   Never Had This Dream   When You Got Love
Changing Times   I Don't Care What People Say   Everything   Before   Witchfinder General

DOUGLAS, Carol
Born on 4/7/48 in Brooklyn. Worked on commercials. Member of The Chantels vocal group in the early '70s.

3/29/75	177	3		1 The Carol Douglas Album	$10	Midland Int. 0931
11/6/76	188	6		2 Midnight Love Affair	$10	Midland Int. 1798
7/16/77	139	10		3 Full Bloom	$10	Midland Int. 2222

All Night Long (1)   Dancing Queen (3)   Hurricane Is Coming   In The Morning (2)   We Do It (3)
Baby Don't Let This Good   **Doctor's Orders (1) 11**   Tonite (1) 81   Lie To Me (2)   We're Gonna Make It (3)
Love Die (1)   Friend In Need (1)   I Fell In Love With Love (1)   Life Time Guarantee (2)   Who, What, When, Where,
Boy, You Know Just What   Full Bloom Suite #2 (3)   I Got You On My Mind (3)   Light My Fire (3)   Why (3)
I'm After (1)   Full Bloom Suite #1 & #2 (3)   I Want To Stay With You (3)   Midnight Love Affair (2)   Will We Make It Tonight (1)
Carol's Theme I & II (2)   Headline News (2)   I'll Take A Chance On Love   Take Me (Make Me Lose
Crime Don't Pay (2)   (3)   Control) (1)

DOUGLAS, Mike
Born Michael Dowd, Jr. in Chicago on 8/11/25. Longtime syndicated TV talkshow host (1961-80). Singer with Kay Kyser's band, 1945-50 (vocalist on Kyser's #1 hit "Ole Buttermilk Sky" in 1946).

| 1/29/66 | 46 | 15 | | The Men In My Little Girl's Life | $15 | Epic 26186 |

"A" - You're Adorable (The   House Of Love   Is There A Baby In The   Let Her Be A Little Girl (A   Sunrise, Sunset
Alphabet Song)   I'd Give A Million Tomorrows   House   Little Longer)   While We're Young
House I Live In (That's   (For Just One Yesterday)   Kids!   **Men In My Little Girl's**
America To Me)   **Life 6**

DOVE, Ronnie
Born on 9/7/40 in Herndon, Virginia. Discovered while singing in Baltimore. Nearly all of Ronnie's hits were produced by Phil Kahl (vice president of Diamond Records).

7/24/65	119	41		1 One Kiss For Old Times' Sake	$25	Diamond 5003
4/2/66	35	21		2 The Best Of Ronnie Dove	[G] $20	Diamond 5005
10/22/66	122	5		3 Ronnie Dove Sings The Hits For You	$20	Diamond 5006
3/4/67	121	12		4 Cry	$20	Diamond 5007

All (1)   I Had To Lose You (To Find   If I Live To Be A Hundred   Little White Cloud That   **Right Or Wrong (2) 14**   Wheel Of Fortune (4)
All Of Me (1)   That I Need You) (1)   (1,2)   Cried (4)   **Say You (2) 40**   **When Liking Turns To**
Almost In Paradise (3)   **I Really Don't Want To**   It's Almost Tomorrow (1)   Long After (3)   She Only Makes Me Love   **Loving (2) 18**
Autumn Rhapsody (4)   **Know (3) 22**   It's The Talk Of The Town (4)   **Mountain Of Love (3) 67**   You More (1)   Where In The World (1,2)
Cry (4) 18   I Won't Cry Anymore (4)   Keep It A Secret (2)   Nevertheless (I'm In Love   Someday (You'll Want Me To   Years Of Tears (4)
Happy Summer Days (3) 27   **I'll Make All Your Dreams**   **Kiss Away (2) 25**   With You) (1,2)   Want You) (3)
Hello Pretty Girl (2) 54   **Come True (2) 21**   Let's Start All Over Again   On A Slow Boat To China (3)   Tell The Lady I Said
I Can't Stop Loving You (4)   I'm The One Who Taught   (3) 20   **One Kiss For Old Times'**   Good-bye (4)
I Found You (Just In Time)   You How (3)   **Little Bit Of Heaven**   **Sake (1,2) 14**   That Empty Feeling (3)
(3)   If I Cried Everytime You   (1,2) 16   **One More Mountain To**   Walkin' My Baby Back
   Hurt Me (1)   **Climb (4) 45**   Home (4)

DOVELLS, The
Vocal group formed at Overbrook High School in Philadelphia. Originally called the Brooktones. Consisted of Leonard Borisoff ("Len Barry"), Arnie Silver, Jerry Gross ("Jerry Summers"), Mike Freda ("Mike Dennis") and Jim Meeley ("Danny Brooks"). Brooks left in 1962. Barry left in late 1963 and recorded solo. Group continued as a trio. Recorded as The Magistrates for MGM in 1968.

| 7/13/63 | 119 | 7 | | You Can't Sit Down | $40 | Parkway 7025 |

Baby Workout   Hey, Beautiful   Lockin' Up My Heart   Miss Daisy De Lite   Summer Job   Wildwood Days
Havin' A Good Time   If You Wanna Be Happy   Maybelline   Short Fat Fannie   36-22-36   **You Can't Sit Down 3**

DOZIER, Lamont
Born on 6/16/41 in Detroit. R&B singer/songwriter/producer. Recorded as Lamont Anthony for Anna in 1961. With the brothers Brian and Eddie Holland in highly successful songwriting/production team for Motown. Trio left Motown in 1968 and formed own Invictus/Hot Wax label. Inducted into the Rock and Roll Hall of Fame in 1990.

| 1/26/74 | 136 | 13 | | 1 Out Here On My Own | $10 | ABC 804 |
| 1/25/75 | 186 | 2 | | 2 Black Bach | $10 | ABC 839 |

All Cried Out (2)   I Wanna Be With You (2)   Put Out My Fire (2)   Thank You For The Dream   We Don't Want Nobody To
Blue Sky And Silver Bird (2)   Let Me Make Love To You (1)   Rose (2)   (2)   Come Between Us (1)
Breaking Out All Over (1)   **Let Me Start Tonite (2) 87**   Shine (2)   **Trying To Hold On To My**
Fish Ain't Bitin' (1) 26   Out Here On My Own (1)   Take Off Your Make-Up (1)   **Woman (1) 15**

DRAGON, Carmen
Carmen conducted the Capitol Symphony Orchestra. Died on 3/28/84 (age 69). Father of Daryl Dragon (of Captain & Tennille). Also see Leonard Pennario.

| 4/14/62 | 36 | 8 | | Nightfall | [I] $20 | Capitol 8575 |

classical melodies

Bizet: Adagietto (From   Grieg: Ases Tod (From "Peer   Herbert: Toyland (From   Rachmaninoff: Vocalise, Op.   Tchaikovsky: Andante
"L'Arlesienne Suite")   Gynt Suite")   "Babes In Toyland")   34, No. 14   Cantabile (From String
Brahms: Lullaby, Op. 49,   Grofe: Old Creole Days   Jarnefelt: Berceuse   Ravel: Pavane For A Dead   Quartet No. 1, Op. 11)
No. 4   (From "Mississippi Suite")   Princess

DEBUT DATE	PEAK POS	WKS CHR	GOLD	ARTIST — Album Title	$	Label & Number

DRAKE, Pete, And His Talking Steel Guitar

Pete was born on 10/8/32 in Atlanta; died on 7/29/88. Was Nashville's top steel guitar sessionman.

5/2/64	**85**	14		Forever	$15	Smash 67053

Danny Boy
For Those That Cry
Forever 25
I'm Just A Guitar
(Everybody Picks On Me)
Making Believe
Melody Of Love
My Bluest Day
Paradise
Red Sails In The Sunset
Sleep Walk
Spook, The
Still

★★434★★ DRAMATICS, The

Soul group from Detroit. First recorded for Wingate as the Dynamics, 1966. Members in 1971: Ron Banks (lead singer), William Howard, Larry Demps, Willie Ford and Elbert Wilkins. Howard and Wilkins replaced by L.J. Reynolds and Lenny Mayes in 1973. Reynolds, formerly of Chocolate Syrup, began solo career in 1981. Banks recorded solo in 1983. Drummer Carl Smalls was a member of Undisputed Truth and Sweat Band.

1/22/72	**20**	24		1	Whatcha See Is Whatcha Get	$12	Volt 6018
10/13/73	**86**	18		2	A Dramatic Experience	$12	Volt 6019
5/4/74	**156**	6		3	The Dells vs. The Dramatics	$12	Cadet 60027
3/22/75	**31**	18		4	The Dramatic Jackpot	$10	ABC 867
11/15/75	**93**	12		5	Drama V	$10	ABC 916
10/30/76+	**103**	25		6	Joy Ride	$10	ABC 955
8/13/77	**60**	19		7	Shake It Well	$10	ABC 1010
5/13/78	**44**	15	●	8	Do What You Wanna Do	$8	ABC 1072
3/8/80	**61**	12		9	10 1/2	$8	MCA 3196

After This Dance (6)
Be My Girl (6) *53*
Be With The One You Love (9)
Beautiful People (2)
Beware Of The Man (With The Candy In His Hand) (2)
California Sunshine (8)
Choosing Up On You (3)
Come Inside (7)
Come Out Of Your Thing (5)
Devil Is Dope (2)
Disco Dance Contest (8)
Do What You Want To Do (8)
Don't Make Me No Promises (3)
Door To Your Heart (3) *62*
Dramatic Theme (medley) (5)
Fall In Love, Lady Love (1)
Fell For You (2) *45*
Finger Fever (6)
Get Up And Get Down (1) *78*
Gimme Some (Good Soul Music) (1)
Good Things Don't Come Easy (4)
Hey You! Get Off My Mountain (1) *43*
Hot Pants In The Summertime (1)
How Do You Feel (4)
I Can't Get Over You (6)
I Cried All The Way Home (4)
I Dig Your Music (4)
I Get Carried Away (6)
I Just Wanna Dance The Night Away (9)
(I Like) Makin' You So Happy (7)
I Want You (8)
I Was The Life Of The Party (5)
I'll Make It So Good (5)
(I'm Going By) The Stars In Your Eyes (4) *81*
I'm Gonna Love You To The Max (5)
If You Feel Like You Wanna Dance, Dance (9)
In The Rain (1) *5*
It Ain't Rainin' (On Nobody's House But Mine) (9)
Jane (8)
Jim, What's Wrong With Him? (2)
Just Shopping (Not Buying Anything) (5)
Love Is Here (9)
Mary Don't Cha Wanna (1)
Me And Mrs. Jones (4) *47*
Me Myself And I (4)
Music Is Forever (7)
Music Is The Peoples Choice (9)
My Ship Won't Sail Without You (7)
Never Let You Go (4)
Now You Got Me Loving You (2)
Ocean Of Thoughts And Dreams (7)
Richest Man Alive (9)
Runnin' From My Love (9)
Say The Word (6)
Shake It Well (7) *76*
She's A Rainmaker (5)
Sing And Dance Your Troubles Away (6)
Spaced Out On You (7)
Stand Up And Move (6)
Stop Your Weeping (8)
Sundown Is Coming (Hold Back The Night) (6)
Thank You For Your Love (1)
That Heaven Kind Of Feeling (7)
Things Are Changing (5)
Thousand Shades Of Blue (4)
Treat Me Like A Man (medley) (5)
Trying To Get Over Losing You (4)
Tune Up (3)
Welcome Back Home (9)
Whatcha See Is Whatcha Get (1) *9*
Why Do You Want To Do Me Wrong (8)
Yo' Love (Can Only Bring Me Happiness) (8)
You Could Become The Very Heart Of Me (2)
You Make The Music (I Just Dance Along) (7)
You're Fooling You (5) *87*

DREAD ZEPPELIN

White reggae band from Pasadena, California covering Led Zeppelin rock classics. Fronted by Elvis Presley imitator Greg "Tortelvis" Tortell. Gary Putman, Carl Haasis, Bruce Fernandez, Paul Masselli and Joe Ramsey masqueraded as Ed Zeppelin, Jah Paul Jo, Carl Jah, Put-Mon and Fresh Cheese & Cheese.

8/25/90	**116**	13		Un-led-Ed	$12	I.R.S. 82048

Black Dog
Black Mountain Side
Bring It On Home
Heartbreaker (At The End Of Lonely Street)
I Can't Quit You Baby
Immigrant Song
Living Loving Maid
Moby Dick
Whole Lotta Love
Your Time Is Gonna Come

DREAM ACADEMY, The

English pop-rock trio: Nick Laird-Clowes (guitar, vocals), Gilbert Gabriel (keyboards) and Kate St. John (vocals).

11/9/85+	**20**	37		1	The Dream Academy	$8	Warner 25265
11/14/87	**181**	3		2	Remembrance Days	$8	Reprise 25625

Ballad In 4/4 (2)
Bound To Be (1)
Doubleminded (2)
Edge Of Forever (1)
Everybody's Gotta Learn Sometime (2)
Hampstead Girl (2)
Here (1)
Humdrum (2)
In Exile (For Rodrigo Rojas) (2)
In Places On The Run (1)
In The Hands Of Love (2)
Indian Summer (2)
(Johnny) New Light (1)
Lesson Of Love (2)
Life In A Northern Town (1) *7*
Love Parade (1) *36*
Moving On (1)
One Dream (1)
Party, The (1)
Power To Believe (2)
This World (1)

DREAMBOY

R&B group formed at Oak Park High School, Michigan, in 1979. Consisted of Jeff Stanton (vocals), Jeff Bass (guitar), Jimi Hunt (keyboards), Paul Stewart, Jr. (bass) and George "Dewey" Twymon (drums).

1/14/84	**168**	11		Dreamboy ....[M]	$8	Qwest 23988

Don't Go
Get Off
I Want To Know Your Name
Let's Go Out
Slow Down
Walk The Streets

DREAMS

Jazz-rock group formed by Mike and Randy Brecker, who later recorded as The Brecker Brothers.

11/28/70	**146**	6		Dreams	$15	Columbia 30225

Devil Lady
Dream Suite Medley
15 Miles To Provo
Holli Be Home
Maryanne, The
New York
Try Me

DREAMS SO REAL

Trio from Athens, Georgia: Barry Marler (vocals), Trent Allen and Drew Worsham.

11/26/88+	**150**	18		Rough Night In Jericho	$8	Arista 8555

Bearing Witness
California
City Of Love
Distance
Heart Of Stone
Love Fall Down
Melanie
Open Your Eyes
Rough Night In Jericho
Victim

DREAM SYNDICATE

Rock quartet — Steve Wynn, lead singer.

8/4/84	**171**	4		Medicine Show	$8	A&M 4990

Armed With An Empty Gun
Bullet With My Name On It
Burn
Daddy's Girl
John Coltrane Stereo Blues
Medicine Show
Merrittville
Still Holding On To You

DREGS — see DIXIE DREGS

DEBUT DATE	PEAK POS	WKS CHR	GOLD	ARTIST — Album Title	$	Label & Number

D.R.I.
D.R.I.: Dirty Rotten Imbeciles. Texas metal/punk band: Kurt Brecht (vocals), Spike Cassidy, Felix Griffin and Josh Pappe (replaced in 1989 by bassist John Menor).

DEBUT DATE	PEAK POS	WKS CHR	GOLD	ARTIST — Album Title	$	Label & Number
7/23/88	116	14		1 Four Of A Kind	$8	Metal Blade 77304
12/23/89+	140	13		2 Thrash Zone	$8	Metal Blade 73407

Abduction (2) Do The Dream (1) Gone Too Long (1) Man Unkind (1) Slum Lord (1) Think For Yourself (1)
All For Nothing (1) Drown You Out (2) Gun Control (2) Manifest Destiny (1) Standing In Line (2) Thrashard (2)
Beneath The Wheel (2) Enemy Within (2) Kill The Words (2) Modern World (1) Strategy (2) Trade, The (2)
Dead In A Ditch (1) Give A Hoot (2) Labeled Uncurable (2) Shut-Up! (1) Suit And Tie Guy (1) Worker Bee (2)

DRIFTERS, The
R&B vocal group formed in 1953 to showcase lead singer Clyde McPhatter, who went solo in 1955. Various lead singers until 1958, when manager George Treadwell disbanded group, brought in The Five Crowns and renamed them The Drifters. Among many personnel changes, lead singers were Ben E. King (1959-60), Rudy Lewis (1961-63; d: summer of 1963) and Johnny Moore (1957, 1964-66). Inducted into the Rock and Roll Hall of Fame in 1988.

DEBUT DATE	PEAK POS	WKS CHR	GOLD	ARTIST — Album Title	$	Label & Number
6/8/63	110	9		1 Up On The Roof - The Best Of The Drifters [G]	$40	Atlantic 8073
8/15/64	40	22		2 Under The Boardwalk	$50	Atlantic 8099
2/6/65	103	6		3 The Good Life With The Drifters	$30	Atlantic 8103
3/16/68	122	8		4 The Drifters' Golden Hits [G]	$25	Atlantic 8153

greatest hits from 1959-64

Another Night With The Boys (1) I'll Take You Home (2) 25 Mexican Divorce (1) **Saturday Night At The Movies** (3,4) 18 There Goes My Baby (1,4) 2 **When My Little Girl Is Smiling** (1) 28
As Long As She Needs Me (1) I've Got Sand In My Shoes (4) 33 More (1) **This Magic Moment** (1,4) 16 Who Can I Turn To (3)
Dance With Me (4) 15 (If You Cry) True Love, True Love (1,4) 33 On Broadway (2,4) 9 **Save The Last Dance For Me** (1,4) 1 Tonight (3)
Desafinado (3) On The Street Where You Live (3) **Some Kind Of Wonderful** (4) 32 **Under The Boardwalk** (2,4) 4
Didn't It (2) If You Don't Come Back (2) One Way Love (2) 56 Stranger On The Shore (1) 73 **Up On The Roof** (1,2,4) 5
Good Life All Over (2) In The Land Of Make Believe (2) Quando Quando Quando (3) Vaya Con Dios (2) 43
I Count The Tears (4) 17 Let The Music Play (2) Rat Race (2) 71 Sweets For My Sweet (1) 16 What Kind Of Fool Am I (3)
I Feel Good All Over (2) Room Full Of Tears (1) 72 Temptation (1) What To Do (1)
I Wish You Love (3) Loneliness Or Happiness (1) Ruby Baby (1)

DRISCOLL, Julie — see AUGER, Brian

DRIVIN' N' CRYIN'
Atlanta-based pop trio: Kevn Kinney (vocals), Tim Nielsen and Jeff Sullivan.

DEBUT DATE	PEAK POS	WKS CHR	GOLD	ARTIST — Album Title	$	Label & Number
4/2/88	130	12		1 Whisper Tames The Lion	$8	Island 90699
1/26/91	90	38		2 Fly Me Courageous	$12	Island 848000

Around The Block Again (2) Catch The Wind (1) For You (2) Let's Go Dancing (2) On A Clear Daze (1) Whisper Tames The Lion (1)
Blue Ridge Way (1) Chain Reaction (2) Friend Song (1) Livin' By The Book (1) Powerhouse (1)
Build A Fire (2) Check Your Tears At The Door (1) Good Day Every Day (1) Look What You've Done To Your Brother (2) Ridin' On The Soul Road (1)
Can't Promise You The World (1) Fly Me Courageous (2) Innocent, The (2) Lost In The Shuffle (2) Rush Hour (2)
Legal Gun (1) Together (2)

"D" TRAIN
R&B duo from Brooklyn: James "D Train" Williams (vocals) and Hubert Eaves III (keyboards).

DEBUT DATE	PEAK POS	WKS CHR	GOLD	ARTIST — Album Title	$	Label & Number
6/26/82	128	9		1 "D" Train	$8	Prelude 14105

"D" Train (Theme) Love Vibrations Tryin' To Get Over You're The One For Me
Keep On Lucky Day Walk On By

DUCHIN, Eddy — see SOUNDTRACKS

DUDEK, Les
Session guitarist/producer. Worked with The Allman Brothers Band and the Steve Miller Band. Formed rock band Black Rose with then-girlfriend Cher.

DEBUT DATE	PEAK POS	WKS CHR	GOLD	ARTIST — Album Title	$	Label & Number
4/23/77	107	12		1 Say No More	$10	Columbia 34397
5/6/78	100	11		2 Ghost Town Parade	$10	Columbia 35088

Avatar (2) Does Anybody Care (2) Ghost Town Parade (2) Lady You're Nasty (1) Tears Turn Into Diamonds (2)
Baby Sweet Baby (1) Down To Nothin' (2) Gonna Move (1) Old Judge Jones (1) What's It Gonna Be (1)
Bound To Be A Change (2) Falling Out (2) I Remember (1) One To Beam Up (1) Zorro Rides Again (1)
Central Park (1) Friend Of Mine (2) Jailabamboozle (1)

★★326★★ **DUKE, George**
Top jazz-rock keyboardist. Born on 1/12/46 in San Rafael, California. Own group in San Francisco during the mid-1950s. With the Don Ellis Big Band and Jean-Luc Ponty. With Mothers Of Invention from 1971-75. Also with Cannonball Adderley from 1972-75. Own group from 1977. With Stanley Clarke in the Clarke/Duke Project.

DEBUT DATE	PEAK POS	WKS CHR	GOLD	ARTIST — Album Title	$	Label & Number
2/1/75	141	6		1 Feel	$10	MPS/BASF 25355
5/31/75	111	10		2 The Aura Will Prevail	$10	MPS/BASF 25613
1/24/76	169	6		3 I Love The Blues, She Heard My Cry	$10	MPS/BASF 25671
10/23/76	99	9		4 "Live"-On Tour In Europe [L]	$8	Atlantic 18194
				THE BILLY COBHAM/GEORGE DUKE BAND		
12/4/76	190	2		5 Liberated Fantasies [I]	$10	MPS/BASF 22835
5/14/77	192	3		6 From Me To You	$10	Epic 34469
10/29/77+	25	24	●	7 Reach For It	$10	Epic 34883
6/3/78	39	14		8 Don't Let Go	$8	Epic 35366
3/17/79	56	11		9 Follow The Rainbow	$8	Epic 35701
11/24/79+	125	11		10 Master Of The Game	$8	Epic 36263
5/31/80	119	9		11 A Brazilian Love Affair	$8	Epic 36483
5/9/81	33	23		12 The Clarke/Duke Project *	$8	Epic 36918
3/6/82	48	12		13 Dream On	$8	Epic 37532
4/30/83	147	7		14 Guardian Of The Light	$8	Epic 38513
11/26/83+	146	10		15 The Clarke/Duke Project II *	$8	Epic 38934
				*STANLEY CLARKE/GEORGE DUKE		
4/20/85	183	5		16 Thief In The Night	$8	Elektra 60398

DEBUT DATE	PEAK POS	WKS CHR	GOLD	ARTIST — Album Title	$	Label & Number

DUKE, George — Cont'd

After The Love (5)
Alien Challenges The Stick (medley) (10)
Alien Succumbs To The Macho Inter-Galactic Funkativity Of The Funkblasters (medley) (10)
Almustafa The Beloved (4)
Alone-6AM (11)
Ao Que Vai Nascer (11)
Atlanta (15)
Aura, The (2)
Back To Where We Never Left (5)
Beginning, The (7)
Born To Love You (14)
Brazilian Love Affair (11)
Brazilian Sugar (11)
Broken Dreams (6)
Carry On (6)
Celebrate (14)
Chariot (3)
Cora Joberge (1)
Corine (9)
Cravo E Cancla (11)
Dawn (2)
Diamonds (7)
Do What Cha Wanna (4)
Dog-Man (10)

Don't Be Shy (5)
Don't Let Go (8)
Down In It (6)
Dream On (13)
Dukey Stick (8)
Echidna's Arf (2)
End, The (7)
Every Little Step I Take (10)
Every Reason To Smile (15)
Everybody's Talkin' (10)
Feel (1)
Festival (9)
Finding My Way (12)
Floop De Loop (2)
Fly Away (14)
Follow The Rainbow (9)
Fools (2)
Foosh (2)
For Love (I Come Your Friend) (2)
Framed (13)
Frankenstein Goes To The Disco (4)
From Me To You (6)
Funkin' For The Thrill (9)
Funny Funk (1)
Future, The (8)
Games (10)

Giant Child Within Us - Ego (3)
Give Me Your Love (14)
Good Times (15)
Great Danes (15)
Heroes (2)
Hip Pockets (4)
Hot Fire (7)
I Am For Real (May The Funk Be With You) (9)
I C'n Hear That (5)
I Just Want To Love You (12)
I Love The Blues, She Heard My Cry (3)
I Love You More (10)
I Need You Now (11)
I Want You For Myself (10)
I Will Always Be Your Friend (13)
In The Distance (10)
Ivory Tattoo (4)
Jam (16)
Juicy (4)
Just For You (7)
La La (16)
Lemme At It (7)
Let Your Love Shine (13)
Let's Get Started (12)

Liberated Fantasies (5)
Light (14)
Look Into Her Eyes (3)
Look What You Find (10)
Louie Louie (12)
Love (1)
Love Mission (16)
Love Reborn (11)
Malibu (8)
Mashavu (3)
Morning Sun (8)
Movin' On (8)
Never Judge A Cover By It's Book (12)
Old Slipper (1)
Omi (Fresh Water) (7)
Once Over (1)
Party Down (9)
Pluck (9)
Positive Energy (13)
Prepare Yourself (3)
Put It On The Line (15)
Rashid (1)
Reach For It (7) *54*
Reach Out (14)
Remembering The Sixties (16)
Ride (16)
Ride On Love (13)

Rokkinrowl, I Don't Know (3)
Say That You Will (9)
'Scuse Me Miss (6)
Searchin' My Mind (7)
Seasons (6)
Seeing You (5)
Shane (14)
Shine On (13) *41*
Silly Fightin' (14)
Sing It (6)
Sister Serene (3)
Someday (3,13)
Son Of Reach For It (The Funky Dream) (13)
Soon (14)
Space Lady (4)
Stand (14)
Starting Again (6)
Statement (1)
Straight From The Heart (9)
Sugar Loaf Mountain (11)
Summer Breezin' (11)
Sunrise (9)
Sweet Baby (12) *10*
Sweet Wine (4)
That's What She Said (3)
Thief In The Night (16)
Touch And Go (12)
Trip You In Love (15)

Try Me Baby (15)
Tryin' & Cryin' (5)
Tzina (1,5)
Uncle Remus (2)
Up From The Sea It Arose And Ate Rio In One Swift Bite (11)
Up On It (6)
War Fugue Interlude (14)
Watch Out Baby! (7)
Way I Feel (8)
We Give Our Love (8)
We're Supposed To Have Fun (16)
What Do They Really Fear? (6)
What The... (5)
Why (16)
Wild Dog (12)
Winners (12)
Yana Aminah (1)
Yeah, We Going (8)
You (13)
You And Me (6)
You (Are The Light) (4)
You're Gonna Love It (15)

DUKE, Patty

Born Anna Marie Duke on 12/14/46 in Elmhurst, New York. Actress. Married actor John Astin. Won an Oscar for her performance in film *The Miracle Worker* (1962). Starred in TV series *The Patty Duke Show* (1963-65), *It Takes Two* (1982-83) and *Hail To The Chief* (1985). Winner of three Emmys.

| 9/18/65 | 90 | 12 | | Don't Just Stand There | $20 | United Art. 3452 |

Danke Schoen
Don't Just Stand There 8
Downtown

End Of The World
Everything But Love
Ribbons And Roses

Save Your Heart For Me
Say Something Funny 22
Too Young

What The World Needs Now Is Love
Why Don't They Understand

World Without Love

DUKE JUPITER

Rock quartet from Rochester, New York — Marshall Styler, lead singer, keyboards.

| 6/2/84 | 122 | 12 | | White Knuckle Ride | $8 | Morocco 6097 |

Backfire
Don't Turn Your Back

(I've Got A) Little Black Book
Little Lady 68

Me And Michelle
Rescue Me

She's So Hot
Top Of The Bay

Woman Like You
Work It Out

DUKES OF DIXIELAND

New Orleans dixieland jazz combo led by Assunto brothers: Fred (trombone; d: 4/21/66) and Frank (trumpet; d: 2/25/74) Assunto.

| 9/9/57+ | 6 | 26 | | 1 **Marching Along With The Dukes Of Dixieland, Vol. 3** ....[I] | $15 | Audio Fidel. 1851 |
| 12/11/61+ | 10 | 21 | | 2 **The Best Of The Dukes Of Dixieland** ....[G-I] | $12 | Audio Fidel. 1956 |

Bill Bailey (2)
Bourbon Street Parade (1,2)
Dixie (2)
Down By The Riverside (2)
Dukes Of Dixieland March (1)
Eyes Of Texas (1,2)

Georgia Camp Meeting (2)
Glory To Old Georgia (1)
Hot Time In The Old Town Tonight (2)
Just A Closer Walk With Thee (1)
Lassus Trombone (1)

McDonough Let The Trombones Blow (1)
Muskrat Ramble (2)
My Home Town (1)
Scobey Strut (1)
South (2)

South Rampart Street Parade (1)
Tromboneum (1)
Wait Till The Sun Shines Nellie (2)
When Johnny Reb Comes Marching Home (1)

When The Saints Go Marching In (2)
With A Pack On My Back (1)
Won't You Come Home Bill Bailey ..see: Bill Bailey

DULFER, Candy

Saxophonist. Born on 9/19/69 in Amsterdam.

| 6/22/91 | 22 | 36 | ● | Saxuality ....[I] | $12 | Arista 8674 |

several tracks feature backing vocals and raps

Donja
Get The Funk
Heavenly City

Home Is Not A House
Jazzid

Lily Was Here [includes 2 versions] *11*

Mr. Lee
Pee Wee

Saxuality
So What

There Goes The Neighbourhood

DUNN, Holly

Country singer/songwriter. Born on 8/22/57 in San Antonio, Texas.

| 8/17/91 | 162 | 1 | | Milestones - Greatest Hits ....[G] | $12 | Warner 26630 |

Are You Ever Gonna Love Me
Daddy's Hands
Face In The Crowd

(It's Always Gonna Be) Someday
Love Someone Like Me

Maybe I Mean Yes
No One Takes The Train Anymore

Only When I Love
Strangers Again
There Goes My Heart Again

You Really Had Me Going

DUPREE, Robbie

Singer/songwriter. Born Robert Dupuis in Brooklyn in 1947.

| 6/14/80 | 51 | 24 | | 1 Robbie Dupree .... | $8 | Elektra 273 |
| 6/13/81 | 169 | 5 | | 2 Street Corner Heroes .... | $8 | Elektra 344 |

All Night Long (2)
Are You Ready For Love? (2)
Brooklyn Girls (2) *54*
Desperation (2)

Free Fallin' (2)
Hot Rod Hearts (1) *15*
I'll Be The Fool Again (2)
I'm No Stranger (1)

It's A Feeling (1)
Lonely Runner (1)
Long Goodbye (2)
Love Is A Mystery (1)

Missin' You (2)
Nobody Else (1)
Saturday Night (2)
Steal Away (1) *6*

Street Corner Heroes (2)
Thin Line (1)
We Both Tried (1)

DUPREES, The

Italian-American vocal quintet from Jersey City: Joseph ("Joey Vann") Canzano (lead singer), Mike Arnone, Tom Bialablow, John Salvato and Joe Santollo. Joey Vann died on 2/28/84 (age 40).

| 12/15/62 | 101 | 5 | | You Belong To Me .... | $90 | Coed 905 |

As Time Goes By
Ginny
I Wish I Could Believe You

Let's Make Love Again
My Dearest One
My Own True Love *13*

September In The Rain
Take Me As I Am

These Foolish Things Remind Me Of You
Things I Love

Why Don't You Believe Me 37
You Belong To Me 7

DEBUT DATE	PEAK POS	WKS CHR	GOLD	ARTIST — Album Title	$	Label & Number

★★259★★ DURAN DURAN

Synth-pop-dance band formed in Birmingham, England in 1980. Consisted of Simon LeBon (b: 10/27/58; vocals), Andy Taylor (b: 2/16/61; guitar), Nick Rhodes (b: 6/8/62; keyboards), John Taylor (b: 6/20/60; bass) and Roger Taylor (b: 4/26/60; drums). None of the Taylors are related. Group named after a villain in the Jane Fonda film *Barbarella*. In 1984, Andy and Roger left group. In 1985, Andy, Nick and Roger recorded with supergroup The Power Station; Simon, Nick and Roger recorded as Arcadia. Duran Duran reduced to a trio in 1986 of Simon, Nick and John. Expanded to a quintet in 1990 with the addition of Warren Cuccurullo (ex-guitarist of Missing Persons) and Sterling Campbell (left by 1993).

DEBUT DATE	PEAK POS	WKS CHR	GOLD	ARTIST — Album Title	$	Label & Number
6/5/82+	6	129	▲²	1 Rio	$8	Harvest 12211
10/2/82	98	15		2 Carnival .... [M]	$8	Harvest 15006
				new mixes of previously released material		
2/19/83	10	87	▲	3 Duran Duran .... [E-R]	$8	Capitol 12158
				their first album, released in 1981		
12/10/83+	8	64	▲²	4 Seven And The Ragged Tiger	$8	Capitol 12310
12/1/84+	4	28	▲²	5 Arena .... [L]	$8	Capitol 12374
12/20/86+	12	34	▲	6 Notorious	$8	Capitol 12540
11/5/88	24	26	●	7 Big Thing	$8	Capitol 90958
				DURANDURAN		
12/9/89+	67	16	●	8 Decade .... [G]	$8	Capitol 93178
9/8/90	46	10		9 Liberty	$13	Capitol 94292

All Along The Water (9)
All She Wants Is (7,8) **22**
American Science (6)
Big Thing (7)
Can You Deal With It (9)
Careless Memories (3,5)
Chauffeur, The (1,5)
Do You Believe In Shame? (7) **72**
Downtown (9)
Drug (It's Just A State Of Mind) (7)
Edge Of America (7)
First Impression (9)

Friends Of Mine (3)
Girls On Film (2,3,8)
Hold Back The Rain (1,2)
Hold Me (6)
Hothead (9)
Hungry Like The Wolf (1,2,5,8) **3**
I Don't Want Your Love (7,8) **4**
I Take The Dice (4)
(I'm Looking For) Cracks In The Pavement (4)
Is There Anyone Out There (3)

Is There Something I Should Know (5,8) **4**
Lake Shore Driving (7)
Land (7)
Last Chance On The Stairway (7)
Liberty (9)
Lonely In Your Nightmare (1)
Matter Of Feeling (6)
Meet El Presidente (6) **70**
My Antarctica (9)
My Own Way (1,2)
New Moon On Monday (4) **10**

New Religion (1,5)
Notorious (6,8) **2**
Of Crime And Passion (4)
Palomino (3)
Planet Earth (3,5,8)
Proposition (9)
Read My Lips (9)
Reflex, The (4,8) **1**
Rio (1,8) **14**
Save A Prayer (1,5,8) **16**
Serious (9)
Seventh Stranger (4,5)
Shadows On Your Side (4)
Skin Trade (6,8) **39**

So Misled (6)
Sound Of Thunder (3)
Tel Aviv (3)
Tiger Tiger (4)
Too Late Marlene (7)
Union Of The Snake (4,5,8) **3**
Venice Drowning (6)
Vertigo (Do The Demolition) (6)
View To A Kill (8) **1**
Violence Of Summer (Love's Taking Over) (9) **64**

(Waiting For The) Night Boat (3)
Wild Boys (5,8) **2**
Winter Marches On (6)

DURANTE, Jimmy

Born on 2/10/1893 in New York City; died on 1/29/80. Much-beloved comedian who started on vaudeville and became star of many Broadway shows and movies as well as his own TV show (1954-56).

DEBUT DATE	PEAK POS	WKS CHR	GOLD	ARTIST — Album Title	$	Label & Number
9/21/63	30	19		September Song	$15	Warner 1506
				serious singing by the great comedian		

Blue Bird Of Happiness
Count Your Blessings Instead Of Sheep

Don't Lose Your Sense Of Humor
I Believe

Look Ahead Little Girl
One Room Home
September Song 51

When The Circus Leaves Town
You'll Never Walk Alone

Young At Heart

DURY, Ian, & The Blockheads

Britain's "poet of punk" was crippled by polio during childhood. The Blockheads featured songwriter/musical director Chaz Jankel who left in mid-1979, replaced by Wilko Johnson.

DEBUT DATE	PEAK POS	WKS CHR	GOLD	ARTIST — Album Title	$	Label & Number
5/6/78	168	5		1 New Boots And Panties!!!	$8	Stiff 0002
7/21/79	126	6		2 Do It Yourself	$12	Stiff 36104
2/7/81	159	4		3 Laughter	$8	Stiff 36998

Billericay Dickie (1)
Blackmail Man (1)
Blockheads (1)
Clevor Trever (1)
Dance Of The Crackpots (3)
Dance Of The Screamers (2)
Delusions Of Grandeur (3)
Don't Ask Me (2)

F---ng Ada (3)
Hey, Hey, Take Me Away (3)
I'm Partial To Your Abracadabra (1)
If I Was With A Woman (1)
Inbetweenies (2)
Lullaby For Francies (2)
Manic Depression (Jimi) (3)

Mischief (2)
My Old Man (1)
Oh Mr. Peanut (3)
Over The Points (3)
Pardon (3)
Plaistow Patricia (1)
Quiet (1)
S-------'s Big Sister (3)

Sex & Drugs & Rock And Roll (1)
Sink My Boats (2)
Sweet Gene Vincent (1)
(Take Your Elbow Out Of The Soup You're Sitting On The Chicken) (3)
This Is What We Find (2)

Uncoolohol (3)
Uneasy Sunny Day Hotsy Totsy (2)
Waiting For Your Taxi (2)
Wake Up And Make Love With Me (1)
What A Waste (1)
Yes & No (Paula) (3)

DYKE AND THE BLAZERS

Band led by Arlester "Dyke" Christian (b: 1943, Brooklyn). With O'Jays' backing band, the Blazers, in the mid-1960s. Dyke was shot to death in 1971.

DEBUT DATE	PEAK POS	WKS CHR	GOLD	ARTIST — Album Title	$	Label & Number
11/4/67	186	4		The Funky Broadway	$30	Original Snd. 8876

Broadway Combination
City Dump

Don't Bug Me

Funky Broadway - Parts 1 & 2 65
So Sharp
Uhh, Parts 1 & 2

Wrong House

★★11★★ DYLAN, Bob

Born Robert Allen Zimmerman on 5/24/41 in Duluth, Minnesota. Singer/songwriter/guitarist/harmonica player. Took stage name from poet Dylan Thomas. To New York City in December 1960. Worked Greenwich Village folk clubs. Signed to Columbia Records in October 1961. Innovator of folk-rock style. Motorcycle crash on 7/29/66 led to short retirement. Films *Don't Look Back* (1965), *Eat The Document* (1969) and *Pat Garrett And Billy The Kid* (1973). Made film *Renaldo And Clara* (1978). Newly-found Christian faith reflected in his recordings of 1979. Co-starred with Fiona in the 1987 film *Hearts Of Fire*. Member of the supergroup Traveling Wilburys. Inducted into the Rock and Roll Hall of Fame in 1988. Won Grammy's Lifetime Achievement Award in 1991. Star players who frequently appeared on his albums include Charlie McCoy, Al Kooper, Jim Keltner, Sly Dunbar, Robbie Shakespeare, Mick Taylor, Mark Knopfler and Tom Petty's Heartbreakers.

DEBUT DATE	PEAK POS	WKS CHR	GOLD	ARTIST — Album Title	$	Label & Number
9/7/63	22	32	●	1 The Freewheelin' Bob Dylan	$30	Columbia 8786
3/7/64	20	21		2 The Times They Are A-Changin'	$30	Columbia 8905
9/19/64	43	41		3 Another Side Of Bob Dylan	$25	Columbia 8993
5/1/65	6	43	●	4 Bringing It All Back Home	$25	Columbia 9128
10/2/65	3	47	●	5 Highway 61 Revisited	$20	Columbia 9189
7/23/66	9	34	●	6 Blonde On Blonde	$25	Columbia 841 [2]
5/6/67	10	94	▲²	7 Bob Dylan's Greatest Hits .... [G]	$25	Columbia 9463
1/27/68	2⁴	52	●	8 John Wesley Harding	$25	Columbia 9604
5/3/69	3	47	▲	9 Nashville Skyline	$12	Columbia 9825
				guests include Johnny Cash and Charlie Daniels		

DEBUT DATE	PEAK POS	WKS CHR	GOLD		ARTIST — Album Title	$	Label & Number
					DYLAN, Bob — Cont'd		
7/4/70	**4**	22	●	10	**Self Portrait**	$15	Columbia 30050 [2]
11/14/70	**7**	23	●	11	**New Morning**	$10	Columbia 30290
12/11/71+	**14**	36	▲	12	Bob Dylan's Greatest Hits, Vol. II.................[G]	$15	Columbia 31120 [2]
8/4/73	**16**	30		13	Pat Garrett & Billy The Kid ....[S]	$10	Columbia 32460
					Dylan appeared as Alias in the film; 3 vocals by Dylan		
12/22/73+	**17**	15	●	14	Dylan ....[K]	$10	Columbia 32747
					outtake recordings from 1969-70		
2/9/74	**1**[4]	21	●	15	**Planet Waves ***	$15	Asylum 1003
7/13/74	**3**	19	●	16	**Before The Flood *** ....[L]	$15	Asylum 201 [2]
2/8/75	**1**[2]	24	▲	17	**Blood On The Tracks**	$12	Columbia 33235
7/26/75	**7**	14		18	**The Basement Tapes *** ....[E]	$15	Columbia 33682 [2]
					***BOB DYLAN AND THE BAND** recorded in 1967 at the Big Pink, a house rented by The Band in West Saugerties, New York		
1/24/76	**1**[5]	35	▲	19	Desire	$10	Columbia 33893
10/2/76	**17**	12	●	20	Hard Rain ....[L]	$10	Columbia 34349
					recorded during Dylan's tour, the *Rolling Thunder Revue*		
7/8/78	**11**	23	●	21	Street-Legal	$10	Columbia 35453
5/12/79	**13**	25		22	Bob Dylan At Budokan ....[L]	$12	Columbia 36067 [2]
					recorded in Japan on 3/1/78		
9/8/79	**3**	26	▲	23	**Slow Train Coming**	$10	Columbia 36120
7/12/80	**24**	11		24	Saved	$8	Columbia 36553
9/5/81	**33**	9		25	Shot Of Love	$8	Columbia 37496
					guests include Ringo Starr, Donald "Duck" Dunn and Ron Wood		
11/19/83	**20**	24	●	26	Infidels	$8	Columbia 38819
1/5/85	**115**	9		27	Real Live ....[L]	$8	Columbia 39944
6/22/85	**33**	17		28	Empire Burlesque...	$8	Columbia 40110
12/7/85+	**33**	22	▲	29	Biograph ....[K]	$25	Columbia 38830 [5]
					consists of a 53-song collection from 1962-81 (18 songs previously unreleased)		
8/2/86	**53**	13		30	Knocked Out Loaded...................................	$8	Columbia 40439
					guests include Tom Petty & The Heartbreakers		
6/18/88	**61**	10		31	Down In The Groove	$8	Columbia 40957
					guests include Eric Clapton, Ron Wood, Mark Knopfler, Paul Simonon (The Clash), Steve Jones (The Sex Pistols) and Grateful Dead members Jerry Garcia, Bob Weir and Brent Mydland		
2/18/89	**37**	11	●	32	Dylan & The Dead ....[L]	$8	Columbia 45056
					BOB DYLAN & GRATEFUL DEAD recordings from 6 concert dates in July 1987		
10/7/89	**30**	23		33	Oh Mercy	$8	Columbia 45281
9/29/90	**38**	11		34	Under The Red Sky......................................	$12	Columbia 46794
					guests include David Crosby, George Harrison, Bruce Hornsby, Elton John, Slash (Guns N' Roses) and Jimmie and Stevie Ray Vaughan		
4/13/91	**49**	6		35	The Bootleg Series - Volumes 1-3 [Rare & Unreleased] 1961-1991 ....[K]	$37	Columbia 47382 [3]
					includes a 69-page booklet		
11/21/92	**51**	9		36	Good As I Been To You.................................	$12	Columbia 53200

Abandoned Love (29)
Absolutely Sweet Marie (6)
Ain't No More Cane (18)
Alberta #1 & #2 (10)
All Along The Watchtower (8,16,22,29,32)
All I Really Want To Do (3,12,22)
All The Tired Horses (10)
Angelina (35)
Apple Suckling Tree (18)
Are You Ready (24)
Arthur McBride (36)
As I Went Out One Morning (8)
Baby, I'm In The Mood For You (8)
Baby, Let Me Follow You Down (29)
Baby Stop Crying (21)
Ballad In Plain D (3)
Ballad Of A Thin Man (5,16,22,27)
Ballad Of Frankie Lee And Judas Priest (8)
Ballad Of Hollis Brown (2)
Ballad Of Ira Hayes (14)
Belle Isle (10)
Bessie Smith (18)
Big Yellow Taxi (14)
Billy *[includes Main Title Theme and versions 1, 4, & 7]* (13)
Black Crow Blues (3)
Black Diamond Bay (19)
Blackjack Davey (36)
Blind Willie McTell (35)
Blowin' In The Wind (1,7,16,22,29)

Blue Moon (10)
Bob Dylan's 115th Dream (4)
Bob Dylan's Blues (1)
Bob Dylan's Dream (1)
Boots Of Spanish Leather (2)
Born In Time (34)
Boxer, The (10)
Brownsville Girl (30)
Buckets Of Rain (17)
Bunkhouse Theme (13)
Call Letter Blues (35)
Can You Please Crawl Out Your Window? (29) **58**
Can't Help Falling In Love (14)
Canadee-I-O (36)
Cantina Theme (Workin' For The Law) (13)
Caribbean Wind (29)
Cat's In The Well (34)
Catfish (35)
Changing Of The Guards (21)
Chimes Of Freedom (3)
Clean Cut Kid (28)
Clothes Line Saga (18)
Copper Kettle (The Pale Moonlight) (10)
Corrina, Corrina (1)
Country Pie (9)
Covenant Woman (24)
Crash On The Levee (Down In The Flood) (12,18)
Dark Eyes (28)
Day Of The Locusts (11)
Days Of 49 (10)
Dead Man, Dead Man (25)
Dear Landlord (8,29)
Death Is Not The End (31)
Desolation Row (5)

Diamond Joe (36)
Dirge (15)
Disease Of Conceit (33)
Do Right To Me Baby (Do Unto Others) (23)
Don't Fall Apart On Me Tonight (26)
Don't Think Twice, It's All Right (1,12,16,22)
Don't Ya Tell Henry (18)
Down Along The Cove (8)
Down In The Flood ..see: Crash On The Levee (Down In The Flood)
Down The Highway (1)
Drifter's Escape (8)
Driftin' Too Far From Shore (30)
Early Mornin' Rain (10)
Emotionally Yours (28)
Endless Highway (16)
Eternal Circle (35)
Every Grain Of Sand (25,29,35)
Everything Is Broken (33)
Farewell, Angelina (35)
Father Of Night (11)
Final Theme (13)
Fool Such As I (14) 55
Foot Of Pride (35)
Forever Young (15,22,29)
4th Time Around (6)
Frankie & Albert (36)
Froggie Went A Courtin' (36)
From A Buick 6 (5)
Gates Of Eden (5)
Girl From The North Country (1,9,27)
God Knows (34)

Goin' To Acapulco (18)
Going Going Gone (15,22)
Golden Loom (35)
Gonna Change My Way Of Thinking (23)
Got My Mind Made Up (30)
Gotta Serve Somebody (23,29,32) **24**
Gotta Travel On (10)
Groom's Still Waiting At The Altar (29)
Had A Dream About You, Baby (31)
Handy Dandy (34)
Hard Rain's A-Gonna Fall (1,12)
Hard Times (36)
Hard Times In New York Town (35)
Hazel (15)
He Was A Friend Of Mine (35)
Heart Of Mine (25,29)
Highway 61 Revisited (5,16,27)
Honey, Just Allow Me One More Chance (1)
House Carpenter (35)
Hurricane (Part I) (19) **33**
I Am A Lonesome Hobo (8)
I And I (26,27)
I Believe In You (23,29)
I Don't Believe You (3,29)
I Dreamed I Saw St. Augustine (8)
I Forgot More Than You'll Ever Know (10)
I Pity The Poor Immigrant (8)
I Shall Be Free (1)

I Shall Be Free No. 10 (3)
I Shall Be Released (12,16,22,29,35)
I Threw It All Away (9,20) **85**
I Wanna Be Your Lover (29)
I Want You (6,7,22,29,32) **20**
I'll Be Your Baby Tonight (8,12,29)
I'll Keep It With Mine (29,35)
I'll Remember You (28)
Idiot Wind (17,20,35)
If Dogs Run Free (11)
If Not For You (11,12,29,35)
If You Gotta Go, Go Now (Or Else You Got To Stay All Night) (35)
If You See Her, Say Hello (17,35)
In Search Of Little Sadie (10)
In The Garden (24)
In The Summertime (25)
Is Your Love In Vain? (21,22)
Isis (19,29)
It Ain't Me Babe (3,7,16,27,29)
It Takes A Lot To Laugh, It Takes A Train To Cry (5,35)
It's All Over Now, Baby Blue (4,12,29)
It's Alright, Ma (I'm Only Bleeding) (4,16,22)
Jet Pilot (35)
Jim Jones (36)
Joey (19,32)
John Wesley Harding (8)
Jokerman (26)

Just Like A Woman (6,7,16,22,29) **33**
Just Like Tom Thumb's Blues (5,12)
Katie's Been Gone (18)
Kingsport Town (35)
Knockin' On Heaven's Door (13,16,22,29,35) **12**
Last Thoughts On Woody Guthrie (35)
Lay Down Your Weary Tune (29)
Lay Lady Lay (9,12,16,20,29) **7**
Lenny Bruce (25)
Leopard-Skin Pill-Box Hat (6) **81**
Let It Be Me (10)
Let Me Die In My Footsteps (35)
Like A Rolling Stone (5,7,10,16,22,29,35) **2**
Lily Of The West (14)
Lily, Rosemary And The Jack Of Hearts (17)
Little Maggie (36)
Little Sadie (10)
Living The Blues (10)
Lo And Behold! (18)
Lonesome Death Of Hattie Carroll (2,29)
Long Distance Operator (18)
Lord Protect My Child (35)
Love Minus Zero/No Limit (4,22)
Maggie's Farm (4,12,20,22,27)

218

DEBUT DATE	PEAK POS	WKS CHR	GOLD	ARTIST — Album Title	$	Label & Number

DYLAN, Bob — Cont'd

Mama, You Been On My Mind (35)
Man Gave Names To All The Animals (23)
Man In Me (11)
Man In The Long Black Coat (33)
Man Of Peace (26)
Man On The Street (35)
Mary Ann (14)
Masters Of War (1,27,29)
Maybe Someday (30)
Meet Me In The Morning (17)
Mighty Quinn (Quinn, The Eskimo) (10,12,29)
Million Dollar Bash (18,29)
Minstrel Boy (10)
Mixed-up Confusion (29)
Moonshiner (35)
Most Likely You Go Your Way (And I'll Be Mine) (6,16,29) **66**
Most Of The Time (33)
Motorpsycho Nitemare (3)
Mozambique (19) **54**
Mr. Bojangles (14)
Mr. Tambourine Man (4,7,22,29)
My Back Pages (3,12)
Nashville Skyline Rag (9)
Need A Woman (35)
Neighborhood Bully (26)
Never Gonna Be The Same Again (28)
Never Say Goodbye (15)
New Morning (11)
New Pony (21)
Night They Drove Old Dixie Down (16)
Ninety Miles An Hour (Down A Dead End Street) (31)
No More Auction Block (35)
No Time To Think (21)
Nobody 'Cept You (35)

North Country Blues (2)
Nothing Was Delivered (18)
Obviously 5 Believers (6)
Odds And Ends (18)
Oh, Sister (19,20,22)
On A Night Like This (15,29) **44**
On The Road Again (4)
One More Cup Of Coffee (19,22)
One More Night (9)
One More Weekend (11)
One Of Us Must Know (Sooner Or Later) (6)
One Too Many Mornings (2,20)
Only A Hobo (35)
Only A Pawn In Their Game (2)
Open The Door, Homer (18)
Orange Juice Blues (Blues For Breakfast) (18)
Outlaw Blues (4)
Oxford Town (1)
Paths Of Victory (35)
Peggy Day (9)
Percy's Song (29)
Please, Mrs. Henry (18)
Pledging My Time (6)
Political World (33)
Positively 4th Street (7,29) **7**
Precious Angel (23)
Precious Memories (30)
Pressing On (24)
Property Of Jesus (25)
Queen Jane Approximately (5,32)
Quit Your Low Down Ways (35)
Rainy Day Women #12 & 35 (6,7,16) **2**
Rambling, Gambling Willie (35)

Rank Strangers To Me (31)
Restless Farewell (2)
Ring Them Bells (33)
River Theme (13)
Romance In Durango (19,29)
Ruben Remus (18)
Sad Eyed Lady Of The Lowlands (6)
Sally Sue Brown (31)
Santa-Fe (35)
Sara (19)
Sarah Jane (14)
Satisfied Mind (24)
Saved (24)
Saving Grace (24)
Seeing The Real You At Last (28)
Senor (Tales Of Yankee Power) (21,29)
Series Of Dreams (35)
Seven Curses (35)
Seven Days (35)
Shape I'm In (16)
She Belongs To Me (4,10,12)
She's Your Lover Now (35)
Shelter From The Storm (17,20,23)
Shenandoah (31)
Shooting Star (33)
Shot Of Love (25)
Sign On The Window (11)
Silvio (31)
Simple Twist Of Fate (17,22)
Sittin' On Top Of The World (36)
Sitting On A Barbed Wire Fence (35)
Slow Train (23,32)
Solid Rock (24,29)
Someone's Got A Hold Of My Heart (35)
Something There Is About You (15)

Something's Burning, Baby (28)
Spanish Harlem Incident (3)
Spanish Is The Loving Tongue (14)
Stage Fright (16)
Step It Up And Go (36)
Stuck Inside Of Mobile With The Memphis Blues Again (6,12,20)
Subterranean Homesick Blues (4,7,29,35) **39**
Sweetheart Like You (26) **55**
T.V. Talkin' Song (34)
Take A Message To Mary (10)
Take Me As I Am (Or Let Me Go) (10)
Talkin' Bear Mountain Picnic Massacre Blues (35)
Talkin' Hava Negeilah Blues (35)
Talkin' John Birch Paranoid Blues (35)
Talking World War III Blues (1)
Tangled Up In Blue (17,27,29,35) **31**
Tears Of Rage (18)
Tell Me (35)
Tell Me That It Isn't True (9)
Temporary Like Achilles (6)
10,000 Men (34)
They Killed Him (30)
This Wheel's On Fire (18)
Three Angels (11)
Tight Connection To My Heart (Has Anybody Seen My Love) (28)
Time Passes Slowly (11,29)
Times They Are A-Changin' (2,7,22,29,35)
Tiny Montgomery (18)

To Be Alone With You (9)
To Ramona (3,29)
Tombstone Blues (5,27,29)
Tomorrow Is A Long Time (12)
Tomorrow Night (36)
Tonight I'll Be Staying Here With You (9,12) **50**
Too Much Of Nothing (18)
Tough Mama (15)
Trouble (25)
True Love Tends To Forget (21)
Trust Yourself (28)
Turkey Chase (13)
2 X 2 (34)
Ugliest Girl In The World (31)
Unbelievable (34)
Under The Red Sky (34)
Under Your Spell (30)
Union Sundown (26)
Up On Cripple Creek (16)
Up To Me (29)
Visions Of Johanna (6,29)
Walkin' Down The Line (35)
Wallflower (35)
Walls Of Red Wing (35)
Watching The River Flow (12) **41**
Watered-Down Love (25)
We Better Talk This Over (21)
Wedding Song (15)
Weight, The (16)
Went To See The Gypsy (11)
What Can I Do For You? (24)
What Good Am I? (33)
What Was It You Wanted (33)
When Did You Leave Heaven? (31)
When He Returns (23)
When I Paint My Masterpiece (12)

When The Night Comes Falling From The Sky (28,35)
When The Ship Comes In (2,35)
When You Awake (16)
When You Gonna Wake Up (23)
Where Are You Tonight? (Journey Through Dark Heat) (21)
Where Teardrops Fall (33)
Who Killed Davey Moore? (35)
Wicked Messenger (8)
Wigwam (10) **41**
Winterlude (11)
With God On Our Side (2)
Woogie Boogie (10)
Worried Blues (35)
Yazoo Street Scandal (18)
Ye Shall Be Changed (35)
Yea! Heavy And A Bottle Of Bread (18)
You Ain't Goin' Nowhere (12,18)
You Angel You (15,29)
You Changed My Life (35)
You Wanna Ramble (30)
You're A Big Girl Now (17,20,29)
You're Gonna Make Me Lonesome When You Go (17)
You're Gonna Quit Me (36)

DYNAMIC SUPERIORS
Soul quintet from Washington, D.C. — Tony Washington, lead singer.

| 8/9/75 | 130 | 10 | | Pure Pleasure .... | $10 | Motown 841 |

Ain't Nothing Like The Real Thing
Better Way
Deception
Don't Give Up On Me Baby
Face The Music
Feeling Mellow
Hit And Run Lovers
Nobody's Gonna Change Me
Pleasure

DYNASTY
Los Angeles R&B group formed by producer/bassist Leon Sylvers III (of the Sylvers). Fronted by vocalists Kevin Spencer, Nidra Beard (Sylvers) and Linda Carriere (DeBlanc, Starfire).

| 8/2/80 | 43 | 21 | | 1 Adventures In The Land Of Music .... | $8 | Solar 3576 |
| 10/10/81 | 119 | 4 | | 2 The Second Adventure .... | $8 | Solar 20 |

Adventures In The Land Of Music (1)
Day and Night (1)
Do Me Right (1)
Give It Up For Love (2)
Give Your Love To Me (2)
Groove Control (1)
Here I Am (2)
High Time (I Left You Baby) (2)
I've Just Begun To Love You (1) **87**
Ice Breaker (1)
Love In The Fast Lane (2)
Man In Love (1)
Pain, Got A Hold On Me (2)
Revenge (2)
Something To Remember (1)
Take Another Look At Love (1)
That Lovin' Feelin' (2)
You're My Angel (2)

DYSON, Ronnie
Soul singer. Born on 6/5/50 in Washington, D.C. and raised in Brooklyn. Leading role in the Broadway musical Putney Swope. In the film Putney Swope. Died on 11/10/90 of heart failure complicated by chronic lung disease.

| 9/5/70 | 55 | 18 | | 1 (If You Let Me Make Love To You Then) Why Can't I Touch You?..... | $10 | Columbia 30223 |
| 4/7/73 | 142 | 7 | | 2 One Man Band .... | $10 | Columbia 32211 |

Band Of Gold (1)
Bridge Over Troubled Water (1)
Do What Your Heart Tells You To Do (1)
Emmie (1)
Fever (1)
Girl Don't Come (2)
Give In To Love (2)
I Don't Wanna Cry (1) **50**
I Just Can't Help Believin' (1)
I Think I'll Tell Her (2)
(If You Let Me Make Love To You Then) Why Can't I Touch You? (1) **8**
Just Don't Want To Be Lonely (2) **60**
Love Of A Woman (2)
Make It With You (1)
One Man Band (Plays All Alone) (2) **28**
Point Of No Return (2)
She's Gone (1)
Something (2)
Touch Of Baby (1)
Wednesday In Your Garden (2)
When You Get Right Down To It (2) **94**

DEBUT DATE	PEAK POS	WKS CHR	GOLD	ARTIST — Album Title	$	Label & Number

E

★★131★★ **EAGLES**

Rock group formed in Los Angeles in 1971. Consisted of Glenn Frey (vocals, guitar), Bernie Leadon (guitar), Randy Meisner (bass) and Don Henley (drums). Meisner founded Poco; Leadon had been in the Flying Burrito Brothers; and Frey and Henley were with Linda Ronstadt. Debut album recorded in England in 1972. Don Felder (guitar) added in 1975. Leadon replaced by Joe Walsh in 1975. Meisner replaced by Timothy B. Schmit in 1977. Frey and Henley were the only members to play on all recordings. Disbanded in 1982.

6/24/72	22	49	●	1 Eagles	$12	Asylum 5054
5/5/73	41	70	●	2 Desperado	$12	Asylum 5068
4/20/74	17	87	●	3 On The Border	$12	Asylum 1004
6/28/75	1⁵	56	●	4 One Of These Nights	$10	Asylum 1039
3/6/76	1⁵	133	▲¹²	5 Eagles/Their Greatest Hits 1971-1975 .... [G]	$10	Asylum 1052
12/25/76+	1⁸	107	▲⁹	6 Hotel California	$10	Asylum 1084
10/20/79	1⁹	57	▲⁴	7 The Long Run	$8	Asylum 508
11/29/80	6	26	▲	8 Eagles Live .... [L]	$10	Asylum 705 [2]
11/13/82+	52	15	●	9 Eagles Greatest Hits, Volume 2 .... [G]	$8	Asylum 60205

After The Thrill Is Gone (4,9)
All Night Long (8)
Already Gone (3,5) *32*
Best Of My Love (3,5) *1*
Bitter Creek (2)
Certain Kind Of Fool (2)
Chug All Night (1)
Desperado (2,5,8)
Disco Strangler (7)
Doolin-Dalton (2,8)
Earlybird (1)
Good Day In Hell (3)

Greeks Don't Want No Freaks (7)
Heartache Tonight (7,8,9) *1*
Hollywood Waltz (4)
Hotel California (6,8,9) *1*
I Can't Tell You Why (7,8,9) *8*
I Wish You Peace (4)
In The City (7)
Is It True? (3)
James Dean (3) *77*
Journey Of The Sorcerer (4)
King Of Hollywood (7)

Last Resort (6)
Life In The Fast Lane (6,8,9) *11*
Life's Been Good (8)
Long Run (7,8,9) *8*
Lyin' Eyes (4,5) *2*
Midnight Flyer (3)
Most Of Us Are Sad (1)
My Man (3)
New Kid In Town (6,8,9) *1*
Nightingale (1)
Ol' '55 (3)
On The Border (3)

One Of These Nights (4,5) *1*
Out Of Control (2)
Outlaw Man (2) *59*
Peaceful Easy Feeling (1,5) *22*
Pretty Maids All In A Row (6)
Sad Cafe (7,9)
Saturday Night (2,8)
Seven Bridges Road (8,9) *21*
Take It Easy (1,5,8) *12*
Take It To The Limit (4,5,8) *4*

Take The Devil (1)
Teenage Jail (7)
Tequila Sunrise (2,5) *64*
Those Shoes (7)
Too Many Hands (4)
Train Leaves Here This Morning (1)
Try And Love Again (6)
Tryin' (1)
Twenty-One (2)
Victim Of Love (6,9)
Visions (4)
Wasted Time (6,8)

Witchy Woman (1,5) *9*
You Never Cry Like A Lover (3)

EARLAND, Charles

R&B-jazz keyboard player born on 5/24/41 in Philadelphia. Played sax while in the Temple University Band. Tenor saxophonist with Jimmy McGriff's trio. Alto saxophonist with Lou Donaldson from 1968-70, then formed his own group.

7/11/70	108	19		1 Black Talk! .... [I]	$8	Prestige 7758
11/21/70+	131	10		2 Black Drops .... [I]	$8	Prestige 7815
5/15/71	176	7		3 Living Black! .... [I-L]	$8	Prestige 10009
4/3/76	155	11		4 Odyssey	$8	Mercury 1049

Aquarius (1)
Black Talk (1)
Buck Green (2)
Cosmic Fever (4)
Don't Say Goodbye (2)

From My Heart To Yours (4)
Here Comes Charlie (1)
Intergalactic Love Song (4)
Journey Of The Soul (4)
Keyclub Cookout (3)

Killer Joe (3)
Lazybird (2)
Letha (4)
Mighty Burner (1)
Milestones (3)

More Today Than Yesterday (1)
Phire (4)
Raindrops Keep Falling On My Head (2)

Sing A Simple Song (4)
Sons Of The Gods (4)
We All Live In The Jungle (4)
Westbound #9 (3)

EARLE, Steve

Born in Fort Monroe, Virginia; raised in Schertz, Texas. Country-rock singer/songwriter/acoustic guitarist.

10/25/86	89	20		1 Guitar Town	$8	MCA 5713
6/13/87	90	14		2 Exit O *	$8	MCA 5998
11/12/88+	56	28		3 Copperhead Road	$8	Uni 7
7/21/90	100	9		4 The Hard Way *	$12	MCA 6430

*STEVE EARLE AND THE DUKES

Angry Young Man (2)
Back To The Wall (3)
Billy Austin (4)
Close Your Eyes (4)
Copperhead Road (3)
Country Girl (4)
Devil's Right Hand (3)
Down The Road (3)
Esmeralda's Hollywood (4)
Even When I'm Blue (3)

Fearless Heart (1)
Good Ol' Boy (Gettin' Tough) (1)
Goodbye's All We've Got Left (1)
Guitar Town (1)
Have Mercy (4)
Hillbilly Highway (1)
Hopeless Romantics (4)
I Ain't Ever Satisfied (2)

I Love You Too Much (2)
It's All Up To You (2)
Johnny Come Lately (3)
Justice In Ontario (4)
Little Rock 'N' Roller (1)
My Old Friend The Blues (1)
Nothing But A Child (3)
Nowhere Road (2)
No. 29 (2)
Once You Love (3)

Other Kind (4)
Promise You Anything (4)
Rain Came Down (2)
Regular Guy (4)
San Antonio Girl (2)
Snake Oil (3)
Someday (1)
Sweet Little '66 (3)
Think It Over (1)

This Highway's Mine (Roadmaster) (4)
Waiting On You (3)
Week Of Living Dangerously (2)
West Nashville Boogie (4)
When The People Find Out (4)
You Belong To Me (3)

EARTH OPERA

Boston rock quartet led by David Grisman and Peter Rowan.

3/22/69	181	4		The Great American Eagle Tragedy	$12	Elektra 74038

Alfie Finney
All Winter Long

American Eagle Tragedy
Home To You *97*

It's Love
Mad Lydia's Waltz

Roast Beef Love
Sanctuary From The Law

EARTHQUAKE

San Francisco rock quintet — John Doukas, lead singer.

9/4/76	151	4		8.5	$10	Beserkley 0047

And He Likes To Hurt You
Don't Want To Go Back

Finders Keepers
Girl Named Jesse James

Hit The Floor
Little Cindy

Motivate Me
Same Old Story

Savin' My Love

DEBUT DATE	PEAK POS	WKS CHR	GOLD	ARTIST — Album Title	$	Label & Number

★★72★★ **EARTH, WIND & FIRE**

Los Angeles-based R&B group formed by Chicago-bred producer/songwriter/vocalist/percussionist/kalimba player Maurice White. In 1969, White, former session drummer for Chess Records and member of The Ramsey Lewis Trio, formed the Salty Peppers; recorded for Capitol. Maurice's brother Verdine White was the group's bassist. Eighteen months later, the brothers hired a new band and recorded as Earth, Wind & Fire — named for the three elements of Maurice's astrological sign. Co-lead singer Philip Bailey joined as lead singer in 1971. Group generally contained eight to 10 members, with frequent personnel shuffling. Appeared in the films *That's the Way of the World* (1975) and *Sgt. Pepper's Lonely Hearts Club Band* (1978). Elaborate stage shows featured an array of magic acts and pyrotechnics. Group members Philip Bailey, Wade Flemons, Ronnie Laws and Maurice White had solo hits.

DEBUT DATE	PEAK POS	WKS CHR	GOLD	#	Album Title	$	Label & Number
5/15/71	172	13		1	Earth, Wind & Fire	$15	Warner 1905
1/15/72	89	13		2	The Need Of Love	$15	Warner 1958
11/25/72+	87	25		3	Last Days And Time	$15	Columbia 31702
6/9/73	27	71	●	4	Head To The Sky	$12	Columbia 32194
3/30/74	15	37	▲	5	Open Our Eyes	$12	Columbia 32712
9/7/74	97	10		6	Another Time [R]	$12	Warner 2798 [2]

reissue of their first 2 albums

DEBUT DATE	PEAK POS	WKS CHR	GOLD	#	Album Title	$	Label & Number
3/15/75	1³	55	▲²	7	That's The Way Of The World [S]	$12	Columbia 33280

group portrayed a rock band in the film

DEBUT DATE	PEAK POS	WKS CHR	GOLD	#	Album Title	$	Label & Number
12/6/75+	1³	54	▲²	8	Gratitude [L]	$15	Columbia 33694 [2]

contains some studio cuts

DEBUT DATE	PEAK POS	WKS CHR	GOLD	#	Album Title	$	Label & Number
10/16/76	2²	30	▲²	9	Spirit	$12	Columbia 34241
12/3/77+	3	47	▲²	10	All 'N All	$12	Columbia 34905
12/2/78+	6	60	▲³	11	The Best Of Earth, Wind & Fire, Vol. I [G]	$10	ARC 35647
6/16/79	3	38	▲²	12	I Am	$10	ARC 35730
11/22/80	10	21	●	13	Faces	$10	ARC 36795 [2]
11/14/81	5	25	▲	14	Raise!	$8	ARC 37548
3/12/83	12	21	●	15	Powerlight	$8	Columbia 38367
12/3/83+	40	16		16	Electric Universe	$8	Columbia 38980
11/21/87	33	28	●	17	Touch The World	$8	Columbia 40596
12/10/88	190	4		18	The Best Of Earth, Wind & Fire, Vol. II [G]	$8	Columbia 45013
2/17/90	70	11		19	Heritage	$12	Columbia 45268

Africano (7,8)
After The Love Has Gone (12,18) *2*
All About Love (7)
And Love Goes On (13) *59*
Anything You Want (19)
Back On The Road (13)
Bad Tune (1,6)
Beauty (2,6)
Be Ever Wonderful (10)
Biyo (6)
Boogie Wonderland (12,18) *6*
Brazilian Rhyme (medley) (10)
Build Your Nest (4)
Burnin' Bush (9)
C'mon Children (1,6)
Can't Hide Love (8,11) *39*
Can't Let Go (12)
Caribou (5)
Celebrate (8)
Changing Times (14)
Close To Home (19)
Clover (4)
Could It Be Right (16)
Daydreamin' (19)
Departure (9)
Devotion (5,8,18) *33*

Drum Stong (5)
Earth, Wind & Fire (9)
Electric Nation (16)
Energy (2,6)
Every Now And Then (17)
Everything Is Everything (2,6)
Evil (4) *50*
Evil Roy (17)
Evolution Orange (14)
Faces (13)
Faith (19)
Fair But So Uncool (5)
Fall In Love With Me (15) *17*
Fan The Fire (1,6)
Fantasy (11,18) *32*
Feelin' Blue (5)
For The Love Of You (19)
Freedom Of Choice (15)
Getaway (9,11) *12*
Good Time (19)
Got To Get You Into My Life (11) *9*
Gratitude (8)
Handwriting On The Wall (6)
Happy Feelin' (7)
Hearts To Heart (15)
Help Somebody (1,6)

Here Today And Gone Tomorrow (17)
Heritage (17)
I Can Feel It In My Bones (2,6)
I Think About Lovin' You (2,6)
I'd Rather Have You (3)
I'll Write A Song For You (19)
I'm In Love (19)
I've Had Enough (14)
Imagination (9)
In The Marketplace (medley) (10)
In The Stone (12) *58*
In Time (13)
Jupiter (medley) (10)
Kalimba Story (5) *55*
Keep Your Head To The Sky (4) *52*
King Of Groove (19)
Lady Sun (14)
Let Me Talk (13) *44*
Let Your Feelings Show (12)
Let's Groove (14,18) *3*
Love Is Life (1,6) *93*
Love Music (11)
Love's Holiday (10,18)
Magic Mind (10)

Magnetic (16) *57*
Make It With You (3)
Mighty Mighty (5,18) *29*
Miracles (15)
Mom (3)
Moment Of Truth (1,6)
Money Tight (17)
Moonwalk (16)
Motor (19)
My Love (14)
New Horizons (17)
New World Symphony (8)
On Your Face (5)
Open Our Eyes (5)
Power (3,8)
Pride (13)
Reasons (7,8,11)
Remember The Children (3)
Rock That! (12)
Runnin' (medley) (10)
Sailaway (13)
Saturday Nite (9,18) *21*
See The Light (7)
September (11) *8*
Serpentine Fire (10,18) *13*
Share Your Love (13)
Shining Star (7,8,11) *1*
Side By Side (15) *76*
Sing A Message To You (8)

Sing A Song (8,11) *5*
Something Special (15)
Song In My Heart (13)
Sparkle (13)
Spasmodic Movements (5)
Speed Of Love (15)
Spirit (9)
Spirit Of A New World (16)
Spread Your Love (15)
Star (12) *64*
Straight From The Heart (15)
Sun Goddess (8) *44*
Sunshine (15)
Sweet Sassy Lady (16)
System Of Survival (17) *60*
Take It To The Sky (13)
Takin' Chances (19)
Tee Nine Chee Bit (5)
That's The Way Of The World (7,11) *67*
They Don't See (3)
Thinking Of You (17) *67*
This World Today (1,6)
Time Is On Your Side (3)
Touch (16)
Touch The World (17)
Turn It Into Something Good (13)
Turn On (The Beat Box) (18)

Victim Of The Modern Heart (17)
Wait (12)
Wanna Be The Man (19)
Wanna Be With You (14) *51*
We're Living In Our Own Time (16)
Welcome (19)
Where Have All The Flowers Gone (13)
Win Or Lose (13)
World's A Masquerade (4)
Yearnin', Learnin' (7,8)
You (13) *48*
You And I (12,17)
You Are A Winner (medley) (14)
You Went Away (13)
Zanzibar (4)

EAST COAST FAMILY

Grouping of artists assembled by Michael Bivins (New Edition, Bell Biv DeVoe). Features Bivins, Another Bad Creation, Boyz II Men, M.C. Brains, and Yo-Yo, plus newcomers Whytgize, Yvette Brown, Hayden Hajdu, Cale Brock, Tam Rock & Lady V, Tom Boyy, 1010, Fruit Punch, Anthony Velasquez, and Mark, Rico & Finesse.

DEBUT DATE	PEAK POS	WKS CHR	GOLD	Album Title	$	Label & Number
8/15/92	54	26↑	●	East Coast Family Volume One	$12	Biv 10 6352

except for "1-4-All-4-1," tracks performed by individual artists

All These Wanna Be's *[Another Bad Creation]*
End Of Road *[Boyz II Men]* *1*

It's So Hard To Say Goodbye To Yesterday *[Boyz II Men]*
Listen Closely *[Tam Rock]*

Motownphilly *[Boyz II Men]*
1-4-All-4-1 *81*

Playground *[Another Bad Creation]*

Pump Ya Fist *[M.C. Brains]*
Sympin' *[Boyz II Men]*

Uhh Ahh *[Boyz II Men]*

EASTON, Elliot

Born Elliot Shapiro on 12/18/53 in Brooklyn. Lead guitarist of the Cars.

DEBUT DATE	PEAK POS	WKS CHR	GOLD	Album Title	$	Label & Number
3/9/85	99	11		Change No Change	$8	Elektra 60393

Change
Fight My Way To Love

Hard Way
Help Me

I Want You
Shayla

(She Made It) New For Me
Tools Of Your Labor

(Wearing Down) Like A Wheel
Wide Awake

★★382★★ **EASTON, Sheena**

Born on 4/27/59 in Glasgow, Scotland. Real last name is Orr. Vocalist/actress. Portrayed a singer in the 1980 BBC-TV documentary *The Big Time*. Won the 1981 Best New Artist Grammy Award. Portrayed Sonny Crockett's wife in five episodes of TV's *Miami Vice*.

DEBUT DATE	PEAK POS	WKS CHR	GOLD	#	Album Title	$	Label & Number
3/14/81	24	38	●	1	Sheena Easton	$8	EMI America 17049
11/28/81+	47	53	●	2	You Could Have Been With Me	$8	EMI America 17061

DEBUT DATE	PEAK POS	WKS CHR	GOLD	ARTIST — Album Title	$	Label & Number
				EASTON, Sheena — Cont'd		
10/16/82	85	12	3	Madness, Money And Music	$8	EMI America 17080
9/17/83	33	38	4	Best Kept Secret	$8	EMI America 17101
10/20/84+	15	35	● 5	A Private Heaven	$8	EMI America 17132
11/23/85	40	19	6	Do You	$8	EMI America 17173
12/3/88+	44	26	● 7	The Lover In Me	$8	MCA 42249
4/27/91	90	7	8	What Comes Naturally	$12	MCA 10131

All By Myself (5)
Almost Over You (4) 25
Are You Man Enough (3)
Back In The City (5)
Best Kept Man (4)
Calm Before The Storm (4) 6
Can't Wait Till Tomorrow (6)
Cool Love (7)
Cry (1)
Days Like This (7)
Devil In A Fast Car (4) 79
Do It For Love (6) 29
Don't Break My Heart (6)
Don't Leave Me This Way (4)
Don't Send Flowers (1)
Don't Turn Your Back (6)
Double Standard (5)

Fire And Rain (7)
First Touch Of Love (8)
Follow My Rainbow (7)
Forever Friends (8)
Half A Heart (8)
Hard To Say It's Over (5)
Hungry Eyes (5)
I Like The Fright (4)
I Wouldn't Beg For Water (3) 64
I'm Not Worth The Hurt (2)
Ice Out In The Rain (3)
If It's Meant To Last (7)
If You Wanna Keep Me (8)
In The Winter (3)
Jimmy Mack (6) 65
Johnny (2)

Just Another Broken Heart (2)
Just One Smile (4)
Kisses (6)
Let Sleeping Dogs Lie (4)
Letter From Joey (7)
Little Tenderness (2)
Love And Affection (5)
Lover In Me (7) 2
Machinery (3) 57
Madness, Money And Music (3)
Magic Of Love (6)
Manic Panic (8)
Modern Girl (1) 18
Money Back Guarantee (6)

Morning Train (Nine To Five) (1) 1
Next Time (8)
No Deposit, No Return (7)
One Love (7)
One Man Woman (1)
101 (7)
Prisoner (1)
Savoir Faire (2)
(She's In Love) With Her Radio (4)
So Much In Love (1)
Somebody (8)
Strut (5) 7
Sugar Walls (5) 9
Swear (5) 80
Sweet Talk (4)

Take My Time (1)
Telefone (Long Distance Love Affair) (4) 9
Telephone Lines (2)
There When I Needed You (3)
Time Bomb (8)
To Anyone (8)
Trouble In The Shadows (2)
Voice On The Radio (1)
Weekend In Paris (3)
What Comes Naturally (8) 19
When He Shines (2) 30
When The Lightning Strikes Again (4)
Wind Beneath My Wings (3)
Without You (7)

You Can Swing It (8)
You Could Have Been With Me (2) 15
You Do It (3)
You Make Me Nervous (5)
Young Lions (6)

EASYBEATS, The
Rock quintet formed in Australia in 1965. To England in 1966. Steven Wright (vocals) & Gordon Fleet (drums) were English. Dick Diamonde (bass) & Harry Vanda (guitar) were Dutch. George Young (guitar; older brother of AC/DC's Angus & Malcolm Young) was Scottish. Young & Vanda formed Flash & The Pan.

| 6/10/67 | 180 | 5 | | Friday On My Mind | $35 | United Art. 6588 |

Do You Have A Soul
Friday On My Mind 16

Happy Is The Man
Made My Bed, Gonna Lie In It

Make You Feel Alright (Women)

Pretty Girl
Remember Sam
River Deep, Mountain High

Saturday Night
See Line Woman

Who'll Be The One
You Me, We Love

EAZY-E
Rapper/producer from Compton, California. Born Eric Wright on 9/7/73. Member of N.W.A.

| 12/10/88+ | 41 | 90 | ▲² | Eazy-Duz-It | $8 | Ruthless 57100 |

Boyz-N-The Hood
Eazy - Chapter 8 Verse 10

Eazy-Duz-It
Eazy-er Said Than Dunn

I'mma Break It Down
No More ?'s

Nobody Move
Radio

Still Talkin'
2 Hard Mutha's

We Want Eazy

EBN/OZN
Male New York duo: "Ebn" Liben (synthesizer) and "Ozn" Rosen (vocals).

| 3/31/84 | 185 | 4 | | Feeling Cavalier | $8 | Elektra 60319 |

AEIOU Sometimes Y
Bag Lady (I Wonder)

Dawn, The
I Want Cash

Kuchenga Pamoja
Pop Art Bop

Rockin' Robin
Stop Stop Give It Up

TV Guide
Video D.J.

EBONEE WEBB
R&B octet from Memphis led by vocalist Michael Winston and guitarist Thomas Brown.

| 9/12/81 | 157 | 7 | | Ebonee Webb | $8 | Capitol 12148 |

Anybody Wanna Dance
Do Me Right (Everybody Needs A Little Love)

Gonna Get Cha'
Keep On Steppin'

Something About You
Stop Teasing Me

Throw Down
Woman

ECHO & THE BUNNYMEN
Rock quartet: Ian McCulloch (vocals), Will Sergent (guitar) and Les Pattinson (bass) are from England. Pete de Freitas, of Trinidad, replaced Echo the drum machine (10/79). In June 1989, de Freitas was killed in a motorcycle accident. McCulloch went solo in 1989, replaced by Noel Burke.

7/25/81	184	2	1	Heaven Up Here	$8	Sire 3569
3/26/83	137	9	2	Porcupine	$8	Sire 23770
2/11/84	188	3	3	Echo and The Bunnymen [M-L]	$8	Sire 23987
6/9/84	87	11	4	Ocean Rain	$8	Sire 25084
1/11/86	158	9	5	Songs To Learn & Sing [K]	$8	Sire 25360
8/8/87	51	37	6	Echo & The Bunnymen	$8	Sire 25597

All I Want (1)
All In Your Mind (6)
All My Colours (1)
All My Life (6)
Back Of Love (2,3,5)
Bedbugs And Ballyhoo (6)
Blue Blue Ocean (6)
Bombers Bay (6)

Bring On The Dancing Horses (5)
Clay (2)
Crystal Days (4)
Cutter, The (2,3,5)
Disease, The (1)
Do It Clean (3,5)
Game, The (6)
Gods Will Be Gods (2)

Heads Will Roll (2)
Heaven Up Here (1)
Higher Hell (2)
In Bluer Skies (2)
It Was A Pleasure (1)
Killing Moon (4,5)
Lips Like Sugar (6)
Lost And Found (6)
My Kingdom (4)

My White Devil (2)
Never Stop (3,5)
New Direction (6)
No Dark Things (1)
Nocturnal Me (4)
Ocean Rain (4)
Over The Wall (1)
Over You (6)
Porcupine (2)

Promise (1,5)
Puppet, The (5)
Rescue (3,5)
Ripeness (3)
Satellite (6)
Seven Seas (4,5)
Show Of Strength (1)
Silver (4,5)
Thorn Of Crowns (4)

Turquoise Days (1)
With A Hip (4)
Yo Yo Man (4)

ECKSTINE, Billy
Born William Clarence Eckstein on 7/8/14 in Pittsburgh. Nickname: "Mr. B." Sang with Earl Hines from 1939-43. Formed own jazz band with Charlie Parker, Dizzy Gillespie, Gene Ammons, Miles Davis and Sarah Vaughan.

| 11/17/62 | 92 | 6 | | Don't Worry 'Bout Me | $20 | Mercury 60736 |

Beauty Of True Love
Don't Worry 'Bout Me

Exodus Song
Guilty

I Want To Talk About You
It Isn't Fair

Jeannie
(Love Is) The Tender Trap

Stranger In Town
Tender Is The Night

Till There Was You
What Kind Of Fool Am I

EDDIE, John
New Jersey rocker.

| 6/21/86 | 83 | 15 | | John Eddie | $8 | Columbia 40181 |

Buster
Cool Walk

Dream House
Hide Out

Jungle Boy 52
Just Some Guy

Living Doll
Please Jodi

Pretty Little Rebel
Romance

Stranded
Waste Me

DEBUT DATE	PEAK POS	WKS CHR	GOLD	ARTIST — Album Title	$	Label & Number

★★330★★ EDDY, Duane

Born on 4/26/38 in Corning, New York. Began playing guitar at age five. At age 13, moved to Tucson, then to Coolidge, Arizona. To Phoenix in 1955, and then began long association with producer/songwriter Lee Hazlewood. Eddy's backing band, The Rebels, included three top sessionmen: Larry Knechtel on piano (later with Bread) and Jim Horn and Steve Douglas on sax. Films *Because They're Young*, *A Thunder Of Drums*, *The Wild Westerners*, *The Savage Seven* and *Kona Coast*. Married to Jessi Colter from 1962-68. Duane originated the "twangy" guitar sound and is the all-time #1 rock and roll instrumentalist. Currently resides in the Nashville area.

DEBUT DATE	PEAK POS	WKS CHR	#	Album Title	$	Label & Number
1/19/59	5	82	1	Have 'Twangy' Guitar-Will Travel [I]	$35	Jamie 3000
8/3/59	24	24	2	Especially For You [I]	$30	Jamie 3006
1/25/60	18	24	3	The "Twangs" The "Thang" [I]	$30	Jamie 3009
12/26/60+	10	21	4	$1,000,000.00 Worth Of Twang [G-I]	$30	Jamie 3014
7/17/61	93	15	5	Girls! Girls! Girls! [I]	$30	Jamie 3019
5/26/62	82	13	6	Twistin' 'N' Twangin' [I]	$25	RCA 2525
10/27/62	72	6	7	Twangy Guitar-Silky Strings [I]	$25	RCA 2576
1/19/63	47	17	8	Dance With The Guitar Man	$25	RCA 2648
10/5/63	93	8	9	"Twangin'" Up A Storm!	$25	RCA 2700
5/16/64	144	2	10	Lonely Guitar	$20	RCA 2798

vocal background on above 3 albums by the Anita Kerr Singers

All You Gave To Me (9)
Along Came Linda (2,10)
Along The Navajo Trail (2)
Angel On My Shoulder (7)
Annette (5)
Annie Laurie (10)
Anytime (1)
Ball Ha'i (7)
Battle, The (3)
Beach Bound (9)
Because They're Young (4) 4
Big 'Liza (5)
Blowin' Up A Storm (9)
Blueberry Hill (3)
Bonnie Came Back (4) 26
Born To Be With You (7)
Brenda Medley (5)
Cannonball (1,4) 15
Carol (5)
Climb, The (8)
Connie (5)
Country Twist (6)

Creamy Mashed Potatoes (8)
Cryin' Happy Tears (10)
(Dance With The) Guitar Man (8) 12
Danny Boy (10)
Dear Lady Twist (6)
Detour (3)
Easy (3)
Exactly Like You (6)
First Love, First Tears (4) 59
Forty Miles Of Bad Road (4) 9
Fuzz (2)
Giddy Goose (9)
Guitar Child (9)
Guitar'd And Feathered (9)
Gunsmoke (10)
Hard Times (2)
He's So Fine (9)
HI-Lill, Hi-Lo (7)
High Noon (7)
Home In The Meadow (10)

I Almost Lost My Mind (1)
I'm So Lonesome I Could Cry (10)
Just Because (2)
Last Minute Of Innocence (3)
Let's Twist Again (6)
Limbo Rock (8)
Loco-Locomotion (8)
Lonely One (1,4) 23
Lonesome Road (1)
Long Lonely Days Of Winter (10)
Love Me Tender (7)
Lover (2)
Loving You (1)
Mary Ann (5)
Memories Of Madrid (7)
Miriam (7)
Miss Twist (8)
Moanin' 'N' Twistin' (6)
Mona Lisa (5)

Moon Children, Theme For (4)
Moon River (7)
Moovin' N' Groovin' (1,4) 72
Mr. Guitar Man (7)
My Baby Plays The Same Old Song On His Guitar All Night Long (9)
My Blue Heaven (3) 50
My Destiny (10)
Nashville Stomp (8)
New Hully Gully (8)
Night Train To Memphis (3)
Only Child (2)
Patricia (5)
Peppermint Twist (6)
Peter Gunn (2) 27
Popeye (The Hitchhiker) (8)
Quiet Three (4) 46
Quiniela (2)
Ramrod (1) 27
Rebel-'Rouser (1,4) 6

Rebel Walk (3)
Route #1 (3)
Scrape, The (8)
Secret Love (7)
Shenandoah (10)
Sioux City Sue (5)
Soldier Boy (9)
Some Kind-A Earthquake (4) 37
Someday The Rainbow (10)
Soul Twist (9)
Spanish Twist (8)
St. Louis Blues (3)
Stalkin' (1)
Sugartime Twist (6)
Summer Kiss (10)
Sweet Cindy (5)
Tammy (7)
Three-30-Blues (1)
Tiger Love & Turnip Greens (3)
Trambone (3)
Trouble In Mind (2)

Tuesday (5)
Tuxedo Junction (2)
Twist, The (6)
Twistin' 'N' Twangin' (6)
Twisting Off A Cliff (6)
Unchained Melody (7)
Walk Right In (9)
Walkin' 'N' Twistin' (I'm Walkin') (6)
Waltz Of The Wind (8)
When I Fall In Love (7)
Wild Watusi (8)
"Yep!" (2) 30
You Are My Sunshine (3)

EDEN'S CHILDREN

Boston-based rock trio led by Richard "Sham" Schamach.

DEBUT DATE	PEAK POS	WKS CHR	#	Album Title	$	Label & Number
3/9/68	196	2	1	Eden's Children	$15	ABC 624

Don't Tell Me
Goodbye Girl
I Wonder Why
If She's Right
Just Let Go
Knocked Out
My Bad Habit
Out Where The Light Fish Live
Stone Fox

EDGE, Graeme, Band featuring Adrian Gurvitz

British rock group led by the Moody Blues' drummer Edge.

DEBUT DATE	PEAK POS	WKS CHR	#	Album Title	$	Label & Number
10/11/75	107	9	1	Kick Off Your Muddy Boots	$10	Threshold 15
7/9/77	164	4	2	Paradise Ballroom	$10	London 686

All Is Fair In Love (2)
Bareback Rider (1)
Caroline (2)
Down, Down, Down (2)
Everybody Needs Somebody (2)
Gew Janna Woman (1)
Have You Ever Wondered (1)
Human (1)
In Dreams (1)
In The Night Of The Light (2)
Lost In The Light (2)
My Life's Not Wasted (1)
Paradise Ballroom (2)
Shotgun (1)
Somethin' We'd Like To Say (1)
Tunnel, The (1)

EDMUNDS, Dave

Born on 4/15/44 in Cardiff, Wales. Singer/songwriter/guitarist/producer. Formed Love Sculpture in 1967. Formed rockabilly band Rockpile in 1976. Produced for Shakin' Stevens, Brinsley Schwarz and Stray Cats.

DEBUT DATE	PEAK POS	WKS CHR	#	Album Title	$	Label & Number
8/4/79	54	15	1	Repeat When Necessary	$10	Swan Song 8507
5/16/81	48	14	2	Twangin	$8	Swan Song 16034
1/9/82	163	5	3	The Best Of Dave Edmunds [G]	$8	Swan Song 8510
5/1/82	46	14	4	D.E. 7th	$8	Columbia 37930
5/21/83	51	20	5	Information	$8	Columbia 38651
10/13/84	140	4	6	Riff Raff	$8	Columbia 39273
1/31/87	106	12	7	I Hear You Rockin' [L]	$8	Columbia 40603

THE DAVE EDMUNDS BAND
recorded live in London, New York City and Passaic, New Jersey

DEBUT DATE	PEAK POS	WKS CHR	#	Album Title	$	Label & Number
3/24/90	146	6	8	Closer To The Flame	$12	Capitol 90372

A. 1. On The Juke Box (3)
Almost Saturday Night (2,3) 54
Baby Let's Play House (2)
Bad Is Bad (1)
Breaking Out (1)
Busted Loose (6)
Can't Get Enough (6)
Cheap Talk, Patter And Jive (2)
Closer To The Flame (8)
Crawling From The Wreckage (1,3,7)
Creature From The Black Lagoon (1,3)

Dear Dad (4)
Deborah (3)
Deep In The Heart Of Texas (4)
Don't Call Me Tonight (4)
Don't Talk To Me (8)
Don't You Double (5)
Dynamite (1)
Every Time I See Her (8)
Fallin' Through A Hole (8)
Far Away (6)
Feel So Right (5)
From Small Things (Big Things One Day Come) (4)
Generation Rumble (4)
Girls Talk (1,3,7) 65

Goodbye Mr. Good Guy (1)
Hang On (6)
Have A Heart (5)
Here Comes The Weekend (3,7)
Home In My Hand (1)
How Could I Be So Wrong (6)
I Got Your Number (1)
I Hear You Knocking (7)
I Knew The Bride (She Used To Rock And Roll) (3,7)
I Want You Bad (5)
(I'm Gonna Start) Living Again If It Kills Me (5)
I'm Only Human (1)

Information (5,7)
It's Been So Long (2)
Juju Man (3,7)
King Of Love (8)
Louisiana Man (4)
Me And The Boys (4)
Never Take The Place Of You (8)
One More Night (4)
Other Guys Girls (4)
Paralyzed (1)
Paula Meet Jeanne (4)
Queen Of Hearts (1,3,7)
Race Is On (2,3)
Rules Of The Game (6)
S.O.S. (6)

Shape I'm In (5)
Sincerely (8)
Singin' The Blues (2,3)
Slipping Away (5,7) 39
Something About You (6)
Something Happens (4)
Stay With Me Tonight (8)
Steel Claw (6)
Stockholm (8)
Sweet Little Lisa (1)
Take Me For A Little While (1)
Test Of Love (8)
Three Time Loser (2)
Trouble Boys (3)
Wait (5)

Wanderer, The (7)
Warmed Over Kisses (Left Over Love) (4)
Watch On My Wrist (5)
We Were Both Wrong (4)
What Have I Got To Do To Win? (5)
You'll Never Get Me Up (In One Of Those) (2)

DEBUT DATE	PEAK POS	WKS CHR	G O L D	ARTIST — Album Title	$	Label & Number

ED O. G & DA BULLDOGS
Rap outfit led by rapper Edward Anderson, a.k.a. ED O. G which stands for Every Day, Other Girls. BULLDOGS stands for Black United Leaders Living Directly On Groovin' Sounds.

| 5/18/91 | 166 | 1 | | Life Of A Kid In The Ghetto .... | $12 | PWL Amer. 848326 |

Be A Father To Your Child
Bug-A-Boo

Dedicated To The Right
Wingers
Feel Like A Nut

Gotta Have Money (If You
Ain't Got Money, You Ain't
Got Jack)

I Got To Have It
I'm Different
Let Me Tickle Your Fancy

Life Of A Kid In The Ghetto
She Said It Was Great

Speak Upon It
Stop (Think For A Moment)

EDWARD BEAR
Pop trio from Toronto — Larry Evoy, lead singer. Took name from a character in *Winnie The Pooh*.

| 2/10/73 | 63 | 16 | 1 | Edward Bear .... | $10 | Capitol 11157 |
| 7/7/73 | 183 | 6 | 2 | Close Your Eyes .... | $10 | Capitol 11192 |

All The Lights (2)
Back Home Again (1)
Best Friend (1)
Black Pete (1)

Cachet County (1)
Close Your Eyes (2) 37
Does Your Mother Know (2)
Ease Me Down (1)

Edgware Station (1)
Fly Across The Sea (1)
Fool (2)
Haven't You Touched Her (2)

I Love Her (You Love Me) (2)
Last Song (1) 3
Masquerade (1)
Nowhere Is Karen Around (2)

Private School Girls (1)
Some Sunny Day (2)
Walking On Back (1)
What You Done (2)

EDWARDS, Dennis
Born on 2/3/43 in Birmingham, Alabama. Lead singer of The Contours until 1968. Lead singer of The Temptations from 1968-77, 1980-84 and 1987-present.

| 3/3/84 | 48 | 27 | | Don't Look Any Further .... | $8 | Gordy 6057 |

Another Place In Time
Can't Fight It

Don't Look Any Further 72
I Thought I Could Handle It

I'm Up For You
Just Like You

Let's Go Up

Shake Hands (Come Out
Dancin')

(You're My) Aphrodisiac

EDWARDS, Jonathan
Born on 7/28/46 in Minnesota. Formed bluegrass band Sugar Creek in 1965.

| 11/20/71+ | 42 | 20 | 1 | Jonathan Edwards .... | $10 | Capricorn 862 |
| 11/18/72 | 167 | 9 | 2 | Honky-Tonk Stardust Cowboy .... | $10 | Atco 7015 |

Athens County (1)
Ballad Of Upsy Daisy (2)
Cold Snow (1)
Don't Cry Blue (1)
Dream Song (2)

Dues Days Bar (2)
Dusty Morning (1)
Emma (1)
Everybody Knows Her (1)
Everything (2)

Give Us A Song (2)
Honky-Tonk Stardust
Cowboy (2)
It's A Beautiful Day (2)
Jesse (1)

King, The (1)
Longest Ride (2)
Morning Train (2)
Paper Doll (2)
Shanty (1)

Sometimes (1)
Stop And Start It All Again
(2)
Sugar Babe (2)
Sunshine (1) 4

That's What Our Life Is (2)
Train Of Glory (1)

EDWARDS, Vincent
Born Vincento Eduardo Zoine on 7/9/28 in New York City. Stage, film and TV actor. Best known as star of the TV series *Ben Casey*.

| 7/7/62 | 5 | 21 | 1 | Vincent Edwards Sings .... | $20 | Decca 4311 |
| 12/29/62+ | 125 | 6 | 2 | Sometimes I'm Happy...Sometimes I'm Blue ...... | $20 | Decca 4336 |

And Now (1)
As Time Goes By (1)
Blue Prelude (2)
Cheek To Cheek (2)
Don't Worry 'Bout Me
(1) 72

Everybody's Got A Home
But Me (1)
Glad To Be Unhappy (2)
Harbor Lights (2)
How Deep Is The Ocean
(How High Is The Sky) (1)

I Got It Bad (And That Ain't
Good) (1)
I Gotta Right To Sing The
Blues (2)
I'll Walk Alone (1)
Lonesome Road (1)
Make Someone Happy (2)

Polka Dots And Moonbeams
(2)
Say It Isn't So (2)
Sometimes I'm Happy (2)
Stormy Weather (Keeps
Rainin' All The Time) (1)
Thrill Is Gone (2)

Try A Little Tenderness (1)
Unchained Melody (1)
When I Fall In Love (1)
You Stepped Out Of A
Dream (2)
You've Changed (2)

EGAN, Walter
Born on 7/12/48 in Jamaica, New York.

5/14/77	137	6	1	Fundamental Roll	$8	Columbia 34679
4/15/78	44	31	2	Not Shy	$8	Columbia 35077
				above 2 feature Stevie Nicks and Lindsey Buckingham		
5/28/83	187	2	3	Wild Exhibitions	$8	Backstreet 5400

Animal Lover (3)
Blonde In The Blue T-Bird (2)
Feel So Good (1)
Finally Find A Girlfriend (2)
Fool Moon Fire (3) 46
Girl Next Door (3)

Hot Summer Nights (2) 55
I Wannit (2)
I'd Rather Have Fun (1)
I'll Be There (3)
Just The Wanting (2)
Like No Other One (3)

Magnet And Steel (2) 8
Make It Alone (1)
Maybe Maybe (3)
Only The Lucky (1) 82
She's So Tough (1)
Star In The Dust (2)

Star Of My Heart (3)
Stay All Night (3)
Such A Shame (3)
Surfin' & Drivin' (1)
Sweet South Breeze (2)
Tammy Ann (3)

Too Much Love (3)
Tunnel O' Love (1)
Unloved (2)
Waitin' (1)
When I Get My Wheels (1)
Where's The Party (1)

Won't You Say You Will (1)
Yes I Guess I Am (1)

EGG CREAM featuring ANDY ADAMS
Rock quartet led by singer/songwriter Andy Adams (b: 3/3/51 in Brooklyn).

| 5/28/77 | 197 | 4 | | Egg Cream .... | $8 | Pyramid 9008 |

Can I Stay
Dark Nite Blue Lite Ladies

Good Strong Hearted Band
I Never Wanted To

I Think It's Time We Met
I Wanna Be With You

Maybe Tonite
My Destruction

Until The End
Woman

EGYPTIAN LOVER
Los Angeles techno-funk vocalist Greg Broussard. Former DJ.

| 2/9/85 | 146 | 10 | | On The Nile .... | $8 | Egyptian E. 0663 |

And My Beat Goes Boom
Computer Love (Sweet
Dreams)

Egypt Egypt
Girls
I Cry (Night After Night)

My House (On The Nile)
Unreal

What Is A D.J. If He Can't
Scratch

8TH DAY, The
Five-man, three-woman group of R&B session musicians from Detroit. Assembled by producers Holland-Dozier-Holland in 1966.

| 8/7/71 | 131 | 16 | | 8th Day .... | $10 | Invictus 7306 |

Enny-Meeny-Miny-Mo
(Three's A Crowd)
I Can't Fool Myself

I'm Worried
I've Come To Save You
Just As Long

La-De-Dah
**She's Not Just Another
Woman** 11

Too Many Cooks (Spoil The
Soup)

**You've Got To Crawl
(Before You Walk)** 28

ELBERT, Donnie
Vocalist/multi-instrumentalist. Born on 5/25/36 in New Orleans; died on 1/26/89. First recorded for DeLuxe in 1957. A&R director for Polygram Records, Canada, in the mid-1980s.

| 1/1/72 | 153 | 9 | | Where Did Our Love Go .... | $12 | All Platinum 3007 |

**Can't Get Over Losing
You 98**
Get Myself Together

If I Can't Have You
Little Piece Of Leather

One Thousand Nine
Hundred Seventy Years
Sweet Baby 92

That's If You Love Me
What Can I Do 61
Where Did Our Love Go 15

Will You Ever Be Mine

DEBUT DATE	PEAK POS	WKS CHR	G O L D	ARTIST — Album Title	$	Label & Number

EL CHICANO
Mexican-American band formed in Los Angeles as the VIP's in 1965, featuring Jerry Salas (lead vocals).

DEBUT DATE	PEAK POS	WKS CHR	GOLD	#	Album Title	$	Label & Number
6/13/70	51	17		1	Viva Tirado .... [I]	$12	Kapp 3632
4/17/71	178	9		2	Revolucion	$12	Kapp 3640
5/6/72	173	13		3	Celebration	$12	Kapp 3663
8/4/73	162	16		4	El Chicano	$10	MCA 312
4/6/74	194	3		5	Cinco	$10	MCA 401

Ahora Si (5)
El Grito (3)
La Cucuracha (3)
(Se Fue Mi) Cha Chita (4)
Viva La Raza (2)
Brown Eyed Girl (3) **45**
Eleanor Rigby (1)
Latin One (5)
Senor Blues (3)
Viva Tirado - Part 1 (1,3) **28**
Cantaloupe Island (1)
Enchanted Forest (4)
Light My Fire (1)
Sometimes I Feel Like A
We've Only Just Begun (4)
Chicano Chant (2)
Gringo En Mexico (5)
Little Sunflower (5)
Motherless Child (1)
What You Don't Know Won't
Children (5)
Hurt So Bad (1)
Look Of Love (1)
Spanish Grease (2)
Hurt You (5)
Coming Home Baby (1)
I Feel Free (3)
Make It All Go (2)
Sugar Sugar (2)
What's Going On (4)
Cubano Chant (2)
I'm A Good Woman (2)
Mas Zacate (3)
Sunday Kind Of Mood (4)
You've Been Wrong So Long
Don't Put Me Down (If I'm
In A Silent Way (3)
Quiet Village (1)
Tell Her She's Lovely (4) **40**
(5)
Brown) (2)
Juntos (3)
Sabor A Mi (4)
Together (4)
El Cayuco (5)
Keep On Moving (2)
Satisfy Me Woman (3)
Un-Mundo (4)

EL COCO
Los Angeles-based disco sextet led by producers Laurin Rinder and Michael Lewis.

DEBUT DATE	PEAK POS	WKS CHR	GOLD		Album Title	$	Label & Number
10/15/77+	82	23			Cocomotion	$8	AVI 6012

Cocomotion 44
Got That Feeling
I'm Mad As Hell
Love To The World
We Call It Disco
You're My Everything

ELECTRIC BOYS
Swedish male rock quartet: Conny Bloom (vocals), Andy Christell, Franco Santunione and Niclas Sigevall.

DEBUT DATE	PEAK POS	WKS CHR	GOLD		Album Title	$	Label & Number
6/2/90	90	20			Funk-O-Metal Carpet Ride	$12	Atco 91337

All Lips N' Hips 76
Change
Electrified
Into The Woods
Rags To Riches
Captain Of My Soul
Cheek To Check
If I Had A Car
Psychedelic Eyes
Who Are You

ELECTRIC FLAG
Chicago rock-blues band formed by Mike Bloomfield and Buddy Miles.

DEBUT DATE	PEAK POS	WKS CHR	GOLD	#	Album Title	$	Label & Number
4/20/68	31	35		1	A Long Time Comin'	$15	Columbia 9597
1/18/69	76	12		2	The Electric Flag	$15	Columbia 9714

Another Country (1)
Killing Floor (1)
Nothing To Do (2)
She Should Have Just (1)
Texas (1)
You Don't Realize (1)
Easy Rider (1)
My Woman That Hangs
Over-Lovin' You (1)
Sittin' In Circles (1)
Wine (1)
Groovin' Is Easy (1)
Around The House (2)
Qualified (2)
Soul Searchin' (2)
With Time There Is Change
Hey, Little Girl (2)
Mystery (2)
See To Your Neighbor (2)
Sunny (2)
(2)

ELECTRIC INDIAN, The
Instrumental group assembled from top Philadelphia studio musicians. Some members later joined MFSB.

DEBUT DATE	PEAK POS	WKS CHR	GOLD		Album Title	$	Label & Number
10/4/69	104	9			Keem-O-Sabe .... [I]	$12	United Art. 6728

Geronimo
Keem-O-Sabe 16
Only The Strong Survive
Storm Warning
I Heard It Through The
My Cherie Amour
Rain Dance
What Does It Take To Win
Grapevine
1-2-3
Spinning Wheel
Your Love

★★147★★ ELECTRIC LIGHT ORCHESTRA
Orchestral rock band formed in Birmingham, England in 1971, by Roy Wood, Bev Bevan and Jeff Lynne of The Move. Wood left after their first album, leaving Lynne as the group's leader. Much personnel shuffling from then on. Among various members: Kelly Groucutt (keyboards) and Mike Kaminski (violin). From a group size of eight in 1971, the 1986 ELO consisted of three members: Lynne (vocals, guitar, keyboards), Bevan (drums) and Richard Tandy (keyboards, guitar). Bevan also recorded with Black Sabbath in 1987. Lynne is a member of the supergroup Traveling Wilburys.

DEBUT DATE	PEAK POS	WKS CHR	GOLD	#	Album Title	$	Label & Number
6/3/72	196	2		1	No Answer	$12	United Art. 5573
3/3/73	172	8		2	Split Ends .... [K]	$12	United Art. 5666
					THE MOVE includes singles releases plus bulk of the 1971 album *Message from the Country*		
4/21/73	62	22		3	Electric Light Orchestra II	$12	United Art. 040
12/29/73+	52	24		4	On The Third Day	$12	United Art. 188
10/19/74	16	32	●	5	Eldorado	$12	United Art. 339
10/25/75+	8	48	●	6	Face The Music	$12	United Art. 546
7/4/76	32	43	●	7	Ole ELO .... [K]	$12	United Art. 630
10/30/76+	5	69	▲	8	A New World Record	$12	United Art. 679
11/26/77+	4	58	▲	9	Out Of The Blue	$15	Jet 823 [2]
6/23/79	5	35	▲	10	Discovery	$10	Jet 35769
12/8/79+	30	15	▲	11	ELO's Greatest Hits .... [G]	$10	Jet 36310
7/12/80	4	36	▲	12	Xanadu .... [S]	$8	MCA 6100
					side 1: Olivia Newton-John; side 2: Electric Light Orchestra		
8/22/81	16	20	●	13	Time	$8	Jet 37371
7/16/83	36	16		14	Secret Messages	$8	Jet 38490
3/1/86	49	15		15	Balance Of Power	$8	CBS Assoc. 40048

Above The Clouds (8)
Can't Get It Out Of My
Ella James (2)
Here Is The News (13)
Kuiama (3,7)
Midnight Blue (10)
Across The Border (9)
Head (5,7,11) **9**
Endless Lies (15)
Hold On Tight (13) **10**
Laredo Tornado (5)
Minister, The (2)
All Over The World (12) **13**
China Town (2)
Evil Woman (6,7,11) **10**
I'm Alive (12) **16**
Last Train To London
Mission (A World Record) (8)
Another Heart Breaks (13)
Confusion (10) **37**
Fall, The (12)
Illusions In G Major (5)
(10) **39**
Mister Kingdom (5)
Battle Of Marston Moor
Danger Ahead (14)
Fire On High (6)
In Old England Town
Letter From Spain (14)
Mr. Blue Sky (9,11) **35**
(July 2nd, 1644) (1)
Daybreaker (4) **87**
First Movement (Jumpin'
(Boogie #2) (3)
Lights Go Down (13)
Mr. Radio (1)
Believe Me Now (9)
Diary Of Horace Wimp (10)
Biz) (1)
In The Hall Of The Mountain
Livin' Thing (8,11) **13**
Need Her Love (10)
Big Wheels (9)
Do Ya (2) **93**
Four Little Diamonds
King (4)
Look At Me Now (1)
Nellie Takes Her Bow (1)
Birmingham Blues (9)
Do Ya (8) **24**
(14) **86**
Is It Alright (15)
Loser Gone Wild (14)
New World (medley) (1)
Bluebird (14)
Don't Bring Me Down (10) **4**
From The End Of The World
It Wasn't My Idea To Dance
Ma-Ma-Ma Belle (4,7,11)
Night In The City (9)
Bluebird Is Dead (4)
Don't Walk Away (12)
(13)
(2)
Mama (3)
Nightrider (6)
Boy Blue (5,7)
Down Home Town (2)
From The Sun To The World
It's Over (9) **75**
Manhattan Rumble (49th
No Time (2)
California Man (2)
Down On The Bay (2)
(Boogie #1) (3)
Jungle (9)
Street Massacre) (1)
Nobody's Child (5)
Calling America (15) **18**
Dreaming Of 4000 (4)
Getting To The Point (15)
King Of The Universe
Message From The Country
Ocean Breakup (medley) (4)
Eldorado (5)
Heaven Only Knows (15)
(medley) (4)
(2)
Oh No Not Susan (4)

225

DEBUT DATE	PEAK POS	WKS CHR	GOLD	ARTIST — Album Title	$	Label & Number

ELECTRIC LIGHT ORCHESTRA — Cont'd

On The Run (10)	Rockaria! (8,11)	So Fine (8)	Sweet Is The Night (9)	Turn To Stone (9,11) 13	Wishing (10)
10538 Overture (1,7)	**Roll Over Beethoven**	So Serious (15)	**Sweet Talkin' Woman**	21st Century Man (13)	Without Someone (15)
One Summer Dream (6)	(3,7) **42**	Sorrow About To Fall (15)	(9,11) **17**	**Twilight** (13) **38**	Words Of Aaron (2)
Poker (6)	Secret Lives (15)	Standin' In The Rain (9)	Take Me On And On (14)	Until Your Mama's Gone (2)	**Xanadu** (12) **8**
Poor Boy (The Greenwood) (5)	Secret Messages (14)	Starlight (9)	**Telephone Line** (8,11) **7**	Waterfall (6)	Yours Truly, 2095 (13)
Queen Of The Hours (1)	Send It (15)	Steppin' Out (9)	Ticket To The Moon (13)	Way Life's Meant To Be (13)	
Rain Is Falling (13)	Shangri-La (8)	**Strange Magic** (6,7,11) **14**	Tightrope (8)	Whale, The (9)	
Rock 'N' Roll Is King	**Shine A Little Love** (10) **8**	Stranger (9)	Tonight (2)	Whisper In The Night (1)	
(14) **19**	**Showdown** (4,7,11) **53**	Summer And Lightning (9)	Train Of Gold (14)	Wild West Hero (9)	

ELECTRIC PRUNES, The
Seattle psychedelic rock quintet — James Lowe, lead singer.

DEBUT	PEAK	WKS		ARTIST — Album Title	$	Label & Number
4/15/67	113	12	1	The Electric Prunes	$25	Reprise 6248
9/2/67	172	4	2	Underground	$25	Reprise 6262
1/6/68	135	13	3	Mass In F Minor [F]	$25	Reprise 6275

electric rock mass, sung in Latin

About A Quarter To Nine (1)	Capt. Glory (1)	Hideaway (2)	King Is In The Counting	Sold To The Highest Bidder
Antique Doll (2)	Children Of Rain (2)	I (2)	House (1)	(1)
Are You Lovin' Me More (But	Dr. Do-Good (2)	**I Had Too Much To Dream**	Long Day's Flight (2)	Train For Tomorrow (1)
Enjoying It Less) (1)	**Get Me To The World On**	**(Last Night)** (1) **11**	Luvin' (1)	Try Me On For Size (1)
Bangles (1)	**Time** (1) **27**	I Happen To Love You (2)	Mass In F Minor (3)	Tunerville Trolley (1)
Big City (2)	Great Banana Hoax (2)	It's Not Fair (2)	Onie (1)	Wind-Up Toys (2)

ELECTRONIC
Collaboration between Manchester, England natives Bernard Sumner (vocalist of New Order) and Johnny Marr (guitarist of The Smiths and The The). Outside contributors include Neil Tennant (Pet Shop Boys) on backing vocals, Anne Dudley (The Art Of Noise) on strings and David Palmer on drums.

DEBUT	PEAK	WKS		ARTIST — Album Title	$	Label & Number
6/15/91	109	15		Electronic	$12	Warner 26387

Feel Every Beat	Get The Message	Idiot Country	Reality	Soviet	Try All You Want
Gangster	**Getting Away With It 38**	Patience Of A Saint	Some Distant Memory	Tighten Up	

ELECTRONIC CONCEPT ORCHESTRA
Studio group directed by Robin McBride.

DEBUT	PEAK	WKS		ARTIST — Album Title	$	Label & Number
10/18/69	175	2		Electric Love [I]	$10	Limelight 86072

featuring Eddie Higgins on the Moog Synthesizer

Goin' Out Of My Head	Je T'Aime...Moi Non Plus	Love Is Blue	Stella By Starlight
I'm Gonna Make You Love	Like A Lover	Misty	This Guy's In Love With You
Me	Look Of Love	Romeo & Juliet Theme	Wichita Lineman

ELEPHANT'S MEMORY
Rock/jazz group formed in New York City's East Village. Backing band on John Lennon's *Some Time In New York City* album, and Yoko Ono's *Approximately Infinite Universe* album.

DEBUT	PEAK	WKS		ARTIST — Album Title	$	Label & Number
5/10/69	200	2		Elephants Memory	$15	Buddah 5033

Band Of Love	Crossroads Of The Stepping	Don't Put Me On Trial No	Hot Dog Man	R.I.P.	Takin' A Walk
Brief Encounter	Stones	More	Jungle Gym At The Zoo	Super Heep	Yogurt Song
			Old Man Willow		

ELEVENTH HOUSE with LARRY CORYELL
Jazz-rock quartet formed by the Texan guitarist.

DEBUT	PEAK	WKS		ARTIST — Album Title	$	Label & Number
4/13/74	163	11	1	Introducing The Eleventh House with Larry Coryell [I]	$10	Vanguard 79342
8/9/75	163	4	2	Level One [I]	$10	Arista 4052

Adam Smasher (1)	Eyes Of Love (2)	Joy Ride (1)	Other Side (1)	Suite Medley (2)
Birdfingers (1)	Funky Waltz (1)	Level One (1)	Right On Y'all (1)	That's The Joint (2)
Diedra (2)	Gratitude "A So Low" (1)	Low-Lee-Tah (1)	Some Greasy Stuff (2)	Yin (1)
Dream, Theme For A (1)	Ism-Ejercicio (1)	Nyctaphobia (2)	Struttin' With Sunshine (2)	

ELFMAN, Danny
Lead singer of Oingo Boingo from Los Angeles.

DEBUT	PEAK	WKS		ARTIST — Album Title	$	Label & Number
6/25/88	118	6	1	Beetlejuice [S]	$8	Geffen 24202

all songs composed and conducted by Elfman except for 2 Harry Belafonte songs: "Day-O" & "Jump in Line (Shake, Shake Senora)"

| 8/26/89 | 30 | 12 | 2 | Batman Original Motion Picture Score [S-I] | $8 | Warner 25977 |

Elfman-composed music performed by the Sinfonia of London Orchestra; songs from and songs inspired by the film *Batman*

| 8/4/90 | 194 | 1 | 3 | Dick Tracy Original Score [S-I] | $12 | Sire 26264 |

Elfman-composed music conducted by Shirley Walker; orchestrations: Steve Bartek

| 1/26/91 | 174 | 3 | 4 | Edward Scissorhands [S-I] | $12 | MCA 10133 |

includes "With These Hands" by Tom Jones; instrumental music composed by Elfman; orchestrations: Steve Bartek

| 7/11/92 | 61 | 5 | 5 | Batman Returns [S-I] | $12 | Warner 26972 |

includes "Face To Face" by Siouxsie And The Banshees

After The "Kid" (3)	Beetlejuice, Main Titles	Descent Into Mystery (2)	Finale, The [Batman	Lydia's Pep Talk (medley) (1)	Story Unfolds (3)
Aftermath, The (1)	From (1)	Dick Tracy, Main Titles	Returns] (5)	Meet The Blank (3)	Storytime (4)
Attack Of The Batwing (2)	Big Boy/Bad Boys (3)	From (4)	First Confrontation (2)	Obituaries (medley) (1)	Tess' Theme (3)
Ballet De Suburbia (Suite) (4)	Birth Of A Penguin (5)	Edwardo The Barber (4)	Flier, The (medley) (1)	Photos (medley) (2)	Tide Turns (Suite) (4)
Bat Cave (2)	Blank Gets The Goods (5)	End, The (4)	Flowers (2)	Rise And Fall From Grace (5)	Travel Music (1)
Batman Returns, End	Book!, The (medley) (1)	Enter..."The Family"	Fly, The (1)	Roasted Dude (2)	Up The Cathedral (2)
Credits (5)	Breathless Comes On (3)	(medley) (1)	Home Sweet Home (medley)	Roof Fight (2)	Waltz To The Death (2)
Batman Theme (2)	Breathless' Theme (3)	Esmeralda (4)	(4)	Rooftops [Dick Tracy] (3)	Wedding, The (1)
Batman To The Rescue (2)	Castle On The Hill (4)	Etiquette Lesson (4)	Ice Dance (4)	Rooftops (medley) [Batman	Wild Ride (medley) (5)
Batman vs. The Circus (5)	Cat Suite (5)	Farewell (1)	In The Model (1)	Returns] (5)	
Beautiful Dreamer (medley)	Cemetery, The (5)	Final Confrontation	Incantation, The (1)	Sand Worm Planet (medley)	
(2)	Charge Of The Batmobile (2)	[Batman] (2)	Joker's Poem (2)	(1)	
Beautiful New World	Chase, The (3)	Final Confrontation [Batman	Juno's Theme (1)	Selina Transforms (5)	
(medley) (4)	Children's Hour (5)	Returns] (5)	Lair, The (5)	Showdown/Reunited (3)	
Beetle-Snake (1)	Clown Attack (2)	Final Confrontation [Edward	Laughs (1)	Showtime! (1)	
Beetlejuice, End Credits	Cookie Factory (4)	Scissorhands] (4)	Love Theme (2)	Slimy D.A. (3)	
From (1)	Crime Spree (3)	Finale [Batman] (2)	Lydia Discovers (1)	Sold (1)	
	Death! (4)		Lydia Strikes A Bargain... (1)	Sore Spots (5)	

226

ELGART, Larry, And His Manhattan Swing Orchestra
Larry was born on 3/20/22 in New London, Connecticut. Alto saxman in brother Les' band and his own band.

6/19/82	24	41 ▲		1 Hooked On Swing .... [I]	$8	RCA 4343
2/12/83	89	14		2 Hooked On Swing 2 .... [I]	$8	RCA 4589

Hooked On A Star Medley (1)	Hooked On Broadway Medley (1)	Hooked On Swing 2 Medley (2)	Hooked On The Roaring '20s Medley (2)	Swing With Bing Medley (2)
Hooked On Astaire Medley (1)	Hooked On Dixie Medley (2)	Hooked On The Blue(s) Medley (1)	Save The Last Dance For Me Medley (2)	Swingin' The Classics Medley (2)
Hooked On Big Bands Medley (1)	Hooked On Swing Medley (1) 31			

ELGART, Les, And His Orchestra
Les was born on 8/3/18 in New Haven, Connecticut. Trumpeter/bandleader since 1945.

11/3/56	13	7		1 The Elgart Touch .... [I]	$20	Columbia 875
8/19/57	14	7		2 For Dancers Also .... [I]	$20	Columbia 1008

Autumn Serenade (1)	For Dancers Also (2)	I Had The Craziest Dream (1)	Stompin' At The Savoy (1)	Where Or When (1)
Boy Next Door (2)	Green Satin (2)	I Hear A Rhapsody (2)	Street Of Dreams (1)	Who Cares (2)
Dancing Sound (1)	High On A Windy Hill (2)	Paradise (2)	Swingin' Down The Lane (1)	Why Do I Love You? (2)
Don't Be That Way (1)	How Long Has This Been Going On? (2)	'S Too Much (2)	Swingy Swan (1)	You Go To My Head (2)
Fascinatin' Rhythm (1)		Slo Roll (1)	Three To Get Ready (1)	You Walk By (2)

ELGART, Les & Larry
Brothers Les and Larry each led his own band in the Forties.

10/10/64	128	5		Command Performance! Les & Larry Elgart Play The Great Dance Hits .... [I]	$15	Columbia 2221

Blues In The Night	My Heart Belongs To Daddy	Sentimental Journey	So Rare	Tuxedo Junction
Jersey Bounce	One O'Clock Jump	Skyliner	Song Of India	Woodchopper's Ball
Mood Indigo				You Made Me Love You (I Didn't Want To Do It)

ELLIMAN, Yvonne
Born on 12/29/51 in Honolulu. Portrayed Mary Magdalene on the concept LP and in the rock opera and film *Jesus Christ Superstar*. Joined with Eric Clapton during his 1974 comeback tour.

3/12/77	68	16		1 Love Me	$8	RSO 3018
3/11/78	40	17		2 Night Flight	$8	RSO 3031
11/10/79	174	6		3 Yvonne	$8	RSO 3038

Baby Don't Let It Mess Your Mind (2)	Greenlight (3)	(I Don't Know Why) I Keep Hangin' On (1)	In A Stranger's Arms (2)	Sally Go 'Round The Roses (2)	Without You (There Ain't No Love At All) (1)
Cold Wind Across My Heart (3)	Hello Stranger (1) 15	I Know (1)	Lady Of The Silver Spoon (2)	Savannah (3)	
Down The Backstairs Of My Life (2)	Hit The Road Jack (medley) (3)	I'd Do It Again (1)	Love Me (1) 14	She'll Be The Home (1)	
Everything Must Change (3)	How Long (3)	I'll Be Around (2)	Love Pains (3) 34	Sticks And Stones (medley) (3)	
Good Sign (1)	I Can't Get You Outa My Mind (1)	I'm Gonna Use What I Got To Get What I Need (3)	Nowhere To Hide (3)	Up To The Man In You (2)	
		If I Can't Have You (2) 1	Prince Of Fools (2)	Uphill Peace Of Mind (1)	
			Rock Me Slowly (3)		
			Sailing Ships (2)		

ELLINGTON, Duke
Born Edward Kennedy Ellington on 4/29/1899 in Washington, D.C. Died on 5/24/74. One of Jazz music's leading bandleader/composer/arrangers. Studied piano since age seven; formed first band around 1918. To New York, in 1923, at Fats Waller's suggestion. In late 1927, began five-year association with the famous Cotton Club. His 50-minute suite, *Black, Brown, and Beige*, was introduced at Carnegie Hall in 1943. Worked with noted arranger/composer Billy Strayhorn from 1939 on. Won Grammy's Lifetime Achievement Award (1966) and Trustees Award (1968).

6/24/57	14	1		1 Ellington At Newport .... [I-L]	$30	Columbia 934
				recorded at the Newport Jazz Festival on 7/7/56		
10/3/64	133	7		2 Ellington '65: Hits of the 60's/This Time By Ellington .... [I]	$20	Reprise 6122
5/14/66	145	3		3 The Duke At Tanglewood .... [I-L]	$15	RCA 2857
				DUKE ELLINGTON/BOSTON POPS/ARTHUR FIEDLER		
2/24/68	78	13		4 Francis A. & Edward K.	$15	Reprise 1024
				FRANK SINATRA & DUKE ELLINGTON		

All I Need Is The Girl (4)	Do Nothin' 'Til You Hear From Me (3)	I Left My Heart In San Francisco (2)	Love Scene (3)	Poor Butterfly (4)
Blowin' In The Wind (2)	Fly Me To The Moon (In Other Words) (2)	I Let A Song Go Out Of My Heart (3)	Mooch, The (3)	Satin Doll (3)
Call Me Irresponsible (2)	Follow Me (4)	I Like The Sunrise (4)	Mood Indigo (3)	Second Time Around (2)
Caravan (3)	Hello, Dolly! (2)	I'm Beginning To See The Light (3)	More (2)	Solitude (3)
Come Back To Me (4)	I Got It Bad And That Ain't Good (3)	Indian Summer (4)	Never On Sunday (2)	Sophisticated Lady (3)
Danke Schoen (2)		Jeep's Blues (1)	Newport Jazz Festival Suite Medley (1)	Stranger On The Shore (2)
Diminuendo And Crescendo In Blue (1)			Peking Theme (So Little Time) (2)	Sunny (4)
				Timon Of Athens March (3)
				Yellow Days (4)

ELLIOT, Cass — see MAMA CASS

EL RAYO-X — see LINDLEY, David

ELY, Joe
Country singer. Born on 2/9/47 in Amarillo, Texas; raised in Lubbock. Member of the Buzzin' Cousins, group that appeared in the 1992 film *Falling from Grace*.

4/11/81	135	11		1 Musta Notta Gotta Lotta	$8	SouthCoast 5183
10/24/81	159	3		2 Live Shots .... [L]	$8	SouthCoast 5262

Bet Me (1)	Fingernails (2)	Hold On (1)	I Keep Gettin' Paid The Same (1)	Midnight Shift (2)	She Never Spoke Spanish To Me (2)
Boxcars (2)	Fools Fall In Love (2)	Honky Tonk Masquerade (2)		Musta Notta Gotta Lotta (1)	Wishin' For You (1)
Dallas (1)	Good Rockin' Tonight (1)	Honky Tonkin' (2)	Johnny's Blues (2)	Road Hawg (1)	
Dam Of My Heart (1)	Hard Livin' (2)	I Had My Hopes Up High (2)	Long Snake Moan (2)	Rock Me My Baby (1)	

EMERSON, Keith
Keyboardist of Emerson, Lake & Palmer and The Nice. Born on 11/1/44 in Lancashire, England. Also see Nice.

5/2/81	183	3		Nighthawks .... [S-I]	$8	Backstreet 5196
				soundtrack produced, composed and performed by Emerson		

Bust, The	Chopper, The	Flight Of A Hawk	I'm Comin' In	Nighthawks - Main Title Theme	Tramway
Chase, The	Face To Face	I'm A Man	Mean Stalkin'		
			Nighthawking		

DEBUT DATE	PEAK POS	WKS CHR	GOLD		ARTIST — Album Title	$	Label & Number

★★186★★ EMERSON, LAKE & PALMER

English classical-oriented rock trio formed in 1969. Consisted of Keith Emerson (with The Nice; keyboards), Greg Lake (King Crimson; vocals, bass, guitars) and Carl Palmer (Atomic Rooster, Crazy World of Arthur Brown; drums). Group split up in 1979, with Palmer joining supergroup Asia. Emerson and Lake re-grouped in 1986 with new drummer Cozy Powell. Palmer returned in 1987, replacing Powell who joined Black Sabbath in 1990.

DEBUT DATE	PEAK POS	WKS CHR	GOLD	#	ARTIST — Album Title	$	Label & Number
2/6/71	18	42	●	1	Emerson, Lake & Palmer	$15	Cotillion 9040
7/3/71	9	26	●	2	Tarkus	$15	Cotillion 9900
1/22/72	10	23	●	3	Pictures At An Exhibition [L]	$12	Cotillion 66666
					based on Mussorgsky's classical composition		
7/29/72	5	37	●	4	Trilogy	$12	Cotillion 9903
12/15/73+	11	47	●	5	Brain Salad Surgery	$10	Manticore 66669
9/7/74	4	24	●	6	Welcome back, my friends, to the show that never ends- Ladies and Gentlemen [L]	$20	Manticore 200 [3]
4/9/77	12	26	●	7	Works, Volume 1	$10	Atlantic 7000 [2]
12/10/77+	37	14	●	8	Works, Volume 2	$8	Atlantic 19147
					above 2 albums feature mostly solo material		
12/9/78+	55	9	●	9	Love Beach	$8	Atlantic 19211
12/1/79	73	10		10	Emerson, Lake & Palmer In Concert [L]	$8	Atlantic 19255
					from the 1978 U.S.A.-Canadian tour		
11/29/80	108	7		11	The Best Of Emerson, Lake & Palmer [G]	$8	Atlantic 19283
6/28/86	23	12		12	Emerson, Lake & Powell	$8	Polydor 829297
					EMERSON, LAKE & POWELL		
6/27/92	78	4		13	Black Moon	$12	Victory 80003

Abaddon's Bolero (4)
Affairs Of The Heart (13)
All I Want Is You (9)
Aquatarkus (2)
Are You Ready Eddy? (2)
Bach: Two Part Invention In D Minor (7)
Barbarian, The (1)
Barrelhouse Shake-Down (8)
Battlefield (2)
Benny The Bouncer (5)
Better Days (13)
Bitches Crystal (2)
Black Moon (13)
Blues Variation (3)
Brain Salad Surgery (8)
Bullfrog (8)
Burning Bridges (13)
C'est La Vie [solo: Greg Lake] (7) **91**
C'est La Vie (10)

Canario (9)
Changing States (13)
Close But Not Touching (8)
Closer To Believing (7)
Close To Home (13)
Curse Of Baba Yaga (3)
End, The (medley) (3)
Endless Enigma (Parts 1 & 2) (4)
Enemy God Dances With The Black Spirits (7,10)
Eruption (2)
Fanfare For The Common Man (7,11)
Farewell To Arms (13)
Food For Your Soul (7)
Footprints In The Snow (13)
For You (9)
From The Beginning (4) **39**
Fugue (4)
Gambler, The (9)

Gnome, The (3)
Great Gates Of Kiev (medley) (3)
Hallowed Be Thy Name (7)
Hoedown (4)
Honky Tonk Blues (8)
Hut Of Baba Yaga (3)
I Believe In Father Christmas [solo: Greg Lake] (8) **95**
Iconoclast (2)
Infinite Space (2)
Jeremy Bender (2,6)
Jerusalem (5,6,11)
Karn Evil 9 (5,6,7,11)
Knife Edge (1,10)
L.A. Nights (7)
Lay Down Your Guns (12)
Learning To Fly (12)
Lend Your Love To Me Tonight (7)

Living Sin (4)
Love Beach (9)
Love Blind (12)
Lucky Man (1,11) **48**
Manticore (2)
Maple Leaf Rag (8)
Mars, The Bringer Of War (12)
Mass (2)
Memoirs Of An Officer And A Gentleman Medley (9)
Miracle, The (12)
New Orleans (7)
Nobody Loves You Like I Do (7)
Nutrocker (medley) (3) **70**
Old Castle (3)
Only Way (2)
Paper Blood (13)
Peter Gunn (10,11)
Piano Concerto No. 1 (7,10)

Piano Improvisations (6)
Pictures At An Exhibition (10)
Pirates (7)
Promenade (3)
Romeo And Juliet (13)
Sage, The (3)
Score, The (12)
Sheriff, The (4,6)
Show Me The Way To Go Home (8)
So Far To Fall (8)
Step Aside (12)
Still....You Turn Me On (5,11)
Stones Of Years (2)
Take A Pebble (1,6)
Tank (1,7)
Tarkus (2)
Taste Of My Love (9)
Three Fates Medley (1)

Tiger In A Spotlight (8,10,11)
Time And A Place (2)
Toccata (5,6)
Touch & Go (12) **60**
Trilogy (4,11)
Watching Over You (8)
When The Apple Blossoms Bloom In The Windmills Of Your Mind I'll Be Your Valentine(8)

EMF

Techno-funk band from Forest of Dean, England: James Atkin (vocals), Ian Dench, Mark Decloedt, Zac Foley and Derry Brownson. EMF stands for the name of New Order groupies called the Epson Mad Funkers.

DEBUT DATE	PEAK POS	WKS CHR	GOLD	#	ARTIST — Album Title	$	Label & Number
6/1/91	12	36	▲		Schubert Dip	$12	EMI 96238

Admit It
Children

Girl Of An Age
I Believe

Lies 18
Long Summer Days

Longtime
Travelling Not Running

Unbelievable 1
When You're Mine

EMOTIONS, The

Black female trio from Chicago, consisting of sisters Wanda (lead), Sheila and Jeanette Hutchinson. First worked as a child gospel group called the Heavenly Sunbeams. Left gospel, became The Emotions in 1968. Jeanette replaced by cousin Theresa Davis in 1970, and later by sister Pamela. Jeanette returned to group in 1978.

DEBUT DATE	PEAK POS	WKS CHR	GOLD	#	ARTIST — Album Title	$	Label & Number
8/28/76	45	27	●	1	Flowers	$10	Columbia 34163
6/25/77	7	33	▲	2	Rejoice	$10	Columbia 34762
12/3/77+	88	15		3	Sunshine [E]	$10	Stax 4100
					reissue of Volt label recordings		
8/26/78	40	12	●	4	Sunbeam	$8	Columbia 35385
12/8/79	96	10		5	Come Into Our World	$8	ARC 36149
9/26/81	168	4		6	New Affair	$8	ARC 37456

Ain't No Doubt About It (4)
Ain't No Sunshine (3)
All Night, Alright (4)
Anyway You Look At It (3)
Baby, I'm Through (3)
Best Of My Love (2) **1**
Blessed (2)
Cause I Love You (5)
Come Into My World (5)
Don't Ask My Neighbors (2) **44**
Feeling Is (2)
Flowers (1) **87**

Gee Whiz (Look At His Eyes) (3)
God Will Take Care Of You (1)
Here You Come Again (6)
How Can You Stop Loving Someone (1)
How'd I Know That Love Would Slip Away (2)
I Don't Wanna Lose Your Love (1) **51**
I Really Miss You (3)
I Should Be Dancing (5)

I Wouldn't Lie (4)
Innocent (3)
Key To My Heart (2)
Layed Back (5)
Long Way To Go (2)
Love Is Right On (4)
Love Lies (6)
Love Vibes (4)
Love's What's Happenin' (2)
Me For You (1)
Movie, The (5)
Music Box (4)
My Everything (4)

New Affair (6)
No Plans For Tomorrow (1)
Now That I Know (6)
On & On (5)
Put A Little Love Away (3) **73**
Rejoice (2)
Runnin' Back (And Forth) (4)
Shouting Out Love (3)
Smile (4)
Special Part (1)
Spirit Of Summer (4)

There'll Never Be Another Moment (6)
Time Is Passing By (4)
Turn It Out (6)
Walking The Line (4)
We Go Through Changes (1)
What's The Name Of Your Love? (5)
When You Gonna Wake Up (6)
Where Is Your Love? (5)
Whole Lot Of Shakin' (4)
Yes, I Am (5)

You've Got The Right To Know (1)

ENCHANTMENT

Soul quintet formed in 1966 at Pershing High School in Detroit. Did soundtrack for the film *Deliver Us From Evil*.

DEBUT DATE	PEAK POS	WKS CHR	GOLD	#	ARTIST — Album Title	$	Label & Number
3/5/77	104	19		1	Enchantment	$10	United Art. 682
1/21/78	46	21		2	Once Upon A Dream	$8	Roadshow 811
3/17/79	145	8		3	Journey To The Land Of...Enchantment	$8	Roadshow 3269

ENCHANTMENT — Cont'd

Angel In My Life (2)
Anyway You Want It (3)
Come On And Ride (1)
Dance To The Music (1)
Forever More (3)
Fun (3)
Future Gonna Get You (3)
Gloria (1) **25**
Hold On (1)
I Wanna Boogie (3)
If You're Ready (Here It Comes) (2)
It's You That I Need (2) **33**
Journey (3)
Let Me Entertain You (3)
Love Melodies (3)
Magnetic Feel (3)
My Rose (1)
Oasis Of Love (3)
Sexy Lady (1)
Silly Love Song (2)
Sunny Shine Feeling (2)
Sunshine (1) **45**
Thank You Girl For Loving Me (1)
Trying To Get Over (With You) (2)
Up Higher (2)
Where Do We Go From Here (3)
You Must Be An Angel (2)
You're The One (2)

ENGLAND DAN & JOHN FORD COLEY
Pop duo from Austin, Texas: Dan Seals (b: 2/8/48) and Coley (b: 10/13/48). In the late '60s, both were members of Southwest F.O.B. Dan, the brother of Jim Seals of Seals & Crofts, charted solo pop hits and is currently a top country artist.

DEBUT DATE	PEAK POS	WKS CHR	G O L D	ARTIST — Album Title	$	Label & Number
8/21/76	17	31	●	1 Nights Are Forever	$10	Big Tree 89517
4/23/77	80	15		2 Dowdy Ferry Road	$10	Big Tree 76000
4/8/78	61	14		3 Some Things Don't Come Easy	$8	Big Tree 76006
4/14/79	106	12		4 Dr. Heckle And Mr. Jive	$8	Big Tree 76015
1/5/80	194	2		5 Best Of England Dan & John Ford Coley	[G] $8	Big Tree 76018

Another Golden Oldie Night For Wendy (4)
Beyond The Tears (3)
Broken Hearted Me (4)
Calling For You Again (3)
Caught Up In The Middle (4)
Children Of The Half-Light (4)
Don't Feel That Way No More (2)
Dowdy Ferry Road (2)
Everything's Gonna Be Alright (1)
Falling Stars (2,5)
Gone Too Far (2,5) **23**
Hold Me (3)
Hollywood Heckle & Jive (4)
I'd Really Love To See You Tonight (1,5) **2**
I'll Stay (1)
If The World Ran Out Of Love Tonight (3)
In It For Love (5) **75**
It's Not The Same (1)
It's Sad To Belong (2,5) **21**
Just The Two Of Us (3)
Lady (1)
Long Way Home (1)
Love Is The Answer (4,5) **10**
Love Is The One Thing We Hide (2)
Lovin' Somebody On A Rainy Night (3)
Nights Are Forever Without You (1,5) **10**
Only A Matter Of Time (4)
Prisoner, The (1)
Rolling Fever (4)
Running After You (4)
Showboat Gambler (1)
Soldier In The Rain (2,5)
Some Things Don't Come Easy (3)
There'll Never Be Another For Me (1)
Wanting You Desperately (3)
We'll Never Have To Say Goodbye Again (3,5) **9**
Westward Wind (1)
What Can I Do With This Broken Heart (4,5) **50**
What's Forever For (4)
Where Do I Go From Here (2)
Who's Lonely Now (3,5)
Why Is It Me (5)
You Can't Dance (3) **49**
You Know We Belong Together (2)

ENGLISH BEAT
Ska (reggae/R&B mix) group formed in Birmingham, England: Dave Wakeling (vocals), Andy Cox (guitar), Dave Steele (bass), Everett Martin (drums), Ranking Roger (Roger Charley; vocals) and Saxa (saxophonist formerly with Prince Buster). Split in 1983. Wakeling and Roger formed General Public. Cox and Steele formed Fine Young Cannibals.

DEBUT DATE	PEAK POS	WKS CHR	G O L D	ARTIST — Album Title	$	Label & Number
8/9/80	142	14		1 I Just Can't Stop It	$8	Sire 6091
6/27/81	126	6		2 Wha'ppen?	$8	Sire 3567
11/13/82+	39	44		3 Special Beat Service	$8	I.R.S. 70032
12/17/83+	87	22		4 What Is Beat?	[K] $8	I.R.S. 70040

Ackee 1 2 3 (3)
All Out To Get You (2)
Best Friend (1,4)
Big Shot (1)
Can't Get Used To Losing You (1,4)
Cheated (2)
Click Click (1)
Doors Of Your Heart (2,4)
Dream Home In NZ (2)
Drowning (2)
End Of The Party (3)
French Toast (Soleil Trop Chaud) (2)
Get-A-Job (2,4)
Hands Off...She's Mine (1)
Hit It (4)
I Am Your Flag (1)
I Confess (3,4)
Jackpot (1)
Jeanette (3)
Limits We Set (2)
Mirror In The Bathroom (1,4)
Monkey Murders (2)
Noise In This World (1)
Over And Over (2)
Pato And Roger A Go Talk (3)
Ranking Full Stop (1)
Rotating Heads (3)
Rough Rider (1)
Save It For Later (3,4)
She's Going (3)
Sole Salvation (3)
Sorry (3)
Spar Wld Me (1)
Stand Down Margaret (1,4)
Sugar & Stress (3)
Tears Of A Clown (1,4)
Too Nice To Talk To (4)
Twist & Crawl (1,4)
Two Swords (1)
Walk Away (1)
What's Your Best Thing? (4)
Whine & Grine (medley) (1)

ENIGMA
Enigma is producer Michael Cretu. Born on 5/18/57 in Bucharest, Romania. Moved to Germany in 1975. Worked with Vangelis and The Art Of Noise. Featured vocalist is Cretu's wife, Sandra.

DEBUT DATE	PEAK POS	WKS CHR	G O L D	ARTIST — Album Title	$	Label & Number
3/2/91	6	102↑ ▲		MCMXC a.D.	$12	Charisma 91642

title is the Roman numeral for the year 1990

Back To The Rivers Of Belief Medley
Callas Went Away
Find Love
Knocking On Forbidden Doors
Mea Culpa
Sadeness Part 1 5
Voice & The Snake
Voice Of Enigma

ENNIS, Ethel
Jazz vocalist/pianist. Born and raised in Baltimore.

DEBUT DATE	PEAK POS	WKS CHR	G O L D	ARTIST — Album Title	$	Label & Number
3/21/64	147	2		This Is Ethel Ennis	$15	RCA 2786

As You Desire Me
Dear Friend
He Loves Me
Joey, Joey, Joey
Love, Don't Turn Away
Moon River (And The Night Was Young)
Night Club
Nobody Told Me
Occasional Man
Starry-Eyed And Breathless
When Did I Fall In Love
Who Will Buy?

ENO, Brian
British rock producer/keyboardist. Founding member of Roxy Music. Production work for Devo, Ultravox and Talking Heads. With Daniel Lanois, co-produced U2's *The Unforgettable Fire* and *The Joshua Tree*.

DEBUT DATE	PEAK POS	WKS CHR	G O L D	ARTIST — Album Title	$	Label & Number
8/24/74	151	6		1 Here Come The Warm Jets	$10	Island 9268
5/27/78	171	5		2 Before And After Science	$8	Island 9478
3/21/81	44	13		3 My Life In The Bush Of Ghosts	[I] $8	Sire 6093

BRIAN ENO-DAVID BYRNE

America Is Waiting (3)
Baby's On Fire (1)
Backwater (2)
Blank Frank (1)
By This River (2)
Carrier, The (3)
Cindy Tells Me (1)
Come With Us (3)
Dead Finks Don't Talk (1)
Driving Me Backwards (1)
Energy Fools The Magician (2)
Help Me Somebody (3)
Here Come The Warm Jets (1)
Here He Comes (2)
Jezebel Spirit (3)
Julie With... (2)
King's Lead Hat (2)
Kurt's Rejoinder (2)
Mea Culpa (3)
Moonlight In Glory (3)
Mountain Of Needles (3)
Needles In The Camel's Eye (1)
No One Receiving (2)
On Some Faraway Beach (1)
Paw Paw Negro Blowtorch (1)
Qu'Ran (3)
Regiment (3)
Secret Life (3)
Some Of Them Are Old (1)
Spider And I (1)
Through Hollow Lands (2)

ENTOUCH
R&B male duo of Eric McCaine (from Mt. Vernon, New York) and Free (from the Bronx, New York). McCaine formed the group Touch in 1987.

DEBUT DATE	PEAK POS	WKS CHR	G O L D	ARTIST — Album Title	$	Label & Number
2/10/90	177	4		All Nite	$12	Vintertn. 60858

All Nite 71
Crazay 4/U
4Ever
Just A Little Bit Of Luv
Scratch My Back
II Hype
II Steps 2 The Right
Whatchagonnado

ENTWISTLE, John
Born on 10/9/44 in London. Bass guitarist of The Who. Musical director for the films *Quadrophenia* and *The Kids Are Alright*.

DEBUT DATE	PEAK POS	WKS CHR	G O L D	ARTIST — Album Title	$	Label & Number
10/23/71	126	9		1 Smash Your Head Against The Wall	$15	Decca 79183

DEBUT DATE	PEAK POS	WKS CHR	G O L D	ARTIST — Album Title	$	Label & Number

ENTWISTLE, John — Cont'd

DEBUT DATE	PEAK POS	WKS CHR	GOLD	ARTIST — Album Title	$	Label & Number
11/18/72+	138	13		2 Whistle Rymes	$10	Track 79190
7/7/73	174	7		3 Rigor Mortis Sets In	$10	Track 321
3/1/75	192	1		4 Mad Dog	$10	Track 2129

JOHN ENTWISTLE'S OX

| 10/10/81 | 71 | 9 | | 5 Too Late The Hero | $8 | Atco 142 |

Apron Strings (2)
Big Black Cadillac (3)
Cell Number Seven (4)
Dancin' Master (5)
Do The Dangle (3)
Drowning (4)
Fallen Angel (5)
Gimme That Rock N' Roll (3)
Heaven And Hell (1)

Hound Dog (3)
I Believe In Everything (1)
I Fall To Pieces (4)
I Feel Better (2)
I Found Out (2)
I Was Just Being Friendly (2)
I Wonder (2)
I'm Coming Back (5)
I'm So Scared (4)

Jungle Bunny (4)
Lady Killer (4)
Love Is A Heart Attack (5)
Lovebird (5)
Lucille (3)
Mad Dog (4)
Made In Japan (3)
Mr. Bass Man (3)
My Size (1)

My Wife (3)
Nightmare (Please Wake Me Up) (2)
No. 29 (External Youth) (1)
Peg Leg Peggy (3)
Pick Me Up (Big Chicken) (1)
Roller Skate Kate (3)
Sleepin Man (5)
Talk Dirty (5)

Ted End (1)
Ten Little Friends (2)
Thinkin' It Over (2)
Too Late The Hero (5)
Try Me (5)
What Are We Doing Here? (1)
What Kind Of People Are They? (1)
Who Cares? (2)

Who In The Hell? (4)
Window Shopper (2)
You Can Be So Mean (4)
You're Mine (1)

ENUFF Z'NUFF

Chicago-based, hard-rock quartet formed by bassist Chip Z'Nuff (former minor league baseball player). Includes vocalist Donnie Vie, guitarist Derek Frigo and drummer Vikki Foxx.

| 9/30/89 | 74 | 34 | | 1 Enuff Z'nuff | $8 | Atco 91262 |
| 4/13/91 | 143 | 6 | | 2 Strength | $12 | Atco 91638 |

Baby Loves You (2)
Blue Island (2)
Coming Home (medley) (2)
Finger On The Trigger (2)
Fly High Michelle (1) 47

For Now (1)
Goodbye (2)
Heaven Or Hell (2)
Holly Wood Ya (2)
Hot Little Summer Girl (1)

I Could Never Be Without You (1)
In Crowd (1)
In The Groove (1)
Kiss The Clown (1)

Little Indian Angel (1)
Long Way To Go (2)
Missing You (2)
Mother's Eyes (2)
New Thing (1) 67

She Wants More (1)
Something For Free (2)
Strength (2)
Time To Let You Go (2)
Way Home (medley) (2)

World Is A Gutter (2)

EN VOGUE

Black female vocal quartet from the San Francisco Bay area. Formed by the production team of Denzil Foster and Thomas McElroy. Consists of Dawn Robinson, Terry Ellis, Cindy Herron and Maxine Jones.

| 4/28/90 | 21 | 69 ▲ | | 1 Born To Sing | $12 | Atlantic 82084 |
| 4/11/92 | 8 | 44↑ ▲² | | 2 Funky Divas | $12 | EastWest 92121 |

Desire (2)
Don't Go (1)
Free Your Mind (2) 8
Give It Up, Turn It Loose (2) 15

Giving Him Something He Can Feel (2) 6
Hip Hop Bugle Boy (2)
Hip Hop Lover (2)
Hold On (1) 2
Hooked On Your Love (2)

It Ain't Over Till The Fat Lady Sings (2)
Just Can't Stay Away (1)
Lies (1) 38
Love Don't Love You (2)
Luv Lines (1)

My Lovin' (You're Never Gonna Get It) (2) 2
Part Of Me (1)
Party (1)
Strange (1)
This Is Your Life (2)

Time Goes On (1)
Waitin' On You (1)
What Is Love (2)
Yesterday (2)
You Don't Have To Worry (1)

ENYA

Born Eithne Ni Bhraonain (Gaelic spelling of Brennan) in Donegal, Ireland. From 1980-82, she was a member of her siblings' folk-rock group Clannad.

| 2/4/89 | 25 | 39 ▲² | | 1 Watermark | $8 | Geffen 24233 |
| 12/7/91+ | 17 | 62↑ ▲² | | 2 Shepherd Moons | $12 | Reprise 26775 |

Afer Ventus (2)
Angeles (2)
Book Of Days (2)
Caribbean Blue (2) 79
Cursum Perficio (1)

Ebudae (2)
Evacuee (2)
Evening Falls... (1)
Exile (1)

How Can I Keep From Singing? (2)
Longships, The (1)
Lothlorien (2)

Marble Halls (2)
Miss Clare Remembers (1)
Na Laetha Geal M'oige (1)
No Holly For Miss Quinn (2)

On Your Shore (1)
Orinoco Flow (Sail Away) (1) 24
River (1)

Shepherd Moons (2)
Smaointe (2)
Storms In Africa (1)
Watermark (1)

EPMD

Long Island rap duo: Erick Sermon and Parrish Smith. EPMD: Erick and Parrish Making Dollars. Parrish was a football tight end at Southern Connecticut State University.

7/9/88	80	23	●	1 Strictly Business	$8	Fresh 82006
8/19/89	53	14	●	2 Unfinished Business	$8	Fresh 92012
2/2/91	36	21	●	3 Business As Usual	$12	Def Jam 47067
8/15/92	14	18	●	4 Business Never Personal	$12	RAL 52848

Big Payback (2)
Boon Dox (4)
Brothers On My Jock (3)
Can't Hear Nothing But The Music (4)
Chill (4)
Crossover (4) 42
Cummin' At Cha (4)
D.J. K La Boss (1)
For My People (3)

Funky Piano (3)
Get Off The Bandwagon (1)
Get The Bozack (2)
Give The People (3)
Gold Digger (3)
Hardcore (3)
Head Banger (4)
Hit Squad Heist (3)
I'm Housin' (1)
I'm Mad (3)

It Wasn't Me, It Was The Fame (2)
It's Going Down (4)
It's My Thing (1)
It's Time To Party (2)
Jane (1)
Jane II (2)
Jane 3 (3)
Knick Knack Patty Wack (2)
Let The Funk Flow (1)

Manslaughter (3)
Mr. Bozack (3)
Nobody's Safe Chump (4)
Play The Next Man (4)
Please Listen To My Demo (2)
Rampage (3)
Rap Is Outta Control (3)
Scratch Bring It Back (Part 2-Mic Doc) (4)
So Wat Cha Sayin' (2)

Steve Martin (1)
Strictly Business (1)
Strictly Snappin' Necks (2)
Total Kaos (2)
Underground (3)
Who Killed Jane (4)
Who's Booty (2)
You Gots To Chill (1)
You Had Too Much To Drink (2)

You're A Customer (1)

EPPS, Preston

Bongo player born in 1931 in Oakland. Discovered by Original Sound owner, Art Laboe.

| 8/15/60 | 35 | 3 | | Bongo Bongo Bongo [I] | $35 | Original Snd. 5002 |

Bongo Bongo Bongo 78
Bongo In The Congo

Bongo Rock 14
Bongos In Pastel

Call Of The Jungle
Doin' The Cha Cha Cha

Jungle Drums

ERASURE

British techno-soul duo of composer/producer/multi-instrumentalist Vince Clarke and lyricist/vocalist Andy Bell. Clarke was a member of Depeche Mode and half of the duo Yaz.

7/18/87	190	3		1 The Circus	$8	Sire 25554
1/16/88	186	3		2 The Two Ring Circus [K]	$10	Sire 25667 [2]
				6 remixes plus 3 re-recordings		
6/18/88	49	50 ▲		3 The Innocents	$8	Sire 25730
5/13/89	73	10		4 Crackers International	$8	Sire 25904
11/11/89	57	23		5 Wild!	$8	Sire 26026
11/2/91	29	17		6 Chorus	$12	Sire 26668
7/18/92	85	22		7 Abba-esque [M]	$6	Mute 61386
12/12/92	112	9↑		8 Pop! - The First 20 Hits [G]	$12	Sire 45153

DEBUT DATE	PEAK POS	WKS CHR	GOLD	ARTIST — Album Title	$	Label & Number

ERASURE — Cont'd

Am I Right? (6,8)
Blue Savannah (5,8)
Breath Of Life (6,8)
Brother And Sister (5)
Chains Of Love (3,8) *12*
Chorus (Fishes In The Sea) (6,8) *83*
Circus, The (1,8)
Crown Of Thorns (5)
Don't Dance (1,2)
Drama! (5,8)

Hallowed Ground (3)
Hardest Part (4)
Heart Of Stone (3)
Heavenly Action (8)
Hideaway (1,2)
Home (6)
How Many Times? (5)
If I Could (1,2)
Imagination (3)
It Doesn't Have To Be (1,2,8)
Joan (6)

Knocking On Your Door (4)
La Gloria (5)
Lay All Your Love On Me (7)
Leave Me To Bleed (1,2)
Little Respect (3,8) *14*
Love To Hate You (6,8)
My Heart...So Blue (2)
Oh L'amour (8)
Perfect Stranger (6)
Phantom Bride (3)
Piano Song (5)

S.O.S. (7)
Sexuality (1)
She Won't Be Home (4)
Ship Of Fools (3,8)
Siren Song (6)
Sixty-Five Thousand (3)
Sometimes (1,2,8)
Spiralling (1,2)
Star (5,8)
Stop! (4,8) *97*
Take A Chance On Me (7,8)

Turns The Love To Anger (6)
2,000 Miles (5)
Victim Of Love (1,2,8)
Voulez Vous (7)
Waiting For The Day (6)
Weight Of The World (3)
Who Needs Love (Like That) (8)
Witch In The Ditch (3)
Yahoo! (3)
You Surround Me (5,8)

ERIC B. & RAKIM

Rap duo: DJ Eric Barrier (from Elmhurst, New York) and rapper William Griffin, Jr. (from Long Island, New York).

DEBUT DATE	PEAK POS	WKS CHR	GOLD	#	ARTIST — Album Title	$	Label & Number
9/12/87	58	38	●	1	Paid In Full ..... [Y]	$8	4th & B'way 4005
8/13/88	22	16	●	2	Follow The Leader	$8	Uni 3
7/7/90	32	14	●	3	Let The Rhythm Hit 'Em	$12	MCA 6416
7/11/92		11		4	Don't Sweat The Technique	$12	MCA 10594

As The Rhyme Goes On (1)
Beats For The Listeners (2)
Casualties Of War (4)
Chinese Arithmetic (1)
Don't Sweat The Technique (4)
Eric B. Is On The Cut (1)
Eric B. Is President (1)
Eric B. Made My Day (3)

Eric B. Never Scared (2)
Extended Beat (2)
Follow The Leader (2)
I Ain't No Joke (1)
I Know You Got Soul (1)
In The Ghetto (3)
Juice (Know The Ledge) (4) *96*
Just A Beat (2)

Keep 'Em Eager To Listen (3)
Keep The Beat (4)
Kick Along (4)
Let The Rhythm Hit 'Em [includes 2 versions] (3)
Lyrics Of Fury (2)
Mahogany (3)
Microphone Fiend (2)
Move The Crowd (1)

Musical Massacre (2)
My Melody (1)
No Competition (2)
No Omega (3)
Paid In Full (1)
Pass The Hand Grenade (3)
Punisher, The (4)
Put Your Hands Together (2)
R, The (2)

Relax With Pep (4)
Rest Assured (4)
Run For Cover (3)
Set 'Em Straight (3)
Step Back (3)
Teach The Children (4)
To The Listeners (2)
Untouchables (3)
What's Going On (4)

What's On Your Mind (4)

ERUPTION

London-based, techno-funk quintet of Jamaican natives featuring lead singers Precious Wilson and Lintel.

DEBUT DATE	PEAK POS	WKS CHR	GOLD	ARTIST — Album Title	$	Label & Number
4/1/78	133	13		Eruption	$10	Ariola 50033

Be Yourself
Computer Love

Do You Know What It Feels Like
I Can't Carry On
I Can't Stand The Rain *18*

I'll Take You There
Movin'

Party, Party
Way We Were

Wayward Love

ESCAPE CLUB, The

London-based rock quartet formed in 1983: Trevor Steel (vocals), John Holliday (guitar), Johnnie Christo (bass) and Milan Zekavica (drums).

DEBUT DATE	PEAK POS	WKS CHR	GOLD	#	ARTIST — Album Title	$	Label & Number
8/27/88	27	38	●	1	Wild Wild West	$8	Atlantic 81871
4/6/91	145	12		2	Dollars And Sex	$12	Atlantic 82198

Blast Off To Heaven (2)
Call It Poison (2) *44*
Come Alive (2)
Edge Of Your Bed (2)

Freedom (2)
Goodbye Joey Rae (1)
I'll Be There (2) *8*
Jealousy (1)

Longest Day (1)
Only The Rain (1)
Shake For The Sheik (1) *28*
Shout The Walls Down (2)

So Fashionable (2)
Staring At The Sun (1)
Sugar Man (2)
This City (2)

Walking Through Walls (1) *81*
Who Do You Love? (1)
Wild, Wild West (1) *1*

Working For The Fatman (1)

ESCOVEDO, Coke

Percussionist from Los Angeles. Prominent session musician, worked with Cal Tjader in the '60s. Toured with Santana in 1971. Uncle of Sheila E.

DEBUT DATE	PEAK POS	WKS CHR	GOLD	#	ARTIST — Album Title	$	Label & Number
3/13/76	195	2		1	Coke	$8	Mercury 1041
5/29/76	190	3		2	Comin' At Ya!	$8	Mercury 1085
2/12/77	195	1		3	Disco Fantasy	$8	Mercury 1132

Backseat (2)
Breeze And I (2)
Diamond Dust (medley) (2)
Disco Fantasy (3)
Doesn't Anybody Want To Hear A Love Song (3)
Easy Come, Easy Go (1)

Everything Is Coming Our Way (2)
Fried Neck Bones And Home Fries (2)
Hall's Delight (1)
Hangin' On (2)
Hot Soul Single (3)

I Wouldn't Change A Thing (2)
If I Ever Lose This Heaven (1)
Life Is A Tortured Love Affair (1)
Love Letters (1)
Make It Sweet (1)
No One To Depend On (1)

Rebirth (1)
Runaway (2)
Somebody's Callin' (2)
Something So Simple (2)
Something Special (3)
Soul Support (3)
Stay With Me (2)
Trash Man (3)

Vida (medley) (2)
What Are You Under (1)
Who Do You Want To Love (3)
Why Can't We Be Lovers (1)
Won't You Gimme The Funk (3)
Your Kind Of Loving (3)

ESQUIRE

British rock trio: Nikki Squire (lead singer), Nigel McLaren (bass) and Charles Olins (keyboards). Nikki is married to Chris Squire of Yes.

DEBUT DATE	PEAK POS	WKS CHR	GOLD	ARTIST — Album Title	$	Label & Number
3/28/87	165	4		Esquire	$8	Geffen 24101

Blossomtime
Hourglass

Knock Twice For Heaven
Moving Together

Silent Future
Special Greeting

Sunshine
To The Rescue

Up Down Turnaround
What You've Been Saying

ESSEX, David

Born David Cook on 7/23/47 in London. Portrayed Christ in the London production of *Godspell*. Star of British films since 1970.

DEBUT DATE	PEAK POS	WKS CHR	GOLD	ARTIST — Album Title	$	Label & Number
1/5/74	32	21		Rock On	$20	Columbia 32560

Bring In The Sun
For Emily, Whenever I May Find Her

Lamplight *71*
Ocean Girl
On And On

Rock On *5*
Sept. 15th
Streetfight

Tell Him No
Turn Me Loose
We All Insane

ESSEX, The

R&B quintet formed by members of U.S. Marine Corps at Camp LeJeune, North Carolina in 1962. Consisted of Anita Humes (lead), Walter Vickers, Rodney Taylor, Billie Hill and Rudolph Johnson.

DEBUT DATE	PEAK POS	WKS CHR	GOLD	ARTIST — Album Title	$	Label & Number
8/3/63	119	5		Easier Said Than Done	$35	Roulette 25234

All In My Mind
Are You Going My Way

Been So Long
Come On To My Party

Conga La Ya
Easier Said Than Done *1*

Every Night
I Have To Cry

I Love Her
We Belong Together

Whenever I Need My Baby
Where Is He

DEBUT DATE	PEAK POS	WKS CHR	GOLD	ARTIST — Album Title	$	Label & Number

★★471★★ ESTEFAN, Gloria/Miami Sound Machine

Latin American-flavored pop music band based in Miami, led by singer Gloria Estefan with her husband, percussionist Emilio Estefan, Jr. Band formed in 1975. Gloria (b: Gloria Fajardo, 12/1/57) came to Miami from Cuba in 1960. Emilio emigrated in 1965. On March 20, 1990, both were involved in a serious crash involving their tour bus, in which Gloria suffered a broken vertebra but fully recovered within a year.

MIAMI SOUND MACHINE:

DEBUT DATE	PEAK POS	WKS CHR	GOLD	ARTIST — Album Title	$	Label & Number
11/23/85+	21	75 ▲²		1 Primitive Love	$8	Epic 40131

GLORIA ESTEFAN and MIAMI SOUND MACHINE:

6/20/87+	6	97 ▲³		**2 Let It Loose**	$8	Epic 40769

GLORIA ESTEFAN:

7/29/89	8	69 ▲²		3 Cuts Both Ways	$8	Epic 45217
				cassette and CD versions contain Spanish versions of 2 tracks		
2/16/91	5	68 ▲		4 Into The Light	$12	Epic 46988
11/21/92	15	12↑ ▲		5 Greatest Hits .... [G]	$12	Epic 53046

Always Tomorrow (5) *81*
Anything For You (2,5) *1*
Ay, Ay, I (3)
Bad Boy (1) *8*
Betcha Say That (2) *36*
Body To Body (1)
Can't Forget You (4) *43*
Can't Stay Away From You (2,5) *6*
Christmas Through Your Eyes (5)

Close My Eyes (4)
Coming Out Of The Dark (4,5) *1*
Conga (1,5) *10*
Cuts Both Ways (3) *44*
Desde La Oscuridad ..see: Coming Out Of The Dark
Don't Wanna Lose You (3,5) *1*
Falling In Love (Uh-Oh) (1) *25*

Get On Your Feet (3,5) *11*
Give It Up (2)
Go Away (5)
Heart With Your Name On It (4)
Here We Are (3,5) *6*
I See Your Smile (5)
I Want You So Bad (2)
Let It Loose (2)
Light Of Love (4)
Live For Loving You (4) *22*

Love Toy (2)
Mama Yo Can't Go (4)
Movies (1)
Mucho Money (1)
Nayib's Song (I Am Here For You) (4)
Nothin' New (3)
1-2-3 (2,5) *3*
Oye Mi Canto (Hear My Voice) (3) *48*
Primitive Love (1)

Remember Me With Love (4)
Rhythm Is Gonna Get You (1,5) *5*
Say (3)
Seal Our Fate (4) *53*
Sex In The 90's (4)
Surrender (2)
Surrender Paradise (1)
Think About You Now (3)
What Goes Around (4)

Words Get In The Way (4)
You Made A Fool Of Me (1)
Your Love Is Bad For Me (3)

ESTUS, Deon

Detroit-born black bassist. Formerly with George Michael, Wham!, Marvin Gaye and Brainstorm.

4/1/89	89	15		Spell	$8	Mika 835713

Blue Envelope
False Start

Heaven Help Me 5
Love Can't Wait

Love Me Over
Me Or The Rumours

Solid Ground
Spell

You're The Only One

ETHERIDGE, Melissa

Singer/guitarist born and raised in Leavenworth, Kansas. Studied guitar at Boston's Berklee College of Music. Discovered in Long Beach, California by Island Records' founder Chris Blackwell.

6/18/88+	22	65 ●		1 Melissa Etheridge	$8	Island 90875
10/7/89	22	58 ●		2 Brave And Crazy	$8	Island 91285
4/4/92	21	26 ●		3 Never Enough	$12	Island 512120

Ain't It Heavy (3)
Angels, The (2)
Boy Feels Strange (3)
Brave And Crazy (2)
Bring Me Some Water (1)
Chrome Plated Heart (1)

Dance Without Sleeping (3)
Don't You Need (1)
I Want You (1)
It's For You (3)
Keep It Precious (3)
Late September Dogs (1)

Let Me Go (2)
Letting Go (3)
Like The Way I Do (1)
Meet Me In The Back (3)
Must Be Crazy For Me (3)
My Back Door (2)

No Souvenirs (2) *95*
Occasionally (1)
Place Your Hand (3)
Precious Pain (1)
Royal Station 4/16 (2)
Similar Features (1) *94*

Skin Deep (2)
Testify (2)
2001 (3)
Watching You (1)
You Can Sleep While I Drive (2)

You Used To Love To Dance (2)

ETZEL, Roy

Trumpet virtuoso from Germany.

12/18/65	140	5		The Silence (Il Silenzio) .... [I]	$10	MGM 4330

El Amor
Goldfinger

La Mama
Melancholy

More
Non Ho L'eta (Per Amarti)

Oh, Warum?
Puerto Rico

Silence (Il Silenzio)
Sonny Boy

Stardust
Sunrise

E.U.

E.U.: Experience Unlimited. Ten-member R&B male group from Washington, D.C. — Gregory "Sugar Bear" Elliott, lead vocals, bass.

4/22/89	158	9		Livin' Large	$8	Virgin 91021

Buck Wild
Come To The Go-Go

Da Butt '89
Don't Turn Around

Express
Livin' Large

Shaka Zulu
Shake It Like A White Girl

Shake Your Thang
Taste Of Your Love

EUROGLIDERS

Australian pop-rock sextet — Grace Knight, lead singer.

12/22/84+	140	11		This Island	$8	Columbia 39588

Another Day In The Big World
Cold Comfort

Heaven (Must Be There) 65
It's The Way
Judy's World

Keep It Quiet
Maybe Only I Dream
Never Say

No Action
Nothing To Say
Someone

Waiting For You

EUROPE

Swedish rock quintet: Joey Tempest (vocals), Kee Marcello (guitar), John Leven (bass), Mic Michaeli (keyboards) and Ian Haugland (drums).

11/1/86+	8	78 ▲²		**1 The Final Countdown**	$8	Epic 40241
8/27/88	19	25 ▲		2 Out Of This World	$8	Epic 44185

Carrie (1) *3*
Cherokee (1) *72*
Coast To Coast (2)
Danger On The Track (1)

Final Countdown (1) *8*
Heart Of Stone (1)
Just The Beginning (2)
Let The Good Times Rock (2)

Lights And Shadows (2)
Love Chaser (1)
More Than Meets The Eye (2)
Never Say Die (2)

Ninja (1)
On The Loose (1)
Open Your Heart (2)
Ready Or Not (1)

Rock The Night (1) *30*
Sign Of The Times (2)
Superstitious (2) *31*
Time Has Come (1)

Tomorrow (1)
Tower's Callin' (2)

★★327★★ EURYTHMICS

Synth/pop duo: Annie Lennox (b: 12/25/54, Aberdeen, Scotland; vocals, keyboards, flute, composer) and David Stewart (b: 9/9/52, England; keyboards, guitar, synthesizer, composer). Both had been in the Tourists from 1977-80. First album recorded in Cologne, Germany, with drummer Clem Burke (formerly of Blondie). Stewart married Siobhan Fahey of Bananarama on 8/1/87. Lennox appeared in TV film *The Room*.

5/28/83	15	59 ●		1 Sweet Dreams (Are Made Of This)	$8	RCA 4681
2/4/84	7	37 ▲		2 Touch	$8	RCA 4917
7/7/84	115	11		3 Touch Dance	$8	RCA 5086
				vocal and instrumental dance remixes of some cuts from above LP		
1/5/85	93	14		4 1984 (for the love of big brother) .... [S]	$8	RCA 5349
5/25/85	9	45 ▲		5 Be Yourself Tonight	$8	RCA 5429

232

DEBUT DATE	PEAK POS	WKS CHR	GOLD	ARTIST — Album Title	$	Label & Number

EURYTHMICS — Cont'd

8/9/86	**12**	33	●	6 Revenge	$8	RCA 5847
12/26/87+	**41**	19		7 Savage	$8	RCA 6794
9/30/89	**34**	28		8 We Too Are One	$8	Arista 8606
6/15/91	**72**	23	●	9 Greatest Hits	[G] $12	Arista 8680

Adrian (5)
Angel (8,9)
Aqua (2)
Beethoven (I Love To Listen To) (7)
Better To Have Lost In Love (Than Never To Have Loved At All) (5)
Brand New Day (7)
Conditioned Soul (5)
Cool Blue (2,3)
Do You Want To Break Up? (7)
Don't Ask Me Why (8,9) **40**
Doubleplusgood (7)
First Cut (2,3)

For The Love Of Big Brother (4)
Greetings From A Dead Man (4)
Heaven (7)
Here Comes That Sinking Feeling (5)
Here Comes The Rain Again (1,2) 9
How Long? (8)
I Could Give You (A Mirror) (1)
I Did It Just The Same (4)
I Love You Like A Ball And Chain (5)
I Need A Man (7,9) **46**
I Need You (7)

I Remember You (6)
I've Got A Lover (Back In Japan) (7)
I've Got An Angel (1)
In This Town (6)
It's Alright (Baby's Coming Back) (5) **78**
Jennifer (1)
Julia (4)
King & Queen Of America (8,9)
Last Time (6)
Let's Go! (6)
Little Of You (6)
Love Is A Stranger (1,9) **23**
Ministry Of Love (4)
Miracle Of Love (7)

Missionary Man (6,9) **14**
(My) My) Baby's Gonna Cry (8)
No Fear, No Hate, No Pain (No Broken Hearts) (2)
Paint A Rumour (2,3)
Put The Blame On Me (7)
Regrets (2,3)
Revival (8)
Right By Your Side (2) **29**
Room 101 (4)
Savage (7)
Sexcrime (Nineteen Eighty-Four) (4) **81**
Shame (7)
Sisters Are Doin' It For Themselves (5,9) **18**

Somebody Told Me (1)
Sweet Dreams (Are Made Of This) (1,9) **1**
Sylvia (8)
Take Your Pain Away (6)
There Must Be An Angel (Playing With My Heart) (5,9) **22**
This City Never Sleeps (1)
This Is The House (1)
Thorn In My Side (6,9) **68**
Walk, The (1)
We Two Are One (8)
When The Day Goes Down (8)
When Tomorrow Comes (6,9)
Who's That Girl? (2,9) **21**

Wide Eyed Girl (7)
Winston's Diary (4)
Would I Lie To You? (5,9) **5**
Wrap It Up (1)
You Have Placed A Chill In My Heart (7) **64**
You Hurt Me (And I Hate You) (8)

EVERETT, Betty — see BUTLER, Jerry

★★398★★ **EVERLY BROTHERS, The**
Donald (real name: Isaac Donald) was born on 2/1/37 in Brownie, Kentucky; Philip on 1/19/39 in Chicago. Vocal duo/guitarists/songwriters. Don (beginning at age eight) and Phil (age six) sang with parents through high school. Invited to Nashville by Chet Atkins and first recorded there for Columbia in 1955. Signed to Archie Bleyer's Cadence Records in 1957. Phil married for a time to the daughter of Janet Bleyer (Chordettes). Duo split up in July 1973 and reunited in September 1983. Inducted into the Rock and Roll Hall of Fame in 1986. Don's daughter Erin was married for a short time to Axl Rose of Guns N' Roses in 1990.

2/10/58	**16**	3		1 The Everly Brothers	$75	Cadence 3003
5/23/60	**9**	10		2 It's Everly Time!	$40	Warner 1381
8/22/60	**23**	19		3 The Fabulous Style Of The Everly Brothers	[K] $65	Cadence 3040
12/5/60+	**9**	24		4 A Date With The Everly Brothers	$40	Warner 1395
8/25/62	**35**	17		5 The Golden Hits Of The Everly Brothers	[G] $30	Warner 1471
9/25/65	**141**	3		6 Beat & Soul	$35	Warner 1605
7/18/70	**180**	8		7 The Everly Brothers' Original Greatest Hits	[G] $12	Barnaby 350 [2]
				original Cadence label hits		
3/10/84	**162**	5		8 The Everly Brothers Reunion Concert	[L] $10	Passport 11001 [2]
				recorded in September 1983 at Albert Hall, London		
10/13/84	**38**	17		9 EB 84	$8	Mercury 822431
2/8/86	**83**	19		10 Born Yesterday	$8	Mercury 826142

Abandoned Love (10)
All I Have To Do Is Dream (7,8) **1**
Always Drive A Cadillac (10)
Always It's You (4) **56**
Amanda Ruth (10)
Arms Of Mary (10)
Asleep (9)
Baby What You Want Me To Do (4)
Be Bop-A-Lula (1,3,7,8) **74**
Bird Dog (7,8) **1**
Born Yesterday (10)
Brand New Heartache (1,3,7)
Bye Bye Love (1,7,8) **2**
Carol Jane (2)
Cathy's Clown (4,5,8) **1**
Change Of Heart (4)
Claudette (8)
Crying In The Rain (5,8) **6**
Danger Danger (9)
Devoted To You (medley) (8)

Don't Blame Me (5) **20**
Don't Say Goodnight (10)
Donna, Donna (4)
Ebony Eyes (5,8) **8**
First In Line (9)
Following The Sun (9)
Girl Can't Help It (6)
Gone Gone Gone (8)
Good Golly Miss Molly (8)
Hey Doll Baby (1,3)
Hi Heel Sneakers (6)
How Can I Meet Her? (5) **75**
I Almost Lost My Mind (9)
I Know Love (10)
I Want You To Know (2)
I Wonder If I Care As Much (1,8) flip
I'm Not Angry (5)
I'm Takin' My Time (9)
Just In Case (2)
Keep A Knockin' (1,7)
Lay, Lady, Lay (4)

Leave My Woman Alone (1,7)
Let It Be Me (3,7,8) **7**
Lightning Express (7,8)
Like Strangers (3,7) **22**
Lonely Avenue (6)
Long Time Gone (7)
Love Hurts (4,8)
Love Is Strange (6,8)
Love Of My Life (7) **40**
Lucille (4,5,8) **21**
Made To Love (4)
Man With Money (6)
Maybe Tomorrow (1,7,8)
Memories Are Made Of This (2)
Money (That's What I Want) (6)
More Than I Can Handle (9)
Muskrat (5) **82**
My Babe (6)
Nashville Blues (2)
Oh, True Love (2)

Oh, What A Feeling (3)
On The Wings Of A Nightingale (9) **50**
People Get Ready (6)
Poor Jenny (3,7) **22**
Price Of Love (8)
Problems (7) **2**
Put My Little Shoes Away (8)
Rip It Up (1,3,7)
Rockin' Alone (In An Old Rocking Chair) (7)
See See Rider (6)
Should We Tell Him (1,7) flip
Sigh, Cry, Almost Die (4)
Since You Broke My Heart (3)
Sleepless Nights (2)
So How Come (No One Loves Me) (4)
So Sad (To Watch Good Love Go Bad) (2,5,8) **7**

Some Sweet Day (2)
Step It Up And Go (8)
Stick With Me Baby (4) **41**
Story Of Me (9)
Take A Message To Mary (3,8) **16**
Temptation (5,8) **27**
That Uncertain Feeling (10)
That's Just Too Much (4)
That's Old Fashioned (That's The Way Love Should Be) (5) **9**
That's What You Do To Me (2)
These Shoes (10)
Thinkin' 'Bout You (10)
This Little Girl Of Mine (1) **26**
('Til) I Kissed You (3,7,8) **4**
Wake Up Little Susie (1,7,8) **1**
Walk Right Back (5,8) **7**

Walking The Dog (6)
What Am I Living For (6)
What Kind Of Girl Are You (2)
When Will I Be Loved (3,8) **8**
Why Worry (10)
You Make It Seem So Easy (9)
You Thrill Me (Through And Through) (2)

EVERY MOTHER'S NIGHTMARE
Nashville hard-rock quartet: Rick Ruhl (vocals), Steve Malone, Mark McMurtry and Jim Phipps.

11/17/90+	**146**	15		Every Mother's Nightmare	$12	Arista 8633

Bad On Love
Dues To Pay

EZ Come, EZ Go
Hard To Hold

Listen Up
Long Haired Country Boy

Lord Willin'
Love Can Make You Blind

Nobody Knows
Walls Come Down

EVERY MOTHERS' SON
Rock quintet formed in Greenwich Village, led by brothers Dennis and Lary Larden.

6/10/67	**117**	10		Every Mothers' Son	$15	MGM 4471

Ain't It A Drag
Ain't No Use
Allison Dozer

Come On Down To My Boat 6
Come On Queenie

Didn't She Lie
For Brandy

I Believe In You
I Won't

Sittin' Here (Peter's Tune)
What Became Of Mary

EVERYTHING BUT THE GIRL
London-based duo: Tracey Thorn and Ben Watt. Group name taken from a furniture store on England's Hull University campus.

3/17/90	**77**	18		The Language Of Life	$12	Atlantic 82057

Driving
Get Back Together

Imagining America
Language Of Life

Letting Love Go
Me And Bobby D

Meet Me In The Morning
My Baby Don't Love Me

Road, The
Take Me

DEBUT DATE	PEAK POS	WKS CHR	GOLD	ARTIST — Album Title	$	Label & Number

EXILE
Band formed in Lexington, Kentucky in 1963 as The Exiles — J.P. Pennington, lead singer. Toured with Dick Clark in 1965. Changed name to Exile in 1973. Pennington left band in early 1989, replaced by Paul Martin. A top country act since 1983.

| 8/19/78 | 14 | 26 ● | | Mixed Emotions .... | $8 | Warner 3205 |

Ain't Got No Time · Don't Do It · **Kiss You All Over 1** · Never Gonna Stop · One Step At A Time · Stay With Me · There's Been A Change · You And Me · **You Thrill Me 40**

EXODUS
San Francisco heavy-metal band formed by drummer Tom Hunting in 1981. Early personnel included guitarist Kirk Hammet, later with Metallica. By mid-1980s, featured vocalist Steve Souza.

11/28/87+	82	20	1	Pleasures Of The Flesh	$8	Combat 8169
2/25/89	82	17	2	Fabulous Disaster	$8	Combat 2001
8/11/90	137	9	3	Impact Is Imminent	$12	Capitol 90379

A.W.O.L. (3) · Brain Dead (1) · Cajun Hell (2) · Changing Of The Guard (3) · Chemi-Kill (1) · Choose Your Weapon (1) · Corruption (2) · Deranged (1) · Fabulous Disaster (2) · Faster Than You'll Ever Live To De (1) · Heads They Win (Tails You Lose) (3) · Impact Is Imminent (3) · Last Act Of Defiance (2) · Like Father, Like Son (3) · Low Rider (2) · Lunatic Parade (3) · Objection Overruled (3) · Only Death Decides (3) · Open Season (2) · Parasite (1) · Pleasures Of The Flesh (1) · Seeds Of Hate (1) · 30 Seconds (1) · Thrash Under Pressure (3) · 'Til Death Do Us Part (1) · Toxic Waltz (2) · Verbal Razors (2) · Within The Walls Of Chaos (3)

EXOTIC GUITARS
Studio group featuring the lead guitar of Al Casey.

8/3/68	155	5	1	The Exotic Guitars ....[I]	$8	Ranwood 8002
1/4/69	167	11	2	Those Were The Days ....[I]	$8	Ranwood 8040
5/31/69	162	6	3	Indian Love Call ....[I]	$8	Ranwood 8051

Alley Cat (1) · Autumn Leaves (2) · Battle Hymn Of The Republic (3) · Bells That Ring For No One (2) · Blue Velvet (2) · Blueberry Hill (1) · C'est Si Bon (1) · Galveston (3) · Green Door (3) · Heartaches (1) · I Walk Alone (2) · I Will Wait For You (1) · Indian Love Call (3) · La Paloma (3) · Love Is Blue (2) · Man And A Woman (2) · Melody Of Love (1) · Moon River (3) · Music To Watch Girls By (2) · My Happiness (1) · Only You (2) · Pearly Shells (3) · Petite Fleur (3) · Red Roses For A Blue Lady (3) · Sabre Dance (from Ballet Gayne) (3) · Sound Of Music (2) · Spanish Eyes (1) · Strangers On The Shore (1) · Taste Of Honey (2) · Those Were The Days (2) · Trying (3) · Twilight Time (2) · Vaya Con Dios (3) · Wonderland By Night (1) · Yellow Bird (1)

EXPOSE
Miami-based, vocal dance trio assembled by producer/songwriter Lewis Martinee. Consists of Miamian Ann Curless, Los Angeles native Jeanette Jurado and Italian-born, New York-raised Gioia Bruno (replaced by Fairbanks, Alaska native Kelly Moneymaker in 1992).

2/21/87+	16	74	▲² 1	Exposure	$8	Arista 8441
7/1/89	33	50	● 2	What You Don't Know	$8	Arista 8532
11/21/92	193	1	3	Expose	$12	Arista 18577

Angel (3) · As Long As I Can Dream (3) · **Come Go With Me (1) 5** · December (1) · Didn't It Hurt To Hurt Me (2) · Exposed To Love (1) · Extra Extra (1) · Face To Face (3) · Give Me All Your Love (3) · I Know You Know (1) · I Specialize In Love (3) · I Think I'm In Trouble (3) · I Wish The Phone Would Ring (3) · I'll Never Get Over You Getting Over Me (3) · In Walked Love (3) · **Let Me Be The One (1) 7** · Let Me Down Easy (2) · Love Don't Hurt (Until You Fall) (2) · Love Is Our Destiny (1) · Now That I Found You (2) · **Point Of No Return (1) 5** · Same Love (3) · **Seasons Change (1) 1** · Still Hung Up On You (1) · Stop, Listen, Look & Think (2) · **Tell Me Why (2) 9** · Touch And Go (3) · Walk Along With Me (2) · **What You Don't Know (2) 8** · **When I Looked At Him (2) 10** · You Don't Know What You Got (1) · You're The One I Need (1) · **Your Baby Never Looked Good In Blue (2) 17**

EXTREME
Boston metal-funk band: Gary Cherone (vocals), Nuno Bettencourt (guitar; born in Portugal), Pat Badger (bass) and Paul Geary (drums).

4/8/89	80	32	1	Extreme	$8	A&M 5238
8/25/90+	10	75	▲² 2	Pornograffitti	$12	A&M 5313
10/10/92	10	18↑	● 3	III Sides To Every Story	$12	A&M 40006

Am I Ever Gonna Change (3) · Big Boys Don't Cry (1) · Color Me Blind (3) · Cupid's Dead (3) · Decadence Dance (2) · Flesh 'N' Blood (1) · Get The Funk Out (2) · God Isn't Dead? (3) · He-Man Woman Hater (2) · **Hole Hearted (2) 4** · It ('S A Monster) (2) · Kid Ego (1) · Li'l Jack Horny (2) · Little Girls (1) · Money (In God We Trust) (2) · **More Than Words (2) 1** · Mutha (Don't Wanna Go To School Today) (1) · Our Father (3) · Peacemaker Die (3) · Politicalamity (3) · Pornograffitti (2) · **Rest In Peace (3) 96** · Rise 'N Shine (3) · Rock A Bye Bye (1) · Seven Sundays (3) · Smoke Signals (1) · Song For Love (2) · Stop The World (3) · Suzi (Wants Her All Day What?) (1) · Teacher's Pet (1) · Tragic Comic (3) · Warheads (3) · Watching, Waiting (1) · When I First Kissed You (2) · When I'm President (2) · Who Cares? (3) · Wind Me Up (1)

EYE TO EYE
Pop duo: vocalist Deborah Berg from Seattle and pianist Julian Marshall (of Marshall Hain) from England.

| 6/19/82 | 99 | 15 | | Eye To Eye .... | $8 | Warner 3570 |

Hunger Pains · Life In Motion · More Hopeless Knowledge · **Nice Girls 37** · On The Mend · Physical Attraction · Progress Ahead · Time Flys

EZO
Four-man, heavy-metal band from Sapporo, Japan led by vocalist Masaki.

| 6/13/87 | 150 | 9 | | E-Z-O .... | $8 | Geffen 24143 |
| | | | | produced by Gene Simmons of Kiss | | |

Big Changes · Desiree · Destroyer · Flashback Heart Attack · Here It Comes · House Of 1,000 Pleasures · I Walk Alone · Kiss Of Fire · Mr. Midnight

F

FABARES, Shelley
Born Michele Fabares on 1/19/44 in Santa Monica, California. Niece of actress Nanette Fabray. Starred with Elvis in three of his movies. Best known as Mary Stone on *The Donna Reed Show*. Married record producer Lou Adler in 1964; later divorced. Cast member of several TV series since 1972, among them *One Day At A Time* (1981-84) and *Coach*. Currently married to actor Mike Farrell.

DEBUT DATE	PEAK POS	WKS CHR	GOLD	ARTIST — Album Title	$	Label & Number
7/21/62	106	11		1 Shelley!	$75	Colpix 426
10/27/62	121	5		2 The Things We Did Last Summer	$60	Colpix 431
5/11/63	48	18		3 Teen-Age Triangle [G]	$40	Colpix 444

JAMES DARREN/SHELLEY FABARES/PAUL PETERSEN
includes 4 cuts by James Darren (see Darren) and 4 by Paul Petersen: "Keep Your Love Locked (Deep In Your Heart)," "Little Boy Sad," "Lollipops And Roses" and "She Can't Find Her Keys"

Boy Of My Own (1)
Breaking Up Is Hard To Do (2)
Funny Face (1)
Hi Lilli, Hi-Lo (1)
I'm Growing Up (1,2,3)
It Keeps Right On A Hurtin' (2)
It's Been A Long, Long Time (1)
Johnny Angel (1,3) *1*
Johnny Get Angry (2)
Johnny Loves Me (2,3) *21*
Loco-Motion (2)
Love Letters (1)
Palisades Park (2)
Picnic (1)
Roses Are Red (2)
Sealed With A Kiss (2)
See You In September (2)
Things We Did Last Summer (2,3) *46*
True Love (1)
Vacation (2)
Very Unlikely (1)
Where's It Gonna Get Me? (1)

FABIAN
Born Fabiano Forte on 2/6/43 in Philadelphia. Discovered at age 14 (because of his good looks and intriguing name) by a chance meeting with Bob Marcucci, owner of Chancellor Records. Began acting career in 1959 with the film *Hound Dog Man*.

DEBUT DATE	PEAK POS	WKS CHR	GOLD	ARTIST — Album Title	$	Label & Number
5/18/59	5	21		1 Hold That Tiger!	$35	Chancellor 5003
12/28/59+	3	19		2 Fabulous Fabian	$35	Chancellor 5005

Ain't Misbehavin' (2)
Any Ole Time (2)
Cuddle Up A Little Closer (1)
Don't You Think It's Time? (1)
Everything Is Just Right (2)
Gimme A Little Kiss (2)
Give (2)
Gonna Get You (1)
Gonna Make You Mine (2)
Gotta Tell Somebody (2)
Hold Me (In Your Arms) (1)
I Don't Know Why (1)
I'm Sincere (2)
Just One More Time (1)
Learnin' (2)
Love Me, Love My Tiger (1)
Lovesick (1)
Ohh What You Do! (1)
Please Don't Stop (1)
Remember Me (2)
Steady Date (1)
Tiger Rag (1)
Turn Me Loose (1) *9*
You Excite Me (2)
You'll Never Tame Me (2)

FABRIC, Bent, & His Piano
Born Bent Fabricius-Bjerre on 12/7/24 in Copenhagen. Head of Metronome Records in Denmark.

DEBUT DATE	PEAK POS	WKS CHR	GOLD	ARTIST — Album Title	$	Label & Number
10/27/62+	13	39		Alley Cat [I]	$15	Atco 148

Across The Alley From The Alamo
Alley Cat 7
Baby Won't You Please Come Home
Catsanova Walk
Comme Ci, Comme Ca
Delilah
Early Morning In Copenhagen
In The Arms Of My Love
Markin' Time
Symphony
Trudie
You Made Me Love You

FABULOUS POODLES
English rock quartet led by Tony DeMeur and Richie Robertson.

DEBUT DATE	PEAK POS	WKS CHR	GOLD	ARTIST — Album Title	$	Label & Number
2/10/79	61	17		1 Mirror Stars	$10	Epic 35666
12/1/79	185	3		2 Think Pink	$10	Epic 36256

Anna Rexia (2)
Any Port In A Storm (2)
B Movies (1)
Bike Blood (2)
Bionic Man (2)
Cherchez La Femme (1)
Chicago Boxcar (1)
Cossack Cowboy (2)
(Hollywood) Dragnet (2)
Man With Money (2)
Mirror Star (1) *81*
Mr. Mike (1)
Oh Cheryl (1)
Pink City Twist (2)
Roll Your Own (1)
Suicide Bridge (2)
Tit Photographer Blues (1)
Toytown People (1)
Vampire Rock (1)
Work Shy (1)
You Wouldn't Listen (2)

FABULOUS RHINESTONES, The
Rock trio led by keyboardist Martin Grebb (of The Buckinghams).

DEBUT DATE	PEAK POS	WKS CHR	GOLD	ARTIST — Album Title	$	Label & Number
7/29/72	193	6		1 The Fabulous Rhinestones	$10	Just Sunshine 1
9/22/73	193	3		2 Freewheelin'	$10	Just Sunshine 9

Big Indian (1)
Do It Like Ya' Mean It (2)
Down To The City (2)
Easy As You Make It (1)
Free (1)
Freewheelin' (2)
Go With Change (2)
Harmonize (1)
Hurt Somebody (2)
Just Can't Turn My Back On You (1)
Live It Out To The End (1)
Living On My Own Time (1)
Nothing New (1)
Positive Direction (1)
Roots With You, Girl (2)
Vicious Circle (2)
What Becomes Of Your Life (2)
What A Wonderful Thing We Have (1) *78*
Whitecaps (2)

FABULOUS THUNDERBIRDS, The
Austin, Texas rock and roll group: Kim Wilson (lead singer), Jimmie Vaughan (guitar; older brother of Stevie Ray Vaughan), Preston Hubbard (bass) and Fran Christina (drums). Vaughan appeared in the 1989 film *Great Balls Of Fire* and recorded in The Vaughan Brothers in 1990. Disbanded in June 1990. Reorganized in 1991 with Wilson, Hubbard, Christina and guitarists Duke Robillard and Kid Bangham.

DEBUT DATE	PEAK POS	WKS CHR	GOLD	ARTIST — Album Title	$	Label & Number
3/28/81	176	7		1 Butt Rockin'	$8	Chrysalis 1319
3/15/86	13	53	▲	2 Tuff Enuff	$8	CBS Assoc. 40304
7/18/87	49	15		3 Hot Number	$8	CBS Assoc. 40818
5/6/89	118	7		4 Powerful Stuff	$8	CBS Assoc. 45094

Amnesia (2)
Cherry Pink And Apple Blossom White (1)
Close Together (4)
Don't Bother Tryin' To Steal Her Love (3)
Down At Antones (2)
Emergency (4)
Give Me All Your Lovin' (1)
Hot Number (3)
How Do You Spell Love (2)
I Believe I'm In Love (1)
I Don't Care (2)
I Hear You Knockin' (1)
I'm Sorry (1)
In Orbit (1)
It Comes To Me Naturally (3)
It Takes A Big Man To Cry (3)
Knock Yourself Out (4)
Look At That (2)
Love In Common (3)
Mathilda (1)
Mistake Number 1 (4)
Now Loosen Up Baby (4)
One Night Stand (1)
One's Too Many (1)
Powerful Stuff (4) *65*
Rainin' In My Heart (4)
Rock This Place (4)
Roll, Roll, Roll (1)
She's Hot (4)
Sofa Circuit (3)
Stand Back (3) *76*
Streets Of Gold (3)
Tell Me (2)
Tell Me Why (1)
Tip On In (1)
True Love (2)
Two Time My Lovin (2)
Wasted Tears (3)
Why Get Up (2)
Wrap It Up (2) *50*

FACES
With the departure of lead singer Steve Marriott who formed Humble Pie, the British rock group Small Faces added, in 1969, former Jeff Beck Group members: Rod Stewart (vocals) and Ron Wood (bass, joined The Rolling Stones in 1976). Other members were Ian McLagen, Kenney Jones (joined The Who in 1978, formed The Law in 1991) and Ronnie Lane (left in 1973, replaced by ex-Free bassist Tetsu Yamauchi). Disbanded in 1975.

DEBUT DATE	PEAK POS	WKS CHR	GOLD	ARTIST — Album Title	$	Label & Number
4/18/70	119	12		1 First Step	$15	Warner 1851

SMALL FACES

DEBUT DATE	PEAK POS	WKS CHR	GOLD	ARTIST — Album Title	$	Label & Number
3/13/71	29	19	2	Long Player	$15	Warner 1892
12/18/71+	6	24	● 3	A Nod Is As Good As A Wink...To A Blind Horse	$15	Warner 2574
4/21/73	21	16	4	Ooh La La	$12	Warner 2665
1/5/74	63	11	5	Rod Stewart/Faces Live - Coast To Coast Overture and Beginners [L]	$12	Mercury 697

ROD STEWART/FACES

Amazing Grace (medley) (5)
Angel (5)
Around The Plynth (1)
Bad 'N' Ruin (2)
Borstal Boys (4,5)
Cindy Incidentally (4) 48
Cut Across Shorty (5)
Debris (3)
Devotion (1)

Every Picture Tells A Story (medley) (5)
Flags And Banners (4)
Fly In The Ointment (4)
Flying (1)
Glad And Sorry (4)
Had Me A Real Good Time (2)
I Feel So Good (2)
I Wish It Would Rain (5)

I'd Rather Go Blind (5)
If I'm On The Late Side (4)
It's All Over Now (5)
Jealous Guy (5)
Jerusalem (2)
Just Another Honky (4)
Last Orders Please (3)
Looking Out The Window (1)
Love Lives Here (3)

Maybe I'm Amazed (2)
Memphis (3)
Miss Judy's Farm (3)
My Fault (4)
Nobody Knows (1)
On The Beach (2)
Ooh La La (4)
Pineapple And The Monkey (1)

Richmond (2)
Shake, Shudder, Shiver (1)
Silicone Grown (4)
Stay With Me (3,5) 17
Stone (1)
Sweet Lady Mary (2)
Tell Everyone (2)
That's All You Need (3)

Three Button Hand Me Down (1)
Too Bad (3,5)
Wicked Messenger (1)
You're So Rude (3)

FACE TO FACE
Boston-based rock quintet. Group appeared as backing band in the film *Streets Of Fire* for which lead singer Laurie Sargent recorded actress Diane Lane's vocals.

DEBUT DATE	PEAK POS	WKS CHR	GOLD	ARTIST — Album Title	$	Label & Number
6/16/84	126	16	1	Face To Face	$8	Epic 38857
6/18/88	176	7	2	One Big Day	$8	Mercury 834376

All Because Of You (1)
As Forever As You (2)
Change In The Wind (?)
Day I Was Born (2)

Don't Talk Like That (1)
Ever Since Eve (Blood Gone Bad) (2)
Face In Front Of Mine (1)

Grass Grows Greener (2)
Heaven On Earth (1)
I Believe In You (2)
Never Had A Reason (2)

Out Of My Hands (1)
Over The Edge (1)
Pictures Of You (1)
Place Called Home (1)

She's A Contradiction (2)
Some Stories (2)
10-9-8 (1)
Under The Gun (1)

Wreckless Heart (1)

FACTS OF LIFE
Soul trio formed by Millie Jackson, originally known as The Gospel Truth: Jean Davis (younger sister of Tyrone Davis), Keith William (Imperials, Flamingos) and Chuck Carter.

DEBUT DATE	PEAK POS	WKS CHR	GOLD	ARTIST — Album Title	$	Label & Number
4/9/77	146	7		Sometimes	$10	Kayvette 802

Bitter Woman
Caught In The Act (Of Getting It On)

Givin' Me Your Love
Hundred Pounds Of Pain
Looks Like We Made It

Lost Inside Of You
Love Is The Final Truth
Sometimes 31

That Kind Of Fire
Uphill Places Of Mind

What Would Your Mama Say?

FAGEN, Donald
Born on 1/10/48 in Passaic, New Jersey. Backup keyboardist/vocalist with Jay & The Americans. At New York's Bard College, formed band with Walter Becker and drummer-turned-comedic actor Chevy Chase. Fagen and Becker formed Steely Dan in 1972.

DEBUT DATE	PEAK POS	WKS CHR	GOLD	ARTIST — Album Title	$	Label & Number
10/30/82	11	27	●	The Nightfly	$8	Warner 23696

an account of one night at the fictional jazz radio station WJAZ

Goodbye Look
Green Flower Street

I.G.Y. (What A Beautiful World) 26

Maxine
New Frontier 70

Nightly, The
Ruby Baby

Walk Between Raindrops

FAIRGROUND ATTRACTION
English-Scottish quartet: female lead singer Eddi Reader with Mark Nevin, Simon Edwards and Roy Dodds.

DEBUT DATE	PEAK POS	WKS CHR	GOLD	ARTIST — Album Title	$	Label & Number
1/21/89	137	11		The First Of A Million Kisses	$8	RCA 8596

Allelujah
Clare

Comedy Waltz
Fairground Attraction

Find My Love
Moon Is Mine

Moon On The Rain
Perfect 80

Smile In A Whisper
Station Street

Whispers
Wind Knows My Name

FAIRPORT CONVENTION
English folk-rock group featuring lead singer Sandy Denny (d: 4/21/78 [age 37]). Varying membership included vocalist Ian Matthews (1967-69) and guitarist Richard Thompson (1967-71).

DEBUT DATE	PEAK POS	WKS CHR	GOLD	ARTIST — Album Title	$	Label & Number
12/4/71	200	1	1	Angel Delight	$12	A&M 4319
3/25/72	195	3	2	"Babbacombe" Lee	$12	A&M 4333
				based on the story of condemned prisoner John Lee		
8/16/75	143	8	3	Rising For The Moon	$10	Island 9313

After Halloween (3)
Angel Delight (1)
Banks Of The Sweet Primroses (1)
Bonny Black Hare (1)

Bridge Over The River Ash (1)
Cuckoo's Nest (medley) (1)
Dawn (3)
Hardiman The Fiddler (medley) (1)

Iron Lion (3)
John Babbacombe Lee (2)
Journeyman's Grace (1)
Let It Go (3)
Lord Marlborough (1)
Night-Time Girl (3)

One More Chance (3)
Papa Stour (medley) (1)
Restless (3)
Rising For The Moon (3)
Sickness & Diseases (1)
Sir William Gower (1)

Stranger To Himself (3)
What Is True? (3)
White Dress (3)
Wizard Of The Worldly Game (1)

★★93★★ FAITH, Percy
Born on 4/7/08 in Toronto; died of cancer on 2/9/76. Orchestra leader. Moved to the United States in 1940. Joined Columbia Records in 1950 as conductor/arranger for their leading singers (Tony Bennett, Doris Day, Rosemary Clooney, Johnny Mathis and others).

DEBUT DATE	PEAK POS	WKS CHR	GOLD	ARTIST — Album Title	$	Label & Number
7/28/56	18	2	1	Passport To Romance [I]	$15	Columbia 880
5/6/57	8	2	2	My Fair Lady [I]	$15	Columbia 895
5/25/59	17	14	3	Porgy And Bess [I]	$15	Columbia 8105
1/11/60	7	17	● 4	Bouquet [I]	$15	Columbia 8124
11/28/60+	7	15	5	Jealousy [I]	$15	Columbia 8292
1/9/61	6	23	6	Camelot [I]	$15	Columbia 8370
10/9/61	38	7	7	Mucho Gusto! More Music Of Mexico [I]	$15	Columbia 8439
4/14/62	26	6	8	Bouquet Of Love [I]	$15	Columbia 8481
9/29/62	105	5	9	The Music Of Brazil! [I]	$15	Columbia 8622
6/22/63	12	36	● 10	Themes for Young Lovers [I]	$12	Columbia 8823
10/19/63	80	15	11	Shangri-La! [I]	$12	Columbia 8824
2/15/64	103	12	12	Great Folk Themes [I]	$12	Columbia 8908
5/30/64	110	7	13	More Themes for Young Lovers [I]	$12	Columbia 8967
12/4/65	101	5	14	Broadway Bouquet [I]	$12	Columbia 9156
5/27/67	152	5	15	The Academy Award Winner and Other Great Movie Themes [I]	$12	Columbia 9450
9/16/67	111	17	16	Today's Themes For Young Lovers [I]	$12	Columbia 9504

DEBUT DATE	PEAK POS	WKS CHR	GOLD	ARTIST — Album Title	$	Label & Number
				FAITH, Percy — Cont'd		
3/23/68	**121**	22	17	For Those In Love	$12	Columbia 9610
9/21/68	**95**	11	18	Angel Of The Morning (Hit Themes For Young Lovers)	$12	Columbia 9706
2/15/69	**88**	14	19	Those Were The Days	$10	Columbia 9762
5/31/69	**194**	4	20	Windmills Of Your Mind .... [I]	$10	Columbia 9835
9/27/69	**134**	11	21	Love Theme From "Romeo & Juliet"	$10	Columbia 9906
2/14/70	**88**	14	22	Leaving On A Jet Plane...............................	$10	Columbia 9983
6/13/70	**196**	2	23	Held Over! Today's Great Movie Themes........ [I]	$10	Columbia 1019
10/17/70	**179**	4	24	The Beatles Album .... [I]	$10	Columbia 30097
1/23/71	**200**	2	25	A Time For Love ....[K]	$10	Columbia 30330 [2]
2/27/71	**198**	2	26	I Think I Love You	$10	Columbia 30502
7/31/71	**184**	5	27	Black Magic Woman .... [I]	$10	Columbia 30800
12/18/71+	**186**	6	28	Jesus Christ, Superstar........................ [I]	$10	Columbia 31042
4/1/72	**176**	6	29	Joy .... [I]	$8	Columbia 31301
9/23/72	**197**	4	30	Day By Day	$8	Columbia 31627

Adios Mariquita Linda (7)
Airport Love Theme (23)
Alfie (15)
All Alone Am I (10)
Amazing Grace (30)
Amorada (Brasileirnho) (9)
Amy (10)
And This Is My Beloved (11)
Angel Of The Morning (18,25)
Anne Of The Thousand Days, Theme From (23)
Anyone Who Had A Heart (13)
April Fools (21)
Aquarius (21,25)
As Long As He Needs Me (14,20)
Ascot Gavotte (2)
Atrevido (Bem Te Vi Atrevido) (9)
Autumn Leaves (4)
Ba-Tu-Ca-Da (9)
Bach's Lunch (30)
Baia (9)
Ballad Of Easy Rider (22,23)
Ballad Of John And Yoko (24)
Bandit, The (9)
Because (24)
Begin The Beguine (5)
Besame Mucho (7)
Bess, Oh Where's My Bess (3)
Bess, You Is My Woman Now (3)
Beyond The Reef (11)
Beyond The Sea (4)
Big Yellow Taxi (27)
Black Magic Woman (27)
Blowin' In The Wind (12)
Blue Moon (8)
Blue On Blue (13)
Bonjour Tristesse (1)
Born Free (15,25)
Both Sides Now (19)
Bouquet (4)
Brand New Morning (17)
Brazil (Aquarela Do Brasil) (9)
Bread, Love And Dreams (Pane, Amore E Fantasia) (1)
Brian's Song (29)
Buzzard Song (3)
Camelot (6)
Can't Get Used To Losing You (10)
Can't Take My Eyes Off You (16)
Candy Man (3)
Canticle ..see: Scarborough Fair
Catfish Row (3)
Cherry Blossom (11,25)
Chitty Chitty Bang Bang (20)
Cielito Lindo (7)
Cocula (7)
Colours (22)
Come Saturday Morning (23)
Conquistador (30)
Dancing On The Ceiling (He Dances On My Ceiling) (5)
Darlin' Corey (12)

Day By Day (30)
Deep Purple (4)
Delicado (9)
Diamonds Are Forever (29)
Do You Know The Way To San Jose (1)
Dr. Zhivago ..see: Somewhere, My Love
Don't Say Goodbye (26)
Don't Sleep In The Subway (17)
Duet (8)
Early In The Morning (22)
Easy Days - Easy Nights (26)
Easy To Love (8)
Ebb Tide (4)
Eleanor Rigby (24)
Elvira's Theme (18,20)
Embassy Waltz (2)
End Of The World (10)
Everybody's Talkin' (22)
Everything's Alright (26,28)
Fascination (4)
Fiddler On The Roof (medley) (14,25,29)
59th Street Bridge Song (Feelin' Groovy) (16,25)
First Time Ever (I Saw Your Face) (30)
Five Hundred Miles (12)
Follow Me (6)
Fool On The Hill (19,24)
For Love Of Ivy (20)
For Once In My Life (19)
For Those In Love (17)
Forget Him (13)
Fox, Theme From The (20)
Funny Girl (20)
Georgy Girl (15)
Get Me To The Church On Time (2)
Gethsemane (I Only Want To Say) (28)
Go Away Little Girl (10)
Godfather, Love Theme From The (30)
Goin' Out Of My Head (17,25)
Golden Boy, Theme From (14)
Good Morning Starshine (21)
Green Grass Starts To Grow (26)
Greenback Dollar (12)
Greenfields (12)
Guenevere (6)
Gypsies, Tramps And Thieves (29)
Hammer Song (12)
Happy Together (16)
He Ain't Heavy, He's My Brother (24)
Heart Is A Lonely Hunter (20)
Heart Of Paris (I Left My Heart In The Heart Of Montmartre) (Coeur De Mon Coeur) (1)
Heaven On Their Minds (28)
Hello, Dolly! (14)
Hello Tomorrow (21,25)
Here, There And Everywhere (24)
Honey (I Miss You) (18,25)

Hosanna (28)
How Are Things In Glocca Morra? (20)
How Can I Be Sure (30)
How High The Moon (8)
How To Handle A Woman (6)
Huapango (7)
Hurting Each Other (29)
I Can Hear The Music (16)
I Concentrate On You (8)
I Could Have Danced All Night (2)
I Don't Know How To Love Him (26,28)
I Got Plenty O' Nuttin' (3)
I Love How You Love Me (19)
I Loved You Once In Silence (6)
I Loves You, Porgy (3)
I Need You (30)
I Only Have Eyes For You (8)
I Say A Little Prayer (17)
I Think I Love You (26)
I Will Follow You (10)
I Wonder What The King Is Doing Tonight (6)
I'll Take You Home (13)
I'm An Ordinary Man (2)
I've Grown Accustomed To Her Face (2)
I've Told Every Little Star (5)
If (2)
If Ever I Would Leave You (6)
If I Loved You (8)
Intermezzo (4)
Invitation (8)
It Ain't Necessarily So (3)
It Must Be Him (17)
Jealousy (Jalousie) (5)
Jean (23)
Joy (29)
Judy (13)
Kahlua (25)
Kashmiri Song (11)
Kisses Sweeter Than Wine (12)
La Chaparrita (7)
La Negra (7)
Lara's Theme ..see: Somewhere, My Love
Las Altenitas (A Gay Ranchero) (7)
Las Mananitas (7)
Laura (4)
Leavin' For The Promised Land (3)
Leaving On A Jet Plane (22)
Lemon Tree (12)
Let Go (Canto De Ossanha) (22)
Let It Be (24)
Lion In Winter (20)
Little Bells And Big Bells (Glocke Und Glockchen) (1)
Little Dreamer (Tutu Maramba) (9)
Little Green Apples (19)
Little Lost Dog (Chiens Perdus Sans Collier) (1)
Live For Life (17)
Long Ago (14)
Look Of Love (17)

Love (Can Make You Happy) (21)
Love Story, Theme From (26)
Love The One You're With (26)
Lucy In The Sky With Diamonds (24)
Lusty Month Of May (6)
MacArthur Park (18,25)
Mack The Knife ..see: Threepenny Opera, Theme From The
Madeira (1)
Make Someone Happy (14)
Man And A Woman (15,25)
Man Without Love (Quando M'Innamoro) (18)
March (6)
March Of Siamese Children (11)
Maria Elena (7)
Mary In The Morning (16)
Mary, Queen Of Scots (This Way Mary), Love Theme From (29)
Maxixe (Dengoza) (9)
Merry-Go-Round (Complainte De La Butte) (1)
Michael Row The Boat (12)
Michelle (24)
Midnight Cowboy (23)
Minute Samba (9)
Moon Of Manakoora (11)
More Than You Know (5)
Most Beautiful Girl In The World (5)
Moulin Rouge, Song From (4)
Mountain High, Valley Low (11)
Mrs. Robinson (16)
Mucho Gusto (7)
Music Until Midnight (Lullaby For Adults Only) (8)
My Coloring Book (10)
My Man's Gone Now (3)
My Special Angel (19)
My Sweet Lord (26)
Never Can Say Goodbye (27)
Never My Love (17)
Norwegian Wood (24)
O Lawd I'm On My Way (3)
Oh I Can't Sit Down (3)
Old Fashioned Love Song (29)
On Broadway (10,25)
On The Street Where You Live (2)
Once Upon A Time (14)
One (21)
Oscar (Maybe September), Song From The (15)
Our Day Will Come (10,25)
Out Of This World (8)
Oye Como Va (27)
Patton Theme (23)
Perfidia (7)
Pilate's Dream (28)
Popsicles And Icicles (13)
Portuguese Washerwomen (Les Lavandieres Du Portugal) (1)

Promises, Promises (19)
Quiet Day (19)
Quiet Thing (14)
Rain In Spain (2)
Raindrops Keep Fallin' On My Head (22,23)
Release Me (16)
Return To Paradise (11)
Reza (Ray-za) (27)
Rhythm Of The Rain (10)
Right As The Rain (5)
Romeo And Juliet, Love Theme From (21)
Rose Garden (26)
Sand Pebbles (And We Were Lovers), Theme From The (15)
Sayonara (1)
Scalinatella (Stay After School) (1)
Scarborough Fair/Canticle (18)
See The Funny Little Clown (13)
Shaft, Theme From (29)
Shangri-La (11)
Show Me (2)
Sierra Madre (Luna Gitana) (1)
Simon Zealotes (28)
Simple Joys Of Maidenhood (6)
Since I Fell For You (13)
Sloop John B. (12)
Soft Lights And Sweet Music (8)
Solitude (4)
Sombra (Merveilleux) (1)
Somethin' Stupid (16)
Something (22,24)
Somewhere (14)
Somewhere, My Love (15)
Song Of India (11)
Song Sung Blue (30)
Sophisticated Lady (5)
Spanish Harlem (25)
Speak Low (8)
Spinning Wheel (21)
Star! (20)
Stella By Starlight (8)
Stormy (19)
Stranger In Paradise (11)
Strawberry Woman And The Crab Man (3)
Sugar Shack (13)
Summer Of '42 (The Summer Knows), Theme From (29)
Summer Place, Theme From A (21) *1*
Summertime (3)
Sun King (27)
Sunny (17,25)
Sunrise, Sunset (medley) (14,25,29)
Superstar (28)
Sweetest Sounds (14)
Tell Her (Every Girl Likes To Be Told) (18)
Temple, The (28)
Temptation (5)
Tenderly (4)
That Old Black Magic (5)

Then You May Take Me To The Fair (6)
There's A Boat That's Leavin' Soon For New York (3)
There's A Kind Of Hush (All Over The World) (16)
This Guy's In Love With You (18)
This Hotel (15)
This Is My Song (15)
This Land Is Your Land (12)
This Train (12)
Those Were The Days (19)
Threepenny Opera (Moritat), Theme From The (1)
Through The Eyes Of A Child (Un Jour, Un Enfant) (21)
Tia Juana (5)
Tico-Tico (9)
Time For Livin' (18)
Time For Love (15,25)
Too Young (30)
Tres (27)
Trial Before Pilate (28)
True Grit (23)
Tu Sabes (9)
Um, Um, Um, Um, Um, Um (13)
Up On The Roof (10,25)
Viva Tirado (27)
Wailing Of The Willow (27)
Waitin' ('Round The Bend) (17)
Wanting You (22)
Wave (27)
Wedding Bell Blues (22)
What Are You Doing The Rest Of Your Life (23)
What Do The Simple Folks Do (6)
What Kind Of Fool Am I? (14,25)
What's The Buzz (28)
Where Or When (5)
Who Can I Turn To (When Nobody Needs Me) (14)
Windmills Of Your Mind (20)
Windy (16,25)
Wishing Doll (15)
With A Little Bit Of Luck (2) *82*
Without Her (21)
Without You (29)
Wives And Lovers (13)
Woman Is A Sometime Thing (3)
World Of Whispers (16)
Wouldn't It Be Lovely (2)
Yellow Days (16)
Yester-Me, Yester-You, Yesterday (17)
Yesterday (24)
You Don't Own Me (13)
Young Lovers, Theme For (10) *35*
"Z" (To Yelasto Pedi), Theme From (23)
Zorba (19)

237

DEBUT DATE	PEAK POS	WKS CHR	GOLD	ARTIST — Album Title	$	Label & Number

FAITHFULL, Marianne

Born on 12/29/46 in Hampstead, London. Discovered by Rolling Stones' manager, Andrew Loog Oldham. Involved in a long, tumultuous relationship with Mick Jagger. Acted in several stage and screen productions. Married British art gallery owner John Dunbar, Vibrators bassist Ben Brierly and American playwright Giorgio Dellaterza.

DEBUT DATE	PEAK POS	WKS CHR	GOLD	ARTIST — Album Title	$	Label & Number
6/5/65	12	31		1 Marianne Faithfull	$20	London 423
12/25/65+	81	16		2 Go Away From My World	$20	London 452
11/19/66	147	2		3 Faithfull Forever	$20	London 482
4/5/69	171	10		4 Marianne Faithfull's Greatest Hits .... [G]	$15	London 547
2/2/80	82	15		5 Broken English	$12	Island 9570
10/17/81	104	9		6 Dangerous Acquaintances	$8	Island 9648
3/26/83	107	7		7 A Child's Adventure	$8	Island 90066
7/7/90	160	9		8 Blazing Away .... [L]	$12	Island 842794

all tracks but one were recorded live on 11/25-26/89 at St. Anne's Cathedral in Brooklyn, New York

As Tears Go By (1,4,8) **22**
Ashes In My Hand (7)
Ballad Of Lucy Jordan (5,8)
Blazing Away (8)
Blue Millionaire (7)
Brain Drain (5)
Broken English (5,8)
Come And Stay With Me (1,4) **26**
Come My Way (2)
Counting (3)
Easy In The City (6)
Eye Communication (6)
Falling From Grace (7)

First Time (3)
For Beautie's Sake (6)
Go Away From My World (2,4) **89**
Guilt (5,8)
He'll Come Back To Me (1)
How Should True Love (2)
I Have A Love (3)
I'm A Loser (1)
I'm The Sky (3)
If I Never Get To Love You (1)
In My Time Of Sorrow (1,4)
In The Night Time (3)
Intrigue (6)

Ireland (7)
Is This What I Get For Loving You? (4)
Last Thing On My Mind (4)
Les Prisons Du Roy (8)
Lucky Girl (3)
Lullabye (2)
Mary Ann (2)
Monday Monday (3,4)
Morning Come (7)
Ne Me Quitte Pas (3)
North Country Maid (4)
Paris Bells (1)
Plaisir D'Amour (3)

Running For Our Lives (7)
Sally Free And Easy (2)
Scarborough Fair (2,4)
She Moved Through The Fair (8)
She's Got A Problem (7)
Sister Morphine (8)
So Sad (6)
Some Other Spring (3)
Strange One (6)
Strange Weather (8)
Summer Nights (2,4) **24**
Sweetheart (6)
Tenderness (6)

That's Right Baby (3)
This Little Bird (1,4) **32**
Time Takes Time (1)
Times Square (7,8)
Tomorrow's Calling (3,4)
Truth Bitter Truth (6)
What Have I Done Wrong (1)
What Have They Done To The Rain (1)
What's The Hurry? (5)
When I Find My Life (8)
Why'd Ya Do It? (5,8)
Wild Mountain Tyme (2)
Witches' Song (5)

With You In Mind (3)
Working Class Hero (5,8)
Yesterday (2,4)

FAITH HOPE & CHARITY

Soul trio from Tampa, Florida: Brenda Hilliard, Albert Bailey and Zulema Cusseaux. Zulema went solo in 1971. Hilliard and Bailey continued as a duo until 1974 when joined by Diane Destry.

DEBUT DATE	PEAK POS	WKS CHR	GOLD	ARTIST — Album Title	$	Label & Number
8/30/75	100	14		Faith, Hope & Charity	$10	RCA 1100

Disco Dan
Don't Go Looking For Love

Find A Way
Just One Look

Let's Go To The Disco
Little Bit Of Love

Mellow Me
Rescue Me

To Each His Own 50

FAITH NO MORE

San Francisco rock quintet: Michael "Vlad Dracula" Patton (vocals), Jim Martin (guitar), Roddy Bottum (keyboards), Billy Gould (bass) and Mike Bordin (drums).

DEBUT DATE	PEAK POS	WKS CHR	GOLD	ARTIST — Album Title	$	Label & Number
2/24/90	11	60	▲	1 The Real Thing	$12	Slash 25878
7/4/92	10	19	●	2 Angel Dust	$12	Slash 26785

Be Aggressive (2)
Caffeine (2)
Crack Hitler (2)
Edge Of The World (1)

Epic (1) **9**
Everything's Ruined (2)
Falling To Pieces (1) **92**
From Out Of Nowhere (1)

Jizzlobber (2)
Kindergarten (2)
Land Of Sunshine (2)
Malpractice (2)

MidLife Crisis (2)
Midnight Cowboy (2)
Morning After (1)
RV (2)

Real Thing (1)
Small Victory (2)
Smaller And Smaller (2)
Surprise! You're Dead! (1)

Underwater Love (1)
War Pigs (1)
Woodpecker From Mars (1)
Zombie Eaters (1)

FALCO

Falco (Johann Holzel) was born on 2/19/57 in Vienna, Austria.

DEBUT DATE	PEAK POS	WKS CHR	GOLD	ARTIST — Album Title	$	Label & Number
5/7/83	64	13		1 Einzelhaft	$8	A&M 4951
3/1/86	3	27	●	2 Falco 3	$8	A&M 5105

America (2)
Auf Der Flucht (1)
Der Kommissar (1)
Einzelhaft (1)
Ganz Wien (1)

Helden Von Heute (1)
Hinter Uns Die Sintflut (1)
It's All Over Now, Baby Blue (2)
Jeanny (2)

Macho Macho (2)
Manner Des Westens - Any Kind Of Land (2)
Maschine Brennt (1)

Munich Girls (Looking For Love) (2)
Nie Mehr Schule (1)
Nothin' Sweeter Than Arabia (2)

Rock Me Amadeus (2) **1**
Siebzehn Jahr (1)
Tango The Night (2)
Vienna Calling (2) **18**
Zuviel Hitze (1)

FALTSKOG, Agnetha

Pronounced: Ag-nyet-ta Felts-kogue. Born on 4/5/50 in Sweden. Member of Abba.

DEBUT DATE	PEAK POS	WKS CHR	GOLD	ARTIST — Album Title	$	Label & Number
9/17/83	102	11		Wrap Your Arms Around Me	$8	Polydor 813242

Can't Shake Loose 29
Heat Is On
I Wish Tonight Could Last Forever

Man
Mr. Persuasion
Once Burned, Twice Shy

Shame
Stand By My Side
Stay

Take Good Care Of Your Children
To Love

Wrap Your Arms Around Me

FAME — see KIDS FROM "FAME" and SOUNDTRACKS

FAME, Georgie

Born Clive Powell on 6/26/43 in Lancashire, England. Began as a pianist with Billy Fury's backup group The Blue Flames.

DEBUT DATE	PEAK POS	WKS CHR	GOLD	ARTIST — Album Title	$	Label & Number
5/1/65	137	3		1 Yeh Yeh	$20	Imperial 12282
5/11/68	185	4		2 The Ballad Of Bonnie And Clyde	$20	Epic 26368

Ask Me Nice (2)
Ballad Of Bonnie And Clyde (2) **7**
Blue Prelude (2)
Bullets La Verne (2)

Exactly Like You (2)
Get On The Right Track, Baby (1)
Gimme That Wine (1)
I Love The Life I Live (1)

I'm In The Mood For Love (1)
Let The Sun Shine In (1)
Mellow Yellow (2)
Monkey Time (1)
Monkeying Around (1)

Pink Champagne (1)
Point Of No Return (1)
Preach And Teach (1)
Pride And Joy (1)
Side By Side (1)

Someone To Watch Over Me (2)
St. James Infirmary (2)
This Is Always (2)
When I'm Sixty-Four (2)

Yeh, Yeh (1) **21**

FAMILY

British quintet led by vocalist Roger Chapman and bassist John Wetton (King Crimson, Uriah Heep, Asia).

DEBUT DATE	PEAK POS	WKS CHR	GOLD	ARTIST — Album Title	$	Label & Number
2/5/72	177	7		1 Fearless	$12	United Art. 5562
10/28/72	183	5		2 Bandstand	$12	United Art. 5644

Between Blue And Me (1)
Blind (1)
Bolero Babe (2)
Broken Nose (2)

Burlesque (2)
Burning Bridges (1)
Children (1)
Coronation (2)

Crinkly Grin (1)
Dark Eyes (2)
Glove (1)
Larf And Sing (1)

My Friend The Sun (2)
Ready To Go (2)
Sat'd'y Barfly (1)
Save Some For Thee (1)

Spanish Tide (1)
Take Your Partners (1)
Top Of The Hill (2)

DEBUT DATE	PEAK POS	WKS CHR	GOLD	ARTIST — Album Title	$	Label & Number

FAMILY, The
Twin Cities quintet featuring Time members St. Paul (Paul Peterson), Jerome Benton and Jellybean Johnson. Female vocalist Susannah is the twin sister of Wendy Melvoin (Prince's Revolution, Wendy & Lisa) and the daughter of jazz pianist Mike Melvoin (The Plastic Cow).

| 9/7/85 | 62 | 22 | | The Family... | $8 | Paisley P. 25322 |

Desire | Mutiny | River Run Dry | Susannah's Pajamas
High Fashion | Nothing Compares 2 U | **Screams Of Passion 63** | Yes

FANNY
Female rock quartet from California: vocalists/sisters June and Jean Millington, with Alice DeBuhr and Nickey Barclay. Jean and Alice left in 1974, replaced by Brie Brandt-Howard and Patti Quatro (sister of Suzi Quatro).

| 10/23/71 | 150 | 7 | | 1 Charity Ball.. | $12 | Reprise 6456 |
| 4/1/72 | 135 | 6 | | 2 Fanny Hill... | $12 | Reprise 2058 |

Ain't That Peculiar (2) **85** | **Charity Ball** (1) **40** | Little While Later (1) | Soul Child (1) | Thinking Of You (1) | You're The One (1)
Blind Alley (2) | First Time (2) | Person Like You (1) | Sound And The Fury (2) | What Kind Of Lover (1) | You've Got A Home (2)
Borrowed Time (2) | Hey Bulldog (2) | Place In The Country (1) | Special Care (1) | What's Wrong With Me? (1) |
Cat Fever (1) | Knock On My Door (2) | Rock Bottom Blues (2) | Think About The Children (2) | Wonderful Feeling (2) |

FANTASTIC FOUR
Soul group formed in Detroit in 1955. Consisted of "Sweet" James Epps, Robert and Joseph Pruitt, and Toby Childs. Robert Pruitt and Childs later replaced by Cleveland Horne and Ernest Newsome. Epps was cousin of the Tilmon brothers of the Detroit Emeralds.

| 6/21/75 | 99 | 16 | | Alvin Stone (The Birth And Death Of A Gangster)............................... | $10 | Westbound 201 |

Alvin Stone (The Birth & | County Line | Let This Moment Last | My Love Won't Stop At | Words
Death Of A Gangster) 74 | Have A Little Mercy | Forever | Nothing |

FANTASY
Rock quintet (ages 16-21 in 1970). Led by guitarist Vincent DeMeo, Jr. and female vocalist Lydia Miller.

| 8/15/70 | 194 | 3 | | Fantasy... | $12 | Liberty 7643 |

Circus Of Invisible Men | Happy | Understand | What's Next
Come | **Stoned Cowboy 77** | Wages Of Sin |

FARGO, Donna
Born Yvonne Vaughan on 11/10/49 in Mt. Airy, North Carolina. Recorded for Ramco in 1969. Worked as a high school teacher until June 1972. Donna was stricken with multiple sclerosis in 1979. Has own music publishing company.

| 7/15/72 | 47 | 43 | ● | 1 The Happiest Girl In The Whole U.S.A. .... | $12 | Dot 26000 |
| 3/17/73 | 104 | 11 | | 2 My Second Album .... | $12 | Dot 26006 |

Awareness Of Nothing (1) | **Happiest Girl In The** | How Close You Came (To | Johnny B. Goode (1) | **Superman** (2) **41**
Daddy Dumplin' (1) | **Whole U.S.A.** (1) **11** | Being Gone) (1) | Little Somethin' (To Hang | You Don't Mess Around
Don't Be Angry (2) | Have Yourself A Time (2) | How Would I (2) | On To) (1) | With Jim (2)
Forever Is As Far As I Could | He Can Have All He Wants | I'd Love You To Want Me (2) | Manhattan, Kansas (1) | **You Were Always There**
Go (2) | (2) | It Would Have Been Just | Society's Got Us (1) | (2) **93**
Funny Face (1) **5** | Hot Diggity Dog (2) | Perfect (1) | Song I Can Sing (2) |

FARQUAHR
Brothers Barnswallow, Hummingbird, Condor and Flamingo Farquahr.

| 12/5/70 | 195 | 3 | | Farquahr... | $10 | Elektra 74083 |

Babe In The Woods | Hanging On By A Thread | Just For Kings | Much Too Nice A Day | Peace In Mind | Start Living
Dear John Deere | Holy Moses | Moonrider | My Island | Silver Spoons | Streets Of Montreal

FARRELL, Eileen
Born on 2/13/20 in Willimantic, Connecticut. Operatic soprano. Major debut came with the San Francisco Opera in 1956. Metropolitan Opera debut in February 1960.

| 2/13/61 | 15 | 17 | | I've Got A Right To Sing The Blues .... | $20 | Columbia 1465 |

Blues In The Night | He Was Too Good To Me | I'm Old Fashioned | On The Sunny Side Of The | Supper Time
Ev'rytime | I Gotta Right To Sing The | Looking For A Boy | Street | Ten Cents A Dance
Glad To Be Unhappy | Blues | Old Devil Moon | September Song |

FARRELL, Joe — see BENSON, George

FARRENHEIT
Boston rock trio: Charlie Farren (guitar, vocals), David Heit (bass) and Muzz (drums).

| 5/9/87 | 179 | 7 | | Farrenheit... | $8 | Warner 25564 |

Bad Habit | Goofy Boy | Lost In Loveland | Shine | Staying Together | Wildness
Fool In Love | Impossible World | New Days | Stand Out | Time Won't Wait |

FASTER PUSSYCAT
Los Angeles-based, hard-rock quintet led by vocalist Taime Downe. Name taken from the 1962 action film *Faster Pussycat! Kill! Kill!.*

8/29/87	97	35		1 Faster Pussycat	$8	Elektra 60730
9/23/89+	48	41	●	2 Wake Me When It's Over	$8	Elektra 60883
8/22/92	90	4		3 Whipped...	$12	Elektra 61124

Ain't No Way Around It (2) | Cat Bash (3) | **House Of Pain** (2) **28** | Mr. Lovedog (3) | Ship Rolls In (1)
Arizona Indian Doll (2) | Cathouse (1) | Jack The Bastard (3) | No Room For Emotion (1) | Shooting You Down (1)
Babylon (1) | City Has No Heart (1) | Little Dove (2) | Nonstop To Nowhere (3) | Slip Of The Tongue (2)
Bathroom Wall (1) | Cryin' Shame (2) | Loose Booty (3) | Only Way Out (3) | Smash Alley (1)
Big Dictionary (3) | Don't Change That Song (1) | Madam Ruby's Love | Out With A Bang (3) | Tattoo (2)
Body Thief (3) | Friends (3) | Boutique (1) | Poison Ivy (2) | Where There's A Whip
Bottle In Front Of Me (1) | Gonna Walk (2) | Maid In Wonderland (3) | Pulling Weeds (2) | There's A Way (2)

FASTWAY
British rock group led by Motorhead's Fast Eddie Clarke (guitar) with David King (vocals), Jerry Shirley (drums) and Charlie McCracken (bass; joined in 1984).

5/28/83	31	32		1 Fastway	$8	Columbia 38662
7/21/84	59	14		2 All Fired Up	$8	Columbia 39373
11/22/86+	156	12		3 Trick Or Treat .... [S]	$8	Columbia 40549

DEBUT DATE	PEAK POS	WKS CHR	GOLD	ARTIST — Album Title	$	Label & Number
4/22/89	135	10	4	On Target	$8	GWR 75411

After Midnight (3)
All Fired Up (2)
All I Need Is Your Love (2)
Another Day (1)
Change Of Heart (4)
Close Your Eyes (4)
Dead Or Alive (4)
Don't Stop The Fight (3)

Easy Livin' (1)
Feel Me, Touch Me (Do Anything You Want) (1)
Fine Line (4)
Get Tough (3)
Give It All You Got (1)
Give It Some Action (1)
Heft! (1,3)

Hold On To The Night (3)
Hung Up On Love (2)
Hurtin' Me (2)
If You Could See (2,3)
Let Him Rock (4)
Misunderstood (2)
Non-Stop Love (2)
Say What You Will (1)

She Is Danger (4)
Show Some Emotion (4)
Stand Up (3)
Station (2)
Steal The Show (2)
Stranger, The (2)
Tear Down The Walls (3)
Telephone (2)

Tell Me (2)
These Dreams (4)
Trick Or Treat (3)
Two Hearts (4)
We Become One (1)
You (4)
You Got Me Runnin' (1)

FATBACK
R&B rock band originally consisted of Johnny King (guitar), Earl Shelton (saxophone), George Williams (trumpet), George Adam (flute), Johnny Flippin (bass) and Bill Curtis (drums). Later included Saunders McCrae (keyboards) and Richard Cromwell (trombone).

| 2/28/76 | 158 | 8 | 1 | Raising Hell | $10 | Event 6905 |
| 8/28/76 | 182 | 5 | 2 | Night Fever | $10 | Spring 6711 |

above 2: THE FATBACK BAND

8/12/78	73	12	3	Fired Up 'N' Kickin'	$8	Spring 6718
9/29/79	89	12	4	Fatback XII	$8	Spring 6723
4/19/80	44	27	● 5	Hot Box	$8	Spring 6726
11/1/80	91	7	6	14 Karat	$8	Spring 6729
6/20/81	102	8	7	Tasty Jam	$8	Spring 6731
1/9/82	148	4	8	Gigolo	$8	Spring 6734

All Day (1)
Angel (2)
(Are You Ready) Do The Bus Stop (1)
At Last (3)
Backstrokin' (5)
Boogie Freak (3)
Booty, The (2)
Can't You See (3)
Chillin' Out (6)
Come And Get The Love (5)

Concrete Jungle (6)
December 1963 (Oh, What A Night) (2)
Disco Bass (4)
Disco Crazy (2)
Disco Queen (4)
Do It ('Til The Feelin' Runs Out) (8)
Get Out On The Dance Floor (3)
Get Ready For The Night (7)
Gigolo (8)

Gimme That Sweet Sweet Lovin' (4)
Gotta Get My Hands On Some (Money) (5)
Groovy Kind Of Day (1)
High Steppin' Lady (7)
Higher (8)
Hot Box (5)
I Can't Help Myself (Sugar Pie, Honey Bunch) (1)
I Like Girls (3)
I'm Fired Up (3)

I'm So In Love (8)
If That's The Way You Want It (2)
Joint (You And Me) (2)
Keep Your Fingers Out The Jam (7)
King Tim III (Personality Jock) (4)
Kool Whip (7)
Lady Groove (6)
Let's Do It Again (6)
Little Funky Dance (2)

Love In Perfect Harmony (4)
Love Spell (5)
Na Na, Hey Hey, Kiss Her Goodbye (8)
Night Fever (2)
No More Room For Dancing (2)
Oh Girl (8)
Party Time (1)
Put Your Love (In My Tender Care) (1)
Rockin' To The Beat (8)

Rub Down (8)
Snake (3)
Spanish Hustle (1)
Street Band (5)
Take It Any Way You Want It (7)
(To Be) Without Your Love (6)
Wanna Dance (Keep Up The Dance) (7)
You're My Candy Sweet (4)
Your Love Is Strange (6)

FAT BOYS
Brooklyn-born rap trio: Darren "The Human Beat Box" Robinson, Mark "Prince Markie Dee" Morales and Damon "Kool Rock-ski" Wimbley. Combined weight of over 750 pounds. Appeared in the 1987 film *Disorderlies*.

1/5/85	48	40	● 1	Fat Boys	$8	Sutra 1015
8/31/85	63	33	● 2	The Fat Boys Are Back!	$8	Sutra 1016
5/24/86	62	19	3	Big & Beautiful	$8	Sutra 1017
6/13/87	8	49	▲ 4	Crushin'	$8	Tin Pan A. 831948
10/3/87	108	10	5	The Best Part of the FAT BOYS	[K] $8	Sutra 1018

10 tunes from 3 earlier Sutra albums

| 7/9/88 | 33 | 24 | ● 6 | Coming Back Hard Again | $8 | Tin Pan A. 835809 |
| 10/28/89 | 175 | 3 | 7 | On And On | $8 | Tin Pan A. 838867 |

All Day Lover (6)
All You Can Eat (6)
Are You Ready For Freddy (6)
Back & Forth (6)
Beat Box Is Rockin' (3)
Between The Sheets (4)
Big And Beautiful (3)
Big Daddy (6)
Boys Will Be Boys (4)
Braggin' (7)
Breakdown (3)

Can You Feel It (1)
Comin' Back Hard Again (6)
Crushin' (4)
Don't Be Stupid (2)
Don't Dog Me (1)
Double-O Fat Boys (3)
Falling In Love (4)
Fat Boys (1,5)
Fat Boys Are Back (2,5)
Fat Boys Dance (1)
Fat Boys Scratch (2)

Get Down (7)
Go For It (3)
Hard Core Reggae (2,5)
Hell, No! (4)
Human Beat Box (1,5)
Human Beat Box #2 (2)
Human Beat Box, Part 3 (3)
If It Ain't One Thing It's Anuddah (Bruddah) (7)
In The House (3,5)
It's Getting Hot (7)

Jail House Rap (1,5)
Jellyroll (6)
Just Loungin' (7)
Knock 'Em Out The Box (7)
Lie-z (7)
Louie, Louie (6) 89
Making Noise (4)
My Nuts (medley) (4)
On And On (7)
Pig Feet (6)
Place To Be (1)

Powerlord (6)
Protect Yourself (medley) (4)
Pump It Up (2)
Rainy, Rainy (7)
Rap Symphony (In C-Minor) (3)
Rock 'N' Roll (2,5)
Rock Ruling (4)
Rock The House, Y'all (6)
School Days (7)
Sex Machine (3,5)

She's Hookin' (7)
Stick 'Em (1,5)
Tings Nah Go So (7)
Trouble (7)
Twist (Yo, Twist!) (6) 16
We Can Do This (6)
Wipeout (4) 12
Yes, Yes, Y'all (2)

FATES WARNING
Heavy-metal quintet from Hartford, Connecticut: vocalist John Arch (replaced by Ray Alder in 1987), Jim Matheos, Vic Arduni (replaced by Frank Aresti in 1985), Steve Zimmerman and Joe DiBiase.

2/7/87	191	4	1	Awaken The Guardian	$8	Enigma 73231
4/23/88	111	13	2	No Exit	$8	Metal Blade 73330
9/16/89	141	9	3	Perfect Symmetry	$8	Metal Blade 73408

Anarchy Divine (2)
Arena, The (3)
At Fates Hands (3)
Chasing Time (3)
Exodus (1)

Fata Morgana (1)
Giant's Lore (Heart Of Winter) (1)
Guardian (1)
In A Word (2)

Ivory Gate Of Dreams Medley (2)
No Exit (2)
Nothing Left To Say (3)
Part Of The Machine (3)

Prelude To Ruin (1)
Shades Of Heavenly Death (2)
Silent Cries (2)
Sorceress, The (1)

Static Acts (3)
Through Different Eyes (3)
Time Long Past (1)
Valley Of The Dolls (1)
World Apart (3)

FATHER M.C.
Dancehall Reggae singer Timothy Brown. Raised in Brooklyn and Queens.

| 12/1/90+ | 62 | 30 | 1 | Father's Day | $12 | Uptown 10061 |
| 9/12/92 | 185↑ | 2↑ | 2 | Close To You | $12 | Uptown 10542 |

Ain't It Funky (1)
All I Want (2)
Baby We Can Do It (2)
Close To You (2)
Dance 4 Me (1)

Do The One, Two (2)
Everything's Gonna Be Alright (2) 42↑
Father's Day (1)
Go Natalie (2)

I Come Correct (1)
I'll Do 4 U (1) 20
I've Been Watching You (1)
Ladies, I Luv 'Em (1)
Lisa Baby (1)

My Body (2)
On The Road Again (2)
One Nite Stand (2)
Red Lace Lingerie (2)
Tell Me Something Good (1)

Treat Them Like They Want To Be Treated (1)
Why U Wanna Hurt Me (1)

FAT MATTRESS
English rock quartet formed by former Jimi Hendrix bassist Noel Redding (lead guitar).

| 11/15/69 | 134 | 10 | | Fat Mattress | $15 | Atco 309 |

All Night Drinker
Bright New Way

Everything's Blue
How Can I Live

I Don't Mind
Magic Forest

Mr. Moonshine
Petrol Pump Assistant

She Came In The Morning
Walking Through A Garden

DEBUT DATE	PEAK POS	WKS CHR	GOLD	ARTIST — Album Title	$	Label & Number

FAZE-O
Chicago R&B quintet consisting of Keith "Chop Chop" Harrison (keyboards), Ralph "Love" Aikens (guitar), Tyrone "Flye" Crum (bass), Roger "Dodger" Parker (drums) and Robert "Bip" Neal Jr. (percussion).

| 3/4/78 | 98 | 17 | | 1 Riding High .... | $8 | She 740 |
| 11/11/78 | 145 | 3 | | 2 Good Thang .... | $8 | She 741 |

Funky Lady (2)	Good Thang (2)	Riding High (1)	Toe Jam (1)	You And I (Belong Together)
Funky Reputation (1)	Love Me Girl (2)	Space People (2)	True Love (1)	(1)
Get Some Booty (1)	Party Time (2)	Test-This Is Faze-O (1)	Who Loves You (2)	

FCC [Funky Communication Committee]
White funk group — Jim "Be-Bop" Evans, leader.

| 9/8/79 | 192 | 2 | | Baby I Want You .... | $8 | Free Flight 3405 |

Ain't Givin' Up No Love	Dreamer	How Great A Love Can Be	Shot From The Saddle	That Didn't Hurt Too Bad
Baby I Want You 47	Ghost Of Love	It Took A Woman Like You	Sunshine	Woman

FEELIES, The
Quintet from Hoboken, New Jersey: Stanley Demeski, Bill Million, Dave Weckerman, Brenda Sauter and Glenn Mercer. Appeared in the 1986 film *Something Wild*. Disbanded in 1992.

| 11/19/88 | 173 | 5 | | Only Life .... | $8 | A&M 5214 |

Away	Final Word	Higher Ground	Too Far Gone	Undertow, The
Deep Fascination	For Awhile	It's Only Life	Too Much	What Goes On

FEITEN, Buzz — see LARSEN/FEITEN BAND

FELDER, Don
Born on 9/21/47 in Gainesville, Florida. Guitarist with the Eagles.

| 12/3/83+ | 178 | 8 | | Airborne .... | $8 | Elektra 60295 |

Asphalt Jungle	Haywire	Night Owl	Who Tonight
Bad Girls	Never Surrender	Still Alive	Winners

FELDER, Wilton
Born in Houston on 8/31/40. Reed player, made debut at age 12. Co-founder of The Crusaders (originally known as The Swingsters, then as the Jazz Crusaders).

12/9/78+	173	14		1 We All Have A Star	$8	ABC 1109
11/8/80	142	13		2 Inherit The Wind	$8	MCA 5144
3/9/85	81	16		3 Secrets .... [I]	$8	MCA 5510

featuring 2 vocal tracks by Bobby Womack

Cycles Of Time (1)	Inherit The Wind (2)	Mr. Scoots (3)	Ride On (1)	We All Have A Star (1)
I Found You (3)	Insight (2)	My Name Is Love (1)	Secrets (3)	Why Believe (1)
I Know Who I Am (1)	L.A. Light (2)	(No Matter How High I Get)	Someday We'll All Be Free (2)	You And Me And Ecstasy (1)
I've Got A Secret I'm Gonna	La Luz (3)	I'll Still Be Lookin' Up To	Truth Song (3)	
Tell (2)	Let's Dance Together (1)	You (3)	Until The Morning Comes (2)	

★★396★★ **FELICIANO, Jose**
Born on 9/8/45 in Lares, Puerto Rico and raised in New York City. Blind since birth. Virtuoso acoustic guitarist. First performed at age nine. First recorded for Spanish language TV series in the mid-1960s. Acted in the TV shows *McMillan & Wife, Lucas Turner, Kung Fu, Chico & The Man* and own specials. Composed score for TV's *Chico & The Man*. Won the 1968 Best New Artist Grammy Award.

7/20/68	2³	59	●	1 Feliciano!	$12	RCA 3957
12/7/68+	24	19		2 Souled	$12	RCA 4045
7/5/69	16	36	●	3 Feliciano/10 To 23	$12	RCA 4185
				featuring a recording by Jose at age 10		
12/20/69+	29	14	●	4 Alive Alive-O! .... [L]	$12	RCA·6021 [2]
				in concert at the London Palladium		
5/30/70	57	20		5 Fireworks	$8	RCA 4370
4/17/71	92	10		6 Encore! Jose Feliciano's Finest Performances .... [G]	$8	RCA 1005
11/13/71	173	9		7 That The Spirit Needs	$8	RCA 4573
5/19/73	156	8		8 Compartments	$8	RCA 0141
12/21/74+	136	7		9 And The Feeling's Good	$8	RCA 0407
9/6/75	165	4		10 Just Wanna Rock 'N' Roll	$8	RCA 1005

Affirmation (10)	Don't Let The Sun Catch	Hitchcock Railway (2,6) 77	Manha de Carnaval (medley)	Pay Day (7)	Take Me To The Pilot (7)
Ain't That Peculiar (10)	You Crying (1,4)	I Can't Get Next To You (10)	(4)	Peace Of Mind (8)	Thank God (10)
Amor Jibaro (3)	El Jenite (4)	(I Can't Get No) Satisfaction	Marie (10)	Pegao (5,6)	(There's) Always Something
And I Love Her (1)	El Voh (4)	(5)	Me And Baby Jane (8)	Rain (3,4,6) 76	There To Remind Me (1)
And The Feeling's Good (9)	Essence Of Your Love (9)	I'll Be Your Baby Tonight (2)	Mellow Feeling (7)	Rock 'N' Roll (10)	Things Are Changing (8)
And The Sun Will Shine (2)	Felicidade (medley) (4)	I'm Leavin' (8)	Miss Otis Regrets (3)	Sad Gypsy (2)	Twilight Time (10)
Blackbird (5)	Find Somebody (8)	I've Got To Convince Myself	Must Be The Breeze (10)	Samba de Orfeu (medley) (4)	Virgo (9)
Border Song (4)	Fireworks (5)	(9)	My Last Farewell (7)	Sea Cruise (8)	Wichita Lineman (6)
By The Time I Get To	First Of May (3)	In My Life (1)	**My World Is Empty**	She Came In Through The	Wild World (7)
Phoenix (4)	God Save The Queen (4)	Just A Little Bit Of Rain (1)	**Without You** (2) 87	Bathroom Window (5)	Windmills Of Your Mind (3)
California Dreamin' (1,4,6)	Golden Lady (9)	La Entrada de Bilboa (Battle	Nature Boy (6)	She Let Me Down (7)	Yes We Can Can (8)
Chico And The Man (9) 96	Gotta Get A Message To You	of Entrada) (4)	Nena Na Na (1)	She's A Woman (3)	Yesterday (5)
Come Down Jesus (7)	(3)	Lady Madonna (3)	No Dogs Allowed (4)	She's Too Good To Me (2)	You're No Good (9)
Comedy Bit (4)	Guantanamera (4)	Last Thing On My Mind (1)	No Jive (10)	Simple Song (8)	You've Got A Lot Of Style (2)
Compartments (8)	Hard Times In El Barrio (9)	Let It Be (5)	Nobody Knows You When	Sleep Late, My Lady Friend	Younger Generation (2)
Day In The Life (4)	Here, There And Everywhere	Life Is That Way (6)	You're Down And Out (4)	(2)	
Day Tripper (4)	(1)	**Light My Fire** (1,4,6) 3	Norwegian Wood (5)	Spirit, The (7)	
Daytime Dreams (7)	**Hey! Baby** (2) 71	Little Red Rooster (3)	Not That Kind Of Guy (Hot	Stay With Me (9)	
Destiny (5,6) 83	Hey Jude (3)	Malaguena (4,6)	Burrito #1) (10)	Sunny (1)	
Differently (9)	Hey Look At The Sun (8)	Mama Don't Allow It (4)	Once There Was A Love (5)	**Susie-Q** (5,6) 84	
Don't Fail (8)	**Hi-Heel Sneakers** (2,4,6) 25		Only Once (7)	Suspicions (10)	

FELONY
Los Angeles rock quintet led by brothers Jeffrey (vocals) and Joe (guitar) Spry.

| 3/26/83 | 185 | 5 | | The Fanatic .... | $8 | Rock 'n' R. 38453 |

Aggravated Man	Girl Ain't Straight	No Room In Heaven	Positively Negative	Teaser
Fanatic, The 42	Kristine	One Step	666 Beware	What A Way To Go

DEBUT DATE	PEAK POS	WKS CHR	GOLD	ARTIST — Album Title	$	Label & Number

FEMME FATALE

Four-man, one-woman, heavy-metal band: Lorraine Lewis (vocals), Mazzi Rawd, Rick Rael, Bill D'Angelo and Bobby Murray.

1/28/89	141	5		Femme Fatale..	$8	MCA 42155

Back In Your Arms Again   Falling In & Out Of Love   Heat The Fire   My Baby's Gun   Touch And Go
Cradle's Rockin'   Fortune & Fame   If   Rebel   Waiting For The Big One

FENDER, Freddy

Born Baldemar Huerta on 6/4/37 in San Benito, Texas. Mexican-American singer/guitarist. First recorded in Spanish under his real name for Falcon in 1956. In the film *The Milagro Beanfield War*. Joined the Texas Tornados in 1990.

4/19/75	20	43	●	1 Before The Next Teardrop Falls..	$10	ABC/Dot 2020
10/18/75	41	18		2 Are You Ready For Freddy...	$10	ABC/Dot 2044
2/28/76	59	11		3 Rock 'n' Country..	$8	ABC/Dot 2050
11/6/76	170	3		4 If You're Ever In Texas..	$8	ABC/Dot 2061
5/21/77	155	7		5 The Best Of Freddy Fender......................................[G]	$8	ABC/Dot 2079

After The Fire Is Gone (1)   I Almost Called Your Name (1)   If You're Ever In Texas (4)   Please Don't Tell Me How The Story Ends (1)   Take Your Time (2)   (You Came In) The Winter Of My Life (2)
Before The Next Teardrop Falls (1,5) *1*   I Can't Help It (If I'm Still In Love With You) (3)   It's All In The Game (4)   Teardrops In My Heart (2)   You Can't Get Here From There (1)
Begging To You (2)   I Can't Put My Arms Around A Memory (2)   It's Too Late (4)   Rains Came (3,5)   Then You Can Tell Me Goodbye (1)   You'll Lose A Good Thing (3,5) *32*
Big Boss Man (3)   Just One Time (4)   Roses Are Red (1)   **Vaya Con Dios** (3,5) *59*
Cielito Lindo Is My Lady (2)   I Love My Rancho Grande (1,5)   Just Out Of Reach Of My Two Open Arms (3)   San Antonio Lady (4)   **Wasted Days And Wasted Nights** (1,5) *8*
Don't Do It Darling (4)   **Living It Down** (4,5) *72*   **Secret Love** (2,5) *20*   What A Difference A Day Made (4)
50's Medley (4)   I Need You So (3)   Loving Cajun Style (2)   **Since I Met You Baby** (3,5) *45*   What'd I Say (2)
Goodbye Clothes (2)   I'm Not A Fool Anymore (1)   Mathilda (3,5)   Sometimes (4)   Wild Side Of Life (1,5)
How Much Is That Doggie In The Window (2)   I'm Not Through Loving You Yet (2)   My Happiness (3)   Sugar Coated Love (5)
Pass Me By (If You're Only Passing Through) (4)   Take Her A Message! I'm Lonely (3)

FENN, Rick — see MASON, Nick

FERGUSON, Jay

Born on 5/10/43 in San Fernando Valley, California. Before going solo, Jay formed and led the rock groups Spirit and Jo Jo Gunne.

3/25/78	72	12		1 Thunder Island	$8	Asylum 1115
4/21/79	86	16		2 Real Life Ain't This Way	$8	Asylum 158
4/17/82	178	5		3 White Noise	$8	Capitol 12196

Baby Come Back (3)   Happy Birthday, Baby (1)   I'm Down (3)   Million $ (3)   Soulin' (1)
Babylon (1)   Happy Too! (1)   Inside Out (3)   Night Shift (1)   **Thunder Island** (1) *9*
City Of Angels (2)   Have You Seen Your Mother, Baby, Standing In The Shadow? (medley) (2)   Let's Spend The Night Together (medley) (2)   No Secrets (2)   Tonite (Fallin' For Ya') (3)
Cozumel (1)   Losing Control (1)   Paying Time (2)   Too Late To Save Your Heart (2)
Davey (3)   Heat Of The Night (3)   Love Is Cold (1)   Real Life Ain't That Way (2)   Turn Yourself In (2)
Do It Again (2)   I Come Alive (3)   Magic Moment (1)   **Shakedown Cruise** (2) *31*   White Noise (3)
Empty Sky (3)   She's Mine Tonight (3)

FERGUSON, Maynard

Jazz trumpeter. Born on 5/4/28 in Verdun, Quebec, Canada. Moved to the U.S. in 1949. Played for Charlie Barnet and then Stan Kenton's Band (1950-56).

7/28/73	128	8		1 M.F. Horn/3 ....[I]	$10	Columbia 32403
4/17/76	75	14		2 Primal Scream ....[I]	$8	Columbia 33953
4/2/77	22	26	●	3 Conquistador ....[I]	$8	Columbia 34457
11/26/77	124	8		4 New Vintage ....[I]	$8	Columbia 34971
10/7/78	113	9		5 Carnival ....[I]	$8	Columbia 35480
9/1/79	188	3		6 Hot ....[I]	$8	Columbia 36124
9/27/80	188	2		7 It's My Time ....[I]	$8	Columbia 36766
5/22/82	185	4		8 Hollywood ....[I]	$8	Columbia 37713

Airegin (4)   Deja Vu (8)   **Gonna Fly Now (Theme From "Rocky")** (3) *28*   Naima (6)   Red Creek (7)   Stella By Starlight (5)
Awright, Awright (1)   Don't Stop 'Til You Get Enough (8)   Nice 'N Juicy (1)   **Rocky II Disco** (6) *82*   Swamp (2)
Baker Street (5)   Here Today (8)   Nine To Five (8)   'Round Midnight (1)   Topa-Topa Woman (6)
Battlestar Galactica, Theme From (5)   El Vuelo (The Flight) (4)   Hollywood (8)   Oasis (4)   S.O.M.F. (1)   Touch And Go (6)
Everybody Loves The Blues (7)   How Ya Doin' Baby? (5)   Offering Of Love - Part 1 (7)   Scheherazade (4)   Valachi Papers, Love Theme From The (1)
Birdland (5)   Invitation (2)   Om Sai Ram (4)   Soar Like An Eagle (3)
Cheshire Cat Walk (2)   Fantasy (5)   It's My Time (7)   Over The Rainbow (5)   Spirit Of St. Frederick (7)   You Can Have Me Anytime (7)
Conquistador (7)   Fly, The (3)   M.F. Carnival (5)   Pagliacci (2)   Star (7)
Dance To Your Heart (7)   For Your Eyes Only (8)   Maria (4)   Pocahontas (1)   Star Trek, Theme From (3,6)
Dayride (6)   Gabriel (6)   Mister Mellow (1)   Portuguese Love (8)   Star Wars, Main Title From (4)
Mother Fingers (1)   Primal Scream (2)

★★78★★   FERRANTE & TEICHER

Piano duo: Arthur Ferrante (b: 9/7/21, New York City) and Louis Teicher (b: 8/24/24, Wilkes-Barre, Pennsylvania). Met as children while attending Manhattan's performing arts academy Juilliard School.

11/20/61+	10	47		1 West Side Story & Other Motion Picture & Broadway Hits ....[I]	$15	United Art. 6166
12/18/61+	23	16		2 Love Themes ....[I]	$15	United Art. 8514
2/10/62	30	27		3 Golden Piano Hits ....[I]	$15	United Art. 8505
3/17/62	11	38		4 Tonight ....[I]	$15	United Art. 6171
6/16/62	61	11		5 Golden Themes From Motion Pictures ....[I]	$15	United Art. 6210
9/29/62	43	7		6 Pianos In Paradise ....[I]	$15	United Art. 6230
12/15/62+	60	11		7 Snowbound ....[I]	$15	United Art. 6233
6/29/63	23	13		8 Love Themes From Cleopatra ....[I]	$15	United Art. 6290
12/14/63+	63	17		9 Concert For Lovers ....[I]	$15	United Art. 6315
3/21/64	128	7		10 50 Fabulous Piano Favorites ....[I]	$15	United Art. 6343
7/18/64	128	5		11 The Enchanted World of Ferrante & Teicher ....[I]	$15	United Art. 6375
11/14/64	145	9		12 My Fair Lady ....[I]	$15	United Art. 6361

DEBUT DATE	PEAK POS	WKS CHR	GOLD	ARTIST — Album Title	$	Label & Number

FERRANTE & TEICHER — Cont'd

DEBUT DATE	PEAK POS	WKS CHR	GOLD		$	Label & Number
11/28/64+	35	20		13 The People's Choice............[I]	$12	United Art. 6385
4/24/65	130	6		14 Springtime............[I]	$12	United Art. 6406
6/12/65	120	4		15 By Popular Demand............[I]	$12	United Art. 6416
9/11/65	49	13		16 Only The Best............[I]	$12	United Art. 6434
1/1/66	134	5		17 The Ferrante And Teicher Concert............[I-L]	$12	United Art. 6444
6/25/66	119	5		18 For Lovers Of All Ages............[I]	$12	United Art. 6483
9/24/66	57	21		19 You Asked For It!............[I]	$12	United Art. 6526
2/18/67	133	5		20 A Man And A Woman & Other Motion Picture Themes............[I]	$12	United Art. 6572
12/2/67	177	2		21 Our Golden Favorites............[I]	$10	United Art. 6556
12/21/68+	198	4		22 A Bouquet Of Hits............[I]	$10	United Art. 6659
10/11/69	93	27	●	23 10th Anniversary - Golden Piano Hits............[G-I]	$10	United Art. 70 [2]
11/22/69+	61	26		24 Midnight Cowboy............[I]	$10	United Art. 6725
5/30/70	97	10		25 Getting Together............[I]	$10	United Art. 5501
12/5/70	188	2		26 Love Is A Soft Touch............[I]	$10	United Art. 6771
3/6/71	134	9		27 The Best Of Ferrante & Teicher............[K-I]	$10	United Art. 73 [2]
				recordings from 1967-70		
5/8/71	172	4		28 The Music Lovers............[I]	$10	United Art. 6792
10/9/71	172	5		29 It's Too Late............[I]	$10	United Art. 5531
1/1/72	186	3		30 Fiddler On The Roof............[I]	$10	United Art. 5552

Ac-cent-tchu-ate The Positive (medley) (10)
Adventures In Paradise (6)
African Echoes (6)
After The Fox (20)
Alfie (23)
All The Way (5)
Alley Cat (21)
Aloha Oe (11)
And I Love Her (13)
Anniversary Song (9)
Antony And Cleopatra Theme (8) 83
Apartment, Theme From The (23) 10
April In Paris (14)
Aquarius (23,24)
Around The World In 80 Days (1)
As Long As He Needs Me (15)
As Time Goes By (5)
Autumn Leaves (3)
Ballad Of Easy Rider (25)
Ballad Of The Green Berets (19)
Basin Street Blues (medley) (10)
Be My Love (5)
Beautiful (9)
Beethoven: Ode To Joy (Symphony No. 9 In D Minor) (28)
Begin The Beguine (3)
Bewitched (3)
Beyond The Blue Horizon (medley) (10)
Bible...In The Beginning, Song Of The (20)
Blue Moon (18)
Born Free (20,21,27)
Borodin: Highlights From Borodin (5)
Brazilian Sleigh Bells (7)
Breeze At I (6)
Bridge Over Troubled Water (26)
Buttons And Bows (medley) (10)
By The Time I Get To Phoenix (22,27)
Caesar & Cleopatra Theme (8)
Call Me Irresponsible (13)
Camelot (2)
Can't Help Lovin' Dat Man (2)
Can't Stop Loving You (27)
Canadian Sunset (3)
Caravan (8)
Carnival, Theme From (1)
Cast Your Fate To The Wind (16)
Champagne Waltz (10)
Charade (13)
Chim Chim Cher-ee (10)
Chopin: Polonaise (21)
Chopsticks (Bossa Nouveau) (21)

Claire De Lune (6,23)
Close To You ..see: (They Long To Be)
Colonel Bogie March (25)
Comedy Tonight (20)
Concerto For A Love's Ending (28)
Country Boy (16)
Crystal Fingers (17)
Days Of Wine And Roses (9)
Dear Heart (15)
Dear Hearts And Gentle People (medley) (10)
Debutante Waltz (15)
Devotion (8)
Do I Hear A Waltz? (16)
Do You Love Me? (30)
Dolores (medley) (10)
Dominique (21)
Downtown (16)
Dream Of Love (Liebestraum) (2,11)
Drifting And Dreaming (medley) (10)
Easter Parade (14)
Ebb Tide (6,18)
El Condor Pasa (27)
Eleventh Hour, Theme From The (9)
Enjoy Yourself (medley) (10)
Everybody Loves Somebody (13)
Exodus (3,17,23) 2
Familiar Concerto (25,27,28)
Fanny (1)
Fascination (8)
Fiddler On The Roof (16,30)
Firebird (19)
Five Minutes More (medley) (10)
Flamingo (6)
Fly Me To The Moon (9)
For All We Know (29)
For Every Man There Is A Woman (medley) (10)
For Once In My Life (25,27)
Gentle On My Mind (24)
Georgia On My Mind (13)
Get Me To The Church On Time (12)
Gigi (1)
Girl From Ipanema (13,23)
Gitchie Goomie (29)
Goin' Out Of My Head (22,27)
Golden Earrings (18)
Goldfinger (15)
Good Morning Starshine (25)
Good, The Bad And The Ugly (22)
Goodbye Again, Theme From (2) 85
Greatest Story Ever Told (15)
Greensleeves (9,23)
Grieg: Piano Concerto (Eddie's Tune), Theme From (21)
Grieg: Piano Concerto In A Minor (28)

Grieg: To Spring (14)
Hair (25)
Half A Sixpence (12)
Happy Sleigh Ride (7,11)
Hawaii (20)
He (9)
He Ain't Heavy, He's My Brother (27)
Heart And Soul (medley) (10)
Hello Dolly (13)
Her Concerto (9)
Hey Look Me Over (medley) (10)
High And The Mighty (5)
Honey (22,27)
Hooray For Love (medley) (10)
Hush...Hush, Sweet Charlotte (16)
I Could Have Danced All Night (12)
I Feel Pretty (1)
I Hear Music (medley) (10)
I Left My Heart In San Francisco (9)
I Remember You (medley) (10)
I Will Wait For You (15)
I'll Be Seeing You (9)
I'll Never Fall In Love Again (26)
I'll Remember April (14)
I'll Walk Alone (medley) (10)
I'm Always Chasing Rainbows (21)
I'm Glad There Is You (medley) (10)
I'm In The Mood For Love (2)
I've Got A Crush On You (2)
I've Got My Love To Keep Me Warm (7)
I've Grown Accustomed To Her Face (12)
I've Heard That Song Before (medley) (10)
If I Ruled The World (16)
If I Were A Rich Man (30)
Imagination (2)
Impossible Dream (23)
Impossible Dream (The Quest) (21)
In A Persian Market (8)
In The Cool Cool Cool Of The Evening (medley) (10)
Is Paris Burning, Love Theme From (20)
Is That All There Is (29)
It Might As Well Be Spring (14)
It's Been A Long Long Time (medley) (10)
It's Impossible (Somos Novios) (29)
It's So Nice To Have A Man Around The House (medley) (10)
It's Too Late (29)
Italian Caprice (The Happy Italian) (28)

James Bond Theme (13)
Japanese Garden (11)
Jean (26)
Jessica (15)
Jingle Bells (7)
Jingle, Jangle, Jingle (medley) (10)
Judith (20)
June In January (7)
Jungle Rhumba (6)
Just One More Chance (medley) (10)
Khartoum (19)
Kids (medley) (10)
King Of Kings (4)
Knack, Main Theme From The (20)
La Strada (4)
Lara's Theme (19,23)
Last Time I Saw Paris (17)
Late Show (18)
Laura (2)
Lay Lady Lay (25,27) 99
Leaving On A Jet Plane (25)
Let It Be (26)
Let It Snow (7)
Letter To My Secret Love (18)
Lili Marlene (4)
Little Green Apples (24,27)
Little Hands (18)
Loch Lomond (11)
Louise (medley) (10)
Love Is A Many Splendored Thing (2)
Love Is A Soft Touch (26)
Love Is Blue (L'Amour Est Bleu) (22)
Love Is Just Around The Corner (medley) (10)
Love Me With All Your Heart (13)
Love Story, Theme From (28,29)
Love's Old Sweet Song (24)
Lover (10)
Lover's Lullaby (4)
Mac Arthur Park (22,27)
Magical Connection (26)
Magnificent Seven (20)
Make Believe Ballroom (medley) (10)
Malaguena (21)
Mame (19)
Man And A Woman (20,23)
Man That Got Away (medley) (10)
Man Without Love (Quando M'Innamoro) (22)
March From The River Kwai ..see: Colonel Bogie March
Maria (1)
Matchmaker (15,30)
Mendelssohn: Spring-Song (14)
Mexican Hat Dance (11)
Midnight Cowboy (24,27) 10
Miracle Of Miracles (30)
Misirlou (3)

Misty (6,23)
Mona Lisa (5)
Moon Of Manakoora (6)
Moon River (4,23)
Moonlight In Vermont (7)
Moonlight On The Ganges (8)
Moonlight Serenade (7)
More (9,23)
More I See You (19)
Moulin Rouge (5)
Mozart: Piano Concerto No. 21 In C Major - K.467 (22,23,27)
Mozart: Symphony No. 40 In G Minor, K550, (1st Movement) (29)
Music Lovers (28)
My Fair Lady Overture (12)
My Foolish Heart (5)
My Funny Valentine (2)
My Ideal (medley) (10)
My Love, Forgive Me (15)
My Silent Love (medley) (10)
My Way (24)
Near You (5)
Nearness Of You (medley) (10)
Negligee (6)
Nocturne In E Flat (3)
Now I Have Everything (30)
Oh! Calcutta! (25)
Oh To Be Young Again (26)
Ole Buttermilk Sky (medley) (10)
Oliver (23)
On A Clear Day (You Can See Forever) (18)
On The Street Where You Live (12)
Once Around The World (29)
One Dozen Roses (medley) (10)
One Eyed Jacks, Love Theme From (2) 37
Orientale (8)
Out Of Nowhere (medley) (10)
Out Of This World (medley) (10)
Paper Mache (26)
Paris In The Spring (14)
Penthouse Serenade (medley) (10)
People (13)
Phaedra, Love Theme From (20)
Picnic (5)
Pieces Of Dreams (26)
Playboy's Theme (medley) (10)
Please (medley) (10)
Popi (24)
Possessed (2,11)
Procession Of Sardar (8,11)
Proud Mary (29)
Put Your Hand In The Hand (29)
Quiet Village (3)
Rachmaninoff: Piano Concerto No. 2 (28)

Rage To Live (18,20)
Rain In Spain (12)
Raindrops Keep Fallin' On My Head (27)
Rainy Days And Mondays (29)
Red Roses For A Blue Lady (16)
Reverie (15)
Rock-A-Bye Baby (24)
Romeo & Juliet, Love Theme From (27)
Rose By Any Other Name (16)
Route 66! (medley) (10)
S'posin (medley) (10)
Samson & Delilah (8,11)
Sands Of Time (8)
Scarborough Fair (24)
Scheherazade (8,11)
Schubert's Serenade (18)
Secret Love (5)
Sentimental Journey (medley) (10)
Seventh Dawn (13)
Shadow Of Your Smile (19)
Shalom (4)
Shangri-La (6)
Show Me (12)
Sirocco (8,11)
Skaters Waltz (7,11)
Sleighride (2)
Smile (4) 94
Smile A Little Smile For Me (26)
Snowbird (26)
Snowbound (7)
Something (25,27)
Somewhere (1)
Somewhere, My Love ..see: Lara's Theme
Sound Of Music (15)
Sound Of Silence (24,27)
Spanish Eyes (23)
Spellbound (5)
Spring Is Here (14)
Spring Will Be A Little Late This Year (14)
Springtime (14)
Stella By Starlight (10)
Stephen Foster Medley (17)
Strangers In The Night (19)
Summer Place, Theme From A (18)
Sunny (22,27)
Sunrise, Sunset (30)
Taboo (6)
Tammy (5)
Tangerine (medley) (10)
Tara's Theme (2,23)
Taste Of Honey (9)
Tchaikovsky: 5th Symphony, E Minor (3rd Movement) (28)
Tchaikovsky: Love Is Now (5th Symphony - 2nd Movement) (28)

DEBUT DATE	PEAK POS	WKS CHR	GOLD	ARTIST — Album Title	$	Label & Number

FERRANTE & TEICHER — Cont'd

Tchaikovsky: Piano Concerto No. 1 In B Flat Minor - (1st Movement) (28)
Tchaikovsky: Swan Lake (Swan Lake Suite, No. 1) (28)
Tchaikovsky: Tchaikovsky Concerto (3)
Temptation (21)
That's Amore (10)
(They Long To Be) Close To You (27)
Those Were The Days (23,24)
Thousand And One Nights (4)
Three Coins In The Fountain (1)
Three Over Four (19)
Tiger Rag (17)
Till (3)
To Life (30)
Tonight (1,4,17,23) 8
True Love (5)
Twilight (4)
Two Different Worlds (22)
Two Sleepy People (medley) (10)
Unchained Melody (17)
Valley Of The Dolls, Theme From (22)
Walk In The Black Forest (21)
Warsaw Concerto (3)
Way You Look Tonight (4)
What Kind Of Fool Am I (9)
What Now My Love (18,23)
When It's Springtime In The Rockies (14)
When Your Hair Has Turned To Silver (10)
Who Can I Turn To (15)
Why (22)
Windmills Of Your Mind (23,24)
Winter Wonderland (7)
Witchcraft (medley) (10)
With A Little Bit Of Luck (12)
With The Wind And The Rain In Your Hair (medley) (10)
Wives And Lovers (13)
Work Song (19)
Wouldn't It Be Lovely (12)
Yellow Bird (21)
Yellow Rolls-Royce, Theme From The (16)
Yesterday (18,23)
You Did It (12)
You Don't Have To Say You Love Me (Lo Che Non Vivo [Senza Te]) (19)
You've Got A Friend (29)
Younger Than Springtime (14)
Z (To Yelasto Pedi), Theme From (25)

FERRY, Bryan
Lead singer of Roxy Music. Born on 9/26/45 in County Durham, England. Married socialite Lucy Helmore on 6/26/82.

10/16/76	160	5		1 Let's Stick Together	$10	Atlantic 18187
4/23/77	126	5		2 In Your Mind	$10	Atlantic 18216
11/4/78	159	5		3 The Bride Stripped Bare	$10	Atlantic 19205
6/29/85	63	25		4 Boys and Girls	$8	Warner 25082
11/21/87+	63	31		5 Bete Noire	$8	Reprise 25598

translation of French title: Black Beast

| 8/26/89 | 100 | 11 | | 6 Street Life-20 Great Hits .... [G] | $10 | Reprise 25857 [2] |

BRYAN FERRY/ROXY MUSIC
Bryan Ferry's solo and Roxy Music hits from 1972-85

All Night Operator (2)
Angel Eyes (6)
Avalon (6)
Bete Noire (5)
Boys And Girls (4)
Can't Let Go (3)
Carrickfergus (3)
Casanova (1)
Chance Meeting (1)
Chosen One (4)
Dance Away (6) *44*
Day For Night (5)
Do The Strand (6)
Don't Stop The Dance (4)
Hard Rain's A-Gonna Fall More Than This (6)
[solo: Bryan] (6)
Heart On My Sleeve (1) *86*
Hold On (I'm Coming) (3)
In The Midnight Hour (6)
In Your Mind (2)
It's Only Love (1)
Jealous Guy (6)
Kiss And Tell (5) *31*
Let's Stick Together (1,6)
Limbo (5)
Love Is The Drug (6) *30*
Love Me Madly Again (2)
Name Of The Game (5)
New Town (3)
Oh Yeah (6)
One Kiss (2)
Over You (6) *80*
Party Doll (2)
Price Of Love (1)
Pyjamarama (6)
Re-Make/Re-Model (1)
Right Stuff (5)
Rock Of Ages (2)
Same Old Blues (3)
Same Old Scene (6)
Sea Breezes (1)
Sensation (4)
Seven Deadly Sins (4)
Shame, Shame, Shame (1)
Sign Of The Times (3,6)
Slave To Love (4,6)
Smoke Gets In Your Eyes [solo: Bryan] (6)
Stone Woman (4)
Street Life (6)
Take Me To The River (3)
That's How Strong My Love Is (3)
These Foolish Things [solo: Bryan] (6)
This Is Tomorrow (2)
This Island Earth (3)
Tokyo Joe (3)
2 HB (1)
Valentine (4)
Virginia Plain (6)
Waste Land (4)
What Goes On (3)
When She Walks In The Room (3)
Windswept (4)
You Go To My Head (1)
Zamba (5)

FESTIVAL
Studio group assembled by producer Boris Midney.

| 2/9/80 | 50 | 18 | | Evita | $8 | RSO 3061 |

a disco version of the Broadway show

Buenos Aires
Don't Cry For Me Argentina *72*
Eva's Theme: Lady Woman
High Flying, Adored
I'd Be Surprisingly Good For You
Rainbow High
She Is A Diamond

FETCHIN BONES
Los Angeles-based, three-man, two-woman band founded by Hope Nicholls (vocals) and Aaron Pitkin (bass).

| 11/18/89 | 175 | 8 | | Monster | $8 | Capitol 90661 |

Bonework
Cross
Deep Blue
I Dig You
(I Feel Like An) Astronaut
Love Crushing
Mr. Bad
Say The Word
Spot
You're So Much

FEVER TREE
Houston psychedelic-rock quintet — Dennis Keller, lead vocals.

5/18/68	156	21		1 Fever Tree	$25	Uni 73024
12/28/68+	83	13		2 Another Time, Another Place	$20	Uni 73040
2/7/70	97	6		3 Creation	$20	Uni 73067

Catcher In The Rye (3)
Come With Me (Rainsong) (1)
Day Tripper (medley) (1)
Death Is The Dancer (2)
Don't Come Crying To Me Girl (2)
Fever (2)
Fever Blue (3)
Filligree & Shadow (1)
God Game (3)
Grand Candy Young Sweet (2)
I've Never Seen Evergreen (2)
Imitation Situation (1,3)
Jokes Are For Sad People (2)
Love Makes The Sunrise (3)
Man Who Paints The Pictures (1)
Man Who Paints The Pictures - Part II (2)
Ninety-Nine And One Half (1)
Nowadays Clancy Can't Even Sing (2)
Peace Of Mind (2)
Run Past My Window (3)
San Francisco Girls (Return Of The Native) (1) *91*
Sun Also Rises (1)
Time Is Now (3)
Unlock My Door (1)
We Can Work It Out (medley) (1)
What Time Did You Say It Is In Salt Lake City? (2)
Where Do You Go? (medley) (1)
Wild Woman Ways (3)
Woman, Woman (Woman) (3)

FIEDLER, Arthur — see BOSTON POPS

FIELD, Sally
Born on 11/6/46 in Pasadena, California. Leading television/film actress. Star of TV's *Gidget* and *The Flying Nun*. Oscar winner for *Norma Rae* and *Places In The Heart*. Emmy winner for TV's *Sybil*.

| 12/23/67+ | 172 | 4 | | The Flying Nun | $20 | Colgems 106 |

Count To Ten
Darkest Before Dawn
Felicidad *94*
Find Yourself A Rainbow
Flying Nun Theme ..see: Who Needs Wings To Fly
Follow The Star
I'm On My Way
I'm So Glad I Can Fly
Louder I Sing (The Braver I Get)
Musicians, The
Optimize
Paint Me A Picture
Turn On The Sunshine
Who Needs Wings To Fly?

FIELDS, Richard "Dimples"
R&B vocalist. Owner of the Cold Duck Music Lounge in San Francisco.

| 7/25/81 | 33 | 17 | | 1 Dimples | $8 | Boardwalk 33232 |
| 3/6/82 | 63 | 20 | | 2 Mr. Look So Good! | $8 | Boardwalk 33249 |

After I Put My Lovin' On You (2)
Baby Work Out (2)
Don't Ever Take Your Love (1)
Earth Angel (1)
I Like Your Lovin (1)
I've Got To Learn To Say No! (1)
If It Ain't One Thing...It's Another (2) *47*
In The Still Of The Night (I'll Remember) (1)
Lady Is Bad (2)
Let Me Take You In My Arms Tonight (1)
Let The Lady Dance (1)
Lovely Lady (1)
Mr. Look So Good (2)
She's Got Papers On Me (1)
Sincerely (2)
Taking Applications (2)
(Woman At Home And) A Freak On The Side (2)

DEBUT DATE	PEAK POS	WKS CHR	G O L D	ARTIST — Album Title	$	Label & Number

FIELDS, W.C.
Born on 2/20/1879 in Philadelphia; died on 12/25/46. Classic comedian of American film.

DEBUT DATE	PEAK POS	WKS CHR	GOLD	ARTIST — Album Title	$	Label & Number
1/4/69	30	29		1 The Original Voice Tracks From His Greatest Movies ....[C]	$12	Decca 79164
10/18/69	197	2		2 W. C. Fields On Radio ....[C]	$10	Columbia 9890

with Edgar Bergen and Charlie McCarthy (comedian/ventriloquist Bergen, father of actress Candice Bergen, was a popular radio personality of the 1940s with his dummy McCarthy)

Chicanery Of W.C. Fields (1)
Children (2)
Feathered Friends (2)
Moths (2)
Old Friends And Old Wine (2)
Pharmacist, The (1)
Philosophy Of W.C. Fields (1)
Promotions Unlimited (2)
Rascality Of W.C. Fields (1)
Skunk Trap (1)
Snake Story (A Commercial) (2)
"Sound" Of W.C. Fields (1)
Spirit Of W.C. Fields (1)
Swim To Catalina Island (2)
Temperance Lecture (2)
W.C. Fields - A Man Against Children, Motherhood, Fatherhood And Brotherhood (1)
W.C. Fields - Creator Of Weird Names (1)
W.C. Fields - The Braggart And Teller Of Tall Tales (1)

FIFTH ANGEL
Heavy-metal band from Bellevue, Washington formed in 1984. Led by singer Ted Pilot. Group name taken from the Book Of Revelations in the Bible.

DEBUT DATE	PEAK POS	WKS CHR	GOLD	ARTIST — Album Title	$	Label & Number
4/16/88	117	13		Fifth Angel	$8	Epic 44201

Call Out The Warning
Cry Out The Fools
Fade To Flames
Fifth Angel
In The Fallout
Night, The
Only The Strong Survive
Shout It Out
Wings Of Destiny

★★161★★ 5TH DIMENSION, The
Los Angeles-based R&B vocal group formed in 1966: Marilyn McCoo, Florence LaRue, Billy Davis, Jr., Lamont McLemore and Ron Townson. McLemore and McCoo had been in the Hi-Fi's; Townson and Davis had been with groups in St. Louis. First called the Versatiles. Davis and McCoo were married in 1969 and recorded as a duo since 1976.

DEBUT DATE	PEAK POS	WKS CHR	GOLD	ARTIST — Album Title	$	Label & Number
6/17/67	8	83	●	1 Up, Up And Away	$12	Soul City 92000
1/13/68	105	31		2 The Magic Garden	$12	Soul City 92001
8/24/68	21	21		3 Stoned Soul Picnic	$12	Soul City 92002
5/31/69	2²	72	●	4 The Age Of Aquarius	$12	Soul City 92005
5/9/70+	20	50	●	5 Portrait	$8	Bell 6045
5/16/70	5	55	●	6 The 5th Dimension/Greatest Hits ....[G]	$10	Soul City 33900
8/15/70	63	8		7 The July 5th Album ....[K]	$10	Soul City 33901
3/13/71	17	23	●	8 Love's Lines, Angles And Rhymes	$8	Bell 6060
10/23/71	32	18	●	9 The 5th Dimension/Live!! ....[L]	$8	Bell 9000 [2]
11/6/71	112	7		10 Reflections ....[K]	$8	Bell 6065
4/1/72	58	32		11 Individually & Collectively	$8	Bell 6073
9/30/72	14	24	●	12 Greatest Hits On Earth ....[G]	$8	Bell 1106

greatest hits from both Soul City and Bell labels

DEBUT DATE	PEAK POS	WKS CHR	GOLD	ARTIST — Album Title	$	Label & Number
3/24/73	108	11		13 Living Together, Growing Together	$8	Bell 1116
8/23/75	136	8		14 Earthbound	$8	ABC 897

All Kinds Of People (11)
Another Day, Another Heartache (1) 45
Aquarius/Let The Sunshine In (4,6,9,12) 1
Ashes To Ashes (13) 52
Band Of Gold (11)
Be Here How (medley) (14)
Black Patch (11)
Blowing Away (4,6,10) 21
Bobbie's Blues (Who Do You Think Of?) (3,7)
Border Song (11)
Broken Wing Bird (3)
California My Way (1,7,10)
California Soul (3,6,10) 25
Carpet Man (2,6,10) 29
Change Is Gonna Come & People Gotta Be Free (5) 60
Day By Day (13)
Declaration, The (medley) (5) 64

Dimension 5ive (5)
Don't Stop For Nothing (14)
Don'tcha Hear Me Callin' To Ya (4,7)
Dreams/Pax/Nepenthe (2)
Earthbound (14)
Eleventh Song (What A Groovy Day!) (3)
Eli's Coming (9)
Every Night (2)
Everything's Been Changed (13) 70
Feelin' Alright? (7)
Girls' Song (2,6,9) 43
Go Where You Wanna Go (1,7) 16
Good News (3)
Guess Who (8)
Half Moon (11)
He's A Runner (8)
Hideaway, The (4)
I Just Wanta Be Your Friend

I Want To Take You Higher (9)
I've Got A Feeling (14)
If I Could Reach You (11) 10
It'll Never Be The Same Again (3,7,10)
It's A Great Life (3)
(Last Night) I Didn't Get To Sleep At All (11,12) 8
Lean On Me Always (14)
Learn How To Fly (1)
Leave A Little Room (11)
Let It Be Me (4,7,10)
Let Me Be Lonely (13)
Light Sings (8) 44
Living Together, Growing Together (13) 32
Love Like Ours (5)
Love Medley (9)
Love's Lines, Angles And Rhymes (8,12) 19
Lovin' Stew (3,7)

Magic Garden (2)
Magic In My Life (14)
Misty Roses (1)
Moonlight Mile (14)
Never Gonna Be The Same (1)
Never My Love (9,12) 12
Ode To Billy Joe (9)
One Less Bell To Answer (5,12) 2
Open Your Window (13)
Orange Air (2)
Paper Cup (2,6,9) 34
Pattern People (1)
Poor Side Of Town (1,7,10)
Puppet Man (5,12) 24
Rainmaker, The (8)
Requiem: 820 Latham (2)
Riverwitch, The (13)
Rosecrans Blvd. (1)
Sailboat Song (3,7)
Save The Country (5,9,12) 27

Shake Your Tambourine (9)
Singer, The (8)
Skinny Man (4)
Sky & Sea (11)
Speaking With My Heart (14)
Stoned Soul Picnic (3,6,9,12) 3
Stoney End (medley) (9)
Summer's Daughter (2)
Sunshine Of Your Love (4,7,10)
Sweet Blindness (3,6,9) 13
There Never Was A Day (13)
There's Nothin' Like Music (13)
This Is Your Life (5,9)
Those Were The Days (4,7,10)
Ticket To Ride (2,7,10)
Time And Love (8)
Together Let's Find Love (9,12) 37

Tomorrow Belongs To The Children (11)
Turn Around To Me (11)
Up-Up And Away (1,6,9,12) 7
Viva Tirado (8)
Walk Your Feet In The Sunshine (14)
Wedding Bell Blues (4,6,9,12) 1
What Do I Need To Be Me (13)
What Does It Take (To Win Your Love? (13)
When Did I Lose Your Love (14)
Which Way To Nowhere (1)
Winds Of Heaven (4)
Workin' On A Groovy Thing (4,6,10) 20
Worst That Could Happen (2,6,9)
Woyaya (13)

50 GUITARS OF TOMMY GARRETT — see GARRETT, Tommy

FINE YOUNG CANNIBALS
Pop trio from Birmingham, England: Roland Gift (vocals) and English Beat members David Steele (bass) and Andy Cox (guitar). Group appeared in the film Tin Men; Gift was in the films Sammy And Rosie Get Laid and Scandal.

DEBUT DATE	PEAK POS	WKS CHR	GOLD	ARTIST — Album Title	$	Label & Number
1/25/86	49	28		1 Fine Young Cannibals	$8	I.R.S. 5683
3/11/89	1⁷	63	▲²	2 The Raw & The Cooked	$8	I.R.S. 6273

As Hard As It Is (2)
Blue (1)
Couldn't Care More (1)
Don't Ask Me To Choose (1)
Don't Let It Get You Down (2)
Don't Look Back (2) 11
Ever Fallen In Love (2)
Funny How Love Is (1)
Good Thing (2) 1
I'm Not Satisfied (2) 90
I'm Not The Man I Used To Be (2) 54
It's OK (It's Alright) (2)
Johnny Come Home (1) 76
Like A Stranger (1)
Move To Work (1)
On A Promise (1)
She Drives Me Crazy (2) 1
Suspicious Minds (1)
Tell Me What (2)
Time Isn't Kind (1)

FINN, Tim
Co-founder/vocalist of The Split Enz. Joined brother Neil Finn's band Crowded House in 1991.

DEBUT DATE	PEAK POS	WKS CHR	GOLD	ARTIST — Album Title	$	Label & Number
9/17/83	161	5		Escapade	$8	A&M 4972

Below The Belt
Fraction Too Much Friction
Growing Pains
I Only Want To Know
In A Minor Key
Made My Day
Not For Nothing
Staring At The Embers
Through The Years
Wait And See

FINNEY, Albert
Oscar-/Tony-nominated actor. Born on 5/9/36 in Salford, England. Star of the 1963 Academy Award-winning Best Picture, Tom Jones.

DEBUT DATE	PEAK POS	WKS CHR	GOLD	ARTIST — Album Title	$	Label & Number
9/3/77	199	1		Albert Finney's Album	$8	Motown 889

DEBUT DATE	PEAK POS	WKS CHR	GOLD	ARTIST — Album Title	$	Label & Number

FINNEY, Albert — Cont'd

Bird Of Paradise	How Do You Know?	Stream Of Life	We'll Be Okay	When It's Gone
But I Was A Child	I'd Like It To Be Me	They Say	What Have They Done (To	
Crazy Song	State Of Grace	Those Other Men	My Home Town?)	

FIONA
Born Fiona Flanagan on 9/13/61 in New York City. Co-starred in the 1987 film *Hearts Of Fire*.

| 3/30/85 | 71 | 18 | | 1 Fiona .... | $8 | Atlantic 81242 |
| 11/25/89+ | 150 | 16 | | 2 Heart Like A Gun .... | $8 | Atlantic 81903 |

Bringing In The Beast (2)	Hang Your Heart On Me (1)	Little Jeannie (Got The Look	Mariel (2)	Talk To Me (1) 64	You're No Angel (1)
Draw The Line (2)	Here It Comes Again (2)	Of Love) (2)	Na Na Song (1)	Victoria Cross (2)	
Everything You Do (You're	James (1)	Look At Me Now (1)	Over Now (1)	When Pink Turns To Blue (2)	
Sexing Me) (2) 52		Love Makes You Blind (1)	Rescue You (1)	Where The Cowboys Go (2)	

FIORILLO, Elisa
Los Angeles-based vocalist raised in Philadelphia. Commercial jingle singer as a child. Winner on TV's *Star Search*. Signed with Chrysalis in 1985 at age 15.

| 2/20/88 | 163 | 8 | | Elisa Fiorillo .... | $8 | Chrysalis 41608 |

Do Something Foolish	Gimme Special Love	How Can I Forget You 60	Lover's Prayer	Two Times Love
Forgive Me For	Headin' For A Heartache	Little Too Good To Me	More Than Love	You Don't Know
Dreaming 49				

FIREBALLET
Jim Como (vocals), Bryan Howe, Ryche Chlanda, Frank Petto and Marlyn Biglin.

| 9/6/75 | 151 | 8 | | Night On Bald Mountain .... | $10 | Passport 98010 |

produced by Ian McDonald (King Crimson, Foreigner)

Atmospheres	Fireballet, The	Night On Bald Mountain
Centurion (Tales Of Fireball	Les Cathedrales	(Suite)
Kids)		

FIREBALLS, The — see GILMER, Jimmy

FIREFALL
Mellow rock group formed in Boulder, Colorado. Original lineup: Rick Roberts (lead singer), Larry Burnett (guitar), Jack Bartley (lead guitar), Mark Andes (Spirit, Jo Jo Gunne; bass) and Mike Clarke (drums). David Muse (keyboards) joined in 1977. Andes joined Heart in 1980. Roberts and Clarke were members of Flying Burrito Brothers.

5/8/76	28	67	●	1 Firefall	$10	Atlantic 18174
8/20/77	27	28	●	2 Luna Sea	$10	Atlantic 19101
10/28/78+	27	24	▲	3 Elan	$8	Atlantic 19183
4/12/80	68	15		4 Undertow	$8	Atlantic 16006
1/10/81	102	13		5 Clouds Across The Sun	$8	Atlantic 16024
12/26/81+	186	4		6 The Best Of Firefall .... [G]	$8	Atlantic 19316
3/12/83	199	3		7 Break Of Dawn	$8	Atlantic 80017

Always (7) **59**	Don't It Feel Empty (5)	I Don't Want To Hear It (5)	Love Isn't All (1)	**So Long** (2,6) **48**	Undertow (4)
Anymore (3)	Don't Tell Me Why (7)	If You Only Knew (4)	**Love That Got Away**	Sold On You (2)	Winds Of Change (3)
Baby (3)	Dreamers (5)	In The Dead Of Night (7)	(4,6) **50**	Some Things Never Change	Wrong Side Of Town (3)
Be In Love Tonight (5)	Even Steven (2)	It Doesn't Matter (1)	Mexico (1,6)	(4)	**You Are The Woman** (1,6) **9**
Body And Soul (7)	Fall For You (7)	It's Not Too Late (7)	No Class (5)	Someday Soon (2)	
Break Of Dawn (7)	Falling In Love (7)	**Just Remember I Love**	No Way Out (1)	Stardust (4)	
Business Is Business (4)	Get You Back (3)	**You** (2,6) **11**	Old Wing Mouth (5)	**Staying With It** (5,6) **37**	
Cinderella (1,6) **34**	Getaway (2)	Just Think (2)	Only A Fool (1)	**Strange Way** (3,6) **11**	
Clouds Across The Sun (5)	**Goodbye, I Love You**	Laugh Or Cry (4)	Only Time Will Tell (4)	Suddenly (7)	
Count Your Blessings (3)	(3,6) **43**	Leave It Alone (3)	Piece Of Paper (2)	Sweet And Sour (3)	
Do What You Want (1)	Head On Home (2)	**Livin' Ain't Livin'** (1) **42**	Quite Like You (5)	Sweet Ann (3)	
Dolphin's Lullaby (1)	**Headed For A Fall** (4,6) **35**	Love Ain't What It Seems (5)	Sad Ol' Love Song (1)	Take Me Back (7)	

FIREHOUSE
Hard-rock quartet from North Carolina: C.J. Snare (vocals), Bill Leverty, Perry Richardson and Michael Foster.

| 3/9/91 | 21 | 76 | ▲ | 1 Firehouse .... | $12 | Epic 46186 |
| 7/4/92 | 23 | 30 | ● | 2 Hold Your Fire .... | $12 | Epic 48615 |

All She Wrote (1) **58**	Hold The Dream (2)	**Love Of A Lifetime** (1) **5**	Oughta Be A Law (1)	Seasons Of Change (1)	**When I Look Into Your**
Don't Treat Me Bad (1) **19**	Hold Your Fire (2)	Lover's Lane (1)	Overnight Sensation (1)	Shake & Tumble (1)	**Eyes** (2) **8**
Don't Walk Away (1)	Home Is Where The Heart Is	Mama Didn't Raise No Fool	**Reach For The Sky** (2) **83**	**Sleeping With You** (2) **78**	You're Too Bad (2)
Get In Touch (2)	(1)	(2)	Rock On The Radio (1)	Talk Of The Town (2)	
Helpless (1)	Life In The Real World (2)	Meaning Of Love (2)	Rock You Tonight (2)		

FIRESIGN THEATRE
Satirical comedy foursome: Phil Austin, Peter Bergman, David Ossman and Philip Proctor.

10/18/69	195	2		1 How Can You Be In Two Places At Once When You're Not Anywhere At All .... [C]	$15	Columbia 9884
9/19/70	106	10		2 Don't Crush That Dwarf, Hand Me The Pliers .... [C]	$15	Columbia 30102
9/25/71	50	14		3 I Think We're All Bozos On This Bus .... [C]	$15	Columbia 30737
2/26/72	75	11		4 Dear Friends .... [K-C]	$12	Columbia 31099 [2]
11/25/72	115	8		5 Not Insane Or Anything You Want To .... [C]	$12	Columbia 31585
3/2/74	172	5		6 The Tale Of The Giant Rat Of Sumatra .... [C]	$10	Columbia 32730
11/2/74	147	6		7 Everything You Know Is Wrong .... [C]	$10	Columbia 33141
6/11/77	184	2		8 Just Folks...A Firesign Chat... [C]	$10	Butterfly 001

Any More Rocket Fuel For	Brickbreaking (4)	Echo Poem (4)	Funny Thing Happened On	How Can You Be In Two	International Youth-Sex On
You Hardhats? (8)	Chinchilla Show (4)	Electrician Exposes Himself	The Way To The	Places At Once When	Parade (4)
Balliol Bros. (4)	Coal! (4)	(6)	Inquisition (4)	You're Not Anywhere At All	Live From The Senate Bar (If
Ben Bland's All-Day	Deputy Dan Has No Friends	Everything You Know Is	Further Adventures Of Nick	(1)	You Call That Living!) (4)
Matinee, Part One (8)	(4)	Wrong (7)	Danger (1)	I Think We're All Bozos On	Mark Time! (4)
Ben Bland's All-Night	Dr. Whiplash (4)	40 Great Unclaimed	Giant Toad (4)	This Bus (3)	Minority Street (4)
Matinee, Part Two (8)	Driving For Dopers (4)	Melodies! (4)	Hello, What's Happening? I	I Was A Cock-Teaser For	Not Insane (5)
Bob's Brazerko Lounge (4)	Duke Of Madness Motors (4)	Freezing Mr. Foster (4)	Die Every Night (8)	Roosterama! (4)	

DEBUT DATE	PEAK POS	WKS CHR	GOLD	ARTIST — Album Title	$	Label & Number

FIRESIGN THEATRE — Cont'd

Not Quite The Solution He Expected (6)
Not Responsible (5)
$100.00 Ben (4)
Other Side (2)

Outrageously Disgusting Disguise (6)
Pass The Indian, Please (8)
Pickles Down The Rat Hole! (6)
Poop's Principles (4)

Praise The Hoove! (4)
Sleep (4)
Small Animal Administration (4)
Sodom And Jubilee (4)
Someday Funnies (4)

Stiff Idiot Is The Worst Kind! (8)
T.B. Guide (4)
T.V. Glide (4)
This Side (2)
Toad Away (4)

Truck Stops Here (8)
Where Did Jonas Go When The Lights Went Out? (6)
Where There's Smoke, There's Work (6)

FIRM, The

British supergroup: Jimmy Page (Led Zeppelin, The Honeydrippers; guitar), Paul Rodgers (Free, Bad Company; vocals), Chris Slade (Manfred Mann; drums) and Tony Franklin (keyboards). Disbanded in 1986. Franklin joined Blue Murder in 1989. Slade joined AC/DC in 1990. Rodgers joined The Law in 1991.

3/2/85	17	33	●	1 The Firm	$8	Atlantic 81239
2/22/86	22	19		2 Mean Business	$8	Atlantic 81628

All The Kings Horses (2) 61
Cadillac (2)
Closer (1)
Dreaming (2)

Fortune Hunter (2)
Free To Live (2)
Live In Peace (2)
Make Or Break (1)

Midnight Moonlight (1)
Money Can't Buy (1)
Radioactive (1) 28

Satisfaction Guaranteed (1) 73
Someone To Love (1)
Spirit Of Love (2)

Tear Down The Walls (2)
Together (1)
You've Lost That Lovin' Feeling (1)

FIRST CHOICE

Female soul trio from Philadelphia, formed as the Debronettes. Consisted of Rochelle Fleming, Annette Guest and Joyce Jones. By 1977, Jones left and Ursula Herring joined. Herring left by 1979 and Debbie Martin joined.

10/27/73	184	4		1 Armed And Extremely Dangerous	$10	Philly Groove 1400
10/26/74	143	7		2 The Player	$10	Philly Groove 1502
10/1/77	103	8		3 Delusions	$8	Gold Mind 7501
3/31/79	135	12		4 Hold Your Horses	$8	Gold Mind 9502

All I Need Is Time (2)
Armed And Extremely Dangerous (1) 28
Boy Named Junior (1)
Chances Go Around (3)
Do Me Again (3)
Doctor Love (3) 41
Double Cross (4)

Gamble On Love (3)
Good Morning Midnight (medley) (4)
Great Expectations (medley) (4)
Guess What Mary Jones Did (2)
Guilty (2)

Hold Your Horses (4)
Hustler Bill (2)
I Love You More Than Before (3)
Indian Giver (3)
Jimmy "D" (3)
Let Me Down Easy (medley) (4)

Let No Man Put Asunder (3)
Love And Happiness (1)
Love Having You Around (3)
Love Thang (4)
Newsy Neighbors (1) 97
One Step Away (1)
Player - Part 1 (2) 70
Runnin' Out Of Fools (1)

Smarty Pants (1) 56
This Is The House (1)
This Little Woman (1)
Wake Up To Me (1)
You Took The Words Right Out Of My Mouth (1)
You've Been Doin' Wrong For So Long (2)

FIRST EDITION, The — see ROGERS, Kenny

FISCHER, Lisa

Native of Fort Greene, Brooklyn, New York. Session singer with Billy Ocean, Melba Moore and others. Touring vocalist with Luther Vandross.

5/18/91	100	14		So Intense	$12	Elektra 60889

Chain Of Broken Hearts
Get Back To Love

How Can I Ease The Pain 11

Last Goodbye
Save Me 74

Send The Message Of Love
So Intense

So Tender
Some Girls
Wildflower

FISHBONE

Los Angeles black funk/thrash band led by Angelo Moore (vocals/sax). Includes Chris Dowd, Kendall Jones, Walter Kibby II, Fish, John Norwood Fisher and Charlie Down (left by 1991, John Bigham added). Formed in 1979 while members were in junior high school. Appeared in the films *Back To The Beach, Tape Heads, Far Out, Man* and *I'm Gonna Git You Sucka*.

10/1/88	153	9		1 Truth And Soul	$8	Columbia 40891
5/11/91	49	10		2 The Reality Of My Surroundings	$12	Columbia 46142

Asswhippin' (2)
Babyhead (2)
Behavior Control Technician (2)
Bonin' In The Boneyard (1)
Change (1)

Deathmarch (1)
Deep Inside (1)
Everyday Sunshine (2)
Fight The Youth (2)
Freddie's Dead (1)
Ghetto Soundwave (1)

Housework (2)
If I Were A ... I'd (2)
Junkies Prayer (2)
Ma And Pa (1)
Mighty Long Way (1)
Naz-tee May'en (2)

One Day (1)
Pouring Rain (1)
Pray To The Junkiemaker (2)
Pressure (2)
Question Of Life (1)

Slow Bus Movin' (Howard Beach Party) (1)
So Many Millions (2)
Subliminal Fascism (1)
Sunless Saturday (2)
Those Days Are Gone (2)

FISHER, Climie — see CLIMIE

FISHER, Eddie

Born Edwin Jack Fisher on 8/10/28 in Philadelphia. Radio work while still in high school. At Copacabana night club in New York at age 17. With Buddy Morrow and Charlie Ventura in 1946. On Eddie Cantor's radio show in 1949. In the Armed Forces Special Services, 1952-53. Married to Debbie Reynolds from 1955-59. Other marriages to Elizabeth Taylor and Connie Stevens. Daughter with Debbie is actress Carrie Fisher. Daughter with Connie is singer Tricia Leigh Fisher. Own *Coke Time* 15-minute TV series, 1953-57. In films *All About Eve* (1950), *Bundle Of Joy* (1956) and *Butterfield 8* (1960). Eddie was the #1 idol of bobbysoxers during the early 1950's.

4/30/55	8	10		1 I Love You	$30	RCA 1097
3/30/63	128	3		2 Eddie Fisher At The Winter Garden [L]	$20	Ramrod 1 [2]
				the Winter Garden is a Broadway theater in New York City		
7/24/65	52	10		3 Eddie Fisher Today!	$15	Dot 25631
11/26/66+	72	10		4 Games That Lovers Play	$12	RCA 3726
7/1/67	193	3		5 People Like You	$12	RCA 3820

Back In Your Own Backyard (2)
Born Free (5)
Call Me Irresponsible (3)
Carnival (Manha De Carnaval) (4)
Come Love! (5)
Dear Heart (4)
Dr. Zhivago ..see: Lara's Theme
Don't Let It Get You Down (2)
Downtown (3)
Games That Lovers Play (4) 45
Girl That I Marry (1)

Hava Naguila (Dance Everyone Dance) (2)
Heart (medley) (2)
Hello, Dolly! (3)
Hit Medley (2)
How Insensitive (Insensatez) (4)
I Can't Give You Anything But Love (1)
I Get Along Without You Very Well (4)
I Haven't Got Anything Better To Do (5)
I Surrender, Dear (1)
I Will Wait For You (5)

If I Loved You (3)
If She Walked Into My Life (5)
It Never Entered My Mind (4)
Jolson Medley No. 1 & 2 (2)
Just Let Me Look At You (4)
Lara's Theme (4)
Let's Fall In Love (1)
Love Sends A Little Gift Of Roses (1)
Love Somebody (1)
Mack The Knife (2)
Makin' Whoopee (2)
Mame (5)
Maybe Today (Le Coeur Trop Tendre) (5)

Mein Shtetele Belz (That Wonderful Girl Of Mine) (2)
Moon River (4)
My Best Girl (5)
My One And Only Love (1)
My Romance (1)
Never On Sunday (2)
Oh My Papa (O Mein Papa) (medley) (2)
Once I Loved (4)
Once Upon A Time (3)
People (3)
People Like You (5) 97
Pretty Baby (1)

Red Roses For A Blue Lady (3)
So In Love (1)
Somebody Loves Me (1)
Somewhere, My Love ..see: Lara's Theme
Sonny Boy (2)
Sunrise, Sunset (3)
Sweetest Sounds (2)
This Nearly Was Mine (4)
Try To Remember (3)
Watch What Happens (5)
West Side Story Medley (2)
What Is This Thing Called Love? (1)

What Kind Of Fool Am I (2)
What Now My Love (Et Maintenant) (3)
Where's That Rainbow (4)
Who Can I Turn To (When Nobody Needs Me) (4)
Wish You Were Here (medley) (4)
Yesterday (4)
You Don't Have To Say You Love Me (Io Che Non Vivo [Senza Te]) (4)
You Made Me Love You (2)
You're Devastating (4)

DEBUT DATE	PEAK POS	WKS CHR	GOLD	ARTIST — Album Title	$	Label & Number

★★368★★ **FITZGERALD, Ella**

The most-honored jazz singer of all time. Born on 4/25/18 in Newport News, Virginia. Discovered after winning on the *Harlem Amateur Hour* in 1934, she was hired by Chick Webb and in 1938 created a popular sensation with "A-Tisket, A-Tasket." Following Chick's death in 1939, Ella took over the band for three years. Appeared in several films. Won the Lifetime Achievement Grammy in 1967. Winner of the Down Beat poll as top female vocalist more than 20 times and winner of 12 Grammys, she remains among the undisputed royalty of 20th century popular music.

DEBUT DATE	PEAK POS	WKS CHR	#	ARTIST — Album Title	$	Label & Number
9/17/55	7	10	1	Songs from Pete Kelly's Blues	$50	Decca 8166

PEGGY LEE & ELLA FITZGERALD
songs from the film in which Ella and Peggy had supporting roles; also see Ray Heindorf and Jack Webb

7/28/56	15	1	2	Ella Fitzgerald sings the Cole Porter Song Book *	$40	Verve 4001 [2]
12/15/56	12	2	3	Ella And Louis	$50	Verve 4003

ELLA FITZGERALD and LOUIS ARMSTRONG
backing by the Oscar Peterson Trio, plus Buddy Rich

3/16/57	11	4	4	Ella Fitzgerald sings the Rodgers and Hart Song Book *	$45	Verve 4002 [2]

*arranged and conducted by Buddy Bregman

9/12/60+	11	51	5	Mack The Knife - Ella In Berlin ....[L]	$20	Verve 4041

accompanied by the Paul Smith Quartet

11/13/61+	35	34	6	Ella In Hollywood ....[L]	$20	Verve 4052
10/19/63	69	20	7	Ella And Basie!	$20	Verve 4061

ELLA FITZGERALD/COUNT BASIE
arranged by Quincy Jones

3/28/64	111	5	8	Ella Fitzgerald sings the George and Ira Gershwin Song Books	$60	Verve V-29-5 [5]

recorded 1958-59; arranged and conducted by Nelson Riddle

8/22/64	146	2	9	Hello, Dolly!	$20	Verve 4064
8/19/67	172	2	10	Brighten The Corner	$15	Capitol 2685

sacred songs; with the Ralph Carmichael Choir and Orchestra

10/18/69	196	2	11	Ella	$12	Reprise 6354

Abide With Me (10)
Ace In The Hole (2)
Ain't Misbehavin' (7)
Airmail Special (6)
All Of You (2)
All Through The Night (2)
Always True To You In My Fashion (2)
Anything Goes (2)
April In Paris (3)
Aren't You Kind Of Glad We Did? (8)
Baby, Won't You Please Come Home (6)
Begin The Beguine (2)
Beginner's Luck (8)
Bewitched (4)
Bidin' My Time (8)
Blue Moon (4,6)
Blue Room (4)
Boy Wanted (8)
Boy! What Love Has Done To Me! (8)
Brighten The Corner (Where You Are) (10)
But Not For Me (8)
By Strauss (8)
Can't Buy Me Love (9)
Can't We Be Friends (3)
Cheek To Cheek (3)
Church In The Wildwood (10)
Clap Yo' Hands (8)
Dancing On The Ceiling (4)
'Deed I Do (7)
Do I Love You (2)
Don't Fence Me In (2)
Dream A Little Dream Of Me (7)
Easy To Love (2)
Ella Hums The Blues [solo: Ella] (1)

Embraceable You (8)
Ev'ry Time We Say Good-bye (2)
Ev'rything I've Got (4)
Fascinating Rhythm (8)
Foggy Day (3,8)
For You, For Me, For Evermore (8)
From This Moment On (2)
Funny Face (8)
Get Out Of Town (2)
Get Ready (11)
Give It Back To The Indians (4)
God Be With You Till We Meet Again (10)
God Will Take Care Of You (10)
Gone With The Wind (5)
Got To Get You Into My Life (11)
Half Of It, Dearie Blues (8)
Hard Hearted Hannah (The Vamp Of Savannah) [solo: Ella] (1)
Have You Met Miss Jones? (4)
He Loves And She Loves (8)
Hello, Dolly! (9)
Here In My Arms (4)
Honeysuckle Rose (7)
How High The Moon (Part 1) (5,9) 76
How Long Has This Been Going On? (8)
Hunter Gets Captured By The Game (11)
I Am In Love (2)
I Can't Be Bothered Now (8)
I Concentrate On You (2)
I Could Write A Book (4)

I Didn't Know What Time It Was (4)
I Get A Kick Out Of You (2)
I Got Rhythm (8)
I Love Paris (2)
I Need Thee Every Hour (10)
I Shall Not Be Moved (10)
I Was Doing All Right (8)
I Wish I Were In Love Again (4)
I Wonder Why (11)
I'll Never Fall In Love Again (11)
I'm Beginning To See The Light (7)
I've Got A Crush On You (8)
I've Got Five Dollars (4)
I've Got The World On A String (8)
I've Got You Under My Skin (2)
In The Garden (10)
In The Still Of The Night (2)
Into Each Life Some Rain Must Fall (7)
Isn't It A Pity? (8)
Isn't It Romantic (4)
Isn't This A Lovely Day (3)
It Might As Well Be Spring (6)
It Never Entered My Mind (4)
It's All Right With Me (2)
It's Delovely (2)
Johnny One Note (4)
Just A Closer Walk With Thee (10)
Just Another Rhumba (8)
Just In Time (6)
Just One Of Those Things (2)
Knock Knock (11)
Lady Is A Tramp (4,5)

Let The Lower Lights Be Burning (10)
Let's Call The Whole Thing Off (8)
Let's Do It (2)
Let's Kiss And Make Up (8)
Little Girl Blue (4)
Looking For A Boy (8)
Lorelei (5,8)
Love For Sale (2)
Love Is Here To Stay (8)
Love Is Sweeping The Country (8)
Love Walked In (8)
Lover (4)
Lullaby Of The Leaves (8)
Man I Love (5,8)
Manhattan (4)
Memories Of You (9)
Miss Otis Regrets (2,9)
Misty (5)
Moonlight In Vermont (3)
Mountain Greenery (4)
My Cousin In Milwaukee (8)
My Funny Valentine (4)
My Heart Stood Still (4)
My Last Affair (7)
My Man (9)
My One And Only (8)
My Romance (4)
Nearness Of You (3)
Nice Work If You Can Get It (8)
Night And Day (2)
Of Thee I Sing (Baby) (8)
Oh, Lady Be Good! (8)
Oh, So Nice (8)
Old Rugged Cross (10)
On The Sunny Side Of The Street (7)

Ooo Baby Baby (11)
Open Your Window (11)
People (9)
Pete Kelly's Blues [solo: Ella] (1,9)
Real American Folk Song (8)
Ridin' High (2)
Rock Of Ages, Cleft For Me (10)
'S Wonderful (8)
Sam And Delilah (8)
Satin Doll (6,7)
Savoy Truffle (11)
Shall We Dance? (8)
Shiny Stockings (7)
Ship Without A Sail (4)
Slap That Bass (8)
So In Love (2)
Somebody From Somewhere (8)
Someone To Watch Over Me (8)
Soon (8)
Spring Is Here (4)
Stairway To The Stars (6)
Stars Fell On Alabama (3)
Stiff Upper Lip (8)
Strike Up The Band (8)
Summertime (5)
Sweetest Sounds (9)
Take The "A" Train (6)
Tea For Two (7)
Ten Cents A Dance (4)
Tenderly (3)
That Certain Feeling (8)
Them There Eyes (7)
There's A Small Hotel (4)
They All Laughed (8)
They Can't Take That Away From Me (3,8)
Things Are Looking Up (8)

This Can't Be Love (4)
This Could Be The Start Of Something Big (6)
Thou Swell (4)
Throw Out The Lifeline (10)
To Keep My Love Alive (4)
Too Darn Hot (2,5)
Treat Me Rough (8)
Under A Blanket Of Blue (3)
Volare (Nel Blu Dipinto Di Blu) (9)
Wait Till You See Her (4)
What A Friend We Have In Jesus (10)
What Is This Thing Called Love (2)
Where Or When (4)
Who Cares? (8)
Why Can't You Behave (2)
With A Song In My Heart (4)
Yellow Man (11)
You Do Something To Me (2)
You Took Advantage Of Me (4)
You'll Have To Swing It Mr. Paganini (6)
You're Driving Me Crazy (6)
You're The Top (2)
You've Got What Gets Me (8)

FIVE AMERICANS, The

Dallas-based rock quintet, originally from Oklahoma, led by vocalist Michael Rabon (later with Gladstone). Keyboardist John Durrill wrote Cher's "Dark Lady" and "I Saw A Man And He Danced With His Wife." Member Jimmy Wright married Robin of Jon & Robin & The In Crowd.

4/30/66	136	5	1	I See The Light	$30	HBR 9503
7/8/67	121	10	2	Western Union	$20	Abnak 2067

Big Cities (2)
Don't You Dare Blame Me (1)
Gimme Some Lovin' (2)
Goodbye (1)

Husbands And Wives (2)
I Know They Lie (1)
I Put A Spell On You (2)
I See The Light (1) 26

I'm So Glad (1)
If I Could (1)
It's A Crying Shame (1)
Losing Game (1)

Now That It's Over (2)
Outcast, The (1)
Reality (2)
See-Saw-Man (2)

She's-A-My Own (1)
Sound Of Love (2) 36
Sympathy (1)
Tell Ann I Love Her (2)

Train, The (1)
Twist And Shout (1)
Western Union (2) 5
What'd I Say (1)

FIVE HEARTBEATS, The — see SOUNDTRACKS

DEBUT DATE	PEAK POS	WKS CHR	GOLD	ARTIST — Album Title	$	Label & Number

FIVE MAN ELECTRICAL BAND
Ontario, Canada rock group — Les Emmerson, lead singer (b: 9/17/44).

7/31/71	148	9		1 Good-Byes & Butterflies	$12	Lionel 1100
2/12/72	199	2		2 Coming Of Age	$12	Lionel 1101

Absolutely Right (2) *26*
All Is Right (With The World) (1)
Coming Of Age (2)
Country Girl (Suite) Medley (2)

Dance Of The Swamp Woman (1)
Find The One (2)
Forever Together (1)
Friends & Family (2)
Hello Melinda Goodbye (1)

Isn't It A Long Hard Road (2)
Julianna (2)
Mama's Baby Child (1)
Man With The Horse And Wagon (1)
Me & Harley Davidson (2)

Moonshine (Friend Of Mine) (1)
Safe And Sound (With Jesus) (1)
Signs (1) *3*

Variations On A Theme Of Lepidoptera (1)
Whole Lotta Heavy (2)
(You And I) Butterfly (1)

FIVE SPECIAL
R&B quintet from Detroit. Lead tenor Bryan Banks is the brother of Ron Banks of The Dramatics.

8/11/79	118	11		Five Special	$8	Elektra 206

Baby
Do It Baby

It's A Wonderful Day

It's Such A Groove Part II - Whatcha Got For Music!

Rock Dancin'
Why Leave Us Alone 55

You're Something Special

FIVE STAIRSTEPS, The
Soul group from Chicago, consisting of brothers Clarence, Jr., James, Kenneth and Dennis Burke with their sister Aloha. Later joined by their five-year-old brother Cubie. Managed by their father and produced by Curtis Mayfield; later became The Invisible Man's Band.

3/25/67	139	4		1 The Five Stairsteps	$15	Windy C 6000
				5 STAIRSTEPS & CUBIE:		
1/27/68	195	3		2 Our Family Portrait	$12	Buddah 5008
4/26/69	198	2		3 Love's Happening	$10	Curtom 8002
				STAIRSTEPS:		
6/13/70	83	12		4 Stairsteps	$10	Buddah 5061
12/12/70	199	2		5 Step by Step by Step ....[K]	$10	Buddah 5068
				9 of 11 cuts are from album #1 above		

(Baby) Make Me Feel So Good (3,5)
Bad News (2)
Because I Love You (4,5) *flip*
Behind Curtains (1,5)
Come Back (1,5) *61*
Danger! She's A Stranger (1,5) *89*

Dear Prudence (4) *66*
Don't Change Your Love (3) *59*
Don't Waste Your Time (1,5)
Find Me (2)
Getting Better (4)
Girl I Love (1)
I Made A Mistake (3)
I Remember You (2)

I'm The One Who Loves You (3)
Little Boy Blue (3)
Little Young Lover (3)
Look Of Love (2)
Loves Happening (3)
Million To One (2) *68*
New Dance Craze (2,3)
O-o-h Child (4,5) *8*

Oooh, Baby Baby (1,5) *63*
Playgirl's Love (1,5)
Something's Missing (2) *88*
Stay Close To Me (3,5) *91*
Sweet As A Peach (1)
Tell Me Who (2)
Touch Of You (1,5)
Under The Spell (2)
Up & Down (4)

Vice The Lights (4)
We Must Be In Love (5) *88*
What About Your Wife (4)
Who Do You Belong To (4)
Windows Of The World (2)
World Of Fantasy (1,5) *49*
You Don't Love Me (1)
You Make Me So Mad (2)

You Waited Too Long (1,5) *94*
Your Love Has Changed (3)

FIVE STAR
Brother/sister R&B quintet from Britain: Deniece (lead singer), Stedman, Doris, Lorraine and Delroy Pearson. Their father, Buster Pearson, was a guitarist with Otis Redding.

9/21/85+	57	47		1 Luxury Of Life	$8	RCA 8052
10/4/86	80	25		2 Silk & Steel	$8	RCA 5901

All Fall Down (1) *65*
Are You Man Enough? (2)
Can't Wait Another Minute (2) *41*
Crazy (1)

Don't You Know I Love It (2)
Find The Time (2)
Hide And Seek (1)
If I Say Yes (2) *67*
Let Me Be The One (1) *59*

Love Take Over (1)
Now I'm In Control (1)
Please Don't Say Goodnight (2)
R.S.V.P. (1)

Rain Or Shine (2)
Say Goodbye (1)
Show Me What You've Got For Me (2)
Slightest Touch (2)

Stay Out Of My Life (2)
System Addict (1)
Winning (1)

FIXX, The
London-based, techno-pop group: Cy Curnin (lead singer, piano), Jamie West-Oram (guitars), Rupert Greenall (keyboards), Adam Woods (drums) and Dan K. Brown (bass).

11/13/82+	106	51		1 Shuttered Room	$8	MCA 5345
5/28/83	8	54	▲	2 **Reach The Beach**	$8	MCA 39001
9/8/84	19	29	●	3 **Phantoms**	$8	MCA 5507
6/14/86	30	21		4 Walkabout	$8	MCA 5705
7/18/87	110	7		5 React ....[L]	$8	MCA 42008
2/11/89	72	18		6 Calm Animals	$8	RCA 8566
3/16/91	111	10		7 Ink.	$12	MCA 10205
				includes a bonus track available on cassette and CD only plus a bonus track available on CD only		

All Is Fair (7)
All The Best Things (7)
Are We Ourselves? (3,5) *15*
Big Wall (5)
Built For The Future (4,5)
Calm Animals (6)
Cameras In Paris (1)
Camphor (4)
Can't Finish (4)
Cause To Be Alarmed (6)
Changing (2)
Chase The Fire (4)
Climb The Hill (7)

Crucified (7)
Deeper And Deeper (5)
Don't Be Scared (5)
Driven Out (6) *55*
Facing The Wind (3)
Falling In Love (7)
Flow, The (4)
Fool, The (1)
Gypsy Feet (4)
How Much Is Enough (7) *35*
I Found You (1)
I Live (1)
I Will (3)

I'm Life (6)
In Suspense (3)
Less Cities, More Moving People (3)
Liner (2)
Lose Face (4)
Lost In Battle Overseas (3)
Lost Planes (1)
Make No Plans (7)
No One Has To Cry (7)
One Jungle (7)
One Look Up (4)

One Thing Leads To Another (2,5) *4*
Opinions (2)
Outside (2)
Phantom Living (3)
Precious Stone (6)
Privilege (2)
Question (3)
Reach The Beach (2)
Read Between The Lines (4)
Red Skies (1,5)
Rules And Schemes (5)
Running (2)

Saved By Zero (2,5) *20*
Secret Separation (4) *19*
Sense The Adventure (4)
Shred Of Evidence (6)
Shut It Out (7)
Shuttered Room (1)
Sign Of Fire (2) *32*
Some People (1)
Stand Or Fall (1,5) *76*
Still Around (7)
Strain, The (1)
Subterranean (6)

Sunshine In The Shade (3) *69*
Treasure It (4)
Walkabout (4)
Wish (3)
Woman On A Train (3)
World Weary (6)
Yesterday, Today (7)

★★130★★ FLACK, Roberta
Born on 2/10/39 in Asheville, North Carolina and raised in Arlington, Virginia. Played piano from an early age. Music scholarship to Howard University at age 15; classmate of Donny Hathaway. Discovered by jazz musician Les McCann. Signed to Atlantic in 1969.

1/31/70+	1 [5]	54	●	1 First Take	$10	Atlantic 8230
8/29/70	33	82	●	2 Chapter Two	$10	Atlantic 1569
12/11/71+	18	48	●	3 Quiet Fire	$10	Atlantic 1594
5/13/72	3	39	●	4 **Roberta Flack & Donny Hathaway**	$10	Atlantic 7216
				ROBERTA FLACK & DONNY HATHAWAY		
9/1/73	3	53	●	5 **Killing Me Softly**	$8	Atlantic 7271

FLACK, Roberta — Cont'd

DEBUT DATE	PEAK POS	WKS CHR	GOLD	ARTIST — Album Title	$	Label & Number
3/29/75	24	26		6 Feel Like Makin' Love	$8	Atlantic 18131
1/7/78	8	32	●	7 **Blue Lights In The Basement**	$8	Atlantic 19149
9/30/78	74	10		8 Roberta Flack	$8	Atlantic 19186
3/29/80	25	24	●	9 Roberta Flack Featuring Donny Hathaway	$8	Atlantic 16013
				features 2 duets by Roberta and Donny, the rest are her solo		
12/20/80+	52	19		10 Live & More [L]	$10	Atlantic 7004 [2]

ROBERTA FLACK & PEABO BRYSON

DEBUT DATE	PEAK POS	WKS CHR	GOLD	ARTIST — Album Title	$	Label & Number
6/27/81	161	11		11 Bustin' Loose [S]	$8	MCA 5141
6/19/82	59	21		12 I'm The One	$8	Atlantic 19354
8/13/83	25	42	●	13 Born To Love	$8	Capitol 12284

PEABO BRYSON/ROBERTA FLACK

DEBUT DATE	PEAK POS	WKS CHR	GOLD	ARTIST — Album Title	$	Label & Number
1/14/89	159	8		14 Oasis	$8	Atlantic 81916
11/9/91	110	10		15 Set The Night To Music	$12	Atlantic 82321

After You (7)
All Caught Up In Love (14)
Always (15)
And So It Goes (14)
And The Feeling's Good (8)
Angelitos Negros (1)
Baby I Love You (4)
Baby I Love You So (8)
Back Together Again (9,10) *56*
Ballad For D. (11)
Ballad Of The Sad Young Men (1)
Be Real Black For Me (4)
Blame It On Me (13)
Born To Love (13)
Bridge Over Troubled Water (3)
Business Goes On As Usual (2)
Can We Find Love Again (13)
Childrens Song (11)
Closer I Get To You (7) *2*
Come Share My Love (8)
Come Ye Disconsolate (4)
Comin' Alive (13)
Compared To What (1)
Conversation Love (5)
Disguises (9)
Do What You Gotta Do (2)

Don't Make Me Wait Too Long (9,10)
Early Ev'ry Midnite (6)
Feel Like Makin' Love (6,10) *1*
Feel The Fire (10)
Feelin' That Glow (6) *76*
Fine, Fine Day (7)
First Time Ever I Saw Your Face (1) *1*
For All We Know (4)
Friend (15)
Go Up Moses (13)
God Don't Like Ugly (9,10)
Gone Away (2)
Happiness (12)
Heaven Above Me (13)
Hey, That's No Way To Say Goodbye (1)
(His Name) Brazil (14)
Hittin' Me Where It Hurts (11)
I Believe In You (medley) (10)
I Can See The Sun In Late December (6)
I Just Came Here To Dance (13)
I Told Jesus (1)
I Wanted It Too (6)
I (Who Have Nothing) (4)

I'd Like To Be Baby To You (7)
I'm The Girl (5)
I'm The One (12) *42*
If Ever I See You Again (8) *24*
If Only For One Night (10)
Impossible Dream (2)
In The Name Of Love (12)
Independent Man (8)
Jesse (5) *30*
Just Like A Woman (2)
Just When I Needed You (11)
Killing Me Softly With His Song (5,10) *1*
Knowing That We're Made For Each Other (8)
Let It Be Me (2)
Let Them Talk (3)
Love (Always Commands) (11)
Love And Let Love (12)
Love In Every Season (medley) (10)
Love Is A Waiting Game (10)
Love Is The Healing (7)
Lovin' You (Is Such An Easy Thang To Do) (11)
Make The World Stand Still (10)

Making Love (12) *13*
Maybe (13)
Mood (4)
More Than Everything (10)
Mr. Magic (6)
My Foolish Heart (15)
My Love For You (12)
My Someone To Love (14)
Natural Thing (15)
Never Loved Before (12)
No Tears (In The End) (5)
Oasis (14)
Old Heartbreak Top Ten (6)
Only Heaven Can Wait (For Love) (9,10)
Ordinary Man (12)
Our Ages Or Our Hearts (1)
Qual E Malindrinho (Why Are You So Bad) (11)
Reachin' For The Sky (10)
Reverend Lee (2)
River (5)
Rollin' On (11)
See You Then (3)
Set The Night To Music (15) *5*
She's Not Blind (9)
Shock To My System (14)
Some Gospel According To Matthew (6)

Something Magic (14)
Something Your Heart Has Been Telling Me (15)
Soul Deep (7)
Stay With Me (9)
Summertime (15)
Sunday And Sister Jones (3)
Suzanne (5)
Sweet Bitter Love (3)
This Time I'll Be Sweeter (7)
'Til The Morning Comes (12)
To Love Somebody (3)
Tonight, I Celebrate My Love (13) *16*
Tryin' Times (1)
25th Of Last December (7)
Uh-Uh Ooh-Ooh Look Out (Here It Comes) (14)
Unforgettable (15)
Until It's Time For You To Go (2)
Waiting Game (15)
What A Woman Really Means (8)
When It's Over (8)
When Love Has Grown (4)
When Someone Tears Your Heart In Two (15)
When Will I Learn (10)
When You Smile (5)

Where I'll Find You (7)
Where Is The Love (4) *5*
Why Don't You Move In With Me (7)
Will You Still Love Me Tomorrow (3) *76*
You Are Everything (8)
You Are My Heaven (9,10) *47*
You Know What It's Like (14)
You Make Me Feel Brand New (15)
You Stopped Loving Me (11)
You Who Brought Me Love (14)
You're Looking Like Love To Me (13) *58*
You've Got A Friend (4) *29*
You've Lost That Lovin' Feelin' (4) *71*

FLAGG, Fannie

TV and film comedienne/author. Real name: Patricia Neal. Born on 9/21/44. Her Pulitzer Prize-nominated novel was made into the 1992 film *Fried Green Tomatoes*.

DEBUT DATE	PEAK POS	WKS CHR	GOLD	ARTIST — Album Title	$	Label & Number
9/23/67	183	3		Rally 'Round The Flagg [C]	$15	RCA 3856

Baseball
Beauty Contest
Bingo
Check Out
Don't Do That John
Let's Cook
Mrs. Johnson Speaks
New Teacher
Renting Agent
Spelling Bee
Susie Sweetwater Local Wedding
Susie Sweetwater Society Wedding
Susie Sweetwater Theatre Review
Telephone Operator
Weather Girl
Winchester Cathedral

FLAME, The

Rock sextet from Brooklyn led by female vocalist Marge Raymond and guitarist Jimmy Crespo.

DEBUT DATE	PEAK POS	WKS CHR	GOLD	ARTIST — Album Title	$	Label & Number
5/14/77	147	5		Queen Of The Neighborhood	$10	RCA 2160

All My Love To You
Angry Times
Beg Me
Everybody Loves A Winner
Grown Up Man
Laugh My Tears Away
Long Time Gone
Queen Of The Neighborhood
You Sit In Darkness

FLAMING EMBER, The

White soul-rock group from Detroit formed as the Flaming Embers: Joe Sladich (guitar), Bill Ellis (piano), Jim Bugnel (bass) and Jerry Plunk (drums).

DEBUT DATE	PEAK POS	WKS CHR	GOLD	ARTIST — Album Title	$	Label & Number
8/29/70	188	3		Westbound #9	$12	Hot Wax 702

Empty Crowded Room
Flashbacks And Reruns
Going In Circles
Heart On (Loving You)
Mind, Body And Soul *26*
Shades Of Green *88*
Spinning Wheel
Stop The World And Let Me Off
This Girl Is A Woman Now
Westbound #9 *24*
Where's All The Joy
Why Don't You Stay

FLAMIN' GROOVIES

San Francisco rock quintet.

DEBUT DATE	PEAK POS	WKS CHR	GOLD	ARTIST — Album Title	$	Label & Number
8/21/76	142	7		Shake Some Action	$15	Sire 7521

produced by Dave Edmunds

Don't You Lie To Me
I Can't Hide
I Saw Her
I'll Cry Alone
Let The Boy Rock 'N' Roll
Misery
Please Please Girl
Shake Some Action
She Said Yeah
Sometimes
St. Louis Blues
Teenage Confidential
Yes It's True
You Tore Me Down

FLASH

English rock quartet led by Peter Banks (Yes; guitar) and Colin Carter (vocals).

DEBUT DATE	PEAK POS	WKS CHR	GOLD	ARTIST — Album Title	$	Label & Number
5/20/72	33	29		1 Flash	$10	Capitol 11040
12/9/72+	121	13		2 Flash In The Can	$10	Capitol 11115
9/1/73	135	8		3 Out Of Our Hands	$10	Capitol 11218

Bishop (3)
Black And White (2)
Children Of The Universe (1)
Dead Ahead (Queen) (3)
Dreams Of Heaven (1)
Farewell Number One (Pawn) (3)
also see: Psychosync (Escape)
Lifetime (2)
Man Of Honour (Knight) (3)
Manhattan Morning (Christmas '72) (3)
Monday Morning Eyes (2)
Morning Haze (1)
None The Wiser (King) (3)
Open Sky (3)
Psychosync (Escape) (Farewell Number Two) (Conclusion) (3)
Shadows (It's You) (3)
Small Beginnings (1) *29*
Stop That Banging (2)
There No More (2)
Time It Takes (1)

DEBUT DATE	PEAK POS	WKS CHR	GOLD	ARTIST — Album Title	$	Label & Number

FLASH AND THE PAN
Pop duo formed in Australia: George Young and Harry Vanda — formerly with The Easybeats. George's younger brothers, Angus and Malcom Young, are members of AC/DC.

5/26/79	**80**	16		1 Flash And The Pan	**$8**	Epic 36018
5/31/80	**159**	6		2 Lights In The Night	**$8**	Epic 36432

African Shuffle (1)   Captain Beware (2)   First And Last (1)   Hole In The Middle (1)   Man In The Middle (1)   Restless (2)
Atlantis Calling (2)   Down Among The Dead Men   Headhunter (2)   Lady Killer (1)   Man Who Knew The Answer   Walking In The Rain (1)
California (1)   (1)   **Hey, St. Peter** (1) 76   Lights In The Night (2)   (1)   Welcome To The Universe (2)
Make Your Own Cross (2)   Media Man (2)

FLATT & SCRUGGS
Influential bluegrass duo. Lester Flatt (guitar) was born on 6/28/14 in Overton County, Tennessee; died in Nashville on 5/11/79. Earl Scruggs (banjo) was born on 1/6/24 in Cleveland County, North Carolina. Duo formed in 1948 while both were members of Bill Monroe's band. Regulars on TV's *Beverly Hillbillies*. Separated in early 1969.

4/13/63	**115**	4		1 Hard Travelin' featuring The Ballad Of Jed Clampett	**$20**	Columbia 8751
9/28/63	**134**	6		2 Flatt And Scruggs At Carnegie Hall! ....[L]	**$20**	Columbia 8845
3/30/68	**194**	4		3 Changin' Times featuring Foggy Mountain Breakdown	**$20**	Columbia 9596
6/8/68	**161**	4		4 Original Theme From Bonnie & Clyde ....[E]	**$15**	Mercury 61162
				their first recordings from 1948-50		
7/6/68	**187**	5		5 The Story Of Bonnie & Clyde	**$15**	Columbia 9649

Another Ride With Clyde (5)   Dig A Hole In The Meadow   Footprints In The Snow (2)   Mr. Tambourine Man (3)   Reunion (5)   Where Have All The Flowers
Ballad Of Jed Clampett   (2)   Four Strong Winds (3)   My Cabin In Caroline (4)   Roll In My Sweet Baby's   Gone (3)
(1) 44   Dixie Home (1)   Get-Away (5)   My Little Girl In Tennessee   Arms (4)   Why Don't You Tell Me So (4)
Bang, You're Alive (5)   Doin' My Time (4)   Hard Travelin' (1)   (4)   Salty Dog Blues (2)   Wreck Of The Old 97 (1)
Barrow Gang Will Get You   Don't Think Twice, It's All   Highway's End (5)   My Native Home (1)   See Bonnie Die, See Clyde   Yonder Stands Little Maggie
Little Man (5)   Right (3)   Hot Corn, Cold Corn (2)   99 Years Is Almost For Life   Die (See Bonnie And Clyde   (2)
Blowin' In The Wind (3)   Down In The Flood (3)   I Wonder Where You Are   (1)   Die) (5)
Bound To Ride (1)   Drowned In The Deep Blue   Tonight (4)   No Mother Or Dad (4)   Story Of Bonnie And Clyde
Bouquet In Heaven (4)   Sea (1)   I'll Be Going To Heaven   Ode To Billie Joe (3)   (5)
Buddy, Don't Roll So Slow (3)   Durham's Reel (2)   Some Time (4)   Over The Hill To The   Take Me In A Lifeboat (4)
Chase, The (5)   Fiddle And Banjo (2)   It Ain't Me Babe (3)   Poorhouse (4)   Take This Hammer (1)
Coal Miner's Blues (1)   Flint Hill Special (2)   Let The Church Roll On (2)   Pastures Of Plenty (1)   This Land Is Your Land (3)
Cora Is Gone (4)   **Foggy Mountain**   Mama Blues (2)   Picture Of Bonnie (5)   When I Left East Virginia (1)
  Breakdown (3,4,5) 55   Martha White Theme (2)   Pike County Breakdown (4)

★★51★★ ## FLEETWOOD MAC
Formed as a British blues band in 1967 by ex-John Mayall's Bluesbreakers Peter Green (guitar), Mick Fleetwood (drums) and John McVie (bass), along with guitarist Jeremy Spencer. Many lineup changes followed as group headed toward rock superstardom. Green and Spencer left in 1970. Christine McVie (keyboards) joined in August 1970. Bob Welch (guitar) joined in April 1971, stayed through 1974. Group relocated to California in 1974, whereupon Americans Lindsey Buckingham (guitar) and Stevie Nicks (vocals) joined in January 1975. Buckingham left in summer of 1987. Guitarists/vocalists Billy Burnette (son of Dorsey Burnette) and Rick Vito joined in July 1987. Christine McVie and Nicks quit touring with the band at the end of 1990. Vito left in 1991.

8/17/68	**198**	3		1 Fleetwood Mac	**$25**	Epic 26402
2/8/69	**184**	6		2 English Rose	**$25**	Epic 26446
12/13/69+	**109**	22		3 Then Play On	**$20**	Reprise 6368
				Peter Green was a member on above albums		
10/31/70	**69**	14		4 Kiln House	**$15**	Reprise 6408
				Christine McVie joins group; Jeremy Spencer quits after this LP		
7/3/71	**190**	6		5 Fleetwood Mac In Chicago ....[E]	**$20**	Blue Horiz. 3801 [2]
				recorded January 1969; featuring various American blues singers		
10/16/71	**143**	7		6 Black Magic Woman ....[R]	**$18**	Epic 30632 [2]
				reissue of albums #1 and 2 above		
10/30/71	**91**	12		7 Future Games	**$15**	Reprise 6465
				Bob Welch joins group (stays through *Heroes* LP)		
4/22/72	**70**	27	▲	8 Bare Trees	**$15**	Reprise 2080
4/28/73	**49**	13		9 Penguin	**$15**	Reprise 2138
11/17/73	**67**	26	●	10 Mystery To Me	**$15**	Reprise 2158
10/5/74	**34**	26		11 Heroes Are Hard To Find	**$12**	Reprise 2196
3/1/75	**138**	9		12 Vintage Years ....[E-K]	**$12**	Sire 3706 [2]
				recordings from 1967-69		
8/2/75+	**1**[1]	148	▲[5]	13 **Fleetwood Mac**	**$10**	Reprise 2225
				Americans Stevie Nicks and Lindsey Buckingham join group		
12/6/75+	**118**	16		14 Fleetwood Mac In Chicago ....[R]	**$12**	Sire 3715 [2]
				new cover is eggplant-colored and not the side of a car door		
2/26/77	**1**[31]	134	▲[13]	15 Rumours	**$10**	Warner 3010
				1977 Grammy winner: Album of the Year		
11/3/79	**4**	37	▲[2]	16 **Tusk**	**$10**	Warner 3350 [2]
12/27/80+	**14**	18	●	17 Fleetwood Mac Live ....[L]	**$10**	Warner 3500 [2]
7/17/82	**1**[5]	45	▲[2]	18 Mirage	**$8**	Warner 23607
5/2/87	**7**	57	▲[2]	19 **Tango In The Night**	**$8**	Warner 25471
12/10/88+	**14**	26	▲	20 Greatest Hits ....[G]	**$8**	Warner 25801
4/28/90	**18**	19	●	21 Behind The Mask	**$12**	Warner 26111

Affairs Of The Heart (21)   Bad Loser (11)   Big Boat (12)   Born Enchanter (11)   Chain, The (15)   Coming Your Way (3)
Albatross (2,6,12)   Bare Trees (8)   **Big Love** (19) 5   Bright Fire (9)   Child Of Mine (8)   Crystal (13)
Although The Sun Is   Beautiful Child (16)   Black Jack Blues (5,14)   Brown Eyes (16)   City, The (10)   Danny's Chant (8)
Shining (3)   Before The Beginning (3)   Black Magic Woman (2,6,12)   Buddy's Song (4)   Closing My Eyes (3)   Derelect The (9)
Angel (11,16)   Behind The Mask (21)   Blood On The Floor (8)   Can't Go Back (18)   Cold Black Night (1,6)   Did You Ever Love Me (9)
As Long As You Follow   Believe Me (10)   Blue Letter (13)   Caroline (19)   Come A Little Bit Closer (11)   Dissatisfied (9)
(20) 43   Bermuda Triangle (11)   Book Of Love (18)   Caught In The Rain (9)   Coming Home (2,6,11,12)   Do You Know (21)

FLEETWOOD MAC — Cont'd

Doctor Brown (2,6,12)
Don't Let Me Down Again (17)
Don't Stop (15,17,20) **3**
Dreams (15,17,20) **1**
Dust (8)
Dust My Broom (12)
Earl Gray (4)
Emerald Eyes (10)
Empire State (18)
Evenin' Boogie (2,6,12)
Everyday I Have The Blues (5,14)
Everywhere (19,20) **14**
Eyes Of The World (18)
Family Man (19) **90**
Farmer's Daughter (17)
Fighting For Madge (3)
Fireflies (60)
For Your Love (10)
Forever (10)
Freedom (21)
Future Games (7)
Ghost, The (8)
Go Your Own Way (15,17,20) **10**
Gold Dust Woman (15)
Got To Move (1,6)
Gypsy (18,20) **12**
Hard Feelings (21)
Hellhound On My Trail (1,6)
Heroes Are Hard To Find (11)
Hi Ho Silver (4)
Hold Me (18,20) **4**

Homeward Bound (8)
Homework (5,14)
Honey Hi (16)
Hungry Country Girl (5,14)
Hypnotized (10)
I Can't Hold Out (5,14)
I Don't Want To Know (15)
I Got The Blues (5,14)
I Held My Baby Last Night (5,14)
I Know I'm Not Wrong (16)
I Need Your Love (5,14)
(I'm A) Road Runner (9)
I'm So Afraid (13,17)
I'm Worried (5,14)
I've Lost My Baby (2,6,12)
If I Loved Another Woman (1,6)
If You Want To Be My Baby (12)
In The Back Of My Mind (21)
Isn't It Midnight (19)
Jewel Eyed Judy (4)
Jigsaw Puzzle Blues (2,6,12)
Just Crazy Love (10)
Just The Blues (12)
Keep On Going (10)
Landslide (13,17)
Last Night (5,14)
Lay It All Down (7)
Lazy Poker Blues (12)
Ledge, The (16)
Like Crying (3)
Like It This Way (5,14)

Little Lies (19,20) **4**
Long Grey Mare (1,6)
Looking For Somebody (1,6,12)
Love In Store (18) **22**
Love Is Dangerous (21)
Love That Burns (2,6,12)
Madison Blues (5,14)
Man Of The World (12)
Merry Go Round (1,6)
Miles Away (10)
Mission Bell (4)
Monday Morning (13,17)
Morning Rain (7)
My Baby's Good To Me (1,6)
My Heart Beat Like A Hammer (1,6)
Mystified (19)
Need Your Love So Bad (12)
Need Your Love Tonight (12)
Never Forget (16)
Never Going Back Again (15,17)
Never Make Me Cry (16)
Night Watch (9)
No Place To Go (1,6)
No Questions Asked (20)
Not That Funny (16,17)
Oh Daddy (15)
Oh Diane (18)
Oh Well - Pt. 1 (3,17) **55**
One More Night (17)
One Sunny Day (2,6)
One Together (17)

Only Over You (18)
Ooh Baby (5,14)
Over & Over (16,17)
Over My Head (13,17) **20**
Prove Your Love (11)
Rambling Pony (12)
Rattlesnake Shake (3)
Red Hot Jam (5,14)
Remember Me (9)
Revelation (9)
Rhiannon (Will You Ever Win) (13,17,20) **11**
Rockin' Boogie (5,14)
Rollin' Man (12)
Safe Harbour (11)
Sands Of Time (7)
Sara (16,17,20) **7**
Save Me (21) **33**
Save Me A Place (16)
Say You Love Me (13,17,20) **11**
Searching For Madge (3)
Second Hand News (15)
Second Time (21)
Sentimental Lady (8)
Seven Wonders (19) **19**
Shake Your Moneymaker (1,6,12)
She's Changing Me (11)
Show-Biz Blues (3)
Show Me A Smile (7)
Silver Heels (11)
Sisters Of The Moon (16) **86**

Skies The Limit (21)
Somebody (10)
Someday Soon Baby (5,14)
Something Inside Of Me (2,6,12)
Sometimes (7)
Songbird (15)
South Indiana (Take 1 & 2) (5,14)
Spare Me A Little Of Your Love (8)
Stand On The Rock (21)
Station Man (4)
Stop Messin' 'Round (2,6,12)
Storms (16)
Straight Back (18)
Sugar Daddy (13)
Sugar Mama (5,14)
Sun Is Shining (12)
Sunny Side Of Heaven (8)
Talk With You (5,14)
Tango In The Night (19)
Tell Me All The Things You Do (4)
That's All For Everyone (16)
That's Alright (18)
That's Enough For Me (16)
Think About Me (16) **20**
This Is The Rock (4)
Thoughts On A Grey Day (8)
Trying So Hard To Forget (12)
Tusk (16,20) **8**
Underway (16)

Walk A Thin Line (16)
Warm Ways (13)
Watch Out (5,14)
Way I Feel (10)
Welcome To The Room...Sara (19)
What A Shame (7)
What Makes You Think You're The One (16)
When I See You Again (19)
When It Comes To Love (21)
When The Sun Goes Down (21)
Why (10)
Wish You Were Here (18)
Without You (2,6)
Woman Of 1000 Years (7)
World Keep On Turning (1,6)
World Turning (13)
Worlds In A Tangle (5,14)
You And I, Part II (19)
You Make Loving Fun (15) **9**

FLEETWOOD, Mick

Founder/drummer of Fleetwood Mac and The Zoo. Born on 6/24/42 in London. Prior to Fleetwood Mac, was a member of Shotgun Express and John Mayall's Bluesbreakers. Appeared in the 1987 film *Running Man* and several episodes of TV's *Wiseguy.*

7/18/81	43	14		The Visitor	$8	RCA 4080

recorded in Ghana, West Africa

Amelle (Come On Show Me Your Heart)
Cassiopeia Surrender

Don't Be Sorry (Just Be Happy)
Not Fade Away

O' Niamali
Rattlesnake Shake

Super Brains
Visitor, The

Walk A Thin Line
You Weren't In Love

FLEETWOODS, The

Pop trio formed while in high school in Olympia, Washington in 1958: Gary Troxel (b: 11/28/39), Gretchen Christopher (b: 2/29/40) and Barbara Ellis (b: 2/20/40).

12/29/62+	71	6		The Fleetwoods' Greatest Hits .... [G]	$30	Dolton 8018

Come Softly To Me *1*
Confidential
Graduation's Here *39*

(He's) The Great Impostor *30*
Last One To Know *96*

Mr. Blue *1*
Outside My Window *28*
Poor Little Girl

Runaround *23*
Tragedy *10*
Truly Do

You Mean Everything To Me *84*

FLESH FOR LULU

British punk band formed in 1983 by Nick Marsh (vocals, guitar) and James Mitchell (drums). In 1987, included Rocco Barker (guitar), Kevin Mills (bass) and Derek Greening (keyboards).

12/12/87+	89	24		Long Live The New Flesh	$8	Capitol 48217

Crash
Dream On Cowboy

Good For You
Hammer Of Love

I Go Crazy
Lucky Day

Postcards From Paradise
Siamese Twist

Sleeping Dogs
Sooner Or Later

Way To Go

FLESHTONES

Peter Zaremba, lead vocalist of New York-based rock quartet.

3/6/82	174	5		Roman Gods	$8	I.R.S. 70018

Chinese Kitchen
Dreg (Fleshtone-77)

Hope Come Back
I've Gotta Change My Life

Let's See The Sun
Ride Your Pony

R-I-G-H-T-S
Roman Gods

Shadow-line (To J. Conrad)
Stop Fooling Around!

World Has Changed

FLOATERS, The

Detroit soul group discovered by the Detroit Emeralds: Charles Clarke (lead), Larry Cunningham, and brothers Paul and Ralph Mitchell.

6/25/77	10	25	▲	**1 Floaters**	$8	ABC 1030
4/22/78	131	8		**2 Magic**	$8	ABC 1047

Anything That Keeps You Satisfied (2)
Everything Happens For A Reason (1)
Float On (1) *2*

Got To Find A Way (1)
I Am So Glad I Took My Time (1)
I Bet You Get The One You Love (1)

I Dedicate My Love To You (2)
I Just Want To Be With You (2)

Let's Try Love (One More Time) (2)
Magic (We Thank You) (2)
No Stronger Love (1)
Take One Step At A Time (1)

Time Is Now (2)
What Ever Your Sign (2)
You Don't Have To Say You Love Me (1)

FLOCK, The

Chicago rock septet: Fred Glickstein (vocals, guitar), Jerry Goodman (violin), Jerry Smith (bass), saxmen Rick Canoff (died June 1988) and Tom Webb, Frank Posa (trumpet) and Ron Karpman (drums).

9/20/69	48	20		**1 The Flock**	$12	Columbia 9911
10/17/70	96	9		**2 Dinosaur Swamps**	$12	Columbia 30007

Big Bird (2)
Clown (1)
Crabfoot (2)

Green Slice (2)
Hornschmeyer's Island (2)
I Am The Tall Tree (1)

Lighthouse (2)
Mermaid (2)

Store Bought - Store Thought (1)
Tired Of Waiting (1)

Truth (1)
Uranian Sircus (2)

DEBUT DATE	PEAK POS	WKS CHR	GOLD	ARTIST — Album Title	$	Label & Number

FLOCK OF SEAGULLS, A
British new wave group formed by brothers Mike (vocals) and Ali (keyboards, drums) Score. Quartet until 1988 when three Philadelphia natives joined the group.

5/22/82	10	50	●	1 A Flock Of Seagulls	$8	Jive 66000
5/28/83	16	23		2 Listen	$8	Jive 8013
8/25/84	66	10		3 The Story Of A Young Heart	$8	Jive 8250

D.N.A. (1)
Don't Ask Me (1)
Electrics (2)
End, The (3)
European (I Wish I Was) (3)
Fall, The (2)
Heart Of Steel (3)

I Ran (So Far Away) (1) *9*
(It's Not Me) Talking (2)
Man Made (1)
Messages (1)
Modern Love Is Automatic (1)
More You Live, The More You Love (3) *56*

Never Again (The Dancer) (3)
Nightmares (2)
Over My Head (3)
Over The Border (2)
Remember David (3)
Space Age Love Song (1) *30*
Standing In The Doorway (1)

Story Of A Young Heart (3)
Suicide Day (3)
Telecommunication (1)
Transfer Affection (2)
Traveller, The (2)
2:30 (2)

What Am I Supposed To Do (2)
Wishing (If I Had A Photograph Of You) (2) *26*
You Can Run (1)

FLOTSAM AND JETSAM
Heavy-metal band formed in Phoenix in 1985 by drummer Kelly Smith and bassist Jason Newstead (who joined Metallica in 1986). 1988 lineup includes: Eric A.K. (vocals), Ed Carlson, Mike Gilbert and Troy Gregory.

6/18/88	143	8		1 No Place For Disgrace	$8	Elektra 60777
7/7/90	174	7		2 When The Storm Comes Down	$12	MCA 6382

Burned Device (2)
Deviation (2)
Dreams Of Death (1)
E.M.T.E.K. (2)

Escape From Within (1)
Greed (2)
Hard On You (1)
I Live You Die (1)

Jones, The (1)
K.A.B. (1)
Master Sleeps (2)
Misguided Fortune (1)

N.E. Terror (1)
No More Fun (2)
No Place For Disgrace (1)
October Thorns (2)

P.A.A.B. (1)
Saturday Night's Alright For Fighting (1)
Scars (2)

6, Six, VI (2)
Suffer The Masses (2)

FLOYD, King
Soul-funk singer/songwriter born on 2/13/45 in New Orleans. First recorded for Original Sound in 1965.

5/29/71	130	5		King Floyd	$12	Cotillion 9047

Baby Let Me Kiss You *29*
Day In The Life Of A Fool

Don't Leave Me Lonely
Groove Me *6*

It's Wonderful
Let Us Be

Messing Up My Mind
So Glad I Found You

What Our Love Needs
Woman Don't Go Astray *53*

FLYING BURRITO BROTHERS
Rock-country band formed by ex-Byrds Gram Parsons (guitar, vocals) and Chris Hillman (guitar, mandolin). Various personnel. Bernie Leadon (later with the Eagles) joined as guitarist in late 1969. Parsons left in 1970; died on 9/19/73. Hillman and steel guitarist Al Perkins (ex-Shiloh) left in 1971 to join Stephen Stills' Manassas. Guitarist Rick Roberts and drummer Mike Clarke left in 1971 and later formed Firefall.

5/3/69	164	7		1 The Gilded Palace Of Sin	$15	A&M 4175
6/12/71	176	9		2 The Flying Burrito Bros.	$12	A&M 4295
6/3/72	171	7		3 Last Of The Red Hot Burritos .... [L]	$12	A&M 4343
7/13/74	158	5		4 Close Up The Honky Tonks .... [K]	$10	A&M 3631 [2]
				recordings from 1968-72		
10/25/75	138	3		5 Flying Again	$10	Columbia 33817
5/22/76	185	4		6 Sleepless Nights .... [E]	$10	A&M 4578

GRAM PARSONS/THE FLYING BURRITO BROS.
9 tracks recorded in 1970; 3 tracks recorded in 1973 for Gram Parsons' album *Grievous Angel*

Ain't That A Lot Of Love (3)
All Alone (2)
Angels Rejoiced Last Night (6)
Beat The Heat (4)
Bon Soir Blues (5)
Bony Moronie (4)
Brand New Heartache (6)
Break My Mind (4)
Building Fires (5)
Can't You Hear Me Calling (2)
Christine's Tune (1,4)

Close Up The Honky Tonks (4,6)
Cody, Cody (4)
Colorado (2)
Crazy Arms (6)
Dark End Of The Street (1)
Devil In Disguise (4)
Did You See (4)
Dim Lights, Thick Smoke (And Loud, Loud Music) (5,6)
Dixie Breakdown (3)
Do Right Woman (1,4)

Do You Know How It Feels (1)
Don't Fight It (3)
Don't Let Your Deal Go Down (3)
Easy To Get On (5)
Four Days Of Rain (2)
God's Own Singer (4)
Green, Green Grass Of Home (6)
Hand To Mouth (2)
Here Tonight (4)
High Fashion Queen (3,4)
Hippie Boy (1)

Honky Tonk Women (6)
Hot Burrito #1 (1,4)
Hot Burrito #2 (1,3,4)
Hot Burrito #3 (5)
If You Gotta Go (4)
Juanita (1)
Just Can't Be (2)
Losing Game (3)
Money Honey (4)
My Uncle (1,3)
Orange Blossom Special (3)
River Road (5)
Roll Over Beethoven (4)
Sin City (1,4)

Sing Me Back Home (4,6)
Six Days On The Road (3)
Sleepless Nights (6)
Sweet Desert Childhood (5)
To Love Somebody (4)
To Ramona (2)
Together Again (6)
Tonight The Bottle Let Me Down (6)
Train Song (4)
Tried So Hard (2)
Wake Up Little Susie (4)
Wheels (1,4)
White Line Fever (2)

Why Are You Crying (2)
Why Baby Why (5)
Wild Horses (4)
Wind And Rain (5)
You Left The Water Running (5)
Your Angel Steps Out Of Heaven (6)

FLYING LIZARDS, The
British electronic production of David Cunningham.

2/23/80	99	8		The Flying Lizards	$8	Virgin 13137

Der Song Von Mandelay
Events During Flood

Flood, The
Her Story

Money *50*
Russia

Summertime Blues
TV

Trouble
Window, The

FLYING MACHINE, The
Studio project of British songwriters/producers Tony Macauley and Geoff Stevens. Touring group featured Tony Newman as lead vocalist.

12/27/69+	179	7		The Flying Machine	$12	Janus 3007

Baby Make It Soon *87*
Broken Hearted Me, Evil Hearted You

Marie Take A Chance
My Baby's Coming Home
Send My Baby Home Again

Smile A Little Smile For Me *5*
That Same Old Feeling

There She Goes
Thing Called Love

Waiting On The Shores Of Nowhere

FOCUS
Dutch progressive rock quartet led by guitar virtuoso Jan Akkerman and flutist Thijs van Leer.

1/20/73	8	38	●	1 Moving Waves .... [I]	$10	Sire 7401
4/14/73	35	22	●	2 Focus 3 .... [I]	$10	Sire 3901 [2]
6/30/73	104	9		3 In And Out Of Focus .... [E]	$10	Sire 7404
				their first album; recorded in 1970		
11/17/73	132	10		4 Live At The Rainbow .... [I-L]	$10	Sire 7408
8/3/74	66	19		5 Hamburger Concerto .... [I]	$8	Atco 100
3/1/75	120	9		6 Dutch Masters - A Selection Of Their Finest Recordings 1969-1973 .... [K-I]	$8	Sire 7505
9/27/75	152	6		7 Mother Focus .... [I]	$8	Atco 117

DEBUT DATE	PEAK POS	WKS CHR	GOLD	ARTIST — Album Title	$	Label & Number
6/4/77	163	7	8	Ship Of Memories .... [K]	$8	Sire 7531

All Together!.....Oh That! (7)
Anonymous (3)
Anonymus II (Part 1) (2)
Answers? Questions!
  Questions? Answers! (2,4)
Bennie Helder (7)
Birth (5)
Black Beauty (3)
Can't Believe My Eyes (8)
Carnival Fugue (2,6)

Crackers (8)
Delitiae Musicae (5)
Elspeth Of Nottingham (2)
Eruption Medley (1,4)
Father Bach (7)
Focus (3,6)
Focus II (1,4,6)
Focus III (2,4,6)
Focus IV (7)
Focus V (8)

Glider (8)
Hamburger Concerto Medley (5)
Happy Nightmare (Mescaline) (8)
Hard Vanilla (7)
Harem Scarem (5)
Hocus Pocus (1,4,6) *9*
House Of The King (2,6)
I Need A Bathroom (7)

Janis (1)
La Cathedrale De Strasbourg (5)
Le Clochard (Bread) (1)
Love Remembered (2,6)
Mother Focus (7)
Moving Waves (1,6)
My Sweetheart (7)
No Hang Ups (7)
Out Of Vesuvius (8)

P'S March (8)
Red Sky At Night (8)
Round Goes The Gossip (2)
Ship Of Memories (8)
Soft Vanilla (7)
Someone's Crying.....What! (7)
Spoke To The Lord Creator (8)
Sylvia (2,4,6) *89*

Tropic Bird (7)
Why Dream (3)

★★216★★ FOGELBERG, Dan

Born on 8/13/51 in Peoria, Illinois. Vocalist/composer. Worked as a folk singer in Los Angeles. With Van Morrison in the early '70s. Session work in Nashville.

DEBUT DATE	PEAK POS	WKS CHR	GOLD	ARTIST — Album Title	$	Label & Number
12/7/74+	17	27	▲²	1 Souvenirs	$10	Full Moon 33137
				Joe Walsh, producer and guitarist		
10/4/75	23	19	▲	2 Captured Angel	$10	Full Moon 33499
6/4/77	13	39	▲	3 Nether Lands	$10	Full Moon 34185
9/16/78	8	35	▲	4 **Twin Sons Of Different Mothers**	$10	Full Moon 35339
				DAN FOGELBERG & TIM WEISBERG		
12/8/79+	3	39	▲	5 Phoenix	$8	Full Moon 35634
9/12/81	6	62	▲	6 **The Innocent Age**	$10	Full Moon 37393 [2]
11/13/82	15	35	▲	7 Dan Fogelberg/Greatest Hits [G]	$8	Full Moon 38308
2/18/84	15	27	●	8 Windows and Walls	$8	Full Moon 39004
5/11/85	30	23		9 High Country Snows	$8	Full Moon 39616
6/20/87	48	19		10 Exiles	$8	Full Moon 40271
9/22/90	103	13		11 The Wild Places	$12	Full Moon 45059

Aireshire Lament (6)
Along The Road (5)
Anastasia's Eyes (11)
As The Raven Flies (1)
Aspen (medley) (2)
Beggar's Game (5)
Believe In Me (8) *48*
Below The Surface (medley) (2)
Better Change (1)
Blind To The Truth (11)
Bones In The Sky (11)
Captured Angel (2)
Changing Horses (1)
Comes And Goes (2)
Crow (2)
Dancing Shoes (3)
Down Road (9)
Empty Cages (6)
Ever On (11)
Exiles (10)
Face The Fire (5)

False Faces (3)
Forefathers (11)
Ghosts (8)
Give Me Some Time (3)
Go Down Easy (9) *85*
Gone Too Far (8)
Guitar Etude No. 3 (4)
Gypsy Wind (5)
Hard To Say (6,7) *7*
Heart Hotels (5,7) *21*
Hearts In Decline (10)
High Country Snows (9)
Higher You Climb (9)
Hurtwood Alley (4)
Illinois (1)
In The Passage (6)
Innocent Age (6)
Intimidation (4)
It Doesn't Matter (10)
Lahaina Luna (4)
Language Of Love (8) *13*
Last Nail (2)

Last To Know (5)
Lazy Susan (4)
Leader Of The Band (6,7) *9*
Lessons Learned (3)
Let Her Go (8)
Lion's Share (6)
Lonely In Love (10)
Long Way (1)
Longer (5,7) *2*
Loose Ends (3)
Lost In The Sun (6)
Love Gone By (3)
Lovers In A Dangerous Time (11)
Loving Cup (8)
Make Love Stay (7) *29*
Man In The Mirror (medley) (2)
Missing You (7) *23*
Morning Sky (1)
Mountain Pass (9)
Nether Lands (3)

Next Time (2)
Nexus (6)
Old Tennessee (2)
Once Upon A Time (3)
Only The Heart May Know (6)
Our Last Farewell (10)
Outlaw, The (9)
Paris Nocturne (4)
Part Of The Plan (1,7) *31*
Phoenix (5)
Power Of Gold (4,7) *24*
Promises Made (3)
Reach, The (6)
Rhythm Of The Rain (11)
Run For The Roses (6,7) *18*
Same Old Lang Syne (6,7) *9*
Sand And The Foam (6)
Scarecrow's Dream (3)
Seeing You Again (10)
Shallow Rivers (9)

She Don't Look Back (10) *84*
Since You've Asked (4)
Sketches (3)
(Someone's Been) Telling You Stories (1)
Song From Half Mountain (1)
Song Of The Sea (3)
Souvenirs (1)
Spirit Trail (11)
Stolen Moments (6)
Sutter's Mill (9)
Sweet Magnolia (And The Travelling Salesman) (8)
Tell Me To My Face (4)
There's A Place In The World For A Gambler (1)
These Days (medley) (2)
Think Of What You've Done (9)
Times Like These (6)
Tucson, Arizona (Gazette) (8)

Tullamore Dew (5)
Twins Theme (9)
Wandering Shepherd (9)
Washington Post March (medley) (9)
Way It Must Be (10)
What You're Doing (10)
Wild Places (11)
Windows And Walls (8)
Wishing On The Moon (5)
Wolf Creek (9)

FOGERTY, John

Lead vocalist of Creedence Clearwater Revival. Born on 5/28/45 in Berkeley, California. Multi-instrumentalist. Wrote "Proud Mary," "Have You Ever Seen The Rain," "Bad Moon Rising," "Lookin' Out My Back Door" and many others. Went solo in 1972 and recorded as one-man band, The Blue Ridge Rangers.

DEBUT DATE	PEAK POS	WKS CHR	GOLD	ARTIST — Album Title	$	Label & Number
5/5/73	47	15		1 The Blue Ridge Rangers	$10	Fantasy 9415
				THE BLUE RIDGE RANGERS		
10/4/75	78	7		2 John Fogerty	$10	Asylum 1046
1/26/85	1¹	51	▲²	3 **Centerfield**	$8	Warner 25203
10/11/86	26	19	●	4 Eye Of The Zombie	$8	Warner 25449

Almost Saturday Night (2) *78*
Big Train (From Memphis) (3)
Blue Ridge Mountain Blues (1)
California Blues (Blue Yodel #4) (1)
Centerfield (3) *44*
Change In The Weather (4)
Dream (medley) (2)

Eye Of The Zombie (4) *81*
Flyin' Away (2)
Goin' Back Home (4)
Have Thine Own Way, Lord (1)
Headlines (4)
Hearts Of Stone (1) *37*
I Ain't Never (1)
I Can't Help Myself (3)
I Saw It On T.V. (3)

Jambalaya (On The Bayou) (1) *16*
Knockin' On Your Door (4)
Lonely Teardrops (2)
Mr. Greed (3)
Old Man Down The Road (3) *10*
Please Help Me I'm Falling (1)
Rock And Roll Girls (3) *20*

Rockin' All Over The World (2) *27*
Sail Away (4)
Sea Cruise (2)
Searchlight (3)
She Thinks I Still Care (1)
Soda Pop (4)
Somewhere Listening (For My Name) (1)
Song (medley) (2)

Today I Started Loving You Again (1)
Travelin' High (2)
Violence Is Golden (4)
Wall, The (2)
Wasn't That A Woman (4)
Where The River Flows (2)
Workin' On A Building (1)
You Rascal You (2)
You're The Reason (1)

Zanz Kant Danz (3)
appeared as "Vanz Kant Danz" on most copies due to legal conflict

FOGERTY, Tom

Born on 11/9/41 in Berkeley, California. Guitarist/vocalist with Creedence Clearwater Revival. Brother of John Fogerty. Went solo in 1970. Member of the group Ruby from 1977-78. Died on 9/6/90 of respiratory failure from tuberculosis.

DEBUT DATE	PEAK POS	WKS CHR	GOLD	ARTIST — Album Title	$	Label & Number
6/3/72	180	6		Tom Fogerty	$10	Fantasy 9407

Beauty Is Under The Skin
Cast The First Stone

Everyman
Here Stands The Clown

Lady Of Fatima
Legend Of Alcatraz

Me Song
My Pretty Baby

Train To Nowhere
Wondering

★★258★★ FOGHAT

British rock quartet: Lonesome Dave Peverett (vocals, guitar; formerly with Savoy Brown), Rod Price (guitar), Tony Stevens (bass) and Roger Earl (drums). Settled in New York City in 1975, many bass player changes since. Price replaced by Erik Cartwright in 1981.

DEBUT DATE	PEAK POS	WKS CHR	GOLD	ARTIST — Album Title	$	Label & Number
7/15/72	127	22		1 Foghat	$10	Bearsville 2077
3/31/73	67	19	●	2 Foghat	$10	Bearsville 2136
				picture of a rock and a roll on the cover		
2/2/74	34	30	●	3 Energized	$10	Bearsville 6950
11/9/74	40	19	●	4 Rock And Roll Outlaws	$10	Bearsville 6956

DEBUT DATE	PEAK POS	WKS CHR	GOLD	ARTIST — Album Title	$	Label & Number
				FOGHAT — Cont'd		
10/11/75+	**23**	52	▲ 5	Fool For The City	**$8**	Bearsville 6959
11/20/76	**36**	21	● 6	Night Shift	**$8**	Bearsville 6962
9/10/77	**11**	29	▲² 7	Foghat Live ...... [L]	**$8**	Bearsville 6971
5/20/78	**25**	23	● 8	Stone Blue	**$8**	Bearsville 6977
10/13/79	**35**	21	9	Boogie Motel	**$8**	Bearsville 6990
6/21/80	**106**	10	10	Tight Shoes	**$8**	Bearsville 6999
7/25/81	**92**	9	11	Girls To Chat & Boys To Bounce	**$8**	Bearsville 3578
11/13/82	**162**	5	12	In The Mood For Something Rude	**$8**	Bearsville 23747
6/25/83	**192**	2	13	Zig-Zag Walk	**$8**	Bearsville 23888

Ain't Livin' Long Like This (12) — And I Do Just What I Want (12) — Baby Can I Change Your Mind (10) — Back For A Taste Of Your Love (12) — Be My Woman (10) — Blue Spruce Woman (4) — Boogie Motel (9) — Burnin' The Midnight Oil (6) — Bustin' Up Or Bustin' Out (12) — Chateau Lafitte '59 Boogie (4) — Chevrolet (8) — Choo Choo Ch'Boogie (13) — Comin' Down With Love (9) — Couldn't Make Her Stay (2) — Dead End Street (10) — Delayed Reaction (11) — Don't Run Me Down (6) — Down The Road A Piece (13) — Dreamer (4) — Drive Me Home (5) — **Drivin' Wheel** (6) *34* — Easy Money (8) — Eight Days On The Road (4) — Feel So Bad (2) — Fly By Night (3) — **Fool For The City** (5,7) *45* — Fool's Hall Of Fame (1) — Full Time Lover (10) — Golden Arrow (3) — Gotta Get To Know You (1) — Hate To See You Go (4) — Helping Hand (2) — High On Love (8) — Highway (Killing Me) (1) — Hole To Hide In (1) — Home In My Hand (3,7) — Honey Hush (3,7) — Hot Shot Love (6) — **I Just Want To Make Love To You** (1) *83* — **I Just Want To Make Love To You** [live] (7) *33* — I'll Be Standing By (6) *67* — It Hurts Me Too (8) — It'll Be Me (13) — It's Too Late (2) — Jenny Don't Mind (13) — Leavin' Again (Again!) (1) — Let Me Get Close To You (11) — Linda Lou (13) — Live Now - Pay Later (11) — Long Way To Go (2) — Loose Ends (10) — Love In Motion (9) — Love Rustler (1) — Love Zone (11) — Maybelline (1) — Midnight Madness (8) — My Babe (5) — Nervous Release (9) — Night Shift (6) — No Hard Feelings (10) — Nothin' I Won't Do (3) — Paradise Alley (9) — Ride, Ride, Ride (2) — Road Fever (2,7) — Rock & Roll Outlaw (4) — Sarah Lee (1) — Save Your Loving (For Me) (5) — Second Childhood (11) — Seven Day Weekend (13) — She's Gone (2) — Shirley Jean (4) — Silent Treatment (1) — Sing About Love (11) — Slipped, Tripped, Fell In Love (12) — **Slow Ride** (5,7) *20* — Somebody's Been Sleepin' In My Bed (9) — Stay With Me (8) — Step Outside (3) — **Stone Blue** (8) *36* — **Stranger In My Home Town** (10) *81* — Sweet Home Chicago (8) — Take It Or Leave It (3) — Take Me To The River (6) — Take This Heart Of Mine (12) — Terraplane Blues (5) — That'll Be The Day (3) — That's What Love Can Do (13) — There Ain't No Man That Can't Be Caught (12) — **Third Time Lucky (First Time I Was A Fool)** (9) *23* — Three Wheel Cadillac (13) — Too Late The Hero (10) — Trouble In My Way (4) — Trouble, Trouble (1) — Weekend Driver (11) — **What A Shame** (2) *82* — Wide Boy (3) — Wild Cherry (3) — Zig-Zag Walk (13)

FOLEY, Ellen
New York-based singer/actress from St. Louis. Vocalist on Meat Loaf's *Bat Out Of Hell* album. Acted in films *Tootsie* and *Hair*; in cast of TV's *Night Court*, *Search For Tomorrow* and *One Life To Live*.

9/29/79	**137**	6	1	Nightout	**$8**	Cleve. I. 36052
4/4/81	**152**	4	2	Spirit Of St. Louis	**$8**	Cleve. I. 36984

produced by Mick Jones of the Clash

Beautiful Waste Of Time (2) — Death Of The Psychoanalyst Of Salvador Dali (2) — Don't Let Go (1) — Game Of A Man (2) — Hideaway (1) — How Glad I Am (2) — In The Killing Hour (2) — Indestructible (2) — M.P.H. (2) — My Legionnaire (2) — Night Out (1) — Phases Of Travel (2) — Sad Song (1) — Shuttered Palace (2) — Stupid Girl (1) — Theatre Of Cruelty (2) — Thunder And Rain (1) — Torchlight (2) — We Belong To The Night (1) — **What's A Matter Baby** (1) *92* — Young Lust (1)

FOLKSWINGERS, The
Instrumental quartet led by Glen Campbell.

9/28/63	**132**	4	1	12 String Guitar! ...... [I]	**$20**	World Pac. 1812

Answer Is Blowin' In The Wind — Black Mountain Rag — Bull Durham — Columbus Stockade Blues — Cottonfields — Dark As A Dungeon — If I Had A Hammer (Hammer Song) — Midnight Special — Rye Whiskey — This Train — Wabash Cannonball — Walk Right In — Wildwood Flower

FONDA, Jane — see AEROBICS section

FONTAINE, Frank
Born on 4/19/20 in Cambridge, Massachusetts. Comedian/singer/actor. Played Crazy Guggenheim on TV's *Jackie Gleason Show*.

2/9/63	**1**⁵	53	● 1	Songs I Sing On The Jackie Gleason Show	**$15**	ABC-Para. 442
8/24/63	**44**	25	2	Sings Like Crazy	**$15**	ABC-Para. 460
3/7/64	**92**	12	3	How Sweet It Is	**$20**	ABC-Para. 470

All I Do Is Dream Of You (3) — Always (1) — Beautiful (1) — Carolina Moon (2) — Daddy's Little Girl (1) — Easter Parade (1) — For All We Know (3) — Galway Bay (3) — (Gang That Sang) Heart Of My Heart (1) — Girl Of My Dreams (2) — Have You Ever Been Lonely (2) — How Sweet It Is (3) — I Don't Know Why (1) — I Want A Girl (2) — I Wonder Who's Kissing Her Now (1) — I'll Get By (2) — I'm Afraid To Love You (3) — I'm Forever Blowing Bubbles (1) — If I Had My Way (1) — If You Were The Only Girl In The World (1) — It's The Talk Of The Town (3) — Let Me Call You Sweetheart (2) — Let The Rest Of The World Go By (3) — Love Letters In The Sand (2) — Mary's A Grand Old Name (2) — Miss You (3) — Oh How I Miss You Tonight (2) — Pretty Baby (3) — R.S.V.P. (3) — Shine On Harvest Moon (2) — Sweet And Lovely (2) — That Old Gang Of Mine (2) — Till We Meet Again (2) — When I Grow Too Old To Dream (3) — When Your Hair Has Turned To Silver (1) — When Your Old Wedding Ring Was New (3)

FONTANA, Wayne — see MINDBENDERS, The

FOOLS, The
Boston-based rock quintet — Mike Girard, lead singer.

4/5/80	**151**	8	1	Sold Out	**$8**	EMI America 17024
3/28/81	**158**	4	2	Heavy Mental	**$8**	EMI America 17046

Alibi (2) — Around The Block (2) — Coming Home With Me (2) — Don't Tell Me (1) — Dressed In White (2) — Easy For You (1) — Fine With Me (1) — I Won't Grow Up (1) — **It's A Night For Beautiful Girls** (1) *67* — Last Cadillac On Earth (2) — Local Talent (2) — Lost Number (2) — Mind Control (2) — Mutual Of Omaha (1) — Night Out (1) — **Running Scared** (2) *50* — Sad Story (1) — Sold Out (1) — Spent The Rent (1) — Tell Me You Love Me (2) — What I Tell Myself (2)

FOOLS GOLD
Dan Fogelberg's backing group — Denny Henson, lead vocals, guitar.

4/24/76	**100**	13		Fools Gold	**$10**	Morning Sky 5500

Choices — Coming Out Of Hiding — I Will Run — Love Me Through And Through — Old Tennessee — One By One — **Rain, Oh Rain** *76* — Rollin' Fields And Meadows — Sailing To Monterey — Way Love Grows

FORBERT, Steve
Born in 1955 in Meridian, Mississippi. Moved to New York City in 1976.

2/10/79	**82**	15	1	Alive On Arrival	**$8**	Nemperor 35538

DEBUT DATE	PEAK POS	WKS CHR	GOLD	ARTIST — Album Title	$	Label & Number
11/10/79+	20	26	2	Jackrabbit Slim	$8	Nemperor 36191
10/11/80	70	9	3	Little Stevie Orbit	$8	Nemperor 36595
7/24/82	159	6	4	Steve Forbert	$8	Nemperor 37434

Baby (2)
Beautiful Diana (4)
Big City Cat (1)
Cellophane City (3)
Complications (2)
Get Well Soon (3)
Goin' Down To Laurel (1)
Grand Central Station, March 18, 1977 (1)
He's Gotta Live Up To His Shoes (4)
I'm An Automobile (3)
I'm In Love With You (2)
If You Gotta Ask You'll Never Know (3)
It Isn't Gonna Be That Way (1)
It Takes A Whole Lotta Help (To Make It On Your Own) (4)
January 23-30, 1978 (2)
Laughter Lou (Who Needs You?) (3)
Listen To Me (4)
Lonely Girl (3)
Lost (4)
Lucky (3)
Make It All So Real (2)
Oh So Close (And Yet So Far Away) (4)
On The Beach (4)
One More Glass Of Beer (3)
Prisoner Of Stardom (4)
Rain (3)
Romeo's Tune (2) *11*
Sadly Sorta Like A Soap Opera (2)
Say Goodbye To Little Jo (2) *85*
Schoolgirl (3)
Settle Down (1)
Song For Katrina (3)
Song for Carmelita (3)
Steve Forbert's Midsummer Night's Toast (1)
Sweet Love That You Give (Sure Goes A Long, Long Way) (2)
Thinkin' (1)
Tonight I Feel So Far Away From Home (1)
Visitor, A (3)
Wait (2)
What Kinda Guy? (1)
When You Walk In The Room (4)
Ya Ya (Next To Me) (4)
You Cannot Win If You Do Not Play (1)
You're Darn Right (4)

FORCE M.D.'S
Staten Island-based, soul-rap quintet. Originally called Dr. Rock & The M.C.'s. M.D. stands for Musical Diversity.

DEBUT DATE	PEAK POS	WKS CHR	GOLD	ARTIST — Album Title	$	Label & Number
12/15/84	185	4	1	Love Letters	$8	Tommy Boy 1003
2/22/86	69	25	2	Chillin'	$8	Tommy Boy 1010
8/15/87	67	16	3	Touch And Go................................	$8	Tommy Boy 25631

Be Mine Girl (1)
Chillin' (2)
Couldn't Care Less (3)
Don't Make Me Dance (All Night Long) (1)
Force M.D.'S Meet The Fat Boys (2)
Forgive Me Girl (1)
Here I Go Again (2)
I Just Wanna Love You (1)
Itchin' For A Scratch (1)
Let Me Love You (1)
Let's Save Tonight (1)
Love Is A House (3) *78*
Midnite Lover (3)
One Plus One (2)
Sweet Dreams (3)
Take Your Love Back (3)
Tears (1)
Tender Love (2) *10*
Touch And Go (3)
Uh Oh! (2)
Walking On Air (2)
Will You Be My Girlfriend? (2)
Would You Love Me? (3)
Your Love Drives Me Crazy (3)

FORD, Lita
Born on 9/23/59 in London. Lead guitarist of Los Angeles-based female rock group The Runaways, 1975-79.

DEBUT DATE	PEAK POS	WKS CHR	GOLD	ARTIST — Album Title	$	Label & Number
8/4/84	66	16	1	Dancin' On The Edge................................	$8	Mercury 818864
2/20/88	29	62 ▲	2	Lita	$8	RCA 6397
6/16/90	52	16	3	Stiletto	$12	RCA 2090
11/30/91	132	4	4	Dangerous Curves	$12	RCA 61025

Aces & Eights (3)
Back To The Cave (2)
Bad Boy (3)
Bad Love (4)
Big Gun (3)
Black Widow (4)
Blueberry (2)
Broken Dreams (2)
Can't Catch Me (2)
Cherry Red (3)
Close My Eyes Forever (2) *8*
Dancin' On The Edge (1)
Dedication (3)
Don't Let Me Down Tonight (1)
Dressed To Kill (1)
Falling In And Out Of Love (2)
Fatal Passion (2)
Fire In My Heart (1)
Gotta Let Go (1)
Hellbound Train (4)
Hit 'N Run (1)
Holy Man (4)
Hungry (3) *98*
Kiss Me Deadly (2) *12*
Lady Killer (4)
Larger Than Life (4)
Lisa (3)
Little Black Spider (4)
Little Too Early (4)
Only Women Bleed (3)
Playin' With Fire (4)
Ripper, The (3)
Run With The $ (1)
Shot Of Poison (4) *45*
Stiletto (3)
Still Waitin' (1)
Tambourine Dream (4)
Under The Gun (2)
What Do Ya Know About Love (4)
Your Wake Up Call (3)

FORD, Robben
Male session guitarist; member of Jimmy Witherspoon's band, 1972-73. Joined Tom Scott's L.A. Express. Founded the Yellowjackets in 1977; departed in 1983.

DEBUT DATE	PEAK POS	WKS CHR	GOLD	ARTIST — Album Title	$	Label & Number
8/6/88	120	13		Talk To Your Daughter................................	$8	Warner 25647

Ain't Got Nothin' But The Blues
Born Under A Bad Sign
Can't Let Her Go
Getaway
Help The Poor
I Got Over It
Revelation
Talk To Your Daughter
Wild About You (Can't Hold Out Much Longer)

★★210★★ FORD, "Tennessee" Ernie
Country singer, known as America's favorite hymn singer. Born Ernest Jennings Ford on 2/13/19 in Bristol, Tennessee; died on 10/17/91 of liver disease. Began career as a DJ. Host of musical variety TV shows, 1955-65. Favorite expression: "Bless your little pea-pickin' hearts."

DEBUT DATE	PEAK POS	WKS CHR	GOLD	ARTIST — Album Title	$	Label & Number
4/28/56	12	3		1 This Lusty Land!	$15	Capitol 700
1/5/57	2³	277 ▲		2 Hymns................................	$15	Capitol 756
5/6/57	5	68 ●		3 Spirituals................................	$15	Capitol 818
6/9/58	5	77 ●		4 Nearer The Cross................................	$15	Capitol 1005
5/2/60	23	26		5 Sing A Hymn With Me................................	$15	Capitol 1332
				includes a hymn book		
1/27/62	67	19		6 Hymns At Home................................	$12	Capitol 1604
				recorded at Ernie's hometown church in Bristol, Tennessee		
5/26/62	110	12		7 Here Comes The Mississippi Showboat................................	$12	Capitol 1684
11/10/62	43	2		8 I Love To Tell The Story................................	$12	Capitol 1751
1/5/63	71	12		9 Book Of Favorite Hymns................................ [K]	$12	Capitol 1794
4/25/70	192	2		10 America The Beautiful................................	$10	Capitol 412
				CHRISTMAS ALBUM:		
12/22/58+	4	3 ▲		11 **The Star Carol**................................ [X]	$15	Capitol 1071
12/28/59+	7	2		12 **The Star Carol**................................ [X-R]	$15	Capitol 1071
12/31/60	28	1		13 The Star Carol................................ [X-R]	$15	Capitol 1071
12/25/61+	110	3		14 The Star Carol................................ [X-R]	$15	Capitol 1071
12/22/62	48	2		15 The Star Carol................................ [X-R]	$15	Capitol 1071
				Christmas charts: 15/'64, 25/'65, 56/'66, 41/'67		

Adeste Fidelis (11)
All Hail The Power (5,9)
America (10)
America, I Love You (10)
America, The Beautiful (10)
Asleep In Jesus (8)
Band Played On (7)
Battle Hymn Of The Republic (10)
Beautiful Isle Of Somewhere (4,9)
Blessed Assurance (8)
Blest Be The Tie That Binds (6)
Break Thou The Bread Of Life (6)
Brighten The Corner Where You Are (5)
Bringing In The Sheaves (5)
Chicken Road (1)
Church In The Wildwood (5)
Comin' Home (6)
Count Your Blessings (5)
Dark As A Dungeon (1)
Day Is Dying In The West (6)
Did You Think To Pray? (6)
Drifting Too Far From The Shore (9)
Face To Face (6)
Fairest Lord Jesus (8)
False Hearted Girl (1)
Farther Along (8)
First Noel (11)
Floatin' Down To Cotton Town (7)
Gaily The Troubador (7)
Get On Board, Little Children (3)
Give To The Winds Thy Fears (8)
God Be With You (4)
God Bless America (10)
God Rest Ye Merry, Gentlemen (11)
Hark! The Herald Angels Sing (11)
He'll Understand And Say "Well Done" (3)
His Amazing Grace (6)
His Eye Is On The Sparrow (4)
Holy Spirit, Faithful Guide (6)
Home Over There (5)
How Great Thou Art (8)
I Gave My Love A Cherry (1)
I Know The Lord Laid His Hands On Me (3)

DEBUT DATE	PEAK POS	WKS CHR	GOLD	ARTIST — Album Title	$	Label & Number

FORD, "Tennessee" Ernie — Cont'd

I Love To Tell The Story (5,8)
I Need Thee Every Hour (4)
I Want To Be Ready (3)
If I Can Help Somebody (8)
In The Garden (2)
In The Pines (1)
In The Shade Of The Old Apple Tree (7)
It Came Upon A Midnight Clear (11)
It Is Well With My Soul (6)
Ivory Palaces (2)
Jesus Loves Me (5)
Jesus Paid It All (6)
Jesus, Savior, Pilot Me (4)
John Henry (1)
Joy To The World (11)

Just A Closer Walk With Thee (3)
Last Letter (1)
Let The Lower Lights Be Burning (2)
Lord, I'm Coming Home (4)
Mary's A Grand Old Name (7)
My Faith Looks Up To Thee (6)
My Jesus, I Love Thee (6)
My Task (2,8)
Nearer, My God, To Thee (4)
Nine Pound Hammer (1)
Ninety And Nine (2,9)
Noah Found Grace In The Eyes Of The Lord (3)
Now The Day Is Over (4)
O Hearken Ye (11)

O Holy Night (11)
O Little Town Of Bethlehem (11)
Oh How I Love Jesus (5)
Old Piano Roll Blues (7)
Old Rugged Cross (2)
Onward Christian Soldiers (5,9)
Others (2,8)
Our Land, O Lord (10)
Paddlin' Madelin' Home (7)
Peace In The Valley (3)
Pledge Of Allegiance (10)
Precious Memories (9)
Rock Of Ages (2,9)
Rovin' Gambler (1) 60
Row, Row, Row (7)
Saved By Grace (8)

Shall We Gather At The River (5)
Silent Night (11)
Sleep, My Little Lord Jesus (11)
Soft Shoe Song (7)
Softly And Tenderly (2,9)
Some Children See Him (11)
Stand By Me (3)
Star Carol (11)
Star-Spangled Banner (10)
Straw Hat And A Cane (7)
Sweet Hour Of Prayer (2,6)
Sweet Peace The Gift Of God's Love (4)
Take My Hand, Precious Lord (3)
Take Time To Be Holy (4)

Take Your Girlie To The Movies (7)
There Is Power In The Blood (5)
There'll Be No New Tunes On This Old Piano (7)
This Is My Country (10)
This Land Is Your Land (10)
Trouble In Mind (1)
Waiting For The Robert E. Lee (7)
Wayfaring Pilgrim (3)
We Three Kings (11)
Were You There? (3)
What A Friend (5)
What A Friend We Have In Jesus (4,9)

When God Dips His Love In My Heart (3)
When The Roll Is Called Up Yonder (5,9)
When They Ring The Golden Bells (2,9)
Whispering Hope (4,9)
Who At My Door Is Standing (2)
Who Will Shoe Your Pretty Little Foot (1)

FORDHAM, Julia

Singer from southern England. Member of Mari Wilson's eclectic Wilsations for two years. Also worked as a backing vocalist for Kim Wilde.

DEBUT DATE	PEAK POS	WKS CHR	GOLD	ARTIST — Album Title	$	Label & Number
12/3/88+	118	25		1 Julia Fordham	$8	Virgin 90955
2/17/90	74	20		2 Porcelain	$12	Virgin 91325

Behind Closed Doors (1)
Cocooned (1)
Comfort Of Strangers (1)
Did I Happen To Mention? (2)

Few Too Many (1)
For You Only For You (2)
Genius (2)
Girlfriend (2)

Happy Ever After (1)
Invisible War (1)
Island (2)
Lock And Key (2)

Manhattan Skyline (2)
My Lover's Keeper (1)
Other Woman (1)
Porcelain (2)

Towerblock (2)
Unconditional Love (1)
Where Does The Time Go? (1)

Woman Of The 80's (1)
Your Lovely Face (2)

★★204★★ FOREIGNER

British-American rock group formed in New York City in 1976. Consisted of Mick Jones (guitar), Lou Gramm (vocals), Ian McDonald (guitar, keyboards), Ed Gagliardi (bass), Al Greenwood (keyboards) and Dennis Elliott (drums). Gagliardi, Gramm and Greenwood are from New York. Most of material written by Jones (Spooky Tooth) and Gramm. Rick Wills (Roxy Music, Small Faces) replaced Gagliardi in 1979. Greenwood and McDonald (King Crimson) left in 1980. Gramm left in 1991 to form Shadow King; replaced by Johnny Edwards. Gramm returned in mid-1992. Wills left in 1992 to join Bad Company; Elliott left to open woodworking business. Jones not to be confused with Mick Jones of The Clash and Big Audio Dynamite.

DEBUT DATE	PEAK POS	WKS CHR	GOLD	ARTIST — Album Title	$	Label & Number
3/26/77	4	113	▲⁴	1 Foreigner	$10	Atlantic 18215
7/8/78	3	88	▲⁵	2 Double Vision	$10	Atlantic 19999
9/29/79	5	41	▲²	3 Head Games	$10	Atlantic 29999
7/25/81	1¹⁰	81	▲⁶	4 4	$8	Atlantic 16999
12/25/82+	10	25	▲³	5 Foreigner Records	[G] $8	Atlantic 80999
1/5/85	4	45	▲²	6 Agent Provocateur	$8	Atlantic 81999
12/26/87+	15	37	▲	7 Inside Information	$8	Atlantic 81808
7/6/91	117	9		8 Unusual Heat	$12	Atlantic 82299
10/10/92	123	17↑		9 The Very Best...And Beyond	[G] $12	Atlantic 89999

At War With The World (1)
Back Where You Belong (2)
Beat Of My Heart (7)
Blinded By Science (3)
Blue Morning, Blue Day (2) 15
Break It Up (4) 26
Can't Wait (7)
Cold As Ice (1,5,9) 6
Counting Every Minute (7)
Damage Is Done (1)
Dirty White Boy (3,5,9) 12
Do What You Like (3)
Don't Let Go (4)
Double Vision (2,5,9) 2
Down On Love (6) 54

Face To Face (7)
Feels Like The First Time (1,5,9) 4
Flesh Wound (8)
Fool For You Anyway (1)
Girl On The Moon (4)
Growing Up The Hard Way (6)
Head Games (3,5,9) 14
Headknocker (1)
Heart Turns To Stone (7) 56
Hot Blooded (2,5,9) 3
I Don't Want To Live Without You (7,9) 5
I Have Waited So Long (2)

I Need You (1)
I Want To Know What Love Is (6,9) 1
I'll Fight For You (8)
I'll Get Even With You (3)
I'm Gonna Win (4)
Inside Information (7)
Juke Box Hero (4,5,9) 26
Lonely Children (2)
Long, Long Way From Home (1,5) 20
Love Has Taken Its Toll (2)
Love In Vain (6)
Love On The Telephone (3)
Lowdown And Dirty (8)
Luanne (4) 75

Modern Day (3)
Moment Of Truth (8)
Mountain Of Love (8)
Night Life (4)
Night To Remember (7)
No Hiding Place (8)
Only Heaven Knows (8)
Out Of The Blue (7)
Prisoner Of Love (9)
Reaction To Action (6) 54
Ready For The Rain (8)
Rev On The Red Line (3,9)
Safe In My Heart (8)
Say You Will (7,9) 6
Seventeen (3)
She's Too Tough (6)

Soul Doctor (9)
Spellbinder (2)
Starrider (1)
Stranger In My Own House (6)
That Was Yesterday (6,9) 12
Tooth And Nail (6)
Tramontane (2)
Two Different Worlds (6)
Unusual Heat (8)
Urgent (4,5,9) 4
Waiting For A Girl Like You (4,5,9) 2
When The Night Comes Down (8)

With Heaven On Our Side (9)
Woman In Black (4)
Woman Oh Woman (1)
Women (3) 41
You're All I Am (2)

FORESTER SISTERS, The

Country family vocal quartet from Lookout Mountain, Georgia: Kathy, Kim, June and Christy Forester.

DEBUT DATE	PEAK POS	WKS CHR	GOLD	ARTIST — Album Title	$	Label & Number
4/20/91	137	7		Talkin' 'Bout Men	$12	Warner 26500

Blues Don't Stand A Chance (1)
It's Gettin' Around

Let Not Your Heart Be Troubled

Men
Somebody Else's Moon

Step In The Right Direction
That Makes One Of Us

Too Much Fun
What About Tonight

You Take Me For Granted

FOREVER MORE

Rock quartet from the U.K.: Alan Gorrie (vocals), Mick Travis (guitar), Onnie Mair (bass) and Stuart Francis (drums). Gorrie later formed Average White Band.

DEBUT DATE	PEAK POS	WKS CHR	GOLD	ARTIST — Album Title	$	Label & Number
3/7/70	180	3		Yours Forever More	$12	RCA 4272

Back In The States Again
Beautiful Afternoon
8 O'Clock & All's Well

Good To Me
Home Country Blues
It's Home

Mean Pappie Blues
Sylvester's Last Voyage
We Sing

You Too Can Have A Body Like Mine
Yours

FORTUNES, The

English pop quintet led by guitarists/vocalists Glen Dale (Garforth) and Barry Pritchard. Dale left in July 1966, replaced by Scotsman Shel MacRae.

DEBUT DATE	PEAK POS	WKS CHR	GOLD	ARTIST — Album Title	$	Label & Number
7/10/71	134	10		Here Comes That Rainy Day Feeling Again	$15	Capitol 809

All My Calendar Is You
Eye For The Main Chance

Hear The Band
Here Comes That Rainy Day Feeling Again 15

I Gotta Dream
Just A Line To Let You Know

Night Started To Cry
Noises (In My Head)

Oh! Babe
Thoughts

DEBUT DATE	PEAK POS	WKS CHR	G O L D	ARTIST — Album Title	$	Label & Number

FOSTER, David
Keyboardist/composer/arranger born in Victoria, British Columbia. Member of the groups Skylark and Attitudes. Wrote hits for Chicago, Barbra Streisand and others.

7/19/86	**195**	3		1 David Foster	$8	Atlantic 81642
2/20/88	**111**	8		2 The Symphony Sessions .... [I-L]	$8	Atlantic 81799

recorded June 26-29, 1987, at the Orpheum Theater in Vancouver

All That My Heart Can Hold (1)	Color Purple (Mailbox/Proud Theme), Theme From The (1)	Elizabeth (1)	Piano Concerto In G (2)	TapDance (1)	Who's Gonna Love You Tonight (1)
Ballet, The (2)	Conscience (2)	Firedance (2)	Playing With Fire (1)	Time Passing (2)	**Winter Games** (2) 85
Best Of Me (1) 80		Flight Of The Snowbirds (1)	Saje (1)	Water Fountain (2)	
		Just Out Of Reach (2)	St. Elmo's Fire, Love	We Were So Close (2)	
		Morning To Morning (2)	Theme From (1) 15		

FOSTER & LLOYD
Country vocal duo of songwriters Radney Foster and Bill Lloyd.

5/13/89	**142**	6		Faster & Llouder..	$8	RCA 9587

Before The Heartache Rolls In	Fair Shake	Fat Lady Sings	I'll Always Be Here Loving You	Lie To Yourself	Suzette
	Faster And Louder	Happy For Awhile		She Knows What She Wants	

FOTOMAKER
New York pop-rock quintet formed by former Rascals' Dino Danelli and Gene Cornish, and former Raspberries' member Wally Bryson.

3/25/78	**88**	13		Fotomaker..	$8	Atlantic 19165

All There In Her Eyes	Can I Please Have Some More	Lose At Love	Pain	Say The Same For You	**Where Have You Been All My Life** 81
All These Years		Other Side	Plaything	Two Can Make It Work	

FOUNDATIONS, The
British interracial R&B-pop group. Lead singer Clem Curtis (from Trinidad) replaced by Colin Young (West Indies) in 1968. Disbanded in 1970.

3/8/69	**92**	11		Build Me Up Buttercup ....[L]	$15	Uni 73043

side 1: live; side 2: studio

Am I Groovin' You	**Back On My Feet Again** 59	Harlem Shuffle	I'm A Whole New Thing	People Are Funny
Any Old Time (You're Lonely And Sad)	**Build Me Up Buttercup** 3	I Can Take Or Leave Your Loving	Love Is All Right	Tomorrow
	Comin' Home Baby		New Direction	

★★285★★   FOUNTAIN, Pete
Born on 7/3/30 in New Orleans. Top jazz clarinetist. With Al Hirt, 1956-57. Performed on Lawrence Welk's weekly TV show, 1957-59. Own club in New Orleans, The French Quarter Inn.

2/22/60	**8**	87		1 Pete Fountain's New Orleans ....[I]	$15	Coral 57282
5/9/60	**31**	4		2 Pete Fountain Day ....[I-L]	$15	Coral 57313
9/11/61	**43**	4		3 Pete Fountain's French Quarter ....[I]	$15	Coral 57359
				Pete's nightclub at 231 Bourbon St. in New Orleans		
2/3/62	**41**	2		4 Bourbon Street ....[I]	$15	Coral 57389
				PETE FOUNTAIN/AL HIRT		
7/28/62	**30**	6		5 Music From Dixie ....[I]	$15	Coral 57401
9/7/63	**91**	9		6 South Rampart Street Parade ....[I]	$15	Coral 57440
6/13/64	**53**	14		7 New Orleans At Midnight..................................[I]	$12	Coral 57429
8/22/64	**48**	44		8 Licorice Stick ....[I]	$12	Coral 57460
1/2/65	**121**	7		9 Pete's Place ....[I-L]	$12	Coral 57453
				recorded at Pete's French Quarter Inn		
5/8/65	**64**	14		10 Mr. Stick Man..[I]	$12	Coral 57473
4/23/66	**100**	8		11 A Taste Of Honey	$12	Coral 57486
				features a 3-woman, 2-man chorus		
6/15/68	**187**	2		12 For The First Time	$15	Decca 74955
				BRENDA LEE & PETE FOUNTAIN		
3/22/69	**186**	6		13 Those Were The Days ....[I]	$12	Coral 57505

Amazon (10)	**Closer Walk** (1) 93	I Got Rhythm (2)	March Through The Streets	Second Line (6)	Tippin' In (8)
American Boys (13)	Cotton Fields (1)	I Gotta Right To Sing The	Of Their City [solo: Pete] (4)	Shadow Of Your Smile (11)	Walking Through New
Another World (10)	Creole Love Call (7)	Blues (12)	March To Peruna (9)	Sheik Of Araby (9)	Orleans (6)
Anything Goes (12)	Cycles (13)	I Know A Place (11)	Marching 'Round The	Shine (2,5)	Washington And Lee Swing
At The Jazz Band Ball (4)	Darktown Strutters' Ball (6)	I Love You So Much It Hurts	Mountain (6)	Show Me A City Like New	(6)
Avalon (2)	Dear Old Southland (3)	(8)	Maria Elena (8)	Orleans (10)	Way Down Yonder In New
Ballin' The Jack (7)	Dear World (13)	I Want To Be Happy (7)	Midnight Boogie (7)	Shrimp Boats (3)	Orleans (1,9)
Basin Street Blues (1,6,9,12)	Dixie (3)	I Wish I Could Shimmy Like	Midnight Pete (7)	Someday Sweetheart (2,3)	(What Did I Do To Be So)
Battle Hymn Of The	Dixie Jubilee (5)	My Sister Kate (5)	Milenberg Joys (5)	Song Of The Wanderer	Black And Blue (3)
Republic (7)	Do You Know What It Means	I'm Henry VIII, I Am (11)	Mood Indigo (12)	(Where Shall I Go?) (5)	(When It's) Darkness On The
Birth Of The Blues (3)	To Miss New Orleans (1)	"In" Crowd (11)	Moonglow (7)	Sound Of Music (10)	Delta (4)
Blues On Bourbon Street	Don't Be That Way (2)	Is It True What They Say	Mr. Stick Man (10)	South Rampart Street	When It's Sleepy Time Down
[solo: Pete] (4)	Estrellita (8)	About Dixie (3)	My Special Angel (13)	Parade (6)	South (1)
Born To Lose (8)	Farewell Blues (4,6)	It's Been A Long, Long Time	Night And Day (12)	St. James Infirmary [solo:	When The Saints Come
Bourbon Street Parade (7)	Fascination (medley) (9)	(11)	Oh, Didn't He Ramble (3)	Pete] (4)	Marching In March (1)
Brahms' Lullaby (7)	59th Street Bridge Song	It's Just A Little While (To	Oh, Lady Be Good! (9)	Stand By Me (11)	When You're Smiling The
Bye Bye Bill Bailey (5)	(Feelin' Groovy) (12)	Stay Here) (9)	Ol' Man River (1)	Struttin' With Some	Whole World Smiles With
Bye Bye Blackbird (3)	Folsom Prison Blues (13)	Ja-Da (2)	On The South Side Of	Barbecue (5)	You) (5)
Cabaret (12)	Fountain Blue (8)	Jambalaya (On The Bayou)	Chicago (13)	Sugar Bowl Parade (6)	Whiffenpoof Song (Baa Baa
California Summer (People	Fountain In The Rain (11)	(10)	On The Street Where You	Summertime (3)	Baa) (10)
Movin' West) (11)	French Quarter, Theme	Jazz Me Blues (4)	Live (10)	Sweethearts On Parade (1)	While We Danced At The
Can't Take My Eyes Off You	From The (3)	King Of The Road (11)	One Of Those Songs (12)	Swing Low (7)	Mardi Gras (1)
(12)	Goodbye (10)	Lazy Bones (3)	Over The Waves (6)	Taste Of Honey (11)	Whipped Cream (10)
Careless Love (6)	Gotta Travel On (10)	Lazy River (1,4)	Poor Butterfly (2)	That Da Da Strain (3)	Wichita Lineman (13)
Cast Your Fate To The Wind	Gravy Waltz (6)	Les Bicyclettes De Belsize	Preacher, The (9)	That's A Plenty (9)	Windy (12)
(11)	Hallelujah (5)	(13)	Puddin' (1)	There's A Kind Of Hush (All	Yearling, Theme From The
China Boy (Go Sleep) (2)	Hello, Dolly! (8)	Licorice Stick (8)	Put On Your Old Grey	Over The World!) (12)	(11)
Chlo-E (Song Of The	High Society (5)	Lucky Pierre (11)	Bonnet (6)	Those Were The Days (13)	Young Maiden's Prayer (8)
Swamp) (5)	Honey-Wind Blows (8)	Makin' Whoopee (7)	Rockin' Chair (7)	Tiger Rag (2)	
Clarinet Strip (8)	Humbug (10)	March Of The Bob Cats (4)	S' Wonderful (2)	Tin Roof Blues (1,9)	

DEBUT DATE	PEAK POS	WKS CHR	GOLD	ARTIST — Album Title	$	Label & Number

4 BY FOUR
Soul quartet from Queens, New York: Damen and Lance Heyward, Steve Gray and Jeraude Jackson.

| 6/27/87 | 141 | 7 | | 4 By Four .... | $8 | Capitol 12560 |

Come Over · Don't Put The Blame On Me · Fingertips · Mommy – Daddy · Problems Too · She's Alright · Smokin' · This Time I Know It's Real · **Want You For My Girlfriend 79** · You Changed

★★463★★ FOUR FRESHMEN, The
Jazz-styled vocal and instrumental group formed in 1948 while at Arthur Jordan Conservatory of Music in Indianapolis. Consisted of brothers Ross and Don Barbour, their cousin Bob Flanigan and Ken Errair.

2/25/56	6	33		1 **Four Freshmen and 5 Trombones**	$30	Capitol 683
10/13/56	11	8		2 Freshmen Favorites ....[G]	$30	Capitol 743
3/2/57	9	7		3 **4 Freshmen and 5 Trumpets**	$30	Capitol 763
11/18/57	25	1		4 Four Freshmen and Five Saxes	$30	Capitol 844
9/29/58	17	1		5 The Four Freshmen In Person ....[L]	$20	Capitol 1008
11/3/58	11	6		6 Voices In Love	$20	Capitol 1074
1/11/60	40	1		7 The Four Freshmen and Five Guitars	$20	Capitol 1255

After You've Gone (3) · Angel Eyes (1) · **Charmaine** (2) *69* · Circus (5) · Come Rain Or Come Shine (7) · **Day By Day** (2,5) *42* · Day Isn't Long Enough (2) · Don't Worry 'Bout Me (7) · East Of The Sun (4) · Easy Street (3) · Ev'ry Time We Say Goodbye (3) · For All We Know (4) · Give Me The Simple Life (3) · Good Night Sweetheart (3) · Good-bye (3) · Got A Date With An Angel (3) · Graduation Day (2) *17* · Guilty (1) · Holiday (5) · How Can I Tell Her (2) · I Get Along Without You Very Well (4) · I Heard You Cried Last Night (And So Did I) (6) · I May Be Wrong (4) · I Never Knew (7) · I Remember You (1) · I Understand (7) · I'll Remember April (6) · I'm Always Chasing Rainbows (6) · In The Still Of The Night (6) · In This Whole Wide World (2,5) · Indian Summer (5) · Invitation (7) · It All Depends On You (7) · It Could Happen To You (6) · It Never Occurred To Me (2) · It's A Blue World (5) · It's A Pity To Say Goodnight (7) · Last Time I Saw Paris (1) · Laughing On The Outside (Crying On The Inside) (3) · Liza (4) · Lonely Night In Paris (2) · Love (1) · Love Is Here To Stay (1) · Love Is Just Around The Corner (1) · Love Turns Winter To Spring (2) · Lullaby In Rhythm (4) · Malaya (5) · Mam'selle (1) · Moonlight (6) · More I See You (7) · Mr. B's Blues (5) · My Heart Stood Still (5) · Nancy (7) · Night We Called It A Day (3) · Now You Know (2) · Oh Lonely Winter (7) · Old Folks (5) · Out Of Nowhere (6) · Poinciana (Song Of The Tree) (2) · Rain (7) · Seems Like Old Times (2) · Somebody Loves Me (1,5) · Someone Like You (3) · Something In The Wind (3) · Sometimes I'm Happy (4) · Speak Low (1) · Sweet Lorraine (5) · Them There Eyes (1) · There Is No Greater Love (6) · There Will Never Be Another You (3) · There's No One But You (4) · This Can't Be Love (4) · This Love Of Mine (4) · This October (7) · Time Was (Duerme) (6) · Very Thought Of You (4) · Warm (6) · While You Are Gone (6) · You Made Me Love You (I Didn't Want To Do It) (1) · You Stepped Out Of A Dream (1) · You're All I See (6) · You've Got Me Cryin' Again (4,5)

FOUR JACKS AND A JILL
South African quintet; Jill is Glenys Lynne (lead singer).

| 6/22/68 | 155 | 6 | | Master Jack .... | $15 | RCA 4019 |

Bobby Blows A Blue Note · Fifi The Flea · Hamba Liliwam · I Looked Back · La La Song · Lonely Desert Boy · **Master Jack 18** · **Mister Nico 96** · Penny Paper · Sunny Side Of Somewhere · Timothy

FOUR LADS, The
Toronto vocal quartet: Bernie Toorish, Jimmie Arnold, Frankie Busseri and Connie Codarini. Backed Johnny Ray on his #1 single "Cry."

| 10/6/56 | 14 | 2 | | On The Sunny Side .... | $30 | Columbia 912 |

Bidin' My Time · Dancing In The Dark · Lazy River · Makin' Whoopee · On The Sunny Side Of The Street · Sentimental Journey · Side By Side · Taking A Chance On Love · These Foolish Things (Remind Me Of You) · Things We Did Last Summer · Way You Look Tonight · Wrap Your Troubles In Dreams (And Dream Your Troubles Away)

FOURPLAY
Quartet of jazz notables: keyboardist Bob James, guitarist Lee Ritenour, drummer Harvey Mason and bassist Nathan East.

| 10/12/91 | 97 | 33 | ● | Fourplay ....[I] | $12 | Warner 26656 |

After The Dance · Bali Run · Foreplay · Max-O-Man · Midnight Stroll · Moonjogger · October Morning · 101 Eastbound · Quadrille · Rain Forest · Wish You Were Here

FOUR PREPS, The
Vocal group formed while at Hollywood High School: Bruce Belland, Glen Larson, Ed Cobb and Marvin Ingraham. Belland, who was later in duo with Dave Somerville of the Diamonds, is the father of Tracey and Melissa Belland of Voice Of The Beehive.

| 8/21/61 | 8 | 26 | | 1 **The Four Preps On Campus** ....[L] | $25 | Capitol 1566 |
| 3/24/62 | 40 | 17 | | 2 Campus Encore ....[L] | $25 | Capitol 1647 |

Big Draft (2) *61* · Come To The Dance (2) · He's Goin' Away (1) · Heart And Soul (1) · In The Good Old Summer Time (1) · Lonesome Town (2) · Lullaby (2) · Moon River (2) · **More Money For You And Me** (1) *17* · Next Man Told His Tale (2) · Preps Hit Medley (1) · Rememb'ring (2) · Rock 'N Roll (1) · Sphinx Won't Tell (2) · Suzy Cocroach (2) · Swing Down Chariot (1) · Their Hearts Were Full Of Spring (1) · Young And Foolish (1)

★★75★★ 4 SEASONS, The
Vocal group formed in Newark, New Jersey. In 1955, lead singer Frankie Valli (Francis Castelluccio) formed the Variatones with the brothers Nick and Tommy DeVito, and Hank Majewski. Changed name to The Four Lovers in 1956. Bob Gaudio (of The Royal Teens) joined as keyboardist/songwriter in 1959, replacing Nick DeVito. Nick Massi replaced Majewski, and their 1961 lineup was set: Valli, Gaudio, Massi and Tommy DeVito. Group had been doing session work for their producer Bob Crewe and took their new name from a New Jersey bowling alley, The Four Seasons. In 1965, Nick Massi was replaced by the group's arranger Charlie Callelo and then by Joe Long. In 1971, Tommy DeVito retired, and Gaudio left (as a performer) the following year. Numerous personnel changes from then on. Inducted into the Rock and Roll Hall of Fame in 1990. Also recorded as The Wonder Who?

10/27/62	6	27		1 **Sherry & 11 others**	$30	Vee-Jay 1053
3/2/63	8	19		2 **Big Girls Don't Cry and Twelve others**	$40	Vee-Jay 1056
7/13/63	47	12		3 Ain't That A Shame and 11 others	$40	Vee-Jay 1059
9/7/63	15	56		4 Golden Hits of the 4 Seasons ....[G]	$40	Vee-Jay 1065
2/29/64	84	9		5 Born To Wander	$20	Philips 129
3/28/64	6	25		6 **Dawn (Go Away) and 11 other great songs**	$20	Philips 124
6/6/64	100	5		7 Stay & Other Great Hits ....[K]	$30	Vee-Jay 1082
				originally titled *Folk-Nanny*		
8/8/64	7	26		8 **Rag Doll**	$20	Philips 146

DEBUT DATE	PEAK POS	WKS CHR	GOLD	ARTIST — Album Title	$	Label & Number
				4 SEASONS, The — Cont'd		
9/5/64	105	5		9 More Golden Hits By The Four Seasons .... [K]	$35	Vee-Jay 1088
10/10/64	142	3		10 The Beatles vs. The Four Seasons .... [R]	$500	Vee-Jay 30 [2]
				Introducing...The Beatles & Golden Hits of the 4 Seasons LPs		
4/10/65	77	13		11 The 4 Seasons Entertain You	$20	Philips 164
12/11/65+	10	88	●	**12 The 4 Seasons' Gold Vault of Hits** .... [G]	$20	Philips 196
12/18/65+	106	10		13 Big Hits by Burt Bacharach...Hal David...Bob Dylan	$50	Philips 193
1/29/66	50	15		14 Working My Way Back To You	$20	Philips 201
12/3/66+	22	53	●	15 2nd Vault Of Golden Hits .... [G]	$20	Philips 221
				9 of 12 cuts are Vee-Jay hits		
12/17/66+	107	9		16 Lookin' Back .... [K]	$20	Philips 222
				recordings from their first 3 Vee-Jay albums		
6/24/67	37	25		17 New Gold Hits	$20	Philips 243
12/28/68+	37	21	●	18 Edizione D'Oro (The 4 Seasons Gold Edition-29 Gold Hits) .... [G]	$25	Philips 6501 [2]
2/15/69	85	11		19 The Genuine Imitation Life Gazette	$35	Philips 290
6/13/70	190	2		20 Half & Half	$20	Philips 341
				5 songs by Frankie Valli, 5 songs by The 4 Seasons		
11/29/75+	38	31		21 Who Loves You	$10	Warner 2900
12/13/75+	51	17		22 The Four Seasons Story .... [G]	$12	Private St. 7000 [2]
				all their top hits 1962-68		
5/14/77	168	5		23 Helicon	$10	Warner 3016

Ain't That A Shame! (3,4,10,18,22) **22**
All I Really Want To Do (13)
Alone (2,9,15,18,22) **28**
Always Something There To Remind Me (13)
American Crucifixion Resurrection (19)
And That Reminds Me (My Heart Reminds Me) (20,22) **45**
Angel Cried (8)
Any Day Now (medley) (18)
Anyone Who Had A Heart (13)
Apple Of My Eye ..see: You're The Apple Of My Eye
Around And Around (Andaroundandaroundandaroundandaround) (17)
Ballad For Our Time (5)
Beggin' (17,18,22) **16**
Betrayed (11,12)
Big Girls Don't Cry (1,2,4,10,15,18,22) **1**
Big Man In Town (11,12,18,22) **20**
Big Man's World (6)
Blowin' In The Wind (13)
Born To Wander (6)
Breaking Up Is Hard To Do (6)
Bye, Bye, Baby (Baby Goodbye) (11,12,18,22) **12**
Can't Get Enough Of You Baby (14)

Candy Girl (3,4,10,15,18,22) **3**
Church Bells May Ring (6)
Circles In The Sand [solo: *Frankie*] (20)
C'mon Marianne (17,18,22) **9**
Comin' Up In The World (14)
Connie-O (4,7,10,15,18)
Cry Myself To Sleep (5,12)
Danger (8)
Dawn (Go Away) (6,12,18,22) **3**
December, 1963 (Oh, What A Night) (21) **1**
Do You Want To Dance (17)
Dody (13)
Don't Cry, Elena (5)
Don't Let Go (6)
Don't Think Twice (13,18,22) **12**
Down The Hall (23) **65**
Dumb Drum (3,9)
Earth Angel (6)
Electric Stories (22) **61**
Emily [solo: *Frankie*] (20)
Emily's (Salle De Danse) (21)
Everybody Knows My Name (14)
Funny Face (8)
Girl Come Running (12,18) **30**
Girl I'll Never Know (Angels Never Fly This Low) [solo: *Frankie*] (20) **52**
Girl In My Dreams (1)
Golden Ribbon (5)

Good-bye Girl (17)
Goodnight My Love (2,7,16)
Happy, Happy Birthday Baby (3,9,16)
Harmony, Perfect Harmony (21)
Helicon (23)
HI-Lili, HI-Lo (2,7,9)
Honey Love (3,9,16)
Huggin' My Pillow (8)
I Believe In You (23)
I Can't Give You Anything But Love (1)
I Woke Up (14)
I'm Gonna Change (17)
I've Cried Before (4,10)
I've Got You Under My Skin (15,18,22) **9**
Idaho (19) **95**
If We Should Lose Our Love (23)
La Dee Dah (1)
Let's Hang On! (12,18,22) **3**
Let's Get It Right (23)
Let's Ride Again (17)
Life Is But A Dream (6)
Like A Rolling Stone (13)
Little Angel (11)
Little Darlin' (1)
Little Pony (Get Along) (5)
Living Just For You (11,14)
Lonesome Road (17) **89**
Long Ago (23)
Long Lonely Nights (3,7,9,16)
Look Up Look Over (19)
Lost Lullabye (1,7)
Lucky Ladybug (2,16)

Make It Easy On Yourself (13)
Marcie (8)
Mariena (3,4,10,15,18,22) **36**
Melancholy (3,7)
Millie (5)
Morning After Loving You [solo: *Frankie*] (20)
Mountain High (6)
Mr. Tambourine Man (13)
Mrs. Stately's Garden (19)
My Prayer (11)
My Sugar (2)
Mystic Mr. Sam (21)
Never On Sunday (1)
New Mexican Rose (3,9) **36**
New Town (5)
New York Street Song (No Easy Way) (23)
No One Cares (8)
No Surfin' Today (5)
Oh, Carol (1,9)
Oh Happy Day (medley) (20)
On Broadway Tonight (8)
One Clown Cried (11,14)
One Song (2,7)
Only Yesterday (6)
Opus 17 (Don't You Worry 'Bout Me) (15,18,22) **13**
Patch Of Blue (20) **94**
Peanuts (1,4,10,15,18)
Pity (14)
Puppet Song (17)
Put A Little Away (23)
Queen Jane Approximately (13)
Rag Doll (8,12,18,22) **1**

Rhapsody (23)
Ronnie (8,12,18,22) **6**
Saturday's Father (19)
Save It For Me (8,12,18,22) **10**
Searching Wind (5)
Setting Sun (8)
She Gives Me Light (20)
Sherry (1,4,10,15,18,22) **1**
Show Girl (11,14)
Silence Is Golden (5,12,18,22)
Silhouettes (2,9,16)
Silver Star (21) **38**
Silver Wings (4,7,10)
Since I Don't Have You (2,16)
Sincerely (2,16) **75**
16 Candles (6)
Slip Away (21)
Something's On Her Mind (19) **98**
Somewhere (11)
Soon (I'll Be Home Again) (3,4,7,10) **77**
Sorry (20)
Soul Of A Woman (19)
Starmaker (4,7,10)
Stay (3,7,9,15,18,22) **16**
Storybook Lovers (21)
Sundown (21)
Teardrops (1,7,16)
Tell It To The Rain (17,18,22) **10**
That's The Only Way (3) **88**
To Make My Father Proud [solo: *Frankie*] (20)
Tonite, Tonite (1)
Too Many Memories (14)

Touch Of You (8)
Toy Soldier (11,12,18,22) **64**
Walk Like A Man (2,4,10,15,18,22) **1**
Walk On By (13)
Wall Street Village Day (19)
Watch The Flowers Grow (18,22) **30**
What The World Needs Now Is Love (13)
What's New Pussycat? (13)
Where Have All The Flowers Gone (5)
Where Is Love? (11)
Who Loves You (21) **3**
Why Do Fools Fall In Love (2,9,16)
Will You Love Me Tomorrow (18,22) **24**
Wonder What You'll Be (19)
Working My Way Back To You (14,15,18,22) **9**
Yes Sir, That's My Baby (1,9,16)
You Send Me (6)
You're The Apple Of My Eye (1) **62**

★★67★★ **FOUR TOPS**

Detroit R&B vocal group formed in 1953 as the Four Aims. Consisted of Levi Stubbs (lead singer), Renaldo "Obie" Benson, Lawrence Payton and Abdul "Duke" Fakir. First recorded for Chess in 1956, then Red Top and Columbia, before signing with Motown in 1963. Group has had no personnel changes since its formation. Stubbs is the voice of Audrey II (the voracious vegetation) in the 1986 film *Little Shop of Horrors*. Group inducted into the Rock and Roll Hall of Fame in 1990.

DEBUT DATE	PEAK POS	WKS CHR	GOLD	ARTIST — Album Title	$	Label & Number
2/27/65	63	27		1 Four Tops	$20	Motown 622
11/13/65+	20	35		2 Four Tops Second Album	$20	Motown 634
8/27/66	32	22		3 4 Tops On Top	$20	Motown 647
12/17/66+	17	43		4 Four Tops Live! .... [L]	$20	Motown 654
4/8/67	79	15		5 4 Tops On Broadway	$20	Motown 657
8/12/67	11	59		6 Four Tops Reach Out	$20	Motown 660
9/30/67	4	73		**7 The Four Tops Greatest Hits** .... [G]	$20	Motown 662
9/28/68	91	16		8 Yesterday's Dreams	$20	Motown 669
7/5/69	74	10		9 Four Tops Now!	$20	Motown 675
12/13/69+	163	6		10 Soul Spin	$10	Motown 695
4/11/70	21	42		11 Still Waters Run Deep	$15	Motown 704
10/17/70	109	12		12 Changing Times	$15	Motown 721
10/17/70	113	16		13 The Magnificent 7 *	$12	Motown 717
6/26/71	154	6		14 The Return Of The Magnificent Seven *	$12	Motown 736
9/25/71	106	10		15 Four Tops Greatest Hits, Vol. 2 .... [G]	$15	Motown 740

DEBUT DATE	PEAK POS	WKS CHR	GOLD	ARTIST — Album Title	$	Label & Number
				FOUR TOPS — Cont'd		
1/8/72	**160**	6		16 Dynamite *	**$12**	Motown 745
				***SUPREMES & FOUR TOPS**		
5/27/72	**50**	28		17 Nature Planned It	**$15**	Motown 748
11/11/72+	**33**	31		18 Keeper Of The Castle	**$10**	Dunhill 50129
5/12/73	**103**	9		19 The Best Of The 4 Tops ....[G]	**$12**	Motown 764 [2]
9/22/73	**66**	14		20 Main Street People	**$10**	Dunhill 50144
4/27/74	**118**	11		21 Meeting Of The Minds	**$10**	Dunhill 50166
10/26/74	**92**	9		22 Live & In Concert ....[L]	**$10**	Dunhill 50188
6/14/75	**148**	5		23 Night Lights Harmony	**$10**	ABC 862
11/13/76	**124**	8		24 Catfish	**$10**	ABC 968
9/12/81	**37**	21		25 Tonight!	**$8**	Casablanca 7258
6/29/85	**140**	9		26 Magic	**$8**	Motown 6130
9/24/88	**149**	7		27 Indestructible	**$8**	Arista 8492

Again (26)
Ain't No Woman (Like The One I've Got) (18,22) **4**
Ain't Nothing Like The Real Thing (13)
All I Do (25)
All My Love (21)
Am I My Brother's Keeper (20)
Are You Man Enough (20,22) **15**
Are You With Me (27)
Ask The Lonely (1,4,7,19) **24**
Baby I Need Your Loving (1,4,7,19,22) **11**
Baby, (You've Got What It Takes) (13)
Barbara's Boy (10)
Bernadette (6,7,19) **4**
Bigger You Love (The Harder You Fall) (16)
Bluesette (3)
Brenda (3)
Bring Me Together (11)
By The Time I Get To Phoenix (8)
California Dreamin' (10)
Call Me (14)
Call On Me (1)
Can't Seem To Get You Out Of My Mind (8)
Catfish (24) **71**
Change Of Heart (27)
Cherish (6)
Climb Ev'ry Mountain (4,5)
Darling, I Hum Our Song (2)
Daydream Believer (8)
Disco Daddy (4)
Do What You Gotta Do (9)
Do You Love Me Just A Little, Honey (16)
Don't Bring Back Memories (9)
Don't Let Him Take Your Love From Me (9,15) **45**
Don't Let Me Lose This Dream (14)
Don't Tell Me That It's Over (26)
Don't Turn Away (1,26)
Don't Walk Away (25)
Easier Said Than Done (26)
Eleanor Rigby (9)
Elusive Butterfly (11)
Everybody's Talking (11)
Everyday People (13)

Feel Free (24)
Fool On The Hill (9)
For Once In My Life (5)
For Your Love (13)
From A Distance (25)
Girl From Ipanema (4)
Good Lord Knows (18)
Good Lovin' Ain't Easy To Come By (16)
Got To Get You Into My Life (10)
Happy (Is A Bumpy Road) (17)
Hello Broadway (5)
Hello Stranger (16)
Helpless (2)
Hey Man (medley) (17)
Honey (10)
How Will I Forget You (17)
I Almost Had Her (But She Got Away) (12)
I Am Your Man (17,22)
I Can Feel The Magic (26)
I Can't Believe You Love Me (14)
I Can't Help Myself (2,4,7,19,22) **1**
I Can't Hold On Much Longer (23)
I Can't Quit Your Love (17)
I Found The Spirit (21)
I Got A Feeling (3)
I Just Can't Get You Out Of My Mind (20) **62**
I Know You Like It (24)
I Left My Heart In San Francisco (4)
I Like Everything About You (2,4)
(I Think I Must Be) Dreaming (18)
I Want To Be With You (5)
I Wish I Were Your Mirror (11)
I Wonder Where We're Going (14)
I'll Never Change (17)
I'll Never Ever Leave Again (25)
I'll Try Not To Cry (14)
I'll Turn To Stone (4,6,19) **76**
I'm A Believer (2)
I'm Glad About It (14)
I'm Glad You Walked Into My Life (23)
I'm Grateful (2)

I'm In A Different World (8,15,19) **51**
I'm Only Wounded (27)
I'm Ready For Love (26)
I've Got What You Need (23)
If (16)
If Ever A Love There Was (27)
If I Could Build The Whole World Around You (16)
If I Had A Hammer (4)
If I Were A Carpenter (6,15,19) **20**
If You Could See Me Now (14)
If You Let Me (17)
In The Still Of The Night (3)
In These Changing Times (12,15,19) **70**
Indestructible (27) **35**
Is There Anything That I Can Do (2)
Is This The Price? (23)
It Won't Be The First Time (10)
(It Would Almost) Drive Me Out Of My Mind (23)
It's All In The Game (11,15,19) **24**
It's Got To Be A Miracle (This Thing Called Love) (13)
It's Impossible (16)
It's Not Unusual (4)
It's The Same Old Song (2,4,7,19) **5**
(It's The Way) Nature Planned It (17,19) **53**
Jubilee With Soul (18)
Just As Long As You Need Me (2)
Just Seven Numbers (Can Straighten Out My Life) (12,15,19) **40**
Keeper Of The Castle (18,22) **10**
Key, The (2)
Knock On My Door (13)
L.A. (My Town) (11)
Last Train To Clarksville (6)
Left With A Broken Heart (1)
Let Me Know The Truth (23)
Let Me Set You Free (25)
Let's Jam (27)
Let's Make Love Now (14)
Light My Fire (10)
Little Green Apples (9)
Loco In Acapulco (27)

Long And Winding Road (medley) (12)
Look At My Baby (24)
Look Of Love (10)
Look Out Your Window (10)
Lost In A Pool Of Red (19)
Love Ain't Easy To Come By (21,22)
Love Don't Come Easy (24)
Love Feels Like Fire (2)
Love Has Gone (1)
Love Is The Answer (11)
Love Makes You Human (18)
Love Music (18,22)
Love The One You're With (2)
Loving You Is Sweeter Than Ever (3,7,19) **45**
MacArthur Park (Part II) (9,19) **38**
Main Street People (20)
Make Someone Happy (5)
Mama You're All Right With Me (23)
Mame (2)
Maria (5)
Matchmaker (3)
Maybe Tomorrow (26)
Meeting Of The Minds (21)
Melodie (16)
Michelle (3)
Midnight Flower (21,22) **55**
My Past Just Crossed My Future (9)
My Way (5)
Never My Love (8)
Next Time (27)
Nice 'N' Easy (5)
No Sad Songs (21)
Nothing (10)
On The Street Where You Live (5)
Once Upon A Time (8)
One Chain Don't Make No Prison (21,22) **41**
One More Bridge To Cross (14)
One Woman Man (20)
Opportunity Knock (For Me) (9)
Peace Of Mind (20)
Place In The Sun (8)
Put A Little Love Away (18)
Quiet Nights Of Quiet Stars (3)
Raindrops Keep Fallin' On My Head (12)

Reach Out And Touch (Somebody's Hand) (13)
Reach Out I'll Be There (4,6,7,19,22) **1**
Reflections (11)
Remember Me (26)
Remember What I Told You To Forget (18)
Remember When (8)
Right Before My Eyes (12)
Right On Brother (21)
River Deep - Mountain High (13) **14**
Sad Souvenirs (1)
Seven Lonely Nights (23) **71**
7 Rooms Of Gloom (6,7,19) **14**
Sexy Ways (26)
Shake Me, Wake Me (When It's Over) (3,7,19) **18**
She's An Understanding Woman (17)
Since You've Been Gone (2)
Sing A Song Of Yesterday (12)
Something About You (2,7,19) **19**
Something To Remember (25)
Something's Tearing At The Edges Of Time (12)
Sound Of Music (5)
Standing In The Shadows Of Love (6,7,19,22) **6**
Stay In My Lonely Arms (2)
Still Water (Love) (11,15,19) **11**
Still Water (Peace) (11,15)
Stoned Soul Picnic (13)
Stop The World (10)
Strung Out For Your Love (24)
Sun Ain't Gonna Shine (27)
Sunny (8)
Sweet Understanding Love (20) **33**
Sweetheart Tree (8)
Taste Of Honey (13)
Tea House In China Town (1)
Tell Me You Love Me (Love Sounds) (21)
Then (3)
There's No Love Left (3)
This Guy's In Love With You (10)

Together We Can Make Such Sweet Music (13)
Tonight I'm Gonna Love You All Over (25)
Too Little Too Late (20)
Try To Remember (12)
Turn On The Light Of Your Love (18)
Until You Love Someone (3)
Walk Away Renee (6,15,19) **14**
Walk With Me, Talk With Me, Darling (17)
We All Gotta Stick Together (17) **97**
We Got To Get You A Woman (medley) (17)
We've Got A Strong Love (On Our Side) (8)
Well Is Dry (24)
What Did I Have That I Don't Have (8)
What Do You Have To Do (To Stay On The Right Side Of Love) (14)
What Else Is There To Do (But Think About You) (6)
What Is A Man (9,15) **53**
When She Was My Girl (25) **11**
When Tonight Meets Tomorrow (18)
When You Dance (27)
Whenever There's Blue (20)
Where Did You Go (1)
Where Would I Be Without You, Baby (14)
Who's Right, Who's Wrong (25)
Wish I Didn't Love You So (9)
Without The One You Love (Life's Not Worth While) (1,7,13,19) **43**
Wonderful Baby (6)
Yesterday's Dreams (8,15,19) **49**
You Can't Hold Back On Love (24)
You Can't Hurry Love (4)
You Gonna Forget Him Darling (17)
You Gotta Have Love In Your Heart (14) **55**
You Keep Running Away (15,19) **19**
Your Love Is Amazing (1)

FOWLEY, Kim
Los Angeles-based producer/songwriter. Born on 7/21/42 in Manila. Son of actor Douglas Fowley and grandson of composer Rudolf Friml. Produced Paul Revere & The Raiders, The Rivingtons, Slade, Johnny Winter, Gene Vincent and others. Assembled girl groups The Murmaids and The Runaways.

4/19/69	**198**	3		Outrageous	**$30**	Imperial 12423

Animal Man
Barefoot Country Boy
Bubble Gum
California Hayride
Caught In The Middle
Chinese Water Torture
Down
Hide And Seek
Inner Space Discovery
Nightrider
Up
Wildfire

FOX, Samantha
British singer born on 4/15/66. Rose to stardom as a topless model for the U.K. *Daily Sun* newspaper.

11/29/86+	**24**	28	●	1 Touch Me	**$8**	Jive 1012
10/24/87+	**51**	25	●	2 Samantha Fox	**$8**	Jive 1061
11/26/88+	**37**	34	●	3 I Wanna Have Some Fun	**$8**	Jive 1150

Baby I'm Lost For Words (1)
Best Is Yet To Come (2)
Confession (3)
Do Ya Do Ya (Wanna Please Me) (1) **87**
Dream City (2)
He's Got Sex (1)
Hold On Tight (3)
Hot For You (3)
(I Can't Get No) Satisfaction (2)
I Only Wanna Be With You (3) **31**
I Promise You (2)
I Surrender (To The Spirit Of The Night) (2)
I Wanna Have Some Fun (3) **8**
I'm All You Need (1)
If Music Be The Food Of Love (2)
Love House (3)

DEBUT DATE	PEAK POS	WKS CHR	GOLD	ARTIST — Album Title	$	Label & Number

FOX, Samantha — Cont'd

Naughty Girls (Need Love Too) (2) 3	Nothing's Gonna Stop Me Now (2) 80	Ready For This Love (3)	That Sensation (2)	Walking On Air (3)	Your House Or My House (3)
Next To Me (3)	One In A Million (3)	Rockin' In The City (1)	**Touch Me (I Want Your**	Want You To Want Me (1)	
	Out Of Our Hands (3)	Suzie, Don't Leave Me With	**Body) (1) 4**	Wild Kinda Love (1)	
		Your Boyfriend (1)	True Devotion (2)	You Started Something (3)	

FOX, Virgil
Organ virtuoso; died on 10/25/80 (age 68).

5/29/71	183	2		Bach Live At Fillmore East.. [I-L]	$10	Decca 75263

Johann Sebastian Bach compositions

Bach: Air For The G String	Bach: Fugue In A Minor	Bach: Passacaglia And	Bach: Prelude And Fugue In	Bach: Vivace: Trio Sonata	Middelschulte: Perpetuum
Bach: Fanfare: Toccata In D Minor	Bach: Now Thank We All Our God	Fugue In C Minor	D Major	No. 6 In G Major	Mobile

FOXX, Redd
Real name: John Elroy Sanford. Born on 12/9/22 in St. Louis. Died on 10/11/91 from a heart attack. Star of TV sitcom *Sanford & Son*, 1972-79; *The Redd Foxx Show*, 1987; and *The Royal Family*, 1991. Dubbed "King of the Party Records."

6/3/72	198	3	1	Sanford & Foxx... [C-E]	$12	Dooto 853

most of these comedy bits were recorded in the '50s

7/29/72	155	8	2	Sanford and Son.. [C-TV]	$10	RCA 4739

actual comedy excerpts from the TV series includes 1 instrumental by Quincy Jones: "Sanford And Son Theme"

1/3/76	87	13	3	You Gotta Wash Your Ass .... [C]	$8	Atlantic 18157

recorded live at the Apollo Theater in Harlem, 1975; no track titles listed on this album

Alligator Dog (1)	Dental Care (1)	Lamont's Wedding (2)	Sales Manners (1)	Ugly Women (1)
Beret, The (2)	Festive Dinner With Donna	Lost Wallet (1)	Scarce Dogmeat (1)	Union Man (1)
Bravery (1)	(2)	Luau Layaway Furniture	Shower Stall (1)	Voting (1)
Cheap Accident (1)	Fiddler On The Roof (2)	Company (2)	Sleepy Deacon (1)	We Were Robbed (2)
Childless Couple (1)	Fred's Birthday (2)	Missionary On The Menu (1)	Social Security (2)	Whiskey Sales (1)
Chinese Restaurant (2)	Funerals (1)	My Son (1)	Television (1)	Wino DTs (1)
Christmas Hardtimes (1)	Gift Pajamas (1)	Parlay, The (1)	That's Poor (2)	
Cigarettes (2)	Happy Couple (1)	Private Eye (1)	Ugly White Woman (2)	

FOXY
Miami-based Latino dance band. Four of five members came to Florida with the Cuban emigres of 1959. Lead vocalist/guitarist Ish Ledesma founded and produced Oxo and Company B. Percussionist Richie Puente is the son of luminary Latin bandleader Tito Puente.

7/22/78	12	27	1	Get Off..	$10	Dash 30005
4/14/79	29	16	2	Hot Numbers...	$10	Dash 30010

Chicapon-Chicapon (2)	Give Me A Break (2)	Head Hunter (2)	Lady (2)	Madamoiselle (1)	Ready For Love (1)
Devil Boogie (2)	Give Me That Groove (2)	**Hot Number (2) 21**	Lady Of The Streets (2)	Nobody Will Ever Take Me	Tena's Song (1)
Get Off (1) 9	Goin' Back To You (1)	It's Happening (1)	Lucky Me (1)	Away From You (2)	You (1)

★★260★★ FRAMPTON, Peter
Born on 4/22/50 in Beckenham, England. Vocalist/guitarist/composer. Joined British band The Herd at age 16, before forming Humble Pie in 1969, which he left in 1971 to form Frampton's Camel. Went solo in 1974. Played Billy Shears in the 1978 film *Sgt. Pepper's Lonely Hearts Club Band*. Near-fatal car crash on 6/29/78 temporarily sidelined his career.

10/7/72	177	6		1	Wind Of Change	$12	A&M 4348
6/9/73	110	22		2	Frampton's Camel	$12	A&M 4389

title refers to Frampton's 4-member band

3/30/74	125	9		3	Somethin's Happening	$10	A&M 3619
3/29/75	32	64	●	4	Frampton	$10	A&M 4512
1/31/76	1¹⁰	97	▲⁶	5	Frampton Comes Alive! .... [L]	$12	A&M 3703 [2]
6/25/77	2⁴	32	▲	6	I'm In You	$10	A&M 4704
6/23/79	19	16	●	7	Where I Should Be	$10	A&M 3710
6/13/81	43	13		8	Breaking All The Rules..	$8	A&M 3722
8/28/82	174	8		9	The Art Of Control	$8	A&M 4905
2/8/86	80	14		10	Premonition	$8	Atlantic 81290
10/14/89	152	6		11	When All The Pieces Fit	$8	Atlantic 82030

All Eyes On You (10)	Doobie Wah (3,5)	**I Can't Stand It No More**	May I Baby (7)	Sail Away (3)	Which Way The Wind Blows
All I Want To Be (Is By Your	Everything I Need (7)	**(7) 14**	Mind Over Matter (11)	Save Me (9)	(2)
Side) (1,5)	Eye For An Eye (9)	I Don't Wanna Let You Go (8)	More Ways Than One (11)	She Don't Reply (7)	White Sugar (2)
All Night Long (2)	Fanfare (4)	I Got My Eyes On You (2)	Moving A Mountain (10)	Shine On (5)	Wind Of Change (1,5)
Alright (1)	Fig Tree Bay (1)	I Read The News (9)	My Heart Goes Out To You	**Show Me The Way (4,5) 6**	Won't You Be My Friend (6)
Apple Of Your Eye (4)	Friday On My Mind (8)	I Wanna Go To The Sun (3,5)	(11)	**Signed, Sealed, Delivered**	You Don't Have To Worry (6)
Baby, I Love Your Way (4,5)	Going To L.A. (8)	(I'll Give You) Money (4,5)	Nassau (medley) (4)	**(I'm Yours) (6) 18**	You Don't Know Like I Know
Baby (Somethin's	Golden Goose (3)	(I'm A) Road Runner (6)	Now And Again (11)	Sleepwalk (9)	(7)
Happening) (3)	Got My Feet Back On The	**I'm In You (6) 2**	Nowhere's Too Far (For My	Something's Happening (5)	You Kill Me (8)
Back To Eden (9)	Ground (7)	Into View (10)	Baby) (4)	St. Thomas (Don't You Know	You Know So Well (10)
Back To The Start (11)	Hard (1)	It's A Plain Shame (1,5)	Oh For Another Day (1)	How I Feel) (6)	
Barbara's Vacation (9)	Hard Earned Love (11)	It's A Sad Affair (7)	One More Time (4)	Stop (10)	
Breaking All The Rules (8)	Heart In The Fire (9)	Jumping Jack Flash (1,5)	Penny For Your Thoughts	Take Me By The Hand (7)	
Call Of The Wild (10)	Here Comes Caroline (9)	Just The Time Of Year (2)	(4,5)	This Time Around (11)	
Crying Clown (4)	Hiding From A Heartache	Lady Lieright (1)	People All Over The World	**Tried To Love (6) 41**	
Day's Dawning (4)	(10)	Lines On My Face (2,5)	(11)	Underhand (3)	
Dig What I Say (8)	Hold Tight (11)	Lodger, The (1)	Premonition (10)	Wasting The Night Away (8)	
Do You Feel Like We Do	Holding On To You (11)	Lost A Part Of You (8)	(Putting My) Heart On The	Waterfall (3)	
(2,5) 10	I Believe (When I Fall In	**Lying (10) 74**	Line (6)	We've Just Begun (7)	
Don't Fade Away (2)	Love With You It Will Be	Magic Moon (Da Da Da Da	Rise Up (8)	Where I Should Be	
Don't Think About Me (9)	Forever) (2)	Da!) (3)	Rocky's Hot Club (6)	(Monkey's Song) (7)	

FRANCHI, Sergio
Italian tenor. Starred in Broadway's *Do I Hear A Waltz?* (1965) and *Nine* (1982). Died of cancer on 5/1/90 (age 57) in Stonington, Connecticut.

11/24/62	17	18		1	Sergio Franchi..	$12	RCA 2640
2/9/63	66	21		2	Our Man From Italy...	$12	RCA 2657

DEBUT DATE	PEAK POS	WKS CHR	GOLD	ARTIST — Album Title	$	Label & Number
7/6/63	103	5	3	Broadway...I Love You...	$12	RCA 2674
1/25/64	97	7	4	The Dream Duet	$12	RCA 2675
				ANNA MOFFO/SERGIO FRANCHI		
3/27/65	114	4	5	Live At The Cocoanut Grove .... [L]	$10	RCA 3310
				with the Freddy Martin Orchestra		

'A Vucchella (1)
Ah! Sweet Mystery Of Life (4)
And This Is My Beloved (medley) (5)
Anema E Core (How Wonderful To Know) (5)
Arrivederci, Roma (Goodbye To Rome) (2)
As Long As She Needs Me (3)
Autumn In Rome (2)
Chicago (5)
Clair De Lune (medley) (5)
Come Facette Mammeta (1)
Core'ngrato (1,5)

Dicitencello Vuie (You Should Tell Her) (2)
E Lucevan Le Stelle (5)
Fenesta Che Lucive (1)
Funiculi-Funicula (1)
Gypsies (Les Gitans) (5)
Hootenanny Medley (5)
I Left My Heart In San Francisco (5)
I Wish You Love (Que Reste-t-il De Nos Amours?) (5)
I'Te Vurria Vasa! (I Want To Kiss You!) (2)
I'll See You Again (5)

I've Grown Accustomed To Her Face (3)
If Ever I Would Leave You (3)
In The Still Of The Night (medley) (5)
Indian Love Call (4)
Just Say I Love Her (Dicitencello Vuie) (5)
Kiss In The Dark (4)
La Strada (Traveling Down A Lonely Road), Love Theme From (2)
La Vilanella (1)
Lover, Come Back To Me! (4)

Luna Rossa (Blushing Moon) (2)
Make Someone Happy (3)
Mamma (2)
Mamma Mia Che Vo'Sape (1)
Marechiare (1)
Mattinata (1)
My Hero (4)
O Sole Mio (1)
O Surdato 'Namorato (1)
One Alone (4)
Quando-Quando-Quando (5)
Santa Lucia (2)
Shalom (3)
She's My Love (3)

Some Day (4)
Somebody, Somewhere (3)
Sound Of Music (3,5)
Souvenir D'Italie (Souvenir Of Italy) (2)
Stella By Starlight (5)
Summertime In Venice (2,5)
Sweetest Sounds (3)
Sweethearts (4)
This Is All I Ask (medley) (3)
Till There Was You (3)
Tonight (3)
Torna A Surriento (1)
Torna, Piccina! (Come Back, My Little Girl) (2)

What Kind Of Fool Am I? (3)
Will You Remember (4)
Woman In Love (5)
You Are Love (4)
Yours Is My Heart Alone (4)

★★91★★ **FRANCIS, Connie**
Born Concetta Rosa Maria Franconero on 12/12/38 in Newark, New Jersey. First recorded for MGM in 1955. From 1961-65, appeared in films *Where The Boys Are, Follow Love* and *When The Boys Meet The Girls.* Connie stopped performing after she was raped on 11/8/74. Began comeback with a performance on *Dick Clark's Live Wednesday* TV show in 1978. Pop music's #1 female vocalist from the late 1950s to the mid-1960s.

DEBUT DATE	PEAK POS	WKS CHR	GOLD	ARTIST — Album Title	$	Label & Number
2/8/60	4	81	1	**Italian Favorites** .... [F]	$25	MGM 3791
2/22/60	17	100	2	Connie's Greatest Hits .... [G]	$25	MGM 3793
12/12/60+	9	20	3	**More Italian Favorites** .... [F]	$25	MGM 3871
5/8/61	65	19	4	Connie Francis At The Copa .... [L]	$25	MGM 3913
5/29/61	69	10	5	Jewish Favorites .... [F]	$25	MGM 3869
7/3/61	39	17	6	More Greatest Hits .... [G]	$25	MGM 3942
10/30/61	11	34	7	Never On Sunday and other title songs from motion pictures	$25	MGM 3965
4/14/62	47	17	8	Do The Twist	$25	MGM 4022
8/25/62	111	9	9	Connie Francis sings .... [G]	$25	MGM 4049
10/13/62	22	14	10	Country Music Connie Style.............................	$25	MGM 4079
2/16/63	103	5	11	Modern Italian Hits .... [F]	$20	MGM 4102
3/30/63	66	11	12	Follow The Boys .... [S]	$20	MGM 4123
				only side 1 features songs from the soundtrack		
6/15/63	108	5	13	Award Winning Motion Picture Hits..................	$20	MGM 4048
10/5/63	94	17	14	Greatest American Waltzes	$20	MGM 4145
10/19/63	70	13	15	Mala Femmena & Connie's Big Hits From Italy .... [K-F]	$20	MGM 4161
11/2/63+	68	23	● 16	The Very Best Of Connie Francis .... [G]	$20	MGM 4167
2/1/64	126	2	17	In The Summer Of His Years	$20	MGM 4210
				a tribute to President John F. Kennedy		
8/1/64	122	9	18	Looking For Love .... [S]	$20	MGM 4229
				includes instrumental by Claus Ogerman: "Whoever You Are I Love You"		
12/5/64	149	2	19	A New Kind Of Connie...	$20	MGM 4253
5/1/65	78	15	20	Connie Francis sings For Mama.......................	$20	MGM 4294
1/29/66	61	9	21	When The Boys Meet The Girls .... [S]	$20	MGM 4334
				includes "Aruba Liberace" by Liberace; "Bidin' My Time" & "Listen People" by Herman's Hermits; "Embraceable You" by Harve Presnell; "I Got Rhythm" & "Throw It Out Your Mind" by Louis Armstrong and "Monkey See, Monkey Do" by Sam The Sham & The Pharoahs		

Addio Addio (11)
Ain't That Better Baby (8)
Al Di La (11) 90
Al Jolson Medley (4)
All The Way (13)
Always (14)
Among My Souvenirs (6,16) 7
Anema E Core (1)
Anna (7)
Anniversary Song (5)
Anniversary Waltz (14)
April Love (7)
Around The World (7)
Arrivederci Roma (1,11)
Aura Lee (17)
Ave Maria (17)
Baby's First Christmas (9) 26
Be My Love (18)
Beautiful Ohio (14)
Bells Of Saint Mary's (17)
Bill Baily, Won't You Please Come Home (medley) (4)
Breakin' In A Brand New Broken Heart (9,16) 7
But Not For Me (21)
C'e Qualcuno ..see: Where The Boys Are
Carolina Moon (2)

Che Bella Notte! ..see: Tonight's My Night
Ciao, Ciao, Bambina (1)
Come Back To Sorrento (1)
Come Prima (For The First Time) (1)
Come Sinfonia (11)
Comm'e Bella A Stagione (1)
Connie Francis-Lady Valet Theme (18)
Danny Boy (17)
Days Of Wine And Roses (13)
Do You Love Me Like You Kiss Me? (Scapricciatiello) (1)
Does Ol' Broadway Ever Sleep (8)
Don't Break The Heart That Loves You [includes English & foreign versions] (9,15,16) 1
Drop It Joe (8)
Embraceable You (21)
Every Night (17)
Everybody's Somebody's Fool (6,16) 1
Fallin' (2) 30
Fascination (14)
Follow The Boys (12,16) 17
For Every Young Heart (12)

For Mama (La Mamma) (20) 48
Frankie (2,16) 9
Funiculi, Funicula (3)
God Bless America (6,17) 36
Gonna Git That Man (9)
Guaglione (3)
Happy Days And Lonely Nights (2)
Hava Nagila (Dance Everyone Dance) (4,5)
He Thinks I Still Care (10) 57
(He's My) Dreamboat (16) 14
Heartaches By The Number (10)
Hey Ring-A-Ding (8)
High Hopes (13)
High Noon (7)
I Can't Believe That You're In Love With Me (18)
I Can't Reach Your Heart (12)
I Can't Stop Loving You (10)
I Don't Hurt Anymore (10)
I Fall To Pieces (10)
I Found Myself A Guy (19)
I Got Rhythm (21)
I Have But One Heart (1)
I Love You Much Too Much (5)

I Really Don't Want To Know (10)
I Walk The Line (10)
I Was Such A Fool [To Fall In Love With You] (20) 24
I Won't Be Home To You (8)
(I'll Be With You) In Apple Blossom Time (14)
I'm A Fool To Care (10)
I'm Glad There Is You (19)
I'm Gonna Be Warm This Winter (16) 18
I'm Movin' On (10)
I'm Sorry I Made You Cry (2) 36
I've Got A Crush On New York Town (19)
If I Didn't Care (2) 22
Il Cielo In Una Stanza (This World We Love In) (1)
In The Summer Of His Years (17) 46
In Your Arms (12)
Intrigue (12)
It All Depends On You (4)
It Happened Last Night (9)
It Takes More (20)
It's Gonna Take Me Some Time (20)
Italian Lullaby (12,15)

Jealous Of You (Tango Della Gelosia) [includes English & foreign versions] (4,6,15) 19
Johnny Darlin' (8)
Just Say I Love Him (3)
Kiss 'N' Twist (Tarantella) (4)
La Paloma (Your Love) (15)
Last Time I Saw Paris (13)
Let's Have A Party (18)
Like Someone In Love (19)
Lipstick On Your Collar (2,16) 5
Looking For Love [includes 2 versions] (18) 45
Lord's Prayer (17)
Love Is A Many Splendored Thing (7)
Love Me Tender (7)
Loveliest Night Of The Year (3)
Lullaby Of Broadway (13)
Luna Caprese (15)
Ma (He's Making Eyes At Me) (19)
Mail Call (21)
Mala Femmena (15)
Malaguena (6) 42
Mama (1,4,6) 8
Many Tears Ago (4,6) 3
Mein Shtetele Belz (5)

Melody Of Love (14)
Mom-E-Le (Mother Dear) (5)
Mommy Your Daughter's Fallin' In Love (8)
Moon River (13)
Moonglow And Picnic (7)
More (19)
Moulin Rouge (Where Is Your Heart), Song From (7)
Mr. Twister (8)
My Buddy (14,17)
My Dearest Possession (12)
My Happiness (2,16) 2
My Heart Has A Mind Of Its Own (6,16) 1
My Kind Of Guy (19)
My Man (19)
My Real Happiness (8)
My Yiddishe Momme (5)
Nessuno Al Mondo (No Arms Can Ever Hold You) (11)
Nessuno E' Solo (No One Is Alone) (15)
Never On Sunday (7)
Nights Of Splendor (3)
No Better Off (20)
No One (6,20) 34
No One Ever Sends Me Roses (20)

263

FRANCIS, Connie — Cont'd

Non Dimenticar (Don't Forget) (T'Ho Voluto Bene) (1)
Nun E Peccato (11)
O Mein Papa (Oh! My Pa-Pa) (5)
Oh, Lonesome Me (10)
Olfen Pripetchik (5)
Ol' Man Mose (4)
On A Little Street In Venice (12)
Over The Rainbow (13)
Picnic ..see: Moonglow
Playin' Games (20)
Plenty Good Lovin' (2) 69
Portami Con Te (Fly Me To The Moon) (In Other Words) (15)
Pretty Little Baby (9)
Quando Quando Quando (Tell Me When) (11)
Red River Valley (17)

Remember (14)
Return To Me (3)
Rock Dem Bells (18)
Roman Guitar (3)
Romantica (11)
Santa Lucia (1)
Second Hand Love (9,16) 7
Secret Love (13)
Senza Mamma (With No One) (3,6) 87
She'll Have To Go (10)
Shein VI De Levone (4,5)
Smack Dab In The Middle (4)
Someday (You'll Want Me To Want You) (10)
Someone Else's Boy (9)
Somewhere Near Someplace (12)
Souvenirs (20)
Stupid Cupid (2,16) 14
Summertime In Venice (3)
Sweetest Sounds (19)

Tammy (14)
Tango Della Gelosia ..see: Jealous Of You
Tango Italiano (11)
Teach Me How To Twist (8)
Telephone Lover (8)
Tell Me You're Mine (3)
That's Amore (That's Love) (3)
There's No Tomorrow (1)
This Is My Happiest Moment (18)
Three Coins In The Fountain (7)
Three O'Clock In The Morning (14)
Till We Meet Again (14)
Together (9) 6
Tonight's My Night [includes English & foreign versions] (12,15)
Too Many Rules (9) 72

Too-Ra-Loo-Ra-Loo-Ral (That's An Irish Lullaby) (17)
Torero (3)
Toward The End Of The Day (1)
True Love (14)
True Love, True Love (17)
24 Mila Baci (11)
Tzena Tzena (5)
Un Desiderio Folle ..see: Don't Break The Heart That Loves You
Un Violina Nel Mio Cuor (A Violin In My Heart) (15)
Vacation (16) 9
Valentino (6)
Violina Tsigano (Gypsy Violin) (15)
Volare (Nel Blu, Dipinto Di Blu) (1)
Vus Geven Is Geven (5)

Waiting For Billy (12)
Way You Look Tonight (13)
What Kind Of Fool Am I? (20)
Whatever Will Be Will Be (Que Sera Sera) (13)
When The Boy In Your Arms (Is The Boy In Your Heart) (9) 10
When The Boys Meet The Girls (21)
When The Clock Strikes Midnight (18)
When The Saints Go Marching In (medley) (4)
When You Wish Upon A Star (13)
Where Can I Go Without You (19)
Where Did Ev'ryone Go? (19)
Where The Boys Are [includes English & foreign versions] (6,15,16) 4

Who's Sorry Now (2,16) 4
Whoever You Are I Love You (18)
Whose Heart Are You Breaking Tonight (20) 43
Will You Still Be Mine? (19)
Won't You Come Home Bill Bailey ..see: Bill Bailey
Yossel, Yossel (5)
You Alone (Solo Tu) (1)
You Always Hurt The One You Love (19)
You Can Take It From Me (19)
You Can't Be True, Dear (14)
You'll Never Know (13)
You're Gonna Miss Me (2) 34
You're The Only One Can Hurt Me (20)
Young At Heart (7)
Zip-A-Dee-Doo-Dah (13)

FRANKE & THE KNOCKOUTS
Soft-rock quintet led by vocalist Franke Previte of New Brunswick, New Jersey.

3/28/81	**31**	27		1 Franke & The Knockouts	$8	Millennium 7755
4/10/82	**48**	18		2 Below The Belt	$8	Millennium 7763

Annie Goes Hollywood (1)
Any Way That You Want Me (2)
Come Back (1)

Don't Stop (1)
Gina (2)
Have No Fear (2)
Just What I Want (2)

Keep On Fighting (1)
Morning Sun (Dream On) (2)
Never Had It Better (2)
One For All (1)

Running Into The Night (1)
Shakedown (2)
She's A Runner (1)
Sweetheart (1) 10

Tell Me Why (1)
Tonight (1)
Without You (Not Another Lonely Night) (2) 24

You're My Girl (1) 27

FRANKIE GOES TO HOLLYWOOD
Dance-rock quintet from Liverpool, England — vocals by William "Holly" Johnson and Paul Rutherford. Group's name inspired by publicity recounting Frank Sinatra's move into the film industry.

11/24/84	**33**	41		1 Welcome To The Pleasuredome	$10	Island 90232 [2]
11/15/86	**88**	13		2 Liverpool	$8	Island 90546

Bang... (1)
Black Night White Light (1)
Born To Run (1)
Ferry (1)
For Heaven's Sake (2)

Is Anybody Out There? (2)
Kill The Pain (1)
Krisco Kisses (1)
Lunar Bay (2)
Maximum Joy (2)

Only Star In Heaven (1)
Power Of Love (1)
Rage Hard (2)
Relax (1) 67
San Jose (1)

Snatch Of Fury (1)
Two Tribes (1) 43
War (1)
Warriors Of The Wasteland (2)

Watching The Wildlife (2)
Welcome To The Pleasure Dome (1)
Well... (1)
Wish The Lads Were Here (1)

World Is My Oyster (1)

★★17★★ FRANKLIN, Aretha
Born on 3/25/42 in Memphis and raised in Buffalo and Detroit. Daughter of Rev. Cecil L. Franklin, pastor of New Bethel Church in Detroit. Taught to sing gospel at age 9 by Rev. James Cleveland (d: 2/9/91, age 59). First recorded for JVB/Battle in 1956. Signed to Columbia Records in 1960 by John Hammond, then dramatic turn in style and success after signing with Atlantic and working with producer Jerry Wexler. Appeared in the 1980 film *The Blues Brothers*. Winner of 15 Grammy Awards. In 1987, became the first woman to be inducted into the Rock and Roll Hall of Fame. Won Grammy's Legends Award in 1990. The all-time Queen of Soul Music.

11/17/62	**69**	12		1 The Tender, The Moving, The Swinging Aretha Franklin	$30	Columbia 8676
12/19/64+	**84**	13		2 Runnin' Out Of Fools	$30	Columbia 9081
7/10/65	**101**	8		3 Yeah!!! ....[L]	$15	Columbia 9151
8/6/66	**132**	4		4 Soul Sister	$15	Columbia 9321
4/8/67	**2**[3]	79	●	5 I Never Loved A Man The Way I Love You	$15	Atlantic 8139
6/10/67	**94**	14		6 Aretha Franklin's Greatest Hits ....[K] featuring her Columbia recordings from 1961-66	$15	Columbia 9473
8/26/67	**5**	41		7 Aretha Arrives	$15	Atlantic 8150
10/21/67	**173**	8		8 Take A Look ....[K] more early Columbia recordings	$15	Columbia 9554
2/24/68	**2**[2]	52	●	9 Aretha: Lady Soul	$15	Atlantic 8176
7/13/68	**3**	35	●	10 Aretha Now	$15	Atlantic 8186
11/23/68+	**13**	20		11 Aretha In Paris ....[L] recorded at the Olympia Theatre in Paris on 5/7/68	$15	Atlantic 8207
2/15/69	**15**	32		12 Aretha Franklin: Soul '69	$15	Atlantic 8212
7/19/69	**18**	33		13 Aretha's Gold ....[G]	$15	Atlantic 8227
2/14/70	**17**	30		14 This Girl's In Love With You	$12	Atlantic 8248
9/12/70	**25**	22		15 Spirit In The Dark	$12	Atlantic 8265
6/5/71	**7**	34	●	16 Aretha Live At Fillmore West ....[L]	$12	Atlantic 7205
9/25/71	**19**	34		17 Aretha's Greatest Hits ....[G]	$12	Atlantic 8295
2/19/72	**11**	31	●	18 Young, Gifted & Black	$12	Atlantic 7213
6/17/72	**7**	23	▲[2]	19 Amazing Grace ....[L] with James Cleveland & The Southern California Comm. Choir	$12	Atlantic 906 [2]
6/24/72	**160**	9		20 In The Beginning/The World Of Aretha Franklin 1960-1967 ....[K]	$10	Columbia 31355 [2]
7/14/73	**30**	20		21 Hey Now Hey (The Other Side Of The Sky)	$10	Atlantic 7265
3/16/74	**14**	25		22 Let Me In Your Life	$10	Atlantic 7292
12/21/74+	**57**	13		23 With Everything I Feel In Me	$10	Atlantic 18116
11/15/75	**83**	11		24 You	$10	Atlantic 18151
6/19/76	**18**	24	●	25 Sparkle ....[S]	$10	Atlantic 18176
12/25/76+	**135**	8		26 Ten Years Of Gold ....[G]	$10	Atlantic 18204

DEBUT DATE	PEAK POS	WKS CHR	GOLD	ARTIST — Album Title	$	Label & Number
				FRANKLIN, Aretha — Cont'd		
6/18/77	**49**	19	27	Sweet Passion	$10	Atlantic 19102
5/13/78	**63**	11	28	Almighty Fire	$10	Atlantic 19161
10/13/79	**146**	6	29	La Diva	$10	Atlantic 19248
10/25/80	**47**	30	30	Aretha	$8	Arista 9538
8/29/81	**36**	17	31	Love All The Hurt Away	$8	Arista 9552
8/14/82	**23**	30	● 32	Jump To It	$8	Arista 9602
7/30/83	**36**	18	33	Get It Right	$8	Arista 8019
				above 2 produced by Luther Vandross		
7/27/85	**13**	51	● 34	Who's Zoomin' Who?	$8	Arista 8286
11/15/86+	**32**	39	● 35	Aretha	$8	Arista 8442
12/26/87+	**106**	16	36	One Lord, One Faith, One Baptism ......[L]	$10	Arista 8497 [2]
				recorded at the New Bethel Baptist Church, Detroit (July 1987); features Rev. Jesse Jackson and Mavis Staples		
5/20/89	**55**	18	37	Through The Storm	$8	Arista 8572
8/10/91	**153**	7	38	What You See Is What You Sweat	$12	Arista 8628

Ain't No Way (9,13) *16*
Ain't Nobody Ever Loved You (34)
Ain't Nobody (Gonna Turn Me Around) (7)
Ain't Nothing Like The Real Thing (22) *47*
All Of These Things (23)
All The King's Horses (18) *26*
Almighty Fire (Woman Of The Future) (28)
Amazing Grace (19)
Angel (21,26) *20*
Angel Cries (35)
Another Night (34) *22*
April Fools (18)
As Long As You Are There (24)
Ave Maria (36)
Baby, Baby, Baby (5)
Baby I Love You (7,11,13,17,26) *4*
Better Friends Than Lovers (33)
Bill Bailey, Won't You Please Come Home? (8)
Blue Holiday (8)
Border Song (Holy Moses) (18) *37*
Brand New Me (18) *flip*
Break It To Me Gently (27) *85*
Bridge Over Troubled Water (16,17) *6*
Bring It On Home To Me (12)
Call Me (14,17) *13*
Can't Turn You Loose (30)
Can't You Just See Me (4) *96*
Chain Of Fools (9,11,13,17) *2*
Change, A (10)
Change Is Gonna Come (5)
Climbing Higher Mountains (19)
Close To You (28)
Come Back Baby (9,11)
Come To Me (30,37) *84*
Crazy He Calls Me (12)
Cry Like A Child (9)
Dark End Of The Street (14)
Day Dreaming (4,6,26) *5*
Didn't I (Blow Your Mind This Time) (11)
Do Right Woman - Do Right Man (5,13,17)
Do You Still Remember (35)
Dr. Feelgood (5,11,13,16,17)
Doctor's Orders (39)
Don't Cry, Baby (1,20) *92*
Don't Go Breaking My Heart (23)
Don't Let Me Lose This Dream (5,11)
Don't Play That Song (15,16,17) *11*
Drown In My Own Tears (5)
Eight Days On The Road (22)
Eleanor Rigby (14,16) *17*
Elusive Butterfly (12)
Ever Changing Times (38)
Every Girl (Wants My Guy) (33)
Every Little Bit Hurts (2,20)

Every Natural Thing (22)
Everyday People (includes 2 versions) (38)
Evil Gal Blues (6,20)
Feeling, The (29)
First Snow In Kokomo (18)
Follow Your Heart (4,8)
Freeway Of Love (34) *3*
Gentle On My Mind (12) *76*
Get It Right (33) *61*
Gimme Your Love (37)
Give Yourself To Jesus (19)
Giving In (33)
God Bless The Child (1,6,20)
God Will Take Care Of You (19)
Going Down Slow (7)
Good Times (5)
Good To Me As I Am To You (9)
Groovin' (9,11)
Half A Love (29)
He'll Come Along (35)
He's The Boy (37)
Hello Sunshine (10)
Hey Now Hey (The Other Side Of The Sky) (21)
Higher Ground (36)
Hold On I'm Comin' (31)
Honest I Do (35)
Honey I Need Your Love (29)
Hooked On Your Love (25)
House That Jack Built (13) *6*
How Deep Is The Ocean (8)
How Glad I Am (2)
How I Got Over (19)
I Apologize (1)
(I Can't Get No) Satisfaction (7,11)
I Can't See Myself Leaving You (10) *28*
I Can't Wait Until I See My Baby's Face (2)
I Don't Know You Anymore (1)
I Dreamed A Dream (38)
I Get High (25)
I Got Your Love (33)
I Knew You Were Waiting (For Me) (35) *1*
I Love Every Little Thing About You (23)
I Needed You Baby (28)
I Never Loved A Man (The Way I Love You) (5,11,13,17,26) *9*
I Say A Little Prayer (10,13,17) *10*
I Take What I Want (10)
I Wanna Make It Up To You (32)
I Was Made For You (29)
I Wish It Would Rain (33)
I Won't Cry Anymore (8)
I Wonder (7)
I'll Keep On Smiling (8)
I'll Never Be Free (12)
I'm In Love (22) *19*
I'm Not Strong Enough To Love You Again (24)
I'm Sitting On Top Of The World (1)
I'm Wandering (1)
I'm Your Speed (28)

I've Been In The Storm Too Long (36)
I've Been Loving You Too Long (18)
I've Got The Music In Me (medley) (27)
If Ever A Love There Was (37)
If Ever I Would Leave You (3)
If I Had A Hammer (3)
If She Don't Want Your Lovin' (32)
If You Don't Think (22)
If You Gotta Make A Fool Of Somebody (12)
If You Need My Love Tonight (35)
Impossible (34)
Integrity (34)
It Ain't Fair (14)
It Isn't, It Wasn't, It Ain't Never Gonna Be (37) *41*
It Only Happens (When I Look At You) (24)
It's Gonna Get A Bit Better (29)
It's Just A Matter Of Time (2)
(It's Just) Your Love (37)
It's My Turn (31)
It's Your Thing (32)
Jesus Hears Every Prayer (36)
Jimmy Lee (35) *28*
Jump (25) *72*
Jump To It (32) *24*
Jumpin' Jack Flash (35) *21*
Just For A Thrill (1,20)
Just My Daydream (32)
Just Right Tonight (21)
Keep On Loving You (28)
Kind Of Man (31)
Ladies Only (29)
Lady, Lady (28)
Lee Cross (8,20)
Let It Be (14,17)
Let Me In Your Life (22)
Living In The Streets (31)
Long And Winding Road (18)
Look For The Silver Lining (1)
Look Into Your Heart (25) *82*
Look To The Rainbow (35)
Lord's Prayer (36)
Love All The Hurt Away (31) *46*
Love For Sale (3)
Love Me Forever (30)
Love Me Right (32)
Love The One You're With (16)
Lover Come Back To Me (1)
Loving You Baby (25)
Make It With You (16)
Mary, Don't You Weep (19)
Mary Goes Round (38)
Masquerade Is Over (22)
Meadows Of Springtime (27)
Mercy (37)
Mister Spain (21)
Misty (3)
Mockingbird (2,20) *94*
Money Won't Change You (9)
Moody's Mood (21)
More (3)

More Than Just A Joy (28)
Mother's Love (4)
Mr. D.J. (5 For The D.J.) (24) *53*
Muddy Water (3)
Mumbles (medley) (27)
My Guy (2)
Natural Woman (You Make Me Feel Like) (9,11,13,17,26) *8*
Never Grow Old (19)
Never Let Me Go (7)
Night Life (7,11)
Night Time Is The Right Time (10)
Niki Hoeky (9)
96 Tears (7)
No Matter Who You Love (28)
(No, No) I'm Losing You (4)
No One Could Ever Love You More (27)
Oh Baby (22)
Oh Happy Day (36)
Oh Me Oh My (I'm A Fool For You Baby) (18) *73*
Oh No Not My Baby (15)
Ol' Man River (4)
Old Landmark (19)
Once In A Lifetime (3)
One Room Paradise (2)
One Step Ahead (6,20)
One Way Ticket (15)
Only Star (29)
Operation Heartbreak (8)
Packing Up, Getting Ready To Go (36)
People (20)
People Get Ready (9)
Pitiful (12)
Precious Lord, Take My Hand (medley) (19)
Precious Memories (19)
Pretender (33)
Prove It (37)
Pullin' (15)
Push (34)
Ramblin' (12)
Reach Out And Touch (Somebody's Hand) (16)
Reasons Why (29)
Respect (5,11,13,16,17,26) *1*
River's Invitation (12)
Rock-A-Bye Your Baby With A Dixie Melody (6) *37*
Rock-A-Lott (35) *82*
Rock Steady (18,26) *9*
Rock With Me (25)
Runnin' Out Of Fools (2,6,20) *57*
Satisfaction ..see: (I Can't Get No)
Save Me (5)
School Days (30)
Search On (31)
See Saw (10,13,26) *14*
Sha-La Bandit (24)
Share Your Love With Me (14) *13*
Shoop Shoop Song (It's In His Kiss) (2)
Since You've Been Gone ..see: (Sweet Sweet Baby)

Sing It Again - Say It Again (23)
Sisters Are Doin' It For Themselves (34) *18*
Sit Down And Cry (14)
Skylark (20)
So Long (12)
So Swell When You're Well (21)
Someone Else's Eyes (38)
Something He Can Feel (25,26) *28*
Somewhere (21)
Song For You (22)
Soul Serenade (5,11)
Soulville (20) *83*
Spanish Harlem (17,26) *2*
Sparkle (25)
Spirit In The Dark (15,16) *23*
Sunshine Will Never Be The Same (27)
Surely God Is Able (36)
Swanee (4)
Sweet Bitter Love (4,6,20,34)
Sweet Passion (27)
(Sweet Sweet Baby) Since You've Been Gone (9,11,13) *5*
Take A Look (4,8,20) *56*
Take It Like You Give It (20)
Take Me With You (30)
Tender Touch (27)
That's All I Want From You (15)
That's Life (7)
That's The Way I Feel About Cha (21)
There Is No Greater Love (3)
There's A Star For Everyone (31)
Think (10,13,26) *7*
Think (1989) (37)
This Could Be The Start Of Something (3)
This Girl's In Love With You (14)
This Is For Real (32)
This You Can Believe (28)
Thrill Is Gone (From Yesterday's Kiss) (15)
Through The Storm (37) *16*
Today I Love Ev'rybody (3)
Today I Sing The Blues (6,12,20)
Together Again (30)
Touch Me Up (27)
Tracks Of My Tears (12) *71*
Trouble In Mind (3) *86*
Truth And Honesty (31)
Try A Little Tenderness (1,6,20) *100*
Try Matty's (15)
Two Sides Of Love (2)
United Together (30) *56*
Until You Come Back To Me (That's What I'm Gonna Do) (22,26) *3*
Until You Say You Love Me (34)
Until You Were Gone (4,8)
Walk In The Light (36)

Walk On By (2)
Walk Softly (24)
We Need Power (36)
Weight, The (14) *19*
What A Fool Believes (30)
What A Friend We Have In Jesus (37)
What Did You Give (38)
What I Did For Love (27)
What If I Should Ever Need You (29)
What You See Is What You Sweat (38)
Whatever It Is (30)
When I Think About You (27)
When The Battle Is Over (15)
When You Get Right Down To It (23)
When You Love Me Like That (33)
Who's Zoomin' Who (34) *7*
Whole Lot Of Me (31)
Wholy Holy (19) *81*
Why I Sing The Blues (15)
With Everything I Feel In Me (23)
With Pen In Hand (23)
Without Love (23) *45*
Without The One You Love (1,3,6,20)
Without You (24)
Won't Be Long (8) *76*
Won't You Come Home Bill Bailey ..see: Bill Bailey
You (24)
You And Me (15) *flip*
You Are My Sunshine (7)
You Brought Me Back To Life (29)
You Can't Always Get What You Want (31)
You Can't Take Me For Granted (38)
You Got All The Aces (24)
You Made Me Love You (I Didn't Want To Do It) (4)
(You Make Me Feel Like) A Natural Woman ..see: Natural Woman
You Make My Life (24)
You Move Me (23)
You Send Me (10,13) *56*
You'll Lose A Good Thing (2)
You'll Never Get To Heaven (23)
You'll Never Walk Alone (19)
You're A Sweet Sweet Man (10)
You're All I Need To Get By (17) *19*
You've Got A Friend (medley) (19)
Young, Gifted And Black (18)

DEBUT DATE	PEAK POS	WKS CHR	G O L D	ARTIST — Album Title	$	Label & Number

FRANKLIN, Erma
Born in 1943 in Memphis. Younger sister of Aretha.

DEBUT DATE	PEAK POS	WKS CHR		ARTIST — Album Title	$	Label & Number
10/18/69	199	2		Soul Sister	$12	Brunswick 754147

Baby I Love You   Can't See My Way   For Once In My Life   Hold On, I'm Comin'   Son Of A Preacher Man
By The Time I Get To   Change My Thoughts From   Gotta Find Me A Lover (24   Light My Fire   You've Been Cancelled
  Phoenix   You   Hours A Day)   Saving My Love For You

FRANKLIN, Rodney
Jazz pianist. Born on 9/16/58 in Berkeley, California. Played alto sax and organ from age six. Toured with Bill Summers in 1977. Tours with Freddie Hubbard, Marlena Shaw and John Handy.

DEBUT DATE	PEAK POS	WKS CHR		ARTIST — Album Title	$	Label & Number
4/19/80	104	13	1	You'll Never Know ....[I]	$8	Columbia 36122
1/22/83	190	3	2	Learning To Love	$8	Columbia 38198
2/25/84	187	3	3	Marathon	$8	Columbia 38953

Don't Wanna Let You Go (2)   God Bless The Blues (1)   Let's Talk (3)   Parkay Man (1)   Stay On In The Groove (3)
Early Morning (medley) (2)   Groove, The (1)   Love Is The Answer (3)   Reflection Of A Dream (3)   That's The Way I Feel 'Bout
Enuff Is Enuff [includes 2   Journey (1)   Lumiere (3)   Return (1)   Your Love (2)
  versions] (2)   Learning To Love (2)   Marathon (3)   Sailing (2)   Watcher, The (1)
Felix Leo (1)   Let There Be Light (medley)   Nature's Way (medley) (2)   Searchin' For (3)   You'll Never Know (1)
Genesis (medley) (2)   (2)   New Day (medley) (2)   Sonshine (2)

★★495★★ FRANKS, Michael
Born on 9/18/44 in La Jolla, California. Florida-based, jazz-pop singer/songwriter. Albums featured as many as 35 guest artists, among them: David Sanborn, Joe Sample, Larry Carlton, the Brecker Brothers, Ron Carter, Flora Purim, Eric Gale, Bonnie Raitt, Luther Vandross, Brenda Russell, Art Garfunkel, Steve Jordan, Earl Klugh, Patti Austin and many others.

DEBUT DATE	PEAK POS	WKS CHR	G	ARTIST — Album Title	$	Label & Number
7/31/76	131	13	● 1	The Art Of Tea...............	$10	Reprise 2230
2/19/77	119	9	2	Sleeping Gypsy	$10	Warner 3004
4/8/78	90	10	3	Burchfield Nines	$10	Warner 3167
3/17/79	68	16	4	Tiger In The Rain	$10	Warner 3294
5/10/80	83	21	5	One Bad Habit	$8	Warner 3427
1/30/82	45	14	6	Objects Of Desire	$8	Warner 3648
10/29/83	141	11	7	Passionfruit	$8	Warner 23962
6/15/85	137	27	8	Skin Dive	$8	Warner 25275
8/1/87	147	11	9	The Camera Never Lies	$8	Warner 25570
7/7/90	121	17	10	Blue Pacific	$12	Reprise 26183

All Dressed Up With   Doctor Sax (9)   Innuendo (9)   Meet Me In The Deerpark (3)   **Popsicle Toes** (1) **43**   Underneath The Apple Tree
  Nowhere To Go (5)   Don't Be Blue (2)   Inside You (5)   Monkey See-Monkey Do (1)   Queen Of The Underground   (4)
All I Need (10)   Don't Be Shy (8)   Island Life (9)   Mr. Blue (1)   (8)   Vincent's Ear (10)
Alone At Night (7)   Down In Brazil (2)   Jardin Botanico (4)   Never Satisfied (7)   Rainy Night In Tokyo (7)   Vivaldi's Song (3)
Amazon (7)   Eggplant (1)   Jealousy (6)   Never Say Die (7)   Read My Lips (8)   When I Give My Love To You
Antonio's Song (The   Face To Face (9)   Jive (1)   Nightmoves (1)   Robinsong, A (3)   (8)
  Rainbow) (2)   Flirtation (9)   Ladies' Nite (6)   No-Deposit Love (6)   Sanpaku (4)   When I Think Of Us (9)
Art Of Love (10)   He Tells Himself He's Happy   Lady Wants To Know (2)   No One But You (6)   Satisfaction Guaranteed (4)   When It's Over (4)
B'wana-He No Home (2)   (5)   Laughing Gas (6)   Now I Know Why (They Call   Sometimes I Just Forget To   When She Is Mine (8)
Baseball (5)   Hideaway (4)   Let Me Count The Ways (8)   It Falling) (8)   Smile (1)   When Sly Calls (Don't Touch
Blue Pacific (10)   How The Garden Grows (7)   Lifeline (4)   Now That Your Joystick's   Speak To Me (10)   That Phone) (7)
Burchfield Nines (3)   I Don't Know Why I'm So   Lip Service (9)   Broke (7)   St. Elmo's Fire (1)   When The Cookie Jar Is
Camera Never Lies (9)   Happy I'm Sad (1)   Living On The Inside (4)   Now You're In My Dreams (9)   Still Life (5)   Empty (3)
Chain Reaction (2)   I Really Hope It's You (2)   Long Slow Distance (10)   On My Way Home To You (5)   Sunday Morning Here With   Woman In The Waves (10)
Chez Nous (10)   I Surrender (8)   Lotus Blossom (5)   On The Inside (10)   You (7)   Wonderland (6)
Crayon Sun (Safe At Home)   In Search Of The Perfect   Love Duet (6)   One Bad Habit (5)   Tahitian Moon (6)   Wrestle A Live Nude Girl (3)
  (10)   Shampoo (3)   Loving You More And More   Please Don't Say Goodnight   Tell Me All About It (7)   Your Secret's Safe With Me
Dear Little Nightingale (3)   In The Eye Of The Storm (1)   (5)   (8)   Tiger In The Rain (4)   (8)

FRATIANNE, Linda — see AEROBICS section

FREBERG, Stan
Born on 8/7/26 in Pasadena, California. Did cartoon voices for the major film studios. Launched highly successful advertising career in the early '60s; winner of 21 Clio awards (outstanding achievement award of the radio and TV ad industry).

DEBUT DATE	PEAK POS	WKS CHR		ARTIST — Album Title	$	Label & Number
7/3/61	34	24		Stan Freberg Presents The United States Of America ....[C]	$25	Capitol 1573

with Jesse White and Paul Frees; musical score by Billy May

Battle Of Yorktown   Boston Tea Party   Declaration Of Independence   Sale Of Manhattan   Washington Crosses The   Yankee Doodle Go Home
Betsy Ross And The Flag   Columbus Discovers America   Pilgrim's Progress   Thanksgiving Story   Delaware

FRED, John, & His Playboy Band
John Fred Gourrier was born on 5/8/41 in Baton Rouge, Louisiana. Formed The Playboys in 1956 as a white band playing R&B music. John played basketball at LSU, and his father, Fred Gourrier, played baseball with the Detroit Tigers.

DEBUT DATE	PEAK POS	WKS CHR		ARTIST — Album Title	$	Label & Number
2/3/68	154	10		Agnes English................................	$20	Paula 2197

AcHenall Riot   **Judy In Disguise (With**   No Good To Cry   Sad Story   Sometimes You Just Can't   Up And Down
Agnes English   **Glasses) 1**   Off The Wall   She Shot A Hole In My Soul   Win   When The Lights Go Out
   Most Unlikely To Succeed   Out Of Left Field

FREDDIE AND THE DREAMERS
Lead singer Freddie Garrity was born on 11/14/40 in Manchester, England. Formed The Dreamers in 1961 with Derek Quinn (lead guitar), Roy Crewsdon (guitar), Peter Birrell (bass) and Bernie Dwyer (drums).

DEBUT DATE	PEAK POS	WKS CHR		ARTIST — Album Title	$	Label & Number
4/17/65	19	19	1	Freddie & The Dreamers	$20	Mercury 61017
5/8/65	86	10	2	I'm Telling You Now.....................	$30	Tower 5003

includes "After Today" & "Low Grades And High Fever" by Linda Laine & The Sinners, "The Beating Of My Heart" & "Questions I Can't Answer" by Heinz, "Bye Bye Bird" & "I'm Gonna Jump" by Toggery Five, "Head Over Heels" & "I'm Leaving You" by Mike Rabon & The Demons and "That's My Baby" & "Things Will Never Be The Same" by Four Just Men

DEBUT DATE	PEAK POS	WKS CHR		ARTIST — Album Title	$	Label & Number
6/19/65	85	12	3	Do The Freddie	$30	Mercury 61026

DEBUT DATE	PEAK POS	WKS CHR	GOLD	ARTIST — Album Title	$	Label & Number

FREDDIE AND THE DREAMERS — Cont'd

Do The Freddie (3) 18	I Understand (Just How You Feel) (1) 36	In My Baby's Arms (3)	Kansas City (1)	Over You (3)	Tell Me When (1)
Don't Do That To Me (3)	I'm Telling You Now (2) 1	It Doesn't Matter Anymore (1)	Little Bitty Pretty One (3)	Sally Anne (1)	Things I'd Like To Say (3)
Early In The Morning (1)	If You Gotta Make A Fool Of Somebody (1)	Johnny B. Goode (1)	Little You (3) 48	Say It Isn't True (1)	What Have I Done To You (2)
Feel So Blue (3)		Just For You (3)	Love Like You (3)	She Belongs To You (3)	Yes I Do (1)
I Don't Love You Anymore (1)			Money (That's What I Want) (1)	Silly Girl (3)	

FREE

British rock band formed in 1968: Paul Rodgers (vocals), Paul Kossoff (guitar), Simon Kirke (drums) and Andy Fraser (bass). Kossoff and Fraser left in 1972, replaced by Tetsu Yamauchi (bass, later with Faces) and John "Rabbit" Bundrick (keyboards). Kossoff (d: 3/19/76 of drug-induced heart failure) formed Back Street Crawler. Rodgers and Kirke formed Bad Company in 1974. Rodgers was lead singer of The Firm (1984-85) and The Law (since 1991).

DEBUT DATE	PEAK POS	WKS CHR	GOLD	ARTIST — Album Title	$	Label & Number
9/13/69	197	2		1 Tons Of Sobs	$15	A&M 4198
9/5/70	17	27		2 Fire And Water	$12	A&M 4268
2/27/71	190	2		3 Highway	$12	A&M 4287
9/11/71	89	8		4 Free Live! ....[L]	$12	A&M 4306
5/27/72	69	16		5 Free At Last	$12	A&M 4349
2/3/73	47	16		6 Heartbreaker	$10	Island 9217
5/24/75	120	7		7 Best Of Free ....[G]	$10	A&M 3663

All Right Now (2,4,7) 4	Don't Say You Love Me (2)	Heavy Load (2)	Mouthful Of Grass (7)	Remember (2)	Sweet Tooth (1)
Be My Friend (3,4)	Easy On My Soul (6)	Highway Song (3,7)	Mr. Big (2,4)	Ride On Pony (3,4)	Travellin In Style (6)
Bodie (3)	Fire And Water (2,4,7)	Hunter, The (1,4,7)	Muddy Water (6)	Sail On (5)	Travellin' Man (5)
Catch A Train (5,7)	Get Where I Belong (4)	I'm A Mover (1,4,7)	My Brother Jake (4,7)	Seven Angels (6)	Walk In My Shadow (1)
Child (5)	Goin' Down Slow (1)	Little Bit Of Love (5,7)	Oh I Wept (2)	Soldier Boy (5)	Wild Indian Woman (1)
Come Together In The Morning (6)	Goodbye (5,7)	Love You So (3)	On My Way (3)	Soon I Will Be Gone (3)	Wishing Well (6)
Common Mortal Man (6)	Guardian Of The Universe (5)	Magic Ship (5)	Over The Green Hills - Parts I & II (1)	Stealer (3,7) 49	Woman (7)
	Heartbreaker (6)	Moonshine (3)		Sunny Day (3)	Worry (1)

FREED, Alan — see VARIOUS - Radio/TV Celebrity Compilations

FREE MOVEMENT, The

Los Angeles-based vocal sextet. Several members formerly with gospel groups.

DEBUT DATE	PEAK POS	WKS CHR	GOLD	ARTIST — Album Title	$	Label & Number
1/29/72	167	8		I've Found Someone Of My Own	$10	Columbia 31136

Coming Home	Harder I Try (The Bluer I Get) 50	I Know I Could Love You Better (The Second Time Around)	I've Found Someone Of My Own 5	Land Where I Live	Where Do We Go From Here
Could You Believe In A Dream			If Only You Believe	Love The One You're With	Your Love Has Grown Cold
				Son Of The Zulu King	

FREHLEY, Ace

Born Paul Frehley on 4/27/51 in the Bronx. Lead guitarist of Kiss until 1983. Prominent sessionman Anton Fig (drummer of TV's Late Night With David Letterman) was with Frehley from 1978-88.

DEBUT DATE	PEAK POS	WKS CHR	GOLD	ARTIST — Album Title	$	Label & Number
10/14/78+	26	23	▲	1 Ace Frehley	$15	Casablanca 7121
5/23/87	43	25		2 Frehley's Comet	$8	Megaforce 81749
2/27/88	84	10		3 Live + 1 ....[L]	$8	Megaforce 81826
6/11/88	81	13		4 Second Sighting	$8	Megaforce 81862
				above 2: FREHLEY'S COMET		
11/11/89	102	9		5 Trouble Walkin'	$8	Megaforce 82042

Acorn Is Spinning (4)	Fractured Mirror (1)	Loser In A Fight (4)	Rocket Ride (3)	Time Ain't Runnin' Out (4)	
Back To School (5)	Fractured Too (2)	Lost In Limbo (5)	Separate (4)	2 Young 2 Die (5)	
Breakout (2,3)	Fractured III (5)	Love Me Right (2)	Shot Full Of Rock (5)	Trouble Walkin' (5)	
Calling To You (2)	Hide Your Heart (5)	New Kind Of Lover (4)	Snow Blind (4)	We Got Your Rock (2)	
Dancin' With Danger (4)	I'm In Need Of Love (4)	New York Groove (1) 13	Something Moved (2,3)	What's On Your Mind? (1)	
Do Ya (5)	Insane (4)	Ozone (1)	Speedin' Back To My Baby (1)	Wiped-Out (1)	
Dolls (2)	Into The Night (4)	Remember Me (5)	Stranger In A Strange Land (2)	Words Are Not Enough (3)	
Fallen Angel (4)	It's Over Now (4)	Rip It Out (1,3)			
Five Card Stud (5)	Juvenile Delinquent (4)	Rock Soldiers (4)			

FREIBERG, David — see KANTNER, Paul, and/or SLICK, Grace

FREY, Glenn

Founding member of the Eagles. Born on 11/6/48 in Detroit. Singer/songwriter/guitarist. Appeared in episodes of TV's Miami Vice and Wiseguy.

DEBUT DATE	PEAK POS	WKS CHR	GOLD	ARTIST — Album Title	$	Label & Number
6/26/82	32	38	●	1 No Fun Aloud	$8	Asylum 60129
7/14/84+	22	65	●	2 The Allnighter	$8	MCA 5501
9/3/88	36	19		3 Soul Searchin'	$8	MCA 6239

All Those Lies (1) 41	I Found Somebody (1) 31	Let's Pretend We're Still In Love (3)	One You Love (1) 15	Some Kind Of Blue (3)	Working Man (3)
Allnighter, The (2) 54	I Got Love (2)	Livin' Right (3) 90	Partytown (1)	Somebody Else (3)	
Better In The U.S.A. (3)	I Volunteer (1)	Living In Darkness (2)	Sea Cruise (1)	Soul Searchin' (3)	
Can't Put Out This Fire (3)	I've Been Born Again (1)	Lover's Moon (2)	Sexy Girl (2) 20	That Girl (1)	
Don't Give Up (1)	It's Your Life (3)	New Love (2)	She Can't Let Go (1)	True Love (2) 13	
I Did It For Your Love (3)	Let's Go Home (2)		Smuggler's Blues (2) 12	Two Hearts (3)	

FRIDA

Born Anni-Frid Lyngstad on 11/15/45 in Narvik, Norway. Member of Abba.

DEBUT DATE	PEAK POS	WKS CHR	GOLD	ARTIST — Album Title	$	Label & Number
11/13/82+	41	28		Something's Going On	$8	Atlantic 80018
				produced by Phil Collins		

Baby Don't You Cry No More	I Know There's Something Going On 13	I See Red	Tell Me It's Over	To Turn The Stone	You Know What I Mean
Here We'll Stay		Strangers	Threnody	Way You Do	
I Got Something					

FRIEDMAN, Dean

Singer/songwriter from New Jersey.

DEBUT DATE	PEAK POS	WKS CHR	GOLD	ARTIST — Album Title	$	Label & Number
6/4/77	192	6		Dean Friedman	$10	Lifesong 6008

Ariel 26	Funny Papers	I May Be Young	Love Is Not Enough	Song For My Mother
Company	Humor Me	Letter, The	Solitaire	Woman Of Mine

DEBUT DATE	PEAK POS	WKS CHR	GOLD	ARTIST — Album Title	$	Label & Number

FRIEDMAN, Kinky
Jewish country singer/satirist. Born Richard Friedman on 10/31/44 in Rio Duckworth, Texas.

| 2/1/75 | 132 | 6 | | Kinky Friedman | $10 | ABC 829 |

Autograph
Before All Hell Breaks Loose
Homo Erectus

Lover Please
Miss Nickelodeon
Popeye The Sailor Man

Rapid City South Dakota
Somethin's Wrong With The Beaver

They Ain't Makin' Jews Like Jesus Anymore

When The Lord Closes The Door (He Opens A Little Window)

Wild Man From Borneo

FRIENDS OF DISTINCTION, The
Los Angeles-based, soul-MOR group. Original lineup: Floyd Butler, Harry Elston, Jessica Cleaves and Barbara Jean Love. Butler and Elston were in the Hi-Fi's with LaMonte McLemore and Marilyn McCoo (later with The 5th Dimension).

5/3/69	35	25	1	Grazin'............	$12	RCA 4149
10/25/69	173	6	2	Highly Distinct............	$12	RCA 4212
3/28/70	68	21	3	Real Friends............	$10	RCA 4313
10/31/70	179	3	4	Whatever............	$10	RCA 4408
8/7/71	166	7	5	Friends & People	$8	RCA 4492

And I Love Him (1)
Any Way You Want Me (3)
Baby I Could Be So Good At Loving You (1)
Bring Us A Better Day (4)
Check It Out (4)
Crazy Mary (3)
Didn't We (4)
Down I Go (5)
Dying To Live (5)
Eli's Comin (1)
Faces On The Bus (5)

Going In Circles (1) **15**
Grazing In The Grass (1) **3**
Great Day (4)
Help Yourself (To All Of My Lovin') (1)
I Can't Get You Out Of My Mind (5)
I Need You (5) **79**
I Really Hope You Do (1)
I've Never Found A Girl (To Love Me Like You Do) (1)
Impressions (2)

It Don't Matter To Me (3)
It's A Wonderful World (2)
It's Just A Game Love (2)
It's Sunday (2)
It's Time To See Each Other (5)
Jenny Wants To Know (3)
Just A Little Lovin' (3)
Lady Mae (3)
Let Me Be (5)
Let Yourself Go (2) **63**
Light My Fire (5)

Lonesome Mood (1)
Long Time Comin' My Way (3)
Love Or Let Me Be Lonely (3) **6**
My Mind Is A Camera (3)
New Mother Nature (4)
Oh, How I Miss You (5)
On & On (3)
Out In The Country (3)
Peaceful (4)
People (5)

People Talkin' And Sayin' Nothin' (4)
Soulful Anthem (4)
Sweet Young Thing Like You (1)
This Generation (3)
Time Waits For No One (4) **60**
We Got A Good Thing Goin' (2)
Why Did I Lose You (2)
Willa Faye (4)

Workin' On A Groovy Thing (2)
You And I (4)

FRIJID PINK
Rock group formed in Detroit: Kelly Green (lead singer), Gary Thompson (guitar), Tom Beaudry (bass) and Rich Stevens (drums).

| 1/24/70 | 11 | 30 | 1 | Frijid Pink............ | $20 | Parrot 71033 |
| 10/31/70 | 149 | 12 | 2 | Defrosted............ | $20 | Parrot 71041 |

Black Lace (2)
Boozin' Blues (1)
Bye Bye Blues (2)
Crying Shame (1)

Drivin' Blues (1)
End Of The Line (1)
God Gave Me You (1)

House Of The Rising Sun (1) **7**
I Haven't Got The Time (2)
I Want To Be Your Lover (1)

I'll Never Be Lonely (2)
I'm Movin' (2)
I'm On My Way (1)
Pain In My Heart (2)

Sing A Song For Freedom (2) **55**
Sloony (2)
Tell Me Why (1)

FRIPP, Robert
Founder of King Crimson. British rock avant-gardist. Born in May of 1946 in Dorset, England.

5/26/79	79	14	1	Exposure............	$10	EG 6201
4/26/80	110	6	2	God Save The Queen/Under Heavy Manners............[I]	$8	Polydor 6266
				features Fripp's "Frippertronics" electronic music		
4/4/81	90	7	3	The League Of Gentlemen............[I]	$8	Polydor 6317
				title also refers to the name of Fripp's eclectic band		

ANDY SUMMERS/ROBERT FRIPP:

| 11/6/82 | 60 | 11 | 4 | I Advance Masked............[I] | $8 | A&M 4913 |
| 10/20/84 | 155 | 5 | 5 | Bewitched............[I] | $8 | A&M 5011 |

Aquarelle (medley) (4)
Begin The Day (5)
Bewitched (5)
Breathless (4)
Chicago (1)
China - Yellow Leader (4)
Cognitive Dissonance (3)
Disengage (1)
Dislocated (3)
Exposure (1)
Eye Needles (3)

Forgotten Steps (5)
Girl On A Swing (4)
God Save The Queen (2)
Guide (5)
H.G. Wells (3)
Haaden Two (1)
Hardy Country (4)
Heptaparaparshinokh (3)
Here Comes The Flood (1)
I Advance Masked (4)

I May Not Have Had Enough Of Me But I've Had Enough Of You (1)
Image And Likeness (5)
In The Cloud Forest (4)
Indiscreet I, II & III (3)
Inductive Resonance (3)
Lakeland (medley) (4)
Maquillage (5)
Mary (1)
Minor Man (3)

New Marimba (4)
NY3 (1)
1983 (2)
North Star (1)
Ochre (3)
Painting And Dance (4)
Parade (5)
Pareto Optimum I & II (3)
Postscript (1)
Red Two Scorer (2)
Seven On Seven (4)

Still Point (4)
Stultified (4)
Train (3)
Trap (3)
Tribe (3)
Truth Of Skies (4)
Under Bridges Of Silence (4)
Under Heavy Manners (2)
Urban Landscape (1)
Water Music I & II (1)

What Kind Of Man Reads Playboy (5)
You Burn Me Up I'm A Cigarette (1)
Zero Of The Signified (2)

FRONT, The
Hard-rock quintet from Kansas City: brothers Michael (vocals) and Bobby Franano, with Mike Greene, Randy Jordan and Shane.

| 2/3/90 | 118 | 14 | | The Front............ | $12 | Columbia 45260 |

Fire
In The Garden

Le Motion
Pain

Ritual
Sin

Sister Moon
Sunshine Girl

Sweet Addiction
Violent World

FRONT 242
Industrial dance foursome from Brussels, Belgium: Daniel B, P. Codenys, J-L De Meyer and Richard JK.

| 2/16/91 | 95 | 12 | | Tyranny For You............ | $12 | Epic 46998 |

Gripped By Fear
Leitmotiv 136

Moldavia
Neurobashing

Rhythm Of Time
Sacrifice

Soul Manager
Tragedy For You

Trigger 2 (Anatomy Of A Shot)

Untold

FROST
Detroit rock quartet: Dick Wagner (lead singer, guitar), Don Hartman (guitar), Gordy Garris (bass) and Bob Riggs (drums).

6/21/69	168	10	1	Frost Music............	$15	Vanguard 6520
11/29/69+	148	8	2	Rock And Roll Music............[L]	$15	Vanguard 6541
				4 of 7 cuts are live		
10/17/70	197	2	3	Through The Eyes Of Love............	$15	Vanguard 6556

Baby Once You Got It (1)
Big Time Spender (3)
Black As Night (3)
Black Train (2)
Donny's Blues (2)

Family, The (1)
Fifteen Hundred Miles (Through The Eye Of A Beatle) (3)
First Day Of May (1)

Help Me Baby (2)
It's So Hard (3)
Jennie Lee (1)
Linda (2)
Little Susie Singer (1)

Long Way Down From Mobile (1)
Long Way From Home (3)
Maybe Tomorrow (3)
Mystery Man (1)

Rock And Roll Music (2)
Stand In The Shadows (1)
Sweet Lady Love (2)
Take My Hand (1)

Through The Eyes Of Love (God Help Us Please) (3)
We Got To Get Out Of This Place (2)
Who Are You? (1)

DEBUT DATE	PEAK POS	WKS CHR	GOLD	ARTIST — Album Title	$	Label & Number

FROZEN GHOST

Canadian pop duo: Arnold Lanni (vocals, guitar, keyboards) and Wolf Hassel (bass). Both were members of the group Sheriff.

4/11/87	107	13		Frozen Ghost	$8	Atlantic 81736

Beware The Masque   Love Like A Fire   Promises   Soldiers Cry   Truth In Lies
End Of The Line   Love Without Lies   **Should I See 69**   Time Is The Answer   Yum Bai Ya

FRYE, David

Comedian/impressionist.

12/27/69+	19	18		1 I Am The President ....[C]	$12	Elektra 75006
3/27/71	123	6		2 Radio Free Nixon ....[C]	$10	Elektra 74085
12/11/71+	60	13		3 Richard Nixon Superstar ....[C]	$10	Buddah 5097
8/11/73	45	15		4 Richard Nixon: A Fantasy ....[C]	$10	Buddah 1600

Addressing The Nation (4)   Dear Henry Cabot (1)   Golda Goes Washington (1)   New Tenants (1)   Rocky Reports (1)   WNIX Sports (2)
Advisors, The (3)   Dick Nixon Show (2)   Historic Words (1)   Nixon Meets The Godfather (4)   Sesame Street (3)   Weather Report (2)
And The Winner Is (1)   Dick Nixon's Solid Gold (4)   Hush, Hush, Sweet Spiro (1)   Soap Opera (2)
Big Four (2)   Dr. Kissinger (4)   Inauguration, The (3)   Nixon Sings The Blues (3)   Southern Strategy (2)
Big House (4)   Early Nixon Medley (3)   Inside Hubert (1)   Oh Dad, Poor Dad (1)   Special Bulletin (2)
Bill Buckley Show (4)   Echoes Of His Mind (1)   It's A Gas (1)   Parable, The (3)   State Of The Union (3)
Blessed Event (1)   Economy, The (3)   Last Mile (4)   Power Politics (3)   Swing Vote (1)
Boss, The (3)   Editorial, An (2)   Late Night At The Office (1)   Presidential Trip (1)   Ten O'Clock Shadow (1)
Break In (4)   Face The Country (3)   Listen To Martha (3)   Press Conference (1)   Thought For Tomorrow (2)
Cellmates, The (4)   Farm Report (2)   Loyal Opposition (3)   Prison Break (4)   Trial, The (4)
Critics Medley (3)   Foreign Affairs (2)   Message, The (2)   Prison Reform (4)   Trip, The (3)
Dear Dick (1)   Funnies, The (2)   My Way (2)   Public Servant Number 1 (3)   Victory Speech (1)

FUGS

New York City "underground" group — Ed Sanders, leader.

7/2/66	95	26		1 The Fugs...	$25	ESP 1028
10/29/66	142	4		2 The Fugs First Album	$25	ESP 1018
10/19/68	167	10		3 It Crawled Into My Hand, Honest..	$25	Reprise 6305

Ah! Sunflower, Weary Of Time (2)   Divine Toe (Part I & II) (medley) (3)   I Feel Like Homemade Shit (2)   Morning, Morning (1)   Swinburne Stomp (2)
Boobs A Lot (2)   Doin' All Right (1)   I Want To Know (1)   National Haiku Contest (medley) (3)   Tuli Visited By Ghost Of Plotinus (medley) (3)
Burial Waltz (3)   Frenzy (3)   Irene (medley) (3)   Nothing (2)   Virgin Forest (1)
Claude Pelleu And J.J. Lebel Discuss The Early Verlaine (medley) (3)   Grope Need (Part I & II) (medley) (3)   Johnny Pissoff Meets The Red Angel (medley) (3)   Ramses II Is Dead, My Love (3)   We're Both Dead Now, Alice (medley) (3)
Bread Crust Fragments (medley) (3)   Group Grope (1)   Kill For Peace (1)   Robinson Crusoe (medley) (3)   When The Mode Of The Music Changes (medley) (3)
Coming Down (1)   How Sweet I Roamed From Field To Field (2)   Leprechaun (medley) (3)   Seize The Day (2)   Whimpers From The Jello (medley) (3)
Crystal Liaison (3)   I Couldn't Get High (2)   Life Is Funny (medley) (3)   Skin Flowers (1)
Dirty Old Man (1)   Life Is Strange (3)   Slum Goddess (2)   Wide Wide River (3)
Marijuana (medley) (3)   Supergirl (2)

FULLER, Bobby, Four

Bobby was born on 10/22/43 in Baytown, Texas. Died mysteriously of asphyxiation in Los Angeles on 7/18/66. Band, formed in El Paso, featured Bobby (lead vocals, guitar) and his brother Randy (bass).

4/2/66	144	2		The Bobby Fuller Four	$50	Mustang 901

Another Sad And Lonely Night   **I Fought The Law 9**   Let Her Dance   Never To Be Forgotten   Only When I Dream   Take My Word
Fool Of Love   Julie   Little Annie Lou   New Shade Of Blue   Saturday Night   You Kiss Me

FULL FORCE

Producing/composing rap sextet from Brooklyn. The George brothers - Brian "B-Fine," Paul Anthony and "Bowlegged" Lou - with their cousins "Baby" Gerry Charles, Junior "Shy Shy" Clark and "Curt-T-T" Bedeau. Appeared in the films *House Party* and *House Party 2*. Assembled and produced Lisa Lisa & Cult Jam. Production work for UTFO, Cheryl "Pepsi" Riley and others.

2/15/86	160	8		1 Full Force	$8	Columbia 40117
8/30/86	141	13		2 Full Force get busy 1 time!	$8	Columbia 40395
12/5/87	126	11		3 Guess Who's Comin' To The Crib?	$8	Columbia 40894

Alice, I Want You Just For Me! (1)   Child's Play (Part I & II) (2)   Katty Women (3)   Low Blow Brenda (3)   Take Care Of Homework (3)   Your Love Is So Def (3)
All In My Mind (3)   Child's Play (Part 3) (3)   Let's Dance Against The Wall (1)   Man Upstairs (1)   Temporary Love Thing (2)
Black Radio (3)   Dream Believer (1)   Never Had Another Lover (2)   3: O'Clock...School's Out! (3)
Body Heavenly (2)   Full Force Git Money $ (3)   Love Is For Suckers (Like Me And You) (3)   Old Flames Never Die (2)   Unfaithful (2)
Chain Me To The Night (2)   Girl If You Take Me Home (1)   Please Stay (1)   United (1)
Half A Chance (1)   Love Scene (2)   So Much (2)   Unselfish Lover (1)

FUN BOY THREE

British trio of former Specials members Terry Hall (vocals), Lynval Golding (guitar) and Neville Staples (vocals).

7/30/83	104	7		Waiting	$8	Chrysalis 41417

produced by David Byrne (Talking Heads)

Farm Yard Connection   More I See (The Less I Believe)   Murder She Said   Pressure Of Life (Takes Weight Off The Body)   Things We Do   We're Having All The Fun
Going Home   Our Lips Are Sealed   Tunnel Of Love   Well Fancy That!

FUNKADELIC

★★362★★

Funk aggregation formed in 1968. Consisted of The Parliaments plus a backing band. While recording for Westbound, group also recorded for Invictus as Parliament in 1971. Formed corporation, "A Parliafunkadelicament Thang," through which they recorded under both names. By 1974, leader/producer George Clinton reorganized the Parliament/Funkadelic corporation to include varying membership. Three of the original members of The Parliaments left the corporation in 1977; recorded as Funkadelic for LAX Records in 1981, not in association with Clinton. Also see Parliament.

3/21/70	126	17		1 Funkadelic..	$30	Westbound 2000
10/31/70	92	11		2 Free Your Mind...And Your Ass Will Follow	$30	Westbound 2001
8/14/71	108	16		3 Maggot Brain	$35	Westbound 2007
6/17/72	123	15		4 America Eats Its Young	$30	Westbound 2020 [2]
7/21/73	112	13		5 Cosmic Slop	$30	Westbound 2022
9/7/74	163	5		6 Standing On The Verge Of Getting It On	$30	Westbound 1001

FUNKADELIC — Cont'd

DEBUT DATE	PEAK POS	WKS CHR	GOLD	ARTIST — Album Title	$	Label & Number
7/19/75	102	16		7 Let's Take It To The Stage	$30	Westbound 215
10/9/76	103	10		8 Tales Of Kidd Funkadelic	$30	Westbound 227
11/27/76	96	12		9 Hardcore Jollies	$10	Warner 2973
10/7/78	16	22	▲	10 One Nation Under A Groove	$8	Warner 3209
10/13/79	18	17	●	11 Uncle Jam Wants You	$8	Warner 3371
8/29/81	105	4		12 The Electric Spanking Of War Babies	$8	Warner 3482

Adolescent Funk (9)
Alice In My Fantasies (6)
America Eats Its Young (4)
Atmosphere (7)
Back In Our Minds (3)
Balance (4)
Be My Beach (7)
Better By The Pound (7) 99
Biological Speculation (4)
Brettino's Bounce (12)
Butt-To-Buttresuscitation (8)
Can You Get To That (3) 93
Can't Stand The Strain (5)
Cholly (Funk Getting Ready To Roll!) (10)
Comin' Round The Mountain (5)
Cosmic Slop (5,9)
Electric Spanking Of War Babies (12)
Electro-Cuties (12)
Eulogy And Light (2)

Everybody Is Going To Make It This Time (4)
Field Maneuvers (11)
Foot Soldiers (Star-Spangled Funky) (11)
Freak Of The Week (11)
Free Your Mind And Your Ass Will Follow (2)
Friday Night, August 14th (12)
Funk Gets Stronger (Part I) (12)
Funky Dollar Bill (2)
Get Off Your Ass And Jam (7)
Good Old Music (1)
Good Thoughts, Bad Thoughts (6)
Good To Your Earhole (7)
Groovallegiance (10)
Hardcore Jollies (9)
Hit It And Quit It (3)
Holly Wants To Go To California (11)
How Do Yeaw View You? (8)

I Got A Thing, You Got A Thing, Everybody's Got A Thing (1) 80
I Owe You Something Good (7)
I Wanna Know If It's Good To You? (2) 81
I'll Bet You (1) 63
I'll Stay (6)
I'm Never Gonna Tell It (8)
Icka Prick (12)
If You Don't Like The Effects, Don't Produce The Cause (4)
If You Got Funk, You Got Style (9)
Into You (10)
Jimmy's Got A Little Bit Of Bitch In Him (6)
Joyful Process (4)
Let's Make It Last (5)
Let's Take It To The People (8)

Let's Take It To The Stage (7)
Loose Booty (4)
Lunchmeataphobia (Think! It Ain't Illegal Yet!) (10)
Maggot Brain (3,10)
March To The Witch's Castle (5)
Miss Lucifer's Love (4)
Mommy, What's A Funkadelic? (1)
Music For My Mother (1)
Nappy Dugout (5)
No Compute (4)
No Head, No Backstage Pass (7)
(Not Just) Knee Deep - Part 1 (11) 77
Oh, I (12)
One Nation Under A Groove - Part 1 (10) 28
P.E. Squad (Doo Doo Chasers) (10)
Philmore (4)

Pussy (4)
Qualify & Satisfy (1)
Red Hot Momma (6)
Sexy Ways (6)
She Loves You (medley) (12)
Shockwaves (12)
Smokey (9)
Some More (2)
Song Is Familiar (7)
Soul Mate (9)
Standing On The Verge Of Getting It On (6)
Stuffs And Things (7)
Super Stupid (3)
Take Your Dead Ass Home! (Say Som'n Nasty) (8)
Tales Of Kidd Funkadelic (Opusdelite Years) (8)
That Was My Girl (4)
This Broken Heart (5)
Trash-A-Go-Go (5)
Uncle Jam (11)
Undisco Kidd (8)

Wake Up (4)
Wars Of Armageddon (3)
We Hurt Too (4)
What Is Soul (1)
Who Says A Funk Band Can't Play Rock?! (10)
You And Your Folks, Me And My Folks (3) 91
You Can't Miss What You Can't Measure (5)
You Hit The Nail On The Head (4)
You Scared The Lovin' Outta Me (0)

FUNKADELIC

Group includes three members of The Parliaments: Clarence Haskins, Calvin Simon and Grady Thomas; no longer in association with George Clinton and the Parliament/Funkadelic corporation.

DEBUT DATE	PEAK POS	WKS CHR	GOLD	ARTIST — Album Title	$	Label & Number
4/11/81	151	4		Connections & Disconnections	$8	LAX 37087

Call The Doctor
Come Back

Connections And Disconnections
Phunklords
Who's A Funkadelic

Witch Medley
You'll Like It Too

FUNKY COMMUNICATION COMMITTEE — see FCC

FURAY, Richie, Band

Born on 5/9/44 in Yello Springs, Ohio. Member of Buffalo Springfield, Poco, and The Souther, Hillman, Furay Band.

DEBUT DATE	PEAK POS	WKS CHR	GOLD	ARTIST — Album Title	$	Label & Number
8/7/76	130	8		I've Got A Reason	$10	Asylum 1067

Gettin' Through
I've Got A Reason

Look At The Sun
Mighty Maker

Over And Over Again
Starlight

Still Rolling Stones
We'll See

You're The One I Love

FU-SCHNICKENS

Brooklyn rap trio: Poc Fu, Chip Fu and Moc Fu. FU stands for "For Unity" and Schnicken is a term invented by the group to signify coalition.

DEBUT DATE	PEAK POS	WKS CHR	GOLD	ARTIST — Album Title	$	Label & Number
4/4/92	64	20		F.U. "Don't Take It Personal"	$12	Jive 41472

Back Off
Bebo

Check It Out
Generals

Heavenly Father
La Schmoove

Movie Scene
Props

Ring The Alarm
True Fuschnick

FUSE ONE

Supergroup of contemporary jazz artists: Stanley Clarke, Ronnie Foster, Ndugu, Tom Browne, Stanley Turrentine, Eric Gale, George Benson, Dave Valentin and Wynton Marsalis.

DEBUT DATE	PEAK POS	WKS CHR	GOLD	ARTIST — Album Title	$	Label & Number
2/13/82	139	8		Silk [I]	$8	CTI 9006

Hot Fire

In Celebration Of The Human Spirit

Silk

Sunwalk

FUZZ, The

Black female trio from Washington, D.C.: Sheila Young, Barbara Gilliam and Val Williams. Originally called the Passionettes.

DEBUT DATE	PEAK POS	WKS CHR	GOLD	ARTIST — Album Title	$	Label & Number
10/2/71	196	3		The Fuzz	$12	Calla 2001

All About Love
I Love You For All Seasons 21

I Think I Got The Making Of A True Love Affair
I'm So Glad 95
It's All Over

Leave It All Behind Me
Like An Open Door 77

Ooh Baby Baby
Search Your Mind

G

★★283★★ **GABRIEL, Peter**

Born on 2/13/50 in London. Lead singer of Genesis from 1966-75. Scored films *Birdy* and *The Last Temptation Of Christ*. In 1982, financed the World of Music Arts and Dance (WOMAD) festival.

DEBUT DATE	PEAK POS	WKS CHR	GOLD	ARTIST — Album Title	$	Label & Number
3/12/77	38	17		1 Peter Gabriel	$12	Atco 147
7/22/78	45	10		2 Peter Gabriel	$10	Atlantic 19181
6/21/80	22	29		3 Peter Gabriel	$8	Mercury 3848
10/2/82	28	31	●	4 Peter Gabriel (Security)	$8	Geffen 2011
6/25/83	44	16	●	5 Peter Gabriel/Plays Live [L]	$10	Geffen 4012 [2]

DEBUT DATE	PEAK POS	WKS CHR	GOLD	ARTIST — Album Title	$	Label & Number
				GABRIEL, Peter — Cont'd		
4/20/85	162	7		6 Birdy .... [S-I]	$8	Geffen 24070
				includes 5 instrumental versions of his previous releases		
6/14/86	2³	93 ▲³		7 So	$8	Geffen 24088
7/1/89	60	14		8 Passion: Music for The Last Temptation Of Christ .... [S-I]	$10	Geffen 24206 [2]
				selections composed by Gabriel for the Martin Scorsese film plus traditional music performed by North African and Eastern musicians		
12/22/90+	48	28	●	9 Shaking The Tree - Sixteen Golden Greats .... [G]	$12	Geffen 24326
10/17/92	2¹	17↑	▲	10 Us .... [G]	$12	Geffen 24473

And Through The Wire (3)
Animal Magic (2)
At Night (6)
Before Night Falls (8)
Big Time (7,9) *8*
Biko (3,5,9)
Birdy's Flight (6)
Blood Of Eden (10)
Bread And Wine (8)
Close Up (6)
Come Talk To Me (10)
D.I.Y. (2,5)
Different Drum (8)
Digging In The Dirt (10) *52*
Disturbed (8)
Don't Give Up (7,9) *72*
Down The Dolce Vita (1)
Dressing The Wound (6)

Excuse Me (1)
Exposure (2)
Family And The Fishing Net (4,5)
Family Snapshot (3,5,9)
Feeling Begins (8)
Floating Dogs (6)
Flotsam And Jetsam (2)
Fourteen Black Paintings (10)
Games Without Frontiers (3,9) *48*
Gethsemane (8)
Heat, The (6)
Here Comes The Flood (1,9)
Home Sweet Home (2)
Humdrum (1,5)
I Don't Remember (3,5,9)

I Go Swimming (5)
I Have The Touch (4,5,9)
In Doubt (8)
In Your Eyes (7) *26*
Indigo (2)
Intruder (3,5)
It Is Accomplished (8)
Kiss Of Life (4)
Kiss That Frog (10)
Lay Your Hands On Me (4)
Lazarus Raised (8)
Lead A Normal Life (3)
Love To Be Loved (10)
Mercy Street (7,9)
Modern Love (1)
Moribund The Burgermeister (1)
Mother Of Violence (2)

No Self Control (3,5)
Not One Of Us (3,5)
Of These, Hope (8)
On The Air (2,5)
Only Us (10)
Open (8)
Passion (8)
Perspective (2)
Powerhouse At The Foot Of The Mountain (6)
Promise Of Shadows (8)
Quiet And Alone (6)
Red Rain (7,9)
Rhythm Of The Heat (4,5)
San Jacinto (4,5,9)
Sandstorm (8)
Secret World (10)
Shaking The Tree (9)

Shock The Monkey (4,5,9) *29*
Sketchpad With Trumpet And Voice (6)
Sledgehammer (7,9) *1*
Slow Marimbas (6)
Slow Water (6)
Slowburn (1)
Solsbury Hill (1,9) *68*
Solsbury Hill [live] (5) *84*
Start (3)
Steam (10) *32↑*
Stigmata (8)
That Voice Again (7)
Troubled (8)
Under Lock And Key (8)
Waiting For The Big One (1)
Wall Of Breath (8)

Wallflower (4)
Washing Of The Water (10)
We Do What We're Told (7)
White Shadow (2)
With This Love [includes 2 versions] (8)
Wonderful Day In A One-Way World (2)
Zaar (8,9)

GALE, Eric
Jazz-soul session guitarist. Worked with Paul Butterfield, Joe Cocker, Felix Pappalardi, Paul Simon and others. Member of Fuse One.

DEBUT DATE	PEAK POS	WKS CHR		ARTIST — Album Title	$	Label & Number
4/9/77	148	12		1 Ginseng Woman .... [I]	$8	Columbia 34421
7/21/79	154	5		2 Part Of You .... [I]	$8	Columbia 35715

De Rabbit (1)
East End, West End (1)

Ginseng Woman (1)
Holding On To Love (2)

Let-Me-Slip-It-To-You (2)
Lookin' Good (2)

Nezumi (2)
Part Of You (2)

Red Ground (1)
Sara Smile (1)

She Is My Lady (1)
Trio (2)

GALLAGHER, Rory
Leader of Taste. Irish blues-rock guitarist/vocalist. Born on 3/2/49.

DEBUT DATE	PEAK POS	WKS CHR		ARTIST — Album Title	$	Label & Number
8/26/72	101	15		1 Rory Gallagher/Live! .... [L]	$10	Polydor 5513
4/21/73	147	7		2 Blueprint	$10	Polydor 5522
12/1/73+	186	7		3 Tattoo	$10	Polydor 5539
9/14/74	110	11		4 Irish Tour '74 .... [L]	$10	Polydor 9501 [2]
2/22/75	156	5		5 Sinner...And Saint	$10	Polydor 6510
11/29/75+	121	13		6 Against The Grain	$8	Chrysalis 1098
10/30/76+	163	11		7 Calling Card	$8	Chrysalis 1124
11/4/78+	116	15		8 Photo-Finish	$8	Chrysalis 1170
10/6/79	140	4		9 Top Priority	$8	Chrysalis 1235

Admit It (3)
Ain't Too Good (6)
All Around Man (6)
As The Crow Flies (4)
At The Bottom (6)
At The Depot (9)
Back On My (Stompin' Ground) (4)
Bad Penny (9)
Banker's Blues (2)
Barley And Grape Rag (7)
Bought And Sold (6)
Brute Force And Ignorance (8)

Bullfrog Blues (1)
Calling Card (7)
Cloak And Dagger (8)
Country Mile (7)
Cradle Rock (3,4)
Crest Of A Wave (5)
Cross Me Off Your List (6)
Cruise On Out (8)
Daughter Of The Everglades (2)
Do You Read Me (7)
Don't Know Where I'm Going (5)
Edged In Blue (7)

Follow Me (9)
For The Last Time (5)
Fuel To The Fire (8)
Going To My Home Town (1)
Hands Off (2)
Hands Up (5)
I Could've Had Religion (1)
I Fall Apart (5)
I Take What I Want (6)
I Wonder Who (Who's Gonna Be Your Sweet Man) (4)
I'll Admit You're Gone (7)
I'm Not Awake Yet (5)
If I Had A Reason (2)

In Your Town (1)
Jackknife Beat (7)
Just A Little Bit (4)
Just Hit Town (9)
Just The Smile (5)
Keychain (9)
Last Of The Independants (8)
Laundromat (1)
Let Me In (6)
Livin' Like A Trucker (3)
Lost At Sea (8)
Messin' With The Kid (1)
Million Miles Away (3,4)
Mississippi Sheiks (8)

Moonchild (7)
Off The Handle (9)
Out On The Western Plain (6)
Overnight Bag (8)
Philby (9)
Pistol Slapper Blues (1)
Public Enemy No. 1 (9)
Race The Breeze (2)
Secret Agent (7)
Seventh Son Of A Seventh Son (2)
Shadow Play (8)
Shin Kicker (8)

Sinner Boy (5)
Sleep On A Clothes-Line (3)
Souped-Up Ford (6)
Tattoo'd Lady (3,4)
There's A Light (6)
They Don't Make Them Like You Anymore (3)
Too Much Alcohol (4)
20:20 Vision (9)
Unmilitary Two-Step (4)
Used To Be (5)
Walk On Hot Coals (2,4)
Wayward Child (9)
Who's That Coming (3,4)

GALLERY
Detroit pop group led by singer/guitarist Jim Gold.

DEBUT DATE	PEAK POS	WKS CHR		ARTIST — Album Title	$	Label & Number
8/5/72	75	15		Nice To Be With You	$12	Sussex 7017

Big City Miss Ruth Ann 23
Gee Whiz

Ginger Haired Man
He Will Break Your Heart

I Believe In Music 22
Louisiana Line

Lover's Hideaway
Nice To Be With You 4

Someone
Sunday And Me

There's An Island
You're Always On My Mind

GALWAY, James
Classical flutist. Born on 12/8/39 in Belfast, Ireland. Prior to going solo in 1975, was a member and principal flutist of several orchestras including the London Symphony, the Royal Philharmonic and the Berlin Philharmonic.

DEBUT DATE	PEAK POS	WKS CHR		ARTIST — Album Title	$	Label & Number
3/3/79	153	5		1 Annie's Song and Other Galway Favorites .... [I]	$8	RCA 3061
				with the National Phil. Orch., Charles Gerhardt, conductor		
7/26/80	150	6		2 Sometimes When We Touch	$8	RCA 3628
				CLEO LAINE & JAMES GALWAY		
12/14/91	144	1		3 The Wind Beneath My Wings .... [I]	$12	RCA 60862

Angel Of Music (3)
Annie's Song (1)
Anyone Can Whistle (2)
Bachianas Brasileiras No. 5: Aria (1)
Basque (3)
Belfast Hornpipe (1)
Berceuse (1)
Bizet: Carmen Fantasy (1)

Brian Boru's March (1)
Ceremony, The (3)
Come To My Garden (3)
Consuelo's Love Theme (2)
Debussy: La Plus Que Lente (1)
Drifting, Dreaming (Gymnopedie No. 1) (2)

El Condor Pasa (If I Could) (3)
Fluter's Ball (2)
From A Distance (3)
How, Where, When? (3)
Irish Medley (3)
Keep Loving Me (2)
La Vie En Rose (3)
Le Basque (1)

Liebesfreud (1)
Like A Sad Song (2)
Lo! Hear The Gentle Lark (3)
Memory (3)
Mozart: Piano Sonata In C.K. 545 - Allegro (1)
Perhaps Love (2)
Play It Again, Sam (1)
Send In The Clowns (3)

Skylark (2)
Smoke Gets In Your Eyes (3)
Sometimes When We Touch (2)
Spanish Love Song (1)
Still Was The Night (2)
Tambourin (1)
Unchained Melody (3)
Wind Beneath My Wings (3)

Windmills Of Your Mind (3)

DEBUT DATE	PEAK POS	WKS CHR	G O L D	ARTIST — Album Title	$	Label & Number

GAMMA

Rock group formed by Ronnie Montrose after breakup of Montrose. Vocals by Davey Pattison. Drummer Denny Carmassi (ex-Montrose) later joined Heart in 1982.

9/22/79	131	17		1 Gamma 1	$15	Elektra 219
9/13/80	65	19		2 Gamma 2	$15	Elektra 288
3/20/82	72	12		3 Gamma 3	$15	Elektra 60034

Cat On A Leash (2)
Condition Yellow (3)
Dirty City (2)
Fight To The Finish (1)
Four Horsemen (2)

I'm Alive (1) 60
Mayday (2)
Mean Streak (2)
Mobile Devotion (3)
Modern Girl (3)

Moving Violation (3)
No Tears (1)
No Way Out (3)
Razor King (1)
Ready For Action (1)

Right The First Time (3) 77
Skin And Bone (2)
Solar Heat (1)
Something In The Air (2)
Stranger (3)

Third Degree (3)
Thunder And Lightning (1)
Voyager (2)
What's Gone Is Gone (3)
Wish I Was (1)

GANG OF FOUR

British new wave band formed in 1980 by lead singer Jon King and guitarist Andy Gill. Disbanded in 1984. King and Gill reunited in 1988.

6/6/81	190	2		1 Solid Gold	$8	Warner 3565
2/13/82	195	2		2 Another Day/Another Dollar ....[M]	$8	Warner 3646
6/26/82	175	3		3 Songs Of The Free	$8	Warner 23683
10/8/83	168	4		4 Hard	$8	Warner 23936

Arabic (4)
Call Me Up (3)
Capital (It Falls Us Now) (2)
Cheeseburger (1,2)
He'd Send In The Army (1)
History Of The World (3)
History's Bunk! (2)

Hole In The Wallet (1)
I Fled (4)
I Love A Man In A Uniform (3)
I Will Be A Good Boy (4)
If I Could Keep It For Myself (1)

In The Ditch (1)
Independence (4)
Is It Love (4)
It Don't Matter (4)
It Is Not Enough (3)
Life! It's A Shame (3)
Man With A Good Car (4)

Muscle For Brains (3)
Of The Instant (3)
Outside The Trains Don't
 Run On Time (1)
Paralysed (1)
Piece Of My Heart (4)
Republic, The (1)

Silver Lining (4)
To Hell With Poverty (2)
We Live As We Dream, Alone (3)
What We All Want (1,2)
Why Theory? (1)
Woman Town (4)

GANG STARR

Brooklyn-based rap duo: D.J. Premier (from Brooklyn) and G.U.R.U. (from Boston, name stands for Gifted Unlimited Rhymes Universal).

| 3/16/91 | 121 | 12 | | 1 Step In The Arena .... | $12 | Chrysalis 21798 |
| 5/23/92 | 65 | 10 | | 2 Daily Operation .... | $12 | Chrysalis 21910 |

As I Read My S-A (1)
B.Y.S. (2)
Beyond Comprehension (1)
Check The Technique (1)
Conspiracy (2)
Daily Operation (2)
Ex Girl To Next Girl (2)
Execution Of A Chump (No
 More Mr. Nice Guy Pt. 2) (1)

Flip The Script (1)
Form Of Intellect (1)
Game Plan (1)
Hardcore Composer (2)
Here Today, Gone Tomorrow
 (1)
I'm The Man (2)
Illest Brother (2)
Just To Get A Rep (1)

Lovesick (1)
Meaning Of The Name (1)
Much Too Much (Mack A
 Mil) (2)
Name Tag (Premier & The
 Guru) (1)
92 Interlude (2)
No Shame In My Game (1)
Place Where We Dwell (2)

Precisely The Right Rhymes
 (1)
Say Your Prayers (1)
Soliloquy Of Chaos (2)
Stay Tuned (1)
Step In The Arena (1)
Street Ministry (1)
Take A Rest (1)
Take It Personal (2)

Take Two And Pass (2)
2 Deep (2)
24-7/365 (2)
What You Want This Time?
 (1)
Who's Gonna Take The
 Weight? (1)

★★414★★ GAP BAND, The

Soul trio from Tulsa, Oklahoma consisting of brothers Charles, Ronnie and Robert Wilson. Named for three streets in Tulsa: Greenwood, Archer and Pine. Cousins of Bootsy Collins. Charles is part of the Eurythmics' backing band.

5/19/79	77	18		1 The Gap Band	$8	Mercury 3758
12/22/79+	42	28	●	2 The Gap Band II	$8	Mercury 3804
12/27/80+	16	37	▲	3 The Gap Band III	$8	Mercury 4003
6/12/82	14	52	▲	4 Gap Band IV	$8	Total Exp. 3001
9/10/83	28	43	●	5 Gap Band V - Jammin'	$8	Total Exp. 3004
1/19/85	58	23		6 Gap Band VI	$8	Total Exp. 5705
3/9/85	103	16		7 Gap Gold/Best of the Gap Band ....[G]	$8	Total Exp. 824343
2/1/86	159	15		8 Gap Band VII	$8	Total Exp. 5714
12/9/89+	189	7		9 Round Trip	$8	Capitol 90799

Addicted To Your Love (9)
All Of My Love (9)
Antidote (To Love) (9)
Are You Living (3)
Automatic Brain (8)
Baby Baba Boogie (1)
Beep A Freak (5)
Boys Are Back In Town (2)
Bumpin' Gum People (8)
**Burn Rubber (Why You
 Wanna Hurt Me)** (3,7) 84
Desire (8)
Disrespect (6)
Don't You Leave Me (6)

Early In The Morning
 (4,7) 24
Gash Gash Gash (3)
Going In Circles (8)
Got To Get Away (1)
Humpin' (3)
I Believe (6)
I Can Sing (1)
I Can't Get Over You (4)
I Don't Believe You Want To
 Get Up And Dance (Oops!)
 (2,7)
I Expect More (5)
I Found My Baby (6)
I Know We'll Make It (8)

I Like It (9)
I Need Your Love (8)
I Want A Real Love (8)
I'm Dreaming (9)
I'm In Love (1)
I'm Ready (If You're Ready)
 (5)
It's Our Duty (9)
Jam (9)
Jam (The Motha' (5)
Jammin' In America (5)
L'il Red Funkin' Hood (8)
Lonely Like Me (4)
Messin' With My Mind (1)
No Easy Out (9)

No Hiding Place (2)
Nothin' Comes To Sleepers
 (3)
Ooh, What A Feeling (8)
Open Up Your Mind (Wide)
 (1)
Outstanding (4,7) 51
Party Lights (2)
Party Train (5,7)
Season's No Reason To
 Change (4,7)
Shake (1,7)
Shake A Leg (5)
Smile (5)
Someday (5)

Stay With Me (4,7)
Steppin' (Out) (2)
Sun Don't Shine Everyday
 [includes 2 versions] (6)
Sweet Caroline (3)
Talkin' Back (4)
Video Junkie (6)
Way, The (3)
We Can Make It Alright (9)
Weak Spot (6)
Wednesday Lover (9)
When I Look In Your Eyes (3)
Where Are We Going? (5)
Who Do You Call (2)

Yearning For Your Love
 (3,7) 60
You Are My High (2)
You Can Count On Me (1)
**You Dropped A Bomb On
 Me** (4,7) 31
You're My Everything (5)
You're Something Special (5)

GARCIA, Jerry

Founder/lead guitarist of the Grateful Dead. Born on 8/1/42 in San Francisco. Prior to forming the Grateful Dead, played banjo in Mother McCree's Uptown Jug Champions. Produced and acted in the film *Hells Angels Forever*. Ben & Jerry's Cherry Garcia ice cream named after him.

1/29/72	35	14		1 Garcia	$30	Warner 2582
6/22/74	49	15		2 Garcia	$20	Round 102
2/14/76	42	14		3 Reflections	$20	Round 565
4/15/78	114	5		4 Cats Under The Stars	$8	Arista 4160
11/20/82	100	8		5 Run For The Roses	$8	Arista 9603
9/14/91	97	5		6 Jerry Garcia Band ....[L]	$19	Arista 18690 [2]

JERRY GARCIA BAND (includes John Kahn, Melvin Seals, David Kemper, Jackie LaBranch and Gloria Jones)

Bird Song (1)
Catfish John (3)
Cats Under The Stars (4)

Comes A Time (3)
Deal (1,6)
Dear Prudence (6)

Don't Let Go (6)
Down Home (4)
Eep Hour (1)

Evangeline (6)
Get Out Of My Life (6)
Gomorrah (4)

He Ain't Give You None (2)
I Saw Her Standing There (5)
I Shall Be Released (6)

I'll Take A Melody (3)
It Must Have Been The
 Roses (3)

DEBUT DATE	PEAK POS	WKS CHR	GOLD	ARTIST — Album Title	$	Label & Number

GARCIA, Jerry — Cont'd

Knockin' On Heaven's Door (5)
Late For Supper (1)
Leave The Little Girl Alone (5)
Let It Rock (2)
Let's Spend The Night Together (2)
Loser (1)
Love In The Afternoon (4)

Midnight Getaway (5)
Midnight Town (2)
Might As Well (3)
Mission In The Rain (3)
Mississippi Moon (2)
My Sisters And Brothers (6)
Night They Drove Old Dixie Down (6)
Odd Little Place (1)
Palm Sunday (4)

Rain (4)
Rhapsody In Red (4)
Rubin And Cherise (4)
Run For The Roses (5)
Russian Lullaby (2)
Senor (Tales Of Yankee Power) (6)
Simple Twist Of Fate (6)
Spidergawd (1)
Stop That Train (6)

Sugaree (1) *94*
Tangled Up In Blue (6)
That Lucky Old Sun (6)
That's What Love Will Make You Do (2)
They Love Each Other (3)
To Lay Me Down (1)
Tore Up Over You (3)
Turn On The Bright Lights (2)

Valerie (5)
Waiting For A Miracle (6)
Way You Do The Things You Do (6)
What Goes Around (2)
Wheel, The (1)
When The Hunter Gets Captured By The Game (2)
Without Love (5)

★★479★★ GARDNER, Dave
Comedian "Brother Dave"; born on 6/11/26 in Jackson, Tennessee. Now deceased.

6/20/60	5	69		1 Rejoice, Dear Hearts! ....[C]	$25	RCA 2083
8/29/60	5	56		2 Kick Thy Own Self ....[C]	$25	RCA 2239
9/18/61	15	30		3 Ain't That Weird? ....[C]	$25	RCA 2335
9/1/62	49	13		4 Did You Ever? ....[C]	$25	RCA 2498
3/9/63	52	10		5 All Seriousness Aside ....[C]	$25	RCA 2628
5/4/63	28	13		6 It Don't Make No Difference ....[C]	$25	Capitol 1867

no track titles listed on any of the albums above

GARFUNKEL, Art
Half of Simon & Garfunkel duo. Born on 10/13/42 in Queens, New York. Appeared in films *Catch 22*, *Carnal Knowledge* and *Bad Timing*. Has masters degree in mathematics from Columbia University.

9/29/73	5	25	●	1 Angel Clare	$12	Columbia 31474
10/25/75	7	28	▲	2 Breakaway	$12	Columbia 33700
2/4/78	19	16	●	3 Watermark	$12	Columbia 34975
4/7/79	67	14		4 Fate For Breakfast	$12	Columbia 35780
9/12/81	113	8		5 Scissors Cut	$8	Columbia 37392
4/16/88	134	8		6 Lefty	$8	Columbia 40942

All I Know (1) *9*
All My Love's Laughter (4)
And I Know (4)
Another Lullaby (1)
Barbara Allen (1)
Beyond The Tears (4)
Break Away (2) *39*
Bright Eyes (4)
Can't Turn My Heart Away (5)
Crying In My Sleep (3)
Disney Girls (2)
Do Space Men Pass Dead Souls On Their Way To The Moon? (medley) (1)

Down In The Willow Garden (1)
Feuilles-Oh (medley) (1)
Finally Found A Reason (4)
French Waltz (5)
Hang On In (5)
Heart In New York (5) *66*
I Believe (When I Fall In Love It Will Be Forever) (2)
I Have A Love (6)
I Only Have Eyes For You (2) *18*
I Shall Sing (1) *38*
I Wonder Why (6)
If Love Takes You Away (6)

In A Little While (I'll Be On My Way) (4)
In Cars (5)
King Of Tonga (5)
Looking For The Right One (2)
Love Is The Only Chain (6)
Marionette (3)
Mary Was An Only Child (1)
Miss You Nights (4)
Mr. Shuck 'N' Jive (3)
My Little Town [duet; Simon & Garfunkel] (2) *9*
99 Miles From L.A. (4)
Oh How Happy (4)

Old Man (1)
Paper Chase (3)
Promise, The (6)
Rag Doll (2)
Sail On A Rainbow (4)
Same Old Tears On A New Background (2)
Saturday Suit (3)
Scissors Cut (5)
She Moved Through The Fair (3)
Shine It On Me (3)
Since I Don't Have You (4) *53*
Slow Breakup (6)

So Easy To Begin (5)
So Much In Love (6)
Someone Else (1958) (3)
Take Me Away (4)
That's All I've Got To Say (5)
This Is The Moment (6)
Traveling Boy (1)
Up In The World (5)
Watermark (4)
Waters Of March (2)
(What A) Wonderful World (3) *17*
When A Man Loves A Woman (6)

When Someone Doesn't Want You (4)
Wooden Planes (3)
Woyaya (1)

★★284★★ GARLAND, Judy
Born Frances Gumm on 6/10/22 in Grand Rapids, Minnesota. Died on 1/22/69. Star of MGM film musicals from 1935-54. Most famous film role was Dorothy in 1939's *Wizard Of Oz*. Hosted own TV variety series, 1963-64. Married to director Vincente Minnelli; their daughter is Liza Minnelli.

10/29/55	5	7		1 Miss Show Business	$40	Capitol 676
11/10/56	17	5		2 Judy	$35	Capitol 734
6/17/57	17	3		3 Alone	$35	Capitol 835
7/31/61	1[13]	95	●	4 Judy At Carnegie Hall ....[L]	$35	Capitol 1569 [2]

1961 Grammy winner: Album of the Year

8/25/62	33	14		5 The Garland Touch	$30	Capitol 1710
5/11/63	45	6		6 I Could Go On Singing ....[S]	$30	Capitol 1861

Judy's first musical film role since 1954's *A Star Is Born*; includes 3 instrumentals by Mort Lindsey: "Overture," "Interlude: Matt's Dilemma" and "Helicopter Ride"

1/4/64	136	2		7 The Best Of Judy Garland ....[G]	$20	Decca 7172 [2]
9/4/65	41	14		8 "Live" At The London Palladium ....[L]	$20	Capitol 2295 [2]
				JUDY GARLAND & LIZA MINNELLI		
9/16/67	174	3		9 Judy Garland At Home At The Palace - Opening Night ....[L]	$15	ABC 620
8/16/69	161	3		10 Judy Garland's Greatest Hits ....[G]	$12	Decca 75150
				condensation of album #7 above		
6/9/73	164	8		11 "Live" At The London Palladium ....[R-L]	$10	Capitol 11191
				JUDY GARLAND & LIZA MINNELLI		
				condensation of album #8 above		

After You've Gone (1,4,8,11)
Almost Like Being In Love (medley) (4,9)
Alone Together (4)
Among My Souvenirs (3)
Any Place I Hang My Hat Is Home (2)
April Showers (3)
Blue Prelude (3)
Bob White (Whatcha Gonna Swing Tonight?) (medley) (8,9)
Boy Next Door (1,7,10)
Brotherhood Of Man (medley) (11)
But Not For Me (7)
By Myself (3,6)

Carolina In The Morning (1)
Chicago (4,8)
Come Rain Or Come Shine (2,4)
Comes Once In A Lifetime (5)
Danny Boy (1)
(Dear Mr. Gable) ...see: You Made Me Love You (I Didn't Want To Do It)
Dirty Hands, Dirty Face (2)
Do I Love You? (5)
Do It Again (4)
F.D.R. Jones (4)
Foggy Day (4)
For Me And My Gal (1,4,7,9,10)

Happiness Is A Thing Called Joe (1,5)
Happy New Year (3)
Have Yourself A Merry Little Christmas (7,10)
He's Got The Whole World In His Hands (8,11)
Hello Bluebird (4)
Hello, Dolly! (8,11)
Hooray For Love (medley) (8,11)
How About Me (3)
How About You (medley) (8,11)
How Long Has This Been Going On? (4)

I Am The Monarch Of The Sea (6)
I Can't Give You Anything But Love (4)
I Could Go On Singing [includes 2 versions] (6)
I Feel A Song Coming On (2,9)
I Get The Blues When It Rains (3)
I Happen To Like New York (5)
I Loved Him, But He Didn't Love Me (9)
I Never Knew (I Could Love Anybody Like I'm Loving You) (7)

I Will Come Back (2)
I'm Always Chasing Rainbows (7,10)
I'm Nobody's Baby (7,10)
If Love Were All (4)
In-Between (7)
It All Depends On You (medley) (8,11)
It Never Was You (6)
It's A Great Day For The Irish (8)
Jamboree Jones (medley) (9)
Judy At The Palace Medley (1,5)
Just A Memory (3)
Just Imagine (2)
Just You, Just Me (4)

Last Night When We Were Young (2)
Life Is Just A Bowl Of Cherries (2)
Little Girl Blue (3)
Love (7)
Lucky Day (2,5)
Make Someone Happy [solo: Judy] (8)
Man That Got Away (4,8,9,11)
Me And My Shadow (3)
Mean To Me (3)
Meet Me In St. Louis, Louis (7,10)
Memories Of You (2)
More Than You Know (5)

GARLAND, Judy — Cont'd

Music That Makes Me Dance [solo: Judy] (8)
Never Will I Marry [solo: Judy] (8)
Ol' Man River (medley) (9)
On The Atchison, Topeka And The Santa Fe (7,10)
On The Sunny Side Of The Street (7)
Our Love Affair (7)
Over The Rainbow (1,4,7,8,9,10,11)

Poor Little Rich Girl (7)
Pretty Girl Milking Her Cow (1,7,10)
Puttin' On The Ritz (4)
Rock-A-Bye Your Baby With A Dixie Melody (1,4,9)
'S Wonderful (medley) [solo: Judy] (8,11)
San Francisco (4,8)
Smile [solo: Judy] (8)
Stormy Weather (4)
Swanee (4,8,11)

Sweet Danger (5)
Sweet Sixteen (7)
That Old Black Magic (7)
That's Entertainment (4,9)
This Can't Be Love (medley) (4,9)
This Is The Time Of The Evening (medley) (1)
Together (Wherever We Go) (8,9,11)
Trolley Song (1,4,7,9,10)

We Could Make Such Beautiful Music (medley) (8)
What Now My Love (8,9,11)
When The Saints Go Marching In (medley) (8,11)
When You Wore A Tulip (And I Wore A Big Red Rose) (7,10)
When You're Smiling (The Whole World Smiles With You) (4)

While We're Young (medley) (1)
Who Cares? (So Long As You Care For Me) (4)
You And The Night And The Music (medley) [solo: Judy] (8,11)
You Go To My Head (4)
You Made Me Love You (I Didn't Want To Do It) (1,4,7,9,10)
You'll Never Walk Alone (5,7)

You're Nearer (4)
Zing! Went The Strings Of My Heart (4,7)

GARNER, Erroll

Jazz pianist/composer born on 6/15/21 in Pittsburgh; died on 1/2/77. No formal training on piano; could not read music. Composer of "Misty," later a hit for Johnny Mathis and others.

DEBUT DATE	PEAK POS	WKS CHR	GOLD	ARTIST — Album Title	$	Label & Number
11/25/57	16	2		1 Other Voices ....[I]	$20	Columbia 1014
3/10/58	12	7		2 Concert By The Sea ....[I-L]	$20	Columbia 883
				recorded in 1956 in Carmel, California		
6/26/61	35	31		3 Dreamstreet ....[I]	$15	ABC-Para. 365
7/6/63	94	6		4 One World Concert ....[I-L]	$15	Reprise 6080
				recorded at Seattle World's Fair		

April In Paris (2)
Autumn Leaves (2)
Blue Lou (3)
Come Rain Or Come Shine (3)
Dancing Tambourine (4)
Dreamstreet (3)
Dreamy (1)
Erroll's Theme (2)

Happiness Is A Thing Called Joe (4)
How Could You Do A Thing Like That To Me (2)
I Didn't Know What Time It Was (1)
I'll Remember April (2)
I'm Getting Sentimental Over You (3)

It Might As Well Be Spring (1)
It's All Right With Me (2)
Just One Of Those Things (3)
Lady Is A Tramp (3)
Lover Come Back To Me (4)
Mack The Knife (4)
Mambo Carmel (2)
Mambo Gotham (3)

Misty (1,4)
Moment's Delight (1)
Movin' Blues (4)
Oklahoma! Medley (3)
On The Street Where You Live (1)
Other Voices (1)
Red Top (2)
Solitaire (1)

Sweet And Lovely (4)
Sweet Lorraine (3)
Teach Me Tonight (2)
Thanks For The Memory (4)
They Can't Take That Away From Me (2)
This Is Always (1)
Very Thought Of You (1)
Way You Look Tonight (4)

When You're Smiling (The Whole World Smiles With You) (3)
Where Or When (2)

GARNETT, Gale

Born on 7/17/42 in Auckland, New Zealand. Came to the U.S. in 1951. Made singing debut in 1960. Worked as an actress from age 15. Appeared on many TV shows including *Hawaiian Eye* and *Bonanza*.

DEBUT DATE	PEAK POS	WKS CHR	GOLD	ARTIST — Album Title	$	Label & Number
9/26/64	43	22		My Kind Of Folk Songs	$15	RCA 2833

Fly Bird
I Came To The City
I Know You Rider

Little Man, Nine Years Old
Malaika

Oh Brandy Leave Me Alone
Pretty Boy

Prism Song
Sleep You Now

Take This Hammer
Wanderin'

We'll Sing In The Sunshine 4

GARRETT, Leif

Born on 11/8/61 in Hollywood. Began film career in 1969. Appeared in all three *Walking Tall* films, *Macon County Line, Bob and Carol and Ted and Alice* and *The Outsiders*.

DEBUT DATE	PEAK POS	WKS CHR	GOLD	ARTIST — Album Title	$	Label & Number
12/17/77+	37	24	●	1 Leif Garrett..	$10	Atlantic 19152
11/25/78+	34	19	●	2 Feel The Need	$8	Scotti Br. 7100
12/15/79+	129	22		3 Same Goes For You	$8	Scotti Br. 16008
12/12/81+	185	7		4 My Movie Of You	$8	Scotti Br. 37625

Bad To Me (1)
California Girls (1)
Every Night With You (4)
Feel The Need (2) 57
Feels So Right (4)
Forget About You (2)
Fun, Fun, Fun (2)
Give In (3)
Groovin' (2)
Guilty (3)

Hungry For Your Love Tonight (3)
I Don't Want To Want You (4)
I Wanna Share A Dream With You (1)
I Was Looking For Someone To Love (3) 78
I Was Made For Dancin' (2) 10
If I Were A Carpenter (3)

Johnny B. Goode (1)
Just Like A Brother (4)
Kicks (3)
Little Things You Do (3)
Living Without Your Love (4)
Memorize Your Number (3) 60
Missin' You (4)
Mo Mo Way (Momoe) (4)
Moonlight Dancin' (3)

Movie Of You (4)
Once A Fool (2)
Put Your Head On My Shoulder (1) 58
Runaround Sue (1) 13
Runaway Rita (4) 84
Same Goes For You (3)
Santa Monica Bay (4)
Sheila (2)
Singin' In The Rain (3)

Special Kind Of Girl (1)
Surfin' USA (1) 20
That's All (1)
This Time (2)
Uptown Girl (4)
Wanderer, The (1) 49
When I Think Of You (2,3) 78

GARRETT, Tommy, 50 Guitars Of

A&R man/producer for Liberty, 1958-66, known as "Snuff" Garrett. Born in 1939 in Dallas. 50 Guitars featured guitar solos by Tommy Tedesco.

DEBUT DATE	PEAK POS	WKS CHR	GOLD	ARTIST — Album Title	$	Label & Number
12/18/61+	36	6		1 50 Guitars Go South Of The Border.................................[I]	$10	Liberty 14005
12/14/63+	94	8		2 Maria Elena ....[I]	$10	Liberty 14030
6/13/64	142	2		3 50 Guitars Go Italiano ....[I]	$10	Liberty 14028
11/26/66	99	5		4 50 Guitars In Love ....[I]	$10	Liberty 14037
7/8/67	168	3		5 More 50 Guitars In Love ....[I]	$10	Liberty 14039
5/3/69	147	9		6 The Best Of The 50 Guitars Of Tommy Garrett..........................[G-I]	$8	Liberty 14045

Adios (1)
Al-Di-La (3)
Amapola (2)
Anema E Core (3)
Anna (2)
Arrivederci, Roma (3)
Be Mine Tonight (1)
Besame Mucho (1)
Brazil (1)
Breeze And I (2)
Cherry Pink And Apple Blossom White (2)
Ciao, Ciao Bambina (3)
Come Back To Sorrento (3)

Come Closer To Me (1)
Courtin' (5)
Dr. Zhivago ..see: Lara's Theme
Dream Theme (4)
El Choclo (2)
El Relicario (6)
Escape To Love (4)
Flamenco Love (4)
Frenesi (1)
Girl From Ipanema (6)
Good, The Bad, And The Ugly (6)
Granada (1)

Guadalajara (1,6)
Guantanamera (6)
Guitar Serenade (5)
Hung Up In Your Eyes (5)
I Left My Heart In San Francisco (4)
If You Go Away (5)
Jungle Drums (2)
La Bamba (1,6)
La Negra (2)
La Strada, Love Theme From (3)
La Virgen De La Macarena (1)

Lara's Theme (4)
Love Me With All Your Heart (6)
Malaguena (6)
Man And A Woman (5)
Maria Elena (2,6)
Mattinata (4)
Mexican Hat Dance (6)
Michelle (4)
Moon Guitar (4)
My Cup Runneth Over (5)
My Love, Forgive Me (5)
My Special Angel (5)
Non Dimenticar (3)

O Sole Mio (3)
Old Cape Cod (5)
Our Day Will Come (4)
Perfidia (1)
Poinciana (4)
Return To Me (3)
Shadow Of Your Smile (4)
Softly, As I Leave You (5)
Someone In Love, Theme For (5)
Somewhere, My Love ..see: Lara's Theme
South Of The Border (1)
Spanish Eyes (6)

Strangers In The Night (4)
Summertime In Venice (4)
Sure Gonna Miss Her (4)
Taboo (2)
Volare (3)
What Now My Love (4)
Without You (2)
You Belong To My Heart (1)
You Don't Have To Say You Love Me (4)
You've Lost That Lovin' Feelin' (5)

★★215★★ GARY, John

Born in Watertown, New York on 11/29/32. Singer on Don McNeill's radio program, *Breakfast Club*.

DEBUT DATE	PEAK POS	WKS CHR	GOLD	ARTIST — Album Title	$	Label & Number
11/9/63+	19	63		1 Catch A Rising Star	$10	RCA 2745
2/22/64	16	46		2 Encore..	$10	RCA 2804
8/15/64	42	28		3 So Tenderly	$10	RCA 2922

GARY, John — Cont'd

DEBUT DATE	PEAK POS	WKS CHR	GOLD	ARTIST — Album Title	$	Label & Number
11/14/64	141	4	4	David Merrick presents Hits From His Broadway Hits	$15	RCA 2947

JOHN GARY/ANN-MARGRET
Merrick is a leading Broadway producer; includes "As Long As He Needs Me," "Is It Really Me?," "Love Makes The World Go 'Round" and "Our Language Of Love" by Ann-Margret; "Hello, Dolly!," "Comes Once In A Lifetime," "Make Someone Happy" and "Take Me Along" by Merrill Staton Voices

DEBUT DATE	PEAK POS	WKS CHR	GOLD	ARTIST — Album Title	$	Label & Number
1/23/65	17	33	5	A Little Bit Of Heaven	$10	RCA 2994
7/24/65	11	29	6	The Nearness Of You	$10	RCA 3349
10/30/65	21	25	7	Your All-Time Favorite Songs	$10	RCA 3411
3/12/66	51	20	8	Your Choice	$10	RCA 3501
7/9/66	65	12	9	Your All-Time Country Favorites	$10	RCA 3570
10/8/66	73	17	10	A Heart Filled With Song	$10	RCA 3666
2/11/67	117	14	11	Especially For You	$10	RCA 3695
5/13/67	90	11	12	Spanish Moonlight	$10	RCA 3785
10/7/67	76	19	13	The John Gary Carnegie Hall Concert [L]	$10	RCA 1139
4/19/69	192	3	14	Love Of A Gentle Woman	$10	RCA 4134

All The Things You Are (7)
And This Is My Beloved (2)
Any Time (9)
Anyone Would Love You [solo: John] (4)
Anywhere I Wander (3)
As Time Goes By (7)
Autumn Leaves (7)
Be My Love (10)
Beautiful (6)
Beautiful Thing (2)
Because of You (10)
Believe Me If All Those Endearing Young Charms (5)
Black Is The Color Of My True Love's Hair (11)
Brown Eyed Baby Boy (3)
Charade (8)
Cockles And Mussels (Molly Malone) (5)
Cold, Cold Heart (9)
Come To Me, Bend To Me (3)
Cu-Cu-Rru-Cu-Cu, Paloma (12)
Danny Boy (3)
Dear Heart (4)
Deep Purple (7)
Don't Blame Me (8)
Ebb Tide (1)
Fanny [solo: John] (4)
Far Away Places (7)
Fascination (7)
Fly Me To The Moon (In Other Words) (10)
Galway Bay (5)

Georgia On My Mind (8)
Granada (Fantasia Espagnola) (12)
Guantanamera (12)
Half As Much (1)
Have I Told You Lately That I Love You? (9)
Hawaiian Wedding Song (Ke Kali Nei Au) (6)
He'll Have To Go (9)
Here I'll Stay (3)
Here In My Heart (14)
How Are Things In Glocca Morra (3)
How Deep Is The Ocean (How High Is The Sky) (8)
How I Learned To Sing Medley (13)
I Ain't Down Yet (3)
I Can't Stop Loving You (9)
I Left My Heart In San Francisco (7)
I Really Don't Want To Know (9)
I Wish You Love (Que Reste-t-il De Nos Amours) (6)
I'll Be Seeing You (8)
I'll Never Fall In Love Again (14)
I'll Remember Her (8)
I'll Rock You In My Mind (14)
I'll Take You Home Again, Kathleen (5)
I'm Sitting On Top Of The World (13)

If (2)
If Ever I Would Leave You (10)
If You Ever Leave Me (14)
If You Go Away (Ne Me Quitte Pas) (14)
If You Love Me (Really Love Me) (3)
Impossible Dream (The Quest) (13)
(It's Been) Grand Knowing You (2)
Kathleen Mavourneen (5)
La Malaguena (Son Huasteco) (12,13)
Let There Be Peace On Earth (Let It Begin With Me) (11)
Little Bit Of Heaven (5)
Love Is A Many Splendored Thing (10)
Love Is Here To Stay (8)
Love Me Tender (3)
Love Me With All Your Heart (Cuando Calienta El Sol) (12)
Love Of A Gentle Woman (14)
Luck Be A Lady (8)
Macushla (5)
Made For Each Other (Tu Felicidad) (12)
Maria Elena (12)
Medley (Finale) (13)
Melodie D'Amour (Melody Of Love) (2)

Michelle (11)
More (1,13)
Most Beautiful Girl In The World (13)
Mother Machree (5)
My Cup Runneth Over (13)
My Foolish Heart (4)
My Kind Of Girl (1)
My Wild Irish Rose (5)
Nearness Of You (6)
Night And Day (7)
No Arms Can Ever Hold You (Like These Arms Of Mine) (10)
Oh, Lonesome Me (9)
Ol' Man River (2)
On The Street Where You Live (6)
Once Upon A Summertime (La Valse Des Lilas) (11)
Once Upon A Time (1)
Opportunity (Poem) (13)
Perfect Day (11)
Poinciana (12)
Possum Song (3)
Red Rosey Bush (3)
Scarborough Fair (14)
Shadow Of Your Smile (10,13)
She Loves Me (13)
Small World [solo: John] (4)
Smilin' Through (3)
Smoke Gets In Your Eyes (7)
Softly, As I Leave You (6)
Some Enchanted Evening (7)

Someday (You'll Want Me To Want You) (9)
Something Simple (3)
Somewhere (8)
Somewhere Along The Way (1)
Song Of The Cuckoo (3)
Sound of Music (6)
Spanish Moonlight (12)
Star Dust (7)
Stella By Starlight (2)
Straight Life (14)
Stranger In Paradise (2)
Sunrise, Sunset (13)
Take Me In Your Arms (2)
Take My Love (3)
Tammy (8)
Ten Girls Ago (3)
Tender Is The Night (2)
Tenderly (3)
Tennessee Waltz (9)
Thank Heaven For Little Girls (1)
That's An Irish Lullaby (Too-Ra-Loo-Ra-Loo-Ral) (5)
They Don't Make Love Like They Used To (14)
This Is All I Ask (1)
'Til Tomorrow (11)
Till The Birds Sing In The Morning (1)
Till There Was You (11)
Till We Meet Again (11)
Time After Time (6)
Tonight (7)

Try To Remember (11)
Two Different Worlds (11)
Unchained Melody (1)
What Kind Of Fool Am I? [solo: John] (4)
What Now My Love (10)
When Irish Eyes Are Smiling (5)
While We're Young (10)
Who Can I Turn To (When Nobody Needs Me) (6)
Windmills Of Your Mind (14)
Without A Song (10)
Without You (Tres Palabras) (12)
Yellow Bird (1)
Yesterday (10)
You Belong To My Heart (Solamente Una Vez) (12)
You Don't Have To Say You Love Me (14)
You Don't Know Me (9)
You Stepped Out Of A Dream (6)
You'll Never Walk Alone (7)
Young At Heart (11)
Younger Than Springtime (8)
Your Cheatin' Heart (1)
Yours (Quiereme Mucho) (12)

GARY'S GANG

Septet from Queens, New York, led by Gary Turnier (drums) and Eric Matthew (guitar).

DEBUT DATE	PEAK POS	WKS CHR	GOLD	ARTIST — Album Title	$	Label & Number
3/31/79	42	10		Keep On Dancin'	$10	Columbia 35793

Do It At The Disco
Keep On Dancin' 41

Let's Lovedance Tonight
Party Tonight!

Showtime

You'll Always Be My Everything

GASCA, Luis

Jazz trumpet player. Born on 3/3/40 in Houston. Worked with Perez Prado, Stan Kenton, Maynard Ferguson, Lionel Hampton, Janis Joplin, Woody Herman, Santana, Count Basie and others.

DEBUT DATE	PEAK POS	WKS CHR	GOLD	ARTIST — Album Title	$	Label & Number
5/27/72	195	3		Luis Gasca [I]	$10	Blue Thumb 37

with Joe Henderson (sax), Carlos Santana (guitar) and Stanley Clarke (bass)

La Raza
Little Mama

Spanish Gypsy
Street Dude

GATES, David

Born on 12/11/40 in Tulsa, Oklahoma. Began career as a session musician, then a songwriter/producer before becoming the lead singer of Bread. Wrote The Murmaids' hit "Popsicles & Icicles."

DEBUT DATE	PEAK POS	WKS CHR	GOLD	ARTIST — Album Title	$	Label & Number
10/27/73	107	10	1	First	$12	Elektra 75066
2/15/75	102	9	2	Never Let Her Go	$12	Elektra 1028
8/12/78	165	4	3	Goodbye Girl	$10	Elektra 148

Angel (2)
Ann (1,3)
California Lady (3)
Chain Me (2)
Clouds (medley) (1,3) 47

Do You Believe He's Comin' (1)
Drifter (3)
Goodbye Girl (3) 15
Greener Days (2)

He Don't Know How To Love You (3)
Help Is On The Way (1)
Light Of My Life (2)
Lorilee (1,3)
Never Let Her Go (2,3) 29

Overnight Sensation (3)
Part Time Love (2,3)
Playin' On My Guitar (2)
Rain (medley) (1,3)
Sail Around The World (1) 50

Sight & Sound (1)
Soap (I Use The) (1)
Someday (2)
Strangers (2)
Sunday Rider (1,3)
Took The Last Train (3) 30

Watch Out (2)

GATLIN, Larry

Country singer/songwriter/guitarist. Born on 5/2/48 in Seminole, Texas. Worked as a staff writer for Dottie West; also wrote for Elvis Presley, Tom Jones, Kris Kristofferson and Glen Campbell. His brothers Steve (b: 4/4/51) and Rudy (b: 8/20/52) joined Larry after finishing college. Own ABC-TV special in 1981.

DEBUT DATE	PEAK POS	WKS CHR	GOLD	ARTIST — Album Title	$	Label & Number
4/1/78	175	5	1	Love Is Just A Game	$10	Monument 7616

GATLIN, Larry — Cont'd

DEBUT DATE	PEAK POS	WKS CHR	GOLD	ARTIST — Album Title	$	Label & Number
7/22/78	140	8		2 Oh! Brother	$10	Monument 7626
12/23/78+	171	9	●	3 Larry Gatlin's Greatest Hits ..... [G]	$10	Monument 7628

LARRY GATLIN & THE GATLIN BROTHERS BAND:

DEBUT DATE	PEAK POS	WKS CHR	GOLD	ARTIST — Album Title	$	Label & Number
11/17/79+	102	16	●	4 Straight Ahead	$8	Columbia 36250
11/1/80	118	4		5 Help Yourself	$8	Columbia 36582
10/17/81	184	2		6 Not Guilty	$8	Columbia 37464

All The Gold In California (4)
Alleluia (1)
Anything But Leavin' (1)
Bitter They Are, Harder They Fall (1)
Broken Lady (3)
Can't Cry Anymore (4)
Can't Take It With You (6)
Cold Day In Hell (2)
Daytime Heroes (5)
Delta Dirt (3) *84*
Do It Again Tonight (2,3)
Everything I Know About Cheatin' (2)
Everytime A Plane Flies Over Our House (1)
Good Wilbur (4)
Gypsy Flower Child (4)
Hard Workin' Hands (6)
Heart, The (3)
Help Yourself To Me (5)
Hold Me Closer (4)
How Much Is A Man Supposed To Take (4)
I Don't Wanna Cry (1,3)
I Just Wish You Were Someone I Love (1,3)
I Still Don't Love You Anymore (5)
I've Done Enough Dyin' Today (2)
I've Got You (2)
If Practice Makes Perfect (1)
In Like With Each Other (6)
It Don't Get No Better Than This (5)
It's Love At Last (1)
Kiss It All Goodbye (1)
L.A. You're A Killer (2)
Love Is Just A Game (1,3)
Midnight Choir (Mogen David) (4)
Must Be All The Same To You (5)
My Last Love Song (6)
Night Time Magic (2,3)
Nothin' You Do (2)
Piece By Piece (4)
Rain (6)
She Used To Sing On Sunday (6)
Someone Else's Day (6)
Songwriters Trilogy (5)
Standin' By Me (2)
Statues Without Hearts (3)
Steps (1)
Straight To My Heart (5)
Sweet Becky Walker (3)
Take Me To Your Lovin' Place (5)
Taking Somebody With Me When I Fall (4)
Tomorrow (1)
Until She Said Goodbye (5)
Way I Did Before (4)
We're Number One (4)
What Are We Doin' Lonesome (6)
Wind Is Bound To Change (5)
You Happened To Me (2)
You Wouldn't Know Love (6)

GATTON, Danny
Rock 'n' roll guitarist from Southeast Washington, D.C. Born in 1945.

DEBUT DATE	PEAK POS	WKS CHR	GOLD	ARTIST — Album Title	$	Label & Number
4/27/91	121	4		88 Elmira St. ..... [I]	$12	Elektra 61032

Blues Newburg
Elmira St. Boogie
Fandingus
Funky Mama
In My Room
Muthaship
Pretty Blue
Quiet Village
Red Label
Simpsons, The
Slidin' Home

★★50★★ GAYE, Marvin
Born Marvin Pentz Gay, Jr. on 4/2/39 in Washington, D.C. Sang in his father's Apostolic church. In vocal groups the Rainbows and Marquees. Joined Harvey Fuqua in the re-formed Moonglows. To Detroit in 1960. Session work as a drummer at Motown; married to Berry Gordy's sister Anna, 1961-75. First recorded under own name for Tamla in 1961. In seclusion for several months following the death of Tammi Terrell, 1970. Problems with drugs and the IRS led to his moving to Europe for three years. Fatally shot by his father after a quarrel on 4/1/84 in Los Angeles. Inducted into the Rock and Roll Hall of Fame in 1987.

DEBUT DATE	PEAK POS	WKS CHR	GOLD	ARTIST — Album Title	$	Label & Number
5/16/64	42	16		1 Together	$30	Motown 613

MARVIN GAYE & MARY WELLS

DEBUT DATE	PEAK POS	WKS CHR	GOLD	ARTIST — Album Title	$	Label & Number
5/30/64	72	14		2 Marvin Gaye/Greatest Hits ..... [G]	$25	Tamla 252
2/27/65	128	10		3 How Sweet It Is To Be Loved By You	$25	Tamla 258
7/16/66	118	10		4 Moods Of Marvin Gaye	$25	Tamla 266
9/30/67	178	5		5 Marvin Gaye/Greatest Hits, Vol. 2 ..... [G]	$20	Tamla 278
10/7/67	69	44		6 United *	$15	Tamla 277
9/21/68	60	21		7 You're All I Need *	$15	Tamla 284
11/2/68+	63	27		8 In The Groove	$15	Tamla 285
6/14/69	33	18		9 M.P.G.	$15	Tamla 292
6/14/69	183	7		10 Marvin Gaye And His Girls ..... [K]	$15	Tamla 293

with Tammi Terrell, Mary Wells and Kim Weston

DEBUT DATE	PEAK POS	WKS CHR	GOLD	ARTIST — Album Title	$	Label & Number
10/18/69	184	2		11 Easy *	$15	Tamla 294

***MARVIN GAYE & TAMMI TERRELL**

DEBUT DATE	PEAK POS	WKS CHR	GOLD	ARTIST — Album Title	$	Label & Number
11/1/69+	189	3		12 That's The Way Love Is	$15	Tamla 299
6/13/70	171	3		13 Marvin Gaye & Tammi Terrell Greatest Hits ..... [G]	$12	Tamla 302
11/7/70	117	6		14 Marvin Gaye Super Hits ..... [G]	$12	Tamla 300
6/12/71	6	53		15 **What's Going On**	$12	Tamla 310
12/30/72+	14	21		16 Trouble Man ..... [S-I]	$12	Tamla 322

includes 1 vocal by Marvin

DEBUT DATE	PEAK POS	WKS CHR	GOLD	ARTIST — Album Title	$	Label & Number
9/15/73	2¹	61		17 Let's Get It On	$12	Tamla 329
11/17/73	26	47		18 Diana & Marvin	$12	Motown 803

DIANA ROSS & MARVIN GAYE

DEBUT DATE	PEAK POS	WKS CHR	GOLD	ARTIST — Album Title	$	Label & Number
4/20/74	61	29		19 Marvin Gaye Anthology ..... [G]	$18	Motown 791 [3]
7/13/74	8	28		20 **Marvin Gaye Live!** ..... [L]	$12	Tamla 333
4/3/76	4	28		21 **I Want You**	$10	Tamla 342
10/2/76	44	8		22 Marvin Gaye's Greatest Hits ..... [G]	$10	Tamla 348
4/2/77	3	26		23 **Marvin Gaye Live At The London Palladium** ..... [L]	$12	Tamla 352 [2]
1/6/79	26	21		24 Here, My Dear	$12	Tamla 364 [2]
2/7/81	32	17		25 In Our Lifetime	$8	Tamla 374
11/20/82	7	41	▲²	26 **Midnight Love**	$8	Columbia 38197
10/22/83+	80	16		27 Every Great Motown Hit Of Marvin Gaye ..... [G]	$8	Motown 6058
6/8/85	41	15		28 Dream Of A Lifetime ..... [K]	$8	Columbia 39916

contains previously released material; 6 tracks from the 1970s; 2 tracks from 1983

DEBUT DATE	PEAK POS	WKS CHR	GOLD	ARTIST — Album Title	$	Label & Number
5/3/86	193	2		29 Motown Remembers Marvin Gaye ..... [E]	$8	Tamla 6172

previously unreleased material recorded from 1963-72

Abraham, Martin And John (12)
After The Dance (21,22) *74*
After The Lights Go Down Low (1)
Ain't It Funny (How Things Turn Around) (28)
Ain't No Mountain High Enough (6,13,19,23) *19*
Ain't Nothing Like The Real Thing (7,13,19,23,27) *8*
Ain't That Peculiar (4,5,14,19,23) *8*
All The Way Around (21,23)
Anger (24)
Anna's Song (24)
Baby Don't You Do It (3,5,14,19) *27*
Baby (Don't You Leave Me) (29)
Baby Don'tcha Worry (7)
Baby I Need Your Loving (11)
Baby I'm Glad That Things Worked Out So Well (29)
Break In (Police Shoot Big) (16)
California Soul (11) *56*
Can I Get A Witness (2,14,19,20,22) *22*
Chained (8,14,19) *32*
Change What You Can (8)
Cleo's Apartment (16)
Cloud Nine (12)
Come Get To This (17,23) *21*
Come Live With Me Angel (21)
Come On And See Me (7)
Dark Side Of The World (29)
Deed I Do (1,10)
Deep In It (16)
Distant Lover (17,20,22,23,27) *28*
Don't Knock My Love (18) *46*
Don't Mess With Mister "T" (16)
Don't You Miss Me A Little Bit Baby (12)
Dream Of A Lifetime (28)
End Of Our Road (9,14,19) *40*
Every Now And Then (8)
Everybody Needs Love (24)
Falling In Love Again (19)
Far Cry (25)
Feel All My Love Inside (21)
Flyin' High (In The Friendly Sky) (15)
Forever (3,5,19)
Funk Me (25)
Funky Space Reincarnation (24)
Give A Little Love (6)
Give In, You Just Can't Win (7)
God Is Love (15,23)
Gonna Give Her All The Love I've Got (12) *67*

GAYE, Marvin — Cont'd

Gonna Keep On Tryin' 'Till I Win Your Love (12)
Good Lovin' Ain't Easy To Come By (10,11,13,19) **30**
Got To Give It Up (Pt. I) (23,27) **1**
Groovin' (12)
Heavy Love Affair (25)
Hello There Angel (2)
Here, My Dear (24)
Hey Diddle Diddle (4,5)
Hitch Hike (2,14,19,23) **30**
Hold Me Oh My Darling (6,13)
How Can I Forget (12,19) **41**
How Sweet It Is To Be Loved By You (3,5,14,19,20,22,23,27) **6**
How You Gonna Keep It (After You Get It) (11)
I Can't Believe You Love Me (11)
I Can't Help But Love You (7,10)
I Got To Get To California (9)
I Gotta Have Your Lovin' (29)
I Heard It Through The Grapevine (8,14,19,22,23,27) **1**
(I Love You) For Sentimental Reasons (1)
I Met A Little Girl (24)
I Wanna Be Where You Are (21)
I Want You (21,22) **15**
I Want You 'Round (10)
I Wish It Would Rain (12)
I Worry 'Bout You (14)
I'll Be Doggone (4,5,14,19,20) **8**

I'll Never Stop Loving You Baby (7)
I'm Crazy 'Bout My Baby (2) **77**
I'm Falling In Love With You (18)
I'm Going Home (29)
I'm In Love With You (29)
I'm Your Puppet (11)
If I Could Build My Whole World Around You (6,13,19,27) **10**
If I Should Die Tonight (17)
If This World Were Mine (6,13,19) **68**
In Our California (18)
Include Me In Your Life (18)
Inner City Blues (Make Me Wanna Holler) (15,19,20,23,27) **9**
Is That Enough (24)
It Don't Take Much To Keep Me (9)
It Hurt Me Too (2)
It Takes Two (10,19,23) **14**
It's A Bitter Pill To Swallow (9)
It's Got To Be A Miracle (This Thing Called Love) (10)
It's Love I Need (8)
It's Madness (28)
Jan (20)
Joy (26)
Just Like A Man (29)
Just Say, Just Say (18)
Just To Keep You Satisfied (17)
Keep Gettin' It On (17)
Keep On Lovin' Me Honey (7,13) **24**

Late Late Show (1)
Let's Get It On (17,20,22,23,27) **1**
Life Is A Gamble (16)
Life Is For Learning (25)
Life's Opera (28)
Little Darling, I Need You (4,5,19,23) **47**
Little Ole Boy, Little Ole Girl (6,10)
Lonely Lover (29)
Love Me Now Or Love Me Later (25)
Love Party (25)
Love Twins (18)
Love Woke Me Up This Morning (11)
Loving And Affection (29)
Loving You Is Sweeter Than Ever (8)
Masochistic Beauty (28)
Me And My Lonely Room (3)
Memories (9)
Memory Chest (7)
Mercy Mercy Me (The Ecology) (15,19,22,27) **4**
Midnight Lady (26)
More, More, More (11)
More Than A Heart Can Stand (9)
My Love Is Waiting (26)
My Mistake (Was To Love You) (18) **19**
Need Somebody (3)
Need Your Lovin' (Want You Back) (3)
Night Life (4)
No Good Without You (3)
No Greater Love (29)
No Time For Tears (12)
Now That You've Won Me (3)
Oh How I'd Miss You (6)

Once Upon A Time (1,10,19) **19**
One For My Baby (And One For The Road) (4)
One More Heartache (4,5,19) **29**
One Of These Days (2,3)
Onion Song (11,13) **50**
Only A Lonely Man Would Know (9)
Please Don't Stay (Once You Go Away) (17)
Pledging My Love (18)
Poor Abbey Walsh (16)
Praise (25)
Pretty Little Baby (5,19) **25**
Pride And Joy (2,14,19,23) **10**
Right On (15)
Rockin' After Midnight (26)
Sad Wedding (6)
Sanctified Lady (28)
Sandman (2)
Satisfied Feelin' (11)
Savage In The Sack (28)
Save The Children (15,19,23)
Seek And You Shall Find (9)
Sexual Healing (26) **3**
Since I Had You (21,23)
So Long (12)
Some Kind Of Wonderful (8)
Somethin' Stupid (6)
Soon I'll Be Loving You Again (21)
Sparrow (24)
Squeeze Me (6)
Stepping Closer To Your Heart (3)
Stop, Look, Listen (To Your Heart) (18)
Stubborn Kind Of Fellow (2,14,19,20,23) **46**

Symphony (28)
'T' Plays It Cool (16)
'T' Stands For Trouble (16)
Take This Heart Of Mine (4,5,19) **44**
Taking My Time (2)
Tear It On Down (8)
That's How It Is (Since You've Been Gone) (7)
That's The Way It Goes (29)
That's The Way Love Is (9,12,14,19,27) **7**
There Goes Mister 'T' (16)
There Goes My Baby (8)
Third World Girl (26)
This Magic Moment (9)
Time To Get It Together (24)
Together (1,10)
Too Busy Thinking About My Baby (9,14,19,23,27) **4**
Trouble Man (16,19,20,22,23,27) **7**
Trouble Man, Theme From (16)
Try It Baby (3,5,14,19,20) **15**
Try My True Love (9)
Turn On Some Music (26)
Two Can Have A Party (6)
Until I Met You (1)
What Good Am I Without You (10,19) **61**
What You Gave Me (11,13) **49**
What's Going On (15,19,20,22,23,27) **2**
What's Happening Brother (15)
What's The Matter With You Baby (1,10,19) **17**

When Did You Stop Loving Me, When Did I Stop Loving You (24)
When Love Comes Knocking At My Heart (7)
Wholly Holy (15)
World Is Rated X (29)
Yesterday (12)
You (8,14,19,23) **34**
You Ain't Livin' Till You're Lovin' (7,13)
You Are Everything (18)
You Came A Long Way From St. Louis (1)
You Can Leave, But It's Going To Cost You (24)
You Got What It Takes (6)
You Sure Love To Ball (17) **50**
You're A Special Part Of Me (18) **12**
You're A Wonderful One (2,3,14,19,20,23) **15**
You're All I Need To Get By (7,13,19,23,27) **7**
You're The Man (19) **50**
You're The One For Me (4)
You're What's Happening (In The World Today) (8)
You've Been A Long Time Coming (4)
Your Precious Love (6,10,13,19,23,27) **5**
Your Unchanging Love (4,5,19) **33**

★★395★★ GAYLE, Crystal
Born Brenda Gail Webb on 1/9/51 in Paintsville, Kentucky and raised in Wabash, Indiana. Youngest sister of Loretta Lynn. First country artist to tour China (1979).

DEBUT DATE	PEAK POS	WKS CHR	GOLD	#	Album Title	$	Label & Number
9/3/77	12	35	▲	1	We Must Believe In Magic	$10	United Art. 771
7/15/78	52	39	▲	2	When I Dream	$10	United Art. 858
8/11/79	128	8		3	We Should Be Together	$10	United Art. 969
9/29/79	36	28	●	4	Miss The Mississippi	$10	Columbia 36203
11/17/79+	62	22	●	5	Classic Crystal	[G]	$10	United Art. 982
5/3/80	149	6		6	Favorites	[K]	$8	United Art. 1034
9/27/80	79	11		7	These Days		$8	Columbia 36512
9/19/81	99	6		8	Hollywood, Tennessee		$8	Columbia 37438
12/4/82+	120	12		9	True Love		$8	Elektra 60200
9/10/83	169	8		10	Crystal Gayle's Greatest Hits	[G]	$8	Columbia 38803
11/12/83	171	6		11	Cage The Songbird		$8	Warner 23958

Ain't No Love In The Heart Of The City (7)
Ain't No Sunshine (1)
All I Want To Do In Life (1,6)
Baby, What About You (9) **83**
Beyond You (3)
Blue Side (4,10) **81**
Cage The Songbird (11)
Come Back (When You Can Stay Forever) (11)
Come Home Daddy (6)
Cry Me A River (2)
Crying In The Rain (8)
Dancing The Night Away (4)
Danger Zone (4)
Deeper In The Fire (9)
Don't Go My Love (4)
Don't It Make My Brown Eyes Blue (1,5) **2**
Don't Treat Me Like A Stranger (2,6)

Easier Said Than Done (9)
Everything I Own (9)
Funny (1)
Going Down Slow (1)
Green Door (1)
Half The Way (4,10) **15**
He Is Beautiful To Me (9)
Heart Mender (2,6)
Hello I Love You (2)
Help Yourselves To Each Other (7)
Hollywood (8)
I Don't Wanna Lose Your Love (11)
I Just Can't Leave Your Love Alone (7)
I Still Miss Someone (2)
I Wanna Come Back To You (1,6)
I'll Do It All Over Again (5)
I'll Get Over You (5) **71**

If You Ever Change Your Mind (7,10)
It's All Right With Me (1)
It's Like We Never Said Goodbye (4,10) **63**
Keepin' Power (8,10)
Lean On Me (8)
Let Your Feelings Show (9)
Little Bit Of The Rain (4)
Livin' In These Troubled Times (8,10)
Love Crazy Love (8)
Lover Man (7)
Make A Dream Come True (1)
Me Against The Night (11)
Miss The Mississippi And You (4)
On Our Way To Love (11)
Other Side Of Me (1)
Our Love Is On The Faultline (9)

Paintin' This Old Town Blue (2)
Ready For The Times To Get Better (5) **52**
Right In The Palm Of Your Hand (4)
River Road (1,6)
Room For One More (4)
Same Old Story (Same Old Song) (7)
Sneakin' Out The Back Door (3)
Somebody Loves You (5)
Someday Soon (2)
Sound Of Goodbye (11) **84**
Take It Easy (7,10)
Take Me Home (11)
Talking In Your Sleep (2,5) **18**
Tennessee (8)
Through Believing In Love Songs (3)

'Til I Gain Control Again (9)
Time Will Prove That I'm Right (3)
Too Deep For Tears (3)
Too Good To Throw Away (2)
Too Many Lovers (7,10)
True Love (9)
Turning Away (11)
Victim Or A Fool (11)
Wayward Wind (2,6)
We Must Believe In Magic (3)
We Should Be Together (3)
What A Little Moonlight Can Do (7)
We Been Needin' (6)
When I Dream (2,5) **84**
Why Have You Left The One You Left Me For (2,5)
Woman In Me (8,10) **76**
Wrong Road Again (5)
You (6)

You Bring Out The Lover In Me (9)
You Made A Fool Of Me (11)
You Never Gave Up On Me (8,10)
You Never Miss A Real Good Thing (Till He Says Goodbye) (5)
You'll Be Loved Someday (3)
You're The Best Thing In My Life (3)
You've Almost Got Me Believin' (7)
Your Kisses Will (3)
Your Old Cold Shoulder (3)

GAYLORD & HOLIDAY
Italian-American duo: Ronnie "Gaylord" Fredianelli and Burt "Holiday" Bonaldi. With pianist/arranger Don Rea. Recorded in the late '50s as The Gaylords.

2/21/76	180	8			Second Generation	$10	Prodigal 10009

Dio Como Ti Amo
Dormi, Dormi, Dormi
Eh! Cumpari 72

From The Vine Came The Grape

Godfather (Speak Softly Love), Love Theme From The

I Will Never Pass This Way Again
Italian Wedding Song

Little Shoemaker
Sempre Tu
Tell Me You're Mine

To The Door Of The Sun

DEBUT DATE	PEAK POS	WKS CHR	GOLD	ARTIST — Album Title	$	Label & Number

GAYNOR, Gloria
Born on 9/7/49 in Newark, New Jersey. Disco singer. With the Soul Satisfiers in 1971.

2/1/75	**25**	15		1 Never Can Say Goodbye	$10	MGM 4982
10/11/75	**64**	21		2 Experience Gloria Gaynor	$10	MGM 4997
8/14/76	**107**	14		3 I've Got You	$10	Polydor 6063
3/19/77	**183**	4		4 Glorious	$10	Polydor 6095
1/6/79	**4**	34	▲	5 **Love Tracks**	$10	Polydor 6184
10/20/79	**58**	11		6 I Have A Right	$10	Polydor 6231
5/24/80	**178**	4		7 Stories	$8	Polydor 6274

Ain't No Bigger Fool (7)
All I Need Is Your Sweet Lovin' (1)
All My Life (7)
Anybody Wanna Party? (5)
As Time Goes By (4)
Be Mine (4)
Can't Fight The Feelin' (6)
Casanova Brown (2)
Do It Right (3)
Don't Read Me Wrong (7)
Don't Stop Us (6)
False Alarm (1)
Goin' Out Of My Head (5)
Honey Bee (1)
How High The Moon (2) 75
I Let Love Slip Right Through My Hands (7)
I Said Yes (5)
I Will Survive (5) 1
I'm Still Yours (2)
I've Got You Under My Skin (3)
(If You Want It) Do It Yourself (2) 98
Let Me Know (I Have A Right) (6) 42
Let's Make A Deal (3)
Let's Make Love (3)
Life Ain't Worth Living (4)
Lock Me Up (3)
Luckiest Girl In The World (7)
Make Me Yours (7)
Midnight Rocker (6)
Most Of All (4)
Never Can Say Goodbye (1) 9
Nothing In This World (3)
On A Diet Of You (7)
One Number One (6)
Please, Be There (5)
Prettiest Face I've Ever Seen (2)
Reach Out, I'll Be There (1) 60
Real Good People (1)
Say Somethin' (6)
Searchin' (1)
So Much Love (4)
Stoplight (5)
Substitute (5)
Sweet Sweet Melody (4)
Talk, Talk, Talk (3)
Tell Me How (2)
This Side Of The Pain (4)
Tonight (6)
Touch Of Lightning (3)
Walk On By (2) 98
We Belong Together (1)
We Can Start All Over Again (4)
What'll I Do (2)
Why Should I Pay (4)
You Can Exit (5)
You Took Me In Again (6)

★★157★★ GEILS, J., Band
Formed in 1967, guitarist Jerome Geils led rock band consisting of Peter "Wolf" Blankfield (vocals), "Magic Dick" Salwitz (harmonica), Seth Justman (keyboards), Danny Klein (bass) and Stephen Jo Bladd (drums). First recorded for Atlantic in 1969. Wolf left for a solo career in the fall of 1983.

1/30/71	**195**	2		1 The J. Geils Band	$12	Atlantic 8275
11/6/71	**64**	17		2 The Morning After	$12	Atlantic 8297
10/21/72	**54**	26	●	3 "Live" - Full House ....[L]	$12	Atlantic 7241
4/28/73	**10**	44	●	4 **Bloodshot**	$12	Atlantic 7260
12/1/73+	**51**	18		5 Ladies Invited	$12	Atlantic 7286
10/19/74	**26**	22		6 Nightmares...and other tales from the vinyl jungle	$10	Atlantic 18107
9/27/75	**36**	9		7 Hotline	$10	Atlantic 18147
5/22/76	**40**	11		8 Live - Blow Your Face Out ....[L]	$12	Atlantic 507 [2]
7/9/77	**51**	17		9 Monkey Island	$10	Atlantic 19103
12/16/78+	**49**	22	●	10 Sanctuary	$10	EMI America 17006
7/21/79	**129**	5		11 Best of the J. Geils Band ....[G]	$8	Atlantic 19234
2/9/80	**18**	42	●	12 Love Stinks	$8	EMI America 17016
11/14/81+	**1**⁴	70	▲	13 **Freeze-Frame**	$8	EMI America 17062
12/4/82+	**23**	19	●	14 Showtime! ....[L]	$8	EMI America 17087
11/24/84	**80**	10		15 You're Gettin' Even While I'm Gettin' Odd ...	$8	EMI America 17137

(Ain't Nothin' But A) House Party (4,8,11)
Angel In Blue (13) 40
Back To Get Ya (4,8)
Be Careful (What You Do) (7)
Believe In Me (7)
Bite From Inside (15)
Californicatin' (15)
Centerfold (13,14) 1
Come Back (12) 32
Concealed Weapons (15) 63
Cruisin' For A Love (1,3)
Cry One More Time (2)
Desire (Please Don't Turn Away) (12)
Detroit Breakdown (6,8,11)
Did You No Wrong (5)
Diddyboppin' (5)
Do You Remember When (13)
Don't Try To Hide It (4)
Easy Way Out (7)
Eenie Meenie Minie Moe (15)
Fancy Footwork (7)
First I Look At The Purse (1,3)
Flamethrower (13)
Floyd's Hotel (2)
Freeze-Frame (13) 4
Funky Judge (6)
Gettin' Out (6)
Give It To Me (4,8,11) 30
Givin' It All Up (5)
Gonna Find Me A New Love (2)
Gotta Have Your Love (5)
Hard Drivin' Man (1,3)
Heavy Petting (15)
Hold Your Loving (4)
Homework (1,3)
I Can't Believe You (10)
I Can't Go On (5)
I Could Hurt You (10)
I Do (9,11,14) 24
I Don't Hang Around Much Anymore (10)
I Don't Need You No More (2)
I Will Carry You Home (1,3)
I'll Be Coming Home (6)
I'm Falling (14)
I'm Not Rough (9)
Ice Breaker (For The Big "M") (1)
Insane, Insane Again (13)
It Ain't What You Do (It's How You Do It) (2)
Jealous Love (7)
Jus' Can't Stop Me (10,14)
Just Can't Wait (12,14) 78
Land Of A Thousand Dances (14) 60
Lay Your Good Thing Down (5)
Look Me In The Eye (6)
Looking For A Love (2,3,8,11) 39
Love Rap (Rap) (14)
Love Stinks (12,14) 38
Love-itis (7,8)
Make Up Your Mind (4) 98
Mean Love (7)
Monkey Island (9)
Must Of Got Lost (6,8,11) 12
My Baby Don't Love Me (5)
Night Time (12)
Nightmares (6)
No Anchovies, Please (12)
No Doubt About It (5)
On Borrowed Time (1)
One Last Kiss (10) 35
Orange Driver (7)
Pack Fair And Square (1,3)
Piss On The Wall (13)
Rage In The Cage (13)
Raise Your Hand (8)
River Blindness (13)
Sanctuary (10,14)
Serves You Right To Suffer (1,3)
Shoot Your Shot (8)
Sno-Cone (1,8)
So Good (9)
So Sharp (2,8)
Somebody (9)
Southside Shuffle (4,8,11)
Start All Over Again (4,8)
Stoop Down #39 (6,14)
Struttin' With My Baby (4)
Surrender (8)
Take A Chance (On Romance) (5)
Take It Back (10) 67
Takin' You Down (12)
Tell 'Em Jonesy (15)
Teresa (11)
That's Why I'm Thinking Of You (5)
Think It Over (7)
Till The Walls Come Tumblin' Down (12,14)
Truck Drivin' Man (8)
Tryin' Not To Think About It (12)
Usual Place (2)
Wait (1,8)
Wasted Youth (15)
Whammer Jammer (2,3,11)
What's Your Hurry (11)
Where Did Our Love Go (8,11) 68
Wild Man (10)
Wreckage (9)
You're Gettin' Even While I'm Gettin' Odd (15)
You're The Only One (9) 83

GELDOF, Bob
Born on 10/5/54 in Dublin, Ireland. Leader of Boomtown Rats. Played Pink in the Pink Floyd film *The Wall*. Organized British superstar benefit group Band Aid and earned a Nobel Peace Prize nomination.

12/13/86+	**130**	12		Deep In The Heart Of Nowhere	$8	Atlantic 81687

August Was A Heavy Month
Beat Of The Night
Deep In The Heart Of Nowhere
I Cry Too
In The Pouring Rain
Love Like A Rocket
Night Turns To Day
This Heartless Heart
This Is The World Calling 82
When I Was Young
Words From Heaven

GENE LOVES JEZEBEL
British techno-rock group led by twin brothers Michael and Jay Aston, from Porthcawl, Wales. Michael left the group in 1988.

10/18/86+	**155**	19		1 Discover	$8	Geffen 24118
11/14/87+	**108**	22		2 The House Of Dolls	$8	Geffen 24171
8/18/90	**123**	14		3 Kiss Of Life	$12	Geffen 24260

Beyond Doubt (1)
Brand New Moon (1)
Desire (1)
Drowning Crazy (2)
Evening Star (3)
Every Door (2)
Gorgeous (2)
Heartache (1)
I Die For You (3)
It'll End In Tears (3)
Jealous (3) 68
Kick (1)
Kiss Of Life (3)
Maid Of Sker (1)
Message (2)
Motion Of Love (2) 87
Over The Rooftops (1)
Set Me Free (2)
Suspicion (2)
Sweetest Thing (1)
Syzygy (3)
Tangled Up In You (3)
Treasure (1)
Twenty Killer Hurts (2)
Two Shadows (3)
Up There (2)
Wait And See (1)
Walk Away (3)
White Horse (1)
Why Can't I? (3)

DEBUT DATE	PEAK POS	WKS CHR	GOLD	ARTIST — Album Title	$	Label & Number

GENERAL PUBLIC

Fronted by former English Beat vocalists Dave Wakeling and Ranking Roger (Roger Charley). Disbanded in March 1987. Roger recorded solo in 1988, Wakeling in 1991.

DEBUT DATE	PEAK POS	WKS CHR	GOLD	Album Title	$	Label & Number
10/27/84+	26	39		1 ...All The Rage	$8	I.R.S. 70046
10/25/86	83	16		2 Hand To Mouth	$8	I.R.S. 5782

Anxious (1) · Are You Leading Me On? (1) · As A Matter Of Fact (1) · Burning Bright (1) · Cheque In The Post (2) · Come Again (2) · Cry On Your Shoulder (2) · Day-To-Day (1) · Faults And All (2) · Forward As One (2) · General Public (1) · Hot You're Cool (1) · In Conversation (2) · Love Without The Fun (2) · Murder (2) · Never All There (2) · Never You Done That (1) · **Tenderness** (1) **27** · Too Much Or Nothing (2) · Where's The Line? (1)

★★133★★ GENESIS

Formed as a progressive rock group in England in 1967. Consisted of Peter Gabriel (lead vocals), Anthony Phillips (guitar), Tony Banks (keyboards), Michael Rutherford (guitar, bass) and Chris Stewart (drums; replaced by John Silver in 1968, then John Mayhew in 1969). Phillips and Mayhew left in 1970, replaced by Steve Hackett (guitar) and Phil Collins (drums). Gabriel left in June 1975, with Collins replacing him as new lead singer. Hackett went solo in 1977, leaving group as a trio: Collins, Rutherford and Banks. Collins also recorded in jazz-fusion group Brand X. Rutherford also in own group, Mike + The Mechanics, formed in 1985. Hackett later formed group GTR.

DEBUT DATE	PEAK POS	WKS CHR	GOLD	Album Title	$	Label & Number
12/15/73+	70	29	●	1 Selling England By The Pound	$12	Charisma 6060
5/18/74	105	14		2 Genesis Live [L]	$12	Charisma 1666
				recorded in Manchester, England, February 1973		
10/12/74	170	4		3 From Genesis To Revelation [E]	$30	London 643
				their first album, released in 1969		
12/14/74+	41	16	●	4 The Lamb Lies Down On Broadway	$12	Atco 401 [2]
3/20/76	31	19	●	5 A Trick Of The Tail	$12	Atco 129
1/22/77	26	21	●	6 Wind & Wuthering	$8	Atco 144
12/3/77	47	16		7 Seconds Out [L]	$10	Atlantic 9002 [2]
4/15/78	14	33	▲	8 And Then There Were Three	$8	Atlantic 19173
				from here on, group consists of Banks, Collins and Rutherford		
4/26/80	11	31	▲	9 Duke	$8	Atlantic 16014
10/17/81	7	66	▲²	10 Abacab	$8	Atlantic 19313
6/26/82	10	25	●	11 Three Sides Live [L]	$10	Atlantic 2000 [2]
				side 4: studio cuts from 1979-81		
10/29/83	9	50	▲³	12 Genesis	$8	Atlantic 80116
6/28/86	3	85	▲⁵	13 Invisible Touch	$8	Atlantic 81641
11/30/91	4	63↑	▲³	14 We Can't Dance	$12	Atlantic 82344
12/5/92	35	10↑	●	15 Live/The Way We Walk - Volume One: The Shorts [L]	$12	Atlantic 82452
				recorded during the 1992 *We Can't Dance* tour		

Abacab (10,11) **26** · After The Ordeal (1) · Afterglow (6,7,11) · Aisle Of Plenty (medley) (1) · All In A Mouse's Night (6) · Alone Tonight (9) · Am I Very Wrong (3) · Another Record (10) · Anything She Does (13) · Anyway (4) · Back In N.Y.C. (4) · Ballad Of Big (8) · Battle Of Epping Forest (1) · Behind The Lines (9,11) · Blood On The Rooftops (6) · Brazilian, The (13) · Broadway Melody Of 1974 (4) · Burning Rope (8) · Carpet Crawlers (4,7) · Chamber Of 32 Doors (4) · Cinema Show (1,7,11) · Colony Of Slippermen Medley (4,11) · Conqueror, The (3) · Counting Out Time (4) · Cuckoo Cocoon (4) · Cul-De-Sac (9) · Dance On A Volcano (5,7)

Dancing With The Moonlit Knight (1) · Deep In The Motherlode (8) · DoDo (10,11) · Domino Medley (13) · Down And Out (8) · Dreaming While You Sleep (14) · Driving The Last Spike (14) · Duchess (9,11) · Duke's End (9) · Duke's Travels (9) · Eleventh Earl Of Mar (6) · Entangled (5,7) · Evidence Of Autumn (11) · Fading Lights (14) · Fireside Song (3) · Firth Of Fifth (1,7) · Fly On A Windshield (4) · Follow You Follow Me (8,11) **23** · Get 'Em Out By Friday (2) · Grand Parade Of Lifeless Packaging (4) · Guide Vocal (9) · Hairless Heart (4) · Heathaze (9)

Hold On My Heart (14,15) **12** · Home By The Sea (12) · **I Can't Dance** (14,15) **7** · I Know What I Like (In Your Wardrobe) (1,7) · **Illegal Alien** (12) **44** · In Hiding (3) · In Limbo (3) · ...In That Quiet Earth (medley) (6) · In The Beginning (3) · In The Cage (4,11) · In The Rapids (4) · In The Wilderness (3) · **In Too Deep** (13,15) **3** · **Invisible Touch** (13,15) **1** · It (4) · It's Gonna Get Better (12) · **Jesus He Knows Me** (14,15) **23** · Just A Job To Do (12) · Keep It Dark (10) · Knife, The (2) · Lady Lies (8) · Lamb Lies Down On Broadway (4,7) · Lamia, The (4)

Land Of Confusion (13,15) **4** · Light Dies Down On Broadway (4) · Like It Or Not (10) · Living Forever (14) · Los Endos (5,7) · Lurker (10) · Mad Man Moon (5) · **Mama** (12,15) **73** · Man Of Our Times (8) · Many Too Many (8) · Me And Sarah Jane (10,11) · Me And Virgil (11) · **Misunderstanding** (9,11) **14** · More Fool Me (1) · Musical Box (2,7) · **Never A Time** (14) **21** · **No Reply At All** (10) **29** · **No Son Of Mine** (14,15) **12** · One Day (3) · One For The Vine (6) · Open Door (11) · **Paperlate** (11) **32** · Place To Call My Own (3) · Please Don't Ask (9) · Ravine (4)

Return Of The Giant Hogweed (2) · Riding The Scree (4) · Ripples (5) · Robbery, Assault & Battery (5,7) · Say It's Alright Joe (8) · Scenes From A Night's Dream (8) · Second Home By The Sea (12) · Serpent, The (3) · Silent Sorrow In Empty Boats (4) · Silent Sun (3) · Silver Rainbow (12) · Since I Lost You (14) · Snowbound (8) · Squonk (5,7) · Supernatural Anaesthetist (4) · Supper's Ready (7) · **Taking It All Too Hard** (12) **50** · Tell Me Why (14) · **That's All!** (12,15) **6** · **Throwing It All Away** (13,15) **4**

Tonight, Tonight, Tonight (13,15) **3** · Trick Of The Tail (5) · **Turn It On Again** (9,11) **58** · Undertow (8) · Unquiet Slumbers For The Sleepers... (medley) (6) · Waiting Room (4) · Watcher Of The Skies (2) · Way Of The World (14) · Where The Sour Turns To Sweet (3) · Who Dunnit? (10) · Window (3) · Wot Gorilla? (6) · You Might Recall (11) · **Your Own Special Way** (6) **62**

GENTLE GIANT

British progressive rock band led by brothers Ray (b: 12/8/49; bass, guitar), Derek (b: 2/2/47; sax, vocals) and Phil (b: 8/27/37; sax, trumpet) Shulman. Phil left after second album.

DEBUT DATE	PEAK POS	WKS CHR	GOLD	Album Title	$	Label & Number
10/21/72	197	5		1 Three Friends	$10	Columbia 31649
3/31/73	170	9		2 Octopus	$10	Columbia 32022
10/12/74	78	13		3 The Power And The Glory	$8	Capitol 11337
8/16/75	48	11		4 Free Hand	$8	Capitol 11428
5/29/76	137	5		5 Interview	$8	Capitol 11532
2/19/77	89	6		6 The Official "Live" Gentle Giant - Playing The Fool [L]	$10	Capitol 11592 [2]
10/15/77	81	7		7 The Missing Piece	$8	Capitol 11696

Advent Of Panurge (2) · Another Show (5) · As Old As You're Young (7) · Aspirations (3) · Betcha Thought We Couldn't Do It (7) · Boys In The Band (2) · Cogs In Cogs (3) · Cry For Everyone (2) · Design (5) · Dog's Life (2) · Empty City (5) · Excerpts From Octopus (6) · Experience (6) · Face, The (3) · For Nobody (7) · Free Hand (4,6) · Funny Ways (6) · Give It Back (5) · His Last Voyage (4) · I Lost My Head (5,6) · I'm Turning Around (7) · Interview (5) · Just The Same (4,6) · Knots (2) · Memories Of Old Days (7) · Mister Class And Quality? (1) · Mobile (4) · Mountain Time (7) · No God's A Man (3) · On Reflection (4,6) · Peel The Paint (1,6) · Playing The Game (3) · Proclamation (3,6) · Raconteur Troubadour (2) · River (4) · Runaway, The (6) · Schooldays (1) · So Sincere (3,6) · Sweet Georgia Brown (Breakdown In Brussels) (6) · Talybont (3) · Think Of Me With Kindness (2) · Three Friends (1)

279

GENTLE GIANT — Cont'd

Time To Kill (4) Two Weeks In Spain (7) Who Do You Think You Are? Winning (7)
Timing (5) Valedictory (3) (7) Working All Day (1)

GENTRY, Bobbie

Born Roberta Streeter on 7/27/44 in Chickasaw County, Mississippi; raised in Greenwood, Mississippi. Guitarist/pianist/bassist/banjo player. Moved to Palm Springs, California while still in high school. Own TV series in England in the late '60s. Own production company in Los Angeles. Married singer Jim Stafford on 10/15/78.

DEBUT DATE	PEAK POS	WKS CHR	GOLD	ARTIST — Album Title	$	Label & Number
9/16/67	1²	30	●	1 Ode To Billie Joe	$15	Capitol 2830
3/23/68	132	12		2 The Delta Sweete	$15	Capitol 2842
10/12/68	11	47	●	3 Bobbie Gentry & Glen Campbell	$15	Capitol 2928

BOBBIE GENTRY & GLEN CAMPBELL

DEBUT DATE	PEAK POS	WKS CHR	GOLD	ARTIST — Album Title	$	Label & Number
8/9/69	164	4		4 Touch 'em With Love	$15	Capitol 155
12/27/69+	180	2		5 Bobbie Gentry's Greatest! .....[G]	$15	Capitol 381
5/9/70	96	17		6 Fancy	$15	Capitol 428

Ace Insurance Man (5) Greyhound Goin' Jessye' Lisabeth (2) Papa, Won't You Let Me Go Sermon (2) You've Made Me So Very
Big Boss Man (2) Somewhere (4) Lazy Willie (1) To Town With You (1) Sittin' Pretty (5) Happy (4)
Bugs (1) He Made A Woman Out Of Less Of Me (3) Papa's Medicine Show (5) Something In The Way He
Canticle ..see: Scarborough Me (6) 71 Let It Be Me (3) 36 Parchman Farm (2) Moves (6)
Fair Heart To Heart Talk (3) Little Green Apples (3) Penduli Pendulum (2,5) Son Of A Preacher Man (4)
Chickasaw County Child (1) Hurry, Tuesday Child (1) Louisiana Man (2) 100 Raindrops Keep Fallin' On Sunday Best (1)
Courtyard (2) I Saw An Angel Die (1) Mississippi Delta (1,5) My Head (6) Sunday Mornin' (3)
Delta Man (6) I Wouldn't Be Surprised (4) Mornin' Glory (2,3) 78 Rainmaker (6) Sweet Peony (5)
Fancy (6) 31 I'll Never Fall In Love Again My Elusive Dreams (3) Refractions (2) Terrible Tangled Web (3)
Find 'Em, Fool 'Em And (4,6) Natural To Be Gone (4) Reunion (2) Tobacco Road (2)
Forget 'Em (6) If You Gotta Make A Fool Of Niki Hoeky (1) Scarborough Fair/Canticle Touch 'Em With Love (4,5)
Gentle On My Mind (3) Somebody (6) **Ode To Billie Joe** (1,5) *1* (3) Wedding Bell Blues (6)
Glory Hallelujah, How (It's Only Your) Imagination **Okolona River Bottom** Seasons Come, Seasons Go Where's The Playground,
They'll Sing (4,5) (3) **Band** (2,5) *54* (4) Johnny (4)

GENTRYS, The

Memphis-based rock band formed in 1963 featuring lead singer Larry Raspberry. Original member Jimmy Hart re-formed the band in 1969 for their Sun recordings, with Hart as lead singer. Hart is currently a professional wrestling manager.

DEBUT DATE	PEAK POS	WKS CHR	GOLD	ARTIST — Album Title	$	Label & Number
12/18/65+	99	10		Keep On Dancing	$25	MGM 4336

Brown Paper Sack Everybody To Their Own Hang On Sloopy Little Girl Next Door So Sad (To Watch Good Love
Do You Love Me Kick Hey Girl Don't Bother Me Make Up Your Mind Go Bad)
Don't Send Me No Flowers Hand Jive **Keep On Dancing** *4* Sometimes

GEORGE, Lowell

Founder of Little Feat. Born on 4/13/45 in Hollywood; died on 6/29/79 of drug-related heart failure. Played with The Standells, The Seeds and briefly a member of Mothers Of Invention.

DEBUT DATE	PEAK POS	WKS CHR	GOLD	ARTIST — Album Title	$	Label & Number
4/14/79	71	9		Thanks I'll Eat It Here	$10	Warner 3194

Can't Stand The Rain Easy Money Himmler's Ring 20 Million Things What Do You Want The Girl
Cheek To Cheek Find A River Honest Man Two Trains To Do

GEORGIA SATELLITES

Rock quartet formed in Atlanta in 1980, led by dual guitarists/vocalists Dan Baird and Rick Richards, with bassist Rich Price and drummer Mauro Magellan. Baird left by 1992.

DEBUT DATE	PEAK POS	WKS CHR	GOLD	ARTIST — Album Title	$	Label & Number
11/1/86+	5	42	▲	1 Georgia Satellites	$8	Elektra 60496
7/2/88	77	13		2 Open All Night	$8	Elektra 60793
11/11/89	130	13		3 In The Land Of Salvation And Sin	$8	Elektra 60887

All Over But The Cryin' (3) Crazy (3) Games People Play (3) Myth Of Love (1) Six Years Gone (3)
Another Chance (3) Dan Takes Five (3) Golden Light (1) Nights Of Mystery (1) Slaughterhouse (3)
Baby So Fine (2) Days Gone By (3) Hand To Mouth (2) Open All Night (2) Stellazine Blues (3)
Battleship Chains (1) *86* Don't Pass Me By (2) I Dunno (3) Over And Over (1) Sweet Blue Midnight (3)
Bottle O' Tears (3) Down And Down (3) **Keep Your Hands To** Railroad Steel (1) Whole Lotta Shakin' (2)
Bring Down The Hammer (3) Dunk 'N' Dine (2) **Yourself** (1) *2* Red Light (1)
Can't Stand The Pain (1) Every Picture Tells A Story Mon Cheri (2) Shake That Thing (3)
Cool Inside (2) (1) My Baby (2) Sheila (2)

GEORGIO

Los Angeles-based singer/songwriter/keyboardist/guitarist Georgio Allentini. Raised in San Francisco; worked as a mobile DJ and dance promoter.

DEBUT DATE	PEAK POS	WKS CHR	GOLD	ARTIST — Album Title	$	Label & Number
4/25/87+	117	52		Sexappeal	$8	Motown 6229

Bed Rock I Won't Change Menage A Trois **Sexappeal** *58*
Hey U **Lover's Lane** *59* 1/4 2 9 **Tina Cherry** *96*

GERARDO

Rapper/actor. Born Gerardo Mejia III in Guayaquil, Ecuador on 4/16/65. To Glendale, California at age 12. Raps in Spanglish (half Spanish, half English). Appeared in films *Can't Buy Me Love* and *Colors*.

DEBUT DATE	PEAK POS	WKS CHR	GOLD	ARTIST — Album Title	$	Label & Number
2/23/91	36	32	●	Mo' Ritmo	$12	Interscope 91619

ritmo is Spanish for rhythm

Brother To Brother Fandango Latin Till I Die (Oye Como **We Want The Funk** *16* You Gotta Hold Of My Soul
Christina Groove Remains The Same Va) **When The Lights Go**
En Mi Barrio (Mo' Ritmo) **Rico Suave** *7* **Out** *98*

GERRY AND THE PACEMAKERS

Pop-rock group formed in Liverpool, England in 1959: Gerry Marsden (b: 9/24/42; vocals, guitar), Leslie Maguire (piano), Les Chadwick (bass) and Freddie Marsden (drums). The Marsden brothers had been in skiffle bands; Gerry had own rock band Mars-Bars. Signed in 1962 by The Beatles' manager Brian Epstein.

DEBUT DATE	PEAK POS	WKS CHR	GOLD	ARTIST — Album Title	$	Label & Number
7/11/64	29	12		1 Don't Let The Sun Catch You Crying	$25	Laurie 2024
11/21/64	129	9		2 Gerry & The Pacemakers Second Album	$25	Laurie 2027
2/27/65	13	20		3 Ferry Cross The Mersey .....[S]	$25	United Art. 6387

group stars in the film which was set in Liverpool; includes "I Gotta Woman" by The Black Knights; "Shake A Tail Feather" by Earl Royce & The Olympics and "Why Don't You Love Me" by The Blackwells

DEBUT DATE	PEAK POS	WKS CHR	GOLD	ARTIST — Album Title	$	Label & Number
2/27/65	120	7		4 I'll Be There!	$25	Laurie 2030

DEBUT DATE	PEAK POS	WKS CHR	G O L D	ARTIST — Album Title	$	Label & Number
5/15/65	44	22	5	Gerry & The Pacemakers Greatest Hits ....[G]	$25	Laurie 2031

Away From You (1,5)
Baby You're So Good To Me (3)
Chills (2,5)
Don't Let The Sun Catch You Crying (1,5) **4**
Don't You Ever (1)
Fall In Love (3)
Ferry Cross The Mersey (3,5) **6**

Here's Hoping (2)
How Do You Do It? (1,5) **9**
I Count The Tears (4)
I Like It (2,5) **17**
I'll Be There (4,5) **14**
I'll Wait For You (3)
I'm The One (1,5) **82**
It'll Be Me (4,5)
It's All Right (2)

It's Gonna Be Alright (3,5) **23**
It's Happened To Me (2)
Jambalaya (1,2)
Mabellene (1)
My Babe (4,5)
Now I'm Alone (4)
Pretend (2,5)
Reelin' And A Rockin' (4)
Rip It Up (4)

She's The Only Girl For Me (3)
Shot Of Rhythm And Blues (2)
Show Me That You Care (1)
Skinny Minnie (4)
Slow Down (1,2)
Summertime (1)
Think About Love (3)
This Thing Called Love (3)

What'd I Say (4)
Where Have You Been (2)
Whole Lotta Shakin' Goin' On (4)
Why Oh Why (3)
Wrong Yo Yo (2)
You Can't Fool Me (2)
You Win Again (4)
You You You (4)

You'll Never Walk Alone (1) **48**
You're The Reason (1)

GETO BOYS, The

Houston-based rap outfit: Richard "Bushwick Bill" Shaw, William "Willie Dee" Dennis, Brad "Scarface" Akshen" Jordan and Collins "DJ Ready Red" Lyaseth (left group in early 1991). Shaw, a Jamaican-born dwarf, lost his right eye in a shooting on 5/10/91.

DEBUT DATE	PEAK POS	WKS CHR	G	ARTIST — Album Title	$	Label & Number
3/24/90	166	10	1	Grip It! On That Other Level	$12	Rap-A-Lot 103
				GHETTO BOYS		
10/20/90	171	7	2	The Geto Boys..	$12	Def Amer. 24306
7/27/91	24	42 ▲	3	We Can't Be Stopped..	$12	Rap-A-Lot 57161
12/5/92	147	6↑	4	Best Uncut Dope...[G]	$12	Rap-A-Lot 57183

Action Speaks Louder Than Words (4)
Ain't With Being Broke (3)
And My Word (4)
Another Nigger In The Morgue (3)
Assassins (2,4)
Chuckie (3,4)

City Under Siege (2)
Damn It Feels Good To Be A Gangsta (4)
Do It Like A G.O. (1,2,4)
F___ A War (3)
F#@* 'Em (2)
Gangster Of Love (1,2)

Gota Let Your Nuts Hang (3,4)
Homie Don't Play That (3)
I'm Not A Gentleman (3)
Let A Ho Be A Ho (1,2)
Life In The Fast Lane (1,2)
Mind Of A Lunatic (1,2,4)

Mind Playing Tricks On Me (3,4) **23**
No Sell Out (3)
Other Level (3)
Punk-B___ Game (3)
Quickie (3)
Read These Nikes (1,2)
Rebel Rap Family (3)

Scarface (1,2,4)
Seek And Destroy (1)
Size Ain't Shit (1,2,4)
Talkin' Loud Ain't Saying Nothin' (1,2)
Trigga Happy Nigga (1,2)
Trophy (3)
Unseen, The (4)

We Can't Be Stopped (3)

★★448★★ GETZ, Stan

Born Stan Gayetsky on 2/2/27 in Philadelphia. Jazz tenor saxophonist. With Stan Kenton (1944-45), Jimmy Dorsey (1945-46), Benny Goodman (1946) and Woody Herman (1947-49). Seventeen-time winner of Down Beat polls as top tenor saxophonist. Leader of the bossa nova movement of the 1960s. Died of liver cancer on 6/6/91.

DEBUT DATE	PEAK POS	WKS CHR	●	ARTIST — Album Title	$	Label & Number
9/15/62+	1[1]	70	1	Jazz Samba...[I]	$25	Verve 8432
				STAN GETZ/CHARLIE BYRD (guitar)		
12/22/62+	13	23	2	Big Band Bossa Nov ....[I]	$25	Verve 8494
				with the Gary McFarland Orchestra		
5/18/63	88	11	3	Jazz Samba Encore!...[I-F]	$25	Verve 8523
				with Luiz Bonfa (guitar) and Maria Toledo (vocals)		
4/11/64	122	6	4	Reflections ....[I]	$20	Verve 8554
6/6/64	2[2]	96 ●	5	Getz/Gilberto..	$20	Verve 8545
				STAN GETZ/JOAO GILBERTO (Brazilian singer/guitarist; married to Astrud Gilberto); 1964 Grammy winner: Album of the Year		
12/19/64+	24	46	6	Getz Au Go Go ....[L]	$20	Verve 8600
				THE NEW STAN GETZ QUARTET featuring ASTRUD GILBERTO		
9/2/67	195	2	7	Sweet Rain ....[I]	$20	Verve 8693
3/1/75	191	1	8	Captain Marvel ....[I]	$15	Columbia 32706
				above 2 feature pianist Chick Corea		

Baia (1)
Balanco No Samba (Street Dance) (2)
Bim Bom (2)
Blowin' In The Wind (4)
Captain Marvel (8)
Charade (4)
Chega De Saudade (Too Much Longing) (2)
Con Alma (7)
Corcovado ..see: Quiet Nights Of Quiet Stars
Day Waves (8)
Desafinado (1,5) **15**

Doralice (5)
E Luxo So (1)
Early Autumn (4)
Ebony Samba (3)
Entre Amigos (Sympathy Between Friends) (2)
Five Hundred Miles High (8)
Girl From Ipanema (1,5) **5**
Here's That Rainy Day (6)
If Ever I Would Leave You (4)
Insensatez (3)
It Might As Well Be Spring (6)
La Fiesta (8)

Litha (7)
Love (4)
Lush Life (8)
Manha De Carnival (Morning Of Carnival) (2)
Mania De Maria (3)
Melancolico (Melancholy) (2)
Menina Flor (3)
Moonlight In Vermont (4)
Nitetime Street (4)
Noite Triste (Night Sadness) (2)
O Grande Amor (5,7)
O Morro Nao Tem Vez (3)

O Pato (1)
One Note Samba ..see: Samba De Uma Nota So
Only Trust Your Heart (6)
Para Machuchar Meu Coracao (To Hurt My Heart) (5)
Penthouse Serenade (4)
Quiet Nights Of Quiet Stars (5,6)
Reflections (4)
Samba De Duas Notas (Two Note Samba) (3)

Samba De Uma Nota So (One Note Samba) (1,2,6)
Samba Dees Days (1)
Samba Triste (1)
Sambalero (3)
Saudade Vem Correndo (3)
Singing Song (6)
Six, Nix Quix, Flix (6)
Sleeping Bee (4)
So Danco Samba (Jazz Samba) (3,5)
Spring Can Really Hang You Up The Most (4)
Summertime (6)

Sweet Rain (7)
Telephone Song (6)
Times Lie (8)
Um Abraco No Getz (A Tribute To Getz) (3)
Vivo Sohando (5)
Voce E Eu (6)
Windows (7)

GHETTO BOYS — see GETO

GIANT

Rock quartet led by Nashville brothers Dann (vocals) and David (drums) Huff. All members are prominent studio musicians.

DEBUT DATE	PEAK POS	WKS CHR		ARTIST — Album Title	$	Label & Number
10/14/89+	80	36		Last Of The Runaways	$8	A&M 5272

Big Pitch
Hold Back The Night

I Can't Get Close Enough
I'll See You In My Dreams 20

I'm A Believer 56
Innocent Days

It Takes Two
Love Welcome Home

No Way Out
Shake Me Up

Stranger To Me

GIANT STEPS

English duo: vocalist Campsie and multi-instrumentalist George McFarlane. Both initially worked together as members of the British band Grand Hotel, then as Quick.

DEBUT DATE	PEAK POS	WKS CHR		ARTIST — Album Title	$	Label & Number
11/12/88	184	5		The Book Of Pride..	$8	A&M 5190

Another Lover 13
Book Of Pride

Dance Away
Do You Still Care

Dream Away
End Of The War

Golden Hours
Into You 58

Same Planet Different World
Steamy

GIBB, Andy

Born Andrew Roy Gibb on 3/5/58 in Manchester, England. Moved to Australia when six months old, then back to England at age nine. Youngest brother of Barry, Robin and Maurice Gibb — The Bee Gees. Hosted TV's *Solid Gold* from 1981-82. Died on 3/10/88 of an inflammatory heart virus in Oxford, England.

DEBUT DATE	PEAK POS	WKS CHR		ARTIST — Album Title	$	Label & Number
7/2/77	19	68 ▲	1	Flowing Rivers	$10	RSO 3019
6/17/78	7	43 ▲	2	Shadow Dancing..	$10	RSO 3034
3/1/80	21	15 ●	3	After Dark	$8	RSO 3069

DEBUT DATE	PEAK POS	WKS CHR	GOLD	ARTIST — Album Title	$	Label & Number

12/6/80+ **46** 18 4 Andy Gibb's Greatest Hits .... [G] **$8** RSO 3091

After Dark (3,4)	Falling In Love With You (3)	In The End (1)	One More Look At The Night (2)	**Time Is Time** (4) **15**	Will You Love Me Tomorrow (4)
Come Home For The Winter (1)	Flowing Rivers (1)	Let It Be Me (1)	**(Love Is) Thicker Than**	Too Many Looks In Your	Words And Music (1)
Dance To The Light Of The	Fool For A Night (2)	**(Love Is) Thicker Than**	**(Our Love) Don't Throw It**	Eyes (1)	
Morning (1)	Good Feeling (2)	**Water** (1,4) **1**	**All Away** (2,4) **9**	Waiting For You (2)	
Desire (3,4) **4**	**I Can't Help It** (3) **12**	**Me (Without You)** (4) **40**	Rest Your Love On Me (3)	Warm Ride (3)	
Dreamin' On (3)	I Go For You (2)	Melody (2)	**Shadow Dancing** (2,4) **1**	Wherever You Are (3)	
Everlasting Love (2,4) **5**	**I Just Want To Be Your**	One Love (3)	Someone I Ain't (3)	Why (2)	
	Everything (1,4) **1**		Starlight (1)		

GIBB, Barry
Born on 9/1/46 in Manchester, England. Eldest brother of The Bee Gees. Appeared in *Sgt. Pepper's Lonely Hearts Club Band.*

10/20/84 **72** 8 Now Voyager .... **$8** MCA 5506

Face To Face	Hunter	Lesson In Love	Shatterproof	**Shine Shine 37**	Temptation
Fine Line	I Am Your Driver	One Night (For Lovers)	She Says	Stay Alone	

GIBBS, Terri
Born on 6/15/54 in Augusta, Georgia. Country singer/pianist, blind since birth.

2/14/81 **53** 25 Somebody's Knockin'... **$8** MCA 5173

I Won't Cry in Dallas	It's True	Plans	Some Days It Rains All	**Somebody's Knockin' 13**	Wasted Love
Anymore	Magic Time	**Rich Man 89**	Night Long	Tell Me That You Love Me	Wishing Well

GIBSON, Debbie
Singer/songwriter/pianist. Born on 8/31/70 in Long Island. Playing piano since age five and songwriting since age six. In 1991, played Eponine in *Les Miserables* on Broadway.

9/5/87+	**7**	89	▲³ 1	Out Of The Blue	**$8**	Atlantic 81780
2/11/89	**1⁵**	51	▲² 2	Electric Youth	**$8**	Atlantic 81932
12/1/90	**41**	17	● 3	Anything Is Possible	**$12**	Atlantic 82167

Another Brick Falls (3)	In His Mind (3)	**No More Rhyme** (2) **17**	Reverse Psychology (3)	Sure (3)
Anything Is Possible (3) **26**	It Must've Been My Boy (3)	One Hand, One Heart (3)	Shades Of The Past (3)	This So-Called Miracle (3)
Between The Lines (1)	Lead Them Home My	One Step Ahead (3)	**Shake Your Love** (1) **4**	Try (3)
Deep Down (3)	Dreams (3)	**Only In My Dreams** (1) **4**	Should've Been The One (2)	Wake Up To Love (1)
Electric Youth (2) **11**	**Lost In Your Eyes** (2) **1**	**Out Of The Blue** (1) **3**	Silence Speaks (A Thousand	**We Could Be Together**
Fallen Angel (3)	Love In Disguise (3)	Over The Wall (2)	Words) (2)	(2) **71**
Foolish Beat (1) **1**	Mood Swings (3)	Play The Field (1)	Stand Your Ground (3)	Where Have You Been? (3)
Helplessly In Love (2)	Negative Energy (3)	Red Hot (1)	**Staying Together** (1) **22**	Who Loves Ya Baby? (2)

GIBSON, Don
Born on 4/3/28 in Shelby, North Carolina. Country singer/songwriter/guitarist. Joined the *Grand Ole Opry* in 1958.

11/2/63 **134** 3 I Wrote A Song.. **$30** RCA 2702

featuring new versions of Don's biggest hits

After The Heartache	Blue, Blue Day	I Can't Stop Loving You	Lonesome Number One	Oh Such A Stranger
Anything New Gets Old	Don't Tell Me Your Troubles	(I'd Be) A Legend In My Time	Love Has Come My Way	
(Except My Love For You)	Give Myself A Party	Just One Time	Oh Lonesome Me	

GIBSON BROTHERS
Paris-based trio of brothers Chris (guitar, percussion), Patrick (vocals, drums) and Alex Gibson (from the West Indies; vocals, keyboards).

7/28/79 **185** 2 Cuba .... **$10** Island 9579

Better Do It Salsa!	Ooh, What A Life...	Que Sera Mi Vida (If You	West Indies
Cuba 81		Should Go)	You

GILBERTO, Astrud
Born on 3/30/40 in Salvador, Brazil. Wife of composer/guitarist Joao Gilberto.

12/19/64+	**24**	46	1	Getz Au Go Go ....[L]	**$20**	Verve 8600

THE NEW STAN GETZ QUARTET featuring ASTRUD GILBERTO

5/15/65	**41**	18	2	The Astrud Gilberto Album	**$15**	Verve 8608

with Antonio Carlos Jobim (guitar)

10/9/65	**68**	18	3	The Shadow Of Your Smile..	**$15**	Verve 8629

Agua De Beber (2)	Dreamer (2)	It Might As Well Be Spring	One Note Samba (1)	So Finha De Ser Com Voce	Who Can I Turn To? (When
All That's Left Is To Say	Funny World (3)	(1)	Only Trust Your Heart (1)	(2)	Nobody Needs Me) (3)
Goodbye (2)	Gentle Rain (3)	Manha De Carnaval (3)	Photograph (2)	Summertime (1)	
And Roses And Roses (2)	Here's That Rainy Day (1)	Meditation (2)	Sandpiper (The Shadow Of	(Take One) Arauanda (3)	
Corcovado (Quiet Nights Of	How Insensitive (2)	Non-Stop To Brazil (3)	Your Smile), Love Theme	Telephone Song (1)	
Quiet Stars) (1)	(In Other Words) Fly Me To	O Ganso (3)	From The (3)	Tristeza (1)	
Day By Day (3)	The Moon (3)	O Morro (Nao Tem Vez) (3)	Singing Song (1)	Voce E Eu (1)	
Dindi (2)		Once I Loved (2)	Six, Nix Quix, Flix (1)		

GILBERTO, Joao — see GETZ, Stan

GILDER, Nick
Born on 11/7/51 in London. Moved to Vancouver, Canada at age 10. Founding member of the rock band Sweeney Todd.

9/23/78	**33**	20	1	City Nights	**$10**	Chrysalis 1202
7/7/79	**127**	8	2	Frequency	**$10**	Chrysalis 1219

All Because Of Love (1)	Frustration (1)	Hold On Me Tonight (2)	**Rock Me** (2) **57**	21st Century (1)
Brightest Star (2)	Got To Get Out (1)	**Hot Child In The City** (1) **1**	Rockaway (1)	Watcher Of The Night (2)
Electric Love (2)	**Here Comes The Night**	Into The 80's (2)	(She's) One Of The Boys (1)	We'll Work It Out (1)
Fly High (1)	(1) **44**	Metro Jets (2)	Time After Time (1)	Worlds Collide (2)

GILL, Johnny
Born in 1965 in Washington, D.C. Sang in family gospel group, Wings Of Faith, from age five. Joined New Edition in 1988.

3/31/84 **139** 8 1 Perfect Combination... **$8** Cotillion 90136

STACY LATTISAW & JOHNNY GILL

5/5/90 **8** 60 ▲² 2 Johnny Gill .... **$12** Motown 6283

DEBUT DATE	PEAK POS	WKS CHR	G O L D	ARTIST — Album Title	$	Label & Number

GILL, Johnny — Cont'd

Baby It's You (1)	**Fairweather Friend** (2) *28*	Fun 'N' Games (1)	Lady Dujour (2)	**Perfect Combination** (1) *75*
Block Party (1)	Falling In Love Again (1)	Giving My All To You (1)	Let's Spend The Night (2)	**Rub You The Right Way**
Come Out Of The Shadows (1)	Feels So Much Better (2)	Heartbreak Look (1)	**My, My, My** (2) *10*	(2) *3*
	50/50 Love (1)	Just Another Lonely Night (2)	Never Know Love (2)	**Wrap My Body Tight** (2) *84*

GILL, Vince
Country singer/guitarist. Born on 4/5/57 in Norman, Oklahoma. Member of Pure Prairie League from 1979-83. Married to Janis Oliver of the Sweethearts Of The Rodeo.

7/28/90	67	78 ▲		1 When I Call Your Name..	$12	MCA 42321
3/23/91+	37	97 ▲		2 Pocket Full Of Gold..	$12	MCA 10140
9/19/92	10	21↑▲		3 I Still Believe In You...	$12	MCA 10630

Don't Let Our Love Start	Little Left Over (2)	Never Knew Lonely (1)	One More Last Chance (3)	Sight For Sore Eyes (1)	Tryin' To Get Over You (3)
Slippin' Away (3)	Liza Jane (1)	No Future In The Past (3)	Pocket Full Of Gold (2)	Sparkle (2)	Under These Conditions (3)
I Quit (2)	Look At Us (3)	Nothing Like A Woman (3)	Pretty Words (3)	Strings That Tie You Down	We Could Have Been (1)
I Still Believe In You (3)	Love Never Broke Anyone's	Oh Girl (You Know Where	Ridin' The Rodeo (1)	(2)	We Won't Dance (1)
If I Didn't Have You In My	Heart (3)	To Find Me) (1)	Rita Ballou (1)	Take Your Memory With You	What's A Man To Do (2)
World (2)	Never Alone (1)	Oklahoma Swing (1)	Say Hello (3)	(2)	When I Call Your Name (1)

GILLAN
Ian Gillan — Deep Purple's lead singer. Born on 12/19/45 in London. Portrayed Jesus in the rock opera *Jesus Christ Superstar*. Joined Black Sabbath for *Born Again* album.

12/6/80	183	3		Glory Road...	$8	RSO/Virgin 1001

Are You Sure?	Nervous	On The Rocks	Time And Again	Your Mother Was Right
If You Believe Me	No Easy Way	Running, White Face, City Boy	Unchain Your Brain	

GILLEY, Mickey
Born on 3/9/36 in Ferriday, Louisiana. Country singer/pianist. First cousin to both Jerry Lee Lewis and Reverend Jimmy Swaggart. Owner of Gilleys nightclub in Pasadena, Texas. Gilley and the club were featured in the film *Urban Cowboy*.

8/30/80	177	3		1 That's All That Matters To Me	$8	Epic 36492
8/22/81	170	6		2 You Don't Know Me	$8	Epic 37416

Blame Lies With Me (1)	Headache Tomorrow (Or A	Lonely Nights (2)	She Left You (A Long Time	We've Watched Another
Blues Don't Care Who's Got	Heartache Tonight) (1)	Lyin' Again (1)	Ago) (2)	Evening Waste Away (2)
'Em (1)	Jukebox Argument (1)	Million Dollar Memories (1)	So Easy To Begin (1)	**You Don't Know Me** (2) *55*
Clinging To A Memory (2)	Ladies Night (2)	More I Turn The Bottle Up (1)	Tears Of The Lonely (2)	
Drinking Old Memories	Learning To Live Without	My Affection (2)	That's All That Matters (1)	
Down (2)	You (2)		True Love Ways (1) *66*	

GILMER, Jimmy, & The Fireballs
Rock and roll band formed while high schoolers in Raton, New Mexico. Lead vocalist Chuck Tharp was replaced in 1960 by Jimmy Gilmer, who was introduced to group by producer Norman Petty at his famed Clovis, New Mexico studio.

11/16/63	26	14		Sugar Shack	$30	Dot 25545

Almost Eighteen	Let's Talk	Lonesome Tears	Red Cadillac And A Black	Suzie Q
I Wonder Why	Linda Lu	Pretend	Mustache	Won't Be Long
Let The Good Times Roll	Little Baby		**Sugar Shack** *1*	

GILMOUR, David
Born on 3/6/47 in Cambridge, England. Guitarist/vocalist with Pink Floyd.

7/1/78	29	18		1 David Gilmour	$10	Columbia 35388
3/17/84	32	28		2 About Face	$8	Columbia 39296

All Lovers Are Deranged (2)	I Can't Breathe Anymore (1)	Mihalis (1)	Out Of The Blue (2)	There's No Way Out Of Here
Blue Light (2) *62*	It's Deafinitely (1)	Murder (2)	Raise My Rent (1)	(1)
Cruise (2)	Let's Get Metaphysical (2)	Near The End (2)	Short And Sweet (1)	Until We Sleep (2)
Cry From The Street (1)	Love On The Air (2)	No Way (1)	So Far Away (1)	You Know I'm Right (2)

GILSTRAP, Jim
Backup singer from Texas; based in Los Angeles.

8/30/75	179	7		Swing Your Daddy..	$10	Roxbury 102

Ain't That Peculiar	One More Heartache	Special Occasion	Swing Your Daddy, Part II
House Of Strangers *93*	Put Out The Fire	**Swing Your Daddy** *55*	Take Your Daddy For A Ride

GIORGIO — see MORODER, Giorgio

GIOVANNI, Nikki, & The New York Community Choir
Black poetess.

8/21/71	165	13		Truth Is On Its Way.. [T]	$8	Right-On 5001

Nikki recites her poems to the music of famous spirituals performed by various gospel artists

Alabama Poem	I Stood On The Banks Of	Must Jesus Bear The Cross	Peace Be Still *[Isaac Douglas]*	Second Rap Poem
All I Gotta Do (poem)	Jordan *[Arthur Freeman]*	Alone *[Edgar Kendricks]*	Poem For A Lady Of Leisure	This Little Light Of Mine
Amazing Grace *[New York	I've Decided To Make Jesus	My Tower (poem)	Now Retired	*[New York Community*
Community Choir]*	My Choice *[New York	Nikki Rosa (poem)	Poem For Aretha	*Choir]*
Ego Tripping (poem)	Community Choir]*	Nobody Knows The Trouble	Pretty Little Baby *[Edgar	Woman Poem
Great Pax Whitey (poem)	It Is Well *[Isaac Douglas]*	I've Seen *[Wilbert Johnson]*	Kendricks]*	

GIPSY KINGS
Six-man band, formed in 1979, made up of members of the related Reyes and Baliardo gypsy families from Montpelier and Arles, France. Andre and Nicholas (lead vocals) Reyes are the sons of famous Flamenco singer Jose Reyes. Lyrics are sung in Gitane, a mixture of Spanish and French.

12/17/88+	57	42	●	1 Gipsy Kings .... [F]	$8	Musician 60845
12/16/89+	95	19		2 Mosaique .... [F]	$8	Musician 60892
8/3/91	120	7		3 Este Mundo .... [F]	$12	Elektra M. 61179

translation of Spanish title: This World

A Mi Manera (My Way) (1)	Bem, Bem, Maria (1)	El Camino (2)	Furia (3)	Liberte (2)	Nina Morena (3)
Amor, Amor (1)	Caminando Por La Calle (2)	El Mauro (3)	Habla Me (3)	Mi Vida (3)	No Volvere (3)
Baila Me (3)	Djobi Djoba (1)	Este Mundo (3)	Inspiration (1)	Moorea (1)	Oh Mai (3)
Bamboleo (1)	Duende (1)	Faena (1)	Lagrimas (3)	Mosaique (2)	Oy (3)

DEBUT DATE	PEAK POS	WKS CHR	G O L D	ARTIST — Album Title	$	Label & Number

GIPSY KINGS — Cont'd

Passion (2)	Serana (2)	Soy (2)	Trista Pena (2)	Un Amor (1)	Viento Del Arena (2)
Quiero Saber (1)	Sin Ella (3)	Ternuras (3)	Tu Quieres Volver (1)	Vamos A Bailar (2)	Volare (2)

GIRLSCHOOL
Heavy-metal female quartet from England: guitarists/vocalists Kelly Johnson and Kim McAuliffe, with bassist Enid Williams and drummer Denise Dufort.

| 5/22/82 | 182 | 5 | | Hit And Run .... | $8 | Stiff 18 |

C'mon Let's Go	Hit And Run	Kick It Down	Race With The Devil	Watch Your Step
Future Flash	Hunter	Not For Sale	Take It All Away	Yeah Right

GIUFFRIA
California-based rock quintet led by Gregg Giuffria (keyboardist with Angel) and David Glen Eisley. Gregg and member Chuck Wright joined House Of Lords in 1988.

| 12/8/84+ | 26 | 29 | 1 | Giuffria .... | $8 | MCA 5524 |
| 5/24/86 | 60 | 14 | 2 | Silk + Steel .... | $8 | MCA 5742 |

Awakening (1)	Dirty Secrets (2)	Heartache (2)	**Lonely In Love** (1) 57	Out Of The Blue (Too Far	Tell It Like It Is (2)
Call To The Heart (1) 15	Do Me Right (1)	**I Must Be Dreaming** (2) 52	Love You Forever (2)	Gone) (1)	Trouble Again (1)
Change Of Heart (2)	Don't Tear Me Down (1)	Lethal Lover (2)	No Escape (2)	Radio (2)	Turn Me On (1)
Dance (1)	Girl (2)	Line Of Fire (1)			

GLASER, Tompall — see CONCEPT ALBUMS

GLASS, Philip
New Age composer. Born on 1/31/37 in Baltimore. Formed seven-piece Philip Glass Ensemble in 1968. Incorporates Eastern musical structures with Western harmony. Scored the 1983 film documentary *Koyaanisqatsi.*

| 4/10/82 | 121 | 6 | 1 | Glassworks ....[I] | $8 | CBS 37265 |
| 4/12/86 | 91 | 13 | 2 | Songs From Liquid Days .... | $8 | CBS 39564 |

music: Glass; lyrics: Paul Simon, Laurie Anderson, Suzanne Vega, David Byrne; Linda Ronstadt on vocals of "Forgetting" & "Freezing"

Changing Opinion (2)	Floe (1)	Freezing (2)	Lightning (2)	Open The Kingdom (Liquid	Rubric (1)
Facades (1)	Forgetting (2)	Islands (1)	Liquid Days (Part I) (2)	Days, Part II) (2)	

GLASS HARP
Ohio rock trio led by Phil Keaggy (guitars, vocals; began noted inspirational career in 1973).

| 11/27/71 | 192 | 3 | | Synergy .... | $15 | Decca 75306 |

Answer	Coming Home	Just Always	Never Is A Long Time	Song Of Hope
Child Of The Universe	Dawn Of A New Day	Mountains	One Day At A Time	Special Friends

GLASS MOON
U.S. rock quartet: Dave Adams, Nestor Nunez, Chris Jones and Jaime Glaser.

| 5/10/80 | 148 | 9 | | Glass Moon .... | $8 | Radio 2003 |

Blue Windows	Easy Life	(I Like) The Way You Play	Only Have To Cry One Time	Sundays And Mondays
Dreamer	Follow Me	Killer At 25	Solsbury Hill	

GLASS TIGER
Canadian rock quintet: Alan Frew (vocals), Sam Reid (keyboards), Al Connelly (guitar), Wayne Parker (bass) and Michael Hanson (drums).

| 7/19/86+ | 27 | 51 | ● 1 | The Thin Red Line .... | $8 | Manhattan 53032 |
| 5/7/88 | 82 | 15 | 2 | Diamond Sun .... | $8 | EMI-Man. 48684 |

Ancient Evenings (1)	Ecstacy (2)	Lifetime Of Moments (2)	**Someday** (1) 7	(Watching) Worlds Crumble
Closer To You (1)	Far Away From Here (2)	Looking At A Picture (1)	Suffer In Silence (2)	(2)
Diamond Sun (2)	**I Will Be There** (1) 34	My Song (2)	Thin Red Line (1)	You're What I Look For (1)
Don't Forget Me (When I'm	**I'm Still Searching** (2) 31	Secret, The (1)	This Island Earth (2)	
Gone) (1) 2	It's Love U Feel (2)	Send Your Love (2)	Vanishing Tribe (1)	

GLAZER, Tom, And The Do-Re-Mi Children's Chorus
Tom (b: 9/3/14 in Philadelphia) is a novelty folk singer. Hosted own ABC radio program, 1945-47. Composed score for 1957 film *A Face In The Crowd.*

| 7/27/63 | 114 | 8 | | On Top Of Spaghetti .... [N] | $15 | Kapp 3331 |

Barbers Anthem	Dance With A Dolly (With A	From The Halls Of	Oh, How I Hate To Get Up In	Webfooted Friends
Battle Hymn Of The Children	Hole In Her Stocking)	Montezuma (To The Shores	The Morning	When The Dust Mops Go
Capital Ship	Dunderbeck	Of P.T.A.)	**On Top Of Spaghetti** 14	Bottom Of The Sea	Rolling Along

★★160★★ GLEASON, Jackie
Born Herbert John Gleason on 2/26/16 in Brooklyn; died of cancer on 6/24/87. Star of stage and screen before enormous popularity on TV's *The Honeymooners* (1955-56) and his own CBS-TV variety series. His albums featured dreamy mood music played by studio orchestras, conducted by Gleason with trumpet solos by Bobby Hackett and Pee Wee Erwin; much of the music was written by Gleason.

3/5/55	5	16		1 **Music To Remember Her**..[I]	$15	Capitol 570
6/25/55	1²	23		2 **Lonesome Echo** ....[I]	$15	Capitol 627
11/12/55	2²	11		3 **Romantic Jazz** ....[I]	$15	Capitol 568
1/28/56	7	7		4 **Music For Lovers Only/Music To Make You Misty**................[I-R]	$15	Capitol 475 [2]

reissue of albums from 1953 and 1954

2/25/56	8	5		5 **Music To Change Her Mind** ....[I]	$15	Capitol 632
6/9/56	10	10		6 **Night Winds** ....[I]	$15	Capitol 717
12/8/56	16	3		7 Merry Christmas..[X-I]	$15	Capitol 758

Christmas charts: 25/63, 70/'66, 32/'67

8/26/57	13	2	●	8 **Music For The Love Hours** ....[I]	$15	Capitol 816
9/9/57	16	10		9 **Velvet Brass** ....[I]	$15	Capitol 859
12/9/57	14	4		10 Jackie Gleason presents "Oooo!" ....[I]	$15	Capitol 905
8/10/63	82	5		11 Movie Themes - For Lovers Only..[I]	$12	Capitol 1877
12/7/63	115	8		12 Today's Romantic Hits/for lovers only..[I]	$12	Capitol 1978
6/6/64	82	10		13 Today's Romantic Hits/for lovers only, Vol. 2 ....[I]	$12	Capitol 2056
2/5/66	141	4		14 Silk 'N' Brass ....[I]	$12	Capitol 2409

DEBUT DATE	PEAK POS	WKS CHR	GOLD	ARTIST — Album Title	$	Label & Number

GLEASON, Jackie — Cont'd

DEBUT DATE	PEAK POS	WKS CHR		ARTIST — Album Title	$	Label & Number
11/26/66	71	11	15	How Sweet It Is for lovers .... [I]	$12	Capitol 2582
6/24/67	200	2	16	A Taste Of Brass for lovers only .... [I]	$12	Capitol 2684
8/23/69	192	2	17	Close-Up .... [I-R]	$12	Capitol 255 [2]

reissue of *Music For Lovers Only* ('53) and *Music, Martinis & Memories* ('54)

African Waltz (16)
All By Myself (5)
Alone (6)
Alone Together (4)
Am I Blue? (9)
Are You Lonesome Tonight (6)
Art Of Love (16)
As Long As He Needs Me (12)
Au Revoir (15)
Autumn Waltz (15)
Begin To Love (14)
Best Things In Life Are Free (3)
Beyond The Blue Horizon (10)
Blue Velvet (13)
Body And Soul (4,17)
But Not For Me (4,9,17)
By The Beautiful Sea (9)
By The Fireside (7)
Call Me (16)
Call Me Irresponsible (11)
Cardinal, Theme From The (13)
Charade (13)
Charmaine (1)
Cherokee (Indian Love Song) (9)
Cherry (1)
Chinatown, My Chinatown (9)
Christmas In Paris (7)
Christmas Song (Merry Christmas To You) (7)
Close As Pages In A Book (6)
Colette (11)
Come Rain Or Come Shine (2)
Coquette (5)
Crazy Rhythm (3)
Dancing In The Dark (2)
Dancing On The Ceiling (2)
Dancing With Tears In My Eyes (6)
Danke Schoen (2)
Darling, Je Vous Aime Beaucoup (2)
Darn That Dream (8)

Days Of Wine And Roses (11)
Deep Purple (2,13)
Desafinado (12)
Diane (1)
Did I Remember (5)
Dinah (1)
Dr. Zhivago ..see: Lara's Theme
Don't Blame Me (3)
Everything's Coming Up Roses (14)
Fly Me To The Moon (12)
Fools Rush In (13)
For You (13)
From Russia With Love (13)
Garden In The Rain (2)
Get Out Of Town (8)
Girl From Ipanema (14)
Girl Of My Dreams (9)
Girls Of The Folies Bergere (14)
Good Life (12)
Good Night, Sweet Nightingale (6)
Guilty (6)
Happy Holiday (7)
Have You Heard (13)
Have Yourself A Merry Little Christmas (7)
Here Lies Love (10)
High On A Windy Hill (10)
Home (7)
Home In The Meadow (11)
House Is Haunted (By The Echo Of Your Last Goodbye) (8)
How About Me (10)
How About You? (3)
How Deep Is The Ocean (2)
How Did She Look (8)
How Sweet It Is (15)
I Apologize (6)
I Can't Believe That You're In Love With Me (9)
I Can't Get Started (17)
I Cover The Waterfront (17)
I Don't Know Why (I Just Do) (2)

I Don't Stand A Ghost Of A Chance With You (8)
I Got It Bad And That Ain't Good (17)
I Guess I'll Have To Change My Plan (4)
I Hadn't Anyone Till I Knew (4)
I Left My Heart In San Francisco (12)
I Love You Much Too Much (8)
I Never Knew (3)
I Only Have Eyes For You (4,17)
I Remember You (17)
I Still Get A Thrill (2)
I Wanna Be Loved By You (15)
I Will Wait For You (15)
I Wished On The Moon (2)
I'll Be Around (10)
I'll Be Home For Christmas (If Only In My Dreams) (7)
I'm Always Chasing Rainbows (2)
I'm Glad There Is You (5)
I'm In The Mood For Love (4,17)
I've Got A Crush On You (10)
I've Got My Love On You (3)
I've Got My Love To Keep Me Warm (7)
I've Got You Under My Skin (15)
If He Walked Into My Life (15)
If I Had You (17)
If I Ruled The World (14)
If I Should Lose You (6)
Imagination (10)
It All Depends On You (4,16)
It Could Happen To You (17)
It Happened In Monterey (4)
It Was So Beautiful (3)
It's All Right With Me (10)
It's Such A Happy Day (14)
It's The Talk Of The Town (5)
Jeannine, I Dream Of Lilac Time (1)

Jingle Bells (7)
Jo Anne (1)
Just A Memory (8)
La Dolce Vita (The Sweet Life) (11)
La Terre (The Earth) (16)
Lady Is A Tramp (3)
Lara's Theme (15)
Laura (1)
Lawrence Of Arabia (11)
Leaves Of Love (16)
Little Girl (17)
Louise (1)
Love Is Here To Stay (4,16,17)
Love Letters In The Sand (6)
Love Locked Out (6)
Love Nest (3)
Love (Your Spell Is Everywhere) (9)
Mad About The Boy (2)
Make Someone Happy (12)
Mame (16)
Man I Love (4,9)
Man That Got Away (11)
Maria Elena (13)
Marie (1)
Marilyn (1)
Me And My Shadow (9)
Memories Of You (6)
Mickey (4)
Midnight Sun (12)
Misty (12)
Moonlight Becomes You (8)
More I See You (10)
More (Theme from Mondo Cane) (12)
Most Beautiful Girl In The World (3)
Mutiny On The Bounty (Follow Me), Love Theme From (11)
My Blue Heaven (3)
My Buddy (9)
My Devotion (10)
My Funny Valentine (4)
My Ideal (17)
My Love For Carmen (16,17)
My Romance (11)

My Sin (5)
Once In A While (17)
Out Of Nowhere (9)
Petite Waltz (3)
Real Live Girl (14)
Remember (2)
Rosanne (1)
Ruby (1)
Santa Claus Is Comin' To Town (7)
Say It Isn't So (4)
Second Time Around (15)
September Song (9)
Serenade In Blue (8)
Shadow Of Your Smile (15)
Shangri-La (14,17)
She's Funny That Way (5)
Since I Fell For You (13)
Skyliner (9)
Sleepy Time Gal (6)
Snowfall (17)
Some Day (17)
Somebody Else Is Taking My Place (14)
Someday I'll Find You (2)
Somewhere, My Love ..see: Lara's Theme
Song Is Ended (17)
Soon (3)
Speak Low (2)
Starry Eyed And Breathless (14)
Stella By Starlight (1)
Story Of A Starry Night (7)
Strangers In The Night (15)
Sweet Lorraine (1)
Sweet Sue Just You (1)
Take Me In Your Arms (5)
Take The "A" Train (9)
Tangerine (1)
Taras Bulba (The Wishing Star), Theme From (11)
Taste Of Honey (16)
There I've Said It Again (13)
There Must Be A Way (2)
There'll Be Some Changes Made (3)
Third Man Theme (11)
Thousand Goodnights (6)

Thrill Is Gone (2)
Time On My Hands (17)
Touch Of Your Lips (6)
Unforgiven, Theme From The (12)
What Can I Say After I Say I'm Sorry (4)
What Kind Of Fool Am I? (12)
What's New (9)
When You're Away (6)
White Christmas (7)
Who Cares? (So Long As You Care For Me) (3)
Willow Weep For Me (10)
Winter Wonderland (7)
World Is Waiting For The Sunrise (3)
Yesterdays (17)
You And The Night And The Music (3)
You Are Too Beautiful (6)
You Brought A New Kind Of Love To Me (10)
You Call It Madness (5)
You Can't Pull The Wool Over My Eyes (3)
You Hit The Spot (15)
You Were Meant For Me (4)
You're All The World To Me (11)
You're Driving Me Crazy! (What Did I Do?) (9)
You're Gonna Hear From Me (15)
You're My Greatest Love (5)
You're Nobody Till Somebody Loves You (14)
You've Changed (5)

GLITTER, Gary

Born Paul Gadd on 5/8/44 in Banbury, England. First recorded as Paul Raven in the early '60s, then as Paul Monday; changed name to Gary Glitter in 1971.

DEBUT DATE	PEAK POS	WKS CHR		ARTIST — Album Title	$	Label & Number
10/28/72	186	8		Glitter	$10	Bell 1108

Ain't That A Shame
Baby Please Don't Go
Clapping Song

Donna
Famous Instigator

I Didn't Know I Loved You (Till I Saw You Rock And Roll) 35
Rock And Roll Part 1
Rock And Roll Part 2 7
Rock On

School Day (Ring! Ring!)
Goes The Bell)

Shakey Sue
Wanderer, The

GLOVER, Roger

Born on 11/30/45 in Brecon, Wales, England. Bass player of Deep Purple and Rainbow.

DEBUT DATE	PEAK POS	WKS CHR		ARTIST — Album Title	$	Label & Number
1/24/76	142	8	1	The Butterfly Ball and the Grasshopper's Feast	$10	UK 56000

with guests: David Coverdale (Deep Purple, Whitesnake), Glenn Hughes (Deep Purple, Black Sabbath) and Ronnie Dio (Black Sabbath, Rainbow)

6/16/84	101	12	2	Mask	$8	21 Records 9009

Aranea (1)
Behind The Smile (1)
Dancin' Again (2)
Dawn (1)
Divided World (2)
Don't Look Down (2)

Dreams Of Sir Bedivere (1)
Fake It (2)
Feast (1)
Fly Away (1)
Get Ready (1)
Getting Stranger (2)

Harlequin Hare (1)
Hip Level (2)
Homeward (1)
Love Is All (1)
Magician Moth (1)
Mask (2)

No Solution (1)
Old Blind Mole (1)
Saffron Dormouse And Lizzy Bee (1)
Sir Maximus Mouse (1)
Sitting In A Dream (1)

Together Again (1)
Waiting (1)
Watch Out For The Bat (1)
(You're So) Remote (2)

GOANNA

Australian rock group — Shane Howard, lead singer.

DEBUT DATE	PEAK POS	WKS CHR		ARTIST — Album Title	$	Label & Number
6/25/83	179	5		Spirit Of Place	$8	Atco 90081

Borderline
Cheatin' Man

Children Of The Southern Land

Factory Man
Four Weeks Gone

On The Platform
Razor's Edge

Scenes (From An Occasional Window)

Solid Rock 71
Stand Yr' Ground

GODFATHERS, The

Rock group formed in London, in early 1986, by brothers Chris and Peter Coyne. Both were members of underground band, The Sid Presley Experience.

DEBUT DATE	PEAK POS	WKS CHR		ARTIST — Album Title	$	Label & Number
2/20/88	91	16	1	Birth, School, Work, Death...	$8	Epic 40946
5/20/89	174	6	2	More Songs About Love & Hate.......................................	$8	Epic 45023

Another You (2)
Birth, School, Work, Death (1)

'Cause I Said So (1)
Halfway Paralysed (2)
How Low Is Low (2)

I Don't Believe In You (2)
I'm Lost And Then I'm Found (2)

If I Only Had Time (1)
It's So Hard (1)
Just Like You (1)

Life Has Passed Us By (2)
Love Is Dead (1)
Obsession (1)

Pretty Girl (2)
S.T.B. (1)
She Gives Me Love (2)

GODFATHERS, The — Cont'd

Strangest Boy (1)	This Is Your Life (2)	Walking Talking Johnny	When Am I Coming Down (1)
Tell Me Why (1)	Those Days Are Over (2)	Cash Blues (2)	

GODFREY, Arthur — see QUINN, Carmel

GODLEY & CREME

Kevin Godley (b: 10/7/45, Manchester, England) and Lol Creme (b: 9/19/47, Manchester, England) formed duo after leaving British group 10cc. Prior to 10cc, both were with Hotlegs.

| 8/17/85 | 37 | 15 | | The History Mix Volume 1 | $8 | Polydor 825981 |

Cry [includes 2 versions] 16 | Englishman In New York | Golden Boy | Light Me Up | Save A Mountain For Me | Wet Rubber Soup Medley

GODZ

Columbus, Ohio rock quartet: Eric Moore, Bob Hill, Glen Cataline and Mark Chatfield.

| 4/8/78 | 191 | 5 | | 1 The Godz | $8 | Millennium 8003 |
| 2/17/79 | 189 | 2 | | 2 Nothing Is Sacred | $8 | Casablanca 7134 |

Baby I Love You (1) | Festyvul Seasun (2) | Gotta Muv (2) | Hey Mama (2) | Luv Kage (2) | Snakin' (2)
Candy's Going Bad (1) | Go Away (1) | Guaranteed (1) | I Don't Wanna Go Home (2) | Rock Yer Sox Auf (2) | Under The Table (1)
Cross Country (1) | Gotta Keep A Runnin' (1) | He's A Fool (2) | I'll Bi Yer Luv (2) | 714 (2)

GOFFIN, Louise

Singer/songwriter. Daughter of Carole King and Gerry Goffin.

| 8/4/79 | 87 | 13 | | Kid Blue | $8 | Asylum 203 |

All I've Got To Do | Hurt By Love | Kid Blue | Red Lite Fever | Remember (Walking In | Singing Out Alone
Angels Ain't For Keeping | Jimmy And The Tough Kids | Long Distance | | The Sand) 43 | Trapeze

GO-GO'S

Female rock group formed in 1978 in Los Angeles, consisting of Belinda Carlisle (vocals), Jane Wiedlin (guitar), Charlotte Caffey (guitar), Kathy Valentine (bass) and Gina Schock (drums). Disbanded in 1984. Reunion tour in 1990. Caffey formed The Graces in 1989.

8/1/81+	1[6]	72	▲2	1 Beauty And The Beat	$8	I.R.S. 70021
8/14/82	8	28	●	2 Vacation	$8	I.R.S. 70031
4/7/84	18	32		3 Talk Show	$8	I.R.S. 70041
11/17/90	127	4		4 Greatest	[G]	$12	I.R.S. 44797

Automatic (1) | Get Up And Go (2,4) 50 | It's Everything But | This Town (1,4) | Yes Or No (3) 84
Beatnik Beach (2,4) | Girl Of 100 Lists (2) | Partytime (2) | Tonite (1) | You Can't Walk In Your
Beneath The Blue Sky (3) | He's So Strange (2) | Lust To Love (1,4) | Turn To You (3,4) 32 | Sleep (If You Can't Sleep)
Can't Stop The World (1) | Head Over Heels (3,4) 11 | Mercenary (3,4) | Vacation (2,4) 8 | (1)
Capture The Light (3) | How Much More (1,4) | Our Lips Are Sealed | Way You Dance (2) | You Thought (3,4)
Cool Jerk (2,4) | I Think It's Me (2) | (1,4) 20 | We Don't Get Along (2)
Fading Fast (1) | I'm The Only One (3,4) | Skidmarks On My Heart (1) | We Got The Beat (1,4) 2
Forget That Day (3) | I'm With You (3) | This Old Feeling (2) | Worlds Away (2)

GOLD, Andrew

Born on 8/2/51 in Burbank, California. Son of soundtrack composer Ernest Gold (Exodus) and singer Marni Nixon. Co-founder of the group Bryndle. Session and arranging work for Linda Ronstadt since early '70s. Member of pop duo Wax, 1986.

1/10/76	190	2		1 Andrew Gold	$8	Asylum 1047
5/7/77	95	16		2 What's Wrong With This Picture?	$8	Asylum 1086
2/25/78	81	14		3 All This And Heaven Too	$8	Asylum 116

Always For You (3) | Hang My Picture Straight (1) | Learning The Game (2) | Note From You (1) | Still You Linger On (3)
Angel Woman (2) | Heartaches In Heartaches (1) | Lonely Boy (2) 7 | Oh Urania (Take Me Away) | Ten Years Behind Me (1)
Do Wah Diddy (2) | Hope You Feel Good (2) | Looking For My Love (3) | (3) | Thank You For Being A
Endless Flight (1) | How Can This Be Love (3) | Love Hurts (1) | One Of Them Is Me (2) | Friend (3) 25
Firefly (2) | I'm A Gambler (1) | Must Be Crazy (2) | Passing Thing (2) | That's Why I Love You
Genevieve (3) | I'm Coming Home (1) | Never Let Her Slip Away | Resting In Your Arms (1) | (1) 68
Go Back Home Again (2) | I'm On My Way (3) | (3) 67 | Stay (2) | You're Free (3)

GOLD, Marty, and His Orchestra

Born on 12/26/15 in New York City. Composer/conductor/pianist.

| 4/13/63 | 10 | 18 | | Soundpower! | [I] | $10 | RCA 2620 |

Harlem Nocturne | I Left My Heart In San | Misty | Shangri-La | String Of Pearls | Till There Was You
I Concentrate On You | Francisco | Moon Was Yellow | Stella By Starlight | Terry Theme From Limelight | Without A Song
| | I'll Remember April |

GOLDDIGGERS

Female singing/dancing troupe from Dean Martin's TV show.

| 8/2/69 | 142 | 7 | | The Golddiggers | $10 | Metromedia 1009 |

Blame It On My Youth | Come Rain Or Come Shine | 59th Street Bridge Song | It Seems Like Yesterday | Kumquat Tree | One Person
Can't Take My Eyes Off Of | (medley) | (Feelin' Groovy) | It's Fun To Be Young | Montage From How Sweet It | Shuffle Off To Buffalo
You (medley) | | I Wanna Be Loved | Just Like An Old Time Movie | Is | There's A Place For Lovers

GOLDEN EARRING

Rock band from The Netherlands: Barry Hay (vocals), George Kooymans (guitars, vocals), Cesar Zuiderwijk (drums) and Rinus Gerritsen (bass, keyboards). Also supported by keyboardist/arranger Robert Jan Stips through 1982.

5/4/74	12	29	●	1 Moontan	$20	Track 396
4/12/75	108	8		2 Switch	$8	Track 2139
2/28/76	156	4		3 To The Hilt	$8	MCA 2183
5/28/77	182	2		4 Mad Love	$8	MCA 2254
12/11/82+	24	30		5 Cut	$8	21 Records 9004
3/17/84	107	9		6 N.E.W.S.	$8	21 Records 9008
11/24/84	158	6		7 Something Heavy Going Down - Live From The Twilight Zone	[L]	$8	21 Records 823717
7/12/86	196	2		8 The Hole	$8	21 Records 90514

DEBUT DATE	PEAK POS	WKS CHR	GOLD	ARTIST — Album Title	$	Label & Number

GOLDEN EARING — Cont'd

Are You Receiving Me (1)
Baby Dynamite (5)
Big Tree, Blue Sea (1)
Bombay (4)
Candy's Going Bad (1) *91*
Chargin' Up My Batteries (5)
Clear Night Moonlight (6)
Con Man (4)
Daddy's Gonna Save My Soul (2)
Devil Made Me Do It (5) *79*

Enough Is Enough (6,7)
Facedancer (3)
Fightin' Windmills (4)
Fist In Glove (6)
Future (5,7)
Have A Heart (8)
I Need Love (4)
I'll Make It All Up To You (6)
It's Over Now (6)
Jane Jane (8)
Jump And Run (8)

Kill Me (Ce Soir) (2)
Last Of The Mohicans (5)
Latin Lightnin' (3)
Lonesome D.J. (2)
Long Blond Animal (7)
Lost And Found (5)
Love In Motion (8)
Love Is A Rodeo (2)
Mad Love's Comin' (4)
Mission Impossible (6,7)
N.E.W.S. (6)

Nomad (3)
Plus Minus Absurdio (2)
Quiet Eyes (8)
Radar Love (1,7) *13*
Save The Best For Later (8)
Secrets (5)
Shout In The Dark (8)
Sleep Walkin' (3)
Something Heavy Going Down (7)
Sueleen (Sweden) (4)

Switch (2)
They Dance (8)
Time's Up (4)
To The Hilt (8)
Tons Of Time (2)
Troubles & Hassles (2)
Twilight Zone (5,7) *10*
Vanilla Queen (1)
Violins (3)
When The Lady Smiles (6) *76*

Why Do I (8)
Why Me? (3)

GOLDEN GATE STRINGS

Studio outfit produced by Stu Phillips and conducted by Sid Feller. Phillips earlier conducted The Hollyridge Strings.

| 5/27/67 | 200 | 2 | | The Monkees Song Book .... [I] | $10 | Epic 26248 |

Auntie Grizelda
I Wanna Be Free

I'm A Believer
(I'm Not Your) Steppin' Stone

Last Train To Clarksville
Mary, Mary

Monkees, (Theme From) The
Saturday's Child

She

This Just Doesn't Seem To Be My Day

GOLDSBORO, Bobby

Born on 1/18/41 in Marianna, Florida. Singer/songwriter/guitarist. To Dothan, Alabama in 1956. Toured with Roy Orbison, 1962-64. Own syndicated TV show from 1972-75, *The Bobby Goldsboro Show*.

5/6/67	165	3	1	Solid Goldsboro - Bobby Goldsboro's Greatest Hits .... [G]	$20	United Art. 6561
4/20/68	5	48	●	2 Honey	$20	United Art. 6642
9/21/68	116	13		3 Word Pictures featuring Autumn Of My Life	$20	United Art. 6657
6/7/69	60	13		4 Today	$20	United Art. 6704
1/17/70	139	11		5 Muddy Mississippi Line	$15	United Art. 6735
7/4/70	103	10		6 Bobby Goldsboro's Greatest Hits .... [G]	$15	United Art. 5502
1/23/71	120	13		7 We Gotta Start Lovin'	$15	United Art. 6777
8/28/71	142	5		8 Come Back Home	$15	United Art. 5516
9/29/73	150	11		9 Summer (The First Time)	$15	United Art. 124
11/16/74	174	3		10 Bobby Goldsboro's 10th Anniversary Album .... [G]	$15	United Art. 311 [2]

About Time (7)
Ain't That Livin' (4)
And I Love You So (8) *83*
Autumn Of My Life (3,6,10) *19*
Beautiful People (2)
Blue Autumn (1,6,10) *35*
Brand New Kind Of Love (10)
Broomstick Cowboy (1,5,10) *9*
By The Time I Get To Phoenix (2)
California Wine (10)
Can You Feel It (6,10) *75*
Come Back Home (8,10) *69*
Danny (3)
Danny Is A Mirror To Me (8)
Dissatisfied Man (3)
Don't It Make You Wanta Go Home (5)
Down On The Bayou (7)

Everybody's Talkin' (7)
For The Very First Time (7)
Gentle Of A Man (8)
Glad She's A Woman (4,6) *61*
Gold Hill Hotel (8)
Graveyard Of My Mind (5)
Hard Luck Joe (3)
He Ain't Heavy, He's My Brother (7)
He's Part Of Us (9)
Heaven Here On Earth (7)
Hoboes And Kings (4)
Honey (2,6,10) *1*
I Am A Rock (3)
I Know You Better Than That (1) *56*
I'll Remember You (8)
I'm A Drifter (4,6,10) *46*
If You Go Away (Ne Me Quitte Pas) (3)

If You Got A Heart (1)
If You Wait For Love (1) *75*
If You've Got A Heart (10) *60*
If'n I Was Good (9)
It Hurts Me (1) *70*
It's Gonna Change (7)
It's Too Late (1,6,10) *23*
It's Up To Us (8)
Jean (3)
Killing Me Softly With Her Song (9)
L&N Don't Stop Here Anymore (9)
Letter To Emily (3)
Lisa Was (5)
Little Green Apples (2)
Little Things (1,10) *13*
Lodi (5)
Look Around You (It's Christmas Time) (3)

Love Arrestor (2)
Maggie (3)
Marlena (9,10)
Mary Jackson (7)
Me Japanese Boy I Love You (1) *74*
Mississippi Delta Queen (9)
Mornin Mornin (5) *78*
Muddy Mississippi Line (5,6,10) *53*
My God And I (7)
Next Girl That I Marry (8)
Pardon Me Miss (3)
Pledge Of Love (2)
Poem For My Little Lady (8)
Proud Mary (5)
Requiem (7)
Richer Men Than I (4)
Run To Me (2)
Saturdays Only (8)
Say It's Not Over (4)

See The Funny Little Clown (1,6,10) *9*
She (9)
Sing Me A Smile (9)
Spread My Wings And Fly (9)
Straight Life (3,6,10) *36*
Summer (The First Time) (9,10) *21*
Sweet Caroline (5)
Throwback (8)
Time Good, Time Bad (5)
Today (1)
Tomorrow Is Forgotten (4)
Voodoo Woman (1,10) *27*
Watching Scotty Grow (7,10) *11*
Water Color Days (7)
We Gotta Start Lovin' (7)
What A Wonderful World (4)
Whenever He Holds You (1) *39*

Why Don't You Believe Me (2)
With Pen In Hand (2,6,10) *94*
Woman (2)
Woman Without Love (4)
World Beyond (3)
World I Used To Know (4)
You're Here (1)
Your Song (8)

GOMM, Ian

Born on 3/17/47 in Ealing, England. Member of London band Brinsley Schwarz, 1972-75.

| 9/22/79 | 104 | 12 | | Gomm With The Wind .... | $8 | Stiff 36103 |

Airplane
Another Year
Black And White

Chicken Run
Come On

Dirty Lies
Hold On *18*

Hooked On Love
Sad Affair

That's The Way I Rock 'N' Roll

24 Hour Service
You Can't Do That

GONZALEZ

British soul-disco band.

| 1/20/79 | 67 | 14 | | Shipwrecked .... | $8 | Capitol 11855 |

Baby, Baby, Baby
Bob Gropes Blues

Haven't Stopped Dancing Yet *26*

Just Let It Lay
Oh I

Rockmaninoff
Shipwrecked

Tear Down The Business

GOODMAN, Benny

Born on 5/30/09 in Chicago. Nicknamed "King of Swing." Clarinetist/big band leader since the 1930s. Fletcher Henderson arranged many of his early '30s hits. Won the Lifetime Achievement Grammy in 1986. Died on 6/13/86 of an apparent heart attack.

| 3/19/55 | 7 | 16 | | 1 B.G. In Hi-Fi .... [I] | $15 | Capitol 565 |
| 3/24/56 | 4 | 10 | | 2 The Benny Goodman Story .... [S-I] | $30 | Decca 8252/3 [2] |

Benny is portrayed by Steve Allen in the film, although Benny and his musicians play the music

| 11/10/62 | 80 | 6 | | 3 Benny Goodman In Moscow .... [L-I] | $15 | RCA 6008 [2] |

recorded during his tour of Russia, July 1962

| 3/7/64 | 90 | 10 | | 4 Together Again! .... [I] | $15 | RCA 2698 |

reunion of his quartet: Gene Krupa, Lionel Hampton and Teddy Wilson

| 4/3/71 | 189 | 7 | | 5 Benny Goodman Today .... [L-I] | $10 | London P. 4 21 [2] |

recorded live in Stockholm

Air Mail Special (1)
And The Angels Sing (2)
Avalon (2,3)
Baubles, Bangles And Beads (5)

Bei Mir Bist Du Schoen (3)
Big John's Special (1,5)
Blue Lou (1)
Blue Skies (5)
Body And Soul (3,5)

Bugle Call Rag (2)
Bye Bye Blackbird (3)
China Boy (1)
Dear Dave (5)
Dearest (4)

Don't Be That Way (2,5)
Down South Camp Meetin' (2)
Feathers (3)
Fontainebleau (3)

Four Once More (4)
Get Happy (1)
Goodbye (3,5)
Goody Goody (2)

I Got It Bad And That Ain't Good (3,4)
I Would Do Most Anything For You (5)
I'll Get By (4)

DEBUT DATE	PEAK POS	WKS CHR	GOLD	ARTIST — Album Title	$	Label & Number

GOODMAN, Benny — Cont'd

I've Found A New Baby (4)
If I Had You (5)
It's Been So Long (2)
Jersey Bounce (1,2)
Jumpin' At The Woodside (1)
King Porter Stomp (2)
Let's Dance (1,2,3,5)
Meadowland (3)
Meet The Band (3)
Memories Of You (2)

Midgets (3)
Mission To Moscow (3)
Moonglow (3)
On The Alamo (3)
One O'Clock Jump (2,3,5)
Poor Butterfly (5)
Rock Rimmon (1)
Roll 'Em (2,5)
Rose Room (medley) (3)
Runnin' Wild (4)

Say It Isn't So (4)
Sent For You Yesterday And
 Here You Come Today (1)
Seven Come Eleven (4)
Shine (1)
Sing, Sing, Sing (With A
 Swing) (2,5)
Slipped Disc (2)
Somebody Loves Me (4)
Somebody Stole My Gal (1)

Sometimes I'm Happy (2)
Stealin' Apples (3,5)
Stompin' At The Savoy (1,2)
String Of Pearls (5)
Sweet Georgia Brown (5)
Swift As The Wind (3)
Titter Pipes (3)
Venus H.B. (Turkish March)
 (5)

What Can I Say After I Say
 I'm Sorry? (1)
When I Grow Too Old To
 Dream (1)
Who Cares (4)
Why You? (3)
Willow Weep For Me (5)
World Is Waiting For The
 Sunrise (medley) (3)

You Brought A New Kind Of
 Love To Me (1)
You Turned The Tables On
 Me (2)
You're A Sweetheart (1)

GOODMAN, Dickie

Born on 4/19/34 in Hewlett, New York. Dickie and partner Bill Buchanan originated the novelty "break-in" recordings featuring bits of the original versions of top 40 hits interwoven throughout the recording. Comedy writer for Jackie Mason and head of music department at 20th Century Fox. Died on 11/6/89 of a self-inflicted gunshot.

| 12/6/75+ | 144 | 8 | | Mr. Jaws and other Fables ....[G-N] | $25 | Cash 6000 |

side 2: Buchanan & Goodman's top hits; includes "Super Fly Meets Shaft" by John & Ernest

Energy Crisis '74 33
Flying Saucer (Parts 1 &
2) 3

Flying Saucer The 2nd 18
Mr. Jaws 4

Santa And The Satellite
(Parts I & II) 32

Touchables, The 60
Touchables In Brooklyn 42

GOODMAN, Jerry, & Jan Hammer

Jazz-rock duo. Violinist Goodman and keyboardist Hammer were formerly with John McLaughlin.

| 2/8/75 | 150 | 3 | | Like Children .... | $10 | Nemperor 430 |

Country And Eastern Music
Earth (Still Our Only Home)

Full Moon Boogie
Giving In Gently (medley)

I Remember Me
I Wonder (medley)

Night
No Fear

Steppings Tones
Topeka

GOODMAN, Steve

Born on 7/25/48 in Chicago. Singer/songwriter/guitarist. Died of leukemia on 9/20/84.

| 8/23/75 | 144 | 6 | | 1 Jessie's Jig & Other Favorites .... | $10 | Asylum 1037 |
| 5/15/76 | 175 | 4 | | 2 Words We Can Dance To .... | $10 | Asylum 1060 |

Banana Republics (2)
Between The Lines (2)
Blue Umbrella (2)
Can't Go Back (2)
Death Of A Salesman (2)

Door Number Three (1)
Glory Of Love (2)
I Can't Sleep (1)
It's A Sin To Tell A Lie (1)

Jessie's Jig (Rob's Romp,
 Beth's Bounce) (1)
Lookin' For Trouble (1)
Mama Don't Allow It (1)
Moby Book (1)

Old Fashioned (2)
Roving Cowboy (Ballad Of
 Dan Moody) (2)
Spoon River (1)

That's What Friends Are For
 (2)
This Hotel Room (1)
Tossin' And Turnin' (1)
Unemployed (2)

GOOSE CREEK SYMPHONY

Country rock septet.

| 6/3/72 | 167 | 8 | | Words Of Earnest.. | $12 | Capitol 11044 |

Broken Creek Goose Down
Gearheart And God

Gospel, The
Guitars Pickin, Fiddles
 Playin

Me And Him
(Oh Lord Won't You Buy
Me A) Mercedes Benz 64

Rush On Love
Speakin' Of

Whupin It
Words Of Earnest

GORDON, Robert

Rockabilly singer. Born in Washington, D.C. in 1947. Own bands, Confidentials and Newports; worked local clubs in the mid-1960s. Moved to New York City in the early '70s and recorded with own punk band, the Tuff Darts. Went solo in 1976.

| 10/1/77 | 142 | 8 | | 1 Robert Gordon with Link Wray .... | $10 | Private St. 2030 |
| 3/18/78 | 124 | 7 | | 2 Fresh Fish Special .... | $10 | Private St. 7008 |

above 2 feature guitarist Link Wray

3/24/79	106	12		3 Rock Billy Boogie	$10	RCA 3294
2/2/80	150	9		4 Bad Boy	$10	RCA 3523
4/18/81	117	15		5 Are You Gonna Be The One	$10	RCA 3773

All By Myself (3)
Am I Blue (3)
Are You Gonna Be The One
 (5)
Bad Boy (4)
Black Slacks (3)
Blue Christmas (3)
Blue Eyes (Don't Run Away)
 (2)
Boppin' The Blues (1)
Born To Lose (4)
But, But (5)

Catman, The (3)
Crazy Man Crazy (4)
Drivin' Wheel (5)
Fire (2)
Five Days, Five Days (2)
Flyin' Saucers Rock & Roll
 (1)
Fool (1)
I Just Found Out (3)
I Just Met A Memory (3)
I Sure Miss You (1)
I Want To Be Free (2)

If This Is Wrong (2)
Is It Wrong (For Loving You)
 (4)
Is This The Way (1)
It's In The Bottle (1)
It's Only Make Believe (3)
Lonesome Train (On A
 Lonesome Track) (2)
Look Who's Blue (5)
Love My Baby (3)
Lover Boy (5)
Need You (4)

Nervous (4)
Picture Of You (4)
Red Cadillac, And A Black
 Mustache (2)
Red Hot (1) 83
Rock Billy Boogie (3)
Sea Cruise (2)
She's Not Mine Anymore (5)
Someday, Someway (5) 76
Standing On The Outside Of
 Her Door (5)
Summertime Blues (1)

Sweet Love On My Mind (4)
Sweet Surrender (1)
Take Me Back (5)
Too Fast To Live, Too Young
 To Die (5)
Torture (4)
Twenty Flight Rock (2)
Uptown (4)
Walk On By (3)
Way I Walk (2)
Wheel Of Fortune (3)

Woman (You're My Woman)
 (1)
Worrying Kind (4)

GORE, Lesley

Born on 5/2/46 in New York City; raised in Tenafly, New Jersey. Discovered by Quincy Jones while singing at a hotel in Manhattan. In films Girls On The Beach, Ski Party and The T.A.M.I. Show. Co-wrote two songs on the Fame soundtrack with her brother Michael, including "Out Here On My Own."

7/13/63	24	15		1 I'll Cry If I Want To	$30	Mercury 60805
1/25/64	125	8		2 Lesley Gore Sings Of Mixed-Up Hearts	$30	Mercury 60849
7/18/64	127	6		3 Boys, Boys, Boys	$30	Mercury 60901
12/12/64	146	2		4 Girl Talk	$30	Mercury 60943
7/17/65	95	24		5 The Golden Hits Of Lesley Gore ....[G]	$30	Mercury 61024
12/4/65	120	4		6 My Town, My Guy & Me	$30	Mercury 61042
5/13/67	169	5		7 California Nights	$25	Mercury 61120

All Of My Life (5) 71
Baby That's Me (6)
Bad (7)
Before And After (6)
Boys (3)
Bubble Broke (7)
California Nights (7) 16
Cry (1)
Cry And You Cry Alone (1)

Cry Like A Baby (7)
Cry Me A River (1)
Danny (3)
Don't Call Me (3)
Fools Rush In (Where
 Angels Fear To Tread) (2)
Girl In Love (6)
Hey Now (4,5) 76
I Died Inside (4)

I Don't Care (6)
I Don't Wanna Be A Loser
 (3,5) 37
I Struck A Match (2)
I Understand (1)
I Would (1)
I'll Hate It Up To You (3)
I'm Coolin', No Foolin' (3)

I'm Going Out (The Same
 Way I Came In) (7)
If That's The Way You Want
 It (2)
It's Gotta Be You (3)
It's Just About That Time (4)
It's My Party (1,5) 1
Judy's Turn To Cry (1,5) 5
Just Another Fool (6)

Just Let Me Cry (1,5)
Leave Me Alone (3)
Let Me Dream (6)
Lilacs And Violets (6)
Little Girl Go Home (4)
Live And Learn (4)
Love Goes On Forever (7)
Maybe I Know (4,5) 14

Maybe Now (7)
Misty (1)
Movin' Away (4)
My Foolish Heart (2)
My Town, My Guy And Me
 (6) 32
No Matter What You Do (6)
No More Tears (1)
Off And Running (7)

288

GORE, Lesley — Cont'd

Old Crowd (2)
Party's Over (1)
Run Bobby, Run (2)
Say Goodbye (4)
She's A Fool (2,5) **5**
Something Wonderful (3)

Sometimes I Wish I Were A Boy (4) **86**
Sunshine, Lollipops And Rainbows (2,5) **13**
That's The Way Boys Are (3,5) **12**

That's The Way The Ball Bounces (3)
Things We Did Last Summer (6)
Time To Go (2)
Treat Me Like A Lady (7)

What Am I Gonna Do With You (6)
What Kind Of Fool Am I (1)
What's A Girl Supposed To Do (6)
Wonder Boy (4)

You Didn't Look 'Round (6)
You Don't Own Me (2,5) **2**
You Name It (3)
You've Come Back (4)
Young And Foolish (2)
Young Lover (2)

GORE, Martin L.
Instrumentalist/songwriter of Depeche Mode. Born on 7/23/61 in Basildon, England.

8/12/89	156	5		Counterfeit e.p.	$8	Sire 25980

Compulsion
Gone

In A Manner Of Speaking
Motherless Child

Never Turn Your Back On Mother Earth

Smile In The Crowd

GORKY PARK
Russian rock group: Nikolai Noskov (vocals), Alexei Belov, Big Sasha Minkov, Jan Ianenkov and Sasha Lvov. Group named after a park in Moscow.

9/9/89	80	21		Gorky Park	$8	Mercury 838628

Bang
Child Of The Wind

Danger
Fortress

Hit Me With The News
My Generation

Peace In Our Time
Sometimes At Night

Try To Find Me 81
Within Your Eyes

★★248★★ GORME, Eydie
Born on 8/16/31 in New York City. Vocalist with the big bands of Tommy Tucker and Tex Beneke in the late 1940s. Featured on Steve Allen's *Tonight Show* from 1953. Married Steve Lawrence on 12/29/57. They recorded as the duo Parker & Penny in 1979.

5/6/57	14	10	1	Eydie Gorme	$25	ABC-Para. 150
10/28/57	19	4	2	Eydie Swings The Blues	$25	ABC-Para. 192
3/31/58	19	4	3	Eydie Gorme Vamps The Roaring 20's	$25	ABC-Para. 218
11/3/58	20	1	4	Eydie In Love	$25	ABC-Para. 246
4/6/63	22	22	5	Blame It On The Bossa Nova	$20	Columbia 8812
2/15/64	143	3	6	Gorme Country Style	$20	Columbia 8920
9/12/64	54	22	7	Amor .... [F]	$20	Columbia 9003
8/28/65	53	11	8	More Amor .... [F]	$20	Columbia 9176

above 2 feature the Trio Los Panchos (South American guitar/vocal trio: Alfredo Gil, Johnny Albino and Chucho Navarro)

6/4/66	22	37	9	Don't Go To Strangers	$20	Columbia 9276
2/18/67	85	18	10	Softly, As I Leave You	$15	Columbia 9394
5/20/67	136	6	11	Together On Broadway *	$15	Columbia 9436
12/2/67+	148	9	12	Eydie Gorme's Greatest Hits .... [G]	$15	Columbia 9564
3/8/69	141	6	13	What It Was, Was Love *	$12	RCA 4115
5/10/69	188	3	14	Real True Lovin' *	$12	RCA 4107

***STEVE LAWRENCE & EYDIE GORME**

3/7/70	105	12	15	Tonight I'll Say A Prayer	$10	RCA 4303

After You've Gone (2)
All Alone (10)
Almost Like Being In Love (5)
Amor (7,12)
Back In Your Own Back Yard (3)
Be Careful, It's My Heart (1)
Blame It On The Bossa Nova (5,12) **7**
Blues In The Night (2)
Boys And Girls (3)
Button Up Your Overcoat (3)
Cabaret (11)
Call Me (14)
Caminito (7)
Can't Help Lovin' Dat Man (2)
Can't Take My Eyes Off You (14)
Chapter One (14)
Chicago (That Toddling Town) (3)
Coffee Song (They've Got An Awful Lot Of Coffee In Brazil) (5)
Come Back To Me (11)
Crazy (6)
Cuando Vuelva A Tu Lado (9)
Cuatro Vidas (Four Lives) (8)
Curtain Falls (11)
Dansero (5)
Day By Day (1)
Desafinado (Slightly Out Of Tune) (5)
Desesperadamente (Desperately) (8)
Di Que Es Verdad (7)
Didn't We (15)

Don't Get Around Much Anymore (2)
Don't Go To Strangers (9,12)
Don't Worry 'Bout Me (10)
End Of The World (6)
Every Time We Say Goodbye (10)
Fine And Dandy (1)
First Impression (1)
Flores Negras (Black Flowers) (8)
For All We Know (10)
Fuego Bajo Tu Piel (Fire Under Your Skin) (8)
Gentleman Is A Dope (1)
Gift! (Recado Bossa Nova) (5)
Glad To Be Unhappy (10)
Guess I Should Have Loved Him More (10)
Guess Who I Saw Today (1)
Guitarra Romana (Roman Guitar) (8)
Gypsy In My Soul (1)
Happy Together (14)
Here I Am In Love Again (4)
Historia De Un Amor (7)
Honeymoon Is Over (11)
How About Me (9)
How Did He Look (9)
How Long Has This Been Going On (1)
I Believe In You (11)
I Can't Help It (If I'm Still In Love With You) (6)
I Can't Stop Loving You (6)
I Got It Bad And That Ain't Good (2)

I Gotta Right To Sing The Blues (2)
I Really Don't Want To Know (6)
I Remember You (5)
I Walk The Line (6)
I Wanna Be Around (9)
I Wanna Be Loved By You (3)
I Wish You Love (9,12)
I'll Be Around (9)
I'll Take Romance (1) **65**
I'm Sorry (6)
Idle Conversation (4)
If He Walked Into My Life (9,12)
Impossible (4)
In Love In Vain (4)
In Other Words (4)
In The Wee Small Hours Of The Morning (4)
It Could Happen To You (4)
It Takes A Fool Like Me (15)
It's Not Unusual (14)
Knowing When To Leave (15)
La Ultima Noche (7)
Let's Do It (Let's Fall In Love) (2)
Love Letters (4)
Luna Lunera (Bright Moon) (8)
Make The World Go Away (6)
Mala Noche (Evil Night) (8)
Mame (11)
Man, A [solo: Eydie] (13)
Man I Love (2)
Mas Amor (More Love) (8,12)
Matchmaker (12)
Media Vuelta (7)

Melodie D'Amour (5)
Message, The (5)
Moon River (5)
My Buddy (3)
My Mama Done 'Tol Me (2)
My Man (3)
Never My Love (14)
Nice People (13)
Nightingale Can Sing The Blues (2)
No One To Cry To (6)
No Te Vayas Sin Mi (Don't Leave Without Me) (8)
Noche De Ronda (7)
Nochecita (Little Night) (8)
Nosotros (7)
Oh Lonesome Me (6)
Old Fashioned Wedding (11)
Old Man (13)
One Note Samba (5)
Oracion Caribe (Caribbean Prayer) (8)
Piel Canela (7)
Quiet Soul (15)
Real True Lovin' (14)
Romeo & Juliet, Love Theme From ..see: Time For Us
Room With The View Inside (8)
Sabor A Mi (7,12)
Saturday Night (Is The Loneliest Night Of The Week) (1)
Save The Last Dance For Me (14)
Secret Place [solo: Eydie] (13)
Singin' In The Rain (3)
Softly, As I Leave You (10,12)

Someday (You'll Want Me To Want You) (6)
Stormy Weather (2)
Sunrise, Sunset (11)
Sweetest Sounds (5)
Tell Him I Said Hello (9)
There Goes The Bride [solo: Eydie] (13)
This Is No Laughing Matter (1)
Time (15)
Time For Us (Love Theme from Romeo & Juliet) (15)
Tip Toe Through The Tulips With Me (3)
To Be In Love (13)
Together Forever (11)
Tonight I'll Say A Prayer (15) **45**
Too Close For Comfort (1) **39**
Toot Toot Tootsie, Goodbye (3)
Vereda Tropical (Tropical Trail) (8)
Walk On By (14)
Walking Happy (11)
We Had It All [solo: Eydie] (13)
What Did I Have That I Don't Have? (9,12)
What Is A Woman? (10)
What It Was, Was Love (13)
What The World Needs Now (14)
What You Say (13)
What's Good About Goodbye? (10)

What's New (9)
When He Leaves You (9)
When I Fall In Love (4)
When The Red Red Robin Comes Bob Bob Bobbin' Along (3)
When The Sun Comes Out (2)
When The World Was Young (4)
When Your Lover Has Gone (2)
Who's Sorry Now (3)
Why Shouldn't I? (4)
Why Try To Change Me Now (4)
With A Little Help From My Friends (14)
Without You (15)
Y... (7)
Yeah, But What If? (13)
Yesterday, When I Was Young (15)
You Don't Know Me (6)
You Don't Know What Love Is (2)
You've Changed (10)
You've Made Me So Very Happy (15)

GOUDREAU, Barry
Lead guitarist of Boston, Orion The Hunter and RTZ. Born on 11/29/51 in Boston.

9/20/80	88	8		Barry Goudreau	$8	Portrait 36542

Cold Cold World
Dreams

Hard Luck
Leavin' Tonight

Life Is What We Make It
Mean Woman Blues

Nothin' To Lose
Sailin' Away

What's A Fella To Do?

GOULD, Morton, And His Orchestra

Born on 12/10/13 in Long Island, New York. Composer of semi-classical music; co-wrote two Broadway musicals. Conductor/arranger on NBC radio for years.

11/9/59	5	52		1 Tchaikovsky: 1812 Overture/Ravel: Bolero ....[I]	$20	RCA 2345
7/18/60	3	41		2 Grofe: Grand Canyon Suite/Beethoven: Wellington's Victory ....[I]	$20	RCA 2433

Beethoven: Wellington's Victory (2)   Grofe: Grand Canyon Suite (2)   Ravel: Bolero (1)   Tchaikovsky: 1812 Overture, Op. 49 (1)

★★164★★ GOULET, Robert

Born on 11/26/33 in Lawrence, Massachusetts. Began concert career in Edmonton, Canada. Broadway/film/TV actor. Launched career as Sir Lancelot in the hit Broadway musical *Camelot*. Won the 1962 Best New Artist Grammy Award.

3/17/62+	43	65		1 Always You................	$15	Columbia 8476
9/1/62	20	55		2 Two Of Us................	$15	Columbia 8626
1/5/63	9	48		3 Sincerely Yours................	$15	Columbia 8731
4/27/63	11	29		4 The Wonderful World Of Love	$15	Columbia 8793
10/19/63	16	23		5 Robert Goulet In Person................[L]	$15	Columbia 8888
				recorded at the Chicago Opera House		
5/2/64	31	22		6 Manhattan Tower/The Man Who Loves Manhattan	$15	Columbia 2450
				composed and conducted by Gordon Jenkins		
10/17/64	72	16		7 Without You	$15	Columbia 9000
12/26/64+	5	29	●	8 My Love Forgive Me................	$15	Columbia 9096
6/5/65	69	16		9 Begin To Love	$15	Columbia 9142
8/14/65	31	19		10 Summer Sounds	$15	Columbia 9180
12/11/65+	33	22		11 Robert Goulet On Broadway	$15	Columbia 9218
4/30/66	73	12		12 I Remember You	$15	Columbia 9282
3/11/67	145	3		13 Robert Goulet On Broadway, Volume 2	$12	Columbia 9386
9/14/68	162	15		14 Woman, Woman	$12	Columbia 9695
4/12/69	135	13		15 Both Sides Now	$12	Columbia 9763
9/6/69	174	3		16 Souvenir d'Italie	$12	Columbia 9874
11/14/70	198	2		17 I Wish You Love ....[K]	$12	Columbia 30011 [2]

All I Do Is Dream Of You (4,17)
All Of Me (4)
All Of You (2)
All Or Nothing At All (1)
Almost Like Being In Love (medley) (5)
Always You (1)
And This Is My Beloved (1)
Another Time, Another Place (3)
As Time Goes By (9,17)
Autumn In Rome (16)
Autumn Leaves (1)
Begin To Love (Cominciamo Ad Amarci) (9)
Blues Are Marching In (5)
Bon Soir Dame (15)
Both Sides Now (15)
Breeze And I (1)
But Beautiful (2)
By The Time I Get To Phoenix (14)
Cabaret (13)
Call Me Irresponsible (12,17)
Choose (8)
Ciao Compare' (13)
Come Back To Me (11)
Come Back To Sorrento (16)
Come Prima (16)
Concentrate On One Thing At A Time (5)
Core'Ngrato (16)
Cycles (15)
Dear Love (11)
Didn't We (17)
Do It Again (4)
Do You Know The Way To San Jose (14)
Don't Blame Me (2)
Don't Worry 'Bout Me (7)
Ebb Tide (3)

Fall Of Love (9)
For Once In My Life (15)
Full Moon And Empty Arms (1)
Gigi (3,5)
Gone With The Wind (12)
Goodbye (2)
Hello, Dolly! (11)
Here (1)
Here In My Heart (15,17)
Here's That Rainy Day (5)
Honey (I Miss You) (14,17)
How Small We Are How Little We Know (15)
I Hadn't Anyone Till You (12)
I Never Get To Paris (9)
I Remember You (12)
I Talk To The Trees (3)
(I Wanna Go Where You Go, Do What You Do) Then I'll Be Happy (4)
I Wish You Love (Que Reste-t-il De Nos Amours?) (2,17)
I'll Be Seeing You (3)
I'll Catch The Sun (15)
I'll Get By (As Long As I Have You) (10)
I'll Remember April (12)
I'll Take Romance (4)
I'm A Fool To Want You (7,17)
I've Got The World On A String (10)
If Ever I Would Leave You (5)
If I Ruled The World (11)
If She Walked Into My Life (If He Walked Into My Life) (13)
If You Are But A Dream (1)

If You Love Me (Really Love Me) (Hymne A L'Amour) (10)
Imagination (12)
Impossible Dream (The Quest) (13)
In The Still Of The Night (1)
It Had To Be You (medley) (5)
It's A Blue World (12)
It's All In The Game (1)
Just Say I Love Her (Dicitencello Vule) (8,16,17)
La Strada (Gelsomina), Love Theme From (16)
Lamp Is Low (1)
Lazy River (medley) (5)
Learnin' My Latin (medley) (6)
Les Bicyclettes De Belsize (15)
Life Is Just A Bowl Of Cherries (4)
Little White Lies (2)
Live For Life (14)
Long Ago (1)
Long Ago And Far Away (1)
Look For Small Pleasures (11)
Love In A Tower (Never Leave Me) (medley) (6)
Love Is Blue (14)
Lush Life (7)
Magical City (medley) (6)
Make Someone Happy (2)
Mala Femmina (16)
Mam'selle (10)
Mame (13)
Man Without Love (Quando M'Innamoro) (14)
Maria (3)
Married I Can Always Get (medley) (6)

Mean To Me (4)
Melinda (3)
Moon Was Yellow (3)
More I See Of Mimi (7)
My Cup Runneth Over (3)
My Ideal (12,17)
My Lady Won't Be Here Tonight (7)
My Love, Forgive Me (Amore, Scusami) (8) 16
My Melancholy Baby (medley) (5)
Nearness Of You (3,17)
Never Leave Me (medley) (6)
New York's My Home (medley) (6)
Night Song (11)
Night They Raided Minsky's (Wait For Me), Love Theme From (15)
No Moon At All (4)
Non Dimenticar (16)
Now That It's Ended (8)
Old Cape Cod (10)
Old Songs Are Really Like Old Friends (medley) (5)
On A Clear Day You Can See Forever (11,17)
Once Upon A Dream (medley) (6)
Once Upon A Summertime (La Valse Des Lilas) (10)
Once Upon A Time (7)
Out Of This World (4)
Party, The (medley) (6)
People (11)
Poinciana (Song Of The Tree) (3)
Quiet Nights Of Quiet Stars (Corcovado) (3)
Real Live Girl (9)
Repeat After Me (medley) (6)

S'posin' (4)
Sad Songs (7)
Shalom (13)
She Touched Me (11)
Skylark (12)
Smile (9)
Softly, As I Leave You (8)
Soliloquy (5)
Something's Gotta Give (2)
Somewhere, My Love (17)
Souvenir D'Italie (16)
Stella By Starlight (3)
Story Of A Starry Night (1)
Strange Music (1)
Take Me In Your Arms (2)
There But For You Go I (13)
These Foolish Things (Remind Me Of You) (12)
They Call The Wind Maria (medley) (5)
Things I Love (1)
Thirty Days Hath September (15)
This Guy's In Love With You (14)
This Is All I Ask (5,8,17)
Those Were The Days (15)
Till (10)
Time After Time (9,17)
Time For Love (17)
Today (9)
Tonight (3)
Too Good (8)
Two Different Worlds (8)
Two Of Us (2)
Two People (3)
Unicorn (14)
Wake Up (5)

Walk Into The Dawn (10)
Walking Happy (13)
Welcome Home Angelina (8)
What A Wonderful World (14)
What Can You Do? (8)
What Is A Woman? (13)
What Kind Of Fool Am I? (5,8) 89
What Now My Love (Et Maintenant) (10,17)
What's New? (7)
When Did I Fall In Love? (13)
When The Red, Red Robin Comes Bob, Bob, Bobbin' Along (medley) (5)
Where Are You? (7)
Where Do I Go From Here? (2)
Where Is The One (7)
Who Can I Turn To (When Nobody Needs Me) (11,17)
With These Hands (9)
Without You (7)
Woman, Woman (14)
Wonderful World Of Love (4)
You Don't Have To Say You Love Me (Io Che Non Vivo [Senza Te]) (3)
You Stepped Out Of A Dream (3)
You're Breaking My Heart (1,17)
You're Nobody Till Somebody Loves You (4,17)
Young Only Yesterday (12)

GO WEST

British duo of Peter Cox (vocals) and Richard Drummie (guitar, vocals).

3/23/85	60	35		1 Go West................	$8	Chrysalis 41495
8/22/87	172	9		2 Dancing On The Couch	$8	Chrysalis 41550

Call Me (1) 54
Chinese Whispers (2)
Crossfire (2)
Dangerous (2)

Don't Look Down (1)
Don't Look Down - The Sequel (2) 39
Eye To Eye (1) 73

From Baltimore To Paris (2)
Goodbye Girl (1)
Haunted (1)

I Want To Hear It From You (2)
Innocence (1)
King Is Dead (2)

Little Caesar (2)
Masque Of Love (2)
Missing Persons (1)
S.O.S. (1)

True Colours (2)
We Close Our Eyes (1) 41

DEBUT DATE	PEAK POS	WKS CHR	G O L D	ARTIST — Album Title	$	Label & Number

GQ

Bronx soul group: Emmanuel Rahiem LeBlanc (lead singer), Keith Crier, Herb Lane and Paul Service. Group became a trio with the departure of Service in 1980.

DEBUT DATE	PEAK POS	WKS CHR			$	Label & Number
4/7/79	13	35 ▲	1	Disco Nights	$8	Arista 4225
4/5/80	46	20	2	Two	$8	Arista 9511
11/14/81	140	8	3	Face To Face	$8	Arista 9547

Boogie Oogie Oogie (1)
Boogie Shoogie Feelin' (3)
Dark Side Of The Sun (3)
Disco Nights (Rock-Freak) (1) *12*

Don't Stop This Feeling (2)
Face To Face (3)
GQ Down (2)
I Do Love You (1) *20*
I Love (The Skin You're In) (3)

Is It Cool (2)
It's Like That (2)
It's Your Love (1)
Lies (2)
Make My Dream A Reality (1)

Reason For The Season (2)
Sad Girl (3) *93*
Shake (3)
Shy Baby (3)
Sitting In The Park (2)

Someday (In Your Life) (2)
Spirit (1)
Standing Ovation (2)
This Happy Feeling (1)
Wonderful (1)

You Put Some Love In My Life (3)
You've Got The Floor (3)

GRACES, The

Female trio: Charlotte Caffey (guitarist of the Go-Go's), Meredith Brooks and Gia Ciambotti.

					$	
9/9/89	147	9		Perfect View	$8	A&M 5265

Fear No Love
50,000 Candles Burning

Lay Down Your Arms *56*
Out In The Fields

Perfect View
Should I Let You In

Time Waits For No One
Tomorrow

We Never Met
When The Sun Goes Down

★★361★★ GRAHAM, Larry

Born on 8/14/46 in Beaumont, Texas. To Oakland at the age of two. Bass player with Sly & The Family Stone from 1966-72. In 1973, formed Hot Chocolate (not to be confused with the English group of the same name); band later renamed Graham Central Station. Consisted of Graham (lead), Hershall Kennedy and Robert Sam (keyboards), Willie Sparks and Patrice Banks (percussion), and David Vega (guitar). Graham went solo in 1980.

GRAHAM CENTRAL STATION:

					$	
2/9/74	48	26	1	Graham Central Station	$8	Warner 2763
10/5/74	51	18	2	Release Yourself	$8	Warner 2814
8/2/75	22	24 ●	3	Ain't No 'Bout-A-Doubt It	$8	Warner 2876
6/26/76	46	16	4	Mirror	$8	Warner 2937
4/23/77	67	10	5	Now Do U Wanta Dance	$8	Warner 3041

LARRY GRAHAM & GRAHAM CENTRAL STATION:

					$	
7/1/78	105	11	6	My Radio Sure Sounds Good To Me	$8	Warner 3175
7/14/79	136	4	7	Star Walk	$8	Warner 3322

LARRY GRAHAM:

					$	
6/21/80	26	24 ●	8	One In A Million You	$8	Warner 3447
8/8/81	46	13	9	Just Be My Lady	$8	Warner 3554
6/26/82	142	9	10	Sooner Or Later	$8	Warner 3668
7/30/83	173	4	11	Victory	$8	Warner 23878

Are You Happy? (6)
Baby (11)
Baby, You Are My Sunshine (9)
Boogie Witcha, Baby (6)
Can You Handle It? (1) *49*
Can't Nobody Take Your Place (9)
Crazy Chicken (5)
Do Yah (4)
Don't Stop When You're Hot (10)
Don't Think Too Long (11)
Earthquake (5)
Easy Love (10)
Easy Rider (3)
Entertainer, The (7)
Entrow (4)
Feel The Need (2)
Feels Like Love (9)

Forever (4)
Forever Yours (8)
G.C.S. (2)
Ghetto (1)
Got To Go Through It To Get To It (2)
Guess Who (9)
Hair (1)
Happ-E-2-C-U-A-Ginn (5)
Have Faith In Me (5)
Hey Mr. Writer (2)
Hold Up Your Hand (10)
I Believe In You (2)
I Can't Stand The Rain (3)
I Feel Good (10)
I Got A Reason (4)
I Just Can't Stop Dancing (8)
I Just Love You (9)
I Never Forgot Your Eyes (11)
I'd Rather Be Loving You (11)

I'm Sick And Tired (11)
I'm So Glad It's Summer Again (4)
Is It Love? (6)
It Ain't No Fun To Me (1)
It Ain't Nothing But A Warner Brothers Party (3)
It's Alright (3) *92*
It's The Engine In Me (6)
Jam, The (3) *63*
Just Call My Name (11)
Last Train (5)
Lead Me On (5)
Let Me Come Into Your Life (10)
Love And Happiness (5)
Love (Covers A Multitude Of Sin) (4)
Loving You Is Beautiful (9)

Luckiest People (3)
Mirror (4)
Movin' Inside Your Love (11)
Mr. Friend (6)
My Radio Sure Sounds Good To Me (6)
No Place Like Home (9)
Now Do-U-Wanta Dance (3)
Ole Smokey (3)
One In A Million You (8) *9*
Our Love Keeps Growing Strong (9)
People (1)
Pow (8)
Priscilla (4)
Release Yourself (2)
Remember When (9)
Save Me (4)
Saving My Love For You (5)
Scream (7)

Sneaky Freak (7)
Sooner Or Later [includes 2 versions] (10)
Stand Up And Shout About Love (8)
Star Walk (7)
Still Thinkin' Of You (10)
Stomped Beat-Up And Whooped (5)
Sunshine, Love And Music (8)
Sweetheart (8)
Tell Me What It Is (1)
There's Something About You (8)
Time For You And Me (8)
'Tis Your Kind Of Music (2)
Today (2)
Tonight (7)
Turn It Out (6)

Victory (11)
Walk Baby Walk (10)
Water (3)
We Be's Gettin' Down (1)
We've Been Waiting (1)
When We Get Married (8) *76*
Why? (1)
(You're A) Foxy Lady (7)
You're My Girl (10)
You've Been (11)
Your Love (3) *38*

GRAMM, Lou

Born on 5/2/50 in Rochester, New York. Lead singer of Foreigner. Member of Black Sheep, 1970-75. Left Foreigner in 1991 to form Shadow King.

					$	
2/28/87	27	26	1	Ready Or Not	$8	Atlantic 81728
11/11/89+	85	23	2	Long Hard Look	$8	Atlantic 81915

Angel With A Dirty Face (2)
Arrow Thru Your Heart (1)
Broken Dreams (2)
Chain Of Love (1)

Day One (2)
Hangin' On My Hip (2)
Heartache (1)
I'll Come Running (2)

I'll Know When It's Over (2)
If I Don't Have You (1)
Just Between You And Me (2) *6*

Lover Come Back (1)
Midnight Blue (1) *5*
Ready Or Not (1) *54*
She's Got To Know (1)

Time (1)
Tin Soldier (2)
True Blue Love (2) *40*
Until I Make You Mine (1)

Warmest Rising Sun (2)

★★104★★ GRAND FUNK RAILROAD

Hard-rock band formed in Flint, Michigan in 1968. Consisted of Mark Farner (guitar), Mel Schacher (bass) and Don Brewer (drums). Brewer and Farner had been in Terry Knight & The Pack; Schacher was former bassist with ? & The Mysterians. Knight became producer and manager for Grand Funk, until he was fired in March 1972. Craig Frost (keyboards) added in 1973. Disbanded in 1976. Re-formed in 1981, with Farner, Brewer and Dennis Bellinger (bass). Disbanded again shortly thereafter. Farner recorded Contemporary Christian music. Also see Terry Knight & The Pack.

					$	
10/11/69	27	55 ●	1	On Time	$15	Capitol 307
1/31/70	11	67 ▲	2	Grand Funk	$12	Capitol 406
7/11/70	6	63 ▲²	3	Closer To Home	$12	Capitol 471
12/5/70	5	62 ▲²	4	Live Album .... [L]	$12	Capitol 633 [2]
5/1/71	6	40 ▲	5	Survival	$12	Capitol 764
12/4/71+	5	30 ▲	6	E Pluribus Funk	$12	Capitol 853
				circular, silver album cover is an imitation of a U.S. coin		
5/13/72	17	27 ●	7	Mark, Don & Mel 1969-71 .... [K]	$12	Capitol 11042 [2]

DEBUT DATE	PEAK POS	WKS CHR	GOLD	ARTIST — Album Title	$	Label & Number

GRAND FUNK RAILROAD — Cont'd

DEBUT DATE	PEAK POS	WKS CHR	GOLD	ARTIST — Album Title	$	Label & Number
10/14/72	7	27	●	8 Phoenix..	$12	Capitol 11099
8/18/73	2²	35	▲	9 We're An American Band *...........................	$10	Capitol 11207
3/30/74	5	29	●	10 Shinin' On...	$10	Capitol 11278
12/21/74+	10	24	●	11 All The Girls In The World Beware!!! *..........	$10	Capitol 11356
				*GRAND FUNK		
9/13/75	21	10		12 Caught In The Act...........................[L]	$12	Capitol 11445 [2]
1/31/76	47	11		13 Born To Die..	$10	Capitol 11482
8/28/76	52	9		14 Good Singin' Good Playin'.......................	$10	MCA 2216
11/20/76	126	5		15 Grand Funk Hits..............................[G]	$8	Capitol 11579
10/17/81	149	5		16 Grand Funk Lives	$8	Full Moon 3625

Aimless Lady (3)
Ain't Got Nobody (9)
All The Girls In The World Beware (11)
All You've Got Is Money (5)
Anybody's Answer (1)
Are You Ready (1,4,7)
Bad Time (11,15) **4**
Big Buns (14)
Black Licorice (9,12)
Born To Die (13)
Call Yourself A Man (1)
Can You Do It (14) **45**
Can't Be Too Long (1)
Can't Be With You Tonight (16)
Carry Me Through (10)
Closer To Home (3,7,12) **22**
Comfort Me (5)
Country Road (5)
Creepin' (9)
Crossfire (14)

Don't Let 'Em Take Your Gun (14)
Dues (13)
Feelin' Alright (5,7) **54**
Flight Of The Phoenix (8)
Footstompin' Music (6,7,12) **29**
Freedom Is For Children (8)
Genevieve (13)
Get It Together (3)
Gettin' Over You (10)
Gimme Shelter (5,12) **61**
Goin' For The Pastor (14)
Good & Evil (11)
Good Things (13)
Good Times (16)
Got This Thing On The Move (2)
Gotta Find Me A Better Day (8)
Greed Of Man (16)
Heartbreaker (1,4,7,12) **72**
High Falootin' Woman (2)

High On A Horse (1)
Hooked On Love (3)
I Can Feel Him In The Morning (5)
I Come Tumblin' (6)
I Don't Have To Sing The Blues (3)
I Fell For Your Love (13)
I Just Gotta Know (8)
I Want Freedom (5)
I'm Your Captain ... see: Closer To Home
In Need (2,4)
Inside Looking Out (2,4,7)
Into The Sun (1,4,7)
Just Couldn't Wait (14)
Life (11)
Little Johnny Hooker (10)
Loco-Motion, The (10,12,15) **1**
Loneliest Rider (9)
Loneliness (6,7)

Look At Granny Run Run (11)
Love Is Dyin' (13)
Mark Say's Alright (4)
Mean Mistreater (3,4,7) **47**
Memories (11)
Miss My Baby (11)
Mr. Limousine Driver (2) **97**
Mr. Pretty Boy (10)
1976 (14)
No Lies (6)
No Reason Why (16)
Nothing Is The Same (3)
Out To Get You (14)
Paranoid (2,4,7)
Pass It Around (14)
People, Let's Stop The War (6)
Please Don't Worry (2)
Please Me (10)
Politician (13)
Queen Bee (16)
Railroad, The (9,12)

Rain Keeps Fallin' (8)
Release Your Love (14)
Responsibility (11)
Rock 'N Roll Soul (8,12,15) **29**
Runnin' (11)
Sally (13,15) **69**
Save The Land (6)
She Got To Move Me (8)
Shinin' On (10,12,15) **11**
Sin's A Good Man's Brother (3)
So You Won't Have To Die (5)
Some Kind Of Wonderful (11,12,15) **3**
Someone (8)
Stop Lookin' Back (9)
Stuck In The Middle (16)
T.N.U.C. (1,4,7,12)
Take (13,15) **53**
Talk To The People (13)
Testify (16)
Time Machine (1,7) **48**

To Get Back In (10,15)
Trying To Get Away (8)
Ups And Downs (1)
Upsetter (6) **73**
Wait For Me (16)
Walk Like A Man (9,15) **19**
We Gotta Get Out Of This Place (1)
We're An American Band (9,12,15) **1**
Wild (11)
Winter And My Soul (5)
Words Of Wisdom (4)
Y.O.U. (16)

GRANDMASTER FLASH

Grandmaster Flash is pioneer rap DJ/producer Joseph Saddler (born in Barbados; raised in the Bronx). Rapper Melle Mel (Melvin Glover) was part of the original Furious Five rap/dance posse with Kidd Creole (Nathaniel Glover — no relation to the August Darnell character), Rahiem (Guy Todd Williams), Cowboy (Keith Wiggins; d: 1990) and Scorpio. In 1984, Melle Mel, Cowboy and Rahiem left; replaced by La Von Dukes, Broadway, Larry "Love" Parker, and Shame. Fluctuating personnel thereafter. Original lineup reunited in late 1987.

DEBUT DATE	PEAK POS	WKS CHR	GOLD	ARTIST — Album Title	$	Label & Number
10/16/82	53	24		1 The Message *..	$8	SugarHill 268
5/17/86	145	6		2 The Source...	$8	Elektra 60476
4/25/87	197	1		3 Ba-Dop-Boom-Bang...............................	$8	Elektra 60723
4/30/88	189	3		4 On The Strength *.................................	$8	Elektra 60769

*GRANDMASTER FLASH & THE FURIOUS FIVE

Ain't We Funkin' Now [includes 2 versions] (3)
All Wrapped Up (3)
Behind Closed Doors (2)
Big Black Caddy (4)
Boy Is Dope (4)
Bus Dis (Wooo) (3)
Cold In Effect (4)
Dreamin (1)

Fastest Man Alive (2)
Fly Girl (4)
Freelance (2)
Get Yours (3)
Gold (4)
House That Rocked (3)
I Am Somebody (3)
It's A Shame (Mt. Airy Groove) (1)

It's Nasty (1)
Kid Named Flash (3)
King, The (4)
Larry's Dance Theme (Part 2) (2)
Leave Here (4)
Lies (2)
Magic Carpet Ride (4)
Message, The (1) **62**

Ms. Thang (2)
On The Strength (4)
P.L.U. (Peace, Love And Unity) (2)
Scorpio (1)
She's Fresh (1)
Street Scene (2)
Style (Peter Gunn Theme) (2)
Tear The Roof Off (3)

Them Jeans (3)
This Is Where You Got It From (4)
Throwin' Down (2)
U Know What Time It Is (3)
Underarms (3)
We Will Rock You (3)
Yo Baby (4)
You Are (1)

GRAND PUBA

Maxwell Dixon, former member of rap group Brand Nubian. Born in New Rochelle, New York.

DEBUT DATE	PEAK POS	WKS CHR	GOLD	ARTIST — Album Title	$	Label & Number
11/7/92	28	12↑		Reel To Reel..	$12	Elektra 61314
				CD includes 2 bonus tracks		

Baby What's Your Name?
Back It Up
Big Kids Don't Play

Check It Out
Check Tha Resume
Honey Don't Front

Lickshot
Proper Education
Reel To Reel

Soul Controller
That's How We Move It
360 Degrees (What Goes Around) [includes 2 versions] **68**

Who Makes The Loot?
Ya Know How It Goes

GRANT, Amy

Born on 11/25/60 in Augusta, Georgia. The first lady of Contemporary Christian music. Married to singer/songwriter Gary Chapman. Her pop-charted, non-holiday albums have all been #1 on the Inspirational charts for 29 weeks or more.

DEBUT DATE	PEAK POS	WKS CHR	GOLD	ARTIST — Album Title	$	Label & Number
4/20/85	133	20	●	1 Straight Ahead.....................................	$8	A&M 5058
				#1 album on Inspirational charts for over a year		
6/15/85	35	38	▲	2 Unguarded...	$8	A&M 5060
9/20/86+	66	33	▲	3 Amy Grant - The Collection...............[G]	$8	A&M 3900
				features her classic Inspirational hits (1979-86)		
7/23/88	71	13	●	4 Lead Me On..	$8	A&M 5199
3/23/91	10	99↑	▲³	5 Heart In Motion..................................	$12	A&M 5321
10/24/92	2¹	14	▲	6 Home For Christmas ....[X]	$12	A&M 31454
				Christmas charts: 1/'92		

All Right (4)
Angels (1,3)
Ask Me (5)
Baby Baby (5) **1**
Breath Of Heaven (Mary's Song) (6)
Doubly Good To You (1)
El Shaddai (3)
Emmanuel (3)

Emmanuel, God With Us (6)
Every Heartbeat (5) **2**
Everywhere I Go (5)
Faithless Heart (4)
Father's Eyes (3)
Fight (2)
Find A Way (2,3) **29**
For Unto Us A Child Is Born [medley] (6)

Galileo (5)
Good For Me (5) **8**
Grown-Up Christmas List (6)
Hats (5)
Have Yourself A Merry Little Christmas (6)
Hope Set High (5)
How Can We See That Far (5)
I Love You (2)

I Will Remember You (5) **20**
I'll Be Home For Christmas (6)
If These Walls Could Speak (4)
It's Not A Song (1)
It's The Most Wonderful Time Of The Year (6)
Jehovah (1)

Jesu, Joy Of Man's Desiring (6)
Joy To The World (medley) (6)
Lead Me On (4) **96**
Love Can Do (3)
Love Of Another Kind (2)
Night Before Christmas (6)
1974 (4)

Now And The Not Yet (1)
O' Come All Ye Faithful (6)
Open Arms (1)
Prodigal, The (2)
Rockin' Around The Christmas Tree (6)
Saved By Love (4)
Say Once More (4)
Shadows (4)

DEBUT DATE	PEAK POS	WKS CHR	GOLD	ARTIST — Album Title	$	Label & Number

GRANT, Amy — Cont'd

Sharayah (2)
Sing Your Praise To The Lord (3)
Stay For Awhile (3)
Stepping In Your Shoes (2)
Straight Ahead (1)
Sure Enough (4)
That's What Love Is For (5) 7
Thy Word (1,3)
Tomorrow (1)
What About The Love (4)
Where Do You Hide Your Heart (1)
Who To Listen To (2)
Winter Wonderland (6)
Wise Up (2) 66
You're Not Alone (5)

GRANT, Earl
Organist/pianist/vocalist born in Oklahoma City in 1931. First recorded for Decca in 1957. In the films *Tender Is The Night, Imitation Of Life* and *Tokyo Night*. Died in an automobile accident on 6/10/70.

DEBUT DATE	PEAK POS	WKS CHR	GOLD	ARTIST — Album Title	$	Label & Number
8/21/61	7	45	●	1 Ebb Tide .... [I]	$15	Decca 74165
4/7/62	17	32		2 Beyond The Reef .... [I]	$15	Decca 74231
12/1/62	92	10		3 Earl Grant At Basin Street East .... [L]	$15	Decca 74299
				the Basin Street East is in New York		
1/4/64	139	5		4 Fly Me To The Moon .... [I]	$15	Decca 74454
7/11/64	149	2		5 Just For A Thrill .... [I]	$15	Decca 74506
5/15/65	143	4		6 Trade Winds .... [I]	$15	Decca 74623
3/23/68	192	2		7 Gently Swingin' .... [I]	$12	Decca 74937

Alfie (7)
Angel Eyes (2)
Because Of Rain (3)
Bewitched (1)
Beyond The Reef (2)
Blue Velvet (5)
Breeze And I (4)
Canadian Sunset (1)
(Carol's Theme) The Eyes Of Love (7)
Climb Ev'ry Mountain (2)
Days Of Wine And Roses (5)
Deep Purple (1)
Don't Sleep In The Subway (7)
Dreamy (1)
Ebb Tide (1)
El Cid, Love Theme From (6)
Eternally (6)
Evening Rain (1) 63
Exodus, Theme From (1)
Fever (3)
Fly Me To The Moon (In Other Words) (4)
Girl From Ipanema (Garota De Ipanema) (6)
Goin' Out Of My Head (7)
Gotta Be This Or That (3)
Hallelujah, I Love Her So (3)
Hava Nagillah (3)
High And The Mighty (4)
How Are Things In Glocca Morra (4)
How High The Moon (6)
I Miss You So (4)
I'll Build A Stairway To Paradise (3)
I'll Never Smile Again (5)
I'm In The Mood For Love (1)
Just For A Thrill (6)
Learnin' The Blues (3)
Let It Be Me (7)
Londonderry Air (2)
Make Someone Happy (2)
Meditation (Meditacao) (6)
Misty (1)
Mood Indigo (2)
Moon Of Manakoora (6)
Moon River (3)
More (4)
My Foolish Heart (1)
Off Shore (4)
One Note Samba (7)
Over The Rainbow (4)
Quiet Village (6)
Release Me (7)
Ruby (6)
Satin Doll (5)
Second Time Around (2)
Snowfall (4)
Someone To Watch Over Me (5)
Something You Got (7)
Spring Is Here (4)
Star Dust (5)
Stella By Starlight (4)
Stormy Weather (Keeps Rainin' All The Time) (1)
Street Of Dreams (6)
Sukiyaki (4)
Summertime In Venice (6)
Sunny (7)
Sweet Leilani (6)
Sweet Sixteen Bars (3) 55
Sweetest Sounds (5)
Swingin' Gently (2) 44
Tender Is The Night (2)
That's All (1)
That's Life (7)
Too Close For Comfort (3)
Trade Winds (6)
Very Thought Of You (2)
Walk On By (7)
When My Sugar Walks Down The Street (3)
When Sunny Gets Blue (2)
Where Are You (5)
Willow Weep For Me (5)
Without A Song (4)
Yellow Bird (2)
You Stepped Out Of A Dream (5)

GRANT, Eddy
Born Edmond Montague Grant on 3/5/48 in Plaisance, Guyana. Moved to London in 1960. Formed group The Equals in London in 1967. Moved to Barbados in 1982.

DEBUT DATE	PEAK POS	WKS CHR	GOLD	ARTIST — Album Title	$	Label & Number
4/23/83	10	30	●	1 Killer On The Rampage	$8	Portrait 38554
6/23/84	64	17		2 Going For Broke	$8	Portrait 39261

Another Revolutionary (1)
Blue Wave (2)
Boys In The Street (2)
Come On Let Me Love You (2)
Drop Baby Drop (1)
Electric Avenue (1) 2
Funky Rock 'N' Roll (1)
I Don't Wanna Dance (1) 53
Ire Harry (2)
It's All In You (1)
Killer On The Rampage (1)
Latin Love Affair (1)
Only Heaven Knows (2)
Political Bassa-Bassa (2)
Rock You Good (2)
Romancing The Stone (2) 26
Telepathy (2)
Till I Can't Take Love No More (2)
Too Young To Fall (1)
War Party (1)

GRANT, Gogi — see SOUNDTRACK "Helen Morgan Story"

GRAPPELLI, Stephane — see GRISMAN, David

GRASS ROOTS, The
Rock group formed in San Francisco in 1964 by drummer Joel Larson and lead singer Bill Fulton. Originally called The Bedouins. New group recruited in 1967 by pop producer Lou Adler and songwriters Steve Barri and P.F. Sloan (known as the Fantastic Baggies). Consisted of Rob Grill (lead singer, bass), Warren Entner and Creed Bratton (guitars), and Rick Coonce (drums). New lineup in 1971 included Entner, Grill, guitarists Reed Kailing and Virgil Webber, and Joel Larson (drums).

DEBUT DATE	PEAK POS	WKS CHR	GOLD	ARTIST — Album Title	$	Label & Number
8/19/67	75	15		1 Let's Live For Today	$15	Dunhill 50020
11/23/68+	25	43	●	2 Golden Grass .... [G]	$15	Dunhill 50047
3/29/69	73	16		3 Lovin' Things	$15	Dunhill 50052
12/6/69	36	21		4 Leaving It All Behind	$15	Dunhill 50067
10/24/70+	152	27		5 More Golden Grass .... [G]	$10	Dunhill 50087
10/2/71	58	20	●	6 Their 16 Greatest Hits .... [G]	$10	Dunhill 50107
6/24/72	86	14		7 Move Along .... [G]	$10	Dunhill 50112

Anyway The Wind Blows (7)
Baby Hold On (5,6) 35
Baby, You Do It So Well (3)
Back To Dreamin' Again (4)
Beatin' Round The Bush (1)
Bella Linda (2,6) 28
City Women (3)
Come On And Say It (5,6) 61
Days Of Pearly Spencer (3)
Don't Remind Me (4)
Face The Music (7)
Feelings (2,6)
Fly Me To Havanna (3)
Get It Together (5)
Glory Bound (7) 34
Heaven Knows (4,5,6) 24
Here's Where You Belong (2)
Hot Bright Lights (2)
House Of Stone (1)
I Can Turn Off The Rain (5,6)
I Can't Help But Wonder, Elisabeth (3)
I Get So Excited (3)
I'd Wait A Million Years (4,5,6) 15
I'm Livin' For You Girl (4)
Is It Any Wonder (1)
Keepin' Me Down (5)
Lady Pleasure (4)
Let It Go (5)
Let's Live For Today (1,2,6) 8
Lovin' Things (3,5,6) 49
Melinda Love (4)
Melody For You (2)
Midnight Confessions (2,6) 5
Monday Love (7)
Move Along (7)
No Exit (1)
One Word (7)
Only One (7)
Out Of This World (4)
Out Of Touch (1)
Pain (3)
River Is Wide (3,5,6) 31
Runnin' Just To Get Her Home Again (7)
Runway (7) 39
Someone To Love (7)
Something's Comin' Over Me (4)
Sooner Or Later (6) 9
Take Him While You Can (4)
Temptation Eyes (5,6) 15
Things I Should Have Said (1,2,6) 23
This Precious Time (1)
Tip Of My Tongue (1)
Truck Drivin' Man (1)
Two Divided By Love (7) 16
Wake Up, Wake Up (1,2) 68
Walking Through The Country (4,5,6) 44
What Love Is Made Of (3)
Where Were You When I Needed You (1,2,6) 28
Won't You See Me (1)
(You Gotta) Live For Love (3)

★★46★★ GRATEFUL DEAD
Legendary psychedelic-rock band formed in San Francisco in 1966. Consisted of Jerry Garcia (lead guitar), Bob Weir (rhythm guitar), Ron "Pigpen" McKernan (organ, harmonica), Phil Lesh (bass) and Bill Kreutzmann (drums). Mickey Hart (2nd drummer) and Tom Constanten (keyboards) added in 1968. Constanten left in 1970; Hart in 1971. Keith Godchaux (piano) and his wife Donna (vocals) joined in 1972. Pigpen died of a liver ailment on 3/8/73. Hart returned in 1975. Brent Mydland (keyboards) added in 1979, replacing Keith and Donna Godchaux. Mydland was a member of Silver. Keith Godchaux died on 7/23/80 from injuries suffered in a automobile accident. Mydland died on 7/26/90 (age 37) of a drug overdose. Tubes keyboardist Vince Welnick replaced Mydland. Incessant touring band with faithful followers known as "Deadheads." Also see Benefit Recordings (*Deadicated*).

DEBUT DATE	PEAK POS	WKS CHR	GOLD	ARTIST — Album Title	$	Label & Number
5/6/67	73	28	●	1 The Grateful Dead	$40	Warner 1689
8/31/68	87	17		2 Anthem Of The Sun	$30	Warner 1749
6/21/69	73	11		3 Aoxomoxoa	$30	Warner 1790

DEBUT DATE	PEAK POS	WKS CHR	GOLD	ARTIST — Album Title	$	Label & Number
				GRATEFUL DEAD — Cont'd		
1/3/70	64	15		4 Live/Dead..[L]	$25	Warner 1830 [2]
6/27/70	27	26	▲	5 Workingman's Dead	$25	Warner 1869
10/31/70	127	10		6 Vintage Dead ....[E-L]	$25	Sunflower 5001
				recorded at San Francisco's Avalon Ballroom in 1966		
12/12/70+	30	19	▲	7 American Beauty	$25	Warner 1893
6/26/71	154	7		8 Historic Dead ....[E-L]	$25	Sunflower 5004
				more recordings from 1966		
10/16/71	25	12		9 Grateful Dead...[L]	$25	Warner 1935 [2]
12/2/72+	24	24	●	10 Europe '72...[L]	$20	Warner 2668 [3]
7/28/73	60	11		11 History Of The Grateful Dead, Vol. 1 (Bear's Choice)..[L]	$15	Warner 2721
				recorded at Fillmore East, February 1970		
10/27/73	18	19		12 Wake Of The Flood	$15	Grateful Dead 01
3/9/74	75	10	▲	13 The Best Of/Skeleton's From The Closet....................[G]	$12	Warner 2764
7/13/74	16	20		14 Grateful Dead From The Mars Hotel	$12	Grateful Dead 102
9/6/75	12	13		15 Blues For Allah	$20	Grateful Dead 494
7/4/76	56	9		16 Steal Your Face ....[L]	$25	Grateful D. 620 [2]
				recorded at Winterland, San Francisco, October 1974		
8/20/77	28	16	●	17 Terrapin Station	$10	Arista 7001
11/12/77	121	8		18 What A Long Strange Trip It's Been: The Best Of The Grateful Dead......................................[G]	$12	Warner 3091 [2]
12/9/78+	41	19	●	19 Shakedown Street..	$8	Arista 4198
5/17/80	23	21		20 Go To Heaven	$8	Arista 9508
4/18/81	43	16		21 Reckoning..[L]	$10	Arista 8604 [2]
9/19/81	29	11		22 Dead Set...[L]	$10	Arista 8606 [2]
				above 2 recorded in New York City and San Francisco in 1980		
7/25/87	6	34	▲	23 In The Dark	$8	Arista 8452
2/18/89	37	11		24 Dylan & The Dead......................................[L]	$8	Columbia 45056
				BOB DYLAN & GRATEFUL DEAD recordings from 6 concert dates in July 1987		
11/18/89	27	15	●	25 Built To Last	$8	Arista 8575
10/13/90	43	12	●	26 Without A Net ....[L]	$26	Arista 8634 [2]
				recorded October 1989 - April 1990		
5/11/91	106	2		27 One From The Vault ....[L]	$12	Grateful D. 40132
				recorded on 8/13/75 at The Great American Music Hall in San Francisco		
5/30/92	119	3		28 Two From The Vault ....[L]	$17	Grate. D. 40162 [2]
				recorded 8/23-24/68 at the Shrine Auditorium in Los Angeles		

Alabama Getaway (20) **68**
All Along The Watchtower (24)
Alligator (2)
Althea (20,26)
And We Bid You Goodnight (4)
Antwerp's Placebo (The Plumber) (20)
Around And Around (16,27)
Attics Of My Life (7)
Beat It On Down The Line (1,16)
Been All Around This World (21)
Bertha (9)
Big Boss Man (9)
Big Railroad Blues (9)
Big River (16,27)
Bird Song (21,26)
Black Muddy River (23)
Black Peter (5,11,18)
Black-Throated Wind (16)
Blow Away (25)
Blues For Allah (15,27)
Born Cross-Eyed (2,18)
Box Of Rain (7)
Brokedown Palace (7,22)
Brown-Eyed Woman (10,18)
Built To Last (25)
Candyman (7,22)
Casey Jones (5,13,16)
Cassidy (21,26)
Caution (Do Not Stop On Tracks) (2)
China Cat Sunflower (3,10,26)
China Doll (14,21)

Cold Rain And Snow (1,16)
Cosmic Charlie (3,18)
Crazy Fingers (15,27)
Cream Puff War (2)
Cumberland Blues (5,10,18)
Dancing In The Street (6,17)
Dark Hollow (11,21)
Dark Star (4,18,28)
Deal (22)
Dear Mr. Fantasy (26)
Death Don't Have No Mercy (4,28)
Deep Elem Blues (21)
Dire Wolf (5,21)
Doin' That Rag (3,18)
Don't Ease Me In (20)
Drums (medley) (27)
Dupree's Diamond Blues (3)
Easy To Love You (20)
Easy Wind (5)
El Paso (16)
Eleven, The (4,28)
Estimated Prophet (17)
Eyes Of The World (12,26,27)
Far From Me (20)
Feedback (2)
Feel Like A Stranger (20,22,26)
Fire On The Mountain (19,22)
Foolish Heart (25)
France (19)
Franklin's Tower (15,22,26,27)
Friend Of The Devil (7,13,22)
From The Heart Of Me (19)
Goin' Down The Road Feeling Bad (9,27)

Golden Road (To Unlimited Devotion) (1,13)
Good Lovin' (19)
Good Morning, Little School Girl (1,8,28)
Gotta Serve Somebody (24)
Greatest Story Ever Told (22)
Hard To Handle (11)
He's Gone (10)
Hell In A Bucket (23)
Help On The Way (15,26,27)
Here Comes Sunshine (12)
High Time (5,18)
Hurts Me Too (10)
I Know You Rider (6,10,26)
I Need A Miracle (19)
I Want You (24)
I Will Take You Home (25)
I've Been All Around This World (11)
If I Had The World To Give (19)
In The Midnight Hour (6)
It Hurts Me Too (6)
It Must Have Been The Roses (16,21,27)
It's All Over Now Baby Blue (6)
Jack-A-Roe (21)
Jack Straw (10,18)
Joey (24)
Johnny B. Goode (9)
Just A Little Light (25)
Katie Mae (11)
King Solomon's Marbles (15,27)
Knockin' On Heaven's Door (24)

Let It Grow (26)
Let Me Sing Your Blues Away (12)
Lindy (8)
Little Red Rooster (22)
Looks Like Rain (26)
Loose Lucy (14)
Loser (22)
Lost Sailor (20)
Mama Tried (9)
Me & Bobby McGee (9)
Me & My Uncle (9,18)
Mexicali Blues (13)
Mississippi Half-Step Uptown Toodeloo (12,16,26)
Money Money (14)
Monkey And The Engineer (21)
Morning Dew (1,10,28)
Mountains Of The Moon (3)
Mr. Charlie (10)
Music Never Stopped (15,27) 81
New, New Minglewood Blues (1,18,19,22)
New Potato Caboose (2,28)
New Speedway Boogie (5,18)
Not Fade Away (medley) (9)
Oh Babe It Ain't No Lie (21)
On The Road Again (21)
One More Saturday Night (10,13,26)
Operator (7)
Other One (9,27,28)
Passenger (17,22)
Picasso Moon (25)
Playing In The Band (9,18)
Pride Of Cucamonga (14)

Promised Land (16)
Queen Jane Approximately (24)
Race Is On (21)
Ramble On Rose (10,18)
Rhythm Devils (22)
Ripple (7,18,21)
Rosalie McFall (21)
Rosemary (3,13)
Row Jimmy (12)
Sage & Spirit (15,27)
Saint Of Circumstance (20)
Same Thing (8)
Samson & Delilah (17,22)
Sand Castles & Glass Camels (15)
Scarlet Begonias (14)
Serengetti (19)
Shakedown Street (19)
Ship Of Fools (14,16)
Sitting On Top Of The World (1)
Slipknot! (15,26)
Slow Train (24)
Smokestack Lightnin (11)
Space (22)
St. Stephen (3,4,13,18,28)
Stagger Lee (19)
Standing On The Moon (25)
Stealin' (8)
Stella Blue (12,16)
Stronger Than Dirt Or Milkin' The Turkey (15)
Sugar Magnolia (7,10,13) 91
Sugaree (16,27)
Sunrise (17)
Tennessee Jed (10,18)
Terrapin Part I Medley (17)

That's It For The Other One Medley (2)
Throwing Stones (23)
Till The Morning Comes (7)
To Lay Me Down (21)
Tons Of Steel (23)
Touch Of Grey (23) **9**
Truckin' (7,10,13,18) **64**
Turn On Your Love Light (4,13,28)
U.S. Blues (14,16,27)
Unbroken Chain (14)
Uncle John's Band (5,13) 69
Unusual Occurances In The Desert (15)
Victim Or The Crime (25,26)
Viola Lee Blues (1)
Wake Up Little Susie (11)
(Walk Me Out In The) ..see: Morning Dew
Walkin' Blues (26)
Weather Report Suite Medley (12)
West L.A. Fadeaway (23)
Wharf Rat (9)
What's Become Of The Baby (3)
When Push Comes To Shove (23)
You Win Again (10)

GRAY, Dobie
Born Leonard Victor Ainsworth on 7/26/42 in Brookshire, Texas. Soul vocalist/composer/actor. To Los Angeles in 1960. Worked as an actor on Broadway, and in the L.A. production of *Hair*. Lead singer of Pollution in 1971.

DEBUT DATE	PEAK POS	WKS CHR	GOLD	ARTIST — Album Title	$	Label & Number
3/10/73	64	21		1 Drift Away	$10	Decca 75397
11/10/73	188	3		2 Loving Arms	$10	MCA 371
2/17/79	174	4		3 Midnight Diamond	$8	Infinity 9001

DEBUT DATE	PEAK POS	WKS CHR	GOLD	ARTIST — Album Title	$	Label & Number

GRAY, Dobie — Cont'd

Caddo Queen (1)	I'll Be Your Hold Me Tight (3) **Loving Arms** (2) *61*	Rose (2)	Time I Love You The Most (1) **You Can Do It** (3) *37*
City Stars (1)	L.A. Lady (1)	Miss You Nights (3)	Sharing The Night Together (3)	We Had It All (1)
Drift Away (1) *5*	Lay Back (1)	Mississippi Rolling Stone (2)		We've Got To Get It On
Eddie's Song (1)	Let This Man Take Hold Of	Now That I'm Without You (1)	Sweet Lovin' Woman (1)	Again (3)
Good Old Song (2)	Your Life (3)		Thank You For Tonight (3)	Weekend Friend (3)
I Can See Clearly Now (3)	Love Is On The Line (2)	Reachin' For The Feeling (2)	There's A Honky Tonk Angel	Who's Lovin' You (3)
I Never Had It So Good (2)	Lovin' The Easy Way (2)	Rockin' Chair (1)	(Who'll Take Me Back In) (2)	You And Me (2)

GRAY, Glen, and the Casa Loma Orchestra

Alto saxophonist/bandleader. Led the Casa Loma Orchestra swing band. Organized in 1927; named for a Toronto nightclub. Gray died on 8/23/63.

2/23/57	18	9		1 Casa Loma In Hi-Fi!.. [I]	$15	Capitol 747
6/29/59	28	2		2 Sounds Of The Great Bands!... [I]	$15	Capitol 1022
2/2/63	63	13		3 Themes Of The Great Bands.. [I]	$12	Capitol 1812
10/19/63	69	15		4 Today's Best... [I]	$12	Capitol 1938

Alley Cat (4)	Dance Of The Lame Duck (1)	I Can't Get Started (3)	Let's Dance (3)	720 In The Books (2)	Symphony In Riffs (2)
Artistry In Rhythm (3)	Days Of Wine And Roses (4)	I Cried For You (1)	Maniac's Ball (1)	Sleepy Time Gal (1)	Take The A Train (2)
Begin The Beguine (2)	Desafinado (4)	I Left My Heart In San	Memories Of You (1)	Smoke Rings (1)	Tenderly (2)
Black Jazz (1)	Elks' Parade (2)	Francisco (4)	Moonlight Serenade (3)	Snowfall (2)	Those Lazy-Hazy-Crazy
Blue Flame (3)	Fly Me To The Moon (In	I Will Follow You (Chariot) (4)	Nightmare (3)	Song Of India (2)	Days Of Summer (4)
Casa Loma Stomp (1)	Other Words) (4)	I'm Gettin' Sentimental Over	No Name Jive (1)	Stranger On The Shore (4)	Tuxedo Junction (3)
Ciribiribin (3)	Flying Home (2)	You (3)	Our Day Will Come (4)	String Of Pearls (2)	What Kind Of Fool Am I? (4)
Come And Get It (1)	For You (1)	Just An Old Manuscript (1)	Quaker City Jazz (3)	Sunrise Serenade (1)	White Jazz (1)
Contrasts (2)	Good Life (3)	Leap Frog (3)	Redskin Rhumba (3)	Sweetest Sounds (4)	Woodchopper's Ball (2)

GREAN, Charles Randolph, Sounde

Charles (b: 10/1/13 in New York City) is a former artist and repertoire director at RCA and Dot Records. Married singer Betty Johnson.

7/26/69	23	15		Quentin's Theme... [I]	$12	Ranwood 8055

title cut is from TV's *Dark Shadows*

Deep Purple	Manolito	On The Trail	**Quentin's Theme** *13*	Shadows Of The Night ..see: Sunset
Forgotten Dreams	#1 At The "Blue Whale"	Perfect Song	Serenade To Summertime	Quentin's Theme
La Golandrina				

GREASE BAND

Joe Cocker's backup band.

4/17/71	190	3		Grease Band	$10	Shelter 8904

All I Wanna Do	Jessie James	Let It Be Gone	My Baby Left Me	Visitor
Down Home Mama	Laugh At The Judge	Mistake No Doubt	To The Lord	Willie And The Pig

GREAT SOCIETY — see SLICK, Grace

GREAT WHITE

Los Angeles hard-rock quintet led by vocalist Jack Russell and guitarist Mark Kendall. Lineup included Lorne Black (bass) and Garry Holland (drums). Audie Desbrow replaced Holland by 1986. Keyboardist Michael Lardie joined by 1987. Tony Montana replaced Black in 1987, left in 1992.

3/24/84	144	12		1 Great White	$8	EMI America 17111
8/16/86	82	13		2 Shot In The Dark..	$8	Capitol 12525
7/18/87	23	53	▲	3 Once Bitten	$8	Capitol 12565
2/13/88	99	12		4 Recovery: Live! .... [L]	$8	Enigma 73295
				previously unreleased live and studio cover versions of material by Jimi Hendrix, Humble Pie and Led Zeppelin		
5/6/89	9	50	▲2	5 Twice Shy	$8	Capitol 90640
3/16/91	18	25	●	6 Hooked	$12	Capitol 95330
10/10/92	107	6		7 Psycho City	$12	Capitol 98835

Afterglow (6)	Doctor Me (7)	**House Of Broken Love**	Money (That's What I Want)	Original Queen Of Sheba (6)	Step On You (7)
All Over Now (3)	Face The Day (2)	(5) *83*	(4)	Out Of The Night (1)	Stick It (1,4)
Angel Song (5) *30*	Fast Road (3)	I Don't Need No Doctor (4)	Move It (5)	Psycho City (7)	Streetkiller (1,4)
Baby's On Fire (5)	Get On Home (7)	I Want You (1)	Never Change Heart (3)	Red House (4)	Substitute (1,4)
Bad Boys (1,4)	Gimme Some Lovin' (3)	Immigrant Song (4)	Never Trust A Pretty Face (7)	**Rock Me** (3) *60*	Waiting For Love (2)
Big Goodbye (7)	Gonna Getcha (3)	Is Anybody There (2)	Nightmares (1)	Rock N Roll (4)	What Do You Do (2)
Call It Rock N' Roll (6) *53*	Hard And Cold (4)	Lady Red Light (3)	No Better Than Hell (1)	Run Away (2)	
Can't Shake It (6)	Heart The Hunter (5)	Love Is A Lie (7)	Old Rose Motel (7)	**Save Your Love** (3) *57*	
Cold Hearted Lovin' (6)	Heartbreaker (6)	Lovin' Kind (6)	On The Edge (3)	She Only (5)	
Congo Square (6)	Hiway Nights (5)	Maybe Someday (7)	On Your Knees (1)	She Shakes Me (2)	
Dead End (1)	Hold On (1)	Mista Bone (3)	**Once Bitten Twice Shy**	Shot In The Dark (2)	
Desert Moon (6)		Mistreater (3)	(5) *5*	South Bay Cities (6)	

GREAVES, R.B.

Born Ronald Bertram Aloysius Greaves on 11/28/44 at the USAF Base in Georgetown, British Guyana. Half American Indian, raised on a Seminole reservation in California. Nephew of Sam Cooke. To England in 1963, as Sonny Childe & The TNT's.

1/3/70	85	14		R.B. Greaves	$20	Atco 311

Ain't That Good News	Ballad Of Leroy	Don't Play That Song (You	Home To Stay	**Take A Letter Maria** *2*
Always Something There	Birmingham, Alabama	Lied)	Oh When I Was A Boy	This Is Soul
To Remind Me *27*	Cupid			

GREBENSHIKOV, Boris

English-fluent songwriter from Leningrad. Former leader of Aquarium, a popular band within the former Soviet Union.

8/26/89	198	2		Radio Silence	$8	Columbia 44364

produced by Dave Stewart (Eurythmics)

China	Fields Of My Love	Postcard, The	Real Slow Today	Time, The	Winter
Death Of King Arthur	Mother	Radio Silence	That Voice Again	Wind, The	Young Lions

DEBUT DATE	PEAK POS	WKS CHR	GOLD	ARTIST — Album Title	$	Label & Number

GRECH, Rick
Bass player with Family, Traffic, Blind Faith, Ginger Baker's Air Force and KGB.

| 9/29/73 | 195 | 3 | | The Last Five Years .... [K] | $10 | RSO 876 |

compiled from his work with groups

| Doin' It | Hey Mr. Policeman | Just A Guest | Rock 'N' Roll Stew | Second Generation Woman |
| Face In The Cloud | How-Hi-The-Li | Kiss The Children | Sea Of Joy | |

GREELEY, George
Guest pianist with the Warner Bros. Orchestra. Also see soundtrack "Parrish."

| 5/22/61 | 29 | 16 | | The Best Of The Popular Piano Concertos .... [I-K] | $10 | Warner 1410 |

Affair To Remember (Our Love Affair)	Come Back To Sorrento	Laura	Moonlight Sonata	Three Coins In The Fountain
Aloha Oe (Farewell To Thee)	Hawaiian War Chant	Love Is A Many Splendored Thing	On The Trail	Tristan And Isolde, Love
			Street Scene	Music From

★★165★★ GREEN, Al
Born on 4/13/46 in Forest City, Arkansas. Soul singer/songwriter. With gospel group the Greene Brothers. To Grand Rapids, Michigan in 1959. First recorded for Fargo in 1960. In group The Creations from 1964-67. Sang with his brother Robert and Lee Virgins in the group Soul Mates from 1967-68. Went solo in 1969. Wrote most of his songs. Returned to gospel music in 1980.

8/28/71+	58	43		1 Al Green Gets Next To You	$12	Hi 32062
2/12/72	8	56	●	2 **Let's Stay Together**	$12	Hi 32070
9/16/72	162	9		3 Al Green .... [E]	$10	Bell 6076

recordings from 1967-68

| 10/21/72 | 4 | 67 | ● | 4 **I'm Still In Love With You** .... | $10 | Hi 32074 |
| 1/6/73 | 19 | 28 | | 5 Green Is Blues .... [E] | $10 | Hi 32055 |

Green's first album on the Hi label

5/19/73	10	41	●	6 **Call Me**	$10	Hi 32077
12/29/73+	24	30	●	7 Livin' For You	$10	Hi 32082
11/23/74+	15	33	●	8 Al Green Explores Your Mind	$10	Hi 32087
3/22/75	17	21		9 Al Green/Greatest Hits .... [G]	$10	Hi 32089
9/13/75	28	23		10 Al Green Is Love	$10	Hi 32092
3/20/76	59	16		11 Full Of Fire	$10	Hi 32097
11/27/76+	93	14		12 Have A Good Time	$10	Hi 32103
7/2/77	134	9		13 Al Green's Greatest Hits, Volume II .... [G]	$10	Hi 32105
12/24/77+	103	12		14 The Belle Album	$10	Hi 6004
5/2/87	131	14		15 Soul Survivor	$8	A&M 5150

a collection of Inspirational songs

All Because (1)
All N All (14)
Always (11)
Are You Lonely For Me Baby (1)
Back Up Train (3) *41*
Belle (14) *83*
Beware (7)
Call Me (Come Back Home) (6,9) *10*
Chariots Of Fire (14)
City, The (8)
Could I Be The One (10)
Don't Hurt Me No More (3)
Don't Leave Me (3)
Dream (14)
Drivin' Wheel (1)
Everything's Gonna Be Alright (15)
Feels Like Summer (14)
For The Good Times (4,13)
Free At Last (7)
Full Of Fire (11,13) *28*
Funny How Time Slips Away (6)
Georgia Boy (14)

Get Back (5)
Get Back Baby (1)
Get Yourself Together (3)
Glory Glory (11)
God Blessed Our Love (8)
God Find A New World (5)
God Is Standing By (1)
Gotta Find A New World (5)
Guilty (3) *69*
Hangin' On (8)
Happy (12)
Have A Good Time (12)
Have You Been Making Out O.K. (6)
He Ain't Heavy (15)
Here I Am (Come And Take Me) (6,9) *10*
Hold On Forever (12)
Home Again (7)
Hot Wire (3) *71*
How Can You Mend A Broken Heart (2,9)
I Can't Get Next To You (1,9) *60*
I Didn't Know (10)
I Feel Good (14)

I Gotta Be More (Take Me Higher) (10)
I Stand Accused (5)
I Tried To Tell Myself (12)
I Wish You Were Here (10)
I'd Fly Away (11)
I'll Be Good To You (3)
I'm A Ram (1)
I'm Glad You're Mine (4)
I'm Hooked On You (8)
I'm Reachin' Out (3)
I'm So Lonesome I Could Cry (6)
I'm Still In Love With You (4,9) *3*
I've Never Found A Girl (Who Loves Me Like Me Do) (2)
It Ain't No Fun To Me (2)
Jesus Is Waiting (6)
Jesus Will Fix It (15)
Judy (2)
Keep Me Cryin' (12,13) *37*
La-La For You (8)
Let It Shine (11)
Let Me Help You (3)

Let's Get Married (7,9) *32*
Let's Stay Together (2,9) *1*
Letter, The (5)
Light My Fire (1)
Livin' For You (7,13) *19*
Look What You Done For Me (4,9) *4*
Love And Happiness (4,13)
L-O-V-E (Love) (10,13) *13*
Love Ritual (10)
Love Sermon (10)
Loving You (14)
My Girl (5)
My God Is Real (8)
My Sweet Sixteen (7)
Nothing Takes The Place Of You (12)
Oh Me, Oh My (Dreams In My Arms) (10) *48*
Oh, Pretty Woman (4)
Old Time Lovin (2)
One Nite Stand (8)
One Of These Good Old Days (4)
One Woman (5)
Rhymes (10,13)

Right Now Right Now (1)
School Days (8)
Sha-La-La (Make Me Happy) (8,13) *7*
Simply Beautiful (4)
Smile A Little Bit More (12)
So Good To Be Here (7)
So Real To Me (15)
So You're Leaving (2)
Something (12)
Soon As I Get Home (11)
Soul Survivor (15)
Stand Up (6)
Stay With Me Forever (8)
Stop And Check Myself (3)
Summertime (5)
Take Me To The River (8,13)
Talk To Me (5)
That's All It Takes (Lady) (3)
That's The Way It Is (11)
There Is Love (10)
There's No Way (11)
Tired Of Being Alone (1,9) *11*
Together Again (11)
Tomorrow's Dream (5)

Truth Marches On (12)
23rd Psalm (15)
Unchained Melody (7)
What A Wonderful Thing Love Is (4)
What Am I Gonna Do With Myself (7)
What Is This Feeling (2)
Yield Not To Temptation (15)
You Know And I Know (15)
You Ought To Be With Me (6,9) *3*
You Say It (1)
You've Got A Friend (15)
Your Love Is Like The Morning Sun (6)

GREEN, Grant
Jazz guitarist. Born on 6/6/31 in St. Louis. Worked with Jimmy Forrest, Jack McDuff, Hank Mobley and Herbie Hancock.

| 10/16/71 | 151 | 9 | | Visions .... [I] | $10 | Blue Note 84373 |

| Blues For Abraham | Does Anybody Really Know What Time It Is | Love On A Two Way Street | Mozart: Symphony No. 40 In G Minor, K550, 1st Movement | Never Can Say Goodbye |
| Cantaloupe Woman | | Maybe Tomorrow | | We've Only Just Begun |

GREEN, Jack
Former lead guitarist of T. Rex and Pretty Things. Born on 3/12/51 in Glasgow.

| 10/18/80 | 121 | 8 | | Humanesque .... | $8 | RCA 3639 |

Babe	Can't Stand It	I Call, No Answer	Murder	This Is Japan
Bout That Girl	Factory Girl	Life On The Line	So Much	Thought It Was Easy
				Valentina

GREEN, Peter
Blues guitarist who co-founded Fleetwood Mac in 1967. Born Peter Greenbaum on 10/29/46 in London. Prior to Fleetwood Mac, was a member of Shotgun Express and replaced Eric Clapton in John Mayall's Bluesbreakers.

| 10/25/80 | 186 | 5 | | Little Dreamer .... | $8 | Sail 0112 |

| Baby When The Sun Goes Down | Born Under A Bad Sign | I Could Not Ask For More | Loser Two Times | One Woman Love |
| | Cryin' Won't Bring You Back | Little Dreamer | Momma Don'tcha Cry | Walkin' The Road |

GREENBAUM, Norman
Born on 11/20/42 in Malden, Massachusetts. Moved to the West Coast in 1965 and formed the psychedelic jug band Dr. West's Medicine Show & Junk Band.

| 2/28/70 | 23 | 25 | | Spirit In The Sky .... | $15 | Reprise 6365 |

Alice Bodine / Good Lookin' Woman / Jubilee / Junior Cadillac / Marcy / Milk Cow / Power, The / Skyline / **Spirit In The Sky 3** / Tars Of India

GREENE, Jack
Born on 1/7/30 in Maryville, Tennessee. Drummer for Ernest Tubb's band, 1962-66. Joined the *Grand Ole Opry* in 1967. Known as the "Jolly Green Giant."

| 2/25/67 | 66 | 21 | | 1 There Goes My Everything .... | $15 | Decca 74845 |
| 7/22/67 | 151 | 12 | | 2 All The Time .... | $15 | Decca 74904 |

All The Time (2) / Almost Persuaded (1) / Crazy (2) / Cryin' Time (2) / Don't You Ever Get Tired (Of Hurting Me) (1) / Ever Since My Baby Went Away (1) / Happy Tracks (2) / Hardest Easy Thing (2) / Here Comes My Baby (1) / Hurt's On Me (1) / I Can't Help It (If I'm Still In Love With You) (2) / I'm A Lonesome Fugitive (2) / Make The World Go Away (1) / Room For One More / Heartache (2) / She's Gone, Gone, Gone (2) / Tender Years (1) / **There Goes My Everything** (1) **65** / Think I'll Go Somewhere And Cry Myself To Sleep (1) / Together Again (1) / Touch My Heart (2) / Walk Through This World With Me (2) / Walking On New Grass (1) / Wanting You But Never Having You (2) / Wound Time Can't Erase (1)

GREENE, Lorne
Born on 2/12/14 in Ottawa, Canada; died on 9/11/87 of cardiac arrest. Chief newscaster for CBC radio, 1940-43. Acted in films *The Silver Chalice* and *Tight Spot*; starred in TV's *Bonanza* and *Battlestar Galactica*.

| 11/28/64+ | 35 | 19 | | Welcome To The Ponderosa .... | $20 | RCA 2843 |

Alamo / Blue Guitar / Bonanza / Endless Prairie / Ghost Riders In The Sky / Ol' Tin Cup (And A Battered Ol' Coffee Pot) / Pony Express / **Ringo 1** / Saga Of The Ponderosa / Sand

GREEN ON RED
Country-rock quintet led by vocalist Dan Stuart.

| 5/3/86 | 177 | 6 | | No Free Lunch .... | $8 | Mercury 826346 |

Ballad Of Guy Fawkes / Funny How Time Slips Away / Honest Man / Jimmy Boy / Keep On Moving / No Free Lunch / Time Ain't Nothing

GREENWOOD, Lee
Born on 10/27/42 in Los Angeles. Country singer/songwriter/multi-instrumentalist. With Felix Cavaliere (later of the Young Rascals) in the Scotties. Worked as a dealer in Vegas casinos until 1981.

5/28/83	73	21	●	1 Somebody's Gonna Love You	$8	MCA 5403
6/9/84	150	20	●	2 You've Got A Good Love Comin'	$8	MCA 5488
9/8/84	89	13		3 Meant For Each Other	$8	MCA 5477

BARBARA MANDRELL/LEE GREENWOOD

| 5/18/85 | 163 | 8 | ▲ | 4 Greatest Hits .... [G] | $8 | MCA 5582 |

Ain't No Trick (It Takes Magic) (4) / Barely Holding On (1) / Call It What You Want To (It's Still Love) (1) / Can't Get Too Much Of A Good Thing (3) / Dixie Road (4) / Even Love Can't Save Us Now (2) / Fool's Gold (2,4) / God Bless The USA (2,4) / Going, Going, Gone (1,4) / Held Over (3) / I Don't Want To Wake You (2) / I Found Love In Time (2) / I'll Never Stop Loving You (3) / I.O.U. (1,4) **53** / It Should Have Been Love By Now (3) / It Turns Me Inside Out (4) / Ladies Love (1) / Lean, Mean, Lovin' Machine (4) / Love Me Like I'm Leavin' Tonight (2) / Love Won't Let Us Say Goodbye (1) / Now You See Us, Now You Don't (3) / One On One, Eye To Eye, Heart To Heart (3) / Ring On Her Finger, Time On Her Hands (4) / She's Lying (4) / Soft Shoulder (3) / **Somebody's Gonna Love You** (1,4) **96** / Someone Who Remembers (1) / Think About The Good Times (1) / To Me (3) / Two Heart Serenade (2) / We Were Meant For Each Other (3) / We're A Perfect Match (3) / Wind Beneath My Wings (1) / Worth It For The Ride (2) / You've Got A Good Love Comin' (2)

GREGGAINS, Joanie — see AEROBICS section

GREGORY, Dick
Black comedian/civil rights activist. Born on 10/12/32 in St. Louis. In the 1980's, became a diet guru.

| 6/5/61 | 23 | 27 | | 1 In Living Black & White .... [C] | $20 | Colpix 417 |
| 8/16/69+ | 182 | 8 | | 2 The Light Side: The Dark Side .... [C] | $15 | Poppy 60001 [2] |

American History (2) / Assassinations (2) / Atmosphere Of Trust (2) / Black Attitudes (2) / Black Progress (2) / Black Rioters (2) / Comedians Of The '60's (1) / Commentary On Affairs Political (1) / Concerned Honky Law (2) / Congo Daily Tribune (1) / Draft Resisters (2) / 50,000 Ft. - And No Insurance (1) / Learning To Live (2) / Middle East (1) / Moral Gap (2) / Not Poor - Just Busted (1) / 100 Proof (1) / Presidential Campaign (2) / Property Rights-Human Rights (2) / Thoughts On Outer Space (1) / White Brother (2) / White Racists Institutions (2) / Young Moral Dedication (2)

GREY & HANKS
Chicago-based vocal/songwriting duo of Zane Grey and Len Ron Hanks. Wrote "Back In Love Again" for L.T.D., "Never Had A Love Like This Before" for Tavares and many others.

| 2/3/79 | 97 | 11 | | 1 You Fooled Me .... | $8 | RCA 3069 |
| 2/23/80 | 195 | 3 | | 2 Prime Time .... | $8 | RCA 3477 |

Closer To Something Real (1) / **Dancin'** (1) **83** / For The People (2) / Gotta Put Something In (1) / How Can You Live Without Love (1) / I Can Tell Where Your Head Is (1) / I'm Calling On You (2) / Love's In Command (2) / Never Let You Down (1) / Prime Time (2) / Since I Found You (Love Is Better Than Ever) (2) / Single Girls (2) / Tired Of Taking Chances (2) / Way Out To Get In (1) / We Need More (2) / You Fooled Me (1)

GRIFFITH, Nanci
Born in Austin, Texas and raised in southern Louisiana and Dallas. "Folkabilly" (term coined by Griffith, fusion of folk and hillbilly music) singer.

| 9/16/89 | 99 | 14 | | 1 Storms .... | $8 | MCA 6319 |
| 10/12/91 | 185 | 1 | | 2 Late Night Grande Hotel .... | $12 | MCA 10306 |

Brave Companion Of The Road (1) / Down 'N' Outer (2) / Drive-In Movies And Dashboard Lights (1) / Fields Of Summer (2) / Heaven (2) / Hometown Streets (2) / I Don't Wanna Talk About Love (1) / If Wishes Were Changes (1) / It's A Hard Life Wherever You Go (1) / It's Just Another Morning Here (2) / It's Too Late (2) / Late Night Grande Hotel (2) / Leaving The Harbor (1) / Listen To The Radio (1) / One Blade Shy Of A Sharp Edge (2) / Power Lines (2) / Radio Fragile (1) / San Diego Serenade (2) / Storms (1) / Sun, Moon, And Stars (2) / You Made This Love A Teardrop (1)

DEBUT DATE	PEAK POS	WKS CHR	GOLD	ARTIST — Album Title	$	Label & Number

GRIM REAPER
Heavy-metal foursome from Droitwich, England. Led by vocalist Steve Grimmet.

DEBUT DATE	PEAK POS	WKS CHR	GOLD	Album	$	Label & Number
8/25/84	73	27		1 See you in Hell	$8	RCA 8038
7/6/85	108	14		2 Fear No Evil	$8	RCA 5431
8/1/87	93	21		3 Rock You To Hell	$8	RCA 6250

All Hell Let Loose (1)
Dead On Arrival (1)
Fear No Evil (2)
Fight For The Last (2)
Final Scream (2)
I Want More (3)
Lay It On The Line (2)
Let The Thunder Roar (2)
Liar (1)
Lord Of Darkness (Your Living Hell) (2)
Lust For Freedom (3)
Matter Of Time (2)
Never Coming Back (2)
Night Of The Vampire (3)
Now Or Never (1)
Rock & Roll Tonight (2)
Rock Me 'Till I Die (3)
Rock You To Hell (3)
Run For Your Life (1)
See You In Hell (1)
Show Must Go On (1)
Suck It And See (3)
Waysted Love (3)
When Heaven Comes Down (3)
Wrath Of The Ripper (1)
You'll Wish That You Were Never Born (3)

GRIN
Rock trio formed by Nils Lofgren (lead guitar, keyboards, vocals). Disbanded in 1973.

DEBUT DATE	PEAK POS	WKS CHR	GOLD	Album	$	Label & Number
8/7/71	192	3		1 Grin	$10	Spindizzy 30321
2/5/72	180	6		2 1 + 1	$10	Spindizzy 31038
3/10/73	186	7		3 All Out	$10	Spindizzy 31701

Ain't Love Nice (3)
All Out (3)
Direction (1)
Don't Be Long (3)
18 Faced Lover (1)
End Unkind (2)
Everybody's Missin' The Sun (1)
Heart On Fire (3)
Heavy Chevy (3)
Hi, Hello Home (2)
I Had Too Much (Miss Dazl) (1)
If I Were A Song (1)
Just A Poem (1)
Like Rain (1)
Lost A Number (2)
Love Again (3)
Love Or Else (3)
Moon Tears (1)
Open Wide (1)
Outlaw (1)
Pioneer Mary (1)
Please Don't Hide (2)
Rusty Gun (3)
Sad Letter (3)
See What A Love Can Do (1)
She Ain't Right (3)
Slippery Fingers (2)
Soft Fun (2)
Sometimes (2)
Take You To The Movies Tonight (1)
We All Sung Together (1)
White Lies (2) 75

GRINDER SWITCH
Southern-rock quintet: Larry Howard, Rick Burnett, Dru Lumbar, Steve Miller and Joe Dan Petty.

DEBUT DATE	PEAK POS	WKS CHR	GOLD	Album	$	Label & Number
11/19/77	144	8		Redwing	$8	Atco 152

Faster And Faster
I Bought All The Lies
Redwing
Taste Of Love
That Special Woman
This Road
Watermelon Time In Georgia
Wings Of An Angel
You And Me

GRISMAN, David
Jazz-bluegrass mandolin player. Formed Boston rock quartet Earth Opera in 1967.

DEBUT DATE	PEAK POS	WKS CHR	GOLD	Album	$	Label & Number
9/13/80	152	8		1 David Grisman - Quintet '80 [I]	$8	Warner 3469
6/6/81	108	10		2 Live [I-L]	$8	Warner 3550

STEPHANE GRAPPELLI/DAVID GRISMAN
jazz violinist Grappelli was born on 1/26/08 in Paris

DEBUT DATE	PEAK POS	WKS CHR	GOLD	Album	$	Label & Number
10/24/81	174	3		3 Mondo Mando [I]	$8	Warner 3618

Albuquerque Turkey (3)
Anouman (3)
Barkley's Bug (1)
Bow Wow (1)
Calinete (3)
Cedar Hill (3)
Dawg Funk (3)
Dawgma (1)
Dawgmatism (1)
Fanny Hill (3)
Fisztorza (medley) (2)
Fulginiti (medley) (2)
Japan (Op. 23) (3)
Misty (2)
Mondo Mando (3)
Mugavero (1)
Naima (1)
Pent-Up House (2)
Satin Doll (2)
Sea Of Cortez (1)
Shine (3)
Sweet Georgia Brown (2)
Swing '42 (2)
Thailand (1)
Tiger Rag (2)
Tzigani (medley) (2)

GROCE, Larry
Born on 4/22/48 in Dallas. Pop-folk singer/songwriter. Wrote children's songs for Walt Disney Records.

DEBUT DATE	PEAK POS	WKS CHR	GOLD	Album	$	Label & Number
3/27/76	187	2		Junkfood Junkie [L]	$8	Warner 2933

At The End Of The Long, Lonely Day
Biggest Whatever
Calhoun County
Coal Tattoo
I Still Miss Someone
Junk Food Junkie 9
Like The Trout Dart About
Little Old Lady In Cowboy Boots
Muddy Boggy Banjo Man
Old Home Place
You Ain't Goin' Nowhere

GROSS, Henry
Rock singer from Brooklyn. Original lead guitarist of Sha-Na-Na.

DEBUT DATE	PEAK POS	WKS CHR	GOLD	Album	$	Label & Number
2/8/75	26	23		1 Plug Me Into Something	$8	A&M 4502
2/14/76	64	28		2 Release	$8	Lifesong 6002
3/12/77	176	7		3 Show Me To The Stage	$8	Lifesong 6010

All My Love (1)
Come Along (3)
Dixie Spider Man (1)
Driver's Engine (1)
Evergreen (1)
Help (3)
Hideaway (3)
I Can't Believe (3)
I'll Love Her (1)
If We Tie Our Ships Together (3)
Juke Box Song (2)
Lincoln Road (2)
Moonshine Alley (2)
One Last Time (2)
One More Tomorrow (1) 93
Only One (1)
Overton Square (2)
Painting My Love Song (3)
Pokey (2)
Shannon (2) 6
Show Me To The Stage (3)
Showboat (3)
Someday (I Didn't Want To Have To Be The One) (2) 85
Something In Between (2)
Southern Band (1)
Springtime Mama (2) 37
String Of Hearts (3)
Tomorrow's Memory Lane (1)
Travelin' Time (1)
What A Sound (3)

GRUSIN, Dave
Jazz pianist. Born on 6/26/34 in Littleton, Colorado. Composer/producer of over 35 film soundtracks, *On Golden Pond* and *Tootsie* among them. Won Academy Award for *Milagro Beanfield War* soundtrack. Composed many TV themes, *Maude* and *Baretta* among them. Pianist/music director/arranger for *The Andy Williams Show*. Formed Grusin/Rosen Productions with drummer Larry Rosen, the forerunner of GRP Records.

DEBUT DATE	PEAK POS	WKS CHR	GOLD	Album	$	Label & Number
1/12/80	52	25	●	1 The Electric Horseman [S]	$8	Columbia 36327

side 1: songs performed by Willie Nelson (see Nelson); side 2: instrumental score by Dave

DEBUT DATE	PEAK POS	WKS CHR	GOLD	Album	$	Label & Number
3/21/81	74	18		2 Mountain Dance [I]	$8	GRP 5010
7/18/81	140	7		3 Dave Grusin and the GRP All-Stars/Live In Japan [I-L]	$8	GRP 5506

with Sadao Watanabe, Dave Valentin and Tom Browne

DEBUT DATE	PEAK POS	WKS CHR	GOLD	Album	$	Label & Number
8/7/82	88	9		4 Out Of The Shadows [I]	$8	GRP 5510
4/16/83	181	6		5 Dave Grusin and the NY/LA Dream Band [I-L]	$8	GRP 1001

with Lee Ritenour, Steve Gadd and Eric Gale

DEBUT DATE	PEAK POS	WKS CHR	GOLD	Album	$	Label & Number
10/5/85	192	2		6 Harlequin [I]	$8	GRP 1015

DAVE GRUSIN/LEE RITENOUR
side 1 features 2 Portuguese songs by Brazil's Ivan Lins: "Before It's Too Late (Antes Que Seja Tarde)" and "Harlequin (Arlequim Desconhecido)"

DEBUT DATE	PEAK POS	WKS CHR	GOLD	Album	$	Label & Number
2/25/89	110	12		7 Dave Grusin Collection [G-I]	$8	GRP 9579

all but one track are instrumental

DEBUT DATE	PEAK POS	WKS CHR	GOLD	Album	$	Label & Number
10/21/89	145	8		8 Migration [I]	$8	GRP 9592

features Branford Marsalis, Omar Hakim and Hugh Masekela

DEBUT DATE	PEAK POS	WKS CHR	GOLD	ARTIST — Album Title	$	Label & Number

| 11/18/89 | **74** | 13 | | **9** The Fabulous Baker Boys..[S-I] | **$8** | GRP 2002 |

includes "Makin' Whoopee" & "My Funny Valentine" by actress Michelle Pfeiffer; "Do Nothin' Till You Hear From Me" by Duke Ellington; "Lullaby Of Birdland" by the Earl Palmer Trio and "Moonglow" by Benny Goodman

| 12/14/91 | **170** | 2 | | **10** The Gershwin Connection .... [I] | **$12** | GRP 2005 |

George and Ira Gershwin-penned classics performed by Grusin with Chick Corea, Lee Ritenour and others; includes a 40-page booklet

Actor's Life (7)
Anthem Internationale (4)
Bess You Is My Woman (medley) (10)
Bird, The (6)
Captain Caribe (2,3)
Cats Of Rio (6)
Champ (What Matters Most), Theme From The (5)
City Lights (2)
Count Down (5)
Crystal Morning (4)
Dancing In The Township (4)
Disco Magic (1)
Don And Dave (3)

Early A.M. Attitude (6)
Either Way (2)
Electric Horseman (1)
Electro-Phantasma (1)
Fabulous Baker Boys, Main Title ..see: Jack's Theme
Fascinating Rhythm (10)
First-Time Love (8)
Five Brothers (4)
Freedom Epilogue (1)
Friends And Strangers (2,3)
Grid-Lock (6)
Hokkaido (4)
How Long Has This Been Going On? (10)

I Loves You Porgy (medley) (10)
I've Got Plenty O' Nuthin' (10)
In The Middle Of The Night (8)
Jack's Theme (9)
Last Train To Paradiso (4)
Maybe (10)
Milagro Beanfield War Suite Medley (8)
Modaji (3)
Moment Of Truth (9)
Mountain Dance (2,7)
My Man's Gone Now (10)

Nice Work If You Can Get It (10)
Number 8 (5)
Our Love Is Here To Stay (10)
Playera (7)
Prelude II (10)
Punta Del Soul (8)
Rag Bag (2)
Rising Star (Love Theme) (1)
River Song (7)
Rondo - "If You Hold Out Your Hand" (2)
'S Wonderful (10)
San Ysidro (6)

Serengeti Walk (Slippin' In The Back Door) (4,5,7)
Shamballa (3)
She Could Be Mine (4,7)
Shop Till You Bop (9)
Shuffle City (5)
Silent Message (6)
Soft On Me (9)
Soon (10)
Southwest Passage (8)
St. Elsewhere (7)
Summer Sketches '82 (5)
Suzie And Jack (3)
Sweetwater Nights (4)
Thankful 'N Thoughtful (7)

Thanksong (2)
That Certain Feeling (10)
There's A Boat Dat's Leavin' Soon For New York (10)
Three Days Of The Condor (5)
Trade Winds (3)
Tumbleweed Morning (1)
Uh, Oh! (3)
Welcome To The Road (9)
Western Women (8)

GTR
British hard-rock quintet featuring superstar guitarists Steve Hackett (Genesis) and Steve Howe (Yes, Asia), and vocalist Max Bacon.

| 5/17/86 | **11** | 26 | ● | GTR.. | **$8** | Arista 8400 |

Hackett To Bits
Here I Wait

Hunter, The *85*
Imagining

Jekyll And Hyde
Reach Out (Never Say No)

Sketches In The Sun
Toe The Line

When The Heart Rules The Mind *14*

You Can Still Get Through

GUADALCANAL DIARY
Rock quartet based in Marietta, Georgia: Murray Attaway (lead vocals), Rhett Crowe, John Poe and Jeff Walls. Band name is the title of a 1943 war film.

| 1/16/88 | **183** | 7 | | **1** 2 X 4 .... | **$8** | Elektra 60752 |
| 3/25/89 | **132** | 13 | | **2** Flip-Flop .... | **$8** | Elektra 60848 |

Always Saturday (2)
Barometer (2)
Everything But Good Luck (2)
Fade Out (2)

Get Over It (1)
Happy Home (1)
Let The Big Wheel Roll (1)
Likes Of You (2)
Lips Of Steel (1)

Litany (Life Goes On) (1)
Little Birds (1)
Look Up! (2)
Newborn (1)
Pretty Is As Pretty Does (2)

Say Please (1)
Ten Laws (2)
Things Fall Apart (1)
3 AM (1)
Under The Yoke (1)

...Vista (2)
Where Angels Fear To Tread (1)
Whiskey Talk (2)
Winds Of Change (1)

GUARALDI, Vince, Trio
Born on 7/17/32 in San Francisco; died of a heart attack on 2/6/76. Pianist/leader of own jazz trio. Formerly with Woody Herman and Cal Tjader. Wrote the music for the *Peanuts* TV specials.

| 2/2/63 | **24** | 28 | | Jazz Impressions of Black Orpheus .... [I] | **$25** | Fantasy 3337 |

features Vince's interpretations of 4 songs from the film *Black Orpheus*

Alma-Ville
Cast Your Fate To The Wind *22*

Generique
Manha De Carnaval

Moon River
O Nusso Amor

Samba De Orpheus
Since I Fell For You

GUARD, Dave, & The Whiskeyhill Singers
Dave was a member of The Kingston Trio from 1957-61. Died on 3/22/91 (age 56) of lymphoma.

| 6/30/62 | **92** | 11 | | Dave Guard & The Whiskeyhill Singers .... | **$25** | Capitol 1728 |

Banks Of The Ohio
Bonnie Ship, The Diamond
Brady And Duncan

Isa Lei
Nobody Knows You When You're Down And Out

Plane Wreck At Los Gatos (Deportees)
Ride On Railroad Bill

Shine The Light On Me (Salomila)
Soy Libre

We're The World's Last Authentic Playboys

When The War Breaks Out In Mexico
Wild Rippling Water

GUCCI CREW II
Miami-based rap trio formed in 1983: Rick Taylor, Cleveland Bell and Victor May.

| 9/23/89 | **173** | 6 | | Everybody Wants Some .... | **$8** | Gucci 3314 |

Beepers
Can We Get Funky

Everybody Wants Some
Five Dollar High ($5↑)

It's All About The Money
N.T.S.

Return The Burn
Straight From The Bottom

Vic's Story
Who's Cadillac

★★220★★ GUESS WHO, The
Rock group formed in Winnipeg, Canada in 1963. Consisted of Allan "Chad Allan" Kobel (guitar, vocals), Randy Bachman (lead guitar), Garry Peterson (drums), Bob Ashley (piano) and Jim Kale (bass). Recorded as The Reflections, and Chad Allan & The Expressions. Ashley replaced by new lead singer Burton Cummings in 1966. Allan left shortly thereafter. Bachman left in July 1970, to form Bachman-Turner Overdrive; replaced by Kurt Winter and Greg Leskiw. Leskiw and Kale left in 1972, replaced by Don McDougall and Bill Wallace. Domenic Troiano replaced both Winter and McDougall in 1974. Group disbanded in 1975; several reunions since then.

4/26/69	**45**	19		**1** Wheatfield Soul...	**$20**	RCA 4141
10/4/69	**91**	17		**2** Canned Wheat Packed by The Guess Who	**$20**	RCA 4157
2/14/70	**9**	55	●	**3** American Woman..	**$20**	RCA 4266
10/17/70	**14**	25	●	**4** Share The Land	**$20**	RCA 4359
4/17/71	**12**	45	●	**5** The Best of The Guess Who.................................[G]	**$15**	RCA 1004
8/21/71	**52**	16		**6** So Long, Bannatyne	**$15**	RCA 4574
3/18/72	**79**	10		**7** Rockin'..	**$15**	RCA 4602
8/19/72	**39**	21		**8** Live At The Paramount (Seattle)..........................[L]	**$15**	RCA 4779
1/20/73	**110**	12		**9** Artificial Paradise	**$15**	RCA 4830
7/14/73	**155**	8		**10** #10...	**$12**	RCA 0130
1/12/74	**186**	4		**11** The Best of The Guess Who, Volume II......................[G]	**$12**	RCA 0269
5/11/74	**60**	26		**12** Road Food	**$12**	RCA 0405
2/1/75	**48**	9		**13** Flavours	**$12**	RCA 0636
7/26/75	**87**	7		**14** Power In The Music	**$12**	RCA 0995
4/30/77	**173**	4		**15** The Greatest of The Guess Who............................[G]	**$10**	RCA 2253

GUESS WHO, The — Cont'd

Albert Flasher (8,11,15) *29*
All Hashed Out (9)
American Woman (3,5,8,15) *1*
Arriverderci Girl (7)
Attila's Blues (12)
Back To The City (7)
Ballad Of The Last Five Years (12)
Broken (11) *55*
Bus Rider (4,5)
Bye Bye Babe (9)
Cardboard Empire (10)
Clap For The Wolfman (12,15) *6*
Coming Down Off The Money Bag (medley) (4)
Coors For Sunday (14)
Dancin' Fool (13,15) *28*
Diggin' Yourself (13)
Dirty (13)
Do You Miss Me Darlin' (4,5)
Don't You Want Me (7,12)

Down And Out Woman (14)
Dreams (14)
8:15 (3)
Eye (13)
Fair Warning (2)
Fiddlin' (6)
Follow Your Daughter Home (9,11) *61*
Friends Of Mine (1)
Get Your Ribbons On (7)
Glace Bay Blues (8)
Glamour Boy (10,11,15)
Goin' A Little Crazy (6)
Grey Day (6)
Guns, Guns, Guns (9,7,11) *70*
Hamba Gahle-Usalang Gahle (9)
Hand Me Down World (4,5,15) *17*
Hang On To Your Life (4,5) *43*
Heartbroken Bopper (7,11) *47*

Heaven Only Moved Once Yesterday (medley) (7)
Herbert's A Loser (7)
Hoe Down Time (13)
Humpty's Blues (medley) (3)
I Found Her In A Star (1)
Just Let Me Sing (10)
Key (2)
Laughing (2,5,15) *10*
Lie Down (10)
Life In The Bloodstream (6,11)
Lightfoot (1)
Long Gone (13)
Lost And Found Town (9)
Love And A Yellow Rose (1)
Loves Me Like A Brother (13)
Maple Fudge (1)
Minstrel Boy (2)
Miss Frizzy (10)
Moan For You Joe (4)
Musicione (10)
New Mother Nature (3,5,8)

969 (The Oldest Man) (3)
No Sugar Tonight (medley) (3,5) *flip*
No Time (2,3,5,15) *5*
Nobody Knows His Name (13)
Of A Dropping Pin (2)
Old Joe (2)
One Divided (6)
One Man Army (6)
One Way Road To Hell (12)
Orly (9,11)
Pain Train (6,8)
Pink Wine Sparkles In The Glass (1)
Pleasin' For Reason (12)
Power In The Music (14)
Proper Stranger (3)
Rain Dance (6,11) *19*
Rich World - Poor World (14)
Road Food (12)
Rock And Roller Steam (9)
Rosanne (14)

Runnin' Back To Saskatoon (8,11) *96*
Running Bear (7)
Samantha's Living Room (9)
Sea Of Love (medley) (7)
Seems Like I Can't Live With You, But I Can't Live Without You (13)
Self Pity (10)
Share The Land (4,5) *10*
She Might Have Been A Nice Girl (6)
Shopping Bag Lady (14)
6 A.M. Or Nearer (2)
Smoke Big Factory (7)
So Long Bannatyne (6)
Song Of The Dog (medley) (4)
Sour Suite (6,11) *50*
Star Baby (12,15) *39*
Straighten Out (12)
Take It Off My Shoulders (10)
Talisman (3)
These Eyes (1,5,15) *6*

Those Show Biz Shoes (9)
Three More Days (4)
Truckin' Off Across The Sky (8)
Undun (2,5,15) *22*
Watcher, The (9)
We're Coming To Dinner (1)
Wednesday In Your Garden (1)
When Friends Fall Out (3)
When The Band Was Singin' "Shakin' All Over" (14,15)
When You Touch Me (1)
Women (14)
Your Nashville Sneakers (7)

GUIDRY, Greg
Singer/songwriter/pianist from St. Louis. Born in 1950.

4/17/82	**147**	7		Over The Line	$8	Badland 37735

Are You Ready For Love (1)
Darlin' It's You

Goin' Down *17*
Gotta Have More Love

(I'm) Givin' It Up
If Love Doesn't Find Us

Into My Love *92*
Over The Line

Show Me Your Love
(That's) How Long

GUN
Rock band from Glasgow, Scotland: Mark Rankin (vocals), Giuliano Gizzi, Baby Stafford, Dante Gizzi and Scott Shields.

3/31/90	**134**	8		Taking On The World	$12	A&M 5285

Better Days
Can't Get Any Lower

Feeling Within
Girls In Love

I Will Be Waiting
Inside Out

Money (Everybody Loves Her)
Shame On You

Something To Believe In
Taking On The World

GUNNE, Jo Jo — see JO JO

★★420★★ **GUNS N' ROSES**
Los Angeles-based, hard-rock band: lead singer W. Axl Rose (born in 1962 in Indiana; real name is William Bailey, natural father's surname is Rose) with bassist Michael "Duff" McKagan, guitarists Izzy Stradlin (Jeffrey Isbell) and Slash (Saul Hudson), and drummer Steven Adler. Axl Rose married Erin Everly (daughter of Don Everly of The Everly Brothers) on 4/27/90, divorced three weeks later. Adler left in 1990, replaced by former Cult drummer Matt Sorum. Keyboardist Dizzy Reed joined in 1990. Stradlin left in late 1991, replaced by Gilby Clarke (of Kills For Thrills). Slash married model Renee Surran in November 1992.

8/29/87+	**1**[5]	147	▲[8]	1 **Appetite For Destruction**	$8	Geffen 24148
12/17/88+	**2**[1]	53	▲[3]	2 G N' R Lies	$8	Geffen 24198
				side A: reissue of their 1986 4-song EP, *Live Like A Suicide*; side B: 4 tracks recorded in 1988		
10/5/91	**1**[2]	71↑ ▲[4]		3 **Use Your Illusion II**	$12	Geffen 24420
10/5/91	**2**[2]	71↑ ▲[4]		4 **Use Your Illusion I**	$12	Geffen 24415

Anything Goes (1)
Back Off Bitch (4)
Bad Apples (4)
Bad Obsession (4)
Breakdown (3)
Civil War (3)
Coma (4)
Dead Horse (4)
Don't Cry (3,4) *10*
Don't Damn Me (4)

Double Talkin' Jive (4)
Dust N' Bones (4)
Estranged (3)
14 Years (3)
Garden, The (4)
Garden Of Eden (4)
Get In The Ring (3)
It's So Easy (1)
Knockin' On Heaven's Door (3)

Live And Let Die (4) *33*
Locomotive (3)
Mama Kin (2)
Move To The City (2)
Mr. Brownstone (1)
My Michelle (1)
My World (3)
Nice Boys (2)
Nightrain (1) *93*
November Rain (4) *3*

One In A Million (2)
Out Ta Get Me (1)
Paradise City (1) *5*
Patience (2) *4*
Perfect Crime (4)
Pretty Tied Up (3)
Reckless Life (2)
Right Next Door To Hell (4)
Rocket Queen (1)
Shotgun Blues (3)

So Fine (3)
Sweet Child O' Mine (1) *1*
Think About You (1)
Used To Love Her (2)
Welcome To The Jungle (1) *7*
Yesterdays (1)
You Ain't The First (4)
You Could Be Mine (3) *29*
You're Crazy (1)

GURVITZ, Adrian — see BAKER GURVITZ ARMY, and EDGE, Graeme, Band

★★384★★ **GUTHRIE, Arlo**
Born on 7/10/47 in Coney Island, New York. Son of legendary folk singer Woody Guthrie. Starred in the 1969 film *Alice's Restaurant* which was based on his 1967 song "Alice's Restaurant Massacree."

11/18/67+	**17**	99	▲	1 Alice's Restaurant	$10	Reprise 6267
				side 1 is the 18-minute tale of "Alice's Restaurant Massacree"		
10/26/68	**100**	12		2 Arlo ....[L]	$10	Reprise 6299
10/18/69	**63**	17		3 Alice's Restaurant ....[S]	$10	United Art. 5195
				includes "Amazing Grace" by Garry Sherman Chorus, "Songs To Aging Children" by Tigger Outlaw and "You're A Fink" by Al Schackman		
10/25/69	**54**	19		4 Running Down The Road	$10	Reprise 6346
11/7/70	**33**	17		5 Washington County	$10	Reprise 6411
6/10/72	**52**	38		6 Hobo's Lullabye	$10	Reprise 2060
4/28/73	**87**	14		7 Last Of The Brooklyn Cowboys...	$8	Reprise 2142
6/8/74	**165**	10		8 Arlo Guthrie	$8	Reprise 2183
5/17/75	**181**	4		9 Together In Concert...[L]	$10	Reprise 2214 [2]
				PETE SEEGER & ARLO GUTHRIE		
10/2/76	**133**	6		10 Amigo	$8	Reprise 2239
				translation of Spanish title: Friend		
6/27/81	**184**	3		11 Power Of Love	$8	Warner 3558

DEBUT DATE	PEAK POS	WKS CHR	GOLD	ARTIST — Album Title	$	Label & Number

GUTHRIE, Arlo — Cont'd

Alice's Restaurant Massacree (1,3)
(hit POS 97 on "Hot 100" as "Alice's Rock & Roll Restaurant")
Anytime (6)
Bling Blang (8)
Children Of Abraham (8)
Chilling Of The Evening (1)
City Of New Orleans (6,9) *18*
Coming In To Los Angeles (4)
Connection (10)
Cooper's Lament (7)
Cowboy Song (7)
Crash Pad Improvs (3)
Creole Belle (4)
Darkest Hour (10)
Days Are Short (6)
Declaration Of Independence (9)
Deportee (Plane Wreck At Los Gatos) (8,9)

Don't Think Twice, It's All Right (9)
Estadio Chile (9)
Every Hand In The Land (4)
Farrell O'Gara (7)
Fence Post Blues (5)
Gabriel's Mother's Hiway Ballad #16 Blues (5)
Garden Song (11)
Gates Of Eden (7)
Get Up And Go (9)
Give It All You Got (11)
Go Down Moses (8)
Golden Vanity (9)
Grocery Blues (10)
Guabi, Guabi (10)
Guantanamera (9)
Gypsy Davy (7)
Hard Times (8)
Harps And Marriage (3)
Henry My Son (9)
Highway In The Wind (1)
Hobo's Lullaby (6)
I Could Be Singing (5)

I Want To Be Around (5)
I'm Going Home (1)
If I Could Only Touch Your Life (11)
If You Would Just Drop By (5)
Jamaica Farewell (11)
Joe Hill (9)
John Looked Down (2)
Last To Leave (8)
Last Train (7)
Lay Down Little Doggies (5)
Let Down (3)
Lightning Bar Blues (6)
Living In The Country (4)
Living Like A Legend (11)
Lonesome Valley (9)
Lovesick Blues (7)
Manzanillo Bay (10)
Mapleview (20%) Rag (4)
Massachusetts (10)
May There Always Be Sunshine (9)
Me And My Goose (8)

Meditation (Wave Upon Wave) (2)
Miss The Mississippi & You (7)
Mother, The Queen Of My Heart (9)
Motorcycle Song (1,2)
My Front Pages (4)
My Love (10)
1913 Massacre (6)
Nostalgia Rag (8)
Now And Then (1)
Ocean Crossing (10)
Oh, In The Morning (4)
Oklahoma Hills (4)
Oklahoma Nights (11)
On A Monday (9)
Patriots' Dream (10)
Pause Of Mr. Claus (2)
Percy's Song (1)
Power Of Love (11)
Presidential Rag (8,9)
Quite Early Morning (9)
Ramblin' 'Round (7)

Ring-Around-A-Rosy Rag (1)
Roving Gambler (9)
Running Down The Road (4)
Sailor's Bonnett (7)
Shackles & Chains (6)
Slow Boat (11)
Somebody Turned On The Light (9)
Standing At The Threshold (2)
Stealin' (4,9)
Sweet Rosyanne (9)
This Troubled Mind Of Mine (7)
Three Rules Of Discipline And The Eight Rules Of Attention (9)
Traveling Music (3)
Trip To The City (3)
Try Me One More Time (2)
Ukulele Lady (6)
Uncle Jeff (7)
Valley To Pray (5)
Victor Jara (10)

Waimanalo Blues (11)
Walkin' Down The Line (9)
Walking Song (10)
Washington County (5)
Way Out There (9)
Week On The Rag (7)
Well May The World Go (9)
Wheel Of Fortune (4)
When I Get To The Border (11)
When The Cactus Is In Bloom (8)
When The Ship Comes In (6)
Won't Be Long (8)
Wouldn't You Believe It (2)
Yodeling (9)

GUTHRIE, Gwen
Soul singer/songwriter from Newark, New Jersey. Background vocalist for many top artists.

8/30/86	89	13		Good To Go Lover	$8	Polydor 829532

Ain't Nothin' Goin' On But The Rent *42*
Good To Go Lover
I Still Want You
Outside In The Rain
Passion Eyes
Stop Holding Back
(They Long To Be) Close To You
You Touched My Life

GUTHRIE, Woody — see VARIOUS ARTISTS-Benefit Recordings

GUY
New York City R&B trio formed and fronted by Teddy Riley. Includes brothers Aaron and Damion Hall. By age 20, in 1988, Riley (ex-member of R&B group Kids At Work) was a renown producer.

| 7/30/88+ | 27 | 70 | ▲ | 1 Guy .... | $8 | Uptown 42176 |
| 12/1/90+ | 16 | 46 | ▲ | 2 The Future............ | $12 | MCA 10115 |

Do Me Right (2)
D-O-G Me Out (2)
Don't Clap...Just Dance (1)
Future, The (2)
Goodbye Love (1)

Gotta Be A Leader (2)
Groove Me (1)
Her (2)
I Like (1) *70*

I Wanna Get With U
[includes 2 versions] (2) *50*
Let's Chill (2) *41*
Let's Stay Together (2)
Long Gone (1)

My Business (1)
Piece Of My Love (1)
'Round And 'Round (Merry Go 'Round Of Love) (1)
Smile (2)

Spend The Night (1)
Tease Me Tonite (2)
Teddy's Jam (1)
Teddy's Jam 2 (2)
Total Control (2)

Where Did The Love Go (2)
Yearning For Your Love (2)
You Can Call Me Crazy (1)

GUY, Buddy
Born George Guy on 7/30/36 in Lettsworth, Louisiana. Singer/self-taught guitarist. To Chicago in 1957. First solo recording for Artistic in 1958. With Junior Wells during the '60s. Owner of the Chicago blues club Buddy Guy's Legends.

10/19/91	136	6		Damn Right, I've Got The Blues	$12	Silvertone 1462

with guests: Jeff Beck, Eric Clapton, Richie Hayward (Little Feat), Mark Knopfler, Pete Wingfield, and The Memphis Horns

Black Night
Damn Right, I've Got The Blues
Early In The Morning
Five Long Years
Let Me Love You Baby
Mustang Sally
Rememberin' Stevie
There Is Something On Your Mind
Too Broke To Spend The Night
Wanna Get With U ..see: I Wanna Get With U
Where Is The Next One Coming From

GUY, Jasmine
Born on 3/10/64 in Boston and raised in Atlanta. Actress/singer. Whitley Gilbert of TV's *A Different World*. Began career in dance. Dancer in TV show *Fame*. Starred in several off-Broadway shows. In films *School Days* and *Harlem Nights*.

11/3/90	143	13		Jasmine Guy	$12	Warner 26021

Another Like My Lover *66*
Don't Want Money
Everybody Knows My Name
I Don't Have To Justify
I Wish You Well
Johnny Come Lately
Just Want To Hold You *34*
More Love
Try Me
Tuff Boy

GWAR
Gore metal band: Beefcake the Mighty, Oderous Urungus, Balsac the Jaws of Death, Jiz Mac the Gusher, Slymenstra Hymen, The Sexicutioner and Flattus Maximus.

4/18/92	177	1		America Must Be Destroyed	$12	Metal Blade 26807

America Must Be Destroyed
Blimey
Crack In The Egg
Gilded Lily
Gor-Gor
Ham On The Bone
Have You Seen Me?
Morality Squad
Poor Ole Tom
Pussy Planet
Road Behind
Rock N Roll Never Felt So Good

GYPSY
Rock band formed and led by James "Owl" Walsh. Re-formed in 1978 as the James Walsh Gypsy Band.

| 10/10/70 | 44 | 20 | | 1 Gypsy............ | $15 | Metromedia 1031 [2] |
| 8/7/71 | 173 | 8 | | 2 In The Garden .... | $15 | Metromedia 1044 |

Around You (2)
As Far As You Can See, As Much As You Can Feel (2)
Blind Man (2)

Dead And Gone (1)
Decisions (1)
Dream If You Can (1)
Gypsy Queen - Part 1 (1) *62*

Gypsy Queen - Part 2 (1)
Here In My Loneliness (1)
Here (In The Garden) Part I & II (2)

I Was So Young (1)
Late December (1)
Man Of Reason (1)
More Time (1)

Reach Out Your Hand (2)
Third Eye (1)
Time Will Make It Better (2)

Tomorrow Is The Last To Be Heard (1)
Vision, The (1)

DEBUT DATE	PEAK POS	WKS CHR	GOLD	ARTIST — Album Title	$	Label & Number

H

HACKETT, Steve
Former guitarist of Genesis (1970-77). Born on 2/12/50 in London. Formed GTR in 1986.

4/17/76	191	4		1 Voyage Of The Acolyte	$10	Chrysalis 1112
4/29/78	103	14		2 Please Don't Touch	$8	Chrysalis 1176
7/7/79	138	4		3 Spectral Mornings	$8	Chrysalis 1223
8/30/80	144	6		4 Defector	$8	Charisma 3103
10/24/81	169	3		5 Cured...	$8	Epic 37632

Ace Of Wands (1)
Air-Conditioned Nightmare (5)
Ballad Of The Decomposing Man (3)
Can't Let Go (5)
Carry On Up The Vicarage (2)
Clocks - The Angel Of Mons (3)
Cradle Of Swans (5)
Every Day (4)
Funny Feeling (5)
Hammer In The Sand (4)
Hands Of The Priestess Part 1 & 2 (1)
Hermit, The (1)
Hope I Don't Wake (5)
Hoping Love Will Last (2)
How Can I (2)
Icarus Ascending (2)
Jacuzzi (4)
Kim (1)
Land Of A Thousand Autumns (2)
Leaving (4)
Lost Time In Cordoba (3)
Lovers, The (1)
Narnia (2)
Overnight Sleeper (5)
Picture Postcard (5)
Please Don't Touch (2)
Racing In A (2)
Red Flower Of Tachai Blooms Everywhere (3)
Sentimental Institution (4)
Shadow Of The Hierophant (1)
Show, The (4)
Slogans (4)
Spectral Mornings (3)
Star Of Sirius (1)
Steppes, The (4)
Tigermoth (3)
Time To Get Out (4)
Toast, The (4)
Tower Struck Down (1)
Turn Back Time (5)
Two Vamps As Guests (4)
Virgin And The Gypsy (3)
Voice Of Necan (2)

★★381★★ HAGAR, Sammy
Born on 10/13/47 in Monterey, California. Rock singer/songwriter/guitarist. Lead singer of Montrose (1973-75). Replaced David Lee Roth as lead singer of Van Halen in 1985. Also see Hagar, Schon, Aaronson, Shrieve.

2/26/77	167	9	●	1 Sammy Hagar	$8	Capitol 11599
1/21/78	100	11	●	2 Musical Chairs	$8	Capitol 11706
8/19/78	89	9		3 All Night Long ....[L]	$8	Capitol 11812
9/8/79	71	13		4 Street Machine	$8	Capitol 11983
6/21/80	85	12		5 Danger Zone	$8	Capitol 12069
1/30/82	28	32	▲	6 Standing Hampton	$8	Geffen 2006
12/25/82+	17	34	●	7 Three Lock Box	$8	Geffen 2021
1/8/83	171	9		8 Rematch ....[K]	$8	Capitol 12238
8/11/84	32	36	▲	9 VOA	$8	Geffen 24043
7/11/87	14	23		10 Sammy Hagar	$8	Geffen 24144

as a result of an MTV contest, album title changed to *I Never Said Goodbye*, however, none were pressed with the new title

Baby, It's You (6)
Baby's On Fire (6)
Back Into You (10)
Bad Motor Scooter (3)
Bad Reputation (5,8)
Boys' Night Out (10)
Burnin' Down The City (9)
Can't Let Loose (6)
Catch The Wind (1)
Child To Man (4)
Crack In The World (2)
Cruisin' & Boozin' (1,8)
Danger Zone (5)
Dick In The Dirt (9)
Don't Make Me Wait (9)
Don't Stop Me Now (2)
Eagles Fly (10) *82*
Eclipse (medley) (1)
Falling In Love (4)
Feels Like Love (4)
Fillmore Shuffle (1)
Free Money (1)
Give To Live (10) *23*
Growing Pains (4)
Growing Up (7)
Hands And Knees (10)
Heartbeat (5)
Heavy Metal (6)
Hey Boys (2)
Hungry (1)
I Can't Drive 55 (9) *26*
I Don't Need Love (7)
I Wouldn't Change A Thing (7)
I'll Fall In Love Again (6) *43*
I've Done Everything For You (3,8)
Iceman, The (5)
In The Night (Entering The Danger Zone) (5)
In The Room (7)
Inside Lookin' In (6)
It's Gonna Be All Right (7)
Little Star (medley) (1)
Love Has Found Me (1)
Love Or Money (8)
Make It Last (medley) (3)
Miles From Boredom (5)
Mommy Says, Daddy Says (5)
Never Give Up (7) *46*
Never Say Die (4)
Piece Of My Heart (6) *73*
Pits, The (1)
Plain Jane (4,8) *77*
Privacy (10)
Reckless (2,3)
Red (1,3,8)
Remember The Heroes (7)
Remote Love (7)
Returning Home (10)
Rise Of The Animal (7)
Rock 'N' Roll Weekend (1,3,8)
Rock Is In My Blood (9)
Run For Your Life (5)
Someone Out There (2)
Standin' At The Same Old Crossroads (10)
Straight From The Hip Kid (2)
Straight To The Top (4)
Surrender (6)
Sweet Hitchhiker (6)
Swept Away (9)
There's Only One Way To Rock (6)
This Planet's On Fire (Burn In Hell) (4,8)
Three Lock Box (7)
Trans Am (Highway Wonderland) (4,8)
Try (Try To Fall In Love) (2)
Turn Up The Music (2,3,8)
20th Century Man (5)
Two Sides Of Love (9) *38*
VOA (9)
What They Gonna Say Now (10)
When The Hammer Falls (10)
Wounded In Love (4)
You Make Me Crazy (2) *62*
Young Girl Blues (3)
Your Love Is Driving Me Crazy (7) *13*

HAGAR, SCHON, AARONSON, SHRIEVE
Sammy Hagar (see above), Neal Schon (Santana, Journey, Bad English), Kenny Aaronson (Stories) and Michael Shrieve (Santana, Automatic Man).

3/31/84	42	18		Through The Fire...[L]	$8	Geffen 4023

Animation
Giza
He Will Understand
Hot And Dirty
Missing You
My Home Town
Top Of The Rock
Valley Of The Kings
Whiter Shade Of Pale *94*

HAGEN, Nina
Born on 3/11/55 in East Berlin. Los Angeles-based, punk-dance vocalist. In late 1970s, was a cult film actress, famous in Holland and East Germany.

6/5/82	184	3		1 Nunsexmonkrock	$8	Columbia 38008
1/28/84	151	8		2 Fearless	$8	Columbia 39214

Antiworld (1)
Born In Xixax (1)
Change, The (1)
Cosma Shiva (1)
Dr. Art (1)
Dread Love (1)
Flying Saucers (1)
Future Is Now (1)
I Love Paul (2)
Iki Maska (1)
My Sensation (2)
New York New York (2)
Silent Love (2)
Smack Jack (1)
Springtime In Paris (2)
T.V. Snooze (2)
Taitschi - Tarot (1)
UFO (1)
What It Is (2)
Zarah (1)

★★219★★ HAGGARD, Merle
Born on 4/6/37 in Bakersfield, California. Country singer/songwriter/guitarist. Served nearly three years in San Quentin prison on a burglary charge, 1957-60. Signed to Capitol Records in 1965 and then formed backing band, The Strangers. One of the top male vocalists of the country charts with 38 #1 country singles.

5/13/67	165	10		1 I'm A Lonesome Fugitive	$20	Capitol 2702
10/21/67	167	4		2 Branded Man	$20	Capitol 2789
3/15/69	189	7		3 Pride In What I Am	$15	Capitol 168
6/14/69	67	18		4 Same Train, A Different Time....................................	$15	Capitol 223 [2]

featuring the songs of Jimmie Rodgers

DEBUT DATE	PEAK POS	WKS CHR	GOLD	ARTIST — Album Title	$	Label & Number

HAGGARD, Merle — Cont'd

DEBUT DATE	PEAK POS	WKS CHR	GOLD	ARTIST — Album Title	$	Label & Number
8/23/69	140	6		5 Close-Up ....[R]	$15	Capitol 259 [2]
				reissue of *Strangers* and *Swinging Doors* albums		
10/18/69	99	11		6 A Portrait Of Merle Haggard..	$15	Capitol 319
1/24/70	46	52 ▲		7 Okie From Muskogee ....[L]	$12	Capitol 384
				recorded in Muskogee, Oklahoma		
7/25/70	68	33 ●		8 The Fightin' Side Of Me ....[L]	$12	Capitol 451
				recorded in Philadelphia		
12/19/70+	58	9		9 A Tribute To The Best Damn Fiddle Player In The World (or, My Salute To Bob Wills)...........................	$12	Capitol 638
				with members of Bob Wills original Texas Playboy's band		
4/17/71	66	15		10 Hag...	$12	Capitol 735
9/18/71	108	10		11 Someday We'll Look Back	$12	Capitol 835
4/8/72	166	8		12 Let Me Tell You About A Song....................................	$12	Capitol 882
10/7/72	137	9 ▲		13 The Best Of The Best Of Merle Haggard ....[G]	$10	Capitol 11082
8/25/73	126	11		14 I Love Dixie Blues...so I recorded "Live" in New Orleans......................................[L]	$10	Capitol 11200
3/23/74	190	3		15 If We Make It Through December.................................	$10	Capitol 11276
6/28/75	129	9		16 Keep Movin' On	$10	Capitol 11365
11/19/77	133	5		17 My Farewell To Elvis	$8	MCA 2314
				Merle sings 9 of Elvis Presley's hits		
11/7/81+	161	28 ●		18 Big City	$8	Epic 37593
9/25/82	123	12		19 A Taste Of Yesterday's Wine	$8	Epic 38203

MERLE HAGGARD & GEORGE JONES

DEBUT DATE	PEAK POS	WKS CHR	GOLD	ARTIST — Album Title	$	Label & Number
2/12/83	37	53 ▲		20 Poncho & Lefty	$8	Epic 37958

MERLE HAGGARD/WILLIE NELSON

After I Sing All My Songs (19)
All Of Me Belongs To You (1)
All The Soft Places To Fall (20)
Always Wanting You (16)
Are The Good Times Really Over (I Wish A Buck Was Still Silver) (18)
Are You Lonesome Tonight (17)
Better Off When I Was Hungry (15)
Big Bad Bill (Is Sweet William Now) (14)
Big City (18)
Big Time Annie's Square (11)
Bill Woods From Bakersfield (12)
Billy Overcame His Size (7)
Blue Christmas (17)
Blue Rock (7)
Blue Suede Shoes (17)
Blue Yodel No. 6 (4)
Bottle Let Me Down (5)
Brain Cloudy Blues (9)
Branded Man (2,7)
Bring It On Down To My House, Honey (12)
Brothers, The (19)
Brown Skinned Gal (9)
C.C. Waterback (19)
California Blues (3,4)
California Cottonfields (11)
Carolyn (11,14) 58
Champagne (14)
Come On Into My Arms (15)
Corrine Corrina (8,9)
Daddy Frank (The Guitar Man) (12,13)
Day The Rains Came (3)
Devil Woman (medley) (8)
Don't Be Cruel (17)
Don't Get Married (2)
Down The Old Road To Home (4)
Drink Up And Be Somebody (1)
Emptiest Arms In The World (14)
Every Fool Has A Rainbow (6,8,13)

Everybody's Had The Blues (14) 62
Falling For You (5)
Farmer's Daughter (10,13)
Fightin' Side Of Me (8,14)
Folsom Prison Blues (medley)
Frankie And Johnny (4)
From Graceland To The Promised Land (17) 58
Funeral, The (12)
Go Home (2)
Gone Crazy (2)
Good Old American Guest (18)
Grandma Harp (12)
Half A Man (20)
Hammin' It Up (8,14)
Harold's Super Service (8)
Heartbreak Hotel (17)
Here In Frisco (16)
High On A Hilltop (5)
Hobo Bill's Last Ride (4,7)
Hobo's Meditation (4)
House Of Memories (1)
Hungry Eyes (6,13)
Huntsville (11)
I Ain't Got Nobody (And Nobody Cares For Me) (14)
I Always Get Lucky With You (18)
I Came So Close To Living Alone (1)
I Can't Be Myself (10)
I Can't Hold Myself In Line (3)
I Can't Stand Me (5)
I Die Ten Thousand Times A Day (6)
I Forget You Every Day (14)
I Haven't Found Her Yet (19)
I Just Want To Look At You One More Time (3)
I Knew The Moment I Lost You (9)
I Made The Prison Band (2)
I Take A Lot Of Pride In What I Am (3,8)
I Think I'm Gonna Live Forever (19)

I Think I've Found A Way (To Live Without You) (19)
I Think We're Livin' In The Good Old Days (3)
I Threw Away The Rose (2)
I Wonder If They Ever Think Of Me (14)
I'd Rather Be Gone (11)
I'd Trade All Of My Tomorrows (5)
I'll Break Out Again Tonight (15)
I'll Look Over You (5)
I'm A Good Loser (10)
I'm A Lonesome Fugitive (1,7)
I'm An Old, Old Man (Tryin' To Live While I Can) (15)
I'm Bringin' Home Good News (3)
I'm Free (3)
I'm Gonna Break Every Heart I Can (5)
I'm Movin' On (medley) (8)
I've Done It All (10)
I've Got A Darlin' (For A Wife) (10)
I've Got A Yearning (16)
If I Could Be Him (5)
If I Had Left It Up To You (5,7)
If We Make It Through December (15) 28
If You Want To Be My Woman (1)
If You've Got Time (To Say Goodbye) (10)
In The Arms Of Love (7)
In The Ghetto (17)
Irma Jackson (12)
It Meant Goodbye To Me When You Said Hello To Him (3)
It's My Lazy Day (20)
Jackson (medley) (8)
Jailhouse Rock (17)
Jesus, Take A Hold (10)
Jimmie Rodgers' Last Blue Yodel (The Women Make A Fool Out Of Me) (4)
Jimmie's Texas Blues (4)
Keep Me From Cryin' Today (5)

Kentucky Gambler (16)
Life In Prison (1)
Life's Like Poetry (16)
Loneliness Is Eating Me Alive (7)
Long Black Limousine (2)
Longer You Wait (5)
Love And Honor (15)
Love Me Tender (17)
Love's Gonna Live Here (medley) (8)
Lovesick Blues (14)
Mama Tried (7,13)
Man Who Picked The Wildwood Flower (12)
Man's Gotta Give Up A Lot (16)
Mary's Mine (1)
Misery (9)
Miss The Mississippi And You (4)
Mixed Up Mess Of A Heart (1)
Mobile Bay (Magnolia Blossoms) (19)
Montego Bay (6)
Mother, The Queen Of My Heart (4)
Movin' On (16)
Mule Skinner Blues (Blue Yodel No. 8) (4)
Must've Been Drunk (19)
My Carolina Sunshine Girl (4)
My Favorite Memory (18)
(My Friends Are Gonna Be) Strangers (5)
My Hands Are Tied (2)
My Life's Been A Pleasure (I Still Love You As I Did In Yesterday) (20)
My Mary (20)
My Old Pal (4)
My Rough And Rowdy Ways (1)
No Hard Times (4,7)
No More You And Me (5)
No Reason To Quit (10,13,20)
No Show Jones (19)
Nobody Knows But Me (4)

Nobody Knows I'm Hurtin' (14)
Okie From Muskogee (7,8,13,14) 41
Old Doc Brown (12)
Old Fashioned Love (9)
One Row At A Time (11)
One Sweet Hello (11)
Only Trouble With Me (11)
Opportunity To Cry (20)
Orange Blossom Special (medley) (8)
Peach Picking Time Down In Georgia (4)
Philadelphia Lawyer (2)
Please Mr. D.J. (5)
Proudest Fiddle In The World (A Maiden's Prayer) (12)
Reasons To Quit (20)
Right Or Wrong (9)
Roly Poly (9)
Sam Hill (5)
San Antonio Rose (9)
September In Miami (16)
Shade Tree (Fix-It-Man) (5)
She Thinks I Still Care (6)
Shelly's Winter Love (10)
Sidewalks Of Chicago (10)
Silver Eagle (19)
Silver Wings (6,7,13)
Sing A Sad Song (5)
Sing Me Back Home (medley) (7)
Skid Row (1)
Soldier's Last Letter (10) 90
Some Of Us Never Learn (2)
Someday We'll Look Back (11)
Someone Else You've Known (5)
Someone Told My Story (1)
Somewhere Between (2)
Somewhere On Skid Row (3)
Stay A Little Longer (9)
Stealin' Corn (8)
Still Water Runs The Deepest (20)
Stop The World (And Let Me Off) (18)

Swinging Doors (5,7)
T.B. Blues (8)
Take Me Back To Tulsa (9)
Texas Fiddle Song (18)
That's All Right (Mama) (17)
There's Just One Way (15)
These Mem'ries We're Making Tonight (16)
They're Tearin' The Labor Camps Down (12)
This Cold War (15)
This Song Is Mine (18)
Time Changes Everything (9)
To Each His Own (15)
Today I Started Loving You Again (8,13)
Train Of Life (11)
Train Whistle Blues (4)
Travelin' Blues (4)
Tulare Dust (11)
Turnin' Off A Memory (12)
Uncle Lem (15)
Waitin' For A Train (4)
Walking The Floor Over You (5)
'Way Down Yonder In New Orleans (14)
What's Wrong With Stayin' Home (6)
Whatever Happened To Me (1)
When Did Right Become Wrong (8)
White Line Fever (7)
Who Do I Know In Dallas (6)
Who'll Buy The Wine (3)
Why Should I Be Lonely? (4)
Workin' Man Blues (6,7,13)
Yesterday's Wine (19)
You Don't Have Very Far To Go (2,5,18)
You'll Always Be Special (16)
You're The Only Girl In The Game (15)

HAIRCUT ONE HUNDRED
British pop-rock sextet founded by vocalist Nick Heyward. Disbanded in 1983.

DEBUT DATE	PEAK POS	WKS CHR	GOLD	ARTIST — Album Title	$	Label & Number
4/24/82	31	37		Pelican West..	$8	Arista 6600

Baked Bean
Calling Captain Autumn
Fantastic Day

Favourite Shirts (Boy Meets Girl)

Kingsize (You're My Little Steam Whistle)

Lemon Firebrigade
Love Plus One 37
Love's Got Me In Triangles

Marine Boy
Milk Farm

Snow Girl
Surprise Me Again

HALEY, Bill, And His Comets

Born William John Clifton Haley, Jr. on 7/6/25 in Highland Park, Michigan. Began career as a singer with a New England country band, the Down Homers. The original Comets band who backed Haley on "Rock Around The Clock" were: Danny Cedrone (lead guitar), Joey D'Ambrose (sax), Billy Williamson (steel guitar), Johnny Grande (piano), Marshall Lytle (bass) and Dick Richards (drums). Comets lineup on subsequent recordings included Williamson, Grande, Rudy Pompilli (sax; d: 2/5/76 [age 47]), Al Rex (bass), Ralph Jones (drums) and Frannie Beecher (lead guitar). Bill died of a heart attack in Harlingen, Texas on 2/9/81. Inducted into the Rock and Roll Hall of Fame in 1987.

| 1/28/56 | 12 | 4 | | 1 Rock Around The Clock .... [G] | $125 | Decca 8225 |
| 10/13/56 | 18 | 5 | | 2 Rock 'n Roll Stage Show .... | $85 | Decca 8345 |

A.B.C. Boogie (1)
Birth Of The Boogie (1) 17
Blue Comet Blues (2)
Burn That Candle (1) 9
Calling All Comets (1)
Choo Choo Ch'Boogie (2) *flip*

Dim, Dim The Lights (I Want Some Atmosphere) (1) 11
Goofin' Around (2)
Happy Baby (1)
Hey Then, There Now (2)
Hide And Seek (2)

Hook, Line And Sinker (2) *flip*
Hot Dog Buddy Buddy (2) 60
Mambo Rock (1) 18
Razzle-Dazzle (1) 15

Rock-A-Beatin' Boogie (1) 23
Rockin' Through The Rye (2) 78
Rocking Little Tune (2)
Rudy's Rock (2) 34
Shake, Rattle And Roll (1)

Thirteen Women (And Only One Man In Town) (1)
Tonight's The Night (2)
Two Hound Dogs (1) *flip*
(We're Gonna) Rock Around The Clock (1) 1

HALL, Arsenio — see CHUNKY A

HALL, Daryl

Born Daryl Franklin Hohl on 10/11/48 in Philadelphia. Half of Hall & Oates duo.

| 3/29/80 | 58 | 12 | | 1 Sacred Songs .... | $8 | RCA 3573 |
| 9/6/86 | 29 | 26 | | 2 Three Hearts in the Happy Ending Machine .... | $8 | RCA 7196 |

Babs And Babs (1)
Don't Leave Me Alone With Her (1)
Dreamtime (2) 5

Farther Away I Am (1)
Foolish Pride (2) 33
For You (2)
I Wasn't Born Yesterday (2)

Let It Out (2)
NYCNY (1)
Next Step (2)
Only A Vision (2)

Right As Rain (2)
Sacred Songs (1)
Someone Like You (2) 57
Something In 4/4 Time (1)

Survive (1)
Urban Landscape (1)
What's Gonna Happen To Us (2)

Why Was It So Easy (1)
Without Tears (1)

★★80★★ HALL, Daryl, & John Oates

Daryl Hall (see previous entry) and John Oates (b: 4/7/49 in New York City) met while students at Temple University in 1967. Hall sang backup for many top soul groups before teaming up with Oates in 1972. In the late 1980s, they passed The Everly Brothers as the #1 charting duo of the rock era.

2/23/74+	33	38	●	1 Abandoned Luncheonette	$10	Atlantic 7269
10/26/74	86	10		2 War Babies	$10	Atlantic 18109
				produced by Todd Rundgren		
9/13/75+	17	76	●	3 Daryl Hall & John Oates...	$10	RCA 1144
8/28/76	13	57	●	4 Bigger Than Both Of Us	$10	RCA 1467
3/26/77	92	6		5 No Goodbyes .... [K]	$8	Atlantic 18213
9/17/77	30	17	●	6 Beauty On A Back Street	$8	RCA 2300
5/27/78	42	10		7 Livetime .... [L]	$8	RCA 2802
9/9/78	27	22	●	8 Along The Red Ledge	$8	RCA 2804
10/27/79	33	24		9 X-Static	$8	RCA 3494
8/16/80+	17	100	▲	10 Voices	$8	RCA 3646
9/26/81+	5	61	▲	11 Private Eyes	$8	RCA 4028
10/30/82+	3	68	▲2	12 H2O	$8	RCA 4383
11/19/83+	7	44	▲2	13 Rock 'N Soul, Part 1 .... [G]	$8	RCA 4858
10/27/84	5	51	▲2	14 Big Bam Boom	$8	RCA 5309
9/28/85	21	18	●	15 Live At The Apollo with David Ruffin & Eddie Kendrick ....[L]	$8	RCA 7035
				recorded at the re-opening of New York's Apollo Theater; side 1 features guest vocalists Ruffin and Kendrick		
5/21/88	24	26	▲	16 ooh yeah!	$8	Arista 8539
10/27/90	61	29	●	17 Change Of Season	$12	Arista 8614

Abandoned Luncheonette (1,7)
Adult Education (13,15) 8
Africa (10)
Ain't Too Proud To Beg (medley) (15)
All American Girl (14)
All You Want Is Heaven (9)
Alley Katz (8)
Alone Too Long (3)
Art Of Heartbreak (12)
At Tension (12)
August Day (8)
Back Together Again (4) 28
Bad Habits And Infections (6)
Bank On Your Love (14)
Beanie G. And The Rose Tattoo (2,5)
Bebop/Drop (9)
Better Watch Your Back (12)
Big Kids (10)
Bigger Than Both Of Us (6)
Camellia (3)
Can't Stop The Music (He Played It Much Too Long) (2,5)
Change Of Season (17)
Cold Dark And Yesterday (14)
Crazy Eyes (4)
Crime Pays (12)
Dance On Your Knees (14)
Delayed Reaction (12)

Did It In A Minute (11) 9
Diddy Doo Wop (I Hear The Voices) (11)
Do What You Want, Be What You Are (4,7) 39
Don't Blame It On Love (8)
Don't Change (6)
Don't Hold Back Your Love (17) 41
Downtown Life (16) 31
Emptiness, The (6,7)
Ennui On The Mountain (3)
Everything Your Heart Desires (16) 3
Everytime I Look At You (1)
Everytime You Go Away (10,15)
Everywhere I Look (17)
Falling (4)
Family Man (12) 6
Friday Let Me Down (11)
Get Ready (medley) (15)
Gino (The Manager) (3)
Girl Who Used To Be (6)
Give It Up (Old Habits) (17)
Go Solo (12)
Going Thru The Motions (14)
Gotta Lotta Nerve (Perfect Perfect) (10)
Grounds For Separation (3)
Guessing Games (12)
Had I Known You Better Then (1)

Halfway Home (17)
Hallofon (9)
Hard To Be In Love With You (10)
Have I Been Away Too Long (8)
Head Above Water (11)
Heavy Rain (17)
How Does It Feel To Be Back (10) 30
I Ain't Gonna Take It This Time (17)
I Can't Go For That (No Can Do) (11,13,15) 1
I Don't Wanna Lose You (8) 42
I Want To Know You For A Long Time (5)
I'm In Pieces (16)
I'm Just A Kid (Don't Make Me Feel Like A Man) (1,7)
I'm Watching You (A Mutant Romance) (2)
Intravino (9)
Is It A Star (9)
It's A Laugh (8) 20
It's Uncanny (5) 80
Italian Girls (12)
Johnny Gore And The "C" Eaters (2)
Keep On Pushin' Love (16)
Kerry (4)
Kiss On My List (10,13) 1

Lady Rain (1)
Las Vegas Turnaround (The Stewardess Song) (1,5)
Last Time (8)
Laughing Boy (1)
Lilly (Are You Happy) (5)
London Luck, & Love (4)
Looking For A Good Sign (11)
Love Hurts (Love Heals) (6)
Love You Like A Brother (5)
Maneater (12,15) 1
Mano A Mano (11)
Melody For A Memory (8)
Method Of Modern Love (14) 5
Missed Opportunity (16) 29
My Girl ..see: Nite At The Apollo Live!
Nite At The Apollo Live! The Way You Do The Things You Do/My Girl (15) 20
Nothing At All (3)
Number One (3)
One On One (12,13,15) 7
Only Love (17)
Open All Night (12)
Out Of Me, Out Of You (3)
Out Of Touch (14) 1
Pleasure Beach (8)
Portable Radio (9)
Possession Obsession (14,15) 30

Private Eyes (11,13) 1
ReaLove (16)
Rich Girl (4,7,13) 1
Rockability (16)
Rocket To God (16)
Room To Breathe (4,7)
Running From Paradise (9)
Sara Smile (3,7,13) 4
Say It Isn't So (13) 2
Screaming Through December (2)
Serious Music (8)
70's Scenario (2,5)
She's Gone (1,5,13) 7
So Close [includes 2 versions] (17) 11
Soldering (8)
Some Men (11)
Some Things Are Better Left Unsaid (14) 18
Sometimes A Mind Changes (17)
Soul Love (16)
Starting All Over Again (17)
Talking All Night (16)
Tell Me What You Want (11)
Unguarded Minute (11)
United State (10)
Wait For Me (9,13) 18
War Baby Son Of Zorro (2)
Way You Do The Things You Do ..see: Nite At The Apollo Live!

When Something Is Wrong With My Baby (15)
When The Morning Comes (1,5)
Who Said The World Was Fair (9)
Why Do Lovers (Break Each Others Heart?) (6) 73
Winged Bull (6)
Woman Comes And Goes (9)
(You Know) It Doesn't Matter Anymore (3)
You Make My Dreams (10,13) 5
You Must Be Good For Something (8)
You'll Never Learn (4)
You're Much Too Soon (2)
You've Lost That Lovin' Feeling (10) 12
Your Imagination (11) 33

DEBUT DATE	PEAK POS	WKS CHR	GOLD	ARTIST — Album Title	$	Label & Number

HALL, Jimmy
Mobile, Alabama native. Leader of the Southern rock band Wet Willie.

DEBUT DATE	PEAK POS	WKS CHR		ARTIST — Album Title	$	Label & Number
11/22/80	183	2		Touch You	$8	Epic 36516

Bad News	I'm Happy That Love Has	Midnight To Daylight	Private Number	Same Old Moon	Touch You
Eazy Street	Found You 27	Never Again	Rock & Roll Soldier	634-5789	

HALL, John, Band
John was born on 10/25/47. Founder/leader of Orleans.

| 12/5/81 | 158 | 13 | | 1 All Of The Above .... | $8 | EMI America 17058 |
| 3/5/83 | 147 | 5 | | 2 Searchparty .... | $8 | EMI America 17082 |

Can't Stand To See You Go (1)	Don't Hurt Me (1)	Ipso Facto (2)	Original Sin (2)	What You Do To Me (1)	
Clouds (1)	Don't Treat Your Woman Like That (2)	Little Miss Maybe (2)	Security (2)	Woman Of The Water (2)	
Crazy (Keep On Falling) (1) 42	Earth Out Tonight (1)	Love Me Again (2) 64	Somebody's Calling (2)	You Sure Fooled Me (1)	
	I'm The One (2)	On Hold (2)	Star In Your Sky (1)		
		Open Up The Door (2)	Touch, The (1)		

HALL, Tom T.
Born on 5/25/36 in Olive Hill, Kentucky. Country music storyteller. Wrote "Harper Valley P.T.A." hit for Jeannie C. Riley. Host of *Pop Goes The Country* TV series.

10/9/71	137	6		1 In Search Of A Song	$12	Mercury 61350
6/9/73	181	4		2 The Rhymer And Other Five And Dimers..	$10	Mercury 668
1/26/74	149	11		3 For The People In The Last Hard Town..	$10	Mercury 687
4/19/75	180	2		4 Songs Of Fox Hollow	$8	Mercury 500

Another Town (2)	I Care (4)	Joe, Don't Let Your Music Kill You (3)	Mysterious Fox Of Fox Hollow (4)	Sneaky Snake (4) 55	Year That Clayton Delaney Died (1) 42
Back When We Were Young (3)	I Flew Over Our House Last Night (2)	Kentucky Feb. 27, '71 (1)	Never Having You (3)	Song For Uncle Curt (2)	
Barn Dance (4)	I Know Who I'll Be Seeing In New Zealand (3)	L.A. Blues (1)	Old Five And Dimers Like Me (2)	Song Of The One Legged Chicken (4)	
Candy In The Window (2)	I Like To Feel Pretty Inside (4)	Last Hard Town (3)	Ole Lonesome George The Basset (4)	Spokane Motel Blues (2)	
Country Cabin-itis (3)	I Love (3,4) 12	Little Lady Preacher (1)	Pay No Attention To Alice (3)	Subdivision Blues (3)	
Don't Forget The Coffee Billy Joe (2)	I Wish I Had A Million Friends (4)	Looking Forward To Seeing You Again (2)	Ramona's Revenge (4)	Too Many Do-Goods (2)	
Everybody Loves To Hear A Bird Sing (4)	It Sure Can Get Cold In Des Moines (1)	Love's Been Good To Me (3)	Ravishing Ruby (2)	Trip To Hyden (1)	
How To Talk To A Little Baby Goat (4)		Man Who Hated Freckles (2)	Running Wild (3)	Tulsa Telephone Book (1)	
		Million Miles To The City (1)	Second Handed Flowers (1)	Who's Gonna Feed Them Hogs (1)	

HAMILTON, Chico
Jazz drummer. Born Foreststorn Hamilton on 9/21/21 in Los Angeles.

| 12/19/64+ | 145 | 4 | | Man From Two Worlds .... [I] | $20 | Impulse! 59 |

with Charles Lloyd (sax), Gabor Szabo (guitar) and Albert Stinson (bass)

Blues For O.T.	Child's Play	Forest Flower - Sunset	Mallet Dance	
Blues Medley	Forest Flower - Sunrise	Love Song To A Baby	Man From Two Worlds	

HAMILTON, George IV
Born on 7/19/37 in Winston-Salem, North Carolina. Country-folk-pop singer/songwriter/guitarist. Toured with Buddy Holly, Gene Vincent and The Everly Brothers. Moved to Nashville in 1959 and joined the *Grand Ole Opry*. Own TV series on ABC in 1959, and in Canada in the late 1970s.

| 10/5/63 | 77 | 8 | | Abilene .... | $15 | RCA 2778 |

Abilene 15	Everglades, The	If You Don't Know I Ain't Gonna Tell You	Little Lunch Box	Tender Hearted Baby
China Doll	(I Want To Go) Where Nobody Knows Me	Jimmy Brown The News Boy	Oh So Many Years	You Are My Sunshine
Come On Home Boy			Roving Gambler	

HAMILTON, JOE FRANK & REYNOLDS
Dan Hamilton, Joe Frank Carollo and Tommy Reynolds. Trio were members of The T-Bones. Reynolds left group in 1972 and was replaced by Alan Dennison. Although Reynolds had left, group still recorded as Hamilton, Joe Frank & Reynolds until July 1976.

6/19/71	59	15		1 Hamilton, Joe Frank & Reynolds	$10	Dunhill 50103
2/19/72	191	4		2 Hallway Symphony..	$10	Dunhill 50113
12/13/75+	82	14		3 Fallin' In Love..	$8	Playboy 407

Ain't No Woman (Like The One I've Got) (2)	Bridge Over Troubled Water (medley) (2)	Everyday Without You (3) 62	Like Monday Follows Sunday (2)	Only Love (Will Break Your Heart) (3)	Winners And Losers (3) 21
Anna, No Can Do (2)	C'est La Vie (2)	Fallin' In Love (3) 1	Long Road (1)	So Good At Lovin' You (3)	You've Got A Friend (medley) (2)
Badman (3)	Don't Be Afraid Of The World (2)	Goin' Down (1)	Love Is (3)	Sweet Pain (1)	Young, Wild And Free (1)
Barroom Blues (3)	Don't Pull Your Love (1) 4	Hallway Symphony (2)	Nora (1)	What Can You Say (1)	
Behold (1)	Don't Refuse My Love (1)	If Every Man (2)	On The Other Hand (2)	What Kind Of Love Is This (3)	
		It Takes The Best (1)	One Good Woman (2)	Who Do You Love (3)	

HAMLISCH, Marvin
Born on 6/2/44 in New York City. Pianist/composer/conductor for numerous soundtracks. 1973's Best Song Oscar and Grammy winner for "The Way We Were." Won the 1974 Best New Artist Grammy Award.

| 1/26/74 | 1⁵ | 41 | ● | 1 The Sting..[S-I] | $10 | MCA 390 |
| 8/31/74 | 170 | 5 | | 2 The Entertainer .... [I] | $10 | MCA 2115 |

includes adaptations of 5 Scott Joplin tunes

Bethena (2)	Glove, The (1)	I Love A Piano (2)	Merry-Go-Round Music Medley (1)	Rag Time Dance (medley) (1)	Solace [includes 2 versions] (1)
Easy Winners (1)	Grandpa's Spells (2)	Little Girl (1)		Ragtime Nightingale (2)	
Entertainer, The (1,2) 3	Heliotrope Bouquet (2)	Luther (1)	Mexican Dreams (2)	Rialto Ripples (2)	Stoptime Rag (2)
Gladiolus Rag (medley) (1)	Hooker's Hooker (1)	Maple Leaf Rag (2)	Pine Apple Rag (medley) (1)		

HAMMER — see M.C. HAMMER

HAMMER, Jan — see BECK, Jeff/GOODMAN, Jerry/SCHON, Neal/TV SOUNDTRACK "Miami Vice"

HAMMOND, Albert
Born on 5/18/42 in London and raised in Gibraltar, Spain. Member of British group Magic Lanterns, 1971.

| 12/9/72+ | 77 | 15 | | 1 It Never Rains In Southern California .... | $10 | Mums 31905 |
| 9/1/73 | 193 | 4 | | 2 The Free Electric Band .... | $10 | Mums 32267 |

DEBUT DATE	PEAK POS	WKS CHR	GOLD	ARTIST — Album Title	$	Label & Number

HAMMOND, Albert — Cont'd

Air That I Breathe (1)
Anyone Here In The Audience (1)
Brand New Day (1)
Day The British Army Lost The War (2)

Down By The River (1) *91*
Everything I Want To Do (2)
For The Peace Of All Mankind (2)
Free Electric Band (2) *48*

From Great Britain To L.A. (1)
I Think I'll Go That Way (2)
If You Gotta Break Another Heart (1) *63*

It Never Rains In Southern California (1) *5*
Listen To The World (1)
Names, Tags, Numbers & Labels (1)
Peacemaker, The (2) *80*

Rebecca (2)
Road To Understanding (1)
Smokey Factory Blues (2)
Who's For Lunch Today? (2)
Woman Of The World (2)

HAMMOND, John Paul — see BLOOMFIELD, Mike

HAMMOND, Johnny

Jazz organist. Born John Robert Smith on 12/16/33 in Louisville, Kentucky.

DEBUT DATE	PEAK POS	WKS CHR	GOLD	ARTIST — Album Title	$	Label & Number
9/11/71	125	14		1 Breakout ....[I]	$12	Kudu 01
5/20/72	174	6		2 Wild Horses/Rock Steady ....[I]	$12	Kudu 04

Blues Selah (1)
Breakout (1)

I Don't Know How To Love Him (1)
It's Impossible (2)

It's Too Late (1)
Never Can Say Goodbye (1)
Peace Train (2)

Rock Steady (2)
Who Is Sylvia? (2)
Wild Horses (2)

Workin' On A Groovy Thing (1)

★★203★★ HANCOCK, Herbie

Born on 4/12/40 in Chicago. Jazz electronic keyboardist. Pianist with the Miles Davis band, 1963-68. Won an Oscar in 1987 for his *Round Midnight* film score. Also scored the 1988 film *Colors*.

DEBUT DATE	PEAK POS	WKS CHR	GOLD	ARTIST — Album Title	$	Label & Number
5/13/67	192	2		1 Blow-Up ....[S-I]	$15	MGM 4447
				includes "Stroll On" by The Yardbirds		
6/2/73	176	6		2 Sextant ....[I]	$10	Columbia 32212
1/12/74	13	47	▲	3 Head Hunters ....[I]	$10	Columbia 32731
10/5/74	13	23		4 Thrust ....[I]	$10	Columbia 32965
10/12/74	158	3		5 Treasure Chest ....[E-I]	$12	Warner 2807 [2]
				tracks from 3 albums, recorded 1969-70		
10/18/75	21	24		6 Man-Child ....[I]	$8	Columbia 33812
9/11/76	49	17		7 Secrets ....[I]	$8	Columbia 34280
5/7/77	79	7		8 V.S.O.P. ....[I-L]	$10	Columbia 34688 [2]
				V.S.O.P.: Very Special Onetime Performance; recorded at the Newport Jazz Festival		
7/8/78	58	13		9 Sunlight	$8	Columbia 34907
				Herbie's vocals are electronically synthesized		
3/17/79	38	22		10 Feets Don't Fail Me Now	$8	Columbia 35764
3/31/79	100	8		11 An Evening With Herbie Hancock & Chick Corea ....[I-L]	$12	Columbia 35663 [2]
				HERBIE HANCOCK & CHICK COREA		
11/24/79	175	2		12 An Evening With Chick Corea & Herbie Hancock ....[I-L]	$12	Polydor 6238 [2]
				CHICK COREA & HERBIE HANCOCK		
				above 2 recorded during their 1978 concert series		
4/19/80	94	18		13 Monster	$8	Columbia 36415
11/29/80	117	6		14 Mr. Hands ....[I]	$8	Columbia 36578
10/3/81	140	6		15 Magic Windows	$8	Columbia 37387
5/29/82	151	6		16 Lite Me Up	$8	Columbia 37928
9/3/83	43	65	●	17 Future Shock ....[I]	$8	Columbia 38814
9/1/84	71	14		18 Sound-System ....[I]	$8	Columbia 39478

Actual Proof (4)
Autodrive (17)
Bed, The (1)
Blow Up (1)
Bomb (16)
Bouquet (12)
Bring Down The Birds (1)
Bubbles (6)
Butterfly (4)
Button Up (11)
Calypso (14)
Can't Hide Your Love (16)
Cantelope Island (7)
Chameleon (3) *42*
Come Running To Me (9)
Crossings (1)
Curiosity (1)
Doin' It (7)

Don't Hold It In (13)
Earth Beat (17)
Everybody's Broke (15)
Eye Of The Hurricane (8)
February Moment (11)
4 AM (14)
Fun Tracks (16)
Future Shock (17)
Gentle Thoughts (7)
Gettin' To The Good Part (16)
Give It All Your Heart (16)
Go For It (13)
Good Question (9)
Hang Up Your Hang Ups (6,8)
Hardrock (18)
Heartbeat (6)
Help Yourself (15)

Hidden Shadows (2)
Homecoming (12)
Honey From The Jar (10)
Hook, The (12)
Hornets (4)
I Thought It Was You (9)
It All Comes Round (13)
Jane's Theme (1)
Junku (8)
Just Around The Corner (14)
Karabali (18)
Kiss, The (1)
Knee Deep (10)
La Fiesta (11,12)
Li'l Brother (5)
Lite Me Up! (16)
Liza (11)
Magic Number (15)

Maiden Voyage (8,11,12)
Making Love (13)
Metal Beat (18)
Motor Mouth (16)
Naked Camera (1)
Nefertiti (8)
No Means Yes (9)
Ostinato (5,12)
Palm Grease (4)
Paradise (16)
People Are Changing (18)
People Music (7)
Quasar (5)
Rain Dance (2)
Ready Or Not (10)
Rockit (17) *71*
Rough (17)
Sansho Shima (7)

Satisfied With Love (15)
Saturday Night (13)
Shiftless Shuffle (14)
Sleeping Giant (5)
Sly (3)
Someday My Prince Will Come (11)
Sound-System (18)
Spank-A-Lee (4)
Spider (7,8)
Spiraling Prism (14)
Stars In Your Eyes (13)
Steppin' In It (6)
Sun Touch (6)
Sunlight (9)
Swamp Rat (7)
TFS (17)
Tell Everybody (10)

Tell Me A Bedtime Story (5)
Textures (14)
Thief, The (1)
Thomas Studies Photos (1)
Tonight's The Night (15)
Toys (8)
Traitor, The (6)
Twilight Clone (15)
Trust Me (10)
Vein Melter (3)
Verushka Part I & II (1)
Watermelon Man (3)
Wiggle Waggle (5)
You Bet Your Love (10)
You'll Know When You Get There (5,8)

HANDY, John

Born on 2/3/33 in Dallas. Jazz saxophonist. Own quintet in the mid-1960s.

DEBUT DATE	PEAK POS	WKS CHR	GOLD	ARTIST — Album Title	$	Label & Number
6/5/76	43	21		1 Hard Work ....[I]	$10	ABC/Impulse 9314
4/16/77	200	2		2 Carnival ....[I]	$10	ABC/Impulse 9324

Afro Wiggle (1)
All The Things You Are (2)
Alvina (2)

Blues For Louis Jordan (1)
Carnival (1)
Christina's Little Song (2)

Didn't I Tell You (1)
Hard Work (1) *46*
I Will Leave You (2)

Love For Brother Jack (1)
Love's Rejoycing (2)
Make Her Mine (1)

Watch Your Money Go (2)
You Don't Know (1)
Young Enough To Dream (1)

HANSSON, Bo

Scandinavian organist.

DEBUT DATE	PEAK POS	WKS CHR	GOLD	ARTIST — Album Title	$	Label & Number
5/5/73	154	8		Lord Of The Rings ....[I]	$10	Charisma 1059
				inspired by the J.R.R. Tolkien classic tale		

At The House Of Elrond (medley)
Battle Of The Pelennor Fields (medley)

Black Riders (medley)
Dreams In The Houses Of Healing
Flight To The Ford (medley)

Fog On The Barrow-Downs
Great Havens
Homeward Bound (medley)
Horns Of Rohan (medley)

Journey In The Dark
Leaving Shire
Lothlorien
Old Forest (medley)

Ring Goes South (medley)
Scouring Out Shire (medley)
Shadowfax
Tom Bombadil (medley)

HAPPENINGS, The

Vocal group from Paterson, New Jersey: Bob Miranda (lead), Tom Giuliano (tenor), Ralph DiVito (baritone) and Dave Libert (bass). Bernie LaPorta replaced DiVito in 1968. Originally the Four Graduates, recorded for Rust in 1963.

DEBUT DATE	PEAK POS	WKS CHR	GOLD	ARTIST — Album Title	$	Label & Number
10/15/66	61	12		1 The Happenings	$25	B.T. Puppy 1001

DEBUT DATE	PEAK POS	WKS CHR	G O L D	ARTIST — Album Title	$	Label & Number

HAPPENINGS, The — Cont'd

7/22/67	134	6		2 Back To Back	$20	B.T. Puppy 1002

TOKENS/HAPPENINGS
side 1: Tokens (see Tokens); side 2: Happenings

8/10/68	156	4		3 The Happenings Golden Hits!......................................[G]	$30	B.T. Puppy 1004
9/6/69	181	2		4 Piece Of Mind	$20	Jubilee 8028

Be My Brother (4)
Breaking Up Is Hard To Do (3) *67*
Cold Water (4)
Don't You Think It's Time (4)
Girl On A Swing (1,3)
Girls On The Go (1)
Go Away Little Girl (1,3) *12*
Goodnight My Love (2,3) *51*

He Thinks He's A Hero (2)
Heartbeat (4)
I Believe In Nothing (2)
I Got Rhythm (2,3) *3*
If You Love Me, Really Love Me (1)
Imagine (4)
Impatient Girl (2)
Let's Do Something (4)

Lillies By Monet (2)
Living In Darkness (4)
Music Music Music (3) *96*
My Mammy (3) *13*
New Day Comin' (4)
Piece Of Mind (4)
Randy (3)
Same Old Story (1)
Sealed With A Kiss (1,3)

See You In September (1,3) *3*
Tea For Two (3)
Tea Time (1)
Tonight I Fell In Love (1)
We're Gonna Make Them Care (4)
What To Do (1)

Where Do I Go/Be-In/Hare Krishna (4) *66*
Why Do Fools Fall In Love (3) *41*
You're Coming On Strong, Babe (1)
You're In A Bad Way (1)

HAPPY MONDAYS
Dance-rock sextet from Manchester, England, led by vocalist Shaun Ryder.

2/23/91	89	13		Pills 'N' Thrills And Bellyaches	$12	Elektra 60986

Bob's Yer Uncle
Dennis And Lois

Donovan
God's Cop
Harmony

Grandbag's Funeral
Holiday
Kinky Afro

Holiday
Loose Fit
Step On

HARBOR, Pearl — see PEARL

HARDCASTLE, Paul
Born in London on 12/10/57. Keyboardist/producer. Formed own company, Total Control Records.

3/23/85	63	25		Rain Forest ....[I]	$8	Profile 1206

A.M.
Forest Fire

King Tut
Loitering With Intent

Panic
Rain Forest *57*

Sound Chaser

HARDEN TRIO, The
Bobby Harden with his sisters Arleen and Robbie from England, Arkansas.

6/25/66	146	5		Tippy Toeing..	$15	Columbia 9306

Dear Brother
Hey Pinnoch

How Long Does It Take
Is It Really Over

Little Boy Walk Like A Man
Little White House

Make The World Go Away
Poor Boy

Race Is On
Tall Green Pines

Tippy Toeing *44*

HARDIN, Tim
Folk-blues singer/songwriter born on 12/23/41 in Eugene, Oregon. Relative of notorious outlaw John Wesley Hardin. Died from a drug overdose on 12/29/80.

4/26/69	129	8		1 Suite For Susan Moore And Damion-We Are-One, One, All In One	$10	Columbia 9787
7/31/71	189	1		2 Bird On A Wire	$10	Columbia 30551

Andre Johray (2)
Bird On The Wire (2)
Country I'm Living In (1)

Everything Good Become More True (1)
First Love Song (1)
Georgia On My Mind (2)

Hoboin' (2)
If I Knew (2)
Last Sweet Moments (1)
Loneliness She Knows (1)

Love Hymn (2)
Magician (1)
Moonshiner (2)
Once-Touched By Flame (1)

One, One, The Perfect Sum (1)
Question Of Birth (1)
Satisfied Mind (2)

Soft Summer Breeze (2)
Southern Butterfly (2)
Susan (1)

HARDY, Hagood
Indiana-born vibraphonist based in Toronto. Sideman for Herbie Mann and George Shearing.

1/3/76	112	14		The Homecoming ....[I]	$8	Capitol 11468

Balloons
Clouds
Cold On The Shoulder

Homecoming, The *41*
I Won't Last A Day Without You

Jennifer's Song
My Elusive Dreams
Quorum

Travellin' On
Trouble With Hello Is Goodbye

Wintertime
You And Me Against The World

HARDY BOYS, The
Vocal group used in the animated cartoon TV series *The Hardy Boys*.

11/15/69	199	2		Here Come The Hardy Boys	$15	RCA 4217

Feels So Good
Here Come The Hardys

(I Want You To) Be My Baby
Love And Let Love

My Little Sweetpea
Namby-Pamby

One Time In A Million
Sha-La-La

Sink Or Swim
That's That

Those Country Girls

HARMONICATS
Harmonica trio formed in 1944: Jerry Murad (born in Turkey), Al Fiore and Don Les.

3/27/61	17	4		Cherry Pink And Apple Blossom White ....[I]	$15	Columbia 8356

Jerry Murad's "Fabulous" HARMONICATS

Cherry Pink And Apple Blossom White *56*
Fascination

I'll Never Smile Again
It Happened In Monterey

It's A Sin To Tell A Lie
Kiss Of Fire

Lonely Love
Mack The Knife

Paradise
Polka Dots And Moonbeams

Ramona
Ruby

HARNELL, Joe, His Piano And Orchestra
Born on 8/2/24 in the Bronx. Conductor/arranger for Frank Sinatra, Peggy Lee and others. Musical director for many TV shows, including *The Mike Douglas Show*.

1/26/63	3	36		Fly Me To The Moon and the Bossa Nova Pops ....[I]	$15	Kapp 3318

Cry Me A River
Early Autumn
Eso Beso

Fly Me To The Moon-Bossa Nova *14*

I Left My Heart In San Francisco
Loads Of Love
Midnight Sun

My One And Only Love
One Note Samba
Senza Fine

What Kind Of Fool Am I?
You'd Be So Nice To Come Home To

HARPERS BIZARRE
Santa Cruz, California quintet led by Ted Templeman, who later produced many albums for The Doobie Brothers and Van Halen.

5/6/67	108	7		1 Feelin' Groovy	$20	Warner 1693
12/9/67+	76	13		2 Anything Goes..	$20	Warner 1716

Anything Goes (2) *43*
Biggest Night Of Her Life (2)
Chattanooga Choo Choo (2) *45*
Come Love (1)

Come To The Sunshine (1) *37*
Debutante's Ball (1)
59th Street Bridge Song (Feelin' Groovy) (1) *13*
Happy Talk (1)

Happyland (1)
Hey, You In The Crowd (2)
High Coin (2)
I Can Hear The Darkness (1)
Jessie (2)

Louisiana Man (2)
Milord (2)
Peter And The Wolf (1)
Pocketful Of Miracles (2)
Raspberry Rug (1)

Simon Smith And The Amazing Dancing Bear (1)
Snow (2)
This Is Only The Beginning (medley) (2)

Two Little Babes In The Wood (2)
Virginia City (2)
You Need A Change (2)

DEBUT DATE	PEAK POS	WKS CHR	GOLD	ARTIST — Album Title	$	Label & Number

★★346★★ **HARRIS, Eddie**
Born on 10/20/36 in Chicago. Jazz tenor saxophonist/vocalist. Noted for experimentation with electronic reed instruments.

DEBUT DATE	PEAK POS	WKS CHR	GOLD	ARTIST — Album Title	$	Label & Number
5/29/61	2¹	37		1 Exodus To Jazz ......[I]	$30	Vee-Jay 3016
4/13/68	36	41		2 The Electrifying Eddie Harris......[I]	$12	Atlantic 1495
8/3/68	120	16		3 Plug Me In......[I]	$12	Atlantic 1506
2/22/69	199	2		4 Silver Cycles......[I]	$12	Atlantic 1517
8/16/69	122	9		5 High Voltage......[I-L]	$12	Atlantic 1529
12/13/69+	29	38		6 Swiss Movement......[I-L]	$12	Atlantic 1537
				LES McCANN & EDDIE HARRIS recorded live at The Montreux Jazz Festival, Switzerland		
4/18/70	191	3		7 The Best Of Eddie Harris......[I-G]	$10	Atlantic 1545
5/29/71	41	27		8 Second Movement......[I]	$10	Atlantic 1583
				EDDIE HARRIS & LES McCANN		
11/27/71	164	10		9 Eddie Harris Live At Newport......[I-L]	$10	Atlantic 1595
7/22/72	185	7		10 Instant Death......[I]	$10	Atlantic 1611
2/16/74	150	11		11 E.H. in the U.K.......[I]	$8	Atlantic 1647
				with Jeff Beck, Stevie Winwood and Albert Lee		
10/12/74	100	11		12 Is It In......[I]	$8	Atlantic 1659
4/19/75	125	9		13 I Need Some Money......[I]	$8	Atlantic 1669
9/27/75	133	6		14 Bad Luck Is All I Have......[I]	$8	Atlantic 1675

A.M. Blues (1)
A.T.C. (1)
Abstractions (14)
Alicia (1)
Baby (1)
Bad Luck Is All I Have (14)
Ballad (For My Love) (3,5)
Bumpin (13)
Carnival (13)
Carry On Brother (8,9)
Children's Song (5,9)
Cold Duck Time (6)
Coltrane's View (4)
Compared To What (6) *85*
Conversations Of Everything And Nothing (11)
Don't You Know The Future's In Space (9)
Electric Ballad (4)
Exodus (1) *36*
Free At Last (4)
Freedom Jazz Dance (7)
Funkaroma (12)
Funky Doo (5)
Generation Gap (6)
Get On Down (13)
Get On Up And Dance (14)
Gone Home (1)
Happy Gemini (12)
He's Island Man (11)
House Party Blues (12)
I Don't Want No One But You (2)
I Don't Want Nobody (13)
I Need Some Money (13)
I Waited For You (11)
I'm Gonna Leave You By Yourself (4)
I've Tried Everything (11)
Infrapolations (4)
Instant Death (10)
Is It In (12)
It's Crazy (3) *88*
It's War (12)
Judie's Theme (2)
Kathleen's Theme (6)
Little Bit (4)
Little Girl Blue (1)
Little Wes (10)
Live Right Now (3,7)
Look Ahere (12)
Lovely Is Today (3)
Movin' On Out (5,7)
Nightcap (10)
1974 Blues (4)
Obnoxious (14)
Samia (8)
Sandpiper, Love Theme From The (7)
Set Us Free (8)
Shadow Of Your Smile ..see: Sandpiper, Love Theme From The
Sham Time (2)
Shorty Rides Again (8)
Silent Majority (9)
Silver Cycles (4)
Smoke Signals (4)
South Side (9)
Space Commercial (12)
Spanish Bull (2)
Summer's On Its Way (10)
Superfluous (10)
Tampion (10)
That's It (13)
Theme In Search Of A Movie (2,7)
Theme In Search Of A T.V. Commercial (3)
These Lonely Nights (12)
Time To Do Your Thing (6)
Tranquility & Antagonistic (12)
Universal Prisoner (8)
Velocity (1)
W.P. (1)
Wait A Little Longer (11)
Walk Soft (9)
Why Must We Part (7)
Winter Meeting (3)
You Got It In Your Soulness (6)
Zambezi Dance (10)

★★180★★ **HARRIS, Emmylou**
Born on 4/2/47 in Birmingham, Alabama. Contemporary country vocalist. Sang backup with Gram Parsons until his death in 1973. Own band from 1975.

DEBUT DATE	PEAK POS	WKS CHR	GOLD	ARTIST — Album Title	$	Label & Number
3/15/75	45	15	●	1 Pieces Of The Sky	$10	Reprise 2213
1/24/76	25	23	●	2 Elite Hotel	$10	Reprise 2236
1/22/77	21	21	●	3 Luxury Liner	$10	Warner 3115
2/4/78	29	18	●	4 Quarter Moon In A Ten Cent Town	$8	Warner 3141
12/2/78+	81	17	●	5 Profile/Best Of Emmylou Harris......[G]	$8	Warner 3258
5/5/79	43	22	●	6 Blue Kentucky Girl	$8	Warner 3318
5/24/80	26	34	●	7 Roses In The Snow	$8	Warner 3422
11/29/80	102	9		8 Light Of The Stable......[X]	$8	Warner 3484
2/21/81	22	24	●	9 Evangeline	$8	Warner 3508
12/12/81+	46	20		10 Cimarron	$8	Warner 3603
11/13/82	65	17		11 Last Date......[L]	$8	Warner 23740
11/19/83+	116	13		12 White Shoes	$8	Warner 23961
10/6/84	176	6		13 Profile II - The Best Of Emmylou Harris......[G]	$8	Warner 25161
5/25/85	171	4		14 The Ballad Of Sally Rose	$8	Warner 25205
3/8/86	157	6		15 Thirteen	$8	Warner 25352
				Emmylou's thirteenth career album		
3/28/87	6	48	▲	16 Trio	$8	Warner 25491
				DOLLY PARTON, LINDA RONSTADT, EMMYLOU HARRIS		
8/1/87	166	4		17 Angel Band	$8	Warner 25585
2/1/92	174	3		18 At The Ryman......[L]	$12	Reprise 26664
				EMMYLOU HARRIS & THE NASH RAMBLERS recorded live at Nashville's Ryman Auditorium (original home of the Grand Ole Opry) on 4/30/91; The Nash Ramblers: Sam Bush (New Grass Revival), Jon Randall Stewart, Al Perkins (Manassas), Larry Atamanuik (Seatrain) and Roy Huskey, Jr.		

Abraham, Martin And John (medley) (18)
Amarillo (2)
Angel Band (17)
Angel Eyes (Angel Eyes) (10)
Another Lonesome Morning (10)
Ashes By Now (9)
Away In A Manger (8)
Baby, Better Start Turnin' 'Em Down (12)
Bad Moon Rising (9)
Bad News (14)
Ballad Of Sally Rose (14)
Beautiful Star Of Bethlehem (8)
Before Believing (1)
Beneath Still Waters (6,13)
Blue Kentucky Girl (6,13)
Bluebird Wine (1)
Born To Run (10,13)
Bottle Let Me Down (1)
Boulder To Birmingham (1,5)
Boxer (7)
Bright Morning Stars (17)
Buckaroo (medley) (18)
Burn That Candle (4)
Calling My Children Home (18)
Cattle Call (18)
Christmas Time's A-Coming (8)
Coat Of Many Colors (1)
Darkest Hour Is Just Before Dawn (7)
Defying Gravity (4)
Devil In Disguise (11)
Diamond In My Crown (14)
Diamonds Are A Girl's Best Friend (12)
Drifting Too Far (17)
Drivin' Wheel (2)
Easy From Now On (4,5)
Evangeline (9)
Even Cowgirls Get The Blues (6)
Everytime You Leave (6)
Farther Along (16)
Feelin' Single - Seein' Double (2)
First Noel (8)
For No One (1)
Get Up John (18)
Gold Watch And Chain (8)
Golden Cradle (8)
Good News (12)
Green Pastures (7)
Green Rolling Hills (9)
Grievous Angel (11)
Guess Things Happen That Way (18)
Guitar Town (18)
Half As Much (18)
Hard Times (18)
Heart To Heart (medley) (14)
Hello Stranger (3,5)
Here, There And Everywhere (2) *65*
Hickory Wind (6)
Hobo's Meditation (16)
Hot Burrito #2 (9)
How High The Moon (9)
I Ain't Living Long Like This (4)
I Don't Have To Crawl (9)
I Had My Heart Set On You (15)
I Think I Love Him (medley) (14)
I'll Be Your San Antone Rose (3)
I'll Go Stepping Too (7)
I'm Movin' On (11,13)
I've Had Enough (16)
If I Be Lifted Up (17)
If I Could Be There (18)
If I Needed You (10)
In My Dreams (12)
It's A Hard Life Wherever You Go (medley) (18)
It's Not Love (But It's Not Bad) (11)
It's Only Rock 'N Roll (12)
If I Could Only Win Your Love (1,5) *58*

308

HARRIS, Emmylou — Cont'd

Jambalaya (2)
Jordan (7)
Juanita (11)
Just Someone I Used To Know (15)
K-S-O-S Medley (14)
Lacassine Special (15)
Last Cheater's Waltz (10)
Leaving Louisiana In The Broad Daylight (4)
Light Of The Stable (8)
Like An Old Fashioned Waltz (12)
Like Strangers (18)
Little Drummer Boy (8)
Lodi (18)
Long May You Run (11)
Long Tall Sally Rose (14)
(Lost His Love) On Our Last Date (11,13)
Love's Gonna Live Here (medley) (11)
Luxury Liner (3)

Making Believe (3,5)
Making Plans (16)
Mansion On The Hill (18)
Millworker (9)
Miss The Mississippi (7)
Mister Sandman (9,13) **37**
Montana Cowgirl (18)
My Dear Companion (16)
My Father's House (15)
My Songbird (4)
Mystery Train (15)
O Little Town Of Bethlehem (8)
Oh Atlanta (9)
On The Radio (12)
One Of These Days (2,5)
One Paper Kid (4)
Ooh Las Vegas (2)
Other Side Of Life (17)
Pain Of Loving You (16)
Pancho & Lefty (3)
Pledging My Love (12,13)
Precious Memories (17)

Price You Pay (10)
Queen Of The Silver Dollar (1)
Racing In The Streets (11)
Restless (11)
Rhythm Guitar (14)
Rose Of Cimarron (10)
Roses In The Snow (7)
Rosewood Casket (16)
Rough And Rocky (6)
Satan's Jewel Crown (7)
Save The Last Dance For Me (6,13)
Scotland (18)
She (3)
Silent Night (8)
Sin City (2)
Sister's Coming Home (6)
Sleepless Nights (1)
Smoke Along The Track (18)
So Sad (To Watch Good Love Go Bad) (11)

Someday My Ship Will Sail (17)
Someone Like You (13)
Son Of A Rotten Gambler (10)
Sorrow In The Wind (6)
Spanish Is A Loving Tongue (10)
Spanish Johnny (9)
Sweet Chariot (14)
Sweet Dreams (2,5)
Sweetheart Of The Pines (15)
Sweetheart Of The Rodeo (14)
Telling Me Lies (16)
Tennessee Rose (10)
Tennessee Waltz (15)
They'll Never Take His Love From Me (6)
Those Memories Of You (16)
Till I Gain Control Again (2)
Timberline (14)
To Daddy (4,5)

To Know Him Is To Love Him (16)
Today I Started Loving You Again (15)
Too Far Gone (1,5)
Tulsa Queen (3)
Two More Bottles Of Wine (4,5)
Walls Of Time (18)
Wayfaring Stranger (7,13)
We Shall Rise (17)
We'll Sweep Out The Ashes (In The Morning) (11)
Wheels (2)
When He Calls (17)
When I Stop Dreaming (3)
When I Was Yours (15)
When They Ring Those Golden Bells (17)
Where Could I Go But To The Lord (17)
White Line (14)

White Shoes (12)
Who Will Sing For Me (17)
Wildflowers (16)
Woman Walk The Line (14)
(You Never Can Tell) C'est La Vie (3,5)
You're Free To Go (15)
You're Learning (7)
You're Supposed To Be Feeling Good (3)
Your Long Journey (15)

HARRIS, Major

Born on 2/9/47 in Richmond, Virginia. Soul singer. With The Jarmels, Teenagers and Impacts in the early 1960s. With The Delfonics from 1971-74.

DEBUT DATE	PEAK POS	WKS CHR		ARTIST — Album Title	$	Label & Number
3/29/75	**28**	22	1	My Way	$10	Atlantic 18119
2/28/76	**153**	6	2	Jealousy	$10	Atlantic 18160

After Loving You (1)
Each Morning I Wake Up (1)
I Got Over Love (2)
It's Got To Be Magic (2)

Jealousy (2) **73**
Just A Thing That I Do (1)
Love Won't Let Me Wait (1) **5**

Loving You Is Mellow (1)
My Way (1)
Ruby Lee (2)
Sideshow (1)

Sweet Tomorrow (1)
Talking To Myself (2)
Two Wrongs (1)
Tynisa (Goddess Of Love) (2)

Walkin' In The Footsteps (2)
What's The Use In The Truth (2)

HARRIS, Richard

Born on 10/1/30 in Limerick, Ireland. Began prolific acting career in 1958. Portrayed King Arthur in the long-running stage production and film version of *Camelot*.

DEBUT DATE	PEAK POS	WKS CHR		ARTIST — Album Title	$	Label & Number
5/18/68	**4**	42	1	A Tramp Shining	$12	Dunhill 50032
11/16/68+	**27**	15	2	The Yard Went On Forever	$12	Dunhill 50042
12/18/71+	**71**	14	3	My Boy	$12	Dunhill 50116
12/16/72+	**181**	6	4	Slides	$10	Dunhill 50133
9/8/73	**25**	27	5	Jonathan Livingston Seagull	[T] $10	Dunhill 50160
				narration from the book; music composed by Terry James		
12/28/74+	**29**	15	6	The Prophet by Kahlil Gibran	[T] $10	Atlantic 18120
				Harris recites Gibran's classic work		

All The Broken Children (3)
Ballad To An Unborn Child (3)
Best Way To See America (4)
Beth (3)
Blue Canadian Rocky Dream (4)
Coming Of The Ship (6)
Dancing Girl (1)
Didn't We (1) **63**
Farewell, The (6)
Gayla (2)
Gin Buddy (4)
Hive (2)

How I Spent My Summer (4)
Hymns From The Grand Terrace (2)
I Don't Have To Tell You (4)
I'm Comin' Home (4)
If You Must Leave My Life (1)
In The Final Hours (1)
Interim (2)
Jonathan Livingston Seagull (5)
Like Father Like Son (3)
Lovers Such As I (1)
Lucky Me (2)
MacArthur Park (1) **2**

My Boy (3) **41**
Name Of My Sorrow (1)
November Song (4)
On Children (6)
On Clothes (6)
On Crime And Punishment (6)
On Death (6)
On Eating And Drinking (6)
On Friendship (6)
On Giving (6)
On Laws (6)
On Love (6)
On Marriage (6)

On Pleasure (6)
On Religion (6)
On Teaching And Self-Knowledge (6)
On Work (6)
Once Upon A Dusty Road (4)
Paper Chase (1)
Prophet (Pleasure Is A Freedom Song), Theme From The (6)
Proposal (3)
Requiem (3)
Roy (4)
Sidewalk Song (3)

Slides (4)
Sunny Jo (4)
That's The Way It Was (2)
There Are Too Many Saviours On My Cross (4)
This Is Our Child (3)
This Is The Way (3)
This Is Where I Came In (3)
Tramp Shining (1)
Trilogy From The Prophet (Love, Marriage, Children) (6)
Watermark (2)
Why Did You Leave Me (3)

Yard Went On Forever (2) **64**

HARRIS, Rolf

Born in Perth, Australia on 3/30/30. Played piano from age nine. Moved to England in the mid-1950s. Developed his unique "wobble board sound" out of a sheet of masonite. Had own BBC-TV series from 1970.

DEBUT DATE	PEAK POS	WKS CHR		ARTIST — Album Title	$	Label & Number
8/3/63	**29**	9		Tie Me Kangaroo Down, Sport & Sun Arise	[N] $25	Epic 26053

Big Black Hat
Ground Hog
Hair Oil On My Ears

I've Been Everywhere
In The Wet
Johnny Day

Living It Up
Mighty Thunderer

Nick Teen And Al K. Hall 95

Someone's Pinched My Winkles
Sun Arise 61

Tie Me Kangaroo Down, Sport 3

HARRIS, Sam

Winner of TV's *Star Search* male vocalist category in 1984.

DEBUT DATE	PEAK POS	WKS CHR		ARTIST — Album Title	$	Label & Number
9/29/84	**35**	29	● 1	Sam Harris	$8	Motown 6103
2/15/86	**69**	14	2	Sam-I-Am	$8	Motown 6165

Always (medley) (2)
Ba-Doom Ba-Doom (2)
Bells (medley) (2)
Don't Look In My Eyes (1)

Don't Want To Give Up On Love (2)
Forever For You (2)
Heart Of The Machine (2)

Hearts On Fire (1)
I Need You (medley) (2)
I Will Not Wait For You (1)
I'd Do It All Again (2) **52**

I've Heard It All Before (1)
In Your Eyes (2)
Inside Of Me (1)
Out Of Control (1)

Over The Rainbow (1)
Pretender (1)
Rescue (2)
Stay With Me (2)

Suffer The Innocent (2)
Sugar Don't Bite (1) **36**
You Keep Me Hangin' On (1)

HARRISON, Don, Band

Members Stu Cook and Doug Clifford were with Creedence Clearwater Revival.

DEBUT DATE	PEAK POS	WKS CHR		ARTIST — Album Title	$	Label & Number
5/1/76	**159**	6		The Don Harrison Band	$10	Atlantic 18171

Barroom Dancing Girl
Bit Of Love

Fame And Fortune
Living Another Day

Rock 'N' Roll Records
Romance

Sixteen Tons 47
Sometimes Loving You

Sweetwater William
Who I Really Am

DEBUT DATE	PEAK POS	WKS CHR	GOLD	ARTIST — Album Title	$	Label & Number

★★132★★   HARRISON, George

Born on 2/25/43 in Liverpool, England. Formed his first group, the Rebels, at age 13. Joined John Lennon and Paul McCartney in The Quarrymen in 1958; group later evolved into The Beatles, with Harrison as lead guitarist. Organized the Bangladesh benefit concerts at Madison Square Garden in 1971. Member of the 1988 supergroup Traveling Wilburys. In 1992, became the first recipient of The Century Award, *Billboard*'s honor for distinguished creative achievement.

DEBUT DATE	PEAK POS	WKS CHR	GOLD	#	ARTIST — Album Title	$	Label & Number
1/11/69	49	16		1	Wonderwall Music .... [S-I]	$35	Apple 3350
					Indian-influenced instrumentals for the unreleased film *Wonderwall*		
7/5/69	191	2		2	Electronic Sound ....[I]	$25	Zapple 3358
					sounds made by a Moog synthesizer		
12/19/70+	1⁷	38	▲²	3	All Things Must Pass	$35	Apple 639 [3]
1/8/72	2⁶	41	●	4	The Concert For Bangla Desh ....[L]	$35	Apple 3385 [3]
					1972 Grammy winner: Album of the Year; Madison Square Garden benefit concert on 8/1/71; with guests Bob Dylan, Eric Clapton, Ringo Starr, Billy Preston and Leon Russell		
6/16/73	1⁵	26	●	5	Living In The Material World	$12	Apple 3410
12/28/74+	4	17	●	6	Dark Horse	$12	Apple 3418
10/11/75	8	11	●	7	Extra Texture (Read All About It)	$10	Apple 3420
11/27/76	31	15	●	8	The Best of George Harrison ....[G]	$10	Capitol 11578
					includes 7 hits by The Beatles: "For You Blue," "Here Comes The Sun," "If I Needed Someone," "Something," "Taxman," "Think For Yourself" and "While My Guitar Gently Weeps"		
12/11/76+	11	21	●	9	Thirty-Three & 1/3	$8	Dark Horse 3005
					33 1/3: record playing speed and George's age		
3/17/79	14	18	●	10	George Harrison	$8	Dark Horse 3255
6/20/81	11	13		11	Somewhere In England	$8	Dark Horse 3492
11/27/82	108	7		12	Gone Troppo	$8	Dark Horse 23734
11/21/87+	8	31	▲	13	Cloud Nine	$8	Dark Horse 25643
					co-producer: Jeff Lynne (Electric Light Orchestra)		
11/4/89	132	6		14	Best Of Dark Horse 1976-1989 ....[G]	$8	Dark Horse 25726
8/1/92	126	2		15	Live In Japan ....[L]	$24	Dark H. 26964 [2]

All Things Must Pass (3)
All Those Years Ago (11,14,15) **2**
Answer's At The End (7)
Apple Scruffs (3)
Art Of Dying (3)
Awaiting On You All (3,4)
Baby Don't Run Away (12)
Ballad Of Sir Frankie Crisp (Let It Roll) (3)
Baltimore Oriole (11)
Bangla-Desh (4,8) **23**
Bangla Dhun (4)
Be Here Now (5)
Beautiful Girl (9)
Behind That Locked Door (3)
Beware Of Darkness (3,4)
Bit More Of You (7)
Blood From A Clone (11)
Blow Away (10,14) **16**
Blowin' In The Wind (4)
Breath Away From Heaven (13)
Bye Bye, Love (6)
Can't Stop Thinking About You (7)
Cheer Down (14,15)
Circles (12)
Cloud 9 (13,14,15)
Cockamamie Business (14)
Congratulations (3)

Cowboy Museum (1)
Crackerbox Palace (9,14) **19**
Crying (medley) (1)
Dark Horse (6,8,15) **15**
Dark Sweet Lady (10)
Day The World Gets 'Round (5)
Dear One (10)
Devil's Radio (13,15)
Ding Dong; Ding Dong (6) **36**
Don't Let Me Wait Too Long (5)
Dream Away (12)
Dream Scene (medley) (1)
Drilling A Home (medley) (1)
Fantasy Sequins (medley) (1)
Far East Man (6)
Faster (10)
Fish On The Sand (13)
Give Me Love - (Give Me Peace On Earth) (5,8,15) **1**
Glass Box (medley) (1)
Gone Troppo (12)
Got My Mind Set On You (13,14,15) **1**
Greasy Legs (medley) (1)
Greece (12)
Grey Cloudy Lies (7)
Guru Vandana (medley) (1)
Hard Rain's Gonna Fall (4)

Hari's On Tour (Express) (6)
Hear Me Lord (3)
Here Comes The Moon (10,14)
Here Comes The Sun (4,15)
His Name Is Legs (Ladies & Gentlemen) (7)
Hong Kong Blues (11)
I Dig Love (3)
I Really Love You (10)
I Remember Jeep (3)
I Want To Tell You (15)
I'd Have You Anytime (3)
If I Needed Someone (15)
If Not For You (3)
If You Believe (10)
In The Park (medley) (1)
Isn't It A Pity (3,15) *flip*
It Don't Come Easy (4)
It Is "He" (Jai Sri Krishna) (6)
It Takes A Lot To Laugh, It Takes A Train To Cry (4)
It's What You Value (9)
Jumping Jack Flash (medley) (4)
Just For Today (13)
Just Like A Woman (4)
Learning How To Love You (9)
Let It Down (3)
Life Itself (11,14)

Light That Has Lighted The World (5)
Living In The Material World (5)
Lord Loves The One (That Loves The Lord) (5)
Love Comes To Everyone (10,14)
Love Scene (medley) (1)
Maya Love (6)
Microbes (1)
Mr. Tambourine Man (4)
My Sweet Lord (3,4,8,15) **1**
Mystical One (12)
No Time Or Space (2)
Not Guilty (10)
Old Brown Shoe (15)
On The Bed (1)
Ooh Baby (You Know That I Love You) (7)
Out Of The Blue (3)
Party Seacombe (1)
Piggies (15)
Plug Me In (3)
Poor Little Girl (14)
Pure Smokey (9)
Red Lady Too (1)
Roll Over Beethoven (15)
Run Of The Mill (3)
Save The World (11)
See Yourself (9)

Simply Shady (6)
Singing OM (1)
Ski-ing And Gat Kirwani (medley) (1)
So Sad (6)
Soft-Hearted Hana (10)
Soft Touch (10)
Someplace Else (13)
Something (4,15)
Sue Me, Sue You Blues (5)
Tabla And Pakavaj (medley) (1)
Taxman (15)
Teardrops (11)
Thanks For The Pepperoni (3)
That Is All (5)
That Which I Have Lost (11)
That's The Way God Planned It (4)
That's The Way It Goes (12,14)
That's What It Takes (13)
This Guitar (Can't Keep From Crying) (7)
This Is Love (13)
This Song (9) **25**
Tired Of Midnight Blue (7)
True Love (9)
Try Some Buy Some (5)
Unconsciousness Rules (11)

Under The Mersey Wall (2)
Unknown Delight (12)
Wah-Wah (3,4)
Wake Up My Love (12,14) **53**
What Is Life (3,8,15) **10**
When We Was Fab (13,14) **23**
While My Guitar Gently Weeps (4,15)
Who Can See It (5)
Woman Don't You Cry For Me (9)
Wonderwall To Be Here (1)
World Of Stone (7)
Wreck Of The Hesperus (13)
Writing's On The Wall (11)
You (7,8) **20**
Youngblood (medley) (4)
Your Love Is Forever (10)

HARRISON, Jerry: Casual Gods

Born on 2/21/49 in Milwaukee. Keyboardist/producer/Harvard graduate. Member of Modern Lovers 1971-74; member of Talking Heads since 1977. Produced albums for The Violent Femmes, BoDeans and others. The Casual Gods are 13 backing musicians.

DEBUT DATE	PEAK POS	WKS CHR	#	ARTIST — Album Title	$	Label & Number
2/6/88	78	20	1	Casual Gods	$8	Sire 25663
6/9/90	188	3	2	Walk On Water...............................	$12	Sire 25943
				CD includes 2 bonus tracks		

A.K.A. Love (1)
Are You Running? (1)
Big Mouth (2)
Bobby (1)

Cherokee Chief (1)
Confess (2)
Cowboy's Got To Go (2)
Doctors Lie (2)

Facing The Fire (2)
Flying Under Radar (2)
I Cry For Iran (2)
I Don't Mind (1)

If The Rains Return (2)
Kick Start (2)
Let It Come Down (1)
Man With A Gun (1)

Never Let It Slip (2)
Perfect Lie (1)
Remain Calm (2)
Rev It Up (1)

Sleep Angel (2)
Song Of Angels (1)
We're Always Talking (1)

HARRISON, Noel

Actor/singer. Son of late actor Rex Harrison. Screen debut in 1962.

DEBUT DATE	PEAK POS	WKS CHR	#	ARTIST — Album Title	$	Label & Number
12/9/67+	135	9		Collage	$15	Reprise 6263

Go Ask Your Man (1)
Just Like A Woman

Lucy In The Sky With Diamonds
Mrs. Williams' Rose

Museum
People In The Rain

Sign Of The Queen
Strawberry Fields Forever

Suzanne 56
When I'm 64

Whiter Shade of Pale
Woman

HARRISON, Wes

Sound effects comedian.

DEBUT DATE	PEAK POS	WKS CHR	#	ARTIST — Album Title	$	Label & Number
11/2/63	83	5		You Won't Believe Your Ears .... [C]	$25	Philips 103

Better Late Than Never

Father, Oh Father

Out At The Outhouse

Saga Of The Duck Hunt

Wes' Car

HARRISON, Wilbert
R&B singer. Born on 1/5/29 in Charlotte, North Carolina. Plays several instruments as a one-man band. Joined W.C. Baker band. First recorded for Glades in 1952.

1/24/70	190	2		Let's Work Together	$20	Sue 8801

Blue Monday / Forgive Me / Kansas City / **Let's Work Together (Part 1) 32** / Louie-Louie / Peepin' & Hidin' / Soul Rattler / Stagger Lee / Stand By Me / Tropical Shakedown / What Am I Living For

HARRY, Debbie
Lead singer of Blondie. Born on 7/1/45 in New York City. In films *Roadie, Union City, Videodrome Tales From The Darkside-The Movie* and *Hairspray*. Appeared in several episodes of TV's *Wiseguy*.

8/29/81	25	12	●	1 KooKoo	$8	Chrysalis 1347
12/13/86+	97	13		2 Rockbird	$8	Geffen 24123
				released with 3 different colored covers		
10/14/89	123	8		3 Def, Dumb & Blonde	$8	Sire 25938
				DEBORAH HARRY		

Backfired (1) 43 / Beyond The Limit (2) / Brite Side (3) / Buckle Up (2) / Bugeye (3) / Calmarie (3) / Chrome (1) / End Of The Run (3) / Free To Fall (2) / **French Kissin (2) 57** / Get Your Way (3) / He Is So (3) / I Want That Man (3) / I Want You (2) / Kiss It Better (3) / Lovelight (3) / Inner City Spillover (1) / **Jam Was Moving (1) 82** / Jump Jump (1) / Now I Know You Know (1) / Oasis (1) / Rockbird (2) / Maybe For Sure (3) / Military Rap (1) / **In Love With Love (2) 70** / Secret Life (2) / Surrender (1) / Sweet And Low (3) / Under Arrest (1) / You Got Me In Trouble (2)

HART, Corey
Born in Montreal, Canada and raised in Spain and Mexico. Singer/songwriter/keyboardist.

7/14/84	31	36	●	1 First Offense	$8	EMI America 17117
7/20/85	20	37	●	2 Boy In The Box	$8	EMI America 17161
10/18/86	55	27	●	3 Fields of Fire	$8	EMI America 17217
7/9/88	121	8		4 Young Man Running	$8	EMI-Man. 48752
4/28/90	134	5		5 Bang!..	$12	EMI 92513

Angry Young Man (3) / Art Of Color (5) / At The Dance (1) / Ballade For Nien Cheng (5) / BANG! (Starting Over) (5) / Blind Faith (3) / **Boy In The Box (2) 26** / Broken Arrow (3) / **Can't Help Falling In Love (3) 24** / Can't Stand Losin' You (5) / Chase The Sun (4,5) / Cheatin' In Public (5) / Chippin' Away (4) / Crossroad Caravan (4) / **Dancin' With My Mirror (3) 88** / Diamond Cowboy (5) / Does She Love You (1) / Don't Take Me To The Racetrack (4) / Eurasian Eyes (2) / **Everything In My Heart (2) 30** / Goin' Home (3) / **I Am By Your Side (3) 18** / Icon (5) / **In Your Soul (4) 38** / Is It Too Late? (3) / **It Ain't Enough (1) 17** / Jenny Fey (1) / Jimmy Rae (3) / Kisses On The Train (5) / Komrade Kiev (2) / Lamp At Midnite (1) / **Little Love (5) 37** / Lone Wolf (5) / **Never Surrender (2) 3** / No Love Lost (4) / Peruvian Lady (1) / Political Cry (3) / Rain On Me (5) / She Got The Radio (1) / Silent Talking (2) / Slowburn (1) / So It Goes... (4) / Spot You In A Coalmine (4) / Still In Love (4) / **Sunglasses At Night (1) 7** / Sunny Place - Shady People (2) / Take My Heart (3) / Truth Will Set You Free (4) / Waiting For You (2) / Water From The Moon (2) / World Is Fire (1)

HART, Freddie
Born Fred Segrest on 12/21/26 in Lochapoka, Alabama. Country singer/songwriter/guitarist.

10/9/71	37	20	●	1 Easy Loving	$10	Capitol 838
3/18/72	89	11		2 My Hang-Up Is You	$10	Capitol 11014
7/1/72	93	16		3 Bless Your Heart	$10	Capitol 11073
9/22/73	188	6		4 Trip To Heaven	$10	Capitol 11197

Bless Your Heart (3) / California Grapevine (1) / Cinderella (3) / Coldest Bed (4) / Conscience Makes Cowards (Of Us All) (3) / Cravin' (3) / **Easy Loving (1) 17** / Everytime He Touches You (3) / Greatest Gift Of All (2) / Heart (2) / House Of Sand (1) / Human Rat Race (3) / Hungry Row (3) / I'm Afraid To Love You ('Fraid I Might Like It) (3) / I'm In Love (2) / I'm No Angel (4) / I'm Not Going Hungry (3) / If Fingerprints Showed Up On Skin (1) / In The Arms Of Love (1) / Jesus Is My Kind Of People (2) / Key's In The Mailbox (2) / Living On Leftovers Of You (4) / Look-A-Here (4) / Love Did This To Me (4) / Love Makes The Difference (2) / Loving Her Through You (2) / My Hang-Up Is You (2) / One More Mountain To Climb (2) / She Belongs To Me (2) / Skid Row Street (4) / That Hurtin' Feeling (1) / Trip To Heaven (4) / Twin Of An Angel (4) / Ugly Duckling (4) / Until Now (3) / Whole World Holding Hands (1) / Without You (1) / Would You Settle For Roses (2) / Write It All In (Put It All In) (1) / You Belong To Me (4)

HART, Mickey
Drummer with the Grateful Dead (1968-71, 1975-present).

10/21/72	190	4		Rolling Thunder	$35	Warner 2635
				with Jerry Garcia, Bob Weir, Grace Slick and Stephen Stills		

Blind John / Chase (Progress) / Deep, Wide And Frequent / Fletcher Carnaby / Granma's Cookies / Hangin' On / Main Ten (Playing In The Band) / Pump Song / Rolling Thunder (medley) / Shoshone Invocation (medley) / Young Man

HARTFORD, John
Born on 12/30/37 in New York City; raised in St. Louis. Plays guitar, banjo and fiddle. Moved to Nashville and worked as a session musician. Wrote "Gentle On My Mind" hit for Glen Campbell. Regular on the Smothers Brothers' TV series.

6/14/69	137	9		1 John Hartford	$12	RCA 4156
11/27/71	193	4		2 Aereo-Plain..	$10	Warner 1916

Back In The Goodle Days (2) / Because Of You (2) / Boogie (2) / Collector, The (1) / Dusty Miller Hornpipe (2) / Fugue In A Major For Strings, Brass And 5-String Banjo (1) / First Girl I Loved (2) / Holding (2) / I Didn't Know The World Would Last This Long (1) / I've Heard That Tearstained Monologue You Do There By The Door Before You Go (1) / Leather Britches (2) / Little Old Lonesome Little Circle Song (1) / Little Piece In D (1) / Mr. Jackson's Got Nothing To Do (1) / Open Road Ode (1) / Orphan Of World War Two (1) / Poor Old Prurient Interest Blues (1) / Presbyterian Guitar (2) / Railroad Street (1) / Short Sentimental Interlude (1) / Station Break (2) / Steam Powered Aereo Plane (2) / Steamboat Whistle Blues (2) / Symphony Hall Rag (2) / Tear Down The Grand Ole Opry (2) / Turn Your Radio On (2) / Up On The Hill Where They Do The Boogie (2) / Wart, The (1) / With A Vamp In The Middle (2)

HARTLEY, Keef, Band
English blues band. Drummer Hartley (b: 1944 in Preston, England) replaced Ringo Starr in his pre-Beatles group, Rory Storm and the Hurricanes, in 1962. In 1967, replaced Aynsley Dunbar in John Mayall's Bluesbreakers.

11/28/70	191	3		The Time Is Near	$12	Deram 18047

Another Time, Another Place / Change / From A Window / Morning Rain / Premonition / Time Is Near / You Can't Take It With You

DEBUT DATE	PEAK POS	WKS CHR	G O L D	ARTIST — Album Title	$	Label & Number

HARTMAN, Dan
Multi-instrumentalist/songwriter/producer from Harrisburg, Pennsylvania. Member of the Edgar Winter Group from 1972-76. Own studio called the Schoolhouse in Westport, Connecticut.

DEBUT DATE	PEAK POS	WKS CHR	GOLD	ARTIST — Album Title	$	Label & Number
12/16/78+	80	19		1 Instant Replay	$8	Blue Sky 35641
3/15/80	189	2		2 Relight My Fire	$8	Blue Sky 36302
11/3/84	55	28		3 I Can Dream About You	$8	MCA 5525

Chocolate Box (1)
Countdown (medley) (1)
Double-O-Love (1)
Electricity (3)
Free Ride (2)

Hands Down (2)
I Can Dream About You (3) *6*
I Can't Get Enough (3)
I Love Makin' Music (2)

I'm Not A Rolling Stone (3)
Instant Replay (1) *29*
Just For Fun (2)
Love Is A Natural (1)
Love Strong (2)

Name Of The Game (3)
Power Of A Good Love (3)
Rage To Live (3)
Relight My Fire (medley) (2)
Second Nature (3) *39*

Shy Hearts (3)
This Is It (medley) (1) *91*
Time And Space (1)
Vertigo (medley) (2)
We Are The Young (3) *25*

HARVEY, Sensational Alex, Band
Harvey, leader of British rock quintet, was born in Glasgow on 2/5/35; died on 2/4/82.

DEBUT DATE	PEAK POS	WKS CHR	GOLD	ARTIST — Album Title	$	Label & Number
3/1/75	197	1		1 The Impossible Dream	$8	Vertigo 2000
11/1/75	100	4		2 "Live" [L]	$8	Atlantic 18148

Anthem (1)
Delilah (2)
Faith Healer (2)

Fanfare (Justly, Skillfully, Magnanimously) (2)

Framed (2)
Give My Compliments To The Chef (2)

Impossible Dream (medley) (1)
Long Hair Music (1)

Man In The Jar (medley) (1)
Money Honey (medley) (1)
River Of Love (1)

Sergeant Fury (1)
Tomahawk Kid (1,2)
Vambo (1,2)
Weights Made Of Lead (1)

HASLAM, Annie
Lead singer of Renaissance.

DEBUT DATE	PEAK POS	WKS CHR	GOLD	ARTIST — Album Title	$	Label & Number
12/24/77+	167	13		Annie In Wonderland	$10	Sire 6046

Going Home
Hunioco

I Never Believed In Love
If I Loved You

If I Were Made Of Music
Inside My Life

Nature Boy
Rockalise

HATHAWAY, Donny
Born on 10/1/45 in Chicago and raised in St. Louis. Committed suicide by jumping from the 15th floor of New York City's Essex House hotel on 1/13/79. R&B singer/songwriter/keyboardist/producer/arranger. Gospel singer since age three. Attended Washington, D.C.'s Howard University on a fine arts scholarship; classmate of Roberta Flack. His wife Eulalah was a classical singer. Their daughter Lalah Hathaway began her solo recording career in 1990. Also see Roberta Flack and soundtrack Come Back Charleston Blue.

DEBUT DATE	PEAK POS	WKS CHR	GOLD	ARTIST — Album Title	$	Label & Number
5/15/71	89	21		1 Donny Hathaway	$10	Atco 360
5/29/71	73	25		2 Everything Is Everything	$10	Atco 332
				Donny's first album		
3/4/72	18	38	●	3 Donny Hathaway Live [L]	$10	Atco 386
5/13/72	3	39	●	4 Roberta Flack & Donny Hathaway	$10	Atlantic 7216
				ROBERTA FLACK & DONNY HATHAWAY		
7/21/73	69	13		5 Extension Of A Man	$10	Atco 7029

Baby I Love You (4)
Be Real Black For Me (4)
Come Little Children (5)
Come Ye Disconsolate (4)
Flying Easy (5)
For All We Know (4)
Ghetto-Part One (2,3) *87*
Giving Up (1) *81*
He Ain't Heavy, He's My Brother (1)

Hey Girl (3)
I Believe In Music (1)
I Believe To My Soul (2)
I Know It's You (5)
I Love The Lord; He Heard My Cry (Parts I & II) (5)
I Love You More Than You'll Ever Know (5) *60*
I Vous Aime (I Love You) (2)

Jealous Guy (3)
Little Ghetto Boy (3)
Little Girl (1)
Love, Love, Love (4) *44*
Magdalena (5)
Magnificent Sanctuary Band (1)
Misty (2)
Mood (4)

Put Your Hand In The Hand (1)
She Is My Lady (1)
Slums, The (5)
Someday We'll All Be Free (5)
Song For You (1)
Sugar Lee (2)
Take A Love Song (1)
Thank You Master (For My Soul) (2)

To Be Young, Gifted And Black (2)
Tryin' Times (2)
Valdez In The Country (5)
Voices Inside (Everything Is Everything) (2,3)
We're Still Friends (3)
What's Goin' On (3)
When Love Has Grown (4)
Where Is The Love (4) *5*

You've Got A Friend (3,4) *29*
You've Lost That Lovin' Feelin' (4) *71*

HATHAWAY, Lalah
Chicago-born daughter of the late Donny Hathaway. Her mother is classical singer Eulalah Hathaway.

DEBUT DATE	PEAK POS	WKS CHR	GOLD	ARTIST — Album Title	$	Label & Number
10/20/90	191	2		Lalah Hathaway	$12	Virgin 91382

Baby Don't Cry
Heaven Knows

I Gotta Move On
I'm Coming Back

Obvious
Sentimental

Smile
Somethin'

Stay Home Tonight
U-Godit Gowin On

HAVANA 3 A.M.
Former bassist of The Clash, Paul Simonon, formed quartet with fellow Englishmen Nigel Dixon (vocals, guitar) and Travis Williams (drums) and American Gary Myrick (guitar).

DEBUT DATE	PEAK POS	WKS CHR	GOLD	ARTIST — Album Title	$	Label & Number
5/4/91	169	3		Havana 3 a.m.	$12	I.R.S. 13069

Blue Gene Vincent
Blue Motorcycle Eyes

Death In The Afternoon
Hardest Game

Hey Amigo
Hole In The Sky

Joyride
Life On The Line

Living In This Town
Reach The Rock

Surf In The City
What About Your Future

HAVENS, Richie
Born on 1/21/41 in Brooklyn. Black folk singer/guitarist. Opening act of 1969 Woodstock concert.

DEBUT DATE	PEAK POS	WKS CHR	GOLD	ARTIST — Album Title	$	Label & Number
2/24/68	184	7		1 Something Else Again	$15	Verve F. 3034
7/6/68	182	2		2 Mixed Bag	$15	Verve Folk. 3006
				Richie's first album for Verve (1967)		
11/30/68	192	3		3 Electric Havens [E]	$15	Douglas 780
				Richie's second album for Douglas (1966)		
1/11/69	80	11		4 Richard P. Havens, 1983	$15	Verve F. 3047 [2]
1/10/70	155	14		5 Stonehenge	$12	Stormy F. 6001
11/7/70	190	2		6 Mixed Bag [R]	$10	MGM 4698
1/9/71	29	34		7 Alarm Clock	$10	Stormy F. 6005
11/13/71	126	11		8 The Great Blind Degree	$10	Stormy F. 6010
9/23/72	55	18		9 Richie Havens On Stage [L]	$12	Stormy F. 6012 [2]
6/9/73	182	4		10 Portfolio	$10	Stormy F. 6013
10/12/74	186	3		11 Mixed Bag II	$10	Stormy F. 6201
10/2/76	157	4		12 The End Of The Beginning	$8	A&M 4598
10/3/87	173	4		13 Simple Things	$8	RBI 400

Adam (2,6)
Alarm Clock (7)
Arrow Through Me (13)
Baby Blue (5)

Band On The Run (11)
Boots And Spanish Leather (3)
C.C. Rider (3)

Cautiously (4)
Daughter Of The Night (12)
Do It Again (12)

Do You Feel Good (medley) (4)
Dolphins, The (9)
Don't Listen To Me (1)

Dreaming As One (12)
Dreaming My Life Away (10)
Drivin' (13)
Eleanor Rigby (2,6)

End Of The Season (7)
Fathers And Sons (8)
Fire And Rain (8)
Follow (2,6)

DEBUT DATE	PEAK POS	WKS CHR	GOLD	ARTIST — Album Title	$	Label & Number

HAVENS, Richie — Cont'd

For Haven's Sake (4)
From The Prison (1,9)
Girls Don't Run Away (7)
God Bless The Child (9)
Handsome Johnny (2,6)
Headkeeper (11)
Here Comes The Sun (7) *16*
High Flyin' Bird (2,6,9)
I Can't Make It Anymore (2,6)
I Don't Need Nobody (10)
I Don't Wanna Know (13)
I Know I Won't Be There (10)
I Pity The Poor Immigrant (4)
I Started A Joke (5)
I Was Educated By Myself (12)
I'm A Stranger Here (3)
I'm Not In Love (12)
If Not For You (12)
In These Flames (8)
Indian Prayer (11)

Indian Rope Man (4)
Inside Of Him (1)
It Could Be The First Day (5)
It Was A Very Good Year (10)
Just Above My Hobby
Horse's Head (4)
Just Like A Woman (2,6,9)
Klan, The (1)
Lady Madonna (1)
Little Help From My Friends (4)
Loner, The (11)
Long Train Running (12)
Maggie's Farm (1)
Makings Of You (11)
Mama Loves You (10)
Minstrel From Gault (5,9)
Missing Train (7)
Morning, Morning (2,6)
My Own Way (3)
My Sweet Lord (9)

New City (1)
900 Miles (3)
No Opportunity Necessary,
No Experience Needed (1,9)
Nobody Knows (9)
Old Friends (9)
Ooh Child (11)
Open Our Eyes (5)
Oxford Town (3)
Parable Of Ramon (4)
Passin' By (13)
Patient Lady (7)
Prayer (5)
Priests (4)
Putting Out The Vibration,
And Hoping It Comes
Home (4)
Ring Around The Moon (5)
Rocky Raccoon (9)
Run, Shaker Life (1,4)
Runner In The Night (3)

Sad Eyed Lady (Of The
Lowlands) (11)
San Francisco Bay Blues
(2,6,9)
Sandy (2,6)
Shadow Town (3)
She's Leaving Home (4)
Shouldn't All The World Be
Dancing (5)
Shouldn't We All Be Having
A Good Time (13)
Simple Things (13)
Some Will Wait (7)
Someone Suite (11)
Somethin' Else Again (1)
Songwriter (13)
Stop Pulling And Pushing
Me (4)
Strawberry Fields Forever (4)
Sugarplums (1)
Teach Your Children (8,9)

There's A Hole In The Future (5)
Think About The Children (8)
Three Day Eternity (2,6)
3:10 To Yuma (3)
Tight Rope (10)
Tiny Little Blues (5)
To Give All Your Love Away (7)
Tommy (8)
Tupelo Honey (9)
23 Days In September (10)
Wake Up & Dream (13)
Wandering Angus (11)
We Can't Hide It Anymore (12)
Wear Your Love Like Heaven (4)
What About Me (8)
What Have We Done (8)

What More Can I Say John (4)
What's Going On (10)
Where Have All The Flowers Gone (9)
Wild Night (12)
With A Little Help From My Friends ..see: Little Help From My Friends
Woman (10)
You Can Close Your Eyes (12)
Younger Men Grow Older (7,9)

HAWKINS, Edwin, Singers

Hawkins (b: August 1943) formed gospel group with Betty Watson in Oakland in 1967 as the Northern California State Youth Choir. Member Dorothy Morrison went on to a solo career.

DEBUT DATE	PEAK POS	WKS CHR		ARTIST — Album Title	$	Label & Number
5/3/69	15	23	1	Let Us Go Into The House Of The Lord	$12	Pavilion 10001
10/18/69	169	4	2	Live At Yankee Stadium ....[L]	$12	T-Neck 3004

side A: Isley Brothers (see Isley Brothers); side B: Edwin Hawkins Singers;side C: Brooklyn Bridge (see Brooklyn Bridge); side D: "Don't ChangeYour Love" by The Five Stairsteps, "Somebody's Been Messin'" by Judy White and "Love Is What You Make It" by Sweet Cherries

| 10/2/71 | 180 | 8 | 3 | Children (Get Together) | $12 | Buddah 5086 |
| 5/27/72 | 171 | 4 | 4 | I'd Like To Teach The World To Sing | $12 | Buddah 5101 |

Children Get Together (3)
Deeper Love (3)
Early In The Morning (1)
Give Me A Star (4)
Grove Of Eucalyptus (4)
Here's The Reason (4)
His Way (3)

I Don't Know How To Love Him (4)
I Hear The Voice Of Jesus (1)
I Shall Be Free (3)
I'd Like To Teach The World To Sing (4)
I'm Going Through (1)

Jesus, Lover Of My Soul (1,2)
Joy, Joy (1,2)
Late In The Evening (4)
Let Us Go Into The House Of The Lord (1)
Long Way To Go (3)
Lord We Try (4)

Oh Happy Day (1,2) *4*
Ooh Child (4)
Shine (4)
Someday (3)
There's A Place For Me (3)
To My Father's House (1)
Together In Peace (3)

Trouble The World Is In (3)
Wake Up To What's Happening (4)
When We Love (4)
World Is Going To Be A Better Place (3)

HAWKINS, Sophie B.

Sophie Ballantine Hawkins, a Manhattan-bred singer. Percussionist in Bryan Ferry's backing band in the early '80s.

| 5/16/92 | 51 | 24 | | Tongues And Tails | $12 | Columbia 46797 |

Before I Walk On Fire
California Here I Come
Carry Me

Damn I Wish I Was Your Lover I
Don't Stop Swaying
I Want You

Listen
Live And Let Love

Mysteries We Understand
Saviour Child

We Are One Body

HAWKWIND

British space-rock band formed in 1969 by lead guitarist/vocalist Dave Brock. Fluctuating lineup included Ginger Baker and Motorhead's Ian "Lemmy" Kilminster.

11/24/73	179	8	1	Space Ritual/Alive In Liverpool And London ....[L]	$15	United Art. 120 [2]
10/5/74	110	12	2	Hall Of The Mountain Grill	$12	United Art. 328
6/14/75	150	5	3	Warrior On The Edge Of Time	$10	Atco 115

Assault & Battery Part I (3)
Awakening, The (1)
Black Corridor (1)
Born To Go (medley) (1)
Brainstorm (1)
D-Rider (2)
Demented Man (3)
Down Through The Night (1)

Dying Seas (3)
Earth Calling (medley) (1)
Electronic No. 1 (1)
Goat Willow (2)
Golden Void Part II (3)
Hall Of The Mountain Grill (2)
Kings Of Speed (3)

Lord Of Light (1)
Lost Johnnie (2)
Magnu (3)
Master Of The Universe (1)
Opa-Loka (3)
Orgone Accumulator (1)
Paradox (2)

Psychedelic Warlords (Disappear In Smoke) (2)
7 X 7 (1)
Sonic Attack (1)
Space Is Deep (1)
Spiral Galaxy 28948 (3)
Standing At The Edge (3)
10 Seconds Of Forever (1)

Time We Left This World Today (1)
Upside Down (1)
Warriors (3)
Web Weaver (2)
Welcome To The Future (1)
Wind Of Change (2)
Wizard Blew His Horn (3)

You'd Better Believe It (2)

HAY, Colin James

Lead singer/guitarist of Men At Work. Born in Scotland on 6/29/53. To Melbourne, Australia in 1967.

| 2/21/87 | 126 | 9 | | Looking For Jack | $8 | Columbia 40611 |

Can I Hold You?
Circles Erratica

Fisherman's Friend
Hold Me *99*

I Don't Need You Anymore
Looking For Jack

Master Of Crime
Puerto Rico

These Are Our Finest Days
Ways Of The World

★★83★★ HAYES, Isaac

Born on 8/20/42 in Covington, Tennessee. Soul singer/songwriter/keyboardist/producer/actor. Session musician for Otis Redding and other artists on the Stax label. Teamed with songwriter David Porter to compose "Soul Man," "Hold On! I'm A Comin'" and many others. Composed film scores for *Shaft*, *Tough Guys* and *Truck Turner*.

DEBUT DATE	PEAK POS	WKS CHR	GOLD		ARTIST — Album Title	$	Label & Number
7/12/69	8	81	●	1	Hot Buttered Soul	$12	Enterprise 1001
4/18/70	8	75		2	The Isaac Hayes Movement	$12	Enterprise 1010
12/5/70	11	56		3	To Be Continued	$12	Enterprise 1014
8/21/71	1[1]	60		4	Shaft ....[S-I]	$12	Enterprise 5002 [2]

3 of 15 tracks feature vocals

| 12/11/71+ | 10 | 34 | | 5 | Black Moses | $12 | Enterprise 5003 [2] |
| 2/26/72 | 102 | 12 | | 6 | In The Beginning ....[E-R] | $10 | Atlantic 1599 |

reissue of his first album *Presenting Isaac Hayes* (1967)

5/19/73	14	26	●	7	Live At The Sahara Tahoe ....[L]	$10	Enterprise 5005 [2]
10/27/73	16	27	●	8	Joy	$10	Enterprise 5007
6/15/74	146	8		9	Tough Guys ....[S-I]	$10	Enterprise 7504

music from the soundtrack *Three Tough Guys*

DEBUT DATE	PEAK POS	WKS CHR	GOLD	ARTIST — Album Title	$	Label & Number
				HAYES, Isaac — Cont'd		
8/3/74	156	9		10 Truck Turner .... [S-I]	$10	Enterprise 7507 [2]
6/21/75	18	19	●	11 Chocolate Chip	$10	HBS 874
8/23/75	165	4		12 The Best Of Isaac Hayes .... [G]	$10	Enterprise 7510
1/17/76	85	17		13 Disco Connection	$8	HBS 923
2/21/76	45	12		14 Groove-A-Thon	$8	HBS 925
7/24/76	124	7		15 Juicy Fruit (Disco Freak)	$8	HBS 953
2/19/77	49	13		16 A Man And A Woman ....[L]	$10	HBS 996 [2]
				ISAAC HAYES & DIONNE WARWICK		
12/17/77+	78	12		17 New Horizon	$8	Polydor 6120
11/18/78+	75	18		18 For The Sake Of Love	$8	Polydor 6164
9/29/79+	39	30	●	19 Don't Let Go	$8	Polydor 6224
10/20/79	80	19		20 Royal Rappin's	$8	Polydor 6229
				MILLIE JACKSON & ISAAC HAYES		
5/17/80	59	15		21 And Once Again	$8	Polydor 6269

After Five (13)
Ain't No Sunshine (7)
Aruba (13)
Be Yourself (4)
Believe In Me (18)
Blue's Crib (10)
Body Language (11,16)
A Brand New Me (medley) (5)
Breakthrough (10)
Bumpy's Blues (4)
Bumpy's Lament (4)
Buns O'Plenty (9)
By The Time I Get To Phoenix (1,12,16) 37
Cafe Regio's (4)
Can't Hide Love (16)
Chocolate Chip (11,16) 92
Choppers (1)
Close To You ..see: (They Long To Be)
Come Live With Me (11,16)
Come On (medley) (7)
Disco Connection (13)
Disco Shuffle (13)
Do You Wanna Make Love (20)
Do Your Thing (4,7,12) 30
Don't Let Go (19) 18
Don't Let Me Be Lonely Tonight (18)
Don't Take Your Love Away (17)
Dorinda's Party (10)
Drinking (10)
Driving In The Sun (10)
Duke, The (10)

Early Sunday Morning (4)
Ellie's Love Theme (4,7,12)
Feelin' Alright (7)
Feeling Keeps On Coming (8)
Feelings (medley) (16)
Feels Like The First Time (20)
Fever (19)
Few More Kisses To Go (19)
First Day Of Forever (13)
First Time Ever I Saw Your Face (7)
For The Good Times (5)
Friend's Place (4)
Get Down Tonight (medley) (16)
Give It To Me (10)
Going In Circles (3)
Going To Chicago Blues (medley) (6)
Good Love 6-9969 (5)
Groove-A-Thon (14)
Have You Never Been Mellow (medley) (16)
Help Me Love (medley) (16)
Hospital Shootout (10)
House Full Of Girls (10)
House Of Beauty (10)
Hung Up On My Baby (10)
Hyperbolicsyllabicsequedalymistic (1)
I Ain't Never (21)
I Can't Turn Around (11)
I Changed My Mind (20)
I Just Don't Know What To Do With Myself (2,16)

I Just Want To Make Love To You (medley) (6)
I Love Music (medley) (16)
I Love You That's All (8)
I Say A Little Prayer (medley) (16)
I Stand Accused (2,12) 42
I Want To Make Love To You (5)
I'll Never Fall In Love Again (5)
I'm Gonna Make It (Without You) (8)
If I Had My Way (20)
If We Ever Needed Peace (18)
If You Had Your Way (20)
Ike's Mood I (3)
Ike's Rap I (3)
Ike's Rap II, III & IV (medley) (5)
Ike's Rap V & VI (medley) (7)
Ike's Rap VII (medley) (21)
Insurance Company (10)
It's All In The Game (21)
It's Heaven To Me (17)
It's Too Late (7)
Joe Bell (9)
Joy - Pt. 1 (8,12) 30
Juicy Fruit (Disco Freak) (15)
Just The Way You Are (18)
Kidnapped (9)
Lady Of The Night (15)
Let's Don't Ever Blow Our Thing (15)
Light My Fire (medley) (16)
Look Of Love (3,7) 79

Love Changes (20)
Love Has Been Good To Us (21)
Love Me Or Lose Me (15)
Love Will Keep Us Together (medley) (16)
Make A Little Love To Me (14)
Man Will Be A Man (8)
Man's Temptation (5)
Men, Theme From The (7)
Misty (medley) (5)
Moonlight Lovin' (Menage A Trois) (17)
Music To Make Love By (15)
My Eyes Adored You (medley) (16)
My Love (16)
Need To Belong To Someone (5)
Never Can Say Goodbye (5,7,12) 22
Never Gonna Give You Up (5)
No Name Bar (4)
Nothing Takes The Place Of You (5)
Now We're One (10)
Once You Hit The Road (16)
One Big Unhappy Family (2)
One Woman (1)
Our Day Will Come (3)
Out Of The Ghetto (17)
Part-Time Love (5)
Precious, Precious (6)
Pursuit Of The Pimpmobile (10)
Randolph & Dearborn (9)

Red Rooster (9)
Rock Me Baby (6,7)
Rock Me Easy Baby (14)
Run Fay Run (9)
Runnin' Out Of Fools (3)
Shaft, Theme From (4,7,9,12) 1
Shaft II (18)
Shaft Strikes Again (4)
Shaft's Cab Ride (4)
Someone Who Will Take The Place Of You (19)
Something (2)
Soulsville (4)
St. Thomas Square (13)
Storm Is Over (15)
Stormy Monday Blues (7)
Stranger In Paradise (17)
Sweet Music, Soft Lights, And You (20)
Thank You Love (15)
That Loving Feeling (11)
That's The Way I Like It (medley) (16)
Then Came You (16)
(They Long To Be) Close To You (5)
This Time I'll Be Sweeter (medley) (21)
This Will Be (An Everlasting Love) (medley) (16)
Truck Turner (10)
Type Thang (7)
Unity (16)
Use Me (7)
Vykkii (13)

Walk From Regio's (4)
Walk On By (1,12,16) 30
Way I Want To Touch You (medley) (16)
We Need Each Other Girl (10)
We've Got A Whole Lot Of Love (14)
What Does It Take (19)
When I Fall In Love (6)
Wherever You Are (21)
Windows Of The World (7)
Wish You Were Here (You Ought To Be Here) (14)
You Don't Know Like I Know (6)
You Needed Me (20)
You Never Cross My Mind (20)
You're In My Arms Again (10)
You've Lost That Lovin' Feelin' (3)
Your Love Is So Doggone Good (medley) (5)
Your Loving Is Much Too Strong (14)
Zeke The Freak (18)

HAYNES, Roy — see METHENY, Pat

HAYWARD, Justin
Lead singer/guitarist of The Moody Blues. Born on 10/14/46 in Swindon, England.

3/29/75	16	23		1 Blue Jays	$12	Threshold 14
				JUSTIN HAYWARD/JOHN LODGE album title also refers to the name of their duo		
3/12/77	37	16		2 Songwriter	$12	Deram 18073
8/9/80	166	5		3 Night Flight	$10	Deram 4801

Bedtime Stories (3)
Country Girl (2)
Crazy Lovers (3)
Doin' Time (2)
Face In The Crowd (3)
I Dreamed Last Night (1) 47

I'm Sorry (3)
It's Not On (3)
Lay It On Me (2)
Maybe (1)
Maybe It's Just Love (3)
My Brother (1)

Nearer To You (3)
Night Flight (3)
Nights, Winters, Years (1)
Nostradamus (2)
One Lonely Room (2)
Penumbra Moon (3)

Raised On Love (3)
Remember Me, My Friend (1)
Saved By The Music (1)
Songwriter (Part 1 & 2) (2)
Stage Door (2)
Suitcase (3)

This Morning (1)
Tight Rope (2)
When You Wake Up (1)
Who Are You Now (1)
You (1)

HAYWOOD, Leon
Born on 2/11/42 in Houston. Soul singer/keyboardist. With Big Jay McNeely and Sam Cooke in the early '60s.

8/16/75	140	13		1 Come And Get Yourself Some	$8	20th Century 476
5/17/80	92	10		2 Naturally	$8	20th Century 613

Believe Half Of What You See (And None Of What You Hear) (1) 94
Come An' Get Yourself Some (1) 83

Consider The Source (1)
Daydream (2)
Don't Push It Don't Force It (2) 49
I Know What Love Is (1)

I Want'a Do Something Freaky To You (1) 15
If You're Lookin' For A Night Of Fun (Look Past Me, I'm Not The One) (2)

Just Your Fool (1)
Love Is What We Came Here For (2)
Lover's Rap (2)
That's What Time It Is (2)

This Feeling's Rated Extra (1)
Who Have You Been Giving It Up To (1,2)
You Need A Friend Like Mine (1)

HAZA, Ofra
Yemenite Jewish singer/composer/actress. Born in Hatika, Israel. Winner of three Israeli Grammy Awards. Survived a 2/3/87 plane crash in which she was rumored to have died.

1/21/89	130	9		1 Shaday	$8	Sire 25816
				translation of Yemenite title: The Divine		
2/10/90	156	5		2 Desert Wind	$12	Sire 25976

Da'Ale Da'Ale (1)
Da'asa (2)
Eshal (1)
Face To Face (1)

Fatamorgana (Mirage) (2)
Galbi (1)
I Want To Fly (2)
Im Nin'Alu (1)

In-Ta (2)
Kaddish (2)
Love Song (1)

MM'MMA (My Brothers Are There) (2)
Middle East (2)
My Aching Heart (1)

Shaday (1)
Slave Dream (2)
Take Me To Paradise (1)
Taw Shi (2)

Wish Me Luck (2)
Ya Ba Ye (2)

DEBUT DATE	PEAK POS	WKS CHR	GOLD	ARTIST — Album Title	$	Label & Number

HAZARD, Robert
Philadelphia-based rocker.

| 3/26/83 | 102 | 11 | | Robert Hazard .... [M] | $8 | RCA 8500 |

Blowin' In The Wind · Change Reaction · **Escalator Of Life 58** · Hang Around With You · Out Of The Blue

HAZLEWOOD, Lee — see SINATRA, Nancy

HEAD, Roy
Born on 1/9/43 in Three Rivers, Texas. Rock-country singer/guitarist.

| 12/4/65+ | 122 | 8 | | Treat Me Right .... | $20 | Scepter 532 |

Convicted · **Get Back 88** · Money · Night Train · Treat Me Right
Feelings Gone · **Just A Little Bit 39** · **My Babe 99** · One More Time

HEADBOYS, The
Scottish rock quartet — Lou Lewis, leader.

| 11/10/79 | 113 | 15 | | The Headboys .... | $8 | RSO 3068 |

Breakout, The · Gonna Do It Like This · Ripper, The · **Shape Of Things To** · Silver Lining · Take It All Down
Changing With The Times · Kickin' The Kans · Schoolgirls · **Come 67** · Stepping Stones
Experiments · My Favourite D.J.

HEAD EAST
St. Louis rock quintet: Roger Boyd (keyboards), Steve Huston (drums), John Schlitt (vocals), Michael Sommerville (guitar) and Dan Birney (bass). The latter three left by 1980, replaced by Dan Odum, Tony Gross and Mark Boatman.

8/30/75	126	17	●	1 Flat As A Pancake	$8	A&M 4537
5/22/76	161	6		2 Get Yourself Up	$8	A&M 4579
4/2/77	136	7		3 Gettin' Lucky	$8	A&M 4624
3/11/78	78	14		4 Head East	$8	A&M 4680
2/3/79	65	14		5 Head East Live! .... [L]	$10	A&M 6007 [2]
11/17/79	96	16		6 A Different Kind Of Crazy	$8	A&M 4795
11/8/80	137	6		7 U.S. 1	$8	A&M 4826

Babie Ruth (7) · Feelin' Is Right (6) · It's For You (5) · Morning (6) · **Since You Been Gone** · Victim, The (2)
Back In My Own Hands (3) · Fight For Your Life (7) · Jailer (2) · **Never Been Any Reason** · (4,5) **46** · When I Get Ready (2,5)
Brother Jacob (1) · Fly By Night Lady (1,5) · Jefftown Creek (1,5) · (1,5) **68** · Sister Sister (7) · You'll Be The One (7)
Call To Arms And Legs (3) · Get Up & Enjoy Yourself · Keep A Secret (6) · Nothing To Lose (4) · Specialty (6)
City Of Gold (1,5) · (4,5) · Lonelier Now (6) · One Against The Other (1) · Susan (7)
Dance Away Lover (4) · Gettin' Lucky (3,5) · Look To The Sky (4) · Open Up The Door (4) · Take A Hand (5)
Dancer Road (3) · Got To Be Real (6) · Love Me Now (7) · Out Of The Blue (7) · Take It On Home (3)
Don't Let Me Sleep In The · Hard Drivin' Days (6) · **Love Me Tonight** (1,5) **54** · Pictures (4) · This Woman's In Love (2)
Morning (3) · I Don't Want The Chance (2) · Love My Blues Away (2) · Sailor (2) · Ticket Back To Georgia (1)
Elijah (4,5) · I Surrender (7) · Lovin' Me Along (1) · Sands Of Time (3) · Time Has A Way (3)
Every Little Bit Of My Heart · I'm Feelin' Fine (4,5) · Man I Wanna Be (4,5) · Separate Ways (2) · Too Late (6)
(3,5) · If You Knew Me Better (6) · Monkey Shine (2,5) · Show Me I'm Alive (3) · Trouble (2)

HEADHUNTERS
Herbie Hancock's super-funk backup band.

| 4/19/75 | 126 | 10 | | Survival Of The Fittest .... [I] | $8 | Arista 4038 |

Daffy's Dance · God Make Me Funky · Here And Now · If You've Got It, You'll Get It · Mugic · Rima

HEADPINS
Canadian rock quartet — Darby Mills, lead singer.

| 1/21/84 | 114 | 9 | | Line Of Fire .... | $8 | Solid Gold 9031 |

Celebration · Don't Stand In The Line Of · Double Trouble · I Know What You're Thinking · **Just One More Time 70**
Fire · Feel It (Feel My Body) · I've Heard It All Before · Mine, All Mine

HEALEY, Jeff, Band
Toronto-based, blues-rock trio: vocalist/guitarist Healey with drummer Tom Stephen and bassist Joe Rockman. Healey, blind since age one and guitarist since three, appeared in the 1989 film Road House.

10/8/88+	22	69	▲	1 See The Light	$8	Arista 8553
6/16/90	27	39	●	2 Hell To Pay	$12	Arista 8632
11/28/92	174	2		3 Feel This	$12	Arista 18706

Angel Eyes (1) **5** · Dreams Of Love (3) · House That Love Built (3) · I Think I Love You Too Much · Let It All Go (2) · See The Light (1)
Baby's Lookin' Hot (3) · Evil And Here To Stay (3) · How Long Can A Man Be · (2) · Life Beyond The Sky (2) · Someday, Someway (1)
Blue Jean Blues (1) · Full Circle (2) · Strong (2) · If You Can't Feel Anything · Lost In Your Eyes (3) · Something To Hold On To (2)
Confidence Man (1) · Heart Of An Angel (3) · How Much (2) · Else (3) · My Kinda Lover (3) · That's What They Say (1)
Cruel Little Number (3) · Hell To Pay (2) · I Can't Get My Hands On · It Could All Get Blown Away · My Little Girl (1) · While My Guitar Gently
Don't Let Your Chance Go · Hideaway (1) · You (2) · (3) · Nice Problem To Have (1) · Weeps (2)
By (1) · Highway Of Dreams (2) · I Need To Be Loved (1) · Leave The Light On (3) · River Of No Return (1) · You're Coming Home (3)

HEAR 'N AID
Collection of 40 hard-rock artists formed to raise money for famine relief efforts in Africa and around the world.

| 7/5/86 | 80 | 7 | | Hear 'N Aid .... | $8 | Mercury 826044 |

Can You See Me [Jimi · Distant Early Warning [Rush] · Heaven's On Fire [Kiss] · On The Road [Motorhead] · Up To The Limit [Accept]
Hendrix] · Go For The Throat [Y&T] · Hungry For Heaven [Dio] · Stars · Zoo, The [Scorpions]

★★148★★ HEART
Rock band formed in Seattle in 1973. Originally known as The Army, then White Heart, shortened to Heart in 1974. Group features Ann Wilson (lead singer) and her sister Nancy (guitar, keyboards). Band moved to Vancouver in 1975 when their manager Mike Fisher was drafted, and signed with the new Mushroom label. When amnesty was declared, group returned to Seattle and signed with the CBS Portrait label in 1976. Joining the Wilsons were guitarists Howard Leese and Roger Fisher (brother of Mike), bassist Steve Fossen and drummer Michael DeRosier. The Fishers left the band in 1979; Roger joined Alias in 1990. Fossen and DeRosier left by 1982, replaced by bassist Mark Andes (ex-Spirit, Jo Jo Gunne and Firefall member) and drummer Denny Carmassi (ex-Gamma). Nancy married film director Cameron Crowe.

| 4/10/76 | 7 | 100 | ▲ | 1 Dreamboat Annie .... | $12 | Mushroom 5005 |
| 5/28/77 | 9 | 41 | ▲² | 2 Little Queen .... | $10 | Portrait 34799 |

DEBUT DATE	PEAK POS	WKS CHR	GOLD	ARTIST — Album Title	$	Label & Number

HEART — Cont'd

DEBUT DATE	PEAK POS	WKS CHR	GOLD	ARTIST — Album Title	$	Label & Number
4/22/78	17	25	▲	3 Magazine	$25	Mushroom 5008
				recorded in 1976, but not released until 1978 because of a legal battle		
10/7/78+	17	36	▲²	4 Dog & Butterfly	$8	Portrait 35555
3/8/80	5	22	●	5 Bebe Le Strange	$8	Epic 36371
12/6/80	13	25	▲²	6 Greatest Hits/Live ....[G-L]	$10	Epic 36888 [2]
				6 of 18 tracks are live		
6/12/82	25	14		7 Private Audition	$8	Epic 38049
9/17/83	39	21		8 Passionworks	$8	Epic 38800
7/13/85	1¹	92	▲⁵	9 Heart...	$8	Capitol 12410
6/13/87	2³	50	▲³	10 Bad Animals	$8	Capitol 12546
4/21/90	3	49	▲²	11 Brigade	$12	Capitol 91820
10/12/91	107	7		12 Rock The House Live! ....[L]	$12	Capitol 95797
				recorded in Worcester, Massachusetts on 11/28/90		

All Eyes (9)
All I Wanna Do Is Make Love To You (11) **2**
Allies (8) **83**
Alone (10) **1**
Ambush (8)
America (7)
Angels (7)
Bad Animals (10)
Barracuda (2,6,12) **11**
(Beat By) Jealousy (8)
Bebe Le Strange (5,6)
Blue Guitar (8)
Break (5)
Bright Light Girl (7)
Call Of The Wild (11,12)
City's Burning (7)
Cook With Fire (4)
Crazy On You (1,6) **35**
Cruel Nights (11)
Cry To Me (2)

Devil Delight (3)
Dog & Butterfly (4,6) **34**
Down On Me (5)
Dream Of The Archer (2)
Dreamboat Annie (1,6) **42**
Easy Target (10)
Even It Up (5,6) **33**
Fallen From Grace (11,12)
Fast Times (7)
Go On Cry (2)
Heartless (3,6) **24**
Heavy Heart (8)
Here Song (3)
Hey Darlin Darlin (7)
High Time (4)
Hijinx (4)
Hit Single (6)
How Can I Refuse (8,12) **44**
How Deep It Goes (1)
I Didn't Want To Need You (11) **23**

I Love You (11)
I Want You So Bad (10) **49**
I Want Your World To Turn (11)
I'm Down (medley) (6)
I've Got The Music In Me (3)
If Looks Could Kill (9,12) **84**
Johnny Moon (8)
Just The Wine (3)
Kick It Out (2) **79**
Language Of Love (8)
Lighter Touch (4)
Little Queen (2) **62**
Long Tall Sally (medley) (6)
Love Alive (2,12)
(Love Me Like Music) I'll Be Your Song (1)
Love Mistake (8)
Magazine (6)
Magic Man (1,6) **9**

Mistral Wind (4,6)
Mother Earth Blues (3)
Nada One (4)
Never (9) **4**
Night, The (11,12)
Nobody Home (9)
Nothin' At All (9) **10**
One Word (7)
Perfect Stranger (7)
Pilot (5)
Private Audition (7)
RSVP (10)
Raised On You (5)
Rock And Roll (6)
Rockin Heaven Down (5)
Say Hello (2)
Secret (11) **64**
Shell Shock (9,12)
Silver Wheels (5,6)
Sing Child (3)
Situation, The (7)

Sleep Alone (8)
Soul Of The Sea (1)
Straight On (4,6) **15**
Stranded (11) **13**
Strange Euphoria (6)
Strange Night (5)
Strangers Of The Heart (10)
Sweet Darlin (5,6)
Sylvan Song (2)
Tall, Dark Handsome Stranger (11,12)
Tell It Like It Is (6) **8**
There's The Girl (10) **12**
These Dreams (9) **1**
This Man Is Mine (7) **33**
Together Now (8)
Treat Me Well (2)
Unchained Melody (6) **83**
Under The Sky (11,12)
Wait For An Answer (10)
Way Back Machine (12)

What About Love? (9) **10**
What He Don't Know (9)
White Lightning & Wine (1)
Who Will You Run To (10,12) **7**
Wild Child (11,12)
Without You (3)
Wolf (9)
You Ain't So Tough (10)
You're The Voice (12)

HEARTSFIELD
Six-man Chicago rock band led by vocalist J.C. Heartsfield.

DEBUT DATE	PEAK POS	WKS CHR	GOLD	ARTIST — Album Title	$	Label & Number
8/16/75	159	7		Foolish Pleasures	$10	Mercury 1034

Another Man Down
As I Look Into The Fire

Drummer Boy
Honest Junkie

Magic Mood
Nashville

Needing Her
Rocking Chair

HEATH, Ted, And His Music
Born Edward Heath on 3/30/1900 in London. Died on 11/18/69. Trombonist/leader of own band since 1945.

DEBUT DATE	PEAK POS	WKS CHR	GOLD	ARTIST — Album Title	$	Label & Number
10/9/61	28	10		1 Big Band Percussion ....[I]	$15	London P. 4 44002
9/15/62	36	2		2 Big Band Bash ....[I]	$15	London P. 4 44017

A-Tisket A-Tasket (2)
Blues In The Night (1)
But Not For Me (1)
Capuccina (2)

Cherokee (2)
Clopin-Clopant (2)
Daddy (1)
Drum Crazy (1)

Harlem Nocturne (2)
Hernando's Hideaway (2)
Hindustan (2)
I Don't Know Why (2)

In A Persian Market (2)
It Ain't Necessarily So (1)
Johnny One Note (1)
Mood Indigo (1)

More Than You Know (1)
Out Of Nowhere (1)
Peanut Vendor (1)
Poinciana (1)

Sabre Dance (2)
Taking A Chance On Love (1)
Thou Swell (1)

HEATHERTON, Joey
Born on 9/14/44 in Rockville Centre, New York. Movie/TV actress.

DEBUT DATE	PEAK POS	WKS CHR	GOLD	ARTIST — Album Title	$	Label & Number
10/21/72	154	13		The Joey Heatherton Album	$12	MGM 4858

Crazy
God Only Knows

Gone 24
I'm Sorry 87

It's Not Easy
Right Or Wrong

Road I Took To You (Pieces)
Say Hello

Shake-A-Hand
Someone To Watch Over Me

HEATWAVE
Multinational, interracial group formed in Germany by brothers Johnnie and Keith Wilder of Dayton, Ohio. Johnnie became a paraplegic due to a car accident in 1979.

DEBUT DATE	PEAK POS	WKS CHR	GOLD	ARTIST — Album Title	$	Label & Number
8/6/77	11	45	▲	1 Too Hot To Handle.........................	$10	Epic 34761
4/22/78	10	26	▲	2 Central Heating	$10	Epic 35260
5/12/79	38	14	●	3 Hot Property	$8	Epic 35970
12/13/80+	71	10		4 Candles	$8	Epic 36873
7/10/82	156	6		5 Current	$8	Epic 38065

Ain't No Half Steppin' (1)
All I Am (4)
All Talked Out (3)
All You Do Is Dial (1)
Always And Forever (1) **18**
Beat Your Booty (1)
Big Guns (5)
Boogie Nights (1) **2**
Central Heating (2)

Disco (3)
Dreamin' You (4)
Eyeballin' (3)
Find It In Your Heart (5)
First Day Of Snow (3)
Gangsters Of The Groove (4)
Goin' Crazy (4)
Groove Line (2) **7**
Happiness Togetherness (2)

Hold On To The One (5)
Jitterbuggin' (4)
Lay It On Me (1)
Leavin' For A Dream (2)
Lettin' It Loose (5)
Look After Love (5)
Mind Blowing Decisions (2)
Mind What You Find (5)
Naturally (5)

One Night Tan (3)
Party Poops (2)
Party Suite (4)
Posin' 'Til Closin' (4)
Put The Word Out (5)
Raise A Blaze (3)
Razzle Dazzle (3)
Send Out For Sunshine (2)
Sho'nuff Must Be Luv (1)

Star Of A Story (2)
State To State (3)
Super Soul Sister (1)
That's The Way We'll Always Say Goodnight (3)
Therm Warfare (3)
This Night We Fell (3)
Too Hot To Handle (1)
Turn Around (4)

Where Did I Go Wrong (4)

HEAVENS EDGE
Rock quintet formed in Philadelphia by Mark Evans (vocals) and Reggie Wu (guitar).

DEBUT DATE	PEAK POS	WKS CHR	GOLD	ARTIST — Album Title	$	Label & Number
6/23/90	141	12		Heavens Edge	$12	Columbia 45262

Bad Reputation
Can't Catch Me

Come Play The Game
Daddy's Little Girl

Don't Stop, Don't Go
Find Another Way

Hold On To Tonight
Is That All You Want?

Play Dirty
Skin To Skin

Up Against The Wall

HEAVEN 17
British electro-pop trio: Glenn Gregory (vocals) and former Human League co-founders/synthesists Martyn Ware and Ian Craig Marsh.

DEBUT DATE	PEAK POS	WKS CHR	GOLD	ARTIST — Album Title	$	Label & Number
2/12/83	68	28		1 Heaven 17	$8	Arista 6606
6/4/83	72	13		2 The Luxury Gap	$8	Arista 8020

DEBUT DATE	PEAK POS	WKS CHR	GOLD	ARTIST — Album Title	$	Label & Number
4/4/87	177	3		**3** Pleasure One	$8	Virgin 90569

Best Kept Secret (2) • Come Live With Me (2) • Contenders (3) • Crushed By The Wheels Of Industry (2) • Free (3) • Geisha Boys And Temple Girls (1) • Height Of The Fighting (1) • I'm Your Money (1) • If I Were You (3) • Key To The World (2) • Lady Ice And Mr. Hex (2) • **Let Me Go** (1) **74** • Let's All Make A Bomb (2) • Look At Me (3) • Low Society (3) • Move Out (3) • Penthouse And Pavement (1) • Play To Win (1) • Red (3) • Somebody (3) • Song With No Name (2) • Temptation (2) • Trouble (3) • (We Don't Need This) Fascist Groove Thang (1) • We Live So Fast (2) • We're Going To Live For A Very Long Time (1) • Who Will Stop The Rain (1)

HEAVY D. & THE BOYZ
Rap quartet from Mt. Vernon, New York: leader Heavy D. (Dwight Meyers), G. Whiz (Glen Parrish), Trouble T-Roy (Troy Dixon) and DJ Eddie F (Edward Ferrell). Dixon died on 7/15/90 (age 22) from an accidental fall in Indianapolis.

11/14/87	92	16		**1** Living Large..	$8	MCA 5986
7/1/89	19	51 ▲		**2** Big Tyme..	$8	Uptown 42302
7/20/91	21	41 ▲		**3** Peaceful Journey	$12	Uptown 10289

CD includes bonus track

Better Land (2) • Big Tyme (2) • Body And Mind (3) • Chunky But Funky (1) • Cuz He'z Alwayz Around (3) • Dedicated (1) • Do Me, Do Me (3) • Don't Curse (3) • Don't You Know (1) • Ez Duz It, Do It Ez (2) • Flexin' (2) • Gyrlz, They Love Me (2) • Here We Go (1) • Here We Go Again, Y'all (2) • I Can Make You Go Oooh (3) • I'm Getting Paid (1) • I'm Gonna Make You Love Me (1) • **Is It Good To You** (3) **32** • Let It Flow (2) • Let It Rain (3) • Letter To The Future (3) • Lover's Got What U Need (3) • Moneyearnin' Mount Vernon (1) • Mood For Love (2) • More Bounce (2) • Mr. Big Stuff (1) • Nike (1) • **Now That We Found Love** (3) **11** • On The Dance Floor (1) • Overweight Lovers In The House (1) • Overweighter (1) • Peaceful Journey (3) • Rock The Bass (1) • Sister Sister (3) • Somebody For Me (2,3) • Swinging With Da Hevster (3) • We Got Our Own Thang (2) • You Ain't Heard Nuttin Yet (2)

HEBB, Bobby
Born on 7/26/41 in Nashville. Singer/songwriter/multi-instrumentalist. Featured on the *Grand Ole Opry* at age 12. His brother Hal was a member of the Marigolds.

9/10/66	103	12		Sunny	$20	Philips 212

Bread • Crazy Baby • For You • Good Good Lovin' • Got You On My Mind • I Am Your Man • Love Love Love • **Satisfied Mind 39** • **Sunny 2** • Where Are You • Yes Or No Or Maybe Not • You Don't Know What You Got Until You Lose It

HEFTI, Neal
Born on 10/29/22 in Hastings, Nebraska. Trumpeter. Gained fame as arranger for Woody Herman (1944-46), Harry James and Count Basie, then as composer of TV themes.

2/5/55	8	2		**1** Music Of Rudolf Friml .... [I]	$15	"X" 3021

NEAL HEFTI AND HIS ORCHESTRA
10" album

3/12/66	41	21		**2** Batman Theme .... [I]	$20	RCA 3573

Allah's Holiday (1) • Batman Chase (2) • **Batman Theme** (2) **35** • Batusi, The (2) • Donkey Serenade (1) • Eivol Ekdol, The Albanian Genius (2) • Evil Plot To Blow Up Batman (2) • Giannina Mia (1) • Holy Diploma, Batman - Straight A's! (2) • Indian Love Call (1) • Jervis (2) • Just A Simple Millionaire (2) • L'Amour-Toujours-L'Amour (Love Everlasting) (1) • Mafista, The (2) • Mr. Freeze (2) • My Fine Feathered Finks (2) • Only A Rose (1) • Rose Marie (1) • Sewer Lady (2) • Sympathy (1)

HEIGHTS, The — see TELEVISION SHOWS

HEINDORF, Ray/Matty Matlock
Longtime Warner Bros. studios musical director, Ray Heindorf, conducting the Warner Bros. Orchestra. Featuring clarinetist Matty Matlock's jazz band (Dick Cathcart, Moe Schneider, Eddie Miller, Ray Sherman, George Van Eps, Jud DeNaut and Nick Fatool) who all appeared in the film *Pete Kelly's Blues*.

9/3/55	9	6		Pete Kelly's Blues .... [I]	$15	Columbia 690

songs from the film; also see vocal recording by Peggy Lee & Ella Fitzgerald, and narrated recording by Jack Webb

Breezin' Along With The Breeze • Bye Bye, Blackbird • Hard-Hearted Hannah (The Vamp Of Savannah) • He Needs Me • I Never Knew • I'm Gonna Meet My Sweetie Now • Oh, Didn't He Ramble • Pete Kelly's Blues • Smiles • Somebody Loves Me • Sugar (That Sugar Baby O'Mine) • (What Can I Say) After I Say I'm Sorry?

HEINTJE
Male vocalist. Born on 8/12/56 in Bleijerheide, Holland. Name pronounced: Hine-hee.

12/5/70+	108	11		Mama	$10	MGM 4739

Happiest Day • I Would Like To Have A Little Fiddle • I'm Your Little Boy • In Grandma's Rocking Chair • Let The Sun Shine • Little Children, Little Sorrows • Mama • Mother's Tears • Only Memories Are Our Friends • Two Little Stars • When High From The Sky Gleaming Stars Look Down

HELIX
Heavy-metal quintet from Waterloo, Canada: vocalist Brian Vollmer, guitarists/vocalists Brent Doerner and Paul Hackman, drummer Greg Hinz and bassist Mike Uzelac (replaced by Daryl Gray in 1984). Doerner left in mid-1990. Hackman was killed in a car crash on 7/6/92.

10/22/83	186	4		**1** No Rest For The Wicked	$8	Capitol 12281
8/18/84	69	16		**2** Walkin' The Razor's Edge	$8	Capitol 12362
6/29/85	103	17		**3** Long Way To Heaven	$8	Capitol 12411
11/7/87	179	2		**4** Wild In The Streets	$8	Capitol 46920
8/18/90	179	6		**5** Back For Another Taste...	$12	Grudge 4521

Ain't No High Like Rock 'N Roll (1) • Animal House (2) • Back For Another Taste (5) • Bangin' Off-A-The Bricks (3) • Breakdown (2) • Check Out The Love (1) • Christine (2) • Deep Cuts The Knife (3) • Dirty Dog (1) • Does A Fool Ever Learn (1) • Don't Get Mad Get Even (1) • Don't Touch The Merchandise (3) • Dream On (4) • Feel The Fire (2) • Gimme Gimme Good Lovin' (2) • Give 'Em Hell (4) • Give It To You (5) • Good To The Last Drop (5) • Heavy Metal Cowboys (5) • Heavy Metal Love (1) • High Voltage Kicks (4) • House On Fire (3) • Kids Are All Shakin' (3) • Kiss It Goodbye (4) • Let's All Do It Tonight (1) • Long Way To Heaven (3) • Love Hungry Eyes (4) • (Make Me Do) Anything You Want (2) • Midnight Express (5) • My Kind Of Rock (2) • Never Gonna Stop The Rock (4) • Never Want To Lose You (1) • No Rest For The Wicked (1) • Ride The Rocket (3) • Rock You (2) • Rockin' Rollercoaster (5) • Running Wild In The 21st Century (5) • School Of Hard Knocks (3) • She's Too Tough (4) • Shot Full Of Love (4) • Six Strings, Nine Lives (4) • Storm, The (5) • That's Life (5) • What Ya Bringin' To The Party (4) • Wheels Of Thunder (5) • When The Hammer Falls (2) • White Lace And Black Leather (1) • Wild In The Streets (4) • Without You (Jasmine's Song) (3) • You Keep Me Rockin' (2) • Young & Wreckless (2)

DEBUT DATE	PEAK POS	WKS CHR	GOLD	ARTIST — Album Title	$	Label & Number

HELLO PEOPLE
White-faced, mime-rock quartet produced by Todd Rundgren.

11/30/74	145	13		The Handsome Devils	$8	Dunhill 50184

Cry Baby   Finger Poppin' Time   Greego   Just One Victory   Ripped Again   Take The Love In Your Body
Destiny   **Future Shock 71**   How High Is The Moon   Listen To Your Heart   Save A Dance For Me

HELLOWEEN
Heavy-metal quintet from Hamburg, Germany: Michael Kiske (vocals), Kai Hansen, Michael Weikath, Markus Grosskopf and Ingo Schwichtenberg.

7/4/87	104	21		1 Keeper Of The Seven Keys - Part I	$8	RCA 6399
10/29/88	108	16		2 Keeper Of The Seven Keys - Part II	$8	RCA 8529
4/22/89	123	7		3 I Want Out - Live ....[L]	$8	RCA 9709

recorded in the U.K. in November 1988

Dr. Stein (2,3)   Halloween (1)   I'm Alive (1)   Little Time (1,3)   Tale That Wasn't Right (1)
Eagle Fly Free (2)   Happy Helloween (medley) (3)   Initiation (1)   March Of Time (2)   Twilight Of The Gods (1)
Follow The Sign (1)   How Many Tears (3)   Invitation (2)   Rise And Fall (2)   We Got The Right (2,3)
Future World (1,3)   I Want Out (2,3)   Keeper Of The Seven Keys (2)   Save Us (2)   You Always Walk Alone (2)

HELM, Levon, & The RCO All-Stars
Drummer/vocalist of The Band. Born on 5/26/43 in Arkansas. Portrayed Loretta Lynn's father in the film *Coal Miner's Daughter*. The RCO All-Stars are Paul Butterfield, Steve Cropper, Duck Dunn, Mac "Dr. John" Rebennack and Booker T. Jones.

11/19/77	142	10		Levon Helm & The RCO All-Stars	$10	ABC 1017

Blues So Bad   Milk Cow Boogie   Rain Down Tears   Sing, Sing, Sing (Let's Make   That's My Home   Washer Woman
Havana Moon   Mood I Was In   A Better World)   Tie That Binds   You Got Me

HELMET
Rock band from New York led by vocalist/guitarist Page Hamilton. With Peter Mengede, Henry Bogdan and John Stanier.

8/22/92	68	25↑		Meantime	$12	Interscope 92162

Better   Give It   In The Meantime   Role Model   Unsung
FBLA II   He Feels Bad   Ironhead   Turned Out   You Borrowed

HENDERSON, Joe
R&B singer. Born in 1938 in Como, Mississippi and raised in Gary, Indiana. Moved to Nashville in 1958. With the Fairfield Four gospel group. Died in 1966.

10/13/62	93	5		Snap Your Fingers	$25	Todd 2701

After Loving You   **Big Love 74**   If You See Me Cry   Love Me   Sad Teardrops At Dawn   Three Steps
Baby Don't Leave Me   Cause We're In Love   Just Call Me   Right Now   **Snap Your Fingers 8**   You Can't Lose

HENDERSON, Michael
Born in 1951 in Yazoo City, Mississippi. Soul singer/bass player. To Detroit in the early '60s. Worked as session musician. Toured with Stevie Wonder and Aretha Franklin. Featured vocalist on Norman Connors' albums.

12/4/76+	173	7		1 Solid	$10	Buddah 5662
8/27/77	49	13		2 Goin' Places	$10	Buddah 5693
7/8/78	38	28	●	3 In The Night-Time	$10	Buddah 5712
8/4/79	64	12		4 Do It All	$8	Buddah 5719
8/30/80	35	18		5 Wide Receiver	$8	Buddah 6001
9/19/81	86	11		6 Slingshot	$8	Buddah 6002
6/4/83	169	5		7 Fickle	$8	Buddah 6004

Am I Special (3)   Feeling Like Myself Once   Love Will Find A Way (7)   Solid (1)   (We Are Here To) Geek You   You're My Choice (5)
Ask The Lonely (5)   Again (7)   Make It Easy On Yourself (6)   Stay With Me This Summer   Up (6)   **Yours Truly, Indiscreetly**
Assault With A Friendly   Fickle (7)   Make Me Feel Better (1)   (1)   We Can Go On (3)   (3) 3
  Weapon (7)   Goin' Places (2)   Make Me Feel Like (5)   Take Care (6)   What I'm Feeling (For You)
At The Concert (2)   Happy (3)   Never Gonna Give You Up (6)   **Take Me I'm Yours** (3) 88   (5)
Be My Girl (1)   I Can't Help It (2)   One Step At A Time (7)   There's No One Like You (5)   Whip It (2,7)
Can't We Fall In Love Again   I Don't Need Nobody Else (5)   One To One (3)   Thin Walls (7)   Whisper In My Ear (3)
  (6)   I'll Be Understanding (2)   Playing On The Real Thing   Time (1)   Wide Receiver (5)
Come To Me (6)   In It For The Goodies (6)   (4)   To Be Loved (4)   Won't You Be Mine (2)
Do It All (4)   In The Night-Time (3)   Prove It (5)   Treat Me Like A Man (1)   You Haven't Made It To The
Everybody Wants To Know   In The Summertime (4)   Reach Out For Me (5)   Valentine Love (1)   Top (1)
  Why (4)   Let Love Enter (1)   Riding (4)   Wait Until The Rain (4)   You Wouldn't Have To Work
   Let Me Love You (2)   Slingshot (6)   At All (7)

HENDERSON, Skitch
Born Lyle Henderson on 1/27/18 in Halstad, Minnesota. Conducted orchestra for *The Steve Allen Show* and Johnny Carson's *Tonight Show*, 1962-66.

10/9/65	103	8		Skitch...Tonight! ....[I]	$20	Columbia 9167

Bill's Blues   Come Thursday   Heart And Soul   Night-Lights   So What Else Is New?   Tootie Flutie
Cleopatra's Asp   Curacao   Night Life   See-Saw   30 Rockefeller Plaza   Try Again

★★64★★ HENDRIX, Jimi
Born on 11/27/42 in Seattle. Died of a drug overdose in London on 9/18/70. Legendary psychedelic-blues guitarist. Began career as a studio guitarist. In 1965 formed own band, Jimmy James & The Blue Flames. Created The Jimi Hendrix Experience in 1966 with Noel Redding on bass and Mitch Mitchell on drums. Formed new group in 1969, Band of Gypsys, with Buddy Miles on drums and Billy Cox on bass.

8/26/67+	5	106	▲²	1 Are You Experienced? *	$50	Reprise 6261
12/30/67+	75	12		2 Get That Feeling ....[E]	$15	Capitol 2856
				Jimi plays guitar; backing vocalist: Curtis Knight (1964)		
2/10/68	3	53	▲	3 Axis: Bold As Love *	$20	Reprise 6281
10/19/68	1²	37	▲	4 Electric Ladyland *	$15	Reprise 6307 [2]
8/2/69	6	35	▲²	5 Smash Hits * ....[G]	$30	Reprise 2025
5/2/70	5	61	▲	6 Band Of Gypsys ....[L]	$12	Capitol 472

with Buddy Miles (drums) and Billy Cox (bass); recorded New Year's Eve in 1969 at New York's Fillmore East

DEBUT DATE	PEAK POS	WKS CHR	GOLD	ARTIST — Album Title	$	Label & Number

HENDRIX, Jimi — Cont'd

DEBUT DATE	PEAK POS	WKS CHR	GOLD	ARTIST — Album Title	$	Label & Number
9/19/70	**16**	20	●	7 Monterey International Pop Festival ....[S-L]	**$10**	Reprise 2029

OTIS REDDING/THE JIMI HENDRIX EXPERIENCE
recorded June 1967 and featured in the film *Monterey Pop*; side 1: songs performed by The Jimi Hendrix Experience; side 2: songs performed by Otis Redding

3/6/71	**3**	39	●	8 **The Cry Of Love**	**$10**	Reprise 2034

Jimi's last self-authorized album

3/20/71	**127**	4		9 Two Great Experiences Together! ....[E-I]	**$25**	Maple 6004

JIMI HENDRIX and LONNIE YOUNGBLOOD
Hendrix was a saxophonist in Youngblood's band in 1965

10/9/71	**15**	21	●	10 Rainbow Bridge ....[S]	**$15**	Reprise 2040

recordings from 1968-70

3/4/72	**12**	19	●	11 Hendrix In The West ....[K-L]	**$15**	Reprise 2049
9/2/72	**82**	11		12 Rare Hendrix	**$10**	Trip 9500

recorded on 6/10/66 with Lonnie Youngblood

12/9/72+	**48**	18		13 War Heroes ....[K]	**$10**	Reprise 2103
7/14/73	**89**	18		14 sound track recordings from the film Jimi Hendrix ....[S-L]	**$15**	Reprise 6481 [2]

featuring interviews from the documentary soundtrack

3/22/75	**5**	20	●	15 **Crash Landing** ....[K]	**$10**	Reprise 2204
11/29/75	**43**	11		16 Midnight Lightning ....[K]	**$10**	Reprise 2229
8/12/78	**114**	15		17 The Essential Jimi Hendrix ....[K]	**$12**	Reprise 2245 [2]
8/18/79	**156**	7		18 The Essential Jimi Hendrix, Volume Two ....[K]	**$50**	Reprise 2293
4/26/80	**127**	7		19 Nine To The Universe ....[I-K]	**$8**	Reprise 2299

jam sessions while working on his last album (1969)

9/25/82	**79**	8		20 The Jimi Hendrix Concerts ....[K-L]	**$10**	Reprise 22306 [2]
11/17/84	**148**	5		21 Kiss The Sky ....[K]	**$8**	Reprise 25119

recordings from 1967-69

3/8/86	**192**	3		22 Jimi Plays Monterey ....[S-L]	**$8**	Reprise 25358

Jimi's complete show at the Monterey Pop Festival on 6/18/67

12/3/88+	**119**	17		23 Radio One * ....[K]	**$10**	Rykodisc 0078 [2]

3-sided album compiled from 5 sessions broadcast on BBC Radio in 1967

*THE JIMI HENDRIX EXPERIENCE

1/5/91	**174**	5		24 Lifelines/The Jimi Hendrix Story ....[K]	**$32**	Reprise 26435 [4]

alternate takes, home demos, rare live performances and narration; 4th CD is the Jimi Hendrix Experience's 4/26/69 concert at the L.A. Forum

Ain't No Telling (3)
All Along The Watchtower (4,5,17,21,24) **20**
All I Want (9)
...And The Gods Made Love (4)
Angel (8,24)
Are You Experienced? (1,17,20,21)
Astro Man (8)
Beginning (13)
Beginnings (16)
Belly Button Window (8)
Bleeding Heart (13)
Bleeding Heart (Blues In C Sharp) (20)
Blue Suede Shoes (11,16)
Bold As Love (3,17,24)
Bring My Baby Back (12)
Burning Of The Midnight Lamp (4,17,23,24)
Can You See Me (5,7,22)
Captain Coconut (15)
Castles Made of Sand (3,17,21)
Catfish Blues (23)
Changes (15)
Cherokee Mist (24)
Come Down Hard On Me (15)
Come On (Part 1) (4,24)
Crash Landing (15)

Crosstown Traffic (4,5,18,21) **52**
Day Tripper (23)
Dolly Dagger (10,17,24) **74**
Drifter's Escape (24)
Drifting (8,17)
Drivin' South (23,24)
Drone Blues (19)
EXP (3)
Earth Blues (10)
Easy Blues (19)
Ezy Ryder (8,17)
Fire (1,5,18,20,23)
Foxey Lady (1,5,18,22,23,24) **67**
Freedom (8,17) **59**
Get That Feeling (2)
Go Go Shoes, Part 1 & 2 (12)
Good Feeling (12)
Good Times (12)
Goodbye (Bessie Mae) (9)
Gotta Have A New Dress (2)
Gypsy Boy (New Rising Sun) (16)
Gypsy Eyes (4,17)
Have You Ever Been (To Electric Ladyland) (4,17)
Hear My Train A Comin' (10,14,16,20,23)
Hey Baby (New Rising Sun) (10)

Hey Joe (1,5,14,18,20,22,23,24)
Highway Chile (13)
Hoochie Koochie Man (23,24)
Hot Trigger (12)
Hound Dog (12)
House Burning Down (4,17)
How Would You Feel (2)
Hush Now (2)
I Don't Live Today (1,18,20,21,24)
I'm A Man (24)
If 6 Was 9 (3,17)
In From The Storm (8,14)
Izabella (13,17)
Jimi/Jimmy Jam (19)
Johnny B. Goode (11,14)
Killing Floor (23)
Lawdy Miss Clawdy (24)
Like A Rolling Stone (7,14,22,24)
Little Miss Lover (3,17)
Little Miss Strange (4)
Little Wing (3,11,17,20,24)
Long Hot Summer Night (4)
Look Over Yonder (10,24)
Love Or Confusion (1,23)
Lover Man (11)
Machine Gun (6,14,16,18,24)
Manic Depression (1,5,24)
May This Be Love (1)

Message To Love (6,15)
Midnight (13)
Midnight Lightning (16)
Mister Bad Luck (medley) (24)
Moon, Turn The Tides...Gently Gently Away (4)
My Friend (8)
Night Bird Flying (8,24)
Nine To The Universe (19)
1983...(A Merman I Should Turn To Be) (4,24)
No Business (2)
Once I Had A Woman (16)
One Rainy Wish (3,24)
Pali Gap (10)
Peace In Mississippi (15)
Peter Gunn (13)
Power Of Soul (6)
Psycho (9)
Purple Haze (1,5,14,17,21,22,23,24) **65**
Queen, The (11)
Radio One Theme (23)
Rainy Day, Dream Away (4)
Rainy Day Shuffle (24)
Red House (5,11,14,20,21,24)
Remember (5)
Rock Me, Baby (7,14,22,24)

Room Full Of Mirrors (10,17,24)
Send My Love To Linda (24)
Sergeant Pepper's Lonely Hearts Club Band (11)
She's So Fine (3)
Simon Says (2)
Somewhere Over The Rainbow (15)
South Saturn Delta (24)
Spanish Castle Magic (3,23,24)
Star Spangled Banner (10,14,18,24)
Stepping Stone (13,17,21)
Still Raining, Still Dreaming (4,17)
Stone Free (5,20,23)
Stone Free Again (15)
Straight Ahead (8)
Strange Things (2)
Sunshine Of Your Love (medley) (7)
Suspicious (12)
Sweat Segway II & III (9)
Table II & III (9)
Tax Free (13,24)
Testify (24)
Things That I Used To Do (24)

Third Stone From The Sun (1,17,21,24)
3 Little Bears (13)
Trash Man (16)
Two In One Goes (9)
Under The Table (9)
Up From The Skies (3) **82**
Valley Of Neptune (24)
Voice In The Wind (12)
Voodoo Chile (4,11,24)
Voodoo Chile (Slight Return) (4,17,20,21,24)
Wait Until Tomorrow (3,24)
We Gotta Live Together (6)
Welcome Home (2)
Who Knows (6)
Wild Thing (7,14,18,20,22)
Wind Cries Mary (1,5,18,22,24)
Wipe The Sweat (9)
With The Power (15)
You Got Me Floatin' (3)
Young/Hendrix (19)

HENDRYX, Nona

Born on 8/18/45 in Trenton, New Jersey. Member of Patti LaBelle & The Blue-Belles from 1961-77.

DEBUT DATE	PEAK POS	WKS CHR	GOLD	ARTIST — Album Title	$	Label & Number
4/23/83	**83**	19		1 Nona	**$8**	RCA 4565
5/5/84	**167**	7		2 The Art of Defense	**$8**	RCA 4999
5/23/87	**96**	13		3 Female Trouble	**$8**	EMI America 17248

B-Boys (1)
Baby Go-Go (3)
Big Fun (3)
Design For Living (1)
Drive Me Wild (3)
Dummy Up (1)

Electricity (2)
Female Trouble (3)
Ghost Love (2)
I Know What You Need (Pygmy's Confession) (3)

I Sweat (Going Through The Motions) (2)
I Want You (2)
Keep It Confidential (1) **91**
Life, The (2)
Living On The Border (1)

Rhythm Of Change (3)
Run For Cover (1)
Soft Targets (2)
Steady Action (1)
To The Bone (2)
Too Hot To Handle (3)

Transformation (1)
Why Should I Cry? (3) **58**
Winds Of Change (Mandela To Mandela) (3)

HENLEY, Don

Born on 7/22/47 in Gilmer, Texas. Singer/songwriter/drummer. Own band, Shiloh, in the early '70s. Worked with Glenn Frey in Linda Ronstadt's backup band, then the two formed the Eagles with Randy Meisner and Bernie Leadon. Went solo in 1982.

DEBUT DATE	PEAK POS	WKS CHR	GOLD	ARTIST — Album Title	$	Label & Number
9/4/82	**24**	35	●	1 I Can't Stand Still	**$8**	Asylum 60048
12/15/84+	**13**	63	▲²	2 Building The Perfect Beast	**$8**	Geffen 24026

CD and cassette include bonus cut

DEBUT DATE	PEAK POS	WKS CHR	GOLD	ARTIST — Album Title	$	Label & Number

7/15/89 — **8** — 148 — ▲³ — **3 The End Of The Innocence** .... **$8** — Geffen 24217

All She Wants To Do Is Dance (2) **9**	End Of The Innocence (3) **8**	Johnny Can't Read (1) **42**	Man With A Mission (2)	Them And Us (1)
Boys Of Summer (2) **5**	Gimme What You Got (3)	La Eile (1)	New York Minute (3) **48**	Unclouded Day (1)
Building The Perfect Beast (2)	Heart Of The Matter (3) **21**	Land Of The Living (2)	Nobody's Business (1)	You Better Hang Up (1)
Dirty Laundry (1) **3**	How Bad Do You Want It? (3) **48**	Last Worthless Evening (3) **21**	Not Enough Love In The World (2) **34**	You Can't Make Love (2)
Drivin' With Your Eyes Closed (2)	I Can't Stand Still (1) **48**	Lilah (1)	Shangri-La (3)	You're Not Drinking Enough (2)
	I Will Not Go Quietly (3)	Little Tin God (3)	**Sunset Grill** (2) **22**	
	If Dirt Were Dollars (3)	Long Way Home (1)	Talking To The Moon (1)	

HENSEL, Carol — see AEROBICS section

HENSLEY, Ken
Keyboardist with Uriah Heep. Born on 8/24/45 in England.

4/7/73 — **173** — 7 — **Proud Words On A Dusty Shelf** .... **$10** — Mercury 661

Black-Hearted Lady	Fortune	Go Down	Last Time	Rain
Cold Autumn Sunday	From Time To Time	King Without A Throne	Proud Words	When Evening Comes

HERMAN, Woody
Born Woodrow Charles Herman on 5/16/13 in Milwaukee. Saxophonist/clarinetist of dance bands beginning in 1929. Formed own band in 1936. Won the Lifetime Achievement Grammy in 1987. Died on 10/29/87 of cardiac arrest. One of the most innovative and contemporary of all big-band leaders.

2/19/55 — **11** — 2 — **1 The 3 Herds** ....[K-I] **$25** — Columbia 592
recordings from 1945-54

8/17/03 — **136** — 4 — **2 Encore: Woody Herman - 1963** ....[I-L] **$15** — Philips 092

3/21/64 — **148** — 2 — **3 Woody Herman: 1964** ....[I] **$15** — Philips 118

After You've Gone (3)	Cousins (3)	Four Brothers (1)	Jazz Hoot (3)	Non-Alcoholic (1)	That's Where It Is (2)
Better Get It In Your Soul (2)	Days Of Wine And Roses (2)	Four Others (1)	Jazz Me Blues (2)	Satin Doll (3)	Third Herd (1)
Blame Boehm (1)	Deep Purple (3)	Good Earth (1)	Keen And Peachy (1)	Sidewalks Of Cuba (1)	Watermelon Man (2)
Body And Soul (2)	Early Autumn (1)	Goof And I (1)	Mulligan Tawny (1)	Strut, The (3)	
Caldonia (1,2)	El Toro Grande (1)	Hallelujah Time (3)	My Wish (3)	Taste Of Honey (3)	

★★252★★ HERMAN'S HERMITS
Formed in Manchester, England in 1964. Name derived from cartoon character Sherman of TV's *The Bullwinkle Show.* Consisted of Peter "Herman" Noone (b: 11/5/47; vocals), Derek Leckenby and Keith Hopwood (guitars), Karl Green (bass) and Barry Whitwam (drums). First called The Heartbeats. Noone left in 1972 for a solo career; formed Los Angeles-based group The Tremblers in late '70s. Hosts own show on music video TV channel VH-1.

2/20/65 — **2⁴** — 40 — ● — **1 Introducing Herman's Hermits** .... **$15** — MGM 4282

6/19/65 — **2⁶** — 39 — ● — **2 Herman's Hermits On Tour** .... **$15** — MGM 4295

11/20/65 — **5** — 105 — ● — **3 The Best Of Herman's Hermits** ....[G] **$15** — MGM 4315

3/26/66 — **14** — 26 — **4 Hold On!** ....[S] **$15** — MGM 4342

8/20/66 — **48** — 21 — **5 Both Sides Of Herman's Hermits** .... **$15** — MGM 4386

12/3/66+ — **20** — 32 — **6 The Best Of Herman's Hermits, Volume 2** ......[G] **$15** — MGM 4416

3/18/67 — **13** — 35 — ● — **7 There's A Kind Of Hush All Over The World** .... **$15** — MGM 4438

10/7/67 — **75** — 9 — **8 Blaze** .... **$12** — MGM 4478

1/13/68 — **102** — 8 — **9 The Best Of Herman's Hermits, Volume III** ......[G] **$12** — MGM 4505

9/28/68 — **182** — 3 — **10 Mrs. Brown, You've Got A Lovely Daughter** ......[S] **$12** — MGM 4548
group stars in the film and in #4 above

Ace, King, Queen, Jack (8)	Gas Light Street (3)	If You're Goin' What I'm Thinkin' (7)	Man With The Cigar (5)	Rattler (7)	What Is Wrong What Is Right (9)
Big Man (9)	George And Dragon (4)		Moonshine Man (8,9)	Saturday's Child (7)	Where Were You When I
Bus Stop (5,6)	Got A Feeling (4)	It's Nice To Be Out In The Morning (10)	Most Beautiful Thing In My Life (10)	Sea Cruise (1,3)	Needed You (4)
Busy Line (8)	Gotta Get Away (4)			Show Me Girl (1)	Wild Love (4)
Can't You Hear My Heartbeat (3)	Green Street Green (8)	Jezebel (7)	Mother-In-Law (1,3)	**Silhouettes** (2,3) **5**	Wings Of Love (9)
	Hold On! (4,6)	**Just A Little Bit Better** (3) **7**	**Mrs. Brown You've Got A Lovely Daughter** (1,3,8) **1**	Story Of My Life (10)	World Is For The Young (10)
Dandy (6,7) **5**	I Call Out Her Name (8)	Kansas City Loving (1)		Take Love, Give Love (6)	**Wonderful World** (3) **4**
Daisy Chain (Part I & II) (10)	I Gotta Dream On (2,3)	L'Autre Jour (5)	Mum And Dad (9)	Tell Me Baby (2)	You Won't Be Leaving (7)
Dial My Number (5)	I Know Why (1)	Last Bus Home (8,9)	**Museum** (8,9) **39**	**There's A Kind Of Hush** (7,9,10) **4**	Your Hand In Mine (1)
Don't Go Out Into The Rain (You're Going To Melt) (8,9) **18**	I Understand (Just How You Feel) (1)	**Leaning On The Lamp Post** (4,6) **9**	**Must To Avoid** (4,6) **8**	Things I Do For You Baby (4)	
	I Wonder (1)	Lemon And Lime (10)	My Old Dutch (5)	Thinking Of You (1)	
Don't Try To Hurt Me (2)	I'll Never Dance Again (2)	**Listen People** (6) **3**	My Reservation's Been Confirmed (5)	**This Door Swings Both Ways** (5,6) **12**	
East West (7,9) **27**	**I'm Henry VIII, I Am** (2,3) **1**	Little Boy Sad (6)	**No Milk Today** (7,9) **35**	Traveling Light (2)	
End Of The World (2,3)	**I'm Into Something Good** (1,3) **13**	Little Miss Sorrow Child Of Tomorrow (7)	Oh Mr. Porter (5)	Two Lovely Black Eyes (5)	
For Love (5)			One Little Packet Of Cigarettes (8)	Upstairs, Downstairs (8)	
For Your Love (2,6)		Make Me Happy (4)	Ooh, She's Done It Again (10)	Walkin' With My Angel (1)	
Future Mrs. 'Awkins (5)					

HERNANDEZ, Patrick
Rock-disco singer. Born in 1949 in Paris of a Spanish father and Austrian/Italian mother.

7/28/79 — **61** — 15 — **Born To Be Alive** .... **$10** — Columbia 36100

Born To Be Alive **16**	Disco Queen	I Give You Rendezvous	It Comes So Easy	Show Me The Way You Kiss	You Turn Me On

HESITATIONS, The
Soul group from Cleveland. Lead singer George "King" Scott was accidentally killed by a bullet from a gun owned by tenor Fred Deal in February 1968.

2/24/68 — **193** — 3 — **The new Born Free** .... **$15** — Kapp 3548

Born Free **38**	I Believe In Love	I've Gotta Find Her	Love Is Everywhere	Push A Little Bit Harder	We Only Have One Life
Don't Go	I Wish It Could Be Me	Let's Groove	Overworked And Underpaid	We Can Do It	Without Your Love

HEWETT, Howard
Lead vocalist of Shalamar, 1979-85. Born and raised in Akron, Ohio. Married singer/actress Nia Peeples in 1989.

11/1/86+ — **159** — 16 — **1 I Commit To Love** .... **$8** — Elektra 60487

4/16/88 — **110** — 12 — **2 Forever and Ever** .... **$8** — Elektra 60779

4/14/90 — **54** — 21 — **3 Howard Hewett** .... **$12** — Elektra 60904

DEBUT DATE	PEAK POS	WKS CHR	GOLD	ARTIST — Album Title	$	Label & Number

HEWETT, Howard — Cont'd

Challenge (2)
Don't Give In (3)
Eye On You (1)
Forever And Ever (2)
Good-bye Good Friend (2)
I Commit To Love (1)
I Do (3)

I Got 2 Go (1)
I Know You'll Be Comin' Back (3)
I'm For Real (1) 90
If I Could Only Have That Day Back (3)
In A Crazy Way (1)

Jesus (3)
Last Forever (1)
Let Me Show You How To Fall In Love (3)
Let's Get Deeper (3)
Let's Try It All Over Again (1)
Love Don't Wanna Wait (1)

More I Get (The More I Want) (3)
Natural Love (2)
Once, Twice, Three Times (2)
Say Amen (1)
Shadow (3)
Shakin' My Emotion (2)

Share A Love (2)
Show Me (3) 62
Stay (1)
Strange Relationship (2)
This Time (2)
When Will It Be (3)
You'll Find Another Man (2)

HEYWARD, Nick
British, founded and fronted the group Haircut One Hundred in 1981. Group disbanded in 1983.

1/14/84	178	4		North of a Miracle..	$8	Arista 8106

Atlantic Monday
Blue Hat For A Blue Day

Club Boy At Sea
Day It Rained Forever

Kick Of Love
On A Sunday

Take That Situation
Two Make It True

When It Started To Begin
Whistle Down The Wind

HEYWOOD, Eddie
Born on 12/4/15 in Atlanta; died on 1/2/89. Black jazz pianist/composer/arranger. Played professionally by age 14. Own band in New York City in 1941. Worked with Billie Holiday. To the West Coast in 1947, with own trio. Active into the '70s.

5/25/59	16	4		Canadian Sunset...[I]	$12	RCA 1529

title song written by Eddie, not the same version as with Hugo Winterhalter in 1956

All About You
Blues In A Happy Mood

Canadian Sunset
Dearest Darling

Heywood's Beguine
I'm Saving Myself For You

Lies
Now You're Mine

Rain
Rendezvous For Two

Subway Serenade
Time To Go Home

HEYWOODS — see DONALDSON, Bo

HIATT, John
Singer/songwriter born and raised in Indiana. To Los Angeles in 1979. Co-founder of Little Village.

7/4/87	107	17	1	Bring The Family..	$8	A&M 5158

with Ry Cooder (guitar), Nick Lowe (bass) and Jim Keltner (drums) — this lineup went on to record as Little Village in 1992

9/24/88	98	31	2	Slow Turning..	$8	A&M 5206

with guests Bernie Leadon (Eagles) & Dennis Locorriere (Dr. Hook)

7/7/90	61	19	3	Stolen Moments...	$12	A&M 5310

with guests Michael Henderson and Russ Taff

Alone In The Dark (1)
Back Of My Mind (3)
Bring Back Your Love To Me (3)
Child Of The Wild Blue Yonder (3)
Drive South (2)
Feels Like Rain (2)

Georgia Rae (2)
Have A Little Faith In Me (1)
Icy Blue Heart (2)
Is Anybody There? (2)
It'll Come To You (2)
Learning How To Love You (1)
Lipstick Sunset (2)

Listening To Old Voices (3)
Memphis In The Meantime (1)
One Kiss (3)
Paper Thin (2)
Real Fine Love (3)
Rest Of The Dream (3)
Ride Along (2)

Rock Back Billy (3)
Seven Little Indians (3)
Slow Turning (1)
Sometime Other Than Now (2)
Stolen Moments (3)
Stood Up (1)
Tennessee Plates (2)

Thank You Girl (1)
Thing Called Love (1)
Thirty Years Of Tears (3)
Through Your Hands (3)
Tip Of My Tongue (1)
Trudy And Dave (2)
Your Dad Did (1)

HIBBLER, Al
Born on 8/16/15 in Little Rock, Arkansas. Blind since birth, studied voice at Little Rock's Conservatory for the Blind. First recorded with Jay McShann for Decca in 1942. With Duke Ellington, 1943-51. Also recorded with Harry Carney, Tab Smith, Mercer Ellington and Billy Strayhorn.

8/4/56	20	2		Starring Al Hibbler..	$20	Decca 8328

After The Lights Go Down Low 10

Count Every Star
I Don't Stand A Ghost Of A Chance With You

Night And Day
Pennies From Heaven
September In The Rain

Shanghai Lil
Stella By Starlight
There Are Such Things

Where Are You
Where Or When
You'll Never Know

HI-C Featuring Tony A
California-raised, Louisiana-born rapper. Backed by Wilmington, California native DJ Tony A.

1/25/92	152	12		Skanless..	$12	Skanless 61235

Bullshit
Compton Hoochies
Ding-a-ling

Froggy Style
Funky Rap Sanga
I'm Not Your Puppet 63

Jack Move
Leave My Curl Alone
Punk Shit

Request Line
Sitting In The Park
2 Drunk Ta F__k

Too Greasy
2 Skanless
2 Ada Time

Yo Dick

HICKS, Dan, & His Hot Licks
California jazzy jug-band group.

10/2/71	195	8	1	Where's The Money?...[L]	$10	Blue Thumb 29
5/20/72	170	5	2	Striking It Rich!..	$10	Blue Thumb 36
6/9/73	67	18	3	Last Train To Hicksville...the home of happy feet...............	$10	Blue Thumb 51
3/25/78	165	3	4	It Happened One Bite	$8	Warner 3158

DAN HICKS

Boogaloo Jones (4)
Boogaloo Plays Guitar (4)
Buzzard Was Their Friend (1)
By Hook Or By Crook (1)
Canned Music (2)
Caught In The Rain (1)
Cheaters Don't Win (3)
Cloud My Sunny Mood (4)
Coast To Coast (1)

Collared Blues (4)
Cowboy's Dream No. 19 (3)
Crazy - 'Cause He Is (4)
Cruizin' (4)
Dig A Little Deeper (3)
Dizzy Dogs (4)
Euphonius Whale (3)
Flight Of The Fly (2)
Fujiyama (2)

Garden In The Rain (4)
I Asked My Doctor (3)
I Feel Like Singing (1)
I Scare Myself (2)
I'm An Old Cowhand (From The Rio Grand) (2)
Is This My Happy Home? (1)
It's Not My Time To Go (3)
Laughing Song (2)

Lonely Madman (3)
'Long Come A Viper (3)
Lovers For Life (4)
Mama, I'm An Outlaw (4)
Moody Richard (The Innocent Bystander) (2)
My Old Timey Baby (3)
News From Up The Street (1)
O'Reilly At The Bar (2)

Payday Blues (3)
Philly Rag (2)
Presently In The Past (3)
Reelin' Down (1)
Reveille Revisited (4)
Shorty Falls In Love (1)
Skippy's Farewell (2)
Success (3)
Sure Beats Me (3)

Sweetheart (3)
Traffic Jam (1)
Vinnie's Lookin' Good (4)
Vivando (3)
Waitin' (4)
Walkin' One And Only (2)
Where's The Money? (1)
Woe, The Luck (2)
You Got To Believe (2)

HI-FIVE
R&B teen vocal quintet from Waco, Texas and Oklahoma City: Tony Thompson, Roderick Clark, Russell Neal, Marcus Sanders and Toriano Easley (left after release of first album, replaced by Treston Irby).

12/8/90+	38	45	●	1	Hi-Five...	$12	Jive 1328
8/29/92	82	24↑		2	Keep It Goin' On	$12	Jive 41474

Fly Away (2)
I Can't Wait Another Minute (1) 8
I Just Can't Handle It (1)

I Like The Way (The Kissing Game) (1) 1
Just Another Girlfriend (1) 88

Know Love (1)
Let's Get It Started (Keep It Goin' On) (2)
Little Bit Older Now (2)

Mary, Mary (2)
Merry-Go-Round (1)
Quality Time (2) 38
Rag Doll (1)

She Said (2)
She's Playing Hard To Get (2) 5
Sweetheart (1)

Too Young (1)
Video Girl (2)
Way You Said Goodbye (1)
Whenever You Say (2)

DEBUT DATE	PEAK POS	WKS CHR	G O L D	ARTIST — Album Title	$	Label & Number

HIGGINS, Bertie
Singer/songwriter. Born in 1946 in Tarpon Springs, Florida. First recorded for ABC in 1964. Worked as a drummer with the Roemans from 1964-66.

| 2/27/82 | 38 | 25 | | Just Another Day In Paradise .... | $8 | Kat Family 37901 |

Candle Dancer · Down At The Blue Moon · **Just Another Day In** · Key Largo 8 · She's Gone To Live On The · Tropics, The
Casablanca · Heart Is The Hunter · **Paradise 46** · Port O Call (Savannah '55) · Mountain · White Line Fever

HIGH INERGY
Female soul group from Pasadena, California: sisters Barbara and Vernessa Mitchell, Linda Howard and Michelle Rumph. Vernessa left in 1978; group continued as a trio.

11/5/77+	28	25		1 Turnin' On	$8	Gordy 978
7/22/78	42	13		2 Steppin' Out	$8	Gordy 982
5/26/79	147	5		3 Shoulda Gone Dancin'.............................	$8	Gordy 987

Ain't No Love Left (In My · Everytime I See You I Go · Let Me Get Close To You (1) · Peaceland (2) · Too Late (The Damage Is · You Captured My Heart (2)
Heart For You) (1) · Wild (2) · Let Yourself Go (3) · Save It For A Rainy Day (1) · Done) (3)
Beware (2) · Fly Little Blackbird (2) · **Love Is All You Need** (1) 89 · Searchin' (I've Got To Find · We Are The Future (2)
Come And Get It (3) · Hi! (2) · Love Of My Life (3) · My Love) (1) · **You Can't Turn Me Off (In**
Could This Be Love (1) · High School (1) · Lovin' Fever (3) · Shoulda Gone Dancin' (3) · **The Middle Of Turning**
Didn't Wanna Tell You (2) · I've Got What You Need (3) · Midnight Music Man (3) · Some Kinda Magic (1) · **Me On)** (1) 12

HIGHWAYMEN, The
Folk quintet formed at Wesleyan University in Middletown, Connecticut: Dave Fisher, Bob Burnett, Steve Trott, Steve Butts and Chan Daniels (d: 8/2/75).

10/9/61	42	22		1 The Highwaymen	$20	United Art. 3125
3/24/62	99	14		2 Standing Room Only!	$20	United Art. 6168
9/7/63	79	9		3 Hootenanny with The Highwaymen ....[L]	$20	United Art. 6294

A La Claire Fontaine (1) · Chanson De Chagrin (3) · Johnny With The Bandy · Passing Through (3) · Shaggy Dog Songs (3) · You're Always Welcome At
Ah Si Mon Moina (1) · Cotton Fields (2,3) 13 · Legs (2) · Pollerita (3) · Sinner Man (1) · Our House (medley) (3)
Au Claire De La Lune (1) · Great Silkie (2) · La Cansone Del Vino (3) · Raise A Ruckus Tonight (3) · Take This Hammer (1)
Big Rock Candy Mountain (1) · Greenland Fisheries (1) · **Michael** (1,3) 1 · Rise Up Shepherd (3) · Tale Of Michael Flynn (3)
Black Eyed Suzie (2) · Gypsy Rover (2) 42 · Mister Noah (3) · Roll On, Columbia, Roll On · Three Jolly Rogues (2)
Calton Weaver (2) · Irish Work Song (Pat Works · Nostalgias Tucumanas (2) · (3) · Turtle Dove (3)
Can Ye Sew Cushions? (3) · On The Railway) (1) · Old Maid's Song (1) · Run Come See Jerusalem (2) · Wildwood Flower (2)
Carni Valito (1) · · One For The Money (3) · Santiano (1)

HILL, Dan
Born on 6/3/54 in Toronto. Author/singer/songwriter.

12/6/75+	104	17		1 Dan Hill	$10	20th Century 500
12/10/77+	21	24	●	2 Longer Fuse	$8	20th Century 547
1/21/78	79	14		3 Hold On	$8	20th Century 526
9/23/78	118	6		4 Frozen In The Night	$8	20th Century 558
8/8/87	90	19		5 Dan Hill	$8	Columbia 40456

All Alone In California (3) · Every Boys Fantasy (5) · Indian Woman (4) · No One Taught Me How To · **Sometimes When We** · You Are All I See (2)
All I See Is Your Face (4) 41 · Fountain (1) · Jean (2) · Lie (4) · **Touch** (2) 3 · You Make Me Want To Be (1)
Blood In My Veins (5) · 14 Today (2) · **Let The Song Last Forever** · Nobody's Right (1) · Sour Whiskey (1) · You Say You're Free (1)
Can't We Try (5) 6 · Friends (4) · (4) 91 · People (1) · Southern California (2) · Your Only Friend (4)
Canada (3) · Frozen In The Night (4) · Longer Fuse (2) · Perfect Love (5) · Still Not Used To (3)
Carmelia (5) · **Growin' Up** (1) 67 · Looking Back (1) · Phonecall (3) · Till The Day I Die (4)
Caroline (5) · Hold On (3) · Lose Control (5) · Pleasure Centre (5) · USA/USSR (5)
City Madness (3) · I Dreamt I Saw Your Face · McCarthy's Day (2) · Proposal (3) · Welcome (1)
Conscience (5) · Last Night (1) · **Never Thought (That I** · Question Marks In Time (3) · When The Hurt Comes (4)
Crazy (5) · I've Been Alone (3) · **Could Love)** (5) 43 · Rain (3) · (Why Did You Have To Go
Dark Side Of Atlanta (4) · In The Name Of Love (2) · · Seed Of Music (1) · And) Pick On Me (4)

HILL, Z.Z.
Born Arzel Hill on 9/30/35 in Naples, Texas. Blues vocalist. First recorded for M.H. in 1963. Formed own Hill Records in 1970. Died of a heart attack on 4/27/84.

| 1/22/72 | 194 | 2 | | 1 The Brand New Z.Z. Hill .... | $10 | Mankind 201 |

side 1 is a mini opera *Blues At The Opera*

| 2/5/83 | 165 | 5 | | 2 The Rhythm & The Blues .... | $8 | Malaco 7411 |
| 1/7/84 | 170 | 9 | | 3 I'm A Blues Man .... | $8 | Malaco 7415 |

Been So Long (3) · Chokin' Kind (1) · I Ain't Buying What You're · Outside Thang (2) · That Fire Is Hot (2) · You're Gonna Be A Woman
Blind Side (3) · Early In The Morning (1) · Selling (3) · Please Don't Let Our Good · Three Into Two Won't Go (3) · (2)
Blues At The Opera · Get A Little, Give A Little (3) · I Think I'd Do It (1) · Thing End (3) · Wang Dang Doodle (2)
(Communication In Regard · Get You Some Business (2) · I'm A Blues Man (3) · Shade Tree Mechanic (3) · What Am I Gonna Tell Her
To Circumstances) Medley · Help Me, I'm In Need (2) · Man Needs A Woman (A · Someone Else Is Steppin' In · (2)
(1) · Hold Back (One Man At A · Woman Needs A Man) (1) · (2) · Who You Been Giving It To
Cheatin' Love (3) · Time) (1) · Open House At My House (2) · Steal Away (3) · (2)

HILLAGE, Steve
British guitarist.

| 1/15/77 | 130 | 9 | | L .... | $8 | Atlantic 18205 |

produced by Todd Rundgren and featuring his group Utopia

Electrick Gypsies · Hurdy Gurdy Glissando · Hurdy Gurdy Man · It's All Too Much · Lunar Musick Suite · Om Nama Shivaya

HILLMAN, Chris
Born on 12/4/44 in San Diego County, California. Member of The Byrds from 1964-68. Formed the Flying Burrito Brothers with Gram Parsons in 1968. Went solo in 1972. Married Connie Pappas, Elton John's former manager and head of his Rocket Records. Formed country group the Desert Rose Band in 1986. Also see McGuinn, Clark & Hillman.

| 6/19/76 | 152 | 6 | | 1 Slippin' Away .... | $10 | Asylum 1062 |
| 9/17/77 | 188 | 3 | | 2 Clear Sailin' .... | $8 | Asylum 1104 |

Ain't That Peculiar (2) · Fallen Favorite (2) · Love Is The Sweetest · Nothing Gets Through (2) · Slippin' Away (1) · Witching Hour (1)
Blue Morning (1) · Falling Again (1) · Amnesty (1) · Playing The Fool (2) · Step On Out (1)
Clear Sailin' (2) · Heartbreaker (2) · Lucky In Love (2) · Quits (2) · Take It On The Run (1)
Down In The Churchyard (1) · Hot Dusty Roads (2) · Midnight Again (1) · Rollin' And Tumblin' (2) · (Take It In Your) Lifeboat (1)

DEBUT DATE	PEAK POS	WKS CHR	GOLD	ARTIST — Album Title	$	Label & Number

HILLSIDE SINGERS, The
Nine-member vocal group assembled by producer/arranger Al Ham.

| 1/8/72 | 71 | 16 | | I'd Like To Teach The World To Sing .... | $12 | Metromedia 1051 |

Amen
Day By Day

I'd Like To Teach The World To Sing (In Perfect Harmony) 13	Night They Drove Old Dixie Down	One Man's Hands	Tomorrow Belongs To Me
Last Night I Had The Strangest Dream	Old Fashioned Love Song	Take Me Home, Country Roads	We're Together 100
Kum Ba Yah			

HI-LO'S, The
Vocal quartet formed in 1953: Gene Puerling, Clark Burroughs, Bob Morse and Bob Strasen. Numerous appearances on Rosemary Clooney's television show.

4/13/57	13	3		1 Suddenly It's The Hi-Lo's	$25	Columbia 952
7/22/57	14	7		2 Ring Around Rosie	$25	Columbia 1006
				ROSEMARY CLOONEY AND THE HI-LO'S		
10/14/57	19	4		3 Now Hear This	$25	Columbia 1023

Basin Street Blues (1)
Brahams' Lullaby (1)
Brown-Skin Gal In The Calico Gown (3)
Camptown Races (3)
Coquette (2)
Deep Purple (1)
Desert Song (1)

Doncha Go 'Way Mad (2)
Down The Old Ox Road (1)
Everything Happens To Me (2)
Heather On The Hill (3)
How About You (2)
I Could Write A Book (2)
I Married An Angel (1)

I'm Glad There Is You (3)
I'm In The Mood For Love (2)
Laura (3)
Life Is Just A Bowl Of Cherries (1)
Little Girl Blue (3)
Love Letters (2)
Love Walked In (1)

Moonlight Becomes You (2)
My Melancholy Baby (3)
My Sugar Is So Refined (1)
My Time Is Your Time (3)
Quiet Girl (3)
Shine On Your Shoes (3)
Solitude (2)
Stormy Weather (1)

Sunnyside Up (3)
Swing Low, Sweet Chariot (1)
Tenderly (1)
There's No You (3)
Together (2)
Two Ladies In De Shade Of De Banana Tree (3)
What Is There To Say (2)

HINDU LOVE GODS
Warren Zevon (vocals) with R.E.M. members: Peter Buck (guitar), Mike Mills (bass) and Bill Berry (drums).

| 11/10/90 | 168 | 10 | | Hindu Love Gods .... | $12 | Giant 24406 |

Battleship Chains
Crosscut Saw

I'm A One Woman Man
Junko Pardner

Mannish Boy
Raspberry Beret

Travelin' Riverside Blues
Vigilante Man

Walkin' Blues
Wang Dang Doodle

HIPSWAY
Scottish quartet led by vocalist Grahame Skinner. Bassist John McElhone (ex-Altered Images) later joined the group Texas.

| 2/21/87 | 55 | 18 | | Hipsway .... | $8 | Columbia 40522 |

Ask The Lord
Bad Thing Longing

Broken Years
Forbidden

Honeythief, The 19
Long White Car

Set This Day Apart
Tinder

Upon A Thread

HIROSHIMA
Multi-ethnic, Los Angeles jazz-pop band founded in 1974 by Dan Kuramoto. Most members are of Japanese ancestry.

12/22/79+	51	27		1 Hiroshima	$8	Arista 4252
11/15/80	72	18		2 Odori	$8	Arista 9541
8/20/83	142	9		3 Third Generation ....[I]	$8	Epic 38708
11/30/85+	79	45		4 Another Place	$8	Epic 39938
8/15/87	75	32		5 Go	$8	Epic 40679
3/25/89	105	19		6 East	$8	Epic 45022

All I Want (2)
Another Place (4)
Come To Me (6)
Crusin' J-Town (2)
Da-Da (1)
Daydreamer (6)
Distant Thoughts (3)
Do What You Can (3)
East (6)

Echoes (2)
Even Then (5)
Fifths (3)
Fortune Teller (2)
From The Heart (3)
Game, The (4)
Go (5)
Golden Age (6)
Hawaiian Electric (5)

Heavenly Angel (3)
Holidays (1)
I Do Remember (4)
I've Been Here Before (5)
Kokoro (1)
Lion Dance (1)
Living In America (6)
Long Time Love (1)
Long Walks (3)

Midtown Higashi (6)
Never, Ever (1)
No. 9 (5)
Obon (5)
Odori (2)
One Wish (4)
Ren (3)
Roomful Of Mirrors (1)
San Say (3)

Save Yourself For Me (4)
Shinto (2)
Stay Away (4)
Streetcorner Paradise (6)
Sukoshi Bit (3)
Tabo (6)
Taiko Song (1)
Thousand Cranes (6)
311 (6)

Touch And Go (4)
Undercover (4)
Warriors (2)
We Are (3)
What's It To Ya (4)
Why Can't I Love You (5)
Winds Of Change (Henka Non Nagare) (2)
You And Me (6)

★★99★★   **HIRT, Al**
Born Alois Maxwell Hirt on 11/7/22 in New Orleans. Trumpet virtuoso. Toured with Jimmy and Tommy Dorsey, Ray McKinley and Horace Heidt. Formed own Dixieland combo (with Pete Fountain) in the late 1950s.

5/15/61	21	32		1 The Greatest Horn In The World ....[I]	$15	RCA 2366
10/9/61	61	11		2 Al (He's the King) Hirt and His Band..................	$15	RCA 2354
2/3/62	41	2		3 Bourbon Street.......................................[I]	$15	Coral 57389
				PETE FOUNTAIN/AL HIRT includes 4 solo hits by Pete Fountain: "Blues On Bourbon Street," "Lazy River," "March Through The Streets Of Their City," "St. James Infirmary"		
2/10/62	24	25		4 Horn A-Plenty ....[I]	$15	RCA 2446
1/19/63	96	7		5 Trumpet and Strings ....[I]	$15	RCA 2584
3/23/63	44	3		6 Our Man In New Orleans ....[I]	$15	RCA 2607
9/21/63+	3	104	●	7 Honey In The Horn...................................[I]	$15	RCA 2733
				Anita Kerr Singers do background vocals on some tracks		
2/29/64	83	9		8 Beauty and the Beard..................................	$15	RCA 2690
				AL HIRT/ANN-MARGRET		
5/23/64	6	53	●	9 Cotton Candy ....[I]	$15	RCA 2917
8/22/64	9	48	●	10 Sugar Lips ....[I]	$15	RCA 2965
9/26/64	18	31		11 "Pops" Goes The Trumpet ....[I]	$15	RCA 2729
				AL HIRT/BOSTON POPS/ARTHUR FIEDLER		
1/30/65	13	43	●	12 The Best Of Al Hirt ....[G-I]	$15	RCA 3309
3/13/65	28	27		13 That Honey Horn Sound	$15	RCA 3337
7/24/65	47	22		14 Live At Carnegie Hall ....[I-L]	$15	RCA 3416
2/12/66	39	18		15 They're Playing Our Song	$15	RCA 3492
7/30/66	125	6		16 The Happy Trumpet ....[I]	$15	RCA 3579
3/18/67	127	5		17 Music To Watch Girls By ....[I]	$15	RCA 3773
2/10/68	116	13		18 Al Hirt Plays Bert Kaempfert ....[I]	$15	RCA 3917

HIRT, Al — Cont'd

Afrikaan Beat (18)
Al Di La (7)
Alley Cat (13)
As Time Goes By (5)
At The Jazz Band Ball (3)
Autumn Leaves (15)
Baby, It's Cold Outside (8)
Baby Won't You Please Come Home (4)
Back Home Again In Indiana (10)
Bad Man (16)
Begin The Beguine (1)
Best Man (8,12)
Big Man (9)
Bill Bailey (8)
Birth Of The Blues (6)
Blow Your Own Horn (17)
Bourbon Street Parade (12)
Bugler's Holiday (11)
Butterball (13)
Bye Bye Blues (14,18)
Candy Man Jones (16)
Carnival Of Venice (11,14)
Cherry Pink And Apple Blossom White (15)
Christopher Columbus (2)
Clarinet Marmalade (6)
Contrary Waltz (13)
Cornet Chop Suey (2)
Cotton Candy (9,12) **15**
Danke Schoen (18)
Danny Boy (13)
Dear Old Southland (6)
Deep Purple (15)
Django's Castle (9)
Do Nothin' Till You Hear From Me (4)
Down By The Riverside (2,14)

Dream, Theme From A (7)
East Of The Sun (And West Of The Moon) (5)
Easy Street (2)
Easy To Love (5)
Eili, Eili (11)
Elmer's Tune (17)
Everybody Loves My Baby (But My Baby Don't Love Nobody But Me) (8)
Fancy Pants (13) **47**
Farewell Blues (3)
Fiddler On The Roof (13)
Flowers And Candy (13)
Fly Me To The Moon (In Other Words) (7)
Fools Rush In (5)
Fox, The (16)
Georgia On My Mind (1)
Girl From Ipanema (10)
Going To Chicago Blues (14)
Gypsy In My Soul (14)
Happy Trumpet (16)
Haydn: Trumpet Concerto (11)
Hello, Dolly! (9)
His Girl (17)
Holiday For Trumpet (4,12)
How Deep Is The Ocean (How High Is The Sky) (5)
I Can't Get Started (7)
I Cried For You (5)
I Had The Craziest Dream (15)
I Love Paris (2,12)
I'll Be Seeing You (15)
I'll Get By (15)
I'll Never Smile Again (4)
I'll Take Romance (4)
I'm Movin' On (7)

I'm On My Way (1)
I've Heard That Song Before (15)
If You Go Away (Ne Me Quitte Pas) (17)
It's Been A Long, Long Time (15)
Ja-Da (6)
Java (7,11,12,14) **4**
Jazz Me Blues (2,3)
Jitterbug Waltz (2)
Just Because (8)
Kansas City (14)
King's Blues (2)
La Virgen De La Macarena (11)
Lady (18)
Last Date (9)
Laura (2)
Let's Do It (Let's Fall In Love) (1)
Limelight (14)
Little Boy (Little Girl) (8)
Little Gold Ring (16)
Long Walk Home (13)
Lookin' For The Blues (10)
Lost Chord (11)
Love For Sale (14)
Love Makes The World Go 'Round (4)
Love Makes The World Go 'Round (Theme from Carnival) (12)
Lover Come Back To Me (2)
Ma (He's Making Eyes At Me) (8)
Magic Trumpet (18)
Malibu (7)
Man With A Horn (7)
March Of The Bob Cats (3)

Mardi Gras (16)
Margie (4)
Mas Que Nada (17)
Melissa (9)
Memories Of You (4)
Milano (10)
Moo Moo (9)
Music To Watch Girls By (17)
Muskrat Ramble (6)
Mutual Admiration Society (8)
My Baby Just Cares For Me (8)
Nature Boy (17)
New Orleans (6)
New Orleans, My Home Town (10)
Night Life (10)
Night Theme (7)
None But The Lonely Heart (13)
Oh Dem Golden Slippers (6)
Ol' Man River (6)
One O'Clock Jump (2)
Out Of Nowhere (1)
Over The Rainbow (13)
Panama (6)
Paper Doll (1)
Pavanne (11)
Personality (8)
Pink Confetti (10)
Pitty Pat (16)
Poor Butterfly (5,12)
Poupee Brisee (Broken Doll) (10)
Pussy Cat (16)
Red Roses For A Blue Lady (18)
Row, Row, Row (8)

Rumpus (4,9)
Sand Pebbles, Theme From The (17)
September Song (10)
Six Long Days (Sechs Tage Lang) (17)
Skokiaan (16)
Sleepless Hours (5)
Sleepy Lagoon (5)
Song From Moulin Rouge (Where Is Your Heart) (15)
Spanish Eyes (18)
Star Dust (13)
Stella By Starlight (1,12)
Stompin' At The Savoy (1)
Stranger In Paradise (5,12)
Strangers In The Night (18)
Sugar Lips (10,12) **30**
Sweet Maria (18)
Sweet Sue - Just You (1)
Swing Low, Sweet Chariot (4)
Swingin' Safari (18)
Syncopated Clock (16)
'Tain't What You Do (8)
Talkin' 'Bout That River (7)
Tansy (7)
Tenderly (10)
Tennessee Waltz (14)
That Old Feeling (4)
There, I've Said It Again (5)
Three Little Words (2)
Till There Was You (4)
To Ava (1)
To Be In Love (7)
Too Late (Trop Tard) (9)
Toy Trumpet (11)
True Love (5)
Trumpet Concerto ..see: Haydn
Trumpeter's Lullaby (11)

12th Street Rag (9)
Twentieth Century Drawing Room (16)
Undecided (1)
Up Above My Head (I Hear Music In The Air) (10,14) **85**
Walk Right In (14)
Walkin' (9)
Walkin' With Mr. Lee (9)
What The World Needs Now Is Love (16)
What's New (1)
When I'm Feelin' Kinda Blue (14)
When It's Sleepy Time Down South (6)
When The Saints Go Marching In (6,12)
Wilkommen (Welcome) (17)
Willow Weep For Me (1)
Wolverine Blues (8)
Won't You Come Home Bill Bailey ..see: Bill Bailey
Wonderland By Night (18)
World We Knew (Over And Over) (18)
Yo-Yo (Puppet Song) (17)
You Took Advantage Of Me (13)
You'll Never Know (15)

HITCHCOCK, Robyn, & The Egyptians

Guitarist/vocalist Hitchcock was born on 3/3/52 in London. Formed band, Soft Boys, with Andy Metcalfe (Squeeze) and Kimberly Rew (Katrina & The Waves). Went solo in 1981.

3/5/88	**111**	15		1 Globe Of Frogs	**$8**	A&M 5182
4/1/89	**139**	9		2 Queen Elvis	**$8**	A&M 5241

Autumn Sea (2)
Balloon Man (1)
Chinese Bones (1)
Devils Coachman (2)

Flesh Number One (Beatle Dennis) (1)
Freeze (2)
Globe Of Frogs (1)
Knife (2)

Luminous Rose (1)
Madonna Of The Wasps (2)
One Long Pair Of Eyes (2)
Shapes Between Us Turn Into Animals (1)

Sleeping With Your Devil Mask (1)
Superman (2)
Swirling (2)
Tropical Flesh Mandala (1)

Unsettled (1)
Veins Of The Queen (2)
Vibrating (1)
Wax Doll (2)

HO, Don, and the Aliis

Don was born on 8/13/30 in Oahu, Hawaii. Nightclub singer/actor.

3/5/66	**117**	5		1 Don Ho-Again! ....[L]	**$10**	Reprise 6186
12/17/66+	**15**	50		2 Tiny Bubbles	**$10**	Reprise 6232
5/27/67	**115**	5		3 East Coast/West Coast ....[L]	**$10**	Reprise 6244
3/22/69	**199**	3		4 Suck 'Em Up ....[L]	**$10**	Reprise 6331
8/23/69	**162**	6		5 Don Ho-Greatest Hits! ....[G]	**$10**	Reprise 6357
10/18/69	**188**	2		6 The Don Ho TV Show	**$10**	Reprise 6367

summer replacement show for *The Kraft Music Hall*

Ain't No Big Thing (1,5)
All That's Left Is The Lemon Tree (3)
Aloha Means (3)
Aquarius/Let The Sunshine In (6)
Beautiful Kauai (2,5)
Beyond The Reef (4)
Born Free (3)
Bring Back The Good Times (6)
Cycles (6)
Day Is Done (6)
Didn't We (4)

Do I Love You? (3)
Down By The Shack, By The Sea (4,5)
E Lei Ka Lei Lei (Beach Party Song) (5)
Following Sea (1,5)
Geev'um (2)
Gentle On My Mind (6)
Girls Of The Summer (4)
Goin' Out Of My Head (3)
Hang On Sloopy (1)
Happy Me (2)
Hawaii (2)
I Love The Simple Folk (2)

I Wish They Didn't Mean Goodbye (1)
I'll Remember You (5)
I'm A Drifter (6)
If I Had It To Do Over Again (1)
Kanaka Pete (4)
Lahaina Luna (1)
Lights Of Home (2)
Lover's Prayer (1,3,5)
Macao (3)
Maka Hilahila (1)
Molokai Nui Ahina (4)
More I Know The Simple Folk (2)

My Way (6)
Night Life (1,5)
One Paddle, Two Paddle (2,3)
Pearly Shells (5)
Please Wait For Me (2)
Remembering (4)
Sands Of Waikiki (4,6)
She's Gone Again (I'll Remember You) (2,3)
Soon It's Gonna Rain (3)
Straight Life (6)
Suck 'Em Up (4)
Sunny Days, Starry Nights (Ke La La) (4)

Sweet Someone (1,5)
This Could Be The Start Of Something (3)
This Town (3)
Tiny Bubbles (2,3,5) **57**
Turn Around, Look At Me (6)
Ukelele Talk (6)
Welcome Pretty Lady (4)
What Now My Love (3)
Windward Side (Of The Island) (5)
You Are Beautiful (1)
You May Go (1)
You'll Never Go Home (2)

You're Gonna Hear From Me (4)
Young Land (2)

HODGES, Johnny/Wild Bill Davis

Jazz saxman Davis (b: 7/25/06 in Cambridge, Massachusetts; d: 5/11/70 from a heart attack) was a member of Duke Ellington's orchestra from 1928-51 and from 1955. Jazz organist Davis (b: 11/24/18 in Glasgow, Missouri) led own trio since 1951.

2/20/65	**148**	2		Blue Rabbit ....[I]	**$20**	Verve 8599

Blues O'Mighty
Creole Love Call
Fiddler's Fancy

I Let A Song Go Out Of My Heart

Mud Pie
Satin Doll

Tangerine
Things Ain't What They Used To Be

Wisteria

HODGSON, Roger

Born on 5/21/50 in London. Founding member/lead singer of Supertramp.

10/27/84	**46**	22		1 In The Eye Of The Storm	**$8**	A&M 5004
10/31/87	**163**	6		2 Hai Hai	**$8**	A&M 5112

HODGSON, Roger — Cont'd

Desert Love (2)	**Had A Dream (Sleeping**	House On The Corner (2)	London (2)	Only Because Of You (1)	Who's Afraid (2)
Give Me Love, Give Me Life (1)	**With The Enemy)** (1) 48	I'm Not Afraid (1)	Lovers In The Wind (1)	Puppet Dance (2)	You Make Me Love You (2)
	Hai Hai (2)	In Jeopardy (1)	My Magazine (2)	Right Place (2)	
	Hooked On A Problem (1)	Land Ho (2)			

HOFFS, Susanna

Born on 1/17/57. Former lead singer of The Bangles. Starred in 1987 film *The Allnighter*. Her mother is film director Tamara Hoffs.

2/16/91	83	11		When You're A Boy	$12	Columbia 46076

Boys Keep Swinging	Made Of Stone	No Kind Of Love	So Much For Love	That's Why Girls Cry	Unconditional Love
It's Lonely Out Here	**My Side Of The Bed** 30	Only Love	Something New	This Time	Wishing On Telstar

HOLIDAY, Billie

"Lady Day" — revered as one of jazz's leading great vocalists. Born Eleanor Gough on 4/7/15 in Philadelphia. Died on 7/17/59 in New York City (drug addiction). Singing at age 15 in Harlem Clubs, heard by producer/jazz critic John Hammond, who arranged for her to record with Benny Goodman in 1933. With Teddy Wilson from 1935-39, Count Basie from 1937-38, Artie Shaw in 1938, then solo work. Final appearance on 5/25/59 in New York City. Subject of the 1972 film *Lady Sings The Blues* starring Diana Ross. Awarded the Lifetime Achievement Grammy in 1987. Also see Diana Ross.

12/23/72+	85	21		1 The Billie Holiday Story .... [K]	$15	Decca 161 [2]
				recordings from 1944-50		
1/13/73	108	16		2 Strange Fruit .... [K]	$10	Atlantic 1614
				recordings from 1939 and 1944		
2/24/73	135	9		3 The Original Recordings .... [K]	$12	Columbia 32060
				recordings from 1935-58		

Ain't Nobody's Business If I Do (1)	Easy Living (1)	(I Got A Man Crazy For Me) (1)	Lover Man (Oh, Where Can You Be?) (1)	Porgy (1)	You're My Thrill (1)
All Of Me (3)	Embraceable You (2)	He's Funny That Way (2)		Solitude (1)	You've Changed (3)
As Time Goes By (2)	Fine And Mellow (2)	I Gotta Right To Sing The Blues (2)	Man I Love (3)	Somebody's On My Mind (1)	
Baby Get Lost (1)	Gimme A Pigfoot And A Bottle Of Beer (1)		Mean To Me (3)	Strange Fruit (2)	
(Billie's Blues) I Love My Man (2)		I'll Be Seeing You (2)	Miss Brown To You (3)	That Ole Devil Called Love (1)	
	Gloomy Sunday (3)	I'll Get By (2)	My Man (1,3)	Them There Eyes (1,3)	
Crazy He Calls Me (1)	God Bless The Child (1,3)	I'll Look Around (1)	My Old Flame (2)	There Is No Greater Love (1)	
Deep Song (1)	Good Morning Heartache (1)	I'm Yours (2)	No More (1)	This Is Heaven To Me (1)	
Do Your Duty (1)	How Am I To Know (2)	Keeps On Rainin' (1)	Now Or Never (1)	What A Little Moonlight Can Do (3)	
Don't Explain (1)	I Cover The Waterfront (2)	Lover Come Back To Me (2)	On The Sunny Side Of The Street (2)	Yesterdays (2)	
	I Cried For You (3)				

HOLLAND, Amy

Daughter of country singer Esmereldy and opera singer Harry Boersma. Married to Michael McDonald.

8/30/80	146	14		Amy Holland...	$8	Capitol 12071

Don't Kid Yourself	Here In The Light	**How Do I Survive** 22	Looking For Love	Stars
Forgetting You	Holding On To You	I'm Wondering	Show Me The Way Home	Strengthen My Love

HOLLAND, Dave — see METHENY, Pat

HOLLIDAY, Jennifer

Born on 10/19/60 in Riverside, Texas. Won 1982 Tony award for best actress in Broadway's *Dreamgirls*. Also in Broadway's *Your Arm's Too Short To Box With God* (1978) and *Sing, Mahalia Sing* (1985).

10/22/83	31	22		1 Feel My Soul	$8	Geffen 4014
9/14/85	110	14		2 Say You Love Me	$8	Geffen 24073
11/9/91	184	1		3 I'm On Your Side	$12	Arista 18578

Change Is Gonna Come (1)	**Hard Times For Lovers** (2) 69	I'm On Your Side (3)	Love Stories (3)	This Day (1)
Come Sunday (2)		Is It Love (3)	More 'N' More (3)	This Game Of Love (I'm Never Coming Down) (1)
Dream With Your Name On It (3)	He's A Pretender (2)	It Will Haunt Me (3)	My Sweet Delight (1)	What Kind Of Love Is This? (2)
Dreams Never Die (2)	**I Am Love** (1) 49	It's In There (3)	**No Frills Love** (2) 87	You're The One (2)
Guilty (3)	I Am Ready Now (1)	Just A Matter Of Time (2)	Raise The Roof (3)	
	I Fall Apart (3)	Just For A While (1)	Say You Love Me (2)	
	I Rest My Case (2)	Just Let Me Wait (1)	Shine A Light (1)	

★★309★★ HOLLIES, The

Formed in Manchester, England in 1962. Consisted of Allan Clarke (lead vocals), Graham Nash and Tony Hicks (guitars), Eric Haydock (bass) and Don Rathbone (drums). Clarke and Nash had worked as a duo, the Guytones, added other members, became the Fourtones, Deltas, then The Hollies. First recorded for Parlophone in 1963. Rathbone left in 1963, replaced by Bobby Elliott. Haydock left in 1966, replaced by Bernie Calvert (first heard on "Bus Stop"). Nash left in December 1968 to join David Crosby and Stephen Stills in new trio, replaced by Terry Sylvester, formerly in the Swinging Blue Jeans. Shuffling personnel since then. Clarke, Nash, Hicks and Elliott regrouped briefly in 1983.

2/12/66	145	3		1 Hear! Here!	$35	Imperial 12299
10/22/66	75	11		2 Bus Stop	$35	Imperial 12330
2/25/67	91	8		3 Stop! Stop! Stop!	$35	Imperial 12339
6/3/67	11	40		4 The Hollies' Greatest Hits...........................[G]	$35	Imperial 12350
8/5/67	43	14		5 Evolution	$20	Epic 26315
4/4/70	32	14		6 He Ain't Heavy, He's My Brother	$15	Epic 26538
2/13/71	183	2		7 Moving Finger	$15	Epic 30255
7/15/72	21	21		8 Distant Light	$15	Epic 30958
1/27/73	84	12		9 Romany	$10	Epic 31992
10/20/73	157	7		10 The Hollies' Greatest Hits.............................[G]	$10	Epic 32061
				includes both Imperial and Epic hits		
5/11/74	28	23		11 Hollies	$10	Epic 32574
3/29/75	123	10		12 Another Night	$10	Epic 33387
7/9/83	90	9		13 What Goes Around..	$8	Atlantic 80076

Air That I Breathe (11) 6	Cable Car (8)	Confessions Of A Mind (7)	Day That Curly Billy Shot Down Crazy Sam McGee (11)	Delaware Taggett And The Outlaw Boys (9)	Don't Give Up Easily (6)
Another Night (12) 71	Candy Man (2)	Courage Of Your Convictions (9)			Don't Let Me Down (11)
Baby That's All (2)	**Carrie-Anne** (5,10) 9	Crusader (3)		Do You Believe In Love? (6)	Don't Run And Hide (2)
Blue In The Morning (9)	Casualty (13)		**Dear Eloise** (10) 50	Do You Even Think About Changing (3)	Down On The Run (11)
Bus Stop (2,4,10) 5	Clown (3)				Down River (9)

DEBUT DATE	PEAK POS	WKS CHR	GOLD	ARTIST — Album Title	$	Label & Number

HOLLIES, The — Cont'd

Down The Line (1)	Isn't It Nice (7)	Look What We've Got (8)	Please Let Me Please (6)	Suspicious Look In Your Eyes (3)	When I Come Home To You (1)

Down The Line (1)
Falling Calling (11)
Frightened Lady (7)
Games We Play (5)
Gasoline Alley Bred (7)
Give Me Time (12)
Goodbye Tomorrow (6)
Have You Ever Loved Somebody (5)
Having A Good Time (13)
He Ain't Heavy, He's My Brother (6,10) **7**
Heading For A Fall (5)
Here I Go Again (4)
High Classed (3)
Hold On (8)
I Am A Rock (2)
I Can't Let Go (4) **42**
I Got What I Want (13)
I'm Alive (1,4)
I'm Down (12)
I've Been Wrong (1)
If The Lights Go Out (13)

Isn't It Nice (7)
It's A Shame, It's A Game (11)
It's You (3)
Jesus Was A Crossmaker (9)
Just One Look (4,10,13) **44**
King Midas In Reverse (10) **51**
Lady Please (7)
Lawdy Miss Clawdy (1)
Life I've Led (8)
Little Girl (7)
Little Love (2)
Little Thing Like Love (8)
Lonely Hobo Lullabye (12)
Long Cool Woman (In A Black Dress) (8,10) **2**
Long Dark Road (8,10) **26**
Look At Life (6)
Look Out Johnny (There's A Monkey On Your Back) (12)
Look Through Any Window (1,4,10) **32**

Look What We've Got (8)
Love Makes The World Go Round (11)
Lucy (12)
Lullaby To Tim (5)
Magic Woman Touch (9) **60**
Man Without A Heart (7)
Marigold Gloria Swansong (7)
Memphis (4)
Mickey's Monkey (2)
My Life Is Over With You (6)
On A Carousel (4,10) **11**
Oriental Sadness (I'll Never Trust In Anybody No More) (2)
Out On The Road (11)
Pay You Back With Interest (3,4,10) **28**
Peculiar Situation (3)
Perfect Lady Housewife (7)
Pick Up The Pieces Again (11)

Please Let Me Please (6)
Please Sign Your Letters (6)
Promised Land (8)
Pull Down The Blind (8)
Put Yourself In My Place (1)
Rain On The Window (5)
Reflections Of A Time Long Past (6)
Romany (9)
Rubber Lucy (11)
Sandy (12) **85**
Say You'll Be Mine (13)
Second Hand Hangups (12)
Slow Down (9)
So Lonely (1)
Someone Else's Eyes (13)
Something Ain't Right (13)
Stop In The Name Of Love (13) **29**
Stop Right There (5)
Stop Stop Stop (3,4,10) **7**
Survival Of The Fittest (7)

Suspicious Look In Your Eyes (3)
Sweet Little Sixteen (2)
Take My Love And Run (13)
Tell Me To My Face (3,4)
That's My Desire (1)
Then The Heartaches Begin (5)
Time Machine Jive (12)
To Do With Love (8)
Too Many People (1)
Too Young To Be Married (7)
Touch (9)
Transatlantic Westbound Jet (11)
Very Last Day (1)
We're Through (4)
What Went Wrong (3)
What's Wrong With The Way I Live (3)
Whatcha Gonna Do About It (2,4)

When I Come Home To You (1)
Why Didn't You Believe (6)
Won't We Feel Good That Morning (9)
Words Don't Come Easy (9)
Ye Olde Toffee Shoppe (5)
You Gave Me Life (With That Look In Your Eyes) (12)
You Know He Did (2)
You Know The Score (8)
You Love 'Cos You Like It (6)
You Must Believe Me (1)
You Need Love (5)

HOLLOWAY, Loleatta
Soul singer from Chicago. Former member of the Caravans gospel troupe.

12/2/78	187	2		Queen Of The Night	$8	Gold Mind 9501

Catch Me On The Rebound
Good Good Feeling

I May Not Be There When You Want Me (But I'm Right On Time)
I'm In Love
Mama Don't, Papa Won't

Only You 87
Two Sides To Every Story

You Light Up My Life

HOLLY, Buddy/The Crickets
Born Charles Hardin Holley on 9/7/36 in Lubbock, Texas. Began recording western and bop demos with Bob Montgomery in 1954. Signed to Decca label in January 1956 and recorded in Nashville as Buddy Holly & The Three Tunes (Sonny Curtis, lead guitar; Don Guess, bass; and Jerry Ivan Allison, drums). In February 1957, Buddy assembled his backing group, The Crickets (Allison; Niki Sullivan, rhythm guitar; and Joe B. Mauldin, bass), for recordings at Norman Petty's studio in Clovis, New Mexico. Signed to Brunswick and Coral labels (subsidiaries of Decca Records). Because of contract arrangements, all Brunswick records were released as The Crickets and all Coral records were released as Buddy Holly. Holly split from The Crickets in autumn of 1958. Buddy, Ritchie Valens and the Big Bopper were killed in a plane crash near Mason City, Iowa on 2/3/59 (age 22). Holly was inducted into the Rock and Roll Hall of Fame in 1986. Also see Bobby Vee.

4/27/59	11	181	●	1 The Buddy Holly Story	[G] $75	Coral 57279
				includes 4 songs with The Crickets		
3/16/63	40	17		2 Reminiscing	[K] $60	Coral 57426
				BUDDY HOLLY instrumental backing by The Fireballs dubbed in (1962)		
8/5/78	55	12	●	3 Buddy Holly/The Crickets 20 Golden Greats	[G] $10	MCA 3040

Baby, Won't You Come Out Tonight (2)
Because I Love You (2)
Bo Diddley (2,3)
Brown Eyed Handsome Man (2,3)

Changing All Those Changes (2)
Early In The Morning (1) **32**
Everyday (1,3)
Heartbeat (1,3) **82**
I'm Gonna Set My Foot Down (2)

It Doesn't Matter Anymore (1,3) **13**
It's Not My Fault (2)
It's So Easy (1,3)
Listen To Me (3)
Maybe Baby (1,3) **17**
Not Fade Away (3)

Oh, Boy! (1,3) **10**
Peggy Sue (1,3) **3**
Peggy Sue Got Married (1)
Raining In My Heart (1,3) **88**
Rave On (1,3) **37**
Reminiscing (2)

Rock-A-Bye-Rock (2)
Slippin' And Slidin' (2)
That'll Be The Day (1,3) **1**
Think It Over (1,3) **27**
True Love Ways (3)
Wait Till The Sun Shines Nellie (2)

Well...Alright (3)
Wishing (3)
Words Of Love (3)

HOLLY & THE ITALIANS
Holly Vincent, leader of Los Angeles rock group.

7/11/81	177	3		The Right To Be Italian	$8	Virgin 37359

Baby Gets It All
Do You Say Love

I Wanna Go Home
Just For Tonight

Just Young
Means To A Den

Miles Away
Rock Against Romance

Tell That Girl To Shut Up
Youth Coup

HOLLYRIDGE STRINGS, The
Arranged and conducted by Stu Phillips, later of the Golden Gate Strings.

6/20/64	15	25		1 The Beatles Song Book	[I] $15	Capitol 2116
10/10/64	82	12		2 The Beach Boys Song Book	[I] $15	Capitol 2156
2/13/65	144	3		3 Hits Made Famous By Elvis Presley	[I] $15	Capitol 2221
4/24/65	136	3		4 The Nat King Cole Song Book	[I] $15	Capitol 2310
6/4/66	142	3		5 The New Beatles Song Book	[I] $15	Capitol 2429

All My Loving (1) **93**
And I Love Her (5)
Answer Me, My Love (4)
Are You Lonesome Tonight? (3)
Ask Me (3)
Bossa Nova, Baby (3)
Can't Buy Me Love (1)
Can't Help Falling In Love (3)
Christmas Song (Merry Christmas To You) (4)

Day Tripper (5)
Do You Want To Know A Secret? (1)
Don't Be Cruel (3)
Don't Worry Baby (2)
From Me To You (1)
Fun, Fun, Fun (2)
Girl (5)
Girls On The Beach (2)
Good Luck Charm (3)
Heartbreak Hotel (3)

Help! (5)
I Get Around (2)
I Saw Her Standing There (1)
I Want To Hold Your Hand (1)
In My Room (2)
It's Only A Paper Moon (4)
Kiss Me Quick (3)
(Let Me Be Your) Teddy Bear (3)
Little Saint Nick (2)

Love (4)
Love Me Do (1)
Love Me Tender (3)
Michelle (5)
Mona Lisa (4)
Nature Boy (4)
Night Before (5)
Norwegian Wood (This Bird Has Flown) (5)
Nowhere Man (5)
P.S. I Love You (1)

Please Please Me (1)
Pretend (4)
Ramblin' Rose (4)
Return To Sender (3)
She Knows Me Too Well (2)
She Loves You (1)
Shut Down (2)
Somewhere Along The Way (4)
Surfin' U.S.A. (2)
Taste Of Honey (1)

Those Lazy-Hazy-Crazy Days Of Summer (4)
Ticket To Ride (5)
Too Young (4)
Unforgettable (4)
Warmth Of The Sun (2)
We Can Work It Out (5)
Wendy (2)
Yesterday (5)

HOLLYWOOD BOWL SYMPHONY ORCHESTRA — see PENNARIO, Leonard

HOLLYWOOD STUDIO ORCHESTRA, The
Conducted by Mitchell Powell.

1/23/61	23	17		Exodus	[I] $20	United Art. 6123
				this is not the original soundtrack album		

Ari
Brothers, The
Conspiracy

Dawn
Escape
Exodus, Theme Of

Fight For Peace
Fight For Survival
Hatikvah

In Jerusalem
Karen
Prison Break

Summer In Cyprus
Valley Of Jezreel

326

HOLMAN, Eddie
Born on 6/3/46 in Norfolk, Virginia. Soul singer/songwriter. Recorded for Leopard in the early 1960s.

2/21/70	**75**	13		I Love You	**$12**	ABC 701

Am I A Loser
Don't Stop Now *48*
Four Walls

Hey There Lonely Girl *2*	I Love You	It's All In The Game	**Since I Don't Have You** *flip*
I Cried	I'll Be Forever Loving You	Let Me Into Your Life	Since My Love Has Gone

HOLMES, Cecil, Soulful Sounds
Cecil was vice-president of Buddah Records. Album arranged and produced by Tony Camillo (Bazuka).

4/28/73	**141**	10		The Black Motion Picture Experience .... [I]	**$10**	Buddah 5129

themes from black film soundtracks

Across 110th Street
Also Sprach Zarathrusta (2001)

Ben	Lady Sings The Blues, Love	Slaughter	T Stands For Trouble (medley)
Freddie's Dead	Theme From Shaft	Superfly	Trouble Man (medley)

HOLMES, Clint
Born on 5/9/46 in Bournemouth, England. Moved to Buffalo, New York as a child.

5/26/73	**122**	12		Playground In My Mind	**$10**	Epic 32269

Come Hell Or High Water
Killing Me Softly With His Song

Like The Fellow Once Said	Neither One Of Us (Wants	**Playground In My Mind** *2*	There's No Future In My Future
Me And America	To Be The First To Say	Sneaking Around Corners	What Will My Mary Say
Miss Lady Loretta	Goodbye)		

HOLMES, Jake
Born John Grier Holmes on 12/28/39 in San Francisco. Singer/songwriter.

11/14/70	**135**	6		So Close, So Very Far To Go	**$12**	Polydor 4034

Django & Friend
Her Song

I Remember Sunshine	Little Comfort	Population	So Very Far To Go
I Sure Like Her Song	Paris Song	**So Close** *49*	We're All We've Got

HOLMES, Leroy
Born Alvin Holmes on 9/22/13 in Pittsburgh; died on 7/27/86. Orchestra conductor/arranger. Music director for MGM and United Artists Records.

9/9/67	**42**	29	1	For A Few Dollars More and other Motion Picture Themes .... [I]	**$8**	United Art. 6608
6/1/68	**138**	8	2	The Good, The Bad And The Ugly and other Motion Picture Themes .... [I]	**$8**	United Art. 6633

Aces High (1)	Down Here On The Ground (2)	Goodbye Colonel (1)	Tara Theme (2)	Valley Of The Dolls, Theme From (2)
Around The World (2)	Fistful Of Dollars (1)	Here We Go Round The Mulberry Bush (2)	Thoroughly Modern Millie (2)	Vice Of Killing (1)
Bonnie And Clyde (2)	For A Few Dollars More (1)	Live For Life (Vivre Pour Vivre) (2)	To Sir, With Love (2)	Viva Maria (1)
Camelot (2)	Good, The Bad And The Ugly (2)	Sixty Seconds To What (1)	Tom Jones (1)	Zorba The Greek, Theme From (1)
Doctor Dolittle (2)			Topkapi (1)	
			Train, Theme From The (1)	

HOLMES, Richard "Groove"
Born on 5/2/31 in Camden, New Jersey. Died of prostate cancer on 6/29/91. Jazz organist. Discovered by Les McCann. Recorded with Joe Pass, Gene Ammons and Clifford Scott.

5/14/66	**89**	26	1	Soul Message .... [I]	**$15**	Prestige 7435
10/29/66	**143**	3	2	Living Soul .... [I-L]	**$15**	Prestige 7468

recorded at Count Basie's club in Harlem

12/24/66+	**134**	6	3	Misty	**$15**	Prestige 7485

Blues For Yna Yna (2)
Dahoud (1)
Gemini (2)
Girl From Ipanema (2)

Groove's Groove (1)	On The Street Where You Live (3)	Song For My Father (1)	There Will Never Be Another You (3)	**What Now My Love** *(3)* *96*
Living Soul (2)	Over The Rainbow (2)	Soul Message (1)	Things We Did Last Summer (1)	
Misty *(1,3)* *44*	Shadow Of Your Smile (3)	Strangers In The Night (3)		
More I See You (3)		Summertime (3)		

HOLMES, Rupert
Born on 2/24/47 in Cheshire, England. Moved to New York at age six. Member of studio group Street People. Wrote and arranged for The Drifters, The Platters and Gene Pitney. Arranged/produced for Barbra Streisand. Wrote The Buoys' hit "Timothy" and the Broadway musical *Drood*.

11/10/79+	**33**	31	●	Partners In Crime	**$8**	Infinity 9020

Answering Machine *32*
Drop It

Escape (The Pina Colada Song) *1*	Get Outta Yourself	In You I Trust	Nearsighted	People That You Never Get To Love
	Him *6*	Lunch Hour	Partners In Crime	

HOMBRES, The
Memphis foursome: B.B. Cunningham, Gary Wayne McEwen, Johnny Will Hunter and Jerry Lee Masters. All but Masters were members of Ronny & The Daytonas touring band. Hunter died in 1976. Cunningham's brother, Bill, was a member of The Box Tops.

12/9/67	**180**	4		Let It Out (Let It All Hang Out)	**$20**	Verve F. 3036

Am I High
Gloria

Hey Little Girl	**Let It Out (Let It All Hang Out)** *12*	Little 2 Plus 2	So Sad	This Little Girl
It's A Gas		Mau Mau Mau	Sorry 'Bout That	Ya Ya

HONDELLS, The
Southern California-based quartet led by Ritchie Burns.

11/28/64	**119**	4		Go Little Honda	**$40**	Mercury 60940

Black Boots And Bikes
Death Valley Run

Guy Without Wheels	Hon-da Beach Party	**Little Honda** *9*	Ridin' Trails	Two Wheel Show Stopper
Haulin' Honda	Hot Rod High	Mean Streak	Rip's Bike	Wild One

HONEYCOMBS, The
English rock quintet featuring Dennis d'Ell (lead singer) and Ann "Honey" Lantree (drums).

1/2/65	**147**	2		Here Are The Honeycombs	**$30**	Interphon 88001

Color Slide
Have I The Right? *5*
How The Mighty Have Fallen

I Want To Be Free	Leslie Ane	Once You Know	This Too Shall Pass Away
It Ain't Necessarily So	Me From You	She's Too Way Out	Without You It Is Night
Just A Face In The Crowd	Nice While It Lasted	That's The Way	

HONEY CONE, The

Female soul trio formed in Los Angeles in 1969. Consisted of prominent backup singers; Carolyn Willis (member of The Girlfriends and Bob B. Soxx & The Blue Jeans), Edna Wright (sister of Darlene Love) and Shellie Clark (former Ikette and regular on the TV series *The Jim Nabors Hour* from 1969-70).

DEBUT DATE	PEAK POS	WKS CHR		ARTIST — Album Title	$	Label & Number
6/19/71	137	8		1 Sweet Replies	$10	Hot Wax 706
12/11/71+	72	20		2 Soulful Tapestry	$10	Hot Wax 707
9/23/72	189	4		3 Love, Peace & Soul	$10	Hot Wax 713

Ace In The Hole (3)
All The King's Horses (All The King's Men) (2)
Are You Man Enough, Are You Strong Enough (1)
Blessed Be Our Love (1)
Day I Found Myself (1,2) *23*
Deaf, Blind, Paralyzed (1)

Don't Count Your Chickens (Before They Hatch) (2)
Don't Send Me An Invitation (3)
Feeling's Gone (1)
How Does It Feel (2)
I Lost My Rainbow (3)

Innocent 'Til Proven Guilty (3)
Little More (2)
My Mind's On Leaving, But My Heart Won't Let Me Go (1)
O-O-O Baby, Baby (3)

One Monkey Don't Stop No Show Part I (2) *15*
One Monkey Don't Stop No Show Part II (2)
Sittin' On A Time Bomb (Waitin' For The Hurt To Come) (3) *96*
Stay In My Corner (3)

Stick-Up (2) *11*
Sunday Morning People (1)
Take Me With You (1)
V.I.P. (2)
Want Ads (1,2) *1*
We Belong Together (1)
When Will It End (1)
Who's It Gonna Be (2)

Who's Lovin' You (3)
Woman Can't Live By Bread Alone (3)
Woman's Prayer (3)
You Made Me Come To You (1)

HONEYDRIPPERS, The

A rock superstar gathering: vocalist Robert Plant (Led Zeppelin), with guitarists Jimmy Page (The Yardbirds, Led Zeppelin, The Firm), Jeff Beck (The Yardbirds) and Nile Rodgers (Chic).

10/20/84	4	31 ▲		Volume One ....[M]	$8	Es Paranza 90220

I Get A Thrill
I Got A Woman

Rockin' At Midnight *25*
Sea Of Love *3*

Young Boy Blues

HONEYMOON SUITE

Rock quintet from Toronto: Johnnie Dee (vocals), Derry Grehan, Gary Lalonde, Dave Betts and Ray Coburn (replaced by Rob Preuss in 1988).

8/25/84	60	17		1 Honeymoon Suite	$8	Warner 25098
3/15/86	61	35		2 The Big Prize	$8	Warner 25293
5/14/88	86	10		3 Racing After Midnight	$8	Warner 25652

All Along You Knew (2)
Bad Attitude (2)
Burning In Love (1)
Cold Look (3)
Face To Face (1)
Fast Company (3)

Feel It Again (2) *34*
Funny Business (1)
Heart On Fire (1)
It's Over Now (3)
It's Your Heart (1)
Lethal Weapon (3)

Long Way Back (3)
Lookin' Out For Number One (3)
Lost And Found (2)
Love Changes Everything (3) *91*

Love Fever (3)
New Girl Now (1) *57*
Now That You Got Me (1)
Once The Feeling (2)
One By One (2)
Other Side Of Midnight (3)

Stay In The Light (1)
Take My Hand (2)
Tears On The Page (3)
Turn My Head (1)
Wave Babies (1)
What Does It Take (2) *52*

Words In The Wind (2)
Wounded (2)

HOODOO GURUS

Australian pop-rock quartet: Dave Faulkner (vocals), Brad Shepherd, Mark Kingsmill and Clyde Bramley. Rick Grossman (former member of The Divinyls) replaced Bramley in 1989.

5/10/86	140	7		1 Mars Needs Guitars!	$8	Elektra 60485
				album originally released on Big Time 009		
5/2/87	120	13		2 Blow Your Cool!	$8	Elektra 60728
8/12/89	101	15		3 Magnum Cum Louder	$8	RCA 9781
5/18/91	172	1		4 Kinky	$12	RCA 3009

All The Way (3)
Another World (3)
Axe Grinder (3)
Baby Can Dance (Parts II-IV) (3)
Bittersweet (1)
Brainscan (4)
Castles In The Air (4)
Come Anytime (3)

Come On (2)
Death Defying (1)
Death In The Afternoon (3)
Desiree (4)
Dressed In Black (4)
Glamourpuss (3)
Good Times (2)
Hallucination (3)
Hayride To Hell (1)

Head In The Sand (4)
Hell For Leather (3)
I Don't Know Anything (3)
I Don't Mind (4)
I Was The One (2)
In The Middle Of The Land (2)
In The Wild (1)
Like Wow - Wipeout (1)

Mars Needs Guitars! (1)
Miss Freelove '69 (4)
My Caravan (3)
On My Street (2)
1000 Miles Away (4)
Other Side Of Paradise (1)
Out That Door (4)
Party Machine (2)
Place In The Sun (4)

Poison Pen (1)
Shadow Me (3)
She (1)
Show Some Emotion (1)
Something's Coming (4)
Too Much Fun (2)
What's My Scene (2)
Where Nowhere Is (4)
Where's That Hit? (3)

HOOKER, John Lee

Born on 8/22/17 in Clarksdale, Mississippi. Internationally-known blues guitarist/singer. Featured in the movie *The Blues Brothers*. Inducted into the Rock and Roll Hall of Fame in 1991.

2/27/71	73	16		1 Hooker 'N Heat	$15	Liberty 35002 [2]
				CANNED HEAT & JOHN LEE HOOKER		
3/27/71	126	13		2 Endless Boogie	$10	ABC 720 [2]
				prominent backing artists include Steve Miller, Billy Ingram, Carl Radle and Jim Gordon of Derek & The Dominos, and Mark Naftalin (Paul Butterfield Blues Band)		
3/18/72	130	6		3 Never Get Out Of These Blues Alive	$10	ABC 736
				features prominent artists Van Morrison, Elvin Bishop and Charlie Musselwhite		
10/7/89+	62	38		4 The Healer	$8	Chameleon 74808
				with special guests Carlos Santana, Bonnie Raitt, Robert Cray, Canned Heat, Los Lobos, George Thorogood and Charlie Musselwhite		
9/28/91	101	11		5 Mr. Lucky	$12	Charisma 91724
				star players include Keith Richards, Van Morrison, Albert Collins, Robert Cray, Ry Cooder, Nick Lowe, Booker T Jones & Carlos Santana		

Alimonia Blues (1)
Baby Face (4)
Backstabbers (5)
Boogie Chillen No. 2 (1)
Boogie With The Hook (3)
Bottle Up And Go (1)
Bumblebee, Bumblebee (3)
Burning Hell (1)
Country Boy (3)
Crawlin' Kingsnake (5)
Cuttin' Out (4)
Doin' The Shout (2)

Drifter (1)
Endless Boogie, Parts 27 And 28 (2)
Father Was A Jockey (5)
Feelin' Is Gone (1)
Good 'Un ..see: (I Got) A
Healer, The (4)
Highway 13 (5)
Hit The Road (3)
House Rent Boogie (2)
I Cover The Waterfront (5)

I Don't Need No Steam Heat (2)
(I Got) A Good 'Un (2)
I Got My Eyes On You (1)
I Want To Hug You (5)
I'm In The Mood (4)
Just You And Me (1)
Kick Hit 4 Hit Kix U (Blues For Jimi And Janis) (2)
Let's Make It (1)
Letter To My Baby (3)
Meet Me In The Bottom (1)

Messin' With The Hook (1)
Mr. Lucky (5)
My Dream (4)
Never Get Out Of These Blues Alive (3)
No Substitute (4)
Peavine (1)
Pots On, Gas On High (2)
Rockin' Chair (4)
Sally Mae (4)
Send Me Your Pillow (1)
Sheep Out On The Foam (2)

Sittin' Here Thinkin' (1)
Sittin' In My Dark Room (2)
Standin' At The Crossroads (2)
Stripped Me Naked (5)
Susie (5)
T.B. Sheets (3)
That's Alright (4)
Think Twice Before You Go (4)
This Is Hip (5)

We Might As Well Call It Through (I Don't Get Married To Your Two-Timing Mother) (2)
Whiskey And Wimmen' (1)
World Today (1)
You Talk Too Much (1)

HOOPER, Stix

Drummer with The Crusaders. Born Nesbert Hooper in 1939 in Houston.

11/10/79	166	5		The World Within ....[I]	$8	MCA 3180

African Spirit
Brazos River Breakdown

Cordon Bleu

Jasmine Breeze

Little Drummer Boy

Passion

Rum Or Tequila??

DEBUT DATE	PEAK POS	WKS CHR	GOLD	ARTIST — Album Title	$	Label & Number

HOOTERS
Philadelphia rock quintet led by Rob Hyman and Eric Bazilian (arrangers/musicians/backing vocalists on Cyndi Lauper's platinum album *She's So Unusual*). Hooter: nickname of their keyboard-harmonica.

5/25/85+	12	74	●	1 Nervous Night	$8	Columbia 39912
8/8/87	27	26	●	2 One Way Home	$8	Columbia 40659
12/2/89+	115	16		3 Zig Zag	$8	Columbia 45058

All You Zombies (1) *58*   Day By Day (1) *18*   Fightin' On The Same Side (2)   Heaven Laughs (3)   Johnny B (2) *61*   South Ferry Road (1)
Always A Place (3)   Deliver Me (3)   500 Miles (3) *97*   Karla With A K (2)   Washington's Day (2)
And We Danced (1) *21*   Don't Knock It 'Til You Try It (3)   Give The Music Back (3)   Mr. Big Baboon (3)   Where Do The Children Go (1) *38*
Beat Up Guitar (3)   Don't Take My Car Out Tonight (3)   Graveyard Waltz (2)   One Way Home (2)   You Never Know Who Your Friends Are (3)
Blood From A Stone (1)   Engine 999 (2)   Hanging On A Heartbeat (1)   Satellite (2) *61*
Brother, Don't You Walk Away (3)   Hard Rockin Summer (2)   She Comes In Colors (1)

HOPE, Bob
Enduring institution of American entertainment. Comedian/radio-TV-film star. Born Leslie Townes on 5/29/03 in London. Moved to Ohio at age four. Began in 1920s vaudeville. Since World War II, has entertained U.S. troops overseas. Recipient of the Presidential Medal of Freedom (1969), an Emmy and an honorary Academy Award.

7/4/76	175	4		America Is 200 Years Old...And There's Still Hope! [C]	$10	Capitol 11538

comedy sketches featuring Jim Backus, Phyllis Diller and Dudley Moore

Betsy Ross - Song: Young Glory   Bunker Hill - Song: You Can't Win A War Without A War Song   Cornwallis' Surrender   Paul Revere's Ride - Song: Paul Revere   Washington Crosses The Delaware - Song: Drink It Down Boys
Boston Commons - Songs: Rapid Robert/The Boston Tea Party   Burning Tree   Declaration Of Independence - Song: Freedom Policy

HOPKIN, Mary
Born on 5/3/50 in Pontardawe, Wales. Discovered by the model Twiggy. Married to producer Tony Visconti (worked with David Bowie) from December 1971 to October 1981.

3/29/69	28	20		Post Card	$15	Apple 3351

produced by Paul McCartney

Game, The   Lord Of The Reedy River   Pebble And The Man (Happiness Runs)   Puppy Song   Those Were The Days 2   Young Love
Honeymoon Song   Love Is The Sweetest Thing   There's No Business Like Show Business   Voyage Of The Moon
Inch Worm   Lullaby Of The Leaves   Prince En Avignon   Y Blodyn Gwyn

HOPKINS, Nicky
Born on 2/24/44 in London. Session pianist for The Rolling Stones, The Who, The Kinks and others.

2/12/72	33	11		1 Jamming With Edward! [I]	$12	Rolling S. 39100
5/5/73	108	10		2 The Tin Man Was A Dreamer	$10	Columbia 32074

jam session with Ry Cooder, Mick Jagger, Bill Wyman and Charlie Watts

Banana Anna (2)   Dolly (2)   Edward's Thrump Up (1)   It Hurts Me Too (1)   Shout It Out (2)   Waiting For The Band (2)
Blow With Ry (1)   Dreamer, The (2)   Highland Fling (1)   Lawyer's Lament (2)   Speed On (2)
Boudoir Stomp (1)   Edward (2)   Interlude A La El Hopo (1)   Pig's Boogie (2)   Sundown In Mexico (2)

HORNE, Jimmy "Bo"
Soul singer/dancer from Miami.

7/1/78	122	10		Dance Across The Floor	$8	Sunshine S. 7801

Ask The Birds And The Bees   Don't Worry About It   Gimme Some   It's Your Sweet Love   Let Me (Let Me Be Your Lover)
Dance Across The Floor *38*   Get Happy   I Wanna Go Home With You

HORNE, Lena
Born on 6/30/17 in Brooklyn. Broadway and movie musical star. Long-married to bandleader Lennie Hayton. Her career reached a new peak in the early 1980s with her one-woman Broadway show. Won the Lifetime Achievement Grammy in 1989.

9/16/57	24	2		1 Lena Horne at the Waldorf Astoria [L]	$35	RCA 1028
11/17/58	20	1		2 Give The Lady What She Wants	$35	RCA 1879
6/22/59	13	22		3 Porgy & Bess	$25	RCA 1507

LENA HORNE/HARRY BELAFONTE

4/14/62	102	8		4 Lena On The Blue Side	$25	RCA 2465
2/9/63	102	5		5 Lena...Lovely And Alive	$25	RCA 2587
5/16/70	162	10		6 Lena & Gabor	$12	Skye 15

LENA HORNE & GABOR SZABO

9/26/81	112	9		7 Lena Horne: The Lady And Her Music [OC-L]	$10	Qwest 3597 [2]

Lena won a Tony in this Broadway musical; "Cotton Club Revue Medley" contains titles performed by various cast members

As Long As I Live (7)   Everybody's Talkin' (6)   I Only Have Eyes For You (5)   It Might As Well Be Spring (4)   Oh, I Got Plenty Of Nothin' (3)   That's What Miracles Are All About (7)
As You Desire Me (4)   Fly (7)   I Surrender Dear (5)   It's A Lonesome Old Town (4)   Paradise (4)   There's A Boat That's Leavin' Soon For New York (3)
At Long Last Love (2)   Fool On The Hill (6)   I Understand (5)   Just In Time (2)   People Will Say We're In Love (2)
Baubles, Bangles And Beads (2)   From This Moment On (1,7)   I Wanna Be Loved (4)   Just One Of Those Things (7)   Push De Button (7)   They Didn't Believe Me (4)
Bess, Oh Where's My Bess (3)   Get Out Of Town (2)   I Want To Be Happy (3,7)   Lady Is A Tramp (7)   Raisin' The Rent (7)   Today I Love Everybody (1)
Bess, You Is My Woman (3)   Honey In The Honeycomb (1)   I Wants To Stay Here (3)   Lady Must Live (7)   Rocky Raccoon (6)   Watch What Happens (6,7)
Bewitched (2)   Honeysuckle Rose (1)   I'm Beginning To See The Light (medley) (7)   Lady With The Fan (7)   Rules Of The Road (4)   What'll I Do (4)
Bewitched, Bothered And Bewildered (7)   How You Say It (1)   I'm Confessin' (That I Love You) (5)   Let Me Love You (1)   Someone To Watch Over Me (4)   Where Or When (7)
Can't Help Lovin' Dat Man (7)   I Ain't Got Nobody (And Nobody Cares For Me) (5)   I'm Glad There Is You (7)   Let's Put Out The Lights And Go To Sleep (5)   Something (6)   Woman Is A Sometime Thing (3)
Cole Porter Medley (1)   I Concentrate On You (5)   I'm Gonna Sit Right Down And Write Myself A Letter (7)   Life Goes On (3)   Speak Low (2)   Yesterday When I Was Young (6,7)
Come Runnin' (1)   I Found A New Baby (2)   I'm Through With Love (4)   Love (2,7)   Stormy Weather (Part I & II) (7)   You'd Better Know It (2)
Darn That Dream (4)   I Get The Blues When It Rains (5)   I've Grown Accustomed To His Face (5)   Message To Michael (6)   Street Calls Medley (3)
Day In - Day Out (1)   I Got A Name (7)   If You Believe (7)   Mood Indigo (medley) (7)   Summertime (3)
Deed I Do (7)   I Got Rhythm (5)   In My Life (6)   My Man's Gone Now (3)   Surrey With The Fringe On Top (7)
Diamonds Are A Girl's Best Friend (2)   I Hadn't Anyone Till You (4)   It Ain't Necessarily So (3)   My Mood Is You (5)   New-Fangled Tango (1)   Nightwind (6)
I Let A Song Go Out Of My Heart (5)   I Love To Love (1)

DEBUT DATE	PEAK POS	WKS CHR	GOLD	ARTIST — Album Title	$	Label & Number

HORNSBY, Bruce, And The Range

Singer/pianist/songwriter/leader of jazz-influenced pop quintet The Range. Born on 11/23/54 in Williamsburg, Virginia. Moved to Los Angeles in 1980. Backing pianist for Sheena Easton's touring band, 1983. Formed The Range in 1984 with Joe Puerta (bass), John Molo (drums), guitarists George Marinelli and David Mansfield (replaced by Peter Harris who left by 1990). Won the 1986 Best New Artist Grammy Award.

DEBUT DATE	PEAK POS	WKS CHR	GOLD	ARTIST — Album Title	$	Label & Number
6/21/86+	3	73	▲³	1 The Way It Is	$8	RCA 5904
				originally released on RCA 8058 (with different cover)		
5/21/88	5	27	▲	2 scenes from the southside	$8	RCA 6686
7/7/90	20	21	●	3 A Night On The Town	$12	RCA 2041

Across The River (3) 18
Another Day (3)
Barren Ground (3)
Carry The Water (3)
Defenders Of The Flag (2)

Down The Road Tonight (1)
Every Little Kiss (1) 14
Fire On The Cross (3)
I Will Walk With You (2)
Jacob's Ladder (1)

Long Race (1)
Look Out Any Window (2) 35
Lost Soul (3) 84
Mandolin Rain (1) 4

Night On The Town (3)
Old PlayGround (2)
On The Western Skyline (1)
Red Plains (1)
River Runs Low (1)

Road Not Taken (2)
Show Goes On (2)
Special Night (3)
Stander On The Mountain (3)
Stranded On Easy Street (3)

These Arms Of Mine (3)
Till The Dreaming's Done (2)
Valley Road (2) 5
Way It Is (1) 1
Wild Frontier (1)

HOROWITZ, Vladimir

Classical pianist. Born Vladimir Gorowicz on 10/3/03 in the U.S.S.R.; died of a heart attack on 11/5/89. In 1925, left the U.S.S.R. Changed his name in 1926. Moved to the U.S. in 1928. Married for 56 years (until his death) to Wanda, the daughter of famed conductor Arturo Toscanini. His last public performance was in 1987. Won the Lifetime Achievement Grammy in 1990 and 23 Grammys.

DEBUT DATE	PEAK POS	WKS CHR	GOLD	ARTIST — Album Title	$	Label & Number
11/10/62	14	22		1 Vladimir Horowitz (Chopin, Schumann, Rachmaninoff, Liszt)	[I] $25	Columbia 6371
6/22/03	129	8		2 The Sound Of Horowitz	[I] $25	Columbia 6411
7/24/65	22	32		3 Horowitz at Carnegie Hall - An Historic Return	[I-L] $20	Columbia 728 [2]
11/16/68	185	4		4 Horowitz On Television	[I-L] $15	Columbia 7106
				a Carnegie Hall performance on 2/1/68		
4/29/78	102	14		5 Golden Jubilee Concert - Rachmaninoff Concerto No. 3	[I-L] $10	RCA 2633
				a Carnegie Hall concert with Eugene Ormandy & The New York Philharmonic		

Bach-Busoni: Organ Toccata In C Major (3)
Chopin: Ballade In G Minor, Op. 23 (3,4)
Chopin: Etude In F Major, Op. 10, No. 8 (3)
Chopin: Mazurka In C-Sharp Minor, Op. 30, No. 4 (3)
Chopin: Nocturne In F Minor, Op. 55, No. 1 (4)

Chopin: Polonaise In F-Sharp Minor, Op. 44 (4)
Chopin: Sonata No. 2 In B-Flat Minor, Op. 35 (1)
Debussy: Serenade For The Doll from Children's Corner (3)
Horowitz: Variations On A Theme from Bizet's Carmen (4)
Liszt: Hungarian Rhapsody No. 19 (1)

Moszkowski: Etude In A-Flat Major, Op. 72, No. 11 (3)
Rachmaninoff: Concerto No. 3 In D Minor, Op. 30 (5)
Rachmaninoff: Etude-Tableau In C Major, Op. 33, No. 2 (1)
Rachmaninoff: Etude-Tableau In E-Flat Minor, Op. 39, No. 5 (1)
Scarlatti: Sonata In A Major, Longo 483 (2)

Scarlatti: Sonata In E Major, Longo 430 (2)
Scarlatti: Sonata In G Major, Longo 209 (2)
Scarlatti: Two Sonatas - E Major (L. 23) G Major (L. 335) (4)
Schubert: Impromptu In G-Flat Major, Op. 90, No. 3 (2)
Schumann: Arabesque, Op. 18 (1,4)

Schumann: Fantasy In C Major, Op. 17 (3)
Schumann: Scenes Of Childhood, Op. 15 (3)
Schumann: Toccata, Op. 7 (2)
Schumann: Traumerei from Kinderszenen, Op. 15 (3,4)
Scriabin: Poem In F-Sharp Major, Op. 32, No. 1 (3)
Scriabin: Etude In C-Sharp Minor, Op. 2, No. 1 (2,3)

Scriabin: Etude In D-Sharp Minor, Op. 8, No. 12 (2,4)
Scriabin: Sonata No. 9, Op. 68 (3)

HORSLIPS

Dublin, Ireland rock quintet: Eamon Carr, Barry Devlin, John Fean, Jim Lockhart and Charles O'Connor.

DEBUT DATE	PEAK POS	WKS CHR	GOLD	ARTIST — Album Title	$	Label & Number
2/25/78	98	9		1 Aliens	$8	DJM 16
3/10/79	155	9		2 The Man Who Built America	$8	DJM 20

Before The Storm (1)
Come Summer (1)
Exiles (1)
Ghosts (1)

Green Star Liner (2)
Homesick (2)
I'll Be Waiting (2)
If It Takes All Night (2)

Letters From Home (2)
Lifetime To Pay (1)
Loneliness (2)
Long Time Ago (2)

Long Week-End (2)
Man Who Built America (2)
New York Wakes (1)
Second Avenue (1)

Speed The Plough (1)
Stowaway (1)
Sure The Boy Was Green (1)
Tonight (You're With Me) (2)

Wrath Of The Rain (1)

HORTON, Johnny

Country singer. Born on 4/30/25 in Los Angeles and raised in Tyler, Texas. Married to Billie Jean Jones, widow of country music superstar Hank Williams. Killed in an auto accident on 11/5/60.

DEBUT DATE	PEAK POS	WKS CHR	GOLD	ARTIST — Album Title	$	Label & Number
2/27/61	8	34	▲	1 Johnny Horton's Greatest Hits	[G] $30	Columbia 8396
4/28/62	104	10		2 Honky-Tonk Man	[K] $30	Columbia 8779

All For The Love Of A Girl (1)
Battle Of New Orleans (1) 1
Comanche (The Brave Horse) (1)
Everytime I'm Kissing You (2)

Goodbye, Lonesome, Hello, Baby Doll (2)
Honky Tonk Hardwood Floor (2)
Honky-Tonk Man (2) 96

I Got A Hole In My Pirogue (2)
I'm A One-Woman Man (2)
I'm Coming Home (2)
I'm Ready, If You're Willing (1)

Jim Bridger (1)
Johnny Freedom (1) 69
Johnny Reb (1) 54
Mansion You Stole (1)
North To Alaska (1) 4

Ole Slew-Foot (2)
She Knows Why (2)
Sink The Bismarck (1) 3
Sleepy-Eyed John (2) 54
They'll Never Take Her Love From Me (2)

When It's Springtime In Alaska (It's Forty Below) (1)
Whispering Pines (2)
Wild One (2)

HOT

Interracial female trio: Gwen Owens, Cathy Carson and Juanita Curiel. First known as Sugar & Spice.

DEBUT DATE	PEAK POS	WKS CHR	GOLD	ARTIST — Album Title	$	Label & Number
5/28/77	125	15		Hot	$8	Big Tree 89522

Angel In Your Arms 6
Don't Let Me Leave You Behind

If You Don't Love Her (When You Gonna Leave Her?)
Just 'Cause I'm Guilty
Mama's Girl

Right Feeling At The Wrong Time 65
Who's Gonna Love You

Why Don't You Believe In Your Man
You Brought The Woman Out Of Me 71

You Can Do It
You're The Reason For All The Songs

HOT BUTTER

Hot Butter is Moog synthesizer player Stan Free.

DEBUT DATE	PEAK POS	WKS CHR	GOLD	ARTIST — Album Title	$	Label & Number
10/21/72	137	7		Popcorn	[I] $15	Musicor 3242

Amazing Grace
Apache

At The Movies
Day By Day

Hot Butter
Pipeline

Popcorn 9
Song Of The Narobi Trio

Telestar
Tomatoes

Tristana

HOT CHOCOLATE

Interracial rock-soul group formed in London by lead singer Errol Brown in 1970. Included Harvey Hinsley (guitar), Larry Ferguson (keyboards), Tony Wilson (bass), Patrick Olive (congas) and Tony Connor (drums). Wilson left in 1975, Olive switched to bass.

DEBUT DATE	PEAK POS	WKS CHR	GOLD	ARTIST — Album Title	$	Label & Number
3/1/75	55	17		1 Cicero Park	$8	Big Tree 89503
11/22/75+	41	21		2 Hot Chocolate	$8	Big Tree 89512
9/18/76	172	6		3 Man To Man	$8	Big Tree 89519
1/6/79	31	16		4 Every 1's A Winner	$8	Infinity 9002

DEBUT DATE	PEAK POS	WKS CHR	GOLD	ARTIST — Album Title	$	Label & Number
7/28/79	112	6	5	Going Through The Motions	$8	Infinity 9010

Amazing Skin Song (2) — Brother Louie (1) — Call The Police (2) — Changing World (1) — Child's Prayer (2) — Cicero Park (1) — Confetti Day (4) — Congas Man (5) — Could Have Been Born In The Ghetto (Theme from Love Head) (1) — Dance (Get Down To It) (5) — **Disco Queen** (1) *28* — Dollar Sign (2) — **Don't Stop It Now** (3) *42* — Dreaming Of You (5) — **Emma** (1) *8* — **Every 1's A Winner** (4) *6* — Funky Rock 'N' Roll (1) — **Going Through The Motions** (5) *53* — Harry (3) — Heaven Is In The Back Seat Of My Cadillac (3) — Hello America (2) — I Just Love What You're Doing (5) — I'll Put You Together Again (4) — I'm Going To Make You Feel Like A Woman (4) — Lay Me Down (2) — Living On A Shoe String (3) — Love Is The Answer One More Time (4) — Love Like Yours (1) — Love's Coming On Strong (2) — Makin' Music (1) — Man To Man (3) — Mindless Boogie (5) — Night Ride (5) — Put Your Love In Me (4) — Seventeen Years Of Age (3) — Sex Appeal (3) — **So You Win Again** (4) *31* — Sometimes It Hurts To Be A Friend (4) — Stay With Me (4) — Street, The (2) — Sugar Daddy (3) — Warm Smile (2) — You Could've Been A Lady (3) — **You Sexy Thing** (2) *3* — You're A Natural High (1)

HOTHOUSE FLOWERS
Irish soul band from Dublin: Liam O Maonlai (vocals), Fiachna O Braonain (guitar), Peter O'Toole (bass), Leo Barnes (sax) and Jerry Fehily (drums).

DEBUT DATE	PEAK POS	WKS CHR	GOLD	ARTIST — Album Title	$	Label & Number
8/27/88	88	33	1	people	$8	London 828101
7/14/90	122	16	2	Home	$12	London 828197

Ballad Of Katie (1) — Christchurch Bells (2) — Dance To The Storm (2) — Don't Go (1) — Eyes Wide Open (1) — Feet On The Ground (1) — Forgiven (1) — Give It Up (2) — Giving It All Away (2) — Hallelujah Jordan (1) — Hardstone City (2) — Home (2) — I Can See Clearly Now (2) — I'm Sorry (1) — If You Go (1) — It'll Be Easier In The Morning (1) — Love Don't Work This Way (1) — Movies (2) — Older We Get (1) — Seoladh na nGamhna (2) — Shut Up And Listen (2) — Sweet Marie (2) — Trying To Get Through (2) — Water (2) — Yes I Was (1)

HOT TUNA
Formed by Jefferson Airplane members Jorma Kaukonen (guitar) and Jack Casady (bass). Various personnel included harmonica player Will Scarlett (1970-71), violinist Papa John Creach (1971-72; later with Jefferson Starship), drummers Sammy Piazza (1971-74) and Bob Steeler (1975-78), and keyboardist Nick Buck (1978).

DEBUT DATE	PEAK POS	WKS CHR	GOLD	ARTIST — Album Title	$	Label & Number
7/18/70	30	19	1	Hot Tuna .... [L]	$15	RCA 4353
6/26/71	43	13	2	First Pull Up Then Pull Down .... [L]	$15	RCA 4550
3/18/72	68	23	3	Burgers	$15	Grunt 1004
2/9/74	148	7	4	The Phosphorescent Rat	$15	Grunt 0348
5/10/75	75	11	5	America's Choice	$15	Grunt 0820
11/29/75	97	9	6	Yellow Fever	$15	Grunt 1238
11/20/76	116	10	7	Hoppkorv	$15	Grunt 1920
4/15/78	92	10	8	Double Dose .... [L]	$20	Grunt 2545 [2]

Baby What You Want Me To Do (6) — Bar Room Crystal Ball (2) — Been So Long (2) — Bowlegged Woman, Knock Kneed Man (7,8) — Candy Man (2) — Come Back Baby (2) — Corners Without Exits (4) — Day To Day Out The Window Blues (4) — Death Don't Have No Mercy (1) — Don't You Leave Me Here (1) — Drivin' Around (7) — Easy Now (4) — Embryonic Journey (8) — Extrication Love Song (7,8) — Free Rein (6) — Funky #7 (5,8) — Genesis (8) — Great Divide: Revisited (5) — Half/Time Saturation (6) — Hesitation Blues (1) — Highway Song (3) — Hot Jelly Roll Blues (6) — Hit Single #1 (5) — How Long Blues (1) — I Can't Be Satisfied (7,8) — I Don't Wanna Go (5) — I See The Light (4,8) — I Wish You Would (7,8) — In The Kingdom (4) — Invitation (5) — It's So Easy (7) — John's Other (2) — Keep On Truckin' (3) — Keep Your Lamps Trimmed And Burning (2,8) — Killing Time In The Crystal City (8) — Know You Rider (1) — Let Us Get Together Right Down Here (3) — Letter To The North Star (4) — Living Just For You (4) — Mann's Fate (1) — Never Happen No More (2) — New Song (For The Morning) (1) — 99 Year Blues (3) — Ode For Billy Dean (3) — Oh Lord, Search My Heart (1) — Sally, Where'd You Get Your Liquor From? (4) — Santa Claus Retreat (7) — Sea Child (3) — Seeweed Strut (4) — Serpent Of Dreams (5,8) — Sleep Song (5) — Soliloquy For 2 (4) — Song For The Fire Maiden (6) — Song From The Stainless Cymbal (7) — Sunny Day Strut (3) — Sunrise Dance With The Devil (6,8) — Surphase Tension (6) — Talking 'Bout You (7,8) — True Religion (3) — Uncle Sam Blues (1) — Walkin' Blues (5) — Want You To Know (2) — Watch The North Wind Rise (7,8) — Water Song (3) — Winin' Boy Blues (1,8)

HOUSEMARTINS, The
Quartet from Hull, England led by vocalist Paul (P.d.) Heaton. Disbanded in June 1988. Heaton and drummer Dave Hemmingway formed The Beautiful South. Bassist Norman Cook formed Beats International.

DEBUT DATE	PEAK POS	WKS CHR	GOLD	ARTIST — Album Title	$	Label & Number
2/7/87	124	14	1	London 0 Hull 4	$8	Elektra 60501
1/16/88	177	6	2	The People Who Grinned Themselves To Death	$8	Elektra 60761

Anxious (1) — Bow Down (2) — Build (2) — Five Get Over Excited (2) — Flag Day (1) — Freedom (1) — Get Up Off Our Knees (1) — Happy Hour (1) — I Can't Put My Finger On It (2) — Johannesburg (2) — Lean On Me (1) — Light Is Always Green (2) — Me And The Farmer (2) — Over There (1) — People Who Grinned Themselves To Death (2) — Pirate Aggro (2) — Reverends Revenge (1) — Sheep (1) — Sitting On A Fence (1) — Think For A Minute (1) — We're Not Deep (2) — We're Not Going Back (2) — World's On Fire (2) — You Better Be Doubtful (2)

HOUSE OF FREAKS
Richmond, Virginia duo: singer/guitarist Bryan Harvey and drummer Johnny Hott.

DEBUT DATE	PEAK POS	WKS CHR	GOLD	ARTIST — Album Title	$	Label & Number
5/6/89	154	10		Tantilla	$8	Rhino 70846

Big Houses — Birds Of Prey — Broken Bones — Family Tree — I Want Answers — Kill The Mockingbird — King Of Kings — Righteous Will Fall — Sun Gone Down — When The Hammer Came Down — White Folks' Blood — World Of Tomorrow

HOUSE OF LORDS
Quintet of hard-rock veterans: keyboardist Gregg Giuffria (Angel, Giuffria), bassist Chuck Wright (Giuffria, Quiet Riot), guitarist Lanny Cordola (Ozzy Osbourne's band, Giuffria), drummer Ken Mary (Alice Cooper's band) and vocalist James Christian. Cordola, replaced by Michael Guy in 1990, went on to record Contemporary Christian rock.

DEBUT DATE	PEAK POS	WKS CHR	GOLD	ARTIST — Album Title	$	Label & Number
11/19/88+	78	27	1	House Of Lords	$8	RCA/Simn. 8530
10/20/90+	121	18	2	Sahara	$12	Simmons 2170

American Babylon (2) — Call My Name (1) — Can't Find My Way Home (2) — Chains Of Love (2) — Edge Of Your Life (1) — Heart On The Line (2) — Hearts Of The World (1) — **I Wanna Be Loved** (1) *58* — It Ain't Love (2) — Jealous Heart (1) — Kiss Of Fire (2) — Laydown Staydown (2) — Lookin' For Strange (1) — Love Don't Lie (1) — Pleasure Palace (1) — **Remember My Name** (2) *72* — Sahara (2) — Shoot (2) — Slip Of The Tongue (1) — Under Blue Skies (1)

HOUSE OF LOVE, The
British pop quartet led by vocalist Guy Chadwick.

DEBUT DATE	PEAK POS	WKS CHR	GOLD	ARTIST — Album Title	$	Label & Number
9/17/88	156	7	1	The House Of Love	$8	Relativity 8245
5/5/90	148	8	2	The House Of Love	$12	Fontana 842293

HOUSE OF LOVE, The — Cont'd

Beatles And The Stones (2)
Blind (2)
Christine (1)
Fisherman's Tale (1)
Hannah (2)
Happy (1)
Hedonist (2)
Hope (1)
I Don't Know Why I Love You (2)
In A Room (2)
Love In A Car (1)
Man To Child (1)
Never (2)
Road (1)
Salome (1)
Se Dest (2)
Shake And Crawl (2)
Shine On (2)
Someone's Got To Love You (2)
Sulphur (1)
32nd Floor (2)
Touch Me (1)

HOUSE OF PAIN

Los Angeles-based rap outfit: Erik "Everlast" Schrody, "Danny Boy" O'Connor and Leor "DJ Lethal" DiMant. Met at Taft High School in Woodland Hills, California. Both Schrody and O'Connor were born in the U.S.A. of Irish parentage. DiMant was born in Latvia.

| 8/15/92 | 14 | 26↑▲ | | House Of Pain .... | $12 | Tommy Boy 1056 |

All My Love
Come And Get Some Of This
Danny Boy, Danny Boy
Feel It
Guess Who's Back
House And The Rising Sun
House Of Pain Anthem
Jump Around 3
Life Goes On
One For The Road
Put On Your Shit Kickers
Put Your Head Out
Salutations
Shamrocks And Shenanigans (Boom Shalock Lock Boom) 65
Top O' The Morning To Ya

HOUSTON, David

Born on 12/9/38 in Bossier City, Louisiana. Country singer/songwriter/guitarist. Godson of 1920s pop singer Gene Austin and a descendant of Sam Houston and Robert E. Lee.

8/6/66	57	20	1	Almost Persuaded	$15	Epic 26213
9/13/69	143	5	2	David	$12	Epic 26482
				an album of spiritual songs		
4/18/70	194	2	3	Baby, Baby	$12	Epic 26539
9/26/70	170	3	4	Wonders Of The Wine	$12	Epic 30108

All My Love (1)
Almost Persuaded (1) 24
Baby, Baby (I Know You're A Lady) (3)
Bridge Over Troubled Water (4)
China Doll (3)
Don't Mention Tomorrow (1,3)
From A Jack To A King (1)
Give All Your Love (3)
Gonna Lay Down My Burdens (2)
Heart, We Did All That We Could (1)
Heavenly Sunshine (4)
Hold That Tear (3)
Homecoming (3)
I Do My Swinging At Home (4)
I Thought I'd Die (3)
I'm Not Man Enough (To Make My Heart Stop Loving You) (4)
(I'm So) Afraid Of Losing You Again (3)
I've Been Had (1)
If God Can Forgive Me (Why Can't You?) (4)
If I Had My Way (4)
Jump Around (1)
Little Pedro (1)
Livin' In A House Full Of Love (1)
Long Lonesome Highway (4)
Mama, Take Me Home (4)
Milky White Way (2)
My Love (4)
Oh Happy Day (2)
Okie From Muskogee (4)
Old Blind Barnabas (2)
Old Time Religion (2)
Ramblin' Rose (1)
Swing Low, Sweet Chariot (2)
This Train (2)
Tonight You Belong To Me (1)
True Love's A Lasting Thing (3)
Watching My World Walk Away (3)
We Got Love (1)
Were You There (2)
When The Saints Go Marching In (2)
Will The Circle Be Unbroken? (2)
Wonders Of The Wine (4)
You're Always The One (3)

HOUSTON, Thelma

Soul singer/actress from Leland, Mississippi. In films *Norman...Is That You?*, *Death Scream* and *The Seventh Dwarf*.

12/25/76+	11	37	1	Any Way You Like It	$10	Tamla 345
6/18/77	53	12	2	Thelma & Jerry	$8	Motown 887
				THELMA HOUSTON & JERRY BUTLER		
11/12/77	64	11	3	The Devil In Me	$8	Tamla 358
5/30/81	144	6	4	Never Gonna Be Another One	$8	RCA 3842

And You've Got Me (2)
Any Way You Like It (3)
Baby, I Love You Too Much (3)
Come To Me (1)
Differently (1)
Don't Know Why I Love You (1)
Don't Leave Me This Way (1) 1
Don't Make Me Over (4)
Don't Make Me Pay (For Another Girl's Mistake) (1)
Give Me Something To Believe In (3)
Hollywood (4)
I Can't Go On Living Without Your Love (3)
I Love You Through Windows (2)
I'm Here Again (3)
I've Got The Devil In Me (3)
If It's The Last Thing I Do (1) 47
If You Feel It (4)
If You Leave Me Now (medley) (2)
It's A Lifetime Thing (2)
It's Just Me Feeling Good (3)
Joy Inside My Tears (4)
Let's Get Together (2)
Let's Pretend ..see: (Play The Game Of)
Love So Right (medley) (2)
Memories (3)
Never Give You Up (4)
Never Gonna Be Another One (4)
96 Tears (4)
Only The Beginning (2)
(Play The Game Of) Let's Pretend (2)
Sharing Something Perfect Between Ourselves (1)
Sweet Love I've Found (2)
There's No Runnin' Away From Love (4)
Too Many Teardrops (4)
Triflin' (3)
Your Eyes (3)

| ★★289★★ | | | | **HOUSTON, Whitney** | | |

Born on 8/9/63 in Newark, New Jersey. Daughter of Cissy Houston and cousin of Dionne Warwick. Began singing career at age 11 with the gospel group New Hope Baptist Junior Choir. As a teen, worked as a backing vocalist for Chaka Khan and Lou Rawls. Pursued modeling career in 1981, appearing in *Glamour* magazine and the cover of *Seventeen*. Married Bobby Brown on 7/18/92.

3/30/85+	1[14]	162	▲[9]	1	Whitney Houston	$8	Arista 8212
6/27/87	1[11]	85	▲[6]	2	Whitney	$8	Arista 8405
11/24/90	3	51	▲[3]	3	I'm Your Baby Tonight	$12	Arista 8616
12/5/92	1[12]↑	13	↑▲[6]	4	The Bodyguard ....[S]	$12	Arista 18699

Whitney co-stars in the film; includes "Even If My Heart Would Break" by Kenny G & Aaron Neville; "Someday (I'm Coming Back)" by Lisa Stansfield; "It's Gonna Be A Lovely Day" by The S.O.U.L. S.Y.S.T.E.M.; "(What's So Funny 'Bout) Peace, Love And Understanding" by Curtis Stigers; "Theme From The Bodyguard" by Alan Silvestri; and "Trust In Me" by Joe Cocker & Sass Jordan.

After We Make Love (3)
All At Once (1)
All The Man That I Need (3) 1
Anymore (3)
Didn't We Almost Have It All (2) 1
For The Love Of You (2)
Greatest Love Of All (1) 1
Hold Me (1) 46
How Will I Know (1) 1
I Belong To You (3)
I Have Nothing (4)
I Know Him So Well (2)
I Wanna Dance With Somebody (Who Loves Me) (2) 1
I Will Always Love You (4) 1
I'm Every Woman (4) 14↑
I'm Knockin' (2)
I'm Your Baby Tonight (3) 1
Jesus Loves Me (4)
Just The Lonely Talking Again (2)
Love Is A Contact Sport (2)
Love Will Save The Day (2) 9
Lover For Life (3)
Miracle (3) 9
My Name Is Not Susan (3) 20
Nobody Loves Me Like You Do (1)
Queen Of The Night (4)
Run To You (4)
Saving All My Love For You (1) 1
So Emotional (2) 1
Someone For Me (1)
Take Good Care Of My Heart (1)
Thinking About You (1)
We Didn't Know (3)
Where Do Broken Hearts Go (2) 1
Where You Are (2)
Who Do You Love (3)
You Give Good Love (1) 3
You're Still My Man (2)

HOWARD, George

Pop-jazz saxophonist from Philadelphia. Played clarinet from age six. Attended the Settlement School Of Music. Toured with Grover Washington. His nearly all-instrumental albums have featured backing vocalists Gwen Guthrie, Philip Ingram, Siedah Garrett, Billy Davis (The 5th Dimension), Johnny Gill, Alfie Silas, Alex Brown, Phil Perry and Syreeta Wright.

9/1/84	178	4	1	Steppin' Out ....[I]	$8	TBA 201
7/27/85	169	4	2	Dancing in the Sun ....[I]	$8	TBA 205
4/19/86	142	11	3	Love Will Follow ....[I]	$8	TBA 210

DEBUT DATE	PEAK POS	WKS CHR	GOLD	ARTIST — Album Title	$	Label & Number

HOWARD, George — Cont'd

DEBUT DATE	PEAK POS	WKS CHR	GOLD	ARTIST — Album Title	$	Label & Number
12/27/86+	109	26		4 A Nice Place To Be ..... [I]	$8	MCA 5855
6/18/88	109	8		5 Reflections ..... [I]	$8	MCA 42145
3/24/90	128	11		6 Personal ..... [I]	$12	MCA 6335
3/16/91	131	10		7 Love And Understanding ..... [I]	$12	GRP 9629
5/2/92	137	9		8 Do I Ever Cross Your Mind ..... [I]	$12	GRP 9669

Attitude (5)
Baby Come To Me (7)
Broad Street Strut (7)
Come With Me (3)
Cross Your Mind (8)
Dancing In The Sun (2)
Dr. Rock (1)
Dream Ride (1)
Everything I Miss At Home (7)
Fakin' The Feeling (6)
Funk It Out (5)
Got It Goin' On (6)
Hopscotch (2)
Human Nature (1)
I Want You For Myself (6)
I'm In Effect (6)
In Love (2)
It Can't Be Forever (3)
Jade's World (4)
Jo Jo (8)
Just The Way I Feel (8)
Late Night (5)
Let's Live In Harmony (4)
Let's Pretend (5)
Love And Understanding (7)
Love Struck (7)
Love Will Conquer All (5)
Love Will Find A Way (2)
Love Will Follow (3)
Mind Bender (5)
Modern Love (8)
Moods (2)
Nice Place To Be (4)
No No (4)
One Love (5)
Only Here For A Minute (7)
Partly Cloudy (8)
Personally (6)
Philly Talk (1)
Piano In The Dark (6)
Pretty Face (6)
Quiet As It's Kept (2)
Raiders, The (3)
Red, Black, 'N' Blue (7)
Reflections (5)
September Rain (3)
Shadow (8)
Shower You With Love (6)
Slow Walking (3)
Spenser For Hire (4)
Spirit (8)
Stanley's Groove (4)
Stay Here With Me (8)
Stay With Me (8)
Steppin' Out (1)
Sweet Dreams (Are Made Of This) (1)
Sweetest Taboo (4)
Talk To The Drum (7)
Tear Of Spring (1)
Telephone (2)
That's Just What It Is (3)
Too Bad (5)
Try Again (8)
Uptown (9)
You And Me (6)
You Only Come Out At Night (6)

HOWARD, Miki

Session singer/songwriter from Chicago. Former lead singer of Side Effect. Portrayed Billie Holiday in the film *Malcolm X*.

DEBUT DATE	PEAK POS	WKS CHR	GOLD	ARTIST — Album Title	$	Label & Number
3/14/87	171	6		1 Come Share My Love	$8	Atlantic 81688
2/20/88	145	16		2 Love Confessions	$8	Atlantic 81810
3/3/90	112	16		3 Miki Howard	$12	Atlantic 82024
10/3/92	110	11		4 Femme Fatale	$12	Giant 24452

Ain't Nobody Like You (4)
Ain't Nuthin' In The World (3)
Baby, Be Mine (2)
Bitter Love (2)
But I Love You (4)
Cigarette Ashes On The Floor (4)
Come Back To Me Lover (1)
Come Home To Me (3)
Come Share My Love (1)
Crazy (2)
Do You Want My Love (1)
Good Morning Heartache (4)
Hope That We Can Be Together Soon (4)
I Can't Wait (To See You Alone) (1)
I Surrender (1)
I Wanna Be There (2)
I'll Be Your Shoulder (3)
I've Been Through It (4)
If You Still Love Her (3)
Imagination (1)
In Too Deep (2)
Just The Way You Want Me To (3)
Love Confession (2)
Love Me All Over (3)
Love Under New Management (3)
Love Will Find A Way (1)
Mister (3)
My Friend (1)
New Fire From An Old Flame (4)
Reasons (2)
Release Me (4)
Shining Through (4)
Thank You For Talkin' To Me Africa (4)
That's What Love Is (2)
This Bitter Earth (4)
Until You Come Back To Me (That's What I'm Gonna Do) (3)
Who Ever Said It Was Love (3)
You Better Be Ready To Love Me (1)
You've Changed (2)

HOWE, Steve

Prominent guitarist. Born on 4/8/47 in London. In the late '60s, member of psychedelic cult band Tomorrow. Lead guitarist of Yes from 1970-81. Co-founded Asia in 1982. Co-founded GTR in 1986.

DEBUT DATE	PEAK POS	WKS CHR	GOLD	ARTIST — Album Title	$	Label & Number
12/20/75+	63	11		1 Beginnings	$8	Atlantic 18154
2/16/80	164	4		2 The Steve Howe Album ..... [I]	$8	Atlantic 19243

All's A Chord (2)
Australia (1)
Beginnings (1)
Break Away From It All (1)
Cactus Boogie (2)
Continental, The (2)
Diary Of A Man Who Vanished (2)
Doors Of Sleep (1)
Double Rondo (2)
Look Over Your Shoulder (2)
Lost Symphony (1)
Meadow Rag (2)
Nature Of The Sea (1)
Pennants (2)
Pleasure Stole The Night (1)
Ram (1)
Surface Tension (2)
Vivaldi: Concerto In D (Second Movement) (2)
Will O' The Wisp (1)

HOWLIN' WOLF

Influential country-blues singer/guitarist/harmonica player. Born Chester Arthur Burnett on 6/10/10 in West Point, Mississippi. Died of cancer on 1/10/76. With Robert Johnson and Sonny Boy Williamson (Alex "Rice Miller" Ford) in the early 1930s. Own band in 1948. Inducted into the Rock and Roll Hall of Fame in 1991.

DEBUT DATE	PEAK POS	WKS CHR	GOLD	ARTIST — Album Title	$	Label & Number
8/21/71	79	15		The London Howlin' Wolf Sessions	$15	Chess 60008
				with Eric Clapton, Steve Winwood, Bill Wyman, Charlie Watts		

Built For Comfort
Do The Do
Highway 49
I Ain't Superstitious
Poor Boy
Red Rooster [includes 2 versions]
Rockin' Daddy
Sittin' On Top Of The World
Wang-Dang-Doodle
What A Woman!
Who's Been Talking?
Worried About My Baby

HUBBARD, Freddie

Jazz trumpeter. Born on 4/7/38 in Indianapolis. Worked with Art Blakey in the early '60s and also with Quincy Jones.

DEBUT DATE	PEAK POS	WKS CHR	GOLD	ARTIST — Album Title	$	Label & Number
3/10/73	165	7		1 Sky Dive ..... [I]	$10	CTI 6018
1/19/74	186	5		2 Keep Your Soul Together ..... [I]	$10	CTI 6036
9/14/74	153	7		3 High Energy ..... [I]	$10	Columbia 33048
1/11/75	127	7		4 The Baddest Hubbard ..... [K-I]	$10	CTI 6047
5/17/75	167	4		5 Polar AC ..... [I]	$10	CTI 6056
7/19/75	149	6		6 Liquid Love ..... [I]	$10	Columbia 33556
9/4/76	85	9		7 Windjammer ..... [I]	$8	Columbia 34166
10/29/77	149	6		8 Bundle Of Joy ..... [I]	$8	Columbia 34902
7/15/78	131	5		9 Super Blue ..... [I]	$8	Columbia 35386

Baraka Sasa (3)
Betcha By Golly, Wow (5)
Black Maybe (3)
Brigitte (2)
Bundle Of Joy (8)
Camel Rise (3)
Crisis (3)
Destiny's Children (2)
Dream Weaver (7)
Ebony Moonbeams (3)
Feelings (4)
First Light (4)
From Behind (8)
From Now On (8)
Godfather, The (1)
Gospel Truth (9)
Here's That Rainy Day (4)
I Don't Want To Lose You (8)
In A Mist (1,4)
Kareem, Theme For (9)
Keep Your Soul Together (2)
Kuntu (6)
Liquid Love (6)
Lost Dreams (6)
Midnight At The Oasis (6)
Naturally (8)
Neo Terra (New Land) (7)
People Make The World Go Round (5)
Polar AC (5)
Portrait Of Jenny (8)
Povo (1)
Put It In The Pocket (6)
Rahsann (8)
Rainy Day Song (8)
Red Clay (4)
Rock Me Arms (7)
Sky Dive (1)
Son Of Sky Dive (5)
Spirits Of Trane (2)
Super Blue (9)
Surest Things Can Change (9)
Take It To The Ozone (9)
To Her Ladyship (9)
Too High (3)
Touch Me Baby (7)
Tucson Stomp (6)
Windjammer (7)
Yesterday's Thoughts (6)

HUDSON, David

R&B singer based in Miami.

DEBUT DATE	PEAK POS	WKS CHR	GOLD	ARTIST — Album Title	$	Label & Number
8/23/80	184	2		To You Honey, Honey With Love	$8	Alston 4412

Ease Up
Honey, Honey 59
I Have Never Loved A Woman (The Way I Love You)
I Must Have Your Love
Let Me Wrap You In My Love
Pump It
Scratch My Back
When I'm Lovin' You

DEBUT DATE	PEAK POS	WKS CHR	GOLD	ARTIST — Album Title	$	Label & Number

HUDSON and LANDRY
Los Angeles DJs Bob Hudson and Ron Landry. Split up in 1976.

4/10/71	30	26		1 Hanging In There .... [C]	$15	Dore 324
11/27/71+	33	23		2 Losing Their Heads .... [C]	$15	Dore 326
1/6/73	147	9		3 Right-Off.. [C]	$15	Dore 329

Ajax Airlines (2) *68*
Ajax Liquor Store (1) *43*
Ajax Mortuary (3)
Ajax Pet Store (3)
Ajax Travel Bureau (2)
Astro Nut (2)
Bruiser LaRue (2)

Bruiser LaRue Meets Count Dracula (3)
Charlie Chin (3)
Doctors, The (1)
Five Points (1)
Frederickism (2)
Friar Shuck (1,2)

Frontier Christmas (Harlow & The Mrs.) (3)
Heads, The (3)
Hippie & The Redneck (1)
Hippo, The (3)
Impossible Dreams (1)
Kearsarge (1)

Loch Ness Monster (1)
Murph Almighty (3)
Obscene Phone Bust (2)
Pierre's Restaurant (1)
Porno Flicks (1)
Prospectors, The (2)

Rising & Falling Of Adolph Hitler (3)
Sir Basil (2)
Soul Bowl (3)
Top Forty D.J.'s (1)

HUDSON BROTHERS
Bill, Brett and Mark Hudson from Portland. Own TV variety show during the summer of 1974; also hosted kiddie TV show *The Hudson Brothers Razzle Dazzle Comedy Show*. Bill was married to actress Goldie Hawn.

11/30/74	179	4		1 Totally Out Of Control	$10	Rocket 460
12/7/74	176	4		2 Hollywood Situation	$10	Casablanca 7004
12/13/75+	165	6		3 Ba-Fa	$10	Rocket 2169

Adventures Of Chucky Margolis (2)
Apple Pie Hero (3)
Be A Man (1)
Dernie Was A Friend Of Ours (3)
Coochie Coochie Coo (2)
Cry, Cry, Cry (2)
Dolly Day (1)

Find Me A Woman (medley) (1)
Hard On Me (3)
Hollywood Situation (2)
Home (medley) (1)
If You Really Need Me (1)
Isn't It Lovely (1)
Killer On The Road (1)
La La Layna (1)
Little Brown Box (medley) (1)

Lonely School Year (3) *57*
Long Long Day (1)
Lover Come Back To Me (1)
Ma Ma Ma Baby (2)
My Career (3)
My Heart Can't Take It (3)
Oh Gabriel (3)
One And The Same (medley) (1)

Out Of The Rainbow (medley) (1)
Playmate (3)
Razzle Dazzle (3)
Rendezvous *26*
Smooth Talker (3)
So You Are A Star (2) *21*
Sometimes The Rain Will Fall (2)
Song For Stephanie (3)

Spinning The Wheel (With The Girl You Love) (3)
Straight Up And Tall (1)
Suike Up The Boys In The Band (2)
Sunday Driver (1)
These Things We Do (medley) (1)
Three Of Us (2)
Truth Of The Matter (1)

With Somebody Else (3)

HUES CORPORATION, The
Black vocal trio formed in Los Angeles in 1969: Bernard Henderson, Fleming Williams and H. Ann Kelley. Williams replaced by Tommy Brown after "Rock The Boat." Brown replaced by Karl Russell in 1975.

6/29/74	20	18		1 Freedom For The Stallion..	$10	RCA 0323
7/5/75	147	5		2 Love Corporation	$10	RCA 0938

All Goin' Down Together (1)
Bound On A Reason (1)
Family, The (1)
Follow The Spirit (2)

Freedom For The Stallion (1) *63*
Go To The Poet (1)
Gold Rush (2)

He's My Home (2)
Live A Lie (1)
Long Road (2)
Love Corporation (2) *62*

Miracle Maker (Sweet Soul Shaker) (1)
Off My Cloud (1)
One Good Night Together (2)

Rock The Boat (1) *1*
Salvation Lady (1-3-5) (1)
Sing To Your Song (2)
Soul Sailin' (2)

When You Look Down The Road (2)
You Showed Me What Love Is (2)

HUGH, Grayson
Soul-styled white singer/songwriter/pianist from Connecticut.

10/15/88+	71	23		Blind To Reason	$8	RCA 7661

Blind Return
Blind To Reason

Bring It All Back *87*
Empty As The Wind

Finally Found A Friend
Hard Life

Romantic Heart
Talk It Over *19*

Tears Of Love
That's Cool

Two Hearts

HUGO & LUIGI
Producers/songwriters/label executives Hugo Peretti and Luigi Creatore. Owned record labels Roulette and Avco/Embassy. Hugo died on 5/1/86 (age 64).

4/27/63	14	13		1 The Cascading Voices of the Hugo & Luigi Chorus	$10	RCA 2641
10/26/63	125	2		2 Let's Fall In Love	$10	RCA 2717

Always (2)
Anniversary Song (2)
As Time Goes By (2)
Can't Help Falling In Love (2)
Falling In Love With Love (2)

For You (1)
Good Night Sweetheart (1)
I Don't Know Why (I Just Do) (2)
I Love You (1)

I'll See You In My Dreams (1)
I'm In The Mood For Love (1)
It Happened In Monterey (1)
Let Me Call You Sweetheart (2)

Let's Fall In Love (2)
Look For The Silver Lining (1)
Marcheta (1)
Melody Of Love (2)

Moonlight And Roses (1)
Paradise (1)
Remembering Time (1)
Tenderly (2)

Three O'Clock In The Morning (1)
True Love (2)
When Day Is Done (1)

HUMAN BEINZ, The
Cleveland bar band.

3/9/68	65	10		Nobody But Me	$25	Capitol 2906

Black Is The Color Of My True Love's Hair
Dance On Through

Flower Grave
Foxey Lady
It's Fun To Be Clean

Nobody But Me *8*
Serenade To Sarah
Shaman, The

Sueno
This Lonely Town

Turn On Your Love Light *80*

HUMAN LEAGUE, The
Electro-pop band formed in 1977 in Sheffield, England by synthesists Martyn Ware and Ian Craig Marsh and lead singer/synthesist Philip Oakey. Vocalists Joanne Catherall and Susanne Sulley joined in October 1980 when Ware and Marsh left to form Heaven 17.

2/27/82	3	38	●	1 Dare	$8	A&M 4892
9/18/82	135	7		2 Love And Dancing...[I]	$8	A&M 3209
				THE LEAGUE UNLIMITED ORCHESTRA		
				instrumental versions of songs from album #1 above		
6/18/83	22	29		3 Fascination! .... [M]	$8	A&M 12501
6/16/84	62	13		4 Hysteria...	$8	A&M 4923
10/4/86	24	25		5 Crash	$8	A&M 5129

Are You Ever Coming Back? (5)
Betrayed (4)
Darkness (1)
Do Or Die (1,2)
Don't You Know I Want You (4)

Don't You Want Me (1,2) *1*
Get Carter (1)
Hard Times (2,3)
Human (5) *1*
I Am The Law (1)
I Love You Too Much (3,4)
I Need Your Loving (5) *44*

I'm Coming Back (4)
Jam (5)
(Keep Feeling) Fascination [includes 2 versions] (3) *8*
Lebanon, The (4) *64*
Life On Your Own (4)
Louise (4)

Love Action (I Believe In Love) (1,2)
Love Is All That Matters (5)
Love On The Run (5)
Mirror Man (3) *30*
Money (5)
Open Your Heart (1,2)

Party (5)
Real Thing (5)
Rock Me Again And Again And Again And And Again And Again (Six Times) (4)
Seconds (1,2)

Sign, The (4)
So Hurt (4)
Sound Of The Crowd (1,2)
Swang (5)
Things That Dreams Are Made Of (1,2)
You Remind Me Of Gold (3)

DEBUT DATE	PEAK POS	WKS CHR	GOLD	ARTIST — Album Title	$	Label & Number

★★390★★ HUMBLE PIE

Hard-rock band formed in late 1968 in Essex, England. Consisted of Peter Frampton (guitar, vocals; The Herd), Steve Marriott (vocals, guitar; Small Faces; d: 4/20/91 [age 44]), Greg Ridley (bass; Spooky Tooth) and Jerry Shirley (drums). Frampton left in October 1971, replaced by Clem Clempson. Disbanded in 1975. Reunited from 1980-81 with Marriott, Shirley, Bobby Tench (guitar) and Anthony Jones (bass).

DEBUT DATE	PEAK POS	WKS CHR	GOLD	#	Title	$	Label & Number
5/8/71	118	23		1	Rock On	$12	A&M 4301
11/6/71	21	32	●	2	Performance-Rockin' The Fillmore [L]	$12	A&M 3506 [2]
4/1/72	6	34	●	3	Smokin'	$12	A&M 4342
9/30/72	37	20		4	Lost And Found [E-R]	$12	A&M 3513 [2]
					re-issue of their first 2 albums *Town And Country* and *As Safe As Yesterday Is*		
3/24/73	13	21		5	Eat It [L]	$12	A&M 3701 [2]
					side 4 recorded live in Glasgow, Scotland		
3/9/74	52	14		6	Thunderbox	$10	A&M 3611
4/26/75	100	8		7	Street Rats	$10	A&M 4514
4/12/80	60	14		8	On To Victory	$8	Atco 122
5/9/81	154	6		9	Go For The Throat	$8	Atco 131

Alabama '69 (4)
All Shook Up (9)
Anna (Go To Him) (6)
As Safe As Yesterday (4)
Baby Don't You Do It (8)
Bang? (4)
Beckton Dumps (5)
Big George (1)
Black Coffee (9)
Buttermilk Boy (4)
Chip Away (The Stone) (9)
Cold Lady (4)
C'mon Everybody (3)
Countryman Stomp (7)
Desperation (4)
Don't Worry, Be Happy (6)
Down Home Again (4)
Drift Away (6)
Drive My Car (7)
Driver (9)

Drugstore Cowboy (5)
Every Mothers Son (4)
Every Single Day (6)
Fixer, The (3)
Fool For A Pretty Face (Hurt By Love) (8) **52**
Four Day Creep (2)
Further Down The Road (8)
Get Down Yo (5)
Get It In The End (8)
Go For The Throat (9)
Good Booze And Bad Women (5)
Groovin' With Jesus (6)
Hallelujah (I Love Her So) (2)
Heartbeat (4)
Home And Away (4)
Honky Tonk Woman (3)
Hot 'N' Nasty (3) **52**
I Believe To My Soul (5)

I Can't Stand The Rain (6)
I Don't Need No Doctor (2) **73**
I Walk On Gilded Splinters (2)
I Wonder (3)
I'll Go Alone (4)
(I'm A) Road Runner (3,5)
I'm Ready (2)
Infatuation (8)
Is It For Love? (5)
Keep It On The Island (9)
Let Me Be Your Lovemaker (7)
Light, The (1)
Light Of Love (4)
Lottie And The Charcoal Queen (9)
My Lover's Prayer (8)
Natural Born Woman (4)

Nifty Little Number Like You (4)
Ninety-Nine Pounds (6)
No Money Down (6)
No Way (6)
Oh La-De-Da (6)
Old Time Feelin' (3)
Ollie, Ollie (4)
Only You Can Say (4)
Over You (8)
Queens And Nuns (7)
Rain (7)
Rally With All (6)
Red Neck Jump (1)
Restless Blood (9)
Road Hog (7)
Road Runner ...see: (I'm A)
Rock And Roll Music (7)
Rollin' Stone (1,2)

Sad Bag Of Shaky Jake (4)
Savin' It (8)
Say No More (5)
Scored Out (7)
79th And Sunset (1)
Shine On (1)
Shut Up And Don't Interrupt Me (5)
Silver Tongue (4)
Song For Jenny (1)
Sour Grain (1)
Stick Shift (4)
Stone Cold Fever (1,2)
Strange Days (1)
Street Rat (7)
Summer Song (5)
Sweet Peace And Time (3)
Take It From Here (8)
Take Me Back (4)
Teenage Anxiety (9)

That's How Strong My Love Is (5)
There Tis (7)
30 Days In The Hole (3)
Thunderbox (6)
Tin Soldier (9)
Up Our Sleeve (5)
We Can Work It Out (7)
What You Will (4)
You Soppy Pratt (8)
You're So Good For Me (3)

★★144★★ HUMPERDINCK, Engelbert

Born Arnold George Dorsey on 5/2/36 in Madras, India. To Leicester, England in 1947. First recorded for Decca in 1958. Met Tom Jones' manager, Gordon Mills, in 1965, who suggested his name change to Engelbert Humperdinck (a famous German opera composer). Starred in his own musical variety TV series in 1970.

DEBUT DATE	PEAK POS	WKS CHR	GOLD	#	Title	$	Label & Number
6/17/67	7	118	●	1	Release Me	$15	Parrot 71012
12/23/67+	10	60	●	2	The Last Waltz	$15	Parrot 71015
8/24/68	12	78	●	3	A Man Without Love	$15	Parrot 71022
3/22/69	12	33	●	4	Engelbert	$15	Parrot 71026
1/3/70	5	41	●	5	Engelbert Humperdinck	$15	Parrot 71030
7/11/70	19	40	●	6	We Made It Happen	$15	Parrot 71038
2/20/71	22	24	●	7	Sweetheart	$15	Parrot 71043
9/11/71	25	15	●	8	Another Time, Another Place	$15	Parrot 71048
1/1/72	45	13		9	Live At The Riviera, Las Vegas [L]	$15	Parrot 71051
8/19/72	72	14		10	In Time	$15	Parrot 71056
8/11/73	113	10		11	King Of Hearts	$12	Parrot 71061
12/21/74+	103	14		12	His Greatest Hits [G]	$12	Parrot 71067
11/27/76+	17	28	▲	13	After The Lovin'	$10	Epic 34381
7/16/77	167	5		14	Miracles by Engelbert Humperdinck	$10	Epic 34730
12/24/77+	156	4	●	15	Christmas Tyme [X]	$10	Epic 35031
5/19/79	164	4		16	This Moment In Time	$8	Epic 35791

After The Lovin' (13) **8**
All This World And The Seven Seas (2)
All You've Gotta Do Is Ask (Una Volta Nella Vita) (5)
Am I That Easy To Forget (2,9,12) **18**
Another Time, Another Place (8) **43**
Aquarius (medley) (5)
Around The World In 80 Days (medley) (9)
Baby I'm A Want You (10)
By The Time I Get To Phoenix (3)
Cafe (Cosa Hai Messo Nel Caffe) (5)
California Maiden (7)
Call On Me (3)
Can't Help Falling In Love (16)
Can't Smile Without You (13)
Can't Take My Eyes Off You (3)
Carol Tyme Medley (15)
Christmas Song (15)
Christmas Time Again (15)
Day After Day (10)
Days Of Icy Fingers (8)

Didn't We (5)
Do I Love You (11)
Don't Say No (Again) (4)
Eternally (11)
Everybody Knows (2)
Everybody's Talkin' (6)
First Time Ever I Saw Your Face (7,10)
First Time In My Life (16)
For The Good Times (7)
From Here To Eternity (3)
From Me To You (14)
Gentle On My Mind (5)
Girl Of Mine (10)
Good Thing Going (4)
Goodbye My Friend (14) **97**
Help Me Make It Through The Night (8,9)
Home Tyme Medley (15)
How Near Is Love (11)
Hungry Years (13)
I Believe In Miracles (14)
I Believe In You (16)
I Can't Live A Dream (13)
I Love Making Love To You (13)
I Never Said Goodbye (10) **61**
I Wish You Love (5)

I'll Be Your Baby Tonight (7)
I'm A Better Man (5) **38**
I'm Holding Your Memory (But He's Holding You) (4)
I'm Leavin' You (11) **99**
I'm Stone In Love With You (11)
If I Were You (2)
If It Comes To That (2)
Il Mondo (1)
In Time (10) **69**
It's Impossible (9)
Jingle Bell Tyme Medley (15)
Just A Little Bit Of You (9)
Just Say I Love Her (6)
Last Waltz (2,9,12) **25**
Leavin' On A Jet Plane (6)
Les Bicyclettes De Belsize (4,9,12) **31**
Let Me Happen To You (13)
Let Me Into Your Life (4)
Let The Sunshine In (medley) (9)
Let's Kiss Tomorrow Goodbye (Un Nuovo Mondo) (9)
Let's Remember The Good Times (13)
Life Goes On (10)

Live And Just Let Live (7)
Long Gone (2)
Look At Me (14)
Love Can Fly (7)
Love For Love (Ciao, My Love) (6)
Love Letters (5)
Love Me With All Your Heart (Quando Caliente El Sol) (6)
Love The One You're With (9)
Love Was Here Before The Stars (4)
Lovin' You Too Long (16)
Loving You, Losing You (14)
Man And A Woman (3)
Man Without Love (3,9,12) **19**
Marry Me (4)
Maybe Tomorrow (16)
Miss Elaine E.S. Jones (2)
Misty Blue (7)
Morning (8)
Most Beautiful Girl (11)
Much, Much Greater Love (16)
My Cherie Amour (6)
My Prayer (8)
My Summer Song (11)
My Wife The Dancer (6,9)

Nashville Lady (8)
Night To Remember (15)
Only Your Love (11)
Our Love Will Rise Again (8)
Peace Of Mind (14)
Place In The Sun (2)
Put A Light In Your Window (14)
Put Your Hand In Mine (7)
Quando, Quando, Quando (3,12)
Quiet Nights (1)
Raindrops Keep Fallin' On My Head (6)
Release Me (And Let Me Love Again) (1,9,12) **4**
Revivin' Old Emotions (8)
Romeo & Juliet, Love Theme From (5)
Santa Lija (Sogno D'Amore) (7)
Shadow Of Your Smile (3)
Signs Of Love (5)
Silent Night (15)
Silver Bells (15)
Sing-A-Long Tyme Medley (15)
Somebody Waiting (11)

Something (2)
Songs We Sang Together (11)
Spanish Eyes (3,12)
Summer Of My Life (14)
Sweetheart (7) **47**
Take Me For Now Love (7)
Take My Heart (8)
Talk It Over In The Morning (8)
Talking Love (1)
Ten Guitars (1)
That's What It's All About (11)
There Goes My Everything (1,9,12) **20**
There's A Kind Of Hush (1)
There's An Island (8)
(They Long To Be) Close To You (10)
This I Find Is Beautiful (13)
This Is My Song (1)
This Is What You Mean To Me (13)
This Moment In Time (16) **58**
Through The Eyes Of Love (4)
Till (medley) (9)
Time After Time (10)

335

HUMPERDINCK, Engelbert — Cont'd

To Get To You (4)
To The Ends Of The Earth (2)
Too Beautiful To Last (10) *86*
Travelin' Boy (16)
True (4)

Twenty Miles From Home (8)
Two Different Worlds (2)
Up, Up And Away (3)
Walk Through This World With Me (1)

Way It Used To Be (4,9,12) *42*
We Made It Happen (6)
We Are So You (3)
What A Wonderful World (3)
What I Did For Love (14)

When There's No You (7,9) *45*
White Christmas (15)
Winter World Of Love (5,12) *16*
Without You (10,14)

Woman In My Life (7)
Wonderland By Night (3)
Words (6)
World Without Music (13)
You Are There (14)
You Know Me (16)

You'll Never Walk Alone (9)
You're Easy To Love (4)
You're Something Special (16)
Yours Until Tomorrow (1)

HUMPHREY, Bobbi

Born Barbara Ann Humphrey on 4/25/50 in Dallas. Jazz flutist. Studied at Southern Methodist and Texas Southern University. First recorded for Blue Note in 1971. Cousin of former Duke Ellington trumpet player Eddie Preston.

3/30/74	84	21		1 Blacks and Blues ....[I]	$10	Blue Note 142
12/7/74+	30	18		2 Satin Doll ....[I]	$10	Blue Note 344
11/29/75	133	5		3 Fancy Dancer ....[I]	$10	Blue Note 550
7/1/78	89	14		4 Freestyle	$8	Epic 35338

Baby's Gone (1)
Blacks And Blues (1)
Chicago, Damn (1)
Fancy Dancer (3)
Freestyle (4)
Fun House (2)

Good Times (4)
Harlem River Drive (1)
Home-Made Jam (4)
I Could Love You More (4)
If You Let Me (4)
If You Want It (4)

Jasper Country Man (1)
Just A Love Child (1)
Ladies Day (2)
Mestizo Eyes (3)
My Destiny (4)
My Little Girl (4)

New York Times (2)
Please Set Me At Ease (3)
Rain Again (2)
San Francisco Lights (2)
Satin Doll (2)
Sunset Burgundy (4)

Sweeter Than Sugar (3)
Trip, The (3)
Uno Esta (3)
You Are The Sunshine Of My Life (2)

You Make Me Feel So Good (3)

HUMPHREY, Paul, & The Cool Aid Chemists

Paul was born on 10/12/35 in Detroit. Black session drummer. Worked with Wes Montgomery, Les McCann, Kai Winding, Charlie Mingus, Lee Konitz and Gene Ammons in the early '60s. The Cool Aid Chemists were Clarence MacDonald, David T. Walker (Afrique) and Bill Upchurch.

6/12/71	170	6		Paul Humphrey & The Cool Aid Chemists ....[I]	$12	Lizard 20106

Ain't That Peculiar
Baby Rice

Cool Aid *29*
Detroit

Dreams
Funky L.A.

Music Talk
Sack Full Of Dreams

Something
Them Changes

HUNTER, Ian

Born on 6/3/46 in Shrewsbury, England. Singer/guitarist. Leader of Mott The Hoople from 1969-74.

5/17/75	50	14		1 Ian Hunter	$10	Columbia 33480
5/22/76	177	7		2 All-American Alien Boy	$10	Columbia 34142
4/28/79	35	24		3 You're Never Alone With A Schizophrenic	$8	Chrysalis 1214
4/26/80	69	17		4 Ian Hunter Live/Welcome To The Club ....[L]	$10	Chrysalis 1269 [2]
8/29/81	62	11		5 Short Back N' Sides	$8	Chrysalis 1326
8/6/83	125	8		6 All Of The Good Ones Are Taken	$8	Columbia 38628
10/28/89+	157	20		7 Y U I ORTA	$8	Mercury 838973

IAN HUNTER/MICK RONSON (British session guitarist, member of Paul Hyde And The Payolas)

All American Alien Boy (2)
All Of The Good Ones Are Taken (6)
All The Way From Memphis (4)
All The Young Dudes (4)
American Music (7)
Angeline (4)
Apathy 83 (2)
Bastard (3,4)
Beg A Little Love (7)
Big Time (7)
Boy (1)
Captain Void 'N' The Video Jets (6)

Central Park N' West (5)
Cleveland Rocks (3,4)
Cool (7)
Death 'N' Glory Boys (6)
Every Step Of The Way (6)
F.B.I. (4)
Fun (6)
God (Take 1) (2)
Gun Control (5)
I Get So Excited (1)
I Need Your Love (5)
I Wish I Was Your Mother (4)
Irene Wilde (2,4)
It Ain't Easy When You Fall (medley) (1)

Just Another Night (3,4) *68*
Keep On Burning (5)
Laugh At Me (4)
Leave Me Alone (5)
Letter To Brittania From The Union Jack (4)
Life After Death (3)
Lisa Likes Rock N' Roll (4)
Livin' In A Heart (7)
Loner, The (4)
Lounge Lizard (1)
Man 'O' War (4)
Noises (5)
Old Records Never Die (5)
Once Bitten Twice Shy (1,4)

Outsider, The (3)
Rain (5)
Rape (2)
Restless Youth (2)
Rock 'N' Roll Queen (medley) (4)
Seeing Double (6)
Shades Off (medley) (1)
Ships (3)
Silver Needles (4)
Slaughter On Tenth Avenue (4)
Somethin's Goin' On (6)
Sons And Daughters (4)
Sons 'N' Lovers (7)

Speechless (6)
Standin' In My Light (3,4)
Sweet Dreamer (7)
Tell It Like It Is (7)
That Girl Is Rock 'N' Roll (6)
Theatre Of The Absurd (5)
3,000 Miles From Here (1)
Truth, The Whole Truth, Nuthin' But The Truth (1)
Walkin' With A Mountain (medley) (4)
We Gotta' Get Out Of Here (4)
When The Daylight Comes (3)

Who Do You Love (1)
Wild East (3)
Womens Intuition (7)
You Nearly Did Me In (2)

HUNTER, John

Rock singer/keyboardist from Chicago.

2/9/85	148	9		Famous At Night	$8	Private I 39626

Crimes Of Passion
Horses

Losin' You Again
Put Yourself On The Line

Sad Songs On The Radio
She Advertises

Take Your Chances
This Is Forever

Tragedy *39*
Valentine

HUNTLEY, Chet, & David Brinkley

Former co-anchors of TV's *NBC Nightly News*, 1955-70. Huntley died in 1974.

3/14/64	115	7		A Time To Keep: 1963 ....[T]	$15	RCA 1088

a recall of the voices and events of 1963

Eventful Summer
Negro Revolution

People And Providence

Terrible Weekend

Torch Is Passed

World Mourns

World Politics

HURRICANE

Hard-rock quartet formed by guitarists Robert Sarzo and Tony Cavazo. (Robert is the brother of Whitesnake's Rudy Sarzo; Tony's brother, Carlos Cavazo, is a member of Quiet Riot.) Includes: Kelly Hansen (vocals) and Jay Schellen (drums). Sarzo left the band in 1989, replaced by Doug Aldrich.

4/30/88	92	36		1 Over The Edge..	$8	Enigma 73320
4/14/90	125	10		2 Slave To The Thrill	$12	Enigma 73511

Baby Snakes (1)
Dance Little Sister (2)
Don't Wanna Dream (2)
Give Me An Inch (1)

I'm Eighteen (1)
I'm Onto You (1)
In The Fire (2)
Insane (1)

Let It Slide (2)
Livin' Over The Edge (1)
Lock Me Up (2)
Messin' With A Hurricane (1)

Next To You (2)
Reign Of Love (2)
Shout (1)
Smiles Like A Child (2)

Spark In My Heart (1)
Temptation (2)
10,000 Years (2)
We Are Strong (1)

Young Man (2)

HUSKER DU

Minneapolis rock trio (pronounced: hoosker doo): Bob Mould (guitars, vocals), Greg Norton (bass) and Grant Hart (drums, vocals). Band name is Swedish for "do you remember." Group split in 1988.

4/12/86	140	10		1 Candy Apple Grey	$8	Warner 25385
2/14/87	117	10		2 Warehouse: Songs And Stories..	$10	Warner 25544 [2]

HUSKER DU — Cont'd

Actual Condition (2)
All This I've Done For You (1)
Back From Somewhere (2)
Bed Of Nails (2)
Charity, Chastity, Prudence, And Hope (1)
Could You Be The One? (2)

Crystal (1)
Dead Set On Destruction (1)
Don't Want To Know If You Are Lonely (1)
Eiffel Tower High (1)
Friend, You've Got To Fall (1)
Hardly Getting Over It (1)

I Don't Know For Sure (1)
Ice Cold Ice (2)
It's Not Peculiar (2)
No Promise Have I Made (1)
No Reservations (2)
She Floated Away (2)

She's A Woman (And Now He Is A Man) (2)
Sorry Somehow (1)
Standing In The Rain (2)
Tell You Why Tomorrow (2)
These Important Years (2)
Too Far Down (1)

Too Much Spice (2)
Turn It Around (2)
Up In The Air (2)
Visionary (2)
You Can Live At Home (2)
You're A Soldier (2)

HUTCH, Willie

Born Willie McKinley Hutchinson in 1946 in Los Angeles and raised in Dallas. Producer/songwriter for Motown from 1970. Debut as performer with *The Mack* soundtrack album in 1973.

DEBUT DATE	PEAK POS	WKS CHR		ARTIST — Album Title		$	Label & Number
6/2/73	114	16	1	The Mack	[S]	$10	Motown 766
10/13/73	183	6	2	Fully Exposed		$10	Motown 784
5/18/74	179	4	3	Foxy Brown	[S]	$10	Motown 811
11/15/75	150	6	4	Ode To My Lady		$10	Motown 838
4/3/76	163	6	5	Concert In Blues		$10	Motown 854

Ain't Nothing Like Togetherness (2)
Ain't That (Mellow, Mellow) (3)
Baby Come Home (5)
Brother's Gonna Work It Out (1) 67
California My Way (2)
Can't Get Ready For Losing You (2)
Chase (3)
Come On Let's Do The Thang (5)

Don't Let A Little Money Keep You Acting Funny (5)
Foxy Brown, Theme Of (3)
Foxy Lady (3)
Getaway, The (medley) (1)
Give Me Some Of That Good Old Love (3)
Have You Ever Asked Yourself Why (All About Money Game) (3)
Hospital Prelude Of Love Theme (3)
I Choose You (1)

I Finally Made The Headlines (5)
I Just Wanted To Make Her Happy (2)
I Wanna Be Where You Are (2)
I Wish You Love (5)
I'll Be There (2)
(I'm Gonna) Hold On (4)
If You Ain't Got No Honey (You Can't Get No Honey) (2)
Just Another Day (4)

Love Me Back (4)
Love Power (4) 41
Mack, Theme Of The (1)
Mack Man (Got To Get Over) (1)
Mack's Stroll (medley) (1)
Mother's Theme (Mama) (1)
Now That It's All Over (1)
Ode To My Lady (4)
Out There (3)
Overture Of Foxy Brown (3)
Party Down (4,5)
Precious Pearl (5)

Shake, Rattle And Roll (5)
Since I Found You Everything's Alright (4)
Slick (1) 65
Stormy Monday (5)
Stormy Weather (5)
Sunshine Lady (2)
Talk To Me (4)
Tell Me Why Has Our Love Turned Cold (2)
Vampin (1)
Way We Were (4)

Whatever You Do (Do It Good) (3)
You Gotta Give Love Up (4)
You Sure Know How To Love Your Man (3)

HUTSON, LeRoy

Born on 6/4/45 in Newark, New Jersey. Lead singer with The Impressions from 1971-73.

DEBUT DATE	PEAK POS	WKS CHR	ARTIST — Album Title	$	Label & Number
3/6/76	170	8	Feel The Spirit	$10	Curtom 5010

Butterfat
Don't Let It Get Next To You

Feel The Spirit (76)
It's The Music

Let's Be Lonely Together
Lover's Holiday

Never Know What You Can Do (Give It A Try)

HYDE, Paul, And The Payolas

Canadian pop-rock quartet: Hyde (vocals), Bob Rock (guitar), Chris Taylor and Alex Boynton. Paul and Bob later recorded as the duo Rock & Hyde.

DEBUT DATE	PEAK POS	WKS CHR	ARTIST — Album Title	$	Label & Number
6/8/85	144	10	Here's The World For Ya	$8	A&M 5025

All That I Want
Cruel Hearted Lovers

Here's The World
It Must Be Love

It Won't Be You
Little Boys

Never Leave This Place
Rhythm Slaves

Stuck In The Rain
You're The Only Love 84

HYLAND, Brian

Born on 11/12/43 in Queens, New York. Own group, the Delphis, at age 12. In production company with Del Shannon in 1970.

DEBUT DATE	PEAK POS	WKS CHR		ARTIST — Album Title	$	Label & Number
4/19/69	160	5	1	Tragedy/A Million To One	$12	Dot 25926
1/30/71	171	4	2	Brian Hyland	$10	Uni 73097

produced by Del Shannon

Be That Someone (1)
Drivin' Me Crazy (2)
Gypsy Woman (2) 3
I'm Without You (2)
It Could All Begin Again (In You) (1)

Lonely Teardrops (2) 54
Lonesome Town (1)
Lorrayne (2)
Mail Order Gun (2)
Maria (medley) (2)
Million To One (1) 90

On The East Side (2)
See The Funny Little Clown (1)
Slow Down (2)
So Sad (To Watch Good Love Go Bad) (1)

Somewhere (medley) (2)
Thrill Is Gone (2)
Tragedy (1) 56
Walk Right Back (1)
When I Fall In Love (1)

Will You Love Me Tomorrow (1)
You (1)
You & Me (2)
You'd Better Stop - And Think It Over (1)

HYMAN, Dick

Born on 3/8/27 in New York City. Piano playing composer/conductor/arranger who toured Europe with Benny Goodman in 1950. Staff pianist at WMCA and WNBC-New York from 1951-57. Music director of *Arthur Godfrey And His Friends* from 1958-62.

DEBUT DATE	PEAK POS	WKS CHR		ARTIST — Album Title		$	Label & Number
11/25/57	21	2	1	60 Great All Time Songs, Vol. 3	[I]	$20	MGM 3537
				groups of medleys played by Dick on the piano			
11/9/63	117	7	2	Electrodynamics	[I]	$15	Command 856
4/4/64	132	5	3	Fabulous	[I]	$15	Command 862
				above 2: DICK HYMAN at the LOWREY ORGAN			
4/27/68	179	2	4	Mirrors - Reflections Of Today	[I]	$15	Command 924
				DICK HYMAN AND "THE GROUP"			
4/19/69	30	30	5	Moog - The Electric Eclectics of Dick Hyman	[I]	$15	Command 938
9/27/69	110	11	6	The Age Of Electronicus	[I]	$15	Command 946
				above 2 feature synthesized songs on the Moog			

Ain't She Sweet Medley (1)
Ain't We Got Fun Medley (1)
Alfie (6)
Aquarius (5)
As Time Goes By Medley (1)
Band Played On Medley (1)
Best Is Yet To Come (3)
Big Ben Bossa (2)
Birth Of The Blues Medley (1)
Blackbird (6)
Both Sides Now (6)

Cuddle Up A Little Closer Medley (1)
Danke Schoen (3)
Do Nothin' Till You Hear From Me (4)
Evening Thoughts (5)
Flower Road (4)
Fly Me To The Moon (4)
Four Duets In Flight (4)
Give It Up Or Turn It Loose (6)
Green Onions (6)

Groovin' (4)
Hit The Road Jack (4)
House Of Mirrors (4)
I Got Rhythm Medley (1)
I Left My Heart In San Francisco (2)
I'll Be Around (3)
I'll Remember April (3)
Improvisation In Fourths (3)
In The Heat Of The Night (4)
In The Wee Small Hours (Of The Morning) (4)

Kolumbo (6)
Legend Of Johnny Pot (5)
Living On Borrowed Time (3)
Mack The Knife (4)
Mercy, Mercy, Mercy (4)
Minotaur, The (5) 38
Moog And Me (5)
Mr. Lucky (6)
Ob-La-Di, Ob-La-Da (6)
Ode To Billy Joe (4)
Paradise (4)
Respect (4)

S'posin' (3)
Satin Doll (2)
Shadowland (2)
Side By Side (2)
Sing Something Simple Medley (1)
So Easy (3)
Sonny Boy (3)
South America Take It Away Medley (1)
Stompin' At The Savoy (2)
Sweetest Sounds (3)

Tap Dance In The Memory Banks (5)
This Is All I Ask (2)
Till We Meet Again (2)
Time Is Tight (6)
Topless Dancers Of Corfu (5)
Total Bells And Tony (5)
Up, Up And Away (4)
Washington Square (4)
Week End Blues (4)
What'd I Say (3)
Wives And Lovers (3)

HYMAN, Phyllis

Philadelphia-born singer/actress/fashion model. Raised in Pittsburgh. Sang in All-City Choir. With the group New Direction in 1971. Toured with Norman Connors. In the Broadway musical *Sophisticated Ladies* in 1981. Also see Norman Connors.

DEBUT DATE	PEAK POS	WKS CHR		ARTIST — Album Title	$	Label & Number
4/30/77	107	14	1	Phyllis Hyman	$8	Buddah 5681

DEBUT DATE	PEAK POS	WKS CHR	GOLD	ARTIST — Album Title	$	Label & Number

HYMAN, Phyllis — Cont'd

DEBUT DATE	PEAK POS	WKS CHR		ARTIST — Album Title	$	Label & Number
2/3/79	70	17	2	Somewhere In My Lifetime	$8	Arista 4202
12/8/79+	50	21	3	You Know How To Love Me	$8	Arista 9509
8/1/81	57	13	4	Can't We Fall In Love Again	$8	Arista 9544
6/18/83	112	12	5	Goddess Of Love	$8	Arista 8021
10/11/86+	78	41	6	Living All Alone	$8	Phil. Int. 53029
8/10/91	117	12	7	Prime Of My Life	$12	Phil. Int. 11006

Ain't You Had Enough Love (6)
Answer Is You (2)
Be Careful (How You Treat My Love) (2)
Beautiful Man Of Mine (1)
But I Love You (3)
Can't We Fall In Love Again (4)
Children Of The World (1)
Complete Me (3)
Deliver the Love (1)
Don't Tell Me, Tell Her (4)
Don't Wanna Change The World (7)

Falling Star (5)
First Time Together (6)
Give A Little More (3)
Goddess Of Love (5)
Gonna Make Changes (2)
Heavenly (3)
Here's That Rainy Day (2)
Hold On (3)
I Ain't Asking (4)
I Can't Take It Anymore (7)
I Don't Want To Lose You (1)
I Found Love (7)
If You Want Me (6)
Just Another Face In The Crowd (4)

Just Me And You (5)
Just Twenty Five Miles To Anywhere (5)
Kiss You All Over (2)
Let Somebody Love You (5)
Living All Alone (6)
Living In Confusion (4)
Living Inside Your Love (2)
Lookin' For A Lovin' (2)
Love Too Good To Last (4)
Loving You-Losing You (1)
Meet Me On The Moon (7)
Night Bird Gets The Love (1)
No One Can Love You More (1)

Old Friend (6)
One Thing On My Mind (1)
Prime Of My Life (7)
Riding The Tiger (5)
Screaming At The Moon (6)
Slow Dancin' (4)
So Strange (2)
Some Way (3)
Somewhere In My Lifetime (2)
Soon Come Again (2)
Sunshine In My Life (4)
This Feeling Must Be Love (2)
Tonight You And Me (4)
Under Your Spell (3)

Walk Away (7)
Was Yesterday Such A Long Time Ago (1)
We Should Be Lovers (5)
What Ever Happened To Our Love (7)
What You Won't Do For Love (6)
When I Give My Love (This Time) (7)
When You Get Right Down To It (7)
Why Did You Turn Me On (5)
You Just Don't Know (6)

You Know How To Love Me (3)
You Sure Look Good To Me (4)
Your Move, My Heart (5)

I

★★490★★ **IAN, Janis**

Born Janis Eddy Fink on 4/7/51 in New York City. Singer/songwriter/pianist/guitarist. Adopted the last name Ian (her brother's middle name) while studying at Manhattan's High School of Music and Art. Retired from performing from 1968-71.

DEBUT DATE	PEAK POS	WKS CHR	GOLD	ARTIST — Album Title	$	Label & Number
6/17/67	29	28		1 Janis Ian	$12	Verve F. 3017
12/30/67+	179	5		2 For All The Seasons Of Your Mind	$12	Verve F. 3024
6/1/74+	83	20		3 Stars	$10	Columbia 32857
3/22/75	1[1]	64	▲	4 Between The Lines	$10	Columbia 33394
1/24/76	12	19		5 Aftertones	$10	Columbia 33919
1/29/77	45	12		6 Miracle Row	$8	Columbia 34440
9/16/78	120	11		7 Janis Ian	$8	Columbia 35325
7/4/81	156	3		8 Restless Eyes	$8	Columbia 37360

Aftertones (5)
And I Did Ma (2)
Applause (3)
At Seventeen (4) 3
Bahimsa (2)
Belle Of The Blues (5)
Between The Lines (4)
Bigger Than Real (8)
Boy I Really Tied One On (5)
Bridge, The (7)
Bright Lights And Promises (4)
Candlelight (6)
Come On (4)
Dance With Me (3)
Dear Billy (8)
Do You Wanna Dance? (7)
Don't Cry, Old Man (5)

Down And Away (8)
Evening Star (2)
From Me To You (4)
Get Ready To Roll (3)
Goodbye To Morning (5)
Hair Of Spun Gold (1)
Honey D'Ya Think? (2)
Hopper Painting (7)
Hotels & One-Night Stands (7)
Hymn (5)
I Believe I'm Myself Again (8)
I Need To Live Alone Again (7)
I Remember Yesterday (8)
I Want To Make You Love Me (6)
I Would Like To Dance (5)

I'll Cry Tonight (6)
I'll Give You A Stone If You'll Throw It (Changing Tymes) (1)
In The Winter (4)
Insanity Comes Quietly To The Structured Mind (2)
Janey's Blues (1)
Jesse (3)
Let Me Be Lonely (6)
Light A Light (4)
Lonely One (2)
Love Is Blind (2)
Lover Be Kindly (1)
Lover's Lullaby (4)
Man You Are In Me (3)
Maria (medley) (6)
Miracle Row (medley) (6)

Mrs. McKenzie (1)
My Mama's House (7)
New Christ Cardiac Hero (1)
Page Nine (3)
Party Lights (6)
Passion Play (8)
Pro-Girl (1)
Queen Merka & Me (2)
Restless Eyes (8)
Roses (5)
Shady Acres (2)
Silly Habits (7)
Slow Dance Romance (6)
Society's Child (Baby I've Been Thinking) (1) 14
Some People (7)
Song For All The Seasons Of Your Mind (2)

Stars (3)
Streetlife Serenaders (7)
Sugar Mountain (8)
Sunflakes Fall, Snowrays Call (2)
Sunset Of Your Life (6)
Sweet Sympathy (3)
Take To The Sky (6)
Tea & Sympathy (4)
Thankyous (3)
That Grand Illusion (7)
Then Tangles Of My Mind (1)
There Are Times (2)
This Must Be Wrong (5)
Tonight Will Last Forever (7)
Too Old To Go 'Way Little Girl (1)
Under The Covers (8) 71

Water Colors (5)
When The Party's Over (4)
Will You Dance? (6)
Without You (3)
You've Got Me On A String (3)
Younger Generation Blues (1)

IAN & SYLVIA

Canadian folk-country duo: Ian Tyson (b: 9/25/33 in Victoria, British Columbia) and wife Sylvia Fricker (b: 9/19/40 in Chatham, Ontario). Began performing together in 1959. Married in 1964.

DEBUT DATE	PEAK POS	WKS CHR		ARTIST — Album Title	$	Label & Number
9/28/63	115	6	1	Four Strong Winds	$15	Vanguard 79133
9/5/64	70	12	2	Northern Journey	$15	Vanguard 79154
6/19/65	77	18	3	Early Morning Rain	$15	Vanguard 79175
5/28/66	142	6	4	Play One More	$15	Vanguard 79215
4/1/67	130	7	5	So Much For Dreaming	$12	Vanguard 79241
7/8/67	148	10	6	Lovin' Sound	$12	MGM 4388

Awake Ye Drowsy Sleepers (3)
Big River (6)
Brave Wolfe (2)
Captain Woodstock's Courtship (2)
Catfish Blues (5)
Changes (4)
Child Apart (5)
Circle Game (5)
Come All Ye Fair And Tender Ladies (5)
Come In Stranger (3)
Cutty Wren (5)
Darcy Farrow (3)

Early Morning Rain (3)
Ella Speed (1)
Every Night When The Sun Goes Down (1)
Every Time I Feel The Spirit (1)
(Find A) Reason To Believe (6)
For Lovin' Me (3)
Four Rode By (2)
Four Strong Winds (1)
French Girl (4)
Friends Of Mine (4)
Ghost Lover (2)
Gifts Are For Giving (4)

Green Valley (2)
Greenwood Sidie (The Cruel Mother) (1)
Grey Morning (5)
Hang On To A Dream (6)
Hey What About Me (4)
Hold Tight (5)
I Don't Believe You (6)
I'll Bid My Heart Be Still (3)
January Morning (5)
Jealous Lover (2)
Jesus Met The Woman At The Well (1)
Katy Dear (1)
Lady Of Carlisle (1)

Little Beggarman (2)
Lonely Girls (4)
Long Lonesome Road (1)
Lovin' Sound (6)
Marlborough Street Blues (3)
Maude's Blues (3)
Molly And Tenbrooks (4)
Moonshine Can (2)
Mr. Spoons (6)
Nancy Whiskey (3)
National Hotel (6)
Nova Scotia Farewell (2)
Pilgrimage To Paradise (6)
Play One More (4)
Poor Lazarus (1)

Red Velvet (3)
Royal Canal (1)
Satisfied Mind (4)
Short Grass (4)
Si Les Bateaux (5)
So Much For Dreaming (5)
Some Day Soon (2)
Song For Canada (3)
Spanish Is A Loving Tongue (1)
Summer Wages (5)
Sunday (4)
Swing Down, Chariot (2)
Texas Rangers (2)
Tomorrow Is A Long Time (1)

Traveling Drummer (3)
Trilogy (6)
Twenty-Four Hours From Tulsa (4)
V'La L'bon Vent (1)
When I Was A Cowboy (4)
Where Did All The Love Go? (6)
Wild Geese (3)
Windy Weather (6)
You Were On My Mind (2)

DEBUT DATE	PEAK POS	WKS CHR	GOLD	ARTIST — Album Title	$	Label & Number

ICE CUBE

O'Shea Jackson — former lyricist of the Los Angeles rap group N.W.A. Native of Los Angeles. Acted in the films *Boyz N The Hood* and *Trespass*.

DEBUT DATE	PEAK POS	WKS CHR	GOLD	Album Title	$	Label & Number
6/2/90	19	26 ▲		1 AmeriKKKa's Most Wanted	$12	Priority 57120
1/5/91	34	43 ▲		2 Kill At Will	$12	Priority 7230
11/16/91	2[1]	33 ▲		3 Death Certificate	$12	Priority 57155
12/5/92	1[1]	10↑▲		4 **The Predator**	$12	Priority 57185

Alive On Arrival (3)
AmeriKKKa's Most Wanted (1)
Better Off Dead (1)
Bird In The Hand (3)
Birth, The (3)
Black Korea (3)
Bomb, The (1)
Check Yo Self (4)
Color Blind (3)
Dead Homiez (2)
Death (3)
Dirty Mack (4)
Doing Dumb Shit (3)
Don't Trust 'Em (4)
Drive-By, The (1)
Endangered Species (Tales From The Darkside) (1,2)
Funeral, The (3)
Gangsta's Fairytale (1)
Gangsta's Fairytale 2 (4)
Get Off My Dick And Tell Yo Bitch To Come Here (1,2)
Givin' Up The Nappy Dug Out (3)
Horny Lil' Devil (3)
I Gotta Say What Up!!! (2)
I Wanna Kill Sam (3)
I'm Only Out For One Thang (1)
It Was A Good Day (4)
It's A Man's World (1)
JD's Gafflin' (Part 2) (1)
Jackin' For Beats (2)
Look Who's Burnin' (3)
Man's Best Friend (3)
My Summer Vacation (3)
Nigga Ya Love To Hate (1)
No Vaseline (3)
Now I Gotta Wet 'Cha (4)
Once Upon A Time In The Projects (1)
Predator, The (4)
Product, The (2)
Robin Lench (3)
Rollin' Wit The Lench Mob (1)
Say Hi To The Bad Guy (4)
Steady Mobbin' (3)
True To The Game (3)
Turn Off The Radio (1)
Us (3)
We Had To Tear This Mothafucka Up (4)
What They Hittin' Foe? (1)
When Will They Shoot? (4)
Who Got The Camera? (4)
Who's The Mack? (1)
Wicked (4) 55
Wrong Nigga To Fuck Wit (3)
You Can't Fade Me (1)

ICEHOUSE

Australian rock quartet led by singer/guitarist Iva Davies. First known as Flowers. "Icehouse" is Australian slang for an insane asylum.

DEBUT DATE	PEAK POS	WKS CHR	GOLD	Album Title	$	Label & Number
7/25/81	82	15		1 Icehouse	$8	Chrysalis 1350
10/9/82	129	6		2 Primitive Man	$8	Chrysalis 1390
5/24/86	55	24		3 Measure For Measure	$8	Chrysalis 41527
10/17/87+	43	44		4 Man of Colours	$8	Chrysalis 41592

Angel Street (3)
Anybody's War (4)
Baby, You're So Strange (3)
Boulevarde (1)
Can't Help Myself (1)
Crazy (4) 14
Cross The Border (3)
Electric Blue (4) 7
Fatman (1)
Flame, The (3)
Girl In The Moon (4)
Glam (2)
Goodnight, Mr. Matthews (1)
Great Southern Land (2)
Heartbreak Kid (1)
Hey' Little Girl (2)
Icehouse (1)
Kingdom, The (4)
Love In Motion (2)
Lucky Me (3)
Man Of Colours (4)
Mr. Big (1)
My Obsession (4) 88
Mysterious Thing (2)
No Promises (3) 79
Not My Kind (1)
Nothing Too Serious (4)
One By One (2)
Paradise (3)
Regular Boys (3)
Sister (1)
Skin (1)
Sons (1)
Spanish Gold (3)
Street Cafe (2)
Sunrise (4)
Trojan Blue (2)
Uniform (1)
Walls (1)
We Can Get Together (1) 62

ICE-T

Los Angeles-based rapper Tracy Morrow. In films *Breakin'*, *Breakin' II*, *New Jack City* and *Trespass*. Formed his own Rhyme Syndicate label in 1988. Formed controversial speed-metal band Body Count in 1992.

DEBUT DATE	PEAK POS	WKS CHR	GOLD	Album Title	$	Label & Number
8/15/87	93	27 ●		1 Rhyme Pays	$8	Sire 25602
10/1/88	35	33 ●		2 Power	$8	Sire 25765
				cover features his common-law wife, Darlene		
10/28/89	37	28 ●		3 Freedom Of Speech...Just Watch What You Say	$8	Sire 26028
				ICE-T The Iceberg		
6/1/91	15	33 ●		4 O.G. Original Gangster	$12	Sire 26492

Bitches 2 (4)
Black 'N' Decker (3)
Body Count (4)
Drama (2)
Ed (4)
Escape From The Killing Fields (4)
Evil E-What About Sex? (4)
First Impression (4)
Fly By (4)
409 (1)
Freedom Of Speech (3)
Fried Chicken (4)
Girl Tried To Kill Me (3)
Girls L.G.B.N.A.F. (2)
Grand Larceny (4)
Heartbeat (2)
High Rollers (4)
Hit The Deck (4)
Home Of The Bodybag (4)
House, The (4)
Hunted Child (3)
I Love Ladies (1)
I'm Your Pusher (2)
Iceberg, The (3)
Lethal Weapon (3)
Lifestyles Of The Rich And Infamous (4)
M.V.P.s (4)
Make It Funky (1)
Mic Contract (4)
Midnight (4)
Mind Over Matter (4)
New Jack Hustler (Nino's Theme) (4) 67
O.G. Original Gangster (4)
Pain (4)
Peel Their Caps Back (3)
Personal (2)
Power (2)
Prepared To Die (4)
Pulse Of The Rhyme (4)
Radio Suckers (2)
Rhyme Pays (1)
Sex (1)
Shut Up, Be Happy (3)
6 'N The Mornin' (1)
Somebody Gotta Do It (Pimpin' Ain't Easy!!!) (1)
Soul On Ice (2)
Squeeze The Trigger (1)
Straight Up Nigga (4)
Street Killer (4)
Syndicate, The (2)
This One's For Me (3)
Tower, The (4)
What Ya Wanna Do? (3)
Ya Shoulda Killed Me Last Year (4)
You Played Yourself (3)
Ziplock (4)

ICICLE WORKS

Liverpool rock trio: Robert Ian McNabb (vocals), Chris Layhe and Chris Sharrock.

DEBUT DATE	PEAK POS	WKS CHR	GOLD	Album Title	$	Label & Number
4/21/84	40	18		Icicle Works	$8	Arista 8202

As The Dragonfly Flies
Chop The Tree
Factory In The Desert
In The Cauldron Of Love
Love Is A Wonderful Colour
Lovers' Day
Nirvana
Out Of Season
Waterline
Whisper To A Scream (Birds Fly) 37

ICON

Phoenix-based rock quintet — Stephen Clifford, lead singer.

DEBUT DATE	PEAK POS	WKS CHR	GOLD	Album Title	$	Label & Number
6/9/84	190	2		icon	$8	Capitol 12336

Hot Desert Night
I'm Alive
Iconoclast
It's Up To You
Killer Machine
On Your Feet
Rock 'N' Roll Maniac
(Rock On) Through The Night
Under My Gun
World War

IDES OF MARCH, The

Rock group formed while classmates at a Chicago high school. Named after a line in Shakespeare's *Julius Caesar*. Lead singer Jim Peterik joined Survivor as keyboardist.

DEBUT DATE	PEAK POS	WKS CHR	GOLD	Album Title	$	Label & Number
6/27/70	55	12		Vehicle	$15	Warner 1863

Aire Of Good Feeling
Bald Medusa
Dharma For One (medley)
Factory Band
Home
One Woman Man
Sky Is Falling
Symphony For Eleanor (Eleanor Rigby)
Time For Thinking
Vehicle 2
Wooden Ships (medley)

★★406★★ IDOL, Billy

Born Willem Wolfe Broad on 11/30/55 in London. Leader of the London punk band Generation X from 1977-81. Suffered serious leg injuries in a motorcycle crash on 2/6/90. Appeared in 1991 film *The Doors*.

DEBUT DATE	PEAK POS	WKS CHR	GOLD	Album Title	$	Label & Number
10/24/81+	71	68		1 Don't Stop	[M] $8	Chrysalis 4000
7/31/82+	45	104 ●		2 Billy Idol	$8	Chrysalis 41377
12/3/83+	6	82 ▲[2]		3 **Rebel Yell**	$8	Chrysalis 41450
11/8/86	6	47 ▲		4 Whiplash Smile	$8	Chrysalis 41514
10/10/87	10	29 ▲		5 Vital Idol	[K] $8	Chrysalis 41620
				remix versions of 8 of Billy's hits		

DEBUT DATE	PEAK POS	WKS CHR	GOLD	ARTIST — Album Title	$	Label & Number

5/19/90   **11**   39 ▲   6   **Charmed Life** .... **$12**   Chrysalis 21735

All Summer Single (4)	Dancing With Myself (1,5)	Fatal Charm (4)	Loveless, The (6)	Right Way (6)	Worlds Forgotten Boy (4)
Baby Talk (1)	Daytime Drama (3)	**Flesh For Fantasy** (3,5) *29*	Man For All Seasons (4)	Shooting Stars (2)	
Beyond Belief (4)	Dead Next Door (3)	Hole In The Wall (2)	Mark Of Caine (6)	Soul Standing By (4)	
Blue Highway (3)	Dead On Arrival (2)	**Hot In The City** (2,5) *23*	Mony Mony (1,5)	**Sweet Sixteen** (4) *20*	
Catch My Fall (3,5) *50*	(Do Not) Stand In The	It's So Cruel (2)	Nobody's Business (2)	**To Be A Lover** (4,5) *6*	
Come On, Come On (2)	Shadows (3)	**L.A. Woman** (6) *52*	One Night, One Chance (4)	Trouble With The Sweet	
Congo Man (2)	**Don't Need A Gun** (4) *37*	License To Thrill (6)	Prodigal Blues (4)	Stuff (4)	
Cradle Of Love (6) *2*	Endless Sleep (6)	Love Calling (2,5)	Pumping On Steel (6)	Untouchables (1)	
Crank Call (3)	**Eyes Without A Face** (3) *4*	Love Unchained (6)	**Rebel Yell** (3) *46*	**White Wedding** (2,5) *36*	

IF
British jazz-rock combo — J.W. Hodkinson, lead vocals.

10/31/70	187	2		1 If	$15	Capitol 539
9/25/71	171	3		2 If 3	$12	Capitol 820
10/28/72	195	4		3 Waterfall	$10	Metromedia 1057

Cast No Shadows (3)	Here Comes Mr. Time (2)	Raise The Level Of Your	Throw Myself To The Wind	What Did I Say About The
Child Of Storm (2)	I'm Reaching Out On All	Conscious Mind (1)	(3)	Box, Jack? (1)
Dockland (1)	Sides (1)	Sector 17 (3)	Upstairs (2)	Woman Can You See (What
Far Beyond (2)	Light Still Shines (3)	Seldom Seen Sam (2)	Waterfall (3)	This Big Thing Is All
Fibonacci's Number (2)	Paint Your Pictures (3)	Sweet January (2)	What Can A Friend Say? (1)	About?) (1)
Forgotten Roads (2)	Promised Land (1)			

IFIELD, Frank — see BEATLES, The
IGGY & THE STOOGES — see POP, Iggy

IGLESIAS, Julio
Spanish singer, immensely popular worldwide. Born on 9/23/43 in Madrid. Soccer goalie for the pro Real Madrid team until temporary paralysis from a car crash.

4/2/83	32	89	▲	1 Julio .... [F]	$8	Columbia 38640
8/25/84	159	9		2 In Concert .... [L-F]	$10	Columbia 39570 [2]
				recorded in London, Paris, Melbourne & Tokyo in 1983		
9/1/84	5	34	▲³	3 1100 Bel Air Place	$8	Columbia 39157
9/1/84	179	6		4 Hey! .... [F]	$8	Columbia 39567
				originally released in 1980 (not in U.S.A.)		
9/1/84	181	6		5 From A Child To A Woman .... [F]	$8	Columbia 39569
				originally released in 1981 (not in U.S.A.)		
9/15/84	191	4		6 Moments .... [F]	$8	Columbia 39568
				originally released in 1982 (not in U.S.A.)		
8/24/85	92	12	●	7 Libra .... [F]	$8	Columbia 40180
6/4/88	52	17	●	8 Non Stop	$8	Columbia 40995
12/1/90+	37	31	●	9 Starry Night	$12	Columbia 46857
6/6/92	186	2		10 Calor .... [F]	$12	Sony Discos 80763
				Calor is Spanish for Hot		

A Cana Y A Cafe (10)	Coracao Apaixonado (7)	If You Go Away (9)	Never, Never, Never ..see:	Que Nadie Sepa Mi Sufrir (I	Vincent (Starry Starry Night)
Abracame (Wrap Your Arms	Cryin' Time (9)	Isla En El Sol (Island In The	Grande, Grande, Grande	Don't Want Anyone To	(9)
Around Me) (1)	De Domingo A Domingo (10)	Sun) (5)	Ni Te Tengo, Ni Te Olvido (7)	Know My Suffering) (5)	Vivir A Dos (Live Together)
Abril En Portugal (Coimbra)	De Nina A Mujer (From A	La Nave Del Olvido (The	Ni Tu Gato Gris, Ni Tu Perro	Quijote (Quixote) (2,6)	(4)
(7)	Child To A Woman) (1,2,5)	Ship Of Forgetfulness) (4)	Fiel (7)	Ron Y Coca Cola (Rum And	Volver A Empezar ..see:
Ae, Ao (8)	Despues De Ti (After You) (5)	La Paloma (The Dove) (1,6)	99 Miles From L.A. (9)	Coca Cola) (4)	Begin The Beguine
Air That I Breathe (3)	Dire (7)	La Quiero Como Es (10)	No Me Vuelvo A Enamorar (I	Samba Da Minha Terra	When I Fall In Love (9)
All Of You (3) *19*	Esa Mujer (That Woman) (6)	Las Cosas Que Tiene La	Won't Fall In Love Again)	(Samba Of My Land) (2)	When I Need You (9)
Amantes (Lovers) (4)	Esos Amores (10)	Vida (The Things Life Has)	(6)	Si El Amor Llama A Tu	Wo Bist Du (Where Are You)
Amor (1,6)	Esta Cobardia (1)	(6)	Non Si Vive Cosi (Can't Live	Puerta (If Love Knocks On	(1)
And I Love Her (9)	Everytime We Fall In Love (8)	Last Time (3)	Like This) (1)	Your Door) (6)	Words And Music (8)
As Time Goes By (De La	Feelings (5)	Lia (10)	Nostalgie (Nostalgia) (1)	Si, Madame (Yes, Madame)	Y Aunque Te Haga Calor (10)
Pelicula Casablanca) (2)	Felicidades (Duo Con D.	Love Has Been A Friend To	O Me Quieres O Me Dejas	(5)	Y Pensar...(And To Think...)
Bambou Medley (3)	Pedro Vargas) (7)	Me (9)	(Devaneos) (Love Me Or	Somos (10)	(5)
Begin The Beguine (1,2,5)	Fidele (Amantes) (2)	Love Is On Our Side Again	Leave Me) (5)	**To All The Girls I've Loved**	Yesterday When I Was
Can't Help Falling In Love (9)	Grande, Grande, Grande	(8)	Ou Est Passee Ma Boheme?	**Before** (3) *5*	Young (9)
Cantando A Francia	(Great, Great, Great) (2,5,8)	Me Ama Mo (10)	(Carefree Days) (1,2)	Todo Y Nada (7)	
(Singing To France Medley)	Hey (1,2,4)	Me Olvide De Vivir (I Forgot	Pajaro Chogui (Chogui Bird)	Too Many Women (8)	
(2)	Homenaje A Cole Porter	To Live) (2)	(4)	Tu Y Yo (7)	
Cantando A Latinoamerica-I	(Homage To Cole Porter)	Me Va, Me Va (3)	Paloma Blanca (White Dove)	Two Lovers (3)	
& II (Singing To Latin	Medley (2)	Milonga Medley (10)	(2,4)	Un Canto A Galicia (A Song	
American Medley) (2)	I Know It's Over (8)	Momentos (Moments) (2,6)	Pensami (Jurame) (Think Of | To Galicia) (2)	
Cantando A Mexico (Singing	I've Got You Under My Skin	Mona Lisa (9)	Me) (2)	Un Sentimental (A	
To Mexico Medley) (2)	(7)	Moonlight Lady (3)	Por Ella (Because Of Her) (4)	Sentimental) (2,4)	
Como Tu (Like You) (5)	If (E Poi) (3)	Morrinas (Homesickness) (4)	Quand Tu N'es Plus La	Uno (10)	
Con La Misma Piedra (With	If I Ever Needed You (I Need	**My Love** (8) *80*	(Caminito) (When You Are	Viejas Tradiciones (Old	
The Same Stone) (6)	You Now) (8)	Nathalie (2,6)	Not Here Anymore) (2)	Traditions) (4)	

ILLINOIS SPEED PRESS
Chicago rock quintet led by Paul Cotton (Poco).

5/24/69	144	4		The Illinois Speed Press	$15	Columbia 9792

Be A Woman	Free Ride	Hard Luck Story	P.N.S. (When You Come	Pay The Price
Beauty	Get In The Wind	Here Today	Around)	Sky Song

ILLUSION
Jazz-rock sextet formed by Renaissance members Jim McCarty (Yardbirds), John Hawken (Nashville Teens) and Jane Relf (sister of Yardbirds vocalist Keith Relf).

7/2/77	163	7		Out Of The Mist	$8	Island 9489

Beautiful Country	Everywhere You Go	Isadora	Solo Flight
Candles Are Burning	Face Of Yesterday	Roads To Freedom	

ILLUSION, The
Rock quintet led by John Vinci.

5/10/69	69	27		The Illusion	$15	Steed 37003

DEBUT DATE	PEAK POS	WKS CHR	GOLD	ARTIST — Album Title	$	Label & Number

ILLUSION, The — Cont'd

Alone				I Love You, Yes I Do	Real Thing (medley)	Talkin' Sweet Talkin' Soul	Willy Gee (Miss Holy Lady)	You Made Me What I Am
Charlena				Just Imagine	Run, Run, Run (medley)	Why, Tell Me Why (medley)	(medley)	
Did You See Her Eyes 32						

IMPELLITTERI

Hard-rock group fronted by vocalist Graham Bonnet (Rainbow) and guitarist Chris Impellitteri, with Chuck Wright (ex-Quiet Riot bassist), Pat Torpey (Ted Nugent's former drummer) and Phil Wolfe (keyboards).

6/25/88	91	20		Stand In Line	$8	Relativity 8225

Goodnight And Goodbye				Playing With Fire	Since You've Been Gone	Somewhere Over The	Stand In Line	White And Perfect
Leviathan				Secret Lover		Rainbow	Tonight I Fly	

★★253★★ IMPRESSIONS, The

Soul group formed in Chicago in 1957, originally known as The Roosters. Consisted of Jerry Butler, Curtis Mayfield, Sam Gooden and brothers Arthur and Richard Brooks. Butler left for a solo career in 1958, replaced by Fred Cash. The Brooks brothers left in 1962, leaving Mayfield as the trio's leader. Mayfield left in 1970 for a solo career, replaced by Leroy Hutson. In 1973, Hutson was replaced by Reggie Torian and Ralph Johnson. Johnson joined Mystique in 1976. Group did film soundtrack for *Three The Hard Way* (1974). Butler, Mayfield, Gooden and Cash reunited for a tour in 1983. Group inducted into the Rock and Roll Hall of Fame in 1991.

8/31/63+	43	33		1 The Impressions	$20	ABC-Para. 450
3/28/64	52	22		2 The Never Ending Impressions	$20	ABC-Para. 468
8/8/64	8	34		3 Keep On Pushing	$20	ABC-Para. 493
3/6/65	23	19		4 People Get Ready	$20	ABC-Para. 505
3/20/65	83	15		5 The Impressions Greatest Hits ....[G]	$20	ABC-Para. 515
9/18/65	104	9		6 One By One	$20	ABC-Para. 523
3/5/66	79	10		7 Ridin' High	$20	ABC-Para. 545
7/15/67	184	11		8 The Fabulous Impressions	$15	ABC 606
3/2/68	35	27		9 We're A Winner	$15	ABC 635
9/21/68+	172	15		10 The Best Of The Impressions ....[G]	$15	ABC 654
12/7/68+	107	13		11 This Is My Country	$10	Curtom 8001
5/24/69	104	18		12 The Young Mods' Forgotten Story	$10	Curtom 8003
3/20/71	180	6		13 16 Greatest Hits ....[G]	$15	ABC 727
4/29/72	192	2		14 Times Have Changed..	$10	Curtom 8012
3/3/73	180	6		15 Curtis Mayfield/His Early Years With The Impressions ....[G]	$12	ABC 780 [2]
7/6/74	176	3		16 Finally Got Myself Together..	$10	Curtom 8019
8/9/75	115	5		17 First Impressions	$10	Curtom 5003
3/13/76	195	3		18 Loving Power	$10	Curtom 5009
2/5/77	199	2		19 The Vintage Years ....[G]	$12	Sire 3717 [2]

featuring 13 hits by Jerry Butler (see Butler for cuts), 13 by The Impressions and 2 by Curtis Mayfield: "Freddie's Dead" and "Superfly"

Amen (3,5,10,13,15,19) 7	How High Is High (17)	If It's In You To Do Wrong	**Meeting Over Yonder**	September Song (2)	**We're Rolling On (Part 1)**
Answer Me, My Love (6)	I Ain't Supposed To (3)	(16)	(19) 48	**Seven Years** (12) 84	(10,13,15) 59
As Long As You Love Me (1)	**I Can't Stay Away From**	If You Have To Ask (18)	Mighty Mighty (Spade &	She Don't Love Me (8,10)	Wherever You Leadeth Me
Aware Of Love (8)	**You** (8) 80	Inner City Blues (14)	Whitey) (12)	Sister Love (2)	(12)
Can't Satisfy (10) 65	I Can't Wait To See You (18)	Isle Of Sirens (8)	Minstrel And Queen (1,5)	So Unusual (11)	Why Must A Love Song Be A
Can't Work No Longer (4,15)	I Gotta Keep On Movin' (2)	It's All Over (8)	Miracle Woman (16)	Somebody Help Me (3)	Sad Song (17)
Choice Of Colors (12) 21	I Love You (Yeah) (3)	**It's All Right**	Mona Lisa (6)	Sometimes I Wonder (4,15)	Without A Song (17)
Dedicate My Song To You (3)	**I Loved And I Lost** (9,10) 61	(1,5,13,15,19) 4	Moonlight Shadows (9)	**Sooner Or Later** (17) 68	Woman Who Loves Me (2)
Don't Forget What I Told	I Made A Mistake (12)	It's Not Unusual (6)	My Deceiving Heart (12)	Soulful Love (12)	**Woman's Got Soul**
You (16)	I Need A Love (7)	Jealous Man (12)	My Prayer (6)	Stay Close To Me (11)	(4,13,15,19) 29
Don't Let It Hide (3)	I Need To Belong To	Just Another Dance (4)	My Woman's Love (11)	Stop The War (14)	**You Always Hurt Me** (8) 96
Emotions (4,15)	Someone (7,14)	**Just One Kiss From You**	Nature Boy (6)	Sunshine (18)	You Always Hurt The One
Falling In Love With You (6)	I Need Your Love (1)	(6) 76	Never Let Me Go (1,5,13,15)	**Talking About My Baby**	You Love (2)
Finally Got Myself	I Thank Heaven (3)	**Keep On Pushing**	No One Else (7)	(3,5,13,15,19) 12	You Can't Be Wrong (All The
Together (I'm A Changed	I Wanna Be Around (6)	(3,5,13,15,19) 10	No One To Love (9)	Ten To One (8)	Time) (18)
Man) (16) 17	I Want To Be With You (6)	Keep On Trying (18)	Nothing Can Stop Me (9)	That's What Love Will Do (2)	**You Must Believe Me**
First Impressions (17)	I Wish I'd Stayed In Bed (18)	Lemon Tree (2)	Old Before My Time (17)	That's What Mama Say (7)	(4,5,13,15,19) 15
Fool For You (11) 22	I'll Always Be Here (16)	Let It Be Me (7)	100 Lbs. Of Clay (8)	They Don't Know (11)	You Ought To Be In Heaven
For Your Precious Love	(I'm A Changed Man) ..see:	Let Me Tell The World (9)	Our Love Goes On And On	**This Is My Country** (11) 25	(8)
(19) 11	Finally Got Myself Together	Little Boy Blue (2)	(14)	This Loves For Real (14)	You Want Somebody Else
Get Up And Move (4,15)	I'm A Tellin' You (7)	Little Brown Boy (9)	**People Get Ready**	This Must End (10)	(11)
Girl I Find (12)	I'm Gettin' Ready (9)	Little Girl (8)	(4,10,13,15,19) 14	Times Have Changed (14)	**You've Been Cheatin'**
Girl You Don't Know Me (2)	I'm Loving Nothing (11)	**Little Young Lover** (1) 96	Potent Love (14)	**Too Slow** (7,10) 91	(10,19) 33
Gone Away (11)	I'm So Glad (17)	Lonely Man (6)	Ridin' High (7,13,15)	Try Me (16)	You've Come Home (1)
Gotta Get Away (7)	**I'm So Proud**	Long Long Winter (3)	Right On Time (5)	Twilight Time (6)	Young Mods' Forgotten
Groove (17)	(2,5,13,15,19) 14	**Love Me** (14) 94	Romancing To The Folk	Twist And Limbo (1)	Story (12)
Grow Closer Together	I'm Still Waitin' (8)	Love's A Comin' (8)	Song (9)	Up Up And Away (9)	
(1,5,13,15) 99	**I'm The One Who Loves**	Love's Miracle (12)	**Sad, Sad Girl And Boy**	We Go Back A Ways (16)	
Guess What I've Got (15)	**You** (1,5,13,15) 73	Loves Happening (15)	(1,5,13,15) 84	**We're A Winner**	
Gypsy Woman	I've Been Trying (3,10)	Loving Power (18)	**Same Thing It Took** (17) 75	(9,10,13,15,19) 14	
(1,5,13,15,19) 20	I've Found That I've Lost (4)	Man's Temptation (7)	Satin Doll (2)	We're In Love (4)	
Hard To Believe (4)			See The Real Me (4)		

INCREDIBLE BONGO BAND, The

Studio band assembled in Canada by producer Michael Viner.

8/18/73	197	2		Bongo Rock .... [I]	$10	Pride 0028

Apache				Bongolia	In-A-Gadda-Da-Vida	Let There Be Drums	
Bongo Rock 57				Dueling Bongos	Last Bongo In Belgium	Raunchy '73	

INCREDIBLE STRING BAND

Eclectic Scottish folk group led by multi-instrumentalists Mike Heron and Robin Williamson.

7/20/68	161	9		1 The Hangman's Beautiful Daughter	$15	Elektra 74021
3/22/69	174	3		2 Wee Tam	$15	Elektra 74036

DEBUT DATE	PEAK POS	WKS CHR	GOLD	ARTIST — Album Title	$	Label & Number

INCREDIBLE STRING BAND — Cont'd

3/22/69	180	3	3	The Big Huge	$15	Elektra 74037

above 2 albums released as a double album set in England

12/6/69	166	3	4	Changing Horses	$15	Elektra 74057
7/25/70	196	2	5	I Looked Up	$12	Elektra 74061
1/23/71	183	3	6	'U'	$15	Elektra 2002 [2]

a surreal parable in song and dance featuring the mime group Stone Monkey

2/19/72	189	3	7	Liquid Acrobat As Regards The Air	$12	Elektra 74112

Adam And Eve (7)
Air (2)
Astral Plane Theme (6)
Bad Sadie Lee (6)
Beyond The See (2)
Big Ted (4)
Black Jack Davy (5)
Bridge Song (6)
Bridge Theme (6)
Circle Is Unbroken (3)
Cosmic Boy (7)
Cousin Caterpillar (3)
Creation (4)
Cutting The Strings (6)
Darling Belle (7)
Dear Old Battlefield (7)
Douglas Traherne Harding (3)
Ducks On A Pond (2)
Dust Be Diamonds (4)
El Wool Suite (6)
Evolution Rag (7)
Fair As You (9)
Fairies' Hornpipe (medley) (6)
Glad To See You (medley) (6)
Greatest Friend (3)
Half-Remarkable Question (4)
Here Till Here Is There (7)
Hiram Pawnitof (medley) (6)
I Know You (6)
Iron Stone (3)
Jigs Medley (7)
Job's Tears (2)
Juggler's Song (6)
Koeeoaddi There (1)
Letter, The (5)
Light In Time Of Darkness (medley) (6)
Log Cabin Home In The Sky (2)
Lordly Nightshade (3)
Maya (3)
Mercy I Cry City (1)
Minotaur's Song (1)
Mountain Of God (3)
Mr. & Mrs. (4)
Nightfall (1)
Painted Chariot (7)
Partial Belated Overture (6)
Pictures In A Mirror (5)
Puppet Song (6)
Puppies (3)
Queen Of Love (6)
Rainbow (6)
Red Hair (7)
Robot Blues (6)
Sleepers, Awake! (4)
Son Of Noah's Brother (3)
Swift As The Wind (1)
Talking Of The End (7)
This Moment (5)
Three Is A Green Crown (1)
Time (6)
Tree (7)
Very Cellular Song (1)
Walking Along With You (6)
Waltz Of The New Moon (1)
Water Song (1)
When You Find Out Who You Are (5)
White Bird (1)
Witches Hat (1)
Worlds They Rise And Fall (7)
Yellow Snake (2)
You Get Brighter (2)

INDECENT OBSESSION

Pop band from Brisbane, Australia: David Dixon (vocals), Michael Szumowski, Andrew Coyne and Darryl Simms. Band's name taken from a Colleen McCullough novel.

9/1/90	148	6		Indecent Obsession	$12	MCA 6426

Believe
Come Back To Me
Dream After Dream
Going Down
Never Gonna Stop
Nowhere To Hide
Say Goodbye
Spoken Words
Survive The Heat
Tell Me Something 31

INDEPENDENTS, The

Soul group consisting of Chuck Jackson, Maurice Jackson, Helen Curry and Eric Thomas. Jackson (no relation to solo singer Chuck Jackson) and Marvin Yancey, Jr. were producers/writers for the group; later teamed in production work, especially for Natalie Cole, to whom Yancey was married for a time.

5/19/73	127	9		The First Time We Met	$10	Wand 694

Baby I've Been Missing You 41
Can't Understand It
Couldn't Hear Nobody Say (I Love You Like You Do)
Here I Am
I Just Want To Be There
I Love You, Yes I Do
Just As Long As You Need Me, Part 1 84
Leaving Me 21
Our Love Has Got To Come Together

INDIGO GIRLS

Duo of singers/songwriters/guitarists Amy Ray and Emily Saliers from Decatur, Georgia.

4/15/89	22	35	▲	1 Indigo Girls	$8	Epic 45044
11/25/89+	159	14		2 Strange Fire	$8	Epic 45427
10/13/90	43	29	●	3 Nomads-Indians-Saints	$12	Epic 46820
5/30/92	21	34	●	4 Rites Of Passage	$12	Epic 48865

Airplane (4)
Blood And Fire (1)
Cedar Tree (4)
Center Stage (1)
Chickenman (4)
Closer To Fine (1) 52
Crazy Game (2)
Galileo (4) 89
Get Together (2)
Ghost (4)
Girl With The Weight Of The World In Her Hands (3)
Hammer And A Nail (4)
Hand Me Downs (3)
Hey Jesus (4)
History Of Us (1)
I Don't Wanna Know (2)
Joking (4)
Jonas & Ezekial (4)
Keeper Of My Heart (3)
Kid Fears (1)
Land Of Canaan (1,2)
Left Me A Fool (2)
Let It Be Me (4)
Love Will Come To You (4)
Love's Recovery (1)
Make It Easier (2)
Nashville (4)
1 2 3 (3)
Prince Of Darkness (1)
Pushing The Needle Too Far (3)
Romeo And Juliet (4)
Secure Yourself (1)
Southland In The Springtime (3)
Strange Fire (2)
Three Hits (4)
Tried To Be True (1)
Virginia Woolf (4)
Walk Away (2)
Watershed (3)
Welcome Me (3)
World Falls (3)
You And Me Of The 10,000 Wars (3)
You Left It Up To Me (3)

INFECTIOUS GROOVES

Funk-punk outfit: Mike Muir (vocals), Robert Trujillo, Dean Pleasants, Adam Siegel, Scott Crago, Stephen Perkins and Dave Dunn. Muir and Trujillo were formerly with Suicidal Tendencies.

2/22/92	198	1		The Plague That Makes Your Booty Move...It's The Infectious Grooves	$12	Epic 47402

Back To The People
Closed Session
Do The Sinister
I Look Funny?
I'm Gonna Be My King
Infectious Blues
Infectious Grooves
Infecto Groovalistic
Mandatory Love Song
Monster Skank
Punk It Up
Stop Funk'N With My Head
Thanx But No Thanx Therapy
Turn Your Head
You Lie...And Yo Breath Stank

INFORMATION SOCIETY

Techno-dance outfit formed in Minneapolis in 1985: songwriter Paul Robb, vocalist Kurt Valaquen, keyboardist Amanda Kramer and bassist James Cassidy. Reduced to a trio in 1990 with departure of Kramer.

8/20/88	25	38	●	1 Information Society	$8	Tommy Boy 25691
11/3/90	77	14		2 Hack	$12	Tommy Boy 26258

Attitude (1)
Can't Slow Down (2)
Chemistry (2)
Come With Me (2)
Fire Tonight (2)
Hack 1 (2)
Hard Currency (2)
How Long (2)
If Only (2)
Knife And A Fork (2)
Lay All Your Love On Me (1) 83
Make It Funky (1)
Mirrorshades (2)
Move Out (2)
Now That I Have You (2)
Over The Sea (1)
Repetition (1) 76
Running (1)
Seek 200 (2)
Slipping Away (2)
Something In The Air (1)
Think (2) 28
Tomorrow (1)
Walking Away (1) 9
What's On Your Mind (Pure Energy) (1) 3

INGRAM, James

R&B vocalist/multi-instrumentalist from Akron, Ohio. Vocalist on Quincy Jones' album *The Dude*.

11/12/83+	46	42	●	1 It's Your Night	$8	Qwest 23970
9/13/86	123	9		2 Never Felt So Good	$8	Qwest 25424
10/6/90	117	10		3 It's Real	$12	Warner 25924
10/19/91	168	3		4 The Power Of Great Music .... [G]	$12	Warner 26700

Always (2)
Baby Be Mine (3)
Baby, Come To Me (4) 1
Call On Me (3)
Get Ready (4)
How Do You Keep The Music Playing (1,4) 45
I Don't Have The Heart (3,4) 1
I Wanna Come Back (3)
It's Real (3)
It's Your Night (1)
Just Once (4) 17
Lately (3)
Love Come Down (3)
Love 1 Day At A Time (3)
Love's Been Here And Gone (2)
Never Felt So Good (2)
One Hundred Ways (4) 14
One More Rhythm (1)
Party Animal (1)
Red Hot Lover (2)
Remember The Dream (4)
Right Back (2)
Say Hey (2)
She Loves Me (The Best That I Can Be) (1)
So Fine (3)
Someday We'll Be Free (3)
Somewhere Out There (4) 2
There's No Easy Way (1,4) 58
Trust Me (2)
Try Your Love Again (1)
Tuff (2)
Whatever We Imagine (1,4)
When Was The Last Time Music Made You Cry (3)
Where Did My Heart Go? (4)
Wings Of My Heart (2)
Yah Mo B There (1,4) 19
(You Make Me Feel Like) A Natural Man (3)

DEBUT DATE	PEAK POS	WKS CHR	GOLD	ARTIST — Album Title	$	Label & Number

INGRAM, Luther
Born on 11/30/44 in Jackson, Tennessee. Soul singer/songwriter. Sang in gospel group with his brothers. First recorded for Smash in 1965. In the film *Wattstax*.

1/15/72	175	11		1 I've Been Here All The Time	$12	Koko 2201
9/30/72	39	21		2 If Loving You Is Wrong I Don't Want To Be Right	$10	Koko 2202

Ain't That Loving You (For More Reasons Than One) (1) **45**   Always (2) **64**   **Be Good To Me Baby** (1) **97**   Dying & Crying (2)

Ghetto Train (1)   Help Me Love (2)   I Can't Stop (2)   I Remember (2)   **I'll Be Your Shelter (In Time Of Storm)** (2) **40**

I'll Just Call You Honey (1)   I'll Love You Until The End (1,2)   I'm Trying To Sing A Message To You (2)

(If Loving You Is Wrong) I Don't Want To Be Right (2) **3**   Love Ain't Gonna Run Me Away (2)

Missing You (1)   **My Honey And Me** (1) **55**   Oh Baby, You Can Depend On Me (1)   Pity For The Lonely (1)

Since You Don't Want Me (1)   To The Other Man (1)   **You Were Made For Me** (1) **93**

INMATES, The
British rock group led by Peter Gunn.

12/1/79+	49	17		First Offence	$8	Polydor 6241

Back In History   **Dirty Water 51**   I Can't Sleep

If Time Could Turn Backwards   Jealousy

Love Got Me   Midnight To Six Man

Mr. Unreliable   Three Time Loser

Walk, The   You're The One That Done It

INNER CITY
Techno-funk group led by Detroit producer/songwriter/mixer Kevin Saunderson and female vocalist Paris Grey (from Glencove, Illinois).

6/24/89	162	4		Big Fun	$8	Virgin 91242

Ain't Nobody Better   And I Do

Big Fun   Do You Love What You Feel

Good Life 73   Inner City Theme

Paradise   Power Of Passion

Secrets Of The Mind   Set Your Body Free

INNOCENCE MISSION, The
Quartet from Lancaster, Pennsylvania: Don Peris (guitar) and his wife Karen (vocals) with Mike Bitts (bass) and Steve Brown (drums).

3/24/90	167	10		The Innocence Mission...	$12	A&M 5274

Black Sheep Wall   Broken Circle   Clear To You

Come Around And See Me   Curious

I Remember Me   Medjugorje

Mercy   Notebook

Paper Dolls   Surreal

Wonder Of Birds   You Chase The Light

INSIDERS
Rock band from Chicago: John Siegle (lead vocals), Ed Breckenfeld, Jim DeMonte, Jay O'Rourke and Gary Yerkins.

10/10/87	167	5		Ghost On The Beach...	$8	Epic 40630

Ghost On The Beach   Love Like Candy

Memory Row   Moondog Howl

Our Last Day   Peace In Time

Price Of Love   Sad Songs   35,000

Stand In Chains

INSTANT FUNK
Large funk ensemble formed in Philadelphia in 1977. Led by singer/percussionist James Carmichael. Former backup band for Bunny Sigler.

2/17/79	12	22	●	1 Instant Funk	$8	Salsoul 8513
12/8/79+	129	13		2 Witch Doctor	$8	Salsoul 8529
10/18/80	130	6		3 The Funk Is On	$8	Salsoul 8536
4/10/82	147	7		4 Looks So Fine	$8	Salsoul 8545

Bodyshine (2)   Can You See Where I'm Coming From (3)   Crying (1)   Dark Vader (1)   Don't You Wanna Party (1)   Everybody (3)

Funk Is On (3)   Funk-N-Roll (3)   Give It To You Baby (4)   Gotta Like That (4)   **I Got My Mind Made Up (You Can Get It Girl)** (1) **20**

I Had A Dream (2)   I Want To Love You (2)   I'll Be Doggone (1)   It's Cool (3)   It's Your Love On My Mind (2)   Jumpin' To Conclusions (4)

Looks So Fine (4)   Never Let It Go Away (1)   Punk Rockin' (4)   Scream And Shout (2)   Slam Dunk The Funk (4)   Slap, Slap, Lickedy Lap (2)   What Can I Do For You (3)

Why Don't You Think About Me (4)   Wide World Of Sports (1)   Witch Doctor (2)   You Say You Want Me To Stay (1)   You Want My Love (3)

You're Not Getting Older (3)

INTERNATIONAL ALL STARS
Directed by Harry Frekin.

12/4/61	47	2		Percussion Around The World .... [I]	$10	London P. 4 44010

April In Portugal   Auf Wiederseh'n Sweetheart   Calcutta

Children's Marching Song   Cielito Lindo   Frenesi

Japanese Sandman   La Montana   Never On Sunday

Poor People Of Paris (Jean's Song)   Third Man Theme

Volare

INTRUDERS, The
Soul group formed in Philadelphia in 1960. Consisted of Sam "Little Sonny" Brown, Eugene "Bird" Daughtry, Phil Terry and Robert "Big Sonny" Edwards. First recorded for Gowen in 1961.

7/27/68	112	9		1 Cowboys To Girls	$15	Gamble 5004
1/25/69	144	6		2 The Intruders Greatest Hits..[G]	$15	Gamble 5005
5/19/73	133	18		3 Save The Children..	$12	Gamble 31991

By The Time I Get To Phoenix (1)   Call Me (1)   **Cowboys To Girls** (1,2) **6**   Everyday Is A Holiday (1)   Friends No More (1,2)   Girls Girls Girls (2)

Good For Me Girl (1)   Hang On In There (3)   **I Wanna Know Your Name** (3) **60**   **I'll Always Love My Mama (Part 1)** (3) **36**   It Must Be Love (1)

(Love Is Like A) Baseball Game (1,2) **26**   **Love That's Real** (2) **82**   Me Tarzan You Jane (2)   Memories Are Here To Stay (2)

Mother And Child Reunion (3)   **Sad Girl** (1) **47**   Save The Children (3)   **Slow Drag** (2) **54**   (So Glad I'm) Yours (1)   Teardrops (3)

To Be Happy Is The Real Thing (3)   **Together** (2) **48**   Turn The Hands Of Time (1)   **(We'll Be) United** (2) **78**   (Who's Your) Favorite Candidate (2)

INVISIBLE MAN'S BAND, The
Group evolved from The Five Stairsteps. Consisted of Clarence, Kenneth, Dennis and James Burke.

5/31/80	90	14		The Invisible Man's Band..	$8	Mango 9537

All Night Thing 45   X-Country

Full Moon

Love Can't Come/Love Has Come

9 X's Out Of Ten   Rent Strike

DEBUT DATE	PEAK POS	WKS CHR	G O L D	ARTIST — Album Title	$	Label & Number

★★338★★ INXS

Rock sextet formed in Sydney, Australia as The Farris Brothers. Members since group's formation in 1977: Michael Hutchence (lead singer), Kirk Pengilly (guitar), Garry Beers (bass), and brothers Tim (guitar), Andy (keyboards, guitar) and Jon (drums) Farriss. Hutchence, who starred in the films *Dogs In Space* and *Frankenstein Unbound*, also co-founded the band Max Q. Jon Farriss married actress Leslie Bega.

DEBUT DATE	PEAK POS	WKS CHR	GOLD	Album Title	$	Label & Number
3/19/83	46	31	●	1 Shabooh Shoobah	$8	Atco 90072
10/1/83	148	6		2 Dekadance ...... [M]	$8	Atco 90115
				4 extended tracks from above album		
5/26/84	52	28	●	3 The Swing	$8	Atco 90160
8/18/84	164	3		4 INXS ...... [E]	$8	Atco 90184
				originally released in 1980 (not in the U.S.A.)		
11/2/85+	11	55	▲	5 Listen Like Thieves	$8	Atlantic 81277
11/14/87+	3	81	▲⁴	6 Kick	$8	Atlantic 81796
10/6/90	5	43	▲	7 X	$12	Atlantic 82140
11/23/91	72	11		8 Live Baby Live ...... [L]	$12	Atlantic 82294
				limited edition package includes a 32-page mini tour program		
8/22/92	16	25	●	9 Welcome To Wherever You Are	$12	Atlantic 82394

All Around (9)
All The Voices (9)
Baby Don't Cry (9)
Back On Line (9)
Beautiful Girl (9)
Biting Bullets (5)
Bitter Tears (7) *46*
Black And White (1,2)
Body Language (4)
Burn For You (3,8)
By My Side (7,8)
Calling All Nations (6)
Communication (9)

Dancing On The Jetty (3)
Devil Inside (6) *2*
Disappear (7) *8*
Doctor (4)
Don't Change (1) *80*
Face The Change (3)
Faith In Each Other (7)
Golden Playpen (1)
Good + Bad Times (5)
Guns In The Sky (6,8)
Hear That Sound (7,8)
Heaven Sent (9)
Here Comes (1,2)

I Send A Message (3) *77*
In Vain (4)
Jan's Song (1)
Johnson's Aeroplane (3)
Jumping (1)
Just Keep Walking (4)
Kick (6)
Kiss The Dirt (Falling Down The Mountain) (5)
Know The Difference (7)
Lately (4)
Learn To Smile (4)
Listen Like Thieves (5) *54*

Love Is (What I Say) (3)
Loved One (6)
Mediate (6,8)
Melting In The Sun (3)
Men And Women (9)
Mystify (6,8)
Need You Tonight (6,8) *1*
Never Tear Us Apart (6,8) *7*
New Sensation (6,8) *3*
Newsreel Babies (4)
Not Enough Time (9) *28*
Old World New World (1)
On A Bus (9)

On My Way (7)
One X One (5,8)
One Thing (1,2,8) *30*
Original Sin (3) *58*
Questions (9)
Red Red Sun (5)
Roller Skating (4)
Same Direction (5)
Shine Like It Does (5)
Shining Star (8)
Soul Mistake (4)
Spy Of Love (1)
Stairs, The (7,8)

Strange Desire (9)
Suicide Blonde (7,8) *9*
Swing, The (3)
Taste It (9)
This Time (5,8) *81*
Three Sisters (5)
Tiny Daggers (6)
To Look At You (1,2)
What You Need (5,8) *5*
Who Pays The Price (7)
Wild Life (6)
Wishing Well (4)
Wishy Washy (4)

IRIS, Donnie

Real name: Dominic Ierace. Singer/songwriter/guitarist/lead of the Pittsburgh rock group The Jaggerz. Native of Beaver Falls, Pennsylvania. Toured briefly with the funk group Wild Cherry.

DEBUT DATE	PEAK POS	WKS CHR	GOLD	Album Title	$	Label & Number
12/13/80+	57	23		1 Back On The Streets	$8	MCA 3272
9/26/81	84	31		2 King Cool	$8	MCA 5237
11/27/82	180	4		3 The High And The Mighty	$8	MCA 5358
7/2/83	127	12		4 Fortune 410	$8	MCA 5427
3/16/85	115	15		5 No Muss...No Fuss	$8	HME 39949

Agnes (1)
Ah! Leah! (1) *29*
Back On The Streets (1)
Broken Promises (2)
Color Me Blue (2)
Cry If You Want To (4)
Daddy Don't Live Here Anymore (1)
Do You Compute? (4) *64*
Don't Cry Baby (5)

Follow That Car (5)
Glad All Over (3)
Headed For A Breakdown (5)
High And The Mighty (3)
Human Evolution (4)
I Belong (4)
I Can't Hear You (1)
I Wanna Tell Her (3)
I Want You Back (5)
I'm A User (4)

Injured In The Game Of Love (5) *91*
Joking (1)
King Cool (2)
Last To Know (2)
L.O.V.E. (5)
Love Is Like A Rock (2) *37*
Love Is Magic (3)
My Girl (2) *25*
Never Did I (4)

Parallel Time (3)
Pretender (2)
Promise, The (2)
Ridin' Thunder (5)
She's So European (4)
She's So Wild (1)
Shock Treatment (1)
Somebody (2)
Stagedoor Johnny (4)
State Of The Heart (5)

Sweet Merilee (2) *80*
Tell Me What You Want (4)
10th Street (1)
That's The Way Love Ought To Be (2)
This Time It Must Be Love (3)
Too Young To Love (1)
Tough World (3) *57*
You're Gonna Miss Me (3)
You're My Serenity (5)

You're Only Dreaming (1)

IRISH ROVERS, The

Irish-born folk quintet. Group formed in Alberta, Canada in 1964. Brothers Will (vocals) and George Millar, their cousin Joe Millar, Jimmy Ferguson and Wilcil McDowell.

DEBUT DATE	PEAK POS	WKS CHR	GOLD	Album Title	$	Label & Number
4/6/68	24	43		1 The Unicorn	$15	Decca 74951
11/9/68	119	8		2 All Hung Up	$15	Decca 75037
5/10/69	182	5		3 Tales To Warm Your Mind	$15	Decca 75081
4/25/81	157	8		4 Wasn't That A Party	$8	Cleve. I. 37107

THE ROVERS

Ally-Bally (3)
Bare Legged Joe (2)
Biplane, Ever More (2) *91*
Black Velvet Band (1)
Bonnie Kellswater (1)
Bridget Flynn (1)
Cold Winter Shadows (2)
Come In (1)
Does Your Chewing Gum Lose Its Flavor On The Bedpost Over Night? (2)

Fireflyte (4)
First Love In Life (1)
Goodbye Mrs. Durkin (1)
Goodnight Irene (2)
Happy Trails (medley) (4)
Henry Joy McCracken (2)
Here's To The Horses (4)
Hiring Fair (1)
Lily The Pink (3)
Liverpool Lou (2)

Matchstalk Men And Matchstalk Cats And Dogs (4)
Mexican Girl (4)
Minstrel Of Cranberry Lane (3)
Movie Cowboys (medley) (4)
Mrs. Crandall's Boardinghouse (3)
My Little Maureen (2)

Oh You Mucky Kid (Liverpool Lullaby) (3)
Orange And The Green (1)
Our Little Boy Blue (3)
Pat Of Mullingar (1)
Penny Whistle Peddler (3)
Pheasant Plucker's Son (4)
Pigs Can't Fly (3)
(Puppet Song) Whiskey On A Sunday (2) *75*
Rovers Fancy (2)

Shamrock Shore (2)
Stolen Child (3)
Stop, Look, Listen (3)
Tara, The Ice Cream Girl (4)
Unicorn, The (1) *7*
Up Among The Heather (2)
Victory Chimes (4)
Village Of Brambleshire Wood (3)
Wasn't That A Party (4) *37*

Wind That Shakes The Corn (1)
Yo Yo Man (4)

★★436★★ IRON BUTTERFLY

San Diego heavy-metal band: Doug Ingle (vocals, keyboards), Erik Braunn (guitar), Lee Dorman (bass) and Ron Bushy (drums). Braunn left in late 1969, replaced by Mike Pinera (leader of Blues Image) and Larry Reinhardt. Split in mid-1971. Braunn and Bushy regrouped in early 1975 with Phil Kramer and Howard Reitzes.

DEBUT DATE	PEAK POS	WKS CHR	GOLD	Album Title	$	Label & Number
3/9/68	78	49		1 Heavy	$20	Atco 227
7/20/68+	4	140	▲⁴	2 In-A-Gadda-Da-Vida	$15	Atco 250
				translation of title: In The Garden Of Life		
2/15/69	3	44	●	3 Ball	$15	Atco 280
5/23/70	20	23		4 Iron Butterfly Live ...... [L]	$15	Atco 318
				side 2 is a 19-minute version of "In-A-Gadda-Da-Vida"		
8/29/70	16	23		5 Metamorphosis	$15	Atco 339
12/25/71+	137	6		6 The Best Of Iron Butterfly/Evolution ...... [G]	$15	Atco 369
2/15/75	138	6		7 Scorching Beauty	$10	MCA 465

DEBUT DATE	PEAK POS	WKS CHR	GOLD	ARTIST — Album Title	$	Label & Number

IRON BUTTERFLY — Cont'd

Am I Down (7)	Filled With Fear (3,4)	**In-A-Gadda-Da-Vida**	Look For The Sun (1)	Searchin' Circles (7)	Unconscious Power (1,6)
Are You Happy (2,4)	Flowers And Beads (2,6)	(2,4,6) **30**	Most Anything You Want (2)	Shady Lady (5)	You Can't Win (1,4)
Before You Go (7)	Free Flight (5)	In The Crowds (3)	My Mirage (2)	Slower Than Guns (5,6)	
Belda-Beast (3,6)	Gentle As It May Seem (1)	**In The Time Of Our Lives**	New Day (5)	So-Lo (1)	
Best Years Of Our Life (5)	Get Out Of My Life, Woman	(3,4) **96**	1975 Overture (7)	Soldier In Our Town (5)	
Butterfly Bleu (5)	(1)	Iron Butterfly Theme (1,6)	Pearly Gates (7)	**Soul Experience** (3,4,6) **75**	
Easy Rider (Let The Wind	Hard Miseree (7)	It Must Be Love (3)	People Of The World (7)	Stamped Ideas (1)	
Pay The Way) (5,6) **66**	Her Favorite Style (3)	Lonely Boy (3)	Possession (1,6)	Stone Believer (5,6)	
Fields Of Sun (1)	High On A Mountain Top (7)	Lonely Hearts (7)	Real Fright (3)	Termination (2,6)	

IRONHORSE

Rock band formed by Bachman-Turner Overdrive founder Randy Bachman.

4/7/79	153	10		Ironhorse	$8	Scotti Br. 7103

Jump Back In The Light	One And Only	**Stateline Blues**	There Ain't No Cure	Watch Me Fly
Old Fashioned	She's Got It	**Sweet Lui-Louise 36**	Tumbleweed	You Gotta Let Go

★★257★★ IRON MAIDEN

Heavy-metal quintet from London. 1981 lineup: Paul Di'anno (lead vocals), Clive Burr, Dave Murray, Steve Harris and Adrian Smith. Burr and Di'anno left in 1982, replaced by Bruce Dickinson (lead vocals) and Nicko McBrain. 1990 lineup: Dickinson, Murray, Harris, McBrain and Janick Gers.

6/6/81	78	23	●	1 Killers	$8	Harvest 12141
10/31/81	89	30		2 Maiden Japan .... [L-M]	$8	Harvest 15000
4/10/82	33	65	▲	3 The Number Of The Beast	$8	Harvest 12202
				features new lead singer Bruce Dickinson		
6/11/83	14	45	▲	4 Piece Of Mind	$8	Capitol 12274
9/29/84	21	34	▲	5 Powerslave	$8	Capitol 12321
11/16/85	19	22	▲	6 Live After Death .... [L]	$10	Capitol 12441 [2]
10/11/86	11	39	▲	7 Somewhere In Time	$8	Capitol 12524
4/30/88	12	23	●	8 Seventh Son Of A Seventh Son	$8	Capitol 90258
10/20/89	17	18	●	9 No Prayer For The Dying	$12	Epic 46905
5/30/92	12	13		10 Fear Of The Dark	$12	Epic 48993

Aces High (5,6)	Children Of The Damned	Genghis Khan (1)	Mother Russia (9)	Revelations (4,6)	22, Acacia Avenue (3,6)
Afraid To Shoot Strangers	(3,6)	Hallowed Be Thy Name (3,6)	Murders In The Rue Morgue	Rime Of The Ancient	Twilight Zone (1)
(10)	Clairvoyant, The (8)	Heaven Can Wait (7)	(1)	Mariner (5,6)	2 Minutes To Midnight (5,6)
Alexander The Great (7)	Deja Vu (1)	Holy Smoke (9)	No Prayer For The Dying (9)	Run Silent Run Deep (9)	Wasted Years (7)
Another Life (1)	Die With Your Boots On (4,6)	Hooks In You (9)	Number Of The Beast (3,6)	Run To The Hills (3,6)	Wasting Love (10)
Apparition, The (10)	Drifter (1)	Ides Of March (1)	Only The Good Die Young (8)	Running Free (2,6)	Weekend Warrior (10)
Assassin, The (9)	Duellists, The (5)	Infinite Dreams (8)	Phantom Of The Opera (6)	Sea Of Madness (7)	Where Eagles Dare (4)
Back In The Village (5)	Evil That Men Do (8)	Innocent Exile (1,2)	Powerslave (5,6)	Seventh Son Of A Seventh	Wrathchild (1,2,6)
Be Quick Or Be Dead (10)	Fates Warning (9)	Invaders (3)	Prisoner, The (3)	Son (8)	
Bring Your Daughter ... To	Fear Is The Key (10)	Iron Maiden (6)	Prodigal Son (1)	Still Life (4)	
The Slaughter (9)	Fear Of The Dark (10)	Judas Be My Guide (10)	Prophecy, The (8)	Stranger In A Strange Land	
Can I Play With Madness (8)	Flash Of The Blade (5)	Killers (1,2)	Public Enema Number One	(7)	
Caught Somewhere In Time	Flight Of Icarus (4,6)	Loneliness Of The Long	(9)	Sun And Steel (4)	
(7)	From Here To Eternity (10)	Distance Runner (7)	Purgatory (1)	Tailgunner (9)	
Chains Of Misery (10)	Fugitive, The (10)	Losfer Words (Big 'Orra) (5)	Quest For Fire (4)	To Tame A Land (4)	
Childhood's End (10)	Gangland (3)	Moonchild (8)	Remember Tomorrow (2)	Trooper, The (4,6)	

ISAAK, Chris

San Francisco-based singer/songwriter/guitarist. Born in Stockton, California on 6/26/56. Attended college in Japan. Cameo appearances in the films *Married To The Mob, Silence Of The Lambs*, others.

4/11/87	194	2		1 Chris Isaak	$8	Warner 25536
7/15/89+	7	74	▲	2 Heart Shaped World	$8	Reprise 25837

Blue Hotel (1)	Fade Away (1)	In The Heat Of The Jungle	Nothing's Changed (2)	Wild Love (1)
Blue Spanish Sky (2)	Forever Young (2)	(2)	This Love Will Last (1)	Wrong To Love You (2)
Cryin' (1)	Heart Full Of Soul (1)	Kings Of The Highway (2)	Waiting For The Rain To Fall	You Owe Me Some Kind Of
Don't Make Me Dream	Heart Shaped World (2)	Lie To Me (1)	(1)	Love (1)
About You (2)	I'm Not Waiting (2)	Lovers Game (1)	**Wicked Game** (2) **6**	You Took My Heart (1)

ISLE OF MAN

Multi-ethnic pop quartet (members are from France, Nicaragua, Italy and U.S.) — Robere Parlez, leader.

7/19/86	110	18		Isle Of Man	$8	Pasha 40319

Afraid Of Heights	Desperate Surrender (Amor	Land Of The Heroes	Rock Of Ages	Speaking English
Am I Forgiven 90	Moriendo)	Only The Brave	Skin Trade	Tenderness
Building Bridges				

ISLEY, Ernie

Member of the Isley Brothers and Isley, Jasper, Isley. Born on 3/7/52 in Cincinnati.

3/31/90	174	11		High Wire	$12	Elektra 60902

Back To Square One	Diamond In The Rough	High Wire	Muses, The	She Takes Me Up
Deal With It	Fare Thee Well,	In Deep	Rising From The Ashes	Song For The Muses
Deep Water	Fair-Weather Friend	Love Situation		

★★60★★ ISLEY BROTHERS, The

R&B trio of brothers from Cincinnati. Formed in early 1950s as a gospel group. Consisted of O'Kelly, Ronald and Rudolph Isley. Moved to New York in 1957 and first recorded for Teenage Records. Trio added their younger brothers Ernie (guitar, drums) and Marvin (bass, percussion) Isley and brother-in-law Chris Jasper (keyboards) in September 1969. Formed own T-Neck label the same year. Ernie, Marvin and Chris began recording as the trio Isley, Jasper, Isley in 1984. O'Kelly died of a heart attack on 3/31/86 (age 48); Ronald and Rudolph continued on as The Isley Brothers through 1989. Ernie, Marvin and Ronald reunited as The Isley Brothers in late 1990.

9/29/62	61	13		1 Twist & Shout	$35	Wand 653
6/18/66	140	5		2 This Old Heart Of Mine	$15	Tamla 269
5/3/69	22	18		3 It's Our Thing	$10	T-Neck 3001

DEBUT DATE	PEAK POS	WKS CHR	G O L D	ARTIST — Album Title	$	Label & Number
				ISLEY BROTHERS, The — Cont'd		
10/18/69	169	4		4 Live At Yankee Stadium ....[L]	$12	T-Neck 3004 [2]
				side A: Isley Brothers; side B: Edwin Hawkins Singers; side C: Brooklyn Bridge; side D: "Don't Change Your Love" by The Five Stairsteps, "Somebody's Been Messin'" by Judy White and "Love Is What You Make It" by Sweet Cherries		
10/18/69	180	3		5 The Brothers: Isley	$10	T-Neck 3002
9/25/71	71	25		6 Givin' It Back	$10	T-Neck 3008
7/1/72	29	33		7 Brother, Brother, Brother..	$10	T-Neck 3009
3/17/73	139	13		8 The Isleys Live ....[L]	$12	T-Neck 3010 [2]
9/8/73	8	37	▲	9 3 + 3	$10	T-Neck 32453
12/22/73	195	5		10 Isleys' Greatest Hits ....[G]	$10	T-Neck 3011
9/7/74	14	28	●	11 Live It Up	$8	T-Neck 33070
6/14/75	1[1]	40	▲	12 The Heat Is On	$8	T-Neck 33536
5/29/76	9	26	●	13 Harvest For The World...	$8	T-Neck 33809
4/16/77	6	34	▲	14 Go For Your Guns	$8	T-Neck 34432
8/27/77	58	11		15 Forever Gold ....[G]	$8	T-Neck 34452
4/22/78	4	21	▲	16 Showdown	$8	T-Neck 34930
6/16/79	14	20	●	17 Winner Takes All	$10	T-Neck 30077 [2]
4/19/80	8	22	▲	18 Go All The Way	$8	T-Neck 36305
3/21/81	28	17	●	19 Grand Slam	$8	T-Neck 37080
10/31/81	45	13		20 Inside You	$8	T-Neck 37533
8/21/82	87	12		21 The Real Deal	$8	T-Neck 38047
6/4/83	19	23	●	22 Between The Sheets	$8	T-Neck 38674
12/7/85+	140	12		23 Masterpiece	$8	Warner 25347
6/20/87	64	17		24 Smooth Sailin'	$8	Warner 25586
				THE ISLEY BROTHERS Featuring RONALD ISLEY:		
9/2/89	89	13		25 Spend The Night	$8	Warner 25940
6/13/92	140	3		26 Tracks Of Life	$12	Warner 26620

Ain't Givin' Up No Love (16)
Ain't I Been Good To You (Part 1 & 2) (11)
All In My Lover's Eyes (21)
Are You With Me? (21)
(At Your Best) You Are Love (13,15)
Baby Come Back Home (25)
Baby Don't You Do It (2)
Baby Hold On (20)
Ballad For The Fallen Soldier (22)
Bedroom Eyes (26)
Belly Dancer (Parts 1 & 2) (18)
Between The Sheets (22)
Black Berries - Pt 1 (5) *79*
Brazilian Wedding Song (Setembro) (26)
Brother, Brother (7,10)
Brown Eyed Girl (11)
(Can't You See) What You Do To Me? (17)
Choosey Lover (22)
Climbin' Up The Ladder (Part 1 & 2) (14)
Cold Bologna (6)
Colder Are My Nights (23)
Come My Way (24)
Come To Me (23)
Come Together (25)
Coolin' Me Out (Part 1 & 2) (16)
Dedicate This Song (26)
Dish It Out (24)
Don't Give It Away (3)
Don't Hold Back Your Love (Part 1 & II) (20)
Don't Let Me Be Lonely Tonight (1)
Don't Let Up (19)
Don't Say Goodnight (It's Time For Love) (Parts 1 & 2) (18) *39*
Don't You Feel (1)

Everything Is Alright (24)
Feel Like The World (3,5)
Fight The Power Part 1 (12,15) *4*
Fire And Rain (6)
First Love (20)
Footsteps In The Dark (Part 1 & 2) (14)
For The Love Of You (Part 1&2) (12,15) *22*
Freedom (10) *72*
Fun And Games (16)
Get Down Off The Train (5)
Get Into Something (10) *89*
Get My Licks In (26)
Gettin' Over (22)
Give The Women What They Want (3)
Go All The Way (Parts 1 & 2) (18)
Go For What You Know (17)
Go For Your Guns (14)
Groove With You (16)
Harvest For The World (13,15) *63*
He's Got Your Love (3)
Heat Is On (Part 1 & 2) (12)
Hello It's Me (11,15)
Here We Go Again (Parts 1 & 2) (18)
Highways Of My Life (9)
Hold On Baby (1)
Holding On (5)
Hope You Feel Better Love (Part 1 & 2) (12,15)
How Lucky I Am (Parts 1 & 2) (17)
Hurry Up And Wait (19) *58*
I Got To Get Myself Together (17)
I Guess I'll Always Love You (2) *61*
I Hear A Symphony (2)
I Know Who You Been Socking It To (3,4,10)

I Must Be Losing Your Touch (3)
I Need Your Body (22)
I Once Had Your Love (And I Can't Let Go) (19)
I Say Love (1)
I Turned You On (4,5,10) *23*
I Wanna Be With You (Parts 1 & 2) (17)
I Wish (24)
I'll Be There 4 U (26)
I'll Do It All For You (21)
If Leaving Me Is Easy (23)
If You Ever Need Somebody (25)
If You Were There (9)
Inside You (Part I & II) (20)
It Takes A Good Woman (24)
It's A Disco Night (Rock Don't Stop) (17) *90*
It's Alright With Me (21)
It's Too Late (7,8)
It's Your Thing (3,4,8,10) *2*
Just Ain't Enough Love (2)
Keep On Doin' (10) *75*
Keep On Walkin' (2)
Koolin' Out (26)
Lay-Away (7,8,10) *54*
Lay Lady Lay (6,8) *71*
Let Me Down Easy (13)
Let Me In Your Life (Parts 1 & 2) (17)
Let's Fall In Love (Parts 1 & 2) (17)
Let's Make Love Tonight (22)
Lets Twist Again (1)
Life In The City (Parts 1 & 2) (17)
Liquid Love (Parts 1 & 2) (17)
Listen To The Music (9)
Live It Up Part 1 (11,15) *52*
Livin' In The Life (14) *40*
Lost In Your Love (26)
Love Comes And Goes (Parts 3 & 10)

Love Fever (Part 1 & 2) (16)
Love Is What You Make It (3)
Love Merry-Go-Round (20)
Love Put Me On The Corner (7)
Love The One You're With (6,8, 0) *18*
Love Zone (20)
Lover's Eve (11)
Machine Gun (6,8)
Make Me Say It Again Girl (Part 1 & 2) (12)
May I? (23)
Midnight Sky (Part 1) (11) *73*
Mind Over Matter (Parts 1 & 2) (17)
Morning Love (26)
Most Beautiful Girl (23)
My Best Was Good Enough (11)
My Little Girl (5)
Need A Little Taste Of Love (11)
Never Leave Me Baby (1)
No Axe To Grind (26)
Nothing To Do But Today (6)
Nowhere To Run (2)
Ohio (6,8)
One Of A Kind (25)
Party Night (17)
Pass It On (Parts 1 & 2) (18)
People Of Today (13)
Pop That Thang (7,8,10) *24*
Pride (Part 1) (14) *63*
Put A Little Love In Your Heart (7)
Put Yourself In My Place (2)
Real Deal (Part I And II) (21)
Real Woman (25)
Red Hot (26)
Release Your Love (23)
Right Now (1)
Rock You Good (22)

Rockin' With Fire (Part 1 & 2) (16)
Rubber Leg Twist (1)
Save Me (3)
Say You Will (Parts 1 & 2) (18)
Searching For A Miracle (26)
Seek And You Shall Find (2)
Send A Message (24)
Sensitive Lover (26)
Sensuality (Part 1 & 2) (12)
Shout - Part 1 (4,10) *47*
Showdown (Part 1 & 2) (16)
Slow Down Children (22)
Smooth Sailin' Tonight (24)
Snake, The (1)
So You Wanna Stay Down (13)
Somebody Been Messin' (3)
Somebody I Used To Know (24)
Spanish Twist (1)
Spend The Night (Ce Soir) (25)
Spill The Wine (6,10) *49*
Stay Gold (23)
Stone Cold Lover (21)
Stop! In The Name Of Love (2)
Summer Breeze (Part 1) (9,15) *60*
Sunshine (Go Away Today) (9)
Sweet Seasons (7)
Take Me To The Next Phase (Part 1 & 2) (16)
Take Some Time Out For Love (2) *66*
Tell Me When You Need It Again (Part 1 & 2) (14)
That Lady (Part 1) (9,15) *6*
There's No Love Left (2)
This Old Heart Of Mine (Is Weak For You) (2) *12*
Time After Time (1)

Tonight Is The Night (If I Had You) (19)
Touch Me (22)
Turn On The Demon (26)
Twist And Shout (1) *17*
Under The Influence (21)
Vacuum Cleaner (5,10)
Voyage To Atlantis (14)
Was It Good To You (5) *83*
Way Out Love (22)
Welcome Into My Heart (20)
What It Comes Down To (9) *55*
Whatever Turns You On (26)
Who Could Ever Doubt My Love (2)
Who Loves You Better-Part 1 (13) *47*
Who Said? (19)
Winner Takes All (17)
Work To Do (7,8,10) *51*
You Better Come Home (1)
You Never Know When You're Gonna Fall In Love (23)
You Still Feel The Need (13)
You Walk Your Way (9)
You'll Never Walk Alone (25)
You're Beside Me (Parts 1 & 2) (17)
You're The Key To My Heart (17)
Young Girls (19)

ISLEY, JASPER, ISLEY

Ernie Isley, Chris Jasper, Marvin Isley. See above Isley Brothers biography.

| 2/9/85 | 135 | 10 | | 1 Broadway's Closer To Sunset Blvd. .... | $8 | CBS Assoc. 39873 |
| 11/2/85 | 77 | 26 | | 2 Caravan Of Love .... | $8 | CBS Assoc. 40118 |

Break This Chain (1)
Broadway's Closer To Sunset Blvd. (1)
Caravan Of Love (2) *51*

Dancin' Around The World (2)
High Heel Syndrome (2)

I Can Hardly Wait (2)
I Can't Get Over Losin' You (1)

If You Believe In Love (2)
Insatiable Woman (2)
Kiss And Tell (1) *63*

Liberation (2)
Look The Other Way (1)
Love Is Gonna Last Forever (1)

Serve You Right (1)
Sex Drive (1)

DEBUT DATE	PEAK POS	WKS CHR	GOLD	ARTIST — Album Title	$	Label & Number

IT'S A BEAUTIFUL DAY
San Francisco-based, folk-rock group led by electric violinist/vocalist David LaFlamme.

DEBUT DATE	PEAK POS	WKS CHR	GOLD	ARTIST — Album Title	$	Label & Number
6/14/69	47	70	●	1 It's A Beautiful Day	$30	Columbia 9768
7/4/70	28	21		2 Marrying Maiden	$20	Columbia 1058
12/11/71+	130	16		3 Choice Quality Stuff/Anytime	$15	Columbia 30734
11/11/72	144	9		4 It's A Beautiful Day At Carnegie Hall .... [L]	$15	Columbia 31338
4/7/73	114	10		5 It's A Beautiful Day...Today	$15	Columbia 32181

Ain't That Lovin' You Baby (5) — Angels And Animals (4) — Anytime (3) — Bitter Wine (3) — Bombay Calling (1,4) — Bulgaria (1) — Burning Low (5) — Bye Bye Baby (3) — Child (5) — Creator (5) — Creed Of Love (3) — Do You Remember The Sun (2) — Dolphins, The (2) — Don And Dewey (2) — Down On The Bayou (5) — Essence Of Now (2) — Galileo (2) — Girl With No Eyes (1) — Give Your Woman What She Wants (4) — Going To Another Party (4) — Good Lovin' (2,4) — Grand Camel Suite (3,4) — Hoedown (2) — Hot Summer Day (1,4) — It Comes Right Down To You (2) — Lady Love (3) — Let A Woman Flow (2) — Lie To Me (5) — Misery Loves Company (3) — Mississippi Delta (5) — No Word For Glad (3) — Oranges & Apples (3) — Place Of Dreams (3) — Ridin' Thumb (5) — Soapstone Mountain (2) — Time (5) — Time Is (1) — Waiting For The Song (2) — Wasted Union Blues (1) — Watching You, Watching Me (5) — White Bird (1,4) — Words (3)

IVES, Burl
Born on 6/14/09 in Huntington Township, Illinois. Actor/author/singer. Played semi-pro football. Began Broadway career in the late 1930s. Own CBS network radio show *The Wayfaring Stranger* in 1944. Appeared in many films, including *East Of Eden* and *Cat On A Hot Tin Roof*. Narrated the kids' TV classic *Rudolph The Red-Nosed Reindeer*. Worked on TV series *The Bold Ones* in the early 1970s.

DEBUT DATE	PEAK POS	WKS CHR	GOLD	ARTIST — Album Title	$	Label & Number
2/17/62	35	34		1 The Versatile Burl Ives!	$20	Decca 4152
6/2/62	24	36		2 It's Just My Funny Way Of Laughin'	$20	Decca 4279
12/5/64+	65	15		3 Pearly Shells	$20	Decca 74578

Almighty Dollar Bill (1) — Brooklyn Bridge (2) — **Call Me Mr. In-Between** (2) *19* — Delia (1) — Don't Let Love Die (3) — Forty Hour Week (1) — **Funny Way Of Laughin'** (2) *10* — Hard Luck And Misery (3) — I Ain't Comin' Home Tonight (2) — I Ain't Missing Nobody (3) — I Walk The Line (1) — In Foggy Old London (2) — Kentucky Turkey Buzzard (3) — Legend Of The 'T' (3) — Lenora, Let Your Hair Hang Down (1) — **Little Bitty Tear** (1) *9* — Long Black Veil (3) — Lower Forty (3) — Lynching Party (3) — Mama Don't Want No Peas An' Rice An' Cocoanut Oil (1) — Mockin' Bird Hill (1) — Mother Wouldn't Do That (2) — Ninety-Nine (2) — Oh, My Side (1) — Okeechobee Ocean (3) — **Pearly Shells** (3) *60* — Poor Little Jimmie (2) — Royal Telephone (1) — Shanghied (1) — Sixteen Fathoms Down (2) — That's All I Can Remember (2) — Thumbin' Johnny Brown (2) — Two Of The Usual (3) — What Little Tears Are Made Of (3) — What You Gonna Do, Leroy? (2) — Who Done It? (3)

J

JACKS, Terry
Native of Winnipeg, Canada. Recorded with wife Susan as The Poppy Family.

DEBUT DATE	PEAK POS	WKS CHR	GOLD	ARTIST — Album Title	$	Label & Number
3/16/74	81	9		1 Seasons In The Sun	$10	Bell 1307

Again And Again — Concrete Sea — Fire On The Skyline — I'm Gonna Love You Too — I'm So Lonely Here Today — It's Been There From The Start — Love Game — Pumpkin Eater — Sail Away — **Seasons In The Sun** *1* — Since You Broke My Heart

JACKSON, Alan
Country singer from Newnan, Georgia.

DEBUT DATE	PEAK POS	WKS CHR	GOLD	ARTIST — Album Title	$	Label & Number
3/31/90+	57	110	▲	1 Here In The Real World	$12	Arista 8623
6/1/91	17	89↑	▲²	2 Don't Rock The Jukebox	$12	Arista 8681
10/24/92	20	16↑		3 A Lot About Livin' (And A Little 'Bout Love)	$12	Arista 18711

Ace Of Hearts (1) — Blue Blooded Woman (1) — Chasin' That Neon Rainbow (1) — Chattahoochee (3) — Dallas (2) — Dog River Blues (1) — Don't Rock The Jukebox (2) — From A Distance (2) — Here In The Real World (1) — Home (1) — I Don't Need The Booze (To Get A Buzz On) (3) — I'd Love You All Over Again (1) — If It Ain't One Thing (It's You) (1) — Just Playin' Possum (2) — Love's Got A Hold On You (2) — Mercury Blues (3) — Midnight In Montgomery (2) — She Don't Get The Blues (2) — She Likes It Too (3) — She's Got The Rhythm (And I Got The Blues) (3) — Short Sweet Ride (1) — Someday (2) — That's All I Need To Know (2) — Tonight I Climbed The Wall (3) — Tropical Depression (3) — Up To My Ears In Tears (3) — Walkin' The Floor Over Me (2) — Wanted (1) — (Who Says) You Can't Have It All (3) — Working Class Hero (2)

JACKSON, Freddie
Soul singer/songwriter. Born on 10/2/56 and raised in Harlem. Backup singer for Melba Moore, Evelyn King and others. Member of R&B group Mystic Merlin.

DEBUT DATE	PEAK POS	WKS CHR	GOLD	ARTIST — Album Title	$	Label & Number
5/25/85	10	62	▲	1 Rock Me Tonight	$8	Capitol 12404
11/15/86+	23	51	▲	2 Just Like The First Time	$8	Capitol 12495
8/13/88	48	30	●	3 Don't Let Love Slip Away	$8	Capitol 48987
11/24/90	59	30	●	4 Do Me Again	$12	Capitol 92217
8/29/92	83	12		5 Time For Love	$12	Capitol 96859

with guests Audrey Wheeler, Will Downing and Najee

All I'll Ever Ask (5) — All Over You (4) — Calling (1) — Can I Touch You (5) — Can We Try (5) — Chivalry (5) — Come With Me Tonight (4) — Crazy (For Me) (3) — Do Me Again (4) — Don't It Feel Good (4) — Don't Let Love Slip Away (3) — Don't Say You Love Me (4) — Good Morning Heartache (1) — **Have You Ever Loved Somebody** (2) *69* — **He'll Never Love You (Like I Do)** (1) *25* — Hey Lover (3) — I Can't Let You Go (2) — I Can't Take It (4) — I Could Use A Little Love (Right Now) (5) — I Don't Want To Lose Your Love (2) — I Wanna Say I Love You (1) — I'll Be Waiting For You (4) — If You Don't Know Me By Now (3) — It Takes Two (4) — It's Gonna Take A Long, Long Time (3) — **Jam Tonight** (2) *32* — Janay (2) — Just Like The First Time (2) — Live For The Moment (5) — Live My Life Without You (5) — Look Around (2) — Love Is Just A Touch Away (1) — Love Me Down (4) — Main Course (4) — Me & Mrs. Jones (5) — **Nice 'N' Slow** (3) *61* — One Heart Too Many (3) — **Rock Me Tonight (For Old Times Sake)** (1) *18* — Second Time For Love (4) — Sing A Song Of Love (1) — Special Lady (3) — Still Waiting (2) — **Tasty Love** (2) *41* — Time For Love Tonight (5) — Trouble (5) — Will You Be There (5) — Yes, I Need You (3) — You And I Got A Thang (3) — **You Are My Lady** (1) *12* — You Are My Love (2)

347

DEBUT DATE	PEAK POS	WKS CHR	GOLD	ARTIST — Album Title	$	Label & Number

JACKSON, Janet
Born on 5/16/66 in Gary, Indiana. Sister of The Jacksons (youngest of nine children). Debuted at age seven at the MGM Grand in Las Vegas with her brothers. At age 10, she played Penny Gordon Woods in the TV series *Good Times* (1977-79); in the cast of *Diff'rent Strokes* (1981-82) and later *Fame*. Married James DeBarge of DeBarge in August 1984; marriage annulled in March 1985. Signed a $32 million contract with Virgin Records in 1991.

DEBUT DATE	PEAK POS	WKS CHR	GOLD	ARTIST — Album Title	$	Label & Number
11/20/82+	63	25		1 Janet Jackson	$8	A&M 4907
10/27/84	147	6		2 Dream Street	$8	A&M 4962
3/8/86	1²	106	▲⁵	3 Control	$8	A&M 5106
10/7/89	1⁴	108	▲⁶	4 **Janet Jackson's Rhythm Nation 1814**	$8	A&M 3920

"1814" refers to the year that Francis Scott Key wrote America's national anthem

All My Love To You (2) | Don't Mess Up This Good | Funny How Time Flies | Livin' In A World (They | Pleasure Principle (3) 14 | When I Think Of You (3) 1
Alright (4) 4 | Thing (1) | (When You're Having Fun) | Didn't Make) (4) | Pretty Boy (2) | You Can Be Mine (3)
Black Cat (4) 1 | Don't Stand Another Chance | (3) | Lonely (4) | **Rhythm Nation** (4) 2 | You'll Never Find (A Love
Come Back To Me (4) 2 | (2) | He Doesn't Know I'm Alive (3) | Love And My Best Friend (4) | Say You Do (1) | Like Mine) (1)
Come Give Your Love To | Dream Street (2) | Hold Back The Tears (2) | **Love Will Never Do** | Someday Is Tonight (4) | **Young Love** (1) 64
Me (1) 58 | **Escapade** (4) 1 | If It Takes All Night (2) | **(Without You)** 1 | State Of The World (4) |
Communication (2) | Fast Girls (2) | Knowledge, The (4) | Magic Is Working (1) | Two To The Power Of Love (2) |
Control (3) 5 | Forever Yours (1) | **Let's Wait Awhile** (3) 2 | **Miss You Much** (4) 1 | **What Have You Done For** |
| | | **Nasty** (3) 3 | Me Lately (4) |

★★348★★ **JACKSON, Jermaine**
Born on 12/11/54 in Gary, Indiana. Fourth oldest of the Jackson family. Vocalist/bassist of The Jackson 5 until group left Motown in 1976. Married Hazel Joy Gordy, daughter of Berry Gordy, Jr., on 12/15/73; later divorced. Rejoined The Jacksons in 1984 for their *Victory* album and tour.

DEBUT DATE	PEAK POS	WKS CHR	GOLD	ARTIST — Album Title	$	Label & Number
8/12/72	27	36		1 Jermaine	$8	Motown 752
6/16/73	152	6		2 Come Into My Life	$8	Motown 775
9/25/76	164	11		3 My Name Is Jermaine	$8	Motown 842
8/27/77	174	3		4 Feel The Fire	$8	Motown 888
4/12/80	6	29	●	5 Let's Get Serious	$8	Motown 928
12/6/80+	44	23		6 Jermaine	$8	Motown 948
9/26/81	86	10		7 I Like Your Style	$8	Motown 952
8/21/82	46	16		8 Let Me Tickle Your Fancy	$8	Motown 6017
5/19/84	19	49	●	9 Jermaine Jackson	$8	Arista 8203
3/22/86	46	22		10 Precious Moments	$8	Arista 8277
12/2/89+	115	16		11 Don't Take It Personal	$8	Arista 8493

Ain't That Peculiar (1) | **Dynamite** (9) 15 | I Miss You So (6) | Little Girl Don't You Worry | Signed, Sealed, Delivered | Two Ships (In The Night) (11)
All Because Of You (6) | Escape From The Planet Of | I Need You More Now Than | (6) | I'm Yours (7) | Uh, Uh, I Didn't Do It (8)
Bass Odyssey (3) | The Ant Men (9) | Ever (2) | Live It Up (1) | Sitting On The Edge Of My | Very Special Part (8)
Beautiful Morning (6) | Faithful (3) | I Only Have Eyes For You (1) | Lonely Won't Leave Me | Mind (7) | Voices In The Dark (10)
Bigger You Love (The Harder | Feel The Fire (Burning From | I **Think It's Love** 16 | Alone (11) | So In Love (2) | We Can Put It Back
You Fall) (1) | Me To You) (4) | I'd Like To Get To Know You | Lovely You're The One (3) | So Right (11) | Together (5)
Burnin' Hot (3) | Feelin' Free (5) | (1) | Look Past My Life (3) | Some Kind Of Woman (4) | Where Are You Now (5)
Can I Change My Mind (6) | First You Laugh, Then You | I'm In A Different World (4) | Ma (2) | Some Things Are Private (9) | Who's That Lady (3)
Climb Out (11) | Cry (6) | I'm My Brother's Keeper (7) | Make It Easy On Me (11) | Stay With Me (3) | Words Into Action (10)
Come Into My Life (2) | Git Up And Dance (4) | If You Don't Love Me (2) | Maybe Next Time (7) | Strong Love (4) | You Belong To Me (8)
(C'mon) Feel The Need (11) | Give A Little Love (10) | If You Say My Eyes Are | Messing Around (8) | Sweetest Sweetest (9) | You Got To Hurry Girl (5)
Come To Me (One Way Or | Got To Get To You Girl (4) | Beautiful (10) | Million To One (2) | Take Good Care Of My Heart | **You Like Me Don't You**
Another) (9) | Happiness Is (4) | If You Were My Woman (1) | My Touch Of Madness (3) | (9) | (6) 50
Daddy's Home (1) 9 | Homeward Bound (1) | Is It Always Gonna Be Like | Next To You (11) | Take Me In Your Arms (Rock | You Moved A Mountain (8)
Do What You Do (9) 13 | I Can't Take No More (7) | This (7) | Oh Mother (9) | Me For A Little While) (1) | You Need To Be Loved (4)
Do You Remember Me? | I Gotta Have Ya (7) | It's Still Undone (7) | Our Love Story (10) | Take Time (4) | You're Givin' Me The
(10) 71 | I Hear Heartbeat (10) | **Let Me Tickle Your Fancy** | Paradise In Your Eyes (7) | Tell Me I'm Not Dreamin' | Runaround (7)
Does Your Mama Know | I Just Want To Take This | (8) 18 | Pieces Fit (6) | (Too Good To Be True) (9) | **You're In Good Hands**
About Me (2) | Time (3) | **Let's Be Young Tonight** | Precious Moments (10) | **That's How Love Goes** | (2) 79
Don't Make Me Wait (11) | I Let Love Pass Me By (1) | (3) 55 | Rise To The Occasion (11) | (1) 46 | **You're Supposed To Keep**
Don't Take It Personal | I Like Your Style (8) | **Let's Get Serious** (5) 9 | Running (8) | There's A Better Way (8) | Your Love For Me (5) 34
(11) 64 | I Love You More (8) | | | This Time (8) | You've Changed (6)

★★247★★ **JACKSON, Joe**
Born on 8/11/55 in Burton-on-Trent, England. Singer/songwriter/pianist, featuring an ever-changing music style. Moved to New York City in 1982.

DEBUT DATE	PEAK POS	WKS CHR	GOLD	ARTIST — Album Title	$	Label & Number
4/7/79	20	39	●	1 Look Sharp!	$8	A&M 4743
10/27/79	22	25		2 I'm The Man	$8	A&M 4794
11/8/80	41	16		3 Beat Crazy	$8	A&M 4837
8/1/81	42	13		4 Joe Jackson's Jumpin' Jive	$8	A&M 4871

featuring jazz classics of the 1940s

7/17/82	4	57	●	5 **Night And Day**	$8	A&M 4906
9/24/83	64	13		6 Mike's Murder [S]	$8	A&M 4931
4/7/84	20	29		7 Body and Soul	$8	A&M 5000
4/19/86	34	25		8 Big World [L]	$10	A&M 6021 [2]

3-sided album from a special live concert set; includes an 8-page booklet with lyrics in 6 different languages

| 5/2/87 | 131 | 8 | | 9 Will Power [I] | $8 | A&M 3908 |
| 5/21/88 | 91 | 12 | | 10 Live 1980/86 [L] | $10 | A&M 6706 [2] |

22 live songs from 4 world tours

| 5/6/89 | 61 | 21 | | 11 Blaze Of Glory | $8 | A&M 5249 |
| 5/18/91 | 116 | 4 | | 12 Laughter & Lust | $12 | Virgin 91628 |

Acropolis Now (11) | Beat Crazy (3,10) | Cancer (5,10) | Don't Wanna Be Like That | Fit (3) | Go For It (7)
Amateur Hour (2) | Best I Can Do (11) | Cha Cha Loco (7) | (2,10) | Five Guys Named Moe (4) | Goin' Downtown (12)
Another World (5) | Biology (3) | Chinatown (5) | Down To London (11) | Fools In Love (1,10) | Got The Time (1,10)
Baby Stick Around (1) | Blaze Of Glory (11) | Cosmopolitan (5) | Drowning (12) | Forty Years (8) | **Happy Ending** (7) 57
Band Wore Blue Shirts (2) | Breakdown (6) | Crime Don't Pay (3) | Evil Empire (11) | Friday (3) | Happy Loving Couples (1)
Battleground (3) | **Breaking Us In Two** | Discipline (11) | Evil Eye (3) | Geraldine And John (2) | Heart Of Ice (7)
Be My Number Two (7,10) | (5,10) 18 | (Do The) Instant Mash (1) | Fifty Dollar Love Affair (8) | Get That Girl (2) | Hit Single (12)

DEBUT DATE	PEAK POS	WKS CHR	GOLD	ARTIST — Album Title	$	Label & Number

JACKSON, Joe — Cont'd

Home Town (8)
How Long Must I Wait For You (4)
Human Touch (11)
I'm The Man (2,10)
In Every Dream Home (A Nightmare) (3)
Is She Really Going Out With Him? (1,10) *21*
Is You Is Or Is You Ain't My Baby (4)
(It's A) Big World (8)
It's All Too Much (12)
It's Different For Girls (2,10)
Jack, You're Dead (4)
Jamie G. (12)

Jet Set (8)
Jumpin' Jive (4,10)
Jumpin' With Symphony Sid (1)
Kinda Kute (2)
Laundromat Monday (6)
Loisaida (7)
Look Sharp! (1,10)
Mad At You (3)
Man In The Street (8)
Me And You (Against The World) (11)
Memphis (6,10) *85*
Moonlight (6)
Moonlight Theme (6)
My House (1)

Nineteen Forever (11)
No Pasaran (9)
Nocturne (9)
Not Here, Not Now (7)
Obvious Song (12)
Oh Well (1)
Old Songs (12)
On Your Radio (2,10)
One More Time (1)
One To One (3,10)
1-2-3- Go (This Town's A Fairground) (6)
Other Me (12)
Precious Time (8)
Pretty Boys (3)
Pretty Girls (1)

Rant And Rave (11)
Real Men (5,10)
Right And Wrong (8)
San Francisco Fan (4)
Sentimental Thing (11)
Shanghai Sky (8)
Slow Song (5,10)
Solitude (9)
Someone Up There (3)
Soul Kiss (8)
Steppin' Out (5,10) *6*
Stranger Than Fiction (12)
Sunday Papers (1,10)
Survival (9)
Symphony In One Movement (9)

T.V. Age (5)
Tango Atlantico (8)
Target (5)
Throw It Away (1)
Tomorrow's World (11)
Tonight And Forever (8)
Trying To Cry (12)
Tuxedo Junction (4)
Verdict, The (7)
We Can't Live Together (8)
We The Cats (Shall Hep Ya) (4)
What's The Use Of Getting Sober (When You're Gonna Get Drunk Again) (4)
When You're Not Around (12)

Wild West (8)
Will Power (9)
You Can't Get What You Want (Till You Know What You Want) (7,10) *15*
You Run Your Mouth (And I'll Run My Business) (4)
You're My Meat (4)
Zemeo (6)

JACKSON, La Toya
Sister of The Jacksons. Born in 1955 in Gary, Indiana. The fifth of nine children.

DEBUT DATE	PEAK POS	WKS CHR		ARTIST — Album Title	$	Label & Number
10/18/80	116	13	1	LaToya Jackson	$8	Polydor 6291
9/12/81	175	3	2	My Special Love	$8	Polydor 6328
6/9/84	149	6	3	Heart Don't Lie	$8	Private I 39361

Are You Ready? (1)
Bet'cha Gonna Need My Lovin' (3)
Camp Kuchi Kaiai (2)
Fill You Up (2)

Frustration (3)
Giving You Up (2)
Heart Don't Lie (3) *56*
Hot Potato (3)
I Don't Want You To Go (2)

I Like Everything You're Doin' (3)
If I Ain't Got It (1)
If You Feel The Funk (1)
Love Song (2)

Lovely Is She (1)
My Love Has Passed You By (1)
Night Time Lover (1)
Private Joy (3)

Save Your Love (1)
Special Love (2)
Stay The Night (2)
Summertime With You (2)

Taste Of You (Is A Taste Of Love) (1)
Think Twice (3)
Without You (3)

JACKSON, Mahalia
Born on 10/26/11 in New Orleans; died of heart failure on 1/27/72. Began recording for Apollo Records in the mid-1940s. One of the world's greatest gospel singers. Won the Lifetime Achievement Grammy in 1972.

DEBUT DATE	PEAK POS	WKS CHR		ARTIST — Album Title	$	Label & Number
1/6/62	130	2		Sweet Little Jesus Boy ....[X]	$20	Columbia 702

Go Tell It On The Mountain
Holy Babe

I Wonder As I Wander
Joy To The World!

No Room At The Inn

O Come, All Ye Faithful (Adeste Fideles)

O Little Town Of Bethlehem
Silent Night, Holy Night

Sweet Little Jesus Boy
White Christmas

JACKSON, Marlon
Born on 3/12/57 in Gary, Indiana. Sixth oldest of the Jackson family. Vocalist/guitarist of his brothers' group, The Jackson 5.

DEBUT DATE	PEAK POS	WKS CHR		ARTIST — Album Title	$	Label & Number
11/28/87	175	7		Baby Tonight	$8	Capitol 46942

Baby Tonight
Don't Go

Life
Lovely Eyes

She Never Cried
Something Coming Down

Talk-2-U
To Get Away

When Will You Surrender
Where Do I Stand

★★87★★ JACKSON, Michael
Born on 8/29/58 in Gary, Indiana. The seventh of nine children. Became lead singer of his brothers' group, The Jackson 5 (later known as The Jacksons), at age five. Played the Scarecrow in the 1978 movie musical *The Wiz*. His 1982 *Thriller* album, with sales of over 40 million copies, is the best-selling album in history. Starred in the 15-minute film *Captain Eo*, which was shown exclusively at Disneyland and Disneyworld. His 1988 autobiography, *Moonwalker*, became a film the same year. Winner of 11 Grammy Awards. Michael signed a $1 billion multimedia contract with Sony Software on 3/20/91.

DEBUT DATE	PEAK POS	WKS CHR	GOLD	ARTIST — Album Title	$	Label & Number
2/19/72	14	23		1 Got To Be There	$10	Motown 747
8/26/72	5	32		2 Ben	$10	Motown 755
5/5/73	92	12		3 Music & Me	$10	Motown 767
2/15/75	101	9		4 Forever, Michael	$10	Motown 825
9/27/75	156	5		5 The Best Of Michael Jackson ....[G]	$8	Motown 851
9/1/79+	3	169	▲6	6 **Off The Wall**	$8	Epic 35745
4/25/81	144	10		7 One Day In Your Life ....[E-K]	$8	Motown 956

recordings from 1973-75; 4 of 10 tracks with The Jackson 5

| 12/25/82+ | 1³⁷ | 122 | ▲21 | 8 **Thriller** | $8 | Epic 38112 |

the best-selling album in history; produced by Quincy Jones; 1983 Grammy winner: Album of the Year

| 6/2/84 | 46 | 15 | | 9 Farewell My Summer Love 1984 ....[E] | $8 | Motown 6101 |

recordings from 1973

| 6/23/84 | 168 | 7 | | 10 Michael Jackson And The Jackson 5 - 14 Greatest Hits ....[G] | $8 | Motown 6099 |

picture disc; 9 cuts by The Jackson 5 (see Jackson 5), 5 cuts by Michael Jackson

| 9/26/87 | 1⁶ | 87 | ▲6 | 11 **Bad** | $8 | Epic 40600 |
| 12/14/91 | 1⁴ | 61↑ | ▲⁴ | 12 **Dangerous** | $12 | Epic 45400 |

Ain't No Sunshine (1)
All The Things You Are (3)
Another Part Of Me (11) *11*
Baby Be Mine (8)
Bad (11) *1*
Beat It (8) *1*
Ben (2,5,10) *1*
Billie Jean (8) *1*
Black Or White (12) *1*
Burn This Disco Out (6)
Call On Me (9)
Can't Let Her Get Away (12)
Cinderella Stay Awhile (4)
Dangerous (12)
Dapper-Dan (4)
Dear Michael (4,7)
Dirty Diana (11) *1*
Doggin' Around (3)
Don't Let It Get You Down (9)
Don't Say Goodbye Again (7)

Don't Stop 'Til You Get Enough (6) *1*
Euphoria (12)
Everybody's Somebody's Fool (2)
Farewell My Summer Love (9) *38*
Get On The Floor (6)
Girl Don't Take Your Love From Me (1)
Girl Is Mine (8) *2*
Girl You're So Together (9)
Give In To Me (12)
Gone Too Soon (12)
Got To Be There (1,5,10) *4*
Greatest Show On Earth (2)
Happy (3,5)
Heal The World (12) *52*
Here I Am (Come And Take Me) (9)

Human Nature (8) *7*
I Can't Help It (6)
I Just Can't Stop Loving You (11) *1*
I Wanna Be Where You Are (1,5,10) *16*
I'll Come Home To You (4,7)
In Our Small Way (1,2)
In The Closet (12) *6*
It's The Falling In Love (6)
It's Too Late To Change The Time (7)
Jam (12) *26*
Johnny Raven (3)
Just A Little Bit Of You (4) *23*
Just Good Friends (11)
Keep The Faith (12)
Lady In My Life (8)
Liberian Girl (11)

Love Is Here And Now You're Gone (1)
Make Tonight All Mine (7)
Man In The Mirror (11) *1*
Maria (You Were The Only One) (1)
Melodie (9)
Morning Glow (3,5)
Music And Me (3,5)
My Girl (2)
Off The Wall (6) *10*
One Day In Your Life (4,5,7,10) *55*
P.Y.T. (Pretty Young Thing) (8) *10*
People Make The World Go Round (2)
Remember The Time (12) *3*
Rock With You (6) *1*
Rockin' Robin (1,5,10) *2*
She Drives Me Wild (12)

She's Out Of My Life (6) *10*
Shoo Be Doo Be Doo Da Day (1)
Smooth Criminal (11) *7*
Speed Demon (11)
Take Me Back (4,7)
Thriller (8) *4*
To Make My Father Proud (9)
Too Young (8)
Touch The One You Love (9)
Up Again (3)
Wanna Be Startin' Somethin' (8) *5*
Way You Make Me Feel (11) *1*
We're Almost There (4,5) *54*
We've Got A Good Thing Going (2)
We've Got Forever (4,7)

What Goes Around Comes Around (2)
Who Is It (12)
Why You Wanna Trip On Me (12)
Will You Be There (12)
Wings Of My Love (1)
With A Child's Heart (3,5) *50*
Working Day And Night (6)
You Are There (4,7)
You Can Cry On My Shoulder (2)
You're My Best Friend, My Love (7)
You've Got A Friend (1)
You've Really Got A Hold On Me (9)

DEBUT DATE	PEAK POS	WKS CHR	GOLD	ARTIST — Album Title	$	Label & Number

★★337★★ JACKSON, Millie
Born on 7/15/44 in Thompson, Georgia. Soul singer/songwriter. To Newark, New Jersey in 1958. Worked as a model in New York City. Professional singing debut at Club Zanzibar in Hoboken, New Jersey in 1964. First recorded for MGM in 1970.

DEBUT DATE	PEAK POS	WKS CHR	GOLD	#	Album Title	$	Label & Number
9/16/72	166	11		1	Millie Jackson	$8	Spring 5703
9/29/73	175	6		2	It Hurts So Good	$8	Spring 5706
11/2/74	21	21	●	3	Caught Up	$8	Spring 6703
7/26/75	112	16		4	Still Caught Up	$8	Spring 6708
2/19/77	175	6		5	Lovingly Yours	$8	Spring 6712
10/22/77+	34	23	●	6	Feelin' Bitchy	$8	Spring 6715
7/22/78	55	14	●	7	Get It Out'cha System	$8	Spring 6719
4/21/79	144	6		8	A Moment's Pleasure	$8	Spring 6722
10/20/79	80	19		9	Royal Rappin's	$8	Polydor 6229

MILLIE JACKSON & ISAAC HAYES

DEBUT DATE	PEAK POS	WKS CHR	GOLD	#	Album Title	$	Label & Number
12/22/79+	94	18		10	Live & Uncensored ....[L]	$10	Spring 6725 [2]
6/21/80	100	10		11	For Men Only	$8	Spring 6727
2/7/81	137	4		12	I Had To Say It	$8	Spring 6730
3/13/82	113	13		13	Live And Outrageous (Rated XXX) ......[L]	$8	Spring 6735
12/27/86+	119	17		14	An Imitation Of Love	$8	Jive 1016

Ain't No Comin' Back (11)
All I Want Is A Fighting Chance (1)
All The Way Lover (6,10)
Angel In Your Arms (6)
Ask Me What You Want (1) 27
Be A Sweetheart (10)
Body Movements (5)
Breakaway (2)
Cheatin' Is (6)
Child Of God (It's Hard To Believe) (1)
Close My Eyes (2)
Da Ya Think I'm Sexy? (10)
Despair (11)
Didn't I Blow Your Mind (10)
Do What Makes You Satisfied (4)
Do You Wanna Make Love (9)
Don't Send Nobody Else (2)
Don't You Ever Stop Lovin' Me (13)
Fancy This (12)
Feelin' Like A Woman (6)
Feels Like The First Time (9)
Fool's Affair (11)

From Her Arms To Mine (5)
Give It Up (10)
Go Out And Get Some (Get It Out'cha System) (7)
Good To The Very Last Drop (2)
He Wants To Hear The Words (7)
Help Me Finish My Song (5)
Help Yourself (2)
Here You Come Again (7)
Hold The Line (10)
Horse Or Mule (13)
Hot! Wild! Unrestricted! (7)
Hurts So Good (2,10) 24
Hypocrisy (3)
I Ain't Giving Up (1)
I Ain't No Glory Story (12)
I Can't Say Goodbye (7)
I Changed My Mind (9)
I Cry (2)
I Fell In Love (14)
I Gotta Get Away (From My Own Self) (1)
I Had To Say It (12,13)
I Just Can't Stand It (1)

I Just Wanna Be With You (7)
I Miss You Baby (1) 95
I Need To Be By Myself (14)
I Still Love You (You Still Love Me) (4,10)
I Wanna Be Your Lover (14)
I Wish That I Could Hurt That Way Again (11)
I'll Be Rolling (With The Punches) (5)
I'll Continue To Love You (5)
I'll Live My Love For You (5)
I'm Through Trying To Prove My Love To You (3)
I'm Tired Of Hiding (3)
If I Had My Way (9)
If Loving You Is Wrong I Don't Want To Be Right (3,10) 42
If That Don't Turn You On (11)
If This Is Love (1)
If You Had Your Way (9)
If You're Not Back In Love By Monday (6) 43
Imitation Of Love (14)

It Hurts So Good ..see: Hurts So Good
It's A Thang (14)
It's All Over But The Shouting (3)
It's Easy Going (3)
It's Gonna Take Some Time This Time (2)
Just When I Needed You Most (1)
Keep The Home Fire Burnin' (7,10)
Kiss You All Over (8)
Ladies First (12)
Leftovers (4) 87
Little Taste Of Outside Love (4)
Logs And Thangs (7,10)
Love Changes (9)
Love Doctor (2)
Love Is A Dangerous Game (14)
Love Of Your Own (5)
Lovers And Girlfriends (13)
Lovin' Your Good Thing Away (6)
Loving Arms (4)

Loving Arms '81 (12)
Making The Best Of A Bad Situation (4)
Memory Of A Wife (4)
Mind Over Matter (14)
Moment's Pleasure (8,10)
My Man, A Sweet Man (1) 42
Never Change Lovers In The Middle Of The Night (8,10)
Not On Your Life (11)
Now That You Got It (2)
Once You've Had It (8)
Passion (13)
Phuck U Symphony (10)
Put Something Down On It (7,10)
Rap, The (3,10)
Rap '81 (medley) (12)
Rising Cost Of Love (8)
Seeing You Again (8)
Soaps, The (10)
Somebody's Love Died Here Last Night (12)
Somethin' Bout Cha (5)
Still (13)
Strange Things (1)

Stranger (medley) (12)
Summer (The First Time) (3)
Sweet Music Man (7,10)
Sweet Music, Soft Lights, And You (9)
Tell Her It's Over (4)
This Is It (11,13)
This Is Where I Came In (11)
Two-Faced World (2)
Ugly Men (13)
We Got To Hit It Off (8)
What Am I Waiting For (10)
What Went Wrong Last Night (Part I & II) (8)
Why Say You're Sorry (7)
You Can't Stand The Thought (4)
You Can't Turn Me Off (In The Middle Of Turning Me On) (5)
You Created A Monster (6)
You Must Have Known I Needed Love (11)
You Needed Me (9)
You Never Cross My Mind (9)
You Owe Me That Much (12)
You're The Joy Of My Life (9)

JACKSON, Rebbie
Born Maureen Jackson on 5/29/50 in Gary, Indiana. Eldest of the nine-sibling Jackson family. Worked with The Jacksons from 1974-77, then went solo.

DEBUT DATE	PEAK POS	WKS CHR	GOLD		Album Title	$	Label & Number
10/27/84	63	18			Centipede	$8	Columbia 39238

Centipede 24

Come Alive It's Saturday Night
Fork In The Road
Hey Boy
I Feel For You
Open Up My Love
Play Me (I'm A Jukebox)
Ready For Love

JACKSON, Walter
Born on 3/19/38 in Pensacola, Florida. Died on 6/20/83 of a cerebral hemorrhage. Soul singer. To Detroit, contracted polio at an early age, performed on crutches. Lead singer in the Velvetones.

DEBUT DATE	PEAK POS	WKS CHR	GOLD	#	Album Title	$	Label & Number
6/24/67	194	5		1	Speak Her Name	$20	Okeh 12120
10/9/76	113	18		2	Feeling Good	$10	Chi-Sound 656
4/30/77	141	5		3	I Want To Come Back As A Song	$10	Chi-Sound 733

After You There Can Be Nothing (1)
Baby, I Love Your Way (3)
Corner In The Sun (1) 83
Everything Must Change (3)
Feelings (2) 93
Gotta Find Me An Angel (3)

I Want To Come Back As A Song (3)
I'll Keep On Trying (1)
I've Got It Bad Feelin' Good (2)
I've Never Been To Me (3)
If You Walked Away (3)

It's All Over (3) 67
It's An Uphill Climb To The Bottom (1) 88
Love Is Lovelier (2)
Love Woke Me Up This Morning (2)

My One Chance To Make It (1)
Not You (1)
Player In The Band (2)
Please Pardon Me (You Remind Me Of A Friend) (2)
She's A Woman (1)

Someone Saved My Life Tonight (3)
Sorry Seems To Be The Hardest Word (3)
Speak Her Name (1) 89
Stay A While With Me (3)
Tear For Tear (1)

They Don't Give Medals (To Yesterday's Heroes) (1)
Too Shy To Say (2)
Welcome Home (2) 95
What Would You Do (3)
Words (Are Impossible) (2)

JACKSON, Willis
Jazz tenor saxophonist. Born on 4/25/32 in Miami. Died on 10/25/87 following heart surgery. Began career with Cootie Williams in the 1940s. Married for eight years to R&B luminary Ruth Brown.

DEBUT DATE	PEAK POS	WKS CHR	GOLD	#	Album Title	$	Label & Number
7/23/66	137	4		1	Together Again! ....[I]	$15	Prestige 7364

WILLIS JACKSON with JACK McDUFF (organ)

DEBUT DATE	PEAK POS	WKS CHR	GOLD	#	Album Title	$	Label & Number
8/30/75	182	3		2	The Way We Were ....[I]	$8	Atlantic 18145

Brown Eyed Girl (2)
Fire (2)
Glad 'A See Ya' (1)

It Might As Well Be Spring (1)
Lady Marmalade (2)

Love's Theme (2)
Lover's Eve (2)
Pick Up The Pieces (2)

Shame, Shame, Shame (2)
Sideshow (2)
Then Came You (2)

This'll Get To Ya' (1)
Three Little Words (1)
Tu'Gether (1)

Way We Were (2)

★★74★★ JACKSON 5/JACKSONS

Quintet of brothers formed and managed by their father beginning in 1966 in Gary, Indiana. Consisted of Sigmund "Jackie" (b: 5/4/51), Toriano "Tito" (b: 10/15/53), Jermaine (b: 12/11/54), Marlon (b: 3/12/57) and lead singer Michael (b: 8/29/58). First recorded for Steeltown in 1968. Known as The Jackson 5 from 1968-75. Jermaine replaced by Randy (b: 10/29/61) in 1976. Jermaine rejoined the group for 1984's highly publicized *Victory* album and tour. Marlon left for a solo career in 1987. Their sisters Rebbie, La Toya and Janet backed the group; each had a string of solo hits. Michael and Janet emerged with superstar solo careers in the '80s. Group lineup since 1989: Jackie, Tito, Jermaine and Randy Jackson. Also see Television Shows.

THE JACKSON 5:

DEBUT DATE	PEAK POS	WKS CHR	GOLD	ARTIST — Album Title	$	Label & Number
1/17/70	5	32		1 **Diana Ross Presents The Jackson 5**	$15	Motown 700
6/6/70	4	50		2 **ABC**	$15	Motown 709
9/26/70	4	50		3 **Third Album**	$15	Motown 718
5/1/71	11	41		4 Maybe Tomorrow	$15	Motown 735
10/9/71	16	26		5 Goin' Back To Indiana [TV]	$15	Motown 742
				TV special with guests Bill Cosby and Tom Smothers		
1/1/72	12	41		6 Jackson 5 Greatest Hits [G]	$15	Motown 741
6/3/72	7	33		7 **Lookin' Through The Windows**	$15	Motown 750
4/14/73	44	16		8 Skywriter	$12	Motown 761
10/6/73	100	29		9 Get It Together	$12	Motown 783
10/5/74	16	21		10 Dancing Machine	$12	Motown 780
6/14/75	36	15		11 Moving Violation	$12	Motown 829
7/17/76	84	9		12 Jackson Five Anthology [G]	$18	Motown 868 [3]
				also includes Michael's and Jermaine's solo hits		

THE JACKSONS:

DEBUT DATE	PEAK POS	WKS CHR	GOLD	ARTIST — Album Title	$	Label & Number
12/4/76+	36	27	●	13 The Jacksons	$8	Epic 34229
10/29/77	63	11		14 Goin' Places	$8	Epic 34835
12/16/78+	11	41	▲	15 Destiny	$8	Epic 35552
10/18/80	10	29	▲	16 **Triumph**	$8	Epic 36424
11/28/81+	30	19		17 Jacksons Live [L]	$10	Epic 37545 [2]
6/23/84	168	7		18 Michael Jackson And The Jackson 5 - 14 Greatest Hits [G]	$8	Motown 6099
				picture disc; 9 cuts by The Jackson 5, 5 cuts by Michael Jackson		
7/21/84	4	30	▲²	19 **Victory**	$8	Epic 38946
6/17/89	59	11		20 2300 Jackson Street	$8	Epic 40911
				title refers to their previous address in Gary, Indiana		

ABC (2,6,12,17,18) *1*
Ain't Nothing Like The Real Thing (7)
All I Do Is Think Of You (11,12)
All Night Dancin' (15)
Alright With Me (20)
Art Of Madness (20)
Be Not Always (19)
Ben *[solo: Michael] (12,17) 1*
Blame It On The Boogie (15) *54*
Bless His Soul (15)
Blues Away (13)
Body (19) *47*
Body Language (Do The Love Dance) (11,12)
Boogie Man (8,12)
Born To Love You (1)
Breezy (11)
Bridge Over Troubled Water (3)
Call Of The Wild (11)
Can I See You In The Morning (3)
Can You Feel It (16,17) *77*
Can You Remember (1)
Chained (1)
Children Of The Light (7)
(Come Round Here) I'm The One You Need (2)
Corner Of The Sky (8,12) *18*
Daddy's Home *[solo: Jermaine] (12) 9*
Dancing Machine (9,10,12,18) *2*
Darling Dear (3)

Day Basketball Was Saved (5)
Destiny (15)
Different Kind Of Lady (14)
Do What You Wanna (14)
Doctor My Eyes (7)
Don't Know Why I Love You (2,12)
Don't Let Your Baby Catch You (7)
Don't Say Good Bye Again (9)
Don't Stop 'Til You Get Enough (17)
Don't Want To See Tomorrow (1)
Dreamer (13)
E-Ne-Me-Ne-Mi-Ne-Moe (The Choice Is Yours To Pull) (7)
Enjoy Yourself (13) *6*
Even Though You're Gone (14)
Everybody (16)
Feeling Alright (5)
Find Me A Girl (14)
Forever Came Today (11,12) *60*
Get It Together (9,12) *28*
Give It Up (16)
Goin' Back To Indiana (3,5,6,12)
Goin' Places (14) *52*
Good Times (13)
Got To Be There *[solo: Michael] (12) 4*
Hallelujah Day (8,12) *28*
Harley (20)
Heartbreak Hotel (16,17) *22*
Heaven Knows I Love You, Girl (14)

Honey Chile (4)
Honey Love (11)
How Funky Is Your Chicken (3)
Hum Along And Dance (3)
Hurt, The (19)
I Am Love (Parts I & II) (10,12) *15*
I Can Only Give You Love (7)
I Can't Quit Your Love (8)
I Found That Girl (2,6,12) *flip*
(I Know) I'm Losing You (1)
I Wanna Be Where You Are *[solo: Michael] (12) 16*
I Want To Take You Higher (5)
I Want You Back (1,5,6,12,17,18) *1*
I Will Find A Way (4)
I'll Be There (3,6,12,17,18) *1*
I'll Bet You (2)
If I Don't Love You This Way (10)
If I Have To Move A Mountain (7)
If You'd Only Believe (20)
It All Begins And Ends With Love (10)
It's Great To Be Here (4)
It's Too Late To Change The Time (9)
Jump For Joy (14)
Just A Little Bit Of You *[solo: Michael] (12) 23*
Keep On Dancing (13)
La-La Means I Love You (2)
Life Of The Party (10)

Little Bitty Pretty One (7,12) *13*
Living Together (13)
Lookin' Through The Windows (7,12,18) *16*
Love Don't Want To Leave (12)
Love I Saw In You Was Just A Mirage (3)
Love You Save (2,5,6,12,17,18) *1*
Lovely One (16,17) *12*
Mama I Gotta Brand New Thing (Don't Say No) (9)
Mama's Pearl (3,6,12,18) *2*
Man Of War (14)
Maria (20)
Maybe Tomorrow (4,5,6,12,18) *20*
Midnight Rendezvous (20)
Mirrors Of My Mind (19)
Moving Violation (11)
Music's Takin' Over (14)
My Cherie Amour (1)
My Little Baby (4)
Never Can Say Goodbye (4,6,12,18) *2*
Never Had A Dream Come True (1)
Nobody (1)
Nothin (That Compares 2 U) (20) *77*
Off The Wall (17)
Oh How Happy (3)
One More Chance (2)
One More Chance (19)
Ooh, I'd Love To Be With You (8)
Petals (4)

Play It Up (20)
Private Affair (20)
Push Me Away (15)
Reach In (3)
Ready Or Not Here I Come (Can't Hide From Love) (3)
Reflections (9)
Rock With You (17)
Rockin' Robin *[solo: Michael] (12) 2*
Shake Your Body (Down To The Ground) (15,17) *7*
She (20)
She's A Rhythm Child (10)
She's Good (4)
She's Out Of My Life (17)
Show You The Way To Go (13) *28*
Sixteen Candles (4)
Skywriter (8,12)
Stand (1,5)
Standing In The Shadows Of Love (1)
State Of Shock (19) *3*
Strength Of One Man (13)
Style Of Life (13)
Sugar Daddy (6,12) *10*
That's How Love Goes *[solo: Jermaine] (12) 46*
That's What You Get (For Being Polite) (15)
Things I Do For You (15,17)
Think Happy (13)
Time Explosion (11)
Time Waits For No One (16)
To Know (7)
Torture (19) *17*
Touch (8)

True Love Can Be Beautiful (2)
2300 Jackson Street (20)
2-4-6-8 (2)
Uppermost (8)
Wait (19)
Walk On (medley) (5)
Walk Right Now (16) *73*
Wall (4)
We Can Change The World (19)
We're Almost There *[solo: Michael] (12) 54*
(We've Got) Blue Skies (4)
What You Don't Know (10)
Whatever You Got, I Want (10,12) *38*
Who's Lovin' You (1,6)
Wondering Who (16)
Working Day And Night (17)
World Of Sunshine (8)
You Made Me What I Am (8)
You Need Love Like I Do (Don't You?) (9)
(You Were Made) Especially For Me (11)
You've Changed (1)
Young Folks (2)
Your Ways (16)
Zip-A-Dee-Doo-Dah (1)

JACKYL

Hard-rock band based in Atlanta: Jesse Dupree (vocals), Jeff Worley, Jimmy Stiff, Chris Worley and Tom Bettini.

DEBUT DATE	PEAK POS	WKS CHR	GOLD	ARTIST — Album Title	$	Label & Number
10/10/92	103↑	18↑		Jackyl	$12	Geffen 24489

Back Off Brother
Brain Drain

Dirty Little Mind
Down On Me

I Stand Alone
Just Like A Devil

Lumberjack, The
Reach For Me

Redneck Punk
She Loves My Cock

When Will It Rain

DEBUT DATE	PEAK POS	WKS CHR	GOLD	ARTIST — Album Title	$	Label & Number

JACOBI, Lou
Actor/comedian. Born on 12/28/13 in Toronto. Acted in several films and TV shows. Also see Comedy section.

11/12/66	134	3		Al Tijuana and his Jewish Brass..[N-I]	$20	Capitol 2596

a Herb Alpert spoof

Chicken Fat	It's Not Unusual	Never On Sunday	Peter Gunn	Taste Of Honey	What Now My Love
Downtown	Malaguena	People	Strangers In The Night	Tsena, Tsena	Yellow Rose Of Texas

JACOBS, Debbie
Disco-oriented singer from Baltimore.

9/1/79	153	8	1	Undercover Lover..	$8	MCA 3156
2/9/80	178	7	2	High On Your Love	$8	MCA 3202

All The Way (1) High On Your Love (2) 70 I Can Never Forget A Friend Make It Love (2) Undercover Lover (1)
Burnin' Desire (1) Hot Hot (Give It All You Got) (2) Think I'm Fallin' In Love (1) What Goes Up (2)
Don't You Want My Love (1) (1,2) Lovin' Spree (2)

JADE WARRIOR
British progressive rock trio led by Glyn Havard (vocals, bass).

5/6/72	194	2		Released	$12	Vertigo 1009

Barazinbar Eyes On You Three-Horned Dragon King We Have Reason To Believe
Bride Of Summer Minnamoto's Dream Water Curtain Cave Yellow Eyes

JAGGER, Chris
Mick Jagger's brother.

11/3/73	186	4		Chris Jagger...	$10	Asylum 5069

All Souls Handful Of Dust Joy Of The Ride Let Me Down Easy Riddle Song
Going Nowhere (medley) Hold On King Of The Fishes My Friend John Something New (medley)

JAGGER, Mick
Born Michael Phillip Jagger on 7/26/43 in Dartford, England. Lead singer of The Rolling Stones. Starred in the 1970 film *Ned Kelly*. Also in 1992 film *Freejack*. Married to Nicaraguan model Bianca Peres Norena de Macias from 1971-80. Married actress/model Jerry Hall on 11/24/90.

3/16/85	13	29 ▲	1	She's The Boss	$8	Columbia 39940
10/3/87	41	20	2	Primitive Cool	$8	Columbia 40919

1/2 A Loaf (1) Let's Work (2) 39 Party Doll (2) Radio Control (2) Secrets (1) **Throwaway** (2) 67
Hard Woman (1) Lonely At The Top (1) Peace For The Wicked (2) Running Out Of Luck (1) She's The Boss (1) Turn The Girl Loose (1)
Just Another Night (1) 12 **Lucky In Love** (1) 38 Primitive Cool (2) Say You Will (2) Shoot Off Your Mouth (2) War Baby (2)
Kow Tow (2)

JAGGERZ, The
Rock group formed in Pittsburgh in 1965, featuring lead singer Donnie Iris.

4/11/70	62	11		We Went To Different Schools Together..	$12	Kama Sutra 2017

At My Window Don't Make My Sky Cry Looking Glass **Rapper, The 2** Things Gotta Get Better With A Little Help From My
Carousel **I Call My Baby Candy 75** Memoirs Of The Traveler That's My World Friends

JAM
British new wave trio formed in 1975: Paul Weller (vocals, bass), Bruce Foxton (guitar) and Rick Buckler (drums). Disbanded in 1982. Weller formed The Style Council.

2/16/80	137	8	1	Setting Sons	$8	Polydor 6249
2/7/81	72	11	2	Sound Affects	$8	Polydor 6315
12/19/81	176	7	3	The Jam ....[M]	$8	Polydor 503
				5 British hit singles		
3/27/82	82	16	4	The Gift	$8	Polydor 6349
11/27/82	135	14	5	The Bitterest Pill (I ever had to swallow) ....[M]	$8	Polydor 506
				4 more British hit singles		
1/15/83	131	9	6	Dig The New Breed ....[L]	$8	Polydor 6365
				live recordings from 1977-82		
4/9/83	171	4	7	Beat Surrender ....[M]	$8	Polydor 810751
				their last studio recording; 5 tracks from 1982		

Absolute Beginners (3) Disguises (3) Happy Together (4) Move On Up (7) Scrape Away (2) Thick As Thieves (1)
All Mod Cons (6) Dream Time (2) In The City (6) Music For The Last Couple Set The House Ablaze (2,6) To Be Someone (6)
Beat Surrender (7) Dreams Of Children (6) In The Crowd (6) (2) Shopping (7) Town Called Malice (4)
Big Bird (6) Eton Rifles (1) It's Too Bad (6) Pity Poor Alfie (medley) (5) Smithers~Jones (1) Trans-Global Express (4)
Bitterest Pill (I Ever Had To Fever (medley) (5) Just Who Is The 5 O'Clock Planner's Dream Goes Standards (6) War (5,7)
Swallow) (5) Funeral Pyre (3) Hero? (4) Wrong (4) Start! (2,6) Wasteland (1)
Boy About Town (2) Ghosts (4,6) Little Boy Soldiers (1) Precious (4) Stoned Out Of My Mind (7)
Burning Sky (1) Gift (4) Liza Radley (3) Pretty Green (2) Strange Town (1)
But I'm Different Now (2) Girl On The Phone (1) (Love Is Like A) Heat Wave (1) Private Hell (1,6) Tales From The Riverbank
Carnation (4) Going Underground (6) Man In The Corner Shop (2) Running On The Spot (4) (3)
Circus (4) Great Depression (6) Monday (2) Saturday's Kids (1) That's Entertainment (2,6)

JAMAL, Ahmad
Born Fritz Jones on 7/2/30 in Pittsburgh. Jazz pianist/leader. With George Hudson. Formed own trio, the Three Strings, with Ray Crawford (guitar) and Eddie Calhoun (bass). Recorded for Okeh in 1951.

9/22/58	3	107	1	But Not For Me/Ahmad Jamal at the Pershing ....[I-L]	$30	Argo 628
11/17/58	11	18	2	Ahmad Jamal, Volume IV ....[I-L]	$30	Argo 636
2/1/60	32	7	3	Jamal At The Penthouse ....[I]	$25	Argo 646
12/30/67+	168	8	4	Cry Young	$15	Cadet 792
				vocal chorus by the Howard Roberts Chorale		
3/15/80	173	5	5	Genetic Walk ....[I-K]	$8	20th Century 600

Ahmad's Blues (3) Call Me Irresponsible (4) Genetic Walk (5) Ivy (3) Nature Boy (4) Seleritus (3)
Autumn In New York (2) Chaser (5) Girl Next Door (2) La Costa (5) Never Never Land (3) Should I (2)
Beautiful Friendship (4) Cheek To Cheek (2) I Like To Recognize The Little Ditty (4) No Greater Love (1) Sophisticated Gentleman (3)
Bellows (5) Comme Ci, Comme Ca (3) Tune (3) Minor Moods (4) Pablo Sierra (5) Spartacus Love Theme (5)
But Not For Me (1) Cry Young (4) I Wish I Knew (2) Moonlight In Vermont (1) Poinciana (1) Squatty Roo (2)
C'est Si Bon (4) Don't Ask My Neighbors (5) I'm Alone With You (3) Music, Music, Music (1) Secret Love (2)

JAMAL, Ahmad — Cont'd

Stompin At The Savoy (2)	Taboo (2)	There Are Such Things (4)	What's New (1)	Who Needs Manhattan (4)
Surrey With The Fringe On Top (1)	Tangerine (3)	Time For Love (5)	Where Is Love (4)	Wood'yn You (1)
	That's All (2)	Tropical Breeze (4)		

★★122★★ **JAMES, Bob**

Jazz fusion keyboardist. Born on 12/25/39 in Marshall, Missouri. Discovered by Quincy Jones in 1962. Was Sarah Vaughan's musical director for four years. In 1973, became arranger of CTI records. In 1976, appointed director of progressive A&R at CBS Records. Formed own label, Tappan Zee, in 1977. Wrote/performed theme for the TV show *Taxi*. Joined the jazz quartet Fourplay in 1991.

11/2/74	85	14		1 One .... [I]	$10	CTI 6043
4/12/75	75	14		2 Two .... [I]	$10	CTI 6057
7/4/76	49	27		3 Three .... [I]	$8	CTI 6063
				guest saxophonist: Grover Washington, Jr.		
4/9/77	38	17		4 BJ4 .... [I]	$8	CTI 7074
11/26/77+	47	31		5 Heads .... [I]	$8	Tappan Zee 34896
12/16/78+	37	29	●	6 Touchdown... [I]	$8	Tappan Zee 35594
8/25/79	42	14		7 Lucky Seven .... [I]	$8	Tappan Zee 36056
11/3/79	23	33	●	8 One On One .... [I]	$8	Tappan Zee 36241

BOB JAMES AND EARL KLUGH

7/12/80	47	18		9 "H" .... [I]	$8	Tappan Zee 36422
2/21/81	66	16		10 All Around The Town .... [I-L]	$10	Tappan Z. 36786 [2]
9/12/81	56	14		11 Sign Of The Times..	$8	Tappan Zee 37495
				features backing vocals by Patti Austin, Luther Vandross & others		
7/17/82	72	17		12 Hands Down .... [I]	$8	Tappan Zee 38067
11/6/82	44	29		13 Two Of A Kind .... [I]	$8	Capitol 12244

EARL KLUGH & BOB JAMES

6/4/83	77	11		14 The Genie (Themes & Variations From The TV Series "Taxi")....... [I]	$8	Columbia 38678
10/8/83	106	13		15 Foxie .... [I]	$8	Tappan Zee 38801
10/27/84	136	10		16 12 .... [I]	$8	Tappan Zee 39580
6/14/86	50	64	●	17 Double Vision .... [I]	$8	Warner 25393

BOB JAMES/DAVID SANBORN

11/22/86+	142	27		18 Obsession .... [I]	$8	Warner 25495
9/10/88	196	2		19 Ivory Coast .... [I]	$8	Warner 25757
8/29/92	170	3		20 Cool .... [I]	$12	Warner 26939

BOB JAMES/EARL KLUGH

Adult Situations (19)	Friends (7)	Karl (8,10)	Night Crawler (5)	Shepherd's Song (9)	Valley Of The Shadows (1)
Afterglow, The (8)	Fugitive Life (20)	Last Chance (14)	Night Moods (14)	Sign Of The Times (11)	Walkman, The (9)
Angela (6,10,14)	Genie (14)	Legacy (16)	Night On Bald Mountain (1)	Since I Fell For You (17)	We're All Alone (5,10)
As It Happens (20)	Golden Apple (2,10)	Look-Alike (7)	Night That Love Came Back (20)	Snowbird Fantasy (9)	Wes (13)
Ashanti (19)	Gone Hollywood (18)	Love Lips (8)	Nights Are Forever Without You (4)	So Much In Common (20)	Westchester Lady (3,10)
Ballade (14)	Groove For Julie (14)	Love Power (11)	No Pay, No Play (16)	Souleo (1)	Where I Wander (13)
Big Stone City (7)	Handara (20)	Ludwig (15)	Obsession (18)	Sponge, The (20)	Where The Wind Blows Free (1)
Blue Lick (14)	Heads (5)	Macumba (12)	One Loving Night (5)	Spunky (12)	Whiplash (13)
Brighton By The Sea (9)	Hello Nardo (14)	Mallorca (8)	One Mint Julep (3)	Steady (18)	Winding River (8)
Brooklyn Heights Boogie (14)	Hypnotique (11)	Maputo (17)	Orpheus (19)	Steamin' Feelin' (11)	Women Of Ireland (3)
Calaban (15)	I Feel A Song (In My Heart) (2)	Marco Polo (15)	Pure Imagination (4)	Stompin' At The Savoy (10)	Yogi's Dream (19)
Caribbean Nights (6)	I Need More Of You (16)	Marilu (14)	Rain (18)	Storm King (3)	You Are So Beautiful (5)
Courtship (15)	I Want To Thank You (Very Much) (6)	Midnight (16)	Reunited (9)	Sun Runner (6)	You Don't Know Me (17)
Dream Journey (2)	I'll Never See You Smile Again (8)	Miniature (20)	Roberta (12)	Take Me To The Mardi Gras (2)	You're As Right As Rain (2)
El Verano (4)	I'm In You (5)	Miranda (15)	Rosalie (20)	Tappan Zee (4)	Zebra Man (15)
Enchanted Forest (11)	In The Garden (1)	Moodstar (19)	Rousseau (18)	Taxi, Theme From ..see:	
Falcon, The (13)	Ingenue (13)	Moon Tune (17)	Ruby, Ruby, Ruby (16)	Angela	
Farandole (L'Arlesienne Suite #2) (2,10)	It's Only Me (12)	Moonbop (17)	Rush Hour (7)	Terpsichore (20)	
Feel Like Making Love (1) **88**	It's You (17)	More Than Friends (17)	San Diego Stomp (20)	Thoroughbred (9)	
Feel The Fire (18)	Jamaica Farewell (3)	Movin' On (20)	Sandstorm (13)	3 A.M. (18)	
Fireball (15)	Janus (12)	Nautilus (1)	Secret Wishes (20)	Touchdown (6,10)	
Fly Away (7)		Never Enough (17)	Shamboozie (12)	Treasure Island (4)	
		New York Mellow (14)		Unicorn (11)	
		New York Samba (20)			

JAMES, Etta

R&B pioneer. Born Jamesetta Hawkins on 1/25/38 in Los Angeles. Nicknamed "Miss Peaches." First recorded for Modern in 1954. Recorded duets with Harvey Fuqua of The Moonglows as Etta & Harvey. Frequent bouts with heroin addiction; finally cured in the late '70s. Still active into the '90s. Inducted into the Rock and Roll Hall of Fame in 1993.

8/21/61	68	12		1 At Last!	$30	Argo 4003
8/24/63	117	4		2 Etta James Top Ten .... [G]	$30	Argo 4025
2/1/64	96	10		3 Etta James Rocks The House .... [L]	$30	Argo 4032
3/9/68	82	13		4 Tell Mama	$15	Cadet 802
9/15/73	154	9		5 Etta James	$12	Chess 50042

All I Could Do Was Cry (1,2) **33**	Don't Lose Your Good Thing (4)	I'm Gonna Take What He's Got (4)	**My Dearest Darling** (1,2) **34**	**Something's Got A Hold On Me** (2,3) **37**	**Trust In Me** (1,2) **30**
All The Way Down (5)	Down So Low (5)	It Hurts Me So Much (4)	My Mother-In-Law (4)	Steal Away (4)	Watch Dog (4)
Anything To Say You're Mine (1)	**Fool That I Am** (2) **50**	Just A Little Bit (4)	Only A Fool (5)	**Stop The Wedding** (2) **34**	What I Say (3)
At Last (1,2) **47**	Girl Of My Dreams (1)	Just One More Day (5)	Ooh Poo Pah Doo (3)	Stormy Weather (1)	Woke Up This Morning (3)
Baby What You Want Me To Do (3) **82**	God's Song (5)	Lay Back Daddy (5)	**Pushover** (2) **25**	Sunday Kind Of Love (1,2)	**Would It Make Any Difference To You** (2) **64**
	I Just Want To Make Love To You (1)	Leave Your Hat On (5)	Same Rope (4)	Sweet Little Angel (4)	Yesterday's Music (5)
	I'd Rather Go Blind (4)	Love Of My Man (4)	**Security** (4) **35**	**Tell Mama** (4) **23**	
		Money (3)	**Seven Day Fool** (3) **95**	Tough Mary (1)	

JAMES, Harry

Born on 3/15/16 in Albany, Georgia; died on 7/5/83. Star trumpet player/bandleader. Achieved fame playing with Benny Goodman in the late 1930s. His own band was very popular during the '40s. Married to movie star Betty Grable from 1943-65.

| 11/12/55 | 10 | 2 | | Harry James in Hi-Fi ....[I] | $25 | Capitol 654 |

5 of 15 tracks feature vocals (4 by Helen Forrest, 1 by Bob Marlo)

Cherry	I'm Beginning To See The Light	It's Been A Long, Long Time	Music Makers	Trumpet Blues	You Made Me Love You (I Didn't Want To Do It)
Ciribiribin	Jalousie	My Silent Love	Two O'Clock Jump	
I Cried For You (Now It's Your Turn To Cry Over Me)	I've Heard That Song Before	James Session	Sleepy Lagoon	Velvet Moon	

JAMES, Jimmy, & The Vagabonds

R&B band from London. Vocals by Jimmy James and Count Prince Miller.

| 11/29/75+ | 139 | 16 | | You Don't Stand A Chance If You Can't Dance .... | $8 | Pye 12111 |

Chains Of Love	Dancin' To The Music Of Love	**I Am Somebody 94**	Let's Have Fun	You Don't Stand A Chance (If You Can't Dance) (Pt. 1 & 2)
Come Lay Some Lovin' On Me	Hey Girl	I Know You Don't Love Me But You Got Me Anyway	Suspicious Love	

JAMES, Melvin

Minneapolis-based singer/songwriter/guitarist raised in Des Moines, Iowa.

| 10/3/87 | 146 | 8 | | The Passenger .... | $8 | MCA 5663 |

Devil With A Halo	Passenger	Sugar Candy	Twisted	Why Won't You Stay (Come In, Come Out Of The Rain)
Loving You Is Strange	She's So Sorry	Telephone	We Hear The Thunder	

★★241★★ JAMES, Rick

Punk-funk singer/songwriter/guitarist. Born James Johnson on 2/1/52 in Buffalo. In Mynah Birds band with Neil Young in the late '60s. To London; formed the band Main Line. Returned to the U.S. and formed Stone City Band; produced Teena Marie, Mary Jane Girls, Eddie Murphy and others.

6/24/78	13	36	●	1 Come Get It!	$8	Gordy 981
2/10/79	16	27	●	2 Bustin' Out Of L Seven	$8	Gordy 984
11/3/79	34	20		3 Fire It Up	$8	Gordy 990
3/22/80	122	8		4 In 'n' Out	$8	Gordy 991
				RICK JAMES presents the STONE CITY BAND		
8/23/80	83	10		5 Garden Of Love	$8	Gordy 995
5/2/81	3	74	▲	6 Street Songs	$8	Gordy 1002
6/5/82	13	23	●	7 Throwin' Down	$8	Gordy 6005
8/27/83	16	29	●	8 Cold Blooded	$8	Gordy 6043
8/25/84	41	19		9 Reflections ....[G]	$8	Gordy 6095
5/11/85	50	26		10 Glow	$8	Gordy 6135
7/5/86	95	12		11 The Flag	$8	Gordy 6185
7/23/88	148	8		12 Wonderful	$8	Reprise 25659

Are You ..see: R U	Fire And Desire (6,9)	Hypnotize (12)	Moonchild (10)	Sha La La La La (Come Back Home) (10)	**Super Freak (Part 1)** (6,9) **16**
Be My Lady (1)	Fire It Up (3)	I Believe In U (12)	Mr. Policeman (6)	Sherry Baby (12)	Sweet And Sexy Thing (11)
Below The Funk (Pass The J) (6)	Fool On The Street (2)	In 'N' Out (4)	My Love (7)	Silly Little Man (medley) (11)	Teardrops (7)
Big Time (5)	Forever And A Day (11)	In The Girls' Room (12)	New York Town (8)	69 Times (7)	Tell Me (What You Want) (8)
Bustin' Out (2,9) **71**	Free To Be Me (11)	Island Lady (5)	Oh What A Night (4 Luv) (9)	Slow And Easy (11)	Throwdown (7)
Call Me Up (6)	Freak Flag (11)	Jefferson Ball (2)	One Mo Hit (Of Your Love) (medley) (2)	So Tight (12)	U Bring The Freak Out (8)
Can't Stop (10) **50**	Funk In America (medley) (11)	Judy (12)	1,2,3 (U, Her And Me) (8)	Somebody (The Girl's Got) (10)	Unity (8)
Cold Blooded (8) **40**	Gettin' It On (In The Sunshine) (5)	Little Runaway (4)	Painted Pictures (11)	South American Sneeze (4)	When Love Is Gone (3)
Come Into My Life (3)	Ghetto Life (6)	Loosey's Rap (12)	Party Girls (4)	Spacey Love (3)	Wonderful (12)
Cop 'N' Blow (2)	**Give It To Me Baby** (6,9) **40**	Love Gun (3)	P.I.M.P. The S.I.M.P. (8)	Spend The Night With Me (10)	**You And I** (1,9) **13**
Dance Wit' Me - Part 1 (7,9) **64**	Glow (10)	Love In The Night (3)	R U Experienced (11)	**Standing On The Top-Part 1** (7) **66**	You Turn Me On (9)
Doin' It (8)	Happy (7)	Love Interlude (2)	Rick's Raga (11)	Stone City Band (1)	
Don't Give Up On Love (5)	Hard To Get (7)	Love's Fire (12)	Rock And Roll Control (10)	Stormy Love (3)	
Dream Maker (1)	Havin' You Around (4)	Lovin' You Is A Pleasure (5)	Save It For Me (11)	Strut Your Stuff (4)	
Ebony Eyes (8) **43**	**High On Your Love Suite** (2) **72**	Make Love To Me (6)	17 (9) **36**	Summer Love (5)	
F.I.M.A. (Funk In Mama Afrika) (4)	Hollywood (1)	Mary-Go-Round (5)	Sexual Luv Affair (12)		
		Mary Jane (1,9) **41**	Sexy Lady (1)		
		Melody Make Me Dance (10)			
		Money Talks (7)			

JAMES, Sonny

Born James Loden on 5/1/29 in Hackleburg, Alabama. Country singer/songwriter/guitarist. Nicknamed "The Southern Gentleman." Brought to Capitol Records in Nashville by Chet Atkins. In the films *Second Fiddle To A Steel Guitar*, *Nashville Rebel*, *Las Vegas Hillbillies* and *Hillbillys In A Haunted House*.

12/24/66+	141	4		1 The Best of Sonny James ....[G]	$15	Capitol 2615
4/12/69	161	3		2 Only The Lonely	$12	Capitol 193
8/23/69	184	3		3 Close-Up ....[R]	$12	Capitol 258 [2]
				reissue of *True Love's A Blessing* and *I'll Never Find Another You* albums		
10/18/69	83	13		4 The Astrodome Presents In Person Sonny James ....[L]	$12	Capitol 320
4/11/70	177	4		5 It's Just A Matter Of Time	$12	Capitol 432
9/19/70	197	2		6 My Love/Don't Keep Me Hangin' On	$12	Capitol 478
11/28/70+	187	4		7 #1	$12	Capitol 629
				featuring BMI's "million performance" Country songs		
4/24/71	150	5		8 Empty Arms	$12	Capitol 734
9/11/71	197	2		9 The Sensational Sonny James	$12	Capitol 804
9/23/72	190	5		10 When The Snow Is On The Roses	$10	Columbia 31646

All My Life, All My Life (3)	Born To Lose (7)	Don't Cut Timber On A Windy Day (7)	Everything Begins And Ends With You (4)	Going Through The Motions (Of Living) (1)	How Great Thou Art (medley) (4)
Amazin' Love (5)	**Bright Lights, Big City** (9) **91**	Don't Keep Me Hangin' On (medley) (4)	Eyes Of Texas Are Upon You (medley) (4)	Goodbye, Maggie, Goodbye (3)	I Can't Stop Loving You (7)
Any Time (7)	Deep In The Heart Of Texas (medley) (4)	Discoveries And Inventions (5)	Fool #1 (2)	Happiness Bound (9)	I Get Fooled, Don't I (3)
Back Door To Heaven (9)			For The Love Of A Woman Like You (8)	Happy Memories (6)	I Know (3)
Behind The Tear (1)		Don't Ask For Tomorrow (3)	**Empty Arms** (8) **93**	He'll Have To Go (7)	I Walk The Line (7)
Blue For You (4)		Endlessly (8)	Free Roamin' Mind (5)	Heaven On Earth (9)	I'll Do The Same Thing For You (5)
Born To Be With You (medley) (4)		Every Day Every Night (10)			

DEBUT DATE	PEAK POS	WKS CHR	GOLD	ARTIST — Album Title	$	Label & Number

JAMES, Sonny — Cont'd

I'll Keep Holding On (Just To Your Love) (1)
I'll Never Find Another You (3,4) *97*
I'll Think About That Tomorrow (4)
I'll Watch Over You (5)
I'm Movin' On (medley) (4)
I've Just Got To Keep On Keepin' On (5)
Is It Wrong (For Loving You) (10)
It Keeps Right On A Hurtin' (9)
It's Gonna Rain Some In My Heart (5)
It's Just A Matter Of Time (5) *87*
It's Worth It All (2)

Jesus Knows (9)
Just A Closer Walk With Thee (medley) (4)
Just Keep On Thinking Of Me (8)
Keep Me In Mind (2)
King Of The Road (7)
Kiss In The Sunshine (6)
Last Time (3)
Let Me Live And Love With You (6)
Love Is A Rainbow (10)
Love Is You (8)
Love Me Like That (3)
Mean Ole Mississippi (2)
Minute You're Gone (1) *95*
Miracles Still Happen (9)
Missing You (10)
My Love (6)

Old Sweetheart Of Mine (3)
On The Fingers Of One Hand (3)
One Day By And By (8)
Only Ones We Truly Hurt (9)
Only The Lonely (2,4) *92*
Out Of This World (2)
Rally 'Round Your Love (5)
Ramblin' Rose (6)
Reach Out Your Hand And Touch Me (8)
Room In Your Heart (1)
Roses Are Red (2)
Running Bear (4) *94*
Scars (3)
She Believes In Me (9)
She Will, I Know (2)
She's Comin' Home (10)

Since I Met You, Baby (4) *65*
'68 Rock Island Line (medley) (4)
Somehow Your Name Comes Up Again (5)
Suddenly There's A Valley (10)
Take Good Care Of Her (1,3)
Tennessee Waltz (7)
There's Always Another Day (3)
This Time (10)
This World Of Ours (5)
Till The Last Leaf Shall Fall (1)
Today Is The End Of The World (3)
Traces (8)

Train Special '69 (4)
True Love Lasts Forever (9)
True Love's A Blessing (1,3,4)
Wake Up To Me Gentle (2)
Waterloo (6)
We're On Our Way (3)
What Am I Living For (8)
When The Snow Is On The Roses (10)
When Your World Stops Turning (3)
Where Did My Love Go (2)
Where Forgotten Things Belong (2)
White Silver Sands (10)
Why Is It I'm The Last To Know (10)
Woodbine Valley (6)
World Of Our Own (4)

You Are All I Love (6)
You Are My Sunshine (7)
You're The Only World I Know (1) *91*
You're The Reason I'm Living (9)
Young Love (1,4,7) *1*
Your Cheatin' Heart (7)

★★500★★ JAMES, Tommy, And The Shondells

Born Thomas Jackson on 4/29/47 in Dayton, Ohio. To Niles, Michigan at age 11. Formed pop group The Shondells at age 12. Recorded "Hanky Panky" on the Snap label in 1963. Tommy relocated to Pittsburgh in 1965 after a DJ there popularized "Hanky Panky." Original master was sold to Roulette, whereupon Tommy recruited Pittsburgh group The Raconteurs to become the official Shondells. Consisted of Mike Vale (bass), Pete Lucia (drums), Eddie Gray (guitar) and Ronnie Rosman (organ). Began recording as a solo artist in 1970.

DEBUT DATE	PEAK POS	WKS CHR	GOLD	ARTIST — Album Title	$	Label & Number
7/30/66	46	15		1 Hanky Panky	$20	Roulette 25336
4/29/67	74	18		2 I Think We're Alone Now	$20	Roulette 25353
2/24/68	174	5		3 Something Special! The Best Of Tommy James & The Shondells [G]	$20	Roulette 25355
7/27/68	193	2		4 Mony Mony	$20	Roulette 42012
2/1/69	8	35		5 Crimson & Clover	$20	Roulette 42023
10/25/69	141	6		6 Cellophane Symphony	$20	Roulette 42030
12/13/69+	21	41		7 The Best Of Tommy James & The Shondells [G]	$20	Roulette 42040
4/11/70	91	9		8 Travelin'	$15	Roulette 42044
				TOMMY JAMES:		
9/11/71	131	8		9 Christian Of The World	$15	Roulette 3001
3/22/80	134	7		10 Three Times In Love	$8	Millennium 7748

Adrienne (9) *93*
Another Hill To Climb (9)
(Baby, Baby) I Can't Take It No More (2,7)
Baby Let Me Down (2)
Ball Of Fire (7) *19*
Bits & Pieces (8)
Bloody Water (8)
Breakaway (8)
California Sun (2)
Candy Maker (8)
Cellophane Symphony (6)
Changes (8)
Christian Of The World (9)
Church Street Soul Revival (9) *62*
Cleo's Mood (1)
Crimson And Clover (5,7) *1*
Crystal Blue Persuasion (5,7) *2*

Do Something To Me (5) *38*
Do Unto Me (4)
Don't Let My Love Pass You By (3)
Don't Throw Our Love Away (1)
Draggin' The Line (9) *4*
Early In The Mornin' (8)
Evergreen (6)
Everything I Am (10)
Get Out Now (4) *48*
Gettin' Together (3) *18*
Gingerbread Man (9)
Gone, Gone, Gone (2)
Good Lovin' (1)
Gotta Get Back To You (8) *45*
I Am A Tangerine (5)
I Believe In People (9)

I Can't Go Back To Denver (4)
I Just Wanna Play The Music (10)
I Know Who I Am (6)
I Like The Way (2,3) *25*
I Think We're Alone Now (2,3,7) *4*
I'll Go Crazy (1)
I'm Alive (5)
I'm Comin' Home (9) *40*
I'm So Proud (1)
(I'm) Taken (4)
It's All Right (For Now) (10)
It's Magic (10)
It's Only Love (3) *31*
Kathleen McArthur (5)
Kelly Told Ann (8)
Lady In White (10)
Let It Slide (10)

Let's Be Lovers (2)
Light Of Day (9)
Long Way Down (10)
Lot's Of Pretty Girls (1)
Love Makes The World Go Round (1)
Love Of A Woman (6)
Love's Closin' In On Me (3)
Loved One (6)
Lover, The (1)
Makin' Good Time (6)
Mirage (2,3,7) *10*
Mony Mony (4,7) *3*
Moses And Me (8)
Nightime (I'm A Lover) (4)
On Behalf Of The Entire Staff & Management (4)
One Two Three And I Fell (4)
Out Of The Blue (3) *43*
Papa Rolled His Own (6)

Real Girl (3)
Red Rover (8)
Rings And Things (9)
Run Away With Me (4)
Run, Run, Baby, Run (2,3)
Sail A Happy Ship (9)
Say I Am (What I Am) (1,3) *21*
Shake A Tail Feather (1)
She (8) *23*
Shout (3)
Silk, Satin, Carriage Waiting (9)
Sing, Sing, Sing (9)
Smokey Roads (3)
Some Kind Of Love (4)
Somebody Cares (4) *53*
Soul Searchin' Baby (1)
Sugar On Sunday (5,7)
Sweet Cherry Wine (6,7) *7*

Talkin' And Signifyin' (8)
Three Times In Love (10) *19*
Travelin' (8)
Trust Each Other In Love (2)
What I'd Give To See Your Face Again (2)
You Got Me (10)

★★333★★ JAMES GANG, The

Cleveland hard-rock band: Joe Walsh (guitar, keyboards, vocals), Jim Fox (drums) and Tom Kriss (bass; replaced by Dale Peters in 1970). Walsh left in late 1971, replaced by Dominic Troiano and Roy Kenner. Troiano left in 1973, replaced by Tommy Bolin (d: 12/4/76 [age 25]). Many personnel changes from 1974 until group disbanded in 1976.

DEBUT DATE	PEAK POS	WKS CHR	GOLD	ARTIST — Album Title	$	Label & Number
11/1/69+	83	24		1 Yer' Album	$15	BluesWay 6034
7/25/70	20	66	●	2 James Gang Rides Again	$12	ABC 711
4/17/71	27	30	●	3 Thirds	$12	ABC 721
9/11/71	24	16	●	4 James Gang Live In Concert [L]	$12	ABC 733
3/18/72+	58	19		5 Straight Shooter	$12	ABC 741
10/7/72	72	15		6 Passin' Thru	$12	ABC 760
2/10/73	79	16		7 The Best Of The James Gang featuring Joe Walsh [G]	$12	ABC 774
12/8/73	181	5		8 16 Greatest Hits [G]	$12	ABC 801 [2]
1/5/74	122	18		9 Bang	$10	Atco 7037
9/14/74	97	10		10 Miami	$10	Atco 102
5/31/75	109	9		11 Newborn	$10	Atco 112

Again (3,8)
Ain't Seen Nothin' Yet (6)
Alexis (9)
All I Have (11)
Ashes The Rain And I (2,4,7,8)
Asshtonpark (2)
Bluebird (9)
Bomber Medley (2,7,8)
Cold Wind (11)
Collage (1,8)

Come With Me (11)
Cruisin' Down The Highway (10)
Devil Is Singing Our Song (1)
Do It (8)
Dreamin' In The Country (3)
Driftin' Dreamer (11)
Drifting Girl (6)
Earthshaker (11)
Everybody Needs A Hero (6)
Fred (medley) (1)

From Another Time (9)
Funk #48 (1,7,8)
Funk #49 (2,7,8) *59*
Garden Gate (2)
Get Her Back Again (5)
Getting Old (5)
Gonna Get By (11)
Got No Time For Trouble (9)
Had Enough (6)
Hairy Hypochondriac (9)
Head Above The Water (9)

Heartbreak Hotel (11)
I Don't Have The Time (1)
I'll Tell You Why (5)
It's All The Same (3)
Kick Back Jack (9)
Let Me Come Home (5)
Live My Life Again (5)
Looking For My Lady (5)
Lost Woman (1,4)
Madness (5)
Merry-Go-Round (8)

Miami Two-Step (10)
Midnight Man (3,7,8) *80*
Must Be Love (9) *54*
My Door Is Open (5)
Mystery (9)
One Way Street (6)
Out Of Control (9)
Praylude (medley) (10)
Rather Be Alone With You (A.K.A. Song For Dale) (9)
Red Satin Lover (11)

Red Skies (medley) (10)
Ride The Wind (9)
Run, Run, Run (9)
Shoulda' Seen Your Face (11)
Sleepwalker (10)
Spanish Lover (10)
Standing In The Rain (9)
Stone Rap (1)
Stop (1,4,7,8)
Summer Breezes (10)
Take A Look Around (1,4,7,8)

DEBUT DATE	PEAK POS	WKS CHR	GOLD	ARTIST — Album Title	$	Label & Number

JAMES GANG, The — Cont'd

Tend My Garden (2,4,8)
Thanks (2,8)
There I Go Again (2,8)

Things I Could Be (3)
Things I Want To Say To You (8)

Tuning Part One (1)
Up To Yourself (6)
Walk Away (3,4,7,8) **51**

Watch It (11)
White Man/Black Man (3,8)
Wildfire (10)

Woman (2,7,8)
Wrapcity In English (medley) (1)

Yadig? (3,7,8)
You're Gonna Need Me (4)

★★379★★ JAN & DEAN

Jan Berry (b: 4/3/41) and Dean Torrence (b: 3/10/40) formed group called the Barons while attending high school in Los Angeles. Jan & Dean and Barons' member Arnie Ginsburg recorded "Jennie Lee" in Jan's garage. Dean left for a six-month Army Reserve stint, whereupon Jan signed with Doris Day's label, Arwin, and the record was released as by Jan & Arnie. Upon Dean's return from the service, Arnie joined the Navy, and Jan & Dean signed with Herb Alpert's Dore label. Jan was critically injured in an auto accident on 4/19/66. Duo made a comeback in 1978, after their biographical film *Dead Man's Curve* aired on TV.

DEBUT DATE	PEAK POS	WKS CHR		# ARTIST — Album Title	$	Label & Number
6/22/63	71	10		1 Jan & Dean take Linda Surfin'	$40	Liberty 7294
8/10/63	32	21		2 Surf City And Other Swingin' Cities	$30	Liberty 7314
1/18/64	22	14		3 Drag City	$30	Liberty 7339
5/23/64	80	21		4 Dead Man's Curve/The New Girl In School	$30	Liberty 7361
10/10/64+	40	20		5 The Little Old Lady From Pasadena	$30	Liberty 7377
10/17/64+	66	19		6 Ride The Wild Surf ....[S]	$30	Liberty 7368
2/27/65	33	16		7 Command Performance/Live In Person ....[L]	$25	Liberty 7403
10/2/65	107	6		8 Jan & Dean Golden Hits, Volume 2 ....[G]	$25	Liberty 7417
1/15/66	145	3		9 Folk 'n Roll	$25	Liberty 7431
5/14/66	127	5		10 Filet Of Soul ....[L]	$25	Liberty 7441

All I Have To Do Is Dream (7)
Anaheim, Azusa & Cucamonga Sewing Circle, Book Review And Timing Association (5,8) **77**
"B" Gas Rickshaw (4)
Barons, West L.A. (4)
Beginning From An End (9)
Best Friend I Ever Had (1)
Bucket "T" (4)
Dead Man's Curve (3,4,7,8,10) **8**
Detroit City (2)
Do Wah Diddy Diddy (2)
Down At Malibu Beach (6)
Drag City (3,8) **10**
Drag Strip Girl (3)
Eve Of Destruction (9)
Everybody Loves A Clown (10)

Folk City (9)
Gonna Hustle You (10)
Gypsy Cried (1)
Hang On Sloopy (My Girl Sloopy) (9,10)
(Here They Come) From All Over The World (7,8) **56**
Hey Little Freshman (4)
Honolulu Lulu (2,8,10) **11**
Horace The Swingin' School-Bus Driver (9)
Hot Stocker (3)
I Can't Wait To Love You (6)
I Found A Girl (9,10) **30**
I Get Around (7)
I Gotta Drive (3)
I Left My Heart In San Francisco (2)
I Should Have Known Better (7)

It Ain't Me Babe (9)
It's A Shame To Say Goodbye (9)
It's As Easy As 1,2,3 (4,5)
Kansas City (2)
Let's Hang On (10)
Let's Turkey Trot (1)
Lightnin' Strikes (10)
Linda (1,4,8) **20**
Little Deuce Coupe (3)
Little Honda (7)
Little Old Lady [From Pasadena] (5,7,8) **3**
Louie, Louie (2)
Manhattan (2)
Memphis (2,5)
Michelle (10)
Move Out Little Mustang (5)
Mr. Bassman (1)
My Foolish Heart (1)
My Mighty G.T.O. (4)

New Girl In School (4,8) **37**
Norwegian Wood (This Bird Has Flown) (10)
Old Ladies Seldom Power Shift (5)
One-Piece Topless Bathingsuit (5)
1-2-3 (10)
Philadelphia, Pa. (2)
Popsicle Truck (9)
Restless Surfer (6)
Rhythm Of The Rain (1)
Rock And Roll Music (2)
Rockin' Little Roadster (4)
Schlock Rod (Part 1 & 2) (3)
School Day (2)
She's My Summer Girl (9)
Sidewalk Surfin' (5,6,7,8) **25**

Skateboarding - Part 1 (6)
Skateboarding - Part 2 (5)
Soul City (3)
Sting Ray (3)
Submarine Races (6)
Summer Means Fun (5)
Surf City (2,7,8) **1**
Surf Route 101 (4)
Surfer's Dream (6)
Surfin' (1)
Surfin' Hearse (3)
Surfin' Safari (1)
Surfin' Wild (6)
T.A.M.I. Show, Theme From ..see: (Here They Come) From All Over The World
Tallahassee Lassie (2)
Tell 'Em I'm Surfin' (6)
Three Window Coupe (4)
Turn! Turn! Turn! (9)

Universal Coward (9)
Waimea Bay (6)
Walk Like A Man (1)
Walk On The Wet Side (6)
Walk Right In (1)
Way Down Yonder In New Orleans (2)
When I Learn How To Cry (1)
When It's Over (5)
Where Were You When I Needed You (9)
Yesterday (9)
You Came A Long Way From St. Louis (2)
You Really Know How To Hurt A Guy (8) **27**
You've Got To Hide Your Love Away (10)

JANE'S ADDICTION

Los Angeles metal/funk band led by vocalist Perry Farrell with Eric Avery, Stephen Perkins and Dave Navarro.

DEBUT DATE	PEAK POS	WKS CHR		# ARTIST — Album Title	$	Label & Number
9/17/88+	103	35	●	1 Nothing's Shocking	$8	Warner 25727
9/8/90	19	60	▲	2 Ritual de lo Habitual	$12	Warner 25993

Ain't No Right (2)
Been Caught Stealing (2)
Classic Girl (2)
Had A Dad (1)

Idiots Rule (1)
Jane Says (1)
Mountain Song (1)
No One's Leaving (2)

Obvious (2)
Ocean Size (1)
Of Course (1)
Stop! (2)

Standing In The Shower...Thinking (1)
Ted, Just Admit It... (1)
Thank You Boys (1)

Summertime Rolls (1)
Then She Did ... (2)
Three Days (2)
Up The Beach (1)

JANKEL, Chas

Former keyboardist/guitarist with Ian Dury & The Blockheads.

DEBUT DATE	PEAK POS	WKS CHR		ARTIST — Album Title	$	Label & Number
3/6/82	126	14		Questionnaire	$8	A&M 4885

Boy
Glad To Know You

Johnny Funk
Magic Of Music

Now You're Dancing
Questionnaire
109
3,000,000 Synths

JANKOWSKI, Horst

Born on 1/30/36 in Berlin. Jazz pianist.

DEBUT DATE	PEAK POS	WKS CHR		# ARTIST — Album Title	$	Label & Number
5/22/65	18	31		1 The Genius Of Jankowski! ....[I]	$15	Mercury 60993
12/4/65+	65	13		2 More Genius Of Jankowski ....[I]	$15	Mercury 61054
12/3/66	107	2		3 So What's New? ....[I]	$15	Mercury 61093

All My Happiness (3)
Bald Klopft Das Gluck Auch Mal An Deine Tur (Soon Luck Will Also Knock On Your Door) (1)
Berlin Stroll (2)
Bossa Novissima (3)
Canadian Sunset (2)

Caroline - Denise (1)
Charming Vienna (2)
Clair De Lune (1)
Cruising Down The Rhine (2)
Donkey Serenade (1)
Dreamers Concerto (3)

Eine Schwarzwaldfahrt ..see: Walk In The Black Forest
Exactly You (3)
Grand Amour (3)
Happy Frankfurt (2)
Heide (2)
Highway At Night (3)

Moonlight Cocktail (3)
My Roman Love Song (3)
My Yiddishe Momme (1)
Nola (1)
Paris Parade (3)
Parlez-Moi D'Amour (Speak To Me Of Love) (1)
Place In The Sun (3)

Play A Simple Melody (2)
Simpel Gimpel (1) **91**
Sing-Song (1)
So What's New? (3)
Strangers In The Night (3)
Sunrise Serenade (2)
Then The Girls Go Marching In (1)

3rd Man Theme (2)
Toselli Serenade (1)
Walk In Bavaria (2)
Walk In The Black Forest (1) **12**

JARRE, Jean-Michel

Electronic keyboard/synthesizer soloist. Born on 8/24/48 in Lyon, France.

DEBUT DATE	PEAK POS	WKS CHR		# ARTIST — Album Title	$	Label & Number
10/15/77	78	19		1 Oxygene ....[I]	$8	Polydor 6112
2/3/79	126	8		2 Equinoxe ....[I]	$8	Polydor 6175
7/11/81	98	12		3 Magnetic Fields ....[I]	$8	Polydor 6325
5/3/86	52	20		4 Rendez-Vous ....[I]	$8	Dreyfus 829125

Equinoxe Part 1-8 (2)
Magnetic Fields Part 1-5 (3)

Oxygene (Part 1-6) (1)
Rendez-Vous (First-Last) (4)

Ron's Piece ..see: Rendez-Vous

★★281★★ JARREAU, Al

Born on 3/12/40 in Milwaukee. Soul-jazz vocalist. Has masters degree in psychology from the University of Iowa. Worked clubs in San Francisco with George Duke.

DEBUT DATE	PEAK POS	WKS CHR		# ARTIST — Album Title	$	Label & Number
8/28/76	132	11		1 Glow	$8	Reprise 2248

DEBUT DATE	PEAK POS	WKS CHR	GOLD	ARTIST — Album Title	$	Label & Number
				JARREAU, Al — Cont'd		
6/25/77	49	15		2 Look To The Rainbow/Live In Europe .... [L]	$10	Warner 3052 [2]
10/14/78	78	28		3 All Fly Home	$8	Warner 3229
6/21/80	27	35	●	4 This Time	$8	Warner 3434
8/22/81	9	103	▲	5 Breakin' Away	$8	Warner 3576
4/16/83	13	43	●	6 Jarreau	$8	Warner 23801
11/24/84	49	35		7 High Crime	$8	Warner 25106
9/21/85	125	9		8 Al Jarreau In London .... [L]	$8	Warner 25331
10/4/86	81	28		9 L Is For Lover	$8	Warner 25477
12/3/88+	75	23	●	10 Heart's Horizon	$8	Reprise 25778
7/4/92	105	9		11 Heaven And Earth	$12	Reprise 26849

Across The Midnight Sky (9)
After All (7) **69**
Agua De Beber (1)
All (3)
All Of My Love (10)
All Or Nothing At All (10)
Alonzo (4)
Better Than Anything (2)
Black And Blues (6,8)
Blue Angel (11)
Blue In Green
 (Tapestry)-Part I & II (11)
Blue Rondo A La Turk ..see:
 (Round, Round, Round)
Boogie Down (6) **77**
Breakin' Away (5) **43**
Brite 'N' Sunny Babe (3)
Burst In With The Dawn (2)
Closer To Your Love (5)

Could You Believe (2)
Distracted (4)
Easy (5)
Fallin' (7)
Fire And Rain (1)
Fly (3)
Gimme What You Got (4)
Give A Little More Lovin' (9)
Glow (1)
Golden Girl (9)
Have You Seen The Child (1)
Heart's Horizon (10)
Heaven And Earth (11)
High Crime (7,8)
Hold On Me (1)
I Do (3)
I Must Have Been A Fool (10)
I Will Be Here For You
 (Nitakungodea Milele) (6,8)

I'm Home (3)
If I Break (11)
(If I Could Only) Change
 Your Mind (4)
Imagination (7)
It's Not Hard To Love You
 (11)
Killer Love (10)
L Is For Lover (9)
Let's Pretend (3)
Letter Perfect (2)
Look To The Rainbow (2)
Love Is Real (4)
Love Is Waiting (6)
Love Of My Life (11)
Love Speaks Louder Than
 Words (7)
Loving You (2)
Milwaukee (1)

More Love (10)
Mornin' (6) **21**
Murphy's Law (7)
My Old Friend (5)
Never Givin' Up (4)
No Ordinary Romance (9)
Not Like This (6)
One Good Turn (2)
One Way (10)
Our Love (5)
Pleasure (10)
Pleasure Over Pain (10)
Raging Waters (7,8)
Rainbow In Your Eyes (1,2)
Real Tight (9)
(Rhyme) This Time (4)
Roof Garden (5,8)
(Round, Round, Round)
 Blue Rondo A La Turk (5)

Save Me (6)
Says (9)
She's Leaving Home (3)
(Sittin' On) The Dock Of The
 Bay (3)
So Good (10)
So Long Girl (2)
Somebody's Watching You
 (1)
Spain (I Can Recall) (4)
Step By Step (6)
Sticky Wicket (7)
Superfine Love (11)
Take Five (9)
Teach Me Tonight (5,8) **70**
Tell Me (7)
Tell Me What I Gotta Do (9)
10K Hi (10)
Thinkin' About It Too (3)

Trouble In Paradise (6) **63**
Wait A Little While (3)
Way To Your Heart (10)
We Got By (2)
(We Got) Telepathy (9)
**We're In This Love
 Together** (5,8) **15**
What You Do To Me (11)
Whenever I Hear Your Name
 (11)
Yo' Jeans (10)
You Don't See Me (2)
Your Song (1)
Your Sweet Love (4)

JARRETT, Keith
Jazz pianist/composer. Born on 5/8/45 in Allentown, Pennsylvania. Worked with Art Blakey (1965), Charles Lloyd (1966) and Miles Davis (1970-71).

8/2/75	160	5		1 El Juicio (The Judgement) .... [I]	$10	Atlantic 1673
3/13/76	195	1		2 In The Light .... [I]	$12	ECM 1033 [2]
7/10/76	179	3		3 Arbour Zena .... [I]	$10	ECM 1070
7/17/76	184	2		4 Mysteries .... [I]	$10	ABC/Impulse 9315
2/12/77	174	4		5 Shades .... [I]	$8	ABC/Impulse 9322
8/6/77	141	12		6 Staircase/Hourglass/Sundial/Sand ..... [I]	$10	ECM 1090 [2]
10/1/77	117	6		7 Byablue .... [I]	$8	ABC/Impulse 9331
9/2/78	174	2		8 My Song .... [I]	$8	ECM 1115

with Jan Garbarek, Palle Danielsson and Jon Christensen

Brass Quintet (2)
Byablue (7)
Country (2)
Crystal Moment (2)
Diatribe (5)
El Juicio (1)
Everything That Lives
 Laments (4)

Fantasm (7)
Flame (4)
Fughata For Harpsichord (2)
Gypsy Moth (1)
Hourglass (Part 1 & 2) (6)
In The Cave, In The Light (2)
Journey Home (8)
Konya (7)

Mandala (8)
Metamorphosis (2)
Mirrors (2)
My Song (8)
Mysteries (4)
Pagan Hymn (2)
Pardon My Rags (1)

Piece For Ornette [includes 2
 versions] (1)
Pre-Judgement Atmosphere
 (1)
Questar (8)
Rainbow (7)
Rose Petals (5)
Rotation (4)

Runes (3)
Sand (Parts 1, 2 & 3) (6)
Shades Of Jazz (5)
Short Piece For Guitar And
 Strings (2)
Solara March (3)
Southern Smiles (5)
Staircase (Parts 1-3) (6)

String Quartet (2)
Sundial (Parts 1-3) (6)
Tabarka (8)
Toll Road (1)
Trieste (7)
Yahllah (7)

JASON & THE SCORCHERS
Nashville rock band: Jason Ringenberg (b: 11/22/59; lead vocals), Warner Hodges, Jeff Johnson and Perry Baggs.

3/10/84	116	23		1 Fervor .... [M]	$8	EMI America 19008
3/30/85	96	15		2 Lost & Found	$8	EMI America 17153
11/22/86+	91	19		3 Still Standing	$8	EMI America 17219

Absolutely Sweet Marie (1)
Blanket Of Sorrow (2)
Both Sides Of The Line (1)
Broken Whiskey Glass (2)
Change The Tune (2)
Crashin' Down (3)

Far Behind (2)
Ghost Town (3)
Golden Ball And Chain (3)
Good Things Come To Those
 Who Wait (3)
Harvest Moon (1)

Help There's A Fire (1)
Hot Nights In Georgia (1)
I Can't Help Myself (1)
I Really Don't Want To Know
 (2)
If Money Talks (2)

Last Time Around (2)
Lost Highway (2)
My Heart Still Stands With
 You (3)
19th Nervous Breakdown (3)
Ocean Of Doubt (3)

Pray For Me, Mama (I'm A
 Gypsy Now) (1)
Shop It Around (2)
Shotgun Blues (3)
Still Tied (2)

Take Me To Your Promised
 Land (3)
White Lies (2)

JASPER, Chris
Member of group, The Isley Brothers, from 1969-84. Formed trio (Isley, Jasper, Isley) with cousins Ernie and Marvin Isley.

3/5/88	182	3		Superbad	$8	CBS Assoc. 44053

Dance For The Dollar
Earthquake

Givin' My All
Like I Do

My Soul Train
One Time Love

Son Of Man
Superbad

JAY & THE AMERICANS
Group formed in late 1959 by New York University students as the Harbor-Lites: John "Jay" Traynor (formerly with the Mystics), Sandy Yaguda, Kenny Vance (later a Hollywood musical director) and Howie Kane. Guitarist Marty Sanders joined during production of their first album in 1961. Traynor left after their first hit and was replaced by lead singer Jay Black (real name: David Blatt; b: 11/2/38) in 1962.

12/12/64	131	4		1 Come A Little Bit Closer	$25	United Art. 6407
6/12/65	113	17		2 Blockbusters	$20	United Art. 6417
11/20/65+	21	20		3 Jay & The Americans Greatest Hits! .... [G]	$20	United Art. 6453
3/19/66	141	4		4 Sunday And Me	$20	United Art. 6474
3/15/69	51	21		5 Sands Of Time	$20	United Art. 6671
2/28/70	105	11		6 Wax Museum	$20	United Art. 6719

JAY & THE AMERICANS — Cont'd

Baby Stop Your Cryin' (4)
Can't We Be Sweethearts (5)
Cara, Mia (2,3) 4
Chilly Winds (4)
Come A Little Bit Closer (1,3) 3
Come Dance With Me (1) 76
Crying (4) 25
Do I Love You (6)
Friday (1)
Girl (3)
Good Lovin' (4)
Goodbye Boys Goodbye (1,3)
Goodnight My Love (5)

Granada (4)
Gypsy Woman (5)
Hang Around (2)
Hushabye (5) 62
I Don't Need A Friend (4)
I Don't Want To Cry (6)
I Miss You (When I Kiss You) (4)
If You Were Mine, Girl (2,3)
Johnny B. Goode (6)
Let It Be Me (6)
Let's Lock The Door (And Throw Away The Key) (2,3) 11

Life Is But A Dream (5)
Lonely Teardrops (6)
Look In My Eyes Maria (1)
Lover's Question (6)
Maria (4)
Mean Woman Blues (5)
Message To Martha (6)
My Prayer (5)
Only In America (1,3) 25
Please Let Me Dream (2)
Pledging My Love (5)
Room Full Of Tears (6)
Run To My Lovin' Arms (2,3)
She Doesn't Know It (1)

She's The Girl (That's Messin' Up My Mind) (4)
Silly Girl, Silly Boy (2)
Since I Don't Have You (5)
So Much In Love (5)
Some Enchanted Evening (3) 13
Some Kind-A Wonderful (4)
Somebody's Gonna Cry (3)
Something In My Eye! (2,3)
Strangers Tomorrow (1)
Sunday And Me (4) 18
Think Of The Good Times (2,3) 57

This Is It (1)
This Is My Love (6)
This Magic Moment (5) 6
Through This Doorway (3)
'Til (4)
To Wait For Love (1)
Tomorrow (1)
Twenty Four Hours From Tulsa (2)
Walkin' In The Rain (6) 19
What's The Use (1)
When It's All Over (2,3)
When You Dance (5) 70

Why Can't You Bring Me Home (4) 63
You Were On My Mind (6)

JAY AND THE TECHNIQUES

Interracial R&B-rock group from Allentown, Pennsylvania: Jay Proctor (lead singer), Karl Landis, Ronnie Goosly, John Walsh, George Lloyd, Chuck Crowl and Dante Dancho.

10/28/67+	129	13		Apples, Peaches, Pumpkin Pie..	$20	Smash 67095

Ain't No Soul (Left In These Old Shoes)

Apples, Peaches, Pumpkin Pie 6
Been So Long (Since I Loved You)
Contact

Here We Go Again
Hey Diddle Diddle
Keep The Ball Rollin' 14

Lovin' For Money
Power Of Love

Stronger Than Dirt
Victory!

JAYE, Jerry

Born Gerald Jaye Hatley on 10/19/37 in Manila, Arkansas.

7/29/67	195	2		My Girl Josephine	$20	Hi 32038

Ain't Got No Home
Ain't That A Shame
Don't Be Cruel

I'm Gonna Be A Wheel
Someday
Kansas City

Let The Four Winds Blow
My Girl Josephine 29
Singing The Blues

What Am I Living For
When My Dreamboat Comes Home

White Silver Sands
Whole Lot Of Shakin' Going On

JAYE, Miles

Soul singer/songwriter born Miles Davis in Brooklyn. Classical violinist until he became lead vocalist of the Air Force Band. Then, commercial jingle singer.

12/12/87+	125	12		1 Miles...	$8	Island 90615
6/10/89	160	9		2 Irresistible...	$8	Island 91235

Come Home (1)
Desiree (1)
Happy 2 Have U (1)

Heaven (2)
I Cry For You (1)
I'll Be There (2)

I've Been A Fool For You (1)
Irresistible (2)
Lazy Love (1)

Let's Start Love Over (1)
Love In The Night (2)
Message (2)

Neither One Of Us (2)
Next Time (1)
Objective (2)

Slo-Dance (2)
Special Thing (1)

JAZZ CRUSADERS — see CRUSADERS, The

JB's, The

James Brown's super-funk backup band led by Fred Wesley.

7/28/73	77	13		1 Doing It To Death	$8	People 5603
6/29/74	197	3		2 Damn Right I Am Somebody	$8	People 6602

FRED WESLEY & the J.B.'s

Blow Your Head (2)
Damn Right I'm Somebody (2)
Doing It To Death (1) 22

Going To Get A Thrill (2)
I'm Payin' Taxes, What Am I Buyin' (2)

If You Don't Get It The First Time, Back Up And Try It Again, Parrty (2)

La Di Da La Di Day (1)
Make Me What You Want Me To Be (2)

More Peas (1)
Same Beat - Part 1 (2)
Sucker (1)

You Can Have Watergate Just Gimme Some Bucks And I'll Be Straight (1)
You Sure Love To Ball (2)

★★31★★ JEFFERSON AIRPLANE/STARSHIP

Formed as Jefferson Airplane (slang for a split paper match used as a marijuana cigarette holder) in San Francisco, 1965. Consisted of Marty Balin and Signe Anderson (vocals), Paul Kantner (vocals, guitar), Jorma Kaukonen (guitar), Jack Casady (bass) and Alexander "Skip" Spence (drums). Grace Slick and Spencer Dryden joined in 1966, replacing Anderson and Spence. Slick had been in the Great Society. Spence then formed Moby Grape. Dryden replaced by Joey Covington in 1970. Casady and Kaukonen left by 1974 to go full time with Hot Tuna. Balin left in 1971, rejoined in 1975, by which time group was renamed Jefferson Starship and consisted of Slick, Kantner, Papa John Creach (Hot Tuna; violin), David Freiberg (bass), Craig Chaquico (pronounced: chuck-ee-so; guitar), Pete Sears (bass) and John Barbata (drums). Slick left group from June 1978 to January 1981. In 1979, singer Mickey Thomas joined (replaced Balin), along with Aynsley Dunbar (John Mayall's Bluesbreakers, Mothers Of Invention, Journey) who replaced Barbata. Don Baldwin (formerly with Snail) replaced Dunbar (later with Whitesnake) in 1982. Kantner left in 1984, and, due to legal difficulties, band's name was shortened to Starship, whose lineup included Slick, Thomas, Sears, Chaquico and Baldwin. Slick left in early 1988. In 1989, the original 1966 lineup — Balin, Slick, Kantner, Kaukonen and Casady — reunited as Jefferson Airplane with Kenny Aronoff (formerly with John Cougar Mellencamp) replacing Dryden. Continuing as Starship were Thomas, Chaquico, Baldwin, Brett Bloomfield (bass) and Mark Morgan (keyboards). Starship disbanded in 1990.

JEFFERSON AIRPLANE:

9/17/66	128	11		1 Jefferson Airplane Takes Off..	$30	RCA 3584
3/25/67	3	56	●	2 **Surrealistic Pillow**	$25	RCA 3766
12/23/67+	17	23		3 After Bathing At Baxter's..	$25	RCA 1511
9/7/68	6	25	●	4 **Crown Of Creation**	$15	RCA 4058
3/1/69	17	20		5 Bless Its Pointed Little Head..[L]	$20	RCA 4133
11/22/69	13	44	●	6 Volunteers	$15	RCA 4238
12/12/70+	12	40	●	7 The Worst Of Jefferson Airplane..[G]	$15	RCA 4459
12/19/70+	20	23	●	8 Blows Against The Empire	$15	RCA 4448

PAUL KANTNER/JEFFERSON STARSHIP
with Grace Slick, Jerry Garcia, David Crosby and Graham Nash

9/18/71	11	21	●	9 Bark	$40	Grunt 1001
8/19/72	20	21	●	10 Long John Silver	$40	Grunt 1007
4/14/73	52	16		11 Thirty Seconds Over Winterland..[L]	$15	Grunt 0147
5/4/74	110	8		12 Early Flight ....[K]	$15	Grunt 0437

includes previously unreleased material (1965-70)

JEFFERSON STARSHIP:

10/26/74	11	37	●	13 Dragon Fly	$15	Grunt 0717

DEBUT DATE	PEAK POS	WKS CHR	GOLD	ARTIST — Album Title	$	Label & Number

JEFFERSON AIRPLANE/STARSHIP — Cont'd

DEBUT DATE	PEAK POS	WKS CHR	GOLD	#	ARTIST — Album Title	$	Label & Number
7/19/75	1[4]	87	●	14	Red Octopus	$15	Grunt 0999
7/10/76	3	38	▲	15	Spitfire	$15	Grunt 1557
1/29/77	37	15	●	16	Flight Log (1966-1976) ...[K]	$20	Grunt 1255 [2]

includes "Hesitation Blues" and "Ja Da (Keep On Truckin')" by Hot Tuna; "Silver Spoon" and "Sketches Of China" by Paul Kantner/Grace Slick; "Genesis" by Jorma Kaukonen & Tom Hobson

DEBUT DATE	PEAK POS	WKS CHR	GOLD	#	ARTIST — Album Title	$	Label & Number
3/18/78	5	34	▲	17	Earth	$10	Grunt 2515
2/17/79	20	14	●	18	Gold ...[G]	$10	Grunt 3247
12/1/79+	10	28	●	19	Freedom At Point Zero	$8	Grunt 3452
4/18/81	26	33	●	20	Modern Times	$8	Grunt 3848
10/30/82	26	31		21	Winds Of Change	$8	Grunt 4372
6/16/84	28	23	●	22	Nuclear Furniture	$8	Grunt 4921

STARSHIP:

DEBUT DATE	PEAK POS	WKS CHR	GOLD	#	ARTIST — Album Title	$	Label & Number
10/5/85+	7	50	●	23	Knee Deep In The Hoopla	$8	Grunt 5488
4/18/87	138	9		24	2400 Fulton Street - An Anthology * ...[K]	$10	RCA 5724 [2]

address of group's 17-room San Francisco mansion; features 25 remastered songs from their first 6 studio albums (1966-71)

DEBUT DATE	PEAK POS	WKS CHR	GOLD	#	ARTIST — Album Title	$	Label & Number
7/25/87	12	25	●	25	No Protection	$8	Grunt 6413
8/19/89	64	18		26	Love Among The Cannibals	$8	RCA 9693
9/23/89	85	7		27	Jefferson Airplane *	$8	Epic 45271

reunion of the 1966-74 lineup

*JEFFERSON AIRPLANE

Aerie (Gang Of Eagles) (10)
Ai Garimasu (There Is Love) (14)
Alexander The Medium (10)
Alien (20)
All Fly Away (13)
All Nite Long (17)
And I Like It (1)
Assassin (22)
Awakening (19)
Baby Tree (8)
Babylon (25)
Ballad Of You & Me & Pooneil (3,7,24) 42
Be My Lady (21) 28
Be Young You (13)
Bear Melt (5)
Beat Patrol (25) 46
Before I Go (23) 68
Big City (15)
Black Widow (21)
Blaze Of Love (26)
Blues From An Airplane (1,7)
Bringing Me Down (1)
Burn, The (26)
Can't Find Love (21)
Caroline (13,18)
Champion (22)
Chauffeur Blues (1)
Child Is Coming (8)
Children, The (5)
Chushingura (4,7)
Clergy (5)
¿Come Again? Toucan [solo: Grace Slick] (16)
Come To Life (13)
Come Up The Years (1,16,24)
Comin' Back To Me (2,16,24)
Common Market Madrigal (27)
Connection (22)
Count On Me (17,18) 8
Crazy Feelin' (17) 54

Crazy Miranda (9)
Crown Of Creation (4,7,11,24) 64
Cruisin' (15)
D.C.B.A.- 25 (2)
Dance With The Dragon (15)
Desperate Heart (23)
Devils Den (13)
Don't Slip Away (1)
Easter? (10)
Eat Starch Mom (10)
Embryonic Journey (2,7,24)
Eskimo Blue Day (6)
Fading Lady Light (19)
Farm, The (6)
Fast Buck Freddie (14,18)
Fat Angel (5)
Feel So Good (9,11,16)
Find Your Way Back (20) 29
Fire (17)
Free (20)
Freedom (27)
Freedom At Point Zero (19)
Girl With The Hungry Eyes (19) 55
Girls Like You (25)
Git Fiddler (14)
Go To Her (12)
Good Shepherd (6,7)
Greasy Heart (4,16) 98
Have You Seen The Saucers (11,12)
Have You Seen The Stars Tonite (8,16)
Healing Waters (26)
Hearts Of The World (Will Understand) (23)
Hey Fredrick (6)
High Flyin' Bird (12)
Hijack (8)
Home (8)
Hot Water (15)
House At Pooneil Corners (4)

How Do You Feel (2)
How Suite It Is Medley (3)
Hyperdrive (13)
I Came Back From The Jaws Of The Dragon (13)
I Didn't Mean To Stay All Night (26) 75
I Don't Know Why (25)
I Want To See Another World (14)
I Will Stay (21)
I'll Be There (26)
Ice Age (27)
Ice Cream Phoenix (4)
If You Feel (4,16)
In The Morning (12)
In Time (4)
It's Alright (12)
It's Not Enough (26) 12
It's Not Over ('Til It's Over) (25) 9
J.P.P. McStep B. Blues (12)
Jane (19) 14
Just The Same (19)
Keep On Dreamin' (21)
Last Wall Of The Castle (medley) (4)
Lather (4,7,24)
Law Man (9)
Layin' It On The Line (22) 66
Let Me In (1)
Let's Get Together (1)
Lets Go Together (8)
Lightning Rose (19)
Live And Let Live (22)
Long John Silver (10)
Love Among The Cannibals (26)
Love Lovely Love (15)
Love Rusts (14)
Love Too Good (17,18)

Madeleine Street (27)
Magician (22)
Martha (3,7,24)
Mary (20)
Mau Mau (Amerikon) (8)
Meadowlands (6)
Mexico (12,24)
Milk Train (10,11,16)
Miracles (14,18) 3
Modern Times (20)
My Best Friend (2,24)
Never Argue With A German If You're Tired Or European Song (9)
No Way Out (22) 23
Nothing's Gonna Stop Us Now (25) 1
Now Is The Time (27)
Other Side Of This Life (5)
Out Of Control (21)
Panda (21)
Planes (27)
Plastic Fantastic Lover (2,5,7,24)
Play On Love (14,18) 49
Please Come Back (live) (16)
Pretty As You Feel (9,16,24) 60
Private Room (23)
Quit Wasting Time (21)
Rejoyce (3,24)
Ride The Tiger (13,16,18) 84
Rock And Roll Island (9)
Rock Me Baby (5)
Rock Music (19)
Rock Myself To Sleep (23)
Rose Goes To Yale (22)
Run Around (1)
Runaway (17,18) 12
Runnin' 'Round This World (12)
Sandalphon (14)

Sara (23) 1
Save Your Love (20)
Send A Message (26)
Set The Night To Music (25)
Share A Little Joke (4)
She Has Funny Cars (2,24)
Shining In The Moonlight (22)
Show Yourself (17)
Showdown (22)
Skateboard (17)
Small Package Of Value Will Come To You, Shortly (3,24)
Solidarity (27)
Somebody To Love (2,5,7,16,24) 5
Son Of Jesus (9)
Song For All Seasons (6)
Song To The Sun Medley (15)
Sorry Me, Sorry You (22)
St. Charles (15,18) 64
Stairway To Cleveland (20)
Star Track (4)
Starship (8)
Stranger (20) 48
Summer Of Love (27)
Sunrise (8)
Sweeter Than Honey (14)
Switchblade (15)
Take Your Time (17)
Thats For Sure (13)
There Will Be Love (14)
Things To Come (19)
Third Week In The Chelsea (9,24)
3/5 Of A Mile In 10 Seconds (2,5)
Thunk (9)
Tobacco Road (1)
Today (2,7,24)
Tomorrow Doesn't Matter Tonight (23) 26

Too Many Years (27)
Transatlantic (25)
Triad (4,24)
Trial By Fire (10,11)
Trouble In Mind (26)
True Love (27)
Tumblin (14)
Turn My Life Down (6)
Turn Out The Lights (8)
Twilight Double Leader (10,11)
Two Heads (medley) (3)
Up Or Down (12)
Upfront Blues (27)
Volunteers (6,7,16,24) 65
War Movie (9)
We Built This City (23) 1
We Can Be Together (6,7,24)
We Dream In Color (26)
Wheel, The (27)
When The Earth Moves Again (9,11)
White Rabbit (2,7,16,24) 3
Wild Eyes (20)
Wild Turkey (9)
Wild Tyme (3,24)
Winds Of Change (21) 38
Wings Of A Lie (25)
With Your Love (15,18) 12
Won't You Try Saturday Afternoon (3,16,24)
Wooden Ships (6,16,24)
X•M (8)
Young Girl Sunday Blues (medley) (3)

JEFFREYS, Garland

R&B-rock-reggae singer from Brooklyn born circa 1944.

DEBUT DATE	PEAK POS	WKS CHR	GOLD	#	ARTIST — Album Title	$	Label & Number
3/26/77	140	10		1	Ghost Writer	$8	A&M 4629
4/15/78	99	10		2	One-Eyed Jack	$8	A&M 4681
9/22/79	151	5		3	American Boy & Girl	$8	A&M 4778
3/21/81	59	18		4	Escape Artist	$8	Epic 36983
10/31/81	163	4		5	Rock & Roll Adult ...[L]	$8	Epic 37436
2/26/83	176	4		6	Guts For Love	$8	Epic 38190

American Backslide (6)
American Boy & Girl (3)
Bad Dream (3)
Been There And Back (2)
Bound To Get Ahead Someday (5)
Bring Back The Love (3)
Christine (4)
City Kids (3)

Cool Down Boy (1,5)
Dance Up (6)
Desperation Drive (6)
El Salvador (6)
Fidelity (6)
Ghost Of A Chance (4)
Ghost Writer (1)
Graveyard Rock (4)
Guts For Love (6)

Haunted House (2)
I May Not Be Your Kind (1,5)
If Mao Could See Me Now (3)
Innocent (4)
Jump Jump (4)
Keep On Trying (2)
Lift Me Up (1)
Livin' For Me (3)
Loneliness (6)

Matador (3,5)
Modern Lovers (4)
Mystery Kids (4)
New York Skyline (1)
Night Of The Living Dead (3)
96 Tears (4,5) 66
No Woman No Cry (2)
Oh My Soul (3)
One-Eyed Jack (2)

Real Man (6)
Rebel Love (6)
Reelin' (2)
R.O.C.K. (4,5)
Rough And Ready (1)
Scream In The Night (2)
She Didn't Lie (2)
Ship Of Fools (3)
Shoot The Moonlight Out (3)

Shout (6)
Spanish Town (6)
Surrender (6)
35 Millimeter Dreams (1,5)
True Confessions (4)
What Does It Take (To Win Your Love) (6)
Why-O (1)
Wild In The Streets (1,5)

DEBUT DATE	PEAK POS	WKS CHR	GOLD	ARTIST — Album Title	$	Label & Number

JELLYBEAN
John Benitez — renown Manhattan club DJ/remixer/producer. Native of the Bronx. Career took off with his "Flashdance" and "Maniac" remixes, later to include many of Madonna's hits.

| 9/5/87 | **101** | 11 | | Just Visiting This Planet.. | **$8** | Chrysalis 41569 |

features vocalists Elisa Fiorillo, Steven Dante and Adele Bertei

Am I Dreaming	Jingo	Little Too Good To Me	Walking In My Sleep
Hypnotized (By Your Touch)	Just A Mirage	**Real Thing** *82*	**Who Found Who** *16*

JELLYFISH
San Francisco band: Jason Falkner (guitar), Andy Sturmer (vocals, drums), and brothers Chris (bass) and Roger Manning (keyboards).

| 11/17/90+ | **124** | 27 | | Bellybutton .... | **$12** | Charisma 91400 |

All I Want Is Everything	Bedspring Kiss	I Wanna Stay Home	Man I Used To Be	She Still Loves Him
Baby's Coming Back *62*	Calling Sarah	King Is Half-Undressed	Now She Knows She's Wrong	That Is Why

JENKINS, Gordon
Born on 5/12/10 in Webster Groves, Missouri; died on 5/1/84. Pianist/arranger in the early 1930s with Isham Jones, Benny Goodman and others. Musical director/conductor for Decca Records beginning in 1945.

| 11/24/56 | **13** | 4 | | Gordon Jenkins complete Manhattan Tower .... | **$25** | Capitol 766 |

a musical narrative originally composed by Jenkins in 1945

Happiness Cocktail	Magic Fire	Married I Can Always Get	New York's My Home	Party, The	Statue Of Liberty
I'm Learnin' My Latin	Magical City	Never Leave Me	Once Upon A Dream	Repeat After Me	This Close To The Dawn

★★128★★ JENNINGS, Waylon
Born on 6/15/37 in Littlefield, Texas. While working as a DJ in Lubbock, Texas, Waylon befriended Buddy Holly. Holly produced Waylon's first record "Jole Blon" in 1958. Waylon then joined with Buddy's backing band as bass guitarist on the fateful "Winter Dance Party" tour in 1959. Established himself in the mid-1970s as a leader of the "outlaw" movement in country music. Married to Jessi Colter since 1969. In the films *Nashville Rebel*, *MacKintosh And T.J.* and *Urban Cowboy*. Also see *The Outlaws* and *Highwayman* in Concept Albums.

| 10/4/69 | **169** | 4 | | 1 Country-Folk .... | **$25** | RCA 4180 |

WAYLON JENNINGS & THE KIMBERLYS

5/16/70	**192**	2		2 Waylon	**$15**	RCA 4260
8/11/73	**185**	5		3 Honky Tonk Heroes	**$10**	RCA 0240
10/5/74	**105**	17		4 The Ramblin' Man..	**$10**	RCA 0734
7/5/75	**49**	21	●	5 Dreaming My Dreams	**$10**	RCA 1062
4/17/76	**189**	4		6 Mackintosh & T.J. ....[S]	**$10**	RCA 1520

includes "(Stay All Night) Stay A Little Longer" by Willie Nelson; "Back In The Saddle Again," "Crazy Arms," "Gardenia Waltz" and "Shopping" by The Waylors

| 7/17/76 | **34** | 35 | ● | 7 Are You Ready For The Country .... | **$10** | RCA 1816 |
| 12/18/76+ | **46** | 17 | ● | 8 Waylon Live ....[L] | **$10** | RCA 1108 |

recorded in Dallas and Austin, Texas (1974)

| 5/21/77 | **15** | 33 | ▲ | 9 Ol' Waylon .... | **$8** | RCA 2317 |
| 2/4/78 | **12** | 29 | ▲² | 10 Waylon & Willie .... | **$8** | RCA 2686 |

WAYLON JENNINGS & WILLIE NELSON

10/21/78	**48**	24	●	11 I've Always Been Crazy	**$8**	RCA 2979
5/5/79	**28**	115	▲³	12 Greatest Hits ....[G]	**$8**	RCA 3378
11/10/79	**49**	28	●	13 What Goes Around Comes Around	**$8**	RCA 3493
6/7/80	**36**	43	●	14 Music Man	**$8**	RCA 3602
3/21/81	**43**	19	●	15 Leather and Lace	**$8**	RCA 3931

WAYLON & JESSI (wife Jessi Colter)

| 3/6/82 | **39** | 23 | | 16 Black On Black .... | **$8** | RCA 4247 |
| 10/30/82 | **57** | 22 | ● | 17 WWII .... | **$8** | RCA 4455 |

WAYLON & WILLIE

| 4/30/83 | **109** | 11 | | 18 It's Only Rock & Roll .... | **$8** | RCA 4673 |
| 5/21/83 | **60** | 16 | | 19 Take It To The Limit .... | **$8** | Columbia 38562 |

WILLIE NELSON with WAYLON JENNINGS

| 8/18/90 | **172** | 5 | | 20 The Eagle .... | **$12** | Epic 46104 |
| 8/3/91 | **193** | 3 | | 21 Clean Shirt .... | **$12** | Epic 47462 |

WAYLON & WILLIE

Ain't No God In Mexico (3)
All Around Cowboy (6)
All Of Me Belongs To You (2)
Amanda (4,12) *54*
Angel Eyes (Angel Eyes) (18)
Another Man's Fool (13)
Are You Ready For The Country (7)
Are You Sure Hank Done It This Way (5,12) *60*
As The 'Billy World Turns (11)
Belle Of The Ball (9)
Billy (11)
Black Rose (3)
Blackjack County Chains (19)
Bob Wills Is Still The King (5,6,8)
Brand New Goodbye Song (9)
Breakin' Down (18)
Brown Eyed Handsome Man (2)
Buddy Holly Hits Medley (3)
But You Know I Love You (1)
Can't You See (7) *97*

Cindy, Oh Cindy (1)
Cloudy Days (4)
Clyde (14,18)
Come Stay With Me (1)
Come With Me (14)
Couple More Years (7)
Do It Again (14)
Don't Cuss The Fiddle (10)
Don't Play The Game (2)
Don't You Think This Outlaw Bit's Done Get Out Of Hand (1,18)
Door Is Always Open (5)
Dreaming My Dreams With You (5)
Drivin' Nails In The Wall (3)
Dukes Of Hazzard (Good Ol' Boys), Theme From (14) *82*
Eagle, The (20)
Elvis Hits Medley (9)
Folsom Prison Blues (16)
Games People Play (1)
Get Naked With Me (18)
Girl I Can Tell (You're Trying To Work It Out) (11)

Gold Dust Woman [solo: Waylon] (10)
Gonna Write A Letter (16)
Good Hearted Woman (8,12,18) *25*
(Good Ol' Boys) ..see: Dukes Of Hazzard
Good Ol' Nights (21)
Guitars That Won't Stay In Tune (21)
He Went To Paris (14)
Her Man (20)
Heroes (17)
High Time (You Quit Your Lowdown Ways) (5)
Homeward Bound (19)
Honky Tonk Blues (16)
Honky Tonk Heroes (3,12)
House Of The Rising Sun (8)
Hunger, The (4)
I Ain't Living Long Like This (13)
I Ain't The One (15)
I Believe You Can (15)
I Can Get Off On You (10)

I Can't Keep My Hands Off Of You (4)
I Could Write A Book About You (21)
I Got The Train Sittin' Waitin' (13)
I May Never Pass This Way Again (2)
I Recall A Gypsy Woman (5)
I Think I'm Gonna Kill Myself (9)
I Walk The Line (11)
I'll Be Alright (15)
I'll Go Back To Her (7)
I'm A Ramblin' Man (4,8,12,18) *75*
I've Always Been Crazy (11,12,18)
I've Been A Long Time Leaving (But I'll Be A Long Time Gone) (5)
If I Can Find A Clean Shirt (21)
If You See Her (13)
If You See Me Getting Smaller (9)

It'll Be Her (4)
It's Alright (14)
It's Only Rock & Roll (18)
It's The World's Gone Crazy (13)
Ivory Tower (13)
Jack A Diamonds (7)
Just Across The Way (21)
Just To Satisfy You (16) *52*
Ladies Love Outlaws (12,18)
Lady In The Harbor [solo: Waylon] (17)
Last Cowboy Song [solo: Waylon] (17)
Last Letter (8)
Let Her Do The Walking (18)
Let Me Tell You My Mind (1)
Let's All Help The Cowboys (Sing The Blues) (5)
Let's Turn Back The Years (5)
Living Legends (A Dyin' Breed) (18)
Lonesome, On'ry And Mean (12)
Long Time Ago (11)

Long Way Back Home (1)
Lookin' For A Feeling [solo: Waylon] (10)
Loves' Legalities (18)
Low Down Freedom (3)
Lucille (9,18)
Luckenbach, Texas (Back To The Basics Of Love) (9,12,18) *25*
MacArthur Park (1,7) *93*
Makin's Of A Song (21)
Mammas Don't Let Your Babies Grow Up To Be Cowboys (10,12) *42*
Mary Ann Regrets (1)
May I Borrow Some Sugar From You (16,17)
Me And Bobby McGee (8)
Me And Paul (8)
Memories Of You And I (4)
Mental Revenge (18)
Midnight Rider (4)
Mr. Shuck And Jive (17)
Nashville Wimmin (14)
No Love At All (19)
No Middle Ground (18)

DEBUT DATE	PEAK POS	WKS CHR	GOLD	ARTIST — Album Title	$	Label & Number

JENNINGS, Waylon — Cont'd

Oklahoma Sunshine (4)
Old Age And Treachery (21)
Old Church Hymns And Nursery Rhymes (20)
Old Five And Dimers (Like Me) (3)
Old Friend (7,19)
Old Love, New Eyes (13)
Old Mother's Locket Trick [solo: Waylon] (17)
Omaha (3)
Only Daddy That'll Walk The Line (12)
Out Among The Stars (13)
Pastels And Harmony (15)
Pick Up The Tempo (8,10)
Precious Memories (7)
Put Me On A Train Back To Texas (21)

Rainy Day Woman (4,8)
Rainy Seasons (15)
Reno And Me (20)
Ride Me Down Easy (3,6)
Rocks From Rolling Stones (21)
Roman Candles [solo: Waylon] (17)
Satin Sheets (9)
She's Looking Good (5)
Shine (16)
Shutting Out The Light (2)
(Sittin' On) The Dock Of The Bay (17)
So Good Woman (7)
Song For The Life (16)
Storms Never Last (14,15)
Sweet Caroline (9)
Sweet Music Man (14)

T For Texas (8)
Take It To The Limit (19)
Teddy Bear Song [solo: Waylon] (17)
Them Old Love Songs (7)
These New Changing Times (1)
Thirty Third Of August (2)
This Is Getting Funny (But There Ain't Nobody Laughing) (9)
This Time (18)
This Time Tomorrow (I'll Be Gone) (2)
Till I Gain Control Again (9,19)
Tonight The Bottle Let Me Down (11)
Too Close To Call (20)

Tryin' To Outrun The Wind (21)
Two Old Sidewinders (21)
Waking Up With You (20)
Waltz Across Texas (4)
Waymore's Blues (5)
We Had It All (3,19)
We Made It As Lovers (We Just Couldn't Make It As Friends) (16)
What About You (14)
What Bothers Me Most (20)
What Goes Around (13)
What's Happened To Blue Eyes (15)
Where Corn Don't Grow (20)
Where Love Has Died (2)
Whistlers And Jugglers (11)
Why Baby Why (19)

Why Do I Have To Choose (19)
Wild Side Of Life (15)
Willy The Wandering Gypsy And Me (3)
Women Do Know How To Carry On (16)
Workin' Cheap (20)
World Of Our Own (1)
Would You Lay With Me (In A Field Of Stone) (19)
Write Your Own Songs (17)
Wrong (20)
Wurlitzer Prize (I Don't Want To Get Over You) [solo: Waylon] (10)
Year That Clayton Delaney Died (17)
Year 2003 Minus 25 (10)

Yellow Haired Woman (2)
Yes, Virginia (2)
You Ask Me To (3)
You Never Can Tell (C'est La Vie) (15)
You're Not My Same Sweet Baby (15)

JEROME, Henry
Bandleader/composer popular in the late '40s and '50s. Born on 11/12/17 in New York City.

| 10/9/61 | 42 | 2 | | Brazen Brass Goes Hollywood .... [I] | $12 | Decca 4085 |

Around The World
Colonel Bogey
Gigi

High Noon (Do Not Forsake Me)
Love Is A Many-Splendored Thing

Man With The Golden Arm, Main Title From
Moonglow And Theme From "Picnic"

Moulin Rouge, Song From
Summer Place, Theme From A
Tammy - Cha Cha Cha

Third Man Theme
Three Coins In The Fountain - Cha Cha

(Where Is Your Heart) ..see: Moulin Rouge

JESUS & MARY CHAIN, The
Scottish rock group led by vocalists/guitarists/brothers James and William Reid with bassist Douglas Hart and rotating drummers.

2/22/86	188	4		1 Psycho Candy	$8	Reprise 25383
10/17/87	161	4		2 Darklands	$8	Warner 25656
6/18/88	192	3		3 Barbed Wire Kisses	$8	Warner 25729
11/25/89+	105	25		4 Automatic	$8	Warner 26015
5/2/92	158	2		5 Honey's Dead	$12	Def Amer. 26830

About You (2)
Almost Gold (5)
April Skies (2)
Between Planets (4)
Blues From A Gun (4)
Catchfire (5)
Cherry Came Too (2)
Coast To Coast (4)
Cut Dead (1)
Darklands (2)
Deep One Perfect Morning (2)

Don't Ever Change (3)
Down On Me (2)
Everything's Alright When You're Down (3)
Fall (2)
Far Gone And Out (5)
Frequency (5)
Gimme Hell (4)
Good For My Soul (5)
Half Way To Crazy (4)
Happy Place (3)

Happy When It Rains (2)
Hardest Walk (1)
Head (3)
Head On (4)
Her Way Of Praying (4)
Here Comes Alice (4)
Hit (3)
I Can't Get Enough (5)
In A Hole (1)
Inside Me (1)
It's So Hard (1)

Just Like Honey (1)
Just Out Of Reach (3)
Kill Surf City (3)
Living End (1)
My Little Underground (1)
Never Understand (1)
Nine Million Rainy Days (2)
On The Wall (2,3)
Psycho Candy (5)
Reverence (5)
Rider (3)

Rollercoaster (5)
Sidewalking (3)
Something's Wrong (1)
Sowing Seeds (1)
Sugar Ray (5)
Sundown (5)
Surfin' USA (3)
Swing (5)
Take It (4)
Taste Of Cindy (1,3)
Taste The Floor (1)

Teenage Lust (5)
Tumbledown (5)
UV Ray (4)
Upside Down (3)
Who Do You Love (3)
You Trip Me Up (1)

JESUS JONES
London quintet: Mike Edwards (vocals, guitar), Jerry De Borg (guitar), Barry D (keyboards), Al Jaworski (bass) and Gen (drums).

| 2/23/91 | 25 | 52 ▲ | | Doubt............... | $12 | SBK 95715 |

Are You Satisfied
Blissed
I'm Burning

International Bright Young Thing
Real, Real, Real 4

Nothing To Hold Me
Right Here, Right Now 2
Stripped

Trust Me
Two And Two

Welcome Back Victoria
Who? Where? Why?

JETBOY
San Francisco heavy-metal band: Mickey Finn (vocals), Fernie Rod, Billy Rowe, Ron Tostenson and Sam Yaffa.

| 11/12/88 | 135 | 10 | | Feel The Shake............... | $8 | MCA 42235 |

Bad Disease
Bloodstone

Feel The Shake
Fire In My Heart

Hard Climb
Hometown Blues

Locked In A Cage
Make Some Noise

Snakebite
Talkin'

★★45★★ JETHRO TULL
Progressive rock group formed in 1968 in Blackpool, England. Consisted of Ian Anderson (b: 8/10/47, Edinburgh, Scotland; lead singer, flutist), Mick Abrahams (guitar), Glenn Cornick (bass) and Clive Bunker (drums). Named band after 18th century agriculturalist/inventor of seed drill Jethro Tull. Recorded several rock opera/concept albums. Abrahams left after recording of first album (in 1968) to form Blodwyn Pig, replaced by Martin Barre. Added keyboardist John Evan in 1970. Cornick replaced by Jeffrey Hammond-Hammond in 1971. Bunker left in late 1971, replaced by Barriemore Barlow. John Glascock replaced Hammond-Hammond by 1976. Glascock died in 1979, replaced by bassist David Pegg. Since 1980, Anderson and Barre have fronted several lineups which have included Pegg and drummer Doane Perry (Maxus).

3/1/69	62	17		1 This Was	$20	Reprise 6336
10/11/69	20	40	●	2 Stand Up	$20	Reprise 6360
5/9/70	11	41	●	3 Benefit	$15	Reprise 6400
5/15/71	7	76	▲³	4 Aqualung	$15	Reprise 2035
5/20/72	1²	46	●	5 Thick As A Brick	$15	Reprise 2072
11/11/72	3	31	●	6 Living In The Past .... [K]	$15	Chrysalis 2106 [2]
				primarily features unreleased material (1968-71); side 3 recorded live in Carnegie Hall		
7/21/73	1¹	32	●	7 A Passion Play	$12	Chrysalis 1040
10/26/74	2³	31	●	8 War Child	$10	Chrysalis 1067
9/27/75	7	14	●	9 Minstrel In The Gallery	$10	Chrysalis 1082
1/24/76	13	23	▲	10 M.U. - The Best Of Jethro Tull .... [G]	$10	Chrysalis 1078
5/29/76	14	21		11 Too Old To Rock 'N' Roll: Too Young To Die!	$10	Chrysalis 1111
3/5/77	8	22	●	12 Songs From The Wood	$8	Chrysalis 1132
12/3/77	94	6		13 Repeat-The Best Of Jethro Tull, Vol. II .... [G]	$8	Chrysalis 1135

DEBUT DATE	PEAK POS	WKS CHR	GOLD	ARTIST — Album Title	$	Label & Number
				JETHRO TULL — Cont'd		
4/29/78	**19**	17	●	14 Heavy Horses	$8	Chrysalis 1175
10/21/78	**21**	15	●	15 Jethro Tull Live - Bursting Out ....[L]	$10	Chrysalis 1201 [2]
10/6/79	**22**	17	●	16 Stormwatch..	$8	Chrysalis 1238
9/13/80	**30**	12		17 "A"	$8	Chrysalis 1301
5/1/82	**19**	17		18 The Broadsword And The Beast	$8	Chrysalis 1380
10/27/84	**76**	12		19 Under Wraps	$8	Chrysalis 41461
10/10/87	**32**	28	●	20 Crest Of A Knave......................................	$8	Chrysalis 41590
8/13/88	**97**	15		21 20 Years Of Jethro Tull ....[K]	$30	Chrysalis 41653 [5]
				features rare recordings plus unreleased and hit material; includes a 24-page booklet		
9/30/89	**56**	18		22 Rock Island	$8	Chrysalis 21708
9/28/91	**88**	5		23 Catfish Rising	$12	Chrysalis 21863
10/10/92	**150**	2		24 A Little Light Music ....[L]	$12	Chrysalis 21954
				live concert performances recorded around the world in May 1992		

Acres Wild (14)
Aeroplane (21)
Alive And Well And Living In (6)
And Further On (17)
And The Mouse Police Never Sleeps (14)
Another Christmas Song (22)
Apogee (19)
Aqualung (4,10,15,21)
Back-Door Angels (8)
Back To The Family (2)
Bad-Eyed And Loveless (11)
Baker St. Muse Medley (9)
Batteries Not Included (17)
Beastie (14)
Beggar's Farm (1)
Beltane (21)
Big Dipper (11)
Big Riff And Mando (21)
Black Satin Dancer (9,21)
Black Sunday (17)
Blues Instrumental (Untitled) (21)
Bouree (2,6,13,15,21,24)
Broadsword (18)
Budapest (20)
Bundle In The Jungle (8,10,21) 12
By Kind Permission Of (6)
Cat's Squirrel (1)
Chateau D'Isaster Tapes Medley (21)
Cheap Day Return (4,21)
Cheerio (18)
Chequered Flag (Dead Or Alive) (11)
Christmas Song (6,24)
Clasp, The (18,21)
Cold Wind To Valhalla (9,21)
Conundrum (15)
Coronach (21)
Crazed Institution (11)
Cross-Eyed Mary (4,13,15)

Crossfire (17)
Crossword (21)
Cup Of Wonder (12)
Dambusters March/Medley (15)
Dark Ages (16)
Dharma For One (1,6)
Dr. Bogenbroom (6)
Doctor To My Disease (23)
Down At The End Of Your Road (21)
Driving Song (6)
Dun Ringill (16,21)
Ears Of Tin (22)
Elegy (16)
European Legacy (19)
Fallen On Hard Times (18,21)
Farm On The Freeway (20,21)
Fat Man (2,10,21)
Fire At Midnight (12)
Flute Solo Improvisation (medley) (15)
Flying Colours (18)
Flying Dutchman (16)
For A Thousand Mothers (21)
For Michael Collins, Jeffrey And Me (1)
4.W.D. (Low Ratio) (17)
From A Dead Beat To An Old Greaser (11,24)
From Later (6)
Fylingdale Flyer (17)
Glory Row (13)
God Rest Ye Merry Gentlemen (medley) (15)
Gold-Tipped Boots, Black Jacket And Tie (23)
Grace (9,21)
Heat (19)
Heavy Horses (14)
Heavy Water (22)
Home (21)

Hunting Girl (12,15)
Hymn 43 (4,6) 91
I'm Your Gun (21)
Inside (3)
It's Breaking Me Up (1)
Jack-A-Lynn (21)
Jack Frost And The Hooded Crow (21)
Jack-In-The-Green (12,15)
Jeffrey Goes To Leicester Square (2)
John Barleycorn (24)
Journey Man (14)
Jump Start (20)
Just Trying To Be (6)
Kelpie (21)
King Henry's Madrigal (21)
Kissing Willie (22)
Ladies (8)
Lap Of Luxury (19)
Later, That Same Evening (19)
Lick Your Fingers Clean (21)
Life Is A Long Song (6,21,24)
Like A Tall Thin Girl (23)
Living In The Past (6,10,21,24) 11
Living In These Hard Times (21)
Locomotive Breath (4,10,15,21,24) 62
Look Into The Sun (2,24)
Love Story (6,21)
March The Mad Scientist (21)
Mayhem, Maybe (21)
Minstrel In The Gallery (9,13,15,21) 79
Mother Goose (4)
Moths (14,21)
Motoreyes (21)
Mountain Men (20)
Move On Alone (1)
My God (4)

My Sunday Feeling (1)
New Day Yesterday (2,13,15,21,24)
No Lullaby (14,15)
Nobody's Car (19)
North Sea Oil (16)
Nothing Is Easy (2,10)
Nothing To Say (3)
Nursie (6,21,24)
Occasional Demons (23)
Old Ghosts (16)
One Brown Mouse (14,15)
One For John Gee (21)
One White Duck (9,21,24)
Only Solitaire (8,21)
Orion (16)
Overhang (21)
Pan Dance (21)
Paparazzi (19)
Part Of The Machine (21)
Passion Play (7)
Passion Play (Edit #8) (10) 80
Passion Play Edit #9 (13)
Pibroch (Cap In Hand3) (12,21)
Pied Piper (21)
Pine Marten's Jig (17)
Play In Time (3)
Protect And Survive (17)
Pussy Willow (18,24)
Quatrain (15)
Queen And Country (8)
Quizz Kid (11)
Radio Free Moscow (19)
Rainbow Blues (10)
Raising Steam (20)
Rattlesnake Trail (22)
Reasons For Waiting (2)
Requiem (9)
Rhythm In Gold (21)
Ring Out, Solstice Bells (12)
Rock Island (22)
Rocks On The Road (23,24)

Roll Yer Own (23)
Round (1)
Rover (14)
Saboteur (19)
Said She Was A Dancer (20)
Salamander (11,21)
Saturation (21)
SeaLion (8)
Seal Driver (18)
Serenade To A Cuckoo (1) 17 (21)
Singing All Day (6)
Skating Away On The Thin Ice Of The New Day (8,10,15)
Sleeping With The Dog (23)
Slipstream (4)
Slow Marching Band (18)
Some Day The Sun Won't Shine For You (1,24)
Something's On The Move (16)
Son (3)
Song For Jeffrey (1,6,21)
Songs From The Wood (12,15,21)
Sossity; You're A Woman (3)
Sparrow On The Schoolyard Wall (21)
Steel Monkey (20)
Still Loving You Tonight (23)
Stitch In Time (21)
Stormy Monday Blues (21)
Story Of The Hare Who Lost His Spectacles (7)
Strange Avenues (22)
Strip Cartoon (21)
Summerday Sands (21)
Sunshine Day (21)
Sweet Dream (6,15,21)
Taxi Grab (21)
Teacher (3,6,10,21)
Thick As A Brick (5,15,21)
Thick As A Brick Edit #1 (10)

Thick As A Brick Edit #4 (13)
Thinking Round Corners (23)
Third Hoorah (8)
This Is Not Love (23,24)
Time For Everything (3)
To Cry You A Song (3,13)
Too Many Too (21)
Too Old To Rock 'N' Roll: Too Young To Die (11,13,15,24)
Two Fingers (8)
Under Wraps (19,21,24)
Undressed To Kill (22)
Uniform (17)
Up The 'Pool (6)
Up To Me (4)
Velvet Green (12,21)
WarChild (8,13)
Warm Sporran (16)
Watching Me Watching You (18)
We Used To Know (2)
Weathercock (14)
Whalers Dues (22)
When Jesus Came To Play (23)
Whistler, The (12) 59
White Innocence (23)
Wind-Up (4)
Witch's Promise (6,21)
With You There To Help Me (3)
Wond'ring Again (6)
Wond'ring Aloud (4,21)
Working John - Working Joe (17)
0[10] = Nothing At All (medley) (9,21)

JETS, The

Minneapolis-based family band consisting of eight brothers and sisters: Leroy, Eddie, Eugene, Haini, Rudy, Kathi, Elizabeth and Moana Wolfgramm. Their parents are from the South Pacific country of Tonga. All members play at least two instruments. Eugene left group and formed duo Boys Club in 1988.

DEBUT DATE	PEAK POS	WKS CHR	GOLD	ARTIST — Album Title	$	Label & Number
4/5/86	**21**	70	▲	1 The Jets	$8	MCA 5667
11/7/87+	**35**	50	●	2 Magic	$8	MCA 42085
9/2/89	**107**	7		3 Believe	$8	MCA 6313

Anytime (2)
Believe In Love (3)
Believe It Or Not, It's Magic (2)
Cross My Broken Heart (2) 7

Crush On You (1) 3
Curiosity (1)
Do You Remember (3)
Emotional (3)
First Time In Love (2)
Heart On The Line (1)

How Can I Be Sure (3)
I Do You (2) 20
In My Dreams (3)
La La Means I Love You (1)
Leave It To Me (3)
Love Umbrella (1)

Make It Real (2) 4
Mesmerized (1)
Only Dance (2)
Private Number (1) 47
Right Before My Eyes (1)
Rocket 2 U (1) 6

Same Love (3) 87
Sendin' All My Love (2) 88
Somebody To Love Me (3)
Under Any Moon (3)
When You're Young And In Love (2)

You Better Dance (3) 59
You Got It All (1) 3
You've Got Another Boyfriend (3)

★★432★★ JETT, Joan, & The Blackhearts

Born on 9/22/60 in Philadelphia. Played guitar with the Los Angeles female rock band The Runaways, 1975-78. Formed her backing band, the Blackhearts, in 1980. Starred in the 1987 film *Light Of Day* as the leader of a rock band called The Barbusters.

DEBUT DATE	PEAK POS	WKS CHR	GOLD	ARTIST — Album Title	$	Label & Number
3/14/81+	**51**	21		1 Bad Reputation	$8	Boardwalk 37065
12/19/81+	**2**[3]	59	▲	2 I Love Rock-n-Roll	$8	Boardwalk 33243
7/16/83	**20**	20	●	3 Album	$8	Blackheart 5437
10/27/84	**67**	21		4 Glorious Results Of A Misspent Youth	$8	Blackheart 5476
10/25/86	**105**	16		5 Good Music	$8	Blackheart 40544
5/28/88	**19**	46	▲	6 Up Your Alley	$8	Blackheart 44146
2/3/90	**36**	18		7 The Hit List	$12	Blackheart 45473
				JOAN JETT		
				Joan's cover versions of rock classics of the last 3 decades		

Back It Up (6)
Bad Reputation (1)

Be Straight (2)
Bits And Pieces (2)

Black Leather (5)
Celluloid Heroes (7)

Cherry Bomb (4)
Coney Island Whitefish (3)

Contact (5)
Crimson And Clover (2) 7

Desire (6)
Dirty Deeds (7) 36

JETT, Joan, & The Blackhearts — Cont'd

Do You Wanna Touch Me (Oh Yeah) (1) *20*	Have You Ever Seen The Rain? (7)
Doing All Right With The Boys (1)	Hold Me (4)
Don't Abuse Me (1)	Hundred Feet Away (3)
Everyday People (3) *37*	I Got No Answers (4)
Fake Friends (3) *35*	**I Hate Myself For Loving You** (6) *8*
French Song (1)	I Love Playin' With Fire (3)
Frustrated (4)	I Love You Love Me Love (4)
Fun, Fun, Fun (5)	I Need Someone (4)
Good Music (5) *83*	I Still Dream About You (6)
Had Enough (3)	I Wanna Be Your Dog (1)
Handyman (3)	

Other columns:
- (I'm Gonna) Run Away (2)
- If Ya Want My Luv (5)
- Jezebel (1)
- Just Like In The Movies (6)
- Just Lust (5)
- Let Me Go (1)
- Little Drummer Boy (2)
- **Little Liar** (6) *19*
- Long Time (4)
- Love Hurts (7)
- Love Is Pain (2)
- Love Like Mine (4)
- Love Me Two Times (7)
- Make Believe (1)
- Nag (2)
- New Orleans (4)
- Outlaw (5)
- Play That Song Again (6)
- Pretty Vacant (7)
- Push And Stomp (4)
- Ridin' With James Dean (4)
- Roadrunner (5)
- Roadrunner USA (7)
- Secret Love (3)
- Shout (1)
- Someday (4)
- Talkin Bout My Baby (4)
- This Means War (5)
- Time Has Come Today (7)
- Too Bad On Your Birthday (1)
- Tossin' & Turnin' (3)
- Tulane (6)
- Tush (7)
- Up From The Skies (7)
- Victim Of Circumstance (2)
- Why Can't We Be Happy (3)
- Wooly Bully (1)
- You Don't Know What You've Got (1)
- You Don't Own Me (1)
- You Got Me Floatin' (5)
- You Want In I Want Out (6)
- You're Too Possessive (2)

JIGSAW
Pop-rock quartet from England: Des Dyer (lead vocals), Clive Scott, Tony Campbell and Barrie Bernard.

12/13/75+	55	19		Sky High	$10	Chelsea 509

- Baby Don't Do It
- Call Collect
- Have You Heard The News
- I've Seen The Film, I've Read The Book
- Listen To The Joker
- **Love Fire 30**
- Mention My Name
- Mystic Harmony
- **Sky High 3**
- Tell Me Why
- That's The Way It Goes

★★485★★ JIMENEZ, Jose
Real name: Bill Dana. Born William Szarthmary on 10/5/24 in Quincy, Massachusetts. Head writer for TV's *Steve Allen Show*. Star of own TV series from 1963-65. Created the Latin American comic character Jose Jimenez for Steve Allen's TV series.

8/1/60	15	29		1 My Name...Jose Jimenez .... [C]	$20	Signature 1013
7/17/61	5	51		**2 Jose Jimenez - The Astronaut (The First Man In Space)**........ [C]	$20	Kapp 1238
12/25/61+	109	9		3 More...Jose Jimenez .... [C]	$20	Kapp 1215
1/13/62	32	22		4 Jose Jimenez In Orbit/Bill Dana On Earth .... [C]	$20	Kapp 1257
10/13/62	16	20		5 Jose Jimenez Talks To Teenagers Of All Ages .... [C]	$20	Kapp 1304
2/23/63	30	14		6 Jose Jimenez - Our Secret Weapon .... [C]	$20	Kapp 1320
12/14/63	128	4		7 Jose Jimenez In Jollywood .... [C]	$20	Kapp 1332

- Admiral, The (6)
- Another History Lesson - George Washington (5)
- Any Questions? (2)
- Artist, The (3)
- **Astronaut (Parts 1 & 2)** (2) *19*
- Baseball Star (5)
- Bob Sled Racer (1)
- Broadway Writer (3)
- Burgemeister, The (1)
- Cheerleader, The (5)
- Child Star (7)
- Civil Defense Director (6)
- Coast Guardsman (6)
- Darling, Je Vous Aime Beaucoup (2)
- Deep Sea Diver (1)
- Dialogue Director (7)
- Director Of The Central Intelligence Agency (6)
- Etiquette Expert (5)
- Everything's A OK (4)
- General, The (6)
- History Lesson - Christopher Columbus (5)
- Hollywood Agent (7)
- Hollywood Columnist (7)
- Infantryman, The (6)
- J.J.J. Salesman (3)
- Jingle Bells (1)
- Jose And Cleopatra (7)
- Judo Expert (3)
- K-9 Corps (3)
- King Of The Surf (7)
- Lance Playboy (7)
- Lion Tamer (4)
- Look Award (1)
- Mail Call (6)
- Man In The Pub (1)
- Marine Drill Instructor (6)
- Marriage Counselor (5)
- Musical Director (1)
- My Alma Mater (5)
- My Funny Valentine (4)
- My Night Club Act (2)
- Paratrooper, The (6)
- Piano Tuner (3)
- Presenting Bill Dana (2)
- Presidential Trip (1)
- Press Conference (1)
- Psychiatrist, The (7)
- Rancher, The (4)
- Sailor, The (6)
- Santa Claus (1)
- Shakespeare (1)
- Shakespearean Actor (7)
- Shine On Harvest Moon (4)
- Skin Diver (1)
- Smog Expert (7)
- Submarine Officer (3)
- Teenage Problems (5)
- Television Engineer (7)
- U.S. Senator (1,4)
- Vocational Guidance Counselor (5)
- Warmup From Spike Jones Show (3)
- What Kind Of Fool Am I (7)
- With Steve (1)

JIVE BUNNY and the Mastermixers
British dance outfit: DJ Les Hemstock and mixers John Pickles, Andy Pickles and Ian Morgan.

1/6/90	26	18	●	The Album	$12	Music Fac. 91322

- Do You Wanna Rock
- Glen Miller Medley
- Hopping Mad
- Lover's Mix
- Rock And Roll Party Mix
- Swing Sisters Swing
- **Swing The Mood 11**
- **That's What I Like 69**

J.J. FAD
Los Angeles female rap trio: M.C.J.B. (Juana Burns), Baby-D (Dania Birks) and Sassy C (Michelle Franklin). J.J. Fad stands for Just Jammin' Fresh And Def.

7/23/88	49	30	●	Supersonic - The Album	$8	Ruthless 90959

- Blame It On The Muzick
- Eenie Meenie Beats
- In The Mix
- **Is It Love 92**
- Let's Get Hyped
- My Dope Intro
- Now Really
- **Supersonic 30**
- Time Tah Get Stupid
- **Way Out 61**

JO, Damita
Born Damita Jo DuBlanc in Austin, Texas. Featured singer with Steve Gibson & The Red Caps (married to Gibson), 1951-53 and 1959-60. Regular on Red Foxx's TV variety series in 1977.

3/27/65	121	4		1 This Is Damita Jo	$15	Epic 26131
5/6/67	169	2		2 If You Go Away	$15	Epic 26244

- Affair To Remember (2)
- Alice Blue Gown (1)
- Bye Bye Love (1)
- Dinner For One Please James (2)
- Happiness Is A Thing Called Joe (1)
- He Loves Me (1)
- I Could Have Told You (1)
- I Had Someone Else Before I Had You (1)
- I'll Get Along Somehow (1)
- If You Are But A Dream (1,2)
- **If You Go Away (2) 68**
- It Could Happen To You (1)
- Love, I Found You (2)
- Love Is Here To Stay (1)
- My Man's Gone Now (1)
- No Guilty Feelings (2)
- Nobody Knows You When You're Down And Out (1)
- Silver Dollar (1)
- Time To Love And A Time To Cry (Petite Fleur) (2)
- What Did I Have That I Don't Have? (2)
- Yellow Days (2)

JOBIM, Antonio Carlos
Brazilian guitarist/pianist/songwriter/vocalist. Writer of hits "Girl From Ipanema" and "Desafinado." Also see Astrud Gilberto.

9/11/65	57	14		1 The Wonderful World Of Antonio Carlos Jobim	$15	Warner 1611
				backing orchestra conducted by Nelson Riddle		
4/15/67	19	28		2 Francis Albert Sinatra & Antonio Carlos Jobim	$15	Reprise 1021
				FRANK SINATRA & ANTONIO CARLOS JOBIM		
1/13/68	114	11		3 Wave .... [I]	$12	A&M 3002
1/9/71	196	2		4 Stone Flower .... [I]	$12	CTI 6002

- Amparo (4)
- Andorinha (4)
- Antigua (3)
- Aqua De Beber (1)
- Batidinha (3)
- Baubles, Bangles And Beads (2)
- Bonita (1)
- Brazil (4)
- Captain Bacardi (3)
- Change Partners (2)
- Children's Games (4)
- Choro (4)
- Dialogo (3)
- Dindi (1,2)
- Favela (1)
- Felicidade, A (1)
- Girl From Ipanema (2)
- God And The Devil In The Land Of The Sun (4)
- How Insensitive (2)
- I Concentrate On You (2)
- If You Never Come To Me (2)
- Lamento (3)
- Look To The Sky (3)
- Meditation (2)
- Mojave (3)
- Once I Loved (2)
- Por Toda A Minha Vida (1)
- Quiet Nights Of Quiet Stars (Corcovado) (2)
- Red Blouse (3)
- Sabia (4)
- Samba Do Aviao (1)
- She's A Carioca (1)
- So' Tinha De Ser Com Voce (1)
- Stone Flower (4)
- Surfboard (1)
- Tereza My Love (4)
- Triste (3)
- Useless Landscape (1)
- Valsa De Porto Das Caixas (1)
- Wave (3)

DEBUT DATE	PEAK POS	WKS CHR	GOLD	ARTIST — Album Title	$	Label & Number

JoBOXERS
London-based pop quintet led by American expatriate Dig Wayne (vocals). Includes Bristol, England natives Rob Marche, Dave Collard, Chris Bostock and Sean McLusky.

| 10/15/83 | 70 | 15 | | Like Gangbusters .... | $8 | RCA 4847 |

Boxerbeat	Crosstown Walk Up	Fully Booked	Johnny Friendly	Not My Night
Crime Of Passion	Curious George	Hide Nor Hair	**Just Got Lucky 36**	She's Got Sex

JODECI
Two pairs of brothers/vocalists from Tiny Grove, North Carolina: Joel "JoJo" and Gedric "K-Ci" Hailey, with Dalvin and Donald "Devante Swing" DeGrate Jr. Group name pronounced: JOE-deh-see.

| 9/14/91+ | 18 | 74↑ ▲² | | Forever My Lady .... | $12 | Uptown 10198 |

Come & Talk To Me *11*	**Forever My Lady** *25*	**I'm Still Waiting** *85*	My Phone	**Stay** *41*	Treat U
(553-NASTY)	Gotta Love	It's Alright	Play Thang	Xs We Share	U & I

JOE & EDDIE
Joe Gilbert and Eddie Brown — black folk duo from Berkeley, California.

| 1/18/64 | 119 | 7 | | 1 There's A Meetin' Here Tonite ....[L] | $15 | Crescendo 86 |
| 2/15/64 | 140 | 4 | | 2 Coast To Coast.. | $15 | Crescendo 96 |

Amen! (2)	I Laid Around (1)	Lonely And A Lonesome	Old Man (1)	There's A Meetin' Here
Children Go! (1)	I Loved A Lass (2)	Traveler (1)	San Francisco Bay Blues (2)	Tonite (1)
Crawfish (2)	Joshua (2)	Make A Long Time Man Feel	Scarlet Ribbons (1)	Water Is Wide (2)
Drinking Gourd (1)	Kisses Sweeter Than Wine	Bad (1)	Sing Hallelujah! (2)	What's That I Hear?
Farewell My Cindy Jane (2)	(1)	Mariah (1)	Summer's Over (1)	(Freedom Calling) (2)
First Time (?)	Laurie (1)	Muddy Old River (1)		Work Song (1)

★★82★★ **JOEL, Billy**
Born William Martin Joel on 5/9/49 in Hicksville, Long Island, New York. Formed his first band, The Echoes, in 1964, which later became The Lost Souls. Member of Long Island group The Hassles in the late 1960s. Later formed rock duo, Attila, with The Hassles' drummer, Jon Small. Signed solo to Columbia Records in 1973. Involved in a serious motorcycle accident on Long Island in 1982. Married supermodel Christie Brinkley on 3/23/85. Toured and recorded in Russia in 1987. Won Grammy's Legends Award in 1990. Joel composed all of his hits.

1/5/74	27	40	▲³	1 Piano Man	$10	Columbia 32544
11/2/74	35	18	●	2 Streetlife Serenade	$10	Columbia 33146
6/5/76	122	12	▲	3 Turnstiles	$10	Columbia 33848
10/8/77+	2⁶	137	▲⁷	4 The Stranger	$10	Columbia 34987
10/28/78	1⁸	76	▲⁶	5 52nd Street	$10	Columbia 35609
				1979 Grammy winner: Album of the Year		
3/22/80	1⁶	73	▲⁵	6 Glass Houses	$10	Columbia 36384
10/3/81	8	27	▲	7 Songs In The Attic..[L]	$10	Columbia 37461
				1980 concert tour recordings of pre-*Stranger* songs		
10/16/82	7	35	▲	8 The Nylon Curtain	$10	Columbia 38200
8/20/83	4	111	▲⁵	9 An Innocent Man	$10	Columbia 38837
1/14/84	158	8		10 Cold Spring Harbor...[E-R]	$10	Columbia 38984
				remix/reissue of Joel's first album (1971)		
7/20/85	6	65	▲⁴	11 Greatest Hits, Volume I & Volume II ....[G]	$12	Columbia 40121 [2]
8/16/86	7	47	▲²	12 The Bridge	$10	Columbia 40402
11/7/87	38	18	●	13 Kohu,ept...[L]	$12	Columbia 40996 [2]
				recorded in Leningrad (St. Petersburg), Russia		
11/4/89	1¹	69	▲³	14 Storm Front	$10	Columbia 44366

Ain't No Crime (1)	Everybody Loves You Now	**Keeping The Faith** (9) *18*	**Piano Man** (1,11) *25*	Stiletto (5,13)	Weekend Song (2)
All For Leyna (6)	(7,10)	Last Of The Big Time	**Pressure** (8,11) *20*	Stop In Nevada (1)	When In Rome (14)
All You Wanna Do Is Dance	Falling Of The Rain (10)	Spenders (7)	Roberta (2)	Storm Front (14)	Where's The Orchestra? (8)
(3)	52nd Street (5)	Laura (8)	Room Of Our Own (8)	**Stranger, The** (4,11)	Why Judy Why (10)
Allentown (8,11,13) *17*	Get It Right The First Time	**Leave A Tender Moment**	Root Beer Rag (3)	Streetlife Serenader (2,7)	**Worse Comes To Worst**
And So It Goes (14) *37*	(4)	**Alone** (9) *27*	Rosalinda's Eyes (5)	Summer, Highland Falls	(1) *80*
Angry Young Man (3,13)	Getting Closer (12)	**Leningrad** (13)	Running On Ice (12)	(3,7)	You Can Make Me Free (10)
Baby Grand (12,13) *75*	**Goodnight Saigon**	**Longest Time** (9,11) *14*	**Say Goodbye To**	Surprises (8)	You Look So Good To Me (10)
Back In The U.S.S.R. (13)	(8,11,13) *56*	Los Angelenos (2,7)	**Hollywood** (3,7,11) *17*	**Tell Her About It** (9,11) *1*	**You May Be Right** (6,11) *7*
Ballad Of Billy The Kid (1,7)	Got To Begin Again (10)	**Matter Of Trust** (12,13) *10*	Scandinavian Skies (8)	Temptation (12)	You're My Home (1,7)
Big Man On Mulberry Street	Great Suburban Showdown	Mexican Connection (3)	Scenes From An Italian	**That's Not Her Style**	**You're Only Human**
(12,13)	(2)	Miami 2017 (Seen The	Restaurant (14)	(14) *77*	**(Second Wind)** (11) *9*
Big Shot (5,11,13) *14*	Half A Mile Away (5)	Lights Go Out On	Shameless (14)	**This Is The Time** (12) *18*	Zanzibar (5)
C'Etait Toi (You Were The	I Don't Want To Be Alone (6)	Broadway) (3,7)	**She's Always A Woman**	This Night (9)	
One) (6)	**I Go To Extremes** (14) *6*	**Modern Woman** (12) *10*	(4,11) *17*	Through The Long Night (6)	
Captain Jack (1,7)	I've Loved These Days (3,7)	**Movin' Out (Anthony's**	**She's Got A Way** (7,10) *23*	Times They Are A Changin'	
Careless Talk (9)	If I Only Had The Words (To	**Song)** (4,11) *17*	She's Right On Time (8)	(13)	
Christie Lee (9)	Tell You) (1)	**My Life** (5,11) *3*	Sleeping With The Television	Tomorrow Is Today (10)	
Close To The Borderline (6)	**Innocent Man** (9,13) *10*	New York State Of Mind	On (6)	**Travelin' Prayer** (1) *77*	
Code Of Silence (12)	It's Still Rock And Roll To	(3,11)	**Sometimes A Fantasy**	Turn Around (10)	
Don't Ask Me Why (6,11) *19*	Me (6,11) *1*	**Night Is Still Young** (11) *34*	(6,13) *36*	Until The Night (5)	
Downeaster "Alexa" (14) *57*	James (3)	Nocturne (10)	Somewhere Along The Line	**Uptown Girl** (9,11,13) *3*	
Easy Money (9)	**Just The Way You Are**	Odoya (13)	(1)	Vienna (4)	
Entertainer, The (2) *34*	(4,11) *3*	**Only The Good Die Young**	Souvenir (2)	**We Didn't Start The Fire**	
Everybody Has A Dream (4)		(4,11,13) *24*	State Of Grace (14)	(14) *1*	

JOE PUBLIC
Four-man band from Buffalo, New York: Kevin "Kev" Scott (vocals), Joe "J.R." Carter, Joseph "Jake" Sayles and Dwight "Dew" Wyatt. Band co-wrote Keith Sweat's "Keep It Comin'."

| 4/11/92 | 111 | 17 | | Joe Public .... | $12 | Columbia 48628 |

Anything	I Gotta Thang	**I Miss You** *55*	**Live And Learn** *4*	Touch You
Do You Everynite *98*	I Like It	I've Been Watchin'	This One's For You	When I Look In Your Eyes

JOHANSEN, David

Born on 1/9/50 in Staten Island. Founder/lead singer of pre-punk group the New York Dolls, 1971-75. In 1987, recorded jazz-pop as Buster Poindexter. Appeared in the films *Married To The Mob*, *Let It Ride*, *Tales From The Darkside: The Movie* and *Freejack*.

DEBUT DATE	PEAK POS	WKS CHR	GOLD	ARTIST — Album Title	$	Label & Number
9/29/79	**177**	4		1 In Style	$8	Blue Sky 36082
7/11/81	**160**	3		2 Here Comes The Night	$8	Blue Sky 36589
7/3/82	**148**	15		3 Live It Up .... [L]	$8	Blue Sky 38004
1/9/88	**90**	15		4 Buster Poindexter	$8	RCA 6633

BUSTER POINDEXTER AND HIS BANSHEES OF BLUE

Are You Lonely For Me Baby (4)	Donna (3)	Hot Hot Hot (4) **45**	Melody (1,3)	She Knew She Was Falling In Love (1)	We Gotta Get Out Of This Place (medley) (3)
Bad Boy (4)	Flamingo Road (1)	House Of The Rising Sun (4)	My Obsession (2)	She Loves Strangers (2)	Whadaya Want? (4)
Big City (1)	Frenchette (3)	In Style (1)	Party Tonight (2)	Smack Dab In The Middle (4)	Wreckless Crazy (1)
Bohemian Love Pad (2,3)	Funky But Chic (3)	Is This What I Get For Loving You (3)	Personality Crisis (3)	Stranded In The Jungle (3)	You Fool You (2)
Build Me Up Buttercup (3)	Good Morning Judge (4)	It's My Life (medley) (3)	Reach Out I'll Be There (3)	Suspicion (2)	You Touched Me Too (1)
Cannibal (4)	Havin' So Much Fun (2)	Justine (1)	Rollin' Job (2)	Swaheto Woman (1)	
Don't Bring Me Down (medley) (3)	Heart Of Gold (2,4)	Marquesa De Sade (2)	Screwy Music (4)		
	Here Comes The Night (2)		She (1)		

★★9★★ JOHN, Elton

Born Reginald Kenneth Dwight on 3/25/47 in Pinner, Middlesex, England. Formed his first group Bluesology in 1966. Group backed visiting U.S. soul artists and later became Long John Baldry's backing band. Took the name of Elton John from the first names of Bluesology members Elton Dean and John Baldry. Teamed up with lyricist Bernie Taupin beginning in 1969. Formed Rocket Records in 1973. Played the Pinball Wizard in the film version of *Tommy*. Also see Concept Albums.

DEBUT DATE	PEAK POS	WKS CHR	GOLD	ARTIST — Album Title	$	Label & Number
10/3/70+	**4**	51	●	1 Elton John	$20	Uni 73090
1/23/71	**5**	37	●	2 Tumbleweed Connection	$20	Uni 73096
3/27/71	**36**	19	●	3 "Friends" .... [S]	$12	Paramount 6004
5/29/71	**11**	23		4 11-17-70 .... [L]	$20	Uni 93105
				title is date of a live New York City concert broadcast on WPLJ-FM		
11/27/71+	**8**	51	●	5 Madman Across The Water	$20	Uni 93120
6/17/72	**1**[5]	61	●	6 Honky Chateau	$20	Uni 93135
2/10/73	**1**[2]	89	●	7 Don't Shoot Me I'm Only The Piano Player	$10	MCA 2100
10/20/73	**1**[8]	103	●	8 Goodbye Yellow Brick Road	$12	MCA 10003 [2]
7/6/74	**1**[4]	54	●	9 Caribou	$10	MCA 2116
11/23/74	**1**[10]	104	●	10 Elton John - Greatest Hits .... [G]	$10	MCA 2128
2/1/75	**6**	18		11 Empty Sky .... [R]	$10	MCA 2130
				Elton's first album originally released in 1969		
6/7/75	**1**[7]	43	●	12 Captain Fantastic And The Brown Dirt Cowboy	$10	MCA 2142
11/8/75	**1**[3]	26	●	13 Rock Of The Westies	$10	MCA 2163
5/22/76	**4**	20	●	14 Here And There .... [L]	$10	MCA 2197
				side 1: live in London; side 2: live in New York (both 1974)		
11/13/76	**3**	22	▲	15 Blue Moves	$12	MCA/Rkt. 11004 [2]
10/22/77	**21**	20	▲	16 Elton John's Greatest Hits, Volume II .... [G]	$8	MCA 3027
11/11/78	**15**	18	▲	17 A Single Man	$8	MCA 3065
6/30/79	**51**	18		18 The Thom Bell Sessions .... [M]	$8	MCA 13921
				3 songs recorded in 1977		
10/27/79	**35**	10		19 Victim Of Love	$8	MCA 5104
5/31/80	**13**	21	●	20 21 At 33	$8	MCA 5121
				his 21st album, released at age 33; his 20th album, *Lady Samantha*, a compilation of his DJM label recordings hit the U.K. charts but not the *Billboard* album charts		
6/6/81	**21**	19		21 The Fox	$8	Geffen 2002
5/8/82	**17**	33	●	22 Jump Up!	$8	Geffen 2013
6/11/83+	**25**	54	●	23 Too Low For Zero	$8	Geffen 4006
7/21/84	**20**	34	●	24 Breaking Hearts	$8	Geffen 24031
11/30/85+	**48**	28	●	25 Ice On Fire	$8	Geffen 24077
12/6/86	**91**	9		26 Leather Jackets	$8	Geffen 24114
7/25/87+	**24**	41	●	27 Live In Australia .... [L]	$10	MCA 8022 [2]
				recorded on 12/14/86 in Sydney with the Melbourne Symphony Orch.		
10/3/87	**84**	23	▲	28 Elton John's Greatest Hits, Volume III, 1979-1987 .... [G]	$8	Geffen 24153
7/9/88	**16**	29	●	29 Reg Strikes Back	$8	MCA 6240
9/16/89	**23**	53	▲	30 Sleeping With The Past	$8	MCA 6321
11/24/90	**82**	13	●	31 To Be Continued... .... [K]	$41	MCA 10110 [4]
				Elton's releases from 1965-90; hits, rarities, previously unreleased recordings and 4 new compositions, plus a 40-page booklet		
7/11/92	**8**	31↑	▲	32 The One	$12	MCA 10614

Act Of War (31)	Bennie And The Jets (8,10,14,31) **1**	Border Song (1,10,14,31) **92**	Captain Fantastic And The Brown Dirt Cowboy (12)	Crystal (23)	Donner Pour Donner (31)
All Quiet On The Western Front (22)		Born Bad (19)		Curtains (12)	Durban Deep (30)
All The Girls Love Alice (8,31)	Between Seventeen And Twenty (15)	Breaking Down Barriers (21)	Carla Etude (21,31)	Dan Dare (Pilot Of The Future) (13)	Easier To Walk Away (31)
All The Nasties (5)	Big Dipper (17)	Breaking Hearts (Ain't What It Used To Be) (24)	Cartier (31)	Chameleon (15)	**Ego** (31) **34**
Amazes Me (30)	Billy Bones And The White Bird (13)	Burn Down The Mission (2,4,27)	Chasing The Crown (20)	Dear God (20)	Elderberry Wine (7)
Amoreena (2)	**Bitch Is Back** (9,16,31) **4**	Burning Buildings (24)	Chloe (21,31) **34**	Dear John (22)	Elton's Song (21)
Amy (6)	**Bite Your Lip (Get Up And Dance!)** (15) **28**	Cage, The (1)	Club At The End Of The Street (30) **28**	Did He Shoot Her? (24)	Emily (32)
Angeline (26)	Bitter Fingers (12)	Camera Never Lies (29)	Come Back Baby (19)	Dirty Little Girl (8)	**Empty Garden (Hey Hey Johnny)** (22,28,31) **13**
Are You Ready For Love (18)	Blue Avenue (30)	Can I Put You On (3,4)	Come Down In Time (2)	Dixie Lily (9)	Empty Sky (11)
Bad Side Of The Moon (4,31)	**Blue Eyes** (22,28,31) **12**	**Candle In The Wind** (8,27,31) **6**	Country Comfort (2,31)	**Don't Go Breaking My Heart** (16,31) **1**	Fanfare (21,31)
Ball & Chain (2)	Blues For Baby And Me (7)	Candy By The Pound (25)	Crazy Water (15)	**Don't Let The Sun Go Down On Me** (9,10,27,31) **2**	Fascist Faces (31)
Ballad Of A Well-Known Gun (2)	Boogie Pilgrim (15)		**Crocodile Rock** (7,10,14,31) **1**	Don't Trust That Woman (26)	Feed Me (13)
Ballad Of Danny Bailey (1909-34) (8)			Cry To Heaven (25)		First Episode At Hienton (1)
					Four Moods (3)
					Fox, The (21)

DEBUT DATE	PEAK POS	WKS CHR	GOLD	ARTIST — Album Title	$	Label & Number

JOHN, Elton — Cont'd

Friends (3,31) 34 (also see Variations)
Funeral For A Friend (medley) (8,14,31)
Georgia (17)
Get Back (medley) (4)
Give Me The Love (20)
Give Peace A Chance (31)
Go It Alone (26)
Goodbye (5)
Goodbye Marlon Brando (29)
Goodbye Yellow Brick Road (8,10,31) 2
(Gotta Get A) Meal Ticket (12)
Greatest Discovery (1,27)
Grey Seal (8,31)
Grimsby (9)
Grow Some Funk Of Your Own (13,16) 14
Gulliver (medley) (11)
Gypsy Heart (26)
Hard Luck Story (13)
Harmony (8,31)
Have Mercy On The Criminal (7,27)
Hay Chewed (medley) (11)
Healing Hands (30) 13
Heart In The Right Place (21)
Heartache All Over The World (26,28) 55
Heavy Traffic (29)
Heels Of The Wind (21)
Hercules (6)
High Flying Bird (7)
Holiday Inn (5)
Honey Roll (13)
Honky Cat (6,10,14,31) 8
Honky Tonk Women (4)
Hoop Of Fire (26)
Hymn 2000 (11)
I Am Your Robot (22)
I Don't Care (17)
I Don't Wanna Go On With You Like That (29,31) 2
I Fall Apart (26)

I Feel Like A Bullet (In The Gun Of Robert Ford) (13,31) *flip*
I Guess That's Why They Call It The Blues (23,28,31) 4
I Meant To Do My Work Today (3)
I Need You To Turn To (1,27)
I Never Knew Her Name (30)
I Saw Her Standing There (31)
I Swear I Heard The Night Talkin' (31)
I Think I'm Gonna Kill Myself (6)
I'm Going To Be A Teenage Idol (7)
I'm Still Standing (28,31) 12
I've Seen That Movie Too (8)
I've Seen The Saucers (9)
Idol (15)
If There's A God In Heaven (What's He Waiting For?) (15)
In Neon (24) 38
Indian Sunset (5)
Island Girl (13,16,31) 1
It Ain't Gonna Be Easy (17)
It's Me That You Need (31)
Jack Rabbit (31)
Jamaica Jerk-Off (8)
Japanese Hands (29)
Johnny B. Goode (19)
Just Like Belgium (21)
King Must Die (1,27)
Kiss The Bride (23,28) 25
Lady Samantha (31)
Lady What's Tomorrow (11)
Last Song (32) 23
Leather Jackets (26)
Legal Boys (22)
Levon (5,16,31) 24
Li'l 'Frigerator (24)
Little Jeannie (20,28,31) 3

Love Lies Bleeding (medley) (8,14,31)
Love Song (2,14)
Lucy In The Sky With Diamonds (16,31) 1
Made For Me (31)
Madman Across The Water (5,27,31)
Madness (17)
Mama Can't Buy You Love (18,28,31) 9
Mellow (6)
Memory Of Love (28)
Michelle's Song (3) (also see: Variations)
Midnight Creeper (7)
Mona Lisas And Mad Hatters (6,31)
Mona Lisas And Mad Hatters (Part Two) (29)
My Baby Left Me (medley) (4)
My Father's Gun (2)
Never Gonna Fall In Love Again (20)
Nikita (25,28,31) 7
No Shoe Strings On Louise (1)
Nobody Wins (21) 21
North, The (32)
On Dark Street (32)
One, The (32) 9
One Day At A Time (31)
One Horse Town (15)
One More Arrow (23)
Out Of The Blue (15)
Paris (26)
Part-Time Love (17) 22
Passengers (24)
Philadelphia Freedom (16,31) 1
Pinball Wizard (16,31)
Pinky (9)
Poor Cow (29)
Princess (22)
Razor Face (5)
Religion (23)

Restless (24)
Retreat, The (31)
Return To Paradise (17)
Reverie (17)
Rock And Roll Madonna (31)
Rocket Man (6,10,14,31) 6
Rotten Peaches (5)
Roy Rogers (8)
Runaway Train (32)
Sacrifice (30,31) 18
Sad Songs (Say So Much) (24,28,31) 5
Sails (11)
Saint (23)
Salvation (6)
(Sartorial Eloquence) Don't Ya Wanna Play This Game No More? (20) 39
Satellite (25)
Saturday Night's Alright For Fighting (8,10,31) 12
Scaffold, The (11)
Seasons (3)
Shine On Through (17)
Shoot Down The Moon (25)
Shooting Star (17)
Shoulder Holster (15)
Since God Invented Girls (29)
Sixty Years On (1,4,27,31)
Skyline Pigeon (11,14)
Slave (6)
Sleeping With The Past (30)
Slow Down Georgie (She's Poison) (24)
Slow Rivers (26)
Social Disease (8)
Solar Prestige A Gammon (9)
Someone Saved My Life Tonight (12,16,31) 4
Someone's Final Song (15)
Son Of Your Father (2)
Song For Guy (17,31)

Sorry Seems To Be The Hardest Word (15,16,27,31) 6
Soul Glove (25)
Spiteful Child (22)
Spotlight (19)
Step Into Christmas (31)
Stinker (9)
Stones Throw From Hurtin' (30)
Street Boogie (19)
Street Kids (13)
Suzie (Dramas) (6)
Sweat It Out (32)
Sweet Painted Lady (8)
Take Me Back (20)
Take Me To The Pilot (1,4,14,27,31)
Talking Old Soldiers (2)
Teacher I Need You (7)
Tell Me What The Papers Say (25)
Tell Me When The Whistle Blows (12)
Texan Love Song (7)
Theme From A Non-Existent TV Series (15)
This Song Has No Title (8)
This Town (25)
Three Way Love Affair (18)
Thunder In The Night (19)
Ticking (9)
Tiny Dancer (5,27,31) 41
Tonight (15,27)
Too Low For Zero (23,28)
Too Young (25)
Tower Of Babel (12)
Town Of Plenty (29)
Two Rooms At The End Of The World (20)
Ugly (medley) (13)
Understanding Women (32)
Valhalla (11)
Variations On "Friends" Theme (The First Kiss) (3)

Variations On Michelle's Song (3)
Victim Of Love (19) 31
Warm Love In A Cold World (19)
We All Fall In Love Sometimes (12)
Wednesday Night (medley) (13)
Western Ford Gateway (11)
When A Woman Doesn't Want You (32)
Whenever You're Ready (We'll Go Steady Again) (31)
Where Have All The Good Times Gone? (22)
Where To Now St. Peter? (2)
Where's The Shoorah? (15)
Whipping Boy (23)
Whispers (30)
White Lady White Powder (20)
Whitewash County (32)
Who Wears These Shoes? (24) 16
Wide-Eyed And Laughing (15)
Word In Spanish (29) 19
Wrap Her Up (25,28) 20
Writing (12)
Yell Help (medley) (13)
You Gotta Love Someone (31) 43
You're So Static (9)
Young Man's Blues (31)
Your Sister Can't Twist (But She Can Rock 'N' Roll) (8)
Your Song (1,10,27,31) 8
Your Starter For... (15)

JOHN, Robert

Born Robert John Pedrick, Jr. in Brooklyn in 1946. First recorded at age 12 for Big Top Records. In 1963, recorded as lead singer with Bobby & The Consoles.

| 8/25/79 | 68 | 14 | | Robert John | $8 | EMI America 17007 |

Am I Ever Gonna Hold You Again | Dance The Night Away | Give A Little More | **Lonely Eyes 41** | Love Of A Woman | Only Time | **Sad Eyes 1** | Stay A Little Longer | Takin' My Love For Granted | That's What Keeps Us Together

JOHNNY & THE DISTRACTIONS

Johnny Koonce, leader of Portland rock quintet.

| 2/20/82 | 152 | 9 | | Let It Rock | $8 | A&M 4884 |

Break These Chains | Complicated Now | Guys Like Me | Let It Rock | Octane Twilight | City Of Angels | Forever | In The Street | My Desire | Shoulder Of The Road

JOHNNY AND THE HURRICANES

Rock and roll instrumental band formed as the Orbits in Toledo in 1958: leader John Pocisk "Paris" (saxophone), Paul Tesluk (organ), Dave Yorko (guitar), Lionel "Butch" Mattice (bass) and Tony Kaye (drums; replaced in late 1959 by Bo Savich). Paris had own Attila label from 1965-70.

| 4/18/60 | 34 | 3 | | Stormsville | [I] $100 | Warwick 2010 |

Beanbag | Cyclone | Hot Fudge | **Reveille Rock 25** | Time Bomb | Catnip | "Hep" Canary (The Hot Canary) | Hungry Eye | Rockin' "T" | Travelin' | Corn Bread | Milk Shake

JOHNNY HATES JAZZ

Englishmen Clark Datchler (vocals) and Calvin Hayes (son of producer Mickie Most) with American Mike Nocito. Datchler left in late 1988, replaced by producer/ex-Cure member Phil Thornalley.

| 4/16/88 | 56 | 25 | | Turn Back The Clock | $8 | Virgin 90860 |

Different Seasons | Don't Say It's Love | Heart Of Gold | **I Don't Want To Be A Hero 31** | Listen | Turn Back The Clock | Don't Let It End This Way | Foolish Heart | **Shattered Dreams 2** | What Other Reason

JOHNS, Sammy

Born on 2/7/46 in Charlotte, North Carolina. Own band, the Devilles, from 1963-73.

| 3/29/75 | 148 | 12 | | Sammy Johns | $10 | GRC 5003 |

America | **Early Morning Love 68** | Hang My Head And Moan | Jenny | Way Out Jesus | **Chevy Van 5** | Friends Of Mine | Holy Mother, Aging Father | **Rag Doll 52** | We Will Shine

JOHNSON, Don

Born on 12/15/49 in Flatt Creek, Missouri. Actor/singer. Played Sonny Crockett on TV's *Miami Vice*. Starred in several films. Remarried his ex-wife, actress Melanie Griffith, in 1989.

| 9/13/86 | 17 | 27 | ● | Heartbeat | $8 | Epic 40366 |

Can't Take Your Memory | Gotta Get Away | **Heartbeat 5** | Lost In Your Eyes | Star Tonight | Coco Don't | **Heartache Away 56** | Last Sound Love Makes | Love Roulette | Voice On A Hotline

DEBUT DATE	PEAK POS	WKS CHR	GOLD	ARTIST — Album Title	$	Label & Number

JOHNSON, Eric
Rock guitarist/singer from Austin, Texas.

| 4/21/90+ | 67 | 60 | ● | Ah Via Musicom ....[I] | $12 | Capitol 90517 |

title loosely translated: By Way Of The Communication Of Music; 7 of 11 tracks are instrumental

Ah Via Musicom	Desert Rose	Forty Mile Town	Nothing Can Keep Me From	Righteous		Steve's Boogie
Cliffs Of Dover	East Wes	High Landrons	You	Song For George		Trademark

JOHNSON, Howard
Born in Miami. First recorded with Tornader, which became Nite Flyte.

| 9/11/82 | 122 | 9 | | Keepin' Love New .... | $8 | A&M 4895 |

Forever Falling In Love	Keepin' Love New	So Fine	Take Me Through The Night	
Jam Song	Say You Wanna	So Glad You're My Lady	This Is Heaven	

JOHNSON, Jesse
Lead guitarist of The Time. Born on 5/29/60 in Rock Island, Illinois.

3/16/85	43	43	●	1 Jesse Johnson's Revue	$8	A&M 5024
10/18/86	70	20		2 Shockadelica..	$8	A&M 5122
4/16/88	79	13		3 Every Shade Of Love	$8	A&M 5188

Addiction (2)	Burn You Up (2)	Do Yourself A Favor (2)	I'm Just Wanting You (3)	She (I Can't Resist) (2)	Stop-Look-Listen (3)
Baby Let's Kiss (2)	Can You Help Me (1)	Every Shade Of Love (3)	I'm The One (3)	She Won't Let Go (1)	Tonite (2)
Be Your Man (1) 61	Change Your Mind (2)	Everybody Wants Somebody	Just Too Much (1)	She's A Doll (1)	
Better Way (2)	Color Shock (3)	To Love (3)	Let's Have Some Fun (1)	So Misunderstood (3)	
Black In America (2)	Crazay (2) 53	I Want My Girl (1) 76	Love Struck (3) 78	Special Love (1)	

JOHNSON, Michael
Born on 7/8/44 in Alamosa, Colorado and raised in Denver. Studied classical guitar in 1966 in Spain.
In the Chad Mitchell Trio with John Denver in 1968.

| 7/15/78 | 81 | 17 | | 1 The Michael Johnson Album .... | $8 | EMI America 17002 |
| 9/15/79 | 157 | 12 | | 2 Dialogue.. | $8 | EMI America 17010 |

Almost Like Being In Love (1) 32	Dialogue (2)	I Just Can't Say No To You (2)	Ridin' In The Sky (1)	This Night Won't Last Forever (1) 19	Very First Time (2)
Blackmail (2)	Doors (2)	I'll Always Love You (2)	Sailing Without A Sail (1)	25 Words Or Less (1)	When You Come Home (1)
Bluer Than Blue (1) 12	Drops Of Water (2)	Let This Be A Lesson To You (2)	She Put The Sad In All His Songs (2)	Two In Love (1)	
Dancin' Tonight (1)	Foolish (1)				
	Gypsy Woman (1)				

JOHNSON, Robert
White Memphis session guitarist. Worked on Stax Records as a teen in the '60s. Member of John Entwistle's group Ox in 1974.

| 1/13/79 | 174 | 8 | | Close Personal Friend.. | $8 | Infinity 9000 |

Debbie's Theme	Guide My Energy (Parts 1 & 2)	I'll Be Waiting	Leslie	Say Girl	Wish Upon A Star
	Kerri	Responsibility	Tell Me About It, "Slim"	Wreck My Mind

JOHNSON, Robert
Influential blues singer/guitarist. Born on 5/8/11 in Hazlehurst, Mississippi. Died on 8/16/38 from strychnine poisoning. Influenced electric bluesmen Elmore James, Robert Nighthawk, Johnny Shines, Muddy Waters and others. Inducted into the Rock and Roll Hall of Fame in 1985.

| 10/13/90+ | 80 | 31 | ● | The Complete Recordings ....[K] | $17 | Columbia 46222 [2] |

includes a 48-page booklet chronicling Johnson's life

Come On In My Kitchen	Honeymoon Blues	Last Fair Deal Gone Down	Phonograph Blues	Sweet Home Chicago	When You Got A Good Friend
Cross Road Blues	I Believe I'll Dust My Broom	Little Queen Of Spades	Preaching Blues (Up Jumped The Devil)	Terraplane Blues	
Dead Shrimp Blues	I'm A Steady Rollin' Man	Love In Vain		They're Red Hot	
Drunken Hearted Man	If I Had Possession Over Judgment Day	Malted Milk	Rambling On My Mind	32-20 Blues	
From Four Till Late		Me And The Devil Blues	Stones In My Passway	Traveling Riverside Blues	
Hellhound On My Trail	Kindhearted Woman Blues	Milkcow's Calf Blues	Stop Breakin' Down Blues	Walking Blues	

JOHNSTON, Tom
Lead singer/guitarist of The Doobie Brothers from 1970-78. Native of Visalia, California.

| 10/20/79 | 100 | 13 | | 1 Everything You've Heard Is True .... | $8 | Warner 3304 |
| 5/16/81 | 158 | 7 | | 2 Still Feels Good .... | $8 | Warner 3527 |

Baby, Take Me In (2)	I Can Count On You (1)	Man On The Stage (1)	Reachin' Out For Lovin' From You (1)	Show Me (1)	Wastin' Time (2)
Down Along The River (1)	Last Desperado (2)	One-Way Ticket (2)		Small Time Talk (1)	Wishing (2)
Excuse Me Ma'am (2)	Madman (2)	Outlaw (1)	Savannah Nights (1) 34	Up On The Stage (2)	

JO JO GUNNE
Los Angeles-based rock quartet formed by Jay Ferguson and Mark Andes (former members of Spirit). Named group after the 1958 Chuck Berry hit.

2/26/72	57	22		1 Jo Jo Gunne	$15	Asylum 5053
3/17/73	75	17		2 Bite Down Hard	$10	Asylum 5065
12/22/73+	169	7		3 Jumpin' The Gunne	$10	Asylum 5071
12/28/74	198	1		4 So...Where's The Show?	$10	Asylum 1022

Academy Award (1)	Big, Busted Bombshell From	High School Drool (3)	99 Days (1)	S & M Blvd. (4)	Take Me Down Easy (2)
Around The World (4)	Bermuda (4)	I Make Love (1)	Ready Freddy (2)	Shake That Fat (1)	To The Island (3)
At The Spa (3)	Broken Down Man (2)	I Wanna Love You (3)	Red Meat (3)	She Said Allright (4)	Turn The Boy Loose (3)
Babylon (1)	Couldn't Love You Better (4)	I'm Your Shoe (4)	Rhoda (2)	Single Man (4)	Wait A Lifetime (2)
Barstow Blue Eyes (1)	Falling Angel (4)	Into My Life (4)	Rock Around The Symbol (2)	60 Minutes To Go (2)	Where Is The Show? (4)
Before You Get Your Breakfast (3)	Flying Home (1)	Monkey Music (3)	Roll Over Me (2)	Special Situations (2)	
	Getaway (3)	Neon City (3)	Run Run Run (1) 27	Take It Easy (1)	

JOLI, France
French Canadian singer born in 1963 in Montreal.

| 9/8/79 | 26 | 17 | | 1 France Joli .... | $8 | Prelude 12170 |
| 6/28/80 | 175 | 3 | | 2 Tonight .... | $8 | Prelude 12179 |

Come To Me (1) 15	Feel Like Dancing (2)	Let Go (1)	Stoned In Love (2)	Tonight (2)	
Don't Stop Dancing (1)	Heart To Break The Heart (2)	Playboy (1)	This Time (I'm Giving All I've Got) (2)	Tough Luck (2)	When Love Hurts Inside (2)

DEBUT DATE	PEAK POS	WKS CHR	G O L D	ARTIST — Album Title	$	Label & Number

JOLLY, Pete, Trio and friends
Hollywood-based jazz pianist. Born Peter Ceragioli on 6/5/32 in New Haven, Connecticut.

| 6/8/63 | 139 | 2 | | Little Bird ....[I] | $20 | Ava 22 |

Alone Together
Falling In Love With Love

Little Bird
My Favorite Things

Never Never Land

Spring Can Really Hang You
Up The Most

Three-Four-Five
To Kill A Mocking Bird

Toot, Toot, Tootsie (Goodbye)

JOLSON, Al
One of the most popular entertainers of the 20th century. Born Asa Yoelson in St. Petersburg, Russia on 3/26/1886 to a Rabbi father. Died on 10/23/50. Raised in Washington, D.C. Broadway star of many musicals, beginning in 1911. Starred in historical part-sound film *The Jazz Singer* in 1927. Provided vocals for autobiographical films *The Jolson Story* (1946) and *Jolson Sings Again* (1949). Married to actress Ruby Keeler from 1928-39.

| 9/22/62+ | 40 | 42 | | The Best Of Jolson ....[G] | $20 | Decca 169 [2] |

Al's recordings for the soundtracks *The Jolson Story* and *Jolson Sings Again*

About A Quarter To Nine
Anniversary Song
April Showers
Avalon
Baby Face (medley)
California, Here I Come
Carolina In The Morning
Dinah (medley)
Easter Parade

I Wish I Had A Girl
I'm Always Chasing Rainbows
I'm Looking Over A Four Leaf Clover (medley)
If I Only Had A Match
Let Me Sing And I'm Happy
Liza (All The Clouds'll Roll Away)

Ma Blushin' Rosie (Ma Posie Sweet)
Ma (She's Makin' Eyes At Me) (medley)
Margie
My Blue Heaven (medley)
My Mammy
My Melancholy Baby (medley)

Ol' Man River
Rockabye Your Baby With A Dixie Melody
She's A Latin From Manhattan
Sonny Boy
Swanee
There's A Rainbow 'Round My Shoulder

Toot, Toot, Tootsie! (Goo'Bye)
When The Red, Red, Robin Comes Bob, Bob, Bobbin' Along
When You Were Sweet Sixteen
You Made Me Love You (I Didn't Want To Do It)

JON & VANGELIS
Jon Anderson (lead singer of Yes) and Greek keyboardist Evangelos Papathanassiou.

5/31/80	125	15		1 Short Stories	$8	Polydor 6272
8/8/81	64	34		2 The Friends Of Mr. Cairo	$8	Polydor 6326
8/13/83	148	7		3 Private Collection	$8	Polydor 813174

And When The Night Comes (3)
Back To School (2)
Beside (2)
Bird Song (medley) (1)

Curious Electric (1)
Deborah (3)
Each And Everyday (medley) (1)
Far Away In Baagad (1)

Friends Of Mr. Cairo (2)
He Is Sailing (3)
Horizon (3)
I Hear You Now (1) **58**
Italian Song (3)

Love Is (medley) (1)
Mayflower (2)
One More Time (medley) (1)
Outside Of This (Inside Of That) (2)

Play Within A Play (1)
Polonaise (3)
Road, The (1)
State Of Independence (2)
Thunder (1)

JONES, Davy
Born on 12/30/45 in Manchester, England. Member of The Monkees.

| 5/27/67 | 185 | 6 | | David Jones .... | $25 | Colpix 493 |

recorded prior to Davy's Monkee career

Any Old Iron
Baby It's Me
Dream Girl

Face Up To It
It Ain't Me Babe

Maybe It's Because I'm A Londoner

My Dad
New Love, Theme For A

Put Me Amongst The Girls
This Bouquet

What Are We Going To Do? 93

JONES, George
Born on 9/12/31 in Saratoga, Texas. Ranks behind Eddy Arnold as the top artist of the country charts according to *Joel Whitburn's Top Country Singles 1944-1988* book. First recorded for Starday in 1954. Married to Tammy Wynette from 1969-75. Recorded rockabilly music under pseudonyms Hank Smith and Thumper Jones. Recorded with Gene Pitney as George & Gene.

| 3/20/65 | 141 | 4 | | 1 George Jones & Gene Pitney | $20 | Musicor 3044 |

GEORGE JONES & GENE PITNEY

6/26/65	149	2		2 The Race Is On	$20	United Art. 3422
8/2/69	185	5		3 I'll Share My World With You	$15	Musicor 3177
11/13/71	169	6		4 We Go Together	$10	Epic 30802

TAMMY WYNETTE & GEORGE JONES

6/13/81	132	14 ▲		5 I Am What I Am	$8	Epic 36586
11/28/81+	115	14 ●		6 Still The Same Ole Me	$8	Epic 37106
9/25/82	123	12		7 A Taste Of Yesterday's Wine	$8	Epic 38203

MERLE HAGGARD & GEORGE JONES

| 11/2/91 | 148 | 10 | | 8 And Along Came Jones .... | $12 | MCA 10398 |
| 11/14/92 | 77 | 13↑ | | 9 Walls Can Fall .... | $12 | MCA 10652 |

After Closing Time (4)
After I Sing All My Songs (7)
Ain't It Funny What A Fool Will Do (2)
Angels Don't Fly (8)
Bone Dry (9)
Bottle Let Me Down (5)
Brother To The Blues (5)
Brothers, The (7)
C.C. Waterback (7)
Come Home To Me (8)
Couldn't Love Have Picked A Better Place To Die (6)
Daddy Come Home (6)
Do What You Think's Best (9)
Don't Let The Stars Get In Your Eyes (2)
Don't Rob Another Man's Castle (1)
Don't Send Me No Angels (9)
Drive Me To Drink (9)
Finally Friday (9)

Girl, You Sure Know How To Say Goodbye (4)
Good Hearted Woman (5)
Good Ones And Bad Ones (6)
Hard Act To Follow (5)
He Stopped Loving Her Today (5)
Heartaches And Hangovers (3)
Heckel And Jeckel (8)
His Lovin' Her Is Gettin' In My Way (5)
Honky Tonk Myself To Death (8)
I Don't Go Back Anymore (8)
I Don't Have Sense Enough (To Come In Out Of The Pain) (2)
I Don't Need Your Rockin' Chair (9)
I Haven't Found Her Yet (7)
I Think I've Found A Way (To Live Without You) (7)

I Won't Need You Anymore (6)
I'll Never Let Go Of You (2)
I'll Share My World With You (3)
I'm A Fool To Care (1)
I'm Not Ready Yet (5)
I'm The One She Missed Him With Today (5)
I've Aged Twenty Years In Five (5)
I've Got A New Heartache (5)
I've Got Five Dollars And It's Saturday Night (1) **99**
If Drinkin' Don't Kill Me (Her Memory Will) (5)
It Scares Me Half To Death (2)
It's So Sweet (4)
King Of The Mountain (8)
Lifetime Left Together (4)
Livin' On Easy Street (4)
Milwaukee Here I Come (3)

Mobile Bay (Magnolia Blossoms) (7)
Must've Been Drunk (7)
My Shoes Keep Walking Back To You (1)
Never Grow Cold (4)
No Show Jones (7)
One Has My Name (1)
Our Happy Home (3)
Race Is On (2,3) **96**
Same Ole Me (6)
She Loved A Lot In Her Time (8)
She's Mine (2)
Silver Eagle (7)
Someday My Day Will Come (6)
Someone I Used To Know (4)
Something To Brag About (4)
Still Doin' Time (6)
Sweeter Than The Flowers (1)
Take Me (4)

Take Me As I Am (2)
There's The Door (9)
They'll Never Take Her Love From Me (2)
Things Have Gone To Pieces [solo: George] (1)
Three's A Crowd (2)
Time Changes Everything (2)
Together Alone (6)
Walls Can Fall (9)
We Go Together (4)
Wearing My Heart Away [solo: George] (1)
What Am I Doing There (9)
When The Grass Grows Over Me (3)
When The Wife Runs Off (3)
When True Love Steps In (4)
Where The Tall Grass Grows (8)

Yesterday's Wine (7)
You Can't Get The Hell Out Of Texas (6)
You Couldn't Get The Picture (8)
You Done Me Wrong (8)
You Must Have Walked Across My Mind Again (9)
You're Everything (4)
You've Become My Everything (3)
Your Heart Turned Left (2)

JONES, Glenn
Vocalist from Jacksonville, Florida. Sang with the gospel group, Bivens Special, from age eight. Had own gospel group, the Modulations, from age 14. In the Broadway musical *Sing Mahalia, Sing*.

| 10/10/87 | 94 | 17 | | Glenn Jones .... | $8 | Jive 1062 |

JONES, Glenn — Cont'd

All I Need To Know	I Love You	It's All In The Game	Oh Girl	We've Only Just Begun
At Last	It Must Be Love	Living In The Limelight	That Night Mood	(The Romance Is Not Over) 66

JONES, Grace

Model/film actress/singer. Born on 5/19/52 in Spanishtown, Jamaica. Moved to Syracuse, New York in 1964. Cover girl in the 1970s of *Vogue*, *Elle* and *Der Stern* magazines. Appeared in the films *Conan The Destroyer*, *A View To A Kill* and *Vamp*.

DEBUT DATE	PEAK POS	WKS CHR	GOLD	#	Album Title	$	Label & Number
10/22/77	109	20		1	Portfolio	$8	Island 9470
8/5/78	97	8		2	Fame	$8	Island 9525
9/1/79	156	7		3	Muse	$8	Island 9538
6/21/80	132	10		4	Warm Leatherette	$8	Island 9592
5/23/81	32	20		5	Nightclubbing	$8	Island 9624
12/11/82	86	20		6	Living My Life	$8	Island 90018
11/23/85	73	20		7	Slave To The Rhythm	$8	Manhattan 53021
1/18/86	161	7		8	Island Life	[G]	Island 90491
12/13/86+	81	16		9	Inside Story	$8	Manhattan 53038

All On A Summers Night (2)	Crossing (Ooh The Action…) (7)	Frog And The Princess (7)	La Vie En Rose (1,8)	Repentence (Forgive Me) (3)	Victor Should Have Been A Jazz Musician (5)
Am I Ever Gonna Fall In Love In NYC (2)	Crush (9)	Hollywood Liar (7)	Ladies And Gentlemen: Miss Grace Jones (7)	Rolling Stone (4)	Walking In The Rain (5,8)
Apple Stretching (6)	Cry Now, Laugh Later (6)	Hunter Gets Captured By The Game (4)	Love Is The Drug (4,8)	Saved (3)	Warm Leatherette (4)
Art Groupie (5)	Demolition Man (5)	I Need A Man (1,8) 83	My Jamaican Guy (6,8)	Scary But Fun (9)	What I Did For Love (1)
Atlantic City Gambler (3)	Do Or Die (2,8)	I'll Find My Way To You (3)	Nightclubbing (5)	Send In The Clowns (1)	White Collar Crime (9)
Autumn Leaves (4)	Don't Cry - It's Only The Rhythm (7)	I'm Not Perfect (But I'm Perfect For You) (9) 69	On Your Knees (3)	Sinning (3)	
Barefoot In Beverly Hills (9)	Don't Mess With The Messer (3)	I've Done It Again (3)	Operattack (7)	Slave To The Rhythm (7,8)	
Below The Belt (La Vieille Fille) (2)	Everybody Hold Still (6)	I've Seen That Face Before (Libertango) (5,8)	Pars (7)	Sorry (1) 71	
Breakdown (4)	Fame (2)	Inside Story (9)	Party Girl (9)	That's The Trouble (1) flip	
Bullshit (4)	Fashion Show (7)	Inspiration (6)	Pride (2)	Tomorrow (1)	
Chan Hitchhikes To Shanghai (9)	Feel Up (5)	Jones The Rhythm (7)	Private Life (4,8)	Unlimited Capacity For Love (6)	
			Pull Up To The Bumper (5,8)	Use Me (5)	

JONES, Howard

Born on 2/23/55 in Southampton, England. Pop singer/songwriter/synth wizard.

DEBUT DATE	PEAK POS	WKS CHR	GOLD	#	Album Title	$	Label & Number
3/24/84	59	43		1	Human's Lib	$8	Elektra 60346
4/20/85	10	45	▲	2	**Dream Into Action**	$8	Elektra 60390
5/3/86	34	24		3	Action Replay	[K-M]	Elektra 60466
					6 tracks; includes 3 remixes and 2 previously unreleased songs		
11/1/86	56	21		4	One To One	$8	Elektra 60499
4/15/89	65	22		5	Cross That Line	$8	Elektra 60794

All I Want (4) 76	Don't Always Look At The Rain (1)	Give Me Strength (4)	Life In One Day (2) 19	Pearl In The Shell (1)	What Is Love? (1) 33
Always Asking Questions (3)	Don't Want To Fight Anymore (4)	Good Luck, Bad Luck (4)	Like To Get To Know You Well (2) 49	Powerhouse (5)	Where Are We Going? (4)
Assault And Battery (2)	Dream Into Action (2)	Guardians Of The Breath (5)	Little Bit Of Snow (4)	Prisoner, The (5) 30	Will You Still Be There? (4)
Automaton (2)		Hide And Seek (1,3)	Look Mama (2,3)	Specialty (3)	You Know I Love You...Don't You? (4) 17
Balance Of Love (Give And Take) (4)	Elegy (2)	Human's Lib (1)	Natural (1)	Step Into These Shoes (4)	
Bounce Right Back (2,3)	Equality (1)	Hunger For The Flesh (2)	New Song (1) 27	Things Can Only Get Better (2) 5	
Conditioning (1)	Everlasting Love (5) 12	Hunt The Self (1)	No One Is To Blame (2,3) 4	Those Who Move Clouds (5)	
Cross That Line (5)	Fresh Air Waltz (5)	Is There A Difference? (2)	Out Of Thin Air (5)	Wanders To You (5)	
		Last Supper (5)			

★★227★★ JONES, Jack

Born on 1/14/38 in Los Angeles. One of the top MOR singers of the '60s. Son of actress Irene Hervey and actor/singer Allan Jones, who had the #8 pop hit "The Donkey Serenade" the year Jack was born.

DEBUT DATE	PEAK POS	WKS CHR	GOLD	#	Album Title	$	Label & Number
6/29/63+	98	25		1	Call Me Irresponsible	$15	Kapp 3328
12/28/63+	18	53		2	Wives And Lovers	$15	Kapp 3352
6/20/64	43	19		3	Bewitched	$15	Kapp 3365
8/29/64	62	23		4	Where Love Has Gone	$15	Kapp 3396
1/9/65	11	25		5	Dear Heart	$15	Kapp 3415
5/8/65	29	22		6	My Kind Of Town	$15	Kapp 3433
9/18/65	86	13		7	There's Love & There's Love & There's Love	$15	Kapp 3435
3/26/66	147	2		8	For The "In" Crowd	$15	Kapp 3465
7/16/66	9	64		9	The Impossible Dream	$15	Kapp 3486
11/26/66+	75	12		10	Jack Jones Sings	$15	Kapp 3500
3/25/67	23	25		11	Lady	$15	Kapp 3511
10/14/67	148	7		12	Our Song	$15	Kapp 3531
12/16/67+	146	7		13	Without Her	$8	RCA 3911
2/24/68	167	6		14	What The World Needs Now Is Love!	[K]	$12	Kapp 3551
4/27/68	198	3		15	If You Ever Leave Me	$8	RCA 3969
9/21/68	195	3		16	Where Is Love?	$8	RCA 4048
8/16/69	183	4		17	A Time For Us	$8	RCA 4209

Afraid To Love (11)	Autumn Leaves (10)	Charade (2)	Embraceable You (7)	Girl Talk (11)	I Can't Believe That You're In Love With Me (7)
After Today (12)	Baby, Don't You Quit Now (15)	Come Rain Or Come Shine (2)	Emily (5)	Goin' Out Of My Head (15)	I Can't Get Started (13)
Afterthoughts (14)	Baby I'm Yours (8)	Day In The Life Of A Fool (10) 62	Ev'ry Time We Say Goodbye (4)	Good Times (16)	I Don't Care Much (10)
Alfie (9)	Beautiful Friendship (11)	Dear Heart (5) 30	Eyes Of Love (14)	Guess I'll Hang My Tears Out To Dry (4)	I Don't Give A Damn (10)
All Or Nothing At All (9)	Bewitched (3)	Don't Give Your Love Away (12)	Face I Love (10)	Gypsies, The Jugglers, And The Clowns (14)	I Keep Leavin' Houses Behind (17)
Along The Way (12)	Brother, Where Are You (11)	Don't Rain On My Parade (3)	Far Away (3)	Here's That Rainy Day (4)	I Must Know (6)
And I Love Her (7)	By Myself (4)	Don't Talk To Me (13)	Feeling Good (9)	Home (17)	I Never Go There Anymore (14)
And I'll Go (17)	By The Time I Get To Phoenix (15)	Dreams Are All I Have Of You (16)	Fly Me To The Moon (In Other Words) (2)	Homeward Bound (13)	I Only Have Eyes For You (14)
And We Were Lovers ..see: Sand Pebbles, Theme From	Call Me Irresponsible (1) 75	Easy To Be Hard (17)	For All We Know (13)	Hushed Whispers (13)	I Really Want To Know You (16)
Angel Eyes (2)	'Cause I Got So Much Lovin' In Me (12)		Free Again (11)	I Can't Believe I'm Losing You (6)	
As Time Goes By (12)			From Russia With Love (3)		

DEBUT DATE	PEAK POS	WKS CHR	GOLD	ARTIST — Album Title	$	Label & Number

JONES, Jack — Cont'd

I See Your Face Before Me (2)
I Want To Meet Her (8)
I Will Wait For You (9)
I Wish You Love (2)
I'll Get By (As Long As I Have You) (5)
I'll Never Fall In Love Again (17)
I'm All Smiles (6)
I'm Falling In Love Again (15)
I'm Getting Sentimental Over You (15)
I'm Glad There Is You (In This World Of Ordinary People) (5)
I'm Indestructible (14) 81
I'm Moody (2)
I'm Old Fashioned (3)
I've Grown Accustomed To Her Face (3)
If You Ever Leave Me (15) 82
If You Go Away (11)
If You Never Come To Me (11)
Impossible Dream (The Quest) (9) 33
"In" Crowd (8)
Isn't It Lonely Together (17)
Isn't It Romantic? (13)
It Never Entered My Mind (4)

It Only Takes A Moment (3)
It's Easy To Remember (11)
It's Nice To Be With You (16)
Josephine For Better Or For Worse (17)
Just Yesterday (8) 73
King Of The Road (6)
Lady (11) 39
(Lara's Theme) ..see: Somewhere, My Love
Last Seven Days (17)
Letter (15)
Light My Fire (16)
Live For Life (13) 99
Lollipops And Roses (1) 66
Lonely Afternoon (16)
Long Ago, Last Night (15)
Look Of Love (13)
Lorelei (4)
Love After Midnight (10)
Love Bug (8) 71
Love Is Here To Stay (5)
Love Letters (1)
Love With The Proper Stranger (3) 62
Lovely Way To Spend An Evening (7)
Luck Be A Lady (3)
Lush Life (4)

Mean To Me (13)
Michelle (12)
Mood I'm In (3)
Moonlight Becomes You (1)
More (6)
More And More (12)
My Best Girl (9)
My Kind Of Town (6)
My Romance (1)
Nice 'N' Easy (11)
Night Is Young And You're So Beautiful (7)
Nina Never Knew (2)
Now I Know (12) 73
(How Much I Love You (Dio Come Ti Amo)) (12)
Old Man River (16)
Once Upon A Time (11)
One I Love Belongs To Somebody Else (6,14)
1 - 2 - 3 (8)
Our Song (12) 92
People (4)
People Will Say We're In Love (10)
Pretty (15)
Race Is On (6) 15
Right As The Rain (3)
Rosalie (3)

Sand Pebbles, Theme From (11)
Seein' The Right Love Go Wrong (14) 46
Shadow Of Your Smile (9)
Shining Sea (10)
Snows Of Yesteryear (10)
Something's Gotta Give (5)
Somewhere (15)
Somewhere Along The Way (6)
Somewhere, My Love (Lara's Theme) (10)
Somewhere There's Someone (10)
Song About Love (2)
Spinning Wheel (7)
Strangers In The Night (9)
Street Of Dreams (10)
Summertime Promises (2)
Sunshine, Lollipops And Rainbows (8)
Suzanne (16)
Sweet Child (17)
Tenderly (10)
Thank Heaven For Little Girls (5)
Then Was Then And Now Is Now (9)
There Comes A Time (15)

There Will Never Be Another You (1)
There's Love & There's Love & There's Love (7)
They Didn't Believe Me (1)
This Is All I Ask (9)
This Was My Love (1)
Time After Time (6)
Time For Us (Love Theme From Romeo And Juliet) (17)
To Love And Be Loved (4)
Travellin' On (6)
True Love (7,14)
True Picture (12)
Valley Of The Dolls (3)
(Waitin') 'Round The Bend (16)
Watch What Happens (8)
Weekend, The (8)
What Now My Love (9)
What The World Needs Now Is Love (8,14)
What's New? (4)
When I Look In Your Eyes (12)
When She Makes Music (5)
Where Is Love? (16)

Where Love Has Gone (4) 62
While We're Young (7)
Wildflower (9)
Willow Weep For Me (4)
Without Her (13)
Wives And Lovers (2) 14
Yes, I Can! (6)
Yesterday (8,14)
You And The Night And The Music (13)
You Better Go Now (9)
You Do Something To Me (7)
You Made Me Love You (I Didn't Want To Do It) (7)
You Stepped Out Of A Dream (1)
You'd Better Love Me (5)
You're My Girl (5)
You're Sensational (5)
You've Got Your Troubles (8)
Young At Heart (7)

JONES, Jesus — see JESUS

JONES, Jonah

Born Robert Jones on 12/31/08 in Louisville, Kentucky. Jazz trumpet player. Worked with Jimmie Lunceford, Stuff Smith, Billie Holiday and Cab Calloway.

DEBUT DATE	PEAK POS	WKS CHR	GOLD	ARTIST — Album Title	$	Label & Number
3/10/58	7	17		1 Muted Jazz ....[I]	$25	Capitol 839
				THE JONAH JONES QUARTET:		
4/28/58	7	19		2 Swingin' On Broadway ....[I]	$25	Capitol 963
9/8/58	14	5		3 Jumpin' With Jonah ....[I]	$25	Capitol 1039

Baby, Won't You Please Come Home (3)
Baubles, Bangles And Beads (2)
Bill Bailey Won't You Please Come Home? (3)
Blues Don't Care (Who's Got 'Em) (3)
Dance Only With Me (3)

Hey There (1)
I Can't Get Started (1)
I Could Have Danced All Night (2)
It's A Good Day (3)
Jumpin' With Jonah (3)
Just A Gigolo (3)
Just In Time (2)
Just My Luck (2)

Kiss To Build A Dream On (3)
Lots Of Luck Charley (3)
Mack The Knife (1)
Man With The Golden Arm, Main Title From (1)
My Blue Heaven (1)
Night Train (1)
No Moon At All (3)

On The Street Where You Live (1)
Party's Over (2)
Rose Room (1)
Royal Garden Blues (3)
Seventy Six Trombones (2)
St. James Infirmary (1)
Surrey With The Fringe On Top (2)

That's A Plenty (3)
Till There Was You (2)
Too Close For Comfort (1)
Undecided (1)
Whatever Lola Wants (2)
You're Just In Love (2)
You're So Right For Me (2)

JONES, Mick

Founding guitarist of Foreigner. Born on 12/27/44 in London. In the late 1960s, did session work and wrote for French pop idols Johnny Halliday and Sylvie Vartan. Formed Wonderwheel with Gary Wright. Guitarist of Spooky Tooth from 1972-74. Production work for Van Halen, Bad Company and many others.

DEBUT DATE	PEAK POS	WKS CHR	GOLD	ARTIST — Album Title	$	Label & Number
9/23/89	184	3		Mick Jones	$8	Atlantic 81991

Danielle
Everything That Comes Around

4 Wheels Turnin'
Johnny (Part 1)

Just Wanna Hold
Save Me Tonight

That's The Way My Love Is
Write Tonight

Wrong Side Of The Law
You Are My Friend

JONES, Oran "Juice"

Born in Houston in 1959 and raised in Harlem. Soul balladeer singer.

DEBUT DATE	PEAK POS	WKS CHR	GOLD	ARTIST — Album Title	$	Label & Number
9/20/86	44	22		Oran "Juice" Jones	$8	Def Jam 40367

Curiosity
Here I Go Again

It's Yours
Love Will Find A Way

1.2.1
Rain, The 9

Two Faces
You Can't Hide From Love

Your Song

★★188★★ JONES, Quincy

Born Quincy Delight Jones, Jr. on 3/14/33 in Chicago and raised in Seattle. Composer/producer/conductor/arranger. Began as a jazz trumpeter with Lionel Hampton, 1950-53. Music director for Mercury Records in 1961, then vice president in 1964. Wrote scores for many films, 1965-73. Scored TV series *Roots* in 1977. Arranger/producer for hundreds of successful singers and orchestras. Produced Michael Jackson's mega-albums *Off The Wall*, *Thriller* and *Bad*. Established own Qwest label in 1981. Line producer for the film *The Color Purple*. Married to actress Peggy Lipton (TV's *Mod Squad*) from 1974-89. Most nominated artist in Grammy history with 76 nominations and 25 wins. Won the Grammy's Trustees Award in 1989. Won Grammy's Legends Award in 1990. His biographical film *Listen Up: The Lives Of Quincy Jones* was released in 1990.

DEBUT DATE	PEAK POS	WKS CHR	GOLD	ARTIST — Album Title	$	Label & Number
12/29/62+	112	8		1 Big Band Bossa Nova ....[I]	$35	Mercury 60751
11/22/69+	56	39		2 Walking In Space ....[I]	$10	A&M 3023
9/5/70	63	16		3 Gula Matari ....[I]	$10	A&M 3030
10/16/71	56	33		4 Smackwater Jack ....[I]	$10	A&M 3037
3/4/72	173	9		5 Ndeda ....[I-K]	$20	Mercury 623 [2]
6/2/73	94	24		6 You've Got It Bad Girl	$10	A&M 3041
5/25/74	6	43	●	7 Body Heat	$10	A&M 3617
8/23/75	16	30		8 Mellow Madness	$10	A&M 4526
				this album introduces The Brothers Johnson		
10/2/76	43	15		9 I Heard That!! ....[K]	$10	A&M 3705 [2]
2/19/77	21	14	●	10 Roots ....[TV]	$8	A&M 4626
6/24/78	15	20	▲	11 Sounds...And Stuff Like That!!	$8	A&M 4685
4/4/81+	10	80	▲	12 The Dude	$8	A&M 3721

DEBUT DATE	PEAK POS	WKS CHR	GOLD	ARTIST — Album Title	$	Label & Number

JONES, Quincy — Cont'd

7/17/82	122	17		13 The Best ....[G]	$8	A&M 3200
12/9/89+	9	40 ▲		14 **Back On The Block**	$8	Qwest 26020

vocals and instrumentation by many of the pop and jazz artists Quincy has worked with, among them: Ray Charles, Miles Davis, Ella Fitzgerald, Dizzy Gillespie, Ice-T, Chaka Khan and Sarah Vaughan

Al No Corrida (12,13) **28**
Air Mail Special (5)
Along Came Betty (7)
Anderson Tapes, Theme From The (4,9)
Back At The Chicken Shack (5)
Back On The Block (14)
Beautiful Black Girl (8)
Behold, The Only Thing Greater Than Yourself (Birth) (10)
Betcha' Wouldn't Hurt Me (12,13)
Birdland (14)
Birth Of A Band (5)
Bluesette (8)
Body Heat (7,9,13)
Boogie Bossa Nova (1)
Boogie Joe, The Grinder (7)
Boy In The Tree (5)
Boyhood To Manhood (Brazilian Wedding Song) ..see: Setembro
Bridge Over Troubled Water (3)
Brown Ballad (4)
Brown Soft Shoe (9)
Carnival (Manha De Carnaval) (1)

Cast Your Fate To The Wind (4)
Chega De Saudade (No More Blues) (1)
Chump Change (6)
Cry Baby (8)
Dead End (2)
Desafinado (1)
Dreamsville (5)
Dude, The (12)
Everything Must Change (7,13)
Eyes Of Love (6)
Free At Last? (The Civil War) (10)
Getaway, Love Theme From The (6)
Golden Boy, Theme From (5)
Gravy Waltz (5)
Guitar Blues Odyssey: From Roots To Fruits (4)
Gula Matari (3,9)
Harlem Drive (5)
Hikky-Burr (4)
Hummin' (3)
(I Can't Get No) Satisfaction (5)
I Don't Go For That (14)
I Had A Ball (5)
I Heard That!! (10)

I Never Told You (2)
I'll Be Good To You (14) **18**
I'm Gonna Miss You In The Morning (11,13)
If I Ever Lose This Heaven (7,9,13)
Ironside (5)
Is It Love That We're Missin' (8,9) **70**
Jazz Corner Of The Word (14)
Jive Samba (5)
Jumpin' De Broom (Marriage Ceremony) (10)
Just A Little Taste Of Me (8)
Just A Man (7)
Just Once (12,13) **17**
Killer Joe (2,9,13) **74**
Lalo Bossa Nova (1,5)
Listen (What It Is) (8)
Love And Peace (2)
Love, I Never Had It So Good (11)
Love Me By Name (11)
Manteca (5)
Many Rains Ago (Oluwa) [includes 2 versions] (10)
Mellow Madness (14)
Middle Passage (Slaveship Crossing) (10)

Midnight Soul Patrol (9)
Midnight Sun Will Never Set (5)
Mirage (5)
Mr. Lucky (5)
My Cherie Amour (8)
Oh Happy Day (2)
Oh Lord, Come By Here (10)
Ole Fiddler (10)
On The Street Where You Live (1)
One Hundred Ways (12) **14**
One Man Woman (14)
One Track Mind (7)
Paranoid (5)
Pawnbroker, Theme From The (5)
Peter Gunn (5)
Places You Find Love (14)
Rack 'Em Up (5)
Razzamatazz (12)
"Roots" Medley (10) **57**
Roots (Mama Aifamberni), Main Title (10)
Samba De Uma Nota So (One Note Samba) (1)
Sanford & Son Theme (The Streetbeater) (6)
Se E Tarde Me, Pardoa (Forgive Me If I'm Late) (1)

Seaweed (5)
Secret Garden (Sweet Seduction Suite) (14) **31**
Serenata (1)
Setembro (Brazilian Wedding Song) (14)
Slender Thread (5)
Smackwater Jack (4)
Somethin' Special (12)
Soul Bossa Nova (1,5)
Soul Saga (Song Of The Buffalo Soldier) (7)
Stuff Like That (11,13) **21**
Summer In The City (6,9)
Superstition (6,9)
Superwoman (Where Were You When I Needed You) (11)
Takin' It To The Streets (11)
Tell Me A Bedtime Story (11)
There's A Train Leavin' (9)
Things Could Be Worse For Me (9)
Tomorrow (A Better You, A Better Me) (14) **75**
Touboob Is Here! (The Capture) (10)
Tribute To A.F. - RO Medley (6)

Tryin' To Find Out About You (8)
Turn On The Action (12)
Velas (12)
Verb To Be (14)
Walkin' (3)
Walking In Space (2,9)
Wee B. Dooinit (14)
What Good Is A Song (9)
What Shall I Do? (Hush, Hush, Somebody's Calling My Name) (10)
What's Going On? (4,13)
Witching Hour (5)
You Have To Do It Yourself (9)
You In Americuh Now, African (10)
You've Got It Bad Girl (6)

JONES, Rickie Lee

Born on 11/8/54 in Chicago. Pop-jazz-styled singer/songwriter. Moved to Los Angeles in 1977. Won the 1979 Best New Artist Grammy Award.

4/7/79	3	36 ▲		1 Rickie Lee Jones	$8	Warner 3296
8/8/81	5	29 ●		2 Pirates	$8	Warner 3432
7/2/83	39	16		3 Girl At Her Volcano ....[M]	$8	Warner 23805

10" album; 2 of the 7 tracks are live performances

10/13/84	44	21		4 The Magazine	$8	Warner 25117
10/14/89	39	25		5 Flying Cowboys	$8	Geffen 24246
10/12/91	121	5		6 Pop Pop	$12	Geffen 24426

After Hours (Twelve Bars Past Goodnight) (1)
Atlas' Marker (4)
Away From The Sky (5)
Ballad Of The Sad Young Men (6)
Bye Bye Blackbird (6)
Chuck E.'s In Love (1) **4**
Comin' Back To Me (6)
Company (1)
Coolsville (1)
Danny's All-Star Joint (1)
Dat Dere (6)

Deep Space (5)
Don't Let The Sun Catch You Crying (5)
Easy Money (1)
Flying Cowboys (5)
Ghetto Of My Mind (5)
Ghost Train (5)
Gravity (4)
Hey, Bub (3)
Hi-Lili Hi-Lo (6)
Horses (5)
I Won't Grow Up (6)
I'll Be Seeing You (6)

It Must Be Love (4)
Juke Box Fury (4)
Just My Baby (5)
Last Chance Texaco (1)
Letters From The 9th Ward (medley) (5)
Living It Up (2)
Love Is Gonna Bring Us Back Alive (5)
Love Junkyard (6)
Lucky Guy (2) **64**
Lush Life (3)
Magazine (4)

My Funny Valentine (6)
My One And Only Love (6)
Night Train (1)
On Saturday Afternoons In 1963 (1)
Pirates (So Long Lonely Avenue) (2)
Pope, Theme For The (medley) (4)
Rainbow Sleeves (3)
Real End (4) **83**
Returns, The (2)
Rodeo Girl (5)

Rorschachs (medley) (4)
Runaround (4)
Satellites (5)
Second Time Around (4)
Skeletons (2)
So Long (3)
Spring Can Really Hang You Up The Most (6)
Traces Of The Western Slopes (2)
Under The Boardwalk (3)
Unsigned Painting (medley) (4)

Up From The Skies (6)
Walk Away Rene (medley) (3)
We Belong Together (2)
Weasel And The White Boys Cool (1)
Weird Beast (medley) (4)
Woody And Dutch On The Slow Train To Peking (2)
Young Blood (1) **40**

JONES, Shirley

Lead singer of The Jones Girls. Born and raised in Detroit.

8/23/86	128	10		Always In The Mood	$8	Phil. Int. 53031

Always In The Mood
Breaking Up

Caught Me With My Guard Down

Do You Get Enough Love
I'll Do Anything For You

Last Night I Needed Somebody

She Knew About Me
Surrender

JONES, Spike

"King of Corn" bandleader. Born on 12/14/11 in Long Beach, California; died on 5/1/64.

11/23/63	113	4		Washington Square ....[I]	$25	Liberty 3338

Alley Cat
Ballad Of Jed Clampett

Blowin' In The Wind
Frankie And Johnnie

Green, Green
If I Had A Hammer

Maria Elena
Puff (The Magic Dragon)

Red Sails In The Sunset
September Song

Washington Square
Whistler's Muddah

JONES, Steve

Former guitarist of legendary punk band The Sex Pistols. Later with The Professionals. Appeared in the 1982 film *Ladies And Gentlemen, The Fabulous Stains*. Film score work for *Sid & Nancy*.

10/21/89	169	4		Fire And Gasoline	$8	MCA 6298

Fire And Gasoline
Freedom Fighter

Get Ready
Gimme Love

God In Louisiana
Hold On

I Did U No Wrong
Leave Your Shoes On

Trouble Maker
We're Not Saints

Wild Wheels

★★116★★ JONES, Tom

Born Thomas Jones Woodward on 6/7/40 in Pontypridd, South Wales. Worked local clubs as Tommy Scott; formed own trio The Senators in 1963. Began solo career in London in 1964. Won the 1965 Best New Artist Grammy Award. Host of own TV musical variety series from 1969-71.

7/3/65	54	42		1 It's Not Unusual	$20	Parrot 71004
9/18/65	114	5		2 What's New Pussycat?	$20	Parrot 71006
3/4/67+	65	45 ●		3 Green, Green Grass Of Home	$20	Parrot 71009
6/15/68+	14	82 ●		4 The Tom Jones Fever Zone	$20	Parrot 71019
2/1/69	5	54 ●		5 **Help Yourself**	$20	Parrot 71025

DEBUT DATE	PEAK POS	WKS CHR	GOLD	ARTIST — Album Title	$	Label & Number
				JONES, Tom — Cont'd		
3/15/69	13	58	●	6 Tom Jones Live! ....[L]	$20	Parrot 71014
				originally recorded and released in 1967		
6/14/69	4	43	●	7 This Is Tom Jones	$20	Parrot 71028
11/15/69	3	51	●	8 Tom Jones Live In Las Vegas ....[L]	$20	Parrot 71031
5/9/70	6	26	●	9 Tom	$20	Parrot 71037
11/14/70	23	40	●	10 I (Who Have Nothing)	$20	Parrot 71039
5/22/71	17	20	●	11 She's A Lady	$20	Parrot 71046
11/6/71	43	14	●	12 Tom Jones Live At Caesars Palace ....[L]	$20	Parrot 71049 [2]
6/17/72	64	20		13 Close Up	$20	Parrot 71055
6/16/73	93	10		14 The Body And Soul of Tom Jones	$15	Parrot 71060
1/5/74	185	4		15 Tom Jones' Greatest Hits ....[G]	$15	Parrot 71062
3/5/77	76	16		16 Say You'll Stay Until Tomorrow	$10	Epic 34468
3/5/77	191	3		17 Tom Jones Greatest Hits ....[G]	$8	London 50002
5/23/81	179	3		18 Darlin'	$8	Mercury 4010

Ain't No Sunshine (14)
All I Can Say Is Goodbye (5)
All I Ever Need Is You (13)
And I Tell The Sea (3)
Anniversary Song (16)
Any Day Now (3)
At Every End There's A Beginning (16)
Autumn Leaves (1)
Ballad Of Billy Joe (14)
Bama Lama Bama Loo (2)
Bed, The (5)
Bridge Over Troubled Water (12)
Bright Lights And You Girl (8)
Brother Can You Spare A Dime (4)
But I Do (18)
Cabaret (12)
Can't Stop Loving You (10) 25
Come Home Rhondda Boy (18)
Come To Me (16)
Dance Of Love (7,12)
Danny Boy (4,8)
Darlin' (18)
Daughter Of Darkness (10,12,15) 13
Daughter's Question (18)
Delilah (4,8,12,15,17) 15
Dime Queen Of Nevada (18)
Do What You Gotta Do (11)
Don't Fight It (4)
Ebb Tide (The Sea) (11)
Elusive Dreams (5)
Endlessly (2)

Fly Me To The Moon (In Other Words) (7)
Funny Familiar Forgotten Feelings (15,17) 49
Funny How Time Slips Away (4)
Georgia On My Mind (3)
Get Ready (4)
God Bless The Children (3)
Good News (6)
Green, Green Grass Of Home (3,6,15,17) 11
Hard To Handle (8)
Have You Every Been Lonely (16)
Hello Young Lovers (6)
Help Yourself (5,8,15,17) 35
Hey Jude (7,8)
Hi Heel Sneakers (12)
Hold On, I'm Coming (4)
House Song (5)
I Believe (6)
I Can't Break The News To Myself (5)
I Can't Stop Loving You (6,8)
I Can't Turn You Loose (9)
I Don't Want To Know You That Well (18)
I Get Carried Away (5)
I Have Dreamed (1)
I Know (4)
I Need Your Loving (1)
I Still Love You Enough (To Love You All Over Again) (14)
I Thank You (9)
I Wake Up Crying (4)
I Was Made To Love Her (4)

I (Who Have Nothing) (10,12) 14
I Won't Be Sorry To See Suzanne Again (13)
I'll Never Fall In Love Again (8,12,15,17) 6
I'll Share My World With You (14)
I'm A Fool To Want You (7)
I'm Coming Home (17) 57
I've Got A Heart (2)
If (13)
If Ever I Would Leave You (3)
If I Promise (5)
If I Ruled The World (9)
If Loving You Is Wrong (I Don't Wanna Be Right) (14)
If You Go Away (5)
If You Need Me (1)
Impossible Dream (9)
In Dreams (11)
It's A Man's Man's World (4)
It's Just A Matter Of Time (1)
It's Not Unusual (1,6,8,12,15,17) 10
It's Up To The Woman (11)
Kansas City (3)
Keep On Running (4)
Kiss An Angel Good Morning (13)
Lady Lay Down (18)
Land Of A Thousand Dances (6)
Laura (1)
Lean On Me (14)
Let It Be Me (7)
Let There Be Love (9)
Letter To Lucille (14) 60

Little By Little (2)
Little Green Apples (7)
Lodi (10)
Love Me Tonight (8,12,15,17) 13
Love's Been Good To Me (10)
Memphis Tennessee (1)
My Girl Maria (5)
My Mother's Eyes (4)
My Prayer (3)
My Way (12)
My Yiddische Momme (6)
No Guarantee (18)
Nothing Rhymed (11)
Once Upon A Time (1)
One Man Woman (16)
One More Chance (2)
One Night (18)
One Night Only Love Maker (11)
Only Once (7)
Papa (16)
Polk Salad Annie (9)
Proud Mary (9)
Puppet Man (11) 26
Resurrection Shuffle (11,12) 38
Rock N' Roll Medley (12)
Rose, The (2)
Runnin' Bear (9)
Say You'll Stay Until Tomorrow (16) 15
See-Saw (10)
Set Me Free (5)
Shake (8)
She's A Lady (11,12,15) 2
Since I Loved You Last (14)

(Sitting On) The Dock Of The Bay (7)
Skye Boat Song (1)
So Afraid (5)
Some Day (You'll Want Me) (3)
Some Other Guy (2)
Soul Man (12)
Spanish Harlem (1)
Sugar Sugar (9)
Take Me Tonight (16)
Taste Of Honey (3)
That Lucky Old Sun (6)
That Old Black Magic (3)
That Wonderful Sound (7)
That's All Any Man Can Say (7)
Things That Matter Most To Me (18)
Til I Can't Take It Anymore (11)
Till (12) 41
Time To Get It Together (13)
Tired Of Being Alone (13)
To Love Somebody (2)
To Wait For Love (Is To Waste Your Life Away) (2)
Today I Started Loving You (14)
Try A Little Tenderness (10)
Turn On Your Love Light (8)
Twist And Shout (8)
Untrue (2)
Venus (2)
Watcha Gonna Do (1)
We Had It All (16)
What In The World's Come Over You (18)

What The World Needs Now (10)
What's New Pussycat? (2,6,15,17) 3
When I Fall In Love (3)
When It's Just You And Me (16)
When The World Was Beautiful (1)
Wichita Lineman (9)
Witch Queen Of New Orleans (13)
With These Hands (2) 27
Without Love (There Is Nothing) (9,17) 5
Without You (Non C'E' Che Lei) (7)
Woman You Took My Life (13)
Worried Man (1)
Yesterday (8)
You Came A Long Way From St. Louis (3)
You Keep Me Hanging On (4)
You're My World (Il Mio Mondo) (11)
You've Got A Friend (13)
You've Lost That Lovin' Feelin' (9)
Young New Mexican Puppeteer (13) 80

JONES GIRLS, The

Detroit soul sister trio: Shirley, Brenda and Valorie Jones. Backup singers for Lou Rawls, Teddy Pendergrass and Aretha Franklin. With Diana Ross from 1975-78. Sang with Le Pamplemousse.

DEBUT DATE	PEAK POS	WKS CHR	GOLD	ARTIST — Album Title	$	Label & Number
6/9/79	50	16		1 The Jones Girls	$8	Phil. Int. 35757
10/18/80	96	24		2 At Peace With Woman	$8	Phil. Int. 36767
12/5/81+	155	15		3 Get As Much Love As You Can	$8	Phil. Int. 37627

ASAP (As Soon As Possible) (3)
At Peace With Woman (2)
Back In The Day (2)
Children Of The Night (2)
Dance Turned Into A Romance (2)

Get As Much Love As You Can (3)
I Close My Eyes (2)
(I Found) That Man Of Mine (3)
I Just Love The Man (2)
I'm At Your Mercy (3)

Let's Be Friends First (Then Lovers) (3)
Let's Celebrate (Sittin' On Top Of The World) (2)
Life Goes On (1)
Love Don't Ever Say Goodbye (3)

Nights Over Egypt (3)
Show Love Today (1)
This Feeling's Killing Me (1)
We're A Melody (1)
When I'm Gone (2)
Who Can I Run To (1)
World Will Sing Our Song (3)

You Gonna Make Me Love Somebody Else (1) 38
You Made Me Love You (1)
You're Breakin' My Heart (3)

JONZUN CREW, The

Electronic instrumentation group formed in Boston by ex-Florida brothers Michael (lead vocals) and Soni Johnson, with Steve Thorpe and Gordy Worthy. Michael recorded solo in 1986.

DEBUT DATE	PEAK POS	WKS CHR	GOLD	ARTIST — Album Title	$	Label & Number
5/14/83	66	20		Lost In Space	$8	Tommy Boy 1001

Electro Boogie Encounter   Ground Control   Pack Jam   Space Cowboy   Space Is The Place   We Are The Jonzun Crew

★★427★★ JOPLIN, Janis

Born on 1/19/43 in Port Arthur, Texas. White blues-rock singer. Nicknamed "Pearl." To San Francisco in 1966, joined Big Brother & The Holding Company. Left band to go solo in 1968. Died of a heroin overdose in Hollywood on 10/4/70. The Bette Midler film The Rose was inspired by Joplin's life.

DEBUT DATE	PEAK POS	WKS CHR	GOLD	ARTIST — Album Title	$	Label & Number
10/11/69	5	28	●	1 I Got Dem Ol' Kozmic Blues Again Mama!	$20	Columbia 9913
1/30/71	1⁹	42	▲3	2 **Pearl**	$15	Columbia 30322
5/13/72	4	27	●	3 Joplin In Concert ....[L]	$15	Columbia 31160 [2]
				side 1: with Big Brother & The Holding Company; side 2: with Full Tilt Boogie Band		
7/14/73	37	22	▲2	4 Janis Joplin's Greatest Hits ....[G]	$15	Columbia 32168
5/17/75	54	9		5 Janis ....[S]	$12	Columbia 33345 [2]
				soundtrack includes her early recordings from 1963-65		

DEBUT DATE	PEAK POS	WKS CHR	GOLD	ARTIST — Album Title	$	Label & Number

JOPLIN, Janis — Cont'd

| 2/13/82 | 104 | 11 | 6 Farewell Song ....[K] | $8 | Columbia 37569 |

recordings from 1967-70

All Is Loneliness (3)
Amazing Grace (medley) (6)
As Good As You've Been To This World (1)
Ball And Chain (3,4,5)
Black Mountain Blues (5)
Buried Alive In The Blues (2)
Bye, Bye Baby (3,4)
Careless Love (5)
Catch Me Daddy (6)
Cry Baby (2,4,5) *42*
Daddy, Daddy, Daddy (5)

Down On Me (3,4) *91*
Ego Rock (3)
Farewell Song (6)
Flower In The Sun (3)
Get It While You Can (2,3,4) *78*
Half Moon (2,3)
Harry (6)
Hi Heel Sneakers (medley) (6)
I'll Drown In My Own Tears (5)
K.C. Blues (5)

Kozmic Blues (1,3) *41*
Little Girl Blue (4)
Magic Of Love (6)
Mary Jane (5)
Maybe (1,5)
Me And Bobby McGee (2,4,5) *1*
Mercedes Benz (2,5)
Mississippi River (5)
Move Over (2,3,4,5)
My Baby (2)

No Reason For Livin' (5)
One Good Man (1)
One Night Stand (6)
Piece Of My Heart (3,4,5) *12*
Raise Your Hand (6)
River Jordan (5)
Road Block (3)
San Francisco Bay Blues (5)
See See Rider (5)
Silver Threads And Golden Needles (5)

Stealin' (5)
Summertime (3,4,5)
Tell Mama (6)
To Love Somebody (1)
Trouble In Mind (5)
Trust Me (2)
Try (Just A Little Bit Harder) (1,3,4,5)
Walk Right In (5)
What Good Can Drinkin' Do (5)
Winin' Boy (5)

Woman Left Lonely (2)
Work Me, Lord (1)

JOPLIN, Scott — see HAMLISCH, Marvin/RIFKIN, Joshua/NEW ENGLAND RAGTIME

JORDAN, Jerry
Country/religious humorist. Born and raised on a farm in Texas.

| 5/31/75 | 79 | 12 | | Phone Call From God..[C] | $8 | MCA 473 |

Air-Conditioned Cars
Hog Story

It All Depends
No Hand To Dismiss

Overdrawn At The Bank
Phone Call From God

Prejudiced People
Tell Me The Story

JORDAN, Lonnie
Born Leroy Jordan on 11/21/48 in San Diego. R&B singer/keyboardist. Member of War.

| 2/25/78 | 158 | 5 | | Different Moods Of Me .... | $8 | MCA 2329 |

Best Way I Can
Different Moods Of Me

Discoland
Grey Rainy Days

He Used To Be A Friend Of Mine

Jungle Dancin'
Junkie To My Music

Nasty

JORDAN, Sass
Female rock singer.

| 8/29/92 | 174 | 7 | | Racine.. | $12 | Impact 10524 |

Cry Baby
Do What Ya Want

Goin' Back Again
I Want To Believe

If You're Gonna Love Me
Make You A Believer

Time Flies
Where There's A Will

Who Do You Think You Are
Windin' Me Up

You Don't Have To Remind Me

JORDAN, Stanley
Jazz guitarist from Palo Alto, California. Uses a unique two-handed, tapping/playing technique. Appeared in the 1987 film *Blind Date*.

| 5/25/85 | 64 | 66 | | 1 Magic Touch ....[I] | $8 | Blue Note 85101 |
| 2/14/87 | 116 | 18 | | 2 Standards, Volume 1...[I] | $8 | Blue Note 85130 |

pop standards, most of which were popular between 1959 and 1979

| 10/15/88 | 131 | 9 | | 3 Flying Home ....[I] | $8 | EMI 48682 |

All The Children (1)
Angel (1)
Because (2)
Brooklyn At Midnight (3)
Can't Sit Down (3)

Child Is Born (1)
Eleanor Rigby (1)
Flying Home (3)
Freddie Freeloader (1)
Fundance (1)

Georgia On My Mind (2)
Guitar Man (2)
Lady In My Life (1)
Moon River (2)
Music's Gonna Change (3)

My Favorite Things (2)
One Less Bell To Answer (2)
Return Expedition (3)
Round Midnight (1)
Send One Your Love (2)

Silent Night (2)
Sound Of Silence (2)
Stairway To Heaven (3)
Street Talk (3)
Sunny (2)

Time Is Now (3)
Tropical Storm (3)
When Julia Smiles (3)

JOSEPH, Margie
Born in 1950 in Gautier, Mississippi. First recorded at Muscle Shoals for Okeh in 1967.

| 2/6/71 | 67 | 14 | | 1 Margie Joseph Makes A New Impression............................. | $12 | Volt 6012 |
| 8/17/74 | 165 | 3 | | 2 Sweet Surrender .... | $10 | Atlantic 7277 |

Baby I'm-A Want You (2)
Come Lay Some Lovin' On Me (2)
Come Tomorrow (1)
Come With Me (2)

He's Got A Way (2)
How Beautiful The Rain (1)
I'm Fed Up (1)
If I'm Still Around Tomorrow (2)

Make Me Believe You'll Stay (1)
Medicine Bend (1)
My Love (2) *69*
Punish Me (1)

Ridin' High (2)
Same Thing (1)
Stop! In The Name Of Love (1) *96*
(Strange) I Still Love You (2)

Sweet Surrender (2)
Sweeter Tomorrow (1)
Temptation's About To Take Your Love (1)

To Know You Is To Love You (2)

★★120★★ JOURNEY
Rock group formed in San Francisco in 1973. Consisted of Neal Schon, George Tickner (guitars), Gregg Rolie (keyboards, vocals), Ross Valory (bass) and Aynsley Dunbar (John Mayall, Mothers Of Invention; drums). Schon and Rolie had been in Santana. Tickner left in 1975. Steve Perry (lead vocals) added by 1978. In 1979, Steve Smith replaced Dunbar who later joined Jefferson Starship, then Whitesnake. Jonathan Cain (ex-keyboardist of The Babys) added in 1981, replacing Rolie. In 1986 group pared down to a three-man core: Perry, Schon and Cain. The latter two hooked up with Bad English in 1989. Smith, Valory and Rolie joined Storm in 1991. Schon with Hardline in 1992.

5/3/75	138	9		1 Journey	$10	Columbia 33388
2/14/76	100	15		2 Look Into The Future...	$10	Columbia 33904
2/19/77	85	10		3 Next..	$8	Columbia 34311
2/11/78	21	123	▲3	4 Infinity	$8	Columbia 34912
4/14/79	20	96	▲3	5 Evolution	$8	Columbia 35797
1/5/80	152	8		6 In The Beginning..[K]	$10	Columbia 36324 [2]

recordings from albums #1, 2 and 3

3/22/80	8	57	▲2	7 Departure	$8	Columbia 36339
2/21/81	9	69	▲	8 Captured ....[L]	$10	Columbia 37016 [2]
8/8/81	1¹	146	▲7	9 Escape...	$8	Columbia 37408
2/19/83	2⁹	85	▲4	10 Frontiers..	$8	Columbia 38504
5/10/86	4	67	▲2	11 Raised On Radio	$8	Columbia 39936
12/3/88+	10	92	▲4	12 Greatest Hits ....[G]	$8	Columbia 44493
12/26/92+	90	4		13 Time³ ....[K]	$42	Columbia 48937 [3]

After The Fall (10,13) *23*
All That Really Matters (13)
Any Way You Want It (7,8,12,13) *23*

Anytime (4,8,13) *83*
Anyway (2,6)
Ask The Lonely (12,13)
Back Talk (10)

Be Good To Yourself (11,12,13) *9*
Can Do (4)
Chain Reaction (10)

City Of The Angels (5)
Conversations (medley) (1,6)
Cookie Duster (13)
Daydream (5)

Dead Or Alive (9)
Departure (7)
Dixie Highway (8,13)
Do You Recall (5,8)

Don't Stop Believin' (9,12,13) *9*
Edge Of The Blade (10)
Escape (9)

JOURNEY — Cont'd

Eyes Of A Woman (11,13)
Faithfully (10,12,13) *12*
Feeling That Way (4,8,13)
For You (13)
Frontiers (10)
Girl Can't Help It (11,12,13) *17*
Good Morning Girl (7,13) *55*
  hit "Hot 100" as a medley with "Stay Awhile"
Good Times (13)
Happy To Give (11,13)
Here We Are (3)
Homemade Love (7,13)
Hustler (3)
I Would Find You (3)
I'll Be Alright Without You (11,12,13) *14*

I'm Cryin' (7)
I'm Gonna Leave You (2,6,13)
In My Lonely Feeling (medley) (1,6)
In The Morning Day (1)
Into Your Arms (13)
It Could Have Been You (11)
It's All Too Much (2,6)
Just The Same Way (5,8,13) *58*
Karma (3)
Keep On Runnin' (9,13)
Kohoutek (1,6,13)
La Do Da (4,8)
La Raza Del Sol (13)
Lady Luck (5)
Lay It Down (9)
Liberty (13)
Lights (4,12) *68*

Lights [live] (8,13) *74*
Line Of Fire (7,8,13)
Little Girl (13)
Look Into The Future (2,6)
Lovin' You Is Easy (5)
Lovin', Touchin', Squeezin' (5,8,12,13) *16*
Majestic (13)
Midnight Dreamer (2)
Mother, Father (9,13)
Mystery Mountain (1,6)
Natural Thing (13)
Next (3)
Nickel & Dime (3,6,13)
Of A Lifetime (1,6,13)
On A Saturday Nite (2,6)
Once You Love Somebody (11,13)
Only Solutions (13)

Only The Young (12,13) *9*
Open Arms (9,12,13) *2*
Opened The Door (4)
Party's Over (Hopelessly In Love) (8,13) *34*
Patiently (4,13)
People (3,6)
People And Places (7)
Positive Touch (11)
Precious Time (7)
Raised On Radio (11)
Rubicon (10)
Send Her My Love (10,12,13) *23*
Separate Ways (Worlds Apart) (10,12,13) *8*
She Makes Me (Feel Alright) (2)
Someday Soon (7,13)

Somethin' To Hide (4)
Spaceman (3,6)
Stay Awhile (7,8,13) *55*
  hit "Hot 100" as a medley with "Good Morning Girl"
Still They Ride (9,13) *19*
Stone In Love (9,13)
Suzanne (11) *17*
Sweet And Simple (5,13)
To Play Some Music (1)
Too Late (5,8,13) *70*
Topaz (1,6)
Troubled Child (10)
Velvet Curtain (medley) (13)
Walks Like A Lady (7,8,13) *32*
Wheel In The Sky (4,8,12,13) *57*

When You're Alone (It Ain't Easy) (5)
Where Were You (7,8,13)
Who's Crying Now (9,12,13) *4*
Why Can't This Night Go On Forever (11,13) *60*
Winds Of March (4)
With A Tear (13)
You're On Your Own (2,6)

JOY DIVISION
Industrial-rock group formed in April 1977 with the name Warsaw. Included Ian Curtis (vocals), Peter Hook, Bernard Albrecht and Stephen Morris. In March 1978, changed name to Joy Division (slang for the prostitutes' wing in World War II Nazi concentration camps). Curtis committed suicide in May 1980; group became New Order, recruiting keyboardist/guitarist Gillian Gilbert in December 1980.

8/27/88	**146**	8		Substance .... [K]	**$8**	Qwest 25747

                        features material from 1977-80

Atmosphere
Autosuggestion

Dead Souls
Digital

Incubation
Leaders Of Men

Love Will Tear Us Apart
She's Lost Control

Transmission
Warsaw

JOY OF COOKING
Berkeley, California country-rock quintet led by female vocalists Terry Garthwaite and Toni Brown.

3/6/71	**100**	17	1	Joy Of Cooking	**$10**	Capitol 661
10/9/71	**136**	7	2	Closer To The Ground	**$10**	Capitol 828
6/10/72	**174**	6	3	Castles	**$10**	Capitol 11050

All Around The Sun And The Moon (3)
Bad Luck Blues (3)
Beginning Tomorrow (3)
Blues For A Friend (2)
Brownsville (medley) (1) *66*
Castles (3)

Children's House (3)
Closer To The Ground (2)
Dancing Couple (1)
Did You Go Downtown (1)
Don't The Moon Look Fat And Lonesome (3)
Down My Dream (3)

First Time, Last Time (2)
Home Town Man (3)
Humpty Dumpty (2)
Hush (1)
If Some God (Sometimes You Gotta Go Home) (1)
Lady Called Love (3)

Laugh, Don't Laugh (2)
Let Love Carry You Along (3)
Mockingbird (medley) (1)
New Colorado Blues (3)
Only Time Will Tell Me (1)
Pilot (2)
Red Wine At Noon (1)

Sometimes Like A River (Loving You) (2)
Thousand Miles (2)
Three-Day Loser (3)
Too Late, But Not Forgotten (1)

Waiting For The Last Plane (3)
War You Left (2)

★★292★★ JUDAS PRIEST
Heavy-metal group formed in Birmingham, England in 1973: vocalist Rob Halford, guitarists K.K. Downing and Glenn Tipton, bassist Ian Hill and drummer Dave Holland (replaced by Scott Travis by 1990). Halford left band in mid-1992.

4/8/78	**173**	3	● 1	Stained Class	**$8**	Columbia 35296
3/31/79	**128**	7	● 2	Hell Bent For Leather	**$8**	Columbia 35706
10/6/79	**70**	11	▲ 3	Unleashed In The East (Live In Japan) .... [L]	**$8**	Columbia 36179
5/31/80	**34**	18	▲ 4	British Steel	**$8**	Columbia 36443
4/4/81	**39**	25	● 5	Point Of Entry	**$8**	Columbia 37052
7/24/82	**17**	53	● 6	Screaming For Vengeance	**$8**	Columbia 38160
2/4/84	**18**	37	▲ 7	Defenders Of The Faith	**$8**	Columbia 39219
4/12/86	**17**	36	▲ 8	Turbo	**$8**	Columbia 40158
6/20/87	**38**	15	9	Priest...Live! .... [L]	**$10**	Columbia 40794 [2]
6/4/88	**31**	19	● 10	Ram It Down	**$8**	Columbia 44244
10/6/90	**26**	20	● 11	Painkiller	**$12**	Columbia 46891

All Guns Blazing (11)
All The Way (5)
Battle Hymn (11)
Before The Dawn (2)
Better By You Better Than Me (1)
Between The Hammer & The Anvil (11)
Beyond The Realms Of Death (1)
Blood Red Skies (10)
Bloodstone (6)
Breaking The Law (4,9)
Burnin' Up (2)
Come And Get It (10)
Defenders Of The Faith (7)
Delivering The Goods (2)
Desert Plains (5)
Devil's Child (6)

Diamonds And Rust (3)
Don't Go (5)
Don't Have To Be Old To Be Wise (4)
Eat Me Alive (7)
Electric Eye (6,9)
Evening Star (4)
Evil Fantasies (2)
Exciter (1,3)
Fever (6)
Freewheel Burning (7,9)
Genocide (3)
Green Manalishi (With The Two-Pronged Crown) (2,3)
Grinder (4)
Hard As Iron (10)
Heading Out To The Highway (5,9)
Heavy Duty (7)

Heavy Metal (10)
Hell Bent For Leather (2)
Hell Patrol (11)
Hellion, The (6)
Heroes End (1)
Hot For Love (8)
Hot Rockin' (5)
I'm A Rocker (10)
Invader (1)
Jawbreaker (7)
Johnny B. Goode (10)
Killing Machine (2)
Leather Rebel (11)
Living After Midnight (4,9)
Locked In (8)
Love Bites (7)
Love You To Death (10)
Love Zone (10)
Metal Gods (4,9)

Metal Meltdown (11)
Monsters Of Rock (10)
Night Comes Down (7)
Night Crawler (11)
On The Run (5)
One Shot At Glory (11)
Out In The Cold (8,9)
Pain And Pleasure (6)
Painkiller (11)
Parental Guidance (8,9)
Private Property (8,9)
Rage, The (4)
Ram It Down (10)
Rapid Fire (4)
Reckless (8)
Riding On The Wind (6)
Ripper (3)
Rock Forever (2)
Rock Hard Ride Free (7)

Rock You All Around The World (11)
Running Wild (2,3)
Saints In Hell (1)
Savage (1)
Screaming For Vengeance (6)
Sentinel, The (7,9)
Sinner (3)
Solar Angels (5)
Some Heads Are Gonna Roll (7,9)
Stained Class (1)
Steeler (4)
Take On The World (2)
(Take These) Chains (6)
Touch Of Evil (11)
Troubleshooter (5)
Turbo Lover (8,9)
Turning Circles (5)

Tyrant (3)
United (4)
Victim Of Changes (3)
White Heat, Red Hot (1)
Wild Nights, Hot & Crazy Days (8)
You Say Yes (5)
You've Got Another Thing Comin' (6,9) *67*

JUDD, Wynonna
Country singer. Half of The Judds duo with her mother, Naomi, from 1983-91. Born Christina Ciminella in 1964. Moved to Hollywood in 1968. Appeared in *More American Graffiti*. To Nashville in 1979.

4/18/92	**4**	43↑ ▲²		Wynonna	**$12**	Curb 10529

All Of That Love From Here
I Saw The Light

It's Never Easy To Say Goodbye

Little Bit Of Love (Goes A Long, Long Way)
Live With Jesus

My Strongest Weakness
No One Else On Earth *83*

She Is His Only Need
What It Takes

When I Reach The Place I'm Goin'

DEBUT DATE	PEAK POS	WKS CHR	GOLD	ARTIST — Album Title	$	Label & Number

★★402★★

JUDDS, The
Country duo from Ashland, Kentucky of Naomi (born Diana Ellen Judd on 1/11/46) and her daughter Wynonna (born Christina Ciminella in 1964). To Hollywood in 1968. Both appeared in film *More American Graffiti*. To Nashville in May 1979. Made stage debut in mid-1984. Naomi's chronic hepatitis forced duo split in late 1991.

12/1/84+	71	26	▲²	1 Why Not Me	$8	RCA 5319
12/8/84+	153	15		2 The Judds .... [M]	$8	RCA 8515
				their first album		
11/16/85+	66	57	▲	3 Rockin' With The Rhythm	$8	RCA 7042
4/4/87	52	31	▲	4 Heartland..	$8	RCA 5916
8/27/88	76	97	▲²	5 Greatest Hits...[G]	$8	RCA 8318
4/22/89	51	20	●	6 River Of Time	$8	RCA/Curb 9595
9/29/90+	62	53	●	7 Love Can Build A Bridge	$12	Curb/RCA 2070
				Bonnie Raitt appears on guitar on one track; CD includes bonus cut		
9/28/91+	54	32	●	8 Greatest Hits Volume Two ....[G]	$12	Curb/RCA 61018

Are The Roses Not Blooming (7)
Blue Nun Cafe (2)
Born To Be Blue (7,8)
Bye Bye Baby Blues (1)
Cadillac Red (6)
Calling In The Wind (7)
Change Of Heart (2,5)
Cow Cow Boogie (4)
Cry Myself To Sleep (3,5)
Don't Be Cruel (4)

Dream Chaser (3)
Drops Of Water (1)
Endless Sleep (1)
Girls Night Out (1,5)
Give A Little Love (5)
Grandpa (Tell Me 'Bout The Good Old Days) (3,5)
Guardian Angel (6,8)
Had A Dream (For The Heart) (2,8)
Have Mercy (3,5)

I Know Where I'm Going (4,8)
I Wish She Wouldn't Treat You That Way (3)
I'm Falling In Love Tonight (4)
If I Were You (3)
In My Dreams (4)
Isn't He A Strange One (2)
John Deere Tractor (2,7,8)
Let Me Tell You About Love (6,8)

Love Can Build A Bridge (7,8)
Love Is Alive (1,5)
Mama He's Crazy (1,2,5)
Maybe Your Baby's Got The Blues (4,8)
Mr. Pain (1)
My Baby's Gone (1)
Not My Baby (6)
Old Pictures (4)
One Hundred And Two (7)

One Man Woman (6)
River Of Time (6)
River Roll On (3)
Rockin' With The Rhythm Of The Rain (3,5)
Rompin' Stompin' Blues (7)
Sleeping Heart (1)
Sleepless Nights (6)
Sweetest Gift (4)
Talk About Love (7)
Tears For You (3)

This Country's Rockin' (7)
Turn It Loose (4,8)
Water Of Love (6)
Why Don't You Believe Me (4)
Why Not Me (1,5)
Working In The Coal Mine (3)
Young Love (6,8)

JULUKA
The first South African interracial pop band, led by Johnny Clegg and Sipho Mchunu, formed in 1979. Juluka (Zulu for "sweat") incorporated different styles of Zulu dancing into their shows. Mchunu returned to his father's cattle farm and the sextet disbanded in late 1985. In 1986, Clegg, with Juluka members Dudu Zulu and Derek De Beer, formed Savuka.

8/13/83	186	5		Scatterlings	$8	Warner 23898

Digging For Some Words
Ijwanasibeki

Kwela Man
Scatterlings Of Africa

Shake My Way
Simple Things

Siyayilanda
Spirit Is The Journey

Two Humans On The Run
Umbaqanga Music

JUNGKLAS, Rob
Memphis rocker. Born in Boston.

6/14/86	102	22		Closer To The Flame..	$8	Manhattan 53017

Back To 17
Big Bouffant

Boystown
Dizzy Blonde

Hello Heaven

Make It Mean
Something 86

Memphis Thing
Not Like The Other Boys

See That Girl
When You Hold Me

JUNIOR
Full name: Junior Giscombe. R&B-funk singer/songwriter from England.

5/8/82	71	16		1 "Ji"	$8	Mercury 4043
7/23/83	177	6		2 Inside Lookin' Out	$8	Mercury 812325

Baby I Want You Back (2)
Communication Breakdown (2)

Darling You (Don't You Know) (1)
Down Down (1)
F.B. Eye (2)

I Can't Help It (1)
Is This Love (1)
Let Me Know (1)
Love Dies (1)

Mama Used To Say (1) 30
Runnin' (2)
Sayin' Something (2)
Story Teller (2)

Tell Me (2)
Too Late (1)
Women Say It (2)
You're The One (2)

JUNKYARD
Los Angeles-based, hard-rock quintet led by Austin, Texas natives Chris Gates (guitar) and David Roach (vocals).

8/12/89	105	11		Junkyard	$8	Geffen 24227

Blooze
Can't Hold Back

Hands Off
Hollywood

Hot Rod
Life Sentence

Long Way Home
Shot In The Dark

Simple Man
Texas

JUPITER, Duke — see DUKE

JUSTIS, Bill
Born on 10/14/26 in Birmingham, Alabama. Died on 7/15/82 in Nashville. Session saxophonist/arranger/producer. Led house band for Sun Records.

11/24/62	94	8		1 Bill Justis plays 12 big instrumental hits (Alley Cat/Green Onions) .... [I]	$20	Smash 67021
2/23/63	89	6		2 Bill Justis plays 12 more big instrumental hits (Telstar/The Lonely Bull)........................... [I]	$20	Smash 67030

Alley Cat (1)
Calcutta (1)
(Dance With) The Guitar Man (2)
Desafinado (2)

Green Onions (1)
I Got A Woman - Part 1 (2)
Last Date (1)
Last Night (2)
Lonely Bull (2)

Melody Of Love (2)
Mexico (1)
Near You (2)
Raunchy (2) 2
Rebel Rouser (2)

Rinky-Dink (1)
Sail Along Silvery Moon (2)
Stranger On The Shore (1)
Stripper, The (1)

Summer Place, Theme From (1)
Swingin' Safari (1)
Take Five (1)

Tel-Star (2)
Wheels (2)
Wonderland By Night (1)

JUVET, Patrick
Swiss-born disco artist.

7/1/78	125	14		Got A Feeling	$8	Casablanca 7101

Another Lonely Man

Got A Feeling

I Love America

Where Is My Woman

DEBUT DATE	PEAK POS	WKS CHR	GOLD	ARTIST — Album Title	$	Label & Number

K

★★138★★ **KAEMPFERT, Bert, And His Orchestra**
Born on 10/16/23 in Hamburg, Germany. Multi-instrumentalist/bandleader/producer/composer/arranger for Polydor Records in Germany. Produced first Beatles recording session. Died on 6/21/80 in Switzerland.

DEBUT DATE	PEAK POS	WKS CHR	GOLD	#	ARTIST — Album Title	$	Label & Number
12/31/60+	1⁵	40	●	1	**Wonderland By Night** ....[I]	$15	Decca 74101
11/20/61	92	6		2	Dancing In Wonderland ....[I]	$15	Decca 74161
4/21/62	82	13		3	Afrikaan Beat and other favorites ....[I]	$15	Decca 74273
9/29/62	14	17		4	That Happy Feeling ....[I]	$15	Decca 74305
7/6/63	87	12		5	Living It Up! ....[I]	$15	Decca 74374
11/30/63	79	6		6	Lights Out, Sweet Dreams ....[I]	$15	Decca 74265
1/23/65	5	55	●	7	**Blue Midnight** ....[I]	$15	Decca 74569
7/10/65	42	22		8	Three O'Clock In The Morning ....[I]	$15	Decca 74670
9/4/65	27	23		9	The Magic Music Of Far Away Places ....[I]	$15	Decca 74616
3/12/66	46	28		10	Bye Bye Blues ....[I]	$15	Decca 74693
7/9/66	39	21		11	Strangers In The Night ....[I]	$15	Decca 74795
10/8/66	30	40	●	12	Bert Kaempfert's Greatest Hits ....[G-I]	$15	Decca 74810
5/13/67	122	7		13	Hold Me ....[I]	$15	Decca 74860
10/7/67	136	7		14	The World We Knew ....[I]	$15	Decca 74925
11/2/68	186	2		15	My Way Of Life ....[I]	$15	Decca 75059
3/29/69	194	5		16	Warm and Wonderful ....[I]	$15	Decca 75089
11/1/69	153	10		17	Traces Of Love ....[I]	$15	Decca 75140
3/28/70	87	7		18	The Kaempfert Touch ....[I]	$15	Decca 75175
2/13/71	140	6		19	Orange Colored Sky ....[I]	$15	Decca 75256
9/25/71	188	2		20	Bert Kaempfert Now! ....[I]	$15	Decca 75305

Afrikaan Beat (3,12) **42**
Aim Of My Desires (1)
All For You (18)
Almost There (7)
Are We Becoming Strangers (17)
As I Love You (1)
Autumn Leaves (Les Feuilles Mortes) (1)
Balkan Melody (9)
Bell Bottoms (20)
Bert's Tune (3)
Black Beauty (4)
Blue Midnight (7)
Blue Moon (2)
Body And Soul (6)
Boo Hoo (11)
But Not Today (11)
Bye Bye Blackbird (19)
Bye Bye Blues (10,12) **54**
Can't Take My Eyes Off You (16)
Cherokee (Indian Love Call) (3)
Cotton Candy (7)
Cracklin' Rosie (19)
Dancing In The Dark (3)
Danke Schoen (5,12)
Daybreak Serenade (6)
Didn't We (18)
Don't Go (19)
Don't Talk To Me (5)
Dream (6)
Dream Baby (How Long Must I Dream) (20)
Dreaming The Blues (1)
Drifting And Dreaming (Sweet Paradise) (1)
Dutch Treat (5)
Easy Going (5)
Every Sunday Morning (11)
Falling Free (20)
Fascination (15)
Fluter's Holiday (5)
Forgive Me (11)
Free As A Bird (7)
Friends (19)

Funny Talk (2)
Games People Play (17)
Gemma (6)
Gentleman Jim (5)
Give And Take (5)
Goodnight Sweet Dreams (7)
Gray Eyes Make Me Blue (20)
Happiness Never Comes Too Late (1)
Happy Trumpeter (4)
Hava Nagila (9)
Headin' Home (18)
Here's My Life (Here's My Love) (17)
Hi-De-Ho (That Old Sweet Roll) (19)
Highland Dream (6)
Hold Back The Dawn (13)
Hold Me (13)
How Deep Is The Ocean (How High Is The Sky) (2)
I Can't Give You Anything But Love (11) **100**
I Can't Help Remembering You (14)
I Love How You Love Me (17)
I May Be Wrong (But I Think You're Wonderful) (16)
I'll Get By (As Long As I Have You) (2)
I'm Beginning To See The Light (10)
I've Gotta Be Me (17)
If I Give My Heart To You (8)
If I Had You (6)
In Apple Blossom Time (19)
In Our Time (A Musical Prayer For Peace) (20)
In The Mood (5)
It Makes No Difference (18)
It's The Talk Of The Town (13)
Japanese Farewell Song (9)
Java (7)
Jean (18)
Just As Much As Ever (3)

Kiss Her Once With Feeling (20)
La Cumparsita (9)
La Vie En Rose (1)
Lady (13)
Let A Smile Be Your Umbrella (On A Rainy Day) (8)
Let's Go Home (8)
Living Easy (20)
Living It Up (5)
Lonely Nightingale (7)
Lonesome (14)
Love (7,12)
Love Comes But Once (7)
Love Letters (6)
Love Me Happy (17)
Lover (14)
Lullaby For Lovers (1)
Magic Trumpet (12)
Magnolia Blossoms (6)
Malaysian Melody (15)
Maltese Melody (16)
Mambossa (9)
Manhattan After Dark (15)
Marjoram (13)
Market Day (4)
Me And My Shadow (20)
Melina (10)
Memories Of Mexico (15)
Mexican Shuffle (11)
Midnight In Moscow (9)
Milica (11)
Mister Sandman (15)
Monte Carlo (9)
Moon Is Making Eyes (8)
Moon Over Naples (9,12) **59**
Moonglow (3)
Moonlight Serenade (14)
My Love (19)
Nightingale Sang In Berkeley Square (8)
Nothing's New (8)
Now And Forever (2) **48**
Oh Woman, Oh Why? (20)
On A Little Street In Singapore (1)

On My Lonely Way (15)
On The Alamo (1)
Once In A While (10)
One Day When You (18)
One Lonely Night (16)
One Morning In May (16)
Only A Fool (Would Lose You) (17)
Only In Your Arms (16)
Only Those In Love (2)
Orange Colored Sky (19)
Our Street Of Love (16)
Out Of Nowhere (10)
Petula (16)
Pony Violins (3)
Proud Mary (20)
Pussy Footin' (13)
Put Your Hand In The Hand (20)
Rain (14)
Rainbow Melody (8)
Raindrops Keep Fallin' On My Head (18)
Red Roses For A Blue Lady (7,12) **11**
Red Sky At Morning (20)
Remember When (We Made These Memories) (10)
Ridin' Rainbows (15)
Rose Of Washington Square (8)
Rose Room (13)
Send Me Home (17)
Sentimental Journey (6)
Serenade In Blue (14)
Sermonette (13)
She Lets Her Hair Down (Early In The Morning) (18)
Show Me The Way To Go Home (1)
Similau (4)
Skoklaan (South African Song) (4)
Sleepy Lagoon (2)
Snowbird (19)
So What's New (13)

Solitude (3)
Some Of These Days (16)
Somebody Loves Me (2)
Somebody Loves You (13)
Someday We'll Be Together (18)
Something (18)
Soul Time (15)
Spanish Eyes ..see: Moon Over Naples
Stardust (3,9)
Stay With Me (1)
Stay With The Happy People (14)
Steady Does It (10)
Stompin' At The Savoy (15)
Strangers In The Night (11,12)
Sunday In Madrid (4)
Sweet Dreams (6)
Sweet Maria (13)
Swingin' Safari (4,12)
Swissy Missy (5)
Tahitian Sunset (10)
Take Me (4)
Take My Heart (8)
Take Seven (13)
Talk (14)
Tammy (1)
Tea And Trumpets (19)
Tell Me Why (6)
That Happy Feeling (4,12) **67**
There I've Said It Again (2)
(There'll Be Bluebirds Over) The White Cliffs Of Dover (8)
This Guy's In Love With You (16)
This Song Is Yours Alone (1)
This Woman Is Mine (18)
Three O'Clock In The Morning (7,8) **33**
Tijuana Taxi (11)
Time (17)
Time On My Hands (You In My Arms) (11)

Tipsy Gypsy (5)
Tootie Flutie (4)
Traces (17)
Treat For Trumpet (7)
Tricky Trombone (5)
Trumpet In The Night (3)
Twilight Time (2)
Two Can Live On Love Alone (11)
Two On A Tune (5)
Unchained Melody (2)
Vat 96 (14)
Wake Up And Live (19)
Way It Used To Be (17)
We Can Make It Girl (18)
Welcome To My Heart (15)
When I Fall In Love (2)
When You're Smiling (The Whole World Smiles With You) (18)
Where Flamingos Fly (3)
Where Or When (3)
While The Children Sleep (19)
Whispering (6)
Wiedersch'n (10,12)
Wimoweh (4)
Wonderland By Night (1,12) **1**
World We Knew (14)
You Are My Sunshine (14)
(You Are) My Way Of Life (15)
You Are There (15)
You Stepped Out Of A Dream (10)
You You You (18)
You're Mine (18)
You're Worth It All (17)
Zambesi (4)

KAJAGOOGOO
English pop-synth quintet led by Limahl (Chris Hamill), who left in late 1983, replaced by Nick Beggs.

DEBUT DATE	PEAK POS	WKS CHR	GOLD	#	ARTIST — Album Title	$	Label & Number
6/11/83	38	20		1	White Feathers	$8	EMI America 17094
4/27/85	185	4		2	Extra Play	$8	EMI America 17157

Big Apple (2)
Ergonomics (1)
Frayo (1)
Hang On Now (1) **78**

Islands (2)
Kajagoogoo (1)
Lies And Promises (1)

Lion's Mouth (2)
Loop, The (2)
Magician Man (1)

Melting The Ice Away (2)
On A Plane (2)
Ooh To Be Ah (1)

Part Of Me (Is You) (2)
Power To Forgive (2)
This Car Is Fast (1)

Too Shy (1) **5**
Turn Your Back On Me (2)
White Feathers (1)

DEBUT DATE	PEAK POS	WKS CHR	GOLD	ARTIST — Album Title	$	Label & Number

KALEIDOSCOPE
Rock/folk band led by David Lindley.

| 6/14/69 | 139 | 8 | | Kaleidoscope .... | $30 | Epic 26467 |

Banjo
Cuckoo

Let The Good Love Flow   Lie To Me   Petite Fleur   Seven-Ate Sweet   Tempe Arizona

KALLMANN, Gunter, Chorus
German chorus.

| 5/1/65 | 97 | 10 | | 1 Serenade For Elisabeth.............................. [F] | $12 | 4 Corners 4209 |
| 12/24/66+ | 126 | 8 | | 2 Wish Me A Rainbow .... | $12 | 4 Corners 4235 |

Annabelle (1)
Bell Serenade (1)
Bells Ring To The Stars (1)
Beyond The Sea (2)
Day The Rains Came (2)

Dream Melody (1)
I'm Always Chasing Rainbows (2)
If You Are But A Dream (2)
Impossible Dream (2)

La Montanara (1)
Lollipops And Roses (2)
More I See You (2)
Music For Falling In Love (1)
O, Mein Papa (1)

Romantica (2)
Round Dance (1)
Serenade For Elisabeth (1)
Serenade From The Millions Of Harlequins (1)

Somewhere, My Love (Lara's Theme) (1)
Strangers In The Night (2)
Toselli Serenade (1)
Waltz Music (1)

Wish Me A Rainbow (2) 63
You're Nobody 'Til Somebody Loves You (2)

KALYAN
Fourteen-man soul/calypso band from Trinidad — Olsop David, lead singer.

| 4/16/77 | 173 | 4 | | Kalyan... | $10 | MCA 2245 |

Disco Reggae (Tony's Groove)
Hello Africa

Hosannah
La La Jam Back

Neighbour, Neighbour   Nice 'N' Slow   Sweet Music   What We Gonna Do Next

KANE, Big Daddy
Antonio M. Hardy from Brooklyn, New York. Rap lyricist for Cold Chillin' Records. Wrote songs for Roxanne Shante and Biz Markie. Toured as Shante's DJ in 1985. Kane is an acronym for King Asiatic Nobody's Equal.

7/16/88	116	19	●	1 Long Live The Kane	$8	Cold Chill. 25731
10/7/89	33	30	●	2 It's A Big Daddy Thing	$8	Cold Chill. 25941
11/17/90	37	16		3 Taste Of Chocolate	$12	Cold Chill. 26303
11/16/91	57	8		4 Prince Of Darkness	$12	Cold Chill. 26715

Ain't No Half-Steppin' (1)
Ain't No Stoppin' Us Now (2)
All Of Me (3)
Another Victory (2)
Big Daddy Vs. Dolemite (3)
Big Daddy's Theme (2)
Brother, Brother (4)
Calling Mr. Welfare (2)
Cause I Can Do It Right (3)
Children R The Future (2)

Come On Down (4)
D.J.s Get No Credit (4)
Dance With The Devil (3)
Day You're Mine (1)
Death Sentence (4)
Down The Line (3)
Float (4)
Get Down (4)
Git Bizzy (4)
Groove With It (4)

House That Cee Built (2)
I Get The Job Done (2)
I'll Take You There (1)
I'm Not Ashamed (4)
It's A Big Daddy Thing (2)
It's Hard Being The Kane (3)
Just Rhymin' With Biz (1)
Keep 'Em On The Floor (3)
Long Live The Kane (1)
Lover In Me (4)

Mister Cee's Master Plan (1)
Mortal Combat (2)
Mr. Pitiful (3)
No Damn Good (3)
On The Bugged Tip (1)
On The Move (2)
Ooh, Aah, Nah-Nah-Nah (4)
Pimpin' Ain't Easy (2)
Prince Of Darkness (4)
Put Your Weight On It (3)

Raw (1)
Raw '91 (3)
Set It Off (1)
Smooth Operator (2)
T.L.C. (4)
Taste Of Chocolate (3)
To Be Your Man (2)
Troubled Man (4)
Warm It Up, Kane (2)
Who Am I (3)

Word To The Mother(Land) (1)
Young, Gifted And Black (2)

KANE GANG, The
English soul-styled pop trio: vocalists Martin Brammer and Paul Woods with guitarist David Brewis. Band's name derived from the film *Citizen Kane*.

| 11/21/87 | 115 | 20 | | Miracle .... | $8 | Capitol 48176 |

Closest Thing To Heaven
Don't Look Any Further 64

Finer Place
King Street Rain

Let's Get Wet
Looking For Gold

Motortown 36
Strictly Love (It Ain't)

Take Me To The World
What Time Is It

KANO
Italian disco band.

| 1/9/82 | 189 | 4 | | New York Cake .... | $8 | Mirage 19327 |

Baby Not Tonight

Can't Hold Back (Your Loving) 89

Don't Try To Stop Me   Party   Round And Round   She's A Star

★★231★★ KANSAS
Progressive rock group formed in Topeka in 1970. Consisted of Steve Walsh (lead vocals, keyboards), Kerry Livgren (guitar, keyboards), Phil Ehart (drums), Robby Steinhardt (violin), Rich Williams (guitar) and Dave Hope (bass). Walsh left in 1981 and was replaced by John Elefante (later a prolific Christian rock producer). Livgren became a Contemporary Christian artist in the '80s. Revised lineup in 1986: Walsh, Ehart, Williams, Steve Morse (guitarist from Dixie Dregs) and Billy Greer (bass).

6/15/74	174	10		1 Kansas	$12	Kirshner 32817
3/22/75	57	15	●	2 Song For America	$12	Kirshner 33385
12/27/75+	70	20	●	3 Masque	$12	Kirshner 33806
11/6/76+	5	42	▲³	4 Leftoverture	$10	Kirshner 34224
10/15/77+	4	51	▲³	5 Point Of Know Return	$10	Kirshner 34929
11/18/78+	32	19	▲	6 Two For The Show .... [L]	$10	Kirshner 35660 [2]
6/9/79	10	24	●	7 Monolith	$8	Kirshner 36008
10/4/80	26	21	●	8 Audio-Visions	$8	Kirshner 36588
6/12/82	16	20		9 Vinyl Confessions	$8	Kirshner 38002
8/13/83	41	21		10 Drastic Measures	$8	CBS Assoc. 38733
9/8/84	154	5	▲	11 The Best of Kansas .... [G]	$8	CBS Assoc. 39283
11/15/86+	35	27		12 Power	$8	MCA 5838
11/5/88	114	6		13 In The Spirit Of Things	$8	MCA 6254

All I Wanted (12) 19
All The World (3)
Andi (10)
Angels Have Fallen (7)
Anything For You (8)
Apercu (1)
Away From You (7)
Back Door (8)

Belexes (1)
Bells Of Saint James (13)
Borderline (9)
Bringing It Back (1)
Can I Tell You (1)
Can't Cry Anymore (12)
Carry On Wayward Son (4,6,11) *11*

Chasing Shadows (9)
Cheyenne Anthem (4)
Child Of Innocence (3)
Closet Chronicles (5,6)
Crossfire (9)
Curtain Of Iron (8)
Death Of Mother Nature Suite (1)

Devil Game (2)
Diamonds And Pearls (9)
Don't Open Your Eyes (8)
Don't Take Your Love Away (10)
Down The Road (2)
End Of The Age (10)

Everybody's My Friend (10)
Face (1)
Fair Exchange (9)
Fight Fire With Fire (10,11) *58*
Get Rich (10)
Ghosts (13)
Glimpse Of Home (7)

Going Through The Motions (10)
Got To Rock On (8) *76*
Hold On (8,11) *40*
Hopelessly Human (5)
House On Fire (13)
How My Soul Cries Out For You (7)

DEBUT DATE	PEAK POS	WKS CHR	G O L D	ARTIST — Album Title	$	Label & Number

KANSAS — Cont'd

I Counted On Love (13)	Lightning's Hand (5)	Once In A Lifetime (13)	Point Of Know Return	Song For America (2,6,11)	What's On My Mind (4)	
Icarus - Borne On Wings Of	Lonely Street (2)	One Big Sky (13)	(5,6,11) **28**	Sparks Of The Tempest (5)	Windows (9)	
Steel (3,6)	**Lonely Wind** (1,6) *60*	One Man, One Heart (13)	**Power** (12) *84*	Spider, The (5)		
Incident On A Bridge (10)	Loner (8)	Opus Insert (4)	**Portrait** (He Knew) (5,6) *64*	Stand Beside Me (13)		
Incomudro-Hymn To The	Magnum Opus Medley (4,6)	Paradox (5,6)	Preacher, The (13)	Stay Out Of Trouble (7)		
Atman (2)	Mainstream (10)	**People Of The South Wind**	Questions Of My Childhood	T.O. Witcher (13)		
Inside Of Me (13)	Miracles Out Of Nowhere (4)	(7) *23*	(4)	Taking In The View (12)		
It Takes A Woman's Love (To	Musicatto (12)	Perfect Lover (11)	Rainmaker (13)	Three Pretenders (12)		
Make A Man) (3)	Mysteries And Mayhem (3,6)	Pilgrimage, The (1)	**Reason To Be** (7) *52*	Tomb 19 (12)		
It's You (5)	No One Together (8,11)	Pinnacle, The (3)	Relentless (8)	Two Cents Worth (3)		
Journey From Mariabronn	No Room For A Stranger (8)	Play On (9)	**Right Away** (9) *73*	Wall, The (4,11)		
(1,6)	Nobody's Home (5)	**Play The Game Tonight**	Secret Service (12)	We're Not Alone Anymore		
Lamplight Symphony (2,6)	On The Other Side (7)	(9,11) *17*	Silhouettes In Disguise (12)	(12)		

KANTNER, Paul

Born on 3/12/42 in San Francisco. Original member of the rock group Jefferson Airplane, later known as Jefferson Starship. Co-founder of KBC.

12/19/70+	20	23	●	1 Blows Against The Empire	$15	RCA 4448

PAUL KANTNER/JEFFERSON STARSHIP
with Grace Slick, Jerry Garcia, David Crosby and Graham Nash

12/25/71+	89	9		2 Sunfighter	$10	Grunt 1002

PAUL KANTNER/GRACE SLICK
with Jerry Garcia, David Crosby and Graham Nash; LP cover features Kantner & Slick's baby daughter, China

6/23/73	120	12		3 Baron von Tollbooth & The Chrome Nun	$10	Grunt 0148

PAUL KANTNER, GRACE SLICK & DAVID FREIBERG

Across The Board (3)	Earth Mother (2)	Hijack (1)	Silver Spoon (2)	Universal Copernican	X•M (1)
Baby Tree (3)	Fat (3)	Holding Together (2)	Sketches Of China (3)	Mumbles (2)	Your Mind Has Left Your
Ballad Of The Chrome Nun	Fishman (3)	Home (1)	Starship (1)	Walkin (3)	Body (3)
(3)	Flowers Of The Night (3)	Lets Go Together (1)	Sunfighter (2)	When I Was A Boy I	
Child Is Coming (1)	Harp Tree Lament (3)	Look At The Wood (2)	Sunrise (1)	Watched The Wolves (2)	
China (2)	Have You Seen The Stars	Mau Mau (Amerikon) (1)	Titanic (2)	White Boy (Transcaucasian	
Diana - Part 1 & 2 (2)	Tonite (1)	Million (2)		Airmachine Blues) (3)	

KAOMA

Paris-based, multi-national outfit of singers, musicians and dancers. Fronted by keyboardist/arranger Jean-Claude Bonaventure.

1/27/90	40	21	●	World Beat	[F]	$12	Epic 46010

1 of 10 tracks sung in English

Dancando Lambada	Lamba Caribe	Lambamor	Melodi : D'Amour	Sindiang
Jambe Finete (Grille)	**Lambada** *46*	Lambareggae	Salsa Nuestra	Sopenala

KaSANDRA

Born John W. Anderson in 1935 in Panama City, Florida. Soul singer/songwriter.

11/23/68	142	8		John W. Anderson Presents KaSandra	$12	Capitol 2957

Don't Pat Me On The Back	Flag, The	Just Look In My Face	My Neighborhood	Wilderness
And Call Me Brother *91*	If A Storm Wind Blows	Mose	Preacher Man	

KASHIF

Techno-funk musician/vocalist. Born Michael Jones in Brooklyn in 1959. In B.T. Express at age 15. Member of Stephanie Mills' touring band.

4/9/83	54	33		1 Kashif	$8	Arista 9620

features Evelyn King, Fonzi Thornton, Lillo Thomas, Freda Payne and Kenny G

7/21/84	51	21		2 Send Me Your Love	$8	Arista 8205

features George Benson, Al Jarreau, Lillo Thomas & Siedah Garrett

12/21/85+	144	14		3 Condition Of The Heart	$8	Arista 8385

features Audrey Wheeler and Meli'sa Morgan

12/5/87	118	19		4 Love Changes	$8	Arista 8447

features Doug E. Fresh, Expose, Kenny G, Meli'sa Morgan, Whitney Houston and Dionne Warwick

All (1)	Condition Of The Heart (3)	Help Yourself To My Love (1)	Love Changes (4)	Ooh Love (2)	Somebody (4)
Are You The Woman (2)	Dancing In The Dark (Heart	I Just Gotta Have Love (Lover	Love Has No End (2)	**Reservations For Two**	Stay The Night (3)
Baby Don't Break Your	To Heart) (3)	Turn Me On) (1)	Love Me All Over (4)	(4) *62*	Stone Love (1)
Baby's Heart (2)	Don't Stop My Love (1)	I Wanna Have Love With	Loving You Only (4)	Rumors (1)	That's How It Goes (2)
Botha Botha (The Apartheid	Edgartown Groove (2)	You (3)	Midnight Mood (4)	Say Something Love (1)	Vacant Heart (4)
Song) (3)	Fifty Ways (To Fall In Love)	I've Been Missin' You (2)	Mood, The (1)	Say You Love Me (3)	Weakness (3)
Call Me Tonight (2)	(4)	It All Begins Again (4)	Movie Song (3)	Send Me Your Love (2)	Who's Getting Serious? (1)

KATRINA And The WAVES

British-based, pop-rock quartet fronted by Kansas-born Katrina Leskanich, with American Vince de la Cruz (bass) and Britons Alex Cooper (drums) and Kimberley Rew (guitar; Soft Boys).

4/13/85	25	32		1 Katrina And The Waves	$8	Capitol 12400
4/12/86	49	16		2 Waves	$8	Capitol 12478
9/2/89	122	8		3 Break Of Hearts	$8	SBK 92649

Break Of Hearts (3)	I Can Dream About It (3)	Lovely Lindsey (2)	Red Wine And Whiskey (1)	Stop Trying To Prove (How	Tears For Me (2)
Can't Tame My Love (3)	(I've Got A) Crush On You (3)	Machine Gun Smith (1)	Riding Shotgun (2)	Much Of A Man You Is) (2)	**That's The Way** (3) *16*
Cry For Me (1)	**Is That It?** (2) *70*	Mexico (1)	Rock Myself To Sleep (3)	Sun Street (2)	To Have And To Hold (3)
Do You Want Crying (1) *37*	Keep Running To Me (3)	Money Chain (2)	Rock N' Roll Girl (3)	Sun Won't Shine Without	**Walking On Sunshine** (1) *9*
Game Of Love (1)	Love Calculator (3)	Mr. Star (2)	Sleep On My Pillow (2)	You (1)	
Going Down To Liverpool (1)	Love That Boy (2)	**Que Te Quiero** (1) *71*			

KAUKONEN, Jorma, & Vital Parts

Lead guitarist of Jefferson Airplane and Hot Tuna. Born on 12/23/40 in Washington, D.C.

2/14/81	163	6		Barbeque King	$8	RCA 3725

KAUKONEN, Jorma, & Vital Parts — Cont'd

Barbeque King	Man For All Seasons	Roads And Roads &	Runnin' With The Fast	Snout Psalm	To Hate Is To Stay Young
Love Is Strange	Milkcow Blues Boogie	Rockabilly Shuffle	Crowd	Starting Over Again	

KAY, John
Born Joachim Krauledat on 4/12/44 in East Germany. Leader of Steppenwolf.

DEBUT DATE	PEAK POS	WKS CHR		ARTIST — Album Title	$	Label & Number
4/29/72	113	11	1	Forgotten Songs & Unsung Heroes	$10	Dunhill 50120
7/14/73	200	2	2	My Sportin' Life	$10	Dunhill 50147

Bold Marauder (1)	Easy Evil (2)	**I'm Movin' On** (1) 52	My Sportin' Life (2)	Sing With The Children (2)	Walk Beside Me (1)
Dance To My Song (2)	Giles Of The River (2)	Many A Mile (1)	Nobody Lives Here Anymore	Somebody (1)	Walkin' Blues (1)
Drift Away (2)	Heroes And Devils (2)	Moonshine (Friend Of Mine)	(2)	To Be Alive (1)	You Win Again (1)
		(2)		Two Of A Kind (1)	

KAYAK
Rock quintet from Holland featuring Max Werner (vocals, mellotron).

1/17/76	199	2	1	Royal Bed Bouncer	$8	Janus 7023
3/4/78	117	9	2	Starlight Dancer	$8	Janus 7034
3/3/79	145	7	3	Phantom Of The Night	$8	Janus 7039

Back To The Front (2)	Do You Care (2)	Journey Through Time (3)	My Heart Never Changed (1)	Poet And The One Man	Still My Heart Cries For You
Ballad For A Lost Friend (2)	First Signs Of Spring (3)	Keep The Change (3)	No Man's Land (3)	Band (3)	(2)
Bury The World (1)	**I Want You To Be Mine**	Land On The Water (2)	Nothingness (2)	Royal Bed Bouncer (1)	Turn The Tide (2)
Chance For A Lifetime (1)	(2) 55	Life Of Gold (1)	Patricia Anglaia (2)	Ruthless Queen (3)	Winning Ways (3)
Crime Of Passion (3)	If This Is Your Welcome (1)	Love Of A Victim (2)	Phantom Of The Night (3)	Said No Word (1)	(You're So) Bizarre (1)
Daphine (Laurel Tree) (3)	Irene (2)	Moments Of Joy (1)		Starlight Dancer (2)	

KAYE, Sammy
Born on 3/13/10 in Rocky River, Ohio; died on 6/2/87 of cancer. Durable leader of popular "sweet" dance band with the slogan "Swing and Sway with Sammy Kaye." Also played clarinet and alto sax.

8/4/56	20	1	1	My Fair Lady (For Dancing)	[I]	$20	Columbia 885
11/17/56	19	1	2	What Makes Sammy Swing and Sway	[I]	$20	Columbia 891
				SAMMY KAYE and his Swinging and Swaying Strings			
5/30/64	97	9	3	Come Dance To The Hits	[I]	$15	Decca 74502

Alley Cat (3)	Dominique (3)	I've Grown Accustomed To	On The Street Where You	Stompin' At The Savoy (2)	You Did It (1)
Ascot Gavotte (1)	Fools Rush In (3)	Her Face (1)	Live (1)	String Of Pearls (2)	
Begin The Beguine (2)	Get Me To The Church On	In The Mood (2)	One O'Clock Jump (2)	There I've Said It Again (3)	
Blue Velvet (3)	Time (1)	Jersey Bounce (2)	Rain In Spain (1)	Tuxedo Junction (2)	
Charade (3) 36	I Can't Get Started (2)	Just You Wait (1)	Red Sails In The Sunset (3)	Washington Square (3)	
Cherokee (2)	I Could Have Danced All	Little Brown Jug (2)	720 In The Books (3)	With A Little Bit Of Luck (1)	
Danke Schoen (3)	Night (1)	Maria Elena (3)	She Loves Me (3)	Without You (1)	
Deep Purple (3)		Mood Indigo (2)	Show Me (1)	Wouldn't It Be Loverly (1)	

KAY-GEES, The
Eight-man, disco outfit formed in Jersey City, New Jersey. Produced by Ronald Bell of Kool & The Gang, and named for that group.

3/1/75	199	1		Keep On Bumpin' & Masterplan	$8	Gang 101

Ain't No Time (Part 1 & 2)	Get Down	Master Plan	Who's The Man? (With The	Wondering	You've Got To Keep On
Anthology	Let's Boogie	My Favorite Song	Master Plan)		Bumpin'

KBC BAND
Group features three founding members of Jefferson Airplane: Paul Kantner (guitar), Marty Balin (vocals) and Jack Casady (bass).

11/8/86+	75	24		KBC Band	$8	Arista 8440

America	Hold Me	Mariel	Sayonara	Wrecking Crew
Dream Motorcycle	**It's Not You, It's Not Me** 89	No More Heartaches	When Love Comes	

KC And The SUNSHINE BAND
Disco-R&B band formed in Florida in 1973 by lead singer/keyboardist Harry "KC" Casey (b: 1/31/51, Hialeah, Florida) and bassist Richard Finch (b: 1/25/54, Indianapolis). Interracial band contained from seven to 11 members. Casey and Finch wrote, arranged and produced all of their hits (except "It's The Same Old Song").

8/2/75	4	47	1	KC And The Sunshine Band	$10	TK 603
10/4/75	131	8	2	The Sound Of Sunshine	[I]	$10	TK 604
				THE SUNSHINE BAND		
10/23/76	13	77	3	Part 3	$8	TK 605
8/19/78	36	13	4	Who Do Ya (Love)	$8	TK 607
7/7/79	50	37	5	Do You Wanna Go Party	$8	TK 611
3/22/80	132	11	6	Greatest Hits	[G]	$8	TK 612
2/4/84	93	18	7	KC Ten	$8	Meca 8301
				KC		

Ain't Nothin' Wrong (1)	Don't Break My Heart (7)	I Love You (2)	Let's Go Party (3)	(Shake, Shake, Shake)	What Makes You Happy (1)
All I Want (6)	Don't Let Go (7)	I Will Love You Tomorrow (4)	Let's Go Rock And Roll (6)	**Shake Your Booty** (3,6) 1	**Who Do Ya Love** (4) 68
Are You Ready? (7)	Funky '75 (2)	I'm So Crazy ('Bout You) (1)	Miss B. (2)	Sho-Nuff (4)	**Wrap Your Arms Around**
Baby I Love You (Yes, I Do)	**Get Down Tonight** (1,6) 1	**I'm Your Boogie Man** (3,6) 1	Nobody Knows (7)	Shotgun Shuffle (2) 88	**Me** (3) 48
(3)	**Give It Up** (7) 18	I've Got The Feeling (5)	On The Top (7)	So Glad (4)	
Boogie Shoes (1,6) 35	Hey J (2)	In My World (7)	Ooh, I Like It (5)	Sound Your Funky Horn (6)	
Come On In (3)	Hooked On Your Love (5)	**It's The Same Old Song**	Please Don't Go (5,6) 1	Sunshine City (2)	
Come To My Island (4)	How About A Little Love (4)	(4) 35	Que Pasa? (7)	Thank You (Falettinme Be	
Do You Feel All Right	I Betcha Didn't Know That	Just A Groove (2)	**Queen Of Clubs** (6) 66	Mice Elf Agin) (7)	
(4) 63	(5)	**Keep It Comin' Love** (3,6) 2	Rock Your Baby (2)	**That's The Way (I Like It)**	
Do You Wanna Go Party	I Get Lifted (1)	Let It Go (Part One & Two) (1)	S.O.S. (2)	(1,6) 1	
(5) 50	**I Like To Do It** (3) 37	Let's Get Together (7)		Too High (7)	

KEEL
Heavy-metal quintet led by Ron Keel (vocals/guitar).

3/9/85	99	21	1	The Right to Rock	$8	Gold Mt. 5041
4/19/86	53	18	2	The Final Frontier	$8	MCA 5727
				above 2 produced by Gene Simmons (Kiss)		
6/27/87	79	13	3	Keel	$8	MCA 42005

DEBUT DATE	PEAK POS	WKS CHR	GOLD	ARTIST — Album Title	$	Label & Number

KEEL — Cont'd

Arm And A Leg (2)
Back To The City (1)
Because The Night (2)
Calm Before The Storm (3)
Cherry Lane (3)
Don't Say You Love Me (3)
Easier Said Than Done (1)

Electric Love (1)
Final Frontier (2)
4th Of July (3)
Get Down (1)
Here Today, Gone Tomorrow (2)

I Said The Wrong Thing To The Right Girl (3)
If Love Is A Crime (I Wanna Be Convicted) (3)
It's A Jungle Out There (3)
Just Another Girl (2)
King Of The Rock (3)

Let's Spend The Night Together (1)
Nightfall (2)
No Pain No Gain (2)
Raised On Rock (2)
Right To Rock (1)
Rock And Roll Animal (2)

So Many Girls, So Little Time (1)
Somebody's Waiting (3)
Speed Demon (1)
Tears Of Fire (2)
United Nations (3)

You're The Victim (I'm The Crime) (1)

KEENE, Tommy
Rock singer/songwriter/guitarist from Bethesda, Maryland. Earned sociology degree from the University Of Maryland.

| 3/29/86 | 148 | 17 | | Songs From The Film .... | $8 | Geffen 24090 |

As Life Goes By
Astronomy
Call On Me

Gold Town
In Our Lives

Kill Your Sons
Listen To Me

My Mother Looked Like Marilyn Monroe

Paper Words And Lies
Places That Are Gone

Story Ends
Underworld

KEITH
Born James Barry Keefer on 5/7/49 in Philadelphia. First recorded as Keith & The Admirations on Columbia in 1965.

| 3/25/67 | 124 | 5 | | 98.6/Ain't Gonna Lie .... | $20 | Mercury 61102 |

Ain't Gonna Lie *39*
I Can't Go Wrong
Mind If I Hang Around

98.6 *7*
Our Love Started All Over Again

Pretty Little Shy One
Sweet Dreams (Do Come True)

Teeny Bopper Song
Tell Me To My Face *37*
To Whom It Concerns

White Lightnin'
You'll Come Running Back To Me

KELLEM, Manny
Record producer from Philadelphia. Produced many hits for Epic artists.

| 4/13/68 | 197 | 2 | | Love Is Blue .... | $10 | Epic 26367 |

And I Love Her
Claudine

Free Again
Here, There And Everywhere

I Will Wait For You
It's Not Unusual

Love Is Blue *96*
Man And A Woman

My Love
Trains And Boats And Planes

What A Wonderful World

KELLY, R., and Public Announcement
Robert Kelly is a singer/multi-instrumentalist from Chicago. Public Announcement is his assembly of backing dancers and singers.

| 2/15/92 | 42 | 51↑ ▲ | | Born Into The 90's .... | $12 | Jive 41469 |

CD includes bonus track

Born Into The 90's
Dedicated
Definition Of A Hottl

Hangin' Out
Hey Love (Can I Have A Word)

Honey Love *39*
I Know What You Need
Keep It Street

She's Got That Vibe *59*
She's Loving Me

Slow Dance (Hey Mr. DJ) *43*

KEMP, Johnny
Singer/dancer/actor/songwriter. Began performing in nightclubs in his native Nassau, Bahamas, at the age of 13. Moved to Harlem in 1979.

| 6/11/88 | 68 | 19 | | Secrets Of Flying .... | $8 | Columbia 40770 |

Dancin' With Myself
Feeling Without Touching

Just Got Paid *10*

Just Like Flyin'

My Only Want Is You

One Thing Led To Another

Urban Times Medley

KEMP, Tara
Singer/songwriter/classically trained pianist from the San Francisco Bay-area.

| 2/16/91 | 109 | 14 | | Tara Kemp .... | $12 | Giant 24408 |

Be My Lover
Hold You Tight *3*

Monday Love
One Love

Piece Of My Heart *7*
Something To Groove To

Tara By The Way
Together

Too Much *95*
Way You Make Me Feel

★★464★★ KENDRICKS, Eddie
Born on 12/17/39 in Union Springs, Alabama and raised in Birmingham. Joined R&B group the Primes in Detroit in the late '50s. Group later evolved into The Temptations; Eddie sang lead from 1960-71. Eddie later dropped letter "s" from his last name. Died of lung cancer on 10/5/92. Also see Hall & Oates.

5/22/71	80	32	1	All By Myself	$10	Tamla 309
6/3/72	131	14	2	People...Hold On	$10	Tamla 315
6/16/73	18	40	3	Eddie Kendricks	$10	Tamla 327
3/16/74	30	17	4	Boogie Down!	$10	Tamla 330
12/7/74+	108	14	5	For You	$10	Tamla 335
7/12/75	63	25	6	The Hit Man	$8	Tamla 338
1/31/76	38	19	7	He's A Friend	$8	Tamla 343
10/9/76	144	7	8	Goin' Up In Smoke	$8	Tamla 346
4/22/78	180	3	9	Vintage '78	$8	Arista 4170

Ain't No Smoke Without Fire (9)
All Of My Love (7)
Any Day Now (3)
Best Of Strangers Now (9)
Body Talk (6)
Boogie Down (4) *2*
Born Again (8)
Can I (1)
Can't Help What I Am (3)
Chains (7)
Darling Come Back Home (3) *67*
Date With The Rain (4)
Day By Day (2)
Deep And Quiet Love (5)
Didn't We (1)

Don't Put Off Till Tomorrow (8)
Don't Underestimate The Power Of Love (9)
Don't You Want Light (8)
Each Day I Cry A Little (3)
Eddie's Love (2) *77*
Fortune Teller (6)
Get It While It's Hot (7)
Get The Cream Off The Top (6) *50*
Girl Of My Dreams (4)
Girl You Need A Change Of Mind (Part 1) (2) *87*
Goin' Up In Smoke (8)
Happy (6) *66*
He's A Friend (7) *36*
Honey Brown (4)

Hooked On Your Love (4)
How's Your Love Life Baby (9)
I Did It All For You (1)
I Won't Take No (7)
I'm On The Sideline (2)
I've Got To Be (6)
If (5)
If Anyone Can (6)
If It Takes All Night (9)
If You Let Me (2) *66*
If You Think (You Can) (5)
It's Not What You Got (7)
It's So Hard For Me To Say Good-Bye (1) *88*
Just Memories (2)
Keep On Truckin' (Part 1) (3) *1*

Let Me Run Into Your Lonely Heart (2)
Let Yourself Go (5)
Let's Go Back To Day One (1)
Love Love Love (9)
Loving You The Second Time Around (4)
Maybe I'm A Fool To Love You (9)
Music Man (8)
My People...Hold On (2)
Never Gonna Leave You (7)
Newness Is Gone (8)
Not On The Outside (3)
On My Way Home (7)
One Of The Poorest People (9)
One Tear (5) *71*

Only Room For Two (3)
Part Of Me (7)
Please Don't Go Away (5)
Shoeshine Boy (5) *18*
Skeleton In Your Closet (8)
Skippin' Work Today (6)
Someday We'll Have A Better World (2)
Something's Burning (1)
Son Of Sagittarius (4) *28*
Sweet Tenderoni (8)
Sweeter You Treat Her (7)
Tell Her Love Has Felt The Need (4) *50*
Thanks For The Memories (8)
Thin Man (4)
This Used To Be The Home Of Johnnie Mae (1)

Time In A Bottle (5)
To You From Me (8)
Trust Your Heart (4)
Where Do You Go (Baby) (3)
Whip (9)
You Are The Melody Of My Life (4)
You Loved Me Then (6)
Your Wish Is My Command (9)

DEBUT DATE	PEAK POS	WKS CHR	G O L D	ARTIST — Album Title	$	Label & Number

KENNEDY, John Fitzgerald
Tributes to President Kennedy who was born on 5/29/17 in Brookline, Massachusetts; assassinated in Dallas on 11/22/63. Also see Leonard Bernstein, and the Boston Symphony Orchestra.

DEBUT DATE	PEAK POS	WKS CHR	GOLD	ARTIST — Album Title	$	Label & Number
12/28/63+	5	15		1 **That Was The Week That Was** .... [T]	$12	Decca 9116
				the BBC telecast tribute to Kennedy on 11/23/63		
12/28/63+	8	14		2 **The Presidential Years 1960-1963** .... [T]	$12	20th Century 3127
				narrated by David Teig		
1/11/64	42	8		3 **JFK The Man, The President** .... [T]	$12	Documentaries Un.
				narrated by Barry Gray		
1/18/64	18	9	●	4 **A Memorial Album** .... [T]	$12	Premier 2099
				narrated by Ed Brown; a broadcast by WMCA, New York on 11/22/63		
1/18/64	109	5		5 **Actual Speeches of Franklin D. Roosevelt and John F. Kennedy** .... [T]	$10	Somerset 16100
				side 1: Kennedy's complete Inaugural Address (1/20/61); side 2: Roosevelt speeches		
1/25/64	101	4		6 **John F. Kennedy - A Memorial Album** .... [T]	$10	Diplomat 10000
1/25/64	119	4		7 **The Presidential Years (1960-1963)** .... [T]	$10	Pickwick 169
2/8/64	29	10		8 **Four Days That Shocked The World** .... [T]	$12	Colpix 2500
				Nov. 22-25, 1963 (complete story narrated by Reid Collins)		
12/26/64+	49	11		9 **The Kennedy Wit** .... [T]	$15	RCA 101
				narrated by David Brinkley; introduction by Adlai E. Stevenson		
12/11/65+	93	8		10 **John Fitzgerald Kennedy...As We Remember Him** .... [T]	$12	Legacy 1017 [2]
				narrated by Charles Kuralt; includes a 240-page book		

Alliance For Progress (7)
Ambassador Adlai Stevenson (6)
American Labor Movement, May, 1963 (2)
Another Prayer Breakfast, Feb., 1963 (2)
Berlin Speech (7)
Birmingham, May, 1963 (2,7)
Campaign In New York, Oct., 1960 (2)
Complete Story - Nov. 22-25, 1963 (8)
Cuba - Another Crisis, Oct., 1962 (2,6,7)
Election Eve (7)

Election Night, Nov., 1960 (2)
Equal Job Opportunities, Nov., 1962 (2)
Eulogy - Taps (6)
Eye Witness Account Of Assassination (6)
Family, The (9)
Final Address, Fort Worth, Nov. 22, 1963 (2,7)
General Dwight D. Eisenhower (6)
His Holiness Pope Paul VI (6)
Houston Speech (6,7)
In The Summer Of His Years (1)

Inaugural Address, Jan., 1961 (2,5,6,7)
J.F.K. Speech Of Space Flight (6)
Newscast Of Assassination (6)
1917 - 1942: John F. Kennedy's Boyhood And Education (10)
1942-1953: Service In The Pacific; Entry Into Politics; Marriage To Jacqueline B. (10)
1952 - 1961: The Senator And Campaigner; The Inauguration (10)

1960 Campaign (9)
1961 - 1963: John Fitzgerald Kennedy, President Of The United States (10)
Nomination Acceptance, July, 1960 (2)
Nuclear Test Speech (7)
Nuclear Tests, Nov., 1961 (2)
Oath Of Office For Presidency By J.F.K. (6,7)
On Labor (7)
Peace Corps Speech (7)
Prayer Breakfast, Feb., 1961 (2)

Pre-Election Speech Of Senator Kennedy (6,7)
Pres. Franklin D. Roosevelt Highlights Of Speeches (5)
Presidency, The (9)
President Johnson's Tribute At Andrews A.F.B., November 22, 1963 (6,7)
Presidential Press Conference (6)
Press Conferences (9)
Prime Minister Sir Alec Home (6)
Report On Berlin, July, 1961 (2)
Senator Barry Goldwater (6)

"So I Go To Khrushchev In Vienna", May, 1961 (2)
State Of The Union Message, Jan., 1961 (2,7)
Steel Crisis, April, 1962 (2,7)
Still Greater Crisis, Feb., 1963 (2)
To Jackie (1)
Tomb Of The Unknown Soldier, Nov., 1961 (2)
U.N. Address, Sept., 1961 (2,7)
Unspoken Credo, Nov. 22, 1963 (2)
Yale Graduation Address, June, 1962 (2)

KENNEDY, Joyce
Vocalist from Chicago. Formed Mother's Finest with husband Glen Murdoch in 1968.

DEBUT DATE	PEAK POS	WKS CHR	GOLD	ARTIST — Album Title	$	Label & Number
9/8/84	79	13		**Lookin' For Trouble**	$8	A&M 4996

Chain Reaction
Chase The Night
Last Time I Made Love 40
Lookin' For Trouble
Love Is A Bet
Stronger Than Before
Tailor Made
Watch My Body
You Can Bet Your Life

KENNEDY, Robert Francis
New York senator. Younger brother of President Kennedy. Born on 11/20/25 in Brookline, Massachusetts; assassinated on 6/5/68 (pronounced dead one day later) in Los Angeles.

DEBUT DATE	PEAK POS	WKS CHR	GOLD	ARTIST — Album Title	$	Label & Number
1/11/69	187	4		**A Memorial** .... [T]	$15	Columbia 792 [2]
				record 1: highlights of speeches 1964-68; record 2: excerpts from the High Requiem Mass at St. Patrick's Cathedral on 6/9/68; includes "Battle Hymn Of The Republic" by Andy Williams		

Excerpts from the High Requiem Mass
Humor
Measure Of A Nation
Memorial To Another Kennedy
On Vietnam
On Violence
On Youth And Its Responsibilities
Presidential Campaign Of 1968
To The Deprived
Toward A Better World

★★433★★ KENNY G
Born Kenny Gorelick on 7/6/56 in Seattle. Fusion saxophonist. Joined Barry White's Love Unlimited Orchestra at age 17. Graduated Phi Beta Kappa and Magna Cum Laude from the University of Washington with an accounting degree. His non-instrumental albums include featured vocalists Freddie Jackson, Lillo Thomas, Kashif, Lenny Williams and others.

DEBUT DATE	PEAK POS	WKS CHR	GOLD	ARTIST — Album Title	$	Label & Number
3/24/84	62	21	●	1 **G Force**	$8	Arista 8192
6/1/85	97	12	●	2 **Gravity**	$8	Arista 8282
				KENNY G & G FORCE		
9/6/86+	6	102	▲³	3 **Duotones**	$8	Arista 8427
10/22/88	8	57	▲³	4 **Silhouette** .... [I]	$8	Arista 8457
12/9/89+	16	122	▲²	5 **Live** .... [L]	$10	Arista 8613 [2]
				recorded August 26-27, 1989 in Seattle		
12/5/92+	2²↑	10↑	▲²	6 **Breathless** .... [I]	$12	Arista 18646
				includes 2 vocal tracks by Peabo Bryson and Aaron Neville		

Against Doctor's Orders (4)
All In One Night (4)
Alone (6)
By The Time This Night Is Over (6)
Champagne (3)
Do Me Right (1)
Don't Make Me Wait For Love (3,5) 15
End Of The Night (6)

Esther (3,5)
Even If My Heart Would Break (6)
Forever In Love (6) 48↑
G-Bop (6)
G Force (1)
Going Home (5) 56
Gravity (2)
Help Yourself To My Love (1)
Hi, How Ya Doin'? (1)

Home (4,5)
Homeland (6)
I Wanna Be Yours (1)
I'll Be Alright (4)
I've Been Missin' You (1,5)
In The Rain (6)
Japan (2)
Joy Of Life (6)
Last Night Of The Year (2)
Let Go (4)

Love On The Rise (2)
Midnight Motion (3,5)
Morning (6)
One Man's Poison (Another Man's Sweetness) (2)
One Night Stand (2)
Pastel (4)
Sade (3,5)
Sax Attack (3)
Sentimental (6)

Silhouette (4,5) 13
Sister Rose (6)
Slip Of The Tongue (3)
Songbird (3,5) 4
Summer Song (4)
Sunset At Noon (1)
Three Of A Kind (3)
Tradewinds (4)
Tribeca (1,5)
Uncle Al (5)

Virgin Island (2)
We've Saved The Best For Last (4) 47
Wedding Song (6)
What Does It Take (To Win Your Love) (3)
Where Do We Take It (From Here) (2)
Year Ago (6)
You Make Me Believe (3)

KENTON, Stan
Progressive jazz bandleader/pianist/composer. Born on 2/19/12 in Wichita, Kansas; died in Los Angeles on 8/25/79. Organized his first jazz band in 1941. Third person named to the Jazz Hall of Fame.

DEBUT DATE	PEAK POS	WKS CHR	GOLD	ARTIST — Album Title	$	Label & Number
9/8/56	13	2		1 **Kenton in Hi-Fi** .... [I]	$25	Capitol 724
9/15/56	17	4		2 **Cuban Fire!** .... [I]	$25	Capitol 731
10/23/61	16	28		3 **Kenton's West Side Story** .... [I]	$20	Capitol 1609

DEBUT DATE	PEAK POS	WKS CHR	GOLD	ARTIST — Album Title	$	Label & Number

KENTON, Stan — Cont'd

| 7/1/72 | 146 | 14 | 4 | Stan Kenton Today .... [I-L] | $10 | Ln. Ph. 4 44179 [2] |

recorded live in London

Ambivalence (4)
America (3)
Artistry In Boogie (1)
Artistry In Percussion (4)
Artistry In Rhythm (4)
Artistry Jumps (1)
Bogota (4)
Chiapas (4)

Collaboration (1)
Concerto To End All
  Concertos (1)
Cool (3)
Eager Beaver (1)
El Congo Valiente (Valiant
  Congo) (4)
Fringe Benefit (4)

Fuego Cubano (Cuban Fire)
  (2)
Gee, Officer Krupke (3)
God Save The Queen (4)
I Feel Pretty (3)
Intermission Riff (1,4)
La Guera Baila (The Fair
  One Dances) (4)

La Suerte De Los Tontos
  (Fortune Of Fools) (2)
Lover (1)
Malaga (4)
Malaguena (4)
Maria (3)
Minor Riff (1)
Opus In Pastels (4)

Painted Rhythm (1)
Peanut Vendor (1,4)
Quien Sabe (Who Knows) (4)
Recuerdos (Reminiscences)
  (2)
Something's Coming (3)
Somewhere (3)
Southern Scandal (1)

Take The "A" Train (4)
Taunting Scene (3)
Tonight (3)
Unison Riff (1)
Walk Softly (4)
What Are You Doing The
  Rest Of Your Life (4)
Yesterdays (4)

KENTUCKY HEADHUNTERS
Rock-country quintet from Edmonton, Kentucky founded by brothers Richard and Fred Young with their cousin Greg Martin. Includes brothers Doug and Ricky Lee Phelps (vocals). Group hosts own show on WLOC-FM radio *The Chitlin' Show*. The Phelps brothers left the band in June 1992.

| 12/16/89+ | 41 | 96 | ▲ | 1 Pickin' On Nashville .... | $8 | Mercury 838744 |
| 4/20/91 | 29 | 30 | ● | 2 Electric Barnyard .... | $12 | Mercury 848054 |

Always Makin' Love (2)
Ballad Of Davy Crockett (2)
Big Mexican Dinner (2)
Diane (2)
Dumas Walker (1)

High Steppin' Daddy (1)
It's Chitlin' Time (2)
Kickin' Them Blues Around
  (2)
Love Bug Crawl (1)

My Daddy Was A Milkman
  (1)
Oh Lonesome Me (1)
Only Daddy That'll Walk The
  Line (2)

Rag Top (1)
Rock 'N' Roll Angel (1)
16 And Single (2)
Skip A Rope (1)
Smooth (1)

Some Folks Like To Steal (1)
Spirit In The Sky (2)
Take Me Back (2)
Walk Softly On This Heart
  Of Mine (1)

Wishin' Well (2)
With Body And Soul (2)

KERR, Anita, Singers
Nashville-based backup singers for many popular artists. Anita was born Anita Jean Grob on 10/13/27 in Memphis. Formed Singers in 1949. Also see The San Sebastian Strings.

| 3/22/69 | 162 | 6 | | 1 The Anita Kerr Singers Reflect on the hits of Burt Bacharach & Hal David | $10 | Dot 25906 |
| 9/20/69 | 172 | 3 | | 2 Velvet Voices And Bold Brass .... | $10 | Dot 25951 |

Alfie (1)
Are You There (With Another
  Girl) (1)
Do You Know The Way To
  San Jose (1)
Don't Make Me Over (1)

God Bless The Child (2)
Goodbye (2)
Happy Heart (2)
House Is Not A Home (1)
I Say A Little Prayer (1)

In Between The Heartaches
  (1)
Lalena (2)
Look Of Love (1)
My Way (2)

Ob-La-Di, Ob-La-Da (2)
Suppose (2)
Walk On By (1)
What The World Needs Now
  Is Love (1)

What's New Pussycat? (1)
When The World Was Young
  (2)
Whoever You Are, I Love You
  (1)

Windmills Of Your Mind (2)
Windows Of The World (1)
You And I (2)
You've Made Me So Very
  Happy (2)

KERSHAW, Nik
Born on 3/1/58 in Bristol, England. Pop singer/songwriter/multi-instrumentalist.

| 5/5/84 | 70 | 20 | | 1 Human Racing .... | $8 | MCA 39020 |
| 4/27/85 | 113 | 10 | | 2 The Riddle .... | $8 | MCA 5548 |

Bogart (1)
Cloak And Dagger (1)
Dancing Girls (1)
Don Quixote (2)

Drum Talk (1)
Easy (2)
Faces (1)
Gone To Pieces (1)

Human Racing (1)
I Won't Let The Sun Go
  Down On Me (1)
Know How (2)

Riddle, The (2)
Roses (2)
Save The Whale (2)
Shame On You (1)

Wide Boy (2)
Wild Horses (2)
Wouldn't It Be Good
  (1,2) 46

You Might (2)

KERSHAW, Sammy
Native of Kaplan, Louisiana. Third cousin of Cajun fiddler Doug Kershaw.

| 1/25/92 | 95 | 55↑ | ● | Don't Go Near The Water .... | $12 | Mercury 510161 |

Anywhere But Here
Cadillac Style

Don't Go Near The Water
Every Third Monday

Harbor For A Lonely Heart
I Buy Her Roses

Kickin' In

Real Old-Fashioned Broken
  Heart

What Am I Worth
Yard Sale

KESNER, Dick, & his Stradivarius Violin
Violin player. A regular on TV's *The Lawrence Welk Show* (1955-59).

| 1/12/59 | 22 | 2 | | Lawrence Welk Presents Dick Kesner .... [I] | $15 | Brunswick 54044 |

All I Want Is Just Your Love
Farewell Juanita

I Love You Truly
I'll Be With You When The
  Roses Bloom In Spring

Kiss In Your Eyes
Lullaby Of Love
Melody Of Love

My Heart Still Remembers
Play Fiddle Play
Silver Moon

When The Harvest Moon Is
  Shining
Zigeuner

KETCHUM, Hal
Country guitarist/singer from Greenwich, New York. Began career as an R&B drummer at age 15.

| 2/1/92 | 45 | 39 | ● | 1 Past The Point Of Rescue .... | $12 | Curb 77450 |
| 10/10/92 | 151 | 10 | | 2 Sure Love .... | $12 | Curb 77581 |

Daddy's Oldsmobile (2)
Don't Strike A Match (To
  The Book Of Love) (1)
Five O'Clock World (1)
Ghost Town (2)

Hearts Are Gonna Roll (2)
I Know Where Love Lives (1)
I Miss My Mary (1)
Long Day Comin' (1)

Mama Knows The Highway
  (2)
Old Soldiers (1)
Past The Point Of Rescue (1)
She Found The Place (1)

Small Town Saturday Night
  (1)
Softer Than A Whisper (2)
Some Place Far Away (2)
Somebody's Love (1)

Sure Love (2)
Till The Coast Is Clear (2)
Trail Of Tears (2)
You Lovin' Me (2)

KGB
Supergroup of Ray Kennedy (vocals), Rick Grech (Family, Traffic, Blind Faith, Ginger Baker; bass), Mike Bloomfield (Paul Butterfield, Electric Flag; guitar; d: 2/15/81 age 36]), Carmine Appice (Cactus, Vanilla Fudge, Blue Murder; drums) and Barry Goldberg (keyboards).

| 3/6/76 | 124 | 6 | | KGB .... | $10 | MCA 2166 |

Baby Should I Stay Or Go
High Roller

I've Got A Feeling
It's Gonna Be A Hard Night

Let Me Love You
Magic In Your Touch

Midnight Traveler
Sail On Sailor

Workin' For The Children
You Got The Notion

★★442★★ KHAN, Chaka
Born Yvette Marie Stevens on 3/23/53 in Great Lakes, Illinois. Became lead singer of Rufus in 1972. Recorded solo and with Rufus since 1978. Sister of vocalists Taka Boom and Mark Stevens (Jamaica Boys). Chaka's daughter Milini is a member of Pretty In Pink.

11/4/78	12	21	●	1 Chaka	$8	Warner 3245
6/21/80	43	16		2 Naughty	$8	Warner 3385
5/9/81	17	18	●	3 What Cha' Gonna Do For Me	$8	Warner 3526
12/18/82+	52	18		4 Chaka Khan	$8	Warner 23729
10/20/84	14	49	▲	5 I Feel For You	$8	Warner 25162
8/23/86	67	12		6 Destiny	$8	Warner 25425
12/17/88	125	12		7 C.K.	$8	Warner 25707

KHAN, Chaka — Cont'd

DEBUT DATE	PEAK POS	WKS CHR	GOLD	ARTIST — Album Title	$	Label & Number
5/2/92	92	9	8	The Woman I Am	$12	Warner 26296

All Night's All Right (2)
And The Melody Still Lingers On (Night In Tunisia) (3)
Any Old Sunday (3)
Baby Me (7)
Be Bop Medley (4)
Be My Eyes (8)
Best In The West (4)
Caught In The Act (5)
Chinatown (5)
Clouds (2)
Coltrane Dreams (6)
Don't Look At Me That Way (8)
Earth To Mickey (6)
End Of A Love Affair (7)
Eternity (7)

Everything Changes (8)
Eye To Eye (5)
Facts Of Love (8)
Fate (3)
Father He Said (3)
Get Ready, Get Set (2)
Give Me All (8)
Got To Be There (4) 67
Heed The Warning (3)
Hold Her (5)
I Can't Be Loved (6)
I Feel For You (5) 3
I Know You, I Live You (3)
I Want (8)
I Was Made To Love Him (1)
I'll Be Around (7)
I'm Every Woman (1) 21

It's My Party (7)
It's You (6)
Keep Givin' Me Lovin' (8)
La Flamme (5)
Life Is A Dance (1)
Love Has Fallen In Me (1)
Love Of A Lifetime (6) 53
Love With No Strings (8)
Love You All My Lifetime (8) 68
Make It Last (7)
Message In The Middle Of The Bottom (1)
Move Me No Mountain (2)
My Destiny (6)
My Love Is Alive (5)
Night Moods (3)

Nothing's Gonna Take You Away (2)
Other Side Of The World (8)
Our Love's In Danger (2)
Papillon (aka Hot Butterfly) (2)
Pass It On (A Sure Thing) (Pasa Lo Esta Seguro) (4)
Roll Me Through The Rushes (1)
Signed, Sealed, Delivered (I'm Yours) (7)
Sleep On It (1)
Slow Dancin' (4)
So Close (6)
So Naughty (2)
So Not To Worry (4)

Some Love (1)
Soul Talkin' (7)
Sticky Wicked (2)
Stronger Than Before (5)
Tearin' It Up (4)
Telephone (8)
This Is My Night (5) 60
This Time (8)
Through The Fire (5) 60
Tight Fit (6)
Too Much Love (2)
Twisted (4)
Watching The World (6)
We Can Work It Out (3)
We Got Each Other (3)
We Got The Love (1)

What Cha' Gonna Do For Me (3) 53
What You Did (2)
Where Are You Tonite (7)
Who's It Gonna Be (6)
Woman I Am (8)
Woman In A Man's World (1)
You Can Make The Story Right (8)

KHAN, Steve

Jazz guitarist/producer. Born on 4/28/47 in Los Angeles. Son of famed songwriter Sammy Cahn. Prominent studio musician in the 1970s. Member of The Brecker Brothers Band.

DEBUT DATE	PEAK POS	WKS CHR	GOLD	ARTIST — Album Title	$	Label & Number
2/4/78	157	5		Tightrope [I]	$8	Tappan Zee 34857

Big Ones

Darlin' Darlin' Baby (Sweet, Tender, Love)
Soft Summer Breeze
Some Punk Funk
Star Chamber
Tightrope (For Folon)
Where Shadows Meet

KICK AXE

George Criston, lead singer of Canadian heavy-metal quintet.

DEBUT DATE	PEAK POS	WKS CHR	GOLD	ARTIST — Album Title	$	Label & Number
6/30/84	126	15		Vices	$8	Pasha 39297

Alive & Kickin'
All The Right Moves

Cause For Alarm
Dreamin' About You
Heavy Metal Shuffle
Just Passin' Through
Maneater
On The Road To Rock
Stay On Top
Vices

KID CREOLE & THE COCONUTS

Born Thomas Augustus Darnell Browder on 8/12/50 in Montreal. Singer/songwriter/producer. With half-brother Stony Browder, Jr. in Dr. Buzzard's Original Savannah Band during the mid-'70s. Formed The Coconuts with his wife, Addy, and Andy "Coati Mundi" Hernandez (appeared in the film Who's That Girl). Band appeared in the film Against All Odds.

DEBUT DATE	PEAK POS	WKS CHR	GOLD	ARTIST — Album Title	$	Label & Number
7/18/81	180	2	1	Fresh Fruit In Foreign Places	$8	Sire 3534
7/3/82	145	12	2	Wise Guy	$8	Sire 3681

Animal Crackers (1)
Annie, I'm Not Your Daddy (2)
Dear Addy (1)

Gina, Gina (1)
Going Places (1)
I Am (1)
I Stand Accused (1)

I'm A Wonderful Thing, Baby (2)
I'm Corrupt (2)
Imitation (2)

In The Jungle (1)
Latin Music (1)
Love We Have (2)

Loving You Made A Fool Out Of Me (2)
Musica Americana (1)
No Fish Today (1)

Schweinerei (1)
Stool Pigeon (2)
Table Manners (1)
With A Girl Like Mimi (1)

KID FROST

Rapper (b: Arturo Molina, Jr., 5/31/64, East Los Angeles); raised on military bases in Guam and Germany.

DEBUT DATE	PEAK POS	WKS CHR	GOLD	ARTIST — Album Title	$	Label & Number
7/28/90	67	14	1	Hispanic Causing Panic	$12	Virgin 91377
5/9/92	73	10	2	East Side Story	$12	Virgin 92097

Another Firme Rola (Bad Cause I'm Brown) (2)
Come Together (1)
East Side Story (2)

Hispanic Causing Panic (1)
Hold Your Own (1)
Home Boyz (2)
Homicide (1)

I Got Pulled Over (2)
In The City (1)
La Raza (1) 42
Man, The (1)

Mi Vida Loca (2)
No More Wars (2)
No Sunshine (2) 95
Penitentiary (2)
Smiling Faces (2)

Smoke (1)
Straight To The Bank (1)
These Stories Have To Be Told (2)

Thin Line (2)
Throwing Q-VO's (2)
Volo, The (1)
Ya Estuvo (1)

KID 'N PLAY

New York-based rap duo: Kid (Christopher Reid) and Play (Christopher Martin). Starred in the films House Party, House Party 2 and Class Act. Stars of own Saturday morning cartoon show.

DEBUT DATE	PEAK POS	WKS CHR	GOLD	ARTIST — Album Title	$	Label & Number
12/17/88+	96	47	● 1	2 Hype	$8	Select 21628
3/31/90	58	12	● 2	Kid 'N Play's Funhouse	$12	Select 21638
10/19/91	144	11	3	Face The Nation	$12	Select 61206

Ain't Gonna Hurt Nobody (3) 51
Back On Wax (3)
Back To Basix (2)
Bill's At The Door (3)
Brother Man Get Hip (1)
Can You Dig That (1)

Can't Get Enuff (2)
Damn That DJ (The Wizard M.E.) (1)
Decisions (2)
Do This My Way (1)
Do Whatcha Want 2 (2)
Energy (2)

Face The Nation (3)
Foreplay (3)
Funhouse (2)
Gittin' Funky (1)
Give It Here (3)
Got A Good Thing Going On (3)

I Don't Know (2)
It's Alright Y'All (3)
Kid 'N Play Kick Step (1)
Last Night (1)
Next Question (3)
Rollin' With Kid 'N Play (1)
Show 'Em How It's Done (2)

Slippin' (3)
Soul Man (1)
Strokin' (2)
Toe To Toe (2,3)
2 Hype (1)
Undercover (1)
Y U Jellin' Me (2)

KID SENSATION

Real name: Steve Spence. Seattle native. Former DJ/keyboardist with Sir Mix-A-Lot.

DEBUT DATE	PEAK POS	WKS CHR	GOLD	ARTIST — Album Title	$	Label & Number
8/4/90	175	8		Rollin' With Number One	$12	Nastymix 70180

Back To Boom
Emergency

Flowin'
Hype It Up

I S.P.I.T.
Legal

Maxin' With E.C.P.
Partners In Rhyme

Prisoner Of Ignorance
Seatown Ballers

Skin To Skin
Two Minutes

KIDS FROM "FAME", The

Studio musicians featuring cast members of the TV series Fame: Debbie Allen, Erica Gimpel, Gene Anthony Ray, Valerie Landsburg, Lee Curreri, Lori Singer, Albert Hague and Carlo Imperato. Singer/actress/director Allen's sister is actress Phylicia Rashad and husband is basketball player Norm Nixon.

DEBUT DATE	PEAK POS	WKS CHR	GOLD	ARTIST — Album Title	$	Label & Number
4/3/82	146	8	1	The Kids From "Fame"	$8	RCA 4249
1/15/83	181	4	2	Songs	$8	RCA 4525
3/26/83	98	11	3	The Kids From "Fame" Live! [L]	$8	RCA 4674

recorded at the Royal Albert Hall in London

Be My Music (1,3)
Be Your Own Hero (2)
Beautiful Dreamer (2)
Bet Your Life It's Me (2)
Body Language (2,3)

Could We Be Magic Like You (2,3)
Dancing Endlessly (2)
Desdemona (1,3)
Fame (3)

Friday Night (3)
Hi-Fidelity (3)
I Can Do Anything Better Than You Can (1)
I Still Believe In Me (1,3)

It's Gonna Be A Long Night (1,3)
Just Like You (2)
Lay Back And Be Cool (2)
Life Is A Celebration (1,3)

Mannequin (2,3)
Secret, The (medley) (3)
Songs (2)
Special Place (medley) (3)
Starmaker (1,3)

Step Up To The Mike (1)
There's A Train (2)
We Got The Power (1,3)

DEBUT DATE	PEAK POS	WKS CHR	GOLD	ARTIST — Album Title	$	Label & Number

KIHN, Greg, Band
Greg is a rock singer/songwriter/guitarist from Baltimore. Formed band in Berkeley, California in 1975.

DEBUT DATE	PEAK POS	WKS CHR		ARTIST — Album Title	$	Label & Number
9/16/78	145	12	1	Next Of Kihn	$8	Beserkley 0056
8/11/79	114	10	2	With The Naked Eye	$8	Beserkley 10063
4/26/80	167	5	3	Glass House Rock	$8	Beserkley 10068
4/11/81	32	32	4	Rockihnroll	$8	Beserkley 10069
4/10/82	33	17	5	Kihntinued	$8	Beserkley 60101
3/12/83	15	24	6	Kihnspiracy	$8	Beserkley 60224
6/16/84	121	9	7	Kihntagious	$8	Beserkley 60354
3/23/85	51	13	8	Citizen Kihn	$8	EMI America 17152

GREG KIHN

Anna Belle Lee (3)
Another Lonely Saturday Night (2)
Beside Myself (2)
Boy's Won't (8)
Breakup Song (They Don't Write 'Em) (4) 15
Can't Have The Highs (Without The Lows) (2)
Can't Love Them All (6)
Can't Stop Hurtin' Myself (4)
Castaway (3)
Cheri Baby (7)
Chinatown (1)
Cold Hard Cash (1)

Confrontation Music (7)
Curious (6)
Dedication (5)
Desire Me (3)
Every Love Song (5) 82
Everybody Else (1)
Everyday/Saturday (5)
Fallen Idol (2)
Family (5)
Fascination (4)
For Your Love (3)
Free Country (8)
Getting Away With Murder (2)
Girl Most Likely (4)

Go Back (8)
Good Life (8)
Happy Man (5) 62
Hard Times (7)
Higher And Higher (5)
How Long (6)
I Fall To Pieces (6)
I'm In Love Again (8)
Imitation Love (8)
In The Naked Eye (2)
Jeopardy (6) 2
Love Never Fails (6) 59
Lucky (8) 30
Make Up (7)

Man Who Shot Liberty Valance (3)
Moulin Rouge (2)
Museum (1)
Night After Night (3)
Nothing's Gonna Change (4)
One Thing About Love (7)
Only Dance There Is (3)
Privacy (8)
Remember (4)
Rendezvous (2)
Reunited (7)
Roadrunner (2)
Rock (7)

Secret Meetings (1)
Seeing Is Believing (5)
Serenade Her (3)
Sheila (4)
Small Change (3)
Someday (6)
Sorry (1)
Sound System (5)
Stand Together (7)
Talkin' To Myself (6)
Tear That City Down (6)
Tell Me Lies (5)
Temper, Temper (8)
Testify (5)

They Rock By Night (8)
Things To Come (3)
Trouble In Paradise (4)
Trouble With The Girl (7)
True Confessions (4)
Understander (1)
Valerie (4)
When The Music Starts (4)
Whenever (8)
Womankind (4)
Work, Work, Work (7)
Worst That Could Happen (7)

KILLER DWARFS
Hard-rock quartet from Toronto: Russ (vocals), Darrell (drums), Ron (bass) and Mike (guitar) Dwarf. Mike was replaced by Jerry Dwarf by 1992.

DEBUT DATE	PEAK POS	WKS CHR		ARTIST — Album Title	$	Label & Number
5/28/88	165	6	1	Big Deal	$8	Epic 44098
4/28/90	151	9	2	Dirty Weapons	$12	Epic 45139

All That We Dream (2)
Appeal (2)
Breakaway (1)
Burn It Down (1)

Comin' Through (2)
Desperados (1)
Dirty Weapons (2)
Doesn't Matter (2)

I'm Alive (1)
Last Laugh (2)
Lifetime (1)
Not Foolin' (2)

Nothin' Gets Nothin' (2)
One Way Out (2)
Power (1)
Startin' To Shine (1)

Tell Me Please (1)
Union Of Pride (1)
Want It Bad (2)
We Stand Alone (1)

KILLING JOKE
English dance-rock quartet led by vocalist Jaz Coleman.

DEBUT DATE	PEAK POS	WKS CHR		ARTIST — Album Title	$	Label & Number
4/11/87	194	1		Brighter Than A Thousand Suns	$8	Virgin/EG 90568

Adorations
Chessboard

Love Of The Masses
Rubicon

Sanity

Southern Sky

Twilight Of The Mortal

Wintergardens

KILZER, John
Memphis-based rock singer. Born in Jackson, Tennessee. An English literature graduate and former basketball player at Memphis State University.

DEBUT DATE	PEAK POS	WKS CHR		ARTIST — Album Title	$	Label & Number
6/11/88	110	15		Memory In The Making	$8	Geffen 24190

Dirty Dishes
Dream Queen

Give Me A Highway
Green, Yellow And Red

Heart And Soul
I Love You

If Sidewalks Talked
Loaded Dice

Memory In The Making
Pick Me Up

Red Blue Jeans
When Fools Say Love

KIM, Andy
Born Andrew Joachim on 12/5/46 in Montreal. His parents were from Lebanon. Pop singer/songwriter. Teamed with Jeff Barry to write "Sugar, Sugar."

DEBUT DATE	PEAK POS	WKS CHR		ARTIST — Album Title	$	Label & Number
8/2/69	82	14	1	Baby I Love You	$15	Steed 37004
9/14/74	21	17	2	Andy Kim	$12	Capitol 11318
12/21/74	190	6	3	Andy Kim's Greatest Hits [G]	$12	Dunhill 50193

And I Will Sing You To Sleep (2)
Baby, I Love You (1,3) 9
Be My Baby (3) 17
By The Time I Get To Phoenix (1)
Didn't Have To Tell Her (1)

Fire, Baby I'm On Fire (2) 28
Friend In The City (3) 90
Good Good Mornin' (2)
Hang Up Those Rock 'N Roll Shoes (2)
Here Comes The Mornin' (2)

How'd We Ever Get This Way (3) 21
I Been Moved (3) 97
I Got To Know (1)
I Wish I Were (3) 62
I'll Make You Mine (1)
If I Were A Carpenter (1)

It's Your Life (3) 85
Let's Get Married (3)
Rainbow Ride (3) 49
Rock Me Gently [includes 2 versions] (2) 1
Rock Me Gently - Part II (2)
Shoot 'Em Up, Baby (3) 31

So Good Together (1,3) 36
Songs I Can Sing Ya (2)
Sunshine (2)
This Guy's In Love With You (1)
This Is The Girl (1)
Tricia Tell Your Daddy (3)

Walkin' My La De Da (1)
You Are My Everything (2)

KIMBERLYS, The — see JENNINGS, Waylon

KIME, Warren, & his Brass Impact orchestra
Chicago orchestra leader/arranger.

DEBUT DATE	PEAK POS	WKS CHR		ARTIST — Album Title	$	Label & Number
4/15/67	89	12	1	Brass Impact [I]	$10	Command 910
11/11/67+	177	7	2	Explosive Brass Impact [I]	$10	Command 919

Baubles, Bangles & Beads (1)
Brasilia (1)
Breeze And I (1)
Constant Rain (Chove Chuva) (2)

Eleanor Rigby (1)
Everybody Loves My Baby (2)
Feeling Good (2)
Foggy Day (1)
Gentle Rain (2)
Georgy Girl (2)

Get Out Of Town (2)
In The Still Of The Night (1)
It's All Right With Me (2)
Lala Ladaia (Reza) (2)
Man And A Woman (2)

Mas Que Nada (Pow, Pow, Pow) (1)
Mr. Lucky (1)
No Moon At All (2)
One Note Samba (Samba De Uma Nota So) (1)

Prelude To A Kiss (1)
So In Love (2)
So What's New (2)
Sweetest Sounds (1)
What Now My Love (1)

KIMMEL, Tom
Rock singer/songwriter originally from Memphis.

DEBUT DATE	PEAK POS	WKS CHR		ARTIST — Album Title	$	Label & Number
7/4/87	104	15		5 To 1	$8	Mercury 832248

A To Z
5 To 1

Heroes
No Tech

On The Defensive
Shake

That's Freedom 64
True Love

Tryin' To Dance
Violet Eyes

KING
British pop-rock quartet led by vocalist Paul King.

DEBUT DATE	PEAK POS	WKS CHR		ARTIST — Album Title	$	Label & Number
8/17/85	140	9		Steps In Time	$8	Epic 40061

And As For Myself
Cherry

Fish
I Kissed The Spikey Fridge

Love & Pride 55
Soul On My Boots

Trouble
Unity Song

Won't You Hold My Hand Now

DEBUT DATE	PEAK POS	WKS CHR	GOLD	ARTIST — Album Title	$	Label & Number

KING, Albert

Born Albert Nelson on 4/25/23 in Indianola, Mississippi. Died on 12/21/92 of a heart attack. Blues-based singer/guitarist/drummer. With Harmony Kings gospel group from 1949-51. First recorded for Parrot in 1953. Formed own band in St. Louis, in 1956.

DEBUT DATE	PEAK POS	WKS CHR	#	Album Title	$	Label & Number
11/16/68	**150**	10	1	Live Wire/Blues Power .... [I-L]	$20	Stax 2003
3/1/69	**194**	5	2	King Of The Blues Guitar..	$20	Atlantic 8213
5/24/69	**133**	4	3	Years Gone By	$15	Stax 2010
7/12/69	**171**	5	4	Jammed Together .... [I]	$12	Stax 2020

ALBERT KING/STEVE CROPPER/POP STAPLES
Pop is Roebuck Staples, leader of family soul group The Staple Singers

7/3/71	**188**	6	5	Lovejoy	$12	Stax 2040
10/7/72	**140**	8	6	I'll Play The Blues For You	$12	Stax 3009
3/20/76	**166**	6	7	Truckload Of Lovin'	$10	Utopia 1387
3/12/77	**182**	3	8	Albert Live .... [L]	$12	Utopia 2205 [2]

Angel Of Mercy (6)
Answer To The Laundromat Blues (6)
As The Years Go Passing By (8)
Baby, What You Want Me To Do (4)
Bay Area Blues (5)
Big Bird (4)
Blues At Sunrise (1,8)
Blues Power (1)
Born Under A Bad Sign (2)
Breaking Up Somebody's Home (6) **91**
Cadillac Assembly Line (7)
Cockroach (3)
Cold Feet (2) **67**

Cold Women With Warm Hearts (7)
Corina Corina (5)
Crosscut Saw (2)
Don't Burn Down The Bridge (6,8)
Don't Turn Your Heater Down (4)
Drowning On Dry Land [includes 2 versions] (3)
Everybody Wants To Go To Heaven (5)
For The Love Of A Woman (5)
Funk-Shun (2)
Going Back To Iuka (5)
Gonna Make It Somehow (7)
Heart Fixing Business (3)

High Cost Of Loving (6)
Hold Hands With One Another (7)
Homer's Theme (4)
Honky Tonk Woman (5)
I Love Lucy (2)
I'll Be Doggone (6)
I'll Play The Blues For You (6,8)
I'm Gonna Call You As Soon As The Sun Goes Down (8)
I'm Your Mate (7)
If The Washing Don't Get You, The Rinsing Will (3)
Jam In A Flat (8)
Kansas City (8)
Killing Floor (3)

Knock On Wood (4)
Laundromat Blues (2)
Like A Road Leading Home (5)
Little Brother (Make A Way) (6)
Lonely Man (3)
Look Out (1)
Lovejoy, Ill. (5)
Matchbox Holds My Clothes (8)
Night Stomp (1)
Nobody Wants A Loser (7)
Oh, Pretty Woman (4)
Opus De Soul (3)
Overall Junction (2,8)
Personal Manager (2)

Please Love Me (1)
Sensation, Communication Together (7)
She Caught The Katy & Left Me A Mule To Ride (5)
Sky Is Crying (3)
Stormy Monday (8)
That's What The Blues Is All About (8)
Trashy Dog (4)
Truckload Of Lovin' (7)
Tupelo (4)
Water (4)
Watermelon Man (1,8)
What'd I Say (4)
Wrapped Up In Love Again (3)

You Don't Love Me (3)
You Sure Drive A Hard Bargain (2)
You Threw Your Love On Me Too Strong (3)
You're Gonna Need Me (2)

★★149★★ KING, B.B.

The most famous blues singer/guitarist in the world today. Born Riley B. King on 9/16/25 in Itta Bena, Mississippi. Moved to Memphis in 1946. Own radio show on WDIA-Memphis, 1949-50, where he was dubbed "The Beale Street Blues Boy," later shortened to "Blues Boy," then simply "B.B." First recorded for Bullet in 1949. Inducted into the Rock and Roll Hall of Fame in 1987. Won the Lifetime Achievement Grammy award in 1987. Appeared in the films *Into The Night* (1985) and *Amazon Women On The Moon* (1987).

10/12/68	**192**	3	1	Lucille..	$15	BluesWay 6016
				Lucille is B.B.'s Gibson guitar		
6/14/69	**56**	34	2	Live & Well .... [L]	$15	BluesWay 6031
				side 1: live; side 2: studio		
12/27/69+	**38**	30	3	Completely Well	$15	BluesWay 6037
4/11/70	**193**	2	4	The Incredible Soul of B.B. King .... [E]	$15	Kent 539
10/17/70	**26**	28	5	Indianola Mississippi Seeds	$10	ABC 713
2/20/71	**25**	33	6	Live In Cook County Jail .... [L]	$10	ABC 723
9/25/71	**78**	8	7	Live At The Regal.. [E-L]	$10	ABC 724
				recorded in Chicago on 11/21/64		
10/16/71	**57**	17	8	B.B. King In London	$10	ABC 730
2/26/72	**53**	17	9	L.A. Midnight...	$10	ABC 743
9/9/72	**65**	20	10	Guess Who	$10	ABC 759
2/24/73	**101**	11	11	The Best Of B.B. King .... [G]	$10	ABC 767
9/8/73	**71**	25	12	To Know You Is To Love You	$10	ABC 794
8/17/74	**153**	6	13	Friends	$10	ABC 825
10/26/74+	**43**	20	● 14	Together For The First Time...Live .... [L]	$12	Dunhill 50190 [2]
				B.B. KING & BOBBY BLAND		
11/8/75	**140**	5	15	Lucille Talks Back	$10	ABC 898
7/17/76	**73**	14	16	Together Again...Live .... [L]	$10	ABC/Impulse 9317
				BOBBY BLAND & B.B. KING		
2/12/77	**154**	7	17	King Size	$8	ABC 977
5/20/78	**124**	24	18	Midnight Believer	$8	ABC 1061
8/25/79	**112**	12	19	Take It Home	$8	MCA 3151
4/26/80	**162**	4	20	"Now Appearing" at Ole Miss .... [L]	$10	MCA 8016 [2]
2/28/81	**131**	10	21	There Must Be A Better World Somewhere....................	$8	MCA 5162
5/15/82	**179**	5	22	Love Me Tender	$8	MCA 5307
7/2/83	**172**	4	23	Blues 'N' Jazz	$8	MCA 5413
				recorded on his 57th birthday (9/16/82)		

Ain't Gonna Worry My Life Anymore (5)
Ain't Nobody Home (8,11) **46**
Alexis' Boogie (8)
Any Other Way (10)
Ask Me No Questions (5) **40**
B.B. King Blues Theme (20)
Baby I'm Yours (13)
Beginning Of The End (19)
Better Lovin' Man (10)
Better Not Look Down (19)
Black Night (medley) (14)
Blue Shadows (8)
Born Again Human (21)
Breaking Up Somebody's Home (15)

Broken Heart (23)
Caldonia (8,11,20)
Can't You Hear Me Talking To You? (9)
Chains And Things (5) **45**
Chains Of Love (medley) (14)
Cherry Red (medley) (14)
Come By Here (4)
Confessin' The Blues (3)
Country Girl (1)
Cryin' Won't Help You Now (19)
Darlin' You Know I Love You (6,20,23)
Don't Answer The Door (2,14,20)
Don't Change On Me (22)

Don't Cry No More (14)
Don't Make Me Pay For His Mistakes (15)
Don't You Lie To Me (17)
Driftin' Blues (14)
Driving Wheel (medley) (14)
Every Day I Have The Blues (medley) (14)
Everybody Lies A Little (9)
Feel So Bad (16)
Five Long Years (10)
Fool Too Long (4)
Found What I Need (10)
Friends (2)
Friends (13)
Get Off My Back Woman (2) **74**

Ghetto Woman (8) **68**
Go Underground (5)
Goin' Down Slow (14)
Gonna Get Me An Old Woman (medley) (14)
Good To Be Back Home (6,7,16)
Got My Mojo Working (17)
Guess Who (10,20) **62**
Happy Birthday Blues (19)
Have Faith (15)
Heed My Warning (23)
Help The Poor (7,9) **90**
Hold On (I Feel Our Love Is Changing) (18,20)
How Blue Can You Get (6,7,11) **97**

Hummingbird (5,11) **48**
I Ain't Gonna Be The First To Cry (medley) (16)
(I Believe) I've Been Blue Too Long (9)
I Can't Leave (12)
I Can't Let You Go (23)
I Got Some Help I Don't Need (9,20) **92**
I Got Them Blues (13)
I Just Can't Leave Your Love Alone (18,20)
I Just Want To Make Love To You (medley) (17)
I Know The Price (15)
I Like To Live The Love (12,14) **28**

I Love You So (4)
I Need Love So Bad (medley) (20)
I Need Your Love (1)
I Want You So Bad (2)
I Wonder Why (17)
(I'd Be) A Legend In My Time (22)
I'll Take Care Of You (14)
I'm Cracking Up Over You (4)
I'm Sorry (14)
I'm With You (1)
I've Always Been Lonely (19)
I've Got Papers On You Baby (4)
Inflation Blues (23)
It Takes A Young Girl (10)

DEBUT DATE	PEAK POS	WKS CHR	GOLD	ARTIST — Album Title	$	Label & Number

KING, B.B. — Cont'd

It's Just A Matter Of Time (17)
It's My Own Fault (7,14)
Just A Little Love (2) 76
Just Can't Please You (10)
Key To My Kingdom (3)
King's Special (5)
Let Me Make You Cry A Little Longer (18)
Let The Good Times Roll (16)
Let's Get Down To Business (2)
Life Ain't Nothing But A Party (21)
Love (12)
Love Me Tender (22)
Lucille (3)
Lucille Talks Back (Copulation) (15)
Lucille's Granny (9)
Make Love To Me (23)
Mean Old World (medley) (16)
Midnight (9)

Midnight Believer (18)
More, More, More (21)
Mother Fuyer (17)
Mother-In-Law Blues (medley) (16)
My Mood (2)
My Silent Prayer (4)
My Song (13)
Neighborhood Affair (10)
Never Make A Move Too Soon (18,20)
Nightlife (medley) (22)
No Good (3)
No Money No Luck (1)
Nobody Loves Me But My Mother (5,11,20)
Oh To Me (12)
One Of Those Nights (22)
Part-Time Love (8)
Philadelphia (13) 64
Please Accept My Love (2,6)
Please Love Me (7)
Please Send Me Someone To Love (medley) (22)

Power Of The Blues (8)
Rainbow Riot (23)
Rainin' All The Time (1)
Reconsider Baby (15)
Respect Yourself (12)
Rock Me Baby (medley) (14,20)
Same Love That Made Me Laugh (17)
Same Old Story (Same Old Song) (19)
Second Hand Woman (19)
Sell My Monkey (23)
Shouldn't Have Left Me (19)
Since I Met You Baby (22)
Slow And Easy (17)
So Excited (3) 54
Stop Putting The Hurt On Me (1)
Stormy Monday Blues (medley) (16)
Story Everybody Knows (19)
Strange Things Happen (medley) (16)

Summer In The City (10)
Sweet Sixteen (6,9,11) 93
Sweet Little Angel (2,7)
Sweet Thing (4)
Take It Home (19)
Teardrops From My Eyes (23)
Thank You For Loving The Blues (12)
That's The Way Love Is (14)
There Must Be A Better World Somewhere (21)
3 O'Clock Blues (6,14,20)
Thrill Is Gone (3,6,11,16,20) 15
Time Is A Thief (22)
Time To Say Goodbye (4)
To Know You Is To Love You (12) 38
Tomorrow Is Another Day (4)
Tonight I'm Gonna Make You A Star (19)
Treat Me Right (4)
Until I'm Dead And Cold (5)
Up At 5 AM (13)

Victim, The (21)
Walkin' In The Sun (17)
Watch Yourself (1)
We Can't Agree (8)
We Can't Make It (4)
Wet Hayshark (8)
What Happened (3)
When Everything Else Is Gone (13)
When I'm Wrong (15,20)
When It All Comes Down (I'll Still Be Around) (18)
Who Are You (12) 78
Why I Sing The Blues (2,11,14) 61
Woke Up This Mornin' (7)
Woman I Love (4) 94
World Full Of Strangers (18)
World I Never Made (22)
Worried Life Blues (medley) (14)
Worry, Worry, Worry (6,7)
You And Me, Me And You (22)

You Don't Know Nothin' About Love (10)
You Done Lost Your Good Thing Now (7,20)
You Move Me So (1)
You Upset Me Baby (7)
You're Going With Me (21)
You're Losin' Me (3)
You're Mean (3)
You're Still My Woman (5)
You've Always Got The Blues (22)
Your Lovin' Turns Me On (medley) (17)

KING, Ben E.

Born Benjamin Earl Nelson on 9/23/38 in Henderson, North Carolina. To New York in 1947. Worked with The Moonglows for six months while still in high school. Joined the Five Crowns in 1957, who became the new Drifters in 1959. Wrote lyrics to "There Goes My Baby," his first lead performance with The Drifters. Went solo in May 1960.

DEBUT DATE	PEAK POS	WKS CHR	GOLD	ARTIST — Album Title	$	Label & Number
8/7/61	**57**	7		1 Spanish Harlem	$40	Atco 133
5/3/75	**39**	14		2 Supernatural	$12	Atlantic 18132
7/23/77	**33**	21		3 Benny And Us	$8	Atlantic 19105

AVERAGE WHITE BAND & BEN E. KING

Amor (1) 18
Besame Mucho (1)
Come Closer To Me (1)
Do It In The Name Of Love (2) 60
Do You Wanna Do A Thing (2)
Drop My Heart Off (2)

Extra-Extra (2)
Fool For You Anyway (3)
Frenesi (1)
Get It Up For Love (3)
Granada (1)
Happiness Is Where You Find It (2)
Imagination (2)

Imagine (3)
Keepin' It To Myself (3)
Love Me, Love Me (1)
Message (3)
Perfidia (1)
Quizas, Quizas, Quizas (Perhaps, Perhaps, Perhaps) (1)

Someday We'll All Be Free (3)
Souvenir Of Mexico (1)
Spanish Harlem (1) 10
Star In The Ghetto (3)
Supernatural Thing-Part I (2) 5
Supernatural Thing-Part II (2)

Sway (1)
Sweet And Gentle (1)
What Do You Want Me To Do (2)
What Is Soul (3)
Your Lovin' Ain't Good Enough (2)

★★84★★ KING, Carole

Born Carole Klein on 2/9/42 in Brooklyn. Singer/songwriter/pianist. Neil Sedaka wrote his 1959 hit "Oh! Carol" about her. Married lyricist Gerry Goffin in 1958; team wrote four #1 hits: "Will You Love Me Tomorrow," "Go Away Little Girl," "Take Good Care Of My Baby," and "The Loco-Motion." Divorced Goffin in 1968. First solo album in 1970. In 1971, won four Grammys. King and Goffin's daughter, Louise, began a solo career in 1979. One of the most successful female songwriters of the rock era. She and Goffin were inducted as a songwriting team into the Rock and Roll Hall of Fame in 1990.

DEBUT DATE	PEAK POS	WKS CHR	GOLD	ARTIST — Album Title	$	Label & Number
4/10/71	**1**[15]	302	●	1 Tapestry	$12	Ode 77009
				1971 Grammy winner: Album of the Year		
5/1/71	**84**	27		2 Writer: Carole King	$12	Ode 77006
				originally released before *Tapestry*		
12/11/71+	**1**[3]	44	●	3 Music	$12	Ode 77013
11/4/72	**2**[5]	31	●	4 Rhymes & Reasons	$12	Ode 77016
6/23/73	**6**	37	●	5 Fantasy	$12	Ode 77018
9/28/74	**1**[1]	29	●	6 Wrap Around Joy	$12	Ode 77024
3/8/75	**20**	15		7 Really Rosie	[TV] $12	Ode 77027
				from the original animated TV soundtrack		
2/7/76	**3**	21	●	8 Thoroughbred	$12	Ode 77034
8/6/77	**17**	14	●	9 Simple Things	$8	Capitol 11667
4/1/78	**47**	13	●	10 Her Greatest Hits	[G] $8	Ode 34967
6/17/78	**104**	8		11 Welcome Home	$8	Avatar 11785
6/23/79	**104**	9		12 Touch The Sky	$8	Capitol 11953
6/7/80	**44**	17		13 Pearls-Songs of Goffin and King	$8	Capitol 12073
4/3/82	**119**	11		14 One To One	$8	Atlantic 19344
5/6/89	**111**	16		15 City Streets	$8	Capitol 90885

Ain't That The Way (15)
Alligators All Around (7)
Ambrosia (8)
Ave. P (7)
Awful Truth (7)
Back To California (3)
Ballad Of Chicken Soup (7)
Beautiful (1)
Been To Canaan (4,10) 24
Being At War With Each Other (5)
Believe In Humanity (5,10) 28
Best Is Yet To Come (6)
Bitter With The Sweet (4)
Brighter (3)
Brother, Brother (3,10)
Can't You Be Real (2)
Carry Your Load (3)
Chains (13)

Change In Mind, Change Of Heart (6)
Changes (11)
Chicken Soup With Rice (7)
Child Of Mine (2)
City Streets (15)
Come Down Easy (4)
Corazon (5,10) 37
Crazy (12)
Dancin' With Tears In My Eyes (13)
Daughter Of Light (8)
Directions (5)
Disco Tech (11)
Down To The Darkness (15)
Dreamlike I Wander (12)
Eagle (12)
Eventually (2)
Everybody's Got The Spirit (11)

Fantasy Beginning (5)
Fantasy End (5)
Feeling Sad Tonight (4)
Ferguson Road (4)
First Day In August (4)
Goat Annie (14)
God Only Knows (9)
Goin' Back (2,13)
Golden Man (14)
Good Mountain People (12)
Goodbye Don't Mean I'm Gone (4)
Gotta Get Through Another Day (4)
Growing Away From Me (3)
Hard Rock Cafe (9) 30
Haywood (5)
Hey Girl (13)
Hi De Ho (13)
High Out Of Time (8) 76

Hold On (9)
Home Again (1)
Homeless Heart (15)
I Can't Hear You No More (2)
I Can't Stop Thinking About You (15)
I Feel The Earth Move (1,10) *flip*
I Think I Can Hear You (4)
I'd Like To Know You Better (8)
In The Name Of Love (9)
It's A War (14)
It's Going To Take Some Time (4)
It's Gonna Work Out Fine (8)
It's Too Late (1,10) 1
Jazzman (6,10) 2
Labyrinth (9)
Legacy (15)

Life Without Love (14)
Little Prince (14)
Locomotion (13)
Lookin' Out For Number One (14)
(Love Is Like A) Boomerang (14)
Lovelight (15)
Main Street Saturday Night (11)
Midnight Flyer (15)
Morning Sun (11)
Move Lightly (12)
Music (3)
My Lovin' Eyes (6)
My My She Cries (4)
My Simple Humble Neighborhood (7)
Night This Side Of Dying (6)
Nightingale (6,10) 9

No Easy Way Down (2)
Oh No Not My Baby (13)
One (9)
One Fine Day (13) 12
One To One (14) 45
One Was Johnny (7)
Only Love Is Real (8,10) 28
Passing Of The Days (12)
Peace In The Valley (7)
Pierre (7)
Quiet Place To Live (5)
Raspberry Jam (2)
Read Between The Lines (14)
Really Rosie (7)
Ride The Music (11)
Screaming And Yelling (7)
Seeing Red (2)
Simple Things (9)
Smackwater Jack (1,10) *flip*

DEBUT DATE	PEAK POS	WKS CHR	GOLD	ARTIST — Album Title	$	Label & Number

KING, Carole — Cont'd

Snow Queen (13)	Still Here Thinking Of You (8)	There's A Space Between Us (8)	Way Over Yonder (1)	Wings Of Love (11)	You've Been Around Too Long (5)
So Far Away (1,10) **14**	Such Sufferin' (7)	Time Alone (9)	We All Have To Be Alone (8)	Wrap Around Joy (6)	You've Got A Friend (1)
So Many Ways (8)	Sunbird (11)	Time Gone By (12)	We Are All In This Together (6)	You Gentle Me (6)	
Some Kind Of Wonderful (3)	Surely (3)	To Know That I Love You (9)	Weekdays (5)	You Go Your Way, I'll Go Mine (6)	
Someone Who Believes In You (15)	Sweet Adonis (6)	To Love (2)	Welcome Home (11)	**You Light Up My Life** (5) **67**	
Someone You Never Met Before (14)	Sweet Life (15)	Too Much Rain (3)	Welfare Symphony (5)	(You Make Me Feel Like) A Natural Woman (4)	
Song Of Long Ago (3)	**Sweet Seasons** (3,10) **9**	Up On The Roof (2)	What Have You Got To Lose (2)	You Still Want Her (12)	
Spaceship Races (2)	Sweet Sweetheart (2)	Venusian Diamond (11)	Where You Lead (1)	You're Something New (6)	
Stand Behind Me (4)	Tapestry (1)	Walk With Me (I'll Be Your Companion) (12)	Will You Love Me Tomorrow? (1)	You're The One Who Knows (9)	
	That's How Things Go Down (5)	Wasn't Born To Follow (13)			

KING, Claude

Born on 2/5/33 in Shreveport, Louisiana. Country singer/songwriter/guitarist. Acted in the TV miniseries *The Blue And The Gray* in 1982.

8/11/62	80	7		Meet Claude King	$20	Columbia 8610

Big River, Big Man 82	Give Me Your Love And I'll Give You Mine	I Can't Get Over The Way You Got Over Me	I'm Here To Get My Baby Out Of Jail	Pistol Packin' Papa	**Wolverton Mountain** *6*
Comancheros, The 71	I Backed Out		Little Bitty Heart	Sweet Lovin'	You're Breaking My Heart
				Tell Me Darlin', Would You Care?	

KING, Evelyn "Champagne"

Born on 6/29/60 in the Bronx. To Philadelphia in 1970. Employed as a cleaning woman at Sigma Studios when discovered.

5/27/78	14	45	●	1	Smooth Talk	$8	RCA 2466
4/14/79	35	17	●	2	Music Box	$8	RCA 3033
10/11/80	124	7		3	Call On Me	$8	RCA 3543
7/25/81	28	18		4	I'm In Love	$8	RCA 3962
9/11/82	27	32	●	5	Get Loose	$8	RCA 4337
					above 2: EVELYN KING		
12/24/83+	91	20		6	Face To Face	$8	RCA 4725
6/25/88	192	3		7	Flirt	$8	EMI-Man. 46968

Action (6) **75**	Flirt (7)	I Think My Heart Is Telling (2)	Make Up Your Mind (2)	Spirit Of The Dancer (4)	When Your Heart Says Yes (7)
Back To Love (5)	Get Loose (5)	**I'm In Love** (4) **40**	Makin' Me So Proud (6)	Steppin' Out (Part I & II) (2)	Whenever You Touch Me (7)
Bedroom Eyes (3)	Get Up Off Your Love (5)	I'm Just Warmin' Up (5)	**Music Box** (2) **75**	Stop It (5)	You Can Turn Me On (7)
Before The Date (7)	Givin' You My Love (What Cha Gonna Do With It) (6)	If You Want My Lovin' (4)	No Time For Fooling Around (2)	Stop That (5)	Your Kind Of Loving (3)
Best Is Yet To Come (4)	Hold On To What You've Got (7)	It's OK (3)	Nobody Knows (1)	Talk Don't Hurt Nobody (3)	
Betcha She Don't Love You (5) **49**	I Can't Stand It (5)	Just A Little Bit Of Love (3)	Other Side Of Love (4)	Teenager (6)	
Call On Me (3)	I Can't Take It (4)	Kisses Don't Lie (7)	Out There (2)	Tell Me Something Good (6)	
Dancin', Dancin', Dancin' (1)	**I Don't Know If It's Right** (1) **23**	Let's Get Crazy (6)	Shake Down (6)	Til I Come Off The Road (3)	
Don't Hide Our Love (4)	I Need Your Love (3)	Let's Get Funky Tonight (3)	**Shame** (1) **9**	Universal Girl (3)	
Don't It Feel Good (6)		Let's Start All Over Again (3)	Show Is Over (1)	We're Going To A Party (1)	
Face To Face (6)		**Love Come Down** (5) **17**	Smooth Talk (1)	What Are You Waiting For (4)	

KING, Freddie

Blues singer/guitarist. Born Freddie Christian on 9/3/34 in Gilmer, Texas. Died of a hepatitis-related heart attack on 12/28/76. Session work for Parrot and Chess. Released singles as Freddy King.

7/21/73	158	8			Woman Across The River	$10	Shelter 8919

Boogie Man	Help Me Through The Day	I'm Ready	Leave My Woman Alone	Woman Across The River	You Don't Have To Go
Danger Zone	Hootchie Cootchie Man	Just A Little Bit	Trouble In Mind	Yonder Wall	

KING, Morgana

Jazz-pop singer/film actress. Born on 6/4/30 in Pleasantville, New York. Played Mama Corleone in *The Godfather* and *The Godfather, Part II*.

8/22/64	118	15		1	With A Taste Of Honey	$25	Mainstream 6015
10/27/73	184	5		2	New Beginnings	$10	Paramount 6067

All In All (2)	Easy To Love (1)	Jennifer Had (2)	Prelude To A Kiss (1)	Taste Of Honey (1)	You Are The Sunshine Of My Life (2)
As Long As He Will Stay (2)	Fascinating Rhythm (1)	Lady Is A Tramp (1)	Sands Of Time And Changes (2)	We Could Be Flying (2)	Young And Foolish (medley) (1)
Corcovado (1)	I Am A Leaf (medley) (1)	Lazy Afternoon (1)	Song For You (2)	When The World Was Young (medley) (1)	
Desert Hush (medley) (2)	I Love Paris (1)	Like A Seed (2)			

KING, Rev. Martin Luther

America's civil rights leader. Born on 1/15/29 in Atlanta. Assassinated on 4/4/68 in Memphis. Nobel prize winner in 1964. The third Monday in January is a principal U.S. holiday: Martin Luther King Day.

10/26/63	141	9		1	The Great March To Freedom [T]	$15	Gordy 906
					King's speech at Detroit's Freedom Rally (6/23/63)		
11/2/63	102	5		2	The March On Washington [T]	$10	Mr. Maestro 1000
					side 1: History of Negro Contributions; side 2: recorded in Washington, D.C. on 8/28/63		
11/9/63	119	5		3	Freedom March On Washington [T]	$10	20th Century 3110
					highlights of the 8/28/63 gathering		
5/4/68	69	8		4	I Have A Dream [T]	$10	Creed 3201
					speeches from the March on Washington (8/28/63)		
5/18/68	173	4		5	The American Dream [T]	$10	Dooto 841
					recorded during a Freedom Rally at the Los Angeles Coliseum; no track titles listed on above 4 albums		
6/8/68	150	3		6	In Search Of Freedom [T]	$10	Mercury 61170
					King's speeches from 1964-68		
6/8/68	154	3		7	In The Struggle For Freedom And Human Dignity [T]	$10	Unart 21033
					King's speech on 12/17/64 in New York City		

Address To American Jewish Committee (6)	Eulogy (A Preacher Leading His Flock) (7)	I Believe I've Got To Go Back To The Valley (7)	Love Your Enemy (1)	Police Brutality Will Backfire (6)	Urgency Of The Moment (1)
Commitment To Non-Violence (6)	Faith In America (6)	**I Have A Dream** (1,6) **88**	Militant Negro (1)	Price Of Freedom (1)	Who Is The Least Of These (7)
Dr. King's Entrance Into Civil Rights Movement (6)	Ground Crew And Mississippi (7)	I've Been To The Mountain Top (excerpt from speech the day before his death) (6)	Must Establish Priorities (6)	Segregation In The North (1)	
			Non-Violent Approach (1)	Segregation Is Wrong (1)	
			100 Years Later (1)	Sense Of Dignity (1)	
			Pilots Of The Movement (7)		

DEBUT DATE	PEAK POS	WKS CHR	G O L D	ARTIST — Album Title	$	Label & Number
				KINGBEES, The Jamie James, lead singer of three-man Los Angeles rock band.		
5/31/80	**160**	12		The Kingbees	**$10**	RSO 3075

Everybody's Gone   Follow Your Heart   **My Mistake** *81*   Once Is Not Enough   Sweet Sweet Girl To Me
Fast Girls   Man Made For Love   No Respect   Shake-Bop   Ting-A-Ling

| | | | | **KING BISCUIT BOY with CROWBAR** Canadian blues-rock band. King Biscuit Boy is Richard Newell. | | |
| 12/26/70+ | **194** | 2 | | Official Music .... | **$15** | Paramount 5030 |

Badly Bent   Cookin' Little Baby   Don't Go No Further   Hoy Hoy Hoy   Key To The Highway   Unseen Eye
Biscuit's Boogie   Corrina, Corrina   Highway 61   I'm Just A Lonely Guy   Shout Bama Lama

				★★**325**★★ **KING CRIMSON** English progressive rock group formed in 1969 by the eccentric guitarist Robert Fripp. Group featured an ever-changing lineup of top British artists, among them Ian McDonald (sax; Foreigner), Greg Lake (bass, vocals; Emerson, Lake & Palmer), Bill Bruford (drums; Yes), Boz Burrell (bass, vocals; Bad Company), John Wetton (bass, vocals; Uriah Heep, U.K., Asia) and American Adrian Belew (vocals, guitar).		
12/13/69+	**28**	25	●	1 In The Court Of The Crimson King - An Observation By King Crimson	**$20**	Atlantic 8245
9/12/70	**31**	13		2 In The Wake Of Poseidon	**$20**	Atlantic 8266
				lead singer is Greg Lake on above 2		
3/20/71	**113**	10		3 Lizard	**$20**	Atlantic 8278
				Gordon Haskell, lead singer		
2/5/72	**76**	12		4 Islands	**$20**	Atlantic 7212
				Boz Burrell, lead singer		
5/5/73	**61**	14		5 Larks' Tongues In Aspic	**$15**	Atlantic 7263
5/4/74	**64**	11		6 Starless And Bible Black	**$15**	Atlantic 7298
11/23/74	**66**	11		7 Red	**$10**	Atlantic 18110
5/24/75	**125**	5		8 USA ....[L]	**$10**	Atlantic 18136
				lead singer is John Wetton on above 4		
10/31/81	**45**	17		9 Discipline	**$8**	Warner 3629
7/3/82	**52**	14		10 Beat	**$8**	Warner 23692
4/7/84	**58**	17		11 Three of a Perfect Pair	**$8**	Warner 25071
				lead singer is Adrian Belew on above 3		

Asbury Park (8)   Fallen Angel (7)   Ladies Of The Road (4)   Matte Kudasai (9)   Red (7)   21st Century Schizoid Man
Book Of Saturday (5)   Formentera Lady (4)   Lady Of The Dancing Water (3)   Mincer, The (6)   Requiem (10)   (1,8)
Cadence And Cascade (2)   Fracture (6)   Lament (6,8)   Model Man (11)   Sailor's Tale (4)   Two Hands (10)
Cat Food (2)   Frame By Frame (9)   Larks' Tongues In Aspic,   Moonchild (1)   Sartori In Tangier (10)   Waiting Man (10)
Cirkus (3)   Great Deceiver (6)   Part One (5)   Neal And Jack And Me (10)   Sheltering Sky (9)   We'll Let You Know (6)
Court Of The Crimson   Happy Family (3)   Larks' Tongues In Aspic,   Neurotica (10)   Sleepless (11)
King-Part 1 (1) *80*   Heartbeat (10)   Part Two (5,8)   Night Watch (6)   Song Of The Gulls (medley)
Devil's Triangle (2)   Howler, The (10)   Larks' Tongues In Aspic,   No Warning (11)   (4)
Dig Me (11)   I Talk To The Wind (1)   Part Three (11)   Nuages (That Which Passes,   Starless (7)
Discipline (9)   In The Wake Of Poseidon (2)   Letters, The (4)   Passes Like Clouds) (11)   Starless And Bible Black (6)
Easy Money (5,8)   Indiscipline (9)   Lizard Medley (3)   One More Red Nightmare (7)   Talking Drum (5)
Elephant Talk (9)   Indoor Games (3)   Man With An Open Heart   Peace (Parts 1-3) (2)   Thela Hun Ginjeet (9)
Epitaph (1)   Industry (10)   (11)   Pictures Of A City (2)   Three Of A Perfect Pair (11)
Exiles (5,8)   Islands (medley) (4)   Providence (7)   Trio (6)

				KING CURTIS Born Curtis Ousley on 2/7/34 in Fort Worth, Texas. Stabbed to death on 8/13/71 in New York City. R&B saxophonist. With Lionel Hampton in 1950. Moved to New York City, did session work. First own recording on Gem in 1953. Played on sessions for Bobby Darin, Aretha Franklin, Brook Benton, Nat King Cole, McGuire Sisters, Andy Williams, The Coasters, The Shirelles and hundreds of others.		
6/13/64	**103**	12		1 Soul Serenade ....[I]	**$20**	Capitol 2095
6/3/67	**185**	12		2 The Great Memphis Hits ....[I]	**$20**	Atco 211
12/9/67+	**168**	9		3 King Size Soul ....[I]	**$20**	Atco 231
8/17/68	**198**	2		4 Sweet Soul ....[I]	**$20**	Atco 247
12/21/68	**190**	4		5 The Best of King Curtis ....[G-I]	**$20**	Atco 266
7/19/69	**160**	3		6 Instant Groove ....[I]	**$20**	Atco 293
				guitar solos by Duane Allman		
8/29/70	**198**	2		7 Get Ready ....[I]	**$20**	Atco 338
8/21/71	**54**	15		8 Live At Fillmore West ....[I-L]	**$20**	Atco 359
				with Billy Preston on organ		
3/25/72	**189**	3		9 Everybody's Talkin' ....[I]	**$20**	Atco 385

Alexander's Ragtime Band (9)   Good To Me (2)   I've Been Loving You Too   Mr. Bojangles (8)   **Spanish Harlem** (5) *89*   Whole Lotta Love (8)
Bridge Over Troubled Water   Green Onions (2)   Long (4)   Night Train (1)   Spooky (4)   Wichita Lineman (6)
(7)   Groove Me (9)   If I Were A Carpenter (9)   **Ode To Billie Joe** (3,5,8) *28*   Sugar Foot (7)   Wiggle Wobble (1)
By The Time I Get To   Harlem Nocturne (1)   In The Midnight Hour (2)   Promenade (7)   Sweet Inspiration (4)   You Don't Miss Your Water
Phoenix (4)   **Harper Valley P.T.A.** (5) *93*   Instant Groove (6)   Ridin' Thumb *(includes 2*   Swingin' Shepherd Blues (1)   (2)
C.C. Rider (3)   Hey Joe (6)   Knock On Wood (2)   *versions)* (9)   Teasin' (7)   You're The One (9)
Central Park (9)   Hey Jude (6)   La Jeanne (6)   Signed Sealed Delivered I'm   Tequila (1)   You've Lost That Lovin'
Changes (8)   Hold Me Tight (6)   Last Night (2)   Yours (8)   To Sir, With Love (3)   Feelin' (5)
Dock Of The Bay ..see: Hold On, I'm Comin' (2)   Let It Be (7)   Sing A Simple Song (6)   Up - Up And Away (4)
(Sittin' On)   Honey (4)   Little Green Apples (6)   **(Sittin' On) The Dock Of**   **Valley Of The Dolls** (4) *83*
Dog, The (2)   Honky Tonk (Parts 1 & 2)   Live For Life (Vivre Pour   **The Bay** (4,5) *84*   Watermelon Man (1)
Everybody's Talkin' (9)   (1,9)   Vivre) (3)   Someday We'll Be Together   Weight, The (6)
Fa-Fa-Fa-Fa-Fa (Sad Song)   **I Heard It Thru The**   Look Of Love (4)   (7)   Wet Funk (Low Down And
(2)   **Grapevine** (4,5) *83*   Love Is All (4)   Something (7)   Dirty) (9)
Floatin' (7)   I Never Loved A Man (The   Love The One You're With (9)   Something On Your Mind (5)   When A Man Loves A
Foot Pattin' (6)   Way I Love You) (3)   Makin' Hey (5)   Somewhere (6)   Woman (3)
For What It's Worth (3) *87*   I Stand Accused (8)   Memphis (1)   **Soul Serenade** (1,4,5,8) *51*   When Something Is Wrong
Games People Play (6)   **I Was Made To Love Her**   **Memphis Soul Stew**   **Soul Twist** (1) *17*   With My Baby (2)
Get Ready (7)   (3,5) *76*   (3,5,8) *33*   Soulin' (7)   Whiter Shade of Pale (3,8)

DEBUT DATE	PEAK POS	WKS CHR	GOLD	ARTIST — Album Title	$	Label & Number

KING DIAMOND
European heavy-metal quintet led by vocalist King Diamond.

7/11/87	123	13		1 Abigail	$8	Roadracer 9622
7/23/88	89	12		2 Them	$8	Roadracer 9550
9/30/89	111	8		3 Conspiracy	$8	Roadracer 9461
12/15/90+	179	8		4 "The Eye"	$12	Roadracer 9346

Abigail (1)
Accusation Chair (2)
"Amon" Belongs To "Them" (3)
Arrival (1)
At The Graves (3)
Behind These Walls (4)
Black Horsemen (1)
Broken Spell (2)
Burn (1)
Bye, Bye Missy (2)
Coming Home (2)
Cremation (2)
Curse, The (4)
Eye Of The Witch (4)
Family Ghost (1)
Father Picard (4)
Funeral (1)
Insanity (4)
Into The Convent (4)
Invisible Guests (2)
Let It Be Done (3)
Lies (3)
Mansion In Darkness (1)
Meetings, The (4)
Mother's Getting Weaker (2)
Omens (1)
Out From The Asylum (2)
Possession, The (1)
7th Day Of July 1777 (1)
1642 Imprisonment (4)
Sleepless Nights (3)
Something Weird (3)
Tea (2)
Them (2)
Trial (Chambre Ardente) (4)
Twilight Symphony (2)
Two Little Girls (4)
Victimized (3)
Visit From The Dead (3)
Wedding Dream (3)
Welcome Home (2)

KINGDOM COME
Hard-rock quintet formed and fronted by Hamburg, Germany native Lenny Wolf (vocals). In 1984, Wolf formed & fronted Stone Fury. Reduced to a one-man band of Wolf in 1991.

3/19/88	12	29	●	1 Kingdom Come	$8	Polydor 835368
5/13/89	49	15		2 In Your Face	$8	Polydor 839192

Do You Like It (2)
Get It On (1) *69*
Gotta Go (Can't Wage A War) (2)
Hideaway (1)
Highway 6 (2)
Just Like A Wild Rose (2)
Living Out Of Touch (1)
Loving You (1)
Mean Dirty Joe (2)
Now "Forever After" (1)
Overrated (2)
Perfect 'O' (2)
Pushin' Hard (1)
17 (1)
Shout It Out (1)
Shuffle, The (1)
Stargazer (2)
What Love Can Be (1)
Who Do You Love (2)
Wind, The (2)

KING FAMILY
The daughters of William King Driggs, Sr. with their families, numbering nearly 40. The extended family had own variety TV series in 1965. Accompanied by the Alvino Rey Orchestra (the husband of Luise Driggs).

7/10/65	34	16		1 The King Family Show!	$10	Warner 1601
10/2/65	142	3		2 The King Family Album	$10	Warner 1613

Amen (1)
America The Beautiful (2)
Battle Hymn Of The Republic (2)
Bluebird Of Happiness (2)
Climb Ev'ry Mountain (1)
Every Man Has A Castle (2)
God Bless The Child (2)
He's Got The Whole World In His Hands (2)
I Don't Know Why (I Just Do) (1)
I Used To Love You (But It's All Over Now) (1)
Irving Berlin Medley (1)
Line The Track (1)
Make Someone Happy (1)
My Favorite Things (1)
Open Up Your Heart (And Let The Sunshine In) (2)
Pass Me By (1)
Shenandoah (2)
Square, The (1)
Stardust (1)
Sunrise, Sunset (1)
Swing Low, Sweet Chariot (2)
Very Last Day (2)
When Are You Going To Learn? (1)
When The Saints Come Marching In (2)
(When There's) Love At Home (1)
You'll Never Walk Alone (2)

KINGFISH
Rock group led by Bob Weir (Grateful Dead; rhythm guitar).

3/27/76	50	9		1 Kingfish	$15	Round 564
5/21/77	103	10		2 Live 'N' Kickin'	[L] $10	Jet 732

Around And Around (2)
Asia Minor (2)
Big Iron (1)
Bye And Bye (1)
Good-Bye Yer Honor (1,2)
Home To Dixie (1)
Hypnotize (1,2)
I Hear You Knocking (2)
Juke (2)
Jump Back (2)
Jump For Joy (1,2)
Lazy Lightnin' (1)
Mule Skinner Blues (2)
Overnight Bag (2)
Shake And Fingerpop (2)
Supplication (2)
This Time (1)
Wild Northland (1)

KING HARVEST
Six-man, pop-rock group based in Olcott, New York. Formed by Ron Altback (piano), Rod Novak (sax), Eddie Tulya (guitar) and Doc Robinson (bass).

1/27/73	136	10		Dancing In The Moonlight	$10	Perception 36

Dancing In The Moonlight *13*
I Can Tell
Lady, Come On Home
Marty And The Captain
Motor Job
Roosevelt And Ira Lee
She Keeps Me High
Smile On Her Face
Think I Better Wait Till Tomorrow
You And I

KINGOFTHEHILL
St. Louis rock-funk band: Frankie (vocals), Jimmy Griffin, George Potsos and Vito Bono.

4/13/91	139	6		Kingofthehill	$12	SBK 95827

Big Groove
Electric Riot
Freak Show
I Do U
If I Say *63*
Party In My Pocket
Place In My Heart
Roses
Something 'Bout You
Take It Or Leave It (Kingadahill)

KING RICHARD'S FLUEGEL KNIGHTS
Instrumental troupe led by Dick (King Richard) Behrke.

1/27/68	198	2		Something Super!	[I] $10	MTA 5005

Bye, Bye Blues
Come On Over
Don't Sleep In The Subway
Georgy Girl
Goin' Outta My Head
Horn Duey
Lay Some Happiness On Me
Some Day My Prince Will Come
Somethin' Stupid
There's A Kind Of Hush
Who's Afraid Of The Big Bad Wolf
Yes Sir That's My Baby

KINGS, The
Rock quartet from Toronto — David Diamond, lead singer.

8/16/80	74	26		1 The Kings Are Here	$15	Elektra 274
9/26/81	170	4		2 Amazon Beach	$8	Elektra 543

All The Way (2)
Amazon Beach (2)
Anti Hero Man (1)
Don't Let Me Know (1)
Equal Noise (2)
Fools Are In Love (1)
Go Away (1)
Got Two Girlfriends (2)
It's Okay (1)
Loading Zone (2)
Love Store (1)
My Habit (1)
Partyitis (1)
Run Shoes Running (1)
Surprises (2)
Switchin' To Glide (1) *43*
This Beat Goes On (1) *flip*
Why Don't Love Do (2)

KINGSMEN, The
Rock band formed in Portland, Oregon in 1957. Consisted of Jack Ely (lead singer, guitar), Lynn Easton (drums), Mike Mitchell (guitar), Bob Nordby (bass) and Don Gallucci (keyboards). After release of "Louie Louie" (featuring lead vocal by Ely), Easton took over leadership of band and replaced Ely as lead singer. One of America's premier '60s garage rock bands.

1/18/64	20	131		1 The Kingsmen In Person	[L] $35	Wand 657
9/26/64	15	37		2 The Kingsmen, Volume II	[L] $35	Wand 659
2/20/65	22	18		3 The Kingsmen, Volume 3	[L] $30	Wand 662
10/30/65+	68	17		4 The Kingsmen On Campus	[L] $25	Wand 670
8/20/66	87	8		5 15 Great Hits	[K] $25	Wand 674

7 cuts from first 3 albums; 8 new recordings

DEBUT DATE	PEAK POS	WKS CHR	GOLD	ARTIST — Album Title	$	Label & Number

KINGSMEN, The — Cont'd

Annie Fanny (4)
Bent Scepter (1)
(C.C. Rider) ..see: Jenny Take A Ride
Climb, The (4) **65**
Come On Baby, Let The Good Times Roll (2)
Comin' Home Baby (3)
David's Mood (2)
Death Of An Angel (2)
Do You Love Me (2,5)

Don't You Just Know It (3)
Fever (1,5)
Genevieve (4)
Good Lovin' (5)
Great Balls Of Fire (2)
Hang On Sloopy (5)
Hard Day's Night (4)
I Go Crazy (3)
I Like It Like That (4)
J.A.J. (1)

Jenny Take A Ride (C.C. Rider) (5)
Jolly Green Giant (3)
Killer Joe (5) **77**
La-Do-Dada (3)
Linda Lu (2)
Little Green Thing (4)
Little Latin Lupe Lu (2)
Long Green (2,3)
Long Tall Texan (1)

Louie Louie (1) **2**
Mashed Potatoes (1)
Mojo Workout (1)
Money (1,5) **16**
Mother In Law (3)
New Orleans (2,5)
Night Train (1)
Ooh Poo Pah Doo (2,5)
Over You (3)
Peter Gunn (4)

Poison Ivy (5)
Quarter To Three (5)
Rosalie (4)
Satisfaction (5)
Searchin' (5)
Searching For Love (3)
Shotgun (4)
Shout (3,5)
Something's Got A Hold On Me (2)

Sometimes (4)
Stand By Me (4)
Sticks And Stones (4)
Tall Cool One (3)
That's Cool, That's Trash (3)
Twist & Shout (1,5)
Waiting, The (1)
Walking The Dog (2)
You Can't Sit Down (1)

KINGS OF THE SUN

Australian hard-rock quartet formed in 1983: brothers Jeffrey (vocals) and Clifford Hoad, Anthony Ragg and Glen Morris.

DEBUT DATE	PEAK POS	WKS CHR	GOLD	ARTIST — Album Title	$	Label & Number
4/30/88	**136**	16		1 Kings Of The Sun	**$8**	RCA 6826
6/9/90	**130**	7		2 Full Frontal Attack	**$12**	RCA 9889

Bad Love (1)
Black Leather (1) **98**
Bottom Of My Heart (1)
Crazy (2)

Cry 4 Love (1)
Drop The Gun (2)
Full Frontal Attack (2)
Get On Up (1)

Haunt You Baby (2)
Hooked On It (2)
Hot To Trot (1)
Howling Wind (1)

I Get Lonely (2)
Jealous (1)
Lock Me Up (2)
Medicine Man (1)

Overdrive (2)
Rescue Me (2)
Serpentine (1)
There Is Danger (2)

Tom Boy (1)
Vampire (2)
Vicious Delicious (1)

★★18★★ KINGSTON TRIO, The

Folk trio formed in San Francisco in 1957: Dave Guard (banjo), Bob Shane and Nick Reynolds (guitars). Big break came at San Francisco's Purple Onion, where they stayed for eight months. Guard left in 1961 to form the Whiskeyhill Singers; John Stewart replaced him. Disbanded in 1968. Shane formed New Kingston Trio. Guard died on 3/22/91 (age 56) of lymphoma. The originators of the folk music craze of the 1960s.

DEBUT DATE	PEAK POS	WKS CHR	GOLD	ARTIST — Album Title	$	Label & Number
11/3/58	**1**[1]	195	●	1 The Kingston Trio	**$25**	Capitol 996
2/16/59	**2**[4]	178	●	2 From The Hungry i [L]	**$25**	Capitol 1107
				The Hungry i is a nightclub in San Francisco		
6/22/59	**1**[15]	118	●	3 The Kingston Trio At Large	**$25**	Capitol 1199
11/9/59	**1**[8]	126	●	4 Here We Go Again!	**$25**	Capitol 1258
4/25/60	**1**[12]	73	●	5 Sold Out	**$25**	Capitol 1352
8/15/60	**1**[10]	60	●	6 String Along	**$25**	Capitol 1407
9/5/60	**15**	15		7 Stereo Concert [L]	**$30**	Capitol 1183
				concert in Liberty Hall, El Paso, Texas		
12/5/60	**11**	4		8 The Last Month Of The Year [X]	**$20**	Capitol 1446
2/27/61	**2**[1]	39		9 Make Way!	**$20**	Capitol 1474
7/3/61	**3**	41		10 Goin' Places	**$20**	Capitol 1564
10/9/61	**3**	46		11 Close-Up	**$20**	Capitol 1642
				John Stewart replaces Dave Guard from here on		
3/10/62	**3**	51		12 College Concert [L]	**$20**	Capitol 1658
				concert on the campus of UCLA		
6/9/62	**7**	105	●	13 The Best Of The Kingston Trio [G]	**$20**	Capitol 1705
8/18/62	**7**	37		14 Something Special	**$20**	Capitol 1747
				with orchestral and chorus background		
12/15/62+	**16**	36		15 New Frontier	**$20**	Capitol 1809
3/30/63	**4**	29		16 The Kingston Trio #16	**$20**	Capitol 1871
8/17/63	**7**	25		17 Sunny Side!	**$20**	Capitol 1935
1/11/64	**69**	14		18 Sing A Song with The Kingston Trio [I]	**$20**	Capitol 2005
2/1/64	**18**	21		19 Time To Think	**$20**	Capitol 2011
5/30/64	**22**	20		20 Back In Town [L]	**$20**	Capitol 2081
				recorded at San Francisco's Hungry i nightclub		
1/16/65	**53**	13		21 The Kingston Trio (Nick-Bob-John)	**$25**	Decca 74613
6/19/65	**126**	10		22 Stay Awhile	**$25**	Decca 74656
7/12/69	**163**	6		23 Once Upon A Time [E-L]	**$20**	Tetragra. 5101 [2]
				recorded at the Sahara-Tahoe Hotel in Las Vegas (1966)		

Across The Wide Missouri (4)
Adios Farewell (15)
Ah, Woe, Ah, Me (20)
All My Sorrows (3)
All Through The Night (8)
Ally Ally Oxen Free (19) **61**
Ann (20)
Away Rio (14)
Babe, You've Been On My Mind (Mama, You Been On My Mind) (23)
Baby Boy (11)
Bad Man Blunder (6,13) **37**
Ballad Of The Quiet Fighter (16)
Ballad Of The Shape Of Things (12,23)
Ballad Of The Thresher (17)
Banua (1,7)
Bay Of Mexico (1)
Beneath The Willow (11)
Big Ball In Town (16)
Billy Goat Hill (10)
Bimini (1)
Blind Date (23)
Blow The Candle Out (9)
Blow Ye Winds (3)
Blowin' In The Wind (17,18)

Blue Eyed Gal (9)
Bonny Hielan' Laddie (9)
Bottle Of Wine (22)
Brown Mountain Light (14)
Buddy Better Get On Down The Line (6)
Bye, Bye, Thou Little Tiny Child (8)
Carrier Pigeon (5)
Chilly Winds (12,18)
Coal Tattoo (19)
Coast Of California (10)
Colorado Trail (6)
Colours (23)
Come All You Fair And Tender Ladies (9)
Coplas (23)
Coplas Revisited (12)
Corey, Corey (3,18)
Day In Our Room (13)
Deportee (19)
Desert Pete (17) **33**
Dogie's Lament (15)
Don't Cry Katie (5)
Don't You Weep, Mary (11)
Dooley (22)
E Inu Tatou E (4)

Early Mornin' (3)
Early Mornin' Rain (23)
El Matador (5) **32**
En El Agua (9)
Escape Of Old John Webb (6)
Everglades (6) **60**
Farewell Adelita (5)
Farewell Captain (20)
Farewell (Fare Thee Well My Own True Love) (21)
Fast Freight (1)
First Time (15)
500 Miles (13)
Follow Now, Oh Shepherds (8)
Genny Glenn (15)
Georgia Stockade (20)
Getaway John (3,23)
Go Where I Send Thee (8)
Goin' Away For To Leave You (12)
Gonna Go Down The River (22)
Goo Ga Gee (17)
Goober Peas (19)
Good News (3)
Goodnight Irene (23)
Goodnight My Baby (8)

Gotta Travel On (21)
Greenback Dollar (15,18,23) **21**
Guardo El Lobo (10)
Gue, Gue (2)
Gypsy Rover (11)
Hangman (9)
Hanna Lee (20)
Hard, Ain't It Hard (1,23)
Hard Travelin' (9,23)
Haul Away (4)
Hobo's Lullaby (19)
Honey, Are You Mad At Your Man? (15)
Hope You Understand (21)
Hunter, The (5)
I Bawled (3)
I'm Going Home (21,23)
If I Had A Ship (22)
If You Don't Look Around (19)
If You See Me Go (21)
Isle In The Water (20)
It Was A Very Good Year (10)
Jackson (17)
Jane, Jane, Jane (14) **93**
Jesse James (11)
Jug Of Punch (9)

Karu (11)
La Bamba (16)
Laredo? (12)
Last Month Of The Year (What Month Was Jesus Born In) (8)
Last Night I Had The Strangest Dream (19)
Leave My Woman Alone (6)
Lemon Tree (19)
Let's Get Together (20)
Little Boy (14)
Little Maggie (1)
Little Play Soldiers (21)
Lonesome Traveler (medley) (2)
Long Black Rifle (3)
Long Black Veil (15)
Love Comes A Trickling Down (7)
Love's Been Good To Me (21)
Low Bridge (14)
M.T.A. (3,12,13,23) **15**
Mangwani Mpulele (5)
Marcelle Vahine (17)
Mark Twain (16)
Mary Mild (8)
Merry Minuet (2,7,13)

Midnight Special (21)
Molly Dee (4)
More Poems (21)
Mountains O'Mourne (5)
My Lord What A Mornin' (15)
My Ramblin' Boy (21)
New Frontier (15)
New York Girls (2)
No One To Talk My Troubles To (19)
O Ken Karenge (11,12)
O Willow Waly (14)
Oh Joe Hannah (16)
Oh, Miss Mary (12)
Oh, Yes, Oh! (9)
Old Joe Clark (14)
Oleanna (4)
One More Round (16)
One More Town (14,18) **97**
One Too Many Mornings (23)
Pastures Of Plenty (10)
Patriot Game (1)
Poor Ellen Smith (15)
Portland Town (14)
Poverty Hill (21)
Pullin' Away (14,18)

KINGSTON TRIO, The — Cont'd

Raspberries, Strawberries (5,7,13) **70** · Salty Dog (20) · Some Fool Made A Soldier Of Me (15) · This Little Light (12) · Unfortunate Miss Bailey (4) · With Her Head Tucked Underneath Her Arm (5)
Razors In The Air (10) · San Miguel (4) · Somerset Gloucestershire Wassail (8) · This Mornin', This Evenin', So Soon (6) · Utawena (9) · With You My Johnny (5)
Remember The Alamo (3) · Santy Anno (1) · This Train (medley) (23) · Walkin' This Road To My Town (20) · World I Used To Know (20)
Reverend Mr. Black (16) **8** · Saro Jane (1) · Song For A Friend (19) · Those Brown Eyes (17) · Wanderer, The (4) · **Worried Man** (4,13,18) **20**
Rider (17) · Scarlet Ribbons (3) · South Coast (2,7) · Those Who Are Wise (17) · We Wish You A Merry Christmas (8) · Wreck Of The John B (1)
River Is Wide (9) · Scotch And Soda (1,13,23) **81** · South Wind (6) · Three Jolly Coachmen (1,7) · When I Was Young (6) · Yes I Can Feel It (22)
River Run Down (16) · Seasons In The Sun (19) · Speckled Roan (9) · Three Song (22) · When My Love Was Here (11) · You Don't Knock (10)
Road To Freedom (16) · Seine, The (3) · Stay Awhile (22) · Tic, Tic, Tic (2) · When The Saints Go Marching In (2,7,18,23) · You're Gonna Miss Me (Frankie And Johnny) (10)
Roddy McCorley (12) · Senora (17) · Stories Of Old (7) · **Tijuana Jail** (13,23) **12** · **Where Have All The Flowers Gone** (12,13,18,23) **21** · Zombie Jamboree (2,7)
Rollin' Stone (4) · Shady Grove (medley) (2) · Strange Day (14) · To Be Redeemed (15)
Round About Christmas (8) · She Was Too Good To Me (14) · Take Her Out Of Pity (11,13) · To Morrow (6) · Where I'm Bound (5)
'Round About The Mountain (4) · Silicone Bust (23) · Tanga Tika (medley) (5) · Toerau (medley) (5) · Wherever We May Go (11)
Rovin' Gambler (medley) (23) · Sing Out (17) · Tattooed Lady (6) · **Tom Dooley** (1,7,13,18,20,23) **1** · White Snows Of Winter (8)
Ruben James (11,18) · Sing We Noel (8) · Tell It On The Mountain (14) · Tomorrow Is A Long Time (23) · Who's Gonna Hold Her Hand (6)
Run Molly, Run (10) · Sloop John B ..see: Wreck Of The John B · Them Poems Medley (20) · Try To Remember (16) · Wimoweh (2,23)
Run The Ridges (16) · So Hi (20) · These Seven Men (4) · Turn Around (19)
Rusting In The Rain (22) · Some Day Soon (21) · They Call The Wind Maria (2,7) · Two-Ten, Six Eighteen (17)
Sail Away (11) · · This Land Is Your Land (10)

KING SWAMP

British quintet: vocalist Walter Wray with Dave Allen (Gang Of Four, Shriekback; bass), Steve Halliwell (Shriekback; guitar), Martyn Barker (Shriekback; drums) and Dominic Miller (World Party; guitar; replaced by Nick Lashley in 1990).

6/3/89	159	14		King Swamp	$8	Virgin 91069

Blown Away · Louisiana Bride · Mirror, The · Original Man · Widders Dump
Is This Love? · Man Behind The Gun · Motherlode · Sacrament, The · Year Zero

KING'S X

Houston-based rock trio formed in Springfield, Missouri: Douglas Pinnick (vocals, bass), Ty Tabor (guitar) and Jerry Gaskill (drums).

5/7/88	144	11	1	Out Of The Silent Planet	$8	Megaforce 81825
8/5/89	123	18	2	Gretchen Goes To Nebraska	$8	Megaforce 81997
11/10/90+	85	24	3	Faith Hope Love By King's X	$12	Megaforce 82145
3/28/92	138	3	4	King's X	$12	Atlantic 82372

Big Picture (4) · Dream In My Life (4) · I Can't Help It (3) · Moanjam (3) · Send A Message (2) · We Are Finding Who We Are (3)
Black Flag (4) · Everybody Knows A Little Bit Of Something (4) · I'll Never Be The Same (2) · Mr. Wilson (3) · Shot Of Love (1) · We Were Born To Be Loved (3)
Burning Down (2) · Everywhere I Go (3) · I'll Never Get Tired Of You (3) · Not Just For The Dead (4) · Silent Wind (4) · What I Know About Love (4)
Chariot Song (4) · Faith Hope Love (3) · In The New Age (1) · Ooh Song (4) · Six Broken Soldiers (3) · What Is This? (1)
Difference (In The Garden Of St. Anne's-On-The-Hill) (2) · Fall On Me (3) · It's Love (3) · Out Of The Silent Planet (1) · Sometimes (4) · Wonder (4)
Don't Believe It (It's Easier Said Than Done) (2) · Far, Far Away (1) · King (1) · Over My Head (2) · Summerland (2) · World Around Me (4)
· Fine Art Of Friendship (3) · Legal Kill (3) · Pleiades (2) · Talk To You (3)
· Goldilox (1) · Lost In Germany (4) · Power Of Love (1) · Visions (1)
· · Mission (2) · Prisoner (4)

KING TEE

Compton, California-based rapper. Born in Los Angeles. Worked at Houston's KTSU and KYOK as a mixer.

1/21/89	125	15	1	Act A Fool	$8	Capitol 90544
10/20/90	175	4	2	At Your Own Risk	$12	Capitol 92359

Act A Fool (1) · Can This Be Real (2) · E Get Swift (2) · Jay Fay Dray (2) · Let's Dance (1) · Ruff Rhyme (Back Again) (2)
At Your Own Risk (2) · Coolest, The (1) · Flirt (1) · Just Clowning (1) · On The Dance Tip (2) · Skanless (2)
Baggin' On Moms (1) · Diss You (2) · Guitar Playin' (1) · King Tee Production (2) · Payback's A Mutha (1) · Take You Home (2)
Bass (1) · Do Your Thing (2) · I Got A Cold (1) · Ko Rock Stuff (1) · Played Like A Piano (2) · Time To Get Out (2)

KINISON, Sam

Born on 12/8/53 in Peoria, Illinois; died on 4/10/92 in a car crash. A Pentecostal preacher who became a shock comic in 1978. Acted in the film *Back To School* and the TV show *Charlie Hoover*.

11/8/86	175	5	1	Louder Than Hell [C]	$8	Warner 25503
11/26/88	43	17	2	Have You Seen Me Lately? [C]	$8	Warner 25748
4/14/90	95	8	3	Leader Of The Banned [C]	$12	Warner 26073

Alphabet (1) · Detox This (3) · Jesus (1) · Manson (1) · Pocket Toys (2) · Sexual Diaries (1)
Big Menu (1) · Devil (1) · Jesus The Miracle Caterer (2) · Mississippi Queen (3) · Relationships (1) · Sexual Therapy (1)
Blind (1) · Gonna Raise Hell (3) · Lenny Bruce's Mom (1) · Mother Mary's Mystery Date (2) · Robo-Pope (1) · Shopping For Pets (1)
Buddies (2) · Grilled Cheese Sandwich (2) · Lesbians Are Our Friends (2) · Old People Must Die (3) · Rock Against Drugs? (1) · Story Of Jim (Bakker) (2)
Butt And The Bible (2) · Heart-Stoppers (2) · Letter From Home (1) · Parties With The Dead (2) · Rubber Love (2) · Under My Thumb (3)
Casual Users Of Terrorism (3) · Highway To Hell (3) · Libya (1) · Phone Call From Hell (3) · Sex, Videotape And Zoo Animals (3) · Wild Thing (1)
· Jerry's Bastard Kid (3) · Love Song (1) · · · World Hunger (1)

★★47★★ KINKS, The

Rock group formed in London in 1963 by Ray Davies (lead singer, guitar) and his brother Dave Davies (lead guitar, vocals). Original lineup also included Peter Quaife (bass) and Mike Avory (drums). Numerous personnel changes during the '70s. Ray appeared in the 1986 film *Absolute Beginners*. 1987 lineup consisted of Ray & Dave Davies, Ian Gibbons (keyboards, left by 1989), Bob Henrit (drums) and Jim Rodford (bass). Henrit and Rodford were members of Argent. Group inducted into the Rock and Roll Hall of Fame in 1990.

12/12/64+	29	26	1	You Really Got Me	$50	Reprise 6143
4/3/65	13	29	2	Kinks-Size	$40	Reprise 6158
8/28/65	60	9	3	Kinda Kinks	$40	Reprise 6173
12/25/65+	47	17	4	Kinks Kinkdom	$40	Reprise 6184
4/30/66	95	12	5	The Kink Kontroversy	$40	Reprise 6197
8/27/66	9	64	● 6	The Kinks Greatest Hits! [G]	$30	Reprise 6217
2/11/67	135	3	7	Face To Face	$25	Reprise 6228
9/9/67	162	4	8	The Live Kinks [L]	$25	Reprise 6260
3/2/68	153	2	9	Something Else By The Kinks	$25	Reprise 6279
11/22/69	105	20	10	Arthur (or the decline and fall of The British Empire)	$20	Reprise 6366

rock opera written for a British TV show

DEBUT DATE	PEAK POS	WKS CHR	GOLD	ARTIST — Album Title	$	Label & Number

KINKS, The — Cont'd

DEBUT DATE	PEAK POS	WKS CHR	GOLD	ARTIST — Album Title	$	Label & Number
12/26/70+	35	12		11 Lola Versus Powerman and The Moneygoround, Part One	$10	Reprise 6423
12/18/71+	100	14		12 Muswell Hillbillies	$15	RCA 4644
4/15/72	94	13		13 The Kink Kronikles ....[K]	$12	Reprise 6454 [2]
9/23/72	70	14		14 Everybody's In Show-Biz ....[L]	$12	RCA 6065 [2]
				record 1: studio recordings; record 2: live recordings		
2/24/73	145	5		15 The Great Lost Kinks Album ....[K]	$35	Reprise 2127
				recordings which were never released in the U.S.		
12/15/73+	177	6		16 Preservation Act 1	$12	RCA 5002
6/15/74	114	11		17 Preservation Act 2	$12	RCA 5040 [2]
5/17/75	51	13		18 Soap Opera	$12	RCA 5081
12/6/75+	45	14		19 Schoolboys In Disgrace	$12	RCA 5102
6/26/76	144	5		20 The Kink's Greatest-Celluloid Heroes ....[K]	$12	RCA 1743
2/26/77	21	16		21 Sleepwalker	$8	Arista 4106
6/3/78	40	21		22 Misfits	$8	Arista 4167
7/28/79	11	18	●	23 Low Budget	$8	Arista 4240
6/28/80	14	33	●	24 One For The Road ....[L]	$10	Arista 8401 [2]
9/20/80	177	4		25 Second Time Around ....[K]	$8	RCA 3520
9/12/81	15	36	●	26 Give The People What They Want	$8	Arista 9567
6/11/83	12	25		27 State of Confusion	$8	Arista 8018
12/15/84+	57	20		28 Word Of Mouth	$8	Arista 8264
7/19/86	159	4		29 Come Dancing With The Kinks - The Best Of The Kinks 1977-1986 ....[G]	$10	Arista 8428 [2]
12/20/86+	81	16		30 Think Visual	$8	MCA 5822
2/6/88	110	7		31 The Road ....[L]	$8	MCA 42107
				recorded during the summer of 1987 in Philadelphia and Maryland		
11/25/89	122	8		32 UK Jive	$8	MCA 6337

DEBUT DATE	PEAK POS	WKS CHR	GOLD	ARTIST — Album Title	$	Label & Number

KINKS, The — Cont'd

Yes Sir No Sir (10)   You Can't Win (5)   You Make It All Worthwhile (18)   You Shouldn't Be Sad (3)   Young And Innocent Days (10)
Yo-Yo (26)   You Don't Know My Name (14)   You're Lookin' Fine (7,8)   Young Conservatives (27)
You Can't Stop The Music (18)   **You Really Got Me** (1,6,8,24,29) **7**

★★55★★   **KISS**

Hard-rock band formed in New York City in 1973. Consisted of Gene Simmons (bass), Paul Stanley (guitar), Ace Frehley (lead guitar) and Peter Criss (drums). Noted for elaborate makeup and highly theatrical stage shows. Criss replaced by Eric Carr in 1981. Frehley replaced by Vinnie Vincent in 1982. Group appeared without makeup for the first time in 1983 on album cover *Lick It Up*. Mark St. John replaced Vincent in 1984. Bruce Kulick replaced St. John in 1985. Carr died of cancer on 11/25/91 (age 41). Drummer Eric Singer joined in 1991.

DEBUT DATE	PEAK POS	WKS CHR	GOLD	# ARTIST — Album Title	$	Label & Number
4/20/74	87	23	●	1 Kiss	$20	Casablanca 9001
11/16/74	100	15	●	2 Hotter Than Hell	$20	Casablanca 7006
4/19/75	32	29	●	3 Dressed To Kill	$15	Casablanca 7016
10/11/75	9	110	●	4 Alive! [L]	$20	Casablanca 7020 [2]
4/3/76	11	78	▲	5 Destroyer	$15	Casablanca 7025
8/21/76	36	17		6 The Originals [R]	$50	Casablanca 7032 [3]
				reissue of their first 3 albums		
11/20/76	11	45	▲	7 Rock And Roll Over	$15	Casablanca 7037
7/9/77	4	26	▲	8 **Love Gun**	$30	Casablanca 7057
11/26/77+	7	33	▲	9 Alive II [L]	$30	Casablanca 7076 [2]
5/20/78	22	24	▲	10 Double Platinum [G]	$30	Casablanca 7100 [2]
				during October 1978, each member of Kiss issued a solo album - see each name for chart details		
6/23/79	9	25	▲	11 Dynasty	$15	Casablanca 7152
6/21/80	35	14	●	12 Kiss Unmasked	$15	Casablanca 7225
12/5/81+	75	11		13 Music From The Elder	$30	Casablanca 7261
				Eric Carr replaces Peter Criss		
11/20/82+	45	19		14 Creatures Of The Night	$15	Casablanca 7270
				Vinnie Vincent replaces Ace Frehley		
10/15/83	24	30	▲	15 Lick It Up	$8	Mercury 814297
				group shown unmasked for the first time		
10/6/84	19	38	▲	16 Animalize	$8	Mercury 822495
10/5/85	20	29	●	17 Asylum	$8	Mercury 826099
10/10/87	18	34	▲	18 Crazy Nights	$8	Mercury 832626
12/3/88+	21	27	▲	19 Smashes, Thrashes & Hits [G]	$8	Mercury 836427
11/4/89	29	36	●	20 Hot In The Shade	$8	Mercury 838913
6/6/92	6	23		21 **Revenge**	$12	Mercury 48037

All American Man (9)   Do You Love Me (5,10)   I Still Love You (14)   Love's A Slap In The Face (20)   Rockin' In The USA (9)   Torpedo Girl (12)
All Hell's Breakin' Loose (15)   Domino (21)   I Stole Your Love (8,9)   Magic Touch (11)   Room Service (3,6)   Tough Love (21)
All The Way (2,6)   Easy As It Seems (18)   I Want You (7,9,10)   Mainline (2,6)   Saint And Sinner (14)   Trial By Fire (17)
Almost Human (8)   Escape From The Island (13)   **I Was Made For Lovin' You** (11,19) **11**   Makin' Love (7,9,10)   Save Your Love (11)   Turn On The Night (18)
And On The 8th Day (15)   Every Time I Look At You (21)   I'll Fight Hell To Hold You (18)   Million To One (15)   Secretly Cruel (17)   Two Sides Of The Coin (12)
Any Way You Slice It (17)   Exciter (15)   I'm Alive (17)   Mr. Blackwell (13)   See You In Your Dreams (7)   2,000 Man (11)
Any Way You Want It (9)   Fanfare (15)   I've Had Enough (Into The Fire) (18)   Mr. Speed (7)   **Shandi** (12) **47**   Two Timer (3,6)
Anything For My Baby (3,6)   Firehouse (1,4,6,10)   Is That You? (12)   Murder In High-Heels (16)   She (3,4,6,10)   Uh! All Night (17)
Baby Driver (7)   Fits Like A Glove (15)   Just A Boy (13)   My Way (18)   She's So European (12)   Under The Gun (16)
Bang Bang You (18)   Flaming Youth (5) 74   Keep Me Comin' (14)   Naked City (12)   Shock Me (8,9)   Under The Rose (13)
Beth (5,9,10,19) 7   Forever (20) 8   Killer (14)   No, No, No (18)   Shout It Out Loud (5,19) 31   Unholy (21)
Betrayed (20)   Get All You Can Take (16)   King Of Hearts (20)   Not For The Innocent (15)   Shout It Out Loud [live] (9) 54   War Machine (14)
Black Diamond (1,4,6,10)   Getaway (3,6)   King Of The Mountain (17)   Nothin' To Lose (1,4,6)   Silver Spoon (20)   Watchin' You (2,4,6)
Boomerang (20)   Gimme More (15)   King Of The Night Time World (5,9)   Oath, The (13)   Somewhere Between (Heaven And Hell) (20)   What Makes The World Go 'Round (12)
Burn Bitch Burn (16)   God Gave Rock 'N' Roll To You II (21)   Kiss, Love Theme From (1,6)   Odyssey (13)   Spit (21)   When Your Walls Come Down (18)
Cadillac Dreams (20)   God Of Thunder (5,9,10)   **Kissin' Time** (6) 83   100,000 Years (1,4,6,10)   Strange Ways (2,6)   While The City Sleeps (16)
Calling Dr. Love (7,9,10,19) 16   Goin' Blind (2,6)   Ladies In Waiting (3,6)   Only You (13)   Street Giveth And The Street Taketh Away (20)   Who Wants To Be Lonely (17)
Charisma (11)   Good Girl Gone Bad (18)   Ladies Room (7,9)   Paralyzed (21)   Strutter (1,4,6,19)   **World Without Heroes** (13) 56
Christine Sixteen (8,9) 25   Got Love For Sale (8)   Larger Than Life (9)   Parasite (2,4,6)   Strutter '78 (10)   X-Ray Eyes (11)
Cold Gin (1,4,6,10)   Got To Choose (2,4,6)   Let Me Go, Rock 'N Roll (2,4,6,10)   Plaster Caster (8)   **Sure Know Something** (11) 47   You Love Me To Hate You (20)
C'mon And Love Me (3,4,6,10)   Great Expectations (5)   Let Me Know (1,6)   Prisoner Of Love (20)   Sweet Pain (5)   (You Make Me) Rock Hard (19)
Comin' Home (2,6)   **Hard Luck Woman** (7,9,10) 15   Let's Put The X In Sex (19) 97   Radar For Love (17)   Take It Off (21)   You're All That I Want (12)
Crazy Crazy Nights (18) 65   Hard Times (11)   **Lick It Up** (15,19) 66   Read My Body (20)   Take Me (7)   Young And Wasted (15)
Creatures Of The Night (14)   Heart Of Chrome (21)   Little Caesar (20)   **Reason To Live** (18) 64   Talk To Me (12)
Dance All Over Your Face (15)   **Heaven's On Fire** (16,19) 49   Lonely Is The Hunter (14)   **Rise To It** (20) 81   **Tears Are Falling** (17,19) 51
Danger (14)   Hell Or High Water (18)   Love 'Em And Leave 'Em (7)   **Rock And Roll All Nite** (3,6,10,19) 68   Then She Kissed Me (8)
Dark Light (14)   Hide Your Heart (20) 66   Love Gun (8,9,10,19) 61   Rock And Roll All Nite [live] (4) 12   Thief In The Night (18)
Detroit Rock City (5,9,10,19) flip   Hooligan (8)   Love Her All I Can (8,9)   Rock And Roll Hell (14)   Thou Shalt Not (21)
Deuce (1,4,6,10,19)   Hotter Than Hell (2,4,6,10)   Love's A Deadly Weapon (17)   Rock Bottom (3,4,6)   Thrills In The Night (16)
Dirty Livin' (11)   I (13) | Rock Hard ..see: (You Make Me)   Tomorrow (12)
| I Just Wanna (21) | | Rocket Ride (9) 39   Tomorrow And Tonight (8,9)
| I Love It Loud (14,19) | | | |

KITARO

Japanese synthesist based in Colorado. Born Masanori Takahashi in 1953 in Toyohashi City, Japan.

DEBUT DATE	PEAK POS	WKS CHR	GOLD	# ARTIST — Album Title	$	Label & Number
11/30/85	191	2		1 Asia [I-L]	$8	Geffen 24087
				recorded in Shanghai		
5/10/86	141	10		2 My Best [I-K]	$8	Gramavision 7016
4/4/87	183	1		3 Tenku [I]	$8	Geffen 24112
5/12/90	159	5		4 Kojiki [I]	$12	Geffen 24255
				translation of title: The Record of Ancient Matters		

KITARO — Cont'd

Aqua (2)	Earth Born (1)	Matsuri (4)	Orochi (4)	Sacred Journey II (2)	Tenku (3)
Aura (3)	Four Changes (2)	Message From The Cosmos (3)	Reimei (4)	Shimmering Light (2)	Theme Of Silk Road (1)
Caravansary (1)	Hajimari (4)		Return To Russia (1)	Silk Road Fantasy (2)	Time (2)
Cloud (1)	Japanese Drums (1)	Milky Way (3)	Revelation (2)	Silver Moon (2)	Time Traveller (3)
Cosmic Love (1)	Koi (4)	Nageki (4)	Rising Sun (2)	Sozo (4)	Westbound (2)
Dawn In Malaysia (1)	Legend Of The Road (3)	Oasis (2)	Romance (3)	Straightaway To Orion (1)	Wings (3)

KIX

Hard-rock quintet from Hagerstown, Maryland led by vocalist Steve Whiteman. Includes Ronnie Younkins, Brian Forsythe, Donnie Purnell and Jimmy Chalfant.

DEBUT DATE	PEAK POS	WKS CHR	GOLD		$	Label & Number
5/28/83	177	8		1 Cool Kids	$8	Atlantic 80056
10/15/88+	46	60	●	2 Blow My Fuse	$8	Atlantic 81877
7/27/91	64	11		3 Hot Wire	$12	EastWest 91714

Blow My Fuse (2)	Cold Chills (3)	Get It While It's Hot (2)	Love Pollution (1)	Piece Of The Pie (2)	She Dropped Me The Bomb (2)
Body Talk (1)	Cool Kids (1)	Get Your Monkeys Out (1)	Luv-A-Holic (3)	Red Lite, Green Lite, TNT (2)	
Boomerang (2)	Dirty Boys (2)	Girl Money (3)	Mighty Mouth (1)	Restless Blood (1)	Tear Down The Walls (3)
Bump The La La (3)	**Don't Close Your Eyes** (2) 11	Hee Bee Jee Bee Crush (3)	Nice On Ice (1)	Rock & Roll Overdose (3)	
Burning Love (1)	For Shame (1)	Hot Wire (3)	No Ring Around Rosie (2)	Same Jane (3)	
Cold Blood (2)		Loco-Emotion (1)	Pants On Fire (Liar, Liar) (3)		

KLAATU

Canadian rock trio: Terry Draper, Dee Long and John Woloschuck. Anonymous first release led to speculation that they were The Beatles. Name taken from a character in the 1951 film *The Day The Earth Stood Still.*

DEBUT DATE	PEAK POS	WKS CHR		$	Label & Number
4/2/77	32	11	1 Klaatu	$15	Capitol 11542
10/15/77	83	7	2 Hope	$10	Capitol 11633

Anus Of Uranus (1)	**Calling Occupants** (1) *flip*	Loneliest Of Creatures (2)	Sir Bodsworth Rugglesby III (1)	**Sub-Rosa Subway** (1) 62
Around The Universe In Eighty Days (2)	Doctor Marvello (1)	Long Live Politzania (2)	So Said The Lighthouse Keeper (2)	True Life Hero (1)
California Jam (1)	Hope (2)	Madman (2)		We're Off You Know (2)
	Little Neutrino (1)	Prelude (2)		

KLEEER

R&B group formed in New York City in 1972 as Pipeline. Consisted of Paul Crutchfield (vocals, percussion), Richard Lee (guitar), Norman Durham (bass) and Woody Cunningham (drums). Became the Jam Band in the mid-1970s; recorded and toured as the Universal Robot Band in 1977.

DEBUT DATE	PEAK POS	WKS CHR		$	Label & Number
4/26/80	140	10	1 Winners	$8	Atlantic 19262
3/7/81	81	16	2 License To Dream	$8	Atlantic 19288
2/20/82	139	8	3 Taste The Music	$8	Atlantic 19334

Affirmative Mood (3)	Get Tough (3)	I've Had Enough (Can't Take Anymore) (1)	Rollin' On (1)	Taste The Music (3)	Your Way (1)
Close To You (1)	Hunger For Your Love (1)	License To Dream (2)	Running Back To You (2)	Wall To Wall (3)	
De Kleeer Ting (2)	Hypnotized (2)	Nothin' Said (1)	Say You Love Me (2)	Where Would I Be (Without Your Love) (2)	
De Ting Continues (3)	I Shall Get Over (3)	Open Your Mind (1)	Sippin' & Kissin' (1)	Winners (1)	
Fella (3)	I Still Love You (1)		Swann (3)		

KLEIN, Robert

Comedian/actor/writer. Born on 2/8/42 in New York City. Appeared in several films and TV shows. Married to opera singer Brenda Boozer from 1973-90.

DEBUT DATE	PEAK POS	WKS CHR			$	Label & Number
4/28/73	191	3	Child Of The 50's	[C]	$12	Brut 6001

All Night Groceries	Commercials	James Abram Garfield	My Little Margie	Public School	Sex Impulse
Athletics	F.M. Disc Jockey	Middle Class Educated Blues	New York City Animals	Public Service Commercials	Starting Your Car
Childhood Myth	Fabulous 50's	Musical Instruments	Our Gang	School Assembly	Substitute School Teacher
Civil Defense (No Talking)	Foreigner, The	My Last Movie	Panhandler, The	School Lunch	Words

KLEMMER, John

Born on 7/3/46 in Chicago. Jazz saxophonist/flutist. Began recording with Don Ellis in the late '60s. Member of Ellis's eclectic big band in the mid-'70s.

DEBUT DATE	PEAK POS	WKS CHR			$	Label & Number
9/13/69	176	5	1 Blowin' Gold	[I]	$20	Cadet Concept 321
12/27/75+	90	40	2 Touch	[I]	$15	ABC 922
9/18/76	66	16	3 Barefoot Ballet	[I]	$10	ABC 950
6/18/77	51	17	4 LifeStyle (Living & Loving)	[I]	$10	ABC 1007
6/17/78	83	10	5 Arabesque	[I]	$8	ABC 1068
11/18/78	178	3	6 Cry	[I]	$8	ABC 1106
6/2/79	172	9	7 Brazilia	[I]	$8	ABC 1116
11/24/79	187	2	8 The Best Of John Klemmer, Volume One/Mosaic	[K-I]	$10	MCA 8014 [2]
8/9/80	146	11	9 Magnificent Madness	[I]	$8	Elektra 284
6/13/81	99	9	10 Hush	[I]	$8	Elektra 527

Adventures In Paradise (9)	Don't Take Your Love Away (9)	Hot (10)	Magic (10)	Rain Dancer (3)	Walk With Me My Love And Dream (2,8)
Arabesque (5)	Ecstasy (6)	Hummingbird Bay (10)	Magnificent Madness (9)	'Round Midnight (6)	Waterfalls (6)
At 17 (3,8)	Excursion #2 (1)	Hush (10)	Mardi Gras (5)	Sleeping Eyes (2)	Waterwheels (2)
Bahia (7)	Falling (5)	I Am (6)	My Heart Sings (1)	Summertime (7)	We Couldn't Start Over (9)
Barefoot Ballet (3,8)	Feelin' Free (10)	I Can't Help It (9)	My Love Has Butterfly Wings (1,7)	Taboo (10)	Whisper To The Wind (3,8)
Body Pulse (2,8)	Forest Child (3,8)	Infinity (6)	Naked (3)	Talking Hands (3,8)	
Brazilia (7)	Forever (4)	Intimacy (6)	Nothing Will Ever Be The Same Again Forever (5,8)	Tender Storm (7,8)	
Caress (4,8)	Free Fall Lover (2,8)	Let's Make Love (10)	Paradise (5)	Third Stone From The Sun (1)	
Children Of The Earth: Flames! (1)	Free Soul (1)	Life Is So Beautiful (10)	Picasso (5)	Tone Row Weaver (2)	
Copacabana (7)	Glass Dolphins (2)	Lifesong (9)	Poem Painter (3,8)	Touch (2)	
Cry (6)	Happiness (6)	Lifestyle (4)	Pure Love (4)	Tough And Tender (4)	
Crystal Fingers (3)	Heart (Summer Song) (9)	Love (6)	Purity (4,8)	Tropical Snowflakes (7)	
Deja Vu (9)	Heartbreak (7,8)	Love Affair (5,8)	Quiet Afternoon (4,8)	Walk In Love (5)	
Desire (5)	Hey Jude (1)	Love You Madly (10)			
		Lovin' Feelings (4)			

DEBUT DATE	PEAK POS	WKS CHR	GOLD	ARTIST — Album Title	$	Label & Number

KLF, The

British duo previously known as The Timelords: Bill Drummond (founding member of Big In Japan/former manager of Echo & The Bunnymen and Teardrop Explodes) & Jimmy Cauty (formerly with Zodiac Mindwarp). KLF stands for Kopyright Liberation Front.

| 6/29/91 | 39 | 50 | ● | The White Room ....[K] | $12 | Arista 8657 |

tracks written and recorded from 1987-91

Build A Fire	Justified And Ancient	Make It Rain	**3 A.M. Eternal 5**	White Room
Church Of The KLF	Last Train To Trancentral	No More Tears	**What Time Is Love? 57**	

KLIQUE

Soul trio: Howard Huntsberry, Isaac Suthers and his sister Deborah Hunter. Huntsberry went solo in 1988.

| 10/8/83 | 70 | 14 | | Try It Out .... | $8 | MCA 39008 |

Burning Hot	Honey (I Want To Be Your	Inside Me	**Stop Doggin' Me Around 50** Try It Out
Flashback	Lover)	Sarah	Tender Footed

KLOWNS, The

Four-man, two-woman group produced by Jeff Barry (half of prolific songwriting partnership with then-wife Ellie Greenwich; ex-Raindrops).

| 12/12/70 | 184 | 2 | | The Klowns .... | $10 | RCA 4438 |

Be A Kid	Fish Tales	Honey Bunny Day	**Lady Love 95**	Movin'	Whole Lotta Love
Dream On	Good News	If You Can't Be A Clown	Love Is The Answer	River Cruisin'	Yellow Sunglasses

★★175★★ KLUGH, Earl

Born on 9/16/53 in Detroit. Jazz acoustic guitarist/pianist. Taught guitar from age 15. Worked Baker's Keyboard Lounge. Toured with Chick Corea's Return To Forever and George Benson. First solo recording for Blue Note in 1976. The Earl Klugh Trio includes Ray Armstrong and Gene Dunlap.

7/10/76	124	6		1 Earl Klugh ....[I]	$8	Blue Note 596
12/11/76	188	2		2 Living Inside Your Love ......[I]	$8	Blue Note 667
7/9/77	84	8		3 Finger Paintings ....[I]	$8	Blue Note 737
7/1/78	139	9		4 Magic In Your Eyes ....[I]	$8	United Art. 877
5/19/79	49	21		5 Heart String ....[I]	$8	United Art. 942
11/3/79	23	33	●	6 One On One ....[I]	$8	Tappan Zee 36241

BOB JAMES AND EARL KLUGH

| 4/19/80 | 42 | 19 | | 7 Dream Come True ....[I] | $8 | United Art. 1026 |
| 9/27/80 | 134 | 4 | | 8 How To Beat The High Cost Of Living ....[S-I] | $8 | Columbia 36741 |

HUBERT LAWS & EARL KLUGH

12/6/80+	98	23		9 Late Night Guitar ....[I]	$8	Liberty 1079
11/14/81	53	27		10 Crazy For You ....[I]	$8	Liberty 51113
11/6/82	44	29		11 Two Of A Kind ....[I]	$8	Capitol 12244

EARL KLUGH & BOB JAMES

5/7/83	38	24		12 Low Ride ....[I]	$8	Capitol 12253
3/31/84	69	23		13 Wishful Thinking ....[I]	$8	Capitol 12323
10/27/84	107	17		14 Nightsongs ....[I]	$8	Capitol 12372
5/11/85	110	17		15 Soda Fountain Shuffle ......[I]	$8	Warner 25262
8/30/86	143	11		16 Life Stories ....[I]	$8	Warner 25478
7/11/87	59	31	●	17 Collaboration ....[I]	$8	Warner 25580

GEORGE BENSON/EARL KLUGH

5/20/89	150	5		18 Whispers And Promises .....[I]	$8	Warner 25902
4/6/91	189	3		19 Midnight In San Juan ....[I]	$12	Warner 26293
8/29/92	170	3		20 Cool ....[I]	$12	Warner 26939

BOB JAMES/EARL KLUGH

Acoustic Lady Part I & II (5)
Afterglow, The (6)
Ain't Misbehavin' (14)
Alicia (4)
All The Time (13)
Amazon (7)
Angelina (1)
Another Time, Another Place (2)
April Fools (2)
April Love (15)
As It Happens (20)
Baby Cakes (15)
Back In Central Park (12)
Balladina (4)
Brazilian Stomp (17)
Broadway Ramble (10)
Cabo Frio (3)
Calypso Breeze (10)
Caper, The (8)
Captain Caribe (2)
Cast Your Fate To The Wind (4)
Catherine (14)
Certain Smile (14)
Christina (12)
Close To Your Heart (15)
Collaboration (17)
Could It Be I'm Falling In Love (1)
Crazy For You (10)
Cry A Little While (4)
Dance With Me (3)
Debra Anne (16)

Doc (7)
Dr. Macumba (3)
Down River (8)
Dream Come True (7)
Dream Something (8)
Dreamin' (17)
Edge, The (8)
Every Moment With You (19)
Falcon, The (11)
Fall In Love (18)
Felicia (2)
For The Love Of You (16)
Frisky Biscuits (18)
Fugitive Life (20)
Good Time Charlie's Got The Blues (4)
Handara (20)
Heart String (5)
I Don't Want To Leave You Alone Anymore (7)
I Heard It Through The Grapevine (2)
I Never Thought I'd Leave You (12)
I'll Never Say Goodbye (The Promise) (9)
I'll Never See You Smile Again (6)
I'll See You Again (5)
I'm Ready For Your Love (10)
If It's In Your Heart (It's In Your Smile) (7)
(If You Want To) Be My Love (12)

If You're Still In Love With Me (12)
Incognito (15)
Ingenue (11)
It's So Easy Loving You (8)
Jamaica (17)
Jamaica Farewell (9)
Jamaican Winds (19)
Jolanta (3)
Julie (9)
Just For Your Love (16)
Just Like Yesterday (12)
Just Pretend (15)
Just You And Me (18)
Kari (6)
Keep Your Eye On The Sparrow (Baretta's Theme) (3)
Kiko (2)
Kissin' On The Beach (19)
Las Manos De Fuego (Hands Of Fire) (1)
Laughter In The Rain (1)
Laura (9)
Like A Lover (9)
Lisbon Antiqua (9)
Living Inside Your Love (2)
Lode Star (4)
Long Ago And Far Away (3)
Look Of Love (14)
Love Lips (6)
Low Ride (12)
Magic In Your Eyes (4)
Mallorca (6)

Master Of Suspense (18)
Mayaguez (4)
Message To Michael (7)
Midnight In San Juan (19)
Mimosa (17)
Miniature (20)
Mirabella (9)
Mobimientos Del Alma (Rhythms Of The Soul) (19)
Mona Lisa (9)
Moon And The Stars (16)
Moonlight Dancing (15)
Movin' On (20)
Mt. Airy Road (17)
Natural Thing (13)
Nature Boy (14)
New York Samba (20)
Nice To Be Around (Nice To Have Around) (9)
Night Drive (12)
Night Moves (8)
Night Song (14)
Night That Love Came Back (20)
Once Again (13)
One Night (Alone With You) (15)
Only One For Me (13)
Outsiders, Theme From The ...see: Stay Gold
Pawnbroker, Theme From The (14)
Piccolo Boogie (8)
Picnic, Theme From (14)

Pretty World (5)
Rainbow Man (15)
Rainmaker (10)
Rainy Day, Theme For A (19)
Rayna (5)
Ready To Run (8)
Return Of The Rainmaker (16)
Right From The Start (13)
Rose Hips (4)
San Diego Stomp (20)
Sandman (16)
Sandstorm (11)
Santiago Sunset (16)
Scuffle, The (8)
Second Chances (16)
Secret Wishes (20)
See See Rider (14)
Shadow Of Your Smile (14)
She Never Said Why (19)
Since You're Gone (17)
Slippin' In The Back Door (1)
Smoke Gets In Your Eyes (9)
So Much In Common (20)
Soda Fountain Shuffle (15)
Soft Stuff (And Other Sweet Delights) (10)
Some Other Time (15)
Song For A Pretty Girl (8)
Spanish Night (5)
Spellbound (7)
Sponge, The (20)
Stay Gold (14)
Strawberry Avenue (18)

Summer Nights (18)
Summer Song (3)
Sweet Rum And Starlight (7)
Take It From The Top (13)
Take You There (19)
Tango Classico (18)
Tenderly (9)
Terpsichore (20)
This Time (3)
Time For Love (9)
Traveler (Part I & II) (16)
Triste (9)
Tropical Legs (13)
Twinkle (10)
Two For The Road (9)
Vonetta (1)
Waiting For Cathy (5)
Waltz For Debby (1)
Water Song (18)
Wes (11)
What Love Can Do (18)
Where I Wander (11)
Whiplash (11)
Whispers And Promises (18)
Wind And The Sea (1)
Winding River (6)
Wishful Thinking (13)

DEBUT DATE	PEAK POS	WKS CHR	GOLD	ARTIST — Album Title	$	Label & Number

KLYMAXX

Black female band founded by drummer/producer Bernadette Cooper in Los Angeles in 1979. Lead vocals by Lorena Porter Shelby and Joyce "Fenderella" Irby. Pared down to a trio of Shelby, Cheryl Cooley (guitar) and Robbin Grider (keyboards) in 1990.

DEBUT DATE	PEAK POS	WKS CHR	GOLD	ARTIST — Album Title	$	Label & Number
2/2/85+	18	67	●	1 Meeting In The Ladies Room	$8	Constellation 5529
12/6/86+	98	31		2 Klymaxx	$8	Constellation 5832
6/23/90	168	4		3 The Maxx Is Back	$12	MCA 6376

Ask Me No Questions (1)
Come Back (2)
Danger Zone (2)
Divas Need Love Too (2)
Don't Mess With My Man (3)
Don't Run Away (3)
Fab Attack (2)
Fashion (2)
Finishing Touch (3)
Girls Chasing Boys (3)
Good Love [includes 2 versions] (3)
I Betcha (1)
I Miss You (1) 5
I'd Still Say Yes (2) 18
Just Our Luck (1)
Lock And Key (1)
Long Distance Love Affair (2)
Love Bandit (1)
Man Size Love (2) 15
Maxx Is Back (3)
Meeting In The Ladies Room (1) 59
Men All Pause (1) 80
Private Party (3)
Sexy (2)
Shame (3)
She's A User (3)
Video Kid (1)
When You Kiss Me (3)

KNACK, The

Rock group formed in Los Angeles in 1978. Consisted of Doug Fieger (lead singer, guitar), Berton Averre (lead guitar), Bruce Gary (drums) and Prescott Niles (bass). Disbanded in 1982. All members but Gary reunited in 1986, replaced by drummer Billy Ward. Fieger was a member of the Detroit rock trio Sky.

DEBUT DATE	PEAK POS	WKS CHR	GOLD	ARTIST — Album Title	$	Label & Number
6/30/79	1[5]	40	▲[2]	1 Get The Knack	$8	Capitol 11948
3/1/80	15	14	●	2 But The Little Girls Understand	$8	Capitol 12045
11/7/81	93	6		3 Round Trip	$8	Capitol 12168

Africa (3)
Another Lousy Day In Paradise (3)
Art War (3)
Baby Talks Dirty (2) 38
Boys Go Crazy (3)
Can't Put A Price On Love (2) 62
End Of The Game (2)
Feeling I Get (2)
Frustrated (1)
Good Girls Don't (1) 11
Hard Way (2)
(Havin') A Rave Up (2)
Heartbeat (1)
Hold On Tight And Don't Let Go (2)
How Can Love Hurt So Much (2)
I Want Ya (2)
It's You (2)
Just Wait And See (3)
Let Me Out (1)
Lil' Cals Big Mistake (3)
Lucinda (1)
Maybe Tonight (1)
Mr. Handleman (2)
My Sharona (1) 1
Oh Tara (1)
Pay The Devil (Ooo, Baby, Ooo) (3) 67
Radiating Love (3)
She Likes The Beat (1)
(She's So) Selfish (1)
Siamese Twins (The Monkey And Me) (1)
Soul Kissin' (3)
Sweet Dreams (3)
Tell Me You're Mine (2)
That's What The Little Girls Do (1)
We Are Waiting (3)
Your Number Or Your Name (1)

KNICKERBOCKERS, The

Rock band formed in Bergenfield, New Jersey in 1964 as the Castle Kings. Lead singer, Buddy Randell, was with the Royal Teens. Member Jimmy Walker replaced Bill Medley, for a time, in The Righteous Brothers. Band named after Knickerbocker Avenue in their hometown.

DEBUT DATE	PEAK POS	WKS CHR	GOLD	ARTIST — Album Title	$	Label & Number
2/12/66	134	5		1 Lies	$55	Challenge 622

Can't You See I'm Trying
Harlem Nocturne
I Believe In Her
I Can Do It Better
Just One Girl
Lies 20
Please Don't Fight It
Wishful Thinking
You'll Never Walk Alone
Your Kind Of Lovin'

KNIGHT, Curtis — see HENDRIX, Jimi

★★61★★ KNIGHT, Gladys, & The Pips

R&B family group from Atlanta, formed in 1952 when lead singer Gladys was eight years old. Consisted of Gladys (b: 5/28/44, Atlanta), her brother Merald "Bubba" Knight and sister Brenda, and cousins William and Eleanor Guest. Named "Pips" for their manager, cousin James "Pip" Woods. First recorded for Brunswick in 1958. Brenda and Eleanor replaced by cousins Edward Patten and Langston George in 1959. Langston left group in 1962 and group has remained a quartet with the same members ever since. Due to legal problems, Gladys could not record with the Pips from 1977-80. Gladys was a cast member of the 1985 TV series *Charlie & Co.*

DEBUT DATE	PEAK POS	WKS CHR	GOLD	ARTIST — Album Title	$	Label & Number
10/14/67	60	24		1 Everybody Needs Love	$15	Soul 706
6/8/68	158	13		2 Feelin' Bluesy	$15	Soul 707
1/11/69	136	16		3 Silk N' Soul	$15	Soul 711
10/25/69	81	10		4 Nitty Gritty	$15	Soul 713
4/4/70	55	16		5 Gladys Knight & The Pips Greatest Hits	[G] $15	Soul 723
5/15/71	35	26		6 If I Were Your Woman	$15	Soul 731
1/8/72	60	24		7 Standing Ovation	$15	Soul 736
3/10/73	9	30		8 Neither One Of Us	$15	Soul 737
7/14/73	70	21		9 All I Need Is Time	$15	Soul 739
10/27/73	9	61	●	10 Imagination	$12	Buddah 5141
2/16/74	77	23		11 Anthology	[G] $15	Motown 792 [2]
3/16/74	139	11		12 Knight Time	[K] $12	Soul 741
3/23/74	35	34	●	13 Claudine	[S] $12	Buddah 5602
				includes one instrumental by Curtis Mayfield: "Claudine Theme"		
11/16/74	17	41	●	14 I Feel A Song	$12	Buddah 5612
4/26/75	164	4		15 A Little Knight Music	[K] $10	Soul 744
10/18/75	24	16	●	16 2nd Anniversary	$10	Buddah 5639
				title refers to their signing with Buddah Records		
2/7/76	36	15		17 The Best Of Gladys Knight & The Pips	[G] $10	Buddah 5653
11/27/76	94	12		18 Pipe Dreams	[S] $10	Buddah 5676
4/23/77	51	21		19 Still Together	$8	Buddah 5689
9/16/78	145	6		20 The One And Only...	$8	Buddah 5701
5/31/80	48	18		21 About Love	$8	Columbia 36387
9/5/81	109	8		22 Touch	$8	Columbia 37086
5/21/83	34	33	●	23 Visions	$8	Columbia 38205
3/23/85	126	12		24 Life	$8	Columbia 39423
12/12/87+	39	27	●	25 All Our Love	$8	MCA 42004
7/20/91	45	15		26 Good Woman	$12	MCA 10329

GLADYS KNIGHT

Add It Up (21)
Ain't No Greater Love (23)
Ain't No Sun Since You've Been Gone (1,4)
Ain't You Glad You Chose Love (2)
Alaskan Pipeline (18)
All I Could Do Was Cry (4)
All I Need Is Time (9) 61
All The Time (20)
All We Need Is A Miracle (15)
And This Is Love (8)
At Every End There's A Beginning (16)
Baby Don't Change Your Mind (19) 52
Baby I Need Your Loving (3)
Be Yourself (20)
Best Thing That Ever Happened To Me (10,17) 3
Better You Go Your Way (14)
Between Her Goodbye And My Hello (12) 57
Billy, Come On Back As Quick As You Can (12)
Bourgie', Bourgie' (21)
Boy From Crosstown (2)
Bridge Over Troubled Water (medley) (7)
Butterfly (20)
Can You Give Me Love With A Guarantee (7,15)
Can't Give It Up No More (8)

DEBUT DATE	PEAK POS	WKS CHR	GOLD	ARTIST — Album Title	$	Label & Number

KNIGHT, Gladys, & The Pips — Cont'd

Changed (22)
Cloud Nine (4)
Come Back And Finish What You Started (20)
Come Together (15)
Complete Recovery (25)
Daddy Could Swear, I Declare (8,11) *19*
Didn't You Know (You'd Have To Cry Sometime) (4,5,11) *63*
Do You Love Me Just A Little, Honey (1)
Do You Wanna Have Some Fun (24)
Don't Burn Down The Bridge (14) *flip*
Don't It Make You Feel Guilty (8)
Don't Let Her Take Your Love From Me (2)
Don't Make Me Run Away (23)
Don't Say No To Me Tonight (20)
Don't Tell Me I'm Crazy (15)
Don't Turn Me Away (2)
Don't You Miss Me A Little Bit Baby (2)
Ease Me To The Ground (12)
End Of Our Road (2,5,11) *15*
Every Beat Of My Heart (5,11) *45*
Every Little Bit Hurts (3,11)
Everybody Is A Star (16)
Everybody Needs Love (1,5,11) *39*
Everybody's Got To Find A Way (18)
Feel Like Makin' Love (16)
Feeling Alright (6)
Fire And Rain (7)
For Once In My Life (8,11)
Forever (24)
Friend Of Mine (22)
Friendly Persuasion (21)
Friendship Train (5,11) *17*
Georgia On My Mind (16)

Get The Love (21)
Give Me A Chance (26)
Giving Up (5,11) *38*
Glitter (24)
God Is (22)
Goin' Out Of My Head (18)
Going Ups And The Coming Downs (14,17)
Good Woman (26)
Got Myself A Good Man (4)
Groovin' (3)
He Ain't Heavy, He's My Brother (medley) (7)
He's My Kind Of Fellow (1)
Heaven Sent (23)
Heavy Makes You Happy (7)
Help Me Make It Through The Night (7,11) *33*
Here I Am Again (6,9)
Hero (23)
Hold On (13)
Home Is Where The Heart Is (19)
How Can You Say That Ain't Love (6,12)
I Can See Clearly Now (10,17)
I Don't Want To Do Wrong (6,11) *17*
I Feel A Song (In My Heart) (14,17) *21*
I Hate Myself For Loving You (15)
I Heard It Through The Grapevine (1,5,11) *2*
I Know Better (2)
(I Know) I'm Losing You (19)
I Love To Feel That Feeling (19)
I Want Him To Say It Again (4)
I Will Fight (22)
I Will Follow My Dream (18)
I Will Survive (22)
I Wish It Would Rain (3,5,11) *41*
I'll Be Here (When You Get Home) (7)
I'll Be Standing By (1)

I'll Miss You (18)
I've Got To Use My Imagination (10,17) *4*
If I Were Your Woman (6,11) *9*
If That'll Make You Happy (22)
If You Gonna Leave (Just Leave) (7)
If You Only Knew (26)
In The Middle Of The Road (15)
In This Life (26)
Is There A Place (In His Heart For Me) (6)
It Should Have Been Me (2,5,11) *40*
It Takes A Whole Lot Of Human Feeling (12)
It Takes A Whole Lotta Man For A Woman Like Me (7)
It's A Better Than Good Time (20)
It's All Over But The Shoutin' (12)
It's Gonna Take All Our Love (25)
It's Gotta Be That Way (8)
It's Summer (4)
It's Time To Go Now (2)
Just Be My Lover (23)
Just Let Me Know (24)
Just Walk In My Shoes (1,11)
Keep An Eye (4)
Keep Givin' Me Love (24)
Landlord (21) *46*
Let It Be (6)
Let Me Be The One (25)
Letter Full Of Tears (5,11) *19*
Life (24)
Little Bit Of Love (19)
Long And Winding Road (4)
Look Of Love (3)
Love Finds It's Own Way (14) *47*
Love Is Always On Your Mind (1)

Love Is Fire (Love Is Ice) (25)
Love Overboard (25) *13*
Love Was Made For Two (22)
Lovin' On Next To Nothin' (25)
Make Me The Woman That You Go Home To (7,11) *27*
Make Yours A Happy Home (13,17)
Makings Of You (13)
Master Of My Mind (7,12)
Meet Me In The Middle (26)
Men (26)
Midnight Train To Georgia (10,17) *1*
Money (16) *50*
Mr. Love (26)
Mr. Welfare Man (13)
My Bed Of Thorns (1)
My Time (7)
Need To Be (14)
Neither One Of Us (Wants To Be The First To Say Goodbye) (8,11) *2*
Nitty Gritty (4,5,11) *19*
No One Could Love You More (7,15)
Nobody But You (18)
Oh La De Da (23)
Oh! What A Love I Have Found (7)
On And On (13,17) *5*
Once In A Lifetime Thing (10)
One And Only (20)
One Less Bell To Answer (6)
One Step Away (6)
Only Time You Love Me Is When You're Losing Me (9)
Overnight Success (25)
Perfect Love (10)
Pipe Dreams (18)
Point Of View (25)
Pot Of Jazz (18)
Part Time Love (16) *22*
Put A Little Love In Your Heart (15)
Reach High (22)
Runnin' Out (4)

Save The Overtime (For Me) (23) *66*
Saved By The Grace Of Your Love (20)
Say What You Mean (25)
Seconds (14,23)
Since I've Lost You (1)
Singer, The (9)
So Sad The Song (18) *47*
Somebody Stole The Sunshine (12)
Sorry Doesn't Make It Right (20)
Still Such A Thing (21)
Storms Of Troubled Times (10)
Straight Up (24)
Stranger, The (4)
Street Brother (16)
Strivin' (24)
Sugar Sugar (15)
Summer Sun (16)
Superwoman (26)
Take Me In Your Arms And Love Me (1,11) *98*
Taste Of Bitter Love (21)
Tenderness Is His Way (14)
Thank You (Falletin Me Be Mice Elf Agin) (9)
That's The Way Love Is (2)
There's A Lesson To Be Learned (9)
Thief In Paradise (25)
This Child Needs Its Father (8)
This Is Love (26)
Till I See You Again (24)
To Be Invisible (13)
To Make A Long Story Short (19)
Together (3)
Tracks Of My Tears (3,11)
Try To Remember ..see: Way We Were
Valley Of The Dolls, Theme From (3)
Waiting On You (26)
Walk Softly (19)

Way We Were/Try To Remember (14,17) *11*
We Need Hearts (21)
We've Got Such A Mellow Love (12)
What Good Am I Without You (2)
What If I Should Ever Need You (20)
When You're Far Away (23)
Where Do I Put His Memory (16)
Where Peaceful Waters Flow (10,17) *28*
Where Would I Be (26)
Who Is She (And What Is She To You) (8)
Window Raisin' Granny (10)
Yes, I'm Ready (1)
Yesterday (3)
You (25)
You And Me Against The World (16)
You Don't Love Me No More (1)
You Need Love Like I Do (Don't You) (5,11) *25*
You Put A New Life In My Body (19)
You're My Everything (3)
You're Number One (In My Book) (23)
You've Lost That Lovin' Feelin' (3)
Your Heartaches I Can Surely Heal (12)
Your Love's Been Good For Me (6)
Your Old Standby (2)

KNIGHT, Jean
Born on 1/26/43 in New Orleans. Soul songstress.

| 8/21/71 | 60 | 11 | | 1 Mr. Big Stuff .... | $15 | Stax 2045 |
| 8/3/85 | 180 | 4 | | 2 My Toot Toot .... | $8 | Mirage 90282 |

Call Me Your Fool (If You Want To) (1)
Don't Talk About Jody (1)
Funny Bone (2)
Isn't Life So Wonderful (2)

Let The Good Times Roll (2)
Little Bit Of Something (Is Better Than All Of Nothing) (1)
Magic (2)

Mr. Big Stuff (1,2) *2*
My Heart Is Willing (2)
My Toot Toot (2) *50*
One Monkey Don't Stop The Show (2)

One-Way Ticket To Nowhere (It's The End Of The Ride) (1)
Take Him (You Can Have My Man) (1)

Think It Over (1)
Why I Keep Living These Memories (1)
Working Your Mojo (2)
You City Slicker (1)

Your Six-Bit Change (1)

KNIGHT, Jerry
Bass player, founding member (with Ray Parker) of Raydio. Born and raised in Los Angeles.

| 5/24/80 | 165 | 7 | | 1 Jerry Knight .... | $8 | A&M 4788 |
| 4/11/81 | 146 | 6 | | 2 Perfect Fit .... | $8 | A&M 4843 |

Easier To Run Away (2)
Freek Show (1)
Good Times (1)

Higher (2)
Joy Ride (1)
Let Me Be The Reason (1)

Monopoly (1)
Now That She's Rockin' (1)
Overnight Sensation (1)

Perfect Fit (2)
Play Sista' (2)
Rainbow (2)

Sweetest Love (1)
Too Busy (2)
Turn It Out (2)

Twilight (2)

KNIGHT, Robert
Born on 4/21/45 in Franklin, Tennessee. Soul singer. Recorded for Dot in 1960.

| 12/16/67 | 196 | 2 | | Everlasting Love .... | $20 | Rising Sons 17000 |

Branded! (1)
Dance Of Love

Everlasting Love *13*
It's Been Worth It All

Letter, The
My Rainbow Valley

Never My Love
Rachel The Stranger

Sandy
Somebody's Baby

Somewhere My Love (Lara's Theme from Dr. Zhivago)

KNIGHT, Terry, and The Pack
Rock quintet from Flint, Michigan. Terry (real name: Richard Terrance Knapp) formed, managed and produced Grand Funk Railroad, which included two former Pack members, Don Brewer and Mark Farner.

| 11/26/66+ | 127 | 13 | | 1 Terry Knight And The Pack .... | $25 | Lucky Eleven 8000 |
| 11/4/72 | 192 | 3 | | 2 Mark, Don & Terry 1966-67 ....[K] | $15 | Abkco 4217 [2] |

Mark Farner, Don Brewer (both of Grand Funk) and Terry Knight

Change On The Way (1,2)
Come With Me (2)
Dimestore Debutante (2)
Dirty Lady (2)
Forever And A Day (2)

Got Love (1,2)
He's A Bad Boy (2)
I (Who Have Nothing) (1,2) *46*
I've Been Told (1,2)

Lady Jane (1,2)
Lizabeth Peach (2)
Love Goddess Of Sunset Strip (2)
Love Love Love (2)

Lovin' Kind (1,2)
Numbers (1,2)
One Monkey Don't Stop No Show (2)
Satisfaction (2)

Shut-In (1,2)
Sleep Talkin' (2)
This Precious Time (2)
What's On Your Mind (1)
Where Do You Go (1)

You're A Better Man Than I (1,2)

K-9 POSSE
Rap group formed at the Fairleigh Dickinson University in Teaneck, New Jersey by Vernon Lynch and Wardell Mahone. DJ Terrence Sheppard joined in 1988.

| 3/4/89 | 98 | 14 | | K-9 Posse .... | $8 | Arista 8569 |

DEBUT DATE	PEAK POS	WKS CHR	GOLD	ARTIST — Album Title	$	Label & Number

K-9 POSSE — Cont'd

Ain't Nothin To It	No Sell Out	Say Who Say What	This Is The Way The Quick
It Gets No Deeper	No Stoppin Or Standin	Somebody's Brother	Cut Goes
	Between The Rhyme	This Beat Is Military	

Tough Cookie
Turn That Down

KNOBLOCK, Fred
Born in Jackson, Mississippi. With the rock band Let's Eat in the late 1970s. Member of the country trios Schuyler, Knobloch & Overstreet (SKO) and Schuyler, Knobloch & Bickhardt (SKB).

| 10/4/80 | 179 | 5 | | Why Not Me .... | $8 | Scotti Br. 7109 |

Bigger Fool	Can't Keep From Crying	It's Over	Let Me Love You	Still Feel The Same Way	Why Not Me 18
Can I Get A Wish	Father	Laugh It Off	Love Isn't Easy	Take A Flight Tonight	

KNOPFLER, Mark
Leader of Dire Straits. Born on 8/12/49 in Glasgow, Scotland and raised in Newcastle, England. Worked as a teacher prior to forming Dire Straits. Recorded film soundtracks of *Local Hero, Cal, Comfort And Joy, The Princess Bride* and *Last Exit To Brooklyn.*

| 11/3/90 | 127 | 25 | | Neck And Neck .... | $12 | Columbia 45307 |

CHET ATKINS/MARK KNOPFLER

I'll See You In My Dreams	Next Time I'm In Town	So Soft, Your Goodbye	Tahitian Skies	There'll Be Some Changes	Yakety Axe
Just One Time	Poor Boy Blues	Sweet Dreams	Tears	Made	

KOKOMO
English jazz-rock, nine-member band.

| 6/7/75 | 159 | 9 | | 1 Kokomo .... | $10 | Columbia 33442 |
| 4/17/76 | 194 | 2 | | 2 Rise And Shine! .... | $10 | Columbia 34031 |

Angel (1)	Feelin' Good (2)	Happy Birthday (2)	It Ain't Cool (To Be Cool No	Little Girl (2)	That's Enough (2)
Angel Love (2)	Feeling This Way (1)	I Can Understand It (1)	More) (1)	Rise And Shine (2)	Use Your Imagination (2)
Anytime (1)	Forever (1)	I'm Sorry Babe (1)	Kitty Sittin' Pretty (1)	Sweet Sugar Thing (1)	Without Me (2)
Do It Right (2)					

KONGAS
A disco production by Cerrone.

| 3/18/78 | 120 | 8 | | Africansim .... | $8 | Polydor 6138 |

Africanism/Gimme Some	Dr. Doo-Dah	Tatoo Woman
Lovin' 84		

★★113★★   KOOL & THE GANG
R&B group formed in Jersey City, New Jersey in 1964 by bass player Robert "Kool" Bell as the Jazziacs. Session work in New York City, 1964-68. First recorded for De-Lite in 1969. Added lead singer James "J.T." Taylor in 1979. Current lineup consists of brothers Robert and Ronald Bell (sax, keyboards), George Brown (drums), Curtis "Fitz" Williams (keyboards) and Charles Smith (guitar). Taylor left in 1988; replaced by lead singers Gary Brown, Odeen Mays and former Dazz Band lead vocalist Skip Martin.

2/27/71	122	19		1 Live At The Sex Machine .... [I-L]	$10	De-Lite 2008
9/25/71	157	8		2 The Best Of Kool And The Gang .... [G]	$10	De-Lite 2009
1/1/72	171	7		3 Live At P.J.'S .... [I-L]	$10	De-Lite 2010
3/17/73	142	7		4 Good Times	$10	De-Lite 2012
10/13/73+	33	60	●	5 Wild And Peaceful	$10	De-Lite 2013
1/12/74	187	4		6 Kool Jazz .... [K-I]	$8	De-Lite 4001
10/5/74	63	34	●	7 Light Of Worlds	$8	De-Lite 2014
3/8/75	81	23		8 Kool & The Gang Greatest Hits! .... [G]	$8	De-Lite 2015
8/30/75	48	14		9 Spirit Of The Boogie	$8	De-Lite 2016
3/20/76	68	20		10 Love & Understanding	$8	De-Lite 2018
				3 of 8 cuts recorded live in London		
11/20/76+	110	18		11 Open Sesame	$8	De-Lite 2023
1/28/78	142	7		12 The Force	$8	De-Lite 9501
9/22/79	13	45	▲	13 Ladies' Night	$8	De-Lite 9513
10/18/80+	10	44	▲	14 Celebrate!	$8	De-Lite 9518
10/17/81	12	67	▲	15 Something Special	$15	De-Lite 8502
10/9/82	29	24	●	16 As One	$8	De-Lite 8505
12/10/83+	29	37	●	17 In The Heart	$8	De-Lite 8508
12/15/84+	13	74	▲	18 Emergency	$8	De-Lite 822943
12/6/86+	25	42	●	19 Forever	$8	Mercury 830398
8/20/88	109	11		20 Everything's Kool & The Gang: Greatest Hits & More ... [G]	$8	Mercury 834780
				includes remixes of 5 hits		

All Night Long (11)	Forever (19)	Home Is Where The Heart Is	**Let The Music Take Your**	N.T. (3)	Ronnie's Groove (3)
Ancestral Ceremony (9)	Free (12)	(17)	**Mind** (1,2) 78	Night People (14)	Sea Of Tranquility (6)
As One (16)	**Fresh** (18,20) 9	I.B.M.C. (19)	**Let's Go Dancin' (Ooh La,**	No Show (15)	September Love (17)
Bad Woman (18)	Fruitman (7)	I Remember John W.	**La, La)** (16) 30	North, East, South, West	Slick Superchick (12)
Be My Lady (15)	**Funky Man** (1,2) 87	Coltrane (4,6)	Life Is What You Make It (5)	(4,6)	Sombrero Sam (3,6)
Big Fun (16) 21	**Funky Stuff** (5,8,20) 29	I Want To Take You Higher	Life's A Song (12)	Oasis (2)	Soul Vibrations (8)
Blowin' With The Wind (6)	**Gangs Back Again** (2) 85	(1)	Light Of Worlds (7)	**Open Sesame - Part 1**	**Special Way** (19) 72
Breeze & Soul (6)	**Get Down On It** (15) 10	If You Feel Like Dancin' (13)	Little Children (11)	(11,20) 55	**Spirit Of The Boogie** (9) 35
Broadway (19)	Gift Of Love (19)	Ike's Mood (medley) (3)	L-O-V-E (11)	Pass It On (15)	Stand Up And Sing (15)
Caribbean Festival (9) 55	Give It Up (2)	In The Heart (17)	Love Affair (14)	Peace Maker (19)	**Steppin' Out** (15) 89
Celebration (14,20) 1	God's Country (19)	Joanna (17,20) 2	**Love And Understanding**	Penguin, The (2)	**Stone Love** (19,20) 10
Cherish (18,20) 2	Good Time Tonight (15)	**Jones Vs. Jones** (14) 39	**(Come Together)** (10) 77	Place For Us (17)	Straight Ahead (17)
Chocolate Buttermilk (1,2)	Good Times (4,8)	Jungle Boogie (5,8,20) 4	Love Festival (14)	Place In Space (12)	Street Corner Symphony (7)
Come Together ..see: Love	Got You Into My Life (13)	Jungle Jazz (9)	Lucky For Me (3,6)	Pneumonia (1,2)	Street Kids (16)
And Understanding	Hangin' Out (13)	Just Be True (12)	Making Merry Music (4)	Pretty Baby (16)	Strong (20)
Cosmic Energy (10)	Heaven At Once (5)	Just Friends (14)	Mighty, Mighty High (12)	Rags To Riches (20)	Sugar (10)
Country Junkey (4)	Here After (7)	**Kool And The Gang** (2) 59	**Misled** (18) 10	Rated X (4,8)	**Summer Madness**
Do It Right Now (10)	Hi De Hi, Hi De Ho (16)	Kool It (Here Comes The	Money And Power (20)	Raw Hamburger (2)	(7,10) *flip*
Dujii (3,6)	Hi De Hi, Hi De Ho (16)	Fuzz) (2)	More Funky Stuff (5,8)	**Rhyme Tyme People** (7) 63	Sunshine (11)
Emergency (18) 18	**Higher Plane** (7,8) 37	Kools Back Again (2)	Morning Star (14)	Ricksonata (3)	Sunshine And Love (9)
Father, Father (4)	**Holiday** (19) 66	**Ladies Night** (13) 8	Mother Earth (9)	Ride The Rhythm (9)	Super Band (11)
Force, The (12)	**Hollywood Swinging**		Music Is The Message (8)	Rollin' (17)	Surrender (18)
	(5,8,10,20) 6				

DEBUT DATE	PEAK POS	WKS CHR	G O L D	ARTIST — Album Title	$	Label & Number

KOOL & THE GANG — Cont'd

Take It To The Top (14)	Tonight (17) *13*	Universal Sound (10)	Whisper Softly (11)	Wild Is Love (4,6)	You've Lost That Lovin'
Take My Heart (You Can Have It If You Want It) (15) *17*	Tonights The Night (13)	**Victory** (19) *10*	Whiting H. & G. (7)	Winter Sadness (9)	Feeling (medley) (3)
	Too Hot (13,20) *5*	Walk On By (1)	Who's Gonna Take The	You Are The One (18)	
Think It Over (16)	Touch Of You (1)	What Would The World Be	Weight - Part 1 & 2 (1,2)	You Can Do It (17)	
This Is You, This Is Me (5)	Trying To Make A Fool Of	Like Without Music	Wichita Lineman (1)	You Don't Have To Change	
	Me (1)	(medley) (1)	Wild And Peaceful (5)	(7)	

KOOL G RAP & D.J. POLO
Kool G Rap (Kool Genius Of Rap) was born Nathaniel Wilson on 7/20/68 in Elmhurst, Queens, New York.

12/12/92	185	1		Live And Let Die	$12	Cold Chill. 5001

Crime Pays	Go For Your Guns	Letters	#1 With A Bullet	Still Wanted Dead Or Alive	Two To The Head
Edge Of Sanity	Home Sweet Home	Live And Let Die	On The Run	Straight Jacket	
Fuck U Man	Ill Street Blues	Nuff Said	Operation CB	Train Robbery	

KOOL MOE DEE
Rapper from Harlem. Real name: Mohandas DeWese. Formerly with the Treacherous Three.

4/18/87	83	21		1	Kool Moe Dee	$8	Jive 1025
11/28/87+	35	50	▲	2	How Ya Like Me Now..	$8	Jive 1079
6/17/89	25	23	●	3	Knowledge Is King	$8	Jive 1182
6/29/91	72	9		4	Funke Funke Wisdom	$12	Jive 1388

All Night Long (3)	Don't Dance (2)	How Kool Can One	Knowledge Is King (3)	Rock Steady (1)
Avenue, The (3)	Dumb Dick (Richard) (1)	Blackman Be (4)	Let's Get Serious (4)	Rock You (2)
Bad, Bad, Bad (4)	50 Ways (2)	How Ya Like Me Now (2)	Little Jon (1)	Stupid (2)
Bad Mutha (1)	Funke Wisdom (4)	I Go To Work (3)	Mo' Better (4)	Suckers (2)
Best, The (1)	Gangster Boogie (4)	I Like It Nasty (4)	Monster Crack (1)	They Want Money (3)
Death Blow (4)	Get Paid (2)	I'm A Player (2)	No Respect (2)	Times Up (4)
Do You Know What Time It	Get The Picture (4)	I'm Blowin' Up (3)	Poetic Justice (4)	To The Beat Y'all (4)
Is? (1)	Go See The Doctor (1) *89*	I'm Hittin' Hard (3)	Pump Your Fist (3)	Way Way Back (2)
Don, The (3)	Here We Go Again (4)	I'm Kool Moe Dee (1)	Rise 'N' Shine (4)	**Wild, Wild West** (2) *62*

KOOPER, Al
Born on 2/5/44 in Brooklyn. Top session keyboardist/guitarist/vocalist. Founded Blood, Sweat & Tears in 1968, left in 1969. A member of The Royal Teens in 1959. Founded The Blues Project in 1967.

8/31/68	12	37	●	1	Super Session	$15	Columbia 9701
					MIKE BLOOMFIELD/AL KOOPER/STEVE STILLS		
2/8/69	18	20		2	The Live Adventures Of Mike Bloomfield And Al Kooper............. [L]	$15	Columbia 6 [2]
					MIKE BLOOMFIELD & AL KOOPER		
2/8/69	54	13		3	I Stand Alone	$15	Columbia 9718
10/11/69	125	6		4	You Never Know Who Your Friends Are....................	$15	Columbia 9855
1/24/70	182	5		5	Kooper Session	$12	Columbia 9951
					AL KOOPER Introduces SHUGGIE OTIS		
9/19/70	105	6		6	Easy Does It	$15	Columbia 30031 [2]
7/3/71	198	3		7	New York City (You're A Woman)	$15	Columbia 30506
5/6/72	200	2		8	A Possible Projection Of The Future/Childhood's End	$15	Columbia 31159
1/8/77	182	5		9	Act Like Nothing's Wrong	$10	United Art. 702

Albert's Shuffle (1)	Dearest Darling (7)	I Bought You The Shoes	Love Is A Man's Best Friend	Possible Projection Of The	This Diamond Ring (9)
Anna Lee (What Can I Do	Don't Know Why I Love You	(You're Walking Away In)	(medley) (8)	Future (8)	Toe Hold (3)
For You) (4)	(4)	(6)	Love Trap (8)	Really (1)	Together 'Til The End Of
Baby Please Don't Go (6)	Don't Throw Your Love On	I Can Love A Woman (3)	Lucille (4)	Refugee (2)	Time (2)
Back On My Feet (7)	Me So Strong (2)	I Forgot To Be Your Lover (9)	Magic In My Socks (4)	Right Now For You (3)	Too Busy Thinking About
Ballad Of The Hard Rock	Double Or Nothing (5)	I Got A Woman (6)	Man In Me (8)	Rose And A Baby Ruth (6)	My Baby (4)
Kid (4)	Easy Does It (6)	I Stand Alone (3)	Man's Temptation (1)	Sad, Sad Sunshine (6)	Turn My Head Towards
Bended Knees (Please Don't	59th Street Bridge Song	I Wonder Who (2)	Mary Ann (9)	Season Of The Witch (1)	Home (9)
Leave Me Now) (8)	(Feelin' Groovy) (2)	I'm Never Gonna Let You	Missing You (9)	She Don't Ever Lose Her	12:15 Slow Goonbash Blues
Blue Moon Of Kentucky (3)	First Time Around (4)	Down (4)	Monkey Time (3)	Groove (9)	(5)
Blues, Part IV (4)	Fly On (8)	In My Own Sweet Way (9)	Mourning Glory Story (4)	She Gets Me Where I Live (6)	Visit To The Rainbow Bar &
Brand New Day (Main	God Sheds His Grace On	Is We On The Downbeat? (9)	New York City (You're A	Shuggie's Old Time	Grill (9)
Theme from The Landlord)	Thee (6)	It Takes A Lot To Laugh, It	Woman) (7)	Dee-Di-Lee-Di-Leet-Deet	Warning (Someone's On The
(6)	Going Quietly Mad (7)	Takes A Train To Cry (1)	Nightmare No. 5 (7)	Slide Boogie (5)	Cross Again) (7)
Buckskin Boy (6)	Great American Marriage	John The Baptist (Holy	No More Lonely Nights (2)	Shuggie's Shuffle (5)	Weight, The (2)
Bury My Body (5)	(medley) (7)	John) (7)	Nothing (medley) (4)	Soft Landing On The Moon	You Don't Love Me (1)
Camille (1)	Green Onions (2)	Landlord, Love Theme From	One (3)	(3)	You Never Know Who Your
Can You Hear It Now (500	Harvey's Tune (1)	The (6)	One Room Country Shack (5)	Song And Dance For The	Friends Are (4)
Miles) (7)	Her Holy Modal Highness (2)	Let The Duchess No (6)	Oo Wee Baby, I Love You	Unborn, Frightened Child	
Childhood's End (8)	Hey, Western Union Man (3)	Let Your Love Shine (8)	(medley) (9)	(3)	
Coloured Rain (1)	His Holy Modal Majesty (1)	Lookin' For A Home (5)	Out Of Left Field (9)	Sonny Boy Williamson (2)	
Come Down In Time (9)	Hollywood Vampire (9)	Loretta (Union Turnpike	(Please Not) One More Time	Stop (1)	
Country Road (6)		Eulogy) (4)	(9)	Swept For You Baby (8)	
Dear Mr. Fantasy (2)			Please Tell Me Why (8)	That's All Right (2)	

KORGIS, The
British pop duo: James Warren and Andy Davis (both formerly with Stackridge).

11/8/80	113	12			Dumb Waiters	$8	Asylum 290

Drawn And Quartered	**Everybody's Got To Learn**	If It's Alright With You Baby	It's No Good Unless You	Love Ain't Too Far Away	Rovers Return
Dumb Waiters	**Sometime** *18*	Intimate	Love Me	Perfect Hostess	Silent Running

KOSSOFF, Paul
British guitarist — member of Free and Back Street Crawler; died on 3/19/76 (age 25).

9/6/75	191	2			Back Street Crawler .... [E-I]	$10	Island 9264
					recorded in 1973; Paul formed new band (named after LP title) in 1975		

Back Street Crawler (Don't	I'm Ready	Molten Gold	Time Away	Tuesday Morning
Need You No More)				

KOSTELANETZ, Andre, & His Orchestra
Born on 12/23/01 in St. Petersburg, Russia; died on 1/13/80. Conductor/arranger on radio and records from the '30s to the '70s. Also saw Beverly Sills.

10/1/55	4	11		1	Meet Andre Kostelanetz .... [K-I]	$15	Columbia KZ 1
5/23/64	68	7		2	New York Wonderland .... [I]	$10	Columbia 2138

DEBUT DATE	PEAK POS	WKS CHR	G O L D	ARTIST — Album Title	$	Label & Number
				KOSTELANETZ, Andre, & His Orchestra — Cont'd		
6/7/69	**200**	2		3 Traces..[I]	$10	Columbia 9823
11/1/69	**194**	2		4 Sounds Of Love...[K-I]	$10	Columbia 10 [2]
4/10/71	**183**	2		5 Love Story...[I]	$10	Columbia 30501

Alfie (4)
Autumn In New York (2)
Bizet: Carmen - Overture (1)
Bowery, The (medley) (2)
(Carol's Theme) The Eyes Of Love (4)
Chitty Chitty Bang Bang (3)
Days Of Wine And Roses (4)
Don't Blame Me (4)
Easy To Love (1)
Ebb Tide (4)
Eyes Of Love ..see: (Carol's Theme)
Fool On The Hill (3)
Funny Girl (4)
Galveston (3)

Games That Lovers Play (4)
Give My Regards To Broadway (medley) (2)
Green Grass Starts To Grow (5)
I Cover The Waterfront (2)
I Don't Know Why (I Just Do) (4)
I Love You (1)
I Want To Be Happy (medley) (5)
I'll Begin Again (medley) (5)
I'll Catch The Sun (3)
I'll Follow My Secret Heart (1)
I'm In The Mood For Love (4)
I've Gotta Be Me (3)

In The Still Of The Night (1)
It's Impossible (5)
Love Is A Many-Splendored Thing (4)
Love Story, Theme From (5)
Lullaby Of Birdland (2)
Lullaby Of Broadway (2)
Man And A Woman (4)
Manhattan (1)
Manhattan Serenade (2)
Moon River (4)
Mr. Bojangles (4)
Nearness Of You (4)
New York, New York (2)
One Less Bell To Answer (5)
People (4)

Prokofiev: Bravo - The Love For Three Oranges - March (1)
Romeo And Juliet, Theme From (3)
Rose Garden (3)
She's A Latin From Manhattan (2)
So In Love (1)
Someone To Watch Over Me (4)
Something Doesn't Happen (5)
Somewhere, My Love (Lara's Theme) (4)
Song Of India (1)

Spanish Harlem (2)
Stella By Starlight (4)
Street Scene (2)
Tales From The Vienna Woods (1)
Tara Theme (4)
Tchaikovsky: Nutcracker Suite, Op. 71a - Waltz Of The Flowers (1)
Tea For Two (medley) (5)
Thank You Very Much (medley) (5)
This Guy's In Love With You (3)
This Is My Song (4)

Thomas Crown Affair (Windmills Of Your Mind), Theme From The (3)
Traces (3)
Try A Little Tenderness (3)
Valse De Rothschild (3)
Verdi: Aida - Celeste Aida (1)
Washington Square (2)
We've Only Just Begun (5)
What Now My Love (4)
Where Or When (1)
(Windmills Of Your Mind) ..see: Thomas Crown Affair
Zorba Theme (Life Is) (3)

KOTTKE, Leo
Acoustic guitarist. Born on 9/11/45 in Athens, Georgia. Suffered hearing loss due to a childhood accident and a firing practice mishap while in the Navy.

DEBUT DATE	PEAK POS	WKS CHR	G O L D	ARTIST — Album Title	$	Label & Number
6/19/71	**168**	7		1 Mudlark..	$10	Capitol 682
2/12/72	**127**	9		2 Greenhouse...	$10	Capitol 11000
4/7/73	**108**	11		3 My Feet Are Smiling ....[I-L]	$10	Capitol 11164
2/2/74	**69**	18		4 Ice Water...	$10	Capitol 11262
11/9/74	**45**	12		5 Dreams and all that stuff..................................[I]	$10	Capitol 11335
10/25/75	**114**	7		6 Chewing Pine..	$10	Capitol 11446
11/27/76	**153**	4		7 Leo Kottke 1971-1976 - Did You Hear Me? ....[K-I]	$10	Capitol 11576
1/29/77	**107**	9		8 Leo Kottke...[I]	$8	Chrysalis 1106
9/2/78	**143**	12		9 Burnt Lips...	$8	Chrysalis 1191

Airproofing (8)
All Through The Night (4,7)
America, The Beautiful (medley) (5)
Bach: Bourree (1)
Bean Time (2,3)
Bill Cheatham (5)
Blue Dot (3)
Born To Be With You (4)
Buckaroo (8)
Bumblebee (1)
Burnt Lips (9)
Busted Bicycle (3)
Can't Quite Put It Into Words (6)
Child Should Be A Fish (4)
Constant Traveler (5)
Cool Water (9)

Credits: Out-Takes From Terry's Movie (9)
Cripple Creek (1,7)
Crow River Waltz (medley) (3)
Death By Reputation (8)
Don't You Think (8)
Easter (3)
Eggtooth (3)
Eight Miles High (1)
Endless Sleep (9)
Everybody Lies (9)
Fisherman, The (3)
Frank Forgets (9)
From The Cradle To The Grave (2)
Good Egg (4)
Grim To The Brim (6,7)
Hayseed Suede (8)
Hear The Wind Howl (1,3)

Hole In The Day (5)
I Called Back (9)
Ice Miner (1)
In Christ There Is No East Or West (2)
Jack Fig (medley) (3)
Jesu, Joy Of Man's Desiring (medley) (3)
June Bug (1,3,7)
Last Steam Engine Train (2)
Living In The Country (3)
Lost John (2)
Louise (2,3)
Low Thud (9)
Lullaby (1)
Machine #2 (1)
Maroon (8)
Mona Ray (5)
Mona Roy (5)

Monkey Lust (1)
Monkey Money (6)
Morning Is The Long Way Home (4,7)
Open Country Joy (Constant Traveler) (7)
Orange Room (9)
Owls (2)
Pamela Brown (4,7)
Poor Boy (1)
Power Failure (6,7)
Quiet Man (9)
Range (1)
Rebecca (6)
Regards From Chuck Pink (6)
Rio Leo (8)
Room 8 (1,7)

San Antonio Rose (medley) (5)
Sand Street (9)
Scarlatti Rip-Off (6,7)
Shadowland (8)
Short Stories (4)
Song Of The Swamp (2)
Sonora's Death Row (9)
Spanish Entomologist (2)
Standing In My Shoes (1,3)
Standing On The Outside (6,7)
Stealing (1,3)
Taking A Sandwich To A Feast (5)
Tilt Billings And The Student Prince (4)
Tiny Island (2)

Train And The Gate: From Terry's Movie (9)
Trombone (4)
Twilight Property (5)
Up Tempo (8)
Venezuela, There You Go (6)
Vertical Trees (5)
Voluntary Target (9)
Waltz (8)
Wheels (8)
When Shrimps Learn To Whistle (5,7)
White Ape (8)
Why Ask Why? (5,7)
You Don't Have To Need Me (2)
You Know I Know You Know (4)
You Tell Me Why (4,7)

KOZ, Dave
Saxophonist born in San Fernando Valley, California. Touring member of Jeff Lorber's band. Member of *The Pat Sajak Show* band.

DEBUT DATE	PEAK POS	WKS CHR	G O L D	ARTIST — Album Title	$	Label & Number
3/23/91	**128**	9		Dave Koz..[I]	$12	Capitol 91643
				3 tracks feature vocals by Joey Diggs and Cole Basque		

Art Of Key Noise
Castle Of Dreams

Emily
Endless Summer Nights

Give It Up
If Love Is All We Have

Love Of My Life
Nothing But The Radio On

Perfect Stranger
So Far From Home

Yesterday's Rain

KRAFTWERK
Synthesizer band formed in 1970 in Dusseldorf, Germany by Ralf Hutter and Florian Schneider. Kraftwerk is German for power station.

DEBUT DATE	PEAK POS	WKS CHR	G O L D	ARTIST — Album Title	$	Label & Number
2/8/75	**5**	22		1 Autobahn..[I]	$10	Vertigo 2003
9/20/75	**160**	5		2 Ralf And Florian..[I]	$10	Vertigo 2006
12/13/75+	**140**	8		3 Radio-Activity...	$10	Capitol 11457
4/16/77	**119**	10		4 Trans-Europe Express...	$10	Capitol 11603
5/13/78	**130**	9		5 The Man-Machine..[I]	$8	Capitol 11728
6/6/81	**72**	42		6 Computer-World...[I]	$8	Warner 3549
11/29/86	**156**	14		7 Electric Cafe..	$8	Warner 25525

Airwaves (3)
Ananas Symphonie (Pineapple Symphony) (2)
Antenna (3)
Autobahn (1) 25
Boing Boom Tschak (7)
Computer Love (6)
Computer-World (6)
Electric Cafe (7)

Elektrisches Roulette (Electric Roulette) (2)
Endless Endless (4)
Europe Endless (4)
Franz Schubert (4)
Geiger Counter (3)
Hall Of Mirrors (4)
Heimatklange (The Bells Of Home) (2)

Home Computer (6)
It's More Fun To Compute (6)
Kometenmelodie 1 & 2 (Comet Melody 1 & 2) (1)
Kristallo (Crystals) (2)
Man-Machine (5)
Metal On Metal (4)
Metropolis (4)
Mitternacht (Midnight) (1)

Model, The (5)
Morgenspaziergang (Morning Walk) (1)
Musique Non Stop (7)
Neon Lights (5)
News (3)
Numbers (6)
Ohm Sweet Ohm (3)
Pocket Calculator (6)

Radio Stars (3)
Radioactivity (3)
Radioland (3)
Robots, The (5)
Sex Object (7)
Showroom Dummies (4)
Spacelab (5)
Tanzmusik (Dance Music) (2)
Techno Pop (7)

Telephone Call (7)
Terminal Board (6)
Tongebirge (Mountain Of Sound) (2)
Trans-Europe Express (4) 67
Transistor (3)
Uranium (3)
Voice Of Energy (3)

KRAMER, Billy J., With The Dakotas
Billy was born William Ashton on 8/19/43 near Liverpool, England. Discovered by The Beatles' manager, Brian Epstein, who teamed him with the group The Dakotas.

DEBUT DATE	PEAK POS	WKS CHR	G O L D	ARTIST — Album Title	$	Label & Number
6/20/64	**48**	15		Little Children	$40	Imperial 12267

Bad To Me 9
Da Doo Ron Ron
Dance With Me

Do You Want To Know A Secret
Great Balls Of Fire

I Know
I'll Keep You Satisfied 30

It's Up To You
Little Children 7

Pride
Tell Me Girl

They Remind Me Of You

DEBUT DATE	PEAK POS	WKS CHR	G O L D	ARTIST — Album Title	$	Label & Number

KRAVITZ, Lenny
Singer/songwriter/multi-instrumentalist raised in New York City and later Los Angeles. Three-year member of the California Boys Choir. Married for a time to actress Lisa Bonet. Son of actress Roxie Roker (played Helen Willis on TV's *The Jeffersons*).

11/25/89+	61	28		1 Let Love Rule	$8	Virgin 91290
4/20/91	39	40	●	2 Mama Said	$12	Virgin 91610

All I Ever Wanted (2) / Always On The Run (2) / Be (1) / Butterfly (2) / Difference Is Why (2) / Does Anybody Out There Even Care (1) / Fear (1) / Fields Of Joy (2) / Flowers For Zoe (2) / Freedom Train (1) / I Build This Garden For Us (1) / **It Ain't Over 'Til It's Over** (2) *2* / **Let Love Rule** (1) *89* / More Than Anything In This World (2) / Mr. Cab Driver (1) / My Precious Love (1) / Rosemary (1) / Sittin' On Top Of The World (1) / **Stand By My Woman** (2) *76* / Stop Draggin' Around (2) / What Goes Around Comes Around (2) / What The .... Are We Saying? (2) / When The Morning Turns To Night (2)

KRIS KROSS
Rap duo of Atlanta junior high students: Chris "Mack Daddy" Kelly (b: in 1978) and Chris "Daddy Mack" Smith (b: 1/10/79).

4/18/92	1²	43↑ ▲⁴		**Totally Krossed Out**	$12	Ruffhouse 48710

Can't Stop The Bum Rush / **I Missed The Bus** *63* / It's A Shame / **Jump** [includes 2 versions] *1* / Lil' Boys In Da Hood / Party [includes 2 versions] / Real Bad Dream / **Warm It Up** *13* / Way Of Rhyme / We're In Da House / You Can't Get With This

★★275★★ KRISTOFFERSON, Kris
Born on 6/22/36 in Brownsville, Texas. Singer/songwriter/actor. Attended England's Oxford University on a Rhodes scholarship. Married to Rita Coolidge from 1973-80. Wrote "Me And Bobby McGee," "For The Good Times" and "Help Make Me Make It Through The Night." Has starred in many films since 1972. Also see *Highwayman* in Concept Albums.

7/31/71	21	28	●	1 The Silver Tongued Devil And I	$12	Monument 30679
9/11/71	43	22	●	2 Me And Bobby McGee	$12	Monument 30817
3/18/72	41	16		3 Border Lord	$12	Monument 31302
11/25/72+	31	54	●	4 Jesus Was A Capricorn	$12	Monument 31909
9/22/73	26	33	●	5 Full Moon *	$12	A&M 4403
5/25/74	78	14		6 Spooky Lady's Sideshow	$10	Monument 32914
12/21/74+	103	12		7 Breakaway *	$10	Monument 33278
12/6/75+	105	11		8 Who's To Bless...And Who's To Blame	$10	Monument 33379
8/21/76	180	2		9 Surreal Thing	$10	Monument 34254
5/7/77	45	18	●	10 Songs Of Kristofferson .... [K]	$10	Monument 34687
4/1/78	86	7		11 Easter Island *	$10	Monument 35310
2/3/79	106	9		12 Natural Act *	$10	A&M 4690
				*KRIS KRISTOFFERSON & RITA COOLIDGE		
11/10/84	152	5		13 Music from SongWriter .... [S]	$8	Columbia 39531
				WILLIE NELSON & KRIS KRISTOFFERSON (co-stars of the film)		

After The Fact (5) / Back In My Baby's Arms (12) / Bad Love Story (9) / Best Of All Possible Worlds (2) / Bigger The Fool (The Harder The Fall) (11) / Billy Dee (1) / Blame It On The Stones (2) / Blue As I Do (12) / Border Lord (3) / Breakdown (A Long Way From Home) (1) / Broken Freedom Song (6) / Burden Of Freedom (3) / Casey's Last Ride (1) / Crippled Crow (7) / Crossing The Border [solo: Kris] (13) / Dakota (The Dancing Bear) (7) / Darby's Castle (2) / Don't Cuss The Fiddle (8) / Down To Her Socks [solo: Kris] (13) / Duvalier's Dream (2) / Easter Island (11) / Easy, Come On (8) / Eddie The Eunuch (9) / Enough For You (4) / Epitaph (Black And Blue) (1) / Eye Of The Storm (13) / Fighter, The (11) / Final Attraction [solo: Kris] (13) / For The Good Times (2,10) / Forever In Your Love (11) / From The Bottle To The Bottom (4) / Gettin' By, High And Strange (3) / Give It Time To Be Tender (4) / Golden Idol (9) / Good Christian Soldier (1) / Hard To Be Friends (5) / Help Me (4) / Help Me Make It Through The Night (2,10) / Hoola Hoop (12) / How Do You Feel (About Foolin' Around) (11,13) / I Fought The Law (12) / I Got A Life Of My Own (9,10) / I Heard The Bluebirds Sing (5) / I May Smoke Too Much (6) / I Never Had It So Good (9) / I'd Rather Be Sorry (7) / I'm Down (But I Keep Falling) (5) / I've Got To Have You (7) / If It's All The Same To You (8) / If You Don't Like Hank Williams (7) / It Sure Was (Love) (4) / It's All Over (All Over Again) (5) / It's Never Gonna Be The Same Again (9) / Jesse Younger (4) / **Jesus Was A Capricorn** (4) *91* / Jody And The Kid (1) / **Josie** (6) / Just The Other Side Of Nowhere (2) / Killing Time (9) / Kiss The World Goodbye (2) / Late Again (Gettin' Over You) (6) / Law Is For Protection Of The People (2) / Lay Me Down (And Love The World Away) (11) / Lights Of Magdala (7) / Little Girl Lost (3) / Living Legend (11) / Love Don't Live Here Anymore (12) / **Loving Arms** (5) *86* / **Loving Her Was Easier (Than Anything I'll Ever Do Again)** (1,10,12) *26* / Me And Bobby McGee (2,10) / Nobody Wins (4) / Not Everyone Knows (12) / Number One (12) / One For The Money (6) / Out Of Mind, Out Of Sight (4) / Part Of Your Life (5) / Pilgrim - Chapter 33 (1,10) / Please Don't Tell Me How The Story Ends (12) / Prisoner, The (9) / Rain (7) / Rescue Mission (6) / Risky Bizness (11) / Rock And Roll Time (6) / Rocket To Stardom (8) / Sabre And The Rose (11) / Same Old Song (6) / Shandy (The Perfect Disguise) (6) / Silver Mantis (12) / Silver (The Hunger) (8) / Silver Tongued Devil And I (1,10) / Slow Down (7) / Smile At Me Again (6) / Smokey Put The Sweat On Me (3) / Somebody Nobody Knows (3) / **Song I'd Like To Sing** (5) *49* / Spooky Lady's Revenge (11) / Stagger Mountain Tragedy (3) / Stairway To The Bottom (6) / Stallion (3) / Star-Spangled Bummer (Whores Die Hard) (6) / Stranger (8,10) / Stranger I Love (9) / Sugar Man (4) / Sunday Mornin' Comin' Down (2,10) / Sweet Susannah (7) / Take Time To Love (5) / Taker, The (1) / Tennessee Blues (5) / Things I Might Have Been (7) / To Beat The Devil (2) / Under The Gun [solo: Kris] (13) / We Must Have Been Out Of Our Minds (7) / What'cha Gonna Do (7) / When I Loved Her (1) / When She's Wrong (3) / Who's To Bless And Who's To Blame (8,10) / **Why Me** (4,10) *16* / Year 2000 Minus 25 (8) / You Show Me Yours (And I'll Show You Mine) (9,10) / You're Gonna Love Yourself (In The Morning) (12)

KROKUS
Heavy-metal band from Zurich, Switzerland. Led by Marc Storace (vocals) and Fernando Von Arb (guitar).

4/4/81	103	12		1 Hardware	$8	Ariola 1508
4/10/82	53	20		2 One Vice At A Time	$8	Arista 9591
4/16/83	25	41	●	3 Headhunter	$8	Arista 9623
9/8/84	31	27	●	4 The Blitz	$8	Arista 8243
5/3/86	45	17		5 Change Of Address	$8	Arista 8402
11/22/86	97	12		6 Alive and Screamin' .... [L]	$8	Arista 8445
5/7/88	87	11		7 Heart Attack	$8	MCA 42087

American Woman (2) / Axx Attack (2) / Bad, Bad Girl (7) / Bad Boys Rag Dolls (2) / Ballroom Blitz (4) / Bedside Radio (6) / Boys Nite Out (4) / Burning Bones (1) / Burning Up The Night (5) / Celebration (1) / Down The Drain (4) / Easy Rocker (1) / Eat The Rich (3,6) / Everybody Rocks (7) / Flyin' High (7) / Hard Luck Hero (5) / Headhunter (3,6) / Hot Shot City (5,6) / Hot Stuff (4) / I'm On The Run (2) / Lay Me Down (6) / Let It Go (7) / Let This Love Begin (5) / Long Stick Goes Boom (2,6) / Long Way From Home (5) / Mad Racket (1) / **Midnite Maniac** (4,6) *71* / Mr. Sixty Nine (1) / Night Wolf (3) / Now (All Through The Night) (7) / Our Love (4) / Out Of Control (4) / Out To Lunch (4) / Playin' The Outlaw (2)

KROKUS — Cont'd

Ready To Burn (3)	Rock 'N' Roll Tonight (7)	Shoot Down The Night (7)	Stayed Awake All Night (3,6)	Winning Man (1,7)
Ready To Rock (4)	Rock The Nation (4)	Smelly Nelly (1)	To The Top (2)	World On Fire (5)
Rock City (1)	Russian Winter (3)	**School's Out (5)** 67	Speed Up (7)	White Din (3)
Rock N' Roll (2)	Save Me (2)	Screaming In The Night (3,6)	Stand And Be Counted (3)	Wild Love (7)
	Say Goodbye (5)	She's Got Everything (1)		

K-SOLO

Born Kevin Madison in Central Islip, New York. As a youth, in rap group with Parrish Smith, later of EPMD. K-Solo stands for Kevin Self Organization Left Others.

6/20/92	135	2		Times Up	$12	Atlantic 82388

Baby Doesn't Look Like Me	I Can't Hold It Back	Letterman	Premonition Of A Black	Who's Killin' Who?
Formula (House Party)	King Of The Mountain	Long Live The Fugitive	Prisoner	
Household Maid			Rock Bottom	
			Sneak Tip	

KUBAN, Bob, And The In-Men

Eight-man, St. Louis pop-rock band formed by drummer Kuban. Lead singer Walter Scott (real name: Walter Notheis, Jr.), disappeared on 12/27/83; his ex-wife and her husband were charged with Scott's murder after his body was found, three years later, with a gunshot wound to the back.

4/23/66	129	5		Look Out For The Cheater	$35	Musicland 3500

All I Want	Get Out	Stop Her On Sight (S.O.S.)	Try Me Baby	You've Got Your Troubles
Batman Theme	Harlem Shuffle	These Boots Were Made For	Virginia Wolfe, Theme From	(I've Got Mine)
Cheater, The 12	In The Midnight Hour	Walking		

KWAME

Rapper from East Elmhurst, Queens, New York, with his backing group A New Beginning

5/27/89	114	18		1 The Boy Genius featuring A New Beginning	$8	Atlantic 81941
6/16/90	113	15		2 "A Day In The Life" A Pokadelick Adventure	$12	Atlantic 82100

KWAME AND A NEW BEGINNING

Boy Genius (1)	Hai (2)	Man We All Know And Love	Ownlee Eue (2)	Sweet Thing (1)	Yes Yes Yall (2)
Da' Man (2)	Itz Oh Kay (2)	(1)	Pushthepanicbutton!!! (1)	Therez A Partee Goinz On (2)
Day In The Life (2)	Keep On Doin' (What You're	Mic Is Mine (1)	Rhythm, The (1)	U Gotz 2 Get Down! (1)
Doin' Ma Thang (2)	Doin') Baby) (1)	Oneovdabigbolz (2)	Skinee Muva (2)	Whoz Dat Guy (2)

KWICK

Memphis vocal group formed at Booker T. Washington High School: Terry Bartlett, Bertram Brown & William Sumlin. Recorded as The Newcomers, 1971-78. Changed name to Kwick with the addition of Vince Williams.

6/7/80	197	2		Kwick	$8	EMI America 17025

Can't Help Myself	I Want To Dance With You	Serious Business	We Ought To Be Dancing	Why Don't We Love Each
Here I Go Again (Another	Let This Moment Be Forever	Tonight Is The Night		Other
Weekend)				

K.W.S.

Dance trio from Nottingham, England: Chris King, Winnie Williams and "Mystic Meg" St. Joseph.

10/17/92	143	5		Please Don't Go (The Album)	$12	Next Plat. 828368

CD includes bonus track

Different Man	I Guess I'll Try It Again	Please Don't Go 6	Rock Your Baby [includes 2	This Time	Where Will You Go When
Hold Back The Night	Keep It Comin' Love	Reach For The Sky	versions]		The Party's Over

KYPER

Rapper. Born Randall Kyper in Baton Rouge, Louisiana.

8/4/90	82	12		Tic Tac Toe	$12	Atlantic 82116

CD contains 2 bonus tracks

Conceited	I Wanna Freak	Throw Down	What Gets Your Body Hyped	What Is This World Comin'	Work It
Dangerous	Let's Rock This Party	**Tic-Tac-Toe** 14	(XTC)	To	
Do It	Satisfaction				

L

★★243★★				**LaBELLE, Patti**		

Born Patricia Holt on 5/24/44 in Philadelphia. Began singing career as leader of the Ordettes which evolved into The Blue Belles. The quartet, formed in Philadelphia in 1962, included Nona Hendryx, Sarah Dash and Cindy Birdsong. Cindy left in 1967 to join The Supremes. Group continued as a trio. In 1971, they shortened their name to LaBelle. Trio disbanded in 1977.

LaBELLE:

12/21/74+	7	28	●	1 Nightbirds	$10	Epic 33075
9/20/75	44	13		2 Phoenix	$10	Epic 33579
9/25/76	94	10		3 Chameleon	$10	Epic 34189

PATTI LaBELLE:

9/24/77	62	16		4 Patti LaBelle	$10	Epic 34847
6/24/78	129	7		5 Tasty	$10	Epic 35335
3/31/79	145	16		6 It's Alright With Me	$10	Epic 35772
4/12/80	114	13		7 Released	$10	Epic 36381
10/3/82	156	4		8 The Spirit's In It	$8	Phil. Int. 37380
1/7/84	40	35	●	9 I'm In Love Again	$8	Phil. Int. 38539
8/10/85	72	29		10 Patti	$8	Phil. Int. 40020
5/24/86	1¹	30	▲	**11 Winner In You**	$8	MCA 5737
7/22/89	86	26		12 Be Yourself	$8	MCA 6292

DEBUT DATE	PEAK POS	WKS CHR	GOLD	ARTIST — Album Title	$	Label & Number

LaBELLE, Patti — Cont'd

DEBUT DATE	PEAK POS	WKS CHR	GOLD	ARTIST — Album Title	$	Label & Number
10/19/91+	71	36	● 13	Burnin'	$12	MCA 10439

CD and cassette contain 2 bonus tracks not available on LP; LP and CD contain bonus track not available on cassette

| 11/28/92 | 135 | 3 | 14 | Live! .... [G-L] | $12 | MCA 10691 |

Action Time (2)
Ain't That Enough (7)
All Girl Band (1)
All Right Now (14)
Are You Lonely? (1)
Be Yourself (12)
Beat My Heart Like A Drum (11)
Black Holes In The Sky (2)
Boats Against The Current (8)
Body Language (9)
Burnin' (The Fire Is Still) Burnin' For You (13)
Can't Bring Me Down (12)
Chameleon (3)
Chances Go Round (2)
Come And Dance With Me (7)
Come Into My Life (3)
Come What May (6)
Cosmic Dancer (2)
Crazy Love (13)
Dan Swit Me (4)
Deliver The Funk (6)
Do I Stand A Chance (4)
Don't Bring Me Down (1)
Don't Let Go (5)

Don't Make Your Angel Cry (7)
Eyes In The Back Of My Head (5)
Family (8)
Far As We Felt Like Goin' (2)
Feels Like Another One (13,14)
Finally We're Back Together Again (11)
Find The Love (7)
Funky Music (9)
Get Ready (Lookin' For Loving) (7)
Get You Somebody New (3)
Give It Up (The Dawning Of Rejection) (7)
Going Down Makes Me Shiver (3)
Good Intentions (2)
Gypsy Moths (3)
Here You Come Again (18)
I Can Fly (12)
I Can't Complain (12)
I Can't Forget You (10)
I Don't Do Duets (13)
I Don't Go Shopping (7)

I Don't Like Goodbyes (medley) (14)
I Fell In Love Without Warning (8)
I Got It Bad (12)
I Hear Your Voice (13)
I See Home (5)
I Think About You (4)
I'll Never, Never Give Up (9)
I'm In Love Again (9)
I'm Scared Of You (12)
If Only You Knew (9,14) 46
If You Asked Me To (12) 79
If You Don't Know Me By Now (10)
Isn't It A Shame (3)
It Took A Long Time (10)
It's Alright With Me (6)
Joy To Have Your Love (4)
Kiss Away The Pain (11)
Lady Marmalade (1,14) 1
Little Girls (5)
Living Double (10)
Look To The Rainbow (10)
Love And Learn (6)
Love Bankrupt (9)
Love 89 (12)

Love Has Finally Come (7)
Love Is Just A Touch Away (6)
Love Lives (8)
Love, Need And Want You (9)
Love, Man (Oh, Where Can You Be?) (9)
Man In A Trenchcoat (Voodoo) (3)
Messin' With My Mind (2)
Monkey See - Monkey Do (3)
Most Likely You Go Your Way (And I'll Go Mine) (4)
Music Is My Way Of Life (6)
My Best Was Good Enough (6)
Need A Little Faith (12)
New Attitude (14)
Nightbird (1)
Oh, People (11) 29
On My Own (11) 1
Over The Rainbow (8,14)
Phoenix (The Amazing Flight Of A Lone Star) (2)
Quiet Time (5)

Release (7)
Release Yourself (13,14)
Rocking Pneumonia And The Boogie Woogie Flu (5)
Save The Last Dance For Me (5)
Shoot Him On Sight (8)
Shy (10)
Since I Don't Have You (4)
Sleep With Me Tonight (11)
Slow Burn (2)
Somebody Loves You Baby (You Know Who It Is) (13,14)
Somebody Somewhere (1)
Something Special (Is Gonna Happen Tonight) (11)
Space Children (1)
Spirit's In It (8)
Still In Love (12)
Take The Night Off (2)
Teach Me Tonight (Me Gusta Tu Baile) (5)
Temptation (13)
There's A Winner In You (11)
Twisted (11)

Up There With You (14)
We're Not Makin' Love Anymore (13)
What Can I Do For You? (1) 48
What Can I Do For You (10)
What'cha Doing To Me (6)
When Am I Gonna Find True Love (9)
When You Love Somebody (I'm Saving My Love For You) (13)
When You've Been Blessed (Feels Like Heaven) (13,14)
Where I Wanna Be (10)
Who's Watching The Watcher? (3)
Wind Beneath My Wings (14)
Yo Mister (12)
You And Me (6)
You Are My Friend (4,14)
You Can't Judge A Book By The Cover (4)
You Make It So Hard (To Say No) (5)
You Turn Me On (1)
You're Mine Tonight (11)

L.A. BOPPERS

R&B-bop quartet led by Vance Tenort (vocals, percussion). Formed in Los Angeles as backup band for Side Effect.

| 3/15/80 | 85 | 11 | | L.A. Boppers .... | $8 | Mercury 3816 |

Are We Wrong
Be-Bop Dancin'

Funk It Out
I Can't Stay

Is This The Best (Bop-Doo-Wah)
Saturday

Life Is What You Make It
You Did It Good

Watching Life

LACE

Black female trio: Lisa Frazier, Vivian Ross and Kathy Merrick.

| 1/23/88 | 187 | 5 | | Shades Of Lace .... | $8 | Wing 833451 |

Don't Get So Emotional
Falling In Love

How Could It Be
Keep It Comin'

My Love Is Deep
Since You Came Over Me

Still In Love
Triple Threat

LADD, Cheryl

Born Cheryl Stoppelmoor on 7/2/51 in Huron, South Dakota. Played Kris Monroe on the TV series Charlie's Angels. Voice on the cartoon series Josie & The Pussycats. Married to David Ladd (son of actor Alan Ladd) from 1973-79. Married producer/songwriter Brian Russell (Brian & Brenda) in 1981.

| 8/12/78 | 129 | 11 | 1 | Cheryl Ladd .... | $12 | Capitol 11808 |
| 4/28/79 | 179 | 3 | 2 | Dance Forever .... | $12 | Capitol 11927 |

Better Days (2)
Dance Forever (2)
Good Good Lovin' (1)
Here Is A Song (1)

I Know I'll Never Love This Way Again (1)
I'll Come Runnin' (1)
Lady Gray (1)
Missing You (2)

On The Run (2)
Rock And Roll Slave (2)
Rose Nobody Knows (1)
SkinnyDippin' (1)
Still Awake (2)

Teach Me Tonight (2)
Think It Over (1) 34
Thunder In The Distance (2)
Walking In The Rain (1)

Whatever Would I Do Without You (2)
You Turn Me Around (1)
You're The Only One I Ever Needed (2)

L.A. DREAM TEAM

West Coast rap group led by Rudy Pardee (from Cleveland) and Chris Wilson (from Watts).

| 9/13/86 | 138 | 7 | 1 | Kings Of The West Coast .... | $8 | MCA 5779 |
| 11/14/87 | 162 | 4 | 2 | Bad To The Bone .... | $8 | MCA 42042 |

And The Orchestra Plays (1)
Calling On The Dream Team (1)

Don't Push Me (2)
Dream Team Is In The House (1)

For Lisa For Love (2)
Hollywood Boulevard (1)
Just Chill'n [includes 2 versions] (2)

Kings Of The West Coast (1)
Nursery Rhymes (1)
Rockberry Jam (1)

Rudy And Snake (2)
She Only Rock And Rolls (2)
Stop To Start (2)

Uhh! Song (2)
What's A Skeezer? (2)
You're Just Too Young (1)

L.A. EXPRESS

Jazz quintet minus leader/saxophonist Tom Scott. Also charted with Tom Scott.

| 3/6/76 | 167 | 8 | | L.A. Express .... [I] | $10 | Caribou 33940 |

Cry Of The Eagle
Down The Middle

It's Happening Right Now
Midnite Flite

Shrug
Stairs

Suavements (Gently)
Transylvania Choo Choo

Western Horizon

LAFLAMME, David

Leader of the San Francisco "flower-rock" group It's A Beautiful Day. Electric violinist/vocalist. Born on 4/5/41 in Salt Lake City.

| 12/25/76+ | 159 | 6 | | White Bird .... | $10 | Amherst 1007 |

Baby Be Wise
Easy Woman

Hot Summer Day

Spirit Of America

Swept Away

This Man

White Bird 89

L.A. GUNS

Hollywood male hard-rock group led by vocalist Philip Lewis and founded by guitarist Tracii Guns. Includes Mick Cripps, Kelly Nickels and Steve Riley. Guns was also a member of Contraband in 1991.

2/6/88	50	33	1	L.A. Guns	$8	Vertigo 834144
9/16/89+	38	56	● 2	Cocked & Loaded	$8	Vertigo 838592
7/13/91	42	18	3	Hollywood Vampires	$12	Polydor 849485

3-D cover includes 3-D glasses

Ballad Of Jayne (2) 33
Big House (3)
Bitch Is Back (1)

Cry No More (1)
Crystal Eyes (3)
Dirty Luv (3)

Down In The City (1)
Electric Gypsy (1)
Give A Little (2)

Here It Comes (3)
Hollywood Tease (1)
I Found You (3)

I'm Addicted (2)
It's Over Now (3) 62
Kiss My Love Goodbye (3)

Letting Go (2)
Magdalaine (2)
Malaria (2)

DEBUT DATE	PEAK POS	WKS CHR	GOLD	ARTIST — Album Title	$	Label & Number

L.A. GUNS — Cont'd

My Koo Ka Choo (3)   One More Reason (1)   Rip And Tear (2)   Shoot For Thrills (1)   Slap In The Face (2)   Some Lie 4 Love (3)
Never Enough (2)   One Way Ticket (1)   17 Crash (2)   Showdown (Riot On Sunset)   Sleazy Come Easy Go (2)   Wheels Of Fire (2)
No Mercy (1)   Over The Edge (3)   Sex Action (1)   (2)   Snake Eyes Boogie (3)   Wild Obsession (3)
Nothing To Lose (1)

LAID BACK

Danish synth-pop duo: Tim Stahl (keyboards) and John Guldberg (guitar). Highly successful in Europe for three years before their U.S. debut.

| 3/31/84 | 67 | 15 | | ...Keep Smiling | $8 | Sire 25058 |

Don't Be Mean   Fly Away (medley)   Slowmotion Girl   Sunshine Reggae   Walking In The Sunshine   **White Horse 26**
Elevator Boy   High Society Girl   So Wie So   (medley)

LAINE, Cleo

Jazz singer. Born Clementina Dinah Campbell in England in 1927 to a Jamaican father and British mother. Joined the Dankworth Seven in 1952. Married bandleader Johnny Dankworth in 1958.

4/6/74	157	8		1 Cleo Laine Live!!! at Carnegie Hall ....[L]	$10	RCA 5015
7/20/74	199	1		2 Day By Day	$10	Buddah 5607
12/28/74+	168	5		3 A Beautiful Thing	$10	RCA 5059
2/7/76	158	10		4 Born On A Friday	$10	RCA 5113
12/4/76	138	11		5 Porgy & Bess	$12	RCA 1831 [2]

RAY CHARLES/CLEO LAINE
includes 7 instrumentals by Frank DeVol: "Summertime," "I Got Plenty O'Nuttin'," "Strawberry Woman," "It Ain't Necessarily So," "There's A Boat Dat's Leavin' Soon For New York," "I Loves You, Porgy" and "Oh, Bess, O Where's My Bess"

| 7/26/80 | 150 | 6 | | 6 Sometimes When We Touch .... | $8 | RCA 3628 |

CLEO LAINE & JAMES GALWAY

All In Love Is Fair (3)   Do You Really Want Him (4)   It Ain't Necessarily So (5)   Play It Again, Sam (6)   Stop And Smell The Roses (1,2)   What You Want Wid Bess? [solo: Cleo] (5)
Any Place I Hang My Hat Is Home (4)   Don't Talk Now (2)   Keep Loving Me (6)   Please Don't Talk About Me When I'm Gone (1)   Strawberry Woman [solo: Cleo] (5)   Wish You Were Here (I Do Miss You) (1)
Anyone Can Whistle (6)   Drifting, Dreaming (Gymnopedie No. 1) (6)   Least You Can Do Is The Best You Can (3)   Prepare Ye The Way Of The Lord (medley) (2)   Streets Of London (4)   You Must Believe In Spring (1)
Beautiful Thing (3)   Feel The Warm (4)   Let Me Be The One (4)   Rainy Day Man (2)   Summer Knows (3)
Bess, You Is My Woman (5)   Fluter's Ball (6)   Life Is A Wheel (3)   Ridin' High (1)   Summertime (5)
Big Best Shoes (1)   Gimme A Pig Foot & A Bottle Of Beer (1)   Like A Sad Song (6)   Send In The Clowns (1,3)   Sunday (4)
Bill (1)   Good, Bad But Beautiful (4)   Living Is Easy (4)   Skip-A-Long Sam (3)   They Needed Each Other (3)
Birdsong (Sambalaya) (4)   Here Come De Honeyman (5)   Lo! Hear The Gentle Lark (6)   Skylark (6)   They Pass By Singin' [solo: Cleo] (5)
Both Sides Now (2)   How, Where, When? (6)   Make It With You (2)   Slow Motion (2)   Traces (2)
Can It Be True (2)   I Got Plenty O'Nuttin' (5)   Music (1)   Something's Wrong (2)   Unlucky Woman (Born On A Friday) (4)
Colours Ran (4)   I Know Where I'm Going (1)   My Man's Gone Now [solo: Cleo] (5)   Sometimes When We Touch (6)   Until It's Time For You To Go (3)
Come Back To Me (4)   I Loves You Porgy (3,5)   Oh, Doctor Jesus [solo: Cleo] (5)   Still Was The Night (6)
Consuelo's Love Theme (6)   I Think It's Gonna Rain Today (4)   Perdido (1)
Control Yourself (1)
Day By Day (medley) (2)

LAINE, Frankie

Born Frank Paul LoVecchio on 3/30/13 in Chicago. To Los Angeles in the early 1940s. First recorded for Exclusive in 1945. With Johnny Moore's Three Blazers. Signed to Mercury label in 1947. Dynamic style found favor with black and white audiences.

4/20/57	13	12		1 Rockin'	$30	Columbia 975
10/23/61	71	37		2 Hell Bent For Leather!	$20	Columbia 8415
5/13/67	16	29		3 I'll Take Care Of Your Cares	$15	ABC 604
10/14/67	162	2		4 I Wanted Someone To Love	$15	ABC 608
3/23/68	127	9		5 To Each His Own	$15	ABC 628
4/19/69	55	11		6 You Gave Me A Mountain	$15	ABC 682

Allegra (6)   Green, Green Grass Of Home (5)   **I'll Take Care Of Your Cares (3) 39**   On The Sunny Side Of The Street (1)   There's Not A Moment To Spare (4)   You Taught Me How To Love
Along The Navajo Trail (2)   Gunfight At O.K. Corral (2)   I'm Free (3)   Place In The Shade (6)   3:10 To Yuma (2)   You Now Teach Me To Forget (4)
Blue Turning Grey Over You (1)   Gypsy (4)   I'm Happy To Hear You're Sorry (5)   Rawhide (2)   **To Each His Own (5) 82**   **You Wanted Someone To Play With (I Wanted Someone To Love) (4) 48**
Born To Be With You (6)   Hanging Tree (2)   I've Got A Right To Cry (3)   Real True Meaning Of Love (4)   Walk On Out Of My Mind (6)
Bowie Knife (2)   Heartless One (3)   If I Didn't Care (3)   Rockin' Chair (1)   Wanted Man (2)   You're Breaking My Heart (3)
By The River Sainte Marie (1)   High Noon (Do Not Forsake Me) (2)   It Don't Mean A Thing To Me (5)   Secret Of Happiness (6)   We'll Be Together Again (1)
City Boy (2)   I Don't Want To Set The World On Fire (1)   Laughing On The Outside (Crying On The Inside) (5)   Shine (1)   West End Blues (1)
Cool Water (3)   I Found You (5)   Sing An Italian Song (6)   (What Did I Do To Be So) Black And Blue (1)
Cry Of The Wild Goose (2)   I Heard You Cried Last Night (4)   **Laura, What's He Got That I Ain't Got (4) 66**   Sometimes (I Just Can't Stand You) (4)   What Do You Do With An Old Old Song? (3)
Don't Make Promises (6)   I Need You (5)   **Making Memories (3) 35**   Somewhere There's Someone (4)   You Always Hurt The One You Love (5)
Ev'ry Street's A Boulevard (In Old New York) (4)   I Wish I Had Someone Like You (5)   Maybe (3)   Story Of My Life (6)   **You Gave Me A Mountain (6) 24**
Fresh Out Of Tears (6)   I Wish You Were Jealous Of Me (3)   Meet Me Half Way (5)   That Ain't Right (1)   **You, No One But You (4) 83**
Give Me A Kiss For Tomorrow (1)   Moment Of Truth (3)   That Lucky Old Sun (1)
Give Me Your Kisses (I'll Give You My Heart) (4)   Mule Train (2)   That's My Desire (1)

LAKE

German progressive rock sextet — James Hopkins-Harrison, lead singer.

| 8/20/77 | 92 | 15 | | Lake .... | $8 | Columbia 34763 |

Between The Lines   Do I Love You   Key To The Rhyme   Sorry To Say
Chasing Colours   Jesus Came Down   On The Run   **Time Bomb 83**

LAKE, Greg

Born on 11/10/48 in Bournemouth, England. Guitarist/bassist with King Crimson and Emerson, Lake & Palmer.

| 10/31/81 | 62 | 17 | | Greg Lake .... | $8 | Chrysalis 1357 |

Black And Blue   It Hurts   Lie, The   Love You Too Much   Retribution Drive
For Those Who Dare   **Let Me Love You Once 48**   Long Goodbye   Nuclear Attack   Someone

DEBUT DATE	PEAK POS	WKS CHR	GOLD	ARTIST — Album Title	$	Label & Number
				LAKESIDE		
				Nine-man funk aggregation from Dayton, Ohio, formed in 1969. Consisted of Tiemeyer McCain, Thomas Oliver Shelby, Otis Stokes and Mark Wood (vocals), Steve Shockley (guitar), Norman Beavers (keyboards), Marvin Craig (bass), Fred Alexander, Jr. (drums) and Fred Lewis (percussion).		
1/6/79	74	19		1 Shot Of Love	$8	Solar 2937
11/3/79	141	18		2 Rough Riders	$8	Solar 3490
11/29/80+	16	35	●	3 Fantastic Voyage	$8	Solar 3720
12/12/81	109	10		4 Keep On Moving Straight Ahead	$8	Solar 3974
1/9/82	58	23		5 Your Wish Is My Command	$8	Solar 26
5/28/83	42	18		6 Untouchables	$8	Solar 60204
7/28/84	68	15		7 Outrageous	$8	Solar 60355

Alibi (6)
All For You (4)
All In My Mind (2)
Anything For You (4)
Baby I'm Lonely (7)
Be My Lady (4)
Eveready Man (3)
Fantastic Voyage (3) 55
From 9:00 Until (2)
Given In To Love (1)
Hold On Tight (1)

Hollywood Story ..see: Tinsel Town Theory
I Can't Get You Out Of My Head (2)
I Love Everything You Do (3)
I Need You (3)
I Want To Hold Your Hand (5)
I'll Be Standing By (5)
I'll Never Leave You (2)
If You Like Our Music (Get On Up And Move) (2)

It's All The Way Live (1)
It's Got To Be Love (4)
It's You (4)
Keep On Moving Straight Ahead (4)
Magic Moments (5)
Make It Right (7)
Make My Day (7)
One Minute After Midnight (1)
Outrageous (7)
Pull My Strings (2)

Raid (6)
Real Love (6)
Restrictions (7)
Rough Rider (2)
Say Yes (3)
Shot Of Love (1)
Show You The Way (7)
So Let's Love (6)
Something About That Woman (5)
Something About You (7)
Songwriter (5)

Special (5)
Strung Out (3)
Time (1)
Tinsel Town Theory (6)
Turn The Music Up (6)
Untouchable (6)
Urban Man (5)
Visions Of My Mind (1)
We Want You (On The Floor) (4)
Worn 'N Torn (7)
Your Love Is On The One (3)

Your Wish Is My Command (5)

				LaMOND, George		
				Born George Garcia on 2/25/67 in Washington, D.C. and raised in the Bronx. With his cousin Joey Kid, formed New York City club band Loose Touch.		
8/18/90	104	10		Bad Of The Heart	$12	Columbia 45488

Bad Of The Heart 25
Look Into My Eyes 63

Love's Contagious
No Matter What 49

Passing Time
Serenade You

Stop That Girl
What Could've Been

Who Needs Love
Without You

				LANCE, Major		
				Born on 4/4/42 in Chicago. Soul singer. First recorded for Mercury in 1959. Lived in Britain, 1972-74. Had own Osiris label with Al Jackson of the MG's in 1975. In prison for selling cocaine, 1978-81.		
10/5/63	113	3		1 The Monkey Time	$20	Okeh 12105
3/28/64	100	9		2 Um, Um, Um, Um, Um, Um/The Best Of Major Lance [G]	$20	Okeh 12106
9/4/65	109	6		3 Major's Greatest Hits [G]	$20	Okeh 12110

Ain't It A Shame (3) 91
Bird, The (1)
Come See (3) 40
Delilah (1)
Girls (3) 68
Gotta Get Away (3)

Gotta Right To Cry (2)
Gypsy Woman (2)
Hey Little Girl (2,3) 13
Hitchhike (1)
I'm The One (1)
It Ain't No Use (3) 68

It's All Right (2)
Just One Look (1)
Keep On Loving You (1)
Land Of A Thousand Dances (1)
Little Young Lover (2)

Mama Didn't Know (1,2)
Matador, The (3) 20
Monkey Time (1,2,3) 8
Pride And Joy (1)
Rhythm (3) 24
Soldierboy (1)

Sometimes I Wonder (3) 64
Sweet Music (3)
That's What Mama Say (2)
Think Nothing About It (3)
Um, Um, Um, Um, Um, Um (2,3) 5

Watusi (1)
What's Happening (1)
You'll Want Me Back (2)

				LANE, Robin, & The Chartbusters		
				Robin is the daughter of Dean Martin's pianist, Ken Lane.		
4/25/81	172	4		Imitation Life	$8	Warner 3537

For You
Idiot

Imitation Life
No Control

Pretty Mala
Rather Be Blind

Say Goodbye
Send Me An Angel

Solid Rock
What The People Are Doing

				LANE, Ronnie — see TOWNSHEND, Pete		
				lang, k.d.		
				Kathryn Dawn Lang from Consort, Alberta, Canada. Born on 11/2/61. Named her group The Reclines, in honor of Patsy Cline. Left country music in 1992.		
5/28/88	73	25	●	1 Shadowland	$8	Sire 25724
				produced by Owen Bradley (producer of Patsy Cline and Brenda Lee)		
6/17/89+	69	56	●	2 Absolute Torch And Twang	$8	Sire 25877
				k.d. lang and THE RECLINES		
4/4/92	44	45↑	●	3 Ingenue	$12	Sire 26840

Big Big Love (2)
Big Boned Gal (2)
Black Coffee (1)
Busy Being Blue (1)
Constant Craving (3) 38
Didn't I (2)
Don't Let The Stars Get In Your Eyes (1)
Full Moon Full Of Love (2)

Honkey Tonk Angels' Medley (1)
I Wish I Didn't Love You So (1)
I'm Down To My Last Cigarette (1)
It's Me (2)
Lock, Stock And Teardrops (1)

Luck In My Eyes (2)
Mind Of Love (3)
Miss Chatelaine (3)
Nowhere To Stand (2)
Outside Myself (3)
Pullin' Back The Reins (2)
Save Me (3)
Season Of Hollow Soul (3)
Shadowland (1)

So It Shall Be (3)
Still Thrives This Love (3)
Sugar Moon (1)
Tears Don't Care Who Cries Them (1)
Tears Of Love's Recall (3)
Three Days (2)
Trail Of Broken Hearts (2)

Walkin' In And Out Of Your Arms (2)
Wallflower Waltz (2)
(Waltz Me) Once Again Around The Dance Floor (1)
Wash Me Clean (3)
Western Stars (1)

				LANGFORD, Frances — see AMECHE, Don		
				LANIN, Lester, And His Orchestra		
				Born on 8/26/11. Raised in Philadelphia. Leader of society dance bands. First five albums below contain medleys of 25-50 songs with a party atmosphere background.		
6/24/57	7	10		1 Dance To The Music Of Lester Lanin [I]	$12	Epic 3340
11/11/57	18	2		2 Lester Lanin And His Orchestra [I]	$12	Epic 3242
2/3/58	17	2		3 Lester Lanin At The Tiffany Ball [I]	$12	Epic 3410
6/9/58	19	3		4 Lester Lanin Goes To College [I]	$12	Epic 3474
11/17/58	12	4		5 Have Band, Will Travel [I]	$12	Epic 3520
1/20/62	37	20		6 Twistin' in High Society! [I]	$10	Epic 3825

Acceleration Waltz (medley) (2)
Adios Muchachos (5)
After The Ball (medley) (1)
After You've Gone (medley) (4)

Alexander's Ragtime Band (medley) (3)
All Of You (medley) (3)
All The Things You Are (medley) (1)
Always (medley) (5)

Always True To You In My Fashion (medley) (3)
Anything Can Happen - Mambo (medley) (4)
Anything Goes (medley) (1)
April In Portugal (medley) (3)

Arrivederci Roma (medley) (5)
Artist's Life (medley) (3)
At The Darktown Strutters' Ball (1,6)

Bali Ha'i (medley) (5)
Ballin' The Jack (medley) (1)
Baubles, Bangles And Beads (medley) (5)
Babes In The Wood (medley) (1)
Best Things In Life Are Free (medley) (1)

Bewitched (medley) (3)
Big "D" (medley) (3)
Bill Bailey, Won't You Please Come Home? (medley) (1)
Blue Moon (4,6)
Blue Skies (medley) (4)

LANIN, Lester, And His Orchestra — Cont'd

Buckle Down, Winsocki (medley) (3)
Button Up Your Overcoat (medley) (1)
C'est Magnifique (medley) (2)
Carioca (4)
Charleston (4,6)
Cheek To Cheek (medley) (2)
Chicago (medley) (5)
Colonel Bogey (medley) (4)
Continental, The (medley) (2)
Dancing In The Dark (medley) (2)
Dancing On The Ceiling (medley) (2)
Deep Purple (medley) (4)
Die Schoenbrunner (3)
Dirty Lady! (medley) (3)
Dixie (medley) (3)
Do I Love You Because You're Beautiful? (medley) (4)
Down Home Rag (medley) (1)
Easy To Love (medley) (4)
Ev'rything I've Got (medley) (4)
Fidgety Feet (medley) (5)
A Fine Romance (medley) (5)
Five Foot Two, Eyes Of Blue (medley) (5)
A Foggy Day (medley) (2)
Frankie & Johnny (medley) (5)
From This Moment On (medley) (2)
Gang That Sang "Heart Of My Heart" (medley) (5)
Get Me To The Church On Time (medley) (1)
Getting To Know You (medley) (3)
Greensleeves (medley) (1)
Guitar Boogie Twist (6)

Guys And Dolls (medley) (5)
Hawaiian War Chant (medley) (4)
Heart (medley) (5)
Hello Ma Baby (medley) (1)
Hello Young Lovers (medley) (3)
Hey, There (medley) (5)
A Hot Time In The Old Town Tonight (medley) (5)
How High The Moon (medley) (5)
I Can't Give You Anything But Love (medley) (4)
I Could Have Danced All Night (medley) (1)
I Could Write A Book (medley) (3)
I Don't Know Why (I Just Do) (5,6)
I Want My Mama (5)
I Wish I Were In Love Again (medley) (4)
I Won't Dance (medley) (3)
I'm In The Mood For Love (medley) (4)
I've Got A Crush On You (medley) (2)
I've Grown Accustomed To Her Face (medley) (5)
If I Loved You (medley) (3)
If I Were A Bell (medley) (5)
If You Knew Susie Like I Know Susie (medley) (1)
In The Mood (medley) (4)
In The Still Of The Night (medley) (2)
It's A Lovely Day Today (medley) (5)
It's All Right With Me (medley) (2)
It's Delovely (medley) (1)

It's Good To Be Alive (medley) (3)
Ja-Da (medley) (5)
Jazz Me Blues (medley) (1)
Johnson Rag (medley) (5)
Josephine (5)
Jubilation T. Cornpone (medley) (5)
June Is Bustin' Out All Over (medley) (3)
Just In Time (medley) (3)
Just One Of Those Things (medley) (2)
La Mer (Beyond The Sea) (medley) (1)
Lady Is A Tramp (medley) (2)
Last Time I Saw Paris (medley) (5)
Laura (medley) (4)
Lester Lanin Cha-Cha (medley) (4)
Linda Mujer (5)
Little Brown Jug (medley) (4)
Love For Sale (medley) (1)
Love Is A Many-Splendored Thing (medley) (4)
Love Is Here To Stay (medley) (4)
Love Walked In (medley) (4)
Mack The Knife (6)
Make Believe (medley) (3)
Mambo Jumbo Samba (1)
Marianne (medley) (1)
Mine (medley) (2)
Mississippi Mud (medley) (2)
Mister Sandman (medley) (4)
Moonglow (medley) (4)
Mountain Greenery (medley) (2)
Music Goes 'Round And 'Round (medley) (3)
Muskrat Ramble (medley) (2,6)

My Blue Heaven (medley) (4)
My Funny Valentine (medley) (1)
My Heart Belongs To Daddy (medley) (3)
Namely You (medley) (5)
Night And Day (medley) (1)
O Sole Mio (medley) (5)
Oh What A Beautiful Morning! (medley) (3)
Oklahoma (medley) (1)
Ol' Man River (medley) (3)
Old Devil Moon (medley) (3)
On The Street Where You Live (medley) (1)
On The Sunny Side Of The Street (medley) (4)
Once In Love With Amy (medley) (5)
Orchids In The Moonlight (medley) (3)
Organ Twist (6)
Over The Rainbow (5)
Panama (medley) (4)
Party's Over (medley) (5)
Peg O' My Heart (medley) (5)
People Will Say We're In Love (medley) (2)
Poor People Of Paris (medley) (5)
Por Favor (medley) (4)
Puttin' On The Ritz (medley) (5)
Rain In Spain (medley) (5)
Rhode Island Is Famous For You (medley) (3)
Ridin' High (medley) (2)
'S Wonderful (medley) (4)
Say Darling (medley) (5)
Sentimental Journey (medley) (4)
September Song (medley) (1)
Seventy-Six Trombones (medley) (5)

Shall We Dance (medley) (3)
Short'nin' Bread (medley) (5)
Smoke Gets In Your Eyes (medley) (3)
So In Love (medley) (3)
Something's Gotta Give (medley) (1)
Sophisticated Swing (medley) (4)
South Pacific Medley (5)
St. Louis Blues (medley) (3)
Standing On The Corner (medley) (5)
Stardust (medley) (4)
Steppin' In Society (medley) (2)
Stumbling (medley) (5)
Sunny (medley) (1)
Sunshine Girl (medley) (3)
Surrey With The Fringe On Top (medley) (3)
Sweet Georgia Brown (2,6)
Taking A Chance On Love (medley) (4)
Tchaikovsky: Waltz From Eugen Onegin (1)
Tenderly (medley) (4)
That Old Black Magic (medley) (4)
There's A Small Hotel (medley) (1)
They Can't Take That Away From Me (medley) (4)
They Say It's Wonderful (medley) (5)
Till There Was You (medley) (5)
Tin Roof Blues (medley) (4)
Too Darn Hot (medley) (3)
Toot, Toot, Tootsie, Goo'bye (medley) (2)
Top Hat, White Tie And Tails (medley) (5)

Toreador Song (medley) (3)
True Love (medley) (4)
Twelfth Street Rag (medley) (3)
Twisting Saints (6)
Waltz From "Der Rosenkavalier" (medley) (2)
Wang, Wang Blues (medley) (3)
'Way Down Yonder In New Orleans (3,6)
Wedding Bells Are Breaking Up That Old Gang Of Mine (medley) (5)
When The Saints Go Marching In (medley) (2)
Whiffenpoof Song (medley) (5)
Who? (medley) (3)
Why Do I Love You (medley) (3)
Wine, Women And Song (medley) (1)
With A Little Bit Of Luck (medley) (1)
A Wonderful Guy (medley) (5)
Wouldn't It Be Lovely (medley) (5)
Wunderbar (medley) (5)
You're Just In Love (medley) (5)
You're Sensational (medley) (4)
You're So Right For Me (medley) (5)

LANOIS, Daniel

Renown producer. Worked with U2 (*The Joshua Tree*), Peter Gabriel (*So*), Bob Dylan (*Oh Mercy*), Robbie Robertson and others. Born in Hull, Canada in 1951.

1/20/90	166	5		Acadie	$12	Opal/War. 25969

among his backing musicians: Brian Eno, Adam Clayton & Larry Mullen, Jr. (U2), Art & Aaron Neville; Acadie was once the French name for Nova Scotia

Amazing Grace
Fisherman's Daughter
Ice
Jolie Louise
Maker, The
O Marie
Silium's Hill
St. Ann's Gold
Still Water
Under A Stormy Sky
Where The Hawkwind Kills
White Mustang II

LANZ, David

Seattle-based New Age synthesist/songwriter. Lanz is pronounced: lahns.

1/30/88	125	12		1 Natural States	[I]	$8	Narada E. 63001

DAVID LANZ & PAUL SPEER

11/5/88	180	6		2 Cristofori's Dream	[I]	$8	Narada L. 61021

title refers to Bartolommeo Cristofori, the inventor of the piano

Allegro/985 (1)
Behind The Waterfall (1)
Cristofori's Dream (2)
Faces Of The Forest Part 1 & 2 (1)
First Light (1)
Free Fall (2)
Green Into Gold (2)
Lento/984 (1)
Miranova (1)
Mountain (1)
Rain Forest (1)
Spiral Dance (2)
Summer's Child (2)
Whiter Shade Of Pale (2)
Wings To Altair (2)

★★408★★ LANZA, Mario

Born Alfredo Cocozza on 1/31/21 in Philadelphia. Became the most popular operatic tenor since Caruso (his voice featured in seven movies, though no theatrical operas) until his death on 10/7/59.

4/28/56	9	6		1 Serenade	[S]	$25	RCA 1996
3/17/58	7	8		2 Seven Hills Of Rome	[S]	$25	RCA 2211

side 1: soundtrack; side 2: various Lanza recordings

11/2/59	5	46		3 For The First Time	[S]	$25	RCA 2338

Mario sings and stars in the above 3 films

12/14/59+	4	4		4 Lanza Sings Christmas Carols	[X]	$20	RCA 2333
5/16/60	4	53		5 Mario Lanza Sings Caruso Favorites	[F]	$20	RCA 2393

recorded in Rome, June 1959

12/18/61+	67	5		6 Lanza Sings Christmas Carols	[X-R]	$20	RCA 2333
10/6/62+	64	41		7 I'll Walk With God	[E]	$20	RCA 2607
8/8/64	87	15		8 The Best Of Mario Lanza	[G]	$15	RCA 2748

And This Is My Beloved (8)
Arrivederci Roma (2,8) **97**
Away In A Manger (4)
Be My Love (8)
Because (7)
Because You're Mine (8)
Cilea: L'Arlesiana: Lamento Di Federico (1)
Come Dance With Me (2)
Come Prima (3)
DeCurtis: Torna A Surriento (1)
Deck The Halls (4)
Di Capua: 'O Sole Mio (3)
Do You Wonder (3)
Earthbound (2) **53**
First Noel (4)
Funiculi' Funicula (8)
Giordano: Fedora: Act II: Amor Ti Vieta (1)
God Rest Ye Merry, Gentlemen (4)
Grieg: Ich Liebe Dich (8)
Guardian Angels (4,7)
Hark! The Herald Angels Sing (4)
Hofbrauhaus Song (3)
I Love Thee (7)
I Saw Three Ships (4)
I'll Walk With God (7)
Ideale (5)
It Came Upon A Midnight Clear (4)
Jezebel (medley) (2)
Joy To The World (4)
Kiss, A (8)
L'Alba Separa Dalla Luce L'Ombra (5)
La Mia Canzone (5)
Leoncavallo: Pagliacci: Vesti La Guibba (3,8)
Lolita (2,5)
Lord's Prayer (7)
Love In A Home (2)
Loveliest Night Of The Year (8)
Luna D'Estate (5)
Mascagni: Addio Alla Madre (7)
Mazurka (3)
Memories Are Made Of This (medley) (2)
Meyerbeer: L'Africana: Act III: O Paradiso (1)
Musica Proibita (5)
My Destiny (1,2)
Neapolitan Dance (3)
Never Till Now (2)
None But The Lonely Heart (7)
O Christmas Tree (4)
O Come, All Ye Faithful (Adeste Fideles) (4)
O Holy Night (7)
O Little Town Of Bethlehem (4)
O, Mon Amour (3)
O Sole Mio ..see: Di Capua
One Alone (4)
Only A Rose (8)
Pineapple Pickers (3)
Pour Un Baiser (5)
Puccini: La Boheme: Act I: O Soave Fanciulla (1)
Puccini: Turandot: Act III: Nessun Dorma (1)
Rossini: La Danza (1)

DEBUT DATE	PEAK POS	WKS CHR	GOLD	ARTIST — Album Title	$	Label & Number

LANZA, Mario — Cont'd

| | | | | | | |

Santa Lucia (5,8)
Schubert: Ave Maria (1,3,7)
Senza Nisciuno (5)
Serenade (1,2)
Serenade (8)
Serenata (5)

Seven Hills Of Rome (2)
Silent Night (4)
Somebody Bigger Than You And I (7)
Strauss, R.: Der Rosenkavalier: Act I: Di Rigori Armato (1)

Tarantella (3)
Temptation (medley) (2)
There's Gonna Be A Party Tonight (2)
Through The Years (7)
Trees (7)

Trembling Of A Leaf (7)
Vaghissima Sembianza (5)
Verdi: Aida: Act I (3)
Verdi: Il Trovatore: Act III: Di Quella Pira (1)
Verdi: Otello: Act III: Dio Ti Gioconda (1)

Verdi: Otello: Finale (3)
Verdi: Questa O Quella (from Rigoletto) (2)
Vieni Sul Mar (5)
Virgin's Slumber Song (7)
We Three Kings Of Orient Are (4)

When The Saints Go Marching In (medley) (2)

LARKIN, Billy, & The Delegates
Soul-funk quartet led by Billy on organ.

| 4/2/66 | 148 | 2 | | Hole In The Wall .... [I] | $15 | World Pac. 1837 |

Agent Double-O-Soul
And I Love Her

Blue Satin
Close Your Eyes

Hole In The Wall
Hot Sauce

Hot Toddy
"In" Crowd

In The Midnight Hour
Little Mama

Soul Beat
Taste Of Honey

LARKS, The
Los Angeles R&B group originally named Don Julian & The Meadowlarks: Don Julian (lead singer), Ted Walters and Charles Morrison.

| 1/23/65 | 143 | 4 | | The Jerk .... | $30 | Money 1102 |

Do The Jerk
Jerk, The 7

Jerk Once More
Jerkin' U.S.A.

Keep Jerkin'
Mickey's East Coast Jerk

Slauson Shuffle #1 & 2
Soul Jerk

You Must Believe Me

LARSEN, Neil
Born on 8/7/48 in Cleveland; raised in Siesta Key, Florida. Keyboardist with George Harrison, Dan Fogelberg, Jimmy Cliff and The Allman Brothers.

| 9/1/79 | 139 | 7 | | High Gear .... [I] | $8 | Horizon 738 |

Demonette
Futurama

High Gear
Night Letter

Nile Crescent
Rio Este

This Time Tomorrow

LARSEN-FEITEN BAND
Top session musicians Neil Larsen (keyboards) and Buzz Feiten (guitar). Feiten, a former member of the Paul Butterfield Blues Band and Stevie Wonder's band, joined Mr. Mister in 1989.

| 9/13/80 | 142 | 10 | | Larsen-Feiten Band .... | $8 | Warner 3468 |

Aztec Legend
Danger Zone

Further Notice
Make It

Morning Star
Over

She's Not In Love

Who'll Be The Fool Tonight 29

LARSON, Nicolette
Born on 7/17/52 in Helena, Montana and raised in Kansas City. To San Francisco in 1974. Session vocalist with Neil Young, Linda Ronstadt, Van Halen and many others.

11/18/78+	15	37	●	1 Nicolette	$8	Warner 3243
11/3/79	47	21		2 In The Nick Of Time	$8	Warner 3370
1/24/81	62	12		3 Radioland	$8	Warner 3502
8/14/82	75	10		4 All Dressed Up & No Place To Go	$8	Warner 3678

Angels Rejoiced (1)
Baby, Don't You Do It (4)
Back In My Arms (2)
Been Gone Too Long (3)
Breaking Too Many Hearts (2)
Can't Get Away From You (1)
Come Early Mornin' (1)

Daddy (2)
Dancin' Jones (2)
Fallen (2)
Fool For Love (3)
French Waltz (1)
Give A Little (1)
How Can We Go On (3)

I Only Want To Be With You (1) 53
I Want You So Bad (4)
I'll Fly Away (Without You) (4)
Isn't It Always Love (2)
Just In The Nick Of Time (2)
Just Say I Love You (4)

Last In Love (1)
Let Me Go, Love (2) 35
Long Distance Love (3)
Lotta Love (1) 8
Love, Sweet, Love (4)
Mexican Divorce (1)
Nathan Jones (4)

Ooo-eee (3)
Radioland (3)
Rhumba Girl (1) 47
Rio De Janeiro Blue (2)
Say You Will (4)
Still You Linger On (4)
Straight From The Heart (3)

Talk To Me (4)
Tears, Tears And More Tears (3)
Trouble (2)
Two Trains (4)
When You Come Around (3)
You Send Me (1)

LaRUE, D.C.
Born David Charles L'Heureux on 4/26/48 in Meriden, Connecticut. Disco singer.

| 6/26/76 | 139 | 13 | | 1 Ca-the-drals .... | $10 | Pyramid 9003 |
| 1/8/77 | 115 | 11 | | 2 The Tea Dance .... | $10 | Pyramid 9006 |

Bad News (2)
Broadway Melody (2)
Cathedrals (1) 94

Deep, Dark, Delicious Night (1)

Don't Keep It In The Shadows (1)
Face Of Love (2)

Fanfare (2)
Going Hollywood (2)
I Don't Want To Lose You (1)

I'll Still Be Here For You (1)
Indiscreet (2)

O Ba Ba (No Reino Da Mae Do Ouro) (2)
Tea Dance (2)

LA'S, The
Liverpool quartet: brothers Lee (vocals) and Neil Mavers with John Power and Cammy. La's is slang for lads.

| 7/6/91 | 196 | 1 | | The La's .... | $12 | London 828202 |

Doledrum
Failure

Feelin'
Freedom Song

I Can't Sleep
I.O.U.

Liberty Ship
Looking Glass

Son Of A Gun
There She Goes 49

Timeless Melody
Way Out

LaSALLE, Denise
Born Denise Craig on 7/16/39 in LeFlore County, Mississippi. Soul singer/songwriter. Moved to Chicago in the early 1950s. First recorded for Tarpen (Chess) in 1967. Had own Crajon Productions with husband Bill Jones from 1969.

| 2/5/72 | 120 | 9 | | Trapped By A Thing Called Love .... | $10 | Westbound 2012 |

Catch Me If You Can
Deeper I Go (The Better It Gets)

Do Me Right
Good Goody Getter
Heartbreaker Of The Year

Hung Up, Strung Out
If You Should Loose Me
It's Too Late

Keep It Coming
Now Run And Tell That 46

Trapped By A Thing Called Love 13

LAST, James
Born on 4/17/29 in Bremen, Germany. Producer/arranger/conductor of big cabaret band.

2/19/72	160	5		1 Music From Across The Way	$10	Polydor 5505
8/16/75	172	3		2 Well Kept Secret .... [I]	$10	Polydor 6040
6/28/80	148	8		3 Seduction .... [I]	$8	Polydor 6283

JAMES LAST BAND

Bolero '75 (2)
Chirpy Chirpy Cheep Cheep (1)
Dancing Shadows (1)
Dock Of The Bay (1)
Falling Star (3)
Fantasy (3)

Glow (3)
Here Comes The Sun (1)
Hot Love (1)
I Am...I Said (1)
I Can't Move No Mountains (2)
Inflight (3)

It's Over (3)
Jamaica Farewell (1)
Joy To The World (1)
Jubilation (2)
Love For Sale (2)
Me And You And A Dog Named Boo (1)

Music From Across The Way (1) 84
Night Drive (3)
On The Beach (1)
Power To The People (1)
Prisoner Of Second Avenue, Theme From (2)

Question (2)
Seduction (Love Theme) (3) 28
Slaughter On 10th Avenue (2)
So Excited (3)

South Of The Border Down Mexico Way (1)
Summertime (2)
Vibrations (3)

DEBUT DATE	PEAK POS	WKS CHR	G O L D	ARTIST — Album Title	$	Label & Number

LAST POETS, The
Black protest quartet: Abiodun Oyewole, Alafia Pudim, Omar Ben Hassen and Nilaja. Oyewole left after first album.

| 6/20/70 | 29 | 30 | | 1 The Last Poets .... | $20 | Douglas 3 |
| 4/3/71 | 104 | 15 | | 2 This Is Madness .... | $20 | Douglas 30583 |

Black Is (2)	Gashman (1)	O.D. (2)	Scared Of Revolution (1)	Two Little Boys (1)	White Man's Got A God
Black People What Y'all Gon'	Jones Comin' Down (1)	On The Subway (1)	Surprises (1)	Wake Up Niggers (1)	Complex (2)
Do (2)	Just Because (1)	Opposites (2)	This Is Madness (2)	When The Revolution Comes	
Black Thighs (1)	Mean Machine (2)	Related To What (2)	Time (2)	(1)	
Black Wish (1)	New York, New York (1)	Run Nigger (1)	True Blues (2)		

LAST POETS, The
Black protest trio: David Nelson, Felipe Luciano and Gylan Kain.

| 3/6/71 | 106 | 6 | | Right On! ....[S] | $15 | Juggernaut 8802 |

THE ORIGINAL LAST POETS

Alley	Die Nigga!!!	James Brown	Library, The	Puerto Rican Rhythms	Tell Me Brother
Been Done Already	Hey Now	Jazz	Little Willie Armstrong Jones	Shalimar, The	Today Is A Killer
Black Woman	Into The Streets	Jibaro/My Pretty Nigger	Poetry Is Black	Soul	Un Rifle/Oracion Rifle Prayer

LATEEF, Yusef
Jazz tenor saxophonist/flutist. Born in 1921 in Chattanooga, Tennessee. Raised in Detroit. After high school graduation, played with Lucky Millinder. Worked with Dizzy Gillespie in 1949, then Charlie Mingus in the early 1960s.

| 8/16/69 | 183 | 5 | | Yusef Lateef's Detroit ....[I] | $15 | Atlantic 1525 |

Belle Isle	Eastern Market	Raymond Winchester	That Lucky Old Sun
Bishop School	Livingston Playground	Russell And Eliot	Woodward Avenue

LATIMORE
Born Benjamin Latimore on 9/7/39 in Charleston, Tennessee. Soul singer. With Steve Alaimo in the '60s.

| 3/26/77 | 181 | 5 | | It Ain't Where You Been... .... | $8 | Glades 7509 |

All The Way Lover	It Ain't Where You Been	Let Me Go	Let's Do It In Slow Motion	**Somethin' 'Bout 'Cha** 37	Sweet Vibrations
I Get Lifted					

LATIN ALLIANCE
Members of rap septet are of various Latin American heritages. Formed by Kid Frost in Los Angeles in 1989. Group members are from the Bronx and Los Angeles. A.L.T. was a member.

| 8/24/91 | 133 | 8 | | Latin Alliance .... | $12 | Virgin 91625 |

Can U Feel It	Latinos Unidos (United	**Low Rider (On The**	No Man's Land	Smooth Roughness	What You See Is What You
Know What I'm Sayin'?	Latins)	**Boulevard) 54**	Runnin'	Valla En Paz (Go In Peace)	Get
				What Is An American?	

LaTOUR
William LaTour — solo artist from Chicago.

| 5/11/91 | 145 | 4 | | LaTour .... | $12 | Smash 848323 |

Allen's Got A New Hi-Fi	Blue	Dark Sunglasses	Involved	**People Are Still Having**	Psych
[includes 2 versions]	Cold	Fantasy Soldiers	Laurie Monster	**Sex** [includes 2 versions] 35	
Amazing You					

LATTISAW, Stacy
Born on 11/25/66 in Washington, D.C. Soul singer. Recorded her first album at age 12. Childhood friend of Johnny Gill.

7/5/80	44	28		1 Let Me Be Your Angel	$8	Cotillion 5219
7/25/81	46	15		2 With You	$8	Cotillion 16049
8/28/82	55	16		3 Sneakin' Out	$8	Cotillion 90002
8/27/83	160	8		4 Sixteen	$8	Cotillion 90106
3/31/84	139	8		5 Perfect Combination	$8	Cotillion 90136

STACY LATTISAW & JOHNNY GILL

| 10/11/86 | 131 | 22 | | 6 Take Me All The Way .... | $8 | Motown 6212 |
| 3/5/88 | 153 | 10 | | 7 Personal Attention .... | $8 | Motown 6247 |

Ain't No Mountain High	Don't Throw It All Away (3)	Guys Like You (Give Love A	Jump Into My Life (6)	Million Dollar Babe (4)	Take Me All The Way (6)
Enough (7)	Don't You Want To Feel It	Bad Name) (7)	Jump To The Beat (1)	**Miracles** (4) 40	Tonight I'm Gonna Make
Attack Of The Name Game	(For Yourself) (1)	Hard Way (6)	**Let Me Be Your Angel**	My Love (1)	You Mine (3)
(3) 70	Dreaming (1)	He's Got A Hold On Me (7)	(1) 21	Nail It To The Wall (6) 48	Ways Of Love (4)
Baby I Love You (2)	Dynamite! (1)	Heartbreak Look (5)	Let Me Take You Down (7)	One More Night (6)	What's So Hot 'Bout Bad
Baby It's You (5)	Electronic Eyes (7)	Hey There Lonely Boy (3)	Little Bit Of Heaven (6)	Over The Top (6)	Boys (4)
Black Pumps And Pink	Every Drop Of Your Love (7)	I Could Love You So Divine	Longshot (6)	**Perfect Combination** (5) 75	With You (2)
Lipstick (4)	Falling In Love Again (5)	(3)	Love Me Like The First Time	Personal Attention (7)	You Ain't Leavin' (6)
Block Party (5)	Feel My Love Tonight	I'm Down For You (3)	(6)	Screamin' Off The Top (2)	You Don't Love Me Anymore
Call Me (7)	(medley) (2)	I've Loved You Somewhere	**Love On A Two Way Street**	Sneakin' Out (3)	(1)
Changes (7)	50/50 Love (5)	Before (4)	(2) 26	Spotlight (2)	You Know I Like It (1)
Come Out Of The Shadows	Find Another Lover (7)	It Was So Easy (2)	Love Town (7)	Stacy Rap (medley) (2)	You Take Me To Heaven (2)
(5)	Fun 'N' Games (5)	Johey! (4)	Memories (3)		Young Girl (2)

LAUPER, Cyndi
Born on 6/20/53 in Queens, New York. Recorded an album for Polydor Records in 1980 with the group Blue Angel. Supported by The Hooters, 1983-84. Won the 1984 Best New Artist Grammy Award. In the 1988 film Vibes. Married actor David Thornton on 11/24/91.

12/24/83+	4	96	▲5	1 She's So Unusual	$8	Portrait 38930
10/4/86	4	44	▲	2 True Colors	$8	Portrait 40313
5/27/89	37	21		3 A Night To Remember	$8	Epic 44318

All Through The Night (1) 5	**Girls Just Want To Have**	**I Drove All Night** (3) 6	Maybe He'll Know (2)	911 (2)	Unconditional Love (1)
Boy Blue (2) 71	**Fun** (1) 2	I'll Kiss You (1)	**Money Changes**	One Track Mind (2)	**What's Going On** (2) 12
Calm Inside The Storm (2)	He's So Unusual (1)	Iko Iko (2)	**Everything** (1) 27	Primitive (1)	When You Were Mine (1)
Change Of Heart (2) 3	Heading West (3)	Insecurious (3)	**My First Night Without**	She Bop (1) 3	Witness (1)
Dancing With A Stranger (3)	I Don't Want To Be Your	Kindred Spirit (3)	**You** (3) 62	**Time After Time** (1) 1	Yeah Yeah (1)
Faraway Nearby (2)	Friend (3)	Like A Cat (3)	Night To Remember (3)	**True Colors** (2) 1	

DEBUT DATE	PEAK POS	WKS CHR	GOLD	ARTIST — Album Title	$	Label & Number

LAW, The

British rock duo: vocalist Paul Rodgers (Free, Bad Company, The Firm) and drummer Kenney Jones (Small Faces, Faces, The Who).

| 4/13/91 | 126 | 6 | | The Law .... | $12 | Atlantic 82195 |

Anything For You / Best Of My Love / Come Save Me (Julianne) / For A Little Ride / Laying Down The Law / Miss You In A Heartbeat / Missing You Bad Girl / Nature Of The Beast / Stone / Stone Cold / Tough Love

LAWRENCE, Steve

Born Sidney Leibowitz on 7/8/35 in Brooklyn. Regular performer on Steve Allen's *Tonight Show* for five years. First recorded for King in 1953. Married singer Eydie Gorme on 12/29/57; they recorded as Parker & Penny in 1979. Steve and Eydie remain a durable nightclub act.

6/2/58	19	2		1 Here's Steve Lawrence	$30	Coral 57204
8/14/61	76	10		2 Portrait Of My Love	$20	United Art. 6150
2/9/63	27	29		3 Winners!	$15	Columbia 8753
2/15/64	135	5		4 Academy Award Losers	$15	Columbia 8921
9/12/64	73	9		5 Everybody Knows	$15	Columbia 9027
12/11/65	133	2		6 The Steve Lawrence Show	$15	Columbia 9219

Steve had an hourly TV variety show from 9/65 to 12/65.

STEVE LAWRENCE & EYDIE GORME:

5/20/67	136	6		7 Together On Broadway	$15	Columbia 9436
3/8/69	141	6		8 What It Was, Was Love	$12	RCA 4115
5/10/69	188	3		9 Real True Lovin'	$12	RCA 4107

All The Way (3) / Around The World (3) / Bluesette (5) / Boys And Girls (8) / Cabaret (7) / Call Me (9) / Can't Get Over (The Bossa Nova) (5) / Can't Take My Eyes Off You (9) / Change Partners (4) / Chapter One (9) / Chattanooga Choo Choo (4) / Cheek To Cheek (4) / Come Back To Me (7) / Come Rain Or Come Shine (1) / Cotton Fields (3) / Curtain Falls (7) / Day In Day Out (1) / Don't Blame Me (2) / Don't Let The Sun Catch You Crying (5)

Don't Take Your Love From Me (2) / Easy To Love (1) / **Everybody Knows (5) 72** / Exactly Like You (3) / For You (2) / Girl From Ipanema (5) / **Go Away Little Girl (3) 1** / Happy Together (9) / Hello, Dolly! (5) / Here's That Rainy Day (5) / Honeymoon Is Over (7) / How About You (4) / I Believe In You (7) / I'll Remember April (4) / I'm Glad There Is You (2) / I've Got You Under My Skin (1,4) / I've Grown Accustomed To Her Face (2) / It's Not For Me To Say (3) / It's Not Unusual (9) / Kansas City (3)

Lazy River (1) / Lollipops And Roses (3) / Long Ago (And Far Away) (4) / Love Letters (4) / Love Me With All Your Heart (5) / Makin' Whoopee (1) / Mame (7) / Millions Of Roses (6) / Misty (3) / Moon River (3) / More Than You Know (2) / More (Theme from Mondo Cane) (1) / Music, Maestro, Please! (1) / My Foolish Heart (4) / Never My Love (9) / Old Fashioned Wedding (7) / Old Man (8) / Once In A Lifetime (6) / People (5) / **Portrait Of My Love (2) 9**

Put 'Em In A Box, Tie 'Em With A Ribbon (And Throw 'Em In The Deep Blue Sea) (1) / Real True Lovin' (9) / Remember (6) / Room With The View Inside (8) / Room Without Windows (6) / Sandpiper, Love Theme From The ..see: Shadow Of Your Smile / Save The Last Dance For Me (9) / Second Time Around (2) / Shadow Of Your Smile (6) / Sunny Side Up (1) / Sunrise, Sunset (7) / Sweetheart Tree (6) / Teach Me Tonight (3) / That Old Feeling (4) / There Will Never Be Another You (2)

They Can't Take That Away From Me (4) / Time Has Come To Say Goodnight (6) / To Be In Love (8) / Together Forever (7) / Volare (3) / Walk On By (9) / Walkin' My Baby Back Home (1) / Walking Happy (7) / Warm Hours (4) / What Now My Love (6) / What The World Needs Now (9) / What You Say (8) / What's New Pussycat? (6) / When She Leaves You (2) / When You're In Love (2) / Where Can I Go (9) / Where You Are [solo: Steve] (8)

Which Way Is Yesterday? [solo: Steve] (8) / Who's Sorry Now (3) / With A Little Help From My Friends (9) / Wives And Lovers (5) / Yeah, But What If? (8) / **Yet...I Know (5) 77** / You Made Me Love You (I Didn't Want To Do It) (1) / You Took Advantage Of Me (1) / You'd Be So Nice To Come Home To (4) / You'll Never Know (6)

LAWRENCE, Tracy

Male country singer. Born in Foreman, Arkansas. In May 1991, he was shot four times in an attempted holdup in Nashville; fully recovered.

| 1/18/92 | 71 | 40 | ● | Sticks And Stones .... | $12 | Atlantic 82326 |

April's Fool / Between Us / Dancin' To Sweet 17 / Froze Over / I Hope Heaven Has A Honky Tonk / Paris, Tennessee / Runnin' Behind / Somebody Paints The Wall / Sticks And Stones / Today's Lonely Fool

LAWRENCE, Vicki

Born on 5/26/49 in Inglewood, California. Regular on Carol Burnett's CBS-TV series from 1967-78. Also starred in TV's *Mama's Family*, 1982-83.

| 4/28/73 | 51 | 14 | | The Night The Lights Went Out In Georgia .... | $10 | Bell 1120 |

Dime A Dance (For A While) / We Helped Each Other Out / Gypsys, Tramps, And Thieves / **He Did With Me 75** / How You Gonna Stand It / It Could Have Been Me / Killing Me Softly With His Song / Little Green Apples / Mr. Allison / **Night The Lights Went Out In Georgia 1** / Sensual Man

LAWS, Debra

Born in Houston. Younger sister of Eloise, Hubert and Ronnie Laws.

| 4/11/81 | 70 | 27 | | Very Special .... | $8 | Elektra 300 |

All The Things I Love / Be Yourself / How Long / Long As We're Together / Meant For You / On My Own / **Very Special 90** / Your Love

LAWS, Eloise

Born in 1949 in Houston. Sister of Debra, Hubert and Ronnie Laws. First recorded for Columbia in 1969.

| 2/4/78 | 156 | 5 | | 1 Eloise .... | $8 | ABC 1022 |
| 2/14/81 | 175 | 7 | | 2 Eloise Laws .... | $8 | Liberty 1063 |

Almost All The Way To Love (2) / Baby You Lied (1) / Forever Now (1) / Got You Into My Life (2) / His House And Me (1) / I'm Just Warmin' Up (2) / If I Don't Watch Out (2) / Let's Find Those Two People Again (2) / Love Comes Easy (1) / Love Is Feeling (1) / Moment To Moment (2) / **Number One (1) 97** / Search. Find (2) / Someone Who Still Needs Me (1) / Strength Of A Woman (2) / **1,000 Laughs (1) 91** / You Are Everything (2) / You're Incredible (1)

LAWS, Hubert

Born in 1939 in Houston. Oldest brother of Ronnie, Eloise and Debra Laws. Jazz flutist. With the Swingsters (later the Jazz Crusaders), in 1954. With Mongo Santamaria from 1958.

2/24/73	148	9		1 Morning Star .... [I]	$12	CTI 6022
6/30/73	175	6		2 Carnegie Hall .... [I-L]	$12	CTI 6025
6/21/77	42	18		3 The Chicago Theme .... [I]	$12	CTI 6058
11/6/76	139	6		4 Romeo & Juliet .... [I]	$12	Columbia 34330
4/8/78	71	18		5 Say It With Silence .... [I]	$8	Columbia 35022
4/28/79	93	8		6 Land Of Passion .... [I]	$8	Columbia 35708

409

DEBUT DATE	PEAK POS	WKS CHR	GOLD	ARTIST — Album Title	$	Label & Number

LAWS, Hubert — Cont'd

9/27/80	134	4		7 How To Beat The High Cost Of Living.............................[S-I]	$8	Columbia 36741
				HUBERT LAWS & EARL KLUGH		
11/8/80	133	13		8 Family ....[I]	$8	Columbia 36396

Amazing Grace (1)	Family (8)	Key, The (8)	No More (1)	Tryin' To Get The Feeling	Wildfire (8)
Bach: Passacaglia In C	Fire & Rain (medley) (2)	Land Of Passion (6)	Piccolo Boogie (7)	Again (4)	Windows (medley) (2)
Minor (2)	Forlane (4)	Let Her Go (1)	Ravel's Bolero (8)	Undecided (4)	You Make Me Feel Brand
Baron, The (5)	Going Home (3)	Love Gets Better (5)	Ready To Run (7)	We Will Be (6)	New (3)
Caper, The (7)	Guatemala Connection (4)	Memory Of Minnie	Romeo & Juliet (4)	We're In Ecstasy (6)	
Chicago Theme (3)	Heartbeats (6)	(Riperton) (8)	Say I'm Yours (8)	What A Night! (8)	
Down River (7)	I Had A Dream (3)	Midnight At The Oasis (3)	Say You're Mine (8)	What Are We Gonna Do (4)	
Dream Something (7)	Inflation Chaser (3)	Morning Star (1)	Scuffle, The (7)	What Do You Think Of This	
Edge, The (7)	It Happens Every Day (5)	Music Forever (6)	Song For A Pretty Girl (7)	World Now? (1)	
False Faces (5)	It's So Easy Loving You (7)	Night Moves (7)		Where Is The Love (1)	

★★499★★   LAWS, Ronnie

Born on 10/3/50 in Houston. R&B-jazz saxophonist. Brother of Debra, Eloise and Hubert Laws. With Earth, Wind & Fire from 1972-73.

9/27/75	73	29		1 Pressure Sensitive ....[I]	$12	Blue Note 452
6/12/76	46	21		2 Fever ....[I]	$12	Blue Note 628
5/7/77	37	28	●	3 Friends And Strangers ....[I]	$10	Blue Note 730
11/4/78	51	22		4 Flame..	$8	United Art. 881
2/16/80	24	19		5 Every Generation...	$8	United Art. 1001
10/10/81	51	19		6 Solid Ground...	$8	Liberty 51087
8/13/83	98	11		7 Mr. Nice Guy...	$8	Capitol 12261

All For You (4)	Good Feelings (6)	Living Love (4)	Nuthin' 'Bout Nuthin' (3)	Strugglin' (2)	Young Child (5)
All The Time (2)	Goodtime Ride (3)	Love Is Here (4)	O.T.B.A. Law (Outta Be A	Summer Fool (6)	Your Stuff (6)
Always There (1)	Grace (4)	Love's Victory (5)	Law) (5)	Tell Me Something Good (1)	
As One (5)	Heavy On Easy (6)	Mis' Mary's Place (1)	Off And On Again (7)	There's A Way (6)	
Big Stars (7)	In The Groove (7)	Momma (1)	Rolling (7)	These Days (4)	
Can't Save Tomorrow (7)	Joy (4)	Mr. Nice Guy (7)	Same Old Story (3)	Third Hour (7)	
Captain Midnite (2)	Just As You Are (6)	Never Be The Same (1)	Saturday Evening (3)	Thoughts & Memories (5)	
Every Generation (5)	Just Love (3)	Never Get Back To Houston	Segue (6)	Tidal Wave (1)	
Fever (2)	Karmen (2)	(5)	Solid Ground (6)	Tomorrow (5)	
Flame (4)	Let's Keep It Together (2)	New Day (3)	**Stay Awake** (6) **60**	What Does It Take (7)	
Friends And Strangers (3)	Life In Paradise (3)	Night Breeze (2)	Stay Still (And Let Me Love	Why Do You Laugh At Me (1)	
From Ronnie With Love (2)	Live Your Life Away (4)	Nothing To Lose (1)	You) (2)	You (7)	

LEAGUE UNLIMITED ORCHESTRA — see HUMAN LEAGUE

LEADERS OF THE NEW SCHOOL

Hip-hop foursome: Uniondale, New York natives MC Charlie Brown ("The Freestyle Wizard"), MC Dinco D. ("The Rhyme Scientist") and MC Busta Rhymes ("The Mighty Infamous...") with Cut Monitor Milo.

| 8/17/91 | 128 | 6 | | A Future Without A Past... .... | $12 | Elektra 60976 |

Case Of The P.T.A.	Just When You Thought It	Show Me A Hero	Teachers, Don't Teach Us	Trains, Planes And	What's The Pinocchio's
Feminine Fatt	Was Safe...	Sobb Story	Nonsense!!	Automobiles	Theory?
International Zone Coaster	My Ding-A-Ling	Sound Of The Zeekers	Too Much On My Mind	Transformers	Where Do We Go From Here?
		@#^**?!			

LEADON, Bernie/Michael Georgiades Band

Guitarist Leadon (b: 7/19/47 in Minneapolis) was a member of the Flying Burrito Brothers, the Eagles and later the Nitty Gritty Dirt Band. With Georgiades on vocals/guitar.

| 8/20/77 | 91 | 6 | | Natural Progressions .... | $10 | Asylum 1107 |

As Time Goes On	Breath	Glass Off	How Can You Live Without	Rotation	Tropical Winter
At Love Again	Callin' For Your Love		Love?	Sparrow, The	You're The Singer

LEAPY LEE

Born Lee Graham on 7/2/42 in Eastbourne, England. Acted on stage and TV in England. Nicknamed "Leapy" in school because "I was always a leaper!"

| 1/18/69 | 71 | 12 | | Little Arrows .... | $15 | Decca 75076 |

Harper Valley P.T.A.	If I Ever Get To Saginaw	Little Green Apples	Roly	So Afraid	Where Has All The Love
I'll Be Your Baby Tonight	Again	My Girl Maria	Senorita Jones	Teresa	Gone
	Little Arrows 16				

LEATHERWOLF

Southern California heavy-metal quintet: Michael Oliveri (vocals, guitars), Carey Howe, Geoffrey Gayer, Dean Roberts and Paul Carmen.

| 3/5/88 | 105 | 12 | | 1 Leatherwolf.. | $8 | Island 90660 |
| 4/29/89 | 123 | 8 | | 2 Street Ready... | $8 | Island 91072 |

Bad Moon Rising (1)	Gypsies And Thieves (1)	Magical Eyes (1)	Rule The Night (1)	Street Ready (2)	Too Much (2)
Black Knight (2)	Hideaway (2)	Princess Of Love (1)	Share A Dream (1)	Take A Chance (2)	Way I Feel (2)
Calling, The (1)	Lonely Road (2)	Rise Or Fall (1)	Spirits In The Wind (2)	Thunder (2)	Wicked Ways (2)
Cry Out (1)					

LEAVES, The

Los Angeles garage-rock quintet: John Beck (lead singer), Robert Lee Reiner, Jim Pons, Tom "Ambrose" Ray and Bobby Arlin.

| 7/30/66 | 127 | 5 | | Hey Joe .... | $40 | Mira 3005 |

Back On The Avenue	Get Out Of My Life Woman	Good-Bye My Lover	**Hey Joe 31**	Tobacco Road	War Of Distortion
Dr. Stone	Girl From The East	He Was A Friend Of Mine	Just A Memory	Too Many People	Words

LeBLANC & CARR

Lenny LeBlanc (b: 6/17/51, Leominster, Massachusetts) and Pete Carr (b: 4/22/50, Daytona Beach). Lenny (bass) and Pete (lead guitar) were both session musicians at Muscle Shoals, Alabama. Lenny later recorded Christian Contemporary music.

| 3/18/78 | 145 | 7 | | Midnight Light .... | $8 | Big Tree 89521 |

Coming And Going	How Does It Feel (To Be In	I Believe That We	Johnny Too Bad	Something About You	
Desperado	Love)	I Need To Know	**Midnight Light 91**	Stronger Love	
Falling 13					

DEBUT DATE	PEAK POS	WKS CHR	GOLD	ARTIST — Album Title	$	Label & Number

★★**65**★★   **LED ZEPPELIN**

British heavy-metal rock supergroup formed in October 1968. Consisted of Robert Plant (lead singer), Jimmy Page (lead guitar), John Paul Jones (bass, keyboards) and John Bonham (drums). First known as the New Yardbirds. Page had been in the Yardbirds, 1966-68. Plant and Bonham had been in a group called Band Of Joy. Led Zeppelin's U.S. tour in 1973 broke many box office records. Formed own Swan Song label in 1974. Plant seriously injured in an auto accident in Greece on 8/4/75. In concert film *The Song Remains The Same* in 1976. Bonham died on 9/25/80 (age 33) of asphyxiation. Group disbanded in December 1980. Plant and Page formed The Honeydrippers in 1984. "Bonham" is the name of group formed by Jason Bonham, John's son, in 1989. Led Zeppelin's most famous recording, "Stairway To Heaven" (on album *Led Zeppelin IV*), was never released as a single.

DEBUT DATE	PEAK POS	WKS CHR	GOLD	#	Album Title	$	Label & Number
2/15/69	10	95	▲4	1	Led Zeppelin	$15	Atlantic 8216
11/8/69	1⁷	98	▲6	2	Led Zeppelin II	$15	Atlantic 8236
10/24/70	1⁴	42	▲3	3	Led Zeppelin III	$12	Atlantic 7201
11/27/71	2⁴	259	▲11	4	Led Zeppelin IV (untitled)	$10	Atlantic 7208
4/14/73	1²	99	▲6	5	Houses Of The Holy	$10	Atlantic 7255
3/15/75	1⁶	41	▲4	6	Physical Graffiti	$12	Swan Song 200 [2]
4/24/76	1²	30	▲2	7	Presence	$10	Swan Song 8416
11/6/76	2³	48	▲2	8	The Soundtrack From The Film "The Song Remains The Same" ..... [S-L] soundtrack recorded live at Madison Square Garden	$12	Swan Song 201 [2]
9/8/79	1⁷	41	▲5	9	In Through The Out Door 6 versions of cover released depicting same bar scene photographed at 6 different angles	$8	Swan Song 16002
12/18/82+	6	16	▲	10	Coda ..... [K] previously unreleased recordings from 1969-78	$8	Swan Song 90051
11/10/90	18	20	▲3	11	Led Zeppelin ..... [K] 54 tracks recorded from 1968-78; includes a 36-page booklet	$50	Atlantic 82144 [4]
3/28/92	47	12	●	12	Remasters ..... [K] 2 CDs feature 26 of group's songs, third CD is an interview with Page, Plant and Jones	$31	Atlantic 82371 [3]

Achilles Last Stand (7,11,12)
All My Love (9,11,12)
Babe I'm Gonna Leave You (1,11,12)
Battle Of Evermore (4,11,12)
Black Country Woman (6)
Black Dog (4,11,12) *15*
Black Mountain Side (1,11)
Bonzo's Montreux (10,11)
Boogie With Stu (6)
Bring It On Home (2)
Bron-Y-Aur Stomp (3,6,11)
Candy Store Rock (7,11)
Carousel Ambra (9)
Celebration Day (3,8,11,12)
Communication Breakdown (1,11,12)
Crunge, The (5)
Custard Pie (6,11)

D'yer Mak'er (5,11,12) *20*
Dancing Days (5,11)
Darlene (10)
Dazed And Confused (1,8,11,12)
Down By The Seaside (6)
Fool In The Rain (9,11) *21*
For Your Life (7,11)
Four Sticks (4)
Friends (3,11)
Gallows Pole (3,11)
Going To California (4,11)
Good Times Bad Times (1,12) *80*
Hats Off To (Roy) Harper (3)
Heartbreaker (2,11,12)
Hey Hey What Can I Do (11)
Hot Dog (9)
Hots On For Nowhere (7)

Houses Of The Holy (6,11,12)
How Many More Times (1)
I Can't Quit You Baby (1,10,11)
I'm Gonna Crawl (9,11)
Immigrant Song (3,11,12) *16*
In My Time Of Dying (6,11)
In The Evening (9,11,12)
In The Light (6,11)
Kashmir (6,11)
Lemon Song (2)
Living Loving Maid (She's Just A Woman) (2) *65*
Misty Mountain Hop (4,11,12)
Moby Dick (2,8,11)
Night Flight (6)
No Quarter (5,8,11,12)

Nobody's Fault But Mine (7,11,12)
Ocean, The (5,11)
Out On The Tiles (3)
Over The Hills And Far Away (5,11) *51*
Ozone Baby (10,11)
Poor Tom (10,11)
Rain Song (5,8,11,12)
Ramble On (2,11,12)
Rock And Roll (4,8,11,12) *47*
Rover, The (6)
Royal Orleans (7)
Sick Again (6)
Since I've Been Loving You (3,11,12)
Song Remains The Same (5,8,11,12)

South Bound Saurez (9)
Stairway To Heaven (4,8,11,12)
Tangerine (3,11)
Tea For One (7)
Ten Years Gone (6,11)
Thank You (2,11)
That's The Way (3)
Trampled Under Foot (6,11,12) *38*
Travelling Riverside Blues (11)
Walter's Walk (10)
Wanton Song (6,11)
We're Gonna Groove (10)
Wearing And Tearing (10,11)
What Is And What Should Never Be (2,11)

When The Levee Breaks (4,11)
White Summer (medley) (11)
Whole Lotta Love (2,8,11,12) *4*
You Shook Me (1)
Your Time Is Gonna Come (1,11)

LeDOUX, Chris

Country singer. Born on 10/2/48 in Biloxi, Mississippi. Inter-Collegiate National Champion Bareback Rider; World Bareback Champion in 1976. Got big break with mention in Garth Brooks' first country hit.

8/15/92	65	26↑		Whatcha Gonna Do With A Cowboy	$12	Liberty 98818

Cadillac Ranch
Call Of The Wild
Hooked On An 8 Second Ride
I'm Ready If You're Willing
Little Long-Haired Outlaw
Look At You Girl
Making Ends Meet
Western Skies
Whatcha Gonna Do With A Cowboy
You Just Can't See Him From The Road

LEE, Alvin

Lead guitarist/vocalist of Ten Years After. Born on 12/19/44 in Nottingham, England.

1/12/74	138	8		1	On The Road To Freedom ALVIN LEE & MYLON LeFEVRE LeFevre is an American gospel singer; with guests Steve Winwood, Jim Capaldi, George Harrison and Ron Wood	$10	Columbia 32729
1/4/75	65	12		2	In Flight ..... [L]	$12	Columbia 33187 [2]
9/6/75	131	5		3	Pump Iron!	$10	Columbia 33796
6/3/78	115	11		4	Rocket Fuel	$10	RSO 3033
5/26/79	158	5		5	Ride On above 2 with new group Ten Years Later	$10	RSO 3049
12/20/80+	198	4		6	Free Fall	$8	Atlantic 19287
8/23/86	124	9		7	Detroit Diesel	$8	21 Records 90517

Ain't Nothin' Shakin' (4,5)
All Life's Trials (2)
Alvin's Blue Thing (4)
Baby, Don't You Cry (4)
Back In My Arms Again (7)
(Battle, The) ..see: Devil's Screaming
Burnt Fungus (3)
Can't Sleep At Nite (5)
Carry My Load (7)
City Lights (6)
Darkest Night (6)
Detroit Diesel (7)
Devil's Screaming - Part 1 & 2 (4)

Don't Be Cruel (2)
Don't Want To Fight (7)
Dustbin City (6)
Every Blues You've Ever Heard (4)
Fallen Angel (1)
Freedom For The Stallion (2)
Friday The 13th (4)
Funny (1)
Going Home (5)
Going Through The Door (2)
Gonna Turn U On (4)
Got To Keep Moving (2)
Have Mercy (3)
Heart Of Stone (7)

Heartache (6)
Hey Joe (5)
How Many Times (2)
I Can't Take It (1)
I Don't Wanna Stop (6)
I'm Writing You A Letter (2)
I've Got Eyes For You Baby (2)
It's A Gaz (3)
It's All Right Now (3)
Julian Rice (3)
Keep A Knockin' (2)
Lay Me Back (1)
Let 'Em Say What They Will (1)

Let The Sea Burn Down (3)
Let's Get Back (2)
Let's Go (7)
Money Honey (2)
Mystery Train (2)
No More Lonely Nights (6)
On The Road To Freedom (1)
One Lonely Hour (6)
One More Chance (3)
Ordinary Man (7)
Ride My Train (3)
Ride On Cowboy (5)
Ridin' Truckin' (6)
Riffin (1)
Rocket Fuel (4)

Rockin' Till The Sun Goes Down (1)
Running Round (2)
Scat Encounter (5)
She's So Cute (7)
Shot In The Dark (7)
Sittin' Here (5)
Slow Down (2)
So Sad (No Love Of His Own) (1)
Somebody Callin' Me (4)
Somebody's Waltz (4)
Sooner Or Later (6)
Stealin' (6)
Take The Money And Run (6)

Talk Don't Bother Me (7)
There's A Feeling (2)
Time And Space (3)
Too Late To Run For Cover (7)
Too Much (5)
Truckin' Down The Other Way (3)
Try To Be Righteous (3)
We Will Shine (1)
World Is Changing (1)
You Need Love Love Love (2)
You Told Me (3)

DEBUT DATE	PEAK POS	WKS CHR	GOLD	ARTIST — Album Title	$	Label & Number

★★169★★ LEE, Brenda

Born Brenda Mae Tarpley on 12/11/44 in Lithonia, Georgia. Professional singer since age six. Signed to Decca Records in 1956. Became known as "Little Miss Dynamite." Successful country singer since 1971.

DEBUT DATE	PEAK POS	WKS CHR		ARTIST — Album Title	$	Label & Number
8/22/60	5	57	1	Brenda Lee	$25	Decca 74039
11/21/60+	4	41	2	This Is.....Brenda	$25	Decca 74082
5/8/61	24	33	3	Emotions	$25	Decca 74104
8/28/61	17	39	4	All The Way	$20	Decca 74176
3/24/62	29	23	5	Sincerely	$20	Decca 74216
11/3/62	20	22	6	Brenda, That's All	$20	Decca 74326
3/9/63	25	31	7	All Alone Am I	$20	Decca 74370
12/21/63+	39	13	8	Let Me Sing	$20	Decca 74439
6/13/64	90	11	9	By Request	$20	Decca 74509
9/25/65	36	14	10	Too Many Rivers	$20	Decca 74684
4/9/66	94	13	11	Bye Bye Blues	$20	Decca 74755
6/25/66	70	14	12	10 Golden Years [G]	$20	Decca 74757
				featuring one hit for each year from 1956-1965		
12/24/66+	94	12	13	Coming On Strong	$15	Decca 74825
6/15/68	187	2	14	For The First Time	$15	Decca 74955

BRENDA LEE & PETE FOUNTAIN

DEBUT DATE	PEAK POS	WKS CHR		ARTIST — Album Title	$	Label & Number
5/24/69	98	9	15	Johnny One Time	$15	Decca 75111

All Alone Am I (7,12) 3
All By Myself (7)
All The Way (4)
Anything Goes (14)
Around The World (3)
As Usual (9,12) *12*
At Last (3)
Basin Street Blues (14)
Be My Love Again (1)
Big Chance (4)
Bill Bailey, Won't You Please Come Home (12)
Blue Velvet (9)
Blueberry Hill (2)
Break It To Me Gently (8) *4*
Bring Me Sunshine (15)
Build A Big Fence (2)
By Myself (7)
Bye Bye Blues (11)
Cabaret (14)
Call Me (1)
Call Me Irresponsible (10)
Can't Take My Eyes Off You (14)
Come Rain Or Come Shine (7)
Coming On Strong (13) *11*
Crazy Talk (3)
Cry (3)
Crying Time (13)
Danke Schoen (9)
Days Of Wine And Roses (9)
Do I Worry (Yes I Do) (4)
Dum Dum (4,12) *4*
Dynamite (1,12) *72*
Emotions (3) *7*
End Of The World (8)
Eventually (4) *56*

Everybody Loves Somebody (10)
59th Street Bridge Song (Feelin' Groovy) (14)
Flowers On The Wall (11)
Fly Me To The Moon (In Other Words) (7)
Fool #1 (6,12) *3*
Fools Rush In (Where Angels Fear To Tread) (5)
For Once In My Life (15)
Georgia On My Mind (3)
Gonna Find Me A Bluebird (6)
Good Life (11)
Grass Is Greener (9) *17*
Hallelujah I Love Him So (2)
Heading Home (1)
Hello, Dolly! (10)
Help Yourself (15)
Hold Me (5)
How Deep Is The Ocean (How High Is The Sky) (5)
I Gotta Right To Sing The Blues (14)
I Hadn't Anyone Till You (7)
I Left My Heart In San Francisco (7)
I Love You Because (9)
I Miss You So (5)
I Wanna Be Around (8)
I Want To Be Wanted (2) *1*
I Wonder (9) *25*
I'll Always Be In Love With You (5)
I'll Be Seeing You (5)
I'm Confessin' (That I Love You) (9)

I'm In The Mood For Love (3)
I'm Learning About Love (3) *33*
I'm Sitting On Top Of The World (7)
I'm Sorry (1,12) *1*
If I Didn't Care (7)
(If I'm Dreaming) Just Let Me Dream (1)
If You Go Away (15)
If You Love Me (Really Love Me) (3)
It's A Lonesome Old Town (When You're Not Around) (6)
It's All Right With Me (7)
It's Not Unusual (10)
It's The Talk Of The Town (5)
Jambalaya (On The Bayou) (1,12)
Johnny One Time (15) *41*
Just A Little (2) *40*
Just Another Lie (3)
Just Out Of Reach (6)
Kansas City (14)
Kiss Away (13)
Lazy River (5)
Let It Be (15)
Let's Jump The Broomstick (1)
Letter, The (15)
Losing You (5) *6*
Love And Learn (2)
Lover (7)
Lover, Come Back To Me (4)
Make The World Go Away (11)
Matelot (15)

Mood Indigo (14)
More (9)
My Baby Likes Western Guys (1)
My Coloring Book (7)
My Prayer (7)
My Whole World Is Falling Down (9) *24*
Night And Day (8,14)
No One (10) *98*
On The Sunny Side Of The Street (2)
One Of Those Songs (Le Bal De Madame De Mortemouille) (14)
Only You (And Only Me) (5)
Organ Grinder's Swing (6)
Our Day Will Come (8)
Out In The Cold Again (9)
Pretend (2)
Remember When (We Made These Memories) (11)
Rusty Bells (11) *33*
Sandpiper, Love Theme From The ..see: Shadow Of Your Smile
Send Me Some Lovin' (5)
September In The Rain (11)
Shadow Of Your Smile (11)
Softly, As I Leave You (11)
Someday You'll Want Me To Want You (6)
Someone To Love Me (The Prisoner's Song) (4)
Somewhere (13)
Speak To Me Pretty (4)
Stormy Weather (Keeps Raining All The Time) (10)

Strangers In The Night (13)
Summer Wind (13)
Swanee River Rock (3)
Sweet Dreams (13)
Sweet Nothin's (1,12) *4*
Sweethearts On Parade (6)
Talkin' 'Bout You (4)
Tammy (9)
Taste Of Honey (11)
Teach Me Tonight (2)
That's All You Gotta Do (1) *6*
There Goes My Heart (8)
There's A Kind Of Hush (All Over The World) (14)
Think (10) *25*
This Girl's In Love With You (15)
Too Many Rivers (10,12) *13*
Traces (15)
Tragedy (4)
Truer Than True (10)
Unforgettable (8)
Uptight (Everything's Alright) (13)
Valley Of Tears (6)
Walk Away (15)
Walkin' To New Orleans (2)
We Three (My Echo, My Shadow And Me) (2)
Wee Wee Willies (1)
Weep No More My Baby (1)
What A Diff'rence A Day Made (11)
What Kind Of Fool Am I? (7)
What Now My Love (13)
When I Fall In Love (3)

When My Dreamboat Comes Home (2)
When Your Lover Has Gone (8)
Where Are You (8)
Whispering (10)
White Silver Sands (6)
Who Can I Turn To (When Nobody Needs Me) (10)
Why Don't You Believe Me (9)
Why Me? (6)
Will You Love Me Tomorrow (3)
Windy (14)
Yesterday (11)
You Always Hurt The One You Love (5)
You Can Depend On Me (6) *4*
You Don't Have To Say You Love Me (13)
You're The Reason I'm Living (4)
You've Got Me Crying Again (5)
You've Got Your Troubles (13)

LEE, Dickey

Born Dickey Lipscomb on 9/21/41 in Memphis. Pop-country singer/songwriter. First recorded for Sun Records in 1957.

DEBUT DATE	PEAK POS	WKS CHR		ARTIST — Album Title	$	Label & Number
11/10/62	50	12		The Tale Of Patches	$25	Smash 67020

Ballad Of A Teenage Queen
Devil Woman
Ebony Eyes
Little Bitty Tear
Miller's Cave
Patches *6*
Roses Are Red
Running Bear
Teen Angel
Tell Laura I Love Her
Travelin' Man
Wolverton Mountain

LEE, Jackie

Earl Nelson, of Bob & Earl. Born on 9/8/28 in Lake Charles, Louisiana. Took name from his wife's middle name, Jackie, and his middle name, Lee. Sang lead on Hollywood Flames' "Buzz-Buzz-Buzz."

DEBUT DATE	PEAK POS	WKS CHR		ARTIST — Album Title	$	Label & Number
2/5/66	85	9		The Duck	$20	Mirwood 7000

Bounce, The
Dancin' In The Street
Do The Temptation Walk
Do You Love Me
Duck, The *14*
Duck - Part II, The
Everybody Jerk
Harlem Shuffle
Hully Gully
Land Of A Thousand Dances
Neighborhood, The
Shotgun And The Duck

LEE, Johnny

Born John Lee Ham on 7/3/46 in Texas City and raised in Alta Loma, Texas. Country singer/songwriter. Married to actress Charlene Tilton from 1982-84.

DEBUT DATE	PEAK POS	WKS CHR		ARTIST — Album Title	$	Label & Number
11/15/80	132	21	●	1 Lookin' For Love	$8	Asylum 309
10/24/81	147	8		2 Bet Your Heart On Me	$8	Full Moon 541

Anni (1)
Be There For Me Baby (2)
Bet Your Heart On Me (2) *54*
Crossfire (2)
Do You Love As Good As You Look (1)
Down And Dirty (1)
Dreams Die Hard (1)
Finally Fallin' (2)
Fool For Love (1)
Highways Run On Forever (2)
How Deep In Love Am I (2)
I've Come A Long Way (But I Got A Long Way To Go) (2)
Little Bit Of Lovin' (2)
Lookin' For Love (1) *5*
Never Lay My Lovin' Down (1)
One In A Million (1)
Prisoner Of Hope (1)
Somebody Like You (2)
Too Damned Old (1)
When You Fall In Love (2)

DEBUT DATE	PEAK POS	WKS CHR	GOLD	ARTIST — Album Title	$	Label & Number

LEE, Laura
Born Laura Lee Rundless in 1945 in Chicago. Soul singer/songwriter. In Meditation Singers gospel group, in Detroit, until 1965.

| 1/29/72 | 117 | 11 | | Women's Love Rights .... | $10 | Hot Wax 708 |

(Don't Be Sorry) Be Careful If You Can't Be Good / Her Picture Matches Mine / I Don't Want Nothing Old (But Money) / It's Not What You Fall For, It's What You Stand For / **Since I Fell For You 76** / That's How Strong My Love Is / Two Lovely Pillows / Wedlock Is A Padlock / **Women's Love Rights 36** / Love And Liberty 94

LEE, Leapy — see LEAPY LEE

★★201★★ **LEE, Peggy**
Born Norma Jean Egstrom on 5/26/20 in Jamestown, North Dakota. Jazz singer with Jack Wardlow band (1936-40), Will Osborne (1940-41) and Benny Goodman (1941-43). Went solo in March 1943. In films *Mister Music* (1950), *The Jazz Singer* (1953) and *Pete Kelly's Blues* (1955). Co-wrote many songs with husband Dave Barbour (married, 1943-52). Awarded nearly $4 million in court for her singing in the animated film *Lady and The Tramp*.

| 9/17/55 | 7 | 10 | 1 | Songs from Pete Kelly's Blues .... | $50 | Decca 8166 |

PEGGY LEE and ELLA FITZGERALD
songs from the film in which Peggy and Ella had supporting roles; also see Ray Heindorf and Jack Webb

| 9/23/57 | 20 | 1 | 2 | The Man I Love .... | $25 | Capitol 864 |

orchestra conducted by Frank Sinatra

7/14/58	15	2	3	Jump For Joy	$25	Capitol 979
12/8/58	16	1	4	Things Are Swingin'	$25	Capitol 1049
4/11/60	11	59	5	Latin ala Lee!	$20	Capitol 1290
9/11/61	77	22	6	Basin Street East ....[L]	$20	Capitol 1520
8/25/62	85	6	7	Bewitching-Lee! ....[G]	$20	Capitol 1743
11/17/62+	40	21	8	Sugar 'N' Spice	$20	Capitol 1772
3/9/63	18	26	9	I'm A Woman	$20	Capitol 1857
7/27/63	42	9	10	Mink Jazz	$20	Capitol 1850
9/26/64	97	6	11	In The Name Of Love	$20	Capitol 2096
5/22/65	145	4	12	Pass Me By	$20	Capitol 2320
7/30/66	130	3	13	Big Spender	$20	Capitol 2475
12/13/69+	55	18	14	Is That All There Is?	$12	Capitol 386
6/6/70	142	9	15	Bridge Over Troubled Water	$12	Capitol 463
12/19/70	194	2	16	Make It With You	$12	Capitol 622

After You've Gone (11) / Ain't That Love (8) / Ain't We Got Fun (3) / Alley Cat Song (9) / Alone Together (4) / **Alright, Okay, You Win** (4,7,13) **68** / As Long As I Live (10) / Back In Your Own Back Yard (3) / Best Is Yet To Come (8) / Bewitched (12) / Big Bad Bill (Is Sweet William Now) (8) / Big Spender (13) / Boy From Ipanema (Garota De Ipanema) (11) / Bridge Over Troubled Water (15) / Brother Love's Traveling Salvation Show (14) / Bye, Bye, Blackbird [solo: *Peggy*] (1) / C'est Magnifique (5) / Cheek To Cheek (5) / Close Your Eyes (10) / Cloudy Morning (10) / Come Back To Me (13) / Come Rain Or Come Shine (9) / Dance Only With Me (5) / Day In - Day Out (6) / Days Of Wine And Roses (10) / Dear Heart (12) / Don't Smoke In Bed (7,14) / Embrasse Moi (8) / **Fever** (6,7) **8** / Folks Who Live On The Hill (2)

Four Or Five Times (3) / Glory Of Love (3) / Golden Earrings (7) / Good-bye (16) / Gotta Travel On (13) / **Hallelujah, I Love Him So** (7) **77** / Happiness Is A Thing Called Joe (2) / Hard Day's Night (12) / Have You Seen My Baby [solo: *Peggy*] (1) / He Needs Me (15) / He Used Me (15) / He's My Guy (2) / Heart (5) / Hey There (5) / I Am In Love (5) / I Believe In You (8) / I Could Have Danced All Night (5) / I Could Write A Book (10) / I Don't Know Enough About You (7) / I Don't Wanna Leave You Now (8) / I Enjoy Being A Girl (5) / I Got A Man (6) / I Hear Music (5) / I Left My Heart In San Francisco (9) / I Love Being Here With You (6) / I Must Know (13) / I Never Had A Chance (10) / I Never Knew [solo: *Peggy*] (1) / I See Your Face Before Me (15) / I Wanna Be Around (12) / I Won't Dance (10)

I'll Get By (As Long As I Have You) (9) / I'll Only Miss Him When I Think Of Him (13) / **I'm A Woman** (9,14) **54** / I'm Beginning To See The Light (4) / I'm Gonna Meet My Sweetie Now [solo: *Peggy*] (1) / I'm Walkin' (3) / I've Got The World On A String (8) / I've Never Been So Happy In My Life (16) / If I Should Lose You (2) / In The Name Of Love (11) / **Is That All There Is** (14) **11** / It's A Big Wide Wonderful World (10) / It's A Good Day (7) / It's A Good, Good Night (4) / It's A Wonderful World (4,13) / It's Been A Long, Long Time (4) / Johnny (Linda) (14) / Joy House (Just Call Me Love Bird), Theme From (11) / Jump For Joy (3) / Just In Time (3) / Just One Way To Say I Love You (2) / Lady Is A Tramp (10) / Let's Fall In Love (13) / Let's Get Lost In Now (16) / Life Is For Livin' (4) / Long And Winding Road (16) / Love (12) / Love Story (14)

Lullaby In Rhythm (4) / Mack The Knife (9) / Make It With You (16) / Mama's Gone, Goodbye (9) / Man I Love (2) / Manana (7) / Me And My Shadow (14) / Moments Like This (6) / Music! Music! Music! (3) / My Heart Stood Still (2) / My Love, Forgive Me (Amore, Scusami) (12) / **My Man** (7) **81** / My Old Flame (14) / My Romance (medley) (6) / My Silent Love (10) / My Sin (11) / No-Color Time Of The Day (16) / Oh Didn't He Ramble [solo: *Peggy*] (1) / Old Devil Moon (3) / On The Street Where You Live (5) / One Kiss (medley) (6) / One More Ride On The Merry-Go-Round (16) / One Note Samba (Samba De Una Nota So) (9) / Party's Over (5) / **Pass Me By** (12) **93** / Passenger Of The Rain (Le Passager De La Pluie) (16) / Peggy Lee Bow Music (6) / Please Be Kind (2) / Quiet Nights (Corcovado) (12) / Raindrops Keep Fallin' On My Head (15) / Ridin' High (4)

Right To Love (Reflections) (11) / See See Rider (8) / Senza Fine (11) / Shangri-La (11) / Sing A Rainbow [solo: *Peggy*] (1) / Sneakin' Up On You (12) / Somebody Loves Me [solo: *Peggy*] (1) / Something (14) / Something Strange (15) / Something Wonderful (2) / Sugar (That Sugar Baby Of Mine) [solo: *Peggy*] (1) / Surrey With The Fringe On Top (5) / Sweetest Sounds (8) / Talk To Me Baby (11) / Taste Of Honey (9) / Teach Me Tonight (8) / Tell All The World About You (8) / That's All (2) / That's What It Takes (12) / That's What Living's About (16) / Them There Eyes (6,7) / Then I'll Be Tired Of You (2) / There Ain't No Sweet Man That's Worth The Salt Of My Tears (9) / There Is No Greater Love (2) / There'll Be Some Changes Made (11) / (There's) Always Something There To Remind Me (15) / Things Are Swingin' (4)

Thrill Is Gone (From Yesterday's Kiss) (15) / Till There Was You (5) / Tribute To Ray Charles Medley (6) / Vagabond King Waltz (medley) (6) / Watch What Happens (13) / What A Little Moonlight Can Do (3) / What Are You Doing The Rest Of Your Life? (15) / What Can I Say After I Say I'm Sorry? [solo: *Peggy*] (1) / When In Rome (11) / When My Sugar Walks Down The Street (All The Little Birdies Go Tweet-Tweet-Tweet) (3) / When The Sun Comes Out (8) / Where Can I Go Without You? (10) / While We're Young (7) / Whisper Not (10) / Whistle For Happiness (14) / Why Don't You Do Right (7) / Wish You Were Here (5) / You Always Hurt The One You Love (12) / You Don't Know (13) / You'll Remember Me (15,16) / You're Getting To Be A Habit With Me (4) / You're Mine, You (4) / You're Nobody 'Til Somebody Loves You (9) / You've Got Possibilities (13)

LeFEVRE, Mylon — see LEE, Alvin

LEFEVRE, Raymond
Conductor/pianist/flutist from Paris.

| 3/30/68 | 117 | 16 | | Soul Coaxing (Ame Caline) ....[I] | $10 | 4 Corners 4244 |

Adios Amor / **Ame Caline (Soul Coaxing) 37** / Dommage, Dommage / Groovin' / If I Were A Carpenter / L'Important De La Rose / Puppet On A String / Quand On Revient / Release Me / Soul Coaxing ..see: Ame Caline / This Is My Song / Time Alone Will Tell (Non Pensare A Me) / Whiter Shade Of Pale

LEFT BANKE, The
Classical-styled New York rock quintet led by Steve Martin (lead singer) and Mike Brown (keyboards).

| 3/25/67 | 67 | 11 | | Walk Away Renee/Pretty Ballerina .... | $35 | Smash 67088 |

DEBUT DATE	PEAK POS	WKS CHR	GOLD	ARTIST — Album Title	$	Label & Number

LEFT BANKE, The — Cont'd

Barterers And Their Wives	I've Got Something On My Mind	Let Go Of You Girl	Shadows Breaking Over My Head	She May Call You Up Tonight	**Walk Away Renee 5**
Evening Gown		**Pretty Ballerina 15**			What Do You Know
I Haven't Got The Nerve	Lazy Day				

LeGRAND, Michel, And His Orchestra

Pianist/composer/conductor/arranger. Born on 2/24/32 in Paris. Scored over 50 motion pictures. Also see soundtracks *Summer Of '42* and *Thomas Crown Affair*.

5/28/55	5	16		1 **Holiday In Rome** ....[I]	$20	Columbia 647
9/17/55	13	2		2 **Vienna Holiday** ....[I]	$20	Columbia 706
6/30/56	9	4		3 **Castles In Spain** ....[I]	$20	Columbia 888
3/11/72	127	10		4 **"Brian's Song" themes & variations** ....[I]	$10	Bell 6071
7/1/72	173	12		5 **Sarah Vaughan/Michel Legrand**	$10	Mainstream 361

SARAH VAUGHAN/MICHEL LEGRAND

Addormentarmi Cosi (1) · Andalucia (3) · Andaluza (3) · Artist's Life Waltz (2) · Aveva Un Bavero (1) · Blue Danube Waltz (2) · Blue, Green, Grey And Gone (5) · **Brian's Song** (4,5) **56** · Cafe Mozart Waltz (2) · Caprice Viennois (2) · Deep Blue C (4) · Dicitencello Vuie! (You Tell Her) (1) · Dis-Moi (4) · El Choclo (3) · El Gato Montes (3) · Emperor Waltz (2) · Espana (3) · Espana Cani (3) · Fiorin Fiorello (In Love) (1) · Funiculi Funicula (1) · Go-Between, Theme From The (4) · Grazie Dei Fiori (1) · Hands Of Time ..see: Brian's Song · His Eyes, Her Eyes (5) · I Was Born In Love With You ..see: Wuthering Heights, Theme From · I Will Say Goodbye (4,5) · Jungle Drums (3) · La Danse Du Feu (3) · La Violetera (3) · Luna Lunera (1) · Luna Rossa (Blushing Moon) (1) · Malaguena (3) · Mattinata (1) · Merry Widow Waltz (2) · Munasterio 'E Santa Chiara (1) · Neapolitan Nights (1) · Non Dimenticar (Don't Forget) (1) · O Sole Mio (My Sunshine) (1) · Old Refrain (2) · Once You've Been In Love (5) · Oriental (3) · Picasso Summer (4) · Pieces Of Dreams (4,5) · Pizzicato Polka (2) · Rondella Aragonesa (3) · Sant Marti Del Canigo (3) · Sentir De La Alhambra (3) · Serenade (2) · Summer Me, Winter Me (5) · Summer Of '42 (The Summer Knows), Theme From (4,5) · Tales From The Vienna Woods (2) · Tango (3) · Third Man Theme (2) · Torna A Surriento (Come Back To Sorrento) (1) · Vieni, Vieni (1) · Vienna, City Of My Dreams (2) · Villa (2) · Vola, Colomba (1) · What Are You Doing The Rest Of Your Life (4,5) · Windmills Of Your Mind (4) · Wuthering Heights, Theme From (4,5)

LEHRER, Tom

Born on 4/9/28 in New York City. Satirist (in song) who performed on the TV show *That Was The Week That Was*. Alumnus of Harvard, where he also taught mathematics.

11/6/65+	18	51		1 **That Was The Year That Was** ....[C]	$20	Reprise 6179
3/26/66	133	8		2 **An Evening wasted With Tom Lehrer** ....[C]	$20	Reprise 6199

recorded March 1959 in Cambridge, Massachusetts

Alma (1) · Bright College Days (2) · Christmas Carol (2) · Clementine (2) · Elements, The (2) · Folk Song Army (1) · George Murphy (1) · In Old Mexico (2) · It Makes A Fellow Proud To Be A Soldier (1) · MLF Lullaby (1) · Masochism Tango (2) · National Brotherhood Week (1) · New Math (1) · Oedipus Rex (2) · Poisoning Pigeons In The Park (1) · Pollution (1) · Send The Marines (1) · She's My Girl (2) · Smut (1) · So Long, Mom (A Song For World War III) (1) · Vatican Rag (1) · We Will All Go Together When We Go (2) · Wernher Von Braun (1) · Whatever Became Of Hubert? (1) · Who's Next? (1)

LEINSDORF, Erich — see BOSTON SYMPHONY ORCHESTRA

LEMON PIPERS, The

Psychedelic/bubblegum rock quintet from Oxford, Ohio — Ivan Browne, lead singer. Member Bill Bartlett was leader of Ram Jam.

2/17/68	90	18		**Green Tambourine**	$15	Buddah 5009

Ask Me If I Care · Blueberry Blue · Fifty Year Void · **Green Tambourine 1** · Rainbow Tree · **Rice Is Nice 46** · Shoemaker Of Leatherwear Square · Shoeshine Boy · Straglin' Behind · Through With You · Turn Around Take A Look

★★90★★ LENNON, John

Born on 10/9/40 in Liverpool, England. Founding member of The Beatles. Married Cynthia Powell on 8/23/62, had son Julian. Divorced Cynthia on 11/8/68. Met Yoko Ono in 1966 and married her on 3/20/69. Formed Plastic Ono Band in 1969. To New York City in 1971. Fought deportation from the U.S., 1972-76, until he was granted a permanent visa. Lennon was shot to death on 12/8/80 in New York City. Won Grammy's Lifetime Achievement Award in 1991.

2/8/69	124	8		1 Unfinished Music No. 1: Two Virgins *	$80	Apple 5001

full frontal and rear nude shots of John and Yoko on front and back cover of album

6/28/69	174	8		2 Unfinished Music No. 2: Life With The Lions *	$25	Zapple 3357
12/13/69	178	3		3 Wedding Album *	$75	Apple 3361

JOHN ONO LENNON & YOKO ONO LENNON
above 3 feature experimental music and avant-garde sounds by John & Yoko

1/10/70	10	32	●	4 **The Plastic Ono Band - Live Peace In Toronto 1969** ....[L]	$30	Apple 3362

THE PLASTIC ONO BAND
9/13/69 concert featuring Eric Clapton on guitar

12/26/70+	6	33	●	5 **John Lennon/Plastic Ono Band **	$15	Apple 3372

Plastic Ono Band: John's backing musicians; also see Yoko Ono/Plastic Ono Band

9/18/71	1[1]	45	●	6 **Imagine ****	$15	Apple 3379
7/1/72	48	17		7 Some Time In New York City **	$18	Apple 3392 [2]

record 1: studio recordings backed by Elephants Memory; record 2: *Live Jam* featuring concert recordings with The Mothers of Invention

11/24/73	9	31	●	8 Mind Games	$12	Apple 3414
10/12/74	1[1]	35	●	9 Walls And Bridges	$12	Apple 3416
3/8/75	6	15	●	10 **Rock 'N' Roll**	$12	Apple 3419
11/8/75	12	32	▲	11 Shaved Fish ** ....[G]	$12	Apple 3421
12/6/80	1[8]	74	▲[3]	12 Double Fantasy *	$8	Geffen 2001

7 songs by John, 7 by Yoko; 1981 Grammy winner: Album of the Year

12/4/82+	33	16		13 The John Lennon Collection * ....[G]	$8	Geffen 2023
1/14/84	94	12		14 Heart Play -unfinished dialogue- * ....[T]	$8	Polydor 817238

excerpts from a Playboy interview done shortly before John's death

2/11/84	11	19	●	15 Milk and Honey *	$8	Polydor 817160

6 songs by John and 6 by Yoko; recorded in 1980

*JOHN LENNON & YOKO ONO
**JOHN LENNON/PLASTIC ONO BAND

DEBUT DATE	PEAK POS	WKS CHR	GOLD	ARTIST — Album Title	$	Label & Number

LENNON, John — Cont'd

DEBUT DATE	PEAK POS	WKS CHR	GOLD	ARTIST — Album Title	$	Label & Number
3/22/86	41	11	16	Live In New York City...............................[L]	$8	Capitol 12451

John's last performance; recorded at Madison Square Garden on 8/30/72; proceeds donated to help handicapped children

| 11/22/86 | 127 | 4 | 17 | Menlove Ave. ....[E] | $8 | Capitol 12533 |

Liverpool street Lennon liveroad on as a child; comprised of outtakes from *Rock 'N' Roll* and *Walls And Bridges* album sessions

| 10/22/88 | 31 | 18 | ▲² 18 | Imagine: John Lennon.......................[S] | $10 | Capitol 90803 [2] |

from the film documentary of Lennon's life; includes 9 cuts by The Beatles: "Ballad Of John & Yoko," "A Day In The Life," "Don't Let Me Down," "Help!," "In My Life," "Julia," "Revolution," "Twist And Shout," and "Strawberry Fields Forever"

Ain't That A Shame (10)
Aisumasen (I'm Sorry) (8)
Amsterdam (3)
Angel Baby (17)
Angela (7)
Attica State (7)
Au (7)
Baby's Heartbeat (2)
Be-Bop-A-Lula (10)
Beautiful Boy (Darling Boy) (12,13,18)
Beef Jerky (9)
Bless You (9,17)
Blue Suede Shoes (4)
Bony Moronie (10)
Born In A Prison (7)
Borrowed Time (15)
Bring It On Home To Me (medley) (10)
Bring On The Lucie (Freeda Peeple) (8)
Cambridge 1969 (2)
Cleanup Time (12)

Cold Turkey (4,7,11,16) *30*
Come Together (16)
Crippled Inside (6)
Dear Yoko (12,13)
Dizzy Miss Lizzie (4)
Do You Want To Dance (10)
Don't Worry Kyoko (Mummy's Only Looking For Her Hand In The Snow) (4,7)
(Forgive Me) My Little Flower Princess (4,7)
Give Me Some Truth (6)
Give Peace A Chance (4,11,13,16,18) *14*
God (18)
Going Down On Love (9)
Grow Old With Me (15)
Happy Xmas (War Is Over) (medley) (11)
Hard Times Are Over (12)
Here We Go Again (17)
Hold On (5)

Hound Dog (16)
How? (6,18)
How Do You Sleep? (6)
I Don't Wanna Face It (15)
I Don't Want To Be A Soldier (6)
I Found Out (8)
I Know (I Know) (8)
I'm Losing You (12,13)
I'm Stepping Out (15) *55*
Imagine (6,11,13,16,18) *3*
Instant Karma (We All Shine On) (11,13,16) *3*
Intuition (8)
Isolation (5)
It's So Hard (6,16)
Jamrag (7)
Jealous Guy (6,13,18) *80*
John & Yoko (3)
John John (Let's Hope For Peace) (7)
John Sinclair (7)
Just Because (10)

(Just Like) Starting Over (12,13,18) *1*
Look At Me (5)
Love (5,13)
Luck Of The Irish (7)
Meat City (8)
Mind Games (8,11,13) *18*
Money (4)
Mother (5,11,16,18) *43*
My Mummy's Dead (5)
New York City (7,16)
No Bed For Beatle John (2)
Nobody Loves You (When You're Down And Out) (9,17)
Nobody Told Me (15) *5*
#9 Dream (9,11,13) *9*
Nutopian International Anthem (6)
Oh My Love (6)
Oh Yoko! (6)
Old Dirt Road (9,17)
One Day (At A Time) (8)

Only People (8)
Out The Blue (8)
Peggy Sue (10)
Power To The People (11,13) *11*
Radio Play (4)
Ready Teddy (medley) (10)
Real Love (18)
Remember (5)
Rip It Up (medley) (10)
Rock And Roll People (17)
Scared (9,17)
Scumbag (7)
Send Me Some Lovin' (medley) (10)
Since My Baby Left Me (17)
Sisters O Sisters (7)
Slippin' And Slidin' (10)
Stand By Me (10,18) *20*
Steel And Glass (9,17)
Sunday Bloody Sunday (7)
Surprise, Surprise (Sweet Bird Of Paradox) (9)

Sweet Little Sixteen (10)
Tight A$ (8)
To Know Her Is To Love Her (17)
Two Minutes Silence (2)
Two Virgins (1)
Watching The Wheels (12,13) *10*
We're All Water (7)
Well (Baby Please Don't Go) (7)
Well Well Well (5,16)
What You Got (9)
Whatever Gets You Thru The Night (9,11,13) *1*
Woman (12,13,18) *2*
Woman Is The Nigger Of The World (7,11,16) *57*
Working Class Hero (5)
Ya Ya (9,10)
Yer Blues (4)
You Are Here (8)
You Can't Catch Me (10)

LENNON, Julian

Born John Charles Julian Lennon on 4/8/63. Son of John and Cynthia Lennon. First child to be born to any of The Beatles.

DEBUT DATE	PEAK POS	WKS CHR	GOLD	ARTIST — Album Title	$	Label & Number
11/10/84+	17	46	● 1	Valotte	$8	Atlantic 80184

title refers to the French studio where album was recorded

| 4/12/86 | 32 | 18 | ● 2 | The Secret Value of DayDreaming.......... | $8 | Atlantic 81640 |
| 4/1/89 | 87 | 15 | 3 | Mr. Jordan .... | $8 | Atlantic 81928 |

Always Think Twice (2)
Angillette (3)
Coward Till The End? (2)
Everyday (3)
I Get Up (3)
I Want You To Know (3)

I've Seen Your Face (2)
Jesse (1) *54*
Let Me Be (1)
Let Me Tell You (2)
Lonely (1)
Make It Up To You (1)

Mother Mary (3)
Now You're In Heaven (3) *93*
O.K. For You (1)
On The Phone (1)
Open Your Eyes (1)

Say You're Wrong (1) *21*
Second Time (3)
Space (1)
Stick Around (2) *32*
Sunday Morning (3)
This Is My Day (1)

Too Late For Goodbyes (1) *5*
Valotte (1) *9*
Want Your Body (2)
Well I Don't Know (1)
You Don't Have To Tell Me (2)

You Get What You Want (2)
You're The One (3)

LENNON SISTERS, The

Four sisters from Venice, California: Dianne, Peggy, Kathy and Janet Lennon. TV debut on Lawrence Welk's Christmas Eve show in 1955. Left Welk in 1967.

DEBUT DATE	PEAK POS	WKS CHR	GOLD	ARTIST — Album Title	$	Label & Number
12/25/61+	95	4	1	Christmas With The Lennon Sisters.................[X]	$15	Dot 25343

Christmas charts: 40/'63, 31/'67

| 5/27/67 | 77 | 18 | 2 | Somethin' Stupid .... | $15 | Dot 25797 |

Adeste Fideles (1)
Away In A Manger (1)
Christmas Island (1)
Dedicated To The One I Love (2)

Georgy Girl (1)
Hark! The Herald Angels Sing (1)
I Saw Mommy Kissing Santa Claus (1)

I'll Be Home For Christmas (1)
Jingle Bells (1)
Joy To The World (1)
Little Drummer Boy (1)

Lover's Concerto (2)
My Cup Runneth Over (2)
O Little Town Of Bethlehem (1)
Rudolph The Red-Nosed Reindeer (1)

Silent Night (1)
Single Girl (1)
Somethin' Stupid (2)
Sure Gonna Miss Him (1)
There's A Kind Of Hush (2)

This Is My Song (2)
White Christmas (1)
Winter Wonderland (1)
You Don't Have To Say You Love Me (2)

LENNOX, Annie

Born on 12/25/54 in Aberdeen, Scotland. Lead singer of the Eurythmics.

DEBUT DATE	PEAK POS	WKS CHR	GOLD	ARTIST — Album Title	$	Label & Number
5/30/92	23	37↑	▲	Diva..........................	$12	Arista 18704

CD includes a bonus track; also available as Arista 18709, a limited edition CD which includes an interview

Cold
Gift, The
Keep Young And Beautiful

Legend In My Living Room
Little Bird *71↑*
Precious

Money Can't Buy It
Primitive
Stay By Me

Walking On Broken Glass *14*

Why *34*

LE PAMPLEMOUSSE

Disco band featuring vocals by The Jones Girls.

DEBUT DATE	PEAK POS	WKS CHR	GOLD	ARTIST — Album Title	$	Label & Number
1/21/78	116	11		Le Spank	$8	AVI 6032

Cafe Au Lait
Come On Inside

Get Your Boom Boom (Around The Room Room)

Le Spank *58*

Monkey See, Monkey Do

When She Smiles

LEROI BROTHERS, The

Texas rock 'n' roll quartet: Steve Doerr (vocals, guitar), Mike Buck (drums), Jackie Newhouse (bass) and Rick "Casper" Rawls (vocals, guitar).

DEBUT DATE	PEAK POS	WKS CHR	GOLD	ARTIST — Album Title	$	Label & Number
3/28/87	181	5		Open All Night	$8	Profile 1224

Alligator Man
Ballad Of The Leroi Brothers

Beat Don't Ever Stop
Chain Of Love

Cindy Cindy
Gusano

Hard Luck Blues
Hey Baby

Maybe Little Baby
Pretty Girls Everywhere

So Much To Say
Wicked Prayer

LE ROUX

Six-man Louisiana rock band — Jeff Pollard, lead singer.

LOUISIANA'S LeROUX:

DEBUT DATE	PEAK POS	WKS CHR	GOLD	ARTIST — Album Title	$	Label & Number
7/8/78	135	15	1	Louisiana's Le Roux	$8	Capitol 11734

DEBUT DATE	PEAK POS	WKS CHR	G O L D	ARTIST — Album Title	$	Label & Number

LE ROUX — Cont'd

| 6/9/79 | 162 | 4 | | 2 Keep The Fire Burnin' .... | $8 | Capitol 11926 |

LE ROUX:

| 8/23/80 | 145 | 6 | | 3 Up .... | $8 | Capitol 12092 |
| 2/6/82 | 64 | 21 | | 4 Last Safe Place .... | $8 | RCA 4195 |

Addicted (4)
Back To The Levee (2)
Backslider (1)
Bridge Of Silence (1)
Call Home The Heart (2)
Crazy In Love (1)
Crying Inside (3)
Fa-Fa-Fa-Fa-Fa (The Sad Song) (2)
Feel It (2)

Get It Right The First Time (3)
Heavenly Days (1)
I Can't Do One More Two-Step (1)
I Know Trouble When I See It (3)
I Won't Be Staying (3)
Inspiration (4)
It Could Be The Fever (3)

It Doesn't Matter (4)
Keep The Fire Burnin' (2)
Last Safe Place On Earth (4) **77**
Let Me Be Your Fantasy (3)
Long Distance Lover (4)
Love Abductor (1)
Make Believe (4)
Midnight Summer Dream (4)
Mystery (3)

New Orleans Ladies (1) **59**
Nobody Said It Was Easy (Lookin' For The Lights) (4) **18**
Rock 'N' Roll Woman (4)
Roll Away The Stone (3)
Say It (With Your Heart) (4)
Slow Burn (1)
Snake Eyes (1)

Take A Ride On A Riverboat (1)
Thunder N' Lightnin' (2)
Waiting For Your Love (3)
When I Get Home (2)
Window Eyes (2)
You Be My Vision (2)
You Know How Those Boys Are (4)

LESTER, Ketty
Born Revoyda Frierson on 8/16/34 in Hope, Arkansas. To Los Angeles in 1955. Acted in several films and TV shows (formerly a cast member of *Days Of Our Lives*, *Rituals* and *Little House On The Prairie*).

| 6/9/62 | 53 | 11 | | Love Letters .... | $30 | Era 108 |

Fallen Angel
Gloomy Sunday

Goin' Home
I'll Never Stop Loving You

I'm A Fool To Want You
Love Letters 5

Moscow Nights
Once Upon A Time

P.S. I Love You
Porgy, I's Your Woman Now

When I Fall In Love
Where Or When

LET'S ACTIVE
North Carolina pop-rock trio: Mitch Easter, Faye Hunter and Sara Romweber.

2/18/84	154	11		1 Afoot .... [M]	$8	I.R.S. 70505
11/10/84	138	16		2 Cypress	$8	I.R.S. 70648
4/26/86	111	10		3 Big Plans For Everybody	$8	I.R.S. 5703

Badger (3)
Blue Line (2)
Co-star (2)
Counting Down (2)
Crows On A Phone Line (2)

Easy Does (2)
Edge Of The World (1)
Every Word Means No (1)
Fell (3)
Flags For Everything (2)

Gravel Truck (2)
In Between (1)
In Little Ways (3)
Last Chance Town (3)
Order Of Men (1)

Lowdown (2)
Make Up With Me (1)
Ornamental (2)
Prey (2)
Reflecting Pool (3)

Ring True (2)
Room With A View (1)
Route 67 (3)
Still Dark Out (3)
Talking To Myself (3)

Waters Part (2)
Whispered News (3)
Won't Go Wrong (3)
Writing The Book Of Last Pages (3)

★★41★★ LETTERMEN, The
Harmonic vocal group formed in Los Angeles in 1960. Consisted of Tony Butala (b: 11/20/40), Jim Pike (b: 11/6/38) and Bob Engemann (b: 2/19/36). First recorded for Warner Bros. Engemann replaced by Gary Pike (Jim's brother) in 1968.

2/24/62	6	55		1 A Song For Young Love	$20	Capitol 1669
6/9/62	30	24		2 Once Upon A Time	$20	Capitol 1711
10/13/62+	59	19		3 Jim, Tony And Bob	$20	Capitol 1761
4/13/63	65	10		4 College Standards	$20	Capitol 1829
8/31/63	76	10		5 The Lettermen in Concert .... [L]	$15	Capitol 1936
2/8/64	31	32		6 A Lettermen Kind Of Love	$15	Capitol 2013
6/20/64	94	10		7 The Lettermen Look At Love	$15	Capitol 2083
11/14/64	41	20		8 She Cried	$15	Capitol 2142
3/13/65	27	23		9 Portrait Of My Love	$15	Capitol 2270
8/21/65	13	24		10 The Hit Sounds Of The Lettermen	$15	Capitol 2359
10/30/65	73	13		11 You'll Never Walk Alone	$15	Capitol 2213
2/19/66	57	17		12 More Hit Sounds Of The Lettermen!	$15	Capitol 2428
6/25/66	52	15		13 A New Song For Young Love	$15	Capitol 2496
10/8/66+	17	27	●	14 The Best Of The Lettermen .... [G]	$15	Capitol 2554
2/4/67	58	17		15 Warm	$15	Capitol 2633
7/8/67	31	26		16 Spring!	$15	Capitol 2711
11/25/67+	10	48	●	17 The Lettermen!!!...and "Live!" .... [L]	$15	Capitol 2758
4/13/68	13	44	●	18 Goin' Out Of My Head	$15	Capitol 2865
9/14/68	82	14		19 Special Request .... [K]	$15	Capitol 2934
12/14/68+	43	21		20 Put Your Head On My Shoulder	$15	Capitol 147
2/22/69	128	10		21 The Best Of The Lettermen, Vol. 2 .... [G]	$12	Capitol 138
4/5/69	74	18		22 I Have Dreamed	$12	Capitol 202
8/23/69	90	8		23 Close-Up .... [R]	$12	Capitol 251 [2]

reissue of albums #6 and 7 above

9/6/69	17	30	●	24 Hurt So Bad	$12	Capitol 269
2/7/70	42	23		25 Traces/Memories	$12	Capitol 390
9/5/70	134	11		26 Reflections	$12	Capitol 496
2/6/71	119	10		27 Everything's Good About You	$10	Capitol 634
6/26/71	192	6		28 Feelings	$10	Capitol 781
10/9/71	88	13		29 Love Book	$10	Capitol 836
3/18/72	136	6		30 Lettermen 1	$10	Capitol 11010
6/23/73	193	7		31 "Alive" Again...Naturally .... [L]	$10	Capitol 11183
2/23/74	186	4		32 All-Time Greatest Hits .... [G]	$10	Capitol 11249

Again (3)
Ain't No Sunshine (29)
All I Do Is Dream Of You (4)
All I Have To Do Is Dream (7,23)
(All Of A Sudden) My Heart Sings (24)
Almost There (9)
Alone Again (Naturally) (31)
And I Love Her (12)

Ane Lisle (4)
Anticipation (30)
Anyone Who Had A Heart (18)
Are You Lonesome Tonight (8)
Baby Don't Get Hooked On Me (31)
Baby, It's You (24)
Be My Girl (6,23)

Big Hurt (27)
Black And White (medley) (31)
Blue Moon (7,23)
Blue Velvet (12)
Blueberry Hill (1)
Born Free (16)
Bridge Over Troubled Water (medley) (31)

By The Time I Get To Phoenix (18)
California Dreamin' (22)
Can't Help Falling In Love With You (6,23)
Canticle ..see: Scarborough Fair
Catch The Wind (25)
Chanson D'Amour (15,21)
Cherish (16,19)

Climb Ev'ry Mountain (11)
Come Back Silly Girl (1) **17**
Come Softly To Me (9)
Crimson And Clover (28)
Crying (8)
Crying In The Chapel (12)
Day After Day (30)
Dear Heart (10)
Dearly Beloved (6)

Dedicated To The One I Love (16)
Don't Blame It On Me (15)
Don't Let The Sun Catch You Crying (8)
Don't Make Over (28)
Don't Pull Your Love (29)
Don't You Know? (25)
Downtown (10)
Dream (4)

DEBUT DATE	PEAK POS	WKS CHR	GOLD	ARTIST — Album Title	$	Label & Number

LETTERMEN, The — Cont'd

Dream Lover (25)
Dreamer (1)
Dreamin' (10)
Elusive Butterfly (24)
End, The (11)
End Of The World (18)
Evening Rain (2)
Everybody Loves Somebody (9)
Everyone's Gone To The Moon (28)
Everything Is Good About You (27) **74**
Exodus (11)
Fast Freight (5)
Feelings (28)
First Time Ever I Saw Your Face (31)
Folk Medley (5)
For Love (25)
For No One (15)
For Your Love (25)
Forget Him (7)
Friendly Persuasion (6,23)
Gentle On My Mind (20)
Georgy Girl (16)
Go Away Little Girl (7,23)
Goin' Out Of My Head/Can't Take My Eyes Off You (17,18,21,32) **7**
Graduation Day (4)
Graduation (13)
Greatest Discovery (28)
Greensleeves (medley) (18)
Groups Are Nothing New Medley (5)
Halls Of Ivy (4)
Hang On Sloopy (25) **93**
Happy Together (16)
Harper Valley PTA (20)
Hawaiian Wedding Song (10)
Heartache Oh Heartache (8)
Hello, I Love You (20)
Here, There And Everywhere (15,24)
Hey, Girl (26)
Hey Jude (20)
Hey, Look Me Over (5)
Holly (18)
How Can You Mend A Broken Heart (29)
How Is Julie? (2) **42**

Hurt So Bad (24,32) **12**
I Believe (11,17,21,32)
I Believe In Music (medley) (31)
I Have Dreamed (22)
I Love How You Love Me (22)
I Only Have Eyes For You (13,19) **72**
I Told The Stars (3)
I Wanna Be Free (18)
I Will Love You (3)
I'll Be Seeing You (1)
I'll Never Stop Loving You (6,23)
I'll See You In My Dreams (4)
I'm Gonna Make You Love Me (22)
I'm Leavin' (29)
I'm Only Sleeping (30)
I'm Sorry (9)
If (29)
If Ever I Would Leave You (10)
If I Loved You (13)
If She Walked Into My Life (17)
Impossible Dream (The Quest) (21)
In The Still Of The Night (1)
It Happened Once Before (1)
It Never Rains In Southern California (31)
It's All In The Game (8)
It's Dark On Observatory Hill (4)
It's One Of Those Nights (30)
It's Over (27)
Jean (25)
Just Say Goodbye (28)
Let It Be Me (3,21)
Light My Fire (20)
Listen People (13)
Listen To The Music (medley) (31)
Lonely Little Girl (3)
Look Of Love (18)
Look To Your Soul (27)
Love (29,32) **42**
Love Is A Hurtin' Thing (28)
Love Is A Many-Splendored Thing (6,14)
Love Is Blue (medley) (18)

Love Is Here And Now You're Gone (24)
Love Letters (13)
Love Letters In The Sand (7,23)
Love Me Tender (3)
Love Means You Never Have To Say You're Sorry) (29)
Love On A Two Way Street (28)
Love Story, Theme From (29)
Lover's Beach (2)
MacArthur Park (31)
Make It With You (26)
Mary's Rainbow (20)
Maybe Tomorrow (29)
Me About You (22)
Meditation (medley) (17)
Michael (3)
Michelle (13)
Moments To Remember (4)
Moon River (13)
More (16,19)
Morning Girl (27)
Mr. Lonely (9)
Mr. Sun (16)
Mr. Tambourine Man (12)
My Cup Runneth Over (16)
My Funny Valentine (2)
My Girl (26)
Never Been To Spain (30)
Never My Love (18)
No Man Is An Island (11)
No Other Love (4,22)
Oh My Love (30)
Ol' Man River (11)
Old Fashioned Love Song (30)
On Broadway (24)
Once Upon A Time (2)
Only Friends (28)
Only You (7,23)
Our Winter Love (15) **72**
Party's Over (4)
People (9)
Place For The Winter (15)
Polka Dots And Moonbeams (2)
Poor Side Of Town (27)
Portrait Of My Love (9,14)
Pretty Blue Eyes (6,23)

Put A Little Love In Your Heart (medley) (31)
Put Away Your Tear Drops (8)
Put Your Head On My Shoulder (20,32) **44**
Quiet Nights (medley) (17)
Red Roses For A Blue Lady (10)
Reflections (26)
Remembering Last Summer (2)
Romeo & Juliet, Love Theme From (24)
Run To Him (8)
Running Scared (9)
Sally Was A Good Old Girl (17)
Save Your Heart For Me (12)
Scarborough Fair/Canticle (20)
Sealed With A Kiss (10,21)
Secret Love (7,19,23)
Secretly (12,14) **64**
Seventh Dawn Theme (8)
Shangri-La (24,32) **64**
She Cried (8,14) **73**
She Don't Want Me Now (16)
Shelter Of Your Arms (7,23)
Sherry Don't Go (19) **52**
Silly Boy (She Doesn't Love You) (8) **81**
Since I'm Alone (13)
Sincerely (7,23)
Sixteen Reasons (Why I Love You) (2)
Smile (1,14)
Smoke Gets In Your Eyes (15)
Softly, As I Leave You (8,19)
Something (27)
Somewhere My Love (16)
Song For Young Love (1,19)
Song From Sleep Walk (15)
Spinning Wheel (25)
Spooky (18)
Suddenly There's A Valley (11)
Summer Place, Theme From (10,14,32) **16**
Summer Song (10,19,31)
Summer's Come And Gone (3)

Summer's Gone (2)
Sun Ain't Gonna Shine Any More (26)
Sunny (24)
Sweet September (12)
(Sweet, Sweet Baby) Since You've Been Gone (26)
Sweetheart Of Sigma Chi (4)
Symphony For Susan (15)
T.K.E. Sweetheart Song (Of All The Girls That I Have Known) (22)
Take Good Care Of My Baby (9)
That Lucky Old Sun (11)
That's Enough For Me (30)
There's Got To Be A Girl (1) (They Long To Be) Close To You (26)
Things We Did Last Summmer (2)
This Guy's In Love With You (20)
This Is My Song (17)
Three Bells (11)
Through A Long And Sleepless Night (7,23)
Till (6,23)
Till Then (7,23)
(Time For Us) ..see: Romeo & Juliet, Love Theme From
Time To Cry (8)
Time Was (Duerme) (2)
To Know Her Is To Love Her (9)
Too Young (6,23)
Touch Me (26,30)
Traces/Memories Medley (22,25,32) **47**
Tree In The Meadow (3)
Try To Remember (13)
Turn Around, Look At Me (2,21)
Turn! Turn! Turn! (12)
Unchained Melody (3)
Until It's Time For You To Go (27)
Up On The Roof (26)
Up, Up And Away (17)
Valley High (1)
Venus (9,19)
Volare (16,21)
Walk Hand In Hand (11)

Walk On By (8,19)
Warm (15,19)
Way You Look Tonight (1,14,32) **13**
Wedding Song (There Is Love) (29)
West Side Story Medley (5)
What Kind Of Fool Am I? (5)
What Now, My Love? (13,17,21)
When I Fall In Love (1,5,14,32) **7**
When Summer Ends (10)
When You Wish Upon A Star (3)
Where Did Our Love Go (27)
(Where Do I Begin) ..see: Love Story, Theme From
Where Is Love? (25)
Where Or When (6,23) **98**
Whiffenpoof Song (4)
White Lies, Blue Eyes (30)
Wichita Lineman (22)
Willow Weep For Me (9)
Windy (17)
Woman, Woman (20)
Wonder Of You (6,23)
Worlds (27)
Worst That Could Happen (22)
Yes, I'm Ready (28)
Yesterday (14)
(You Make Me Feel Like) A Natural Man (22)
You Showed Me (22)
You Were On My Mind (12)
You'll Be Needin' Me (13)
You'll Never Walk Alone (5,11,14)
You've Got A Friend (medley) (31)
You've Lost That Lovin' Feelin' (10,21)
Young And Foolish (2)
Young Girl (20)
Young Love (6,23)

LEVEL 42

Band from Manchester, England: Mark King (lead vocals), Mike Lindup, and brothers Phil and Boon Gould. The brothers left the band in October 1987; replaced by Alan Murphy (guitar) and Gary Husband (drums). Murphy died on 10/19/89 of AIDS. Alan Holdsworth joined in 1991.

DEBUT DATE	PEAK POS	WKS CHR	GOLD		ARTIST — Album Title	$	Label & Number
3/22/86	18	36		1	World Machine	$8	Polydor 827487
4/11/87	23	34		2	Running In The Family	$8	Polydor 831593
10/29/88	128	7		3	Staring At The Sun	$8	Polydor 837247

Chant Has Begun (1)
Children Say (2)
Fashion Fever (2)
Good Man In A Storm (2)
Heaven In My Hands (3)

Hot Water (1) **87**
I Don't Know Why (3)
It's Not The Same For Us (1)
It's Over (2)
Leaving Me Now (1)

Lessons In Love (2) **12**
Lying Still (1)
Man (1)
Over There (3)
Physical Presence (1)

Running In The Family (2) **83**
Silence (3)
Sleepwalkers (2)
Something About You (1) **7**

Staring At The Sun (3)
Take A Look... (3)
To Be With You Again (2)
Tracie (3)
Two Hearts Collide (3)

Two Solitudes (1)
World Machine (1)

LEVERT

Soul trio from Ohio: Gerald and Sean Levert (sons of the O'Jays' Eddie Levert), and Marc Gordon.

DEBUT DATE	PEAK POS	WKS CHR	GOLD		ARTIST — Album Title	$	Label & Number
10/25/86	192	3		1	Bloodline	$8	Atlantic 81669
9/5/87	32	24	●	2	The Big Throwdown	$8	Atlantic 81773
11/26/88+	79	31	●	3	Just Coolin'	$8	Atlantic 81926
12/1/90	122	34	●	4	Rope A Dope Style	$12	Atlantic 82164

Absolutely Positive (4)
All Season (4)
Baby I'm Ready (4)
Casanova (2) **5**
Don't U Think It's Time (2)
Fascination (4)
Feel Real (3)

Give A Little Love (4)
Good Stuff (2)
Gotta Get The Money (3)
Grip (1)
Hey Girl (4)
I Start You Up, You Turn Me On (1)

I've Been Waiting (4)
In N Out (2)
Join In The Fun (3)
Just Coolin' (3)
Kiss And Make Up (1)
Let's Get Romantic (3)
Let's Go Out Tonight (1)

Looking For Love (1)
Love The Way U Love Me (3)
Loveable (3)
My Forever Love (2)
Nobody Does It Better (4)
Now You Know (4)

(Pop, Pop, Pop, Pop) Goes My Mind (1)
Pose (1)
Pull Over (3)
Rain (4)
Rope A Dope Style (4)

Smilin' (3)
Start Me Up Again (3)
Sweet Sensation (2)
Take Your Time (3)
Temptation (2)
Throwdown (2)

LEVERT, Gerald

Lead singer of the Ohio trio Levert. Son of The O'Jays' Eddie Levert. Also discovered Troop.

DEBUT DATE	PEAK POS	WKS CHR	GOLD	ARTIST — Album Title	$	Label & Number
11/2/91+	48	40	●	Private Line	$12	EastWest 91777

CD includes bonus track

Baby Hold On To Me 37
Can You Handle It
Hugs & Kisses

Hurting For You
I Wanna Be Bad
Just A Little Something

Just Because I'm Wrong
Private Line *(includes 2 versions)*

School Me
Shootin' The Breeze

You Oughta Be With Me

DEBUT DATE	PEAK POS	WKS CHR	GOLD	ARTIST — Album Title	$	Label & Number

LEWIS, Barbara

Born on 2/9/43 in South Lyon, Michigan. R&B singer/multi-instrumentalist/songwriter (since age nine). First recorded in Chicago in 1961. Inactive since the early 1970s.

| 9/25/65 | 118 | 7 | | Baby, I'm Yours .... [G] | $35 | Atlantic 8110 |

Baby, I'm Yours **11**	How Can I Say Goodbye	**Puppy Love 38**	Someday We're Gonna Love	Straighten Up Your
Come Home	If You Love Her	**Snap Your Fingers 71**	Again	Heart 43
Hello Stranger **3**	My Heart Went Do Da Dat		Stop That Girl	Think A Little Sugar

★★422★★ LEWIS, Gary, And The Playboys

Pop group formed in Los Angeles in 1964. Consisted of Gary (vocals, drums), Al Ramsey, John West (guitars), David Walker (keyboards) and David Costell (bass). Lewis (b: Cary Levitch on 7/31/45, name changed at age two) is the son of comedian Jerry Lewis. Group worked regularly at Disneyland in 1964. Lewis inducted into the Army on New Year's Day in 1967, resumed career after discharge in 1968.

3/27/65	26	25		1 This Diamond Ring	$30	Liberty 7408
9/18/65	18	20		2 A Session With Gary Lewis And The Playboys	$30	Liberty 7419
12/4/65+	44	16		3 Everybody Loves A Clown	$30	Liberty 7428
3/12/66	71	17		4 She's Just My Style	$25	Liberty 7435
5/28/66	47	24		5 Hits Again!	$25	Liberty 7452
10/22/66	10	46	●	6 Golden Greats .... [G]	$25	Liberty 7468
2/11/67	79	16		7 (You Don't Have To) Paint Me A Picture	$20	Liberty 7487
7/8/67	185	4		8 New Directions	$20	Liberty 7519
8/17/08	150	9		9 Gary Lewis Now!	$20	Liberty 7568

All Day And All Of The Night (1)
All I Have To Do Is Dream (4)
Autumn (5)
Barefootin' (7)
Best Man (1)
Birds And The Bees (1)
Chip Chip (3)
Concrete And Clay (2)
Count Me In (2,6) **2**
Daydream (5)
Double Good Feeling (8)
Down In The Boondocks (4)
Down On The Sloop John B. (7)
Dream Lover (1)
Dreamin' (3)
Elusive Butterfly (9)
Everybody Loves A Clown (3,6) **4**
Face In The Crowd (5)

For Your Love (2)
Forget Him (1)
Free Like Me (2)
Girls In Love 39
Go To Him (1)
Green Grass (5,6) **8**
Heart Full Of Soul (4)
Hello Sunshine (8)
Here I Am (8)
How Can I Thank You (9)
Hundred Pounds Of Clay (4)
I Can Read Between The Lines (5)
I Gotta Find Cupid (3)
I Won't Make That Mistake Again (4,6)
I Wonder What She's Doing Tonight? (9)
It's Too Late (5)
Judy In Disguise (With Glasses) (9)

Keep Searchin' (1)
Keepin' Company (8)
Let Me Tell Your Fortune (3)
Let's Be More Than Friends (8)
Lies (4)
Linda Lu (7)
Little Love From You (8)
Little Miss Go-Go (2,6)
Look Through Any Window (5)
Looking For The Stars (7)
Love Potion Number Nine (1)
Me About You (8)
Moonshine (8)
Mr. Blue (3)
My Heart's Symphony (7) **13**
My Special Angel (3)
Needles And Pins (1)

Neighborhood Rock 'N Roll Band (8)
New In Town (8)
Night Has A Thousand Eyes (1)
One Track Mind (3)
Palisades Park (2)
Pretty Thing (9)
Rubber Ball (5)
Run For Your Life (4)
Runaway (2)
Sara Jane (9)
Save Your Heart For Me (2,6) **2**
Sealed With A Kiss (9) **19**
Sha La La (3)
She's Just My Style (4,6) **3**
Sloop John B ..see: Down On The Sloop John B.
Slow Movin' Man (8)
Someone I Used To Know (4)

String Along (7)
Sunny (9)
Sure Gonna Miss Her (5,6) **9**
Sweet Little Rock And Roller (1)
Take Good Care Of My Baby (4)
This Diamond Ring (1,6) **1**
(Till) I Kissed You (3)
Time Stands Still (3,6)
Tina (I Held You In My Arms) (6,7)
Tossin' And Turnin' (3)
Travelin' Man (2)
Voodoo Woman (2)
Walk Right Back (2)
We'll Work It Out (3)
Well Respected Man (5)
What Am I Gonna Do (9)
When Summer Is Gone (7)

Where Will The Words Come From (7) **21**
Wild Thing (7)
Windy (9)
Without A Word Of Warning (2,6)
You Baby (5)
You Didn't Have To Be So Nice (4)
(You Don't Have To) Paint Me A Picture (7) **15**
You're Sixteen (7)
You've Got To Hide Your Love Away (4)
Young Girl (9)

★★443★★ LEWIS, Huey, and the News

Born Hugh Cregg, III on 7/5/50 in New York City. Joined the country-rock band Clover in the late '70s. Formed his six-man, pop-rock band, the News, in San Francisco in 1980: Huey (lead singer), Chris Hayes (lead guitar), Mario Cipollina (bass; brother of Quicksilver Messenger Service guitarist John Cipollina), Bill Gibson (drums), Sean Hopper (keyboards) and Johnny Colla (sax, guitar).

2/27/82	13	59	●	1 Picture This	$8	Chrysalis 1340
10/8/83+	1¹	158	▲⁷	2 Sports	$8	Chrysalis 41412
9/13/86	1¹	61	▲³	3 Fore!	$8	Chrysalis 41534
8/20/88	11	30	▲	4 Small World	$8	Chrysalis 41622
5/25/91	27	27	●	5 Hard At Play	$12	EMI 93355

Attitude (5)
Bad Is Bad (2)
Best Of Me (5)
Better Be True (4)
Bobo Tempo (4)
Build Me Up (5)
Buzz Buzz Buzz (1)
Change Of Heart (1)
Couple Days Off (5) **11**
Do You Believe In Love (1) **7**

Do You Love Me, Or What? (5)
Doing It All For My Baby (3) **6**
Don't Look Back (5)
Finally Found A Home (2)
Forest For The Trees (3)
Give Me The Keys (And I'll Drive You Crazy) (4) **47**
Giving It All Up For Love (1)
He Don't Know (5)

Heart And Soul (2) **8**
Heart Of Rock & Roll (2) **6**
Hip To Be Square (3) **3**
Honky Tonk Blues (2)
Hope You Love Me Like You Say You Do (1) **36**
I Know What I Like (3) **9**
I Never Walk Alone (3)
I Want A New Drug (2) **6**
If This Is It (2) **6**
Is It Me (1)

It Hit Me Like A Hammer (5) **21**
Jacob's Ladder (3) **1**
Naturally (3)
Old Antone's (4)
Only One (4)
Perfect World (4) **3**
Simple As That (3)
Slammin' (3)
Small World (4) **25**
Stuck With You (3) **1**

Tell Me A Little Lie (1)
That's Not Me (5)
Time Ain't Money (5)
Walking On A Thin Line (2) **18**
Walking With The Kid (4)
We Should Be Making Love (5)
Whatever Happened To True Love (1)
Whole Lotta Lovin' (3)

Workin' For A Livin' (1) **41**
World To Me (4)
You Crack Me Up (2)

LEWIS, Jerry

Comedian/actor. Born Joseph Levitch on 3/16/25 in Newark, New Jersey. Formed comedy duo with Dean Martin in 1946, in Atlantic City, that lasted 16 films and 10 years. Film debut in 1949 in *My Friend Irma*. His son Gary was a '60s pop star. National chairman in campaign against muscular dystrophy.

| 12/22/56+ | 3 | 19 | | Jerry Lewis Just Sings .... | $25 | Decca 8410 |

Back In Your Own Back Yard
Birth Of The Blues
By Myself
Bye Bye Baby

Come Rain Or Come Shine
Get Happy
How Long Has This Been Going On

I'm Sitting On Top Of The World

I've Got The World On A String

Rock-A-Bye Your Baby **With A Dixie Melody 10**

Shine On Your Shoes
Sometimes I'm Happy

★★278★★ LEWIS, Jerry Lee

Born on 9/29/35 in Ferriday, Louisiana. Played piano since age nine, professionally since age 15. First recorded for Sun in 1956. Appeared in the film *Disc Jockey Jamboree* in 1957. Career waned in 1958 after marriage to 13-year-old cousin, Myra Gale Brown, daughter of his bass player. Made comeback in country music beginning in 1968. Nicknamed "The Killer," Lewis has been surrounded by personal tragedies in the past two decades, survived several serious illnesses. Cousin to country singer Mickey Gilley and TV evangelist Jimmy Swaggart. Inducted into the Rock and Roll Hall of Fame in 1986. Jerry's early career is documented in the 1989 film *Great Balls Of Fire* starring Dennis Quaid.

| 3/28/64 | 116 | 8 | | 1 The Golden Hits Of Jerry Lee Lewis .... | $25 | Smash 67040 |
| | | | | 1963 recordings of Jerry's biggest Sun hits | | |

DEBUT DATE	PEAK POS	WKS CHR	GOLD	ARTIST — Album Title	$	Label & Number
				LEWIS, Jerry Lee — Cont'd		
12/5/64+	71	17		2 The Greatest Live Show On Earth ....[L]	$25	Smash 67056
				recorded on 7/1/64 in Birmingham, Alabama		
6/5/65	121	5		3 The Return Of Rock	$25	Smash 67063
5/14/66	145	3		4 Memphis Beat	$25	Smash 67079
6/29/68	160	12		5 Another Place Another Time	$15	Smash 67104
2/8/69	149	7		6 She Still Comes Around (To Love What's Left Of Me)	$15	Smash 67112
5/10/69	127	10		7 Jerry Lee Lewis Sings The Country Music Hall Of Fame Hits, Vol. 1	$15	Smash 67117
5/10/69	124	10		8 Jerry Lee Lewis Sings The Country Music Hall Of Fame Hits, Vol. 2	$15	Smash 67118
9/27/69	119	4		9 Original Golden Hits - Volume 1 ....[G]	$8	Sun 102
9/27/69	122	5		10 Original Golden Hits - Volume 2 ....[G]	$8	Sun 103
2/28/70	186	2		11 She Even Woke Me Up To Say Goodbye.............	$15	Smash 67128
5/9/70	114	14		12 The Best Of Jerry Lee Lewis ....[G]	$15	Smash 67131
				Jerry's Country hits from 1968-70		
10/10/70	149	6		13 Live At The International, Las Vegas ....[L]	$15	Mercury 61278
				includes "Take These Chains From My Heart" by Linda Gail Lewis		
1/30/71	190	6		14 There Must Be More To Love Than This	$15	Mercury 61323
7/24/71	152	3		15 Touching Home..	$15	Mercury 61343
11/27/71	115	12		16 Would You Take Another Chance On Me?.............	$15	Mercury 61346
4/22/72	105	12		17 The "Killer" Rocks On	$10	Mercury 637
3/17/73	37	19		18 The Session..	$15	Mercury 803 [2]
				recorded in London with Peter Frampton, Rory Gallagher, Albert & Alvin Lee and others		
4/28/79	186	3		19 Jerry Lee Lewis	$8	Elektra 184
7/22/89	62	10		20 Great Balls Of Fire!......................................[S]	$8	Polydor 839516
				film based on early part of Lewis' career; includes 8 newly recorded classics by Lewis plus: "Big Legged Woman" by Booker T. Laury, "Rocket 88" by Jackie Brenston & The Delta Cats, and "Whole Lot Of Shakin' Going On" by Valerie Wellington		

All Night Long (5)
All The Good Is Gone (5,12)
Another Hand Shakin' Goodbye (16)
Baby, Hold Me Close (8)
Baby What You Want Me To Do (18)
Bad Moon Rising (18)
Ballad Of Forty Dollars (13)
Before The Next Teardrop Falls (5)
Big Blon' Baby (16)
Big Boss Man (4,18)
Born To Lose (5)
Bottles And Barstools (14)
Break My Mind (5)
Break-Up (10) **52**
Breathless (1,9,20) **7**
Brown-Eyed Handsome Man (11)
Burning Memories (8)
C.C. Rider (17)
Chantilly Lace (17) **43**
Cold Cold Heart (8)
Comin' Back For More (15)
Corine, Corina (3)
Crazy Arms (1,9,20)
Don't Be Cruel (17)
Don't Let Go (3,19)
Drinkin' Champagne (13)
Drinking Wine Spo-Dee O'Dee (4,18) **41**
Early Morning Rain (18)
Echoes (6,11)
End Of The Road (1,9)
Every Day I Have To Cry (19)
Flip, Flop And Fly (3,13)
Foolaid (14)
Foolish Kind Of Man (15)
Fools Like Me (1,10)
For The Good Times (16)

Four Walls (7)
Fraulein (8)
Games People Play (17)
Good Golly Miss Molly (medley) (18)
Goodbye Of The Year (16)
Got You On My Mind (3)
Great Balls Of Fire (1,9,20) **2**
Hallelujah, I Love Her So (4)
He'll Have To Go (8)
Heartaches By The Number (7)
Hearts Were Made For Beating (15)
Help Me Make It Through The Night (15)
Herman The Hermit (3)
High Heel Sneakers (2) **91**
High School Confidential (1,10,18,20) **21**
Home Away From Home (14)
Hound Dog (2)
How's My Ex Treating You (10)
Hurtin' Part (16)
I Believe In You (3)
I Can't Get Over You (6)
I Can't Stop Loving You (5)
I Could Never Be Ashamed Of You (10)
I Forgot More Than You'll Ever Know (14)
I Get The Blues When It Rains (8)
I Like It Like That (19)
I Love You Because (7)
I Wish I Was Eighteen Again (19)
I Wonder Where You Are Tonight (7)

I'd Be Talkin' All The Time (14)
I'll Make It All Up To You (1,10) **85**
I'll Sail My Ship Alone (10) **93**
I'm A Lonesome Fugitive (5)
I'm On Fire (20) **98**
I'm So Lonesome I Could Cry (7)
I'm Walkin (17)
It Makes No Difference Now (8)
It'll Be Me (9)
Jackson (7)
Jambalaya (7,13)
Jenny Jenny (2,18)
Johnny B. Goode (3,18)
Jukebox (9)
Just Because (4)
Let's Talk About Us (6,12)
Lewis Boogie (9)
Life's Little Ups And Downs (14)
Lincoln Limousine (4)
Listen, They're Playing My Song (6)
Little Queenie (9)
Lonely Weekends (17)
Lonesome Fiddle Man (16)
Long Tall Sally (2,18)
Louisiana Man (6,12)
Mathilda (8)
Maybelline (3)
Me And Bobby McGee (16,17) **40**
Mean Woman Blues (10)
Memphis (2,18)
Memphis Beat (4)
Mom And Dad's Waltz (7)
Money (10)
More And More (8)

Mother, The Queen Of My Heart (15)
Move On Down The Line (9,18)
Music To The Man (18)
My Only Claim To Fame (11)
No Headstone On My Grave (18)
No Particular Place To Go (2)
Number One Lovin' Man (19)
Oh Lonesome Me (7)
On The Back Row (5)
Once More With Feeling (11,12,13)
One Has My Name (The Other Has My Heart) (8,12)
One More Time (14)
Out Of My Mind (6)
Pick Me Up On Your Way Down (8)
Play Me A Song I Can Cry To (5)
Please Don't Talk About Me When I'm Gone (15)
Pledging My Love (18)
Release Me (6)
Reuben James (14)
Rita May (19)
Rockin' My Life Away (19)
Rocking Little Angel (18)
Roll Over Beethoven (3)
San Antonio Rose (13)
Save The Last Dance For Me (10)
Sea Cruise (18)
Sexy Ways (3)
She Even Woke Me Up To Say Goodbye (11,12,13)
She Still Comes Around (To Love What's Left Of Me) (6,12,13)
She Thinks I Still Care (4)
Shotgun Man (17)

Since I Met You Baby (11)
Sixty-Minute Man (18)
Slipping Around (12)
Sticks And Stones (4)
Sweet Dreams (7)
Sweet Georgia Brown (14)
Sweet Thang (8)
Swinging Doors (16)
Teen-Age Letter (9)
That Lucky Old Sun (20)
There Must Be More To Love Than This (14)
There Stands The Glass (6)
Things That Matter Most To Me (16)
Thirteen At The Table (16)
Time Changes Everything (15)
To Make Love Sweeter For You (6,12)
Today I Started Loving You Again (6)
Together Again (2)
Too Young (4)
Touching Home (15)
Trouble In Mind (18)
Turn On Your Love Light (17) **95**
Tutti Frutti (medley) (18)
Urge, The (4)
Waiting For A Train (11)
Walk A Mile In My Shoes (17)
Walking The Floor Over You (5)
We Live In Two Different Worlds (5)
What'd I Say (10,18) **30**
What's Made Milwaukee Famous (Has Made A Loser Out Of Me) (5,12) **94**
When Baby Gets The Blues (15)

When He Walks On You (Like You Have Walked On Me) (15)
When The Grass Grows Over Me (11)
When You Wore A Tulip And I Wore A Big Red Rose (13)
Whenever You're Ready (4)
Who Will The Next Fool Be (2,19)
Whole Lot Of Shakin' Going On (1,2,9,18,20) **3**
Why Don't You Love Me (Like You Used To Do) (8)
Wild One (20)
Wine Me Up (11)
Woman, Woman (Get Out Of Our Way) (14)
Workin' Man Blues (11)
Would You Take Another Chance On Me (18)
You Can Have Her (17)
You Don't Miss Your Water (17)
You Helped Me Up (When The World Let Me Down) (15)
You Went Back On Your Word (8)
You Went Out Of Your Way (To Walk On Me) (11)
You Win Again (1,9) **95**
(You've Got) Personality (19)
You've Still Got A Place In My Heart (7)
Your Cheating Heart (1)

★★79★★ **LEWIS, Ramsey**

Ramsey (b: 5/27/35, Chicago; piano) formed the Gentlemen Of Swing, a jazz-oriented trio, in 1956 in Chicago. Consisted of Ramsey, Eldee Young (bass) and Isaac "Red" Holt (drums). All had been in The Clefs in the early '50s. First recorded for Chess/Argo in 1956. Disbanded in 1965; Young and Holt then formed the Young-Holt Trio. Lewis re-formed his own trio with Cleveland Eaton (bass) and Maurice White (later with Earth, Wind & Fire; drums). Reunited with Young and Holt in 1983.

THE RAMSEY LEWIS TRIO:

DEBUT DATE	PEAK POS	WKS CHR	GOLD	ARTIST — Album Title	$	Label & Number
12/22/62	129	2		1 Sound Of Christmas.................................[X-I]	$30	Argo 687
				Christmas charts: 20/'63, 7/'64, 4/'65, 12/'66, 8/'67, 13/'68, 6/'69		
7/4/64	125	7		2 Bach To The Blues ....[I]	$25	Argo 732
10/17/64	103	13		3 The Ramsey Lewis Trio At The Bohemian Caverns...........[I-L]	$25	Argo 741
8/14/65	2[1]	47		4 The In Crowd ....[I-L]	$25	Argo 757

DEBUT DATE	PEAK POS	WKS CHR	GOLD	ARTIST — Album Title	$	Label & Number
				LEWIS, Ramsey — Cont'd		
11/6/65+	54	19		5 Choice! The Best Of The Ramsey Lewis Trio ....[G-I]	$15	Cadet 755
2/19/66	15	27		6 Hang On Ramsey! ....[I-L]	$15	Cadet 761
				above albums are by the original trio		
				RAMSEY LEWIS:		
9/10/66	16	34		7 Wade In The Water............[I]	$15	Cadet 774
3/25/67	95	16		8 Goin' Latin ....[I]	$15	Cadet 790
7/22/67	124	5		9 The Movie Album ....[I]	$15	Cadet 782
10/28/67+	59	16		10 Dancing In The Street............[I-L]	$15	Cadet 794
3/9/68	52	31		11 Up Pops Ramsey Lewis ....[I]	$15	Cadet 799
7/20/68	55	20		12 Maiden Voyage ....[I]	$15	Cadet 811
3/29/69	156	14		13 Mother Nature's Son ....[I]	$15	Cadet 821
				all tunes composed by John Lennon and Paul McCartney		
9/6/69	139	14		14 Another Voyage ....[I]	$15	Cadet 827
3/14/70	172	12		15 The Best Of Ramsey Lewis ....[G-I]	$15	Cadet 839
3/21/70	157	8		16 Ramsey Lewis, The Piano Player ....[I]	$15	Cadet 836
10/24/70	177	7		17 Them Changes ....[I-L]	$15	Cadet 844
6/19/71	163	9		18 Back To The Roots ....[I]	$15	Cadet 6001
6/24/72	79	21		19 Upendo Ni Pamoja ....[I]	$10	Columbia 31096
3/3/73	117	10		20 Funky Serenity ....[I]	$10	Columbia 32030
10/13/73	198	3		21 Ramsey Lewis' Newly Recorded All-Time, Non-Stop Golden Hits ....[I]	$10	Columbia 32490
12/28/74+	12	30	●	22 Sun Goddess	$10	Columbia 33194
				with Earth, Wind & Fire on 2 of 6 cuts		
10/4/75	46	22		23 Don't It Feel Good	$10	Columbia 33800
5/22/76	77	11		24 Salongo ....[I]	$10	Columbia 34173
5/28/77	79	10		25 Love Notes	$8	Columbia 34696
12/24/77+	111	9		26 Tequila Mockingbird............[I]	$8	Columbia 35018
10/28/78	149	5		27 Legacy ....[I]	$8	Columbia 35483
8/23/80	173	8		28 Routes ....[I]	$8	Columbia 36423
6/20/81	152	5		29 Three Piece Suite ....[I]	$8	Columbia 37153
9/8/84	144	9		30 The Two Of Us............[I]	$8	Columbia 39326
				RAMSEY LEWIS & NANCY WILSON		

African Boogaloo Twist (12)
Ain't That Peculiar (7)
Alfie (11)
All My Love Belongs To You (6)
All The Way Live (27)
And I Love Her (6)
Aufu Oodu (24)
Bach To The Blues (2)
Back In The USSR (13)
Back To The Roots (18)
Bearmash (11)
Betcha By Golly Wow! (20)
Billy Boy (medley) (6)
Black Bird (13)
Blue Bongo (8)
Blue Spring (5)
Blues For The Night Owls (5,21)
Bold And Black (14)
Brazilica (24)
Breaker Beat *[solo: Ramsey]* (30)
C C Rider (5)
Camino El Bueno (26)
Can't Function (23)
Can't Wait Till Summer (29)
Candida (18)
Caribbean Blue (28)
Caring For You (26)
Carmen (5,21)
Cast Your Fate To The Wind (8)
Caves, The (3)
Cecile (14)
Chili Today, Hot Tamale (25)
China Gate (9)
Christmas Blues (1)
Christmas Song (1)
Close Your Eyes And Remember (16)
Closer Than Close *[solo: Ramsey]* (30)
Collage (19)
Colors In Space (28)
Come Back Jack (28)
Come Sunday (4)
Concierto de Aranjuez (19)
Crescent Noon (18)
Cry Baby Cry (13)
Crystals 'N Sequence (28)

Dance Mystique (2)
Dancing In The Street (10,15) **84**
Day Tripper (7) **74**
Dear Prudence (13)
Delilah (5,21)
Didn't We (16)
Distant Dreamer (16)
Django (10)
Do I Love Her (16)
Do What You Wanna (14)
Do Whatever Sets You Free (17)
Do You Know The Way To San Jose (14)
Don't Ever Go Away (29)
Don't Feel Good (27)
Don't Look Back (27)
Down By The Riverside (8)
Dreams (20)
Drown In My Own Tears (17)
Emily (9)
Eternal Journey (12)
Everybody's Got Something To Hide Except Me And My Monkey (13)
Everybody's Talkin' (16)
Expansions (29)
Felicidade (Happiness) (4,10)
Fish Bite (23)
Fly Me To The Moon (In Other Words) (3)
Fool On The Hill (18)
For The Love Of A Princess (2)
Free Again (8)
From Russia With Love (8,15)
Function At The Junction (8,15)
Gemini Rising (22)
Gentle Rain (5)
Girl Talk (9)
God Rest Ye Merry Gentlemen (1)
Goin' Hollywood (9)
Goin' Out Of My Head (11)
Golden Slumber (16)
Got To Be There (19)
Hang On Sloopy (6,15,21) **11**

Hard Day's Night (6) **29**
He Ain't Heavy, He's My Brother (11)
He's A Real Gone Guy (6)
Hell On Wheels (28)
Hello, Cello! (5)
Here Comes Santa Claus (1)
Hey Mrs. Jones (8)
Hi Heel Sneakers - Pt. 1 (6,21) **70**
High Point (28)
Hold It Right There (7)
Hot Dawgit (22) **50**
How Beautiful Is Spring (14)
Hurt So Bad (7)
I Dig You (23)
I Love To Please You (27)
I Was Made To Love Her (14)
I'll Wait For You (8)
If Loving You Is Wrong I Don't Want To Be Right (20)
If You've Got It, Flaunt It (Part 1 & 2) (14)
"In" Crowd (4,15,21) **5**
In The Heat Of The Night (12)
Intimacy (15)
Jade East (11,15)
Juaacklyn (23)
Julia (13,15) **76**
Jungle Strut (22)
Kufanya Mapenzi (Making Love) (20) **93**
Lady Madonna (12)
Lakeshore Cowboy (29)
Lara's Theme ..see: Somewhere, My Love
Legacy (27)
Les Fleur (12,15)
Little Liza Jane (5)
Living For The City (22)
Lonely Avenue (5)
Look-A-Here (5)
Look Of Love (11)
Looking Glass (28)
Love I Feel For You (16)
Love Is (29)
Love Notes (25)
Love Now On (18)
Love Song (22)
Maiden Voyage (12,15)

Manha De Carnaval (medley) (10)
Matchmaker, Matchmaker (9)
Memphis In June (5)
Merry Christmas Baby (1)
Message To Michael (7)
Mi Compasion (7)
Michelle (29)
Midnight Rendezvous (30)
Mighty Quinn (Quinn The Eskimo) (12)
Misty Days, Lonely Nights (2)
Money In The Pocket (9)
Mood For Mendes (10)
Moogin' On (27)
More I See You (6)
Mother Nature's Son (13)
Movin' Easy (6)
My Angel's Smile (26)
My Babe (3)
My Bucket's Got A Hole In It (5)
My Cherie Amour (14)
My Love For You (20)
Never Wanna Say Goodnight (30)
Nicole (24)
Nights In White Satin (20)
Ode (12)
Oh Happy Day (17)
One, Two, Three (8) 67
Only When I'm Dreaming (12)
Opus V (14)
Party Time (11)
Pawnbroker (9,15)
Peace And Tranquility (2)
People (3)
People Make The World Go Round (19)
Please Send Me Someone To Love (19)
Put Your Hand In The Hand (19)
Quiet Nights (Corcovado) (10)
Quiet Storm *[solo: Ramsey]* (30)
Rainy Day In Centreville (16)
Ram *[solo: Ramsey]* (30)

Respect (11)
Return To Paradise (9,15)
Rocky Raccoon (13)
Romance Me (29)
Rubato (24)
Sadness Done Come (2)
Salongo (24)
Samba De Orpheus (medley) (10)
Santa Claus Is Coming To Town (1)
Satin Doll (8)
Saturday Night After The Movies (9)
See The End From The Beginning, Look Afar (17)
Serene Funk (20)
Seventh Fold (24)
Sexy Sadie (13)
Shadow Of Your Smile (9)
She's Out Of My Life (29)
Shelter Of Your Arms (3)
Shining (25)
Since I Fell For You (4,18)
Since You've Been Gone (12) **98**
Skippin' (26)
Sleigh Ride (1)
Slick (24)
Slippin' Away (30)
Slipping Into Darkness (19,21)
So Much More (29)
Something (17)
Something About You (23)
Something You Got (3,5,21) **63**
Somewhere, My Love (Song Of) Delilah ..see: Delilah
Song Without Words (Remembering) *[solo: Ramsey]* (30)
Soul Man (11,15) **49**
Sound Of Christmas (1)
Spanish Grease (8)
Spartacus, Love Theme From (4)
Spring High (25)
Star Is Born (Evergreen), Love Theme From (25)

Stash Dash (25)
Struttin' Lightly (10)
Summer Samba (8)
Sun Goddess (22) **44**
Sweet Rain (12)
Tambura (22)
Tennessee Waltz (4)
Tequila Mockingbird (26)
That Ole Bach Magic (26)
That's The Way Of The World (23)
(Them) Changes (17)
Time And Space (16)
Tobacco Road (7)
Tondelayo (28)
Travel On (2,5)
Trilogy Medley (19)
Two Of Us (30)
Uhuru (14)
Unsilent Minority (17)
Up In Yonder (18)
Up Tight (7,15) **49**
Upendo Ni Pamoja (Love Is Together) (19)
Wade In The Water (7,15,21) **19**
Wanderin' Rose (14,26)
We've Only Just Begun (18)
Well, Well, Well! (27)
West Side Story Medley (3)
What Are You Doing New Year's Eve (1)
What It Is! (20)
What Now My Love (10)
What's The Name Of This Funk (Spider Man) (23) **69**
Whenever, Wherever (16)
Where Is The Love (20)
Whisper Zone (28)
Why Am I Treated So Bad (11)
Why Don't You Do Right (2)
Will You (29)
Winter Wonderland (1)
You Are The Reason (28)
You Been Talkin' 'Bout Me Baby (4)
You Don't Know Me (14)
You'll Love Me Yet (2)
You've Made Me So Very Happy (16)

DEBUT DATE	PEAK POS	WKS CHR	G O L D	ARTIST — Album Title	$	Label & Number

LEWIS, Webster
Baltimore keyboardist. Toured with Dionne Warwick, Sonny Rollins and Dizzy Gillespie. Former conductor for Lola Falana. Leader of the 65-piece New England Conservatory Post-Pop Orchestra.

DEBUT DATE	PEAK POS	WKS CHR	GOLD	ARTIST — Album Title	$	Label & Number
3/15/80	114	9		8 For The 80's	$8	Epic 36197

Fire   Go For It   I Want To Blow (My Horn)   Love You Give To Me   Mild Wind   You Deserve To Dance
Give Me Some Emotion   Heavenly

LIEBERMAN, Lori
Folk singer/songwriter. Wrote "Killing Me Softly With His Blues" about Don McLean which became Roberta Flack's #1 pop hit "Killing Me Softly With His Song."

DEBUT DATE	PEAK POS	WKS CHR	GOLD	ARTIST — Album Title	$	Label & Number
8/18/73	192	6		Becoming..	$10	Capitol 11203

Becoming   House Full Of Women   It Didn't Come Easy   Seed First   Song Of The Seventies
Eleazar   I Go Along   No Way Of Knowing   Someone Come And Take It   Sweet Morning After

LIEBERT, Ottmar
Santa Fe-based flamenco guitarist. Born in Cologne, Germany. Luna Negra (Spanish for Black Moon) are bassist Jon Gagan and drummer Dave Bryant.

DEBUT DATE	PEAK POS	WKS CHR	GOLD	ARTIST — Album Title	$	Label & Number
5/26/90	134	18	●	1 Nouveau Flamenco.. [I]	$12	Higher O. 7026
1/5/91	170	2		2 Poets & Angels...[X-I]	$12	Higher O. 7030
7/6/91	176	5		3 Borrasca .... [I]	$12	Higher O. 7036
4/11/92	94	25		4 Solo Para Ti .... [I]	$12	Epic 47840

above 2: **OTTMAR LIEBERT + Luna Negra**
translation of Spanish title: Only For You; features Carlos Santana on guitar; includes one vocal track

After The Rain (1)   Cloudless Sky (medley) (3)   Festival (Of 7 Lights) (4)   La Rosa Negra (3)   Poets + Angels (2)   Starry Nite (March Of Kings) (2)
Angels We Have Heard On High (medley) (2)   Cry Of Faith (medley) (3)   1st Nowell (2)   Lilac Sun (4)   Promise (Beyond The Mountains) (4)   Storm Sings (4)
Arrow W/O Destination (4)   Dancing Under The Moon (3)   1st Rain (medley) (3)   Little Drummer Boy (medley) (2)   Reaching Out 2 U (Todos Bajo La Misma Luna) (4)   Surrender 2 Love (1)
August Moon (3)   Danza Viva (My Heart Grows Wings) (4)   Flowers Of Romance (4 Bok Yun) (1)   Luna Negra Beat (medley) (2)   Road 2 Her (medley) (4)   3 Women Walking (1)
Away In A Manger (medley) (2)   Dawn In A New World (4)   Heart Still (medley) (1)   Merengue De Alegrias (Candy 4 My Soul) (4)   Samba Pa Ti (Thru Every Step In Life U Find Freedom From Within) (4)   Thru The Trees (medley) (3)
Bajo La Luna Mix (3)   Deck The Halls (2)   High On Hope (medley) (2)   Moon Over Trees (1)   2 The Night (Fast Cars/4 Frank) (1)
Barcelona Nights (1)   Deep In Your Heart (4)   Home (Bulerias) (medley) (1)   Morning Glory (3)   Santa Fe (1)   Twilight In Galisteo (3)
Beating (4 Berlin) (medley) (1)   Driving 2 Madrid (B4 The Storm) (3)   In The Hands Of Love (3)   Night In Granada (3)   Santa Fe X'mas (medley) (2)   Waiting 4 Stars 2 Fall (1)
Black Hair In The Wind (4)   Duende Del Amor (Day) (4)   Isla Del Sol (3)   O X'mas Tree (4 Anna + Bartholomaus) (2)   Shadows (1)   We 3 Kings (Of Orient R) (medley) (2)
Borrasca (3)   Duende Del Amor (Night) (4)   Island X'mas (4 Bok Yun) (medley) (2)   O Holy Nite (2)   Shepherd's Nite Watch (2)   When I'm With U (medley) (4)
Bullfighter's Dream (3)   Everything I Ever Needed (medley) (4)   Jingle Bells (3)   Passing Storm (1)   Silent Nite (4)   Whispering Hills (4)
La Aurora (3)

★★54★★ LIGHT, Enoch, & The Light Brigade
Enoch was born on 8/18/07 in Canton, Ohio. Died in New York City on 7/31/78. Conductor of own orchestra, The Light Brigade, since 1935. President of Grand Award label and managing director for Command Records, for whom he produced a long string of hit stereo percussion albums in the '60s. Enoch's studio musicians variously billed as Terry Snyder And The All-Stars (Terry died on 3/15/63 [age 47]), and The Command All-Stars. Also see Charleston City All-Stars, Los Admiradores, and Tony Mottola.

DEBUT DATE	PEAK POS	WKS CHR	GOLD	ARTIST — Album Title	$	Label & Number
6/15/59	38	4		1 I Want To Be Happy Cha Cha's .... [I]	$25	Grand Award 388
1/25/60	1[13]	124	●	2 Persuasive Percussion .... [I]	$15	Command 800
1/25/60	2[5]	97		3 Provocative Percussion .... [I]	$15	Command 806
8/22/60	3	53		4 Persuasive Percussion, Volume 2 .... [I]	$15	Command 808
9/19/60	4	46		5 Provocative Percussion, Volume 2 .... [I]	$15	Command 810
4/24/61	3	20		6 Persuasive Percussion, Volume 3 .... [I]	$15	Command 817
10/9/61	1[7]	57		7 Stereo 35/MM .... [I]	$15	Command 826
				35/MM: magnetic film used in recording process		
2/17/62	8	27		8 Stereo 35/MM, Volume Two .... [I]	$15	Command 831
2/24/62	34	8		9 Persuasive Percussion, Volume 4 .... [I]	$15	Command 830
4/21/62	27	13		10 Great Themes From Hit Films .... [I]	$15	Command 835
11/3/62	44	4		11 Enoch Light And His Orchestra At Carnegie Hall Play Irving Berlin .... [I]	$15	Command 840
12/15/62+	8	33		12 Big Band Bossa Nova .... [I]	$15	Command 844
11/2/63	133	3		13 1963-The Year's Most Popular Themes .... [I]	$15	Command 854
4/4/64	121	7		14 Rome 35/MM .... [I]	$15	Command 863
5/30/64	78	9		15 Dimension "3" .... [I]	$15	Command 867
6/13/64	129	4		16 Command Performances ....[K-I]	$15	Command 868
10/3/64	143	4		17 Great Themes From Hit Films .... [I]	$15	Command 871
11/7/64+	84	15		18 Discotheque Dance...Dance...Dance .... [I]	$15	Command 873
9/11/65	105	10		19 Magnificent Movie Themes .... [I]	$15	Command 887
5/21/66	144	6		20 Persuasive Percussion 1966............................ [I]	$15	Command 895
4/15/67	173	2		21 Film On Film - Great Movie Themes .... [I]	$10	Project 3 5005
4/22/67	163	4		22 Spanish Strings .... [I]	$10	Project 3 5000
4/26/69	192	7		23 Enoch Light & The Brass Menagerie .... [I]	$10	Project 3 5036
3/21/70	191	4		24 Spaced Out .... [I]	$10	Project 3 5043
7/24/71	176	5		25 Big Band Hits Of The 30's & 40's! .... [I]	$10	Project 3 5056

Adios (15)   Am I Blue (9)   Autumn In New York (6)   Bond Street (24)   Cara Mia Cha Cha (Ciribiribin) (1)   Come On, Come On, Come On, Don't Be Timido (22)
Ain't Misbehavin' (3)   Amorous Adventures Of Moll Flanders, Theme From (19)   Autumn Leaves (20)   Born Free (21)   Caravan (20)   Come Rain Or Come Shine (6)
Alexander's Ragtime Band (11)   And I Love Her (18)   Besame Mucho (9,12)   Both Sides Now (23)   Carpetbaggers, Love Theme From The (17)   Days Of Wine And Roses (13)
Alfie (21)   Anna (11)   Bingo Bango Bongo Baby (6)   Brazil (4,12)   Carribe (15)   Dear Heart (19)
All I Do Is Dream Of You (15)   Antony And Cleopatra Theme (13)   Blowin' In The Wind (23)   Breeze And I (2)   Cheek To Cheek (11)   Dearly Beloved (4)
All The Way (6,7)   April In Paris (25)   Blue Is The Night (4)   Bye Bye Blues (medley) (20)   Cherokee (2)   Deep Purple (8)
All The Way Home (17)   April In Portugal (22)   Blue Max, Love Theme From The (21)   California Dreamin' (23)   Chim Chim Cher-ee (19)   Desafinado (12)
Aloha Oe (2)   Army Medley (11,16)   Blue Skies (11)   Call Me Irresponsible (17)   Ciumachella (14)   Diga Diga Do (8)
Alphabet Murders (21)   Arrivederci, Roma (14)   Blue Tango (4,22)   Can't Get Enough For My Baby (9)   C'mon And Swim (18)   Do It Again (8)
Always (11)   Blues In The Night (3)

LIGHT, Enoch, & The Light Brigade — Cont'd

Don't Get Around Much Anymore (25)
Don't Worry 'Bout Me (6)
Down By The Riverside (18)
Dream Lover (18)
E Luxo So (12)
El Cid, Love Theme From (10)
Eleanor Rigby (24)
Everything's Coming Up Roses (20)
Exodus (10)
Fascinating Rhythm (3)
Fate Is The Hunter (17)
Fly Me To The Moon (16)
Flying Home (25)
Foggy Day Cha Cha (5)
Fool On The Hill (23)
For All We Know (15)
Forget Domani (Forget Tomorrow) (19)
Four Brothers (25)
Four Horsemen Of The Apocalypse, Theme From (10)
From Russia With Love (17)
Galanura (12)
Get Back (24)
Goldfinger (19)
Goodnight Sweetheart-Cha Cha (5)
Got A Date With An Angel (9)
Guaglione (1)
Gypsy In My Soul (8)
Happy Ever After (23)
Hard Day's Night (17)
Hawaii (17)
Hawaiian War Chant (6)
Hawaiian Wedding Song (15)
Heat Wave (7)
Hello, Dolly! (Bossa Nova) (18)
Hello Young Lovers (9)
Hernando's Hideaway (5)
Hey There (15)
Hold Me (9)
How Deep Is The Ocean? (1)
How High The Moon (1)
How Insensitive (22)
How The West Was Won (13)

Hud (13)
Hustler, Theme From The (10)
I Can't Get Started With You (25)
I Could Go On Singing (13)
I Could Have Danced All Night (17)
I Love, I Live, I Love (22)
I May Be Wrong (9)
I Remember Her So Well (19)
I See Your Face Before Me (7)
I Still Get A Thrill (8)
I Surrender Dear (2)
I Want To Be Happy (8,18)
I Want To Be Happy Cha Cha (1) **48**
I Want To Hold Your Hand (18)
I'll Never Smile Again (25)
I'll See You Again (7)
I'm Gonna Make You Love Me (23)
I'm In The Mood For Love (2)
I've Got A Crush On You (7)
I've Got A Right To Sing The Blues (5)
I've Got My Love To Keep Me Warm (11)
I've Gotta Be Me (3)
If I Had A Hammer (18)
In A Little Spanish Town (4)
In A Persian Market (4)
In The Mood (5)
Istanbul (20)
It Had Better Be Tonight (17)
It's De Lovely (9)
It's Only A Paper Moon (15)
Japanese Sandman (2)
Jersey Bounce (25)
Just One Of Those Things (8)
Kashmiri Song (6)
Khartoum (21)
King Of Kings, Theme From (10)
Knowing When To Leave (24)
La Cucaracha (4)
La Dolce Vita (10,16)
La Mentira (22)

La Puerta Del Sol (12)
Lady Is A Tramp (5)
Lady L., Theme From (21)
Lady Of Spain (4)
Lawrence Of Arabia Theme (13)
Lemon Merengue (18)
Life Is Just A Bowl Of Cherries (15)
Light In The Piazza (10)
Lisbon Antigua (22)
A Little Fugue For You And Me (24)
Lolita Cha Cha (1)
Love And Marriage (15)
Love Is A Many-Splendored Thing (2)
Love Me Now (19)
Lover (1)
Lover's Concerto (24)
Lullaby Of Birdland (12)
Mack The Knife (1)
Mad About The Boy (3)
Mambo Jambo (4)
Man I Love (3,7)
Maria My Own (22)
Marie (25)
Matilda (5)
Miami Beach Rhumba (4)
Mirror, Mirror, Mirror (21)
Misirlou (2)
Moments To Remember (6)
Mondo Cane No. 2 (17)
Mood Indigo (4)
Moon River (10)
Moonlight Sonata (25)
More (Theme From Mondo Cane) (13)
Mutiny On The Bounty, Theme From (13)
My Blue Heaven (9)
My Favorite Things (23)
My Heart Belongs To Daddy (2)
My Old Flame (15)
My Romance (7)
My Silent Love (24)
'Na Voce, 'Na Chitarra, E'O Poco 'E Luna (14)

Natives Are Restless Tonight (5)
Never On Sunday (10,20)
Night Train (18)
Nina (14)
Non Dimenticar (Don't Forget) (14)
Norwegian Wood (24)
O Sole Mio (14)
Ob-La-Di, Ob-La-Da (24)
Of Thee I Sing (8)
Oh Lady Be Good (9,16)
One For My Baby (6)
One Note Samba (12)
Orchids In The Moonlight (2)
Out Of Nowhere (4)
Paris Smiles (21)
Parlami D'Amore, Mariu (Tell Me That You Love Me) (14)
Patricia (1)
Peking Theme (So Little Time) (14)
People (20)
Per Tutta La Vita (I Want To Be Wanted) (14)
Perdido (6,12)
Perhaps, Perhaps, Perhaps (3,22)
Petite Paulette (24)
Polovetzian Dances, Theme From (6)
Pretty Girl Is Like A Melody (11)
Put On A Happy Face (13)
Put Your Head On My Shoulder (23)
Rain (medley) (20)
Red Roses For A Blue Lady (20)
Remember (11)
Rio Junction (Bossa Nova) (12,16)
Rock-A-Bongo Boogie (4)
S'Wonderful (3)
Sand Pebbles, Theme From The (21)
Sandpiper, Love Theme From The ..see: Shadow Of Your Smile

Satan Never Sleeps (10)
Say It Isn't So (11)
Scalinatella (Stairway To The Sea) (14,16)
Sem Saudades De Voce (12)
Sentimental Journey (17)
September In The Rain (17)
September Song (8,16)
Seventh Dawn (17)
Shadow Of Your Smile (19)
Sheik, The (1)
Ship Of Fools (19)
Sing, Sing, Sing Part 1 & 2 (25)
Somebody Loves Me (3)
Someone To Light Up My Life (22)
Someone To Watch Over Me (7)
Song Of India (3)
Soulful Strut (Am I The Same Girl) (23)
Sound Of Music (19)
Speak Low (5)
Speak Not A Word (12)
Speak To Me Of Love-Cha Cha (5)
Spencer's Mountain (13)
Swamp-Fire (15)
Sweet And Gentle (1)
Tabu (2)
Take The "A" Train (12)
Tango Delle Rose (14)
Tea For Two Cha Cha (1)
Temptation (3)
Tender Is The Night (10)
That Old Black Magic (16)
That's My Desire (16)
There's No Business Like Show Business (11)
Third Man Theme (16)
This Can't Be Love (20)
Thrill Is Gone (8)
Tintarella Di Luna (Magic Color Of The Moonlight) (18)
Tom Jones (Main Theme & Love Song) (17)
Tonight (10,16,20)

Top Hat, White Tie And Tails (11)
Touch Me (23)
Tremendo Cha Cha (1)
Tuxedo Junction (25)
Two Lovers (21)
Very Thought Of You (8)
Via Veneto (14)
Von Ryan March (19)
Walk On By (24)
Was She Prettier Than I? (15)
Watermelon Man (18)
What A Difference A Day Made (22)
What Is This Thing Called Love (5)
What The World Needs Now Is Love (24)
Whatever Lola Wants (2)
When Your Lover Has Gone (6)
Who Can I Turn To (When Nobody Needs Me) (20)
Who's Afraid Of Virginia Woolf? (21)
Wichita Lineman (23)
With A Song In My Heart (7)
Without You (Tres Palabras) (22)
Ya Ya (18)
Yes Sir, That's My Baby (1)
You Brought A New Kind Of Love To Me (9)
You Do Something To Me (7)
You're The Top (3)
Yours Is My Heart Alone (4)
Zing Went The Strings Of My Heart (7,16)
Zorba The Greek, Theme From (19)

LIGHTER SHADE OF BROWN, A

Hispanic rap duo of ODM ("One Dope Mexican," Robert Guitterez) and DTTX ("Don't Try To Xerox," Bobby Ramirez), from Riverside, California.

2/8/92	**184**	4		Brown & Proud	**$12**	Pump 15154

Bouncin'
Brown & Proud
El Varrio
Latin Active 59
On A Sunday Afternoon **39**
Pancho Villa
Paquito Soul
Spill The Wine
T.J. Nights (Includes 2 versions)

★★195★★ LIGHTFOOT, Gordon

Born on 11/17/38 in Orillia, Ontario, Canada. Folk-pop-country singer/songwriter/guitarist. Worked on *Country Hoedown*, CBC-TV series. Teamed with Jim Whalen as the Two Tones in the mid-1960s. Wrote hit "Early Mornin' Rain" for Peter, Paul and Mary. First recorded for Chateau in 1965.

DEBUT DATE	PEAK POS	WKS CHR	GOLD	#	Album Title	$	Label & Number
11/15/69	143	6		1	Sunday Concert .... [L]	$10	United Art. 6714
					recorded in Massey Hall, Toronto, Canada		
5/30/70+	12	37	●	2	Sit Down Young Stranger	$12	Reprise 6392
					later reissued as *If You Could Read My Mind*		
5/29/71	38	20		3	Summer Side Of Life	$12	Reprise 2037
6/26/71	178	5		4	Classic Lightfoot (The Best Of Lightfoot/Volume 2) .... [K]	$10	United Art. 5510
3/25/72	42	17		5	Don Quixote	$12	Reprise 2056
11/18/72	95	12		6	Old Dan's Records	$12	Reprise 2116
2/2/74	1²	42	▲	7	Sundown	$12	Reprise 2177
7/27/74+	155	9		8	The Very Best Of Gordon Lightfoot .... [K]	$10	United Art. 243
3/1/75	10	20		9	Cold On The Shoulder	$12	Reprise 2206
11/22/75+	34	24	▲	10	Gord's Gold .... [G]	$15	Reprise 2237 [2]
					first record features re-recordings of his '60s songs		
6/26/76	12	41	▲	11	Summertime Dream	$12	Reprise 2246
2/4/78	22	20	●	12	Endless Wire	$8	Warner 3149
4/5/80	60	11		13	Dream Street Rose	$8	Warner 3426
2/20/82	87	12		14	Shadows	$8	Warner 3633
8/13/83	175	5		15	Salute	$8	Warner 23901
8/9/86	165	6		16	East Of Midnight	$8	Warner 25482

Affair On Eighth Avenue (4,8,10)
Alberta Bound (5)
All I'm After (14)
All The Lovely Ladies (9)
Anything For Love (16)
Apology (1)

Approaching Lavender (2)
Auctioneer, The (13)
Baby It's Alright (2)
Baby Step Back (14) **50**
Ballad Of Yarmouth Castle (1,4)
Beautiful (5,10) **58**

Bells Of The Evening (9)
Bend In The Water (9)
Biscuit City (15)
Bitter Green (1,10)
Black Day In July (8)
Blackberry Wine (14)
Boss Man (1)

Brave Mountaineers (5)
Broken Dreams (15)
Cabaret (3)
Can't Depend On Love (6)
Canadian Railroad Trilogy (1,8,10)
Carefree Highway (7,10) **10**

Cherokee Bend (9)
Christian Island (Georgian Bay) (5)
Circle Is Small (I Can See It In Your Eyes) (12) **33**
Circle Of Steel (7,10)
Cobwebs & Dust (2)

Cold On The Shoulder (9,10)
Cotton Jenny (5,10)
Daylight Katy (12)
Did She Mention My Name (8,10)
Don Quixote (5,10)
Dream Street Rose (13)

DEBUT DATE	PEAK POS	WKS CHR	GOLD	ARTIST — Album Title	$	Label & Number

LIGHTFOOT, Gordon — Cont'd

Dreamland (12)
Early Morning Rain (8,10)
East Of Midnight (16)
Ecstasy Made Easy (16)
Endless Wire (12)
Farewell To Annabel (6)
Fine As Fine Can Be (9)
For Lovin' Me (8,10)
14 Karat Gold (14)
Ghosts Of Cape Horn (13)
Go My Way (3)
Gotta Get Away (15)
Hangdog Hotel Room (12)
Heaven Help The Devil (14)
Hey You (13)
High And Dry (7)
Hi'Way Songs (6)
Home From The Forest (14)
House You Live In (11)
I'd Do It Again (14)
I'll Do Anything (14)
I'll Tag Along (16)
I'm Not Sayin' (1,8,10)

I'm Not Supposed To Care (11)
If Children Had Wings (12)
If I Could (4,8)
If There's A Reason (12)
If You Could Read My Mind (2,10) **5**
If You Need Me (13)
In A Windowpane (1)
In My Fashion (14)
Is There Anyone Home (7)
It's Worth Believin' (6)
Knotty Pine (15)
Last Time I Saw Her (4,8)
Lazy Mornin' (6)
Leaves Of Grass (1)
Lesson In Love (16)
Let It Ride (16)
List, The (1)
Long Way Back Home (4)
Looking At The Rain (5)
Lost Children (1)
Love & Maple Syrup (3)

Make Way For The Lights (2)
Me And Bobby McGee (2)
Miguel (3)
Minstrel Of The Dawn (2,10)
Mister Rock Of Ages (13)
Morning Glory (16)
Mother Of A Miner's Child (6)
Mountains And Marian (4)
My Pony Won't Go (6)
Never Too Close (11)
Now And Then (9)
Ode To Big Blue (5)
Old Dan's Records (6,10)
On Susan's Floor (5)
On The High Seas (13)
Ordinary Man (5)
Passing Ship (16)
Patriot's Dream (5)
Pony Man (2)
Poor Little Allison (2)
Protocol (11)
Pussy Willows, Cat-Tails (1)

Race Among The Ruins (11) **65**
Rainbow Trout (9)
Rainy Day People (9,10) **26**
Redwood Hill (3)
Ribbon Of Darkness (medley) (1,10)
Romance (15)
Rosanna (4)
Salute (A Lot More Livin' To Do) (5)
Same Old Loverman (3)
Saturday Clothes (2)
Sea Of Tranquility (13)
Second Cup Of Coffee (5)
Seven Island Suite (7)
Shadows (14)
She's Not The Same (14)
Sit Down Young Stranger (2)
Slide On Over (9)
Softly (1,10)
Someone To Believe In (15)
Something Very Special (4)

Sometimes I Don't Mind (12)
Somewhere U.S.A. (7)
Song For A Winter's Night (10)
Songs The Minstrel Sang (12)
Soul Is The Rock (9)
Spanish Moss (11)
Stay Loose (16)
Steel Rail Blues (10)
Summer Side Of Life (3,10) **98**
Summertime Dream (11)
Sundown (7,10) **1**
Sweet Guinevere (12)
Talking In Your Sleep (3) **64**
Tattoo (15)
10 Degrees & Getting Colder (3)
Thank You For The Promises (14)
That Same Old Obsession (6)
Too Late For Prayin' (7)

Too Many Clues In This Room (11)
Tree Too Weak To Stand (9)
Triangle (14)
Walls (4,8)
Watchman's Gone (7)
Way I Feel (8)
Wherefore And Why (8,10)
Whisper My Name (13)
Whispers Of The North (15)
Without You (15)
Wreck Of The Edmund Fitzgerald (11) **2**
You Are What I Am (6)
You Just Gotta Be (16)
Your Love's Return (Song For Stephen Foster) (2)

LIGHTHOUSE
Rock band from Toronto — Bob McBride, lead singer.

DEBUT DATE	PEAK POS	WKS CHR			$	Label & Number
5/9/70	133	3		1 Peacing It All Together	$15	RCA 4325
7/24/71	80	21		2 One Fine Morning	$12	Evolution 3007
1/29/72	157	7		3 Thoughts Of Movin' On	$12	Evolution 3010
7/29/72	178	7		4 Lighthouse Live! .... [L]	$12	Evolution 3014 [2]
				recorded at Carnegie Hall on 2/6/72		
1/13/73	190	9		5 Sunny Days	$12	Evolution 3016

Beneath My Woman (5)
Broken Guitar Blues (5)
Country Song (1)
Daughters And Sons (1)
Eight Miles High (4)
1849 (2,4)
Every Day I Am Reminded (1)
Fiction Of Twenty-Six Million (1)

Fly My Airplane (3)
Hats Off (To The Stranger) (2)
I Just Wanna Be Your Friend (3,4) **93**
I'd Be So Happy (3)
I'm Gonna Try To Make It (3)
Insane (3,4)
Just A Little More Time (1)

Let The Happiness Begin (medley) (1)
Letter Home (5)
Little Kind Words (2)
Little People (medley) (1)
Lonely Places (5)
Love Of A Woman (2)
Merlin (5)
Mr. Candleman (2)

Nam Myoho Renge' Kyo (1)
Old Man (2,4)
On My Way To L.A. (1)
Rockin' Chair (3,4)
Sausalito (1)
Show Me The Way (2)
Silver Bird (5)
Sing, Sing, Sing (2)

Step Out On The Sea (2)
Sunny Days (5) **34**
Sweet Lullaby (2,4)
Take It Slow (Out In The Country) (3,4) **64**
Walk Me Down (3)
What Gives You The Right (3)
You And Me (3,4)
You Girl (5)

You Give To Me (5)

LIGHTNING SEEDS, The
Band with fluctuating lineup spearheaded by U.K. producer/vocalist Ian Broudie (former member of Big In Japan who produced Echo & The Bunnymen and others).

DEBUT DATE	PEAK POS	WKS CHR			$	Label & Number
5/5/90	46	27		1 Cloudcuckooland	$12	MCA 6404
				CD and cassette include bonus track		
3/14/92	154	6		2 Sense	$12	MCA 10388

All I Want (1)
Blowing Bubbles (2)
Bound In A Nutshell (1)
Control The Flame (1)
Cool Place (2)

Don't Let Go (1)
Fools (1)
Frenzy (1)
Happy (2)
Joy (1)

Life Of Riley (2) **98**
Love Explosion (1)
Marooned (2)
Nearly Man (1)
Price, The (1)

Pure (1) **31**
Sense (2)
Small Slice Of Heaven (2)
Sweet Dreams (1)

Thinking Up Looking Down (2)
Tingle Tangle (2)
Where Flowers Fade (2)

LIMAHL
Real name: Chris Hamill (Limahl is an anagram of his last name). Ex-lead singer of Kajagoogoo.

DEBUT DATE	PEAK POS	WKS CHR			$	Label & Number
4/27/85	41	20		Don't Suppose	$8	EMI America 17142

Don't Suppose
I Was A Fool

Never Ending Story 17
Oh Girl

Only For Love 51
Tar Beach

That Special Something
Too Much Trouble

Waiting Game
Your Love

★★295★★ LIMELITERS, The
Folk trio formed in Hollywood in 1959. Consisted of Glen Yarbrough (tenor), Lou Gottlieb (bass) and Alex Hassilev (baritone). Yarbrough went solo in 1963.

DEBUT DATE	PEAK POS	WKS CHR			$	Label & Number
2/27/61	5	74		1 Tonight: In Person .... [L]	$20	RCA 2272
				recorded at the Ash Grove in Hollywood		
9/4/61	40	18		2 The Limeliters	$20	Elektra 7180
10/2/61+	8	36		3 The Slightly Fabulous Limeliters .... [L]	$20	RCA 2393
2/3/62	14	31		4 Sing Out!	$20	RCA 2445
6/9/62	25	29		5 Through Children's Eyes .... [L]	$20	RCA 2512
				featuring 70 children from Berkeley, California		
9/29/62	21	12		6 Folk Matinee...	$20	RCA 2547
2/2/63	37	25		7 Our Men In San Francisco .... [L]	$20	RCA 2609
5/25/63	83	6		8 Makin' A Joyful Noise	$20	RCA 2588
9/28/63	73	8		9 Fourteen 14K Folk Songs	$20	RCA 2671
5/9/64	118	5		10 More Of Everything!	$20	RCA 2844
				Glen Yarbrough replaced by Ernie Sheldon		

Amazing Grace (8)
America The Beautiful (medley) (1)
Aravah, Aravah (3)
B-A Bay (3)
Battle At Gandessa (2)
Bear Chase (2)
Best Is Yet To Come (10)
Betty And Dupree (9)
Blow The Candles Out (9)
Blue Mountain Lake (6)

Bound For The Promised Land (8)
Bring Me A Rose (10)
Burro (2)
By The Risin' Of The Moon (7)
Casinha Pequenina (Little House) (10)
Charlie, The Midnight Marauder (2)
Charmin' Betsy (4)

Civil War Medley (7)
Come And Dine (8)
Corn Whiskey (7)
Curima (3)
Die Gedanken Sind Frei (6)
Down By The Riverside (medley) (8)
Drill Ye Tarriers (9)
Everywhere I Look This Mornin' (7)
Far Side Of The Hill (1)

Farethewell (Dink's Song) (9)
Funk (6)
Gambler's Blues (9)
Gari Gari (2)
Gilgarry Mountain (Darlin' Sportin' Jenny) (4)
God Save The People (8)
Golden Bell (2)
Goodnight Ladies (medley) (7)

Gotta Travel On (4)
Grace Darling (5)
Gunslinger (3)
Hammer Song (2)
Hangman, Hangman (9)
Hard Ain't It Hard (3)
Hard Travelin' (medley) (3)
Harry Pollitt (3)
Headin' For The Hills (1)
Hey Jimmy Joe John Jim Jack (5)

Hey Li Lee Li Lee (1)
Hold On (8)
How Bright Is The Day (8)
I Had A Mule (5)
I'm Goin' Away (2)
I'm Goin' Back (7)
Jam On Jerry's Rock (7)
Jehosephat (4)
John Henry, The Steel Driving Man (9)
John Riley (9)

LIMELITERS, The — Cont'd

Join Into The Game (5)
Joy Across The Land (4)
Just A Closer Walk With Thee (8)
La Llorona (10)
Lass From The Low Country (3)
Last Class Seaman (10)
Leaving A Song (medley) (7)
Lily Of The Valley (8)
Lion And The Lamb (4)
Little Land (4)
Lollipop Tree (5)
Lonesome Traveler (2)
Lute Player (7)
Madeira, M'Dear (1)

Malaguena Salerosa (2)
Mama Don't 'Low (3)
March On (medley) (8)
Marty (5)
Marvin (4)
Max Goolis (7)
Midnight Special (9)
Minneapolis - St. Paul (10)
Minstrel Boy (6)
Molly Malone (1)
Monks Of St. Bernard (1)
Mornington Ride (5)
Mount Zion (medley) (3)
No Man Is An Island (10)
No More Cane (9)

Old Time Religion (medley) (8)
Pretty Far Out (4)
Proshchai (1)
Reedy River (6)
Remember Me (When The Candlelights Are Gleaming) (10)
Revive Us Again (8)
Riddle Song (5)
Rumania, Rumania (1)
Run, Little Donkey (5)
Seven Daffodils (1)
Sing Hallelujah (6)
Sleep Soft (Lullaby) (7)

Spanish Is The Loving Tongue (9)
Stay On The Sunny Side (5)
Sweet Betsy From Pike (9)
Sweet Water Rolling (6)
Take My True Love By The Hand (2)
Tamborito (6)
There's A Meetin' Here Tonight (1)
There's Many A River (10)
This Land Is Your Land (medley) (5)
This Train (5)
Those Were The Days (6)
Time Of Man (3)

To Everything There Is A Season (Turn! Turn! Turn!) (6)
Uncle Benny's Celebration (6)
Vikki Dougan (3)
Wabash Cannonball (7)
Wake Up, Dunia (6)
Wayfaring Stranger (4)
We Will Overcome (8)
Western Wind (3)
Whale, The (5)
When I First Came To This Land (2)
Where Shall I Be? (8)
Whistling Gypsy (3)

Who Will Join? (8)
Whoopee Ti Yi Yo (9)
Why Don't You Come Home (10)
Wild Colonial Boy (10)
Willow Tree (10)
Wondrous Love (medley) (8)
Yerakina (7)
Youth Of The Heart (9)
Zhankoye (2)

LIND, Bob
Born on 11/25/44 in Baltimore. Folk-rock singer/songwriter.

| 4/16/66 | 148 | 2 | | Don't Be Concerned .... | $15 | World Pac. 1841 |

Cheryl's Goin' Home
Counting
Dale Anne

Drifter's Sunrise
Elusive Butterfly 5
I Can't Walk Roads Of Anger

It Wasn't Just The Morning
Mister Zero

Truly Julie's Blues (I'll Be There) 65

Unlock The Door
World Is Just A "B" Movie

You Should Have Seen It

LINDLEY, David
Multi-instrumentalist from San Marino, California. Leader of Kaleidoscope/prominent session musician. Worked with James Taylor, Linda Ronstadt and Jackson Browne. Film score work solo and with Ry Cooder. In 1980, formed El Rayo-X with Jorge Calderon, Walfredo Reyes, William Smith and Ray Woodbury.

| 5/16/81 | 83 | 18 | | 1 El Rayo-X .... | $8 | Asylum 524 |
| 9/24/88 | 174 | 6 | | 2 Very Greasy .... | $8 | Elektra 60768 |

DAVID LINDLEY & EL RAYO X
produced by Linda Ronstadt

Ain't No Way (1)
Bye Bye, Love (1)
Do Ya' Wanna Dance? (2)
Don't Look Back (1)
El Rayo-X (1)

Gimme Da' Ting (2)
I Just Can't Work No Longer (2)
Mercury Blues (1)

Never Knew Her (2)
Papa Was A Rolling Stone (2)
Pay The Man (1)
Petit Fleur (1)

Quarter Of A Man (1)
She Took Off My Romeos (1)
Talk About You (2)
Talkin' To The Wino Too (2)

Texas Tango (2)
Tiki Torches At Twilight (2)
Tu-ber-cu-lucas And The Sinus Blues (1)

Twist And Shout (1)
Werewolves Of London (2)
Your Old Lady (1)

LINDSAY, Mark
Born on 3/9/42 in Cambridge, Idaho. Lead singer/saxophonist of Paul Revere & The Raiders. Also recorded with Raider, Keith Allison, and Steve Alaimo as The Unknowns.

3/7/70	36	19		1 Arizona..	$15	Columbia 9986
9/5/70	82	10		2 Silverbird..	$12	Columbia 30111
10/9/71	180	2		3 You've Got A Friend..	$12	Columbia 30735

All I Really See Is You (3)
And The Grass Won't Pay No Mind (2) 44
Arizona (1) 10
Been Too Long On The Road (3) 98
Bookends (2)
Come Saturday Morning (2)

Feel The Warm (2)
First Hymn From Grand Terrace (1) 81
Funny How Little Men Care (2)
Help Me Make It Through The Night (3)

I'll Never Fall In Love Again (1)
If You Could Read My Mind (3)
It's Too Late (3)
Leaving On A Jet Plane (1)
Long And Winding Road (medley) (2)

Love's Been Good To Me (1)
Man From Houston (1)
Miss America (1) 44
Name Of My Sorrow (1)
Need A Little Time (3)
Never Can Say Goodbye (3)
Old Man At The Fair (3)
Pretty, Pretty (3)

Silver Bird (2) 25
Small Town Woman (1)
So Hard To Leave You (2)
Something (1)
Sunday Mornin' Comin' Down (1)
We've Only Just Begun (1)
Windy Wakefield (2)

Yesterday (medley) (2)
You've Got A Friend (3)

LINEAR
Pronounced: lin-EAR. Miami-based male trio: New Yorkers Charlie "Steele" Pennachio (vocals) and Joey Restivo (percussion) with Ecuadoran Wyatt Pauley (guitar).

| 4/28/90 | 52 | 20 | | Linear.. | $12 | Atlantic 82090 |
| | | | | CD includes bonus mix | | |

Don't You Come Cryin' 70
Dream About Me

Heartache

I Never Felt This Way
Lies

Sending All My Love *[includes 2 versions]* **5**

Something Going On
Still In Love

You're My Lady

LINKLETTER, Art
Born on 7/17/12 in Moose Jaw, Canada. Popular radio and TV personality. Hosted own shows *Art Linkletter's House Party* (later known as *The Linkletter Show*) and several others.

| 12/31/66+ | 143 | 3 | | For The Children Of The World, Art Linkletter narrates "The Bible..In The Beginning" .... [S-T] | $15 | 20th Century 3187 |
| | | | | Art adds narration to music, dialogue and sound effects from the soundtrack | | |

Abraham

Adam And Eve

Cain And Abel

Creation, The

Noah And The Ark

Tower Of Babel

LINX
British funk group led by David Grant (vocals) and Peter "Sketch" Martin (bass).

| 6/20/81 | 175 | 4 | | Intuition .... | $8 | Chrysalis 1332 |

Count On Me
Don't Get In My Way

I Won't Forget
Intuition

Rise And Shine
There's Love

Throw Away The Key
Together We Can Shine

Wonder What You're Doing Now

You're Lying

LIONS & GHOSTS
Rock quartet formed in Hollywood, led by Rick Parker.

| 10/24/87 | 187 | 3 | | Velvet Kiss, Lick of the Lime .... | $8 | EMI America 46959 |

Contradiction
Girl On A Swing

Love & Kisses From The Gutter

Man In A Car
Mary Goes 'Round

One Theme
Passion

Stay
Street Angel

When The Moon Is Full
Wilton House

LIPPS, INC.
Pronounced: lip-synch. Funk project from Minneapolis formed by producer/songwriter/multi-instrumentalist Steven Greenberg. Vocals by Miss Black Minnesota U.S.A. of 1976, Cynthia Johnson.

| 4/19/80 | 5 | 26 | ● | 1 Mouth To Mouth .... | $8 | Casablanca 7197 |
| 10/11/80 | 63 | 9 | | 2 Pucker Up .... | $8 | Casablanca 7242 |

All Night Dancing (1)
Always Lookin' (2)

Funkytown (1) 1
Gossip Song (2)

How Long (2)
Jazzy (2)

Power (1)
Rock It (1) 64

There They Are (2)
Tight Pair (2)

DEBUT DATE	PEAK POS	WKS CHR	GOLD	ARTIST — Album Title	$	Label & Number

LISA LISA AND CULT JAM
Harlem trio: Lisa Velez (lead vocals), Mike Hughes and Alex "Spanador" Moseley. Assembled and produced by Full Force.

DEBUT DATE	PEAK POS	WKS CHR	GOLD	ARTIST — Album Title	$	Label & Number
8/31/85	52	66 ▲		1 Lisa Lisa & Cult Jam with Full Force *	$8	Columbia 40135
				LISA LISA & CULT JAM with FULL FORCE		
5/9/87	7	48 ▲		2 Spanish Fly *	$8	Columbia 40477
5/13/89	77	13		3 Straight To The Sky *	$8	Columbia 44378
				*all songs written, arranged and produced by Full Force		
9/7/91	133	6		4 Straight Outta Hell's Kitchen	$12	Columbia 46035

tracks 1-6 produced, arranged & mixed by Robert Clivilles & David Cole (C&C Music Factory); tracks 7-12 produced & arranged by Full Force

All Cried Out (1) *8*
Behind My Eyes (1)
Can You Feel The Beat (1) *69*
Dance Forever (3)
Do It Like That (4)
Don't Say Goodbye (medley) (4)
Everything Will B-Fine (2)

Face In The Crowd (2)
Fool Is Born Everyday (2)
Forever (4)
Give Me Some Of Your Time (3)
Gotta Find Somebody New (3)
Head To Toe (2) *1*
I Can't Take No More (3)

I Like It, I Like It (4)
I Love What You Do To Me (3)
I Promise You (2)
I Wonder If I Take You Home (1) *34*
Just Git It Together (3)
Kiss Your Tears Away (3)
Let It Go (4)

Let The Beat Hit 'Em (4) *37*
Let The Music Play (4)
Little Jackie Wants To Be A Star (3) *29*
Lost In Emotion (2) *1*
Love Will Get Us By (4)
Playing With Fire (2)
Private Property (1)

Rainstorm Interlude (medley) (4)
Sensuality (4)
Someone To Love Me For Me (2) *78*
Something 'Bout Love (4)
Straight To The Sky (3)
Take Me Home (Rap) (1)

This Is Cult Jam (1)
Where Were You When I Needed You (4)
U Never Nu How Good U Had It (3)
You + Me = Love (4)
You'll Never Change (1)

LITTER
Detroit hard-rock quintet — Mark Gallagher, lead singer.

| 8/16/69 | 175 | 5 | | Emerge .... | $35 | Probe 4504 |

Blue Ice
Breakfast At Gardenson's

Feeling
For What It's Worth

Future Of The Past

Journeys

Little Red Book

Silly People

LITTLE, Rich
Born on 11/26/38 in Ottawa, Canada. Comedian/impressionist. Made first U.S. television appearance on *The Judy Garland Show* in 1964.

| 2/13/82 | 29 | 13 | | The First Family Rides Again ....[C] | $8 | Boardwalk 33248 |

with Melanie Chartoff, Michael Richards, Shelley Hack, Jenilee Harrison, Earle Doud (producer) and Vaughn Meader

Air Force One
Big Game
Bugs

Funeral, The
God
Happening, The

Happy Birthday
Integration
Late Night Phone Call

Lincoln Room
Mr. Bill
Preparing The President

Press Conference
Psychiatrist, The
Reaganomics

Wake Up
Washington Portrait
White House Tour

LITTLE AMERICA
Los Angeles-based rock quartet: Mike Magrisi (vocals), Custer, John Hussey and Andy Logan.

| 4/25/87 | 102 | 14 | | Little America .... | $8 | Geffen 24113 |

Conversations
Heroes

Lies
Lost Along The Way

Out Of Bounds
Perfect World

Standin' On Top
That's The Way It Stays

Underground
Walk On Fire

Walk The Land
You Were Right

LITTLE ANTHONY AND THE IMPERIALS
R&B group formed in 1957 in Brooklyn. Consisted of Anthony Gourdine (b: 1/8/40), Ernest Wright, Jr., Tracy Lord, Glouster Rogers and Clarence Collins. Anthony first recorded on Winley in 1955 with The DuPonts. Formed The Chesters in 1957, then changed name to The Imperials in 1958. Sammy Strain, who joined group in 1964, left in 1975 to join The O'Jays. Gourdine became an Inspirational artist in 1980.

1/16/65	135	4		1 I'm On The Outside (Looking In)	$20	DCP 6801
				includes a new version of "Tears On My Pillow"		
2/20/65	74	13		2 Goin' Out Of My Head	$20	DCP 6808
3/5/66	97	23		3 The Best Of Little Anthony & The Imperials ....[G]	$20	DCP 6809
10/4/69	172	5		4 Out Of Sight, Out Of Mind	$15	United Art. 6720

Easy To Be Hard (4)
Exodus (1)
Funny (1)
Get Out Of My Life (2,3)
Girl From Ipanema (1)
Goin' Out Of My Head (2,3) *6*
Goodbye Goodtimes (4)

Hurt (2,3) *51*
Hurt So Bad (2,3) *10*
I Look At You (4)
I Miss You So (2,3) *34*
I'm On The Outside (Looking In) (1,3) *15*
It's Just A Matter Of Time (2)
Let The Sunshine In (4)

Letter A Day (1)
Love That Dies (4)
Make It Easy On Yourself (1)
Never Again (2,3)
Our Song (1,3)
Out Of Sight, Out Of Mind (4) *52*
People (1)

Please Go (1)
Reputation (2,3)
Ride, The (4)
Shimmy Shimmy Ko-Ko Bop (3)
Summer's Comin' In (4)
Take Me Back (2,3) *16*
Tears On My Pillow (1,3)

Ten Commandments Of **Love** (4) *82*
What A Difference A Day Made (2)
Where Are You (2)
Where Did Our Love Go? (1)
Who's Sorry Now? (2)

You Bring Me Down (4)

LITTLE CAESAR
Los Angeles-based, hard-rock band: Ron Young (vocals), Louren Molinare, Fidel Angel Paniagua, Tom Morris and Apache. Group named after a 1930 gangster film. Young had cameo in film *Terminator 2*.

| 6/30/90 | 139 | 8 | | Little Caesar .... | $12 | DGC 24288 |

Cajun Panther
Chain Of Fools *88*

Down-N-Dirty
Drive It Home

From The Start
Hard Times

I Wish It Would Rain
In Your Arms *79*

Little Queenie
Midtown

Rock-N-Roll State Of Mind
Wrong Side Of The Tracks

LITTLE EVA
Born Eva Narcissus Boyd on 6/29/45 in Bellhaven, North Carolina. Discovered by songwriters Carole King and Gerry Goffin while babysitting their daughter Louise.

| 11/3/62 | 97 | 6 | | Lllllloco-Motion .... | $100 | Dimension 6000 |

Breaking Up Is Hard To Do
Down Home
He Is The Boy

I Have A Love
Keep Your Hands Off My Baby *12*

Loco-Motion *1*
Run To Her
Sharing You

Some Kind-A Wonderful
Up On The Roof
Uptown

Where Do I Go
Will You Love Me Tomorrow

| ★★360★★ | | | | **LITTLE FEAT** | | |

Los Angeles seminal rock band formed in 1969, fronted by guitarist Paul Barrere and vocalist Lowell George (ex-Mothers Of Invention) with Bill Payne, Richie Hayward, Kenny Gradney and Sam Clayton. Frank Zappa named group after George's shoe size. George died on 6/29/79 (age 34) of drug-related heart failure. Reunited briefly in 1985. Regrouped in 1988 with Craig Fuller (formerly with Pure Prairie League) as lead singer; Fred Tackett also added to lineup.

9/7/74	36	16 ●		1 Feats Don't Fail Me Now	$10	Warner 2784
11/15/75	36	15		2 The Last Record Album	$10	Warner 2884
5/14/77	34	18 ●		3 Time Loves A Hero	$8	Warner 3015
3/11/78	18	25 ▲		4 Waiting For Columbus ....[L]	$10	Warner 3140 [2]
12/8/79+	29	21		5 Down On The Farm	$8	Warner 3345

425

DEBUT DATE	PEAK POS	WKS CHR	G O L D	ARTIST — Album Title	$	Label & Number
				LITTLE FEAT — Cont'd		
8/22/81	**39**	13		6 Hoy-Hoy! .... [K]	$10	Warner 3538 [2]
8/20/88	**36**	33	●	7 Let It Roll	$8	Warner 25750
4/28/90	**45**	16		8 Representing The Mambo	$12	Warner 26163
10/12/91	**126**	6		9 Shake Me Up	$12	Morgan Cr. 20005

All That You Dream (2,4,6)
Apolitical Blues (4)
Be One Now (5)
Boom Box Car (9)
Business As Usual (7)
Cajun Girl (7)
Changin' Luck (7)
China White (6)
Clownin' (7)
Cold Cold Cold (medley) (1)
Daily Grind (8)
Day At The Dog Races (3)
Day Or Night (2,4)
Dixie Chicken (4)
Don't Bogart That Joint (4)
Don't Try So Hard (9)

Down Below The Borderline (2)
Down In Flames (9)
Down On The Farm (5)
Down The Road (1)
Easy To Slip (6)
Fan, The (1,6)
Fast & Furious (9)
Fat Man In The Bathtub (4)
Feats Don't Fail Me Now (1,4,6)
Feel The Groove (5)
Feelin's All Gone (8)
Forty-Four Blues (6)
Framed (6)
Front Page News (5,6)

Gringo (6)
Hangin' On To The Good Times (7)
Hate To Lose Your Lovin' (7)
Hi Roller (3)
Ingenue, The (8)
Join The Band (4)
Keepin' Up With The Joneses (3)
Kokomo (5)
Let It Roll (7)
Listen To Your Heart (7)
Livin' On Dreams (9)
Lonesome Whistle (6)
Long Distance Love (2)

Long Time Till I Get Over You (7)
Loved And Lied To (9)
Mercenary Territory (2,4)
Missin' You (3)
Mojo Haiku (9)
New Delhi Freight Train (3)
Oh Atlanta (1,4)
Old Folks Boogie (3,4)
One Clear Moment (7)
One Love Stand (2)
Over The Edge (6)
Perfect Imperfection (7)
Rad Gumbo (6)
Red Streamliner (3,6)
Representing The Mambo (8)

Rock And Roll Doctor (1,6)
Rocket In My Pocket (3,4,6)
Romance Dance (2)
Sailin' Shoes (4)
Shake Me Up (9)
Silver Screen (8)
Six Feet Of Snow (5)
Skin It Back (1,6)
Somebody's Leavin' (2)
Spanish Moon (1,4)
Spider's Blues (Might Need It Sometime) (9)
Straight From The Heart (5)
Strawberry Flats (6)
Teenage Nervous Breakdown (6)

Teenage Warrior (8)
That's Her, She's Mine (8)
Things Happen (9)
Those Feat'll Steer Ya Wrong Sometimes (8)
Time Loves A Hero (3,4)
Tripe Face Boogie (1,4)
Two Trains (6)
Voices On The Wind (7)
Wake Up Dreaming (5)
Willin' (4)
Woman In Love (8)

LITTLE MILTON

Born Milton Campbell, Jr. on 9/7/34 in Inverness, Mississippi. Blues singer/guitarist. Recorded with Ike Turner at Sun Records, 1953-54. In concert film *Wattstax*, 1972.

6/5/65	**101**	14		1 We're Gonna Make It	$30	Checker 2995
6/14/69	**159**	7		2 Grits Ain't Groceries	$15	Checker 3011
3/28/70	**197**	2		3 If Walls Could Talk	$15	Checker 3012

Ain't No Big Deal On You (1)
Baby I Love You (3) *82*
Believe In Me (1)
Blind Man (1) *86*
Blues Get Off My Shoulder (3)
Blues In The Night (1)

Can't Hold Back The Tears (1)
Country Style (1)
Did You Ever Love A Woman (2)
Good To Me As I Am To You (3)

Grits Ain't Groceries (All Around The World) (2) *73*
I Can't Quit You, Baby (1)
I Don't Know (3)
I Play Dirty (2)
I'll Always Love You (2)

I'm Gonna Move To The Outskirts Of Town (1)
If Walls Could Talk (3) *71*
Just A Little Bit (2) *97*
Kansas City (3)
Let's Get Together (3)
Life Is Like That (1)

Poor Man (3)
So Blue (Without You) (2)
Spring (2)
Stand By Me (1)
Steal Away (3)
Things That I Used To Do (3)
Twenty-Three Hours (2)

We're Gonna Make It (1) *25*
Who's Cheating Who? (1) *43*
You're The One (3)
You're Welcome To The Club (1)
Your Precious Love (3)

LITTLE RICHARD

Born Richard Wayne Penniman on 12/5/32 in Macon, Georgia. R&B-rock and roll singer/pianist. Talent contest win led to first recordings for RCA-Victor in 1951. Worked with the Tempo Toppers, 1953-55. Appeared in three early rock and roll films: *Don't Knock The Rock*, *The Girl Can't Help It* and *Mister Rock 'n' Roll* and the 1986 comedy *Down And Out In Beverly Hills*. Earned theology degree in 1961 and was ordained a minister. Left R&B for gospel music, 1959-62, and again in the mid-1970s. One of the key figures in the transition from R&B to rock and roll. Inducted into the Rock and Roll Hall of Fame in 1986.

8/5/57	**13**	5		1 Here's Little Richard .... [G]	$100	Specialty 2100
8/19/67	**184**	3		2 Little Richard's Greatest Hits .... [L]	$20	Okeh 14121
11/13/71	**193**	4		3 King Of Rock And Roll	$15	Reprise 6462

Anyway You Want Me (2)
Baby (1)
Born On The Bayou (3)
Brown Sugar (3)
Can't Believe You Wanna Leave (1)
Dancing In The Street (3)

Get Down With It (2)
Girl Can't Help It (2)
Good Golly Miss Molly (2)
Green Power (3)
I'm So Lonesome I Could Cry (3)
In The Name (3)

Jenny, Jenny (1,2) *10*
Joy To The World (3)
Lucille (2)
Long Tall Sally (1,2) *6*
Midnight Special (3)
Miss Ann (1) *56*

Oh Why? (1)
Ready Teddy (1) *44*
Rip It Up (1)
Send Me Some Lovin' (2)
Settlin' The Woods On Fire (3)
She's Got It (1)

Slippin' And Slidin' (Peepin' And Hidin') (1) *33*
True, Fine Mama (1,2) *68*
Tutti-Frutti (1,2) *17*
Way You Do The Things You Do (3)

Whole Lotta Shakin' Goin' On (2)
You Gotta Feel It (1)

★★318★★   LITTLE RIVER BAND

Pop-rock group formed in Australia in 1975. Consisted of Glenn Shorrock (lead singer), Rick Formosa, Beeb Birtles and Graham Goble (guitars), Roger McLachlan (bass) and Derek Pellicci (drums). McLachlan replaced by George McArdle in 1977 and Formosa replaced by David Briggs in 1978. American bassist Wayne Nelson replaced McLachlan in 1980. In 1983, Shorrock replaced by John Farnham and Briggs replaced by Steve Housden. By 1985, Pellicci replaced by Steven Prestwich, and Birtles had left and keyboardist David Hirschfelder joined. Pellicci and Shorrock returned in 1987. By 1992, Goble had left and Peter Beckett, ex-leader of Player, had joined. Band named after a resort town near Melbourne.

10/2/76	**80**	24		1 Little River Band	$8	Harvest 11512
6/25/77	**49**	48	●	2 Diamantina Cocktail	$8	Harvest 11645
				title is an Australian rum drink made with an emu's egg		
6/17/78	**16**	61	▲	3 Sleeper Catcher	$8	Harvest 11783
8/4/79	**10**	33	▲	4 First Under The Wire	$8	Capitol 11954
4/19/80	**44**	10		5 Backstage Pass .... [L]	$10	Capitol 12061 [2]
9/19/81	**21**	50	●	6 Time Exposure	$8	Capitol 12163
12/4/82+	**33**	30	▲²	7 Greatest Hits .... [G]	$8	Capitol 12247
6/18/83	**61**	21		8 The Net	$8	Capitol 12273
2/9/85	**75**	14		9 Playing To Win	$8	Capitol 12365

LRB

Another Runway (2)
Ballerina (6)
Blind Eyes (9)
Broke Again (2)
By My Side (4)
Cool Change (4,7) *10*
Count Me In (9)
Curiosity (Killed The Cat) (1)
Danger Sign (8)
Days On The Road (2)
Don't Blame Me (9)
Don't Let The Needle Win (6)
Down On The Border (7,8)
Easy Money (8)

Emma (1)
Every Day Of My Life (2)
Fall From Paradise (3,5)
Falling (8)
Full Circle (6)
Guiding Light (6)
Happy Anniversary (2,7) *16*
Hard Life (4,5)
Help Is On Its Way (2,5,7) *14*
Home On Monday (2)
I Don't Worry No More (5)
I Know It (1)

I'll Always Call Your Name (1) *62*
Inner Light (2)
It's A Long Way There (1,5,7) *28*
It's Not A Wonder (4,5) *51*
Just Say That You Love Me (5)
Lady (3,7) *10*
Let's Dance (5)
Light Of Day (3,5)
Lonesome Loser (4,7) *6*
Love Will Survive (6)
Man In Black (1,3)

Man On The Run (4,5)
Man On Your Mind (6,7) *14*
Meanwhile (2)
Middle Man (4)
Mistress Of Mine (4,5)
Mr. Socialite (9)
My Lady And Me (9)
Net, The (8)
Night Owls (6,7) *6*
No More Tears (8)
One For The Road (3)
One Shot In The Dark (9)
Orbit Zero (6)
Other Guy (7) *11*

Piece Of The Dream (9)
Playing To Win (9) *60*
Reappear (9)
Red-Headed Wild Flower (3)
Red Shoes (5)
Relentless (9)
Reminiscing (3,5,7) *3*
Rumor, The (4,5)
Sanity's Side (9)
Shut Down Turn Off (3)
Sleepless Nights (8)
So Many Paths (3,5)
Statue Of Liberty (1,5)
Suicide Boulevard (6)

Sweet Old Fashioned Man (5)
Take It Easy On Me (6,7) *10*
Take Me Home (2)
Through Her Eyes (9)
Too Lonely Too Long (5)
We Two (8) *22*
When Cathedrals Were White (9)
You're Driving Me Out Of My Mind (8) *35*

DEBUT DATE	PEAK POS	WKS CHR	GOLD	ARTIST — Album Title	$	Label & Number

LITTLE STEVEN and the DISCIPLES OF SOUL

Guitarist/producer Miami Steve Van Zandt. Born in Boston and raised in New Jersey. Formed Southside Johnny & the Asbury Jukes with co-lead singer Johnny Lyon in 1974. Joined Bruce Springsteen's E Street Band in 1975. Organized Artists United Against Apartheid.

DEBUT DATE	PEAK POS	WKS CHR			$	Label & Number
12/4/82+	118	18	1	Men Without Women	$8	EMI America 17086
6/9/84	55	17	2	Voice Of America	$8	EMI America 17120
6/13/87	80	12	3	Freedom No Compromise	$8	Manhattan 53048

LITTLE STEVEN

Among The Believers (2)
Angel Eyes (1)
Bitter Fruit (3)
Can't You Feel The Fire (1)
Checkpoint Charlie (2)
Fear (2)

Forever (1) *63*
Freedom (3)
I Am A Patriot (And The River Opens For The Righteous) (1)
I've Been Waiting (1)

Inside Of Me (1)
Justice (2)
Los Desaparecidos (The Disappeared Ones) (2)
Lyin' In A Bed Of Fire (1)
Men Without Women (1)

Native American (3)
No More Party's (3)
Out Of The Darkness (2)
Pretoria (3)
Princess Of Little Italy (1)
Sanctuary (3)

Save Me (1)
Solidarity (2)
Trail Of Broken Treaties (3)
Undefeated (Everybody Goes Home) (2)
Under The Gun (1)

Until The Good Is Gone (1)
Voice Of America (2)

LITTLE TEXAS

Six-man group: Texans Tim Rushlow (vocals), Dwayne O'Brien, Porter Howell and Duane Propes, with Brady Seals (nephew of songwriter Troy Seals and cousin of singer Dan Seals) and Del Gray.

3/21/92	99	12		First Time For Everything	$12	Warner 26820

Better Way
Cry On

Dance
Down In The Valley

First Time For Everything
I'd Rather Miss You

Just One More Night

Some Guys Have All The Love

What Were You Thinkin'
You And Forever And Me

LITTLE VILLAGE

Supergroup of John Hiatt (vocals), Nick Lowe (bass), Ry Cooder (guitar) and Jim Keltner (drums; Attitudes). Lineup first came together for Hiatt's 1987 solo album *Bring The Family*.

3/7/92	66	12		Little Village	$12	Reprise 26713

Action, The
Big Love
Do You Want My Job

Don't Bug Me When I'm Working
Don't Go Away Mad

Don't Think About Her When You're Trying To Drive
She Runs Hot

Fool Who Knows
Inside Job

Solar Sex Panel
Take Another Look

LIVE

York, Pennsylvania foursome: Edward Kowalczyk (vocals), Chad Taylor, Patrick Dalheimer and Chad Gracey.

1/18/92	73	24		Mental Jewelry	$12	Radioactive 10346

produced by Jerry Harrison (Talking Heads)

Beauty Of Gray
Brothers Unaware
Good Pain

Mirror Song
Mother Earth Is A Vicious Crowd

Operation Spirit (The Tyranny Of Tradition)

Pain Lies On The Riverside
Take My Anthem

10,000 Years (Peace Is Now)
Tired Of "Me"

Waterboy
You Are The World

LIVING COLOUR

Black rock quartet from New York City. London-born, Brooklyn-raised lead guitarist/songwriter Vernon Reid, with vocalist Corey Glover (appeared in the film *Platoon*), bassist Muzz Skillings and drummer William Calhoun. Skillings left in early 1992, replaced by Doug Wimbush (ex-Tackhead).

9/3/88+	6	76 ▲	1	Vivid	$8	Epic 44099
9/15/90	13	35 ●	2	Time's Up	$12	Epic 46202
8/3/91	110	5	3	Biscuits	[M] $6	Epic 47988

6 tracks recorded from April 1989 - May 1991, 2 of which are live

Broken Hearts (1)
Burning Of The Midnight Lamp (2)
Cult Of Personality (1) *13*
Desperate People (1,3)
Elvis Is Dead (2)
Fight The Fight (2)

Funny Vibe (1)
Glamour Boys (1) *31*
History Lesson (2)
I Want To Know (1)
Information Overload (2)
Love And Happiness (3)
Love Rears Its Ugly Head (2)

Memories Can't Wait (1,3)
Middle Man (1)
Money Talks (3)
New Jack Theme (2)
Ology (2)
Open Letter (To A Landlord) (1) *82*

Pride (2)
Solace Of You (2)
Someone Like You (2)
Tag Team Partners (3)
Talkin' Loud And Sayin' Nothing (3)
This Is The Life (2)

Time's Up (2)
Type (2)
Under Cover Of Darkness (2)
What's Your Favorite Color? (Theme Song) (1)
Which Way To America? (1)

LIVING IN A BOX

Soul-styled pop trio from England: Richard Darbyshire (vocals), Marcus Vere (keyboards) and Anthony "Tich" Critchlow (drums).

8/8/87	89	13		Living In A Box	$8	Chrysalis 41547

Can't Stop The Wheel
From Beginning To End

Generate The Wheel
Going For The Big One

Human Story
Living In A Box *17*

Love Is The Art

Scales Of Justice

So The Story Goes *81*

LIVING STRINGS

European orchestra.

2/27/61	26	6	1	Living Strings Play All The Music From Camelot	[I] $10	RCA Camden 657

arranged and conducted by Hill Bowen

2/27/61	42	7	2	Living Strings Play Music Of The Sea	[I] $10	RCA Camden 639

arranged and conducted by Johnny Douglas

A-Roving (medley) (2)
Aloha Oe (Farewell To Thee) (medley) (2)
Around The World (medley) (2)
Banana Boat Song (medley) (2)

C'est Moi (1)
Camelot (medley) (1)
Come Back To Sorrento (medley) (2)
Come To Capri (medley) (2)
Ebb Tide (2)
Far Away Places (medley) (2)

Fie On Goodness (medley) (1)
Follow Me (1)
Guinevere (medley) (1)
How To Handle A Woman (1)
I Loved You Once In Silence (1)

I Wonder What The King Is Doing Tonight (medley) (1)
If Ever I Would Leave You (1)
Isle Of Capri (medley) (2)
Jamaica Farewell (medley) (2)

Jousts, The (medley) (1)
La Mer (medley) (2)
Lusty Month Of May (1)
Quests, The (medley) (1)
Rio Grande (2)
Shenandoah (medley) (2)

Simple Joys Of Maidenhood (medley) (1)
Sleepy Lagoon (medley) (2)
What Do Simple Folks Do (1)

LIZZY BORDEN

Hard-rock group led by male vocalist Lizzy Borden.

11/1/86	144	10	1	Menace To Society	$8	Enigma 73224
5/2/87	188	6	2	Terror Rising	[M] $8	Enigma 73254
9/26/87	146	7	3	Visual Lies	$8	Enigma 73288
8/26/89	133	10	4	Master Of Disguise	$8	Metal Blade 73413

American Metal (2)
Be One Of Us (4)
Bloody Mary (1)
Brass Tactics (1)
Catch Your Death (2)
Den Of Thieves (3)
Don't Touch Me There (2)

Eyes Of A Stranger (3)
Generation Aliens (1)
Give 'Em The Axe (2)
Lord Of The Flies (3)
Love Is A Crime (4)
Love Kills (1)
Master Of Disguise (4)

Me Against The World (3)
Menace To Society (1)
Never Too Young (4)
Notorious (4)
One False Move (1)
Outcast (3)
Phantoms (4)

Psychodrama (4)
Rod Of Iron (2)
Roll Over And Play Dead (4)
Shock (3)
Sins Of The Flesh (4)
Stiletto (Voice Of Command) (1)
Visual Lies (3)

Terror On The Town (3)
Terror Rising (2)
Ultra Violence (1)
Under The Rose (4)
Ursa Minor (3)
Visions (3)

Voyeur (I'm Watching You) (3)
Waiting In The Wings (4)
We Got The Power (4)
White Rabbit (2)

DEBUT DATE	PEAK POS	WKS CHR	GOLD	ARTIST — Album Title	$	Label & Number

L.L. COOL J
Real name: James Todd Smith. Rapper from Queens, New York. Stage name is abbreviation for Ladies Love Cool James. Appeared in the films *Krush Groove* and *The Hard Way*.

DEBUT DATE	PEAK POS	WKS CHR	GOLD	#	Album Title	$	Label & Number
1/11/86	46	38	▲	1	Radio	$8	Columbia 40239
6/20/87	3	53	▲²	2	Bigger And Deffer	$8	Def Jam 40793
7/1/89	6	21	▲	3	Walking With A Panther	$8	Def Jam 45172
					LP features 16 tracks, 18 on the CD and 20 on the cassette		
10/6/90	16	76	▲²	4	Mama Said Knock You Out	$12	Def Jam 46888

Ahh, Let's Get Ill (2)
Around The Way Girl (4) *9*
Big Ole Butt (3)
Boomin' System (4) *48*
Breakthrough, The (2)
Bristol Hotel (2)
Cheesy Rat Blues (4)
Clap Your Hands (3)
Dangerous (1)
Dear Yvette (1)

Def Jam In The Motherland (3)
Do Wop (2)
Droppin' Em (3)
Eat Em Up L Chill (4)
Farmers Blvd. (Our Anthem) (4)
Fast Peg (3)
Get Down (2)
Go Cut Creator Go (2)
I Can Give You More (1)

I Can't Live Without My Radio (1)
I Need A Beat (1)
I Need Love (2) *14*
I Want You (1)
I'm Bad (2) *84*
I'm That Type Of Guy (3) *15*
Illegal Search (4)
It Gets No Rougher (3)
Jealous (3)

Jingling Baby (3,4)
Kanday (2)
Mama Said Knock You Out (4) *17*
Milky Cereal (4)
Mr. Good Bar (4)
Murdergram (4)
My Rhyme Ain't Done (2)
Nitro (3)
On The Ill Tip (2)
1-900 L.L. Cool J (3)

One Shot At Love (3)
Power Of God (4)
Rock The Bells (1)
6 Minutes Of Pleasure (4) *95*
Smokin', Dopin' (3)
That's A Lie (1)
.357 - Break It On Down (2)
To Da Break Of Dawn (4)
Two Different Worlds (3)

Why Do You Think They Call It Dope? (3)
You Can't Dance (1)
You'll Rock (1)
You're My Heart (2)

LLOYD, Charles, Quartet
Jazz tenor saxophonist. Born on 3/15/38 in Memphis. Played with Chico Hamilton from 1961-64 and Cannonball Adderley from 1964-65, then own groups. First jazz musician to play San Francisco's Fillmore West. With Mike Love of The Beach Boys, formed Lovesongs record company in the mid-1970s.

DEBUT DATE	PEAK POS	WKS CHR	#	Album Title		$	Label & Number
7/15/67	188	4	1	Forest Flower	[I-L]	$15	Atlantic 1473
				recorded at the Monterey Jazz Festival on 9/18/66			
8/19/67	171	7	2	Love-In	[I-L]	$15	Atlantic 1481
				recorded at the Fillmore in San Francisco			

East Of The Sun (1)
Forest Flower - Sunrise (1)
Forest Flower - Sunset (1)

Here There And Everywhere (2)
Is It Really The Same? (2)

Island Blues (medley) (2)
Love-In (2)
Song Of Her (1)

Memphis Dues Again (medley) (2)

Sorcery (1)
Sunday Morning (2)

Temple Bells (2)
Tribal Dance (2)

LOBO
Pop singer/songwriter/guitarist. Born Roland Kent Lavoie on 7/31/43 in Tallahassee, Florida. Played with the Legends in Tampa in 1961. The Legends included Jim Stafford, Gerald Chambers, Gram Parsons and Jon Corneal. Lobo is Spanish for wolf. Lavoie formed own publishing company, Boo Publishing, in 1974.

DEBUT DATE	PEAK POS	WKS CHR	#	Album Title		$	Label & Number
6/5/71	178	10	1	Introducing Lobo		$12	Big Tree 2003
10/14/72+	37	31	2	Of A Simple Man		$12	Big Tree 2013
5/5/73	163	5	3	Introducing Lobo	[R]	$12	Big Tree 2100
				new cover features a picture of Lobo			
6/30/73	128	14	4	Calumet		$12	Big Tree 2101
8/10/74	183	4	5	Just A Singer		$12	Big Tree 89501
4/5/75	151	7	6	A Cowboy Afraid Of Horses		$12	Big Tree 89505

Albatross, The (1,3)
All For The Love Of A Girl (5)
Am I True To Myself (2)
Another Hill To Climb (medley) (1,3)
Armstrong (5)
Big Red Kite (2)
Country Feelings (medley) (1,3)
Cowboy Afraid Of Horses (6)
Daydream Believer (5)
Don't Expect Me To Be Your Friend (2) *8*

Don't Tell Me Goodnight (6) *27*
Everyday Is My Way (6)
Goodbye Is Just Another Word (1)
Gypsy And The Midnight Ghost (2)
Hope You're Proud Of Me Girl (4)
How Can I Tell Her (4) *22*
However... (6)
I'd Love You To Want Me (2) *2*
I'm Only Sleeping (5)

I'm The Only One (1,3) *flip*
It Sure Took A Long, Long Time (4) *27*
Let Me Down Easy (2)
Let's Get Together (5)
Little Different (1,3)
Little Joe (They're Out To Get Ya) (1,3)
Lodi (5)
Love Me For What I Am (4) *86*
Me And You And A Dog Named Boo (1,3) *5*
Morning Sun (4)

My Momma Had Soul (6)
One And The Same Thing (4)
Pee-ro Juan Valdez Sam Quixote (3)
Reaching Out For Someone (1,3)
Reason To Believe (5)
Recycle Sally (4)
Rings (5) *43*
Rock And Roll Days (4)
Running Deer (2)
She Didn't Do Magic (1,3) *46*
Shelter Of Your Eyes (5)

Simple Man (2) *56*
Something To See Me Through (6)
Standing At The End Of The Line (4) *37*
Stoney (4)
Then I Met You (6)
There Ain't No Way (2) *68*
Thinking Of You (6)
Three Pick-Ups (6)
Try (4)
Universal Soldier (5)
War To End All Wars (6)

We'll Be One By Two Today (1,3)
We'll Make It...I Know We Will (1,3)
Would I Still Have You (6)

LODGE, John
The Moody Blues' bassist. Born on 7/20/45 in Birmingham, England.

DEBUT DATE	PEAK POS	WKS CHR	#	Album Title	$	Label & Number
3/29/75	16	23	1	Blue Jays	$12	Threshold 14
				JUSTIN HAYWARD/JOHN LODGE		
				album title also refers to the name of their duo		
4/23/77	121	9	2	Natural Avenue	$8	London 683

Broken Dreams, Hard Road (2)
Carry Me (2)
Children Of Rock 'N' Roll (2)

I Dreamed Last Night (1)
Maybe (1)
My Brother (1)
Natural Avenue (2)

Nights, Winters, Years (1)
Piece Of My Heart (2)
Rainbow (2)
Remember Me, My Friend (1)

Saved By The Music (1)
Say You Love Me (2)
Summer Breeze (2)
This Morning (1)

When You Wake Up (1)
Who Are You Now (1)
Who Could Change (2)
You (1)

LOFGREN, Nils
Born in 1952 in Chicago; raised in Maryland. Pop-rock singer/guitarist/pianist. Leader of Grin (1969-1974). Member of Bruce Springsteen's E Street Band, 1984-85.

DEBUT DATE	PEAK POS	WKS CHR	#	Album Title		$	Label & Number
3/22/75	141	9	1	Nils Lofgren		$10	A&M 4509
4/17/76	32	16	2	Cry Tough		$10	A&M 4573
3/19/77	36	12	3	I Came To Dance		$8	A&M 4628
10/29/77	44	10	4	Night After Night	[L]	$10	A&M 3707 [2]
7/21/79	54	14	5	Nils		$8	A&M 4756
9/26/81	99	11	6	Night Fades Away		$8	Backstreet 5251
6/22/85	150	5	7	Flip		$8	Columbia 39982
3/30/91	153	8	8	Silver Lining		$12	Rykodisc 10170

Ancient History (6)
Anytime At All (1)
Back It Up (1,4)
Baltimore (5)
Be Good Tonight (1)
Beggars Day (4)
Bein' Angry (8)

Big Tears Fall (7)
Can't Buy A Break (1)
Can't Get Closer (WCGC) (2)
Code Of The Road (3,4)
Cry Tough (2,4)
Delivery Night (7)
Dirty Money (6)

Don't Touch Me (7)
Dreams Die Hard (7)
Duty (1)
Empty Heart (6)
Flip Ya Flip (7)
Fool Like Me (5)
For Your Love (2)

From The Heart (7)
Girl In Motion (8)
Goin' Back (1,4)
Goin' South (3,4)
Gun And Run (8)
Happy (3)
Happy Ending Kids (3)

Home Is Where The Hurt Is (3)
I Came To Dance (3,4)
I Don't Want To Know (3)
I Found Her (5)
I Go To Pieces (6)
I'll Cry Tomorrow (5)

If I Say It, It's So (1)
In Motion (6)
Incidentally...It's Over (2,4)
It's Not A Crime (2,4)
Jailbait (2)
Jealous Gun (3)

428

DEBUT DATE	PEAK POS	WKS CHR	GOLD	ARTIST — Album Title	$	Label & Number

LOFGREN, Nils — Cont'd

Keith Don't Go (Ode To The Glimmer Twin) (1,4)
King Of The Rock (7)
Kool Skool (5)
Like Rain (4)
Little Bit O' Time (8)

Live Each Day (8)
Moon Tears (4)
Mud In Your Eye (4)
New Holes In Old Shoes (7)
Night Fades Away (6)
No Mercy (5)

One More Saturday Night (1)
Rock And Roll Crook (1,4)
Rock Me At Home (3)
Sailor Boy (6)
Secrets In The Street (7)
Share A Little (2)

Shine Silently (5)
Silver Lining (8)
Steal Away (8)
Sticks And Stones (8)
Streets Again (6)

Sun Hasn't Set On This Boy Yet (1)
Sweet Midnight (7)
Take You To The Movies (4)
To Be A Dreamer (3)
Trouble's Back (8)

Two By Two (1)
Valentine (8)
Walkin' Nerve (8)
You Lit A Fire (2)
You're So Easy (5)
You're The Weight (4)

LOGGINS, Dave

Born on 11/10/47 in Mountain City, Tennessee. Pop-country singer/songwriter. Cousin of Kenny Loggins.

| 11/2/74 | 54 | 16 | | Apprentice (In A Musical Workshop) .... | $10 | Epic 32833 |

Girl From Knoxville
Let Me Go Now

My Father's Fiddle
My Lover's Keeper

Please Come To Boston 5
Second Hand Lady

So You Couldn't Get To Me
Someday 57

Sunset Woman
Wonder'n As The Days Go By

★★340★★ LOGGINS, Kenny

Born on 1/7/47 in Everett, Washington. Raised in Alhambra, California. Pop-rock singer/songwriter/guitarist. Cousin of Dave Loggins. In band Gator Creek with producer Michael Omartian (later with Rhythm Heritage), later in Second Helping. Worked as a songwriter for Wingate Music; wrote Nitty Gritty Dirt Band's "House At Pooh Corner." Signed as a solo artist with Columbia in 1971 where he met and recorded with Jim Messina from 1972-76.

5/7/77	27	33	▲	1 Celebrate Me Home	$8	Columbia 34655
7/22/78	7	31	▲	2 Nightwatch	$8	Columbia 35387
10/20/79+	16	43	▲	3 Keep The Fire	$8	Columbia 36172
10/4/80	11	31	●	4 Kenny Loggins Alive .... [L]	$10	Columbia 36738 [2]
9/25/82	13	44	●	5 High Adventure	$8	Columbia 38127
4/20/85	41	31	●	6 Vox Humana	$8	Columbia 39174
				title is Latin for Human Voice		
8/20/88	69	14		7 Back To Avalon	$8	Columbia 40535
9/28/91	71	58	●	8 Leap Of Faith	$12	Columbia 46140

All Alone Tonight (4)
Angelique (2,4)
At Last (6)
Blue On Blue (7)
Celebrate Me Home (1,4)
Cody's Song (8)
Conviction Of The Heart (8) 65
Daddy's Back (1)
Down In The Boondocks (2)
Down 'N Dirty (2,4)
Easy Driver (2,4) 60
Enter My Dream (1)

Forever (6) 40
Give It Half A Chance (3)
Heart To Heart (5) 15
Heartlight ..see: Welcome To Heartlight
Here There And Everywhere (4)
Hope For The Runaway (7)
I Believe In Love (1,4) 66
I Gotta Try (5)
I Would Do Anything (8)
I'll Be There (6) 88
I'm Alright (4)
I'm Gonna Do It Right (6)
I'm Gonna Miss You (4) 82

I've Got The Melody (Deep In My Heart) (1)
If It's Not What You're Looking For (5)
If You Be Wise (1)
If You Believe (7)
Isabella's Eyes (7)
It Must Be Imagination (5)
Junkanoo Holiday (Fallin'-Flyin') (3,4)
Keep The Fire (3,4) 36
Lady Luck (1)
Leap Of Faith (8)
Let There Be Love (6)
Loraine (8)

Love Has Come Of Age (3,4)
Love Will Follow (6)
Meet Me Half Way (7) 11
More We Try (5)
Mr. Night (3)
My Father's House (8)
Nightwatch (2)
No Lookin' Back (6)
Nobody's Fool (7) 8
Now And Then (3,4)
Now Or Never (8)
One Woman (7)
Only A Miracle (5)
Real Thing (8)
Set It Free (1)

She's Dangerous (7)
Somebody Knows (2)
Swear Your Love (5)
Sweet Reunion (8)
Tell Her (7) 76
This Is It (3,4) 11
Too Early For The Sun (8)
True Confessions (7)
Vox Humana (6) 29
Wait A Little While (4)
Welcome To Heartlight (5) 24
What A Fool Believes (2,4)
Whenever I Call You "Friend" (2,4) 5

Who's Right, Who's Wrong (3)
Why Do People Lie (1,4)
Will It Last (3)
Will Of The Wind (8)
You Don't Know Me (1,4)

★★290★★ LOGGINS & MESSINA

Duo of Kenny Loggins and Jim Messina. Messina (Buffalo Springfield, Poco) was originally hired as a producer for Loggins, however, they formed a partnership that lasted five years.

3/18/72	70	113	▲	1 Sittin' In	$10	Columbia 31044
11/11/72+	16	61	▲	2 Loggins And Messina	$10	Columbia 31748
11/10/73+	10	49	▲	3 Full Sail	$10	Columbia 32540
5/11/74	5	37	●	4 On Stage .... [L]	$12	Columbia 32848 [2]
11/9/74	8	29	●	5 Mother Lode	$10	Columbia 33175
9/13/75	21	13		6 So Fine	$10	Columbia 33810
				featuring popular '50s tunes		
1/31/76	16	17	●	7 Native Sons	$10	Columbia 33578
12/11/76+	61	12	▲	8 The Best Of Friends .... [G]	$10	Columbia 34388
11/12/77	83	8		9 Finale .... [L]	$10	Columbia 34167 [2]

Angry Eyes (2,4,8)
Another Road (4)
Back To Georgia (1,4)
Be Free (5,8,9)
Boogie Man (7,9)
Brighter Days (5,9)
Changes (5,9) 84
Coming To You (4)
Danny's Song (1,4,8,9)
Didn't I Know You When (3)
Fever Dream (5)
Fox Fire (7)
Get A Hold (5)
Golden Ribbons (2,4)

Good Friend (2)
Growin' (5,9) 52
Hello Mary Lou (6)
Hey, Good Lookin' (6)
Holiday Hotel (4)
Honky Tonk - Part II (9)
House At Pooh Corner (1,4,8,9)
I Like It Like That (6) 84
I'm Movin' On (6,9)
It's Alright (7)
Just Before The News (2,4)
Keep Me In Mind (5,9)
Lady Of My Heart (2,4)

Lahaina (3)
Lately My Love (5,9)
Listen To A Country Song (1,4,9)
Long Tail Cat (2,4)
Love Song (3,9)
Lover's Question (6) 89
Lovin' Me (medley) (1,4)
Motel Cowboy (9)
Move On (5)
My Baby Left Me (6)
My Lady, My Love (7)
My Music (3,8,9) 16
Native Son (7)

Nobody But You (1,4) 86
Oh, Lonesome Me (6,9)
Oklahoma, Home Of Mine (9)
Pathway To Glory (3)
Peace Of Mind (1,4,8)
Peacemaker (7,9)
Pretty Princess (7,9)
Rock 'N Roll Mood (1)
Sailin' The Wind (3)
Same Old Wine (1)
So Fine (6)
Splish Splash (6,9)
Sweet Marie (7)
Thinking Of You (2,8,9) 18

Till The Ends Meet (2)
Time To Space (5)
To Make A Woman Feel Wanted (medley) (1,4)
Travelin' Blues (3,9)
Vahevala (1,4,8) 84
Wake Up Little Susie (6)
Wasting Our Time (7)
Watching The River Run (3,8) 71
When I Was A Child (7)
Whiskey (2)
You Could Break My Heart (4)

You Need A Man (3,9)
You Never Can Tell (6)
Your Mama Don't Dance (2,4,8) 4

LO-KEY?

Midwest funk fivesome: prof t., Dre, Lance "L.A." Alexander, "D" and T-Bone.

| 11/14/92 | 124↑ | 11↑ | | Where Dey At? .... | $12 | Perspective 1003 |

Attention: Shawanda's Soulful Mix
Attention: The Shawanda Story

Autumn Love
Don't You Know By Now
Hey There Pretty Lady

I Got A Thang 4 Ya! 27↑
I Wanna Make U Mine

Lo-Key?...Where Dey At?!
Milkshake

More Ways Than One
Stay Awhile

Sweet On U
Ya Gots 2 B True

LOMAX, Jackie

Born on 5/10/44 in Liverpool, England. Male singer/songwriter.

| 6/21/69 | 145 | 9 | | Is This What You Want? .... | $20 | Apple 3354 |
| | | | | produced by George Harrison; with Eric Clapton, Paul McCartney and Ringo Starr | | |

Baby You're A Lover
Eagle Laughs At You

Fall Inside Your Eyes
I Just Don't Know

Is This What You Want?
Little Yellow Pills

New Day
Sour Milk Sea

Speak To Me
Sunset

Take My Word
You've Got Me Thinking

DEBUT DATE	PEAK POS	WKS CHR	GOLD	ARTIST — Album Title	$	Label & Number

LOMBARDO, Guy, And His Royal Canadians
Born on 6/19/02 in London, Ontario, Canada; died on 11/5/77. Leader of the #1 dance band of the '30s and '40s. Known for his classic theme "Auld Lang Syne," which he traditionally played to climax his annual New Year's Eve broadcasts.

| 1/19/57 | **18** | 2 | | **1** Your Guy Lombardo Medley ....[I] | **$15** | Capitol 739 |

medley of 40 tunes

| 7/28/58 | **12** | 4 | | **2** Berlin By Lombardo ....[I] | **$15** | Capitol 1019 |

medley of 40 Irving Berlin songs

All Alone (medley) (2)
All By Myself (medley) (2)
Always (medley) (2)
April In Paris (medley) (1)
April Showers (medley) (1)
Auld Lang Syne (medley) (1)
Be Careful, It's My Heart (medley) (1)
Be My Love (medley) (1)
Best Thing For You (medley) (2)
Birth Of The Blues (medley) (1)
Blue Room (medley) (1)
Blue Skies (medley) (2)
Body And Soul (medley) (1)
Coquette (medley) (1)
Crinoline Days (medley) (2)
Dancing On The Ceiling (medley) (1)
Deep Purple (medley) (1)

Did I Remember (medley) (1)
Dinner At Eight (medley) (1)
Easter Parade (medley) (1)
Ebb Tide (medley) (1)
Girl That I Marry (medley) (2)
God Bless America (medley) (2)
Good Night Sweetheart (medley) (1)
Hold Me (medley) (1)
Honey (medley) (1)
How Deep Is The Ocean (How High Is The Sky) (medley) (2)
I Don't Know Why (medley) (1)
I Love A Piano (medley) (2)
I Want To Go Back To Michigan (Down On The Farm) (medley) (1)

I'll See You In My Dreams (medley) (1)
I'm In The Mood For Love (medley) (1)
I'm Putting All My Eggs In One Basket (medley) (2)
If You Were Only Mine (medley) (1)
Isn't This A Lovely Day (medley) (2)
It Had To Be You (medley) (1)
It's A Lovely Day Today (medley) (2)
It's Only A Paper Moon (medley) (1)
Josephine (medley) (1)
Just A Cottage Small (medley) (1)
Just A Memory (medley) (1)
Lady Of The Evening (medley) (2)

Lazy (medley) (2)
Let's Face The Music And Dance (medley) (2)
Love Is The Sweetest Thing (medley) (1)
Love Nest (medley) (1)
Mandy (medley) (2)
Marie (medley) (1)
Maybe It's Because (I Love You Too Much) (medley) (2)
Night And Day (medley) (1)
Night Is Filled With Music (medley) (2)
Nobody Knows (And Nobody Seems To Care) (medley) (2)
Paradise (medley) (1)
Play A Simple Melody (medley) (2)
A Pretty Girl Is Like A Melody (medley) (2)
Rain (medley) (1)

Reaching For The Moon (medley) (2)
Remember (medley) (2)
Rose Room (medley) (1)
Russian Lullaby (medley) (2)
Say It Isn't So (medley) (2)
Say It With Music (medley) (2)
September In The Rain (medley) (1)
Serenade (medley) (1)
Sleepy Time Gal (medley) (1)
Snuggled On Your Shoulder (medley) (1)
Soft Lights And Sweet Music (medley) (2)
Some Sunny Day (medley) (2)
Song Is Ended (medley) (2)
They Say It's Wonderful (medley) (2)

Very Thought Of You (medley) (1)
What Is This Thing Called Love? (medley) (1)
What'll I Do (medley) (2)
When Day Is Done (medley) (1)
When I Lost You (medley) (2)
White Christmas (medley) (2)
You Go To My Head (medley) (1)
You Keep Coming Back Like A Song (medley) (2)
You'd Be Surprised (medley) (2)
You're A Sweetheart (medley) (1)

LONDON, Julie
Born on 9/26/26 in Santa Rosa, California. Singer/actress. Played Dixie McCall on the TV series *Emergency*. Married to Jack Webb, 1945-53.

1/28/56	**2**[2]	14		**1** Julie Is Her Name	**$30**	Liberty 3006
8/11/56	**16**	8		**2** Lonely Girl	**$30**	Liberty 3012
12/15/56+	**18**	6		**3** Calendar Girl...	**$30**	Liberty 9002
7/22/57	**15**	4		**4** About The Blues	**$30**	Liberty 3043
6/1/63	**127**	3		**5** The End Of The World	**$20**	Liberty 7300
11/23/63	**136**	4		**6** The Wonderful World Of Julie London	**$20**	Liberty 7324

About The Blues (4)
All Alone (2)
Basin Street Blues (4)
Blues In The Night (4)
Blues Is All I Ever Had (4)
Bouquet Of Blues (4)
Bye, Bye Blues (4)
Call Me Irresponsible (5)
Can't Get Used To Losing You (6)
Can't Help Lovin' That Man (1)
Chances Are (5)
Cry Me A River (1) *9*
Days Of Wine And Roses (5)

Don't Take Your Love From Me (2)
Easy Street (1)
End Of The World (5)
Fly Me To The Moon (In Other Words) (5)
Fools Rush In (2)
Get Set For The Blues (4)
Gone With The Wind (1)
Good Life (5)
Guilty Heart (6)
How Can I Make Him Love Me (4)
How Deep Is The Ocean (1)

I Gotta Right To Sing The Blues (4)
I Left My Heart In San Francisco (5)
I Lost My Sugar In Salt Lake City (2)
I Love You (1)
I Love You And Don't You Forget It (6)
I Remember You (5)
I Should Care (1)
I Wanna Be Around (5)
I'll Remember April (3)
I'm Coming Back To You (6)
I'm Glad There Is You (1)

I'm In The Mood For Love (1)
In The Still Of The Night (6)
Invitation To The Blues (4)
It's The Talk Of The Town (2)
June In January (3)
Laura (1)
Little Things Mean A Lot (6)
Lonely Girl (2)
Love For Sale (6)
Mean To Me (2)
Meaning Of The Blues (4)
Melancholy March (3)
Memphis In June (3)
Moments Like This (5)

My Coloring Book (5)
Nightingale Can Sing The Blues (4)
No Moon At All (1)
November Twilight (3)
Our Day Will Come (5)
People Who Are Born In May (3)
Remember (2)
S'Wonderful (1)
Say It Isn't So (1)
Say Wonderful Things (6)
September In The Rain (3)
Sleigh Ride In July (3)

Slightly Out Of Tune (Desafinado) (5)
Soft Summer Breeze (6)
Sunday Blues (4)
Taste Of Honey (6)
Thirteenth Month (3)
This October (3)
Time For August (3)
Warm December (3)
What'll I Do (2)
When Snow Flakes Fall In The Summer (6)
When Your Lover Has Gone (2)
Where Or When (2)

LONDONBEAT
Britain-based soul outfit. Vocal trio of Americans Jimmy Helms and George Chandler, with Trinidad native Jimmy Chambers. Backed by British producer/multi-instrumentalist Willy M.

| 3/2/91 | **21** | 25 | ● | In The Blood | **$12** | Radioactive 10192 |

CD includes bonus track

Better Love *18*
Crying In The Rain
Getcha Ya Ya

I've Been Thinking About You *1*
In An I Love You Mood

It's In The Blood
No Woman No Cry

She Broke My Heart (In 36 Places)

She Said She Loves Me
Step Inside My Shoes

This Is Your Life
You Love And Learn

LONDON FESTIVAL ORCHESTRA — see ALDRICH, Ronnie, and BLACK, Stanley
LONDON PHILHARMONIC ORCHESTRA — see ZADORA, Pia
LONDON QUIREBOYS, The
British hard-rock group featuring bassist Nigel Mogg and lead singer Spike.

| 5/5/90 | **111** | 21 | | A Bit Of What You Fancy .... | **$12** | Capitol 93177 |

Hey You
I Don't Love You Anymore *76*

Long Time Comin'
Man On The Loose

Misled
Roses & Rings

7 O'Clock
Sex Party

Sweet Mary Ann
Take Me Home

There She Goes Again
Whippin' Boy

LONDON SYMPHONY ORCHESTRA
Performed on many of the top soundtrack scores. Also see Benjamin Britten/Antal Dorati/Rock Operas *Tommy*.

4/21/79	**185**	2		**1** Classic Rock - Volume One ....[I]	**$8**	RSO 3043
3/5/83	**145**	3		**2** Hooked On Rock Classics ....[I]	**$8**	RCA 4608
1/11/86	**93**	13		**3** A Classic Case - The London Symphony Orchestra Plays The Music Of Jethro Tull ....[I]	**$8**	RCA 7067

featuring Jethro Tull's Ian Anderson

Aqualung (3)
Baker Street (3)
Bohemian Rhapsody (1)
Bourree (3)
Bungle In The Jungle (medley) (3)

Elegy (3)
Eye Of The Tiger (2)
First Time Ever I Saw Your Face (2)
Fly By Night (3)
Get Back (2)

I'm Not In Love (1)
Layla (2)
Living In The Past (3)
Locomotive Breath (3)
Lucy In The Sky With Diamonds (1)

Nights In White Satin (1)
Paint It Black (1,2)
Rainbow Blues (medley) (3)
Reach Out I'll Be There (2)
Rhapsody In Black (2)
Rock Classics Medley (2)

Ruby Tuesday (2)
Standing In The Shadows Of Love (2)
Teacher (medley) (3)
Thick As A Brick (3)

Too Old To Rock 'N' Roll; Too Young To Die (3)
War Child (3)
Whiter Shade Of Pale (1)
Whole Lotta Love (1)
Without You (1)

DEBUT DATE	PEAK POS	WKS CHR	GOLD	ARTIST — Album Title	$	Label & Number

LONE JUSTICE
Los Angeles country-rock quartet — Maria McKee (b: 1964), lead singer. Guitarist Tony Gilkyson (son of singer Terry Gilkyson), a member in 1985, left in 1986 to join X.

5/11/85	**56**	25		1 Lone Justice................................	**$8**	Geffen 24060
11/29/86+	**65**	30		2 Shelter......................................	**$8**	Geffen 24122

After The Flood (1)
Beacon (2)
Belfry (2)
Dixie Storms (2)

Don't Toss Us Away (1)
Dreams Come True (Stand Up And Take It) (2)
East Of Eden (1)

Gift, The (2)
I Found Love (2)
Inspiration (2)
Pass It On (1)

Reflected (On My Side) (2)
Soap, Soup And Salvation (1)

Sweet, Sweet Baby (I'm Falling) (1) 73
Wait Til We Get Home (1)
Ways To Be Wicked (1) 71

Wheels (2)
Working Late (1)
You Are The Light (1)

LONG, Loretta — see CHILDRENS section

LONGET, Claudine
Born on 1/29/42 in France. Singer/actress. Formerly married to Andy Williams. Jailed, for a time, for fatally shooting skier Spider Savich.

4/15/67	**11**	54	●	1 Claudine...................................	**$10**	A&M 4121
10/14/67	**33**	29		2 The Look Of Love......................	**$10**	A&M 4129
4/13/68	**29**	21		3 Love Is Blue.............................	**$10**	A&M 4142
2/1/69	**155**	7		4 Colours...................................	**$10**	A&M 4163

Am I Blue? (4)
Both Sides Now (4)
Catch The Wind (4)
Colours (4)
Creators Of Rain (2)
Dindi (Jin~Jee) (3)
End Of The World (2)
Falling In Love Again (Can't Help It) (3)

Felicidade, A (1)
For Bobbie (For Baby) (4)
Good Day Sunshine (2) 100
Happy Talk (3)
Hello, Hello (1) 91
Here, There And Everywhere (1)
Holiday (3)
How Insensitive (Insensatez) (2)

Hurry On Down (4)
I Believed It All (4)
I Love How You Love Me (2)
I Think It's Gonna Rain Today (4)
It's Hard To Say Goodbye (3)
Let It Be Me (Je T'Appartiens) (4)
Look Of Love (2)

Love Is Blue (L'Amour Est Bleu) (3) 71
Man And A Woman (1)
Man In A Raincoat (2)
Manha De Carnaval (2)
Meditation (Meditacao) (1) 98
My Guy (1)
Pussywillows, Cat-Tails (4)

Scarborough Fair/Canticle (4)
Small Talk (3)
Snow (3)
Sunrise, Sunset (1)
Think Of Rain (2)
Tu As Beau Sourire (1)
Until It's Time For You To Go (1)
Walk In The Park (3)

Wanderlove (1)
When I Look In Your Eyes (3)
When I'm Sixty-Four (2)
Who Needs You (3)

LOOKING GLASS
Rock quartet formed by singer/guitarist Elliot Lurie while at Rutgers University in New Jersey.

7/1/72	**113**	18		Looking Glass..........................	**$12**	Epic 31320

Brandy (You're A Fine Girl) 1

Catherine Street
Dealin' With The Devil

Don't It Make You Feel Good
From Stanton Station

Golden Rainbow
Jenny-Lynne

One By One

LOOSE ENDS
London R&B trio formed in 1985: Carl McIntosh (lead vocals, guitar), Steve Nichol and Jane Eugene.

7/6/85	**46**	19		1 A Little Spice...........................	**$8**	MCA 5588
4/4/87	**59**	14		2 Zagora.....................................	**$8**	MCA 5745
7/23/88	**80**	15		3 The Real Chuckeeboo...............	**$8**	MCA 42196
12/8/90+	**124**	16		4 Look How Long........................	**$12**	MCA 10044

Be Thankful (Mama's Song) (2)
Cheap Talk (4)
Choose Me (1)
Dial 999 (1)
Don't Be A Fool (4)
Don't You Ever (Try To Change Me) (4)

Easier Said Than Done (3)
Hangin' On A String (Contemplating) (1) 43
Hold Tight (3)
Hungry (3)
I Can't Wait (Another Minute) (2)
I Don't Need To Love (4)

Is It Ever Too Late? (3)
Let's Get Back To Love (2)
Let's Rock (1)
Let's Wax A Fatty (4)
Life (3)
Little Spice (1)
Look How Long (4)
Love Controversy Pt. 1 (4)

Love's Got Me (4)
Music Takes Me Higher (1)
Nights Of Pleasure (4)
Ooh, You Make Me Feel (4)
Real Chuckeeboo Medley (3)
Remote Control (1)
Slow Down (2)
So Much Love (1)

Stay A Little While, Child (2)
Sweetest Pain (2)
Symptoms Of Love (4)
Tell Me What You Want (1)
(There's No) Gratitude (3)
Time Is Ticking (4)
Try My Love (4)
Watching You (3)

What Goes Around (3)
Who Are You? (2)
You Can't Stop The Rain (2)

LOPEZ, Denise
Dance singer born in Queens, New York. Recorded under the name "Neecy Dee" in 1984.

11/26/88	**184**	4		Truth In Disguise.....................	**$8**	A&M 5226

Causa' U
I Wanna Fall In Love With You

If You Feel It 94
Power Of Suggestion

Sayin' Sorry (Don't Make It Right) 31
Tell Me What It Is

Stop The Fight
Too Much Too Late
Truth In Disguise

★★185★★ LOPEZ, Trini
Born Trinidad Lopez, III on 5/15/37 in Dallas. Pop-folk singer/guitarist. Discovered by Don Costa while performing at PJs nightclub in Los Angeles. Portrayed Pedro Jiminez in the film *The Dirty Dozen*.

7/20/63	**2**⁶	101	●	1 Trini Lopez At PJ'S.................. [L]	**$12**	Reprise 6093
12/7/63+	**11**	19		2 More Trini Lopez At PJ'S.......... [L]	**$12**	Reprise 6103
4/11/64	**32**	33		3 On The Move........................... [L]	**$12**	Reprise 6112
8/22/64	**18**	24		4 The Latin Album...................... [F]	**$12**	Reprise 6125
10/24/64	**30**	22		5 Live At Basin St. East.............. [L]	**$12**	Reprise 6134
1/30/65	**18**	23		6 The Folk Album........................	**$12**	Reprise 6147
6/12/65	**32**	19		7 The Love Album.......................	**$12**	Reprise 6165
8/28/65	**46**	12		8 The Rhythm & Blues Album.......	**$12**	Reprise 6171
12/18/65+	**101**	10		9 The Sing-Along World Of Trini Lopez	**$12**	Reprise 6183
5/7/66	**54**	16		10 Trini...................................	**$12**	Reprise 6196
8/27/66	**110**	8		11 The Second Latin Album.......... [F]	**$12**	Reprise 6215
11/26/66+	**47**	11		12 Greatest Hits!...................... [G]	**$12**	Reprise 6226
3/4/67	**114**	6		13 Trini Lopez In London.............	**$12**	Reprise 6238
9/2/67	**162**	7		14 Trini Lopez - Now!.................	**$12**	Reprise 6255

Adalita (4)
Alla En El Rancho Grande (medley) (3)
Alright, Okay, You Win (4)
A-me-ri-ca (1,12)
Amor (Love) (11)
(And We Were Lovers) ..see: Sand Pebbles, Theme From
Angelito (2)
Are You Sincere (7,12) 85

Around The World (9)
Ay! Jalisco, No Te Rajes (medley) (3)
Baby, The Rain Must Fall (10)
Be Careful, It's My Heart (5)
Besame Mucho (4)
Bill Bailey, Won't You Please Come Home (5)
Blowin' In The Wind (6)

Blue Velvet (7)
Born Free (14)
Bye Bye Blackbird (1)
Bye Bye Love (3)
Call Me (10)
Chamaka (4)
Cielito Lindo (1)
Corazon De Melon (Watermelon Heart) (2)
Cotton Fields (3)

Crooked Little Man (6)
Cu Cu Rru Cu Cu, Paloma (4)
Cuando Calienta El Sol (9)
Dear Heart (7)
Dixie Belle (9)
Don't Let Go (8)
Don't Think Twice, It's All Right (6)
Double Trouble (8)

Down By The Riverside (medley) (1)
El Reloj (4)
Eyes Of Love (14)
Fever (13)
Fly Me To The Moon (10)
Go Into The Mountains (2)
Gonna Get Along Without Ya' Now (13) 93
Goody Goody (2)

Gotta Travel On (medley) (1)
Granada (1,4)
Green, Green (2)
Greenback Dollar (6)
Guantanamera (Lady Of Guantanamo) (14)
Hall Of Fame (12)
Hallelujah, I Love Her So (5)
Happy (13)
Heart Of My Heart (2)

DEBUT DATE	PEAK POS	WKS CHR	GOLD	ARTIST — Album Title	$	Label & Number

LOPEZ, Trini — Cont'd

Hello, Dolly! (5)
Hold Me Now And Forever (14)
Hurtin' Inside (8)
I Got A Woman (8)
I Love Your Beautiful Brown Eyes (6)
I Wanna Be Around (13)
I Wanna Be Free (14)
I Will Wait For You (10)
I'm Comin' Home, Cindy (10,12) **39**
I'm Gonna Be A Wheel Someday (14)
If I Had A Hammer (1,5,12) **3**
If You Wanna Be Happy (2)
If You Were Me (10)
In The Land Of Plenty (14)
Irresistible You (3)
It Had To Be You (13)

Jailer, Bring Me Water (3) **94**
Jezebel (5)
Kansas City (2,12) **23**
La Bamba - Part I (1,5,12) **86**
La Malaguena (4)
Lady Jane (13)
Laura (7)
Lemon Tree (6,12) **20**
Let The Four Winds Blow (8)
Little Miss Happiness (8)
Lonesome Road (3)
Lonesome Traveler (2)
Love Letters (13)
Mame (13)
Marianne (medley) (1)
Michael (6,12) **42**
Moon River (7)
My Love, Forgive Me (11)
My Melancholy Baby (9)

Never On Sunday (2)
Oh, Lonesome Me (2)
Once I Wondered (14)
One Of Those Songs (10)
Ooh Poo Pah Doo (8)
Our Day Will Come (7)
Pancho Lopez (11)
People (7)
Perfidia (4)
Personality (5)
Piel Canela (4)
Pretty Eyes (6)
Puff (The Magic Dragon) (4)
Put Your Arms Around Me, Honey (9)
Quizas, Quizas, Quizas (4)
Return To Me (7)
Sad Tomorrows (7,12) **94**
Saints, The (9)
San Francisco De Asisi (4)

Sand Pebbles, Theme From (14)
Scarlet Ribbons (For Her Hair) (6)
Shadow Of Your Smile (10)
She's About A Mover (8)
Shout (8)
Side By Side (9)
Sin Ti (Without You) (11)
Sinner Man (12) **54**
Smile (9)
So Fine (8)
Spanish Harlem (11)
Stagger Lee (5)
Story Of Love (11)
Strangers In The Night (13)
Sunny (14)
Sweet And Lovely (9)
Sweet Georgia Brown (9)
Takin' The Back Roads (13)
Tammy (7)

Taste Of Honey (7)
Tengo Nada (11)
That's What Makes The World Go Round (13)
There's A Kind Of Hush (All Over The World) (14)
32nd Of May (10)
This Land Is Your Land (1)
This Little Girl Of Mine (3)
This Train (6)
Trini Dice Te Amo (Trini Says He Loves You) (11)
Trini's Tune (10)
Unchain My Heart (1)
Volare (medley) (1)
Walk Right In (2)
Watch What Happens (11)
Watermelon Man (8)
We'll Sing In The Sunshine (6)
Wee Wee Hours (8)

What Have I Got Of My Own (3,12) **43**
What'd I Say (1,5)
When The Saints Go Marching In (medley) (1)
Where's The Love (14)
Wherever You Are (3)
Ya Ya (3)
Yeah (2)
Yesterday (10)
You Are My Sunshine (9)
You Belong To My Heart (11)
You Can't Say Good-by (3)
You Know (9)
You Need Hands (5)
You Talk Too Much (14)
You'll Be Sorry (7)
You'll Never Know (9)
Your Ever Changin' Mind (13)
Yours (11)

LORBER, Jeff
Jazz fusion keyboardist.

THE JEFF LORBER FUSION:

9/8/79	**119**	14		1 Water Sign ....[I]	$8	Arista 4234
5/31/80	**123**	12		2 Wizard Island ....[I]	$8	Arista 9516
4/18/81	**77**	15		3 Galaxian	$8	Arista 9545

guest vocals by Donnie Gerrard

JEFF LORBER:

3/27/82	**73**	13		4 It's A Fact	$8	Arista 9583
5/5/84	**106**	7		5 In The Heat Of The Night	$8	Arista 8025
3/9/85	**90**	16		6 Step By Step	$8	Arista 8269
11/15/86+	**68**	26		7 Private Passion	$8	Warner 25492

featuring vocals by Karyn White and Michael Jeffries

Above The Clouds (4)
Always There (4)
Back In Love (7)
Best Part Of The Night (6)
Blast Off (5)
Bright Sky (3)
Can't Get Enough (2)
City (2)
Country (1)
Delevans (4)
Don't Say Yes (5)
Double Bad (5)

Every Woman Needs It (6)
Facts Of Love (7) **27**
Full Moon (3)
Fusion Juice (2)
Galaxian (3)
Groovacious (6)
In The Heat Of The Night (5)
It Takes A Woman (6)
It's A Fact (4)
Jamaica (3)
Keep On Lovin' Her (7)
Kristen (7)

Lava Lands (2)
Lights Out (1)
Magic Lady (3)
Magician, The (4)
Midnight Snack (7)
Monster Man (3)
Night Love (3)
On The Wild Side (6)
Pacific Coast Highway (6)
Private Passion (7)
Rain Dance (1)
Really Scarey (5)

Reflections (2)
Right Here (1)
Rock II (5)
Rooftops (2)
Sand Castles (7)
Seventh Heaven (5)
Seventh Mountain (3)
Shadows (2)
Sparkle (1)
Spur Of The Moment (3)
Step By Step (6)
Sushi Monster (5)

Sweet (2)
Think Back And Remember (3)
This Is The Night (6)
Tierra Verde (4)
Toad's Place (1)
Tropical (5)
True Confessions (7)
Tune 88 (1)
Warm Springs (4)
Water Sign (1)
Waterfall (5)

When You Gonna Come Back Home (6)
Wizard Island (2)
Your Love Has Got Me (4)

LORDS OF THE NEW CHURCH
British rock quartet led by Cleveland native Stiv Bator (dropped "s" from surname). Bator (former lead singer of the Dead Boys) died on 6/4/90 [age 40], after being hit by a car.

4/27/85	**158**	7		The Method To Our Madness	$8	I.R.S. 70049

Do What Thou Wilt
I Never Believed

Kiss Of Death
Method To My Madness

Murder Style
My Kingdom Come

Pretty Baby Scream
S.F. & T.

Seducer, The
When Blood Runs Cold

LORD SUTCH & Heavy Friends
Outrageous rock vocalist. Born David Sutch in 1942 in Harrow, Middlesex, England. Formed the Savages in 1958 which included, at times throughout the mid-1960s, Nicky Hopkins, Ritchie Blackmore and Paul Dean (later known as Paul Nicholas).

2/21/70	**84**	13		Lord Sutch and Heavy Friends	$25	Cotillion 9015

Friends: Jimmy Page, Jeff Beck, John Bonham, Nicky Hopkins and Noel Redding

Baby, Come Back
Brightest Light

'Cause I Love You
Flashing Lights

Gutty Guitar
L-o-n-d-o-n

One For You, Baby
Smoke And Fire

Thumping Beat
Union Jack Car

Wailing Sounds
Would You Believe

LORENZ, Trey
Born on 1/19/69 in Florence, South Carolina. Attended New York's Fairleigh Dickinson University; earned advertising degree. Sang backup on Mariah Carey's first two albums; male vocal on her hit "I'll Be There."

10/24/92	**111**	8		Trey Lorenz	$12	Epic 47840

Always In Love
Baby I'm In Heaven

Find A Way
How Can I Say Goodbye

It Only Hurts When It's Love
Just To Be Close To You

Photograph Of Mary
Run Back To Me

Someone To Hold 19
When Troubles Come

Wipe All My Tears Away

LORING, Gloria
Born on 12/10/46 in New York City. Portrayed Liz Curtis on TV's soap opera *Days Of Our Lives*. Formerly married to TV actor/host Alan Thicke.

9/6/86	**61**	14		Gloria Loring	$8	Atlantic 81679

Changes Of Heart
Close My Eyes

Don't Let Me Change The Way You Are

Friends And Lovers 2
Goodbye, The

If You Remember Me
Since I Don't Have You

Smokin'
What's One More Time

You Always Knew

LOS ADMIRADORES
Percussion group produced by Enoch Light.

8/29/60	**2¹**	50		1 Bongos Bongos Bongos .... [I]	$15	Command 809
10/24/60	**3**	34		2 Bongos/Flutes/Guitars .... [I]	$15	Command 812

All Of Me (1)
Between The Devil & The Deep Blue Sea (1)
Bidin' My Time (2)
Birth Of The Blues (2)

Blue Moon (1)
By The River St. Marie (2)
C'est Si Bon (2)
Caravan (1)
Don't Blame Me (1)

East Of The Sun (2)
Friendly Persuasion (2)
Golden Earrings (1)
Greensleeves (1)
How High The Moon (2)

I Can Dream, Can't I (2)
Laura (1)
Londonderry Air (1)
Making Whoopie (2)
My Funny Valentine (2)

Sylvie (1)
Tenderly (1)
Unchained Melody (1)
Very Thought Of You (1)

You & The Night & The Music (1)

LOS BRAVOS
Rock quintet consisting of four members from Spain and one from Germany — Mike Kogel (Kennedy), leader.

| 11/12/66 | 93 | 7 | | Black Is Black | $25 | Press 83003 |

Baby, Baby
Baby, Believe Me
Black Is Black 4
Don't Be Left Out In The Cold
I Don't Care
I Want A Name
I'm Cuttin' Out
Make It Easy For Me
She Believes In Me
Stop That Girl
Trapped
You Won't Get Far

LOS INDIOS TABAJARAS
Brazilian Indian brothers: Natalicio and Antenor Lima.

| 11/16/63+ | 7 | 31 | 1 | Maria Elena ...... [I] | $15 | RCA 2822 |
| 5/16/64 | 85 | 10 | 2 | Always In My Heart ...... [I] | $15 | RCA 2912 |

A La Orilla Del Lago (1)
Always In My Heart (2) 82
Amapola (2)
Ay Maria (1)
Baion Bon (1)
Central Park (2)
Jungle Dream (1)
Los Indios Danzan (1)
Magic Is The Moonlight (2)
Maran Cariua (1)
Maria Elena (1) 6
Maria My Own (2)
Moonlight And Shadows (2)
Moonlight Serenade (1)
More Brandy - Please (2)
New Orleans (2)
Over The Rainbow (2)
Pajaro Campana (1)
¿Por Que Eres Asi? (2)
Star Dust (1)
Ternura (1)
Vals Criollo (1)
Wide Horizon (2)
You Belong To My Heart (2)

LOS LOBOS
Hispanic-American rock quintet formed in East Los Angeles in 1973 by David Hidalgo (lead vocals), Cesar Rosas, Conrad Lozano and Louie Perez. Former Blasters' saxophonist, Steve Berlin, joined in 1983.

12/15/84+	47	34	1	How Will The Wolf Survive?	$8	Slash 25177
2/14/87	47	32	2	By The Light Of The Moon	$8	Slash 25523
7/25/87	1²	44	▲² 3	La Bamba ...... [S]	$8	Slash 25605

includes 8 cuts by Los Lobos; plus "Crying, Waiting, Hoping" by Marshall Crenshaw, "Lonely Teardrops" by Howard Huntsberry, "Who Do You Love" by Bo Diddley and "Summertime Blues" by Brian Setzer.

| 11/5/88 | 179 | 4 | 4 | La Pistola Y El Corazon | $8 | Slash 25790 |

translation of Spanish title: The Pistol and The Heart

| 9/22/90 | 103 | 9 | 5 | The Neighborhood | $12 | Slash 26131 |
| 6/13/92 | 143 | 10 | 6 | Kiko | $12 | Slash 26786 |

All I Wanted To Do Was Dance (2)
Angel Dance (5)
Angels With Dirty Faces (6)
Arizona Skies (6)
Be Still (5)
Breakdown, The (1)
Charlena (3)
Come On, Let's Go (3) 21
Corrida #1 (1)
Deep Dark Hole (5)
Don't Worry Baby (1)
Donna (3)
Down On The Riverbed (5)
Dream In Blue (6)
El Canelo (4)
El Gusto (4)
Emily (5)
Estoy Sentado Aqui (4)
Evangeline (1)
Framed (3)
Georgia Slop (5)
Giving Tree (5)
Goodnight My Love (3)
Hardest Time (6)
I Can't Understand (5)
I Got Loaded (5)
I Got To Let You Know (1)
I Walk Alone (5)
Is This All There Is? (2)
Jenny's Got A Pony (5)
Just A Man (6)
Kiko And The Lavender Moon (6)
La Bamba (3) 1
La Guacamaya (4)
La Pistola Y El Corazon (4)
Las Amarillas (4)
Lil' King Of Everything (1)
Little John Of God (6)
Matter Of Time (1)
Mess We're In (2)
My Baby's Gone (2)
Neighborhood, The (5)
One Time One Night (2)
Ooh! My Head (2)
Our Last Night (1)
Peace (6)
Prenda Del Alma (2)
Que Nadie Sepa Mi Sufrir (4)
Reva's House (6)
Rio De Tenampa (6)
River Of Fools (2)
Saint Behind The Glass (6)
Serenata Nortena (1)
Set Me Free (Rosa Lee) (2)
Shakin' Shakin' Shakes (2)
Short Side Of Nothing (6)
Si You Quisiera (4)
(Sonajas) Mananitas Michoacanas (4)
Take My Hand (3)
Tears Of God (2)
That Train Don't Stop Here (6)
Two Janes (6)
Wake Up Dolores (6)
We Belong Together (6)
When The Circus Comes (6)
Whiskey Trail (6)
Wicked Rain (6)
Will The Wolf Survive? (1) 78

LOUDNESS
Japanese hard-rock quartet: Munetaka Higuchi, Akira Takasaki, Masayoshi Yamashita and Minoru Niihara (vocals). Connecticut-born American Mike Vescera replaced Niihara in 1989.

3/2/85	74	24	1	Thunder In The East	$8	Atco 90246
5/31/86	64	16	2	Lightning Strikes	$8	Atco 90512
8/15/87	190	4	3	Hurricane Eyes	$8	Atco 90619

Ashes In The Sky (2)
Black Star Oblivion (2)
Clockwork Toy (1)
Complication (2)
Crazy Nights (1)
Dark Desire (2)
Face To Face (2)
Heavy Chains (1)
Hungry Hunter (3)
In My Dreams (3)
In This World Beyond (3)
Let It Go (2)
Like Hell (1)
Lines Are Down (1)
Never Change Your Mind (1)
No Way Out (1)
1000 Eyes (3)
Rock 'N Roll Gypsy (3)
Rock This Way (3)
Run For Your Life (1)
S.D.I. (3)
So Lonely (3)
Street Life Dream (3)
Strike Of The Sword (3)
Take Me Home (3)
This Lonely Heart (3)
We Could Be Together (1)
Who Knows (2)

LOUIE LOUIE
Singer/dancer/songwriter Louie Cordero from Southern California. Played Madonna's boyfriend in her "Borderline" video.

| 6/2/90 | 136 | 10 | | The State I'm In | $12 | WTG 45285 |

Hurt Baby
I Wanna Get Back With You 69
I'm Sorry That It Happened To You
Let Me Divorce You
Mata Hari
Penny Lady
Rodeo Clown
Sittin' In The Lap Of Luxury 19
State I'm In
Stop Lookin' For Someone Else
Variety Is The Spice Of Life

LOUISIANA'S LE ROUX — see LE ROUX

LOVE
Los Angeles-based rock group led by singer/guitarist Arthur Lee (from Memphis).

5/14/66	57	18	1	Love	$20	Elektra 74001
2/11/67	80	11	2	Da Capo	$20	Elektra 74005
1/6/68	154	10	3	Forever Changes	$20	Elektra 74013
9/6/69	102	12	4	Four Sail	$15	Elektra 74049
12/27/69+	176	5	5	Out Here	$15	Blue Th. 9000 [2]
9/5/70	142	7	6	Revisited ...... [G]	$15	Elektra 74058
12/26/70	184	3	7	False Start	$15	Blue Thumb 8822

Abalony (5)
Alone Again Or (3,6) 99
Always See Your Face (4)
And More (1)
Andmoreagain (3,6)
Anytime (7)
August (4)
Between Clark And Hilldale (3)
Bummer In The Summer (3)
Can't Explain (1)
Car Lights On In The Day Time Blues (5)
Castle, The (2)
Colored Balls Falling (1)
Daily Planet (3)
Discharged (5)
Doggone (5)
Dream (4)
Emotions (1)
Everlasting First (7)
Feel Daddy Feel Good (7)
Flying (7)
Gather Round (5)
Gazing (1)
Gimi A Little Break (7)
Good Humor Man (3)
Good Times (4,6)
Hey Joe (1,6)
House Is Not A Motel (3)
I Still Wonder (5)
I'll Pray For You (5)
I'm Down (5)
I'm With You (4)
Instra-Mental (5)
Keep On Shining (7)
Listen To My Song (5)
Live And Let Live (3)
Love Is Coming (1)
Love Is More Than Words Or Better Late Than Never (5)
Message To Pretty (1)
Mushroom Clouds (1)
My Flash On You (1)
My Little Red Book (1,6) 52
Nice To Be (5)
No Matter What You Do (1)
Nothing (4)
Old Man (3)
Orange Skies (2,6)
Que Vida (2)
Red Telephone (3)
Revelation (5)
Ride That Vibration (7)
Robert Montgomery (4)
Run To The Top (5)
7 And 7 Is (2,6) 33
She Comes In Colors (2,6)
Signed D.C. (1,5,6)
Singing Cowboy (4)
Slick Dick (7)
Softly To Me (1,6)
Stand Out (5,7)
Stephanie Knows Who (2)
Talking In My Sleep (4)
Willow Willow (5)
You Are Something (5)
You I'll Be Following (1)
You Set The Scene (3,6)
Your Friend And Mine - Nell's Song (4,6)
Your Mind And We Belong Together (6)

DEBUT DATE	PEAK POS	WKS CHR	GOLD	ARTIST — Album Title	$	Label & Number

LOVE, Monie
Simone Wilson, a London-born female rapper based in Brooklyn. Featured on Queen Latifah's single "Ladies First." Nineteen years old in 1990.

11/24/90+	**109**	12		Down To Earth	**$12**	Warner 26358

R U Single *(1)*
Dettrimentally Stable
Don't Funk Wid The Mo

| Down 2 Earth | I Do As I Please | Just Don't Give A Damn | Pups Lickin' Bone | Ring My Bell |
| Grandpa's Party | **It's A Shame (My Sister)** 26 | Monie In The Middle | Read Between The Lines | Swiney Swiney |

LOVE AND KISSES
Studio group assembled by European disco producer Alec Costandinos. Consisted of vocalists Don Daniels, Elaine Hill, Dianne Brooks and Jean Graham.

7/30/77	**135**	14		1 Love And Kisses	**$8**	Casablanca 7063
5/13/78	**85**	17		2 How Much, How Much I Love You	**$8**	Casablanca 7091

Accidental Lover (1)
Beauty And The Beast (2)

| How Much, How Much I | I Found Love (Now That I've | Maybe (2) |
| Love You (2) | Found You) (1) | |

LOVE and MONEY
Scottish pop trio: James Grant (guitar, vocals), Bobby Paterson (bass) and Paul McGeechan (keyboards). Drummer Stuart Kerr of the group Texas was an early member.

3/25/89	**175**	7		Strange Kind Of Love	**$8**	Mercury 836498

Avalanche
Axis Of Love

| **Hallelujah Man** 75 | Jocelyn Square | Shape Of Things To Come | Up Escalator |
| Inflammable | Razorsedge | Strange Kind Of Love | Walk The Last Mile |

LOVE AND ROCKETS
British trio: Daniel Ash (guitar, vocals), Kevin Haskins (drums) and David J. (bass). All were members of Bauhaus, 1979-83. Band name taken from the title of an underground comic book. Ash went solo in 1991.

11/1/86+	**72**	30		1 Express	**$8**	Big Time 6011
10/31/87+	**64**	28		2 Earth.Sun.Moon.	**$8**	Big Time 6058
5/20/89	**14**	26	●	3 Love And Rockets	**$8**	Begr. B. 9715

All In My Mind *[includes 2 versions]* (1)
American Dream (1)
Ball Of Confusion (1)
Bound For Hell (3)

Everybody Wants To Go To	Kundalini Express (1)	Motorcycle (3)	Rock And Roll Babylon (3)	Welcome Tomorrow (2)
Heaven (2)	Lazy (2)	**No Big Deal** (3) *82*	**So Alive** (3) *3*	Yin And Yang The Flower
Here On Earth (2)	Life In Laralay (1)	No New Tale To Tell (2)	Sun, The (2)	Pot Man (1)
I Feel Speed (3)	Light, The (2)	No Words No More (3)	Teardrop Collector (3)	Youth (2)
It Could Be Sunshine (1)	Love Me (1)	Purest Blue (3)	Telephone Is Empty (2)	
****(Jungle Law) (3)	Mirror People (2)	Rain Bird (2)	Waiting For The Flood (2)	

LOVE CHILDS AFRO CUBAN BLUES BAND
Studio group assembled by New York disco producer Michael Zager.

7/12/75	**168**	5		Out Among 'Em ....[I]	**$8**	Roulette 3016

Ask Me
Bang Bang

| Black Skin Blue Eyed Boys | Honeybee | **Life And Death In G&A** *90* | Where Do We Go From Here |
| Get Dancin' | Jerry's Theme | Once You Get Started | |

LOVE/HATE
Male rock quartet: Jizzy Pearl (vocals), Jon E. Love, Skid and Joey Gold.

7/14/90	**154**	5		Blackout In The Red Room	**$12**	Columbia 45263

Blackout In The Red Room
Fuel To Run
Hell, Ca.. Pop. 4

| Mary Jane | Rock Queen | Slave Girl | Straightjacket | Why Do You Think They |
| One More Round | She's An Angel | Slutsy Tipsy | Tumbleweed | Call It Dope? |

LOVELESS, Patty
Country singer. Born Patricia Ramey on 1/4/57 in Pikesville, Kentucky. Married producer Emory Gordy Jr. in February 1989.

9/28/91	**151**	11		Up Against My Heart	**$12**	MCA 10336

Can't Stop Myself From
Loving You
God Will

He Hurt Me Bad	I Came Straight To You	Jealous Bone	Waitin' For The Phone To
I Already Miss You (Like	If It's The Last Thing I Do	Nobody Loves You Like I Do	Ring
You're Already Gone)	If You Don't Want Me		

★★467★★ LOVERBOY
Rock quintet formed in Vancouver, Canada in 1978: Mike Reno (lead singer), Paul Dean (lead guitar), Scott Smith (bass), Matt Frenette (drums) and Doug Johnson (keyboards, left by 1989).

1/31/81	**13**	105	▲2	1 Loverboy	**$8**	Columbia 36762
11/14/81+	**7**	122	▲3	2 Get Lucky	**$8**	Columbia 37638
7/2/83	**7**	39	▲2	3 Keep It Up	**$8**	Columbia 38703
9/14/85	**13**	44	▲	4 Lovin' Every Minute Of It	**$8**	Columbia 39953
9/12/87	**42**	21	●	5 Wildside	**$8**	Columbia 40893
12/23/89	**189**	6		6 Big Ones ....[G]	**$8**	Columbia 45411

Ain't Looking For Love (6)	Don't Let Go (5)	It's Your Life (2)	Lucky Ones (2,6)	Read My Lips (4)	**Too Hot** (6) *84*
Always On My Mind (1)	Emotional (2)	Jump (2)	Meltdown (3)	Steal The Thunder (4)	Too Much Too Soon (4)
Break It To Me Gently (5)	For You (6)	**Kid Is Hot Tonite** (1,6) *55*	**Notorious** (5,6) *38*	Strike Zone (3)	**Turn Me Loose** (1,6) *35*
Bullet In The Chamber (4)	Friday Night (4)	Lady Of The 80's (1)	One-Sided Love Affair (3)	Take Me To The Top (2)	Walkin' On Fire (5)
Can't Get Much Better (5)	Gangs In The Street (2)	**Lead A Double Life** (4) *68*	Passion Pit (3)	Teenage Overdose (1)	Watch Out (2)
Chance Of A Lifetime (3)	Hometown Hero (5)	Little Girl (1)	Prime Of Your Life (3)	That's Where My Money	**When It's Over** (2) *26*
D.O.A. (1)	**Hot Girls In Love** (3,6) *11*	Love Will Rise Again (5)	Prissy Prissy (1)	Goes (5)	Wildside (5)
Dangerous (4) *65*	It Don't Matter (3)	**Lovin' Every Minute Of It**	Queen Of The Broken	**This Could Be The Night**	**Working For The Weekend**
Destination Heartbreak (4)	It's Never Easy (3)	(4,6) *9*	Hearts (3) *34*	(4) *10*	(2,6) *29*

LOVETT, Lyle
Country singer born on 11/1/57 in Klein, Texas. Graduate of Texas A&M with degrees in German and journalism. Acted in the film *The Player*.

2/20/88	**117**	14		1 Pontiac	**$8**	MCA 42028
2/18/89	**62**	21	●	2 Lyle Lovett and his Large Band	**$8**	MCA/Curb 42263
				LYLE LOVETT and his Large Band		
4/18/92	**57**	31		3 Joshua Judges Ruth	**$12**	Curb 10475

All My Love Is Gone (3)
Baltimore (3)
Black And Blue (1)
Blues Walk (2)

Church (3)	Flyswatter/Ice Water (Monty	Good Intentions (2)	I Married Her Just Because	If You Were To Wake Up (3)
Cryin' Shame (2)	Trenckmann's Blues) (3)	Here I Am (2)	She Looks Like You (3)	L.A. County (3)
Family Reserve (3)	Give Back My Heart (1)	I Know You Know (2)	I've Been To Memphis (3)	M-o-n-e-y (1)
	Glory Of Love (medley) (2)	I Loved You Yesterday (1)	If I Had A Boat (1)	Nobody Knows Me (2)

LOVETT, Lyle — Cont'd

North Dakota (3)
Once Is Enough (2)
Pontiac (1)
She Makes Me Feel Good (3)

She's Already Made Up Her Mind (3)
She's Hot To Go (1)

She's Leaving Me Because She Really Wants To (3)
She's No Lady (1)
Simple Song (1)

Since The Last Time (3)
Stand By Your Man (2)
Walk Through The Bottomland (1)

What Do You Do (medley) (2)
Which Way Does That Old Pony Run (2)

You've Been So Good Up To Now (3)

LOVE UNLIMITED

Female soul trio from San Pedro, California: sisters Glodean and Linda James, and Diane Taylor. Barry White, who married Glodean on 7/4/74, was their manager and producer.

4/29/72	151	12		1 Love Unlimited	$10	Uni 73131
9/8/73+	3	44	●	2 Under The Influence Of....	$10	20th Century 414
10/12/74	85	27		3 In Heat	$10	20th Century 443
2/26/77	192	3		4 He's All I've Got	$8	Un. Gold 101

Another Chance (1)
Are You Sure (1)
Fragile - Handle With Care (1)
He's All I've Got (4)
He's Mine (No, You Can't Have Him) (4)
I Belong To You (3) 27
I Can't Let Him Down (4)

I Did It For Love (4)
I Guess I'm Just Another Girl In Love (4)
I Love You So, Never Gonna Let You Go (3)
I Needed Love - You Were There (1)
I Should Have Known (1)
I'll Be Yours Forever More (1)

If This World Were Mine (1)
Is It Really True Boy - Is It Really Me (1)
It May Be Winter Outside, (But In My Heart It's Spring) (2) 83
Love's Theme (2,3) 1
Lovin' You, That's All I'm After (2)

Move Me No Mountain (3)
Never, Never Say Goodbye (4)
Oh I Should Say It's Such A Beautiful Day (3)
Oh Love, Well We Finally Made It (2)
Say It Again (2)
Share A Little Love In Your Heart (3)

Someone Really Cares For You (2)
Together (1)
Under The Influence Of Love (2) 76
Walkin' In The Rain With The One I Love (1) 14
Whisper You Love Me (2)
Yes, We Finally Made It (2)

LOVE UNLIMITED ORCHESTRA

Studio orchestra conducted and arranged by Barry White.

2/9/74	8	25	●	1 Rhapsody In White [I]	$10	20th Century 433
7/6/74	96	10		2 Together Brothers [I-S]	$10	20th Cent. ST-101
				includes 2 vocals by Barry White and 1 by Love Unlimited		
11/9/74+	28	27	●	3 White Gold [I]	$10	20th Century 458
1/10/76	92	15		4 Music Maestro Please [I]	$10	20th Century 480
10/30/76	123	8		5 My Sweet Summer Suite [I]	$10	20th Century 517

Alive And Well (1)
Always Thinking Of You (3)
Are You Sure (5)
Baby Blues (1)
Barry's Love (Part I & II) (3)
Barry's Theme (1)
Blues Concerto (5)
Brazilian Love Song (5)
Bring It On Up (4)
Can't Seem To Find Him (2)
Do Drop In (2)

Don't Take It Away From Me (1)
Dream On (2)
Dreamin' (2,3)
Find The Man Bros. (2)
Forever In Love (4)
Get Away (2)
Give Up Your Love Girl (4)
Here Comes The Man (2)
Honey, Please Can't Ya See [vocal: Barry] (2)
I Feel Love Coming On (1)

I Wanna Stay (4)
I'm Falling In Love With You (5)
It's Only What I Feel (4)
Just Like A Baby (3)
Just Living It Up (3)
Killer Don't Do It (2)
Killer's Back (2)
Killer's Lullaby (2)
Love's Theme (1) 1
Makin' Believe That It's You (4)

Midnight And You (1)
Midnight Groove (4)
My Sweet Summer Suite (5) 48
Only You Can Make Me Blue (3)
People Of Tomorrow Are The Children Of Today [vocal: Love Unlimited] (2)
Power Of Love (3)
Rhapsody In White (1) 63
Rip, The (2)

Satin Soul (3) 22
So Nice To Hear (1)
Somebody's Gonna Off The Man (2)
Spanish Lei (3)
Stick Up (2)
Strange Games & Things (5)
Together Brothers, Theme From (2)
What A Groove (1)
You Gotta Case (2)
You I Adore (5)

You Make Me Feel Like This (When You Touch Me) (3)
You're All I Want (4)
You've Given Me Something (5)

LOVICH, Lene

New wave singer/actress. Born in Detroit; moved to England at age 13. Acted in the films *Cha-Cha* and *Mata Hari*.

8/4/79	137	10		1 Stateless	$8	Stiff 36102
3/8/80	94	8		2 Flex	$8	Stiff 36308
1/15/83	188	4		3 No-Man's-Land	$8	Stiff 38399

Angels (2)
Bird Song (2)
Blue Hotel (3)
Egg Head (2)
Faces (3)
Freeze, The (2)

Home (1)
I Think We're Alone Now (1)
It's You, Only You (Mein Schmerz) (3)
Joan (2)
Lucky Number (1)

Maria (3)
Momentary Breakdown (1)
Monkey Talk (2)
Night, The (2)
One In 1,000,000 (1)
Rocky Road (3)

Savages (3)
Say When (1)
Sister Video (3)
Sleeping Beauty (1)
Special Star (3)
Telepathy (1)

Tonight (1)
Too Tender (To Touch) (1)
Walking Low (3)
What Will I Do Without You (2)
Wonderful One (2)

Writing On The Wall (1)
You Can't Kill Me (2)

★★474★★ LOVIN' SPOONFUL, The

Jug-band rock group formed in New York City in 1965. Consisted of John Sebastian (lead vocals, songwriter, guitarist, harmonica), Zal Yanovsky (lead guitar), Steve Boone (bass) and Joe Butler (drums). Sebastian had been with the Even Dozen Jug Band; did session work at Elektra. Yanovsky and Sebastian were members of the Mugwumps with Cass Elliot and Denny Doherty (later with The Mamas & The Papas). Yanovsky replaced by Jerry Yester (keyboards) in 1967. Disbanded in 1968.

12/4/65+	32	35		1 Do You Believe In Magic	$20	Kama Sutra 8050
4/2/66	10	31		2 Daydream	$20	Kama Sutra 8051
9/24/66	126	9		3 What's Up, Tiger Lily? [S]	$20	Kama Sutra 8053
				The Lovin' Spoonful appear in this Woody Allen film		
12/17/66+	14	26		4 Hums Of The Lovin' Spoonful	$20	Kama Sutra 8054
3/18/67	3	52	●	5 The Best Of The Lovin' Spoonful [G]	$15	Kama Sutra 8056
4/15/67	160	5		6 You're A Big Boy Now [S]	$15	Kama Sutra 8058
1/20/68	118	7		7 Everything Playing	$15	Kama Sutra 8061
3/30/68	156	5		8 The Best Of The Lovin' Spoonful, Volume 2 [G]	$15	Kama Sutra 8064
4/24/76	183	3		9 The Best...Lovin' Spoonful [G]	$15	Kama Sutra 2608 [2]

Bald Headed Lena (2)
Barbara's Theme (6)
Bes' Friends (4)
Big Noise From Speonk (2)
Blues In The Bottle (1,5)
Boredom (7,8)
Butchie's Tune (2,5)
Close Your Eyes (7)
Coconut Grove (4,9)
Cool Million (3)
Darlin' Companion (4,8)
Darling Be Home Soon (6,8,9) 15
Day Blues (3)
Daydream (2,5,9) 2

Did You Ever Have To Make Up Your Mind? (1,5,9) 2
Didn't Want To Have To Do It (2,5,9)
Dixieland Big Boy (6)
Do You Believe In Magic (1,5,9) 9
Fishin' Blues (1,3)
Forever (7)
4 Eyes (4,9)
Full Measure (4,8) 87
Girl, Beautiful Girl (Barbara's Theme) (6)
Gray Prison Blues (3)

Henry Thomas (4)
It's Not Time Now (2)
Jug Band Music (2,5,9)
Kite Chase (6)
Let The Boy Rock And Roll (2)
Letter To Barbara (6)
Lonely (Amy's Theme) (6)
Lookin' To Spy (3)
Lovin' You (4,8,9)
March (6)
Miss Thing's Thang (6)
Money (7,8,9) 48
My Gal (1)
Nashville Cats (4,8,9) 8

Never Going Back (9) 73
Night Owl Blues (1,5,9)
Old Folks (7,8)
On The Road Again (1)
Only Pretty, What A Pity (1)
Other Side Of This Life (1)
POW (7)
POW Revisited (3)
Peep Show Percussion (6)
Phil's Love Theme (3)
Priscilla Millionaira (7)
Rain On The Roof (4,8,9) 10
Respoken (3)
She Is Still A Mystery (7,8,9) 27

Six O'Clock (7,8,9) 18
Speakin' Of Spoken (3)
Sportin' Life (1)
Summer In The City (4,5,9) 1
There She Is (2)
Till I Run With You (9)
Try A Little Bit (7)
Try And Be Happy (6)
Unconscious Minuet (2)
Voodoo In My Basement (4)
Warm Baby (2,9)
Wash Her Away (6)
What's Up, Tiger Lily? (End Title) (3)

Wild About My Lovin' (1,5)
You Baby (1)
You Didn't Have To Be So Nice (2,5,9) 10
You're A Big Boy Now (6)
Younger Generation (7,8,9)
Younger Girl (1,5,9)

DEBUT DATE	PEAK POS	WKS CHR	GOLD	ARTIST — Album Title	$	Label & Number

LOWE, Nick

Born on 3/25/49 in Woodbridge, Suffolk, England. With Brinsley Schwarz (1970-75) and Rockpile. Married Carlene Carter on 8/18/79; later divorced. Produced albums for Elvis Costello, Graham Parker & The Rumour and others. Co-founder of Little Village.

DEBUT DATE	PEAK POS	WKS CHR	GOLD	ARTIST — Album Title	$	Label & Number
4/29/78	127	10		1 Pure Pop For Now People	$8	Columbia 35329
7/14/79	31	22		2 Labour Of Lust	$8	Columbia 36087
2/20/82	50	14		3 Nick The Knife	$8	Columbia 37932
4/2/83	129	7		4 The Abominable Showman	$8	Columbia 38589

NICK LOWE & HIS COWBOY OUTFIT:

DEBUT DATE	PEAK POS	WKS CHR	GOLD	ARTIST — Album Title	$	Label & Number
6/23/84	113	12		5 Nick Lowe and his Cowboy Outfit	$8	Columbia 39371
9/21/85	119	12		6 The Rose Of England	$8	Columbia 39958
4/7/90	182	3		7 Party Of One	$12	Reprise 26132

All Men Are Liars (7)
American Squirm (2)
Awesome (5)
Ba Doom (3)
Big Kick, Plain Scrap (4)
Bobo Ska Diddle Daddle (6)
Born Fighter (2)
Break Away (5)
Burning (3)
Chicken And Feathers (4)
Cool Reaction (4)
Couldn't Love You (Any More Than I Do) (3)
Cracking Up (2)
Cruel To Be Kind (2) 12
Darlin' Angel Eyes (6)
Dose Of You (2)
Everyone (6)

Gai-Gin Man (7)
Gee And The Rick And The Three Card Trick (5)
God's Gift To Women (5)
Half A Boy And Half A Man (5)
Heart (3)
Heart Of The City (1)
(Hey Big Mouth) Stand Up And Say That (5)
Honeygun (7)
(Hope To God) I'm Right (6)
How Do You Talk To An Angel (4)
I Can Be The One You Love (6)
I Don't Know Why You Keep Me On (7)

I Knew The Bride (When She Use To Rock And Roll) (6) 77
(I Love The Sound Of) Breaking Glass (1)
(I Want To Build A) Jumbo Ark (7)
Indoor Fireworks (6)
L.A.F.S. (5)
Let Me Kiss Ya (3)
Little Hitler (1)
Live Fast, Love Hard, Die Young (1)
Long Walk Back (6)
Love Like A Glove (5)
Love So Fine (2)
Lucky Dog (6)
Man Of A Fool (4)

Marie Provost (1)
Maureen (5)
Mess Around With Love (4)
Music For Money (1)
My Heart Hurts (3)
No Reason (1)
Nutted By Reality (1)
One's Too Many (And A Hundred Ain't Enough) (3)
Paid The Price (4)
Queen Of Sheba (3)
Raging Eyes (4)
Raining Raining (3)
Refrigerator White (7)
Rocky Road (7)
Rollers Show (1)
Rose Of England (6)
Saint Beneath The Paint (4)

7 Nights To Rock (6)
She Don't Love Nobody (6)
Shting-Shtang (7)
Skin Deep (2)
So It Goes (1)
Stick It Where The Sun Don't Shine (3)
Switch Board Susan (2)
Tanque-Rae (4)
They Called It Rock (1)
36 Inches High (1)
Time Wounds All Heels (4)
Tonight (1)
Too Many Teardrops (3)
We Want Action (4)
What's Shakin' On The Hill (7)
Who Was That Man? (7)

Wish You Were Here (4)
Without Love (2)
You Got The Look I Like (7)
You Make Me (2)
You'll Never Get Me Up (In One Of Those) (5)
Zulu Kiss (3)

L7

Female rock band: Dee Plakas, Jennifer Finch, Donita Sparks and Suzi Gardner.

DEBUT DATE	PEAK POS	WKS CHR	GOLD	ARTIST — Album Title	$	Label & Number
8/8/92	160	7		Bricks Are Heavy	$12	Slash 26784

Diet Pill
Everglade

Monster
Mr. Integrity

One More Thing
Pretend We're Dead

Scrap
Shitlist

Slide
This Ain't Pleasure

Wargasm

L.T.D.

Ten-man, R&B-funk band from Greensboro, North Carolina — Jeffrey Osborne, lead singer. Osborne left in 1980, replaced by Leslie Wilson and Andre Ray. L.T.D. stands for Love, Togetherness and Devotion.

DEBUT DATE	PEAK POS	WKS CHR	GOLD	ARTIST — Album Title	$	Label & Number
8/21/76	52	30		1 Love To The World	$10	A&M 4589
8/13/77+	21	34	●	2 Something To Love	$8	A&M 4646
6/17/78	18	26	▲	3 Togetherness	$8	A&M 4705
7/21/79	29	24	●	4 Devotion	$8	A&M 4771
9/6/80	28	28		5 Shine On	$8	A&M 4819
11/28/81+	83	12		6 Love Magic	$8	A&M 4881

Age Of The Showdown (2)
April Love (6)
Burnin' Hot (6)
Concentrate On You (3)
Cuttin' It Up (6)
Dance 'N' Sing 'N' (4)
Don't Stop Loving Me Now (3)
Don'tcha Know (5)
(Every Time I Turn Around) Back In Love Again (2) 4

Feel It (4)
Get Your It Together (1)
Getaway (5)
Holding On (When Love Is Gone) (3) 49
If You're In Need (2)
It Must End (6)
It's Time To Be Real (3)
Jam (3)
Kickin' Back (6)
Lady Love (5)

Let The Music Keep Playing (1)
Let's All Live And Give (1)
Let's All Live And Give
Love Ballad (1) 20
Love Is What You Need (5)
Love Magic (6)
Love To The World (1) 91
Love To The World Prayer (1)
Lovers Everywhere (5)

Make Someone Smile, Today! (2)
Material Things (2)
Never Get Enough Of Your Love (2) 56
Now (6)
One On One (4)
Promise You'll Stay (4)
Say That You'll Be Mine (4)
Share My Love (4)

Shine On (5) 40
Sometimes (4)
Stand Up L.T.D. (4)
Stay On The One (6)
Stranger (4)
Time For Pleasure (1)
Together Forever (3)
We Both Deserve Each Other's Love (3)
We Party Hearty (2)

Where Did We Go Wrong (5)
Will Love Grow (5)
(Won't Cha) Stay With Me (2)
Word, The (1)
You Come First At Last (2)
You Fooled Me (3)
You Gave Me Love (5)
You Must Have Known I Needed Love (3)

L'TRIMM

Miami-based, female rap duo of 18-year-olds (in 1988): Tigra (from New York) and Bunny D. (Chicago).

DEBUT DATE	PEAK POS	WKS CHR	GOLD	ARTIST — Album Title	$	Label & Number
11/5/88	132	16		Grab It!	$8	Atlantic 81925

originally released on Time-X 3307

Better Yet L'Trimm
Cars With The Boom 54

Cuttie Pie
Don't Come To My House

Grab It
He's A Mutt

Sexy
We Can Rock The Beat

LUBOFF, Norman, Choir

Born on 5/14/17 in Chicago; died of cancer on 9/22/87. Composer/conductor; formed own choral group.

DEBUT DATE	PEAK POS	WKS CHR	GOLD	ARTIST — Album Title	$	Label & Number
10/15/55	15	3		1 Songs Of The West	$15	Columbia 657
7/14/56	19	2		2 Songs Of The South	$15	Columbia 860
5/27/57	19	4		3 Calypso Holiday	$15	Columbia 1000
1/13/58	22	1		4 Songs Of Christmas	[X]	Columbia 926

Christmas charts: 57/'65, 44/'66

A La Nanita Nana (medley) (4)
Balance (3)
Ballad Of The Boll Weevil (4)
Baloo Lammy (medley) (4)
Bamboo-Tamboo (3)
Black Is The Color Of My True Love's Hair (2)
Bury Me Not On The Lone Prairie (1)
Calypso Carnival (3)
Carry Me Back To Old Virginny (2)
Colorado Trail (1)
Cool Water (1)

Coventry Carol (medley) (4)
Dance De Limbo (3)
Dansez Calenda (3)
Deck The Hall With Boughs Of Holly (medley) (4)
Deep River (2)
Dixie (2)
Doney Gal (1)
Down In The Valley (2)
First Nowell (medley) (4)
Fisherman's Song (3)
God Rest Ye Merry, Gentlemen (medley) (4)
Hark! The Herald Angels Sing (medley) (4)

Holly And The Ivy (medley) (4)
Home On The Range (1)
I Must Walk That Lonesome Valley (2)
I Ride An Old Paint (1)
I Saw Three Ships (medley) (4)
Joseph Dearest Joseph Mine (medley) (4)
Joy To The World (medley) (4)
Kemo Kimo (2)
Like My Heart (3)
My Old Kentucky Home (2)

Night Herding Song (1)
Nobody Knows The Trouble I've Seen (2)
O Come, All Ye Faithful (Adeste Fideles) (medley) (4)
O Holy Night (medley) (4)
O Little Town Of Bethlehem (medley) (4)
Oh Tannenbaum (medley) (4)
Old Chisholm Trail (1)
Pig Knuckles And Rice (3)
Poor Lonesome Cowboy (1)
Proposal, The (3)
Red River Valley (1)
Salangadou (2)

Silent Night, Holy Night (medley) (4)
Sound De Fire Alarm (3)
Streets Of Laredo (Cowboy's Lament) (1)
Sweet Lorena (2)
Swing Low Sweet Chariot (4)
Tender Love (2)
Tumbling Tumbleweeds (1)
Twelve Days Of Christmas (medley) (4)
Un Deux Trois (3)
Wassail Song (Here We Come A Wassailing) (medley) (4)

Wassail, Wassail All Over The Town (medley) (4)
Water (3)
We Three Kings Of Orient Are (medley) (4)
What Child Is This? (medley) (4)
Whence Comes This Rush Of Wings (medley) (4)
Whoopie Ti Yi Yo (1)
Yellow Bird (2)

DEBUT DATE	PEAK POS	WKS CHR	GOLD	ARTIST — Album Title	$	Label & Number

LUCAS, Carrie
Los Angeles soul-disco stylist. Sang backup with The Whispers.

DEBUT DATE	PEAK POS	WKS CHR			$	Label & Number
4/23/77	**183**	5		1 Simply Carrie	$8	Soul Train 2220
5/19/79	**119**	10		2 Carrie Lucas In Danceland	$8	Solar 3219
1/31/81	**185**	3		3 Portrait Of Carrie.....................................	$8	Solar 3579
9/11/82	**180**	3		4 Still In Love	$8	Solar 60008

Are You Dancing (2) • Career Girl (3) • **Dance With You** (2) 70 • Danceland (2) • Dreamer (4) • Fashion (3) • I Gotta Get Away From Your Love (1) • **I Gotta Keep Dancin'** (1) 64 • I Just Can't Do Without Your Love (4) • I'll Close Loves Door (1) • I'm Gonna Make You Happy (2) • Is It A Dream (4) • It's Not What You Got (It's How You Use It) (3) • Jammin' Tenderly (Tender Part II) • Just A Memory (3) • Keep Smilin' (3) • Lovin' Is On My Mind (3) • Me For You (1) • Men (4) • Men Kiss And Tell (1) • Play By Your Rule (1) • Rockin' For Your Love (4) • Show Me Where You're Coming From (4) • Sometimes A Love Goes Wrong (2) • Southern Star (2) • Still In Love (4) • Sweet Love (4) • Tender (1) • Use It Or Lose It (3) • What's The Question (1)

LUKE
Rapper Luther Campbell, member of the Miami rap group The 2 Live Crew and owner of Luke Records.

DEBUT DATE	PEAK POS	WKS CHR			$	Label & Number
2/29/92	**52**	17		1 I Got Shit On My Mind	$12	Luke 91830

also released clean version *I Got Sumthin' On My Mind*

Ain't That A Bitch Part I & II • Breakdown • Cisco • Fakin' Like Gangsters • Head Head And More Head • I Ain't Bullshittin' Part IV • **I Wanna Rock 73** • Megamix • Menage A Trois • One Black And A Bunch Of Dirty White Boys • Pussy Ass Kid And Hoe Ass Play (Payback Is A Mutha Fucker) • Sonia • You And Me

LULU
Born Marie Lawrie on 11/3/48 near Glasgow, Scotland. Married to Maurice Gibb (Bee Gees) from 1969-73. Starred in the 1967 film *To Sir With Love*. Hosted own U.K. TV show in 1968.

DEBUT DATE	PEAK POS	WKS CHR			$	Label & Number
11/11/67	**24**	20		1 To Sir With Love	$15	Epic 26339
				also see soundtrack of same title		
2/21/70	**88**	14		2 New Routes	$12	Atco 310
9/26/81	**126**	10		3 Lulu	$8	Alfa 11006

After All (I Live My Life) (2) • **Best Of Both Worlds** (1) 32 • Boat That I Row (1) • Can't Hold Out On Love (3) • Day Tripper (1) • Dirty Old Man (2) • Don't Take Love For Granted (3) • Feelin' Alright (2) • **I Could Never Miss You (More Than I Do)** (3) 18 • **If I Were You** (3) 44 • If You're Right (3) • In The Morning (3) • Is That You Love (2) • Last Time (3) • Let's Pretend (1) • Love Loves To Love Love (1) • Loving You (3) • Marley Purt Drive (2) • **Morning Dew** (1) 52 • Mr. Bojangles (2) • **Oh Me Oh My (I'm A Fool For You Baby)** (2) 22 • People In Love (2) • Rattler (1) • Sweep Around Your Own Back Door (2) • Take Me In Your Arms (And Love Me) (1) • To Love Somebody (1) • **To Sir With Love** (1) 1 • Where's Eddie (2) • Who's Foolin' Who (3) • You And I (1) • You Are Still A Part Of Me (3) • You Win, I Lose (3)

LYMAN, Arthur
Born on the island of Kauai, Hawaii in 1934. Plays vibraphone, guitar, piano and drums. Formerly with the Martin Denny Trio.

DEBUT DATE	PEAK POS	WKS CHR			$	Label & Number
5/12/58+	**6**	62		1 Taboo .... [I]	$15	HiFi 806
7/24/61	**10**	30		2 Yellow Bird .... [I]	$12	HiFi 1004
3/30/63	**36**	6		3 I Wish You Love .... [I]	$12	HiFi 1009

Adventures In Paradise (2) • Akaka Falls (1) • Andalusia (2) • Arrivederci Roma (2) • Autumn Leaves (2) • Bamboo Tamboo (2) • Bolero (2) • Caravan (1) • China Clipper (1) • Dahil Sayo (1) • Granada (2) • Havah Nagilah (2) • Hilo March (1) • I Wish You Love (3) • It's So Right To Love (3) • John Henry (2) • Kalua (1) • Katsumi Love Theme (3) • Love (3) • Love Dance (3) • **Love For Sale** (3) 43 • Love Is A Many Splendored Thing (3) • Misirlou (1) • Mutiny On The Bounty, Love Song From (3) • Pagan Love Song (3) • Ringo Oiwake (1) • Sea Breeze (1) • Secret Love (3) • Sentimental Journey (3) • September Song (1) • Sim Sim (1) • Sweet And Lovely (2) • **Taboo** (1) 55 • To You My Love (3) • When I Fall In Love (3) • **Yellow Bird** (2) 4

LYMON, Frankie, and The Teenagers
R&B group formed as The Premiers in the Bronx in 1955. Lead singer Lymon was born on 9/30/42 in New York City; died of a drug overdose on 2/28/68. Other members included Herman Santiago & Jimmy Merchant (tenors), Joe Negroni (baritone; d: 9/5/78) and Sherman Garnes (bass; d: 2/26/77). Group appeared in the films *Rock, Rock, Rock* and *Mister Rock 'n' Roll*. Inducted into the Rock and Roll Hall of Fame in 1993.

DEBUT DATE	PEAK POS	WKS CHR			$	Label & Number
1/19/57	**19**	1		The Teenagers featuring Frankie Lymon	$175	Gee 701

ABC's Of Love 77 • Am I Fooling Myself Again • Baby, Baby • I Promise To Remember 57 • **I Want You To Be My Girl 13** • I'm Not A Juvenile Delinquent • I'm Not A Know It All • Love Is A Clown • Please Be Mine • Share • **Who Can Explain** flip • **Why Do Fools Fall In Love 6**

LYNCH, Ray
New Age keyboardist/guitarist raised in West Texas. Lute player with New York's Renaissance Quartet for seven years.

DEBUT DATE	PEAK POS	WKS CHR			$	Label & Number
6/24/89	**197**	2		No Blue Thing .... [I]	$8	Music West 103

Clouds Below Your Knees • Drifted In A Deeper Land • Evenings, Yes • Here & Never Found • Homeward At Last • No Blue Thing • True Spirit Of Mom & Dad

LYNCH MOB
Hard-rock foursome: George Lynch (guitars), Oni Logan (vocals), Anthony Esposito (bass) and Mick Brown (drums). Lynch and Brown were members of Dokken. Esposito was a member of Beggars & Thieves.

DEBUT DATE	PEAK POS	WKS CHR			$	Label & Number
11/10/90	**46**	23		1 Wicked Sensation	$12	Elektra 60954
5/16/92	**56**	9		2 Lynch Mob	$12	Elektra 61322

All I Want (1) • Cold Is The Heart (2) • Dance Of The Dogs (1) • Dream Until Tomorrow (2) • For A Million Years (1) • Heaven Is Waiting (2) • Hell Child (1) • I Want It (2) • Jungle Of Love (2) • No Bed Of Roses (1) • No Good (1) • Rain (1) • River Of Love (1) • Secret, The (2) • She's Evil But She's Mine (1) • Street Fightin' Man (1) • Sweet Sister Mercy (1) • Tangled In The Web (2) • Through These Eyes (1) • Tie Your Mother Down (2) • When Darkness Calls (2) • Wicked Sensation (1)

LYNN, Cheryl
Born on 3/11/57 in Los Angeles. Soul singer. Discovered on TV's *Gong Show*. Cousin of soul singer D'La Vance.

DEBUT DATE	PEAK POS	WKS CHR	GOLD		$	Label & Number
11/18/78+	**23**	30	●	1 Cheryl Lynn...	$8	Columbia 35486
1/19/80	**167**	4		2 In Love	$8	Columbia 36145
7/11/81	**104**	13		3 In The Night	$8	Columbia 37034
7/17/82	**133**	20		4 Instant Love	$8	Columbia 38057
4/28/84	**161**	5		5 Preppie	$8	Columbia 38961

DEBUT DATE	PEAK POS	WKS CHR	GOLD	ARTIST — Album Title	$	Label & Number

LYNN, Cheryl — Cont'd

All My Lovin' (1)
Baby (3)
Believe In Me (4)
Chances (2)
Change The Channel (5)
Come In From The Rain (1)
Day After Day (4)
Daybreak (Storybook Children) (1)
Don't Let It Fade Away (2)
Encore (5) ***69***
Feel It (2)
Fix It (5)
Fool A Fool (5)
Free (5)
Give My Love To You (1)
Got To Be Real (1) ***12***
Hide It Away (2)
Hurry Home (3)
I Just Wanna Be Your Fantasy (4)
I'm On Fire (3)
I've Got Faith In You (2)
I've Got Just What You Need (2)
If This World Were Mine (4)
If You'll Be True To Me (3)
In Love (2)
In The Night (3)
Instant Love (4)
Keep It Hot (2)
Life's Too Short (5)
Look Before You Leap (4)
Love Bomb (2)
Love Rush (5)
No One Else Will Do (5)
Nothing To Say (1)
Preppie (5)
Say You'll Be Mine (4)
Shake It Up Tonight (3) ***70***
Show You How (3)
Sleep Walkin' (4)
Star Love (1) ***62***
This Time (5)
What's On Your Mind (3)
With Love On Our Side (3)
You Saved My Day (1)
You're The One (1)

★★475★★ LYNN, Loretta

Born Loretta Webb on 4/14/34 in Butcher Holler, Kentucky. Country singer/songwriter/guitarist. Sister of Crystal Gayle and country singers Jay Lee Webb and Peggy Sue. The movie *Coal Miner's Daughter* of 1980 was based on Loretta's autobiography.

DEBUT DATE	PEAK POS	WKS CHR	GOLD	ARTIST — Album Title	$	Label & Number
3/4/67	**140**	9		1 You Ain't Woman Enough	$20	Decca 74783
4/8/67	**80**	20	●	2 Don't Come Home A Drinkin'	$20	Decca 74842
4/5/69	**168**	5		3 Your Squaw Is On The Warpath	$20	Decca 75084
8/9/69	**148**	4		4 Woman Of The World/To Make A Man	$20	Decca 75113
2/28/70	**146**	11		5 Wings Upon Your Horns	$20	Decca 75163
2/13/71	**81**	17	●	6 Coal Miner's Daughter also see Soundtrack *Coal Miner's Daughter*	$20	Decca 75253
3/13/71	**78**	14		7 We Only Make Believe *	$10	Decca 75251
6/26/71	**110**	7		8 I Wanna Be Free	$20	Decca 75282
3/4/72	**106**	13	●	9 Lead Me On *	$10	Decca 75326
4/8/72	**109**	9		10 One's On The Way	$15	Decca 75334
8/25/73	**153**	9		11 Louisiana Woman-Mississippi Man * *CONWAY TWITTY and LORETTA LYNN	$10	MCA 335
9/22/73	**183**	2		12 Love Is The Foundation	$10	MCA 355
4/19/75	**182**	2		13 Back To The Country	$10	MCA 471

After The Fire Is Gone (7) ***56***
Another Man Loved Me Last Night (6)
Another You (13)
Any One, Any Worse, Any Where (6)
As Good As A Lonely Girl Can Be (11)
Back Street Affair (9)
Back To The Country (13)
Before Your Time (11)
Big Ole Hurt (5)
Big Sister, Little Sister (4)
Blueberry Hill (10)
Bye Bye Love (11)
Coal Miner's Daughter (6) ***83***
Darkest Day (1)
Devil Gets His Dues (2)
Don't Come Home A Drinkin' (With Lovin' On Your Mind) (2)
Don't Tell Me You're Sorry (7)
Drive You Out Of My Mind (8)
Easy Loving (9)
Five Fingers Left (12)
For Heavens Sake (11)
For The Good Times (6)
Get Some Loving Done (9)
Get What 'Cha Got And Go (2)
God Gave Me A Heart To Forgive (1)
Hands Of Yesterday (13)
Hangin' On (7)
Harper Valley P.T.A. (3)
He's All I Got (10)
He's Somewhere Between You And Me (3)
Hello Darlin' (6)
Help Me Make It Through The Night (8)
Hey Loretta (12)
How Far Can We Go (9)
I Can Help (13)
I Can't Keep Away From You (2)
I Can't See Me Without You (10)
I Gave Everything (That A Girl In Love Should Never Give) (12)
I Got Caught (2)
I Love You, I Love You (12)
I Only See The Things I Wanna See (5)
I Really Don't Want To Know (2)
I Started Loving You Again (4)
I Walk Alone (3)
I Wanna Be Free (8) ***94***
I Wonder If You Told Her About Me (9)
I'd Rather Be Gone (5)
I'll Still Be Missing You (5)
I'm Dynamite (5)
I'm Living In Two Worlds (2)
I'm Lonesome For Trouble Tonight (4)
I'm Losing My Mind (10)
I'm One Man's Woman (8)
I'm So Used To Loving You (7)
If I Never Love Again (It'll Be Too Soon) (8)
If You Handle The Merchandise (5)
If You Touch Me, (You've Got To Love Me) (11)
If You Were Mine To Lose (4)
Is It Wrong (For Loving You) (1)
It'll Be Open Season On You (6)
It'll Feel Good When It Quits Hurtin' (10)
It's Another World (1)
It's Not The Miles You Traveled (10)
It's Only Make-Believe (7)
It's Time To Pay The Fiddler (13)
Jimmy On My Mind (13)
Johnny One Time (4)
Just To Satisfy (The Weakness In A Man) (12)
Kaw-Liga (3)
Keep Your Change (1)
Lead Me On (9)
Less Of Me (6)
Let Me Go, You're Hurtin' Me (3)
Let's Get Back Down To Earth (5)
Living My Lifetime For You (3)
Living Together Alone (11)
Louisiana Woman, Mississippi Man (11)
Love Is The Foundation (12)
L-o-v-e, Love (10)
Love's On The Loose (10)
Mad Mrs. Jesse Brown (13)
Making Plans (2)
Man I Hardly Know (1)
Man Of The House (6)
Me And Bobby McGee (8)
Morning After Baby Let Me Down (10)
Never Ending Song Of Love (9)
No One Will Ever Know (4)
One I Can't Live Without (7)
One Little Reason (4)
One's On The Way (10)
Only Time I Hurt (4)
Our Conscience You And Me (11)
Paper Roses (13)
Pickin' Wild Mountain Berries (7)
Pill, The (13) ***70***
Playing House Away From Home (9)
Put It Off Until Tomorrow (1)
Put Your Hand In The Hand (8)
Release Me (11)
Rose Garden (8)
Saint To A Sinner (2)
Satin Sheets (12)
See That Mountain (8)
Shoe Goes On The Other Foot Tonight (2)
Sneakin' In (3)
Snowbird (6)
Someone Before Me (1)
Stand By Your Man (4)
Take Me (7)
Taking The Place Of My Man (3)
Talking To The Wall (1)
There Goes My Everything (2)
There's More To Leaving Than Just Saying Goodbye (12)
These Boots Are Made For Walkin' (1)
This Stranger (My Little Girl) (5)
Tippy Toeing (1)
To Make A Man (Feel Like A Man) (4)
Tomorrow Never Comes (2)
Too Far (6)
Too Wild To Be Tamed (10)
We've Closed Our Eyes To Shame (7)
What Are We Gonna Do About Us (11)
What Makes Me Tick (6)
What Sundown Does To You (12)
When I Reach The Bottom (You'd Better Be There) (5)
When I Turn Off My Lights (Your Memory Turns On) (9)
When You Leave My World (8)
When You're Poor (8)
Why Me (12)
Will You Be There (13)
Will You Visit Me On Sunday (7)
Wings Upon Your Horns (5)
Woman Of The World (Leave My World Alone) (4)
Working Girl (7)
You Ain't Woman Enough (1)
You Blow My Mind (9)
You Lay So Easy On My Mind (11)
You Love Everybody But You (13)
You Wouldn't Know An Angel (If You Saw One) (5)
You're Still Lovin' Me (12)
You're The Reason (9)
You've Just Stepped In (From Stepping Out On Me) (3)
Your Squaw Is On The Warpath (3)

★★450★★ LYNNE, Gloria

Born on 11/23/31 in New York City. Jazz-styled vocalist.

DEBUT DATE	PEAK POS	WKS CHR	GOLD	ARTIST — Album Title	$	Label & Number
9/18/61	**51**	13		1 I'm Glad There Is You with the Earl May Trio	$25	Everest 5126
10/16/61	**101**	7		2 He Needs Me	$25	Everest 5128
10/30/61	**57**	18		3 This Little Boy Of Mine	$25	Everest 5131
4/7/62	**58**	22		4 Gloria Lynne at Basin Street East [L]	$25	Everest 5137
2/9/63	**39**	27		5 Gloria Lynne at the Las Vegas Thunderbird [L] with the Herman Foster Trio	$25	Everest 5208
9/21/63+	**27**	22		6 Gloria, Marty & Strings arranged and conducted by Marty Paich (Emmy-winning songwriter and father of Toto's David Paich)	$25	Everest 5220
6/6/64	**43**	19		7 I Wish You Love	$25	Everest 5226
6/5/65	**82**	10		8 Soul Serenade	$18	Fontana 27541

All Alone (8)
All Night Long (1)
And This Is My Beloved (4,7)
Autumn Leaves (4)
Baby Won't You Please Come Home (8)
Be My Love (7)
Birth Of The Blues (1)
But Beautiful (5)
But Not For Me (3)
Condemned Without Trial (3)
Don't Go To Strangers (8)
Don't Take Your Love From Me (6) ***76***
Don't Worry About Me (6)
Dreamy (3)
Drinking Again (4)
End Of A Love Affair (5,7)
Folks That Live On The Hill (6)
Getting To Know You (3)
Greensleeves (2)
He Needs Me (2)
Here Today, Gone Tomorrow (5)
Home (2)
Humming Blues (3)
I Believe In You (5)
I Can't Give You Anything But Love (7)
I Get A Kick Out Of You (4)
I Got Rhythm (4)
I Know Love (3,7)
I See Your Face Before Me (1)

DEBUT DATE	PEAK POS	WKS CHR	GOLD	ARTIST — Album Title	$	Label & Number

LYNNE, Gloria — Cont'd

I Should Care (6) *64*	In Other Words (4)	My Romance (3)	Soul Serenade (8)	This Little Boy Of Mine (3)	You're Mine You (2)
I Thought About You (2)	Indian Love Call (7)	Night Has A Thousand Eyes (6)	Stella By Starlight (1)	Through A Long And Sleepless Night (6)	Young And Foolish (1)
I Wish You Love (6,7) *28*	It Could Happen To You (8)	Old Man River (1)	Sunday, Monday And Always (5)	Trouble Is A Man (1)	
I'll Be Around (8)	It Just Happened To Me (4)	On Christmas Day (1)	Sweet Pumpkin' (1)	**Watermelon Man** (8) *62*	
I'll Buy You A Star (5)	It Never Entered My Mind (4)	Out Of This World (6)	Tall Hope (4)	What Is There To Say (6)	
I'll Take Romance (2)	Jazz In You (3)	People Will Say We're In Love (8)	Teach Me Tonight (8)	What Kind Of Fool Am I (5)	
I'm Glad There Is You (1)	Joey, Joey, Joey (8)		That's My Desire (8)	What'll I Do (1)	
I've Got It Bad And That Ain't Good (2)	Just In Time (3)	Record Company Blues (5)	That's No Joke (1)	Whispering Grass (6)	
If I Loved You (8)	Lamp Is Low (2)	Second Time Around (4)	There Is No Greater Love (3,7)	Wild Is The Wind (2)	
If You Love Me (2,7)	Love, I've Found You (7)	Serenade In Blue (6)	This Could Be The Start Of Something Big (5)	Wouldn't It Be Lovely (4,7)	
Impossible (3) *95*	Mack The Knife (4)	So This Is Love (5)		You Don't Know What Love Is (2,7)	
In Love In Vain (5)	Make The Man Love Me (2)	Something Wonderful (5)			
	My Devotion (6)				

LYNNE, Jeff
Born on 12/30/47 in Birmingham, England. Leader of Electric Light Orchestra and The Move. Otis Wilbury of the Traveling Wilburys. Production work for George Harrison, Roy Orbison, Tom Petty and Del Shannon.

| 6/30/90 | 83 | 9 | | Armchair Theatre .... | $12 | Reprise 26184 |

Blown Away	Don't Say Goodbye	Lift Me Up	Now You're Gone	September Song	What Would It Take
Don't Let Go	Every Little Thing	Nobody Home	Save Me Now	Stormy Weather	

★★209★★ LYNYRD SKYNYRD
Southern-rock band formed by Ronnie Van Zant (b: 1/15/49; lead singer), Gary Rossington (guitar) and Allen Collins (guitar) while they were in junior high in Jacksonville, Florida in 1965. Named after their gym teacher Leonard Skinner. Changing lineup featured drummers Bob Burns, Rick Medlocke (later of Blackfoot) and Artimus Pyle; bassists Larry Junstrom (later of 38 Special), Greg Walker (later of Blackfoot), Leon Wilkeson and Ed King (ex-Strawberry Alarm Clock); pianist Billy Powell; and guitarist Steve Gaines. Plane crash on 10/20/77 in Gillsburg, Mississippi killed Van Zant and members Steve and his sister Cassie Gaines (vocals). Gary and Allen formed the Rossington Collins Band in 1980; split in 1982. Rossington and vocalist Johnny Van Zant (the younger brother of Ronnie and Donnie [lead singer of 38 Special] Van Zant) regrouped with old and new band members for the 1987 Lynyrd Skynyrd Tribute Tour. Collins (paralyzed in a car accident in 1986) died of pneumonia on 1/23/90 (age 37). Rossington, Van Zant, Pyle, Wilkeson, King, Powell regrouped in 1991 with Randall Hall (guitar) and Custer (drums).

9/22/73+	27	79	▲²	1 Lynyrd Skynyrd (pronounced leh-nerd skin-nerd)	$15	MCA/Sounds 363
5/4/74	12	45	▲²	2 Second Helping	$15	MCA/Sounds 413
4/12/75	9	20	▲	3 Nuthin' Fancy	$10	MCA 2137
2/21/76	20	16	●	4 Gimme Back My Bullets	$10	MCA 2170
10/2/76	9	43	▲³	5 One More From The Road .... [L]	$12	MCA 6001 [2]
11/5/77	5	34	▲²	6 Street Survivors	$30	MCA 3029
				album released 3 days after the plane crash		
9/23/78	15	18	▲	7 Skynyrd's First And...Last .... [E]	$8	MCA 3047
				recordings from 1970-72		
12/15/79+	12	65	▲³	8 Gold & Platinum .... [G]	$12	MCA 11008 [2]
11/20/82	171	7		9 Best Of The Rest .... [K]	$8	MCA 5370
10/10/87	41	17		10 Legend .... [L]	$8	MCA 42084
				live concert versions of previously unreleased material featuring the vocals of the late Ronnie Van Zant		
4/16/88	68	11		11 Southern By The Grace Of God/Lynyrd Skynyrd Tribute Tour - 1987 .... [L]	$10	MCA 8027 [2]
6/29/91	64	16		12 Lynyrd Skynyrd 1991	$12	Atlantic 82258

Ain't No Good Life (6)	End Of The Road (12)	I Need You (2)	One In The Sun (10)	**Sweet Home Alabama** (2,5,8,11) *8*	Whiskey Rock-A-Roller (3,5,8)
All I Can Do Is Write About It (4)	Every Mother's Son (4)	I Never Dreamed (6,9)	One More Time (6)	Sweet Little Missy (10)	White Dove (7)
Am I Losin' (3)	Four Walls Of Raiford (10)	I'm A Country Boy (3,9)	Poison Whiskey (1)	T For Texas (5,9)	Wino (7)
Backstreet Crawler (12)	**Free Bird** (1) *19*	I've Been Your Fool (9)	Preacher's Daughter (7)	Take Your Time (10)	Workin' For MCA (2,5,9,11)
Ballad Of Curtis Loew (2)	**Free Bird** [live] (5,8,11) *38*	I've Seen Enough (12)	Pure & Simple (12)	That Smell (6,8,11)	**You Got That Right** (6,8,11) *69*
Call Me The Breeze (2,5,9,11)	Georgia Peaches (10)	It's A Killer (12)	Railroad Song (3)	Things Goin' On (1,7)	
Cheatin' Woman (3)	Gimme Back My Bullets (4,8,11)	Keeping The Faith (12)	Roll Gypsy Roll (4)	Travellin' Man (5)	
Comin' Home (7,8,11)	Gimme Three Steps (1,5,8)	Lend A Helpin' Hand (7)	**Saturday Night Special** (3,5,8) *27*	Truck Drivin' Man (10)	
Crossroads (5)	Good Thing (12)	Made In The Shade (3)	Searching (4,5)	Trust (4)	
Cry For The Bad Man (4)	Gotta Go (9)	Mama (Afraid To Say Goodbye) (12)	Seasons, The (7)	Tuesday's Gone (1,5,8)	
Dixie (medley) (11)	Honky Tonk Night Time Man (6)	Mississippi Kid (1)	Simple Man (1,8,10)	Was I Right Or Wrong (7)	
Don't Ask Me No Questions (2)	I Ain't The One (1,5,8)	Money Man (12)	Smokestack Lightning (12)	**What's Your Name** (6,8,11) *13*	
Double Trouble (4,9) *80*	I Got The Same Old Blues (4)	Mr. Banker (10)	Southern Women (12)	When You Got Good Friends (10)	
Down South Jukin' (7,8)	I Know A Little (6,8,11)	Needle And The Spoon (2,5)	Swamp Music (2,11)		
		On The Hunt (3,8)			

LYTLE, Johnny
Born on 10/13/32 in Springfield, Ohio. Jazz vibraphonist.

| 2/26/66 | 141 | 2 | | The Village Caller! .... [I] | $20 | Riverside 480 |

Can't Help Loving Dat Man	On Green Dolphin Street	Solitude	Village Caller	You Don't Know What Love Is
Kevin Devin	Pedro Strodder	Unhappy Happy Soul		

M

M
M is British pop musician Robin Scott (b: 4/1/47).

| 12/22/79+ | 79 | 8 | | New York-London-Paris-Munich .... | $8 | Sire 6084 |

Cowboys And Indians	Moderne Man (medley)	**Pop Muzik** *1*	That's The Way The Money Goes	Unite Your Nation
Made In Munich	Moonlight And Muzak	Satisfy Your Lust (medley)		Woman Make Man

DEBUT DATE	PEAK POS	WKS CHR	GOLD	ARTIST — Album Title	$	Label & Number

MA, Yo-Yo
Classical cellist. Born on 10/7/55 in Paris of Chinese parentage. Attended Juilliard and graduated from Harvard. Prominent player by age 19.

| 2/15/92 | 93 | 18 | | Hush .... | $12 | Sony 48177 |

YO-YO MA & BOBBY McFERRIN

Bach: Air		Coyote		Grace		Hush Little Baby		Rimsky-Korsakov: Flight Of		Stars
Bach: Musette · Good-Bye · Hoedown! · Rachmaninoff: Vocalise · The Bumblebee · Vivaldi: Andante
Barriere: Allegro Prestissimo · Gounod/Bach: Ave Maria

★★**291**★★ **MABLEY, Moms**
Born Loretta Mary Aiken on 3/19/1894 in Brevard, North Carolina; died on 5/23/75. Bawdy comedienne/actress. In the films *Boarding House Blues*, *Emperor Jones* and *Amazing Grace*.

5/1/61	16	57		1 Moms Mabley At The "UN" .... [C]	$15	Chess 1452
7/10/61	121	5		2 Moms Mabley Onstage .... [C]	$15	Chess 1447
10/30/61	39	27		3 Moms Mabley at The Playboy Club .... [C]	$15	Chess 1460
3/31/62	28	24		4 Moms Mabley At Geneva Conference .... [C]	$15	Chess 1463
9/1/62	27	21		5 Moms Mabley Breaks It Up .... [C]	$15	Chess 1472
1/12/63	19	18		6 Young Men, Si - Old Men, No .... [C]	$15	Chess 1477
6/29/63	41	16		7 I Got Somethin' To Tell You! .... [C]	$15	Chess 1479
1/4/64	134	5		8 The Funny Sides Of Moms Mabley .... [C]	$15	Chess 1482
2/29/64	48	24		9 Out On A Limb .... [C]	$12	Mercury 60889
7/18/64	118	10		10 Moms Wows .... [E-C]	$15	Chess 1486

recorded 1961 at the Playboy Club, Chicago

9/19/64	128	4		11 Moms The Word .... [C]	$12	Mercury 60907
11/13/65	133	3		12 Now Hear This .... [C]	$12	Mercury 61012
9/6/69	173	3		13 The Youngest Teenager .... [C]	$12	Mercury 61229

no track titles listed on albums #1-10 & 12-13

Help The Bear (11) · Lullaby Of The Leaves (11) · Pray, Little Children, Pray (11) · Skitty-Poo (11)
If I Had Money (11) · That Don't Pay My Rent (11)

MacALPINE, Tony
Black hard-rock guitarist.

| 7/4/87 | 146 | 11 | | Maximum Security .... | $8 | Squawk 832249 |

Autumn Lords · Etude #4 Opus #10 · Key To The City · Porcelain Doll · Tears Of Sahara · Vision, The
Dreamstate · Hundreds Of Thousands · King's Cup · Sacred Wonder · Time And The Test

MAC BAND Featuring THE McCAMPBELL BROTHERS
Dallas-based, eight-member group from Flint, Michigan. Vocalist brothers Charles, Derrick, Kelvin and Ray McCampbell, backed by musicians Ray Flippin, Rodney Frazier, Slye Fuller and Mark Harper.

| 7/23/88 | 109 | 14 | | Mac Band .... | $8 | MCA 42090 |

Girl Your Love's So Fine · Jealous · Roses Are Red · Stuck · That's The Way I Look At · You Plus Me
Got To Get Over You · Midnight Lady · Stalemate · Love

MacDONALD, Jeanette, & Nelson Eddy
Top movie duo of the 1930s. Jeanette was born on 6/18/01 in Philadelphia; died on 1/14/65. Nelson was born on 6/29/01 in Providence, Rhode Island; died on 3/6/67.

| 5/25/59 | 40 | 3 | ● | Favorites In Hi-Fi .... | $25 | RCA 1738 |

Ah, Sweet Mystery Of Life · Breeze And I [solo: Jeanette] · Italian Street Song [solo: · Rose-Marie [solo: Nelson] · Wanting You · Will You Remember
Beyond The Blue Horizon · Giannina Mia [solo: Jeanette] · Jeanette] · Stouthearted Men [solo: · While My Lady Sleeps [solo: · (Sweetheart)
[solo: Jeanette] · Indian Love Call · Rosalie [solo: Nelson] · Nelson] · Nelson]

MacDONALD, Ralph
Session percussionist/bandleader. Formerly with Roberta Flack, and the jazz sextet, The Writers.

9/25/76	114	16		1 Sound Of A Drum .... [I]	$10	Marlin 2202
3/4/78	57	17		2 The Path .... [I]	$10	Marlin 2210
7/14/79	110	10		3 Counterpoint	$8	Marlin 2229
10/13/84	108	10		4 Universal Rhythm	$8	Polydor 823323

Always Something Missing (3) · I Cross My Heart (2) · (It's) The Game (4) · Outcasts (Another Time, · Smoke Rings And Wine (2) · You Are In Love (3)
Calypso Breakdown (1) · I Need Someone (3) · Jam On The Groove (1) · Another Place), Theme · Sound Of A Drum (1)
Discolypso (3) · If I'm Still Around Tomorrow · Mister Magic (1) · From The (4) · Tell The Truth (3)
East Dry River (3) · (2) · Only Time You Say You Love · Park Plaza (4) · Tradewinds (4)
Game ..see: (It's The) · In The Name Of Love (4) 58 · Me (Is When We're Making · Path, The (2) · Universal Rhythm (4)
| | | | | It Feels So Good (2) · Love) (1) · Playpen (4) · Where Is The Love (1)

MacGREGOR, Mary
Born on 5/6/48 in St. Paul, Minnesota. Pop singer.

| 1/15/77 | 17 | 19 | | Torn Between Two Lovers .... | $10 | Ariola Am. 50015 |

For A While 90 · It's Too Soon (To Let Our · Mama · This Girl (Has Turned Into · Torn Between Two · Why Did You Wait (To Tell
Good Together · Love End) · Take Your Love Away · A Woman) 46 · Lovers 1 · Me)
I Just Want To Love You · Lady I Am

MACHO
Disco production by Mauro Malavasi.

| 10/7/78 | 101 | 14 | | I'm A Man .... | $8 | Prelude 12160 |

Because There Is Music In · Hear Me Calling · I'm A Man
The Air

MACK, Lonnie
Born Lonnie McIntosh on 7/18/41 in Aurora, Indiana. Singer/guitarist (since age five). Own country band in 1954. With Troy Seals in the early '60s. Rediscovered in 1968. Retired from music, 1971-85.

| 11/30/63 | 103 | 9 | | 1 The Wham Of That Memphis Man! .... | $40 | Fraternity 1014 |
| 6/15/85 | 130 | 21 | | 2 Strike Like Lightning .... | $8 | Alligator 4739 |

with guest guitarist Stevie Ray Vaughan

DEBUT DATE	PEAK POS	WKS CHR	GOLD	ARTIST — Album Title	$	Label & Number

MACK, Lonnie — Cont'd

Baby, What's Wrong (1) *93*
Bounce, The (1)
Double Whammy (2)
Down And Out (1)
Down In The Dumps (1)
Falling Back In Love With You (2)
Hound Dog Man (2)
I'll Keep You Happy (1)
If You Have To Know (2)
Long Way From Memphis (2)
Memphis (1) **5**
Oreo Cookie Blues (1)
Satisfied (1)
Satisfy Susie (2)
Stop (2)
Strike Like Lightning (2)
Suzie-Q (1)
Wham! (1) **24**
Where There's A Will (1)
Why (1)
You Ain't Got Me (2)

MADAME X

West Coast-based black female trio created by producer Bernadette Cooper (founding member of Klymaxx): Iris Parker, Valerie Victoria and Alisa Randolph. Madame X is the code name of the 45 rpm record development project in the 1940s.

| 10/10/87 | 162 | 5 | | Madame X .... | $8 | Atlantic 81774 |

Cherries In The Snow
Flirt
I Want Your Body
I Wonder
I'm Weak For You
Just That Type Of Girl
Madame X
Marry Me (If You Really Love Me)

MAD COBRA

Reggae rapper Ewart Everton Brown. Born on 3/31/68 in Kingston and raised in St. Mary's, Jamaica.

| 11/7/92 | 125 | 13↑ | | Hard To Wet, Easy To Dry .... | $12 | Columbia 52751 |

CD contains 3 bonus tracks

Dead End Street
Elbow
Flex *13*
Glue
Good Body Gal
Hard To Wet, Easy To Dry
If Looks Could Kill
Legacy
Mate A Talk
Mi Sorry
Minute To Pray
Really Do It
Release
Run Him
Wet Dream

MADHOUSE

Jazz-fusion quartet led by Eric Leeds (sax man in Prince's band, The Revolution).

| 2/21/87 | 107 | 11 | | 8 .... [I] | $8 | Paisley P. 25545 |

One
Two
Three
Four
Five
Six
Seven
Eight

MAD LADS, The

Consisted of John Gary Williams, Julius Green, William Brown and Robert Phillips. Williams and Brown replaced by Sam Nelson and Quincy Clifton Billops, Jr. (later with Ollie & The Nightingales, The Ovations) from 1966-69. Brown's brother Bertrand was a member of The Newcomers (later known as Kwick).

| 8/9/69 | 180 | 2 | | The Mad, Mad, Mad, Mad, Mad Lads .... | $15 | Volt 6005 |

By The Time I Get To Phoenix *84*
Cry Baby
I Just Can't Forget
I've Never Found A Girl
It's Loving Time
Love Is Here Today And Gone Tomorrow
Make Room (In Your Heart)
Make This Young Lady Mine
Monkey Time '69
No Strings Attached
So Nice
These Old Memories

MADNESS

Septet from North London, England — Graham "Suggs" McPherson, vocals. Formed as a ska-pop band in 1978, split up in 1986.

3/8/80	128	9		1 One Step Beyond	$8	Sire 6085
11/22/80	146	4		2 Absolutely	$8	Sire 6094
4/30/83	41	29		3 Madness	$8	Geffen 4003
3/17/84	109	8		4 Keep Moving	$8	Geffen 4022

Baggy Trousers (2)
Bed & Breakfast Man (1)
Believe Me (1)
Blue Skinned Beast (3)
Brand New Beat (4)
Cardiac Arrest (3)
Chipmunks Are Go! (1)
Close Escape (2)
Disappear (2)
Embarrassment (2)
E.R.N.I.E. (2)
Give Me A Reason (4)
Grey Day (3)
House Of Fun (3)
In The Middle Of The Night (1)
In The Rain (2)
Keep Moving (4)
Land Of Hope & Glory (1)
Madness (1)
Madness (Is All In The Mind) (3)
March Of The Gherkins (4)
Michael Caine (4)
Mummy's Boy (1)
My Girl (1)
Night Boat To Cairo (1,3)
Not Home Today (2)
On The Beat Pete (2)
One Better Day (4)
One Step Beyond... (1)
Our House (3) **7**
Overdone (1)
Primrose Hill (3)
Prince, The (1)
Prospects (4)
Razor Blade Alley (1)
Return Of The Los Palmas 7 (2)
Rise And Fall (3)
Rockin' In A (1)
Samantha (4)
Shadow Of Fear (2)
Shut Up (3)
Solid Gone (2)
Sun And The Rain (4) **72**
Swan Lake (1)
Take It Or Leave It (2)
Tarzan's Nuts (1)
Tomorrow's Just Another Day (3)
Turning Blue (4)
Victoria Gardens (4)
Wings Of A Dove (A Celebratory Song) (4)
You Said (2)

★★140★★ MADONNA

Born Madonna Louise Ciccone on 8/16/58 in Bay City, Michigan. To New York in the late '70s; performed with the Alvin Ailey dance troupe. Short-lived member of the Breakfast Club, early '80s. Married to actor Sean Penn from 1985-89. Acted in the films *Desperately Seeking Susan, Dick Tracy, A League Of Their Own* and *Body Of Evidence* among others. Appeared in Broadway's *Speed-The-Plow*. Released concert tour documentary film *Truth Or Dare* in 1991. Released adults-only picture book *Sex* in 1992. The top female pop artist since 1984.

9/3/83+	8	168	▲⁴	1 Madonna	$8	Sire 23867
12/1/84+	1³	108	▲⁷	2 Like A Virgin	$8	Sire 25157
7/19/86	1⁵	82	▲⁵	3 True Blue	$8	Sire 25442
8/15/87	7	28	▲	4 Who's That Girl .... [S]	$8	Sire 25611

includes "Best Thing Ever" by Scritti Politti, "El Coco Loco (So So Bad)" by Coati Mundi, "Step By Step" by Club Nouveau, "Turn It Up" by Michael Davidson and "24 Hours" by Duncan Favre

| 12/5/87+ | 14 | 22 | ▲ | 5 You Can Dance .... [K] | $8 | Sire 25535 |

features 7 extended remixes of Madonna's dance hits

| 4/8/89 | 1⁶ | 77 | ▲³ | 6 Like A Prayer .... | $8 | Sire 25844 |
| 6/9/90 | 2³ | 25 | ▲² | 7 I'm Breathless .... [S] | $12 | Sire 26209 |

songs from and songs inspired by the film *Dick Tracy*

| 12/1/90+ | 2² | 115↑ | ▲³ | 8 The Immaculate Collection .... [G] | $12 | Sire 26440 |
| 11/7/92 | 2¹ | 14↑ | ▲² | 9 Erotica .... | $12 | Maverick 45031 |

Act Of Contrition (6)
Angel (2) **5**
Back In Business (7)
Bad Girl (9)
Borderline (1,8) *10*
Burning Up (1)
Bye Bye Baby (9)
Can't Stop (4)
Causing A Commotion (4) *2*
Cherish (3,6) **2**
Crazy For You (8) *1*
Cry Baby (7)
Dear Jessie (6)
Deeper And Deeper (9) *7*
Dress You Up (2) **5**
Erotica (9) *3*
Everybody (1,5)
Express Yourself (6,8) *2*
Fever (9)
Hanky Panky (7) *10*
He's A Man (7)
I Know It (1)
I'm Going Bananas (7)
In This Life (9)
Into The Groove (5,8)
Jimmy Jimmy (3)
Justify My Love (8) *1*
Keep It Together (6) *8*
La Isla Bonita (3,8) *4*
Like A Prayer (6,8) *1*
Like A Virgin (2,8) *1*
Live To Tell (3,8) *1*
Look Of Love (3)
Love Don't Live Here Anymore (2)
Love Makes The World Go Round (3)
Love Song (6)
Lucky Star (1,8) *4*
Material Girl (2,8) *2*
More (7)
Now I'm Following You (Part I & II) (7)
Oh Father (6) *20*
Open Your Heart (3,8) *1*
Over And Over (2,5)
Papa Don't Preach (3,8) *1*
Physical Attraction (1,5)
Pretender (2)
Promise To Try (6)
Rain (9)
Rescue Me (8) *9*
Secret Garden (9)
Shoo-Bee-Doo (2)
Something To Remember (7)
Sooner Or Later (7)
Spanish Eyes (9)
Spotlight (5)
Stay (2)
Thief Of Hearts (9)
Think Of Me (1)
Till Death Do Us Part (6)
True Blue (3) *3*
Vogue (7,8) *1*
Waiting (7)
What Can You Lose (7)
Where Life Begins (9)
Where's The Party (3,5)
White Heat (3)
Who's That Girl (4) *1*
Why's It So Hard (9)
Words (9)

MAD RIVER
Folk-rock quartet from Berkeley, California: David Robinson, Rick Bockner, Greg Dewey and Laurence Hammond.

| 8/9/69 | 192 | 2 | | Paradise Bar And Grill.. | $20 | Capitol 185 |

Academy Cemetery / Cherokee Queen / Copper Plates / Equinox / Harfy Magnum / Leave Me (medley) / Love's Not The Way To Treat A Friend / Paradise Bar And Grill / Revolution's In My Pockets / Stay (medley) / They Brought Sadness

MADURA
Folk-rock trio — Alan DeCarlo, lead singer.

| 10/30/71 | 186 | 2 | | Madura.. | $15 | Columbia 30794 [2] |

Damnation / Don't Be Afraid / Dreams / Drinking No Wine / Free From The Devil / Hawk Piano / I Think I'm Dreaming / It's A Good Time For Loving / Johnny B. Goode / Joy In Old Age By Way Of Self Observation / Man's Rebirth Through Childbirth - Part I & II / My Love Is Free / My My What A World / Plain As Day / Realization / See For Yourself / Stimulation / Talking To Myself / Trapped

MAGGARD, Cledus, And The Citizen's Band
Cledus' real name: Jay Huguely; born in Quick Sand, Kentucky.

| 3/13/76 | 135 | 8 | | The White Knight... [N] | $10 | Mercury 1072 |

novelty "C.B." songs

C.B. Rock / C.B. '76 / Cledus's C.B. Lingo Dictionary / Dad I Gotta Go / Jaw Jackin' / **Kentucky Moonrunner 85** / Mercy Day / **White Knight 19** / Who We Got On That End? (You're The Only Friend I Got)

MAGIC ORGAN, The
Jerry Smith plays the organ.

| 5/6/72 | 135 | 7 | | Street Fair.. [I] | $8 | Ranwood 8092 |

All In The Family ..see: Those Were The Days / Beautiful Dishwasher / It's A Small World / Liechtensteiner Polka / Pennsylvania Polka / Ranger's Waltz / Street Fair / Sweet 'N Sassy / Those Were The Days / Truck Stop / Under The Double Eagle / Wheels / When In Rome

MAGNIFICENT MEN, The
White R&B-styled group from Harrisburg, Pennsylvania: Bob Angelucci, David Bupp (vocals), Terry Crousore, Tommy Hoover, Tom Pane, Jimmy Seville and Buddy King.

| 4/8/67 | 171 | 2 | 1 | The Magnificent Men... | $15 | Capitol 2678 |
| 7/29/67 | 89 | 9 | 2 | The Magnificent Men "Live!"................................. [L] | $15 | Capitol 2775 |

Cry With Me Baby (1) / Do A Justice To Your Heart (1) / Doin' The Philly Dog (2) / Function At The Junction (2) / I Got News (1) / I Wish You Love (1) / I'm Gonna Miss You (2) / I've Been Trying (2) / Just Be True (2) / Just Walk In My Shoes (1) / Keep On Climbing (1) / Maybe, Maybe Baby (1) / Misty (1,2) / Much, Much, More Of Your Love (1) / Peace Of Mind (1,2) / Show Me (2) / Stormy Weather (1,2) / **Sweet Soul Medley - Part 1 (2) 90** / Whispers (2) / You Don't Know Like I Know (2)

MAHAL, Taj
Born on 5/17/40 in New York City. Real name: Henry Fredericks. Blues guitarist/vocalist. Acted in the film *The Man Who Broke A 1,000 Chains*.

2/22/69	160	14	1	The Natch'l Blues..	$15	Columbia 9698
10/11/69	85	9	2	Giant Step/De Ole Folks At Home..............................	$15	Columbia 18 [2]
6/12/71	84	13	3	The Real Thing... [L]	$12	Columbia 30619 [2]
1/15/72	181	6	4	Happy Just To Be Like I Am..	$12	Columbia 30767
11/4/72	177	4	5	Recycling The Blues & Other Related Stuff................. [L]	$10	Columbia 31605

side 1: live; with The Pointer Sisters on 2 cuts

12/1/73	190	5	6	Oooh So Good 'N Blues..	$10	Columbia 32600
10/12/74	165	6	7	Mo' Roots...	$10	Columbia 33051
10/18/75	155	7	8	Music Keeps Me Together...	$10	Columbia 33801
1/29/77	134	8	9	Music Fuh Ya' (Musica Para Tu).....................................	$10	Warner 2994

Ain't Gwine To Whistle Dixie (Anymo') (2,3) / Ain't That A Lot Of Love (1) / Annie's Lover (2) / Aristocracy (8) / Baby, You're My Destiny (9) / Bacon Fat (2) / Big Kneed Gal (3) / Big Mama (7) / Black Spirit Boogie (4) / Blackjack Davey (7) / Blind Boy Rag (2) / Bound To Love Me Some (5) / Brown-Eyed Handsome Man (8) / Buck Dancer's Choice (6) / Built For Comfort (6) / Cajun Tune (2) / Cajun Waltz (7) / Cakewalk Into Town (5) / Candy Man (2) / Chevrolet (4) / Clara (St. Kitts Woman) (7) / Cluck Old Hen (2) / Colored Aristocracy (2) / Corinna (1,5) / Country Blues #1 (2) / Cuckoo, The (1) / Curry (9) / Dear Ladies (8) / Desperate Lover (7) / Diving Duck Blues (3) / Done Changed My Way Of Living (1) / Dust My Broom (6) / Eighteen Hammers (4) / Farther On Down The Road (You Will Accompany Me) (2) / Fishing Blues (2,3) / Four Mills Brothers (9) / Frankie And Albert (6) / Free Song (Rise Up Children Shake The Devil Out Of Your Soul) (5) / Freight Train (9) / Further On Down The Road (8) / Gitano Negro (5) / Give Your Woman What She Wants (2) / Going Up To The Country, Paint My Mailbox Blue (1,3) / Good Morning Little School Girl (2) / Good Morning Miss Brown (1) / Happy Just To Be Like I Am (4) / Honey Babe (9) / I Ain't Gonna Let Nobody Steal My Jellyroll (1) / John, Ain't It Hard (3) / Johnny Too Bad (7) / Kalimba (5) / Keep Your Hands Off Her (2) / Light Rain Blues (2) / Linin' Track (2) / Little Red Hen (6) / Little Soulful Tune (2) / Music Keeps Me Together (8) / My Ancestors (8) / Oh Mama Don't You Know (6) / Oh Susanna (4) / Railroad Bill (6) / Ricochet (4) / Roll, Turn, Spin (8) / Sailin' Into Walker's Cay (9) / She Caught The Katy And Left Me A Mule To Ride (1) / Six Days On The Road (4) / Slave Driver (7) / Stagger Lee (2) / Stealin' (4) / Sweet Home Chicago (5) / Sweet Mama Janisse (3) / Take A Giant Step (2) / Teacup's Jazzy Blues Tune (6) / Texas Woman Blues (5) / Tom And Sally Drake (3) / Tomorrow May Not Be Your Day (4) / Truck Driver's Two-Step (9) / West Indian Revelation (4,8) / When I Feel The Sea Beneath My Soul (8) / Why?...And We Repeat Why?...And We Repeat! (8) / Why Did You Have To Desert Me? (7) / Wild Ox Moan (2) / You Ain't No Street Walker Mama, Honey But I Do Love The Way You Strut Your Stuff (3) / You Don't Miss Your Water ('Til Your Well Runs Dry) (1) / You Got It (9) / You're Gonna Need Somebody On Your Bond (2,3)

MAHARIS, George
Born on 9/1/28 in New York City. Film/TV actor. Played Buz Murdock on TV's *Route 66*.

6/2/62	10	30	1	George Maharis Sings!..	$15	Epic 26001
9/8/62	32	24	2	Portrait In Music..	$15	Epic 26021
3/30/63	129	10	3	Just Turn Me Loose!..	$15	Epic 26037
9/14/63	77	7	4	Where Can You Go For A Broken Heart?.........................	$15	Epic 26064

After The Lights Go Down Low (1) / All Of You (3) / Alright, Okay, You Win (3) / **Baby Has Gone Bye Bye (3) 62** / Can't Help Falling In Love (1) / **Don't Fence Me In (3) 93** / End Of A Love Affair (4) / Fool Such As I ..see: (Now And Then There's) A / Fools Rush In (Where Angels Fear To Tread) (4) / (Get Your Kicks On) Route 66! (1) / Good-Bye (4) / Here's That Rainy Day (2) / How Do You Keep From Cryin' (4) / Hurt (1) / I Can't Believe That You're In Love With Me (3) / I Can't Stop Loving You (2) / I Remember You (1) / I Wanna Be Loved (3) / I Want To Be Wanted (1) / I'll Be Around (4) / I'll Be Here Waiting For You (4) / I'll Never Smile Again (1) / I'll Walk Alone (1) / I'm Gonna Laugh You Out Of My Life (3) / If Love Were All (2) / It All Adds Up To Me (4)

DEBUT DATE	PEAK POS	WKS CHR	GOLD	ARTIST — Album Title	$	Label & Number

MAHARIS, George — Cont'd

It's All In The Game (1)
Laughing On The Outside (3)
Little Girl (3)
Little White Lies (3)
Lollipops And Roses (2)

Love Could Change My Mind (2)
Love Me As I Love You (2) **54**
Moon River (1)
More I See You (2)

My Kind Of Girl (1)
(Now And Then, There's) A Fool Such As I (4)
Oh Lonesome Me (4)
Route 66 ..see: (Get Your Kicks On)

Take Me In Your Arms (3)
Talk To Me (2)
Teach Me Tonight (1) **25**
They Knew About You (2)
What A Diff'rence A Day Made (2)

What Kind Of Fool Am I? (3)
Where Are You? (2)
Where Can You Go (For A Broken Heart) (4)
Witchcraft (1)

You Don't Know What Love Is (4)
You Must Have Been A Beautiful Baby (1)

MAHAVISHNU ORCHESTRA — see McLAUGHLIN, John

MAHOGANY RUSH

Heavy-metal rock formed in Montreal — Frank Marino (guitar, vocals), Paul Harwood (bass), Jim Ayoub (drums). Frank's brother Vince (rhythm guitar) joined in 1980.

DEBUT DATE	PEAK POS	WKS CHR	GOLD	ARTIST — Album Title	$	Label & Number
8/24/74	74	15		1 Child Of The Novelty	$30	20th Century 451
3/1/75	159	4		2 Maxoom	$35	20th Century 463
6/21/75	84	13		3 Strange Universe	$25	20th Century 482
6/5/76	175	3		4 Mahogany Rush IV	$20	Columbia 34190

FRANK MARINO & MAHOGANY RUSH:

DEBUT DATE	PEAK POS	WKS CHR	GOLD	ARTIST — Album Title	$	Label & Number
5/28/77	184	2		5 World Anthem	$15	Columbia 34677
3/11/78	129	11		6 Frank Marino & Mahogany Rush Live [L]	$15	Columbia 35257
5/12/79	129	10		7 Tales Of The Unexpected [L]	$15	Columbia 35753
				side 1: studio; side 2: live		
3/8/80	88	9		8 What's Next	$15	Columbia 36204
8/14/82	185	4		9 Juggernaut	$15	Columbia 38023

FRANK MARINO

All Along The Watchtower (7)
All In Your Mind (2)
Answer, The (4,6)
Back Door Man (medley) (6)
Back On Home (2)
Blues (2)
Boardwalk Lady (2)
Bottom Of The Barrel (7)
Broken Heart Blues (5)
Buddy (2)
Chains Of (S) Pace (1)
Changing (1)
Child Of The Novelty (1)
Dancing Lady (3)
Dear Music (3)
Ditch Queen (9)

Door Of Illusion (7)
Down, Down, Down (7)
Dragonfly (4,6)
Electric Reflections Of War (medley) (6)
Finish Line (4)
IV...(The Emperor) (4)
For Your Love (9)
Free (9)
Funky Woman (2)
Gult War (1)
Hey, Little Lover (5)
I'm A King Bee (medley) (6)
I'm Going Away (4)
In My Ways (5)
It's Begun To Rain (4)

Jive Baby (4)
Johnny B. Goode (6)
Juggernaut (9)
King Who Stole (...The Universe) (3)
Lady (5)
Land Of 1000 Nights (3)
Little Sexy Annie (4)
Look At Me (5)
Look Outside (1)
Loved By You (8)
Madness (2)
Magic Man (2)
Makin' My Wave (1)
Man At The Back Door (4)
Maxoom (2)

Maybe It's Time (9)
Midnight Highway (9)
Mona (8)
Moonlight Lady (3)
Moonwalk (4)
New Beginning (2)
New Rock And Roll (1,6)
Norwegian Wood (This Bird Has Flown) (7)
Once Again (3)
Plastic Man (1)
Purple Haze (6)
Requiem For A Sinner (5)
Roadhouse Blues (8)
Rock Me Baby (8)
Rock 'N' Roll Hall Of Fame (8)

Satisfy Your Soul (3)
Sister Change (7)
Something's Comin' Our Way (8)
Strange Dreams (9)
Strange Universe (3)
Tales Of The Spanish Warrior (3)
Tales Of The Unexpected (7)
Talkin' 'Bout A Feelin' (medley) (6)
Talking 'Bout A Feelin' (6)
Thru The Milky Way (1)
Try For Freedom (5)
Tryin' Anyway (3)

Who Do Ya Love (medley) (6)
Woman (7)
World Anthem (5,6)
You Got Livin' (8)

MAIN INGREDIENT, The

New York soul trio formed as the Poets in 1964. Consisted of Donald McPherson (d: 7/4/71), Luther Simmons, Jr. and Tony Sylvester. First recorded as the Poets for Red Bird in 1965. McPherson replaced by Cuba Gooding in 1971; Gooding's son, Cuba Jr., starred in the 1991 film *Boyz N The Hood.*

DEBUT DATE	PEAK POS	WKS CHR	GOLD	ARTIST — Album Title	$	Label & Number
8/22/70	200	1		1 The Main Ingredient L.T.D.	$10	RCA 4253
3/13/71	146	9		2 Tasteful Soul	$10	RCA 4412
10/2/71	176	5		3 Black Seeds	$10	RCA 4483
6/24/72	79	27		4 Bitter Sweet	$10	RCA 4677
5/5/73	132	13		5 Afrodisiac	$10	RCA 4834
				with guest Stevie Wonder		
3/9/74	52	31		6 Euphrates River	$10	RCA 0335
5/10/75	90	12		7 Rolling Down A Mountainside	$10	RCA 0644
12/13/75+	158	8		8 Shame On The World	$10	RCA 1003
3/5/77	177	3		9 Music Maximus	$8	RCA 1558

Another Day Has Come (3)
Baby Change Your Mind (3)
Black Seeds Keep On Growing (3) **97**
Broken Heart Don't Really Break (7)
Brotherly Love (1)
By The Time I Get To Phoenix (medley) (1)
California My Way (6) **75**
Can't Get Ready (For Losing You) (9)
Car Of Love (9)
Comes The Night (9)
Don't Wonder Why (3)
Don't You Worry 'Bout A Thing (4)
Euphrates (6)
Everybody Plays The Fool (4) **3**

Family Man (7)
Fly Baby Fly (4)
Get Back (1)
Girl Blue (5)
Girl I Left Behind (1)
Good Old Days (7)
Goodbye My Love (5)
Half A Chance (9)
Happiness Is Just Around The Bend (6) **35**
Have You Ever Tried It (6)
I Am Yours (5)
I Can't See Me Without You (4)
I Can't Stand Your Love (9)
I Gotta Know You (9)
I Want To Make You Glad (7)
I Was Born To Lose (1)
I'm Better Off Without You (2) **91**

I'm Leaving This Time (3)
I'm So Proud (2) **49**
I've Fallen For You (3)
If I'm Gonna Be Sad (8)
Instant Love (9)
It's So Sweet (Loving You) (8)
Jamaica (Let Me Go Home) (8)
Just Don't Want To Be Lonely (6) **10**
Just Say It Again (3)
Laughing Song (9)
Let Me Prove My Love To You (8)
Life Won't Be The Same (Without You) (1)
Lillian (8)
Look At Me (2)
Looks Like Rain (6)
Love Of My Life (5)

Magic Shoes (1,2)
Make It With You (2)
Many Women In My Life (9)
Movin' On (3)
Need Her Love (Mr. Bugler) (2)
No Tears (In The End) (4)
Of This I'm Sure (7)
Old Greyhound (8)
Over You (8)
Put Your Love In My Hands (8)
Rolling Down A Mountainside (7) **92**
Searching (2)
Shame On The World (8)
Somebody's Been Sleeping (2)
Something 'Bout Love (5)
Something Lovely (5)

Spinning Around (I Must Be Falling In Love) (2) **52**
Summer Breeze (6)
Superwoman (5)
Thanks For The Laughs (7)
That Ain't My Style (7)
That's What Fate Will Do (2)
Traveling (4)
Una Bella Melodia Brazilania (1)
Where Are You? (4)
Where Do Broken Hearted Lovers Go? (4)
Where Were You When I Needed You (5)
Whirl-Wind (9)
Who Can I Turn To (When Nobody Needs Me) (4)
Who You Really Are (9)
Why Can't We All Unite (7)

Wichita Lineman (medley) (1)
Work To Do (5)
You Ain't Got It No Way (3)
You And Me - Me And You (7)
You Can Call Me Rover (5)
You've Been My Inspiration (1) **64**
You've Got To Take It (If You Want It) (4) **46**

MAKEBA, Miriam

Born Zensi Miriam Makeba on 3/4/32 in Johannesburg, South Africa. Folk singer. Her five husbands included Hugh Masekela (1964-66) and black-power activist Stokeley Carmichael (married in 1968).

DEBUT DATE	PEAK POS	WKS CHR	GOLD	ARTIST — Album Title	$	Label & Number
11/16/63	86	10		1 The World Of Miriam Makeba	$18	RCA 2750
5/30/64	122	4		2 The Voice Of Africa	$15	RCA 2845
7/10/65	85	11		3 An Evening With Belafonte/Makeba	$15	RCA 3420

HARRY BELAFONTE/MIRIAM MAKEBA

DEBUT DATE	PEAK POS	WKS CHR	GOLD	ARTIST — Album Title	$	Label & Number
11/18/67	182	4		4 Miriam Makeba In Concert! [L]	$15	Reprise 6253
12/9/67+	74	22		5 Pata Pata	$15	Reprise 6274

DEBUT DATE	PEAK POS	WKS CHR	GOLD	ARTIST — Album Title	$	Label & Number

MAKEBA, Miriam — Cont'd

Amampondo (1)
Banoyi (4)
Beware, Verwoerd! [solo: Miriam] (3)
Cannon [solo: Miriam] (3)
Click Song #1 (5)
Click Song #2 (4)
Come To Glory (2)
Dubula (1)

Forbidden Games (1)
Ha Po Zamani (5)
Hurry, Mama, Hurry! [solo: Miriam] (3)
Ibabalazie (4)
In The Land Of The Zulus [solo: Miriam] (3)
Into Yam (1)
Jolinkomo (4,5)

Kwedini (1)
Langa More (2)
Le Fleuve (2)
Little Boy (1)
Lovely Lies (2)
Mamorini (2)
Maria Fulo (5)
Mas Que Nada (4)
Mayibuye (5)

Mommy (4)
My Angel (3)
Nomthini (2)
Pata Pata (5) 12
Piece Of Ground (4,5)
Pole Mze (1)
Qhude (2)
Reza (4)
Ring Bell, Ring Bell (5)

Saduva (5)
Shihibolet (2)
To Those We Love [solo: Miriam] (3)
Tonados De Media Noche (Song At Midnight) (1)
Train Song (3)
Tuson (3)
Umhome (1)

Uyadela (2)
Vamos Chamar Ovento (1)
West Wind (5)
What Is Love (5)
When I've Passed On (4)
Where Can I Go? (1)
Willow Song (2)
Wonders And Things (1)
Yetentu Tizaleny (5)

MAKEM, Tommy — see CLANCY BROTHERS

MALICE

Los Angeles heavy-metal quintet formed in 1982 — James Neal, lead singer.

| 4/11/87 | 177 | 6 | | License To Kill.. | $8 | Atlantic 81714 |

Against The Empire
Breathin' Down Your Neck

Chain Gang Woman
Christine

Circle Of Fire
License To Kill

Murder
Sinister Double

Vigilante

MALMSTEEN, Yngwie

Swedish; former lead guitarist of Alcatrazz. Backed by his band Rising Force: Anders Johansson, Joe Lynn Turner (vocals) and Jens Johansson.

5/4/85	60	43		1 Rising Force *..	$8	Polydor 825324
9/7/85	52	28		2 Marching Out *..	$8	Polydor 825733
10/11/86	44	23		3 Trilogy..	$8	Mercury 831073
				YNGWIE J. MALMSTEEN		
4/23/88	40	18		4 Odyssey *..	$8	Polydor 835451
				*YNGWIE J. MALMSTEEN'S RISING FORCE		
11/11/89	128	8		5 Trial By Fire: Live In Leningrad ....[L]	$8	Polydor 839726
				performances from January 18-22 and 24-29, 1989 in Moscow and February 1-5 and 7-10, 1989 in Leningrad, U.S.S.R.		
5/26/90	112	6		6 Eclipse	$12	Polydor 843361
2/29/92	121	5		7 Fire And Ice	$12	Elektra 61137

All I Want Is Everything (7)
Anguish And Fear (2)
As Above, So Below (1)
Bedroom Eyes (6)
Bite The Bullet (4)
Black Star (1,5)
C'est La Vie (7)
Caught In The Middle (2)
Cry No More (7)
Crying (3)
Crystal Ball (4)
Dark Ages (3)
Deja Vu (4,5)

Demon Driver (6)
Devil In Disguise (6)
Disciples Of Hell (2)
Don't Let It End (2)
Dragonfly (7)
Dreaming (Tell Me) (4,5)
Eclipse (6)
Evil Eye (1)
Far Beyond The Sun (1,5)
Farewell (1)
Faster Than The Speed Of Light (4)
Faultline (6)

Final Curtain (7)
Fire (3)
Fire And Ice (7)
Forever Is A Long Time (7)
Fury (3)
Golden Dawn (4)
Heaven Tonight (4,5)
Hold On (4)
How Many Miles To Babylon (7)
I Am A Viking (2)
I'll See The Light Tonight (1)
I'm My Own Enemy (7)

Icarus' Dream Suite Opus 4 (1)
Judas (6)
Krakatau (4)
Leviathan (7)
Liar (3)
Little Savage (1)
Magic Mirror (3)
Making Love (6)
Marching Out (2)
Memories (4)
Motherless Child (6)
No Mercy (7)

Now Is The Time (4)
Now Your Ships Are Burned (1)
On The Run Again (2)
Overture 1383 (2)
Perpetual (7)
Queen In Love (3,5)
Riot In The Dungeons (4)
Rising Force (4)
Save Our Love (6)
See You In Hell (Don't Be Late) (6)
Soldier Without Faith (2)

Spanish Castle Magic (5)
Spasebo Blues (5)
Teaser (7)
Trilogy Suite Op:5 (3)
What Do You Want (6)
You Don't Remember, I'll Never Forget (3,5)

MALO

Latin-rock band formed by Jorge Santana (brother of Carlos). Malo is Spanish for Bad.

2/12/72	14	31		1 Malo..	$10	Warner 2584
11/11/72	62	14		2 Dos	$10	Warner 2652
4/28/73	101	11		3 Evolution	$10	Warner 2702
3/23/74	188	3		4 Ascencion	$10	Warner 2769

A La Escuela (4)
All For You (3)
Cafe (1)
Chevere (4)
Close To Me (4)
Dance To My Mambo (3)

Entrance To Paradise (3)
Everlasting Night (4)
Hela (2)
I Don't Know (3)
I'm For Real (3)
Just Say Goodbye (1)

Latin Bugaloo (2)
Latin Woman (4)
Love Will Survive (4)
Merengue (3)
Midnight Thoughts (2)
Momotombo (2)

Moving Away (3)
Nena (1)
No Matter (4)
Offerings (4)
Oye Mama (2)
Pana (1)

Peace (1)
Street Man (3)
Suavecito (1) 18
Think About Love (4)
Tiempo De Recordar (4)

MAMA CASS

Born Ellen Naomi Cohen on 9/19/41 in Baltimore. Died of a heart attack on 7/29/74 in London. Cass Elliot of The Mamas & The Papas.

10/19/68	87	10		1 Dream A Little Dream....................................	$20	Dunhill 50040
7/5/69	91	14		2 Bubble Gum, Lemonade & ....Something For Mama	$20	Dunhill 50055
12/6/69+	169	6		3 Make Your Own Kind Of Music ....[R]	$20	Dunhill 50071
				MAMA CASS ELLIOT		
				reissue of Bubble Gum LP plus song "Make Your Own Kind Of Music"		
3/13/71	49	7		4 Dave Mason & Cass Elliot	$15	Blue Thumb 25
				DAVE MASON & CASS ELLIOT		
3/13/71	194	1		5 Mama's Big Ones ....[G]	$15	Dunhill 50093
				includes "Words Of Love" by The Mamas & The Papas		

Ain't Nobody Else Like You (5)
Blow Me A Kiss (2,3)
Blues For Breakfast (1)
Burn Your Hatred (1)
California Earthquake (1) **67**
Don't Let The Good Life Pass You By (5)

Dream A Little Dream Of Me (1,5) **12**
Easy Come, Easy Go (2,3,5)
Glittering Facade (5)
Good Times Are Coming (5)
He's A Runner (2,3)
Here We Go Again (4)
I Can Dream, Can't I (2,3)
It's Getting Better (2,3,5) **30**

Jane, The Insane Dog Lady (1)
Lady Love (2,3)
Long Time Loving You (1)
Make Your Own Kind Of Music (3,5) **36**
Move In A Little Closer, Baby (2,3,5) **58**
New World Coming (5) **42**
Next To You (4)

On And On (4)
One Way Ticket (3)
Pleasing You (4)
Room Nobody Lives In (1)
Rubber Band (4)
Sit And Wonder (4)
Something To Make You Happy (4)
Song That Never Comes (5) **99**

Sour Grapes (2,3)
Sweet Believer (1)
Talkin' To Your Toothbrush (1)
To Be Free (4)
Too Much Truth, Too Much Love (4)
Walk To The Point (4)
Welcome To The World (2,3)
What Was I Thinking Of (1)

When I Just Wear My Smile (2,3)
Who's To Blame (2,3)
You Know Who I Am (1)

DEBUT DATE	PEAK POS	WKS CHR	GOLD	ARTIST — Album Title	$	Label & Number

★★263★★   MAMAS & THE PAPAS, The

Quartet formed in New York City in 1963. Consisted of John Phillips (b: 8/30/35, Paris Island, South Carolina); Holly Michelle Gilliam Phillips (b: 6/4/45, Long Beach, California); Dennis Doherty (b: 11/29/41, Halifax, Nova Scotia, Canada) and Cass Elliot (see Mama Cass above). John Phillips had been in the Journeymen, married Michelle Gilliam in 1962. Elliot had been in the Mugwumps with Doherty and future Lovin' Spoonful member Zal Yanovsky. Group moved to Los Angeles in 1964. Disbanded in 1968, reunited briefly in 1971. Michelle Phillips acted in films *Dillinger* and *Valentino*, and is a cast member of TV's *Knots Landing*; married for eight days to actor Dennis Hopper in 1970. New Mamas & Papas group formed in 1982: John and daughter actress MacKenzie Phillips, Dennis Doherty and Spanky McFarlane of Spanky & Our Gang. Michelle and John's daughter, Chynna, is a member of the trio Wilson Phillips.

DEBUT DATE	PEAK POS	WKS CHR	GOLD	ARTIST — Album Title	$	Label & Number
3/12/66	1¹	105	●	1 If You Can Believe Your Eyes And Ears	$15	Dunhill 50006
10/1/66	4	76	●	2 The Mamas & The Papas	$15	Dunhill 50010
3/18/67	2⁷	55	●	3 The Mamas & The Papas Deliver	$15	Dunhill 50014
11/11/67	5	65	●	4 Farewell To The First Golden Era	[G] $15	Dunhill 50025
5/25/68	15	34		5 The Papas & The Mamas	$15	Dunhill 50031
9/28/68	53	13		6 Golden Era, Vol. 2	[G] $12	Dunhill 50038
9/27/69	61	26		7 16 Of Their Greatest Hits	[G] $12	Dunhill 50064
11/6/71	84	8		8 People Like Us	$12	Dunhill 50106
3/3/73	186	4		9 20 Golden Hits	[G] $15	Dunhill 50145 [2]

Blueberries For Breakfast (8)
Boys & Girls Together (3)
California Dreamin' (1,4,7,9) 4
Creeque Alley (3,4,7,9) 5
Dancing Bear (2) 51
Dancing In The Street (2,4,7,9) 73
Dedicated To The One I Love (3,4,7,9) 2
Did You Ever Want To Cry (3)
Do You Wanna Dance (1,6) 76

Dream A Little Dream Of Me [solo: Mama Cass] (5,6,7,9) 12
European Blueboy (8)
Even If I Could (5,6,7,9) 81
For The Love Of Ivy (5,6,7,9) 81
Free Advice (3)
Frustration (3)
Gemini Childe (5)
Glad To Be Unhappy (6) 26
Go Where You Wanna Go (1,4,7,9)
Got A Feelin' (1,4,9)

Grasshopper (8)
Hey Girl (1,6)
I Call Your Name (1,4,7,9)
I Can't Wait (2)
I Saw Her Again (2,4,7,9) 5
I Wanna Be A Star (8)
In Crowd (1)
John's Music Box (3)
Lady Genevieve (8)
Look Through My Window (3,4,7,9) 24
Mansions (5)

Meditation Mama (Transcendental Woman Travels) (5)
Midnight Voyage (5)
Monday, Monday (1,4,7,9) 1
My Girl (3,6,7,9)
My Heart Stood Still (2)
No Dough (8)
No Salt On Her Tail (2,6)
Nothing's Too Good For My Little Girl (5,6)
Once Was A Time I Thought (2)
Pacific Coast Highway (8)

Pearl (8)
People Like Us (8,9)
Right Somebody To Love (5)
Rooms (5)
Safe In My Garden (5) 53
Shooting Star (8)
Sing For Your Supper (3,6)
Snowqueen Of Texas (6)
Somebody Groovy (1)
Spanish Harlem (1)
Step Out (8) 81
Straight Shooter (1,9)
Strange Young Girls (2)
String Man (3)

That Kind Of Girl (2)
Too Late (5)
Trip, Stumble & Fall (2,6,7,9)
Twelve Thirty (Young Girls Are Coming To The Canyon) (4,5,7,9) 20
Twist And Shout (3,6,7,9)
Words Of Love (2,4,7,9) 5
You Baby (1,6,9)

MAMA'S BOYS

British rock trio: brothers Pat, John and Tommy McManus.

DEBUT DATE	PEAK POS	WKS CHR	GOLD	ARTIST — Album Title	$	Label & Number
8/11/84	172	8		1 Mama's Boys	$8	Jive 8214
6/15/85	151	6		2 Power And Passion	$8	Jive 8285

Crazy Daisy's House Of Dreams (1)
Don't Tell Mama (2)
Gentlemen Rogues (1)

Hard 'N' Loud (2)
In The Heat Of The Night (1)
Let's Get High (2)
Lettin' Go (2)

Lonely Soul (1)
Mama We're All Crazee Now (1)
Midnight Promises (1)

Needle In The Groove (2)
Power And Passion (2)
Professor, The (1)
Professor II, The (2)

Run (2)
Runaway Dreams (1)
Straight Forward (No Looking Back) (1,2)

MANASSAS — see STILLS, Stephen

★★268★★   MANCHESTER, Melissa

Born on 2/15/51 in the Bronx. Vocalist/pianist/composer. Father is a bassoon player with the New York Metropolitan Opera Orchestra. She studied songwriting under Paul Simon at the University School of the Arts in the early '70s. Former backup singer for Bette Midler.

DEBUT DATE	PEAK POS	WKS CHR	GOLD	ARTIST — Album Title	$	Label & Number
6/23/73	156	13		1 Home To Myself	$12	Bell 1123
5/4/74	159	5		2 Bright Eyes	$12	Bell 1303
3/1/75	12	41	●	3 Melissa	$10	Arista 4031
2/21/76	24	17		4 Better Days & Happy Endings	$10	Arista 4067
11/20/76+	60	13		5 Help Is On The Way	$10	Arista 4095
7/23/77	60	11		6 Singin'	$10	Arista 4136
12/9/78+	33	27		7 Don't Cry Out Loud	$8	Arista 4186
11/3/79	63	21		8 Melissa Manchester	$8	Arista 9506
9/13/80	68	11		9 For The Working Girl	$8	Arista 9533
5/15/82	19	39		10 Hey Ricky	$8	Arista 9574
2/26/83	43	21	●	11 Greatest Hits	[G] $8	Arista 9611
12/3/83	135	9		12 Emergency	$8	Arista 8094
5/18/85	144	6		13 Mathematics	$8	MCA 5587

All Tied Up (13)
Almost Everything (7)
Alone (2)
Any Kind Of Fool (9)
Bad Weather (7)
Be Happy Now (1)
Be Somebody (7)
Better Days (4) 71
Boys In The Back Room (3)
Bright Eyes (2)
Caravan (2)
City Nights (12)
Come In From The Rain (4,10,13)
Dirty Work (5)
Doing The Best (That He Can) (1)
Don't Cry Out Loud (7,11) 10
Don't Want A Heartache (8)
Dream, The (13)
Easy (1)
Emergency (12)
End Of The Affair (12)

Energy (13)
Fire In The Morning (8) 32
Fool In Love (5)
Fool's Affair (7)
Funny That Way (1)
Good News (4)
Happier Than I've Ever Been (9)
Happy Endings (4)
He Is The One (2)
Headlines (5)
Help Is On The Way (5)
Hey Ricky (You're A Low-Down Heel) (10)
Holdin' On To The Lovin' (8)
Home To Myself (1)
How Does It Feel Right Now (8)
I Can't Get Started (2)
I Don't Care What The People Say (12)
I Don't Want To Hear It Anymore (3)
I Got Eyes (3)

I Know Your Love Won't Let Me Down (8)
I Wanna Be Where You Are (6)
I'll Always Love You (10)
Ice Castles (Through The Eyes Of Love), Theme From (11) 76
If It Feels Good (Let It Ride) (1)
If This Is Love (9)
Inclined (2)
It's All In The Sky Above (8)
It's Gonna Be Alright (3)
Jenny (1)
Johnny And Mary (12)
Just One Lifetime (13)
Just Too Many People (3,11) 30
Just You And I (4,11) 27
Knowin' My Love's Alive (7)
Let Me Serenade You (6)
Lights Of Dawn (8)

Looking For The Perfect Ahh (10)
Love Havin' You Around (3)
Love Of Your Own (6)
Lovers After All (9) 54
Mathematics (13) 74
Midnight Blue (3,11) 6
Monkey See, Monkey Do (5)
My Boyfriend's Back (medley) (11)
My Love Is All I Know (6)
My Sweet Thing (4)
Nice Girls (11) 42
Night Creatures (13)
No One Can Love You More Than Me (12) 78
No One's Ever Seen This Side Of Me (6)
No. 1 (Ahwant Gimmeh) (2)
O Heaven (How You've Changed To Me) (2)
Ode To Paul (2)
One More Mountain To Climb (1)

Party Music (3)
Pick Up The Good Stuff (1)
Pretty Girls (8) 39
Race To The End (10)
Rescue Me (4) 78
Restless Love (13)
Ruby And The Dancer (2)
Runaway (medley) (11)
Sad Eyes (6)
Shine Like You Should (7)
Shocked (13)
Sing, Sing, Sing (4)
Singing From My Soul (5,7)
Slowly (10)
So's My Old Man (5)
Someone To Watch Over Me (10)
Something To Do With Loving You (1)
Stand (6)
Stand Up Woman (3)
Stevie's Wonder (3)

Stop Another Heart Breakin' (12)
Such A Morning (7)
Talk (9)
Talkin' To Myself (5)
Tears Of Joy (9)
That Boy (12)
There's More Where That Came From (5)
This Lady's Not Home Today (3)
Through The Eyes Of Grace (7)
(Through The Eyes Of Love) ..see: Ice Castles, Theme
Thunder In The Night (13)
Time (6,12)
To Make You Smile Again (7)
Victims Of The Modern Heart (13)

MANCHESTER, Melissa — Cont'd

Warmth Of The Sun (6)	Whenever I Call You Friend (8,11)	Wish We Were Heroes (10)
We've Got Time (3)	Without You (9)	
When We Loved (8)	White Rose (12)	Working Girl (For The) (9)

You And Me (9) · You Can Make It All Come True (4) · You Make It Easy (6) · **You Should Hear How She Talks About You** (10,11) **5** · Your Place Or Mine (10)

MANCHILD
Formed in Indianapolis in 1974 by Reggie Griffin (reeds) and Anthony "A.J." Johnson (bass). In 1977, group included Kenneth Edmonds (later with The Deele and recorded solo as "Babyface"), Chuckie Bush, Daryl Simmons, Robert Parson and Flash Ferrell (vocals).

10/15/77	154	6		Power And Love	$10	Chi-Sound 765

Especially For You · Funky Situation · (I Want To Feel Your) Power And Love · Red Hot Daddy · Takin' It To The Streets · These Are The Things That Are Special To Me · We Need We · You Get What You Give

★★19★★ MANCINI, Henry
Born on 4/16/24 in Cleveland and raised in Aliquippa, Pennsylvania. Leading film and TV composer/arranger/conductor. Staff composer for Universal Pictures, 1952-58. Won more Oscars (four) and Grammys (20) than any other pop artist. Married to Ginny O'Connor, an original member of Mel Torme's Mel-Tones.

DEBUT DATE	PEAK POS	WKS CHR	GOLD	ARTIST — Album Title	$	Label & Number
2/9/59	1[10]	119	●	1 **The Music From Peter Gunn** .... [TV-I]	$25	RCA 1956
				1958 Grammy winner: Album of the Year		
6/22/59	7	35		2 **More Music From Peter Gunn** .... [TV-I]	$25	RCA 2040
3/28/60	2[1]	70		3 **Music From Mr. Lucky** .... [TV-I]	$25	RCA 2198
5/8/61	28	26		4 Mr. Lucky Goes Latin .... [I]	$20	RCA 2360
10/9/61+	1[12]	96	●	5 **Breakfast At Tiffany's** .... [S-I]	$25	RCA 2362
3/3/62	28	14		6 Combo! .... [I]	$20	RCA 2258
				recorded June 1960		
6/2/62	37	12		7 Experiment In Terror .... [S-I]	$30	RCA 2442
7/21/62	4	50		8 **Hatari!** .... [S-I]	$20	RCA 2559
2/16/63	12	40		9 Our Man In Hollywood	$15	RCA 2604
6/29/63	5	22		10 **Uniquely Mancini** .... [I]	$15	RCA 2692
12/28/63+	6	42		11 **Charade** .... [S-I]	$20	RCA 2755
4/11/64	8	88	●	12 **The Pink Panther** .... [S-I]	$20	RCA 2795
8/1/64	15	19		13 The Concert Sound of Henry Mancini .... [I]	$15	RCA 2897
				medleys of 30 tunes; with a 70-piece orchestra		
8/8/64	42	35	●	14 **The Best Of Mancini** .... [G]	$15	RCA 2693
1/30/65	11	25		15 Dear Heart And Other Songs About Love ..... [I]	$15	RCA 2990
6/26/65	46	17		16 The Latin Sound of Henry Mancini .... [I]	$15	RCA 3356
10/2/65	63	22		17 The Great Race .... [S-I]	$15	RCA 3402
3/12/66	74	13		18 The Academy Award Songs	$15	RCA 6013 [2]
				features the Oscar-winning songs from 1934-64		
9/10/66	142	4		19 Arabesque .... [S-I]	$15	RCA 3623
9/10/66	148	2		20 What Did You Do In The War, Daddy? .... [S-I]	$15	RCA 3648
12/17/66+	121	19		21 Music of Hawaii .... [I]	$15	RCA 3713
3/18/67	65	13		22 Mancini '67 .... [I]	$12	RCA 3694
10/28/67	183	3		23 Two For The Road .... [S-I]	$12	RCA 3802
12/9/67+	126	12		24 Encore! More Of The Concert Sound Of Henry Mancini .... [I]	$15	RCA 3887
				medleys of 21 songs; featuring medley of 6 Beatles' tunes		
5/3/69	5	42	●	25 **A Warm Shade Of Ivory** .... [I]	$10	RCA 4140
11/1/69	91	16		26 Six Hours Past Sunset .... [I]	$10	RCA 4239
4/25/70	111	17		27 Theme From "Z" and Other Film Music .... [I]	$10	RCA 4350
9/26/70	196	2		28 This Is Henry Mancini .... [G]	$15	RCA 6029 [2]
12/19/70+	91	17		29 Mancini Country .... [I]	$10	RCA 4307
1/23/71	26	22		30 Mancini plays the Theme From Love Story ... [I]	$10	RCA 4466
7/31/71	85	11		31 Mancini Concert .... [I]	$10	RCA 4542
				medleys of 23 tunes		
1/29/72	109	15		32 Big Screen - Little Screen .... [I]	$10	RCA 4630
4/29/72	74	19		33 Brass On Ivory * .... [I]	$10	RCA 4629
9/23/72	195	5		34 The Mancini Generation .... [I]	$10	RCA 4689
6/9/73	185	3		35 Brass, Ivory & Strings * .... [I]	$10	RCA 0098
				***HENRY MANCINI & DOC SEVERINSEN**		
2/14/76	159	6		36 Symphonic Soul .... [I]	$10	RCA 1025
9/18/76	161	4		37 A Legendary Performer .... [G]	$10	RCA 1843
6/11/77	126	8		38 Mancini's Angels .... [I]	$10	RCA 2290
1/10/87	197	2		39 The Hollywood Musicals	$8	Columbia 40372
				JOHNNY MATHIS & HENRY MANCINI		

Adventurers, Love Theme From The (27) · Adventures In Paradise (21) · African Symphony (36) · Airport Love Theme (27) · All His Children (32) · All The Way (5) · Almost Persuaded (29) · Aloha Oe (Farewell To Thee) (21) · Amazing Grace (34) · Aquarium Scene (medley) (19) · Arabesque (31) · Artistry In Rhythm (medley) (31) · As Time Goes By (27)

Ascot (19) · Autumn Nocturne (22) · Baby Elephant Walk (8,14,28,37) · Bachelor In Paradise (9) · Bagdad On Thames (19) · Baia (16) · **Banzai Pipeline** (10) **93** · Bateau Mouche (11) · Ben (35) · Beyond The Reef (21) · Big Band Bwana (8) · Big Blow Out (5) · Big Heist (5) · Bistro (11) · Blue Flame (medley) (31)

Blue Hawaii (21) · Blue Mantilla (4) · Blue Satin (3) · Blue Steel (2) · Blues For Mother's (2) · Bluish Bag (34) · Borsalino, Theme From (30) · Brass On Ivory (33) · Breeze And I (16) · Brian's Song (33) · Brief And Breezy (1) · Brothers Go To Mother's (1,28) · Buon Giorno (Good Morning) (20) · But Beautiful (medley) (39)

Butterfly (36) · Buttons And Bows (13,18) · By The Time I Get To Phoenix (25) · Bye Bye Charlie (11) · C Jam Blues (10) · Cade's County, Theme From (32) · Call Me Irresponsible (18) · Can't Buy Me Love (15) · Car Wash (38) · Carnavalito (16) · Castle Rock (6) · Cat, The (22) · Champagne And Quail (12) · **Charade** (11,14) **36** · Charade (Carousel) (11)

Charade (Main Title) (11,24,34,37) · Charleston Alley (6) · **Charlie's Angels, Theme From** (38) **45** · Chaser, The (23) · Cheers! (10) · Chelsea Bridge (10) · Cherokee (Indian Love Song) (22) · Chim Chim Cher-ee (18) · Chime Time (3) · Cirifiribin (medley) (31) · Cold Finger (17) · Come To The Mardi Gras (16) · Congaroca (23) · Conquest (22)

Continental (You Kiss While You're Dancing) (18) · Cortina (12) · Cow Bells And Coffee Beans (4) · Crazy World (39) · Crocodile, Go Home! (8) · Cycles (25) · Day In The Life Of A Fool (25) · Dancing Cat (4) · **Days Of Wine And Roses** (9,14,18,24,28,37) **33** · **Dear Heart** (15,28,37) **77** · Didn't We (26) · Doc, Theme For (35) · Domain St. Juste (Din-Din Music) (23)

MANCINI, Henry — Cont'd

Donk, The (23)
Down By The Wharf (7)
Dream (15)
Dream A Little Dream Of Me (25)
Dream Of You (6)
Dream Street (19)
Dreamsville (1,9,13,28,35)
Driftwood And Dreams (21)
Drink More Milk (9)
Drip-Dry Waltz (11)
Eager Beaver (34)
Echoes Of Sicily (20)
End Of The World (29)
Evergreen (38)
Everybody Blow! (6)
Experiment In Terror (7,14)
Facade (19)
Fallout! (1,14)
Far East Blues (6)
Festa! (20)
Final Out At Candlestick Park (7)
Floater, The (1)
Floating Pad (3)
Fluters' Ball (7)
(Follow Me) ..see: Mutiny On The Bounty
Foreign Film Festival Medley (24)
Fox, Theme From The (26)
French Provincial (23)
Gigi (18)
Gina (20)
Girl From Ipanema (15)
Girl Talk (26)
Girls Up-A-Stairs (20)
Golden Gate Twist (7)
Gonna Fly Now (Theme From Rocky) (38)
Good Old Days (7)
Goofin' At The Coffee House (2)
Great Race March (31)
Great Race March (A Patriotic Medley) (17)
Green Onions (10)
Guarare (Cumbieras) (18)
Happy Barefoot Boy (23)
Happy Carousel (11)
Harmonica Man (30)
Hatari!, Theme From (8,14,37) **95**
Hawaii (Main Title) (21)
Hawaiian War Chant (3)
Hawaiian Wedding Song (21)
Hawaiians, Theme From The (30)
He Shouldn't-A, Hadn't-A, Oughtn't-A Swang On Me! (17)
Help Me Make It Through The Night (35)
High Hopes (18)
High Noon (13,18)

Hills Of Yesterday (27)
Holly (8)
Hot Canary (10)
House Of The Rising Sun (22)
How Soon (15)
Hub Caps And Tail Lights (5)
I Can't Get Started (35)
I Can't Stop Loving You (29)
I Had The Craziest Dream (39)
(I Love You And) Don't You Forget It (15)
I'm Gettin' Sentimental Over You (medley) (31)
If (33)
In The Arms Of Love (20)
In The Cool, Cool, Cool Of The Evening (18)
Inspector Clouseau Theme (38)
(also see: Pink Panther Theme)
Ironside Theme (32)
It Could Happen To You (medley) (39)
It Had Better Be Tonight (12)
It Might As Well Be Spring (18,39)
Jean (27)
Jesus Christ, Superstar Medley (31)
Joanna (2,13)
Johnny's Theme (32)
Joy (28)
Just For Tonight (8)
Kelly's Tune (7)
Killer Joe (34)
La Raspa (16)
Last Date (29)
Last Time I Saw Paris (18)
Latin Golightly (5)
Latin Snowfall (11)
Laura, Love Theme For (35)
Leap Frog (medley) (31)
Let It Be Me (29)
Let's Dance (medley) (31)
Life Is What You Make It (32)
Lightly (2)
Lightly Latin (3,13,28)
Little Man Theme (2)
Lonely Princess (12)
Lonesome (10)
Long Ago (And Far Away) (18)
Loose Caboose (3)
Loss Of Love (30)
Love Is A Many-Splendored Thing (13,18)
Love Story, Theme From (30) **13**
Lovely Wife (23)
Lover Man (Oh, Where Can You Be?) (35)
Lujon (4,14)
Lullaby Of Birdland (10)

Lullaby Of Broadway (18)
Make It With You (35)
Make The World Go Away (29)
Mambo Parisienne (11)
Man, A Horse, And A Gun (27)
Man's Favorite Sport (15)
Mancini Generation, Theme From The (34)
March Of The Cue Balls (3,13,14,28,31)
M*A*S*H, Song From (30)
Masterpiece, The (34)
Meditation (25)
Megeve (11)
Memphis Underground (34)
Midnight Cowboy (26,28)
Misty (28,33)
Moanin' (6)
Molly Maguires, Theme From The (27)
Moment To Moment (25,37)
Mona Lisa (18)
Moneychangers (38)
Moon Of Manakoora (21)
Moon River (5,13,14,18,24,28,37) **11**
Moonlight Becomes You (medley) (39)
Moonlight Serenade (10,31)
Moonlight Sonata (26) **87**
Mostly For Lovers (28)
Mr. Hobbs Theme (9)
Mr. Lucky (3,13,14,15,28,37) **21**
Mr. Lucky (Goes Latin) (4)
Mr. Yunioshi (5)
Music From Hollywood Medley (24)
Music Of David Rose Medley (13)
Music To Become King By (17)
Mutiny On The Bounty (Follow Me), Love Song From (1)
My Friend Andamo (3,13,28)
My Manne Shelly (2)
My One And Only Love (28)
Mystery Movie Theme (32)
Nancy (7)
Natalie (26)
Never My Love (33)
Never On Sunday (13,18)
New Frankie And Johnnie Song (15)
Nicholas And Alexandra, Theme From (32)
Night Flower (3)
Night, Night Sweet Prince (17)
Night Side (8)
Night Train (10)

Night Visitor, Theme From The (30)
Nightmare (medley) (31)
No-Cal Sugar Loaf (4)
Not From Dixie (1)
Odd Ball (2)
On The Atchison, Topeka And The Santa Fe (18)
One Eyed Cat (3)
Orange Tamoure (11)
Over The Rainbow (13,18)
Overture From Tommy (A Rock Opera) (31)
Patton Theme (27)
Pearly Shells (21)
Perhaps, Perhaps, Perhaps (16)
Peter Gunn (1,13,14,28,36,37)
Phaedra, Love Theme From (9)
Phone Call To The Past (29)
Piano And Strings (12)
Pick Up The Pieces (36)
Pie-In-The-Face Polka (17)
Pink Panther Theme (12) **31**
(also see: Inspector Clouseau Theme)
Playboy's Theme (6)
Poor Butterfly (33)
Portrait Of Simon And Garfunkel Medley (31)
Portrait Of The Beatles Medley (24)
Powdered Wig (6)
Preciosa (16)
Profound Gass (1)
Punch And Judy (11)
Push The Botton, Max! (17)
Quentin's Theme (26)
Quiet Gass (2)
Quiet Nights Of Quiet Stars (Corcovado) (16)
Quiet Village (21)
Rain Drops In Rio (4)
Raindrops Keep Fallin' On My Head (27)
Release Me (29)
Rhapsody In Blue (10,37)
Robbin's Nest (28)
Romeo & Juliet, Love Theme From (25,28,37) **1**
Roots Medley (38)
'Round Midnight (22,35)
Royal Blue (12)
Royal Waltz (17)
Sally's Tomato (5)
Sandpiper, Theme From The ..see: Shadow Of Your Smile
Satin Doll (22)
Satin Soul (36)
Scandinavian Shuffle (6)
Secret Love (18)

"Senor" Peter Gunn (16)
Session At Pete's Pad (1)
Seventy Six Trombones (9)
Shades Of Sennett (12)
Shadow Of Your Smile (22)
Shaft, Theme From (32)
Shower Of Paradise (19)
Sicily Forever (20)
Sidewalks Of Cuba (6)
Siesta (4)
Silver Streak (38)
Six Hours Past Sunset (26)
Slow And Easy (1)
Slow Hot Wind (36)
Snowfall (28)
Soft Sounds (1)
Soft Touch (8)
Softly (3)
Softly, As I Leave You (26,28)
Soldier In The Rain (15,33)
Something For Audrey (23)
Something For Cat (5)
Something For Sellers (12)
Something For Sophia (19)
Something Loose (23)
Sometimes (33)
Song About Love (15)
Sorta Blue (1)
Soul Saga (Song Of The Buffalo Soldier) (36)
Sound Of Silver (4)
Sounds Of Hatari (8)
Speedy Gonzales (4)
Spook! (2)
Stairway To The Stars (10)
Stand By Your Man (29)
Stockholm Sweetnin' (22)
Stolen Sweets (22)
Summer Knows (Theme From Summer Of '42) (32)
Sun Goddess (36)
Sweet Leilani (18)
Sweetheart Tree (17,28)
Swing Lightly (6)
Swing March (20,31)
Swingin' On A Star (18)
Swingin' Shepherd Blues (34)
Symphonic Soul (36)
Take Me To Your World (29)
Take The "A" Train (medley) (31)
Taking A Chance On Love (39)
Tango Americano (4)
Tarantella Mozzarella (20)
Taras Bulba (The Wishing Star), Theme From (9)
Tavern In Valerno (20)
Teen-age Hostage (7)
Tender Thieves (20)
Tequila (6)
Thank You Very Much (30)
Thanks For The Memory (18)
That's It And That's All (3)

They're Off! (17)
Those Were The Days (32)
Three, Theme For (30)
Three Coins In The Fountain (18)
Tiber Twist (12)
Tico-Tico (Tico-Tico No Fuba) (16)
Tijuana Taxi (22)
Time After Time (39)
Timothy (2,13,14,31)
Tinpanola (4)
Tiny Bubbles (21)
Tipsy (3)
Tommy (A Rock Opera) ..see: Overture
Tomorrow Is My Friend (30)
Too Little Time (9)
Tooty Twist (7)
Traces (26)
Tribute To Victor Young Medley (13)
True Love (39)
Turtles (22)
Two For The Road (23,26,37)
Two For The Road (Main Title) (23)
Vereda Tropical (16)
Village Inn (12)
Walk On The Wild Side (9)
Walkin' Bass (2)
Watch What Happens (25)
Wave (35)
Way You Look Tonight (18)
We've Loved Before (Yasmin's Theme) (19)
We've Only Just Begun (33)
What's Happening!! Theme (38)
Whatever Will Be, Will Be (Que Sera, Sera) (18)
When I Look In Your Eyes (25)
When You Wish Upon A Star (18,39)
Whistling Away The Dark (30,39)
White Christmas (18)
White On White (7)
Willow Weep For Me (33)
Windmills Of Your Mind (25)
Wine And Women (4)
Without You (35)
Wonderful World Of The Brothers Grimm, Theme From The (9)
You Don't Know Me (29)
You Stepped Out Of A Dream (39)
You'll Never Know (18)
Your Father's Feathers (8)
Z (Life Goes On), Theme From (27)
Zip-A-Dee Doo Dah (18)

MANDEL, Harvey

Born in 1946 in Detroit. Guitarist for Canned Heat, 1969-74.

5/10/69	187	3		1 Righteous .... [I]	$12	Philips 306
9/20/69	169	4		2 Cristo Redentor .... [I]	$12	Philips 281
7/22/72	198	3		3 The Snake .... [I]	$10	Janus 3037

Before Six (2)
Bite The Electric Eel (3)
Boo-Bee-Doo (1)
Bradley's Barn (2)
Campus Blues (1)

Cristo Redentor (2)
Divining Rod (3)
Jive Samba (3)
Just A Hair More (1)
Lark, The (2)

Levitation (3)
Lights Out (2)
Long Wait (2)
Love Of Life (1)
Lynda Love (3)

Nashville 1 A.M. (2)
Ode To The Owl (3)
Pegasus (3)
Peruvian Flake (2)
Poontang (1)

Righteous (1)
Short's Stuff (1)
Snake (2,3)
Summer Sequence (1)
Uno Ino (3)

Wade In The Water (2)
You Can't Tell Me (2)

MANDELL, Howie

Born on 11/29/55 in Toronto. Comedian/actor. Played Dr. Wayne Fiscus on TV's *St. Elsewhere* (1982-88).

6/21/86	148	6		Fits Like a Glove .... [C]	$8	Warner 25427

Being From Canada
Bernadette

Bill
Bobby

Danny
Going To School

I Became A Dad
I Do The Watusi

Missy & Mom
My Name Is Ernest

Restaurant

MANDELL, Steve — see WEISSBERG, Eric

M+M — see MARTHA & THE MUFFINS

MANDRE

Disco-funk artist Andre Lewis; formerly with Maxayn, Buddy Miles and Frank Zappa.

9/17/77	64	13		Mandre	$8	Motown 886

Dirty Love
Keep Tryin'

Masked Marauder
Masked Music Man

Money (That's What I Want)
Solar Flight (Opus I)

Third World Calling (Opus II)
Wonder What I'd Do

DEBUT DATE	PEAK POS	WKS CHR	G O L D		ARTIST — Album Title	$	Label & Number

MANDRELL, Barbara

Born on 12/25/48 in Houston and raised in Oceanside, California. Country singer. Moved to Nashville in 1971. Host of own TV variety series *Barbara Mandrell & The Mandrell Sisters*, 1980-82. Suffered severe injuries in an auto accident in 1984, from which she fully recovered.

DEBUT DATE	PEAK POS	WKS CHR	G	#	ARTIST — Album Title	$	Label & Number
2/24/79	170	4	●	1	The Best of Barbara Mandrell .... [G]	$8	ABC 1119
5/26/79	132	9		2	Moods..	$8	ABC 1088
10/13/79	166	5		3	Just For The Record	$8	MCA 3165
9/27/80	175	6		4	Love Is Fair	$8	MCA 5136
9/5/81	86	24	●	5	Barbara Mandrell Live ....[L]	$8	MCA 5243
5/29/82	153	6		6	...in Black & White	$8	MCA 5295
9/3/83	140	4		7	Spun Gold	$8	MCA 5377
9/8/84	89	13		8	Meant For Each Other	$8	MCA 5477

BARBARA MANDRELL/LEE GREENWOOD

After The Lovin' (1)
As Well As Can Be Expected (7)
Bad Boys (7)
Battle Hymn Of The Republic (5)
Best Of Strangers (4)
Black And White (6)
Can't Get Too Much Of A Good Thing (8)
Coming On Strong (4)
Country Girl (5)
Crackers (4)
Cryin' All The Way To The Bank (7)
Darlin' (3)
Doin' It Right (5)
Don't Bother To Knock (2)
Dreams Don't Lie (6)
Early Fall (2)

Fireball Mail (medley) (5)
Fooled By A Feeling (3) 89
Getting Over A Man (6)
He's Out Of My Life (4)
Held Over (8)
Hey Good Lookin' (5)
Hold Me (1)
I Believe You (2)
I Feel The Hurt Coming On (2)
I Was Country When Country Wasn't Cool (3)
I'll Never Stop Loving You (8)
I'm Afraid He'll Find You (Somewhere In My Heart) (4)
(If Loving You Is Wrong) I Don't Want To Be Right (2) 31
In My Heart (5)

In Times Like These (7)
Is It Love Yet (3)
It Can Wait (3)
It Should Have Been Love By Now (8)
It's A Crying Shame (2)
Just One More Of Your Goodbyes (2)
Long Time No Love (4)
Love Is Fair (4,5)
Love Is Thin Ice (1)
Love Takes A Long Time To Die (3)
Loveless (7)
Man's Not A Man ('Til He's Loved By A Woman) (7)
Married But Not To Each Other (1)
Midnight Angel (1)
Mountain Dew (medley) (5)

My Bonnie Lies Over And Over (4)
My Love Can Do No Wrong (3)
No Walls, No Ceilings, No Floors (2)
Not Tonight I've Got A Heartache (4)
Now You See Us, Now You Don't (8)
Old Joe Clark (medley) (5)
One Of A Kind Pair Of Fools (7)
One On One, Eye To Eye, Heart To Heart (8)
Only Now And Then (7)
Operator, Long Distance Please (6)
Overnight Sensation (7)
Pity Party (2)

Rolling Stone (6)
Selfish (3)
She's Out There Dancin' Alone (3,5)
Sleeping Single In A Double Bed (1,2,5)
Soft Shoulder (4)
Some Things Never Change (6)
Sometime, Somewhere, Somehow (4)
Standing Room Only (1)
That's What Friends Are For (1)
Thrill Is Gone (6)
'Till You're Gone (6)
To Me (8)
Tonight (1)
Uncle Joe's Boogie (medley) (5)

Unsung Heros (5)
Using Him To Get To You (3)
We Were Meant For Each Other (8)
We're A Perfect Match (8)
Why Am I Still In Love (6)
Wish You Were Here (5)
Woman To Woman (1) 92
Years (3,5)
You Are No Angel (7)
You're Not Supposed To Be Here (6)

MANDRILL

Brooklyn Latin jazz-rock septet formed in 1968 by the Wilson brothers: Louis "Sweet Lou," Richard "Dr. Ric" and Carlos "Mad Dog." Included Omar, Mesa, Claude "Coffee" Cave, Charlie Pardo and Fudgie Kae.

DEBUT DATE	PEAK POS	WKS CHR	G	#	ARTIST — Album Title	$	Label & Number
4/24/71	48	22		1	Mandrill	$12	Polydor 4050
4/29/72	56	24		2	Mandrill Is	$12	Polydor 5025
2/17/73	28	30		3	Composite Truth	$12	Polydor 5043
10/13/73	82	15		4	Just Outside Of Town	$12	Polydor 5059
4/26/75	92	14		5	Solid	$10	United Art. 408
7/26/75	194	2		6	The Best Of Mandrill ....[G]	$10	Polydor 6047
2/7/76	143	8		7	Beast From The East	$10	United Art. 577
11/12/77	124	10		8	We Are One	$8	Arista 4144
1/13/78	154	5		9	New Worlds	$8	Arista 4195

Afrikus Retrospectus (4)
Ape Is High (2,6)
Aqua-Magic (7)
Aspiration Flame (4)
Can You Get It (Suzie Caesar) (8)
Central Park (2)
Children Of The Sun (2,6)
Closer To You (8)
Cohelo (2,6)
Dirty Ole Man (7)
Disco Lypso (7)
Don't Mess With People (3)

Don't Stop (9)
Fat City Strut (4)
Fencewalk (3,6) 52
Funky Monkey (8)
Gilly Hines (8)
Git It All (2,6)
Golden Stone (3)
Hagalo (3)
Hang Loose (3,6) 83
Happy Beat (8)
Having A Love Attack (9)
Here Today Gone Tomorrow (2)

Holiday (8)
Honey-Butt (7)
House Of Wood (6)
I Refuse To Smile (2,6)
It's So Easy Lovin' You (9)
Koñjahm (2)
Livin' It Up (7)
Lord Of The Golden Baboon (2)
Love Is Happiness (7)
Love One Another (8)
Love Song (4)

Mango Meat (4,6)
Mean Streets (9)
Moroccan Nights (3)
Never Die (4)
Out With The Boys (3)
Panama (7)
Peace And Love (Amani Na Mapenzi) Medley (1)
Peaceful Atmosphere (7)
Peck Ya Neck (5)
Polk Street Carnival (3)
Ratchet (Como Se Va La Cosa) (7)

Rollin' On (1)
She Ain't Lookin' Too Tough (4)
Silk (5)
Solid (5)
Stay Tonite (9)
Stop & Go (5)
Sun Must Go Down (2)
Symphonic Revolution (1,6)
Synthia Song (7)
Tee Vee (5)
Third World Girl (9)
Too Late (9)

Two Sisters Of Mystery (4)
Universal Rhythms (2)
Warning Blues (1)
When You Smile (9)
Wind On Horseback (5)
Yucca Jump (5)

MANFRED MANN — see MANN, Manfred

★★196★★

MANGIONE, Chuck

Born on 11/29/40 in Rochester, New York. Flugelhorn/bandleader/composer. Recorded with older brother Gaspare ("Gap") as The Jazz Brothers for Riverside in 1960. To New York City in 1965; played with Maynard Ferguson, Kai Winding, and Art Blakey's Jazz Messengers.

DEBUT DATE	PEAK POS	WKS CHR	G	#	ARTIST — Album Title	$	Label & Number
7/3/71	116	11		1	Friends & Love...a Chuck Mangione Concert ....[I-L]	$12	Mercury 800 [2]
11/20/71	194	4		2	Together: A New Chuck Mangione Concert................[I-L]	$12	Mercury 7501 [2]
					above 2 with the Rochester Philharmonic Orchestra		
7/15/72	180	6		3	The Chuck Mangione Quartet ....[I]	$12	Mercury 631
12/8/73+	157	12		4	Land Of Make Believe ....[L]	$12	Mercury 684
					with the Hamilton Philharmonic Orchestra		
4/26/75	47	19	●	5	Chase The Clouds Away ....[I]	$10	A&M 4518
11/29/75+	68	15		6	Bellavia...[I]	$10	A&M 4557
					Bellavia: Chuck Mangione's mother's maiden name		
12/6/75+	102	10		7	Encore/The Chuck Mangione Concerts ....[K-L]	$10	Mercury 1050
					excerpts from albums #1, 2 and 4 above		
11/20/76+	86	24		8	Main Squeeze ....[I]	$10	A&M 4612
10/29/77+	2²	88	▲²	9	Feels So Good ....[I]	$10	A&M 4658
9/16/78	105	6		10	The Best Of Chuck Mangione ....[K-L]	$10	Mercury 8601 [2]
					same as album #7 above, only full-length recordings		
9/23/78	14	44	●	11	Children of Sanchez ....[S-I]	$10	A&M 6700 [2]
6/30/79	27	23		12	An Evening Of Magic - Chuck Mangione Live At The Hollywood Bowl..[I-L]	$10	A&M 6701 [2]

DEBUT DATE	PEAK POS	WKS CHR	GOLD	ARTIST — Album Title	$	Label & Number

MANGIONE, Chuck — Cont'd

| 2/23/80 | 8 | 23 | ● | 13 **Fun and Games** .... [I] | $8 | A&M 3715 |
| 5/16/81 | 55 | 15 | | 14 **Tarantella** .... [I-L] | $10 | A&M 6513 [2] |

benefit concert for Italy's earthquake victims; with guests Dizzy Gillespie, Chick Corea and brother Gap Mangione

7/17/82	83	10		15 **Love Notes** .... [I]	$8	Columbia 38101
6/25/83	154	7		16 **Journey To A Rainbow** .... [I]	$8	Columbia 38686
9/15/84	148	8		17 **Disguise**	$8	Columbia 39479

All Blues (14)
And In The Beginning (1,7,10)
As Long As We're Together (4,7,10)
B'bye (11,12)
Bellavia (6,11,14)
Buttercorn Lady (16)
Can't We Do This All Night (5)
Carousel (6)
Chala's Theme (music composed for The Larry King TV Show) (16)
Chase The Clouds Away (5,12) *96*
Children Of Sanchez Finale (11,12)
Children Of Sanchez (Main Theme) (12)
Children Of Sanchez Medley (11)

Children Of Sanchez Overture (11)
Come Take A Ride With Me (6)
Consuelo's Love Theme (11)
Dance Of The Windup Toy (6)
(Day After) Our First Night Together (8,12)
Diana "D" (17)
Do I Dare To Fall In Love (16)
Doin' Everything With You (8,12)
Echano (5,11)
El Gato Triste (4)
XIth Commandment (9,12)
XIth Commandment Suite (14)
Fanfare (11)
Feel Of A Vision (1)
Feelin' (2)
Feels So Good (9,12) *4*

Feels So Good (Encore) (12)
Firewatchers (2)
Floating (3)
Freddie's Walkin' (2,10)
Friends & Love (7)
Friends & Love Medley (1,10)
Fun And Games (13)
Give It All You Got (13) *18*
Give It All You Got, But Slowly (13)
Gloria From The Mass Of St. Bernard (4)
He Was A Friend Of Mine (5)
Hide And Seek (9,12)
Hill Where The Lord Hides (1,2,7,10,12,14) *76*
Hot Consuelo (11)
I Get Crazy (When Your Eyes Touch Mine) (8,12)
I Never Missed Someone Before (13)

If You Know Me Any Longer Than Tomorrow (8)
Josephine (17)
Journey To A Rainbow (16)
Lake Placid Fanfare (14)
Land Of Make Believe (3,4,7,10,12) *86*
Last Dance (9)
Legacy Medley (2)
Legend Of The One-Eyed Sailor (4,7,10,14)
Leonardo's Lady (17)
Listen To The Wind (6)
Little Sunflower (3)
Look To The Children (2,7)
Love Bug Boogie (16)
Love Note (15)
Love The Feelin' (8,12)
Love Theme From London & Davis In New York (17)
Love Wears No Disguise (17)

Lullaby For Nancy Carol (2,4,10)
Lullabye (11)
Main Squeeze (8,12)
Manha De Carnival (3)
Manteca (14)
Market Place (11)
Maui-Waui (9)
Memories Of Scirocco (15)
My One And Only Love (14)
No Problem (15)
Pages From A Journal In America (2)
Pilgrimage (Part I & II) (11)
Pina Colada (13)
Places Warm (2)
Please Stay The Night (16)
'Round Midnight (14)
Self Portrait (3)
She's Not Mine To Love (No More) (17)
Shirley MacLaine (17)

Side Street, Theme From (9)
Sixty-Miles-Young (2)
Soft (5)
Song For A Latin Lady (16)
Song Of The New Moon (5)
Songs From The Valley Of The Nightingale (1)
Steppin' Out (15)
Sun Shower (2,7,10)
Tarantellas Medley (14)
Things To Come (14)
To The 80's (15)
Torreano (6)
You're The Best There Is (13)

★★428★★ MANHATTANS, The — Soul vocal group from Jersey City, New Jersey. Consisted of George "Smitty" Smith (d: 1970, spinal meningitis; lead vocals), Winfred "Blue" Lovett (bass), Edward "Sonny" Bivins and Kenneth "Wally" Kelly (tenors) and Richard Taylor (baritone). First recorded for Piney in 1962. Taylor (aka Abdul Rashid Talhah) left in 1976; died on 12/7/87 (age 47) following lengthy illness. Featured female vocalist Regina Belle began solo career in 1987. Alston went solo in 1988.

8/11/73	150	8		1 **There's No Me Without You**	$10	Columbia 32444
3/1/75	160	4		2 **That's How Much I Love You**	$10	Columbia 33064
5/1/76	16	27	●	3 **The Manhattans**	$10	Columbia 33820
2/26/77	68	20	●	4 **It Feels So Good**	$8	Columbia 34450
3/4/78	78	12		5 **There's No Good In Goodbye**	$8	Columbia 35252
4/14/79	141	7		6 **Love Talk**	$8	Columbia 35693
4/19/80	24	26	●	7 **After Midnight**	$8	Columbia 36411
12/13/80+	87	10		8 **Manhattans Greatest Hits** .... [G]	$8	Columbia 36861
8/8/81	86	10		9 **Black Tie**	$8	Columbia 37156
8/6/83	104	8		10 **Forever By Your Side**	$8	Columbia 38600
4/13/85	171	6		11 **Too Hot To Stop It**	$8	Columbia 39277

After You (6)
Am I Losing You (5)
Angel Of The Night (11)
Blackbird (2)
C'est La Vie (11)
Change Is Gonna Come (2)
Closer You Are (7)
Cloudy, With A Chance Of Tears (7)
Crazy (10) *72*
Day The Robin Sang To Me (1)
Deep Water (9)
Devil In The Dark (6)
Do You Really Mean Goodbye? (7)
Don't Say No (11)
Don't Take Your Love (2,8) *37*
Dreamin' (11)
Everybody Has A Dream (5)
Falling Apart At The Seams (1)
Fever (1)

Forever By Your Side (10)
Girl Of My Dream (7)
Goodbye Is The Saddest Word (5)
Happiness (5)
Here Comes The Hurt Again (6)
Honey, Honey (9)
How Can Anything So Good Be So Bad For You? (3)
Hurt (3,8) *97*
I Don't Want To Pay The Price Of Losing You (2)
I Just Wanna Be The One In Your Life (6)
I Kinda Miss You (4,8) *46*
I Wanta Thank You (9)
I Was Made For You (9)
I'll Never Find Another (Find Another Like You) (8)
I'll Never Run Away From Love Again (7)
I'll See You Tomorrow (4)
I'm Not A Run Around (1)

I'm Ready To Love You Again (10)
If My Heart Could Speak (medley) (7)
If You're Ever Gonna Love Me (3)
It Couldn't Hurt (7)
It Feels So Good To Be Loved so Bad (4,8) *66*
It Just Can't Stay This Way (4)
It's Not The Same (7)
It's So Hard Loving You (1)
Just As Long As I Have You (7)
Just Can't Seem To Get Next To You (9)
Just One Moment Away (9)
Just The Lonely Talking Again (10)
Kiss And Say Goodbye (3,8) *1*

La La La Wish Upon A Star (3)
Let Your Love Come Down (9)
Let's Start It All Over Again (4)
Locked Up In Your Love (10)
Love Is Gonna Find You (10)
Love Talk (6)
Lover's Paradise (10)
Memories (medley) (6)
Mind Your Business (4)
Movin' (12)
New York City (6)
Nursery Rhymes (2)
One Life To Live (medley) (7)
Other Side Of Me (1)
Reasons (3)
Right Feeling At The Wrong Time (6)
Save Our Goodbyes (2)
Searching For Love (3)
Share My Life (5)
Shining Star (7,8) *5*
Soul Train (1)

Start All Over Again (10)
Strange Old World (2)
Summertime In The City (3)
Take It Or Leave It (3)
That's How Much I Love You (2)
That's Not Part Of The Show (6)
Then You Can Tell Me Goodbye (5)
There's No Good In Goodbye (5)
There's No Me Without You (1,8) *43*
Tired Of The Single Life (7)
Tomorrow (6)
Too Hot To Stop It (11)
Too Much For Me To Bear (4)
Up On The Street (Where I Live) (4)
Way We Were (medley) (6)
We Made It (1)
We Never Danced To A Love Song (4,8) *93*

We Tried (6)
We'll Have Forever To Love (3)
When I Leave Tomorrow (9)
When We Are Made As One (11)
When You See Me Laughing (9)
Wish That You Were Mine (1)
Wonderful World Of Love (3)
You Send Me (11) *81*
You Stand Out (9)
You'd Better Believe It (1) *77*
You're Gonna Love Being Loved By Me (11)
You're My Life (5)

★★301★★ MANHATTAN TRANSFER, The — Versatile vocal harmony quartet formed in New York City in 1972: Tim Hauser, Alan Paul, Janis Siegel and Cheryl Bentyne (replaced Laurel Masse in 1979).

5/3/75	33	38	●	1 **The Manhattan Transfer**	$10	Atlantic 18133
9/18/76	48	9		2 **Coming Out**	$10	Atlantic 18183
2/18/78	66	10		3 **Pastiche**	$8	Atlantic 19163
12/8/79+	55	37		4 **Extensions**	$8	Atlantic 19258
6/13/81	22	27		5 **Mecca For Moderns**	$8	Atlantic 16036
12/12/81+	103	11	●	6 **The Best Of The Manhattan Transfer** .... [G]	$8	Atlantic 19319
10/8/83	52	27		7 **Bodies And Souls**	$8	Atlantic 80104
1/5/85	127	11		8 **Bop doo-wopp** .... [L]	$8	Atlantic 81233

6 of 10 cuts are live

DEBUT DATE	PEAK POS	WKS CHR	GOLD	ARTIST — Album Title	$	Label & Number
				MANHATTAN TRANSFER — Cont'd		
8/10/85	**74**	40	9	Vocalese	$8	Atlantic 81266
				features the lyrics of Jon Hendricks		
5/30/87	**187**	3	10	Live .... [L]	$8	Atlantic 81723
				recorded in Toyko in 1986		
12/5/87+	**98**	19	11	Brasil	$8	Atlantic 81803
9/21/91	**179**	2	12	The Offbeat Of Avenues	$12	Columbia 47079
12/12/92	**120**	4	13	The Christmas Album .... [X]	$12	Columbia 52968
				Christmas charts: 25/'92		

Agua (11)
Airegin (9,10)
American Pop (7)
Another Night In Tunisia (9)
Baby Come Back To Me (The Morse Code Of Love) (8) **83**
Birdland (4,6)
Blee Blop Blues (9)
Blue Champagne (1)
Blue Serenade (12)
Blues For Pablo (12)
Body And Soul (4,6)
Boy From New York City (5,6) **7**
Candy (1,6)
Capin (11)
Caroling, Caroling (13)
Chanson D'amour (3)
Christmas Love Song (13)
Christmas Song (Chestnuts Roasting On An Open Fire) (13)
Clap Your Hands (1)
Code Of Ethics (7)
Confide In Me (12)

Coo Coo U (4)
Don't Let Go (2)
Down South Camp Meetin' (7)
Duke Of Dubuque (8,10)
Foreign Affair (4)
Four Brothers (3,6,10)
Gal In Calico (3)
Gentleman With A Family (12)
Gloria (1,6,10)
Goodbye Love (7)
Goodnight (13)
Happy Holiday (medley) (13)
Have Yourself A Merry Little Christmas (13)
Hear The Voices (11)
Heart's Desire (1,8)
Helpless (4)
Holiday Season (medley) (13)
How High The Moon (8)
In A Mellow Tone (3)
It Came Upon The Midnight Clear (13)
It Wouldn't Have Made Any Difference (2)

It's Not The Spotlight (3)
Java Jive (1,6)
Je Voulais (Te Dire Que Je T'Attends) (3)
Jeannine (3)
Jungle Pioneer (11)
Kafka (1)
Let It Snow, Let It Snow, Let It Snow (13)
Love For Sale (3)
Malaise En Malaisie (7)
Metropolis (11)
Move (9,10)
My Cat Fell In The Well (Well! Well! Well!) (8)
Mystery (7)
Night That Monk Returned To Heaven (7)
Nightingale Sang In Berkeley Square (5,6)
Notes From The Underground (11)
Nothin' You Can Do About It (4)
Occapella (1)
Offbeat Of Avenues (12)

Oh Yes, I Remember Clifford (9)
On A Little Street In Singapore (3)
On The Boulevard (5,10)
Poinciana (The Song Of The Tree) (2)
Pieces Of Dreams (3)
Popsicle Toes (2)
Quietude (Encuentro De Animales) (12)
Rambo (9,10)
Ray's Rockhouse (9,10)
Route 66 (8) **78**
S.O.S. (2)
Safronia B (8)
Santa Claus Is Coming To Town (medley) (13)
Santa Man (medley) (13)
Sassy (12)
Scotch And Soda (2)
Shaker Song (4,10)
Silent Night, Holy Night (13)
Sing Joy Spring (9,10)
Smile Again (5)

Snowfall (13)
So You Say (11)
Soldier Of Fortune (7)
Soul Food To Go (11)
Speak Up Mambo (Cuentame) (2)
Spice Of Life (7) **40**
Spies In The Night (5)
Sweet Talking Guy (1)
10 Minutes Till The Savages Come (12)
That Cat Is High (1)
That's Killer Joe (9,10)
That's The Way It Goes (8)
This Independence (7)
Thought Of Loving You (2)
To You (9,10)
Trickle Trickle (4,6) **73**
Tuxedo Junction (1,4)
Twilight Zone/Twilight Tone (4,6) **30**
Unchained Melody (8)
Until I Met You (Corner Pocket) (5)
Wacky Dust (4)
Walk In Love (3)

(Wanted) Dead Or Alive (5)
What Goes Around Comes Around (12)
Where Did Our Love Go (3)
Who, What, When, Where, Why (3)
Why Not! (7)
Women In Love (12)
(Word Of) Confirmation (5)
World Apart (12)
You Can Depend On Me (1)
(You Should) Meet Benny Bailey (9,10)
Zindy Lou (2)
Zoo Blues (11)

★★57★★ MANILOW, Barry

Born Barry Alan Pincus on 6/17/46 in Brooklyn. Vocalist/pianist/composer. Studied at New York's Juilliard School. Music director for the WCBS-TV series *Callback*. Worked at New York's Continental Baths bathhouse/nightclub in New York as Bette Midler's accompanist in 1972; later produced her first two albums. First recorded solo as Featherbed. Wrote and sang jingles for Dr. Pepper, Pepsi and McDonald's ("You Deserve A Break Today").

DEBUT DATE	PEAK POS	WKS CHR	GOLD	ARTIST — Album Title	$	Label & Number
11/23/74+	**9**	58	▲	1 **Barry Manilow II** .... [R]	$10	Arista 4016
				first released on Bell 1314 in 1973		
8/2/75	**28**	51	●	2 **Barry Manilow I** .... [R]	$10	Arista 4007
				first released on Bell 1129 in 1972		
11/8/75+	**5**	87	▲²	3 **Tryin' To Get The Feeling**	$10	Arista 4060
8/21/76+	**6**	60	▲²	4 **This One's For You**	$10	Arista 4090
5/28/77	**1¹**	67	▲³	5 **Barry Manilow/Live** .... [L]	$10	Arista 8500 [2]
2/25/78	**3**	58	▲³	6 **Even Now**	$8	Arista 4164
12/2/78+	**7**	75	▲³	7 **Greatest Hits** .... [G]	$10	Arista 8601 [2]
10/20/79	**9**	25	▲	8 **One Voice**	$8	Arista 9505
12/13/80+	**15**	20	▲	9 **Barry**	$8	Arista 9537
10/17/81	**14**	25	●	10 **If I Should Love Again**	$8	Arista 9573
9/25/82	**69**	9		11 **Oh, Julie!** .... [M]	$8	Arista 2500
12/18/82+	**32**	27	●	12 **Here Comes The Night**	$8	Arista 9610
12/3/83+	**30**	19	●	13 **Barry Manilow/Greatest Hits, Vol. II** .... [G]	$8	Arista 8102
12/15/84+	**28**	20	●	14 **2:00 AM Paradise Cafe**	$8	Arista 8254
				with jazz greats Sarah Vaughan, Gerry Mulligan and Mel Torme		
6/29/85	**100**	12	●	15 **The Manilow Collection - Twenty Classic Hits** .... [G]	$8	Arista 8274
11/30/85	**42**	24		16 **Manilow**	$8	RCA 7044
12/12/87+	**70**	21		17 **Swing Street**	$8	Arista 8527
				features Stan Getz, Phyllis Hyman, Kid Creole and Diane Schuur		
5/20/89	**64**	16		18 **Barry Manilow**	$8	Arista 8570
6/30/90	**196**	1		19 **Live On Broadway** .... [L]	$12	Arista 8638
				recorded live on 12/2-3/89 at the Chicago Theatre; Barry tells the story of his life through song		
12/1/90	**40**	8	●	20 **Because It's Christmas** .... [X]	$12	Arista 8644
				Christmas charts: 1/'90, 8/'91, 28/'92		
10/12/91	**68**	8		21 **Showstoppers**	$12	Arista 18687
				spans 87 years of Broadway show tunes		

Ain't Nothing Like The Real Thing (16)
All I Need Is The Girl (21)
All The Time (4,7)
Anyone Can Do The Heartbreak (18)
As Sure As I'm Standin' Here (3)
At The Dance (16)
Avenue C (1,5)
Baby, It's Cold Outside (20)
Bandstand Boogie (3,5,7)
Beautiful Music (3,7)
Beautiful Music (Part I-III) (5)

Because It's Christmas (For All The Children) (medley) (20)
Bells Of Christmas (medley) (20)
Bermuda Triangle (9)
Best Seat In The House (19)
Big City Blues (14)
Big Fun (17)
Black And Blue (17)
Blue (14)
Bobbie Lee (What's The Difference, I Gotta Live) (8)
Break Down The Door (10)
Bring Him Home (21)

Brooklyn Blues (17,19)
But The World Goes 'Round (21)
Can't Smile Without You (6,7,15) **3**
Carol Of The Bells (medley) (20)
Christmas Song (20)
Cloudburst (2,5)
Copacabana (At The Copa) (6,15) **8**
Copacabana (Disco) (7)
Could It Be Magic (2,5,7,15) **6**
Dance Away (9)

Dancing In The Dark (21)
Daybreak (4,5,7) **23**
Do Like I Do (19)
Don't Fall In Love With Me (10)
Early Morning Strangers (1)
Even Now (6,7,15) **19**
First Noel (medley) (20)
Flashy Lady (2)
Fools Get Lucky (10)
Friends (2)
Fugue For Tinhorns (21)
Getting Over Losing You (12)
Give My Regards To Broadway (21)

God Bless The Other 99 (19)
Gonzo Hits Medley (19)
Good-bye My Love (14)
Handel's Messiah, Excerpt From (medley) (20)
Have Yourself A Merry Little Christmas (medley) (20)
He Doesn't Care (But I Do) (16)
Heart Of Steel (12)
Heaven (11)
Here Comes The Night (12)
Hey Mambo (17) **90**
Home Again (1)
I Am Your Child (2)

I Don't Want To Walk Without You (8) **36**
I Guess There Ain't No Santa Claus (medley) (20)
I Haven't Changed The Room (10)
I Just Want To Be The One In Your Life (6)
I Made It Through The Rain (9,13,15) **10**
I Wanna Do It With You (12)
I Want To Be Somebody's Baby (1)
I Was A Fool (To Let You Go) (6)

MANILOW, Barry — Cont'd

I Write The Songs (3,5,7,15) *1*
I'll Be Seeing You (21)
I'm Gonna Sit Right Down And Write Myself A Letter (11,12)
I'm Your Man (16) *86*
I've Never Been So Low On Love (14)
If I Can Dream (19)
If I Should Love Again (10)
If We Only Have Love (Quand On N'a Que L'amour) (21)
If You Remember Me (19)
If You Were Here With Me Tonight (16)
In Another World (18)
In Search Of Love (16)
It's A Long Way Up (16,19)
It's A Miracle (1,5,7,15,19) *12*
It's All Behind Us Now (16)
It's Just Another New Year's Eve (5,20)
Jingle Bells (20)
Joy To The World (medley) (20)
Jump Shoot Boogie (4,5,7)

Jumpin' At The Woodside (medley) (5)
Keep Each Other Warm (18)
Kid Inside (21)
Last Duet (9)
Lay Me Down (3,5)
Leavin' In The Morning (14)
Let Me Go (4)
Let's Get On With It (9)
Let's Hang On (10,13) *32*
Let's Take All Night (To Say Goodbye) (10)
Life Will Go On (9)
Linda Song (6)
Little Travelling Music, Please (18)
London (9)
Lonely Together (9) *45*
Look To The Rainbow (21)
Looks Like We Made It (4,5,7,15) *1*
Losing Touch (6)
Luck Be A Lady (21)
Mandy (1,5,7,15,19) *1*
Memory (12,13,15,19) *39*
My Baby Loves Me (1)
My Moonlight Memories Of You (18)

Never Met A Man I Didn't Like (21)
New York City Rhythm (3,5,7)
Nice Boy Like Me (3)
Night Song (14)
No Other Love (10)
Oh Julie (11) *38*
Oh My Lady (4)
Old Friends (21)
Old Songs (10,13) *15*
Once And For All (18)
Once In Love With Amy (21)
Once When You Were Mine (17)
One More Time (17)
One Of These Days (2)
One That Got Away (18)
One Voice (8,13,15)
Only In Chicago (9)
Overture Of Overtures (21)
Paradise Cafe (4)
Please Don't Be Scared (14)
Put A Quarter In The Jukebox (13)
Rain (8)
Read 'Em And Weep (13,15) *18*

Ready To Take A Chance Again (7,15) *11*
Real Live Girl (21)
Riders To The Stars (4,5)
Run To Me (15)
Sandra (1)
Say No More (14)
Say The Words (4)
See The Show Again (4)
Seven More Years (2)
She's A Star (3)
Ships (8,13) *9*
Silent Night (medley) (20)
Sing It (2)
Some Girls (12)
Some Good Things Never Last (18,19)
Some Kind Of Friend (11,12,13,15) *26*
Some Sweet Day (16)
Something's Comin' Up (1)
Somewhere Down The Road (10,13) *21*
Somewhere In The Night (6,7,15) *9*
Stardust (17)
Starting Again (6)
Stay (12)
Stompin' At The Savoy (17)

Studio Musician (5)
Summertime (17)
Sunday Father (8)
Sunrise (16)
Sweet Heaven (I'm In Love Again) (16)
Sweet Life (2,19)
Sweetwater Jones (2)
Swing Street (17)
This One's For You (4,5,7,15) *29*
Tryin' To Get The Feeling Again (3,7,15) *10*
Twenty Four Hours A Day (9)
Two Of Us (1)
Up Front (19)
Very Strange Medley (V.S.M.) (9)
We Still Have Time (Theme from Tribute) (9)
We Wish You A Merry Christmas (medley) (20)
Weekend In New England (4,5,7,15) *10*
What Am I Doin' Here (14)
When I Wanted You (8) *20*
When Love Is Gone (14)
When October Goes (14,15)

When The Good Times Come Again (18)
When The Meadow Was Bloomin' (medley) (20)
Where Are They Now (8)
Where Do I Go From Here (6)
Where Have You Gone (14)
Where Or When (21)
White Christmas (20)
Who's Been Sleeping In My Bed (8)
Why Don't We Live Together (3,5)
(Why Don't We Try) A Slow Dance (9)
You Begin Again (18)
You Can Have The TV (21)
You Could Show Me (8)
You Oughta Be Home With Me (4)
You're Leaving Too Soon (3)
You're Lookin' Hot Tonight (13)

★★176★★ MANN, Herbie

Born Herbert Jay Solomon on 4/16/30 in Brooklyn. Renowned jazz flutist. First recorded with Mat Mathews Quintet for Brunswick in 1953. First recorded as a solo for Bethlehem in 1954.

DEBUT DATE	PEAK POS	WKS CHR	GOLD	#	ARTIST — Album Title	$	Label & Number
7/28/62	30	41		1	Herbie Mann at the Village Gate .... [I-L]	$20	Atlantic 1380
11/24/62	100	4		2	Right Now .... [I]	$20	Atlantic 1384
3/2/63	86	7		3	Do The Bossa Nova With Herbie Mann .... [I]	$20	Atlantic 1397
					recorded in Rio De Janeiro, Brazil		
12/21/63+	104	8		4	Herbie Mann Live At Newport .... [I-L]	$20	Atlantic 1413
11/27/65	143	3		5	Standing Ovation At Newport .... [I-L]	$20	Atlantic 1445
10/8/66	139	6		6	Our Mann Flute .... [I]	$20	Atlantic 1464
2/3/68	151	12		7	Glory Of Love .... [I]	$12	A&M 3003
5/24/69	20	44		8	Memphis Underground .... [I]	$12	Atlantic 1522
					with Roy Ayers (vibes) and Larry Coryell (guitar)		
11/22/69	139	10		9	Live At The Whisky A Go Go .... [I-L]	$12	Atlantic 1536
3/7/70	184	3		10	Stone Flute .... [I]	$12	Embryo 520
3/28/70	189	2		11	The Best Of Herbie Mann .... [G-I]	$12	Atlantic 1544
4/17/71	137	3		12	Memphis Two-Step .... [I]	$12	Embryo 531
10/30/71	119	23		13	Push Push .... [I]	$12	Embryo 532
					featuring guitar solos by Duane Allman		
2/3/73	172	8		14	The Evolution Of Mann .... [K-I]	$12	Atlantic 300 [2]
6/16/73	163	6		15	Hold On, I'm Comin' .... [I-L]	$12	Atlantic 1632
9/22/73	146	8		16	Turtle Bay .... [I]	$12	Atlantic 1642
3/30/74	109	10		17	London Underground .... [I]	$10	Atlantic 1648
					recorded in London with guests Albert Lee, Mick Taylor, Ian McDonald and Stephane Grappelli		
8/17/74	141	11		18	Reggae .... [I]	$10	Atlantic 1655
					recorded in London with Mick Taylor and Albert Lee (guitars)		
4/19/75	27	18		19	Discotheque .... [I]	$10	Atlantic 1670
9/27/75	75	7		20	Waterbed .... [I]	$10	Atlantic 1676
5/8/76	178	2		21	Surprises .... [I]	$10	Atlantic 1682
					featuring vocalist Cissy Houston		
2/12/77	132	7		22	Bird In A Silver Cage .... [I]	$8	Atlantic 18209
10/1/77	122	7		23	Herbie Mann & Fire Island	$8	Atlantic 19112
5/27/78	165	5		24	Brazil-Once Again .... [I]	$8	Atlantic 19169
2/24/79	77	13		25	Super Mann	$8	Atlantic 19221

DEBUT DATE	PEAK POS	WKS CHR	GOLD	ARTIST — Album Title	$	Label & Number

MANN, Herbie — Cont'd

O Barquinho (2)
O Meu Amor Chorou (Cry Of Love) (24)
Ob-La-Di, Ob-La-Da (18)
Oh, How I Want To Love You (7,24)
Once I Had A Love (23)
One Note Samba (Samba De Uma Nota So) (3)
Ooh Baby (9)
Our Man Flint (6)
Paper Sun (17)

Paradise Beach (medley) (10)
Paradise Music (20)
Patato (5,14)
Pele (24)
Pendulum (10)
Philly Dog (6,9,11) 93
Pick Up The Pieces (19)
Piper, The (2)
Please Send Me Someone To Love (14)
Push Push (13)
Rainy Night In Georgia (16)

Respect Yourself (15)
Reverend Lee (16)
Rhythmatism (23)
Right Now (2)
Rivers Of Babylon (18)
Rock Freak (25)
Samba De Orfeu (4)
Scratch (6,14)
Skip To My Lou (6)
Soft Winds (4)
Something In The Air (17)
Soul Man (12)

Sound Of Windwood (21)
Spin Ball (17)
Spirit In The Dark (13)
Stolen Moments (5)
Stomp Your Feet (25)
Summer Strut (23)
Summertime (1)
Superman (25) 26
Swingin' Shepherd Blues (18)
This Is My Beloved, Theme From (6)

This Little Girl Of Mine (11)
Turkish Coffee (14)
Turtle Bay (16)
Unchain My Heart (7) 81
Upa, Neguinho (7)
Violet Don't Be Blue (20)
Voce E Eu (You And I) (3)
Waltz For My Son (10)
Waterbed (20)
Welcome Sunrise (23)
What'd I Say (13)
What's Going On (13)

Whiter Shade Of Pale (17)
Why Don't You Do Right (14)
Years Of Love (22)
Yesterday's Kisses (14)
You Are The Song (23)
You Never Give Me Your Money (17)

MANN, Johnny, Singers
Born on 8/30/28 in Baltimore. Johnny was musical director for Joey Bishop's TV talk show.

10/12/63	90	4		1 Golden Folk Song Hits, Volume Two	$15	Liberty 7296
10/3/64	77	15		2 Invisible Tears	$15	Liberty 7387
7/15/67	51	23		3 We Can Fly! Up-Up And Away	$15	Liberty 7523

Al-Di-La (2)
Blue Velvet (2)
Dedicated To The One I Love (3)
Everybody Loves Somebody (2)
Foggy Foggy Dew (1)

Girl From Ipanema (2)
Go Where You Wanna Go (3)
Gotta Travel On (1)
Green Leaves Of Summer (1)
Greenback Dollar (1)
Hello, Dolly! (2)
Honeycomb (1)

I Got Rhythm (3)
If I Had A Hammer (1)
Invisible Tears (2)
Joey Is The Name (3)
Love Me With All Your Heart (?)
Monday, Monday (3)

People (2)
Portrait Of My Love (3)
Puff (The Magic Dragon) (1)
Release Me (3)
Shangri-La (2)
Somethin' Stupid (3)
Thievin' Stranger (1)

This Is My Song (3)
Today (2)
Up-Up And Away (3) 91
Walk Right In (1)
Waltzing Matilda (1)
Wimoweh (1)

World I Used To Know (2)
World Without Love (2)
Yellow Balloon (3)

★★378★★ MANN, Manfred
Rock group formed in England in 1964: Manfred Mann (b: Michael Lubowitz, 10/21/40, Johannesburg, South Africa; keyboards), Paul Jones (vocals), Mike Hugg (drums), Michael Vickers (guitar) and Tom McGuinness (bass). Manfred Mann formed his new Earth Band in 1971, featuring Mick Rogers (vocals), Colin Pattenden (bass) and Chris Slade (drums). Mick replaced by Chris Thompson (vocals, guitar) in 1976. Thompson also recorded with own group Night in 1979. McGuinness left to form McGuinness Flint in 1970.

11/21/64+	35	18		1 the Manfred Mann album	$40	Ascot 16015
3/6/65	141	4		2 the five faces of Manfred Mann	$40	Ascot 16018
6/1/68	176	5		3 The Mighty Quinn	$20	Mercury 61168

MANFRED MANN'S EARTH BAND:

2/26/72	138	6		4 Manfred Mann's Earth Band	$15	Polydor 5015
6/23/73	196	2		5 Get Your Rocks Off	$12	Polydor 5050
3/2/74	96	15		6 Solar Fire	$12	Polydor 6019
11/30/74	157	3		7 The Good Earth	$8	Warner 2826
9/13/75	120	10		8 Nightingales & Bombers	$8	Warner 2877
9/25/76+	10	37	●	9 The Roaring Silence	$8	Warner 2965
3/11/78	83	6		10 Watch	$8	Warner 3157
5/12/79	144	13		11 Angel Station	$8	Warner 3302
1/24/81	87	16		12 Chance	$8	Warner 3498
1/28/84	40	21		13 Somewhere In Afrika	$8	Arista 8194

Adolescent Dream (12)
Angelz At My Gate (11)
As Above So Below (live) (8)
Be Not Too Hard (7)
"Belle" Of The Earth (11)
Big Betty (3)
Blinded By The Light (9) 1
Bring It To Jerome (1)
Brothers And Sisters Of Africa (medley) (13)
Brothers And Sisters Of Azania (medley) (13)
Buddah (5)
California (10)
California Coastline (4)
Can't Believe It (2)
Captain Bobby Stout (4)
Chicago Institute (10)
Circles (10)
Cloudy Eyes (5)
Come Tomorrow (2) 50
Countdown (8)
Country Dancing (3)
Crossfade (8)
Cubist Town (3)

Dashing Away With The Smoothing Iron (2)
Davy's On The Road Again (10)
Demolition Man (13)
Did You Have To Do That (2)
Do Wah Diddy Diddy (1) 1
Don't Ask Me What I Say (1)
Don't Kill It Carol (11)
Down The Road Apiece (1)
Drowning On Dry Land (1)
Each And Every Day (3)
Earth Hymn (Part 1 & 2) (7)
Earth, The Circle (6)
Everyday Another Hair Turns Grey (4)
Eyes Of Nostradamus (13)
Fat Nelly (8)
Father Of Day, Father Of Night (6)
For You (12)
Fritz The Blank (12)
Get Your Rocks Off (5)
Give Me The Good Earth (7)
Got My Mojo Working (1)

Groovin' (2)
Ha Ha Said The Clown (3)
Heart On The Street (12)
Hello, I Am Your Heart (12)
Hollywood Town (1)
Hubble Bubble (Toil And Trouble) (2)
I'll Be Gone (1)
I'm Up And I'm Leaving (4)
I'm Your Hoochie Coochie Man (1)
I'm Your Kingpin (2)
In The Beginning, Darkness (6)
It's Gonna Work Out Fine (1)
It's So Easy Falling (3)
John Hardy (2)
Joybringer (6)
Jump Sturdy (4)
Koze Kobenini (How Long Must We Wait?) (medley) (13)
Lalela (13)
Launching Place (7)
Lies (Through The 80's) (12)

Living Without You (4) 69
Mardi Gras Day (5)
Martha's Madman (10)
Messin' (5)
Mighty Quinn (Quinn The Eskimo) (3,10) 10
Nightingales And Bombers (8)
No Better, No Worse (3)
No Guarantee (12)
On The Run (12)
Part Time Man (4)
Platform End (11)
Please Mrs. Henry (4)
Pluto The Dog (6)
Prayer (4)
Pretty Good (5)
Questions (9)
Quinn The Eskimo ..see: Mighty Quinn
Quit Your Low Down Ways (8)
Rebel (13)
Redemption Song (No Kwazulu) (13)

Resurrection (11)
Road To Babylon (9)
Runner (13) 22
Sack O'Woe (1)
Sadjoy (5)
Saturn, Lord Of The Ring
Mercury, The Winged Messenger (2)
Semi-Detached Suburban Mr. James (3)
Sha La La (2) 12
She (2)
Singing The Dolphin Through (9)
Sky High (2)
Sloth (4)
Smokestack Lightning (1)
Solar Fire (6)
Somewhere In Africa (13)
Spirit In The Night (8) 97
Starbird (9)
Stranded (12)
Third World Service (13)
This Side Of Paradise (9)
Time Is Right (8)

To Bantustan? (medley) (13)
Tribal Statistics (13)
Tribute (4)
Untie Me (1)
Vicar's Daughter (3)
Visionary Mountains (8)
Waiter, There's A Yawn In My Ear (9)
Waiting For The Rain (11)
Watermelon Man (1)
What You Gonna Do? (1)
Without You (1)
You Angel You (11) 58
You Are - I Am (11)
You've Got To Take It (2)

MANNA, Charlie
Comedian from New York.

| 7/24/61 | 27 | 14 | | Manna Overboard!! .... [C] | $20 | Decca 4159 |

Astronaut, The

Breakfast At The White House

Hey, Bud!

Inside You

Perfect Squelch

War At Sea

MANNHEIM STEAMROLLER
Classical-rock group from Omaha, Nebraska. Best known for their Fresh Aire albums. Under the direction of composer/producer/drummer Chip Davis, who founded American Gramaphone Records in 1974. Gained recognition through performance on a series of "Old Home Bread" TV commercials. Davis wrote C.W. McCall's "Convoy." Group's personnel fluctuated; named after Europe's mid-18th century Mannheim School.

| 12/13/86+ | 155 | 14 | | 1 Fresh Aire VI .... [I] | $8 | American G. 386 |
| 12/19/87+ | 118 | 19 | ● | 2 Classical Gas .... [I] | $8 | American G. 800 |

MASON WILLIAMS & MANNHEIM STEAMROLLER
features new arrangement of Williams' 1968, #2 hit "Classical Gas"

DEBUT DATE	PEAK POS	WKS CHR	GOLD	ARTIST — Album Title	$	Label & Number

MANNHEIM STEAMROLLER — Cont'd

DEBUT DATE	PEAK POS	WKS CHR	GOLD	ARTIST — Album Title	$	Label & Number
2/17/90	167	8		3 Yellowstone - The Music of Nature .... [I]	$12	American G. 3089
				features members of Mannheim Steamroller and the Yellowstone Symphony; compositions by Chip Davis, Respighi, Vivaldi and Grofe		
12/1/90	77	16		4 Fresh Aire 7 .... [I]	$12	American G. 777
				includes one vocal track		

CHRISTMAS ALBUMS:

DEBUT DATE	PEAK POS	WKS CHR	GOLD	ARTIST — Album Title	$	Label & Number
12/22/84+	110	6	▲²	5 Mannheim Steamroller Christmas .... [X-I]	$8	American G. 1984
12/21/85	117	5		6 Mannheim Steamroller Christmas .... [X-I-R]	$8	American G. 1984
12/20/86	126	5		7 Mannheim Steamroller Christmas .... [X-I-R]	$8	American G. 1984
11/26/88+	50	8		8 Mannheim Steamroller Christmas .... [X-I-R]	$8	American G. 1984
12/2/89+	54	8		9 Mannheim Steamroller Christmas .... [X-I-R]	$8	American G. 1984
12/1/90+	59	7		10 Mannheim Steamroller Christmas .... [X-I-R]	$8	American G. 1984
				Christmas charts: 3/'84, 2/'85, 2/'87, 2/'88, 3/'89, 2/'90, 1/'91, 6/'92		
11/26/88	36	8	▲²	11 A Fresh Aire Christmas .... [X-I]	$8	American G. 1988
12/2/89+	43	8		12 A Fresh Aire Christmas .... [X-I-R]	$8	American G. 1988
12/1/90+	47	8		13 A Fresh Aire Christmas .... [X-I-R]	$8	American G. 1988
				Christmas charts: 1/'88, 2/'89, 3/'90, 1/'91, 5/'92		

Allegro 1 & 3 (3)
Ballade (3)
Baroque-A-Nova (2)
Bring A Torch, Jeannette, Isabella (5)
Cantique De Noel (O Holy Night) (11)
Carol Of The Bells (11)
Carol Of The Birds (5)
Classical Gas (2)
Come Home To The Sea (1,3)
Conjuring The Number 7 (4)
Country Idyll (2)

Coventry Carol (5)
Deck The Halls (5)
Doot-Doot (2)
Earthrise (3)
God Rest Ye Merry, Gentlemen (5)
Good King Wenceslas (5)
Grand Canyon Suite (3)
Greensleeves (2,11)
Hark! The Herald Angels Sing (11)
Hark! The Herald Trumpets Sing (11)

Holly And The Ivy (11)
I Saw Three Ships (5)
I. Pini Di Villa Borghese (3)
III. Pini Del Gianicolo (3)
In Dulci Jubilo (11)
Katydid's Ditty (2)
La Chanson De Claudine (2)
Little Drummer Boy (11)
Lo How A Rose E'er Blooming (11)
McCall (2)
Morning (3)
Nepenthe (1,3)

Night Festival At Rhodes (medley) (1)
Olympics, The (1)
Orpheus Suite Medley (1)
Return To The Earth (3)
Samba Beach (2)
Saturday Night At The World (2)
7 C's (4)
7 Chakra's Of The Body Medley (4)
7 Colours Of The Rainbow (4)
7 Metals Of Alchemy (4)

7 Stars Of The Big Dipper (4)
Shady Dell (2)
Sirens (1)
Sky, The (3)
Still Still Still (11)
Stille Nacht (Silent Night) (5)
Sunday The 7th Day (4)
Sunflower (2)
Sunrise At Rhodes (1,3)
Traditions Of Christmas (11)
Twilight At Rhodes (medley) (1)
Vancouver Island (2)

Veni Veni (O Come O Come Emanuel) (11)
Wassil (5)
We Three Kings (5)

★★7★★ MANTOVANI

Born Annunzio Paolo Mantovani on 11/15/05 in Venice, Italy; died on 3/29/80. Played classical violin in England before forming his own orchestra in the early 1930s. Had first U.S. chart hit in 1935, "Red Sails In The Sunset" (POS 2). Achieved international fame 20 years later with his 40-piece orchestra and distinctive "cascading strings" sound. His arrangements of favorite classical and pop tunes made him America's favorite orchestra conductor from 1952-72.

DEBUT DATE	PEAK POS	WKS CHR	GOLD	ARTIST — Album Title	$	Label & Number
2/19/55	13	2		1 The Music Of Rudolf Friml .... [I]	$15	London 1150
3/19/55	14	2		2 Waltz Time .... [I]	$15	London 1094
7/9/55	8	8	●	3 **Song Hits From Theatreland** .... [I]	$15	London 1219
5/26/56	12	7		4 Waltzes Of Irving Berlin .... [I]	$15	London 1452
5/27/57+	1¹	231	●	5 **Film Encores** .... [I]	$15	London 1700
3/24/58	22	1		6 Mantovani Plays Tangos * .... [I]	$15	London 768
5/19/58	5	104	●	7 **Gems Forever...** .... [I]	$15	London 3032
11/24/58+	7	68	●	8 **Strauss Waltzes** * .... [I]	$15	London 685
				*released in 1953		
2/16/59+	13	46		9 Continental Encores .... [I]	$15	London 3095
6/1/59	6	11		10 **Mantovani Stereo Showcase** .... [K-I]	$12	London SS1
6/15/59	14	26		11 Film Encores, Vol. 2 .... [I]	$12	London 3117
1/4/60	8	18		12 **All-American Showcase** .... [K-I]	$12	London 3122 [2]
				one side each: Sigmund Romberg/Victor Herbert/Irving Berlin/Rudolf Friml		
3/28/60	11	30		13 The American Scene .... [I]	$12	London 3136
				side 1 features the music of Stephen Foster		
7/25/60	21	53		14 Songs To Remember .... [I]	$12	London 3149
12/5/60+	2⁵	71	●	15 **Mantovani plays music from Exodus and other great themes** . [I]	$12	London 3231
2/20/61	22	12		16 Operetta Memories .... [I]	$10	London 3181
5/29/61	8	50		17 **Italia Mia** .... [I]	$10	London 3239
8/14/61	29	10		18 Themes From Broadway .... [I]	$10	London 3250
1/13/62	83	8		19 Songs Of Praise .... [I]	$10	London 245
6/9/62	8	26		20 **American Waltzes** .... [I]	$10	London 248
10/27/62	24	15		21 Moon River and other great film themes .... [I]	$10	London 249
1/5/63	136	4		22 Stop The World-I Want To Get Off/Oliver! .... [I]	$10	London 270
6/1/63	10	18		23 **Latin Rendezvous** .... [I]	$10	London 295
6/8/63	41	12		24 Classical Encores .... [I]	$10	London 269
11/9/63+	51	22		25 Mantovani/Manhattan .... [I]	$10	London 328
3/14/64	134	3		26 Kismet	$10	London 44043
				with opera stars Robert Merrill and Regina Resnik and chorus		
4/18/64	135	6		27 Folk Songs Around The World .... [I]	$10	London 360
11/7/64	37	43		28 The Incomparable Mantovani .... [I]	$10	London 392
3/20/65	26	31		29 The Mantovani Sound - Big Hits From Broadway And Hollywood . [I]	$10	London 419
10/23/65	41	21		30 Mantovani Ole .... [I]	$10	London 422
3/5/66	23	26		31 Mantovani Magic .... [I]	$10	London 448
10/8/66	27	35		32 Mr. Music...Mantovani .... [I]	$10	London 474
3/11/67	53	33	●	33 Mantovani's Golden Hits .... [G-I]	$10	London 483
9/23/67	49	22		34 Mantovani/Hollywood .... [I]	$10	London 516
3/2/68	64	25		35 The Mantovani Touch .... [I]	$10	London 526

DEBUT DATE	PEAK POS	WKS CHR	GOLD	ARTIST — Album Title	$	Label & Number
				MANTOVANI — Cont'd		
6/15/68	148	7	36	Mantovani/Tango ....[I]	$10	London 532
				includes new versions of 4 tunes from album #6 above		
11/9/68	143	7	37	Mantovani...Memories ....[I]	$10	London 542
4/5/69	73	17	38	The Mantovani Scene ....[I]	$10	London 548
11/1/69	92	17	39	The World Of Mantovani ....[I]	$10	London 565
4/4/70	77	24	40	Mantovani Today ....[I]	$10	London 572
11/7/70	167	3	41	Mantovani in Concert ....[I-L]	$10	London 578
				from the Royal Festival Hall, London		
3/27/71	105	15	42	From Monty, With Love ....[K-I]	$10	London 585 [2]
10/30/71	150	9	43	To Lovers Everywhere U.S.A. ....[I]	$10	London 598
5/27/72	156	12	44	Annunzio Paolo Mantovani ....[I]	$10	London 610
				album celebrates his 25th Anniversary with London Records		
				CHRISTMAS ALBUM:		
12/9/57	4	6	● 45	**Christmas Carols** ....[X-I]	$12	London 913
				originally released in 1953		
12/22/58	3	3	46	**Christmas Carols** ....[X-I-R]	$12	London 913
12/21/59	16	3	47	Christmas Carols ....[X-I-R]	$12	London 913
12/19/60	8	3	48	**Christmas Carols** ....[X-I-R]	$12	London 913
12/18/61+	36	6	49	Christmas Carols ....[X-I-R]	$12	London 913

Abide With Me (19)
Accelerations (8)
Adeste Fideles (45)
Adios (30)
Adios Muchachos (6,36)
Advise And Consent (21)
Affair To Remember ..see:
    Our Love Affair
Ah! Sweet Mystery Of Life
    (12)
Albeniz: Tango In D (24)
Alfie (35)
Alice Blue Gown (20)
All Alone (4)
All Of A Sudden (43)
All The Things You Are (7)
All Through The Night (27)
Almost Like Being In Love (3)
Almost There (35)
Always (4,12)
Amapola (23)
And This Is My Beloved (26)
Andalucia (The Breeze And
    I) (23)
Anema E Core (With All My
    Heart And Soul) (9)
Annie Laurie (medley) (27)
Anniversary Waltz (37)
Answer Me (9)
Apartment, The (21)
April In Portugal (9)
April Love (11)
Aquarius (39,41)
Arana De La Noche (6)
Around The World
    (11,33) *12*
Arrivederci Roma (9)
As Long As He Needs Me
    (22,29)
As Time Goes By (28)
Ascot Gavotte (18)
Auf Wiederseh'n Sweetheart
    (31)
Aura Lee (medley) (27,42)
Autumn In New York (25)
Autumn Leaves (9,41)
Ay-Ay-Ay (30)
Babette (29)
Bach: Air For The G String
    (24,42)
Bach-Gounod: Ave Maria
    (24)
Barabbas (21)
Baubles, Bangles And Beads
    (26)
Be Mine Tonight (23)
Be My Love (18)
Beautiful Dreamer (13)
Beautiful Isle Of Somewhere
    (19)
Beautiful Ohio (20)
Because I Love You (4)
Belle Of New York (25)
Ben Hur (24)
Besame Mucho (6,36)
Bewitched (18)
Beyond The Sea (9)
Bible, The (34)
Big Country (21)

Blaue Himmel (Blue Sky)
    (6,36)
Blowin' In The Wind (40)
Blue Danube (8,42)
Blue Star (14)
Blue-Tail Fly (medley) (27)
Blue Tango (36)
Born Free (34)
Both Sides Now (38)
Bowery, The (25)
Brahms: Cradle Song (24)
Brahms: Hungarian Dance
    No. 5 (24)
By The Time I Get To
    Phoenix (23)
C'est Magnifique (3)
Camptown Races (13)
Capriccio Italien, Op. 45,
    Theme From (17,41)
Cara Mia (31)
Carmen Fantasy (30)
Carnival, Theme From (18)
Carnival Of Venice (17)
Carousel Waltz (15)
Catari, Catari (17)
Catch A Falling Star (28)
Certain Smile (11)
Charade (29)
Charmaine (2,33,41)
Chim Chim Cher-ee (31)
Chiquita Mia (6)
Chitty Chitty Bang Bang (38)
Chopin: Etude No. 3 (24)
Cielito Lindo (23)
Clementine (20)
Climb Ev'ry Mountain (29)
Come Back To Sorrento (17)
Come Prima (For The First
    Time) (9,10)
Come September (I'll
    Remember) (38)
Consider Yourself (22)
Count Of Luxembourg -
    Waltz (16)
Day In The Life Of A Fool (33)
Days Of Wine And Roses (35)
Dear Heart (29)
Dear Love, My Love (1)
Delilah (38)
Desert Song (12)
Deserted Shore (40)
Diane (2,33)
Die Fledermaus - Overture
    (16,41)
Do-Re-Mi (18)
Dr. Zhivago ..see: Lara's
    Theme
Donkey Serenade (1,12)
Door Of Her Dreams (1)
Dvorak: Slavonic Dance No.
    2 (24)
E Bersaglieri (17)
Early One Morning (medley)
    (27)
Ebb Tide (32)
Edelweiss (35)
El Choclo (Kiss Of Fire) (6)
El Relicario (30)
Elvira Madigan, Theme
    From (39,42)

Embraceable You (37)
Emperor Waltz (8)
Espana (23,42)
Estrellita (23)
Eternal Father Strong To
    Save (19)
Everybody's Talkin' (40)
**Exodus (Ari's Theme),
    Main Theme From**
    (15,33) *31*
Fanny (21)
Fantasy On Italian Melodies
    (41)
Faraway Places (14)
Fascination (11)
Fate (26)
Fiddler On The Roof (29,44)
Finale Act II (26)
First Nowell (45)
Fledermaus Waltz (Du Und
    Du) (8)
Fly Me To The Moon (28)
Folk Songs From European
    Countries Medley (27)
For Once In My Life (38)
For The Very First Time
    (4,12)
For You (2)
Four Horsemen Of The
    Apocalypse (21)
Friendly Persuasion (Thee I
    Love) (11)
From Russia With Love (32)
Games That Lovers Play (33)
Gesticulate (26)
Giannina Mia (1)
Gigi (14)
Girl That I Marry (4,12)
Give My Regards To
    Broadway (25)
God Rest Ye Merry,
    Gentlemen (45)
Goldfinger (34)
Gone With The Wind ..see:
    Tara's Theme
Gonna Build A Mountain
    (22)
Good King Wenceslas (45)
Good Morning Starshine (40)
Goodbye Again (21)
Goodnight Irene (13)
Goodnight, Sweetheart (31)
Granada (23)
Grandfather's Clock (13)
Green Cockatoo (30)
Green Leaves Of Summer
    (15)
Greensleeves (10,27,33,41)
Grieg: Solveig's Song (from
    Peer Gynt) (24)
Gwendolyn (42)
Gypsy Baron - Waltz (Your
    Eyes Shine In My Own) (16)
Gypsy Carnival (17)
Gypsy Flower Girl (42)
Gypsy Love - Waltz (16)
Gypsy Princess - Waltz (16)
Handel: Largo (24)
Hark! The Herald Angels
    Sing (45)

Harlem Nocturne (25)
Hava Nagila (27)
He Who Loves And Runs
    Away (1)
He's In Love (26)
Hello Dolly (29)
Hello Young Lovers (3)
Hernando's Hideaway (36)
Hey There (7)
Hi-Lili, Hi-Lo (5)
High And The Mighty (11)
High Noon (5)
Holy City (19)
Home On The Range (13)
Honey (38)
Hora Staccato (41)
How Are Things In Glocca
    Morra (37)
How Soon (32)
I Can't Remember (4)
I Can't Stop Loving You (43)
I Could Have Danced All
    Night (7,10)
I Dream Of Jeannie (13,42)
I Feel Pretty (18)
I Have Dreamed (29)
I Know About Love (18)
(I Left My Heart) In San
    Francisco (28)
I Live For You (2)
I Love Paris (15)
I Only Know I Love You (9)
I Talk To The Trees (3)
I Wanna Be Rich (22)
I Will Wait For You (43)
I Wish You Love (33)
I Wonder Who's Kissing Her
    Now (28)
I'd Do Anything (22)
I'll Be Seeing You (28)
I'll Get By (28)
I'll Never Fall In Love Again
    (40)
I'm A Better Man (39)
I'm Falling In Love With
    Someone (12)
I've Grown Accustomed To
    Her Face (29)
I've Never Been In Love
    Before (3)
If Ever I Would Leave You
    (18)
If I Loved You (3)
If I Only Had Time (42)
If I Were A Rich Man (38,44)
Impossible Dream (35)
In The Still Of The Night (37)
Indian Love Call (1,12)
Indian Summer (12)
Intermezzo (5)
Irma La Douce (15)
It's Impossible (42)
Italia Mia (17)
Italian Fantasia Medley (17)
Jamaica Farewell (14)
Jealousy (6,30)
Jesu Joy Of Man's Desiring
    (19)
Jesu Lover Of My Soul (19)
Joy To The World (45)

Judgment At Nuremberg (21)
Just A Wearyin' For You (13)
Just For A While (2)
Karen (15)
Kiss In The Dark (12)
Kiss Me Again (12)
Kisses In The Dark (3)
La Cumparsita (6)
La Paloma (23)
La Vie En Rose (9,33)
Lara's Theme (34)
Last Summer (42)
Laura (5)
Lawrence Of Arabia (34)
Leaving On A Jet Plane (40)
Lemon Tree (40)
Les Bicyclettes De Belsize
    (38)
Let Me Call You Sweetheart
    (20)
Limelight, Theme From
    (5,10)
Little Brown Church In The
    Vale (19)
Little Green Apples (42)
Little Swiss Waltz (2)
Long Ago (28)
Lord's My Shepherd (19)
Loss Of Love (22)
Love And Marriage (32)
Love Everlasting (1,12)
Love Is A Many Splendored
    Thing (5)
Love Is All (40)
Love Is Blue (38)
Love Is Like A Firefly (1)
Love Letters (7)
Love Me Tonight (39)
Love Me With All Your Heart
    (31)
Love Story, Theme From (42)
Lover (31)
Lover, Come Back To Me (12)
Lumbered (22)
Magnificent Seven (34)
Theme From From Exodus
    ..see: Exodus
Malaguena (23)
Man And A Woman (35)
Man Without Love (38)
Manhattan Lullaby (25)
Manhattan Serenade (25)
Marcheta (20)
Maria Elena (23)
Marie (4,12)
Mattinata (17)
May Each Day (42)
Me And My Shadow (43)
Media Luz (6)
Meet Me In St. Louis, Louis
    (20)
Meilinki Meilchick (22)
Melba Waltz (2)
Mendelssohn: On Wings Of
    Song (24)
Merry Widow - Waltz (16)
Mexican Hat Dance (30,42)
Midnight Cowboy (40)
Midnight Waltz (45)

Mighty Fortress Is Our God
    (19)
Minstrel Boy (27)
Missouri Waltz (20)
Misty (31)
Mona Lisa (31)
Mondo Cane ..see: More
Moon On The Ruined Castle
    (27)
Moon River (31,33,41)
More (28)
Morgen Blatter (8)
Most Beautiful Girl In The
    World (31)
Moulin Rouge Theme (33)
Mr. Wonderful (15)
My Cherie Amour (39)
My Cup Runneth Over (35)
My Foolish Heart (5)
My Heart Is So Full Of You
    (18)
My Hero (16)
My Old Kentucky Home (13)
My Prayer (42)
My Way (39)
Nadia's Theme (21)
Nazareth (45)
Nearer My God To Thee (19)
Nearness Of You (7)
Nessun Dorma (17)
Never On Sunday (21)
New Fangled Tango (36)
Night Of My Nights (26)
No Other Love (14)
Not Since Ninevah (26)
O Holy Night (45)
O Little Town Of Bethlehem
    (45)
O Maiden, My Maiden (16)
O Mein Papa (Oh My Papa)
O Tannenbaum (45)
Offenboch: Barcarolle (24)
Oh! Susanna (medley) (27)
Old Folks At Home (13)
Olive Tree (8)
Oliver (22)
On A Clear Day (35)
Once In A Lifetime (22)
Once Upon A Time (37)
Onedin Line Theme (44)
Only A Rose (1,12)
Onward Christian Soldiers
    (19)
Oom-Pah-Pah (22)
Orange Vendor (36)
Oscar, Theme From The (32)
Our Dream Waltz (2)
Our Love Affair (7)
Out Of My Dreams (3)
Over The Rainbow (5)
People (29)
Perfidia (Tonight) (23)
Perhaps, Perhaps, Perhaps
    (30)
Piccolo Bolero (30)
Play Gypsies, Dance Gypsies
    (16)
Poppa Piccolino (9)
Puppet On A String (35)

DEBUT DATE	PEAK POS	WKS CHR	GOLD	ARTIST — Album Title	$	Label & Number

MANTOVANI — Cont'd

Quando, Quando, Quando (43)
Queen Elizabeth Waltz (2)
Quentin's Theme (39)
Rahadlakum (26)
Rain In Spain (36)
Reaching For The Moon (4)
Red Petticoats (6,36)
Red River Valley (medley) (27)
Red Roses For A Blue Lady (31)
Release Me (35)
Return To Me (17)
Return To Peyton Place (21)
Reviewing The Situation (22)
Rhymes Have I (medley) (26)
Ring De Banjo (13)
Rock Of Ages (19)
Romeo And Juliet, Theme From (39)
Rose Marie (1,12)
Roses From The South (8)
Rosy's Theme (42)
Russian Lullaby (4)
Samaris Dance (26)
Sands Of Time (medley) (26)
Schon Rosmarin (10)
Scottish Rhapsody (44)
Secret Love (11)
Separate Tables (11)
September In The Rain (28)
September Song (5,43)
Serenade (12)

Serenade (16)
76 Trombones (15,41)
Shadow Of Your Smile (32)
Shall We Dance (18)
Shenandoah (medley) (27)
Siboney (23)
Sidewalks Of New York (20)
Silent Night, Holy Night (45)
Skaters Waltz (45)
Skip To My Lou (medley) (27,42)
Slaughter On Tenth Avenue (25)
Smile (32)
Smoke Gets In Your Eyes (37)
Snow Frolic (44)
So In Love (18)
Softly As I Leave You (32)
Softly, As In A Morning Sunrise (12)
Some Enchanted Evening (3,10,33)
Someday (1)
Someone Nice Like You (22)
Something To Remember You By (7)
Song Is Ended (4)
Song Of The Vagabonds (1)
Song Without End (15)
Sound Of Music (15)
Spanish Eyes (44)
Spanish Flea (32)
Spanish Gypsy Dance (19)

Stardust (18)
Stranger In Paradise (3,26)
Strangers In The Night (32)
Streets Of Laredo (medley) (27)
Summer Place, Theme From A (15)
Summertime (7)
Summertime In Venice (5,33)
Sundowners, Theme From The (15) 93
Sunrise, Sunset (37,44)
Swan Lake, Theme From (42)
Swedish Rhapsody (33)
Sweet Leilani (37)
Sweetest Sounds (29)
Sweetheart Of Sigma Chi (20)
Sweethearts (12)
Sympathy (1,12)
Take The "A" Train (25)
Takes Two To Tango (33)
Tales From The Vienna Woods (8)
Tammy (10,11)
Tango De La Luna (6)
Tango Delle Rose (6,36)
Tara's Theme (34)
Taste Of Honey (34)
Tchaikovsky: None But The Lonely Heart (24)
Tea For Two (43)
Tenderly (14)
Tenement Symphony (25)

Theme For A Western (44)
They Say It's Wonderful (3)
This Is My Song (34)
This Nearly Was Mine (7)
This Way Mary (44)
Those Were The Days (38)
Thousand And One Nights (8)
Three Coins In The Fountain (5)
Three O'Clock In The Morning (32)
Thunder And Lightning Polka (42)
Tico-Tico (30)
Till (44)
Till There Was You (18)
Till Tomorrow (18)
Tonight (14)
Totem Tom Tom (1)
Treasure Waltz (8)
Trees (40)
Trolley Song (37)
True Love (7)
Try To Remember (37,42)
Turkey In The Straw (13)
Two Different Worlds (14)
Two Guitars (27)
Unchained Melody (5)
Under Paris Skies (9)
Under The Roofs Of Paris (2)
Up, Up And Away (40)
Valencia (30)
Vaya Con Dios (14)

Very Precious Love (14)
Village Swallows (8,10)
Virginian, Theme From The (39,41)
Vissi D'Arte (17)
Voices Of Spring (8)
Waltz You Saved For Me (20)
Wand'ring Star (40)
Was I Wazir? (26)
Way You Look Tonight (43)
West Side Story Medley (25)
What A Wonderful World (37)
What Kind Of Fool Am I (22,29)
What Now My Love (35)
What'll I Do (4,12)
Whatever Lola Wants (34)
Whatever Will Be, Will Be (Que Sera, Sera) (11)
When I Fall In Love (14)
When I Grow Too Old To Dream (12)
When Love Is Kind (medley) (27)
When The Moon Comes Over The Mountain (20)
When You Wish Upon A Star (11)
Where Are You (28)
Where Did Our Summers Go (39)
Where Have All The Flowers Gone (42)
Where Is Love? (22,39)

Whiffenpoof Song (20)
Whispering (43)
Whispering Hope (19)
White Christmas (45)
Who Can I Turn To (29)
Who Will Buy? (22)
Wi' A Hundred Pipers (medley) (27)
Will You Remember? (2,12)
Windmills Of Your Mind (39)
Wine, Women And Song (8)
Winter World Of Love (43)
With ..also see: Wi'
With These Hands (14)
Without Love (There Is Nothing) (40)
Woman In Love (7)
Wunderbar (3)
Wyoming (2)
Yellow Bird (43)
Yellow Rose Of Texas (13)
Yesterday (32)
Yesterdays (28)
You Are Beautiful (18)
(You Forgot To) Remember (4,12)
You Keep Coming Back Like A Song (7)
You Only Live Twice (34)
You'll Never Walk Alone (37)
You've Got To Pick A Pocket Or Two (22)
Zorba, The Greek (34)
Zubbediya (26)

MANTRONIX
New York City rap outfit fronted by producer/instrumentalist Curtis "Mantronik" Kahleel (born in Jamaica, raised in Canada and New Jersey). Formed as a duo in 1987 with rapper M.C. Tee, who left in 1989; replaced by Bryce Luvah and D.J. D.

DEBUT	PEAK	WKS		TITLE	$	LABEL
4/9/88	108	8		1 In Full Effect	$8	Capitol 48336
3/17/90	161	7		2 This Should Move Ya	$12	Capitol 91119

Do You Like...Mantronik (?) (1)
Don't You Want More (2)
Gangster Boogie (Walk Like Sex...Talk Like Sex) (1)
Get Stupid (Part III) (1)

Get Stupid Part IV (Get On Up '90) (2)
Got To Have Your Love (2) 82
I Get Lifted (2)

I Like The Way (You Do It!) (2)
(I'm) Just Adjustin My Mic [includes 2 versions] (2)
In Full Effect (1)

Join Me Please...(Home Boys - Make Some Noise) (1)
King Of The Beats Lesson #1 (2)
Love Letter (Dear Tracy) (1)

Mega-Mix ('88) (1)
Sex-N-Drugs And Rock-N-Roll (2)
Simple Simon (You Gotta Regard) (1)

Sing A Song (Break It Down) (1)
Stone Cold Roach (2)
This Should Move Ya (2)
Tonight Is Right (2)

MANZANERA, Phil
Born on 1/31/51 in London. Lead guitarist of Roxy Music, 1972-83.

2/10/79	176	3		K-Scope	$8	Polydor 6178

Cuban Crisis
Gone Flying

Hot Spot
K-Scope

N-Shift
Numbers

Remote Control
Slow Motion TV

Walking Through Heaven's Door
You Are Here

MANZAREK, Ray
Born on 2/12/35 in Chicago. Keyboardist of The Doors.

2/8/75	150	6		The Whole Thing Started With Rock & Roll Now It's Out Of Control	$8	Mercury 1014

Art Deco Fandango
Begin The World Again

Bicentennial Blues (Love It Or Leave It)

Gambler, The
I Wake Up Screaming

Perfumed Garden
Whirling Dervish

Whole Thing Started With Rock & Roll Now It's Out Of Control

MARCH, Little Peggy
Born Margaret Battavio on 3/7/48 in Lansdale, Pennsylvania. Lived in Germany from 1969-81. Youngest female singer to have a #1 single on the pop charts.

8/17/63	139	3		I Will Follow Him	$40	RCA 2732

As Young As We Are
Dream World
I Will Follow Him 1

I Wish I Were A Princess 32
I'll Never Forget Last Night
John, John

Johnny Cool
My Teenage Castle (Is Tumblin' Down)
Teasin'

Oh-Oh, I'm Falling In Love Again
You Make Me Laugh

Wind-Up Doll

MARDONES, Benny
Savage, Maryland native.

6/7/80	65	24		Never Run Never Hide	$8	Polydor 6263

with the 1989 popularity of "Into The Night," the album was re-released on Polydor 839532

American Bandstand
Crazy Boy

Hey Baby
Hold Me Down

Hometown Girls
Into The Night 11

Mighta Been Love
She's So French

Too Young

MARIACHI BRASS featuring Chet Baker
Brass band led by trumpet player Baker (b: 12/23/29; d: 5/13/88).

2/26/66	120	4		A Taste Of Tequila	[I] $12	World Pac. 21839

Come A Little Bit Closer
Cuando Calienta El Sol

El Paso
Flowers On The Wall

Hot Toddy
La Bamba

Mexico
Speedy Gonzales

Tequila

Twenty Four Hours From Tulsa

★★400★★ MARIE, Teena
White funk singer/composer/keyboardist/guitarist/producer/actress. Born Mary Christine Brockert in Santa Monica in 1957; raised in Venice, California. Produced the group Ozone.

5/5/79	94	20		1 Wild and Peaceful	$8	Gordy 986
				backed by Rick James & The Stone City Band		
3/15/80	45	23		2 Lady T	$8	Gordy 992
9/13/80	38	29		3 Irons In The Fire	$8	Gordy 997

DEBUT DATE	PEAK POS	WKS CHR	GOLD	ARTIST — Album Title	$	Label & Number

MARIE, Teena — Cont'd

DEBUT DATE	PEAK POS	WKS CHR	GOLD	ARTIST — Album Title	$	Label & Number
6/13/81	23	25	● 4	It Must Be Magic	$8	Gordy 1004
11/26/83+	119	24	5	Robbery	$8	Epic 38882
12/15/84+	31	35	● 6	Starchild	$8	Epic 39528
7/5/86	81	11	7	Emerald City	$8	Epic 40318
4/16/88	65	13	8	Naked To The World	$8	Epic 40872
10/13/90	132	10	9	Ivory	$12	Epic 45101

Aladdin's Lamp (2) / Alibi (6) / Ask Your Momma (5) / Ball, The (8) / Ballad Of Cradle Rob And Me (4) / Batucada Suite (7) / Behind The Groove (2) / Call Me (I Got Yo Number) (8) / Can It Be Love (2) / Cassanova Brown (5) / Chains (3) / Cradle Rob And Me ..see: Ballad Of / Crocodile Tears (8) / Cupid Is A Real Straight Shooter (9)

De Ja Vu (I've Been Here Before) (1) / Dear Lover (5) / Don't Look Back (1) / Emerald City (7) / First Class Love (3) / Fix It (5) / Help Youngblood Get To The Freaky Party (6) / Here's Looking At You (9) / How Can You Resist It (9) / I Can't Love Anymore (1) / **I Need Your Lovin'** (3) *37* / I'm A Sucker For Your Love (1) / I'm Gonna Have My Cake (And Eat It Too) (1)

If I Were A Bell (9) / Irons In The Fire (3) / It Must Be Magic (4) / Ivory (A Tone Poem) (9) / **Jammin** (6) *81* / Just Us Two (9) / Light (6) / Lips To Find You (7) / Lonely Desire (2) / Love Me Down Easy (7) / **Lovergirl** (6) *4* / Midnight Magnet (5) / Miracles Need Wings To Fly (9) / Mr. Icecream (9) / My Dear Mr. Gaye (6) / Naked To The World (8)

Now That I Have You (2) / Once And Future Dream (8) / Once Is Not Enough (7) / **Ooo La La La** (8) *85* / Opus III - The Second Movement (8) / Opus III (Does Anybody Care) (4) / Out On A Limb (6) / Playboy (5) / Portuguese Love (4) / Red Zone (9) / Revolution (4) / Robbery (5) / Shadow Boxing (5) / Shangri-La (7) / Since Day One (9)

Snap Your Fingers (9) / **Square Biz** (4) *50* / Starchild (6) / Stop The World (5) / Sugar Shack (9) / Sunny Skies (7) / Surrealistic Pillow (8) / 365 (4) / Too Many Colors (Tee's Interlude) (2) / Trick Bag (8) / Tune In Tomorrow (3) / Turnin' Me On (1) / We've Got To Stop (Meeting Like This) (6) / Where's California (4)

Why Did I Fall In Love With You (2) / Work It (8) / Yes Indeed (4) / You Make Love Like Springtime (3) / You So Heavy (7) / You're All The Boogie I Need (2) / Young Girl In Love (2) / Young Love (3)

MARILLION
Rock quintet formed in Aylesbury, England as Silmarillion (the title of a J.R.R. Tolkein novel). Lead vocalist Fish (real name: Derek William Dick) left in late 1988, replaced by Steve Hogarth.

DEBUT DATE	PEAK POS	WKS CHR	GOLD	ARTIST — Album Title	$	Label & Number
6/25/83	175	7	1	Script For A Jester's Tear	$8	Capitol 12269
8/24/85	47	35	2	Misplaced Childhood	$8	Capitol 12431
3/22/86	67	10	3	Brief Encounter ....[L-M]	$8	Capitol 15023
				3 of 5 tracks were recorded live in London in early 1986		
7/11/87	103	11	4	Clutching At Straws	$8	Capitol 12539

Bitter Suite Medley (2) / Blind Curve (2) / Chelsea Monday (1) / Childhoods End? (2) / Forgotten Sons (1) / Freaks (3)

Fugazi (3) / Garden Party (1) / He Knows, You Know (1) / Heart Of Lothian Medley (3) / Hotel Hobbies (4) / Incommunicado (4)

Just For The Record (4) / **Kayleigh** (2,3) *74* / Lady Nina (3) / Last Straw (4) / Lavender (2) / Lords Of The Backstage (2)

Pseudo Silk Kimono (2) / Script For A Jester's Tear (1,3) / Slàinte Mhath (4) / Sugar Mice (4) / That Time Of The Night (The Short Straw) (4) / Torch Song (4) / Warm Wet Circles (4) / Waterhole (Expresso Bongo) (2)

Web, The (1) / White Feather (2) / White Russian (4)

MARINO, Frank — see MAHOGANY RUSH

MARK-ALMOND
British sessionmen Jon Mark and Johnny Almond (b: 7/20/46, Enfield, Middlesex, England). Former musicians with John Mayall.

DEBUT DATE	PEAK POS	WKS CHR	GOLD	ARTIST — Album Title	$	Label & Number
6/5/71	154	15	1	Mark-Almond	$12	Blue Thumb 27
1/15/72	87	16	2	Mark-Almond II	$12	Blue Thumb 32
10/21/72	103	14	3	Rising	$10	Columbia 31917
5/26/73	177	7	4	The Best of Mark-Almond ....[G]	$10	Blue Thumb 50
8/25/73	73	14	5	Mark-Almond 73 ....[L]	$10	Columbia 32486
				side 1: live; side 2: studio		
7/31/76	112	14	6	To The Heart	$8	ABC 945

Ballad Of A Man (medley) (2) / Bay, The (medley) (2) / Bridge, The (medley) (2) / Busy On The Line (6) / City Medley (1,4) / Clowns (The Demise Of The European Circus With No Thanks To Fellini) (5)

Everybody Needs A Friend (6) / Friends (2,4) / Get Yourself Together (5) / Ghetto, The (1,4) / Here Comes The Rain (Part One & Two) (6) / Home To You (5) / I'll Be Leaving Soon (3)

Little Prince (3) / Lonely Girl (3) / Love Medley (1) / Monday Bluesong (3) / Neighborhood Man (5) / New York State Of Mind (medley) (6) / One More For The Road (6)

One Way Sunday (2,4) *94* / Organ Grinder (3) / Phoenix, The (3) / Return To The City (medley) (6) / Riding Free (3) / Solitude (2,4) / Song For A Sad Musician (3)

Song For You (1,4) / Sunset (medley) (2) / Trade Winds (6) / Tramp And The Young Girl (1,4) / What Am I Living For (3,5)

MARKETTS, The
Hollywood instrumental surf quintet led by Tommy Tedesco.

DEBUT DATE	PEAK POS	WKS CHR	GOLD	ARTIST — Album Title	$	Label & Number
2/8/64	37	14	1	Out Of Limits! ....[I]	$25	Warner 1537
3/12/66	82	12	2	The Batman Theme ....[I]	$25	Warner 1642

Bat Cape (2) / Bat Cave (2) / Bat (Dance) (2) / Bat Signal (2)

Batman Theme (2) *17* / Batmobile (2) / Bell Star (1) / Bella Dalena (1)

Borealis (1) / Cat Woman (2) / Collision Course (1) / Dr. Death (2)

Hyper-Space (1) / Joker, The (2) / Limits Beyond (1) / Love 1985 (1)

Other Limits (1) / **Out Of Limits** (1) *3* / Penguin, The (2) / Re-Entry (1)

Riddler, The (2) / Robin, The Boy Wonder (2) / Saturn (1) / Twilight City (1)

MAR-KEYS — see BOOKER T. & THE MG's

MARKHAM, Pigmeat
Born Dewey Markham in Durham, North Carolina, in 1906; died on 12/13/81. Stage and TV comedian.

DEBUT DATE	PEAK POS	WKS CHR	GOLD	ARTIST — Album Title	$	Label & Number
7/20/68	109	9		Here Come The Judge ....[C]	$18	Chess 1523
				comedy sketches, except for the title song		

Fast News / Frisco Kate

Here Come The Judge / **Here Comes The Judge** *19*

I Got The Number / My Wife, I Ain't Seen Her

News Reporter / Trial, The

MARKY MARK AND THE FUNKY BUNCH
Marky Mark is Mark Wahlberg, the younger brother of Donnie Wahlberg of New Kids On The Block. Native of Boston. In 1991, 20 years old. The Funky Bunch is DJ Terry Yancey and three male and two female dancers.

DEBUT DATE	PEAK POS	WKS CHR	GOLD	ARTIST — Album Title	$	Label & Number
8/10/91+	21	45	▲ 1	Music For The People	$12	Interscope 91737
10/3/92	67	14	2	You Gotta Believe	$12	Interscope 92203

Ain't No Stoppin' The Funky Bunch (2) / American Dream (2) / Bout Time I Funk You (1)

Don't Ya Sleep (2) / Get Up (2) / Go On (2) / Gonna Have A Good Time (2)

Good Vibrations (1) *1* / **I Need Money** (1) *61* / I Run Rhymes (2) / I Want You (1)

Last Song On Side B (1) / Loungin' (2) / M, The (2) / Make Me Say Ooh! (1)

Marky Mark Is Here (1) / Music For The People (1) / On The House Tip (1) / Peace (1)

So What Chu Sayin (2) / Super Cool Mack Daddy (2) / **Wildside** (1) *10* / **You Gotta Believe** (2) *49*

DEBUT DATE	PEAK POS	WKS CHR	GOLD	ARTIST — Album Title	$	Label & Number
★★199★★				**MARLEY, Bob, & The Wailers**		
				Singer/guitarist born on 2/6/45 in Rhoden Hall, Jamaica. Died of brain cancer on 5/11/81. Bob and his Jamaican band, The Wailers, are considered the masters of reggae. Band included Peter Tosh and Bunny Wailer; both left in 1974. Wrote Eric Clapton's hit "I Shot The Sheriff." Father of Ziggy Marley.		
5/10/75	92	28		1 Natty Dread	$10	Island 9281
10/11/75	151	6		2 Burnin'	$10	Island 9256
				THE WAILERS		
11/8/75	171	5		3 Catch A Fire	$10	Island 9241
5/15/76	8	22		4 Rastaman Vibration	$10	Island 9383
10/23/76	90	9		5 Live! ....[L]	$10	Island 9376
6/11/77	20	24		6 Exodus	$8	Island 9498
4/22/78	50	17		7 Kaya	$8	Island 9517
12/16/78+	102	16		8 Babylon By Bus ....[L]	$10	Island 11 [2]
11/17/79	70	14		9 Survival	$8	Island 9542
8/9/80	45	23		10 Uprising	$8	Island 9596
10/31/81	117	6		11 Chances Are ....[E]	$8	Cotillion 5228
				BOB MARLEY recorded 1968-72		
7/2/83	55	15		12 Confrontation	$8	Island 90085
8/18/84	54	113	▲³	13 Legend ....[K]	$8	Island 90169
				recordings from 1972-81		
9/6/86	140	9		14 Rebel Music ....[K]	$8	Island 90520
2/23/91	103	13		15 Talkin' Blues ....[L]	$12	Tuff Gong 848243
				most tracks from radio broadcast, on KSAN-San Francisco, of The Wailers' first American tour in 1973, plus 4 rarities		
10/24/92	86	15	▲	16 Songs Of Freedom ....[K]	$38	Tuff G. 512280 [4]
				BOB MARLEY		

Acoustic Medley (16)
Africa Unite (9,16)
Am-A-Do (15)
Ambush In The Night (9)
Baby We've Got A Date (Rock It Baby) (3)
Babylon System (9,16)
Back Out (16)
Bad Card (10,16)
Bend Down Low (1,15,16)
Blackman Redemption (12)
Buffalo Soldier (12,13)
Burnin' And Lootin' (2,5,15,16)
Bus Dem Shut (16)
Caution (16)
Chances Are (11)
Chant Down Babylon (12)
Coming In From The Cold (10,16)
Concrete Jungle (3,8,16)
Could You Be Loved (10,13,16)
Craven Choke Puppy (16)

Crazy Baldhead (4,14,16)
Crisis (7)
Cry To Me (4)
Dance Do The Reggae (11)
Do It Twice (16)
Don't Rock The Boat (16)
Duppy Conqueror (2,16)
Easy Skanking (7,16)
Exodus (6,8,13,16)
Forever Loving Jah (10,16)
400 Years (3)
Get Up, Stand Up (2,5,13,14,15,16)
Give Thanks (12)
Give Thanks And Praise (16)
Gonna Get You (11)
Guava Jelly (16)
Guiltiness (6)
Hallelujah Time (2)
Hammer (16)
Heathen, The (6,8)
High Tide Or Low Tide (16)
Hypocrites (16)
I Know (12)

I Shot The Sheriff (2,5,13,15,16)
(I'm) Hurting Inside (11,16)
I'm Still Waiting (16)
Iron Lion Zion (16)
Is This Love (7,8,13,16)
Jah Live (16)
Jamming (6,8,13,16)
Johnny Was (4,16)
Judge Not (16)
Jump Nyabinghi (12)
Kaya (7)
Keep On Moving (16)
Kinky Reggae (3,8,15)
Lick Samba (16)
Lively Up Yourself (1,5,8,16)
Mellow Mood (11,16)
Midnight Ravers (16)
Misty Morning (7)
Mix Up, Mix Up (12)
Mr Brown (16)
Natural Mystic (6,16)
Nice Time (16)

Night Shift (4)
No More Trouble (3,8,14,16)
No Woman, No Cry (1,5,13,16)
One Cup Of Coffee (16)
One Drop (9,16)
One Dub (16)
One Foundation (2)
One Love (medley) (6,13,16)
Pass It On (2)
People Get Ready (medley) (6,13,16)
Pimper's Paradise (10)
Positive Vibration (4,8)
Punky Reggae Party (8)
Put It On (2,16)
Rasta Man Chant (2,15,16)
Rastaman Live Up! (12,16)
Rat Race (4,8,14,16)
Real Situation (10,16)
Rebel Music (3 O'Clock Road Block) (1,8,14)
Redemption Song (10,13,16)
Reggae On Broadway (11)

Revolution (1)
Ride Natty Ride (9,14,16)
Roots (14)
Roots, Rock, Reggae (4) 51
Running Away (7,16)
Satisfy My Soul (7,13)
Screw Face (16)
She's Gone (7)
Simmer Down (16)
Slave Driver (3,14,15,16)
Small Axe (2,16)
Smile Jamaica (16)
So Jah Seh (1)
So Much Things To Say (6)
So Much Trouble In The World (9,14,16)
Soul Rebel (11,16)
Soul Shake Down Party (16)
Stay With Me (11)
Stiff Necked Fools (12)
Stir It Up (3,8,13,16)
Stop That Train (3)
Sun Is Shining (7,16)
Survival (9,16)

Talkin' Blues (1,15)
Thank You Lord (16)
Them Belly Full (But We Hungry) (1,5,14)
Three Little Birds (6,13,16)
Time Will Tell (7,16)
Top Rankin' (9)
Trench Town (12)
Trenchtown Rock (5,16)
Turn Your Lights Down Low (6)
Waiting In Vain (6,13,16)
Wake Up And Live (9)
Walk The Proud Land (15)
Want More (4)
War (4,8,14,16)
We And Dem (10)
Who The Cap Fit (4,16)
Why Should I (16)
Work (10)
You Can't Blame The Youth (15)
Zimbabwe (9,16)
Zion Train (10)

MARLEY, Ziggy, And The Melody Makers
Kingston, Jamaica family reggae group. Children of the late reggae master Bob Marley: David ("Ziggy"), Stephen, Cedella and Sharon Marley.

4/23/88	23	42	▲	1 Conscious Party	$8	Virgin 90878
8/12/89	26	18		2 One Bright Day	$8	Virgin 91256
6/15/91	63	19		3 Jahmekya	$12	Virgin 91626

All Love (2)
Black My Story (Not History) (2)
Conscious Party (1)
Drastic (3)
Dreams Of Home (1)
First Night (3)

Generation (3)
Good Time (3) 85
Have You Ever Been To Hell (1)
Herbs An' Spices (3)
Jah Is True And Perfect (3)
Justice (2)

Kozmik (3)
Lee And Molly (1)
Look Who's Dancing (2)
Love Is The Only Law (2)
Namibia (3)
New Love (1)
New Time & Age (3)

One Bright Day (2)
Pains Of Life (3)
Problem With My Woman (3)
Rainbow Country (3)
Raw Riddim (3)
Small People (3)
So Good So Right (3)

Tomorrow People (1) 39
Tumblin' Down (1)
Urb-an Music (2)
We Propose (1)
What Conquers Defeat (3)
What's True (1)

When The Lights Gone Out (2)
Who A Say (1)
Who Will Be There (2)
Wrong Right Wrong (3)

MARLEY MARL
Prominent rap producer born Marlon Williams in Queens, New York on 9/30/62. Producer of Roxanne Shante, Salt-N-Pepa, Eric B & Rakim, Force M.D.'s and many others. Host of the weekly *Rap Attack* radio program on New York City's WBLS-FM. Cousin of M.C. Shan.

10/8/88	163	5		1 In Control, Volume 1	$8	Cold Chill. 25783
10/19/91	152	2		2 In Control Volume II - For Your Steering Pleasure	$12	Cold Chill. 26257
				featuring rappers Big Daddy Kane, Kool G Rap, Chuck D, Heavy D., L.L. Cool J, Def Jef, Chubb Rock, King Tee and others		

America Eats The Young (2)
Another Hooker (2)
At The Drop Of A Dime (2)
Buffalo Soldier (2)
Cheatin' Days Are Over (2)
Check The Mirror (2)

Droppin' Science (1)
Duck Alert (1)
Fools In Love (2)
Freedom (1)
Girl, I Was Wrong (2)
I Be Gettin' Busy (2)

Keep Control (2)
Keep Your Eye On The Prize (1)
Level Check (2)
Live Motivator (1)
Mobil Phone (2)

No Bullshit (2)
Out For The Count (2)
Reach Out (2)
Rebel, The (1)
Scanning The Dial (2)
Simon Says (1)

Something Funky To Listen To (2)
Sweet Tooth (2)
Symphony, The (1)
Symphony, Pt. II (2)
Wack Itt (1)

We Write The Songs (1)

MARMALADE, The
Scottish pop quintet led by vocalist Dean Ford (real name: Thomas McAleese).

6/20/70	71	13		Reflections Of My Life	$15	London 575

And Yours Is Piece Of Mine
Carolina In My Mind

Dear John
Fight Say The Mighty

I'll Be Home (In A Day Or So)
Kaleidoscope

Life Is

Some Other Guy
Super Clean Jean

Reflections Of My Life 10

DEBUT DATE	PEAK POS	WKS CHR	G O L D	ARTIST — Album Title	$	Label & Number

MARRINER, Neville
Born on 4/15/24 in Lincoln, England. Conductor of English chamber orchestra, Academy Of St. Martin-In-The-Fields, formed by Marriner in 1959.

11/24/84+	56	78		Amadeus ....[S]	$10	Fantasy 1791 [2]

Bubak And Hungaricus: Early 18th Century Gypsy Music
Giovanni Battista Pergolesi: Stabat Mater: Quando Corpus Morietur And Amen
Mozart: Concerto For Two Pianos, K. 365 (III)

Mozart: Don Giovanni, Act II, Commendatore Scene
Mozart: Mass In C Minor, K. 427, Kyrie
Mozart: Piano Concerto In D Minor, K. 466 (II)
Mozart: Piano Concerto In E Flat, K. 482 (III)

Mozart: Requiem, K. 626 Medley
Mozart: Serenade For Winds, K. 361 (III)
Mozart: Symphonie Concertante, K. 364 (I)
Mozart: Symphony No. 29 in A.K. 201 (I)

Mozart: Symphony No. 25 In G Minor, K. 183 (I)
Mozart: The Abduction From The Seraglio, Turkish Finale
Mozart: The Marriage Of Figaro, Act III, Ecco La Marcia

Mozart: The Marriage Of Figaro, Act IV, Ah Tutti Contenti
Mozart: Zaide, Aira, Ruhe Sanft

MARSALIS, Branford
Born on 8/26/60 in New Orleans. Jazz saxophonist — brother of trumpeter Wynton Marsalis and oldest of pianist Ellis Marsalis' six sons. Popular sessionman. Member of Sting's band. Became leader of the *Tonight Show with Jay Leno* band on 5/25/92. Appeared in the films *Bring On The Night*, *Throw Mama From The Train* and *School Daze*.

5/19/84	164	7		1 Scenes in the City ....[I]	$8	Columbia 38951
8/25/90	63	14		2 Mo' Better Blues ....[S]	$12	Columbia 46792

THE BRANFORD MARSALIS QUARTET FEATURING TERENCE BLANCHARD
quartet: Blanchard, Kenny Kirkland, Robert Hurst and Jeff Watts

Again Never (2)
Beneath The Underdog (2)
Harlem Blues *[includes 2 versions]* (2)

Jazz Thing (2)
Knocked Out The Box (2)
Mo' Better Blues (2)

No Backstage Pass (1)
No Sidestepping (1)
Parable (1)
Scenes In The City (1)

Pop Top (2)
Say Hey (2)

Solstice (1)
Waiting For Tain (1)

MARSALIS, Wynton
Born on 10/18/61 in New Orleans. Jazz-classical trumpeter — son of pianist Ellis Marsalis and younger brother of saxophonist Branford Marsalis. Member of Fuse One.

3/6/82	165	5		1 Wynton Marsalis ....[I]	$8	Columbia 37574
7/9/83+	102	27		2 Think Of One ....[I]	$8	Columbia 38641
10/13/84	90	39		3 Hot House Flowers ....[I]	$8	Columbia 39530
10/19/85	118	10		4 Black Codes (From the Underground) ....[I]	$8	Columbia 40009
11/1/86	185	4		5 J Mood ....[I]	$8	Columbia 40308
9/26/87	153	5		6 Marsalis Standard Time - Volume 1 ....[I]	$8	Columbia 40461
7/7/90	101	16		7 Standard Time Vol. 3 - The Resolution Of Romance ....[I]	$12	Columbia 46143
				features his father Ellis on piano		
4/13/91	112	6		8 Standard Time Vol. 2 - Intimacy Calling ....[I]	$12	Columbia 47346
				pianist Marcus Roberts appears on a track on which Marsalis does not appear		

After (5)
April In Paris (6)
Aural Oasis (4)
Autumn Leaves (6)
Bell Ringer (2)
Big Butter And Egg Man (7)
Black Codes (4)
Blues (4)
Bona And Paul (7)
Bourbon Street Parade (8)
Caravan (6)
Chambers Of Tain (4)
Cherokee (6)
Crepuscule With Nellie (8)
Delfeayo's Dilemma (4)
Django (3)

East Of The Sun (West Of The Moon) (8)
Embraceable You (8)
End Of A Love Affair (8)
Everything Happens To Me (7)
Father Time (1)
Flamingo (7)
Foggy Day (6)
For All We Know (3)
For Wee Folks (4)
Fuchsia (2)
Goodbye (6)
Hesitation (1)
Hot House Flowers (3)
How Are Things In Glocca Morra? (7)

I Cover The Waterfront (7)
I Gotta Right To Sing The Blues (7)
I'll Be There When The Time Is Right (1)
I'll Remember April (8)
I'm Confessin' (That I Love You) (3)
In The Afterglow (6)
In The Court Of King Oliver (7)
In The Wee Small Hours Of The Morning (7)
Indelible And Nocturnal (8)
Insane Asylum (5)
It's Easy To Remember (7)
It's Too Late Now (7)

J Mood (5)
Knozz-Moe-King (2)
Later (2)
Lazy Afternoon (3)
Lover (8)
Melancholia (2,3)
Melodique (5)
Memories Of You (6)
Much Later (5)
My Ideal (2)
My Romance (7)
Never Let Me Go (7)
New Orleans (8)
Phryzzinian Man (4)
Presence That Lament Brings (5)
RJ (7)

Seductress, The (7)
Sister Cheryl (1)
Skain's Domain (5)
Skylark (7)
Sleepin' Bee (7)
Song Is You (6)
Soon All Will Know (6)
Stardust (3)
Street Of Dreams (7)
Taking A Chance On Love (7)
Think Of One (2)
Twilight (1)
Very Thought Of You (7)
What Is Happening Here (Now)? (2)
What Is This Thing Called Love? (7)

When It's Sleepytime Down South (8)
When You Wish Upon A Star (3)
Where Or When (7)
Who Can I Turn To (When Nobody Needs Me) (1)
Yesterdays (8)
You Don't Know What Love Is (8)
You're My Everything (7)

★★230★★ MARSHALL TUCKER BAND, The
Southern-rock band formed in South Carolina in 1971: Doug Gray (lead singer), brothers Toy (lead guitarist) and Tommy (bass; d: 4/28/80 in auto accident [age 30]; replaced by Franklin Wilkie) Caldwell, George McCorkle (rhythm guitar), Paul Riddle (drums) and Jerry Eubanks (sax, flute).

7/7/73	29	40	●	1 The Marshall Tucker Band	$12	Capricorn 0112
3/9/74	37	28	●	2 A New Life	$12	Capricorn 0124
12/21/74+	54	14	●	3 Where We All Belong ....[L]	$12	Capricorn 0145 [2]
				record 1: studio; record 2: live		
9/13/75	15	34		4 Searchin' For A Rainbow	$12	Capricorn 0161
6/26/76	32	20	●	5 Long Hard Ride	$8	Capricorn 0170
2/26/77	23	36	▲	6 Carolina Dreams	$8	Capricorn 0180
5/13/78	22	16	●	7 Together Forever	$8	Capricorn 0205
10/21/78	67	32	●	8 Greatest Hits ....[G]	$8	Capricorn 0214
5/5/79	30	22		9 Running Like The Wind	$8	Warner 3317
3/22/80	32	15		10 Tenth	$8	Warner 3410
5/23/81	53	12		11 Dedicated	$8	Warner 3525
				in memory of bassist Tommy Caldwell		
6/12/82	95	7		12 Tuckerized	$8	Warner 3684

AB's Song (1)
Ace High Love (12)
Am I The Kind Of Man (5)
Another Cruel Love (2)
Answer To Love (9)
Anyway The Wind Blows Rider (3)
Asking Too Much Of You (7)
Blue Ridge Mountain Sky (2)
Bob Away My Blues (4)

Bound And Determined (4)
Can't You See (1,4,8) 75
Cattle Drive (10)
Change Is Gonna Come (7)
Desert Skies (6)
Disillusion (10)
Dream Lover (7) 75
Even A Fool Would Let Go (12)

Everybody Needs Somebody (7)
Everyday (I Have The Blues) (3)
Fire On The Mountain (4,8) **38**
Fly Eagle Fly (2)
Fly Like An Eagle (6)
Foolish Dreaming (10)
Gospel Singin' Man (10)

Heard It In A Love Song (6,8) **14**
Heartbroke (12)
Hillbilly Band (11)
Holding On To You (5)
How Can I Slow Down (3)
I Should Have Never Started Lovin' You (6)
I'll Be Loving You (7)

If You Think You're Hurtin' Me (Girl You're Crazy) (12)
In My Own Way (3)
It Takes Time (10) **79**
Jimi (1)
Keeps Me From All Wrong (4)
Last Of The Singing Cowboys (9) **42**
Life In A Song (6)
Long Hard Ride (5,8)

Losing You (1)
Love Is A Mystery (7)
Love Some (11)
Low Down Ways (3)
Melody Ann (9)
Mr. President (12)
My Best Friend (9)
My Jesus Told Me So (1)
Never Trust A Stranger (6)
New Life (2)

DEBUT DATE	PEAK POS	WKS CHR	GOLD	ARTIST — Album Title	$	Label & Number

MARSHALL TUCKER BAND, The — Cont'd

Now She's Gone (3)	Save My Soul (10)	Singing Rhymes (3)	Tell The Blues To Take Off	24 Hours At A Time (2,3,8)	Without You (10)
Pass It On (9)	Sea, Dreams & Fairy Tales	Something's Missing In My	The Night (11)	Unforgiven (12)	You Ain't Foolin' Me (2)
Property Line (5)	(12)	Life (11)	This Ol' Cowboy (3,8) 78	Unto These Hills (9)	You Don't Live Forever (5)
Ramblin' (1,3,8)	Searchin' For A Rainbow	Southern Woman (2)	This Time I Believe (11)	Virginia (4)	You Say You Love Me (5)
Reachin' For A Little Bit	(4,8)	Special Someone (11)	Time Has Come (11)	Walkin' And Talkin' (4)	
More (12)	See You Later, I'm Gone (1)	Sweet Elaine (2)	Tonight's The Night (For	Walkin' The Streets Alone (5)	
Ride In Peace (11)	See You One More Time (10)	Take The Highway (1,3)	Making Love) (11)	Where A Country Boy	
Rumors Are Raging (11)	Silverado (11)	Tell It To The Devil (6)	Too Stubborn (2)	Belongs (3)	
Running Like The Wind (9)	Sing My Blues (10)		Try One More Time (3)	Windy City Blues (5)	

MARTHA & THE MUFFINS

Canadian group led by vocalist Martha Johnson. Member Jocelyn Lanois is the sister of Daniel Lanois, noted producer of U2 and Peter Gabriel.

9/13/80	186	3		1 Metro Music	$8	Virgin 13145
5/21/83	184	4		2 Danseparc	$8	RCA 4664
7/28/84	163	4		3 Mystery Walk	$8	Current 3

M+M

Alibi Room (3)	Cooling The Medium (3)	In Between Sleep And	Revenge (Against The World)	Sins Of Children (2)
Big Trees (3)	Danseparc (Every Day It's	Reason (3)	(1)	Terminal Twilight (1)
Black Stations/White	Tomorrow) (2)	Indecision (1)	Rhythm Of Life (3)	Walking Into Walls (2)
Stations (3) 63	Echo Beach (1)	Monotone (1)	Saigon (1)	What People Do For Fun (2)
Boys In The Bushes (2)	Garden In The Sky (3)	Nation Of Followers (3)	Several Styles Of Blonde	Whatever Happened To
Cheesies And Gum (1)	Hide And Seek (1)	Obedience (2)	Girls Dancing (2)	Radio Valve Road? (2)
Come Out And Dance (3)	I Start To Stop (3)	Paint By Number Heart (1)	Sinking Land (1)	World Without Borders (2)

MARTHA & THE VANDELLAS

Soul group from Detroit, organized by Martha Reeves (b: 7/18/41, Alabama) in 1962 with Annette Beard and Rosalind Ashford. Reeves had been in The Del-Phis, recorded for Checkmate. Worked as A&R secretary, sang backup. Vandellas did backup on several of Marvin Gaye's hits. Beard left group in 1964, replaced by Betty Kelly (formerly from The Velvelettes). Group disbanded from 1969-71, re-formed with Martha and sister Lois Reeves, and Sandra Tilley in 1971. Martha Reeves went solo in late 1972.

11/23/63	125	5		1 Heat Wave	$50	Gordy 907
5/29/65	139	3		2 Dance Party	$45	Gordy 915
6/11/66	50	15		3 Greatest Hits ....[G]	$30	Gordy 917
1/21/67	116	8		4 Watchout!	$30	Gordy 920
10/7/67	140	5		5 Martha & The Vandellas Live!.......................................[L]	$30	Gordy 925

MARTHA REEVES & THE VANDELLAS:

6/1/68	167	8		6 Ridin' High	$20	Gordy 926
4/1/72	146	7		7 Black Magic	$20	Gordy 958

Anyone Who Had A Heart (7)	Hello Stranger (1)	(I've Given You) The Best	Love Like Yours (Don't Come	Quicksand (3) 8	(We've Got) Honey Love
Benjamin (7)	Hey There Lonely Boy (1)	Years Of My Life (7)	Knocking Everyday) (3)	Respect (medley) (5)	(6) 56
Bless You (7) 53	Hitch Hike (1)	If I Had A Hammer (1)	Love (Makes Me Do	Show Me The Way (6)	What Am I Going To Do
Come And Get These	Honey Chile (6) 11	In And Out Of My Life (7)	Foolish Things) (3,5) 70	Something (7)	Without Your Love (4) 71
Memories (3) 29	Hope I Don't Get My Heart	In My Lonely Room (3) 44	Mickey's Monkey (1)	Sweet Soul Music (medley)	Wild One (2,3) 34
Dance Party (2)	Broke (7)	Jerk, The (2)	Mobile Lil The Dancing	(5)	Without You (6)
Dancing In The Street	I Can't Help Myself (Sugar	Jimmy Mack (4,5) 10	Witch (2)	Tear It On Down (7)	You've Been In Love Too
(2,3,5) 2	Pie, Honey Bunch)	Just One Look (1)	Mocking Bird (1)	Tell Me I'll Never Be Alone (4)	Long (3,5) 36
Dancing Slow (2)	(medley) (5)	Keep It Up (1)	More (1)	Then He Kissed Me (1)	Your Love Makes It All
Danke Schoen (1)	I Found A Love (5)	Leave It In The Hands Of	Motoring (2)	There He Is - At My Door (6)	Worthwhile (7)
Do Right Woman (medley) (5)	I Promise To Wait My Love	Love (1)	My Baby Loves Me (3,5) 22	(There's) Always Something	
For Once In My Life (5)	(6) 62	Let This Day Be (4)	My Boyfriend's Back (1)	There To Remind Me (6)	
Forget Me Not (6) 93	I Say A Little Prayer (6)	Live Wire (3) 42	No More Tearstained Make	To Sir, With Love (6)	
Go Ahead And Laugh (4)	I Want You Back (7)	Love Bug Leave My Heart	Up (4)	Uptight (Everything's	
Happiness Is Guaranteed (4)	I'll Follow You (4)	Alone (5,6) 25	No One There (7)	Alright) (medley) (5)	
He Doesn't Love Her	I'm In Love (And I Know It)	Love Is Like A Heat Wave	Nobody'll Care (2)	Wait Till My Bobby Gets	
Anymore (4)	(6)	(3,5)	Nowhere To Run (2,3,5) 8	Home (1)	
Heat Wave (1) 4	I'm Ready For Love (4,5) 9	One Way Out (4)			

MARTIKA

Born Martika Marrero in 1970. Los Angeles-based, Cuban-American singer/writer/actress/dancer. Starred in TV program Kids, Incorporated. Appeared in the 1982 film musical Annie.

2/4/89	15	39	●	1 Martika	$8	Columbia 44290
9/14/91	111	9		2 Martika's Kitchen	$12	Columbia 46827

Alibis (1)	I Feel The Earth Move	Love...Thy Will Be Done	More Than You Know (1) 18	Take Me To Forever (2)
Broken Heart (2)	(1) 25	(2) 10	Pride & Prejudice (2)	Temptation (2)
Coloured Kisses (2)	If You're Tarzan, I'm Jane (1)	Magical Place (2)	Safe In The Arms Of Love (2)	Toy Soldiers (1) 1
Cross My Heart (1)	It's Not What You're Doing	Martika's Kitchen (2) 93	See If I Care (1)	Water (1)
Don't Say U Love Me (2)	(1)	Mi Tierra (2)	Spirit (2)	You Got Me Into This (1)

MARTIN, Bobbi

Born Barbara Anne Martin on 11/29/43 in Brooklyn; raised in Baltimore. Toured the Far East with Bob Hope's Christmas shows.

3/6/65	127	5		1 Don't Forget I Still Love You	$15	Coral 57472
5/30/70	176	5		2 For The Love Of Him	$10	United Art. 6700

Anytime (1)	Everybody Loves Somebody	I Walk The Line (2)	Livin' In A House Full Of	Someday (You'll Want Me To
Crazy Arms (2)	(1)	I'm A Fool (To Go On Loving	Love (2)	Want You) (1)
Dear Heart (1)	For The Love Of Him (2) 13	You) (1)	Long Line Of Fools (2)	Tennessee Waltz (2)
Don't Forget I Still Love	Here Comes My Baby Back	I'm So Lonesome I Could	Lovesick Blues (2)	This Love Of Mine (1)
You (1) 19	Again (2)	Cry (2)	Loving You (1)	We'll Sing In The Sunshine
Don't Touch Me, Jimmy	I Can't Stop Loving You (1)	Kiss Me Goodnight (1)	Million Thanks To You	(1)
Brown (2)	I Fall To Pieces (1)		(Kung Di Lang Sa Lyo) (1)	Your Cheatin' Heart (2)

★★59★★ MARTIN, Dean

Born Dino Crocetti on 6/7/17 in Steubenville, Ohio. Vocalist/actor. To California in 1937, worked local clubs. Teamed with comedian Jerry Lewis in Atlantic City in 1946. First film, My Friend Irma in 1949. Team broke up after 16th film Hollywood Or Bust in 1956. Appeared in many films since then; own TV series from 1965-74.

5/12/62	73	16		1 Dino - Italian love songs	$20	Capitol 1659

DEBUT DATE	PEAK POS	WKS CHR	GOLD	ARTIST — Album Title	$	Label & Number
				MARTIN, Dean — Cont'd		
1/26/63	99	5		2 Dino Latino	$15	Reprise 6054
3/30/63	109	4		3 Country Style	$15	Reprise 6061
8/15/64	2[4]	49	●	4 Everybody Loves Somebody..	$15	Reprise 6130
8/29/64	15	31	●	5 Dream With Dean	$15	Reprise 6123
11/14/64	9	30	●	6 The Door Is Still Open To My Heart	$12	Reprise 6140
2/13/65	13	29	●	7 Dean Martin Hits Again	$12	Reprise 6146
8/28/65	12	39	●	8 (Remember Me) I'm The One Who Loves You...................................	$12	Reprise 6170
11/20/65+	11	34	●	9 Houston	$12	Reprise 6181
3/12/66	40	27	●	10 Somewhere There's A Someone	$12	Reprise 6201
7/2/66	108	3		11 The Silencers ....[S]	$15	Reprise 6211
				Dean's first film as secret agent Matt Helm; includes 4 instrumentals by the Ernie Freeman and Gene Page Orchestras: "Anniversary Song," "Lord, You Made The Night Too Long," "Lovey Kravezit" and "The Silencers"		
8/27/66	50	25		12 The Hit Sound Of Dean Martin...	$12	Reprise 6213
12/3/66+	34	31		13 The Dean Martin TV Show	$12	Reprise 6233
12/17/66+	95	13		14 The Best Of Dean Martin ....[G]	$12	Capitol 2601
5/13/67	46	25		15 Happiness Is Dean Martin	$12	Reprise 6242
9/2/67	20	48	●	16 Welcome To My World	$12	Reprise 6250
6/1/68	26	39	●	17 Dean Martin's Greatest Hits! Vol. 1 ....[G]	$10	Reprise 6301
9/7/68	83	21	●	18 Dean Martin's Greatest Hits! Vol. 2 ....[G]	$10	Reprise 6320
1/4/69	14	25	●	19 Gentle On My Mind	$10	Reprise 6330
2/22/69	145	7		20 The Best Of Dean Martin, Vol. 2 ....[G]	$10	Capitol 140
10/4/69	90	17		21 I Take A Lot Of Pride In What I Am	$10	Reprise 6338
9/12/70	97	12		22 My Woman, My Woman, My Wife	$10	Reprise 6403
2/27/71	113	15		23 For The Good Times	$10	Reprise 6428
2/5/72	117	4		24 Dino	$10	Reprise 2053

Ain't Gonna Try Anymore (3,12)
(Alla En) El Rancho Grande (2)
Always In My Heart (2)
Always Together (6)
Any Time (3,10,12)
April Again (19)
Arrivederci, Roma (1,20)
Baby-O (4)
Baby Won't You Please Come Home (5,13)
Besame Mucho (3)
Birds And The Bees (8,17)
Blue, Blue Day (3,10)
Blue Memories (24)
Blue Moon (5)
Born To Lose (8)
Bouquet Of Roses (10)
Bumming Around (8,17)
By The Time I Get To Phoenix (19)
Canadian Sunset (20)
Candy Kisses (10)
Cha Cha Cha D'Amour (Melodie D'Amour) (20)
Clinging Vine (6)
Come Back To Sorrento (14)
Come Running Back (12,17) **35**
Corrine Corrina (4)
Crying Time (21)
Detour (9)
Detroit City (22)
Do You Believe This Town (21)
Don't Let The Blues Make You Bad (12)
Door Is Still Open To My Heart (6,18) **6**
Down Home (9)
Drowning In My Tears (19)
Empty Saddles In The Old Corral (11)
Every Minute, Every Hour (6,17)
Everybody But Me (9)
Everybody Loves Somebody (4,5,17) **1**
Face In A Crowd (3,4)

First Thing Ev'ry Morning (And The Last Thing Ev'ry Night) (9)
Fools Rush In (5)
For Once In My Life (23)
For The Good Times (23)
From Lover To Loser (4)
Gentle On My Mind (19)
Georgia Sunshine (23)
Gimme A Little Kiss Will Ya Huh? (5)
Glory Of Love (6)
Green, Green Grass Of Home (16)
Guess Who (24)
Hammer And Nails (9)
Hands Across The Table (5)
Have A Heart (7)
He's Got You (15)
Heart Over Mind (22)
Here Comes My Baby (8)
Here We Go Again (22)
Hey Brother Pour The Wine (14)
Hey, Good Lookin' (3)
Home (13)
Honey (19)
Houston (9,17) **21**
I Can Give You What You Want Now (24)
I Can't Help It (10)
I Can't Help Remembering You (16,17)
I Don't Know What I'm Doing (24)
I Don't Know Why (I Just Do) (5)
I Don't Think You Love Me Anymore (8)
I Have But One Heart (1)
I Take A Lot Of Pride In What I Am (21) **75**
I Will (9,18) **10**
I'll Be Seeing You (4)
I'll Buy That Dream (5)
I'll Hold You In My Heart ('Till I Can Hold You In My Arms) (7)

I'm Confessin' (That I Love You) (5)
I'm Gonna Change Everything (6)
I'm Living In Two Worlds (12)
I'm Not The Marrying Kind (Matt Helm's Theme from Murderer's Row) (15)
I'm So Lonesome I Could Cry (3,10)
I'm Yours (14)
I've Grown Accustomed To Her Face (13,20)
If I Ever Get Back To Georgia (15)
If I Had You (13)
If Love Is Good To Me (20)
If You Ever Get Around To Loving Me (21)
If You Knew Susie (11)
If You Were The Only Girl (5)
In A Little Spanish Town (2)
In The Chapel In The Moonlight (7,16,17) **25**
In The Misty Moonlight (6,18) **46**
Invisible Tears (23)
It Just Happened That Way (15)
It Keeps Right On-A-Hurtin' (22)
It's The Talk Of The Town (13)
Just A Little Lovin' (10)
Just Close Your Eyes (4)
Just Friends (13)
Just In Time (14)
Just Say I Love Her (1,20)
Just The Other Side Of Nowhere (24)
King Of The Road (8,18)
Kiss The World Goodbye (24)
La Paloma (2)
Last Round-Up (11)
Lay Some Happiness On Me (15,18) **55**
Little Green Apples (23)
Little Lovely One (9)
Little Ole Wine Drinker, Me (16,18) **38**

Little Voice (4)
Love, Love, Love (9)
Magic Is The Moonlight (2)
Make It Rain (21)
Make The World Go Away (22)
Manana (2)
Marry Me (23)
Memories Are Made Of This (14) **1**
Middle Of The Night Is My Cryin' Time (6)
Million And One (12) **41**
My Heart Cries For You (3,4)
My Heart Is An Open Book (7)
My Heart Reminds Me (1)
My Melancholy Baby (5)
My One And Only Love (20)
My Shoes Keep Walking Back To You (8)
My Sugar's Gone (6)
My Woman, My Woman, My Wife (22)
Nobody But A Fool (Would Love You) (12)
Nobody's Baby Again (15,17) **60**
Non Dimenticar (1)
Not Enough Indians (19) **43**
Old Yellow Line (9,18)
On An Evening In Roma (1) **59**
On The Sunny Side Of The Street (11)
Once A Day (22)
One Cup Of Happiness (And One Peace Of Mind) (13)
One I Love (Belongs To Somebody Else) (13)
One Lonely Boy (12)
(Open Up The Door) Let The Good Times In (15,18) **55**
Pardon (1)
Party Dolls And Wine (24)
Perfect Mountain (19)
Place In The Shade (16)
Pretty Baby (20)
Pride (16)

Rainbows Are Back In Style (19)
Raindrops Keep Fallin' On My Head (23)
Raining In My Heart (23)
Red Roses For A Blue Lady (8)
Red Sails In The Sunset (11)
Release Me (And Let Me Love Again) (10)
(Remember Me) I'm The One Who Loves You (8,17) **32**
Return To Me (1,14) **4**
Right Kind Of Woman (7)
Room Full Of Roses (3,10)
S'posin' (13)
Second Hand Rose (Second Hand Heart) (10)
Send Me Some Lovin' (7)
Send Me The Pillow You Dream On (7,18) **22**
Shades (12)
She's A Little Bit Country (23)
Shutters And Boards (3,4)
Side By Side (11)
Siesta Fiesta (4)
Singing The Blues (3)
Small Exception Of Me (24)
Smile (5)
Snap Your Fingers (9)
Sneaky Little Side Of Me (21)
So Long Baby (9)
Somewhere There's A Someone (10,18) **32**
South Of The Border (2,11)
Standing On The Corner (20) **22**
Sun Is Shinin' (On Everybody But Me) (21)
Supposin' ..see: S'posin'
Sway (14)
Sweet, Sweet Lovable You (15)
Sweetheart (23)
Take Me (6)
Take Me In Your Arms (1)
Take These Chains From My Heart (8)

Tangerine (2)
Terrible, Tangled Web (12)
That Old Clock On The Wall (10)
That Old Time Feelin' (19)
That's Amore (14)
That's When I See The Blues (In Your Pretty Brown Eyes) (19)
There's No Tomorrow (O Sole Mio) (1)
Things (3,4)
Things We Did Last Summer (13)
Think About Me (15)
Thirty More Miles To San Diego (15)
Tips Of My Fingers (22)
Today Is Not The Day (12)
Together Again (22)
Turn The World Around (22)
Turn To Me (16)
Vieni Su (1,20)
Volare (Nel Blu Dipinto Di Blu) (14) **12**
Walk On By (8)
Wallpaper Roses (16)
We'll Sing In The Sunshine (6)
Wedding Bells (7)
Welcome To My Heart (19)
Welcome To My World (8,16)
What A Diff'rence A Day Made (2)
What Can I Say After I Say I'm Sorry? (13)
What's Yesterday (24)
Where The Blue And Lonely Go (21)
You'll Always Be The One I Love (7,17) **64**
You're Breaking My Heart (1)
You're Nobody Till Somebody Loves You (6,7,14,17) **25**
You're The Reason I'm In Love (9)
You've Still Got A Place In My Heart (15,18) **60**
Your Other Love (4)

MARTIN, Eric, Band
Born on 10/10/60 in San Francisco. Pop-rock vocalist. Joined rock group Mr. Big as lead singer in 1988.

| 9/24/83 | 191 | 2 | | Sucker For A Pretty Face .... | $8 | Elektra 60238 |

Catch Me If You Can
Don't Stop
Just Another Pretty Boy
Letting It Out
Love Me
One More Time
Private Life
Sucker For A Pretty Face
Ten Feet Tall
Young At Heart

DEBUT DATE	PEAK POS	WKS CHR	GOLD	ARTIST — Album Title	$	Label & Number

MARTIN, George
Born on 1/3/26 in London. The Beatles' producer from 1962-70. Also produced Billy J. Kramer, Gerry And The Pacemakers, America, Jeff Beck and others. Also see *Yellow Submarine* by The Beatles.

| 9/5/64 | 111 | 10 | | Off The Beatle Track ....[I] | $40 | United Art. 3377 |

instrumental versions of The Beatles' hits

All I've Got To Do	Don't Bother Me	I Saw Her Standing There	Little Child	**Ringo's Theme (This**	She Loves You
All My Loving	From Me To You	I Want To Hold Your Hand	Please Please Me	**Boy) 53**	There's A Place
Can't Buy Me Love					

MARTIN, Marilyn
Raised in Louisville. Background vocalist for Stevie Nicks, Tom Petty, Kenny Loggins and Joe Walsh.

| 2/22/86 | 72 | 11 | | Marilyn Martin .... | $8 | Atlantic 81292 |

Beauty Or The Beast	Dream Is Always The Same	Move Closer	One Step Closer	Turn It On
Body And The Beat	Here Is The News	**Night Moves 28**	Too Much Too Soon	Wildest Dreams

MARTIN, Moon
Real name: John Martin. Pop-rock singer/songwriter/guitarist from Oklahoma. Wrote Robert Palmer's hit "Bad Case Of Loving You." Moved to Los Angeles in 1968. Lead guitarist of group Southwind.

| 9/8/79 | 80 | 11 | | 1 Escape From Domination .... | $8 | Capitol 11933 |
| 11/15/80 | 138 | 15 | | 2 Street Fever .... | $8 | Capitol 12099 |

Bad News (2)	Dangerous (1)	Gun Shy (1)	**No Chance** (1) *50*	Rollin' In My Rolls (2)	Whispers (2)
Bootleg Woman (1)	Dreamer (1)	Hot House Baby (1)	No Dice (2)	She Made A Fool Of You (1)	
Breakout Tonight (2)	Feeling's Right (1)	I've Got A Reason (1)	Pushed Around (2)	Signal For Help (2)	
Cross Your Fingers (2)	Five Days Of Fever (1)	Love Gone Bad (2)	**Rolene** (1) *30*	Stranded (2)	

MARTIN, Ray, & His Orchestra
British conductor.

| 8/14/61 | 43 | 6 | | Dynamica ....[I] | $15 | RCA 2287 |

Bye Bye Blues	Flight Of The Bumble Bee	Indian Summer	Malaguena	Moon Was Yellow	Shadrack
Cry Me A River	Humoresque	Lullaby Of The Leaves	Mood Indigo	Pagan Love Song	Stormy Weather

MARTIN, Steve
Born on 6/8/45 in Waco, Texas; raised in California. Popular TV and film comedian. Comedy writer for the *Smothers Brothers Comedy Hour* TV show and others. Films include *The Jerk, All Of Me, Roxanne, Planes, Trains And Automobiles, L.A. Story* and *Leap Of Faith* among many others. Married actress Victoria Tennant.

10/8/77	10	68	▲	1 Let's Get Small ....[C]	$8	Warner 3090
11/4/78	2⁶	26	▲	2 A Wild And Crazy Guy ....[C]	$8	Warner 3238
10/6/79	25	22	●	3 Comedy Is Not Pretty! ....[C]	$8	Warner 3392
11/14/81	135	4		4 The Steve Martin Brothers ....[C-I]	$8	Warner 3477

side 1: comedy; side 2: banjo music by Steve

All Being (3)	Drop Thumb Medley (3)	Hostages (3)	Mad At My Mother (1)	Ramblin' Man (1)	Vegas (1)
American Photography (4)	Excuse Me (1)	How To Meet A Girl (3)	Make The Rent (4)	Real Me (4)	Waterbound (4)
Banana Banjo (4)	Expose, An (2)	I'm Feelin' It (2)	McDonald's (3)	Religion (2)	What I Believe (3)
Born To Be Wild (3)	Freddie's Lilt, Parts I And II	I'm In The Mood For Love (2)	Men's Underwear (3)	Rubberhead (3)	Wild And Crazy Guy (2)
Cat Handcuffs (2)	(4)	Jackie O. And Farrah F. (3)	My Real Name (2)	Saga Of The Old West (4)	You Can Be A Millionaire (3)
Charitable Kind Of Guy (2)	Funny Comedy Gags (1)	John Henry (4)	One Way To Leave Your	Sally Goodin' (4)	You Naive Americans (2)
College (2)	Googlephonics (3)	**King Tut** (2) *17*	Lover (1)	Scientific Question (4)	
Comedy Is Not Pretty (4)	Gospel Maniacs (4)	Language (1)	Philosophy (2)	Show Biz Moment (4)	
Creativity In Action (2)	**Grandmother's Song** (1) *72*	Let's Get Small (1)	Pitkin County Turn Around	Smoking (1)	
Cruel Shoes (3) *91*	Hoedown At Alice's (4)	Love God (1)	(4)	Song Of Perfect Spaces (4)	

MARTINEZ, Nancy
Dance singer/actress born in Quebec.

| 2/21/87 | 178 | 3 | | Not Just The Girl Next Door .... | $8 | Atlantic 81720 |

Crazy Love	Hurt Me Twice (Shame On	I'll Be There	It Happens All The Time	Rhythm Of Your Heart
For Tonight *32*	You)	In The Heat Of The Night	Move Out	Without Love

★★88★★ MARTINO, Al
Born Alfred Cini on 10/7/27 in Philadelphia. Encouraged by success of boyhood friend, Mario Lanza. Winner on *Arthur Godfrey's Talent Scouts* in 1952. Portrayed singer Johnny Fontane in the 1972 film *The Godfather*.

12/1/62	109	6		1 The Exciting Voice Of Al Martino	$15	Capitol 1774
6/15/63	7	60		2 I Love You Because	$15	Capitol 1914
10/12/63	9	44		3 Painted, Tainted Rose	$15	Capitol 1975
2/8/64	13	28		4 Living A Lie	$15	Capitol 2040
4/18/64	57	15		5 The Italian Voice Of Al Martino	$15	Capitol 1907

Al's second Capitol album

6/27/64	31	25		6 I Love You More And More Every Day/ Tears And Roses....................	$15	Capitol 2107
2/6/65	41	15		7 We Could	$15	Capitol 2200
6/19/65	42	12		8 Somebody Else Is Taking My Place	$15	Capitol 2312
9/11/65+	19	47		9 My Cherie	$15	Capitol 2362
2/19/66	8	73	●	10 Spanish Eyes	$15	Capitol 2435
6/18/66	116	6		11 Think I'll Go Somewhere And Cry Myself To Sleep	$12	Capitol 2528
10/29/66+	57	13		12 This Is Love	$12	Capitol 2592
3/25/67	99	12		13 This Love For You	$12	Capitol 2654
6/24/67	23	21		14 Daddy's Little Girl	$12	Capitol 2733
10/14/67+	63	21		15 Mary In The Morning	$12	Capitol 2780
3/30/68	129	4		16 This Is Al Martino	$10	Capitol 2843
4/20/68	56	17		17 Love Is Blue	$10	Capitol 2908
8/31/68	108	16		18 The Best Of Al Martino ....[G]	$10	Capitol 2946
7/19/69	189	4		19 Sausalito...	$10	Capitol 180
12/20/69	196	2		20 Jean	$10	Capitol 379

DEBUT DATE	PEAK POS	WKS CHR	GOLD	ARTIST — Album Title	$	Label & Number

MARTINO, Al — Cont'd

DEBUT DATE	PEAK POS	WKS CHR			$	Label & Number
4/11/70	184	5		21 Can't Help Falling In Love	$10	Capitol 405
11/28/70	172	6		22 My Heart Sings	$10	Capitol 497
6/3/72	138	10		23 Love Theme From "The Godfather"	$10	Capitol 11071
2/8/75	129	8		24 To The Door Of The Sun	$10	Capitol 11366

Adios Mexico (11)
Affair To Remember (13)
Al Di La (5)
All (13)
All My Dreams (6)
(All Of A Sudden) My Heart Sings (22)
Always Together (7) *33*
Am I Losing You? (6)
And That Reminds Me (16)
Anita, You're Dreaming (11)
Are You Lonesome Tonight? (4)
Autumn Leaves (13)
Because You're Mine (1)
Born Free (14)
Bouquet Of Roses (2)
By The River Of The Roses (10)
Call, The (22)
Call Me (17)
Can't Help Falling In Love (21) *51*
Can't Take My Eyes Off You (15)
Careless (4)
Careless Hands (6)
Chitarra Romana (5)
Close To You (13)
Come Into My Life (24)
Crying In The Chapel (9)
Crying Time (11)
Cuore Di Mamma (5)
Daddy's Little Girl (14,18) *42*
Dear Heart (7)
Devotion (13)
Dicitencello Vuie ..see: Just Say I Love Her
Don't Cry Joe (Let Her Go, Let Her Go Let Her Go) (4)
Don't Leave Me Now (5)
Don't Take Your Love From Me (1)
End Of The World (10)
Every Day Of My Life (23)
Everybody's Talkin' (20)
Exodus Song (1)
Fascination (9)
Fenesta Che Lucive (The Window) (5)
For All We Know (12)
Forgive Me (10) *61*
Georgia On My Mind (17)
Glad She's A Woman (19)
Glory Of Love (16)

Godfather, Love Theme From The ..see: Speak Softly Love
Godfather Waltz (Come Live Your Life With Me) (23)
Goin' Out Of My Head (17)
Got To Live It Up To Live You Down (11)
Granada (1)
Gypsy In You (23)
Happy Time (16)
Harbor Lights (3)
Have I Told You Lately That I Love You? (3)
Hello Memory (10)
Here In My Heart (1) *86*
Hold Back The Dawn (13)
Honey Come Back (21)
Husbands And Wives (11)
Hush...Hush, Sweet Charlotte (8,18)
I Can't Stop My Lovin' You (11)
I Don't See Me In Your Eyes Any More (3)
I Don't Want To See Tomorrow (7)
I Dream Of You (More Than You Dream I Do) (15)
I Have But One Heart (2)
I Love You And You Love Me (14)
I Love You Because (2,18) *3*
I Love You More And More Every Day (6,18) *9*
I Love You Truly (3)
I Really Don't Want To Know (2)
I Will Wait For You (13)
I Wish You Love (9)
I Won't Forget You (1)
I'll Always Be In Love With You (6)
I'll Hold You In My Heart (Till I Can Hold You In My Arms) (10)
I'll Never Find Another You (9)
I'm A Better Man (20)
I'm Carryin' The World On My Shoulders (17)
I'm In The Mood For Love (4)
I'm Living My Heaven With You (6)
I'm Saving All My Love For You (11)

I'm Still Not Thru Missin' You (23,24)
If Ever I Would Leave You (16)
If I Loved You (8)
If I Never Get To Heaven (2)
If I Were A Carpenter (21)
If Tears Were Roses (20)
If You Go Away (13)
In The Arms Of Love (13)
It Only Hurts For A Little While (9)
It's A Sin (2)
Jealous Heart (7)
Jean (20)
Joanne (22)
Just As Much As Ever (17)
Just Call Me Lonesome (2)
Just Loving You (17)
Just Say I Love Her (1,23)
Just Yesterday (12) *77*
La Strada Del Bosco (5)
Less Than Tomorrow (7)
Let It Be Me (17)
Let Me Stay Awhile With You (7)
Letter, The (19)
Lies (4)
Lili Marlene (17) *87*
Living A Lie (4,18) *22*
Lonely Drifter (2)
Long Long Time (22)
Losing You (2)
Love Is A Many-Splendored Thing (16)
Love Is Blue (17,18) *57*
Love Letters (1)
Love Letters In The Sand (15)
Love Me Tender (15)
Love, Where Are You Now (1)
Love Will Conquer All (24)
Loveliest Night Of The Year (1)
Lovely Lady Of Arcadia (24)
Loving You (22)
Make Me Believe (1)
Make The World Go Away (10)
Making Memories (15)
Man Without Love (23)
Many Tears Ago (6)
Maria Mari (Ah! Marie) (5)
Mary Go Lightly (24)
Mary In The Morning (14,18) *27*
Mattinata (1)
Melody Of Love (9)

Memories (19)
Merry-go-round (2)
Mexicali Rose (4)
Minute You're Gone (11)
Moon Over Naples ..see: Spanish Eyes
More (3)
More I See You (4)
More Than The Eye Can See (16) *54*
My Cherie (9) *88*
My Cherie Amour (20)
My Cup Runneth Over (14)
My Darling, I Love You (7)
My Foolish Heart (10)
My Heart Sings ..see: (All Of A Sudden)
My Heart Would Know (8) *52*
My Love, Forgive Me (6)
My Love Is Stronger Than My Pride (15)
My Way (21)
Nessun Dorma (1)
Never My Love (14)
New World In The Morning (22)
No More (1)
No One Will Ever Know (6)
No Other Arms, No Other Lips (8)
Non Ti Scordar Di Me (1)
Now (Before Another Day Goes By) (15)
Once Upon A Time (14)
One Has My Name...The Other Has My Heart (10)
One More Mile (And Darlin', I'll Be Home) (21)
One Pair Of Hands (22)
Oscuritta (19)
Painted, Tainted Rose (3,18) *15*
Pardon Me (8)
Raindrops Keep Fallin' On My Head (21)
Ramona (3)
Red Is Red (15)
Red Roses For A Blue Lady (8,18)
Release Me (15)
Rise And Fall Of A Fool (23)
Rondine Al Nido (5)
Room Full Of Roses (4)
Sandy When She's Sleepin' (19)
Sausalito (19) *99*

Senza Nisciuno (5)
Shadow Of Your Smile (16)
Shadows (24)
She'll Always Love You (14)
Snowbird (22)
Somebody Else Is Taking My Place (8) *53*
Something In Our Hearts (13)
Somewhere (12)
Somewhere In This World (14)
Somewhere In Your Heart (8)
Somewhere, My Love (12)
Song Of Joy (24)
Spanish Eyes (9,10,18) *15*
Speak Softly Love (23) *80*
Stay (20)
Still (2)
Strangers In The Night (12)
Sunrise To Sunrise (7)
Sweet Caroline (Good Times Never Seemed So Good) (21)
Take My Hand For A While (19)
Take These Chains From My Heart (2)
Tears And Roses (6) *20*
That's My Desire (4)
That's The Way It's Got To Be (3)
Then I'll Be Over You (19)
Then You Can Tell Me Goodbye (7)
There Are Such Things (16)
There Must Be A Way (3)
There's No Such Thing As Love (20)
These Things I Offer You (12)
They'll Never Take Her Love From Me (6)
Think I'll Go Somewhere And Cry Myself To Sleep (10,11) *30*
This Guy's In Love With You (20)
This Is My Song (10)
This Love Of Mine (12)
Three Coins In The Fountain (9)
Till (9)
Till Then (3)
Till Then, My Love (10)
To Each His Own (3)

To The Door Of The Sun (Alle Porte Del Sole) (24) *17*
Today I Found You (24)
Together Again (11)
Torna (6)
Torna A Sorriento (Come Back To Sorrento) (5)
Traces (19)
True Love (13)
True Love Is Greater Than Friendship (22)
Two Different Worlds (12)
Unchained Melody (15)
Until It's Time For You To Go (19)
Vaya Con Dios (4)
Vurria (I Would Like) (5)
Walk Away (16)
Walkin' In The Sand (And The Seasons Come And Go) (24)
Watch What Happens (17)
Way It Used To Be (19)
We Could (7) *41*
What Kind Of Girl Are You (17)
What Now, My Love (9)
Whatever Happened (Baby) To You And I (21)
Wheel Of Hurt (14) *59*
Where Do You Go (22)
White Rose Of Athens (10)
Who Can I Turn To (When Nobody Needs Me) (12)
Wiederseh'n (11) *57*
With All My Heart (19)
Woman In Love (14)
Words (21)
Year Ago Tonight (6)
Yesterday (16)
Yesterday, When I Was Young (20)
You Always Hurt The One You Love (3)
You Can't Hide The Truth (From Your Eyes) (4)
You Don't Know Me (7)
You Hurt Me (11)
You Win Again (2)
You'll Never Know (8)
You're All The Woman That I Need (21)
You're Breaking My Heart (23)

MARVELETTES, The

R&B group from Inkster High School, Inkster, Michigan. Formed in 1960 by Gladys Horton, with Georgeanna Marie Tillman Gordon (married Billy Gordon of The Contours), Wanda Young (married Bobby Rogers of The Miracles), Katherine Anderson and Juanita Cowart. Young and Horton both sang lead. Cowart left in 1962. Gordon left in 1965; died on 1/6/80 of lupus. Horton left in 1967, replaced by Anne Bogan (later a member of Love, Peace & Happiness and New Birth). Disbanded in 1969. Also recorded as The Darnells.

DEBUT DATE	PEAK POS	WKS CHR	GOLD		$	Label & Number
3/19/66	84	16		1 Greatest Hits	[G] $25	Tamla 253
4/8/67	129	8		2 The Marvelettes	$25	Tamla 274

As Long As I Know He's Mine (1) *47*
Barefootin' (2)
Beechwood 4-5789 (1) *17*
Danger Heartbreak Dead Ahead (1) *61*

Day You Take One (You Have To Take The Other) (2)
Don't Mess With Bill (1) *7*
Forever (1) *78*
He Was Really Sayin' Somethin' (2)

Hunter Gets Captured By The Game (2) *13*
I Can't Turn Around (2)
I Know Better (2)
I Need Someone (2)
Keep Off, No Trespassing (2)
Locking Up My Heart (1) *44*

Message To Michael (2)
Playboy (1) *7*
Please Mr. Postman (1) *1*
Strange I Know (1) *49*
This Night Was Made For Love (2)

Too Many Fish In The Sea (1) *25*
Twistin' Postman (1) *34*
When I Need You (2)
When You're Young And In Love (2) *23*
You're My Remedy (1) *48*

MARX, Groucho

Born Julius Henry Marx on 10/2/1890 in New York City; died on 8/19/77. Popular TV/film comedian.

DEBUT DATE	PEAK POS	WKS CHR			$	Label & Number
10/11/69	155	3		1 The Marx Bros. (The Original Voice Tracks From Their Greatest Movies)	[C] $12	Decca 79168

THE MARX BROTHERS
narration by Gary Owens

DEBUT DATE	PEAK POS	WKS CHR			$	Label & Number
11/25/72+	160	15		2 An Evening With Groucho	[C] $15	A&M 3515 [2]

transcription of his one-man concert tour; no track titles listed on this album

Chico In Recital (1)

Collected Speeches Of Groucho (1)

Groucho Marx Does His Thing (1)

Implausible Chico (1)
Inimitable Groucho (1)

Meet The Brothers Marx (1)
Sounds Of Harpo (1)

Zaniness Of The Marx Brothers (1)

462

DEBUT DATE	PEAK POS	WKS CHR	GOLD	ARTIST — Album Title	$	Label & Number

MARX, Richard
Born on 9/16/63 in Chicago. Pop-rock singer/songwriter. Professional jingle singer since age five. Backing singer for Lionel Richie. Co-wrote Kenny Rogers' hit "What About Me." On 1/8/89, married Cynthia Rhodes, lead singer of Animotion.

DEBUT DATE	PEAK POS	WKS CHR	GOLD	ARTIST — Album Title	$	Label & Number
6/20/87+	8	86	▲²	1 Richard Marx	$8	EMI-Man. 53049
5/20/89	1¹	66	▲³	2 Repeat Offender	$8	EMI 90380
11/23/91+	35	59	▲	3 Rush Street	$12	Capitol 95874

Angelia (2) 4
Big Boy Now (3)
Calling You (3)
Chains Around My Heart (3) 44
Children Of The Night (2) 13
Don't Mean Nothing (1) 3

Endless Summer Nights (1) 2
Flame Of Love (1)
Hands In Your Pocket (3)
Have Mercy (1)
Hazard (3) 9
Heart On The Line (2)
Heaven Only Knows (1)

Hold On To The Nights (1) 1
I Get No Sleep (3)
If You Don't Want My Love (2)
Keep Coming Back (3) 12
Lonely Heart (1)
Love Unemotional (3)

Nothin' You Can Do About It (2)
Playing With Fire (3)
Real World (2)
Remember Manhattan (1)
Rhythm Of Life (1)
Right Here Waiting (1) 1
Satisfied (2) 1

Should've Known Better (1) 3
Streets Of Pain (3)
Superstar (3)
Take This Heart (3) 20
Too Late To Say Goodbye (2) 12
Wait For The Sunrise (2)

Your World (3)

MARY JANE GIRLS
Female "funk & roll" quartet: Joanne McDuffie, Candice Ghant, Kim Wuletich and Yvette Marina. Formed and produced by Rick James. Marina is the daughter of disco singer Pattie Brooks.

DEBUT DATE	PEAK POS	WKS CHR	GOLD	ARTIST — Album Title	$	Label & Number
5/14/83	56	41	●	1 Mary Jane Girls	$8	Gordy 6040
3/16/85	18	38		2 Only Four You	$8	Gordy 6092

All Night Long (1)
Boys (1)
Break It Up (2)

Candy Man (1)
Girlfriend (2)
I Betcha (1)

In My House (2) 7
Jealousy (1)
Leather Queen (2)

Lonely For You (2)
Musical Love (1)
On The Inside (1)

Prove It (1)
Shadow Lover (2)

Wild And Crazy Love (2) 42
You Are My Heaven (1)

MAS, Carolyne
Rock singer/guitarist from the Bronx, New York.

DEBUT DATE	PEAK POS	WKS CHR	GOLD	ARTIST — Album Title	$	Label & Number
9/22/79	172	3		Carolyne Mas	$8	Mercury 3783

Baby Please
Call Me (Crazy To)

Do You Believe I Love You
It's No Secret

Never Two Without Three
Quote Goodbye Quote

Sadie Says
Sittin' In The Dark

Snow
Stillsane 71

MASEKELA, Hugh
Born Hugh Ramapolo Masekela on 4/4/39 in Wilbank, South Africa. Trumpeter/bandleader/arranger. Played trumpet since age 14. To England in 1959; New York City in 1960. Formed own band in 1964. Married to Miriam Makeba from 1964-66.

DEBUT DATE	PEAK POS	WKS CHR	GOLD	ARTIST — Album Title	$	Label & Number
8/5/67	151	10		1 Hugh Masekela's Latest	$12	Uni 73010
1/6/68	90	10		2 Hugh Masekela Is Alive And Well At The Whisky [L]	$12	Uni 73015
6/8/68	17	22		3 The Promise of a Future	$12	Uni 73028
3/29/69	195	2		4 Masekela	$12	Uni 73041
9/28/74	149	4		5 I Am Not Afraid	$10	Blue Thumb 6015
8/9/75	132	9		6 The Boy's Doin' It	$10	Casablanca 7017
2/11/78	65	19		7 Herb Alpert/Hugh Masekela [I]	$8	Horizon 728

HERB ALPERT/HUGH MASEKELA

African Secret Society (5)
African Summer (7)
Ain't No Mountain High Enough (3)
Almost Seedless (3)
Arrastao (1)
Ashiko (6)
Baby, Baby, Baby (1)
Bajabula Bonke (The Healing Song) (3)
Been Such A Long Time Gone (5)
Blues For Huey (4)

Boeremusiek (4)
Boy's Doin' It (6)
Coincidence (2)
Excuse Me Please (6)
Extra Added Attraction (4)
Fuzz (4)
Gafsa (4)
Gold (4)
Grazing In The Grass (3) 1
Groove Me (1)
Ha Lese Le Di Khanna (2)
Happy Hanna (7)
Head Peepin' (4)

Here, There And Everywhere (1)
I Just Wasn't Meant For These Times (1)
I'll Be There For You (7)
If There's Anybody Out There (4)
In The Jungle (6)
In The Market Place (5)
Jungle Jim (5)
Lily The Fox (4)
Little Miss Sweetness (2)
Lobo (7)

MRA (Christopher Columbus) (2)
Mace And Grenades (4)
Madonna (3)
Mago (1)
Mama (6)
Mazeze (1)
Moonza (7)
Night In Tunisia (5)
Nina (5)
No Face, No Name And No Number (3)
Otis (4)

Person Is A Sometime Thing (6)
Reza (Laia Ladaia) (1)
Ring Bell (7)
Riot (4) 55
Senor Coraza (2)
Skokiaan (7)
Sobukwe (4)
Society's Child (Baby I've Been Thinking) (1)
Son Of Ice Bag (4)
Stimela (Coaltrain) (5)
Stop (3)

There Are Seeds To Sow (3)
Thula (1)
Up-Up And Away (2) 71
Vuca (Wake Up) (3)
Whiter Shade Of Pale (2)

MASKED MARAUDERS, The
Canadian group masquerading as Bob Dylan, Mick Jagger, John Lennon and Paul McCartney.

DEBUT DATE	PEAK POS	WKS CHR	GOLD	ARTIST — Album Title	$	Label & Number
1/3/70	114	12		The Masked Marauders	$18	Deity 6378

Book Of Love
Cow Pie
Duke Of Earl

I Am The Japanese Sandman (Rang Tang Ding Dong)

I Can't Get No Nookie Later

More Or Less Hudson's Bay Again

Saturday Night At The Cow Palace

Season Of The Witch

MASON, Barbara
Born on 8/9/47 in Philadelphia. First recorded for Crusader in 1964. Wrote all of her Arctic hits.

DEBUT DATE	PEAK POS	WKS CHR	GOLD	ARTIST — Album Title	$	Label & Number
10/2/65	129	8		1 Yes, I'm Ready	$20	Arctic 1000
2/3/73	95	12		2 Give Me Your Love	$10	Buddah 5117
2/22/75	187	2		3 Love's The Thing	$10	Buddah 5628

Bed And Board (2) 70
Come See About Me (1)
Come To Me (1)
Everything I Own (2)
From His Woman To You (3) 28
Girls Have Feelings Too (1)

Give Me Your Love (2) 31
Got To Get You Off My Mind (1)
(He Wants) The Two Of Us (3)
I Call Out Your Name (3)
Keep Him (1)
Let Me In Your Life (2)

Misty (1)
Moon River (1)
One-Two-Three (You Her Or Me) (3)
Out Of This World (2)
Sad, Sad Girl (1) 27
Shackin' Up (3) 91

So He's Yours Now (3)
Something You Got (1)
(There's) One Man Between Us (3)
Trouble Child (1)
What Am I Gonna Do (3)
What Do You Say (3)

When I Fall In Love (2)
Who Will You Hurt Next (2)
Yes, I'm Ready (1,2) 5
You Can Be With The One You Don't Love (2)
You Got What It Takes (1)
Your Sweet Love (3)

★★249★★ MASON, Dave
Born on 5/10/46 in Worcester, England. Vocalist/composer/guitarist. Original member of Traffic from March-December 1967 and from June-October 1968. Joined Delaney & Bonnie for a short time in 1970.

DEBUT DATE	PEAK POS	WKS CHR	GOLD	ARTIST — Album Title	$	Label & Number
7/4/70	22	25	●	1 Alone Together	$12	Blue Thumb 19
				with guests Leon Russell, Jim Capaldi, Rita Coolidge and Delaney & Bonnie		
3/13/71	49	7		2 Dave Mason & Cass Elliot	$15	Blue Thumb 25
				DAVE MASON & CASS ELLIOT		
2/26/72	51	14		3 Headkeeper [L]	$12	Blue Thumb 34
				side 1: studio; side 2: live		
4/21/73	116	11		4 Dave Mason is Alive! [L]	$12	Blue Thumb 54

DEBUT DATE	PEAK POS	WKS CHR	GOLD	ARTIST — Album Title	$	Label & Number
				MASON, Dave — Cont'd		
11/10/73	50	28		5 It's Like You Never Left	$10	Columbia 31721
				with guests Graham Nash and Stevie Wonder		
6/29/74	183	9		6 The Best Of Dave Mason .... [G]	$10	Blue Thumb 6013
11/2/74	25	25	●	7 Dave Mason	$10	Columbia 33096
3/22/75	133	3		8 Dave Mason At His Best .... [K]	$10	Blue Thumb 880
				same as album #6 except for one song		
10/18/75	27	17		9 Split Coconut	$10	Columbia 33698
				with guests The Manhattan Transfer, David Crosby and Graham Nash		
11/27/76+	78	17		10 Certified Live .... [L]	$10	Columbia 34174 [2]
4/30/77	37	49	●	11 Let It Flow	$8	Columbia 34680
7/1/78	41	19	●	12 Mariposa de Oro	$8	Columbia 35285
				title is Spanish for Gold Butterfly		
10/28/78	179	4		13 Very Best Of Dave Mason .... [K]	$8	Blue Thumb 6032
6/14/80	74	10		14 Old Crest On A New Wave	$8	Columbia 36144

All Along The Watchtower (7,10)
All Gotta Go Sometime (12)
Baby...Please (5)
Bird On The Wind (13)
Bring It On Home To Me (7,10)
Can't Stop Worrying, Can't Stop Loving (1,3,6,8,13)
Crying, Waiting, Hoping (9)
Don't It Make You Wonder (12)
Every Woman (5,7,10)
Feelin' Alright? (3,4,10,13)
Get Ahold On Love (7)
Get It Right (14)
Gimme Some Lovin' (13)
Give Me A Reason Why (9,10)
Glittering Facade (2)
Goin' Down Slow (10)
Gotta Be On My Way (14)
Harmony & Melody (7)
Headkeeper (3,5,8,13)
Heartache, A Shadow, A Lifetime (3,6,8)
Here We Go Again (2,3,6,8)
I'm Missing You (11)
If You've Got Love (5)
In My Mind (3,6,8)
It Can't Make Any Difference To Me (7)
It's Like You Never Left (5)
Just A Song (1,3,4,13)
Let It Go, Let It Flow (11) 45
Life Is A Ladder (14)
Lonely One (5)
Long Lost Friend (9)
Look At You Look At Me (1,4,6,8,10)
Maybe (5)
Misty Morning Stranger (5)
Mystic Traveler (11)
Next To You (1)
No Doubt About It (12)
Old Crest On A New Wave (14)
On And On (2)
Only You Know And I Know (1,4,6,8,10,13) 42
Paralyzed (14)
Pearly Queen (3,10,13)
Pleasing You (2)
Relation Ships (7)
Sad And Deep As You (1,4,10,13)
Save Me (14) 71
Save Your Love (9)
Searchin' (For A Feeling) (12)
Seasons (11)
Share Your Love (12)
She's A Friend (9)
Shouldn't Have Took More Than You Gave (1,4,6,8,13)
Show Me Some Affection (7,10)
Side Tracked (5)
Silent Partner (5)
Sit And Wonder (2)
So Good To Be Home (12)
So High (Rock Me Baby And Roll Me Away) (11) 89
Something To Make You Happy (2)
Spend Your Life With Me (11)
Split Coconut (9)
Sweet Music (9)
Take It To The Limit (10)
Takin' The Time To Find (11)
Talk To Me (14)
Then It's Alright (9)
To Be Free (2,3,6,8)
Too Much Truth, Too Much Love (2)
Tryin' To Get Back To You (14)
Two Guitar Lovers (9)
Waitin' On You (1,13)
Walk To The Point (2,4,6)
Warm And Tender Love (12)
Warm Desire (12)
We Just Disagree (11) 12
What Do We Got Here? (11)
Will You Still Love Me Tomorrow (12) 39
Words, The (1)
World In Changes (1,3,10,13)
You Can Lose It (9)
You Can't Take It When You Go (7)
You Just Have To Wait Now (11)
You're A Friend Of Mine (14)

MASON, Harvey

Born on 2/22/47 in Atlantic City, New Jersey. Drummer/percussionist. Much session and production work, including Esther Phillips, Herbie Hancock, Deodata, Shirley Brown and Stanley Clarke. Joined jazz quartet Fourplay in 1991.

DEBUT DATE	PEAK POS	WKS CHR	GOLD	ARTIST — Album Title	$	Label & Number
4/28/79	149	8		1 Groovin' You	$8	Arista 4227
5/30/81	186	3		2 M.V.P.	$8	Arista 4283

Don't Doubt My Lovin' (2)
Going Through The Motions (2)
Groovin' You (1)
Here Today, Gone Tomorrow (1)
How Does It Feel (2)
I'd Still Be There (1)
Kauai (1)
Never Give You Up (1)
On And On (2)
Race, The (1)
Say It Again (1)
Spell (2)
Universal Rhyme (2)
Wave (1)
We Can (1)
We Can Start Tonight (1)
You And Me (2)

MASON, Jackie

Born Jacob Maza on 6/9/31 in Sheboygan, Wisconsin. Comedian/actor. Was a Jewish rabbi in the early '60s.

DEBUT DATE	PEAK POS	WKS CHR	GOLD	ARTIST — Album Title	$	Label & Number
7/14/62	77	7		1 I'm The Greatest Comedian In The World Only Nobody Knows It Yet .... [C]	$18	Verve 15033
				no track titles listed on this album		
1/9/88	146	9		2 The World According To Me! .... [C]	$8	Warner 25603

Beverly Hills: Producers/Mercedes (2)
Jews And Gentiles (2)
One Man Show: Sex/Hookers/Psychiatry (2)
Soliloquy (2)
World And Politics: Armies/ Nationalities/Reagan And Other Great Men (2)

MASON, Nick

Born on 1/27/45 in Birmingham, England. Drummer of Pink Floyd.

DEBUT DATE	PEAK POS	WKS CHR	GOLD	ARTIST — Album Title	$	Label & Number
7/4/81	170	3		1 Nick Mason's Fictitious Sports	$8	Columbia 37307
8/31/85	154	5		2 Profiles .... [I]	$8	Columbia 40142
				NICK MASON & RICK FENN (guitarist of 10cc) vocals on 2 of 11 tracks		

And The Address (2)
At The End Of The Day (2)
Black Ice (2)
Boo To You Too (1)
Can't Get My Motor To Start (1)
Do Ya? (1)
Hot River (2)
I Was Wrong (1)
I'm A Mineralist (1)
Israel (2)
Lie For A Lie (2)
Malta (2)
Mumbo Jumbo (2)
Profiles Parts 1-3 (2)
Rhoda (2)
Siam (1)
Wervin' (1)
Zip Code (2)

MASON PROFFIT

Chicago country-rock band led by brothers Terry and John Talbot (now inspirational artists).

DEBUT DATE	PEAK POS	WKS CHR	GOLD	ARTIST — Album Title	$	Label & Number
4/17/71	177	8		1 Movin' Toward Happiness	$12	Happy Tiger 1019
11/6/71+	186	14		2 Last Night I Had The Strangest Dream ...	$10	Ampex 10138
5/19/73	198	5		3 Bareback Rider	$10	Warner 2704

Belfast (medley) (3)
Black September (medley) (3)
Children (3)
Cottonwood (3)
Dance Hall Girl (3)
Eugene Pratt (2)
Everybody Was Wrong (1)
Five Generations (3)
500 Men (2)
Flying Arrow (1)
Freedom (2)
Good Friend Of Mary's (1)
Hard Luck Woman (1)
He Loves Them (1)
Hokey Joe Pony (1)
Hope (1)
I Saw The Light (3)
In The Country (medley) (3)
Jewel (2)
Last Night I Had The Strangest Dream (2)
Let Me Know Where You're Goin' (1)
Lilly (3)
Melinda (1)
Michael Dodge (1)
Mother (2)
My Country (2)
Old Joe Clark (1)
Sail Away (3)
Setting The Woods On Fire (3)
Sparrow (medley) (3)
Stoney River (3)
To Be A Friend (3)
24 Hour Sweetheart (2)

MASS PRODUCTION

Ten-member, disco-funk group. Agnes "Tiny" Kelly and Larry Marshall, lead singers.

DEBUT DATE	PEAK POS	WKS CHR	GOLD	ARTIST — Album Title	$	Label & Number
1/8/77	142	10		1 Welcome To Our World	$8	Cotillion 9910
8/27/77	83	9		2 Believe	$8	Cotillion 9918
7/21/79	43	17		3 In The Purest Form	$8	Cotillion 5211
3/29/80	133	9		4 Massterpiece	$8	Cotillion 5218
5/16/81	166	6		5 Turn Up The Music	$8	Cotillion 5226

DEBUT DATE	PEAK POS	WKS CHR	GOLD	ARTIST — Album Title	$	Label & Number

MASS PRODUCTION — Cont'd

Angel (4)
Being Here (2)
Bopp (5)
Can't You See I'm Fired Up (3)
Clinch Quencher (5)
Come Back Hot (4)
Cosmic Lust (2)

Diamond Chips (5)
Eknuf (4)
Eyeballin' (3)
Firecracker (medley) (3) *43*
Forever (4)
Free And Happy (2)
Fun In The Sun (1)
Galaxy (1)

Gonna Make You Love Me (4)
I Believe In Music (2)
I Can't Believe You're Going Away (5)
I Got To Have Your Love (5)
I Like To Dance (1)
Just A Song (1)
Keep My Heart Together (2)

Love You (medley) (3)
Magic (1)
Nature Lover (4)
Next Year (3)
Our Thought (Purity) (3)
Our Thought (To The World) (1)
Our Thought (Tomorrow) (5)

People Get Up (2)
Please Don't Leave Me (4)
Saucey (5)
Shante (4)
Strollin' (3)
Sunshine (5)
Superlative (2)

Turn Up The Music (5)
We Love You (2)
Welcome To Our World (Of Merry Music) (1) *68*
Wine-Flow Disco (1)
With Pleasure (3)
Your Love (4)

MATERIAL ISSUE
Chicago pop trio: guitarist/vocalist Jim Ellison, bassist Ted Ansani and drummer Mike Zelenko.

| 3/16/91 | 86 | 11 | | International Pop Overthrow .... | $12 | Mercury 848155 |

Chance Of A Lifetime
Crazy
Diane

International Pop Overthrow
Li'l Christine
Out Right Now

Renee Remains The Same
There Was A Few

This Far Before
This Letter

Trouble
Valerie Loves Me

Very First Lie
Very Good Idea

MATHIESON, Muir
Born on 1/24/11 in Sterling, England; died on 8/2/75. Musical director of over 500 British films.

| 5/29/61 | 50 | 21 | | Gone With The Wind ....[I] | $20 | Warner 1322 |

newly recorded version of the Max Steiner original score

Ashley (medley)
Ashley And Melanie (Love Theme) (medley)

Belle Watling (medley)
Bonnie Blue Flag (medley)
Bonnie's Death (medley)

Bonnie's Theme (medley)
Invitation To The Dance (medley)
Prayer, The (medley)

Melanie's Theme (medley)
Oath, The (medley)
Return To Tara (medley)
Rhett Butler (medley)
Scarlet O'Hara (medley)

Scarlet's Agony (medley)
Tara's Theme (medley)
War (medley)

MATHIEU, Mireille
French female singer.

| 10/4/69 | 118 | 8 | | Mireille Mathieu ....[F] | $12 | Capitol 306 |

Celui Que J'Aime (The One I Love)
Ensemble (Sometimes)
Et Merci Quand Meme (And Thanks Just The Same)

Je Ne Suis Rien Sans Toi (I'm Coming Home)
Les Bicyclettes De Belsize (The Bicycles Of Belsize)

Quand Tu T'en Iras (Non Pensare A Me) (Don't Think Of Me)
Tous Les Amoureux (All The Loves)

Un Homme Et Une Femme (A Man And A Woman)

Une Rose Au Coeur De L'Hiver (If You Change Your Mind)

Viens Dans Ma Rue (Come To My Street)

★★★4★★ MATHIS, Johnny
Born on 9/30/35 in San Francisco. Studied opera from age 13. Track scholarship at the San Francisco State College. Invited to Olympic try-outs, chose singing career instead. Discovered by George Avakian of Columbia Records. To New York City in 1956. Initially recorded as jazz-styled singer. Columbia A&R executive Mitch Miller switched him to singing pop ballads, subsequently became young America's favorite MOR male vocalist.

DEBUT DATE	PEAK POS	WKS CHR	GOLD	ARTIST — Album Title	$	Label & Number
9/9/57	4	26		1 **Wonderful Wonderful**	$25	Columbia 1028
12/23/57+	2⁴	113	●	2 **Warm**	$25	Columbia 1078
4/7/58	10	12		3 **Good Night, Dear Lord**	$25	Columbia 1119
4/14/58	1³	490	▲	4 **Johnny's Greatest Hits** ....[G]	$25	Columbia 1133
9/8/58	6	16		5 **Swing Softly**	$25	Columbia 1165
2/9/59	4	96	●	6 **Open Fire, Two Guitars**	$25	Columbia 1270
7/27/59	2²	93	●	7 **More Johnny's Greatest Hits** ....[G]	$15	Columbia 1344
9/21/59	1⁵	295	▲	8 **Heavenly**	$15	Columbia 1351
1/18/60	2¹	75	●	9 **Faithfully**	$15	Columbia 8219
8/29/60	4	65		10 **Johnny's Mood**	$15	Columbia 8326
10/3/60	6	27		11 **The Rhythms And Ballads Of Broadway**	$20	Columbia 803 [2]
5/15/61	38	23		12 I'll Buy You A Star	$15	Columbia 8423
8/28/61	2⁷	63		13 **Portrait Of Johnny** ....[G]	$15	Columbia 8444
2/24/62	14	39		14 Live It Up!	$15	Columbia 8511
10/27/62	12	37		15 Rapture	$15	Columbia 8715
4/20/63	6	45		16 **Johnny's Newest Hits** ....[G]	$15	Columbia 8816
8/24/63	20	27		17 Johnny	$15	Columbia 8844
12/28/63+	23	27		18 Romantically	$15	Columbia 8898
2/15/64	13	28		19 Tender Is The Night	$15	Mercury 60890
5/9/64	35	16		20 I'll Search My Heart and Other Great Hits ....[K]	$15	Columbia 8943
7/25/64	75	10		21 The Wonderful World Of Make Believe	$15	Mercury 60913
8/1/64	88	10		22 The Great Years ....[G]	$15	Columbia 834 [2]
10/17/64	40	20		23 This Is Love	$15	Mercury 60942
3/20/65	52	11		24 Love Is Everything	$15	Mercury 60991
10/16/65	71	26		25 The Sweetheart Tree	$15	Mercury 61041
4/2/66	9	45		26 **The Shadow Of Your Smile**	$15	Mercury 61073
10/8/66+	50	18		27 So Nice	$15	Mercury 61091
4/1/67	103	11		28 Johnny Mathis Sings	$15	Mercury 61107
12/23/67+	60	20		29 Up, Up And Away	$15	Columbia 9526
4/13/68	26	40		30 Love Is Blue	$12	Columbia 9637
12/14/68+	60	21		31 Those Were The Days	$12	Columbia 9705
8/16/69	163	4		32 The Impossible Dream	$12	Columbia 9872
9/13/69	192	2		33 People	$12	Columbia 9871
9/20/69	52	24		34 Love Theme From "Romeo And Juliet"	$12	Columbia 9909
4/4/70	38	26		35 Raindrops Keep Fallin' On Your Head	$12	Columbia 1005
10/10/70	61	9		36 Close To You	$12	Columbia 30210
1/23/71	169	7		37 Johnny Mathis sings the music of Bacharach & Kaempfert	$12	Columbia 30350 [2]
3/13/71	47	18		38 Love Story	$12	Columbia 30499
9/4/71	80	10		39 You've Got A Friend	$12	Columbia 30740

DEBUT DATE	PEAK POS	WKS CHR	GOLD	ARTIST — Album Title	$	Label & Number
				MATHIS, Johnny — Cont'd		
2/5/72	128	7		40 Johnny Mathis In Person ....[L]	$12	Columbia 30979 [2]
				recorded at Caesar's Palace in Las Vegas		
6/10/72	71	15		41 The First Time Ever (I Saw Your Face)................	$12	Columbia 31342
6/24/72	141	15	▲	42 Johnny Mathis' All-Time Greatest Hits ....[G]	$12	Columbia 31345 [2]
10/21/72	83	18		43 Song Sung Blue	$12	Columbia 31626
2/17/73	83	14		44 Me And Mrs. Jones	$10	Columbia 32114
6/30/73	120	7		45 Killing Me Softly With Her Song	$10	Columbia 32258
11/17/73+	115	22		46 I'm Coming Home	$10	Columbia 32435
12/28/74+	139	7		47 The Heart Of A Woman	$10	Columbia 33251
4/19/75	99	13		48 When Will I See You Again	$10	Columbia 33420
11/8/75+	97	21	●	49 Feelings..	$10	Columbia 33887
6/26/76	79	15		50 I Only Have Eyes For You	$10	Columbia 34117
3/19/77	139	5		51 Mathis Is..	$10	Columbia 34441
4/1/78	9	24	▲	52 **You Light Up My Life**	$8	Columbia 35259
7/29/78	19	16	●	53 That's What Friends Are For	$8	Columbia 35435
				JOHNNY MATHIS & DENIECE WILLIAMS		
2/24/79	122	7		54 The Best Days Of My Life	$8	Columbia 35649
8/9/80	164	5		55 Different Kinda Different...........................	$8	Columbia 36505
12/27/80+	140	7		56 The Best Of Johnny Mathis 1975-1980 ....[G]	$8	Columbia 36871
7/25/81	173	4		57 The First 25 Years - The Silver Anniversary Album ...[G]	$8	Columbia 37440 [2]
5/8/82	147	9		58 Friends In Love	$10	Columbia 37748
3/10/84	157	19		59 A Special Part Of Me	$8	Columbia 38718
1/10/87	197	2		60 The Hollywood Musicals	$8	Columbia 40372
				JOHNNY MATHIS & HENRY MANCINI		
1/11/92	189	1		61 Better Together - The Duet Album	$12	Columbia 47982
				duets with Deniece Williams, Dionne Warwick, Take 6 and others		
				CHRISTMAS ALBUM:		
12/15/58+	3	4	▲²	62 **Merry Christmas** ....[X]	$25	Columbia 1195
12/21/59+	10	3		63 **Merry Christmas** ....[X-R]	$15	Columbia 1195
12/26/60	10	2		64 **Merry Christmas** ....[X-R]	$15	Columbia 8021
12/18/61+	31	7		65 Merry Christmas ....[X-R]	$15	Columbia 8021
12/8/62	12	4		66 Merry Christmas ....[X-R]	$15	Columbia 8021
				Christmas charts: 2/'63, 2/'64, 7/'65, 2/'66, 2/'67, 5/'68, 15/'69, 3/'73, 18/'88, 20/'89, 16/'90, 17/'91, 12/'92		

Ace In The Hole (14)
Affair To Remember (Our Love Affair) (24)
Alfie (35,37)
Alice In Wonderland (21)
All Is Well (13)
All I Ever Need (52)
All That Is Missing (18)
All The Sad Young Men (20)
All The Things You Are (57)
All The Time (4,42) *21*
All Through The Night (1)
Alone Again (Naturally) (43)
And Her Mother Came Too (40)
And I Love You So (45)
And I Think That's What I'll Do (46)
And This Is My Beloved (9)
April In Paris (10,40)
April Love (19)
Aquarius (medley) (34)
Arianne (45)
Arrivederci Roma (25)
As Long As We're Together (51)
As Time Goes By (54,57)
At The Crossroads (29)
Aubrey (45)
Autumn In New York (18)
Autumn Leaves (25,33)
Ave Maria *[includes 2 versions]* (3)
Baby, Baby, Baby (2)
Baby's Born (46)
Baubles, Bangles And Beads (27)
Begin The Beguine (54,57)
Best Days Of My Life (54,56)
Best Is Yet To Come (12,59)
Best Of Everything (20) *62*
Betcha By Golly Wow (41)
Better Together (61)
Beyond The Blue Horizon (21)
Beyond The Sea (La Mer) (21)
Blue Christmas (62)
Blue Gardenia (9)
Bottom Line (54)
Break Up To Make Up (45)
Brian's Song (41)

Bridge Over Troubled Water (35)
But Beautiful (medley) (60)
By Myself (2)
By The Time I Get To Phoenix (30)
Bye Bye Blackbird (6)
Call Me (7) *21*
Call Me Irresponsible (19)
Camelot (21)
Can't Get Out Of This Mood (5,22)
Carnival, Theme From (18)
Certain Smile (7,22,42) *14*
Chances Are (4,22,40,42,57) *1*
Cherie (13)
Christmas Song (Merry Christmas To You) (62)
Clock Without Hands (20)
Clopin Clopant (25)
Cock-Eyed Optimist (11)
Come Back To Me (26)
Come Ride The Wind With Me (24)
Come Runnin' (40)
Come Saturday Morning (36)
Come To Me (4,42) *22*
(Corcovado) ..see: Quiet Nights of Quiet Stars
Corner Of The Sky (44)
Corner To Corner (10)
Crazy In The Heart (14)
Crazy World (60)
Dancing In The Dark (24)
Dancing On The Ceiling (11)
Danke Schoen (37)
Danny Boy (37)
Day In Day Out (1,40)
Deep Purple (55,57)
Deep River (3,22)
Didn't We (34,57)
Different Kinda Different (55)
Do Me Wrong, But Do Me (50)
(Do You Know Where You're Going To) Theme From Mahogany (50)
Don't Blame Me (11)
Don't Go Breakin' My Heart (30,37)

Don't Let Me Be Lonely Tonight (44)
Don't Stay (37)
Dream, Dream, Dream (21)
Dream Is A Wish Your Heart Makes (19)
Dreamy (medley) (40)
Drifting (19)
Dulcinea (27,40)
Each Time We Kiss (20)
Early Autumn (1)
Easy Does It (1)
Easy To Say (But So Hard To Do) (5)
Eleanor Rigby (28,32)
Eli Eli (3)
Elusive Butterfly (27,33)
Embraceable You (6)
Emotion (52)
End Of A Love Affair (23)
End Of The World (31)
Every Step Of The Way (20,22) *30*
Every Time I Dream Of You (31)
Every Time You Touch Me (I Get High) (50)
Everybody's Talkin' (35)
Everything Is Beautiful (36)
Everything's Coming Up Roses (11)
Evil Ways (36)
Faithfully (9,37)
Fantastic (23)
Far Above Cayuga's Waters (29)
Feel Like Makin' Love (47)
Feelings (49)
59th Street Bridge Song (Feelin' Groovy) (31)
First Noel (62)
First Time Ever (I Saw Your Face) (41)
Flame Of Love (7)
Fly Me To The Moon (In Other Words) (22)
Folks Who Live On The Hill (10)
Follow Me (9)
Foolish (46)
For All We Know (39)

For The Good Times (38)
Forget Me Not (19)
Friendly Persuasion (Thee I Love) (18)
Friends In Love (58,61) *38*
Fun To Be Fooled (11)
Get Me To The Church On Time (5)
Getting To Know You (18)
Gina (16,22,42) *6*
Go Away Little Girl (24,32)
Godfather, Love Theme From The (41)
Gone, Gone, Gone (54,56)
Good Morning Heartache (45)
Good Night, Dear Lord (3)
Goodbye To Love (43)
Goodnight My Love (10)
Got You Where I Want You (58)
Greatest Gift (49)
Guys And Dolls (11)
Handful Of Stars (2)
Happy (44)
He Ain't Heavy...He's My Brother (43)
Heart Of A Woman (47)
Heaven Must Have Made You Just For Me (51)
Heaven Must Have Sent You (53)
Heavenly (8,37)
Hello, Young Lovers (8)
Help Me Make It Through The Night (39)
Here I'll Stay (15)
Here, There And Everywhere (30)
Hey, Look Me Over (14)
Hey Love (13)
Hi-Lili, Hi-Lo (18)
Honey Come Back (35)
House For Sale (47)
House Of Flowers (21)
How Can I Be Sure (43)
How Can I Make It On My Own (54)
How Can You Mend A Broken Heart? (39)
How Deep Is Your Love (52)

How High The Moon (10)
How To Handle A Woman (13,22) *64*
Hung Up In The Middle Of Love (51)
Hungry Years (50)
Hurry! It's Lovely Up Here (27)
Hurry Mother Nature (49)
I Am In Love (11)
I Can't Believe That You're In Love With Me (17)
I Can't Give You Anything But Love (19)
I Concentrate On You (6)
I Could Have Danced All Night (11)
I Don't Want To Say No (51)
I Dream Of You (27)
I Got Love (40)
I Had The Craziest Dream (60)
I Have Dreamed (11)
I Heard A Forest Praying (3)
I Just Can't Get Over You (53)
I Just Found Out About Love (11)
I Just Wanted To Be Me (46)
(I Left My Heart) In San Francisco (26)
I Look At You (4)
I Love Her That's Why (16)
I Love You (17)
I Married An Angel (11)
I Need You (41)
I Only Have Eyes For You (50)
I Remember You And Me (58)
I Say A Little Prayer (30,37)
I Thought Of You Last Night (29)
I Was Born In Love With You (medley) (44)
I Was Telling Her About You (15)
I Was There (38)
I Will Survive (55)
I Will Wait For You (27,32)
I Wish I Were In Love Again (11)

I Wish I Love You (28)
I Won't Cry Anymore (29)
I Won't Dance (14)
I Won't Last A Day Without You (medley) (48)
I Write The Songs (50)
I Wrote A Symphony On My Guitar (52)
I'd Rather Be Here With You (46)
I'll Be Easy To Find (8)
I'll Be Home For Christmas (62)
I'll Be Seeing You (6)
I'll Buy You A Star (12)
I'll Close My Eyes (25)
I'll Do It All For You (55)
I'll Make You Happy (51)
I'll Never Be Lonely Again (16)
I'll Never Fall In Love Again (34,37)
I'll Search My Heart (20) *90*
I'm Always Chasing Rainbows (21)
I'm Coming Home (46,57) *75*
I'm Glad There Is You (2)
I'm Gonna Laugh You Out Of My Life (10)
I'm In Love For The Very First Time (26)
I'm In The Mood For Love (10)
I'm Just A Boy In Love (6)
I'm So Lost (10)
I'm Stone In Love With You (44)
I've Got The World On A String (16)
I've Grown Accustomed To Her Face (2)
If (39)
If I Could Reach You (44)
If There's A Way (37)
If We Only Have Love (39,40,42)
If You Believe (52)
If You Could Read My Mind (39)

466

MATHIS, Johnny — Cont'd

(If You Let Me Make Love To You Then) Why Can't I Touch You? (36)
Impossible Dream (27,32,40)
In Return (10)
In The Morning (40)
In The Still Of The Night (6,61)
In The Wee Small Hours Of The Morning (1)
In Wisconsin (18)
Isn't It A Pity (11)
It Came Upon The Midnight Clear (62)
It Could Happen To You (1,60)
It Doesn't Have To Hurt Everytime (57)
It Might As Well Be Spring (60)
It Was Almost Like A Song (52)
It's All In The Game (61)
It's De-Lovely (5)
It's Gone (47)
It's Impossible (38)
It's Not For Me To Say (4,22,40,42,57) **5**
It's Only A Paper Moon (18)
It's Too Late (39)
Jean (35)
Jenny (13)
Joey, Joey, Joey (17)
Johnny One Note (14)
Joy Of Loving You (20)
Jump For Joy (17)
Just Friends (14)
Just Move Along, Meadow Lark (23)
Just Once In My Life (medley) (44)
Just The Way You Are (53,56)
Killing Me Softly With Her Song (45)
Kol Nidre (3)
Lady (37)
Lady Sings The Blues ..see: Happy
Lady Smiles (37)
Lament (Love, I Found You Gone) (15)
Lara's Theme ..see: Somewhere, My Love
(Last Night) I Didn't Get To Sleep At All (41)
Last Time I Felt Like This (54,56,61)
Lately (58)
Laughter In The Rain (48)
Laura (19,33)
Lead Me To Your Love (59)
Lean On Me (43)
Let It Rain (7)
Let Me Be The One (medley) (48)
Let Me Love You (1)
Let The Sunshine In (medley) (44)
Let's Do It (11)
Let's Love (7) **44**
Let's Misbehave (11)
Life And Breath (41)
Life Is A Song Worth Singing (46) **54**
Life Is What You Make It (41)
Light My Fire (31)
Lights Of Rio (55)
Like Someone In Love (5)
Limehouse Blues (23)
Little Green Apples (31)
Live For Life (34)
Live It Up (14)
Long Ago (And Far Away) (24,39,60)
Long And Winding Road (36)
Look Of Love (30,37)
Looking At You (1)
Loss Of Love (38)
Lost In Loveliness (15)
Love (14,37)

Love Eyes (11)
Love Is A Gamble (11)
Love Is Blue (30)
Love Is Everything (24)
Love Look Away (12,22)
Love Me As Though There Were No Tomorrow (15)
Love Me Tonight (34)
Love Nest (15)
Love Never Felt So Good (59)
Love Story ..see: (Where Do I Begin)
Love Walked In (5)
Love Without Words (55)
Love Won't Let Me Wait (59,61)
Lovely Things You Do (2)
Lovely Way To Spend An Evening (8)
Lovers In New York (28)
Loving You - Losing You (51)
Lullaby Of Love (51)
Magic Garden (12)
Main Title From Same Time, Next Year ..see: Last Time I Felt Like This
Make It Easy On Yourself (43)
Man And A Woman (35)
Man Of La Mancha (I, Don Quixote) (27)
Mandy (48)
Maria (9,22,40,42) **78**
Marianna (16) **86**
May The Good Lord Bless And Keep You (3)
Me And Mrs. Jones (44)
Me For You, You For Me (53)
Melinda (26)
Memories Don't Leave Like People Do (47)
Memory (58)
Michelle (26)
Midnight Blue (49)
Midnight Cowboy (35)
Miracles (17)
Mirage (25)
Misty (8,22,40,42,57) **12**
Misty Roses (29,42)
Moanin' Low (11)
Moment To Moment (26,32)
Moments Like This (15)
Mondo Cane ..see: More
Moon River (30)
Moonlight Becomes You (8,60)
Moonlight In Vermont (18)
More (23,33)
More I See You (29)
More Than You Know (8)
Morningside Of The Mountain (29)
Most Beautiful Girl In The World (17)
Music That Makes Me Dance (27)
My Darling, My Darling (15)
My Favorite Dream (20)
My Funny Valentine (6,42)
My Heart And I (12)
My Love For You (13) **47**
My One And Only Love (2)
My Romance (11)
My Sweet Lord (38)
Neither One Of Us (Wants To Be The First To Say Goodbye) (45)
Never Can Say Goodbye (39)
Never Givin' Up On You (55)
Never Let Me Go (24)
Never My Love (30)
Never Never Land (17)
Nice To Be Around (48)
99 Miles From L.A. (49,56)
No Love (But Your Love) (4) **21**
No Man Can Stand Alone (17)
No Strings (19)
Nobody Knows (How Much I Love You) (9)

Nothing Between Us But Love (57)
O Holy Night (62)
Odds And Ends (35,37)
Oh How I Try (12)
Oh That Feeling (13)
On A Clear Day You Can See Forever (26,32) **98**
On A Cold And Rainy Day (14)
On The Sunny Side Of The Street (11)
Once (10)
One Day In Your Life (49)
One God (3)
One Look (16)
One Love (59)
One More Mountain (24)
One Starry Night (9)
1000 Blue Bubbles (24)
Only You (And You Alone) (48)
Ooh What We Do (50)
Open Fire (6)
Over The Weekend (23)
Paradise (55)
Party's Over (11)
People (24,33)
Pieces Of Dreams (36)
Play Me (43)
Please Be Kind (6)
Poinciana (Song Of The Tree) (23)
Poor Butterfly (17)
Priceless (59)
Put On A Happy Face (23)
(Quest, The) ..see: Impossible Dream
Quiet Girl (16)
Quiet Nights Of Quiet Stars (26,33)
Raindrops Keep Fallin' On My Head (35)
Rapture (15)
Ready Or Not (53,57)
Remember (44)
Remember When (We Made These Memories) (7)
Ride On A Rainbow (8)
Right Here And Now (59)
Ring The Bell (12)
Riviera, The (14)
Romeo And Juliet (A Time For Us), Love Theme From (34,40,42,57) **96**
Rosary, The (31)
Rose Garden (38)
Run To Me (43)
Sail On White Moon (67)
Same Time, Next Year ..see: Last Time I Felt Like This
Sandpiper, Love Theme From The ..see: Shadow Of Your Smile
Sands Of Time (21)
Saturday Sunshine (28)
Second Time Around (28)
Secret Love (9)
Send In The Clowns (50)
September Song (18,22)
Shadow Of Your Smile (26,33)
Shangri-La (21)
Ship Without A Sail (19)
Should I Wait (Or Should I Run To Her) (13)
Show And Tell (45)
Silent Night, Holy Night (62)
Silver Bells (62)
Simple (59) **81**
Since I Fell For You (41)
Sing (45)
Sky Full Of Rainbows (21)
Skye Boat Song (Scotch Folk Song) (25)
Sleigh Ride (62)
Small World (7,22,42) **20**
Smile (5)
So Nice (Summer Samba) (27,32)
Solitaire (49)

Someone (7) **35**
Somethin's Goin' On (58)
Something (35)
Something I Dreamed Last Night (8)
Something's Coming (26)
Somewhere (19)
Somewhere, My Love (28,32)
Song Of Joy (36)
Song Sung Blue (43)
Sooner Or Later (20) **84**
Soul And Inspiration (medley) (44)
Sound Of Music (18)
Spanish Eyes (37)
(Speak Softly Love) ..see: Godfather, Love Theme From The
Spring Is Here (11)
Stairway To The Sea (7)
Stairway To The Stars (12,22)
Starbright (13,20) **25**
Stardust (49,57)
Stars Fell On Alabama (15)
Stay Warm (10)
Stella By Starlight (15,22)
Stop Look And Listen To Your Heart (46)
Story Of Our Love (13) **93**
Stranger In Paradise (9)
Strangers In Dark Corners (47)
Strangers In The Night (28,32,37)
Street Of Dreams (21)
Sudden Love (12)
Summer Breeze (44)
Summer Me, Winter Me (medley) (44)
Summer Of '42 (The Summer Knows), Theme From (41)
(Summer Samba) ..see: So Nice
Sunny (28,33)
Sweet Child (46)
Sweet Lorraine (5)
Sweet Love Of Mine (51)
Sweet Surrender (44)
Sweet Thursday (16,22) **99**
Sweetheart Tree (25)
Swing Low, Sweet Chariot (3)
Symphony (25)
Taking A Chance On Love (11,60)
Taste Of Honey (26)
Teacher, Teacher (7) **21**
Temptation (55)
Ten Times Forever More (38)
Tender Is The Night (19)
Tenderly (6)
That Old Black Magic (1)
That's All (8)
That's All She Wrote (49)
That's The Way It Is (16)
That's What Friends Are For (53)
Then I'll Be Tired Of You (12)
There Goes My Heart (2)
There! I've Said It Again (57)
There You Are (16,54)
(There's) Always Something There To Remind Me (28)
There's No You (10)
They Long To Be Close To You (36,40)
They Say It's Wonderful (8)
Things I Might Have Been (48)
This Guy's In Love With You (31,37)
This Heart Of Mine (5)
This Is All I Ask (24)
This Is Love (25)
Those Were The Days (31)
Three Times A Lady (57)
Till Love Touches Your Life (52)
Time After Time (60)

(Time For Us) ..see: Romeo And Juliet
Times Will Change (37)
To Be In Love (A Fantastical Love Song) (5)
Tomorrow Song (19)
Tonight (9,22,40)
Too Close For Comfort (1)
Too Much, Too Little, Too Late (52,56,57,61) **1**
Too Much Too Soon (14)
Too Young (43)
Too Young To Go Steady (18)
Touch Of Your Lips (23)
Touching Me With Love (53)
Traces (38)
True Love (60)
Turn Around Look At Me (31)
Twelfth Of Never (4,22,40,42) **22**
Unaccustomed As I Am (16,22)
Under A Blanket Of Blue (23)
Until It's Time For You To Go (36)
Until You Come Back To Me (That's What I'm Gonna Do) (53)
Up, Up And Away (29)
Venus (30,42)
Very Much In Love (7)
Very Thought Of You (25,32)
Wake The Town And Tell The People (28)
Walk On By (30,37)
Warm (2,58)
Warm And Tender (4)
Warm And Willing (12)
Wasn't The Summer Short? (16) **89**
Watch What Happens (35)
Wave (36)
Way We Planned It (47)
Way We Were (48)
Way You Look Tonight (57)
We (34)
We Can Work It Out (39)
We're In Love (54)
We've Only Just Begun (38,40)
Weaver Of Dreams (17)
Wendy (47)
What Are You Doing The Rest Of Your Life (38)
What Child Is This (62)
What To Do You Do With The Love (58)
What Do You Feel In Your Heart (23)
What I Did For Love (49,56)
What Now My Love (27)
What The World Needs Now Is Love (27,33)
What To Do About Love (20)
What Will Mary Say (16,22,42) **9**
What'll I Do (2)
What's Forever For (58)
When A Child Is Born (50,56)
When I Am With You (4)
When I Fall In Love (6,22)
When I Look In Your Eyes (29)
When My Sugar Walks Down The Street (12)
When Sunny Gets Blue (4,40,42,57)
When The Lovin' Goes Out Of The Lovin' (58)
When The World Was Young (17)
When Will I See You Again (48)
When You Wish Upon A Star (1,60)
Where Are The Words (29)
Where Are You? (9)
Where Can I Go? (3)
(Where Do I Begin) Love Story (38,40,42)

Where Do You Think You're Going (9)
Where Is Love? (19)
Where Is The Love (43)
Where Or When (52)
Wherever You Are It's Spring (20)
While We're Young (2)
While You're Young (13)
Whistling Away The Dark (60)
White Christmas (62)
Who Can I Turn To? (28)
Who Can Say (28)
Who's Counting Heartaches (61)
Why Not (14)
Wild Is The Wind (4,40,42) **22**
Wildflower (45)
Will I Find My Love Today (1)
Windmills Of Your Mind (34)
Winter Wonderland (62)
With You I'm Born Again (55,56)
Without Her (34)
Without You (41)
Woman, Woman (47)
Wonderful Day Like Today (25,33)
Wonderful! Wonderful! (4,22,40,42,57) **14**
Wonderful World Of Make-Believe (21)
Wonderland By Night (37)
World I Threw Away (34)
World I Used To Know (31)
World Of Laughter (51)
Would You Like To Spend The Night With Me (54)
Year After Year (1)
Yellow Days (36)
Yellow Roses On Her Gown (50)
Yesterday (26)
Yesterday When I Was Young (34)
You And Me Against The World (48)
You Are Beautiful (7) **60**
You Are Everything To Me (7)
You Are The Sunshine Of My Life (45)
You Better Go Now (9)
You Brought Me Love (61)
You Do Something To Me (11)
You Hit The Spot (5)
You Light Up My Life (52,56)
You Love Me (23)
You Make Me Think About You (31)
You Set My Heart To Music (13)
You Stepped Out Of A Dream (1,60)
You'd Be So Nice To Come Home To (5)
You're A Lady (44)
You're A Special Part Of Me (59,61)
You're A Special Part Of My Life (53)
You're All I Need To Get By (53,61) **47**
You're As Right As Rain (48)
You've Come Home (15)
You've Got A Friend (39)
Young And Foolish (24)

MATLOCK, Matty — see HEINDORF, Ray, and WEBB, Jack

DEBUT DATE	PEAK POS	WKS CHR	G O L D	ARTIST — Album Title	$	Label & Number

MATTEA, Kathy
Born on 6/21/59 in Cross Lane, West Virginia. Country singer/guitarist. Toured with Bobby Goldsboro, Don Williams, Oak Ridge Boys and Gary Morris.

3/3/90	82	19	●	1 Willow In The Wind	$12	Mercury 836950
9/22/90	80	34	●	2 A Collection Of Hits ... [G]	$12	Mercury 842330
				Kathy's hits on the Country charts		
4/13/91	72	25		3 Time Passes By	$12	Mercury 846975
10/24/92	182	4		4 Lonesome Standard Time	$12	Mercury 512567

Amarillo (4)
Asking Us To Dance (3)
Battle Hymn Of Love (2)
Burnin' Old Memories (1)
Come From The Heart (1)
Eighteen Wheels And A Dozen Roses (2)
Few Good Things Remain (2,3)
Forgive And Forget (4)
From A Distance (3)
Goin' Gone (2)
Harley (3)
Here's Hopin' (1)
Hills Of Alabam' (1)
I Wear Your Love (3)
I'll Take Care Of You (1)
Last Night I Dreamed Of Loving You (4)
Life As We Knew It (2)
Listen To The Radio (4)
Lonely At The Bottom (4)
Lonesome Standard Time (4)
Love At The Five & Dime (2)
Love Chooses You (1)
Quarter Moon (3)
Ready For The Storm (4)
Seeds (4)
She Came From Fort Worth (1)
Slow Boat (4)
Standing Knee Deep In A River (Dying Of Thirst) (4)
Summer Of My Dreams (3)
33, 45, 78 (Record Time) (4)
Time Passes By (3)
Train Of Memories (2)
True North (1)
Untold Stories (2)
Walk The Way The Wind Blows (2)
What Could Have Been (3)
Where've You Been (1,2)
Whole Lotta Holes (3)
Willow In The Wind (1)

MATTHEWS, David
Born on 4/3/42 in Sonora, Kentucky. Jazz arranger/songwriter/pianist.

| 9/3/77 | 169 | 7 | | Dune ... [I] | $8 | CTI 5005 |
| | | | | with Hiram Bullock, Eric Gale, David Sanborn and Grover Washington, Jr. | | |

Dune Medley
Princess Leia's Theme
Silent Running
Space Oddity
Star Wars, Main Theme From

MATTHEWS, Ian
Born Ian Matthew MacDonald in Lincolnshire, England in June 1946. Founder of Fairport Convention and Matthews' Southern Comfort. From 1984-87, in A&R for Island and Windham Hill record labels.

4/17/71	72	15		1 Later That Same Year	$10	Decca 75264
				MATTHEWS' SOUTHERN COMFORT		
2/12/72	196	3		2 Tigers Will Survive	$10	Vertigo 1010
9/22/73	181	7		3 Valley Hi	$10	Elektra 75061
11/11/78+	80	24		4 Stealin' Home	$10	Mushroom 5012

And Me (1)
And When She Smiles (She Makes The Sun Shine) (1)
Blue Blue Day (3)
Brand New Tennessee Waltz (1)
Carefully Taught (4)
Close The Door Lightly (2)
Da Doo Ron Ron (When He Walked Me Home) (2) 96
Don't Hang Up Your Dancing Shoes (4)
For Melanie (1)
Gimme An Inch (4)
Hope You Know (2)
House Of Unamerican Blues Activity Dream (2)
Keep On Sailing (3)
King Of The Night (4)
Leaving Alone (3)
Let There Be Blues (4)
Man In The Station (4)
Mare, Take Me Home (1) 96
Midnight On The Water (4)
Morning Song (2)
My Lady (1)
Never Again (2)
Old Man At The Mill (3)
Only Dancer (2)
Please Be My Friend (2)
Propinquity (3)
Right Before My Eyes (2)
Road To Ronderlin (1)
Sail My Soul (3)
Save Your Sorrows (3)
7 Bridges Road (3)
Shady Lies (3)
Shake It (4) 13
Slip Away (4)
Smile (medley) (4)
Stealin' Home (4)
Sylvie (1)
Tell Me Why (1) 96
These Days (3)
Tigers Will Survive (2)
To Love (1)
What Are You Waiting For (3)
Woodstock (1) 23
Yank & Mary (medley) (4)

MAURIAT, Paul
French conductor/arranger; born in 1925. Moved to Paris at age 10. Formed own touring orchestra at 17.

12/16/67+	1⁵	50	●	1 **Blooming Hits** ... [I]	$12	Philips 248
3/30/68	122	22		2 More Mauriat ... [I]	$12	Philips 226
6/8/68	71	18		3 Mauriat Magic ... [I]	$12	Philips 270
10/12/68	142	7		4 Prevailing Airs ... [I]	$12	Philips 280
3/1/69	77	18		5 Doing My Thing ... [I]	$12	Philips 292
5/3/69	157	8		6 The Soul Of Paul Mauriat ... [I]	$12	Philips 299
11/1/69	186	3		7 L.O.V.E. ... [I]	$12	Philips 320
9/19/70	184	3		8 Gone Is Love ... [I]	$12	Philips 345
5/29/71	180	3		9 El Condor Pasa ... [I]	$12	Philips 352
				title is Spanish for The Condor Passes By		

Abraham, Martin & John (5)
Adieu A La Nuit (Adieu To The Night) (1)
Angelica (3)
Aquarius (7)
Banda (Parade) (3)
Bang Bang (My Baby Shot Me Down) (1)
Black Harlem (9)
Black Is Black (2)
Bridge Over Troubled Water (8)
Burning Bridges (9)
Catherine (7)
Cent Mille Chansons (100,000 Songs) (5)
Chitty Chitty Bang Bang (5) 76
Classical Gas (8)
Comme Un Garcon (What A Guy) (8)
Could This Be Me (3)
Delilah (4)
Dr. Zhivago ..see: Lara's Theme
El Condor Pasa (9)
Eleanor Rigby (4)
Elenore (5)
En Bandouliere (2)
Etude In The Form Of Rhythm & Blues (9)
Gentle On My Mind (9)
Get Back (7)
Go Away (Un Adieu) (8)
Gone Is Love (8)
Goodbye (7)
Guantanamera (2)
Hey Jude (5)
Home Again (8)
Honey (7)
I Gotta Get Back To Lovin' You (8)
I Heard It Through The Grapevine (6)
I Never Loved A Man (6)
I Say A Little Prayer (5)
I Waited For You (3)
I'm Coming Home (4)
I'm Gonna Make You Love Me (6)
I've Been Loving You Too Long (6)
In The Midnight Hour (6)
Inch Allah (1)
Irresistiblement (Irresistibly) (5)
Is Paris Burning, Theme From (2)
Isadora's Theme From The Loves Of Isadora (7)
It's A Man's World (6)
L'Amour Te Ressemble (Love Is The Image Of You) (4)
La Source (The Spring) (4)
Lady Madonna (4)
Lara's Theme (2)
Last Waltz (3)
Let It Be (8)
Live For Life (3)
Lonely Days (9)
Love Child (6)
Love In Every Room (3) 60
Love Is Blue (1) 1
Love Me, Please Love Me (2)
Love Story (9)
Ma Maison Et La Riviere (My House And The River) (5)
Mama (1)
Melancholy Man (9)
Merci Cherie (3)
Michelle (3)
Mrs. Robinson (4)
My Girl (6)
My House And The River (8)
My Sweet Lord (9)
Ne Sois Pas Triste (Don't Be Sad) (5)
Oh Happy Day (7)
Penny Lane (1)
Ponteio (3)
Puppet On A String (1)
Rain And Tears (4)
Raindrops Keep Fallin' On My Head (8)
Reach Out I'll Be There (2)
Respect (6)
San Francisco (Wear Some Flowers In Your Hair) (3)
Serenade To Summertime (7)
Seuls Au Monde (Alone In The World) (1)
She Is A Little Bit Sweeter (8)
Siffler Sur La Colline (Whistle On The Hill) (5)
Silver Fingertips (7)
Somethin' Stupid (1)
Somewhere, My Love ..see: Lara's Theme
There's A Kind Of Hush (All Over The World) (1)
This Guy's In Love With You (4)
This Is My Song (1)
Those Were The Days (5)
To Be The One You Love (9)
Tonta Gafay Boba (9)
Un Jour Un Enfant (Through The Eyes Of A Child) (7)
When A Man Loves A Woman (6)
Winchester Cathedral (2)
Windmills Of Your Mind (7)
World We Knew (1)
You Keep Me Hangin' On (6)
You, Love, And Me (7)

MAX DEMIAN BAND, The
Rock quintet — named after musician in the novel *Demian*.

| 3/3/79 | 159 | 5 | | Take It To The Max | $8 | RCA 3273 |

Burnin' Up Inside
Havin' Such A Good Day
Hear My Song
High School Star
Lizard Song
Paradise
See Me Comin' Down
Still Hosed
Through The Eye Of A Storm

TOP 500 ARTISTS

This section ranks the Top 500 album artists from 1955-1992, and features a picture section of the Top 100 artists. The pictures are reproductions of actual albums charted by these artists.

Below each name is an accumulated point total. The point system used to create this total is explained on the next page. The points are totaled through the January 16, 1993 chart.

Special symbols:

★ = **Hot Artist**

Hot artists achieved either of the following from 1990-1992:
a) charted a Top 40 album (compilation albums are not counted, unless they made the Top 10)
b) charted three albums — at least two of which were studio albums

■ = **Deceased Artist** (or group member)

In the case of a group, the total number of square symbols indicates the total number of deceased members.

POINT SYSTEM

Points are awarded according to the following formula:

1. Each artist's charted albums are given points based on their highest charted position:

$$\#1 \; = \; 200 \text{ points for its first week at \#1, plus 20 points}$$
for each additional week at #1

$$\#2 \; = \; 190 \text{ points for its first week at \#2, plus 10 points}$$
for each additional week at #2

$$\#3 \; = \; 180 \text{ points for its first week at \#3, plus 5 points}$$
for each additional week at #3

#4-5	=	170 points	#101-110	=	100 points
#6-10	=	160 points	#111-120	=	90 points
#11-20	=	150 points	#121-130	=	80 points
#21-30	=	145 points	#131-140	=	70 points
#31-40	=	140 points	#141-150	=	60 points
#41-50	=	135 points	#151-160	=	50 points
#51-60	=	130 points	#161-170	=	40 points
#61-70	=	125 points	#171-180	=	30 points
#71-80	=	120 points	#181-190	=	20 points
#81-90	=	115 points	#191-200	=	10 points
#91-100	=	110 points			

2. Total weeks charted are added in.

In the case of a tie, the artist listed first is determined by the following tie-breaker rules:

1) Most charted albums
2) Most Top 40 albums
3) Most Top 10 albums

When two artists combine for a hit album, such as Kenny Rogers and Dolly Parton, the full point value is given to both artists. A duo, such as Simon & Garfunkel, Hall & Oates, and Loggins & Messina are considered regular recording teams, and their points are not shared by either artist individually.

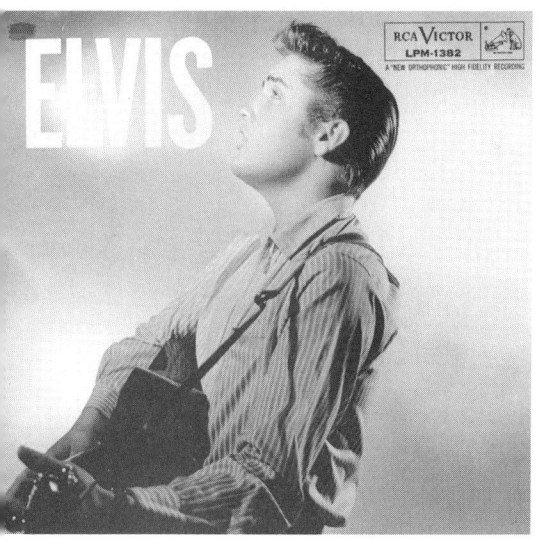

1. Elvis Presley ■
15,422

2. Frank Sinatra
12,076

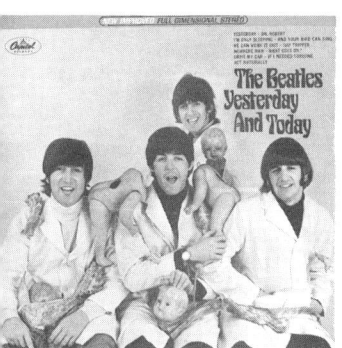

3. The Beatles ■
10,224

4. Johnny Mathis
9,938

5. Barbra Streisand
8,654

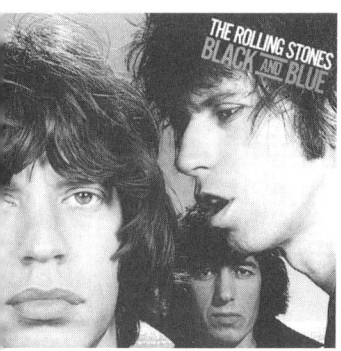

★ **6. The Rolling Stones** ■
8,575

7. Mantovani ■
7,157

8. Ray Conniff
6,998

★ **9. Elton John**
6,902

10. The Temptations ■ ■ ■
6,814

★ **11. Bob Dylan**
6,695

12. The Beach Boys ■
6,498

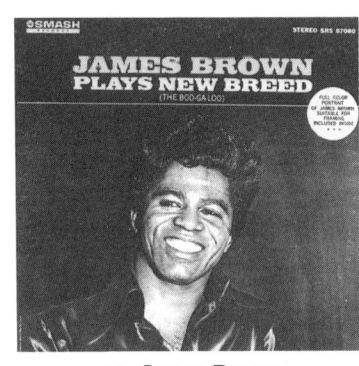

13. James Brown
6,113

14. Lawrence Welk ■
6,112

★ **15. Neil Diamond**
6,028

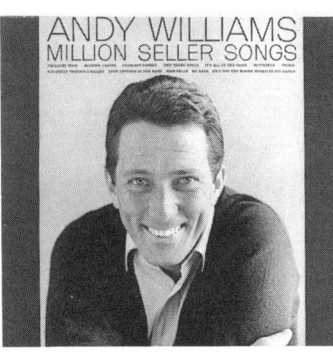

16. Andy Williams
5,858

17. Aretha Franklin
5,837

18. The Kingston Trio ■
5,817

19. Henry Mancini
5,797

20. Ray Charles
5,703

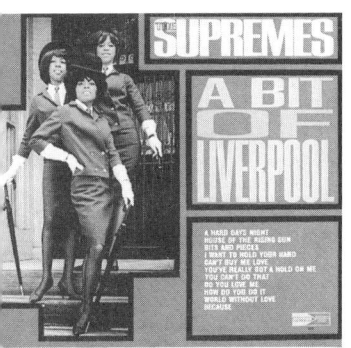

21. The Supremes ■
5,689

22. Herb Alpert/Tijuana Brass
5,577

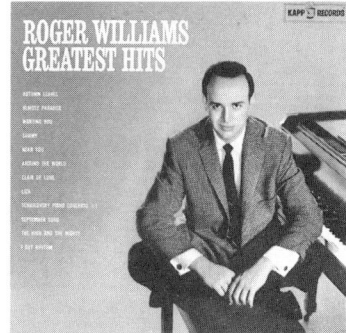

23. Roger Williams
5,377

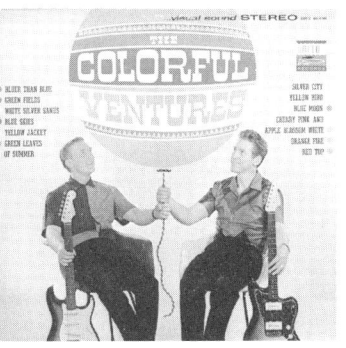

24. The Ventures ■
5,130

25. Billy Vaughn ■
4,936

26. Kenny Rogers
4,914

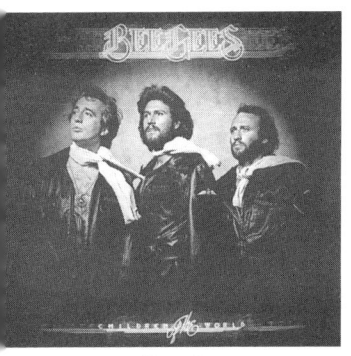

27. Bee Gees
4,888

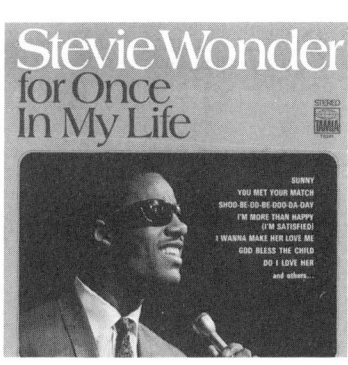

★ **28. Stevie Wonder**
4,845

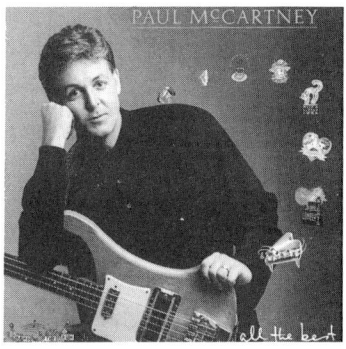

★ **29. Paul McCartney/
Wings** ■
4,806

30. Chicago ■
4,758

31. Jeffeson Airplane/Starship
4,747

★ **32. Eric Clapton**
4,706

33. Dionne Warwick
4,659

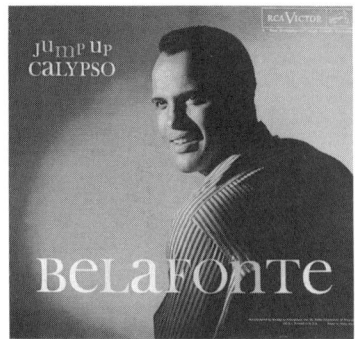

34. Harry Belafonte
4,604

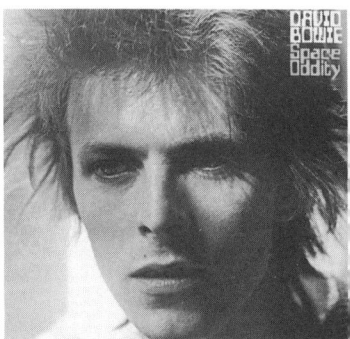

35. David Bowie
4,591

36. Willie Nelson
4,566

37. Diana Ross
4,523

38. Mitch Miller
4,517

39. Nat "King" Cole ■
4,513

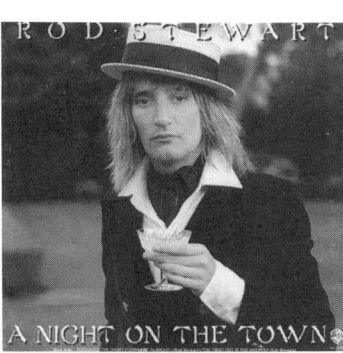

★ 40. Rod Stewart
4,451

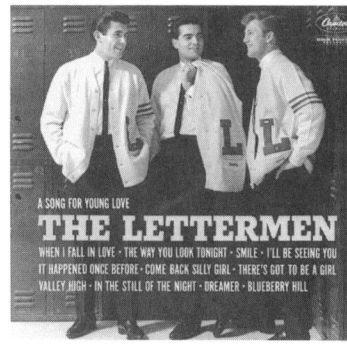

41. The Lettermen
4,320

★ 42. Neil Young
4,318

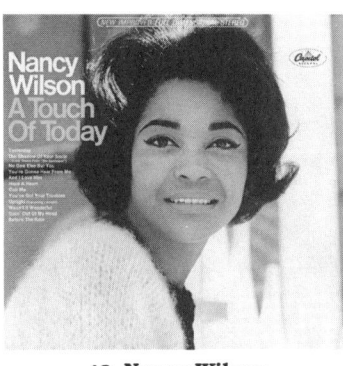

43. Nancy Wilson
4,297

44. Linda Ronstadt
4,269

45. Jethro Tull ■
4,103

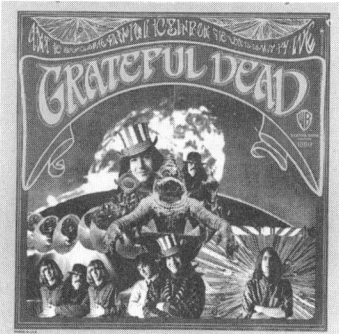

★ **46. Grateful Dead** ■ ■ ■
3,994

47. The Kinks
3,971

48. John Denver
3,962

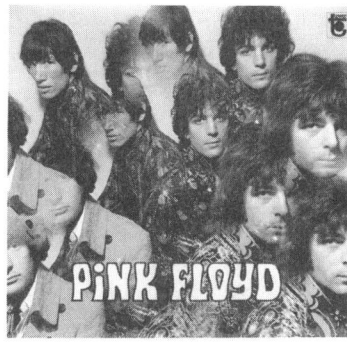

49. Pink Floyd
3,901

50. Marvin Gaye ■
3,889

★ **51. Fleetwood Mac**
3,861

52. Frank Zappa
3,833

53. Joan Baez
3,830

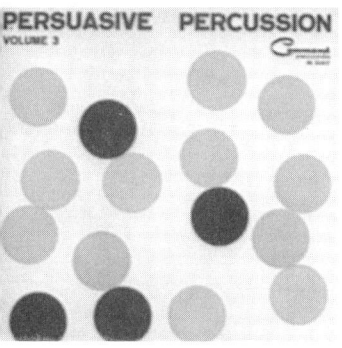

54. Enoch Light ■
3,771

★ **55. Kiss** ■
3,726

56. The Monkees
3,678

★ **57. Barry Manilow**
3,661

58. Glen Campbell
3,657

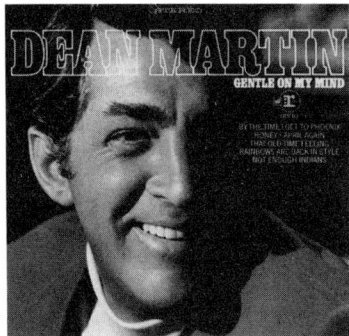

59. Dean Martin
3,644

60. The Isley Brothers ■
3,586

61. Gladys Knight & The Pips
3,582

★ **62. The Doors** ■
3,515

63. Santana
3,504

64. Jimi Hendrix ■
3,497

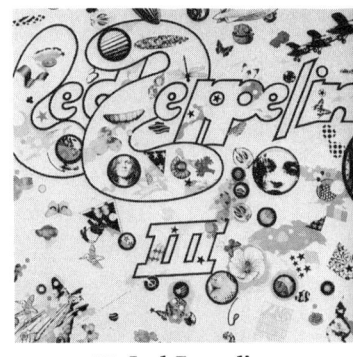

65. Led Zeppelin ■
3.476

66. Bill Cosby
3,472

67. Four Tops
3,470

★ **68. Prince**
3,467

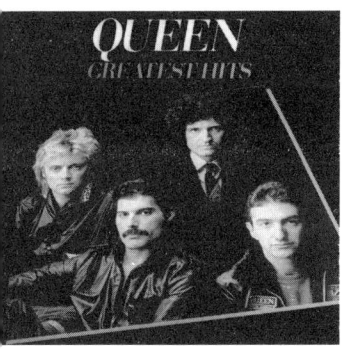

★ 69. Queen ■
3,429

70. The Who ■
3,420

71. The Moody Blues
3,419

72. Earth, Wind & Fire
3,384

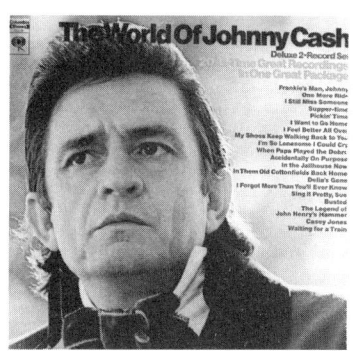

73. Johnny Cash
3,380

74. The Jackson 5/Jacksons
3,368

75. The 4 Seasons
3,282

76. The Miracles
3,240

★ 77. Van Morrison
3,238

78. Ferrante & Teicher
3,219

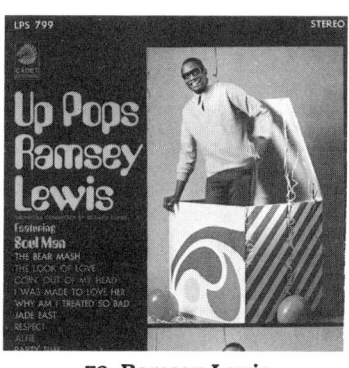

79. Ramsey Lewis
3,209

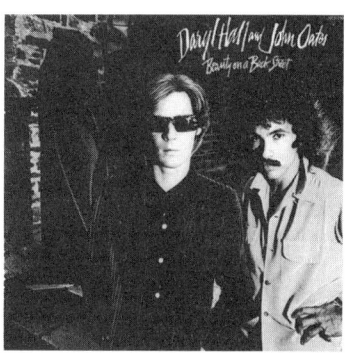

80. Daryl Hall & John Oates
3,202

81. Anne Murray
3,188

82. Billy Joel
3,181

83. Isaac Hayes
3,179

84. Carole King
3,159

85. Perry Como
3,139

★ **86. Rush**
3,100

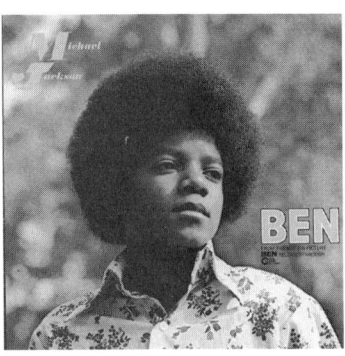

★ **87. Michael Jackson**
3,034

88. Al Martino
3,030

89. Carly Simon
2,999

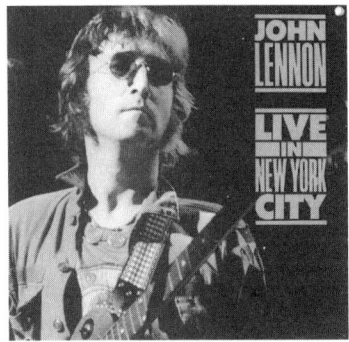

90. John Lennon ■
2,973

91. Connie Francis
2,972

★ **92. Bruce Springsteen**
2,971

93. Percy Faith ■
2,970

94. Bobby Vinton
2,955

95. Peter, Paul & Mary
2,954

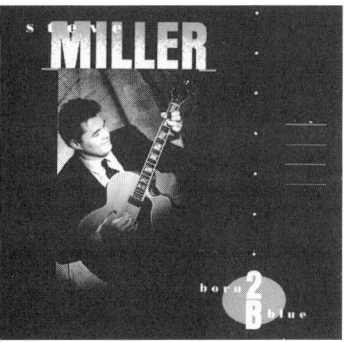

96. Steve Miller Band
2,950

97. Tony Bennett
2,891

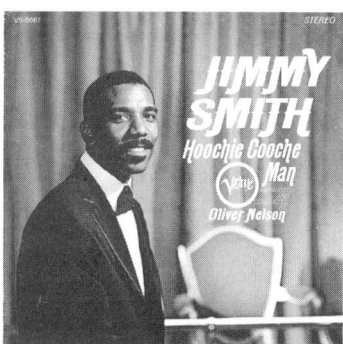

98. Jimmy Smith
2,882

99. Al Hirt
2,874

100. Olivia Newton-John
2,874

TOP 500 ARTISTS RANKING (#101-#302)

Rank		Points
101.	Donna Summer	2,869
102.	Alice Cooper	2,865
★103.	James Taylor	2,864
104.	Grand Funk Railroad	2,844
★105.	Hank Williams, Jr.	2,821
★106.	AC/DC ■	2,805
107.	Chubby Checker	2,799
108.	Aerosmith	2,788
109.	George Benson	2,786
110.	Lou Rawls	2,783
★111.	Yes	2,769
112.	The Doobie Brothers	2,764
113.	Kool & The Gang	2,750
114.	Commodores	2,745
★115.	Alabama	2,735
116.	Tom Jones	2,726
117.	Deep Purple ■	2,725
118.	Grover Washington, Jr.	2,693
119.	Joni Mitchell	2,682
120.	Journey	2,656
121.	Jimmy Buffett	2,653
122.	Bob James	2,648
123.	Black Sabbath	2,639
124.	The O'Jays ■	2,633
★125.	Allman Brothers Band ■ ■	2,630
126.	War ■	2,625
127.	Three Dog Night	2,616
128.	Waylon Jennings	2,606
129.	Dave Brubeck Quartet	2,586
130.	Roberta Flack	2,584
131.	Eagles	2,580
132.	George Harrison	2,579
★133.	Genesis	2,571
134.	Poco	2,565
135.	Creedence Clearwater Revival ■	2,564
136.	Simon & Garfunkel	2,550
137.	Donovan	2,526
138.	Bert Kaempfert ■	2,524
★139.	Dolly Parton	2,523
★140.	Madonna	2,523
141.	Cher	2,520
★142.	Bob Seger ■	2,489
143.	Pat Boone	2,463
144.	Engelbert Humperdinck	2,456
★145.	U2	2,447
146.	REO Speedwagon ■	2,444
147.	Electric Light Orchestra	2,438
★148.	Heart	2,412
149.	B.B. King	2,409
150.	The Righteous Brothers	2,397
151.	Judy Collins	2,394
★152.	Van Halen	2,392
153.	Smokey Robinson	2,372
154.	The Band ■	2,370
155.	Joe Cocker	2,367
156.	Elvis Costello	2,346
157.	The J. Geils Band	2,334
158.	Peter Nero	2,333
159.	Johnny Rivers	2,326
160.	Jackie Gleason ■	2,323
161.	The 5th Dimension	2,323
★162.	Bette Midler	2,318
163.	The Crusaders	2,302
164.	Robert Goulet	2,302
165.	Al Green	2,296
166.	America	2,295
167.	Carpenters ■	2,288
168.	Ohio Players	2,280
169.	Brenda Lee	2,279
170.	The Byrds ■ ■	2,254
★171.	Natalie Cole	2,244
172.	Sergio Mendes/Brasil '66	2,243
173.	Lou Reed	2,241
174.	Barry White	2,236
175.	Earl Klugh	2,235
176.	Herbie Mann	2,233
177.	Cat Stevens	2,231
178.	Ricky Nelson ■	2,227
179.	Miles Davis ■	2,215
180.	Emmylou Harris	2,204
★181.	ZZ Top	2,199
182.	Styx	2,193
183.	Pointer Sisters	2,173
184.	Steppenwolf	2,162
185.	Trini Lopez	2,156
186.	Emerson, Lake & Palmer	2,146
187.	Otis Redding ■	2,143
188.	Quincy Jones	2,143
189.	Cameo	2,138
190.	Eddy Arnold	2,136
191.	Crosby, Stills & Nash	2,134
192.	Jerry Vale	2,129
193.	The Animals	2,128
★194.	Paul Simon	2,103
195.	Gordon Lightfoot	2,092
196.	Chuck Mangione	2,090
197.	Leon Russell	2,089
198.	Chet Atkins	2,080
199.	Bob Marley & The Wailers ■	2,078
200.	Spinners ■	2,076
201.	Peggy Lee	2,069
★202.	Pat Benatar	2,067
203.	Herbie Hancock	2,064
204.	Foreigner	2,038
205.	Paul Anka	2,032
★206.	Tom Petty & The Heartbreakers	2,030
207.	Spyro Gyra	2,028
208.	Paul Revere & The Raiders	2,026
209.	Lynyrd Skynyrd ■ ■ ■	2,021
210.	Tennessee Ernie Ford ■	2,014
211.	John Mayall	2,009
212.	Bobby Darin ■	1,992
213.	Ted Nugent	1,984
214.	Charley Pride	1,981
215.	John Gary	1,974
216.	Dan Fogelberg	1,968
★217.	Bad Company	1,967
218.	The Dave Clark Five	1,964
219.	Merle Haggard ■	1,953
220.	The Guess Who	1,953
221.	Cheap Trick	1,952
222.	The Alan Parsons Project	1,942
223.	Boston Pops Orchestra ■	1,937
224.	Teddy Pendergrass	1,934
★225.	John Cougar Mellencamp	1,932
★226.	Bonnie Raitt	1,932
227.	Jack Jones	1,928
★228.	R.E.M.	1,928
229.	Stephen Stills	1,926
230.	Marshall Tucker Band ■	1,921
231.	Kansas	1,916
232.	Talking Heads	1,915
233.	Peabo Bryson	1,911
234.	Blue Oyster Cult	1,910
235.	Roy Orbison ■	1,909
236.	Seals & Crofts	1,908
237.	The Police	1,906
★238.	Ozzy Osbourne	1,901
239.	Curtis Mayfield	1,875
240.	Jeff Beck	1,864
241.	Rick James	1,852
★242.	Dire Straits	1,842
243.	Patti LaBelle	1,841
244.	Pat Metheny	1,823
245.	Robin Trower	1,811
246.	Traffic ■	1,808
247.	Joe Jackson	1,807
248.	Eydie Gorme	1,803
249.	Dave Mason	1,798
250.	Blood, Sweat & Tears	1,786
251.	Sammy Davis, Jr. ■	1,774
252.	Herman's Hermits	1,773
253.	The Impressions	1,758
★254.	Garth Brooks	1,75?
255.	Sonny & Cher	1,746
256.	Robert Palmer	1,744
★257.	Iron Maiden	1,732
258.	Foghat	1,727
259.	Duran Duran	1,724
260.	Peter Frampton	1,722
261.	Jackson Browne	1,718
262.	The Whispers	1,717
263.	The Mamas & The Papas ■	1,716
264.	Petula Clark	1,708
265.	Cream	1,707
266.	Johnny Winter	1,706
267.	New Christy Minstrels	1,69?
268.	Melissa Manchester	1,694
269.	Bar-Kays ■ ■ ■	1,69?
270.	Helen Reddy	1,68?
271.	Rufus Feat. Chaka Khan	1,68?
272.	Joe Walsh	1,68?
273.	Supertramp	1,68?
274.	Charlie Daniels Band	1,68?
275.	Kris Kristofferson	1,68?
276.	Rita Coolidge	1,68?
★277.	George Strait	1,67?
278.	Jerry Lee Lewis	1,67?
279.	Donny Osmond	1,67?
280.	Ten Years After	1,67?
281.	Al Jarreau	1,66?
282.	Steely Dan ■	1,66?
★283.	Peter Gabriel	1,66?
284.	Judy Garland ■	1,66?
285.	Pete Fountain	1,65?
286.	Todd Rundgren	1,64?
★287.	Bon Jovi	1,64?
★288.	Phil Collins	1,64?
★289.	Whitney Houston	1,64?
290.	Loggins & Messina	1,63?
291.	Moms Mabley ■	1,63?
★292.	Judas Priest	1,63?
★293.	Def Leppard ■	1,63?
294.	Weather Report	1,63?
295.	The Limeliters	1,61?
★296.	Scorpions	1,61?
★297.	Randy Travis	1,60?
298.	Ronnie Milsap	1,60?
299.	Uriah Heep	1,60?
300.	Wilson Pickett	1,60?
301.	The Manhattan Transfer	1,59?
302.	David Sanborn	1,59?

TOP 500 ARTISTS RANKING (#303-#500)

Rank	Points
303. The Rascals	1,588
304. Ashford & Simpson	1,573
★305. Luther Vandross	1,571
306. Nilsson	1,570
307. Procol Harum ■	1,564
308. Ray Parker Jr./Raydio	1,564
309. The Hollies	1,559
310. The Smothers Brothers	1,558
311. The Cars	1,551
★312. Steve Winwood	1,550
313. Average White Band ■	1,547
314. Sam Cooke ■	1,541
315. Rick Springfield	1,536
316. John McLaughlin	1,530
317. Nazareth	1,530
318. Little River Band	1,521
319. Bachman-Turner Overdrive	1,518
320. The Association ■	1,514
321. Joan Armatrading	1,513
322. Abba	1,507
323. The Osmonds	1,504
324. Bobby Womack	1,500
325. King Crimson	1,494
326. George Duke	1,492
327. Eurythmics	1,484
328. Bread	1,484
329. Allan Sherman ■	1,481
330. Duane Eddy	1,477
331. The Stylistics	1,469
★332. Motley Crue	1,467
333. The James Gang ■	1,463
334. Maze Feat. Frankie Beverly	1,453
335. Stephanie Mills	1,440
336. Eddie Money	1,440
337. Millie Jackson	1,439
★338. INXS	1,430
339. George Thorogood & The Destroyers	1,425
340. Kenny Loggins	1,420
341. Gene Pitney	1,419
342. Charlie Rich	1,417
343. Jean-Luc Ponty	1,410
344. Tower Of Power	1,410
345. Sly & The Family Stone	1,410
346. Eddie Harris	1,407
347. Nitty Gritty Dirt Band	1,407
348. Jermaine Jackson	1,406
★349. George Michael/Wham!	1,406
350. Dawn feat. Tony Orlando	1,404
★351. The B-52's ■	1,404
352. Con Funk Shun	1,398
353. Richard Pryor	1,397
354. Harry Chapin ■	1,385
355. Boz Scaggs	1,385
356. Nancy Sinatra	1,385
357. Bob Newhart	1,385
358. Rainbow	1,381
359. Outlaws	1,376
360. Little Feat ■	1,373
361. Larry Graham/Graham Central Station	1,369
362. Funkadelic	1,368
363. Bobby Vee	1,367
★364. The Chipmunks ■	1,364
365. 38 Special	1,358
366. Toto ■	1,351
367. Canned Heat ■ ■	1,349
368. Ella Fitzgerald	1,348

Rank	Points
369. Triumph	1,337
370. Ed Ames	1,336
371. Atlanta Rhythm Section	1,334
372. Cheech & Chong	1,333
373. Stanley Turrentine	1,324
374. The Brothers Four	1,310
375. Roy Ayers/Ubiquity	1,309
376. Rusty Warren	1,309
377. Billy Preston	1,307
378. Manfred Mann/Earth Band	1,306
379. Jan & Dean	1,305
380. Vikki Carr	1,303
381. Sammy Hagar	1,303
382. Sheena Easton	1,303
383. Jim Croce ■	1,292
384. Arlo Guthrie	1,289
★385. Metallica ■	1,286
386. Ringo Starr	1,285
387. Parliament	1,284
388. Stanley Clarke	1,280
389. Oak Ridge Boys	1,279
390. Humble Pie ■	1,277
391. Wes Montgomery ■	1,273
★392. The Cure	1,272
393. The Pretenders ■ ■	1,269
394. Rare Earth	1,268
395. Crystal Gayle	1,266
396. Jose Feliciano	1,266
397. Booker T. & The MG's ■	1,265
398. The Everly Brothers	1,265
399. Utopia	1,261
400. Teena Marie	1,260
401. Pete Townshend	1,260
402. The Judds	1,260
403. Boots Randolph	1,256
404. Atlantic Starr	1,256
405. Pure Prairie League	1,255
★406. Billy Idol	1,254
407. Graham Nash	1,249
408. Mario Lanza ■	1,248
409. Jerry Butler	1,245
410. Quicksilver Messenger Service ■	1,244
411. Mac Davis	1,243
412. Deniece Williams	1,242
413. Roxy Music	1,239
414. The Gap Band	1,239
415. Doris Day	1,234
416. Jim Nabors	1,233
417. Village People	1,232
418. UFO	1,226
419. Gino Vannelli	1,226
★420. Guns N' Roses	1,226
421. George Carlin	1,224
422. Gary Lewis & The Playboys	1,222
423. Graham Parker	1,221
★424. Stevie Ray Vaughan ■	1,220
★425. Depeche Mode	1,215
426. Bill Withers	1,211
427. Janis Joplin ■	1,209
428. The Manhattans ■ ■	1,208
429. Tavares	1,208
430. Lionel Richie	1,208
431. The Partridge Family	1,207
★432. Joan Jett & Blackhearts	1,206
★433. Kenny G	1,206
434. The Dramatics	1,204
435. Tammy Wynette	1,202

Rank	Points
436. Iron Butterfly	1,201
437. Sandy Nelson	1,198
★438. New Kids On The Block	1,196
★439. UB40	1,187
440. The Dells	1,186
★441. M.C. Hammer	1,186
442. Chaka Khan	1,185
★443. Huey Lewis & the News	1,180
444. Count Basie ■	1,179
★445. Ratt	1,179
446. Buddy Miles	1,178
447. Buck Owens	1,168
448. Stan Getz ■	1,165
★449. Michael Bolton	1,165
450. Gloria Lynne	1,163
451. The Tubes	1,162
452. B.J. Thomas	1,156
453. Air Supply	1,153
454. Ramones	1,150
455. Melanie	1,146
456. Dr. Hook	1,140
457. Jim Reeves ■	1,138
458. Deodato	1,125
459. The Platters ■ ■ ■	1,120
460. The Brothers Johnson	1,118
461. Blondie	1,115
462. Shalamar	1,112
463. The Four Freshmen	1,112
464. Eddie Kendricks ■	1,111
465. Billy Squier	1,111
466. Shelley Berman	1,110
467. Loverboy	1,108
468. Dion/The Belmonts	1,106
469. Phoebe Snow	1,106
470. Ike & Tina Turner	1,104
★471. Gloria Estefan/Miami Sound Machine	1,103
472. Roger Miller ■	1,102
473. Stevie Nicks	1,102
474. The Lovin' Spoonful	1,098
475. Loretta Lynn	1,097
476. The Chad Mitchell Trio	1,094
477. Squeeze	1,094
478. Captain & Tennille	1,091
479. Dave Gardner ■	1,091
480. Donald Byrd	1,090
★481. Harry Connick, Jr.	1,090
482. Savoy Brown	1,089
483. Harold Melvin & The Blue Notes	1,086
484. Jr. Walker & The All Stars	1,085
485. Jose Jimenez	1,084
486. The Chi-Lites	1,082
487. Devo	1,080
488. Neil Sedaka	1,078
489. Johnnie Taylor	1,077
490. Janis Ian	1,077
★491. Bryan Adams	1,075
492. Dinah Washington ■	1,072
493. The Clash	1,071
494. Edgar Winter	1,071
495. Michael Franks	1,069
496. "Cannonball" Adderley ■ ■	1,064
497. Paul Butterfield ■	1,061
★498. Queensryche	1,061
499. Ronnie Laws	1,059
500. Tommy James/The Shondells	1,056

A-Z — TOP 500 ARTISTS

DEBUT DATE	PEAK POS	WKS CHR	GOLD	ARTIST — Album Title	$	Label & Number

MAX Q
Melbourne, Australia band formed and fronted by INXS vocalist Michael Hutchence and Ian "Ollie" Olsen, the leader of the underground band No. Olsen also worked with Hugo Kiang and Whirlywirld. Max Q is the name of Olsen's dog.

| 10/7/89 | 182 | 8 | | Max Q .... | $8 | Atlantic 82014 |

Buckethead · Concrete · Everything · Ghost Of The Year · Monday Night By Satellite · Ot-ven-rot · Sometimes · Soul Engine · Tight · Way Of The World · Zero-2-0

MAXWELL, Robert, His Harp and Orchestra
Born on 4/19/21 in New York City. Jazz harpist/composer. With NBC Symphony under Toscanini at age 17. Also recorded as Mickey Mozart.

| 4/18/64 | 17 | 24 | | Shangri-La...[I] | $12 | Decca 74421 |

Bewitched · Breeze And I · It's Magic · Magic Is The Moonlight (Te Quiero Dijiste) · Nature Boy · Old Devil Moon · Poinciana (Song Of The Tree) · **Shangri-La 15** · Sounds Of Summer · Strange Music · Tears · That Old Black Magic

MAY, Billy, And His Orchestra
Born on 1/10/16 in Pittsburgh. Arranger/conductor/sideman for many of the big bands. After leading his own band in early '50s, Billy went on to arrange/conduct for Frank Sinatra and compose movie scores.

| 3/5/55 | 7 | 6 | | Sorta-May...[I] | $15 | Capitol 562 |

All You Want To Do Is Dance · Blues In The Night · Chicago · Deep Purple · Donkey Serenade · In A Persian Market · Just One Of Those Things · Soon · They Didn't Believe Me · Thou Swell · You Go To My Head · You're The Top

MAY, Brian, & Friends
Brian was born on 7/19/47 in London. Lead guitarist of Queen.

| 11/19/83 | 125 | 9 | | Star Fleet Project ....[M] | $8 | Capitol 15014 |
| | | | | with Eddie Van Halen, Alan Gratzer (REO Speedwagon), Phil Chen and Fred Mandel | | |

Blues Breaker · Let Me Out · Star Fleet

★★211★★ MAYALL, John
Born on 11/29/43 in Macclesfield, Cheshire, England. Bluesman John Mayall & his Bluesbreakers band spawned many of Britain's leading rock musicians. Also see Eric Clapton's *History Of Eric Clapton* and *Crossroads* albums.

2/17/68	136	14		1 John Mayall's Blues Breakers Crusade *	$15	London 529
				with Mick Taylor, John McVie and Keef Hartley		
6/15/68	128	5		2 The Blues Alone	$15	London 534
				all instruments (except drums) played by Mayall		
9/14/68	59	19		3 Bare Wires *	$15	London 537
				*JOHN MAYALL'S BLUES BREAKERS		
2/22/69	68	17		4 Blues From Laurel Canyon	$15	London 545
				John's first album after disbanding the Bluesbreakers		
9/13/69	79	12		5 Looking Back ....[K]	$15	London 562
				featuring Bluesbreakers greats Eric Clapton and Mick Fleetwood (1964-67)		
9/20/69	32	55	●	6 The Turning Point ....[L]	$12	Polydor 4004
				featuring Jon Mark and Johnny Almond		
2/28/70	93	11		7 The Diary Of A Band ....[E-L]	$12	London 570
				recordings taped by Mayall in clubs during 1967		
3/14/70	33	19		8 Empty Rooms	$12	Polydor 4010
10/24/70	22	22		9 USA Union	$12	Polydor 4022
				featuring Harvey Mandel and other American artists		
4/17/71	52	15		10 Back To The Roots	$12	Polydor 3002 [2]
				reunion of Bluesbreaker's alumni including Eric Clapton and Mick Taylor		
5/1/71	146	8		11 John Mayall-Live In Europe ....[E-L]	$12	London 589
				volume 2 of album #7 above		
11/13/71	164	7		12 Thru The Years ....[K]	$12	London 600 [2]
11/13/71	179	5		13 Memories	$12	Polydor 5012
				with Jerry McGee (guitar) and Larry Taylor (bass)		
6/17/72	64	18		14 Jazz Blues Fusion ....[L]	$12	Polydor 5027
10/28/72	116	11		15 Moving On	$12	Polydor 5036
2/10/73	158	7		16 Down The Line...[K-L]	$10	London 618 [2]
				record 1: studio cuts 1965-68; record 2: 1964 live concert (Mayall's first British LP)		
10/6/73	157	7		17 Ten Years Are Gone	$10	Polydor 3005 [2]
				last 3 Polydor albums feature Blue Mitchell (trumpet) and Freddy Robinson (guitar)		
3/15/75	140	4		18 New Year, New Band, New Company	$10	Blue Thumb 6019
				featuring female vocalist Dee McKinnie		
8/25/90	170	8		19 A Sense Of Place	$12	Island 842795
				featuring The Bluesbreakers: Coco Montoya, Freebo, Joe Yuele and guest slide guitarist Sonny Landreth		

Accidental Suicide (10) · Alabama March (12) · All My Life (19) · Anzio Ann (medley) (7) · Back From Korea (13) · Bare Wires (3) · Bear, The (4,12) · Better Pass You By (17) · Black Cat Moan (19) · Blood On The Night (7) · Blue City Shakedown (5) · Blue Fox (10) · Blues In B (11) · Boogie Albert (10) · Brand New Start (2) · Broken Wings (2,16) · Brown Sugar (2) · Burning Sun (17)

California (6) · California Campground (17) · Can't Get Home (18) · Cancelling Out (2) · Catch That Train (9) · Change Your Ways (14) · Checking On My Baby (1) · Chicago Line (16) · Christmas 71 (15) · City, The (13) · Congo Square (19) · Counting The Days (8) · Country Road (14) · Crawling Up A Hill (16) · Crocodile Walk (16) · Crying (9) · Crying Shame (11) · Curly (12)

Dark Of The Night (17) · Death Of J.B. Lenoir (1) · Deep Blue Sea (9) · Devil's Tricks (10) · Do It (15) · Don't Hang Me Up (17) · Don't Kick Me (2,13) · Don't Pick A Flower (8) · **Don't Waste My Time (8) 81** · Doreen (16) · Double Trouble (5) · Down The Line (2) · Dream With Me (10) · Drifting (17) · Driving On (18) · Driving Sideways (1)

Driving Till The Break Of Day (17) · Dry Throat (14) · Edmonton-Cooks Ferry Inn (7) · Exercise In C Major (14) · Fighting Line (13) · Fire (3,16) · First Time Alone (4,16) · Fly Tomorrow (4,16) · Force Of Nature (10) · Full Speed Ahead (10) · God Save The Queen (7) · Good Looking Stranger (17) · Good Times Boogie (9) · Goodbye December (10) · Got To Be This Way (14) · Grandad (13)

Greeny (12) · Groupie Girl (10) · Harmonica Free Form (17) · Harp Man (2) · Hartley Quits (3) · Have You Heard (12) · Heartache (16) · Help Me (11) · Hide And Seek (12) · Hideaway (16) · High Pressure Living (15) · Home Again (10) · Home In A Tree (13) · Hoot Owl (16) · I Can't Complain (19) · I Can't Quit You Baby (1,7) · I Know Now (3) · I Need Your Love (16)

I Started Walking (3,16) · I Still Care (17) · I Wanna Teach You Everything (16) · I Want To Go (19) · I'm A Stranger (3,12) · I'm Gonna Fight For You J.B. (7) · It Hurts Me Too (5) · Jacksboro Highway (19) · Jenny (5) · Keep Our Country Green (15) · Key To Love (12) · Killing Time (3) · Knockers Step Forward (12) · Laurel Canyon Home (4) · Laws Must Change (6) · Lesson, The (medley) (7)

484

DEBUT DATE	PEAK POS	WKS CHR	GOLD	ARTIST — Album Title	$	Label & Number

MAYALL, John — Cont'd

Let's Work Together (19)
Local Boy Makes Good (11)
Long Gone Midnight (4)
Look In The Mirror (3)
Looking At Tomorrow (1)
Looking Back (5)
Lying In My Bed (8)
Mama, Talk To Your Daughter (12)
Man Of Stone (1,16)
Many Miles Apart (8)
Marriage Madness (10)
Marsha's Mood (3)
Me And My Woman (1,12)
Medicine Man (4)
Memories (13)
Messin' Around (14)
Miss James (4)
Missing You (12)
Moving On (15)

Mr Censor Man (10)
Mr. James (5)
My Children (10)
My Own Fault (7)
My Pretty Girl (9)
My Time After A While (1)
My Train Time (18)
Nature's Disappearing (9)
Night Flyer (9)
No More Tears (2)
No Reply (3,12)
Nobody Cares (13)
Off The Road (9)
Oh, Pretty Woman (1,16)
Open Up A New Door (3)
Out Of Reach (12)
People Cling Together (8)
Picture On The Wall (5)
Plan Your Revolution (8)
Play The Harp (13)

Please Don't Tell (2,12)
Possessive Emotions (9)
Prisons On The Road (10)
R And B Time Medley (16)
Ready To Ride (4)
Reasons (15)
Red Sky (15)
Respectfully Yours (18)
Room To Move (6)
Runaway (16)
Sandy (3)
Saw Mill Gulch Road (6)
Send Me Down To Vicksburg (19)
Sensitive Kind (9)
Separate Ways (13)
She's Too Young (3)
Sitting Here Thinking (17)
Sitting In The Rain (5)
Sitting On The Outside (18)

Snowy Wood (1,7)
So Hard To Share (6)
So Many Roads (5)
So Much To Do (13)
Somebody Acting Like A Child (4)
Someday After A While (You'll Be Sorry) (16)
Something New (8)
Sonny Boy Blow (2,12)
Soul Of Short, Fat Man (11)
Stand Back Baby (1,12)
Step In The Sun (18)
Stormy Monday Blues (5,16)
Streamline (9)
Sugarcane (19)
Supernatural, The (1)
Suspicions - Part 1 (12)
Suspicions - Part 2 (5)
Sweet Scorpio (18)

Taxman Blues (18)
Tears In My Eyes (1)
Television Eye (10)
Ten Years Are Gone (17)
Things Go Wrong (15)
Thinking Of My Woman (8)
Thoughts About Roxanne (6)
To A Princess (8)
To Match The Wind (18)
Took The Car (9)
Train, The (11)
Travelling (10)
2401 (4)
Unanswered Questions (10)
Undecided (17)
Vacation (4)
Waiting For The Right Time (8)
Walking On Sunset (4)

What's The Matter With You (16)
When I Go (8)
When I'm Gone (16)
Where Did I Belong? (3)
Where Did My Legs Go (9)
Wish I Knew A Woman (13)
Without Her (19)
Worried Mind (15)
You Must Be Crazy (9)
Your Funeral And My Trial (12)

★★239★★ MAYFIELD, Curtis

Born on 6/3/42 in Chicago. Soul singer/songwriter/producer. With Jerry Butler in the gospel group Northern Jubilee Singers. Joined The Impressions in 1957. Wrote most of the hits for The Impressions, Jerry Butler and himself. Own labels: Windy C, Mayfield and Curtom. Went solo in 1970. Scored films *Superfly*, *Claudine*, *A Piece Of The Action* and *Short Eyes*. Appeared in *Short Eyes*. Paralyzed from the chest down when a stage lighting tower fell on him prior to a concert on 8/13/90.

DEBUT DATE	PEAK POS	WKS CHR	GOLD	#	ARTIST — Album Title	$	Label & Number
10/3/70	19	49	●	1	Curtis	$12	Curtom 8005
5/29/71	21	38		2	Curtis/Live! ....[L]	$12	Curtom 8008 [2]
11/6/71	40	19		3	Roots	$12	Curtom 8009
8/26/72	1⁴	46	●	4	Superfly ....[S]	$12	Curtom 8014
3/3/73	180	6		5	Curtis Mayfield/His Early Years With The Impressions ....[G]	$12	ABC 780 [2]
6/9/73	16	26	●	6	Back To The World	$12	Curtom 8015
11/17/73	135	10		7	Curtis In Chicago ....[L]	$12	Curtom 8018

includes "Once In My Life" & "Preacher Man" by The Impressions, "Duke Of Earl" by Gene Chandler and "Love Oh Love" by Leroy Hutson

5/25/74	39	22		8	Sweet Exorcist	$10	Curtom 8601
11/16/74	76	7		9	Got To Find A Way	$10	Curtom 8604
6/7/75	120	11		10	There's no place like America Today	$10	Curtom 5001
7/4/76	171	8		11	Give, Get, Take And Have	$10	Curtom 5007
3/26/77	173	3		12	Never Say You Can't Survive	$10	Curtom 5013
8/11/79	42	16		13	Heartbeat	$8	RSO 3053
7/19/80	180	4		14	The Right Combination	$8	RSO 3084

LINDA CLIFFORD/CURTIS MAYFIELD

| 7/26/80 | 128 | 10 | | 15 | Something To Believe In | $8 | RSO 3077 |

Ain't No Love Lost (9,14)
All Night Long (12)
Amen (5,7)
Back To The World (6)
Beautiful Brother Of Mine (3)
Between You Baby And Me (13,14)
Billy Jack (10)
Blue Monday People (10)
Can't Say Nothin' (6) *88*
Can't Work No Longer (5)
Cannot Find A Way (9)
Check Out Your Mind (2)
(Don't Worry) If There's A Hell Below We're All Going To Go (1,2) *29*
Eddie You Should Know Better (4)
Emotions (5)
For Your Precious Love (7)
Freddie's Dead (Theme From "Superfly") (4) *4* (also see: Superfly)
Future Shock (6) *39*

Future Song (Love A Good Woman, Love A Good Man) (6)
Get A Little Bit (Give, Get, Take And Have) (11)
Get Down (3) *69*
Get Up And Move (5)
Give It Up (1)
Give Me Your Love (Love Song) (4)
Grow Closer Together (5)
Gypsy Woman (2,5)
Hard Times (10)
Heartbeat (13)
I Plan To Stay A Believer (2)
I'm Gonna Win Your Love (12)
I'm So Proud (5,7,14)
I'm The One Who Loves You (5)
If I Were Only A Child Again (6,7) *71*
In Your Arms Again (Shake It) (11)

It's All Right (5,15)
It's Lovin' Time (Your Baby's Home) (14)
Jesus (10)
Junkie Chase (4)
Just Want To Be With You (12)
Keep On Keeping On (3)
Keep On Pushing (5)
Keep On Trippin' (6)
Kung Fu (8) *40*
Little Child Runnin' Wild (4)
Love Me, Love Me Now (15)
Love Me (Right In The Pocket) (9)
Love To Keep You In My Mind (3)
Love To The People (10)
Love's Sweet Sensation (14)
Make Me Believe In You (8)
Makings Of You (1,2)
Mighty Mighty (Spade And Whitey) (2)
Miss Black America (1)

Mothers' Son (9)
Move On Up (1)
Mr. Welfare Man (1)
Never Let Me Go (5,15)
Never Say You Can't Survive (12)
Never Stop Loving Me (15)
No Thing On Me (Cocaine Song) (4)
Now You're Gone (3)
Only You Babe (11)
Other Side Of Town (1)
Over The Hump (13)
P.S. I Love You (11)
Party Night (11)
People Get Ready (2,5)
People Never Give Up (15)
Power To The People (3)
Prayer, A (9)
Pusherman (4)
Ridin' High (5)
Right Combination (14)
Right On For The Darkness (6)

Rock You To Your Socks (14)
Sad, Sad Girl And Boy (5)
Show Me Love (9)
So In Love (10) *67*
So You Don't Love Me (9)
Something To Believe In (5)
Sometimes I Wonder (5)
Soul Music (11)
Sparkle (12)
Stare And Stare (2)
Stone Junkie (4)
Suffer (8)
Superfly (4,7) *8* (also see: Freddie's Dead)
Sweet Exorcist (8)
Talking About My Baby (5)
Tell Me, Tell Me (How Ya Like To Be Loved) (13)
Think (4)
This Love Is Sweet (11)
To Be Invisible (8)
Tripping Out (15)
Underground (13)
Victory (13)

We Got To Have Peace (3)
We The People Who Are Darker Than Blue (1,2)
We're A Winner (2,5)
We're Rolling On (5)
We've Only Just Begun (2)
What Is My Woman For? (13)
When Seasons Change (10)
When We're Alone (12)
When You Used To Be Mine (12)
Wild And Free (1)
Woman's Got Soul (5)
You Better Stop! (13)
You Must Believe Me (5)
You're So Good To Me (13)

MAYS, Lyle — see METHENY, Pat

MAZARATI

Minneapolis funk-rock septet — Sir Casey Terry, lead singer. Group formed and produced by Prince's bassist, Brownmark.

| 4/19/86 | 133 | 8 | | | Mazarati | $8 | Paisley P. 25368 |

I Guess It's All Over
Lonely Girl On Bourbon Street
100 MPH
Players' Ball
She's Just That Kind Of Lady
Strawberry Lover
Stroke
Suzy

★★334★★ MAZE Featuring Frankie Beverly

Soul group formed in Philadelphia as The Butlers (later, Raw Soul); moved to San Francisco in 1972. Nucleus consisted of Frankie Beverly (vocals), Wayne Thomas, Sam Porter, Robin Duhe, Roame Lowry and McKinley Williams.

2/26/77	52	45	●	1	Maze featuring Frankie Beverly	$8	Capitol 11607
2/4/78	27	22	●	2	Golden Time Of Day	$8	Capitol 11710
4/7/79	33	22	●	3	Inspiration	$8	Capitol 11912
8/2/80	31	23	●	4	Joy And Pain	$8	Capitol 12087

DEBUT DATE	PEAK POS	WKS CHR	GOLD	ARTIST — Album Title	$	Label & Number

MAZE Featuring Frankie Beverly — Cont'd

DEBUT DATE	PEAK POS	WKS CHR	GOLD	ARTIST — Album Title	$	Label & Number
7/4/81	34	27	●	5 Live In New Orleans ....[L]	$10	Capitol 12156 [2]
				side 4 contains new studio recordings		
5/28/83	25	26		6 We Are One	$8	Capitol 12262
3/30/85	45	30	●	7 Can't Stop The Love	$8	Capitol 12377
9/20/86	92	11		8 Live In Los Angeles ....[L]	$10	Capitol 12479 [2]
				sides 1-3: Live; side 4: new studio recordings		
9/23/89	37	22	●	9 Silky Soul...	$8	Warner 25802

Ain't It Strange (3)
Back In Stride (7,8) *88*
Before I Let Go (5,8)
Call On Me (3)
Can't Get Over You (9)
Can't Stop The Love (7)
Change Our Ways (9)
Changing Times (4,5)
Color Blind (1)
Dee's Song (8)
Family (4)

Feel That You're Feelin' (3,5,8) *67*
Freedom (South Africa) (8)
Golden Time Of Day (2)
Happiness (4)
Happy Feelin's (1,5,8)
I Love You Too Much (6)
I Need You (2)
I Wanna Be With You (8)
I Wanna Thank You (6,8)

I Want To Feel I'm Wanted (7,8)
I Wish You Well (2)
Joy And Pain (4,5,8)
Just Us (9)
Lady Of Magic (1)
Look At California (1,5)
Look In Your Eyes (4,5)
Love Is The Key (6) *80*
Love's On The Run (9)
Lovely Inspiration (3)

Magic (7)
Mandela (9)
Metropolis (6)
Never Let You Down (6)
Place In My Heart (7)
Reaching Down Inside (7)
Reason (5)
Right On Time (6)
Roots (4)
Running Away (5,8)
Silky Soul (9)

Somebody Else's Arms (9)
Song For My Mother (2)
Songs Of Love (9)
Southern Girl (4,5)
Time Is On My Side (1)
Timin' (3)
Too Many Games (7,8)
Travelin' Man (2)
We Are One (6,8)
We Need Love To Live (5)
Welcome Home (3)

When You Love Someone (8)
While I'm Alone (1) *89*
Woman Is A Wonder (3)
Workin' Together (2)
You (1,5,8)
You're Not The Same (2)
Your Own Kind Of Way (6)

MBULU, Letta
Singer from South Africa. Toured with Harry Belafonte for four years. Background vocals by her husband, Caiphus Semenya.

DEBUT DATE	PEAK POS	WKS CHR	GOLD	ARTIST — Album Title	$	Label & Number
3/19/77	192	3		There's Music In The Air...................................	$8	A&M 4609
				produced by Herb Alpert		

Ain't No Way To Treat A Lady
Feelings
Let's Go Dancing (medley)

Maru A Pula (Clouds Of Rain)
Music Man

Rainy Day Music
Sacred Drum
There's Music In The Air

Tristeza (Reuniao De Tristeza)

You've Lost That Lovin' Feeling (medley)

McAULEY SCHENKER GROUP — see SCHENKER, Michael, Group

M.C. BRAINS
Born James De Shannon Davis in Cleveland. Rapper discovered by Michael Bivins (New Edition, Bell Biv DeVoe). In 1992, age 17.

DEBUT DATE	PEAK POS	WKS CHR	GOLD	ARTIST — Album Title	$	Label & Number
4/4/92	47	17		Lovers Lane	$12	Motown 6342

"B" Is Dumb
Boyz II Men (The Sequel)
Brains Goin' Cra-ze

Brainstorming *69*
Don't Let Me Get Loose

Everybody's Talking About
M.C. Brains
G-String

Oochie Coochie *21*
Strawberry Lane

M.C. BREED & DFC
Eric Breed, nineteen-year-old (in 1991) male rapper from Flint, Michigan.

DEBUT DATE	PEAK POS	WKS CHR	GOLD	ARTIST — Album Title	$	Label & Number
8/31/91	142	10		1 M.C. Breed & DFC	$12	S.D.E.G. 4103
5/30/92	155	4		2 20 Below..	$12	Wrap 8109
				MC BREED		

Ain't No Future In Yo' Frontin' (1) *66*
Ain't To Be F...ed With (2)
Ain't Too Much Worried (2)
Be Myself (2)

Better Terms (1)
Black For Black (1)
Dis Mode (2)
Flash's Groove (2)
Get Loose (1)

Great Depression (2)
Guanja (1)
I Will Excell (1)
Jealous Pimp (2)
Job Corp (1)

Just Kickin' It (1)
Life Of A Flintstone (2)
Little Child Running Wild (2)
More Power (1)
No Frontin' Allowed (2)

Shout Out (2)
That's Life (1)
20 Below (2)
Underground Slang (1)
Whenever You Want Me (2)

McBRIDE & THE RIDE
Country trio of notable Nashville session musicians: Terry McBride (vocals, bass), Ray Herndon (guitar) and Billy Thomas (drums). McBride is the son of country singer Dale McBride.

DEBUT DATE	PEAK POS	WKS CHR	GOLD	ARTIST — Album Title	$	Label & Number
6/29/91	180	8		1 Burnin' Up The Road	$12	MCA 42343
5/16/92	144	10		2 Sacred Ground	$12	MCA 10540

Ain't No Big Deal (1)
All I Have To Offer You Is Me (2)
Baby I'm Loving You Now (2)

Burnin' Up The Road (1)
Can I Count On You (1)
Chains Of Memory (1)
Every Step Of The Way (1)

Felicia (1)
Going Out Of My Mind (2)
I'm The One (2)
Just One Night (2)

Love's On The Line (2)
Makin' Real Good Time (2)
Nobody's Fool (2)
Sacred Ground (2)

Same Old Star (1)
Stone Country (1)
Trick Rider (1)
Turn To Blue (1)

Your One And Only (2)

McCALL, C.W.
Born William Fries on 11/15/28 in Audubon, Iowa. The character "C.W. McCall" was created for the Mertz Bread Company. Fries was their advertising man. Elected mayor of Ouray, Colorado in the early '80s.

DEBUT DATE	PEAK POS	WKS CHR	GOLD	ARTIST — Album Title	$	Label & Number
4/12/75	143	9		1 Wolf Creek Pass	$10	MGM 4989
11/29/75+	12	19	●	2 Black Bear Road	$10	MGM 5008
5/8/76	143	4		3 Wilderness	$8	Polydor 6069

Aurora Borealis (3)
Black Bear Road (2)
Classified (3)
Columbine (3)
Convoy (2) *1*
Crispy Critters (3)
Four Wheel Cowboy (3)
Four Wheel Drive (1)

Ghost Town (2)
Glenwood Canyon (1)
Green River (3)
I've Trucked All Over This Land (1)
Jackson Hole (3)
Lewis And Clark (2)

Little Brown Sparrow And Me (3)
Long Lonesome Road (2)
Mountains On My Mind (2)
Night Rider (1)
Old Home Filler-Up An' Keep On-A-Truckin' Cafe (1) *54*

Old 30 (1)
Oregon Trail (1)
Riverside Slide (3)
Rocky Mountain September (1)
Roy (3)
Silver Iodide Blues (3)
Silverton, The (2)

Sloan (1)
Telluride Breakdown (3)
There Won't Be No Country Music (There Won't Be No Rock 'N' Roll) (3) *73*
Wilderness (3)
Wolf Creek Pass (1) *40*

Write Me A Song (2)

McCALLUM, David
Born on 9/19/33 in Glasgow, Scotland. Studio orchestra conductor. Son of a concert violinist. Portrayed secret agent Illya Kuryakin on TV's The Man From U.N.C.L.E.

DEBUT DATE	PEAK POS	WKS CHR	GOLD	ARTIST — Album Title	$	Label & Number
2/26/66	27	24		1 Music - A Part Of Me ....[I]	$15	Capitol 2432
6/11/66	79	12		2 Music: A Bit More Of Me ....[I]	$15	Capitol 2498

Batman Theme (2)
Call Me (2)
Downtown (1)
Edge, The (2)
Far Away Blue (1)
Far Side Of The Moon (1)

Final (2)
5 O'Clock World (2)
I Can't Get No Satisfaction (1)
"In" Crowd (1)
Insomnia (1)

Isn't It Wonderful (2)
It Won't Be Wrong (2)
Louise (1)
Michelle (2)
My World Is Empty Without You (1)

1-2-3 (1)
Shadow Of Your Smile (Love Theme From The Sandpiper) (2)
Sugar Cane (1)
Taste Of Honey (1)

Turn, Turn, Turn (1)
Uptight (Everything's Alright) (2)
We Gotta Get Out Of This Place (1)
Yesterday (1)

McCAMPBELL BROTHERS — see MAC BAND

McCANN, Les

Born on 9/23/35 in Lexington, Kentucky. Jazz keyboardist/vocalist. First recorded with Leroy Vinnegar (bass) and Ron Jefferson (drums), as Les McCann Ltd, for Pacific Jazz in 1959.

DEBUT DATE	PEAK POS	WKS CHR		#	Album Title		$	Label & Number
3/29/69	169	10		1	Much Les	[I]	$10	Atlantic 1516
12/13/69+	29	38		2	Swiss Movement	[I-L]	$12	Atlantic 1537
					LES McCANN & EDDIE HARRIS recorded live at the Montreux Jazz Festival, Switzerland			
5/29/71	41	27		3	Second Movement	[I]	$10	Atlantic 1583
					EDDIE HARRIS & LES McCANN			
4/8/72	141	6		4	Invitation To Openness	[I]	$10	Atlantic 1603
10/7/72	181	6		5	Talk To The People		$10	Atlantic 1619
1/18/75	166	4		6	Another Beginning		$10	Atlantic 1666
11/22/75	161	4		7	Hustle To Survive		$10	Atlantic 1679

Beaux J. Poo Boo (4)
Benjamin (1)
Burnin' Coal (1)
Butterflies (medley) (7)
Carry On Brother (3)
Changing Seasons (7)
Cold Duck Time (2)
Compared To What (2) 85
Doin' That Thing (1)

Everytime I See A Butterfly (medley) (7)
Generation Gap (2)
Go On And Cry (6)
Got To Hustle To Survive (7)
Kathleen's Theme (2)
Let It Lay (5)
Let Your Learning Be Your Eyes (7)

Love For Sale (1)
Lovers, The (4)
Maybe You'll Come Back (6)
Morning Song (6)
My Soul Lies Deep (6)
North Carolina (5)
Poo Pye McGoochie (And His Friends) (4)
Roberta (1)

Samia (3)
Says Who Says What? (7)
Seems So Long (5)
Set Us Free (3)
Shamading (5)
She's Here (5)
Shorty Rides Again (3)
Somebody's Been Lying 'Bout Me (6)

Someday We'll Meet Again (6)
Song Of Love (6)
Talk To The People (5)
Universal Prisoner (3)
Us (7)
Well, Cuss My Daddy (7)
What's Going On (5)
When It's Over (6)
Why Is Now (7)

Will We Ever Find Our Fathers (7)
With These Hands (1)
You Got It In Your Soulness (2)

McCANN, Peter

Connecticut native; staffwriter with ABC Music. Wrote Jennifer Warnes' hit "Right Time Of The Night."

DEBUT DATE	PEAK POS	WKS CHR		Album Title		$	Label & Number
7/30/77	82	12		Peter McCann		$8	20th Century 544

Broken White Line
Do You Wanna Make Love 5

Everybody's Got To Hold On To Something
I Can't Live Without You

If You Can't Find Love
It's Easy

Right Time Of The Night
Save Me Your Love

Suicide And Vine
Things You Left Behind

★★29★★ McCARTNEY, Paul/Wings

Born James Paul McCartney on 6/18/42 in Liverpool, England. Writer of over 50 top 10 singles. Founding member/bass guitarist of The Beatles. Married Linda Eastman on 3/12/69. First solo album in 1970. Formed group Wings in 1971 with wife Linda (keyboards, backing vocals), Denny Laine (ex-Moody Blues; guitar) and Denny Seiwell (drums). Henry McCullough (guitar) joined in 1972. Seiwell and McCullough left in 1973. In 1975, Joe English (drums) and ex-Thunderclap Newman guitarist Jimmy McCulloch (d: 9/27/79 [age 26] of heart failure); both left in 1977. Wings officially disbanded in April 1981. McCartney starred in own film *Give My Regards To Broad Street* (1984). Won Lifetime Achievement Grammy in 1990.

DEBUT DATE	PEAK POS	WKS CHR	GOLD	#	Album Title		$	Label & Number
					PAUL McCARTNEY:			
5/9/70	1³	47	▲²	1	McCartney		$15	Apple 3363
					recorded at home by Paul as a one-man band			
					PAUL AND LINDA McCARTNEY:			
6/5/71	2²	37	▲	2	RAM		$15	Apple 3375
					WINGS:			
12/25/71+	10	18	●	3	Wild Life		$12	Apple 3386
5/12/73	1³	31	●	4	Red Rose Speedway		$12	Apple 3409
12/22/73+	1⁴	116	▲³	5	Band On The Run		$12	Apple 3415
					above 2: PAUL McCARTNEY & WINGS			
6/14/75	1¹	77	▲	6	Venus And Mars		$12	Capitol 11419
4/10/76	1⁷	51	▲	7	Wings At The Speed Of Sound		$10	Capitol 11525
12/25/76+	1¹	86	▲	8	Wings Over America	[L]	$15	Capitol 11593 [3]
					30 tracks from their 1976 U.S. tour			
4/15/78	2⁶	28	▲	9	London Town		$12	Capitol 11777
12/9/78+	29	18	▲	10	Wings Greatest	[G]	$8	Capitol 11905
6/30/79	8	24	▲	11	Back To The Egg		$8	Columbia 36057
					PAUL McCARTNEY:			
6/14/80	3	19	●	12	McCartney II		$12	Columbia 36511
					recorded solely by Paul at his home			
1/31/81	158	3		13	The McCartney Interview	[T]	$10	Columbia 36987
					no track titles listed on this album			
5/15/82	1³	29	▲	14	Tug Of War		$8	Columbia 37462
11/19/83	15	24	▲	15	Pipes Of Peace		$8	Columbia 39149
					above 2 produced by George Martin			
11/10/84	21	18	●	16	Give my regards to Broad Street	[S]	$8	Columbia 39613
					13 of 16 cuts are re-recordings of Beatles/McCartney hits			
9/13/86	30	22		17	Press To Play		$8	Capitol 12475
12/19/87+	62	17		18	All The Best!	[G]	$12	Capitol 48287 [2]
6/24/89	21	49	●	19	Flowers In The Dirt		$8	Capitol 91653
11/24/90	26	16		20	Tripping The Live Fantastic	[L]	$23	Capitol 94778 [2]
					30 Beatles, Wings and solo McCartney songs performed on Paul's 1989-90 world tour			
12/15/90+	141	9	▲	21	Tripping The Live Fantastic - highlights!	[L]	$12	Capitol 95379
					17 tracks from the above album: 13 Beatles songs and 4 solo songs			
6/22/91	14	8		22	Unplugged (The Official Bootleg)	[L]	$12	Capitol 96413
					live acoustic music from the MTV program *Unplugged*, recorded at Limehouse Studios in Wembley, London on 1/25/91 features Linda McCartney, Paul "Wix" Wickens, Blair Cunningham, Hamish Stuart and Robbie McIntosh			
11/16/91	109	3		23	CHOBA B CCCP - The Russian Album		$12	Capitol 97615
					released exclusively in the U.S.S.R. on vinyl in 1988 on the Melodiya label; CD includes bonus track; translation of title (pronounced snova v'ess ess ess ar): Again In USSR			

DEBUT DATE	PEAK POS	WKS CHR	GOLD	ARTIST — Album Title	$	Label & Number

McCARTNEY, Paul/Wings — Cont'd

| 11/16/91 | 177 | 6 | 24 | Paul McCartney's Liverpool Oratorio Conducted by Carl Davis .... | $22 | EMI 54371 [2] |

Kiri Te Kanawa/Sally Burgess/Jerry Hadley/Willard White; cd: Carl Davis; pf: Royal Liverpool Philharmonic Orchestra & Choir and Choristers Of Liverpool Cathedral; McCartney's first classical recording

After The Ball (medley) (11)
Again And Again And Again (11)
Ain't No Sunshine (22)
Ain't That A Shame (20,23)
And I Love Her (22)
Angry (17)
Another Day (10,18) *5*
Arrow Through Me (11) *29*
Average Person (7)
Baby's Request (11)
Back In The U.S.S.R. (20,21)
Back Seat Of My Car (2)
Backwards Traveller (medley) (9)
Ballroom Dancing (14,16)
Band On The Run (5,8,10,18,20) *1*
Be-Bop-A-Lula (22)
Be What You See (14)
Beware My Love (7,8)
Big Barn Bed (4)
Bip Bop (3)
Birthday (20,21)
Blackbird (8,22)
Blue Moon Of Kentucky (22)
Bluebird (5,8)
Bogey Music (12)
Bring It On Home To Me (23)
Broadcast, The (17)
C Moon (18)
Cafe On The Left Bank (9)
Call Me Back Again (6,8)
Can't Buy Me Love (20,21)
Carry That Weight (medley) (20,21)
Children Children (9)
Coming Up (Live At Glasgow) (12,18,20,21) *1*
Cook Of The House (7)
Corridor Music (16)
Crackin' Up (20,23)
Crises (24)
Crossroads Theme (6)
Crypt (24)
Cuff Link (medley) (9)
Darkroom (12)
Dear Boy (2)
Dear Friend (3)

Deliver Your Children (9)
Distractions (19)
Don't Be Careless Love (19)
Don't Get Around Much Anymore (23)
Don't Let It Bring You Down (9)
Don't Let The Sun Catch You Crying (20)
Dress Me Up As A Robber (14)
Eat At Home (2)
Ebony And Ivory (14,18,20) *1*
Eleanor Rigby (16,20,21)
Eleanor's Dream (medley) (16)
End, The (medley) (20,21)
Every Night (1,22)
Famous Groupies (9)
Father (24)
Feel The Sun (medley) (17)
Figure Of Eight (19,20) *92*
Fool On The Hill (20)
Footprints (17)
For No One (16)
Front Parlour (12)
Frozen Jap (12)
Get It (14)
Get On The Right Thing (4)
Getting Closer (11) *20*
Girlfriend (9)
Glasses (medley) (1)
Go Now (8)
Golden Slumbers (medley) (20,21)
Good Day Sunshine (16)
Good Rockin' Tonight (22)
Good Times Coming (medley) (17)
Goodnight Tonight (18) *5*
Got To Get You Into My Life (20,21)
Hands Of Love (medley) (4)
Heart Of The Country (2)
Helen Wheels (5) *10*
Here, There And Everywhere (16,22)

Here Today (14)
Hey Hey (15)
Hey Jude (20,21)
Hi-Heel Sneakers (22)
Hi, Hi, Hi (8,10) *10*
Hold Me Tight (medley) (4)
Hot As Sun (medley) (1)
How Many People (19)
However Absurd (17)
I Am Your Singer (3)
I Lost My Little Girl (22)
I Saw Her Standing There (20,21)
I'm Carrying (9)
I'm Gonna Be A Wheel Someday (23)
I'm In Love Again (23)
I've Had Enough (9) *25*
I've Just Seen A Face (8,22)
If I Were Not Upon The Stage (20)
Inner City Madness (20)
Jet (5,8,10,18,20) *7*
Junk (1,22)
Just Because (23)
Kansas City (23)
Keep Under Cover (15)
Kreen-Akrore (1)
Lady Madonna (8)
Lawdy Miss Clawdy (23)
Lazy Dynamite (medley) (4)
Let 'Em In (7,8,10,18) *3*
Let It Be (20,21)
Let Me Roll It (5,8)
Listen To What The Man Said (6,8,18) *1*
Little Lamb Dragonfly (4)
Live And Let Die (8,10,18,20) *2*
London Town (9) *39*
Long And Winding Road (8,16,20,21)
Long Haired Lady (2)
Loup (1st Indian On The Moon) (4)
Love Awake (medley) (11)

Love Is Strange (3)
Lovely Linda (1)
Lucille (23)
Magneto And Titanium Man (6,8)
Mamunia (5)
Man, The (15)
Man We Was Lonely (1)
Matchbox (20)
Maybe I'm Amazed (1,8,20) *10*
Medicine Jar (6,8)
Midnight Special (23)
Million Miles (medley) (11)
Momma Miss America (1)
Monkberry Moon Delight (2)
Morse Moose And The Grey Goose (9)
Motor Of Love (19)
Move Over Busker (17)
Mrs. Vandebilt (5)
Mull Of Kintyre (10)
Mumbo (1)
Must Do Something About It (7)
My Brave Face (19,20,21) *25*
My Love (4,8,10,18) *1*
Name And Address (9)
Nineteen Hundred And Eighty Five (5)
No More Lonely Nights (16,18) *6*
No Values (16)
No Words (5)
Nobody Knows (12)
Not Such A Bad Boy (16)
Note You Never Wrote (7)
Old Siam, Sir (11)
On The Way (12)
One More Kiss (4)
One Of These Days (12)
Only Love Remains (17)
Oo You (1)
Other Me (15)
Peace (24)
Picasso's Last Words (Drink To Me) (5,8)
Pipes Of Peace (15)

Pound Is Rising (14)
Power Cut (medley) (4)
Press (17) *21*
Pretty Little Head (17)
Put It There (19,20,21)
Ram On (2)
Reception (11)
Richard Cory (8)
Rockestra Theme (11)
Rough Ride (19,20)
Sally (20)
San Ferry Anne (7)
San Francisco Bay Blues (22)
Say Say Say (15,18) *1*
School (24)
Sgt. Pepper's Lonely Hearts Club Band (20,21)
She's A Woman (22)
She's My Baby (7)
Showtime (20)
Silly Love Songs (7,8,10,16,18) *1*
Singalong Junk (1)
Singing The Blues (22)
Single Pigeon (4)
Smile Away (2)
So Bad (15) *23*
So Glad To See You Here (11)
Solly (8)
Some People Never Know (3)
Somebody Who Cares (14)
Spin It On (11)
Spirits Of Ancient Egypt (6,8)
Stranglehold (17) *81*
Summer's Day Song (12)
Summertime (23)
Sweetest Little Show (15)
Take It Away (14) *10*
Talk More Talk (17)
Teddy Boy (1)
Temporary Secretary (12)
That Day Is Done (19)
That Would Be Something (1,22)
That's All Right Mama (23)
Things We Said Today (20,21)
This One (19,20) *94*
3 Legs (2)

Through Our Love (15)
Time To Hide (7,8)
To You (11)
Together (20)
Tomorrow (2)
Too Many People (2)
Treat Her Gently - Lonely Old People (6)
Tug Of Peace (15)
Tug Of War (14) *53*
Twenty Flight Rock (20,23)
Uncle Albert/Admiral Halsey (2,10,18) *1*
Valentine Day (1)
Venus And Mars Rock Show (6,8) *12*
Wanderlust (14,16)
War (24)
Warm And Beautiful (7)
Waterfalls (12)
We Can Work It Out (22)
We Got Married (19,20,21)
We're Open Tonight (11)
Wedding (24)
What's That You're Doing? (14)
When The Night (4)
Wild Life (3)
Wino Junko (7)
Winter Rose (medley) (11)
With A Little Luck (9,10,18) *1*
Work (24)
Yesterday (8,16,20)
You Gave Me The Answer (6,8)
You Want Her Too (19)

McCLAIN, Alton, & Destiny

Black female trio. Destiny: D'Marie Warren and Robyrda Stiger.

| 3/31/79 | 88 | 16 | | Alton McClain & Destiny .... | $8 | Polydor 6163 |

Crazy Love

God Said, "Love Ye One Another"
It Must Be Love *32*
My Empty Room

Power Of Love
Push And Pull

Sweet Temptation
Taking My Love For Granted

McCLINTON, Delbert

Born on 11/4/40 in Lubbock, Texas. Played harmonica on Bruce Channel's hit "Hey Baby." Leader of the Ron-Dels.

6/30/79	146	6		1 Keeper Of The Flame	$8	Capricorn 0223
11/22/80+	34	28		2 The Jealous Kind	$8	Capitol 12115
12/5/81+	181	9		3 Plain' From The Heart	$8	Capitol 12188
5/30/92	118	13		4 Never Been Rocked Enough	$12	Curb 77521

Baby Ruth (2)
Be Good To Yourself (3)
Blues As Blues Can Get (4)
Bright Side Of The Road (2)
Can I Change My Mind (4)
Cease And Desist (4)
Everytime I Roll These Dice (4)
Fool In Love (3)

Giving It Up For Your Love (2) *8*
Going Back To Louisiana (2)
Good Man, Good Woman (4)
Have A Little Faith In Me (4)
Have Mercy (1)
Heartbreak Radio (3)
I Can't Quit You (2)

I Don't Want To Hear It Anymore (3)
I Feel So Bad (3)
I Received A Letter (1)
I Used To Worry (4)
I Wanna Thank You Baby (3)
I'm Talking About You (1)

I've Got Dreams To Remember (3)
In The Midnight Hour (3)
Jealous Kind (2)
Just A Little Bit (1)
Lipstick Traces (On A Cigarette) (3)
Mess Of Blues (1)

Miss You Fever (4)
My Sweet Baby (3)
Never Been Rocked Enough (4)
Plain Old Makin' Love (1)
Rooster Blues (3)
Sandy Beaches (3)
Seesaw (1)

Shaky Ground (2)
Shot From The Saddle (1)
Shotgun Rider (2) *70*
Stir It Up (4)
Take Me To The River (2)
Two More Bottles Of Wine (1)
Why Me? (4)

McCOO, Marilyn, & Billy Davis, Jr.

Marilyn (b: 9/30/43, Jersey City, New Jersey) and husband Billy (b: 6/26/39, St. Louis) were members of The 5th Dimension. Marilyn co-hosted TV's *Solid Gold* from 1981-84.

9/18/76+	30	38	●	1 I Hope We Get To Love In Time	$10	ABC 952
8/20/77	57	8		2 The Two Of Us	$8	ABC 1026
10/7/78	146	6		3 Marilyn & Billy	$8	Columbia 35603

Carry Me (3)
Easy Way Out (1)
Hard Road Down (2)
I Got Love For You (3)
I Got The Words, You Got The Music (3)

I Hope We Get To Love In Time (1) *91*
Look What You've Done To My Heart (2) *51*
I Still Will Be With You (1)
I Thank You (3)
I Thought It Took A Little Time (But Today I Fell In Love) (3)

In My Lifetime (2)
My Love For You (Will Always Be The Same) (1)
My Reason To Be Is You (2)
My Very Special Darling (2)

Never Gonna Let You Go (1)
Nightsong (2)
Nothing Can Stop Me (1)
Saving All My Love For You (3)
Shine On Silver Moon (3)
So Many Things For Free (3)

Stay With Me (3)
Times, The (2)
Two Of Us (3)
We've Got To Get It On Again (1)
Wonderful (2)

You Can't Change My Heart (1)
You Don't Have To Be A Star (To Be In My Show) (1) *1*
You Got The Love (3)
Your Love (1) *15*

DEBUT DATE	PEAK POS	WKS CHR	G O L D	ARTIST — Album Title	$	Label & Number

McCORMICK, Gayle
Born in St. Louis. Former lead singer of the group Smith.

| 10/16/71 | 198 | 3 | | Gayle McCormick .... | $12 | Dunhill 50109 |

C'est La Vie   **Gonna Be Alright Now 84**   Natural Woman   Save Me   **You Really Got A Hold On**
Everything Has Got To Be   If Only You Believe   Rescue Me   Superstar   **Me 98**
Free   **It's A Cryin' Shame 44**

McCOY, Charlie
Born on 3/28/41 in Oak Hill, West Virginia. Top Nashville harmonica player and session musician.

5/6/72	98	25		1 The Real McCoy .... [I]	$10	Monument 31359
11/25/72	120	13		2 Charlie McCoy .... [I]	$10	Monument 31910
7/21/73	155	6		3 Good Time Charlie .... [I]	$10	Monument 32215

Danny Boy (2)   Grade A (2)   I'm So Lonesome I Could   Loving Her Was Easier   Real McCoy (1)   To Get To You (2)
Delta Dawn (2)   Hangin' On (1)   Cry (2)   (Than Anything I'll Ever Do   Rocky Top (2)   Today I Started Loving You
Don't Touch Me (3)   Help Me Make It Through   Is Anybody Goin' To San   Again) (1)   Shenandoah (3)   Again (1)
Easy Lovin' (1)   The Night (1)   Antone (3)   Me And Bobby McGee (2)   Something (3)   Woman (Sensuous Woman)
First Time Ever (I Saw Your   How Can I Unlove You (1)   Jackson (1)   Minor Miner (3)   Soul Song (3)   (2)
Face) (2)   I Can't Stop Loving You (1)   John Henry (3)   Only Daddy That'll Walk The   Take Me Home Country
Good Time Charlie's Got The   I Really Don't Want To Know   Louisiana Man (3)   Line (1)   Roads (1)
Blues (3)   (2)   Orange Blossom Special (1,3)   'Till I Get It Right (3)

McCOY, Van
Pianist/producer/songwriter/singer. Born on 1/6/44 in Washington, D.C.; died on 7/6/79 of a heart attack. Formed own Rock'N label in 1960. A&R man at Scepter/Wand from 1961-64. Own MAXX label, mid-1960s. Produced The Shirelles, Gladys Knight, The Stylistics and Brenda & The Tabulations.

| 4/26/75 | 12 | 23 | | 1 Disco Baby .... | $10 | Avco 69006 |

VAN McCOY & The Soul City Symphony

| 8/16/75 | 181 | 4 | | 2 From Disco To Love .... [E] | $10 | Buddah 5648 |

originally released in 1972

10/18/75	80	7		3 The Disco Kid	$10	Avco 69009
5/8/76	106	17		4 The Real McCoy	$8	H&L 69012
1/8/77	193	2		5 The Hustle And Best Of Van McCoy .... [G]	$8	H&L 69016

African Symphony (4)   Earthquake (3)   I'm Gonna Love You (3)   Love Child (3)   So Many Mountains (2)   Turn This Mother Out (1)
Change With The Times   Fire (1)   I'm In Love With You Baby   Love Is The Answer (5)   Soul Cha Cha (5)   Walk, The (3)
(3,5) **46**   Get Dancin' (1)   (2)   **Night Walk** (4) **96**   Soul Improvisations (2)   Words Spoken Softly At
Disco Baby (1,5)   Good Night, Baby (3)   Jet Setting (4)   Now That You're Gone (2)   Spanish Boogie (1)   Midnight (3)
Disco Kid (3,5)   Hey Girl, Come And Get It   Just In Case (2)   **Party** (4,5) **69**   Star Trek, Theme From (4,5)
Doctor's Orders (1)   (1,5)   Keep On Hustlin' (3)   Pick Up The Pieces (1)   Sweet, Sweet Rhythm (4)
Don't Hang Me Up (2)   **Hustle, The** (1,5) **1**   Let Me Down Easy (4)   Roll With The Punches (3)   (To Each His Own) That's
Don't Rock The Boat (2)   I Would Love To Love You (2)   Love At First Sight (4)   Shakey Ground (1)   My Philosophy (4)

McCOYS, The
Rock band formed in Union City, Indiana. Rick Derringer (real name: Zehringer; vocals, guitar), brother Randy Zehringer (drums), Randy Hobbs (bass) and Ronnie Brandon (keyboards). Rick went solo in 1974.

| 11/20/65+ | 44 | 19 | | Hang On Sloopy .... | $30 | Bang 212 |

All I Really Want To Do   High Heel Sneakers   I Can't Help Fallin In Love   If You Tell A Lie   Papa's Got A Brand New Bag   Stormy Monday Blues
Fever 7   I Can't Explain It   I Can't Mind   Meet The McCoys   Sorrow   Stubborn Kind Of Fellow
Hang On Sloopy 1

McCRAE, George
Born on 10/19/44 in West Palm Beach, Florida. Duets with wife Gwen McCrae; became her manager.

| 8/3/74 | 38 | 15 | | 1 Rock Your Baby .... | $10 | TK 501 |
| 7/5/75 | 152 | 5 | | 2 George McCrae .... | $10 | TK 602 |

above 2 produced by KC with background music by The Sunshine Band

Baby Baby Sweet Baby (2)   **I Can't Leave You Alone**   I Need Somebody Like You   **Look At You** (1) **95**   Take This Love Of Mine (2)   You Got My Heart (1)
Honey I (2) **65**   (1) **50**   (1)   Make It Right (1)   When I First Saw You (2)   You Got To Know (2)
I Ain't Lyin' (2)   **I Get Lifted** (1) **37**   It's Been So Long (2)   **Rock Your Baby** (1) **1**   You Can Have It All (1)   You Treat Me Good (2)
      Sing A Happy Song (2)

McCRAE, Gwen
Born on 12/21/43 in Pensacola, Florida. Married George McCrae, who later became her manager. First recorded with George for Alston in 1969.

| 6/28/75 | 121 | 10 | | Rockin' Chair .... | $10 | Cat 2605 |

For Your Love   He Keeps Something Groovy   It Keeps On Raining   Let Them Talk   90% Of Me Is You
He Don't Ever Lose His   Goin' On   It's Worth The Hurt   Move Me Baby   **Rockin' Chair 9**
Groove

McCRARYS, The
R&B group consisting of siblings Linda, Charity, Alfred and Sam McCrary.

| 9/9/78 | 138 | 9 | | Loving Is Living .... | $8 | Portrait 34764 |

Don't Wear Yourself Out   Here's That Feeling   Loving Is Living   Thinking About You   **You 45**
Givin' It Up   Looking Ahead   Take Me To Your Leader   Wonderful Feeling   You Are The Key

McCULLOCH, Ian
Born on 5/5/59 in Liverpool, England. Lead singer of Echo & The Bunnymen. In late 1970s, in The Crucial Three with Julian Cope.

| 11/25/89 | 179 | 1 | | Candleland .... | $8 | Sire 26012 |

Candleland   Faith And Healing   Horse's Head   In Bloom   Start Again
Cape, The   Flickering Wall   I Know You Well   Proud To Fall   White Hotel

McDONALD, Country Joe — see COUNTRY JOE

McDONALD, Kathi
Backing vocalist for Joe Cocker, Leon Russell and others.

| 4/6/74 | 156 | 11 | | Insane Asylum .... | $12 | Capitol 11224 |

All I Want To Be   Down To The Wire   Heartbreak Hotel   Insane Asylum   Somethin' Else   To Love Somebody
Bogart To Bowie   Freak Lover   If You Need Me   (Love Is Like A) Heat Wave   Threw My Love Away

McDONALD, Michael
Born on 12/2/52 in St. Louis, Missouri. Vocalist/keyboardist. First recorded for RCA in 1972. Formerly with Steely Dan and The Doobie Brothers. Married to singer Amy Holland.

DEBUT DATE	PEAK POS	WKS CHR	GOLD	ARTIST — Album Title	$	Label & Number
8/28/82	6	32	●	1 If That's What It Takes	$8	Warner 23703
9/7/85	45	15		2 No Lookin' Back	$8	Warner 25291
6/2/90	110	14		3 Take It To Heart	$12	Reprise 25979

All We Got (3)
Any Foolish Thing (2)
Bad Times (2)
Believe In It (1)
By Heart (2)
Don't Let Me Down (2)
Get The Word Started (3)

Homeboy (3)
I Can Let Go Now (1)
I Gotta Try (1) **44**
(I Hang) On Your Every Word (2)
I Keep Forgettin' (Every Time You're Near) (1) **4**

(I'll Be Your) Angel (2)
If That's What It Takes (1)
Lonely Talk (3)
Losin' End (1)
Lost In The Parade (2)
Love Can Break Your Heart (3)

Love Lies (1)
No Amount Of Reason (3)
No Lookin' Back (2) **34**
No Such Luck (1)
One Step Away (3)
Our Love (2)
Playin' By The Rules (1)

Searchin' For Understanding (3)
Take It To Heart (3) **98**
Tear It Up (3)
That's Why (1)
You Show Me (3)

McDUFF, Brother Jack
Born Eugene McDuffy on 9/17/26 in Champaign, Illinois. R&B/jazz-styled organist. With Schoolboy Porter in 1946, Jimmy Coe, Willis Jackson, 1958-59. First recorded for Prestige in 1960.

DEBUT DATE	PEAK POS	WKS CHR	GOLD	ARTIST — Album Title	$	Label & Number
6/15/63	101	4		1 Screamin'	[I] $30	Prestige 7259
11/9/63	81	14		2 Live!	[I-L] $30	Prestige 7274
				with George Benson (guitar)		
7/23/66	137	4		3 Together Again!	[I] $15	Prestige 7364
				WILLIS JACKSON with JACK McDUFF		
12/13/69+	192	6		4 Down Home Style	[I] $12	Blue Note 84322

After Hours (1)
As She Walked Away (4)
Butter (For Yo Popcorn) (4)
Down Home Style (4)

Electric Surfboard, Theme From (4) **95**
Glad 'A See Ya' (3)
Groovin' (4)
He's A Real Gone Guy (1)

I Cover The Waterfront (1)
It Ain't Necessarily So (2)
It Might As Well Be Spring (3)
It's All A Joke (4)

Memphis In June (4)
One O'Clock Jump (1)
Real Good'un (2)
Rock Candy (2)
Sanctified Samba (2)

Screamin' (1)
Soulful Drums (1)
This'll Get To Ya' (3)
Three Little Words (3)
Tu'Gether (3)

Undecided (2)
Vibrator, The (4)
Whistle While You Work (1)

McENTIRE, Reba
Born on 3/28/54 in Chockie, Oklahoma. Country singer. Sang with older brother Pake and younger sister Susie at rodeos as the Singing McEntires while a teenager. Competed in rodeos as a horseback barrel rider. Discovered by country singer Red Steagall when she sang the National Anthem at the National Rodeo Finals in Oklahoma City in 1974. Married rodeo champion Charlie Battles on 6/21/76; divorced in 1987. First worked on the *Grand Ole Opry* in 1977, became a member in 1985. Acted in the film *Tremors*.

DEBUT DATE	PEAK POS	WKS CHR	GOLD	ARTIST — Album Title	$	Label & Number
6/6/87	139	23	▲	1 Reba McEntire's Greatest Hits	[G] $8	MCA 5979
10/10/87	102	20	●	2 The Last One To Know	$8	MCA 42030
5/21/88	118	10	●	3 Reba	$8	MCA 42134
6/3/89	78	18	▲	4 Sweet Sixteen	$8	MCA 6294
				her 16th album		
10/14/89	124	8	●	5 Live	[L] $8	MCA 8034
				recorded in Palm Desert, California on 4/2-4/89		
9/22/90+	39	89	▲	6 Rumor Has It	$12	MCA 10016
10/19/91	13	69↑	▲²	7 For My Broken Heart	$12	MCA 10400

All Dressed Up (With Nowhere To Go) (7)
Am I The Only One Who Cares (7)
Bobby (7)
Buying Her Roses (7)
Can't Stop Now (5)
Cathy's Clown (4,5)
Climb That Mountain High (6)
Do Right By Me (3)
Everytime You Touch Her (3)
Fallin' Out Of Love (6)
Fancy (6)
For My Broken Heart (7)
Girl Who Has Everything (2)

Greatest Man I Never Knew (7)
Have I Got A Deal For You (1)
He Broke Your Memory Last Night (1)
He's In Dallas (7)
How Blue (1)
I Don't Want To Be Alone (2)
I Don't Want To Mention Any Names (2)
I Know How He Feels (3,5)
I Wouldn't Go That Far (7)
I've Still Got The Love We Made (2)
If I Had Only Known (7)
Is There Life Out There (7)

It Always Rains On Saturday (4)
Jolene (5)
Just A Little Love (1)
Just Across The Rio Grande (2)
Last One To Know (2)
Let The Music Lift You Up (5)
Little Girl (4,5)
Little Rock (1,5)
Love Will Find Its Way To You (2)
Mama Tried (5)
New Fool At An Old Game (3,5)
New Love (4)

Night Life (5)
Night The Lights Went Out In Georgia (7)
Now You Tell Me (6)
One Promise Too Late (1,5)
Only In My Mind (1)
Respect (3,5)
Rumor Has It (6)
San Antonio Rose (5)
Say The Word (4)
Silly Me (3)
So, So, So Long (3,5)
Somebody Should Leave (1)
Somebody Up There Likes Me (4,5)
Someone Else (2)

Stairs, The (2)
Sunday Kind Of Love (3,5)
Sweet Dreams (5)
That's All She Wrote (6)
This Picture (6)
'Til Love Comes Again (4)
Waitin' For The Deal To Go Down (4)
Walk On (4)
What Am I Gonna Do About You (1)
What You Gonna Do About Me (2)
Whoever's In New England (1,5)
Wish I Were Only Lonely (3)

You Lie (6)
You Must Really Love Me (4,5)
You Remember Me (6)
You're The One I Dream About (3)

McFADDEN & WHITEHEAD
R&B duo of Gene McFadden and John Whitehead from Philadelphia. Wrote songs for many Philadelphia soul acts; defined "The Sound Of Philadelphia." Whitehead recorded solo in 1988.

DEBUT DATE	PEAK POS	WKS CHR	GOLD	ARTIST — Album Title	$	Label & Number
6/2/79	23	17	●	1 McFadden & Whitehead	$8	Phil. Int. 35800
10/4/80	153	6		2 I Heard It In A Love Song	$8	TSOP 36773

Ain't No Stoppin' Us Now (1) **13**
Always Room For One More (2)
Do You Want To Dance (1)

Don't Feel Bad (2)
Got To Change (1)
I Got The Love (1)
I Heard It In A Love Song (2)

I Know What I'm Gonna Do (2)
I've Been Pushed Aside (1)
Just Wanna Love You Baby (2)

Love Song Number 690 (Life's No Good Without You) (2)
Mr. Music (1)

That Lets Me Know I'm In Love (2)
This Is My Song (2)
Why Oh Why (2)

You're My Someone To Love (1)

McFARLAND, Gary
Born on 10/23/33 in Los Angeles. Jazz arranger/composer/conductor. Co-founder of Skye Records.

DEBUT DATE	PEAK POS	WKS CHR	GOLD	ARTIST — Album Title	$	Label & Number
4/19/69	189	3		America The Beautiful	[I] $12	Skye 8
				a jazz lament for America		

Due To A Lack Of Interest, Tomorrow Has Been Cancelled

80 Miles An Hour Through Beer-Can Country
If I'm Elected

Last Rites For The Promised Land

On This Site Shall Be Erected...

Suburbia - Two Poodles And A Plastic Jesus

McFERRIN, Bobby
Born on 3/11/50 in New York City. Unaccompanied, jazz-styled improvisation vocalist. Sang the 1987 *Cosby Show* theme and the Levi's 501 Blues jingle. Father was a baritone with the New York Metropolitan Opera.

DEBUT DATE	PEAK POS	WKS CHR	GOLD	ARTIST — Album Title	$	Label & Number
3/21/87	103	19		1 Spontaneous Inventions	$8	Blue Note 85110
				featuring Herbie Hancock, The Manhattan Transfer & Robin Williams		
4/23/88	5	55	▲	2 Simple Pleasures	$8	EMI-Man. 48059

DEBUT DATE	PEAK POS	WKS CHR	GOLD	ARTIST — Album Title	$	Label & Number
				McFERRIN, Bobby — Cont'd		
11/24/90	146	22	3	Medicine Music	$12	EMI 92048
2/15/92	93	18	4	Hush	$12	Sony 48177
				YO-YO MA & BOBBY McFERRIN		

All I Want (2)
Angry (3)
Baby (3)
Bach: Air (4)
Bach: Musette (4)
Barriere: Allegro Prestissimo (4)
Beverly Hills Blues (1)
Cara Mia (1)

Come To Me (2)
Common Threads (3)
Coyote (4)
Discipline (3)
Don't Worry Be Happy (2) 1
Drive (2)
Drive My Car (2)
From Me To You (1)
Garden, The (3)
Good-Bye (4)

Good Lovin' (2)
Gounod: Ave Maria (4)
Grace (4)
He Ran All The Way (3)
Hoedown! (4)
Hush Little Baby (4)
I Hear Music (1)
Manana Iguana (1)
Medicine Man (3)
Opportunity (1)

Rachmaninoff: Vocalise (4)
Rimsky-Korsakov: Flight Of The Bumblebee (4)
Simple Pleasures (2)
Soma So De La De Sase (2)
Stars (4)
Sunshine Of Your Love (2)
Susie Q (2)
Sweet In The Mornin' (3)
Them Changes (2)

There Ya Go (1)
Thinkin' About Your Body (1)
Train, The (3)
Turtle Shoes (1)
23rd Psalm (3)
Vivaldi: Andante (4)
Walkin' (1)
Yes, You (3)

MC5
Detroit hard-rock quintet — Rob Tyner, lead singer (b: Robert Derminer; d: 9/17/91 [age 46] from a heart attack). Guitarist Fred "Sonic" Smith married Patti Smith. MC5 is short for Motor City Five.

3/8/69	30	23	1	Kick Out The Jams ....[L]	$35	Elektra 74042
2/21/70	137	7	2	Back In The USA	$20	Atlantic 8247
				produced by rock critic Jon Landau		

American Ruse (2)
Back In The USA (2)
Borderline (1)
Call Me Animal (2)

Come Together (1)
High School (1)
Human Being Lawnmower (2)

I Want You Right Now (1)
Kick Out The Jams (1) 82
Let Me Try (2)
Looking At You (2)

Motor City Is Burning (1)
Ramblin' Rose (1)
Rocket Reducer No. 62 (Rama Lama Fa Fa Fa) (1)

Shakin' Street (2)
Starship (1)
Teenage Lust (2)
Tonight (2)

Tutti-Frutti (2)

McGOVERN, Maureen
Born on 7/27/49 in Youngstown, Ohio. Pop singer. Sang theme of TV show *Angie*. Cameo roles in *The Towering Inferno* and *Airplane* (as Sister Angelina). Starred in Broadway's *Pirates Of Penzance* for 14 months.

7/28/73	77	16	1	The Morning After...	$10	20th Century 419
9/8/79	162	10	2	Maureen McGovern	$8	Warner 3327

And This I Find Is Beautiful (1)
Can You Read My Mind (2) 52
Can't Take My Eyes Off You (2)

Can't You Hear The Song (1)
Carolina Moon (2)
Darlene (1)
Different Worlds (2) 18
Don't Try To Close A Rose (1)

He's A Rebel (2)
I Won't Last A Day Without You (1) 89
I'm Happy Just To Dance With You (1)

If I Wrote You A Song (1)
In Too Deep (2)
It Might As Well Stay Monday (From Now On) (1)
Life's A Long Way To Run (2)

Midnight Storm (1)
Morning After (1) 1
Until It's Time For You To Go (1)
Very Special Love (2)

Yes, I'm Ready (2)

McGRATH, Bob — see CHILDRENS section

McGRIFF, Jimmy
Born on 4/3/36 in Philadelphia. Jazz-R&B organist/multi-instrumentalist.

12/1/62+	22	27	1	I've Got A Woman ....[I]	$25	Sue 1012
11/21/64	146	2	2	Topkapi ....[I]	$25	Sue 1033
5/29/65	130	6	3	Blues For Mister Jimmy ....[I]	$25	Sue 1039
12/28/68+	161	19	4	The Worm ....[I]	$15	Solid State 18045

After Hours (1)
All About My Girl (1) 50
Blue Juice (4)
Blue Star (2)
Blues For Joe (3)
Blues For Mr. Jimmy (3)
Bump De Bump (3)
Cash Box (3)
Discotheque U.S.A. (3)

Dog (You Dog) (3)
Exodus Song (2)
Flying Home (1)
From Russia With Love (2)
Girl Talk (4)
Heavyweight (4)
I've Got A Woman Part I (1) 20
Keep Loose (4)

Lock It Up (4)
M.G. Blues (1) 95
Man With The Golden Arm, Theme From The (2)
Mr. Lucky (2)
On The Street Where You Live (1)
Party's Over (3)
People (2)

Pink Panther (2)
Rawhide (1)
'Round Midnight (1)
Satin Doll (1)
Sermon (1)
Sho' Nuff (3)
Take The "A" Train (1)
Taste Of Honey (2)
That's The Way I Feel (1)

Think (4)
Topkapi (2)
Turn Blue (2)
Woman Of Straw (1)
World Of Suzie Wong, Love Theme From The (2)
Worm, The (4) 97

McGUFFEY LANE
Country-rock sextet from Columbus, Ohio. Group name taken from a street in Athens, Ohio. Lead singer Bob McNelley died from a self-inflicted gunshot wound on 1/7/87 (age 36). Keyboardist Stephen Douglass died on 1/12/84 (age 33) in an auto accident.

1/23/82	193	6		Aqua Dream..	$8	Atco 144

Bag Of Rags Medley (1)
Don't You Think About Me (When I'm Gone)

Dream About You (2)
Fair Weather Friends (1)

Fallin' Timber (2)
It Comes From The Heart (4)

New Beginning (2)
Outlaw Rider (4)

Start It All Over 97
Tennessee (4)

McGUINN, Roger
Founder/lead singer/guitarist of The Byrds. Born James McGuinn on 7/13/42 in Chicago. Changed name to Roger in 1968. Had been with Bobby Darin's band and The Chad Mitchell Trio, prior to forming The Byrds.

7/14/73	137	9	1	Roger McGuinn	$10	Columbia 31946
9/28/74	92	6	2	Peace On You	$10	Columbia 32956
7/5/75	165	5	3	Roger McGuinn & Band	$10	Columbia 33541
1/26/91	44	17	4	Back From Rio	$12	Arista 8648
				featuring all-star lineup of Elvis Costello, Stan Ridgway, David Crosby, Chris Hillman, John Jorgenson, Tom Petty & Tim B. Schmitt		

Bag Full Of Money (1)
Better Change (2)
Born To Rock And Roll (3)
Bull Dog (3)
Car Phone (4)
Circle Song (3)
Do What You Want To (2)
Draggin' (1)
Easy Does It (3)

Gate Of Horn (2)
Going To The Country (2)
Hanoi Hannah (1)
Heave Away (1)
I'm So Restless (1)
If We Never Meet Again (4)
King Of The Hill (4)
Knockin' On Heaven's Door (3)

Lady, The (2)
Lisa (3)
Lost My Drivin' Wheel (1)
Lover Of The Bayou (3)
M' Linda (1)
My New Woman (1)
Painted Lady (3)
Peace On You (1)

(Please Not) One More Time (2)
Same Old Sound (2)
So Long (3)
Somebody Loves You (3)
Someone To Love (4)
Stone (1)
Suddenly Blue (4)
Time Cube (1)

Time Has Come (4)
Together (2)
Trees Are All Gone (4)
Water Is Wide (1)
Without You (2)
Without Your Love (4)
You Bowed Down (4)
Your Love Is A Gold Mine (4)

McGUINN, CLARK & HILLMAN
Roger McGuinn (b: 7/13/42; vocals, guitar), Gene Clark (b: 11/17/44; d: 5/24/91; guitar) and Chris Hillman (b: 6/4/42; bass). All are former members of The Byrds.

2/24/79	39	19	1	McGuinn, Clark & Hillman	$8	Capitol 11910

DEBUT DATE	PEAK POS	WKS CHR	GOLD	ARTIST — Album Title	$	Label & Number

McGUINN, CLARK & HILLMAN — Cont'd

| 2/16/80 | 136 | 7 | 2 | City .... | $8 | Capitol 12043 |

ROGER McGUINN and CHRIS HILLMAN FEATURING GENE CLARK

Backstage Pass (1)	Don't You Write Her Off (1) 33	Let Me Down Easy (2)	Painted Fire (2)	Skate Date (2)	Surrender To Me (1)

Backstage Pass (1)
Bye Bye, Baby (1)
City (2)
Deeper In (2)

Don't You Write Her Off (1) 33
Feelin' Higher (1)
Givin' Herself Away (2)

Let Me Down Easy (2)
Little Mama (1)
Long Long Time (1)
One More Chance (2)

Painted Fire (2)
Release Me Girl (1)
Sad Boy (1)

Skate Date (2)
Stopping Traffic (1)
Street Talk (2)

Surrender To Me (1)
Who Taught The Night (2)
Won't Let You Down (2)

McGUINNESS FLINT
British rock group led by Tom McGuinness (b: 12/2/41) and Hughie Flint (b: 3/15/42). Both formerly with Manfred Mann.

| 1/30/71 | 155 | 8 | 1 | McGuinness Flint .... | $12 | Capitol 625 |
| 9/11/71 | 198 | 2 | 2 | Happy Birthday, Ruthy Baby .... | $12 | Capitol 794 |

Bodang Buck (1)
Brother Pysche (1)
Changes (2)
Conversation (2)
Dream Darling Dream (1)

Faith And Gravy (2)
Fixer (2)
Friends Of Mine (2)
Happy Birthday, Ruthy Baby (2)

Heritage (1)
I'm Letting You Know (1)
International (1)
Jimmy's Song (2)
Klondike (2)

Lazy Afternoon (1)
Let It Ride (1)
Mister, Mister (1)
Piper Of Dreams (2)
Reader To Writer (2)

Sparrow (2)
When I'm Alone With You (2)
When I'm Dead And Gone (1) 47
Who You Got To Love (1)

McGUIRE, Barry
Born on 10/15/37 in Oklahoma City. Member of The New Christy Minstrels. Currently records Contemporary Christian music.

| 9/25/65 | 37 | 21 | | Eve Of Destruction .... | $30 | Dunhill 50003 |

Ain't No Way I'm Gonna Change My Mind
Baby Blue

Eve Of Destruction 1
Mr. Man On The Street - Act One

She Belongs To Me
Sins Of A Family
Sloop John B.

Try To Remember
What Exactly's The Matter With Me

Why Not Stop And Dig It While You Can

You Never Had It So Good
You Were On My Mind

McGUIRE SISTERS, The
Sisters Christine (b: 7/30/29), Dorothy (b: 2/13/30) and Phyllis (b: 2/14/31) from Middletown, Ohio. Replaced the Chordettes on *Arthur Godfrey And His Friends* show in 1953. Phyllis went solo in 1964. Reunited in 1986.

| 3/5/55 | 11 | 6 | | By Request...[M] | $50 | Coral 56123 |

10" album of 8 songs

Goodnight, Sweetheart, Goodnight

Melody Of Love
Muskrat Ramble

Naughty Lady Of Shady Lane
No More 17

Open Up Your Heart (And Let The Sunshine In)

Seems Like Old Times
Sincerely 1

★★441★★ **M.C. HAMMER**
Born Stanley Kirk Burrell on 3/30/63 in Oakland. Rapper/producer/founder/leader of The Posse, an eight-member group of dancers, DJs and singers. Burrell was an Oakland A's batboy in the 1970s; his nickname "The Little Hammer" stemmed from his resemblance to baseball great Hank "The Hammer" Aaron. Oaktown's 3-5-7 and Ace Juice are members of The Posse. Dropped the M.C. from his name in mid-1991.

12/3/88+	30	80	▲² 1	Let's Get It Started	$8	Capitol 90924
3/10/90	1²¹	108	▲¹⁰ 2	Please Hammer Don't Hurt 'Em	$12	Capitol 92857
11/16/91	2²	54	▲³ 3	Too Legit To Quit	$12	Capitol 98151

HAMMER
cassette includes bonus track not available on CD

Black Is Black (2)
Brothers Hang On (3)
Cold Go M.C. Hammer (1)
Count It Off (3)
Crime Story (2)
Dancin' Machine (2)
Do Not Pass Me By (3) 62
Feel My Power (1)

Find Yourself A Friend (3)
Gaining Momentum (3)
Good To Go (3)
Have You Seen Her (2) 4
Help The Children (3)
Here Comes The Hammer (2) 54
It's Gone (1)

Let's Get It Started (1)
Lets Go Deeper (2)
Living In A World Like This (3)
Lovehold (3)
On Your Face (2)
Pray (2) 2

Pump It Up (Here's The News) (1)
Releasing Some Pressure (3)
Ring 'Em (1)
She's Soft And Wet (2)
Son Of The King (1)
Street Soldiers (3)

Tell Me (Why Can't We Live Together) (3)
That's What I Said (1)
They Put Me In The Mix (1)
This Is The Way We Roll (3) 86
2 Legit 2 Quit (3) 5

Turn This Mutha Out (1)
U Can't Touch This (2) 8
Work This (2)
Yo!! Sweetness (2)
You're Being Served (1)

McKEE, Maria
Born in 1964. Former lead singer of Lone Justice from Los Angeles.

| 7/1/89 | 120 | 15 | | Maria McKee .... | $8 | Geffen 24229 |

Am I The Only One (Who's Ever Felt This Way?)
Breathe

Can't Pull The Wool Down (Over The Little Lamb's Eyes)

Has He Got A Friend For Me?
I've Forgotten What It Was In You (That Put The Need In Me)

More Than A Heart Can Hold
Nobody's Child
Panic Beach

This Property Is Condemned
To Miss Someone

McKENDREE SPRING
Folk-pop quintet led by Fran McKendree.

11/28/70	192	2	1	Second Thoughts...	$15	Decca 75230
5/20/72	163	7	2	McKendree Spring 3	$15	Decca 75332
5/3/75	118	8	3	Get Me To The Country	$10	Pye 12108
3/27/76	193	3	4	Too Young To Feel This Old..	$10	Pye 12124

Because It's Time (1)
Cairo Hotel (1)
Clown (4)
Divide & Concord (4)
Down By The River (2)
Easier Things Have Been Done (3)
Fading Lady (2)

Feeling Bad Ain't Good Enough (2)
Fire And Rain (1)
Flying Dutchman (2)
For What Was Gained (1)
Friends Die Easy (1)
Get Me To The Country (3)

Give All You've Got To Give (3)
Give It Some Time (3)
God Bless The Conspiracy (2)
Got No Place To Fall (1)
Heart Is Like A Wheel (2)
Hobo Lady (2)
Hold On (3)

Hustler, The (3)
I'm Gonna Lose That Game Again (4)
I'm In Love (4)
I've Been On The Mountain (3)
'Lani (1)
Meeting In Paris (3)

My Kind Of Life (4)
Oh In The Morning (2)
Oh Now My Friend (1)
Oh, What A Feeling (4)
Run Like The Wind (4)
She'd Never Leave Chicago (3)

(She's A Housewife) No More Rock 'N' Roll (4)
So Long Daddy-O (3)
Susie, Susie (1)
Take It From The Heart (4)
Too Young To Feel This Old (4)

McKENZIE, Bob & Doug
Canadian comedians Rick Moranis and Dave Thomas of *SCTV*. Both featured in the film *Strange Brew*. Moranis later starred in *Ghostbusters*, *Spaceballs*, *Honey, I Shrunk The Kids* and many others. Thomas, the brother of singer Ian Thomas, hosted own CBS-TV series in 1990.

| 1/9/82 | 8 | 21 | ● | Great White North ....[C] | $8 | Mercury 4034 |

Beerhunter, The
Black Holes
Coffee Sandwich

Doug's Mouth
Elron McKenzie
Ernie's Mom

Gimme A Smoke
Miracle Of Music
O.K., This Is The End, Eh?

Peter's Donuts
Ralph The Dog
School Announcements

Take Off 16
This Is Our Album, Eh?
Twelve Days Of Christmas

Welcome To Side Two
You Are Our Guest (See Page 11 Of Daily Hoser)

492

DEBUT DATE	PEAK POS	WKS CHR	GOLD	ARTIST — Album Title	$	Label & Number

McKENZIE, Scott
Born Philip Blondheim in Jacksonville, Florida on 1/10/39 and raised in Virginia. Sang with John Phillips (Mamas & Papas) in The Journeymen. Co-wrote The Beach Boys' 1988 #1 hit "Kokomo."

| 12/9/67 + | 127 | 7 | | The Voice of Scott McKenzie .... | $20 | Ode 44002 |

Celeste
Don't Make Promises
It's Not Time Now

Like An Old Time Movie 24
No, No, No, No, No

Reason To Believe
Rooms

San Francisco (Be Sure To Wear Flowers In Your Hair) 4

Twelve-Thirty
What's The Difference (Chapter I & II)

McKINLEY, Ray — see MILLER, Glenn

McKNIGHT, Brian
R&B singer/composer from Buffalo, New York. His older brother is Claude McKnight of Take 6.

| 9/12/92 | 149 | 5 | | Brian McKnight .... | $12 | Mercury 848605 |

After The Love
Goodbye My Love
I Can't Go For That

I Couldn't Say
Is The Feeling Gone

Love Me, Hold Me
My Prayer

Never Felt This Way
Oh Lord

One Last Cry
Stay The Night

Way Love Goes
Yours

McKUEN, Rod
Born on 4/29/33 in Oakland, California. Poet/singer/songwriter/producer/actor. Wrote songs for films, 20th Century-Fox and Universal, 1950s and 1960s. Also see San Sebastian Strings and Glenn Yarbrough.

1/27/68	178	6		**1** Listen To The Warm	$15	RCA 3863
11/16/68	175	5		**2** Lonesome Cities	$12	Warner 1758
3/1/69	149	10		**3** Greatest Hits Of Rod McKuen ....[K]	$12	Warner 1772
8/16/69	175	4		**4** The Best Of Rod McKuen ....[K]	$12	RCA 4127
10/11/69	96	16		**5** Rod McKuen At Carnegie Hall ....[L]	$12	Warner 1794 [2]
3/14/70	126	13		**6** New Ballads	$12	Warner 1837
9/19/70	148	8		**7** Rod McKuen's Greatest Hits-2 ....[K]	$12	Warner 2560
3/20/71	182	4		**8** Pastorale..	$12	Warner 1894 [2]
				with The Westminster Symphony Orchestra		
11/6/71	177	3		**9** Rod McKuen Grand Tour ....[L]	$12	Warner 1947 [2]

Ain't You Glad You're Livin', Joe (4)
All I Need (6)
Ally, Ally Oxen Free (3,5)
Along The Coasts Of France - Cannes (2)
Amsterdam (5)
And To Each Season (9)
And Tonight (6)
April People (9)
Art Of Catching Trains (2,5)
As I Love My Own (6,7)
Atlantic Crossing (2)
Beautiful Strangers (7,9)
Before I Loved No One (6)
Before The Monkeys Came (8,9)
Bend Down And Touch Me (5)
Blessings In Shades Of Green (3)
Boat Ride - Los Angeles (2)
Boy Named Charlie Brown (7)
Brown October (1)
Cat Named Sloopy (1,5)
Celebrations - Gstaad (2)
Champion Charlie Brown (7)
Channing Way (4)
Children One And All (9)

Church Windows - San Francisco (2)
Concerto For Four Hands - Gstaad (2)
Cowboys - Cheyenne (2,9)
Dandelion Days (1)
Do It Yourself Protest Songs & Don't Ban The Bomb (5)
Do You Like The Rain? (4)
Doesn't Anybody Know My Name? (5)
Ducks On The Millpond (1)
Each Of Us Alone (9)
Earth, Song From The (9)
El Monte (medley) (9)
Ever Constant Sea (7)
Everybody's Rich But Us (5)
Fields Of Wonder (1)
Find Another Rainbow (8)
First Encounter (medley) (9)
Fly Me To The North (8)
Friendly Sounds (9)
Gee, It's Nice To Be Alone (5)
Gifts From The Sea (4)
Gone With The Cowboys (6,9)
Green Hills Of England (8)
Happy Birthday (medley) (5)
He Ain't Heavy, He's My Brother (8)

Hit 'Em In The Head With Love (6,9)
I Live Alone (1,4)
I Looked At You A Long Time (6)
I Think If You (8,9)
I'll Catch The Sun (3,5)
I'll Fly Northward (medley) (8)
I'll Never Be Alone (1)
I'm Not Afraid (6)
I've Been To Town (5)
I've Saved The Summer (8)
If You Go Away (3,5,9)
Importance Of The Rose (4,5)
In Someone's Shadow (6)
Inside Of Me (7)
It's Raining (1)
Ivy That Clings To The Wall (3,5)
Jean (5,7)
Jef (medley) (9)
Joanna (5)
Kaleidoscope (3,5)
Kelly And Me (medley) (9)
Kill The Wind (8)
Language Of Hello - Paris (2)
Listen To The Warm (1,4,5,7)
Lonesome Cities (2,3)
Long, Long Time (8)
Love, Let Me Not Hunger (8)

Love's Been Good To Me (5,7)
Lovers, The (3)
Make It With You (8)
Man Alone (7)
Manhattan Beach (2)
Marvelous Clouds (3)
Merci Beaucoup (5)
Midnight Walk (1)
Mister Kelly (7, 9)
Morning - San Francisco (2)
Moving Day (8)
Natalie (7)
Not So Greatest Hits Medley (9)
Nothin's Going To Change My World (Across The Universe) (9)
Of Monarchs And Pretenders (9)
One By One (3)
One Day I'll Follow The Birds (1)
One Day Soon (9)
Pastorale: Part 1 (8)
Pastures Green (medley) (8,9)
Pavements Gray (medley) (8)
People On Their Birthdays (5)
Philadelphia (6)
Railroad Song (8)

Rock Gently (6)
Round, Round, Round (1,9)
Royal Albert Hall Overture Medley (9)
Scandalous John, Themes From (9)
Seasons In The Sun (3,5)
She (7)
Silver Apples Of The Moon (8)
Singing Of The Wind (1)
Single Man (4,8)
So Long San Francisco (2)
So Long, Stay Well (5)
So Many Others (9)
Soldiers Who Want To Be Heroes (9)
Some (8)
Some Of Them Fall (medley) (9)
Some Trust In Chariots (4,7)
Something (8)
Stanyan Street (3,5)
Summer Come Down Easy (9)
Summer In My Eye (4)
Sun Is A Moveable Target - Venice (2)
Thank You For Christmas (6)
Things Men Do (5)

Three (8)
Three Poems From Sea Cycle (Numbers 1, 4, And 14) (9)
To Share The Summer Sun (1)
To Watch The Trains (2,5)
Tomorrow And Today (6)
Trashy (5)
Up (9)
Vienna (medley) (9)
Waiting For What? - London (2)
We (5)
Weekend (1)
When Am I Ever Going Home? (8)
Where Are We Now? (1)
While More With You (6)
Wind Of Change (8)
Without A Worry In The World (9)
World I Used To Know (3,5)
Yet Another Sunset (8)
Zangra (medley) (9)

McLACHLAN, Sarah
Twenty-year-old (in 1989) vocalist/guitarist born in Halifax, Nova Scotia, Canada.

| 4/29/89 | 132 | 12 | | **1** Touch .... | $8 | Arista 8594 |
| 4/25/92 | 167 | 4 | | **2** Solace .... | $12 | Arista 18631 |

Back Door Man (2)
Ben's Song (1)
Black (2)
Drawn To The Rhythm (2)

Home (2)
I Will Not Forget You (2)
Into The Fire (2)
Lost (2)

Mercy (2)
Out Of The Shadows (1)
Path Of Thorns (2)
Sad Clown (1)

Shelter (2)
Steaming (1)
Strange World (1)
Touch (1)

Trust (1)
Uphill Battle (1)
Vox (1)

Wear Your Love Like Heaven (2)

McLAGAN, Ian
Born on 5/12/45 in London. Keyboardist of Small Faces and Faces.

| 1/19/80 | 125 | 9 | | Troublemaker... | $8 | Mercury 3786 |

Headlines
Hold On

If It's Alright
La De La

Little Troublemaker
Movin' Out

Mystifies Me
Sign

Somebody
Truly

McLAREN, Malcolm
British entrepeneur. Former manager of the New York Dolls. Put together the Sex Pistols at his London clothing boutique, SEX.

2/18/84	173	6		**1** D'ya Like Scratchin' ....[M]	$8	Island 90124
				with The World Famous Supreme Team		
2/2/85	190	6		**2** Fans	$8	Island 90242
				features adaptations of music from the operas Madam Butterfly, Turandot, Carmen and Gianni Scicchi		

Boys' Chorus (2)
Buffalo Gals (1)
Carmen (2)

D'ya Like Scratchin' (1)
Death Of Butterfly (2)

Fans (2)
Hobo (1)

Lauretta (2)
Madam Butterfly (2)

She's Looking Like A Hobo (1)

World's Famous (1)

DEBUT DATE	PEAK POS	WKS CHR	GOLD	ARTIST — Album Title	$	Label & Number
	★★316★★			**McLAUGHLIN, John**		
				Born on 1/4/42 in Yorkshire, England. Jazz-fusion guitar virtuoso. Formed his Mahavishnu Orchestra in 1971 with Billy Cobham, Jan Hammer, Rick Laird and Jerry Goodman. Original group disbanded in 1973.		
1/29/72	89	26		1 The Inner Mounting Flame ....[I]	$10	Columbia 31067
				MAHAVISHNU ORCHESTRA With JOHN McLAUGHLIN		
7/1/72	194	4		2 My Goal's Beyond ....[I]	$10	Douglas 30766
				MAHAVISHNU JOHN McLAUGHLIN		
10/21/72	152	6		3 Extrapolation ....[E-I]	$10	Polydor 5510
				John's first album, recorded in 1969		
2/10/73	15	37	●	4 Birds Of Fire * ....[I]	$10	Columbia 31996
7/7/73	14	24	●	5 Love Devotion Surrender ....[I]	$10	Columbia 32034
				CARLOS SANTANA/MAHAVISHNU JOHN McLAUGHLIN		
12/22/73+	41	14		6 Between Nothingness & Eternity * ....[I-L]	$10	Columbia 32766
6/1/74	43	14		7 Apocalypse * ....[I]	$10	Columbia 32957
				with the London Symphony Orchestra conducted by Michael Tilson Thomas		
3/22/75	68	11		8 Visions Of The Emerald Beyond * ....[I]	$10	Columbia 33411
2/21/76	118	7		9 Inner Worlds	$10	Columbia 33908
				MAHAVISHNU ORCHESTRA JOHN McLAUGHLIN		
6/12/76	194	2		10 Shakti with John McLaughlin ** ....[I]	$10	Columbia 34162
4/2/77	168	4		11 A Handful Of Beauty ** ....[I]	$8	Columbia 34372
5/27/78	105	14		12 Electric Guitarist ....[I]	$8	Columbia 35326
				JOHNNY McLAUGHLIN		
				reunited with Carlos Santana, Tony Williams, Jack Bruce, Chick Corea, Stanley Clarke, Jerry Goodman and Billy Cobham.		
4/28/79	147	5		13 Electric Dreams ....[I]	$8	Columbia 35785
				JOHN McLAUGHLIN with THE ONE TRUTH BAND		
5/30/81	97	13		14 Friday Night In San Francisco *** ....[I-L]	$8	Columbia 37152
12/12/81	172	4		15 Belo Horizonte ....[I]	$8	Warner 3619
8/20/83	171	5		16 Passion, Grace & Fire *** ....[I]	$8	Columbia 38645
				*MAHAVISHNU ORCHESTRA		
				**SHAKTI with JOHN McLAUGHLIN		
				***JOHN McLAUGHLIN/AL DI MEOLA/PACO DE LUCIA		

All Bliss-All Bliss (medley) (10)
All In The Family (9)
Are You The One? Are You The One? (12)
Argen's Bag (3)
Aspan (16)
Awakening (1)
Be Happy (8)
Belo Horizonte (15)
Binky's Beam (3)
Birds Of Fire (4)
Blue In Green (2)
Can't Stand Your Funk (8)
Celestial Terrestrial Commuters (4)
Chiquito (3)
Cosmic Strut (8)
Dance Of Maya (1)
Dark Prince (13)
David (16)
Dawn (1)
Desire And The Comforter (13)

Do You Hear The Voices That You Left Behind? (12)
Dream (6)
Earth Ship (8)
Electric Dreams, Electric Sighs (13)
Eternity's Breath Part 1 & 2 (8)
Every Tear From Every Eye (12)
Extrapolation (3)
Faith (4)
Fantasia Suite (14)
Follow Your Heart (2)
Frevo Rasgado (14)
Friendship (12)
Gita (9)
Goodbye Pork-Pie Hat (2)
Guardian Angels (13,14)
Hearts And Flowers (2)
Hope (4)
Hymn To Him (7)
I Am Dancing At The Feet Of The Lord (medley) (10)

If I Could See (8)
In My Life (9)
India (11)
Inner Worlds Part 1 & 2 (9)
Isis (11)
It's Funny (3)
Joy (10)
Kriti (11)
La Baleine (15)
La Danse Du Bonheur (11)
La Mere De La Mer (medley) (6)
Lady L (11)
Let Us Go Into The House Of The Lord (5)
Life Divine (5)
Lila's Dance (9)
Lotus Feet (9,10)
Lotus On Irish Streams (1)
Love And Understanding (4)
Love Supreme (5)
Manitas D'oro (For Paco De Lucia) (15)
Meditation (5)

Mediterranean Sundance (medley) (14)
Meeting Of The Spirits (1)
Miles Beyond (Miles Davis) (4,13)
Miles Out (9)
Morning Calls (9)
My Foolish Heart (12)
Naima (5)
New York On My Mind (12)
Noonward Race (1)
On The Way Home To Earth (8)
One Melody (15)
One Word (4)
Open Country Joy (4)
Opus 1 (8)
Orient Blue Suite (Part I, II, III) (16)
Passion, Grace & Fire (16)
Pastoral (8)
Peace One (2)
Peace Two (2)
Peace Piece (3)

Pegasus (8)
Pete The Poet (3)
Phenomenon: Compulsion (12)
Phillip Lane (2)
Planetary Citizen (9)
Power Of Love (7)
Really You Know (3)
Resolution (4)
Rio Ancho (medley) (14)
River Of My Heart (9)
Sanctuary (4)
Sapphire Bullets Of Pure Love (4)
Short Tales Of The Black Forest (14)
Singing Earth (13)
Sister Andrea (4)
Smile Of The Beyond (7)
Something Spiritual (2)
Song For My Mother (2)
Spectrum (3)
Stardust On Your Sleeve (15)

Sunlit Path (medley) (6)
This Is For Us To Share (3)
Thousand Island Park (4)
Tomorrow's Story Not The Same (medley) (6)
Two For Two (3)
Two Sisters (11)
Unknown Dissident (13)
Very Early (Homage To Bill Evans) (15)
Vision Is A Naked Sword (7)
Vital Transformation (1)
Waltz For Bill Evans (2)
Waltz For Katia (15)
Way Of The Pilgrim (9)
What Need Have I For This-What Need Have I For That (medley) (10)
Wings Of Karma (7)
You Know You Know (1)
Zamfir (15)

McLAUGHLIN, Pat
Singer/songwriter/mandolin player from Waterloo, Iowa.

DEBUT DATE	PEAK POS	WKS CHR	GOLD	ARTIST — Album Title	$	Label & Number
4/16/88	195	1		Pat McLaughlin	$8	Capitol 48033

Heartbeat From Havin' Fun In The Mood
Is That My Heart Breakin' Lynda
Moment Of Weakness No Problem
Prisoner Of Your Love Real Thing
Without A Melody Wrong Number
You Done Me Wrong

McLEAN, Don
Born on 10/2/45 in New Rochelle, New York. Singer/songwriter/poet. The hit "Killing Me Softly With His Song" was inspired by Don.

DEBUT DATE	PEAK POS	WKS CHR	GOLD	ARTIST — Album Title	$	Label & Number
11/13/71+	1[7]	48	●	1 American Pie	$12	United Art. 5535
2/12/72	111	10		2 Tapestry ....[R]	$12	United Art. 5522
				Don's first album release		
12/23/72+	23	19		3 Don McLean	$12	United Art. 5651
11/23/74	120	8		4 Homeless Brother	$10	United Art. 315
2/14/81	28	21		5 Chain Lightning	$8	Millennium 7756
11/28/81+	156	11		6 Believers	$8	Millennium 7762

American Pie - Parts I & II (1) **1**
And I Love You So (2)
Babylon (1)
Bad Girl (2)
Believers (6)
Birthday Song (5)
Bronco Bill's Lament (3)
Castles In The Air (2) *flip*
Castles In The Air (6) **36**
Chain Lightning (5)
Circus Song (2)
Crazy Eyes (6)

Crossroads (1)
Crying (5) **5**
Crying In The Chapel (4)
Did You Know (4)
Dreidel (3) **21**
Empty Chairs (1)
Everybody Loves Me, Baby (1)
Falling Through Time (3)
General Store (2)
Genesis (In The Beginning) (5)
Grave, The (1)

Great Big Man (4)
Homeless Brother (4)
I Tune The World Out (6)
If We Try (3) **58**
Isn't It Strange (6)
It Doesn't Matter Anymore (5)
It's A Beautiful Life (5)
It's Just The Sun (5) **83**
Jerusalem (5)
La La Love You (4)
Left For Dead On The Road Of Love (6)

Legend Of Andrew McGrew (4)
Lotta Lovin' (5)
Love Hurts (6)
Love Letters (6)
Magdalene Lane (2)
More You Pay (The More It's Worth) (3)
Narcissma (3)
No Reason For Your Dreams (2)
Oh My What A Shame (3)
On The Amazon (3)

Orphans Of Wealth (2)
Pride Parade (3)
Respectable (3)
Sea Cruise (6)
Sea Man (6)
Since I Don't Have You (5) **23**
Sister Fatima (1)
Sunshine Life For Me (Sail Away Raymond) (4)
Tangled (Like A Spider In Her Hair) (4)
Tapestry (2)

Three Flights Up (2)
Till Tomorrow (1)
Vincent (1) **12**
Winter Has Me In Its Grip (4)
Winterwood (1)
Wonderful Baby (4) **93**
Wonderful Night (5)
Words And Music (5)
You Have Lived (1)
Your Cheating Heart (5)

MC LYTE
Female rapper born in Queens and raised in Brooklyn.

10/21/89	86	20		1 Eyes On This	$8	First Pri. 91304
10/5/91	102	16		2 Act Like You Know	$12	First Pri. 91731

Absolutely Positively.....Practical Jokes (2) — Act Like You Know (2) — All That (2) — Beyond The Hype (2) — Big Bad Sister (2) — Can You Dig It (2) — Cappucino (1) — Cha Cha Cha (1) — Eyes Are The Soul (2) — Funky Song (1) — I Am The Lyte (1) — K-Rock's The Man (2) — K-Rocks Housin' (1) — Kamikaze (1) — Like A Virgin (2) — Lola From The Copa (2) — Not Wit' A Dealer (1) — Please Understand (1) — **Poor Georgie** (2) *83* — Rhyme Hangover (1) — Search 4 The Lyte (2) — Shut The Eff Up! (Hoe) (1) — Slave 2 The Rhythm (1) — Stop, Look, Listen (1) — Survival Of The Fittest (1) — Take It Off (2) — Throwin' Words At U (1) — 2 Young 4 What (2) — When In Love (2)

M.C. MADNESS — see D.J. MAGIC MIKE

McMURTRY, James
Born on 3/18/62 in Fort Worth, Texas. Folk/rock guitarist. Son of novelist Larry McMurtry, the writer of *Lonesome Dove*. Appeared in the 1974 film *Daisy Miller*. Member of the Buzzin' Cousins who appeared in the 1992 film *Falling from Grace* (written by his father).

10/14/89	125	9		Too Long In The Wasteland	$8	Columbia 45229

Angeline — Crazy Wind — I'm Not From Here — Outskirts — Painting By Numbers — Poor Lost Soul — Shining Eyes — Song For A Deck Hand's Daughter — Talkin' At The Texaco — Terry — Too Long In The Wasteland

McNICHOL, Kristy And Jimmy
Los Angeles-born TV/film stars: Kristy (b: 9/11/62), a cast member of TV's *Family* and *Empty Nest*, and her brother Jimmy (b: 7/2/61). Each starred in several films.

8/19/78	116	4		Kristy & Jimmy McNichol	$8	RCA 2875

Box On Wheels — Girl You Really Got Me Goin' — Go For It — He's A Dancer — **He's So Fine** *70* — Hot Tunes — My Boyfriend's Back — Page By Page — Rock & Roll Is Here To Stay — Slow Dance

M.C. POOH
Rapper M.C. Pooh is Lawrence Thomas.

3/28/92	158	6		Funky As I Wanna Be	$12	Jive 41476

POOH-MAN (MC POOH)

Big Gangster — Don't Cost A Dime — Eatin' Pussy — Fuckin' Wit Dank — Funky As I Wanna Be — Mellow Man *[includes 2 versions]* — Niggas Ain't Playin' — Player Haters — Projects, The — Racia — Sex, Money And Murder — Your Dick

McRAE, Carmen
Born on 4/8/20 in New York City. Jazz singer/pianist. Active into the 1990s.

1/14/67	150	2		Alfie	$20	Mainstream 56084

Alfie — And I Love Him — Don't Ever Leave Me — He Loves Me — Music That Makes Me Dance — Night Has A Thousand Eyes — Once Upon A Summertime — Shadow Of Your Smile — Sweetest Sounds — Who Can I Turn To?

MC REN
Rapper Lorenzo Patterson, former member of N.W.A.

7/18/92	12	13 ▲		Kizz My Black Azz	$12	Ruthless 53802

Behind The Scenes — Check It Out Y'all — Final Frontier — Hound Dogz — Kizz My Black Azz — Right Up My Alley

MC SERCH
Half of rap duo 3rd Bass. White rapper Michael Berrin from Queens, New York.

9/12/92	103	11		Return Of The Product	$12	Def Jam 52964

Back To The Grill — Can You Dig It — Daze In A Weak — Don't Have To Be — Hard But True — **Here It Comes** *[includes 2 versions]* *71* — Hits The Head — Return Of The Product — Scenes From The Mind — Social Narcotics

MC SHY D
Rapper born Peter Jones in the Bronx; cousin of Afrika Bambaataa.

6/27/87	197	1		Got To Be Tough	$8	Luke Sky. 1004

Bust This — DJ Man Cuts It Up (Part II) — Don't Take Me Seriously — I Will Go Off — I'm Not A Star — I've Got To Be Tough — Paula's On Crack — Rap Will Never Die (Part II) — Shy-D's Theme — So Take That — We Don't Play (live) — Yes Yes Y'All

MC SKAT KAT And The Stray Mob
MC Skat Kat is an animated character featured in Paula Abdul's "Opposites Attract" video. Created by Michael Patterson and Candace Reckinger. The Stray Mob are Fatz, Taboo, Leo, Micetro, Katleen and Silk.

9/28/91	197	2		The Adventures Of MC Skat Kat And The Stray Mob	$12	Captive 91396

Big Time — Gotta Get Up — I Ain't No Kitty — I Go Crazy — Kat In The Casino — Kat Stories — New Kat Swing — No Dogs Allowed — On The Prowl — Skat Kat's Theme — **Skat Strut** *80* — So Sweet So Young

McVIE, Christine
Born Christine Perfect on 7/12/43 in Birmingham, England. Vocalist with Fleetwood Mac since 1970. Married to Fleetwood Mac bassist John McVie, 1968-77. Quit touring with group after 1990.

8/14/76	104	10		1 The Legendary Christine Perfect Album	$12	Sire 7522

recorded in 1969 under her maiden name, after her departure from Chicken Shack

2/18/84	26	23		2 Christine McVie	$8	Warner 25059

And That's Saying A Lot (1) — Ask Anybody (2) — Challenge, The (2) — Close To Me (1) — Crazy 'Bout You (2) — For You (1) — **Got A Hold On Me** (2) *10* — I Want You (1) — I'd Rather Go Blind (1) — I'm On My Way (1) — I'm The One (2) — I'm Too Far Gone (To Turn Around) (1) — Keeping Secrets (2) — Let Me Go (Leave Me Alone) (1) — **Love Will Show Us How** (2) *30* — No Road Is The Right Road (1) — One In A Million (2) — Smile I Live For (2) — So Excited (2) — Wait And See (1) — When You Say (1) — Who's Dreaming This Dream (2)

MEADER, Vaughn
Born on 3/20/36 in Boston. President John F. Kennedy impersonator.

12/8/62	1¹²	49 ●		1 The First Family	[C] $12	Cadence 3060

1962 Grammy winner: Album of the Year

5/25/63	4	17		2 The First Family, volume two	[C] $20	Cadence 3065

above albums feature Naomi Brossart as Jackie Kennedy

After Dinner Conversation (1) — Announcement, The (2) — Astronauts (1) — Auld Lang Syne (1) — Bedtime Story (1) — Biography (2) — Brothers Three (2) — But Vote !! (1) — Caroline's First Date (2) — Concert, The (2) — Crisis, The (2) — Decision, The (1) — Dress, The (1) — Economy Lunch (1) — Equal Time (2) — Evening With JFK (2) — Experiment, The (1) — First Daughter, The (2)

DEBUT DATE	PEAK POS	WKS CHR	GOLD	ARTIST — Album Title	$	Label & Number

MEADER, Vaughn — Cont'd

First Family March (2)	Motorcade (1)	1996 (2)	Relatively Speaking (1)	Stop The World (2)	Trail, The (2)
Law, The (2)	Movie, The (2)	Party, The (1)	Saturday Night, Sunday	Taxes (2)	White House Visitor (1)
Malayan Ambassador (1)	1958 (2)	Press Conference (1)	Morning (1)	Tour, The (1)	

MEAT LOAF

Born Marvin Lee Aday on 9/27/47 in Dallas. Rock singer. Sang lead vocals on Ted Nugent's 1976 *Free-For-All* LP. Played Eddie in the Los Angeles production and film of *The Rocky Horror Picture Show*. Appeared in films *Americathon, Roadie, Out Of Bounds* and *The Squeeze*.

10/29/77+	14	82	▲7	1 Bat Out Of Hell..	$8	Cleve. I. 34974
9/19/81	45	11		2 Dead Ringer	$8	Cleve. I. 36007
5/18/85	74	10		3 Bad Attitude	$8	RCA 5451

All Revved Up With No Place To Go (1)	Don't Leave Your Mark On Me (3)	I'll Kill You If You Don't Come Back (2)	More Than You Deserve (2)	Peel Out (2)	**Two Out Of Three Ain't Bad** (1) 11
Bad Attitude (3)	Everything Is Permitted (2)	**I'm Gonna Love Her For Both Of Us** (2) 84	Nocturnal Pleasure (2)	Piece Of The Action (3)	**You Took The Words Right Out Of My Mouth** (1) 39
Bat Out Of Hell (1)	For Crying Out Loud (1)	Jumpin' The Gun (3)	Nowhere Fast (3)	Read 'Em And Weep (2)	
Cheatin' In Your Dreams (3)	Heaven Can Wait (1)	Modern Girl (3)	**Paradise By The Dashboard Light Medley** (1) 39	Sailor To A Siren (3)	
Dead Ringer For Love (2)				Surf's Up (3)	

MECO

Disco producer Meco Monardo; born on 11/29/39 in Johnsonburg, Pennsylvania. Played trombone in Cadet Band at West Point. Later moved to New York and became a session musician and arranger. Co-produced Gloria Gaynor's hit "Never Can Say Goodbye."

8/6/77	13	28	▲	1 Star Wars And Other Galactic Funk............................[I]	$8	Millennium 8001
1/14/78	62	13		2 Encounters Of Every Kind.....................................[I]	$8	Millennium 8004
9/23/78	68	12		3 The Wizard Of Oz..[I]	$8	Millennium 8009
				the single "Themes From The Wizard Of Oz" made the *Hot 100* (POS 35)		
8/2/80	140	8		4 Meco Plays Music From The Empire Strikes Back ....[M-I]	$8	RSO 3086
				10" album		
12/13/80	61	6		5 Christmas In The Stars/Star Wars Christmas Album ....[X]	$8	RSO 3093
4/3/82	68	9		6 Pop Goes The Movies ....[I]	$8	Arista 9598
				medleys of 28 movie themes; the single "Pop Goes The Movies" made the *Hot 100* (POS 35)		

Apartment, Theme From The (medley) (6)	Delirious Escape (medley) (3)	Hooray For Hollywood (medley) (6)	Magnificent Seven (medley) (6)	R2-D2 We Wish You A Merry Christmas (5)	Topsy (2)
As Time Goes By (medley) (6)	Desert And The Robot Auction (1)	Hot In The Saddle (2)	March Of The Winkies (3)	Roman Nights (3)	20th Century Fox Trademark (medley) (6)
Asteroid Field (medley) (4)	Ding-Dong! The Witch Is Dead (3)	Icebound (2)	Meaning Of Christmas (5)	Secret Love (medley) (6)	We're Off To See The Wizard (The Wonderful Wizard Of Oz) (3)
Atchison, Topeka And The Santa Fe (medley) (6)	Dorothy's Rescue (3)	If I Were King Of The Forest (3)	Meco's Theme (medley) (6)	Shadow Of Your Smile (medley) (6)	**What Can You Get A Wookie For Christmas (When He Already Owns A Comb?)** (5) 69
Battle In The Snow (6)	Empire Strikes Back Medley (4) 18	Imperial Attack (1)	Merry-Go-Round Broke Down (medley) (6)	Sleigh Ride (5)	
Bells, Bells, Bells (5)	Force Theme (4)	In The Beginning (2)	Merry, Merry Christmas (5)	Spell, The (3)	
Chariots Of Fire, Theme From (medley) (6)	Funk (1)	James Bond Theme (medley) (6)	Merry Old Land Of Oz (3)	**Star Wars Theme/Cantina Band** (1) 1	Windmills Of Your Mind (medley) (6)
Christmas In The Stars (5)	Galactic (1)	Lady Marion (2)	Munchkinland (3)	Strike Up The Band (medley) (6)	Zorba The Greek (medley) (6)
Christmas Sighting (Twas The Night Before Christmas) (5)	Godfather, Theme From The (medley) (6)	Land Of The Sand People (1)	Never On Sunday (medley) (6)	Tara's Theme (medley) (6)	
Close Encounters, Theme From (2) 25	Goldfinger (medley) (6)	Last Battle (1)	Odds Against Christmas (5)	Three Coins In The Fountain (medley) (6)	
Crazy Rhythm (2)	Good, The Bad And The Ugly (medley) (6)	Laura (medley) (6)	Optimistic Voices (3)	Other (1)	3 W. 57 (medley) (2)
Cyclone (3)	Hatari (medley) (6)	Love Is A Many Splendored Thing (medley) (6)	Over The Rainbow (3)	Throne Room And End Title (1)	
Days Of Wine And Roses, Theme From (medley) (6)	Haunted Forest (3)	Love Story, Theme From (medley) (6)	Pink Panther (medley) (6)	Time Machine (2)	
	High And The Mighty (medley) (6)	M.A.S.H., Theme From (medley) (6)	Poppies (3)	Tom Jones (medley) (6)	
			Princess Appears (1)		
			Princess Leia's Theme (1)		

MEDEIROS, Glenn

Born on 6/24/70 and raised in Hawaii. Discovered through a local radio station talent search.

| 6/13/87 | 83 | 17 | | 1 Glenn Medeiros .... | $8 | Amherst 3313 |
| 6/23/90 | 82 | 18 | | 2 Glenn Medeiros .... | $12 | MCA 6399 |

All I'm Missing Is You (2) 32	Cracked Up (2)	Knocking At Your Door (1)	Me - U = Blue (2) 78	She Ain't Worth It (2) 1	Wings Of My Heart (1)
Best Man (2)	Doesn't Matter Anymore (2)	**Lonely Won't Leave Me Alone** (1) 67	Niki (2)	Stranger Tonight (1)	You Left The Loneliest Heart (1)
Boyfriend (2)	Fool's Affair (1)	Lovelylittlelady (2)	**Nothing's Gonna Change My Love For You** (1) 12	**Watching Over You** (1) 80	
	Just Like Rain (2)			What's It Gonna Take (1)	

MEDLEY, Bill

Born on 9/19/40 in Santa Ana, California. Baritone of The Righteous Brothers duo. Co-owner of a Las Vegas nightclub named Kicks with Paul Revere of The Raiders.

| 10/12/68 | 188 | 4 | | 1 Bill Medley 100%.. | $15 | MGM 4583 |
| 4/5/69 | 152 | 4 | | 2 Soft And Soulful .... | $15 | MGM 4603 |

Any Day Now (2)	Let The Good Times Roll (1)	Reaching Back (2)	That's Life (1)	Who Can I Turn To (When Nobody Needs Me) (1)	You Don't Have To Say You Love Me (1)
Brown Eyed Woman (1) 43	One Day Girl (1)	Run To My Loving Arms (1)	Then You Can Tell Me Goodbye (1)	Winter Won't Come This Year (2)	You're Nobody 'Till Somebody Loves You (1)
For Your Precious Love (2)	100 Years (2)	Show Me (1)	When Something Is Wrong With My Baby (2)		
Goin' Out Of My Head (1)	**Peace Brother Peace** (2) 48	Softly, As I Leave You (2)			
I Can't Make It Alone (1) 95	Quest (The Impossible Dream) (1)	Something's So Wrong (2)			
I'm Gonna Die Me (2)		Street Of Dirt (2)			

MEGADETH

Heavy-metal group formed in Southern California by Dave Mustaine (vocals, guitar; former guitarist of Metallica) and Dave Ellefson (bass).

10/25/86	76	47	▲	1 Peace Sells...But Who's Buying?	$8	Capitol 12526
2/6/88	28	23	●	2 so far, so good...so what!	$8	Capitol 48148
10/20/90	23	30	●	3 Rust In Peace	$12	Capitol 91935
8/1/92	2¹	28↑	▲	4 Countdown To Extinction	$12	Capitol 98531

Anarchy In The U.K. (2)	Conjuring, The (1)	Good Mourning (medley) (1)	In My Darkest Hour (2)	Poison Was The Cure (3)	Take No Prisoners (3)
Architecture Of Aggression (4)	Countdown To Extinction (4)	Hangar 18 (3)	Into The Lungs Of Hell (2)	Psychotron (4)	This Was My Life (4)
Ashes In Your Mouth (4)	Dawn Patrol (3)	High Speed Dirt (4)	Liar (2)	Rust In Peace...Polaris (3)	Tornado Of Souls (3)
Bad Omen (1)	Devils Island (1)	Holy Wars...The Punishment Due (3)	Lucretia (3)	Set The World Afire (2)	Wake Up Dead (1)
Black Friday (medley) (1)	Five Magics (3)	Hook In Mouth (2)	Mary Jane (2)	Skin O' My Teeth (4)	
Captive Honour (4)	Foreclosure Of A Dream (4)	I Ain't Superstitious (2)	My Last Words (1)	Sweating Bullets (4)	
	502 (2)		Peace Sells (1)	Symphony Of Destruction (4)	

DEBUT DATE	PEAK POS	WKS CHR	GOLD	ARTIST — Album Title	$	Label & Number

MEHTA, Zubin

Born on 4/29/36 in Bombay, India. Conductor of the Los Angeles Philharmonic Orchestra. Also see soundtrack *Manhattan*.

6/10/72	175	10		1 Gustav Holst: The Planets .... [I]	$8	London 6734
3/4/78	130	8		2 Star Wars and Close Encounters Of The Third Kind .... [I]	$8	London 1001

Battle, The (2)
Cantina Band (2)
Throne Room (2)
Jupiter, The Bringer Of Jollity (1)

Little People (2)
Mars, The Bringer Of War (1)
Mercury, The Winged Messenger (1)

Neptune, The Mystic (1)
Princess Leia's Theme (2)
Saturn, The Bringer Of Old Age (1)

Star Wars, End Title From (2)
Star Wars, Main Title From (2)

Suite From "Close Encounters Of The Third Kind" (2)

Uranus, The Magician (1)
Venus, The Bringer Of Peace (1)

MEISNER, Randy

Born on 3/8/46 in Scottsbluff, Nebraska. Bassist/vocalist of Poco (1968), Rick Nelson's Stone Canyon Band (1969-71) and the Eagles (1971-77).

11/1/80+	50	33		1 One More Song	$8	Epic 36748
8/21/82	94	11		2 Randy Meisner	$8	Epic 38121

Anyway Bye Bye (1)
Come On Back To Me (1)
Darkness Of The Heart (2)
Deep Inside My Heart (1) *22*

Doin' It For Delilah (2)
Gotta Get Away (1)
Hearts On Fire (1) *19*
I Need You Bad (1)

Jealousy (2)
Never Been In Love (2) *28*
Nothing Is Said ('Til The Artist Is Dead) (2)

One More Song (1)
Playin' In The Deep End (2)
Still Runnin' (2)
Strangers (2)

Tonight (2)
Trouble Ahead (1)
White Shoes (1)

MELACHRINO, George, And His Orchestra

Born on 5/1/09 in London of Greek parentage; died on 6/18/65. Multi-instrumentalist. First to use masses of strings to produce sentimental mood music.

1/8/55	10	2		1 **Christmas in High Fidelity** .... [X-I]	$20	RCA 1045
5/25/59	30	1		2 Under Western Skies .... [I]	$20	RCA 1676

Adeste Fideles (1)
Colorado River (2)
Cool Water (2)
Empty Saddles (2)
Fairy On The Christmas Tree (1)

First Noel (1)
Good King Wenceslas (1)
Hark! The Herald Angels Sing (1)
Home On The Range (2)

I Saw Mommy Kissing Santa Claus (1)
Jingle Bells (1)
Last Round-Up (2)
Little Brown Jug (1)
Mrs. Santa Claus (1)

Northwest Trail (2)
Once More It's Christmas (1)
One-Armed Bandit (Nevada) (2)
Red River Valley (2)
Riders In The Sky (2)

Rudolph The Red Nosed Reindeer (1)
San Francisco (2)
Silent Night (1)
Skaters Waltz (1)
Sleigh Ride (1)

Tumbling Tumbleweeds (2)
Wagon Wheels (2)
White Christmas (1)
Winter Wonderland (1)

MEL AND TIM

Cousins Mel Hardin and Tim McPherson, from Holly Springs, Mississippi.

1/6/73	175	7		Starting All Over Again	$15	Stax 3007

Carry Me
Don't Mess With My Money, My Honey Or My Woman

Free For All
Heaven Knows
I May Not Be What You Want

I'm Your Puppet
Starting All Over Again *19*

Too Much Wheelin' And Dealin'

What's Your Name
Wrap It Up

★★455★★ MELANIE

Born Melanie Safka on 2/3/47 in Queens, New York. Neighborhood Records formed by Melanie and her husband/producer Peter Schekeryk.

11/15/69	196	2		1 Melanie	$15	Buddah 5041
5/9/70	17	37	●	2 Candles In The Rain	$12	Buddah 5060
9/26/70	33	19		3 Leftover Wine .... [L]	$12	Buddah 5066
2/27/71	80	10		4 The Good Book	$12	Buddah 95000
11/13/71+	15	27	●	5 Gather Me	$10	Neighbor. 47001
12/4/71+	115	12		6 Garden In The City	$10	Buddah 5095
4/1/72	103	9		7 Four Sides Of Melanie .... [K]	$10	Buddah 95005 [2]
11/11/72	70	20		8 Stoneground Words	$10	Neighbor. 47005
5/12/73	109	11		9 Melanie At Carnegie Hall .... [L]	$12	Neighbor. 49001 [2]
5/11/74	192	4		10 Madrugada	$15	Neighbor. 48001

Actress (9,10)
Again (1)
Alexander Beetle (2)
Animal Crackers (3,7)
Any Guy (1,7,9)
Babe Rainbow (4,7,9)
Baby Day (5)
Baby Guitar (1,9)
Beautiful People (1,3,7,9)
Between The Road Signs (4)
Birthday Of The Rain (4)
Bitter Bad (9) *36*
Brand New Key (5,9) *1*
Candles In The Rain (2)
Carolina In My Mind (2,7)
Center Of The Circle (5)
Chords Of Fame (4)
Christopher Robin (7)

Citiest People (2)
Close To It All (3)
Deep Down Low (1)
Do You Believe (8)
Don't You Wait By The Water (1)
For My Father (1)
Garden In The City (6)
Good Book (4,7)
Good Guys (2)
Happy Birthday (3)
Hearing The News (medley) (9)
Here I Am (8)
Holding Out (10)
I Am Being Guided (10)
I Am Not A Poet (Night Song) (8)

I Don't Eat Animals (3,7)
I Really Loved Harold (7)
I Think It's Going To Rain Today (1)
I'm Back In Town (1,7)
In The Hour (7)
Isn't It A Pity (4)
It's Me Again (9)
Jigsaw Puzzle (4)
Johnny Boy (1,7)
Kansas (5)
Lay Down (Candles In The Rain) (2,7) *6*
Lay Lady Lay (6,7)
Lay Your Hands Across The Six Strings (9)
Leftover Wine (2,3,7)
Little Bit Of Me (9)

Love In My Mind (6)
Love To Lose Again (10)
Lover's Cross (10)
Lovin Baby Girl (2)
Maybe I Was (A Golf Ball) (9)
Maybe Not For A Lifetime (10)
Momma Momma (3)
Mr. Tambourine Man (7)
My Father (4)
My Rainbow Race (8,9)
Nickel Song (4,7) *35*
Peace Will Come (According To Plan) (3,7,9) *32*
People In The Front Row (6)
Pine And Feather (10)
Poet (9)

Pretty Boy Floyd (9,10)
Prize, The (4)
Psychotherapy (3,7,9)
Railroad (5)
Ring Around The Moon (5)
Ring The Living Bell Medley (5,9) *31*
Ruby Tuesday (2,7) *52*
Saddest Thing (3,4)
Seasons To Change (medley) (9)
Sign In The Window (4,7)
Some Day I'll Be A Farmer (5,9)
Some Say (I Got Devil) (5,9)
Somebody Loves Me (6,7)
Song Of The South (9)
Soul Sister Annie (1)

Steppin' (5)
Stoneground Words (8)
Stop I Don't Want To Hear It Anymore (6)
Summer Weaving (8)
Take Me Home (1)
Tell Me Why (5)
Together Alone (8,9) *86*
Tuning My Guitar (1,3)
Uptown Down (1,3)
We Don't Know Where We're Going (6)
What Have They Done To My Song Ma (2,7)
What Wondrous Love (5)
Wild Horses (10)
You Can Go Fishin' (4)

★★225★★ MELLENCAMP, John Cougar

Born on 10/7/51 in Seymour, Indiana. Rock singer/songwriter/producer. Worked outside of music until 1975. Given name Johnny Cougar by David Bowie's manager, Tony DeFries. First recorded for MCA in 1976. Directed and starred in the 1992 film *Falling from Grace*; leader of the Buzzin' Cousins group that appeared in the film. Married model Elaine Irwin on 9/5/92.

JOHN COUGAR:

8/18/79+	64	29		1 John Cougar..	$8	Riva 7401
10/4/80+	37	55		2 Nothin' Matters And What If It Did	$8	Riva 7403
5/8/82	1⁹	120	▲³	3 **American Fool**...	$8	Riva 7501

JOHN COUGAR MELLENCAMP:

11/5/83+	9	66	▲	4 **Uh-Huh**...	$8	Riva 7504
9/14/85	2³	75	▲³	5 **Scarecrow**..	$8	Riva 824865

MELLENCAMP, John Cougar — Cont'd

DEBUT DATE	PEAK POS	WKS CHR	GOLD	ARTIST — Album Title	$	Label & Number
9/19/87	6	53	▲²	6 The Lonesome Jubilee	$8	Mercury 832465
5/27/89	7	23	▲	7 Big Daddy	$8	Mercury 838220

JOHN MELLENCAMP:

| 10/26/91 | 17 | 46 | ▲ | 8 Whenever We Wanted | $12 | Mercury 510151 |

Again Tonight (8) *36* — Cry Baby (2) — Hotdogs and Hamburgers (6) — Mansions In Heaven (7) — Rooty Toot Toot (6) *61* — Tonight (2)
Ain't Even Done With The Night (2) *17* — Danger List (3) — Hurts So Good (3) *2* — Martha Say (7) — Rumbleseat (5) *28* — Void In My Heart (7)
Authority Song (4) *15* — Do You Think That's Fair (1) — I Ain't Ever Satisfied (7) — Melting Pot (8) — Serious Business (4) — Warmer Place To Sleep (4)
Between A Laugh And A Tear (5) — Don't Misunderstand Me (2) — I Need A Lover (1) *28* — Miami (1) — Small Paradise (1) *87* — We Are The People (6)
Big Daddy Of Them All (7) — Down And Out In Paradise (6) — J.M.'s Question (7) — Minutes To Memories (5) — Small Town (5) *6* — Weakest Moments (3)
Can You Take It (3) — Empty Hands (6) — Jack & Diane (1) *1* — Now More Than Ever (8) — Sometimes A Great Notion (7) — Welcome To Chinatown (1)
Cheap Shot (2) — Face Of The Nation (5) — Jackie Brown (7) *48* — Paper In Fire (6) *9* — Sugar Marie (1) — Whenever We Wanted (8)
Check It Out (6) *14* — Get A Leg Up (8) *14* — Jackie O (4) — Peppermint Twist (2) — Taxi Dancer (1) — Wild Angel (2)
Cherry Bomb (6) *8* — Golden Gates (4) — Justice And Independence '85 (5) — Pink Houses (4) *8* — Theo And Weird Henry (7) — You've Got To Stand For Somethin' (5)
China Girl (3) — Grandma's Theme (5) — Last Chance (8) — Play Guitar (4) — They're So Tough (8)
Close Enough (3) — Great Mid-West (1) — Little Night Dancin' (1) — Pop Singer (9) *15* — This Time (2) *27*
Country Gentleman (7) — Hand To Hold On To (3) *19* — Lonely Ol' Night (5) *6* — Pray For Me (1) — Thundering Hearts (3)
Crazy Ones (8) — Hard Times For An Honest Man (5) — Love And Happiness (8) — Rain On The Scarecrow (5) *21* — To Live (7)
Crumblin' Down (4) *9* — Hot Night In A Cold Town (2) — Lovin' Mother Fo Ya (4) — Real Life (6) — To M.G. (Wherever She May Be) (2)
Make Me Feel (4) — R.O.C.K. In The U.S.A. (5) *2*

MELLOW MAN ACE

Black Hispanic rapper. Born Ulpiano Sergio Reyez in Cuba on 4/12/67. Moved to the U.S. at age four. Raised in Southgate, California. His brother "Sen Dog" is a member of Cypress Hill.

| 6/2/90 | 69 | 16 | | Escape From Havana | $12 | Capitol 91295 |

B-Boy In Love — Enquentren Amor — Hip Hop Creature — Mas Pingon — Rap Guanco — River Cubano
En La Casa — Gettin' Stupid — If You Were Mine — Mentirosa *14* — Rhyme Fighter — Talkapella

★★483★★ MELVIN, Harold, And The Blue Notes

Philadelphia soul group, The Blue Notes, formed in 1954: Harold Melvin, Bernard Williams, Jesse Gillis, Jr., Franklin Peaker and Roosevelt Brodie. First recorded for Josie in 1956. Numerous personnel changes until 1970, when Teddy Pendergrass joined as drummer and lead singer. Pendergrass went solo in 1976, replaced by David Ebo.

9/2/72	53	31		1 Harold Melvin & The Blue Notes	$10	Phil. Int. 31648
11/10/73+	57	20		2 Black & Blue	$10	Phil. Int. 32407
3/1/75	26	32	●	3 To Be True	$10	Phil. Int. 33148
12/13/75+	9	24	●	4 Wake Up Everybody	$10	Phil. Int. 33808
7/4/76	51	14		5 All Their Greatest Hits!	[G] $10	Phil. Int. 34232
2/5/77	56	10		6 Reaching For The World	$8	ABC 969
3/22/80	95	20		7 The Blue Album	$8	Source 3197

featuring Sharon Paige on 2 songs

After You Love Me, Why Do You Leave Me (6) — Hope That We Can Be Together Soon (3,5) *42* — If You're Looking For Somebody To Love (7) — Prayin' (7) — Tell The World How I Feel About 'Cha Baby (4) *94* — Yesterday I Had The Blues (1) *63*
Baby I'm Back (7) — Hostage Part 1 & 2 (6) — Is There A Place For Me (2) — Pretty Flower (3) — To Be Free To Be Who We Are (4) — You Know How To Make Me Feel So Good (4)
Bad Luck (Part 1) (3,5) *15* — I Miss You (Part 1) (1,5) *58* — It All Depends On You (2) — Reaching For The World (6) *74* — To Be True (3) — Your Love Is Taking Me On A Journey (7)
Be For Real (1,5) — I Should Be Your Lover (7) — It's All Because Of A Woman (3) — Sandman (3) — Tonight's The Night (7)
Big Singing Star (6) — I'm Comin' Home Tomorrow (2) — Keep On Lovin' You (4) — Satisfaction Guaranteed (Or Take Your Love Back) (2) *58* — Wake Up Everybody (Part 1) (4,5) *12*
Cabaret (2) — I'm Searching For A Love (4) — Let It Be Real (1) — Somewhere Down The Line (3) — Where Are All My Friends (3,5) *80*
Concentrate On Me (2) — I'm Weak For You (2) — Let Me Into Your World (1) — Stay Together (6) — Where There's A Will - There's A Way (6)
Don't Leave Me This Way (4) — If You Don't Know Me By Now (1,5) *3* — Love I Lost (Part 1) (2,5) *7*
Ebony Woman (1) — Nobody Could Take Your Place (3)
He Loves You And I Do Too (6)

MEMPHIS HORNS, The

Studio group including Wayne Jackson, Andrew Love, Floyd Newman, Jimmy Brown, Don Chandler, Charlie Freeman, Tommy McClure and Sammy Creason. Jackson was a member of The Mar-Keys. Also see Jackie Moore.

| 6/10/78 | 163 | 9 | | The Memphis Horns Band II | $8 | RCA 2643 |

guest vocalists: Michael McDonald, Anita Pointer, James Gilstrap, Bobby Kimball and Bill Champlin

Don't Change It — Hold On — Livin' For The Music — New Beginning — Party Line
Give It To Me — (Let's Go) All The Way — Minute By Minute — Our Love Will Survive — You

MEN AT WORK

Melbourne, Australia rock quintet formed in 1979. Colin Hay (lead singer, guitar), Ron Strykert (lead guitar), Greg Ham (sax, keyboards), Jerry Speiser (drums) and John Rees (bass). Won the 1982 Best New Artist Grammy Award. Speiser and Rees left in 1984. Hay went solo as Colin James Hay in 1987.

7/3/82	1¹⁵	90	▲⁵	1 Business As Usual	$8	Columbia 37978
5/7/83	3	49	▲²	2 Cargo	$8	Columbia 38660
6/22/85	50	13	●	3 Two Hearts	$12	Columbia 40078

Be Good Johnny (1) — Down By The Sea (1) — High Wire (2) — No Restrictions (2) — Settle Down My Boy (2) — Underground (1)
Blue For You (2) — Down Under (1) *1* — I Can See It In Your Eyes (1) — No Sign Of Yesterday (2) — Snakes And Ladders (3) — Upstairs In My House (2)
Catch A Star (1) — Everything I Need (3) *47* — I Like To (2) — Overkill (2) *3* — Stay At Home (3) — Who Can It Be Now? (1) *1*
Children On Parade (3) — Giving Up (3) — It's A Mistake (2) *6* — People Just Love To Play With Words (1) — Still Life (3)
Dr. Heckyll & Mr. Jive (2) *28* — Hard Luck Story (3) — Man With Two Hearts (3) — Sail To You (3) — Touching The Untouchables (1)
Helpless Automation (1) — Maria (3)

★★172★★ MENDES, Sergio, & Brasil '66

Sergio was born on 2/11/41 in Niteroi, Brazil. Pianist/leader of Latin-styled group originating from Brazil. Member Lani Hall (vocals) married Herb Alpert.

9/10/66	7	126	●	1 Sergio Mendes & Brasil '66	$12	A&M 4116
4/29/67	24	46	●	2 Equinox	$12	A&M 4122
3/9/68	5	51	●	3 Look Around	$12	A&M 4137
6/8/68	197	4		4 Sergio Mendes' Favorite Things *	[E-I] $15	Atlantic 8177
12/7/68+	3	30	●	5 Fool On The Hill	$12	A&M 4160
8/16/69	33	17		6 Crystal Illusions	$12	A&M 4197

DEBUT DATE	PEAK POS	WKS CHR	GOLD	ARTIST — Album Title	$	Label & Number
				MENDES, Sergio, & Brasil '66 — Cont'd		
12/13/69+	**71**	16		7 Ye-Me-Le	$10	A&M 4236
7/4/70	**101**	20		8 Greatest Hits ....[G]	$10	A&M 4252
1/9/71	**130**	9		9 Stillness	$10	A&M 4284
				SERGIO MENDES & BRASIL '77:		
10/16/71	**166**	6		10 Pais Tropical	$10	A&M 4315
7/15/72	**164**	5		11 Primal Roots	$10	A&M 4353
6/2/73	**116**	15		12 Love Music	$10	Bell 1119
5/18/74	**176**	5		13 Vintage 74	$10	Bell 1305
2/15/75	**105**	10		14 Sergio Mendes *	$10	Elektra 1027
3/27/76	**180**	2		15 Homecooking	$10	Elektra 1055
8/20/77	**81**	12		16 Sergio Mendes And The New Brasil '77	$8	Elektra 1102
5/7/83	**27**	27		17 Sergio Mendes *	$8	A&M 4937
5/19/84	**70**	22		18 Confetti *	$8	A&M 4984

*SERGIO MENDES

After Midnight (10)
After Sunrise (11)
Agua De Beber (1)
Alibis (18) 29
All In Love Is Fair (14)
Asa Branca (10)
Banda (Parade) (4)
Batucada (The Beat) (3)
Berimbau (1)
Bim-Bom (2)
Boa Palavra (The Good Word) (4)
Cancao Do Nosso Amor (Far Away Today) (4)
Canto De Ubiratan (11)
Canto Triste (5)
Carnaval (17)
Casa Forte (5)
Celebration Of The Sunrise (9)
Chelsea Morning (5)
Cinnamon And Clove (2)
Circle Game (11)
Comin' Home Baby (4)
Constant Rain (Chove Chuva) (2) 71
Crystal Illusions (6)
Cut That Out (15)
Dance Attack (18)
Davy (14)
Daytripper (1,8)
Dois Dias (6)

Don't Let Me Be Lonely Tonight (12)
Don't You Worry 'Bout A Thing (13)
Double Rainbow (13)
Dream Hunter (17)
Easy To Be Hard (7)
Emorio (5)
Empty Faces (6)
Festa (2)
Fool On The Hill (5,8) *6*
For Me (2) 98
For What It's Worth (9)
Frog, The (3)
Funny You Should Say That (13)
Gente (2)
Going Out Of My Head (1,8)
Gone Forever (18)
Here Comes The Sun (14)
Hey Look At The Sun (12)
Hey People Hey (15)
Homecooking (15)
I Believe (When I Fall In Love It Will Be Forever) (14)
I Can See Clearly Now (12)
I Know You (10)
I Say A Little Prayer (4)
I Won't Last A Day Without You (12)
Iemanja (11)

If I Ever Lose This Heaven (14)
If You Leave Me Now (16)
If You Really Love Me (13)
It's So Obvious That I Love You (15)
It's Up To You (15)
Joker, The (1)
Killing Me Softly With His Song (12)
Kisses (18)
Laia Ladaia (Reza) (5)
Lapinha (5)
Let Them Work It Out (14)
Let's Give A Little More This Time (18)
Life (16)
Life In The Movies (17)
Like A Lover (3,8)
Lonely Sailor (13)
Look Around (3,8)
Look Who's Mine (7)
Lookin' For Another Pure Love (14)
Lost In Paradise (9)
Love City (16)
Love Is Waiting (17)
Love Me Tomorrow (16)
Love Music (12)
Mas Que Nada (1,8) *47*
Masquerade (7)
Moanin' (7)

Morrer De Amor (To Die Of Love) (18)
Morro Velho (10)
Mozambique (16)
My Favorite Things (4)
My Summer Love (17)
Never Gonna Let You Go (17) *4*
Night And Day (2,8) *82*
Norwegian Wood (7)
O Mar E Meu Chao (The Sea Is My Soil) (4)
O Pato (1)
Olympia (18) *58*
One Note Samba (medley) (1)
P-Ka-Boo (16)
Pais Tropical (Tropical Land) (10)
Peninsula (16)
Pomba Gira (11)
Ponteio (4)
Pradizer Adeua (To Say Goodbye) (3)
Pretty World (6,8) *62*
Promise Of A Fisherman (11)
Put A Little Love Away (12)
Rainbow's End (17) *52*
Real Life (18)
Real Thing (16)
Righteous Life (9)
Roda (3)
Salt Sea (6)
Say It With Your Body (18)

Scarborough Fair (5,8) *16*
Shakara (15)
Si Senor (17)
(Sittin' On) The Dock Of The Bay (5) *66*
Slow Hot Wind (1)
So Danco Samba (Jazz 'N' Samba) (2)
So Many People (10)
So Many Stars (3,8)
So What's New (4)
Some Time Ago (7)
Someday We'll All Be Free (14)
Sometimes In Winter (9)
Song Of No Regrets (6)
Sound Of One Song (18)
Spanish Flea (medley) (1)
Stillness (9)
Sunny Day (15)
Superstition (13)
Tell Me In A Whisper (15)
Tempo Feliz (Happy Times) (4)
This Masquerade (13)
Tim Dom Dom (1)
Tonga (1)
Triste (2)
Tristeza (Goodbye Sadness) (3)
Trouble With Hello Is Goodbye (14)
Upa, Neguinho (5)

Veleiro (The Sailboat) (4)
Viola (6)
Viramundo (9)
Voce Abusou (13)
Voo Doo (17)
Waiting For Love (13)
Walk The Way You Talk (12)
Watch What Happens (2)
Waters Of March (13)
Wave (2)
What The World Needs Now (7)
When Summer Turns To Snow (5)
Where Are You Coming From? (7)
Where Is The Love (12)
Where To Now St. Peter (15)
Why (16)
Wichita Lineman (7) *95*
With A Little Help From My Friends (3,8)
Ye-Me-Le (7)
You Been Away Too Long (14)
You Can't Dress Up A Broken Heart (7)
You Stepped Out Of A Dream (6)
Zanzibar (10)

MENUDO

Puerto Rican teen quintet. The superstar group of Latin America. Many personnel changes due to rule that members must retire at age 16.

DEBUT DATE	PEAK POS	WKS CHR	GOLD	ARTIST — Album Title	$	Label & Number
3/10/84	**108**	12		1 Reaching Out...	$8	RCA 4993
				9 of 10 songs are English versions of their Spanish hits		
5/25/85	**100**	19		2 Menudo	$8	RCA 5420

Because Of Love (1)
Chocolate Candy (2)
Come Home (2)
Don't Hold Back (2)

Explosion (2)
Fly Away (1)
Gimme Rock (1)
Gotta Get On Movin' (1)

Heavenly Angel (1)
Hold Me (2) *62*
If You're Not Here (By My Side) (1)

Indianapolis (1)
Like A Cannonball (1)
Motorcycle Dreamer (1)
Oh, My Love (2)

Please Be Good To Me (2)
That's What You Do (1)
Transformation (2)
When I Dance With You (2)

You And Me All The Way (2)

MENUHIN, Yehudi — see SHANKAR, Ravi

MEN WITHOUT HATS

Nucleus of techno-rock band from Montreal consists of Ivan Doroschuk (singer/songwriter) with his brother Stefan (guitar). Fluctuating personnel included their brother Colin (1983-84).

DEBUT DATE	PEAK POS	WKS CHR	GOLD	ARTIST — Album Title	$	Label & Number
8/6/83	**13**	26	●	1 Rhythm Of Youth	$8	Backstreet 39002
10/6/84	**127**	4		2 Folk Of The '80s (Part III)..........................	$8	MCA 5487
11/14/87+	**73**	25		3 Pop Goes The World	$8	Mercury 832730

Antarctica (1)
Ban The Game (1)
Bright Side Of The Sun (3)
Cocoricci (Le Tango Des Voleurs) (3)
End (Of The World) (3)

Eurotheme (3)
Folk Of The '80s (Part III) (2)
Great Ones Remember (1)
I Got The Message (1)
I Know Their Name (2)

I Sing Last (medley) (2)
Ideas For Walls (1)
In The Name Of Angels (3)
Jenny Wore Black (3)
La Valese D'Eugenie (2)

Messlahs Die Young (2)
Moonbeam (3)
Mother's Opinion (2)
No Dancing (2)
Not For Tears (medley) (2)

On Tuesday (3)
Pop Goes The World (3) *20*
Real World (3)
Safety Dance (1) *3*
Things In My Life (1)

Walk On Water (medley) (3)
Where Do The Boys Go? (2)

I Like (1) *84*
Lose My Way (3)
O Sole Mio (3)
Unsatisfaction (2)

MERCURY, Freddie

Born Frederick Bulsara on 9/5/46 in Zanzibar, Tanzania. Died on 11/24/91 of AIDS. Lead singer of Queen. Also recorded as Larry Lurex.

DEBUT DATE	PEAK POS	WKS CHR	GOLD	ARTIST — Album Title	$	Label & Number
5/18/85	**159**	6		1 Mr. Bad Guy	$8	Columbia 40071

Foolin' Around
I Was Born To Love You 76
Let's Turn It On

Living On My Own
Love Me Like There's No Tomorrow

Made In Heaven
Man Made Paradise
Mr. Bad Guy

My Love Is Dangerous
There Must Be More To Life Than This

Your Kind Of Lover

MERCY

Florida group led by Jack Sigler, Jr.

DEBUT DATE	PEAK POS	WKS CHR	GOLD	ARTIST — Album Title	$	Label & Number
6/21/69	**38**	15		The Mercy & Love (Can Make You Happy)	$20	Sundi 803

Back In My Arms Again
Daydream

Hey Jude
Hooked On A Feeling

I've Been Lonely Too Long

Love (Can Make You Happy) 2

My Girl
Our Winter Love

Tracks Of My Tears
Worst That Could Happen

DEBUT DATE	PEAK POS	WKS CHR	GOLD	ARTIST — Album Title	$	Label & Number

MERRILL, Robert — see MANTOVANI

MERRY-GO-ROUND, The
Emitt Rhodes, lead singer/songwriter of Los Angeles-area pop quartet, with Joel Larson (drums; later with The Grass Roots), Bill Rinehart (bass; formerly with Leaves) and Gary Kato (guitar).

| 11/18/67 | 190 | 2 | | The Merry-Go-Round .... | $25 | A&M 4132 |

Clown's No Good | Gonna Leave You Alone | Low Down | Time Will Show The Wiser | Where Have You Been All Of | You're A Very Lovely
Early In The Morning | Had To Run Around | On Your Way Out | We're In Love | My Life | Woman 94
Gonna Fight The War | Live 63

MERRYWEATHER & FRIENDS
San Francisco-based guitarist Neil Merryweather.

| 10/4/69 | 199 | 2 | | Word Of Mouth .... | $15 | Capitol 278 [2] |

with guests Steve Miller, Dave Mason and Barry Goldberg

Dr. Mason | Hooker Blues | Licked The Spoon | News | Sun Down Lady | We Can Make It
Hard Times | I Found Love | Mrs. Roberts' Son | Rough Dried Woman | Teach You How To Fly | Where I Am
Hello Little Girl | Just A Little Bit

MESSINA, Jim
Born on 12/5/47 in Maywood, California; raised in Harlingen, Texas. Member of Buffalo Springfield, 1967-68, then Poco 1968-70. Formed duo with Kenny Loggins from 1971-76. Joined the re-formed Poco in 1989.

| 10/20/79 | 58 | 14 | | 1 Oasis .... | $8 | Columbia 36140 |

JIMMY MESSINA

| 6/20/81 | 95 | 11 | | 2 Messina .... | $8 | Warner 3559 |

Break The Chain (2) | (Is This) Lovin' You Lady (1) | Magic Of Love (1) | Seeing You (For The First | Talk To Me (1)
Child Of My Dreams (2) | It's All Right Here (2) | Money Alone (2) | Time) (1) | Waitin' On You (1)
Do You Want To Dance (1) | Love Is Here (1) | Move Into Your Heart (2) | Stay The Night (2) | Whispering Waters (2)
Free To Be Me (1) | Lovin' You Every Minute (2) | New And Different Way (1) | Sweet Love (2)

METAL CHURCH
Heavy-metal quintet based in Kent, Washington. Nucleus of band: Craig Wells (guitar), Kirk Arrington (drums) and Duke Erikson (bass).

| 11/8/86+ | 92 | 23 | | 1 The Dark .... | $8 | Elektra 60493 |
| 3/11/89 | 75 | 15 | | 2 Blessing In Disguise .... | $8 | Elektra 60817 |

Anthem To The Estranged (2) | Dark, The (1) | Method To Your Madness (1) | Psycho (1) | Start The Fire (1)
Badlands (2) | Fake Healer (2) | Of Unsound Mind (2) | Rest In Pieces (April 15, | Ton Of Bricks (1)
Burial At Sea (1) | It's A Secret (2) | Over My Dead Body (1) | 1912) (2) | Watch The Children Pray (1)
Cannot Tell A Lie (1) | Line Of Death (1) | Powers That Be (2) | Spell Can't Be Broken (2) | Western Alliance (1)

★★385★★ **METALLICA**
Speed-metal quartet formed by Lars Ulrich (drums) and James Hetfield (vocals) in Los Angeles in 1981. Early rhythm guitarist Dave Mustaine (now the leader of Megadeth) was replaced by Kirk Hammett in 1982. Bassist Cliff Burton was killed in a bus crash in Sweden on 9/27/86 (age 24); replaced by Jason Newsted.

| 9/29/84+ | 100 | 50 | ▲² | 1 Ride The Lightning .... | $8 | Megaforce 769 |

reissued on Elektra 60396 in November 1984

| 3/29/86 | 29 | 72 | ▲² | 2 Master Of Puppets .... | $8 | Elektra 60439 |
| 4/5/86 | 155 | 10 | | 3 Kill 'Em All.. | [R] $8 | Megaforce 069 |

reissue of their 1983 debut album

| 9/12/87 | 28 | 30 | ▲ | 4 The $5.98 E.P.: Garage Days Re-Revisited .... | [M] $8 | Elektra 60757 |
| 2/13/88 | 120 | 8 | ▲ | 5 Kill 'Em All.. | [R] $8 | Elektra 60766 |

features 2 bonus tracks not included on original release

| 9/24/88 | 6 | 83 | ▲³ | 6 ...And Justice For All .... | $10 | Elektra 60812 [2] |
| 8/31/91 | 1⁴ | 76↑ | ▲⁶ | 7 Metallica... | $12 | Elektra 61113 |

Am I Evil? (5) | Damage, Inc. (2) | Frayed Ends Of Sanity (6) | Metal Militia (3,5) | Seek & Destroy (3,5) | Welcome Home (Sanitarium)
...And Justice For All (6) | Disposable Heroes (2) | God That Failed (7) | Motorbreath (3,5) | Shortest Straw (6) | (2)
(Anesthesia)-Pulling Teeth | Don't Tread On Me (7) | Green Hell (medley) (4) | My Friend Of Misery (7) | Small Hours (4) | Wherever I May Roam
(3,5) | Dyers Eve (6) | Harvester Of Sorrow (6) | No Remorse (3,5) | Struggle Within (7) | (7) 82
Battery (2) | Enter Sandman (7) 16 | Helpless (4) | Nothing Else Matters (7) 34 | Thing That Should Not Be (2) | Whiplash (3,5)
Blackened (6) | Escape (1) | Hit The Lights (3,5) | Of Wolf And Man (7) | Through The Never (7)
Blitzkrieg (5) | Eye Of The Beholder (6) | Holler Than Thou (7) | One (6) 35 | To Live Is To Die (6)
Call Of Ktulu (1) | Fade To Black (1) | Jump In The Fire (3,5) | Orion (2) | Trapped Under Ice (1)
Crash Course In Brain | Fight Fire With Fire (1) | Last Caress (medley) (4) | Phantom Lord (3,5) | Unforgiven, The (7) 35
Surgery (4) | For Whom The Bell Tolls (1) | Leper Messiah (2) | Ride The Lightning (1) | Wait, The (4)
Creeping Death (1) | Four Horsemen (3,5) | Master Of Puppets (2) | Sad But True (7) 98

METERS, The
R&B instrumental group formed in New Orleans in 1966 featuring keyboardist Arthur Neville (brother of Aaron Neville). Group disbanded in 1977, when Art, Aaron, and brothers Charles and Cyril formed The Neville Brothers.

6/21/69	108	15		1 The Meters	[I] $20	Josie 4010
1/24/70	198	2		2 Look-Ka Py Py	[I] $20	Josie 4011
7/18/70	200	2		3 Struttin'...	[I] $15	Josie 4012
9/6/75	179	3		4 Fire On The Bayou	$15	Reprise 2228

also see The Neville Brothers' Fiyo On The Bayou

Ann (1) | Dry Spell (2) | Hey! Last Minute (3) | Mardi Gras Mambo (4) | Rigor Mortis (2) | Talkin' 'Bout New Orleans (4)
Art (1) | Ease Back (1) 61 | Joog (3) | Middle Of The Road (4) | Running Fast (4) | They All Ask'd For You (4)
Britches (3) | Fire On The Bayou (4) | Liar (4) | Mob, The (2) | Same Old Thing (3) | Thinking (2)
Can You Do Without? (4) | Funky Miracle (2) | Little Old Money Maker (2) | 9 Till 5 (2) | Sehorns Farm (1) | This Is My Last Affair (2)
Cardova (1) | Go For Yourself (3) | Live Wire (1) | Oh, Calcutta! (2) | Simple Song (1) | Tippi-Toes (3)
Chicken Strut (3) 50 | Hand Clapping Song (3) 89 | Liver Splash (3) | Out In The Country (4) | 6V6 LA (1) | Wichita Lineman (3)
Cissy Strut (1) 23 | Here Comes The Meter Man | Look-Ka Py Py (2) 56 | Pungee (2) | Sophisticated Cissy (1) 34 | Yeah, You're Right (4)
Darlin' Darlin' (3) | (1) | Love Slip Upon Ya (4) | Ride Your Pony (3) | Stormy (1) | You're A Friend Of Mine (4)

★★244★★ **METHENY, Pat, Group**
Pat was born on 8/12/55 in Kansas City, Missouri. Jazz guitarist. In 1989, group included Lyle Mays (piano), Steve Rodby (bass), Pedro Aznar and Armando Marcal (percussion).

| 8/26/78 | 123 | 12 | | 1 Pat Metheny Group... | [I] $8 | ECM 1114 |

DEBUT DATE	PEAK POS	WKS CHR	GOLD	ARTIST — Album Title	$	Label & Number
				METHENY, Pat, Group — Cont'd		
5/5/79	44	22		2 New Chautauqua * .... [I]	$8	ECM 1131
11/24/79+	53	24		3 American Garage .... [I]	$8	ECM 1155
11/1/80	89	14		4 80/81 * .... [I]	$8	ECM 1180 [2]
				with Charlie Haden, Jack DeJohnette, Dewey Redman and Mike Brecker		
6/20/81	50	21		5 As Falls Wichita, So Falls Wichita Falls	$8	ECM 1190
				PAT METHENY & LYLE MAYS (keyboards)		
5/22/82	50	28		6 Offramp .... [I]	$8	ECM 1216
6/25/83	62	17		7 Travels .... [I-L]	$8	ECM 23791 [2]
5/12/84	116	9		8 Rejoicing * .... [I]	$8	ECM 25006
				with Charlie Haden and Billy Higgins		
10/13/84	91	35		9 First Circle .... [I]	$8	ECM 25008
3/9/85	54	10		10 The Falcon And The Snowman .... [S-I]	$8	EMI America 17150
8/22/87	86	15	●	11 Still Life (Talking) .... [I]	$8	Geffen 24145
7/22/89	66	18		12 Letter From Home .... [I]	$8	Geffen 24245
7/7/90	154	6		13 Question and Answer * .... [I]	$12	Geffen 24293
				with Dave Holland and Roy Haynes		
8/1/92	110	17		14 Secret Story *	$12	Geffen 24468
				*PAT METHENY		

Above The Treetops (14)
Airstream
All The Things You Are (13)
Always And Forever (14)
American Garage (3)
Antonia (14)
April Joy (1)
Aprilwind (1)
Are We There Yet (12)
Are You Going With Me? (6,7)
As A Flower Blossoms (I Am Running To You) (14)
As Falls Wichita, So Falls Wichita Falls (5,7)
Au Lait (6)
Barcarole (6)
Bat, The (4)
Bat Part II (6)
Beat 70 (12)
Better Days Ahead (12)

Blues For Pat (8)
Calling, The (8)
Capture (10)
Cathedral In A Suitcase (14)
Change Of Heart (13)
Chris (1)
Country Poem (2)
(Cross The) Heartland (3)
Daulton Lee (10)
Daybreak (2)
Distance (11)
Dream Of The Return (12)
Eighteen (6)
80/81 (4)
End Of The Game (9)
Epic, The (3)
Estupenda Graca (5)
Every Day (I Thank You) (14)
Every Summer Night (12)
Extent Of The Lie (10)
Extradition (9)

Facing West (14)
Falcon, The (10)
Fallen Star (medley) (2)
Farmer's Trust (7)
Fields, The Sky (7)
Finding And Believing (14)
First Circle (9)
5-5-7 (12)
Flight Of The Falcon (medley) (10)
Forward March (9)
Goin' Ahead (4,7)
Goodbye (7)
H & H (13)
Have You Heard (12)
Hermitage (2)
Humpty Dumpty (8)
If I Could (9)
In Her Family (11)
It's For You (5)

(It's Just) Talk (11)
Jaco (1)
James (6)
Last Train Home (11)
Law Years (13)
Letter From Home (12)
Level Of Deception (10)
Lone Jack (1)
Lonely Woman (8)
Long-Ago Child (medley) (2)
Longest Summer (14)
Mas Alla (Beyond) (9)
Minuano (Six Eight) (11)
Never Too Far Away (13)
New Chautauqua (2)
Not To Be Forgotten (Our Final Hour) (14)
Offramp (6)
Old Folks (13)
Open (4)
Ozark (5)

Phase Dance (1,7)
Praise (9)
Pretty Scattered (4)
Psalm 121 (10)
Question And Answer (13)
Rain River (14)
Rejoicing (8)
San Lorenzo (1,7)
Search, The (3)
See The World (14)
September Fifteenth (5)
Slip Away (12)
So May It Secretly Begin (11)
Solar (13)
Song For Bilbao (7)
Spring Ain't Here (12)
Story From A Stranger (8)
Straight On Red (7)
Sueno Con Mexico (2)
Sunlight (14)
Tears Inside (8)

Tell Her You Saw Me (14)
Tell It All (9)
Third Wind (11)
This Is Not America (10) 32
Three Flights Up (13)
Travels (7)
Truth Will Always Be (14)
Turnaround (4)
Two Folk Songs (4)
Vidala (12)
Waiting For An Answer (8)
Yolanda, You Learn (9)

MFSB
Large interracial studio band formed by producers Kenny Gamble and Leon Huff. Also recorded as The James Boys, and Family. Name means "Mothers, Fathers, Sisters, Brothers."

4/21/73	131	10		1 MFSB .... [I]	$10	Phil. Int. 32046
1/19/74	4	35	●	2 Love Is The Message .... [I]	$10	Phil. Int. 32707
6/14/75	44	13		3 Universal Love .... [I]	$10	Phil. Int. 33158
12/6/75+	39	12		4 Philadelphia Freedom .... [I]	$10	Phil. Int. 33845
7/10/76	106	9		5 Summertime	$10	Phil. Int. 34238

Back Stabbers (1)
Bitter Sweet (1)
Brothers And Sisters (4)
Cheaper To Keep Her (2)
Family Affair (1)
Ferry Avenue (4)
Freddie's Dead (1)
Get Down With The Philly Sound (4)

Hot Summer Nights (5)
Human Machine (3)
I Hear Music (medley) (2)
I'm On Your Side (5)
I'm Over Here (3)
K-Jee (3)
Lay In Low (1)
Let's Go Disco (3)
Love Has No Time Or Place (3)

Love Is The Message (medley) (2) **85**
MFSB (3)
Morning Tears (4)
My Mood (3)
My One And Only Love (2)
Philadelphia Freedom (4)
Picnic In The Park (5)
Plenty Good Lovin' (5)

Poinciana (1)
Sexy (3) **42**
Smile Happy (4)
Something For Nothing (1)
South Philly (4)
Summertime (5)
Summertime And I'm Feelin' Mellow (5)
Sunnin' And Funnin' (5)

T.L.C. (Tender Lovin' Care) (5)
TSOP (The Sound Of Philadelphia) (2) **1**
Touch Me In The Morning (medley) (2)
We Got The Time (5)
When Your Love Is Gone (4)
Zip, The (4) **91**

MIAMI SOUND MACHINE — see ESTEFAN, Gloria

★★349★★ MICHAEL, George/Wham!
Born Georgios Kyriacos Panayiotou on 6/26/63 in Bushey, England. Wham!, formed in early 80s, centered around George's vocals and songwriting, and included Andrew Ridgeley (b: 1/26/63, Bushey, England) on guitar. Their association ended in 1986. Ridgeley pursued race car driving, then solo career in 1990.

				WHAM! U.K.:		
8/20/83	83	44	●	1 Fantastic	$8	Columbia 38911
				WHAM!:		
11/10/84+	1³	80	▲⁵	2 Make It Big	$8	Columbia 39595
7/19/86	10	28	▲	3 Music From The Edge Of Heaven	$8	Columbia 40285
				GEORGE MICHAEL:		
11/21/87+	1¹²	87	▲⁸	4 Faith	$8	Columbia 40867
				1988 Grammy winner: Album of the Year		
9/29/90	2¹	42	▲	5 Listen Without Prejudice	$12	Columbia 46898

Bad Boys (1) **60**
Battlestations (1)
Blue (3)
Careless Whisper (2) **1**
Club Tropicana (1)
Come On (1)
Cowboys And Angels (5)
Credit Card Baby (2)
Different Corner (3) **7**

Edge Of Heaven (3) 10
Everything She Wants (2) **1**
Faith (4) **1**
Father Figure (4) **1**
Freedom (2) **3**
Freedom (5) **8**
Hand To Mouth (4)
Hard Day (4)
Heal The Pain (5)

Heartbeat (2)
I Want Your Sex (4) **2**
I'm Your Man (3) **3**
If You Were There (2)
Kissing A Fool (4) **5**
Last Christmas (3)
Like A Baby (2)
Look At Your Hands (4)
Love Machine (1)

Monkey (4) **1**
Mother's Pride (5) **46**
Nothing Looks The Same In The Light (1)
One More Try (4) **1**
Praying For Time (5) **1**
Ray Of Sunshine (1)
Something To Save (5)
Soul Free (5)

They Won't Go When I Go (5)
Waiting For That Day (5) **27**
Wake Me Up Before You Go-Go (2) **1**
Wham! Rap '86 (3)
Wham Rap (Enjoy What You Do) (1)
Where Did Your Heart Go? (3) **50**

Young Guns (Go For It!) (1)

MICHAELS, Lee
Born on 11/24/45 in Los Angeles. Rock organist/vocalist.

8/30/69	53	26		1 Lee Michaels	$15	A&M 4199
8/1/70	51	19		2 Barrel	$12	A&M 4249
6/5/71	16	36		3 "5th"	$12	A&M 4302
3/25/72	78	13		4 Space & First Takes	$12	A&M 4336
4/7/73	135	8		5 Lee Michaels Live [L]	$12	A&M 3518 [2]
6/2/73	172	5		6 Nice Day For Something	$12	Columbia 32275

As Long As I Can (2)
Bell (6)
Call It Stormy Monday (5)
Can I Get A Witness (3) *39*
Day Of Change (2,5)
Didn't Have To Happen (3)
Didn't Know What I Had (2)
Do You Know What I Mean (3) *6*
(Don't Want No) Woman (medley) (1)

Drum Solo (5)
First Names (4)
Forty Reasons (5)
Frosty's (medley) (1)
Games (2)
Heighty Hi (1,5)
High Wind (6)
Hold On To Freedom (4,5)
I Don't Want Her (3)
Keep The Circle Turning (3)
Mad Dog (2,5)

Murder In My Heart (For The Judge) (2)
My Friends (medley) (1)
My Lady (5)
Nothing Matters (But It Doesn't Matter) (6)
Oak Fire (3,5)
Olson Arrives At Two Fifty-Five (5)
Other Day (The Other Way) (6)

Own Special Way (As Long As) (4)
Rock & Roll Community (6)
Rock Me Baby (3,5)
Same Old Song (6)
So Hard (6)
Space And First Takes (4)
Stormy Monday (1)
Tell Me How Do You Feel (medley) (1)
Think I'll Cry (2)

Think I'll Go Back (medley) (1)
Thumbs (2,5)
Uummmm My Lady (2)
Want My Baby (1)
War (5)
Went Saw Mama (4)
What Now America (2)
When Johnny Comes Marching Home (2)
Who Could Want More (1)

Willie & The Hand Jive (3)
Ya Ya (3)
You Are What You Do (3)
Your Breath Is Bleeding (6)

MICHEL'LE
Michel'le (pronounced: mee-shell-LAY) Toussant is an 18-year-old (in 1990) black singer from Los Angeles. Former backing singer of the World Class Wreckin Cru.

1/13/90	35	43	●	Michel'le	$12	Ruthless 91282

Close To Me
If?

Keep Watchin
Never Been In Love

Nicety *29*
No More Lies *7*

100% Woman
Silly Love Song

Something In My Heart *31*
Special Thanks

★★162★★ MIDLER, Bette
Born on 12/1/45 in Paterson, New Jersey. Vocalist/actress. Raised in Hawaii. In the Broadway show *Fiddler On The Roof* for three years. Won the 1973 Best New Artist Grammy Award. Barry Manilow was her arranger/accompanist in early years. Nominated for an Oscar for performance in *The Rose* (1979). Also in films *Down And Out In Beverly Hills, Ruthless People, Outrageous Fortune, Beaches* and others.

12/9/72+	9	76	▲	1 The Divine Miss M	$8	Atlantic 7238
12/8/73+	6	27	●	2 Bette Midler	$8	Atlantic 7270
				above 2 co-produced by Barry Manilow		
1/31/76	27	15		3 Songs For The New Depression	$8	Atlantic 18155
5/28/77	49	11		4 Live At Last [L]	$10	Atlantic 9000 [2]
12/17/77+	51	14		5 Broken Blossom	$8	Atlantic 19151
9/22/79	65	17		6 Thighs And Whispers	$8	Atlantic 16004
12/22/79+	12	45	▲	7 The Rose [S-L]	$8	Atlantic 16010
11/29/80	34	14		8 Divine Madness [S-L]	$8	Atlantic 16022
				film captures a live concert at Pasadena Civic Auditorium		
8/27/83	60	13		9 No Frills	$8	Atlantic 80070
12/21/85+	183	6		10 Mud Will Be Flung Tonight! [C]	$8	Atlantic 81291
1/21/89	2³	176	▲³	11 Beaches [S]	$8	Atlantic 81933
10/13/90+	6	73	▲²	12 Some People's Lives	$12	Atlantic 82129
11/30/91	22	21		13 For The Boys [S]	$12	Atlantic 82329

Alabama Song (medley) (4)
All I Need To Know (9) *77*
All Of A Sudden (12)
Am I Blue (1)
Around The World (medley) (4)
Baby It's Cold Outside (13)
Baby Mine (11)
Backstage (4)
Bang, You're Dead (4)
Beast Of Burden (9) *71*
Big Noise From Winnetka (6,8)
Billy-A-Dick (13)
Birds (3)
Boogie Woogie Bugle Boy (1,8) *8*
Breaking Up Somebody's Home (2)
Buckets Of Rain (3)
Camellia (7)
Chapel Of Love (1,8) *flip*
Come Back Jimmy Dean (9)
Come Rain Or Come Shine (13)
Coping (10)
Cradle Days (4)
Da Doo Run Run (medley) (2)
Daytime Hustler (1)
Delta Dawn (1,4)
Dixie's Dream (medley) (13)

Do You Want To Dance? (medley) (1,4) *17*
Don't Say Nothin' Bad (About My Baby) (medley) (2)
Dream Is A Wish Your Heart Makes (5)
Dreamland (13)
Drinking Again (2,4)
E Street Shuffle (medley) (8)
Empty Bed Blues (5)
Every Road Leads Back To You (13) *78*
Favorite Waste Of Time (9) *78*
Fiesta In Rio (medley) (4)
Fire Down Below (8)
Fit Or Fat - Fat As I am (10)
For All We Know (13)
Fried Eggs (4)
Friends (1,4) *40*
Friendship Theme (11)
From A Distance (12) *2*
Gift Of Love (12)
Girl Friend Of The Whirling Dervish (13)
Girl Is On To You (12)
Glory Of Love (11)
Hang On In There Baby (4)
Hawaiian War Chant (medley) (4)

He Was Too Good To Me (medley) (12)
Heart Over Head (9)
Hello In There (1,4)
Higher & Higher (Your Love Keeps Lifting Me) (2)
Hurricane (6)
Hurry On Down (4)
I Don't Want The Night To End (3)
I Know You By Heart (11)
I Never Talk To Strangers (5)
I Remember You (13)
I Shall Be Released (2,8)
I Think It's Going To Rain Today (11)
I've Still Got My Health (11)
In My Life (13)
In The Mood (2,4) *51*
Is It Love (3)
Istanbul (medley) (4)
La Vie En Rose (5)
Leader Of The Pack (1,8)
Let Me Call You Sweetheart (7)
Let Me Drive (9)
Let Me Just Follow Behind (3)
Long John Blues (4)
Love Me With A Feeling (7)

Love Says It's Waiting (3)
Lullaby Of Broadway (medley) (2,4)
Make Yourself Comfortable (5)
Marahauna (3)
Marriage, Movies, Madonna And Mick (10)
Married Men (6) *40*
Medley (Finale) (4)
Midnight In Memphis (7)
Millworker (6)
Miss Otis Regrets (12)
Moonlight Dancing (12)
Mr. Rockefeller (4)
My Eye On You (9)
My Knight In Black Leather (6)
My Mother's Eyes (8) *39*
Nanette (medley) (4)
Night And Day (12) *62*
No Jestering (3)
Oh Industry (11)
Oh My My (medley) (4)
Old Cape Cod (3)
One More Round (12)
Only In Miami (9)
Optimistic Voices (medley) (2)
Otto Titsling (10)
P.S. I Love You (13)

Paradise (5,8)
Rain (6)
Ready To Begin Again (medley) (4)
Red (5)
Rose, The (7) *3*
Samedi Et Vendredi (medley) (3)
Say Goodbye To Hollywood (5)
Shiver Me Timbers (3,4,8)
Since You Stayed Here (medley) (12)
Skylark (2)
Soda And A Souvenir (9)
Sold My Soul To Rock 'N' Roll (7)
Some People's Lives (12)
Soph (10)
Spring Can Really Hang You Up The Most (12)
Stay With Me (7)
Storybook Children (Daybreak) (5) *57*
Strangers In The Night (3)
Stuff Like That There (13)
Summer (The First Time) (medley) (8)
Superstar (1)
Surabaya Johnny (2)
Taking Aim (10)

Tragedy (3)
Twisted (2)
Under The Boardwalk (11)
Unfettered Boob (10)
Uptown (medley) (2)
Vickie And Mr. Valves (13)
Vickie Eydie - I'm Singing Broadway (10)
When A Man Loves A Woman (7) *35*
Whose Side Are You On (7)
Why Bother? (10)
Wind Beneath My Wings (11) *1*
Yellow Beach Umbrella (4)
You Can't Always Get What You Want (medley) (2)
You Don't Know Me (5)
You're Movin' Out Today (4) *42*

MIDNIGHT OIL
Australian rock quintet: Peter Garrett (lead vocals), Peter Gifford, Martin Rotsey, James Moginie and Rob Hirst (replaced by bassist Bones Hillman in 1987). Garrett ran for the Australian Senate in 1984.

2/4/84	178	5		1 10,9,8,7,6,5,4,3,2,1	$8	Columbia 38996
8/3/85	177	6		2 Red Sails In The Sunset	$8	Columbia 39987
2/13/88	21	55	▲	3 Diesel And Dust	$8	Columbia 40967
3/17/90	20	29	●	4 Blue Sky Mining	$12	Columbia 45398

DEBUT DATE	PEAK POS	WKS CHR	GOLD	ARTIST — Album Title	$	Label & Number

MIDNIGHT OIL — Cont'd

| 5/30/92 | 141 | 3 | 5 | Scream In Blue Live .... [L] | $12 | Columbia 52731 |

Antarctica (4)
Arctic World (3)
Bakerman (2)
Bedlam Bridge (4)
Beds Are Burning (3,5) **17**
Bells And Horns In The
 Back Of Beyond (2)
Best Of Both Worlds (2)
Blue Sky Mine (4) **47**

Brave Faces (5)
Bullroarer (5)
Dead Heart (3) **53**
Dreamworld (3,5)
Forgotten Years (4)
Harrisburg (2)
Helps Me Helps You (2)
Hercules (5)
Jimmy Sharman's Boxers (2)

King Of The Mountain (4)
Kosciusko (2)
Maralinga (1)
Minutes To Midnight (2)
Mountains Of Burma (4)
One Country (4)
Only The Strong (1,5)
Outside World (1)
Powderworks (5)

Power And The Passion (1)
Progress (5)
Put Down That Weapon (3)
Read About It (1,5)
River Runs Red (4)
Scream In Blue (1,5)
Sell My Soul (3,5)
Shakers And Movers (4)

Shipyards Of New Zealand (2)
Short Memory (1)
Sleep (2)
Somebody's Trying To Tell
 Me Something (1)
Sometimes (3,5)
Stars Of Warburton (4,5)

Tin Legs And Tin Mines (1)
US Forces (1)
Warakurna (3)
When The Generals Talk (3)
Who Can Stand In The Way (2)
Whoah (3)

MIDNIGHT STAR

R&B-funk group formed in 1976 at Kentucky State University. Lead vocals by Belinda Lipscomb. Until 1988, band led by brothers Reginald (trumpet) and Vincent (trombone) Calloway. Reginald and Vincent produced many artists in the mid-1980s; formed own duo Calloway in 1988.

7/30/83+	27	96	▲²	1 No Parking On The Dance Floor	$8	Solar 60241
12/8/84+	32	32	●	2 Planetary Invasion	$8	Solar 60384
6/14/86	56	27	●	3 Headlines	$8	Solar 60454
11/5/88	96	15		4 Midnight Star	$8	Solar 72564

Body Snatchers (2)
Can You Stay With Me (2)
Close Encounter (3)
Close To Midnight (3)
Curious (2)
Dead End (3)
Don't Rock The Boat (4)

Electricity (1)
Engine No. 9 (3)
Feels So Good (1)
Freak-A-Zoid (1) **66**
Get Dressed (3)
Headlines (3) **69**
Heartbeat (4)

I Don't Wanna Be Lonely (4)
Let's Celebrate (2)
Love Song (4)
Midas Touch (3) **42**
Night Rider (1)
90 Days (Same As Cash) (4)

**No Parking (On The Dance
 Floor)** (1) **81**
Operator (2) **18**
Pamper Me (4)
Planetary Invasion (2)
Playmates (1)
Request Line (4)

Scientific Love (2) **80**
Searching For Love (3)
Slow Jam (1)
Snake In The Grass (4)
Stay Here By My Side (3)
Today My Love (2)
Wet My Whistle (1) **61**

MIDNIGHT STRING QUARTET

A Snuff Garrett production (The Renaissance).

11/19/66+	17	59		1 Rhapsodies For Young Lovers .... [I]	$10	Viva 6001
4/8/67	76	12		2 Spanish Rhapsodies For Young Lovers .... [I]	$10	Viva 36004
7/29/67	67	15		3 Rhapsodies For Young Lovers, Volume Two .... [I]	$10	Viva 36008
3/30/68	129	17		4 Love Rhapsodies .... [I]	$10	Viva 36013
8/17/68	194	3		5 The Look Of Love And Other Rhapsodies For Young Lovers ... [I]	$10	Viva 36015

Alfie (3)
Apologize (5)
Blue Star (The Medic
 Theme) (1)
Born Free (3)
By The Time I Get To
 Phoenix (5)
Can't Take My Eyes Off You (4)
Clair De Lune (3)
Classical Gas (5)
Cuando Calienta El Sol
 (Love Me With All Your
 Heart) (2)

Dr. Zhivago ..see: Lara's
 Theme
El Relicario (2)
Fascination (4)
Girl From Ipanema (2)
Goin' Out Of My Head (4)
Gone With The Wind ..see:
 Tara's Theme
Good, The Bad And The
 Ugly (5)
Guantanamera (2)
I Hear A Symphony (3)
Impossible Dream (4)
Kiss Me Goodbye (5)

La Paloma (2)
Lara's Theme (2)
Lonely Bull (2)
Look Of Her (4)
Look Of Love (5)
Love Is Blue (5)
Love Sonata (5)
Lover's Concerto (4)
MacArthur Park (5)
Maria Elena (2)
Meditation (2)
Michelle (3)
Midnight Memories (5)
Misty Night (4)

Moonlight Sonata (1)
My Cup Runneth Over (3)
My Heart's Symphony (1)
My Prayer (1)
Never My Love (4)
Our Day Will Come (2)
Please Love Me Forever (4)
Portrait Of My Love (3)
Prelude To Love (3)
Prophesy Of Love (3)
Quiet Nights Of Quiet Stars (2)

Shadow Of Your Smile (Love
 Theme From The
 Sandpiper) (1)
Softly (4)
Somewhere, My Love ..see:
 Lara's Theme
Spanish Eyes (2)
Strangers In The Night (1)
Strangers No More (3)
Summer Samba (2)
Tara's Theme (4)
This Is My Song (3)

Tonight's Dream (1)
Twilight Sonata (4)
Valley Of The Dolls, Theme
 From (5)
What Now My Love (1)
Yesterday (1)
You Don't Have To Say You
 Love Me (1)
Young Girl (5)
Young Lovers' Rhapsody (1)

MIGHTY CLOUDS OF JOY

Gospel group formed in Los Angeles in 1960. Nucleus consisted of Willie Joe Ligon and Johnny Martin (leads), Elmo Franklin and Richard Wallace. Later joined by Leon Polk and David Walker.

| 10/26/74 | 165 | 5 | | 1 It's Time.. | $8 | Dunhill 50177 |
| 1/24/76 | 168 | 6 | | 2 Kickin'... | $8 | ABC 899 |

Everything Is Going Up (1)
Everything Is Love (2)
Heart Full Of Love (1)

I've Got The Music In Me
 (medley) (2)
Laugh (2)
Leanin' (2)

Master Plan (1)
Mighty Cloud Of Joy (1)
Mighty High (2) **69**
Millionaire (2)

Standing On The Real Side (2)
Stoned World (1)
Superstition (medley) (2)

Time (1)
Touch My Soul (2)
You Are So Beautiful (2)

(You Think) You're Doin' It
 On Your Own (1)

MIGHTY LEMON DROPS, The

Pop quartet formed in 1985 in Wolverhampton, U.K.: Paul Marsh (vocals), David Newton, Keith Rowley and Tony Linehan (replaced by bassist Marcus Williams in 1989).

| 3/10/90 | 195 | 2 | | Laughter .... | $12 | Sire 26017 |

All That I Can Do
At Midnight
Beautiful Shame

Heartbreak Thing
Into The Heart Of Love

One In A Million
Real World

Rumbletrain?
Second Time Around

Where Do We Go From
 Heaven

Written In Fiction

MIKE + THE MECHANICS

Rock quintet consisting of bassist Mike Rutherford (Genesis), vocalists Paul Carrack (Ace, Squeeze) and Paul Young (Sad Cafe), drummer Peter Van Hooke (Van Morrison) and keyboardist Adrian Lee.

11/23/85+	26	53	●	1 Mike + The Mechanics	$8	Atlantic 81287
11/19/88+	13	37	●	2 Living Years	$8	Atlantic 81923
4/20/91	107	5		3 Word Of Mouth	$12	Atlantic 82233

All I Need Is A Miracle (1) **5**
Beautiful Day (2)
Before (The Next Heartache
 Falls) (3)
Black & Blue (2)
Blame (2)
Call To Arms (1)

Don't (2)
Everybody Gets A Second
 Chance (3)
Get Up (3)
Hanging By A Thread (1)
I Get The Feeling (1)

Let's Pretend It Didn't
 Happen (3)
Living Years (2) **1**
My Crime Of Passion (3)
Nobody Knows (2)
Nobody's Perfect (2) **63**
Par Avion (1)

Poor Boy Down (2)
Seeing Is Believing (2) **62**
**Silent Running (On
 Dangerous Ground)** (1) **6**
Stop Baby (3)
Take The Reins (1)
Taken In (1) **32**

Time And Place (3)
Way You Look At Me (3)
Why Me? (2)
Word Of Mouth (3) **78**
Yesterday, Today, Tomorrow (3)
You Are The One (1)

★★446★★ MILES, Buddy

Born George Miles on 9/5/46 in Omaha. R&B vocalist/drummer. Prominent session musician. Lead singer of The Fidelity's in 1958. Worked as sideman in the Dick Clark Revue, 1963-64. With Wilson Pickett, 1965-66. In Michael Bloomfield's Electric Flag, 1967. In Jimi Hendrix's Band Of Gypsys, 1969-70. In 1987, was the voice of The California Raisins, the claymation TV ad characters.

| 6/7/69 | 145 | 4 | | 1 Electric Church * .... | $15 | Mercury 61222 |

co-produced by Jimi Hendrix

DEBUT DATE	PEAK POS	WKS CHR	GOLD	ARTIST — Album Title	$	Label & Number
				MILES, Buddy — Cont'd		
7/4/70	35	74		2 Them Changes	$12	Mercury 61280
11/14/70	53	26		3 We Got To Live Together	$12	Mercury 61313
4/10/71	60	24		4 A Message To The People	$12	Mercury 608
10/2/71	50	24		5 Buddy Miles Live [L]	$12	Mercury 7500 [2]
7/8/72	8	33	▲	6 Carlos Santana & Buddy Miles! Live! [L]	$10	Columbia 31308
				CARLOS SANTANA & BUDDY MILES		
3/10/73	123	9		7 Chapter VII	$10	Columbia 32048
				THE BUDDY MILES BAND		
1/19/74	194	3		8 Booger Bear *	$10	Columbia 32694
				*BUDDY MILES EXPRESS		
8/23/75	68	11		9 More Miles Per Gallon	$10	Casablanca 7019

Blues City (9)
Booger Bear (8)
Cigarettes & Coffee (1)
Crazy Love (8)
Crossfire (7)
Destructive Love (1)
Do It To Me (9)
Don't Keep Me Wondering (4)
Down By The River (2,5) 68
Dreams (2) 86
Easy Greasy (3)
Elvira (7)
Evil Ways (6) 84

Faith Interlude (6)
Free Form Funkafide Filth (6)
Hear No Evil (7)
Heart's Delight (2)
I Still Love You, Anyway (2)
Joe Tex (4,5)
L.A. Resurrection (7)
Lava (6)
Life Is What You Make It Part 1 & 2 (7)
Livin' In The Right Space (9)
Louie's Blues (8)

Love (8)
Love Affair (7)
Marbles (6)
Memphis Train (2) 100
Midnight Rider (4)
Miss Lady (1)
My Chant (1)
My Last Words Of Love (9)
Nasty Disposition (9)
Nichols Canyon Fuunk (9)
No Time For Sorrow (9)
Paul B. Allen, Omaha, Nebraska (2)

Place Over There (4,5)
Rockin' And Rollin' On The Streets Of Hollywood (9) 91
Runaway Child (Little Miss Nothin') (3)
Segment, The (4,5)
69 Freedom Special (1)
Sudden Stop (4)
Take It Off Him And Put It On Me (3,5)
Texas (1)
That's The Way Life Is (4)

Them Changes (2,5) 81
Them Changes (6) *flip*
There Was A Time (7)
Thinking Of You (8)
United Nations Stomp (8)
Visions (7)
Walkin' Down The Highway (3)
Way I Feel Tonight (1)
We Got To Live Together - Part 1 (3,5) 86
Wholesale Love (4) 71
Why (8)

Wrap It Up (1,5)
You Are Everything (8)
You Don't Have A Kind Word To Say (9)
You Really Got Me (8)
Your Feeling Is Mine (2)

MILES, John
Born on 4/23/49 in Jarrow, England. Rock vocalist/guitarist/keyboardist. Guest vocalist with the Alan Parsons Project.

DEBUT DATE	PEAK POS	WKS CHR	GOLD	ARTIST — Album Title	$	Label & Number
5/22/76	171	4		1 Rebel	$8	London 669
3/19/77	93	15		2 Stranger In The City	$8	London 682

Do It Anyway (2)
Everybody Wants Some More (1)
Glamour Boy (2)

Highfly (1) 68
Lady Of My Life (1)
Manhattan Skyline (2)
Music (1) 88

Music Man (2)
Pull The Damn Thing Down (1)
Rebel (1)

Remember Yesterday (2)
Slowdown (2) 34
Stand Up (And Give Me A Reason) (2)

Stranger In The City (2)
Time (2)
When You Lose Someone So Young (1)

You Have It All (1)

MILLER, Frankie
Born in Glasgow, Scotland, circa 1950. Blues-tinged rock singer.

DEBUT DATE	PEAK POS	WKS CHR	GOLD	ARTIST — Album Title	$	Label & Number
6/18/77	124	12		1 Full House	$8	Chrysalis 1128
5/13/78	177	10		2 Double Trouble	$8	Chrysalis 1174
6/26/82	135	9		3 Standing On The Edge	$8	Capitol 12206

Angels With Dirty Faces (3)
Be Good To Yourself (1)
Danger Danger (3)
Don't Stop (3)
Doodle Song (1) 71
Double Heart Trouble (2)

Down The Honkytonk (1)
Firin' Line (3)
Good Time Love (2)
Goodnight Sweetheart (2)
Have You Seen Me Lately Joan (2)

(I Can't) Breakaway (2)
(I'll Never) Live In Vain (1)
It's All Coming Down Tonight (3)
Jealous Guy (1)
Jealousy (3)

Let The Candlelight Shine (1)
Love Is All Around (2)
Love Letters (1)
Love Waves (2)
On My Way (3)
Searching (1)

Standing On The Edge (3)
Stubborn Kind Of Fellow (2)
Take Good Care Of Yourself (1)
This Love Of Mine (1)
To Dream The Dream (3) 62

Train, The (2)
You'll Be In My Mind (2)
Zap Zap (3)

MILLER, Glenn
Born on 3/1/04 in Clarinda, Iowa. Leader of most popular big band of all time. Played trombone for Ben Pollack, Red Nichols, Benny Goodman and the Dorsey Brothers, became de facto leader of Ray Noble's 1935 American band, and did arrangements for Glen Gray and others before starting his own band in 1937. Glenn disappeared on a plane flight from England to France on 12/15/44.

DEBUT DATE	PEAK POS	WKS CHR	GOLD	ARTIST — Album Title	$	Label & Number
9/16/57	16	6		1 Marvelous Miller Moods [E]	$20	RCA 1494
				GLENN MILLER ARMY AIR FORCE BAND with Johnny Desmond (vocals); from radio broadcasts during 1943-44		
12/9/57	17	4		2 The New Glenn Miller Orchestra In Hi Fi	$20	RCA 1522
				directed by Ray McKinley (leader of the orchestra after Glenn's death)		
2/24/58	19	3		3 The Glenn Miller Carnegie Hall Concert [E-L]	$20	RCA 1506
				recorded on 10/06/39		
1/25/75	115	9		4 A Legendary Performer [E]	$10	RCA 0693 [2]
				previously unreleased performances from 1939-42		

Accentuate The Positive (2)
Anything Goes (2)
At Last (4)
Blue Is The Night (1)
Bugle Call Rag (medley) (3)
Chattanooga Choo Choo (4)
Danny Boy (3,4)
Don't Be That Way (2)
Elmer's Tune (4)
Everything I Love (4)
FDR Jones (medley) (3)
Farewell Blues (1)

Hallelujah, I Just Love Her So (2)
Hold Tight (medley) (3)
Holiday For Strings (1)
I Almost Lost My Mind (2)
I Love You (1)
I'm Thrilled (2)
I've Got A Gal In Kalamazoo (4)
In The Mood (3,4)
Jack And Jill (4)
Jim Jam Jump (medley) (3)

Jingle Bells (4)
Juke Box Saturday Night (4)
Little Brown Jug (3,4)
Londonderry Air ...see: Danny Boy
Long Ago And Far Away (1)
Lovely Way To Spend An Evening (1)
Lullaby Of Birdland (2)
Mine (2)
Moonlight Cocktail (4)
Moonlight Serenade (3,4)

My Ideal (1)
My Melancholy Baby (4)
My Prayer (2)
On The Street Where You Live (2)
One O'Clock Jump (3)
Pearls On Velvet (1)
Pennsylvania 6-5000 (4)
People Will Say We're In Love (1)
Running Wild (medley) (3)
Sentimental Me (4)

Slumber Song (2)
So You're The One (4)
Song Of The Volga Boatmen (4)
Stairway To The Stars (medley) (3)
Star Dust (1,4)
String Of Pearls (4)
Suddenly It's Spring (1)
Sunrise Serenade (3,4)
Take The "A" Train (4)

Tchaikovsky's Piano Concerto (4)
To You (medley) (3)
Tuxedo Junction (4)
Whistle Stop (2)

MILLER, Jody
Born in Phoenix on 11/29/41 and raised in Blanchard, Oklahoma. Pop-country singer.

DEBUT DATE	PEAK POS	WKS CHR	GOLD	ARTIST — Album Title	$	Label & Number
6/26/65	124	6		1 Queen Of The House	$15	Capitol 2349
8/28/71	117	8		2 He's So Fine	$10	Epic 30659

Baby, I'm Yours (2) 91
Don't Be Cruel (2)
Don't Throw Your Love To The Wind (2)
Everybody's Somebody's Fool (1)

Good Lovin' (Makes It Right) (2)
Greatest Actor (1)
He Walks Like A Man (1) 66
He's So Fine (2) 53

I Walk The Line (1)
I'm Gonna Write A Song (2)
If I (1)
Let Him Have It (2)
Make Me Your Kind Of Woman (2)

Odds And Ends (1)
Queen Of The House (1) 12
Race Is On (1)
Sea Of Heartbreak (1)
Silver Threads And Golden Needles (1) 54

Soft And Gentle Ways (1)
These Are The Years (1)
We Had Love All The Way (2)
Woman Left Lonely (2)
You've Got A Friend (2)

DEBUT DATE	PEAK POS	WKS CHR	GOLD	ARTIST — Album Title	$	Label & Number

★★38★★ **MILLER, Mitch, & The Gang**
Born on 7/4/11 in Rochester, New York. Producer/conductor/arranger. Oboe soloist with the CBS Symphony from 1936-47. A&R executive for both Columbia and Mercury Records. Best known for his sing-along albums and TV show (1961-64).

DEBUT DATE	PEAK POS	WKS CHR	GOLD	#	Album Title	$	Label & Number
7/14/58	1[8]	204	●	1	**Sing Along With Mitch**	$12	Columbia 1160
11/10/58+	4	171	●	2	**More Sing Along With Mitch**............................	$12	Columbia 1243
3/23/59	4	130	●	3	**Still More! Sing Along With Mitch**	$10	Columbia 1283
6/1/59+	11	89	●	4	**Folk Songs Sing Along With Mitch**	$10	Columbia 1316
8/31/59+	7	100	●	5	**Party Sing Along With Mitch**	$10	Columbia 1331
12/28/59+	10	91	●	6	**Fireside Sing Along With Mitch**	$10	Columbia 1389
4/4/60+	8	89	●	7	**Saturday Night Sing Along With Mitch**	$10	Columbia 1414
6/27/60	5	107	●	8	**Sentimental Sing Along With Mitch**	$10	Columbia 1457
10/10/60	40	16		9	March Along With Mitch .... [I]	$10	Columbia 1475
10/31/60	5	78	●	10	**Memories Sing Along With Mitch**	$10	Columbia 8342
3/13/61	5	73	●	11	**Happy Times! Sing Along With Mitch**	$10	Columbia 8368
3/13/61	9	27		12	**Mitch's Greatest Hits** ....[G]	$10	Columbia 8344
5/29/61	3	46		13	**TV Sing Along With Mitch**	$10	Columbia 8428
9/18/61	6	44		14	**Your Request Sing Along With Mitch**	$10	Columbia 8471
3/10/62	21	23		15	Rhythm Sing Along With Mitch	$10	Columbia 8527
6/9/62	27	15		16	Family Sing Along With Mitch	$10	Columbia 8573
					CHRISTMAS ALBUMS:		
12/8/58	1[2]	5	●	17	**Christmas Sing-Along With Mitch** ....[X]	$10	Columbia 1205
12/14/59	8	4		18	**Christmas Sing-Along With Mitch** ....[X-R]	$10	Columbia 1205
12/19/60	6	3		19	**Christmas Sing-Along With Mitch** ....[X-R]	$10	Columbia 8027
12/4/61+	9	8		20	**Christmas Sing-Along With Mitch** ....[X-R]	$10	Columbia 8027
12/22/62	37	2		21	Christmas Sing-Along With Mitch ....[X-R]	$10	Columbia 8027
11/6/61+	1[1]	18	●	22	**Holiday Sing Along With Mitch** ....[X]	$10	Columbia 8501
12/8/62	33	4		23	Holiday Sing Along With Mitch ....[X]	$10	Columbia 8501

Christmas charts: 9/'63, 15/'64, 22/'65, 14/'66, 17/'67, 37/'68

After The Ball (medley) (7)
Ain't She Sweet (medley) (7)
Ain't We Got Fun (15)
Alabamy Bound (medley) (11)
All I Do Is Dream Of You (medley) (8)
All Through The Night (medley) (6)
Alouette March (9)
Annie Laurie (medley) (6)
Anniversary Song (11)
At Sundown (medley) (13)
Auf Wiedersehen, My Dear (13)
Auld Lang Syne (medley) (6)
Aunt Rhody (The Old Gray Goose) (4)
Aura Lee (medley) (13)
Avalon (medley) (13)
Away In A Manger (Luther's Carol) (17)
Baby Face (7)
Back In Your Own Back Yard (14)
Band Played On (medley) (3)
Bandit, The (9)
Barney Google (15)
Battle Hymn Of The Republic (10)
Be Kind To Your Web-Footed Friends (medley) (1)
Be My Little Baby Bumble Bee (2)
Bear Went Over The Mountain (medley) (4)
Beautiful Ohio (5)
Beer Barrel Polka (3)
Believe Me If All Those Endearing Young Charms (medley) (6)
Bell Bottom Trousers (medley) (1)
Bicycle Built For Two (medley) (3)
Bidin' My Time (15)
Bill Bailey, Won't You Please Come Home (medley) (10)
Billy Boy (medley) (11)
Bird In A Gilded Cage (medley) (12)
Black Bottom (15)
Blue Tail Fly (4)
Bonnie Eloise (12)
Bowery, The (medley) (10)
Bowery Grenadiers (12)

Breezin' Along With The Breeze (13)
By The Beautiful Sea (14)
By The Light Of The Silvery Moon (1)
Bye Bye Blackbird (7)
California (medley) (13)
Camptown Races (medley) (4)
Carolina In The Morning (2)
Cecilia (14)
Children's Marching Song (12) *16*
Chinatown, My Chinatown (15)
Christmas Song (Merry Christmas To You) (medley) (11)
Collegiate (medley) (11)
Comin' Through The Rye March (9)
Coventry Carol (17)
Cuddle Up A Little Closer (medley) (5)
Dancing With Tears In My Eyes (7)
Deck The Hall With Boughs Of Holly (17)
Deep Purple (16)
Diane (16)
Did You Ever See A Dream Walking? (7)
Dixie (9,10)
Do-Re-Mi (9,12) *70*
Do You Ever Think Of Me (16)
Don't Fence Me In (1)
Don't Sit Under The Apple Tree (With Anyone Else But Me) (16)
Down By The Old Mill Stream (1)
Down In The Valley (4)
Drifting And Dreaming (14)
Drink To Me Only With Thine Eyes (medley) (6)
Drunk Last Night (6)
First Noel (17)
Five Foot Two, Eyes Of Blue (medley) (10)
For Me And My Gal (medley) (2)
Forty-Second Street (15)
Frere Jacques March (9)
Frosty The Snowman (22)
Funiculi, Funicula (6)
Gang That Sang Heart Of My Heart (8)

Girl I Left Behind Me (medley) (9)
Give My Regards To Broadway (medley) (8)
God Rest Ye Merry, Gentlemen (17)
Good Night Sweetheart (3)
Goodnight, Irene (4)
Goodnight, Ladies (medley) (5)
Happy Days Are Here Again (13)
Harbor Lights (14)
Hark! The Herald Angels Sing (17)
Harrigan (medley) (5)
Has Anybody Here Seen Kelly (medley) (13)
Hello! My Baby (5)
Hey, Betty Martin (13)
Hey Little Baby (12)
Hinky Dinky Parlezvous (medley) (3)
Home On The Range (10)
Home, Sweet Home (medley) (5)
Honey (medley) (10)
I Found A Million Dollar Baby (In A Five And Ten Cent Store) (13)
I Love A Lassie (medley) (15)
I Love My Baby - My Baby Loves Me (medley) (11)
I Love You (10)
I Love You Truly (5)
I Saw Mommy Kissing Santa Claus (22)
(I Wanna Go Where You Go, Do What You Do) Then I'll Be Happy (14)
I Want To Be Happy (15)
I Wonder What's Become Of Sally? (medley) (7)
I Wonder Who's Kissing Her Now (5)
I'll Be With You In Apple Blossom Time (3)
I'll See You In My Dreams (8)
I'll Take You Home Again, Kathleen (5)
I'm Forever Blowing Bubbles (15)
I'm Going Back To Dixie (9,10)
I'm Just Wild About Mary (I'm Just Wild About Harry) (medley) (3)

I'm Looking Over A Four Leaf Clover (7)
I'm Nobody's Baby (medley) (10)
I'm Sitting On Top Of The World (16)
I've Been Working On The Railroad (medley) (1)
I've Got Rings On My Fingers (medley) (13)
I've Got Sixpence (medley) (1)
Ida (medley) (8)
If I Could Be With You (One Hour Tonight) (medley) (11)
If You Knew Susie (Like I Know Susie) (medley) (11)
If You Were The Only Girl (2)
In A Shanty In Old Shanty Town (3)
In The Evening By The Moonlight (2)
In The Gloaming (medley) (6)
In The Good Old Summertime (medley) (5)
In The Shade Of The Old Apple Tree (medley) (5)
Indiana (11)
Irish Medley (8)
It Came Upon The Midnight Clear (17)
It Happened In Monterey (16)
It's Been A Long, Long Time (14)
It's Only A Paper Moon (13)
Ja-Da (16)
Jeanie With The Light Brown Hair (8)
Jeannine (I Dream Of Lilac Time) (8)
Jeepers Creepers (15)
Jingle Bells (22)
Joy To The World (17)
Juanita (medley) (6)
June Night (Just Give Me A June Night, The Moonlight And You) (16)
Just A-Wearyin' For You (9)
K-K-K-Katy (16)
Kerry Dancer March (9)
Last Night On The Back Porch (I Loved Her Best Of All) (medley) (11)
Let It Snow! Let It Snow! Let It Snow! (22)
Let Me Call You Sweetheart (medley) (2)

Let The Rest Of The World Go By (1)
Let's Put Out The Lights And Go To Sleep (15)
Linger Awhile (16)
Listen To The Mocking Bird (4)
Little Annie Rooney (medley) (8)
Little Brown Jug (medley) (7)
Little Shepherd's March (9)
Loch Lomond March (9)
Love Nest (13)
Love's Old Sweet Song (6)
Mairzy Doats (16)
Man On The Flying Trapeze (medley) (7)
March From The River Kwai and Colonel Bogey (12) *20*
Meet Me In St. Louis, Louis (medley) (10)
Meet Me Tonight In Dreamland (5)
Memories (3)
Moonlight And Roses (2)
Moonlight Bay (medley) (13)
Mother Machree (medley) (7)
Must Be Santa (22)
My Blue Heaven (10)
My Bonnie Lies Over The Ocean (6)
My Buddy (2)
My Darling Clementine (4)
My Gal Sal (medley) (5)
My Melancholy Baby (11)
(Nel Blu Dipinto Di Blu) ..see: Volare
Now Is The Hour (7)
O Come, All Ye Faithful (Adeste Fideles) (17)
O, Katharina! (4)
O Little Town Of Bethlehem (17)
Oh Dear, What Can The Matter Be (medley) (6)
Oh Marie (16)
Oh Susanna! (medley) (5)
Oh! What A Pal Was Mary (medley) (5)
Oh, Where, Oh Where Has My Little Dog Gone (6)
Oh! You Beautiful Doll (medley) (6)
Old Friends (1)
Old Grey Mare (medley) (6)

On Top Of Old Smoky (4)
Our Boys Will Shine Tonight (medley) (8)
Paddlin' Madelin' Home (14)
Peg O' My Heart (medley) (10)
Peggy O'Neil (medley) (11)
Polly Wolly Doodle (medley) (6)
Poor Butterfly (7)
Pop! Goes The Weasel (medley) (4)
Pretty Baby (medley) (11)
Prisoner's Song (11)
Put On Your Old Grey Bonnet (medley) (3)
Ramblin' Wreck From Georgia Tech (11)
Ramona (2)
Red River Valley (4)
Roamin' In The Gloamin' (medley) (15)
Rudolph, The Red-Nosed Reindeer (22)
San Francisco (16)
Santa Claus Is Comin' To Town (22)
School Days (medley) (5)
She Wore A Yellow Ribbon (1)
She'll Be Coming 'Round The Mountain (medley) (3)
Shine On Harvest Moon (medley) (1)
Show Me The Way To Go Home (medley) (1)
Shuffle Off To Buffalo (13)
Side By Side (11)
Sidewalks Of New York (medley) (5)
Silent Night, Holy Night (17)
Silly Little Tune (12)
Silver Bells (22)
Silver Moon (7)
Silver Threads Among The Gold (medley) (3)
Sing Along (7,12)
Singin' In The Rain (medley) (8)
Skip To My Lou (medley) (4)
Sleepy Time Gal (medley) (10)
Sleigh Ride (22)
Smiles (3)
Somebody Stole My Gal (16)
Song For A Summer Night, Theme Song From (12) *8*
Sunny Side Up (14)

505

DEBUT DATE	PEAK POS	WKS CHR	GOLD	ARTIST — Album Title	$	Label & Number

MILLER, Mitch, & The Gang — Cont'd

Swanee (15)
Sweet Adeline (medley) (2)
Sweet And Low (medley) (6)
Sweet Genevieve (medley) (6)
Sweet Rosie O'Grady (medley) (5)
Sweet Violets (1)
Sweetest Story Ever Told (5)
Sweetheart Of Sigma Chi (14)
Ta-Ra-Ra-Boom-De-E (medley) (7)
Tea For Two (15)
That Old Gang Of Mine (1)
That's My Weakness Now (medley) (11)
That's Where My Money Goes (1)

There Is A Tavern In The Town (medley) (1)
There's A Long, Long Trail (2)
There's Yes! Yes! In Your Eyes (medley) (13)
Three O'Clock In The Morning (8)
Till We Meet Again (1)
Tip-Toe Thru The Tulips With Me (3)
Too-Ra-Loo-Ra-Loo-Ral (That's An Irish Lullaby) (medley) (7)
Toot, Toot, Tootsie! (Goodbye) (medley) (8)
Trail Of The Lonesome Pine (11)

Twelve Days Of Christmas (22)
Under The Bamboo Tree (14)
Vive L'Amour (medley) (6)
Volare (Nel Blu Dipinto Di Blu) (16)
Wagon Wheels (11)
Wait For The Wagon (medley) (6)
Wait Till The Sun Shines Nellie (medley) (5)
Walkin' Down To Washington (1)
We Three Kings Of Orient Are (17)
We're In The Money (15)
What Child Is This (17)
When Day Is Done (3)

When I Grow Too Old To Dream (8)
When It's Springtime In The Rockies (16)
When Johnny Comes Marching Home (4)
When The Red, Red Robin Comes Bob, Bob Bobbin' Along (14)
When The Saints Come Marching In (8)
When You And I Were Young, Maggie (6)
When You Were Sweet Sixteen (medley) (3)
When You Wore A Tulip (And I Wore A Big Red Rose) (16)

Where Do You Work-A, John (medley) (11)
Whiffenpoof Song (Baa! Baa! Baa!) (2)
While Strolling Through The Park One Day (medley) (8)
Whistler And His Dog (9)
White Christmas (22)
Winter Wonderland (22)
Would You Like To Take A Walk? (13)
Yankee Doodle (medley) (9)
Yankee Doodle Boy (medley) (10)
Yellow Rose Of Texas (12) *1*
Yes! We Have No Bananas (medley) (11)
You Are My Sunshine (1)

You Must Have Been A Beautiful Baby (medley) (13)
You Tell Me Your Dream, I'll Tell You Mine (2)
You Were Meant For Me (medley) (10)
You're An Old Smoothie (15)
You're The Cream In My Coffee (14)

MILLER, Mrs.

Mrs. Elva Miller. Tone-deaf singer from Claremont, California.

DEBUT DATE	PEAK POS	WKS CHR	GOLD	ARTIST — Album Title	$	Label & Number
5/7/66	15	17		Mrs. Miller's Greatest Hits .... [N]	$25	Capitol 2494

Catch A Falling Star
Chim Chim Cher-ee
Dear Heart
Downtown *82*
Gonna Be Like That
Hard Day's Night
Let's Hang On
Lover's Concerto *95*
My Love
Shadow Of Your Smile
These Boots Are Made For Walkin'

MILLER, Ned

Born Henry Ned Miller on 4/12/25 in Rains, Utah. Country singer/songwriter. To California in 1956. Signed with Fabor in 1956. Wrote the Gale Storm and Bonnie Guitar hit "Dark Moon."

DEBUT DATE	PEAK POS	WKS CHR	GOLD	ARTIST — Album Title	$	Label & Number
3/30/63	50	13		From A Jack To A King	$30	Fabor 1001

Billy Carino
Cry Of The Wild Goose
From A Jack To A King *6*
Just Before Dawn
Lights In The Street
Loving Shadow
Man Behind The Gun
Mona Lisa
One Among The Many
Stagecoach
Sunday Morning Tears
You Belong To My Heart

★★472★★ MILLER, Roger

Country vocalist/humorist/guitarist/composer. Born on 1/2/36 in Fort Worth, Texas and raised in Erick, Oklahoma. To Nashville in the mid-1950s, began songwriting career. With Faron Young as writer/drummer in 1962. Won six Grammys in 1965. Own TV show in 1966. Songwriter of 1985's Tony Award-winning Broadway musical *Big River*. Died of cancer on 10/25/92.

DEBUT DATE	PEAK POS	WKS CHR	GOLD	#	Album Title	$	Label & Number
6/27/64	37	46	●	1	Roger And Out .... [N]	$12	Smash 67049
2/6/65	4	47	●	2	The Return Of Roger Miller	$12	Smash 67061
7/24/65	13	24		3	The 3rd Time Around	$12	Smash 67068
11/13/65+	6	57	●	4	Golden Hits .... [G]	$12	Smash 67073
11/19/66+	108	13		5	Words And Music	$12	Smash 67075
7/1/67	118	8		6	Walkin' In The Sunshine	$12	Smash 67092
8/24/68	173	8		7	A Tender Look At Love	$12	Smash 67103
8/30/69	163	7		8	Roger Miller	$12	Smash 67123
2/14/70	200	2		9	Roger Miller 1970	$12	Smash 67129

Absence (6)
Ain't That Fine (2)
All Fall Down (9)
As Long As There's A Shadow (4)
Atta Boy Girl (2,4)
Best Of All Possible Worlds (8)
Big Harlan Taylor (3)
Billy Bayou (5)
Boeing Boeing 707 (8)
By The Time I Get To Phoenix (7)
Chug-A-Lug (1,4) *9*
Colonel Maggie (8)
Crystal Day (9)
Dad Blame Anything A Man Can't Quit (5)
Dang Me (1,4) *7*
Darby's Castle (8)
Dear Heart (7)
Do-Wacka-Do (2,4) *31*

Engine Engine #9 (3,4) *7*
England Swings (4) *8*
Every Which-A-Way (5)
Everybody's Talkin' (9)
Feel Of Me (1)
Fool, The (9)
Gentle On My Mind (7)
Good Old Days (3)
Got 2 Again (1)
Green Green Grass Of Home (6)
Hard Headed Me (2)
Heartbreak Hotel (5) *84*
Hey Good Lookin' (6)
Home (5)
Honey (7)
Husbands And Wives (5) *26*
I Ain't Comin' Home Tonight (1)
I Know Who It Is (And I'm Gonna Tell On 'Em) (9)
I'd Come Back To Me (1)

I'll Pick Up My Heart (And Go Home) (5)
I'm Gonna Teach My Heart To Bend (Instead Of Breaking) (8)
I've Been A Long Time Leavin' (But I'll Be A Long Time Gone) (5)
If You Want Me To (1)
In The Summertime (You Don't Want My Love) (2,4)
It Happened Just That Way (3,4)
It Takes All Kinds To Make A World (1)
Jody And The Kid (9)
Kansas City Star (3,4) *31*
King Of The Road (2,4) *4*
Last Word In Lonesome Is Me (3)
Less And Less (5)
Less Of Me (5)

Little Green Apples (7) *39*
Lou's Got The Flu (1)
Love Is Not For Me (2)
Man Who Stayed In Monterey (9)
Me And Bobby McGee (8)
Meanwhile Back In Abilene (8)
Million Years Or So (6)
Moon Is High (1)
My Elusive Dreams (7)
My Uncle Used To Love Me But She Died (5) *58*
Mystery Train (9)
One Dyin' And A Buryin' (3,4) *34*
Our Hearts Will Play The Music (2)
Our Little Love (6)
Pardon This Coffin' (6)
Precious Baby (9)
Private John Q (1)

Reincarnation (2)
Riddle, The (6)
Ruby (Don't Take Your Love To Town) (6)
Shame Bird (4)
Squares Make The World Go Round (1)
Swing Low Swingin' Chariot (3)
Swiss Cottage Place (8)
Swiss Maid (3)
T.J.'s Last Ride (9)
That's The Way It's Always Been (2)
That's Why I Love You Like I Do (1)
There I Go Dreamin' (2)
This Town (3)
Tolivar (7)
Tom Green County Fair (9)
Train Of Life (5)
Twelfth Of Never (7)

Vance (8) *80*
Walkin' In The Sunshine (6) *37*
Water Dog (3)
What I'd Give (To Be The Wind) (7)
Where Have All The Average People Gone (8)
With Pen In Hand (7)
Workin' Girl (9)
You Can't Roller Skate In A Buffalo Herd (2,4) *40*
You Didn't Have To Be So Nice (6)
You're My Kingdom (5)

★★96★★ MILLER, Steve, Band

Born on 10/5/43 in Milwaukee and raised in Dallas. Blues-rock singer/songwriter/guitarist. Formed band in high school, The Marksmen, which included Boz Scaggs. While at the University of Wisconsin-Madison, Steve led the blues-rock band the Ardells, later known as the Fabulous Night Trains, featuring Scaggs. After graduating, studied literature at the University of Copenhagen. To San Francisco in 1966; formed the Steve Miller Band, which featured a fluctuating lineup.

DEBUT DATE	PEAK POS	WKS CHR	GOLD	#	Album Title	$	Label & Number
6/15/68	134	18		1	Children Of The Future	$15	Capitol 2920
11/2/68	24	17		2	Sailor	$15	Capitol 2984
6/28/69	22	26		3	Brave New World	$12	Capitol 184
11/29/69+	38	14		4	Your Saving Grace	$12	Capitol 331
7/25/70	23	26		5	Number 5	$12	Capitol 436
10/9/71	82	9		6	Rock Love	$12	Capitol 748
4/1/72	109	10		7	Recall The Beginning...A Journey From Eden	$12	Capitol 1022
11/18/72+	56	39	●	8	Anthology .... [K]	$12	Capitol 11114 [2]
10/20/73	2[1]	38	▲	9	The Joker	$10	Capitol 11235
5/29/76	3	97	▲[4]	10	Fly Like An Eagle	$10	Capitol 11497
5/21/77	2[2]	68	▲[3]	11	Book Of Dreams	$8	Capitol 11630

MILLER, Steve, Band — Cont'd

DEBUT DATE	PEAK POS	WKS CHR	GOLD	ARTIST — Album Title	$	Label & Number
12/9/78+	18	18	▲⁶ 12	Greatest Hits 1974-78 ....[G]	$8	Capitol 11872
11/14/81	26	17	● 13	Circle Of Love	$8	Capitol 12121
6/26/82	3	33	▲ 14	**Abracadabra**	$8	Capitol 12216
4/30/83	125	7	15	Steve Miller Band - Live! ....[L]	$8	Capitol 12263
11/10/84	101	10	16	Italian X Rays	$8	Capitol 12339
11/15/86+	65	23	17	Living In The 20th Century	$8	Capitol 12445
10/8/88	108	10	18	Born 2B Blue	$8	Capitol 48303

STEVE MILLER
features Milt Jackson (vibes) and Phil Woods (sax)

Abracadabra (14,15) *1*
Ain't That Lovin' You Baby (17)
Babes In The Wood (11)
Baby Wanna Dance (13)
Baby's Callin' Me Home (1)
Baby's House (4,8)
Beauty Of Time Is That It's Snowing (Psychedelic B.B.) (1)
Behind The Barn (17)
Big Boss Man (17)
Blue Odyssey (10)
Blues With Out Blame (6)
Bongo Bongo (16) *84*
Born To Be Blue (18)
Brave New World (3)
Can't You Hear Your Daddy's Heartbeat (3)
Caress Me Baby (17)
Celebration Song (3,8)
Children Of The Future (1)
Circle Of Love (13) *55*
Come On In My Kitchen (9)
Cool Magic (14) *57*
Dance, Dance, Dance (10,12)
Daybreak (17)
Dear Mary (2)
Deliverance (6)

Dime-A-Dance Romance (2)
Don't Let Nobody Turn You Around (4,8)
Electro Lux Imbroglio (11)
Enter Maurice (7)
Evil (9)
Fandango (7)
Fanny Mae (1)
Feel So Glad (4)
Filthy McNasty (18)
Fly Like An Eagle (10,12,15) *2*
Gangster Is Back (9)
Gangster Of Love (2,15)
Get On Home (13)
Give It Up (14) *60*
God Bless The Child (18)
Going To Mexico (5,8)
Going To The Country (5,8) *69*
Golden Opportunity (16)
Good Morning (5)
Goodbye Love (14)
Got Love 'Cause You Need It (3)
Harbor Lights (6)
Harmony Of The Spheres 1 & 2 (16)
Heal Your Heart (7)

Heart Like A Wheel (13) *24*
High On You Mama (7)
Hollywood Dream (16)
Hot Chili (5)
I Love You (5,8)
I Wanna Be Loved (But By Only You) (17)
I Want To Make The World Turn Around (17) *97*
In My First Mind (1)
Industrial Military Complex Hex (5)
Italian X Rays (16)
Jackson-Kent Blues (5)
Jet Airliner (11,12,15) *8*
Joker, The (9,12,15) *1*
Journey From Eden (7,8)
Jungle Love (11,12,15) *23*
Junior Saw It Happen (1)
Just A Little Bit (9)
Just A Passin' Fancy In A Midnite Dream (4)
Keeps Me Wondering Why (14)
Key To The Highway (1)
Kow Kow (3,8)
LT's Midnight Dream (3)
Last Wombat In Mecca (4)
Let Me Serve You (6)

Little Girl (4,8)
Living In The 20th Century (17)
Living In The U.S.A. (2,8,15) *49*
Love Shock (6)
Love's Riddle (7)
Lovin' Cup (9)
Lucky Man (2)
Macho City (13)
Maelstrom (17)
Mary Ann (18)
Mary Lou (9)
Mercury Blues (10,15)
Motherless Children (4,8)
My Babe (17)
My Dark Hour (3,8)
My Friend (2)
My Own Space (11)
Never Kill Anther Man (5,8)
Never Say No (14)
Nobody But You Baby (17)
Nothing Lasts (7)
One In A Million (16)
Out Of The Night (16)
Overdrive (2)
Pushed Me To It (1)
Quicksilver Girl (2)
Radio 1 & 2 (16)

Red Top (18)
Rock Love (6)
Rock'n Me (10,12,15) *1*
Roll With It (1)
Sacrifice (11)
Seasons (3,8)
Serenade (10,12)
Shangri-La (16) *57*
Shu Ba Da Du Ma Ma Ma Ma (9)
Slinky (17)
Somebody Somewhere Help Me (7)
Something Special (14)
Something To Believe In (9)
Song For Our Ancestors (2)
Space Cowboy (3,8)
Stake, The (11,12)
Steppin' Stone (1)
Steve Miller's Midnight Tango (5)
Sugar Babe (9)
Sun Is Going Down (7)
Sweet Maree (10)
Swingtown (11,12) *17*
Take The Money And Run (10,12,15) *11*
Things I Told You (14)
Tokin's (5)

True Fine Love (11,12)
Welcome (7)
When Sunny Gets Blue (18)
While I'm Waiting (14)
Who Do You Love (16)
Wild Mountain Honey (10,12)
Willow Weep For Me (18)
Window, The (10)
Winter Time (11,12)
Wish Upon A Star (11)
Ya Ya (18)
You Send Me (10)
You're So Fine (2)
You've Got The Power (1)
Young Girl's Heart (3)
Your Cash Ain't Nothin' But Trash (9) *51*
Your Saving Grace (4,8)
Zip-A-Dee-Doo-Dah (18)

MILLIONS LIKE US
British duo: John O'Kane and Jeep. Jeep toured with Talk Talk.

DEBUT DATE	PEAK POS	WKS CHR	GOLD	ARTIST — Album Title	$	Label & Number
12/19/87+	171	12		...Millions Like Us	$8	Virgin 90602

Beautiful Enemy
Chain
Guaranteed For Life *69*
Heart To Heart
Heaven And The Sky
Ideal World
In Love With Yourself
Million Voices
Waiting For The Right Time
What You Want Is What You Get

MILLI VANILLI
Europop act formed in Germany by producer Frank Farian (creator of Boney M and Far Corporation). Milli Vanilli is Turkish for Positive Energy. Originally thought to be Rob Pilatus (from Germany) and Fabrice Morvan (from France). Stripped of their 1989 Best New Artist Grammy Award when it was revealed that they did not sing on their debut album. Actual vocalists are Charles Shaw, John Davis and Brad Howe.

DEBUT DATE	PEAK POS	WKS CHR	GOLD	ARTIST — Album Title	$	Label & Number
3/25/89	1⁸	78	▲⁶ 1	**Girl You Know It's True**	$8	Arista 8592
6/16/90	32	20	● 2	The Remix Album ....[K]	$12	Arista 8622

5 of 9 tracks are remixes from the above album

All Or Nothing (1,2) *4*
Baby Don't Forget My Number (1,2) *1*
Blame It On The Rain (1,2) *1*
Boy In The Tree (2)
Can't You Feel My Love (2)
Dreams To Remember (1)
Girl I'm Gonna Miss You (1,2) *1*
Girl You Know It's True (1,2) *2*
Hush (2)
It's Your Thing (2)
Money (2)
More Than You'll Ever Know (1)
Take It As It Comes (1)

MILLS, Frank
Born in Toronto in 1943. Pianist/composer/producer/arranger.

DEBUT DATE	PEAK POS	WKS CHR	GOLD	ARTIST — Album Title	$	Label & Number
3/17/79	21	16	● 1	Music Box Dancer ....[I]	$8	Polydor 6192
11/24/79+	149	9	2	Sunday Morning Suite ....[I]	$8	Polydor 6225

After You Mister Trumpet Man (2)
Ballet Russe (2)
Blackfoot Country (1)
From A Sidewalk Cafe (1)
Hennessey's Island (1)
Love's Like That (1)
Mama, Won't You Boogie With Me? (2)
Mary, Queen Of Scots (2)
Most People Are Nice (2)
Music Box Dancer (1) *3*
Peter Piper (2) *48*
Piano Lesson (2)
Poet And I (1)
Silver Broom, Theme From The (1)
Ski Fever (2)
Spanish Coffee (1)
Sunday Morning Suite (2)
Valse Classique (1)
When You Smile (1)
Wherever You Go (2)
You Don't Love No More (1)

MILLS, Stephanie
★★335★★

Born in 1957 in Brooklyn. In 1967, appeared for four weeks at the Apollo Theater with The Isley Brothers. Appeared in the 1968 Broadway musical *Maggie Flynn*. First recorded for ABC in 1974. At age 15, she won starring role of Dorothy in the hit Broadway show *The Wiz*. Played role for four years. Briefly married to Jeffrey Daniels of Shalamar in 1980.

DEBUT DATE	PEAK POS	WKS CHR	GOLD	ARTIST — Album Title	$	Label & Number
5/19/79	22	34	● 1	Whatcha Gonna Do...With My Lovin'?	$8	20th Century 583
5/3/80	16	44	● 2	Sweet Sensation	$8	20th Century 603
5/16/81	30	23	● 3	Stephanie	$8	20th Century 700
8/7/82	48	19	4	Tantalizingly Hot	$8	Casablanca 7265
9/17/83	104	19	5	Merciless	$8	Casablanca 811364
10/13/84	73	15	6	I've Got The Cure	$8	Casablanca 822421
3/29/86	47	22	7	Stephanie Mills	$8	MCA 5669
6/27/87	30	36	● 8	If I Were Your Woman	$8	MCA 5996
7/22/89	82	38	● 9	Home	$8	MCA 6312

Ain't No Cookin' (9)
Automatic Passion (7)
Can't Change My Ways (8)
Comfort Of A Man (9)
D-A-N-C-I-N' (2)
Deeper Inside Your Love (1)
Do You Love Him? (2)
Don't Stop Dancin' (1)
Don't Stop Doin' What 'Cha Do (3)
Edge Of The Razor (6)
Eternal Love (5)
Everlasting Love (6)
Fast Talk (9)
Feel The Fire (1)
Give It Half A Chance (9)
Good Girl Gone Bad (9)
Here I Am (9)
His Name Is Michael (5)
Hold On To Midnight (7)
Home (9)
How Come U Don't Call Me Anymore? (5)
I Believe In Love Songs (3)
I Can't Give Back The Love I Feel For You (4)
I Come To You (9)
I Feel Good All Over (8)

MILLS, Stephanie — Cont'd

I Have Learned To Respect The Power Of Love (7) · Medicine Song (6) **65** · Outrageous (6) · So Good, So Right (9) · Touch Me Now (8) · Wish That You Were Mine (2)
I Just Wanna Say (2) · Mixture Of Love (2) · Pilot Error (5) · Something In The Way (You Make Me Feel) (9) · True Love Don't Come Easy (4) · You And I (1)
If I Were Your Woman (8) · My Body (5) · Put Your Body In It (1) · Stand Back (7) · Try My Love (2) · You Can Get Over (1)
In My Life (6) · My Love's Been Good To You (3) · Real Love (9) · Starlight (1) · Under Pressure (6) · You Can't Run From My Love (4)
Jesse (8) · Never Get Enough Of You (5) · Rising Desire (7) · Still Lovin' You (4) · Undercover (6) · You Just Might Need A Friend (6)
Just You (7) · **Never Knew Love Like This Before** (2) **6** · Rough Trade (6) · Still Mine (2) · Winner (3) · **(You're Puttin') A Rush On Me** (8) **85**
Keep Away Girls (4) · Night Games (3) · Running For Your Love (8) · **Sweet Sensation** (2) **52** · **What Cha Gonna Do With My Lovin'** (1) **22** · Your Love Is Always New (2)
Last Night (4) · 'Ole Love (4) · Secret Lady (8) · Time Of Your Life (7)
Magic (3) · Since We've Been Together (5) · Top Of My List (3)

MILLS BROTHERS, The

Smooth family vocal group from Piqua, Ohio. Consisted of John, Jr. (b: 1911; d: 1936), Herbert (b: 1912; d: 4/12/89 [age 77]), Harry (b: 1913; d: 6/28/82 [age 68]) and Donald (b: 1915). Originally featured unusual vocal style of imitating instruments. Achieved national fame via radio broadcasts and appearances in films. Father, John, Sr., joined group in 1936, replacing John, Jr.; remained in group until 1956 (d: 12/8/67). Group continued as a trio until 1982. Donald and his son John, III continued singing as a duo.

DEBUT DATE	PEAK POS	WKS CHR	GOLD		ARTIST — Album Title	$	Label & Number
3/16/68	21	26		1	Fortuosity	$15	Dot 25809
4/6/68	145	6		2	The Board Of Directors	$10	Dot 25838
					COUNT BASIE & THE MILLS BROTHERS		
8/10/68	190	3		3	My Shy Violet	$15	Dot 25872
5/24/69	184	5		4	Dream	$15	Dot 25927

Am I That Easy To Forget (3) · December (3) · Guy On The Go (4) · Lazy River (2) · Sherry (1) · When, When, When (4)
April In Paris (2) · Didn't We (4) · Hallelujah Baby! (1) · Let Me Dream (2) · Straight Down The Middle (3) · Whiffenpoof Song (2)
Baby Dream Your Dream (4) · Dig Rock And Roll Music (2) · Happy Go Lucky Me (4) · Long Long Ago (1) · Straight Life (4)
Bramble Bush (1) · Down - Down - Down (2) · Happy Together (1) · More And More (1) · Sugar Boat (3)
Bring Me Sunshine (3) · Dream (4) · I Found A Love (1) · **My Shy Violet** (3) **73** · This Is The Last Time (I'll Cry Over You) (3)
But For Love (3) · Everybody's Friend (1) · I May Be Wrong But I Think You're Wonderful (2) · Ol' Race Track (3) **83** · Tiny Bubbles (3)
By The Time I Get To Phoenix (3) · Flit Around (1) · I Want To Be Happy (2) · Release Me (3) · What Have I Done For Her Lately (4)
Cab Driver (1) **23** · Flower Road (1) · Jimtown Road (4) · Rose (A Ring To The Name Of Rose) (3)
· Fortuosity (1)

★★298★★ MILSAP, Ronnie

Born on 1/16/46 in Robbinsville, North Carolina. Country singer/pianist/guitarist. Blind since birth; multi-instrumentalist by age 12. With J.J. Cale band; own band from 1965.

DEBUT DATE	PEAK POS	WKS CHR	GOLD		ARTIST — Album Title	$	Label & Number
2/15/75	138	7		1	A Legend In My Time	$15	RCA 0846
11/29/75	191	2		2	Night Things	$15	RCA 1223
9/10/77	97	15	●	3	It Was Almost Like A Song	$8	RCA 2439
6/24/78	109	12	●	4	Only One Love In My Life	$8	RCA 2780
6/16/79	98	15		5	Images	$8	RCA 3346
4/5/80	137	13		6	Milsap Magic	$8	RCA 3563
10/25/80+	36	41	▲²	7	Greatest Hits	[G]	$8	RCA 3772
4/18/81	89	29		8	Out Where The Bright Lights Are Glowing	$8	RCA 3932
9/5/81	31	31	●	9	There's No Gettin' Over Me	$8	RCA 4060
7/3/82	66	14		10	Inside Ronnie Milsap	$8	RCA 4311
4/30/83	36	19		11	Keyed Up	$8	RCA 4670
6/2/84	180	3		12	One More Try For Love	$8	RCA 5016
8/31/85	102	20	▲	13	Greatest Hits, Vol. 2	[G]	$8	RCA 5425
5/3/86	121	12	●	14	Lost In The Fifties Tonight	$8	RCA 7194
5/25/91	172	2		15	Back To The Grindstone	$12	RCA 2375

(After Sweet Memories) Play Born To Lose Again (8) · Future Is Not What It Used To Be (3) · (I'd Be) A Legend In My Time (1,7) · Jesus Is Your Ticket To Heaven (9) · Old Habits Are Hard To Break (15) · Stranger In My House (11,13) **23**
All Good Things Don't Have To End (5) · **Get It Up** (5) **43** · I'll Be There (If You Ever Want Me) (2) · Just Because It Feels Good (5) · Once I Get Over You (4) · Suburbia (12)
All Is Fair In Love And War (15) · Happy, Happy Birthday Baby (14) · I'll Leave This World Loving You (1) · Just In Case (2) · One More Try For Love (12) · Too Big For Words (9)
Am I Losing You (8,13) · Hate The Lies - Love The Liar (10) · I'll Take Care Of You (12) · Let My Love Be Your Pillow (7) · **Only One Love In My Life** (4) **63** · Too Late To Worry, Too Blue To Cry (1)
Any Day Now (10,13) **14** · **He Got You** (10) **59** · (I'm A) Stand By My Woman Man (7) · Let's Take The Long Way Around The World (4,7) · Out Where The Bright Lights Are Glowing (8) · Too Soon To Know (4)
Are You Lovin' Me Like I'm Lovin' You (15) · He'll Have To Go (8) · I'm Beginning To Forget You (8) · Like Children I Have Known (11) · **Please Don't Tell Me How The Story Ends** (7) **95** · Turn That Radio On (15)
Back On My Mind Again (4,7) · Here In Love (3) · I'm Getting Better (8) · Long Distance Memory (3) · Pride Goes Before A Fall (8) · Two Hearts Don't Always Make A Pair (9)
Back To The Grindstone (15) · Hi-Heel Sneakers (8) · I'm Just A Redneck At Heart (11) · Lost In The Fifties Tonight (In The Still Of The Night) (13,14) · Prisoner Of The Highway (12) · Watch Out For The Other Guy (11)
Biggest Lie (1) · How Do I Turn You On (14) · I'm No Good At Goodbyes (2) · Love Certified (15) · Pure Love (7) · We're Here To Love (11)
Borrowed Angel (2) · I Ain't Gonna Cry No More (15) · I'm Not Trying To Forget (4) · Love Takes A Long Time To Die (2) · Remember To Remind Me (I'm Leaving) (2) · **What A Difference You've Made In My Life** (3,7) **80**
Busiest Memory In Town (1) · I Guess I Just Missed You (12) · I'm Still Not Over You (1) · Lovin' Kind (3) · Santa Barbara (4) · What's One More Time (4)
Carolina Dreams (10) · I Guess I'm Crazy (8) · I've Got The Music In Me (4) · (Lying Here With) Linda On My Mind (4) · Selfish (3) · When The Hurt Comes Down (1)
Clap Your Hands (1) · I Hate You (7) · If You Don't Want Me To (6) · Misery Loves Company (6) · She Came Here For The Change (1) · When Two Worlds Collide (8)
Country Cookin' (1) · I Heard It Through The Grapevine (14) · In Love (14) · Money (That's What I Want) (14) · She Keeps The Home Fires Burning (13) · Who'll Turn Out The Lights (In Your World Tonight) (2)
Crystal Fallin' Rain (2) · I Honestly Love You (1) · In No Time At All (5) · My Heart (6) · **She Loves My Car** (12) **84** · Who's Counting (10)
Daydreams About Night Things (2,7) · I Let Myself Believe (6) · Inside (10,13) · Nashville Moon (14) · She Thinks I Still Care (4) · Why Don't You Spend The Night (6)
Dear Friend (8) · I Live My Whole Life At Night (9) · Is It Over (11) · Night By Night (12) · She's Always In Love (12) · Wrong End Of The Rainbow (10)
Delta Queen (5) · I Love New Orleans Music (10) · It Don't Hurt To Dream (3) · No One Will Ever Know (3) · Silent Night (After The Fight) (6) · Yesterday's Lovers Never Make Good Friends (4)
Don't Take It Tonight (3) · I Might Have Said (12) · It Happens Every Time (I Think Of You) (9) · No Relief In Sight (4) · Since I Don't Have You (15) · You Don't Look For Love (5)
Don't You Know How Much I Love You (11,13) **58** · I Only Remember The Good Times (14) · **It Was Almost Like A Song** (3,7) **16** · Nobody Likes Sad Songs (5) · **Smoky Mountain Rain** (7) **24** · You Took Her Off My Hands (Now Take Her Off My Mind) (10)
Don't Your Mem'ry Ever Sleep At Night (11) · I Really Don't Want To Know (5) · It's A Beautiful Thing (6) · Old Fashioned Girl Like You (14) · Spare The Rod (Love The Child) (1)
Everywhere I Turn (There's Your Memory) (11) · I Won't Forget You (8) · It's All I Can Do (9) · · Still In Love With You (6)
Feelings Change (11) · **I Wouldn't Have Missed It For The World** (9,13) **20** · It's Already Taken (13) · · Still Losing You (12)
Four Walls (8) · · It's Just A Room (10)
· It's Written All Over Your Face (9)

DEBUT DATE	PEAK POS	WKS CHR	GOLD	ARTIST — Album Title	$	Label & Number

MIMMS, Garnet, & The Enchanters

Garnet was born Garrett Mimms on 11/16/33 in Ashland, West Virginia. Sang in gospel groups the Evening Norfolk Four, Harmonizing Four. Formed group the Gainors in 1958. The Enchanters (Zola Pearnell, Sam Bell and Charles Boyer) were formed in 1961.

11/23/63	**91**	5		Cry Baby And 11 Other Hits	**$30**	United Art. 3305

Anytime You Need Me   **Cry Baby** 4   Don't Change Your Heart   I Keep Wanting You   **Quiet Place** 78   So Close
Baby Don't You Weep 30   Cry To Me   **For Your Precious Love** 26   Nobody But You   Runaway Lover   Until You Were Gone

MINDBENDERS, The

Rock group from Manchester, England: Wayne Fontana (born Glyn Geoffrey Ellis on 10/28/45; lead singer), Eric Stewart (lead guitar, vocals), Bob Lang (bass) and Ric Rothwell (drums). Fontana left in October 1965. Graham Gouldman joined in 1968. Stewart and Gouldman were later members of Hotlegs and 10cc.

5/1/65	**58**	9	1	The Game Of Love	**$25**	Fontana 27542
				WAYNE FONTANA & THE MINDBENDERS		
7/16/66	**92**	9	2	A Groovy Kind Of Love	**$25**	Fontana 27554

All Night Worker (2)   **Game Of Love** (1) *1*   Jaguar And Thunderbird (2)   One Fine Day (2)   Way You Do The Things You
Can't Live With You, Can't   Girl Can't Help It (1)   Just A Little Bit (2)   One More Time (1)   Do (2)
   Live Without You (2)   Git It! (1)   Keep Your Hands Off My   Seventh Son (2)   You Don't Know About Love
Certain Girl (1)   **Groovy Kind Of Love** (2) *2*   Baby (1)   She's Got The Power (1)   (2)
Cops & Robbers (1)   I'm Gonna Be A Wheel   Little Nightingale (2)   Too Many Tears (1)   You Don't Know Me (1)
Don't Cry No More (2)   Someday (1)   Love Is Good (2)   Trickie Dickie (2)

MINISTRY

An assemblage of musicians spearheaded by Chicago-based producers/performers Alain Jourgensen and Paul Barker. Formed by Jourgensen in 1981. Barker joined Ministry in 1986. Varying personnel are members of The Tribe, an affiliation of musicians from various groups.

6/25/83	**96**	14	1	With Sympathy	**$8**	Arista 6608
				features Al Jourgenson and Stephen George		
4/5/86	**194**	3	2	Twitch	**$8**	Sire 25309
11/5/88	**164**	4	3	The Land Of Rape And Honey	**$8**	Sire 25799
12/9/89	**163**	10↑	4	The Mind Is A Terrible Thing To Taste	**$8**	Sire 26004
8/1/92	**27**	28↑ ●	5	Psalm 69	**$12**	Sire 26727

Abortive (3)   Deity (3)   Hero (5)   N.W.O. (5)   Should Have Known Better   Twitch (Version II) (medley)
All Day Remix (2)   Destruction (3)   I Wanted To Tell Her (1)   Never Believe (4)   (1)   (2)
Angel, The (2)   Effigy (1)   Jesus Built My Hotrod (5)   Over The Shoulder (2)   So What (4)   We Believe (2)
Breathe (4)   Faith Collapsing (4)   Just Like You (2)   Psalm 69 (5)   Stigmata (3)   What He Say (1)
Burning Inside (4)   Flashback (3)   Just One Fix (5)   Revenge (1)   TV II (5)   Where You At Now? (medley)
Cannibal Song (4)   Golden Dawn (3)   Land Of Rape And Honey (3)   Say You're Sorry (1)   Test (4)   (2)
Corrosion (5)   Grace (3)   Missing, The (3)   Scare Crow (5)   Thieves (4)   Work For Love (1)
Crash And Burn (medley) (2)   Here We Go (1)   My Possession (2)   She's Got A Cause (1)   You Know What You Are (3)

MINK DeVILLE

R&B-styled, punk-rock band formed by vocalist Willy DeVille (b: William Boray, 8/27/53, New York City).

8/13/77	**186**	2	1	Mink DeVille	**$8**	Capitol 11631
6/10/78	**126**	5	2	Return To Magenta	**$8**	Capitol 11780
9/13/80	**163**	3	3	Le Chat Bleu	**$8**	Capitol 11955
10/24/81	**161**	5	4	Coup De Grace	**$8**	Atlantic 19311

"A" Train Lady (2)   Guardian Angel (2)   Just To Walk That Little Girl   Maybe Tomorrow (4)   Slow Drain (3)   Turn You Every Way But
Bad Boy (3)   Gunslinger (2)   Home (3)   Mixed Up, Shook Up Girl (1)   So In Love Are We (4)   Loose (2)
Cadillac Walk (1)   Heaven Stood Still (4)   Just Your Friends (2)   One Way Street (4)   Soul Twist (2)   Venus Of Avenue D (1)
Can't Do Without It (1)   Help Me To Make It (Power   Lipstick Traces (3)   Party Girls (1)   Spanish Stroll (1)   You Better Move On (4)
Confidence To Kill (2)   Of A Woman's Love) (4)   Little Girl (1)   Rolene (4)   Steady Drivin' Man (2)   You Just Keep Holding On
Desperate Days (2)   I Broke That Promise (2)   Love & Emotion (4)   Savoir Faire (3)   Teardrops Must Fall (4)   (3)
Easy Slider (2)   Just Give Me One Good   Love Me Like You Did Before   She Was Made In Heaven (4)   That World Outside (3)
End Of The Line (4)   Reason (1)   (4)   She's So Tough (1)   This Must Be The Night (3)

MINNELLI, Liza

Born on 3/12/46 in Los Angeles. Singer and Broadway/film actress. Daughter of Judy Garland and film director Vincente Minnelli. Starred in many films (*Arthur*, among them) and in Broadway productions. Won the 1972 Best Actress Oscar for *Cabaret*. Winner of three Tony Awards. Married to Peter Allen from 1967-73. Married film producer Jack Haley, Jr. on 9/15/74. Won Grammy's Living Legends Award in 1989.

11/21/64	**115**	8	1	Liza! Liza!	**$20**	Capitol 2174
9/4/65	**41**	14	2	"Live" At The London Palladium * .... [L]	**$20**	Capitol 2295 [2]
11/28/70	**158**	3	3	New Feelin'	**$20**	A&M 4272
9/30/72	**19**	23	4	Liza With A "Z" .... [TV-L]	**$12**	Columbia 31762
3/24/73	**38**	20	5	Liza Minnelli The Singer	**$12**	Columbia 32149
6/9/73	**164**	8	6	"Live" At The London Palladium * .... [L]	**$10**	Capitol 11191
				***JUDY GARLAND & LIZA MINNELLI**		
				condensation of album #2 above		
5/18/74	**150**	4	7	Live At The Winter Garden .... [L]	**$12**	Columbia 32854
11/14/87	**156**	8	8	Liza Minnelli At Carnegie Hall .... [L]	**$10**	Telarc 15502 [2]
				recorded at Carnegie Hall from May 28 to June 18, 1987		
11/11/89	**128**	10	9	Results	**$8**	Epic 45098
				features backing and co-production by the Pet Shop Boys		

Alexander's Ragtime Band (8)   Brotherhood Of Man   City Lights (medley) (8)   Gypsy In My Soul [solo: Liza]   How Could You Believe Me   I Don't Want To Know (8)
All I Need Is One Good   (medley) (6)   Come Back To Me (medley)   (2,6)   When I Said I Love You   I Gotcha (4)
   Break (medley) (8)   Buckle Down Winsocki (8)   (7)   He's Got The Whole World In   When You Know I've Been   I Happen To Like New York
And I In My Chair (Et Moi   But, The World Goes 'Round   Come Rain Or Come Shine   His Hands (medley) (2,6)   A Liar All My Life [solo: (8)
   Dans Mon Coin) (7)   (medley) (8)   (3)   Hello, Dolly! (2,6)   Liza] (2)   I Knew Him When (1)
Anywhere You Are (medley)   By Myself (medley) [solo: Dancing In The Moonlight (5)   Here I'll Stay (medley) (8)   How Deep Is The Ocean (8)   I Never Has Seen Snow (8)
   (7)   Liza] (2,6)   Don't Drop Bombs (9)   Hooray For Love (medley)   How Long Has This Been   I Want You Now (9)
Baby Don't Get Hooked On   Bye Bye Blackbird (4)   Don't Ever Leave Me (1)   (2,6)   Goin' On? (3)   (I Wonder Where My) Easy
   Me (5)   Cabaret (4,7,8)   Don't Let Me Be Lonely   How About You (medley)   I Believe In Music (5)   Rider's Gone (3)
Blue Moon (1)   Can't Help Lovin' That Man   Tonight (7)   (2,6)   I Believe You (medley) (7)   I'd Love You To Want Me (5)
Bob White (Whatcha Gonna   Of Mine (3)   Exactly Like Me (7)   How Do You (medley)   I Can See Clearly Now (7,8)   I'm All I've Got (1)
   Swing Tonight?) (medley)   Chicago (medley) (2)   God Bless The Child (3,4)   I Can See It (medley) (8)   I'm One Of The Smart Ones
   Circle, The (7)   I Can't Say Goodnight (9)   (7,8)

MINNELLI, Liza — Cont'd

If I Were In Your Shoes (1)
If There Was Love (9)
If You Could Read My Mind (medley) (7)
If You Hadn't, But You Did (8)
It All Depends On You (medley) (2,6)
It Was A Good Time (4)
It's Just A Matter Of Time (1)
Lazy Bones (3)
Liza (medley) (4)
Liza With A "Z" (4,7,8)
Liza's Medley (2)
Lonely Feet (8)

Losing My Mind (9)
Love For Sale (3)
Love Pains (9)
Lover, Come Back To Me (medley) [solo: Liza] (2,6)
Man I Love (3)
Married (medley) (4,8)
Maybe Soon (1)
Maybe This Time (1,3,4,7,8)
Meantime (1)
Mein Herr (medley) (8)
Money, Money (medley) (4,8)
More Than You Know (7)
My Mammy (4)
Natural Man (7)

New York, New York (8)
Oh, Babe, What Would You Say? (5)
Old Friends (8)
Our Love Is Here To Stay (medley) (8)
Pass That Peace Pipe [solo: Liza] (2)
Quiet Thing (7,8)
Rent (9)
Ring Them Bells (4,7,8)
San Francisco (medley) (2)
Shine On Harvest Moon (7)
Sing Happy (medley) (8)
Singer, The (5)

So Sorry, I Said (9)
Some People (8)
Somewhere Out There (8)
Son Of A Preacher Man (4)
Stormy Weather (3)
Swanee (2,6)
Sweetest Sounds (8)
There Is A Time (Le Temps) (7)
Time Heals Everything (medley) (8)
Together Wherever We Go (1,2,6)
Tonight Is Forever (8)
Toot Toot Tootsie (8)

Travelin' Life (1,2)
Try To Remember (1)
Twist In My Sobriety (9)
Use Me (5)
We Could Make Such Beautiful Music (medley) (2,6)
When The Saints Go Marching In (medley) (2,6)
Where Is The Love (5)
Who's Sorry Now? [solo: Liza] (2,6)
Willkommen (medley) (4)
Yes (4,8)
You Are The Sunshine Of My Life (5)

You Better Sit Down, Kids (medley) (8)
You Can Have Him (medley) (8)
You're So Vain (5)
You've Let Yourself Go (4)

MINOGUE, Kylie

Singer/actress from Melbourne, Australia. Born on 5/28/68. Began TV acting career at age 11. Was a longtime cast member of the popular Australian soap *Neighbours*.

9/10/88+	53	28 ●		Kylie	$8	Geffen 24195

Got To Be Certain
I Miss You

I Should Be So Lucky 28
I'll Still Be Loving You

It's No Secret 37
Je Ne Sais Pas Pourquoi

Loco-Motion 3
Look My Way

Love At First Sight
Turn It Into Love

MINOR DETAIL

Irish duo: brothers John and Willie Hughes.

10/1/83	187	2		Minor Detail	$8	Polydor 815004

Ask The Kids
Canvas Of Life 92

Columbia
Hold On

I'll Always Love You
I've Got A Friend

Others Need You
20th Century

We Are Winners (Once We Try)

Why Take It Again

MINT CONDITION

Funk sextet from Minneapolis: Stokley Williams (vocals), Homer O'Dell, Larry Weddell, Jeffrey Allen, Keri Lewis and Ricky Kinchen.

2/8/92	63	22		Meant To Be Mint	$12	Perspective 1001

Are You Free
Breakin' My Heart (Pretty Brown Eyes) 6

Do U Wanna
Forever In Your Eyes 81

Here We Go Again
I Wonder If She Likes Me

Outta Time, Outta Mind
Sensuous Appeal

She's A Honey
Single To Mingle

True To Thee
Try My Love

MIRABAI

Female folk singer.

8/30/75	128	6		Mirabai	$8	Atlantic 18144

Cosmic Overload
Dedication, A

Determination
Exactly What You Are

Magical Time
Mirabai

Schumann's Song
Stairway To Heaven

Strength Of My Soul
To Be Young

You Are My Reason

★★76★★ MIRACLES, The

R&B group formed at Northern High School in Detroit in 1955. Consisted of William "Smokey" Robinson (lead), Emerson and Bobby Rogers (tenors), Ronnie White (baritone) and Warren "Pete" Moore (bass). Emerson left in 1956 for U.S. Army, replaced by Claudette Rogers Robinson, Smokey's future wife. First recorded for End in 1958. Bobby married Wanda Young of The Marvelettes. Claudette retired in 1964. Smokey wrote many hit songs for the group and other Motown artists. Smokey went solo in 1972, replaced by William Griffin.

6/8/63	118	8	1	The Fabulous Miracles	$125	Tamla 238
10/5/63	139	5	2	The Miracles On Stage [L]	$75	Tamla 241
1/4/64	113	4	3	doin' Mickey's Monkey	$75	Tamla 245
4/17/65	21	25	4	Greatest Hits From The Beginning [G]	$35	Tamla 254 [2]

SMOKEY ROBINSON & THE MIRACLES:

11/27/65+	8	40	5	Going To A Go-Go	$20	Tamla 267
12/17/66+	41	27	6	Away We A Go-Go	$20	Tamla 271
9/30/67	28	23	7	Make It Happen	$20	Tamla 276
2/24/68	7	44	8	Greatest Hits, Vol. 2 [G]	$20	Tamla 280
10/5/68+	42	23	9	Special Occasion	$20	Tamla 290
2/15/69	71	14	10	Live! [L]	$20	Tamla 289
8/9/69	25	19	11	Time Out for Smokey Robinson & The Miracles	$20	Tamla 295
12/6/69+	78	12	12	Four In Blue	$20	Tamla 297
5/30/70	97	11	13	What Love Has...Joined Together	$15	Tamla 301
10/24/70	56	11	14	A Pocket Full Of Miracles	$15	Tamla 306
12/26/70+	143	12	15	The Tears Of A Clown [R]	$15	Tamla 276

reissue (new title) of album #7 above

9/25/71	92	10	16	One Dozen Roses	$15	Tamla 312
8/19/72	46	22	17	Flying High Together	$15	Tamla 318
1/6/73	75	16	18	1957-1972 [L]	$15	Tamla 320 [2]

THE MIRACLES:

6/2/73	174	4	19	Renaissance	$15	Tamla 325
2/16/74	97	17	20	Smokey Robinson & The Miracles' Anthology [G]	$18	Motown 793 [3]

SMOKEY ROBINSON & THE MIRACLES

9/14/74	41	21	21	Do It Baby	$15	Tamla 334
2/8/75	96	9	22	Don't Cha Love It	$12	Tamla 336
10/25/75+	33	30	23	City Of Angels	$12	Tamla 339
10/16/76	178	3	24	The Power Of Music	$12	Tamla 344
3/19/77	117	5	25	Love Crazy	$10	Columbia 34460

Abraham, Martin And John (11,18,20) **33**

After You Put Back The Pieces (I'll Still Have A Broken Heart) (7,15)

Ain't Nobody Straight In L.A. (23)
All I Want Is You (4)
All That's Good (5)

And I Love Her (13)
Baby, Baby (6)
Baby, Baby Don't Cry (11,20) **8**

Backfire (14)
Bad Girl (4,18,20) **93**
Beauty Is Only Skin Deep (6)
Betcha By Golly Wow (17)

Better Way To Live (25)
Bird Must Fly Away (25)
Bridge Over Troubled Water (14)

DEBUT DATE	PEAK POS	WKS CHR	GOLD	ARTIST — Album Title	$	Label & Number

MIRACLES, The — Cont'd

Brokenhearted Girl-Brokenhearted Boy (22)
California Soul (12)
Calling Out Your Name (21)
Can I Pretend (24)
Can You Love A Poor Boy (3)
Can't Get Ready For Losing You (21)
Cecilia (16)
Choosey Beggar (5,8,20)
City Of Angels (23)
Come On Do The Jerk (8,20) **50**
(Come 'Round Here) I'm The One You Need (6,8,20) **17**
Composer, The (11)
Crazy About The La La La (16) **56**
Dance What You Wanna (3)
Dancin' Holiday (3)
Dancing's Alright (7,15)
Darling Dear (14,20) **100**
Do It Baby (21) **13**
Do You Love Me (3)
Doggone Right (11,20) **32**
Don't Cha Love It (22) **78**
Don't Let It End ('Til You Let It Begin) (19) **56**
Don't Say You Love Me (12)
Don't Take It So Hard (14)
Don't Think It's Me (7,15)
Dreams, Dreams (12)
Everybody Needs Love (9)
Faces (15)
Flower Girl (14)
Flying High Together (17)
Foolish Thing To Say (21)
For Once In My Life (11)
Fork In The Road (5)
Free Press (23)
From Head To Toe (5)
Gemini (22)
Get Ready (14)
Give Her Up (9)

Give Me Just Another Day (21)
Going To A Go-Go (5,8,10,18,20) **11**
Gonna Tell The World (Wedding Song) (22)
Gossip (24)
Got A Job (4,20)
Got Me Goin' (Again) (22)
Got To Be There (17,18)
Groovey Thing (3)
Happy Landing (1,2)
Here I Go Again (11,18,20) **37**
Hey Jude (12)
Hunter Gets Captured By The Game (16)
Hurt Is Over (11)
I Can Take A Hint (1)
I Can Touch The Sky (25)
I Can't Stand To See You Cry (17,20) **45**
I Cry (4)
I Didn't Realize The Show Was Over (19)
I Like It Like That (4,20) **27**
I Love You Dear (16)
I Love You Secretly (19)
I Love Your Baby (4)
I Need A Change (4)
(I Need Some) Money (4)
I Second That Emotion (8,10,20) **4**
I Wanna Be With You (19)
I'll Take You Any Way That You Come (1)

I'll Try Something New (4,20) **39**
I'm On The Outside (Looking In) (7,15)
I've Been Good To You (1,2,4,20)
If This World Were Mine (13)
If You Can Want (9,10,20) **11**
If You're Ever In The Neighborhood (3)
In Case You Need Love (5)
It Will Be Alright (3)
It's A Good Feeling (7,15)
Just Losing You (9)
Keep On Keepin' On (Doin' What You Do) (22)
Land Of 1000 Dances (3)
Legend In Its Own Time (12)
Let Me Have Some (5)
Let The Children Play (24)
Little Piece Of Heaven (22)
Love Crazy (25)
Love I Saw In You Was Just A Mirage (7,8,15,20) **20**
Love Machine (Part 1) (23) **1**
Love She Can Count On (1,2,4,20) **31**
Love Story, Theme From (17)
Love To Make Love (14)
Mama Done Told Me (4)
Mickey's Monkey (3,4,10,18,20) **8**
Mighty Good Lovin' (3)
Monkey Time (3)
More Love (7,8,15,18,20) **23**
More, More, More Of Your Love (6)
Much Better Off (9)
My Baby Changes Like The Weather (5)
My Cherie Amour (13)
My Girl (11)

My Girl Has Gone (5,8,20) **14**
My Love For You (7,15)
My Love Is Your Love (Forever) (7,15)
My Name Is Michael (2)
My World Is Empty Without You (12)
Night Life (23)
No Wonder Love's A Wonder (16)
Nowhere To Go (19)
Oh Baby Baby I Love You (16)
Oh Be My Love (6)
Oh Girl (17)
Once I Got To Know You (Couldn't Help But Love You) (11)
Once In A Lifetime (medley) (10)
Ooo Baby Baby (5,8,10,18,20) **16**
Poinciana (10)
Point It Out (14,20) **37**
Poor Charlotte (23)
Power Of Music (24)
Reel Of Time (14)
Satisfaction (16,18,20) **49**
Save Me (6,8,20)
Shop Around (4,18,20) **2**
Since You Won My Heart (5)
Smog (23)
Something (medley) (14)
Something You Got (medley) (14)
Soulful Shack (7,15)
Special Occasion (9,20) **26**
Spy For Brotherhood (25)
Street Of Love (24)
Such Is Love, Such Is Life (1)
Sweet Sweet Lovin' (22)
Swept For You Baby (6)
Take It All (22)
Tears Of A Clown (7,15,16,18,20) **1**

That Girl (16)
That's What Love Is Made Of (4,20) **35**
This Guy's In Love With You (13)
Tomorrow Is Another Day (12)
Too Young (25)
Tracks Of My Tears (5,8,10,18,20) **16**
Twist, The (3)
Twist And Shout (3)
Up Again (21)
Up, Up And Away (10)
Valley Of The Dolls, Theme From (10)
Wah-Watusi (3)
Waldo Roderick DeHammersmith (23)
Walk On By (6,10)
Way Over There (2,4,20) **94**
We Can Make It We Can (12)
We Feel The Same (21)
We Had A Love So Strong (17)
We've Come Too Far To End It Now (17,18,20) **46**
What Is A Heart Good For (19,21)
What Love Has Joined Together (13)
What's So Good About Good-By (2,4,20) **35**
Whatever Makes You Happy (1)
When Nobody Cares (12)
When Sundown Comes (16)
Where Are You Going To My Love (21)
Who's Gonna Take The Blame (14,20) **46**
Who's Lovin' You (4,20)
Whole Lot Of Shakin' In My Heart (Since I Met You) (6,8) **46**
Wichita Lineman (11)

Wigs And Lashes (19)
Wish I Knew (12)
Wishful Thinking (14)
With Your Love Came (17)
Women (Make The World Go 'Round) (23)
Won't You Take Me Back (1)
Would I Love You (4)
Yester Love (9,10,20) **31**
Yesterday (9,10)
You Ain't Livin' Till You're Lovin' (17)
You And The Night And The Music (medley) (10)
You Are Love (21,22)
(You Can) Depend On Me (4,20)
You Don't Have To Say You Love Me (6)
You Must Be Love (7,15)
You Need A Miracle (24)
You Only Build Me Up To Tear Me Down (9)
You Send Me (With Your Good Lovin') (12)
You've Got The Love I Need (14)
You've Lost That Lovin' Feelin' (1)
You've Made Me So Very Happy (13)
You've Really Got A Hold On Me (1,2,4,20) **8**
Your Love (1)
Your Mother's Only Daughter (9)

MISSETT, Judi Sheppard — see AEROBICS section

MISSING PERSONS

New wave quintet formed in Los Angeles in 1980: Dale Bozzio (lead singer; former Playboy bunny from Boston), her then-husband Terry Bozzio (drummer with Roxy Music and U.K.), Warren Cuccurulo (joined Duran Duran in 1990), Patrick O'Hearn and Chuck Wild. All but Wild were from Frank Zappa's band. Disbanded in 1986. Terry Bozzio worked with Jeff Beck in 1989.

DEBUT DATE	PEAK POS	WKS CHR	GOLD	ARTIST — Album Title	$	Label & Number
5/15/82	46	47		1 Missing Persons .... [M]	$8	Capitol 15001
10/30/82+	17	40	●	2 Spring Session M	$8	Capitol 12228
				title is an anagram of group's name		
3/31/84	43	16		3 Rhyme & Reason	$8	Capitol 12315
8/9/86	86	11		4 Color In Your Life	$8	Capitol 12465

All Fall Down (3)
Bad Streets (2)
Boy I Say To You (4)
Clandestine People (3)
Closer That Out (3)
Color In Your Life (4)
Come Back For More (4)

Destination Unknown (1,2) **42**
Face To Face (4)
Flash Of Love (4)
Give (3) **67**
Go Against The Flow (4)
Here And Now (2)

I Can't Think About Dancin' (4)
I Like Boys (1)
If Only For The Moment (3)
It Ain't None Of Your Business (2)
Mental Hopscotch (1)

No Secrets (4)
No Way Out (2)
Noticeable One (2)
Now Is The Time (For Love) (3)
Racing Against Time (3)
Right Now (3)

Rock And Roll Suspension (2)
Surrender Your Heart (3)
Tears (2)
U.S. Drag (2)
Waiting For A Million Years (3)

Walking In L.A. (2) **70**
We Don't Know Love At All (4)
Windows (2) **63**
Words (1,2) **42**

MISSION U.K., The

Rock quartet formed in Leeds, England: Wayne Hussey (vocals, guitar, ex-Sisters Of Mercy), Craig Adams (bass), Mick Brown (ex-drummer Red Lorry Yellow Lorry) and Simon Hinkler (guitar).

DEBUT DATE	PEAK POS	WKS CHR	GOLD	ARTIST — Album Title	$	Label & Number
3/7/87	108	18		1 Gods Own Medicine	$8	Mercury 830603
4/30/88	126	10		2 Children	$8	Mercury 834263
3/17/90	101	16		3 Carved In Sand	$12	Mercury 842251

Amelia (3)
And The Dance Goes On (1)
Belief (3)
Beyond The Pale (2)
Black Mountain Mist (2)
Breathe (2)

Bridges Burning (1)
Butterfly On A Wheel (3)
Child's Play (2)
Dance On Glass (1)
Deliverance (3)
Garden Of Delight (1)

Grapes Of Wrath (3)
Heat (2)
Heaven On Earth (2)
Hungry As The Hunter (3)
Hymn (For America) (3)
Into The Blue (3)

Kingdom Come (2)
Let Sleeping Dogs Die (1)
Love Me To Death (1)
Lovely (3)
Paradise (Will Shine Like The Moon) (3)

Sacrilege (1)
Sea Of Love (3)
Severina (3)
Shamera Kye (2)
Stay With Me (1)
Tower Of Strength (2)

Wasteland (1)
Wing And A Prayer (2)

MISSOURI

Rock quintet led by singer/guitarist Ron West.

DEBUT DATE	PEAK POS	WKS CHR	GOLD	ARTIST — Album Title	$	Label & Number
6/23/79	174	4		Welcome Two Missouri	$8	Polydor 6206

Can't Stop
Got Me Goin'

Gotta Be Me
Hangin' On

I Really Love You
Love On The Run

Movin' On
So Far Away

Sunshine Girl
Walk Like A Man

MR. BIG

Rock quartet: Eric Martin (vocals), Pat Torpey (former drummer of Ted Nugent's band and Impellitteri), Billy Sheehan (bass) and Paul Gilbert (guitar). Group took their name from the title of a song by Free.

DEBUT DATE	PEAK POS	WKS CHR	GOLD	ARTIST — Album Title	$	Label & Number
7/22/89	46	18		1 Mr. Big	$8	Atlantic 81990
4/20/91+	15	38	▲	2 Lean Into It	$12	Atlantic 82209

MR. BIG — Cont'd

Addicted To That Rush (1)
Alive And Kickin' (2)
Anything For You (1)
Big Love (1)
Blame It On My Youth (1)

CDFF-Lucky This Time (2)
Daddy, Brother, Lover, Little Boy (The Electric Drill Song) (2)
Green-Tinted Sixties Mind (2)

Had Enough (1)
How Can You Do What You Do (1)
Just Take My Heart (2) *16*
Little Too Loose (2)

Merciless (1)
My Kinda Woman (2)
Never Say Never (2)
Road To Ruin (2)
Rock & Roll Over (1)

Take A Walk (1)
To Be With You (2) *1*
Voodoo Kiss (2)
Wind Me Up (1)

MR. MISTER

Los Angeles-based, pop-rock quartet: Richard Page (vocals), Steve George, Pat Mastelotto and Steve Farris (left in 1989; replaced by Buzz Feiten, ex-guitarist of Paul Butterfield Blues Band, Stevie Wonder's band, and the Larsen-Feiten Band).

4/14/84	170	7		1 I Wear The Face	$8	RCA 4864
8/31/85+	1¹	58 ▲		2 Welcome To The Real World	$8	RCA 8045
9/26/87	55	17		3 Go On...	$8	RCA 6276

Black/White (2)
Border, The (3)
Broken Wings (2) *1*
Code Of Love (1)
Control (3)
Don't Slow Down (2)

Dust (3)
Healing Waters (3)
Hunters Of The Night (1) *57*
I Get Lost Sometimes (1)
I Wear The Face (1)

I'll Let You Drive (1)
Into My Own Hands (3)
Is It Love (2) *8*
Kyrie (2) *1*
Life Goes On (1)

Man Of A Thousand Dances (3)
Partners In Crime (1)
Power Over Me (3)
Run To Her (2)
Runaway (1)

Something Real (Inside Me/Inside You) (3) *29*
Stand And Deliver (3)
Talk The Talk (3)
Tangent Tears (3)
32 (1)

Tube, The (3)
Uniform Of Youth (2)
Watching The World (3)
Welcome To The Real World (2)

MISTRESS

Rock group — Charlie Williams, lead singer.

9/15/79	100	14		Mistress	$8	RSO 3059

China Lake
Cinnamon Girl

Dixie Flyer
High On The Ride

Letter To California
Mistrusted Love *49*

Situations
Tellin' Me Lies

Whose Side Are You On?
You Got The Love

★★476★★ MITCHELL, Chad, Trio

Leader of folk-pop trio which included Mike Kobluk and Joe Frazier. Formed while sophomores at Gonzaga University in Spokane, Washington.

3/24/62	39	21		1 Mighty Day On Campus [L]	$20	Kapp 3262
9/1/62	81	9		2 The Chad Mitchell Trio At The Bitter End [L]	$20	Kapp 3281
				above 2 feature guitarist Jim McGuinn (Byrds)		
4/13/63	87	30		3 Blowin' In The Wind	$20	Kapp 3313
9/28/63	63	28		4 The Best Of Chad Mitchell Trio [G]	$20	Kapp 3334
11/9/63	39	22		5 Singin' Our Mind	$20	Mercury 60838
3/7/64	29	30		6 Reflecting	$20	Mercury 60891
				THE MITCHELL TRIO:		
11/14/64+	128	11		7 The Slightly Irreverent Mitchell Trio	$20	Mercury 60944
5/1/65	130	3		8 Typical American Boys	$20	Mercury 60992

Adios Mi Corazon (3)
African Song (On That Great Civilized Morning) (7)
Ain't No More Cane On This Brazos (5)
Alabama Song (7)
Alberta (2)
Alice Revisited (3)
Alice; Sequel (3)
Alma Mater (5)
Ballad Of The Greenland Whalers (6)
Banks Of Sicily (6)
Barry's Boys (6)
Blowin' In The Wind (3)
Blues Around My Head (2)
Bonny Streets Of Fyve-io (5)
Cherry Tree Carol (8)

Come Along Home (Tom's Song) (2)
Don't Fence Me In (medley) (3,4)
Dona Dona Dona (1)
Draft Dodger Rag (7)
Dubarry Done Gone Again (5)
Dying Business (7)
First Time Ever (6)
Four Strong Winds (5)
Golden Vanity (2)
Gorpus Morpus (8)
Great Historical Bum (The Bragging Song) (2,4)
Green Grow The Lilacs (3,4)
Greenland Whalers ..see: Ballad Of

Hang On The Bell, Nellie (1,4)
Hello Susan Brown (2,4)
Hip Song (It Does Not Pay To Be Hip) (6)
I Can't Help But Wonder (7)
I Feel So Good About It (5)
Ides Of Texas (medley) (3,4)
If I Gave You (7)
In The Summer Of His Years (medley) (6)
Irish Song (5)
James James Morrison Morrison (2,4)
Jesse James (8)
John Birch Society (2,4) *99*
Johnnie (1)
Last Night I Had The Strangest Dream (2)

Last Thing On My Mind (8)
Leave Me If You Want To (3)
Lizzie Borden (1,4) *44*
Maladiozhenaya (The Young Ones) (5)
Mandy Lane (7)
Marvelous Toy (5) *43*
Me Voy Pa Bete (3)
Mighty Day (1)
Moscow Nights (2)
My Guitar (3)
My Name Is Morgan (8)
Natural Girl For Me (8)
Nobody Knows You (5)
On My Journey (1)
One Day When I Was Lost (Easter Morn) (3)
One Man's Hands (8)
Pride Of Petrovar (7)

Puttin' On The Style (1)
Queen Elinor's Confession (6)
Rally Round The Flag (medley) (6)
Rhymes For The Irreverent Medley (7)
Rum By Gum (1)
Run Run Run (3)
Sinking Of Reuben James (6)
Stewball (6)
Stewball And Griselda (7)
Story Of Alice - Part 1 (3)
Super Skier (1,4)
Tail Toddle (1)
Tarriers Song (6)
Tell Old Bill (1)
Twelve Days (5)
Unfortunate Man (2,4)

Virgin Mary (6)
Waves On The Sea (8)
What Did You Learn In School Today (6)
When I Was A Young Man (7)
Which Hat Shall I Wear (8)
Whistling Gypsy (1)
Whup Jamboree (1)
Willie Seton (5)
With God On Our Side (8)
You Can Tell The World (2,4)
You Were On My Mind (8)
Yowzah (8)

★★119★★ MITCHELL, Joni

Born Roberta Joan Anderson on 11/7/43 in Fort McLeod, Alberta, Canada and raised in Saskatoon, Saskatchewan. Singer/songwriter/guitarist/pianist. Moved to New York in 1966. Wrote the hits "Both Sides Now" and "Woodstock." Married her producer/bassist, Larry Klein, in 1982.

5/18/68	189	9		1 Joni Mitchell	$20	Reprise 6293
6/14/69	31	36		2 Clouds	$20	Reprise 6341
4/11/70	27	33 ▲		3 Ladies Of The Canyon	$15	Reprise 6376
7/3/71	15	28 ▲		4 Blue	$15	Reprise 2038
12/2/72+	11	28 ●		5 For The Roses	$10	Asylum 5057
2/9/74	2⁴	64 ●		6 Court And Spark	$10	Asylum 1001
12/14/74+	2¹	22 ●		7 Miles Of Aisles [L]	$10	Asylum 202
				with Tom Scott & The L.A. Express		
12/6/75+	4	17 ●		8 The Hissing Of Summer Lawns	$10	Asylum 1051
12/11/76+	13	18 ●		9 Hejira	$10	Asylum 1087
1/7/78	25	13 ●		10 Don Juan's Reckless Daughter	$8	Asylum 701 [2]
7/7/79	17	18		11 Mingus	$8	Asylum 505
				music composed by Charles Mingus (jazz pianist; d: 1/5/79 [age 56])		
10/4/80	38	16		12 Shadows And Light [L]	$8	Asylum 704 [2]
				with guests Pat Metheny, Michael Brecker and Jaco Pastorius		
11/20/82	25	21		13 Wild Things Run Fast	$8	Geffen 2019
11/23/85	63	19		14 Dog Eat Dog	$8	Geffen 24074
4/9/88	45	16		15 Chalk Mark In A Rain Storm	$12	Geffen 24172
3/23/91	41	14		16 Night Ride Home	$12	Geffen 24302

DEBUT DATE	PEAK POS	WKS CHR	GOLD	ARTIST — Album Title	$	Label & Number

MITCHELL, Joni — Cont'd

All I Want (4,7)
Amelia (9,12)
Arrangement, The (3)
Banquet (5)
Barangrill (5)
Be Cool (13)
Beat Of Black Wings (15)
Big Yellow Taxi (3) **67**
Big Yellow Taxi (7) **24**
Bird That Whistles (15)
Black Crow (9,12)
Blonde In The Bleachers (5)
Blue (4,7)
Blue Boy (3)
Blue Motel Room (9)
Boho Dance (8)
Both Sides Now (2,7)
Cactus Tree (1,7)
California (4)
Car On A Hill (6)
Carey (4,7) **93**
Case Of You (4,7)
Centerpiece (medley) (8)
Chair In The Sky (11)
Chelsea Morning (2)
Cherokee Louise (16)
Chinese Cafe (medley) (13)
Circle Game (3,7)
Coin In The Pocket (Rap) (11)
Cold Blue Steel And Sweet Fire (5,7)

Come In From The Cold (16)
Conversation (3)
Cool Water (15)
Cotton Avenue (10)
Court And Spark (6)
Coyote (9,12)
Dancin' Clown (15)
Dawntreader, The (1)
Dog Eat Dog (14)
Don Juan's Reckless Daughter (10)
Don't Interrupt The Sorrow (8)
Down To You (6)
Dreamland (10,12)
Dry Cleaner From Des Moines (11,12)
Edith And The Kingpin (8,12)
Electricity (5)
Ethiopia (14)
Fiction (14)
Fiddle And The Drum (2)
For Free (3)
For The Roses (5)
Free Man In Paris (6,12) **22**
Funeral (Rap) (11)
Furry Sings The Blues (9,12)
Gallery, The (2)
God Must Be A Boogie Man (11,12)
Good Friends (14) **85**

Goodbye Pork Pie Hat (11,12)
Happy Birthday 1975 (Rap) (11)
Harry's House (medley) (8)
Hejira (9,12)
Help Me (6) **7**
Hissing Of Summer Lawns (8)
I Don't Know Where I Stand (2)
I Had A King (1)
I Think I Understand (2)
I's A Muggin' (Rap) (11)
Impossible Dreamer (14)
In France They Kiss On Main Street (8,12) **66**
Jericho (7,10)
Judgement Of The Moon And Stars (Ludwig's Tune) (5)
Jungle Line (8)
Just Like This Train (6)
Ladies' Man (13)
Ladies Of The Canyon (3)
Lakota (5)
Last Time I Saw Richard (4,7)
Lesson In Survival (5)
Let The Wind Carry Me (5)
Little Green (4)
Love (13)

Love Or Money (7)
Lucky Girl (14)
Lucky (Rap) (11)
Man To Man (13)
Marcie (1)
Michael From Mountains (1)
Moon At The Window (13)
Morning Morgantown (3)
My Old Man (4)
My Secret Place (15)
Nathan La Franeer (1)
Night In The City (1)
Night Ride Home (16)
Nothing Can Be Done (16)
Number One (15)
Off Night Backstreet (10)
Only Joy In Town (16)
Otis And Marlena (10)
Paprika Plains (10)
Passion Play (When All The Slaves Are Free) (16)
People's Parties (6,7)
Pirate Of Penance (1)
Priest, The (3)
Rainy Night House (3,7)
Raised On Robbery (6) **65**
Ray's Dad's Cadillac (16)
Real Good For Free (7)
Refuge Of The Roads (9)
Reoccurring Dream (15)
River (4)

Roses Blue (2)
Same Situation (6)
See You Sometime (5)
Shades Of Scarlet Conquering (8)
Shadows And Light (8,12)
Shiny Toys (14)
Silky Veils Of Ardor (10)
Sisotowbell Lane (1)
Slouching Towards Bethlehem (16)
Smokin' (Empty, Try Another) (14)
Snakes And Ladders (15)
Solid Love (13)
Song For Sharon (9)
Song To A Seagull (1)
Songs To Aging Children Come (2)
Strange Boy (9)
Sweet Bird (8)
Sweet Sucker Dance (11)
Talk To Me (10)
Tax Free (14)
Tea Leaf Prophecy (Lay Down Your Arms) (15)
Tenth World (10)
That Song About The Midway (2)
This Flight Tonight (4)
Three Great Stimulants (14)

Tin Angel (2)
Trouble Child (6)
Twisted (6)
Two Grey Rooms (16)
Unchained Melody (medley) (13)
Underneath The Streetlight (13)
Why Do Fools Fall In Love (12)
Wild Things Run Fast (13)
Willie (3)
Windfall (Everything For Nothing) (16)
Wolf That Lives In Lindsey (11)
Woman Of Heart And Mind (5,7)
Woodstock (3,7,12)
You Dream Flat Tires (13)
You Turn Me On, I'm A Radio (5,7) **25**
(You're So Square) Baby, I Don't Care (13) **47**

MITCHELL, Kim
Male Canadian rock guitarist/vocalist. Leader of Canadian group Max Webster.

| 5/18/85 | 106 | 15 | | Akimbo Alogo | $8 | Bronze 90257 |

All We Are
Called Off

Caroline
Diary For Rock 'N Roll Men

Feel It Burn
Go For Soda **86**

Lager & Ale
Love Ties

Rumour Has It
That's A Man

MITCHELL, Rubin
Jazz-pop pianist.

| 4/15/67 | 164 | 2 | | Presenting Rubin Mitchell | [I] $15 | Capitol 2658 |

Cherish
Flamingo

Jitterbug Waltz
Mas Que Nada

My Liza Jane
My Love Forgive Me

Slaughter On 10th Avenue
Somewhere

Spanish Eyes
Summer Wind

That's All
What Now, My Love

MITCHELL, Willie
Born in Ashland, Mississippi in 1928. Trumpeter/keyboardist/composer/arranger/producer. To Memphis at an early age. With Tuff Green and Al Jackson in the early '50s. Formed own band in 1954, became house band at Home Of The Blues and Hi Records. Eventually became president of Hi Records.

| 3/16/68 | 172 | 5 | 1 | Willie Mitchell Live | [I-L] $15 | Hi 32042 |

recorded at the Manhattan Club in Memphis

| 5/11/68 | 151 | 7 | 2 | Soul Serenade | [I] $15 | Hi 32039 |
| 11/7/70 | 188 | 2 | 3 | Robbin's Nest | [I] $15 | Hi 32058 |

Boot-leg (1)
Bum Daddy (1)
Chilly Chilly (1)
Cleo's Mood (2)
Greasy Spoon (3)
Have You Ever Had The Blues (2)
Honky Tonk (1)

I'll Be In Trouble (1)
Last Date (3)
Late Date (1)
Mercy Mercy Mercy (1)
Mustang Sally (1)
My Girl (1)
On The Other Side (3)

Ooh Baby, You Turn Me On (2)
Papa's Got A Brand New Bag (2)
Pearl Time (2)
Pin Head (1)
Raindrops Keep Fallin' On My Head (3)

Respect (2)
Robbin's Nest (3)
Sing A Simple Song (3)
Sleepy Lagoon (3)
Slippin' & Slidin' (2) **96**
Smokie (1)
Soul Finger (2)
Soul Serenade (2) **23**

Sunny (2)
Tails Out (3)
Tequila (3)
This Guys In Love With You (3)
Toddlin' (2)
Turn Back The Hands Of Time (3)

20-75 (1)
Wade In The Water (3)
Willie's Mood (2)

MOBY GRAPE
Rock group from San Francisco. Original lineup: Bob Mosley, Jerry Miller, Don Stevenson, Peter Lewis and guitarist/lead vocalist Alexander "Skip" Spence (ex-drummer of Jefferson Airplane).

| 7/1/67 | 24 | 27 | 1 | Moby Grape | $35 | Columbia 9498 |

10 of 13 cuts released simultaneously on 45s

| 5/4/68 | 20 | 28 | 2 | Wow | $18 | Columbia 9613 [2] |

includes bonus LP titled *Grape Jam* (jam sessions with Al Kooper and Mike Bloomfield)

3/1/69	113	10	3	Moby Grape '69	$15	Columbia 9696
9/20/69	157	6	4	Truly Fine Citizen	$15	Columbia 9912
9/18/71	177	5	5	20 Granite Creek	$12	Reprise 6460

About Time (5)
Ain't No Use (1)
Ain't That A Shame (3)
Apocalypse (5)
Beautiful Is Beautiful (4)
Bitter Wind (5)
Black Currant Jam (2)
Boysenberry Jam (2)
Can't Be So Bad (2)
Captain Nemo (3)
Changes (1)

Changes, Circles Spinning (4)
Chinese Song (5)
Come In The Morning (1)
8:05 (1)
Fall In You (1)
Funky-Tunk (2)
Goin' Down To Texas (5)
Going Nowhere (3)
Gypsy Wedding (5)
He (2)
Hey Grandma (1)

Hoochie (5)
Horse Out In The Rain (5)
I Am Not Willing (3)
I'm The Kind Of Man That Baby You Can Trust (5)
If You Can't Learn From My Mistakes (5)
Indifference (1)
It's A Beautiful Day Today (5)
Just Like Gene Autry: A Foxtrot (2)
Lake (2)

Lazy Me (1)
Looper (4)
Love Song, Part One & Two (4)
Marmalade (2)
Miller's Blues (2)
Motorcycle Irene (2)
Mr. Blues (1)
Murder In My Heart For The Judge (2)
Naked, If I Want To (1,2)
Never (2)

Now I Know High (4)
Ode To The Man At The End Of The Bar (5)
Omaha (1) **88**
Ooh Mama Ooh (3)
Open Up Your Heart (4)
Place And The Time (2)
Right Before My Eyes (4)
Road To The Sun (5)
Rose Colored Eyes (2)
Roundhouse Blues (5)
Seeing (3)

Sitting By The Window (1)
Someday (1)
Three-Four (2)
Tongue-Tied (4)
Treat Me Bad (4)
Trucking Man (3)
Truly Fine Citizen (4)
What's To Choose (3)
Wild Oats Moan (5)

MOCEDADES
Sextet from Bilbao, Spain, featuring the Amezaga sisters, Amaya and Izaskum.

| 3/16/74 | 152 | 7 | | Eres Tu "Touch The Wind" | $10 | Tara 53000 |

Adios Amor
Dime Senor

Eres Tu (Touch The Wind) **9**
Himno

I Ask The Lord
If You Miss Me From The Back Of The Bus

Mary Ann
Recuerdos De Mocedad

Rin Ron
Yesterday (It Was A Happy Day)

DEBUT DATE	PEAK POS	WKS CHR	GOLD	ARTIST — Album Title	$	Label & Number

M.O.D.
Hardcore-metal foursome led by vocalist Billy Milano, with Tim McMurtrie, Keith Davis and Ken Ballone. All but Milano left in 1988; replaced by Louie Svitek, Tim Mallare and John Monte. M.O.D. stands for Method Of Destruction.

DEBUT DATE	PEAK POS	WKS CHR	GOLD	ARTIST — Album Title	$	Label & Number
11/7/87	153	5		1 U.S.A. for M.O.D.	$8	Megaforce 1344
9/17/88	186	6		2 Surfin' With M.O.D.	$8	Caroline 1359
				sides A & B feature the same 7 tunes, except side A includes dialogue between songs		
3/11/89	151	8		3 Gross Misconduct	$8	Megaforce 1360

Accident Scene (3)
A.I.D.S. (1)
Aren't You Hungry (1)
Ballad Of Dio (1)
Bubble Butt (1)
Bushwackateas (1)
Captain Crunch (medley) (1)
Color My World (2)
Come As You Are (3)
Confusion (1)
Dead Men (medley) (1)
Dio ..see: Ballad Of
Don't Feed The Bears (1)
E Factor (3)
Get A Real Job (1)
Godzula (3)
Goldfish From Hell (2)
Gross Misconduct (1)
Hate Tank (1)
I Executioner (1)
Imported Society (1)
In The City (3)
Jim Gordon (1)
Let Me Out (1)
Man Of Your Dreams (1)
Most (medley) (1)
Mr. Oofus (2)
No Glove No Love (3)
No Hope (3)
Ode To Harry (1)
P.B.M. (3)
Parents (1)
Party Animal (2)
Ride, The (3)
Ruptured Nuptials (1)
Sargent Drexell Theme (2)
Satan's Cronies (3)
Short But Sweet (1)
Shout (2)
Spandex Enormity (1)
Surf's Up (2)
Surfin' U.S.A. (2)
That Noise (1)
Theme (3)
Thrash Or Be Thrashed (1)
True Colors (3)
Vents (3)
You're Beat (1)
You're X'ed (1)

MODELS
Pop-rock quintet from Melbourne, Australia. Led by vocalists/guitarists James Freud and Sean Kelly.

DEBUT DATE	PEAK POS	WKS CHR	GOLD	ARTIST — Album Title	$	Label & Number
5/3/86	84	18		Out Of Mind Out Of Sight	$8	Geffen 24100

Barbados
Big On Love
Cold Fever
I Hear Motion
King Of Kings
Out Of Mind Out Of Sight 37
Ringing Like A Bell
Sooner In Heaven
Stormy Tonight
These Blues

MODERN ENGLISH
British new wave group led by Robbie Grey (vocals).

DEBUT DATE	PEAK POS	WKS CHR	GOLD	ARTIST — Album Title	$	Label & Number
3/19/83	70	28	●	1 After The Snow	$8	Sire 23821
3/24/84	93	12		2 Ricochet Days	$8	Sire 25066
4/5/86	154	7		3 Stop Start	$8	Sire 25343
6/30/90	135	12		4 Pillow Lips	$12	TVT 2810

After The Snow (1)
Beautiful People (4)
Beauty (4)
Blue Waves (2)
Border, The (3)
Breaking Away (3)
Care About You (4)
Carry Me Down (1)
Chapter 12 (2)
Coming Up For Air (4)
Dawn Chorus (1)
Face Of Wood (1)
Greatest Show (3)
Hands Across The Sea (2) 91
Heart (2)
I Don't Know The Answer (3)
I Melt With You (1) 78
I Melt With You (4) 76
Ink And Paper (3)
Let's All Dream (4)
Life In The Gladhouse (1)
Life's Rich Tapestry (4)
Love Breaks Down (3)
Love Forever (3)
Machines (2)
Night Train (3)
Pillow Lips (4)
Rainbow's End (2)
Ricochet Days (2)
Someone's Calling (1)
Spinning Me Round (2)
Start Stop/Stop Start (3)
Tables Turning (1)
Take Me Away (4)
You're Too Much (4)

MODUGNO, Domenico
Born on 1/9/28 in Polignano a Mare, Italy. Singer/actor.

DEBUT DATE	PEAK POS	WKS CHR	GOLD	ARTIST — Album Title	$	Label & Number
9/15/58	8	6		**Nel Blu Dipinto Di Blu (Volare) and other Italian favorites**	[F] $30	Decca 8808

Don Fifi
La Cicoria
Mariti In Citta
Nel Blu Dipinto Di Blu (Volare) 1
O Ccafe
O Specchio
Pasqualino Maraglia
Pizza C' 'A Pummarola
Resta Cu Mme
Strade 'Nfosa
Vecchio Frak
Ventu D'Estati

MOFFO, Anna — see FRANCHI, Sergio

MOLLY HATCHET
Southern hard-rock sextet from Jacksonville, Florida. Original lineup: Danny Joe Brown (lead singer), Bruce Crump, Bonner Thomas, Duane Roland, Dave Hlubek and Steve Holland. Jimmy Farrar replaced Brown in 1980; Brown returned and replaced Farrar in 1983.

DEBUT DATE	PEAK POS	WKS CHR	GOLD	ARTIST — Album Title	$	Label & Number
11/11/78+	64	42	▲	1 Molly Hatchet	$8	Epic 35347
9/29/79	19	48	▲²	2 Flirtin' With Disaster	$8	Epic 36110
9/20/80	25	21	●	3 Beatin' The Odds	$8	Epic 36572
12/5/81+	36	14		4 Take No Prisoners	$8	Epic 37480
3/26/83	59	20		5 No Guts...No Glory	$8	Epic 38429
11/24/84	117	13		6 The Deed Is Done	$8	Epic 39621
12/7/85	130	9		7 Double Trouble Live	[L] $8	Epic 40137 [2]

Ain't Even Close (5)
All Mine (4)
Backstabber (6)
Beatin' The Odds (3,7)
Big Apple (1)
Bloody Reunion (4,7)
Boogie No More (2,7)
Both Sides (5)
Bounty Hunter (1,7)
Cheatin' Woman (1)
Creeper, The (1)
Dead And Gone (3)
Dead Giveaway (4)
Don't Leave Me Lonely (4)
Don't Mess Around (4)
Double Talker (3)
Dreams I'll Never See (1,7)
Edge Of Sundown (7)
Fall Of The Peacemakers (5,7)
Few And Far Between (1)
Flirtin' With Disaster (2,7) 42
Freebird (7)
Gator Country (1,7)
Get Her Back (3)
Good Rockin' (2)
Good Smoke And Whiskey (6)
Gunsmoke (2)
Heartbreak Radio (6)
I Ain't Got You (6)
I'll Be Running (1)
It's All Over Now (2)
Jukin' City (2)
Kinda Like Love (5)
Lady Luck (4)
Let The Good Times Roll (3)
Long Tall Sally (5)
Long Time (4)
Loss Of Control (4)
Man On The Run (6)
On The Prowl (5)
One Man's Pleasure (2)
Penthouse Pauper (3)
Poison Pen (4)
Power Play (4) 96
Price You Pay (1)
Rambler, The (3) 91
Respect Me In The Morning (4)
Sailor (3)
Satisfied Man (6,7) 81
She Does She Does (6)
Song For The Children (6)
Stone In Your Heart (6,7)
Straight Shooter (6)
Sweet Dixie (5)
Trust Your Old Friend (1)
Under The Gun (5)
Walk On The Side Of The Angels (7)
Walk With You (7)
What Does It Matter? (5)
What's It Gonna Take? (5)
Whiskey Man (2,7)

MOM & DADS, The
Polka band from Spokane, Washington: Quentin Ratliff, Harold Hendren, Les Welch and Doris Crow.

DEBUT DATE	PEAK POS	WKS CHR	GOLD	ARTIST — Album Title	$	Label & Number
11/13/71+	85	23		1 The Rangers Waltz	[I] $8	GNP Cres. 2061
5/6/72	165	6		2 In The Blue Canadian Rockies	$8	GNP Cres. 2063

Across The Alley From The Alamo (1)
Alabama Jubilee (1)
Anytime (1)
Blue Skirt Waltz (2)
Cab Driver (2)
Ever True Evermore (2)
Georgianna Moon (1)
In The Blue Canadian Rockies (2)
Judy (1)
Just A Closer Walk With Thee (1)
Marie (1)
Mom And Dads Schottische (2)
Moon Wink (2)
Oh Lonesome Me (2)
Quentin's B Flat Boogie (1)
Ragtime Annie (1)
Rangers Waltz (1)
Roses Of Picardy (2)
Silver Moon (1)
Skirts (2)
Somewhere My Love (1)
St. Louis Blues (2)
Till We Meet Again (2)
White Silver Sands (2)

MOMENTS, The
Soul trio from Hackensack, New Jersey featuring Mark Greene (falsetto lead). Greene left after first record, replaced by William Brown (lead) and Al Goodman. Harry Ray joined after "Love On A Two-Way Street" in 1970. Became Ray, Goodman & Brown in 1978. Ray died on 10/1/92 (age 45) of a stroke.

DEBUT DATE	PEAK POS	WKS CHR	GOLD	ARTIST — Album Title	$	Label & Number
3/27/71	184	7		1 Moments Greatest Hits	[G] $15	Stang 1004

DEBUT DATE	PEAK POS	WKS CHR	G O L D	ARTIST — Album Title	$	Label & Number
				MOMENTS, The — Cont'd		
5/15/71	147	8		2 The Moments Live at the New York State Womans Prison ....[L]	$15	Stang 1006
7/12/75	132	8		3 Look At Me	$12	Stang 1026
				RAY, GOODMAN & BROWN:		
1/26/80	17	23	●	4 Ray, Goodman & Brown	$8	Polydor 6240
10/4/80	84	12		5 Ray, Goodman & Brown II	$8	Polydor 6299
1/9/82	151	7		6 Stay...	$8	Polydor 6341

Another Day (4)
Beautiful Woman (3)
Come Away With Me (3)
Deja Vu (4)
Dolly My Love (3)
Each Time Is Like The First Time (5)
Friends (medley) (4)
Girls [includes 2 versions] (3)
Going In Circles (2)
Good Ole' Days (6)
Got To Get To Know You (3)
Happy Anniversary (5)

Heaven In The Rain (6)
Here I Go Again (medley) (2)
How Can Love So Right (Be So Wrong) (6)
I Do (1,2) 62
I Feel So Good Again (3)
I Won't Do Anything (1)
I'll Remember You With Love (5)
I'm So Lost (1)
I've Got The Need (3)
If I Didn't Care (1) 44
Inside Of You (4) (2)

Just Having Your Love (3)
Letter (2)
Look At Me (I'm In Love) (1,2) 57
[includes 2 versions] (3) 39
Love On A Two-Way Street (1) 3
Lovely Way She Loves (1)
Lovers Night (Rain In May) (6)
Me (5)
Midnight Lady (6)
More Today Than Yesterday (5)

My Prayer (5) 47
Not On The Outside (1,2) 57
Only You (And You Alone) (6)
Oo Baby, Baby (medley) (2)
Part Of You (5)
Pool Of Love (6)
Shoestrings (5)
Slipped Away (4)
Somebody Loves You Baby (1)
Special Lady (4) 5
Stay (6)

Sunday (1,2) 90
Sweet Sexy Woman (5)
Thrill (medley) (4)
Till The Right One Comes Along (6)
Treat Her Right (4)
Way It Should Be (4)
When The Lovin' Goes Out Of The Lovin' (6)
When The Morning Comes (3)
Where (1)
Wichita Lineman (2)

Yesterday (2)
You (5)

★★336★★				**MONEY, Eddie**		
				Born Edward Mahoney on 3/2/49 in Brooklyn, New York. Rock singer discovered and subsequently managed by the late West Coast promoter Bill Graham. Formerly an officer with the New York Police Department.		
1/7/78	37	49	▲²	1 Eddie Money	$8	Columbia 34909
1/27/79	17	26	●	2 Life For The Taking...	$8	Columbia 35598
8/9/80	35	17		3 Playing For Keeps	$8	Columbia 36514
7/10/82	20	44	▲	4 No Control	$8	Columbia 37960
11/5/83	67	19		5 Where's The Party?...	$8	Columbia 38862
8/30/86	20	58	▲	6 Can't Hold Back	$8	Columbia 40096
10/22/88	49	29		7 Nothing To Lose	$8	Columbia 44302
12/2/89+	53	18	●	8 Greatest Hits Sound Of Money ....[G]	$8	Columbia 45381
				not available on vinyl		
2/1/92	160	10		9 Right Here	$12	Columbia 46756

Another Nice Day In L.A. (9)
Baby Hold On (1,8) 11
Back On The Road (5)
Backtrack (5)
Bad Boy (7)
Bad Girls (5)
Big Crash (5) 54
Boardwalk Baby (7)
Bring On The Rain (6)
Call On Me (3)
Calm Before The Storm (6)
Can't Keep A Good Man Down (2) 63
Club Michelle (5) 66
Dancing With Mr. Jitters (7)
Don't Let Go (5)
Don't Worry (1)
Drivin' Me Crazy (4)

Endless Nights (6) 21
Fall In Love Again (9) 54
Far Cry From A Heartache (7)
Fire And Water (9)
Forget About Love (7)
Gamblin' Man (1)
Get A Move On (3) 46
Gimme Some Water (2)
Got To Get Another Girl (1)
Hard Life (4)
Heaven In The Back Seat (9) 58
I Can't Hold Back (6)
I Wanna Go Back (6,8) 14
I'll Get By (9) 21
It Could Happen To You (4)
Jealousys (1)

Keep My Motor Runnin' (4)
Leave It To Me (5)
Let Me In (7) 60
Let's Be Lovers Again (3) 65
Life For The Taking (2)
Looking Through The Eyes Of A Child (8)
Love In Your Eyes (7) 24
Love The Way You Love Me (2)
Magic (7)
Maureen (3)
Maybe I'm A Fool (2) 22
Maybe Tomorrow (5)
Million Dollar Girl (3)
My Friends, My Friends (4)
Nightmare (2)

No Control (4,8)
Nobody (2)
Nobody Knows (3)
One Chance (6)
One Love (6)
Passing By The Graveyard (Song For John B.) (4)
Peace In Our Time (8) 11
Prove It Every Night (9)
Pull Together (7)
Rock And Roll The Place (5)
Run Right Back (9)
Runnin' Away (4)
Running Back (3) 78
Satin Angel (3)
Save A Little Room In Your Heart For Me (1)
Shakin' (4,8) 63

She Takes My Breath Away (9)
So Good To Be In Love Again (1)
Stop Steppin' On My Heart (8)
Stranger In A Strange Land (6)
Take A Little Bit (4)
Take Me Home Tonight (6,8) 4
Things Are Much Better Today (9)
Think I'm In Love (4,8) 16
Think Twice (9)
Trinidad (2)
Two Tickets To Paradise (1,8) 22

Walk On Water (7,8) 9
Wanna Be A Rock 'N' Roll Star (1)
We Should Be Sleeping (6,8) 90
When You Took My Heart (3)
Where's The Party? (5,8)
Wish, The (3)
You've Really Got A Hold On Me (1) 72

				MONK, Thelonious		
				Born on 10/10/20 in Rocky Mount, North Carolina; died on 2/17/82. Legendary jazz pianist.		
11/30/63	127	3		Criss-Cross..[I]	$20	Columbia 8838

Crepuscule With Nellie
Criss-Cross

Don't Blame Me
Eronel

Hackensack
Rhythm-a-ning

Tea For Two
Think Of One

				MONK, T.S.		
				Thelonious Monk Jr. (son of the legendary jazz artist), with sister Boo Boo, and Yvonne Fletcher.		
1/31/81	64	22		1 House Of Music	$8	Mirage 19291
1/9/82	176	8		2 More Of The Good Life	$8	Mirage 19324

Bon Bon Vie (Gimme The Good Life) (1) 63
Can't Keep My Hands To Myself (1)

Candidate For Love (1)
Everybody Get On Up And Dance (1)
Falling In Love With You (2)

First Lady Of Love (2)
Hot Night In The City (1)
House Of Music (1)

Last Of The Wicked Romancers (1)
More To Love (2)
Oh! Oh! Speedo (2)

Stay Free Of His Love (1)
Too Much Too Soon (2)
You're Askin' Me, I'm Askin' You (Buggin' Me Out) (2)

★★56★★				**MONKEES, The**		
				Formed in Los Angeles in 1965. Chosen from over 400 applicants for new Columbia TV series. Consisted of Davy Jones (b: 12/30/45, Manchester, England; vocals), Michael Nesmith (b: 12/30/42, Houston; guitar, vocals), Peter Tork (b: 2/13/44, Washington, D.C.; bass, vocals) and Micky Dolenz (b: 3/8/45, Tarzana, California; drums, vocals). Dolenz had appeared in TV series *Circus Boy*, using the name Mickey Braddock in 1956. Jones was a racehorse jockey, and appeared in London musicals *Oliver* and *Pickwick*. Tork had been in the Phoenix Singers; Nesmith had done session work for Stax/Volt. Group starred in the film *Head* (1968). TV show dropped after 58 episodes, 1966-68. Tork left in 1968. Group disbanded in 1969; re-formed (minus Nesmith) in 1986.		
10/8/66	1¹³	78	●	1 The Monkees	$20	Colgems 101
2/4/67	1¹⁸	70	●	2 More Of The Monkees...	$15	Colgems 102
6/10/67	1¹	51	●	3 Headquarters	$15	Colgems 103
11/25/67	1⁵	47	●	4 Pisces, Aquarius, Capricorn & Jones Ltd.	$15	Colgems 104
5/11/68	3	39	●	5 The Birds, The Bees & The Monkees	$20	Colgems 109
12/21/68+	45	15		6 Head ....[S]	$40	Colgems 5008
				The Monkees starred in the film		
3/1/69	32	15		7 Instant Replay	$40	Colgems 113
6/28/69	89	12		8 The Monkees Greatest Hits ....[G]	$40	Colgems 115

DEBUT DATE	PEAK POS	WKS CHR	GOLD	ARTIST — Album Title	$	Label & Number

MONKEES, The — Cont'd

11/1/69	100	14		9 The Monkees Present	$65	Colgems 117
8/7/76	58	30 ▲		10 The Monkees Greatest Hits .... [G]	$10	Arista 4089
				later released on Arista 8313		
7/26/86	21	34 ▲		11 Then & Now...The Best Of The Monkees .... [G]	$8	Arista 8432
				includes 3 new songs by Micky Dolenz and Peter Tork		
8/16/86	92	24		12 The Monkees .... [R]	$8	Rhino 70140
				originally charted on 10/8/66 (POS #1)		
8/16/86	96	26		13 More Of The Monkees .... [R]	$8	Rhino 70142
				originally charted on 2/4/67 (POS #1)		
8/16/86	121	17		14 Headquarters .... [R]	$8	Rhino 70143
				originally charted on 6/10/67 (POS #1)		
8/16/86	124	17		15 Pisces, Aquarius, Capricorn & Jones Ltd. .... [R]	$8	Rhino 70141
				originally charted on 11/25/67 (POS #1)		
9/13/86	145	11		16 The Birds, The Bees & The Monkees .... [R]	$8	Rhino 144
				originally charted on 5/11/68 (POS #3)		
11/8/86	152	4		17 Changes .... [E]	$8	Rhino 70148
				group reduced to duo of Micky Dolenz and Davy Jones; originally released on Colgems 119 in 1970		
9/19/87	72	9		18 Pool It!	$8	Rhino 70706

Acapulco Sun (17)
All Alone In The Dark (17)
Anytime, Anyplace, Anywhere (11)
As We Go Along (6)
Auntie's Municipal Court (5,16)
Band 6 (3,14)
Bye Bye Baby Bye Bye (9)
Can You Dig It (6)
Circle Sky (6)
Counting On You (18)
Cuddly Toy (4,8,15)
Daddy's Song (6)
Daily Nightly (4,15)
Day We Fall In Love (2,13)
Daydream Believer (5,8,10,11,16) *1*
Ditty Diego - War Chant (6)
Do You Feel It Too? (17)
Don't Bring Me Down (18)
Don't Call On Me (4,15)
Don't Listen To Linda (7)
Don't Wait For Me (7)
Door Into Summer (4,15)
Dream World (5,16)
Early Morning Blues And Greens (3,14)

Every Step Of The Way (18)
For Pete's Sake (3,14)
Forget That Girl (3,14)
French Song (9)
Gettin' In (18)
Girl I Knew Somewhere (11) *39*
Girl I Left Behind Me (7)
Gonna Buy Me A Dog (1,12)
Good Clean Fun (9) *82*
Hard To Believe (4,15)
Heart And Soul (18) *87*
Hold On Girl (2,13)
I Can't Get Her Off My Mind (3,14)
I Love You Better (17)
I Never Thought It Peculiar (17)
I Wanna Be Free (1,8,10,12)
I Won't Be The Same Without Her (7)
(I'd Go There) Whole Wide World (18)
I'll Be Back Up On My Feet (5,16)
I'll Be True To You (1,12)
(I'll) Love You Forever (18)

I'll Spend My Life With You (3,14)
I'm A Believer (2,8,10,11,13) *1*
(I'm Not Your) Steppin' Stone (2,8,10,11,13) *20*
If I Knew (9)
It's Got To Be Love (17)
Just A Game (7)
Kicks (11)
Kind Of Girl I Could Love (2,13)
Ladies Aid Society (9)
Last Train To Clarksville (1,8,10,11,12) *1*
Laugh (2,13)
Let's Dance On (1,12)
Listen To The Band (9,10) *63*
Little Bit Me, A Little Bit You (8,10,11) *2*
Little Girl (9)
Long Title: Do I Have To Do This All Over Again (6)
Long Way Home (18)
Look Out (Here Comes Tomorrow) (2,13)

Looking For The Good Times (9)
Love Is Only Sleeping (4,15)
Magnolia Simms (5,16)
Man Without A Dream (7)
Mary, Mary (2,8,13)
Me Without You (7)
Midnight (18)
Midnight Train (17)
Mommy And Daddy (9)
Monkees, (Theme From) The (1,10,11,12)
Mr. Webster (3,14)
Never Tell A Woman Yes (9)
99 Pounds (17)
No Time (3,14)
Oh My My (17) *98*
Oklahoma Backroom Dancer (9)
P.O. Box 9847 (5,16)
Papa Gene's Blues (1,12)
Peter Percival Patterson's Pet Pig Porky (medley) (4,15)
Pillow Time (9)
Pleasant Valley Sunday (4,8,10,11,15) *3*
Porpoise Song (6) *62*

Poster, The (5,16)
Randy Scouse Git (3,8,14)
Salesman (4,15)
Saturday's Child (1,12)
Secret Heart (18)
Shades Of Gray (3,8,10,14)
She (2,8,10,13)
She Hangs Out (4,15)
She's Movin' In With Rico (18)
Shorty Blackwell (7)
Since You Went Away (18)
Sometime In The Morning (2,13)
Star Collector (4,15)
Sunny Girlfriend (3,14)
Sweet Young Thing (1,12)
Tapioca Tundra (5,16) *34*
Take A Giant Step (1,11,12)
Tear Drop City (7) *56*
Tell Me Love (17)
That Was Then, This Is Now (11) *20*
This Just Doesn't Seem To Be My Day (1,12)
Through The Looking Glass (7)
Ticket On A Ferry Ride (17)

Tomorrow's Gonna Be Another Day (1,12)
Valleri (5,8,11,16) *3*
We Were Made For Each Other (5,16)
What Am I Doing Hangin' 'Round? (4,11,15)
When Love Comes Knockin' (At Your Door) (2,13)
While I Cry (7)
Words (4,15) *11*
Writing Wrongs (5,16)
You And I (7)
You Just May Be The One (3,14)
You Told Me (3,14)
You're So Good To Me (17)
Your Auntie Grizelda (2,13)
Zilch (3,14)
Zor And Zam (5,8,16)

MONRO, Matt
Born Terrence Parsons on 12/1/32 in London; died of liver cancer on 2/7/85. Sang with Cyril Stapleton's Orchestra before going solo.

10/2/61	87	14		1 My Kind Of Girl	$30	Warwick 2045
3/13/65	126	3		2 Walk Away	$15	Liberty 7402
5/13/67	86	22		3 Invitation To The Movies/Born Free	$12	Capitol 2730

Alfie (3)
April Fool (1)
Born Free (3)
Cheek To Cheek (1)
Come Sta (1)
Georgia On My Mind (2)
Georgy Girl (3)
Going Places (2)

Gonna Build A Mountain (2)
Here And Now (2)
How Soon (2)
I Get Along Without You Very Well (2)
I Will Wait For You (3)
I'll Dream Of You (1)
I've Got Love (2)

In The Arms Of Love (3)
It's A Breeze (2)
Let's Face The Music And Dance (1)
Love Is The Same Anywhere (1)
Man And A Woman (3)
Mirage (1)

Moment To Moment (3)
My Friend, My Friend (2)
My Kind Of Girl (1) *18*
No One Will Ever Know (1)
Portrait Of My Love (1)
Sand Pebbles (And We Were Lovers), Theme From The (3)

Softly As I Leave You (2)
Strangers In The Night (3)
There Are No Words For Love (1)
Thing About Love (3)
Time For Love (3)
Walk Away (2) *23*
Wednesday's Child (3)

Who Can I Turn To (2)

MONROE, Marilyn
Born Norma Jean Baker on 6/1/26 in Los Angeles; died on 8/5/62 of an apparent barbiturate overdose. Legendary Hollywood actress/sex symbol. Married to baseball player Joe DiMaggio (1954) and playwright Arthur Miller (1956-61).

| 10/20/62 | 111 | 10 | | Marilyn .... | $50 | 20th Fox 5000 |
| | | | | comprised of songs Marilyn sang in films *There's No Business Like Show Business*, *River Of No Return* and *Gentlemen Prefer Blondes* | | |

After You Get What You Want You Don't Want It
Bye Bye Baby

Diamonds Are A Girl's Best Friend
Heat Wave
I'm Going To File My Claim

Lazy
Little Girl From Little Rock
River Of No Return

One Silver Dollar

When Love Goes Wrong

MONROE, Michael
Former lead singer of heavy-metal group Hanoi Rocks.

| 10/7/89 | 161 | 8 | | Not Fakin' It .... | $8 | Mercury 838627 |

All Night With The Lights On
Dead, Jail Or Rock 'N' Roll

Love Is Thicker Than Blood
Man With No Eyes

Not Fakin' It
Shakedown

She's No Angel
Smoke Screen

Thrill Me

While You Were Looking At Me

MONROES, The
Five-man rock band from San Diego — Jesus Ortiz, lead singer.

| 6/19/82 | 109 | 9 | | The Monroes .... [M] | $8 | Alfa 15015 |

Blind Faith
Hungry Stranger

Pay Pay Pay
Somewhere In The Night

What Do All The People Know *59*

DEBUT DATE	PEAK POS	WKS CHR	GOLD	ARTIST — Album Title	$	Label & Number

MONTANA ORCHESTRA
Studio group conducted by Vincent Montana, Jr. (b: 2/12/28). Also see Salsoul Orchestra.

| 12/19/81+ | 195 | 4 | | Merry Christmas/Happy New Year's ....[X] | $8 | MJS 3302 |

side 1: Christmas medley; side 2: New Year's eve party medley

Get Down New Years Eve Medley   Montana Christmas Medley

MONTE, Lou
Born on 4/2/17 in Lyndhurst, New Jersey. Vocalist/guitarist.

| 12/22/62+ | 9 | 25 | | **Pepino The Italian Mouse & Other Italian Fun Songs**............[N] | $20 | Reprise 6058 |

Calypso Italiano	Mala Femmena	Please Mr. Columbus (Turn	Show Me The Way To Go	Tici Ti-Tica To-Tici Ta	What Did Washington Say
Eh Marie, Eh Marie	Oh, Tessie	The Ship Around)	Home	Twist Italiano	(When He Crossed The
Good Man Is Hard To Find	**Pepino The Italian Mouse 5**		Sixteen Tons		Delaware)

MONTENEGRO, Hugo
Born in 1925 and raised in New York City; died on 2/6/81. Conductor/composer. Also see soundtrack *Hurry Sundown.*

1/29/66	52	20		1 Original Music from The Man From U.N.C.L.E. ....[I]	$35	RCA 3475
2/17/68	9	39	●	2 Music From "A Fistful Of Dollars" & "For A Few Dollars More" & "The Good, The Bad And The Ugly" ....[I]	$15	RCA 3927
9/21/68	166	5		3 Hang 'Em High ....[I]	$15	RCA 4022
8/30/69	182	4		4 Moog Power ....[I]	$15	RCA 4170

Aces High (2)	Fistful Of Dollars, Theme	Illya (1)	Martini Built For Two (1)	Square Dance (2)	Watch Out! (1)
Aquarius (medley) (4)	From A (2)	In The Heat Of The Night (3)	Meet Mr. Solo (1)	Story Of A Soldier (2)	Wild Bike (1)
Bandolero! (1)	For A Few Dollars More (2)	Invaders, The (1)	Moog Power (4)	Three, Theme For (3)	Wish I Knew (3)
Bitter Love (3)	For Love Of Ivy (3)	Keystone Kop (3)	More Today Than Yesterday	Titoli (2)	You Showed Me (4)
Bye, Bye Jill (1)	Fox, Theme From The (3)	MacArthur Park (Allegro	(4)	Tomorrow's Love (3)	
Dizzy (4)	**Good, The Bad And The**	Part III) (4)	My Love (3)	Touch Me (4)	
Don't Leave Me (4)	**Ugly** (2) 2	Man From Thrush (1)	My Way (4)	Traces (4)	
Ecstacy Of Gold (2)	Greatest Love (4)	Man From U.N.C.L.E.,	Sixty Seconds To What? (2)	Valley Of The Dolls, Theme	
Fiddlesticks (1)	Hair (medley) (4)	Theme From The (1)	Solo On A Raft (1)	From (3)	
	Hang 'Em High (3) 82	March With Hope (2)	Solo's Samba (1)	Vice Of Killing (2)	

MONTEZ, Chris
Born Ezekiel Christopher Montanez on 1/17/43 in Los Angeles. Protege of Ritchie Valens.

| 7/2/66 | 33 | 24 | | 1 The More I See You/Call Me ....[I] | $15 | A&M 4115 |
| 1/14/67 | 106 | 11 | | 2 Time After Time ....[I] | $15 | A&M 4120 |

Call Me (1) 22	Going Out Of My Head (2)	Keep Talkin' (2)	Our Day Will Come (2)	**Time After Time** (2) 36	You, I Love You (1)
Day By Day (1)	Hey Baby (1)	Lil' Red Riding Hood (2)	Shadow Of Your Smile (1)	Very Thought Of You (1)	
Elena (2)	How High The Moon (1)	Little White Lies (1)	Sunny (2)	What A Diff'rence A Day	
Fly Me To The Moon (1)	I Wish You Love (1)	**More I See You** (1) 16	**There Will Never Be**	Made (2)	
Girl From Ipanema (2)	Just Friends (2)	One Note Samba (1)	**Another You** (1) 33	Yesterday (2)	

★★391★★ MONTGOMERY, Wes
Born John Leslie Montgomery on 3/6/25 in Indianapolis; died on 6/15/68. Jazz guitarist. His brother Monk plays bass and brother Buddy plays piano.

12/11/65+	116	13		1 Bumpin' ....[I]	$15	Verve 8625
9/3/66	51	32		2 Tequila ....[I]	$15	Verve 8653
3/25/67	65	32		3 California Dreaming ....[I]	$15	Verve 8672
5/20/67	129	23		4 Jimmy & Wes The Dynamic Duo......................................[I]	$20	Verve 8678
				JIMMY SMITH AND WES MONTGOMERY		
10/7/67	13	67	●	5 A Day In The Life ....[I]	$15	A&M 3001
12/9/67+	56	38		6 The Best Of Wes Montgomery ....[K-I]	$15	Verve 8714
5/4/68	38	30		7 Down Here On The Ground ....[I]	$15	A&M 3006
9/7/68	187	8		8 The Best Of Wes Montgomery, Vol. 2 ....[K-I]	$15	Verve 8757
11/16/68	94	16		9 Road Song ....[I]	$15	A&M 3012
				album recorded one month before his death		
4/4/70	175	9		10 Greatest Hits ....[G-I]	$15	A&M 4247

Angel (5)	Fly Me To The Moon (5)	Joker, The (5)	Quiet Thing (5)	13 (Death March) (4)	Winds Of Barcelona (3,8)
Baby, It's Cold Outside (4)	Fox, Theme From The (7)	Know It All (7)	Road Song (9,10)	Thumb, The (2)	**Windy** (5,10) 44
Big Hurt (2,8)	**Georgia On My Mind**	Little Child (Daddy Dear) (2)	Sandpiper, Love Theme	Trust In Me (5)	Without You (3)
Bumpin' (1,8)	(7,10) 91	Mi Cosa (1)	From The ..see: Shadow Of	Twisted Blues (8)	Yesterday (9,10)
Bumpin' On Sunset (2,6)	Goin' On To Detroit (7)	Midnight Mood (2,8)	Your Smile	Up And At It (7)	
California Dreaming (8)	Goin' Out Of My Head (6)	More, More, Amor (3)	Scarborough Fair (Canticle)	Watch What Happens (4)	
California Nights (5)	Green Leaves Of Summer (9)	Movin' Wes (Part 1) (6)	(9,10)	What The World Needs Now	
Caravan (6)	Green Peppers (3)	Mr. Walker (3)	Serene (4)	Is Love (2,8)	
Con Alma (1,6)	Greensleeves (9)	Musty (1)	Shadow Of Your Smile (1,6)	When A Man Loves A	
Day In The Life (5,10)	Here's That Rainy Day (1)	Naptown Blues (6)	South Of The Border (Down	Woman (5,10)	
Down By The Riverside (4)	How Insensitive (Insensatez)	Night Train (4)	Mexico Way) (3)	When I Look In Your Eyes (7)	
Down Here On The Ground	(2,6)	O Morro (8)	Sun Down (3)	Where Have All The Flowers	
(7,10)	I Say A Little Prayer (7,10)	Oh You Crazy Moon (3)	Sunny (4)	Gone? (9)	
Eleanor Rigby (5,10)	I'll Be Back (9)	Other Man's Grass Is	Tear It Down (1)	Willow Weep For Me (5)	
End Of A Love Affair (6)	James And Wes (4)	Always Greener (7)	Tequila (2,6)	Wind Song (7)	

MONTROSE
Heavy-metal band led by guitarist Ronnie Montrose. Sammy Hagar was lead vocalist for the first two albums. Ronnie formed the group Gamma in 1979 during hiatus of Montrose.

5/11/74	133	12	▲	1 Montrose	$10	Warner 2740
11/16/74	65	14		2 Paper Money	$10	Warner 2823
10/18/75	79	7		3 Warner Bros. presents Montrose!	$10	Warner 2892
9/25/76	118	7		4 Jump On It	$10	Warner 2963
2/11/78	98	10		5 Open Fire	$8	Warner 3134
				RONNIE MONTROSE produced by Edgar Winter		
5/30/87	165	7		6 Mean	$8	Enigma 73264

DEBUT DATE	PEAK POS	WKS CHR	GOLD	ARTIST — Album Title	$	Label & Number

MONTROSE — Cont'd

All I Need (3)
Bad Motor Scooter (1)
Black Train (3)
Clown Woman (3)
Connection (2)
Crazy For You (4)
Dancin' Feet (3)
Don't Damage The Rock (6)
Dreamer, The (2)

Flesh And Blood (6)
Game Of Love (6)
Good Rockin' Tonight (1)
Hard Headed Woman (6)
Heads Up (5)
I Don't Want It (1)
I Got The Fire (2)
Jump On It (4)
Leo Rising (5)

Let's Go (4)
M For Machine (6)
Make It Last (1)
Man Of The Hour (6)
Mandolinia (5)
Matriarch (3)
Merry-Go-Round (4)
Music Man (4)
My Little Mystery (5)

No Beginning/No End (5)
O Lucky Man (3)
One And A Half (3)
One Thing On My Mind (1)
Open Fire (5)
Openers (Overture) (5)
Paper Money (2)
Pass It On (6)
Ready Willing And Able (6)

Rich Man (4)
Rock Candy (1)
Rock The Nation (1)
Rocky Road (5)
Space Station #5 (1)
Spaceage Sacrifice (2)
Stand (6)
Starliner (2)
Town Without Pity (5)

Tuft-Sedge (4)
Twenty Flight Rock (3)
Underground (2)
We're Going Home (2)
Whaler (3)
What Are You Waitin' For? (4)

MONTY PYTHON

British comedy troupe: Eric Idle, John Cleese, Terry Jones, Graham Chapman (died of cancer on 10/4/89 [age 48]), Michael Palin and Terry Gilliam.

DEBUT DATE	PEAK POS	WKS CHR	GOLD	ARTIST — Album Title	$	Label & Number
5/24/75	48	13		1 Matching Tie & Handkerchief .... [C]	$12	Arista 4039
8/2/75	83	15		2 Monty Python's Flying Circus .... [C]	$12	Pye 12116
8/23/75	87	11		3 The Album Of The Soundtrack Of The Trailer Of The Film Of "Monty Python And The Holy Grail" .... [S-C]	$12	Arista 4050
6/5/76	186	3		4 Monty Python Live! At City Center .... [C]	$12	Arista 4073
11/10/79	155	2		5 Life Of Brian .... [S-C]	$12	Warner 3396
				individual skit names not shown on above 2 albums		
11/15/80	164	9		6 Monty Python's Contractual Obligation Album .... [C]	$12	Arista 9536

Adventures Of Ralph Melish (1)
All Things Dull And Ugly (6)
Announcement (6)
Background To History (1)
Barber, The (2)
Bells (6)
Bishop (6)
Bishop On The Landing (1)
Bookshop (6)
Bring Me The Head Of Alfredo Garcia (3)
Bruces (1)
Buying A Bed (2)

Cheese Shop (1)
Children's Stories (2)
Cinema, The (2)
Crocodile (4)
Decomposing Composers (6)
Do Wot John (3)
Elephantoplasty (1)
Farewell To John Denver (1)
Fight Of The Century (1)
Finland (6)
Flying Sheep (2)
Great Actor (1)

Greater London Re-Development Plan For Haringey (3)
Henry Kissinger (6)
Herbie Rides Again (3)
Here Comes Another One (6)
Hot Dogs And Knickers (1)
I Bet You They Won't Play This Song On The Radio (6)
I Like Chinese (6)
I'm So Worried (6)
Interesting People (2)
Interviews (2)
King Arthur (3)

Martyrdom Of St. Victor (6)
Me, Doctor (2)
Medical Love Song (6)
Minister For Overseas Development (1)
More Television Interviews (2)
Mouse Problem (2)
Muddy Knees (6)
Never Be Rude To An Arab (6)
North Minehead Bye-Election (2)
Nudge Nudge (2)

Oscar Wilde And Friends (1)
Pet Shop (2)
Phone-in, The (1)
Rock Notes (6)
Scottish Farewell (6)
Self Defense (2)
Sir Kenneth Clash (3)
Sit On My Face (6)
String (6)
Taking In The Terrier (1)
Television Interviews (2)
Tiger Talk (1)
Towering Inferno (3)
Trade Description Act (2)

Traffic Lights (6)
Visitors (2)
Wide World Of Novel Writing (1)
Word Association (1)
World War Noises In 4 (1)

★★71★★ MOODY BLUES, The

Formed in Birmingham, England in 1964. Consisted of Denny Laine (guitar, vocals), Ray Thomas (flute, vocals), Mike Pinder (keyboards, vocals), Clint Warwick (bass) and Graeme Edge (drums). Laine and Warwick left in the summer of 1966, replaced by Justin Hayward (lead vocals, lead guitar) and John Lodge (vocals, bass). Laine joined Wings in 1971. Switzerland-born Patrick Moraz (former keyboardist of Yes) replaced Pinder in 1978; left group in early 1992.

DEBUT DATE	PEAK POS	WKS CHR	GOLD	ARTIST — Album Title	$	Label & Number
5/4/68+	3	106	▲	1 Days Of Future Passed	$15	Deram 18012
				with The London Festival Orchestra		
9/14/68	23	29	●	2 In Search Of The Lost Chord	$15	Deram 18017
5/31/69	20	136	●	3 On The Threshold Of A Dream	$10	Deram 18025
1/10/70	14	44	●	4 To Our Children's Children's Children	$10	Threshold 1
9/12/70	3	74	●	5 A Question Of Balance	$10	Threshold 3
8/21/71	2³	43	●	6 Every Good Boy Deserves Favour	$10	Threshold 5
11/18/72	1⁵	44	●	7 Seventh Sojourn	$10	Threshold 7
11/23/74+	11	25	●	8 This Is The Moody Blues .... [G]	$10	Threshold 12/13 [2]
6/4/77	26	15		9 Caught Live +5 .... [L]	$10	London 690/1 [2]
				first 3 sides recorded live at the Royal Albert Hall in 1969; side 4: previously unreleased studio recordings		
7/1/78	13	30	▲	10 Octave	$8	London 708
6/13/81	1³	39	▲	11 Long Distance Voyager	$8	Threshold 2901
9/10/83	26	22		12 The Present	$8	Threshold 2902
3/23/85	132	9		13 Voices in the Sky/The Best Of The Moody Blues .... [G]	$8	Threshold 820155
5/17/86	9	42	●	14 The Other Side Of Life	$8	Threshold 829179
6/25/88	38	19		15 Sur la mer	$8	Polydor 835756
				title is French for On The Sea		
12/9/89+	113	16		16 Greatest Hits .... [G]	$8	Threshold 840659
7/13/91	94	11		17 Keys Of The Kingdom	$12	Polydor 849433

Actor, The (2,8)
After You Came (6)
And The Tide Rushes In (5,8)
Are You Sitting Comfortably (3,9)
Balance, The (5)
Best Way To Travel (2)
Beyond (4)
Bless The Wings (That Bring You Back) (17)
Blue World (12) **62**
Breaking Point (15)
Candle Of Life (4)
Celtic Sonant (17)
Dawn - Dawn Is A Feeling (1)
Dawning Is The Day (5)
Day Begins (1)
Day We Meet Again (10)
Dear Diary (3,8)
Deep (15)
Departure (2)
Dr. Livingstone, I Presume (2,9)

Don't You Feel Small (5)
Dream, The (3,8,9)
Driftwood (10,13) **59**
Emily's Song (6)
Eternity Road (4)
Evening - The Sun Set: Twilight Time (1)
Eyes Of A Child - Part I (4,8)
Eyes Of A Child - Part II (4)
Floating (4)
For My Lady (7,8)
Gemini Dream (11,13,16) **12**
Gimme' A Little Somethin' (9)
Going Nowhere (12)
Gypsy (Of A Strange And Distant Time) (4,9)
Had To Fall In Love (10)
Have You Heard - Part 1 & 2 (3,8,9)
Here Comes The Weekend (15)
Higher And Higher (4)

Hole In The World (12)
Hope And Pray (17)
House Of Four Doors (Part 1 & 2) (2)
How Is It (We Are Here) (5)
I Am (12)
I Just Don't Care (14)
I Know You're Out There Somewhere (15,16) **30**
I Never Thought I'd Live To Be A Hundred (4)
I Never Thought I'd Live To Be A Million (4)
I'll Be Level With You (10)
I'm Just A Singer (In A Rock And Roll Band) (7,8,13,16) **12**
I'm Your Man (10)
In My World (11)
In The Beginning (3,8)
Is This Heaven? (17)
Isn't Life Strange (7,8,13,16) **29**

It May Be A Fire (14)
It's Cold Outside Of Your Heart (12)
It's Up To You (5)
King And Queen (9)
Land Of Make-Believe (7)
Late Lament (8)
Lazy Day (3)
Lean On Me (Tonight) (17)
Legend Of A Mind (2,8,9)
Long Summer Days (9)
Lost In A Lost World (7)
Love Is On The Run (13)
Lovely To See You (3,8)
Lunch Break - Peak Hour (1)
Magic (17)
Meanwhile (11)
Meet Me Halfway (12)
Melancholy Man (5,8)
Minstrel's Song (5)
Miracle (15)
Morning - Another Morning (1)

My Song (6)
Nervous (11)
Never Blame The Rainbows For The Rain (17)
Never Comes The Day (3,8,9) **91**
New Horizons (7,8)
Nice To Be Here (6)
Nights In White Satin (1,8,9,13,16) **2**
No More Lies (15)
OM (2)
Once Is Enough (17)
One More Time To Live (6)
One Step Into The Light (10)
Other Side Of Life (14) **58**
Our Guessing Game (6)
Out And In (4)
Painted Smile (11)
Peak Hour (1)
Please Think About It (9)
Procession (6)
Question (5,8,13,16) **21**

Reflective Smile (11)
Ride My See-Saw (2,8,9,13,16) **61**
River Of Endless Love (15)
Rock 'N' Roll Over You (14)
Running Out Of Love (14)
Running Water (12)
Say It With Love (17)
Say What You Mean (Parts I & II) (17)
Send Me No Wine (3)
Shadows On The Wall (17)
Simple Game (8)
Sitting At The Wheel (12,13) **27**
Slings And Arrows (14)
So Deep Within You (3)
Sorry (12)
Spirit, The (14)
Steppin' In A Slide Zone (10) **39**
Story In Your Eyes (6,8,16) **23**

DEBUT DATE	PEAK POS	WKS CHR	GOLD	ARTIST — Album Title	$	Label & Number

MOODY BLUES, The — Cont'd

Sun Is Still Shining (4)
Sunset, The (9)
Survival (10)
Talkin' Talkin' (14)
Talking Out Of Turn (11) *65*
To Share Our Love (3)

Top Rank Suite (10)
Tortoise And The Hare (5)
Tuesday Afternoon
(Forever Afternoon)
(1,8,9,16) *24*
22,000 Days (11)

Under Moonshine (10)
Under My Feet (12)
Veteran Cosmic Rocker
(11,13)
Vintage Wine (15)
Visions Of Paradise (2)

Voice, The (11,13,16) *15*
Voices In The Sky (2)
Voyage, The (3,8,9)
Want To Be With You (15)
Watching And Waiting (4,8)
What Am I Doing Here? (9)

When You're A Free Man (7)
Word, The (2,8)
You And Me (7)
You Can Never Go Home (6)
Your Wildest Dreams
(14,16) *9*

MOOG MACHINE, The
Kenny Ascher (b: 10/26/44) plays the Moog Synthesizer.

| 9/27/69 | 170 | 8 | | Switched-On Rock...[I] | $10 | Columbia 9921 |

Aquarius (medley)
59th Street Bridge Song
(Feelin' Groovy)

Get Back
Hey Jude
Jumpin' Jack Flash

Let The Sunshine In (medley)
Spinning Wheel

Time Of The Season
Weight, The

You Keep Me Hangin' On
Yummy Yummy Yummy

MOON, Keith
Born on 8/23/47 in London; died on 9/7/78 of a drug overdose. Drummer of The Who.

| 4/5/75 | 155 | 3 | | Two Sides Of The Moon.. | $25 | Track 2136 |

with guests Ringo Starr, Joe Walsh, Harry Nilsson and Rick Nelson

Back Door Sally
Crazy Like A Fox

Don't Worry Baby
In My Life

Kids Are Alright
Move Over Ms. L

One Night Stand
Solid Gold

Teenage Idol
Together

MOONGLOWS, The
R&B group from Louisville. Consisted of lead singers Bobby Lester (d: 10/15/80 of cancer [age 50]) and Harvey Fuqua, with Alexander "Pete" Graves, Prentiss Barnes and Billy Johnson.

| 8/5/72 | 193 | 4 | | The Return Of The Moonglows... | $15 | RCA 4722 |

Beat Of My Heart
I Was Wrong

I'll Stop Wanting You
Love Is A River

Most Of All
Penny Arcade

Sincerely
Ten Commandments

When I'm With You
You've Chosen Me

MOORE, Bob, and His Orchestra
Born on 11/30/32 in Nashville. Top session bass player. Led the band on Roy Orbison's sessions for Monument Records. Also worked as sideman for Elvis Presley, Brenda Lee, Pat Boone and others.

| 11/13/61 | 33 | 18 | | Mexico and Other Great Hits!..[I] | $20 | Monument 4005 |

Blue Tango
Cielito Lindo

Corazon D'Oro
El Picador

La Paloma
Mexicali Rose

Mexico *7*
My Adobe Hacienda

Neuvo Laredo
Ninita Linda

South Of The Border
Vaya Con Dios

MOORE, Dorothy
Born in Jackson, Mississippi in 1946. Lead singer of The Poppies. Also a popular gospel artist.

| 5/29/76 | 29 | 23 | | 1 Misty Blue.. | $8 | Malaco 6351 |
| 8/6/77 | 120 | 13 | | 2 Dorothy Moore... | $8 | Malaco 6353 |

Ain't That A Mother's Luck
(1)
Daddy's Eyes (2)
Dark End Of The Street (1)

Enough Woman Left (To Be
Your Lady) (1)
For Old Time's Sake (2)
Funny How Time Slips
Away (1) *58*

I Believe You (2) *27*
I Don't Want To Be With
Nobody But You (1)
It's So Good (1)
Laugh It Off (1)

Let The Music Play (2)
Love Me (2)
Loving You Is Just An Old
Habit (2)
Make It Soon (2)

Misty Blue (1) *3*
1-2-3 (You And Me) (2)
Only Time You Ever Say You
Love Me (1)
Too Blind To See (2)

Too Much Love (1)
With Pen In Hand (2)

MOORE, Gary
Guitarist from Belfast, Ireland. Brief member of Thin Lizzy.

4/23/83	149	13		1 Corridors Of Power...	$8	Mirage 90077
6/9/84	172	5		2 Victims Of The Future..	$8	Mirage 90154
3/15/86	146	7		3 Run For Cover..	$8	Mirage 90482
5/16/87	139	15		4 Wild Frontier..	$8	Virgin 90588
3/25/89	114	9		5 After The War...	$8	Virgin 91066
7/14/90+	83	42		6 Still Got The Blues..	$12	Charisma 91369
3/28/92	145	8		7 After Hours...	$12	Charisma 91825

special guests: B.B. King and Albert Collins

After The War (5)
All Messed Up (3)
All Your Love (6)
Always Gonna' Love You (1)
As The Years Go Passing By
(6)
Blood Of Emeralds (5)
Blues Is Alright (7)
Cold Day In Hell (6)
Cold Hearted (1)
Devil In Her Heart (2)
Don't Take Me For A Loser
(1)

Don't You Lie To Me (I Get
Evil) (7)
Empty Rooms (2,3)
End Of The World (1)
Falling In Love With You (1)
Friday On My Mind (4)
Gonna' Break My Heart
Again (1)
Hold On To Love (2)
Hurt Inside (7)
I Can't Wait Until Tomorrow
(1)
Johnny Boy (4)

Jumpin' At Shadows (7)
Key To Love (7)
King Of The Blues (6)
Law Of The Jungle (2)
Led Clones (5)
Listen To Your Heartbeat (3)
Livin' On Dreams (5)
Loner, The (4)
Midnight Blues (6)
Military Man (3)
Moving On (6)
Murder In The Skies (2)
Nothing To Lose (3)

Nothing's The Same (7)
Oh Pretty Woman (6)
Once In A Lifetime (3)
Only Fool In Town (7)
Out In The Fields (3)
Over The Hills And Far
Away (3)
Reach For The Sky (3)
Ready For Love (5)
Rockin' Every Night (1)
Run For Cover (3)
Running From The Storm (5)
Separate Ways (7)

Shapes Of Things (2)
Since I Met You Baby (7)
Speak For Yourself (5)
Still Got The Blues (6) *97*
Stop Messin' Around (6)
Story Of The Blues (7)
Strangers In The Darkness
(4)
Take A Little Time (4)
Teenage Idol (2)
Texas Strut (6)
That Kind Of Woman (6)
This Thing Called Love (5)

Thunder Rising (4)
Too Tired (6)
Victims Of The Future (2)
Walking By Myself (6)
Wild Frontier (4)
Wishing Well (1)

MOORE, Melba
Born Melba Hill on 10/29/45 in New York City. Soul singer/actress. Appeared in the Broadway and film productions of *Hair*; Tony Award-winning performer as Lutiebelle in the musical *Purlie*.

2/20/71	157	5		1 Look What You're Doing To The Man..................................	$12	Mercury 61321
7/5/75	176	4		2 Peach Melba...	$10	Buddah 5629
5/8/76	145	5		3 This Is It...	$10	Buddah 5657
12/25/76+	177	7		4 Melba..	$10	Buddah 5677
11/18/78+	114	18		5 Melba..	$8	Epic 35507
11/13/82+	152	19		6 The Other Side Of The Rainbow.......................................	$8	Capitol 12243
12/24/83+	147	14		7 Never Say Never...	$8	Capitol 12305
4/27/85	130	10		8 Read My Lips..	$8	Capitol 12382
8/23/86+	91	29		9 A Lot Of Love...	$8	Capitol 12471

Ain't No Love Lost (4)
Blood Red Roses (4)
Brand New (3)
Don't Go Away (6,9)
Dreams (8)

Falling (9)
Free (3)
Get Into My Mind (2)
Good Love Makes
Everything Alright (4)

Got To Have Your Love (7)
Greatest Feeling (4)
Green Birds Fly (2)
Happy (5)

He Ain't Heavy He's My
Brother (1)
Heaven Help Us All (1)
How's Love Been Treatin'
You (6)

I Am His Lady (2)
I Can't Believe It (It's Over)
(8)
I Can't Help Myself (Sugar
Pie-Honey Bunch) (6)

(I Need) Someone (4)
I Promise To Love You (5)
I'm Not Gonna Let You Go (9)
If I Had A Million (1)
If I Lose (2)

MOORE, Melba — Cont'd

If You Can Believe (2)
It's Been So Long (9)
It's Hard Not To Like You (5)
It's Really Love (7)
Keepin' My Lover Satisfied (7)
King Of My Heart (8)
Knack For Me (6)
Lean On Me (3,7)
Little Bit More (9)
Livin' For Your Love (7)
Long And Winding Road (4)
Look What You're Doing To The Man (1)

Love Can Be Good To You (2)
Love Me Right (7)
Love Of A Lifetime (8)
Love The One I'm With (A Lot Of Love) (9)
Love's Comin' At Ya (6)
Lovin' Touch (7)
Loving You Comes So Easy (1)
Make Me Believe In You (3)
Mighty Clouds Of Joy (4)
Million Years Before This Time (2)

Mind Over Matter (8)
Mind Up Tonight (6)
Must Be Dues (2)
My Soul Is Satisfied (2)
Natural Part Of Everything (2)
Never Say Never (7)
One Less Morning (3)
Other Side Of The Rainbow (1)
Patience Is Rewarded (1)
Pick Me Up, I'll Dance (5)
Play Boy Scout (3)

Read My Lips (8)
Searchin' For A Dream (1)
So Many Mountains (4)
Stay (9)
Stay Awhile (3)
Sunshine Superman (2)
There I Go Falling In Love Again (9)
There's No Other Like You (9)
This Is It (3) *91*
Thrill Is Gone (From Yesterday's Kiss) (1)
To Those Who Wait (8)

Together Forever (5)
Twenty Five Miles (medley) (1)
Underlove (6)
Walk A Mile In My Shoes (medley) (1)
Way You Make Me Feel (4)
When We Touch (It's Like Fire) (9)
When You Love Me Like This (8)
Where Did You Ever Go (5)
Winner (8)

You Got The Power (To Make Me Happy) (1)
You Stepped Into My Life (5) *47*
You Trip Me Out (9)

MOORE, Tim
Pop singer/songwriter/guitarist/keyboardist from New York City.

| 10/12/74 | 119 | 9 | | 1 Tim Moore .... | $10 | Asylum 1019 |
| 8/2/75 | 181 | 3 | | 2 Behind The Eyes .... | $10 | Asylum 1042 |

Aviation Man (1)
Bye Bye Man (2)
Charmer (1) *91*
Fool Like You (1) *93*
For The Minute (2)

High Feeling (1)
I Can Almost See The Light (1)
(I Think I Wanna) Possess You (2)

I'll Be Your Time (1)
If Somebody Needs It (2)
Kaptain Kidd (2)
Lay Down A Line To Me (2)
Love Enough (1)

Night We First Sailed Away (2)
Now I See (2)
Rock And Roll Love Letter (2)
Second Avenue (1) *58*

Sister Lilac (1)
Sweet Navel Lightning (2)
When You Close Your Eyes (1)

MOORE, Vinnie
Heavy-metal guitarist from Newcastle, Delaware. Age 24 in 1988.

| 6/18/88 | 147 | 7 | | Time Odyssey ....[I] | $8 | Squawk 834634 |

April Sky
As Time Slips By

Beyond The Door
Into The Future

Message In A Dream
Morning Star

Pieces Of A Picture
Race With Destiny

Tempest, The

While My Guitar Gently Weeps

MORALES, Michael
Born on 4/25/63. Native of San Antonio, Texas.

| 6/17/89 | 113 | 20 | | Michael Morales .... | $8 | Wing 835810 |

Cry, Cry, Cry
Eighteen
Hey Lori!

I Don't Know *81*
I Don't Want You No More

I Only Want To Look In Your Eyes

Romeo
Way To Go Baby

What I Like About You *28*

Who Do You Give Your Love To? *15*

MORAZ, Patrick
Born on 6/24/48 in Morges, Switzerland. Keyboardist for Yes (1974-78) and The Moody Blues (1978-92).

| 6/5/76 | 132 | 5 | | i .... | $10 | Atlantic 18175 |

Best Years Of Our Lives
Cachaca (Baião)
Dancing Now

Descent
Impact
Impressions (The Dream)

Incantation-Procession
Indoors

Intermezzo
Like A Child In Disguise

Rise And Fall
Storm, The

Symphony In The Space
Warmer Hands

MORGAN, Jane
Born Jane Currier in Boston and raised in Florida. Popular singer in France before achieving U.S. fame via TV and nightclub entertaining.

| 12/9/57 | 13 | 3 | | 1 Fascination .... | $25 | Kapp 1066 |

JANE MORGAN and THE TROUBADORS

| 11/26/66 | 134 | 4 | | 2 Fresh Flavor .... | $13 | Epic 26211 |

Affair To Remember (1)
Around The World (1)
Daydream (2)
Elusive Butterfly (2)
Fascination (1) *7*

Good Lovin' (2)
Intermezzo (1)
It's Not For Me To Say (1)
Message To Michael (2)
Midnight In Athens (1)

Monday, Monday (2)
My Heart Reminds Me (And That Reminds Me) (1)
River Seine (1)
Sounds Of Silence (2)

Speak Low (1)
Stars In My Eyes (1)
Strangers In The Night (2)
These Boots Are Made For Walkin' (2)

Two Different Worlds (1) *41*
When A Woman Loves A Man (2)
(You're My) Soul And Inspiration (2)

Yours Is My Heart Alone (1)

MORGAN, Lee
Jazz trumpeter. Born on 7/10/38 in Philadelphia; fatally shot on 2/19/72.

10/10/64+	25	30		1 The Sidewinder ....[I]	$20	Blue Note 84157
11/26/66	143	3		2 Search For The New Land ....[I]	$20	Blue Note 84169
3/1/69	190	3		3 Caramba! ....[I]	$20	Blue Note 84289

Boy, What A Night (1)
Caramba (3)
Cunning Lee (3)

Gary's Notebook (1)
Helen's Ritual (3)
Hocus-Pocus (1)

Joker, The (2)
Melancholee (1)
Morgan The Pirate (2)

Mr. Kenyatta (2)
Search For The New Land (2)

Sidewinder, Part 1 (1) *81*
Soulita (3)

Suicide City (3)
Totem Pole (1)

MORGAN, Lorrie
Born Loretta Lynn Morgan on 6/27/60. Country singer. Youngest daughter of country singer George Morgan. Worked on the *Grand Ole Opry* since 1984. Married Keith Whitley (d: 5/9/89) in November 1986.

1/27/90	117	33	●	1 Leave The Light On	$12	RCA 9594
5/25/91+	53	89	▲	2 Something In Red	$12	RCA 3021
10/31/92	65	15↑	●	3 Watch Me	$12	BNA 66047

Autumn's Not That Cold (2)
Behind His Last Goodbye (3)
Best Woman Wins (3)
Dear Me (1)
Eight Days A Week (1)
Except For Monday (2)
Faithfully (2)

Far Side Of The Bed (1)
Five Minutes (1)
From Our House To Yours (3)
Gonna Leave The Light On (1)
Half Enough (3)
Hand Over Your Heart (2)

He Talks To Me (1)
I Guess You Had To Be There (3)
I'll Take The Memories (1)
If I Didn't Love You (1)
In Tears (2)
It's A Heartache (3)

It's Too Late (To Love Me Now) (1)
Out Of Your Shoes (1)
Picture Of Me (Without You) (2)
She's Takin' Him Back Again (3)

Someone To Call Me Darling (3)
Something In Red (2)
Tears On My Pillow (2)
Trainwreck Of Emotion (1)
Watch Me (3)
We Both Walk (2)

What Part Of No (3)
You Leave Me Like This (3)

MORGAN, Meli'sa
Meli'sa (pronounced: me-lee-say) is a Queens, New York native. Backup singer for Melba Moore, Whitney Houston, Kashif and Chaka Khan. Formal training at New York's Juilliard School.

| 2/8/86 | 41 | 36 | | 1 Do Me Baby .... | $8 | Capitol 12434 |
| 12/19/87+ | 108 | 19 | | 2 Good Love .... | $8 | Capitol 46943 |

Do Me Baby (1) *46*
Do You Still Love Me? (1)
Fool's Paradise (1)

Getting To Know You Better (1)
Good Love (2)

Heart Breaking Decision (1)
Here Comes The Night (2)
I Still Think About You (2)

I'll Give It When I Want It (1)
I'll Love No More (2)
If You Can Do It: I Can Too!! (2)

Just For Your Touch (2)
Lies (1)
Love Changes (2)

Now Or Never (1)
Think It Over (2)
You're All I Got (2)

DEBUT DATE	PEAK POS	WKS CHR	GOLD	ARTIST — Album Title	$	Label & Number

MORMON TABERNACLE CHOIR, The
Three hundred and seventy-five-voice choir directed by Richard P. Condie (died on 12/22/85).

DEBUT DATE	PEAK POS	WKS CHR	GOLD	Album Title	$	Label & Number
10/19/59+	1[1]	80	●	1 The Lord's Prayer	$10	Columbia 6068
12/28/59	5	2		2 The Spirit Of Christmas ....[X]	$15	Columbia 6100
10/30/61	47	1		3 Songs Of The North & South 1861-1865.........	$10	Columbia 6259
12/25/61+	118	3		4 The Spirit Of Christmas ....[X-R]	$10	Columbia 6100
				Christmas charts: 26/'63, 26/'65, 60/'67		
1/5/63	49	8		5 The Lord's Prayer, Volume II	$12	Columbia 6367
				albums #1 & 5 feature The Philadelphia Orchestra, Eugene Ormandy, conductor		

Aura Lee (3)
Bach: Come Sweet Death (5)
Battle Cry Of Freedom (3)
Battle Hymn Of The Republic (1,3) *13*
Bethlehem Night (2)
Blessed Are They That Mourn (1)
Bonnie Blue Flag (3)
Break Forth, O Beauteous Heavenly Light (2)
Carol Of The Bells (2)

Christmas Day (2)
Come, Come Ye Saints (1)
Coventry Carol (2)
David's Lamentation (1)
Dixie (3)
For Christ Is Born (2)
For Unto Us A Child Is Born (1)
Glory To God In The Highest (2)
Gounod: Unfold, Ye Portals (5)

Handel: Hallelujah Amen (5)
Hark! The Herald Angels Sing (2)
He's Gone Away (3)
Holy, Holy, Holy (1)
How Great The Wisdom And The Love (1)
Kathleen Mavourneen (3)
Lo, How A Rose E'er Blooming (2)
Londonderry Air (1)
Lord's Prayer (1,5)

Lorena (3)
Mighty Fortress Is Our God (5)
Mozart: Give Unto The Meek (5)
My Shepherd Will Supply My Need (5)
O Be Joyful (5)
O Come, All Ye Faithful (2)
O Little Town Of Bethlehem (2)
O, My Father (1)

148th Psalm (1)
Robertson: Old Things Are Done Away (5)
Schubert: Heavenly Father! (Ave Maria) (5)
Shepherds' Story (2)
Silent Night, Holy Night (2)
Snow Lay On The Ground (2)
Sometimes I Feel Like A Motherless Child (3)
Sweet Evelina (3)
Tell Us, Shepherd Maids (2)

Tenting On The Old Camp Ground (3)
Three Kings (2)
Tramp, Tramp, Tramp (3)
Verdi: Lord, Hear Our Prayer (5)
What Perfume This? O Shepherds, Say! (2)
When Johnny Comes Marching Home (3)
While Shepherds Watched Their Flocks (2)

MORODER, Giorgio
Born on 4/26/40 in Ortisei, Italy. Electronic composer/conductor/producer for numerous soundtracks. Produced seven of Donna Summer's albums.

DEBUT DATE	PEAK POS	WKS CHR	GOLD	Album Title	$	Label & Number
10/29/77	130	7		GIORGIO		
				From Here To Eternity	$8	Casablanca 7065

Faster Than The Speed Of Love

First Hand Experience In Second Hand Love

From Here To Eternity

I'm Left, You're Right, She's Gone

Lost Angeles
Too Hot To Handle

Utopia - Me Giorgio

MORRIS, Gary
Country singer/songwriter from Ft. Worth, Texas. Lead in the Broadway musical *Les Misérables* (1987).

DEBUT DATE	PEAK POS	WKS CHR	GOLD	Album Title	$	Label & Number
10/15/83	174	8	●	Why Lady Why	$8	Warner 23738

Again
I Can Feel The Fire Going Out

I'd Be The First To Fall In Love Again
Love She Found In Me

Mama You Can't Give Me No Whippin'
Runaway Hearts

Velvet Chains
Way I Love You Tonight

Why Lady Why
Wind Beneath My Wings

★★77★★ MORRISON, Van
Born George Ivan on 8/31/45 in Belfast, Ireland. Blue-eyed soul singer/songwriter. Leader of Them. Wrote the classic hit "Gloria." Inducted into the Rock and Roll Hall of Fame in 1993.

DEBUT DATE	PEAK POS	WKS CHR	GOLD	Album Title	$	Label & Number
10/7/67	182	7		1 Blowin' Your Mind!	$20	Bang 218
3/14/70	29	22	▲	2 Moondance	$12	Warner 1835
12/26/70+	32	17		3 His Band And The Street Choir	$12	Warner 1884
10/30/71	27	24	●	4 Tupelo Honey	$12	Warner 1950
8/5/72	15	28		5 Saint Dominic's Preview	$12	Warner 2633
8/11/73	27	19		6 Hard Nose The Highway	$12	Warner 2712
1/26/74	181	4		7 T.B. Sheets ....[E]	$15	Bang 400
				previously unreleased takes from same sessions as album #1		
3/16/74	53	17		8 It's Too Late To Stop Now..............[L]	$12	Warner 2760 [2]
				featuring The Caledonia Soul Orchestra		
11/9/74	53	10		9 Veedon Fleece	$12	Warner 2805
5/7/77	43	11		10 A Period Of Transition	$8	Warner 2987
				featuring Dr. John (Mac Rebennack) on keyboards		
10/14/78	28	23		11 Wavelength	$8	Warner 3212
9/8/79	43	13		12 Into The Music	$8	Warner 3390
9/20/80	73	10		13 Common One	$8	Warner 3462
3/6/82	44	11		14 Beautiful Vision	$8	Warner 3652
4/9/83	116	8		15 Inarticulate Speech Of The Heart	$8	Warner 23802
3/9/85	61	17		16 A Sense Of Wonder	$8	Mercury 822895
8/16/86	70	13		17 No Guru, no Method, no Teacher	$8	Mercury 830077
10/10/87	90	22		18 Poetic Champions Compose	$8	Mercury 832585
7/23/88	102	13		19 Irish Heartbeat	$8	Mercury 834496
				VAN MORRISON & THE CHIEFTAINS		
				traditional folk songs arranged by Morrison and Paddy Moloney (leader of The Chieftains)		
7/1/89	91	39		20 Avalon Sunset	$8	Mercury 839262
5/26/90	41	141↑	▲	21 The Best Of Van Morrison ....[G]	$12	Mercury 841970
				Van's hits solo and with Them		
11/24/90+	62	25		22 Enlightenment	$12	Mercury 847100
10/12/91	99	17	●	23 Hymns To The Silence	$27	Polydor 849026 [2]

Across The Bridge Where Angels Dwell (14)
Ain't Nothin' You Can Do (8)
Alan Watts Blues (18)
All Saints Day (23)
Allow Me (18)
Almost Independence Day (5)
Ancient Of Days (16)
And It Stoned Me (2,21)
And The Healing Has Begun (12)
Angeliou (12)
Aryan Mist (14)
Autumn Song (6)
Avalon Of The Heart (22)

Baby Please Don't Go (21)
Be Thou My Vision (23)
Beautiful Obsession (medley) (11)
Beautiful Vision (14)
Beside You (7)
Blue Money (3) *23*
Boffyflow And Spike (14)
Brand New Day (2)
Bright Side Of The Road (12,21)
Bring It On Home To Me (8)
Brown Eyed Girl (1,7,21) *10*
Bulbs (9)
By His Grace (23)

Call Me Up In Dreamland (3) *95*
Caravan (2,8)
Carrickfergus (19)
Carrying A Torch (23)
Celtic Excavation (18)
Celtic Ray (14,19)
Celtic Swing (15)
Checkin' It Out (11)
Cleaning Windows (14,21)
Cold Wind In August (10)
Come Here My Love (9)
Come Running (2) *39*
Comfort You (9)
Coney Island (20)

Connswater (15)
Contacting My Angel (20)
Country Fair (9)
Crazy Face (3)
Crazy Love (2)
Cry For Home (15)
Cul De Sac (9)
Cypress Avenue (8)
Daring Night (20)
Did Ye Get Healed? (18,21)
Domino (3,8,21) *9*
Dweller On The Threshold (14,21)

Evening Meditation (16)
Everyone (2)
Fair Play (9)
Flamingos Fly (10)
Foreign Window (17)
Full Force Gale (12,21)
Give A Kiss (3)
Give Me My Rapture (18)
Glad Tidings (2)
Gloria (8,21)
Goodbye Baby (Baby Goodbye) (1)
Got To Go Back (17)
Great Deception (9)
Green (6)

Green Mansions (23)
Gypsy (5)
Gypsy Queen (3)
Hard Nose The Highway (6)
Haunts Of Ancient Peace (13)
Have I Told You Lately (20,21)
He Ain't Give You None (1,7)
Heavy Connection (10)
Help Me (8)
Here Comes The Night (8,17,21)
Higher Than The World (15)
Hungry For Your Love (11)
Hymns To The Silence (23)

MORRISON, Van — Cont'd

I Believe To My Soul (8)
I Can't Stop Loving You (23)
I Forgot That Love Existed (18)
I Just Want To Make Love To You (8)
I Need Your Kind Of Loving (23)
I Wanna Roo You (Scottish Derivative) (4)
I Will Be There (5)
I'd Love To Write Another Song (20)
I'll Be Your Lover, Too (3)
I'll Tell Me Ma (19)
I'm Not Feeling It Anymore (23)
I'm Tired Joey Boy (20)
I've Been Working (3,8)
If I Ever Needed Someone (3)
If You Only Knew (16)
In The Days Before Rock 'N' Roll (22)
In The Garden (17)
Inarticulate Speech Of The Heart No. 1 & 2 (15)
Into The Mystic (2,8)
Irish Heartbeat (15,19)
It Fills You Up (10)
It Must Be You (23)

It's All In The Game (12)
It's All Right (7)
Ivory Tower (17)
Jackie Wilson Said (I'm In Heaven When You Smile) (5,21) **61**
Joyous Sound (10)
Just A Closer Walk With Thee ..see: See Me Through
Kingdom Hall (11)
Let The Slave (16)
Lifetimes (11)
Linden Arden Stole The Highlights (9)
Listen To The Lion (5,8)
Madame George (7)
Marie's Wedding (19)
Master's Eyes (16)
Memories (22)
Midnight Special (1)
Moondance (2,21) **92**
Moonshine Whiskey (4)
My Lagan Love (19)
Mystery, The (18)
Natalia (11)
New Kind Of Man (16)
Northern Muse (Solid Ground) (14)
Oh The Warm Feeling (17)
Old Old Woodstock (4)

On Hyndford Street (23)
One Irish Rover (17)
Orangefield (20)
Ordinary Life (23)
Pagan Streams (23)
Professional Jealousy (23)
Purple Heather (6)
Quality Street (23)
Queen Of The Slipstream (18,21)
Raglan Road (19)
Rave On, John Donne (15)
Real Real Gone (22)
Redwood Tree (5) **98**
River Of Time (15)
Ro Ro Rosey (1,7)
Rolling Hills (12)
Saint Dominic's Preview (5,8)
Santa Fe (medley) (11)
Satisfied (13)
Scandinavia (14)
See Me Through (22)
See Me Through Part II (Just A Closer Walk With Thee) (23)
Sense Of Wonder (16)
September Night (15)
She Gives Me Religion (14)
She Moved Through The Fair (19)

She's My Baby (22)
Snow In San Anselmo (6)
So Complicated (23)
So Quiet In Here (22)
Some Peace Of Mind (23)
Someone Like You (18)
Sometimes I Feel Like A Motherless Child (18)
Spanish Rose (1)
Spanish Steps (18)
Spirit (13)
Star Of The County Down (19)
Start All Over Again (22)
Starting A New Life (4)
Stepping Out Queen (12)
(Straight To Your Heart) Like A Cannonball (4)
Street Choir (3)
Street Only Knew Your Name (15)
Streets Of Arklow (9)
Summertime In England (13)
Sweet Jannie (3)
Sweet Thing (1,7)
T.B. Sheets (1,7)
Ta Mo Chleamhnas Deanta (19)
Take It Where You Find It (11)

Take Me Back (23)
Take Your Hand Out Of My Pocket (8)
Thanks For The Information (17)
These Are The Days (20)
These Dreams Of You (2,8)
Tir Na Nog (17)
Tore Down A La Rimbaud (16)
Town Called Paradise (17)
Troubadours (12)
Tupelo Honey (4) **47**
Vanlose Stairway (14)
Venice U.S.A. (11)
Village Idiot (23)
Virgo Clowns (3)
Warm Love (6,8,21)
Wavelength (11) **42**
What Would I Do Without You (16)
When Heart Is Open (13)
When That Evening Sun Goes Down (4)
When Will I Ever Learn To Live In God (20)
Whenever God Shines His Light (20,21)
Who Drove The Red Sports Car (1,7)

Who Was That Masked Man (9)
Why Must I Always Explain (23)
Wild Children (6,8)
Wild Honey (13)
Wild Night (4,21) **28**
Wonderful Remark (21)
You Don't Pull No Punches, But You Don't Push The River (9)
You Gotta Make It Through The World (10)
You Know What They're Writing About (12)
You Make Me Feel So Free (12)
You're My Woman (4)
Youth Of 1,000 Summers (22)

MORRISSEY

Born Stephen Morrissey on 5/22/59 in Manchester, England. Former lead singer/songwriter of The Smiths.

DEBUT DATE	PEAK POS	WKS CHR	GOLD	ARTIST — Album Title	$	Label & Number
4/9/88	48	20		1 Viva Hate	$8	Sire 25699
11/24/90	59	16		2 Bona Drag	$12	Sire 26221
3/23/91	52	10		3 Kill Uncle	$12	Sire 26514
8/15/92	21	14		4 Your Arsenal	$12	Sire 26994

produced by Mick Ronson

Alsatian Cousin (1)
Angel, Angel, Down We Go Together (1)
Asian Rut (3)
Bengali In Platforms (1)
Break Up The Family (1)
Certain People I Know (4)
Dial-A-Cliche (1)
Disappointed (2)
Driving Your Girlfriend Home (3)

Everyday Is Like Sunday (1,2)
Found Found Found (3)
Glamorous Glue (4)
Hairdresser On Fire (2)
Harsh Truth Of The Camera Eye (3)
He Knows I'd Love To See Him (2)
I Don't Mind If You Forget Me (1)

I Know It's Gonna Happen Someday (4)
(I'm) The End Of The Family Line (3)
Interesting Drug (2)
King Leer (3)
Last Of The Famous International Playboys (2)
Late Night, Maudlin Street (1)
Little Man, What Now? (1)

Lucky Lisp (2)
Margaret On The Guillotine (1)
Mute Witness (3)
National Front Disco (4)
November Spawned A Monster (2)
Ordinary Boys (1)
Ouija Board, Ouija Board (2)
Our Frank (3)
Piccadilly Palare (2)

Seasick, Yet Still Docked (4)
Sing Your Life (3)
Such A Little Thing Makes Such A Big Difference (2)
Suedehead (1,2)
There's A Place In Hell For Me And My Friends (3)
Tomorrow (4)
Tony The Pony (3)

We Hate It When Our Friends Become Successful (4)
We'll Let You Know (4)
Will Never Marry (2)
Yes, I Am Blind (2)
You're Gonna Need Someone On Your Side (4)
You're The One For Me, Fatty (4)

MORSE, Steve, Band

Lead guitarist of the Dixie Dregs. Also a backing guitarist with Kansas.

DEBUT DATE	PEAK POS	WKS CHR	GOLD	ARTIST — Album Title	$	Label & Number
9/1/84	101	12		1 The Introduction ... [I]	$8	Musician 60369
6/24/89	182	3		2 High Tension Wires ... [I]	$8	MCA 6275

STEVE MORSE

Country Colors (2)
Cruise Missile (1)
Endless Waves (2)
General Lee (1)

Ghostwind (2)
Highland Wedding (2)
Huron River Blues Medley (1)
Introduction, The (1)

Leprechaun Promenade (2)
Looking Back (2)
Modoc (2)
Mountain Waltz (1)

On The Pipe (1)
Road Home (2)
Third Power (2)
Tumeni Notes (2)

V.H.F. (Vertical Hair Factor) (1)
Whistle, The (1)

MOSBY, Johnny and Jonie

Husband-and-wife team of Johnny (b: Fort Smith, Arkansas) and Jonie (real name: Janice Irene Shields; b: 8/10/40 in Van Nuys, California) Mosby.

DEBUT DATE	PEAK POS	WKS CHR	GOLD	ARTIST — Album Title	$	Label & Number
10/11/69	197	1		Hold Me	$12	Capitol 286

Gentle On My Mind
Hold Me, Thrill Me, Kiss Me
I Can Tell

Jackson
Johnny One Time

Let The World Keep On A Turnin'

One Has My Name (The Other Has My Heart)

Souvenirs Of Love
Sweet Thang
Walkin' Papers

MOTELS, The

Los Angeles-based quintet led by vocalist Martha Davis. Formed in Berkeley. To Los Angeles in the early '70s. Re-formed in 1978, signed to Capitol in 1979. Disbanded in 1987.

DEBUT DATE	PEAK POS	WKS CHR	GOLD	ARTIST — Album Title	$	Label & Number
12/1/79	175	2		1 Motels	$8	Capitol 11996
7/12/80	45	20		2 Careful	$8	Capitol 12070
4/24/82	16	41	●	3 All Four One	$8	Capitol 12177
10/15/83	22	24	●	4 Little Robbers	$8	Capitol 12288
8/17/85	36	16		5 Shock	$8	Capitol 12378

Annie Told Me (5)
Anticipating (1)
Apocalypso (3)
Art Fails (3)
Atomic Cafe (1)
Bonjour Baby (2)
Careful (2)
Celia (1)
Change My Mind (3)
Closets & Bullets (1)
Counting (1)

Cries And Whispers (5)
Cry Baby (2)
Danger (2)
Days Are O.K. (But The Nights Were Made For Love) (2)
Dressing Up (1)
Envy (2)
Footsteps (4)
Forever Mine (3) **60**

He Hit Me (And It Felt Like A Kiss) (3)
Hungry (4)
Icy Red (5)
Into The Heartland (4)
Isle Of You (4)
Kix (4)
Little Robbers (4)
Love Don't Help (4)
Mission Of Mercy (3)
Monday Shut Down (4)

My Love Stops Here (5)
New York Times (5)
Night By Night (5)
Only The Lonely (3) **9**
Party Professionals (2)
People, Places And Things (2)
Porn Reggae (1)
Remember The Nights (4) **36**
Shame (5) **21**
Shock (5) **84**

Slow Town (4)
So L.A. (3)
State Of The Heart (5)
Suddenly Last Summer (4) **9**
Tables Turned (4)
Take The L. (3) **52**
Total Control (1)
Tragic Surf (3)
Trust Me (4)

Where Do We Go From Here (Nothing Sacred) (4)
Whose Problem? (2)

MOTHER EARTH
Tracy Nelson, lead singer of Nashville sextet.

DEBUT DATE	PEAK POS	WKS CHR		ARTIST — Album Title	$	Label & Number
2/22/69	144	8		1 Living With The Animals	$20	Mercury 61194
8/23/69	95	9		2 Make A Joyful Noise	$15	Mercury 61226
5/15/71	199	2		3 Bring Me Home	$12	Reprise 6431

Blues For The Road (2)
Bring Me Home (3)
Come On And See (2)
Cry On (1)
Deliver Me (3)
Down So Low (1)

Goodnight Nelda Grebe, The Telephone Company Has Cut Us Off (1)
I Did My Part (1)
I Need Your Love So Bad (2)
I, The Fly (2)

I Wanna Be Your Mama Again (2)
I'll Be Long Gone (3)
It Won't Be Long (1)
Kingdom Of Heaven (Is Within You) (1)
Living With The Animals (1)

Lo And Behold (3)
Marvel Group (1)
Mother Earth (1)
My Love Will Never Die (1)
Seven Bridges Road (3)
Soul Of Sadness (3)
Soul Of The Man (2)

Stop The Train (2)
Temptation Took Control Of Me And I Fell (2)
Then I'll Be Moving On (2)
There Is No End (3)
Tonight The Sky's About To Cry (3)

Wait, Wait, Wait (2)
What Are You Trying To Do (2)
You Win Again (2)

MOTHERLODE
Canadian pop quartet led by keyboardist William "Smitty" Smith.

DEBUT DATE	PEAK POS	WKS CHR		ARTIST — Album Title	$	Label & Number
10/4/69	93	12		When I Die	$15	Buddah 5046

Can't You Find Love
Child Without Mother
Dear Old Daddy Bill

Hard Life
Help Me Find Peace Of Mind
Living Life

Memories Of A Broken Promise
Oh! See The White Light

Soft Shell
What Does It Take (To Win Your Love)

When I Die *18*
You Ain't Lookin' In The Right Place Baby

MOTHER LOVE BONE
Seattle rock band: vocalist Andrew Wood (d: 1990 of heroin overdose), guitarists Bruce Fairweather and Stone Gossard, bassist Jeff Ament and drummer Greg Gilmore. Gossard and Ament recorded with other Seattle notables as Temple Of The Dog, in tribute to Wood, then formed Pearl Jam.

DEBUT DATE	PEAK POS	WKS CHR		ARTIST — Album Title	$	Label & Number
10/10/92	77	12		Mother Love Bone	$13	Stardog 512884 [2]
				bonus CD includes 2 songs		

Bone China
Capricorn Sister (includes 2 versions)
Captain Hi-Top

Chloe Dancer (medley)
Come Bite The Apple
Crown Of Thorns
Gentle Groove

Half Ass Monkey Boy
Heartshine
Holy Roller
Lady Godiva Blues

Man Of Golden Words
Mindshaker Meltdown
Mr. Danny Boy

Stardog Champion
Stargazer

This Is Shangrila
Thru Fade Away

MOTHER'S FINEST
R&B sextet led by vocalists (husband-and-wife) Glenn Murdoch and Joyce Kennedy.

DEBUT DATE	PEAK POS	WKS CHR		ARTIST — Album Title	$	Label & Number
9/11/76	148	8		1 Mother's Finest	$8	Epic 34179
9/17/77	134	8		2 Another Mother Further	$8	Epic 34699
9/30/78	123	21		3 Mother Factor	$8	Epic 35546
5/23/81	168	8		4 Iron Age	$8	Atlantic 19302

All The Way (4)
Baby Love (2) *58*
Burning Love (2)
Can't Fight The Feeling (3)
Dis Go Dis Way, Dis Go Dat Way (2)
Don't Wanna Come Back (3)
Dontcha Wanna Love Me (1)

Earthling (4)
Evolution (4)
Fire (1) *93*
Fly With Me (Feel The Love) (1)
Give It Up (3)
Give You All The Love (Inside Of Me) (4)

Gone With Th' Rain (4)
Hard Rock Lover (2)
I Can't Believe (3)
Illusion (C'mon Over To My House) (4)
Love Changes (3)
Luv Drug (4)
Mickey's Monkey (2)

More And More (4)
Movin' On (4)
Mr. Goodbar (3)
My Baby (1)
Niggizz Can't Sang Rock & Roll (1)
Piece Of The Rock (2)
Rain (1)

Rock N' Roll 2 Nite (4)
Tell Me (3)
Thank You For The Love (2)
Time (4)
Truth'll Set You Free (2)
U Turn Me On (4)
Watch My Stylin' (3)

MOTHERS OF INVENTION, The — see ZAPPA, Frank

★★332★★ **MOTLEY CRUE**
Los Angeles-based, hard-rock band: "Vince Neil" Wharton (lead vocals), Mick Mars (real name: Bob Deal; guitar), Nikki Sixx (Frank Ferranno; bass) and "Tommy Lee" Bass (drums; married actress Heather Locklear). Neil left band in February of 1992.

DEBUT DATE	PEAK POS	WKS CHR	GOLD	ARTIST — Album Title	$	Label & Number
10/15/83+	17	111	▲³	1 Shout At The Devil	$8	Elektra 60289
12/17/83+	77	62	▲	2 Too Fast For Love ...[R]	$8	Elektra 60174
				their first album		
7/13/85	6	72	▲²	3 Theatre Of Pain	$8	Elektra 60418
6/13/87	2¹	46	▲²	4 Girls, Girls, Girls	$8	Elektra 60725
9/23/89	1²	109	▲⁴	5 Dr. Feelgood	$8	Elektra 60829
10/19/91	2¹	37	▲	6 Decade Of Decadence - '81-'91	$12	Elektra 61204

All In The Name Of... (4)
Anarchy In The U.K. (6)
Angela (6)
Bad Boy Boogie (4)
Bastard (1)
City Boy Blues (3)
Come On And Dance (2)
Dancing On Glass (4)
Danger (1)
Dr. Feelgood (5,6) *6*
Don't Go Away Mad (Just Go Away) (5) *19*

Fight For Your Rights (3)
Five Years Dead (4)
Girls, Girls, Girls (4,6) *12*
God Bless The Children Of The Beast (1)
Helter Skelter (1)
Home Sweet Home (3) *89*
Home Sweet Home '91 (6) *37*
In The Beginning (1)
Jailhouse Rock (4)

Keep Your Eye On The Money (3)
Raise Your Hands To Rock (3)
Kickstart My Heart (5,6) *27*
Knock 'Em Dead, Kid (1)
Live Wire (2,6)
Looks That Kill (1,6) *54*
Louder Than Hell (3)
Merry-Go-Round (2)
Nona (4)
On With The Show (2)
Piece Of Your Action (2,6)
Primal Scream (6) *63*

Public Enemy #1 (2)
Raise Your Hands To Rock (3)
Rattlesnake Shake (5)
Red Hot (1)
Rock N' Roll Junkie (6)
Same Ol' Situation (S.O.S.) (5) *78*
Save Our Souls (3)
She Goes Down (5)
Shout At The Devil (1,6)
Slice Of Your Pie (5)

Smokin' In The Boys Room (3,6) *16*
Starry Eyes (2)
Sticky Sweet (5)
Sumthin' for Nuthin' (4)
T.N.T. (Terror 'N Tinseltown) (5)
Take Me To The Top (2)
Teaser (6)
Ten Seconds To Love (1)
Time For Change (5)
Tonight (We Need A Lover) (3)

Too Fast For Love (2)
Too Young To Fall In Love (1) *90*
Use It Or Lose It (3)
Wild Side (4,6)
Without You (5) *8*
You're All I Need (4) *83*

MOTORHEAD
British heavy-metal band formed by Ian "Lemmy" Kilminster (vocals; ex-Hawkwind) in 1975. Trio from 1976 with guitarist "Fast Eddie" Clarke and drummer "Philthy Animal" Taylor. Clarke left in May 1982 (later formed Fastway), replaced by Brian Robertson (ex-Thin Lizzy). Taylor and Robertson left in August 1983. Kilminster then organized new foursome with guitarists Phil Campbell and Wurzel, and drummer Pete Gill (ex-Saxon). Taylor replaced Gill in 1991.

DEBUT DATE	PEAK POS	WKS CHR		ARTIST — Album Title	$	Label & Number
5/22/82	174	6		1 Iron Fist	$8	Mercury 4042
7/23/83	153	7		2 Another Perfect Day	$8	Mercury 811365
11/29/86	157	11		3 Orgasmatron	$8	GWR/Profile 1223
10/24/87	150	6		4 Rock 'N' Roll	$8	GWR/Profile 1240
3/23/91	142	9		5 1916	$12	WTG 46858

Ain't My Crime (3)
All For You (4)
America (1)
Angel City (5)
Another Perfect Day (2)

Back At The Funny Farm (2)
Bang To Rights (1)
Blackheart (4)
Boogeyman (4)
Built For Speed (3)

Claw (3)
Dancing On Your Grave (2)
Deaf Forever (3)
Die You Bastard (2)
Doctor Rock (3)

Dogs (4)
(Don't Let 'Em) Grind Ya Down (1)
(Don't Need) Religion (1)
Eat The Rich (4)

Go To Hell (1)
Going To Brazil (5)
Heart Of Stone (5)
I Got Mine (2)

I'm So Bad (Baby I Don't Care) (5)
I'm The Doctor (1)
Iron Fist (1)
Loser (1)

DEBUT DATE	PEAK POS	WKS CHR	GOLD	ARTIST — Album Title	$	Label & Number

MOTORHEAD — Cont'd

Love Me Forever (5)
Make My Day (5)
Marching Off To War (2)
Mean Machine (3)

Nightmare/The Dreamtime (5)
1916 (5)
No Voices In The Sky (5)
Nothing Up My Sleeve (3)

One To Sing The Blues (5)
One Track Mind (2)
Orgasmatron (3)
Ramones (5)
Riding With The Driver (3)

Rock It (2)
Rock 'N' Roll (4)
Sex And Outrage (1)
Shine (2)
Shut It Down (1)

Shut You Down (5)
Speedfreak (1)
Stone Deaf In The USA (4)
Tales Of Glory (2)
Traitor (4)

Wolf, The (4)

MOTORS, The

British duo: Andy McMaster and Nick Garvey. Peter Bramall (later of Bram Tchaikovsky) was an early group member through 1978.

| 4/12/80 | 174 | 8 | | Tenement Steps | $8 | Virgin 13139 |

Here Comes The Hustler (5)
Love And Loneliness 78

Metropolis
Modern Man

Nightmare Zero
Slum People

Tenement Steps
That's What John Said

MOTTOLA, Tony

Born on 4/18/18 in Kearney, New Jersey. Latin-style guitarist. Produced by Enoch Light.

4/7/62	26	26		1 Roman Guitar .... [I]	$15	Command 816
7/21/62	41	6		2 Roman Guitar, Volume Two .... [I]	$15	Command 836
12/11/65+	85	13		3 Love Songs - Mexico/S.A. .... [I]	$15	Command 889
12/2/67	198	3		4 A Latin Love-In .... [I]	$10	Project 3 5010
5/16/70	189	3		5 Tony Mottola's Guitar Factory .... [I]	$10	Project 3 5044

All (4)
Anema E Core (2)
Anna (1)
Arrivederci, Roma (1)
Autumn In Rome (2)
Besame Mucho (3)
Bewitched (5)
Black Orpheus (Manha De Carnaval), Theme From (3)
Bluesette (5)
Brasilia (3)
Call Me (4)

Carnival Of Venice (2)
Chewy-Chewy Gum-Gum (5)
Come Together (5)
Curacao (3)
Dream Theme From Act I (4)
Funiculi Funicula (2)
Girl From Ipanema (3)
Guadalajara (3)
Guaglione (2)
Guitar Thing (3)
I Love, I Live, I Love (4)
I Love You (4)

Italian Serenade (1)
La Bamba (3)
La Montana (4)
La Strada (1)
Lay, Lady, Lay (5)
Maria Elena (3)
Mexican Hat Dance (3)
Mexican Medley (3)
Na Voce (1)
Neopolitan Tarantella (1)
Nina (2)
Noche De Ronda (4)

Non Dimenticar (1)
Piel Canela (3)
Roman Guitar (1)
Sabor A Mi (Be True To Me) (3)
Samba De Orfeu (4)
Scalinatella (2)
Scapricciatiello (2)
So Nice (Summer Samba) (4)
Something (5)
Sorrento (1)
Souvenir D'Italie (2)

Spanish Harlem (4)
Spinning Wheel (5)
Sugar, Sugar (5)
Summertime In Venice (2)
Te Volo Ben (2)
Tequila (3)
Tra Veglia E Sono (2)
Violetta (1)
Volare (1)
What Now My Love (4)
Windy (3)
Woodpecker Song (1)

World Of Your Embrace (4)
Yester-Me, Yester-You, Yesterday (5)

MOTT THE HOOPLE

British glitter-rock group led by vocalist Ian Hunter. Group name taken from a Willard Manus novel. Various personnel included guitarist Mick Ralphs (left in 1973 to form Bad Company). Hunter left in 1976; members Pete "Overend" Watts, Morgan Fisher and Dale "Buffin" Griffin formed the British Lions.

7/4/70	185	2		1 Mott The Hoople	$15	Atlantic 8258
11/11/72+	89	19		2 All The Young Dudes	$10	Columbia 31750
				produced by David Bowie		
8/25/73	35	29		3 Mott	$10	Columbia 32425
4/27/74	28	23		4 The Hoople	$10	Columbia 32871
6/15/74	112	11		5 Rock And Roll Queen .... [E-K]	$12	Atlantic 7297
11/30/74+	23	13		6 Mott The Hoople Live .... [L]	$10	Columbia 33282
11/1/75	160	5		7 Drive On	$10	Columbia 33705
				MOTT		

After Lights (medley) (2)
Alice (4)
All The Way From Memphis (3,6)
All The Young Dudes (2,6) 37
Apologies (7)
At The Crossroads (1)
Backsliding Fearlessly (1)
Born Late '58 (4)
By Tonight (7)
Crash Street Kidds (4)

Death May Be Your Santa Claus (5)
Drivin' Sister (3)
El Camino Dolo Roso (medley) (3)
Get Back (medley) (6)
Golden Age Of Rock 'N' Roll (4) 96
Great White Wail (7)
Half Moon Bay (1)
Here We Are (7)
Honaloochie Boogie (3)

Hymn For The Dudes (3)
I Can Show You How It Is (7)
I Wish I Was Your Mother (3)
I'll Tell You Something (7)
I'm A Cadillac (medley) (3)
It Takes One To Know One (7)
Jerkin' Crocus (2,6)
Keep A Knockin' (3)
Laugh At Me (1)
Love Now (7)
Marionette (4)

Midnight Lady (5)
Momma's Little Jewel (2)
Monte Carlo (7)
Mottle The Hoople (March 26, 1972 - Zurich), Ballad Of (3)
One Of The Boys (2,6) 96
Pearl 'N' Roy (England) (4)
Rabbit Foot And Toby Time (1)
Ready For Love (medley) (2)
Rest In Peace (6)

Rock And Roll Queen (1,5,6)
Roll Away The Stone (4)
Rose (6)
Sea Diver (2)
She Does It (7)
Soft Ground (2)
Stiff Upper Lip (7)
Sucker (2,6)
Sweet Angeline (6)
Sweet Jane (2)
Through The Looking Glass (4)

Thunderbuck Ram (5)
Trudi's Song (4)
Violence (3,6)
Walkin' With A Mountain (5,6)
Wheel Of The Quivering Meat Conception (5)
Whizz Kid (3)
Whole Lotta Shakin' Goin' On (medley) (6)
Wrath And Wroll (1)
You Really Got Me (1,5)

MOULD, Bob

Minneapolis-based singer/songwriter/guitarist. Former member of Husker Du.

| 5/27/89 | 127 | 14 | | 1 Workbook .... | $8 | Virgin 91240 |
| 9/15/90 | 123 | 10 | | 2 Black Sheets Of Rain .... | $12 | Virgin 91395 |

Black Sheets Of Rain (2)
Brasilia Crossed With Trenton (1)
Compositions For The Young And Old (1)

Disappointed (2)
Dreaming, I Am (1)
Hanging Tree (2)
Hear Me Calling (2)
Heartbreak A Stranger (1)

It's Too Late (2)
Last Night (2)
Let There Be Peace (medley) (2)
Lonely Afternoon (1)

One Good Reason (2)
Out Of Your Life (2)
Poison Years (1)
Sacrifice (medley) (2)
See A Little Light (1)

Sinners And Their Repentances (1)
Stand Guard (2)
Stop Your Crying (2)
Sunspots (1)

Whichever Way The Wind Blows (1)
Wishing Well (1)

MOUNTAIN

New York power-rock group led by Leslie West (b: Leslie Weinstein, 10/22/45, New York City) and Felix Pappalardi (b: 1939, the Bronx; fatally shot on 4/17/83 [age 44] in New York City). Group formed after Pappalardi produced West's solo album *Mountain*. Also see Leslie West and West, Bruce & Laing.

3/14/70	17	39	●	1 Mountain Climbing!	$12	Windfall 4501
2/6/71	16	29	●	2 Nantucket Sleighride	$12	Windfall 5500
12/18/71+	35	16		3 Flowers Of Evil	$12	Windfall 5501
5/13/72	63	18		4 Mountain Live (the road goes ever on) .... [L]	$12	Windfall 5502
2/24/73	72	16	●	5 The Best Of Mountain .... [G]	$10	Columbia 32079
3/9/74	142	8		6 Twin Peaks .... [L]	$12	Columbia 32818 [2]
				recorded live at Osaka, Japan on 8/30/73		
8/10/74	102	9		7 Avalanche	$10	Columbia 33088
4/27/85	166	6		8 Go For Your Life	$8	Scotti Br. 40006

Alisan (7)
Animal Trainer And The Toad (2,5) 76
Babe In The Woods (8)

Back Where I Belong (7)
Bardot Damage (8)
Blood Of The Sun (6)
Boys In The Band (1,5)

Crossroader (3,4,5,6)
Don't Look Around (2,5)
Dreams Of Milk And Honey (medley) (3)

Flowers Of Evil (3)
For Yasgur's Farm (1,5)
Great Train Robbery (2)
Guitar Solo (3,6)

Hard Times (8)
I Love To See You Fly (7)
I Love Young Girls (8)

Imaginary Western, Theme For An (1,5,6)
King's Chorale (3,5)
Laird, The (1)

MOUNTAIN — Cont'd

Last Of The Sunshine Days (7)	My Lady (2)	Satisfaction (7)	Sittin' On A Rainbow (1)	To My Friend (1)	You Better Believe It (7)
Little Bit Of Insanity (8)	Nantucket Sleighride (2,4,5,6)	She Loves Her Rock (And She Loves It Hard) (8)	Spark (8)	Travelin' In The Dark (2)	You Can't Get Away (2)
Long Red (4)	Never In My Life (1,5,6)	Shimmy On The Footlights (8)	Swamp Boy (7)	Variations (medley) (3)	
Makin' It In Your Car (8)	One Last Cold Kiss (3)		Swan Theme (medley) (3)	Waiting To Take You Away (4)	
Mississippi Queen (1,3,5,6) *21*	Pride And Passion (3)	Silver Paper (1,6)	Taunta (Sammy's Tune) (2,5)	Whole Lotta Shakin' Goin' On (7)	
	Roll Over Beethoven (3,5,6)	Sister Justice (7)	Thumbsucker (7)		
			Tired Angels (2)		

MOUSKOURI, Nana
Female songstress, superstar in her native Greece. Born on 10/10/36 in Athens.

4/9/66	124	8		1 An Evening With Belafonte/Mouskouri	$15	RCA 3415

HARRY BELAFONTE/NANA MOUSKOURI

10/5/91	141	6		2 Only Love - The Very Best Of Nana Mouskouri ....[K]	$12	Philips 510229

And I Love You So (2)	Even Now (2)	First Time Ever I Saw Your Face (2)	If You Love Me (2)	Only Love (2)	Train, The [solo: Nana] (1)
Baby Snake [solo: Nana] (1)	Every Time We Say Goodbye (2)	I Have A Dream (2)	Irene (1)	Power Of Love (2)	Why Worry (2)
Both Sides Now (2)		If You Are Thirsty (1)	Love Changes Everything (2)	Time After Time (2)	Your Love, My Love (2)
Dream [solo: Nana] (1)			Love Me Tender (2)	Town Crier [solo: Nana] (1)	

MOUTH & MACNEAL
Dutch duo: Willem Duyn and Maggie Macneal (real name: Sjoukje Van't Spijker).

7/1/72	77	16		How Do You Do?	$12	Philips 700

A.B.C.	I Almost Lost My Mind	Isolation	Remember (Walking In The Sand)	Rosianna
Hey, You Love *87*	I Heard It Through The Grapevine	It Happened Long Ago		Tell Me World
How Do You Do? *8*		Land Of Milk And Honey		Why Did You, Why?

MOUZON, Alphonse
Born on 11/21/48 in Charleston, South Carolina. Singer/pianist/drummer. With Chubby Checker in 1965, Freddie Hubbard and Roy Ayers in 1970, Weather Report in 1971. Also with Les McCann, Roberta Flack and Stevie Wonder. Own recordings from 1971.

12/4/82+	146	11		Distant Lover	$8	Highrise 100

Everybody Party	I Don't Want To Lose This Feeling	Lady In Red	Step Into The Funk	When We Were Young
Get Up And Dance		Saving My Love For You	That's Right	

MOVE, The — see ELECTRIC LIGHT ORCHESTRA

MOVING PICTURES
Australian six-man pop group led by Alex Smith (vocals). Member Garry Frost later formed the group 1927.

12/4/82+	101	16		Days Of Innocence	$8	Network 60202

Angel And The Madman	Joni And The Romeo	Round Again	Streetheart	**What About Me** *29*
Bustin' Loose	Nothing To Do	So Tired	Sweet Cherie	Wings

MOYET, Alison
Born Genevieve Alison-Jane "Alf" Moyet on 6/18/61 in Basildon, Essex, England. Female vocalist of Yaz.

4/6/85	45	25		1 Alf	$8	Columbia 39956
6/20/87	94	17		2 Raindancing	$8	Columbia 40653

All Cried Out (1)	Honey For The Bees (1)	Money Mile (1)	Steal Me Blind (1)	When I Say (No Giveaway) (2)
Blow Wind Blow (2)	**Invisible** (1) *31*	Ordinary Girl (2)	Twisting The Knife (1)	Where Hides Sleep (1)
For You Only (1)	Is This Love? (2)	Sleep Like Breathing (2)	Weak In The Presence Of Beauty (2)	Without You (2)
Glorious Love (2)	**Love Resurrection** (1) *82*	Stay (2)		You Got Me Wrong (2)

MSG — see SCHENKER, Michael, Group

MTUME
Progressive funk band, led by Philadelphian James Mtume (pronounced: EM-too-may), featuring female vocalist Tawatha Agee. Mtume (keyboards/vocals) was a percussionist with Miles Davis in the early '70s.

10/18/80	119	4		1 In Search Of The Rainbow Seekers	$8	Epic 36017
5/28/83	26	22		2 Juicy Fruit	$8	Epic 38588
9/15/84	77	19		3 You, Me And He	$8	Epic 39473
7/5/86	135	8		4 Theater Of The Mind	$8	Epic 40262

Anticipatin' (1)	Deep Freeze (Tree's Thing) Part II (4)	I Don't Believe You Heard Me (A Tribute To James Brown) (4)	P.O.P. Generation (4)	Theater Of The Mind, Theme For (4)	Would You Like To (Fool Around) (2)
Body & Soul (Take Me) (4)	Everything Good To Me (1)		Prime Time (3)	Tie Me Up (3)	You Are My Sunshine (3)
Breathless (4)	Give It On Up (If You Want To) (1)	I Simply Live (4)	Ready For Your Love (2)	To Be Or Not To Bop That Is The Question (Whether We Funk Or Not) (3)	You Can't Wait For Love (1)
C.O.D. (I'll Deliver) (3)	Green Light (2)	I'd Rather Be With You (4)	She's A Rainbow Dancer (1)		**You, Me And He** (3) *83*
Dance Around My Navel (Doesn't Have To Make Sense, Just Cents) (1)	Hip Dip Skippedabeat (2)	**Juicy Fruit** (2) *45*	So You Wanna Be A Star (1)	We're Gonna Make It This Time (1)	Your Love's Too Good (To Spread Around) (2)
Deep Freeze (Rap-A-Song) Part I (4)	Hips (2)	Juicy Fruit Part II (2)	Spirit Of The Dance (1)		
		Mrs. Sippi (1)	Sweet For You And Me (Monogamy Mix) (3)		
		New Face Deli (4)			

MUDHONEY
Seattle rock band: Mark Arm (vocals), Steve Turner, Dan Peters and Matt Lukin.

10/31/92	189	1		Piece Of Cake	$12	Reprise 45090

Acetone	Let Me Let You Down	No End In Sight	Suck You Dry	Thirteenth Floor Opening	Youth Body Expression Explosion
Blinding Sun	Living Wreck	Ritzville	Take Me There	When In Rome	
I'm Spun	Make It Now				

MUHAMMAD, Idris
Born Leo Morris in New Orleans in 1939. Prolific session drummer since early '60s.

6/18/77	127	19		Turn This Mutha Out ....[I]	$8	Kudu 34

4 of 7 tracks are instrumental, the rest feature guest vocalists

Camby Bolongo	**Could Heaven Ever Be Like This (Part 1)** *76*	Crab Apple	Say What	Turn This Mutha Out
		Moon Hymn	Tasty Cakes	

MULDAUR, Maria
Born Maria D'Amato on 9/12/43 in New York City. Member of Jim Kweskin's Jug Band with former husband Geoff Muldaur (divorced in 1972). Maria later became an Inspirational recording artist.

9/22/73+	3	56	●	1 Maria Muldaur	$10	Reprise 2148
11/9/74+	23	26		2 Waitress In The Donut Shop	$10	Reprise 2194

DEBUT DATE	PEAK POS	WKS CHR	GOLD	ARTIST — Album Title	$	Label & Number

MULDAUR, Maria — Cont'd

| 3/13/76 | 53 | 12 | | 3 Sweet Harmony | $8 | Reprise 2235 |
| 4/8/78 | 143 | 5 | | 4 Southern Winds | $8 | Warner 3162 |

Any Old Time (1)
As An Eagle Stirreth In Her Nest (3)
Back By Fall (3)
Brickyard Blues (2)
Cajun Moon (4)
Cool River (2)
Don't You Make Me High (1)
Gringo En Mexico (2)

Here Is Where Your Love Belongs (4)
Honey Babe Blues (3)
I Can't Say No (4)
I Can't Stand It (3)
I Got A Man (4)
I Never Did Sing You A Love Song (1)
I'll Keep My Light In My Window (4)

I'm A Woman (2) 12
If You Haven't Any Hay (2)
It Ain't The Meat It's The Motion (2)
Jon The Generator (3)
Joyful Noise (4)
Long Hard Climb (1)
Lying Song (3)
Mad Mad Me (1)
Make Love To The Music (4)

Midnight At The Oasis (1) 6
My Sisters And Brothers (4)
My Tennessee Mountain Home (1)
Oh Papa (2)
Rockin' Chair (3)
Sad Eyes (3)
Say You Will (4)
Squeeze Me (2)
Sweet Harmony (3)

Sweetheart (2)
That's The Way Love Is (4)
Three Dollar Bill (2)
Travelin' Shoes (2)
Vaudeville Man (1)
Walkin' One & Only (1)
We Just Couldn't Say Goodbye (3)
Wild Bird (3)
Work Song (1)

MULL, Martin

Born in Chicago on 8/18/43. Comedian/TV-film actor. Acted in films *Mr. Mom*, *FM*, *Clue* and others.

| 3/26/77 | 184 | 2 | | 1 I'm Everyone I've Ever Loved | [C] $8 | ABC 997 |
| 6/17/78 | 157 | 3 | | 2 Sex & Violins | [C] $8 | ABC 1064 |

Artist Relations (Or Don't Write Me At Home) (1)
Best Of You (2)
Birds Gotta Swim (Vinyl World, Pt. I) (2)
Bombed Anyway (1)
Boogie Man (1)
Buy Me A Drink (1)
Cleveland (Revisited) (2)

Dogs (2)
Get Up, Get Down (1)
Goodnight (2)
Half Hour Of Heaven (And Eight Hours Of Sleep) (2)
Honor Roll (1)
Humming Song (1)
I Haven't Got The Vegas Idea (2)

I'll Do The Samba (2)
I'm Everyone I've Ever Loved (1)
It's Downtime, Folks (1)
It's Folktime, Folks (1)
It's Meantime, Folks (1)
It's Showtime, Folks (1)
Martin Goes And Does Where It's At (1)

Martin Reveals Where He's At (1)
Martin Touches The President's Very Desk (1)
Men (1)
Michelle (1)
Mother-in-law Song (1)
Now Martin Suggests Where He's At (1)

Playtentype Shows Martin Where It's At (1)
They Never Met (1)
Trailer Waltz (2)
Truth, The (1)
Vinyl World, Pt. II (2)
Westward Ho! (2)

MULLIGAN('S), Gerry, Jazz Combo

Born on 4/6/27 in New York City. West Coast-based jazz baritone saxophonist. Teamed with trumpeter Chet Baker in 1951. Combo included Shelly Manne (drums), Art Farmer (trumpet), Bud Shank (sax), Frank Rosolino (trombone), Pete Jolly (piano) and Red Mitchell (bass).

| 5/25/59 | 39 | 10 | | I Want To Live! | [S-I] $20 | United Art. 5006 |

arranged and composed by Johnny Mandel

Barbara's Theme

Black Nightgown

Frisco Club

I Want To Live, Theme From

Life's A Funny Thing

Night Watch

MUNCH, Charles — see BOSTON SYMPHONY ORCHESTRA

MUNGO JERRY

British skiffle quartet: Ray Dorset (lead vocals), Colin Earl, Paul King and Mike Cole.

| 9/12/70 | 64 | 11 | | Mungo Jerry | $15 | Janus 7000 |

Baby Let's Play House
In The Summertime 3

Johnny B. Badde
Maggie

Mother *!*!*! Boogie
Movin' On

My Friend
Peace In The Country

Sad Eyed Joe
San Francisco Bay Blues

See Me
Tramp

MUNICH MACHINE

A Giorgio Moroder/Pete Bellotte electronic disco production.

| 7/1/78 | 190 | 3 | | A Whiter Shade Of Pale | $8 | Casablanca 7090 |

featuring vocals by Chris Bennett

In Love With Love

It's All Wrong (But It's Alright)

It's For You
La Nuit Blanche

Love Fever
Whiter Shade Of Pale

MUPPETS — see CHILDRENS section

MURAD, Jerry — see HARMONICATS

MURDOCK, Shirley

Former gospel singer from Toledo. Discovered by Roger Troutman (aka Roger) who hired her as backup singer for his family funk group, Zapp.

| 2/14/87 | 44 | 26 | ● | 1 Shirley Murdock! | $8 | Elektra 60443 |
| 7/23/88 | 137 | 15 | | 2 A Woman's Point Of View | $8 | Elektra 60791 |

produced by Roger Troutman (Zapp)

And I Am Telling You I'm Not Going (2)
As We Lay (1) 23
Be Free (1)

Danger Zone (1)
(Everybody Wants) Somethin' For Nothin' (2)
Found My Way (2)

Go On Without You (1)
Husband (2)
I Still Love You (2)
If I Know (2)

Instrument Of Praise (2)
Modern Girl (2)
No More (1)
Oh What A Feeling (2)

One I Need (1)
Spend My Whole Life (2)
Teaser (2)
Tribute (1)

Truth Or Dare (1)
Woman's Point Of View (2)

MURPHEY, Michael

Born Michael Martin Murphey in Dallas. Progressive country singer/songwriter. Toured as Travis Lewis of The Lewis & Clarke Expedition in 1967. Worked as a staff writer for Screen Gems. Lived in Austin from 1971-74; Colorado from 1974-79. Based in Taos, New Mexico since 1979.

9/23/72	160	9		1 Geronimo's Cadillac	$10	A&M 4358
6/16/73	196	2		2 Cosmic Cowboy Souvenir	$10	A&M 4388
2/22/75	18	38	●	3 Blue Sky-Night Thunder	$10	Epic 33290
12/6/75+	44	13		4 Swans Against The Sun	$10	Epic 33851
11/20/76	130	5		5 Flowing Free Forever	$10	Epic 34220
4/1/78	99	6		6 Lonewolf	$8	Epic 35013

MICHAEL MARTIN MURPHEY:

| 9/4/82 | 69 | 16 | | 7 Michael Martin Murphey | $8 | Liberty 51120 |
| 10/29/83 | 187 | 3 | | 8 The Heart Never Lies | $8 | Liberty 51150 |

with guests Charlie Daniels, John Denver and Willie Nelson

Alleys Of Austin (2)
Arrows In The Darkness (6)
Backslider's Wine (1)
Blessing In Disguise (2)
Blue Sky Riding Song (3)
Boy From The Country (1)
Buffalo Gun (4)

Calico Silver (2)
Carolina In The Pines (3) 21
Changing Woman (5)
Cherokee Fiddle (5)
Cosmic Cowboy (Part One) (2)

Crack In Las Cruces (1)
Crazy Blue (8)
Crystal (7)
Dancing In The Meadow (4)
Desert Rat (3)
Disenchanted (8)

Don't Count The Rainy Days (8)
Drunken Lady Of The Morning (2)
First Taste Of Freedom (7)
Flowing Free Forever (5)
Geronimo's Cadillac (1) 37

Goodbye Money Mountain (8)
Harbor For My Soul (1)
Hard To Live Together (6)
Heart Never Lies (8)
Hearts In The Right Places (7)
High Country Caravan (aka Song For Stephen Stills) (5)

Honolulu (2)
Lights Of The City (1)
Loners (6)
Lost River (7)
Love Affairs (7)
Loving Time (6)
Mansion On The Hill (4)

DEBUT DATE	PEAK POS	WKS CHR	GOLD	ARTIST — Album Title	$	Label & Number

MURPHEY, Michael — Cont'd

Maybe This Time (8)
Medicine Man (3)
Michael Angelo's Blues (Song For Hogman) (1)
Natchez Trace (1)
Natural Bridges (4)
Night Patrol (6)
Night Thunder (3)
No Man's Land (6)

North Wind And A New Moon (5)
Nothing Is Your Own (6)
Our Lady Of Santa Fe (5)
Paradise Tonight (6)
Pink Lady (4)
Prometheus Busted (2)
Radio Land (8)
Rainbow Man (1)
Renegade (4) *39*

Rhythm Of The Road (4)
Ring Of Truth (7)
Rings Of Life (3)
Rolling Hills (2)
Running Wide Open (5)
Sacred Heart (8)
Seasons Change (4)
Secret Mountain Hideout (3)
See How All The Horses Come Dancing (5)

Showdown (8)
Song Dog (6)
South Canadian River Song (2)
Still Taking Chances (7) *76*
Swans Against The Sun (4)
Take It Like A Man (7)
Temperature Train (2)
Temple Of The Sun (4)
Two-Step Is Easy (7)

Waking Up (1)
Wandering Minstrel (5)
What Am I Doin' Hangin' Around? (1)
What's Forever For (7) *19*
Wild Bird (3)
Wild West Show (4)
Wildfire (3) *3*
Will It Be Love By Morning (8)

Without My Lady There (3)
Yellow House (5)

MURPHY, Eddie

Born on 4/3/61 in Hempstead, New York. Comedian/actor. Former cast member of TV's *Saturday Night Live*. Starred in the films *Beverly Hills Cop (I & II)*, *Trading Places*, *48 Hrs.*, *Coming To America*, *Boomerang* and many others.

8/14/82	52	53	▲	1 Eddie Murphy .... [C]	$8	Columbia 38180
11/19/83+	35	44	▲	2 Eddie Murphy: Comedian .... [C]	$8	Columbia 39005
10/12/85+	26	26		3 How Could It Be	$8	Columbia 39952
8/26/89	70	9		4 So Happy	$8	Columbia 40970

Barbecue, The (2)
Black Movie Theaters (1)
Boogie In Your Butt (1)
Bubble Hill (4)
Buckwheat (1)
C-o-n Confused (3)
Christmas Gifts (1)
Do I (3)

Doo-Doo (1)
Drinking Fathers (1)
Effrom (1)
Enough Is Enough (1)
Everything's Coming Up Roses (3)
Faggots (1)
Faggots Revisited (2)

Fart Game (2)
Hit By A Car (1)
How Could It Be (3)
I Got It (4)
I, Me, Us, We (3)
I Wish (I Could Tell You When) (1)
Ice Cream Man (2)

Languages (2)
Let's Get With It (4)
Little Chinese (1)
Love Moans (4)
Modern Women (2)
My God Is Color Blind (3)
Myths (1)
Party All The Time (3) *2*

Politics (2)
Pope And Ronald Reagan (1)
Pretty Please (4)
Put Your Mouth On Me (4) *27*
Racism (2)
Sexual Crime (2)
Shoe Throwin' Mothers (2)

Singers (2)
So Happy (4)
TV (2)
Talking Cars (1)
Till The Money's Gone (4)
Tonight (4)
With All I Know (4)

MURPHY, Peter

Singer/songwriter. Former leader of British post-punk cult quartet Bauhaus; the other three members later formed Love And Rockets.

5/14/88	135	19		1 Love Hysteria	$8	Begr. B. 7634
2/3/90	44	22		2 Deep	$12	Begr. B. 9877
5/2/92	108	3		3 Holy Smoke	$12	Begr. B. 66007

All Night Long (1)
Blind Sublime (1)
Crystal Wrists (2)
Cuts You Up (2) *55*
Deep Ocean Vast Sea (2)
Dragnet Drag (1)

Dream Gone By (3)
Funtime (1)
His Circle And Hers Meet (1)
Hit Song (3)
Indigo Eyes (1)
Keep Me From Harm (3)

Kill The Hate (3)
Let Me Love You (3)
Line Between The Devil's Teeth (And That Which Cannot Be Repeat) (2)
Low Room (3)

Marlene Dietrich's Favorite Poem (2)
My Last Two Weeks (1)
Our Secret Garden (3)
Roll Call (2)
Seven Veils (2)

Shy (3)
Socrates The Python (1)
Strange Kind Of Love (2)
Sweetest Drop (4)
Time Has Got Nothing To Do With It (1)

You're So Close (3)

MURPHY, Walter

Born in 1952 in New York City. Studied classical and jazz piano at Manhattan School of Music. Former arranger for Doc Severinsen and *The Tonight Show* orchestra.

9/4/76	15	29	●	1 A Fifth Of Beethoven	$8	Private St. 2015
				THE WALTER MURPHY BAND		
7/16/77	175	3		2 Rhapsody In Blue	$8	Private St. 2028

California Strut (1)
Could It Be The Music (2)
Fifth Of Beethoven (1) *1*
Flight '76 (1) *44*

Get A Little Lovin' (1)
It Ain't Necessarily So (2)
Just A Love Song (1)
Love Eyes (2)

Midnight Express (1)
New York City Suite Medley (2)
Night Fall (1)

Only Two People In The World (2)
Rhapsody In Blue (2)
Russian Dressing (1)

Suite Love Symphony (1)
Sunflower (2)
You Are On My Mind (2)

(You've Got To) Be Your Own Best Friend (1)

★★81★★ MURRAY, Anne

Born Morna Anne Murray on 6/20/45 in Springhill, Nova Scotia. High school teacher for one year after college. With CBC-TV show *Sing Along Jubilee*. First recorded for ARC in 1969. Regular on Glen Campbell's *Goodtime Hour* TV series. Currently resides in Toronto.

10/3/70	41	31	●	1 Snowbird	$10	Capitol 579
4/3/71	121	9		2 Anne Murray	$10	Capitol 667
10/9/71	179	4		3 Talk It Over In The Morning	$10	Capitol 821
12/11/71+	128	8		4 Anne Murray/Glen Campbell.......................	$12	Capitol 869
				ANNE MURRAY/GLEN CAMPBELL		
5/20/72	143	8		5 Annie	$10	Capitol 11024
4/28/73	39	24		6 Danny's Song	$10	Capitol 11172
3/9/74	24	33		7 Love Song	$10	Capitol 11266
8/31/74	32	16	●	8 Country .... [K]	$10	Capitol 11324
12/14/74+	70	13		9 Highly Prized Possession	$10	Capitol 11354
12/6/75+	142	11		10 Together	$10	Capitol 11433
10/2/76	96	6		11 Keeping In Touch	$10	Capitol 11559
3/4/78	12	52	▲	12 Let's Keep It That Way	$8	Capitol 11743
2/17/79	23	29	▲	13 New Kind Of Feeling	$8	Capitol 11849
11/3/79+	24	23	●	14 I'll Always Love You	$8	Capitol 12012
2/9/80	73	9		15 A Country Collection .... [K]	$8	Capitol 12039
5/3/80	88	15		16 Somebody's Waiting	$8	Capitol 12064
10/4/80	16	64	▲⁴	17 Anne Murray's Greatest Hits .... [G]	$8	Capitol 12110
5/2/81	55	15	●	18 Where Do You Go When You Dream	$8	Capitol 12144
11/28/81+	54	8	▲²	19 Christmas Wishes............................... [X]	$8	Capitol 16232
				Christmas charts: 4/'83, 6/'84, 21/'88, 20/'91, 19/'92		
8/28/82	90	12		20 The Hottest Night Of The Year	$8	Capitol 12225
10/15/83+	72	24		21 A Little Good News	$8	Capitol 12301
10/27/84	92	25	●	22 Heart Over Mind	$8	Capitol 12363
2/15/86	68	23	●	23 Something To Talk About........................	$8	Capitol 12466
6/20/87	149	6		24 Harmony	$8	Capitol 12562

MURRAY, Anne — Cont'd

Ain't No Way To Rise Above (Fallin' In Love) (20)
Another Pot O' Tea (7)
Another Sleepless Night (18) **44**
Anyone Can Do The Heartbreak (24)
Are You Still In Love With Me (24)
Away In A Manger (19)
Backstreet Lovin' (7)
Beautiful (5)
Beginning To Feel Like Home (16)
Bitter They Are, Harder They Fall (18)
Blessed Are The Believers (18) **34**
Blue-Finger Lou (10)
Break My Mind (1,8)
Bring Back The Love (3,4)
Broken Hearted Me (14,17) **12**
Call, The (10) **91**
Call Me With The News (18)
Call Us Fools (23)
Canadian Sunset (4)
Caress Me Pretty Music (11)
Carolina Sun (11)
Child Of Mine (2)
Children Of My Mind (7)
Christmas Wishes (19)
Come On Love (21)
Come To Me (21)
Cotton Jenny (3,8) **71**
Could I Have This Dance (17) **33**
Dancin' All Night Long (11)
Danny's Song (6,8,17) **7**
Day Tripper (9) **59**
Daydream Believer (14,17) **12**
Days Of The Looking Glass (2)
Destiny (3)
Do You Think Of Me? (15,16)
Dream Lover (9)

Drown Me (5)
Ease Your Pain (4,6)
Easy Does It (20)
Easy Love (14)
Everything Has Got To Be Free (5)
Everything Old Is New Again (10)
Everything's Been Changed (5)
Fallin' In Love (Fallin' Apart) (20)
Falling Into Rhyme (5)
Fire And Rain (1)
For No Reason At All (13,15)
French Waltz (16)
Get Together (1)
Give Me Your Love (24)
Go Tell It On The Mountain (19)
Golden Oldie (11)
Good Old Song (14)
Gotcha (23)
Great Divide (24)
Harmony (24)
(He Can't Help It It) He's Not You (13,15)
He Thinks I Still Care (6,8)
Heart On The Line (20)
Heart Stealer (21)
Heartaches (23)
Heaven Is Here (13,15)
Hey! Baby! (20)
Highly Prized Possession (9)
Hold Me Tight (12)
Hottest Night Of The Year (20)
I Don't Think I'm Ready For You (22)
I Just Fall In Love Again (13,17) **12**
I Know (3,6)
I Like Your Music (5)
I Say A Little Prayer/By The Time I Get To Phoenix (4) **81**
I Should Know By Now (22)

I Still Wish The Very Best For You (12)
I'll Always Love You (14)
I'll Be Home (6)
I'll Be Home For Christmas (19)
I'll Be Your Baby Tonight (1)
I'll Never Fall In Love Again (2)
I'm Happy Just To Dance With You (16) **64**
I'm Not Afraid Anymore (21)
If A Heart Must Be Broken (18)
If It's Alright With You (10)
It Happens All The Time (24)
It Should Have Been Easy (18)
It Takes Time (2)
It's All I Can Do (18) **53**
Joy To The World (19)
Just Another Woman In Love (21)
Just Bidin' My Time (1,8)
Just One Look (7) **86**
Just To Feel This Love From You (12,15)
Killing Me Softly With His Song (6)
Lady Bug (10)
Lay Me Down (Roll Me Out To Sea) (11)
Let Me Be The One (3,4)
Let Sunshine Have Its Day (6)
Let Your Heart Do The Talking (22)
Let's Keep It That Way (12,15)
Lift Your Hearts To The Sun (8)
Little Drummer Boy (19)
Little Good News (21) **74**
Love Song (7,17) **12**
Love Story (You & Me) (4)
Love You Out Of Your Mind (22)

Lover's Knot (14)
Lucky Me (16) **42**
Lullaby (20)
Million More (11)
Moon Over Brooklyn (16)
More We Try (21)
Most Of All (3)
Musical Friends (1)
My Ecstasy (4)
My Life's A Dance (23)
Natural Love (24)
Nevertheless (I'm In Love With You) (16)
Night Owl (3)
Nobody Loves Me Like You Do (22)
Now And Forever (You And Me) (23) **92**
O Holy Night (19)
On And On (23)
Once You've Had It (22)
One Day I Walk (2,6)
Only Love (18)
Our Love (22)
Out On The Road Again (10)
Part-Time Love (10)
People's Park (2)
Perfect Strangers (24)
Player In The Band (10)
Please Don't Sell Nova Scotia (9)
Please Smile (3)
Put Your Hand In The Hand (1,6,8)
Rain (1)
Rainin' In My Heart (13)
Reach For Me (23)
Real Emotion (17)
Robbie's Song For Jesus (5)
Running (1)
Saved By The Grace Of Your Love (9)
Send A Little Love My Way (7) **72**
Sentimental Favorite (21)
Shadows In The Moonlight (13,17) **25**

Shine (11)
Silent Night (19)
Silver Bells (19)
Sing High - Sing Low (2) **83**
Slow Fall (9)
Snowbird (1,8,17) **8**
Somebody's Always Saying Goodbye (20)
Somebody's Waiting (16)
Son Of A Rotten Gambler (7,8)
Song For The Mira (23)
Stranger At My Door (14)
Stranger In My Place (2,8)
Sunday School To Broadway (11)
Sunday Sunrise (10) **98**
Sweet Music Man (11)
Sycamore Slick (2)
Take Good Care Of My Heart (22)
Take This Heart (13)
Talk It Over In The Morning (3) **57**
Tennessee Waltz (12,15)
That'll Keep Me Dreamin' (20)
That's Not The Way (It's S'posed To Be) (21)
That's Why I Love You (13)
There's Always A Goodbye (12)
They Don't Call It Magic For Nothing (20)
Things (11) **89**
Time Don't Run Out On Me (22)
Together (10)
Tonight (I Want To Be In Love) (24)
United We Stand (4)
Uproar (9)
Walk Right Back (12,15)
Watching The River Run (7)
We All Pull The Load (4)
We Don't Have To Hold Out (18)

We Don't Make Love Anymore (12,15)
What's Forever For (16)
What About Me (6,8) **64**
When I Can't Have You (21)
When We Both Had The Time To Love (9)
When You're Gone (23)
Where Do You Go When You Dream (18)
Who's Leaving Who (23)
Why Don't You Stick Around (14)
Winter Wonderland (19)
Wintery Feeling (14,15)
Wishing Smiles Made It All True (2)
Without You (24)
You Can't Go Back (5)
You Can't Have A Hand On Me (5)
You Haven't Heard The Last Of Me (22)
You Made My Life A Song (5)
You Needed Me (12,17) **1**
You Never Know (23)
You Set My Dreams To Music (16)
You Won't See Me (7,17) **8**
You're A Part Of Me (12)
You're Easy To Love (4)
You've Got A Friend (5)
You've Got Me To Hold On To (14)
You've Got What It Takes (13)
Yucatan Cafe (13)

MURRAY THE "K" — see VARIOUS - Radio/TV Celebrity Compilations

MUSCLE SHOALS HORNS
Studio band from Muscle Shoals, Alabama.

| 7/4/76 | 154 | 8 | | Born To Get Down .... | $10 | Bang 403 |

Born To Get Down (Born To Mess Around)
Break Down
Bump De Bump Yo Boodie
Get It Up
Give It To Me
Hustle To The Music
Open Up Your Heart
Where I'm Coming From
Who's Gonna Love You

MUSICAL YOUTH
Five schoolboys (ages 11 to 16 in 1983) from Birmingham, England: Dennis Seaton (lead), with brothers Kelvin (guitar) & Michael (keyboards) Grant, and Patrick (bass) & Junior (drums) Waite.

| 1/8/83 | 23 | 22 | 1 | The Youth Of Today .... | $8 | MCA 5389 |
| 12/17/83+ | 144 | 12 | 2 | Different Style! .... | $8 | MCA 5454 |

Air Taxi (2)
Blind Boy (1)
Children Of Zion (1)
Heartbreaker (1)
Incommunicado (2)
Mash It The Youth Man, Mash It (2)
Mirror Mirror (1)
Never Gonna Give You Up (1)
No Strings (2)
Pass The Dutchie (1) **10**
Rockers (1)
Schoolgirl (1)
Shanty Town (007) (2)
She's Trouble (2) **65**
Sixteen (2)
Tell Me Why (2)
Whatcha Talking 'Bout (2)
Yard Stylee (2)
Young Generation (1)
Youth Of Today (1)

MUSIC EXPLOSION, The
Jamie Lyons, lead singer of quintet from Mansfield, Ohio. Produced by Jerry Kasenetz and Jeff Katz.

| 8/26/67 | 178 | 2 | | Little Bit O' Soul .... | $25 | Laurie 2040 |

Everybody
Good Time Feeling (Hey) La, La, La
I Can't Stop Now
I See The Light
Let Yourself Go
Little Bit O'Soul 2
Love, Love, Love, Love, Love
96 Tears
One Potato Two
Patches Dawn
What Did I Do To Deserve Such A Fate

MUSIC MACHINE, The
Los Angeles rock quintet — Sean Bonniwell, lead singer/songwriter.

| 1/21/67 | 76 | 16 | | (Turn On) The Music Machine .... | $35 | Original Snd. 5015 |

Cherry Cherry
Come On In
Hey Joe
Masculine Intuition
96 Tears
People In Me 66
See See Rider
Some Other Drum
Talk Talk 15
Taxman
Trouble
Wrong

MUSIQUE
Disco trio: Christine Wiltshire, Gina Tharps and Mary Seymour.

| 9/30/78 | 62 | 17 | | Keep On Jumpin' .... | $8 | Prelude 12158 |

In The Bush 58
Keep On Jumpin'
Summer Love
Summer Love Theme

MYERS, Alicia
Former lead singer of One Way.

| 12/8/84 | 186 | 5 | | I Appreciate .... | $8 | MCA 5485 |

Appreciation
Don't Do Me This Way
Just Can't Stay Away
Just Praying
My Guy
Say That
You Get The Best From Me (Say, Say, Say)

DEBUT DATE	PEAK POS	WKS CHR	GOLD	ARTIST — Album Title	$	Label & Number

MYLES, Alannah
Rock singer born in Toronto and raised in Buckhorn, Canada.

1/13/90	5	36 ▲		Alannah Myles	$12	Atlantic 81956

Black Velvet 1
Hurry Make Love

If You Want To
Just One Kiss

Kick Start My Heart
Love Is 36

Lover Of Mine
Rock This Joint

Still Got This Thing
Who Loves You

MYRICK, Gary
Texan guitarist; joined British group Havana 3 A.M. in 1991.

8/6/83	186	3		Language .... [M]	$8	Epic 38637

Glamorous

Guitar, Talk, Love & Drums

Lost In Clubland

Message Is You

Time To Win

MYSTIC MOODS, The
Hollywood studio orchestra produced by Brad Miller.

4/30/66	63	14		1 One Stormy Night .... [I]	$8	Philips 205
10/8/66	110	10		2 Nighttide .... [I]	$8	Philips 213
3/25/67	157	4		3 More Than Music .... [I]	$8	Philips 231
11/25/67	164	3		4 Mexican Trip .... [I]	$8	Philips 250
2/24/68	182	4		5 The Mystic Moods Of Love .... [I]	$8	Philips 260
11/9/68	194	3		6 Emotions .... [I]	$8	Philips 277
5/3/69	155	9		7 Extensions .... [I]	$8	Philips 301
11/22/69+	165	8		8 Love Token .... [I]	$8	Philips 321
5/23/70	165	15		9 Stormy Weekend .... [I]	$8	Philips 342
11/28/70+	174	9		10 English Muffins .... [I]	$8	Philips 349
4/29/72	184	3		11 Love The One You're With .... [I]	$8	Warner 2577
5/5/73	190	4		12 Awakening .... [I]	$8	Warner 2690

Aja Toro (1)
And The Sun Will Shine (8)
Another Dawn (With You) (11)
Autumn Leaves (1)
Awakening, The (12)
Born Free (3)
Both Sides Now (8)
California Dreamin' (7)
Can't Take My Eyes Off You (5)
Carry That Weight (medley) (10)
Cielito Lindo (4)
Cloudy (6)
Colour Of My Love (10)
Come Saturday Morning (9)
Cosmic Sea (12) 83
Daphne's Theme (2)
Days Of Wine And Roses (2)
Do You Know The Way To San Jose (6)
Don't Remind Me Now Of Time (8)
Dream (1)
Early In The Morning (10)
Early Mornin' Rain (6)
Eleanor Rigby (6)

England Swings (10)
Far From The Madding Crowd (5)
Fire Island (1)
First Day Of Forever (12)
First Of May (10)
Four Square City Medley (12) 4:22 A.M. (9)
Friendly Persuasion (Thee I Love) (5)
Gay Ranchero (4)
Glory Of Love (5)
Golden Slumbers (medley) (10)
Good Feelings (11)
Grand Prix, Theme From (3)
Here There And Everywhere (10)
Holly On My Mind (8)
Homeward Bound (6)
Hot Bagel (1)
How Do I Love You (11)
Hurt So Bad (8)
I Am, It Is (12)
I Can't Get Away From You (9)
If You Go Away (9)
If You Must Leave My Life (7)

In Your Arms (1)
Invitation (2)
Jim Webb Collage Medley (8)
Just 'Round The River Bend (3)
La Golondrina (4)
La Virgena De La Macarena (4)
Lalena (7)
Lara's Theme (Somewhere My Love) (2)
Las Chiapanecas (4)
Last Thing On My Mind (7)
Lay Lady Lay (11)
Listen To The Warm (6)
Live For Life (5)
Living Is Giving (11)
Local Freight (1)
Look Of Love (5)
Love (11)
Love Grows (Where My Rosemary Goes) (10)
Love Is Blue (9)
Love The One You're With (11)
Love Token (8)
Lovers Lullaby (9)
Malaguena Salerosa (4)

Maman (6)
Man And A Woman (3)
Maria Elena (4)
Massachusetts (10)
Mexican Hat Dance And Soliloquy (4)
Minstrel Boy (1)
Moments Ago (medley) (7)
Monday, Monday (9)
Moon River (2)
Moonlight (5)
My Own True Love (2)
Ne Dis Rien (Say No More) (9)
Nevada Smith (2)
New Testament, Theme From (3)
Norwegian Wood (7)
Nothing On My Mind (medley) (7)
One Stormy Night (1)
Paris Smiles (3)
Paul Simon Montage Medley (7)
Puerte De Manzanillo (4)
Queretaro-Tula Fast Freight (4)
Rhapsody, Love Theme From A (5)

Romeo & Juliet (8)
Sand Pebbles, Theme From The (3)
Sayonara (1)
Scarborough Fair/Canticle (medley) (6)
Sensuous Woman (11)
Seventh Plane (12)
Shane (2)
Shoes Of The Fisherman, Theme From (7)
Singin' In The Rain (2)
Soldier In The Rain (6)
Something (10)
Somewhere, My Love ..see: Lara's Theme
Sound Of Silence (medley) (6)
Stormy Weekend, Theme From (9)
Stragglers & Newcomers (12)
Strangers In The Night (2)
Summer Place, Theme From A (2)
Summertime (2)
Sunny Googe Street (6)
Sunshower (8)
Sweet Rollin' (11)
Symphony (3)

There's A Good Earth Out Tonight (7)
Ti-Pi-Tin (4)
Ticket To Ride (10)
Traces (8)
Trains, Boats & Planes (6)
Tristan And Isolde, Love Theme From (5)
Universal Mind (12)
Very Precious Love (5)
Visions (9)
Waltz For Tricia (9)
Warm Lovin' (11)
Webb Of Jim Collage Medley (7)
Wednesdays' Child (3)
When You Are There (3)
Words (10)

N

★★416★★ NABORS, Jim
Born on 6/12/32 in Sylacauga, Alabama. Gomer Pyle on TV's *Andy Griffith Show* (1963-64) and *Gomer Pyle-U.S.M.C.* (1964-69). Own TV variety series *The Jim Nabors Hour* (1969-71).

10/15/66	24	56 ●		1 Jim Nabors Sings Love Me With All Your Heart	$15	Columbia 9358
5/20/67	50	40		2 Jim Nabors By Request	$15	Columbia 9465
9/16/67	147	6		3 The Things I Love	$15	Columbia 9503
				adaptations of classical music		
7/13/68	153	26		4 Kiss Me Goodbye	$15	Columbia 9620
11/16/68	173	12 ●		5 The Lord's Prayer And Other Sacred Songs	$15	Columbia 9716
6/14/69+	145	19		6 Galveston	$15	Columbia 9817
6/27/70	34	23		7 The Jim Nabors Hour	$15	Columbia 1020
9/5/70	124	26		8 Everything Is Beautiful	$15	Columbia 30129
3/27/71	75	13		9 For The Good Times/The Jim Nabors Hour .... [L]	$15	Columbia 30449
7/24/71	122	10		10 Help Me Make It Through The Night	$15	Columbia 30810
10/23/71	136	4		11 How Great Thou Art	$15	Columbia 30671
6/17/72	157	8		12 The Way Of Love	$15	Columbia 31336

Abide With Me (11)
Almost Persuaded (10)
Amazing Grace (5)
And This Is My Beloved (3)

Anytime (9)
(At) The End (Of A Rainbow) (12)
Ave Maria (5,11)

Battle Hymn Of The Republic (5)
Blessed Assurance (11)
Born Free (4)

Bridge Over Troubled Water (8)
By The Time I Get To Phoenix (4)

Cabaret (2)
(Cuando Calienta El Sol) ..see: Love Me With All Your Heart

Cycles (6)
Day In The Life Of A Fool (7)
Detroit City (9)
Didn't We (6)

NABORS, Jim — Cont'd

Dr. Zhivago ..see: Somewhere, My Love
Don't You Know (3)
Everything Is Beautiful (8)
First Time Ever (I Saw Your Face) (12)
For Once In My Life (6)
For The Good Times (9)
Full Moon And Empty Arms (3)
Galveston (6)
Games People Play (7)
God Be With You (11)
God Is Love (11)
Godfather (Speak Softly Love), Love Theme From The (12)
Green Green Grass Of Home (6)
Hasta Luego (2)
Have A Little Faith (10)
Have I Stayed Away Too Long (10)
Help Me Make It Through The Night (10)
Hi-Lili, Hi-Lo (8)
Holy City (5)
Holy, Holy, Holy (5)

Honey (I Miss You) (4)
How Great Thou Art (11)
I Can't Help It (If I'm Still In Love With You) (7)
I Can't Stop Loving You (8)
I Love Paris (9)
I Must Have Been Out Of My Mind (4)
I Really Don't Want To Know (7)
I Walk With God (11)
I Will Wait For You (4)
I Won't Mention It Again (10)
I'd Like To Teach The World To Sing (In Perfect Harmony) (12)
I'll Begin Again (9)
I'm Yours (1)
I've Gotta Be Me (6)
If I Never Laugh Again (8)
Impossible Dream (1)
In The Garden (5)
In The Sweet Bye And Bye (11)
It Hurts To Say Goodbye (2)
It's Impossible (12)
It's My Life (7)
Jean (7)

Just A Closer Walk With Thee (5)
Kiss Me Goodbye (4)
Lamp Is Low (3)
Lara's Theme ..see: Somewhere, My Love
Les Bicyclettes De Belsize (6)
Little Green Apples (6)
Living In A House Divided (12)
Lord's Prayer (5)
Louisiana Lady (9)
Love Is Blue (4)
Love Me With All Your Heart (1)
Love Story, Theme From ..see: (Where Do I Begin)
Make The World Go Away (10)
Mama, A Rainbow (8)
Mame (2)
More (2)
My Cup Runneth Over (2)
My Elusive Dreams (10)
My Reverie (3)
My Rosary (11)
My Woman, My Woman, My Wife (10)

Old Rugged Cross (5)
On A Clear Day You Can See Forever (1)
Our Love (3)
Panis Angelicus (O Lord Most Holy) (5)
Release Me (9)
Rock-A-Bye Your Baby With A Dixie Melody (1)
Rock Of Ages (5)
Romeo & Juliet, Love Theme From ..see: Time For Us
Rose Garden (10)
San Francisco (7)
Softly And Tenderly (11)
Something (9)
Somewhere, My Love (1)
Story Of A Starry Night (3)
Stranger In Paradise (3)
Strangers In The Night (1)
Summer Of '42 (The Summer Knows), Theme From (12)
Sunrise, Sunset (2)
Swanee (1)
Sweetheart Tree (8)
Take My Hand, Precious Lord (7)

Tennessee Waltz (10)
There Goes My Everything (10)
There's A Kind Of Hush (All Over The World) (4)
Things I Love (3)
This Is My Song (2)
Thomas Crown Affair, Theme From ..see: Windmills Of Your Mind
Till The End Of Time (3)
Time After Time (2)
Time For Us (Love Theme From Romeo And Juliet) (8)
To Give (4)
Tomorrow Never Comes (4,7)
Try To Remember (4)
Turn Around Look At Me (6)
Until It's Time For You To Go (9)
Way Of Love (12)
What A Friend We Have In Jesus (5)
What Now My Love (1)
When The Roll Is Called Up Yonder (11)
(Where Do I Begin) Love Story (12)

Wichita Lineman (6)
Windmills Of Your Mind (8)
With Pen In Hand (9)
With These Hands (9)
Without You (12)
World I Used To Know (8)
Yesterday When I Was Young (8)
You Don't Have To Say You Love Me (2)
You Don't Know Me (1)
You Gave Me A Mountain (6)
You Know You Don't Want Me (2)
You Must Have Faith (1)
You'll Never Walk Alone (7)
You're Gonna Hear From Me (1)
You've Got A Friend (12)

NAILS, The
New York-based rock sextet led by singer/lyricist Marc Campbell.

8/23/86	194	2		Dangerous Dreams	$8	RCA 5831

Dangerous Dream
Darkness Grows Uncivilized

Dig Myself A Hole
First Time

Hello Janine
Ocean

Save Me
Things You Left Behind

Veil, The
Voices

NAJEE
Jazz saxophonist. Born in Manhattan and raised in Queens, New York. Session work for George Benson, Kashif and Lillo Thomas. Also see Vaneese Thomas.

2/28/87	56	45	●	1 Najee's Theme ....[I]	$8	EMI America 17241
7/9/88	76	21		2 Day By Day	$8	EMI-Man. 90096
				vocals by Audrey Wheeler, Janice Dempsey and Cindy Mizell		
4/28/90	63	17		3 Tokyo Blue ....[I]	$12	EMI 92248
				all tracks instrumental except for 2 with vocals by Vesta Williams and Freddie Jackson		
7/18/92	107	13		4 Just An Illusion	$12	EMI 99400
				includes guest vocals by Freddie Jackson, Jeffrey Osborne and Caron Wheeler		

All I Ever Ask (4)
Betcha Don't Know (1)
Breezy (2)
Buenos Aires (3)
Burn It Up (4)
Can't Hide Love (1)
Cruise Control (3)
Day By Day (2)
Deep Inside Your Love (4)

Feel So Good To Me (1)
For The Love Of You (1)
Gina (2)
(He's) Armed 'N Dangerous (2)
Here We Go (4)
I Adore Mi Amor (4)
I'll Be Good To You (3)
Just An Illusion (4)

Loving Every Moment (4)
My Old Friend (3)
Mysterious (1)
Najee's Nasty Groove (2)
Najee's Theme (1)
Nation's Call (3)
Noah's Ark (4)
Only At Night (3)
Personality (2)

Skyline (4)
So Hard To Let Go (2)
Stand Up (2)
Stay (3)
(Superwoman) Where Were You When I Needed You (4)
Sweet Love (1)
Sweet Sensation (2)
Talkin' (3)

That's The Way Of The World (2)
Tokyo Blue (3)
Tonight I'm Yours (2)
Touch Of Heaven (4)
Until We Meet Again (4)
We're Still Family (1)
What You Do To Me (1)
Whenever We're Together (4)

NAKED EYES
English duo: Pete Byrne (vocals) and Rob Fisher (keyboards, synthesizer). Split in 1984. Fisher later in duo Climie Fisher.

4/16/83	32	42		1 Naked Eyes	$8	EMI America 17089
9/8/84	83	10		2 Fuel For The Fire	$8	EMI America 17116

Always Something There To Remind Me (1) *8*
Answering Service (1)
Burning Bridges (1)

Could Be (1)
Emotion In Motion (1)
Eyes Of A Child (2)
Flag Of Convenience (2)

Flying Solo (2)
Fortune And Fame (1)
I Could Show You How (1)
Low Life (1)

Me I See In You (2)
New Hearts (2)
No Flowers Please (2)
Once Is Enough (2)

Promises, Promises (1) *11*
Sacrifice (2)
Voices In My Head (1)

(What) In The Name Of Love (2) *39*
When The Lights Go Out (1) *37*

★★407★★   NASH, Graham
Born on 2/2/42 in Blackpool, England. Co-founding member/guitarist of The Hollies. Formed Crosby, Stills & Nash in 1970.

6/19/71	15	24	●	1 Songs For Beginners	$10	Atlantic 7204
4/22/72	4	26	●	2 **Graham Nash/David Crosby** *	$12	Atlantic 7220
1/26/74	34	14		3 Wild Tales	$10	Atlantic 7288
10/11/75	6	31	●	4 **Wind On The Water** *	$10	ABC 902
7/24/76	26	15	●	5 **Whistling Down The Wire** *	$10	ABC 956
11/19/77	52	8		6 Crosby/Nash - Live * ....[L]	$10	ABC 1042
10/28/78	150	4		7 The Best Of Crosby/Nash * ....[G]	$10	ABC 1102
				*DAVID CROSBY/GRAHAM NASH		
3/8/80	117	5		8 Earth & Sky	$8	Capitol 12014
4/26/86	136	7		9 Innocent Eyes	$8	Atlantic 81633

And So It Goes (3)
Another Sleep Song (3)
Barrel Of Pain (Half-Life) (8)
Be Yourself (1)
Better Days (1)
Bittersweet (4,7)
Blacknotes (2)
Broken Bird (5)
Carry Me (4,7) *52*
Chicago (1,7) *35*

Chippin' Away (9)
Cowboy Of Dreams (4)
Dancer (4)
Deja Vu (6)
Don't Listen To The Rumours (4)
Earth & Sky (8)
Fieldworker (4)
Foolish Man (5,6)
Frozen Smiles (2)

Games (2)
Girl To Be On My Mind (2)
Glass And Steel (9)
Grave Concern (3)
Helicopter Song (8)
Hey You (Looking At The Moon) (3)
Homeward Through The Haze (4)
I Got A Rock (9)

I Miss You (3)
I Used To Be A King (1,6)
Immigration Man (2,6) *36*
In The 80's (8)
It's All Right (8)
J.B.'s Blues (5)
Keep Away From Me (9)
Laughing (1)
Leeshore, The (6)

Love Has Come (8)
Love Work Out (4,7)
Low Down Payment (4)
Magical Child (8)
Mama Lion (4,6)
Man In The Mirror (1)
Marguerita (5)
Military Madness (1) *73*
Mutiny (5)
Naked In The Rain (4)

Newday (9)
Oh! Camil (The Winter Soldier) (3)
On The Line (3)
Out Of The Darkness (5,7) *89*
Out On The Island (8)
Over The Wall (9)
Page 43 (2,6)
Prison Song (3)

NASH, Graham — Cont'd

Sad Eyes (9)
See You In Prague (9)
Simple Man (1,6)
Skychild (8)
Sleep Song (9)
Southbound Train (2,7) *99*
Spotlight (5)
Strangers Room (2)
T.V. Guide (9)
Take The Money And Run (4)
Taken At All (5)
There's Only One (1)
Time After Time (5)
To The Last Whale Medley (4,7)
Wall Song (2,7)
We Can Change The World (1)
Where Will I Be? (2)
Whole Cloth (2)
Wild Tales (3,7)
Wounded Bird (1)
You'll Never Be The Same (3)

NASH, Johnny

Born on 8/19/40 in Houston. Vocalist/guitarist/actor. Appeared on local TV from age 13. With Arthur Godfrey's TV and radio shows from 1956-63. In the film *Take A Giant Step* in 1959. Own JoDa label in 1965. Began recording in Jamaica in the late '60s.

DEBUT DATE	PEAK POS	WKS CHR			$	Label & Number
11/23/68+	109	12	1	Hold Me Tight	$15	JAD 1207
10/7/72	23	31	2	I Can See Clearly Now	$12	Epic 31607
7/14/73	169	6	3	My Merry-Go-Round	$12	Epic 32158

Comma Comma (2)
Cream Puff (2)
Cupid (1) *39*
Don't Cry (1)
Don't Look Back (1)
Gonna Open Up My Heart Again (3)
Groovin' (1)
Guava Jelly (1)
How Good It Is (2)
I Can See Clearly Now (2) *1*
(It Was) So Nice While It Lasted (2)
Love (1)
Love Is Not A Game (3)
Lovey Dovey (1)
Loving You (3) *91*
My Merry-Go-Round (3) *77*
Nice Time (3)
(Oh Jesus) We're Trying To Get Back To You (3)
Ooh Baby You've Been Good To Me (2)
Ooh What A Feeling (3)
People In Love (1)
Salt Annie Ginger Tree (3)
Stir It Up (2) *12*
That's The Way We Get By (2)
There Are More Questions Than Answers (2)
We're All Alike (2)
Yellow House (3)
You Better Stop (Messing Around) (3)
You Got Soul (1) *58*
You Got To Change Your Ways (1)
You Poured Sugar On Me (2)

NASHVILLE BRASS — see DAVIS, Danny

NATIONAL LAMPOON

Comedy troupe spawned from the magazine of the same name. Also see soundtrack *Animal House*.

DEBUT DATE	PEAK POS	WKS CHR			$	Label & Number
9/2/72	132	12	1	Radio Dinner	[C] $15	Banana 38

featuring Christopher Guest and Melissa Manchester

| 6/23/73 | 107 | 13 | 2 | Lemmings | [C] $12 | Banana 6006 |

satirical rock revue recorded at New York's Village Gate

| 3/16/74 | 118 | 8 | 3 | Missing White House Tapes | [C] $15 | Banana 6008 |

above 2 feature John Belushi and Chevy Chase

Admission Speech (3)
All Kidding Aside (1)
All Star Dead Band (2)
Calendar (3)
Catch It And You Keep It (1)
Checkers (3)
Colorado (2)
Concert In Bangla Desh (1)
Constitution Game (3)
Crowd Rain Chant (2)
Deteriorata (1) *91*
Energy Crisis (3)
FBI, The (3)
Farmer Yassir (2)
Gerry Ford Show (3)
Hearings (3)
Hell's Angel (2)
Highway Toes (2)
Impeachment Parade (3)
Impeachment, Swearing Out (3)
Inspiration (3)
It's Obvious (1)
Lemmings Lament (2)
Lonely At The Bottom (2)
Magical Misery Tour (1)
Megadeath (2)
Megagroupie (2)
Mission: Impeachable (3)
New VP (3)
Ng Asi (1)
Oval Office (3)
Papa Was A Running Dog Lackey Of The Bourgeoisie (2)
Pennsylvania Avenue (3)
Phono Funnies (1)
Pigeons (1)
Pizza Man (2)
Plumber Commercial (3)
Positively Wall Street (2)
President's Qualities (3)
Profiles In Chrome (1)
Pull The Tregros (1)
'Quinas 'N' Rasmus (1)
Richie Havens (2)
Senate Hearings (3)
Send Money (3)
Support Your Local Police (1)
Teenyrap (1)
Those Fabulous Sixties (1)
Tooth Commercial (3)
Weather Person (2)
Wrap Up (3)

NATURAL FOUR

Soul group led by Chris James, formed in 1967 in San Francisco.

DEBUT DATE	PEAK POS	WKS CHR			$	Label & Number
7/5/75	182	3		Heaven Right Here On Earth	$12	Curtom 5004

Baby Come On
Count On Me
Give This Love A Try
Heaven Right Here On Earth
Love's So Wonderful
What Do You Do
What's Happening Here
While You're Away

NATURE'S DIVINE

Ten-member soul group from Detroit.

DEBUT DATE	PEAK POS	WKS CHR			$	Label & Number
11/10/79	91	8		In The Beginning	$8	Infinity 9013

Just Can't Control Myself *65*
I Never Felt This Way Before
Love Is You
Nature Divine
Questions
Success
Summer Nights

NAUGHTY BY NATURE

Rap trio from East Orange, New Jersey: Anthony "Treach" Criss, Vincent Brown and Kier "dj KG" Gist.

DEBUT DATE	PEAK POS	WKS CHR			$	Label & Number
9/21/91	16	54 ▲		Naughty By Nature	$12	Tommy Boy 1044

Everyday All Day
Ghetto Bastard
Guard Your Grill
Let The Ho's Go
O.P.P. *6*
1,2,3
Pin The Tail On The Donkey
Rhyme'll Shine On
Strike A Nerve
Thankx For Sleepwalking
Wickedest Man Alive
Yoke The Joker

★★317★★ NAZARETH

Hard-rock group formed in Scotland in 1969: Dan McCafferty (lead singer), Manny Charlton (lead guitar), Pete Agnew (bass) and Darrell Sweet (drums). Billy Rankin (lead guitar) and John Locke (keyboards) added in 1981.

DEBUT DATE	PEAK POS	WKS CHR			$	Label & Number
8/18/73	157	13	1	Razamanaz	$8	A&M 4396
3/9/74	150	8	2	Loud 'N' Proud	$8	A&M 3609
7/13/74	157	9	3	Rampant	$8	A&M 3641
4/26/75+	17	40 ▲	4	Hair Of The Dog	$8	A&M 4511
5/8/76	24	14	5	Close Enough For Rock 'N' Roll	$8	A&M 4562
12/4/76	75	9	6	Play 'N' The Game	$8	A&M 4610
7/2/77	120	6	7	Hot Tracks	[G] $8	A&M 4643
11/19/77+	82	16	8	Expect No Mercy	$8	A&M 4666
2/3/79	38	14	9	No Mean City	$8	A&M 4741
2/16/80	41	19	10	Malice In Wonderland	$8	A&M 4799
2/14/81	70	13	11	The Fool Circle	$8	A&M 4844
10/10/81	83	9	12	'Snaz	[L] $10	A&M 6703 [2]
7/2/82	122	10	13	2XS	$8	A&M 4901

Alcatraz (1)
All The King's Horses (8)
Another Year (11)
Back To The Trenches (13)
Bad, Bad Boy (1)
Ballad Of Hollis Brown (1)
Beggars Day (4,12)
Big Boy (10,12)
Born To Love (6,7)
Born Under The Wrong Sign (5)
Boys In The Band (1)
Broken Down Angel (1,7)
Busted (8)
Carry Out Feelings (5,7)
Changin' Times (4)
Child In The Sun (9)
Claim To Fame (9)
Cocaine (11,12)
Down Home Girl (6)
Dream On (13)
Dressed To Kill (11,12)
Every Young Man's Dream (11,12)
Expect No Mercy (8,12)
Fallen Angel (10)
Fast Cars (10)
Flying (6)
Freewheeler (2)
Games (13)
Gatecrash (13)
Gimme What's Mine (8)
Glad When You're Gone (3)
Go Down Fighting (2,7)
Gone Dead Train (8)
Hair Of The Dog (4,7,12)
Heart's Grown Cold (10,12)
Holiday (10,12) *87*
Homesick Again (5)
I Don't Want To Go On Without You (6)
I Want To (Do Everything For You) (6,7,12)
Java Blues (12)
Jet Lag (3)
Juicy Lucy (12)
Just To Get Into It (9)
Kentucky Fried Blues (8)
L.A. Girls (6)
Let Me Be Your Leader (11,12)
Lift The Lid (5)
Light My Way (11)
Little Part Of You (11)

DEBUT DATE	PEAK POS	WKS CHR	G O L D	ARTIST — Album Title	$	Label & Number

NAZARETH — Cont'd

Lonely In The Night (13)	New York Broken Toy (8)	Rose In The Heather (4)	Sold My Soul (1)	Telegram Medley (5,12)	We Are The People (11)
Loretta (5)	Night Woman (1)	Shanghai'd In Shanghai (3,7)	Somebody To Roll (6)	This Flight Tonight (2,7,12)	What's In It For Me (9)
Love Hurts (4,7,12) **8**	No Mean City (Parts 1 & 2) (9)	Shapes Of Things (3,12)	Space Safari (medley) (3)	Too Bad, Too Sad (1)	Whatever You Want Babe (9)
Love Leads To Madness (13)	Not Faking It (2)	Ship Of Dreams (10)	Star (9)	Turn On Your Receiver (2)	Whiskey Drinkin' Woman (4)
Loved And Lost (3)	Place In Your Heart (8)	Shot Me Down (8)	Sunshine (9)	Turning A New Leaf (10)	Wild Honey (6)
May The Sunshine (9)	Please Don't Judas Me (4)	Showdown At The Border (10)	Take The Rap (13)	Tush (12)	Woke Up This Morning (1)
Mexico (13)	Pop The Silo (11)	Silver Dollar Forger (Parts 1 And 2) (9)	Talkin' 'Bout Love (10)	Vancouver Shakedown (5,7)	You Love Another (13)
Miss Misery (4)	Preservation (13)	Simple Solution (Parts 1 & 2) (9)	Talkin' To One Of The Boys (10)	Vicki (5)	You're The Violin (5)
Moonlight Eyes (11)	Razamanaz (1,7,12)		Teenage Nervous Breakdown (2)	Victoria (11)	
Morning Dew (12)	Revenge Is Sweet (8)			Vigilante Man (1)	
My White Bicycle (7)				Waiting For The Man (6)	

NAZZ

Philadelphia rock quartet featuring Todd Rundgren (guitar) and Stewkey (real name: Robert Antoni; vocals). Rundgren left in 1970 and replaced by Rick Nielsen and Tom Petersson (later members of Cheap Trick).

DEBUT DATE	PEAK POS	WKS CHR		ARTIST — Album Title	$	Label & Number
10/19/68+	118	26	1	Nazz	$35	SGC 5001
5/10/69	80	15	2	Nazz Nazz	$35	SGC 5002

Back Of Your Mind (1)	Forget All About It (2)	If That's The Way You Feel (1)	Letters Don't Count (2)	Rain Rider (1)	When I Get My Plane (1)
Beautiful Song (2)	Gonna Cry Today (2)	Kiddie Boy (2)	Meridian Leeward (2)	See What You Can Be (1)	Wildwood Blues (1)
Crowded (1)	Hang On Paul (2)	Lemming Song (1)	Not Wrong Long (2)	She's Goin' Down (1)	
Featherbedding Lover (2)	**Hello It's Me** (1) **66**		Open My Eyes (1)	Under The Ice (2)	

NED'S ATOMIC DUSTBIN

British rock quintet: Jonathan Penney (vocals), Garath Pring, Alexander Griffin, Matthew Cheslin and Daniel Worton. Took name from the script of a BBC comedy TV series The Goon Show.

DEBUT DATE	PEAK POS	WKS CHR		ARTIST — Album Title	$	Label & Number
1/11/92	91	14	1	God Fodder	$12	Columbia 47929
11/28/92	183	1	2	Are You Normal?	$12	Chaos 53154

Capital Letters (1)	Intact (2)	Less Than Useful (1)	Suave And Suffocated (2)	Until You Find Out (1)	You Don't Want To Do That (2)
Cut Up (1)	Kill Your Television (1)	Not Sleeping Around (2)	Swallowing Air (2)	Walking Through Syrup (1)	Your Complex (1)
Fracture (2)	Leg End In His Own Boots (2)	Nothing Like (1)	Tantrum (2)	What Gives My Son? (1)	
Grey Cell Green (1)	Legoland (2)	Selfish (1)	Throwing Things (1)	Who Goes First? (2)	
Happy (1)		Spring (1)	Two And Two Made Five (2)	You (1)	

NEELY, Sam

Born on 8/22/48 in Cuero, Texas. Performing since age 11. Worked with local rock groups. Played clubs in Corpus Christi, especially at The Rogue, in the late '60s. Long residency at the Electric Eel in Corpus Christi in the late '70s.

DEBUT DATE	PEAK POS	WKS CHR		ARTIST — Album Title	$	Label & Number
9/16/72	147	11	1	Loving You Just Crossed My Mind	$10	Capitol 11097
2/10/73	175	6	2	Sam Neely-2	$10	Capitol 11143

Ain't It Good To Be Home (2)	Can't Help Wondering (1)	Gentle People (2)	Long Road To Texas (1)	Neither Do I (2)	Take Me Back Wife (2)
Before Your Eyes (1)	Cry Me A Song (1)	It's Another Day (2)	**Loving You Just Crossed My Mind** (1) **29**	Pray (1)	Young And Free (2)
Bless Me Miss America (2)	Every Day Is The Same As Today (1)	Jesse California (1)	Molly Bee (1)	**Rosalie** (2) **43**	
Blue Time (1)		Kiss The Morning Sunshine (2)		Sweet Country Child (2)	

NEKTAR

English art-rock quartet based in Germany — Roye Albrighton, lead singer.

DEBUT DATE	PEAK POS	WKS CHR		ARTIST — Album Title	$	Label & Number
7/20/74	19	28	1	Remember The Future	$10	Passport 98002
2/15/75	32	20	2	Down To Earth	$10	Passport 98005
4/3/76	89	14	3	Recycled	$8	Passport 98011
9/18/76	141	4	4	A Tab In The Ocean	[I] $8	Passport 98017
11/5/77	172	3	5	Magic Is A Child	$8	Polydor 6115

Astral Man (2) **91**	Early Morning Clown (2)	Listen (1)	Oh Willy (2)	Remember The Future (1)	Train From Nowhere (5)
Automaton Horrorscope (3)	Eerie Lackawanna (5)	Little Boy (2)	On The Run (The Trucker) (5)	Returning Light (1)	Unendless Imaginations? (3)
Away From Asgard (5)	Fidgety Queen (2)	Love To Share (Keep Your Worries Behind You) (5)	Path Of Light (1)	Sao Paolo Sunrise (3)	Waves (4)
Confusion (3)	Flight To Reality (3)	Magic Is A Child (5)	Questions And Answers (1)	Show Me The Way (2)	Wheel Of Time (1)
Costa Del Sol (3)	Images Of The Past (1)	Marvellous Moses (3)	Recognition (1)	Spread Your Wings (5)	
Cryin' In The Dark (4)	It's All Over (3)	Midnite Lite (5)	Recycle (1)	Tab In The Ocean (4)	
Cybernetic Consumption (3)	King Of The Twilight (4)	Nelly The Elephant (2)	Recycle Countdown (3)	That's Life (1)	
Desolation Valley (4)	Let It Grow (1)		Recycling (3)	Tomorrow Never Comes (1)	

NELSON

Gunnar (vocals, bass) and Matthew Nelson (vocals, rhythm guitar), the identical twin sons (b: 9/20/67) of the late Ricky Nelson. Their sister is actress Tracy Nelson of TV's Father Dowling Mysteries.

DEBUT DATE	PEAK POS	WKS CHR		ARTIST — Album Title	$	Label & Number
7/21/90	17	64 ▲		After The Rain	$12	DGC 24290

After The Rain 6	(Can't Live Without Your) **Love And Affection** 1	Fill You Up	(It's Just) Desire	Only Time Will Tell	Tracy's Song (medley)
Bits And Pieces	Everywhere I Go	I Can Hardly Wait	**More Than Ever 14**	(medley) 28	Will You Love Me?

★★178★★ NELSON, Ricky

Born Eric Hilliard Nelson on 5/8/40 in Teaneck, New Jersey. Died on 12/31/85 in a plane crash in DeKalb, Texas. Son of bandleader Ozzie Nelson and vocalist Harriet Hilliard. Rick and brother David appeared on Nelson's radio show from March 1949, later on TV, 1952-66. Formed own Stone Canyon Band in 1969. In films Rio Bravo, Wackiest Ship In The Army and Love And Kisses. Married Kristin Harmon (sister of actor Mark Harmon) in 1963; divorced in 1982. Their daughter Tracy is a film/TV actress. Their twin sons began recording as Nelson in 1990. Ricky was one of the first teen idols of the rock era. Inducted into the Rock and Roll Hall of Fame in 1987.

DEBUT DATE	PEAK POS	WKS CHR		ARTIST — Album Title	$	Label & Number
11/11/57+	1[2]	33	1	Ricky	$75	Imperial 9048
7/28/58	7	9	2	Ricky Nelson	$75	Imperial 9050
2/2/59	14	19	3	Ricky Sings Again	$75	Imperial 9061
9/28/59+	22	26	4	Songs By Ricky	$75	Imperial 9082
8/29/60	18	22	5	More Songs By Ricky	$40	Imperial 9122
				RICK NELSON:		
5/29/61	8	49	6	Rick Is 21	$30	Imperial 9152
4/14/62	27	20	7	Album Seven By Rick	$30	Imperial 9167

DEBUT DATE	PEAK POS	WKS CHR	GOLD	ARTIST — Album Title	$	Label & Number
				NELSON, Ricky — Cont'd		
3/2/63	112	4	8	Best Sellers By Rick Nelson [G]	$30	Imperial 9218
5/4/63	128	5	9	It's Up To You [K]	$30	Imperial 9223
6/8/63	20	19	10	For Your Sweet Love	$25	Decca 74419
1/4/64	14	22	11	Rick Nelson sings "For You"	$25	Decca 74479
2/21/70	54	19	12	Rick Nelson In Concert [L]	$20	Decca 75162
				recorded at The Troubadour Club in Los Angeles		
11/7/70	196	2	13	Rick Sings Nelson	$20	Decca 75236
12/9/72+	32	18	14	Garden Party	$20	Decca 75391
2/23/74	190	4	15	Windfall	$15	MCA 383
				above 2: **RICK NELSON & THE STONE CANYON BAND**		
2/21/81	153	6	16	Playing To Win	$8	Capitol 12109

Again (5,9) / Ain't Nothin' But Love (5) / Almost Saturday Night (16) / Am I Blue (1) / Anytime (13) / Are You Really Real? (14) / Baby I'm Sorry (1,8) / Baby Won't You Please Come Home (5,9) / Baby You Don't Know (7) / Back To Schooldays (16) / **Be-Bop Baby** (1,8) **3** / Be True To Me (3) / **Believe What You Say** (3,8,12,16) **4** / Blood From A Stone (4) / Boppin' The Blues (6,9) / Break My Chain (6,9) / California (13) / Call It What You Want (16) / Come On In (12) / **Congratulations** (7) **63** / Do The Best You Can (16) / Do You Know What It Means To Miss New Orleans (6) / Don't Leave Me (4) / Don't Leave Me Here (15) / Don't Leave Me This Way (2) / Don't Let Your Goodbye Stand (14) / Don't Look At Me (16)

Down Along The Bayou Country (13) / Down Home (11) / Down The Line (2) / **Easy To Be Free** (12) **48** / Everybody But Me (6) / Everytime I See You Smiling (10) / Everytime I Think About You (10) / Evil Woman Child (15) / Excuse Me Baby (7) / Flower Opens Gently By (14) / **Fools Rush In** (11) **12** / **For You** (11) **6** / For Your Sweet Love (10) / **Garden Party** (14) **6** / **Gypsy Woman** (10) **62** / Half Breed (4,9) / **Have I Told You Lately That I Love You?** (1,8) **29** / **Hello Mary Lou** (6,12) **9** / Hello Mister Happiness (11) / Here I Go Again (5) / Hey Pretty Baby (5) / Hey There, Little Miss Tease (11) / History Of Love (7) / Honeycomb (1) / How Long (13) / How Many Times (15)

I Can't Help It (3) / I Can't Stop Loving You (7) / I Can't Take It No More (16) / I Don't Want To Be Lonely Tonight (15) / **I Got A Woman** (10) **49** / **I Need You** (9) **83** / I Rise, I Fall (11) / I Shall Be Released (12) / I Wanna Be With You (14) / I Will Follow You (10) / I'd Climb The Highest Mountain (5,9) / I'll Make Believe (6) / I'll Walk Alone (2) / I'm All Through With You (5) / I'm Confessin' (1) / I'm Feelin' Sorry (2) / **I'm In Love Again** (2,8) **67** / **I'm Not Afraid** (5) **27** / I'm Talking About You (14) / I'm Walkin' (12) / I've Been Thinkin' (4) / **If You Can't Rock Me** (1,9) **100** / If You Gotta Go, Go Now (12) / It Hasn't Happened Yet (16) / It's All In The Game (3) / **It's Late** (3) **9** / **It's Up To You** (9) **6**

Just A Little Too Much (4,8) **9** / Just Take A Moment (11) / Legacy (15) / Legend In My Time (11) / Let It Bring You Along (14) / Let's Talk The Whole Thing Over (10) / Lifestream (15) / Little Miss American Dream (16) / **Lonesome Town** (3,8) **7** / Long Vacation (4) / Look At Mary (13) / Loser Babe Is You (16) / Louisiana Man (13) / Lucky Star (6) / Mad Mad World (7) / Make Believe (5) / Mr. Dolphin (13) / My Babe (5) / My One Desire (6) / My Woman (13) / Nearness Of You (11) / **Never Be Anyone Else But You** (3) **6** / Nightime Lady (14) / Oh Yeah, I'm In Love (6) / **Old Enough To Love** (3) **94** / One Boy Too Late (10) / One Minute To One (4)

One Night Stand (15) / One Of These Mornings (3) / **Palace Guard** (14) **65** / Pick Up The Pieces (10) / **Poor Little Fool** (2,8) **1** / Poor Loser (7) / Proving My Love (5) / Reason Why (13) / Red Balloon (12) / Restless Kid (3) / **She Belongs To Me** (12) **33** / Shirley Lee (2,9) / So Long (4) / So Long Mama (14) / Someday (2) / Someone To Love (15) / Stars Fell On Alabama (6,9) / **Stood Up** (2) / Stop Sneakin' 'Round (7) / **String Along** (10) **25** / **Summertime** (7) **89** / Sure Fire Bet (6) / Sweet Mary (13) / **Sweeter Than You** (4) **9** / Teenage Doll (13) / Thank You Darling (7) / That Same Old Feeling (11) / That Warm Summer Night (6) / **That's All** (4,8) **48** / That's All She Wrote (11) / There Goes My Baby (9)

There's Good Rockin' Tonight (2) / There's Not A Minute (7) / Time After Time (5) / **Today's Teardrops** (7) **54** / **Travelin' Man** (6) **1** / True Love (1) / Tryin' To Get To You (3,9) / Unchained Melody (2) / Violets Of Dawn (12) / **Waitin' In School** (3) **18** / We've Got A Long Way To Go (13) / What Comes Next? (10) / When Your Lover Has Gone (5) / Who Cares About Tomorrow - Promises (12) / Whole Lotta Shakin' Goin' On (1) / Wild Nights In Tulsa (15) / Windfall (15) / **You Don't Love Me Anymore (And I Can Tell)** (10) **47** / You Tear Me Up (3) / You'll Never Know What You're Missin' (4) / You're Free To Go (11) / You're So Fine (4) / Your True Love (1)

★★437★★ NELSON, Sandy

Born Sander Nelson on 12/1/38 in Santa Monica, California. Rock 'n' roll drummer. Became prominent studio musician. Heard on "Alley Oop," "To Know Him Is To Love Him," "A Thousand Stars" and many others. Lost portion of right leg in a motorcycle accident in 1963. Returned to performing in 1964.

DEBUT DATE	PEAK POS	WKS CHR		ARTIST — Album Title	$	Label & Number
1/20/62	6	48	1	**Let There Be Drums** [I]	$20	Imperial 9159
4/14/62	29	24	2	Drums Are My Beat! [I]	$20	Imperial 9168
7/14/62	55	11	3	Drummin' Up A Storm [I]	$20	Imperial 9189
11/3/62	141	3	4	Compelling Percussion [I]	$20	Imperial 9204
12/1/62	106	3	5	Golden Hits [I]	$20	Imperial 9202
11/21/64+	122	11	6	Live! In Las Vegas [I-L]	$20	Imperial 12272
3/6/65	135	5	7	Teen Beat '65 [I]	$20	Imperial 12278
7/10/65	120	8	8	Drum Discotheque [I]	$20	Imperial 12283
10/2/65	118	11	9	Drums A Go-Go [I]	$20	Imperial 12287
1/8/66	126	7	10	Boss Beat [I]	$20	Imperial 12298
4/23/66	148	2	11	"In" Beat [I]	$20	Imperial 12305

Alexes (4) / All Around The World With Drums (3) / **All Night Long** (3) **75** / **And Then There Were Drums** (4) **65** / Batman (4) / Be Bop Baby (5) / Beat From Another World (7) / Big Noise From Winnetka (1) / **Birth Of The Beat** (1) **75** / Bongo Rock (7) / Bony Moronie (5) / Boot-Le (7) / Boss Beat (10) / Bouncy (1) / C Jam Blues (3) / Caravan (2) / Casbah (9) / Castle Rock (3) / Chicka Boom (4) / City, The (2)

Civilization (4) / Clapping Song (9) / Come On, Do The Jerk (7) / Day Drumming (2) / Day Tripper (1) / Do The Boomerang (9) / Down In The Boondocks (10) / Drum Bay (6) / Drum Dance (8) / Drum Discotheque (8) / Drum Roll (2) / **Drum Stomp** (2) **86** / Drum Stuff (6) / **Drummin' Up A Storm** (3) **67** / Drums - For Drummers Only (4) / Drums - For Strippers Only (4) / Drums A Go-Go (9) / **Drums Are My Beat** (2) **29** / Drums In A Sea Cave (10)

Duck, The (11) / Early In The Morning (5) / El Bandido (6) / El Pussycat (8) / Get With It (1) / Go-Go A Go-Go (8) / Hang On Sloopy (My Girl Sloopy) (10) / Hard Day's Night (11) / Hawaiian War Chant (2) / Here We Go Again (3) / Honky Tonk (5) / Honky Tonk '65 (7) / Hum Drum (2) / (I Can't Get No) Satisfaction (9) / I Like It Like That (9) / I Want To Walk You Home (5) / I'm Gonna Be A Wheel Someday (5) / I'm In Love Again (3) / "In" Beat (11)

"In" Crowd (10) / Jenny Take A Ride (11) / Jerk, The (7) / Johnny B. Goode (6) / Jolly Green Giant (8) / Jump Time (4) / Just Like Me (1) / Kansas City (5) / Kitty's Theme (9) / Land Of A Thousand Dances (8) / **Let There Be Drums** (1,6,8) **7** / Live It Up (5) / Louie, Louie (10) / Lover's Concerto (10) / Memphis (5) / Mr. John Lee (Part I & II) (6) / My Blue Heaven (2) / My Girl Josephine (1) / My Love (11)

My World Is Empty Without You (11) / No Matter What Shape (Your Stomach's In) (11) / Papa's Got A Brand New Bag (10) / Quite A Beat (1) / Raunchy '65 (7) / Rock House (5) / Sandy (3) / Scratchy (7) / Secret Agent Man (11) / Shotgun (8) / Sidewinder (8) / Skokiaan (6) / Slippin' And Slidin' (1) / Slow Down (10) / Soul Drums (9) / Splish Splash (5) / Taste Of Honey (10) / Teen Beach (8) / **Teen Beat '65** (6,7) **44**

Tequila (1) / 3rd Man Theme (10) / Tim Tom Drum (8) / Time After Time (5) / Topsy (1) / Treat Her Right (10) / Tub-Thumpin' (3) / 20 - 75 (7) / Twine Time (8) / Twisted (2) / Uptight (Everything's Alright) (11) / Walking To New Orleans (5) / What'd I Say (5) / Whittier Blvd. (9) / Wipe-Out (5) / Wooly Bully (9) / You Turn Me On (9)

NELSON, Tracy

Lead singer of Mother Earth.

DEBUT DATE	PEAK POS	WKS CHR	ARTIST — Album Title	$	Label & Number
10/19/74	145	5	Tracy Nelson	$10	Atlantic 7310

After The Fire Is Gone / Down So Low / Hold An Old Friend's Hand / I Wish Someone Would Care / It Takes A Lot To Laugh, It Takes A Train To Cry / Lay Me Down Easy / Lean On Me / Love Has No Pride / Rock Me In Your Cradle / Slow Fall

DEBUT DATE	PEAK POS	WKS CHR	GOLD	ARTIST — Album Title	$	Label & Number

★★36★★ NELSON, Willie

Born on 4/30/33 in Ft. Worth, Texas; raised in Abbott, Texas. Prolific country singer/songwriter (writer of Patsy Cline's "Crazy" and Faron Young's "Hello Walls"). Played bass for Ray Price. Moved to Nashville in 1960. Moved back to Texas in 1970. Pioneered the "outlaw" country movement. Appeared in several films including *The Electric Horseman* (1979), *Honeysuckle Rose* (1980) and *Barbarosa* (1982). Won Grammy's Living Legends Award in 1989. Also see Concept Albums - *The Outlaws* and *Highwayman*.

DEBUT DATE	PEAK POS	WKS CHR	GOLD	ARTIST — Album Title	$	Label & Number
7/26/75	28	43	▲²	1 Red Headed Stranger	$15	Columbia 33482
11/8/75	196	3		2 What Can You Do To Me Now [E]	$12	RCA 1234
3/20/76	48	15	●	3 The Sound In Your Mind	$10	Columbia 34092
5/8/76	149	7		4 Willie Nelson Live [E-L-R] originally released in 1966 as *Country Music Concert*	$10	RCA 1487
6/5/76	187	3		5 Phases And Stages [E] recorded in 1964; produced by Jerry Wexler	$12	Atlantic 7291
10/16/76	60	7	●	6 The Troublemaker gospel songs; title song refers to Christ	$10	Columbia 34112
5/21/77	78	15		7 Before His Time [E] remix by Waylon Jennings of earlier recordings3	$8	RCA 2210
7/9/77	91	12		8 To Lefty From Willie a tribute to Lefty Frizzell who died in 1975	$8	Columbia 34695
2/4/78	12	29	▲	9 Waylon & Willie **WAYLON JENNINGS & WILLIE NELSON**	$8	RCA 2686
5/13/78	30	117	▲⁴	10 Stardust an album of pop standards from 1926-55 (produced by Booker T. Jones)	$8	Columbia 35305
12/2/78+	32	55	▲²	11 Willie and Family Live [L] recorded at Harrah's, Lake Tahoe, Nevada	$10	Columbia 35642 [2]
3/3/79	154	5		12 Sweet Memories [E]	$8	RCA 3243
6/30/79	25	18	●	13 One For The Road **WILLIE NELSON AND LEON RUSSELL**	$10	Columbia 36064 [2]
11/17/79+	42	25	▲	14 Willie Nelson sings Kristofferson songs written by Kris Kristofferson	$8	Columbia 36188
12/1/79+	73	8	▲	15 Pretty Paper [X] Christmas charts: 9/'83	$8	Columbia 36189
1/12/80	52	25	●	16 The Electric Horseman [S] side 1: songs performed by Willie; side 2: instrumental score by Dave Grusin	$8	Columbia 36327
3/15/80	150	5		17 Danny Davis & Willie Nelson with The Nashville Brass [E] **DANNY DAVIS & WILLIE NELSON** new instrumental backing for earlier recordings by Willie	$8	RCA 3549
6/14/80	70	25	●	18 San Antonio Rose **WILLIE NELSON and RAY PRICE**	$8	Columbia 36476
9/6/80	11	36	▲²	19 Honeysuckle Rose [S-L] **WILLIE NELSON & FAMILY** includes "Fiddlin' Around" and "Jumpin' Cotton Eyed Joe" by Johnny Gimble; "Working Man Blues" by Jody Payne; "I Don't Do Windows" by Hank Cochran; "Coming Back To Texas" by Kenneth Threadgill; "If You Want Me To Love You I Will" by Amy Irving; "So You Think You're A Cowboy" by Emmylou Harris; "Two Sides To Every Story" by Dyan Cannon; and "Make The World Go Away" by Hank Cochran/Jeannie Seely	$10	Columbia 36752 [2]
3/21/81	31	23	▲	20 Somewhere Over The Rainbow	$8	Columbia 36883
8/1/81	148	7		21 The Minstrel Man [E]	$8	RCA 4045
9/19/81	27	93	▲³	22 Willie Nelson's Greatest Hits (& Some That Will Be) [G]	$10	Columbia 37542 [2]
3/20/82	2⁴	99	▲³	**23 Always On My Mind**	$8	Columbia 37951
10/30/82	57	22	●	24 WWII **WAYLON & WILLIE**	$8	RCA 4455
2/12/83	37	53	▲	25 Poncho & Lefty **MERLE HAGGARD/WILLIE NELSON**	$8	Epic 37958
3/19/83	39	20		26 Tougher Than Leather	$8	Columbia 38248
4/23/83	60	16	●	27 Take It To The Limit **WILLIE NELSON with WAYLON JENNINGS**	$8	Columbia 38562
11/26/83+	54	34	●	28 Without A Song	$8	Columbia 39110
12/3/83	182	5		29 My Own Way [E]	$8	RCA 4819
6/16/84	116	7		30 Angel Eyes featuring the guitar of Jackie King	$8	Columbia 39363
8/4/84	69	26	●	31 City Of New Orleans	$8	Columbia 39145
11/10/84	152	5		32 Music from SongWriter [S] **WILLIE NELSON & KRIS KRISTOFFERSON** (co-stars of the film)	$8	Columbia 39531
3/30/85	152	7		33 Me & Paul title refers to Willie and his drummer Paul English	$8	Columbia 40008
10/12/85	178	3	●	34 Half Nelson duets with 10 superstar artists	$8	Columbia 39990
8/3/91	193	3		35 Clean Shirt **WAYLON & WILLIE**	$12	Epic 47462

All Of Me (10)
All The Soft Places To Fall (25)
Always (13)
Always Late (With Your Kisses) (8)
Always On My Mind (23) 5
Am I Blue (13)
Amazing Grace (3,11)
Angel Eyes (19,30)

Angel Flying Too Close To The Ground (19,22)
Are There Any More Real Cowboys (34)
As Time Goes By (28)
Autumn Leaves (28)
Bandera (1)
Because Of You (13)
Beer Barrel Polka (26)
Black Rose (33)

Blackjack County Chain (21,27)
Bloody Mary Morning (5,11,17,19)
Blue Christmas (15)
Blue Eyes Crying In The Rain (1,11,19,22) 21
Blue Rock Montana (medley) (1,11)
Blue Skies (10)
Both Sides Now (12,29)

Bridge Over Troubled Water (23)
Buddy (12)
Can I Sleep In Your Arms (1)
Changing Skies (26)
Christmas Blues (15)
City Of New Orleans (31)
Convict And The Rose (26)
Couple More Years [solo: Willie] (9)
Crazy (3,11)

Crazy Arms (18)
Cry (31)
Danny Boy (13)
December Day (12,17)
Deep Water (18)
Denver (1)
Detour (13)
Do Right Woman, Do Right Man (23)
Don't Cuss The Fiddle (9)
Don't Fence Me In (13)

Don't Get Around Much Anymore (10)
Don't You Ever Get Tired Of Hurting Me) (18)
Down At The Corner Beer Joint (medley) (5)
Down Yonder (2)
Dreamer's Holiday (28)
Everybody's Talkin' (12)
Exactly Like You (20)
Eye Of The Storm (32)

NELSON, Willie — Cont'd

Faded Love (18,22)
Far Away Places (13)
Fire And Rain (2)
For The Good Times (14)
Forgiving You Was Easy (33)
Frosty The Snowman (15)
Funny How Time Slips Away (3,11,17,18,29)
Georgia On My Mind (10,11,22) **84**
Golden Earrings (28)
Good Hearted Woman (11,17,22) **25**
Good Ol' Nights (35)
Good Time Charlie's Got The Blues (31)
Good Times (21,32)
Guitars That Won't Stay In Tune (35)
Gypsy, The (30)
Half A Man (4,25,34)
Hands On The Wheel (1,16)
Harbor Lights (28)
Healing Hands Of Time (3)
Heartaches Of A Fool (22)
Heartbreak Hotel (13,22)
Heaven And Hell (5,19)
Hello Walls (4,11,17,29)
Help Me Make It Through The Night (12,14,22)
Here Comes Santa Claus (15)
Heroes (24)
Homeward Bound (27)
Honky Tonk Women (34)
How Do You Feel About Foolin' Around (32)
How Long Have You Been There (7)
How Long Is Forever (4)
(How Will I Know) I'm Falling In Love Again (5)
I Am The Forest (26)
I Been To Georgia On A Fast Train (33)
I Can Get Off On You (9,11)
I Can't Begin To Tell You (28)
I Could Write A Book About You (35)
I Couldn't Believe It Was True (1,11)
I Fall In Love Too Easily (30)
I Fall To Pieces (18)
I Gotta Get Drunk (2,4,11)
I Guess I've Come To Live Here In Your Eyes (19)
I Just Can't Let You Say Goodbye (4)
I Let My Mind Wander (33)

I Love You A Thousand Ways (8)
I Never Cared For You (4,33)
I Never Go Around Mirrors (8)
I Saw The Light (13)
I Still Can't Believe You're Gone (5)
I Told A Lie To My Heart (34)
I Want To Be With You Always (8)
I'd Have To Be Crazy (3,22)
I'd Trade All Of My Tomorrows (For Just One Yesterday) (7)
I'll Be There (If You Ever Want Me) (18)
I'm A Memory (2,7,11,29,33)
I'm Confessin' (That I Love You) (20)
I'm Gonna Sit Right Down And Write Myself A Letter (20)
I've Seen That Look On Me (A Thousand Times) (2)
If I Can Find A Clean Shirt (35)
If You Could Touch Her At All [solo: Willie] (9,11,19,22)
If You've Got The Money I've Got The Time (3,11,22)
In The Garden (6)
It Should Be Easier Now (7,21)
It Turns Me Inside Out (31)
It Wouldn't Be The Same (Without You) (20)
It's My Lazy Day (25)
It's Not Supposed To Be That Way (5,9,19)
Jingle Bells (15)
Just As I Am (1,11)
Just Out Of Reach (31)
Last Letter (medley) (4)
Last Thing I Needed First This Morning (23)
Laying My Burdens Down (21)
Let It Be Me (23) **40**
Let The Rest Of The World Go By (13)
Little Old Fashioned Karma (26)
Little Things (7,12)
Little Unfair (8)
Local Memory (17)
Look What Thoughts Will Do (8,22)

Loving Her Was Easier (Than Anything I'll Ever Do Again) (14,19)
Makin's Of A Song (13)
Mammas Don't Let Your Babies Grow Up To Be Cowboys (9,11,16,22) **42**
Me And Bobby McGee (14)
Me And Paul (33)
Midnight Rider (16)
Minstrel Man (21)
Mom And Dad's Waltz (8)
Mona Lisa (20)
Moonlight In Vermont (10)
Mountain Dew (21)
Mr. Record Man (4,11)
Mr. Shuck And Jive (24)
My Heroes Have Always Been Cowboys (16,22) **44**
My Life's Been A Pleasure (I Still Love You As I Did In Yesterday) (25)
My Love For The Rose (26)
My Mary (25)
My Mother's Eyes (20)
My Own Peculiar Way (2,4,17,29)
My Window Faces The South (30)
Night Life (3,11,17,18)
No Love Around (medley) (5)
No Love At All (27)
No Reason To Quit (25)
Nobody Said It Was Going To Be Easy [solo: Willie] (32)
Nobody Slides, My Friend (26)
O Little Town Of Bethlehem (15)
O'er The Waves (1)
Old Age And Treachery (35)
Old Five & Dimers Like Me (33)
Old Fords And A Natural Stone (23)
Old Friends (27)
On The Road Again (19,22) **20**
On The Sunny Side Of The Street (10)
Once In A While (28)
Once More With Feeling (2)
One Day At A Time (4,11,33)
One For My Baby And One More For The Road (13)
One In A Row (7,29)
Only Daddy That'll Walk The Line (11)
Opportunity To Cry (4,25)

Over The Rainbow (20)
Party's Over (23)
Penny For Your Thoughts (3)
Permanently Lonely (2,4,23)
Phases And Stages (medley) (5)
Pick Up The Tempo (5,9,19)
Pilgrim: Chapter 33 (14)
Pins And Needles (In My Heart) (29)
Please Come To Boston (31)
Please Don't Tell Me How The Story Ends (14)
Poncho And Lefty (25,34)
Precious Memories (6)
Pretend I Never Happened (5,33)
Pretty Paper (15)
Put Me On A Train Back To Texas (35)
Railroad Lady (8,22)
Rainy Day Blues (17,29)
Reasons To Quit (25)
Red Headed Stranger (1,11)
Release Me (18)
Remember Me (1) **67**
Ridin' Down The Canyon (13)
Rocks From Rolling Stones (35)
Roll In My Sweet Baby's Arms (11)
Rudolph The Red-Nosed Reindeer (15)
Samba For Charlie (30)
San Antonio Rose (18)
Santa Claus Is Coming To Town (15)
Senses (21)
September Song (10)
Seven Spanish Angels (34)
Shall We Gather (6)
She's Gone (33)
She's Gone, Gone, Gone (8)
She's Not For You (7)
She's Out Of My Life (31)
Silent Night, Holy Night (15)
Sioux City Sue (13)
Sister's Coming Home (medley) (5)
(Sittin' On) The Dock Of The Bay (24)
Slow Movin' Outlaw (34)
So You Think You're A Cowboy (16)
Someone To Watch Over Me (10)
Something To Think About (4)

Somewhere In Texas (Part I & II) (26)
Song For You (11,19)
Songwriter (solo: Willie) (32)
Sound In Your Mind (3)
Stardust (10)
Staring Each Other Down (23)
Stay A Little Longer (11,22)
Stay Away From Lonely Places (7,29)
Still Water Runs The Deepest (25)
Stormy Weather (13)
Summer Of Roses (26)
Summertime (13)
Sunday Mornin' Comin' Down (4)
Sweet Bye & Bye (6)
Sweet Memories (12)
Take It To The Limit (27)
Take This Job And Shove It (11)
Tenderly (13)
Texas On A Saturday Night (34)
Thank You (30)
Thanks Again (3)
That Lucky Old Sun (3,13)
That's The Way Love Goes (8)
There Is A Fountain (6)
There Will Never Be Another You (30)
They All Went To Mexico (34)
This Cold War With You (18)
Till I Gain Control Again (11,22,27)
Time Of The Preacher (1,11)
To All The Girls I've Loved Before (34) **5**
To Each His Own (28)
To Make A Long Story Short (She's Gone) (7)
Touch Me (4)
Tougher Than Leather (26)
Trouble In Mind (13)
Troublemaker, The (6)
Tryin' To Outrun The Wind (35)
Tumbling Tumbleweed (30)
Twinkle, Twinkle Little Star (20)
Two Old Sidewinders (35)
Unchained Melody (10)
Uncloudy Day (6,11,19,22)
Under The Double Eagle (11)
Until It's Time For You To Go (31)

Wake Me When It's Over (2,12)
Walkin' (medley) (5)
Washing The Dishes (medley) (5)
We Had It All (27)
What Can You Do To Me Now? (2)
When The Roll Is Called Up Yonder (6)
Where Do You Stand? (21)
Where The Soul Never Dies (6)
Whiskey River (11,19,22)
Whispering Hope (6)
White Christmas (15)
Whiter Shade Of Pale (23)
Who'll Buy My Memories [solo: Willie] (32)
Who's Sorry Now? (20)
Why Are You Pickin' On Me (31)
Why Baby Why (27)
Why Do I Have To Choose (27)
Why Me (14)
Wild Side Of Life (13)
Will The Circle Be Unbroken (6,11)
Will You Remember? (12,21)
Wind Beneath My Wings (31)
Winter Wonderland (15)
Without A Song (28)
Won't You Ride In My Little Red Wagon (20)
Wonderful Future (12)
Would You Lay With Me (In A Field Of Stone) (27)
Write Your Own Songs (24,32)
Year That Clayton Delaney Died (24)
Year 2003 Minus 25 (9)
Yesterday (4)
Yesterday's Wine (17)
You Are My Sunshine (13)
You Left A Long, Long Time Ago (2,21)
You Ought To Hear Me Cry (7)
You Show Me Yours (And I'll Show You Mine) (14,19)
You Wouldn't Cross The Street (To Say Goodbye) (33)
You'll Never Know (28)

NEMESIS

Rap trio from Dallas: The Snake, Big Al and M.C. Azim.

7/13/91	183	2		Munchies For Your Bass	$12	Profile 1411

All English And The 40 Oz. Thieves
Bitches And Money
Dallas We Come From
Dis-N-Dat
Droppin' The Bass
Grind
I Want Your Sex
Let's Have A Good Time
Life In The 90's
Munchies For Your Bass
Nemesis To The Future
On The One
Settin' The Record Straight
S.O.U.L.

NENA

Gabriele "Nena" Kerner (b: 3/26/60) with four-member backup group from Hagen, Germany.

3/24/84	27	14		99 Luftballons	$8	Epic 39294

Das Land Der Elefanten
Hangin' On You
Just A Dream
Kino
Let Me Be Your Pirate
Leuchtturm
99 Luftballons 2
99 Red Balloons
?
Rette Mich
Uner Kannt Durch's Marchenland

★★158★★ NERO, Peter

Born on 5/22/34 in Brooklyn. Pop-jazz-classical pianist. Won the 1961 Best New Artist Grammy Award.

7/10/61	34	22		1 Piano Forte .... [I]	$12	RCA 2334
9/18/61	32	62		2 New Piano In Town .... [I]	$12	RCA 2383
3/17/62	22	23		3 Young And Warm And Wonderful .... [I]	$12	RCA 2484
7/7/62	16	38		4 For The Nero-Minded .... [I]	$12	RCA 2536
2/2/63	40	9		5 The Colorful Peter Nero .... [I]	$12	RCA 2638
3/30/63	5	28		6 Hail The Conquering Nero .... [I]	$12	RCA 2638
9/7/63	31	23		7 Peter Nero In Person .... [I-L]	$12	RCA 2710
2/29/64	133	4		8 Sunday In New York .... [S-I]	$12	RCA 2827
6/6/64	38	26		9 Reflections .... [I]	$12	RCA 2853
10/10/64	42	21		10 Songs You Won't Forget .... [I]	$12	RCA 2935
2/20/65	123	4		11 The Best Of Peter Nero .... [G-I]	$12	RCA 2978
5/29/65	147	3		12 Career Girls .... [I]	$12	RCA 3313
10/23/65	86	16		13 Nero Goes "Pops" .... [I]	$15	RCA 2821

PETER NERO/BOSTON POPS/ARTHUR FIEDLER

DEBUT DATE	PEAK POS	WKS CHR	G O L D	ARTIST — Album Title	$	Label & Number

NERO, Peter — Cont'd

2/19/66	114	6		14 The Screen Scene ....[I]	$12	RCA 3496
7/16/66	141	3		15 Peter Nero-Up Close ....[I]	$12	RCA 3550
5/13/67	193	2		16 Peter Nero plays Born Free and others...................................[I]	$12	RCA Camden 2139
4/20/68	180	4		17 Peter Nero plays Love Is Blue and ten other great songs ....[I]	$12	RCA 3936
5/10/69	193	3		18 I've Gotta Be Me ....[I]	$12	Columbia 9800
11/27/71+	23	27	●	19 Summer of '42 ....[I]	$10	Columbia 31105
7/8/72	172	9		20 The First Time Ever (I Saw Your Face) ....[I]	$10	Columbia 31335

All The Things You Are (3)
America (medley) (7)
And I Love Her (15)
Anna (6)
Are My Dreams Real? (7)
As Long As He Needs Me (9)
Autumn (10)
Baby I'm A Want You (20)
Bess, You Is My Woman (2)
Best Is Yet To Come (9)
Best Thing For You (15)
Bidin' My Time (13)
Black Is The Color Of My True Love's Hair (5)
Bluesette (9)
Body And Soul (2)
Born Free (16)
Boy Like That (medley) (7)
Brian's Song (20)
Button Up Your Overcoat (7)
Call Me Irresponsible (10)
Career Girl (12)
Certain Smile (12)
Cherokee (1)
Chim Chim Cheree (14)
Continental Holiday (6)
Cookie Crumbles (8)
Cute (7)
Dancing On The Ceiling (4)
Days Of Wine And Roses (9)
Deep Purple (5)
Don't Blame Me (3)
Don't Get Around Much Anymore (4)
Don't Speak Of Love (8,16)
Easy To Love (12)
Eileen's Theme (8)
Embraceable You (13)
England Swings (15)
Ev'rything I've Got (4)
Everything I Own (20)
First Time Ever (I Saw Your Face) (20)
Flick, The (14)

For All We Know (19)
For Once In My Life (18)
Forget Domani (Forget Tomorrow) (14)
Fox, Theme From The (17)
Free Again (19)
Get Me To The Church On Time (1)
Girl From Ipanema (10)
Gloomy Sunday (6)
Glory Of Love (17)
Go Away Little Girl (19)
Godfather, Love Theme From (20)
Golden Earrings (5)
Gone With The Wind (16)
Got To Be There (20)
Granada (6)
Green Leaves Of Summer (7)
Happy Time (17)
Harlow (Lonely Girl), Theme From (14)
Hello (8)
Hello, Dolly! (10)
Hello Hop (8)
Help! (14)
Here's That Rainy Day (15)
Hey Jude (18)
How Can You Mend A Broken Heart? (19)
Hurting Each Other (20)
I Can't Get Started (1)
I Could Have Danced All Night (12)
I Feel Pretty (medley) (7)
I Got Plenty O' Nuttin' (7,16)
I Got Rhythm (13)
I Love How You Love Me (18)
I Say A Little Prayer (17)
I Want To Hold Your Hand (10)
I Wish You Love (10)
I'm Gonna Make You Love Me (8)

I'm Gonna Sit Right Down And Write Myself A Letter (12)
I've Gotta Be Me (18)
I've Grown Accustomed To Her Face (1,11)
In Other Words (Fly Me To The Moon) (1)
Isn't It Romantic (4)
It's A Darn Good Thing (16)
It's All Right With Me (7,11)
Journey To Red Rocks (5)
Just One Of Those Things (2)
Just Squeeze Me (3)
Let's Not Waste A Moment (4)
Little Girl Blue (4)
Lo Mucho Que Te Quiero (All I Need Is Time) (18)
Londonderry Air (16)
Long Ago And Far Away (2)
Look For The Silver Lining (5)
Lot Of Livin' To Do (15)
Love (19)
Love Is A Many-Splendored Thing (7)
Love Is A Simple Thing (4)
Love Is Blue (17)
Love Is Here To Stay (13)
Love Story, Theme From (19)
Love That Never Ends (20)
Mack The Knife (6)
Made For Each Other, Theme From (20)
Make It With You (19)
Man I Love (13)
Maria (2,7,11)
Midnight In Moscow (6,11)
Moment Of Truth (9)
Mood Indigo (5,11)
Moon River (4,11)
More (9)
More In Love (8,11)

Most Beautiful Girl In The World (12)
Mountain Greenery (2,11)
My Bonnie Lies Over The Ocean (6)
My Coloring Book (9)
My Favorite Things (14)
My Funny Valentine (7)
My Man's Gone Now (4)
My Ship (17)
Never Can Say Goodbye (20)
Never My Love (19)
Never On Sunday (6)
Night And Day (1,11)
No Moon At All (15)
Ob-La-Di Ob-La-Da, Variations On The Theme (18)
On Frantic Fifth (8)
On Green Dolphin Street (5,11)
On The Street Where You Live (2)
Orange Colored Sky (5)
Out Of This World (12)
Over The Rainbow (1)
People (10)
Personality (12)
Philosopher, The (8)
Pick Yourself Up (15)
Pink Panther Theme (10)
Rain In My Heart (18)
Reflections (9)
Rhapsody In Blue (13)
Room Without Windows (10)
Sandpiper, Love Theme From The ..see: Shadow Of Your Smile
Scarborough Fair/Canticle (18)
Scarlet Ribbons (5)
Scratch My Bach (1)
Secret Love (3,11)
Serenade In Blue (5)

Shadow Of Your Smile (14)
Shangri-La (10)
She Loves Me (9)
Shelter Of Your Arms (10)
Ship Of Fools (14)
Show Me (12)
Silencers, Theme From The (14)
Slow Boat To China (2)
Someone To Watch Over Me (12)
Something's Coming (4,7)
Somewhere (medley) (7)
Soulful Strut (18)
Speak Low (12)
Spring Concerto (15)
Spring Is Here (1)
Spy Who Came In From The Cold, Theme From (14)
St. Louis Blues (2)
Star Eyes (12)
Stella By Starlight (16)
Stormy Weather (2)
Strange Music (6)
Summer Of '42, Theme From (19) **21**
Sunday In New York (8,16)
Sunny (17)
Surrey With The Fringe On Top (1)
Sweetest Sounds (16)
Take The "A" Train (15)
Tangerine (5)
Taxi! (8)
Tea For Two (2)
Tender Is The Night (10)
That's All (1)
Then I'll Be Tired Of You (15)
They Can't Take That Away From Me (13)
(They Long To Be) Close To You (19)
This Is All I Ask (9)
Thou Swell (14)

Three Coins In The Fountain (2)
Thunderball (14)
Tonight (medley) (7)
Too Late Now (4)
Try To Remember (17)
Variations ..see: Ob-La-Di Ob-La-Da
Walk Right In (9)
Warm (3)
Wasn't The Summer Short (3)
Way You Look Tonight (3)
We've Only Just Begun (19)
What Kind Of Fool Am I? (6)
What's New Pussycat? (14)
When I Fall In Love (3)
When My Dream Boat Comes Home (15)
When The World Was Young (6,11)
Who Will Answer? (17)
Who's Afraid Of Virginia Woolf? (16)
Wichita Lineman (18)
Windy (17)
Without You (20)
Wives And Lovers (9)
Wonderful You (3,8,16)
Yellow Rose Of Texas (5)
Yesterday (15)
Yesterdays (4)
You Are Too Beautiful (3)
You've Got A Friend (19)
Young And Warm And Wonderful (3)

NESMITH, Michael, & The First National Band

Born on 12/30/43 in Houston. Michael was a professional musician before joining The Monkees. Wrote Linda Ronstadt's hit "Different Drum." Formed own video production company, Pacific Arts, in 1977; produced films *Elephant Parts*, *Repo Man* and others. Also see The Wichita Train Whistle.

10/17/70	143	3		1 Magnetic South	$30	RCA 4371
1/2/71	159	4		2 Loose Salute	$25	RCA 4415
8/4/79	151	9		3 Infinite Rider On The Big Dogma	$15	Pacific Arts 130

MICHAEL NESMITH

Beyond The Blue Horizon (1)
Bye, Bye, Bye (2)
Calico Girlfriend (1)
Capsule (Hello People A Hundred Years From Now) (3)
Carioca (Blue Carioca) (3)

Conversations (2)
Crippled Lion (1)
Cruisin' (Lucy And Ramona And Sunset Sam) (3)
Dance (Dance & Have A Good Time) (3)
Dedicated Friend (2)

Factions (The Daughter Of Rock N' Roll) (3)
First National Rag (1)
Flying (Silks & Satins) (3)
Hello Lady (2)
Hollywood (1)

Horserace (Beauty And The Magnum Force) (3)
I Fall To Pieces (2)
Keys To The Car (1)
Lady Of The Valley (2)
Light (The Eclectic Light) (3)

Listen To The Band (2)
Little Red Rider (1)
Magic (This Night Is Magic) (3)
Mama Nantucket (1)
Nine Times Blue (1)
One Rose (1)

Silver Moon (2) **42**
Tengo Amor (2)
Thanx For The Ride (2)
Tonite (The Television Song) (3)

Joanne (1) **21**

NEVIL, Robbie

Pop singer/songwriter/guitarist from Los Angeles.

| 11/29/86+ | 37 | 46 | | 1 Robbie Nevil .... | $8 | Manhattan 53006 |
| 11/26/88+ | 118 | 21 | | 2 A Place Like This .... | $8 | EMI 48359 |

Back On Holiday (2) **34**
Back To You (1)
C'est La Vie (1) **2**
Can I Count On You (2)

Dominoes (1) *14*
Getting Better (2)
Here I Go Again (2)
Holding On (2)

Just A Little Closer (1)
Limousines (2)
Look Who's Alone Tonight (1)
Love And Money (2)

Love Is Only Love (2)
Mary Lou (2)
Neighbors (1)

Simple Life (Mambo Luv Thang) (1)
Somebody Like You (2) **63**
Too Soon (2)

Walk Your Talk (1)
Wot's It To Ya (1) *10*

NEVILLE, Aaron

Born on 1/24/41 in New Orleans. Member of the New Orleans family group The Neville Brothers. Brother Art was keyboardist of The Meters. Bassist/singer Ivan Neville is his son. Also see Linda Ronstadt.

| 6/29/91 | 44 | 41 | ● | Warm Your Heart .... | $12 | A&M 5354 |

co-produced by Linda Ronstadt

Angola Bound
Ave Maria
Close Your Eyes

Don't Go Please Stay
Everybody Plays The Fool *8*

I Bid You Goodnight
It Feels Like Rain

La Vie Dansante
Louisiana 1927

Somewhere, Somebody
That's The Way She Loves

Warm Your Heart
With You In Mind

DEBUT DATE	PEAK POS	WKS CHR	GOLD	ARTIST — Album Title	$	Label & Number

NEVILLE, Ivan

New Orleans bassist. Son of singer Aaron Neville (of The Neville Brothers). Formerly with Bonnie Raitt's band. Played on The Rolling Stones' *Dirty Work* album.

| 11/12/88+ | **107** | 23 | | If My Ancestors Could See Me Now .... | **$8** | Polydor 834896 |

After All This Time   **Falling Out Of Love 91**   Never Should Have Told Me   Out In The Streets   Sun
Another Day's Gone By   Money Talks   **Not Just Another Girl 26**   Primitive Man   Up To You

NEVILLE BROTHERS, The

New Orleans quintet formed in 1977: Art (b: 12/17/37; keyboards), Charles (b: 1939; sax), Aaron (b: 1/24/41; percussion) and Cyril (b: 1949; percussion) Neville. All share vocals. In the early '50s, Art joined The Hawketts (recorded the Carnival standard "Mardi Gras Mambo"), which Charles and Aaron later joined. Aaron's solo chart career began in the '60s. Art was a member of The Meters from 1966-77. Cyril was with The Meters from 1975-77. Charles and Aaron also contributed to The Meters, 1976-77.

| 8/29/81 | **166** | 3 | | 1 Fiyo On The Bayou .... | **$8** | A&M 4866 |
| 4/11/87 | **178** | 3 | | 2 Treacherous: A History Of The Neville Brothers 1955-1985 ....[K] | **$10** | Rhino 71494 [2] |

includes solo recordings by Art and Aaron, a 1955 recording by Art's first group, The Hawketts, and a 1976 recording with the Wild Tchoupitoulas Mardi Gras Indian tribe

| 5/2/87 | **155** | 9 | | 3 Uptown .... | **$8** | EMI America 17249 |

guest musicians: Jerry Garcia, Branford Marsalis, Ronnie Montrose, Keith Richards and Carlos Santana

4/8/89	**66**	24		4 Yellow Moon	**$8**	A&M 5240
8/25/90	**60**	15		5 Brother's Keeper	**$12**	A&M 5312
5/23/92	**103**	9		6 Family Groove	**$12**	A&M 5384

All These Things (2)
Amazing Grace (medley) (2)
Amen (medley) (2)
Arianne (2)
Ballad Of Hollis Brown (4)
Bird On A Wire (5)
Brother Blood (5)
Brother Jake (5)
Brother John (1,2)
  recorded as The Wild
  Tchoupitoulas on LP #2
Cha Dooky-Do (2)
Change Is Gonna Come (4)
Dancing Jones (2)
Day To Day Thing (6)
Down By The Riverside (medley) (2)

Drift Away (3)
Fallin' Rain (5)
Family Groove (6)
Fear, Hate, Envy, Jealousy (2)
Fearless (5)
Fever (2)
Fire And Brimstone (4)
Fire On The Bayou (1,2)
Fly Like An Eagle (6)
Forever...For Tonight (3)
Greatest Love (2)
Healing Chant (4)
Hercules (2)
Hey Pocky Way (1,2)
I Can See It In Your Eyes (6)
I Love Her Too (2)

I Never Needed No One (3)
Iko Iko (medley) (1)
It Takes More (6)
Jah Love (5)
Let My People Go (6)
Let's Live (2)
Line Of Fire (6)
Maori Chant (6)
Mardi Gras Mambo (2)
  recorded as The Hawketts
Meet De Boys On The Battlefront (2)
  recorded as The Wild Tchoupitoulas
Midnight Key (3)
Mona Lisa (1)

Money Back Guarantee (My Love Is Guaranteed) (3)
My Blood (4)
My Brother's Keeper (5)
Mystery Train (5)
Old Habits Die Hard (3)
On The Other Side Of Paradise (6)
One More Day (6)
Over You (2)
River Of Life (5)
Run Joe (1)
Saxafunk (6)
Shek-A-Na-Na (3)
Sister Rosa (4)
Sitting In Limbo (1,2)
Sons And Daughters (5)

Spirits Of The World (3)
Steer Me Right (5)
Sweet Honey Dripper (1)
Take Me To Heart (6)
Tell It Like It Is [solo: Aaron] (2) **2**
Ten Commandments Of Love (1)
True Love (6)
Voodoo (4)
Waiting At The Station (2)
Wake Up (2)
Washable Ink (2)
Whatever It Takes (3)
Where Is My Baby (2)
Wild Injuns (4)

Will The Circle Be Unbroken (4)
With God On Our Side (4)
Witness (5)
Wrong Number (I Am Sorry, Goodbye) (2)
Yellow Moon (4)
You're The One (3)
Zing, Zing (2)

NEWBEATS, The

Pop trio: Larry Henley (b: 6/30/41, Arp, Texas; lead singer) with brothers Dean and Marc Mathis (b: Hahira, Georgia on 3/17/39 and 2/9/42, respectively).

| 10/3/64 | **56** | 19 | | 1 Bread & Butter .... | **$50** | Hickory 120 |
| 1/22/66 | **131** | 4 | | 2 Run Baby Run .... | **$50** | Hickory 128 |

Ain't That Lovin' You, Baby (1)
Bread And Butter (1) **2**
Bye, Bye, Love (1)
Come See About Me (2)

Everything's Alright (1) **16**
Hang On Sloopy (2)
Help (2)
(I Can't Get No) Satisfaction (2)

I'm Blue (The Gong-Gong Song) (1)
It's Really Goodbye (2)
Little Child (2)
Looking For Love (2)

Mean Wooly Willie (2)
Oh, Girls, Girls (2)
Oh, Pretty Woman (2)
Patent On Love (1)
Pink Dally Rue (1)

Run, Baby Run (Back Into My Arms) (2) **12**
Shoop Shoop Song (It's In His Kiss) (1)
So Fine (1)

There Oughta Be A Law (Bout The Stuff I Saw) (1)
This Old Heart (2)
Thou Shalt Not Steal (1)
Tough Little Buggy (1)

NEW BIRTH, The

R&B vocal group portion of New Birth, Inc. (see Nite-Liters). Original group consisted of vocalists Londee Loren, Bobby Downs, Melvin Wilson, Leslie Wilson, Ann Bogan and soloist Alan Frye, with instrumental backing by The Nite-Liters. Melvin, Leslie and Ann recorded as Love, Peace & Happiness in 1972. Ann was also a member of The Marvelettes and in duo, Harvey & Ann, with Harvey Fuqua.

10/30/71	**189**	2		1 Ain't No Big Thing, But It's Growing	**$12**	RCA 4526
3/10/73	**31**	29		2 Birth Day	**$10**	RCA 4797
11/17/73+	**50**	31	●	3 It's Been A Long Time	**$10**	RCA 0285
8/17/74	**56**	15		4 Comin' From All Ends	**$10**	RCA 0494
5/24/75	**57**	17		5 Blind Baby	**$10**	Buddah 5636
7/19/75	**175**	2		6 The Best Of The New Birth ....[G]	**$10**	RCA 1021
8/28/76	**168**	4		7 Love Potion	**$10**	Warner 2953
12/10/77+	**164**	6		8 Behold The Mighty Army	**$8**	Warner 3071

Ain't It Something (8)
Ain't No Change (3)
Blind Baby (5)
Blind Man (5)
Buck & The Preacher, Theme From (2)
Come On And Dream Some Paradise (3)
Comin' From All Ends (4)
Deeper (8)
Do It Again (4,6)
Dream Merchant (5) **36**

Easy, Evil (2)
Echoes Of My Mind (4)
End To End (4)
Fallin' In Love (7)
Fire & Rain (1)
Forever (4)
Got To Get A Knutt (2,6)
Granddaddy (Part 1) (5) **95**
Heaven Says (3)
Honeybee (3)
How Good It Feels (1)
How Will I Live (8)

Hurry Hurry (7)
I Can Understand It (2,6) **35**
I Never Felt This Way Before (7)
I Remember Well (5)
I Want To Make It With You (1)
I Wash My Hands Of The Whole Damn Deal, Part I (4) **88**

I'd Spend My Whole Life Loving You (3)
It's Been A Long Time (3,6) **66**
It's Impossible (1,6) **52**
Keep On Doin' It (3)
Lady Love (4)
Let It Be Me (1)
Long And Winding Road (7)
Mighty Army (8)
Never Can Say Goodbye (1,6)
Oh What A Feeling (1)

O-o-h Child (1)
Pains Of Love (3)
Patiently (4)
Pretty Music (4)
Slow Driving (7)
Squeezing Too Much Living (8)
Stop, Look, Listen (To Your Heart) (2)
Sure Thing (7)
Take This Train To Freedom (4)

Until It's Time For You To Go (2) **97**
Up Against The Wall (8)
We Are All God's Children (7)
Why Did I (5)
Wildflower (3,6) **45**
You Are What I'm All About (2)
Your Love Is (8)
Your Love Is In My Veins (8)

NEWBURY, Mickey

Born Milton S. Newbury, Jr. on 5/19/40 in Houston. Moved to Nashville in 1963, worked as staff writer for Acuff-Rose. Wrote "Just Dropped In (To See What Condition My Condition Was In)."

11/13/71+	**58**	15		1 'Frisco Mabel Joy	**$10**	Elektra 74107
3/10/73	**173**	5		2 Heaven Help The Child	**$10**	Elektra 75055
4/5/75	**172**	3		3 Lovers	**$10**	Elektra 1030

American Trilogy (1) **26**
Apples Dipped In Candy (3)
Cortelia Clark (2)

Frisco Depot (1)
Future's Not What It Used To Be (1)

Good Morning Dear (2)
Good Night (3)
Heaven Help The Child (2)

How I Love Them Old Songs (1)

How Many Times (Must The Piper Be Paid For His Song) (1)

How's The Weather (3)
If You Ever Get To Houston (3)

NEWBURY, Mickey — Cont'd

Lead On (3)
Let Me Sleep (3)
Lovers (3)
Mobile Blue (1)

Remember The Good (1)
Sail Away (3)
San Francisco Mabel Joy (2)
Song For Susan (2)

Sunshine (2) 87
Sweet Memories (2)
Swiss Cottage Place (1)

When Do We Stop Starting Over (3)
Why You Been Gone So Long (2)

You're Not My Same Sweet Baby (1)
You've Always Got The Blues (3)

NEW CACTUS BAND — see CACTUS

★★267★★ NEW CHRISTY MINSTRELS, The

Folk/balladeer troupe named after the Christy Minstrels (formed in 1842 by Edwin "Pop" Christy). Group founded and led by Randy Sparks — Barry McGuire, lead singer. Kenny Rogers was briefly a member in 1966.

DEBUT DATE	PEAK POS	WKS CHR	GOLD	ARTIST — Album Title	$	Label & Number
10/20/62	19	92		1 The New Christy Minstrels	$20	Columbia 8672
2/23/63	30	20		2 The New Christy Minstrels In Person [L]	$20	Columbia 8741
5/25/63	20	22		3 Tall Tales! Legends & Nonsense	$20	Columbia 8817
8/24/63	15	77	●	4 Ramblin' featuring Green, Green	$20	Columbia 8855
4/18/64	9	34		5 Today [S]	$20	Columbia 8959
				featuring songs from the film *Advance To The Rear*		
8/29/64	48	23		6 Land Of Giants	$20	Columbia 8987
2/13/65	62	11		7 Cowboys And Indians	$20	Columbia 9103
6/26/65	22	22		8 Chim Chim Cher-ee	$20	Columbia 9109
10/16/65	125	9		9 The Wandering Minstrels	$20	Columbia 9184
6/18/66	76	16		10 Greatest Hits [G]	$20	Columbia 9279
11/28/70	195	2		11 You Need Someone To Love	$10	Gregar 102

Ambush At Teton Pass (7)
Anything Love Can Buy (5)
Appleseed John (6)
Beaucatcher Mountain (3)
Because (11)
Betsy From Pike (7)
Billy's Mule (3)
Bits And Pieces Medley (2)
Blacksmith Of Brandywine (6)
Brackenby's Music Box (5)
Brother (11)
California (1)
Can You Do The Can-Can? (9)
Casey Jones (6)
Cat, The (3)
Charleston Town (5)
Chim, Chim, Cheree (8,10) 81
Company Of Cowards (5)
Corn Whiskey (7)
Cotton Fields (8,10)
Cotton Pickers' Song (1)
Deep Blue Sea (1)

Denver (2)
Don't Cry, Suzanne (1)
Down The Ohio (4)
Down To Darby (3)
Downtown (8,10)
Drinkin' Gourd (The Muddy Road To Freedom) (4,10)
Dying Convict (2)
East & West (11)
El Camino Real (6)
Everybody Loves Saturday Night (9,10)
Fire (1)
Freedom (4)
Girl From Ipanema (9)
Go, Lassie, Go (9)
Golden Bells (2)
Green, Green (4,10) 14
Guadalajara (1)
Hard To Be Without You (11)
He's A Loser (8)
Hi Jolly (4)
I Know Where I'm Goin' (1)
Ida Red (7,10)
In The Hills Of Shiloh (3)

In The Pines (1)
Invalids, The (2)
It's Gonna Be Fine (8)
Jimmy Grove And Barbara Ellen (3)
Joe Magarac (6)
John Henry And The Steam Drill (6)
Julianne (3)
Kisses Sweeter Than Wine (8)
Ladies (5)
Land Of Giants (Theme) (6)
Lark Day (8)
Last Farewell (4)
Lily Langtry (7)
Little Bit Of Happiness (8,10)
Live! Live! (Havah Nagilah) (9)
Liza Lee (2)
Louisiana Lou (2)
Lovely Greensleeves (9)
Make It With You (11)
Massacre (9)
Mighty Big Ways (6)

Mighty Mississippi (4,10)
Mount Rushmore (6)
My Dear Mary Anne (4)
My Last Gold Dollar Is Gone (7)
My Name Is Liberty (6)
Natural Man (6)
Nine Hundred Miles (5)
Oh! Shenando (1)
Old-Timer (3)
Paul Bunyan (6)
Railroad Bill (1)
Ramblin' (4)
Red Clay Country (7)
Red River Shore (7)
Ride, Ride, Ride (4)
Rounder, The (5)
Rovin' Gambler (4)
Saints' Train (2)
Song Of The Pious Itinerant (Hallelujah, I'm A Bum) (3)
Song Of The Wandering Minstrels (9)

South American Get Away (11)
Springfield Fair (1)
Springtime (8)
Stormy (6)
(Story Of) The Preacher And The Bear (2)
Susanna (3)
Sweet Sorrento (9)
That Big Rock Candy Mountain (1)
They Gotta Quit Kickin' My Dog Around (7)
(They Long To Be) Close To You (11)
This Land Is Your Land (1) 93
This Ol' Riverboat (includes 2 versions) (5)
Three Wheels On My Wagon (3)
Tie Me Kangaroo Down, Sport (9)
Today (5,10) 17
Travelin' Man (4)

Treasury Of Nonsense Medley (3)
Turtles And Trees (11)
Wagoner's Song (Land Of The Sacramento) (8)
Way Down In Arkansas (5)
We'll Sing In The Sunshine (8,10)
Wellinbrook Well (1)
Whistle (1)
Whistlin' Dixie (5)
Wigwam (11)
Wimoweh (The Lion Sleeps Tonight) (9)
Yamao Toko No Uta (9)
You Know My Name (2)
You Need Someone To Love (11)

NEWCLEUS

New York rap group.

DEBUT DATE	PEAK POS	WKS CHR	GOLD	ARTIST — Album Title	$	Label & Number
9/8/84	74	28		Jam On Revenge	$8	Sunnyview 4901

Auto-Man

Computer Age (Push The Button)

Destination Earth (1999)
I'm Not A Robot

Jam On It 56
Jam On Revenge

No More Runnin'
Where's The Beat

NEW COLONY SIX, The

Soft-rock group from Chicago: Patrick McBride, Ronnie Rice, Gerry Van Kollenburg, Les Kummel, Chuck Jobes and William Herman. Ray Graffia joined in 1969. Kummel died on 12/18/78 (age 33).

DEBUT DATE	PEAK POS	WKS CHR	GOLD	ARTIST — Album Title	$	Label & Number
9/2/67	172	7		1 Colonization	$35	Sentar 3001
7/20/68	157	6		2 Revelations	$20	Mercury 61165
11/1/69	179	4		3 Attacking A Straw Man	$20	Mercury 61228

Accept My Ring (1)
Barbara, I Love You (3) 78
Blue Eyes (3)
Can't You See Me Cry (2) 52
Come And Give Your Love To Me (3)
Come Away With You (3)

Dandy Handy Man (2)
Elf Song (Ballad Of The Wingbat Marmaduke) (1)
Free (3)
Girl Unsigned (2)
Hello Lonely (1)
Hold Me With Your Eyes (2)

I Could Never Lie To You (3) 50
I Want You To Know (3) 65
I Will Always Think About You (2) 22
I'm Here Now (1)
I'm Just Waitin' (Anticipatin' For Her To Show Up) (1)

Just Feel Worse (1)
Let Me Love You (1)
Love, That's The Best I Can Do (3)
Love You So Much (1) 61
Mister You're A Better Man Than I (1)

My Dreams Depend On You (1)
Power Of Love (1)
Prairie Grey (3)
Ride The Wicked Wind (3)
Summertime's Another Name For Love (2)
Sun Within You (3)

Things I'd Like To Say (2) 16
Treat Her Groovy (2)
Warm Baby (1)
We Will Love Again (2)
Woman (1)
You Know Better (2)
You're Gonna Be Mine (1)

NEW EDITION

Boston R&B teen vocal quintet (ages 13 to 15 in 1983): Ralph Tresvant, Ronald DeVoe, Michael Bivins, Ricky Bell and Bobby Brown. Formed in 1982 by future New Kids On The Block and Perfect Gentlemen producer, Maurice Starr. Brown left for solo career in 1986; replaced by Johnny Gill in 1988. Bell, Bivins and DeVoe recorded as Bell Biv DeVoe in 1990. Tresvant and Gill recorded solo in the '90s.

DEBUT DATE	PEAK POS	WKS CHR	GOLD	ARTIST — Album Title	$	Label & Number
9/3/83	90	33		1 Candy Girl	$8	Streetwise 3301
10/13/84+	6	54	▲	2 New Edition	$8	MCA 5515
12/7/85+	32	48	▲	3 All For Love	$8	MCA 5679
12/20/86+	43	23	●	4 Under The Blue Moon	$8	MCA 5912
				features standards from the '50s and '60s		
7/9/88	12	50	▲	5 Heart Break	$8	MCA 42207
10/19/91	99	6		6 New Edition's Greatest Hits, Volume One [G]	$12	MCA 10434

All For Love (3)
Baby Love (2)
Blue Moon (4)
Boys To Men (5,6)
Bring Back The Memories (4)

Can You Stand The Rain (5,6) 44
Candy Girl (1,6) 46
Competition (5)
Cool It Now (2,6) 4

Count Me Out (3,6) 51
Crucial (5)
Delicious (2)
Duke Of Earl (4)
Earth Angel (4) 21

Gimme Your Love (1)
Gotta Have Your Lovin' (1)
Hey There Lonely Girl (4)
Hide And Seek (2)
I'm Comin' Home (5)

I'm Leaving You Again (2)
If It Isn't Love (5,6) 7
Is This The End (1,6) 85
Jealous Girl (1)
Kickback (3)

Kinda Girls We Like (5)
Let's Be Friends (3)
Little Bit Of Love (Is All It Takes) (3,6) 38
Lost In Love (2,6) 35

DEBUT DATE	PEAK POS	WKS CHR	GOLD	ARTIST — Album Title	$	Label & Number

NEW EDITION — Cont'd

Maryann (2)
Million To One (4)
Mr. Telephone Man (2,6) *12*
My Secret (Didja Gitit Yet?) (2)

N.E. Heart Break (5)
Ooh Baby (1)
Pass The Beat (1)
Popcorn Love (1,6)
School (3)

She Gives Me A Bang (1)
Should Have (1)
Since I Don't Have You (4)
Sweet Thing (3)
Tears On My Pillow (4)

That's The Way We're Livin' (5)
Thousand Miles Away (4)
Tonight's Your Night (3)
What's Your Name (4)

Where It All Started (5)
Whispers In Bed (3)
Who Do You Trust (3)
With You All The Way (3) *51*

You're Not My Kind Of Girl (5) *95*

NEW ENGLAND
East Coast melodic-rock quartet: John Fannon, Jimmy Waldo, Hirsh Gardner and Gary Shea.

| 5/19/79 | **50** | 17 | | 1 New England .... | $8 | Infinity 9007 |
| 7/18/81 | **176** | 4 | | 2 Walking Wild .... | $8 | Elektra 346 |

produced by Todd Rundgren

Alone Tonight (1)
DDT (2)
Don't Ever Let Me Go (2)
Don't Ever Wanna Lose Ya (1) *40*

Elevator (2)
Encore (1)
Get It Up (2)
Hello, Hello, Hello (1) *69*
Holdin' Out On Me (2)

L-5 (2)
Last Show (1)
Love's Up In The Air (2)
Nothing To Fear (1)

P.U.N.K. (Puny Undernourished Kid) (1)
Shall I Run Away (1)
She's Gonna Tear You Apart (2)

Shoot (1)
Turn Out The Light (1)
Walking Wild (2)
You're There (2)

NEW ENGLAND CONSERVATORY RAGTIME ENSEMBLE
Gunther Schuller, conductor.

| 5/19/73+ | **65** | 36 | | Scott Joplin: The Red Back Book .... [I] | $8 | Angel 36060 |

Red Back Book: collection of famous Joplin rags

Cascades, The
Chrysanthemum, The

Easy Winners
Entertainer, The

Maple Leaf Rag
Rag Time Dance

Sugar Cane
Sun Flower Slow Drag

NEW GRASS REVIVAL — see RUSSELL, Leon

★★357★★ NEWHART, Bob
Born on 9/5/29 in Oak Park, Illinois. Enduring deadpan comedian/TV actor. Bob starred in three TV situation comedies: *The Bob Newhart Show* (1972-78), *Newhart* (1982-90) and *Bob* (since 1992).

| 5/16/60 | **1**[14] | 108 | ● | 1 The Button-Down Mind Of Bob Newhart .... [C] | $30 | Warner 1379 |

1960 Grammy winner: Album of the Year

11/14/60+	**1**[1]	70	●	2 The Button-Down Mind Strikes Back! .... [C]	$30	Warner 1393
10/30/61	**10**	30		3 Behind The Button-Down Mind Of Bob Newhart .... [C]	$30	Warner 1417
9/8/62	**28**	26		4 The Button-Down Mind On TV .... [C]	$30	Warner 1467

Bob hosted a comedy variety show from 1961-62

| 2/29/64 | **113** | 11 | | 5 Bob Newhart Faces Bob Newhart (faces Bob Newhart) ...... [C] | $30 | Warner 1517 |
| 4/24/65 | **126** | 5 | | 6 The Windmills Are Weakening .... [C] | $30 | Warner 1588 |

Abe Lincoln Vs. Madison Avenue (1)
African Movie (3)
Amateur Show Contestants (5)
Automation and A Private In Washington's Army (2)
Ben Franklin In Analysis (6)
Bus Drivers School (2)
Buying A House (6)

Cruise Of The U.S.S. Codfish (3)
Defusing A Bomb (4)
Driving Instructor (1)
Edison's Most Famous Invention (4)
Expectant Father (5)
Friend With A Dog (4)
General Chariot Corp. (4)

Grace L. Ferguson Airline (And Storm Door Co.) (2)
Herb Philbrick - Counter Spy (3)
Hold Out Huns (4)
Infinite Number Of Monkeys (2)
Introducing Tobacco To Civilization (2)
King Kong (6)

Krushchev Landing Rehearsal (1)
Ledge Psychology (2)
Man Who Looked Like Hitler (5)
Merchandising The Wright Brothers (1)
Nobody Will Ever Play Baseball (1)
Nudist Camp Expose (5)

On Poodles And Planes (5)
Reflections On TV Commercials (5)
Retirement Party (2)
Returning A Gift (6)
Rocket Scientist (1)
Seven Lost Cities Of The Incas (3)
Siamese Cat (4)

Superman And The Dry Cleaner (6)
TV Commercials (3)
Tourist Meets Khrushchev (3)
Uncle Freddie Show (3)
Upset Stomach Commercial (6)

★★438★★ NEW KIDS ON THE BLOCK
Boston teen vocal quintet: Joe McIntyre (b: 12/31/72), Donny Wahlberg (b: 8/17/69), Danny Wood (b: 5/14/69), and brothers Jordan (b: 5/17/70) and Jon Knight (b: 11/29/68). Formed in the summer of 1984 by New Edition's founder/producer, Maurice Starr. Wahlberg is the older brother of Marky Mark.

| 8/27/88+ | **1**[2] | 132 | ▲[8] | 1 Hangin' Tough .... | $8 | Columbia 40985 |
| 8/5/89+ | **25** | 80 | ▲[3] | 2 New Kids On The Block .... [E] | $8 | Columbia 40475 |

their first album, originally released in 1987

10/14/89	**9**	18	▲[2]	3 Merry, Merry Christmas .... [X]	$8	Columbia 45280
6/23/90	**1**[1]	49	▲[3]	4 Step By Step	$12	Columbia 45129
11/17/90+	**48**	10		5 Merry, Merry Christmas .... [X-R]	$8	Columbia 45280

Christmas charts: 1/'89, 4/'90

| 12/8/90+ | **19** | 32 | ● | 6 No More Games/The Remix Album .... [K] | $12 | Columbia 46959 |

remixes of their hits; all of above produced by Maurice Starr

Angel (2)
Are You Down? (2)
Baby, I Believe In You (4,6)
Be My Girl (2)
Call It What You Want (4,6)
Christmas (Chestnuts Roasting On An Open Fire) (3)
Cover Girl (1,6) *2*
Didn't I (Blow Your Mind) (2) *8*

Don't Give Up On Me (2)
Funky, Funky, Xmas (3)
Funny Feeling (4)
Games (4,6)
Hangin' Tough (1,6) *1*
Happy Birthday (4)
Hold On (1)
I Need You (1)
I Remember When (1)
I Still Believe In Santa Claus (3)

I Wanna Be Loved By You (2)
I'll Be Loving You (Forever) (1) *1*
I'll Be Missin You Come Christmas (A Letter To Santa) (3)
Last Night I Saw Santa Claus (3)
Let's Try It Again (4) *53*
Little Drummer Boy (3)
Merry, Merry Christmas (3)

My Favorite Girl (1,6)
Never Gonna Fall In Love Again (4,6)
New Kids On The Block (2)
Please Don't Go Girl (1,6) *10*
Popsicle (2)
Right Stuff ..see: You Got It (The Right Stuff)
Stay With Me Baby (4)
Step By Step (4,6) *1*

Stop It Girl (2)
This One's For The Children (3) *7*
Time Is On Our Side (4)
Tonight (4) *7*
Treat Me Right (2)
Valentine Girl (6)
What'cha Gonna Do (About It) (1,6)
Where Do I Go From Here? (4)

White Christmas (3)
You Got It (The Right Stuff) (1,6) *3*

NEWMAN, Randy
Born on 11/28/43 in New Orleans. Singer/composer/pianist. Nephew of composers Alfred, Emil and Lionel Newman. Scored the films *Ragtime*, *The Natural* and *Avalon*.

10/2/71	**191**	3		1 Randy Newman/Live .... [L]	$10	Reprise 6459
6/17/72	**163**	18		2 Sail Away	$10	Reprise 2064
10/5/74	**36**	23		3 Good Old Boys	$10	Reprise 2193

background vocals by the Eagles' Glenn Frey and Don Henley

| 10/22/77+ | **9** | 29 | ● | 4 Little Criminals .... | $8 | Warner 3079 |

guest appearances by members of the Eagles

| 9/1/79 | **41** | 11 | | 5 Born Again .... | $8 | Warner 3346 |

vocal harmonies by Stephen Bishop

| 2/12/83 | **64** | 13 | | 6 Trouble In Paradise .... | $8 | Warner 23755 |

guests include Bob Seger, Linda Ronstadt, Paul Simon and Christine McVie

| 10/15/88 | **80** | 19 | | 7 Land Of Dreams .... | $8 | Reprise 25773 |

NEWMAN, Randy — Cont'd

Back On My Feet Again (3)
Bad News From Home (7)
Baltimore (4)
Birmingham (3)
Blues, The (6) *51*
Burn On (2)
Christmas In Capetown (3)
Cowboy (1)
Davy The Fat Boy (1)
Dayton, Ohio - 1903 (2)
Dixie Flyer (7)
Every Man A King (3)
Falling in Love (7)
Follow The Flag (7)
Four Eyes (7)
Ghosts (5)
Girls In My Life (Part 1) (5)

God's Song (That's Why I Love Mankind) (2)
Guilty (3)
Half A Man (5)
He Gives Us All His Love (2)
I Love L.A. (6)
I Think It's Going To Rain Today (1)
I Want You To Hurt Like I Do (7)
I'll Be Home (1,4)
I'm Different (6)
In Germany Before The War (4)
It's Money That I Love (5)
It's Money That Matters (7) *60*

Jolly Coppers On Parade (4)
Kathleen (Catholicism Made Easier) (4)
Kingfish (3)
Last Night I Had A Dream (1,2)
Little Criminals (4)
Living Without You (1)
Lonely At The Top (1,2)
Louisiana 1927 (3)
Lover's Prayer (1)
Mama Told Me Not To Come (1)
Marie (3)
Masterman And Baby J (7)
Maybe I'm Doing It Wrong (1)
Memo To My Son (2)

Miami (6)
Mikey's (6)
Mr. President (Have Pity On The Working Man) (3)
Mr. Sheep (5)
My Life Is Good (6)
Naked Man (3)
New Orleans Wins The War (7)
Old Kentucky Home (1)
Old Man (2)
Old Man On The Farm (4)
Political Science (2)
Pretty Boy (5)
Real Emotional Girl (6)
Red Bandana (7)

Rednecks (3)
Rider In The Rain (4)
Roll With The Punches (7)
Rollin' (3)
Sail Away (2)
Same Girl (6)
Short People (4) *2*
Sigmund Freud's Impersonation Of Albert Einstein In America (4)
Simon Smith And The Amazing Dancing Bear (2)
So Long Dad (4)
Something Special (7)
Song For The Dead (6)
Spies (5)

Story Of A Rock And Roll Band (5)
Take Me Back (6)
Texas Girl At The Funeral Of Her Father (4)
There's A Party At My House (6)
They Just Got Married (5)
Tickle Me (1)
Wedding In Cherokee County (3)
William Brown (5)
Yellow Man (1)
You Can Leave Your Hat On (2)
You Can't Fool The Fat Man (4)

NEW ORDER

Techno-dance quartet from Manchester, England. Evolved from the industrial-rock group Warsaw, formed in April 1977. Changed name to Joy Division. After suicide of vocalist Ian Curtis (May 1980), name changed to New Order. Lineup since 1986: Bernard Sumner, Stephen Morris, Peter Hook and Gillian Gilbert. Sumner was also a member of Electronic; Hook also with Revenge; and Morris and Gilbert with Tasty Fish.

DEBUT DATE	PEAK POS	WKS CHR	GOLD	ARTIST — Album Title	$	Label & Number
6/8/85	94	22		1 Low-life	$8	Qwest 25289
10/25/86	117	21		2 Brotherhood	$8	Qwest 25511
9/5/87+	36	60	▲	3 Substance .....[G]	$10	Qwest 25621 [2]
2/11/89	32	28	●	4 Technique	$8	Qwest 25845

All Day Long (2)
All The Way (4)
Angel Dust (2)
As It Is When It Was (2)
Bizarre Love Triangle (2,3)
Blue Monday 1988 (3) *68*

Broken Promise (2)
Ceremony (3)
Confusion (3)
Dream Attack (4)
Elegia (1)
Every Little Counts (2)

Everything's Gone Green (3)
Face Up (1)
Fine Time (4)
Guilty Partner (4)
Love Less (4)
Love Vigilantes (1)

Mr. Disco (4)
Paradise (2)
Perfect Kiss (1,3)
Round & Round (4) *64*
Run (4)
Shellshock (3)

Sooner Than You Think (1)
State Of The Nation (3)
Subculture (1,3)
Sunrise (1)
Temptation (3)
Thieves Like Us (3)

This Time Of Night (1)
True Faith (3) *32*
Vanishing Point (4)
Way Of Life (2)
Weirdo (2)

NEW RIDERS OF THE PURPLE SAGE

San Francisco country-rock band formed in 1969 by Jerry Garcia as an offshoot of the Grateful Dead. Garcia left after first album in 1971.

DEBUT DATE	PEAK POS	WKS CHR	GOLD	ARTIST — Album Title	$	Label & Number
9/11/71	39	15		1 New Riders Of The Purple Sage	$15	Columbia 30888
5/6/72	33	18		2 Powerglide	$15	Columbia 31284
12/9/72+	85	13		3 Gypsy Cowboy	$15	Columbia 31930
10/20/73	55	18	●	4 The Adventures of Panama Red	$12	Columbia 32450
4/27/74	68	12		5 Home, Home on the Road .....[L]	$12	Columbia 32870
11/2/74	68	9		6 Brujo	$12	Columbia 33145
				Brujo is Spanish for Sorcerer		
11/8/75	144	4		7 Oh, What A Mighty Time	$12	Columbia 33688
6/12/76	145	8		8 New Riders	$12	MCA 2196

All I Ever Wanted (1)
Annie May (8)
Ashes Of Love (6)
Big Wheels (6)
California Day (2)
Can't Get Over You (8)
Cement, Clay And Glass (4)
Contract (2)
Crooked Judge (6)
Dead Flowers (5,8)
Death And Destruction (3)
Dim Lights, Thick Smoke (And Loud, Loud Music) (2)
Dirty Business (1)
Don't Put Her Down (8)
Duncan And Brady (2)

Farewell Angelina (7)
Fifteen Days Under The Hood (8)
Garden Of Eden (1)
Glendale Train (1)
Going Round The Horn (7)
Groupie (3,5)
Gypsy Cowboy (3)
Hard To Handle (8)
Hello Mary Lou (2,5)
Henry (1,5)
Hi, Hello, How Are You (5)
Honky Tonkin' (I Guess I Done Me Some) (8)
I Don't Know You (1)

I Don't Need No Doctor (2) *81*
I Heard You Been Layin' My Old Lady (7)
Important Exportin Man (4)
Instant Armadillo Blues (6)
It's Alright With Me (4)
Kick In The Head (4,5)
L.A. Lady (4)
La Bamba (7)
Last Lonely Eagle (1)
Linda (3)
Little Old Lady (7)
Lochinvar (4)
Lonesome L.A. Cowboy (4)
Long Black Veil (3)

Louisiana Lady (1)
Mighty Time (7)
Neon Rose (4)
Old Man Noll (6)
On My Way Back Home (3)
On The Amazon (6)
On Top Of Old Smoky (7)
One Too Many Stories (4)
Over & Over (7)
Panama Red (4)
Parson Brown (6)
Portland Woman (1)
Rainbow (4)
Runnin' Back To You (2)
Sailin' (3)
School Days (5)

She's Looking Better Every Beer (8)
She's No Angel (3,5)
Singing Cowboy (6)
Strangers On A Train (7)
Sunday Susie (5)
Superman (3)
Sutter's Mill (3,5)
Sweet Lovin' One (2)
Swimming Song (8)
Take A Letter, Maria (7)
Teardrops In My Eyes (4)
Thank The Day (4)
Truck Drivin' Man (5)
Up Against The Wall, Redneck (3)

Whatcha Gonna Do (1)
Whiskey (3)
Willie And The Hand Jive (3)
Workingman's Woman (6)
You Angel You (6)
You Never Can Tell (8)
You Should Have Seen Me Runnin (4)

NEW SEEKERS, The

British-Australian group formed by former Seekers' member Keith Potger after disbandment of The Seekers in 1969. Consisted of Eve Graham, Lyn Paul, Peter Doyle, Marty Kristian and Paul Layton.

DEBUT DATE	PEAK POS	WKS CHR	GOLD	ARTIST — Album Title	$	Label & Number
4/3/71	136	6		1 Beautiful People	$12	Elektra 74088
12/25/71+	37	14		2 We'd Like To Teach The World To Sing	$12	Elektra 74115
7/15/72	166	10		3 Circles	$12	Elektra 75034
5/19/73	190	4		4 Pinball Wizards	$10	MGM/Verve 5098

Ain't Love Easy (1)
Allright My Love (1)
Beautiful People (1) *67*
Beg, Steal Or Borrow (3) *81*
Blackberry Way (1)
Boom Town (2)
Brand New Song (4)
Changes IV (3)
Child Of Mine (2)
Cincinnati (1)
Circles (3) *87*

Dance, Dance, Dance (3) *84*
Eighteen Carat Friend (1)
Evergreen (2)
Feelin' (2)
Further We Reach Out (4)
Good Old Fashioned Music (2)
Holy Rollin' (3)
I Can Say You're Beautiful (3)

I'd Like To Teach The World To Sing (In Perfect Harmony) (2) *7*
I'll Be Home (1)
Jean's Little Street Cafe (1)
Just An Old Fashioned Love Song (2)
Lay Me Down (2)
Look Cool (4)
Look What They've Done To My Song Ma (1) *14*

Mystic Queen (3)
Never Ending Song Of Love (1)
Nickel Song (2) *81*
No Man's Land (2)
One (1)
Out On The Edge Of Beyond (3)
Perfect Love (3)
Pinball Wizard/See Me, Feel Me (4) *29*

Reaching Out For Someone (4)
Somebody Somewhere (4)
Sweet Louise (2)
That's My Guy (4)
Time Limit (4)
Tonight (2)
Too Many Trips To Nowhere (2)
Utah (4)
Wanderer's Song (2)

When There's No Love Left (1)
With Everything Changing (4)
World I Wish For You (3)
Your Song (1)

NEWTON, Juice

Born Judy Kay Newton on 2/18/52 in New Jersey; raised in Virginia Beach. Pop/country singer. Performed folk music from age 13. Moved to Los Angeles with own Silver Spur band in 1974; recorded for RCA in 1975. Group disbanded in 1978. Juice is an accomplished equestrian.

DEBUT DATE	PEAK POS	WKS CHR	GOLD	ARTIST — Album Title	$	Label & Number
3/7/81+	22	86	▲	1 Juice	$8	Capitol 12136
5/29/82	20	46	●	2 Quiet Lies	$8	Capitol 12210

DEBUT DATE	PEAK POS	WKS CHR	GOLD	ARTIST — Album Title	$	Label & Number
				NEWTON, Juice — Cont'd		
9/10/83	**52**	15		3 Dirty Looks	**$8**	Capitol 12294
7/14/84	**128**	10		4 Can't Wait All Night..................................	**$8**	RCA 4995
7/21/84	**178**	5	●	5 Greatest Hits ....[G]	**$8**	Capitol 12353

Adios Mi Corazon (2) — Don't Bother Me (3) — I'm Dancing As Fast As I Can (2) — **Queen Of Hearts** (1,5) *2* — **Sweetest Thing (I've Ever Known)** (1,5) *7* — (You Don't Hear) The One That Gets You (4)
All I Have To Do Is Dream (1) — Easy Way Out (4) — Restless Heart (4) — **Tell Her No** (3,5) *27* — You Don't Know Me (4)
Angel Of The Morning (1,5) *4* — Ever True (2) — I'm Gonna Be Strong (2,5) — Ride 'Em Cowboy (1,5) — River Of Love (1) — Texas Heartache (1)
Break It To Me Gently (2,5) *11* — Eye Of A Hurricane (4) — Keeping Me On My Toes (3) — Runaway Hearts (3) — Til I Loved You (3)
Can't Wait All Night (4) *66* — Falling In Love (2) — Let's Dance (4) — Shot Full Of Love (1,5) — Trail Of Tears (2)
Country Comfort (1) — For Believers (3) — **Little Love** (4) *44* — Slipping Away (3) — Twenty Years Ago (3)
Dirty Looks (3) *90* — He's Gone (4) — Love Sail Away (2) — Stranger At My Door (3) — Waiting For The Sun (4)
Headin' For A Heartache (1) — **Love's Been A Little Bit Hard On Me** (2,5) *7*
Heart Of The Night (2,5) *25*

NEWTON, Wayne

Born on 4/3/42 in Roanoke, Virginia. Singer/multi-instrumentalist. Top Las Vegas entertainer. Began singing career with regular appearances on Jackie Gleason's TV variety show in 1962. Appeared in the 1990 film *The Adventures Of Ford Fairlane*.

DEBUT DATE	PEAK POS	WKS CHR	GOLD	ARTIST — Album Title	$	Label & Number
10/12/63	**55**	9		1 Danke Schoen	**$20**	Capitol 1973
5/1/65	**17**	20		2 Red Roses For A Blue Lady	**$20**	Capitol 2335
10/23/65	**114**	6		3 Summer Wind	**$20**	Capitol 2389
6/4/66	**80**	21		4 Wayne Newton - Now!................................	**$20**	Capitol 2445
2/4/67	**131**	13		5 It's Only The Good Times	**$20**	Capitol 2635
10/7/67	**194**	4		6 The Best Of Wayne Newton ....[G]	**$20**	Capitol 2797
6/1/68	**186**	5		7 One More Time	**$12**	MGM 4549
8/31/68	**196**	3		8 Walking On New Grass	**$12**	MGM 4523
6/17/72	**34**	21		9 Daddy Don't You Walk So Fast	**$12**	Chelsea 1001
11/18/72+	**164**	11		10 Can't You Hear The Song?.........................	**$12**	Chelsea 1003

After The Laughter (4,6) — Echo Valley 2-6809 (9) — I'm Looking Over A Four Leaf Clover (2) — My Shoes Keep Walking Back To You (8) — Somewhere (7) — Walking On New Grass (8)
All Alone Am I (10) — Everybody Loves Somebody (3) — I've Got The World On A String (1) — My Special Angel (5) — Song Sung Blue (10) — We'll Sing In The Sunshine (9)
All The Time (8) — Fool (10) — In The Name Of Love (3) — Nothing Matters But You (5) — Superstar (9) — What's He Doing In My World (3)
All This World And Seven Seas (7) — For Once In My Life (9) — It's Only The Good Times (5) — Ol' Man Mose (1) — Take Good Care Of Yourself (9) — When I Lost You (7)
Alone Again, Naturally (10) — Fraulein (3) — It's Such A Pretty World Today (8) — One Kiss For Old Times' Sake (3) — Talking In Your Sleep (10) — Wiedersehn (4,6)
Anthem (10) *65* — **Games That Lovers Play** (5,6) *86* — Lady (7) — One More Memory (2) — That Funny Feeling (5) — Without You (9)
Baby I'm-a Want You (9) — Half A World Away (5) — Last Waltz (8) — One More Time (7) — That's Life (7) — Wolverton Mountain (7)
Believe In Me (10) — **Heart! (I Hear You Beating)** (2) *82* — Laughing On The Outside (Crying On The Inside) (2) — **Red Roses For A Blue Lady** (2) *23* — They Can't Take That Away From Me (1) — Wonderland By Night (4)
Bill Bailey (6) — Hello Ma Baby (7) — Laura Lee (2,6) — Release Me (8) — They'll Never Know (2) — Yo-Yo Puppet Song (4)
But Not For Me (1) — How Did It Get So Late So Early (3) — Like Everything Else (9) — Remember Me, I'm The One Who Loves You (3) — Those Lazy-Hazy-Crazy Days Of Summer (3) — You Don't Have To Ask (10)
Bye Bye Blackbird (1) — I Believe In Music (9) — Little Bit Of Heaven (3) — **Remember When** (4) *69* — Tip Of My Fingers (8) — You Just Don't Know (4)
Can't You Hear The Song? (10) *48* — I Cried For You (1) — Looking Through A Tear (2) — Rock-A-Bye Your Baby With A Dixie Melody (7) — To Each His Own (5) — You Made Me Love You (1)
Crazy Arms (8) — I Believe In Music (9) — L-o-v-e (4) — Smile Is Just A Frown (Turned Upside-Down) (4) — Together (10) — You're Nobody 'Til Somebody Loves You (6)
Daddy Don't You Walk So Fast (4) *4* — I'll Be Standing By (3) — Love Doesn't Live Here Anymore (9) — So Long Lucy (2) — Toot, Toot, Tootsie! (1) — You've Got Your Troubles (10)
Danke Schoen (1,4,6) *13* — **I'll Be With You In Apple Blossom Time** (2,6) *52* — Minute You're Gone (4) — Some Sunday Morning (3) — Volare (1) — You've Let Yourself Go (5)
Days Of Wine And Roses (1,6) — I'll Meet You Halfway (9) — Moon Over Naples (4) — Somebody To Love (5) — Walkin' In The Sand (And The Seasons Come And Go) (9) — Your Cheatin' Heart (7)
Don't Talk To Me (2,4) — I'll Remember April (1) — My Prayer (3)
Don't Touch Me (8)

★★100★★ NEWTON-JOHN, Olivia

Born on 9/26/48 in Cambridge, England. To Australia in 1953. At age 16, won talent contest trip to England; sang with Pat Carroll as Pat & Olivia. With the group Toomorrow, in a British film of the same name. Granddaughter of Nobel Prize-winning German physicist Max Born. In films *Grease*, *Xanadu* and *Two Of A Kind*. Married actor Matt Lattanzi in 1984. Opened own chain of clothing boutiques (Koala Blue) in 1984. Battled breast cancer in 1992.

DEBUT DATE	PEAK POS	WKS CHR	GOLD	ARTIST — Album Title	$	Label & Number
11/27/71	**158**	4		1 If Not For You	**$50**	Uni 73117
12/29/73+	**54**	20	●	2 Let Me Be There	**$12**	MCA 389
6/8/74	**1**¹	61	●	3 If You Love Me, Let Me Know	**$12**	MCA 411
2/22/75	**1**¹	31	●	4 Have You Never Been Mellow	**$10**	MCA 2133
10/11/75	**12**	22	●	5 Clearly Love	**$10**	MCA 2148
3/20/76	**13**	24	●	6 Come On Over	**$10**	MCA 2186
11/6/76	**30**	28	●	7 Don't Stop Believin'	**$10**	MCA 2223
7/9/77	**34**	16		8 Making A Good Thing Better	**$8**	MCA 2280
11/12/77+	**13**	19	▲	9 Olivia Newton-John's Greatest Hits ....[G]	**$8**	MCA 3028
12/9/78+	**7**	39	▲	10 Totally Hot	**$8**	MCA 3067
7/12/80	**4**	36	▲²	11 Xanadu ....[S]	**$8**	MCA 6100
				side 1: Olivia; side 2: Electric Light Orchestra		
10/31/81	**6**	57	▲	12 Physical	**$8**	MCA 5229
10/9/82	**16**	86	▲	13 Olivia's Greatest Hits, Vol. 2 ....[G]	**$8**	MCA 5347
11/2/85	**29**	16		14 Soul Kiss	**$8**	MCA 6151
9/3/88	**67**	9		15 The Rumour	**$8**	MCA 6245
12/2/89+	**124**	13		16 Warm And Tender	**$8**	Geffen 24257
				collection of lullabies		
6/27/92	**121**	8		17 Back To Basics - The Essential Collection 1971-1992 ....[G]	**$12**	Geffen 24470

Air That I Breathe (4) — Blue Eyes Crying In The Rain (6) — Carried Away (12) — Crying, Laughing, Loving, Lying (5) — **Deeper Than The Night** (10,17) *11* — Driving Music (14)
All The Pretty Little Horses (16) — Boats Against The Current (10) — Changes (3,9) — Culture Shock (14) — Don't Ask A Friend (8) — Emotional Tangle (14)
Angel Of The Morning (4) — Borrowed Time (10) — Clearly Love (5) — Dancin' (11) — Don't Cry For Me Argentina (8) — **Every Face Tells A Story** (7) *55*
Angel Of The Morning (2) — Can't We Talk It Over In Bed (15) — **Come On Over** (6,9) *23* — **Dancin' 'Round And 'Round** (10) *82* — **Don't Stop Believin'** (7,9) *33* — Falling (12)
Banks Of The Ohio (1,2) *94* — Car Games (15) — Compassionate Man (7) — Deeper Than A River (17) — **Don't Stop Believin'** (7,9) *33* — Flower That Shattered The Stone (16)
Big And Strong (15) — Coolin' Down (8) — Country Girl (3) — — Don't Throw It All Away (6) — Follow Me (4)

DEBUT DATE	PEAK POS	WKS CHR	GOLD	ARTIST — Album Title	$	Label & Number

NEWTON-JOHN, Olivia — Cont'd

Free The People (3)
Get Out (15)
Gimme Some Lovin' (10)
God Only Knows (3)
Goodbye Again (16)
Greensleeves (6)
Have You Never Been Mellow (4,9,17) *1*
He Ain't Heavy...He's My Brother (5) *flip*
He's My Rock (5)
Heart Attack (13) *3*
Help Me Make It Through The Night (1,2)
Hey Mr. Dreammaker (7)
Home Ain't Home Anymore (3)
Hopelessly Devoted To You (13,17) *3*
I Honestly Love You (3,9,17) *1*
I Need Love (17) *96*
I Never Did Sing You A Love Song (4)

I Think I'll Say Goodbye (8)
I Want To Be Wanted (17)
I'll Bet You A Kangaroo (7)
If (1)
If I Could Read Your Mind (1,2)
If I Gotta Leave (1)
If Love Is Real (6)
If Not For You (1,2,9) *25*
If You Love Me (Let Me Know) (3,9,17) *5*
In A Station (1)
It'll Be Me (6)
It's Not Heaven (15)
It's So Easy (4)
Jenny Rebecca (16)
Jolene (6)
Just A Little Too Much (2)
Just A Lot Of Folk (The Marshmallow Song) (5)
Landslide (12) *52*
Last Time You Loved (7)
Let It Shine (5,9) *30*
Let Me Be There (2,9) *6*

Let's Talk About Tomorrow (15)
Lifestream (4)
Little More Love (10,13,17) *3*
Long And Winding Road (6)
Love And Let Live (15)
Love Make Me Strong (12)
Love Song (1,2)
Love You Hold The Key (7)
Lovers (3)
Loving Arms (4)
Lullaby (4)
Lullaby Lullaby My Lovely One (16)
Magic (11,13,17) *1*
Make A Move On Me (12,13) *3*
Making A Good Thing Better (8) *87*
Mary Skeffington (3)
Me And Bobby McGee (1,2)
Moth To A Flame (14)
Never Enough (10)

New-Born Babe (7)
No Regrets (1)
Not Gonna Be The One (17)
Over The Rainbow (16)
Overnight Observation (14)
Physical (12,13,17) *1*
Please Don't Keep Me Waiting (10)
Please Mr. Please (4,9,17) *3*
Pony Ride (6)
Promise (The Dolphin Song) (12)
Queen Of The Publication (14)
Reach Out For Me (16)
Recovery (12)
Right Moment (14)
Ring Of Fire (8)
River's Too Wide (3)
Rock A Bye Baby (16)
Rocking (16)
Sad Songs (8)
Rumour, The (15) *62*
3all Into Tomorrow (5)

Sam (7,9,17) *20*
Silvery Rain (12)
Sleep My Princess (16)
Slow Dancing (8)
Slow Down Jackson (5)
Small Talk And Pride (6)
Smile For Me (6)
So Easy To Begin (8)
Something Better To Do (5,9) *13*
Soul Kiss (14) *20*
Stranger's Touch (12)
Suddenly (11,13) *20*
Summer Nights (17)
Summertime Blues (5)
Suspended In Time (11)
Take Me Home, Country Roads (2)
Talk To Me (10)
Thousand Conversations (7)
Tied Up (13) *38*
Totally Hot (10) *52*
Toughen Up (14)
Tutta La Vita (15)

Twelfth Of Never (16)
Twinkle Twinkle Little Star (16)
Twist Of Fate (17)
Walk Through Fire (15)
Warm And Tender (16)
Water Under The Bridge (4)
Way You Look Tonight (16)
When You Wish Upon A Star (16)
Whenever You're Far Away From Me (11)
Where Are You Going To My Love? (1)
Who Are You Now? (7)
Wrap Me In Your Arms (6)
Xanadu (11,13) *8*
You Ain't Got The Right (16)
You Were Great, How Was I? (14)
You Won't See Me Cry (8)
You'll Never Walk Alone (16)
You're The One That I Want (13,17) *1*

NEW VAUDEVILLE BAND, The
Creation of British composer/record producer Geoff Stephens (b: 10/1/34, London).

| 12/10/66+ | 5 | 31 | ● | **Winchester Cathedral** | $15 | Fontana 27560 |

Diana Goodbye
I Can't Go Wrong
Lilli Marlene

Nightingale Sang In Berkeley Square

Tap Your Feet (And Go Bo-De-Do-De-Doo)

That's All For Now, Sugar Baby
There's A Kind Of Hush

Whatever Happened To Phyllis Puke?
Whispering

Winchester Cathedral *1*
Your Love Ain't What It Used To Be

NEW WORLD THEATRE ORCHESTRA, The — see SOUNDTRACK: Around The World In 80 Days

NEW YORK CITY
New York City R&B quartet: Tim McQueen, John Brown, Ed Shell and Claude Johnston. First recorded for Buddah as Triboro Exchange. Name changed in 1972.

| 6/16/73 | 122 | 10 | | I'm Doin' Fine Now | $12 | Chelsea 0198 |

Ain't It So
By The Time I Get To Phoenix

Hang On Sloopy
Hang Your Head In Shame
I'm Doin' Fine Now *17*

Make Me Twice The Man *93*
Quick, Fast, In A Hurry *79*

Reach Out
Sanity

Set The Record Straight
Uncle James

NEW YORK DOLLS
Glitter-rock band led by David Johansen and Sylvain Sylvain. Managed by British entrepeneur Malcolm McLaren who later formed the Sex Pistols. Guitarist Johnny "Thunders" Genzale died on 4/23/91 (age 38).

| 9/1/73 | 116 | 12 | | 1 New York Dolls | $25 | Mercury 675 |

produced by Todd Rundgren

| 6/1/74 | 167 | 5 | | 2 in Too Much Too Soon | $20 | Mercury 1001 |

Babylon (2)
Bad Detective (2)
Bad Girl (1)
Chatterbox (2)

Don't Start Me Talkin' (2)
Frankenstein (Orig.) (1)
Human Being (2)
It's Too Late (2)

Jet Boy (1)
Lonely Planet Boy (1)
Looking For A Kiss (1)
Personality Crisis (1)

Pills (1)
Private World (1)
Puss 'N' Boots (2)
Stranded In The Jungle (2)

Subway Train (1)
(There's Gonna Be A) Showdown (2)
Trash (1)

Vietnamese Baby (1)
Who Are The Mystery Girls? (2)

NEW YORK PHILHARMONIC — see BERNSTEIN, Leonard

NICE, The
British classical-rock trio led by keyboardist Keith Emerson (Emerson, Lake and Palmer).

| 8/29/70 | 197 | 5 | | 1 Five Bridges | [I-L] | $12 | Mercury 61295 |

with the Sinfonia of London Orchestra

| 2/26/72 | 152 | 8 | | 2 Keith Emerson with The Nice | [R] | $15 | Mercury 6500 [2] |

KEITH EMERSON WITH THE NICE
reissue of *Five Bridges* and *Elegy* albums

America (2)
Bach: Brandenburg Concerto No. 6 (medley) (1,2)

Bridge (1st-5th) (1,2)
Country Pie (medley) (1,2)

Hang On To A Dream (2)
Intermezzo Karelia Suite (1,2)

My Back Pages (2)
One Of Those People (1,2)

Tchaikovsky: Pathetique Symphony No. 6, 3rd Movement (1,2)

NICE & SMOOTH
Rap duo from New York City: Gregg Nice (Greg Mays) and Smooth Bee (Daryl Barnes).

| 10/5/91 | 141 | 19 | | Ain't A Damn Thing Changed | $12 | RAL 47373 |

Billy-Gene
Cake & Eat It Too
Down The Line

Harmonize
Hip Hop Junkies
How To Flow

One, Two And One More Makes Three
Paranoia

Pump It Up
Sex, Sex, Sex

Sometimes I Rhyme Slow *44*
Step By Step

NICHOLS, Mike, & Elaine May
Improvisational comedy team. Nichols (born Michael Peschkowsky on 11/6/31 in Berlin) is a premier Broadway/film director. Films: *The Graduate*, *Catch-22*, *Silkwood* and others. Married to network newscaster Diane Sawyer. Elaine (b: 4/21/32, Pennsylvania) is a film writer/director/actress. Wrote screenplay for *California Suite* and *Heaven Can Wait*.

| 6/1/59 | 39 | 7 | | 1 Improvisations To Music | [C] | $30 | Mercury 20376 |

with Marty Rubenstein at the piano

| 1/23/61 | 10 | 32 | | 2 An evening with Mike Nichols and Elaine May | [OC-C] | $20 | Mercury 2200 |

opened on Broadway on 10/8/60

| 2/24/62 | 17 | 29 | | 3 Mike Nichols & Elaine May Examine Doctors | [C] | $20 | Mercury 20680 |

Adultery (2)
Bach To Bach (1)
Bedside Manner (3)
Calling Dr. Marx (3)
Chopin (1)

Cocktail Piano (1)
Disc Jockey (2)
Everybody's Doing It (1)
Interrupted Hour (3)
Little More Gauze (3)

Merry Christmas, Doctor (3)
Morning Rounds (3)
Mother And Son (2)
Mysterioso (1)
Nichols And May At Work (3)

Out Of Africa (3)
Physical (3)
Second Piano Concerto (3)
Sonata For Piano And Celeste (1)

Tango (1)
Telephone (2)
Thank You Very Much (3)
Transference (3)
Von Brauns At Home (3)

DEBUT DATE	PEAK POS	WKS CHR	GOLD	ARTIST — Album Title	$	Label & Number

★★473★★ NICKS, Stevie

Born Stephanie Nicks on 5/26/48 in Phoenix; raised in California. Became vocalist of Bay-area group Fritz and subsequently met guitarist Lindsey Buckingham. Teamed up and recorded album *Buckingham-Nicks* in 1973. Vocalist with Fleetwood Mac since January 1975. Quit touring with band after 1990.

8/15/81	1¹	145	▲⁴	1 Bella Donna	$8	Modern 139
7/2/83	5	52	▲	2 The Wild Heart	$8	Modern 90048
12/14/85+	12	35	▲	3 Rock A Little	$8	Modern 90479
6/10/89	10	21	●	4 The Other Side Of The Mirror...................................	$8	Modern 91245
9/21/91	30	24	●	5 TimeSpace - The Best Of Stevie Nicks ....[G]	$12	Modern 91711

After The Glitter Fades (1) *32* — Alice (4) — Beauty And The Beast (2,5) — Bella Donna (1) — Cry Wolf (4) — Desert Angel (5) — Doing The Best That I Can (Escape From Berlin) (4)

Edge Of Seventeen (Just Like The White Winged Dove) (1,5) *11* — Enchanted (4) — Fire Burning (4) — Gate And Garden (4) — Ghosts (4) — **Has Anyone Ever Written Anything For You** (3,5) *60* — Highwayman, The (1)

How Still My Love (1) — **I Can't Wait** (3,5) *16* — I Sing For The Things (3) — I Still Miss Someone (Blue Eyes) (4) — I Will Run To You (2) — **If Anyone Falls** (2,5) *14* — If I Were You (3) — Imperial Hotel (3) — Juliet (4)

Kind Of Woman (1) — **Leather And Lace** (1,5) *6* — Long Way To Go (4) — Love's A Hard Game To Play (5) — **Nightbird** (2) *33* — Nightmare, The (3) — No Spoken Word (3) — Nothing Ever Changes (3) — Ooh My Love (4)

Outside The Rain (1) — Rock A Little (Go Ahead Lily) (3) — **Rooms On Fire** (4,5) *16* — Sable On Blond (3) — Sister Honey (3) — Some Become Strangers (3) — **Sometimes It's A Bitch** (5) *56* — **Stand Back** (2,5) *5*

Stop Draggin' My Heart Around (1,5) *3* — **Talk To Me** (3,5) *4* — Think About It (1) — Two Kinds Of Love (4) — Whole Lotta Trouble (4,5) — Wild Heart (2)

NIGHT

Sextet led by female vocalist Stevie Lange and Chris Thompson, lead singer/guitarist of Manfred Mann's Earth Band.

| 8/11/79 | 113 | 10 | | Night .... | $8 | Planet 2 |

second pressings of LP (on Planet 3) include Thompson's "If You Remember Me"

Ain't That Peculiar — Cold Wind Across My Heart — Come Around (If You Want Me) — **Hot Summer Nights** *18* — If You Gotta Make A Fool Of Somebody — **If You Remember Me** *17* — Love Message — Party Shuffle — Shocked — You Ain't Pretty Enough

NIGHTHAWKS, The

Blues-rock quartet formed in Washington, D.C. in 1972: Mark Wenner (vocals), Jim Thackery, Jan Zukowski and Pete Ragusa.

| 7/26/80 | 166 | 4 | | The Nighthawks .... | $8 | Mercury 3833 |

Back To The City — Brand New Man — Don't Go No Further — Everynight And Everyday — I Wouldn't Treat A Dog (The Way You Treated Me) — Little Sister — Mainline — One Nite Stand — Pretty Girls And Cadillacs — Teen-age Letter — Upside Your Head

NIGHTINGALE, Maxine

Born on 11/2/52 in Wembly, England. First recorded in 1968. In productions of *Hair*, *Jesus Christ Superstar*, *Godspell* and *Savages* in the early '70s.

5/29/76	65	9		1 Right Back Where We Started From	$10	United Art. 626
7/21/79	45	18		2 Lead Me On	$8	Windsong 3404
1/8/83	176	4		3 It's A Beautiful Thing	$8	Highrise 101

Anyone Who Had A Heart (3) — Ask Billy (They Tell Me) (2) — Bless You (1) — **(Bringing Out) The Girl In Me** (2) *73* — Darlin' Dear (2)

Everytime I See A Butterfly (1) — Give A Little Love (To Me) (3) — Good-Bye Again (1) — **Gotta Be The One** (1) *53* — Hideaway (1)

I Don't Miss You At All (3) — (I Think I Wanna) Possess You (1) — If I Ever Lose This Heaven (1) — In Love We Grow (1) — **Lead Me On** (2) *5*

Life Has Just Begun (1) — Love Enough (1) — Love Me Like You Mean It (2) — Never Gonna Be Another One (3) — No One Like My Baby (2)

One Last Ride (1) — Reasons (1) — **Right Back Where We Started From** (1) *2* — Shakin' Me Up (3) — So Right (3)

Stand Up For Your Heart (3) — Turn To Me (3) — You Are The Most Important Person In Your Life (1) — You Got The Love (1) — You Got To Me (2)

NIGHT RANGER

Rock group from California: lead singers Kelly Keagy (drums) and Jack Blades (bass), with guitarists Jeff Watson and Brad Gillis, and keyboardist Alan "Fitz" Gerald. Blades and Gillis were members of Rubicon. Gerald left in 1988; band split up in early 1989. Blades joined supergroup Damn Yankees.

12/25/82+	38	69		1 Dawn Patrol	$8	Boardwalk 33259
11/19/83+	15	69	▲	2 Midnight Madness	$8	MCA 5456
6/8/85	10	45	▲	3 7 Wishes	$8	MCA/Camel 5593
4/11/87	28	18	●	4 Big Life	$8	MCA 5839
10/22/88	81	8		5 Man In Motion	$8	Camel 6238

At Night She Sleeps (1) — Better Let It Go (4) — Big Life (4) — Call My Name (1) — Can't Find Me A Thrill (1) — Carry On (4) — Chippin' Away (2) — Color Of Your Smile (4) — Don't Start Thinking (I'm Alone Tonight) (5)

Don't Tell Me You Love Me (1) *40* — Eddie's Comin' Out Tonight (1) — Faces (3) — **Four In The Morning (I Can't Take Any More)** (3) *19* — Goodbye (3) *17* — Halfway To The Sun (5) — **Hearts Away** (4) *90*

Here She Comes Again (5) — **I Did It For Love** (5) *75* — I Know Tonight (4) — I Need A Woman (3) — I Will Follow You (3) — Interstate Love Affair (3) — Kiss Me Where It Hurts (5) — Let Him Run (2) — Love Is Standing Near (4) — Love Shot Me Down (5) — Man In Motion (5)

Night Machine (3) — Night Ranger (2) — Passion Play (2) — Penny (1) — Play Rough (1) — Rain Comes Crashing Down (4) — Reason To Be (5) — Restless Kind (5) — Right On You (5) — Rumours In The Air (2)

Secret Of My Success (4) *64* — **Sentimental Street** (3) *8* — Seven Wishes (3) — **Sing Me Away** (1) *54* — **Sister Christian** (2) *5* — This Boy Needs To Rock (3) — Touch Of Madness (2) — **When You Close Your Eyes** (2) *14*

Why Does Love Have To Change (2) — Woman In Love (5) — **(You Can Still) Rock In America** (2) *51* — Young Girl In Love (1)

NILE, Willie

Rock singer/songwriter from Buffalo, New York. Real name: Robert Noonan.

| 4/12/80 | 145 | 6 | | 1 Willie Nile .... | $8 | Arista 4260 |
| 5/2/81 | 158 | 8 | | 2 Golden Down .... | $8 | Arista 4284 |

Across The River (1) — Behind The Cathedral (1) — Dear Lord (1) — Golden Down (2) — Grenade (2) — Hide Your Love (2) — I Can't Get You Off Of My Mind (2) — I Like The Way (2) — I'm Not Waiting (1) — It's All Over (1) — Les Champs Elysees (2) — Old Men Sleeping On The Bowery (1) — Poor Boy (2) — She's So Cold (1) — Shine Your Light (2) — Shoulders (2) — Sing Me A Song (1) — That's The Reason (1) — They'll Build A Statue Of You (1) — Vagabond Moon (1)

★★306★★ NILSSON

Born Harry Edward Nelson, III on 6/15/41 in Brooklyn. Wrote Three Dog Night's hit "One"; scored the film *Skidoo* and TV's *The Courtship Of Eddie's Father*. Close friend of John Lennon and Ringo Starr.

| 8/23/69 | 120 | 15 | | 1 Harry .... | $12 | RCA 4197 |
| 3/6/71 | 25 | 32 | | 2 The Point!...[TV] | $10 | RCA 1003 |

songs and narration from his animated TV special

| 7/17/71 | 149 | 3 | | 3 Aerial Pandemonium Ballet....................................[K] | $10 | RCA 4543 |

selections from *Pandemonium Shadow Show* and *Aerial Ballet* LPs

DEBUT DATE	PEAK POS	WKS CHR	GOLD	ARTIST — Album Title	$	Label & Number
				NILSSON — Cont'd		
12/4/71+	**3**	46	● ⁴	**Nilsson Schmilsson**	$10	RCA 4515
7/22/72	**12**	31	● ⁵	**Son Of Schmilsson**	$10	RCA 4717
6/23/73	**46**	17	⁶	A Little Touch Of Schmilsson In The Night	$10	RCA 0097
				with orchestra conducted by Gordon Jenkins		
5/4/74	**106**	9	⁷	Son Of Dracula ....[S]	$10	Rapple 0220
				the film stars Nilsson and Ringo Starr		
9/7/74	**60**	12	⁸	Pussy Cats	$10	RCA 0570
				produced by John Lennon		
4/5/75	**141**	7	⁹	Duit On Mon Dei	$10	RCA 0817
2/7/76	**111**	7	¹⁰	Sandman	$8	RCA 1031
7/10/76	**158**	6	¹¹	...That's The Way It Is	$8	RCA 1119
8/6/77	**108**	10	¹²	Knnillssonn	$8	RCA 2276
6/17/78	**140**	5	¹³	Greatest Hits ....[G]	$8	RCA 2798

Abdication Of Count Down (7)
All I Think About Is You (12)
All My Life (8)
Always (6)
Ambush (5)
Are You Sleeping? (2)
As Time Goes By (6,13) *80*
At My Front Door (5,7)
Baby I'm Yours (medley) (11)
Bath (3)
Birds, The (2)
Black Sails (8)
Blanket For A Sail (12)
City Life (1)
Clearing In The Woods (2)
Coconut (4,13) *8*
Count Down Meets Merlin And Amber (7)
Counts Vulnerability (7)
Daddy's Song (3)
Daybreak (7,13) *39*
Daylight Has Caught Me (1)
Don't Forget Me (8)
Don't Leave Me (3)
Down (4,7)

Down By The Sea (9)
Driving Along (4)
Early In The Morning (4)
Easier For Me (9)
Everybody's Talkin' (3,13) *6*
Everything's Got 'Em (1)
Fairfax Rag (1)
Flying Saucer Song (10)
For Me And My Gal (1)
Frankenstein, Merlin And The Operation (7)
Game, The (2)
Goin' Down (12)
Good For Good (9)
Good Old Desk (4)
Gotta Get Up (4)
Home (9)
How To Write A Song (10)
I Need You (11)
I Never Thought I'd Get This Lonely (12)
I Wonder Who's Kissing Her Now (6)

I'd Rather Be Dead (5)
I'll Never Leave You (4)
I'll Take A Tango (10)
It Had To Be You (6)
It Is He Who Will Be King (7)
It's A Jungle Out There (9)
Ivy Covered Walls (10)
Jesus Christ You're Tall (9,10)
Joy (5)
Jump Into The Fire (4,7,13) *27*
Just One Look (medley) (11)
Kojak Columbo (9)
Laughin' Man (12)
Lazy Moon (6)
Lean On Me (12)
Let The Good Times Roll (5)
Life Line (9)
Loop De Loop (8)
Lottery Song (5)
Lullaby In Ragtime (6)
Makin' Whoopee! (6)
Many Rivers To Cross (8)
Marchin' Down Broadway (1)
Maybe (1)

Me And My Arrow (2,13) *34*
Moonbeam (4,7)
Moonshine Bandit (11)
Most Beautiful World In The World (5)
Mother Nature's Son (1)
Mt. Elga (medley) (8)
Mournin' Glory Story (1)
Mr. Bojangles (1)
Mr. Richland's Favorite Song (3)
Mucho Mungo (medley) (8)
Nevertheless (I'm In Love With You) (6)
1941 (8)
Nobody Cares About The Railroad Anymore (1)
Oblio's Return (2)
Old Bones (12)
Old Forgotten Soldier (8)
One (3,13)
Open Your Window (11)
P.O.V. Waltz (2)
Perfect Day (12)
Perhaps This Is All A Dream (7)

Pointed Man (2)
Poli High (2)
Pretty Soon There'll Be Nothing Left For Everybody (10)
Puget Sound (9)
Puppy Song (1)
Rainmaker (1)
Remember (Christmas) (5,7,13) *53*
River Deep-Mountain High (3)
Rock Around The Clock (8)
Sail Away (11)
Salmon Falls (9)
Save The Last Dance For Me (8)
She Sits Down On Me (11)
Simon Smith And The Amazing Dancing Bear (1)
Sleep Late, My Lady Friend (3)
Something True (10)
Spaceman (5,13) *23*
Subterranean Homesick Blues (8)

Sweet Surrender (12)
Take 54 (5)
That Is All (11)
Think About Your Troubles (2)
This Is All I Ask (6)
Thousand Miles Away (11)
Thursday Or, Here's Why I Did Not Go To Work Today (10)
Together (3)
Town, The (3)
Trial & Banishment (2)
Turn On Your Radio (5)
Turn Out The Light (9)
What'll I Do (6)
What's Your Sign (9)
Who Done It? (12)
Will She Miss Me (10)
Without Her (3,13)
Without You (4,7,13) *1*
You Made Me Love You (I Didn't Want To Do It) (8)
You're Breakin' My Heart (5)
Zombie Jamboree (Back To Back) (11)

NIMOY, Leonard
Born on 3/26/31 in Boston. TV and film actor/director. Portrayed Mr. Spock on *Star Trek*.

6/10/67	**83**	25	¹	Mr. Spock's Music From Outer Space	$50	Dot 25794
				Leonard sings 3 songs and narrates 3 others; also includes 5 instrumentals by Charles Green: "Beyond Antares," "Mission Impossible," "Music To Watch Space Girls By," "Theme From Star Trek" and "Where No Man Has Gone Before"		
2/24/68	**97**	13	²	Two Sides Of Leonard Nimoy	$50	Dot 25835
				side 1: performs as Mr. Spock; side 2: performs as Leonard Nimoy		

Alien (1)
Amphibious Assault (2)
Ballad Of Bilbo Baggins (2)
By Myself (2)

Cotton Candy (On A Summer Day) (2)
Difference Between Us (2)
Follow Your Star (2)

Gentle On My Mind (2)
Highly Illogical (2)
If I Were A Carpenter (2)
Lost In The Stars (1)

Love Of The Common People (2)
Miranda (2)
Once I Smiled (2)

Spock Thoughts (2)
Twinkle, Twinkle Little Earth (1)
Visit To A Sad Planet (1)

Where Is Love (1)
You Are Not Alone (1)

NINE INCH NAILS
Industrial rock, one-man band Trent Reznor. The Cleveland-based, classically-trained pianist is from rural Pennsylvania.

2/10/90+	**75**	100↑	● ¹	Pretty Hate Machine	$12	TVT 2610
10/10/92	**7**	18↑	▲ ²	**Broken**	$12	Nothing/TVT 92213
				includes a mini CD with 2 tracks		

Down In It (1)
Gave Up (2)
Happiness In Slavery (2)

Head Like A Hole (1)
Help Me I Am In Hell (2)
Kinda I Want To (1)

Last (2)
Only Time (1)
Pinion (1)

Ringfinger (1)
Sanctified (1)
Sin (1)

Something I Can Never Have (1)
Terrible Lie (1)

That's What I Get (1)
Wish (2)

9.9
Black trio from Boston: Margot Thunder, Leslie Jones, Wanda Perry.

9/14/85	**79**	22		9.9	$8	RCA 8049

All Of Me For All Of You 51
Feel The Fire

Hooked On You
Hypnotized

I Like The Way You Dance

I'll Help You Forget About Him

Little Bitty Woman (Owch!) Hot Blood Pressure

999
Nick Cash, lead singer of British new wave quintet.

2/23/80	**177**	3	¹	The Biggest Prize In Sport	$8	Polydor 6256
6/27/81	**192**	2	²	Concrete	$8	Polydor 6323

Biggest Prize In Sport (1)
Boiler (1)
Bongos On The Nile (2)
Boys In The Gang (1)
Break It Up (1)

Don't You Know I Need You (2)
English Wipe-Out (1)
Fortune Teller (1)
Found Out Too Late (1)

Fun Thing (1)
Hollywood (1)
Inside Out (1)
Lil' Red Riding Hood (2)
Mercy Mercy (2)

Obsessed (2)
Public Enemy No. 1 (2)
Silent Anger (2)
So Greedy (2)
So Long (1)

Stop Stop (1)
Stranger (1)
Taboo (2)
That's The Way It Goes (2)
Trouble (1)

1910 FRUITGUM CO.
New Jersey bubblegum quintet: Mark Gutkowski, Floyd Marcus, Pat Karwan, Steve Mortkowitz and Frank Jeckell. Produced by The Music Explosion and Ohio Express producers Jerry Kasenetz and Jeff Katz.

4/20/68	**162**	8	¹	Simon Says	$15	Buddah 5010
10/5/68	**163**	12	²	1,2,3 Red Light	$15	Buddah 5022
4/5/69	**147**	8	³	Indian Giver	$15	Buddah 5036

DEBUT DATE	PEAK POS	WKS CHR	GOLD	ARTIST — Album Title	$	Label & Number

1910 FRUITGUM CO. — Cont'd

Blue Eyes And Orange Skies (2) · Book, The (2) · Bubble Gum World (1) · Candy (3) · Game Of Love (3) · Good Good Lovin' (3) · Groovy Groovy (3) · Happy Little Teardrops (1) · I've Got To Have Your Love (3) · **Indian Giver** (3) *5* · Keep Your Thoughts On The Bright Side (1) · Let's Make Love (3) · Lookin' Back (2) · Magic Windmill (1) · **May I Take A Giant Step (Into Your Heart)** (1) *63* · Mighty Quinn (2) · 9,10, Let's Do It Again (3) · 1910 Cotton Candy Castle (3) · No Good Annie (3) · **1, 2, 3, Red Light** (2) *5* · (Poor Old) Mr. Jensen (1) · Pop Goes The Weasel (1) · Shirley Applegate (3) · **Simon Says** (1) *4* · Sister John (2) · Song Song (2) · Soul Struttin' (1) · **Special Delivery** (3) *38* · Story Of Flipper (1) · Sweet Lovin' (3) · Take Away (2) · Year 2001 (1) · Yummy Yummy Yummy (2)

NIRVANA

Punk group from Aberdeen, Washington led by Kurt Cobain (vocals) and Chris Novoselic (bass). By 1991, guitarist Jason Everman left and drummer Chad Channing was replaced by Dave Grohl. Cobain married Courtney Love, lead singer of punk group Hole, on 2/24/92.

DEBUT DATE	PEAK POS	WKS CHR	GOLD	ARTIST — Album Title	$	Label & Number
10/12/91+	1²	70↑ ▲⁴		1 Nevermind	$12	DGC 24425
				an uncredited track, "Endless Nameless," is hidden at the end of the CD; produced by Butch Vig (Firetown)		
1/4/92	89	20		2 Bleach ....[E]	$12	Sub Pop 34

About A Girl (2) · Big Cheese (2) · Blew (2) · Breed (1) · **Come As You Are** (1) *32* · Downer (2) · Drain You (1) · Floyd The Barber (2) · In Bloom (1) · Lithium (1) · Lounge Act (1) · Love Buzz (2) · Mr. Moustache (2) · Negative Creep (2) · On A Plain (1) · Paper Cuts (2) · Polly (1) · School (2) · Scoff (2) · Sifting (2) · **Smells Like Teen Spirit** (1) *6* · Something In The Way (1) · Stay Away (1) · Swap Meet (2) · Territorial Pissings (1)

NITE-LITERS, The

R&B band formed in Louisville in 1963 by Harvey Fuqua and Tony Churchill. Expanded to 17 members with two vocal groups and band. Renamed New Birth, Inc., with The Nite-Liters making up the instrumental section. Also see New Birth.

DEBUT DATE	PEAK POS	WKS CHR	GOLD	ARTIST — Album Title	$	Label & Number
7/24/71	167	13		1 Morning, Noon & The Nite-Liters ....[I]	$10	RCA 4493
5/20/72	198	2		2 Instrumental Directions ....[I]	$10	RCA 4580

Afro-Strut (2) *49* · Bakers Instant (2) · Brand X (2) · Cherish Every Precious Moment (2) · Funky-Doo (1) · Fuqua's Theme (medley) (2) · Hang-Up (1) · I've Got Dreams To Remember (2) · If I Were Your Woman (1) · **K-Jee** (1) *39* · Kool-Pick (1) · Listen Here (medley) (1) · MacArthur Park (medley) (1) · Respect To The Other Man (2) · Shaft, Theme From (2) · Stinkin' Charlie (1) · Tanga Boo Gonk (1) · (Them) Changes (2) · Traveling (medley) (1) · (We've Got To) Pull Together (1) · We've Only Just Begun (1) · What's Going On (medley) (2) · Wichita Lineman (2)

NITRO

Heavy-metal quartet led by vocalist Jim Gillette.

DEBUT DATE	PEAK POS	WKS CHR	GOLD	ARTIST — Album Title	$	Label & Number
8/12/89	140	9		O.F.R.	$8	Rhino 70894

Bring It Down · Double Trouble · Fighting Mad · Freight Train · Long Way From Home · Machine Gunn Eddie · O.F.R. · Nasty Reputation · Shot Heard 'Round The World

★★347★★ NITTY GRITTY DIRT BAND

Country-folk-rock group from Long Beach, California. Led by Jeff Hanna (b: 7/11/47; vocals, guitar) and John McEuen (b: 12/19/45; banjo, mandolin). Changed name to Dirt Band in 1976 when Hanna left the group. Resumed using Nitty Gritty Dirt Band name in 1982. Various members included ex-Eagle Bernie Leadon who replaced McEuen briefly in early 1987. Revamped quartet since late 1987: Hanna, Jimmy Ibbotson, Bob Carpenter and Jimmie Fadden. In the films For Singles Only and Paint Your Wagon.

DEBUT DATE	PEAK POS	WKS CHR	GOLD	ARTIST — Album Title	$	Label & Number
4/8/67	151	8		1 The Nitty Gritty Dirt Band	$15	Liberty 7501
12/5/70+	66	32		2 Uncle Charlie & His Dog Teddy	$15	Liberty 7642
2/5/72	162	10		3 All The Good Times	$10	United Art. 5553
12/30/72+	68	32	●	4 Will The Circle Be Unbroken	$18	United Art. 9801 [3]
				with Mother Maybelle Carter, Earl Scruggs, Doc Watson, Roy Acuff and Merle Travis		
7/13/74	28	21		5 Stars & Stripes Forever...................[L]	$15	United Art. 184 [2]
10/4/75	66	9		6 Dream	$10	United Art. 469
12/18/76+	77	13		7 Dirt, Silver & Gold...................[K]	$18	United Art. 670 [3]
				THE DIRT BAND:		
7/8/78	163	6		8 The Dirt Band	$8	United Art. 854
1/26/80	76	14		9 An American Dream	$8	United Art. 974
7/19/80	62	16		10 Make A Little Magic	$8	United Art. 1042
9/5/81	102	9		11 Jealousy	$8	Liberty 1106
				NITTY GRITTY DIRT BAND:		
5/27/89	95	12		12 Will The Circle Be Unbroken, Volume Two....................	$10	Univers. 12500 [2]
				with Roy Acuff, Chet Atkins, Paulette Carlson, The Carter Family, Johnny Cash, June Carter Cash, Rosanne Cash, John Denver, Emmylou Harris, Levon Helm, John Hiatt, Chris Hillman, Bruce Hornsby, Roy Huskey, Jr., Bernie Leadon, Jimmy Martin, Roger McGuinn, Michael Martin Murphey, New Grass Revival, John Prine, Earl Scruggs, Randy Scruggs, Ricky Skaggs		

(All I Have To Do Is) Dream (6,7) *66* · Amazing Grace (12) · **American Dream** (9) *13* · And So It Goes (12) · Angel (8) · Anxious Heart (10) · Avalanche (10) · Badlands (10) · Baltimore (3) · Battle Of New Orleans (5,6,7) *72* · Bayou Jubilee (6,7,12) · Billy In The Low Ground (2) · Black Mountain Rag (4) · Blues Berry Hill (2) · Both Sides Now (4) · Bowleg's (7) · **Buy For Me The Rain** (1,5,7) *45* · Candy Man (1) · Cannonball Rag (4) · Catch The Next Dream (11) · Chicken Reel (medley) (2) · Circular Man (11) · Civil War Trilogy (3) · Classical Banjo I & II (medley) (6) · Clinch Mountain Backstep (medley) (2) · Collegiana (1) · Cosmic Cowboy (Part 1) (5,7) · Crazy Words, Crazy Tune (1) · Creepin' Round Your Back Door (3,7) · Cripple Creek (5) · Crossfire (11) · Cure, The (2,7) · Daddy Play A Sailor (6) · Daisy (3) · Dance The Night Away (9) · Dark As A Dungeon (4) · Diggy Liggy Lo (3,5) · Dismal Swamp (1) · Dixie Hoedown (5) · Do It! (Party Lights) (10) · Do You Feel It Too (3) · Do You Feel The Way That I Do (9) · Doc's Guitar (7) · Don't You Hear Jerusalem Moan (12) · Down In Texas (3) · Down Yonder (4) · Earl's Breakdown (2) · Easy Slow (11) · End, The (medley) (2) · End Of The World (4) · Escaping Reality (8) · Euphoria (8) · Falling Down Slow (7) · **Fire In The Sky** (11) *76* · Fish Song (3,5,7) · Flint Hill Special (4) · Foggy Mountain Breakdown (7) · For A Little While (8) · Forget It! (11) · Gavotte No. 2 (7) · Glocoat-Blues (5) · Gotta Travel On (6) · Grand Ole Opry Song (4) · Grandpa Was A Carpenter (12) · Happy Feet (9) · Hard Hearted Hannah (The Vamp Of Savannah) (1) · Harmony (10) · Hey Good Lookin' (6) · High School Yearbook (10) · Holding (1) · Honky Tonk Blues (4) · Honky Tonkin' (4,5,7) · Hoping To Say (3) · **House At Pooh Corner** (2,5,7) *53* · I Am A Pilgrim (4) · I Saw The Light (4) · I Wish I Could Shimmy Like My Sister Kate (1) · I'm Sittin' On Top Of The World (12) · I'm Thinking Tonight Of My Blue Eyes (4) · **In For The Night** (8) *86* · In Her Eyes (9) · It Came From The 50's (Blast From The Past) (5) · Jamaica Lady (7) · Jamaica, Say You Will (3) · **Jambalaya (On The Bayou)** (3,5) *84* · Jas'Moon (9) · Jealousy (11) · Jesse James (medley) (2) · Joshua Come Home (medley) (6) · Keep On The Sunny Side (4) · Leigh Anne (10) · Life's Railway To Heaven (12) · Lights (8) · Listen To The Mockingbird (5) · Little Mountain Church House (12) · Livin' Without You (2,7) · Losin' You (Might Be The Best Thing Yet) (4) · Lost Highway (medley) (4) · Lost River (12) · Love Is The Last Thing (11) · Lovin' On The Side (12) · **Make A Little Magic** (10) *25* · Malaguena (medley) (6)

545

NITTY GRITTY DIRT BAND — Cont'd

Mary Danced With Soldiers (12)
Melissa (1,7)
Moon Just Turned Blue (6)
Mother Earth (Provides For Me) (7)
Mother Of Love (6)
Mountain Whippoorwill (Or How Hillbilly Jim Won The Great Fiddler's Prize) (5)
Mournin' Blues (7)
Mr. Bojangles (2,5,7) *9*
Mullen's Farewell To America (10)
My True Story (5)
My Walkin' Shoes (4)
Nashville Blues (4)
New Orleans (9)

Nine-Pound Hammer (4)
Oh Boy (5)
On The Loose (8)
One Step Over The Line (12)
Opus 36, Clementi (John) (2,7)
Orange Blossom Special (4)
Pins And Needles (In My Heart) (4)
Precious Jewel (4)
Prodigal's Return (2)
Propinquity (2)
Raleigh-Durham Reel (medley) (6)
Randy Lynn Rag (2,7)
Rave On (2)
Resign Yourself To Me (5)
Riding Alone (10,12)

Ripplin' Waters (6,7)
Rocky Top (7)
Sailin' On To Hawaii (4)
Sally Was A Goodun (6,7)
Santa Monica Pier (6)
Santa Rosa (2)
Sheik Of Araby (5)
Sixteen Tracks (3,7)
Sleeping On The Beach (6)
Slim Carter (3)
So You Run (11)
Soldier's Joy (4,7)
Solstice (medley) (6)
Some Of Shelly's Blues (2,7) *64*
Song To Jutta (1)
Spanish Fandango (medley) (2)

Stars And Stripes Forever (5)
Sunny Side Of The Mountain (4)
Swanee River (medley) (2)
Symphonion Montage (medley) (6)
Take Me Back (9)
Teardrops In My Eyes (5)
Tennessee Stud (4)
Togary Mountain (4,7)
Too Close For Comfort (11)
Too Good To Be True (10)
Travelin' Mood (medley) (2)
Turn Of The Century (12)
Uncle Charlie (medley) (2)
Valley Road (12)
Visiting An Old Friend (7)
Wabash Cannonball (4)

Way Downtown (4)
What's On Your Mind (9)
When I Get My Rewards (12)
When It's Gone (8)
White Russia (8)
Whoa Babe (8)
Wild Nights (8)
Wildwood Flower (4)
Will The Circle Be Unbroken (4,7,12)
Willie The Weeper (7)
Win Or Lose (7)
Winterwhite (medley) (6)
Wolverton Mountain (9)
Woody Woodpecker (7)
Wreck On The Highway (4)
You Ain't Going Nowhere (12)
You Are My Flower (4,7)

You Can't Stop Loving Me Now (8)
You Don't Know My Mind (4)
You Took The Happiness (Out Of My Head) (1)
You're Gonna Get It In The End (1)
Yukon Railroad (2)

NITZER EBB
Pronounced: night-zer ebb. Dance synth duo of Douglas McCarthy and Bon Harris from Chelmford, Essex, England.

| 11/16/91 | 146 | 2 | | Ebbhead. | $12 | Geffen 24456 |

Ascend
DJVD

Family Man
Godhead

I Give To You
Lakeside Drive

Reasons
Sugar Sweet

Time
Trigger Happy

NITZINGER
Rock trio led by John Nitzinger.

| 9/2/72 | 170 | 8 | | Nitzinger. | $10 | Capitol 11091 |

Boogie Queen
Enigma

Hero Of The War
L.A. Texas Boy

Louisiana Cock Fight
My Last Goodbye

Nature Of Your Taste
No Sun

Ticklelick
Witness To The Truth

NIX, Don
Born on 9/27/41 in Memphis. Singer/guitarist/saxophonist. Formerly in the Mar-Keys.

| 9/11/71 | 197 | 3 | | Living By The Days. | $10 | Elektra 74101 |

Going Back To luka
I Saw The Light

Living By The Days
Mary Louise

My Train's Done Come And Gone
Shape I'm In

Olena 94

She Don't Want A Lover (She Just Needs A Friend)
Three Angels

NIXON, Mojo, & SKID ROPER
San Diego-based duo formed in 1983. Mojo, a Virginia state champion bicycle racer as a teenager, appeared in the 1989 film *Great Balls Of Fire*.

| 10/10/87 | 189 | 2 | | **1** Bo-Day-Shus!!! ... [N] | $8 | Enigma 73272 |
| 5/6/89 | 151 | 7 | | **2** Root Hog Or Die | $8 | Enigma 73335 |

B.B.Q. U.S.A. (1)
Burn Your Money (2)
Chicken Drop (2)
Circus Mystery (2)

Debbie Gibson Is Pregnant With My Two Headed Love Child (2)
Elvis Is Everywhere (1)
Gin Guzzlin' Frenzy (1)

I Ain't Gonna Piss In No Jar (1)
I'm A Wreck (2)
I'm Gonna Dig Up Howlin' Wolf (1)

Legalize It (2)
Lincoln Logs (1)
Louisiana Liplock (2)
Pirate Radio (2)
Polka Polka (1)

Positively Bodies Parking Lot (1)
She's Vibrator Dependent (2)
(619) 239-K.I.N.G. (2)
This Land Is Your Land (2)

Wash No Dishes No More (1)
We Gotta Have More Soul! (1)
Wide Open (1)

NOBLES, Cliff, & Co.
Cliff was born in Mobile, Alabama in 1944. Soul bandleader/singer. Moved to Philadelphia in 1965.

| 9/21/68 | 159 | 3 | | The Horse. | $20 | Phil-L.A. S. 4001 |

Boogaloo Down Broadway Theme
Burning Desire

Camel, The
Dry Your Eyes

Heartaches, I Can't Take
Horse, The 2

Judge Baby, I'm Back
Let's Have A Good Time

Love Is All Right
More I Do For You Baby

Mule, The
Yes, I'm Ready

NOEL
Real name: Noel Pagan; 21-year-old (in 1988) Latin singer from the Bronx.

| 10/22/88 | 126 | 13 | | Noel. | $8 | 4th & B'way 4009 |

Change
City Streets

Fallen Angel
Fire To Ice

Like A Child 67
Out Of Time

Silent Morning 47
To Be With You

What I Feel For You

NOLAN, Kenny
Los Angeles-based singer/songwriter. Wrote "My Eyes Adored You," "Lady Marmalade" and "Get Dancin'." Fronted studio group The Eleventh Hour.

| 3/26/77 | 78 | 16 | | Kenny Nolan. | $8 | 20th Century 532 |

I Like Dreamin' 3
If You Ever Stopped Callin' Me Baby

Love's Grown Deep 20
Monette

My Eyes Get Blurry 97
My Jole

My World Will Wait For You
Time Ain't Time Enough

Today I Met The Girl I'm Gonna Marry

Wakin' Up To Love

NORMA JEAN
Born Norma Jean Wright in Elyria, Ohio. Sang in female trio, the Topettes. Attended Ohio State University. Toured for a short time with the Spinners. Moved to New York. Former lead singer of Chic.

| 8/26/78 | 134 | 11 | | Norma Jean. | $8 | Bearsville 6983 |

Having A Party
I Believe In You

I Like Love
Saturday

So I Get Hurt Again
Sorcerer

This Is The Love

NORMAN, Jessye — see BATTLE, Kathleen

NORTH, Freddie
Black vocalist from Nashville. Worked in sales and promotion for Nashboro Records. DJ on *Night Train*, WLAC-Nashville.

| 1/1/72 | 179 | 5 | | Friend. | $12 | Mankind 204 |

Ain't Nothing In The News (But The Blues)

Did I Come Back Too Soon (Or Stay Away Too Long)

I Did The Woman Wrong
Laid Back And Easy

Raining On A Sunny Day
She's All I Got 39

Sidewalks Fences And Walls
Sweeter Than Sweetness

You And Me Together Forever
Yours Love

DEBUT DATE	PEAK POS	WKS CHR	GOLD	ARTIST — Album Title	$	Label & Number

NOTTING HILLBILLIES, The
Quartet of rock 'n' roll roots guitarists: Mark Knopfler and Guy Fletcher (both of Dire Straits), with Brendan Croker and Steve Phillips. Recorded at Knopfler's studio in London's Notting Hill Gate.

| 3/31/90 | 52 | 13 | | Missing...Presumed Having A Good Time | $12 | Warner 26147 |

Bewildered / Feel Like Going Home / Please Baby / Run Me Down / Weapon Of Prayer / Your Own Sweet Way
Blues Stay Away From Me / One Way Gal / Railroad Worksong / That's Where I Belong / Will You Miss Me

NOVA, Aldo
Born Aldo Scarporuscio in Montreal. Rock singer/songwriter/guitarist/keyboardist.

2/20/82	8	37 ▲		1 Aldo Nova	$8	Portrait 37498
10/15/83	56	20		2 Subject: Aldo Nova	$8	Portrait 38721
6/8/91	124	7		3 Blood On The Bricks	$12	Jambco 848513

Africa (Primal Love) (2) / Bright Lights (3) / Hey Ronnie (Veronica's Song) (2) / Monkey On Your Back (2) / Touch Of Madness (3)
All Night Long (2) / Can't Stop Lovin' You (1) / Hold Back The Night (2) / Paradise (2) / Under The Gun (1)
Always Be Mine (2) / Cry Baby Cry (2) / Hot Love (1) / Prelude To Paradise (2) / Victim Of A Broken Heart (2)
Armageddon (Race Cars) (2) / **Fantasy** (1) 23 / It's Too Late (1) / See The Light (1) / War Suite (2)
Ball And Chain (1) / Foolin' Yourself (1) 65 / Medicine Man (3) / Someday (3) / You're My Love (1)
Bang Bang (3) / Heart To Heart (1) / Modern World (3) / Subject's Theme (2) / Young Love (3)
Blood On The Bricks (3) / Hey Operator (3) / / This Ain't Love (3) /

NOVO COMBO
New York-based rock quartet led by Michael Shrieve (Santana, Automatic Man).

| 10/10/81 | 167 | 6 | | Novo Combo | $8 | Polydor 6331 |

Axis Will Turn / Do You Wanna Shake? / Hard To Say Goodbye / Long Road / Tattoo / We Need Love
City Bound ("E" Train) / Don't Do That / Light Of The World / Sorry (For The Delay) / Up Periscope

NRBQ
Multi-styled group formed as the New Rhythm & Blues Quartet in Miami in 1967 by keyboardist Terry Adams. Bassist Joey Spampinato married country singer Skeeter Davis.

| 7/19/69 | 162 | 4 | | 1 NRBQ | $15 | Columbia 9858 |
| 1/6/90 | 198 | 2 | | 2 Wild Weekend | $12 | Virgin 91291 |

Boozoo, That's Who! (2) / Fireworks (2) / Ida (1) / Like A Locomotive (2) / One And Only (2) / This Love Is True (2)
Boy's Life (2) / Fraction Of Action (2) / If I Don't Have You (2) / Little Floater (2) / Poppin' Circumstance (2) / You Can't Hide (1)
C'mon Everybody (1) / Hey! Baby (1) / Immortal For A While (1) / Liza Jane (1) / Rocket Number 9 (1)
C'mon If You're Comin' (1) / Hymn Number 5 (1) / It's A Wild Weekend (2) / Mama Get Down Those / Stay With Me (1)
Fergie's Prayer (1) / I Didn't Know Myself (1) / Kentucky Slop Song (1) / Rock And Roll Shoes (1) / Stomp (1)

N2DEEP
White rap outfit from Vallejo, California put together by producer "Johnny Z." Zunino with rappers "Jay Tee" Trujillo and "TL." Lyon.

| 7/11/92 | 55 | 31↑ | | Back To The Hotel | $12 | Profile 1427 |

Back To The Hotel 14 / Get Mine / N2Deep (We're Who?) / Shakedown / V-Town / What The F**k Is Goin' On?
Comin' Legit / Mack Daddyz / Revenge Of Starchild / Toss-Up / Weekend, The / Ya Gotta Go
Do Tha Crew

NUCLEAR ASSAULT
Heavy-metal quartet formed in 1984 by ex-Anthrax bassist Dan Lilker. Includes John Connelly (vocals), Glenn Evans and Anthony Bramante.

| 8/13/88 | 145 | 11 | | 1 Survive | $8 | I.R.S. 42195 |
| 11/18/89+ | 126 | 24 | | 2 Handle With Care | $8 | In-Effect 3010 |

Brainwashed (1) / F sharp (1) / Good Times Bad Times (1) / Mothers' Day (2) / Search & Seizure (2) / Torture Tactics (2)
Critical Mass (2) / F sharp (Wake Up) (2) / Got Another Quarter (1) / New Song (2) / Surgery (2) / Trail Of Tears (2)
Emergency (2) / Fight To Be Free (1) / Great Depression (2) / PSA (1) / Survive (1) / When Freedom Dies (2)
Equal Rights (1) / Funky Noise (2) / Inherited Hell (2) / Rise From The Ashes (1) / Technology (1) / Wired (1)

NUCLEAR VALDEZ
Miami rock band: Froilan Sosa (vocals), Jorge Barcala, Juan Diaz and Robert Slade LeMont.

| 2/24/90 | 175 | 5 | | I Am I | $12 | Epic 45354 |
CD includes bonus track

Apache / If I Knew Then / Run Through The Fields / Summer / Unsung Hero (Song For / Where Do We Go From Here
Eve / Rising Sun / Strength / Trace The Thunder / Lenny Bruce)
Hope

| ★★213★★ | | | | **NUGENT, Ted** | | |

Born on 12/13/48 in Detroit. Heavy-metal rock guitarist; leader of The Amboy Dukes. Currently a member of the supergroup Damn Yankees.

11/22/75+	28	62 ▲²		1 Ted Nugent	$10	Epic 33692
10/2/76	24	32 ▲²		2 Free-For-All	$10	Epic 34121
				featuring vocals by Meat Loaf		
6/25/77	17	39 ▲²		3 Cat Scratch Fever	$8	Epic 34700
2/11/78	13	22 ▲		4 Double Live Gonzo! [L]	$10	Epic 35069 [2]
11/11/78	24	20 ▲		5 Weekend Warriors	$8	Epic 35551
6/2/79	18	18 ●		6 State Of Shock	$8	Epic 36000
5/31/80	13	18 ●		7 Scream Dream	$8	Epic 36404
3/21/81	51	10		8 Intensities In 10 Cities [L]	$8	Epic 37084
11/28/81	140	8		9 Great Gonzos! The Best Of Ted Nugent [G]	$8	Epic 37667
7/17/82	51	14		10 Nugent	$8	Atlantic 19365
2/18/84	56	15		11 Penetrator	$8	Atlantic 80125
3/22/86	76	14		12 Little Miss Dangerous	$8	Atlantic 81632
8/22/88	112	7		13 If You Can't Lick 'Em...Lick 'Em	$8	Atlantic 81812

Alone (6) / Blame It On The Night (11) / **Cat Scratch Fever** / Death By Misadventure (3) / Don't Push Me (10) / Fist Fightin' Son Of A Gun
Angry Young Man (12) / Bound And Gagged (10) / (3,4,9) 30 / Dog Eat Dog (2,9) 91 / Don't You Want My Love (11) / (3)
Baby, Please Don't Go (4,9) / Can't Live With 'Em (13) / Come And Get It (7) / Don't Cry (I'll Be Back / Ebony (10) / Flesh & Blood (7)
Bite Down Hard (6) / Can't Stop Me Now (10) / Crazy Ladies (12) / Before You Know It Baby) / Fightin' Words (10) / Flying Lip Lock (8)
Bite The Hand (13) / / Cruisin' (5) / (7) / / Free-For-All (2,9)

547

NUGENT, Ted — Cont'd

Funlover (13)	I Gotta Move (7)	Live It Up (3)
Go Down Fighting (11)	I Love You So I Told You A	Motor City Madhouse (1,4,9)
Gonzo (4)	Lie (7)	My Love Is Like A Tire Iron
Good And Ready (10)	I Take No Prisoners (8)	(8)
Good Friends And A Bottle	I Want To Tell You (6)	Name Your Poison (5)
Of Wine (5)	If You Can't Lick 'Em...Lick	**Need You Bad** (5) *84*
Great White Buffalo (4)	'Em (7)	No Man's Land (11)
Habitual Offender (10)	It Don't Matter (6)	No, No, No (10)
Hammerdown (2)	Jailbait (8)	One Woman (5)
Hard As Nails (7)	Just What The Doctor	Out Of Control (3)
Harder They Come (The	Ordered (1,4,9)	Painkiller (12)
Harder I Get) (13)	Knockin' At Your Door (11)	Paralyzed (6,9)
Heads Will Roll (8)	Land Of A Thousand Dances	Put Up Or Shut Up (8)
Hey Baby (1) *72*	(8)	Queen Of The Forest (1)
Hibernation (4)	Lean Mean R&R Machine	Saddle Sore (6)
High Heels In Motion (12)	(11)	Satisfied (6)
Home Bound (3) *70*	Light My Way (2)	Savage Dancer (12)
I Am A Predator (8)	Little Miss Dangerous (12)	Scream Dream (7)
I Got The Feelin' (5)	Little Red Book (1)	

Separate The Men From The	Take Me Away (12)	(Where Do You) Draw The
Boys, Please (13)	Take Me Home (11)	Line (11)
She Drives Me Crazy (13)	Terminus Eldorado (7)	Where Have You Been All
Skintight (13)	That's The Story Of Love (13)	My Life (1)
Smokescreen (5)	Thousand Knives (3)	Workin' Hard, Playin' Hard
Snake Charmer (6)	Thunder Thighs (11)	(3)
Snakeskin Cowboys (1)	Tied Up In Love (11)	Writing On The Wall (2)
Spit It Out (7)	Tight Spots (5)	**Yank Me, Crank Me** (4) *58*
Spontaneous Combustion (8)	Together (2)	You Make Me Feel Right At
Spread Your Wings (13)	Turn It Up (2)	Home (1)
State Of Shock (6)	Venom Soup (5)	
Stormtroopin' (1,4,9)	Violent Love (7)	
Strangers (12)	Wang Dang Sweet Poontang	
Stranglehold (1,4,9)	(3,4,9)	
Street Rats (2)	**Wango Tango** (7,9) *86*	
Sweet Sally (3)	We're Gonna Rock Tonight	
TNT Overture (8)	(10)	
Tailgunner (10)	Weekend Warriors (5)	
Take It Or Leave It (6)	When Your Body Talks (12)	

NUMAN, Gary

Born Gary Webb on 3/8/58 in Hammersmith, England. Synthesized techno-rock artist.

9/15/79	124	10		1 Replicas	$8	Atco 117

GARY NUMAN & TUBEWAY ARMY

2/2/80	16	30		2 The Pleasure Principle	$8	Atco 120
10/4/80	64	10		3 Telekon	$8	Atco 103
10/24/81	167	4		4 Dance	$8	Atco 143

Aircrash Bureau (3)	Cry The Clock Said (4)	I'm An Agent (3)
Airlane (2)	Down In The Park (1)	It Must Have Been Years (1)
Are 'Friends' Electric? (1)	Engineers (2)	Joy Circuit (3)
Boys Like Me (4)	Films (2)	Machman, The (1)
Cars (2) *9*	I Die: You Die (3)	M.E. (2)
Complex (2)	I Dream Of Wires (3)	Me! I Disconnect From You
Conversation (2)	I Nearly Married A Human	(1)
Crash (4)	(1)	Metal (2)

Moral (4)	Replicas (1)	When The Machines Rock (1)
My Brother's Time (4)	She's Got Claws (4)	You Are In My Vision (1)
Night Talk (4)	Slowcar To China (4)	You Are You Are (4)
Observer (2)	Stories (4)	
Please Push No More (3)	Subway Called You (4)	
Praying To The Aliens (1)	Telekon (3)	
Remember I Was Vapour (3)	This Wreckage (3)	
Remind Me To Smile (3)	Tracks (2)	

NUNN, Bobby

Vocalist/keyboardist from Buffalo, New York. Performed on Rick James' debut LP *Come Get It*. Moved to Los Angeles, formed own band, Splendor.

10/23/82	148	8		Second To Nunn	$8	Motown 6022

Get It While You Can	Never Seen Anything Like	Party's Over	She's Just A Groupie
Got To Get Up On It	You	Sexy Sassy	You Need Non-Stop Lovin'

NU SHOOZ

Portland, Oregon group centered around husband-and-wife team of guitarist/songwriter John Smith and lead singer Valerie Day.

5/31/86	27	32	●	1 Poolside	$8	Atlantic 81647
4/23/88	93	14		2 Told U So	$8	Atlantic 81804

Are You Lookin' For	Don't You Be Afraid (1)	If That's The Way You Want	**Point Of No Return** (1) *28*	Told U So (2)
Somebody Nu (2)	Driftin' (2)	It (2)	Savin' All My Time (2)	Wonder (2)
Doin' Alright (2)	Goin' Thru The Motions (1)	Lost Your Number (1)	Secret Message (1)	You Put Me In A Trance (1)
Don't Let Me Be The One (1)	**I Can't Wait** (1) *3*	Montecarlo Nite (2)	**Should I Say Yes?** (2) *41*	

N.W.A.

Los Angeles-based rap outfit: Eric "Eazy-E" Wright, Lorenzo "M.C. Ren" Patterson, Andre "Dr. Dre" Young, Oshea "Ice Cube" Jackson and DJ Antoine "Yella" Carraby. N.W.A. stands for Niggas With Attitude. Wright, Patterson and Young are successful solo artists. Young and Carraby are also members of World Class Wreckin Cru and produce others. Ice Cube left by 1990.

3/4/89	37	81	▲²	1 Straight Outta Compton	$8	Ruthless 57102
9/1/90	27	25	▲	2 100 Miles And Runnin'	$6	Ruthless 7224
6/15/91	1¹	44	▲	3 EFIL4ZAGGIN ... [M]	$12	Ruthless 57126

title actually appears on LP as an inverse image of NIGGAZ4LIFE

Alwayz Into Somethin' (3)	Don't Drink That Wine (3)	I Ain't Tha 1 (1)	Niggaz 4 Life (3)	Straight Outta Compton (1)
Appetite For Destruction (3)	Dopeman (1)	I'd Rather Fuck You (3)	100 Miles And Runnin' (2)	To Kill A Hooker (3)
Approach To Danger (3)	Express Yourself (1)	If It Ain't Ruff (1)	One Less Bitch (3)	
Automobile (3)	Findum, Fuckum & Flee (3)	Just Don't Bite It (2)	1-900-2-COMPTON (3)	
Compton's N The House (3)	___ Tha Police (1)	Kamurshol (3)	Parental Discretion Iz	
Dayz Of Wayback (3)	Gangsta Gangsta (1)	Message To B.A. (3)	Advised (1)	
			Protest (3)	
			Quiet On Tha Set (1)	
			Real Niggaz (2,3)	
			Real Niggaz Don't Die (3)	
			Sa Prize (Part 2) (2)	
			She Swallowed It (3)	

NYLONS, The

Canadian a cappella quartet formed in 1979: Marc Connors, Paul Cooper, Claude Morrison and Arnold Robinson. Connors died on 3/25/91 (age 41).

3/29/86	133	16		1 Seamless	$8	Open Air 0304
5/23/87	43	24		2 Happy Together	$8	Open Air 0306
6/10/89	136	10		3 Rockapella	$8	Windham Hill 1085

all of above contain vocals and percussion only

(All I Have To Do Is) Dream	Count My Blessings (3)	Grown Man Cry (2)	No Stone Unturned (3)	Rise Up (3)	Touch Of Your Hand (2)
(3)	Crazy In Love (Morning	**Happy Together** (2) *75*	Oo-Wee, Oh Me, Oh My (1)	Stars Are Ours (1)	Up On The Roof (1)
Another Night Like This (3)	Comes Early) (2)	It's What They Call Magic (2)	Perpetual Emotion (3)	Stepping Stone (1)	Wildfire (3)
Busy Tonight (3)	Dance Of Love (2)	**Kiss Him Goodbye** (2) *12*	Poison Ivy (3)	Take Me To Your Heart (1)	
Chain Gang (2)	Drift Away (1)	Lion Sleeps Tonight (1)	Remember (Walking In The	This Boy (1)	
Combat Zone (1)	Face In The Crowd (2)	Love This Is Love (3)	Sand) (1)	This Island Earth (2)	

NYRO, Laura

Born Laura Nigro on 10/18/47 in the Bronx, New York. White soul-gospel singer/songwriter. Wrote "Stoned Soul Picnic," "Wedding Bell Blues," "And When I Die" and "Stoney End."

8/10/68	181	7		1 Eli And The Thirteenth Confession	$15	Columbia 9626
11/1/69	32	17		2 New York Tendaberry	$10	Columbia 9737

NYRO, Laura — Cont'd

12/26/70+	51	14	3	Christmas And The Beads Of Sweat..	$10	Columbia 30259
12/25/71+	46	17	4	Gonna Take A Miracle...	$10	Columbia 30987
				backing vocals by LaBelle		
2/3/73	97	11	5	The First Songs.. [E-R]	$10	Columbia 31410
				reissue of her first album *More Than A New Discovery*		
3/13/76	60	14	6	Smile..	$10	Columbia 33912
7/2/77	137	5	7	Season of Lights...Laura Nyro in Concert..................................... [L]	$8	Columbia 34786
3/10/84	182	3	8	Mother's Spiritual..	$8	Columbia 39215

And When I Die (5,7)
Beads Of Sweat (3)
Been On A Train (3)
Bells, The (4)
Billy's Blues (5)
Blackpatch (3)
Blowing Away (5)
Brighter Song (8)
Brown Earth (3)
Buy And Sell (5)
California Shoeshine Boys (5)
Captain For Dark Mornings (2)
Captain Saint Lucifer (2,7)
Cat-Song (6,7)

Children Of The Junks (6)
Christmas In My Soul (3)
Confession, The (1,7)
Dancing In The Street (medley) (4)
December's Boudoir (1)
Desiree (4)
Eli's Comin (1)
Emmie (1,7)
Flim Flam Man (5)
Free Thinker (8)
Gibson Street (2)
Good By Joe (5)
He's A Runner (5)
I Am The Blues (6)
I Met Him On A Sunday (4)

I Never Meant To Hurt You (5)
It's Gonna Take A Miracle (4)
Jimmy Mack (4)
Late For Love (8)
Lazy Susan (5)
Lonely Women (1)
Lu (1)
Luckie (8)
Man In The Moon (8)
Man Who Sends Me Home (2)
Map To The Treasure (3)
Melody In The Sky (8)
Mercy On Broadway (2)
Midnite Blue (6)

Money (6,7)
Monkey Time (medley) (4)
Mother's Spiritual (8)
New York Tendaberry (2)
Nowhere To Run (4)
Once It Was Alright Now (Farmer Joe) (1)
Poverty Train (1)
Refrain (8)
Right To Vote (8)
Roadnotes (8)
Save The Country (2)
Sexy Mama (6)
Smile (6)
Sophia (8)
Spanish Harlem (4)

Stoned Soul Picnic (1)
Stoney End (5)
Stormy Love (6)
Sweet Blindness (1,7)
Sweet Lovin' Baby (2)
Talk To A Green Tree (8)
Time And Love (2)
Timer (1,7)
To A Child (8)
Tom Cat Goodbye (2)
Trees Of The Ages (8)
Up On The Roof (3) *92*
Upstairs By A Chinese Lamp (3,7)
Wedding Bell Blues (5)

When I Was A Freeport And You Were The Main Drag (3,7)
Wilderness (8)
Wind, The (4)
Woman's Blues (1)
You Don't Love Me When I Cry (2)
You've Really Got A Hold On Me (4)

★★389★★ OAK RIDGE BOYS

Country-pop vocal group formed as a gospel quartet in 1940 in Oak Ridge, Tennessee. Disbanded after World War II; re-formed in 1957. Many personnel changes. Lineup since early 1970s: Duane Allen (lead), Joe Bonsall (tenor), Richard Sterban (bass) and Bill Golden (baritone; left for a solo career in 1987, replaced by the group's guitarist, Steve Sanders).

2/18/78	120	9	●	1 Y'all Come Back Saloon..	$8	ABC/Dot 2093
6/17/78	164	11	●	2 Room Service..	$8	ABC 1065
3/29/80	154	6	●	3 Together..	$8	MCA 3220
11/22/80	99	21	▲	4 Greatest Hits... [G]	$8	MCA 5150
6/13/81	14	48	▲²	5 Fancy Free...	$8	MCA 5209
2/20/82	20	21	●	6 Bobbie Sue..	$8	MCA 5294
12/4/82+	73	7	●	7 Christmas.. [X]	$8	MCA 5365
2/26/83	51	23	●	8 American Made...	$8	MCA 5390
11/19/83	121	14	●	9 Deliver...	$8	MCA 5455
9/8/84	71	24	●	10 Greatest Hits 2.. [G]	$8	MCA 5496
4/20/85	156	5		11 Step On Out..	$8	MCA 5555

Ain't No Cure For The Rock And Roll (9)
Alice In Wonderland (9)
American Made (8,10) *72*
Amity (8)
Another Dream Just Came True (8)
Any Old Time You Choose (8)
Back In Your Arms Again (6)
Beautiful You (3,10)
Bobbie Sue (6) *12*
Break My Mind (9)
But I Do (2)
Callin' Baton Rouge (2)
Christmas Carol (7)
Christmas Is Paintin' The Town (7)
Class Reunion (11)
Come On In (2,4,11)
Cryin' Again (2,4)

Didn't She Really Thrill Them (Back In 1924) (1)
Doctor's Orders (6)
Down Deep Inside (9)
Down The Hall (8)
Dream Of Me (5)
Dream On (4)
Easy (1)
Elvira (5,10) *5*
Emmylou (1)
Everyday (10)
Fancy Free (5,10)
Freckles (1)
Happy Christmas Eve (7)
Heart Of Mine (3,4)
Heart On The Line (Operator, Operator) (8)
Holdin' On To You (3)
How Long Has It Been (5)
I Can Love You (2)

I Can't Imagine Laying Down (With Anyone But You) (3)
I Guess It Never Hurts To Hurt Sometimes (9,10)
I Wish You Could Have Turned My Head (And Left My Heart Alone) (6)
I Wish You Were Here (Oh My Darlin') (5)
I Would Crawl All The Way (To The Heart) (5)
I'll Be True To You (1,2,4)
I'm So Glad I'm Standing Here Today (8)
If There Were Only Time For Love (2)
If You Can't Find Love (2)
In The Pines (9)
It Could Have Been Ten Years Ago (2)

Jesus Is Born Today (It Is His Birthday) (7)
Lay Down Your Sword And Shield (2)
Leaving Louisiana In The Broad Daylight (4)
Let Me Be The One (6)
Little More Like Me (The Crucifixion) (3)
Little One (7)
Little Things (11)
Lots Of Matchbooks (2)
Love Is Everywhere (11)
Love Song (8,10)
Love Takes Two (3)
Make My Life With You (10)
Mary Christmas (7)
Oh Holy Night (7)
Old Kentucky Song (10)
Old Time Family Bluegrass Band (1)

Old Time Lovin' (1)
Only One I Love (11)
Ophelia (11)
Ozark Mountain Jubilee (9,10)
Ready To Take My Chances (3)
Roll Tennessee River (11)
Sail Away (11)
Santa's Song (7)
She's Gone To L.A. Again (5)
She's Not Just Another Pretty Face (8)
Silent Night (7)
Silver Bells (7)
So Fine (6) *76*
Somewhere In The Night (5)
Staying Afloat (11)
Step On Out (11)
Still Holding On (9)
Take This Heart (8)

Thank God For Kids (7,10)
Through My Eyes (9)
Touch A Hand, Make A Friend (11)
Trying To Love Two Women (3,4)
Until You (6)
Up On Cripple Creek (6)
When I'm With You (5)
When Love Calls You (5)
When You Get To The Heart (9)
Whiskey Lady (3)
White Christmas (7)
Would They Love Him Down In Shreveport (7)
Y'all Come Back Saloon (1,4)
You Made It Beautiful (8)
You're The One (1,4,8)

OAKTOWN'S 3-5-7

Female rap group from Oakland, California: Djuana "Sweet L.D." Johnican, Tabatha "Terrible T" King, Vicious C and Sweet Pea (former Oakland Raiders cheerleader). By 1991, reduced to a duo of Johnican and King who were dancers with M.C. Hammer's touring posse.

5/13/89	126	16		Wild & Loose..	$8	Capitol 90926

I Betcha Wanna Take It
It's A Shame

Juicy Gotcha Krazy
Rock 'N' Soul

Say That Then
Stupid Def Ya'll

3.5.7 Straight At You
We Like It

Yeah, Yeah, Yeah

O'BANION, John

Pop singer from Kokomo, Indiana.

5/16/81	164	4		John O'Banion..	$8	Elektra 342

Come To My Love
If You Love Me

Love Is Blind
Love Is In Your Eyes

Love You Like I Never Loved Before *24*

Our Love Can Make It
She's Not For You

Take A Chance On Love
Walk Away Renee

You're In My Life Again

DEBUT DATE	PEAK POS	WKS CHR	GOLD	ARTIST — Album Title	$	Label & Number

O'BRYAN
Born O'Bryan Burnett II. R&B singer from Sneads Ferry, North Carolina.

4/10/82	80	12		1 Doin' Alright	$8	Capitol 12192
3/12/83	87	27		2 You And I	$8	Capitol 12256
5/26/84	64	21		3 Be My Lover	$8	Capitol 12332

Be My Lover (3)
Breakin' Together (3)
Can't Live Without Your Love (1)
Dazzlin' Lady (2)

Doin' Alright (1)
Gigolo, The (1) 57
Go On And Cry (3)
I'm Freaky (2)
I'm In Love Again (2)

It's Over (1)
Lady I Love You (3)
Love Has Found It's Way (1)
Lovelite (3)
Mother Nature's Callin' (1)

Right From The Start (1)
Shake (2)
Soft Touch (2)
Soul Train's A'Comin' (2)
Still Water (Love) (1)

Together Always (2)
Too Hot (3)
You And I (2)
You Gotta Use It (3)

You're Always On My Mind

OCASEK, Ric
Born Richard Otcasek on 3/23/49 in Baltimore. Lead singer/guitarist/songwriter of The Cars. Appeared in the 1987 film *Made In Heaven*. Married supermodel/actress Paulina Porizkova in 1989. His son Christopher Otcasek is leader of Glamour Camp.

| 1/29/83 | 28 | 16 | | 1 Beatitude .... | $8 | Geffen 2022 |
| 10/11/86 | 31 | 23 | | 2 This Side Of Paradise .... | $8 | Geffen 24098 |

Coming For You (2)
Connect Up To Me (1)
Emotion In Motion (2) 15
Hello Darkness (2)

I Can't Wait (1)
Jimmy Jimmy (1)
Keep On Laughin' (2)
Look In Your Eyes (2)

Mystery (2)
Out Of Control (1)
P.F.J. (2)
Prove (1)

Quick One (1)
Sneak Attack (1)
Something To Grab For (1) 47

Take A Walk (1)
This Side Of Paradise (2)
Time Bomb (1)
True Love (2)

True To You (2) 75

OCEAN
Canadian pop quintet: Janice Morgan (vocals), David Tamblyn, Greg Brown, Jeff Jones and Charles Slater.

| 5/29/71 | 60 | 13 | | Put Your Hand In The Hand .... | $10 | Kama Sutra 2033 |

Deep Enough For Me 73
No Other Woman

One Who's Left
Pleasure Of Your Company

Put Your Hand In The Hand 2
We Got A Dream 82

Stones I Throw

Will The Circle Be Unbroken

OCEAN, Billy
Born Leslie Sebastian Charles on 1/21/50 in Trinidad. Raised in England, worked as a tailor. Did session work in London. Moved to the U.S. in the late '70s.

7/25/81	152	3		1 Nights (Feel Like Getting Down)	$8	Epic 37406
8/25/84	9	86	▲²	2 Suddenly	$8	Jive 8213
5/17/86	6	48	▲²	3 Love Zone	$8	Jive 8409
3/19/88	18	31	▲	4 Tear Down These Walls	$8	Jive 8495
11/4/89	77	16	●	5 Greatest Hits .... [G]	$8	Jive 1271

Another Day Won't Matter (1)
Are You Ready (1)
Because Of You (4)
Bitter Sweet (3)
Calypso Crazy (4)
Caribbean Queen (No More Love On The Run) (2,5) 1
Colour Of Love (4,5) 17
Dancefloor (2)

Don't Say Stop (1)
Everlasting Love (1)
Get Outta My Dreams, Get Into My Car (4,5) 1
Gun For Hire (4)
Here's To You (4,5)
I Sleep Much Better (In Someone Else's Bed) (5)
If I Should Lose You (2)

It's Never Too Late To Try (3)
Licence To Chill (5) 32
Long And Winding Road (2)
Love Is Forever (3) 16
Love Zone (3,5) 10
Loverboy (2,5) 2
Lucky Man (2)
Mystery Lady (2) 24

Nights (Feel Like Getting Down) (1)
Pleasure (4)
Promise Me (3)
Showdown (3)
Soon As You're Ready (4)
Stand And Deliver (4)
Stay The Night (4)
Suddenly (2,5) 4

Syncopation (2)
Taking Chances (1)
Tear Down These Walls (4)
There'll Be Sad Songs (To Make You Cry) (3,5) 1
Whatever Turns You On (1)
When The Going Gets Tough, The Tough Get Going (3,5) 2

Who's Gonna Rock You (1)
Without You (3)

OCEAN BLUE, The
Band from Hershey, Pennsylvania: Dave Schelzel (vocals), Steve Lau (keyboards), Bobby Mittan (bass) and Rob Minnig (drums).

| 2/3/90 | 155 | 8 | | The Ocean Blue .... | $12 | Sire 25906 |

Ask Me Jon
Awaking To A Dream

Between Something And Nothing
Circus Animals

Drifting, Falling
Familiar Face

Frigid Winter Days
Just Let Me Know

Love Song
Myron

Office Of A Busy Man
Vanity Fair

OCHS, Phil
Born on 12/19/40 in El Paso, Texas; hanged himself on 4/9/76. Folk-protest singer/songwriter; part of the early '60s Greenwich Village folk scene.

7/9/66	149	2		1 Phil Ochs In Concert .... [L]	$25	Elektra 7310
12/9/67	168	5		2 Pleasures Of The Harbor	$20	A&M 4133
6/14/69	167	7		3 Rehearsals For Retirement	$20	A&M 4181
3/14/70	194	2		4 Phil Ochs Greatest Hits	$20	A&M 4253

album contains all new recordings

Another Age (3)
Bach, Beethoven, Mozart & Me (4)
Basket In The Pool (4)
Boy In Ohio (4)
Bracero (1)
Canons Of Christianity (1)
Changes (1)
Chords Of Fame (4)

Cops Of The World (1)
Cross My Heart (2)
Crucifixion, The (2)
Doesn't Lenny Live Here Anymore (3)
Doll House (3)
Flower Lady (2)
Gas Station Women (4)
I Kill Therefore I Am (3)

I'm Going To Say It Now (1)
I've Had Her (2)
Is There Anybody Here? (1)
Jim Dean Of Indiana (4)
Love Me, I'm A Liberal (1)
Miranda (2)
My Kingdom For A Car (4)
My Life (3)
No More Songs (4)

One Way Ticket Home (4)
Outside Of A Small Circle Of Friends (2)
Party, The (2)
Pleasures Of The Harbor (2)
Pretty Smart On My Part (4)
Rehearsals For Retirement (3)
Ringing Of Revolution (1)

Santo Domingo (1)
Scorpion Departs, But Never Returns (3)
Ten Cents A Coup (4)
There But For Fortune (1)
When I'm Gone (1)
William Butler Yeats Visits Lincoln Park And Escapes Unscathed (3)

World Began In Eden And Ended In Los Angeles (3)

O'CONNOR, Carroll
Born on 8/2/24 in New York City. TV/film actor. Portrayed Archie Bunker on TV's *All In The Family* and Chief Bill Gillespie on *In The Heat Of The Night*.

| 6/17/72 | 118 | 13 | | Remembering You .... | $10 | A&M 4340 |

About A Quarter To Nine
Can't We Talk It Over

I Get Along Without You Very Well
I'll Never Be The Same

Just A Memory
Last Night When We Were Young
So Rare

Love Is Here Stay
Remembering You

Sweet And Lovely
What Is There To Say

Would You Like To Take A Walk

O'CONNOR, Sinead
Pronounced: shin-NAYD. Born on 12/8/67 in Dublin, Ireland. Female singer/songwriter.

2/6/88	36	38	●	1 The Lion And The Cobra	$8	Chrysalis 41612
4/7/90	1⁶	52	▲²	2 I Do Not Want What I Haven't Got	$12	Ensign 21759
10/10/92	27	9		3 Am I Not Your Girl?	$12	Ensign 21952

DEBUT DATE	PEAK POS	WKS CHR	GOLD	ARTIST — Album Title	$	Label & Number

O'CONNOR, Sinead — Cont'd

Bewitched, Bothered And Bewildered (3)	Emperor's New Clothes (2) *60*	I Do Not Want What I Haven't Got (2)	Jerusalem (1)	Love Letters (3)	Success Has Made A Failure Of Our Home (3)
Black Boys On Mopeds (2)	Feel So Different (2)	I Want To Be Loved By You (3)	Jump In The River (2)	Mandinka (1)	Three Babies (2)
Black Coffee (3)	Gloomy Sunday (3)	I Want Your (Hands On Me) (1)	Just Call Me Joe (1)	Never Get Old (1)	Troy (1)
Don't Cry For Me Argentina [includes 2 versions] (3)	How Insensitive (3)	Jackie (1)	Just Like U Said It Would B (1)	**Nothing Compares 2 U** (2) *1*	Why Don't You Do Right? (3)
Drink Before The War (1)	I Am Stretched On Your Grave (1)		Last Day Of Our Acquaintance (1)	Scarlet Ribbons (3)	You Cause As Much Sorrow (2)
				Secret Love (3)	

O'DAY, Alan
Born on 10/3/40 in Hollywood. Singer/songwriter/pianist. Wrote Helen Reddy's #1 hit "Angie Baby" and the Righteous Brothers' "Rock And Roll Heaven."

9/3/77	109	9		Appetizers	$8	Pacific 4300

Angie Baby	Catch My Breath	Gifts	Slot Machine	**Started Out Dancing,**	*Undercover Angel 1*
Caress Me Pretty Music	Do Me Wrong, But Do Me	Satisfied	Soldier Of Fortune	**Ended Up Making Love 73**	

ODETTA
Folk singer Odetta Holmes. Born on 12/31/30 in Birmingham, Alabama.

9/28/63	75	8		Odetta sings Folk Songs	$18	RCA 2643

All My Trials	Blowing In The Wind	I Never Will Marry	900 Miles	Shenandoah	Why Oh Why
Anthem Of The Rainbow	Golden Vanity	Maybe She Go	Roberta	This Little Light Of Mine	Yes I See

ODYSSEY
New York soul-disco trio: Manila-born Tony Reynolds, and sisters Lillian and Louise Lopez, originally from the Virgin Islands.

10/8/77	36	38		1 Odyssey	$8	RCA 2204
11/11/78	123	5		2 Hollywood Party Tonight	$8	RCA 3031
6/14/80	181	4		3 Hang Together	$8	RCA 3526
7/18/81	175	5		4 I Got The Melody	$8	RCA 3910

Baby That's All I Want (4)	Hang Together (3)	If You're Lookin' For A Way Out (3)	Rooster Loose In The Barnyard (3)	What Time Does The Balloon Go Up (medley) (2)
Comin' Back For More (2)	Hey Bill (Last Night Was Really A Thrill) (2)	It Will Be Alright (4)	Roots Suite Medley (4)	Woman Behind The Man (1)
Don't Tell Me, Tell Her (3)	Hold De Mota Down (medley) (1)	Lilly And Harvey, Late To The Party Again (2)	Single Again (medley) (2)	You Keep Me Dancin' (1)
Down Boy (3)	Hold On To Love (4)	Lucky Star (2)	Thank You God For One More Day (1)	You Wouldn't Know A Real Live True Love If It Walked
Easy Come, Easy Go (medley) (1)	I Can't Keep Holding Back My Love (4)	**Native New Yorker** (1) *21*	Use It Up And Wear It Out (3)	Right Up, Kissed You On The Cheek And Said Hello
Ever Lovin' Sam (1)	I Dare Ya (2)	Never Had It At All (3)	**Weekend Lover** (1) *57*	Baby (2)
Follow Me (Play Follow The Leader) (3)	I Got The Melody (4)	Oh No Not My Baby (4)		
Golden Hands (1)		Pride (2)		

OFF BROADWAY usa
Rock quintet from Oak Park, Illinois — Cliff Johnson, lead singer.

2/16/80	101	11		On	$15	Atlantic 19263

Bad Indication	Full Moon Turn My Head Around	Hang On For Love	New Little Girl	**Stay In Time** *51*
Bully Bully		Money's No Good	Oh, Boy!	You Belong To You
Drop Me A Line				

OHIO EXPRESS
Bubblegum group from Mansfield, Ohio. Produced by Jerry Kasenetz and Jeff Katz (worked with The Music Explosion and 1910 Fruitgum Co.). Joey Levine (later with Reunion) was lead singer on most of the hits.

| 7/6/68 | 126 | 11 | | 1 Ohio Express .... | $15 | Buddah 5018 |
| 2/8/69 | 191 | 2 | | 2 Chewy, Chewy .... | $15 | Buddah 5026 |

Chewy Chewy (2) *15*	Fun (2)	Little Girl (2)	She's Not Comin' Home (1)	Vacation (1)
Down At Lulu's (1) *33*	Into This Time (1)	Mary-Ann (1)	Simon Says (2)	Winter Skies (1)
Down In Tennessee (2)	It's A Sad Day (It's A Sad Time) (1)	Nothing Sweeter Than My Baby (2)	So Good, So Fine (2)	Yes Sir (2)
Firebird (2)	Let It Take You (2)	1,2,3 Red Light (2)	Time You Spent With Me (1)	**Yummy Yummy Yummy** (1) *4*
First Grade Reader (1)			Turn To Straw (1)	

★★168★★ OHIO PLAYERS
Originally an R&B instrumental group called the Ohio Untouchables, formed in Dayton in 1959. Backup on The Falcons' records. First recorded for Lupine in 1962. Members during prime (1974-79): Marshall Jones, Clarence "Satch" Satchell, Jimmy "Diamond" Williams, Marvin "Merv" Pierce, Billy Beck, Ralph "Pee Wee" Middlebrook and Leroy "Sugarfoot" Bonner.

3/4/72	177	7		1 Pain	$10	Westbound 2015
2/24/73	63	22		2 Pleasure	$10	Westbound 2017
9/29/73	70	19		3 Ecstasy	$10	Westbound 2021
4/27/74	11	48	●	4 Skin Tight	$10	Mercury 705
11/2/74	102	8		5 Climax .... [K]	$10	Westbound 1003
11/23/74+	1[1]	29	●	6 Fire	$10	Mercury 1013
2/22/75	92	7		7 Ohio Players Greatest Hits .... [G]	$10	Westbound 1005
8/23/75	2[1]	36	●	8 Honey	$10	Mercury 1038
12/20/75+	61	14		9 Rattlesnake .... [K]	$10	Westbound 211
6/12/76	12	20	●	10 Contradiction	$8	Mercury 1088
11/13/76	31	17	●	11 Ohio Players Gold .... [G]	$8	Mercury 1122
4/9/77	41	27		12 Angel	$8	Mercury 3701
12/24/77+	68	10		13 Mr. Mean	$8	Mercury 3707
9/9/78	69	9		14 Jass-Ay-Lay-Dee	$8	Mercury 3730
4/14/79	80	14		15 Everybody Up	$8	Arista 4226
4/11/81	165	3		16 Tenderness	$8	Boardwalk 37090

Ain't Givin' Up No Ground (8)	Body Vibes (12)	Don't Fight My Love (12)	**Feel The Beat (Everybody Disco)** (11) *61*	Funk-O-Nots (14)	Hard To Love Your Brother (16)
Alone (14)	Call Me (16)	Don't Say Goodbye (15)	Feelings (medley) (6)	**Funky Worm** (2,7) *15*	Heaven Must Be Like This (4)
Angel (12)	Can You Still Love Me (12)	**Ecstasy** (3,7) *31*	Fight Me, Chase Me (13)	Glad To Know You're Mine (12)	Hollywood Hump (9)
Bi-Centennial (10)	Climax (5,7)	Everybody Up (15)	**Fire** (6,11) *1*	Gone Forever (9)	Honey (8)
Big Score (13)	Contradiction (10)	Faith (12)	Food Stamps Y'all (3,5)	Good Luck Charm (13)	Hustle Bird (9)
Black Cat (3)	Controller's Mind (13)	Far East Mississippi (10,11)	**Fopp** (8,11) *30*		I Wanna Hear From You (1,7)
Boardwalkin' (16)	Dance (If Ya Wanta) (14)				

551

DEBUT DATE	PEAK POS	WKS CHR	GOLD	ARTIST — Album Title	$	Label & Number

OHIO PLAYERS — Cont'd

(I Wanna Know) Do You Feel It (3)
I Want To Be Free (6,11) **44**
Introducing The Players (9)
Is Anybody Gonna Be Saved? (4)
It Takes A While (16)
It's All Over (6)
It's Your Night (medley) (4)
Jass-Ay-Lay-Dee (14)
Jive Turkey (Part 1) (4,11) **47**
Laid It (2,9)
Let's Love (8)
Little Lady Maria (10)

Love Rollercoaster (8,11) **1**
Magic Trick (13)
Make Me Feel (15)
Merry Go Round (12)
Mr. Mean (13)
My Ladies Run Me Crazy (10)
My Life (10)
Never Had A Dream (1)
Not So Sad And Lonely (3)
Nott Enuff (14)
O-H-I-O (12) **45**
Only A Child Can Love (11)
Our Love Has Died (2)
Pack It Up (5)
Pain (Part II) (7)

Pain (Part I) (1,7) **64**
Paint Me (2)
Players Balling (Players Doin' Their Own Thing) (1,5)
Pleasure (2,7)
Precious Love (10)
Pride And Vanity (2)
Proud Mary (5)
Rattlesnake (9) **90**
Reds, The (1)
Rooster Poot (9)
Ruffell Foot (5)
Runnin' From The Devil (6)
Say It (15)

She Locked It (9)
Shoot Yer Shot (medley) (14)
Short Change (3)
Silly Billy (3)
Singing In The Morning (1)
Sitting On The Dock Of The Bay (16)
Skin Tight (4,11) **13**
Skinny (16)
Sleep Talk (3,5,7)
Sleepwalkin' (14)
Smoke (6)
Something Special (15)
Sometimes I Cry (16)
Speak Easy (13)

Spinning (3,9)
Streakin' Cheek To Cheek (4)
Sweet Sticky Thing (8,11) **33**
Take De Funk Off, Fly (15)
Tell The Truth (5)
Time Slips Away (medley) (14)
Together (6)
Try A Little Tenderness (16)
Try To Be A Man (16)
Varee Is Love (2,7,9)
Walked Away From You (2)
Walt's First Trip (2,7)
What It Is (9)

What The Hell (6)
What's Going On (5)
Who'd She Coo? (10,11) **18**
Words Of Love (medley) (4)
You And Me (3)

OINGO BOINGO

Eight-man new wave rock group from Los Angeles led by vocalist Danny Elfman. Group appeared in the 1986 film *Back To School*. Elfman scored the films *Beetlejuice*, *Batman*, *Dick Tracy* and others.

DEBUT DATE	PEAK POS	WKS CHR	GOLD	#	Album Title	$	Label & Number
10/25/80	163	5		1	Oingo Boingo [M] 10" 4-song E.P.	$8	I.R.S. 70400
8/15/81	172	5		2	Only A Lad	$8	A&M 4863
9/4/82	148	9		3	Nothing To Fear	$8	A&M 4930
9/10/83	144	7		4	Good For Your Soul	$8	A&M 4959
11/16/85	98	16	●	5	Dead Man's Party	$8	MCA 5665
3/21/87	77	16		6	Boi-ngo	$8	MCA 5811
10/22/88	90	11		7	Boingo Alive [L] recorded on a sound stage in July 1988	$10	MCA 8030 [2]
2/11/89	150	5		8	Skeletons In The Closet: The Best Of Oingo Boingo [G]	$8	A&M 5217
3/10/90	72	14		9	Dark At The End Of The Tunnel [G] CD and cassette include bonus track	$12	MCA 6365

Ain't This The Life (1)
Capitalism (2)
Cinderella Undercover (7)
Controller (2)
Cry Of The Vatos (4)
Dead Man's Party (5,7)
Dead Or Alive (4,7)
Dream Somehow (9)
Elevator Man (6)
Fill The Void (4)
Flesh 'N Blood (9)
Fool's Paradise (5)
Glory Be (9)
Good For Your Soul (4)

Goodbye - Goodbye (7)
Gratitude (7)
Grey Matter (3,7,8)
Heard Somebody Cry (5)
Help Me (5)
Home Again (6)
I'm So Bad (1)
Imposter (2)
Insects (3,8)
Is This (9)
Islands (3)
Just Another Day (5,7) **85**
Little Girls (2,8)
Little Guns (4)

Long Breakdown (9)
My Life (6,7)
Nasty Habits (2,8)
New Generation (6)
No One Lives Forever (5)
No Spill Blood (4,7)
Not My Slave (6,7)
Nothing Bad Ever Happens (4,8)
Nothing To Fear (But Fear Itself) (3,7,8)
On The Outside (2,7,8)
Only A Lad (1,2,7,8)
Only Makes Me Laugh (7)

Out Of Control (9)
Outrageous (6)
Pain (6)
Perfect System (2)
Pictures Of You (4)
Private Life (3,7,8)
Reptiles And Samurai (3)
Right To Know (9)
Run Away (The Escape Song) (9)
Running On A Treadmill (3)
Same Man I Was Before (5)
Skin (9)
Stay (5,7)

Sweat (4,7)
Try To Believe (9)
Violent Love (1,7)
Wake Up (It's 1984) (4,8)
We Close Our Eyes (6)
Weird Science (5) **45**
What You See (2)
When The Lights Go Out (9)
Where Do All My Friends Go (6)
Who Do You Want To Be (4,7,8)
Whole Day Off (3,8)
Why'd We Come (3)

Wild Sex (In The Working Class) (3,7)
Winning Side (7)
You Really Got Me (2)

★★124★★ O'JAYS, The

R&B group from Canton, Ohio formed in 1958 as the Triumphs. Consisted of Eddie Levert, Walter Williams, William Powell, Bobby Massey and Bill Isles. Recorded as the Mascots for the King label in 1961. Renamed by Cleveland DJ, Eddie O'Jay. Isles left in 1965. Massey left to become a record producer in 1971; Levert, Williams and Powell continued as a trio. Powell retired from touring due to illness in late 1975 (d: 5/26/77; replaced by Sammy Strain, formerly with Little Anthony & The Imperials. Levert's sons Gerald and Sean, are members of the trio Levert.

DEBUT DATE	PEAK POS	WKS CHR	GOLD	#	Album Title	$	Label & Number
9/9/72	10	44	●	1	**Back Stabbers**	$10	Phil. Int. 31712
4/28/73	156	8		2	The O'Jays In Philadelphia [E] recordings from 1969 (Neptune label)	$10	Phil. Int. 32120
11/10/73+	11	48	▲	3	Ship Ahoy	$10	Phil. Int. 32408
6/29/74	17	24	●	4	The O'Jays Live In London [L]	$10	Phil. Int. 32953
4/26/75	11	24	●	5	Survival	$10	Phil. Int. 33150
11/29/75+	7	34	▲	6	**Family Reunion**	$10	Phil. Int. 33807
10/2/76	20	22	●	7	Message In The Music	$10	Phil. Int. 34245
6/4/77	27	16	●	8	Travelin' At The Speed Of Thought	$8	Phil. Int. 34684
1/7/78	132	6		9	The O'Jays: Collectors' Items [G]	$10	Phil. Int. 35024 [2]
4/29/78	6	28	▲	10	**So Full Of Love**	$8	Phil. Int. 35355
9/15/79	16	30	▲	11	Identify Yourself	$8	Phil. Int. 36027
8/30/80	36	12		12	The Year 2000	$8	TSOP 36416
5/15/82	49	13		13	My Favorite Person	$8	Phil. Int. 37999
8/13/83	142	5		14	When Will I See You Again	$8	Epic 38518
10/19/85	121	12		15	Love Fever	$8	Phil. Int. 53015
10/10/87	66	25		16	Let Me Touch You	$8	EMI-Man. 53036
5/27/89	114	17		17	Serious	$8	EMI 90921
2/16/91	73	20	●	18	Emotionally Yours	$12	EMI 93390

Ain't Nothin' Wrong With Good Lovin' (14)
All Eyes On Africa (15)
Answer's In You (12)
Back Stabbers (1,4,9) **3**
Betcha Don't Know (What Comes After That) (14)
Branded Bad (2)
Brandy (79)
Can't Slow Down (15)
Cause I Want You Back Again (11)
Closer To You (18)

Cry Together (10)
Darlin' Darlin' Baby (Sweet, Tender, Love) (7,9) **72**
Deeper (In Love With You) (2) **64**
Desire Me (7)
Dollar Bill (15)
Don't Call Me Brother (3)
Don't Let Me Down (18)
Don't Let The Dream Get Away (16)

Don't Take Your Love Away (16)
Don't Walk Away Mad (13)
Don't You Know True Love (18)
Emotionally Yours [includes 2 versions] (18)
Fading (17)
Family Reunion (6,9)
Feelings (8)
For The Love Of Money (3,9) **9**
Forever Mine (11) **28**

Friend Of A Friend (17)
Get On Out And Party (14)
Girl, Don't Let It Get You Down (12) **55**
Give The People What They Want (5,9) **45**
Have You Had Your Love Today (17)
Help (Somebody Please) (10)
House Of Fire (10)
How Time Flies (5)
Hurry Up & Come Back (11)
I Can't Stand The Pain (14)

I Just Want Somebody To Love Me (16)
I Just Want To Satisfy You (13)
I Like To See Us Get Down (13)
I Love America (15)
I Love Music (Part 1) (6,9) **5**
I Should Be Your Lover (2)
I Swear, I Love No One But You (7)
I Wanna Be With You Tonight (15)

I Want You Here With Me (11)
I've Got The Groove (2)
Identify (11)
If I Find Love Again (18)
It's Too Strong (2)
Just Another Lonely Night (15)
Just Can't Get Enough (2)
Keep On Lovin' Me (18)
Keep On Pleasin' Me (18)
Leave It Alone (17)
Let Life Flow (7)

552

DEBUT DATE	PEAK POS	WKS CHR	GOLD	ARTIST — Album Title	$	Label & Number

O'JAYS, The — Cont'd

Let Me In Your World (2)
Let Me Make Love To You (5,9) **75**
Let Me Touch You (16)
Let's Spend Some Time Together (4)
Letter To My Friends (14)
Lies (18)
Listen To The Clock On The Wall (1)
Little Green Apples (medley) (2)
Livin' For The Weekend (6,9) **20**
Looky Looky (Look At Me Girl) (2) 98
Love & Trust (18)
Love Fever (15)
Love Train (1,4,9) 1
Lovin' You (16)

Make A Joyful Noise (7)
Make It Feel Good (18)
Message In Our Music (7) **49**
My Favorite Person (13)
Never Been Better (18)
Never Break Us Up (5)
Nice And Easy (14)
992 Arguments (1) 57
No Lies To Cloud My Eyes (16)
Now That We Found Love (3)
Once Is Not Enough (12)
One Night Affair (2) 68
One On One (13)
Out In The Real World (13)
Out Of My Mind (17)
Paradise (7)
People Keep Tellin' Me (3)

Pot Can't Call The Kettle Black (17)
Prayer, A (7)
Put Our Heads Together (14)
Put Your Hands Together (3,4) **10**
Rainbow (17)
Respect (18)
Rich Get Richer (5)
Serious Hold On Me (17)
She's Only A Woman (6)
Shiftless, Shady, Jealous Kind Of People (1)
Ship Ahoy (8)
Sing A Happy Song (11)
Sing My Heart Out (10)
So Glad I Got You, Girl (8)
So Nice I Tried It Twice (1)
Something (medley) (2)
Something For Nothing (18)

Stairway To Heaven (6,9)
Stand Up (8)
Still Missing (16)
Strokey Stroke (10)
Sunshine Part II (1,4,9) **48**
Survival (5,9)
Take Me To The Stars (10)
That's How Love Is (18)
(They Call Me) Mr. Lucky (1)
This Air I Breathe (3)
This Time Baby (10)
Those Lies (Done Caught Up With You This Time) (8)
Time To Get Down (1) 33
To Prove I Love You (12)
Travelin' At The Speed Of Thought (8)
True Love Never Dies (16)
Undercover Lover (10)
Unity (6)

Use Ta Be My Girl (10) 4
We're All In This Thing Together (8)
We're Still Together (15)
What A Woman (15)
What Am I Waiting For (5)
What Good Are These Arms Of Mine (15)
When The World's At Peace (1,4)
When Will I See You Again (14)
Where Did We Go Wrong (5)
Who Am I (1)
Wildflower (4,9)
Work On Me (8)
Year 2000 (12)
You And Me (6)
You Got Your Hooks In Me (3,9)

You Won't Fail (12)
You'll Never Know (All There Is To Know 'Bout My Love) (12)
You're The Best Thing Since Candy (2)
You're The Girl Of My Dreams (Sho Nuff Real) (12)
Your Body's Here With Me (But Your Mind's On The Other Side Of Town) (13)
Your True Heart (And Shining Star) (13)

O'KAYSIONS, The
R&B sextet from Wilson, North Carolina: Donny Weaver (lead singer), Ron Turner, Jim Spidel, Wayne Pittman, Jimmy Hennant and Bruce Joyner. Originally called The Kays.

| 11/9/68 | 153 | 4 | | Girl Watcher | $20 | ABC 664 |

Deal Me In
Dedicated To The One I Love

Girl Watcher 5
How Are You Fixed For Love?

Little Miss Flirt
Love Machine 76

My Baby's Love
My Song (Poor Man's Son)

Soul Clap

Sunday Will Never Be The Same

O'KEEFE, Danny
Singer/songwriter born in Spokane, Washington.

| 9/2/72 | 87 | 16 | | 1 O'Keefe | $10 | Signpost 8404 |
| 8/11/73 | 172 | 9 | | 2 Breezy Stories | $10 | Atlantic 7264 |

American Dream (1)
Angel Spread Your Wings (2)
Babe, The (medley) (2)
Catfish (2)
Edge, The (2)

Farewell To Storyville (Good Time Flat Blues) (2)
Good Time Charlie's Got The Blues (1) **9**
Grease It (1)
Honky Tonkin' (1)

I Know You Really Love Me (1)
I'm Sober Now (1)
If Ya Can't Boogie, Woogie (You Sure Can't Rock & Roll) (2)

Junkman (2)
Louie The Hook Vs. The Preacher (1)
Mad Ruth (medley) (2)
Magdalena (2)
Portrait In Black Velvet (2)

Question (Obviously) (1)
Road, The (1)
Roseland Taxi Dancer (1)
She Said "Drive On, Driver" (2)
Shooting Star (1)

Steppin' Out Tonight (2)
Valentine Pieces (1)

OLD & IN THE WAY
Bluegrass band: Jerry Garcia (Grateful Dead), David Grisman, Peter Rowan, John Kahn and Vassar Clements.

| 3/29/75 | 99 | 8 | | Old & In The Way | [L] $20 | Round 103 |

Hobo Song
Kissimmee Kid

Knockin' On Your Door
Land Of The Navajo

Midnight Moonlight
Old And In The Way

Panama Red
Pigs In The Pen

White Dove
Wild Horses

OLDFIELD, Mike
Born on 5/15/53 in Reading, England. Classical-rock, multi-instrumentalist/composer.

11/10/73+	3	45	●	1 **Tubular Bells**	[I] $10	Virgin 105
9/21/74	87	10		2 Hergest Ridge	[I] $10	Virgin 109
12/20/75+	146	7		3 Ommadawn	[I] $10	Virgin 33913
7/4/81	174	3		4 QE2	[I] $8	Epic 37358
5/8/82	164	5		5 Five Miles Out	$8	Epic 37983
2/27/88	138	8		6 Islands	$8	Virgin 90645

features various vocalists including Bonnie Tyler

Arrival (4)
Celt (4)
Conflict (4)
Family Man (5)
Five Miles Out (5)

Flying Start (6)
Hergest Ridge (2)
Islands (6)
Magic Touch (6)
Mirage (4)

Molly (4)
Mount Teidi (5)
North Point (6)
Ommadawn - Part One & Two (3)

Orabidoo (5)
QE2 (4)
Sheba (4)
Taurus 1 (4)
Taurus II (5)

Time Has Come (6)
Tubular Bells (1) **7**
Wind Chimes Part One & Two (6)
Wonderful Land (4)

OLIVER
Born William Oliver Swofford on 2/22/45 in North Wilkesboro, North Carolina.

| 8/2/69 | 19 | 38 | | 1 Good Morning Starshine | $12 | Crewe 1333 |
| 5/16/70 | 71 | 13 | | 2 Oliver Again | $12 | Crewe 1344 |

Angelica (2) 97
Arrangement, The (1)
Both Sides Now (Clouds) (1)
Buddy (2)

Can't You See (1)
Comfort Me (2)
Good Morning Starshine (1) **3**

I Can Remember (2)
If You Go Away (2)
In My Life (1)
Jean (1) 2

Leaving On A Jet Plane (2)
Letmekissyouwithadream (1)
Picture Of Kathleen Dunne (2)

Ruby Tuesday (1)
Twelfth Of Never (2)
Until It's Time For You To Go (2)

Where Is Love (1)
Who Will Buy (1)
Young Birds Fly (2)

OLIVER, David
Singer from Florida. Teamed with Gene Godfrey (piano). Moved to Los Angeles in 1967, worked with Five Days And Three Nights. Toured with Mighty Joe Hicks from 1973-75.

| 5/27/78 | 128 | 8 | | David Oliver | $8 | Mercury 1183 |

Friends & Strangers
Let's Make Happiness

Love So Strong
Ms.

Munchies
Playin' At Bein' A Winner

What Kinda Woman
You And I

OLIVOR, Jane
Lyrical stylist from New York City.

10/22/77	86	8		1 Chasing Rainbows	$8	Columbia 34917
7/8/78	108	12		2 Stay The Night	$8	Columbia 35437
2/23/80	58	12		3 The Best Side Of Goodbye	$8	Columbia 36355
5/29/82	144	6		4 In Concert	[L] $8	Columbia 37938

recorded at Berkley School Of Music, Boston

Annie's Song (4)
Beautiful Sadness (1)
Best Side Of Goodbye (3)

Better Days (Looks As Though We're Doing Somethin' Right) (4)
Big Parade (1)

Can't Leave You 'Cause I Love You (2)
Can't We Make It Right Again (2)
Carousel Of Love (4)

Come In From The Rain (1)
Daydreams (4)
Don't Let Go Of Me (3)
French Waltz (1)
Golden Pony (3)

Greatest Love Of All (3)
He's So Fine (2) 77
Honesty (2)
I'm Always Chasing Rainbows (1)

It's Over Goodbye (1)
Lalena (1)
Let's Make Some Memories (2)
Long And Lasting Love (3)

OLIVOR, Jane — Cont'd

Love This Time (3)
Manchild Lullaby (3)
Marigold Wings (Earthbound) (4)

Pretty Girl (4)
Race To The End (4)
Right Garden (2)
Run For The Roses (4)

Seasons (4)
Solitaire (4)
Song For My Father (2)
Stay The Night (2,4)

To Love Again (3)
Vagabond (3)
Weeping Willows, Cattails (3,4)

Where There Is Love (4)
You (1)
You Wanna Be Loved (1)
You're The One I Love (2)

OLSSON, Nigel
Born on 2/10/49 in Merseyside, England. Drummer for Elton John's band from 1971-76.

| 3/24/79 | 140 | 5 | | Nigel | $8 | Bang 35792 |

All It Takes
Au Revoir (medley)

Cassey Blue (medley)
Dancin' Shoes *18*

Little Bit Of Soap *34*
Living In A Fantasy

Part Of The Chosen Few
Say Goodbye To Hollywood

Thinking Of You

You Know I'll Always Love You

OMAR & THE HOWLERS
Austin, Texas rock group led by vocalist Omar Dykes, with Bruce Jones, Gene Brandon and Eric Scortia.

| 6/27/87 | 81 | 19 | | Hard Times In The Land Of Plenty | $8 | Columbia 40815 |

Border Girl
Dancing In The Canebrake

Don't Rock Me The Wrong Way
Don't You Know

Hard Times In The Land Of Plenty
Lee Anne

Mississippi Hoo Doo Man
Same Old Grind

Shadow Man
You Ain't Foolin' Nobody

O'NEAL, Alexander
Minneapolis-based R&B vocalist. Born on 11/15/53 in Natchez, Mississippi. Own band, Alexander, in the late 1970s. Lead singer of Flyte Tyme which included Jimmy "Jam" Harris, Terry Lewis and Monte Moir and later evolved into The Time. Went solo in 1980. Co-producer of Janet Jackson's hit "Control."

4/27/85	92	18		1 Alexander O'Neal	$8	Tabu 39331
8/22/87	29	40	●	2 Hearsay	$8	Tabu 40320
12/17/88+	149	5		3 My Gift To You	[X] $8	Tabu 45016
				Christmas charts: 9/'88		
2/25/89	185	5		4 All Mixed Up	$8	Tabu 44492
2/16/91	49	15	●	5 All True Man	$12	Tabu 45349

Alex 9000 (medley) (1)
All True Man (5) *43*
Broken Heart Can Mend (1)
Christmas Song (Chestnuts Roasting On An Open Fire) (3)
Criticize (2,4) *70*
Crying Overtime (2)
Do You Wanna Like I Do (1)

Every Time I Get Up (5)
Fake (2) *25*
Fake 89 (4)
Hang On (5)
Hearsay (5)
If You Were Here Tonight (1)
Innocent (1,4)
Innocent II (medley) (1)
Little Drummer Boy (3)

Look At Us Now (1)
Lovers, The (2,4)
Midnight Run (5)
Morning After (5)
My Gift To You (3)
Never Knew Love Like This (2,4) *28*
Our First Christmas (3)

Remember Why (It's Christmas) (3)
Sentimental (3)
Shame On Me (5)
Sleigh Ride (3)
Somebody (Changed Your Mind) (5)
Sunshine (2)

Thank You For A Good Year (3)
This Christmas (3)
Time Is Running Out (5)
Used (5)
(What Can I Say) To Make You Love Me (2,4)
What Is This Thing Called Love? (5)

What's Missing (1)
When The Party's Over (2)
Winter Wonderland (3)
Yoke (G.U.O.T.R.) (5)
You Were Meant To Be My Lady (Not My Girl) (1,4)

101 STRINGS
European orchestra under the direction of D.L. Miller.

5/25/59+	9	58		1 **The Soul of Spain**	[I] $10	Somerset 6600
				this album was #1 for 46 of the 47 weeks that *Billboard* published a special Best Selling Low Price LP's chart (2/19/60-1/8/61)		
1/9/61	21	19		2 The Soul of Spain, Volume II	[I] $10	Somerset 9900
1/9/61	46	15		3 101 Strings Play The Blues	[I] $10	Somerset 5800
				a tribute to W.C. Handy		
1/9/61	104	13		4 Concerto Under The Stars	[I] $10	Somerset 6700
				featuring Harry Heineman at the piano		

Basin Street Blues (3)
Birth Of The Blues (3)
Blues In The Night (3)
Blues Pizzacato (3)
Breeze And I (2)
Cantina Toreros (2)

Chopin's Nocturne (4)
Chopin's Study In E Major (4)
Claire De Lune (4)
Cornish Rhapsody, Theme From (4)

Domingo En Seville (Sunday In Seville) (1)
El Relicario (2)
Espana (1)
Espana Cani (1)
Frankie And Johnny (3)

Granada (2)
La Violetera (1)
Le Cid (2)
Liebestraum (4)
Macarenas (Patron Saint Of The Matadors) (1)

Malaguena (1)
Matador (2)
Meditation From Thais (4)
Shades Of Blues (3)
St. Louis Blues (3)

Swedish Rhapsody, Theme From (4)
Symphony For Blues (3)
Valencia (2)

100 PROOF Aged in Soul
Soul group from Detroit: Clyde Wilson ("Steve Mancha"; lead), Joe Stubbs and Eddie Anderson ("Eddie Holiday"). Stubbs, brother of Levi Stubbs of the Four Tops, had been in the Contours and The Falcons.

| 12/12/70+ | 151 | 7 | | Somebody's Been Sleeping In My Bed | $12 | Hot Wax 704 |

Age Ain't Nothing But A Number
Ain't That Lovin' You (For More Reasons Than One)

Backtrack
I Can't Sit And Wait ('Til Johnny Comes Marching Home)

I've Come To Save You
Love Is Sweeter (The Second Time Around)
Not Enough Love To Satisfy

One Man's Leftovers (Is Another Man's Feast) *96*
She's Not Just Another Woman

Somebody's Been Sleeping *8*
Too Many Cooks (Spoil The Soup) *94*

ONE WAY
Detroit-based soul group led by vocalist Al Hudson. Recorded from 1976-79 as Al Hudson & The Soul Partners. Signed with MCA in 1979, name changed to One Way.

11/17/79	181	5		1 One Way featuring Al Hudson	$8	MCA 3178
8/2/80	128	12		2 One Way Featuring Al Hudson	$8	MCA 5127
3/7/81	157	8		3 Love Is...One Way	$8	MCA 5163
9/26/81	79	19		4 Fancy Dancer	$8	MCA 5247
4/3/82	51	23		5 Who's Foolin' Who	$8	MCA 5279
8/20/83	164	6		6 Shine On Me	$8	MCA 5428
5/26/84	58	20		7 Lady	$8	MCA 5470
8/10/85	156	9		8 Wrap Your Body	$8	MCA 5552

Age Ain't Nothing But A Number (5)
All Over Again (3)
Be Serious (3)
Believe In Me (8)
Bring It Down (6)
Burn It (4)
Can't Get Enough Of Your Love (7)
Come Dance With Me (1)
Come Give Me Your Love (4)
Condemned (8)

Copy This (2)
Cutie Pie (5) *61*
Didn't You Know It (6)
Do Your Thang (2)
Don't Give Up On Love (8)
Don't Stop (7)
Dynomite (4)
Get It Over (3)
Get Up (4)
Give Me One More Chance (5)
Guess You Didn't Know (1)

He Is My Friend (4)
Hold It (4)
I Am Under Your Spell (1)
I Didn't Mean To Break Your Heart (3)
I Wanna Be With You (2)
I'll Make It Up To You (7)
I'm In Love With Lovin' You (4)
If I Knew (8)
If Only You Knew (7)
Lady You Are (7)

Let's Get Together (6)
Let's Go Out Tonite (2)
Let's Talk (8)
Love Is (3)
More Than Friends, Less Than Lovers (8)
Mr. Groove (7)
Music (1)
My Lady (3)
Now That I Found You (1)
Pop It (2)
Pull Fancy Dancer/Pull (4)

Push (3)
Runnin' Away (5)
Serving It (8)
Shake It Till It's Tight (6)
Shine On Me (6)
Slow Me (4)
Smile (7)
So Afraid It's Over (6)
Something In The Past (2)
Sugar Rock (6)
Sweet Lady (5)
Together Forever (6)

Wait Until Tomorrow (3)
Who's Foolin' Who (5)
Wrap Your Body (8)
You (5)
You Can Do It (1)
You're So Very Special (5)
You're The One (2)
Your Love Is All I Need (4)

DEBUT DATE	PEAK POS	WKS CHR	GOLD	ARTIST — Album Title	$	Label & Number

ONO, Yoko

Born in Tokyo on 2/18/33. Moved to New York at age 14. Avant-garde artist/poet in the late 1960s. Married John Lennon in Gibraltar on 3/20/69. Also see John Lennon.

DEBUT DATE	PEAK POS	WKS CHR	GOLD	ARTIST — Album Title	$	Label & Number
2/6/71	182	3		1 Yoko Ono/Plastic Ono Band	$15	Apple 3373
				front cover identical to *John Lennon/Plastic Ono Band*		
11/13/71	199	2		2 Fly	$18	Apple 3380 [2]
2/24/73	193	4		3 Approximately Infinite Universe	$18	Apple 3399 [2]
				backed by Elephant's Memory		
12/6/80	1⁸	74	▲³	4 Double Fantasy	$8	Geffen 2001
				JOHN LENNON & YOKO ONO		
				7 songs by John, 7 by Yoko; 1981 Grammy winner: Album of the Year		
6/27/81	49	9		5 Season Of Glass	$8	Geffen 2004
				recorded shortly after John's death		
12/25/82+	98	13		6 It's Alright (I See Rainbows)	$8	Polydor 6364
2/11/84	11	19	●	7 Milk and Honey	$8	Polydor 817160
				JOHN LENNON & YOKO ONO		
				6 songs by John, 6 by Yoko; recorded in 1980		

Air Male (Tone Deaf Jam) (2)
Air Talk (3)
Aos (1)
Approximately Infinite Universe (3)
Beautiful Boys (4)
Catman (The Rosies Are Coming) (3)
Death Of Samantha (3)
Dogtown (3)
Don't Be Scared (7)
Don't Count The Waves (2)
Don't Worry Kyoko (2)
Dream Love (6)
Even When You're Far Away (5)
Every Man Has A Woman Who Loves Him (4)
Extension 33 (5)
Fly (2)
Give Me Something (4)
Goodbye Sadness (5)
Greenfield Morning I Pushed An Empty Baby Carriage All Over The City (1)
Hard Times Are Over (4)
Have You Seen A Horizon Lately (3)
Hirake (2)
I Don't Know Why (5)
I Felt Like Smashing My Face In A Clear Glass Window (3)
I Have A Woman Inside My Soul (3)
I See Rainbows (6)
I Want My Love To Rest Tonight (3)
I'm Moving On (4)
I'm Your Angel (4)
Is Winter Here To Stay? (3)
It's Alright (6)
Kiss Kiss Kiss (4)
Kite Song (3)
Let Me Count The Ways (4)
Let The Tears Dry (6)
Loneliness (6)
Looking Over From My Hotel Window (3)
Midsummer New York (2)
Mind Holes (2)
Mindtrain (2)
Mindweaver (5)
Mother Of The Universe (5)
Move On Fast (3)
Mrs. Lennon (2)
My Man (6)
Never Say Goodbye (6)
No, No, No (5)
Nobody Sees Me Like You Do (5)
Now Or Never (3)
O'Sanity (7)
O'Wind (Body Is The Scar Of Your Mind) (2)
Paper Shoes (1)
Peter The Dealer (3)
She Gets Down On Her Knees (3)
Shiranakatta (I Didn't Know) (3)
Silver Horse (5)
Sleepless Night (7)
Song For John (3)
Spec Of Dust (6)
Telephone Piece (2)
Toilet Piece (medley) (2)
Tomorrow May Never Come (6)
Touch Me (1)
Toyboat (7)
Turn Of The Wheel (5)
Unknown (medley) (2)
Waiting For The Sunrise (3)
Wake Up (6)
What A Bastard The World Is (3)
What A Mess (3)
What Did I Do! (3)
Why (1)
Why Not (1)
Will You Touch Me (5)
Winter Song (3)
Yang Yang (3)
You (7)
You're The One (7)
Your Hands (7)

OPUS

Pop-rock quintet from Austria led by vocalist Herwig Rudisser.

DEBUT DATE	PEAK POS	WKS CHR	GOLD	ARTIST — Album Title	$	Label & Number
3/1/86	64	16		Up And Down	$8	Polydor 827952

Again And Again
End Of The Show
Flyin' High
Live Is Life *32*
No Job
Opuspocus
Positive
She Loves You
Up And Down
Vivian

★★235★★ ORBISON, Roy

Born on 4/23/36 in Vernon, Texas. Had own band, the Wink Westerners, in 1952. Attended North Texas University with Pat Boone. First recorded for Je-Wel in early 1956 as leader of The Teen Kings. Toured with Sun Records shows to 1958. Toured with The Beatles in 1963. Wife Claudette killed in a motorcycle accident on 6/7/66; two sons died in a fire in 1968. Resurgence in career beginning in 1985. Inducted into the Rock and Roll Hall of Fame in 1987. Member of the supergroup Traveling Wilburys in 1988. Died of a heart attack on 12/6/88 in Madison, Tennessee.

DEBUT DATE	PEAK POS	WKS CHR	GOLD	ARTIST — Album Title	$	Label & Number
4/7/62	21	31		1 Crying	$75	Monument 4007
9/1/62	13	140	●	2 Roy Orbison's Greatest Hits .... [G]	$35	Monument 4009
8/17/63	35	23	●	3 In Dreams	$45	Monument 18003
8/22/64	19	30		4 More Of Roy Orbison's Greatest Hits ..... [G]	$30	Monument 18024
10/17/64	101	11		5 Early Orbison .... [K]	$35	Monument 18023
				selections from *Lonely & Blue* and *Crying* albums		
9/4/65	55	17		6 There Is Only One Roy Orbison	$20	MGM 4308
11/6/65+	136	11		7 Orbisongs .... [K]	$25	Monument 18035
3/5/66	128	3		8 The Orbison Way	$20	MGM 4322
8/13/66	94	9		9 The Very Best Of Roy Orbison .... [G]	$20	Monument 18045
1/7/89	95	15		10 In Dreams: The Greatest Hits .... [K]	$10	Virgin 90604 [2]
				18 of the 19 hits were rerecorded in 1985; the track "In Dreams" was rerecorded in April 1987		
1/7/89	110	13		11 For The Lonely: A Roy Orbison Anthology, 1956-1965 .... [G]	$10	Rhino 71493 [2]
2/18/89	5	27	▲	12 Mystery Girl	$8	Virgin 91058
12/2/89	123	12		13 A Black And White Night Live .... [L-S]	$8	Virgin 91295
				ROY ORBISON AND FRIENDS		
				soundtrack from the September 1987 Coconut Grove concert, aired as a Cinemax special in December 1988; backing group includes Bruce Springsteen, Elvis Costello, Jackson Browne, Tom Waits, T-Bone Burnett and Bonnie Raitt		
12/19/92	179	2		14 King Of Hearts .... [E]	$12	Virgin 86520
				unissued and posthumously completed tracks		

Afraid To Sleep (6)
After The Love Has Gone (14)
(All I Can Do Is) Dream You (12,13)
All I Have To Do Is Dream (3)
Beautiful Dreamer (3)
Big As I Can Dream (6)
Blue Angel (2,9,10,11) *9*
Blue Bayou (3,4,10,11,13) *29*
Borne On The Wind (4)
Breakin' Up Is Breakin' My Heart (8) *31*
Bye Bye Love (5)
California Blue (12)
Candy Man (2,9,10,11,13) *25*
Careless Heart (12,14)
Claudette (6,10)
Come Back To Me (My Love) (5)
Comedians, The (12,13)
Coming Home (14)
Crawling Back (8) *46*
Crowd, The (2,11) *26*
Cry (5)
Crying (1,2,9,10,11,13,14) *2*
Dance (5)
Devil Doll (11)
Dream (3)
Dream Baby (How Long Must I Dream) (2,9,10,11,13) *4*
Dream You (3)
Evergreen (2)
Falling (4,10,11) *22*
Go Away (8)
Go! Go! Go! (11)
Goodnight (7,11) *21*
Great Pretender (1,5)
Heartbreak Radio (14)
House Without Windows (3)
I Can't Stop Loving You (5)
I Drove All Night (14)
(I Get So) Sentimental (7)
I'd Be A Legend In My Time (7)
I'll Say It's My Fault (5)
I'm Hurtin' (2,10,11) *27*
I'm In A Blue, Blue Mood (6)
If You Can't Say Something Nice (6)
In Dreams (3,4,9,10,11,13) *7*
In The Real World (12)
Indian Wedding (4)
It Ain't No Big Thing (8)
It Wasn't Very Long Ago (8)
It's Over (4,9,10,11,13) *9*
Lana (1,4,10)
Leah (4,10,11,13) *25*
Let The Good Times Roll (7) *81*
Let's Make A Memory (1)
Loneliness (1)
Lonely Wine (3)
Loner, The (8)
Love In Time (8)
Love So Beautiful (12)
Love Star (2)
Love Hurts (1,5)
Mama (2)
Maybe (8)
Mean Woman Blues (4,9,10,11,13) *5*
Move On Down The Line (13)
My Prayer (1)
Never (8)
New Star (8)
Nightlife (1,7)
No One Will Ever Know (3)
Oh, Pretty Woman (7,9,10,11,13) *1*
Only One (12)
Only The Lonely (Know How I Feel) (2,9,10,11,13) *2*
Ooby Dooby (10,11,13) *59*
Pretty One (5)
Pretty Paper (4,11) *15*
Raindrops (5)
Ride Away (6) *25*
Rockhouse (11)
Running Scared (1,2,9,10,11,13) *1*

DEBUT DATE	PEAK POS	WKS CHR	GOLD	ARTIST — Album Title	$	Label & Number

ORBISON, Roy — Cont'd

(Say) You're My Girl (7,11) *39*
Shahdaroba (3)
She Wears My Ring (1,5)
She's A Mystery To Me (12)
Sleepy Hollow (7)
Sugar And Honey (6)
Summer Love (6)
Summer Song (1,5)
Sunset (3)
(They Call You) Gigolette (3)
This Is My Land (8)
This Is Your Song (6)
Time Changed Everything (8)
22 Days (7)
Two Of A Kind (6)
Up Town (2,10,11,13) *72*
We'll Take The Night (14)
Wedding Day (1,7)
What'd I Say (4)
Why Hurt The One Who Loves You (8)
Wild Hearts Run Out Of Time (14)
Windsurfer (12)
Wondering (6)
Workin' For The Man (4,10,11) *33*
Yo Te Amo Maria (7)
You Fool You (6)
You Got It (12) *9*
You're The One (14)

ORCHESTRAL MANOEUVRES IN THE DARK
English electro-pop quartet: keyboardists/vocalists Paul Humphreys and Andrew McCluskey, with drummer Malcolm Holmes and multi-instrumentalist Martin Cooper. Humphreys left band in 1991.

DEBUT DATE	PEAK POS	WKS CHR	GOLD	ARTIST — Album Title	$	Label & Number
2/6/82	144	12		1 Architecture & Morality	$8	Epic 37721
4/23/83	162	6		2 Dazzle Ships	$8	Epic 38543
11/24/84	182	6		3 Junk Culture	$8	A&M 5027
7/27/85	38	53		4 Crush	$8	A&M 5077
10/18/86	47	23		5 The Pacific Age	$8	A&M 5144
3/26/88	46	29	●	6 in the dark/the best of OMD .... [G]	$8	A&M 5186

ABC (Auto Industry) (2)
All Wrapped Up (3)
Apollo (3)
Architecture & Morality (1)
Beginning And The End (1)
Bloc Bloc Bloc (4)
Crush (4)
Dazzle Ships (2)
Dead Girls (5)
Dreaming (6) *16*
88 Seconds In Greensboro (4)
Electricity (6)
Enola Gay (6)
Flame Of Hope (5)
(Forever) Live And Die (5,6) *19*
Genetic Engineering (2)
Georgia (1)
Goddess Of Love (5)
Hard Day (3)
Hold You (4)
If You Leave (6) *4*
International (2)
Joan Of Arc (1,6)
Joan Of Arc (Maid Of Orleans) (1,6)
Junk Culture (3)
La Femme Accident (4)
Lights Are Going Out (4)
Locomotion (3,6)
Love And Violence (3)
Maid Of Orleans ..see: Joan Of Arc
Messages (6)
Native Daughters Of The Golden West (4)
Never Turn Away (3)
New Stone Age (1)
Of All The Things We've Made (2)
Pacific Age (5)
Radio Prague (2)
Radio Waves (2)
Romance Of The Telescope (2)
Sealand (1)
Secret (4,6) *63*
Shame (5)
She's Leaving (1)
Silent Running (2)
So In Love (4,6) *26*
Southern (5)
Souvenir (1,6)
Stay (The Black Rose And The Universal Wheel) (5)
Talking Loud And Clear (3,6)
Telegraph (5)
Tesla Girls (3,6)
This Is Helena (2)
Time Zones (2)
Watch Us Fall (5)
We Love You (5)
White Trash (3)
Women iii (4)

ORIGINAL LAST POETS — see LAST POETS, The

ORIGINALS, The
Soul group formed in Detroit in 1966. Consisted of Freddie Gorman (bass), Crathman Spencer and Henry Dixon (tenors) and Walter Gaines (baritone). Spencer replaced by Ty Hunter in 1971.

DEBUT DATE	PEAK POS	WKS CHR	GOLD	ARTIST — Album Title	$	Label & Number
1/17/70	174	4		1 Baby, I'm For Real	$12	Soul 716
7/11/70	198	2		2 Portrait Of The Originals	$12	Soul 724

Aquarius (medley) (2)
Baby, I'm For Real (1) *14*
Bells, The (2) *12*
Don't Stop Now (2)
Green Grow The Lilacs (1)
I Like Your Style (2)
I'll Wait For You (2)
I've Never Begged Before (1)
Just Another Morning (2)
Let The Sunshine In (medley) (2)
Love Is A Wonder (1)
Moment Of Truth (1)
My Way (2)
One Life We Live (1)
Red Sails In The Sunset (1)
Since I Fell For You (2)
There's A Place We'd Like To Know (2)
We've Got A Way Out Love (1)
When Will We Learn (1)
Why When Love Is Gone (1)
Wichita Lineman (2)
You May Not Like The Change (1)
You, Mysterious You (1)
You Want Hearts And Flowers (2)
You're The One (1)

ORION THE HUNTER
Rock quartet led by Barry Goudreau, former guitarist of the rock group Boston and later with RTZ.

DEBUT DATE	PEAK POS	WKS CHR	GOLD	ARTIST — Album Title	$	Label & Number
5/19/84	57	14		Orion The Hunter	$8	Portrait 39239

All Those Years
Dark And Stormy
Dreamin'
Fast Talk
I Call It Love
Joanne
So You Ran *58*
Stand Up
Too Much In Love

ORLANDO, Tony — see DAWN

ORLEANS
Rock group founded in New York City by John Hall with the Hoppen brothers (Lawrence and Lance), Wells Kelly and Jerry Marotta. Hall and Marotta left in 1977, replaced by Bob Leinbach and R.A. Martin.

DEBUT DATE	PEAK POS	WKS CHR	GOLD	ARTIST — Album Title	$	Label & Number
3/29/75	33	32		1 Let There Be Music	$10	Asylum 1029
8/28/76	30	16		2 Waking And Dreaming	$10	Asylum 1070
5/5/79	76	13		3 Forever	$8	Infinity 9006

Bum, The (2)
Business As Usual (1)
Cold Spell (1)
Dance With Me (1) *6*
Don't Throw Our Love Away (3)
Ending Of A Song (1)
Everybody Needs Some Music (3)
Flame And The Moth (3)
Forever (3)
Fresh Wind (1)
Give One Heart (1)
Golden State (2)
I Never Wanted To Love You (3)
If I Don't Have You (2)
Isn't It Easy (3)
Keep On Rollin' (3)
Let There Be Music (1) *55*
Love Takes Time (3) *11*
Path, The (2)
Reach (2) *51*
Sails (2)
Slippin' Away (3)
Spring Fever (2)
Still The One (2) *5*
Time Passes On (1)
Waking And Dreaming (2)
What I Need (1)
You've Given Me Something (1)
Your Life My Friend (1)

ORLONS, The
R&B group from Philadelphia. Consisted of lead Rosetta Hightower (b: 6/23/44), Marlena Davis (b: 10/4/44), Steve Caldwell (b: 11/22/42) and Shirley Brickley (b: 12/9/44; d: 10/13/77 [gunshot]). Davis and Caldwell left in 1964 and were replaced by Audrey Brickley. Disbanded in 1968.

DEBUT DATE	PEAK POS	WKS CHR	GOLD	ARTIST — Album Title	$	Label & Number
9/1/62	80	10		1 The Wah-Watusi	$40	Cameo 1020
7/6/63	123	5		2 South Street	$40	Cameo 1041

Between 18th & 19th On Chestnut Street (2)
Big Daddy (2)
Cement Mixer (2)
Charlie Brown (2)
Dedicated To The One I Love (1)
Don't Let Go (2)
Gather 'Round (2)
Gravy (For My Mashed Potatoes) (1)
(Happy Birthday) Mr. Twenty-One (1)
He's Gone (1)
I Met Him On A Sunday (Ronde Ronde) (1)
I'll Be True (1)
Let Me In (1)
Mashed Potato Time (1)
Mister Sandman (2)
Muskrat Ramble (2)
Over The Mountain, Across The Sea (1)
Plea, The (1)
Pokey Lou (2)
South Street (2) *3*
Tonight (1)
Wah Watusi (1) *2*
Walk Right In (2)
We Got Love (2)

ORMANDY, Eugene — see PHILADELPHIA ORCHESTRA

ORPHEUS
Boston soft-rock quartet: Bruce Arnold, Jack McKenes, John Eric Gulliksen and Harry Sandler.

DEBUT DATE	PEAK POS	WKS CHR	GOLD	ARTIST — Album Title	$	Label & Number
3/9/68	119	14		1 Orpheus	$15	MGM 4524
9/28/68	159	12		2 Ascending	$15	MGM 4569
10/11/69	198	1		3 Joyful	$15	MGM 4599

As They All Fall (3)
Borneo (2)
Brown Arms In Houston (3) *91*
By The Size Of My Shoes (3)
Can't Find The Time (1) *80*
Congress Alley (1)
Don't Be So Serious (2)
Door Knob Song (1)
Dream, The (1)
I Can Make The Sun Rise (3)
I'll Fly (1)
I'll Stay With You (1)
I've Never Seen Love Like This (1)
Joyful (3)

DEBUT DATE	PEAK POS	WKS CHR	GOLD	ARTIST — Album Title	$	Label & Number

ORPHEUS — Cont'd

Just A Little Bit (2)	Love Over There (2)	May I Look At You (3)	Music Machine (1)	Roses (2)		To Touch Our Love Again (3)
Just Got Back (2)	Lovin' You (3)	Me About You (3)	Never In My Life (1)	She's Not There (2)		Walk Away Renee (2)
Lesley's World (1)	Magic Air (2)	Mine's Yours (2)	Of Enlightenment (3)	So Far Away In Love (2)		

ORR, Benjamin
Born Benjamin Orzechowski in Cleveland. Bassist/vocalist of The Cars.

11/8/86+	86	22		The Lace	$8	Elektra 60460

Hold On	Lace, The	Spinning	That's The Way	Too Hot To Stop	
In Circles	Skyline	Stay The Night 24	This Time Around	When You're Gone	

ORRALL, Robert Ellis
Singer/songwriter/pianist from Boston.

4/16/83	146	9		Special Pain	[M]	$8	RCA 8502

Facts And Figures	Senseless	(You've Had) Too Much To	
I Couldn't Say No 32	Tell Me If It Hurts	Think	

OSBORNE, Jeffrey
Born on 3/9/48 in Providence, Rhode Island. Soul singer/songwriter/drummer. Lead singer of L.T.D. until 1980.

6/19/82	49	43		1 Jeffrey Osborne	$8	A&M 4896
8/6/83+	25	89	●	2 Stay With Me Tonight	$8	A&M 4940
10/20/84	39	37	●	3 Don't Stop	$8	A&M 5017
6/28/86	26	26	●	4 Emotional	$8	A&M 5103
8/27/88	86	16		5 One Love-One Dream	$8	A&M 5205
12/15/90+	95	23		6 Only Human	$12	Arista 8620

CD and cassette include bonus track

Ain't Nothin' Missin' (1)	Don't You Get So Mad	I Really Don't Need No	My Heart Can Wait Forever	Sending You A Love Song (6)	Who Would Have Guessed
All Because Of You (5)	(2) 25	Light (1) 39	(5)	She's On The Left (5) 48	(4)
Baby (1)	Eenie Meenie (1) 76	I'll Make Believe (2)	New Love (1)	Soweto (4)	Who You Talkin' To? (1)
Baby Wait A Minute (6)	Emotional (4)	If My Brother's In Trouble (3)	Nitetime (6)	Stay With Me Tonight	You Can't Be Serious (3)
Back In Your Arms (6)	Family, The (5)	In Your Eyes (4)	On The Wings Of Love	(2) 30	(You Can't Get) Love From A
Borderlines, The (3) 38	Feel Like Making Love (6)	Is It Right (3)	(1) 29	True Believers (5)	Stone (5)
Can't Go Back On A Promise	Forever Mine (2)	La Cuenta, Por Favor (5)	One Love - One Dream (5)	Two Wrongs Don't Make A	You Should Be Mine (The
(5)	Getting Better All The Time	Lay Your Head (4)	Only Human (6)	Right (2)	Woo Woo Song) (4) 13
Cindy (5)	(6)	Let Me Know (3)	Other Side Of The Coin (2)	We Belong To Love (4)	You Were Made To Love (1)
Come Midnight (4)	Good Things Come To Those	Live For Today (3)	Plane Love (2)	We're Going All The Way	
Congratulations (1)	Who Wait (6)	Love's Not Ready (4)	Power, The (3)	(2) 48	
Crazy 'Bout Cha (3)	Greatest Love Affair (2)	Morning After I Made Love	Ready For Your Love (1)	When Are You Comin' Back?	
Don't Stop (3) 44	Hot Coals (3)	To You (6)	Room With A View (4)	(2)	
			Second Chance (4)		

OSBORNE BROTHERS, The
Bluegrass trio from Hyden, Kentucky. Led by brothers Bobby Van and Sonny Osborne with Benny Birchfield.

7/4/70	193	1		Ru-beeeee	$15	Decca 75204

Fightin' Side Of Me	Listening To The Rain	Put It Off Until Tomorrow	Somebody's Back In Town	Thanks For All The	World Of Forgotten People
Let Me Be The First To Know	Mid Night Angel	Ruby, Are You Mad	Tennessee Hound Dog	Yesterdays	
		Siempre			

★★238★★ OSBOURNE, Ozzy
Born John Michael Osbourne on 12/3/48 in Birmingham, England. Heavy-metal artist; former lead singer of Black Sabbath. Appeared in the 1986 film *Trick Or Treat*.

4/18/81	21	104	▲²	1 Blizzard Of Ozz	$8	Jet 36812
11/21/81	16	73	▲²	2 Diary Of A Madman	$8	Jet 37492
5/8/82	120	18		3 Mr. Crowley	[M-L]	$8	Jet 37640
				live EP picture disk		
12/11/82+	14	20	▲	4 Speak Of The Devil	[L]	$10	Jet 38350 [2]
				recorded at The Ritz, New York		
12/10/83+	19	29	▲²	5 Bark At The Moon		$8	CBS Assoc. 38987
2/15/86	6	39	▲	6 The Ultimate Sin		$8	CBS Assoc. 40026
5/9/87	6	23	▲	7 Tribute	[L]	$10	CBS As. 40714 [2]

OZZY OSBOURNE/RANDY RHOADS
live recordings from 1981 featuring Ozzy's guitarist, Randy Rhoads, who was killed in an airplane crash on 3/19/82 (age 25)

10/22/88	13	27	▲	8 No Rest For The Wicked		$8	CBS Assoc. 44245
3/3/90	58	13		9 Just Say Ozzy	[M]	$6	CBS Assoc. 45451

Ozzy backed on his solo and Black Sabbath material by former Black Sabbath bandmates Geezer Butler, Zakk Wylde and Randy Castillo

8/18/90	163	2		10 Ten Commandments	[K]	$12	Priority 57129
10/5/91	7	71↑	▲²	11 No More Tears		$12	Epic 46795

A.V.H. (11)	Diary Of A Madman (2,10)	Mama, I'm Coming Home	Paranoid (4,7)	Steal Away (The Night)	You Can't Kill Rock And Roll
Bark At The Moon (5,10)	Fairies Wear Boots (4)	(11) 28	Revelation (Mother Earth)	(1,7,10)	(2)
Believer (2,7)	Fire In The Sky (8)	Miracle Man (8,9)	(1,7)	Suicide Solution (1,3,7)	You Said It All (3)
Black Sabbath (4)	Flying High Again (2,7,10)	Mr. Crowley (1,3,7)	Road To Nowhere (11)	Sweet Leaf (4,9)	You're No Different (5)
Bloodbath In Paradise (8,9)	Fool Like You (6)	Mr. Tinkertrain (11)	Rock 'N' Roll Rebel (5)	Symptom Of The Universe (4)	Zombie Stomp (11)
Breaking All The Rules (8)	Goodbye To Romance (1,7)	N.I.B. (4)	S.A.T.O. (2)	Tattooed Dancer (8,9)	
Centre Of Eternity (5)	Hellraiser (11)	Never (6)	Sabbath, Bloody Sabbath (4)	Thank God For The Bomb	
Children Of The Grave (4,7)	I Don't Know (1,7)	Never Know Why (6)	Secret Loser (6)	(6,10)	
Crazy Babies (8)	I Don't Want To Change The	Never Say Die (4)	Shot In The Dark	Time After Time (11)	
Crazy Train (1,7,10)	World (11)	No Bone Movies (1,7)	(6,9,10) 68	Tonight (2,10)	
Dee (1,7)	Iron Man (4,7)	No More Tears (11) 71	S.I.N. (11)	Ultimate Sin (6)	
Demon Alcohol (8)	Killer Of Giants (6)	Now You See It (Now You	Slow Down (5)	Waiting For Darkness (5)	
Desire (11)	Lightning Strikes (6)	Don't) (5)	Snowblind (4)	War Pigs (4,9)	
Devil's Daughter (8)	Little Dolls (2,10)	Over The Mountain (2)	So Tired (5,10)	Wizard, The (4)	

DEBUT DATE	PEAK POS	WKS CHR	GOLD	ARTIST — Album Title	$	Label & Number

OSIBISA

Britain-based band founded by Ghanaians Teddy Osei (reeds, percussion), Sol Amarifo (drums), Mac Tontoh (bass, percussion) and West Indian Wendell Richardson (guitar). Evolving personnel in the mid-1970s.

DEBUT DATE	PEAK POS	WKS CHR	GOLD	#	Album Title	$	Label & Number
7/3/71	55	19		1	Osibisa	$12	Decca 75285
2/12/72	66	17		2	Wcyaya	$12	Decca 75327
10/28/72	125	8		3	Heads	$12	Decca 75368
7/21/73	159	7		4	Super Fly T.N.T. [S]	$10	Buddah 5136
9/28/74	175	4		5	Osibirock	$10	Warner 2802
4/24/76	200	2		6	Welcome Home	$10	Island 9355

African Jive (5) • Akwaaba (1) • Atinga Bells (5) • Ayiko Bia (1) • Beautiful 7 (2) • Brotherhood (4) • Che Che Kule (3) • Chooboi (Heave Ho!) (6) • Come Closer (If You're A Man) (4) • Dawn, The (1) • Densu (6) • Do It (Like It Is) (6) • Do You Know (3) • Home Affairs (5) • Kangaroo (5) • Kelele (4,5) • Kokorokoo (3) • Kolomashie (6) • Komfo (High Priest) (5) • La Ila I La La (4) • Mentumi (3) • Move On (2) • Music For Gong Gong (1) • Oranges (1) • Osibirock (5) • Oye Mama (4) • Phallus C (1) • Prophets (4) • Rabiato (3) • Right Now (6) • Seaside - Meditation (6) • So So Mi La So (3) • Spirits Up Above (2) • Sunshine Day (6) • Superfly Man (4) • Survival (2) • Sweet America (3) • Sweet Sounds (3) • T.N.T. (4) • Think About The People (1) • Uhuru (6) • Vicarage, The (4) • Wango Wango (3) • Wcyaya (2) • We Belong (5) • Welcome Home (6) • Who's Got The Paper (5) • Why (5) • Y Sharp (3) • Ye Tie Wo (3)

OSKAR, Lee

Born on 3/24/48 in Copenhagen, Denmark. Harmonica player. Studio musician in Los Angeles. Original member of War.

DEBUT DATE	PEAK POS	WKS CHR	GOLD	#	Album Title	$	Label & Number
4/3/76	29	24		1	Lee Oskar [I] (includes 2 vocal tracks)	$10	United Art. 594
9/16/78	86	12		2	Before The Rain	$8	Elektra 150
8/1/81	162	6		3	My Road Our Road	$8	Elektra 526

BLT (1) 59 • Before The Rain (2) • Blisters (1) • Children's Song (You Can Find Your Way) (3) • Down The Nile (1) • Feelin' Happy (2) • Haunted House (2) • I Remember Home (A Peasant's Symphony) • Medley (1) • More Than Words Can Say (2) • My Road (3) • Our Road Medley (3) • San Francisco Bay (2) • Sing Song (2) • Song For My Son (3) • Starkite (1) • Steppin' (2) • Sunshine Keri (1) • Up All Night (3) • Yes, I'm Singing (3)

OSLIN, K.T.

Country singer/songwriter Kay Toinette Oslin was born in Crossitt, Arkansas and raised in Mobile, Alabama. Former backup vocalist and commercial jingle singer.

DEBUT DATE	PEAK POS	WKS CHR	GOLD	#	Album Title	$	Label & Number
12/12/87+	68	32	▲	1	80's Ladies	$8	RCA 5924
9/24/88	75	52	▲	2	This Woman	$8	RCA 8369
11/24/90+	76	26	●	3	Love In A Small Town	$12	RCA 2365

Come Next Monday (3) • Cornell Crawford (3) • Didn't Expect It To Go Down This Way (2) • Do Ya' (1) • Dr., Dr. (1) • 80's Ladies (1) • Hey Bobby (2) • Hold Me (2) • I'll Always Come Back (1) • Jealous (2) • Lonely But Only For You (1) • Love Is Strange (3) • Mary And Willi (3) • Momma Was A Dancer (3) • Money (2) • New Way Home (3) • Old Pictures (1) • Oo-Wee (3) • Round The Clock Lovin' (2) • Still On My Mind (3) • This Woman (2) • Truly Blue (2) • Two Hearts (1,3) • Wall Of Tears (1) • Where Is A Woman To Go (2) • You Call Everybody Darling (3) • Younger Men (1)

★★279★★ OSMOND, Donny

Born on 12/9/57 in Ogden, Utah. Seventh son of George and Olive Osmond, Donny became a member of The Osmonds in 1963. Owner of production company Night Star. Burst back on to pop charts in March 1989.

DEBUT DATE	PEAK POS	WKS CHR	GOLD	#	Album Title	$	Label & Number
7/10/71	13	37	●	1	The Donny Osmond Album	$10	MGM 4782
11/6/71	12	33	●	2	To You With Love, Donny	$10	MGM 4797
5/27/72	6	36	●	3	**Portrait Of Donny**	$10	MGM 4820
7/22/72	11	30	●	4	Too Young	$10	MGM 4854
12/16/72+	29	20	●	5	My Best To You [G]	$10	MGM 4872
3/24/73	26	29		6	Alone Together	$10	MGM 4886
12/8/73+	58	13		7	A Time For Us	$10	MGM 4930
12/7/74+	57	17		8	Donny	$10	MGM 4978
8/21/76	145	8		9	Disco Train	$8	Polydor 6067
9/3/77	169	5		10	Donald Clark Osmond	$8	Polydor 6109
5/13/89	54	23		11	Donny Osmond	$8	Capitol 92354
11/17/90	177	2		12	Eyes Don't Lie	$12	Capitol 94051

All I Have To Do Is Dream (3) • **Are You Lonesome Tonight** (7) 14 • Before It's Too Late (12) • Big Man (7) • Boy Is Waiting (7) • Bye Bye Love (7) • **C'mon Marianne** (9) 38 • Disco Dancin' (9) • Disco Train (9) • Do Want Me (6) • (also see: We Can Make It Together) • Don't Need No Money (9) • Don't Say No (1) • Donna (9) • Eyes Don't Lie (12) • Faces In The Mirror (11) • Flirtin' (10) • Fly Into The Wind (10) • Go Away Little Girl (2,5) 1 • Going Going Gone (To Somebody Else) (3) • Groove (11) • Guess Who (7) • Hawaiian Wedding Song (Ke Kali Nei Au) (7) • **Hey Girl** (3,5) 9 • Hey Little Girl (1) • Hey Little Johnny (2) • Hey There, Lonely Girl (3) • **Hold On** (11) 73 • I Believe (9) • I Can't Put My Finger On It (9) • I Can't Stand It (10) • I Discovered You, You Discovered Me (10) • I Follow The Music (Disco Donny) (9) • I Got Your Lovin' (9) • **I Have A Dream** (8) 50 • I Haven't Had A Heartache All Day (10) • **I Knew You When** (2,5) flip • I'll Be Good To You (11) • I'm Dyin' (8) • I'm Into Something Good (2) • I'm So Lonesome I Could Cry (8) • I'm Sorry (10) • I'm Your Puppet (1,5) • I've Got Plans For You (3) • If It's Love That You Want (11) • If Someone Ever Breaks Your Heart (8) • Inner Rhythm (11) • It Takes A Lot Of Love (6) • It's Hard To Say Goodbye (6) • Just Between You And Me (12) • Last Of The Red Hot Lovers (4) • Let My People Go (3) • Life Is Just What You Make It (6) • Little Bit (2) • Little Bit Mo, A Little Bit You (2) • Lollipops, Lace And Lipstick (1) • **Lonely Boy** (4,5) flip • Love Me (3) • Love Will Survive (12) • Make It Last Forever (12) • **Million To One** (7) 23 • Mona Lisa (8) • More I Live (More I Love) (10) • **My Love Is A Fire** (12) 21 • My Secret Touch (11) • Never Gonna Let You Go (9) • Never Too Late For Love (12) • Oh, It Must Be Love (10) • Old Man Auctioneer (9) • Only Heaven Knows (11) • Other Side Of Me (6) • Ours (8) • Pretty Blue Eyes (4) • Private Affair (6) • Promise Me (3) • **Puppy Love** (3,5) 3 • Reachin' For The Feeling (9) • Run To Him (4) • **Sacred Emotion** (11) 13 • Sit Down, I Think I Love You (2) • Sixteen Candles (8) • So Shy (1) • **Soldier Of Love** (11) 2 • Standin' In The Need Of Love (12) • Sunshine Rose (6) • **Sure Lookin'** (12) 54 • **Sweet And Innocent** (1,5) 7 • Swingin' City Gal (9) • Take Another Try (At Love) (12) • Take Good Care Of My Baby (4) • Tears On My Pillow (6) • Teenager In Love (4) • This Guy's In Love With You (3) • This Time (8) • Time For Us (7) • To Run Away (4) • **Too Young** (4,5) 13 • **Twelfth Of Never** (6) 8 • Unchained Melody (7) • Wake Up, Little Susie (1) • We Can Make It Together (Do You Want Me?) (2,5) • (also see: Do You Want Me) • What's He Doing In My World (8) • **When I Fall In Love** (7) 55 • Where Did All The Good Times Go (8) • Who Can I Turn To (When Nobody Needs Me) (6) • **Why** (4,5) 13 • Wild Rover (Time To Ride) (1) • You Are The Music In My Life (10) • You'll Be Glad (10) • You've Got Me Dangling On A String (10) • Young And In Love (7) • **Young Love** (6) 25

OSMOND, Donny And Marie

Brother and sister co-hosts of own musical/variety TV series from 1976-78. Starred in the film *Goin' Coconuts* (1978).

9/7/74	**35**	30	●	1 I'm Leaving It All Up To You	$10	MGM 4968
6/28/75	**133**	6	●	2 Make The World Go Away	$10	MGM 4996
4/3/76	**60**	38	●	3 Donny & Marie - Featuring Songs From Their Television Show	$8	Polydor 6068
11/27/76+	**85**	14	●	4 Donny & Marie - New Season	$8	Polydor 6083
1/7/78	**99**	12	●	5 Winning Combination	$8	Polydor 6127
11/11/78	**98**	8	●	6 Goin' Coconuts ....[S]	$8	Polydor 6169

4 of 12 songs are from the film (starring Donny and Marie)

"A" My Name Is Alice (3)
Ain't Nothing Like The Real Thing (4) *21*
Angel Love (Heaven Is Where You Are) (5)
Anytime Sunshine (4)
Baby, I'm Sold On You (5)
Baby, Now That I've Found You (6)
Best Of Me (5)
Butterfly (3)
C'mon Marianne [solo: Donny] (3) *38*
Dandelion (3)
Day Late And A Dollar Short (1)
Deep Purple (3) *14*
Doctor Dancin' (6)
Don't Play With The One Who Loves You (6)
Everything Good Reminds Me Of You (1)
Fallin' In Love Again (6)
Gimme Some Time (6)
Gone (1)
Hold Me, Thrill Me, Kiss Me (4)
I Can't Do Without You (5)
I Want To Be In Your World (5)
I Want To Give You My Everything (5)
I Will (2)
I'm Leaving It (All) Up To You (1) *4*
It Takes Two (1,3)
It's All Been Said Before (4)
It's All In The Game (2)
Jigsaw (2)
Let It Be Me (1)
Let's Fall In Love (6)
Little Bit Country, A Little Bit Rock 'N Roll (3)
Living On My Suspicion (2)
Make The World Go Away (2) *44*
Mama Didn't Lie (2)
May Tomorrow Be A Perfect Day (3,6)
Morning Side Of The Mountain (1) *8*
Now We're Together (4)
Oh, Sweet Lovin' (5)
On The Shelf (6) *38*
One Of These Days (2)
Show Me (4)
Sing (4)
Sunshine Lady (3)
Sure Would Be Nice (5)
Take Me Back Again (1,3)
Together (2)
True Love (1)
Umbrella Song (1)
We Got Love (4)
Weeping Willow (3)
When Somebody Cares For You (2)
(When You're) Young And In Love (2)
Which Way You Goin' Billy (4)
Winning Combination (5)
You Bring Me Sunshine (6)
You Broke My Heart (4)
You Don't Have To Say You Love Me (6)
You Never Can Tell (6)
You Remind Me (5)
(You're My) Soul And Inspiration (5) *38*

OSMOND, Little Jimmy

Born on 4/16/63 in Canoga Park, California. Youngest member of the Osmond family.

12/2/72+	**105**	14		1 Killer Joe	$10	MGM 4855

If My Dad Were President
Killer Joe
Let Me Be Your Teddy Bear
Little Girls Are Fun
Long Haired Lover From Liverpool *38*
Mama'd Know What To Do
Mother Of Mine
My Girl
Rubber Ball
Tweedlee Dee *59*

OSMOND, Marie

Born Olive Marie Osmond on 10/13/59 in Ogden, Utah. Began performing in concert with her brothers at age 14. Co-hosted the TV series *Ripley's Believe It Or Not* from 1985-86. Emerged as a top country artist in the '80s.

9/22/73	**59**	23		1 Paper Roses	$10	MGM 4910
7/20/74	**164**	9		2 In My Little Corner Of The World	$10	MGM 4944
3/8/75	**152**	6		3 Who's Sorry Now	$10	MGM 4979

above 3 produced and arranged by Sonny James

4/30/77	**152**	6		4 This Is The Way That I Feel	$8	Polydor 6099

All He Did Was Tell Me Lies (To Try To Woo Me) (4)
Among My Souvenirs (3)
Anytime (3)
Big Hurts Can Come (From Little White Lies) (2)
Clinging Vine (3)
Crazy Arms (4)
Cry, Baby, Cry (4)
Didn't I Love You, Boy? (4)
Everybody's Somebody's Fool (2)
Everything Is Beautiful (1)
Fool No. 1 (1)
I Love You Because (2)
I Love You So Much It Hurts (2)
In My Little Corner Of The World (2)
Invisible Tears (2)
It's Just The Other Way Around (2)
It's Such A Pretty World Today (1)
It's The Little Things (3)
Jealous Heart (3)
Least Of All You (1)
Louisiana Bayou (1)
Love Letters In The Sand (3)
Making Believe (3)
Miss You Nights (4)
Paper Roses (1) *5*
Play The Music Loud (4)
Please Tell Him That I Said Hello (4)
Run To Me (4)
Singing The Blues (3)
Sweet Dreams (1)
Things I Tell My Pillow (3)
This I Promise You (3)
This Is The Way That I Feel (4) *21*
Too Many Rivers (1)
True Love Lasts Forever (1)
True Love's A Blessing (2)
Where Did Our Love Go (4)
Who's Sorry Now (3) *40*
You're My Superman (You're My Everything) (4)
You're The Only World I Know (1)

★★323★★ OSMONDS, The

Family group from Ogden, Utah. Alan (b: 6/22/49), Wayne (b: 8/28/51), Merrill (b: 4/30/53), Jay (b: 3/2/55) and Donny (b: 12/9/57). Began as a quartet in 1959, singing religious and barbershop-quartet songs. Regulars on Andy Williams' TV show from 1962-67. Alan, Wayne, Merrill and Jay turned to country music as The Osmond Brothers in the early '80s.

1/30/71	**14**	43	●	1 Osmonds	$10	MGM 4724
6/26/71	**22**	34	●	2 Homemade	$10	MGM 4770
1/29/72	**10**	35	●	3 **Phase-III**	$10	MGM 4796
6/17/72	**13**	29	●	4 The Osmonds "Live" ....[L]	$12	MGM 4826 [2]
10/14/72	**14**	22	●	5 Crazy Horses	$10	MGM 4851
7/7/73	**58**	20		6 The Plan	$10	MGM 4902
11/2/74	**47**	14		7 Love Me For A Reason	$10	MGM 4939
8/30/75	**160**	5		8 The Proud One	$10	MGM 4993
12/20/75+	**148**	8		9 Around The World - Live In Concert ...[L]	$12	MGM 5012 [2]
10/23/76	**145**	6		10 Brainstorm	$8	Polydor 6077
12/18/76+	**127**	5		11 The Osmond Christmas Album ......[X]	$10	Polydor 8001 [2]
1/14/78	**192**	3		12 The Osmonds Greatest Hits ......[G]	$10	Polydor 9005 [2]

Ain't Nothing Like The Real Thing [duet: Donny & Marie] (12) *21*
And You Love Me (5)
Are You Lonesome Tonight? [solo: Donny] (9,12) *14*
Are You Up There? (6)
At The Rainbows End (10)
Back On The Road Again (10,12)
Ballin' The Jack (7)
Before The Beginning (medley) (6)
Big Finish (9)
Blue Christmas (11)
Boogie Down (10)
Business (7)
Caroling Medley (11)
Carrie (2)
Catch Me Baby (1)
Check It Out (10)
Chilly Winds (2)
Christmas Song (11)
Christmas Waltz (11)
C'mon Marianne [solo: Donny] (12) *38*
Crazy Horses (5,9,12) *14*
Darlin' (6)
Don't Panic (8)
Don't Take It Too Easy (medley) (6)
Double Lovin' (2,4) *14*
Down By The Lazy River (3,4,9,12) *4*
Everytime I Feel The Spirit (medley) (4)
Feelin' All Right (9)
Fever (7)
50's Medley (9)
Find'em, Fool'em And Forget'em (4)
Flirtin' (1)
Free (medley) (4)
Frightened Eyes (8)
Gabrielle (7)
Girl (5)
Girl I Love (7,9)
Go Away Little Girl [solo: Donny] (4,9,12) *1*
Goin' Home (6,12) *36*
Gotta Get Love (10)
Having A Party (7)
He Ain't Heavy...He's My Brother (1)
He's The Light Of The World (3)
Hey Girl (4)
Hey Look Me Over (medley) (9)
Hey, Mr. Taxi (5)
Hold Her Tight (5,9,12) *14*
Honey Bee Song (2)
I Can See Love In You And Me (7)
I Can't Get Next To You (4,7,9)
I Can't Live A Dream (10) *46*
I Got A Woman (medley) (4)
I'll Be Home For Christmas (11)
I'm Gonna Make You Love Me (medley) (4)
I'm Leaving It (All) Up To You [duet: Donny & Marie] (9,12) *4*
I'm Sorry (medley) (6)
I'm Still Gonna Need You (8)
If Santa Was My Daddy (11)
If You're Gonna Leave Me (2)
In The Rest Of My Life (3)
It Never Snows In L.A. (11)
It Takes Two (medley) [duet: Donny & Marie] (9)
It'll Be Me (10)
It's All Up To You (medley) (6)
It's Alright (6)
It's Beginning To Look A Lot Like Christmas (medley) (11)
It's You Babe (3)
Julie (5)
Kay Thompson's Jingle Bells (11)
Kind Of A Woman That A Man Wants (8)
Last Day Is Coming (8)
Last Days (6)

OSMONDS, The — Cont'd

Learnin' How To Love Again (10)
Let It Snow! Let It Snow! Let It Snow! (11)
Let Me In (6,12) **36**
Life Is Hard Enough Without Goodbyes (5)
Lonesome They Call Me, Lonesome I Am (1)
Long Haired Lover From Liverpool [solo: Jimmy] (9,12) **38**
Love Is (3)
Love Me For A Reason (7,9,12) **10**
Make The World Go Away (9)
Medicine Man (10)
Merrill's Banjo Medley (9)
Mirror, Mirror (6)

Mona Lisa (9)
Morning Side Of The Mountain [duet: Donny & Marie] (9,12) **8**
Most Of All (1)
Motown Special (1,4)
Movie Man (medley) (6)
Music Makin' (medley) (9)
My Drum (3)
My World Is Empty Without You (medley) (4)
Never Can Say Goodbye (medley) [solo: Jimmy] (9)
Old Fashioned Christmas (11)
One Bad Apple (1,4,12) **1**
One Way Ticket To Anywhere (6)

Paper Roses [solo: Marie] (9,12) **5**
Peace (7)
Pine Cones And Holly Berries (medley) (11)
Promised Land (2)
Proud Mary (medley) (4)
Proud One (8,9) **22**
Puppy Love [solo: Donny] (9,12) **3**
Send A Little Love (7)
She Makes Me Warm (2)
Sho Would Be Nice (2)
Shuckin' And Jivin' (2)
Silent Night (11)
Silver Bells (11)
Sleigh Ride (11)
Some Kind Of Wonderful (9)
Someone To Go Home To (8)

Sometimes I Feel Like A Motherless Child (medley) (4)
Stevie Wonder Medley (9)
Sun, Sun, Sun (7)
Sweet And Innocent (1,4,12)
Take Love If Ever You Find Love (8)
Taste Of Rhythm And Blues (3)
Thank You (8)
That's My Girl (5)
Think (1)
This Christmas Eve (11)
This Is The Way That I Feel [solo: Marie] (12) **39**
Too Young [solo: Donny] (12) **13**

Traffic In My Mind (medley) (6)
Trouble (medley) (4)
Twelfth Of Never [solo: Donny] (12) **8**
Utah (5)
Very Merry Christmas (11)
Walkin' In The Jungle (10)
We All Fall Down (5)
We Gotta Live Together (4)
We Never Said Forever (2)
What Are You Doing On New Year's Eve (11)
What Could It Be (5)
When He Comes Again (11)
Where Are You Going To My Love (8)
Where Could I Go But To The Lord (medley) (4)

Where Would I Be Without You (8)
White Christmas (11)
Who's Sorry Now (medley) [solo: Marie] (9)
Winter Wonderland (11)
Yo-Yo (3,4,12) **3**
You Are So Beautiful (medley) [solo: Jimmy] (9)
You've Lost That Lovin' Feelin' (4)
Your Mama Don't Dance (9)
Your Song (4)

O'SULLIVAN, Gilbert

Born Raymond O'Sullivan on 12/1/46 in Waterford, Ireland.

DEBUT DATE	PEAK POS	WKS CHR	GOLD	ARTIST — Album Title	$	Label & Number
8/12/72	9	29		1 Gilbert O'Sullivan-Himself	$12	MAM 4
1/6/73	48	19		2 Back To Front	$10	MAM 5
10/13/73	101	10		3 I'm A Writer, Not A Fighter	$10	MAM 7

Alone Again (Naturally) (1) **1**
But I'm Not (2)
Bye Bye (1)
Can I Go With You (2)
Clair (2) **2**
Friend Of Mine (3)
Get Down (3) **7**

Golden Rule (2)
Houdini Said (1)
I Have Never Loved You As Much As I Love You Today (3)
I Hope You'll Stay (2)
I'm A Writer, Not A Fighter (3)

I'm In Love With You (2)
I'm Leaving (2)
If I Don't Get You (Back Again) (1)
If You Love Me Like You Love Me (3)
In My Hole (2)
Independent Air (1)

January Git (1)
Matrimony (1)
Not In A Million Years (3)
Nothing Rhymed (1)
Ooh Baby (3) **25**
Out Of The Question (2) **17**
Permissive Twit (1)
That's Love (2)

They've Only Themselves To Blame (3)
Thunder And Lightning (1)
Too Much Attention (1)
We Will (1)
What Could Be Nicer (Mum The Kettle's Boiling) (2)

Where Peaceful Waters Flow (3)
Who Knows, Perhaps Maybe (3)
Who Was It (2)

OTHER ONES, The

Rock sextet consisting of Australian siblings Jayney (lead vocals), Alf and Johnny Klimek, and Germans Andreas Schwarz-Ruszczynski, Stephan Gottwald and Uwe Hoffmann.

DEBUT DATE	PEAK POS	WKS CHR	GOLD	ARTIST — Album Title	$	Label & Number
5/16/87	139	6		The Other Ones	$8	Virgin 90576

All Day, All Night
All The Love

He's A Man
Holiday 29

It Makes Me Higher
Losing It

Moments

Stay With Me (It's Not Forever)

Stranger
We Are What We Are 53

OTIS, Shuggie

Born on 11/30/53 in Los Angeles. Multi-instrumentalist. Son of R&B legend Johnny Otis. Professional debut in 1965.

DEBUT DATE	PEAK POS	WKS CHR	GOLD	ARTIST — Album Title	$	Label & Number
1/24/70	182	5		1 Kooper Session	$12	Columbia 9951
				AL KOOPER Introduces SHUGGIE OTIS		
3/7/70	199	2		2 Here Comes Shuggie Otis	$12	Epic 26511
3/22/75	181	3		3 Inspiration Information	$10	Epic 33059

Aht Uh Mi Hed (3)
Baby, I Needed You (2)
Bootie Cooler (2)
Bury My Body (1)
Double Or Nothing (1)

Funky Thithee (2)
Gospel Groove (2)
Happy House (3)
Hawks, The (3)
Hurricane (2)

Inspiration Information (3)
Island Letter (3)
Jennie Lee (2)
Knowing (That You Want Him) (2)

Lookin' For A Home (3)
Not Available (3)
One Room Country Shack (1)
Oxford Gray (3)
Pling! (3)

Rainy Day (3)
Shuggie's Boogie (2)
Shuggie's Old Time (1)
Dee-Di-Lee-Di-Leet-Deet (1)
Slide Boogie (1)

Shuggie's Shuffle (1)
Sparkle City (3)
12:15 Slow Goonbash Blues (1)
XL-30 (3)

OUTFIELD, The

British pop-rock trio: Tony Lewis (lead singer; bass), John Spinks (guitar, keyboards, vocals) and Alan Jackman (drums). Jackman left by 1990; Lewis and Spinks continued as a duo.

DEBUT DATE	PEAK POS	WKS CHR	GOLD	ARTIST — Album Title	$	Label & Number
11/2/85+	9	66	▲²	1 Play Deep	$8	Columbia 40027
7/4/87	18	21	●	2 Bangin'	$8	Columbia 40619
4/15/89	53	23		3 Voices Of Babylon	$8	Columbia 44449
11/24/90+	90	16		4 Diamond Days	$12	MCA 10111

After The Storm (4)
All The Love In The World (1) **19**
Alone With You (2)
Bangin' On My Heart (2)
Better Than Nothing (2)
Burning Blue (4)

Everytime You Cry (1) **66**
Eye To Eye (4)
For You (4) **21**
I Don't Need Her (1)
Inside Your Skin (3)
John Lennon (4)
Long Way Home (2)

Magic Seed (4)
Main Attraction (2)
Makin' Up (3)
Moving Target (2)
My Paradise (3) **72**
Mystery Man (1)
Nervous Alibi (1)

Night Ain't Over (3)
No Point (3)
No Surrender (2)
One Night In Heaven (4)
Part Of Your Life (3)
Playground (2)
Raintown Boys (4)

Reach Out (3)
Say It Isn't So (1)
Shelter Me (3)
Since You've Been Gone (2) **31**
61 Seconds (1)
Somewhere In America (2)

Take It Away (3)
Taken By Surprise (3)
Taking My Chances (1)
Talk To Me (1)
Unrespectable (4)
Voices Of Babylon (3) **25**
Your Love (1) **6**

★★359★★ OUTLAWS

Southern-rock band formed in Tampa in 1974. Consisted of guitarists Hughie Thomasson, Billy Jones and Henry Paul, with drummer Monte Yoho and bassist Frank O'Keefe (replaced by Harvey Arnold in 1977). Paul, Yoho and Arnold left by 1980.

DEBUT DATE	PEAK POS	WKS CHR	GOLD	ARTIST — Album Title	$	Label & Number
8/9/75	13	16	●	1 Outlaws	$8	Arista 4042
4/10/76	36	12		2 Lady In Waiting	$8	Arista 4070
5/28/77	51	27		3 Hurry Sundown	$8	Arista 4135
3/25/78	29	21	●	4 Bring It Back Alive [L]	$10	Arista 8300 [2]
11/25/78	60	18		5 Playin' To Win	$8	Arista 4205
11/3/79	55	18		6 In The Eye Of The Storm	$8	Arista 9507
12/13/80+	25	26	●	7 Ghost Riders	$8	Arista 9542
5/1/82	77	9		8 Los Hombres Malo	$8	Arista 9584
				title is Spanish for The Bad Men		
11/27/82+	136	9		9 Greatest Hits Of The Outlaws/High Tides Forever [G]	$8	Arista 9614
11/8/86	160	10		10 Soldiers Of Fortune	$8	Pasha 40512

DEBUT DATE	PEAK POS	WKS CHR	GOLD	ARTIST — Album Title	$	Label & Number

OUTLAWS — Cont'd

Ain't So Bad (2)
All Roads (8)
Angels Hide (7)
Back From Eternity (8)
Blueswater (6)
Breaker - Breaker (2) *94*
Cold And Lonesome (3,4)
Cold Harbor (10)
(Come On) Dance With Me (6)
Comin' Home (6)
Cry No More (1)
Cry Some More (5)
Devil's Road (7)
Dirty City (5)

Don't Stop (8)
Easy Does It (8)
Falling Rain (5)
Foxtail Lilly (8)
Freeborn Man (2,4)
Freedom Walk (7)
(Ghost) Riders In The Sky (7,9) *31*
Girl From Ohio (2)
Goodbye (8)
Green Grass & High Tides (1,4,9)
Gunsmoke (3)
Hearin' My Heart Talkin' (3)
Heavenly Blues (3)

Holiday (3,4,9)
Hurry Sundown (3,4,9) *60*
I Can't Stop Loving You (7)
I Hope You Don't Mind (4)
I'll Be Leaving Soon (6)
If Dreams Came True (5)
It Follows From Your Heart (1)
It's All Right (6)
Just For You (2)
Just The Way I Like It (10)
Keep Prayin' (1)
Knoxville Girl (1)
Lady Luck (10)

Lights Are On (But Nobody's Home) (6)
Long Gone (6)
Love At First Sight (5)
Lover Boy (2,4)
Man Of The Hour (3)
Miracle Man (6)
Night Cries (10)
Night Wines (3)
One Last Ride (9)
Outlaw, The (10)
Prisoner (2,4)
Racin' For The Red Light (10)
Real Good Feelin' (5)
Rebel Girl (8)

Running (8)
Saved By The Bell (10)
So Afraid (3)
Soldiers Of Fortune (10)
Song For You (1,4)
Song In The Breeze (1)
South Carolina (2)
Stay With Me (1)
Stick Around For Rock & Roll (2,4,9)
Sunshine (7)
Take It Anyway You Want It (5,9)
There Goes Another Love Song (1,4,9) *34*

Too Long Without Her (6)
Waterhole (1)
Whatcha Don't Do (10)
White Horses (7)
Wishing Wells (7)
Won't Come Out Of The Rain (8)
You Are The Show (5,9)
You Can Have It (5)

OUTSIDERS, The

Cleveland rock quintet: Sonny Geraci (lead singer), Tom King (guitar), Bill Bruno (lead guitar), Mert Madsen (bass) and Rick Baker (drums). Geraci later led band Climax.

DEBUT DATE	PEAK POS	WKS CHR		ARTIST — Album Title	$	Label & Number
5/28/66	37	16	1	Time Won't Let Me	$20	Capitol 2501
9/17/66	90	10	2	The Outsiders Album #2	$20	Capitol 2568
8/26/67	103	10	3	Happening 'Live!' [L]	$20	Capitol 2745

Ain't Too Proud To Beg (3)
Backwards, Upside Down (2)
Chase Away The Tears (1)
Come On Up (3)
Cool Jerk (2)
Girl In Love (1,3) *21*
Gloria (3)

Good Lovin' (3)
Hanky Panky (2)
Help Me Girl (3) *37*
I Will Love You (3)
(Just Like) Romeo & Juliet (2)
Keep On Running (1)

Listen People (1)
Lonely Man (2)
Lost In My World (2)
Love Makes The World Go 'Round (3)
Maybe Baby (1)
Michelle (1)

My Girl (1)
Oh How It Hurts (2)
Respectable (2,3) *15*
Rockin' Robin (1)
She Cried (1)
Show Me (3)
Since I Lost My Baby (2)

Time Won't Let Me (1,3) *5*
Was It Really Real (1)
What Makes You So Bad You Weren't Brought Up That Way (1)
Wine Wine Wine (2)

OVERKILL

New York-based, heavy-metal quartet: Bobby "Blitz" Ellsworth (vocals), Bobby Gustafson, D.D. Verni and Sid Falck.

DEBUT DATE	PEAK POS	WKS CHR		ARTIST — Album Title	$	Label & Number
4/11/87	191	1	1	Taking Over	$8	Megaforce 81735
7/30/88	142	13	2	Under The Influence	$8	Megaforce 81865
11/18/89+	155	8	3	The Years Of Decay	$8	Megaforce 82045

Birth Of Tension (3)
Brainfade (2)
Deny The Cross (1)
Drunken Wisdom (2)
Electro-Violence (1)
Elimination (3)

End Of The Line (2)
E.vil N.ever D.ies (3)
Fatal If Swallowed (3)
Fear His Name (1)
Head First (2)
Hello From The Gutter (2)

I Hate (1)
In Union We Stand (1)
Mad Gone World (2)
Never Say Never (2)
Nothing To Die For (3)

Overkill II (The Nightmare Continues) (1)
Overkill III (Under The Influence) (2)
Playing With Spiders (medley) (3)

Powersurge (1)
Shred (2)
Skullrusher (medley) (3)
Time To Kill (3)
Use Your Head (1)
Who Tends The Fire (3)

Wrecking Crew (1)
Years Of Decay (3)

OVERSTREET, Paul

Singer/songwriter from VanCleave, Mississippi. Wrote "Same Ole Me" for George Jones and "A Long Line Of Love" for Michael Martin Murphey. Part of Schuyler, Knobloch & Overstreet (SKO). Went solo, 1987. Briefly married to Dolly Parton's sister, Freida.

DEBUT DATE	PEAK POS	WKS CHR		ARTIST — Album Title	$	Label & Number
2/23/91	163	6		Heroes	$12	RCA 2459

Ball & Chain
Billy Can't Read

Calm At The Center Of My Storm
Daddy's Come Around

Heroes
I'm So Glad I Was Dreaming

If I Could Bottle This Up
Love Lives On

She Supports Her Man
Straight And Narrow

'Til The Mountains Disappear

★★447★★ OWENS, Buck

Country singer/guitarist/songwriter. Has charted 21 #1 country hits. Born Alvis Edgar Owens on 8/12/29 in Sherman, Texas; raised in Mesa, Arizona. Moved to Bakersfield, California in 1951. Co-host of TV's Hee Haw, 1969-86. Backing group: The Buckaroos.

DEBUT DATE	PEAK POS	WKS CHR	GOLD	ARTIST — Album Title	$	Label & Number
7/18/64	46	31	●	1 The Best Of Buck Owens [G]	$20	Capitol 2105
9/5/64	88	18		2 Together Again/My Heart Skips A Beat	$20	Capitol 2135
12/12/64	135	5		3 I Don't Care	$20	Capitol 2186
4/3/65	43	22		4 I've Got A Tiger By The Tail	$20	Capitol 2283
3/12/66	106	10		5 Roll out the red carpet for Buck Owens and his Buckaroos	$20	Capitol 2443
9/24/66	114	10		6 Carnegie Hall Concert [L]	$15	Capitol 2556
9/30/67	177	7		7 Your Tender Loving Care	$15	Capitol 2760
2/15/69	199	2		8 I've Got You On My Mind Again	$12	Capitol 131
7/5/69	113	5		9 Buck Owens In London [L]	$12	Capitol 232
8/16/69	185	5		10 Close-Up [R]	$15	Capitol 257 [2]
				reissue of Together Again and No One But You albums		
11/8/69	122	10		11 Tall Dark Stranger	$12	Capitol 212
2/7/70	141	6		12 Big In Vegas [L]	$12	Capitol 413
				includes "Lodi" by Buddy Alan; "Let Me Get My Message Thru" by The Sanland Brothers; "Maybe If I Close My Eyes (It'll Go Away)" by Susan Raye; "Goin' Home To Your Mother" and "With Lonely" by The Hagers; "I'm A Natural Loser" by Doyle Holly; "Catfish Capers" by Don Rich; and "Cold Cold Wind" by Ira Allen		
4/25/70	198	2		13 Your Mother's Prayer	$12	Capitol 439
5/16/70	154	6		14 We're Gonna Get Together	$12	Capitol 448
				BUCK OWENS & SUSAN RAYE		
9/19/70	196	2		15 The Kansas City Song	$12	Capitol 476
11/28/70	190	2		16 I Wouldn't Live In New York City	$12	Capitol 628

A-11 (2,10)
Abilene (3)
Above And Beyond (1,6)
Across This Town And Gone (11)
Act Naturally (1,6,9)
After You Leave Me (5)
Ain't It Amazin' Gracie (2)

Alabama, Louisiana, Or Maybe Tennessee (8)
Along Came Jones (12)
Amsterdam (15)
Band Keeps Playin' On (4)
Before You Go (10) *83*
Big In Vegas (12,16) *100*
Black Texas Dirt (15)

Bring Back My Peace Of Mind (15)
Buck's Polka (3)
Buckaroo (6) *60*
Bud's Bounce (3)
But You Know I Love You (11)
Cajun Fiddle (5,9)

Charlie Brown (10)
Cinderella (5)
Close Up The Honky Tonks (2,10)
Cryin' Time (4,6,9,14)
Dang Me (3)
Darlin', You Can Depend On Me (11)

Diggy Liggy Lo (medley) (9)
Don't Ever Tell Me Goodbye (7)
Don't Let Her Know (3,6)
Don't Let True Love Slip Away (8)
Down In New Orleans (16)
Dust On Mother's Bible (9)

Everybody Needs Somebody (14)
Excuse Me (I Think I've Got A Heartache) (1,6)
Fallin' For You (4,14)
Foolin' Around (1,6,14)
Full Time Daddy (15)

DEBUT DATE	PEAK POS	WKS CHR	GOLD	ARTIST — Album Title	$	Label & Number

OWENS, Buck — Cont'd

Getting Used To Losing You (2,10)
Getting Used To Loving You (10)
Gonna Have Love (6,10)
Gonna Roll Out The Red Carpet (5)
Great Judgment Day (13)
Hangin' On To What I Got (5)
Happening In London Town (9)
Happy Times Are Here Again (9)
He Don't Deserve You Anymore (5)
Hello Trouble (2,6,10)
High As The Mountains (1)
House Of Memories (7)
Houston-Town (16)
Hurry, Come Running Back To Me (8)
Hurtin' Like I've Never Hurt Before (11)
I Ain't A Gonna Be Treated This A Way (8)
I Betcha Didn't Know (10)
I Can't Stop (My Lovin' You) (1)
I Don't Care (Just As Long As You Love Me) (3,6) 92

I Don't Hear You (2,10)
I Wanna Be Wild And Free (8)
(I Want) No One But You (10)
I Would Do Anything For You (11)
I Wouldn't Live In New York City (If They Gave Me The Whole Dang Town) (16)
I'd Love To Be Your Man (15)
(I'll Love You) Forever And Ever (5,8)
I'm Layin' It On The Line (5)
I've Got A Tiger By The Tail (4,6,9) 25
I've Got You On My Mind Again (8)
If I Had You Back Again (7)
If You Fall Out Of Love With Me (4)
If You Want A Love (10)
In God I Trust (13)
In The Middle Of A Teardrop (11)
In The Palm Of Your Hand (medley) (6)
It Takes People Like You (To Make People Like Me) (9)
(It's A Long Way To) Londontown (15,16)

Jesus, Jesus, Hold To Me (13)
Johnny B. Goode (9)
Just A Few More Days (13)
Kansas City Song (15,16)
Kickin' Our Hearts Around (1)
Las Vegas Lament (12)
Let The Sad Times Roll On (4)
Let The World Keep On A Turnin' (8)
Lonesome Valley (13)
Loose Talk (3)
Louisiana Man (3,9)
Love Is Me (1)
Love Is Strange (14)
Love's Gonna Live Here (1,6,9)
Maiden's Prayer (4)
Maybe If I Close My Eyes (It'll Go Away) (11)
Memphis (4)
My Heart Skips A Beat (2,6,10) 94
My Savior Leads The Way (13)
No Fool Like An Old Fool (10)
No Milk And Honey In Baltimore (16)

Nobody's Fool But Yours (1)
Number One Heel (10)
Only You And You Alone (7)
Only You (Can Break My Heart) (6,7)
Open Up Your Heart (medley) (9)
Over And Over Again (2,10)
Playboy (3)
Reno Lament (16)
Rocks In My Head (7)
Rovin' Gambler (12)
Santo Domingo (16)
Save The Last Dance For Me (2)
Scandinavian Polka (15)
Second Fiddle (1)
Sing A Happy Song (8)
Sing Me Back Home (9)
Sing That Kind Of Song (11)
Someone With No One To Love (7)
Somewhere Between (14)
Song And Dance (7)
Storm Of Love (2,10)
Streets Of Laredo (4,6)
Sweet Rosie Jones (9)
Tall Dark Stranger (11)
That Old Time Religion (13)

That Sunday Feeling (13)
That's All Right With Me (If It's All Right With You) (8)
That's What I'm Like Without You (5)
There Never Was A Fool (5)
There's Gonna Come A Day (10)
There's Gotta Be Some Changes Made (11)
This Ol' Heart (3)
Together Again (2,6,9,10,12,14)
Togetherness (14)
Trouble And Me (4)
Truck Drivin' Man (2,6,10)
Under The Influence Of Love (1)
Under Your Spell Again (1,6)
Understand Your Man (3)
Wait A Little Longer Please, Jesus (13)
Waitin' In Your Welfare Line (6) 57
We Split The Blanket (5)
We Were Made For Each Other (14)
We're Gonna Get Together (14)

We're Gonna Let The Good Times Roll (4,12)
Wham Bam (4)
What A Liar I Am (7)
When The Roll Is Called Up Yonder (13)
Where Has Our Love Gone? (8)
White Satin Bed (11)
Who's Gonna Mow Your Grass (9)
Wind Blows Every Day In Chicago (16)
Wind Blows Every Day In Oklahoma (15)
You Can't Make Nothin' Out Of That But Love (15)
You Made A Monkey Out Of Me (7)
You're Welcome Anytime (3)
Your Mother's Prayer (13)
Your Tender Loving Care (7)

OXO
West Coast pop-rock quartet led by former Foxy member Ish "Angel" Ledesma.

| 4/30/83 | 117 | 7 | | Oxo .... | $8 | Geffen 4001 |

Back In Town
Dance All Night

I'll Take You Back
In The Stars

Love I Need Her
My Ride

Runnin' Low
Waiting For You

Wanna Be Your Love
Whirly Girl 28

You Make It Sound So Easy

OZARK MOUNTAIN DAREDEVILS
Country-rock group from Springfield, Missouri. Nucleus: Larry Lee (keyboards, guitar), Steve Cash (harp), John Dillon (guitar) and Michael Granda (bass).

2/16/74	26	28	●	1 The Ozark Mountain Daredevils	$10	A&M 4411
12/14/74+	19	31		2 It'll Shine When It Shines	$10	A&M 3654
11/8/75	57	15		3 The Car Over The Lake Album	$10	A&M 4549
10/2/76	74	10		4 Men From Earth	$10	A&M 4601
11/19/77+	132	10		5 Don't Look Down	$8	A&M 4662
9/30/78	176	3		6 It's Alive ....[L]	$10	A&M 6006 [2]
5/24/80	170	4		7 Ozark Mountain Daredevils	$8	Columbia 36375

Arroyo (4)
Backroads (5)
Beauty In The River (1)
Black Sky (1,6)
Breakaway (From Those Chains) (4)
Chicken Train (1,6)
Cobblestone Mountain (3)
Colorado Song (1)
Commercial Success (1)
Country Girl (1)
Crazy Lovin' (5)
E.E. Lawson (2)
Empty Cup (7)

Fly Away Home (4,6)
Following The Way That I Feel (5,6)
Fool's Gold (7)
Fox, The (5)
From Time To Time (3)
Giving It All To The Wind (5)
Gypsy Forest (3)
Homemade Wine (4,6)
Horse Trader (6)
If I Only Knew (3) 65
If You Wanna Get To Heaven (1,6) 25
It Couldn't Be Better (2)

It Probably Always Will (2)
It'll Shine When It Shines (2)
It's All Over Now (6)
It's How You Think (4)
Jackie Blue (2,6) 3
Jump At The Chance (7)
Kansas You Fooler (2)
Keep On Churnin' (3)
Leatherwood (3)
Look Away (2)
Love Makes The Lover (5)
Lovin' You (7)
Lowlands (2)
Moon On The Rise (5)

Mountain Range (4)
Mr. Powell (3)
Noah (4,6)
Oh, Darlin' (7)
Ooh Boys (It's Hot) (6)
Out On The Sea (3)
Red Plum (4)
River To The Sun (5,6)
Road To Glory (1)
Rosalie (7)
Runnin' Out (7)
Sailin' Around The World (7)
Satisfied Mind (6)
Snowbound (5)

Southern Cross (3)
Spaceship Orion (1)
Standin' On The Rock (1)
Stinghead (5)
Take You Tonight (7) 67
Thin Ice (3)
Tidal Wave (2)
True Believer (5)
Tuff Luck (7)
Walkin' Down The Road (2,6)
Watermill (4)
What's Happened Along In My Life (2)
Whippoorwill (3)

Within Without (1)
You Know Like I Know (4,6) 74
You Made It Right (2)

OZONE
Nashville-based band produced by Teena Marie: Thomas Bumpass, William White, Ray Woodard, Greg Hargrove, Benny Wallace, Jimmy Stewart, Charles Glenn and Paul Hines. Stewart, Wallace and Glenn had been in the Endeavors.

| 9/4/82 | 152 | 6 | | Li'l Suzy .... | $8 | Motown 6011 |

Aerobic Jamercise
Ain't Got Far To Go
Comin' After Your Love

Funkin' On The One (Make Your Body Move)
I'm Not Easy

Let The Ozone Take Your Mind
Li'l Suzy

Shake It Down
She's A Ten

You'll Never Know How Much (I Love You)

P

PABLO CRUISE
San Francisco pop-rock quartet formed in 1973: Dave Jenkins (vocals, guitar), Bud Cockrell (member of It's A Beautiful Day; vocals, bass), Cory Lerios (keyboards) and Stephen Price (drums). Cockrell replaced by Bruce Day in 1977. John Pierce replaced Day, and guitarist Angelo Rossi joined in 1980.

8/16/75	174	4		1 Pablo Cruise	$10	A&M 4528
4/17/76+	139	13		2 Lifeline	$10	A&M 4575
3/5/77	19	46	▲	3 A Place In The Sun	$8	A&M 4625

DEBUT DATE	PEAK POS	WKS CHR	GOLD	ARTIST — Album Title	$	Label & Number

PABLO CRUISE — Cont'd

DEBUT DATE	PEAK POS	WKS CHR	GOLD	ARTIST — Album Title	$	Label & Number
6/17/78	6	43 ▲	4	Worlds Away	$8	A&M 4697
11/17/79	39	17	5	Part Of The Game	$8	A&M 3712
7/18/81	34	18	6	Reflector	$8	A&M 3726

Always Be Together (4)
Atlanta June (3)
Can't You Hear The Music? (3)
Cool Love (6) *13*
Crystal (2)
Denny (1)
Don't Believe It (2)
Don't Let The Magic Disappear (6)

Don't Want To Live Without It (4) *21*
Drums In The Night (6)
El Verano (3)
Family Man (4)
For Another Town (5)
Givin' It Away (5)
Good Ship Pablo Cruise (2)
How Many Tears? (4)
I Go To Rio (4) *46*

I Just Wanna Believe (3)
(I Think) It's Finally Over (2)
I Want You Tonight (5) *19*
In My Own Quiet Way (1)
Inside/Outside (6)
Island Woman (1)
Jenny (6)
Lifeline (2)
Lonely Nights (5)
Look To The Sky (2)

Love Will Find A Way (4) *6*
Never Had A Love (3) *87*
Never See That Girl Enough (2)
Not Tonight (1)
Ocean Breeze (1)
One More Night (6)
Paradise (Let Me Take You Into) (6)
Part Of The Game (5)

Place In The Sun (3) *42*
Raging Fire (3)
Rock N' Roller (1)
Runnin' (4)
Sailing To Paradise (4)
Sleeping Dogs (1)
Slip Away (6) *75*
Tearin' Down My Mind (2)
Tell Me That You Love Me (5)
That's When (6)

This Time (6)
Tonight My Love (3)
What Does It Take (1)
Whatcha Gonna Do? (3) *6*
When Love Is At Your Door (5)
Who Knows (2)
Worlds Away (4)
You're Out To Lose (4)
Zero To Sixty In Five (2)

PACIFIC GAS & ELECTRIC

West Coast blues-rock quintet — Charles Allen, lead singer (died on 5/7/90 [age 48] in Los Angeles). Through 1970 included guitarists Glenn Schwartz and Tom Marshall, bassist Brent Block and drummer Frank Cook. Allen spearheaded a new lineup in 1971, group name shortened to PG&E.

DEBUT DATE	PEAK POS	WKS CHR	GOLD	ARTIST — Album Title	$	Label & Number
2/1/69	159	12	1	Get It On	$15	Power 701
9/13/69	91	8	2	Pacific Gas And Electric	$12	Columbia 9900
7/4/70	101	11	3	Are You Ready	$12	Columbia 1017
8/28/71+	182	8	4	PG&E	$12	Columbia 30362

PG&E

Are You Ready? (3) *14*
Blackberry (3)
Bluesbuster (2)
Cry, Cry, Cry (1)
Death Row #172 (2,4)
Elvira (2)
Hawg For You (3)

Hunter (1)
Jelly, Jelly (1)
Live Love (1)
Long Handled Shovel (1)
Love, Love, Love, Love, Love (3)
Miss Lucy (2)

Mother, Why Do You Cry? (3)
Motor City's Burning (1)
My Women (2)
One More River To Cross (4)
PG&E Suite Medley (2)
Recall (4)
Redneck (2)

Rock And Roller's Lament (4)
Screamin' (3)
See The Monkey Run (4)
She's Long And She's Tall (3)
Short Dogs And Englishmen (4)
Staggolee (3)

Stormy Times (1)
Thank God For You Baby (4) *97*
Time Has Come (To Make Your Peace) (4)
Wade In The Water (1)

When A Man Loves A Woman (3)
When The Sun Shines (4)

PAGE, Gene

Keyboardist/arranger/conductor from Los Angeles. Staff arranger with Reprise and Motown Records.

DEBUT DATE	PEAK POS	WKS CHR	GOLD	ARTIST — Album Title	$	Label & Number
2/1/75	156	4		Hot City	[I] $10	Atlantic 18111

produced by Barry White

All Our Dreams Are Coming True
Cream Corner (Get What You Want)
Don't Play That Song
Gene's Theme
I Am Living In A World Of Gloom
Jungle Eyes
Satin Soul
She's My Main Squeeze
To The Bone

PAGE, Jimmy

Prominent guitarist. Born on 1/9/44 in London. Member of The Yardbirds, 1966 to July 1968. In October 1968, formed The New Yardbirds, which evolved into rock supergroup Led Zepplin. Page produced all of their music. Joined The Honeydrippers in 1984, also co-founded The Firm with vocalist Paul Rodgers.

DEBUT DATE	PEAK POS	WKS CHR	GOLD	ARTIST — Album Title	$	Label & Number
4/3/82	50	10		1 Death Wish II	[S-I] $8	Swan Song 8511

9 of 12 tracks are instrumental; vocals by Chris Farlowe and Gordon Edwards

DEBUT DATE	PEAK POS	WKS CHR	GOLD	ARTIST — Album Title	$	Label & Number
7/9/88	26	20	●	2 Outrider	$8	Geffen 24188

vocals by Chris Farlowe, Robert Plant and John Miles

Big Band, Sax, And Violence (1)
Blues Anthem (2)
Carole's Theme (1)

Chase, The (1)
City Sirens (1)
Emerald Eyes (2)
Hotel Rats And Photostats (1)

Hummingbird (1)
Hypnotizing Ways (Oh Mamma) (1)
Jam Sandwich (1)

Jill's Theme (1)
Liquid Mercury (2)
Only One (2)
Prelude (1)

Prison Blues (2)
Release, The (1)
Shadow In The City (1)
Wanna Make Love (2)

Wasting My Time (2)
Who's To Blame (1)
Writes Of Winter (2)

PAGE, Patti

Born Clara Ann Fowler on 11/8/27 in Muskogee, Oklahoma. One of 11 children. Raised in Tulsa. On radio KTUL with Al Klauser & His Oklahomans, as "Ann Fowler," late 1940s. Another singer was billed as "Patti Page" for the Page Milk Company show on KTUL. When she left, Fowler took her place and name. With the Jimmy Joy band in 1947. On *Breakfast Club*, Chicago radio in 1947; signed by Mercury Records. Used multi-voice effect on records from 1947. Own TV series *The Patti Page Show*, 1955-58 and *The Big Record*, 1957-58. In the 1960 film *Elmer Gantry*.

DEBUT DATE	PEAK POS	WKS CHR	GOLD	ARTIST — Album Title	$	Label & Number
11/24/56	18	2		1 Manhattan Tower	$25	Mercury 20226

a version of Gordon Jenkins' musical narrative

DEBUT DATE	PEAK POS	WKS CHR	GOLD	ARTIST — Album Title	$	Label & Number
9/1/62	115	5		2 Golden Hits Of The Boys	$20	Mercury 20712

Patti's versions of male vocalist hits

DEBUT DATE	PEAK POS	WKS CHR	GOLD	ARTIST — Album Title	$	Label & Number
9/21/63	83	6		3 Say Wonderful Things	$15	Columbia 8849
5/22/65	27	26		4 Hush, Hush, Sweet Charlotte	$15	Columbia 9153
7/27/68	168	6		5 Gentle On My Mind	$15	Columbia 9666

...m I That Easy To Forget (5)
Big Bad John (2)
Black Is The Color Of My True Love's Hair (4)
Call Me Irresponsible (3)
Can't Get Used To Losing You (3)
Can't Help Falling In Love (4)
Croce Di Oro (Cross Of Gold) (4) *16*
Danny Boy (4)
Days Of Wine And Roses (3)

Don't Be Cruel (To A Heart That's True) (2)
Don't Worry (2)
End Of The World (3)
Fly Me To The Moon (In Other Words) (4)
Four Walls (5)
Gentle On My Mind (5) *66*
Georgia On My Mind (3)
Good Life (3)
Green Green Grass Of Home (5)
Green Leaves Of Summer (4)

Happiness Cocktail (1)
Have A Little Faith (5)
Honey (I Miss You) (5)
Hush, Hush, Sweet Charlotte (4) *8*
I Almost Lost My Mind (3)
I Wanna Be Around (3)
I'm Walkin' (2)
If And When (3)
Indian Giver (2)
It's Just A Matter Of Time (2)
Jamaica Farewell (4)
Learnin' My Latin (1)

Little Green Apples (5) *96*
Longing To Hold You Again (4)
Love Letters (3)
Mack The Knife (2)
March Marches On (1)
Married I Can Always Get (1)
Moon River (3)
Never Leave Me (1)
New York's My Home (1)
Once Upon A Dream (1)
Our Day Will Come (3)
Party (Noah) (1)

Poor Little Fool (2)
Put Your Head On My Shoulder (2)
Release Me (5)
Repeat After Me (1) *53*
Say Wonderful Things (3) *81*
Scarlet Ribbons (For Her Hair) (4)
Skip A Rope (5)
Take Me To Your World (5)
This Close To The Dawn (1)
This House (5)

Try To Remember (4)
Twist, The (2)
Who's Gonna Shoe My Pretty Little Feet (4)
(You've Got) Personality (2)

PAGE, Tommy

Born on 5/24/69 in West Caldwell, New Jersey.

DEBUT DATE	PEAK POS	WKS CHR	GOLD	ARTIST — Album Title	$	Label & Number
5/6/89	166	5		1 Tommy Page	$8	Sire 25740
3/24/90	38	23		2 Paintings In My Mind	$12	Sire 26148
6/15/91	192	2		3 From The Heart	$12	Sire 26583

African Sunset (1)
Can't Get You Outta My Mind (3)

Don't Give Up On Love (2)
Don't Walk Away (2)
Hard To Be Normal (1)

I Break Down (2)
I Love London (1)

I Still Believe In You And Me (3)
I Think I'm In Love (1)

I'll Be Your Everything (2) *1*
I'll Never Forget You (3)

Just Before (I Was Gonna Say I Love You) (2)
Love Takes Over (1)

DEBUT DATE	PEAK POS	WKS CHR	G O L D	ARTIST — Album Title	$	Label & Number

PAGE, Tommy — Cont'd

Madly In Love (3)
Making My Move (1)
Minetta Lane (1)
My Shining Star (3)

Never Gonna Fall In Love Again (3)
Paintings In My Mind (2)
Shoulder To Cry On (1) **29**

Till The End Of Time (2)
Turn On The Radio (2)
Turning Me On (1)
Under The Rainbow (3)

When I Dream Of You (2) **42**
Whenever You Close Your Eyes (3)

Written All Over My Heart (3)
You Are My Heaven (3)
You're The Best Thing (That Ever Happened To Me) (2)

Zillion Kisses (1)

PAIGE, Kevin
White soul-pop singer from Memphis.

| 9/23/89 | 107 | 31 | | Kevin Paige | $8 | Chrysalis 21683 |

Anything I Want 29
Believe In Yourself

Black And White
Don't Shut Me Out 18

Hypnotize
I Realize

Love Of The World
Stop Messin' With Me

Touch Of Paradise

(You Put Me In) Another World

PALM BEACH BAND BOYS, The
Vocal trio led by Roger Rigney and arranged by Billy Mure.

| 1/28/67 | 149 | 1 | | Winchester Cathedral | $10 | RCA 3734 |

Bend It
Boo-Hoo
Gypsy Caravan

I Don't Want To Set The World On Fire

I'm Gonna Sit Right Down And Write Myself A Letter
Ida, Sweet As Apple Cider

It Looks Like Rain in Cherry Blossom Lane
Let A Smile Be Your Umbrella

Little Bit Independent
Winchester Cathedral

★★256★★ PALMER, Robert
Born Alan Palmer on 1/19/49 in Batley, England and raised on the Mediterranean island of Malta. Formed first band, Mandrake Paddle Steamer, in 1969. Lead singer of short-lived supergroup The Power Station.

6/14/75	107	15		1 Sneakin' Sally Through The Alley	$8	Island 9294
11/22/75	136	8		2 Pressure Drop	$8	Island 9372
10/23/76	68	16		3 Some People Can Do What They Like	$8	Island 9420
4/1/78	45	25		4 Double Fun	$8	Island 9476
7/21/79	19	24		5 Secrets	$8	Island 9544
10/11/80	59	17		6 Clues	$8	Island 9595
5/15/82	148	5		7 Maybe It's Live	[L] $8	Island 9665
				6 of 10 tracks are live		
4/30/83	112	19		8 Pride	$8	Island 90065
11/23/85+	8	90	▲	9 Riptide	$8	Island 90471
7/16/88	13	44	▲	10 Heavy Nova	$8	EMI-Man. 48057
11/25/89+	79	17		11 "Addictions" Volume I	[G] $8	Island 91318
12/1/90	88	28		12 Don't Explain	$12	EMI 93935
				guest appearances by UB40, Steve Stevens and Brent Bourgeois		
11/14/92	173	1		13 Ridin' High	$12	EMI 98923
				features several classics by Cole Porter, Gus Kahn and others		

Addicted To Love (9,11) **1**
Aeroplane (12,13)
Baby It's Cold Outside (13)
Back In My Arms (2)
Bad Case Of Loving You (Doctor, Doctor) (5,7,11) **14**
Best Of Both Worlds (4,7)
Between Us (10)
Blackmail (1)
Can We Still Be Friends (5) **52**
Casting A Spell (10)
Chance (13)
Change His Ways (10)
Come Over (4)
Dance For Me (8)
Deadline (8)
Discipline Of Love (Why Did You Do It) (9) **82**
Disturbing Behaviour (10)
Do Nothin' Till You Hear From Me (13)
Don't Explain (12,13)

Dreams To Remember (12)
Early In The Morning (10) **19**
Every Kinda People (4,7,11) **16**
Fine Time (2)
Flesh Wound (9)
Found You Now (6)
From A Whisper To A Scream (1)
Get It Through Your Heart (9)
Get Outside (1)
Give Me An Inch Girl (5)
Goody Goody (13)
Gotta Get A Grip On You (Part II) (3)
Happiness (12)
Hard Head (3,13)
Have Mercy (8)
Here With You Tonight (2)
Hey Julia (1)
History (12)
Honeysuckle Rose (13)

Housework (12)
How Much Fun (1)
Hyperactive (9) **33**
I Didn't Mean To Turn You On (9) **2**
I Dream Of Wires (6)
I'll Be Your Baby Tonight (12)
In Walks Love Again (5)
It Could Happen To You (10)
It's Not Difficult (8)
Jealous (3)
Johnny And Mary (6,11)
Keep In Touch (3)
Light-Years (12)
Looking For Clues (6,11)
Love Can Run Faster (4)
(Love Is) The Tender Trap (13)
Love Me Or Leave Me (13)
Love Stop (5)
Man Smart, Woman Smarter (3) **63**
Maybe It's You (7)
Mean Old World (5)

Mercy Mercy Me (The Ecology)/I Want You (12) **16**
Mess Around (12)
More Than Ever (10)
Night People (4)
No Not Much (13)
Not A Second Time (6)
Not A Word (12)
Off The Bone (3)
One Last Look (3)
People Will Say We're In Love (12)
Pressure Drop (2)
Pride (8,11)
Remember To Remember (5)
Ridin' High (13)
Riptide (12)
Riverboat (2)
Sailing Shoes (1)
Say You Will (8)
She Makes My Day (10)
Si Chatouillieux (7)
Silver Gun (8)

Simply Irresistible (10,11) **2**
Sneakin' Sally Through The Alley (1,7)
Some Guys Have All The Luck (7,11)
Some Like It Hot (Power Station) (11) **6**
Some People Can Do What They Like (3)
Spanish Moon (3)
Style Kills (7,11)
Sulky Girl (6)
Sweet Lies (11) **94**
Tell Me I'm Not Dreaming (5,10) **60**
Through It All There's You (1)
Top 40 (12)
Trick Bag (9)
Trouble (2)
Under Suspicion (5)
Want You More (8,13)
What A Little Moonlight Can Do (13)
What Can You Bring Me (3)

What Do You Care (6,7)
What You Waiting For (8)
What's It Take? (5,7,11)
Where Can It Go? (1)
Which Of Us Is The Fool (2)
Witchcraft (13)
Woke Up Laughing (6,11)
Woman You're Wonderful (5)
Work To Make It Work (2)
You Are In My System (8) **78**
You Can Have It (Take My Heart) (8)
You Can't Get Enough Of A Good Thing (12)
You Really Got Me (4)
You're Amazing (12) **28**
You're Gonna Get What's Coming (4)
You're My Thrill (12,13)
You're So Desirable (13)
Your Mother Should Have Told You (12)

PANTERA
Heavy-metal band: Philip Anselmo (vocals), Diamond Darrell (guitar), Rex (bass) and Vinnie Paul (drums). Darrell and Paul are brothers. Group name is Spanish for Panther.

| 3/14/92 | 44 | 48↑ | | Vulgar Display Of Power | $12 | Atco 91758 |

By Demons Be Driven
Fucking Hostile

Hollow
Live In A Hole

Mouth For War
New Level

No Good (Attack The Radical) (3)
Regular People (Conceit)

Rise
This Love

Walk

PAPER LACE
English quintet formed in 1969: Phil Wright (b: 4/9/48; lead singer, drums), Cliff Fish (bass), Michael Vaughan (lead guitar) and Chris Morris (guitar). Morris later replaced by Carlo Santanna.

| 9/7/74 | 124 | 8 | | Paper Lace | $12 | Mercury 1008 |

Billy-Don't Be A Hero 96
Black-Eyed Boys 41
Cheek To Cheek

Dreams Are Ten A Penny
Happy Birthday Sweet Sixteen
Hitchin' A Ride
I Did What I Did For Maria
Love Song

Love - You're A Long Time Coming
Mary In The Morning

Night Chicago Died 1
Sealed With A Kiss

PARAMOR, Norrie, His Strings and Orchestra
Born in England in 1914; died on 9/9/79 (age 65). Conductor/composer/arranger. A&R man for EMI Columbia; guided the careers of Cliff Richard, Frank Ifield and many others.

| 9/8/56 | 18 | 3 | | In London, Love | [I] $15 | Capitol Int. 10025 |

All The Things You Are
Dearly Beloved

Deep Purple
Embraceable You

I'll Get By
Nearness Of You

Someone To Watch Over Me
Stairway To The Stars

Stardust
Stars Fell On Alabama

Touch Of Your Lips
Very Thought Of You

DEBUT DATE	PEAK POS	WKS CHR	GOLD	ARTIST — Album Title	$	Label & Number

PARIS
British rock trio: Bob Welch (ex-Fleetwood Mac; guitar), Glenn Cornick (ex-Jethro Tull; bass) and Thom Mooney (ex-Nazz; drums). Hunt Sales (later with Tin Machine) replaced Mooney in 1976.

2/7/76	**103**	9		1 Paris	**$10**	Capitol 11464
9/11/76	**152**	6		2 Big Towne, 2061	**$10**	Capitol 11560

Beautiful Youth (1)	Breathless (1)	Narrow Gate (1)	Outlaw Game (2)	Rock Of Ages (1)
Big Towne, 2061 (2)	Heart Of Stone (2)	Nazarene (1)	Pale Horse, Pale Rider (2)	Slave Trader (2)
Black Book (1)	Janie (2)	New Orleans (1)	Red Rain (1)	Solitaire (1)
Blue Robin (2)	Money Love (2)	1 In 10 (2)	Religion (1)	Starcage (1)

PARIS
San Francisco-based male rapper. Graduated in 1990 from the University of California with an economics degree.

12/22/90+	**158**	8		1 The Devil Made Me Do It	**$12**	Tommy Boy 1030
				CD includes 4 bonus tracks unavailable on vinyl LP (2 of which are unavailable on cassette)		
12/12/92	**182**	3		2 Sleeping With The Enemy	**$12**	Scarface 100
				CD includes bonus track		

Assata's Song (2)	Check It Out Ch'All (2)	Ebony (2)	House Niggas Bleed Too (2)	Panther Power (1)
Break The Grip Of Shame	Coffee, Donuts & Death (2)	Enema, The (2)	I Call Him Mad (1)	Rise (2)
[includes 2 versions] (1)	Conspiracy Of Silence (2)	Escape From Babylon (1)	Long Hot Summer (2)	Scarface Groove (1)
Brutal (1)	Days Of Old (2)	Funky Lil' Party (2)	Make Way For A Panther (2)	Sleeping With The Enemy (2)
Bush Killa [includes 2	Devil Made Me Do It	Guerrillas In The Mist (2)	Mellow Madness (1)	Thinka 'Bout It (2)
versions] (2)	[includes 2 versions] (1)	Hate That Hate Made (1)	On The Prowl (1)	This Is A Test (1)

Warning (1)
Wretched (1)

PARIS, Mica
Mica (pronounced: MEE-sha) was born on 4/27/69 in London. Real name: Michelle Wallen.

5/13/89	**86**	23		So Good	**$8**	Island 90970

Breathe Life Into Me	Great Impersonation	**My One Temptation 97**	So Good
Don't Give Me Up	I'd Hate To Love You	Nothing Hits Your Heart	Sway (Dance The Blues
	Like Dreamers Do	Like Soul Music	Away)

Where Is The Love

★★423★★ PARKER, Graham
Born on 11/18/50 in East London. Pub-rock vocalist/guitarist/songwriter. The Rumour featured guitarists Brinsley Schwarz and Martin Belmont, bassist Andrew Bodnar, keyboardist Bob Andrews (left by 1980) and drummer Stephen Goulding.

1/29/77	**169**	7		1 Heat Treatment	**$8**	Mercury 1117
				GRAHAM PARKER AND THE RUMOUR:		
11/5/77	**125**	5		2 Stick To Me	**$8**	Mercury 3706
7/1/78	**149**	3		3 The Parkerilla .... [L]	**$10**	Mercury 100 [2]
				sides 1,2 & 3: live; side 4: 12" single studio recording		
4/14/79	**40**	24		4 Squeezing Out Sparks	**$8**	Arista 4223
5/31/80	**40**	15		5 The Up Escalator	**$8**	Arista 9517
				Bruce Springsteen sings on one track		
				GRAHAM PARKER:		
4/10/82	**51**	16		6 Another Grey Area	**$8**	Arista 9589
8/20/83	**59**	14		7 The Real Macaw	**$8**	Arista 8023
4/20/85	**57**	21		8 Steady Nerves	**$8**	Elektra 60388
				GRAHAM PARKER AND THE SHOT		
5/28/88	**77**	19		9 The Mona Lisa's Sister	**$8**	RCA 8316
2/24/90	**165**	9		10 Human Soul	**$12**	RCA 9876
3/23/91	**131**	8		11 Struck By Lightning	**$12**	BMG 3013

And It Shook Me (11)	Dark Side Of The Bright	I Don't Know (9)	My Love's Strong (10)	Soultime (10)
Anniversary (7)	Lights (7)	I Was Wrong (10)	New York Shuffle (2,3)	Sounds Like Chains (7)
Back Door Love (1)	Devil's Sidewalk (5)	I'm Gonna Tear Your	No Holding Back (5)	Stick To Me (2)
Back In Time (9)	Discovering Japan (4)	Playhouse Down (5)	No More Excuses (6)	Strong Winds (11)
Back To Schooldays (1)	Don't Ask Me Questions (3)	I'm Just Your Man (9)	Nobody Hurts You (4)	Stupefaction (5)
Beating Of Another Heart (5)	Don't Get Excited (4)	It's All Worth Nothing Alone	OK Hieronymus (9)	Success (9)
Beyond A Joke (7)	Don't Let It Break You Down	(6)	Over The Border (To	Sugar Gives You Energy (10)
Big Fat Zero (6)	(9)	Jolie Jolie (5)	America) (11)	Sun Is Gonna Shine Again
Big Man On Paper (10)	Empty Lives (5)	Just Like A Man (7)	Paralyzed (5)	(11)
Black Honey (1)	Endless Night (5)	Kid With The Butterfly Net	Passion Is No Ordinary	Take Everything (8)
Black Lincoln Continental (8)	Everyone's Hand Is On The	(11)	Word (4)	Temporary Beauty (6)
Blue Highways (9)	Switch (8)	Lady Doctor (3)	Passive Resistance (7)	Ten Girls Ago (11)
Brand New Book (11)	Everything Goes (10)	Last Couple On The Dance	Pourin' It All Out (1)	Thankless Task (6)
Break Them Down (8)	Fear Not (6)	Floor (7)	Problem Child (2)	That's What They All Say (1)
Call Me Your Doctor (10)	Fools' Gold (1,3)	Life Gets Better (7) 94	Protection (4)	That's Where She Ends Up
Can't Waste A Minute (6)	Get Started, Start A Fire (9)	Little Miss Understanding	Raid, The (2)	(9)
Canned Laughter (8)	Girl Isn't Ready (9)	(10)	Saturday Nite Is Dead (4)	They Murdered The Clown
Children And Dogs (11)	Glass Jaw (7)	Local Girls (4)	She Wants So Many Things	(11)
Clear Head (2)	Green Monkeys (10)	Locked Into Green (8)	(11)	Thunder And Rain (2)
Crying For Attention (6)	Guardian Angels (11)	Love Gets You Twisted (4)	Silly Thing (3)	(Too Late) The Smart Bomb
Cupid (9)	Gypsy Blood (3)	Love Without Greed (5)	Slash And Burn (10)	(7)
Daddy's A Postman (10)	Heat In Harlem (2,3)	Lunatic Fringe (8)	Something You're Going	Turned Up Too Late (1)
Dancing For Money (10)	Heat Treatment (1,3)	Maneuvers (5)	Through (1)	Under The Mask Of
	Help Me Shake It (1)	Mighty Rivers (8)	Soul On Ice (2)	Happiness (9)
	Hotel Chambermaid (1)	Miracle A Minute (7)	Soul Shoes (3)	Waiting For The UFO's (4)

Wake Up (Next To You)
(8) 39
Watch The Moon Come
Down (2,3)
Weekend's Too Short (8)
Weeping Statues (11)
When I Was King (11)
When You Do That To Me (8)
Wrapping Paper (11)
You Can't Be Too Strong (4)
You Can't Take Love For
Granted (7)
You Got The World (Right
Where You Want It) (10)
You Hit The Spot (6)

★★308★★ PARKER, Ray Jr./Raydio
Born on 5/1/54 in Detroit. Prominent session guitarist in California; worked with Stevie Wonder, Barry White and others. Formed band Raydio in 1977 with Arnell Carmichael, Jerry Knight, Larry Tolbert, Darren Carmichael and Charles Fearing. Parker went solo in 1982. Knight later recorded in duo Ollie & Jerry.

				RAYDIO:		
2/11/78	**27**	23	●	1 Raydio..	**$8**	Arista 4163
4/14/79	**45**	30	●	2 Rock On	**$8**	Arista 4212
				RAY PARKER JR. & RAYDIO:		
4/12/80	**33**	21	●	3 Two Places At The Same Time	**$8**	Arista 9515

DEBUT DATE	PEAK POS	WKS CHR	GOLD	ARTIST — Album Title	$	Label & Number
				PARKER, Ray Jr./Raydio — Cont'd		
4/18/81	13	26	●	4 A Woman Needs Love	$8	Arista 9543
				RAY PARKER JR.:		
4/24/82	11	27	●	5 The Other Woman..	$8	Arista 9590
12/18/82+	51	22		6 Greatest Hits .... [G]	$8	Arista 9612
11/26/83+	45	23		7 Woman Out Of Control	$8	Arista 8087
12/15/84+	60	15	●	8 Chartbusters .... [G]	$8	Arista 8266
10/26/85	65	13		9 Sex And The Single Man.............................	$8	Arista 8280
10/10/87	86	9		10 After Dark	$8	Geffen 24124

After Dark (10)
After Midnite (10)
All In The Way You Get Down (4)
Bad Boy (6) **35**
Betcha You Can't Love Me Just Once (1)
Can't Keep From Cryin' (3)
Christmas Time Is Here (8)
Electronic Lover (7)
Everybody Makes Mistakes (3)
Everybody Wants Someone (9)
For Those Who Like To Groove (3,6)
Get Down (1)

Ghostbusters (8) **1**
Girls Are More Fun (9) **34**
Goin' Thru School And Love (2)
Good Time Baby (9)
Honey I'm A Star (2)
Honey I'm Rich (1)
Hot Stuff (2)
I Don't Think That Man Should Sleep Alone (10) **68**
I Don't Wanna Know (7)
I Love Your Daughter (10)
I Still Can't Get Over Loving You (7,8) **12**
I'm A Dog (9)
I'm In Love (9)

I've Been Diggin You (8)
In The Heat Of The Night (7)
Is This A Love Thing (1)
It's Our Own Affair (9)
It's Time To Party Now (3)
It's Your Night (4)
Jack And Jill (1,6) **8**
Jamie (8) **14**
Just Havin' Fun (5)
Let Me Go (5,6) **38**
Let's Get Off (5)
Let's Go All The Way (1)
Little Bit Of You (3)
Lovin' You (10)
Me (1)
Men Have Feelings Too (9)

More Than One Way To Love A Woman (2)
N2U2 (7)
Old Pro (4)
One Sided Love Affair (9)
Other Woman (5,6,8) **4**
Over You (10)
Past, The (10)
People Next Door (6)
Perfect Lovers (10)
Rock On (2)
Sex And The Single Man (9)
She Still Feels The Need (7)
So Into You (4)
Stay The Night (5)
Still In The Groove (4)

Stop, Look Before You Love (5)
Streetlove (5)
That Old Song (4,6) **21**
Tonight's The Night (3)
Two Places At The Same Time (3,6) **30**
Until The Morning Comes (3)
What You Waitin' For (2)
When You're In Need Of Love (2)
Woman Needs Love (Just Like You Do) (4,0,8) **4**
Woman Out Of Control (7,8)
You Can't Change That (2,6) **9**

You Can't Fight What You Feel (4)
You Make My Nature Dance (10)
You Need This (To Satisfy That) (1)
You Shoulda Kept A Spare (10)

PARKS, Michael
Born on 4/4/38 in Corona, California. Film and TV actor/singer. In films *The Man Who Came To Dinner*, *Night Must Fall*, *Wild Seed* and *Back In Town*. Starred in the 1963 TV series *Channing*; portrayed Jim Bronson in the 1969 TV series *Then Came Bronson*.

11/8/69+	35	46		1 Closing The Gap	$12	MGM 4646
5/23/70	24	21		2 Long Lonesome Highway	$12	MGM 4662
10/10/70	71	8		3 Blue	$12	MGM 4717
3/13/71	195	1		4 Lost And Found	$12	Verve 5079

Beautiful Means You (3)
Big "T" Water (2)
Born To Lose (3)
California's Fine (2)
Cold, Cold Heart (3)
Farther Along (medley) (4)
I Can't Help It (If I'm Still In Love With You) (3)
I Come To The Garden (3)
I Let You Take Advantage (4)

I Think Of You (2)
I Was Born In Kentucky (4)
I'm Lonely And Blue (4)
I'm So Lonesome I Could Cry (medley) (4)
It's You (medley) (4)
Long Lonesome Highway (2) **20**
Look Down That Lonesome Road (4)

Lost And Found (4)
Midnight Wind (1)
Mountain High (2)
My Little Buckaroo (1)
My Melancholy Baby (2)
No One To Cry To (3)
Oklahoma Hills (1)
Pretty Piece Of Paper (1)
Re-Enlistment Blues (2)
Ride 'Em Cowboy (1)

Sally (Was A Gentle Woman) (3)
San Antonio Rose (1)
Save A Little, Spend A Little (Give A Little Away) (3)
Sneakin' In The Back Door Of Love (1)
Softly And Tenderly (1)
Soldier's Last Letter (1)
Statue Of A Fool (4)

Summer Days (2)
Sunshine Showers (2)
Sweet Misery (4)
There's Been A Change In Me (3)
Tie Me To Your Apron Strings Again (1)
Treasure Untold (1)
Turn Around Little Mama (4)
Wayfarin' Stranger (1)

When I've Learned (medley) (4)
Won't You Ride In My Little Red Wagon (1)
Yonder Comes The Blues (2)

★★387★★ PARLIAMENT
The funk group Funkadelic, which evolved from the Detroit-based group The Parliaments, recorded under the name Parliament for Invictus in 1971. The original members of The Parliaments, led by producer/singer/songwriter George Clinton, founded the corporation "A Parliafunkadelicament Thang." By the time Parliament signed to Casablanca in 1974, Clinton had reorganized the New York-based corporation to include a varying roster of nearly 40 musicians which recorded under the names of Parliament and Funkadelic. Three original members of The Parliaments split from Clinton in 1977. Parliament/Funkadelic spawned various offshoots: Bootsy's Rubber Band, The Brides Of Funkenstein, Parlet and the P.Funk All Stars.

5/3/75	91	18		1 Chocolate City	$15	Casablanca 7014
2/21/76	13	37	▲	2 Mothership Connection...............................	$15	Casablanca 7022
10/16/76	20	22	●	3 The Clones Of Dr. Funkenstein	$15	Casablanca 7034
5/21/77	29	19	●	4 Parliament Live/P. Funk Earth Tour ....[L]	$20	Casablanca 7053 [2]
12/24/77+	13	34	▲	5 Funkentelechy Vs. The Placebo Syndrome	$15	Casablanca 7084
12/16/78+	23	18	●	6 Motor-Booty Affair	$15	Casablanca 7125
12/22/79+	44	19	●	7 Gloryhallastoopid (Or Pin The Tale On The Funky)...	$15	Casablanca 7195
1/10/81	61	7		8 Trombipulation	$15	Casablanca 7249

Agony Of Defeat (8)
Aqua Boogie (A Psychoalphadiscobetabioaquadooloop) (6) **89**
Big Bang Theory (7)
Big Footin' (1)
Black Hole, Theme From (7)
Body Language (8)
Bop Gun (Endangered Species) (5)
Children Of Production (3,4)
Chocolate City (1) **94**
Colour Me Funky (7)
Crush It (8)
Deep (6)
Do That Stuff (3,4)

Dr. Funkenstein (3,4)
Dr. Funkenstein's Supergroovalisticprosifunksotication Medley (4)
Everything Is On The One (3)
Fantasy Is Reality (4)
Flash Light (5) **16**
Freeze (Sizzaleenmean) (7)
Funkentelechy (5)
Funkin' For Fun (3)
Gamin' On Ya (3,4)
Get Off Your Ass And Jam (medley) (4)
Getten' To Know You (3)

Give Up The Funk ..see:
Tear The Roof Off The Sucker (Give Up The Funk)
(Gloryhallastoopid) Pin The Tale On The Funky (7)
Handcuffs (2)
I Misjudged You (1)
I've Been Watching You (Move Your Sexy Body) (3)
If It Don't Fit (Don't Force It) (1)
Landing (Of The Holy Mothership) (4)
Let Me Be (1)
Let's Play House (8)
Liquid Sunshine (6)

Long Way Around (8)
May We Bang You? (7)
Mothership Connection (Star Child) (2,4)
Motor-Booty Affair (6)
Mr. Wiggles (8)
New Doo Review (8)
Night Of The Thumpasorus Peoples (2,4)
One Of Those Funky Things (6)
P. Funk (Wants To Get Funked Up) (4)
Party People (7)
Peek-A-Groove (8)
Placebo Syndrome (5)

Ride On (1)
Rumpofsteelskin (6)
Side Effects (7)
Sir Nose D'Voidoffunk (Pay Attention - B3M) (5)
Supergroovalisticprosifunkstication (The Thumps Bump) (2)
Swing Down, Sweet Chariot (4)
Tear The Roof Off The Sucker (Give Up The Funk) (2,4) **15**
This Is The Way We Funk With You (4)
Together (1)

Trombipulation (8)
Undisco Kidd (The Girl Is Bad!) (4)
Unfunky UFO (2)
What Comes Funky (1)
Wizard Of Finance (3)
(You're A Fish And I'm A) Water Sign (6)

PARR, John
Singer/songwriter, born in Nottingham, England.

12/15/84+	48	26		John Parr	$8	Atlantic 80180

Don't Leave Your Mark On Me

Heartbreaker
Love Grammar 89

Magical 73
Naughty Naughty 23

Revenge

She's Gonna Love You To Death

Somebody Stole My Thunder
Treat Me Like An Animal

DEBUT DATE	PEAK POS	WKS CHR	GOLD	ARTIST — Album Title	$	Label & Number

★★222★★ PARSONS, Alan, Project

Duo formed in London in 1975. Consisted of producer Alan Parsons (guitar, keyboards) and lyricist Eric Woolfson (vocals, keyboards). Both had worked at the Abbey Road Studios; Parsons was an engineer, Woolfson a songwriter. Parsons engineered Pink Floyd's *Dark Side Of The Moon* and The Beatles' *Abbey Road* albums. Project features varying musicians and vocalists.

DEBUT DATE	PEAK POS	WKS CHR	GOLD	#	Album Title	$	Label & Number
5/15/76	38	46		1	Tales Of Mystery And Imagination - Edgar Allan Poe	$15	20th Century 508
					musical interpretation of Poe's most notable works		
7/16/77	9	54	▲	2	I Robot	$10	Arista 7002
7/1/78	26	25	●	3	Pyramid	$8	Arista 4180
9/15/79	13	27	●	4	Eve	$8	Arista 9504
11/15/80+	13	58	▲	5	The Turn Of A Friendly Card	$8	Arista 9518
6/19/82	7	41	▲	6	Eye In The Sky	$8	Arista 9599
11/19/83	53	29	●	7	The Best Of The Alan Parsons Project [G]	$8	Arista 8193
3/17/84	15	26	●	8	Ammonia Avenue	$8	Arista 8204
3/9/85	46	19		9	Vulture Culture	$8	Arista 8263
2/1/86	43	18		10	Stereotomy	$8	Arista 8384
2/7/87	57	14		11	Gaudi	$8	Arista 8448
					inspired by the life & works of Spanish architect Antonio Gaudi		

Ace Of Swords (medley) (5)
Ammonia Avenue (8)
Beaujolais (10)
Breakdown (2)
Can't Take It With You (3,7)
Cask Of Amontillado (1)
Children Of The Moon (6)
Chinese Whispers (10)
Closer To Heaven (11)
Damned If I Do (4,7) **27**
Dancing On A High Wire (9)
Day After Day (The Show Must Go On) (2)
Days Are Numbers (The Traveller) (9) **71**
Don't Answer Me (8) **15**
Don't Hold Back (4)
Don't Let It Show (2,7) **92**

Dream Within A Dream (1)
Eagle Will Rise Again (3)
Eye In The Sky (6,7) **3**
Fall Of The House Of Usher Medley (1)
Gemini (6)
Genesis Ch. 1. V.32 (2)
Gold Bug (5)
Hawkeye (8)
Hyper-Gamma-Spaces (3)
I Don't Wanna Go Home (5)
I Robot (2)
I Wouldn't Want To Be Like You (2,7) **36**
I'd Rather Be A Man (4)
If I Could Change Your Mind (4)

In The Lap Of The Gods (3)
In The Real World (10)
Inside Looking Out (11)
La Sagrada Familia (11)
Let Me Go Home (8)
Let's Talk About Me (9) **56**
Light Of The World (10)
Limelight (10)
Lucifer (4,7)
Mammagamma (6)
May Be A Price To Pay (5)
Money Talks (11)
Nothing Left To Lose (medley) (5)
Nucleus (2)
Old And Wise (6,7)
One Good Reason (8)
One More River (3)

Paseo De Gracia (11)
Pipeline (8)
Prime Time (8) **34**
Psychobabble (6,7) **57**
Pyramania (3,7)
Raven, The (1) **80**
Same Old Sun (9)
Secret Garden (4)
Separate Lives (9)
Shadow Of A Lonely Man (3)
Silence And I (6)
Since The Last Goodbye (8)
Sirius (6)
Snake Eyes (medley) (5) **67**
Some Other Time (2)
Somebody Out There (9)
Sooner Or Later (9)

Standing On Higher Ground (11)
Step By Step (6)
Stereotomy (10) **82**
Stereotomy Two (10)
(System Of) Doctor Tarr And Professor Fether (1) **37**
Tell-Tale Heart (1)
Time (5,7) **15**
To One In Paradise (1)
Too Late (11)
Total Eclipse (2)
Turn Of A Friendly Card (Part One & Two) (medley) (5)
Urbania (10)
Voice (2)

Voyager (3)
Vulture Culture (9)
What Goes Up (3) **87**
Where's The Walrus? (10)
Winding Me Up (4)
You Don't Believe (7,8) **54**
You Lie Down With Dogs (4)
You Won't Be There (4)
You're Gonna Get Your Fingers Burned (6)

PARSONS, Gram

Born on 11/5/46 in Winter Haven, Florida; died on 9/19/73 of a heroin overdose. Country-rock singer. Member of The Byrds (1968) and the Flying Burrito Brothers (1968-70).

DEBUT DATE	PEAK POS	WKS CHR	GOLD		Album Title	$	Label & Number
2/16/74	195	3			Grievous Angel	$10	Reprise 2171
					with Emmylou Harris		

Brass Buttons
Cash On The Barrelhead (medley)

Hearts On Fire
Hickory Wind (medley)
I Can't Dance

In My Hour Of Darkness
Las Vegas
$1000 Wedding

Love Hurts

Return Of The Grievous Angel

PARTLAND BROTHERS

Canadian duo: Chris (vocals, guitars) and G.P. (vocals, percussion) Partland.

DEBUT DATE	PEAK POS	WKS CHR	GOLD		Album Title	$	Label & Number
6/27/87	146	5			Electric Honey	$8	Manhattan 53050

Best Love
Electric Honey

Heat Up The Feel
One Chance

Outside The City
Reason, The

Soul City 27
That's The Way It Will Be

This One's For You
Walk With Me

★★139★★ PARTON, Dolly

Born on 1/19/46 in Sevier County, Tennessee. Leading female artist of the Country charts. Worked on Knoxville radio show at age 11. First recorded for Gold Band in 1957. To Nashville in 1964. Replaced Norma Jean on the Porter Wagoner TV show, 1967-74. Joined the *Grand Ole Opry* in 1969. Starred in the films *9 To 5*, *The Best Little Whorehouse In Texas*, *Steel Magnolias* and *Straight Talk*. Hosted own TV variety show in 1987. Also see Soundtrack *Best Little Whorehouse In Texas*.

DEBUT DATE	PEAK POS	WKS CHR	GOLD	#	Album Title	$	Label & Number
3/22/69	184	4		1	Just The Two Of Us *	$15	RCA 4039
8/16/69	162	5		2	Always, Always *	$15	RCA 4186
11/22/69	194	2		3	My Blue Ridge Mountain Boy	$15	RCA 4188
4/4/70	137	7		4	Porter Wayne And Dolly Rebecca *	$12	RCA 4305
8/15/70	154	2		5	A Real Live Dolly [L]	$15	RCA 4387
					recorded at her alma mater, Sevier County High School, Tennessee (with Porter Wagoner on 4 songs)		
10/10/70	191	2		6	Once More *	$15	RCA 4388
3/13/71	142	3		7	Two Of A Kind *	$12	RCA 4490
					PORTER WAGONER & DOLLY PARTON		
6/12/71	198	1		8	Joshua	$12	RCA 4507
4/2/77	71	21		9	New Harvest...First Gathering	$8	RCA 2188
10/29/77+	20	47	▲	10	Here You Come Again	$8	RCA 2544
8/12/78	27	34	●	11	Heartbreaker	$8	RCA 2797
6/23/79	40	17	●	12	Great Balls Of Fire	$8	RCA 3361
5/3/80	71	13		13	Dolly Dolly Dolly	$8	RCA 3546
12/6/80+	11	34	●	14	9 to 5 and Odd Jobs	$8	RCA 3852
4/24/82	106	12		15	Heartbreak Express	$8	RCA 4289
10/16/82	77	23	▲	16	Greatest Hits [G]	$8	RCA 4422
6/4/83	127	11		17	Burlap & Satin	$8	RCA 4691
2/18/84	73	14		18	The Great Pretender	$8	RCA 4940
					featuring Dolly's versions of 50's & 60's hits		

DEBUT DATE	PEAK POS	WKS CHR	GOLD	ARTIST — Album Title	$	Label & Number

PARTON, Dolly — Cont'd

| 7/21/84 | 135 | 7 | | 19 Rhinestone ....[S] | $8 | RCA 5032 |

includes "Too Much Water" by Randy Parton; "The Day My Baby Died" by Rusty Buchanan; "Goin' Back To Heaven" by Stella Parton & Kin Vassy; "Drinkin' Stein" by Sylvester Stallone; and "Waltz Me To Heaven" by Floyd Parton

| 12/8/84+ | 31 | 8 ▲² | | 20 Once Upon A Christmas ....[X] | $8 | RCA 5307 |

KENNY ROGERS & DOLLY PARTON
Christmas charts: 1/'84, 4/'85, 10/'87, 16/'88, 15/'89, 14/'90, 14/'91, 19/'92

| 3/28/87 | 6 | 48 ▲ | | 21 Trio .... | $8 | Warner 25491 |

DOLLY PARTON, LINDA RONSTADT, EMMYLOU HARRIS

12/19/87+	153	8		22 Rainbow	$8	Columbia 40968
4/6/91	24	47 ▲		23 Eagle When She Flies ....[S]	$12	Columbia 46882
4/25/92	138	3		24 Straight Talk ....[S]	$12	Hollywood 61303

Act Like A Fool (15)
Afraid To Love Again (1)
All I Need Is You (7)
Almost In Love (12)
Always, Always (2)
Anything's Better Than Nothing (2)
Appalachian Memories (17)
Applejack (9,16)
As Much As Always (15)
As Soon As I Touched Him (10)
Baby Come Out Tonight (10)
Baby I'm Burnin' (11) **25**
Barbara On Your Mind (15)
Be There (19)
Before Our Weakness Gets Too Strong (6)
Best Woman Wins (23)
Big Wind (11)
Bloody Bones (5)
Blue Grace (24)
Blue Me (24)
Burning (24)
Burning To Burned (24)
But You Know I Love You (14,16) **41**
Butterflies (19)
Calm On The Water (17)
Chicken Every Sunday (8)
Christmas Song (20)
Christmas To Remember (20)
Christmas Without You (20)
Closer By The Hour (1)
Could I Have Your Autograph (22)
Country Road (23)
Cowboy's Ways (17)
Cowgirl & The Dandy (10)
Curse Of The Wild Weed Flower (7)
Daddy (3)
Daddy Was An Old Time Preacher Man (6)
Daddy's Moonshine Still (8)
Dark As A Dungeon (14)
Dark End Of The Street (1)
Deportee (Plane Wreck At Los Gatos) (14)
Detroit City (14)
Dirty Job (24)

Do I Ever Cross Your Mind (15,16)
Do You Think That Time Stands Still (12)
Down (2)
Downtown (18) **80**
Dreams Do Come True (23)
Dumb Blonde (medley) (5)
Dump The Dude (22)
Each Season Changes You (4)
Eagle When She Flies (23)
Elusive Butterfly (18)
Even A Fool Would Let Go (13)
Evening Shade (3)
Everyday Hero (22)
Family (23)
Farther Along (24)
Fight And Scratch (6)
Fighting Kind (7)
Fire's Still Burning (8)
Fish Out Of Water (24)
Flame, The (7)
Fool For Your Love (13)
Forty Miles From Poplar Bluff (17)
Gamble Either Way (17)
Games People Play (3)
Getting In My Way (9)
God Won't Get You (19)
God's Coloring Book (10)
Good As Gold (2)
Good Understanding (6)
Great Balls Of Fire (12)
Great Pretender (18)
Greatest Gift Of All (20) **81**
Gypsy, Joe And Me (3)
Hard Candy Christmas (16)
Heartbreak Express (15,16)
Heartbreaker (11) **37**
Help! (12)
Here You Come Again (10,16) **3**
Hobo's Meditation (21)
Holdin' On To You (9)
Holding On To Nothin' (1)
Hollywood Potters (15)
Home For Pete's Sake (3)
House Of The Rising Sun (14) **77**

House Where Love Lives (2)
How Does It Feel (9)
How Great Thou Art (5)
Hush-A-Bye Hard Times (14)
I Believe In Santa Claus (20)
I Can (1)
I Can't Help Myself (Sugar Pie, Honey Bunch) (18)
I Don't Believe You've Met My Baby (2)
I Knew You When (13)
I Know You By Heart (22)
I Know You're Married But I Love You Still (6)
I Really Don't Want To Know (17)
I Really Got The Feeling (11)
I Walk The Line (18)
I Wanna Fall In Love (11)
I Washed My Face In The Morning Dew (1)
I Will Always Love You (16) **53**
I'm Fed Up With You (3)
I'm Wasting Your Time And You're Wasting Mine (4)
I've Had Enough (21)
If You Need Me (23)
In The Ghetto (3)
Is It Real (7)
It Ain't Fair That It Ain't Right (8)
It Might As Well Be Me (4)
It's All Wrong, But It's All Right (10,16)
It's Not My Affair Anymore (12)
It's Too Late To Love Me Now (11)
J.J. Sneed (8)
Jealous Heart (17)
Jeannie's Afraid Of The Dark (1,5)
Joshua (8)
Just Someone I Used To Know (4)
Just The Two Of Us (1)
Last One To Touch Me (8)
Let's Live For Tonight (6)
Letter To Heaven (8)

Light Of A Clear Blue Morning (9,24) **87**
Livin' A Lie (24)
Lovin' You (10)
Make Love Work (22)
Making Plans (21)
Malena (18) **45**
Man, The (11)
Me And Little Andy (10,16)
Mendy Never Sleeps (4)
Milwaukee, Here I Come (3)
Monkey's Tale (3)
More Than I Can Say (22)
My Blue Ridge Mountain Boy (3,5,15)
My Dear Companion (21)
My Girl (My Love) (9)
My Hands Are Tied (2)
Nickels And Dimes (11)
9 To 5 (14,16) **1**
No Love Left (4)
No Reason To Hurry Home (2)
Oh, The Pain Of Loving You (7)
Old Flames Can't Hold A Candle To You (13,16)
Once More (6)
Once Upon A Christmas (20)
One Day At A Time (6)
One Emotion After Another (19)
One Of Those Days (17)
Ooo-Eee (17)
Packin' It Up (13)
Pain Of Loving You (21)
Party, The (1)
Poor Folks Town (14)
Possum Holler (7)
Potential New Boyfriend (17)
Prime Of Our Love (15)
Put It Off Until Tomorrow (medley) (5)
Ragged Angel (6)
Red Hot Screaming Love (22)
Release Me (15)
River Unbroken (22)
Rockin' Years (23)
Rosewood Casket (21)
Run That By Me One More Time (4,5)

Runaway Feelin' (23)
Same Old Fool (13)
Sandy's Song (12)
Save The Last Dance For Me (18) **45**
Savin' It For You (22)
Say Goodnight (13)
Send Me The Pillow You Dream On (17)
She Don't Love You (Like I Love You) (18)
Silent Night (20)
Silver And Gold (23)
Silver Sandals (4)
Sing For The Common Man (14)
Single Women (15)
Sleigh Ride (medley) (20)
Slip Away Today (1)
Something Fishy (medley) (5)
Somewhere Between (1)
Star Of The Show (7)
Starting Over Again (13) **36**
Stay Out Of My Bedroom (19)
Straight Talk (24)
Sure Thing (11)
Sweet Agony (13)
Sweet Lovin' Friends (19)
Sweet Music Man (10)
Sweet Summer Lovin' (12) **77**
Tall Man (5)
Telling Me Lies (21)
Tennessee Homesick Blues (19)
There (9)
There Never Was A Time (2)
There'll Be Love (7)
Those Memories Of You (21)
Thought I Couldn't Dance (24)
Thoughtfulness (1)
'Til Death Do Us Part (3)
To Know Him Is To Love Him (21)
Today, Tomorrow And Forever (7)
Tomorrow Is Forever (4,5)
Turn! Turn! Turn! (To Everything There Is A Season) (18)

Two Doors Down (10,16) **19**
Two Lovers (22)
Two Of A Kind (7)
Two Sides To Every Story (5)
Wabash Cannon Ball (5)
Walls Of My Mind (8)
We Can't Let This Happen To Us (4)
We Had All The Good Things Going (3)
We Had It All (18)
We'll Get Ahead Someday (1)
We'll Sing In The Sunshine (18)
We're Through Forever ('Til Tomorrow) (11)
What A Heartache (19,23)
Where Beauty Lives In Memory (9)
White Christmas (20)
Why Don't You Haul Off & Love Me (2)
Wildest Dreams (23)
Wildflowers (21)
Winter Wonderland (medley) (20)
With Bells On (20)
With You Gone (11)
Woke Up In Love (19)
Working Girl (14)
You All Come (Y'all Come) (18)
You Are (9)
You Can't Reach Me Anymore (4)
You Gotta Be My Baby (5)
You're The Only One (12) **59**
You're The Only One I Ever Needed (13)
(Your Love Has Lifted Me) Higher And Higher (9)
Yours Love (2)

★★**431**★★ **PARTRIDGE FAMILY, The**
Popularized through *The Partridge Family* TV series, broadcast from 1970-74. Recordings by series stars David Cassidy (lead singer) and real-life stepmother Shirley Jones (backing vocals). David, son of actor Jack Cassidy, was born on 4/12/50 in New York City; raised in California. Shirley, born on 3/31/34 in Smithton, Pennsylvania, starred in the film musicals *Oklahoma* and *The Music Man*; married David's father in 1956.

THE PARTRIDGE FAMILY Starring Shirley Jones Featuring David Cassidy:

10/31/70+	4	68 ●		1 The Partridge Family Album	$15	Bell 6050
4/3/71	3	53 ●		2 Up To Date	$15	Bell 6059
8/28/71	9	35 ●		3 The Partridge Family Sound Magazine	$15	Bell 6064
3/25/72	18	17 ●		4 The Partridge Family Shopping Bag............................	$20	Bell 6072
9/16/72	21	23 ●		5 The Partridge Family at home with their Greatest Hits ....[G]	$15	Bell 1107
12/16/72+	41	16		6 The Partridge Family Notebook	$15	Bell 1111
7/7/73	167	5		7 Crossword Puzzle	$15	Bell 1122

Am I Losing You (4,5) **59**
As Long As There's You (7)
As Long As You're There (6)
Bandala (1)
Brand New Me (1)
Breaking Up Is Hard To Do (5) **28**
Brown Eyes (3,5)
Come On Love (7)
Doesn't Somebody Want To Be Wanted (2,5) **6**

Echo Valley 2-6809 (3,5)
Every Little Bit O' You (4)
Every Song Is You (4)
Friend And A Lover (6) **99**
Girl, You Make My Day (4)
Hello, Hello (4)
I Can Feel Your Heartbeat (1,5)
I Got Your Love All Over Me (7)

I Really Want To Know You (4)
I Think I Love You (1,5) **1**
I Woke Up In Love This Morning (3,5) **13**
I Would Have Loved You Anyway (1)
I'll Leave Myself A Little Time (2)
I'll Meet You Halfway (2,5) **9**

I'm Here, You're Here (2)
I'm On My Way Back Home (3)
I'm On The Road (1)
If You Ever Go (4)
It Means I'm In Love With You (7)
It Sounds Like You're Saying Hello (7)
It's A Long Way To Heaven (7)

It's All In Your Mind (4)
It's One Of Those Nights (Yes Love) (4,5) **20**
It's You (7)
Last Night (4)
Lay It On The Line (7)
Let Your Love Go (7)
Looking Through The Eyes Of Love (3) **39**
Love Is All That I Ever Needed (3)

Love Must Be The Answer (6)
Maybe Someday (1)
Morning Rider On The Road (2)
Now That You Got Me Where You Want Me (1)
One Day At A Time (7)
One Night Stand (3)
Only A Moment Ago (1)
Point Me In The Direction Of Albuquerque (1)

DEBUT DATE	PEAK POS	WKS CHR	GOLD	ARTIST — Album Title	$	Label & Number

PARTRIDGE FAMILY, The — Cont'd

Rainmaker (3)
She'd Rather Have The Rain (2,5)
Singing My Song (1)

Somebody Wants To Love You (1)
Something New Got Old (4)
Something's Wrong (6)
Storybook Love (6)

Summer Days (3)
Sunshine (7)
Take Good Care Of Her (6)
That'll Be The Day (2)
There'll Come A Time (4)

There's No Doubt In My Mind (2)
To Be Lovers (1)
Together We're Better (6)
Twenty-Four Hours A Day (3)

Umbrella Man (2)
Walking In The Rain (6)
We Gotta Get Out Of This Place (6)

You Are Always On My Mind (2)
You Don't Have To Tell Me (3)

PARTY, The

Dance quintet from Central Florida: Albert Fields, Chase Hampton, Damon Pampolina, Dee Dee Magno and Tiffini Hale (lead singer). All were cast members of TV's *The Mickey Mouse Club* in 1988.

10/6/90	116	20		1 The Party	$12	Hollywood 60980
10/5/91	77	12		2 In The Meantime, In Between Time	$12	Hollywood 61225
				features a hologram card of the group		
9/12/92	163	4		3 Free..	$12	Hollywood 61358

Adult Decision (2)
All About Love (3)
At All Times (3)
Cappuccino And Bacon (3)
Change On Me (3)
Coulda Shoulda Woulda (1)
Dancing In The City (1)

Free (3)
Frontin' (3)
I Found Love (1) 79
I Gotcha (3)
I Know What Boys Like (2)
I Wanna Be Your Boyfriend (1)

I Want You (3)
I'm Just Wishin' (1)
In My Dreams (2) 34
In My Life (3)
Independent Woman (3)
It's Out Of My Heart (3)
Let's Get Right Down To It (3)

Life Ain't Nothin' But A Party (3)
My Generation (2)
Needin' Someone (3)
Peace, Love And Understanding (2)
Private Affair (2)

Rodeo (1)
Spiders And Snakes (2)
Storm Me (1)
Sugar Is Sweet (1,2)
Summer Vacation (1) 72
That's Why (1,2) 55
Ton Of Bricks (1)

Walking In The Rain (1)
Where Is My Romeo [includes English & foreign versions] (3)

PASADENAS, The

U.K. five-man R&B vocal group: Michael and David Milliner, their brother Jeff Aaron Brown, with John Andrew Banfield and Hammish Seelochan.

3/18/89	89	12		To Whom It May Concern	$8	Columbia 45065

Enchanted Lady
Funny Feeling

Give A Little Peace
I Really Miss You

Justice For The World

Living In The Footsteps Of Another Man
Riding On A Train

New Love
Something Else
Tribute (Right On) 52

PASSPORT

German jazz-fusion group led by Klaus Doldinger (sax, keyboards). Varying personnel.

3/15/75	137	7		1 Cross-Collateral .... [I]	$10	Atco 107
4/23/77	191	3		2 Iguacu .... [I]	$8	Atco 149
6/3/78	140	7		3 Sky Blue .... [I]	$8	Atlantic 19177
4/5/80	163	4		4 Oceanliner .... [I]	$8	Atlantic 19265
8/29/81	175	3		5 Blue Tattoo .... [I]	$8	Atlantic 19304

Aguamarinha (1)
Albatros Song (1)
Alegria (1)
Allegory (4)
Ancient Saga (4)
Ataraxia Part 1 & 2 (3)
Bahia Do Sol (2)
Bassride (4)

Bird Of Paradise (2)
Blue Tattoo (5)
Cross-Collateral (1)
Damals (1)
Daybreak Delight (5)
Departure (4)
Guna Guna (2)
Heavy Weight (2)

Homunculus (1)
Iguacu (2)
In A Melancholy Way (5)
Jadoo (4)
Loco-Motive (3)
Louisiana (5)
Mandrake (3)
Oceanliner (4)

Piece For Rock Orchestra (5)
Praia Leme (2)
Radiation (5)
Ragtag And Bobtail (5)
Rambling (5)
Reng Ding Dang Dong (3)
Riding On A Cloud (5)
Rub-A-Dub (4)

Sambukada (2)
Scope (4)
Seaside (4)
Secret, The (3)
Sky Blue (3)
Uptown Rendezvous (4)
Will-O'-The-Wisp (1)

PASTORIUS, Jaco

Born on 12/1/51 in Norristown, Pennsylvania. Bassist of jazz/rock group Weather Report. Died on 9/22/87 (age 35) from injuries received in a beating on 9/12/87.

8/15/81	161	3		Word Of Mouth .... [I]	$8	Warner 3535

Blackbird
Chromatic Fantasy

Crisis
John And Mary

Liberty City

3 Views Of A Secret
Word Of Mouth

PATTON, Robbie

English singer/songwriter. Toured with Fleetwood Mac as a guest in 1979.

8/15/81	162	6		Distant Shores	$8	Liberty 1107
				co-produced by Fleetwood Mac's Christine McVie		

Alright
Boulevard

Distant Shores
Don't Give It Up 26

Heartache
How I Feel

Last Night
One On One

She
When Love Disappears

PAUL, Billy

Born Paul Williams on 12/1/34 in Philadelphia. Soul singer; sang on Philadelphia radio broadcasts at age 11. First recorded for Jubilee in 1952.

8/22/70	183	5		1 Ebony Woman	$15	Neptune 201
10/16/71	197	2		2 Going East	$12	Phil. Int. 30580
11/25/72+	17	27	●	3 360 Degrees Of Billy Paul	$10	Phil. Int. 31793
4/28/73	186	3		4 Ebony Woman .... [R]	$12	Phil. Int. 32118
				new cover features a photo of a woman		
11/17/73+	110	26		5 War Of The Gods	$10	Phil. Int. 32409
7/6/74	187	4		6 Live In Europe .... [L]	$10	Phil. Int. 32952
3/15/75	140	9		7 Got My Head On Straight	$10	Phil. Int. 33157
12/27/75+	139	20		8 When Love Is New	$10	Phil. Int. 33843
1/22/77	88	18		9 Let 'Em In	$8	Phil. Int. 34389
1/28/78	152	4		10 Only The Strong Survive	$8	Phil. Int. 34923

Am I Black Enough For You (3) 79
America (We Need The Light) (8)
Be Truthful To Me (7)
Billy's Back Home (7)
Black Wonders Of The World (7)
Brown Baby (3,6)
Compared To What (2)
Don't Give Up On Us (10)
East (2)
Ebony Woman (1,4)
Enlightenment (7)

Everybody's Breakin' Up (10)
Everyday People (1,4)
Everything Must Change (7)
How Good Is Your Game (9)
I See The Light (5)
I Think I'll Stay Home Today (9)
I Trust You (9)
I Want 'Cha Baby (8)
I Was Married (5)
I Wish It Were Yesterday (2)
I'm Gonna Make It In Time (3)
I'm Just A Prisoner (3)

I've Got So Much To Live For (7)
(If You Let Me Make Love To You Then) Why Can't I Touch You? (2)
It's Too Late (3)
Jesus Boy (You Only Look Like A Man) (2)
July, July, July, July (7)
Let 'Em In (9)
Let The Dollar Circulate (8)
Let's Fall In Love All Over (1,4)
Let's Make A Baby (8) 83

Let's Stay Together (3)
Love Buddies (2)
Love Won't Come Easy (9)
Magic Carpet Ride (2)
Malorie (8)
Me And Mrs. Jones (3,6) 1
Mrs. Robinson (1,4)
My Head's On Straight (7)
One Man's Junk (10)
Only The Strong Survive (10)
Peace Holy Peace (8)
People Power (8)
Proud Mary (1,4)
Psychedelic Sally (1,4)

Sooner Or Later (10)
Takin' It To The Streets (10)
Thanks For Saving My Life (5,6) 37
There's A Small Hotel (2)
This Is Your Life (7)
Times Of Our Lives (10)
Traces (3)
War Of The Gods (5,6)
We All Got A Mission (9)
When It's Your Time To Go (7)
When Love Is New (8)
Where I Belong (10)

Whole Town's Talking (5)
Windmills Of Your Mind (1,4)
Windy (1,4)
Without You (9)
Word Sure Gets Around (9)
Your Song (3,6)

DEBUT DATE	PEAK POS	WKS CHR	GOLD	ARTIST — Album Title	$	Label & Number
				PAUL, Henry, Band		
				Southern-rock band led by former Outlaws' guitarist, Henry Paul.		
6/2/79	107	12		1 Grey Ghost	$8	Atlantic 19232
8/2/80	120	8		2 Feel The Heat	$8	Atlantic 19273
12/26/81+	158	8		3 Anytime	$8	Atlantic 19325

All I Need (1)
Anytime (3)
Brown Eyed Girl (3)
Crazy Eyes (3)
Crossfire (1)
Distant Riders (3)

Feel The Heat (2)
Foolin' (1)
Go Down Rockin' (2)
Grey Ghost (1)
Hollywood Paradise (3)
I Can See It (2)

I Don't Need You No More (1)
Keeping Our Love Alive (3) *50*
Living Without Your Love (3)
Lonely Dreamer (1)
Longshot (3)

Night City (2)
One-Night Stands (1)
Outa My Mind (3)
Rising Star (In The Southern Sky) (3)
Running Away (2)

766-2623 (Rom-ance) (3)
Shot To Hell (2)
So Long (1)
Turn It Up (2)
Whiskey Talkin' (2)
Wood Wind (1)

You Really Know (What I Mean) (1)

				PAUL, Les, and Mary Ford		
				Les was born Lester Polfus on 6/9/16 in Waukesha, Wisconsin. Mary was born Colleen Summer on 7/7/28 in Pasadena; died on 9/30/77. Self-taught guitarist Les is an innovator in electric guitar and multi-track recordings. Les and vocalist Mary married on 12/29/49; divorced in 1963. Les won the Grammy's Trustees Award in 1983 and he was inducted into the Rock and Roll Hall of Fame in 1988. Also see Chet Atkins.		
5/14/55	15	6		Les and Mary	$50	Capitol 577
				10 songs feature Mary's vocals; 6 are instrumentals by Les		

Baby, Won't You Please Come Home
Best Things In Life Are Free
Dangerous Curves

Falling In Love With Love
Farewell For Just Awhile
I'm Movin' On
Just One Of Those Things

Lies
Moritat (Theme from "Three Penny Opera") *49*
Nuevo Laredo *91*

On The Sunny Side Of The Street
Some Of These Days
Swing Low, Sweet Chariot

Tico Tico
Turista
Twelfth Street Rag

				PAUL & PAULA		
				Real names: Ray Hildebrand (b: 12/21/40, Joshua, Texas) and Jill Jackson (b: 5/20/42, McCaney, Texas). Formed duo at Howard Payne College, Brownwood, Texas.		
2/23/63	9	25		1 **Paul & Paula Sing For Young Lovers**	$30	Philips 078
8/10/63	99	5		2 We Go Together	$30	Philips 089

All The Love (1)
Average Boy And Average Girl (2)
Ba-Hey-Be (1)
Beginning Of Love (2)

Blue Roller Rink (2)
Come Softly To Me (1)
Don't Let It End (1)
Flipped Over You (1)
Gee Baby (1)

Hey Baby (1)
Hey Paula (1) *1*
Love Comes Once (2)
My Happiness (1)
Oh What A Love (2)

Pledging My Love (2)
So Fine (2)
Something Old, **Something New** (2) *77*
Stepping Stone (2)

Sweet Baby (1)
Two People In The World (1)
We Go Together (2)
We Two Forever Shall Be One (2)

You Send Me (1)
Young Lovers (1) *6*

				PAULSEN, Pat		
				Born on 7/6/27 in South Bend, Washington. Regular comedian on TV's *Smothers Brothers Comedy Hour*.		
10/19/68	71	10		Pat Paulsen For President	[C] $18	Mercury 61179
				with commentary by Ralph Story		

Age Of Reason
Bandwagon, The
Big Shot
Counter-Attack

Critics Attack
Formal Announcement
Freedom To Censor
Humble Beginning

I Will Not Run
I Will Not Serve
In Your Gourd, You Know
He's Good

Meet The Candidate
Meet The Prez
Messing Around
Questions And Evasions

Ruthless Denial
Simple Savior
Slip Of The Tongue
Soldiers' Lament

Two Cows
Victory Rally

				PAUPERS, The		
				Folk-rock quartet from Toronto — Skip Prokop, lead singer.		
11/11/67	178	2		Magic People	$12	Verve F. 3026

Black Thank You Package
It's Your Mind

Let Me Be
Magic People

My Love Hides Your View
One Rainy Day

Simple Deed
Think I Care

Tudor Impressions
You And Me

				PAVAROTTI, Luciano		
				Born on 10/12/35 in Modena, Italy. World-renown operatic tenor. Former teacher and insurance salesman. Operatic debut in 1961 in *La Boheme*.		
11/24/79+	77	21	●	1 O Sole Mio - Favorite Neapolitan Songs	[F] $8	London 26560
6/7/80	94	18		2 Pavarotti's Greatest Hits	[F-G] $10	London 2003-4 [2]
4/24/82	141	7		3 Luciano	[F-K] $8	London 2013
11/6/82	158	3		4 Yes, Giorgio	[S] $8	London 9001
9/8/84	103	14		5 Mamma	[F] $8	London 411959
				popular Italian songs arranged and conducted by Henry Mancini		
10/6/90+	35	89	▲	6 CARRERAS DOMINGO PAVAROTTI in concert	[L] $12	London 460433
				CARRERAS DOMINGO PAVAROTTI concert on 7/7/90 of opera tenors: Jose Carreras, Placido Domingo, Luciano Pavarotti with orchestra conducted by Zubin Mehta at the Baths of Caracalla in Rome		
1/4/92	173	1		7 Pavarotti Songbook	[F] $12	London 433513

Addio, Sogni Di Gloria (5)
Amapola (medley) (6)
Bellini: I Puritani - A Te O Cara (2)
Bellini: Vanne, O Rosa Fortunata (2,3)
Bizet: Carmen - Flower Song (2)
Caminito (medley) (6)
Cantate Con Me (7)
Capaldo: Comme Facette Mammeta - Tarantella (4)
Chitarra Romana (5)
Cielito Lindo (medley) (6)
De Crescenzo: Rondine Al Nido (5,6)
De Curtis: Torna A Surriento (1,2,3,6,7)
Denza: Funiculi, Funicula (1,2)
Di Capua: Maria, Mari (1,3)

Di Capua: 'O Sole Mio (1,4,6,7)
Did I Remember (medley) (4)
Donizetti: L'Elisir D'Amore - Una Furtiva Lagrima (2)
Donizetti: La Favorita - Spirto Gentil (2)
Donizetti: La Fille Du Regiment - O Mes Amis...Pour Mon Ame (2,3)
Donizetti: Una Furtiva Lagrima (1)
Fenesta Vascia (1)
Firenze Sogna (5)
Franck: Panis Angelicus (2,3)
Giorgio's Bedroom (medley) (4)
Gounod: Faust - Salut! Demeure (2)
(I Left My Heart) In San Francisco (medley) (4)
If We Were In Love (4)

In Un Palco Della Scala (5)
La Campana Di San Giusto (5)
La Ghirlandeina (5)
La Mia Canzone Al Vento (5,7)
La Vie En Rose (medley) (6)
Leoncavallo: Mattinata (5)
Leoncavallo: Mattinata (2,4)
Leoncavallo: Pagliacci - Vesti La Giubba (3)
Leoncavallo: Pagliacci - Vesti La Guibba (2)
Lolita (5,7)
Malinconia D'Amore (7)
Mamma (5,7)
Maria (medley) (6)
Mattinata (medley) (6)
Memory (medley) (6)
Musica Proibita (5,7)
Non Ti Scordar Di Me (5,7)
'O Marenariello (1)

'O Paese D' 'O Sole (1,6)
O Sole Mio (6)
'O Surdato 'Nnammurato (1)
Ochi Tchorniye (medley) (6)
Parlami D'Amore, Mariu (5)
Pecche? (1)
Piscatore 'E Pusilleco (1)
Ponchielli: La Gioconda - Cielo E Mar (2,4)
Puccini: Donna Non Vidi Mai - Manon Lescaut (4)
Puccini: La Boheme - Che Gelida Manina (2,3)
Puccini: Tosca - E Lucevan Le Stelle (2,3)
Puccini: Tosca - Recondita Armonia (2,6)
Puccini: Turandot - Nessun Dorma (2,4)
Rossini: La Danza (2)
Santa Lucia (4)
Schubert: Ave Maria (2,4)

Strauss: Der Rosenkavalier - Di Rigori Armato (2)
This Heart Of Mine (medley) (4)
Tonight (medley) (6)
Tosti: 'A Vucchella (1,3,7)
Tosti: Aprile (3,7)
Tosti: Chanson De L'Adieu (7)
Tosti: L'Ultima Canzone (7)
Tosti: La Serenata (7)
Tosti: Luna D'Estate (3)
Tosti: Marechiare (1,3,7)
Tu, Ca Nun Chiagne! (1)
Verdi: Aida - Ballet Music (4)
Verdi: Aida - Celeste Aida (2,3)
Verdi: Il Trovatore - Di Qual Tetra...Ah, Si Ben Mio (2)
Verdi: Il Trovatore - Di Quella Pira (2,3)
Verdi: La Donna E Mobile (4)

Verdi: Requiem - Ingemisco (2)
Verdi: Rigoletto - La Donna E Mobile (2)
Verdi: Rigoletto - Questo O Quella (2)
Vieni Sul Mar (5)
Vivere (5)
Voglio Vivere Cosi (5)
Volare (7)
Wien, Wien, Nur Du Allein (medley) (6)

DEBUT DATE	PEAK POS	WKS CHR	GOLD	ARTIST — Album Title	$	Label & Number

PAVLOV'S DOG
New York rock septet — David Surkamp, lead singer.

| 4/5/75 | 181 | 6 | | Pampered Menial.. | $10 | ABC 866 |

Episode · Fast Gun · Julia · Late November · Natchez Trace · Of Once And Future Kings · Preludin · Song Dance · Subway Sue, Theme From

PAVONE, Rita
Pop singer born in Torino, Italy.

| 6/20/64 | 60 | 14 | | Rita Pavone.. | $15 | RCA 2900 |

Big Deal · Boy Most Likely To Succeed · Don't Tell Me Not To Love You · I Can't Hold Back The Tears · Just Once More · Kissin' Time · Like I Did · Little By Little · **Remember Me 26** · Say Goodbye To Bobby · Too Many Wait And See

PAXTON, Tom
Born on 10/31/37 in Chicago. Folk singer/songwriter.

8/16/69	155	4	1	The Things I Notice Now	$15	Elektra 74043
6/6/70	184	4	2	Tom Paxton 6	$12	Elektra 74066
8/14/71	120	3	3	How Come The Sun	$12	Reprise 6443
8/26/72	191	4	4	Peace Will Come...	$12	Reprise 2096

About The Children (1) · All Night Long (1) · Angeline Is Always Friday (2) · Annie's Going To Sing Her Song (2) · Bishop Cody's Last Request (1) · California (4) · Cindy's Cryin' (2) · Crazy John (2) · Dance In The Shadows (4) · Dogs At Midnight (2) · Forest Lawn (2) · General Custer (3) · Hostage, The (4) · How Come The Sun (3) · I Give You The Morning (1) · I Had To Shoot That Rabbit (3) · I Lost My Heart On A 747 (4) · I've Got Nothing But Time (2) · Icarus (3) · Iron Man (1) · Jesus Christ S.R.O. (Standing Room Only) (4) · Jimmy Newman (3) · Little Lost Child (3) · Louise (3) · Molly Bloom (2) · Out Behind The Gypsy's (4) · Peace Will Come (4) · Prayin' For Snow (3) · Retrospective (4) · Sailor's Life (3) · Saturday Night (2) · She's Far Away (3) · Things I Notice Now (1) · Uncle Jack (2) · What A Friend You Are (4) · Whose Garden Was This (2) · Wish I Had A Troubadour (1) · You Came Throwing Colors (4) · You Should Have Seen Me Throw That Ball (4)

PAYCHECK, Johnny
Born Donald Eugene Lytle on 5/31/41 in Greenfield, Ohio. Country singer/guitarist/steel guitarist.

| 2/18/78 | 72 | 14 | ● | Take This Job And Shove It .... | $8 | Epic 35045 |

Barstool Mountain · Colorado Cool-Aid · Fool Strikes Again · 4 "F" Blues · From Cotton To Satin (From Birmingham To Manhattan) · Georgia In A Jug · Man From Bowling Green · Spirits Of St. Louis · Take This Job And Shove It · When I Had A Home To Go To

PAYNE, Freda
Born on 9/19/45 in Detroit. Sister of The Supremes' Scherrie Payne. Attended the Institute of Musical Arts. To New York in 1963. Performed with Pearl Bailey, Duke Ellington and Quincy Jones. First recorded for Impulse in 1965. Hosted the syndicated TV talk show *For You, Black Woman* in the early '80s.

8/22/70	60	13	1	Band Of Gold	$12	Invictus 7301
6/12/71	76	18	2	Contact	$12	Invictus 7307
4/15/72	152	8	3	The Best Of Freda Payne...[G]	$12	Invictus 9804

Band Of Gold (1,3) 3 · **Bring The Boys Home** (2,3) 12 · **Cherish What Is Dear To You (While It's Near To You)** (2,3) 44 · Come Back (3) · **Deeper & Deeper** (1,3) 24 · Easiest Way To Fall (1) · Happy Heart (1) · He's In My Life (3) · How Can I Live Without My Life (3) · I Left Some Dreams Back There (1) · I Shall Not Be Moved (2) · I'm Not Getting Any Better (2) · Just A Woman (3) · Love On Borrowed Time (1) · Mama's Gone (2) · Now Is The Time To Say Goodbye (1,3) · Odds And Ends (2) · **Road We Didn't Take** (2,3) 100 · Rock Me In The Cradle (1) · Suddenly It's Yesterday (2) · This Girl Is A Woman Now (1) · Through The Memory Of My Mind (1,3) · Unhooked Generation (1) · World Don't Owe You A Thing (1) · **You Brought The Joy** (2) 52 · You're The Only Bargain I've Got (3) · You've Got To Love Somebody (Let It Be Me) (2)

PEACHES & HERB
Soul duo from Washington, D.C.: Herb Fame (born Herbert Feemster, 1942) and Francine Barker (born Francine Hurd, 1947). Fame had been recording solo, Francine sang in vocal group Sweet Things. Marlene Mack filled in for Francine from 1968-69. Re-formed with Fame and Linda Green in 1977.

3/25/67	30	25	1	Let's Fall In Love	$15	Date 4004
9/2/67	135	12	2	For Your Love..	$15	Date 4005
9/21/68	187	3	3	Peaches & Herb's Greatest Hits ....[G]	$15	Date 4012
11/25/78+	2⁶	46	▲	4 2 Hot!	$8	Polydor 6172
11/10/79	31	30	●	5 Twice The Fire	$8	Polydor 6239
10/11/80	120	6		6 Worth The Wait	$8	Polydor 6298
9/12/81	168	2		7 Sayin' Something!	$8	Polydor 6332

All-Night Celebration (6) · All Your Love (Give It Here) (4) · Answer Me My Love (2) · Because Of You (1) · Bluer Than Blue (7) · **Close Your Eyes** (1,3) 8 · Count On Me (2) · Discover You (6) · Door Is Still Open To My Heart (2) · Dream Come True (7) · Easy As Pie (4) · Embraceable You (2) · Everybody Loves A Lover (2) · **For Your Love** (2,3) 20 · Four's A Traffic Jam (4) · Freeway (7) · Funtime (6) · Gettin' Down, Gettin' Down (5) · Go With The Flow (7) · Gypsy Lady (5) · Hearsay (6) · Howzabout Some Love (5) · I Love How You Love Me (2) · I Need Your Love So Desperately (2,3) · **I Pledge My Love** (5) 19 · (I Want Us) Back Together (5) · I Will Watch Over You (1) · I Wish I Could Be A Kid Again (7) · I'm In The Mood For Love (1) · It's True I Love You (2,3) · Just One Look (1) · **Let's Fall In Love** (1,3) 21 · **Love Is Strange** (3) 13 · Love It Up Tonight (4) · Love Lift (5) · Love Stealers (6) · Lovey Dovey (Girl & Guy) (6) · My Life (2) · One Child Of Love (6) · Picking Up The Pieces (7) · Put It There (5) · Red Hot Lover (7) · **Reunited** (4) 1 · **Roller-Skatin' Mate (Part I)** (5) 66 · **Shake Your Groove Thing** (4) 5 · Star Of My Life (4) · Star Steppin' (7) · Surrender (6) · Ten Commandments Of **Love** (3) 55 · Things I Want To Hear (Pretty Words) (2) · Time After Time (1) · True Love (1) · **Two Little Kids** (3) 31 · **United** (3) 46 · We Belong Together (1) · **We've Got Love** (4) 44 · We've Got To Love One Another (3) · Wear You Out (7) · What A Lovely Way (To Say Goodnight) (3) · When I Fall In Love (2) · Will You Love Me Tomorrow (1)

PEANUT BUTTER CONSPIRACY, The
California psychedelic rock quintet — Sandi Robinson, lead singer.

| 5/20/67 | 196 | 3 | | The Peanut Butter Conspiracy Is Spreading .... | $20 | Columbia 2654 |

Dark On You Now · **It's A Happening Thing 93** · Market Place · Most Up Till Now · Second Hand Man · Then Came Love · Twice Is Life · Why Did I Get So High · You Can't Be Found · You Should Know · You Took Too Much

PEARL HARBOR & THE EXPLOSIONS
San Francisco-based rock group, led by German-born Pearl E. Gates.

| 1/26/80 | 107 | 11 | 1 | Pearl Harbor And The Explosions .... | $8 | Warner 3404 |

DEBUT DATE	PEAK POS	WKS CHR	G O L D	ARTIST — Album Title	$	Label & Number

PEARL HARBOR & THE EXPLOSIONS — Cont'd

| 2/21/81 | 170 | 3 | | 2 Don't Follow Me, I'm Lost Too .... | $8 | Warner 3515 |

PEARL HARBOUR

Alone In The Dark (2)	Don't Come Back (1)	Fujiyama Mama (2)	Let's Go Upstairs (2)	So Much For Love (1)
At The Dentist (2)	Drivin' (1)	Get A Grip On Yourself (1)	Losing To You (2)	Up And Over (1)
Big One (1)	Everybody's Boring But My	Heaven Is Gonna Be Empty	Out With The Girls (2)	You Got It (Release It) (1)
Cowboys & Indians (2)	Baby (2)	(2)	Rough Kids (2)	You're In Trouble Again (2)
Do Your Homework (2)	Filipino Baby (2)	Keep Going (1)	Shut Up And Dance (1)	

PEARL JAM

Seattle punk-rock band: Eddie Vedder (vocals), Mike McCready, Stone Gossard, Jeff Ament and Dave Krusen. Gossard and Ament were members of Mother Love Bone. All except Krusen recorded with Temple Of The Dog. Members of the band acted in the film *Singles* as Matt Dillon's band, Citizen Dick. Group name taken from the nickname of New Jersey Nets basketball player Mookie Blaylock.

| 1/4/92 | 2⁴ | 58↑ ▲⁴ | | Ten .... | $12 | Epic/Assc. 47857 |

Alive	Deep	Garden	Oceans	Porch	Why Go
Black	Even Flow	Jeremy	Once	Release	

PEARLS BEFORE SWINE

New York underground folk quartet led by Tom Rapp.

| 9/27/69 | 200 | 2 | | These Things Too .... | $15 | Reprise 6364 |

Footnote	I Shall Be Released	If You Don't Want To (I Don't	Man In The Tree	Sail Away	When I Was A Child
Frog In The Window	I'm Going To City	Mind)	Mon Amour	These Things Too	Wizard Of Is
Green And Blue		Look Into Her Eyes			

PEARSON, Duke

Real name: Calvin Columbus Pearson. Jazz trumpeter/pianist. Died on 8/4/80 (age 48).

| 4/5/69 | 193 | 2 | | The Phantom .... | $15 | Blue Note 84293 |

featuring Bobby Hutcherson (vibes) and Jerry Dodgion (flute)

Blues For Alvina	Bunda Amerela (Little	Los Ojos Alegres (The Happy	Moana Surf	Phantom, The	Say You're Mine
	Yellow Streetcar)	Eyes)			

PEASTON, David

Native of St. Louis. Former grade school teacher in Brownsville, New York. Won TV competition *Showtime At The Apollo* seven consecutive times. His aunt is Fontella Bass. His mother, Martha Bass, was a member of Clara Ward's Gospel Troupe.

| 8/5/89 | 113 | 18 | | Introducing...David Peaston .... | $8 | Geffen 24228 |

Can I?	Eyes Of Love	Take Me Now	Tonight	Two Wrongs (Don't Make It	We're All In This Together
Don't Say No	God Bless The Child	Thank You For The Moment		Right)	

PEBBLES

Born Perri Alette McKissack. Native of Oakland. Nicknamed "Pebbles" by her family for her resemblance to cartoon character Pebbles Flintstone. Worked with Con Funk Shun in the early '80s while still a teenager. Married to singer/songwriter/producer L.A. Reid of The Deele. Her cousin is vocalist Cherrelle. Put together/managed the female rap group TLC.

| 2/13/88 | 14 | 38 | ▲ | 1 Pebbles........... | $8 | MCA 42094 |
| 9/29/90 | 37 | 36 | ● | 2 Always .... | $12 | MCA 10025 |

Always (2)	First Step (In The Right	Give Me Your Love (1)	**Love Makes Things**	Say A Prayer For Me (2)	Two Hearts (2)
Baby Love (1)	Direction) (1)	**Giving You The Benefit**	**Happen** (2) 13	Slip Away (1)	Why Do I Believe (2)
Backyard (2) 73	**Girlfriend** (1) 5	[includes 2 versions] (2) 4	Love/Hate (1)	Stay With Me (2)	
Do Me Right (1)	Give It To Me (2)	Good Thang (2)	**Mercedes Boy** (1) 2	Take Your Time (1)	

PEEBLES, Ann

Born on 4/27/47 in East St. Louis. Sang in family gospel group, the Peebles Choir, from age eight.

| 4/22/72 | 188 | 3 | | 1 Straight From The Heart .... | $10 | Hi 32065 |
| 3/9/74 | 155 | 7 | | 2 I Can't Stand The Rain .... | $10 | Hi 32079 |

Breaking Up Somebody's	**I Pity The Fool** (1) 85	If We Can't Trust Each	Slipped, Tripped, Fell In	Until You Came Into My Life
Home (1)	I Take What I Want (1)	Other (2)	Love (1)	(2)
Do I Need You (2)	I'm Gonna Tear Your	Love Vibration (2)	Somebody's On Your Case (1)	What You Laid On Me (1)
How Strong Is A Woman (1)	Playhouse Down (2)	99 Pounds (1)	Trouble, Heartaches &	You Got To Feed The Fire (2)
I Can't Stand The Rain	I've Been There Before (1)	One Way Street (2)	Sadness (1)	(You Keep Me) Hangin' On (2)
(2) 38		Run, Run, Run (2)		

PEEL, David, & The Lower East Side

New York-based rock group led by vocalist Peel.

| 5/24/69 | 186 | 3 | | 1 Have A Marijuana .... | $12 | Elektra 74032 |

recorded live on the streets of New York

| 5/27/72 | 191 | 3 | | 2 The Pope Smokes Dope .... | $12 | Apple 3391 |

produced by John Lennon and Yoko Ono

Alphabet Song (1)	Chicago Conspiracy (2)	Hip Generation (2)	I'm A Runaway (2)	Mother Where Is My Father?	Up Against The Wall (1)
Ballad Of Bob Dylan (2)	Everybody's Smoking	Hippie From New York City	I'm Gonna Start Another	(1)	We Love You (1)
Ballad Of New York	Marijuana (2)	(2)	Riot (2)	Pope Smokes Dope (2)	
City/John Lennon - Yoko	F Is Not A Dirty Word (2)	I Do My Bawling In The	I've Got Some Grass (1)	Show Me The Way To Get	
Ono (2)	Happy Mother's Day (1)	Bathroom (1)	McDonalds Farm (2)	Stoned (1)	
Birth Control Blues (2)	Here Comes A Cop (1)	I Like Marijuana (1)			

PEEPLES, Nia

Born on 12/10/61. Singer/actress. Played Nicole Chapman for three seasons on the TV series *Fame*. Hosted *Top Of The Pops* TV show and own syndicated music video dance TV program, *Party Machine*. Married Howard Hewett in 1989.

| 5/14/88 | 97 | 21 | | Nothin' But Trouble........... | $8 | Mercury 834303 |

Be My Lover	High Time	I Know How (To Make You	Is This Really Love	Poetry In Motion	This Time I'll Be Sweeter
For The Sake Of Loving		Love Me)	Never Gonna Get It	Star Crossed Lovers	**Trouble 35**

★★224★★ PENDERGRASS, Teddy

Born on 3/26/50 in Philadelphia. Worked local clubs, became drummer for Harold Melvin's Blue Notes in 1969; lead singer with same group in 1970. Went solo in 1976. In the 1982 film *Soup For One*. Auto accident on 3/18/82 left him partially paralyzed.

| 3/19/77 | 17 | 35 | ▲ | 1 Teddy Pendergrass .... | $8 | Phil. Int. 34390 |

DEBUT DATE	PEAK POS	WKS CHR	GOLD	ARTIST — Album Title	$	Label & Number
				PENDERGRASS, Teddy — Cont'd		
7/1/78	11	35	▲	2 Life Is A Song Worth Singing..	$8	Phil. Int. 35095
6/23/79	5	31	▲	3 Teddy	$8	Phil. Int. 36003
12/22/79+	33	15	●	4 Teddy Live! Coast To Coast .... [L]	$10	Phil. Int. 36294 [2]
				side 4: interviews and new studio recordings		
8/23/80	14	34	▲	5 TP	$8	Phil. Int. 36745
10/3/81	19	27	●	6 It's Time For Love	$8	Phil. Int. 37491
8/21/82	59	15		7 This One's For You	$8	Phil. Int. 38118
1/7/84	123	9		8 Heaven Only Knows	$8	Phil. Int. 38646
6/16/84	38	35	●	9 Love Language	$8	Asylum 60317
12/7/85+	96	23		10 Workin' It Back	$8	Asylum 60447
5/28/88	54	24	●	11 Joy	$8	Elektra 60775
3/23/91	49	16		12 Truly Blessed	$12	Elektra 60891

All I Need Is You (3)
And If I Had (1)
Bad Luck (medley) (4)
Be Sure (1)
Can We Be Lovers (11)
Can't We Try (5) *52*
Close The Door (2,4) *25*
Cold, Cold World (2)
Come Go With Me (3,4)
Crazy About Your Love (8)
Do Me (3,4)
Don't Ever Stop (Giving Your Love To Me) (8)
Don't Leave Me Out Along The Road (7)
Don't You Ever Stop (12)
Easy, Easy, Got To Take It Easy (1)
Feel The Fire (5)
Get Up, Get Down, Get Funky, Get Loose (2,4)
Girl You Know (5)
Glad To Be Alive (12)

Good To You (1)
Heaven Only Knows (8)
Hold Me (9) *46*
Hot Love (9)
How Can You Mend A Broken Heart (12)
I Can't Leave Your Love Alone (6)
I Can't Live Without Your Love (6)
I Can't Win For Losing (7)
I Don't Love You Anymore (1) *41*
I Find Everything In You (12)
I Just Called To Say (5)
I Want My Baby Back (8)
I'll Never See Heaven Again (3)
I'm Ready (11)
If You Don't Know Me By Now (medley) (4)
If You Know Like I Know (3)
In My Time (9)

Is It Still Good To Ya (5)
It Don't Hurt Now (2)
It Should've Been You (12)
It's Over (12)
It's Time For Love (6)
It's Up To You (What You Do With Your Life) (7)
It's You I Love (4)
Joy (11) *77*
Judge For Yourself (8)
Just Because You're Mine (8)
Keep On Lovin' Me (6)
Let Me Be Closer (10)
Let Me Love You (5)
Life Is A Circle (3)
Life Is A Song Worth Singing (2,4)
Life Is For Living (8)
Lonely Color Blue (10)
Love (9)
Love Emergency (10)
Love 4/2 (10)
Love I Lost (medley) (4)

Love Is The Power (11)
Love T.K.O. (5) *44*
Loving You Was Good (1)
More I Get, The More I Want (1)
Never Felt Like Dancin' (10)
Nine Times Out Of Ten (6)
Now Tell Me That You Love Me (7)
One Of Us Fell In Love (10)
Only To You (7)
Only You (2,4)
Set Me Free (3)
She Knocks Me Off My Feet (12)
She's Over Me (6)
Shout And Scream (4)
So Sad The Song (9)
Somebody Told Me (1)
Spend The Night (12)
Stay With Me (9)
Take Me In Your Arms Tonight (5)

This Gift Of Life (7)
This Is The Last Time (11)
This One's For You (7)
This Time Is Ours (9)
Through The Falling Rain (Love Story) (11)
Truly Blessed (12)
Turn Off The Lights (3,4) *48*
2 A.M. (11)
Wake Up Everybody (medley) (4)
Want You Back In My Life (10)
We Can't Keep Going On (Like This) (12)
When Somebody Loves You Back (2,4)
Where Did All The Lovin' Go (4)
Whole Town's Laughing At Me (1)
With You (12)

Workin' It Back (10)
You And Me For Right Now (8)
You Can't Hide From Yourself (1)
You Must Live On (6)
You're My Choice Tonight (Choose Me) (9)
You're My Latest, My Greatest Inspiration (6) *43*

PENISTON, Ce Ce
Born on 9/6/69 in Dayton, Ohio. Moved to Phoenix in 1977. In 1989, crowned Miss Black Arizona.

2/15/92	70	36	●	Finally..	$12	A&M 5381

Crazy Love *97*
Finally *5*

I See Love
Inside That I Cried *94*

It Should Have Been You
Keep On Walkin'

Lifeline
Virtue

We Got A Love Thang *20*
You Win, I Win, We Lose

PENN, Michael
Los Angeles-based singer/songwriter. Older brother of actors Sean and Christopher Penn. Son of actor/director Leo Penn and actress Eileen Ryan.

11/25/89+	31	34		1 March	$8	RCA 9692
10/3/92	160	2		2 Free-For-All	$12	RCA 61113

Battle Room (1)
Bedlam Boys (medley) (1)
Big House (1)
Brave New World (1)
Bunker Hill (2)

By The Book (2)
Coal (2)
Cupid's Got A Brand New Gun (1)

Disney's A Snow Cone (medley) (1)
Drained (2)
Evenfall (1)
Free Time (2)

Half Harvest (1)
Innocent One (1)
Invisible (1)
Long Way Down (Look What The Cat Drug In) (2)

No Myth (1) *13*
Now We're Even (2)
Seen The Doctor (2)
Slipping My Mind (2)
Strange Season (2)

This & That (1) *53*

PENNARIO, Leonard
Born on 7/9/24 in Buffalo, New York. Classical pianist. To Los Angeles at age 10 and appeared on Bing Crosby's *Kraft Music Hall*. Debuted at age 12 with the Dallas Symphony. Has performed with nearly every prestigious international orchestra.

6/8/59	29	13		Concertos under the Stars .... [I]	$20	Capitol 8326
				with The Hollywood Bowl Symphony Orchestra, conducted by Carmen Dragon		

Addinsell: Warsaw Concerto
Rath: Cornish Rhapsody

Beethoven: Adagio From Moonlight Sonata
Liszt: Liebestraum

Litolff: Scherzo From Concerto Symphonique

Rachmaninoff: Prelude In C Sharp Minor
Wildman: Swedish Rhapsody

PENSE, Lydia — see COLD BLOOD

PENTANGLE
Traditional English folk quintet featuring Bert Jansch and John Renbourn (acoustic guitars) and Jacqui McShee (vocals).

12/21/68	192	3		1 The Pentangle	$15	Reprise 6315
1/31/70	200	2		2 Basket Of Light	$12	Reprise 6372
3/13/71	193	1		3 Cruel Sister	$12	Reprise 6430
12/4/71	183	3		4 Reflection	$12	Reprise 6463
10/28/72	184	4		5 Solomon's Seal	$12	Reprise 2100

Bells (1)
Bruton Town (1)
Cherry Tree Carol (5)
Cruel Sister (3)
Cuckoo, The (2)
Hear My Call (1)
Helping Hand (4)
High Germany (5)

House Carpenter (2)
Hunting Song (2)
Jack Orion (3)
Jump Baby Jump (5)
Lady Of Carlisle (5)
Let No Man Steal Your Thyme (1)
Light Flight (2)

Lord Franklin (3)
Lyke-Wake Dirge (2)
Maid That's Deep In Love (3)
Mirage (1)
No Love Is Sorrow (5)
Omie Wise (4)
Once I Had A Sweetheart (2)
Pentangling (1)

People On The Highway (5)
Rain And Snow (4)
Reflection (4)
Sally Free And Easy (5)
Sally Go Round The Roses (2)
Snows, The (5)
So Clear (4)

Springtime Promises (2)
Train Song (2)
Waltz (1)
Way Behind The Sun (1)
Wedding Dress (4)
When I Get Home (4)
When I Was In My Prime (3)

Will The Circle Be Unbroken? (4)
Willy Of Winsbury (5)

PENTHOUSE PLAYERS CLIQUE
Male rap duo produced by DJ Quik: Playa Hamm and Tweed Cadillac.

5/16/92	76	10		Paid The Cost	$12	Ruthless 57181

DEBUT DATE	PEAK POS	WKS CHR	GOLD	ARTIST — Album Title	$	Label & Number

PENTHOUSE PLAYERS CLIQUE — Cont'd

Blak Iz A Poet	Handle Yo Bizness	N-Trance	P.S. Phuk U 2	They Don't Know	Undaground Boss
Chekmate	Jealous Knukle Heads	Nathen's Changed	Pimp Lane	Trust No Bitch	X-It
Explanation Of A Playa	Jus 2 Kep Yo Attenchun	P.L.F.	Smooth	U Cain't Check Me	

PEOPLE
San Jose, California pop-rock sextet founded by lead guitarist Jeff Levin.

7/27/68	128	8		I Love You	$30	Capitol 2924

Ashes Of Me	Epic, The	Nothing Can Stop The	We Need A Whole Lot More
Crying Shoes	**I Love You** *14*	Elephants	Jesus (And A Lot Less
		1,000 Years B.C.	Rock 'N' Roll)

PEOPLE'S CHOICE
Philadelphia soul group formed in 1971: Frankie Brunson (vocals), Guy Fiske, Roger Andrews, Dave Thompson and Leon Lee. Lee left in 1973, replaced by Darnell Jordan and Donald Ford.

9/6/75	56	15		1 Boogie Down U.S.A.	$8	TSOP 33154
6/26/76	174	3		2 We Got The Rhythm	$8	TSOP 34124

Are You Sure (1)	Do It Any Way You Wanna	I'm Leaving You (1)	Mellow Mood (2)	**Nursery Rhymes (Part I)**	Party Is A Groovy Thing (1)
Boogie Down U.S.A. (1)	(1) *11*	If You Want Me Back (1)	Mickey D's (1)	(1) *93*	Sooner You Get Here (1)
Cold Blooded &	Don't Send Me Away (1)	Jam, Jam, Jam (All Night	Movin' In All Directions (2)	Opus-De-Funk (2)	We Got The Rhythm (2)
Down-Right-Funky (2)	Here We Go Again (2)	Long) (2)			

PEPPERMINT RAINBOW, The
Three-man, two-woman vocal group put together by producer Paul Leka (Steam).

8/2/69	106	9		Will You Be Staying After Sunday	$15	Decca 75129

And I'll Be There	Green Tambourine	Pink Lemonade	Sierra (Chasin' My Dream)	**Will You Be Staying After**
Don't Wake Me Up In The	I Found Out I Was A Woman	Rosemary	Walking In Different Circles	**Sunday** *32*
Morning, Michael *54*	Jamais	Run Like The Devil		

PEPSI AND SHIRLIE
Pepsi DeMacque and Shirlie Holliman of the U.K. — former Wham! backing singers. Pepsi also sang backup for Andy Taylor, Fine Young Cannibals and Spandau Ballet. Shirlie was a classmate of Andrew Ridgley.

2/27/88	133	9		All Right Now	$8	Polydor 833724

All Right Now *66*	Crime Of Passion	High Time	What's Going On Inside
Can't Give Me Love	Goodbye Stranger	Lovers' Revolution	Your Head
	Heartache *78*	Surrender	

PERFECT GENTLEMEN
Boston teen trio produced by New Edition and New Kids On The Block producer, Maurice Starr: Corey Blakely, Maurice Starr, Jr. (Starr's son) and Tyrone Sutton. All were between the ages of 11-13 years old in 1990.

5/26/90	72	14		Rated PG	$12	Columbia 46070
				CD includes bonus track		

Birthday Girl	Girl In My Dreams	Move Me Groove Me	**Ooh La La (I Can't Get**	Perfect Intro	Rings Around The Moon
	Mama	One More Chance	**Over You)** *10*	Rated PG	Tell Me Again

PERLMAN, Itzhak — see PREVIN, Andre

PERRY, Joe, Project
Joe (lead guitarist of Aerosmith) was born on 9/10/50 in Lawrence, Massachusetts.

4/12/80	47	13		1 Let The Music Do The Talking	$8	Columbia 36388
7/4/81	100	10		2 I've Got The Rock 'N' Rolls Again	$8	Columbia 37364

Break Song (1)	Discount Dogs (1)	Let The Music Do The	Mist Is Rising (1)	Ready On The Firing Line (1)	South Station Blues (2)
Buzz Buzz (2)	East Coast, West Coast (2)	Talking (1)	No Substitute For Arrogance	Rockin' Train (1)	TV Police (2)
Conflict Of Interest (1)	I've Got The Rock 'N' Rolls	Life At A Glance (1)	(2)	Shooting Star (1)	
Dirty Little Things (2)	Again (2)	Listen To The Rock (2)	Play The Game (2)	Soldier Of Fortune (2)	

PERRY, Phil
Native of East St. Louis, Illinois. Member of the Montclairs. Later a top Los Angeles session singer. Recorded in duo with Kevin Sanlin — Perry & Sanlin.

5/18/91	191	1		The Heart Of The Man	$12	Capitol 92115

Amazing Love	Call Me	(Forever In The) Arms Of	God's Gift To The World	More Nights	Who Do You Love
Best Of Me	Forever	Love	Good-bye	Say Anything	Woman

PERRY, Steve
Born on 1/22/49 in Hanford, California. Lead singer of Journey since 1978.

4/28/84	12	60	▲²	Street Talk	$8	Columbia 39334

Captured By The Moment	Go Away	It's Only Love	Running Alone	**Strung Out** *40*
Foolish Heart *18*	I Believe	**Oh Sherrie** *3*	**She's Mine** *21*	You Should Be Happy

PERSUADERS, The
Soul group formed in New York City in 1969. Consisted of lead Douglas "Smokey" Scott, Willie Holland, James "B.J." Barnes and Charles Stodghill.

3/11/72	141	7		1 Thin Line Between Love And Hate..	$12	Win Or Lose 387
4/7/73	178	4		2 The Persuaders	$10	Atco 7021

Bad Bold And Beautiful Girl	If This Is What You Call	Love Goes Good When	Please Stay (2)	What Is The Definition Of
(2)	Love (I Don't Want Any	Things Go Bad (2)	Thanks For Loving Me (1)	Love (2)
Blood Brothers (1)	Part Of It) (1)	**Love Gonna Pack Up (And**	Thigh Spy (1)	You Musta Put Something
Can't Go No Further And Do	If You Feel Like I Do (2)	**Walk Out)** (1) *64*	**Thin Line Between Love &**	In Your Love (1)
No Better (1)	Is It Too Heavy For You (2)	Mr. Sunshine (1)	**Hate** (1) *15*	You Still Love Me (After All
I Want To Make It With You	Let's Get Down Together (1)	Peace In The Valley Of Love	Trying Girls Out (2)	You've Been Through) (2)
(2)		(2)		

PERSUASIONS, The
A cappella quintet from Bedford-Stuyvesant, New York, formed in 1966. Consisted of Jerry Lawson (lead), Joseph "Jesse" Russell and Jayotis Washington (tenors), Herbert "Tubo" Rhoad (baritone, d: 12/8/88 [44] of a stroke) and Jimmy "Bro" Hayes (bass).

9/18/71	189	3		1 We Came To Play	$20	Capitol 791
2/12/72	88	12		2 Street Corner Symphony	$15	Capitol 872

DEBUT DATE	PEAK POS	WKS CHR	GOLD	ARTIST — Album Title	$	Label & Number

PERSUASIONS, The — Cont'd

| 11/18/72 | 195 | 3 | | 3 Spread The Word.. | $15 | Capitol 11101 |
| 6/9/73 | 178 | 3 | | 4 We Still Ain't Got No Band........................ | $12 | MCA 326 |

Another Night With The Boys (1)
Any More (4)
Baby What You Want Me To Do (You Got Me Running) (medley) (4)
Be Good To Me Baby (2)
Bright Lights, Big City (medley) (4)

Buffalo Soldier (2)
Chain Gang (1)
Chapel Of Love (4)
Christian's Automobile (2)
Dance With Me (4)
Don't It Make You Want To Go Home (1)
Don't Know Why I Love You (1)

Good Old Acappella (4)
Good Times (2)
Gypsy Woman (1)
He Ain't Heavy, He's My Brother (medley) (2)
Heaven Help Us All (3)
Hymn #9 (3)
I Could Never Love Another (After Loving You) (2)

Idol With The Golden Head (4)
It's You That I Need (1)
Lean On Me (3)
Let It Be (1)
Lord's Prayer (3)
Love You Most Of All (4)
Man In Me (2)
Man, Oh Man (1)

People Get Ready (2)
Send Me Some Lovin' (4)
So Much In Love (2)
Steal Away (4)
Sun, The (1)
T.A. Thompson (3)
Tempts Jam Medley (2)
Ten Commandments Of Love (3)

Three Angels (3)
Walk On The Wild Side (1)
When I Leave These Prison Walls (3)
When Jesus Comes (3)
Without A Song (3)
You Must Believe Me (4)
You've Got A Friend (medley) (2)

PETER AND GORDON

Pop duo formed in London in 1963: Peter Asher (b: 6/22/44, London) and Gordon Waller (b: 6/4/45, Braemar, Scotland). Peter's sister Jane was Paul McCartney's girlfriend, and Paul wrote their first three chart hits. Toured the U.S. in 1964, appeared on *Shindig, Hullabaloo* and Ed Sullivan TV shows. Disbanded in 1967. Asher went into production and management, including work with Linda Ronstadt, James Taylor and 10,000 Maniacs.

7/4/64	21	14		1 A World Without Love..............................	$20	Capitol 2115
1/2/65	95	11		2 I Don't Want To See You Again................	$20	Capitol 2220
5/22/65	51	15		3 I Go To Pieces..	$20	Capitol 2324
8/14/65	49	13		4 True Love Ways......................................	$20	Capitol 2368
4/16/66	60	14		5 Woman...	$20	Capitol 2477
7/30/66	72	12		6 The Best Of Peter And Gordon.............[G]	$20	Capitol 2549
2/4/67	80	13		7 Lady Godiva..	$20	Capitol 2664

All My Trials (1)
All Shook Up (3)
Any Day Now (My Wild Beautiful Bird) (4)
As Long As I Have You (5)
Baby I'm Yours (7)
Broken Promises (4)
Brown, Black And Gold (5)
Cry To Me (4)
Crying In The Rain (4)
Don't Pity Me (4,6) 83
Exodus Song (7)
Five Hundred Miles (1)
Freight Train (1)

Good Morning Blues (3)
Green Leaves Of Summer (5)
High Noon (5)
Hurtin' Is Lovin' (4)
I Don't Care What They Say (3)
I Don't Want To See You Again (2,6) 16
I Go To Pieces (3,6) 9
I Know A Man (5)
I Still Love You (3)
I Told You So (4)
If I Fell (7)
If I Were In You (1,6)

If You Wish (3,6)
Lady Godiva (7) 6
Land Of Oden (5)
Last Night I Woke (1)
Leave Me Alone (5)
Leave My Woman Alone (1)
Let It Be Me (5)
Lonely Avenue (1)
Love Is A Many-Splendored Thing (7)
Love Me, Baby (2,6)
Lucille (7)
Mess Of Blues (3)
Morning's Calling (7)

My Babe (2)
Nobody I Know (2) 12
Pretty Mary (1)
Sleepless Nights (3)
Soft As The Dawn (5)
Someone Ain't Right (3)
Somewhere (5)
Start Trying Someone Else (7)
Taste Of Honey (5)
Tears Don't Stop (3)
Tell Me How (1)
There's No Living Without Your Loving (5) 50

3:10 To Yuma (5)
Till There Was You (7)
To Know You Is To Love You (4,6) 24
Trouble In Mind (1)
Two Little Love Birds (3)
Whatcha Gonna Do 'Bout It (3)
When I Fall In Love (7)
When The Black Of Your Eyes Turns To Grey (5)
Who's Lovin' You (4)
Willow Garden (2)

Woman (5,6) 14
World Without Love (1,6) 1
Wrong From The Start (5)
You Don't Have To Tell Me (1)
Young And Beautiful (7)

★★95★★ PETER, PAUL & MARY

Folk group formed in New York City in 1961. Consisted of Mary Travers (b: 11/7/37, Louisville); Peter Yarrow (b: 5/31/38, New York City); and Paul Stookey (b: 11/30/37, Baltimore). Yarrow had worked the Newport Folk Festival in 1960. Stookey had done TV work, and Travers had been in the Broadway musical *The Next President*. Disbanded in 1971, reunited in 1978.

4/28/62	1[7]	185	▲[2]	1 Peter, Paul and Mary...............................	$20	Warner 1449
1/19/63	2[9]	99	●	2 (Moving)...	$20	Warner 1473
10/26/63	1[5]	80	●	3 In The Wind..	$20	Warner 1507
8/15/64	4	54	●	4 Peter, Paul and Mary In Concert.............[L]	$20	Warner 1555 [2]
4/10/65	8	38	●	5 A Song Will Rise......................................	$20	Warner 1589
10/30/65	11	39	●	6 See What Tomorrow Brings.....................	$20	Warner 1615
8/27/66	22	53		7 Peter, Paul and Mary Album...................	$20	Warner 1648
9/2/67	15	82	●	8 Album 1700..	$12	Warner 1700
9/14/68	14	22		9 Late Again...	$12	Warner 1751
6/14/69	12	25		10 Peter, Paul and Mommy.........................	$12	Warner 1785
6/20/70	15	40	▲	11 10 Years Together/The Best Of Peter, Paul and Mary...............[G]	$12	Warner 2552
10/21/78	106	7		12 Reunion...	$8	Warner 3231
3/14/87	173	5		13 No Easy Walk To Freedom.....................	$8	Gold Castle 171001

All My Trials (3)
All Through The Night (10)
And When I Die (7)
Apologize (9)
Autumn To May (1)
Ballad Of Spring Hill (Spring Hill Disaster) (5)
Bamboo (1)
Because All Men Are Brothers (6)
Best Of Friends (12)
Betty & Dupree (6)
Big Boat (1) 93
Blowin' In The Wind (3,4,1) 2
Blue (4)
Boa Constrictor (10)
Bob Dylan's Dream (8)
Brother, (Buddy) Can You Spare A Dime? (4)
By Surprise (12)
Car, Car (4)
Christmas Dinner (10)
Come And Go With Me (5)
Cruel War (1) 52
Cuckoo, The (5)
Day Is Done (10,11) 21

Don't Think Twice, It's All Right (3,11) 9
Early In The Morning (1)
Early Morning Rain (6,11) 91
El Salvador (10)
First Time Ever I Saw Your Face (11)
500 Miles (1,4,11)
Flora (2)
For Baby (For Bobbie) (7)
For Lovin' Me (5,11) 30
Forever Young (12)
Freight Train (3)
Gilgarry Mountain (5)
Going To The Zoo (10)
Gone The Rainbow (2)
Good Times We Had (7)
Great Mandella (The Wheel Of Life) (8)
Greenland Whale Fisheries (13)
Greenwood (13)
Hangman (6)
House Song (8)
Hurry Sundown (7)
Hush-A-Bye (3)
Hymn (9)

I Dig Rock And Roll Music (8,11) 9
I Have A Song To Sing, O! (10)
I Need Me To Be For Me (12)
I Shall Be Released (8)
I'd Rather Be In Love (13)
I'm In Love With A Big Blue Frog (8)
If I Had A Hammer (The Hammer Song) (1,4,11) 10
If I Had My Way (1,4)
If I Had Wings (8)
If I Were Free (6)
It's Raining (1,4,10)
Jane, Jane (6)
Jesus Met The Woman (4)
Jimmy Whalen (5)
King Of Names (7)
Kisses Sweeter Than Wine (7)
Last Thing On My Mind (6)
Le Deserteur (4)
Leatherwing Bat (10)
Leaving On A Jet Plane (8,11) 1
Lemon Tree (1,11) 35
Light One Candle (13)

Like The First Time (12)
Long Chain On (3)
Love City (Postcards To Duluth) (9)
Make-Believe Town (10)
Man Come Into Egypt (2)
Marvelous Toy (10)
Mockingbird (10)
Moments Of Soft Persuasion (9)
Mon Vrai Destin (5)
Monday Morning (5)
Morning Train (2)
Motherless Child (5)
Ms. Rheingold (12)
No Easy Walk To Freedom (13)
No Other Name (8)
Norman Normal (7)
Oh, Rock My Soul (Part 1) (4) 93
Old Coat (3)
On A Desert Island (With You In My Dreams) (6)
One Kind Favor (4)
Other Side Of This Life (7) 100

Polly Von (3)
Pretty Mary (3)
Puff The Magic Dragon (2,4,10,11) 2
Quit Your Low Down Ways (3)
Reason To Believe (9)
Rich Man Poor Man (9)
Right Field (13)
Rising Of The Moon (6)
Rocky Road (3)
Rolling Home (8)
San Francisco Bay Blues (5)
Settle Down (Goin' Down That Highway) (2) 56
She Dreams (9)
Single Girl (4)
'Soalin', A (2,4)
Sometime Lovin' (9)
Song Is Love (8)
Sorrow (1)
State Of The Heart (13)
Stewball (3,11) 35
Summer Highland Falls (12)
Sweet Survivor (12)
Talkin' Candy Bar Blues (5)
Tell It On The Mountain (3) 33

There Is A Ship (4)
There's Anger In The Land (9)
This Land Is Your Land (2)
This Train (1)
Three Ravens (4)
Times They Are A Changin' (4)
Tiny Sparrow (2)
Too Much Of Nothing (9,11) 35
Tramp On The Street (9)
Tryin' To Win (6)
Unicorn Song (12)
Very Last Day (5)
Wasn't That A Time (5)
Weave Me The Sunshine (13)
Weep For Jamie (5)
Well, Well, Well (7)
Whatshername (8)
When The Ship Comes In (5) 91
Where Have All The Flowers Gone (1)
Whispered Words (13)
Yesterday's Tomorrow (9)

PETERS, Bernadette

Born Bernadette Lazzara on 2/28/44 in Queens, New York. Broadway/TV/film star. Appeared in the films *The Jerk* and *Annie* among others, and the TV series *All's Fair* (1976-77).

5/3/80	114	14		1 Bernadette Peters	$12	MCA 3230
10/3/81	151	9		2 Now Playing	$12	MCA 5244

Broadway Baby (2)
Carrying A Torch (2)
Chico's Girl (1)
Dedicated To The One I Love (2) 65

Don't (2)
Gee Whiz (1) 31
Heartquake (1)
I Don't Know Why (I Just Do) (medley) (2)

I Never Thought I'd Break (1)
If You Were The Only Boy (1)
Maybe My Baby Will (2)
Mean To Me (medley) (2)
Only Wounded (1)

Other Lady (1)
Pearl's A Singer (1)
Should've Never Let Him Go (1)
Sweet Alibis (2)

Tears On My Pillow (2)
Weekend Of A Private Secretary (2)
You'll Never Know (1)

PETERSEN, Paul — see DARREN, James

PETERSON, Oscar, Trio

Jazz trio: Oscar (b: 8/15/25 in Montreal; piano), Ray Brown (bass) and Ed Thigpen (drums).

2/9/63	145	2		1 Bursting Out With The All Star Big Band! ....[I]	$25	Verve 8476
6/8/63	127	2		2 Affinity ....[I]	$25	Verve 8516
10/31/64	81	12		3 Oscar Peterson Trio + One ....[I]	$25	Mercury 60975

with Clark Terry (trumpet)

Baubles, Bangles And Beads (2)
Blues For Big Scotia (1)
Blues For Smedley (3)
Brotherhood Of Man (3)
Daahoud (1)

Gravy Waltz (2)
Here's That Rainy Day (1)
I Love You (1)
I Want A Little Girl (3)
I'm A Fool To Want You (2)
I'm Old Fashioned (1)

Incoherent Blues (3)
Jim (3)
Mack The Knife (3)
Manteca (1)
Mumbles (3)
Roundalay (3)

Six And Four (2)
Squeaky's Blues (3)
Tangerine (3)
They Didn't Believe Me (3)
This Could Be The Start Of Something (2)

Tricrotism (1)
Waltz For Debbie (2)
West Coast Blues (1)
Young And Foolish (1)
Yours Is My Heart Alone (2)

PET SHOP BOYS

British duo: Neil Tennant (vocals) and Chris Lowe (keyboards). Tennant was a writer for the British fan magazine *Smash Hits*. In 1989, Tennant also recorded with the group Electronic.

4/19/86	7	31	▲	1 Please	$8	EMI America 17193
12/27/86+	95	12		2 Disco ....[K]	$8	EMI America 17246
				4 of 6 tracks are dance remixes of tracks from above album		
10/3/87	25	45	●	3 Pet Shop Boys, actually..	$8	EMI-Man. 46972
11/5/88	34	22	●	4 Introspective	$8	EMI-Man. 90868
11/17/90	45	25		5 Behavior.	$12	EMI 94310
11/23/91	111	14		6 Pet Shop Boys Discography - The Complete Singles Collection ....[G]	$12	EMI 97097

their British and American hits

Always On My Mind (4,6) 4
Being Boring (5,6)
DJ Culture (6)
Domino Dancing (4,6) 18
End Of The World (5)
Heart (3,6)
Hit Music (3)
How Can You Expect To Be Taken Seriously? (5) 93

I Want A Dog (4)
I Want A Lover (1)
I Want To Wake Up (3)
I'm Not Scared (4)
In My House (medley) (3)
In The Night (2)
It Couldn't Happen Here (3)
It's A Sin (3,6) 9
It's Alright (4,6)
Jealousy (5,6)

King's Cross (3)
Later Tonight (1)
Left To My Own Devices (4,6) 84
Love Comes Quickly (1,2,6) 62
My October Symphony (5)
Nervously (5)
One More Chance (3)
Only The Wind (5)

Opportunities (Let's Make Lots Of Money) (1,2,6) 10
Paninaro (3,6)
Rent (3,6)
Shopping (2)
So Hard (5,6) 62
Suburbia (1,2,6) 70
This Must Be The Place I Waited Years To Leave (5)
To Face The Truth (5)

Tonight Is Forever (1)
Two Divided By Zero (1)
Violence (1)
Was It Worth It? (6)
West End Girls (1,2,6) 1
What Have I Done To Deserve This? (3,6) 2
Where The Streets Have No Name (I Can't Take My Eyes Off You) (6) 72

Why Don't We Live Together? (1)

★★206★★ PETTY, Tom, And The Heartbreakers

Rock group formed in Los Angeles in 1975. Consisted of Petty (b: 10/20/53, Gainesville, Florida; guitar, vocals), Mike Campbell (guitar), Benmont Tench (keyboards), Ron Blair (bass) and Stan Lynch (drums). Petty, Campbell and Tench had been in Florida group Mudcrutch, early '70s. Backed Stevie Nicks on solo LP *Bella Donna*. Blair left in 1982, replaced by Howard Epstein. Toured with Bob Dylan in 1986. Petty appeared in the 1987 film *Made In Heaven*. Member of the supergroup Traveling Wilburys.

9/24/77+	55	42	●	1 Tom Petty & The Heartbreakers	$12	Shelter 52006
6/10/78	23	24	●	2 You're Gonna Get It!	$12	Shelter 52029
11/10/79+	2⁷	66	▲²	3 Damn The Torpedoes	$8	Backstreet 5105
5/23/81	5	31	▲	4 Hard Promises	$8	Backstreet 5160
11/20/82+	9	32	●	5 Long After Dark	$8	Backstreet 5360
4/13/85	7	32	▲	6 Southern Accents	$8	MCA 5486
12/14/85+	22	26		7 Pack Up The Plantation - Live! ....[L]	$10	MCA 8021 [2]
5/9/87	20	20	●	8 Let Me Up (I've Had Enough)	$8	MCA 5836
5/13/89	3	71	▲³	9 Full Moon Fever	$8	MCA 6253
				TOM PETTY		
				backing by all of The Heartbreakers except drummer Stan Lynch		
7/20/91	13	41	▲	10 Into The Great Wide Open	$12	MCA 10317

above 2 co-produced by Jeff Lynne

Ain't Love Strange (8)
All Mixed Up (8)
All Or Nothin' (10)
All The Wrong Reasons (10)
Alright For Now (9)
American Girl (1,7)
Anything That's Rock 'N' Roll (1)
Apartment Song (9)
Baby's A Rock 'N' Roller (2)
Best Of Everything (6)
Between Two Worlds (5)
Breakdown (1,7) 40
Built To Last (10)
Century City (3)
Change Of Heart (5) 21
Criminal Kind (4)
Damage You've Done (8)
Dark Of The Sun (10)

Deliver Me (5)
Depending On You (9)
Dogs On The Run (9)
Don't Bring Me Down (1)
Don't Come Around Here No More (6) 13
Don't Do Me Like That (3) 10
Even The Losers (3)
Face In The Crowd (9) 46
Feel A Whole Lot Better (9)
Finding Out (5)
Fooled Again (I Don't Like It) (1)
Free Fallin' (9) 7
Here Comes My Girl (3) 59
Hometown Blues (1)
How Many More Days (8)
Hurt (2)

I Need To Know (2,7) 41
I Won't Back Down (9) 12
Insider (4)
Into The Great Wide Open (10) 92
It Ain't Nothin' To Me (6,7)
It'll All Work Out (8)
Jammin' Me (8) 18
Kings Highway (10)
Learning To Fly (10) 28
Let Me Up (I've Had Enough) (8)
Letting You Go (4)
Listen To Her Heart (2) 59
Louisiana Rain (3)
Love Is A Long Road (9)
Luna (1)
Magnolia (2)

Make It Better (Forget About Me) (6) 54
Makin' Some Noise (10)
Mary's New Car (6)
Mind With A Heart Of Its Own (9)
My Life/Your World (8)
Mystery Man (1)
Needles And Pins (7) 37
Nightwatchman (4)
No Second Thoughts (2)
One Story Town (5)
Out In The Cold (10)
Rebels (6,7) 74
Refugee (3,7) 15
Restless (2)
Rockin' Around (With You) (1,7)
Runaway Trains (8)

Runnin' Down A Dream (9) 23
Same Old You (5)
Self-Made Man (8)
Shadow Of A Doubt (A Complex Kid) (3)
Shout (3)
So You Want To Be A Rock & Roll Star (7)
Something Big (4)
Southern Accents (6,7)
Spike (8)
Stories We Could Tell (7)
Straight Into Darkness (5)
Strangered In The Night (1)
Thing About You (4)
Think About Me (8)
Too Good To Be True (10)
Too Much Ain't Enough (2)

Two Gunslingers (10)
Waiting, The (4,7) 19
Wasted Life (5)
We Stand A Chance (5)
What Are You Doin' In My Life? (3)
When The Time Comes (2)
Wild One, Forever (1)
Woman In Love (It's Not Me) (4) 79
Yer So Bad (9)
You And I Will Meet Again (10)
You Can Still Change Your Mind (4)
You Got Lucky (5,7) 20
You Tell Me (5)
You're Gonna Get It (2)
Zombie Zoo (9)

DEBUT DATE	PEAK POS	WKS CHR	GOLD	ARTIST — Album Title	$	Label & Number

P.F.M.
P.F.M.: Premiata Forneria Marconi. Italian progressive rock quintet led by vocalist Bernardo Lanzetti.

10/20/73	180	6		1 Photos Of Ghosts	$10	Manticore 66668
				PREMIATA FORNERIA MARCONI		
12/28/74+	151	8		2 P.F.M. 'Cook' .... [I-L]	$10	Manticore 502

Alta Loma Nine Till Five (2)   Dove....Quando.... (2)   Il Banchetto (1)   Mr. Nine Till Five (1,2)   Photos Of Ghosts (1)   River Of Life (1)
Celebration (1,2)   Four Holes In The Ground (2)   Just Look Away (1)   Old Rain (1)   Promenade The Puzzle (1)

PHANTOM, ROCKER & SLICK
Rock trio featuring Stray Cats' Slim Jim Phantom (drums) and Lee Rocker (vocals, bass), and Silver Condor's Earl Slick (guitar).

10/26/85	61	23		1 Phantom, Rocker & Slick	$8	EMI America 17172
10/18/86	181	2		2 Cover Girl	$8	EMI America 17229

Can't Get It Right (2)   Going South (2)   It's Good To Be Alive (2)   Men Without Shame (1)   Runnin' From The Hounds   Still Got Time (2)
Cover Girl (2)   Hollywood Distractions (1)   Lonely Actions (1)   My Mistake (1)   (1)   Time Is On My Hands (1)
Dressed In Dirt (2)   I Found Someone Who   Long Cool Woman (In A   No Regrets (1)   Sidewalk Princess (2)   Well Kept Secret (1)
Enough Is Enough (2)   Loves Me (2)   Black Dress) (2)   Only Way To Fly (1)   Sing For Your Supper (1)   What You Want (1)

PHILADELPHIA ORCHESTRA, The
Conducted by Eugene Ormandy (b: 11/18/1899, Budapest, Hungary; d: 3/12/85). Came to the U.S. in 1921; conducted orchestra from 1938-1980. Also see Mormon Tabernacle Choir.

5/19/62	17	13		1 The Magnificent Sound Of The Philadelphia Orchestra ....[K-I]	$12	Columbia 1 [2]
				compiled from 16 of their albums		
12/22/62	109	2	●	2 The Glorious Sound Of Christmas ....[X]	$12	Columbia 6369
				with The Temple University Concert Choir; Christmas charts: 17/'63, 45/'64, 19/'67		
5/6/78	136	8		3 David Bowie narrates Prokofiev's "Peter and The Wolf"	$12	RCA 2743
				side 1: above title; side 2: Britten: Young Person's Guide to the Orchestra - both sides feature The Philadelphia Orch.		

Bach: Air On The G String   Borodin: Polovtsian Dance   Glinka: Russlan And   Liszt: Hungarian Rhapsody   O Sanctissima (O Du   Sibelius: The Swan Of
(1)   No. 2 from Prince Igor (1)   Ludmilla Overture (1)   No. 2 (1)   Frohliche) (2)   Tuonela (1)
Bach: Toccata And Fugue In   Britten: Young Person's   God Rest Ye Merry,   O Come, All Ye Faithful   Prokofiev: Peter And The   Silent Night, Holy Night (2)
D Minor (1)   Guide To The Orchestra,   Gentlemen (2)   (Adeste Fideles) (2)   Wolf, Op. 67 (A Musical   Strauss, J.: Voices Of Spring
Beethoven: The Worship Of   Op. 34 (3)   Grieg: Anitra's Dance from   O Come, Little Children (2)   Tale For Children) (3)   (1)
God (2)   Debussy: Prelude To The   Peer Gynt Suite No. 1 (1)   O Come, O Come, Emanuel   Ravel: Alborada Del   Tchaikovsky: Waltz from
Berlioz: March To The   Afternoon Of A Faun (1)   Handel: Air from Water   (2)   Graciose (1)   Sleeping Beauty (1)
Scaffold from Symphonie   Deck The Hall With Boughs   Music Suite (1)   O Holy Night (Cantique De   Saint-Saens: Danse   Tchaikovsky: Waltz from
Fantastique (1)   Of Holly (2)   Hark! The Herald Angels   Noel) (2)   Macabre (1)   Swan Lake, Act 1 (1)
Bizet: Les Toreadors from   First Noel (2)   Sing (2)   O Little Town Of Bethlehem   Schubert: Ave Maria (2)
Carmen Suite (1)   Joy To The World (2)   (2)

PHILLIPS, Anthony
Guitarist of Genesis from 1967-70.

3/26/77	191	3		The Geese & The Ghost..	$10	Passport 98020
				with Mike Rutherford and Phil Collins (both of Genesis)		

Chinese Mushroom Cloud   Geese And The Ghost (Parts   God If I Saw Her Now   Henry, Portraits from Tudor   Sleepfall: The Geese Fly West   Wind-Tales
Collections   I & II)   Times Medley   Which Way The Wind Blows

PHILLIPS, Esther
Born Esther Mae Jones on 12/23/35 in Galveston, Texas. One of the first female superstars of R&B. Vocalist/multi-instrumentalist. Moved to Los Angeles in 1940. Recorded and toured with The Johnny Otis Orchestra as "Little Esther," 1948-54; scored seven top 10 hits on the R&B charts in 1950. Bouts with drug addiction interrupted her career and led to her death on 8/7/84 (liver, kidney failure).

1/5/63	46	14		1 Release Me!	$50	Lenox 227
				"LITTLE ESTHER" PHILLIPS with the Anita Kerr Singers		
1/2/71	115	15		2 Burnin' ....[L]	$20	Atlantic 1565
				recorded at Freddie Jett's Pied Piper Club, Los Angeles		
3/18/72	137	15		3 From A Whisper To A Scream	$10	Kudu 05
12/30/72+	177	8		4 Alone Again, Naturally	$10	Kudu 09
8/2/75	32	17		5 What A Diff'rence A Day Makes	$10	Kudu 23
				with jazz guitarist Joe Beck		
1/31/76	170	4		6 Confessin' The Blues ....[L]	$15	Atlantic 1680
				side 2: live recording at same club as in album #2 above		
1/8/77	150	4		7 Capricorn Princess	$8	Kudu 31

After You Love You (1)   Confessin' The Blues (6)   I Can't Help It (1)   I've Never Found A Man (To   No Headstone On My Grave   To Lay Down Beside You (3)
All The Way Down (7)   Cry Me A River Blues (2)   I Don't Want To Do Wrong (4)   Love Me Like You Do) (4)   (1)   Turn Around, Look At Me (5)
Alone Again (Naturally) (4)   Do Right Woman, Do Right   I Haven't Got Anything   If It's The Last Thing I Do (2)   Oh Papa (5)   Use Me (4)
Am I That Easy To Forget (1)   Man (4)   Better To Do (7)   In The Evenin' (6)   One Night Affair (5)   **What A Diff'rence A Day**
And I Love Him (2) 54   Don't Let Me Lose This   I Love Paris (6)   It Could Happen To You (6)   Please Send Me Someone To   **Makes** (5) 20
Baby, I'm For Real (3)   Dream (7)   **I Really Don't Want To**   Jelly Jelly Blues (medley) (6)   Love (2)   Why Should We Try
Beautiful Friendship (7)   Dream (7)   **Know** (1) 61   Just Out Of Reach (1)   **Release Me** (1,2) 8   Anymore (1)
Be Honest With Me (1)   From A Whisper To A   I Wonder (6)   Let Me In Your Life (4)   Romance In The Dark (6)   You And Me Together
Blow Top Blues (medley) (6)   Scream (3)   I'd Fight The World (1)   Let's Move & Groove (4)   Scarred Knees (3)   Forever (4)
Boy, I Really Tied One On (7)   Georgia Rose (4)   I'm Gettin' 'Long Alright (2,6)   Long John Blues (medley) (6)   Shangri-La (4)   You're Coming Home (5)
Bye Bye Blackbird (3)   Home Is Where The Hatred   I've Forgotten More Than   Magic's In The Air (7)   Sweet Touch Of Love (3)   (Your Love Has Lifted Me)
C.C. Rider (6)   Is (3)   You'll Ever Know About   Makin' Whoopee (2)   That's All Right With Me (3)   Higher & Higher (5)
Candy (7)   Hurtin' House (5)   Him (1)   Mister Magic (5)   'Til My Back Ain't Got No   Your Love Is So Doggone
Cherry Red (4,6)   I Can Stand A Little Rain (5)   Bone (3)   Good (3)

PHILLIPS, John
Born on 8/30/35 in Paris Island, South Carolina. Co-founder of The Mamas & The Papas. Father of actress MacKenzie Phillips and singer Chynna Phillips. Co-wrote The Beach Boys' 1988 #1 hit "Kokomo."

5/2/70	181	9		John Phillips (John The Wolfking of L.A.)...	$15	Dunhill 50077

April Anne   Down The Beach   Holland Tunnel   Malibu People   Someone's Sleeping
Captain   Drum   Let It Bleed, Genevieve   **Mississippi 32**   Topanga Canyon

DEBUT DATE	PEAK POS	WKS CHR	GOLD	ARTIST — Album Title	$	Label & Number

PHILLIPS, Shawn
Born on 2/3/43 in Fort Worth, Texas. Soft-rock vocalist.

12/2/72+	**57**	20		1 Faces	$10	A&M 4363
				includes 3 recordings from 1969		
12/15/73+	**72**	13		2 Bright White	$10	A&M 4402
11/30/74+	**50**	12		3 Furthermore	$10	A&M 3662
9/13/75	**101**	9		4 Do You Wonder	$8	A&M 4539

All The Kings And Castles (2)
Anello (Where Are You) (1)
As All Is Played (4)
Believe In Life (4)
Blunt And Frank (4)
Breakthrough (3)
Bright White (2)
Cape Barras (3)

Chorale (1)
City To City (4)
Do You Wonder (4)
Dream Queen (2)
Furthermore (3)
Golden Flower (4)
Hey Miss Lonely (1)
(I Took) A Walk (1)

It's A Beautiful Morning (2)
January First (3)
'L' Ballade (1)
Lady Of The Blue Rose (1)
Landscape (2)
Lasting Peace Of Mind (4)
Looking At The Angel (4)
Mr. President (3)

Ninety Two Years (3)
Parisian Plight II (1)
Planned "O" (2)
Planscape (3)
Salty Tears (2)
See You (3)
Song For Northern Ireland (2)

Starbright (3)
Summer Vignette (4)
Talking In The Garden (4)
Technotronic Lad (2)
Troof (3)
Victoria Emmanuele (2)
We (1) **89**
Xasper (4)

PHOTOGLO, Jim
Pop vocalist from the South Bay area of Los Angeles.

5/24/80	**194**	3		1 Photoglo	$8	20th Century 604
				PHOTOGLO		
6/6/81	**119**	11		2 Fool In Love With You	$8	20th Century 621

Angelina (2)
Beg, Borrow Or Steal (1)
Best That I Can Be (1)
Don't Be Afraid To Love Somebody (1)

Faded Blue (1)
Fool In Love With You (2) **25**
I Can't Let Go Of You (2)

I Don't Want To Be In This Movie (1)
More To Love (2)
Ruled By My Heart (1)
Run To Me (1)

Steal Away (1)
There's Always Another Chance Left For Love (2)
Tonight Will Last Forever (2)
Try It Again (2)

20th Century Fool (1)
We Were Meant To Be Lovers (1) **31**
When Love Is Gone (1)
Won't Let You Do It To Me (2)

Young Girl (1)

PICKETT, Bobby "Boris", And The Crypt-Kickers
Born on 2/11/40 in Somerville, Massachusetts. Began recording career in Hollywood while aspiring to be an actor. A member of The Stompers in early 1962. Leon Russell, Johnny MacCrae (Ronny & The Daytonas), Rickie Page (The Bermudas) and Gary Paxton (Hollywood Argyles) were Crypt-Kickers.

11/3/62	**19**	13		1 The Original Monster Mash	[N]	$50	Garpax 57001
9/29/73	**173**	4		2 The Original Monster Mash	[N-R]	$20	Parrot 71063
				reissue of Garpax album, less 4 songs		

Bella's Bash (1,2)
Blood Bank Blues (1,2)
Graveyard Shift (1,2)

Irresistible Igor (1,2)
Let's Fly Away (1,2)
Me & My Mummy (1,2)

Monster Mash (1,2) **1**
Monster Mash Party (1,2)
Monster Minuet (1,2)

Monster Motion (1)
Monsters' Holiday (2) **30**

Rabian-The Fiendage Idol (1,2)
Sinister Stomp (1,2)

Skully Gully (1)
Transylvania Twist (1,2)
Wolfbane (1)

★★300★★ PICKETT, Wilson
Soul singer/songwriter. Born on 3/18/41 in Prattville, Alabama. Sang in local gospel groups. To Detroit in 1955. With the Falcons, 1961-63. Career took off after recording in Memphis with guitarist/producer Steve Cropper. Inducted into the Rock and Roll Hall of Fame in 1991.

10/30/65	**107**	6		1 In The Midnight Hour	$30	Atlantic 8114
8/27/66	**21**	29		2 The Exciting Wilson Pickett	$20	Atlantic 8129
1/21/67	**42**	31		3 The Wicked Pickett	$20	Atlantic 8138
8/12/67	**54**	11		4 The Sound Of Wilson Pickett	$20	Atlantic 8145
11/11/67+	**35**	54		5 The Best Of Wilson Pickett	[G]	$20	Atlantic 8151
2/24/68	**70**	15		6 I'm In Love	$20	Atlantic 8175
7/13/68	**91**	13		7 The Midnight Mover	$20	Atlantic 8183
3/1/69	**97**	14		8 Hey Jude	$12	Atlantic 8215
4/4/70	**197**	3		9 Right On	$12	Atlantic 8250
10/3/70	**64**	19		10 Wilson Pickett In Philadelphia	$12	Atlantic 8270
5/22/71	**73**	13		11 The Best Of Wilson Pickett, Vol. II	[G]	$12	Atlantic 8290
12/25/71+	**132**	14		12 Don't Knock My Love	$12	Atlantic 8300
2/10/73	**178**	8		13 Wilson Pickett's Greatest Hits	[G]	$12	Atlantic 501 [2]
4/28/73	**187**	3		14 Mr. Magic Man	$10	RCA 4858

Ain't No Doubt About It (10)
Baby Man (14)
Back In Your Arms (8)
Barefootin' (2)
Born To Be Wild (8,11) **64**
Bring It On Home To Me (6)
Bumble Bee (Sting Me) (10)
Call My Name, I'll Be There (12) **52**
Cole, Cooke & Redding (11) **91**
Come Home Baby (1)
Come Right Here (10)
Covering The Same Old Ground (12)
Danger Zone (2)
Days Go By (10)
Don't Cry No More (6)
Don't Fight It (1,5,13) **53**
Don't Knock My Love - Pt. 1 (12,13) **13**
Don't Knock My Love - Pt. 2 (12)
Don't Let The Green Grass Fool You (10,11,13) **17**
Down By The Sea (7)

Engine Number 9 (10,11,13) **14**
Everybody Needs Somebody To Love (3,5,13) **29**
Fire And Water (12) **24**
For Better Or Worse (1,7)
Funky Broadway (4,5,13) **8**
Funky Way (9)
Get Me Back On Time, Engine Number 9 ..see: Engine Number 9
Groovy Little Woman (9)
Hello Sunshine (6)
Help The Needy (10)
Hey Joe (9,11) **59**
Hey Jude (8,11,13) **23**
Hot Love (12)
I Can't Let My True Love Slip Away (14)
I Found A Love - Part 1 (1,4,5,13) **32**
I Found A Love, Part 2 (4)
I Found A True Love (7,11,13) **42**
I Found The One (4)
I Keep Walking Straight Ahead (14)

I Need A Lot Of Loving Every Day (4)
I Sho' Love You (14)
I'm A Midnight Mover (7,11,13) **24**
I'm Drifting (2)
I'm Gonna Cry (1,7)
I'm In Love (6,11,13) **45**
I'm Not Tired (1)
I'm Sorry About That (4)
I've Come A Long Way (6)
If You Need Me (5,13,14) **64**
In The Midnight Hour (1,2,5,13) **21**
International Playboy (10)
It's A Groove (7)
It's All Over (2)
It's Still Good (9)
It's Too Late (5,13) **49**
Jealous Love (6) **50**
Knock On Wood (3)
Land Of 1000 Dances (2,5,13) **6**
Let's Get An Understanding (7)
Let's Kiss And Make Up (1)
Lord Pity Us All (9)
Love Is A Beautiful Thing (4)

Love Is Beautiful (14)
Mama Told Me Not To Come (12,13) **99**
Man And A Half (8,11,13) **42**
Mercy, Mercy (4)
Mojo Mamma (4)
Mr. Magic Man (14) **98**
Mustang Sally (3,5,13) **23**
My Own Style Of Loving (8)
New Orleans (3)
Night Owl (8)
Ninety-Nine And A Half (Won't Do) (2,5,13) **53**
Not Enough Love To Satisfy (12)
Nothing You Can Do (1)
Only I Can Sing This Song (14)
Ooh Poo Pah Doo (3)
People Make The World (8)
Pledging My Love (12)
Remember, I Been Good To You (7)
Run Joey Run (10)
Save Me (8)
Search Your Heart (8)
She Ain't Gonna Do Right (3)

She Said Yes (9) **68**
She's Lookin' Good (6,11,13) **15**
She's So Good To Me (2)
Sin Was The Blame (14)
Sit Down And Talk This Over (8)
634-5789 (Soulsville, U.S.A.) (2,5,13) **13**
Something Within Me (4)
Something You Got (2)
Soul Dance Number Three (4,5,13) **55**
Stag-O-Lee (6) **22**
Steal Away (9)
Sugar Sugar (9,11,13) **25**
Sunny (3)
Sweet Inspiration (9)
Take A Little Love (1)
Take This Love I've Got (1)
Teardrops Will Fall (1)
That Kind Of Love (9)
That's A Man's Way (1)
This Old Town (9)
Three Time Loser (3)
Time Is On My Side (1)
Toe Hold (5)
Trust Me (7)

Up Tight Woman (3)
We've Got To Have Love (6)
What It Is (14)
Woman Let Me Be Down Home (12)
Woman Likes To Hear That (9)
You Can't Judge A Book By Its Cover (12)
You Can't Stand Alone (4) **70**
You Keep Me Hanging On (9,11,13) **92**
You Left The Water Running (3)
You're So Fine (2)
(Your Love Has Brought Me) A Mighty Long Way (12)

DEBUT DATE	PEAK POS	WKS CHR	GOLD	ARTIST — Album Title	$	Label & Number

PIECES OF A DREAM
Jazz trio from Philadelphia, formed in 1975 as Touch Of Class. Consisted of James Lloyd (keyboards), Cedric Napoleon (bass) and Curtis Harmon (drums). Ages in 1981 were 17, 19 and 19, respectively. Worked as house band for *City Lights* TV series at KYW-Philadelphia.

DEBUT DATE	PEAK POS	WKS CHR		ARTIST — Album Title	$	Label & Number
10/31/81	170	6	1	Pieces Of A Dream	$8	Elektra 350
8/28/82	114	15	2	We Are One	$8	Elektra 60142
2/25/84	90	15	3	Imagine This	$8	Elektra 60270

above 3 produced by Grover Washington, Jr.

| 8/2/86 | 102 | 12 | 4 | Joyride .... | $8 | Manhattan 53023 |

produced by Maurice White

All About Love (1)	For The Fun Of It (3)	Joyride (4)	Please Don't Do This To Me (2)	Sunshine (4)	Winning Streak (4)
Body Magic (1)	Foreverlasting Love (3)	Love Of My Life (4)	Pop Rock (2)	Tell Me A Bedtime Story (3)	Yo Frat (2)
Careless Whisper (4)	I Can Give You What You	Lovers (1)	Save Some Time For Me (4)	Touch Me In The Spring (1)	You Know I Want You (2)
Don't Be Sad (2)	Want (4)	Mt. Airy Groove (2)	Say La La (4)	Warm Weather (1)	
Easy Road Home (1)	Imagine This (3)	Outside In (4)	Shadow Of Your Smile (3)	We Are One (2)	
Fo-Fi-Fo (3)	It's Getting Hot In Here (3)	Pieces Of A Dream (1)	Steady Glide (1)	When You Are Here With Me (2)	
For Ramsey (2)	It's Time For Love (3)				

PILOT
Scottish trio: David Paton (lead singer, guitar), Bill Lyall (keyboards) and Stuart Tosh (drums).

5/31/75	82	14		Pilot	$10	EMI 11368

produced by Alan Parsons

Auntie Iris	Girl Next Door	**Just A Smile 90**	Lucky For Some	Never Give Up	Sky Blue
Don't Speak Loudly	High Into The Sky	Lovely Lady Smile	**Magic 5**	Over The Moon	Sooner Or Later

PINDER, Michael
Born on 12/27/41 in Birmingham, England. Keyboardist of The Moody Blues.

5/1/76	133	8		The Promise	$10	Threshold 18

Air	Free As A Dove	Message	Seed, The	You'll Make It Through
Carry On	I Only Want To Love You	Promise, The	Someone To Believe In	

★★49★★ PINK FLOYD
English progressive rock band formed in 1965: David Gilmour (b: 3/6/46; guitar; replaced Syd Barrett in 1968), Roger Waters (b: 9/6/44; bass), Nick Mason (b: 1/27/45; drums) and Rick Wright (b: 7/28/45; keyboards). Wright left in early 1982; Waters went solo in 1984. Band inactive, 1984-86. Gilmour, Mason and Wright regrouped in 1987. Group name taken from Georgia bluesmen Pink Anderson and Floyd Council.

12/2/67+	131	11		1	Pink Floyd	$75	Tower 5093

a condensation of their first British album, *The Piper At The Gates Of Dawn*

| 1/3/70 | 74 | 27 | ● | 2 | Ummagumma .... [L] | $30 | Harvest 388 [2] |

record 1: live; record 2: studio

| 11/7/70 | 55 | 13 | | 3 | Atom Heart Mother .... | $15 | Harvest 382 |

with the John Aldiss Choir on side 1

| 7/31/71 | 152 | 7 | | 4 | Relics .... [K] | $12 | Harvest 759 |

recordings from 1967-69

| 11/6/71 | 70 | 73 | ● | 5 | Meddle .... | $12 | Harvest 832 |
| 6/24/72 | 46 | 25 | | 6 | Obscured By Clouds .... [S] | $10 | Harvest 11078 |

music from the film *The Valley*

| 3/17/73 | 1¹ | 741 | ▲¹² | 7 | The Dark Side Of The Moon .... | $10 | Harvest 11163 |

set the all-time record for longevity; no album in the history of any chart has charted longer

| 9/1/73 | 153 | 7 | | 8 | More .... [S-R] | $10 | Harvest 11198 |

soundtrack originally released in 1969

| 12/22/73+ | 36 | 17 | | 9 | A Nice Pair .... [E-R] | $10 | Harvest 11257 [2] |

reissue of their first 2 British albums *The Piper At The Gates Of Dawn* and *A Saucerful Of Secrets*

9/27/75	1²	39	▲⁴	10	Wish You Were Here	$10	Columbia 33453
2/19/77	3	28	▲³	11	Animals	$8	Columbia 34474
12/15/79+	1¹⁵	123	▲⁸	12	The Wall	$10	Columbia 36183 [2]

concept album released as a film in the early 1980s

12/12/81+	31	16	▲	13	A Collection Of Great Dance Songs .... [G]	$8	Columbia 37680
4/9/83	6	23	▲	14	The Final Cut	$8	Columbia 38243
6/18/83	68	9		15	Works .... [K]	$8	Capitol 12276

Harvest label recordings (1968-73)

| 9/26/87 | 3 | 56 | ▲³ | 16 | A Momentary Lapse Of Reason .... | $8 | Columbia 40599 |
| 12/10/88+ | 11 | 21 | ▲ | 17 | Delicate Sound Of Thunder .... [L] | $10 | Columbia 44484 [2] |

recorded in August 1988; CD contains bonus track

Absolutely Curtains (6)	Careful With That Axe,	Fletcher Memorial Home (14)	In The Flesh? (12)	Obscured By Clouds (6)	Remember A Day (4,9)
Alan's Psychedelic Breakfast	Eugene (2,4)	Free Four (6,15)	Interstellar Overdrive (1,4,9)	On The Run (7)	Round And Around (16,17)
Medley (3)	Chapter 24 (1,9)	Get Your Filthy Hands Off	Is There Anybody Out	On The Turning Away	**Run Like Hell** (12,17) **53**
Another Brick In The Wall	Childhood's End (6)	My Desert (14)	There? (12)	(16,17)	San Tropez (5)
(Part I) (12)	Cirrus Minor (4,8)	Gnome, The (1,9)	Jugband Blues (9)	One Of My Turns (12)	Saucerful Of Secrets (9)
Another Brick In The Wall	Comfortably Numb (12,17)	Goodbye Blue Sky (12)	Julia Dream (4)	One Of The Few (14)	Saucerful Of Secrets Medley
(Part II) (12,13,17) **1**	Corporal Clegg (9)	Goodbye Cruel World (12)	**Learning To Fly** (16,17) **70**	One Of These Days	(2)
Another Brick In The Wall	Crying Song (8)	Grand Vizier's Garden Party:	Let There Be More Light (9)	(5,13,15,17)	Scarecrow, The (1,9)
(Part III) (12)	Cymbaline (8)	Pts. 1 - 3 (2)	Lucifer Sam (1,9)	One Slip (16)	Seamus (5)
Any Colour You Like (7)	Dogs (11)	Grantchester Meadows (2)	Matilda Mother (1,9)	Outside The Wall (12)	See Emily Play (1,4,15)
Arnold Layne (4,15)	Dogs Of War (16,17)	Great Gig In The Sky (7)	**Money** (7,13,17) **13**	Paint Box (4)	See-Saw (9)
Astronomy Domine (2,9)	Don't Leave Me Now (12)	Green Is The Colour (8)	More, Main Theme From (8)	Paranoid Eyes (14)	Set The Controls For The
Atom Heart Mother Suite	Dramatic Theme (8)	Gunners Dream (14)	More Blues (8)	Party Sequence (8)	Heart Of The Sun (2,9,15)
Medley (3)	Echoes (5)	Happiest Days Of Our Lives	Mother (12)	Pigs On The Wing (Part One	Several Species Of Small
Biding My Time (4)	Eclipse (7,15)	(12)	Mudmen (8)	& Two) (11)	Furry Animals Gathered
Bike (4,9)	Embryo (15)	Have A Cigar (10)	Narrow Way - Parts 1, 2 & 3	Pigs (Three Different Ones)	Together In A Cave And
Brain Damage (7,15)	Empty Spaces (12)	Hero's Return (14)	(2)	(11)	Grooving With A Pict (2,15)
Breathe (7)	Fat Old Sun (3)	Hey You (12)	New Machine Part 1 & 2 (16)	Pillow Of Winds (5)	Sheep (11,13)
Bring The Boys Back Home	Fearless (5,15)	Ibizar Bar (8)	Nile Song (4,8)	Post War Dream (14)	Shine On You Crazy
(12)	Final Cut (14)	If (3)	Nobody Home (12)	Pow R Toc H (1,9)	Diamond - Part I, II, III, IV,
Burning Bridges (6)	Flaming (9)		Not Now John (14)	Quicksilver (8)	V (10,13,17)

579

DEBUT DATE	PEAK POS	WKS CHR	GOLD	ARTIST — Album Title	$	Label & Number

PINK FLOYD — Cont'd

Show Must Go On (12)
Signs Of Life (16)
Sorrow (16,17)
Southampton Dock (14)
Spanish Piece (8)
Speak To Me (7)

Stay (6)
Stop (12)
Summer '68 (3)
Sysyphus - Parts 1, 2, 3 & 4 (2)

Take Up Thy Stethoscope And Walk (1,9)
Terminal Frost (16)
Thin Ice (12)
Time (7,17)
Trial, The (12)

Two Suns In The Sunset (14)
Up The Khyber (8)
Us And Them (7)
Vera (12)
Waiting For The Worms (12)

Welcome To The Machine (10)
When You're In (6)
Wish You Were Here (10,13,17)

Wots...Uh The Deal (6)
Yet Another Movie (16,17)
Young Lust (12)
Your Possible Pasts (14)

PIPKINS, The

British vocal duo: Roger Greenaway and Tony Burrows (low voice). Worked together in studio group White Plains.

| 8/8/70 | 132 | 4 | | Gimme Dat Ding! .... [N] | $15 | Capitol 483 |

All You'll Ever Get From Me
Are You Cookin' Goose?

Busy Line
Gimme Dat Ding 9
My Baby Loves Lovin'

Here Come De Kins
People Dat You Wanna Phone Ya!

Sunny Honey Girl
Yakety Yak

You Can't Go Wrong

PIRATES OF THE MISSISSIPPI

Five-man Country band featuring lead singer Bill McCorvey (from Montgomery, Alabama).

| 5/18/91 | 80 | 23 | | Pirates Of The Mississippi .... | $12 | Capitol 94389 |

Anything Goes
Down And Out In Birmingham

Feed Jake
Honky Tonk Blues

I Take My Comfort In You
Jolly Roger (medley)

Pirates Of The Mississippi (medley)
Redneck Rock N' Roll
Rollin' Home

Speak Of The Devil
Talkin' 'Bout Love

PISCOPO, Joe

Born on 6/17/51 in Passaic, New Jersey. Actor/comedian. Cast member of TV's *Saturday Night Live*, 1980-84.

| 7/27/85 | 168 | 3 | | New Jersey .... [C] | $8 | Columbia 40046 |

Biography
Candid Radio
Fat Boy

Good Morning America
Honeymooners Rap
Late Night

I Wanna Sound Like A Black Man
Music Minus One
MTV

My Oh My
New Jersey

Nightclub, The
Witchcraft

★★341★★ PITNEY, Gene

Born on 2/17/41 in Hartford, Connecticut and raised in Rockville, Connecticut. Own band at Rockville High School. Recorded for Decca in 1959, with Ginny Arnell as Jamie & Jane. Recorded for Blaze in 1960 as Billy Bryan. First recorded under own name for Festival in 1960. Wrote "Hello Mary Lou," "He's A Rebel" and "Rubber Ball." Recorded with George Jones as George & Gene.

12/1/62	48	15	1	Only Love Can Break A Heart................................	$25	Musicor 3003
5/18/63	85	7	2	Gene Pitney Sings Just For You	$25	Musicor 3004
8/3/63	41	31	3	World-Wide Winners .... [G]	$25	Musicor 3005
11/23/63	105	6	4	Blue Gene	$25	Musicor 3006
4/4/64	87	9	5	Gene Pitney's Big Sixteen .... [G]	$15	Musicor 3008
11/14/64	42	17	6	It Hurts To Be In Love	$15	Musicor 3019
3/20/65	141	4	7	George Jones & Gene Pitney	$15	Musicor 3044
				GEORGE JONES & GENE PITNEY		
7/17/65	112	9	8	I Must Be Seeing Things....................................	$15	Musicor 3056
9/18/65	43	24	9	Looking Through The Eyes Of Love	$15	Musicor 3069
3/19/66	123	8	10	Big Sixteen, Vol. 3 .... [G]	$15	Musicor 3085
12/17/66+	61	51	11	Greatest Hits Of All Times .... [G]	$15	Musicor 3102
9/14/68	193	3	12	She's A Heartbreaker..	$12	Musicor 3164

Aladdin's Lamp (2,5)
All The Way (9,10)
Amor Mio (10)
Angels Got Together (2)
Answer Me, My Love (4)
Anywhere I Wander (9)
As Long As She Needs Me (9)
Autumn Leaves (4)
Backstage (11) *25*
Blue Gene (4)
Born To Lose [solo: Gene] (7,10)
Close To My Heart (10)
Cornflower Blue (2)
Cry Your Eyes Out (1,5)
Don't Let The Neighbors Know (2)
Don't Rob Another Man's Castle (7)
Don't Take Candy From A Stranger (8)
Donna Means Heartbreak (1,5)
Down In The Subway (8)
E Se Domani (If Tomorrow) (6)

Every Breath I Take (3,11) *42*
Follow The Sun (6)
Garden Of Love (3)
Going To Church On Sunday (1)
Half Heaven - Half Heartache (1,3,5,11) *12*
Half The Laughter, Twice The Tears (4)
Hate (12)
Hawaii (6)
Heaven Held (12)
Hello Mary Lou (3)
House Without Windows (2,4)
I Can't Run Away (4)
I Can't Stop Loving You (10)
I Lost Tomorrow (Yesterday) (8)
I Love You More Today (6)
I Must Be Seeing Things (8,11) *31*
I Really Don't Want To Know [solo: Gene] (7,10)
I Should Try To Forget (1)

(I Wanna) Love My Life Away (3) *39*
I'll Be Seeing You (4)
I'm A Fool To Care (7)
I'm Afraid To Go Home (10)
I'm Gonna Be Strong (6,11) *9*
I'm Gonna Find Myself A Girl (6)
I've Got A New Heartache (7)
I've Got Five Dollars And It's Saturday Night (7) *99*
If I Didn't Have A Dime (To Play The Jukebox) (1,3) *58*
If I Only Had Time (12)
If Mary's There (8)
It Hurts To Be In Love (6,11) *7*
Just One Smile (8) *64*
Keep Tellin' Yourself (4,5)
Last Chance To Turn Around (10,11) *13*
Last Two People On Earth (6)
Lips Are Redder On You (6)
Little Betty Falling Star (1)

Lonely Night Dreams (Of Far Away Arms) (4)
Looking Through The Eyes Of Love (8,9,10,11) *28*
Louisiana Mama (3)
Love Grows (12)
(Man Who Shot) Liberty Valance (1,3,5,11) *4*
Maria (9)
Marianne (8)
Maybe You'll Be There (4)
Mecca (2,5) *12*
Misty (9)
More (9)
Mr. Moon, Mr. Cupid And I (3)
My Heart, Your Heart (1)
My Shoes Keep Walking Back To You (7)
Not Responsible (2,5)
On The Street Where You Live (9,10)
One Day (8)
One Has My Name (7)
(1-2-3-4-5-6-7) Count The Days (12)

Only Love Can Break A Heart (1,3,5,11) *2*
Peanuts, Popcorn And Crackerjacks (2)
Princess In Rags (10) *37*
Rags To Riches (9,10)
Remind My Baby Of Me (10)
Run, Run, Roadrunner (12)
Save Your Love (8)
She's A Heartbreaker (12) *16*
She's Still There (8)
Ship True Love Goodbye (2,5)
Small Town, Bring Down (12)
Somewhere In The Country (12)
Stay (10)
Sweeter Than The Flowers (7)
Take Me Tonight (3)
Teardrop By Teardrop (2,5)
Tell The Moon To Go To Sleep (2)
That Girl Belongs To Yesterday (6) *49*

There's No Livin' Without Your Lovin' (8,10)
Time And The River (2)
Tonight (9)
Tower Tall (1,3,5)
Town Without Pity (3,5,11) *13*
True Love Never Runs Smooth (1,5) *21*
Twenty Four Hours From Tulsa (4,5,11) *17*
Unchained Melody (9,10)
Walk (6)
Who Needs It (6)
Wreck On The Highway (7)
Yesterday's Hero (4) *64*
Yours Until Tomorrow (12)

PIXIES

Three-man, one-woman group from Boston: Charles "Black Francis" Kitridge Thompson IV (vocals), Joey Santiago (guitar), Kim "Mrs. John Murphy" Deal (bass) and David Lovering (drums).

5/6/89	98	27	1	Doolittle	$8	Elektra 60856
9/1/90	70	12	2	Bossanova	$12	Elektra 60963
10/26/91	92	8	3	Trompe Le Monde	$12	Elektra 61118

translation of French title: Fooling The World

Alec Eiffel (3)
All Over The World (2)
Allison (2)
Ana (2)
Bird Dream Of The Olympus Mons (3)

Blown Away (2)
Cecilia Ann (2)
Crackity Jones (1)
Dead (1)
Debaser (1)

Dig For Fire (2)
Distance Equals Rate Times Time (3)
Down To The Well (2)
Gouge Away (1)

Hang Wire (2)
Happening, The (2)
Havalina (2)
Head On (3)
Here Comes Your Man (1)

Hey (1)
I Bleed (1)
Is She Weird (2)
La La Love You (1)
Letter To Memphis (3)

Lovely Day (3)
Monkey Gone To Heaven (1)
Motorway To Roswell (3)
Mr. Grieves (1)

DEBUT DATE	PEAK POS	WKS CHR	GOLD	ARTIST — Album Title	$	Label & Number

PIXIES — Cont'd

Navajo Know (3)   Planet Of Sound (3)   Silver (1)   Subbacultcha (3)   Trompe Le Monde (3)   Wave Of Mutilation (1)
No. 13 Baby (1)   Rock Music (2)   Space (I Believe In) (3)   Tame (1)   U-Mass (3)
Palace Of The Brine (3)   Sad Punk (3)   Stormy Weather (2)   There Goes My Gun (1)   Velouria (2)

PLANET P
Session musicians assembled by German producer Peter Hauke — Tony Carey, lead singer.

| 3/26/83 | 42 | 23 | | 1 Planet P | $8 | Geffen 4000 |
| 12/1/84+ | 121 | 14 | | 2 Pink World | $10 | MCA 8019 [2] |

PLANET P PROJECT

Adam And Eve (1)   Breath (2)   March Of The Artemites (2)   Requiem (2)   To Live Forever (Part 1 & 2) (2)
Armageddon (2)   I Won't Wake Up (2)   One Star Falling (2)   Send It In A Letter (1)   Top Of The World (1)
Baby's At The Door (2)   In The Forest (2)   Only You And Me (1)   Shepherd, The (2)   What Artie Knows (2)
Behind The Barrier (Part 1 & 2) (2)   In The Woods (2)   Pink World (2)   Static (1)   What Artie Knows (Part 2) (2)
In The Zone (2)   Pink World Coming Down (2)   Stranger, The (2)   What I See (Part 1 & 2) (2)
Boy Who Can't Talk (Part 1 & 2) (2)   King For A Day (1)   Power (2)   This Perfect Place (Part 1 & 2) (2)   **Why Me?** (1) 64
Letter From The Shelter (2)   Power Tools (1)

PLANT, Robert
Born on 8/20/48 in West Bromwich, England. Lead singer of Led Zeppelin and The Honeydrippers.

7/17/82	5	53	▲	1 **Pictures At Eleven**	$8	Swan Song 8512
7/30/83	8	40	▲	2 **The Principle Of Moments**	$8	Es Paranza 90101
6/15/85	20	19	●	3 Shaken 'N' Stirred	$8	Es Paranza 90265
3/12/88	6	48	▲	4 **Now And Zen**	$8	Es Paranza 90863
4/7/90	13	25	●	5 Manic Nirvana	$12	Es Paranza 91336

Anniversary (5)   Fat Lip (1)   Kallalou Kallalou (3)   Pink And Black (3)   **Tall Cool One** (4) 25   Worse Than Detroit (1)
Big Log (2) 20   Heaven Knows (4)   Liars Dance (5)   **Pledge Pin** (1) 74   Thru' With The Two Step (2)   Wreckless Love (2)
Big Love (4)   Helen Of Troy (4)   Like I've Never Been Gone (1)   S S S & Q (5)   Tie Dye On The Highway (5)   Your Ma Said You Cried In
Billy's Revenge (4)   Hip To Hoo (3)   **Little By Little** (3) 36   She Said (5)   Too Loud (3)   Your Sleep Last Night (5)
Burning Down One Side (1) 64   Horizontal Departure (2)   Messin' With The Mekon (1)   **Ship Of Fools** (4) 84   Trouble Your Money (3)
Hurting Kind (I've Got My Eyes On You) (5) 46   Moonlight In Samosa (1)   Sixes And Sevens (3)   Watching You (5)
Dance On My Own (4)   Mystery Title (1)   Slow Dancer (1)   Way I Feel (4)
Doo Doo A Do Do (3)   I Cried (5)   Nirvana (5)   Stranger Here...Than Over   White, Clean And Neat (4)
Easily Lead (3)   **In The Mood** (2) 39   Other Arms (2)   There (2)   Why (4)

PLASMATICS
New York punk-rock quintet led by former porn star Wendy O. Williams. Williams appeared in the film *Reform School Girls*. Guitarist Jean Beauvoir began solo career in 1986.

2/21/81	134	10		1 New Hope For The Wretched	$8	Stiff 9
6/6/81	142	9		2 Beyond The Valley Of 1984	$8	Stiff 11
12/5/81	177	3		3 Metal Priestess	[M] $8	Stiff 666

Black Leather Monster (3)   Dream Lover (1)   Living Dead (1,2)   Pig Is A Pig (2)   Summer Nite (2)   Won't You (1)
Butcher Baby (1)   Fast Food Service (2)   Lunacy (3)   Plasma Jam (2)   Test Tube Babies (1)
Concrete Shoes (1)   Headbanger (2)   Masterplan (2,3)   Sex Junkie (2,3)   Tight Black Pants (1)
Corruption (1)   Hitman (2)   Monkey Suit (1)   Sometimes I (1)   12 Noon (1)
Doom Song (3)   Incantation (2)   Nothing (2)   Squirm (1)   Want You Baby (1)

PLASTIC COW, The
Jazz pianist/studio musician Mike Melvoin performs on the Moog Synthesizer. Wendy Melvoin (Prince's Revolution, Wendy & Lisa) and Susannah Melvoin (The Family) are his twin daughters.

| 11/8/69 | 184 | 2 | | The Plastic Cow Goes Mooooooog | [I] $10 | Dot 25961 |

Ballad Of John And Yoko   Brown Arms In Houston   Lay Lady Lay   One   Plastic Cow   Sunshine Of Your Love
Born To Be Wild   Lady Jane   Medicine Man   One Man, One Volt   Spinning Wheel   Tomorrow Tomorrow

PLASTIC ONO BAND — see LENNON, John

★★459★★ PLATTERS, The
R&B group formed in Los Angeles in 1953. Consisted of Tony Williams (lead), David Lynch (tenor), Paul Robi (baritone), Herb Reed (bass) and Zola Taylor. Group first recorded for Federal in 1954, with Alex Hodge instead of Robi, and without Zola Taylor. Hit "Only You" was written by manager Buck Ram (d: 1/1/91; age 83) and first recorded for Federal, who did not want to use it. In Mercury in 1955, re-recorded "Only You." Williams left to go solo, replaced by Sonny Turner in 1961. Taylor replaced by Sandra Dawn; Robi replaced by Nate Nelson (formerly in The Flamingos) in 1959. Lynch died of cancer on 1/2/81 (age 61). Robi died of cancer on 2/1/89. Williams died on 8/14/92 of diabetes and emphysema. Group inducted into the Rock and Roll Hall of Fame in 1990. Several unrelated groups use The Platters' famous name today.

7/14/56	7	26		1 The Platters	$35	Mercury 20146
1/19/57	12	8		2 The Platters, Volume Two	$30	Mercury 20216
3/30/59	15	8		3 Remember When?	$20	Mercury 20410
3/14/60	6	174	●	4 **Encore Of Golden Hits**	[G] $20	Mercury 20472
11/14/60+	20	18	●	5 More Encore Of Golden Hits	[G] $20	Mercury 20591
7/9/66	100	6		6 I Love You 1,000 Times	$15	Musicor 3091

A-Tisket A-Tasket (3)   I Don't Know Why (2)   **If I Didn't Care** (3) 30   **On My Word Of Honor** (1) 20   Sound And The Fury (5)   You Can Depend On Me (2)
At Your Beck And Call (1)   I Give You My Word (2)   If I Had A Love (6)   **One In A Million** (4) 20   Take Me In Your Arms (2)   You've Changed (2)
Bewitched, Bothered And Bewildered (1)   **I Love You 1000 Times** (6) 31   If I Had You (6)   **Only You (And You Alone)** (4,6) 5   Temptation (2)   **(You've Got) The Magic Touch** (4,6) 4
Thanks For The Memory (3)
Don't Blame Me (5)   I Love You Because (6)   In The Still Of The Night (2)   It's Raining Outside (5) 93   Prisoner Of Love (3)   That Old Feeling (5)
Enchanted (4) 12   **I Wanna** (1) *flip*   Love In Bloom (3)   Remember When (1,3,4) 41   **To Each His Own** (5) 21
Glory Of Love (1)   **I Wish** (5) 42   Lovely (4)   September In The Rain (2)   **Twilight Time** (4) 1
Great Pretender (4) 1   I'd Climb The Highest Mountain (2)   Magic Touch ..see: (You've Got) The   **Sleepy Lagoon** (5) 65   Until The Real Thing Comes Along (3)
Harbor Lights (5,6) 8   My Blue Heaven (5)   **Smoke Gets In Your Eyes** (3,4,6) 1   Wagon Wheels (2)
Have Mercy (3)   **I'll Be Home** (6) 97   **My Dream** (4) 24   Somebody Loves Me (3)   What Does It Matter (5)
Heart Of Stone (2)   I'll Get By (2)   **My Prayer** (1,4) 1   Someone To Watch Over Me (1)   **Where** (5) 44
Heaven On Earth (1,4,6) 39   **I'll Never Smile Again** (3) 25   My Secret (5)   Why Should I? (1)
I Can't Get Started With You (3)   **I'm Sorry** (1,4) 11   **Wish It Were Me** (5) 61

includes new versions of 4 of their top 10 hits

DEBUT DATE	PEAK POS	WKS CHR	GOLD		ARTIST — Album Title	$	Label & Number

PLAYER
Pop-rock group formed in Los Angeles: Peter Beckett (vocals, guitar), John Crowley (vocals, guitar), Ronn Moss (bass), John Friesen (drums) and Wayne Cooke (keyboards). Moss plays Ridge Forrester on the TV soap *The Bold & The Beautiful*. Crowley began solo country career in 1988. Beckett joined Little River Band by 1992.

DEBUT DATE	PEAK POS	WKS CHR	GOLD		Title	$	Label & Number
11/5/77+	26	34	●	1	Player	$8	RSO 3026
9/9/78	37	23	●	2	Danger Zone	$8	RSO 3036
2/6/82	152	7		3	Spies Of Life	$8	RCA 4186

Baby Come Back (1) *1* | Goodbye (That's All I've Ever Heard) (1) | If Looks Could Kill (3) *48* | Love In The Danger Zone (2) | Prisoner Of Your Love (2) *27* | Thank You For The Use Of Your Love (3)
Born To Be With You (3) | I Just Wanna Be With You (2) | In Like Flynn (3) | Love Is Where You Find It (1) | Silver Lining (2) *62* | This Time I'm In It For Love (1) *10*
Cancellation (1) | | It Only Hurts When I Breathe (3) | Melanie (1) | Some Things Are Better Left Unsaid (3) | Tryin' To Write A Hit Song (1)
Come On Out (1) | I'd Rather Be Gone (3) | Join In The Dance (2) | Movin' Up (1) | | Wait Until Tomorrow (2)
Every Which Way (1) | I've Been Thinkin' (2) | Let Me Down Easy (2) | My Mind's Made Up (3) | Take Me Back (3) |
Forever (2) | | | My Survival (3) | |

PLEASURE
R&B group from Portland, Oregon — Sherman Davis, lead singer.

DEBUT DATE	PEAK POS	WKS CHR		Title	$	Label & Number
8/28/76	162	5	1	Accept No Substitutes	$8	Fantasy 9506
4/23/77	113	11	2	Joyous	$8	Fantasy 9526
5/13/78	119	13	3	Get To The Feeling	$8	Fantasy 9550
8/11/79	67	29	4	Future Now	$8	Fantasy 9578
7/12/80	97	14	5	Special Things	$8	Fantasy 9600
5/15/82	164	6	6	Give It Up	$8	RCA 4209

All The Way (6) | Future Now (4) | Law Of The Raw (5) | Pleasure For Your Pleasure (1) | Stone Love (6) | Yearnin' Burnin' (5)
Beginnings (6) | Get To The Feeling (3) | Let Me Be The One (2) | Real Thing (4) | Strong Love (4) | You Are My Star (5)
Can't Turn You Loose (2) | Ghettos Of The Mind (1) | Let's Dance (1) | Sassafras Girl (2) | Take A Chance (5) | Your Love Means Life (Memories) (3)
Carolyn (6) | Give It Up (6) | Living Without You (5) | Sassy Baby (4) | Take It To The Streets (6) |
Celebrate The Good Things (3) | Glide (4) *55* | Love Of My Life (1) | Selim (3) | Thanks For Everything (3) |
Dance To The Music (2) | Happiness (3) | Moonchild, Theme For The (1) | Sending My Love (6) | Thoughts Of Old Flames (4) |
Dedication To The Past (4) | I'm Mad (1) | | Space Is The Place (4) | Tune In (2) |
Departure (4) | It's So Hard (6) | No Matter What (3) | Special Things (5) | 2 For 1 (1) |
Farewell, Goodbye (3) | Jammin' With Pleasure (1) | Nothin' To It (4) | Spread That Feelin' (All Around) (5) | Universal (4) |
Foxy Lady (3) | Joyous (2) | Now You Choose Me (5) | | We Have So Much (1) |
| | Ladies Night Out (3) | Only You (2) | | What's It Gonna Be (6) |

PLIMSOULS, The
Los Angeles rock quartet led by vocalist Peter Case. Plimsouls: British slang for gym shoes.

DEBUT DATE	PEAK POS	WKS CHR		Title	$	Label & Number
4/4/81	153	4	1	The Plimsouls	$8	Planet 13
7/23/83	186	4	2	Everywhere At Once	$8	Geffen 4002

Everyday Things (1) | I Want What You Got (1) | Inch By Inch (2) | Magic Touch (2) | Nickels And Dimes (1) | Shaky City (2)
Everywhere At Once (2) | I Want You Back (1) | Lie, Beg, Borrow And Steal (2) | Million Miles Away (2) *82* | Now (1) | Women (1)
How Long Will It Take? (2) | I'll Get Lucky (2) | | Mini-Skirt Minnie (1) | Oldest Story In The World (1) | Zero Hour (1)
Hush, Hush (1) | In This Town (2) | Lost Time (1) | My Life Ain't Easy (2) | Play The Breaks (2) |

PM DAWN
Jersey City, New Jersey rap duo of brothers Attrell and Jarrett Cordes — nicknamed Prince Be and DJ Minutemix. PM Dawn means "from the darkest hour comes the light."

DEBUT DATE	PEAK POS	WKS CHR	GOLD	Title	$	Label & Number
10/19/91+	48	28	●	Of The Heart, Of The Soul And Of The Cross: The Utopian Experience	$12	Gee St. 510276

Beautiful, The | If I Wuz U | Paper Doll *28* | Set Adrift On Memory Bliss *1* | To Serenade A Rainbow
Comatose | In The Presence Of Mirrors | Reality Used To Be A Friend Of Mine | Shake | Watcher's Point Of View (Don't 'Cha Think)
Even After I Die | On A Clear Day | | |

POCKETS
R&B group from Baltimore, Maryland — Al McKinney, lead singer.

DEBUT DATE	PEAK POS	WKS CHR		Title	$	Label & Number
10/22/77	57	24	1	Come Go With Us	$8	Columbia 34879
10/28/78	85	6	2	Take It On Up	$8	Columbia 35384

Come Go With Me (1) *84* | Got To Find My Way (2) | In Your Eyes (2) | One Day At A Time (1) | Tell Me Why (2)
Doin' The Do (1) | Happy For Love (2) | Lay Your Head (On My Shoulder) (2) | Pasado (1) | Wizzard Wuzzit (1)
Elusive Lady (1) | Heaven Only Knows (1) | | Sphinx (2) | You And Only You (2)
Funk It Over (2) | In The Pocket (1) | Nothing Is Stronger (1) | Take It On Up (2) |

★★134★★ POCO
Country-rock band formed in Los Angeles by Rusty Young (pedal steel guitar) and Buffalo Springfield members Richie Furay (rhythm guitar) and Jim Messina (lead guitar). Randy Meisner (later of the Eagles) left in 1969, replaced by bassist Timothy B. Schmit. As of second album, group consisted of Furay, Messina, Young, Schmit and George Grantham (drums). Messina left in 1970, replaced by Paul Cotton, and Furay left in 1973. Grantham and Schmit (joined Eagles) left in 1977; replacements: Charlie Harrison, Kim Bullard and Steve Chapman. Disbanded in 1984. In 1989, Young, Furay, Messina, Grantham and Meisner reunited. Poco is Spanish for Small.

DEBUT DATE	PEAK POS	WKS CHR		Title	$	Label & Number
6/28/69	63	21	1	Pickin' Up The Pieces	$15	Epic 26460
6/6/70	58	19	2	Poco	$12	Epic 26522
2/6/71	26	21	3	Deliverin' [L]	$12	Epic 30209
9/25/71	52	11	4	From The Inside	$12	Epic 30753
11/25/72+	69	20	5	A Good Feelin' To Know	$10	Epic 31601
9/15/73	38	23	6	Crazy Eyes	$10	Epic 32354
5/11/74	68	13	7	Seven	$10	Epic 32895
11/30/74+	76	11	8	Cantamos	$10	Epic 33192
				title is Spanish for We Sing		
7/19/75	43	18	9	Head Over Heels	$8	ABC 890
8/2/75	90	8	10	The Very Best Of Poco [G]	$10	Epic 33537 [2]
4/3/76	169	4	11	Live [L]	$8	Epic 33336
				recorded November 1974		
5/29/76	89	15	12	Rose Of Cimarron	$8	ABC 946
5/14/77	57	18	13	Indian Summer	$8	ABC 989

DEBUT DATE	PEAK POS	WKS CHR	GOLD	ARTIST — Album Title	$	Label & Number
				POCO — Con'td		
11/25/78+	**14**	52	● 14	Legend	**$8**	ABC 1099
7/26/80	**46**	16	15	Under The Gun	**$8**	MCA 5132
7/25/81	**76**	10	16	Blue And Gray	**$8**	MCA 5227
2/20/82	**131**	8	17	Cowboys & Englishmen	**$8**	MCA 5288
12/4/82	**195**	3	18	Ghost Town	**$8**	Atlantic 80008
5/19/84	**167**	6	19	Inamorata	**$8**	Atlantic 80148
				title is Italian for In Love		
9/23/89	**40**	28	● 20	Legacy...	**$8**	RCA 9694

All Alone Together (12)
All The Ways (8)
And Settlin' Down (5,10)
Angel (7,11)
Another Time Around (8,10)
Anyway Bye Bye (2)
Ashes (medley) (17)
Bad Weather (4,10,11)
Barbados (14)
Bitter Blue (8)
Blue And Gray (16)
Blue Water (6,11)
Boomerang (14)
Brass Buttons (6)
Break Of Hearts (18)
Brenda X (19)
Cajun Moon (17)
Calico Lady (1)
Call It Love (20) **18**
Child's Claim To Fame (medley) (3)
C'mon (3,10) **69**
Company's Comin' (12)
Consequently So Long (1,3,10)
Cowboy's Desire (14)
Crazy Eyes (6)
Crazy Love (14) **17**
Cry No More (18)
Dallas (13)
Dance Medley (13)
Daylight (19)
Days Gone By (19) **80**
Do You Feel It Too (4)

Don't Let It Pass By (2)
Down In The Quarter (9)
Down On The River Again (16)
Down To The Wire (15)
Downfall (13)
Drivin' Wheel (7)
Early Times (4)
El Tonto De Nadie, Regresa (medley) (2)
Everlasting Kind (15)
Faith In The Families (7,10)
Feudin' (medley) (17)
Find Out In Time (13)
First Love (1)
Flyin' Solo (9)
Follow Your Dreams (20)
Fool's Paradise (15)
Fools Gold (6,10,11)
Footsteps Of A Fool (Shaky Ground) (15)
Foreword (medley) (1)
Friends In The Distance (15)
From The Inside (4)
Georgia, Bind My Ties (9)
Ghost Town (18)
Glorybound (16)
Go And Say Goodbye (5)
Good Feelin' To Know (5,10,11)
Grand Junction (1,3,10)
Hard Luck (medley) (3)
Hear That Music (3)
Heart Of The Night (14) **20**

Here Comes That Girl Again (16)
Here We Go Again (6,10)
High And Dry (8,11)
High Sierra (18)
Hoe Down (4)
Honky Tonk Downstairs (17)
How Many Moons (19)
How Will You Feel Tonight (18)
Hurry Up (2)
I Can See Everything (5)
I Guess You Made It (3)
I'll Be Back Again (9)
If It Wasn't For You (20)
If You Could Read My Mind (17)
Indian Summer (13) **50**
Just Call My Name (7)
Just For Me And You (4,10)
Just In Case It Happens, Yes Indeed (1,3,10)
Just Like Me (7)
Keep On Believin' (2)
Keep On Tryin' (9) **50**
Keeper Of The Fire (5)
Kind Woman (3)
Krikkit's Song (Passing Through) (7)
Land Of Glory (16)
Last Goodbye (14)
Legend (14)
Let Me Turn Back To You (9)
Let's Dance Tonight (6)

Little Darlin' (14)
Living In The Band (13)
Love Comes Love Goes (14)
Love's So Cruel (18)
Lovin' Arms (9)
Lovin' You Every Minute (20)
Made Of Stone (15)
Magnolia (6)
Make Me A Smile (medley) (1)
Makin' Love (9)
Man Like Me (3,10)
Me And You (13)
Midnight Rain (15) **74**
Midnight Rodeo (In The Lead Tonight) (18)
Nature Of Love (20)
No Relief In Sight (17)
Nobody's Fool (1,2)
Nothin' To Hide (20) **39**
Odd Man Out (19)
Oh Yeah (4)
Ol' Forgiver (4)
One Horse Blue (8)
P.N.S. (When You Come Around) (12)
Pickin' Up The Pieces (1,3,10)
Please Wait For Me (16)
Price Of Love (17)
Railroad Days (4,10)
Reputation (15)
Restrain (5,11)
Ribbon Of Darkness (17)
Ride The Country (5,11)

Right Along (6,10)
Rocky Mountain Breakdown (7,10,11)
Rose Of Cimarron (12) **94**
Rough Edges (20)
Sagebrush Serenade (8)
Save A Corner Of Your Heart (19)
Sea Of Heartbreak (17)
Shoot For The Moon (18) **50**
Short Changed (medley) (1)
Sittin' On A Fence (9)
Skatin' (7,10)
Slow Poke (12)
Sometimes (We Are All We Got) (16)
Special Care (18)
Spellbound (14)
Standing In The Fire (19)
Starin' At The Sky (12)
Stay (Night Until Noon) (13)
Stealaway (12)
Storm, The (19)
Streets Of Paradise (16)
Susannah (8)
Sweet Lovin' (5,10)
There Goes My Heart (17)
This Old Flame (19)
Tomorrow (1)
Too Many Nights Too Long (12)
Tulsa Turnaround (12)
Twenty Years (13)

Under The Gun (15) **48**
Us (9)
Western Waterloo (8)
What A Day (medley) (1)
What Am I Gonna Do (4)
What Do People Know (20)
What If I Should Say I Love You (4)
Whatever Happened To Your Smile (8)
When Hearts Collide (18)
When It All Began (20)
When You Love Someone (19)
While We're Still Young (15)
While You're On Your Way (17)
Who Else (20)
Widowmaker (16)
Win Or Lose (13)
Writing On The Wall (16)
You Are The One (4)
You Better Think Twice (2,3,10) **72**
You've Got Your Reasons (7)

POGUES, The
Punk-folk octet from Kings Cross, London founded by Jem Finer, Spider Stacy and Shane MacGowan (vocals). Appeared as the McMahon family in the 1987 film *Straight To Hell*. Bassist Cait O'Riordan, wife of Elvis Costello, left the band in late 1986. MacGowan left band in mid-1991.

2/27/88	**88**	16	1	If I Should Fall From Grace With God	**$8**	Island 90872
8/12/89	**118**	9	2	Peace & Love	**$8**	Island 91225
12/15/90	**187**	3	3	Hell's Ditch..	**$12**	Island 422846
				produced by Joe Strummer (The Clash)		

Birmingham Six (medley) (1)
Blue Heaven (2)
Boat Train (2)
Bottle Of Smoke (1)
Broad Majestic Shannon (1)
Cotton Fields (2)
Down All The Days (2)
Fairytale Of New York (1)
Fiesta (1)

Five Green Queens And Jean (3)
Galway Races (medley) (1)
Gartloney Rats (2)
Ghost Of A Smile (3)
Gridlock (2)
Hell's Ditch (3)
House Of The Gods (3)
If I Should Fall From Grace With God (1)

London You're A Lady (2)
Lorca's Novena (3)
Lorelei (1)
Lullaby Of London (1)
Maidrin Rua (3)
Metropolis (1)
Misty Morning, Albert Bridge (1)
Night Train To Lorca (2)
Rain Street (3)

Rainbow Man (3)
Recruiting Sergeant (medley) (1)
Rocky Road (medley) (1)
Sayonara (3)
Sit Down By The Fire (1)
Six To Go (3)
Streets Of Sorrow (medley) (1)
Summer In Siam (3)

Sunnyside Of The Street (3)
Thousands Are Sailing (1)
Tombstone (3)
Turkish Song Of The Damned (1)
USA (3)
Wake Of The Medusa (3)
White City (2)
Worms (1)
Young Ned Of The Hill (2)

POINDEXTER, Buster — see JOHANSEN, David

POINT BLANK
Six-man rock band from Texas — John O'Daniel, lead singer (replaced by Bubba Keith by 1981).

9/11/76	**175**	3	1	Point Blank	**$8**	Arista 4087
8/18/79	**175**	9	2	Airplay	**$8**	MCA 3160
5/31/80	**110**	13	3	The Hard Way	**$8**	MCA 5114
4/25/81	**80**	24	4	American Exce$$	**$8**	MCA 5189
4/17/82	**119**	17	5	On A Roll	**$8**	MCA 5312

Bad Bees (2)
Cadillac Dragon (4)
Changed My Mind (2)
Danger Zone (4)
Distance (1)
Do It All Night (4)
Don't Look Down (5)
Free Man (1)

Getaway, The (4)
Go On Home (4)
Gone Hollywood (5)
Great White Line (5)
Guessing Game (3)
Hard Way (3)
Highway Star (3)
I Just Want To Know (5)

In This World (1)
Let Her Go (5)
Let Me Stay With You Tonight (4)
Lone Star Fool (1)
Louisiana Leg (2)
Love On Fire (5)
Man To Your Queenie (2)

Moving (1)
Nicole (4) **39**
On A Roll (5)
On The Run (3)
Penthouse Pauper (2)
Restless (4)
Rock 'N Roll Soldier (3)
Shine On (2)

Take Me Up (5)
Takin' It Easy (2)
Thank You Mama (3)
That's The Law (1)
Thunder And Lightning (4)
Turning Back (3)
Two Time Loser (2)
Walk Across The Fire (4)

Wandering (1)
Way You Broke My Heart (4)
Wrong To Cry (3)

POINTER, Bonnie
Born on 7/11/51 in East Oakland, California. Member of the Pointer Sisters, 1971-78.

12/16/78+	**96**	15	1	Bonnie Pointer	**$8**	Motown 911
12/22/79+	**63**	14	2	Bonnie Pointer	**$8**	Motown 929

Ah Shoot (1)
Come See About Me (2)
Deep Inside My Soul (2)

Free Me From My Freedom/Tie Me To A Tree (Handcuff Me) (1) **58**

Heaven Must Have Sent You (1) **11**
I Can't Help Myself (Sugar Pie, Honey Bunch) (2) **40**

I Love To Sing To You (1)
I Wanna Make It (In Your World) (1)
Jimmy Mack (1)

More And More (1)
My Everything (1)
Nowhere To Run (Nowhere To Hide) (2)

When I'm Gone (1)
When The Lovelight Starts Shining Through His Eyes (2)

POINTER, Noel

Jazz-fusion violin prodigy from Brooklyn.

DEBUT DATE	PEAK POS	WKS CHR		ARTIST — Album Title	$	Label & Number
6/18/77	144	8		1 Phantazia [I]	$8	Blue Note 736
3/18/78	95	13		2 Hold-On	$8	United Art. 848
9/1/79	138	7		3 Feel It [I]	$8	United Art. 973
8/16/80	167	4		4 Calling	$8	United Art. 1050

As Long As I Know (4)
Calling (4)
Cappriccio Stravagante (2)
Captain Jarvis (3)
Feel It (3)
Fiddler On The Roof (1)
For You (A Disco Concerto) (3)
Higher Than Heaven (4)
Hold On (2)
I Don't Care (4)
Living For The City (4)
Love Is (4)
Mirabella (1)
Morning Song (4)
Movin' In (2)
Night Song (1)
Niteroi (2)
Peace On Earth (4)
Phantazia (1)
Precious Pearl (4)
Rainstorm (1)
Roots Suite Medley (2)
Stardust Lady (2)
Staying With You (4)
Superwoman (Where Were You When I Needed You) (2)
Take A Look (4)
There's A Feeling (When You Touch Me) (3)
'Tween The Lines (4)
Wayfaring Stranger (1)

★★183★★ POINTER SISTERS

Soul group formed in Oakland in 1971, consisting of sisters Ruth, Anita, Bonnie and June Pointer. Parents were ministers. Group was originally a trio, joined by youngest sister June in the early '70s. First recorded for Atlantic in 1971. Backup work for Cold Blood, Elvin Bishop, Boz Scaggs, Grace Slick and many others. Sang in nostalgic 1940s style, 1973-77. In the 1976 film *Car Wash*. Bonnie went solo in 1978, group continued as trio in new musical style.

DEBUT DATE	PEAK POS	WKS CHR	GOLD	ARTIST — Album Title	$	Label & Number
6/23/73	13	37	●	1 The Pointer Sisters	$10	Blue Thumb 48
3/9/74	82	10	●	2 That's A Plenty	$10	Blue Thumb 6000
9/14/74	96	15		3 Live At The Opera House [L]	$12	Blue Th. 8002 [2]
				includes instrumental "Prelude To Islandia" by Tom Salisbury		
6/14/75	22	22		4 Steppin	$10	Blue Thumb 6021
12/4/76	164	6		5 The Best Of The Pointer Sisters [G]	$10	Blue Th. 6026 [2]
12/24/77+	176	3		6 Having A Party	$8	Blue Thumb 6023
12/2/78+	13	32	●	7 Energy	$8	Planet 1
9/22/79	72	8		8 Priority	$8	Planet 9003
8/30/80	34	24		9 Special Things	$8	Planet 9
7/11/81	12	22	●	10 Black & White	$8	Planet 18
7/17/82	59	28		11 So Excited!	$8	Planet 4355
11/13/82	178	3		12 Pointer Sisters' Greatest Hits [G]	$8	Planet 60203
11/26/83+	8	105	▲²	**13 Break Out**	$8	Planet 4705
				second pressings of LP substitute "I'm So Excited" for "Nightline"		
8/10/85	24	34	▲	14 Contact	$8	RCA 5487
11/29/86	48	18		15 Hot Together	$8	RCA 5609
3/19/88	152	6		16 Serious Slammin'	$8	RCA 6562

All I Know Is The Way I Feel (15) *93*
All Of You (11)
All Your Love (8)
American Music (11) *16*
Angry Eyes (7)
As I Come Of Age (7)
Automatic (13) *5*
Baby Come And Get It (13) *44*
Back In My Arms (14)
Bangin' On The Pipes (medley) (2)
Bei Mir Bist Du Schoen (medley) (2)
Black Coffee (2,3,5)
Blind Faith (8)
Bodies And Souls (14)
Bring Your Sweet Stuff Home To Me (8)
Burn Down The Night (14)
Chainey Do (4)
Cloudburst (1,3,5)
Come And Get Your Love (7)
Contact (14)
Could I Be Dreaming (9,12) *52*
Dance Electric (13)
Dare Me (14) *11*
Dirty Work (7)
Don't It Drive You Crazy (6)
Don't Let A Thief Steal Into Your Heart (8)
Dreaming As One (8)
Easy Days (4,5)
Easy Persuasion (13)
Echoes Of Love (7)
Everybody Is A Star (7)
Evil (9)
Eyes Don't Lie (15)
Fairytale (2,3,5) *13*
Fall In Love Again (10)
Fire (7,12) *2*
Flirtatious (16)
Freedom (14) *59*
Going Down Slowly (4,5) *61*
Goldmine (15) *33*
Got To Find Love (10)
Grinning In Your Face (2)
Hands Up (medley) (3)
Happiness (7,12) *30*
Happy (8)
Having A Party (6)
He Turned Me Out (16)
He's So Shy (9,12) *3*
Heart Beat (1)
Heart To Heart (11)
Here Is Where Your Love Belongs (9)
Hey You (14)
Hot Together (15)
How Long (Betcha' Got A Chick On The Side) (4,5) *20*
Hypnotized (7)
I Ain't Got Nothin' But The Blues Medley (4)
I Feel For You (11)
I Need A Man (6)
I Need You (13) *48*
I Will Be There (16)
I'll Get By Without You (6)
I'm In Love (16)
I'm So Excited (11) *30*
I'm So Excited (remix) (13) *9*
If You Wanna Get Back Your Lady (11) *67*
Jada (1,3,5)
Jump (For My Love) (13) *3*
Lay It On The Line (7)
Let It Be Me (8)
Little Pony (2,5)
Lonely Gal (6)
Love In Them There Hills (2,3)
Love Too Good To Last (9,12)
Mercury Rising (15)
Moonlight Dancing (16)
My Life (15,16)
Naked Foot (1)
Nightline (13)
Neutron Dance (13) *6*
Old Songs (1,3)
Operator (13)
Pains And Tears (1)
Pound, Pound, Pound (14)
Pride (16)
River Boulevard (1)
Salt Peanuts (2,3,5)
Save The Bones For Henry Jones (4)
Save This Night For Love (15)
Say The Word (15)
See How The Love Goes (11)
Serious Slammin' (16)
Set Me Free (15)
Sexual Power (15)
Shaky Flat Blues (2,3,5)
Shape I'm In (8)
(She's Got) The Fever (8)
Should I Do It (10,12) *13*
Shut Up And Dance (16)
Sleeping Alone (4,5)
Slow Hand (10,12) *2*
Someday We'll Be Together (10,12)
Special Things (9,12)
Steam Heat (2,3,5)
Sugar (1,5)
Surfeit, U.S.A. (medley) (2,5)
Sweet Lover Man (10)
Take My Heart, Take My Soul (10,12)
Taste (1,5)
Telegraph Your Love (13)
That's A Plenty (medley) (2,3,5)
That's How I Feel (1)
Twist My Arm (14) *83*
Uh Uh (16)
Waiting On You (6)
Wang Dang Doodle (1,3,5) *61*
Wanting Things (4)
We're Gonna Make It (10)
We've Got The Power (9)
What A Surprise (10)
Where Did The Time Go (9)
Who Do You Love (8)
You Gotta Believe (8)
Yes We Can Can (1,3,5) *11*

POISON

Hard-rock quartet formed in Harrisburg, Pennsylvania: Bret Michaels (vocals), Bobby Dall (bass), Rikki Rockett (drums) and CC DeVille (guitar; left band in early 1992).

DEBUT DATE	PEAK POS	WKS CHR	GOLD	ARTIST — Album Title	$	Label & Number
8/2/86+	3	101	▲³	**1 Look What The Cat Dragged In**	$8	Capitol 12523
5/21/88	2¹	70	▲⁵	**2 Open Up and Say...Ahh!**	$8	Enigma 48493
7/28/90	2¹	63	▲³	**3 Flesh & Blood**	$12	Capitol 918132
11/30/91	51	13		4 Swallow This Live [L]	$12	Capitol 98046
				includes 4 studio tracks		

Back To The Rocking Horse (2)
Bad To Be Good (2)
Ball And Chain (3)
Blame It On You (1)
Come Hell Or High Water (3)
Cry Tough (1)
Don't Give Up An Inch (3)
Every Rose Has Its Thorn (2,4) *1*
Fallen Angel (2,4) *12*
(Flesh & Blood) Sacrifice (3)
Good Love (2,4)
I Want Action (1,4) *50*
I Won't Forget You (1) *13*
Let It Play (3,4)
Let Me Go To The Show (1)
Life Goes On (3,4) *35*
Life Loves A Tragedy (3)
Look But You Can't Touch (2,4)
Look What The Cat Dragged In (1,4)
Love On The Rocks (2,4)
No More Lookin' Back (4)
Nothin' But A Good Time (2,4) *6*
#1 Bad Boy (1)
Only Time Will Tell (4)
Play Dirty (4)
Poor Boy Blues (3,4)
Ride The Wind (3,4) *38*
So Tell Me Why (4)
Something To Believe In (3,4) *4*
Souls On Fire (4)
Strange Days Of Uncle Jack (3)
Swampjuice (Soul-O) (3)
Talk Dirty To Me (1,4) *9*
Tearin' Down The Walls (1)
Unskinny Bop (3,4) *3*
Valley Of Lost Souls (3)
Want Some, Need Some (1)
Your Mama Don't Dance (2,4) *10*

★★237★★ POLICE, The

Rock trio formed in England in 1977: Gordon "Sting" Sumner (b: 10/2/51; vocals, bass), Andy Summers (b: 12/31/42; guitar) and Stewart Copeland (b: 7/16/52; drums). First guitarist was Henri Padovani, replaced by Summers in 1977. Copeland had been with Curved Air. Inactive as a group since appearance at "Amnesty '86." Sting began recording solo in 1985. Copeland formed group Animal Logic in 1989.

DEBUT DATE	PEAK POS	WKS CHR	GOLD	ARTIST — Album Title	$	Label & Number
3/3/79	23	63	▲	1 Outlandos d'Amour	$8	A&M 4753

DEBUT DATE	PEAK POS	WKS CHR	GOLD	ARTIST — Album Title	$	Label & Number
				POLICE, The — Cont'd		
11/3/79	25	100	●	2 Reggatta de Blanc..	$8	A&M 4792
10/25/80+	5	153	▲	3 Zenyatta Mondatta..	$8	A&M 4831
10/24/81	2⁶	109	▲²	4 Ghost In The Machine	$8	A&M 3730
7/2/83	1¹⁷	75	▲⁴	5 Synchronicity..	$8	A&M 3735
11/22/86	7	26	▲³	6 Every Breath You Take - The Singles ....[G]	$8	A&M 3902

Be My Girl (medley) (1)
Bed's Too Big Without You (2)
Behind My Camel (3)
Bombs Away (3)
Born In The 50's (1)
Bring On The Night (2)
Can't Stand Losing You (1,6)
Canary In A Coalmine (3)
Contact (2)
Darkness (4)
De Do Do Do, De Da Da Da (3,6) *10*

Deathwish (2)
Demolition Man (4)
Does Everyone Stare (2)
Don't Stand So Close To Me (3) *10*
Don't Stand So Close To Me '86 (6) *46*
Driven To Tears (3)
Every Breath You Take (5,6) *1*
Every Little Thing She Does Is Magic (4,6) *3*
Hole In My Life (1)

Hungry For You (J'Aurais Toujours Faim De Toi) (4)
Invisible Sun (4,6)
It's Alright For You (2)
King Of Pain (5,6) *3*
Man In A Suitcase (4)
Masoko Tanga (1)
Message In A Bottle (2,6) *74*
Miss Gradenko (5)
Mother (5)
Next To You (1)
No Time This Time (2)

O My God (5)
Omegaman (4)
On Any Other Day (2)
One World (Not Three) (4)
Other Way Of Stopping (3)
Peanuts (1)
Reggatta De Blanc (2)
Rehumanize Yourself (4)
Roxanne (1,6) *32*
Sally (medley) (2)
Secret Journey (4) *46*
Shadows In The Rain (3)
So Lonely (1)

Spirits In The Material World (4,6) *11*
Synchronicity I (5)
Synchronicity II (5) *16*
Tea In The Sahara (5)
Too Much Information (4)
Truth Hits Everybody (1)
Voices Inside My Head (3)
Walking In Your Footsteps (5)
Walking On The Moon (2,6)

When The World Is Running Down, You Make The Best Of What's Still Around (3)
Wrapped Around Your Finger (5,6) *8*

POLNAREFF, Michel
Pop vocalist/keyboardist/guitarist.

2/21/76	117	13		Michel Polnareff	$10	Atlantic 18153

Come On Lady Blue
Fame A La Mode
Holding On To Smoke

If You Only Believe (Jesus For Tonite) *48*

Jesus For Tonite ..see: If You Only Believe
No No No No Not Now

Rainy Day Song
Since I Saw You

So Long Beauty
Wandering Man

★★343★★ PONTY, Jean-Luc
Classically-trained, jazz-rock violinist. Born on 9/29/42 in Normandy, France. First American appearance at the 1967 Monterey Jazz Festival. Worked with Frank Zappa and Elton John. Emigrated to the U.S. in 1973. Member of Mahavishnu Orchestra, 1973-75.

7/26/75	158	5		1 Upon The Wings Of Music ....[I]	$10	Atlantic 18138

with Patrice Rushen (keyboards) and Ray Parker, Jr. (guitar)

4/10/76	123	13		2 Aurora ....[I]	$10	Atlantic 18165
12/4/76+	67	23		3 Imaginary Voyage ....[I]	$10	Atlantic 18195
10/1/77	35	16		4 Enigmatic Ocean ....[I]	$8	Atlantic 19110
9/2/78	36	28		5 Cosmic Messenger ....[I]	$8	Atlantic 19189
5/19/79	68	10		6 Jean-Luc Ponty: Live ....[I-L]	$8	Atlantic 19229
10/27/79	54	21		7 A Taste For Passion ....[I]	$8	Atlantic 19253
10/18/80	73	18		8 Civilized Evil ....[I]	$8	Atlantic 16020
2/13/82	44	14		9 Mystical Adventures ....[I]	$8	Atlantic 19333
8/27/83	85	15		10 Individual Choice ....[I]	$8	Atlantic 80098
12/8/84	171	13		11 Open Mind ....[I]	$8	Atlantic 80185

with guests Chick Corea and George Benson

11/2/85	166	4		12 Fables ....[I]	$8	Atlantic 81276

Art Of Happiness (5)
As (9)
Aurora - Part I, II (2,6)
Beach Girl (7)
Between You And Me (2)
Bowing - Bowing (1)
Cats Tales (12)
Computer Incantations For World Peace (10)
Cosmic Messenger (5)
Demagomania (8)
Don't Let The World Pass You By (5)
Dreamy Eyes (7)
Echoes Of The Future (1)

Egocentric Molecules (5,6)
Elephants In Love (12)
Enigmatic Ocean - Part I, II, III, IV (4)
Ethereal Mood (5)
Eulogy To Oscar Romero (10)
Fake Paradise (5)
Far From The Beaten Paths (10)
Farewell (7)
Fight For Life (1)
Final Truth - Part I, II (9)
Forms Of Life (4)
Gardens Of Babylon (3)
Give Us A Chance (7)

Good Guys, Bad Guys (8)
Happy Robots (8)
I Only Feel Good With You (5)
Imaginary Voyage - Part I, II, III, IV (3)
Imaginary Voyage - Part III, IV (6)
In Case We Survive (8)
In Spiritual Love (10)
In The Kingdom Of Peace (12)
Individual Choice (10)
Infinite Pursuit (12)

Intuition (11)
Is Once Enough? (2)
Jig (9)
Life Cycles (5)
Lost Forest (2)
Mirage (4,6)
Modern Times Blues (11)
Mystical Adventures (Suite) - Part I, II, III, IV, V (9)
New Country (3)
No Strings Attached (6)
Nostalgia (10)
Nostalgic Lady (4)
Now I Know (1)
Obsession (7)

Once A Blue Planet (8)
Once Upon A Dream (3)
Open Mind (11)
Orbital Encounters (11)
Passenger Of The Dark (7)
Peace Crusaders (8)
Perpetual Rondo (12)
Plastic Idols (12)
Polyfolk Dance (11)
Puppets' Dance (5)
Question With No Answer (1)
Radioactive Legacy (12)
Reminiscence (2)
Renaissance (2)
Rhythms Of Hope (9)

Shape Up Your Mind (8)
Solitude (11)
Stay With Me (7)
Struggle Of The Turtle To The Sea - Part I, II, III (4)
Sunset Drive (7)
Tarantula (8)
Taste For Passion (7)
Trans-Love Express (4)
Upon The Wings Of Music (1)
Waking Dream (2)
Wandering On The Milky Way (3)
Watching Birds (11)
Waving Memories (1)

POOH-MAN — see M.C. POOH

POOR RIGHTEOUS TEACHERS
Rap trio from Trenton, New Jersey: Wise Intelligent, Culture Freedom and DJ Father Shaheed.

6/16/90	142	22		1 Holy Intellect	$12	Profile 1289
9/21/91	155	3		2 Pure Poverty	$12	Profile 1415

Butt Naked Booty Bless (1)
Can I Start This? (1)
Each One Teach One (2)
Easy Star (2)
Freedom Or Death (2)

Holy Intellect (1)
Hot Damn I'm Great (2)
I'm Comin' Again (2)
Just Servin' Justice (2)
Lessons Taught (medley) (1)

Methods Of Droppin' Mental (2)
Nation's Anthem (2)
Poor Righteous Teachers (1)
Pure Poverty (2)

Rappin' Black (2)
Rock Dis Funky Joint (1)
Self-Styled Wisdom (2)
Shakiyla (1,2)
So Many Teachers (1)

Speaking Upon A Blackman (1)
Strictly Ghetto (1)
Strictly Mash'ion (1)
Style Dropped (medley) (1)

Time To Say Peace (1)
Word From The Wise (1)

POP, Iggy
Punk-rock pioneer. Born James Jewel Osterberg on 4/21/47 in Ann Arbor, Michigan. Leader of The Stooges from 1969-74. Acted in the films *Cry Baby* and *Hardware*. Adopted nickname Iggy from his first band, The Iguanas.

8/23/69	106	11		1 The Stooges..	$20	Elektra 74051
				THE STOOGES		
4/28/73	182	3		2 Raw Power...	$15	Columbia 32111
				IGGY AND THE STOOGES		
4/9/77	72	13		3 The Idiot...	$8	RCA 2275
9/17/77	120	6		4 Lust For Life..	$8	RCA 2488
10/6/79	180	4		5 New Values...	$8	Arista 4237
3/8/80	125	7		6 Soldier	$8	Arista 4259

DEBUT DATE	PEAK POS	WKS CHR	GOLD	ARTIST — Album Title	$	Label & Number

POP, Iggy — Cont'd

9/19/81	166	5	7	Party	$8	Arista 9572
10/18/86	75	27	8	Blah-Blah-Blah	$8	A&M 5145
7/23/88	110	12	9	Instinct	$8	A&M 5198

features guitarist Steve Jones (formerly of The Sex Pistols)

| 7/28/90 | 90 | 37 | 10 | Brick By Brick .... | $12 | Virgin 91381 |

African Man (5)
Ambition (6)
Angel (5)
Ann (1)
Baby (3)
Baby, It Can't Fall (8)
Bang Bang (7)
Billy Is A Runaway (5)
Blah-Blah-Blah (8)
Brick By Brick (10)
Butt Town (10)
Candy (10) *28*
China Girl (3)
Cold Metal (9)
Cry For Love (8)
Curiosity (5)
Death Trip (2)
Dog Food (6)

Don't Look Down (5)
Dum Dum Boys (3)
Easy Rider (9)
Eggs On Plate (7)
Endless Sea (5)
Fall In Love With Me (4)
Fire Girl (8)
Five Foot One (5)
Funtime (3)
Get Up And Get Out (8)
Gimme Danger (2)
Girls (5)
Happy Man (7)
Hideaway (8)
High On You (9)
Home (10)
Houston Is Hot Tonight (7)

How Do Ya Fix A Broken Part (5)
I Need More (6)
I Need Somebody (2)
I Snub You (6)
I Wanna Be Your Dog (1)
I Won't Crap Out (10)
I'm A Conservative (6)
I'm Bored (5)
Instinct (9)
Isolation (8)
Knocking 'Em Down (In The City) (6)
Little Doll (1)
Loco Mosquito (6)
Lowdown (9)
Lust For Life (4)
Main Street Eyes (10)

Mass Production (3)
Moonlight Lady (6)
Mr. Dynamite (6)
My Baby Wants To Rock & Roll (10)
Neighborhood Threat (4)
Neon Forest (10)
New Values (5)
Nightclubbing (3)
1969 (1)
No Fun (1)
Not Right (1)
Passenger, The (4)
Penetration (2)
Play It Safe (6)
Pleasure (7)
Power & Freedom (4)
Pumpin' For Jill (7)

Pussy Power (10)
Raw Power (2)
Real Cool Time (1)
Real Wild Child (Wild One) (8)
Rock And Roll Party (7)
Sea Of Love (7)
Search And Destroy (2)
Shades (8)
Shake Appeal (2)
Sincerity (7)
Sister Midnight (3)
Sixteen (4)
Some Weird Sin (4)
Something Wild (10)
Squarehead (9)
Starry Night (10)
Strong Girl (9)

Success (4)
Take Care Of Me (6)
Tell Me A Story (5)
Time Won't Let Me (7)
Tiny Girls (3)
Tom Tom (9)
Tonight (4)
Tuff Baby (9)
Turn Blue (4)
Undefeated, The (10)
We Will Fall (1)
Winners & Losers (8)
Your Pretty Face Is Going To Hell (2)

POPE JOHN XXIII
Angelo Roncalli. Born on 11/25/1881 in Italy; died on 6/3/63. Served as Pope from 1958-63.

| 8/3/63 | 126 | 3 | | Pope John XXIII ....[T] | $15 | Mercury 200 |

excerpts of the Pope's voice and events during his reign

Canonization

Closing Ceremonies, 2nd Vatican Ecumenical Council

Coronation, His Holiness Pope John XXIII

Election, His Holiness Pope John XXIII
Papal Audience

Papal Blessing, St. Peter's Square

POPE JOHN PAUL II
Karol Wojtyla. Born on 5/18/20 in Poland. Has served as Pope since 1978.

| 11/3/79 | 126 | 4 | | Pope John Paul II Sings At The Festival Of Sacrosong .... | $8 | Infinity 9899 |

recorded during the Pope's return to Poland, June 1979

Brown Madonna
Do Not Be Afraid, Mary, You
Lily

Fanfare For The Pope
Huzulen Song
Little Cantata

Moment Of The Entire Life
Oh, God, I Place My Trust In You
On A December Night
Our Father; Blessing
Peter's Song

Prayer To The Mother Of God
Queen, Black Madonna
Raftsmen, The

Temple Is Our House
We Are Never Alone Like Skipping Stones

POPPY FAMILY Featuring Susan Jacks
Canadian pop quartet: Susan (vocals) and husband Terry Jacks (guitar, composer), Craig MacCaw (guitar) and Satwan Singh (percussion). Group and marriage broke up in 1973; Susan and Terry began solo careers.

| 6/20/70 | 76 | 11 | | Which Way You Goin' Billy? .... | $12 | London 574 |

Beyond The Clouds
For Running Wild
Free From The City

Good Thing Lost
Happy Island
Of Cities And Escapes

Shadows On My Wall
That's Where I Went Wrong *29*

There's No Blood In Bone
What Can The Matter Be?

Which Way You Goin' Billy? *2*

You Took My Moonlight Away

POP WILL EAT ITSELF
Psychedelic-metal-rap-rock quartet from Stourbridge, England: vocalists Clint Mansell and Graham Crabb with guitarist Adam Mole and bassist Richard March.

| 8/26/89 | 169 | 6 | | This Is The Day...This Is The Hour...This Is This! .... | $8 | RCA 9742 |

Can U Dig It?
Def Con One
Fuses Have Been Lit
Inject Me

Not Now James, We're Busy
PWEI Is A Four Letter Word
Poison To The Mind
Preaching To The Perverted

Radio P.W.E.I.
Satellite Ecstatica

Shortwave Transmission On "Up To The Minuteman Nine"

Sixteen Different Flavours Of Hell

Wake Up, Time To Die
Wise Up Sucker

PORTER, David
Born on 11/21/41 in Memphis. Songwriter, teamed with Isaac Hayes, wrote "Hold On I'm Coming," "B-A-B-Y," "I Got To Love Somebody's Baby," and many others.

| 3/28/70 | 163 | 10 | 1 | Gritty, Groovy, & Gettin' It .... | $10 | Enterprise 1009 |
| 1/30/71 | 104 | 9 | 2 | David Porter...Into A Real Thing .... | $10 | Enterprise 1012 |

Can't See You When I Want To (1)
Grocery Man (2)

Guess Who (1)
Hang On Sloopy (2)

I Don't Know Why I Love You (1)
I'm A-Tellin' You (1)
I Don't Want To Cry (2)
Just Be True (1)

I Only Have Eyes For You (1)

One Part - Two Parts (1)
Ooo-Wee Girl (2)
Thirty Days (2)

Too Real To Live A Lie (2)
Way You Do The Things You Do (1)

POSEY, Sandy
Born on 6/18/47 in Jasper, Alabama; raised in West Memphis, Arkansas. Worked as a session singer in Nashville and Memphis in the early '60s. Left music from 1968-70. Backup singer on the Nashville Network.

| 12/17/66+ | 129 | 7 | 1 | Born A Woman .... | $12 | MGM 4418 |
| 9/30/67 | 182 | 4 | 2 | I Take It Back .... | $12 | MGM 4480 |

Arms Full Of Sin (1)
Big Hurt (2)
Blue Is My Best Color (1)
Born A Woman (1) *12*
Boy I Love (2)

Bread And Butter (1)
Caution To The Wind (1)
Come Softly To Me (2)
Halfway To Paradise (2)

I Can Show You How To Live (2)
I Take It Back (2) *12*
If Tears Had Color In Them (1)

It's All In The Game (1)
It's Wonderful To Be In Love (2)
Just Out Of Reach (1)

Love Of The Common People (2)
Miss Lonely (1)
Satin Pillows (2)
Standing In The Rain (1)

Strangers In The Night (1)
Sunglasses (1)
This Time (1)
You Got To Have Love To Be Happy (1)

POST, Mike
Born on 9/29/44 in Los Angeles. Record producer/composer of numerous TV and film scores. Orchestra leader for two TV variety shows: *The Andy Williams Show* (1969-71) and *The Mac Davis Show* (1974-76).

| 11/8/75 | 195 | 3 | 1 | Railhead Overture ....[I] | $10 | MGM 5005 |
| 2/27/82 | 70 | 17 | 2 | Television Theme Songs ....[I] | $8 | Elcktra 60028 |

Blade (1)
Georgia On My Mind (1)
Greatest American Hero (Believe It Or Not), Theme From (2) *2*

Hill Street Blues, Theme From (2) *10*
Lay Back Lafayette (1)
Magnum P.I., Theme From (2) *25*

Manhattan Spiritual (1) *56*
Pictures At An Exhibition (1)
Railhead Overture (1)

Rockford Files (1,2) *10*
School's Out (1)
Viking (1)

White Shadow, Theme From (2)
Will The Circle Be Unbroken (1)
Wouldn't It Be Nice (1)

DEBUT DATE	PEAK POS	WKS CHR	GOLD	ARTIST — Album Title	$	Label & Number

POTLIQUOR
Southern-rock quartet: George Ratzlaff (lead singer), Jerry Amoroso, Guy Scheffler and Les Wallace.

2/19/72	**168**	7		Levee Blues	**$12**	Janus 3033

Beyond The River Jordan	**Cheer 65**	Levee Blues	Train, The	When God Dips His Love In	You're No Good
Chattanooga	Lady Madonna	Rooster Blues		My Heart	

POUSETTE-DART BAND
Country-pop quartet — Jon Pousette-Dart, leader.

3/19/77	**143**	7		**1** Amnesia..	**$8**	Capitol 11608
6/10/78	**161**	5		**2** Pousette-Dart Band 3	**$8**	Capitol 11781

Amnesia (1)	I Stayed Away Too Long (2)	Louisiana (2)	Next To You (2)	Who's That Knockin' (1)
County Line (1)	I Think I Know (1)	Love Is My Belief (2)	Stand By Me (2)	Winterness (1)
Fall On Me (1)	Listen To The Spirit (1)	May You Dance (1)	Too Blue To Be True (2)	Yaicha (1)
I Don't Know Why (1)	Lord's Song (2)	Mr. Saturday Night (1)	Where Are You Going (2)	

POWELL, Adam Clayton
Congressman from Harlem, New York (1944-70); died in 1972 (age 64).

2/25/67	**112**	9		Keep The Faith, Baby! ....[T]	**$10**	Jubilee 2062

a message from Powell, recorded in a studio, January 1967

Burn, Baby, Burn	Death Of Anyman	Handwriting On The Wall	Keep The Faith, Baby!	My Dear Colleagues	One Day

POWER STATION, The
Superstar quartet: Robert Palmer (lead singer), Chic's Tony Thompson (drums) and Duran Duran's John Taylor (bass) and Andy Taylor (guitar). Formed as a one-album studio project. Michael Des Barres replaced Palmer for the group's 1985 concert tour.

4/13/85	**6**	44 ▲		**The Power Station**..	**$8**	Capitol 12380

Communication 34	Go To Zero	Lonely Tonight	**Some Like It Hot 6**
Get It On 9	Harvest For The World	Murderess	Still In Your Heart

POZO-SECO SINGERS
Native Texan trio: Susan Taylor, Lofton Kline and country star Don Williams (lead singer).

7/30/66	**127**	6		**1** Time..	**$15**	Columbia 9315
2/4/67	**81**	10		**2** I Can Make It With You	**$15**	Columbia 9400

Almost Persuaded (2)	Forget His Name (2)	**I'll Be Gone** (1) **92**	Johnny (2)	She Understands Me (1)	You've Lost That Lovin'
Blue Eyes (2)	Guantanamera (1)	If I Fell (1)	**Look What You've Done**	Silver Threads And Golden	Feelin' (1)
Changes (2)	House Of The Rising Sun (1)	If I Were A Carpenter (2)	(2) **32**	Needles (1)	
Come A Little Bit Closer (1)	**I Can Make It With You**	It Ain't Worth The Lonely	Mary Jenkins (2)	**Time** (1) **47**	
Diet (2)	(2) **32**	Road Back (1)	Ribbon Of Darkness (2)	Tomorrow Is A Long Time (1)	

PRADO, Perez
Born Damaso Perez Prado on 12/11/16 in Mantanzas, Cuba. Bandleader/organist. Moved to Mexico City in 1949 and formed a big band. Toured and worked in the U.S. beginning in 1954. In the film *Underwater!*. "The King Of Mambo" died on 9/14/89 after suffering a stroke in Colonia del Valle, Mexico.

5/25/59	**22**	3		"Prez" ....[I]	**$18**	RCA 1556

Adios Mi Chaparrita	Come Back To Sorrento	Cu-Cu-Rru-Cu-Cu Paloma	La Borrachita (I'll Never Love	Lullaby Of Birdland	Maria Bonita
(Goodbye My Little Angel)	(Torna A Sorrento)	Fireworks	Again)	Machaca	Marta
		Flight Of The Bumblebee	Leo's Special		

PRATT, Andy
Born on 1/25/47 in Boston. Great-grandson of Standard Oil's co-founder. Soft-rock singer/songwriter/keyboardist/guitarist.

5/12/73	**192**	4		**1** Andy Pratt	**$10**	Columbia 31722
7/10/76	**104**	10		**2** Resolution	**$8**	Nemperor 438
8/27/77	**90**	9		**3** Shiver In The Night	**$8**	Nemperor 443

All I Want Is You (3)	Deer Song (1)	If You Could See Yourself	Love Song (2)	Sittin' Down In The Twilight	Summer, Summer (1)
All The King's Weight (3)	Dreams (3)	(Through My Eyes) (2)	Mama's Getting Love (3)	(1)	That's When Miracles Occur
Avenging Annie (1) **78**	Everything Falls Into Place	Inside Me Wants Out (1)	My Love Is So Tender (3)	So Faint (3)	(2)
Born To Learn (3)	(Lillian's Song) (2)	It's All Behind You (1)	Rainbow (3)	So Fine (It's Frightening) (1)	Treasure That Canary (1)
Call Up That Old Friend (1)	Give It All To Music (1)	Karen's Song (2)	Resolution (2)	Some Things Go On Forever	What's Important To You (3)
Can't Stop My Love (2)	I Want To See You Dance (3)	Keep Your Dream Alive (3)	Set Your Sights (2)	(2)	Who Am I Talking To (1)
Constant Heat (2)		Landscape (1)			

PRATT & McCLAIN
Truett Pratt and Jerry McClain, with backing group Brother Love.

7/10/76	**190**	2		Pratt & McClain Featuring "Happy Days"	**$10**	Reprise 2250

California Cowboy	**Happy Days 5**	One Way Or The Other	Raised On Rock	Tonight We're Gonna Fall In	Who Needs It
Devil With A Blue Dress 71	Midnight Ride	Our Last Song Together	Summertime In The City	Love	

PREFAB SPROUT
Pop quartet from Britain: brothers Paddy (vocals, guitar) and Martin (bass) McAloon with Wendy Smith (vocals) and Neil Conti (drums).

11/2/85	**178**	5		Two Wheels Good..	**$10**	Epic 40100

Appetite	Bonny	Faron	Hallelujah	Moving The River	When The Angels
Blueberry Pies	Desire As	Goodbye Lucille #1	Horsin' Around	When Love Breaks Down	

PRELUDE
English folk-based trio: Ian Vardy with Brian and Irene Hume (husband-and-wife).

12/7/74	**94**	7		**1** After The Gold Rush	**$10**	Island 9282
11/22/75+	**111**	14		**2** Owlcreek Incident	**$10**	Pye 12120

Adventures On The Way (1)	Dear Jesus (1)	**For A Dancer** (2) **63**	Me And The Boy (2)	Owlcreek Incident (2)	To Hell With The War (1)
After The Goldrush (1) **22**	Faites Vos Jeux (2)	Hotel Room (1)	Meet On The Ledge (2)	Rock Dreams (1)	
Amsterdam (2)	Fly (1)	Lady From A Small Town (1)	Old Sam (2)	Rufus (1)	
Best Of A Bad Time (2)	Follow Me Down (1)	Love Song (2)	Open Book (1)	Shalle (2)	

PREMIATA FORNERIA MARCONI — see P.F.M.

DEBUT DATE	PEAK POS	WKS CHR	GOLD	ARTIST — Album Title	$	Label & Number

PRESIDENTS, The
East Coast soul group consisting of Archie Powell, Bill Shorter and Tony Boyd.

| 1/30/71 | 158 | 6 | | 5-10-15-20-25-30 years of love .... | $12 | Sussex 7005 |

Fiddle De De	For You	How Can You Say You're	It's All Over	**Triangle Of Love (Hey**
5-10-15-20 (25-30 Years	Girl You Cheated On Me	Leavin'	Sweet Magic	**Diddle Diddle)** *68*
Of Love) *11*	Gotta Keep Movin'	I'm Still Dancing	This Is My Dream World	Why Are You So Good To Me

★★1★★ **PRESLEY, Elvis**
"The King of Rock & Roll." Born on 1/8/35 in Tupelo, Mississippi. Died at Graceland mansion in Memphis on 8/16/77 (age 42) of heart failure caused by prescription drug abuse. Won talent contest at age eight, singing "Old Shep." Moved to Memphis in 1948. First recorded for Sun in 1954. Signed to RCA Records on 11/22/55. In U.S. Army from 3/24/58 to 3/5/60. Starred in 33 films (beginning with *Love Me Tender* in 1956). Married Priscilla Beaulieu on 5/1/67; divorced on 10/11/73. Priscilla pursued acting in the 1980s beginning with a role on TV's *Dallas*. Their only child Lisa Marie was born on 2/1/68. Elvis' last live performance was in Indianapolis on 6/26/77. Won the Lifetime Achievement Grammy in 1971. Inducted into the Rock and Roll Hall of Fame in 1986. The U.S. Postal Service issued an Elvis commemorative stamp on 1/8/93.

3/31/56	1[10]	48	●	1 Elvis Presley	$100	RCA LPM-1254
				includes 5 Sun studio recordings		
11/10/56	1[5]	32	●	2 Elvis..	$100	RCA LPM-1382
5/13/57	3	9		3 Peace In The Valley .... [EP]	$75	RCA EPA-4054
				7" EP of sacred songs		
7/22/57	1[10]	29	●	4 Loving You .... [S]	$100	RCA LPM-1515
				only side 1 has the soundtrack recordings		
9/2/57	18	1		5 Loving You, Vol. II.............................. [EP-S]	$75	RCA EPA 2-1515
				7" EP: 4 songs from the soundtrack of previous album		
9/2/57	22	1		6 Love Me Tender .... [EP-S]	$75	RCA EPA-4006
				7" EP of songs from his first film		
9/30/57	16	1		7 Just For You .... [EP]	$75	RCA EPA-4041
				7" EP; 3 of 4 songs from side 2 of *Loving You*; in addition to the above 4 charted E.P.'s, 10 other Elvis E.P.'s made *Billboard*'s pop singles charts, including 5 from soundtracks: "Flaming Star," "Follow That Dream," "Kid Galahad," "Viva Las Vegas" and "Tickle Me"		
12/2/57	1[4]	7	●	8 Elvis' Christmas Album .... [X]	$200	RCA LOC-1035
				gatefold with 10 pages of bound-in color photos of Elvis; includes all 4 songs from *Peace In The Valley* EP; see special Christmas section for more details		
4/21/58	3	50	▲	9 Elvis' Golden Records .... [G]	$100	RCA LPM-1707
9/15/58	2[1]	15		10 King Creole .... [S]	$100	RCA LPM-1884
3/23/59	19	8		11 For LP Fans Only .... [E]	$100	RCA LPM-1990
				includes 4 Sun studio recordings; others from 1956		
9/21/59	32	8		12 A Date With Elvis .... [E]	$150	RCA LPM-2011
				includes 5 Sun studio recordings; others from 1956-57		
2/15/60	31	6	●	13 50,000,000 Elvis Fans Can't Be Wrong - Elvis' Gold Records-Volume 2 .... [G]	$100	RCA LPM-2075
5/9/60	2[3]	56		14 Elvis Is Back!	$115	RCA LSP-2231
				recorded shortly after his March 5th release from the Army		
10/31/60	1[10]	111	●	15 G.I. Blues .... [S]	$100	RCA LSP-2256
12/31/60	33	1		16 Elvis' Christmas Album .... [X-R]	$90	RCA LPM-1951
				repackage of LOC-1035 album (no gatefold or photos)		
1/9/61	13	20	●	17 His Hand in Mine	$90	RCA LSP-2328
				Elvis' first full album of sacred songs		
7/10/61	1[3]	25		18 Something for Everybody........................	$90	RCA LSP-2370
10/23/61	1[20]	79	●	19 Blue Hawaii .... [S]	$90	RCA LSP-2426
1/6/62	120	2		20 Elvis' Christmas Album .... [X-R]	$90	RCA LPM-1951
7/14/62	4	31		21 Pot Luck	$90	RCA LSP-2523
12/8/62+	3	32	●	22 Girls! Girls! Girls! .... [S]	$90	RCA LSP-2621
12/8/62	59	4		23 Elvis' Christmas Album .... [X-R]	$90	RCA LPM-1951
4/20/63	4	26		24 It Happened At The World's Fair .... [S]	$90	RCA LSP-2697
9/14/63	3	63	●	25 Elvis' Golden Records, Volume 3 .... [G]	$65	RCA LSP-2765
12/21/63+	3	24		26 Fun in Acapulco .... [S]	$65	RCA LSP-2756
				includes 2 bonus songs not in the film		
4/11/64	6	30		27 Kissin' Cousins .... [S]	$65	RCA LSP-2894
				includes 2 bonus songs not in the film		
11/14/64+	1[1]	27	●	28 Roustabout .... [S]	$40	RCA LSP-2999
4/17/65	8	31		29 Girl Happy .... [S]	$40	RCA LSP-3338
				includes one bonus song not in the film		
8/14/65	10	27		30 Elvis For Everyone! .... [K]	$40	RCA LSP-3450
				recordings from 2/57 to 1/64 (plus one Sun studio recording)		
11/13/65+	8	23		31 Harum Scarum .... [S]	$60	RCA LSP-3468
				includes 2 bonus songs not in the film		
4/23/66	20	19		32 Frankie And Johnny.............................. [S]	$60	RCA LSP-3553
7/16/66	15	19		33 Paradise, Hawaiian Style .... [S]	$40	RCA LSP-3643
				includes one bonus song not in the film		
10/29/66	18	32		34 Spinout .... [S]	$60	RCA LSP-3702
				includes 3 bonus songs not in the film		
3/25/67	18	29	●	35 How Great Thou Art...............................	$40	RCA LSP-3758
				Elvis' second full album of sacred songs		
6/24/67	47	20		36 Double Trouble .... [S]	$40	RCA LSP-3787
				includes 4 bonus songs (3 from '63) not in the film		
12/2/67+	40	14		37 Clambake .... [S]	$60	RCA LSP-3893
				includes 2 bonus songs not in the film		
3/2/68	33	22		38 Elvis' Gold Records, Volume 4 .... [G]	$40	RCA LSP-3921

DEBUT DATE	PEAK POS	WKS CHR	G O L D	ARTIST — Album Title	$	Label & Number
				PRESLEY, Elvis — Cont'd		
7/6/68	**82**	13		39 Speedway...[S] includes 5 bonus songs not in the film; includes "Your Groovy Self" by Nancy Sinatra	**$40**	RCA LSP-3989
12/21/68+	**8**	32	●	40 **Elvis**...[TV-L] NBC-TV special; Elvis' first live album	**$20**	RCA LPM-4088
4/19/69	**96**	16		41 Elvis sings Flaming Star..[K] only the title song is from the film; others recorded 1963-68	**$20**	RCA Camden 2304
6/14/69	**13**	34	●	42 From Elvis In Memphis... first Memphis sessions since his 1955 Sun recordings	**$25**	RCA LSP-4155
11/29/69	**12**	24	●	43 From Memphis To Vegas/From Vegas To Memphis.......................[L] record 1: Elvis in Person at the International Hotel, Las Vegas; record 2: Elvis Back In Memphis (studio)	**$30**	RCA LSP-6020 [2]
5/9/70	**105**	11		44 Let's Be Friends ....[K] recordings from 1962-69	**$18**	RCA Camden 2408
6/20/70	**13**	20	●	45 On Stage-February, 1970 ....[L] recorded at the International Hotel, Las Vegas	**$20**	RCA LSP-4362
8/22/70	**45**	36	●	46 Worldwide 50 Gold Award Hits, Vol. 1 ....[G] includes all 18 of Elvis' #1 hits	**$65**	RCA LPM-6401 [4]
11/21/70	**65**	18		47 Almost In Love ....[K] recordings from 1966-69 (all but 2 are from films)	**$30**	RCA Camden 2440
11/21/70	**183**	3		48 Elvis Back In Memphis ....[R] previously issued as record 2 of #43 above	**$20**	RCA LSP-4429
12/12/70+	**21**	23	●	49 Elvis-That's The Way It Is..[S-L] 5 of 12 songs are live (Las Vegas)	**$20**	RCA LSP-4445
1/23/71	**12**	21	●	50 Elvis Country ("I'm 10,000 Years Old")...............................	**$20**	RCA LSP-4460
3/20/71	**69**	12		51 You'll Never Walk Alone ....[R-K] reissue of all 4 songs on Peace In The Valley, plus 5 sacred songs recorded 1966-69	**$20**	RCA Camden 2472
6/26/71	**33**	15		52 Love Letters from Elvis... all songs recorded in Nashville during June 1970	**$20**	RCA LSP-4530
7/24/71	**70**	11		53 C'mon Everybody...[K] selections from 4 of Elvis' films (1961-66)	**$20**	RCA Camden 2518
8/28/71	**120**	7		54 The Other Sides - Worldwide Gold Award Hits, Vol. 2.................[G] 22 of 50 songs are from 6 E.P.s released 1956-58	**$70**	RCA LPM-6402 [4]
11/27/71	**104**	8		55 I Got Lucky ....[K] more selections from the same 4 films as in album #53	**$20**	RCA Camden 2533
2/12/72	**43**	19		56 Elvis Now...[K]	**$20**	RCA LSP-4671
4/22/72	**79**	10		57 He Touched Me .... new sacred recordings	**$20**	RCA LSP-4690
7/8/72	**11**	34	▲	58 Elvis As Recorded At Madison Square Garden ....[L] the entire show of 6/10/72	**$20**	RCA LSP-4776
7/8/72	**87**	15		59 Elvis sings hits from his movies, volume 1 ....[K] songs from 4 of Elvis' films (1963-67) plus 2 bonus songs	**$20**	RCA Camden 2567
11/11/72+	**22**	25		60 Burning Love and hits from his movies, volume 2 ....[K] featuring songs from 8 of Elvis' films (1960-67)	**$20**	RCA Camden 2595
1/27/73	**46**	18		61 Separate Ways ....[K] recordings from 1956-63 plus 2 from 1972	**$20**	RCA Camden 2611
2/24/73	**1**[1]	52	▲[2]	62 **Aloha from Hawaii via Satellite** ....[TV-L] RCA's first QuadraDisc; recorded on 1/14/73	**$75**	RCA VPSX-6089 [2]
7/21/73	**52**	13		63 Elvis..	**$50**	RCA APL-0283
11/24/73+	**50**	13		64 Raised On Rock/For Ol' Times Sake.....................................	**$20**	RCA APL-0388
2/2/74	**43**	28	●	65 Elvis-A Legendary Performer, Volume 1 ....[K] unreleased recordings, big hits and interviews (1954-61)	**$25**	RCA CPL-0341
4/6/74	**90**	8		66 Good Times	**$20**	RCA CPL-0475
7/27/74	**33**	13		67 Elvis Recorded Live On Stage In Memphis...............................[L]	**$20**	RCA CPL-0606
11/2/74	**130**	7		68 Having Fun with Elvis On Stage ....[T] excerpts of dialogue from Elvis' live concerts; no track titles listed on this album	**$20**	RCA CPM-0818
2/1/75	**47**	12		69 Promised Land	**$20**	RCA APL-0873
6/7/75	**57**	13		70 Today..	**$20**	RCA APL-1039
2/7/76	**46**	17	●	71 Elvis-A Legendary Performer, Volume 2 ....[K] unreleased recordings, big hits and interviews (1954-68)	**$25**	RCA CPL-1349
4/17/76	**76**	11		72 The Sun Sessions ....[E] Elvis' first commercial recordings (July 1954-July 1955)	**$15**	RCA APM-1675
6/5/76	**41**	17	●	73 From Elvis Presley Boulevard, Memphis, Tennessee .... recorded at Elvis' home, Graceland	**$15**	RCA APL-1506
4/16/77	**44**	25	▲	74 Welcome To My World ....[K-L] recordings from 1969-73 (1 from 1958); 6 of 10 cuts are live	**$15**	RCA APL-2274
7/23/77	**3**	31	▲	75 **Moody Blue**..[K] recordings from 1974-77 (4 live; 6 recorded at Graceland); Elvis' last album release before his death	**$12**	RCA AFL-2428
10/29/77	**5**	18	▲	76 **Elvis In Concert**..[TV-L] record 1: from the CBS-TV Special; record 2: from Elvis' final tour, June 1977	**$20**	RCA APL-2587 [2]
5/13/78	**113**	8		77 He Walks Beside Me ....[K] inspirational recordings from 1966-72	**$10**	RCA AFL-2772
8/5/78	**130**	11		78 Elvis Sings for Children and Grownups Too!...........................[K] featuring recordings from 7 Elvis movies	**$10**	RCA CPL-2901
11/4/78	**86**	7		79 Elvis-A Canadian Tribute ....[K] featuring 3 hits from 1957 plus songs by Canadian composers	**$12**	RCA KKL-7065
1/6/79	**113**	11	●	80 Elvis-A Legendary Performer, Volume 3 ....[K] unreleased recordings, big hits and an interview (1956-70)	**$12**	RCA CPL-3082
3/10/79	**132**	7		81 Our Memories of Elvis ....[K]	**$10**	RCA AQL-3279

DEBUT DATE	PEAK POS	WKS CHR	GOLD		ARTIST — Album Title	$	Label & Number
					PRESLEY, Elvis — Cont'd		
8/25/79	157	5		82	Our Memories of Elvis, Volume 2 .... [K]	$10	RCA AQL-3448
					above 2 albums feature Elvis studio recordings with no additional mixing		
8/23/80	27	14		83	Elvis Aron Presley .... [K]	$80	RCA CPL-3699 [8]
					boxed set: side 1: An Early Live Performance/Monolog; 2: An Early Benefit Performance; 3: Collectors' Gold From The Movie Years; 4: The TV Specials; 5: The Las Vegas Years; 6: Lost Singles; 7: Elvis At The Piano/The Concert Years-Part 1; 8: The Concert Years-Concluded		
2/14/81	49	12		84	Guitar Man .... [K]	$12	RCA AAL-3917
					remixed versions of previously released recordings		
4/25/81	115	10		85	This Is Elvis .... [S-K]	$14	RCA CPL-4031 [2]
					film and records are a documentation of Elvis' career		
12/19/81+	142	7		86	Elvis-Greatest Hits, Volume One............................ [K-L]	$12	RCA AHL-2347
					includes only 3 top 10 hits; 5 cuts are live		
11/27/82	133	9		87	The Elvis Medley .... [K]	$10	RCA AHL-4530
					4-minute medley, plus 9 full-length top hits		
5/21/83	103	6		88	I Was The One... [K]	$10	RCA AHL-4678
					11 rockabilly tracks from 1956-60		
3/17/84	163	4		89	Elvis: The First Live Recordings .... [E-L]	$10	Music Works 3601
					5 performances from the *Louisiana Hayride* (1955-56)		
11/17/84+	80	19		90	Elvis - A Golden Celebration:.................................. [K-L]	$50	RCA CPM-5172 [6]
					boxed set: 1: The Sun Sessions-Outtakes ('54-'55)/The Dorsey Bros. Stage Show ('56); 2: The Dorsey Bros. Stage Show/The Milton Berle Show/The Steve Allen Show ('56); 3: The Mississippi-Alabama Fair And Dairy Show ('56); 4: The Mississippi-Alabama Fair And Dairy Show/The Ed Sullivan Show ('56); 5: The Ed Sullivan Show/Elvis At Home ('57-'60); 6: Collector's Treasures (dates unknown)/Elvis In Burbank ('68)		
12/8/84+	154	13		91	Rocker .... [K]	$8	RCA AFM-5182
					12 of Elvis' best rock 'n roll songs from 1956-57		
3/2/85	154	3		92	A Valentine Gift For You .... [K]	$8	RCA AFL1-5353
					13 of Elvis' classic love songs from 1956-66		
12/28/85	178	2		93	Elvis' Christmas Album... [X-R]	$10	RCA AFM1-5486
					includes the gatefold jacket and full-color photo booklet as in the original 1957 release; Christmas charts: 5/'63, 3/'64, 2/'65, 2/'66, 3/'67, 3/'68, 2/'69, 2/'70, 9/'72, 6/'85, 11/'87, 10/'88, 22/'89, 22/'90, 29/'92, 29/'93		
8/8/87	143	9		94	The Number One Hits .... [G]	$8	RCA 6382
					commemorative issue featuring all 18 of Elvis' #1 hits		
8/15/87	117	8		95	The Top Ten Hits .... [G]	$10	RCA 6383 [2]
					commemorative issue featuring all 38 of Elvis' top 10 hits		
8/29/92	159	2 ▲		96	The King Of Rock 'N' Roll - The Complete 50's Masters .... [K]	$66	RCA 66050 [5]
					boxed set: contains every studio master take of Presley, released during the 1950s as well as alternate takes, early live takes and previously unreleased material plus a 92-page booklet		

Adam And Evil (34)
After Loving You (42,84)
Ain't That Loving You Baby (38,46,96) **16**
All I Needed Was The Rain (41)
All Shook Up (9,40,43,46,58,83,94,95,96) **1**
All That I Am (34) **41**
Almost (44)
Almost Always True (19)
Almost In Love (47) **95**
Aloha Oe (19)
Always On My Mind (61,85,87)
Am I Ready (34,60)
Amazing Grace (57)
Amen (medley) (76,83)
America The Beautiful (83)
American Trilogy (58,62,67,83,85) **66**
And I Love You So (70,76)
And The Grass Won't Pay No Mind (43,48)
Angel (53,78)
Animal Instinct (31)
Any Day Now (42,54)
Anyone (Could Fall In Love With You) (27)
Anyplace Is Paradise (2,96)
Anything That's Part Of You (25,46) **31**
Anyway You Want Me (That's How I Will Be) (9,46,96) **20**
Are You Lonesome To-night? (25,43,46,65, 76,83,85,90,92,94,95) **1**
Are You Sincere (64,81)
As Long As I Have You (10,54,96)
Ask Me (38,54) **12**
Baby, If You'll Give Me All Of Your Love (36)
Baby Let's Play House (12,72,88,89,90,96)
Baby What You Want Me To Do (40,71,83,90)

Barefoot Ballad (27)
Beach Boy Blues (19)
Beach Shack (34)
Because Of Love (22)
Beginner's Luck (32)
Beyond The Bend (24)
Beyond The Reef (83)
Big Boots (15,78)
Big Boss Man (37,40,59) **38**
Big Hunk O' Love (13,46,62,86,94,95,96) **1**
Big Love Big Heartache (28)
Bitter They Are, Harder They Fall (73)
Blue Christmas (8,16,40,71,83,90,93,96)
Blue Eyes Crying In The Rain (73)
Blue Hawaii (19,71)
Blue Moon (1,72,96) **55**
Blue Moon Of Kentucky (12,72,90,96)
Blue River (36) **95**
Blue Suede Shoes (1,15,43,62,71,83,85,90, 91,96) **20**
Blueberry Hill (4,7,67,96)
Bosom Of Abraham (57)
Bossa Nova Baby (26,46,95) **8**
Boy Like Me, A Girl Like You (22)
Bridge Over Troubled Water (49)
Bringing It Back (70) **65**
Britches (80)
Bullfighter Was A Lady (26)
Burning Love (60,62,83,86,87,95) **2**
By And By (35)
Can't Help Falling In Love (19,40,43,46,58,62,65, 67,76,83,92,95) **2**
Cane And A High Starched Collar (71)
Carny Town (28)
Catchin' On Fast (27)
Change Of Habit (44)
Charro (47)

Chesay (32)
Cindy, Cindy (52)
City By Night (36)
Clambake (37)
Clean Up Your Own Back Yard (47,84) **35**
Come Along (32)
C'mon Everybody (53)
Confidence (37,59)
Cotton Candy Land (24,78)
Could I Fall In Love (36)
Crawfish (10,54,96)
Cross My Heart And Hope To Die (29)
Crying In The Chapel (35,46,80,95) **3**
Danny (80,96)
Danny Boy (73,90)
Dark Moon (90)
Datin' (33,83)
Didja' Ever (15)
Dirty, Dirty Feeling (14)
Dixieland Rock (10,54,96)
Do The Clam (29) **21**
Do The Vega (41)
Do You Know Who I Am? (43,48)
Dog's Life (33,83)
Doin' The Best I Can (15)
Don't (13,46,88,94,95,96) **1**
Don't Ask Me Why (10,54,96) **25**
Don't Be Cruel (9,46,58,65,76,83,85,87, 90,94,95,96) **1**
Don't Cry Daddy (46,86,95) **6**
Don't Leave Me Now (4,96)
Don't Think Twice, It's All Right (63,82)
Doncha' Think It's Time (13,54,96) **15**
Double Trouble (36)
Down By The Riverside (medley) (32,59)
Down In The Alley (34)
Drums Of The Islands (33)

Early Morning Rain (56,76,79)
Earth Angel (Will You Be Mine) (90)
Earth Boy (22)
Easy Come, Easy Go (53)
Echoes Of Love (27)
Edge Of Reality (47)
El Toro (26)
Elvis Medley (87) **71**
Evening Prayer (57,77)
Everybody Come Aboard (32)
Eyes Of Texas (medley) (41)
Faded Love (50,84)
Fair's Moving On (43,48)
Fairytale (70,76)
Fame And Fortune (25,54,80,92) **17**
Farther Along (35)
Fever (14,62,92)
Find Out What's Happening (64,82)
Finders Keepers, Losers Weepers (29)
First In Line (2,96)
First Time Ever I Saw Your Face (83)
Five Sleepyheads (39,78)
Flaming Star (80,96) **14**
Flip, Flop And Fly (67,85,90)
Follow That Dream (53,83) **15**
Fool (63,83) *flip*
Fool, The (50,90)
Fool, Fool, Fool (96)
Fools Fall In Love (55)
Fools Rush In (Where Angels Fear To Tread) (54)
For Ol' Times Sake (64) *flip*
For The Good Times (58,74)
For The Heart (73,82) *flip*
For The Millionth And The Last Time (30)
Forget Me Never (30,61)
Fort Lauderdale Chamber Of Commerce (29)
Fountain Of Love (21)
Frankfort Special (15,80)

Frankie And Johnny (32,59) **25**
From A Jack To A King (43,48)
Fun In Acapulco (26)
Funny How Time Slips Away (50,58,83)
G.I. Blues (15,85)
Gentle On My Mind (42,74)
Gently (18)
Get Back (medley) (83)
Girl Happy (29)
Girl I Never Loved (37)
Girl Next Door Went A'Walking (14)
Girl Of Mine (64,81)
Girl Of My Best Friend (14)
Girls! Girls! Girls! (22)
Give Me The Right (18,92)
Go East Young Man (31)
Goin' Home (39)
Golden Coins (31)
Gonna Get Back Home Somehow (21)
Good Luck Charm (25,46,94,95) **1**
Good Rockin' Tonight (12,72,96)
Good Time Charlie's Got The Blues (66)
Got A Lot O' Livin' To Do! (4,5,54,96)
Got My Mojo Working (52)
Green Green Grass Of Home (70,82)
Guadalajara (26,60,80)
Guitar Man (37,40,59) **43**
Guitar Man (re-mix) (84) **28**
Happy Ending (24)
Harbor Lights (71,90,96)
Hard Headed Woman (10,46,87,94,95,96) **1**
Hard Knocks (28)
Hard Luck (32)
Harem Holiday (31)
Have A Happy (44,78)
Have I Told You Lately That I Love You? (4,7,96)
Hawaiian Sunset (19)

(Hawaiian Sweetheart) ..see: Ku-u-i-po
Hawaiian Wedding Song (19,76)
He Is My Everything (57,77)
He Touched Me (57)
He'll Have To Go (75)
He's Only A Prayer Away (90)
He's Your Uncle Not Your Dad (39)
Heart Of Rome (52)
Heartbreak Hotel (9,40,46,58,65,83,85,87, 90,94,95,96) **1**
Help Me (67,69)
Help Me Make It Through The Night (56,74)
Here Comes Santa Claus (Right Down Santa Claus Lane) (8,16,93,96)
Hey, Hey, Hey (37)
Hey Jude (56)
Hey Little Girl (31)
Hi-Heel Sneakers (83)
His Hand In Mine (17)
Home Is Where The Heart Is (55)
Hot Dog (4,5,54,96)
Hound Dog (9,40,43,46,58,62,67,76, 80,83,85,87,89,90,91,94, 95,96) **1**
House Of Sand (33)
House That Has Everything (37)
How Can You Lose What You Never Had (37)
How Do You Think I Feel (2,96)
How Great Thou Art (35,67,71,76,77,83)
How The Web Was Woven (49)
How Would You Like To Be (24,59,78)
How's The World Treating You (2,96)
Hurt (73,76) **28**
I Beg Of You (13,46,95,96) **8**

PRESLEY, Elvis — Cont'd

Believe (3,8,16,51,93,96)
Believe In The Man In The Sky (17,54)
Can Help (70,82)
Can't Stop Loving You (43,58,62,67,74)
Don't Care If The Sun Don't Shine (72,90,96) **74**
Don't Wanna Be Tied (22)
Don't Want To (22)
Feel So Bad (25,46,95) **5**
Feel That I've Known You Forever (21)
Forgot To Remember To Forget (12,72,96)
Got A Feelin' In My Body (66,82)
Got A Woman (1,67,76,83,90,91,96)
Got Lucky (55)
Got Stung (13,46,95,96) **8**
Gotta Know (25,46) **20**
, John (57)
Just Can't Help Believin' (49)
Love Only One Girl (36,60)
Love You Because (1,65,72,96)
Met Her Today (30,61)
Miss You (64)
Need Somebody To Lean On (55,92)
Need You So (4,7,96)
Need Your Love Tonight (13,54,83,85,95,96) **4**
Really Don't Want To Know (50,54,74,76) **21**
Slipped, I Stumbled, I Fell (18,61)
Think I'm Gonna Like It Here (26)
Wanna Play House With You ..see: Baby Let's Play House
Want To Be Free (12,54,96)
Want You, I Need You, I Love You (9,46,71,90,94,95,96) **1**
Want You With Me (18)
Was Born About Ten Thousand Years Ago (50,56)
Was The One (11,46,88,90,92,96) **19**
Washed My Hands In Muddy Water (50)
Will Be Home Again (14)
Will Be True (63,83)
ll Be Back (34)
ll Be Home For Christmas (8,16,93,96)
ll Be There (If You Ever Want Me) (44)
ll Hold You In My Heart (Till I Can Hold You In My Arms) (42)
ll Never Fall In Love Again (73,81)
ll Never Know (52)
ll Never Let You Go (Little Darlin') (1,72,90,96)
ll Take Love (53)
ll Take You Home Again Kathleen (63,83)
m Comin' Home (18)
m Counting On You (1,96)
m Falling In Love Tonight (24,83)
m Gonna Sit Right Down And Cry (Over You) (1,96)
m Gonna Walk Dem Golden Stairs (17)
m Leavin' (83) **36**
m Left, You're Right, She's Gone (11,72,90,96)
m Movin' On (42,79,84)
m Not The Marrying Kind (53)
m So Lonesome I Could Cry (62,74)
m Yours (21) **11**
ve Got A Thing About You Baby (66,85) **39**

I've Got Confidence (57)
I've Got To Find My Baby (29)
I've Lost You (49,54) **32**
If I Can Dream (40,46,71,77) **12**
If I Were You (52)
If I'm A Fool (For Loving You) (44)
If That Isn't Love (66)
If The Lord Wasn't Walking By My Side (35)
If We Never Meet Again (17)
If You Don't Come Back (44)
If You Love Me (Let Me Know) (75,76,83)
If You Talk In Your Sleep (69) **17**
If You Think I Don't Need You (55)
Impossible Dream (The Quest) (58,77)
In My Father's House (17)
In My Way (30,61)
In The Garden (35)
In The Ghetto (42,43,48,46,80,83,95) **3**
In Your Arms (18)
Indescribably Blue (38) **33**
Inherit The Wind (43,48)
Is It So Strange (7,12,61,96)
Island Of Love (19)
It Ain't No Big Thing (But It's Growing) (52)
It Feels So Right (14,92) **55**
It Hurts Me (38,54,80) **29**
It Is No Secret (What God Can Do) (3,8,16,51,93,96)
It Keeps Right On A-Hurtin' (42)
It Won't Be Long (36)
(It's A) Long Lonely Highway (27)
It's A Matter Of Time (60)
It's A Sin (18)
It's A Wonderful World (28)
It's Carnival Time (28)
It's Easy For You (75)
It's Impossible (63)
It's Midnight (69,81)
It's Now Or Never (25,46,71,76,83,94,95) **1**
It's Only Love (83) **51**
It's Over (62)
It's Still Here (63,83)
It's Your Baby, You Rock It (50)
Ito Eats (19)
Jailhouse Rock (9,40,46,67,71,76,79,83, 85,87,91,94,95,96) **1**
Jesus Knows What I Need (17)
Johnny B. Goode (43,62,76,83)
Joshua Fit The Battle (17)
Judy (18) **78**
Just A Little Bit (64)
Just Because (1,72,96)
Just Call Me Lonesome (37,84)
Just For Old Time Sake (21)
Just Pretend (49)
Just Tell Her Jim Said Hello (38,54) **55**
Kentucky Rain (46,83) **16**
King Creole (10,54,96)
King Of The Whole Wide World (30) **30**
Kismet (31)
Kiss Me Quick (21) **34**
Kissin' Cousins (27,46) **12**
Kissin' Cousins (Number 2) (27)
Known Only To Him (17,77)
Ku-u-i-po (Hawaiian Sweetheart) (19)
Last Farewell (73)
Lawdy Miss Clawdy (11,40,67,83,90,91,96)
Lead Me, Guide Me (17)
Let It Be Me (45,80)
Let Me (6,54,96)
Let Me Be There (67,75,83)

(Let Me Be Your) Teddy Bear (4,9,46,58,76,78,79,83, 85,87,94,95,96) **1**
Let Us Pray (51)
Let Yourself Go (39,80) **71**
Let's Be Friends (44)
Let's Forget About The Stars (44)
Life (52) **53**
Like A Baby (14)
Little Bit Of Green (43,48)
Little Cabin On The Hill (50)
Little Darlin' (75,79,83)
Little Egypt (28,40)
Little Less Conversation (47) **69**
Little Sister (25,46,76,83,88,95) **5**
Lonely Man (38,54) **32**
Lonesome Cowboy (4,5,54,96)
Long Black Limousine (42)
Long Legged Girl (With The Short Dress On) (36,47,59) **63**
Long Live Rock And Roll (83)
Long Tall Sally (2,62,67,83,90,91,96)
Look Out, Broadway (32)
Love Coming Down (73)
Love Letters (38,52,92) **19**
Love Machine (55)
Love Me (2,9,54,58,62,65,67,76, 83,90,95,96) **2**
Love Me, Love The Life I Lead (63)
Love Me Tender (6,9,40,46,58,65,83,85, 90,94,95,96) **1**
Love Me Tonight (26)
Love Song Of The Year (69)
Lover Doll (10,54,96)
Lovin' Arms (66,84)
Loving You (4,9,46,79,96) **20**
Make Me Know It (14)
Make The World Go Away (50,74)
Mama (44)
Mama Don't Dance (medley) (67)
Mansion Over The Hilltop (17)
Marguerita (26)
(Marie's The Name) His Latest Flame (25,54,85,95) **4**
Mary In The Morning (49)
Maybellene (29)
Mean Woman Blues (4,5,54,85,96)
Meanest Girl In Town (29)
Memories (36,47,59) **35**
Memphis, Tennessee (30)
Merry Christmas Baby (85)
Mess Of Blues (38,46) **32**
Mexico (26)
Milkcow Blues Boogie (12,72,96)
Milky White Way (17)
Mine (39)
Miracle Of The Rosary (56,77)
Mirage (31)
Money Honey (1,83,90,91,96) **76**
Moody Blue (75,85) **31**
Moonlight Swim (19)
Mr. Songman (69)
My Babe (43,83)
My Baby Left Me (11,54,67,85,88,96) **31**
My Boy (66,81) **20**
My Desert Serenade (31)
My Happiness (96)
My Heart Cries For You (90)
My Little Friend (96)
My Way (62,76,79,83,85) **22**
My Wish Came True (13,54,96) **12**
Mystery Train (11,43,72,83,96)

Never Again (73,81)
Never Been To Spain (58)
Never Ending (36)
Never Say Yes (34)
New Orleans (10,54,96)
Next Step Is Love (49,54) flip
Night Life (41)
Night Rider (21)
No More (19,60)
Nothingville (medley) (40)
(Now And Then There's) A Fool Such As I (13,46,65,83,95,96) **2**
Oh Little Town Of Bethlehem (8,16,93,96)
Old MacDonald (36,59,78)
Old Shep (2,61,78,96) **47**
Once Is Enough (27)
One Boy Two Little Girls (27)
One Broken Heart For Sale (24,46) **11**
One Night (13,40,54,83,90,95,96) **4**
One Night Of Sin (96)
One-Sided Love Affair (1,96)
One Track Heart (28)
Only Believe (52) flip
Only The Strong Survive (42)
Padre (63,77)
Paradise, Hawaiian Style (33)
Paralyzed (2,54,88,96) **59**
Party (4,96)
Patch It Up (49,54) flip
Peace In The Valley ..see: (There'll Be)
Petunia, The Gardener's Daughter (32)
Pieces Of My Life (70)
Playing For Keeps (11,46,92,96) **21**
Please Don't Drag That String Around (38,54)
Please Don't Stop Loving Me (32) **45**
Pledging My Love (75)
Pocketful Of Rainbows (15)
Poison Ivy League (28)
Polk Salad Annie (45,58,83)
Poor Boy (6,11,54,96) **24**
Power Of My Love (42)
Promised Land (69,85) **14**
Proud Mary (45,58)
Puppet On A String (29,54,78) **14**
Put The Blame On Me (18)
Put Your Hand In The Hand (56,79)
Queenie Wahine's Papaya (33)
Rags To Riches (83) flip
Raised On Rock (64) **41**
Reach Out To Jesus (57)
Ready Teddy (2,88,90,91,96)
Reconsider Baby (14,83,96)
Relax (24)
Release Me (And Let Me Love Again) (45,74)
Return To Sender (22,46,95) **2**
Riding The Rainbow (55)
Rip It Up (2,54,88,91,96)
Rock-A-Hula Baby (19,46) **23**
Roustabout (28)
Rubberneckin' (47) flip
Run On (35)
Runaway (45)
Sand Castles (33)
Santa Bring My Baby Back (To Me) (8,16,93,96)
Santa Claus Is Back In Town (8,16,93,96)
Santa Lucia (30,60)
Saved (medley) (40)
Scratch My Back (Then I'll Scratch Yours) (33)
See See Rider (45,62,67,76,83)
Seeing Is Believing (57)
Sentimental Me (54)
Separate Ways (61) **20**
Shake A Hand (70)

Shake, Rattle And Roll (11,85,90,91,96)
Shake That Tambourine (31)
She Thinks I Still Care (75,81,84) flip
She Wears My Ring (66,82)
She's A Machine (41)
She's Not You (25,46,95) **5**
Shoppin' Around (15,83)
Shout It Out (32)
Silent Night (8,16,93,96)
Sing You Children (51)
Singing Tree (37)
Slicin' Sand (19)
Slowly But Surely (26)
Smokey Mountain Boy (27)
Smorgasbord (34)
Snowbird (50,79)
So Close, Yet So Far (From Paradise) (31)
So Glad You're Mine (2,96)
So High (35)
Softly, As I Leave You (83)
Soldier Boy (14,90)
Solitaire (73,81)
Somebody Bigger Than You And I (35,77)
Something (62)
Something Blue (21)
Song Of The Shrimp (22)
Sound Advice (19)
Sound Of Your Cry (86)
Spanish Eyes (66,81)
Speedway (39)
Spinout (34) **40**
Spring Fever (29)
Stand By Me (35)
Startin' Tonight (29)
Starting Today (18)
Stay Away (44,47) **67**
Steadfast, Loyal And True (10,96)
Steamroller Blues (62,86) **17**
Steppin' Out Of Line (21)
Stop, Look And Listen (34)
Stop Where You Are (33)
Stranger In My Own Home Town (43,48)
Stranger In The Crowd (49)
Stuck On You (25,46,94,95) **1**
Such A Night (14,71,83) **16**
(Such An) Easy Question (21) **11**
Summer Kisses, Winter Tears (30)
Suppose (39,90)
Surrender (25,46,80,94,95) **1**
Susan When She Tried (70)
Suspicion (21)
Suspicious Minds (43,46,58,62,83,85,86, 87,94,95) **1**
Sweet Angeline (64)
Sweet Caroline (45,83)
Swing Down Sweet Chariot (17,83)
Sylvia (36)
Take Good Care Of Her (66,81) flip
Take Me To The Fair (24)
Take My Hand, Precious Lord (3,8,16,51,93,96)
Talk About The Good Times (66)
Teddy Bear ..see: (Let Me Be Your)
Tell Me Why (54,92,96) **33**
Tender Feeling (27,60)
Thanks To The Rolling Sea (22,83)
That's All Right (11,58,65,72,76,83,85, 89,90,96)
That's Someone You Never Forget (21) **92**
(That's What You Get) For Lovin' Me (63,79)
That's When Your Heartaches Begin (9,46,96) **58**

There Ain't Nothing Like A Song (39)
There Goes My Everything (50,54,86) flip
There Is No God But God (57)
There Is So Much World To See (36)
(There'll Be) Peace In The Valley (For Me) (3,8,16,51,65,90,93,96) **25**
There's A Brand New Day On The Horizon (28)
There's A Honky Tonk Angel (Who Will Take Me Back In) (69,82)
There's Always Me (18) **56**
There's Gold In The Mountains (27)
(There's) No Room To Rhumba In A Sports Car (26)
They Remind Me Too Much Of You (24,54,59,83) **53**
Thing Called Love (57)
Thinking About You (69,82)
This Is Living (53)
This Is My Heaven (33)
This Is Our Dance (52)
This Is The Story (43,48)
Three Corn Patches (64)
Thrill Of Your Love (14)
Tiger Man (41,43,83,90)
Today, Tomorrow And Forever (52)
Tomorrow Is A Long Time (34,92)
Tomorrow Never Comes (50)
Tomorrow Night (30,96)
Tonight Is So Right For Love (15,60,65,83)
Too Much (9,46,90,94,95,96) **1**
Too Much Monkey Business (41,84,85)
Treat Me Nice (9,46,96) **18**
T-R-O-U-B-L-E (70,83) **35**
Trouble (10,40,54,96)
True Love (4,96)
True Love Travels On A Gravel Road (42)
Tryin' To Get To You (1,65,67,72,76,83,90,96)
Tutti Frutti (1,90,91,96)
Tweedle Dee (89,96)
Twenty Days And Twenty Nights (49)
U.S. Male (47) **28**
Unchained Melody (75,83)
Until It's Time For You To Go (56,79) **40**
Up Above My Head (medley) (40)
Vino, Dinero Y Amor (26)
Viva Las Vegas (46,85) **29**
Walk A Mile In My Shoes (45)
Walls Have Ears (22)
Way Down (75,82) **18**
We Call On Him (51)
We Can Make The Morning (56)
We'll Be Together (22,60)
We're Coming In Loaded (22)
We're Gonna Move (6,12,54,96)
Wear My Ring Around Your Neck (13,46,88,95,96) **2**
Wearin' That Loved On Look (42)
Welcome To My World (62,74,83)
Western Union (39)
What A Wonderful Life (50)
What Every Woman Lives For (32)
What Now My Love (62)
What Now, What Next, Where To (36,61)
What'd I Say (38,76,86) **21**
What's She Really Like (15)
Wheels On My Heels (28)
When I'm Over You (52)

PRESLEY, Elvis — Cont'd

When It Rains, It Really Pours (30,90,96)	Where Do You Come From (22,46) **99**	Wild In The Country (54,83) **26**
When My Blue Moon Turns To Gold Again (2,54,90,96) **19**	Where No One Stands Alone (35)	Wisdom Of The Ages (31)
When The Saints Go Marching In (medley) (32,59)	Whistling Tune (53)	**Witchcraft** (38,54) **32**
Where Could I Go But To The Lord (35,40)	White Christmas (8,16,93,96)	Without Him (35)
Where Did They Go, Lord (77) **33**	Who Am I? (51,77)	Without Love (There Is Nothing) (43,48)
Where Do I Go From Here (63)	Who Are You? (Who Am I?) (39)	Wolf Call (29)
	Who Needs Money (37)	Woman Without Love (70)
	Whole Lot-ta Shakin' Goin' On (50,62,67)	**Wonder Of You** (45,54,83,86,95) **9**
	Why Me Lord (67,83)	Wonderful World (41)
		Wooden Heart (15,46,78)
		Words (43)

Working On The Building (17)	**You Don't Know Me** (37,59) **44**	(You're the) Devil In Disguise (38,46,95) **3**
World Of Our Own (24)	You Gave Me A Mountain (62,76,83)	You've Lost That Lovin' Feelin' (49,58,83)
Write To Me From Naples (90)	You Gotta Stop (55)	Young And Beautiful (12,54,88,92,96)
Yellow Rose Of Texas (medley) (41)	You'll Be Gone (29)	Young Dreams (10,54,96)
Yesterday (45,83)	**You'll Never Walk Alone** (51,86) **90**	Your Cheatin' Heart (30,74,96)
Yoga Is As Yoga Does (55)	You'll Think Of Me (43,48,54)	Your Love's Been A Long Time Coming (69,81)
You Asked Me To (69,84)	You're A Heartbreaker (11,72,96)	**Your Time Hasn't Come Yet, Baby** (39) **72**
You Can't Say No In Acapulco (26)	(You're So Square) Baby I Don't Care (12,54,88,91,96)	
You Don't Have To Say You Love Me (49,54,58) **11**		

★★377★★ PRESTON, Billy

Born on 9/9/46 in Houston. R&B vocalist/keyboardist. To Los Angeles at an early age. With Mahalia Jackson in 1956. Played piano in film *St. Louis Blues*, 1958. Regular on *Shindig* TV show. Recorded with The Beatles on "Get Back" and "Let It Be"; worked Concert For Bangladesh in 1969. Prominent session man, played on Sly & The Family Stone hits. With The Rolling Stones U.S. tour in 1975.

DEBUT DATE	PEAK POS	WKS CHR		ARTIST — Album Title	$	Label & Number
6/12/65	143	3	1	The Most Exciting Organ Ever ....[I]	$20	Vee-Jay 1123
7/9/66	118	6	2	Wildest Organ In Town! ....[I]	$20	Vee-Jay 2532
1/22/72	32	38	3	I Wrote A Simple Song	$10	A&M 3507
6/10/72	127	12	4	That's The Way God Planned It .... [R]	$10	Apple 3359
				originally released in 1969; produced by George Harrison		
12/23/72+	32	35	5	Music Is My Life	$10	A&M 3516
10/27/73	52	18	6	Everybody Likes Some Kind Of Music........................	$10	A&M 3526
9/21/74	17	14	7	The Kids & Me	$10	A&M 3645
7/19/75	43	14	8	It's My Pleasure	$10	A&M 4532
3/8/80	49	18	9	Late At Night	$8	Motown 925
8/8/81	127	9	10	Billy Preston & Syreeta	$8	Motown 958

BILLY PRESTON & SYREETA

Advice (2)	If I Had A Hammer (1)	Long And Lasting Love (10)	One Time Or Another (5)	That's Life (8)

Advice (2)	Free Funk (2)	If I Had A Hammer (1)	Long And Lasting Love (10)	One Time Or Another (5)	That's Life (8)
Ain't Got No Time To Play (2)	Give It Up, Hot (9)	"In" Crowd (9)	Looner Tune (3)	Outa-Space (3) **2**	**That's The Way God Planned It** (4) **62**
Ain't That Nothin' (5)	God Is Great (3)	In The Midnight Hour (2)	Love (10)	Sad Sad Song (7)	
All I Wanted Was You (9)	God Loves You (5)	It Doesn't Matter (4)	Love Makes Me Do Foolish Things (2)	Searchin' (10)	This Is It (1)
All Of My Life (8)	Hard Day's Night (2)	It Will Come In Time (9)	Lovely Lady (9)	She Belongs To Me (4)	Uptight (Everything's Alright) (2)
Billy's Bag (1)	Heart Full Of Sorrow (5)	It's Alright Ma (I'm Only Bleeding) (6)	Low Down (1)	Should've Known Better (3)	We're Gonna Make It (5)
Blackbird (5)	Hey Brother (4)	It's Got To Happen (2)	Make The Devil Mad (Turn On To Jesus) (5)	Slippin' And Slidin' (1)	What About You (4)
Bus, The (3)	Hey You (10)	It's My Pleasure (8)	Masquerade Is Over (1)	Sister Sugar (4)	What We Did For Love (10)
Creature Feature (7)	How Long Has The Train Been Gone (6)	It's So Easy (10)	Minuet For Me (6)	Sock-It, Rocket (1)	**Will It Go Round In Circles** (5) **1**
Do It While You Can (8)	I Am Coming Through (1)	John Henry (3)	Morning Star (4)	Someone Special (10)	**With You I'm Born Again** (9) **4**
Do What You Want (4)	(I Can't Get No) Satisfaction (2)	John The Baptist (7)	Music's My Life (5)	Sometimes I Love You (7)	Without A Song (3)
Do You Love Me? (6)	I Can't Stand It (8)	Just For You (10)	My Country 'Tis Of Thee (3)	Song Of Joy (8)	You (9)
Don't Let The Sun Catch You Crying (1)	I Come To Rest In You (9)	Keep It To Yourself (4)	My Soul Is A Witness (4)	Soul Meetin' (1)	You Are So Beautiful (7)
Drown In My Tears (1)	I Got You (I Feel Good) (2)	Late At Night (9)	New Way To Say I Love You (10)	Space Race (6) **4**	You Done Got Older (3)
Duck, The (2)	I Want To Thank You (4)	Let Me Know (1)		St. Elmo (3)	**You're So Unique** (4) **48**
Everybody Likes Some Kind Of Music (6)	I Wonder Why (5)	Let Us All Get Together Right Now (4)	Nigger Charlie (5)	Steady Gettin' It (1)	You've Got Me For Company (6)
Everything's All Right (4)	**I Wrote A Simple Song** (3) **77**	Listen To The Wind (6)	**Nothing From Nothing** (7) **1**	**Struttin'** (7) **22**	
Fancy Lady (8) **71**	I'm So Tired (6)	Little Black Boys And Girls (7)	Octopus, The (1)	Sunday Morning (6)	
Found The Love (8)			One More Try (1)	Swing Down Chariot (3)	
				Tell Me You Need My Loving (3)	

★★393★★ PRETENDERS, The

Rock quartet featuring lead singer/songwriter/guitarist Chrissie Hynde (b: 9/7/51, Akron, Ohio). Formed in 1978, early British lineup included guitarist James Honeyman-Scott (d: 6/16/82; replaced by Robbie MacIntosh), bassist Pete Farndon (d: 4/14/83; replaced in 1982 by Malcolm Foster) and drummer Martin Chambers. Hynde was married to Jim Kerr of Simple Minds. With the exception of Hynde, numerous personnel changes since 1985.

DEBUT DATE	PEAK POS	WKS CHR			ARTIST — Album Title	$	Label & Number
1/26/80	9	78	▲	1	Pretenders...	$8	Sire 6083
4/18/81	27	29		2	Extended Play ....[M]	$8	Sire 3563
8/29/81	10	19		3	Pretenders II	$8	Sire 3572
2/4/84	5	42	▲	4	Learning To Crawl	$8	Sire 23980
11/15/86	25	29	●	5	Get Close..	$8	Sire 25488
12/5/87	69	15		6	The Singles ....[G]	$8	Sire 25664
6/9/90	48	17		7	packed!...	$12	Sire 26219

Adultress, The (3)	**Don't Get Me Wrong** (5,6) **10**	I Hurt You (4)	Millionaires (7)	Sense Of Purpose (7)	Up The Neck (1)
Back On The Chain Gang (4,6) **5**	Downtown (Akron) (7)	I Remember You (5)	**My Baby** (5,6) **64**	**Show Me** (4,6) **28**	Wait, The (1)
Bad Boys Get Spanked (3)	English Roses (3)	Jealous Dogs (3)	My City Was Gone (4)	Space Invader (1)	Waste Not Want Not (3)
Birds Of Paradise (3)	Hold A Candle To This (7)	Kid (1,6)	Mystery Achievement (1)	**Stop Your Sobbing** (1,6) **65**	Watching The Clothes (4)
Brass In Pocket (I'm Special) (1,6) **14**	How Do I Miss You (7)	Let's Make A Pact (7)	Never Do That (7)	Talk Of The Town (2,3,6)	When I Change My Life (7)
Chill Factor (5)	How Much Did You Get For Your Soul? (5)	Light Of The Moon (5)	No Guarantee (7)	Tattooed Love Boys (1)	When Will I See You (7)
Criminal (7)	Hymn To Her (5,6)	Louie Louie (3)	Pack It Up (3)	**Thin Line Between Love And Hate** (4,6) **83**	
Cuban Slide (2)	I Go To Sleep (3,6)	Lovers Of Today (1)	Phone Call (7)	Thumbelina (4)	
Dance! (5)	**I Got You Babe** [UB40 with Chrissie Hynde] (6) **28**	May This Be Love (7)	Porcelain (2)	Time The Avenger (4)	
Day After Day (3,6)		Message Of Love (2,3,6)	Precious (1,2)	Tradition Of Love (5)	
		Middle Of The Road (4,6) **19**	Private Life (1)	2000 Miles (4,6)	
			Room Full Of Mirrors (5)		

PRETTY BOY FLOYD

Male hard-rock quartet: Steve Summers (vocals), Kristy Majors, Vinnie Chas and Kari Kane.

DEBUT DATE	PEAK POS	WKS CHR		ARTIST — Album Title	$	Label & Number
3/24/90	130	9		Leather Boyz With Electric Toyz	$12	MCA 6341

48 Hours	Leather Boyz With Electric Toyz	Rock & Roll (Is Gonna Set The Night On Fire)	Rock And Roll Outlaws	Wild Angels
I Wanna Be With You	Only The Young		Toast Of The Town	Your Mama Won't Know
Last Kiss				

DEBUT DATE	PEAK POS	WKS CHR	GOLD	ARTIST — Album Title	$	Label & Number
				PRETTY MAIDS Hard-rock quintet from Denmark formed in 1981 by Ronnie Atkins (vocals) and Ken Hammer (guitar).		
6/20/87	**165**	8		Future World	**$8**	Epic 40713

Eye Of The Storm   Long Way To Go   Love Games   Rodeo   Yellow Rain
Future World   Loud 'N' Proud   Needles In The Dark We Came To Rock

| | | | | **PRETTY POISON** Philadelphia dance band founded by Camden, New Jersey natives Jade Starling (vocals) and Whey Cooler. | | |
| 4/30/88 | **104** | 8 | | Catch Me I'm Falling .... | **$8** | Virgin 90885 |

Catch Me (I'm Falling) 8 Don't Cry Baby Hold Me Look, The Shine
Closer   Heaven   Let Freedom Ring **Nightime** 36 When I Look Into Your Eyes

				PRETTY THINGS British rock sextet led by vocalist Phil May and guitarist Peter Tolson. Ex-T. Rex guitarist Jack Green joined group for *Savage Eye* album.		
3/1/75	**104**	9	1	Silk Torpedo	**$8**	Swan Song 8411
2/21/76	**163**	6	2	Savage Eye	**$8**	Swan Song 8414

Atlanta (1)   Come Home Momma (1) Is It Only Love (1) L.A.N.T.A. (1) Remember That Boy (2)
Belfast Cowboys (1) Dream (1)   It Isn't Rock 'N' Roll (2) Maybe You Tried (1) Sad Eye (1)
Bridge Of God (1)   Drowned Man (2)   It's Been So Long (2) Michelle, Theme For (2) Singapore Silk Torpedo (1)
Bruise In The Sky (1) I'm Keeping (2)   Joey (1)   My Song (2)   Under The Volcano (2)

				PREVIN, Andre Born on 4/6/29 in Berlin. Pianist/conductor/arranger/composer. Became musical director for MGM movies by the age of 21. Composed and arranged background music for *Gigi* and many other films. In the 1970s, served as resident conductor of the London Symphony Orchestra. Married to actress Mia Farrow from September 1970 to February 1979.		
6/29/59	**16**	21	1	Secret Songs For Young Lovers .... [I]	**$15**	MGM 3716
				with David Rose & His Orchestra		
7/4/60+	**25**	28	2	Like Love .... [I]	**$15**	Columbia 1437
10/16/61	**118**	9	3	A Touch Of Elegance .... [I]	**$15**	Columbia 8449
				the music of Duke Ellington		
11/30/63	**130**	4	4	Andre Previn in Hollywood .... [I]	**$15**	Columbia 8834
				music from motion pictures (1929-63)		
12/19/64	**147**	4	5	My Fair Lady .... [I]	**$15**	Columbia 8995
				jazz version of the film score		
3/14/81	**149**	9	6	A Different Kind Of Blues .... [I]	**$8**	Angel 37780
				ITZHAK PERLMAN/ANDRE PREVIN jazz album featuring classical violinist Perlman		

At Long Last Love (2) I Could Have Danced All In Love In Vain (2) **Like Young** (1) 46 Portrait Of Bert Williams (3) What Am I Here For (3)
Best Years Of Our Lives,   Night (5)   Irma La Douce (Look Again), Little Face (6) Prelude To A Kiss (3) When I Fall In Love (2)
 Theme From (4)   I Got It Bad (And That Ain't   Theme From (4) Look At Him Go (6) Rain In Spain (5) While We're Young (1)
Blame It On My Youth (1)   Good) (3)   It Don't Mean A Thing (If It Looking For Love (4) Satin Doll (3) Who Reads Reviews (6)
Chocolate Apricot (6)   I Let A Song Go Out Of My   Ain't Got That Swing) (2) Love Is For The Very Young Second Time Around (4) With A Little Bit Of Luck (5)
Different Kind Of Blues (6)   Heart (3)   It Might As Well Be Spring   (1)   Solitude (3) Without You (5)
Falling In Love Again (2) I Love A Piano (2)   (4)   Love Is Here To Stay (2) Sophisticated Lady (3) Wouldn't It Be Loverly (5)
Fascination (4)   I Wish I Were In Love Again Last Night When We Were Love Me Or Leave Me (2) Too Young To Be True (1) Year Of Youth (1)
Five Of Us (6)   (2)   Young (1)   Make Up Your Mind (6) Too Young To Go Steady (1) You Did It (5)
Get Me To The Church On I'm A Dreamer, Aren't We Last Time I Saw Paris (4) Night Thoughts (6) Touch Of Elegance (3) You Make Me Feel So Young
 Time (5)   All? (4)   Laura (4)   Nothin' To Do With Love (3) Two For The Seesaw (A   (1)
Gigi (4)   I'm An Ordinary Man (5) Le Sucrier Velours (3) On The Street Where You   Second Chance), Song Young And Tender (1)
Hi-Lili, Hi-Lo (4)   I've Grown Accustomed To Like Love (2)   Live (5)   From (4) Young Man's Lament (1)
       Her Face (5)   Like Someone In Love (2) Perdido (3) We Kiss In A Shadow (4) Younger Than Springtime (1)

				PRICE, Alan Born on 4/19/42 in Fairfield, Durham, England. Organist with the original Animals; left in 1965; rejoined group in 1983.		
8/11/73	**117**	14	1	O Lucky Man! .... [S]	**$12**	Warner 2710
11/19/77	**187**	3	2	Alan Price	**$8**	Jet 809

Arrival (1)   I've Been Hurt (2)   Let Yourself Go (2) O Lucky Man! (1) Rainbow's End (2)
Changes (1)   Is It Right (2)   Life Is Good (2) Pastoral (1) Same Love (2)
I Wanna Dance (2)   Just For You (2)   Look Over Your Shoulder (1) Poor Boy (2) Sell Sell (1)
I'm A Gambler (2)   Justice (1)   My Home Town (1) Poor People (1) Thrill, The (2)

				PRICE, Leontyne Born on 2/10/27 in Laurel, Mississippi. One of the great sopranos of opera. Career took off after touring Europe in *Porgy And Bess* during the mid-1950s. Won the Lifetime Achievement Grammy in 1989.		
12/18/61+	**55**	5	1	A Christmas Offering .... [X]	**$20**	London 25280
				with Herbert von Karajan conducting the Vienna Philharmonic Orchestra		
12/29/62	**128**	1	2	A Christmas Offering .... [X-R]	**$20**	London 25280
				Christmas charts: 23/'63		
4/27/63	**29**	12	3	Giacomo Puccini: Madama Butterfly .... [F]	**$20**	RCA 6160 [3]
				with Richard Tucker (tenor), Rosalind Elias (mezzo-soprano), Philip Maero (baritone) and Erich Leinsdorf (conductor)		
9/7/63	**79**	6	4	Giacomo Puccini: Tosca .... [F]	**$20**	RCA 7022 [2]
				with Giuseppe Taddei, Giuseppi Di Stefano and Herbert Von Karajan (conductor)		
10/5/63	**66**	16	5	Great Scenes from Gershwin's "Porgy And Bess"	**$20**	RCA 2679
				with William Warfield (baritone) and Skitch Henderson (conductor)		
10/31/64	**147**	3	6	Georges Bizet: Carmen .... [F]	**$20**	RCA 6164 [3]
				with Franco Corelli (tenor), Robert Merrill (baritone) and Herbert von Karajan conducting the Vienna Philharmonic Orchestra		

Angels We Have Heard On Bizet: Carmen [includes Acts I Got Plenty O' Nuttin' (5) O Tannenbaum (1) Puccini: Tosca [includes Acts There's A Boat Dat's Leavin
 High (1)   I thru IV] (6)   I Loves You, Porgy (5) Oh Bess, Oh Where's My   I thru III] (4)   Soon For New York (5)
Bach, Gounod: Ave Maria (1) God Rest Ye Merry, It Ain't Necessarily So (5)   Bess (5)   Schubert: Ave Maria (1) We Three Kings Of Orient
Bach, Luther: Vom Himmel   Gentlemen (1)   It Came Upon The Midnight Oh Lawd, I'm On My Way (5) Silent Night (1)   Are (1)
 Hoch (1)   Gone, Gone, Gone (5)   Clear (1)   Puccini: Madama Butterfly Summertime (medley) (5) What You Want Wid Bess? (5)
Bess, You Is My Woman (5) Hark! The Herald Angels Mozart: Alleluja (K.165) (1)   [includes Acts I thru III] (3) Sweet Little Jesus Boy (1) Woman Is A Sometime
       Sing (1)   O Holy Night (1)   Thing (medley) (5)

DEBUT DATE	PEAK POS	WKS CHR	GOLD	ARTIST — Album Title	$	Label & Number

PRICE, Ray

Country singer. Born on 1/12/26 in Perryville, Texas and raised in Dallas. Ray charted over 80 top 40 singles on *Billboard*'s country charts. Known as "The Cherokee Cowboy."

DEBUT DATE	PEAK POS	WKS CHR	GOLD	#	ARTIST — Album Title	$	Label & Number
3/4/67	129	12		1	Touch My Heart	$20	Columbia 9406
6/10/67	106	17		2	Danny Boy	$20	Columbia 9477
9/12/70+	28	59	●	3	For The Good Times	$10	Columbia 30106
6/12/71	49	24		4	I Won't Mention It Again	$10	Columbia 30510
12/4/71	146	5		5	Welcome To My World ...... [K]	$12	Columbia 30878 [2]
7/29/72	145	12		6	The Lonesomest Lonesome	$12	Columbia 31546
9/9/72	165	10		7	Ray Price's All-Time Greatest Hits ...... [G]	$12	Columbia 31364 [2]
4/21/73	161	7		8	She's Got To Be A Saint	$10	Columbia 32033
6/14/80	70	25	●	9	San Antonio Rose	$8	Columbia 36476

WILLIE NELSON & RAY PRICE

Across The Wide Missouri (2)
Am I That Easy To Forget (1)
April's Fool (7)
Black And White Lies (3)
Born To Lose (2)
Bridge Over Troubled Water (4,7)
Burden Of Freedom (4)
Burning Memories (5)
But I Was Lying (6)
By The Time I Get To Phoenix (5,7)
City Lights (5) *71*
Cold, Cold Heart (5)
Cold Day In July (8)
Crazy (2)
Crazy Arms (3,5,7,9) *67*
Danny Boy (2,7) *60*
Deep Water (9)
Don't You Ever Get Tired (Of Hurting Me) (9)

Empty Chairs (6)
Enough For You (8)
Enough To Lie (1)
Everything That's Beautiful (Reminds Me Of You) (8)
Faded Love (9)
For The Good Times (3,7) *11*
Forgive Me Heart (4)
Funny How Time Slips Away (5,9)
Goin' Away (8)
Gonna Burn Some Bridges (3)
Grazin' In Greener Pastures (8)
Greensleeves (2)
Heartaches By The Number (3,5,7)
Help Me (8)

Help Me Make It Through The Night (3,5)
I Can't Help It (If I'm Still In Love With You) (5)
I Fall To Pieces (9)
I Keep Looking Back (8)
I Lie A Lot (1)
I Won't Mention It Again (4,7) *43*
(I'd Be) A Legend In My Time (5)
I'd Rather Be Sorry (4,7) *70*
I'll Be There (If You Ever Want Me) (6)
I'll Go To A Stranger (1)
It's Only Love (1)
Jesse Younger (4)
Just For The Record (1)
Just The Other Side Of Nowhere (6)
Kiss The World Goodbye (4)

Last Letter (5)
Little Green Apples (5,7)
Lonely World (3,7)
Lonesomest Lonesome (6)
Loving Her Was Easier (4,7)
Make The World Go Away (5) *100*
My Baby's Gone (8)
Night Life (5,9)
Nobody Wins (8)
Oh, Lonesome Me (5)
One Night To Remember (6)
Over (6)
Pretend (2)
Pride (5)
Release Me (9)
Same Two Lips (1)
San Antonio Rose (9)
She Wears My Ring (7)
She's Got To Be A Saint (8) *93*

Soft Rain (2)
Spanish Eyes (2)
Sunday (8)
Sunday Morning Comin' Down (4,7)
Sweet Memories (4,7)
Sweetest Tie (8)
Sweetheart Of The Year (7)
Swinging Doors (Swang In Doors) (1)
Take Me As I Am (Or Let Me Go) (7)
Take These Chains From My Heart (5)
That's What Leaving's About (6)
There Goes My Everything (1)
This Cold War With You (9)
This House (6)

Time (Old Faithful Friend Of Mine) (6)
Touch My Heart (1)
Turn Around, Look At Me (8)
Unloved, Unwanted (5)
Vaya Con Dios (2,5)
Wake Up Yesterday (6)
Way To Survive (1)
Welcome To My World (5)
What's Come Over My Baby (2)
When I Loved Her (4,7)
Yesterday (5,7)
You Can't Take It With You (3)
You Took My Happy Away (1)
You Wouldn't Know Love (7)

★★214★★ PRIDE, Charley

Born on 3/18/38 in Sledge, Mississippi. The most successful black country performer. Discovered by Red Sovine in 1963. Charley has charted 29 #1 singles on the country charts.

DEBUT DATE	PEAK POS	WKS CHR	GOLD	#	ARTIST — Album Title	$	Label & Number
3/30/68	199	2	●	1	The Country Way	$15	RCA 3895
2/15/69	62	43	●	2	Charley Pride-In Person ...... [L]	$15	RCA 4094
					recorded at Panther Hall, Fort Worth, Texas		
6/28/69	44	39	●	3	The Sensational Charley Pride	$15	RCA 4153
11/1/69	24	65	●	4	The Best Of Charley Pride ...... [G]	$12	RCA 4223
2/28/70	22	27	●	5	Just Plain Charley	$12	RCA 4290
7/18/70	30	38	●	6	Charley Pride's 10th Album	$12	RCA 4367
2/6/71	42	26	●	7	From Me To You	$12	RCA 4468
4/17/71	76	15	●	8	Did You Think To Pray	$12	RCA 4513
7/24/71	50	19	●	9	I'm Just Me	$12	RCA 4560
12/4/71+	38	26	●	10	Charley Pride Sings Heart Songs	$12	RCA 4617
3/18/72	50	15	●	11	The Best Of Charley Pride, Volume 2 ...... [G]	$12	RCA 4682
8/19/72	115	15		12	A Sunshiny Day with Charley Pride	$12	RCA 4742
1/6/73	189	8		13	The Incomparable Charley Pride ...... [K]	$10	RCA Camden 2584
2/17/73	149	8		14	Songs of Love by Charley Pride	$10	RCA 4837
7/28/73	166	6		15	Sweet Country	$10	RCA 0217
1/22/77	188	2		16	The Best Of Charley Pride, Vol. III ...... [G]	$8	RCA 2023
11/21/81	185	7		17	Greatest Hits ...... [G]	$8	RCA 4151
					hits from 1976-81		

Able Bodied Man (6)
Act Naturally (1)
All I Have To Offer You (Is Me) (4) *91*
Along The Mississippi (15)
Amazing Love (16)
Angel Band (8)
Anywhere (Just Inside Your Arms) (10,13)
Back To The Country Roads (12)
Before I Met You (4)
Billy Bayou (3)
Brand New Bed Of Roses (5)
Burgers And Fries (17)
Church In The Wildwood (8)
Come On Home And Sing The Blues To Daddy (3)
Cotton Fields (2)
Crystal Chandelier (1,2)
(Darlin' Think Of Me) Every Now And Then (14)
Day The World Stood Still (1,4)
Did You Think To Pray (1,4)
Does My Ring Hurt Your Finger (1,4)
Don't Fight The Feelings Of Love (15,16)

Easy Part's Over (4)
Even After Everything She's Done (3)
Fifteen Years Ago (7)
Give A Lonely Heart A Home (14)
Gone, Gone, Gone (5)
Gone, On The Other Hand (1,4)
Good Chance Of Tear-Fall Tonight (5)
Good Hearted Woman (14)
Got Leavin' On His Mind (2)
Happiest Song On The Jukebox (15)
Happiness Of Having You (16)
Happy Street (5)
Hello Darlin' (9)
Honky Tonk Blues (17)
Hope You're Feelin' Me (Like I'm Feelin' You) (16)
I Ain't All Bad (16)
I Can't Believe That You've Stopped Loving Me (7) *71*
I Don't Deserve A Mansion (16)
I Know One (2,4)

I Love You More In Memory (14)
I Think I'll Take A Walk (6)
I Threw Away The Rose (1)
I'd Rather Love You (9,11,13) *79*
I'll Fly Away (8)
I'll Wander Back To You (1)
I'm A Lonesome Fugitive (5)
I'm Beginning To Believe My Own Lies (10)
I'm Building Bridges (14)
I'm Just Me (9,11) *94*
I'm Learning To Love Her (15)
(I'm So) Afraid Of Losing You Again (5,11) *74*
If You Had Only Taken The Time (5)
Image Of Me (2)
(In My World) You Don't Belong (9,11)
Instant Loneliness (9,13)
Is Anybody Goin' To San Antone (6,11) *70*
It's All Right (5)
It's Gonna Take A Little Bit Longer (12)
(It's Just A Matter Of) Making Up My Mind (3)

It's The Little Things (3)
Jeanie Norman (10,13)
Jesus, Don't Give Up On Me (8)
Just Between You And Me (2,4)
Just To Be Loved By You (15)
Kaw-Liga (2,4)
Kiss An Angel Good Mornin' (10,11) *21*
Last Thing On My Mind (2)
Let Me Live (8,11)
Let Me Live Again (3)
Let The Chips Fall (3,4)
Life Turned Her That Way (1)
Little Folks (1)
Lord, Build Me A Cabin In Glory (8)
Louisiana Man (3)
Love Unending (15)
Lovesick Blues (2)
Mama Don't Cry For Me (1)
Me And Bobby McGee (5)
Miracles, Music And My Wife (17)
Missin' You (17)
Mississippi Cotton Picking Delta Town (16) *70*

My Eyes Can Only See As Far As You (16)
My Love Is Deep, My Love Is Wide (14)
Never Been So Loved (In All My Life) (17)
Never More Than I (3)
No One Could Ever Take Me From You (10)
Nothin' Left But Leavin' (12)
Oklahoma Morning (16)
On The Southbound (9)
Once Again (10)
One More Year (12)
One Time (5)
Pass Me By (15)
Piroque Joe (7,13)
Place For The Lonesome (9,11)
Poor Boy Like Me (6)
Pretty House For Sale (10)
Put Back My Ring On Your Hand (12)
Roll On Mississippi (17)
Searching For The Morning Sun (16)
Sentimental 'Ol Me (5)
Seven Years With A Wonderful Woman (12)

She's Helping Me Get Over You (12)
She's Just An Old Love Turned Memory (17)
She's Still Got A Hold On You (3)
She's That Kind (14)
She's Too Good To Be True (14)
Shelter Of Your Eyes (15)
Shoulder To Cry On (15)
Shutters And Boards (2)
Six Days On The Road (2)
Snakes Crawl At Night (4)
Someone Loves You Honey (17)
Special (6)
Streets Of Baltimore (2)
Sunshiny Day (12)
Sweet Promises (7)
Take Care Of The Little Things (3)
Tennessee Girl (15)
That's My Way (9)
That's The Only Way Life's Good To Me (7)
That's Why I Love You So Much (5)
Then Who Am I (16)

DEBUT DATE	PEAK POS	WKS CHR	G O L D	ARTIST — Album Title	$	Label & Number

PRIDE, Charley — Cont'd

(There's) Nobody Home To Go Home To (6) · (There's) Still Someone I Can't Forget (7,11) · Things Are Looking Up (6) · This Highway Leads To Glory (8,13) · This Is My Year For Mexico (6) · Thought Of Losing You (6) · Through The Years (6) · Time Out For Jesus (8,13) · Time (You're Not A Friend Of Mine) (7,13) · Today Is That Tomorrow (7) · Too Hard To Say I'm Sorry (1,4) · Too Weak To Let You Go (14) · Was It All Worth Losing You (7,13) · We Had All The Good Things Going (3) · What Money Can't Buy (10) · When I Stop Leaving (I'll Be Gone) (17) · When The Trains Come In (12,13) · Where Do I Put Her Memory (17) · Whispering Hope (8) · Whole Lotta Things To Sing About (17) · **Wonder Could I Live There Anymore** (7) *87* · You Can Tell The World (1) · You Never Gave Up On Me (9) · You Were All The Good In Me (14) · You'll Still Be The One (10,11) · You're My Jamaica (17) · You're Still The Only One I'll Ever Love (9) · You're Wanting Me To Stop Loving You (12)

PRIEST, Maxi

Born Max Elliott in London to Jamaican parents. Dancehall reggae singer.

12/3/88+	108	17		1 Maxi Priest	$8	Virgin 90957
8/4/90	47	37	●	2 Bonafide	$12	Charisma 91384
12/7/91	189	2		3 Best Of Me	[G] $12	Charisma 91804
12/12/92	191	1		4 fe Real	$12	Charisma 86500

Amazed Are We (4) · Best Of Me (2,3) · Can't Turn Away (4) · Caution (3) · **Close To You** (2,3) *1* · Crazy Love (3) · Goodbye To Love Again (1) · **Groovin' In The Midnight** (4) *63* · Hard To Get (4) · **Housecall (Your Body Can't Lie To Me)** (3) *37* · How Can We Ease The Pain? (1,3) · Human Work Of Art (2) · I Know Love (3) · In The Springtime (3) · It Ain't Easy (1) · **Just A Little Bit Longer** (2,3) *62* · Just Wanna Know (4) · Let Me Know (3) · Life (2) · Make My Day (4) · Marcus (1) · Never Did Say Goodbye (2) · One More Chance (4) · Peace Throughout The World (2,3) · Prayer For The World (2) · Problems (1) · Promises (4) · Same Old Story (1) · Should I (3) · Some Guys Have All The Luck (1,3) · Space In My Heart (2) · Strollin' On (3) · Sublime (4) · Sure Fire Love (2) · Suzie - You Are (1) · Temptress (2) · Ten To Midnight (4) · **Wild World** (1,3) *25* · Woman In You (3) · You (2)

PRIMA, Louis, & Keely Smith

Born on 12/7/11 in New Orleans. Vocalist/trumpeter/composer/leader Louis was married to jazz-styled vocalist Dorothy "Keely" Smith (b: 3/9/32 in Norfolk, Virginia) from 1952-61. The popular Las Vegas duo was backed by Sam Butera & The Witnesses. Louis was the voice of King Louis in animated Disney film *Jungle Book*. Surgery from a brain tumor in 1975 left him in a coma until his death on 8/24/78.

| 6/23/58 | 12 | 4 | | 1 Las Vegas Prima Style | [L] $20 | Capitol 1010 |
| 5/25/59 | 37 | 2 | | 2 Hey Boy! Hey Girl! | [S] $20 | Capitol 1160 |

Louis and Keely portray Las Vegas entertainers in the film

| 11/2/59 | 43 | 4 | | 3 Louis and Keely! | $15 | Dot 3210 |
| 1/16/61 | 9 | 11 | | 4 **Wonderland By Night** | [I] $15 | Dot 25352 |

LOUIS PRIMA

All I Do Is Dream Of You (3) · And The Angels Sing (3) · Autumn Leaves (2) · Banana Split For My Baby (2) · **Bei Mir Bist Du Schon** (3) *69* · By The Light Of The Silvery Moon (4) · Cheek To Cheek (3) · Embraceable You (medley) (1) · Fever (2) · Goodnight My Love (4) · Greenback Dollar Bill (1) · Hey, Boy! Hey, Girl! (2) · Holiday For Strings (1) · Honeysuckle Rose (medley) (1) · I Can't Believe That You're In Love With Me (medley) (1) · I Could Have Danced All Night (1) · I Don't Know Why (3) · I Got It Bad And That Ain't Good (medley) (1) · I Want Some Lovin' (4) · I'm Confessin' (That I Love You) (1) · I've Grown Accustomed To Her Face (3) · Lazy River (2) · Love Of My Life (O Sole Mio) (1) · Lovely Way To Spend An Evening (4) · Make Love To Me (3) · Moonlight Becomes You (4) · Moonlight In Vermont (4) · Night And Day (3) · Night Is Young (And You're So Beautiful) (4) · Nitey-Nite (4) · Oh, Marie (1) · Polka Dots And Moonbeams (4) · Should I (medley) (1) · Tea For Two (3) · Them There Eyes (medley) (1) · Tiger Rag (1) · Too Marvelous For Words (1) · Twilight Time (4) · When The Saints Go Marching In (2) · White Cliffs Of Dover (1) · Why Do I Love You (3) · **Wonderland By Night** (4) *15* · You And The Night And The Music (4) · You Are My Love (2) · You're My Everything (3)

PRIMITIVES, The

Quartet from Coventry, England: female lead singer Tracey Tracey, Paul Court, Steve Dullaghan and Tig Williams. By 1989, Dullaghan left and bassist Paul Sampson added.

| 9/10/88 | 106 | 9 | | 1 Lovely | $8 | RCA 8443 |

later pressings include the track "Way Behind Me"

| 12/23/89+ | 113 | 15 | | 2 Pure | $8 | RCA 9934 |

CD includes 4 bonus tracks

All The Way Down (2) · Buzz Buzz Buzz (1) · Can't Bring Me Down (2) · Carry Me Home (1) · Crash (1) · Dizzy Heights (2) · Don't Want Anything To Change (1) · Dreamwalk Baby (1) · I'll Stick With You (1) · Keep Me In Mind (2) · Lonely Streets (2) · Never Tell (2) · Nothing Left (1) · Ocean Blue (1) · Out Of Reach (1) · Outside (2) · Run Baby Run (1) · Secrets (2) · Shadow (1) · Shine (2) · Sick Of It (2) · Spacehead (1) · Stop Killing Me (1) · Summer Rain (2) · Thru' The Flowers (1) · Way Behind Me (1,2)

PRIMUS

San Francisco thrash-jazz-rock trio: Les Claypool (vocals, bass), Larry LaLoude (guitar) and Tim Alexander (drums).

| 6/1/91 | 116 | 36 | | Sailing The Seas Of Cheese | $12 | Interscope 91659 |

American Life · Eleven · Fish On · Grandad's Little Ditty · Here Come The Bastards · Is It Luck? · Jerry Was A Race Car Driver · Los Bastardos · Sathington Waltz · Seas Of Cheese · Sgt. Baker · Those Damned Blue-Collar Tweekers · Tommy The Cat

★★68★★ PRINCE

Born Prince Roger Nelson on 6/7/58 in Minneapolis. Vocalist/multi-instrumentalist/composer/producer/ actor. Named for the Prince Roger Trio, led by his father. Self-taught musician; own band, Grand Central, in junior high school. Self-produced first album in 1978. Starred in the films *Purple Rain*, *Under The Cherry Moon*, *Sign 'O' The Times* and *Graffiti Bridge*. Founded own label, Paisley Park. The Revolution featured Lisa Coleman (keyboards), Wendy Melvoin (guitar), Bobby Z (percussion), Matt "Dr." Fink (keyboards), Eric Leeds (saxophone) and Andre Cymone (bass; replaced by Brownmark in 1981). In 1986, Brownmark founded Mazarati (who also backed Prince). Leeds formed Madhouse in 1987. Coleman and Melvoin formed duo Wendy & Lisa in 1987. Sheila E. (drums) joined Prince's band in 1986. Prince's sister Tyka Nelson began recording in 1988. Prince formed new band, New Power Generation (named for the oldest Prince fan club in Britain), in 1990, featuring Levi Seacer, Jr. (guitar), Sonny T. (bass), Tommy Barbarella (keyboard), dancer/percussionists Kirk Johnson and Damon Dickson, Michael Bland (drums), rapper Tony M. and Rosie Gaines (keyboards, vocals; replaced by Mayte [pronounced: my-tie] by 1992).

10/28/78	163	5		1 Prince-For You	$8	Warner 3150
11/17/79+	22	28	▲	2 Prince	$8	Warner 3366
11/8/80	45	52	●	3 Dirty Mind	$8	Warner 3478
11/7/81	21	64	▲	4 Controversy	$8	Warner 3601

DEBUT DATE	PEAK POS	WKS CHR	GOLD	ARTIST — Album Title	$	Label & Number

PRINCE — Cont'd

| 11/20/82+ | 9 | 153 | ▲³ | 5 Prince **1999** | $10 | Warner 23720 [2] |

PRINCE and the REVOLUTION:

| 7/14/84 | 1²⁴ | 72 | ▲¹⁰ | 6 Purple Rain ....[S] | $8 | Warner 25110 |

film is a semi-autobiographical story about Prince's career

| 5/11/85 | 1³ | 40 | ▲² | 7 Around the World in a Day | $8 | Paisley P. 25286 |
| 4/19/86 | 3 | 28 | ▲ | 8 Parade ....[S] | $8 | Paisley P. 25395 |

music from the film *Under The Cherry Moon*

PRINCE:

4/18/87	6	54	▲	9 Sign "O" The Times	$10	Paisley P. 25577 [2]
5/28/88	11	21		10 Lovesexy	$8	Paisley P. 25720
7/8/89	1⁶	34	▲²	11 Batman ....[S]	$8	Warner 25936
9/8/90	6	24	●	12 Graffiti Bridge ....[S]	$12	Paisley P. 27493

includes "Round And Round" by Tevin Campbell; "Melody Cool" by Mavis Staples; "We Can Funk" by George Clinton; and "Release It", "Latest Fashion," "Love Machine" & "Shake!" by The Time

PRINCE & THE NEW POWER GENERATION:

| 10/19/91 | 3 | 45 | ▲² | 13 Diamonds And Pearls | $12 | Paisley P. 25379 |

LP cover is a hologram

| 10/31/92 | 5 | 15↑ | ▲ | 14 ♀ (untitled) | $12 | Paisley P. 45037 |

released on Paisley Park 45123 with inexplicit edit of "Sexy M.F."

Adore (9)
All The Critics Love U In New York (5)
Alphabet St. (10) *8*
America (7) *46*
And God Created Woman (14)
Anna Stesia (10)
Annie Christian (4)
Anotherloverholenyohead (8) *63*
Arms Of Orion (11) *36*
Around The World In A Day (7)
Arrogance (14)
Automatic (5)
Baby (1)
Baby I'm A Star (6)
Ballad Of Dorothy Parker (9)
Bambi (2)
Batdance (11) *1*
Beautiful Ones (6)
Blue Light (14)
Can't Stop This Feeling I Got (12)
Christopher Tracy's Parade (8)
Computer Blue (6)
Condition Of The Heart (7)
Continental, The (14)

Controversy (4) *70*
Crazy You (1)
Cream (13) *1*
Cross, The (9)
D.M.S.R. (5)
Daddy Pop (13)
Damn U (14)
Dance On (10)
Darling Nikki (4)
Delirious (5) *8*
Diamonds And Pearls (13) *3*
Dirty Mind (3)
Do It All Night (3)
Do Me, Baby (4)
Do U Lie? (8)
Electric Chair (11)
Elephants & Flowers (12)
Flow, The (14)
For You (1)
Forever In My Life (9)
Free (5)
Future, The (11)
Gett Off (13) *21*
Girls & Boys (8)
Glam Slam (10)
Gotta Broken Heart Again (3)
Graffiti Bridge (12)
Head (3)
Hot Thing (9) *63*
Housequake (9)

I Could Never Take The Place Of Your Man (9) *10*
I Feel For You (2)
I No (10)
I Wanna Be Your Lover (2) *11*
I Wanna Melt With U (14)
I Wish U Heaven (10)
I Wonder U (8)
I Would Die 4 U (6) *8*
I'm Yours (1)
If I Was Your Girlfriend (9) *67*
In Love (1)
Insatiable (13) *77*
International Lover (5)
It (9)
It's Gonna Be A Beautiful Night (9)
It's Gonna Be Lonely (2)
Jack U Off (4)
Joy In Repetition (12)
Jughead (8)
Just As Long As We're Together (1)
Kiss (8) *1*
Ladder, The (7)
Lady Cab Driver (5)
Lemon Crush (11)
Let's Go Crazy (6) *1*

Let's Pretend We're Married (5) *52*
Let's Work (4)
Life Can Be So Nice (8)
Little Red Corvette (5) *6*
Live 4 Love (13)
Love 2 The 9's (14)
Lovesexy (10)
Max, The (14)
Money Don't Matter 2 Night (13) *23*
Morning Papers (14)
Mountains (8) *23*
My Love Is Forever (1)
My Name Is Prince (14) *36*
New Position (8)
New Power Generation (12) *64*
New Power Generation (Pt. II) (12)
1999 (5) *12*
Paisley Park (7)
Partyman (11) *18*
Partyup (3)
Play In The Sunshine (9)
Pop Life (7) *7*
Positivity (10)
Private Joy (4)
Purple Rain (6) *2*
Push (13)

Question Of U (12)
Raspberry Beret (7) *2*
Ronnie, Talk To Russia (4)
Sacrifice Of Victor (14)
Scandalous (11)
7 (14) *8↑*
Sexuality (4)
Sexy Dancer (2)
Sexy M.F. (14) *66*
Sign 'O' The Times (9) *3*
Sister (3)
Slow Love (9)
So Blue (1)
Soft And Wet (1) *92*
Something In The Water (Does Not Compute) (5)
Sometimes It Snows In April (8)
Starfish And Coffee (9)
Still Waiting (2)
Still Would Stand All Time (12)
Strange Relationship (9)
Strollin' (13)
Sweet Baby (14)
Take Me With U (6) *25*
Tamborine (7)
Temptation (7)
Thieves In The Temple (12) *6*

3 Chains O' Gold (14)
Thunder (13)
Tick, Tick, Bang (12)
Trust (11)
U Got The Look (9) *2*
Under The Cherry Moon (8)
Uptown (3)
Venus De Milo (8)
Vicki Waiting (11)
Walk Don't Walk (13)
When Doves Cry (6) *1*
When 2 R In Love (10)
When We're Dancing Close And Slow (2)
When You Were Mine (3)
Why You Wanna Treat Me So Bad? (2)
Willing And Able (13)
With You (2)

PRINE, John

Born on 10/10/46 in Chicago. Country-folk singer/songwriter. Member of the Buzzin' Cousins, group that appeared in the 1992 film *Falling from Grace*.

2/26/72	154	3		1 John Prine	$10	Atlantic 8296
10/28/72	148	10		2 Diamonds In The Rough	$10	Atlantic 7240
11/24/73	135	11		3 Sweet Revenge	$10	Atlantic 7274
4/26/75	66	10		4 Common Sense	$10	Atlantic 18127
1/15/77	196	2	●	5 Prime Prine-The Best Of John Prine ....[G]	$8	Atlantic 18202
7/8/78	116	13		6 Bruised Orange	$8	Asylum 139
9/8/79	152	7		7 Pink Cadillac	$8	Asylum 222
8/30/80	144	7		8 Storm Windows	$8	Asylum 286

Accident (Things Could Be Worse) (3)
All Night Blue (8)
Angel From Montgomery (1)
Automobile (7)
Aw Heck (6)
Baby Let's Play House (4)
Baby Ruth (6)
Billy The Bum (2)
Blue Umbrella (3)
Bruised Orange (Chain Of Sorrow) (6)
Chinatown (7)
Christmas In Prison (3)
Clocks And Spoons (2)
Cold War (This Cold War With You) (7)

Come Back To Us Barbara Lewis Hare Krishna Beauregard (4,5)
Common Sense (4)
Crooked Piece Of Time (7)
Dear Abby (3,5)
Diamonds In The Rough (2)
Donald And Lydia (1,5)
Down By The Side Of The Road (7)
Everybody (2)
Far From Me (1)
Fish And Whistle (6)
Flashback Blues (1)
Forbidden Jimmy (4)
Frying Pan (2)
Good Time (3)

Grandpa Was A Carpenter (3,5)
Great Compromise (2,5)
He Was In Heaven Before He Died (4)
Hello In There (1,5)
Hobo Song (6)
How Lucky (7)
I Had A Dream (8)
If You Don't Want My Love (6)
Illegal Smile (1,5)
Iron Ore Betty (6)
It's Happening To You (8)
Just Wanna Be With You (8)
Killing The Blues (7)
Late John Garfield Blues (2)
Living In The Future (8)

Mexican Home (3)
Middle Man (4)
My Own Best Friend (4)
Nine Pound Hammer (3)
No Name Girl (7)
Often Is A Word I Seldom Use (3)
One Red Rose (8)
Onomatopoeia (3)
Paradise (1)
Please Don't Bury Me (3,5)
Pretty Good (1)
Quiet Man (1)
Rocky Mountain Time (2)
Sabu Visits The Twin Cities Alone (6)
Saddle In The Rain (4,5)
Saigon (7)

Sam Stone (1,5)
Shop Talk (8)
Six O'Clock News (1)
Sleepy Eyed Boy (8)
Sour Grapes (7)
Souvenirs (1)
Spanish Pipedream (1)
Storm Windows (8)
Sweet Revenge (3,5)
Take The Star Out Of The Window (2)
That Close To You (4)
That's The Way That The World Goes 'Round (6)
There She Goes (6)
Torch Singer (2)
Ubangi Stomp (3)
Way Down (4)

Wedding Day In Funeralville (4)
Yes I Guess They Oughta Name A Drink After You (2)
You Never Can Tell (4)
Your Flag Decal Won't Get You Into Heaven Anymore (1)

PRISM

Canadian rock group — Ron Tabak, lead singer (replaced by Henry Small in 1981).

10/1/77	137	10		1 Prism	$10	Ariola 50020
7/29/78	158	8		2 See Forever Eyes	$15	Ariola 50034
2/6/82	53	20		3 Small Change	$8	Capitol 12184

DEBUT DATE	PEAK POS	WKS CHR	GOLD	ARTIST — Album Title	$	Label & Number

PRISM — Cont'd

Amelia (1)
Crime Wave (2)
Don't Let Him Know (3) *39*
Flyin' (2) *53*
Freewill (1)
Heart And Soul (3)

Hello (2)
Hole In Paradise (3)
I Ain't Lookin' Anymore (1)
In The Jailhouse Now (3)
It's Over (1)
Julie (1)

Just Like Me (2)
N-N-N-No! (2)
Nickles And Dimes (2)
Open Soul Surgery (1)
Rain (3)
See Forever Eyes (2)

Spaceship Superstar (1) *82*
Stay (3)
Take Me Away (2)
Take Me To The Kaptin (1) *59*
Turn On Your Radar (3) *64*

Vladivostok (1)
When Love Goes Wrong (You're Not Alone) (3)
When Will I See You Again (3)
Wings Of Your Love (3)

You're Like The Wind (2)
You're My Reason (2)

PROCLAIMERS, The
Singer/songwriter duo of twin brothers Craig and Charlie Reid from Edinburgh, Scotland.

| 4/8/89 | 125 | 11 | | Sunshine On Leith | $8 | Chrysalis 41668 |

Cap In Hand
Come On Nature

I'm Gonna Be (500 Miles)
I'm On My Way

It's Saturday Night
My Old Friend The Blues

Oh Jean
Sean

Sunshine On Leith
Teardrops

Then I Met You
What Do You Do

★★307★★ PROCOL HARUM
British rock group formed in 1967 by Gary Brooker (vocals, piano) and lyricist Keith Reid. Included Matthew Fisher (organ), Dave Knights (bass), Ray Royer (guitar) and Bobby Harrison (drums). The latter two left after recording of "Whiter Shade Of Pale," replaced by Robin Trower and Barry J. Wilson (d: 1989). Knights and Fisher left in early 1969; bassist Chris Copping added. Trower left in mid-1971, replaced by Dave Ball; bassist Alan Cartright added while Copping switched to keyboards. Ball left in mid-1972, replaced by Mick Grabham (ex-Cochise). Cartright left in mid-1976; Copping moved to bass and keyboardist Pete Solley joined. Band split up in 1977. Reunited in 1991 with Brooker, Reid, Fisher and Trower. Translation of Latin "procol": beyond these things.

9/23/67	47	16		1 Procol Harum	$30	Deram 18008
10/12/68	24	20		2 Shine On Brightly	$12	A&M 4151
5/10/69	32	20		3 A Salty Dog	$12	A&M 4179
7/11/70	34	15		4 Home	$12	A&M 4261
5/8/71	32	20		5 Broken Barricades	$12	A&M 4294
5/13/72	5	28	●	6 Procol Harum Live In Concert with the Edmonton Symphony Orchestra [L]	$12	A&M 4335
3/31/73	21	22		7 Grand Hotel	$10	Chrysalis 1037
10/20/73	131	10		8 The Best Of Procol Harum [G]	$10	A&M 4401
4/20/74	86	9		9 Exotic Birds and Fruit	$10	Chrysalis 1058
8/23/75	52	8		10 Procol's Ninth	$10	Chrysalis 1080
3/26/77	147	6		11 Something Magic	$8	Chrysalis 1130

About To Die (4)
All This And More (3,6)
As Strong As Samson (9)
Barnyard Story (4)
Beyond The Pale (9)
Boredom (3)
Bringing Home The Bacon (7)
Broken Barricades (5)
Butterfly Boys (9)
Cerdes (Outside The Gates Of) (1)
Christmas Camel (1)
Conquistador (1,6,8) *16*
Crucifiction Lane (3)
Dead Man's Dream (4)
Devil Came From Kansas (3)
Eight Days A Week (10)

Final Thrust (10)
Fires (Which Burnt Brightly) (7)
Fools Gold (10)
For Liquorice John (7)
Fresh Fruit (9)
Grand Hotel (7)
Homburg (8) *34*
I Keep Forgetting (10)
Idol, The (9)
In Held Twas In I (2,6)
(In The Wee Small Hours Of) Sixpence (8)
Juicy John Pink (3)
Kaleidoscope (1)
Lime Street Blues (8)
Long Gone Geek (8)

Luskus Delph (5)
Mabel (1)
Magdalene (My Regal Zonophone) (2)
Mark Of The Claw (11)
Memorial Drive (5)
Milk Of Human Kindness (3)
Monsieur R. Monde (9)
New Lamps For Old (9)
Nothing But The Truth (9)
Nothing That I Didn't Know (4)
Pandora's Box (10)
Piggy Pig Pig (4)
Pilgrims Progress (3)
Piper's Tune (10)
Playmate Of The Mouth (5)

Poor Mohammed (7)
Power Failure (5)
Quite Rightly So (2,8)
Rambling On (2)
Repent Walpurgis (1)
Robert's Box (7)
Rum Tale (7)
Salad Days (Are Here Again) (1)
Salty Dog (3,6,8)
She Wandered Through The Garden Fence (1)
Shine On Brightly (2,8)
Simple Sister (5,8)
Skating On Thin Ice (11)
Skip Softly (My Moonbeams) (2)

Something Following Me (1)
Something Magic (11)
Song For A Dreamer (5)
Souvenir Of London (7)
Still There'll Be More (4)
Strangers In Space (11)
T.V. Ceasar (7)
Taking The Time (10)
Thin End Of The Wedge (9)
Too Much Between Us (3)
Toujours L'Amour (7)
Typewriter Torment (10)
Unquiet Zone (10)
Whaling Stories (4,6)
Whisky Train (4,8)
Whiter Shade Of Pale (1,8) *5*

Wish Me Well (2)
Without A Doubt (10)
Wizard Man (11)
Worm & The Tree Medley (11)
Wreck Of The Hesperus (3)
Your Own Choice (4)

PRODUCERS, The
Pop-rock quartet from Atlanta: Van Temple, Kyle Henderson, Wayne Famous and Bryan Holmes.

| 6/6/81 | 163 | 2 | | The Producers | $8 | Portrait 37097 |

Body Language
Boys Say When/Girls Say Why

Certain Kinda Girl
End, The
Here's To You

I Love Lucy
Life Of Crime

Sensations
What She Does To Me (The Diana Song) *61*

What's He Got?
Who Do You Think You Are?
You Go Your Way

PROFESSOR GRIFF and THE LAST ASIATIC DISCIPLES
Professor Griff is Richard Griffin. Former member of Public Enemy.

| 4/14/90 | 127 | 8 | | Pawns In The Game | $12 | Skyywalker 111 |

5th Amendment
Interview, The
It's A Blax Thanx

L.A.D.
Love Thy Enemy
1-900 Stereotype

Pass The Ammo
Pawns In The Game
Rap Terrorist

Real African People Pt. 1 & 2
Suzi Wants To Be A Rock Star

Verdict, The
Word Of God

PROPHET
Hard-rock quintet led by vocalist Russell Arcara.

| 3/12/88 | 137 | 7 | | Cycle Of The Moon | $8 | Megaforce 81822 |

As One
Asylum

Can't Hide Love
Cycle Of The Moon

Frontline
Hands Of Time

Hyperspace
Red Line Rider

Sound Of A Breaking Heart
Tomorrow Never Comes

PROVINE, Dorothy
Born on 1/20/37 in Deadwood, South Dakota. Portrayed songstress Pinky Pinkham in the TV series *The Roaring Twenties* (1960-62).

| 5/15/61 | 34 | 66 | | The Roaring 20's | $20 | Warner 1394 |

medleys of 30 songs from the 1920s

Am I Blue? (medley)
Avalon (medley)
Barney Google (medley)
Black Bottom (medley)
Bye Bye Blackbird (medley)
Charleston (medley)
Clap Hands! Here Comes Charley! (medley)

Crazy Words-Crazy Tune (medley)
Cup Of Coffee, A Sandwich And You (medley)
Do-Do-Do (medley)
Doin' The Racoon (medley)
Don't Bring Lulu (medley)
Girl Friend (medley)

I Wanna Be Loved By You (medley)
I'm Forever Blowing Bubbles (medley)
I'm Looking Over A Four Leaf Clover (medley)
It Had To Be You (medley)
Just A Memory (medley)

Laugh! Clown! Laugh! (medley)
Let's Do It (medley)
Let's Misbehave (medley)
Limehouse Blues (medley)
Mountain Greenery (medley)
Nagasaki (medley)

O-oo Ernest (Are You Earnest With Me) (medley)
Poor Butterfly (medley)
Roaring Twenties (medley)
Someone To Watch Over Me (medley)
Sweet Georgia Brown (medley)

Tea For Two (medley)
Whisper Song (When The Pussywillow Whispers To The Catnip) (medley)

PRUETT, Jeanne
Born Norma Jean Bowman on 1/30/37 in Pell City, Alabama. Country singer/songwriter. Moved to Nashville in 1956 with husband Jack Pruett (guitarist for Marty Robbins). Songwriter for Marty Robbins since 1963.

| 7/7/73 | 122 | 9 | | Satin Sheets .... | $10 | MCA 338 |

Baby's Gone   I've Been So Wrong, For So   Is Her Love Any Better Than   Only Way To Hold Your Man   Walking Piece Of Heaven   Your Memory's Comin' On
Hold On Woman   Long   Mine   Sweet Sweetheart   What My Thoughts Do All
  Lonely Women Cryin'   **Satin Sheets 28**   The Time

★★353★★ PRYOR, Richard
Born on 12/1/40 in Peoria, Illinois. Ribald comedian/actor. In films *Stir Crazy*, *Silver Streak*, *Superman III* and many others. Revealed that he has muscular sclerosis in the early 1990s.

6/15/74	29	53	●	1 That Nigger's Crazy .... [C]	$10	Partee 2404
8/23/75	12	25	▲	2 Is It Something I Said? .... [C]	$8	Reprise 2227
10/9/76	22	19	●	3 Bicentennial Nigger .... [C]	$8	Warner 2960
5/28/77	58	9		4 Are You Serious??? .... [E-C]	$8	Laff 196
6/4/77	114	5		5 L.A. Jail .... [E-C]	$8	Tiger Lily 14023
6/25/77	68	12	▲	6 Richard Pryor's Greatest Hits .... [C-K]	$8	Warner 3057
12/16/78+	32	20	●	7 Wanted .... [C]	$10	Warner 3364 [2]
9/8/79	176	4		8 Outrageous .... [E-C]	$8	Laff 206
4/17/82	21	17		9 Richard Pryor Live On The Sunset Strip .... [C-S]	$8	Warner 3660
				filmed live at the Hollywood Palladium		
11/12/83	71	13		10 Richard Pryor: Here And Now .... [C-S]	$8	Warner 23981
				filmed live at the Saenger Theater in New Orleans		

Acid (3)
Africa (9)
All (6,7)
Arrested (5)
Back Down (1)
Bad Breath (4)
Bathroom (8)
Bathrooms (5)
Being Born (4)
Being Famous (10)
Being Sensitive (7)
Bicentennial Nigger (3)
Bicentennial Prayer (3)
Big Daddy (5)
Black & White Life Styles (1)
Black & White Women (3)
Black Funerals (3)
Black Hollywood (3)
Black Jack (5)
Black Man/White Woman (1)
Brick Eight (5)

Chain Gang (5)
Chinese Food (9)
Chinese Restaurant (3)
Chow Line (5)
Cocaine (2,6)
Country Singer (5)
Craps (6)
Deer Hunter (7)
Deodorant (4)
Discipline (7)
Dogs And Horses (7)
Eulogy (3)
Exorcist (1,6)
Farting Smells (5)
Fighting (8)
Fire Exit (10)
Flying Saucers (1)
Freebase (9)
Funky People (5)
G - D (4)
Good Night Kiss (2)

Grandmothers (4)
Groovy Feelings (5)
Hair (5)
Have Your Ass Home By 11:00 (1,6)
Heart Attacks (7)
Here And Now (10)
Hi Way 16 (8)
Hillbilly (3,4)
Hospital (9)
I Feel (8)
I Hope I'm Funny (1)
I Like Women (10)
I Met The President (10)
I Remember (10)
Improvisation (8)
Inebriated (10)
Jail (8)
Jesse (4)
Jim Brown (7)
Judgement Day (5)

Just Us (2)
Keeping In Shape (7)
Kids (7)
Leon Spinks (7)
Leroy (4)
Looters (8)
Mafia (10)
Mafia Club (9)
Mankind (4)
Moses (3)
Monkeys (7)
Motherland (10)
Mudbone (9,10)
Mudbone - Little Feets (2,6)
Mudbone Goes To Hollywood (3)
My Father (6)
My Neighborhood (6)
Nature (7)
New Niggers (2)
New Year's Eve (7)

Nigger Babys' (4)
Nigger With A Seizure (1,6)
Niggers Vs. Police (1)
9 Pound Pill (4)
One Day At A Time (10)
One Night Stands (10)
Operation, The (8)
Our Gang (3)
Our Text For Today (7)
Pimples (5)
Prison (5)
Processed Hair (4)
Shortage Of White People (2)
Slavery (10)
Southern Hospitality (10)
State Park (5)
Things In The Woods (7)
Throw Up (8)
True Story Of J.C. (8)
2001 (5)
Virgins (4)

War Movies (4)
When Your Woman Leaves You (2,6)
White And Black People (7)
White Chicks (8)
Wino & Junkie (1)
Wino Dealing With Dracula (1,6)
Women (2)
Women Are Beautiful (2)

PRYSOCK, Arthur
Born on 1/2/29 in Spartanburg, South Carolina. R&B Singer. First recorded with Buddy Johnson, 1944. Solo, 1952. Popular nightclub act, often appearing with brother, saxophonist Wilbert "Red" Prysock.

7/13/63	138	7		1 Coast To Coast	$25	Old Town 2005
12/28/63+	97	7		2 A Portrait Of Arthur Prysock	$25	Old Town 2006
8/15/64	131	8		3 Everlasting Songs For Everlasting Lovers	$25	Old Town 2007
7/17/65	116	7		4 A Double Header with Arthur Prysock	$25	Old Town 2009
3/26/66	107	13		5 Arthur Prysock/Count Basie	$15	Verve 8646
				ARTHUR PRYSOCK/COUNT BASIE		
1/29/77	153	4		6 All My Life	$8	Old Town 12-004

Ain't No Use (5)
All I Need Is You Tonight (6)
All My Life (6)
All Or Nothing At All (4)
Am I Asking Too Much (2)
April Showers (1)
Are You Ready For A Laugh (2)
Autumn Leaves (2)
Baby I'm The One (6)
Because (2)
Blue Velvet (1)
Close Your Eyes (3)
Come Home (5)

Come Rain Or Come Shine (5)
Don't Go To Strangers (5)
Ebb Tide (2)
Fly Me To The Moon (1)
For Your Love (3)
Gone Again (5)
Goodnight My Love (Pleasant Dreams) (4)
Hard Day's Night (4)
I Could Have Told You (5)
I Could Write A Book (5)
I Left My Heart In San Francisco (1)
I Live My Love (4)

I Love Makin' Love To You (6)
I Wantcha Baby (6)
I Wonder Where Our Love Has Gone (2)
I Worry 'Bout You (5)
I'll Be Around (2)
I'll Follow You (1)
I'm A Fool To Want You (3)
I'm Gonna Sit Right Down And Write Myself A Letter (5)
I'm Lost (5)
Jet (2)
Let It Be Me (4)

Let Me Call You Sweetheart (4)
Let There Be Love (3)
Let's Start All Over Again (3)
Love Look Away (1)
Make Someone Love You (3)
My Everlasting Love (3)
My Wish (2)
One Broken Heart (6)
Open Up Your Heart (4)
Stella By Starlight (2)
Stranger In Town (3)
Sun, The Sand And The Sea (4)
There Goes My Heart (4)

There Will Never Be Another You (2)
They All Say I'm The Biggest Fool (1)
They Say You're Laughing At Me (4)
This Is What You Mean To Me (6)
What Kind Of Fool Am I (1)
What Will I Tell My Heart (5)
What's New (1)
When Love Is New (6) 64
Where Can I Go (2)
Where Or When (3)

Who Can I Turn To (When Nobody Needs Me) (4)
Without The One You Love (3)
You Are Too Beautiful (1)
You Don't Know What Love Is (3)
You'll Never Know (1)
You're Nothing But A Girl (4)
You've Changed (3)

PSEUDO ECHO
Techno-rock quartet from Melbourne, Australia — Brian Canham, lead singer.

| 3/21/87 | 54 | 27 | | Love An Adventure .... | $8 | RCA 5730 |
| | | | | second pressings of LP substitute "Funky Town" for "Don't Go" | | |

Beat For You
Destination Unknown

Don't Go
Funky Town 6

I Will Be You
Lies Are Nothing

Listening
Living In A Dream 57

Lonely Without You
Love An Adventure

Try

PSYCHEDELIC FURS
New York-based, British techno-rock group. Formed in 1978 by brothers Richard (vocals) and Tim Butler (bass), and John Ashton (guitar).

11/22/80	140	7		1 The Psychedelic Furs	$8	Columbia 36791
6/27/81	89	14		2 Talk Talk Talk	$8	Columbia 37339
11/13/82+	61	32	●	3 Forever Now	$8	Columbia 38261
				produced by Todd Rundgren		
5/26/84	43	27		4 Mirror Moves	$8	Columbia 39278

DEBUT DATE	PEAK POS	WKS CHR	GOLD	ARTIST — Album Title	$	Label & Number
				PSYCHEDELIC FURS — Cont'd		
3/7/87	**29**	27		5 Midnight To Midnight	$8	Columbia 40466
9/24/88	**102**	8		6 All Of This And Nothing...............................[G]	$8	Columbia 44377
11/25/89	**138**	4		7 Book Of Days...	$8	Columbia 45412

Alice's House (4)   Forever Now (3)   Imitation Of Christ (1,6)   No Release (5)   She Is Mine (2)   We Love You (1)
All Of The Law (5)   **Ghost In You** (4,6) *59*   India (1)   No Tears (2)   Shine (7)   Wedding (7)
All Of This & Nothing (2,6)   Goodbye (3)   Into You Like A Train (2)   One More Word (5)   Shock (5)   Wedding Song (1)
All That Money Wants (6)   Heartbeat (4)   It Goes On (2)   Only A Game (4)   Should God Forget (7)   Yes I Do (3)
Angels Don't Cry (5)   **Heartbreak Beat** (5,6) *26*   Like A Stranger (4)   Only You And I (3)   Sister Europe (1,6)
Book Of Days (7)   Heaven (4,6)   **Love My Way** (3,6) *44*   Parade (7)   Sleep Comes Down (3)
Danger (3)   Here Come Cowboys (4)   Midnight To Midnight (5)   President Gas (3,6)   So Run Down (2)
Dumb Waiters (2,6)   Highwire Days (4,6)   Mother - Son (2)   **Pretty In Pink** (2,6) *41*   Soap Commercial (1)
Entertain Me (7)   House (7)   Mr. Jones (2)   Pulse (1)   Susan's Strange (1)
Fall (1)   I Don't Mine (7)   My Time (4)   Run And Run (3)   Torch (7)
Flowers (1)   I Wanna Sleep With You (2)   No Easy Street (3)   Shadow In My Heart (5)   Torture (7)

PUBLIC ENEMY

Rap group led by Chuck D. (Carlton Ridenhauer). Includes MC Flavor-Flave (William Drayton), DJ Terminator X (Norman Rogers) and Professor Griff (Richard Griffin). Disbanded briefly in June 1989 due to controversy over anti-semitic remarks Griff made. Griff left band at the end of 1989.

1/23/88	**125**	12		1 Yo! Bum Rush The Show	$8	Def Jam 40658
7/23/88	**42**	51	▲	2 It Takes A Nation Of Millions To Hold Us Back	$8	Def Jam 44303
4/28/90	**10**	27	▲	3 **Fear Of A Black Planet**	$12	Def Jam 45413
10/19/91	**4**	37	▲	4 **Apocalypse 91...The Enemy Strikes Black**	$12	Def Jam 47374
10/3/92	**13**	14	●	5 Greatest Misses	$12	Def Jam 53014
				CD includes a bonus track		

Air Hoodlum (5)   Cold Lampin' With Flavor (2)   How To Kill A Radio   More News At 11 (4)   Reggie Jax (3)   Timebomb (1)
Anti-Nigger Machine (3)   Contract On The World Love   Consultant (4,5)   Move! (4)   Revolutionary Generation (3)   Too Much Posse (1)
B. Side Wins Again (3)   Jam (3)   I Don't Wanna Be Called Yo   Night Of The Living   Rightstarter (Message To A   War At 33 1/3 (3)
Black Steel In The Hour Of   Countdown To Armageddon   Niga (4)   Baseheads (2)   Black Man) (1)   Welcome To The Terrordome
Chaos (2)   (2)   Incident At 66.6 FM (3)   Nighttrain (4)   Security Of The First World   (3)
Bring The Noise (2,4)   Don't Believe The Hype (2)   Leave This Off Your Fu*kin   911 Is A Joke (3)   (2)   Who Stole The Soul? (3,5)
Brothers Gonna Work It Out   Fear Of A Black Planet (3)   Charts (3)   1 Million Bottlebags (4)   She Watch Channel Zero?!   Yo! Bum Rush The Show (1)
(3)   Fight The Power (3)   Letter To The NY Post (4)   Party For Your Right To   (2)   You're Gonna Get Yours (1,5)
Burn Hollywood Burn (3)   Final Count Of The Collision   Lost At Birth (4)   Fight (2,5)   Show 'Em Whatcha Got (4)
By The Time I Get To   Between Us And The   Louder Than A Bomb (2,5)   Pollywanacraka (3)   Shut Em Down (4,5)
Arizona (4)   Damned (3)   M.P.E. (1)   Power To The People (3)   Sophisticated Bitch (1)
Can't Do Nuttin' For Ya Man   Get The F___ Outta Dodge (4)   Meet The G That Killed Me   Prophets Of Rage (2)   Terminator X Speaks With
(3)   Gett Off My Back (3)   (3)   Public Enemy No. 1 (1)   His Hands (1)
Can't Truss It (4) *50*   Gotta Do What I Gotta Do (5)   Megablast (1,5)   Raise The Roof (1)   Terminator X To The Edge
Caught, Can We Get A   Hazy Shade Of Criminal (5)   Mind Terrorist (2)   Rebel Without A Pause (2)   Of Panic (2)
Witness? (2)   Hit Da Road Jack (5)   Miuzi Weighs A Ton (1)   Rebirth (4)   Tie Goes To The Runner (5)

PUBLIC IMAGE LTD.

Post-punk outfit formed in 1978 led by former Sex Pistols lead singer Johnny Lydon (earlier known as Johnny Rotten). Features varying membership.

5/10/80	**171**	3		1 Second Edition..	$10	Island 3288 [2]
5/30/81	**114**	4		2 The Flowers Of Romance	$8	Warner 3536
3/8/86	**115**	16		3 Album	$8	Elektra 60438
				cassette release entitled *Cassette*		
10/24/87	**169**	10		4 Happy?	$8	Virgin 90642
				PUBLIC IMAGE LIMITED		
6/3/89	**106**	23		5 9	$8	Virgin 91062

Albatross (1)   Careering (1)   Four Enclosed Walls (2)   Like That (5)   Round (3)   Swan Lake (1)
Angry (4)   Chant (1)   Francis Massacre (2)   Memories (1)   Rules And Regulations (4)   Track 8 (2)
Armada (5)   Disappointed (5)   Go Back (2)   No Birds (1)   Same Old Story (5)   U.S.L.S. 1 (5)
Bad Baby (1)   Ease (3)   Graveyard (1)   Open And Revolving (4)   Sand Castles In The Snow (5)   Under The House (2)
Bags (3)   FFF (3)   Happy (5)   Phenagen (2)   Save Me (4)   Warrior (5)
Banging The Door (2)   Fat Chance Hotel (4)   Hard Times (4)   Poptones (1)   Seattle (4)   Worry (5)
Body, The (4)   Fishing (3)   Home (3)   Radio 4 (1)   Socialist (1)
Brave New World (5)   Flowers Of Romance (2)   Hymie's Him (2)   Rise (3)   Suit, The (1)

PUCKETT, Gary, And The Union Gap

Singer/guitarist Puckett (b: 10/17/42, Hibbing, Minnesota) formed The Union Gap in San Diego in 1967; named after the town of Union Gap, Washington. Included Kerry Chater (bass), Paul Whitebread (drums), Dwight Bement (sax) and Gary Withem (keyboards).

2/17/68	**22**	45		1 Woman, Woman	$15	Columbia 9612
				THE UNION GAP Featuring Gary Puckett		
5/18/68	**21**	39	●	2 Young Girl	$15	Columbia 9664
11/2/68+	**20**	20		3 Incredible	$15	Columbia 9715
12/6/69+	**50**	14		4 The New Gary Puckett And The Union Gap Album	$15	Columbia 9935
7/11/70	**50**	33	▲	5 Gary Puckett & The Union Gap's Greatest Hits...................[G]	$15	Columbia 1042
10/16/71	**196**	2		6 The Gary Puckett Album	$15	Columbia 30862
				GARY PUCKETT		

All That Matters (6)   **Don't Give In To Him**   Honey (I Miss You) (2)   Kiss Me Goodbye (2)   Paindrops (1)   To Love Somebody (1)
Angelica (6)   (4,5) *15*   **I Just Don't Know What**   Lady Madonna (2)   Pleasure Of You (2)   Wait Till The Sun Shines On
Beggar, The (5)   Don't Make Promises (1,5)   **To Do With Myself** (6) *61*   **Lady Willpower** (3,5) *2*   Reverend Posey (3)   You (2)
By The Time I Get To   Dreams Of The Everyday   I Want A New Day (1)   **Let's Give Adam And Eve**   Say You Don't Need Me (2)   **Woman, Woman** (1,5) *4*
Phoenix (6)   Housewife (6)   I'm Just A Man (3)   **Another Chance** (5) *41*   Shimmering Eyes (6)   You Better Sit Down Kids (1)
Can You Tell (3)   Feeling Bad (6)   I'm Losing You (2)   Lullaby (4)   Simple Man (4)   **Young Girl** (2,5) *2*
Common Cold (3)   Gentle Woman (6)   I've Done All I Can (3)   M'Lady (1)   Stay Out Of My World (4)
Delta Lady (6)   Give In (3)   If The Day Would Come (3)   Mighty Quinn (2)   (Sweet, Sweet Baby) Since
Do You Really Have A Heart   Hard Tomorrow (4)   If We Only Have Love (6)   My Son (1,4)   You've Been Gone (2)
(6)   Hello Morning (4)   **Keep The Customer**   Now And Then (3)   Take Your Pleasure (3)
  His Other Woman (4)   **Satisfied** (6) *71*   Out In The Cold Again (4)   **This Girl Is A Woman Now**
  Home (4,5)   Kentucky Woman (1)   **Over You** (3,5) *7*   (4,5) *9*

DEBUT DATE	PEAK POS	WKS CHR	GOLD	ARTIST — Album Title	$	Label & Number

PURE LOVE & PLEASURE
Quintet featuring lead vocalists David McAnally and Pegge Ann May, plus Bob Bohanna (guitar), John Allair (keyboards) and Dick Rogers (drums).

DEBUT DATE	PEAK POS	WKS CHR	GOLD	ARTIST — Album Title	$	Label & Number
4/25/70	195	2		A Record Of Pure Love & Pleasure	$12	Dunhill 50076

All In My Mind	Joyce	Love, Love, Love You	My Lies	Too Scared To Go	
Hard Times	Lord's Prayer (Liturgical Text)	Mama Said	Relax	What'cha Gonna Do	

★★405★★ PURE PRAIRIE LEAGUE
Country-rock group formed in Cincinnati in 1971. Numerous personnel changes. Country singer Vince Gill was lead singer from late 1979-83.

DEBUT DATE	PEAK POS	WKS CHR	GOLD	ARTIST — Album Title	$	Label & Number
2/8/75	34	24	●	1 Bustin' Out............	$8	RCA 4769
6/7/75	24	14		2 Two Lane Highway............	$8	RCA 0933
2/7/76	33	16		3 If The Shoe Fits............	$8	RCA 1247
11/20/76	99	14		4 Dance	$8	RCA 1924
9/10/77	68	11		5 Live!! Takin' The Stage ....[L]	$10	RCA 2404 [2]
5/13/78	79	11		6 Just Fly	$8	RCA 2590
6/23/79	124	6		7 Can't Hold Back	$8	RCA 3335
5/17/80	37	24		8 Firin' Up	$8	Casablanca 7212
5/2/81	72	15		9 Something In The Night	$8	Casablanca 7255

All The Lonesome Cowboys (4,5)	Early Morning Riser (1)	I Can't Hold Back (7)	Leave My Heart Alone (1)	Pickin' To Beat The Devil (2,5)	Tornado Warning (4)
All The Way (4)	Fade Away (4,5)	**I Can't Stop The Feelin'** (8) 77	**Let Me Love You Tonight** (8) 10	Place In The Middle (6)	**Two Lane Highway** (2,5) 97
Amie (1,5) 27	Falling In And Out Of Love (1)	I Wanna Know Your Name (9)	Lifetime (6)	Restless Woman (7)	White Line (7)
Angel (1)	Feel The Fire (9)	I'll Be Damned (8)	Lifetime Of Nighttime (8)	Rude Rude Awakening (7)	Working In The Coal Mine (6)
Angel #9 (1)	Feelin' Of Love (5)	I'll Change Your Flat Tire, Merle (2,5)	Livin' Each Day At A Time (4)	Runner (4)	You Are So Near To Me (3)
Aren't You Mine (3)	Fool Fool (7)	I'm Almost Ready (8) 34	Livin' It Alone (7)	San Antonio (4)	You Don't Have To Be Alone (6)
Bad Dream (6)	Gimme Another Chance (3)	I'm Goin' Away (7)	Long Cold Winter (3)	She's All Mine (8)	You're Mine Tonight (9) 68
Boulder Skies (1)	Give Us A Rise (2)	In The Morning (4)	Louise (What I Did) (5)	Sister's Keeper (2)	You're My True Love (8)
Call Me, Tell Me (1)	Goin' Home (3)	Janny Lou (8)	Love Is Falling (6)	Slim Pickin's (6)	
Came Through (5)	Goodbye So Long (7)	Jazzman (1)	Love Me Again (9)	Something In The Night (9)	
Catfishin' (4)	Harvest (2,5)	Jerene (7)	Love Will Grow (4)	**Still Right Here In My Heart** (9) 28	
Country Song (5)	Heart Of Her Own (5)	Just Can't Believe It (2)	Lucille Crawfield (3,5)	Sun Shone Lightly (3,5)	
Dance (4,5)	Help Yourself (4)	Just Fly (6)	Memories (2)	Tell Me One More Time (9)	
Dark Colours (5)	Hold On To Our Hearts (9)	Kansas City Southern (2,5)	Misery Train (7)	That'll Be The Day (3,5)	
Do You Love Me Truly, Julie (9)	I Can Only Think Of You (3)	Kentucky Moonshine (2,5)	My Young Girl (6)	Too Many Heartaches In Paradise (8)	
Don't Keep Me Hangin' (9)	I Can't Believe (7)		Out In The Street (3,5)		

PURIM, Flora
Born in Rio de Janeiro on 3/6/42. Married to Brazilian jazz artist Airto Moreira.

DEBUT DATE	PEAK POS	WKS CHR	GOLD	ARTIST — Album Title	$	Label & Number
2/15/75	172	5		1 Stories To Tell	$8	Milestone 9058
3/13/76	59	15		2 Open Your Eyes You Can Fly	$8	Milestone 9065
10/16/76	146	5		3 500 Miles High ....[L]	$8	Milestone 9070
				recorded at the Montreux Jazz Festival (7/6/74)		
3/26/77	163	4		4 Nothing Will Be As It Was...Tomorrow............	$8	Warner 2985
8/13/77	194	3		5 Encounter	$8	Milestone 9077
6/3/78	174	4		6 Everyday, Everynight............	$8	Warner 3168
				accompaniment on all albums by a host of famous jazz musicians		

Above The Rainbow (5)	Cravo E Canela (Cinnamon And Cloves) (3)	I Just Want To Be Here (medley) (1)	Nothing Will Be As It Was — Nada Sera Como Antes (4)	Time's Lie (2)
Andei (I Walked) (2)	Dedicated To Bruce (5)	I'm Coming For Your Love (4)	O Cantador (1,3)	To Say Goodbye (1)
Angels (1)	Encounter (5)	In Brasil (6)	Open Your Eyes You Can Fly (2)	Tomara (I Wish) (5)
Baia (3)	Everyday, Everynight (6)	Ina's Song (Trip To Bahia) (medley) (2)	Samba Michel (6)	Transition (medley) (2)
Black Narcissus (5)	Fairy Tale Song (4)	Insensatez (1)	San Francisco River (2)	Uri (The Wind) (3,5)
Blues Ballad (6)	Five-Four (5)	Jive Talk (3)	Search For Peace (1)	Vera Cruz (Empty Faces) (1)
Bridge (3)	500 Miles High (3)	Las Olas (6)	Silver Sword (1)	Walking Away (6)
Bridges (4)	Hope, The (6)	Latinas (5)	Sometime Ago (2)	White Wing/Black Wing (2)
Casa Forte (1)	I Just Don't Know (6)	Mountain Train (1)	Stories To Tell (1)	Why I'm Alone (6)
Conversation (2)				Windows (5)
Corre Nina (4)				You Love Me Only (4)

PURSELL, Bill
Pianist from Tulare, California. Appeared with the Nashville Symphony Orchestra. Taught musical composition at Vanderbilt University.

DEBUT DATE	PEAK POS	WKS CHR	GOLD	ARTIST — Album Title	$	Label & Number
4/6/63	28	14		Our Winter Love............[I]	$15	Columbia 1992
				arrangements by Bill Justis; orchestra directed by Grady Martin		

Born To Lose	Four Walls	I Walk The Line	Stranger	There'll Be No Teardrops Tonight
Bye Bye Love	I Can't Help It (If I'm Still In Love With You)	Love Can't Wait	That Which Is Loved	Wound Time Can't Erase
Dark Alley	Love Can't Wait	Our Winter Love 9		

PURSUIT OF HAPPINESS, The
Toronto-based quintet: Moe Berg (lead vocals, guitar), Dave Gilby, Johnny Sinclair, Kris Abbott and Leslie Stanwyck. Sinclair and Stanwyck left in 1990, replaced by Brad Barker and Susan Murumets.

DEBUT DATE	PEAK POS	WKS CHR	GOLD	ARTIST — Album Title	$	Label & Number
12/17/88+	93	21		Love Junk	$8	Chrysalis 41675

Beautiful White Consciousness Raising As A Social Tool	Hard To Laugh	Looking For Girls	Ten Fingers	Walking In The Woods
	I'm An Adult Now	Man's Best Friend	Tree Of Knowledge	When The Sky Comes Falling Down
	Killed By Love	She's So Young		

PYRAMIDS, The
Surf band from Long Beach, California: Skip Mercer, Willie Glover, Steve Leonard, Ron McMullen and Tom Pittman.

DEBUT DATE	PEAK POS	WKS CHR	GOLD	ARTIST — Album Title	$	Label & Number
3/14/64	119	6		The Original Penetration! and other favorites	$100	Best 16501

Do The Slauson	Here Comes Marsha	Long Tall Texan	Out Of Limits	**Penetration** 18	Road Runnah
Everybody	Koko Joe	Louie Louie	Paul	Pyramid Stomp	Sticks And Skins

DEBUT DATE	PEAK POS	WKS CHR	GOLD	ARTIST — Album Title	$	Label & Number

PYTHON LEE JACKSON
Australian rock quintet led by keyboardist David Bentley.

| 10/7/72 | 182 | 6 | | In A Broken Dream ....[E] | $12 | GNP Cres. 2066 |

recorded in 1968; Rod Stewart sings lead on 3 tracks

Blues, The   If It's Meant To Be A Party   **In A Broken Dream 56**   Sweet Consolation   Your Wily Ways
Boogie Woogie Joe   If The World Stopped Still   Second Time Around The   Turn The Music Down
Doin' Fine   Tonight   Wheel

Q

Q
Pop quartet from Beaver Falls, Pennsylvania. Led by ex-Jaggerz members Robert Peckman and Don Garvin.

| 6/18/77 | 140 | 2 | | Dancin' Man .... | $8 | Epic 34691 |

Dancin' Man 23   Feel It In Your Backbone.   Feelin' That Rhythm To The   If It Ain't One Thing, It's   Jump For Joy   Make Us One Again
Do I Love You?   Got It In Your Feet   Bone   Another   Knee Deep In Love   Sweet Summertime
   Have I Sinned

QUARTERFLASH
Rock group from Portland, Oregon led by the husband-and-wife team of Marv (guitar) and Rindy (vocals, saxophone) Ross. Originally known as Seafood Mama.

10/31/81+	8	52 ▲		1 Quarterflash	$8	Geffen 2003
7/9/83	34	21		2 Take Another Picture..	$8	Geffen 4011
10/5/85	150	5		3 Back Into Blue..	$8	Geffen 24078

Back Into Blue (3)   **Find Another Fool** (1) **16**   Just For You (3)   One More Round To Go (2)   Take Me To Heart (2) **14**   Williams Avenue (1)
Caught In The Rain (3)   Grace Under Fire (3)   Love Should Be So Kind (1)   **Right Kind Of Love** (1) **56**   Talk To Me (3) **83**
Come To Me (3)   **Harden My Heart** (1) **3**   Love Without A Net (You   Shakin' The Jinx (2)   Try To Make It True (1)
Cruisin' With The Deuce (1)   I Want To Believe It's You (3)   Keep Falling) (3)   Shane (2)   Valerie (1)
Eye To Eye (2)   It All Becomes Clear (2)   Make It Shine (2)   **Take Another Picture**   Walking On Ice (3)
   It Don't Move Me (2)   Nowhere Left To Hide (2)   (2) **58**   Welcome To The City (3)

QUATEMAN, Bill
Pop vocalist/guitarist/pianist/composer from Chicago.

| 2/12/77 | 129 | 8 | | Night After Night .... | $8 | RCA 2027 |

Au Claire   Carolina   Doncha Wonder   Mama Won't You Roll Me   You're The One
Back By The River   Dance Baby Dance   Down To The Bone   Night After Night   Your Money Or Your Life

QUATRO, Suzi
Rock singer born on 6/3/50 in Detroit. Moved to England in 1970, signed with Mickie Most's RAK label. Played Leather Tuscadero on TV's *Happy Days* in 1977. Her older sister Patti was a bassist with Fanny.

3/30/74	142	13		1 Suzi Quatro	$15	Bell 1302
10/5/74	126	10		2 Quatro	$15	Bell 1313
5/10/75	146	6		3 Your Mama Won't Like Me................................	$8	Arista 4035
3/24/79	37	20		4 If You Knew Suzi..	$8	RSO 3044
10/6/79	117	14		5 Suzi...And Other Four Letter Words..................	$8	RSO 3064
11/1/80	165	5		6 Rock Hard..	$8	Dreamland 5006

All Shook Up (1) **85**   Hit The Road Jack (2)   Love Hurts (5)   Race Is On (4)   State Of Mind (6)   You Can Make Me Want You
Breakdown (4)   Hollywood (4)   Love Is Ready (6)   Rock And Roll Hoochie Koo   Sticks And Stones (1)   (3)
Can The Can (1) **56**   I Bit Off More Than I Could   Mama's Boy (5)   (4)   Strip Me (3)   Your Mama Won't Like Me
Can't Trust Love (3)   Chew (3)   Michael (3)   Rock Hard (6)   **Stumblin' In** (4) **4**   (3)
Cat Size (2)   I Wanna Be Your Man (1)   Mind Demons (5)   Savage Silk (6)   Suicide (4)
Devil Gate Drive (2)   **I've Never Been In Love**   Move It (2)   Shakin' All Over (1)   Tired Of Waiting (4)
Don't Change My Luck (4)   (5) **44**   New Day Woman (3)   **She's In Love With You**   Too Big (2)
Ego In The Night (6)   **If You Can't Give Me Love**   Non-Citizen (4)   (5) **41**   Trouble (2)
Ever (3)   (4) **45**   Official Suburban   Shine My Machine (1)   Wild One (2)
48 Crash (1)   Keep A Knockin' (2)   Superman (1)   Shot Of Rhythm And Blues   Wiser Than You (4)
Four Letter Words (5)   Klondyke Kate (2)   Paralysed (2)   (2)   Wish Upon Me (6)
Glad All Over (6)   Lay Me Down (6)   Primitive Love (1)   Skin Tight Skin (1)   Woman Cry (6)
Glycerine Queen (1)   **Lipstick** (6) **51**   Prisoner Of Your   Space Cadets (5)   You Are My Lover (5)
Hard Headed (6)   Lonely Is The Hardest (6)   Imagination (3)   Starlight Lady (5)

QUAZAR
Band from New Jersey: Kevin Goins, Harvey Banks, Monica Peteres, Darryl "Major D" Dixon, Gregory Fitz, Richard "Shiadi" Banks, Eugene "Moochie" Jackson, Jeffrey Adams, Darryl de Lomberto and Peachena.

| 1/11/78 | 121 | 5 | | Quazar .... | $8 | Arista 4187 |

Funk 'N Roll (Dancin' In   Funk With A Big Foot   Love Me Baby   Savin' My Love For A Rainy   Shades Of Quaze   Workin' On The Buildin'
The "Funkshine")   Funk With A Capital "G"   Day   Starlight Circus   Your Lovin' Is Easy

★★69★★ QUEEN
Rock group formed in England in 1972: Freddie Mercury (born Fred Bulsara on 9/5/46 in Zanzibar; d: 11/24/91 of AIDS; vocals), Brian May (guitar), John Deacon (bass) and Roger Taylor (drums). May and Taylor had been in the group Smile. Mercury had recorded as Larry Lurex.

11/3/73+	83	22	●	1 Queen	$12	Elektra 75064
5/11/74	49	13		2 Queen II..	$8	Elektra 75082
2/14/74+	12	32	●	3 Sheer Heart Attack	$8	Elektra 1026
2/27/75+	4	56	●	4 A Night At The Opera	$8	Elektra 1053
1/15/77	5	19	●	5 A Day At The Races	$8	Elektra 101
1/26/77+	3	37	▲	6 News Of The World	$8	Elektra 112
12/9/78+	6	18	▲	7 Jazz...	$8	Elektra 166
7/7/79	16	14	●	8 Queen Live Killers ....[L]	$10	Elektra 702 [2]

DEBUT DATE	PEAK POS	WKS CHR	GOLD	ARTIST — Album Title	$	Label & Number
				QUEEN — Cont'd		
7/19/80	1⁵	43 ▲	9	**The Game**	$8	Elektra 513
12/27/80+	23	15	10	Flash Gordon ....[S]	$8	Elektra 518
11/14/81	14	26 ▲	11	Greatest Hits ....[G]	$8	Elektra 564
5/29/82	22	21 ●	12	Hot Space	$8	Elektra 60128
3/17/84	23	20 ●	13	The Works	$8	Capitol 12322
7/19/86	46	13	14	A Kind of Magic.....................................	$8	Capitol 12476
6/24/89	24	14	15	The Miracle	$8	Capitol 92357
				CD includes 3 bonus tracks		
2/23/91	30	17 ●	16	Innuendo...	$12	Hollywood 61020
3/28/92	4	46↑▲	17	**Classic Queen** ....[G]	$12	Hollywood 61311
				U.S. version of the U.K. release *Greatest Hits II*		
6/20/92	53	15	18	Live At Wembley....................................[L]	$12	Hollywood 61104
10/3/02	11	19↑▲	19	Greatest Hits ....[G]	$12	Hollywood 61265

Action This Day (12)
All Dead, All Dead (6)
All God's People (16)
Another One Bites The Dust (9,11,18,19) *1*
Arboria (Planet Of The Tree Man) (10)
Back Chat (12)
Battle Theme (10)
Bicycle Race (7,8,11,19) *24*
Big Spender (18)
Bijou (16)
Body Language (12,19) *11*
Bohemian Rhapsody (4,8,11,17,18) *2*
Breakthru (15)
Brighton Rock (3,8,18)
Bring Back That Leroy Brown (3)
Calling All Girls (12) *60*
Coming Soon (9)
Cool Cat (12)
Crash Dive On Ming City (10)
Crazy Little Thing Called Love (9,11,18,19) *1*
Dancer (12)
Dead On Time (7)
Dear Friends (3)
Death On Two Legs (Dedicated To...) (4,8)
Delilah (16)
Doing All Right (1)
Don't Stop Me Now (7,8,19) *86*
Don't Try So Hard (16)
Don't Try Suicide (9)
Dragon Attack (9)
Dreamer's Ball (7,8)
Drowse (16)
Escape From The Swamp (10)
Execution Of Flash (10)
Fairy Feller's Master-Stroke (2)
Fat Bottomed Girls (7,11,19) *flip*
Father To Son (2)
Fight From The Inside (6)
Flash To The Rescue (10)
Flash's Theme aka Flash (10,11) *42*
Flick Of The Wrist (3)
Football Fight (10)
Friends Will Be Friends (14,18)
Fun It (7)
Funny How Love Is (2)
Get Down, Make Love (6,8)
Gimme Some Lovin' (18)
Gimme The Prize (Kurgan's Theme) (14)
God Save The Queen (4,8,18)
Good Company (4)
Good Old-Fashioned Lover Boy (5,19)
Great King Rat (1)
Hammer To Fall (13,17,18)
Headlong (16,17)
Hello Mary Lou (Goodbye Heart) (18)
Hero (10)
Hitman (16)
I Can't Live With You (16)
I Want It All (15,17) *50*
I Want To Break Free (13,18,19) *45*
I'm Going Slightly Mad (16,17)
I'm In Love With My Car (4,8)
If You Can't Beat Them (7)
Impromptu (18)
In Only Seven Days (7)
In The Death Cell (Love Theme Reprise) (10)
In The Lap Of The Gods (3,18)
In The Space Capsule (The Love Theme) (10)
Innuendo (16)
Invisible Man (15)
Is This The World We Created...? (13,18)
It's A Hard Life (13) *72*
It's Late (6) *74*
Jealousy (7)
Jesus (1)
Keep Passing The Open Windows (13)
Keep Yourself Alive (1,8,11,17)
Khashoggi's Ship (15)
Killer Queen (3,8,11,19) *12*
Kind Of Magic (14,17,18) *42*
Kiss (Aura Resurrects Flash) (10)
Las Palabras De Amor (The Words Of Love) (12)
Lazing On A Sunday Afternoon (4)
Leaving Home Ain't Easy (7)
Let Me Entertain You (7,8)
Liar (1)
Life Is Real (Song For Lennon) (12)
Lily Of The Valley (3)
Long Away (5)
Loser In The End (2)
Love Of My Life (4,8,18)
Machines (or Back To Humans) (13)
Man On The Prowl (13)
March Of The Black Queen (2)
Marriage Of Dale And Ming (And Flash Approaching) (10)
Millionaire Waltz (5)
Ming's Theme (In The Court Of Ming The Merciless) (10)
Miracle, The (15,17)
Misfire (3)
Modern Times Rock 'N' Roll (1)
More Of That Jazz (7)
Mustapha (7)
My Baby Does Me (15)
My Fairy King (1)
My Melancholy Blues (6)
Need Your Loving Tonight (9) *44*
Nevermore (2)
Night Comes Down (1)
Now I'm Here (3,8,18,19)
Ogre Battle (2)
One Vision (14,17,18) *61*
One Year Of Love (14,17)
Pain Is So Close To Pleasure (14)
Party (15)
Play The Game (9,11,18,19) *42*
Princes Of The Universe (14)
Procession (2)
Prophet's Song (4)
Put Out The Fire (12)
Radio Ga-Ga (13,17,18) *16*
Rain Must Fall (15)
Ride The Wild Wind (16)
Ring (Hypnotic Seduction Of Dale) (10)
Rock It (Prime Jive) (9)
Sail Away Sweet Sister (9)
Save Me (9,19)
Scandal (15)
Seaside Rendezvous (4)
Seven Seas Of Rhye (1,2,18,19)
She Makes Me (Stormtrooper In Stilettoes) (3)
Sheer Heart Attack (6,8)
Show Must Go On (16,17)
Sleeping On The Sidewalk (6)
Some Day One Day (2)
Somebody To Love (5,11,19) *13*
Son And Daughter (1)
Spread Your Wings (6,8)
Staying Power (12)
Stone Cold Crazy (3,17)
Sweet Lady (4)
Tear It Up (13,18)
Tenement Funster (3)
Teo Torriatte (Let Us Cling Together) (5)
These Are The Days Of Our Lives (16,17)
Tie Your Mother Down (5,8,17,18) *49*
Tutti Frutti (18)
Under Pressure (11,12,17,18) *29*
Vultan's Theme (Attack Of The Hawk Men) (10)
Was It All Worth It (15)
We Are The Champions (6,8,11,18,19) *4*
We Will Rock You (6,8,11,18,19) *52* charted at POS 52 as "We Will Rock You/We Are The Champions" in 1992
Wedding March (10)
White Man (5)
White Queen (As It Began) (2)
Who Needs You (6)
Who Wants To Live Forever (14,17,18)
You And I (5)
You Take My Breath Away (4
You're My Best Friend (4,8,11,19) *16*
(You're So Square) Baby I Don't Care (18)

QUEEN LATIFAH
Female rapper. Born Dana Owens in Newark, New Jersey; raised in nearby East Orange. Appeared in films *Jungle Fever* and *House Party 2*. Latifah is Arabic for delicate and sensitive.

12/16/89+	124	17	1	All Hail The Queen	$8	Tommy Boy 1022
9/21/91	117	23	2	Nature Of A Sista'	$12	Tommy Boy 1035

Bad As A Mutha (2)
Come Into My House (1)
Dance For Me (1)
Evil That Men Do (1)
Fly Girl (2)
Give Me Your Love (2)
How Do I Love Thee (2)
If You Don't Know (2)
Inside Out (1)
King And Queen Creation (1)
Ladies First (1)
Latifah's Had It Up 2 Here (2)
Latifah's Law (1)
Love Again (2)
Mama Gave Birth To The Soul Children (1)
Nature Of A Sista' (2)
Nuff Of The Ruff 'Stuff (2)
One Mo' Time (2)
Princess Of The Posse (1)
Pros, The (1)
Queen Of Royal Badness (1)
Sexy Fancy (2)
That's The Way We Flow (2)
Wrath Of My Madness (1)

★★498★★ **QUEENSRYCHE**
Heavy-metal quintet formed in 1981, in Bellevue, Washington, by high school classmates: Geoff Tate (vocals), Chris DeGarmo, Michael Wilton, Eddie Jackson and Scott Rockenfield.

9/17/83	81	22	1	Queensryche ....[M]	$8	EMI America 1900
10/13/84	61	23 ●	2	The Warning	$8	EMI America 1713
7/26/86	47	21 ●	3	Rage For Order	$8	EMI America 1719
5/21/88	50	52 ▲	4	Operation:mindcrime	$8	EMI-Man. 48640
9/22/90	7	125↑▲²	5	Empire	$12	EMI 92806
11/23/91	38	11	6	Operation:livecrime ....[L]	$12	EMI 97048
				package includes CD, a one-hour video and a 44-page booklet; *Operation:mindcrime* performances filmed on location in Wisconsin		

Anarchy-X (4,6)
Another Rainy Night (Without You) (5)
Anybody Listening? (5)
Before The Storm (4)
Best I Can (5)
Blinded (1)
Breaking The Silence (4,6)
Chemical Youth (We Are Rebellion) (3)
Child Of Fire (2)
Deliverance (2)
Della Brown (5)
Electric Requiem (4,6)
Empire (5)
En Force (2)
Eyes Of A Stranger (4,6)
Gonna Get Close To You (3)
Hand On Heart (5)
I Don't Believe In Love (4,6)
I Dream In Infrared (3)
I Remember Now (4,6)
I Will Remember (5)
Jet City Woman (5)
Killing Words (3)
Lady Wore Black (1)
London (3)
Mission, The (4,6)
My Empty Room (5)
NM 156 (2)
Needle Lies (4,6)
Neue Regel (3)
Nightrider (1)
No Sanctuary (2)
One And Only (5)
Operation:Mindcrime (4,6)
Queen Of The Reich (1)
Resistance (5)
Revolution Calling (4,6)
Roads To Madness (4,6)
Screaming In Digital (3)
Silent Lucidity (5) *9*
Speak (4,6)
Spreading The Disease (4,6)
Suite Sister Mary (4,6)
Surgical Strike (3)
Take Hold Of The Flame (2)
Thin Line (5)
Waiting For 22 (4,6)
Walk In The Shadows (3)
Warning (2)
Whisper, The (3)

? (QUESTION MARK) & THE MYSTERIANS
Early punk-rock quintet. Lead singer Rudy Martinez was born in Mexico and raised in Saginaw, Michigan.

11/19/66	66	15		96 Tears	$50	Cameo 2004

DEBUT DATE	PEAK POS	WKS CHR	GOLD	ARTIST — Album Title	$	Label & Number

? (QUESTION MARK) & THE MYSTERIANS — Cont'd

Don't Break This Heart Of Mine				"8" Teen		Midnight Hour

Don't Break This Heart Of Mine   "8" Teen   Midnight Hour   Set Aside   Ten O'Clock   Why Me

Don't Tease Me   I Need Somebody 22   96 Tears 1   Stormy Monday   nd Side   You're Telling Me Lies

★★410★★ QUICKSILVER MESSENGER SERVICE

San Francisco acid-rock group featuring guitarist John Cipollina (brother of Huey Lewis & The News' bassist Mario Cipollina; d: 5/29/89 [age 45] of emphysema) and bassist David Freiberg (joined Jefferson Starship in 1973). Many personnel changes.

DEBUT DATE	PEAK POS	WKS CHR	GOLD	ARTIST — Album Title	$	Label & Number
6/22/68	63	25		1 Quicksilver Messenger Service	$30	Capitol 2904
3/29/69	27	30	●	2 Happy Trails .... [L]	$20	Capitol 120
				includes several studio tracks		
1/24/70	25	24		3 Shady Grove	$12	Capitol 391
8/22/70	27	24		4 Just For Love	$12	Capitol 498
1/23/71	26	20		5 What About Me	$12	Capitol 630
12/4/71+	114	9		6 Quicksilver	$12	Capitol 819
5/6/72	134	10		7 Comin' Thru	$12	Capitol 11002
5/19/73	108	10		8 Anthology .... [K]	$12	Capitol 11165 [2]
11/15/75	89	12		9 Solid Silver	$10	Capitol 11462

All In My Mind (5)   Don't Cry My Lady Love (6,8)   Good Old Rock And Roll (5)   Letter, The (9)   Spindrifter (5,8)   Won't Kill Me (5)
Baby Baby (5)   Don't Lose It (7)   Gypsy Lights (9)   Light Your Windows (1)   Subway (5)   Words Can't Say (3)
Bears (8)   Edward, The Mad Shirt Grinder (3,8)   Happy Trails (9)   Local Color (5,8)   They Don't Know (9)   Worryin' Shoes (9)
Bittersweet Love (9)   Fire Brothers (6,8)   Hat, The (4)   Long Haired Lady (5)   Three Or Four Feet From Home (3,8)
California State Correctional Facility Blues (7)   Flames (9)   Heebie Jeebies (9)   Maiden Of The Cancer Moon (2)   Too Far (3)
Call On Me (5)   Flashing Lonesome (3)   Holy Moly (3)   Mojo (7)   Truth, The (6)
Calvary (2)   Flute Song (3)   Hope (6,8)   Mona (2,8)   What About Me (5,8) 100
Changes (7)   Fool, The (1,8)   How You Love (2)   Out Of My Mind (6)   When You Love (2)
Chicken (7)   Forty Days (7)   I Found Love (6,8)   Play My Guitar (6)   Where You Love (2)
Cobra (4)   Freeway Flyer (4)   I Heard You Singing (9)   Pride Of Man (1,8)   Which Do You Love (2)
Cowboy On The Run (9)   Fresh Air (4,8) 49   It's Been Too Long (1)   Rebel (6)   Who Do You Love (2) 91
Dino's Song (1,8)   Gold And Silver (1)   Joseph's Coat (3)   Shady Grove (3)   Witch's Moon (9)
Doin' Time In The U.S.A. (7)   Gone Again (4)   Just For Love (Part 1 & 2) (4,8)   Song For Frisco (6)   Wolf Run (Part 1 & 2) (4)

QUIET RIOT

Heavy-metal rock quartet from Los Angeles: Kevin DuBrow (lead singer), Carlos Cavazo (guitar), Frankie Banali (drums) and Rudy Sarzo (bass; replaced by Chuck Wright in 1985. DuBrow and Wright left group in 1987; replaced by Paul Shortino (vocals) and Sean McNabb (bass).

DEBUT DATE	PEAK POS	WKS CHR	GOLD	ARTIST — Album Title	$	Label & Number
4/23/83	1¹	81	▲⁴	1 Metal Health	$8	Pasha 38443
8/4/84	15	28	▲	2 Condition Critical	$8	Pasha 39516
8/2/86	31	27		3 QR III	$8	Pasha 40321
11/19/88	119	11		4 Quiet Riot	$8	Pasha 40981

Bad Boy (2)   Cum On Feel The Noize (1) 5   In A Rush (4)   Metal Health ..see: Bang Your Head   Scream And Shout (2)   Twilight Hotel (3)
Bang Your Head (Metal Health) (1) 31   Don't Wanna Be Your Fool (4)   Joker, The (4)   Party All Night (2)   Sign Of The Times (4)   (We Were) Born To Rock (2)
Bass Case (3)   Don't Wanna Let You Go (1)   King Of The Hill (4)   Pump, The (3)   Slave To Love (3)   Wild And The Young (3)
Battle Axe (1)   Down And Dirty (3)   Let's Get Crazy (1)   Put Up Or Shut Up (3)   Slick Black Cadillac (1)   Winners Take All (2)
Breathless (1)   Empty Promises (4)   Love's A Bitch (1)   Red Alert (2)   Stay With Me Tonight (4)
Callin' The Shots (4)   Helping Hands (3)   Lunar Obsession (4)   Rise Or Fall (3)   Still Of The Night (3)
Condition Critical (2)   I'm Fallin' (4)   Main Attraction (3)   Run For Cover (1)   Stomp Your Hands, Clap Your Feet (2)
Coppin' A Feel (4)   Mama Weer All Crazee Now (2) 51   Run To You (4)   Thunderbird (1)

QUINN, Carmel

Irish female singer.

DEBUT DATE	PEAK POS	WKS CHR	GOLD	ARTIST — Album Title	$	Label & Number
4/2/55	4	10		Arthur Godfrey presents Carmel Quinn	$20	Columbia 629

Ballymaquilty Band   Galway Bay   Humour Is On Me Now   Isle Of Innisfree   Spinning Wheel   With My Shillelagh Under My Arm
Cuttin' The Corn In Creeshla   Green Glens Of Antrim   If I Were A Blackbird   Mick McGilligan's Ball   Whistling Gypsy
Doonaree

R

RABBITT, Eddie

Born Edward Thomas Rabbitt on 11/27/44 in Brooklyn; raised in East Orange, New Jersey. Country singer/songwriter/guitarist. First recorded for 20th Century in 1964. Moved to Nashville in 1968. Became established after Elvis Presley recorded his song "Kentucky Rain."

DEBUT DATE	PEAK POS	WKS CHR	GOLD	ARTIST — Album Title	$	Label & Number
6/24/78	143	7		1 Variations	$12	Elektra 127
6/9/79	91	20		2 Loveline	$8	Elektra 181
11/24/79+	151	12	●	3 The Best of Eddie Rabbitt .... [G]	$8	Elektra 235
7/12/80+	19	54	▲	4 Horizon	$8	Elektra 276
8/22/81	23	34	●	5 Step By Step	$8	Elektra 532
11/6/82+	31	25		6 Radio Romance	$8	Elektra 60160
10/1/83	131	11		7 Greatest Hits, Volume II .... [G]	$8	Warner 23925

All My Life, All My Love (6)   Do You Right Tonight (3)   Gone Too Far (2,7) 82   I Don't Know Where To Start (5) 35   I Love A Rainy Night (4,7) 1   Just The Way It Is (4)
Amazing Love (2)   Drinkin' My Baby (Off My Mind) (3)   Good Night For Falling In Love (6)   I Don't Wanna Make Love (With Anyone Else But You) (2)   I Need To Fall In Love Again (4)   Kentucky Rain (1)
Bedroom Eyes (6)   Drivin' My Life Away (4,7) 5   Hearts On Fire (1,3)   I Will Never Let You Go Again (2)   Laughing On The Outside (6)
Bring Back The Sunshine (5)   Early In The Mornin' (5)   Hurtin' For You (1)   I Just Want To Love You (1,3)   It's Always Like The First Time (2)   Loveline (2)
Caroline (1)   Every Which Way But Loose (3) 30   I Can't Help Myself (3) 77   My Only Wish (5)
Crossin' The Mississippi (1)   Nobody Loves Me Like My Baby (5)
Dim Dim The Lights (5)

DEBUT DATE	PEAK POS	WKS CHR	GOLD	ARTIST — Album Title	$	Label & Number

RABBITT, Eddie — Cont'd

Nothing Like Falling In Love (7)	Pretty Lady (4)	747 (4)	Song Of Ireland (1)	We Can't Go On Living Like This (3)	**You Don't Love Me Anymore** (1,3) **53**
One And Only One (2)	Rivers (5)	Short Road To Love (4)	**Step By Step (5,7) 5**	What Will I Write (4)	You Got Me Now (6)
Our Love Will Survive (6)	Rockin' With My Baby (4)	Skip-A-Beat (5)	Stranger In Your Eyes (6)	Years After You (6)	**You Put The Beat In My Heart** (7) **81**
Plain As The Pain On My Face (1)	**Rocky Mountain Music** (3) **76**	So Deep In Your Love (4)	**Suspicions** (2,7) **13**	**You And I** (6,7) **7**	
Pour Me Another Tequila (2)	Room At The Top Of The Stairs (1)	So Fine (2)	Two Dollars In The Jukebox (3)	**You Can't Run From Love** (6,7) **55**	
		Someone Could Lose A **Heart Tonight** (5,7) **15**			

RABIN, Trevor

Rock guitarist/singer/songwriter. Born and raised in Johannesburg, South Africa. Formed and fronted South African band Rabbitt. Member of Yes since 1983. Wrote their #1 hit "Owner Of A Lonely Heart."

12/9/78	192	4		1 Trevor Rabin	$8	Chrysalis 1196
8/19/89	111	10		2 Can't Look Away	$8	Elektra 60781

All I Want Is Your Love (1)	Eyes Of Love (2)	Getting To Know You Better (1)	I Didn't Think It Would Last (2)	Love Life (1)	Sludge (2)
Cape, The (2)	Fantasy (1)	Hold On To Me (2)	I Miss You Now (2)	Painted Picture (1)	Something To Hold On To (2)
Cover Up (2)	Finding Me A Way Back Home (1)	I Can't Look Away (2)	Live A Bit (1)	Promises (2)	Sorrow (Your Heart) (2)
Etoile Noir (2)				Red Desert (1)	Stay With Me (1)

RACING CARS

British rock quintet led by guitarist/vocalist Ray Ennis.

4/2/77	198	3		Downtown Tonight	$8	Chrysalis 1099

Calling The Tune	Four Wheel Drive	Hard Working Woman	Moonshine Fandango	They Shoot Horses Don't
Downtown Tonight	Get Out And Get It	Ladee-Lo	Pass The Bottle	They

RADIATORS, The

Six-man New Orleans band; known for their "Fishhead Music" — a blend of blues, funk, Cajun, calypso and bluegrass.

12/19/87+	139	16		1 Law Of The Fish	$8	Epic 40888
4/1/89	122	11		2 Zigzagging Through Ghostland	$8	Epic 44343

Boomerang (1)	Fall Of Dark (2)	Law Of The Fish... (1)	Mood To Move (1)	Squeeze Me (2)
But It's Alright (2)	Hard Time Train (1)	Like Dreamers Do (1)	Oh Beautiful Loser (1)	Suck The Head (1)
Confidential (2)	Hardcore (2)	Love Grows On Ya (2)	Raw Nerve (2)	This Wagon's Gonna Roll (1)
Dedicated To You (2)	Holiday (1)	Love Is A Tangle (1)	Red Dress (2)	Zigzagging Through
Doctor Doctor (1)	I Want To Live (2)	Memories Of Venus (2)	Sparkplug (1)	Ghostland (2)

RADNER, Gilda

Born on 6/28/46 in Detroit; died on 5/20/89 of cancer. Actress/comedienne. Cast member of TV's *Saturday Night Live*, 1975-80. Married actor Gene Wilder in 1984.

12/1/79+	69	12		Live From New York .... [C]	$8	Warner 3320

Emily Litella	Goodbye Saccharine	Honey (Touch Me With My	I Love To Be Unhappy	Let's Talk Dirty To The	Roseanne Roseannadanna
Gimme Mick (medley)		Clothes On)	If You Look Close (medley)	Animals	Way We Were

RAES, The

Canadian husband-and-wife disco duo: Robbie and Cherrill Rae.

3/24/79	161	5		Dancing Up A Storm	$8	A&M 4754

Don't Make Waves	Gonna Burn My Boogie	Honest I Do	I Only Wanna Get Up And	**Little Lovin' (Keeps The**	School
Don't Turn Around	Shoes		Dance	**Doctor Away) 61**	

RAFFERTY, Gerry

Born on 4/16/47 in Paisley, Scotland. Singer/songwriter/guitarist. Co-leader of Stealers Wheel.

5/6/78	1[1]	49	▲	1 City to City	$8	United Art. 840
6/16/79	29	21	●	2 Night Owl	$8	United Art. 958
6/14/80	61	9		3 Snakes And Ladders	$8	United Art. 1039

Already Gone (2)	**Days Gone Down (Still Got**	Get It Right Next Time	Johnny's Song (3)	Stealin' Time (1)	Welcome To Hollywood (3)
Ark, The (1)	**The Light In Your Eyes)**	(2) **21**	Look At The Moon (3)	Syncopatin Sandy (3)	Whatever's Written In Your
Baker Street (1) **2**	(2) **17**	Home And Dry (1) **28**	Mattie's Rag (1)	Take The Money And Run (2)	Heart (1)
Bring It All Home (3)	Didn't I (3)	I Was A Boy Scout (3)	Night Owl (2)	Tourist, The (2)	Why Won't You Talk To Me?
Cafe In Cabotin (3)	Don't Close The Door (3)	Island (1)	**Right Down The Line** (1) **12**	Waiting For The Day (1)	(2)
City To City (1)	Family Tree (2)	It's Gonna Be A Long Night	**Royal Mile (Sweet Darlin')**	Wastin' Away (3)	
	Garden Of England (3)	(2)	(3) **54**	Way That You Do It (2)	

RAGING SLAB

Manhattan four-man, one-woman, hard-rock band: Gregory Strzempka (vocals), Elyse Steinman, Alec Morton, Mark Middleton and Bob Pantella.

10/28/89	113	15		Raging Slab	$8	RCA 9680

Bent For Silver	Don't Dog Me	Get Off My Jollies	Love Comes Loose	Shiny Mama	Waiting For The Potion
Dig A Hole	Geronimo	Joy Ride	San Loco	Sorry's All I Got	

RAIDERS, The — see REVERE, Paul

RAIL

Hard-rock quartet led by vocalist Terry Young.

8/25/84	143	10		Rail .... [M]	$8	EMI America 19010

Fantasy	Hard Girl To Love	1-2-3-4 Rock And Roll	You've Got To Give

★★358★★ RAINBOW

Hard-rock band led by British guitarist Ritchie Blackmore and bassist Roger Glover, both members of Deep Purple. Fluctuating lineup included vocalists Ronnie James Dio and Joe Lynn Turner, keyboardist Tony Carey and drummer Cozy Powell. Group split up upon re-formation of Deep Purple in 1984. Turner joined Deep Purple in 1990.

BLACKMORE'S RAINBOW:

9/6/75	30	15		1 Ritchie Blackmore's R-A-I-N-B-O-W	$10	Oyster 6049
6/5/76	48	17		2 Rainbow Rising	$10	Oyster 1601

RAINBOW:

7/16/77	65	9		3 On Stage .... [L]	$10	Oyster 1801 [2]
5/6/78	89	11		4 Long Live Rock 'n' Roll	$8	Polydor 6143
8/25/79	66	15		5 Down To Earth	$8	Polydor 6221

DEBUT DATE	PEAK POS	WKS CHR	GOLD	ARTIST — Album Title	$	Label & Number
				RAINBOW — Cont'd		
3/7/81	**50**	16		6 Difficult To Cure	$8	Polydor 6316
11/14/81	**147**	4		7 Jealous Lover .... [M]	$8	Polydor 502
5/8/82	**30**	23		8 Straight Between The Eyes...	$8	Mercury 4041
10/1/83	**34**	21		9 Bent Out Of Shape	$8	Mercury 815305
3/15/86	**87**	10		10 Finyl Vinyl .... [L]	$10	Mercury 827987 [2]
				recordings from 1978-84; 12 of 14 tracks are live		

All Night Long (5)		Difficult To Cure (6,10)		L.A. Connection (4)		No Release (6)		Sixteenth Century	Tite Squeeze (8)
Anybody There (9)		Do You Close Your Eyes (2)		Lady Of The Lake (4)		No Time To Lose (5)		Greensleeves (1,3)	Vielleicht Das Nachster Zeit
Bad Girl (10)		Drinking With The Devil (9)		Light In The Black (4)		Over The Rainbow (medley)		Snake Charmer (1)	(Maybe Next Time) (6)
Black Sheep Of The Family (1)		Eyes Of Fire (8)		Long Live Rock 'N' Roll (4,10)		(3)		Snowman (9)	Weiss Heim (7,10)
Blues (medley) (3)		Eyes Of The World (5)		Lost In Hollywood (9)		Power (8,10)		Spotlight Kid (6,10)	
Bring On The Night (Dream Chaser) (4)		Fire Dance (9)		Love's No Friend (5)		Rainbow Eyes (4)		Stargazer (5)	
Can't Happen Here (6,7,10)		Fool For The Night (9)		Magic (6)		Rock Fever (8)		Starstruck (2,3)	
Can't Let You Go (9)		Freedom Fighter (6)		Make Your Move (9)		Run With The Wolf (2)		Still I'm Sad (1,3)	
Catch The Rainbow (1,3)		Gates Of Babylon (4)		Makin' Love (5)		Self Portrait (1)		**Stone Cold** (8,10) **40**	
Danger Zone (5)		I Surrender (6,7,10)		Man On The Silver Mountain (1,3,10)		Sensitive To Light (4)		Stranded (9)	
Death Alley Driver (8)		If You Don't Like Rock 'N' Roll (1)		Midtown Tunnel Vision (6)		Shed (Subtle) (4)		**Street Of Dreams** (9) **60**	
Desperate Heart (9)		Jealous Lover (7,10)		Miss Mistreated (8,10)		**Since You Been Gone** (5,10) **57**		Tarot Woman (2)	
		Kill The King (3,4)		Mistreated (3)				Tearin' Out My Heart (8,10)	
								Temple Of The King (1)	

				RAINMAKERS, The		
				Kansas City, Missouri rock quartet led by vocalist Bob Walkenhorst.		
9/13/86	**85**	22		1 The Rainmakers	$8	Mercury 830214
11/28/87	**116**	19		2 Tornado	$8	Mercury 832795

Big Fat Blonde (1)	Government Cheese (1)	Let My People Go-Go (1)	One More Summer (2)	Rockin' At The T-Dance (1)	Wages Of Sin (2)
Doomsville (1)	I Talk With My Hands (2)	Long Gone Long (1)	One That Got Away (1)	Small Circles (2)	
Downstream (1)	Information (1)	No Romance (2)	Other Side Of The World (2)	Snakedance (2)	
Drinkin' On The Job (1)	Lakeview Man (1)	Nobody Knows (1)	Rainmaker (2)	Tornado Of Love (2)	

				★★226★★ RAITT, Bonnie		
				Born on 11/8/49 in Burbank, California. Veteran blues-rock singer/guitarist. Daughter of Broadway actor/ singer John Raitt. Winner of four Grammys for her 1989 album *Nick Of Time*. Married actor Michael O'Keefe (*Caddyshack* film and TV's *Against The Law*) on 4/28/91.		
10/21/72	**138**	15		1 Give It Up	$12	Warner 2643
10/27/73	**87**	20		2 Takin My Time	$12	Warner 2729
11/2/74	**80**	8		3 Streetlights	$12	Warner 2818
10/11/75	**43**	12		4 Home Plate	$10	Warner 2864
4/23/77	**25**	22	●	5 Sweet Forgiveness...	$8	Warner 2990
10/13/79	**30**	21		6 The Glow	$8	Warner 3369
3/6/82	**38**	18		7 Green Light	$8	Warner 3630
8/30/86	**115**	11		8 Nine Lives	$8	Warner 25486
4/15/89+	**1**³	185	▲³	9 Nick Of Time	$8	Capitol 91268
				1989 Grammy winner: Album of the Year		
7/28/90	**61**	15		10 The Bonnie Raitt Collection .... [K]	$12	Warner 26242
7/13/91	**2**²	83↑	▲⁴	11 Luck Of The Draw	$12	Capitol 96111

About To Make Me Leave Home (7)		Gamblin' Man (5)		I Thank You (6)		**Not The Only One** (11) **34**	Takin' My Time (5)	You Got To Be Ready For Love (If You Wanna Be Mine) (1)
Ain't Nobody Home (3)		Give It Up Or Let Me Go (1,10)		I Thought I Was A Child (2)		Nothing Seems To Matter (1)	Talk To Me (7)	You Got To Know How (1)
All At Once (11)		Glow, The (6,10)		I Will Not Be Denied (9)		One Part Be My Lover (11)	Tangled And Dark (11)	You Told Me Baby (1)
All Day, All Night (8)		Goin') Wild For You Baby (6,10)		I'm Blowin' Away (4)		Papa Come Quick (Jody And Chico) (11)	That Song About The Midway (3)	**You're Gonna Get What's Coming** (6) **73**
Angel (8)		Good Enough (4)		If You Gotta Make A Fool Of Somebody (1)		Pleasin' Each Other (4)	Thing Called Love (9)	You've Been In Love Too Long (1)
Angel From Montgomery (3,10)		Good Man, Good Woman (11)		Keep This Heart In Mind (7)		Rainy Day Man (3)	Three Time Loser (5)	Your Good Thing (Is About To End) (6)
Baby Come Back (7)		Got You On My Mind (3)		Kokomo Blues (medley) (2)		Real Man (9)	Too Long At The Fair (7)	Your Sweet And Shiny Eyes (4)
Boy Can't Help It (6)		Green Lights (7)		Let Me In (2)		River Of Tears (7)	Too Soon To Tell (9)	
Bye Bye Baby (6)		Guilty (2,10)		Let's Keep It Between Us (7)		Road's My Middle Name (9)	True Love Is Hard To Find (8,10)	
Can't Get Enough (7)		Have A Heart (9) **49**		Louise (5,10)		Run Like A Thief (4)	Two Lives (5)	
Come To Me (11)		Home (5)		Love Has No Pride (1,10)		Runaway (5,10) **57**	Under The Falling Sky (1,10)	
Crime Of Passion (8)		I Ain't Gonna Let You Break My Heart Again (9)		Love Letter (9)		Runnin' Back To Me (5)	Wah She Go Do (2)	
Cry Like A Rainstorm (2)		I Can't Help Myself (7)		Love Me Like A Man (1,10)		Sleep's Dark And Silent Gate (6)	Walk Out The Front Door (4)	
Cry On My Shoulder (9)		Me And The Boys (7)		Luck Of The Draw (11)		Slow Ride (11)	What Do You Want The Boy To Do (4)	
Everybody's Cryin' Mercy (3)		**I Can't Make You Love Me** (11) **18**		My First Night Alone Without You (4,10)		**Something To Talk About** (11) **5**	What Is Success (3,10)	
Everything That Touches You (3)		(I Could Have Been Your) Best Old Friend (6)		My Opening Farewell (5)		Stand Up To The Night (8)	Who But A Fool (Thief Into Paradise) (8)	
Excited (8)		I Feel The Same (2,10)		Nick Of Time (9) **92**		Standin' By The Same Old Love (6)	Willya Wontcha (7,10)	
Finest Lovin' Man (7)		I Gave My Love A Candle (2)		No Business (11)		Streetlights (3)	Women Be Wise (10)	
Fool Yourself (4)		I Got Plenty (3)		No Way To Treat A Lady (8,10)		Sugar Mama (4,10)	Write Me A Few Of Your Lines (medley) (2)	
Freezin' (For A Little Human Love) (8)		I Know (1)		Nobody's Girl (9)		Sweet Forgiveness (5)		

				RAMATAM		
				Rock quintet led by guitarist Mike Pinera (Iron Butterfly, Blues Image and Cactus).		
9/2/72	**182**	7		Ramatam	$10	Atlantic 7236

Ask Brother Ask	Changing Days	Strange Place	What I Dream I Am	Wild Like Wine
Can't Sit Still	Heart Song	Wayso	Whiskey Place	

				RAMBEAU, Eddie		
				Born Edward Flurie on 6/30/43 in Hazleton, Pennsylvania. Pop singer/songwriter.		
7/24/65	**148**	2		Concrete And Clay	$20	DynoVoice 9001

Baby, Baby Me	Girl Don't Come	It's Not A Game Anymore	(Look For The) Rainbow	Save The Last Dance For Me
Concrete And Clay 35	I Fell In Love So Easily	It's Not Unusual	My Name Is Mud	Yesterday's Newspapers
Don't Believe Him	I Just Need Your Love	King Of The Road	Same Old Room	

DEBUT DATE	PEAK POS	WKS CHR	GOLD	ARTIST — Album Title	$	Label & Number

RAMIN, Sid, and Orchestra
Born on 1/22/24 in Boston. Conductor/composer/arranger. Won Oscar in 1961 for collaberation on *West Side Story* soundtrack. Music director for TV's *Patty Duke Show, Milton Berle Show* and *Candid Camera.*

5/25/63	34	6		New Thresholds in Sound ....[I]	$15	RCA 2658

April In Paris	Granada	Life Is Just A Bowl Of	Strike Up The Band	Sweetest Sounds
Bewitched	Hernando's Hideaway	Cherries	Swanee	Varsity Drag
Embraceable You	I Believe In You	Spring Is Here		

RAM JAM
East Coast rock quartet led by Bill Bartlett (lead guitarist of The Lemon Pipers). Member Howie Blauvelt played bass in Billy Joel's group, The Hassles.

9/10/77	34	12		Ram Jam	$8	Epic 34885

All For The Love Of Rock N' Roll	Black Betty 18 404	Hey Boogie Woman High Steppin'	Keep Your Hands On The Wheel	Let It All Out Overloaded	Right On The Money Too Bad On Your Birthday

★★454★★ RAMONES
Punk rock quartet formed in August 1974 in New York City. All members have taken Ramone as their last name: lead singer Joey (Jeffrey Hyman), Johnny (John Cummings), Dee Dee (Douglas Colvin), and Tommy (Tom Erdelyi). Tommy became the band's co-producer in 1978, replaced by Marky (Marc Bell). Richie "Beau Ramone" replaced Marky in 1983. Marky returned in 1988. Bassist C.J. "Ramone" was added in 1989. Group appeared in the 1979 film *Rock 'n' Roll High School.*

6/5/76	111	18		1 Ramones	$15	Sire 7520
2/12/77	148	10		2 Leave Home	$15	Sire 7528
11/26/77+	49	25		3 Rocket To Russia	$12	Sire 6042
10/21/78	103	11		4 Road To Ruin	$8	Sire 6063
2/23/80	44	14		5 End Of The Century .... produced by Phil Spector	$8	Sire 6077
8/8/81	58	11		6 Pleasant Dreams	$8	Sire 3571
3/26/83	83	9		7 Subterranean Jungle	$8	Sire 23800
11/3/84	171	6		8 Too Tough To Die	$8	Sire 25187
6/21/86	143	6		9 Animal Boy	$8	Sire 25433
10/10/87	172	3		10 Halfway To Sanity	$8	Sire 25641
6/25/88	168	5		11 Ramones Mania ....[G]	$10	Sire 25709 [2]
6/17/89	122	6		12 Brain Drain	$8	Sire 25905
9/26/92	190	1		13 Mondo Bizarro	$12	Radioactive 10615

All Screwed Up (12)
All The Way (5)
All's Quiet On The Eastern Front (6)
Animal Boy (9,11)
Anxiety (13)
Apeman Hop (9)
Baby, I Love You (5)
Bad Brain (4)
Beat On The Brat (1,11)
Blitzkrieg Bop (1,11)
Bop 'Til You Drop (10,11)
Bye Bye Baby (10)
Cabbies On Crack (13)
California Sun (2)
Can't Get You Outta My Mind (12)
Censorshit (13)
Chain Saw (1)
Chasing The Night (8)
Chinese Rock (5,11)
Come Back, Baby (12)
Come On Now (9)
Commando (2,11)
Cretin Hop (3,11)
Crummy Stuff (9)
Danger Zone (8)
Danny Says (5)
Daytime Dilemma (Dangers Of Love) (8)
Death Of Me (10)

Do You Remember Rock 'N' Roll Radio? (5,11)
Do You Wanna Dance (3) 86
Don't Bust My Chops (12)
Don't Come Close (4)
Don't Go (6)
Durango 95 (8)
Eat That Rat (9)
Endless Vacation (8)
Everytime I Eat Vegetables It Makes Me Think Of You (7)
53rd & 3rd (1)
Freak Of Nature (9)
Garden Of Serenity (10)
Gimme Gimme Shock Treatment (2,11)
Glad To See You Go (2)
Go Lil' Camaro Go (10)
Go Mental (4)
Hair Of The Dog (9)
Havana Affair (1)
Heidi Is A Headcase (13)
Here Today, Gone Tomorrow (3)
High Risk Insurance (5)
Highest Trails Above (9)
Howling At The Moon (Sha-La-La) (8,11)
Human Kind (8)
I Believe In Miracles (12)
I Can't Give You Anything (5)

I Can't Make It On Time (5)
I Don't Care (3)
I Don't Wanna Go Down To The Basement (1)
I Don't Wanna Walk Around With You (1)
I Don't Want You (4)
I Just Want To Have Something To Do (4,11)
I Know Better Now (10)
I Lost My Mind (10)
I Need Your Love (7)
I Remember You (2)
I Wanna Be Sedated (4,11)
I Wanna Be Well (3)
I Wanna Be Your Boyfriend (1,11)
I Wanna Live (10,11)
I Wanted Everything (4)
I Won't Let It Happen (13)
I'm Affected (5)
I'm Against It (4)
I'm Not Afraid Of Life (8)
I'm Not Jesus (10)
Ignorance Is Bliss (12)
In The Park (7)
Indian Giver (11)
It's A Long Way Back (4)
It's Gonna Be Alright (13)
It's Not My Place (In The 9 To 5 World) (6)
Job That Ate My Brain (13)

Judy's A Punk (1)
KKK Took My Baby Away (6,11)
Learn To Listen (12)
Let's Dance (1)
Let's Go (5)
Listen To My Heart (1)
Little Bit O' Soul (7)
Locket Love (3)
Loudmouth (1)
Love Kills (9)
Main Man (13)
Mama's Boy (8,11)
Mental Hell (9)
Merry Christmas (I Don't Want To Fight Tonight) (12)
My Brain Is Hanging Upside Down (Bonzo Goes To Bitburg) (9,11)
My-My Kind Of A Girl (9)
Needles & Pins (4,11)
No Go (8)
Now I Wanna Be A Good Boy (2)
Now I Wanna Sniff Some Glue (1)
Oh Oh I Love Her So (2)
Outsider (7,11)
Palisades Park (12)
Pet Sematary (12)
Pinhead (2,11)
Planet Earth 1988 (8)

Poison Heart (13)
Psycho Therapy (7,11)
Punishment Fits The Crime (12)
Questioningly (4)
Ramona (3)
Real Cool Time (10)
Return Of Jackie And Judy (5)
Rock 'N' Roll High School (5,11)
Rockaway Beach (3,11) 66 7-11 (6)
She Belongs To Me (9)
She's A Sensation (6)
She's The One (4)
Sheena Is A Punk Rocker (2,3,11) 81
Sitting In My Room (6)
Somebody Like Me (7)
Somebody Put Something In My Drink (9,11)
Something To Believe In (9)
Strength To Endure (13)
Surfin' Bird (3)
Suzy Is A Headbanger (2)
Swallow My Pride (2)
Take It As It Comes (13)
Teenage Lobotomy (3,11)
This Ain't Havana (5)
This Business Is Killing Me (6)

Time Bomb (7)
Time Has Come Today (7)
Today Your Love, Tomorrow The World (1)
Tomorrow She Goes Away (13)
Too Tough To Die (8)
Touring (13)
Wart Hog (8,11)
We Want The Airwaves (6,11)
We're A Happy Family (3,11)
Weasel Face (10)
What'd Ya Do? (7)
What's Your Game (2)
Why Is It Always This Way (3)
Worm Man (10)
You Didn't Mean Anything To Me (6)
You Should Have Never Opened That Door (2)
You Sound Like You're Sick (6)
You're Gonna Kill That Girl (2)
Zero Zero UFO (12)

RAMPAL, Jean-Pierre/Claude Bolling
Both Rampal (flute) and Bolling (pianist/composer) are natives of France.

1/31/76	173	4	●	Suite for Flute and Jazz Piano ....[I] Rampal's first non-classical recording	$8	Columbia 33233

Baroque And Blue	Irlandaise	Javanaise	Sentimentale	Veloce	Versatile
Fugace				

★★403★★ RANDOLPH, Boots
Born Homer Louis Randolph, III on 6/3/27 in Paducah, Kentucky. Premier Nashville session saxophonist.

6/15/63+	79	49	●	1 Boots Randolph's Yakety Sax ....[I]	$18	Monument 18002
11/13/65	118	5		2 Boots Randolph plays More Yakety Sax! ....[I]	$18	Monument 18037
1/14/67	36	47	●	3 Boots with Strings ....[I]	$18	Monument 18066
2/3/68	189	5		4 Boots Randolph with the Knightsbridge Strings & Voices ....[I]	$18	Monument 18082
3/23/68	76	12		5 Sunday Sax ....[I] gospel songs	$18	Monument 18092
8/31/68	60	24		6 The Sound Of Boots ....[I]	$18	Monument 18099
5/10/69	82	17		7 ...with love/The Seductive Sax of Boots Randolph ....[I]	$18	Monument 18111

DEBUT DATE	PEAK POS	WKS CHR	GOLD	ARTIST — Album Title	$	Label & Number

RANDOLPH, Boots — Cont'd

DEBUT DATE	PEAK POS	WKS CHR		ARTIST — Album Title	$	Label & Number
1/10/70	113	18	8	Yakety Revisited .... [I]	$18	Monument 18128
10/10/70	157	9	9	Hit Boots 1970 .... [I]	$18	Monument 18144
1/9/71	168	3	10	Boots With Brass .... [I]	$18	Monument 18147
6/12/71	141	11	11	Homer Louis Randolph, III .... [I]	$12	Monument 30678
11/27/71	144	8	12	The World Of Boots Randolph .... [K-I]	$12	Monum. 30963 [2]
12/2/72	192	3	13	Boots Randolph Plays The Great Hits Of Today .... [I]	$12	Monument 31908

All The Time (6)
Am I That Easy To Forget? (8)
Amazing Grace (11)
Amen (5)
Aquarius - Let The Sunshine In (9)
Ave Maria (5)
Baby, I'm-A Want You (13)
Battle Of New Orleans (8)
Because Of You (7)
Big Daddy (8)
Black Orpheus (Manha De Carnaval), Theme From (4,12)
Born To Lose (8)
Both Sides Now (9)
Bridge Over Troubled Water (9,12)
By The Time I Get To Phoenix (6,12)
C.C. Rider (10)
Cacklin' Sax (1)
Cast Your Fate To The Wind (4)
Charade (4)
Charlie Brown (1)
Cotton Fields (1)
Crackety Jacks (6)
Days Of Wine And Roses (3)

Dear Hearts (10)
Desafinado (12)
Do You Know The Way To San Jose? (9)
Don't Touch Me (6)
Down Yonder (9)
Drowning In A Sea Of Love (13)
Elusive Butterfly (6,12)
Ev'ry Day Of My Life (13)
Fire And Rain (10)
Flowers On The Wall (6)
For The Good Times (13)
Funny How Time Slips Away (2)
Games People Play (8)
Gentle On My Mind (6,12)
Godfather, Love Theme From The (13)
Gotta Travel On (2)
Green Green Grass Of Home (6)
He'll Have To Go (2)
Help Me Make It Through The Night (11)
Here Comes My Baby (2)
Hi Heel Sneakers (10)
I Believe (5)
I Can't Stop Loving You (1)
I Fall To Pieces (1)

I Left My Heart In San Francisco (3)
I Really Don't Want To Know (1)
I'll Be There (10)
I'll Just Walk Away (6)
I'm Glad There Is You (7)
I'm Gonna Be A Wheel Someday (2)
I'm In The Mood For Love (7)
I'm Walking The Floor (Over You) (2)
If You've Got The Money (I've Got The Time) (1)
It Keeps Right On A Hurtin' (1)
It's Impossible (11)
It's Not Unusual (4,12)
Jackson (6)
Just A Closer Walk With Thee (5)
King Of The Road (12)
Last Date (10)
Let It Be Me (7)
Letter, The (10)
Light My Fire (10)
Little Band Of Gold (8)
Lonely Street (1)
Look Of Love (7,12)
Lookin' (13)

Lord's Prayer (5)
Love Is Blue (7,12)
Love Letters (4)
Love Story, Theme From (11)
Love's Been Good To Me (9)
Make The World Go Away (6)
May The Good Lord Bless And Keep You (5)
Me And Bobby McGee (11)
Me And Julio Down By The Schoolyard (13)
Meditation (7)
Michelle (3)
Mickey's Tune (6)
Misty (4,12)
Moon River (3)
More (4,12)
My Sweet Lord (11)
Nearness Of You (7,12)
(Now And Then There's) A Fool Such As I (2)
Peace In The Valley (5)
People (4,12)
Proud Mary (9)
Race Is On (9,12)
Raindrops Keep Fallin' On My Head (9,12)
Rainy Night In Georgia (9)
Release Me (8,12)
Rocky Top (13)

Rose Garden (11)
Shadow Of Your Smile (3) *93*
Smoke Gets In Your Eyes (1)
Snowbird (13)
Somewhere My Love (Lara's Theme from Dr. Zhivago) (4)
Spinning Wheel (10)
Stranger On The Shore (3)
Strangers In The Night (7)
Summer Of '42, Theme From (13)
Sunday Mornin' Comin' Down (9)
Sunshine (13)
Sweet Caroline (11)
Take A Letter Maria (10)
Temptation (4) *93*
Tenderly (7,12)
(They Long To Be) Close To You (10)
Those Were The Days (9)
Tragedy (8)
25 Or 6 To 4 (10)
Unchained Melody (3)
Viva Tirado (10)
Walk Right In (1)
Walking On New Grass (8)
Waterloo (2)

We've Only Just Begun (10)
What A Diff'rence A Day Made (7)
What Kind Of Fool Am I? (8)
What Now My Love (3)
When The Saints Go Marching In (5)
Who Can I Turn To (4,12)
Wichita Lineman (8,12)
Will The Circle Be Unbroken (5)
Without Love (There Is Nothing) (8)
Without You (13)
Y'all Come (2)
Yakety Sax (1) *35*
Yesterday (3)
Yesterday, When I Was Young (8)
You Don't Have To Say You Love Me (11)
You Don't Know Me (2,12)
You'll Never Walk Alone (5)
You've Lost That Lovin' Feelin' (3)

RANK & FILE
Country-rock quartet led by brothers Chip and Tony Kinman.

DEBUT DATE	PEAK POS	WKS CHR		ARTIST — Album Title	$	Label & Number
5/7/83	165	5		Sundown	$8	Slash 23833

Amanda Ruth
Conductor Wore Black

Coyote
(Glad I'm) Not In Love

I Don't Go Out Much Anymore
I Went Walking

I Went Walking
Lucky Day

Rank And File
Sundown

RANKIN, Billy
Born on 4/25/59 in Glasgow, Scotland. Lead guitarist with Nazareth, 1981-82.

DEBUT DATE	PEAK POS	WKS CHR		ARTIST — Album Title	$	Label & Number
3/24/84	119	11		Growin' Up Too Fast	$8	A&M 4977

Baby Come Back *52*
Baby's Got A Gun

Burning Down
Call Me Automatic

Day In The Life
I Wanna Be Alone Tonight

Never In A Million Years
Rip It Up

Think I'm In Love
Where Are You Now

RANKIN, Kenny
Singer/songwriter/acoustic guitarist.

DEBUT DATE	PEAK POS	WKS CHR		ARTIST — Album Title	$	Label & Number
9/9/72	184	8	1	Like A Seed	$10	Little David 1003
11/16/74+	63	25	2	Silver Morning	$10	Little David 3000
12/13/75+	81	15	3	Inside	$8	Little David 1009
3/12/77	99	23	4	The Kenny Rankin Album	$8	Little David 1013
6/28/80	171	6	5	After The Roses	$8	Atlantic 19271

After The Roses (5)
Bad Times Make You Strong (1)
Birembau (2)
Blackbird (2)
Catfish (2)
Comin' Down (1)
Creepin' (3)
Cue #1 (5)
Cue #2 (5)

Down The Backstairs Of My Life (3)
Eartheart (1)
Feeling, The (3)
Groovin' (4)
Haven't We Met (2)
Here's That Rainy Day (4)
House Of Gold (4)
I Love You (4)
I Was Born (1)

If I Should Go To Pray (1)
In The Name Of Love (2)
Inside (3)
Killed A Cat (2)
Like A Seed (1)
Lost Up In Loving You (3)
Lyin' Eyes (5)
Make Believe (4)
Marie (3)
On And On (4)

One More Goodbye, One More Hello (5)
Peaceful (1)
Penny Lane (3)
People Get Ready (2)
Pussywillows, Cat-Tails (2)
Regrets (5)
Roll-A-Round (A Warmup Lick) (3)
She's A Lady (3)

Silver Morning (2)
Sometimes (1)
Stringman (1)
Strings (5)
Sunday Kind Of Love (3)
Through The Eye Of The Eagle (4)
To A Wild Rose (5)
Up From The Skies (3)
What Matters Most (5)

When Sunny Gets Blue (4)
While My Guitar Gently Weeps (4)
With A Little Help From My Friends (5)
Woman, Woman (5)
Yesterday's Lies (1)
You (3)
You Are My Woman (1)
You Are So Beautiful (4)

RANKING ROGER
Former lead vocalist of English Beat and General Public. Roger Charley from Birmingham, England. Born on 2/21/61.

DEBUT DATE	PEAK POS	WKS CHR		ARTIST — Album Title	$	Label & Number
8/13/88	151	7		Radical Departure	$8	I.R.S. 42197

Falling Down
I Told You
I'll Be There

In Love With You
Mono Gone To Stereo

One Minute Closer (To Death)
Point Of View

Smashing Down Another Door
So Excited

Time To Mek A Dime
Your Problems

RANKS, Shabba
Born Rawlston Fernando Gordon on 1/17/66 in Sturgetown, Jamaica. Dancehall reggae singer. Formerly known as Jamaican DJ Don.

DEBUT DATE	PEAK POS	WKS CHR		ARTIST — Album Title	$	Label & Number
6/22/91	89	51	●	1 As Raw As Ever	$12	Epic 47310
8/1/92	78	11		2 Rough & Ready - Vol. 1	$12	Epic 52443
10/17/92	64	17↑	●	3 X-tra Naked	$12	Epic 52464

Ambi Get Scarce (1)
Another One Program (3)
Bad & Wicked (2)
Bedroom Bully (3)
Ca'an Dun (2)
Cocky Rim (3)
Fist-A-Ris (1)

5-F Man (3)
Flesh Axe (1)
Gal Yuh' Good (2)
Gone Up (1)
Gun Pon Me (1)
Hard And Stiff (2)

Housecall (Your Body Can't Lie To Me) (1) *37*
Jam, The (1)
Just Reality (3)
Mi Di Girls Dem Love (1)
Mr. Loverman (2) *40*
Muscle Grip (3)

Park Yu Benz (1)
Pirates Anthem (2)
Raggamuffin (2)
Ready-Ready, Goody-Goody (3)
Rude Boy (3)
Slow And Sexy (3) *33*

Ting-A-Ling (3)
Trailor Load A Girls (1)
Two Breddrens (3)
What 'Cha Gonna Do? (3)
Where Does Slackness Come From (1)
Wicked In Bed (2)

Will Power (3)
Woman Tangle (1)
Woodtop (2)

DEBUT DATE	PEAK POS	WKS CHR	GOLD	ARTIST — Album Title	$	Label & Number

RARE BIRD
British rock group — Steve Gould, lead singer. Gould later formed the group Runner.

3/7/70	117	13		1 Rare Bird	$20	Probe 4514
8/18/73	194	2		2 Epic Forest	$15	Polydor 5530

Baby Listen (2)
Beautiful Scarlet (1)
Bird On A Wing (1)
Epic Forest (2)
Fears Of The Night (2)
God Of War (1)
Her Darkest Hour (2)
Hey Man (2)
House In The City (2)
Iceberg (1)
Melanie (1)
Natures Fruit (1)
Sympathy (1)
Times (1)
Title No. 1 Again (Birdman) (2)
Turn It All Around (2)
Turning The Lights Out (2)
You Went Away (1)

★★394★★ **RARE EARTH**
Nucleus of Detroit rock group: Gil Bridges (saxophone, flute), John Persh (trombone, bass) and Pete Rivera (drums). Worked as the Sunliners in the '60s. In 1970, added Ed Guzman (percussion) and Ray Monette (replaced guitarist Rob Richards). Mark Olson replaced Kenneth James (keyboards) in 1971. Many changes thereafter.

12/6/69+	12	77		1 Get Ready	$12	Rare Earth 507
				side 2 is a 21 1/2-minute version of the title song		
7/11/70	15	49		2 Ecology	$10	Rare Earth 514
7/17/71	28	25		3 One World	$10	Rare Earth 520
1/1/72	29	21		4 Rare Earth In Concert ....[L]	$10	Rare Earth 534 [2]
11/25/72+	90	20		5 Willie Remembers	$10	Rare Earth 543
6/16/73	65	23		6 Ma	$10	Rare Earth 546
7/12/75	59	11		7 Back To Earth	$10	Rare Earth 548
10/1/77	187	6		8 Rare Earth	$8	Prodigal 10019
6/3/78	156	6		9 Band Together	$8	Prodigal 10025

Ah Dunno (8)
Any Man Can Be A Fool (3)
Big John Is My Name (6)
Boogie With Me Children (7)
Born To Wander (2,4) 17
City Life (7)
Come With Me (6)
Come With Your Lady (5)
Crazy Love (8)
Delta Melody (9)
Dreamer (9)
Eleanor Rigby (2)
Every Now And Then We Get To Go On Down To Miami (5)
Feeling Alright (1)
Foot Loose And Fancy Free (5)
Get Ready (1,4) 4
Good Time Sally (5) 67
Got To Get Myself Back Home (5)
Happy Song (5)
Hey Big Brother (4) 19
Hum Along And Dance (6)
I Couldn't Believe What Happened Last Night (5)
I Just Want To Celebrate (3,4) 7
(I Know) I'm Losing You (2,4) 7
I Really Love You (8)
If I Die (3)
In Bed (1)
Is Your Teacher Cool? (8)
It Makes You Happy (But It Ain't Gonna Last Too Long) (7)
Keeping Me Out Of The Storm (7)
Let Me Be Your Sunshine (7)
Long Time Leavin' (2)
Love Do Me Right (9)
Love Has Lifted Me (8)
Love Is What You Get (If Love Is What You Give Me) (9)
Love Music (9)
Ma (6)
Magic Key (1)
Maybe The Magic (9)
Mota Molata (9)
Nice Place To Visit (2)
Nice To Be With You (4)
No. 1 Man (2)
Road, The (8)
Rock 'N' Roll Man (9)
Satisfaction Guaranteed (2)
Seed, The (3)
Share My Love (8)
Smiling Faces Sometimes (6)
Someone To Love (3)
Think Of The Children (5)
Thoughts (4)
Tin Can People (8)
Tobacco Road (1)
Train To Nowhere (1)
Under God's Light (3)
Walking Schtick (7)
Warm Ride (9) 39
We're Gonna Have A Good Time (5) 93
What'd I Say (3,4) 61
When I Write (8)
Would You Like To Come Along (5)
You (9)

★★303★★ **RASCALS, The**
Blue-eyed, soul-pop quartet formed in New York City in 1964. Consisted of Felix Cavaliere, Dino Danelli, Eddie Brigati and Gene Cornish. All except Danelli had been in Joey Dee's Starliters. Brigati and Cornish left in 1971, replaced by Robert Popwell, Buzzy Feiten and Ann Sutton. Group disbanded in 1972. Cavaliere, Cornish and Danelli reunited in June 1988. Also see Bulldog and Fotomaker.

THE YOUNG RASCALS:

5/7/66	15	84	●	1 The Young Rascals	$20	Atlantic 8123
1/21/67	14	74	●	2 Collections	$20	Atlantic 8134
8/12/67	5	59	●	3 Groovin'	$20	Atlantic 8148

THE RASCALS:

3/2/68	9	30		4 Once Upon A Dream	$15	Atlantic 8169
7/13/68	1[1]	58	●	5 Time Peace/The Rascals' Greatest Hits .....[G]	$15	Atlantic 8190
3/29/69	17	16	●	6 Freedom Suite	$20	Atlantic 901 [2]
				record 2, entitled Music Music, is all instrumental		
1/10/70	45	16		7 See	$15	Atlantic 8246
3/20/71	198	1		8 Search And Nearness	$12	Atlantic 8276
6/5/71	122	12		9 Peaceful World	$10	Columbia 30462 [2]
5/13/72	180	3		10 The Island Of Real	$10	Columbia 31103

Adrian's Birthday (6)
Almost Home (8)
America The Beautiful (6)
Any Dance'll Do (6)
Away Away (7)
Baby I'm Blue (6)
Baby Let's Wait (1)
Be On The Real Side (10)
Beautiful Morning (5) 3
Bells (2)
Bit Of Heaven (9)
Boom (6)
Brother Tree (10)
Buttercup (10)
Carry Me Back (7) 26
Come On Up (2,5) 43
Cute (9)
Death's Reply (7)
Do You Feel It (1)
Easy Rollin' (4,5)
Echoes (10)
Find Somebody (3)
Fortunes (8)
Getting Nearer (9)
Girl Like You (3,5) 10
Glory Glory (8) 58
Good Lovin' (1,5) 1
Groovin' (3,5) 1
Happy Song (9)
Heaven (9)
Hold On (7) 51
How Can I Be Sure (3,5) 4
Hummin' Song (10)
I Ain't Gonna Eat Out My Heart Anymore (1,5) 52
I Believe (1,8)
I Don't Love You Anymore (3)
I'd Like To Take You Home (7)
I'm Blue (7)
I'm Gonna Love You (4)
I'm So Happy Now (3)
I've Been Lonely Too Long (2,5) 16
Icy Water (3)
If You Knew (3)
In And Out Of Love (9)
In The Midnight Hour (1,5)
Island Of Love (6)
Island Of Real (10)
It's Love (3)
It's Wonderful (4,5) 20
Jungle Walk (10)
Just A Little (1)
Lament (8)
Land Of 1000 Dances (2)
Letter, The (8)
Like A Rolling Stone (1)
Little Dove (9)
Look Around (6)
Love Is A Beautiful Thing (2,5)
Love Letter (9)
Love Lights (medley) (2)
Love Me (9) 95
Love Was So Easy To Give (4)
Lucky Day (10)
Me & My Friends (6)
Mickey's Monkey (medley) (2)
More (2)
Mother Nature Land (9)
Mustang Sally (1,5)
My Hawaii (4)
My World (4)
Nama (8)
Nineteen Fifty-Six (3)
No Love To Give (2)
Nubia (7)
Of Course (6)
Once Upon A Dream (4)
Peaceful World (9)
People Got To Be Free (6) 1
Place In The Sun (8)
Please Love Me (4)
Rainy Day (4)
Ray Of Hope (6) 24
Ready For Love (8)
Real Thing (7)
Remember Me (7)
Right On (8)
Saga Of New York (10)
Sattva (4)
See (7) 27
Silly Girl (4)
Since I Fell For You (2)
Singin' The Blues Too Long (4)
Sky Trane (9)
Slow Down (1)
Sound Effect (4)
Stop And Think (7)
Sueno (3)
Temptation's 'Bout To Get Me (7)
Thank You Baby (8)
Time Will Tell (10)
Too Many Fish In The Sea (2)
Visit To Mother Nature Land (9)
What Is The Reason (7)
You Better Run (3,5) 20
You Don't Know (8)

RASPBERRIES
Pop-rock band formed in Mentor, Ohio in 1971: Eric Carmen (lead singer, guitar), Wally Bryson (lead guitar), David Smalley (bass) and Jim Bonfanti (drums). Smalley and Bonfanti replaced by Scott McCarl and Michael McBride in 1974. Carmen went solo in 1975.

5/20/72	51	30		1 Raspberries	$20	Capitol 11036
12/9/72+	36	16		2 Fresh	$20	Capitol 11123
10/6/73	128	7		3 Side 3	$15	Capitol 11220

DEBUT DATE	PEAK POS	WKS CHR	GOLD	ARTIST — Album Title	$	Label & Number

RASPBERRIES — Cont'd

10/19/74	143	6	4	Starting Over	$15	Capitol 11329
6/12/76	138	4	5	Raspberries' Best Featuring Eric Carmen ....[G]	$10	Capitol 11524

All Through The Night (4)
Come Around And See Me (1)
Cruisin Music (4)
Cry (4)
Don't Want To Say Goodbye (1,5) *86*
Drivin' Around (2,5)
Ecstacy (3,5)

Every Way I Can (2)
Get It Moving (1)
Go All The Way (1,5) *5*
Goin' Nowhere Tonight (2)
Hands On You (4)
Hard To Get Over A Heartbreak (3)

I Can Hardly Believe You're Mine (4)
I Can Remember (1,5)
I Don't Know What I Want (4)
I Reach For The Light (2)
I Saw The Light (1)
I Wanna Be With You (2,5) *16*

I'm A Rocker (3) *94*
If You Change Your Mind (2)
It Seemed So Easy (2)
Last Dance (3)
Let's Pretend (2,5) *35*
Making It Easy (4)
Might As Well (2)
Money Down (3)

Nobody Knows (2)
On The Beach (3)
Overnight Sensation (Hit Record) (4,5) *18*
Party's Over (4)
Play On (4)
Rock & Roll Mama (1)
Rose Coloured Glasses (4)

Should I Wait (3)
Starting Over (4,5)
Tonight (3,5) *69*
Waiting (1)
With You In My Life (1)

RATCHELL
Rock quartet featuring Chris and Pat Couchois.

4/15/72	176	3		Ratchell	$12	Decca 75330

And If I Will
Here On My Face

Home
How Many Times

Julie My Woman
Lazy Lady

My My
Out Of Hand

Peace Of Mind
Problems

Saycus
Warm And Tender Love

★★445★★ **RATT**
Los Angeles hard-rock quintet: Stephen Pearcy (lead singer), Warren DeMartini (guitar), Robbin Crosby (guitar), Juan Croucier (bass) and Bobby Blotzer (drums; also a member of Contraband in 1991. Pearcy left band in early 1992.

3/24/84	7	56	▲³ 1	**Out Of The Cellar**	$8	Atlantic 80143
6/30/84	133	19	2	Ratt ....[M-R]	$8	Time Coast 2203
				first released in 1983		
6/29/85	7	42	▲ 3	**Invasion Of Your Privacy**	$8	Atlantic 81257
10/25/86	26	40	▲ 4	Dancin' Undercover	$8	Atlantic 81683
11/19/88	17	27	▲ 5	Reach For The Sky	$8	Atlantic 81929
9/8/90	23	17	● 6	Detonator	$12	Atlantic 82127
9/21/91	57	18	7	Ratt & Roll 8191 ....[G]	$12	Atlantic 82260
				19 remastered tracks from 1981-91		

All Or Nothing (6)
Back For More (1,2,7)
Between The Eyes (3)
Body Talk (4,7)
Bottom Line (5)
Can't Wait On Love (6)
Chain Reaction (5)
City To City (5)
Closer To My Heart (3)
Dance (4,7) *59*

Dangerous But Worth The Risk (3)
Don't Bite The Hand That Feeds (5)
Drive Me Crazy (4)
Enough Is Enough (4)
Give It All (3)
Givin' Yourself Away (6,7)
Got Me On The Line (3)
Hard Time (6)

Heads I Win, Tails You Lose (6,7)
I Want A Woman (5,7)
I Want To Love You Tonight (5)
I'm Insane (1)
In Your Direction (1)
It Doesn't Matter (4)
Lack Of Communication (1,7)
Lay It Down (3,7) *40*
Looking For Love (4)

Lovin' You's A Dirty Job (6,7)
Morning After (1)
Never Use Love (3)
No Surprise (5)
Nobody Rides For Free (7)
One Good Lover (4)
One Step Away (6,7)
Round And Round (1,7) *12*
Scene Of The Crime (1)
Scratch That Itch (6)
7th Avenue (5)

Shame Shame Shame (6,7)
She Wants Money (1)
Slip Of The Lip (4,7)
Sweet Cheater (2)
Take A Chance (4)
Tell The World (2,7)
Top Secret (6)
U Got It (2)
Walkin' The Dog (5)
Wanted Man (1,7) *87*
Way Cool Jr. (5,7) *75*

What I'm After (5)
What You Give Is What You Get (3)
What's It Gonna Be (5)
You Should Know By Now (3)
You Think You're Tough (2,7)
You're In Love (3,7) *89*
You're In Trouble (1)

RAVAN, Genya
Born Goldie Zelkowitz in Lodz, Poland in 1940; raised in New York City. Lead singer of Ten Wheel Drive.

9/2/78	147	6	1	Urban Desire	$8	20th Century 562
9/29/79	106	6	2	...And I Mean It!	$8	20th Century 595

Aye Co'orado (1)
Back In My Arms Again (1) *92*
Cornered (1)

Darling, I Need You (1)
Do It Just For Me (1)
I Won't Sleep On The Wet Spot No More (1)

I'm Wired, Wired, Wired (2)
It's Me (2)
Jerry's Pigeons (1)
Junkman (2)

Knight Ain't Long Enough (1)
Love Isn't Love (2)
Messin Around (1)
Night Owl (2)

Pedal To The Metal (2)
Roto Root Her (2)
Shadowboxing (1)
Shot In The Heart (1)

Steve... (2)
Stubborn Kinda Girl (2)
Sweetest One (1)

RAVEN
Heavy-metal trio from Newcastle, England: John (vocals) and Mark Gallagher (guitar) and Wacko! (drums).

3/23/85	81	15	1	Stay Hard	$8	Atlantic 81241
3/8/86	121	10	2	The Pack Is Back	$8	Atlantic 81629

All I Want (2)
Bottom Line (1)
Don't Let It Die (2)
Extract The Action (1)

Get Into Your Car (2)
Get It Right (1)
Gimme Some Lovin' (2)
Hard Ride (1)

Hyperactive (2)
Nightmare Ride (2)
On And On (1)
Pack Is Back (2)

Power And The Glory (1)
Pray For The Sun (1)
Restless Child (2)
Rock Dogs (2)

Screamin' Down The House (2)
Stay Hard (1)

When The Going Gets Tough (1)
Young Blood (2)

★★110★★ **RAWLS, Lou**
Born on 12/1/35 in Chicago. With the Pilgrim Travelers gospel group, 1957-59. Summer replacement TV show *Lou Rawls & The Golddiggers* in 1969. In films *Angel Angel, Down We Go* and *Believe In Me*. Voice of many Budweiser beer ads and featured singer in the *Garfield* TV specials.

4/6/63	130	3	1	Black And Blue	$20	Capitol 1824
5/7/66	4	74	● 2	Lou Rawls Live! ....[L]	$15	Capitol 2459
9/10/66	7	51	● 3	Lou Rawls Soulin'	$15	Capitol 2566
1/21/67	20	31	4	Lou Rawls Carryin' On!	$15	Capitol 2632
5/6/67	18	22	5	Too Much!	$15	Capitol 2713
8/26/67	29	20	6	That's Lou	$15	Capitol 2756
3/9/68	103	22	7	Feelin' Good	$15	Capitol 2864
7/20/68	165	6	8	You're Good For Me	$15	Capitol 2927
8/31/68	103	16	9	The Best Of Lou Rawls ....[G]	$15	Capitol 2948
6/14/69	71	23	10	The way it was - The way it is	$12	Capitol 215
8/23/69	191	3	11	Close-Up ....[R]	$12	Capitol 261 [2]
				reissue of *Black And Blue* and *Tobacco Road* albums		
12/20/69	200	2	12	Your Good Thing	$12	Capitol 325
4/18/70	172	3	13	You've Made Me So Very Happy	$12	Capitol 427
9/4/71+	68	24	14	Natural Man	$10	MGM 4771
2/26/72	186	4	15	Silk & Soul	$10	MGM 4809 [2]
6/5/76	7	35	▲ 16	**All Things In Time**	$8	Phil. Int. 33957
4/16/77	41	29	● 17	Unmistakably Lou	$8	Phil. Int. 34488
12/10/77+	41	34	● 18	When You Hear Lou, You've Heard It All	$8	Phil. Int. 35036

DEBUT DATE	PEAK POS	WKS CHR	GOLD	ARTIST — Album Title	$	Label & Number

RAWLS, Lou — Cont'd

11/11/78	108	8	19	Lou Rawls Live ....[L]	$10	Phil. Int. 35517 [2]
6/2/79	49	15	20	Let Me Be Good To You	$8	Phil. Int. 36006
1/12/80	81	18	21	Sit Down And Talk To Me	$8	Phil. Int. 36304
1/10/81	110	6	22	Shades Of Blue	$8	Phil. Int. 36774
5/14/83	163	4	23	When The Night Comes	$8	Epic 38553

Ain't That Loving You (21)
All God's Children (13)
All The Way (17)
Autumn Leaves (3)
Baby I Could Be So Good At Lovin' You (8)
Baby What You Want Me To Do (22)
Bark, Bite (Fight All Night) (20)
Be Anything (But Be Mine) (22)
Beautiful Friendship (8)
Believe In Me (15)
Blues For A Four String Guitar (11)
Breaking My Back (Instead Of Using My Mind) (15)
Bye Bye Blackbird (medley) (19)
Chained And Bound (12)
Cottage For Sale (22)
Cotton Fields (11)
Couple More Years (23)
Dead End Street (5,9,19) 29
Devil In Your Eyes (4)
Did You Ever Love A Woman (22)
Dixieland Joe (medley) (19)
Dollar Green (18)
Don't Explain (3)
Down Here On The Ground (8) 69
Early Morning Love (17,19)
Encore (7)
Even When You Cry (7)
Everyday I Have The Blues (1,11)
Everywhere I Go (14)
Evil Woman (7)
Fa Fa Fa Fa Fa (Sad Song) (10)
Feelin' Alright (13)
Feelin' Good (7)
Find Out What's Happening (4)
For What It's Worth (7)
From Now On (16)
Gentle On My Mind (10)
Georgia On My Mind (11)
Girl From Ipanema (2)

Give Me Your Love (12)
Goin' To Chicago Blues (1,2,11)
Golden Slumbers (15)
Got A Lotta Love (14)
Got To Get You Into My Life (14)
Gotta Find A Way (7)
Groovy People (16,19) 64
Hallelujah For A Friend (15)
Hang-Ups (7)
Hard To Get Thing Called Love (6)
Heartaches (Just When You Think You're Loved) (21)
Hello Dolly (medley) (19)
Here's That Rainy Day (15)
His Song Shall Be Sung (15)
Hoochie Coochie Man (22)
How Can That Be (13)
(How Do You Say) I Don't Love You Anymore (6)
How Long, How Long Blues (1,11)
How Thoughtless I've Become (14)
Hurtin' (13)
I Been Him (23)
I Can't Make It Alone (12) 63
I Go Crazy (22)
I Got It Bad And That Ain't Good (2)
I Just Want To Make Love To You (5)
I Love You Yes I Do (10)
I Wanna Little Girl (5)
I Want To Be Loved (But Only By You) (12)
I Want To Hear It From You (8)
I Wish It Were Yesterday (18)
I Wonder (10)
I Wonder Where Our Love Has Gone (12)
I'd Rather Drink Muddy Water (1,2,11)
I'll Take Time (5)
I'm A King Bee (14)
I'm Gonna Use What I Got (To Get What I Need) (17)

I'm Satisfied (8)
I'm Waiting (15)
If I Coulda, Woulda, Shoulda (18)
If You're Gonna Love Me (23)
In The Evening When The Sun Goes Down (2,19)
It Was A Very Good Year (3,9)
It's An Uphill Climb To The Bottom (5)
It's Our Anniversary Today (17)
It's You (10)
Just Squeeze Me (But Don't Tease Me) (12)
Kansas City (1,11)
Lady Love (18,19) 24
Let Me Be Good To You (20)
Let's Burn Down The Cornfield (13)
Let's Fall In Love All Over Again (16)
Letter, The (17)
Life That I Lead (4)
Life Time (8)
Love Is A Hurtin' Thing (3,9,19) 13
Love That I Give (6)
Lovely Way To Spend An Evening (19)
Lover's Holiday (20)
Mack The Knife (medley) (19)
Make The World Go Away (12)
Mama Told Me Not To Come (13)
Mean Black Snake (4)
Memory Lane (3)
Midnight Sunshine (23)
Mona Lisa (medley) (19)
My Ancestors (7,9)
My Son (7)
Natural Man (14,19) 17
Need You Forever (16)
No More (15)
Not The Staying Kind (18)
Oh, What A Beautiful Mornin' (14)
Ol' Man River (8,11)
Old Folks (3)

Old Times (21)
On A Clear Day (You Can See Forever) (3)
On Broadway (4)
One Day Soon You'll Need Me (21)
One For My Baby (And One More For The Road) (8)
One I Sing My Love Songs To (23)
One Life To Live (18)
Please Give Me Someone To Love (6)
Problems (6)
Pure Imagination (16,19)
Red Top (12)
Rockin' Chair (11)
Roll 'Em Pete (1)
Sandpiper, Love Theme From ...see: Shadow Of Your Smile
Season Of The Witch (10)
Secret Tears (17)
See You When I Git There (17,19) 66
Send In The Clowns (19)
Sentimental Journey (11)
Shadow Of Your Smile (17)
Show Business (6) 45
Sir Duke (medley) (19)
Sit Down And Talk To Me (21)
Six Cold Feet Of Ground (1,11)
So Hard To Laugh, So Easy To Cry (3)
Some Day You'll Be Old (17)
Some Folks Never Learn (17)
Something (15)
Something Stirring In My Soul (4)
Sophisticated Lady (15,19)
Soul Serenade (8)
Spring Again (17)
St. James Infirmary (1,2)
St. Louis Blues (11)
Stay Awhile With Me (19)
Stormy Down (2,19)
Stormy Weather (11)
Strange Fruit (1,11)
Street Of Dreams (6)

Summertime (11)
Sweet Tender Nights (20)
Take The "A" Train (medley) (19)
That Would Do It For Me (18)
That's When The Magic Begins (23)
Then You Can Tell Me Goodbye (5)
There Will Be Love (18)
They Don't Give Medals (To Yesterday's Heroes) (6)
Think (22)
This One's For You (19)
This Song Will Last Forever (16,19)
Three O'Clock In The Morning (9) 83
Till Love Touches Your Life (14)
Time (16)
Time Will Take Care Of Everything (20)
Tobacco Road (2,9,11,19)
Tomorrow (20)
Trade Winds (18)
Trouble Down Here Below (4,9) 92
Trouble In Mind (1,11)
Trying Just As Hard As I Can (10)
Twelfth Of Never (5)
Unforgettable (18,19)
Upside Down (23)
Walking Proud (4)
Watch What Happens (15)
We Keep Getting Closer (To Being Further Apart) (20)
We Understand Each Other (17,19)
Wee Baby Blues (12)
What Are You Doing About Today (6)
(What Did I Do To Be So) Black And Blue (1,11)
What Now My Love (3)
What's The Matter With The World (20)
When A Man Loves A Woman (10)
When I Fall In Love (14)

When Love Goes Wrong (6)
When She Speaks (12)
When Someone Comes Along (13)
When The Night Comes (23)
When You Get Home (21)
When You Say Budweiser, You've Said It All (19)
Whole Lotta Sunlight (13)
Whole Lotta Woman (3)
Why (Do I Love You So) (5)
Will Someone Carry The Ball (13)
Wind Beneath My Wings (23) 65
Woman Who's A Woman (4)
World Of Trouble (1,2,9,11)
Yes It Hurts (Doesn't It?) (5)
Yesterday (4)
Yesterday's Dreams (13)
You Are (21)
You Can Bring Me All Your Heartaches (4) 55
You Can't Hold On (14)
You Can't Take It With You (23)
You'll Never Find Another Love Like Mine (16,19) 2
You're Always On My Mind (5)
You're Gonna Hear From Me (4)
You're Good For Me (3)
You're My Blessing (21) 77
You're Takin' My Bag (5)
You're The One (3,16)
You've Lost That Lovin' Feelin' (22)
You've Made Me So Very Happy (13) 95
Your Good Thing (Is About To End) (10,12) 18

RAY, Don
German disco producer/arranger/composer.

9/23/78	113	11		The Garden Of Love	$8	Polydor 6150

Body And Soul
Garden Of Love
Got To Have Loving 44
Midnight Madness
My Desire
Standing In The Rain

RAY, Johnnie
Born on 1/10/27 in Dallas, Oregon. Wore hearing aid since age 14. First recorded for Okeh in 1951. Famous for emotion-packed delivery, with R&B influences. Appeared in three films. Died on 2/25/90 of liver failure.

3/2/57	19	2		The Big Beat	$35	Columbia 961

Everyday (Everyday I Have The Blues)
How Long, How Long Blues
I Miss You So
I Want To Be Loved (But Only By You)
I'll Never Be Free
I'm Gonna Move To The Outskirts Of Town
Lotus Blossom
Pretty-Eyed Baby
Sent For You Yesterday
Shake A Hand
So Long
Trouble In Mind

RAYDIO — see PARKER, Ray Jr.

RAYE, Collin
Native of Texarkana, Arkansas. Country singer.

11/30/91+	54	43	●	1 All I Can Be	$12	Epic 47468
9/12/92	42	22↑		2 In This Life	$12	Epic 48983

All I Can Be (Is A Sweet Memory) (1)
Any Old Stretch Of Blacktop (1)
Big River (2)
Blue Magic (1)
Every Second (1)
Faithful Old Flame (1)
I Want You Bad (And That Ain't Good) (2)
If I Were You (2)
In This Life (2)
It Could've Been So Good (1)
Latter Day Cowboy (2)
Let It Be Me (1)
Love, Me (1)
Many A Mile (2)
Sadly Ever After (1)
'Scuse Moi, My Heart (1)
Somebody Else's Moon (2)
That Was A River (2)
What They Don't Know (2)
You Can't Take It With You (2)

RAYE, Susan
Born on 10/8/44 in Eugene, Oregon. Country singer; regular on TV's Hee-Haw.

5/16/70	154	6		1 We're Gonna Get Together	$12	Capitol 448
				BUCK OWENS & SUSAN RAYE		
9/26/70	190	2		2 One Night Stand	$12	Capitol 543

Cryin' Time (1)
Everybody Needs Somebody (1)
Fallin' For You (1)
Foolin' Around (1,2)
Heartaches Have Just Started (2)
I Ain't A Gonna Be Treated This Way (2)
I've Carried This Torch Much Too Long (2)
Living Tornado (2)

DEBUT DATE	PEAK POS	WKS CHR	GOLD	ARTIST — Album Title	$	Label & Number

RAYE, Susan — Cont'd

Love Is Strange (1)
Maybe If I Close My Eyes (It'll Go Away) (2)
One Night Stand (2)
Put A Little Love In Your Heart (2)
Rocks In My Head (2)
She Don't Deserve You Anymore (2)
Somewhere Between (1)
Together Again (1)
Togetherness (1)
We Were Made For Each Other (1)
We're Gonna Get Together (1)

RAY, GOODMAN & BROWN — see MOMENTS, The

REA, Chris
Born on 3/4/51 in Middlesborough, England. Pop singer/songwriter.

8/12/78	49	12	●	1 Whatever Happened To Benny Santini?	$8	United Art. 879
3/4/89	92	13		2 New Light Through Old Windows	$8	Geffen 24232
3/17/90	107	19		3 The Road To Hell	$12	Geffen 24276
5/18/91	176	1		4 Auberge	$12	Atco 91662

Ace Of Hearts (2)
And You My Love (4)
Auberge (4)
Bows And Bangles (1)
Because Of You (1)
Candles (2)
Closer You Get (1)
Dancing With Charlie (1)
Daytona (3)
Every Second Counts (4)
Fires Of Spring (1)
Fool (If You Think It's Over) (1) 12
Gone Fishing (4)
Heaven (4)
I Can Hear Your Heartbeat (2)
I Just Wanna Be With You (3)
Josephine (2)
Just One Of Those Days (1)
Let's Dance (2,3) 81
Looking For A Rainbow (3)
Looking For The Summer (4)
Mention Of Your Name (4)
On The Beach (2)
Red Shoes (4)
Road To Hell (Part I & II) (3)
Set Me Free (4)
Sing A Song Of Love To Me (4)
Stainsby Girls (2)
Standing In Your Doorway (1)
Steel River (2)
Tell Me There's A Heaven (3)
Texas (3)
That's What They Always Say (3)
Three Angels (1)
Whatever Happened To Benny Santini? (1) 71
Windy Town (2)
Working On It (2) 73
You Must Be Evil (3)
You're Not A Number (4)
Your Warm And Tender Love (3)

READY FOR THE WORLD
Black sextet from Flint, Michigan, formed in 1982: Melvin Riley, Jr. (lead singer), Gordon Strozier, Gregory Potts, Willie Triplett, John Eaton and Gerald Valentine.

6/22/85	17	48	▲	1 Ready For The World	$8	MCA 5594
12/6/86+	32	26	●	2 Long Time Coming	$8	MCA 5829
10/15/88	65	10		3 Ruff 'N' Ready	$8	MCA 42198

Baby (Let Me Love You) (2)
Ceramic Girl (1)
Cowboy (3)
Darlin', Darlin' (3)
Deep Inside Your Love (1)
Digital Display (1) 21
Do You Get Enough (2)
Don't You Wanna (With Me) (3)
Gently (3)
Here I Am (2)
Human Toy (1)
I'm The One Who Loves You (1)
In My Room (4)
It's All A Game (2)
It's Yours (3)
Late Saturday Night (3)
Long Time Coming (2)
Love You Down (2) 9
Mary Goes 'Round (2)
Money (3)
My Girly (3)
Oh Sheila (1) 1
Out Of Town Lover (1)
Shame (3)
Slide Over (1)
So In Love (2)
Some People Don't Care (2)
Tonight (1)

REAL LIFE
Australian quartet — David Sterry, lead singer.

1/7/84	58	24		1 Heart Land	$8	Curb 5459
7/1/89	191	3		2 Send Me An Angel '89	[K] $8	Curb 10614

Always (1,2)
Babies (2)
Breaking Point (1)
Broken Again (1)
Burning Blue (1)
Catch Me I'm Falling (1,2) 40
Exploding Bullets (1)
Face To Face (2)
Hammer Of Love (2)
Heartland (1)
Let's Fall In Love (2)
No Shame (2)
One Blind Love (2)
Openhearted (1)
Send Me An Angel (1) 29
Send Me An Angel '89 (2) 26
Under The Hammer (1)

REBELS, The — see ROCKIN' REBELS

RECORDS, The
British rock quartet: John Wicks, Huw Gower, Phil Brown and Will Birch. Jude Cole replaced Gower in 1979, left in 1981.

8/25/79	41	14		The Records	$8	Virgin 13130

includes special edition 4-track EP record

Affection Rejected
All Messed Up And Ready To Go
Another Star Girl
Girls That Don't Exist
Insomnia
Phone, The
Starry Eyes 56
Teenarama
Up All Night

REDBONE
American Indian "swamp-rock" group formed in Los Angeles in 1968. Consisted of brothers Lolly (lead vocals, guitar) and Pat Vegas (lead vocals, bass), Anthony Bellamy (guitar) and Peter De Poe (drums). The Vegas brothers had been session musicians and worked the *Shindig* TV show.

11/7/70+	99	17		1 Potlatch	$12	Epic 30109
2/5/72	75	9		2 Message From A Drum	$12	Epic 30815
3/16/74	66	16		3 Wovoka	$12	Epic 32462
10/26/74	174	3		4 Beaded Dreams Through Turquoise Eyes	$12	Epic 33053

Alcatraz (1)
Bad News Ain't No News At All (1)
(Beaded Dreams Through) Turquoise Eyes (4)
Beautiful Illusion (4)
Blood Sweat And Tears (4)
Clouds In My Sunshine (3)
Come And Get Your Love (3) 5
Cookin' With D'Redbone (4)
Day To Day Life (medley) (3)
Drinkin' And Blo (1)
Emotions (4)
Fate (2)
I'll Never Stop Loving You (4)
Interstate Highway 101 (4)
Jerico (2)
Judgment Day (1)
Light As A Feather (1)
Liquid Truth (4)
Maggie (1) 45
Maxsplivitz (2)
Message From A Drum (2)
Moon When Four Eclipse (4)
New Blue Sermonette (1)
Niji Trance (2)
One Monkey (2)
One More Time (4)
Only You And Rock And Roll (4)
Perico (2)
Someday (A Good Song) (3)
Sun Never Shines On The Lonely (2)
Suzi Girl (4)
Sweet Lady Of Love (3)
13th Hour (1)
23rd And Mad (3)
When You Got Trouble (2)
Who Can Say? (1)
Witch Queen Of New Orleans (2) 21
Without Reservation (1)
Wovoka (3)

REDBONE, Leon
Mysterious performer of 1920s and 1930s blues and ragtime. Rose to fame in the mid-1970s with appearances on TV's *Saturday Night Live*. Baritone voice of several TV commercials.

7/31/76	87	15		1 On The Track	$10	Warner 2888
1/22/77	38	13		2 Double Time	$10	Warner 2971
9/16/78	163	4		3 Champagne Charlie	$10	Warner 3165
4/11/81	152	11		4 From Branch To Branch	$8	Emerald City 136

Ain't Misbehavin' (I'm Savin' My Love For You) (1)
Alabama Jubilee (3)
Big Bad Bill (Is Sweet William Now) (3)
Big Time Woman (4)
Champagne Charlie (3)
Crazy Blues (2)
Desert Blues (Big Chief Buffalo Nickel) (1)
Diddy Wa Diddie (2)
Extra Blues (4)
Haunted House (1)
Hot Time In The Old Town Tonight (4)
I Hate A Man Like You (3)
If Someone Would Only Love Me (3)
If We Never Meet Again This Side Of Heaven (2)
Lazybones (4)
Lulu's Back In Town (1)
(Mama's Got A Baby Named) Te Na Na (4)
Marie (1)
Mississippi Delta Blues (2)
Mississippi River Blues (2)
Mr. Jelly Roll Baker (2)
My Blue Heaven (4)
My Melancholy Baby (2)
My Walking Stick (1)
Nobody's Sweetheart (2)
One Rose (That's Left In My Heart) (3)
Please Don't Talk About Me When I'm Gone (3)
Polly Wolly Doodle (1)
Prairie Lullaby (4)
Seduced (4) 72
Sheik Of Araby (2)
Shine On Harvest Moon (2)
Some Of These Days (1)
Step It Up And Go (4)
Sweet Mama Hurry Home Or I'll Be Gone (1)
Sweet Mama Papa's Getting Mad (4)
Sweet Sue (Just You) (3)
T.B. Blues (3)
When You Wish Upon A Star (4)
Why (4)
Winin' Boy Blues (2)
Yearning (Just For You) (3)
Your Cheatin' Heart (4)

DEBUT DATE	PEAK POS	WKS CHR	GOLD	ARTIST — Album Title	$	Label & Number

★★187★★ REDDING, Otis

Born on 9/9/41 in Dawson, Georgia. Killed in a plane crash in Lake Monona in Madison, Wisconsin on on 12/10/67. Soul singer/songwriter/producer/pianist. First recorded with Johnny Jenkins & The Pinetoppers on Confederate in 1960. Own label, Jotis. Plane crash also killed four members of the Bar-Kays. Otis was inducted into the Rock and Roll Hall of Fame in 1989.

DEBUT DATE	PEAK POS	WKS CHR		ARTIST — Album Title	$	Label & Number
5/2/64	103	8		1 Pain In My Heart	$50	Atco 161
4/10/65	147	3		2 The Great Otis Redding Sings Soul Ballads	$40	Volt 411
10/16/65+	75	34		3 Otis Blue/Otis Redding Sings Soul	$30	Volt 412
4/30/66	54	29		4 The Soul Album	$30	Volt 413
11/26/66+	73	15		5 Complete & Unbelievable....The Otis Redding Dictionary Of Soul	$30	Volt 415
4/22/67	36	31		6 King & Queen .... OTIS REDDING & CARLA THOMAS	$25	Stax 716
8/19/67	32	42		7 Otis Redding Live In Europe .... [L]	$20	Volt 416
12/2/67+	9	50		8 History Of Otis Redding .... [G]	$20	Volt 418
3/23/68	4	42		9 The Dock Of The Bay	$20	Volt 419
7/20/68	58	21		10 The Immortal Otis Redding	$15	Atco 252
11/30/68+	82	17		11 Otis Redding In Person At The Whisky A Go Go ....[L] recorded April 1966	$15	Atco 265
7/19/69	46	14		12 Love Man .... [K]	$15	Atco 289
8/29/70	200	2		13 Tell The Truth .... [K] albums #9,10,12 & 13 consist of Otis' last recordings from 1967	$12	Atco 333
9/19/70	16	20	●	14 Monterey International Pop Festival .... [S-L] OTIS REDDING/THE JIMI HENDRIX EXPERIENCE recorded June 1967 and featured in the film Monterey Pop; side 1: songs performed by The Jimi Hendrix Experience; side 2: songs performed by Otis Redding	$10	Reprise 2029
9/16/72	76	15		15 The Best Of Otis Redding .... [G]	$15	Atco 801 [2]

Amen (10) 36
Any Ole Way (4,11)
Are You Lonely For Me Baby (6)
Bring It On Home To Me (6)
Can't Turn You Loose ..see: I Can't Turn You Loose
Chain Gang (4,15)
Chained And Bound (2) 70
Champagne And Wine (10)
Change Is Gonna Come (3,15)
Cigarettes And Coffee (4,15)
Come To Me (2) 69
Day Tripper (5,7)
Demonstration (13)
Direct Me (12)
Dock Of The Bay ..see: (Sittin' On)
Dog, The (1)
Don't Mess With Cupid (9)
Down In The Valley (3,15)
Everybody Makes A Mistake (4)
Fa-Fa-Fa-Fa-Fa (Sad Song) (5,7,8,15) 29
Fool For You (10)

For Your Precious Love (2)
Free Me (12)
Give Away None Of My Love (12)
Glory Of Love (9) 60
Good To Me (4,15)
Got To Get Myself Together (12)
Groovin' Time (12)
Happy Song (Dum-Dum) (10) 25
Hard To Handle (10) 51
Hawg For You (5)
Hey Hey Baby (1)
Home In Your Heart (2)
Huckle-Buck (9)
(I Can't Get No) Satisfaction ..see: Satisfaction
I Can't Turn You Loose (7,8,11,15)
I Got The Will (13)
I Love You More Than Words Can Say (9) 78
I Need Your Lovin' (1)
I Want To Thank You (2)
I'll Let Nothing Separate Us (12)

I'm A Changed Man (12)
I'm Coming Home (9)
I'm Depending On You (11)
I'm Sick Y'all (5)
I've Been Loving You Too Long (To Stop Now) (3,7,8,14,15) 21
I've Got Dreams To Remember (10) 41
It Takes Two (6)
It's Growing (4)
It's Too Late (13)
Johnny's Heartbreak (13)
Just One More Day (4,11,15) 85
Keep Your Arms Around Me (2)
Knock On Wood (6) 30
Let Me Be Good To You (4)
Let Me Come On Home (9)
Little Time (13)
Look At That Girl (12)
Louie Louie (9)
Love Have Mercy (5)
Love Man (12) 72
Lover's Question (12) 48
Lovey Dovey (6) 60

Lucille (1)
Match Game (13)
Mr. Pitiful (2,8,11) 41
My Girl (3,7,15)
My Lover's Prayer (5,8,15) 61
New Year's Resolution (6)
Nobody Knows You (When You're Down And Out) (4,9)
Nobody's Fault But Mine (10)
Nothing Can Change This Love (2)
Ole Man Trouble (3,9,15)
Ooh Carla, Ooh Otis (6)
Open The Door (9)
Out Of Sight (13)
Pain In My Heart (1,8,11,15) 61
Papa's Got A Brand New Bag (11) 21
Respect (3,7,8,11,14,15) 35
Rock Me Baby (3,15)
Satisfaction (3,7,8,11,14,15) 31
Scratch My Back (4)
Security (1,8) 97
Shake (3,7,8,14,15) 47

She Put The Hurt On Me (5)
(Sittin' On) The Dock Of The Bay (9,15) 1
634-5789 (4)
Slippin' And Slidin' (13)
Snatch A Little Piece (13)
Something Is Worrying Me (1)
Stand By Me (1)
Sweet Lorene (5)
Swingin' On A String (13)
Tell It Like It Is (6)
Tell The Truth (13,15)
Tennessee Waltz (5)
That's A Good Idea (12)
That's How Strong My Love Is (2,15) 74
That's What My Heart Needs (1)
These Arms Of Mine (1,7,8,11,15) 85
Think About It (10)
Thousand Miles Away (10)
Ton Of Joy (5)
Tramp (6,9,15) 26
Treat Her Right (4)

Try A Little Tenderness (5,7,8,14,15) 25
Waste Of Time (10)
When Something Is Wrong With My Baby (6)
Wholesale Love (13)
Woman, Lover, A Friend (2)
Wonderful World (3)
You Don't Miss Your Water (3,15)
You Made A Man Out Of Me (10)
You Send Me (1)
You're Still My Baby (5)
(Your Love Has Lifted Me) Higher And Higher (12)
Your Feeling Is Mine (12)
Your One And Only Man (2)

REDDINGS, The

Consisted of Otis Redding's sons Dexter (vocals, bass) and Otis III (guitar), and cousin Mark Locket (vocals, drums, keyboards).

DEBUT DATE	PEAK POS	WKS CHR		ARTIST — Album Title	$	Label & Number
12/20/80	174	12		1 The Awakening	$8	Believe 36875
8/1/81	106	5		2 Class	$8	Believe 37175
5/29/82	153	12		3 Steamin' Hot	$8	Believe 37974

Awakening Pt. 1 & 2 (1)
Class (Is What You Got) (2)
Come In Out The Rain (1)
Doin' It (1)
Follow Me (3)

For You (3)
Funkin' On The One (1)
Hurts So Bad (2)
I Know You Got Another (Don't Matter) (2)

I Want It (1)
If You Feel It (2)
It's Friday Night (1)
Lady Be My Lovesong (1)
Love Dance (2)

Love Is Over (2)
Main Nerve (2)
Remote Control (1) 89
Seriously (2)

(Sittin' On) The Dock Of The Bay (3) 55
Steamin' Hot (3)
Time Won't Wait (3)

You Bring Me Joy (3)
You Can Be A Star (3)
You're The Only One (2)

★★270★★ REDDY, Helen

Born on 10/25/41 in Melbourne, Australia. Family was in show business; Helen made stage debut at age four. Own TV series in the early '60s. Migrated to New York in 1966. To Los Angeles in 1968. Acted in the films Airport 1975, Pete's Dragon and Sgt. Pepper's Lonely Hearts Club Band.

DEBUT DATE	PEAK POS	WKS CHR		ARTIST — Album Title	$	Label & Number
6/5/71+	100	37	●	1 I Don't Know How To Love Him	$10	Capitol 762
12/4/71+	167	7		2 Helen Reddy	$10	Capitol 857
12/9/72+	14	62	▲	3 I Am Woman	$10	Capitol 11068
8/11/73	8	43	●	4 Long Hard Climb	$10	Capitol 11213
4/20/74	11	35	●	5 Love Song For Jeffrey	$10	Capitol 11284
11/2/74+	8	28	●	6 Free And Easy	$10	Capitol 11348
7/12/75	11	34	●	7 No Way To Treat A Lady	$10	Capitol 11418
12/6/75+	5	51	▲²	8 Helen Reddy's Greatest Hits .... [G]	$10	Capitol 11467
8/14/76	16	13	●	9 Music, Music	$10	Capitol 11547
5/21/77	75	19		10 Ear Candy	$8	Capitol 11640

Ah, My Sister (5)
Ain't No Way To Treat A Lady (7,8) 8

And I Love You So (3)
Angie Baby (6,8) 1
Aquarius Miracle (10)

Baby, I'm A Star (10)
Best Friend (1)
Birthday Song (7)

Bit O.K. (4)
Bluebird (7) 35
Come On John (2)

Crazy Love (1) 51
Delta Dawn (4,8) 1

Don't Let It Mess Your Mind (7)
Don't Make Promises (1)

REDDY, Helen — Cont'd

Don't Mess With A Woman (4)
Emotion (6,8) 22
Free And Easy (6)
Get Off Me Baby (9)
Gladiola (9)
Happy Girls (10) 57
Hit The Road, Jack (3)
Hold Me In Your Dreams Tonight (9)
How? (2)
How Can I Be Sure (1)
I Am Woman (1,3,8) 1
I Believe In Music (1)
I Can't Hear You No More (9) 29

I Didn't Mean To Love You (3)
I Don't Know How To Love Him (1,8) 13
I Don't Remember My Childhood (2)
I Got A Name (5)
I Think I'll Write A Song (6)
I Think It's Going To Rain Today (2)
I'll Be Your Audience (6)
I've Been Wanting You So Long (6)
If It's Magic (10)
If We Could Still Be Friends (4)
Keep On Singing (5,8) 15

L.A. Breakdown (3)
Ladychain (9)
Laissez Les Bontemps Rouler (10)
Last Blues Song (3)
Leave Me Alone (Ruby Red Dress) (4,8) 3
Loneliness (6)
Long Distance Love (10)
Long Hard Climb (4)
Long Time Looking (7)
Love Song For Jeffrey (5)
Lovin' You (4)
Mama (9)
Midnight Skies (10)

More Than You Could Take (2)
Music Is My Life (9) flip
Music, Music (9)
New Year's Resovolution (2)
Nice To Be Around (9)
No Sad Song (2) 62
Nothing Good Comes Easy (7)
Old Fashioned Way (4)
One More Night (10)
Our House (1)
Peaceful (3,8) 12
Pretty, Pretty (5)
Raised On Rock (6)
Showbiz (9)

Somewhere In The Night (7) 19
Song For You (1)
Songs (5)
Stella By Starlight (5)
Summer Of '71 (2)
Ten To Eight (7)
Thank You (10)
That Old American Dream (5)
This Masquerade (3)
Time (2)
Tulsa Turnaround (2)
Until It's Time For You To Go (4)
West Wind Circus (4)
What Would They Say (3)

Where Is My Friend (3)
Where Is The Love (3)
You And Me Against The World (5,8) 9
You Don't Need A Reason (7)
You Have Lived (6)
You Know Me (7)
You Make It So Easy (9)
You're My Home (5)
You're My World (10) 18

REDEYE

Rock quartet led by Dave Hodgkins and Douglas "Red" Mark.

| 12/12/70+ | 113 | 12 | | Redeye | $12 | Pentagram 10003 |

Collections Of Yesterday And Now
Dadaeleus' Unfinished Dream
Down Home Run
Empty White Houses
Games 27
Green Grass
Mississippi Stateline
199 Thoughts Too Late
Oregon Bound
Your Train Is Leaving

RED FLAG

Brothers Chris and Mark Reynolds from Liverpool, England. To California in 1980. Keyboardist Chris and vocalist Mark are classically-trained pianists.

| 9/23/89 | 178 | 4 | | Naive Art | $8 | Enigma 73523 |

All Roads Lead To You
Broken Heart
Count To Three
Fur Michelle
Give Me Your Hand
I Don't Know Why
If I Ever
Pretty In Pity
Rain
Russian Radio
Save Me Tonight

REDHEAD KINGPIN and the FBI

Real name: David Guppy. Rapper from Englewood, New Jersey. Members of backing outfit, The F.B.I., included D.J. Wildstyle, Bo Roc, Lt. Squeak, Buzz and Poochie.

| 4/27/91 | 182 | 1 | | The Album With No Name | $12 | Virgin 91608 |

All About Red
Dave & Kwame (Gimme Dat Girl)
Get It Together
Got 2 Go
Harlem Brown
It's A Love Thang (Word)
Nice & Slow
No Reason
Soap
Song With No Name
3-2-1-Pump 52
We Don't Have A Plan B
What Do U Hate

RED HOT CHILI PEPPERS

Los Angeles-based, rap-styled rock foursome: Anthony Kiedis (vocals), Michael "Flea" Balzary (bass), Hillel Slovak (guitar) and Jack Irons (drums). Slovak died of a heroin overdose on 6/25/88 (age 26); replaced by John Frusciante. Irons left in 1988; replaced by Chad Smith. Frusciante left in May 1992; replaced by Zander Schloss (Thelonious Monster). Kiedis appeared in film Point Break.

11/21/87+	148	18		1 The Uplift Mofo Party Plan	$8	EMI-Man. 48036
9/16/89	52	42	●	2 Mother's Milk	$8	EMI 92152
10/12/91	3	70↑	▲³	3 Blood Sugar Sex Magik	$12	Warner 26681
10/17/92	22	17↑		4 What Hits!?	[K] $12	EMI 94762

Apache Rose Peacock (3)
Backwoods (1,4)
Behind The Sun (1,4)
Blood Sugar Sex Magik (3)
Breaking The Girl (3)
Brothers Cup (4)
Catholic School Girls Rule (4)
Fight Like A Brave (1,4)
Fire (2,4)
Funky Crime (1)

Funky Monks (3)
Get Up And Jump (4)
Give It Away (3) 73
Good Time Boys (2)
Greeting Song (3)
Higher Ground (2,4)
Hollywood (4)
I Could Have Lied (3)
If You Have To Ask (3)
If You Want Me To Stay (4)

Johnny Kick A Hole In The Sky (2,4)
Jungle Man (4)
Knock Me Down (2,4)
Love Trilogy (4)
Magic Johnson (2)
Me And My Friends (1,4)
Mellowship Slinky In B Major (3)
My Lovely Man (3)

Naked In The Rain (3)
No Chump Love Sucker (1)
Nobody Weird Like Me (2)
Organic Anti-Beat Box Band (1)
Power Of Equality (3)
Pretty Little Ditty (2)
Punk Rock Classic (2)
Righteous & The Wicked (3)
Sexy Mexican Maid (2)

Show Me Your Soul (4)
Sir Psycho Sexy (3)
Skinny Sweaty Man (1)
Special Secret Song Inside (1)
Stone Cold Bush (2)
Subterranean Homesick Blues (1)
Subway To Venus (2)
Suck My Kiss (3)

Taste The Pain (2,4)
They're Red Hot (3)
True Men Don't Kill Coyotes (1)
Under The Bridge (3,4) 2
Walkin' On Down The Road (1)

REDMAN

Rapper from New Jersey.

| 10/24/92 | 49 | 16↑ | | Whut? Thee Album | $12 | RAL 52967 |

Blow Your Mind [includes 2 versions]
Da Funk
Day Of Sooperman Lover
Encore
Funky Uncles
Hardcore
How To Roll A Blunt
I'm A Bad
Jam 4 U
Psycho Ward
Rated "R"
Redman Meets Reggie Noble
So Ruff
Time 4 Sum Aksion
Tonight's Da Night
Watch Yo Nuggets

RED RIDER — see COCHRANE, Tom

RED ROCKERS

New Orleans foursome — John Griffith, lead singer.

| 5/14/83 | 71 | 16 | | Good As Gold | $8 | Columbia 38629 |

Answers To The Questions
Change The World Around
China 53
(Come On Into) My House
Dreams Fade Away
Fanfare For Metropolis
Good As Gold
Home Is Where The War Is
Running Away From You
'Til It All Falls Down

RED 7

Rock trio: Gene Stashuk (lead singer), Michael Becker and Paul Revelli.

| 5/25/85 | 105 | 10 | | 1 Red 7 | $8 | MCA 5508 |
| 5/30/87 | 175 | 3 | | 2 When The Sun Goes Down | $8 | MCA 5792 |

Big Boys (Talk Tuff) (2)
Can't Much Anymore (1)
Condition Red (2)
Heartbeat (1)
Hearts In Flames (2)
I'm On Your Side (2)
Inspiration (2)
Less Than Perfect (1)
Let Me Use You (1)
No Sorry (1)
Questions And Answers (1)
Relentless (1)
Rise And The Fall (2)
Say You Will (2)
Shades Of Grey (1)
This Dark Hour (1)
True Confessions (2)
Under The Water (2)
Way, The (1)
When The Sun Goes Down (2)

RED SIREN

Vocalist Kristin Massey with Robert Haas, Gregg Potter and Jon Brant. Changed name from Siren to Red Siren in April 1989.

| 4/8/89 | 124 | 12 | | All Is Forgiven | $8 | Mercury 836776 |
originally released under the name Siren

All Is Forgiven
Don't Let Go
Good Kid
How Dare A Woman
Love Shut Down
Master Of The Land
One Good Lover
Rock-A-Bye
So Far Away
Stand Up

REED, Dan, Network
Portland-based, funk-rock quintet led by singer/composer Dan Reed.

4/2/88	95	19		1 Dan Reed Network	$8	Mercury 834309
10/21/89	160	6		2 Slam	$8	Mercury 838868

All My Lovin' (2)
Baby Don't Fade (1)
Come Back Baby (2)
Cruise Together (2)
Doin' The Love Thing (2)

Forgot To Make Her Mine (1)
Get To You (1)
Halfway Around The World (1)
Human (1)

I'm Lonely, Please Stay (1)
I'm So Sorry (1)
Lover (2)
Make It Easy (2)
Rainbow Child (2)

Resurrect (1)
Ritual (1) 38
Rock You All Night Long (1)
Seven Sisters Road (2)
Slam (2)

Stronger Than Steel (2)
Tamin' The Wild Nights (1)
Tiger In A Dress (2)
Under My Skin (2)
World Has A Heart Too (1)

REED, Jerry
Born Jerry Reed Hubbard on 3/20/37 in Atlanta. Country singer/guitarist/songwriter/actor. Among his many films, co-starred in *Gator* and *Smokey & The Bandit I* and *II*. Own TV series *Concrete Cowboys*. Elvis Presley recorded two of Reed's songs: "U.S. Male" and "Guitar Man."

5/16/70	194	2		1 Cookin'	$10	RCA 4293
3/6/71	102	11		2 Georgia Sunshine	$10	RCA 4391
5/1/71	45	20		3 When You're Hot, You're Hot	$10	RCA 4506
9/18/71	153	5		4 Ko-Ko Joe	$10	RCA 4596
4/1/72	196	2		5 Smell The Flowers	$10	RCA 4660
7/15/72	116	12		6 The Best Of Jerry Reed	[G]	$10	RCA 4729
8/11/73	183	4		7 Lord, Mr. Ford	$10	RCA 0238

Alabama Jubilee (1)
Amos Moses (2,3,6) 8
Another Puff (4) 65
Aunt Maudie's Fun Garden (1)
Big Daddy (3)
Brand New Day (4)
Claw, The (6)
Country Boy's Dream (4)
Don't Get Heavy (5)
Don't Let The Good Life Pass You By (5)
Don't Think Twice It's All Right (1)
Dream Sweet Dreams About Me (2)

Early Morning Rain (4)
Eight More Miles To Louisville (2)
Endless Miles Of Highway (5)
Folsom Prison Blues (7)
Framed (4)
Georgia On My Mind (6)
Georgia Sunshine (2,6)
Gomyeyonyo (1)
Good Friends And Neighbors (2)
Guitar Man (6)
How Many Tomorrows (1)
I Shoulda Stayed Home (1)
I'll Be Around (In All The Old Places) (3)

I'm Gonna Write A Song (7)
If I Ever (Love Again) (4)
It Ain't Home, But It Ain't Bad (5)
It Don't Work That Way (5)
Just To Satisfy You (1)
Ko-Ko Joe (4,6) 51
Lady Is A Woman (7)
Lord, Mr. Ford (7) 68
(Love Is) A Stranger To Me (4)
Mule Skinner Blues (Blue Yodel No. 8) (2)
My Guitar And My Song (5)
My Kinda Love (3)
My Next Impersonation (1)

Not As A Sweetheart (But Just As A Friend) (4) (5)
One Sweet Reason (7)
Pave Your Way Into Tomorrow (5)
Pickle, Pickle, Pickle (7)
Plastic Saddle (1)
Preacher And The Bear (2)
Rainbow Ride (7)
Ruby, Don't Take Your Love To Town (3)
Seasons Of My Mind (4)
Semi-Great Predictor (1)
She Understands Me (3)
Smell The Flowers (5)
Sometimes Feelin' (1)

Take It Easy (In Your Mind) (5)
Talk About The Good Times (2)
Thank You Girl (3)
That Lucky Old Sun (Just Rolls Around Heaven All Day) (7)
That's All Part Of Losing (2)
Thing Called Love (6)
Today Is Mine (6)
Tupelo Mississippi Flash (6)
Turn It Around In Your Mind (1)
Turned On (3)
Two-Timin' (7)

U.S. Male (6)
Ugly Woman (2)
When You're Hot, You're Hot (3,6) 9
With You (Missing You) (3)
You Can't Keep Me Here In Tennessee (7)
You'll Never Walk Alone (4)

REED, Jimmy
Born Mathis James Reed on 9/6/25 in Dunleith, Mississippi; died from an epileptic seizure on 8/29/76. Distinctive, influential blues singer/guitarist/harmonica player/songwriter, active until his death. Afflicted with epilepsy since 1957. Inducted into the Rock and Roll Hall of Fame in 1991.

10/16/61	46	31		1 Jimmy Reed at Carnegie Hall	[G]	$40	Vee-Jay 1035 [2]
				record 1: studio re-creation of his Carnegie Hall program; record 2: The Best of Jimmy Reed		
10/20/62	103	6		2 Just Jimmy Reed	$35	Vee-Jay 1050
				side 2 is an unrehearsed recording session		

Ain't That Lovin' Baby (1)
Aw Shucks, Hush Your Mouth (1) 93
Baby What You Want Me To Do (1) 37
Back Home At Noon (2)

Big Boss Man (1) 78
Blue Blue Water (1)
Blue Carnegie (1)
Boogie In The Dark (1)
Bright Lights Big City (1) 58

Found Joy (1)
Found Love (1) 88
Going To New York (1)
Good Lover (2) 77
Hold Me Close (1)
Honest I Do (1) 32

Hush-Hush (1) 75
I'll Change That Too (2)
I'm A Love You (1)
I'm Mr. Luck (1)
In The Morning (2)
Kansas City Baby (2)

Kind Of Lonesome (1)
Let's Get Together (2)
Oh John (2)
Sun Is Shining (1) 65
Take It Slow (2)
Take Out Some Insurance (1)

Tell Me You Love Me (1)
Too Much (2)
What's Wrong Baby? (1)
You Can't Hide (2)
You Don't Have To Go (1)
You Got Me Dizzy (1)

★★173★★ REED, Lou
Born Louis Firbank on 3/2/42 in Freeport, Long Island, New York. Lead singer/songwriter of the New York seminal-rock band, Velvet Underground. Appeared in the film *One Trick Pony*.

6/24/72	189	2		1 Lou Reed	$15	RCA 4701
				with Steve Howe (guitar) and Rick Wakeman (piano)		
12/16/72+	29	31		2 Transformer	$12	RCA 4807
				produced by David Bowie		
10/20/73	98	11		3 Berlin	$12	RCA 0207
3/2/74	45	27	●	4 Rock N Roll Animal	[L]	$10	RCA 0472
				recorded at New York's Academy of Music		
10/5/74	10	14		5 Sally Can't Dance	$10	RCA 0611
4/5/75	62	10		6 Lou Reed Live	[L]	$10	RCA 0959
				from same live sessions as album #4		
2/7/76	41	14		7 Coney Island Baby	$10	RCA 0915
11/13/76	64	8		8 Rock And Roll Heart	$8	Arista 4100
4/16/77	156	6		9 Walk On The Wild Side-The best of Lou Reed	[G]	$8	RCA 2001
4/8/78	89	9		10 Street Hassle	$8	Arista 4169
6/2/79	130	4		11 The Bells	$8	Arista 4229
5/10/80	158	5		12 Growing Up In Public	$8	Arista 9522
12/20/80	178	4		13 Rock And Roll Diary 1967-1980	[K]	$10	Arista 8603 [2]
				record 1: all cuts but one are with The Velvet Underground		
2/27/82	169	4		14 The Blue Mask	$8	RCA 4221
4/9/83	159	7		15 Legendary Hearts	$8	RCA 4568
6/16/84	56	32		16 New Sensations	$8	RCA 4998
5/24/86	47	21		17 Mistrial	$8	RCA 7190
1/28/89	40	22		18 New York	$8	Sire 25829
5/12/90	103	8		19 Songs For Drella	$12	Sire 26140
				LOU REED/JOHN CALE		
				songs comprise a fictitious account of artist Andy Warhol's life		
2/1/92	80	7		20 Magic And Loss	$12	Sire 26662

DEBUT DATE	PEAK POS	WKS CHR	GOLD	ARTIST — Album Title	$	Label & Number

REED, Lou — Cont'd

All Through The Night (11,13)
Andy's Chest (2)
Animal Language (5)
Average Guy (14)
Baby Face (8)
Banging On My Drum (8)
Bed, The (3)
Beginning Of A Great Adventure (18)
Beginning To See The Light (13)
Bells, The (11)
Berlin (1,3,13)
Betrayed (15)
Billy (5)
Blue Mask (14)
Bottoming Out (15)
Busload Of Faith (18)
Caroline Says I (3)
Caroline Says II (3)
Charley's Girl (7)
Chooser And The Chosen (8)
City Lights (11)
Claim To Fame (8)
Coney Island Baby (7,9,13)
Crazy Feeling (7)
Cremation (20)
Day John Kennedy Died (14)
Dime Store Mystery (18)
Dirt (10)
Dirty Blvd. (18)
Disco Mystic (11)
Doin' The Things That We Want To (16)
Don't Hurt A Woman (17)

Don't Talk To Me About Work (15)
Dorita (20)
Dream, A (19)
Dreamin' (20)
Endless Cycle (18)
Endlessly Jealous (16)
Ennui (5)
Faces And Names (19)
Families (11)
Femme Fatale (13)
Fly Into The Sun (16)
Follow The Leader (8)
Forever Changed (19)
Gassed And Stoked (20)
Gift, A (7)
Gimmie Some Good Times (10)
Going Down (1)
Good Evening Mr. Waldheim (18)
Goodby Mass (20)
Goodnight Ladies (2)
Great Defender (Down At The Arcade) (16)
Growing Up In Public (12)
Gun, The (14)
Halloween Parade (18)
Hangin' 'Round (2)
Harry's Circumcision (20)
Heavenly Arms (14)
Hello It's Me (19)
Heroin (4,13,14)
High In The City (16)
Hold On (18)
Home Of The Brave (15)

How Do You Speak To An Angel (12,13)
How Do You Think It Feels (3,9)
I Believe (19)
I Believe In Love (8)
I Can't Stand It (1)
I Heard Her Call My Name (13)
I Love You (1,9)
I Love You, Suzanne (16)
I Remember You (17)
I Wanna Be Black (10)
I Want To Boogie With You (11)
I'm So Free (2)
I'm Waiting For The Man (6)
Images (19)
It Wasn't Me (19)
Keep Away (12,13)
Kicks (7)
Kids, The (3,13)
Kill Your Sons (5)
Ladies Pay (8)
Lady Day (3,4)
Last Great American Whale (18)
Last Shot (15)
Leave Me Alone (10)
Legendary Hearts (15)
Lisa Says (1)
Looking For Love (11)
Love Is Here To Stay (12)
Love Makes You Feel (1)
Magic And Loss (20)
Magician (20)

Make Up (2)
Make Up Mind (15)
Mama's Got A Lover (17)
Martial Law (15)
Men Of Good Fortune (3,13)
Mistral (17)
My Friend George (16)
My House (14)
My Old Man (12)
My Red Joystick (16)
New Sensations (16)
N.Y. Stars (5)
New York Telephone Conversation (2,9)
No Chance (20)
No Money Down (17)
Nobody But You (19)
Nobody's Business (7)
Nowhere At All (9)
Ocean (1)
Oh Jim (3,6)
Ooohhh Baby (7)
Open House (19)
Original Wrapper (17)
Outside (17)
Pale Blue Eyes (13)
Perfect Day (2)
Pow Wow (15)
Power And Glory (Parts I & II) (20)
Power Of Positive Drinking (12)
Real Good Time Together (10)
Ride Into The Sun (1)
Ride Sally Ride (5)
Rock And Roll Heart (8)

Rock 'N' Roll (4,13)
Romeo Had Juliette (18)
Rooftop Garden (15)
Sad Song (3,6)
Sally Can't Dance (5,9)
Satellite Of Love (2,6,9)
Senselessly Cruel (8)
She's My Best Friend (7)
Sheltered Life (8)
Shooting Star (10)
Sick Of You (18)
Slip Away (A Warning) (10,19)
Smalltown (19)
Smiles (12)
So Alone (12,13)
Spit It Out (17)
Standing On Ceremony (12)
Starlight (19)
Strawman (18)
Street Hassle (medley) (10,13)
Stupid Man (11)
Style It Takes (19)
Sweet Jane (4,9,13)
Sword Of Damocles (20)
Teach The Gifted Children (12)
Tell It To Your Heart (17)
Temporary Thing (8,13)
There Is No Time (18)
Think It Over (12)
Trouble With Classicists (19)
Turn Out The Light (15)
Turn To Me (16)
Underneath The Bottle (14)

Vicious (2,6)
Vicious Circle (8)
Video Violence (17)
Wagon Wheel (2)
Wait (10)
Waiting For The Man (13)
Walk And Talk It (1)
Walk On The Wild Side (2,6,9,13) **16**
Waltzing Matilda (medley) (10)
Warrior King (20)
Waves Of Fear (14)
What Becomes A Legend Most (16)
What's Good (20)
White Light/White Heat (4,9,13)
Wild Child (1,9)
With You (11)
Women (14)
Work (19)
Xmas In February (18)
You Wear It So Well (8)

REESE, Della
Born Delloreese Patricia Early on 7/6/31 in Detroit. With Mahalia Jackson gospel troupe from 1945-49, and Erskine Hawkins in the early '50s. Solo since 1957. Actress/singer on many TV shows. Appeared in the 1958 *Let's Rock* and the 1989 film *Harlem Nights*. Own series *Della* in 1970. Played "Della Rogers" on the TV series *Chico & The Man* from 1976-78. On TV's *The Royal Family*.

3/7/60	35	2		1 Della	$20	RCA 2157
10/23/61	113	6		2 Special Delivery	$15	RCA 2391
4/7/62	94	6		3 The Classic Della	$15	RCA 2419
10/22/66	149	2		4 Della Reese Live .... [L]	$12	ABC 569

with Bill Doggett (organ) and Shelly Manne (drums)

And The Angels Sing (1)
Baby, Won't You Please Come Home (1)
Blue Skies (1)
But Beautiful (4)
Detour Ahead (4)
Don't You Know (3) **2**
Driftin' Blues (4)
Girl Talk (4)
Gone (3)
Good Morning Blues (4)
Goody Goody (1)

Gotta Travel On (1)
Have You Ever Been Lonely? (2)
I Got It Bad And That Ain't Good (4)
I Used To Love You (But It's All Over Now) (2)
I'll Get By (1)
I'm Always Chasing Rainbows (2)
I'm Beginning To See The Light (1)

I'm Just A Lucky So And So (2)
If I Could Be With You One Hour Tonight (1)
If You Are But A Dream (3)
Ill Wind (4)
Lady Is A Tramp (1)
Let's Get Away From It All (1)
Moon Love (4)
My Reverie (3)
Please Don't Talk About Me When I'm Gone (2)

Serenade (3)
Softly My Love (3)
Someday Sweetheart (2)
Someday (You'll Want Me To Want You) (1) **56**
Story Of A Starry Night (3)
Stranger In Paradise (3)
Take My Heart (3)
There Will Never Be Another You (4)
These Are The Things I Love (3)

Thou Swell (1)
Three O'Clock In The Morning (2)
Till The End Of Time (3)
Until The Real Thing Comes Along (2)
What's The Reason I'm Not Pleasin' You (2)
Who Can I Turn To? (When Nobody Needs Me) (4)
Won'cha Come Home, Bill Bailey (2) **98**

You Made Me Love You (I Didn't Want To Do It) (2)
You're Driving Me Crazy (1)
You're Nobody 'Til Somebody Loves You (2)

REEVES, Dianne
Jazz singer. Born in Detroit in 1956; raised in Denver. Niece of jazz bassist Charles Burrell.

4/23/88	172	12		1 Dianne Reeves	$8	Blue Note 46906
3/10/90	81	14		2 Never Too Far	$12	EMI 92401

Better Days (1)
Bring Me Joy (2)
Chan's Song (Never Said) (1)
Come In (2)

Company (2)
Eyes On The Prize (2)
Fumilayo (2)
Harvest Time (1)

Hello (Haven't I Seen You Before) (2)
How Long (2)
I'm O.K. (1)

I've Got It Bad And That Ain't Good (1)
More To Love (2)
Never Too Far (2)

Sky Islands (1)
That's All (1)
We Belong Together (2)
Yesterdays (1)

★★457★★ REEVES, Jim
Prominent Country singer. Born James Travis Reeves on 8/20/24 in Panola County, Texas. Killed in a plane crash on 7/31/64. Joined the *Grand Ole Opry* in 1955. Own TV series in 1957. In the film *Kimberly Jim* in 1963. Posthumously, continued to have country hits into the 1980s.

5/23/60	18	26		1 He'll Have To Go...............................	$25	RCA 2223
6/16/62	97	11		2 A Touch Of Velvet	$20	RCA 2487
6/13/64	30	30		3 Moonlight and Roses	$20	RCA 2854
8/8/64	9	43	●	4 **The Best Of Jim Reeves** .... [G]	$20	RCA 2890
3/6/65	45	13		5 The Jim Reeves Way	$20	RCA 2968
2/12/66	100	6		6 The Best Of Jim Reeves, Vol. II....... [G]	$20	RCA 3482
6/4/66	21	29	●	7 Distant Drums .... [K]	$20	RCA 3542
7/15/67	185	5		8 Blue Side Of Lonesome .... [K]	$20	RCA 3793

According To My Heart (6)
Adios Amigo (4) **90**
After Awhile (1)
All Dressed Up And Lonely (1)
Am I Losing You (4) **31**
Am I That Easy To Forget (2)
Anna Marie (4) **93**

Be Honest With Me (2)
Billy Bayou (1,4) **95**
Blizzard, The (4) **62**
Blue Boy (4) **45**
Blue Side Of Lonesome (8) **59**
Blue Skies (2)
Blue Without My Baby (8)

Bolandse Nooientjie (5)
Carolina Moon (3)
Crying Is My Favorite Mood (8)
Danny Boy (4)
Deep Dark Water (8)
Distant Drums (7) **45**
Drinking Tequila (6)

Ek Verlang Na Jou (5)
Four Walls (4) **11**
Gods Were Angry With Me (7)
Good Morning Self (7)
Guilty (4) **91**
Have You Ever Been Lonely (Have You Ever Been Blue) (2)

He'll Have To Go (1,4) **2**
Home (1,6)
Honey, Won't You Please Come Home (1)
I Can't Stop Loving You (5)
I Catch Myself Crying (8)
I Fall To Pieces (1)
I Guess I'm Crazy (6) **82**

I Know One (8) **82**
I Love You More (1)
I Missed Me (7) **44**
I Won't Come In While He's There (8)
I Won't Forget You (6) **93**
I'd Like To Be (1)
I'm A Fool To Care (2)

REEVES, Jim — Cont'd

I'm Beginning To Forget You (1)
I'm Gettin' Better (4) 37
If Heartache Is The Fashion (1)
In The Misty Moonlight (5)
Is It Really Over? (7) 79
Is This Me? (6)
It Hurts So Much (To See You Go) (5)
(It's No) Sin (2)

It's Only A Paper Moon (3)
Just Walking In The Rain (2)
Letter To My Heart (7)
Losing Your Love (7) 89
Love (I Love To Say, "I Love You"), Theme Of (1)
Make The World Go Away (1)
Maureen (5)
Mexicali Rose (3)
Mexican Joe (6)
Moon River (3)

Moonlight And Roses (Bring Mem'ries Of You) (3)
My Lips Are Sealed (6)
Nickel Piece Of Candy (5)
Not Until The Next Time (1)
Oh What It Seemed To Be (3)
One Dozen Roses (3)
Overnight (7)
Partners (1)
Penny Candy (6)
Rosa Rio (3)

Roses (3)
Seabreeze (8)
Snow Flake (7) 66
Somewhere Along The Line (5)
Stand At Your Window (3)
Teardrops On The Rocks (8)
Then I'll Stop Loving You (6)
There's A New Moon Over My Shoulder (3)
There's Always Me (2)

There's That Smile Again (5)
This Is It (7) 88
Trying To Forget (8)
Welcome To My World (2,6)
What's In It For Me (3)
When I Lost You (3)
Where Do I Go To Throw A Picture Away (5)
Where Does A Broken Heart Go? (7)
Wild Rose (2)

Wishful Thinking (1)
Yonder Comes A Sucker (6)
You'll Never Know (5)

REEVES, Martha — see MARTHA & THE VANDELLAS

RE-FLEX
British techno-rock quartet founded by keyboardist Paul Fishman

| 12/24/83+ | 53 | 28 | | The Politics Of Dancing .... | $8 | Capitol 12314 |

Couldn't Stand A Day
Hit Line

Hurt 82
Jungle

Keep In Touch
Pointless

Politics Of Dancing 24
Praying To The Beat

Sensitive
Something About You

REGINA
New York native Regina Richards.

| 10/4/86 | 102 | 8 | | Curiosity .... | $8 | Atlantic 81671 |

Baby Love 10
Beat Of Love

Bring Me All Your Love
Curiosity

Head On
Just Like You

Love Time
Say Goodbye

Sentimental Love

REID, Terry
English rock singer/guitarist. Based in Los Angeles.

12/21/68+	153	8	1	bang, bang you're Terry Reid	$15	Epic 26427
10/18/69	147	5	2	Terry Reid	$15	Epic 26477
4/7/73	172	8	3	River	$10	Atlantic 7259

Avenue (3)
Bang, Bang (My Baby Shot Me Down) (1)
Dean (3)
Dream (3)
Erica (1)

Friends (medley) (2)
Highway 61 Revisited (medley) (2)
July (2)
Live Life (3)
Loving Time (1)

Marking Time (2)
May Fly (2)
Milestones (3)
Rich Kid Blues (2)
River (3)
Season Of The Witch (1)

Silver White Light (2)
Something's Gotten Hold Of My Heart (1)
Speak Now Or Forever Hold Your Peace (2)
Stay With Me Baby (2)

Summertime Blues (medley) (1)
Super Lungs (Supergirl) (2)
Sweater (1)
Things To Try (3)
Tinker Taylor (1)

When You Get Home (1)
Without Expression (1)
Writing On The Wall (medley) (1)

REINER, Carl, & Mel Brooks
Actor/writer/director Reiner was born on 3/20/22 in New York City. Appeared in many TV shows and films. Father of actor/director Rob Reiner. Actor/writer/director Brooks was born Melvin Kaminsky on 6/28/26 in New York City. Directed and starred in several films. Married to actress Anne Bancroft.

| 11/24/73+ | 150 | 12 | | 2000 and Thirteen .... [C] | $15 | Warner 2741 |
revival of the 1961 2000 Year Old Man act

America's Economic Plight
Ancient Poetry
Asparagus
Dolly Madison
Fig Leaf

Generals
Great Inventions
Greatest Invention
Hope For Mankind
Intro

Jesus And The Apostles
Jolson
Lord Byron
Ma And Pa
Miracle Fruits

Natural Foods
Origin Of Words
Paul Revere
Phil
Slow Growth

Strawberries
21,000 Doctors
War Of The Roses
Will To Live
Winston Churchill

★★228★★ R.E.M.
Athens, Georgia rock quartet formed in 1980: Michael Stipe (vocals), Peter Buck (guitar), Mike Mills (bass) and Bill Berry (drums). R.E.M. is abbreviation for Rapid Eye Movement, the dream stage of sleep. Developed huge following with college audiences in the early 1980s as one of the first "alternative rock" bands. Buck, Mills and Berry recorded with Warren Zevon as the Hindu Love Gods in 1990.

5/14/83	36	30	●	1	Murmur	$8	I.R.S. 70604
5/5/84	27	53	●	2	Reckoning	$8	I.R.S. 70044
6/29/85	28	42	●	3	Fables Of The Reconstruction	$8	I.R.S. 5592
8/23/86	21	32	●	4	Lifes Rich Pageant	$8	I.R.S. 5783
5/16/87	52	14		5	Dead Letter Office .... [K]	$8	I.R.S. 70054
mostly B-sides of their singles
9/26/87	10	33	▲	6	R.E.M. No. 5: Document	$8	I.R.S. 42059
10/22/88	44	19		7	Eponymous .... [G]	$8	I.R.S. 6262
new mixes of 12 of their hits
11/26/88+	12	40	▲	8	Green	$8	Warner 25795
3/30/91	1²	98↑ ▲⁴		9	Out Of Time	$12	Warner 26496
10/24/92	2²	16↑ ▲²		10	Automatic For The People	$12	Warner 45138
jewel-box-only CD and cassette catalog number is 45055

Ages Of You (5)
Auctioneer (Another Engine) (3)
Bandwagon (5)
Begin The Begin (4)
Belong (9)
Burning Down (5)
Burning Hell (5)
Camera (2)
Can't Get There From Here (3,7)
Catapult (1)
Country Feedback (9)
Crazy (5)
Cuyahoga (4)
Disturbance At The Heron House (7)
(Don't Go Back To) Rockville (2,7)
Drive (10) 28

Driver 8 (3,7)
Endgame (9)
Everybody Hurts (10)
Exhuming McCarthy (6)
Fall On Me (4,7) 94
Feeling Gravitys Pull (3)
Femme Fatale (5)
Find The River (10)
Finest Worksong (6,7)
Fireplace (6)
Flowers Of Guatemala (4)
Gardening At Night (7)
Get Up (8)
Good Advices (8)
Green Grow The Rushes (3)
Hairshirt (8)
Half A World Away (9)
Harborcoat (2)
Hyena (4)
I Believe (4)

I Remember California (8)
Ignoreland (10)
Its The End Of The World As We Know It (And I Feel Fine) (7) 69
Just A Touch (4)
King Of The Birds (6)
King Of The Road (5)
Kohoutek (3)
Laughing (1)
Letter Never Sent (2)
Life And How To Live It (3)
Lightnin' Hopkins (6)
Little America (2)
Losing My Religion (9) 4
Low (9)
Man On The Moon (10) 93↑
Maps And Legends (3)
Me In Honey (9)
Monty Got A Raw Deal (10)

Moral Kiosk (1)
Near Wild Heaven (9)
New Orleans Instrumental No. 1 (10)
Nightswimming (10)
9-9 (1)
Oddfellows Local 151 (6)
Old Man Kensey (3)
One I Love (6,7) 9
Orange Crush (8)
Pale Blue Eyes (5)
Perfect Circle (1)
Pilgrimage (1)
Pop Song 89 (8) 86
Pretty Persuasion (2)
Radio Free Europe (1,7) 78
Radio Song (9)
Romance (7)
Rotary Ten (5)
Second Guessing (2)

7 Chinese Bros. (2)
Shaking Through (1)
Shiny Happy People (9) 10
Sidewinder Sleeps Tonite (10)
Sitting Still (1)
so. Central Rain (I'm Sorry) (2,7) 85
Stand (8) 6
Star Me Kitten (10)
Strange (4)
Superman (4)
Swan Swan H (4)
Sweetness Follows (10)
Talk About The Passion (1,7)
Texarkana (9)
There She Goes Again (5)
These Days (4)
Time After Time (Annelise) (2)
Toys In The Attic (5)

Try Not To Breathe (10)
Turn You Inside - Out (8)
Underneath The Bunker (4)
Voice Of Harold (5)
Walters Theme (5)
We Walk (1)
Welcome To The Occupation (6)
Wendell Gee (3)
West Of The Fields (1)
What If We Give It Away? (4)
White Tornado (5)
Windout (5)
World Leader Pretend (8)
Wrong Child (9)
You Are The Everything (8)

REMBRANDTS, The
Duo of Danny Wilde and Phil Solem. Both were members of the L.A. pop band Great Buildings.

1/19/91	88	24		The Rembrandts...	$12	Atco 91412

Burning Timber	Everyday People	Goodnight	Moonlight On Mt. Hood	Show Me Your Love
Confidential Information	Follow You Down	If Not For Misery	**Just The Way It Is,**	New King	**Someone 78**
Every Secret Thing			**Baby 14**	Save Me	

RENAISSANCE
British classical-rock group. Founded in 1969 by Yardbirds Keith Relf and Jim McCarty, and former Nashville Teens member John Hawken. Entirely new lineup in 1972 featured lead vocalist Annie Haslam. McCarty, Hawken and Relf's sister Jane (an original Renaissance member) were with Illusion in 1977.

9/22/73	171	4		1 Ashes Are Burning...	$10	Sovereign 11216
8/3/74	94	21		2 Turn Of The Cards	$10	Sire 7502
8/30/75	48	13		3 Scheherazade and other stories	$10	Sire 7510
				side 2: contemporary version of Rimsky-Korsakov's *Scheherazade*		
6/5/76	55	20		4 Live At Carnegie Hall ....[L]	$12	Sire 3902 [2]
				with the New York Philharmonic, conducted by Tony Cox		
2/5/77	46	16		5 Novella	$8	Sire 7526
3/25/78	58	14		6 A Song For All Seasons	$8	Sire 6049
6/16/79	125	9		7 Azure d'or..	$8	Sire 6068
				title is French for Blue Gold		
12/12/81	196	4		8 Camera Camera	$8	I.R.S. 70019

Ashes Are Burning (1,4)	Carpet Of The Sun (1,4)	Friends (7)	Mother Russia (2,4)	Running Hard (2,4)	Touching Once (Is So Hard To Keep) (5)
At The Harbour (1)	Closer Than Yesterday (6)	Golden Key (7)	Northern Lights (6)	Scheherazade (3,4)	Trip To The Fair (3)
Back Home Once Again (6)	Cold Is Being (2)	I Think Of You (2)	Ocean Gypsy (3,4)	Secret Mission (7)	Tyrant-Tula (8)
Black Flame (2)	Day Of The Dreamer (6)	Jekyll And Hyde (7)	Okichi-San (8)	She Is Love (6)	Ukraine Ways (8)
Bonjour Swansong (8)	Discovery, The (7)	Jigsaw (8)	On The Frontier (1)	Sisters, The (5)	Vultures Fly High (3)
Camera Camera (8)	Faeries (Living In The	Kalynda (A Magical Isle) (7)	Only Angels Have Wings (7)	Song For All Seasons (6)	Winter Tree (7)
Can You Hear Me? (5)	Bottom Of The Garden) (6)	Kindness (At The End) (6)	Opening Out (6)	Things I Don't Understand	
Can You Understand? (1,4)	Flood At Lyons (7)	Let It Grow (1)	Remember (8)	(2)	
Captive Heart (5)	Forever Changing (7)	Midas Man (7)	Running Away From You (8)		

RENAISSANCE, The
Studio group produced by Snuff Garrett (Midnight String Quartet).

1/9/71	198	2		Bacharach Baroque................................[I]	$8	Ranwood 8084
				baroque treatments of Burt Bacharach songs		

Alfie	I Say A Little Prayer	Raindrops Keep Fallin' On	(There's) Always Something	(They Long To Be) Close To	Walk On By
Blue On Blue	I'll Never Fall In Love Again	My Head	There To Remind Me	You	What The World Needs Now
Do You Know The Way To	Look Of Love				Is Love
San Jose?					

RENAY, Diane
Philadelphian Renee Diane Kushner.

4/4/64	54	11		Navy Blue...	$40	20th Century 3133

Bell Bottom Trousers	Hello Heartaches	Man Of Mystery	Please Forget Me	Soft-Spoken Guy	Sooner Or Later
He Promised Me Forevermore	Kiss Me Sailor 29	Navy Blue 6	Present From Eddie	Soldier Boy	Unbelievable Guy

RENE AND ANGELA
Los Angeles-based R&B duo: Rene Moore and Angela Winbush. Formed in 1978.

8/22/81	100	8		1 Wall To Wall	$8	Capitol 12161
7/6/85+	64	70	●	2 Street Called Desire	$8	Mercury 824607

Come My Way (1)	**I'll Be Good (2) 47**	Love's Alright (1)	Secret Rendezvous (1)	Wanna Be Close To You (1)	**You Don't Have To Cry**
Drive My Love (2)	Imaginary Playmates (1)	No How - No Way (2)	Street Called Desire (2)	Who's Foolin' Who (2)	**(2) 75**
I Love You More (1)	Just Friends (1)	Save Your Love (For #1) (2)	Wall To Wall (1)		**Your Smile** (2) 62

RENE & RENE
Mexican-American duo from Laredo, Texas: Rene Ornelas (b: 8/26/36) and Rene Herrera (b: 10/2/35).

1/11/69	129	9		Lo Mucho Que Te Quiero...................................	$12	White Whale 7119
				translation of Spanish title: The More That I Love You		

Cuando Llegue A Phoenix	Day Tripper	Hand Me Down	Las Cosas	**Lo Mucho Que Te Quiero**	Mornin'
(By The Time I Get To	Enchilada Jose	Hidin' In The Shadows	Lloraras	**(The More I Love You) 14**	Relampago
Phoenix)	Far Away				

★★146★★ REO SPEEDWAGON
Rock quintet from Champaign, Illinois: Kevin Cronin (lead vocals, rhythm guitar), Gary Richrath (lead guitar), Neal Doughty (keyboards), Bruce Hall (bass) and Alan Gratzer (drums). Gratzer left in 1988, replaced by former Santana drummer Graham Lear. 1990 lineup: Cronin, Doughty and Hall joined by new members Bryan Hitt, Dave Amato and Jesse Harms (left by 1991). Group named after a 1911 fire truck.

1/12/74+	171	8	▲	1 Ridin' The Storm Out..	$10	Epic 32378
11/16/74+	98	14		2 Lost In A Dream	$10	Epic 32948
8/2/75	74	10		3 This Time We Mean It	$10	Epic 33338
				above 3 feature lead vocals by Mike Murphy		
6/19/76	159	5		4 R.E.O.	$10	Epic 34143
3/19/77	72	50	▲	5 REO Speedwagon Live/You Get What You Play For ....[L]	$10	Epic 34494 [2]
4/22/78	29	48	▲²	6 You can Tune a piano, but you can't Tuna fish	$8	Epic 35082
8/11/79	33	23	●	7 Nine Lives	$8	Epic 35988
4/19/80	55	34	▲	8 A Decade Of Rock And Roll 1970 To 1980 ....[K]	$10	Epic 36444 [2]
12/13/80+	1¹⁵	101	▲⁷	9 Hi Infidelity	$8	Epic 36844
7/10/82	7	24	▲	10 Good Trouble	$8	Epic 38100
11/24/84+	7	49	▲²	11 Wheels are turnin'	$8	Epic 39593
2/28/87	28	48	●	12 Life As We Know It	$8	Epic 40444
6/25/88	56	22	▲	13 The Hits ....[G]	$8	Epic 44202
8/18/90	129	8		14 The Earth, A Small Man, His Dog And A Chicken	$12	Epic 45246

DEBUT DATE	PEAK POS	WKS CHR	GOLD	ARTIST — Album Title	$	Label & Number

REO SPEEDWAGON — Cont'd

Accidents Can Happen (12)
All Heaven Broke Loose (14)
Any Kind Of Love (4,5)
Back In My Heart Again (10)
Back On The Road Again (7,8)
Being Kind (Can Hurt Someone Sometimes) (5)
Blazin' Your Own Trail Again (6)
Break His Spell (11)
Breakaway (4,8)
Can't Fight This Feeling (11,13) *1*
Can't Get You Out Of My Heart (12)
Can't Lie To My Heart (14)
Candalera (3)
Dance (3)
Do You Know Where Your Woman Is Tonight (6)
Do Your Best (2)
Don't Let Him Go (9,13) *24*
Down By The Dam (2)
Dream Weaver (3)

Drop It (An Old Disguise) (7)
Easy Money (7)
Every Now And Then (10)
Find My Fortune (1)
Flying Turkey Trot (4,5,8)
Follow My Heart (9)
Gambler (3)
Girl With The Heart Of Gold (10)
Give Me A Ride (Roller Coaster) (2)
Go For Broke (14)
Golden Country (5,8)
Good Trouble (10)
Gotta Feel More (11)
Half Way (14)
Headed For A Fall (3)
Heart Survives (14)
Heavy On Your Love (7)
Here With Me (13) *20*
(I Believe) Our Time Is Gonna Come (4,5,8)
I Do'wanna Know (11) *29*
I Don't Want To Lose You (13)

I Need You Tonight (3)
I Wish You Were There (9)
I'll Follow You (10)
I'm Feeling Good (2)
In My Dreams (12,13) *19*
In Your Letter (9) *20*
It's Everywhere (1)
Keep On Loving You (9,13) *1*
Keep Pushin' (4,5,8,13)
Keep The Fire Burnin' (10) *7*
Key, The (10)
L.I.A.R. (14)
Lay Me Down (13)
Let's Be-Bop (10)
Lies (3)
Lightning (4,8)
Like You Do (5,8)
Little Queenie (5)
Live Every Moment (11) *34*
Live It Up (1)
Lost In A Dream (2,8)
Love In The Future (14)
Love Is A Rock (14) *65*

Love To Hate (14)
Lucky For You (6)
Meet Me On The Mountain (7)
Movin' (1)
Music Man (5,8)
New Way To Love (12)
Oh Woman (1)
157 Riverside Avenue (5,8)
One Lonely Night (11) *19*
One Too Many Girlfriends (12)
(Only A) Summer Love (4,5)
Only The Strong Survive (7,8)
Open Up (1)
Out Of Control (1)
Out Of Season (9)
Over The Edge (12)
Reelin' (3,8)
Ridin' The Storm Out (1,5,8,13) *94*
River Of Life (3)
Rock & Roll Music (7)
Rock 'N Roll Star (11)

Roll With The Changes (6,8,13) *58*
Runnin' Blind (4)
Say You Love Me Or Say Goodnight (6,8)
Screams And Whispers (12)
Shakin' It Loose (9)
Sing To Me (6)
Sky Blues (2)
Someone Tonight (9)
Son Of A Poor Man (1,5,8)
Sophisticated Lady (8)
Start A New Life (9)
Stillness Of The Night (10)
Sweet Time (10) *26*
Take It On The Run (9,13) *5*
Take Me (7)
That Ain't Love (12,13) *16*
They're On The Road (4)
Throw The Chains Away (2)
Thru The Window (11)
Time For Me To Fly (6,8,13) *56*
Tired Of Gettin' Nowhere (12)

Tonight (4)
Tough Guys (9)
Unidentified Flying Tuna Trot (6)
Variety Tonight (12) *60*
Wheels Are Turnin' (11)
Whiskey Night (1)
Wild As The Western Wind (2)
Without Expression (Don't Be The Man) (1)
You Better Realize (3)
You Can Fly (2)
You Won't See Me (14)

REPLACEMENTS, The

Minneapolis rock quartet: Paul Westerberg (vocals), Tommy Stinson, Chris Mars and Slim Dunlap. Originally known as The Impediments. Mars (drums) left in 1990, replaced by Steve Foley. Disbanded in early 1991.

DEBUT DATE	PEAK POS	WKS CHR		#	Album Title	$	Label & Number
2/1/86	183	7		1	Tim	$8	Sire 25330
5/30/87	131	19		2	Pleased To Meet Me	$8	Sire 25557
2/18/89	57	19		3	Don't Tell A Soul	$8	Sire 25831
10/13/90	69	14		4	All Shook Down	$12	Sire 26298

Achin' To Be (3)
Alex Chilton (2)
All Shook Down (4)
Anywhere's Better Than Here (3)
Asking Me Lies (3)
Attitude (2)
Back To Back (3)

Bastards Of Young (1)
Bent Out Of Shape (4)
Can't Hardly Wait (2)
Darlin' One (3)
Dose Of Thunder (1)
Happy Town (4)
Here Comes A Regular (1)
Hold My Life (1)

I Don't Know (2)
I Won't (3)
I'll Be You (3) *51*
I'll Buy (1)
I.O.U. (2)
Kiss Me On The Bus (1)
Last, The (4)
Lay It Down Clown (3)

Ledge, The (2)
Left Of The Dial (1)
Little Mascara (1)
Merry Go Round (4)
My Little Problem (4)
Never Mind (2)
Nightclub Jitters (2)
Nobody (4)

One Wink At A Time (4)
Red Red Wine (2)
Rock 'N' Roll Ghost (3)
Sadly Beautiful (4)
Shooting Dirty Pool (2)
Skyway (3)
Someone Take The Wheel (4)
Swingin Party (1)

Talent Show (3)
They're Blind (3)
Torture (4)
Valentine (2)
Waitress In The Sky (1)
We'll Inherit The Earth (3)
When It Began (4)

RESTLESS HEART

Nashville country-rock quintet consisting of former session musicians Larry Stewart (vocals), David Innis, Greg Jennings, Paul Gregg and John Dittrich. Stewart went solo in early 1992. Keyboardist Innis left in early 1993. Remaining three continued on with two backing musicians.

DEBUT DATE	PEAK POS	WKS CHR	GOLD	#	Album Title	$	Label & Number
4/11/87	73	25	●	1	Wheels	$8	RCA 5648
8/27/88	114	11	●	2	Big Dreams In A Small Town	$8	RCA 8317
2/24/90	78	17	●	3	Fast Movin' Train	$12	RCA 9961
11/16/91+	144	12		4	The Best Of Restless Heart	[G] $12	RCA 61041
11/7/92	119↑	14↑		5	Big Iron Horses	$12	RCA 66049

As Far As I Can Tell (5)
Big Dreams In A Small Town (2)
Big Iron Horses (5)
Blame It On Love (5)
Bluest Eyes In Texas (2,4)
Born In A High Wind (5)
Boy's On A Roll (5)
Calm Before The Storm (2)

Dancy's Dream (3)
Eldorado (2)
Familiar Pain (4)
Fast Movin' Train (3,4)
Hard Time (1)
Hummingbird (1)
I'll Still Be Loving You (1,4) *33*
I've Never Been So Sure (3)

Jenny Come Back (2)
Just In Time (5)
Lady Luck (3)
Little More Coal On The Fire (3)
Long Lost Friend (3)
Meet Me On The Other Side (5)
Mending Fences (5)

New York (Hold Her Tight) (1)
No Way Out (2)
River Of Stone (3)
Say What's In Your Heart (2)
Sweet Auburn (3)
Tender Lie (2,4)
That Rock Won't Roll (1,4)
This Time (2)
Til I Loved You (4)

Truth Hurts (3)
Victim Of The Game (1)
We Got The Love (5)
We Owned This Town (1)
We're Gonna Be OK (5)
Wheels (1,4)
When She Cries (5) *11*
When Somebody Loves You (3)

Why Does It Have To Be (Wrong Or Right) (1,4)
You Can Depend On Me (4)

RETURN TO FOREVER

Jazz-rock band: Chick Corea (keyboards), Stanley Clarke (bass), Lenny White (drums) and Al DiMeola (guitar).

DEBUT DATE	PEAK POS	WKS CHR	GOLD	#	Album Title	$	Label & Number
12/8/73	124	15		1	Hymn Of The Seventh Galaxy	[I] $10	Polydor 5536
9/28/74	32	23		2	Where Have I Known You Before	[I] $10	Polydor 6509
3/15/75	39	13		3	No Mystery	[I] $10	Polydor 6512
4/3/76	35	15	●	4	Romantic Warrior	[I] $8	Columbia 34076
4/2/77	38	17		5	Musicmagic	$8	Columbia 34682
3/3/79	155	4		6	Return To Forever Live	[L] $8	Columbia 35281

recorded May 1977

After The Cosmic Rain (1)
Beyond The Seventh Galaxy (2)
Captain Senor Mouse (1)
Celebration Suite Part II (3)
Celebration Suite Part I & II (3)
Come Rain Or Come Shine (6)

Dayride (2)
Do You Ever (5)
Duel Of The Jester And The Tyrant (Part I & Part II) (4)
Earth Juice (2)
Endless Night (Part 1 & 2) (5,6)
First Movement Of Heavy Metal, Excerpt From The (3)

Flight Of The Newborn (3)
Game Maker (1)
Hello Again (5)
Hymn Of The Seventh Galaxy (1)
Interplay (3)
Jungle Waterfall (3)
Magician, The (4)
Majestic Dance (4)

Medieval Overture (4)
Moorish Warrior And Spanish Princess (6)
Mothership, Theme To The (1)
Musician, The (5,6)
Musicmagic (5,6)
No Mystery (3)
Romantic Warrior (4)

Shadow Of Lo (2)
So Long Mickey Mouse (5,6)
Sofistifunk (3)
Song To The Pharaoh Kings (2)
Sorceress (4)
Space Circus Part I & II (medley) (1)
Vulcan Worlds (2)

Where Have I Danced With You Before (2)
Where Have I Known You Before (2)
Where Have I Loved You Before (2)

REVENGE

Manchester, England trio formed by New Order bassist Peter Hook. Joined by guitarist Dave Hicks and keyboardist Chris "CJ" Jones.

DEBUT DATE	PEAK POS	WKS CHR			Album Title	$	Label & Number
9/1/90	190	2			One True Passion	$12	Capitol 94053

Big Bang
Bleachman
Fag Hag

It's Quiet
Kiss The Chrome
Pineapple Face

7 Reasons
Slave
Surf Nazi

DEBUT DATE	PEAK POS	WKS CHR	GOLD	ARTIST — Album Title	$	Label & Number

REVERBERI
Italian composer Gian Piero Reverberi.

| 2/21/76 | **169** | 7 | | Reverberi & Schumann, Chopin, Liszt..[I] | $8 | Pausa 7003 |

contemporary stylings of above named classical composers

Chopin: Preludio Op. 28 N.4	Chopin: Studio Op. 10 N.3	Liszt: Studio Da Concerto	Schumann: Carnaval Op.	Schumann: Carnaval Op.	Schumann: Carnaval Op.
Chopin: Preludio Op. 28 N.20	Chopin: Studio Op. 10 N.12	No. 6	9/1	9/2	9/3

★★208★★ REVERE, Paul, And The Raiders
Pop-rock group formed in Portland, Oregon in 1960. Group featured Paul Revere (b: 1/7/42, Boise, Idaho; keyboards) and Mark Lindsay (lead singer). To Los Angeles in 1965. On daily ABC-TV show *Where The Action Is* in 1965. Own TV show *Happening* in 1968. Lindsay and Raider member, Keith Allison, recorded with Steve Alaimo as The Unknowns. Group had many personnel changes.

7/3/65+	**71**	45		1 Here They Come!..	$25	Columbia 9107
2/5/66	**5**	43	●	2 Just Like Us!..	$25	Columbia 9251
6/11/66	**9**	43	●	3 **Midnight Ride**...	$25	Columbia 9308
12/31/66+	**9**	33	●	4 **The Spirit Of '67**..	$25	Columbia 9395
5/13/67	**9**	47	●	5 **Greatest Hits**...[G]	$20	Columbia 9462
9/2/67	**25**	21		6 Revolution!...	$20	Columbia 9521

Freddy Weller joins group as lead guitarist

3/2/68	**61**	23		7 Goin' To Memphis..	$20	Columbia 9605
9/14/68	**122**	14		8 Something Happening...	$20	Columbia 9665
4/5/69	**51**	19		9 Hard 'N' Heavy (With Marshmallow)..................................	$20	Columbia 9753
8/23/69	**48**	12		10 Alias Pink Puzz..	$20	Columbia 9905
11/8/69	**166**	4		11 Two All-Time Great Selling LP's......................................[R]	$20	Columbia 12 [2]

reissue of albums #4 & 6 above

RAIDERS:

4/11/70	**154**	9		12 Collage...	$20	Columbia 9964
6/19/71	**19**	20		13 Indian Reservation..	$15	Columbia 30768
7/8/72	**143**	8		14 All-Time Greatest Hits..[G]	$15	Columbia 31464 [2]

PAUL REVERE AND THE RAIDERS

Action (2)
Ain't Nobody Who Can Do It Like Leslie Can (6,11)
All About Her (4,11)
All I Really Need Is You (3)
Baby, Please Don't Go (2)
Ballad Of A Useless Man (3)
Big Boy Pete (1)
Birds Of A Feather (13) **23**
Boogaloo Down Broadway (7)
Boys In The Band (12)
Burn Like A Candle (8)
Call On Me (9)
Catch The Wind (2)
Cinderella Sunshine (9,14) **58**
Come In, You'll Get Pneumonia (13)
Communication (Part 1 & 2) (8)
Cry On My Shoulder (7)
Do Unto Others (14)
Do You Love Me (1)
Dr. Fine (12)
Doggone (2)
Don't Take It So Hard (8,14) **27**

Down In Amsterdam (7)
Eve Of Destruction (13)
Every Man Needs A Woman (7)
Fever (1)
Frankfort Side Street (10)
Free (8)
Freeborn Man (10)
Get It On (3)
Get Out Of My Mind (8)
Goin' To Memphis (7)
Gone (1)
Gone - Movin' On (6,11,12)
Good Thing (4,5,11,14) **4**
Good Times (8)
Great Airplane Strike (4,5,11,14) **20**
Happening '68 (8)
Happens Every Day (4)
Hard And Heavy 5 String Soul Banjo (9)
Heaven Help Us All (13)
Here Comes The Pain (10)
Hey Babro (10)
Him Or Me - What's It Gonna Be? (6,11,14) **5**
Hungry (4,5,11,14) **6**

I Can't Get No Satisfaction (2)
I Don't Know (10)
I Don't Want Nobody (To Lead Me On) (7)
I Had A Dream (6,11,14) **17**
I Hear A Voice (6,11)
I Know (2)
I Need You (10)
I'm A Loser Too (7)
I'm Crying (2)
I'm Not Your Stepping Stone (2)
In My Community (4,11)
Indian Reservation (The Lament Of The Cherokee Reservation Indian) (1)
Interlude (To Be Forgotten) (12)
Just Like Me (2,5,14) **11**
Just Remember You're My Sunshine (13)
Just Seventeen (12,14) **82**
Kicks (3,5,14) **4**
Kiss To Remember You By (1)
Legend Of Paul Revere (5,14)

Let Me (10,14) **20**
Little Girl In The 4th Row (3)
Louie, Go Home (3,5)
Louie, Louie (1,5,14)
Louise (4,11)
Louisiana Redbone (10)
Love Makes The World Go Round (Don't You Let It Stop) (8)
Love You So (7)
Make It With Me (6,11)
Melody For An Unknown Girl (3,5)
Mo'reen (6,11)
Money Can't Buy Me (9)
Money (That's What I Want) (1)
Mr. Sun, Mr. Moon (9,14) **17**
My Way (7)
New Orleans (2)
Night Train (2)
No Sad Songs (7)
Observation From Flight 285 (In 3/4 Time) (8)
Oh! To Be A Man (4,11)
One Night Stand (7)

1001 Arabian Nights (4,11)
Oo Poo Pah Doo (1)
Original Handy Man (10)
Our Candidate (4,11)
Out Of Sight (9)
Out On That Road (9)
Peace Of Mind (7,14) **42**
Prince Of Peace (13)
Reno (6,11)
Ride On My Shoulder (9)
Save The Country (12)
Shape Of Things To Come (13)
Sometimes (1)
Sorceress With Blues Eyes (12)
Soul Man (7)
Steppin' Out (2,5,14) **46**
Take A Look At Yourself (3)
Take Me Home (13)
Thank You (10)
There She Goes (3)
There's Always Tomorrow (3)
These Are Bad Times (For Me And My Baby) (1)
Think Twice (12)
Tighter (6,11,12)

Time After Time (9)
Time Is On My Side (1)
Too Much Talk (8,14) **19**
Trishalana (9)
Turkey, The (13)
Undecided Man (4,11)
Upon Your Leaving (6,11)
Ups And Downs (5,14) **22**
Wanting You (6,11)
We Gotta All Get Together (12,14) **50**
Wednesday's Child (12)
Where You Goin' Girl (9)
Why? Why? Why? (Is It So Hard) (4,11)
Without You (9)
You Can't Sit Down (1)

REYNOLDS, Debbie
Born Mary Reynolds on 4/1/32 in El Paso, Texas. Leading lady of '50s musicals and later in comedies. Married Eddie Fisher on 9/26/55; divorced in 1959. Mother of actress Carrie Fisher.

| 4/30/66 | **23** | 25 | | The Singing Nun...[S] | $25 | MGM 7 |

film is a fictionalized story about the late Soeur Sourire

Alleluia (medley)
Avec Toi (With You I Shall Walk) (medley)

Beyond The Stars (Entre Les Etoiles)
Brother John

Dibwe Diambula Kabanda (medley)
Dominique

I'd Like To Be (Je Voudrais) (medley)
It's A Miracle (Une Fleur)
Kyrie (medley)

Lovely
Pied Piper (Petit Pierrot)
Put On Your Pretty Skirt (Mets Ton Joli Jupon)

Raindrops
Sister Adele (Soeur Adele)

RHEIMS, Robert
Los Angeles-based arranger/conductor.

| 1/5/59 | **25** | 1 | | 1 Merry Christmas in Carols ....[X-I] | $12 | Rheims 6006 |

Christmas charts: 16/'63, 67/'66, 23/'67

| 1/4/60 | **39** | 1 | | 2 We Wish You A Merry Christmas ....[X] | $12 | Rheims 6008 |

The ROBERT RHEIMS Choraliers

Angels We Have Heard On High (medley) (1,2)
Away In A Manger (medley) (1,2)
Bells Of Christmas (medley) (2)
Bring A Torch, Jeannette Isabella (medley) (1,2)
Christmas Chimes Are Pealing (medley) (1,2)

Coventry Carol (medley) (2)
Deck The Halls (medley) (1,2)
Firl Noel (medley) (1,2)
From Every Spire On Christmas Eve (medley) (1)
God Rest Ye Merry, Gentlemen (medley) (1,2)
Good King Wenceslas (medley) (1)

Hark! The Herald Angels Sing (1,2)
Here We Come A Caroling (medley) (2)
I Heard The Bells On Christmas Day (medley) (1,2)
I Saw Three Ships (medley) (1,2)

It Came Upon A Midnight Clear (medley) (1,2)
Joy To The World (medley) (1,2)
O Christmas Tree (medley) (1)
O Come All Ye Faithful (1,2)
O Holy Night (1,2)
O Little Town Of Bethlehem (1,2)

Shepherd Shake Off Your Drowsy Sleep (medley) (2)
Silent Night (1,2)
We Three Kings Of Orient Are (medley) (1,2)
We Wish You A Merry Christmas (medley) (2)
What Child Is This (medley) (2)

While Shepherds Watched Their Flocks By Night (medley) (2)

DEBUT DATE	PEAK POS	WKS CHR	GOLD	ARTIST — Album Title	$	Label & Number

RHINOCEROS
Los Angeles-based rock group — John Finley, lead singer.

DEBUT DATE	PEAK POS	WKS CHR	GOLD	ARTIST — Album Title	$	Label & Number
12/28/68+	115	22		1 Rhinoceros	$20	Elektra 74030
9/27/69	105	9		2 Satin Chickens	$12	Elektra 74056
7/11/70	178	6		3 Better Times Are Coming	$10	Elektra 74075

Along Comes Tomorrow (1) **Apricot Brandy** (1) *46* Back Door (2) Belbuekus (1) Better Times (3) Chicken (2) Don't Come Crying (2)

Find My Hand (2) Funk Butt (2) Happiness (3) I Need Love (1) I Will Serenade You (1) I've Been There (1) In A Little Room (2)

Insanity (3) It's A Groovy World (3) It's The Same Thing (2) Just Me (3) Lady Of Fortune (3) Let's Party (3) Monkee Man (2)

Old Age (3) Rain Child (3) Same Old Way (1) Satin Doll (2) Somewhere (3) Sugar Foot Rag (2) Sweet, Nice 'N' High (3)

That Time Of The Year (1) Top Of The Ladder (2) When You Say You're Sorry (1) You're My Girl (I Don't Want To Discuss It) (1)

RHODES, Emitt
Lead singer of The Merry-Go-Round; from Hawthorne, California.

DEBUT DATE	PEAK POS	WKS CHR	GOLD	ARTIST — Album Title	$	Label & Number
12/12/70	29	20		1 Emitt Rhodes	$10	Dunhill 50089
4/17/71	194	1		2 The American Dream .....[E]	$15	A&M 4254
				recorded 1967-68		
11/27/71	182	4		3 Mirror	$10	Dunhill 50111

Emitt plays all instruments on albums #1 & 3 above

Better Side Of Life (3) Birthday Lady (3) Bubblegum The Blues (medley) (3) Come Ride, Come Ride (2) Ever Find Yourself Running? (1)

Fresh As A Daisy (1) *54* Golden Child Of God (3) Holly Park (3) I'm A Cruiser (medley) (3) In Days Of Old (2) Let's All Sing (2) Live Till You Die (1)

Long Time No See (1) Love Will Stone You (3) Lullabye (3) Man He Was (2) Mary Will You Take My Hand (2) Mirror (3)

Mother Earth (2) My Love Is Strong (3) Pardon Me (2) Promises I've Made (1) Really Wanted You (3) She's Such A Beauty (1) Side We Seldom Show (3)

Somebody Made For Me (1) Someone Died (2) Take You Far Away (3) Textile Factory (2) 'Til The Day After (2) With My Face On The Floor (1)

You Must Have (1) You Should Be Ashamed (1) You Take The Dark Out Of The Night (1) You're A Very Lovely Woman (2)

RHYTHM CORPS
Detroit rock band formed in 1981: Michael Persh (vocals), Davey Holmbo, Greg Apro and Richie Lovsin.

DEBUT DATE	PEAK POS	WKS CHR	GOLD	ARTIST — Album Title	$	Label & Number
8/13/88	104	14		Common Ground	$8	Pasha 44159

Cold Wire Common Ground

Faith & Muscle Father's Footsteps

Giants I Surrender

Perfect Treason Revolution Man

Solidarity Streets On Fire

RHYTHM HERITAGE
Los Angeles studio group assembled by prolific producers Steve Barri and Michael Omartian (keyboards). Vocals by Oren and Luther Waters. Omartian was in band Gator Creek with Kenny Loggins.

DEBUT DATE	PEAK POS	WKS CHR	GOLD	ARTIST — Album Title	$	Label & Number
3/6/76	40	17		1 Disco-Fied .....[I]	$8	ABC 934
2/19/77	138	6		2 Last Night On Earth	$8	ABC 987

Baretta's Theme ("Keep Your Eye On The Sparrow") (1) *20* Blockbuster (1)

Caravan (2) Cisco Kid (medley) (2) Dance The Night Away (2) Disco-Fied (1)

Disco Queen (2) Do It Again (medley) (2) (It's Time To) Boogie Down (2) Lipstick, Theme From (2) My Cherie Amour (1)

Last Night On Earth Medley (2) **Rocky, Theme From** (2) *94* Three Days Of The Condor (1)

S.W.A.T., Theme From (1) *1*

RICH, Buddy
Born Bernard Rich on 6/30/17 in New York City; died on 4/2/87. All-time great jazz drummer. With Tommy Dorsey, 1939-46.

DEBUT DATE	PEAK POS	WKS CHR	GOLD	ARTIST — Album Title	$	Label & Number
12/31/66+	91	27		1 Swingin' New Big Band .....[I-L]	$20	Pacific Jz. 20113
7/15/67	97	21		2 Big Swing Face .....[I-L]	$20	Pacific Jz. 20117
11/30/68	186	6		3 Mercy, Mercy .....[I-L]	$15	World Pac. 20133
9/13/69	186	3		4 Buddy & Soul .....[I-L]	$15	World Pac. 20158
5/20/72	180	5		5 Rich In London .....[I-L]	$12	RCA 4666

Acid Truth (3) Alfie (3) Basically Blues (1) Beat Goes On (2) Big Mama Cass (3) Big Swing Face (2) Bugle Call Rag (2) Channel 1 Suite (3)

Comin' Home Baby (4) Critic's Choice (1) Dancing Men (5) Goodbye Yesterday (3) Greensleeves (4) Hello I Love You (4) Little Train (5) Love And Peace (4)

Love For Sale (2) Love Story, Theme From (5) Meaning Of The Blues (4) Mercy, Mercy, Mercy (3) Mexicali Nose (2) Monitor Theme (2) More Soul (1) My Man's Gone Now (1)

Norwegian Wood (This Bird Has Flown) (2) Ode To Billy Joe (3) Preach And Teach (3) Readymix (1) Ruth (4) Sister Sadie (1) Soul Kitchen (4)

Soul Lady (4) St. Marks Square (A Special Day) (5) St. Petersberg Race (4) That's Enough (5) Time Being (5) Two Bass Hit (5)

Uptight (Everything's Alright) (1) Wack Wack (2) West Side Story Medley (1) Willowcrest (2) Wonderbag (4) Word, The (5)

★★342★★ RICH, Charlie
Born on 12/14/32 in Colt, Arkansas. Rockabilly-country singer/pianist/songwriter. First played jazz and blues. Own jazz group, the Velvetones, mid-'50s, while in U.S. Air Force. Session work with Sun Records in 1958. Known as the "Silver Fox."

DEBUT DATE	PEAK POS	WKS CHR	GOLD	ARTIST — Album Title	$	Label & Number
5/19/73+	8	105	▲	1 Behind Closed Doors	$10	Epic 32247
2/23/74	36	27	●	2 There Won't Be Anymore .....[E]	$10	RCA 0433
3/23/74	24	31	●	3 Very Special Love Songs	$10	Epic 32531
4/27/74	89	19		4 The Best Of Charlie Rich	$10	Epic 31933
				new recordings of early non-Epic hits		
10/19/74	177	4		5 Charlie Rich Sings the Songs of Hank Williams & Others .....[R]	$10	Hi 32084
				previously released as *Charlie Rich Sings Country & Western*		
10/26/74	84	15		6 She Called Me Baby .....[E]	$10	RCA 0686
12/7/74+	25	17		7 The Silver Fox	$10	Epic 33250
6/21/75	54	20		8 Every Time You Touch Me (I Get High)	$10	Epic 33455
6/21/75	162	4		9 Greatest Hits .....[E-K]	$10	RCA 0857
				includes 4 original Sun recordings		
4/3/76	160	6		10 Silver Linings	$10	Epic 33545
				gospel songs		
7/4/76	148	6		11 Greatest Hits .....[G]	$10	Epic 34240
10/29/77	180	3		12 Rollin' With The Flow	$8	Epic 34891

All Over Me (8,11) Almost Persuaded (3) Amazing Grace (10)

America, The Beautiful (1976) (11) Are You Still My Baby (6) Beautiful Woman (12)

Behind Closed Doors (1,7,11) *15* Big Jack (6) Big Boss Man (4,9) Big Build Up (2)

Big Jack (6) Break-Up (medley) (7) Caught In The Middle (9) Charlie's Swing (medley) (7)

Cold Cold Heart (5) Daddy Don't You Walk So Fast (4)

Don't Put No Headstone On My Grave (medley) (7) Down By The Riverside (10)

DEBUT DATE	PEAK POS	WKS CHR	GOLD	ARTIST — Album Title	$	Label & Number

RICH, Charlie — Cont'd

Every Time You Touch Me (I Get High) (8,11) *19*
Field Of Yellow Daisies (3)
Half As Much (5)
He Follows My Footsteps (3)
Hey Good Lookin' (5)
I Can't Help It (5)
I Do My Swingin' At Home (4)
I Don't See Me In Your Eyes Anymore (2,9) *47*
I Feel Like Going Home (medley) (7)
I Love My Friend (7,11) *24*
I Need A Thing Called Love (6)
I Take It On Home (1,4)
I'm Not Going Hungry Anymore (1)
I'm Right Behind You (6)
I'm So Lonesome I Could Cry (5)

If I Knew Then What I Know Now (1)
If You Wouldn't Be My Lady (5)
It Just Goes To Show (You Never Know About Love) (2)
It's All Over Now (2)
Just A Closer Walk With Thee (10)
Let Me Go My Merry Way (6)
Life Has Its Little Ups And Downs (4,11)
Little Bit Here (A Little Bit There) (8)
Lonely Weekends (9) *22*
Love Survived (12)
Mellow Melody (8)
Midnight Blues (8)
Milky White Way (10)
Most Beautiful Girl (1,11) *1*

My Elusive Dreams (7,11) *49*
My Heart Would Know (5)
My Mountain Dew (9)
Nice 'N' Easy (2,4)
Night Talk (12)
No Room To Dance (2)
Nobody's Lonesome For Me (5)
Nothing In The World (To Do With Me) (1)
Ol' Man River (6)
Old Time Religion (10)
Part Of Your Life (4)
Pass On By (8)
Peace On You (1)
Pieces Of My Life (7)
Pretty People (3)
Rendezvous (8)
Rollin' With The Flow (12)
Rondo A La Charlie (medley) (7)

Satisfied Man (3)
Set Me Free (4)
Share Your Love With Me (6)
She (8)
She Called Me Baby (6,9) *47*
Since I Fell For You (8,11) *71*
Sittin' And Thinkin' (4,9)
Somebody Wrote That Song For Me (12)
Sometimes I Feel Like A Motherless Child (10)
Somewhere In My Lifetime (12)
Stay (3)
Sunday Kind Of Woman (1)
Swing Low, Sweet Chariot (10)
Take These Chains From My Heart (5)
Take Time To Love (3)

Ten Dollars And A Clean White Shirt (6)
That's The Way A Cowboy Rocks And Rolls (12)
That's What Love Is (12)
There Won't Be Anymore (2,3,9) *18*
They'll Never Take Her Love From Me (5)
'Til I Can't Take It Anymore (1)
To Sing A Love Song (12)
Tomorrow Night (9)
Too Many Teardrops (2)
Tragedy (6)
Turn Around And Face Me (2)
Very Special Love Song (3,11) *11*
We Love Each Other (1)
Wedding Bells (5)

Were You There? (10)
Whatever Happened (7)
Who Will The Next Fool Be (9)
Why Don't We Go Somewhere And Love (3)
Why Me (10)
Why, Oh Why (3)
Will The Circle Be Unbroken? (10)
Windsong (12)
Woman Left Lonely (4)
You And I (8)
You Never Really Wanted Me (1)
You Win Again (5)
Your Cheatin' Heart (5)
Your Place Is Here With Me (7)

RICHARD, Cliff

Born Harry Rodger Webb on 10/14/40 in Lucknow, India, of British parentage. Vocalist/actor/guitarist. To England in 1948. Worked in skiffle groups, mid-1950s. Backing band: The Drifters (later: The Shadows). Cliff also recorded Inspirational music since 1967. The Shadows disbanded in 1969. Superstar in England, with over 80 charted hits, including 10 #1 singles. British films *Expresso Bongo*, *The Young Ones*, *Summer Holiday* and *Wonderful Life*.

4/18/64	115	7		1 It's All In The Game	$25	Epic 26089
8/7/76	76	15		2 I'm Nearly Famous	$10	Rocket 2210
12/8/79+	93	15		3 We Don't Talk Anymore	$8	EMI America 17018
10/11/80	80	34		4 I'm No Hero	$8	EMI America 17039
10/17/81	132	4		5 Wired For Sound	$8	EMI America 17059

Anything I Can Do (4)
Better Than I Know Myself (5)
Broken Doll (5)
Carrie (3) *34*
Cos I Love That Rock 'N' Roll (5)
Daddy's Home (5) *23*
Devil Woman (2) *6*
Doing Fine (3)
Dreaming (4) *10*
Everyman (4)

Fallin' In Luv (3)
Fly Me To The Moon (In Other Words) (1)
Give A Little Bit More (4) *41*
Heart Will Break Tonight (4)
Here (4)
Hot Shot (3)
I Can't Ask For Anymore Than You (2) *80*
I Found A Rose (1)

I Only Came To Say Goodbye (1)
I Only Have Eyes For You (1)
I Only Know I Love You (1)
I Wish You'd Change Your Mind (2)
I'm In The Mood For Love (1)
I'm Nearly Famous (2)
I'm No Hero (4)
If You Walked Away (2)
In The Night (4)
It's All In The Game (1) *25*

It's Alright Now (2)
It's No Use Pretending (2)
Junior Cowboy (2)
Kiss (1)
Language Of Love (3)
Lost In A Lonely World (5)
Lovers (2)
Magic Is The Moonlight (1)
Miss You Nights (4)
Monday Thru Friday (3)
Oh No, Don't Let Go (5)

Once In A While (5)
Rock N Roll Juvenile (3)
Sci-Fi (3)
Secret Love (3)
Since I Lost You (1)
Such Is The Mystery (2)
Summer Rain (3)
Take Another Look (4)
We Don't Talk Anymore (3) *7*
Where The Four Winds Blow (1)

Wired For Sound (5) *71*
You Know That I Love You (3)
You've Got To Give Me All Your Lovin' (2)
Young Love (5)

RICHARDS, Keith

Born on 12/18/43 in Dartford, England. Lead guitarist of The Rolling Stones. Dropped the "s" from his last name in the '60s and '70s. Married model Patti Hansen on 12/18/83.

10/22/88	24	23	●	1 Talk Is Cheap	$8	Virgin 90973
11/7/92	99	8↑		2 Main Offender	$12	Virgin 86499

Big Enough (1)
Bodytalks (2)
Demon (2)
Eileen (2)

Hate It When You Leave (2)
How I Wish (1)
I Could Have Stood You Up (1)

It Means A Lot (1)
Locked Away (1)
Make No Mistake (1)
999 (2)

Rockawhile (1)
Runnin' Too Deep (2)
Struggle (1)
Take It So Hard (1)

Whip It Up (1)
Wicked As It Seems (2)
Will But You Won't (2)
Words Of Wonder (2)

Yap Yap (2)
You Don't Move Me (1)

★★430★★ RICHIE, Lionel

Born on 6/20/49 in Tuskegee, Alabama. Grew up on the campus of Tuskegee Institute where his grandfather worked. Former lead singer of the Commodores. Appeared in the film *Thank God It's Friday* (1978).

10/23/82	3	140	▲⁴	1 Lionel Richie	$8	Motown 6007
11/12/83	1³	161	▲⁸	2 Can't Slow Down	$8	Motown 6059
				1984 Grammy winner: Album of the Year		
8/30/86	1²	58	▲⁴	3 Dancing On The Ceiling	$8	Motown 6158
5/23/92	19	29	▲	4 Back To Front	[G] $12	Motown 6338
				includes 4 top 5 hits while with the Commodores		

All Night Long (All Night) (2,4) *1*
Ballerina Girl (3) *7*
Can't Slow Down (2)
Dancing On The Ceiling (3) *2*
Deep River Woman (3) *71*

Do It To Me (3) *21*
Don't Stop (3)
Easy (4) *4*
Endless Love (4) *1*
Hello (2,4) *1*
Just Put Some Love In Your Heart (1)

Love, Oh Love (4)
Love Will Conquer All (3) *9*
Love Will Find A Way (2)
My Destiny (4)
My Love (1) *5*
Only One (2)
Penny Lover (2,4) *8*

Round And Round (1)
Running With The Night (2,4) *7*
Sail On (4) *4*
Say You, Say Me (3,4) *1*
Se La (3) *20*
Serves You Right (1)

Still (4) *1*
Stuck On You (2) *3*
Tell Me (1)
Three Times A Lady (4) *1*
Tonight Will Be Alright (3)
Truly (1,4) *1*
Wandering Stranger (1)

You Are (1) *4*
You Mean More To Me (1)

RICHTER, Sviatoslav

Classical pianist from Russia.

12/12/60+	5	26		**Brahms: Piano Concerto No. 2**	[I] $20	RCA 2466
				with the Chicago Symphony Orchestra conducted by Erich Leinsdorf		

Brahms: Concerto No. 2, In B-Flat, Op. 83

RICKLES, Don

Born on 5/8/26 in New York City. Master of insulting comedy. Appeared in many TV shows and films.

6/15/68	54	29		1 Hello Dummy!	[C] $15	Warner 1745
				no track titles listed on this album		
4/12/69	180	4		2 Don Rickles Speaks!	[C] $15	Warner 1779

Capsule Comments (2)
Current Events (2)

Famous Men And Women (2)
Names In The News (2)

Night Clubs (2)
Show Biz And Travel (2)

Sinatra (2)
Some Big Stars (2)

Some Good Friends (2)
Sports (2)

Television (2)
Thoughts (2)

DEBUT DATE	PEAK POS	WKS CHR	GOLD	ARTIST — Album Title	$	Label & Number

RIDDLE, Nelson
Born on 6/1/21 in Oradell, New Jersey; died on 10/6/85. Trombonist/arranger with Charlie Spivak and Tommy Dorsey in the '40s. One of the most in-demand of all arranger/conductors for many top artists, including Frank Sinatra (several classic '50s albums), Nat King Cole, Ella Mae Morse, and more recently, Linda Ronstadt; also arranger/musical director for many films.

DEBUT DATE	PEAK POS	WKS CHR	GOLD	#	ARTIST — Album Title	$	Label & Number
5/27/57	20	1		1	Hey...Let Yourself Go! ....[I]	$15	Capitol 814
2/17/58	20	1		2	C'mon...Get Happy! ....[I]	$15	Capitol 893
10/20/62	48	9		3	Route 66 Theme and Other Great TV Themes ....[I]	$15	Capitol 1771

Alvin Show Theme (3)
Am I Blue? (2)
Andy Griffith Theme (3)
Ben Casey, Theme From (3)
Darn That Dream (1)
Defenders Theme (3)
Diga Diga Doo (2)
Dr. Kildare, Theme From (3)
For All We Know (2)
Get Happy! (2)
Have You Got Any Castles, Baby? (1)
I Can't Escape From You (1)
I Get Along Without You Very Well (1)
I'll Get By (As Long As I Have You) (2)
Jeannine (I Dream Of Lilac Time) (2)
Let Yourself Go (1)
Let's Face The Music And Dance (1)
My Three Sons (3)
Naked City Theme (3)
Rain (2)
Route 66 Theme (3) 30
S'posin' (2)
Sam Benedict, Theme From (3)
September In The Rain (2)
Sing Along (3)
Something To Remember You By (2)
Then I'll Be Happy (1)
This Could Be The Start Of Something (3)
Time Was (2)
Untouchables, The (3)
Without A Song (2)
You And The Night And The Music (1)
You Are My Lucky Star (1)
You Leave Me Breathless (1)
You're An Old Smoothie (3)
Younger Than Springtime (1)

RIDGELEY, Andrew
Born on 1/26/63 in Bushey, England. Former guitarist of Wham!.

DEBUT DATE	PEAK POS	WKS CHR	GOLD	ARTIST — Album Title	$	Label & Number
6/16/90	130	3		Son Of Albert	$12	Columbia 46188

Baby Jane
Big Machine
Flame
Hangin'
Kiss Me
Mexico
Price Of Love
Red Dress
Shake [includes 2 versions] 77

RIDGWAY, Stan
Lead singer of Wall Of Voodoo from 1977-83. Raised in the San Gabriel Valley, California.

DEBUT DATE	PEAK POS	WKS CHR	GOLD	ARTIST — Album Title	$	Label & Number
4/12/86	131	9		The Big Heat	$8	I.R.S. 5637

Big Heat
Camouflage
Can't Stop The Show
Drive She Said
Pick It Up (And Put It In Your Pocket)
Pile Driver
Salesman
Twisted
Walkin' Home Alone

RIFF
Male vocal quintet from Paterson, New Jersey formed at Eastside High School: Kenny Kelly, Steven Capers, Jr., Anthony Fuller, Dwayne Jones and Michael Best. Appeared as themselves (singing the alma mater) in the 1989 film *Lean On Me*, which was based on their school.

DEBUT DATE	PEAK POS	WKS CHR	GOLD	ARTIST — Album Title	$	Label & Number
5/25/91	177	3		Riff	$12	SBK 95828

All Or Nothing
April's Fool
Baby It's Wonderful
Everytime My Heart Beats
I Can't Believe We Just Met
If You're Serious 88
Little Girls
My Heart Is Falling Me 25
Read My Eyes
Temporary Insanity

RIFKIN, Joshua
Born on 4/22/44 in New York City. Classical/jazz/ragtime pianist.

DEBUT DATE	PEAK POS	WKS CHR	GOLD	#	ARTIST — Album Title	$	Label & Number
12/11/65+	83	17		1	The Baroque Beatles Book ....[I]	$15	Elektra 7306
					classical variations of Beatles' tunes; Rifkin conducts the Baroque Ensemble Of The Merseyside Kammermusikgesellschaft		
6/22/74	75	15		2	Piano Rags By Scott Joplin, Volumes I & II * ....[I]	$10	Nonesuch 73026 [2]
12/14/74	126	5		3	Piano Rags By Scott Joplin, Volume III * ....[I]	$8	Nonesuch 71305
					*music written by Joplin between 1899 and 1914		

Bethena (2)
Cascades, The (3)
Chrysanthemum, The (3)
Country Club (3)
Eight Days A Week (1)
Elite Syncopations (2)
Entertainer (2)
Eugenia (2)
Euphonic Sounds (2)
Fig Leaf Rag (2)
Gladiolus Rag (2)
Hard Day's Night (medley) (1)
Help! (1)
Hold Me Tight (1)
I Want To Hold Your Hand (1)
I'll Be Back (1)
I'll Cry Instead (1)
Leola (2)
Magnetic Rag (2)
Maple Leaf Rag (2)
Nonpareil, The (3)
Original Rags (3)
Paragon Rag (2)
Pine Apple Rag (2)
Please Please Me (1)
Ragtime Dance (2)
Rose Leaf Rag (2)
Scott Joplin's New Rag (2)
She Loves You (medley) (1)
Solace (2)
Stoptime Rag (3)
Sugar Cane (3)
Thank You Girl (medley) (1)
Things We Said Today (1)
Ticket To Ride (1)
Weeping Willow (3)
You've Got To Hide Your Love Away (1)

★★150★★ **RIGHTEOUS BROTHERS, The**
Blue-eyed soul duo: Bill Medley (b: 9/19/40, Santa Ana, California; baritone) and Bobby Hatfield (b: 8/10/40, Beaver Dam, Wisconsin; tenor). Formed duo in 1962. First recorded as the Paramours for Smash in 1962. On *Hullabaloo* and *Shindig* TV shows. Split up from 1968-74. Medley went solo, replaced by Jimmy Walker; rejoined Hatfield in 1974.

DEBUT DATE	PEAK POS	WKS CHR	GOLD	#	ARTIST — Album Title	$	Label & Number
1/2/65	11	21		1	Right Now! * ....[E]	$30	Moonglow 1001
1/16/65	14	20		2	Some Blue-Eyed Soul * ....[E]	$30	Moonglow 1002
1/23/65	4	67		3	You've Lost That Lovin' Feelin'	$30	Philles 4007
5/29/65	9	41		4	Just Once In My Life...	$30	Philles 4008
6/19/65	39	20		5	This Is New! * ....[E]	$30	Moonglow 1003
12/25/65+	16	26		6	Back To Back	$30	Philles 4009
4/30/66	7	32	●	7	Soul & Inspiration	$20	Verve 5001
5/21/66	130	11		8	The Best Of The Righteous Brothers * ....[E-K]	$25	Moonglow 1004
					*recorded from 1962-63		
9/3/66	32	20		9	Go Ahead And Cry	$20	Verve 5004
4/8/67	155	15		10	Sayin' Somethin'.	$20	Verve 5010
9/16/67	21	50	●	11	Greatest Hits ....[G]	$20	Verve 5020
					Philles and Moonglow label hits; a CD reissue of album, with 10 additional cuts on Verve 823119, re-entered chart in 1990		
10/28/67	198	2		12	Souled Out	$20	Verve 5031
12/14/68	187	2		13	One For The Road ....[L]	$20	Verve 5058
4/5/69	126	5		14	Greatest Hits, Vol. 2 ....[G]	$20	Verve 5071
					Verve, Philles and Moonglow label hits		
8/31/74	27	18		15	Give It To The People	$12	Haven 9201
8/25/90	31	81		16	Greatest Hits ....[G-R]	$12	Verve 823119
					contains their entire 1967 *Greatest Hits* album plus 10 more songs		
10/27/90	178	3	●	17	Anthology (1962-1974) ....[K]	$12	Rhino 71488 [2]
11/24/90	161	3	▲	18	Best Of The Righteous Brothers ....[G]	$12	Curb 77381

RIGHTEOUS BROTHERS, The — Cont'd

All The Way (16)
Along Came Jones (10)
American Rock And Roll (18)
And I Thought You Loved Me (15)
Angels Listened In (3)
At My Front Door (5,8)
Baby She's Mine (6)
Baby, What You Want Me To Do (2)
Been So Nice (12)
Big Boy Pete (4)
Big Time Ben (9)
Blues, The (4)
Bring It On Home To Me (7)
Bring Your Love To Me (2,17) *83*
Brown Eyed Woman [solo: Bill] (17) *43*
Burn On Love (9)
Bye Bye Love (1,8,14)
Change Is Gonna Come (7)
Come Rain Or Come Shine (16)
Country Boy (16)
Cryin' Blues (5)
Dr. Rock And Roll (15)
Don't Fight It (10)
Dream On (15,17) *32*
Drown In My Own Tears (9)
Ebb Tide (6,11,16,17,18) *5*
Fannie Mae (2,8)

Fee-Fi-Fidily-I-Oh (1)
For Sentimental Reasons ...see: (I Love You)
For Your Love (2,8)
Georgia On My Mind (1,8,11,16,17,18) *62*
Give It To The People (15,17) *20*
Go Ahead And Cry (9,14,17) *30*
God Bless The Child (6)
Gospel Medley (13)
Gotta Tell You How I Feel (5)
Great Pretender (4,11,16)
Guess Who (4,11,16)
Hallelujah I Love Her So (6)
Hang Ups (17)
Harlem Shuffle (10)
He (7) *91*
He Will Break Your Heart (7) *91*
Here I Am (12)
Hey Girl (7)
Hold On I'm Comin' (10)
Hot Tamales (6)
Hung On You (6,11,16,17) *47*
I Believe (9)
I Can't Make It Alone [solo: Bill] (17) *95*
I Don't Believe In Losing (12)
I Just Wanna Be Me (15)

I Just Want To Make Love To You (2,8,14,17)
(I Love You) For Sentimental Reasons (6,11,16)
I Need A Girl (3)
(I Need) Someone Like You (12)
I Still Love You (5)
I Who Have Nothing (17)
I'm Leaving It Up To You (7)
I'm So Lonely (1)
I've Got The Beat (9)
If I Ruled The World (16)
If Loving You Is Wrong (I'm Sorry) (12)
If You're Lying, You'll Be Crying (5)
In That Great Gettin' Up Mornin' (1)
In The Midnight Hour (3)
Island In The Sun (9)
It's Up To You (12)
Jimmy's Blues (10)
Just Once In My Life (4,11,16,17,18) *9*
Justine (5,8,14,17) *85*
Ko Ko Mo (3)
Koko Joe (1,17)
Late Late Night (6)
Let It Be Me (9)
Let The Good Times Roll (1,8,13,14)
Lines (15)

Little Latin Lupe Lu (1,8,13,14,17,18) *49*
Look At Me (3)
Love Is Not A Dirty Word (15)
Love Keeps Callin' My Name (12)
Love Or Magic (1)
Loving You (6,14)
Man Without A Dream (10,17)
Melancholy Music Man (17) *43*
Mine All Mine (7)
My Babe (1,13,17,18) *75*
My Darling Clementine (16)
My Girl (10)
My Prayer (1,8,14)
My Tears Will Go Away (2)
Night Owl (2)
Old Man River (3)
Oldies But Goodies Medley (13)
On This Side Of Goodbye (10,17) *47*
Ooh Poo Pah Doo (4,13)
Over And Over (3)
Rat Race (7)
Rock And Roll Heaven (15,17) *3*
Save The Last Dance For Me (9)
Secret Love (16)
See That Girl (4,11,16,17)

Sick And Tired (3)
Since I Fell For You (16)
So Many Lonely Nights Ahead (12)
Something You Got (9)
Something's Got A Hold On Me (2,8)
Somewhere (16)
Soul City (3)
Soulville (10)
Stagger Lee (9)
Stand By (7,17)
Sticks And Stones (4)
Stranded In The Middle Of Noplace (12,17) *72*
Summertime (3)
That Lucky Old Sun (Just Rolls Around Heaven All Day) (13)
That's All (16)
There She Goes (5,17)
There's A Woman (3)
Things Didn't Go Your Way (9)
This Little Girl Of Mine (2,8,14,17)
Together Again (15)
Try To Find Another Man (Woman) (2,8,17,18)
Turn On Your Love Lights (7)
Unchained Melody (4,11,13,16,17) *4*
Unchained Melody (18) *19*

What Now My Love (9,14)
What'd I Say (3)
White Cliffs Of Dover (6,11,16,17)
Will You Love Me Tomorrow (10)
Without A Doubt (6)
Without A Song (16)
Without You I'd Be Lost (12)
Yes Indeed (10)
You Are My Sunshine (4)
You Bent My Mind (12)
You Can Have Her (5,8,17) *67*
You Turn Me Around (15)
You'll Never Walk Alone (4,11,13,16)
(You're My) Soul And Inspiration (7,13,14,17,18) *1*
You've Lost That Lovin' Feelin' (3,11,13,16,17,18) *1*

RIGHT SAID FRED

British trio: brothers Fred (guitar) and Richard Fairbrass (vocals) with Rob Manzoli (lead guitar). The brothers run a fitness gym in South London. Group name was the title of a song by Bernard Cribbins popular in Britain in 1962.

3/21/92	46	20 ●		Up	$12	Charisma 92107

Deeply Dippy
Do Ya Feel

Don't Talk Just Kiss *76*
I'm Too Sexy *1*

Is It True About Love
Love For All Seasons

No-One On Earth
Swan

Those Simple Things
Upon My Heart

RILEY, Cheryl Pepsii

R&B singer. Native of Brooklyn. Discovered by the group Full Force.

11/12/88	128	11		Me, Myself And I	$8	Columbia 44409

produced by Full Force

Every Little Thing About You
Falling From The Floor

He Said - She Said
Life Goes On

Me, Myself And I
Seein' Is Believin'

Sister Knows What She Wants

Sisters
Thanks For My Child *32*

RILEY, Jeannie C.

Born Jeanne Carolyn Stephenson on 10/19/45 in Anson, Texas. Country singer.

10/12/68	12	27 ●	1	Harper Valley P.T.A.	$12	Plantation 1

all songs about characters mentioned in the title song

3/15/69	187	5	2	Yearbooks and Yesterdays	$12	Plantation 2
9/13/69	142	7	3	Things Go Better With Love	$12	Plantation 3

Artist, The (2)
Back Side Of Dallas (3)
Back To School (2)
Ballad Of Louise (1)
Box Of Memories (2)
Cotton Patch (1)
Edna Burgoo (2)

Girl Most Likely (2) *55*
Harper Valley P.T.A. (1) *1*
I'm Only A Woman (3)
I'm The Woman (3)
Little Town Square (1)
Louise ...see: Ballad Of
Mr. Harper (1)

My Scrapbook (2)
No Brass Band (1)
Our Minnie (3)
Part Of Honey (2)
Real Woman (3)
Rib, The (3)
Run Jeannie Run (1)

Satan Place (1)
Shed Me No Tears (1)
Sippin' Shirley Thompson (1)
Sunday After Church (3)
Taste Of Tears (3)
Teardrops On Page Forty-Three (2)

That's How It Is With Him And Me (2)
There Never Was A Time (3) *77*
Thin Ribbon Of Smoke (3)
Things Go Better With Love (3)

Wedding Cake (3)
What Ever Happened To Charlie Brown (2)
What Was Her Name (2)
Widow Jones (1)
Yearbooks And Yesterdays (2)

RINGS, The

Rock quartet from Boston: Mark Sutton, Mike Baker, Bob Gifford and Matt Thurber.

2/21/81	164	6		The Rings	$8	MCA 5165

Got My Wish
I Need Strange

Let Me Go *75*
My Kinda Girl

Opposites Attract
Third Generation

This One's For The Girls
Too Much Of Nothin'

Watch You Break
Who's She Dancin' With

RIOS, Miguel

Born in Granada, Spain in 1944.

8/22/70	140	4		A Song Of Joy	$12	A&M 4267

orchestra directed by Waldo de Los Rios

Life I Knew (Mi Vida Fue)
Like An Old Time Movie (El Viaje)

Look To Your Soul (Mira Hacia Ti)

River, The
Second Glance (Despierta)

She's Gone (Ella Se Fue)
Soledad

Song Of Joy [includes English & foreign versions] *14*

Vuelvo A Granada

RIOS, Waldo de los

Spanish conductor/composer; died on 3/28/77.

6/5/71	53	16		Sinfonias .... [I]	$10	United Art. 6802

contemporary stylings of classical symphonies

Beethoven: Ode To Joy, Ninth Symphony In D Minor, Choral, 4th Movement
Brahms: Third Symphony In F Major, 3rd Movement

Dvorak: Symphony No. 9, Opus 95, New World, 4th Movement, 2nd Movement
Mendelssohn: Fourth Symphony In A Major, "Italian," 1st Movement

Haydn: Symphony Of The Toys In C Major, 2nd Movement

Mozart: Symphony No. 40 In G Minor K.550, 1st Movement *67*

Schubert: Eighth Symphony In C Minor, "Incomplete," 1st Movement

Tchaikovsky: Symphony No. 5 In E Minor, 2nd Movement

RIOT

New York-based, heavy-metal band led by guitarist Mark Reale. Varying personnel since 1981.

9/12/81	99	11	1	Fire Down Under	$8	Elektra 546

DEBUT DATE	PEAK POS	WKS CHR	GOLD	ARTIST — Album Title	$	Label & Number

RIOT — Cont'd

DEBUT DATE	PEAK POS	WKS CHR		ARTIST — Album Title	$	Label & Number
1/14/84	175	6	2	Born In America	$8	Quality 1008
5/14/88	150	10	3	Thundersteel	$8	CBS Assoc. 44232

Altar Of The King (1)
Bloodstreets (3)
Born In America (2)
Buried Alive (Tell Tale Heart) (3)

Devil Woman (2)
Don't Bring Me Down (1)
Don't Hold Back (1)
Feel The Same (1)
Fight Or Fall (3)

Fire Down Under (1)
Flashbacks (1)
Flight Of The Warrior (3)
Gunfighter (2)
Heavy Metal Machine (2)

Johnny's Back (3)
No Lies (1)
On Wings Of Eagles (3)
Outlaw (1)
Promised Land (2)

Run For Your Life (1,3)
Running From The Law (2)
Sign Of The Crimson Storm (3)
Swords And Tequila (1)

Thundersteel (3)
Vigilante Killer (2)
Where Soldiers Rule (2)
Wings Of Fire (2)
You Burn In Me (2)

RIP CHORDS, The

California group featuring the duo of Terry Melcher (Doris Day's son — produced The Byrds, Paul Revere & The Raiders) and Bruce Johnston (Beach Boys). Touring group featured a different foursome.

2/22/64	56	17		Hey Little Cobra and other Hot Rod Hits	$30	Columbia 8951

Ding Dong
Drag City

'40 Ford Time
409

Gone 88
Here I Stand 51

Hey Little Cobra 4
Little Deuce Coupe

Queen, The
She Thinks I Still Care

Shut Down
Trophy Machine

RIPERTON, Minnie

Born on 11/8/47 in Chicago; died of cancer on 7/12/79 in Los Angeles. Recorded as "Andrea Davis" on Chess in 1966. Lead singer of the rock-R&B sextet Rotary Connection from 1967-70. In Stevie Wonder's backup group Wonderlove in 1973.

DEBUT DATE	PEAK POS	WKS CHR	GOLD	ARTIST — Album Title	$	Label & Number
8/17/74+	4	47	● 1	Perfect Angel	$10	Epic 32561
11/16/74	160	4	2	Come To My Garden ... [E]	$10	Janus 7011
				recorded in 1969		
5/31/75	18	23	3	Adventures In Paradise	$10	Epic 33454
3/19/77	71	10	4	Stay In Love	$10	Epic 34191
5/19/79	29	27	5	Minnie	$8	Capitol 11936
9/6/80	35	15	6	Love Lives Forever	$8	Capitol 12097

recordings from 1978 with new accompaniment featuring George Benson, Peabo Bryson, Roberta Flack, Michael Jackson, Patrice Rushen, Stevie Wonder and many others

Adventures In Paradise (3)
Alone In Brewster Bay (3)
Baby, This Love I Have (3)
Can You Feel What I'm Saying? (4)
Close Your Eyes And Remember (2)
Come To My Garden (2)
Completeness (2)
Could It Be I'm In Love (4)
Dancin' & Actin' Crazy (5)

Don't Let Anyone Bring You Down (3)
Edge Of A Dream (1)
Every Time He Comes Around (1)
Expecting (2)
Feelin' That Your Feelin's Right (3)
Gettin' Ready For Your Love (4)
Give Me Time (6)

Here We Go (6)
How Could I Love You More (4)
I'm A Woman (5)
I'm In Love Again (6)
Inside My Love (3) 76
Island In The Sun (4)
It's So Nice (To See Old Friends) (1)
Les Fleur (2)
Light My Fire (5)

Love And Its Glory (3)
Love Hurts (5)
Lover And Friend (5)
Lovin' You (1) 1
Memory Band (2)
Memory Lane (5)
Minnie's Lament (3)
Never Existed Before (5)
Oh, By The Way (2)
Oh Darlin'...Life Goes On (4)
Only When I'm Dreaming (2)

Our Lives (1)
Perfect Angel (1)
Rainy Day In Centerville (2)
Reasons (1)
Return To Forever (3)
Seeing You This Way (1)
Simple Things (4)
Song Of Life (La-La-La) (6)
Stay In Love (4)
Stick Together (4)
Strange Affair (6)

Take A Little Trip (1)
When It Comes Down To It (3)
Whenever-Wherever (2)
Wouldn't Matter Where You Are (4)
You Take My Breath Away (6)
Young, Willing And Able (4)

RIPPINGTONS featuring RUSS FREEMAN

Jazz-pop combo assembled in 1987 by composer/producer/guitarist Russ Freeman (b: 2/11/60, raised in Nashville).

DEBUT DATE	PEAK POS	WKS CHR		ARTIST — Album Title	$	Label & Number
5/7/88	110	15	1	Kilimanjaro ... [I]	$8	Passport J. 88042
6/10/89	85	12	2	Tourist In Paradise ... [I]	$8	GRP 9588
8/31/91	148	7	3	Curves Ahead ... [I]	$12	GRP 9651
9/5/92	147	3	4	Weekend In Monaco ... [I]	$12	GRP 9681

Aruba! (2)
Aspen (3)
Backstabbers (1)
Carnival! (4)
Curves Ahead (3)
Destiny (2)
Dreams Of The Sirens (1)

Earthbound (2)
Highroller (4)
Indian Summer (4)
Jupiter's Child (2)
Katrina's Dance (1)
Kilimanjaro (1)
Let's Stay Together (2)

Los Cabos (1)
Love Notes (1)
Miles Away (3)
Moka Java (4)
Morning Song (3)
Morocco (1)
Nature Of The Beast (3)

North Star (3)
Northern Lights (1)
Oceansong (1)
One Ocean Way (2)
One Summer Night In Brazil (2)
Place For Lovers (4)

Princess, The (2)
Santa Fe Trail (3)
Snowbound (3)
St. Tropez (3)
Take Me With You (3)
Tourist In Paradise (2)
Vienna (4)

Weekend In Monaco (4)
Where The Road Will Lead Us (4)

RITCHARD, Cyril — see CHILDRENS

RITCHIE FAMILY, The

Philadelphia disco group named for arranger/producer Ritchie Rome. Group featured various session singers and musicians.

DEBUT DATE	PEAK POS	WKS CHR		ARTIST — Album Title	$	Label & Number
10/4/75	53	12	1	Brazil	$10	20th Century 498
7/24/76	30	25	2	Arabian Nights	$8	Marlin 2201
2/12/77	100	10	3	Life Is Music	$8	Marlin 2203
7/30/77	164	12	4	African Queens	$8	Marlin 2206
9/2/78	148	6	5	American Generation	$8	Marlin 2215

African Queens (4)
American Generation (medley) (5)
Arabian Nights Medley (2)
Baby I'm On Fire (2)
Best Disco In Town (2) 17
Big Spender (medley) (5)

Brazil (1) 11
Cleopatra, Theme Of (4)
Disco Blues (1)
Frenesi (1)
Good In Love (medley) (5)
I Feel Disco Good (medley) (5)

I Want To Dance With You (Dance With Me) (1) 84
Lady Champagne (1)
Lady Luck (3)
Let's Pool (1)
Liberty (3)
Life Is Fascination (1)

Life Is Music (3)
Long Distance Romance (3)
Music Man (5)
Nefertiti, Theme Of (4)
Peanut Vendor (1)
Pinball (1)

Queen Of Sheba, Theme Of The (4)
Quiet Village (4)
Romantic Love (2)
Summer Dance (4)
Super Lover (3)
Voodoo (4)

RITENOUR, Lee

Born on 1/11/52 in Los Angeles. Guitarist/composer/arranger. Top session guitarist, has appeared on more than 200 albums. Nicknamed "Captain Fingers." Member of jazz outfits Brass Fever and Fourplay.

DEBUT DATE	PEAK POS	WKS CHR		ARTIST — Album Title	$	Label & Number
6/4/77	178	5	1	Captain Fingers ... [I]	$8	Epic 34426
6/24/78	121	7	2	The Captain's Journey ... [I]	$8	Elektra 136
6/16/79	136	6	3	Feel The Night ... [I]	$8	Elektra 192
5/9/81	26	23	4	"Rit"	$8	Elektra 331
4/17/82	163	6	5	Rio ... [I]	$8	Musician 60024
12/4/82	99	14	6	Rit/2	$8	Elektra 60186
6/23/84	145	8	7	Banded Together	$8	Elektra 60358

DEBUT DATE	PEAK POS	WKS CHR	GOLD	ARTIST — Album Title	$	Label & Number

RITENOUR, Lee — Cont'd

| 10/5/85 | **192** | 2 | | 8 Harlequin .... [I] | **$8** | GRP 1015 |

DAVE GRUSIN/LEE RITENOUR
side 1 features 2 Portuguese songs by Brazil's Ivan Lins: "Before It's Too Late (Antes Que Seja Tarde)" and "Harlequin (Arlequim Desconhecido)"

| 1/21/89 | **156** | 8 | | 9 Festival .... [I] | **$8** | GRP 9570 |

Amaretto (7)	Feel The Night (3)	Keep It Alive (6)	Night Rhythms (9)	San Juan Sunset (5)	Wicked Wine (3)
Be Good To Me (7)	Fly By Night (1)	Latin Lovers (9)	No Sympathy (4)	San Ysidro (8)	(You Caught Me) Smilin' (4)
Bird, The (8)	French Roast (3)	Linda (Voce E Linda) (9)	Odile, Odila (9)	Shadow Dancing (7)	You Make Me Feel Like
Captain Fingers (1,4)	Good Question (4)	Little Bit Of This And A	On The Boardwalk (6)	Silent Message (8)	Dancing (3)
Captain's Journey Medley (2)	Grid-Lock (8)	Little Bit Of That (5)	On The Slow Glide (4)	Simplicidad (5)	
Cats Of Rio (8)	Heavenly Bodies (7)	Malibu (6)	Operator (Thief On The Line)	Space Glide (1)	
Cross My Heart (6) 69	Humana (9)	Mandela (7)	(7)	Sugarloaf Express (2)	
Dolphin Dreams (1)	I'm Not Responsible (7)	Margarita (1)	Other Love (7)	Sun Song (1)	
Dreamwalk (4)	Inner Look (9)	Market Place (3)	Promises, Promises (6)	Sunset Drivers (7)	
Dreamwalkin' (Along With	Japanica Sol (5)	Matchmakers (2)	Rainbow (5)	That's Enough For Me (2)	
Me) (6)	Is It You (4) 15	Midnight Lady (3)	Rio Funk (5)	Tied Up (4)	
Early A.M. Attitude (8)	Isn't She Lovely (1)	Morning Glory (2)	Rio Sol (9)	Uh Oh! (3)	
Etude (2)	It Happens Everyday (5)	Mr. Briefcase (4)	Rit Variations II (7)	Voices (6)	
Fantasy, A (6)	(Just) Tell Me Pretty Lies (4)	New York/Brazil (9)	Road Runner (6)	What Do You Want? (2)	

RIVERS, Joan

Born on 6/8/33 in New York City. Popular comedienne. Guest host for Johnny Carson, 1983-86; host of *The Late Show*, 1986-87. Currently hosts own TV talk show. Directed the 1978 film *Rabbit Test*.

| 4/23/83 | **22** | 21 | | What Becomes A Semi-Legend Most? .... [C] | **$8** | Geffen 4007 |

Anchors Aweigh	Being Married	Great Movie Star	Men She Dated	Nurses And Stewardesses
Battle Hymn Of The Republic	Childbirth	Heidi Abromowitz	Men Vs. Women	Rock Stars
Before And After Marriage	Drugs	How God Divides	National Enquirer And	Royal Family
Being A Bridesmaid	Going To The Gynecologist	Living In New York	U.F.O. Sightings	

★★159★★ RIVERS, Johnny

Born John Ramistella on 11/7/42 in New York City; raised in Baton Rouge. Rock and roll singer/guitarist/songwriter/producer. Recorded with the Spades for Suede in 1956. Named Johnny Rivers by DJ Alan Freed in 1958. To Los Angeles in 1961. Began own Soul City label in 1966. Recorded Christian music in the early 1980s.

6/20/64	**12**	45		1 Johnny Rivers At The Whisky a Go Go .... [L]	**$20**	Imperial 12264
10/17/64	**38**	23		2 Here We a Go Go Again! .... [L]	**$20**	Imperial 12274
2/20/65	**42**	14		3 Johnny Rivers In Action! .... [L]	**$20**	Imperial 12280
6/26/65	**21**	19		4 Meanwhile Back At The Whisky a Go Go .... [L]	**$20**	Imperial 12284
9/25/65	**91**	18		5 Johnny Rivers Rocks The Folk	**$20**	Imperial 12293
4/16/66	**52**	21		6 "...and I know you wanna dance" .... [L]	**$20**	Imperial 12307
9/24/66	**29**	36	●	7 Johnny Rivers' Golden Hits .... [G]	**$20**	Imperial 12324
12/17/66+	**33**	46		8 Changes	**$20**	Imperial 12334
6/24/67	**14**	21		9 Rewind	**$20**	Imperial 12341
6/29/68	**5**	41	●	10 Realization	**$20**	Imperial 12372
6/14/69	**26**	25	●	11 A Touch Of Gold .... [G]	**$20**	Imperial 12427
8/8/70	**100**	9		12 Slim Slo Slider	**$15**	Imperial 16001
9/11/71	**148**	4		13 Home Grown	**$12**	United Art. 5532
11/4/72+	**78**	20		14 L.A. Reggae	**$12**	United Art. 5650
9/20/75	**147**	6		15 New Lovers and Old Friends	**$10**	Epic 33681
1/14/78	**142**	8		16 Outside Help	**$8**	Big Tree 76004

Apple Tree (12)	Do You Wanna Dance? (8)	Into The Mystic (12) 51	Muddy Water ..see: (I	Seventh Son (4,7) 7	Uptight (Everything's
Ashes And Sand (16) 96	Eleventh Song (9)	It Wouldn't Happen With Me	Washed My Hands In)	Shadow Of Your Smile (8)	Alright) (6)
Baby I Need Your Lovin'	Enemies And Friends (12)	(1,7)	Multiplication (1)	Sidewalk Song (medley) (9)	Use The Power (14)
(9,11) 3	Every Day I Have To Cry (6)	It'll Never Happen Again (9)	My New Life (12)	Silver Threads And Golden	Walk Myself On Home (2)
Baby What You Want Me To	Fire And Rain (13) 94	It's All Over Now (3)	New Lovers And Old Friends	Needles (4)	Walkin' The Dog (1)
Do (2)	500 Miles (5)	It's The Same Old Song (15)	(15)	Slim Slo Slider (12)	Way We Live (10)
Better Life (11)	Flying Away With You (16)	Jailer Bring Me Water (5)	New York City Dues (14)	Snake, The (6)	What Am I Doin' Here With
Blowin' In The Wind (5)	Foolkiller (9)	Jesus Is A Soul Man (12)	Ode To John Lee (11)	So Far Away (13)	You (3)
Brass Buttons (12)	For Emily, Whenever I May	John Lee Hooker (7)	Oh Lonesome Me (1)	Softly As I Leave You (8)	What's The Difference (10)
Break Up (4)	Find Her (9)	Johnny B. Goode (2)	Oh, Pretty Woman (3)	Something Strange (10)	Where Have All The
Brother Where Are You (10)	For You (16)	Josephine (2)	On The Borderline (14)	Song For Michael (13)	Flowers Gone (5,7) 26
Brown-Eyed Girl (14)	Gettin' Ready For Tomorrow	Keep A-Knockin' (3)	One Last Dance (For The	Spare Me A Little (15)	Whisky-A-Go-Go (1)
Brown Eyed Handsome Man	(8)	Knock On Wood (14)	Melody) (16)	Stagger Lee (4)	Whiter Shade Of Pale (10)
(1)	Glory Train (12)	La Bamba (medley) (1,7)	Our Lady Of The Well (13)	Stop! In The Name Of Love	Whole Lotta Shakin' Goin'
By The Time I Get To	Going Back To Big Sur	Land Of A Thousand Dances	Outside Help (16)	(4)	On (2)
Phoenix (1)	(10,11)	(4)	Parchman Farm (4)	Stories To A Child (14)	Work Song (2)
California Dreamin' (8)	Green, Green (5)	Lawdy Miss Clawdy (1)	People Get Ready (13)	Strangers In The Night (8)	Wrote A Song For Everyone
Can I Change My Mind (15)	Greenback Dollar (4)	Life Is A Game (14)	Permanent Change (13)	Summer Rain (10,11) 14	(12)
Can't Buy Me Love (2)	He Don't Love You, Like I	Long Time Man (5)	Poor Side Of Town (8,11) 1	Susie Q (4)	You Better Move On (11,15)
Carpet Man (9)	Love You (3)	Look At The Sun (13)	Positively 4th Street (10)	Swayin' To The Music	You Can Get It If You Really
Cast Your Fate To The Wind	Help Me Rhonda (15) 22	Look To Your Soul	Postcards From Hollywood	(Slow Dancin') (16) 10	Want (15)
(8)	Hey Joe (10)	(10,11) 49	(15)	Sweet Smiling Children (9)	You Can Have Her (I Don't
Catch The Wind (5)	High Heel Sneakers (2)	Maybelline (2,7) 12	Promised Land (3)	Tall Oak Tree (5)	Want Her) (1)
City Ways (11)	I Can't Help Myself (Sugar	Memphis (1,7,14) 2	Rainy Night In Georgia (12)	Taste Of Honey (8)	You Dig (6)
Come Home America (14)	Pie Honey Bunch) (1)	Michael (Row The Boat	Respect (7)	Think His Name (13) 65	You Must Believe (6)
Crazy Mama (14)	I Should Have Known Better	Ashore) (5)	Resurrection (12)	Tom Dooley (5)	You've Lost That Lovin'
Cupid (3) 76	(1)	Midnight Special (2,7) 20	Rhythm Of The Rain (13)	Tracks Of My Tears	Feelin' (6)
Curious Mind (Um, Um,	(I Washed My Hands In)	Monkey Time (13)	Rock Me On Water (13)	(9,11) 10	
Um, Um, Um, Um) (16) 41	Muddy Water (7) 19	Moody River (3)	Rockin' Pneumonia -	Tunesmith (9)	
Dancin' In The Moonlight	I'll Cry Instead (4)	Mother And Child Reunion	Boogie Woogie Flu (14) 6	27th Street (medley) (9)	
(15)	I'm In Love Again (3)	(14)	Roll Over Beethoven (2)	Twist And Shout (medley)	
Dang Me (2)	I've Got A Woman (2)	Mountain Of Love (3,7) 9	Rosecrans Boulevard (9)	(1,7)	
Days Of Wine And Roses (8)	If I Had A Hammer (5)	Moving To The Country (13)	Rotation (16)	U.F.O. (15)	
Do What You Gotta' Do	If I Were A Carpenter (8)	Mr. Tambourine Man (5)	Run For Your Life (6)	Un-Square Dance (4)	
(9,11)	In The Midnight Hour (6)	Muddy River (12) 41	Secret Agent Man (6,7) 3		

DEBUT DATE	PEAK POS	WKS CHR	GOLD	ARTIST — Album Title	$	Label & Number

RIVIERAS, The
Teenage rock and roll band. Evolved from a South Bend, Indiana high school group known as The Playmates. Lead singer, Marty Fortson, left for Marines after recording "California Sun." Band's manager, Bill Dobslaw, was the lead singer on recordings of subsequent hits.

| 6/13/64 | 115 | 5 | | Let's Have A Party.. | $75 | U.S.A. 102 |

California Sun 5	Danny Boy	Keep A Knockin	**Let's Have A Party 99**	Oh, Boy	Twist & Shout
Church Key	H.B. Goose Step	Killer Joe	**Little Donna 93**	**Rockin' Robin 96**	When The Saints

ROACHFORD
British-based, soul-rock band: Andrew Roachford (vocals, keyboards), Hawi Gondwe (guitar), Derrick Taylor (bass) and Chris Taylor (drums).

| 5/20/89 | 109 | 12 | | Roachford... | $8 | Epic 45097 |

Cuddly Toy (Feel For Me) 25	Find Me Another Love	Kathleen	No Way	Shotgun (Crazy World We Live In)	Since
Family Man	Give It Up	Lying Again	Nobody But You		

ROAD, The
Pop-rock group led by brothers Jerry and Phil Hudson.

| 1/31/70 | 199 | 2 | | The Road... | $15 | Kama Sutra 2012 |

Dance To The Music	I Can Only Give You Everything	Love Is All	Mr. Soul	Rock & Roll Woman	She's Not There
Grass Looks Greener On The Other Side	In Love	Love-it-is	Never Gonna Give You Up	See You There	Taste Of Honey

ROB BASE & D.J. E-Z ROCK
Harlem rap duo: Robert Ginyard with DJ Rodney "Skip" Dryce.

| 10/8/88 | 31 | 81 ▲ | 1 | It Takes Two .... | $8 | Profile 1267 |
| 12/9/89+ | 50 | 26 ● | 2 | The Incredible Base .... | $8 | Profile 1285 |

ROB BASE

Ain't Nothing Like The Real Thing (1)	Crush (1)	Get Up And Have A Good Time (2)	If You Really Want To Party (2)	**Joy And Pain** (1) 58	Rumors (2)
Check This Out (1)	Don't Sleep On It (1)	Hype It Up (2)	Incredible Base (2)	Keep It Going Now (1)	Times Are Gettin' Ill (1)
Creativity (1)	Dope Mix (2)		Make It Hot (1)	Turn It Out (Go Base) (2)
	Get On The Dance Floor (1)	**It Takes Two** (1) 36		Outstanding (2)	War (1)

ROBBINS, Marty
Born Martin David Robinson on 9/26/25 in Glendale, Arizona; died of a heart attack on 12/8/82. Country singer/guitarist/songwriter. Own radio show with K-Bar Cowboys, late 1940s. Own TV show, Western Caravan, KPHO-Phoenix, 1951. First recorded for Columbia in 1952. Regular on the *Grand Ole Opry* since 1953. Own Robbins label in 1958. Raced stock cars. Films: *Road To Nashville* and *Guns Of A Stranger*.

12/28/59+	6	57 ▲	1	**Gunfighter Ballads and Trail Songs**	$20	Columbia 1349
1/9/61	21	12	2	More Gunfighter Ballads and Trail Songs	$20	Columbia 1481
11/3/62+	35	22	3	Devil Woman	$20	Columbia 1918
12/14/68	160	7	4	I Walk Alone	$15	Columbia 9725
7/19/69	194	4	5	It's A Sin	$15	Columbia 9811
5/23/70	117	16	6	My Woman, My Woman, My Wife	$12	Columbia 9978
5/8/71	143	10	7	Marty Robbins' Greatest Hits, Vol. III .... [G]	$12	Columbia 30571
9/18/71	175	6	8	Today...	$12	Columbia 30816
1/22/83	170	9	9	Biggest Hits .... [G]	$12	Columbia 38309

except for "El Paso" all hits are from 1966-81

Ain't Life A Crying Shame (3)	Hello Daily News (5)	In The Valley (1)	Master's Touch (6)	Seventeen Years (8)	Time Can't Make Me Forget (3)
Another Day Has Gone By (8)	Hundred And Sixty Acres (1)	It's A Sin (5,7)	My Greatest Memory (9)	She Thinks I Still Care (4)	Times Have Changed (5)
Begging To You (4) 74	I Can't Help It (If I'm Still In Love With You) (4)	Jenny (9)	My Happy Heart Sings (6)	She Was Young And She Was Pretty (2)	Tonight Carmen (7)
Big Iron (1) 26		Jolie Girl (8)	My Love (2)		Too Many Places (8)
Billy The Kid (1)	I Can't Say Goodbye (5)	Kinda Halfway Feel (3)	**My Woman My Woman, My Wife** (6,7) 42	Song Of The Bandit (2)	Utah Carol (1)
Can't Help Falling In Love (6)	I Feel Another Heartbreak Coming On (4)	Last Letter (4)		She's Just A Drifter (9)	Very Special Way (6)
Chair, The (8)		Late Great Lover (8)	Occasional Rose (9)	Strawberry Roan (1)	We're Getting Mighty Close (5)
Completely Out Of Love (9)	I Started Loving You Again (4)	Let Me Live In Your World (4)	Padre (7,9)	Streets Of Laredo (2)	
Cool Water (1)		Lily Of The Valley (4)	Prairie Fire (2)	Teardrops In My Heart (9)	When My Turn Comes Around (5)
Devil Woman (3,7) 16	**I Walk Alone** (4,7) 65	Little Green Valley (1)	Progressive Love (3)	Thanks, But No Thanks, Thanks To You (8)	Windows Have Pains (9)
Early Morning Sunshine (8)	I'm Beginning To Forget (3)	Little Joe The Wrangler (2)	Put A Little Rainbow In Your Pocket (8)	They'll Never Take Her Love From Me (4)	Wine Flowed Freely (3)
El Paso (1,9) 1	I'm Not Blaming You (8)	Little Rich Girl (3)	Quiet Shadows (8)	They're Hanging Me Tonight (1)	Without You To Love (6)
Five Brothers (2) 74	I've Got A Woman's Love (6)	Love Is A Hurting Thing (3)	Rainbows (3)		Worried (3)
Fresh Out Of Tears (5)	I've Got No Use For The Women (2)	Love Is Blue (7)	Ribbon Of Darkness (7,9)	This Peaceful Sod (2)	You Gave Me A Mountain (5,7,9)
Girl With Gardenias In Her Hair (7)	If I Want To (5)	Love Me Tender (6)	Ride, Cowboy Ride (2)	This Song (5)	You Say It's Over (8)
Hands You're Holding Now (3)	In The Ashes Of An Old Love Affair (3)	Maria (If I Could) (9)	Running Gun (1)	Three Little Words (6)	
		Martha Ellen Jenkins (6)	San Angelo (2)		
		Master's Call (1)			

ROBBINS, Rockie
Black vocalist born Edward W. Robbins, Jr. in Minneapolis. Inactive in music from 1981-85.

| 6/7/80 | 71 | 16 | 1 | You And Me .... | $8 | A&M 4805 |
| 9/12/81 | 147 | 6 | 2 | I Believe In Love .... | $8 | A&M 4869 |

Act Of Love (1)	For You, For Love (2)	I Believe In Love (2)	Lost In Love Again (1)	Talk To Me (2)
After Loving You (1)	Girl I'm Gonna Get Ya (1)	I Never Knew (1)	My Old Friend (2)	Time To Think (2)
For The Sake Of A Memory (1)	Give Our Love A Chance (2)	I'll Turn To You (2)	Nothing Like Love (2)	Together (1)
	Hang Tough (1)	Look Before You Leap (2)	Point Of View (1)	**You And Me** (1) 80

ROBBS, The
Rock quartet of brothers from Oconomowoc, Wisconsin: Dee (lead vocals), Craig, Joe and Bruce Donaldson. Backing band for Del Shannon in early '60s. To West Coast in late '60s, replaced Paul Revere And The Raiders as house band for TV show *Where The Action Is*. Owners of Cherokee recording studio.

| 1/13/68 | 200 | 1 | | The Robbs .... | $25 | Mercury 61130 |

Bittersweet	Girls, Girls	Jolly Miller	Race With The Wind	See Jane Run
Cynthia Loves	In A Funny Sort Of Way	Next Time You See Me	Rapid Transit	Violets Of Dawn

ROBERTINO
Robertino Loreti — 15-year-old from Italy.

| 12/1/62 | 96 | 6 | | The Young Italian Singing Sensation ....[F] | $15 | Kapp 3293 |

DEBUT DATE	PEAK POS	WKS CHR	G O L D	ARTIST — Album Title	$	Label & Number

ROBERTINO — Cont'd

Anema E Core   La Paloma   Luna Rossa   Parlami D'Amore Mariu (Tell   Serenade   Silenzio Cantatore
Buon Anno-Buona Fortuna   Lullaby   Oh! My Papa (O Mein Papa)   Me That You Love Me)   Signora Fortuna   Torna
Francesina

ROBERTSON, Robbie

Born Jaime Robbie Robertson on 7/5/44 in Toronto, Canada. Vocalist/bassist/composer/producer. Joined Ronnie Hawkins' Hawks in 1960 which evolved into The Band in 1967. Group disbanded Thanksgiving Day, 1976. Produced film soundtracks. Appeared in the film *Carny*. Wrote Joan Baez's 1971 hit "The Night They Drove Old Dixie Down."

11/14/87	38	34	●	1 Robbie Robertson	$8	Geffen 24160
				guest musicians: BoDeans, Peter Gabriel, Maria McKee (Lone Justice) and U2		
10/19/91	69	10		2 Storyville	$12	Geffen 24303
				guest musicians: David Baerwald, Bruce Hornsby, Mike Mills (REM), Aaron, Art, Cyril & Ivan Neville and Neil Young; Storyville was a notorious section of New Orleans in the 1900s		

American Roulette (1)   Day Of Reckoning (Burnin   Hell's Half Acre (1)   Shake This Town (2)   Somewhere Down The Crazy   Sweet Fire Of Love (1)
Breakin The Rules (2)   For You) (2)   Hold Back The Dawn (2)   Showdown At Big Sky (1)   River (1)   Testimony (1)
Broken Arrow (1)   Fallen Angel (1)   Night Parade (2)   Sign Of The Rainbow (2)   Sonny Got Caught In The   What About Now (2)
   Go Back To Your Woods (2)   Resurrection (2)   Soap Box Preacher (2)   Moonlight (1)

ROBINSON, Freddy

Born on 2/24/39 in Memphis. Jazz-rock guitarist. With Little Walter's Band, Howling Wolf and John Mayall.

| 9/19/70 | 133 | 7 | | The Coming Atlantis .... [I] | $12 | Pacific Jz. 20162 |

Before Six   Coming Atlantis   (I'm A) Fool For You   Oogum Boogum Song
Black Fox 56   Freddy's Sermon   Monkin' Around   Rita

★★153★★ ROBINSON, Smokey

Born William Robinson on 2/19/40 in Detroit. Formed The Miracles (then called the Matadors) at Northern High School in 1955. First recorded for End in 1958. Married Miracles' member Claudette Rogers in 1963. Left The Miracles on 1/29/72. Wrote dozens of hit songs for Motown artists. Vice President of Motown Records, 1961-1988. Inducted into the Rock and Roll Hall of Fame in 1987. Won Grammy's Living Legends Award in 1989.

7/14/73	70	19		1 Smokey	$10	Tamla 328
4/13/74	99	17		2 Pure Smokey	$10	Tamla 331
4/19/75	36	42		3 A Quiet Storm	$10	Tamla 337
3/6/76	57	15		4 Smokey's Family Robinson	$10	Tamla 341
2/19/77	47	14		5 Deep In My Soul	$8	Tamla 350
4/15/78	75	19		6 Love Breeze	$8	Tamla 359
1/20/79	165	6		7 Smokin' .... [L]	$10	Tamla 363 [2]
6/30/79+	17	47		8 Where There's Smoke...	$8	Tamla 366
3/15/80	14	21		9 Warm Thoughts	$8	Tamla 367
3/14/81	10	28	●	**10 Being With You**	$8	Tamla 375
2/20/82	33	17		11 Yes It's You Lady	$8	Tamla 6001
1/29/83	50	17		12 Touch The Sky	$8	Tamla 6030
9/3/83	124	7		13 Blame It On Love & All The Great Hits .... [G]	$8	Tamla 6064
6/30/84	141	11		14 Essar	$8	Tamla 6098
2/15/86	104	13		15 Smoke Signals	$8	Tamla 6156
3/28/87	26	58	●	16 One Heartbeat	$8	Motown 6226
3/17/90	112	11		17 Love, Smokey	$12	Motown 6268

CD includes 2 bonus tracks

Agony And The Ecstasy (3,7) *36*   All My Life's A Lie (12)   And I Don't Love You (14)   Are You Still Here (11)   As You Do (10)   Asleep On My Love (2)   **Baby Come Close** (1,7,13) *27*   **Baby That's Backatcha** (3,7) *26*   Bad Girl (medley) (7)   Be Kind To The Growing Mind (1)   Because Of You (It's The Best It's Ever Been) (15)   **Being With You** (13) *48*   **Blame It On Love** (13) *48*   Can't Fight Love (10)   Castles Made Of Sand (4)   Close Encounters Of The First Kind (14)   Coincidentally (3)   Come To Me Soon (17)   **Cruisin'** (8,13) *4*   **Daylight And Darkness** (6,7) *75*   Destiny (11)   Do Like I Do (4)   Don't Play Another Love Song (13)

Don't Wanna Be Just Physical (17)   Driving Thru Life In The Fast Lane (14)   Dynamite (12)   Easy (17)   Even Tho' (12)   Ever Had A Dream (8)   Everything You Touch (17)   Family Song (1)   Feeling You, Feeling Me (6)   Food For Thought (10)   Fulfill Your Need (5)   Get Out Of Town (4)   Get Ready (8)   Gimme What You Want (12)   Girl I'm Standing There (14)   Gone Again (12)   Gone Forever (14)   Hanging On By A Thread (15)   Happy (Love Theme From Lady Sings The Blues) (3)   Heavy On Pride (Light On Love) (9)   Here I Go Again (7)   Hold On To Your Love (15)   Holly (1)   Humming Song (Lost For Words) (5)   Hurt's On You (8)   **I Am I Am** (2) *56*

I Can't Find (14,17)   I Hear The Children Singing (10)   I Love The Nearness Of You (8)   I Second That Emotion (7)   I Want To Be Your Love (9)   I'll Try Something New (11)   I'm Loving You Softly (6)   I've Made Love To You A Thousand Times (12)   If You Wanna Make Love (Come 'Round Here) (10,13)   If You Want My Love (5)   In My Corner (5)   International Baby (11)   Into Each Rain Some Life Must Fall (9)   It's A Good Night (8)   **It's Been A Long Time (Since I Been In Love)** (5)   **It's Her Turn To Live** (2) *82*   (It's The) Same Old Love (17)   It's Time To Stop Shoppin' Around (16)   Jasmin (1)   Just A Touch Away (13)   Just Another Kiss (17)   Just Like You (13)   Just My Soul Responding (1)   Just Passing Through (2)

Just To See Her (16) *8*   Keep Me (16)   **Let Me Be The Clock** (9,13) *31*   Let's Do The Dance Of Life Together (5)   Like Nobody Can (4)   Little Girl Little Girl (14)   Love Between Me And My Kids (2)   Love Brought Us Here Tonight (16)   Love Don't Give No Reason (16)   Love Is The Light (17)   Love Letters (3)   Love 'N Life (17)   Love So Fine (6,7)   Melody Man (9)   Merry-Go-Ride (5)   Mickey's Monkey (7)   Never Can Say Goodbye (medley) (1)   Never My Love (medley) (1)   No Time To Stop Believing (15)   **Old Fashioned Love** (11) *60*   **One Heartbeat** (16) *10*   Only Game In Town (11)   Ooo Baby Baby (7)

Open (4) *81*   Photograph In My Mind (15)   **Quiet Storm** (3,7) *61*   Sad Time (8)   Share It (8)   She's Only A Baby Herself (2)   Shoe Soul (6,7)   Silent Partner In A Three-Way Love Affair (1)   Sleepless Nights (15)   So In Love (4)   Some People (Will Do Anything For Love) (15)   **Sweet Harmony** (1) *48*   Take Me Through The Night (17)   Tattoo, A (2)   Te Quiero Como Si No Hubiera Un Manana (I'mGonnaLoveYouLikeThere 'sNoTomorrow) (7)   Tears Of A Clown (7)   **Tell Me Tomorrow - Part I** (11,13) *33*   **There Will Come A Day (I'm Gonna Happen To You)** (5) *42*   Touch The Sky (12)   Tracks Of My Tears (7)   Train Of Thought (14)   Travelin' Through (9)

Trying It Again (6)   Unless You Do It Again (17)   **Virgin Man** (2) *56*   Vitamin U (5,7)   Wanna Know My Mind (1)   Wedding Song (3)   What's In Your Life For Me (9)   **What's Too Much** (16) *79*   When You Came (4)   Who's Sad (10)   Why Are You Running From My Love (14)   Why Do Happy Memories Hurt So Bad (16)   Why You Wanna See My Bad Side (7)   Will You Love Me Tomorrow? (1)   Wine, Women And Song (9)   Wishful Thinking (15)   Yes It's You Lady (11)   **You Are Forever** (10) *59*   (You Can) Depend On Me (medley) (7)   You Cannot Laugh Alone (5)   You Don't Know What It's Like (16)   You Made Me Feel Love (17)   You've Really Got A Hold On Me (7)

ROBINSON, Tom, Band

British rock band led by political/gay rights activist Robinson.

| 7/15/78 | 144 | 8 | | 1 Power In The Darkness.. | $10 | Harvest 11778 [2] |

ROBINSON, Tom, Band — Cont'd

DEBUT DATE	PEAK POS	WKS CHR	GOLD	ARTIST — Album Title	$	Label & Number
5/12/79	163	7	2	TRB Two..	$8	Harvest 11930

produced by Todd Rundgren

Ain't Gonna Take It (1)
All Right All Night (2)
Better Decide Which Side You're On (1)
Black Angel (2)
Blue Murder (2)
Bully For You (2)
Crossing Over The Road (2)
Days Of Rage (2)
Don't Take No For An Answer (1)
Glad To Be Gay (1)
Grey Cortina (1)
Hold Out (2)
I Shall Be Released (1)
I'm Alright Jack (1)
Law & Order (1)
Let My People Be (2)
Long Hot Summer (1)
Man You Never Saw (1)
Martin (1)
Power In The Darkness (1)
Right On Sister (1)
Sorry Mr. Harris (2)
Too Good To Be True (1)
2-4-6-8 Motorway (1)
Up Against The Wall (1)
Why Should I Mind (2)
Winter Of '79 (1)
You Gotta Survive (1)

ROBINSON, Vicki Sue

Born in Philadelphia in 1955. Disco vocalist. Appeared in the original Broadway productions of *Hair* and *Jesus Christ Superstar*.

DEBUT DATE	PEAK POS	WKS CHR	GOLD	ARTIST — Album Title	$	Label & Number
4/10/76	49	39	1	Never Gonna Let You Go	$8	RCA 1256
10/23/76	45	16	2	Vicki Sue Robinson	$8	RCA 1829
2/11/78	110	9	3	Half And Half	$8	RCA 2294

Act Of Mercy (1)
After All This Time (2)
Can't Find No Love (2)
Common Thief (1)
Daylight (2) *63*
Don't Try To Win Me Back Again (3)
Falling In Love (2)
Feels So Good It Must Be Wrong (3)
Freeway Song (3)
Half And Half (3)
Hold Tight (3) *67*
How About Me (3)
I Won't Let You Go (medley) (2)
Jealousy (3)
Lack Of Respect (1)
Let Me Down Easy (2)
Never Gonna Let You Go (1)
Should I Stay (medley) (2)
Something Like A Dream (2)
Trust In Me (3)
Turn The Beat Around (1) *10*
We Can Do Almost Anything (1)
We Found Each Other (3)
When You're Lovin' Me (1)
Wonderland Of Love (1)

ROBINSON, Wanda

Born on 11/18/49 in Baltimore. Black poetess.

DEBUT DATE	PEAK POS	WKS CHR	GOLD	ARTIST — Album Title	$	Label & Number
10/16/71+	186	13		Black Ivory ....[T]	$10	Perception 18

Wanda recites her poems to a musical background

Black Oriented Love Poem
Celebration
Compromise
Final Hour
First Time I Saw Loneliness
Good Things Come
Great American Passtime
Grooving
Instant Replay
John Harvey's Blues
Meeting Place
Parting Is Such
Read St. Festival
Tragedy No. 456
Trouble With Dreams
Word To The Wise

ROCHES, The

Sisters Maggie, Suzzy and Terre Roche.

DEBUT DATE	PEAK POS	WKS CHR	GOLD	ARTIST — Album Title	$	Label & Number
6/16/79	58	11	1	The Roches *	$8	Warner 3298
11/22/80	130	7	2	Nurds...	$8	Warner 3475
11/13/82	183	3	3	Keep On Doing *	$8	Warner 23735

*produced by Robert Fripp (King Crimson)

Boat Family (2)
Bobby's Song (2)
Damned Old Dog (1)
Death Of Suzzy Roche (2)
Factory Girl (1)
Hallelujah Chorus (3)
Hammond Song (1)
I Fell In Love (3)
It's Bad For Me (2)
Jerks On The Loose (medley) (3)
Keep On Doing What You Do (medley) (3)
Largest Elizabeth In The World (3)
Losing True (3)
Louis (3)
Married Men (1)
Mr. Sellack (1)
My Sick Mind (2)
Nurds (2)
On The Road To Fairfax County (2)
One Season (2)
Pretty And High (1)
Quitting Time (1)
Runs In The Family (1)
Scorpion Lament (3)
Sex Is For Children (3)
Steady With The Maestro (3)
This Feminine Position (2)
Train, The (1)
Troubles, The (1)
Want Not Want Not (3)
We (1)

ROCK, Pete, & C.L. Smooth

Producer/DJ Pete Rock and rapper C.L. Smooth are from Mt. Vernon, New York. Worked with Johnny Gill.

DEBUT DATE	PEAK POS	WKS CHR	GOLD	ARTIST — Album Title	$	Label & Number
6/27/92	43	15		Mecca & The Soul Brother	$12	Elektra 60948

Act Like You Know
Anger In The Nation
Basement, The
Can't Front On Me
For Pete's Sake
Ghettos Of The Mind
If It Ain't Rough, It Ain't Right
It's Like That
Lots Of Lovin
On And On
Return Of The Mecca
Skinz
Soul Brother #1
Straighten It Out
They Reminisce Over You (T.R.O.Y.) *58*
Wig Out

ROCK AND HYDE

Vancouver, Canada pop-rock duo: Paul Hyde (lead singer) and Bob Rock (guitar, keyboards). Both formerly with Paul Hyde & The Payolas.

DEBUT DATE	PEAK POS	WKS CHR	GOLD	ARTIST — Album Title	$	Label & Number
5/2/87	94	15		Under The Volcano	$8	Capitol 12569

Blind, The Deaf And The Lame
Dirty Water *61*
I Will
It's Always Raining
Knocking On Closed Doors
Middle Of The Night
Oh Ruby
Talk To Me
There's Always Someone Tougher
What Children Say

ROCKETS

Detroit rock band led by David Gilbert (vocals), Jim McCarty (guitar) and John Badanjek (drums).

DEBUT DATE	PEAK POS	WKS CHR	GOLD	ARTIST — Album Title	$	Label & Number
4/14/79	56	26	1	Rockets	$8	RSO 3047
2/2/80	53	15	2	No Ballads	$8	RSO 3071
8/8/81	165	5	3	Back Talk	$8	Elektra 351

American Dreams (3)
Back Talk (3)
Can't Sleep (1) *51*
Desire (2) *70*
Don't Hold On (2)
Feel Alright (1)
I Can't Get Satisfied (3)
I Want You To Love Me (2)
I'll Be Your Lover (3)
Is It True (3)
Jealous (3)
Lie To Me (3)
Lift You Up (3)
Long Long Gone (1)
Lost Forever - Left For Dreaming (1)
Love For Hire (3)
Love Me Once Again (1)
Lucille (1)
Oh Well (1) *30*
Restless (3)
Sad Songs (2)
Sally Can't Dance (2)
Shanghaied (3)
Something Ain't Right (1)
Takin' It Back (2)
Time After Time (2)
Tired Of Wearing Black (3)
Troublemaker (2)
Turn Up The Radio (1)

ROCKIN' REBELS

Buffalo DJ Tom Shannon and producer Phil Todaro (Shan-Todd label) recorded as the Hot-Toddys featuring Bill Pennell on sax, from Port Colborne, Canada, in 1959. Then in 1960 they brought in the Buffalo group, The Rebels, to record Shannon's theme song "Wild Weekend." After the song's success in 1963, they re-released the original Hot-Toddys' single as by the Rockin' Rebels.

DEBUT DATE	PEAK POS	WKS CHR	GOLD	ARTIST — Album Title	$	Label & Number
3/23/63	53	19		Wild Weekend ....[I]	$100	Swan 509

Honky Tonk
Hully Gully Rock
Ram-Bunk-Shus
Rockin' Crickets *57*
Rumble
Stripper, The
Sweet Little Sixteen
Telstar
Tequila
Whole Lotta Shakin' Goin On
Wild Rebel
Wild Weekend *8*

ROCKIN' SIDNEY

Sidney Simien, born in Lebeau, Louisiana on 4/9/38. Recorded blues and soul as Count Rockin' Sidney in the early '60s. Own Zydeco band, the Dukes.

DEBUT DATE	PEAK POS	WKS CHR	GOLD	ARTIST — Album Title	$	Label & Number
8/24/85	166	4		My Toot-Toot ....[M]	$8	Epic 40153

4 song mini-album of previously released material

Dance And Show Off
Joe Pete Is In The Bed
My Toot-Toot
My Zydeco Shoes

DEBUT DATE	PEAK POS	WKS CHR	GOLD	ARTIST — Album Title	$	Label & Number

ROCKPILE
British pop-rock quartet: Dave Edmunds, Nick Lowe, Billy Bremner, Terry Williams.

| 11/15/80 | 27 | 19 | | 1 Seconds Of Pleasure .... | $12 | Columbia 36886 |

includes a 7" EP of Edmunds and Lowe singing 4 Everly Brothers tunes

Crying In The Rain	If Sugar Was As Sweet As	Now And Always	Play That Fast Thing (One	Take A Message To Mary	When Will I Be Loved
Fool Too Long	You	Oh What A Thrill	More Time)	**Teacher Teacher 51**	Wrong Again (Let's Face It)
Heart	Knife And A Fork	Pet You And Hold You	Poor Jenny	When I Write The Book	You Ain't Nothin' But Fine

ROCKWELL
Born Kennedy Gordy on 3/15/64 in Detroit. Son of Motown chairman, Berry Gordy, Jr.

| 2/11/84 | 15 | 30 | ● | 1 Somebody's Watching Me .... | $8 | Motown 6052 |
| 2/23/85 | 120 | 9 | | 2 Captured .... | $8 | Motown 6122 |

Captured (By An Evil Mind)	Don't It Make You Cry (2)	**Obscene Phone Caller**	**Somebody's Watching Me**	Tokyo (2)
(2)	Foreign Country (2)	(1) **35**	(1) **2**	Wasting Away (1)
Change Your Ways (1)	He's A Cobra (2)	Peeping Tom (2)	T.V. Psychology (2)	We Live In A Jungle (2)
Costa Rica (2)	Knife (1)	Runaway (1)	Taxman (1)	

RODGERS, Jimmie
Born James Frederick Rodgers on 9/18/33 in Camas, Washington. Vocalist/guitarist/pianist. Formed first group while in the Air Force. Own NBC-TV variety series in 1959. Career hampered following mysterious assault on the San Diego Freeway on 12/1/67, which left him with a fractured skull. Returned to performing a year later. Starred in films *The Little Shepherd From Kingdom Come* and *Back Door To Hell.*

12/16/57	15	3		1 Jimmie Rodgers	$20	Roulette 25020
7/30/66	145	4		2 It's Over	$15	Dot 25717
1/6/68	162	4		3 Child Of Clay	$12	A&M 4130
8/30/69	183	4		4 Windmills Of Your Mind	$12	A&M 4187

Ballad Of Black Gold (1)	Hey Little Baby (1)	I'm Just A Country Boy (1)	Let's Stay Together (2)	Scarlet Ribbons (For Her	Windows Of The World (4)
Better Loved You'll Never Be	**Honeycomb** (1) **1**	If I Were The Man (3)	Little Boy Born (2)	Hair) (1)	Woman From Liberia (1)
(1)	How Do You Say Goodbye (4)	**It's Over** (2) **37**	Lonely Tears (2)	Sloop John B (2)	You Pass Me By (3)
Black Gold ..see: Ballad Of	I Believed It All (3)	**Kisses Sweeter Than Wine**	Lovers, The (3)	Suzanne (4)	
Both Sides Now (4)	I Keep Thinking (You'll	(1) **3**	Mating Call (1)	Time (2)	
Child Of Clay (3) **31**	Come Back To Me) (4)	L.A. Breakdown (And Let Me	Me About You (1)	Today (3)	
Cycles (4)	I Wanna Be Free (3)	In) (4)	Morning Means Tomorrow (2)	Try To Remember (3)	
Girl In The Wood (1)	I'll Never Fall In Love Again	La-De-Da (2)	My Love Is A Wanderer (3)	Turnaround (3)	
Good Times Are Gone (4)	(4)	Land Of Milk And Honey (2)	Preacher, The (1)	Water Boy (1)	
Grass Is Greener (2)	I'll Say Goodbye (3)	Let's Go Away (1)		Windmills Of Your Mind (4)	

RODGERS, Paul
Born in Middlesbrough, Cleveland, England on 12/17/49. Lead singer of Free (1969-73), Bad Company (1974-82), The Firm (1984-86) and The Law (since 1991).

| 11/26/83+ | 135 | 10 | | 1 Cut Loose .... | $8 | Atlantic 80121 |

| Boogie Mama | Fragile | Morning After The Night | Northwinds | Superstar Woman | Talking Guitar Blues |
| Cut Loose | Live In Peace | Before | Rising Sun | Sweet Sensation | |

RODNEY-O JOE COOLEY
Los Angeles rap trio: Rodney Oliver, Joe Cooley and "General" Jeff Page.

| 3/4/89 | 187 | 2 | | 1 Me And Joe .... | $8 | Egyptian E. 00777 |
| 3/31/90 | 128 | 9 | | 2 Three The Hard Way .... | $12 | Atlantic 82082 |

Beat Blaster (2)	Everlasting Bass (1)	Let's Have Some Fun (1)	Say It Loud (2)	We're Gonna Kick It Once (2)
Can U Back It Up (2)	Fun, Fun, Fun (2)	Me And Joe (1)	See Ya... (1)	We've Arrived (Oh! But Yes)
Cooley High (1)	Give Me The Mic (1)	Nobody Disses Me (1)	Supercuts (1)	(1)
DJ's & MC's Part II (2)	Hocus Pocus (2)	Once Again (2)	This Is For The Homies (1)	When He Plays (2)
Down Goes Another (2)	It's My Rope (1)	Party (2)	Three The Hard Way (2)	When The Beats Come In (2)

RODRIGUEZ, Johnny
Born on 12/10/51 in Sabinal, Texas. Mexican-American country singer.

| 4/7/73 | 156 | 14 | | 1 introducing Johnny Rodriguez .... | $10 | Mercury 61378 |
| 10/27/73 | 174 | 4 | | 2 All I Ever Meant To Do Was Sing .... | $10 | Mercury 686 |

All I Ever Meant To Do Was	I Wonder Where You Are	Jimmy Was A Drinkin' Kind	Love And Honor (2)	Release Me (2)	**You Always Come Back**
Love You (2)	Tonight (1)	Of Man (2)	Music City Band (2)	**Ridin' My Thumb To**	**(To Hurting Me)** (1) **86**
Answer To Your Letter (1)	I'll Just Have To Learn To	Leavin' Somethin' Left To Do	One More Chance To Be	**Mexico** (2) **70**	You Go Around (1)
Easy Come Easy Go (1)	Stay Away From You (2)	With You (1)	With You (1)	That's The Way Love Goes (2)	
Good Lord Knows I Tried (2)	Jealous Darlin' (1)	Love Ain't Such An Easy	Pass Me By (If You're Only	We Had A Good Time Trying	
I Really Don't Want To Know	Jealous Heart (1)	Thing To Find (2)	Passing Through) (1)	(1)	
(2)					

ROE, Tommy
Born on 5/9/42 in Atlanta. Pop-rock singer/guitarist/composer. Formed band The Satins at Brown High School, worked local dances in the late 1950s. Group recorded for Judd in 1960. Moved to Britain in the mid-1960s, returned in 1969.

11/10/62	110	3		1 Sheila	$40	ABC-Para. 432
11/5/66+	94	13		2 Sweet Pea ....[K]	$20	ABC-Para. 575
4/22/67	159	3		3 It's Now Winters Day	$15	ABC 594
4/12/69	25	18		4 Dizzy	$15	ABC 683
12/27/69+	21	29		5 12 In A Roe/A Collection of Tommy Roe's Greatest Hits...............[G]	$15	ABC 700
10/31/70	134	6		6 We Can Make Music	$15	ABC 714

Aggravation (3)	**Folk Singer** (2,5) **84**	**Jam Up Jelly Tight** (5) **8**	Moon Talk (3)	Stir It Up And Serve It	Think About The Good
Blue Ghost (1)	Golden Girl (3)	Kick Me Charlie (2)	Nightime (3)	(6) **50**	Things (3)
Brush A Little Sunshine	Gotta Keep Rolling Along (4)	King Of Fools (6)	No Sad Songs (6)	Stormy (4)	Traffic Jam (6)
And Love (6)	Greatest Love (6)	Leave Her (3)	**Party Girl** (2,5) **85**	**Susie Darlin'** (1) **35**	Under My Thumb (3)
Carol (5) **61**	Have Pity On Me (3)	Little Hollywood Girl (4)	**Pearl** (6) **50**	**Sweet Pea** (2,5) **8**	**We Can Make Music** (6) **49**
Cinnamon (4)	Heart Beat (1)	Long Live Love (3)	Piddle De Pat (4)	Sweet Sounds (3)	Where Were You When I
Cry On Crying Eyes (3)	**Heather Honey** (4,5) **29**	Look At Me (1)	Pleasing You Pleases Me (2)	There Will Be Better Years (1)	Needed You (2)
Dizzy (4,5) **1**	**Hooray For Hazel** (2,5) **6**	Look Out Girl (4)	Pretty Flamingo (2)	There's A Great Day A	Wild Thing (2)
Dollar's Worth Of Pennies (4)	I Found A Love (1)	Makin' Music (4)	Proud Mary (4)	Coming (1)	
Evergreen (2,5) **3**	**It's Now Winters Day**	Maybellene (3)	Raining In My Heart (4)	(They Long To Be) Close To	
Everybody (2,5) **3**	(3,5) **23**	Misty Eyes (3)	**Sheila** (1,2,5) **1**	You (6)	
Firefly (6)	**Jack And Jill** (5) **53**	Money Is My Pay (3)	**Sing Along With Me** (3) **91**		

DEBUT DATE	PEAK POS	WKS CHR	GOLD	ARTIST — Album Title	$	Label & Number

ROGER

Born Roger Troutman from Hamilton, Ohio. Leader of the family group Zapp. Worked with Sly Stone and George Clinton. Father of male singer, Lynch.

DEBUT DATE	PEAK POS	WKS CHR	GOLD	ARTIST — Album Title	$	Label & Number
10/3/81	26	25	●	1 The Many Facets Of Roger	$8	Warner 3594
6/2/84	64	14	●	2 The Saga Continues	$8	Warner 23975
11/28/87+	35	24	●	3 Unlimited!	$8	Reprise 25496

Been This Way Before (3)
Blue (A Tribute To The Blues) (1)
Break Song (2)
Bucket Of Blood (2)
Chunk Of Sugar (1)

Composition To Commemorate (May 30, 1918) (3)
Do It Roger (1)
Girl, Cut It Out (2)

I Heard It Through The Grapevine (Part 1) (1) 79
I Keep Trying (2)
I Really Want To Be Your Man (3)

I Want To Be Your Man (3) 3
If You're Serious (3)
In The Mix (2)
Maxx Axe (1)
Midnight Hour (2)

Night And Day (3)
Papa's Got A Brand New Bag (3)
Play Your Guitar, Brother Roger (2)
Private Lover (3)

So Ruff, So Tuff (1)
TC Song (2)
Tender Moments (3)
Thrill Seekers (3)

ROGERS, D.J.

DeWayne Julius Rogers — R&B vocalist/keyboardist/composer from Los Angeles.

DEBUT DATE	PEAK POS	WKS CHR	GOLD	ARTIST — Album Title	$	Label & Number
9/18/76	175	5		On The Road Again	$10	RCA 1697

Girl I Love You
Holding On To Love

Let My Life Shine (Part I & II)
Love Can Be Found

On The Road Again
One More Day

Only While It Lasts
Say You Love Me 98

Secret Lady

ROGERS, Eric, and his Orchestra

British conductor.

DEBUT DATE	PEAK POS	WKS CHR	GOLD	ARTIST — Album Title	$	Label & Number
12/4/61	37	8		1 The Percussive Twenties	[I] $15	London P. 4 44006
11/12/66	114	3		2 Vaudeville!	[L] $10	London P. 4 44083

re-creation of a vaudeville show, complete with a Master of Ceremonies

Ain't She Sweet (1)
Birth Of The Blues (1,2)
Black Bottom (1)
Charleston (1)

Chicago (1)
Coast-To-Coast Medley (2)
Fascinating Rhythm (1)
Finale Medley (2)

Hearts And Flowers (2)
Light Cavalry (2)
Me And My Shadow (1)
Minstrels Medley (2)

Mooners Medley (2)
She's Funny That Way (1)
Sing Along Medley (2)
Swan, The (2)

Tea For Two (1)
Tiger Rag (1)
Tillies From Tucson Medley

Whispering (1)
Who? (1)
Ziegfield Medley (2)

★★26★★ **ROGERS, Kenny/First Edition**

Born Kenneth Donald Rogers on 8/21/38 in Houston. With high school band the Scholars in 1958. Bass player of jazz group the Bobby Doyle Trio, recorded for Columbia. In Kirby Stone Four and The New Christy Minstrels, mid-1960s. Formed and fronted The First Edition in 1967. Original lineup included Thelma Camacho, Mike Settle, Terry Williams and Mickey Jones. All but Jones were members of the New Christy Minstrels. Group hosted own syndicated TV variety show *Rollin* in 1972. Rogers split from group in 1973. Starred in films *The Gambler, The Gambler II, Gambler III, Coward Of The County* and *Six Pack.*

THE FIRST EDITION:

DEBUT DATE	PEAK POS	WKS CHR	GOLD	ARTIST — Album Title	$	Label & Number
1/13/68	118	15		1 The First Edition	$20	Reprise 6276
3/22/69	164	4		2 The First Edition 69	$20	Reprise 6328

KENNY ROGERS & THE FIRST EDITION:

DEBUT DATE	PEAK POS	WKS CHR	GOLD	ARTIST — Album Title	$	Label & Number
10/11/69	48	18		3 Ruby, Don't Take Your Love To Town	$20	Reprise 6352
4/18/70	26	24		4 Something's Burning	$15	Reprise 6385
10/31/70	61	16		5 Tell It All Brother	$15	Reprise 6412
2/20/71	57	16	●	6 Greatest Hits	[G] $15	Reprise 6437
9/25/71	155	3		7 Transition	$15	Reprise 2039
2/5/72	118	14		8 The Ballad Of Calico	$15	Reprise 6476 [2]

inspired by the 1889 mining town of Calico, California

KENNY ROGERS:

DEBUT DATE	PEAK POS	WKS CHR	GOLD	ARTIST — Album Title	$	Label & Number
5/7/77	30	25	●	9 Kenny Rogers	$8	United Art. 689
8/20/77	39	21	●	10 Daytime Friends	$8	United Art. 754
2/4/78	33	103	▲	11 Ten Years Of Gold	[G] $8	United Art. 835
				side 1: new versions of his First Edition hits		
7/29/78	53	12	●	12 Love Or Something Like It	$8	United Art. 903
12/16/78+	12	112	▲	13 The Gambler	$8	United Art. 934
4/14/79	82	23	●	14 Classics *	$8	United Art. 946
9/29/79+	5	53	▲	15 Kenny	$8	United Art. 979
1/5/80	186	3		16 Every Time Two Fools Collide *	$8	United Art. 864

*KENNY ROGERS & DOTTIE WEST

DEBUT DATE	PEAK POS	WKS CHR	GOLD	ARTIST — Album Title	$	Label & Number
4/12/80	12	34	▲	17 Gideon	$8	United Art. 1035
10/18/80	1²	183	▲	18 Kenny Rogers' Greatest Hits	[G] $8	Liberty 1072
7/11/81	6	60	▲	19 Share Your Love	$8	Liberty 1108
				produced by Lionel Richie		
11/21/81+	34	9	▲	20 Christmas	[X] $8	Liberty 51115
7/24/82	34	24	●	21 Love Will Turn You Around	$8	Liberty 51124
12/25/82+	149	4	▲	22 Christmas	[X-R] $8	Liberty 51115
				Christmas charts: 1/'83, 3/'84, 27/'88		
3/12/83	18	27	●	23 We've Got Tonight	$8	Liberty 51143
9/24/83	6	38	▲	24 Eyes That See In The Dark	$8	RCA 4697
				produced by Barry Gibb		
11/12/83+	22	30	▲	25 Twenty Greatest Hits	[G] $8	Liberty 51152
5/5/84	85	11		26 Duets	[K] $8	Liberty 51154
				with Dottie West (8 of 10 cuts), Kim Carnes and Sheena Easton		
9/22/84	31	31	▲	27 What About Me?	$8	RCA 5043
12/8/84+	31	8	▲²	28 Once Upon A Christmas	[X] $8	RCA 5307

KENNY ROGERS & DOLLY PARTON

Christmas charts: 1/'84, 4/'85, 10/'87, 16/'88, 15/'89, 14/'90, 14/'91, 19/'92

DEBUT DATE	PEAK POS	WKS CHR	GOLD	ARTIST — Album Title	$	Label & Number
4/20/85	145	7		29 Love Is What We Make It	[E] $8	Liberty 51157
				all previously unreleased recordings		
10/19/85	51	28		30 The Heart of The Matter	$8	RCA 7023

ROGERS, Kenny/First Edition — Cont'd

DEBUT DATE	PEAK POS	WKS CHR	GOLD	ARTIST — Album Title	$	Label & Number
12/13/86+	137	15		31 They Don't Make Them Like They Used To	$8	RCA 5633
9/26/87	163	4		32 I Prefer The Moonlight	$8	RCA 6484
5/27/89	141	8	●	33 Something Inside So Strong	$8	Reprise 25792
12/16/89+	119	6	●	34 Christmas In America ....[X]	$8	Reprise 25973

Christmas charts: 12/'89, 28/'91

After All (I Live My Life) (5)
After All This Time (31)
All God's Lonely Children (7)
All I Ever Need Is You (14,26)
All My Life (23) **37**
All That I Am (1)
Always Leaving, Always Gone (3)
Am I Too Late (10)
Anyone Who Isn't Me Tonight (16,26)
Anything At All (31)
Away In A Manger (34)
Baby I'm-A Want You (16,26)
Bad Enough (23)
Beautiful Lies (16)
Best Of Me (30)
Blaze Of Glory (19) **66**
Born To Love Me (29)
Buckeroos, The (17)
Buried Treasure (24)
Buried Treasures (12)
But You Know I Love You (2,6,11) **19**
Calico Saturday Night (8)
Calico Silver (8)
Call Me Up (The Phone Is In The Cradle) (17)
Camptown Ladies (5)
Carol Of The Bells (20)
Christmas Everyday (20)
Christmas In America (34)
Christmas Is My Favorite Time Of The Year (20)
Christmas Song (28)
Christmas To Remember (28)
Christmas Without You (28)
Church Without A Name (1)
Coward Of The County (15,18,25) **3**
Crazy (27) **79**
Daytime Friends (10,11,25) **28**
Desperado (10)
Didn't We? (27)
Don't Fall In Love With A Dreamer (17,18,25,26) **4**
Don't Look In My Eyes (30)
Dorsey, The Mail-Carrying Dog (8)
Dream Dancin' (27)
Dream On (1)
Elvira (4)
Empty Handed Compadres (8)
Even A Fool Would Let Go (12)
Evening Star (24)
Every Time Two Fools Collide (16,18,26)
Eyes That See In The Dark (24) **79**
Factory, The (32)
Farther I Go (23)
Fightin' Fire With Fire (21)
First Noel (34)
Fool In Me (21)

For The Good Times (7)
Gambler, The (13,18,25) **16**
Ghost of Another Man (10)
Gideon Tanner (17)
Girl, Get A Hold Of Yourself (3)
God Rest Ye Merry Gentlemen (34)
Goin' Back To Alabama (19)
Goin' Home To The Rock (17)
Good Lady of Toronto (7)
Good Life (19)
Good Time Liberator (8)
Goodbye Marie (15)
Greatest Gift Of All (28) **81**
Green Green Grass Of Home (9)
Grey Beard (19)
Harbor For My Soul (8)
Have Yourself A Merry Little Christmas (34)
Heart Of The Matter (30)
Heart To Heart (27)
Heed The Call (5,6) **33**
(Hey Won't You Play) Another Somebody Done Somebody Wrong Song (14,26)
Highway Flyer (12)
Hold Me (24)
Homemade Lies (1)
Hoodooin' Of Miss Fannie Deberry (13)
How Long (23)
Hurry Up Love (1)
I Believe In Music (6)
I Believe In Santa Claus (28)
I Can't Believe Your Eyes (30)
I Could Be So Good For You (12)
I Don't Call Him Daddy (32)
I Don't Need You (19,25) **3**
I Don't Wanna Have To Worry (30)
I Don't Want To Know Why (27)
I Found A Reason (1)
I Get A Funny Feeling (1)
I Just Wanna Give My Love To You (2)
I Prefer The Moonlight (32)
I Want A Son (21)
I Want To Make You Smile (15)
I Was The Loser (1)
I Wasn't Man Enough (9)
I Will Always Love You (24)
I Wish That I Could Hurt That Way Again (13)
I'll Be Home For Christmas (34)
I'll Just Write My Music And Sing My Songs (10)
I'll Take Care Of You (21)
I'm Gonna Sing You A Sad Song Susie (5)

If I Could Hold On To Love (31)
If I Ever Fall In Love Again (33)
If I Knew Then What I Know Now (33)
If Wishes Were Horses (1)
If You Can Lie A Little Bit (21)
In And Out Of Your Heart (15)
Islands In The Stream (24) **1**
It Happened In The Best Of Dreams (29)
It Turns Me Inside Out (29)
It's A Crazy Afternoon (4)
It's Gonna Be Better (2)
It's Raining In My Mind (2)
Joy To The World (34)
Just Dropped In (To See What Condition My Condition Was In) (1,6,11) **5**
Just Remember You're My Sunshine (4)
Just The Thought Of Losing You (31)
Just The Way You Are (14)
Kentucky Homemade Christmas (20)
Kids (20)
King Of Oak Street (5,13)
Lady (18,25) **1**
Last Few Threads Of Love (2)
Laura (What's He Got That I Ain't Got) (9)
Lay Down Beside Me (9)
Lay It Down (7)
Let It Be Me (14)
Let Me Sing For You (10)
Let's Take The Long Way Around The World (14)
Life Is Good, Love Is Better (31)
Listen To The Music (3)
Little More Like Me (The Crucifixion) (13)
Living With You (24)
Long Arm Of The Law (18)
Love Is What We Make It (29)
Love Lifted Me (11,25) **97**
Love, Love, Love (2)
Love Or Something Like It (12,25) **32**
Love Song (21) **47**
Love The Way You Do (33)
Love The World Away (18) **14**
Love Will Turn You Around (21,25) **13**
Love Woman (5,6)
Loving Gift (18)
Lucille (9,11,18,25) **5**
Lying Again (10)
Madame De Lil And Diabolical Bill (8)

Make No Mistake, She's Mine (32)
Makes Me Wonder If I Ever Said Goodbye (19)
Making Music For Money (13)
Man Came Up From Town (8)
Marcia: 2 A.M. (1)
Maybe (33)
Maybe In The End (29)
Maybe You Should Know (21)
Me And Bobby McGee (3)
Midnight Flyer (14)
Midsummer Nights (24)
Molly (5)
Momma's Waiting (4,6,12)
Morgana Jones (13)
Morning Desire (30) **72**
Mother Country Music (9)
My Favorite Things (20)
My Washington Woman (4)
My World Begins And Ends With You (10)
New Design (3)
Night Goes On (27)
No Dreams (23)
No Good Texas Rounder (17)
Now And Forever (32)
O' Holy Night (20)
O Little Town Of Bethlehem (34)
Old Folks (15)
Old Mojave Highway (8)
Once Again She's All Alone (3)
Once Upon A Christmas (28)
One Lonely Room (8)
One Man's Woman (15)
One More Day (32)
One Night (33)
One Place In The Night (7)
Our Perfect Song (30)
People In Love (3)
Planet Texas (33)
Poem For My Little Lady (7)
Puttin' In Overtime At Home (9)
Road Agent (8)
Rock And Roll Man (10)
Rockin' Chair Theme (8)
Ruben James (3,6,11,18,25) **26**
Ruby, Don't Take Your Love To Home (2,3,6,11,18,25) **6**
Run Through Your Mind (2)
Sail Away (12)
Sally Grey's Epitaph (8)
San Francisco Mabel Joy (13)
Santiago Midnight Moonlight (15)
Sayin' Goodbye (17)
Scarlet Fever (23,25) **94**
School Teacher (8) **91**
Shadow In The Corner Of Your Mind (1)

Share Your Love With Me (19) **14**
She Believes In Me (13,18,25) **5**
She Even Woke Me Up To Say Goodbye (4)
She's A Mystery (15)
She's Ready For Someone To Love Her (32)
Shine On Ruby Mountain (5)
Silent Night (28,34)
Silver Bells (34)
Sleep Comes Easy (2)
Sleep Tight, Goodnight Man (13)
Sleigh Ride (medley) (28)
So In Love With You (19)
Somebody Help Me (17)
Somebody Took My Love (27)
Something About Your Song (12)
(Something Inside) So Strong (33)
Something's Burning (4,6,11,25) **11**
Somewhere Between Lovers And Friends (21)
Son Of Hickory Holler's Tramp (9)
Starting Again (12)
Starting Today, Starting Over (29)
Still Hold On (29)
Stranger, The (27)
Stranger In My Place (4,29)
Sunrise Overture (8)
Sunshine (3)
Sunshine Joe (4)
Sweet Little Jesus Boy (20)
Sweet Music Man (10) **44**
Take My Hand (7) **91**
Take This Heart (21)
Tell It All Brother (5,6) **17**
Tennessee Bottle (13)
That's The Way It Could Have Been (16,26)
Then I Miss You (4)
There Lies The Difference (33)
There's A Lot Of That Going Around (12)
These Chains (17)
They Don't Make Them Like They Used To (31)
This Love We Share (31)
This Woman (24) **23**
Through The Years (19,25) **13**
Ticket To Nowhere (1)
Tie Me To Your Heart Again (29)
'Til I Can Make It On My Own (14,25,26)
Till I Get It Right (9)
Time For Love (31)
Today I Started Loving You Again (1)

Together Again (14,26)
Tomb Of The Unknown Love (30)
Trigger Happy Kid (8)
Trying Just As Hard As I Can (2)
Tulsa Turnaround (7,15)
Twentieth Century Fool (29)
Twenty Years Ago (31)
Two Hearts One Love (27)
Two Little Boys (7)
Vachel Carling's Rubilator (8)
Vows Go Unbroken (Always True To You) (33)
Way It Used To Be (8)
We All Got To Help Each Other (5)
We Could Have Been The Closest Of Friends (12)
We Don't Make Love Anymore (10)
We Fell In Love Anyway (32)
We Love Each Other (16)
We're Doin' Alright (32)
We've Got Tonight (23,25,26) **6**
What About Me? (27) **15**
What Am I Gonna Do (7)
What Child Is This (34)
What I Learned From Loving You (23)
What's Wrong With Us Today (11)
When A Child Is Born (20)
When You Put Your Heart In It (33)
Where Does Rosie Go (7)
While I Play The Fiddle (9)
While The Feeling's Good (11)
White Christmas (20,28)
Why Don't We Go Somewhere and Love (9,16)
Winter Wonderland (28,34)
With Bells On (28)
Without You In My Life (19)
Write Me Down (Don't Forget My Name) (1)
You And I (24)
You And Me (16)
You Are So Beautiful (23)
You Can't Say (You Don't Love Me Anymore) (32)
You Decorated My Life (15,18,25) **7**
You Made Me Feel Love (30)
You Needed Me (1)
You Turn The Light On (15)
You Were A Good Friend (17,25)
You're My Love (31)
You've Lost That Lovin' Feelin' (14)

ROGERS, Roy

"King Of The Cowboys." Born Leonard Slye on 11/5/11 in Cincinnati. Original member of the famous western group, the Sons Of The Pioneers. Roy starred in close to 100 movie Westerns, then in a popular radio and TV series with his wife Dale Evans.

DEBUT DATE	PEAK POS	WKS CHR	GOLD	ARTIST — Album Title	$	Label & Number
11/9/91	113	9		Roy Rogers Tribute	$12	RCA 3024

Roy performs with Clint Black, K.T. Oslin, The Oak Ridge Boys, Lorrie Morgan, Restless Heart, Kentucky Headhunters, Emmylou Harris, Ricky Van Shelton, Kathy Mattea, Willie Nelson and others; includes one solo track by Dusty Rogers: "King Of The Cowboys"

Alive And Kickin'
Don't Fence Me In

Final Frontier
Happy Trails

Here's Hopin'
Hold On Partner

Little Joe The Wrangler
Rodeo Road

That's How The West Was Swung

Tumbling Tumbleweeds
When Pay Day Rolls Around

★★6★★ **ROLLING STONES, The**

British R&B-influenced rock group formed in London in January 1963. Consisted of Mick Jagger (b: 7/26/43; vocals), Keith Richards (b: 12/18/43; lead guitar), Brian Jones (b: 2/28/42; guitar), Bill Wyman (b: 10/24/36; bass) and Charlie Watts (b: 6/2/41; drums). Jagger was the lead singer of Blues, Inc. Group took name from a Muddy Waters song. Promoted as the bad boys in contrast to The Beatles. First UK tour, with Ronettes, in 1964. Jones left group shortly before drowning on 7/3/69. Replaced by Mick Taylor (b: 1/17/48). In 1975, Ron Wood (ex-Jeff Beck Group, ex-Faces) replaced Taylor. Film *Gimme Shelter* is a documentary of their controversial Altamont concert on 12/6/69 at which a concertgoer was murdered by a member of the Hell's Angels. Won Lifetime Achievement Grammy in 1986. Inducted into the Rock and Roll Hall of Fame in 1989. Wyman left band in late 1992. Considered by many as the world's all-time greatest rock band.

6/27/64	11	35	●	1 England's Newest Hit Makers/The Rolling Stones	$20	London 375
11/14/64	3	38	●	2 12 x 5	$20	London 402
3/20/65	5	53	●	3 The Rolling Stones, Now!	$20	London 420
8/7/65	1³	66	▲	4 Out Of Our Heads	$20	London 429
12/11/65+	4	33	●	5 December's Children (and everybody's)	$20	London 451
4/16/66	3	99	▲²	6 Big Hits (High Tide And Green Grass)	$25	London 1
7/9/66	2²	50	▲	7 Aftermath	$20	London 476
12/17/66+	6	48	●	8 got Live if you want it!...[L]	$20	London 493
				recorded at the Royal Albert Hall, London		
2/18/67	2⁴	47	●	9 Between The Buttons	$20	London 499
7/22/67	3	35	●	10 Flowers...[G]	$20	London 509
12/23/67+	2⁰	30	●	11 Their Satanic Majesties Request	$30	London 2
12/14/68+	5	32	▲	12 Beggars Banquet	$15	London 539
9/13/69	2²	32	▲	13 Through The Past, Darkly (Big Hits Vol. 2)...[G]	$10	London 3
12/6/69	3	44	▲²	14 Let It Bleed	$10	London 4
				Brian Jones' last appearance/Mick Taylor's first with band		
10/17/70	6	23	▲	15 'Get Yer Ya-Ya's Out!'...[L]	$10	London 5
				recorded at New York's Madison Square Garden, November 1969		
5/15/71	1⁴	62	●	16 Sticky Fingers	$10	Rolling S. 59100
1/8/72	4	243	▲⁵	17 Hot Rocks 1964-1971...[G]	$12	London 606/7 [2]
				reissued on CD on Abkco 6667 during its chart run in 1989		
6/10/72	1⁴	43	●	18 Exile On Main St.	$12	Rolling S. 2900 [2]
12/30/72+	9	29	●	19 More Hot Rocks (big hits & fazed cookies)...[G]	$12	London 626/7 [2]
9/29/73	1⁴	37	●	20 Goats Head Soup	$10	Rolling S. 59101
11/2/74	1¹	20	●	21 It's Only Rock 'N Roll	$10	Rolling S. 79101
6/21/75	6	17	●	22 Made In The Shade...[G]	$10	Rolling S. 79102
6/21/75	8	13		23 Metamorphosis...[K]	$12	Abkco 1
				collection of old and new songs		
5/8/76	1⁴	24	▲	24 Black And Blue	$10	Rolling S. 79104
				Ron Wood's first appearance with band		
10/8/77	5	17	●	25 Love You Live...[L]	$12	Rolling S. 9001 [2]
6/24/78	1²	82	▲⁴	26 Some Girls	$8	Rolling S. 39108
7/19/80	1⁷	51	▲	27 Emotional Rescue	$8	Rolling S. 16015
4/4/81	15	12	●	28 Sucking In The Seventies...[G]	$8	Rolling S. 16028
9/12/81	1⁹	58	▲³	29 Tattoo You	$8	Rolling S. 16052
6/26/82	5	23	●	30 "Still Life" (American Concert 1981)...[L]	$8	Rolling S. 39113
11/26/83	4	23	●	31 Undercover	$8	Rolling S. 90120
7/28/84	86	11		32 Rewind (1971-1984)...[G]	$8	Rolling S. 90176
				CD includes bonus track		
4/12/86	4	25	▲	33 Dirty Work	$8	Rolling S. 40250
9/9/89	91	22	▲	34 Singles Collection* The London Years...[G]	$30	Abkco 1218 [4]
				all of their singles released on the London label plus a 72-page booklet		
9/16/89	3	36	▲²	35 Steel Wheels	$8	Rolling S. 45333
4/20/91	16	17	●	36 Flashpoint...[L]	$12	Rolling S. 47456
				recorded during the 1989-90 Steel Wheels/Urban Jungle World Tour		

Ain't Too Proud To Beg (21) *17*
All About You (27)
All Down The Line (18)
All Sold Out (9)
All The Way Down (31)
Almost Hear You Sigh (35) *50*
Angie (20,22,32) *1*
Around And Around (2,25)
As Tears Go By (5,6,17,34) *6*
Back Street Girl (10)
Back To Zero (33)
Beast Of Burden (26,28,32) *8*
Before They Make Me Run (26)
Bitch (16,22)
Black Limousine (29)
Blinded By Love (35)
Blue Turns To Grey (5)
Break The Spell (35)
Brown Sugar (16,17,22,25,32,34,36) *1*
Bye Bye Johnnie (19)

Can I Get A Witness (1)
Can You Hear The Music (20)
Can't Be Seen (35,36)
Can't You Hear Me Knocking (16)
Carol (1,15)
Casino Boogie (18)
Cherry Oh Baby (24)
Child Of The Moon (19,34)
Citadel (11)
Come On (19,34)
Coming Down Again (20)
Complicated (9)
Confessin' The Blues (2)
Congratulations (2,34)
Connection (9)
Continental Drift (35,36)
Cool, Calm And Collected (9)
Country Honk (14)
Crackin' Up (29)
Crazy Mama (24,28)
Cry To Me (4)
Dance Little Sister (21,22)
Dance (Pt. 1) (27)
(also see: If I Was A Dancer)
Dancing With Mr. D. (20)

Dandelion (13,19,34) *14*
Dead Flowers (16)
Dear Doctor (12)
Dirty Work (33)
Don't Lie To Me (23)
Doncha Bother Me (7)
Doo Doo Doo Doo Doo (Heartbreaker) (20,22) *15*
Down Home Girl (3)
Down In The Hole (27)
Down The Road Apiece (3)
Downtown Suzie (23)
Each And Everyday Of The Year (23)
Emotional Rescue (27,32) *3*
Empty Heart (2)
Everybody Needs Somebody To Love (3)
Everything Is Turning To Gold (34)
Factory Girl (12,36)
Family (23)
Far Away Eyes (26)
Feel On Baby (31)
Fight (33)
Fingerprint File (21,25)

Flight 505 (7)
Fool To Cry (24,28,32) *10*
Fortune Teller (8,19)
Get Off Of My Cloud (5,6,8,17,25,34) *1*
Gimme Shelter (14,17)
Goin' Home (7)
Going To A Go-Go (30) *25*
Gomper (11)
Good Times (4)
Good Times, Bad Times (2,6,19,34)
Gotta Get Away (5,34)
Grown Up Wrong (2)
Had It With You (33)
Hand Of Fate (24)
Hang Fire (29,32) *20*
Happy (18,22,25) *22*
Harlem Shuffle (33) *5*
Have You Seen Your Mother, Baby, Standing In The Shadow? (8,10,13,19,34) *9*
Heart Of Stone (3,6,17,23,34) *19*
Hearts For Sale (35)

Heaven (29)
Hey Negrita (24)
Hide Your Love (20)
Highwire (36) *57*
Hitch Hike (4)
Hold Back (33)
Hold On To Your Hat (35)
Honest I Do (1)
Honky Tonk Women (13,15,17,25,34) *1*
Hot Stuff (24,25,28) *49*
I Am Waiting (7)
I Can't Be Satisfied (19)
(I Can't Get No) Satisfaction (4,6,8,17,30,34,36) *1*
I Don't Know Why (23,34) *42*
I Got The Blues (16)
I Just Want To Make Love To You (1,34)
I Just Want To See His Face (18)
I Wanna Be Your Man (34)
I Want To Be Loved (34)

I'd Much Rather Be With The Boys (23)
I'm A King Bee (1)
I'm All Right (4,8)
I'm Free (5,19,34)
I'm Going Down (33)
I'm Moving On (5)
I've Been Loving You Too Long (8)
If I Was A Dancer (Dance Pt 2) (28)
(also see: Dance)
If You Can't Rock Me (21,25)
If You Let Me (23)
If You Need Me (2)
If You Really Want To Be My Friend (21)
In Another Land (11,34)
Indian Girl (27)
It Must Be Hell (31)
It's All Over Now (2,6,19,34) *26*
It's Not Easy (7)
It's Only Rock 'N Roll (But I Like It) (21,22,25) *16*
Jig-Saw Puzzle (12)

ROLLING STONES, The — Cont'd

Jiving Sister Fanny (23,34)
Jumpin' Jack Flash (13,15,17,25,34,36) **3**
Just My Imagination (Running Away With Me) (26,30)
Lady Jane (7,8,10,19,34) 24
Lantern, The (11,34)
Last Time (4,6,8,19,34) **9**
Let It Bleed (14,19)
Let It Loose (18)
Let Me Go (27,30)
Let's Spend The Night Together (9,10,13,17,30,34) **55**
Lies (26)
Little By Little (1,34)
Little Queenie (15)
Little Red Rooster (3,25,34,36)
Little T & A (29)
Live With Me (14,15)
Long Long While (19,34)
Look What You've Done (5)
Love In Vain (14,15)
Loving Cup (18)
Luxury (21)
Mannish Boy (25,28)
Melody (24)
Memo From Turner (23,34)
Memory Motel (24)
Mercy Mercy (4)
Midnight Rambler (14,15,17)
Miss Amanda Jones (9)

Miss You (26,32,36) **1**
Mixed Emotions (35) **5**
Mona (I Need You Baby) (3)
Money (19)
Monkey Man (14)
Moonlight Mile (16)
Mothers Little Helper (10,13,17,34) **8**
My Girl (10)
My Obsession (9)
Neighbors (29)
19th Nervous Breakdown (6,8,17,34) **2**
No Expectations (12,19,34)
No Use In Crying (29)
Not Fade Away (1,6,8,19,34) **48**
Now I've Got A Witness (1)
Off The Hook (3,34)
Oh Baby (We Got A Good Thing Goin') (3)
On With The Show (11)
One Hit (To The Body) (33) **28**
100 Years Ago (20)
One More Try (4)
Out Of Time (10,19,23,34) **81**
Pain In My Heart (3)
Paint It, Black (7,13,17,34,36) **1**
Parachute Woman (12)
Play With Fire (4,6,17,34) **96**

Please Go Home (10)
Poison Ivy (19)
Pretty Beat Up (31)
Prodigal Son (12)
Respectable (26)
Ride On Baby (10)
Rip This Joint (18,22)
Rock And A Hard Place (35,36) **23**
Rocks Off (18)
Route 66 (1)
Ruby Tuesday (9,10,13,17,34,36) **1**
Sad Day (34)
Sad Sad Sad (35,36)
Salt Of The Earth (12)
Satisfaction ..see: (I Can't Get No)
Send It To Me (27)
Sex Drive (36)
Shake Your Hips (18)
She Said Yeah (5)
She Smiled Sweetly (9)
She Was Hot (31) **44**
She's A Rainbow (11,13,19,34) **25**
She's So Cold (27) **26**
Shine A Light (18)
Short And Curlies (21)
Silver Train (20)
Sing This All Together (11)
Sing This All Together (See What Happens) (11)

Singer Not The Song (5,34)
Sister Morphine (16)
Sittin' On A Fence (10,19)
Slave (29)
Sleep Tonight (33)
Slipping Away (35)
Some Girls (26)
Something Happened To Me Yesterday (9)
Soul Survivor (18)
Spider And The Fly (4,34)
Star Star (20,25)
Start Me Up (29,30,32,36) **2**
Stoned (34)
Stop Breaking Down (18)
Stray Cat Blues (12,15)
Street Fighting Man (12,13,15,17,34) **48**
Stupid Girl (7,34)
Summer Romance (27)
Surprise, Surprise (3,34)
Susie Q (2)
Sway (16)
Sweet Black Angel (18)
Sweet Virginia (18)
Sympathy For The Devil (12,15,17,25,34,36)
Take It Or Leave It (10)
Talkin' About You (5)
Tell Me (You're Coming Back) (1,6,19,34) **24**
Terrifying (35)
That's How Strong My Love Is (4)

Think (7)
Tie You Up (The Pain Of Love) (31)
Till The Next Goodbye (21)
Time Is On My Side (2,6,8,17,30,34) **6**
Time Waits For No One (21,28)
Too Much Blood (31)
Too Rude (33)
Too Tough (31)
Tops (29)
Torn And Frayed (18)
Try A Little Harder (23,34)
Tumbling Dice (18,22,25,32) **7**
Turd On The Run (18)
Twenty Flight Rock (30)
2120 South Michigan Avenue (2)
2,000 Light Years From Home (11,13,19,34)
2,000 Man (11)
Under Assistant West Coast Promotion Man (4,34)
Under My Thumb (7,8,17,30)
Under The Boardwalk (3)
Undercover Of The Night (31,32) **9**
Ventilator Blues (18)
Waiting On A Friend (29,32) **13**
(Walkin' Thru The) Sleepy City (23)

Walking The Dog (1)
Wanna Hold You (31)
We Love You (19,34) **50**
What A Shame (3,34)
What To Do (19)
When The Whip Comes Down (26,28)
Where The Boys Go (27)
Who's Been Sleeping Here (9)
Who's Driving Your Plane? (34)
Wild Horses (16,17,22,34) **28**
Winning Ugly (33)
Winter (20)
Worried About You (29)
Yesterday's Papers (9)
You Better Move On (5)
You Can Make It If You Try (1)
You Can't Always Get What You Want (14,17,25,34,36) **42**
You Can't Catch Me (3)
You Got The Silver (14)
You Gotta Move (16,25)

ROLLINS BAND

Henry Rollins (b: 2/13/61 in Washington, D.C.) was lead singer of hard-core punk band Black Flag from July 1981 to July 1986. Formed Rollins Band in April 1987 with guitarist Chris Haskett, bassist Andrew Weiss, drummer Sim Cain and soundman Theo Van Rock. An accomplished poet, Rollins also tours as a spoken word performer since 1983.

4/25/92	160	4		The End Of Silence	$12	Imago 21006

Almost Real
Another Life

Blues Jam
Grip

Just Like You
Low Self Opinion

Obscene
Tearing

What Do You Do
You Didn't Need

ROMAN HOLIDAY

Seven-man, jive-rock band from London — Steve Lambert, lead singer.

9/3/83	142	11		1 Roman Holliday .... [M]	$8	Jive 8086
10/22/83	116	6		2 Cookin' On The Roof	$8	Jive 8101

Beat My Time (1)
Don't Try To Stop It (1,2) **68**

Furs And High Heels (2)
I.O.U. (1,2)
Jive Dive (2)

Midnight Bus (2)
Motor Mania (1,2)

No Ball Games (2)
One More Jilt (2)

Serious Situation (2)
Stand By (1,2) **54**

ROMANTICS, The

Rock quartet from Detroit formed in 1977. Original lineup: Wally Palmar (lead singer, guitar), Mike Skill (lead guitar), Richard Cole (bass) and Jimmy Marinos (drums).

2/2/80	61	15		1 The Romantics	$8	Nemperor 36273
12/6/80	176	7		2 National Breakout	$8	Nemperor 36881
11/14/81	182	2		3 Strictly Personal	$8	Nemperor 37435
10/22/83+	14	36	●	4 In Heat	$8	Nemperor 38880
9/21/85	72	11		5 Rhythm Romance	$8	Nemperor 40106

All That I Want (3)
Be My Everything (5)
Better Make A Move (5)
Bop (3)
C'mon Girl (Work Out With Me) (3)
Can't Get Over You (3)
Diggin' On You (4)
Do Me Anyway You Wanna (4)

Don't You Put Me On Hold (3)
First In Line (1)
Forever Yours (2)
Friday At The Hideout (1)
Gimme One More Chance (1)
Girl Next Door (1)
Got Me Where You Want Me (4)
Hung On You (1)

I Can't Tell You Anything (2)
I Got It If You Want It (5)
I'm Hip (4)
In The Nighttime (3)
Keep In Touch (1)
Let's Get Started (5)
Little White Lies (1)
Look At Her (3)
Love Me To The Max (4)
Make It Last (5)

Mystified (5)
National Breakout (2)
Never Thought It Would Be Like This (5)
New Cover Story (2)
Night Like This (2)
No One Like You (3)
One In A Million (4) 37
Open Up Your Door (4)
Poison Ivy (5)

Poor Little Rich Girl (2)
Rhythm Romance (5)
Rock You Up (4)
Shake A Tail Feather (4)
She's Got Everything (1)
She's Hot (3)
Spend A Little Love On Me (3)
Stone Pony (3)
Take Me Out Of The Rain (2)

Talking In Your Sleep (4) **3**
Tell It To Carrie (1)
Test Of Time (5) **71**
Till I See You Again (1)
Tomboy (3)
21 And Over (2)
What I Like About You (1) **49**
When I Look In Your Eyes (1)
Why'd You Leave Me (3)

ROMEO'S DAUGHTER

British rock trio: Leigh Matty (vocals), Craig Joiner (guitars, vocals) and Tony Mitman (keyboards).

11/19/88	191	2		Romeo's Daughter	$8	Jive 1135

Colour You A Smile
Don't Break My Heart 73

Heaven In The Back Seat
Hymn (Look Through Golden Eyes)

I Cry Myself To Sleep At Night
I Like What I See

Inside Out
Stay With Me Tonight
Wild Child

Velvet Tongue

ROMEO VOID

San Francisco new-wave quintet formed in 1979 — Debora Iyall, lead singer.

3/6/82	147	6		1 Never Say Never .... [M]	$8	415 Records 0007

produced by Ric Ocasek (Cars)

9/4/82	119	13		2 Benefactor	$8	Columbia 38182
8/25/84	68	19		3 Instincts	$8	Columbia 39155

Billy's Birthday (3)
Chinatown (2)
Flashflood (2)

Girl In Trouble (Is A Temporary Thing) (3) **35**
Going To Neon (3)
In The Dark (1)

Instincts (3)
Just Too Easy (3)
Never Say Never (1,2)
Not Safe (1)

Orange (3)
Out On My Own (3)
Present Tense (1)
S.O.S. (2)

Say No (3)
Shake The Hands Of Time (2)
Six Days And One (3)
Undercover Kept (2)

Ventilation
Wrap It Up (2)
Your Life Is A Lie (3)

DEBUT DATE	PEAK POS	WKS CHR	GOLD	ARTIST — Album Title	$	Label & Number

RON "C"
Rapper Ron Pierre Carey. Raised in Oakland, California. Moved to Dallas at age 17. In spring of 1990, received a 20-year sentence for possession of a controlled dangerous substance with intent.

5/19/90	170	7		1 "C" Ya	$12	Profile 1284
7/25/92	183	3		2 Back On The Street	$12	Profile 1431

RON C

And I'm Ron C (2)	Dookie Booty (2)	Lock Down Tight (2)	On And On (2)	They Can't Handle It (2)
Anotha Trick (2)	Funky Lyrics (1)	MMM There It Is (1)	Pimpin' Lyrics (2)	Trendsetter (1)
Back On The Street (2)	Funky Lyrics II (2)	Mad Man (2)	Ron "C" (1)	Trendsetter Jam (2)
Capping (1)	Good To Go (1)	Make It Funky (1)	Smooth Attack (2)	We Outta Here (2)
Do Dat Danz (1)	It's On (2)	Mary Had A Pimp (2)	South Dallas Drop (1)	What's Tha Tip? (1)

RONETTES, The
New York City female vocal trio formed in 1958 as the Darling Sisters: Veronica "Ronnie" Bennett Spector, her sister Estelle Bennett Vann and cousin Nedra Talley Ross. Sang professionally since junior high school. Ronnie was married to superproducer Phil Spector from 1968-74.

12/26/64+	96	8		...presenting the fabulous Ronettes featuring Veronica	$150	Philles 4006

Baby, I Love You 24	(Best Part Of) Breakin'	Do I Love You? 34	I Wonder	Walking In The Rain 23	When I Saw You
Be My Baby 2	Up 39	How Does It Feel?	So Young	What'd I Say	You Baby
	Chapel Of Love				

RONNY & THE DAYTONAS
Nashville group specializing in hot-rod music. Ronny is John "Bucky" Wilkin (b: 4/26/46, Tulsa: vocals; son of country songwriter Marijohn Wilkin). Backed on recordings by well-known sessionmen Bobby Russell (wrote "Little Green Apples"), Chips Moman (prolific producer) and Johnny MacRae (member of Bobby "Boris" Pickett's Crypt-Kickers), among others. The touring group, which featured an entirely different lineup, later charted as The Hombres.

12/5/64	122	6		G.T.O.	$60	Mala 4001

Antique '32 Studebaker	Bucket "T" 54	G.T.O. 4	Hot Rod Baby	Little Rail Job	Little Sting Ray That Could
Dictator Coupe	California Bound 72	Hey Little Girl	Hot Rod City	Little Scrambler	Surfin' In The Summertime
Back In The U.S.A.					

RONSON, Mick
English — guitarist with David Bowie and Mott The Hoople.

4/6/74	156	5		1 Slaughter On 10th Avenue	$10	RCA 0353
2/8/75	103	9		2 Play Don't Worry	$10	RCA 0681
10/28/89+	157	20		3 Y U I ORTA	$8	Mercury 838973

IAN HUNTER/MICK RONSON
Ian on vocals with Mick on guitar

American Music (3)	Cool (3)	Hazy Days (2)	Love Me Tender (1)	Slaughter On Tenth Avenue	This Is For You (2)
Angel No. 9 (2)	Empty Bed (Io Me Ne	Hey Ma Get Papa (medley)	Music Is Lethal (1)	(1)	White Light/White Heat (2)
Beg A Little Love (3)	Andrei) (2)	I'm The One (1)	Only After Dark (1)	Sons 'N' Lovers (3)	Woman (2)
Big Time (3)	Girl Can't Help It (2)	Livin' In A Heart (3)	Play Don't Worry (2)	Sweet Dreamer (3)	Womens Intuition (3)
Billy Porter (2)	Growing Up And I'm Fine (1)	Loner (3)	Pleasure Man (medley) (1)	Tell It Like It Is (3)	

★★**44**★★ **RONSTADT, Linda**
Born on 7/15/46 in Tucson, Arizona. While in high school formed folk trio The Three Ronstadts (with sister and brother). To Los Angeles in 1964. Formed the Stone Poneys with Bobby Kimmel (guitar) and Ken Edwards (keyboards). Went solo in 1968. In 1971 formed backing band with Glenn Frey, Don Henley, Randy Meisner and Bernie Leadon (later became the Eagles). In *Pirates Of Penzance* operetta in New York City in 1980, also in film of same name in 1983.

12/2/67+	100	15		1 Evergreen, Vol. 2	$25	Capitol 2763
				THE STONE PONEYS		
10/24/70	103	10		2 Silk Purse	$12	Capitol 407
2/12/72	163	10		3 Linda Ronstadt	$12	Capitol 635
				backing by all 4 of the original Eagles		
10/20/73+	45	56	●	4 Don't Cry Now	$8	Asylum 5064
2/2/74	92	15		5 Different Drum .... [K]	$8	Capitol 11269
				5 of 10 songs are with The Stone Poneys		
12/7/74+	1¹	51	▲²	6 Heart Like A Wheel	$8	Capitol 11358
6/14/75	172	4		7 The Stone Poneys Featuring Linda Ronstadt .... [E-R]	$8	Capitol 11383
				THE STONE PONEYS Featuring Linda Ronstadt reissue of Linda's first album (released January 1967)		
10/4/75	4	28	▲	8 Prisoner In Disguise	$8	Asylum 1045
8/28/76	3	36	▲	9 Hasten Down The Wind	$8	Asylum 1072
12/18/76+	6	80	▲⁴	10 Greatest Hits .... [G]	$8	Asylum 1092
				includes her hits on Capitol		
5/21/77	46	9	●	11 A Retrospective .... [K]	$10	Capitol 11629 [2]
9/24/77	1⁵	47	▲³	12 Simple Dreams	$8	Asylum 104
10/7/78	1¹	32	▲	13 Living In The USA	$8	Asylum 155
3/15/80	3	36	▲	14 Mad Love	$8	Asylum 510
11/8/80	26	21	▲	15 Greatest Hits, Volume Two .... [G]	$8	Asylum 516
10/16/82	31	28	●	16 Get Closer	$8	Asylum 60185
10/1/83	3	81	▲²	17 What's New	$8	Asylum 60260
12/8/84+	13	26	▲	18 Lush Life	$8	Asylum 60387
10/11/86	46	27	●	19 For Sentimental Reasons	$8	Asylum 60474
10/11/86	124	17		20 'Round Midnight	$15	Asylum 60489 [3]
				deluxe set of *What's New*, *Lush Life* and *For Sentimental Reasons*; above 4 albums arranged and conducted by Nelson Riddle		
3/28/87	6	48	▲	21 Trio	$8	Warner 25491
				DOLLY PARTON, LINDA RONSTADT, EMMYLOU HARRIS		
12/12/87+	42	35	▲	22 Canciones de mi Padre .... [F]	$8	Elektra 60765
				13 traditional Mexican songs sung in Spanish; translation of Spanish title: My Father's Songs		

DEBUT DATE	PEAK POS	WKS CHR	GOLD	ARTIST — Album Title	$	Label & Number

RONSTADT, Linda — Cont'd

| 10/21/89+ | 7 | 58 | ▲² 23 | **Cry Like A Rainstorm - Howl Like The Wind** .... | $8 | Elektra 60872 |

LINDA RONSTADT featuring Aaron Neville
includes 4 duets with Aaron Neville

| 12/7/91+ | 88 | 13 | 24 | Mas Canciones .... [F] | $12 | Elektra 61239 |

translation of Spanish title: More Songs

| 10/3/92 | 193 | 1 | 25 | Frenesi .... [F] | $12 | Elektra 61383 |

with Ray Santos & His Orchestra; Frenesi is Spanish for Frenzy

Adios (23)
Alison (13)
All My Life (23) *11*
All That You Dream (13)
All The Beautiful Things (7)
Alma Adentro (25)
Am I Blue (19,20)
Are My Thoughts With You? (2)
Autumn Afternoon (1)
Back Home (7)
Back In The U.S.A. (13,15) *16*
Back On The Street Again (1)
Bewitched Bothered & Bewildered (19,20)
Bicycle Race (Soon Now) (7)
Birds (3,11)
Blowing Away (13)
Blue Bayou (12,15) *3*
But Not For Me (19,20)
Can't We Be Friends (18,20)
Carmelita (12)
Colorado (3)
Corrido De Cananea (22)
Cost Of Love (14)
Crazy (9)
Crazy Arms (3,11)
Crazy He Calls Me (17,20)
Cry Like A Rainstorm (23)
Cuando Me Querias Tu (25)
Dark End Of The Street (6)
December Dream (1)
Desperado (4,10)
Despojos (25)
Different Drum (1,5,10,11) *13*
Don't Cry Now (4)
Don't Know Much (23) *2*
Dos Arbolitos (22)
Down So Low (9)
Driftin' (1)
Easy For You To Say (16) *54*
El Camino (24)
El Crucifijo De Piedra (24)
El Gustito (24)
El Sol Que Tu Eres (22)

El Sueno (24)
El Toro Relajo (24)
En Mi Soledad (25)
Entre Abismos (25)
Evergreen Part One & Two (1)
Everybody Loves A Winner (4)
Faithless Love (6,11)
Falling In Love Again (18,20)
Farther Along (21)
Fast One (4)
Frenesi (25)
Get Closer (16) *29*
Girls Talk (14)
Give One Heart (9)
Good-bye (17,20)
Goodbye My Friend (23)
Gritenme Piedras Del Campo (24)
Guess I'll Hang My Tears Out To Dry (17,20)
Hasten Down The Wind (9)
Hay Unos Ojos (22)
He Dark The Sun (2)
Heart Like A Wheel (16)
Heat Wave (8,10) *5*
Hey Mister, That's Me Up On The Jukebox (8)
Hobo (5,11)
Hobo's Meditation (21)
How Do I Make You (14,15) *10*
Hurt So Bad (14,15) *8*
I Ain't Always Been Faithful (3)
I Believe In You (4)
I Can Almost See It (4)
I Can't Help It (If I'm Still In Love With You) (6,11)
I Can't Let Go (14,15) *31*
I Don't Stand A Ghost Of A Chance With You (17,20)
I Fall To Pieces (3,11)
I Get Along Without You Very Well (19,20)
I Keep It Hid (23)
I Knew You When (16) *37*

I Love You For Sentimental Reasons (19,20)
I Need You (23)
I Never Will Marry (12)
I Still Miss Someone (3)
I Think It's Gonna Work Out Fine (16)
I Will Always Love You (8)
I Won't Be Hangin' Round (3)
I'll Be Your Baby Tonight (5,11)
I'm A Fool To Want You (18,20)
I'm Leavin' It All Up To You (2)
I've Got A Crush On You (17,20)
I've Got To Know (1)
I've Had Enough (21)
If He's Ever Near (9)
If I Were You (7)
In My Reply (3,5)
It Doesn't Matter Anymore (6,10,11) *47*
It Never Entered My Mind (18,20)
It's So Easy (12,15) *5*
Just A Little Bit Of Rain (7,11)
Just One Look (13,15) *44*
Justine (14)
Keep Me From Blowing Away (6)
La Barca De Guaymas (22)
La Calandria (22)
La Charreada (22)
La Cigarra (22)
La Mariquita (24)
Lies (16)
Life Is Like A Mountain Railway (2)
Little Girl Blue (19,20)
Lo Siento Mi Vida (9)
Long Long Time (2,5,10,11) *25*
Long Way Around (11) *flip*
Look Out For My Love (14)
Los Laureles (22)

Lose Again (9) *76*
Louise (2,11)
Love Has No Pride (4,10) *51*
Love Is A Rose (8,10) *63*
Love Me Tender (13)
Lover Man (Oh Where Can You Be) (17,20)
Lovesick Blues (2,11)
Lush Life (18,20)
Mad Love (14)
Making Plans (21)
Many Rivers To Cross (8)
Maybe I'm Right (12)
Mean To Me (18,20)
Mental Revenge (2)
Mentira Salome (25)
Meredith (On My Mind) (7)
Mi Ranchito (24)
Mohammed's Radio (13)
Moon Is A Harsh Mistress (16)
Mr. Radio (16)
My Blue Tears (16)
My Dear Companion (21)
My Funny Valentine (19,20)
My Old Flame (18,20)
New Hard Times (1)
Nobody's (2)
Old Paint (21)
One For One (1)
Ooh Baby Baby (13,15) *7*
Orion (7)
Pain Of Loving You (21)
Palomita De Ojos Negros (24)
Party Girl (14)
Pena De Los Amores (24)
People Gonna Talk (16)
Perfidia (25)
Piel Canela (25)
Piensa En Mi (25)
Poor Poor Pitiful Me (12,15) *31*
Por Un Amor (22)
Prisoner In Disguise (8)
Quiereme Mucho (25)
Ramblin' Round (3,11)
Rescue Me (3,11)
Rivers Of Babylon (9)

Rock Me On The Water (3,5,11) *85*
Rogaciano El Huapanguero (22)
Roll Um Easy (8)
Rosewood Casket (21)
'Round Midnight (19,20)
Sail Away (4)
Shattered (23)
Siempre Hace Frio (24)
Silver Blue (8)
Silver Threads And Golden Needles (4,10,11) *67*
Simple Man, Simple Dream (12)
Skylark (18,20)
So Right, So Wrong (23)
Some Of Shelly's Blues (5,11)
Someone To Lay Down Beside Me (9,15) *42*
Someone To Watch Over Me (17,20)
Sometimes You Just Can't Win (16)
Song About The Rain (1)
Sophisticated Lady (18,20)
Sorrow Lives Here (12)
Still Within The Sound Of My Voice (23)
Stoney End (5)
Straighten Up And Fly Right (19,20)
Sweet Summer Blue And Gold (5)
Sweetest Gift (8)
Talk To Me Of Mendocino (16)
Talking In The Dark (14)
Tata Dios (24)
Tattler, The (9)
Te Quiero Dijiste (25)
Tell Him (16)
Telling Me Lies (21)
That'll Be The Day (9,10) *11*
Those Memories Of You (21)
To Know Him Is To Love Him (21)

Toys In Time (1)
Tracks Of My Tears (8,10) *25*
Train And The River (7)
Trouble Again (23)
Try Me Again (9)
Tu Solo Tu (22)
Tumbling Dice (12,15) *32*
2:10 Train (9)
Up To My Neck In High Muddy Water (5) *93*
Verdad Amarga (25)
What'll I Do (17,20)
What's New (17,20) *53*
When I Fall In Love (18,20)
When I Grow Too Old To Dream (13)
When Something Is Wrong With My Baby (23) *78*
When Will I Be Loved (6,10,11) *2*
When You Wish Upon A Star (19,20)
When Your Lover Has Gone (18,20)
White Rhythm & Blues (13)
Wild About My Lovin' (7)
Wildflowers (21)
Will You Love Me Tomorrow? (2,5,11)
Willing (6)
Y Andale (22)
You Can Close Your Eyes (6)
You Go To My Head (19,20)
You Tell Me That I'm Falling Down (8)
You Took Advantage Of Me (18,20)
You're No Good (6,10,11) *1*

ROOFTOP SINGERS, The

Folk trio from New York City: Erik Darling, Willard Svanoe and Lynne Taylor (d: 1982). Disbanded in 1967. Darling was a member of The Tarriers in 1956 and The Weavers, 1958-62. Taylor was a vocalist with Benny Goodman and Buddy Rich.

| 2/16/63 | 15 | 20 | | Walk Right In! .... | $15 | Vanguard 9123 |

Brandy Leave Me Alone
Cool Water
Ha Ha Thisaway

Ham And Eggs
Hey, Boys

Houston Special
Rained Five Days

Shoes
Somebody Came Home

Stagolee
Tom Cat 20

Walk Right In *1*
You Don't Know

ROPER, Skid — see NIXON, Mojo

ROS, Edmundo

Born on 12/7/10 in Venezuela. London-based bandleader/drummer.

5/25/59	28	2	1	Hollywood Cha Cha Cha .... [I]	$15	London 152
12/4/61	41	4	2	Bongos From The South .... [I]	$15	London P. 4 44003
9/22/62	31	6	3	Dance Again .... [I]	$15	London P. 4 44015

Around The World (1)
As Time Goes By (1)
Blue Tango (3)
Brazil (2)
Carnival Procession (La Comparsa) (1)
Cherry Pink And Apple Blossom White (3)
Cocktails For Two (3)

Colonel Bogey (3) *75*
Deep In The Heart Of Texas (2)
Dixie (medley) (2)
El Cumbanchero (2)
Fascination (1)
High Noon (1)
I Came, I Saw, I Conga'd (3)
In A Little Spanish Town (2)

It's Magic (3)
Lady Of Spain (2)
Lisbon Antigua (2)
Love Is A Many-Splendored Thing (1)
Mambo Number Five (3)
Miami Beach Rumba (3)
Moon Over Miami (2)

Moonglow and Theme From "Picnic" (1)
Moulin Rouge Theme (1)
My Old Kentucky Home (2)
Patricia (3)
Roses From The South (2)
Taboo (3)
Tammy (1)
Tea For Two (3)

3rd Man Theme (1)
Three Coins In The Fountain (1)
Tropical Merengue (3)
True Love (1)
Wedding Samba (3)
When The Moon Comes Over The Mountain (3)

When The Saints Go Marching In (medley) (2)

ROSE, Biff

Singer/songwriter/pianist.

| 2/8/69 | 75 | 14 | 1 | The Thorn In Mrs. Rose's Side .... | $12 | Tetragramm. 103 |
| 7/12/69 | 181 | 7 | 2 | Children Of Light .... | $12 | Tetragramm. 116 |

Ain't No Great Day (2)
American Waltz (2)
Angel Tension (1)
Ballad Of Cliches (2)
Buzz The Fuzz (1)

Children Of Light (2)
Color Blind Blues (2)
Communist Sympathizer (2)
Evolution (2)
Fill Your Heart (1)

Gentle People (1)
I've Got You Covered (medley) (2)
It's Happening (1)
Just Like A Man (2)

Mama's Boy (1)
Man, The (1)
Molly (1)
Paradise Almost Lost (poem) (1)

Son In Moon (2)
Spaced Out (medley) (2)
Stars, The (1)
To Baby (2)
What's Gnawing At Me (1)

DEBUT DATE	PEAK POS	WKS CHR	GOLD	ARTIST — Album Title	$	Label & Number

ROSE, David, And His Orchestra

David was born on 6/15/10 in London; died on 8/23/90 of heart disease. Moved to Chicago at an early age. Conductor/composer/arranger for numerous films. Scored many TV series, such as *The Red Skelton Show*, *Bonanza* and *Little House On The Prairie*. Married to Martha Raye (1938-41) and Judy Garland (1941-43).

6/30/62	3	50 ●		The Stripper and other fun Songs for the family ....[I]	$15	MGM 4062

Banned In Boston   Harlem Nocturne   My Heart Belongs To Daddy   Soft Lights And Sweet Music   St. James Infirmary   What Is This Thing Called
Black And Tan Fantasy   Mood Indigo   Night Train   Sophisticated Lady   **Stripper, The** *1*   Love?
Blue Prelude

ROSE GARDEN, The

West Virginia quintet: Diana Di Rose (lead singer), Johnny Noreen (lead guitar), James Groshong (guitar), William Fleming (bass, piano) and Bruce Boudin (drums).

3/16/68	176	2		The Rose Garden	$15	Atco 225

Coins Of Fun   Flower Town   Long Time   **Next Plane To London** *17*   She Belongs To Me
February Sunshine   I'm Only Second   Look What You've Done   Rider   Till Today

ROSELLI, Jimmy

Italian singer.

6/26/65	96	11	1	Life & Love Italian Style ....[F]	$12	United Art. 6429
9/11/65	145	2	2	The Great Ones!	$12	United Art. 6438
11/18/67	191	3	3	There Must Be A Way	$12	United Art. 6611
6/21/69	184	3	4	Core Spezzato ....[F]	$12	United Art. 6698

'A Tazza 'E Cafe (1)   Famme Sunna (Parlami   Just Say I Love Her   Purtatele'sti Rrose (4)   There Goes My Everything   You Make Me Feel So Young
All The Time (3)   D'Amore, Mariu) (4)   (Dicitencello Vule) (1)   Rock-A-Bye Your Baby (2)   (3)   (2)
Anema E Core (1)   Get Out Of My Heart (3)   Little Pal (2)   Senza Mamma E   **There Must Be A Way** (3) *93*   You Wanted Someone To
Anema Nera (1)   Guaglione (1)   Maria, Mari (Oh Marie) (1)   Nnamurata! (4)   There's No Tomorrow (O   Play With, I Wanted
Because You're Mine (1)   I Apologize (2)   Moments To Remember (3)   Silenzio Cantatore (4)   Sole Mio) (1)   Someone To Love (3)
Chapel In The Moonlight (3)   I Don't Want To Walk   My Mother's Eyes (2)   Somewhere Along The Way   Torna (1)
Core Spezzato (4)   Without You (3)   Na Sera 'E Maggio (1)   (2)   Vurria (1)
Cry (2)   I Surrender Dear (1)   Oh What It Seemed To Be (3)   Sweet Lorraine (2)   Walkin' My Baby Back
Dooje Stelle So' Cadute (1)   I'te Vurria Vasa! (4)   Piscatore 'E Pusilleco (1)   Te Purtavo'na Rosa (4)   Home (3)
'E Rrose Parlano (4)   Ida (2)   Prisoner Of Love (2)   That's My Desire (1)

ROSE ROYCE

Eight-member backing band formed in Los Angeles in early '70s. Backed Edwin Starr as Total Concept Unlimited in 1973. Backed The Temptations, became regular band for Undisputed Truth. Lead vocalist Gwen Dickey added, name changed to Rose Royce in 1976.

10/9/76+	14	40 ●	1	Car Wash ....[S]	$10	MCA 6000 [2]
8/27/77	9	33 ▲	2	Rose Royce II/In Full Bloom	$8	Whitfield 3074
9/9/78	28	24 ●	3	Rose Royce III/Strikes Again!	$8	Whitfield 3227
9/8/79	74	8	4	Rose Royce IV/Rainbow Connection	$8	Whitfield 3387
1/24/81	160	7	5	Golden Touch	$8	Whitfield 3512

And You Wish For Yesterday   Doin' What Comes Naturally   I Wanna Make It With You   Let Me Be The First To   Righteous Rhythm (1)   You Can't Please Everybody
(5)   (1)   (5)   Know (3)   Shine Your Light (4)   (2)
Angel In The Sky (3)   First Come, First Serve (3)   I Wonder Where You Are   Lock It Down (4)   6 O'Clock DJ (Let's Rock) (1)   You Can't Run From
Bad Mother Funker (4)   Funk Factory (2)   Tonight (4)   **Love Don't Live Here**   Sunrise (1)   Yourself (4)
Born To Love You (1)   Funkin' Around (3)   **I'm Going Down** (1) *70*   **Anymore** (1) *32*   That's What's Wrong With   You Gotta Believe (1)
Car Wash (1) *1*   Get Up Off Your Fat (3)   I'm In Love (And I Love The   Love Is In The Air (5)   Me (3)   You're A Winner (5)
Crying (1)   Golden Touch (5)   Feeling) (3)   Love, More Love (2)   Water (1)   You're My World Girl (2)
Daddy Rich (1)   Help (3)   Is It Love You're After (4)   Mid Day DJ Theme (1)   What You Waitin' For (4)   You're On My Mind (1)
Do It, Do It (3)   Help Yourself (5)   It Makes You Feel Like   **Ooh Boy** (2) *72*   Wishing On A Star (2)   Zig Zag (1)
Do Your Dance - Part 1   **I Wanna Get Next To You**   Dancin' (2)   Pazazz (4)   Would You Please Be Mine
(2) *39*   (1) *10*   Keep On Keepin' On (1)   Put Your Money Where Your   (5)
         Mouth Is (1)   Yo Yo (1)

ROSE TATTOO

Australian heavy-metal rock quintet — Angry Anderson, leader.

11/29/80	197	3		Rock 'N' Roll Outlaw	$8	Mirage 19280

Astra Wally   Butcher And Fast Eddy   One Of The Boys   Rock 'N' Roll Outlaw   T.V.
Bad Boy For Love   Nice Boys   Remedy   Stuck On You   Tramp

★★37★★ ROSS, Diana

Born Diane Earle on 3/26/44 in Detroit. In vocal group The Primettes, first recorded for LuPine in 1960. Lead singer of The Supremes from 1961-69. Went solo in late 1969. Oscar nominee for the 1972 film *Lady Sings The Blues*. Appeared in the films *Mahogany* and *The Wiz*. Own Broadway show *An Evening With Diana Ross*, 1976.

7/11/70	19	28	1	Diana Ross	$12	Motown 711
11/21/70	42	16	2	Everything Is Everything	$12	Motown 724
4/24/71	46	15	3	Diana! ....[TV]	$12	Motown 719
				includes 2 medleys by the Jackson 5: "Mama's Pearl"/"Walk On By"/"The Love You Save" and "I'll Be There"/"Feeling Alright"		
8/7/71	56	17	4	Surrender	$12	Motown 723
11/25/72+	1²	54	5	Lady Sings The Blues ....[S]	$15	Motown 758 [2]
				Diana portrayed Billie Holiday in the film; includes 2 instrumentals by Michel Legrand: "Love Theme" and "Closing Theme"; "Had You Been Around" by Michele Aller; "T'Ain't Nobody's Bizness If I Do" by Blinky Williams		
7/14/73	5	28	6	Touch Me In The Morning	$12	Motown 772
11/17/73	26	47	7	Diana & Marvin	$12	Motown 803
				DIANA ROSS & MARVIN GAYE		
12/29/73+	52	17	8	Last Time I Saw Him	$12	Motown 812
6/15/74	64	17	9	Diana Ross Live At Caesars Palace ....[L]	$10	Motown 801
3/6/76	5	32	10	Diana Ross	$10	Motown 861
8/7/76	13	23	11	Diana Ross' Greatest Hits ....[G]	$10	Motown 869
2/12/77	29	14	12	An Evening With Diana Ross ....[L]	$12	Motown 877 [2]
				recorded at the Ahmanson Theatre, Los Angeles		

ROSS, Diana — Cont'd

DEBUT DATE	PEAK POS	WKS CHR	GOLD	ARTIST — Album Title	$	Label & Number
10/8/77	18	19		13 Baby It's Me	$8	Motown 890
10/21/78	49	17		14 Ross	$8	Motown 907
6/16/79	14	37	●	15 The Boss	$8	Motown 923
6/14/80	2²	52	▲	16 Diana	$8	Motown 936
3/14/81	32	14		17 To Love Again [K]	$8	Motown 951
10/24/81	37	32	●	18 All The Great Hits [G]	$12	Motown 960 [2]
				includes medleys with The Supremes		
11/7/81	15	33	▲	19 Why Do Fools Fall In Love	$8	RCA 4153
10/23/82	27	24	●	20 Silk Electric	$8	RCA 4384
6/11/83	63	12		21 Diana Ross Anthology [G]	$15	Motown 6049 [2]
7/16/83	32	17		22 Ross	$8	RCA 4677
9/29/84	26	45	●	23 Swept Away	$8	RCA 5009
10/12/85	45	20		24 Eaten Alive	$8	RCA 5422
5/30/87	73	14		25 Red Hot Rhythm & Blues	$8	RCA 6388
6/24/89	116	6		26 Workin' Overtime	$8	Motown 6274
9/28/91	102	3		27 The Force Behind The Power	$12	Motown 6316
				CD includes bonus track		

After You (10)
Ain't No Mountain High Enough
(1,3,9,11,12,18,21) *1*
Ain't No Sad Song (2)
Ain't Nothin' But A Maybe (10)
All For One (15)
All Night Lover (13)
All Of Me (5)
All Of My Life (6)
All Of You (23) *19*
All The Befores (4)
And If You See Him (4)
Anywhere You Run To (20)
Aux Iles Hawaii (12)
Baby, I Love Your Way (21)
Baby It's Me (13)
Baby It's Love (2)
Baby Love (9,12)
Battlefield (27)
Behind Closed Doors (8)
Being Green (9)
Big Mable Murphy (9)
Blame It On The Sun (27)
Boss, The (15,18,21) *19*
Bottom Line (26)
Brown Baby (medley) (6,21)
Can't It Wait Until Tomorrow (1)
Chain Reaction (24) *95*
Change Of Heart (27)
Come In From The Rain (13)
Come Together (2)
Confide In Me (12)
Corner Of The Sky (9)
Crime Of Passion (24)
Cross My Heart (25)
Cryin' My Heart Out For You (17)
Dance: Ten, Looks: Three (12)
Dark Side Of The World (1)
Did You Read The Morning Paper? (4)
Didn't You Know (You'd Have To Cry Sometime) (4)
Dirty Looks (25)
Don't Explain (5)
Don't Give Up On Each Other (24)
Don't Knock My Love (7) *46*
Don't Rain On My Parade (3,9)

Doobedood'ndoobe, Doobedood'ndoobe, Doobedood'ndoo (2)
Eaten Alive (24) *77*
Endless Love (18,19,21) *1*
Everybody's Got 'Em (12)
Everything Is Everything (2)
Experience (24)
Fine And Mellow (5)
Fingertips (12)
Fool For Your Love (20)
Force Behind The Power (27)
Forever Young (23)
Friend To Friend (16)
Gettin' Ready For Love (13,21) *27*
Gimme A Pigfoot And A Bottle Of Beer (5)
Girls (12,22)
Give Up (16)
God Bless The Child (5,9)
Goin' Through The Motions (26)
Good Morning Heartache (5,9,11,21) *34*
Have Fun (Again) (16)
Heart (Don't Change My Mind) (27)
Heavy Weather (27)
Here I Am (12)
How About You (2)
I Ain't Been Licked (15)
I Am Me (20)
I Can't Give Back The Love I Feel For You (4)
I Cried For You (5,12)
I Hear A Symphony (9,12,18)
I Heard A Love Song (But You Never Made A Sound) (8)
(I Love) Being In Love With You (24)
I Love You (Call Me) (2,3)
I Loves Ya Porgy (9)
I Need A Little Sugar In My Bowl (12)
I Thought It Took A Little Time (But Today I Fell In Love) (10,11,17) *47*
I Want You Back (12)
I Won't Last A Day Without You (6)
I Wouldn't Change A Thing (12)

I Wouldn't Change The Man He Is (1)
I'll Settle For You (4)
I'm A Winner (4)
I'm Coming Out (16,18,21) *5*
I'm Falling In Love With You (7)
I'm In The World (15)
I'm Still Waiting (2,21) *63*
I'm Watching You (24)
If We Hold On Together (27)
Imagine (6,21)
Improvisations (12)
In Your Arms (20)
Include Me In Your Life (7)
It's Hard For Me To Say (25)
It's My House (15,18)
It's My Turn (17,18,21) *9*
It's Never Too Late (19)
It's Your House (12)
Jump In The Pot (And Let's Get Hot) (12)
Just Say, Just Say (7)
Keep An Eye (1)
Keep On (Dancin') (26)
Kiss Me Now (10)
Lady Is A Tramp (9,12)
Lady Sings The Blues (5,9,12)
Last Time I Saw Him (8,11,21) *14*
Leave A Little Room (6)
Let's Go Up (22) *77*
Lifeline (12)
Little Girl Blue (6)
Long And Winding Road (2)
Love Child (medley) (18)
Love Hangover (10,11,12,18,21) *1*
Love Is Here And Now You're Gone (medley) (18)
Love Is Here To Stay (5)
Love Lies (20)
Love Me (8)
Love On The Line (24)
Love Or Loneliness (22)
Love Story (9)
Love Twins (7)
Love Will Make It Right (22)
Love You Save (medley) (3)
Lover Man (Oh Where Can You Be?) (5)
Lovin', Livin' & Givin' (14)

Mahogany (Do You Know Where You're Going To), Theme From (10,11,12,17,18,21) *1*
Man I Love (5)
Me And My Arrow (12)
Mean To Me (5)
Mirror, Mirror (19) *8*
Missing You (23) *10*
Money (That's What I Want) (12)
More And More (24)
Muscles (20) *10*
Music In The Mirror (12)
My Baby (My Baby My Own) (6)
My Man (5,9,12)
My Mistake (Was To Love You) (7) *19*
My Old Piano (16,18)
My Place (12)
My World Is Empty Without You (9,12,18)
Never Say I Don't Love You (14)
No One Gets The Prize (15)
No One's Gonna Be A Fool Forever (8,17)
Nobody Makes Me Crazy Like You Do (23)
Now That There's You (1)
Now That You're Gone (16)
Oh Teacher (24)
Once In The Morning (15)
One Love In My Lifetime (10,11) *25*
One More Chance (17) *79*
One Shining Moment (27)
Paradise (26)
Pieces Of Ice (22) *31*
Please Mr. Postman (12)
Pledging My Love (7)
Reach Out And Touch (Somebody's Hand) (1,9,11,12,18,21) *20*
Reach Out I'll Be There (4,14,21) *29*
Reflections (12,18)
Remember Me (3,4,11,18,21) *16*
Rescue Me (23)
Same Love That Made Me Laugh (13)
Save The Children (medley) (6,21)

Say We Can (26)
Selfish One (25)
Send In The Clowns (medley) (12)
Shine (25)
Shockwaves (25)
Simple Thing Like Cry (4)
Sleepin' (8) *70*
So Close (20) *40*
Someday We'll Be Together (12,18)
Something On My Mind (1)
Sorry Doesn't Always Make It Right (14)
Sparkle (15)
Stay With Me (17)
Still In Love (20)
Stone Liberty (8)
Stop! In The Name Of Love (9,12)
Stop, Look, Listen (To Your Heart) (7)
Stormy Weather (12)
Strange Fruit (5)
Stranger In Paradise (25)
Summertime (25)
Surrender (4,21) *38*
Sweet Nothings (19)
Sweet Surrender (19)
Swept Away (23) *19*
T'Ain't Nobody's Bizness If I Do (5,9,12)
Take The Bitter With The Sweet (26)
Telephone (23)
Tell Me Again (25)
Tenderness (16,18)
That's How You Start Over (22)
Them There Eyes (5)
There Goes My Baby (25)
These Things Will Keep Me Loving You (1)
(They Long To Be) Close To You (2,3)
Think I'm In Love (19)
This House (26)
To Love Again (14,17)
Together (14)
Too Shy To Say (13,21)
Top Of The World (13)
Touch By Touch (23)
Touch Me In The Morning (6,11,12,17,18,21) *1*

Turn Around (8)
Turn Me Over (20)
Two Can Make It (19)
Up Front (22)
Upside Down (16,18,21) *1*
Waiting In The Wings (27)
We Are The Children Of The World (23)
We Need You (6)
We Stand Together (26)
What A Little Moonlight Can Do (5)
What Can One Person Do (26)
What I Did For Love (12)
What You Gave Me (14)
When Will I Come Home To You (8)
When You Tell Me That You Love Me (27)
Where Did We Go Wrong (14)
Where There Was Darkness (1)
Who (20)
Why Do Fools Fall In Love (19) *7*
Work That Body (19) *44*
Workin' Overtime (26)
You (8)
You Are Everything (7)
You Can't Hurry Love (12,18)
You Do It (22)
You Got It (13) *49*
You Keep Me Hangin' On (12,18)
You Were The One (14)
You're A Special Part Of Me (7) *12*
You're All I Need To Get By (1)
You're Gonna Love It (27)
You're Good My Child (10)
You've Changed (5)
Young Mothers (21)
Your Love Is So Good For Me (13) *48*

ROSSINGTON COLLINS BAND

Band formed by four surviving members of Lynyrd Skynyrd, featuring Gary Rossington and Allen Collins (paralyzed in a 1986 car crash). Disbanded in 1982. Gary and wife Dale Krantz-Rossington (vocals), Jay Johnson, Tim Lindsey, Ronnie Eades, Tim Sharpton and Mitch Rigel recorded as the Rossington Band in 1988. Collins died of pneumonia on 1/23/90 (age 37).

DEBUT DATE	PEAK POS	WKS CHR	GOLD	ARTIST — Album Title	$	Label & Number
7/12/80	13	29	●	1 Anytime, Anyplace, Anywhere	$8	MCA 5130
10/10/81	24	16		2 This Is The Way	$8	MCA 5207
7/16/88	140	4		3 Love Your Man	$8	MCA 42166

THE ROSSINGTON BAND

Call It Love (3)
Don't Misunderstand Me (1) *55*
Don't Stop Me Now (2)
Fancy Ideas (2)
Getaway (1)

Gonna Miss It When It's Gone (2)
Gotta Get It Straight (2)
Holdin' My Own (3)
I Don't Want To Leave You (3)

I'm Free Today (2)
Losin' Control (3)
Love Your Man (3)
Means Nothing To You (2)
Misery Loves Company (1)
Next Phone Call (2)

Nowhere To Run (3)
One Good Man (1)
Opportunity (1)
Pine Box (2)
Prime Time (1)
Rock On (3)

Say It From The Heart (3)
Seems Like Every Day (2)
Sometimes You Can Put It Out (1)
Stay With Me (3)
Tashauna (2)

Three Times As Bad (1)
Welcome Me Home (3)
Winners And Losers (1)

DEBUT DATE	PEAK POS	WKS CHR	GOLD	ARTIST — Album Title	$	Label & Number

ROTARY CONNECTION
Canadian rock-R&B sextet — Minnie Riperton, lead singer.

| 3/16/68 | 37 | 31 | | 1 Rotary Connection... | $20 | Cadet Concept 312 |
| 10/19/68 | 176 | 5 | | 2 Aladdin... | $20 | Cadet Concept 317 |

Aladdin (2)
Amen (1)
Black Noise (1)
Didn't Want To Have To Do It (1)
I Feel Sorry (2)
I Must Be There (2)
I Took A Ride (Caravan) (2)
Lady Jane (1)
Let Them Talk (2)
Life Could (2)
Like A Rolling Stone (1)
Magical World (2)
Memory Band (1)
Paper Castle (2)
Pink Noise (1)
Rapid Transit (1)
Rotary Connection (1)
Ruby Tuesday (1)
Soul Man (1)
Sursum Mentes (1)
Teach Me How To Fly (2)
Turn Me On (1)
V.I.P. (2)

ROTH, David Lee
Born on 10/10/55 in Bloomington, Indiana. Former lead singer of Van Halen.

2/23/85	15	33	▲	1 Crazy From The Heat...[M]	$8	Warner 25222
7/26/86	4	36	▲	2 Eat 'Em And Smile..	$8	Warner 25470
				also released as a Spanish version *Sonrisa Salvaje*		
2/13/88	6	27	▲	3 Skyscraper..	$8	Warner 25671
2/2/91	18	19	●	4 A Little Ain't Enough..	$12	Warner 26477

Baby's On Fire (4)
Big Trouble (2)
Bottom Line (3)
Bump And Grind (2)
California Girls (1) *3*
Coconut Grove (1)
Damn Good (3)
Dogtown Shuffle (4)
Drop In The Bucket (4)
Easy Street (1)
Elephant Gun (2)
40 Below (4)
Goin' Crazy! (2) *66*
Hammerhead Shark (4)
Hina (3)
Hot Dog And A Shake (3)
I'm Easy (2)
It's Showtime! (4)
Just A Gigolo/I Ain't Got Nobody (1) *12*
Just Like Paradise (3) *6*
Knucklebones (3)
Ladies' Nite In Buffalo? (2)
Lady Luck (4)
Last Call (4)
Lil' Ain't Enough (4)
Perfect Timing (3)
Sensible Shoes (4)
Shoot It (4)
Shyboy (2)
Skyscraper (3)
Stand Up (3) *64*
Tell The Truth (4)
That's Life (2) *85*
Tobacco Road (2)
Two Fools A Minute (3)
Yankee Rose (2) *16*

ROUGH DIAMOND
English rock quintet — David Byron (Uriah Heep), lead singer.

| 5/7/77 | 103 | 8 | | Rough Diamond... | $8 | Island 9490 |

By The Horn
End Of The Line
Hobo
Link, The
Lock & Key
Lookin' For You
Rock 'N' Roll
Scared
Seasong

ROUSSOS, Demis
Greek singer; born on 6/15/47 in Alexandria, Egypt. Formed rock band, Aphrodites Child, in France with Vangelis, 1968 to early '70s.

| 6/17/78 | 184 | 6 | | Demis Roussos.. | $8 | Mercury 3724 |

Feel Like I'll Never Feel This Way Again
Hey Friend
I Just Don't Know What To Do With Myself
I Just Live
Life In The City
L.O.V.E. Got A Hold Of Me
Loving Arms
Other Woman
That Once In A Lifetime *47*
This Song

ROUTERS, The
Rock and roll instrumental quintet led by Mike Gordon.

| 3/2/63 | 104 | 4 | | Let's Go! with The Routers ....[I] | $20 | Warner 1490 |

Bucket Seats
Grandstand Stomp
Half Time
Let's Dance
Let's Go *19*
Limbo Rock
Make It Snappy
Mashy
Mating Call
Pep Rally
Snap Happy
Sting Ray *50*

ROVERS — see IRISH ROVERS

ROWLES, John
Native of New Zealand.

| 3/20/71 | 197 | 1 | | Cheryl Moana Marie... | $12 | Kapp 3637 |

Another Tear Falls
Cheryl Moana Marie *64*
Come On Back And Get It
Heaven Here On Earth
House Is Not A Home
In The Name Of Heaven
Love I Had With You
One Room World
Salty Tears
Time For Love
What Greater Love

ROXETTE
Male/female Swedish pop-rock duo: Marie Fredriksson (vocals) and Per Gessle (songwriter).

4/22/89+	23	71	▲	1 Look Sharp!	$8	EMI 91098
4/20/91	12	56	▲	2 Joyride	$12	EMI 94435
10/24/92	117	8		3 Tourism ....[K]	$12	EMI 99929
				old and new tracks recorded live on stage or in studio or hotel rooms during their *Join The Joyride 1991-92 world tour*		

Big L. (2)
Chances (1)
Church Of Your Heart (2) *36*
Cinnamon Street (3)
Come Back (Before You Leave) (3)
Cry (1)
Dance Away (1)
Dangerous (1) *2*
(Do You Get) Excited? (2)
Dressed For Success (1) *14*
Fading Like A Flower (Every Time You Leave) (2) *2*
Fingertips (3)
Half A Woman, Half A Shadow (1)
Heart Shaped Sea (3)
Here Comes The Weekend (3)
Hotblooded (2)
How Do You Do! (3) *58*
It Must Have Been Love (3)
Joyride (2,3)
Keep Me Waiting (3)
Knockin' On Every Door (2)
Listen To Your Heart (1) *1*
Look, The (1,3) *1*
Never Is A Long Time (3)
Paint (1)
Perfect Day (2)
Physical Fascination (2)
Queen Of Rain (3)
Rain, The (3)
Shadow Of A Doubt (1)
Silver Blue (3)
Sleeping Single (1)
Small Talk (2)
So Far Away (3)
Soul Deep (2)
Spending My Time (2) *32*
Things Will Never Be The Same (2,3)
View From A Hill (1)
Watercolours In The Rain (2)

★★413★★ ROXY MUSIC
English art-rock band. Nucleus consisted of Bryan Ferry (vocals, keyboards), Phil Manzanera (guitar) and Andy Mackay (horns).

7/28/73	193	2		1 For Your Pleasure...	$20	Warner 2696
5/18/74	186	4		2 Stranded..	$10	Atco 7045
1/25/75	37	15		3 Country Life..	$10	Atco 106
11/29/75+	50	20		4 Siren...	$10	Atco 127
				model on cover is Ferry's then-girlfriend, Jerry Hall, later married to Mick Jagger		
8/7/76	81	7		5 Viva! Roxy Music..[L]	$8	Atco 139
3/31/79	23	16		6 Manifesto	$8	Atco 114
6/28/80	35	19		7 Flesh + Blood...	$8	Atco 102
6/19/82	53	27	▲	8 Avalon..	$8	Warner 23686
4/9/83	67	22		9 Musique/The High Road ....[M-L]	$8	Warner 23808
				recorded at the Apollo Theatre, Glasgow, Scotland		
1/21/84	183	6		10 The Atlantic Years 1973-1980 ....[K]	$8	Atco 90122

DEBUT DATE	PEAK POS	WKS CHR	GOLD	ARTIST — Album Title	$	Label & Number

ROXY MUSIC — Cont'd

| 8/26/89 | 100 | 11 | 11 | Street Life: 20 Great Hits ....[G] | $10 | Reprise 25857 [2] |

BRYAN FERRY/ROXY MUSIC
includes 6 of Bryan Ferry's solo hits (see Ferry for tracks) and Roxy Music hits from 1972-85

Ain't That So (6,10)
All I Want Is You (3)
Amazona (2)
Angel Eyes (6,10,11)
Avalon (8,11)
Beauty Queen (1)
Bitter-Sweet (3)
Bogus Man (1,5)
Both Ends Burning (4,5)
Can't Let Go (9)
Casanova (3)
Chance Meeting (5)
Could It Happen To Me? (4)
Cry, Cry, Cry (6)

Dance Away (6,10,11)
Do The Strand (1,5,10,11)
Editions Of You (1)
Eight Miles High (7)
End Of The Line (4)
Flesh And Blood (7)
For Your Pleasure (1)
Grey Lagoons (1)
If It Takes All Night (3)
If There Is Something (5)
In Every Dream Home A Heartache (1,5)
In The Midnight Hour (7,10,11)

India (8)
Jealous Guy (9,11)
Just Another High (4)
Just Like You (2)
Like A Hurricane (9)
Love Is The Drug (4,10,11) 30
Main Thing (8)
Manifesto (5,11)
More Than This (8,11)
Mother Of Pearl (2)
My Little Girl (6)
My Only Love (7,9,10)
Nightingale (4)

No Strange Delight (7)
Oh Yeah (7,10,11)
Out Of The Blue (3,5)
Over You (7,10,11) 80
Prairie Rose (3)
Psalm (2)
Pyjamarama (5,11)
Rain Rain Rain (7)
Really Good Time (3)
Running Wild (7)
Same Old Scene (7,11)
Sentimental Fool (4)
Serenade (2)
She Sells (4)

Song For Europe (2)
Space Between (8)
Spin Me Round (6)
Still Falls The Rain (6,10)
Street Life (2,11)
Strictly Confidential (1)
Stronger Through The Years (6)
Sunset (2)
Take A Chance With Me (8)
Tara (8)
Three And Nine (3)
Thrill Of It All (3)
To Turn You On (8)

Trash (6)
Triptych (3)
True To Life (8)
Virginia Plain (11)
While My Heart Is Still Beating (8)
Whirlwind (8)

ROYAL, Billy Joe

Born on 4/3/42 in Valdosta, Georgia; raised in Marietta, Georgia. Guitarist/pianist/drummer. Own band, the Corvettes, while in high school. First recorded in 1962. Moved to Cincinnati in 1963.

| 9/18/65 | 96 | 7 | 1 | Down In The Boondocks .... | $25 | Columbia 9203 |
| 1/3/70 | 100 | 9 | 2 | Cherry Hill Park .... | $20 | Columbia 9974 |

Ain't It The Truth (2)
Burning A Hole (2)
Cherry Hill Park (2) 15
Children (2)
Down Home Lovin' (2)

Down In The Boondocks (1) 9
Funny How Time Slips Away (2)
Heartaches And Teardrops (1)

Helping Hand (2)
I Knew You When (1) 14
I've Got To Be Somebody (1) 38
If I Had It To Do Again (2)

King Of Fools (1)
Leaning On You (1)
Mama' Song (2)
My Fondest Memories (1)
Oh, What A Night (1)

Pick Up The Pieces (2)
Pollyanna (1)
Steal Away (1)
Those Railroad Tracks In Between (1)

You Can Make Me Feel Good (2)
You Can't Manufacture Love (2)

ROYAL GUARDSMEN, The

Novelty-pop sextet from Ocala, Florida. Consisted of Barry Winslow (vocals, guitar), Chris Nunley (vocals), Tom Richards (lead guitar), Bill Balough (bass) and Billy Taylor (organ).

| 2/11/67 | 44 | 22 | 1 | Snoopy vs. The Red Baron .... | $20 | Laurie 2038 |
| 12/23/67+ | 46 | 11 | 2 | Snoopy And His Friends .... [N-X] | $20 | Laurie 2042 |

Christmas charts: 6/'67, 19/'68

| 8/31/68 | 189 | 2 | 3 | Snoopy For President .... | $25 | Laurie 2046 |

Airplane Song (My Airplane) (2) 46
Alley-Oop (1)
Baby Let's Wait (1) 35
Battle Of New Orleans (1)
Bears (1)
Biplane Evermore (3)
Bo Diddley (1)

Bonnie & Clyde (3)
Bottle Of Wine (3)
By The Time I Get To Phoenix (3)
Come On Down To My Boat (3)
Cry Like A Baby (medley) (3)
Down Behind The Lines (2)

Honey (3)
I Say Love (2) 72
It Kinda Looks Like Christmas (2)
It's Sopwith Camel Time (2)
Jolly Green Giant (1)
Letter, The (medley) (3)
Li'l Red Riding Hood (1)

Liberty Valance (1)
Peanut Butter (1)
Return Of The Red Baron (2) 15
Road Runner (1)
Simon Says (3)
Snoopy For President (3) 85

Snoopy Vs. The Red Baron (1,2) 2
So Right (To Be In Love) (2)
Story Of Snoopy's Christmas (2)
Sweetmeats Slide (1)
Yummy, Yummy, Yummy (3)

ROYAL PHILHARMONIC ORCHESTRA, The

British — Louis Clark, conductor (born in Birmingham, England; arranger for ELO). Also see Glen Campbell, Crusaders and Deep Purple.

11/14/81+	4	68 ▲	1	Hooked On Classics .... [I]	$8	RCA 4194
8/28/82	33	41 ●	2	Hooked On Classics II (Can't Stop the Classics) .... [I]	$8	RCA 4373
4/23/83	89	14	3	Hooked On Classics III (Journey Through the Classics) ...... [I]	$8	RCA 4588

Also Sprach Zarathustra (3)
Can't Stop The Classics (Part 1 & 2) (1)
Dance Of The Furies (3)
Hooked On A Can Can (1)
Hooked On A Song (1)
Hooked On America (2)

Hooked On Bach (1)
Hooked On Baroque (1)
Hooked On Classics (1) 10
Hooked On Classics Part 3 (1)
Hooked On Haydn (3)
Hooked On Marching (3)

Hooked On Mendelssohn (1)
Hooked On Mozart (1)
Hooked On Rodgers & Hammerstein (3)
Hooked On Romance (1)
Hooked On Romance (Opus 3) (3)

Hooked On Romance (Part 2) (2)
Hooked On Tchaikovsky (1)
If You Knew Sousa (2)
If You Knew Sousa (And Friends) (2)
Journey Through America (3)

Journey Through The Classics (Part 1 & 2) (3)
Journey Through The Classics (Part 2) (3)
Night At The Opera (3)
Scotland The Brave (Hookery Jiggery Jock) (3)

Symphony Of The Seas (3)
Tales Of The Vienna Waltz (2)
Viva Vivaldi (3)

ROYAL SCOTS DRAGOON GUARDS, The

The Pipes and Drums and The Military Band of Scotland's armored regiment. Led by Pipe Major Tony Crease.

| 6/24/72 | 34 | 15 | | Amazing Grace .... [I] | $8 | RCA 4744 |

Abide With Me
Amazing Grace 11
Cornet Carillon

Going Home
Jubilant

March, Strathspeys, Reels & March Medley
Marches Medley

Quick Marches Medley
Reveille
Russian Imperial Anthem

Scotland The Brave
Slow Air & Jigs Medley

Slow March & Walk Medley
Trot & Canter Medley

R*S*F (RIGHT SAID FRED) — see RIGHT SAID FRED

RTZ

Boston-based rock quintet spearheaded by Brad Delp (vocals) and Barry Goudreau (guitar), former members of the group Boston. Goudreau was also a member of Orion The Hunter. RTZ stands for Return To Zero.

| 3/7/92 | 169 | 5 | | Return To Zero .... | $12 | Giant 24422 |

All You've Got 56
Devil To Pay
Every Door Is Open

Face The Music 49
Hard Time (In The Big House)

Livin' For The Rock 'N' Roll
Rain Down On Me

Return To Zero
There's Another Side
This Is My Life

Until Your Love Comes Back Around 26

RUBBER BAND, The

Studio group assembled by producer Michael Lloyd.

| 8/2/69 | 135 | 6 | 1 | Cream Songbook .... [I] | $15 | GRT 10000 |
| 9/6/69 | 116 | 8 | 2 | Hendrix Songbook .... [I] | $15 | GRT 10007 |

All Along The Watch Tower (2)
Dance The Night Away (1)

Deserted Cities Of The Heart (1)
Fire (2)
Foxey Lady (2)

Little Miss Lover (2)
Manic Depression (2)
Purple Haze (2)
Rubber Jam (2)

Strange Brew (1)
Sunshine Of Your Love (1)
Sweet Wine (1)
Those Were The Days (1)

Toad (1)
We're Going Wrong (1)
White Room (1)
Wind Cries Mary (2)

DEBUT DATE	PEAK POS	WKS CHR	GOLD	ARTIST — Album Title	$	Label & Number

RUBICON
Bay area septet led by horn player Jerry Martini (member of Sly & The Family Stone, 1966-76). Group included Jack Blades and Brad Gillis of Night Ranger.

3/25/78	**147**	7		Rubicon	**$8**	20th Century 552

And The Moon's Out Tonight	Closely	I Want To Love You	**I'm Gonna Take Care Of**	It's All For The Show	Vanilla Gorilla
Cheatin'	Far Away		**Everything 28**	That's The Way Things Are	

RUBINSTEIN, Arthur
Born on 1/28/1887 in Lodz, Poland; died on 12/20/82. Classical pianist.

1/9/61	**117**	15	1	Rachmaninoff: Piano Concerto No. 2/ Liszt: Piano Concerto No. 1 ....[I]	**$15**	RCA 2068
2/13/61	**30**	12	2	Heart of the Piano Concerto ....[I]	**$15**	RCA 2495

favorite movements from 6 piano concertos

Beethoven: Concerto No. 3, In C Minor, Op. 37 (2)	Chopin: Concerto No. 2 In F Minor (2)	Grieg: Concerto In A Minor, Op. 16 (2)	Liszt: Concerto No. 1, In E-Flat (1,2)	Rachmaninoff: Concerto No. 2, C Minor, Op. 18 (1,2)	Saint-Saens: Concerto No. 2, In G Minor, Op. 22 (2)

RUBY AND THE ROMANTICS
Akron, Ohio R&B quintet: Ruby Nash Curtis (b: 11/12/39, New York City; lead), Ed Roberts and George Lee (tenors), Ronald Mosley (baritone) and Leroy Fann (bass; d: 1973).

5/11/63	**120**	6		Our Day Will Come	**$20**	Kapp 3323

By The Way	Heartaches	(I'm Afraid) The Masquerade Is Over	Lonely People Do Foolish Things	My Prayer
Day Dreaming	I Don't Know Why (I Just Do)			**Our Day Will Come 1**
End Of The World	I'm Sorry	Moonlight And Music		Stranger On The Shore

RUDE BOYS
Cleveland vocal quartet: Larry Marcus, Melvin Sephus, and brothers Edward Lee "Buddy" Banks and Joe'l Little III. Marcus is the cousin of B.B. King. Group discovered by Levert.

2/23/91	**68**	16		Rude Awakenings	**$12**	Atlantic 82121

CD includes 2 bonus tracks

Are You Lonely For Me	Fool For You	I Feel For You	I'm Going Thru	Pressure	**Written All Over Your Face 16**
Come On Let's Do This	Heaven	I Need You	Never Get Enough Of It		

RUDY, Ed — see BEATLES, The

RUFFIN, David
Born Davis Eli Ruffin on 1/18/41 in Meridian, Mississippi. Brother of Jimmy Ruffin. With the Dixie Nightingales gospel group. Recorded for Anna in 1960. Co-lead singer of The Temptations from 1963-68. Died of a drug overdose on 6/1/91. Also see Hall & Oates.

6/21/69	**31**	17	1	My Whole World Ended	**$15**	Motown 685
12/13/69+	**148**	7	2	Feelin' Good	**$15**	Motown 696
3/17/73	**160**	7	3	David Ruffin	**$10**	Motown 762
11/15/75+	**31**	27	4	Who I Am	**$10**	Motown 849
6/12/76	**51**	12	5	Everything's Coming Up Love	**$10**	Motown 866

6 of 8 cuts written by Van McCoy

Blood Donors Needed (Give All You Can) (3)	First Round Knock-Out (5)	I Pray Everyday You Won't Regret Loving Me (2)	It Takes All Kinds Of People To Make A World (4)	**My Whole World Ended (The Moment You Left Me)** (1) 9	Statue Of A Fool (4)
Common Man (3)	Flower Child (1)		Let's Get Into Something (5)		There Will Always Be Another Song To Sing (3)
Day In The Life, Of A Working Man (3)	Forgotten Man (2)	Go On With Your Bad Self (3)	Letter, The (2)	On And Off (5)	Until We Said Goodbye (5)
Discover Me (5)	Good Good Times (3)	**I'm So Glad I Fell For You (2) 53**	Little More Trust (3)	One More Hurt (2)	**Walk Away From Love (4) 9**
Double Cross (1)	**Heavy Love (4) 47**	I've Got Nothing But Time (4)	Love Can Be Hazardous To Your Health (4)	Pieces Of A Man (1)	We'll Have A Good Thing Going On (1)
Everlasting Love (1)	I Could Never Be President (2)	I've Got To Find Myself A Brand New Baby (1)	Loving You (Is Hurting Me) (2)	Put A Little Love In Your Heart (2)	What You Gave Me (2)
Everything's Coming Up Love (5) 49	I Don't Know Why I Love You (2)	**I've Lost Everything I've Ever Loved (1) 58**	Message From Maria (1)	Ready, Willing And Able (5)	Who I Am (4)
Feeling Alright (2)	I Let Love Slip Away (2)	(If Loving You Is Wrong) I	My Love Is Growing Stronger (1)	Rovin' Kind (3)	Wild Honey (4)
Finger Pointers (4)	I Miss You (Part 1) (3)	Don't Want To Be Right (3)		Somebody Stole My Dream (1)	World Of Darkness (1)

RUFFIN, Jimmy
Born on 5/7/39 in Collinsville, Mississippi. Brother of David Ruffin. Backup work at Motown in the early '60s. First recorded for Miracle in 1961.

5/13/67	**133**	11	1	Top Ten	**$15**	Soul 704
4/19/69	**196**	2	2	Ruff'N Ready	**$15**	Soul 708
5/31/80	**152**	6	3	Sunrise	**$8**	RSO 3078

As Long As There Is L-O-V-E Love (1)	**Don't You Miss Me A Little Bit Baby (2) 68**	Gonna Keep On Tryin' Till I Win Your Love (2)	**I've Passed This Way Before (1) 17**	Night Of Love (3)	Two People (3)
Black Is Black (1)	Everybody Needs Love (2)	Halfway To Paradise (1)	It's Wonderful (To Be Loved By You) (2)	96 Tears (2)	**What Becomes Of The Brokenhearted (1) 7**
Bless You (1)	Farewell Is A Lonely Sound (2)	**Hold On To My Love (3) 10**		Sad And Lonesome Feeling (2)	Where Do I Go (3)
Changin' Me (3)	Forever (3)	How Can I Say I'm Sorry (1)	Jealousy (3)	Searchin' (3)	World So Wide, Nowhere To Hide (From Your Heart) (1)
Don't Let Him Take Your Love From Me (2)	**Gonna Give Her All The Love I've Got (1) 29**	I Want Her Love (1)	Lonely Lonely Man Am I (2)	Since I've Lost You (1)	You Got What It Takes (2)
		I'll Say Forever My Love (2) 77	Love Gives, Love Takes Away (2)	Songbird (3)	
				Tomorrow's Tears (1)	

RUFFIN BROTHERS, The
Jimmy and David Ruffin (d: 6/1/91 of drug overdose at age 50).

11/7/70	**178**	3		I Am My Brother's Keeper	**$12**	Soul 728

Didn't I (Blow Your Mind This Time)	He Ain't Heavy, He's My Brother	**Stand By Me 61**	True Love Can Be Beautiful	When My Love Hand Comes Down
Got To See If I Can't Get Mommy (To Come Back Home)	Lo And Behold	Steppin' On A Dream	Turn Back The Hands Of Time	Your Love Was Worth Waiting For
	Set 'Em Up (Move In For The Thrill)	Things We Have To Do		

RUFFNER, Mason
Rock singer/songwriter/guitarist from Fort Worth, Texas. Formed own band, The Blues Rockers, in New Orleans in 1979.

6/13/87	**80**	16		Gypsy Blood	**$8**	CBS Assoc. 40601

produced by Dave Edmunds

Ain't Gonna Get It	Courage	Distant Thunder	Gypsy Blood	Runnin'
Baby, I Don't Care No More	Dancin' On Top Of The World	Fightin' Back	Red Hot Lover	Under Your Spell

DEBUT DATE	PEAK POS	WKS CHR	GOLD	ARTIST — Album Title	$	Label & Number

★★271★★ RUFUS Featuring Chaka Khan

Soul group from Chicago. First known as Smoke, then Ask Rufus. Varying membership included Chaka Khan (vocals), Tony Maiden (guitar), Nate Morgan, Kevin Murphy (keyboards), Bobby Watson (bass), Andre Fischer (drums; ex-American Breed; later married to Natalie Cole) and Moon Calhoun. Khan has been recording solo and with Rufus since 1978. After 1978, Maiden and David Wolinski also sang lead.

DEBUT DATE	PEAK POS	WKS CHR	GOLD	#	Album Title	$	Label & Number
8/4/73	175	6		1	Rufus *	$10	ABC 783
6/29/74	4	30	●	2	Rags To Rufus *	$10	ABC 809
1/4/75	7	24	●	3	Rufusized	$8	ABC 837
12/6/75+	7	32	●	4	Rufus featuring Chaka Khan	$8	ABC 909
2/5/77	12	25	▲	5	Ask Rufus	$8	ABC 975
2/11/78	14	26	●	6	Street Player	$8	ABC 1049
2/10/79	81	9		7	Numbers *	$8	ABC 1098
11/17/79	14	26	●	8	Masterjam	$8	MCA 5103
3/28/81	73	11		9	Party 'Til You're Broke *	$8	MCA 5159

*RUFUS

| 10/31/81 | 98 | 14 | | 10 | Camouflage | $8 | MCA 5270 |
| 9/3/83 | 50 | 33 | | 11 | Live-Stompin' At The Savoy | [L] | $10 | Warner 23679 [2] |

recorded at the Savoy Theatre, New York (February 1982); side 4: newly-recorded studio cuts

A-Flat Fry (medley) (5)
Afterwards (9)
Ain't Nobody (11) 22
Ain't Nobody Like You (7)
Ain't Nothin' But A Maybe (2)
Any Love (8)
Are We? (7)
At Midnight (My Love Will Lift You Up) (5,11) 30
Best Of Your Heart (6)
Bet My Dreams (7)
Better Days (5)
Better Together (10)
Blue Love (6)
Body Heat (8)
Can I Show You (9)
Change Your Ways (6)
Circles (4)
Close The Door (5)
Dance Wit Me (4,11) 39
Dancin' Mood (7)

Destiny (6)
Do You Love What You Feel (8,11) 30
Don't Go To Strangers (11)
Don't You Sit Alone (7)
Earth Song (5)
Egyptian Song (6)
Everlasting Love (5)
Everybody Has An Aura (4)
Feel Good (1)
Fool's Paradise (4)
Half Moon (3)
Haulin' Coal (1)
Have A Good Time (8)
Heaven Bound (8)
Highlight (10)
Hold On To A Friend (9)
Hollywood (5) 32
I Finally Found You (1)
I Got The Right Street (But The Wrong Direction) (2)

I'm A Woman (I'm A Backbone) (3,11)
I'm Dancing For Your Love (8)
In Love We Grow (2)
Jigsaw (10)
Jive Talkin' (4)
Keep It Coming (1)
Keep It Together (Declaration Of Love) (7)
Life In The City (7)
Lilah (10)
Little Boy Blue (4)
Live In Me (8)
Look Through My Eyes (2)
Loser In Love (10)
Love Is Taking Over (9)
Love The One You're With (medley) (1)
Magic In Your Eyes (5)
Masterjam (8)
Maybe Your Baby (1)

Music Man (The D.J. Song) (10)
On Time (4)
Once You Get Started (3,11) 10
One Million Kisses (11)
Ooh I Like Your Loving (4)
Pack'd My Bags (3,11)
Party 'Til You're Broke (9)
Please Pardon Me (You Remind Me Of A Friend) (3) 48
Pleasure Dome (7)
Quandary (11)
Rags To Rufus (2)
Red Hot Poker (7)
Right Is Right (3)
Rufusized (3)
Satisfied (3)
Secret Friend (10)
Secret Love (9)
Sharing The Love (10) 91

Sideways (2)
Sit Yourself Down (medley) (1)
Slip 'N Slide (7)
Slow Screw Against The Wall (medley) (5)
Smokin' Room (2)
Somebody's Watching You (3)
Stay (6,11) 38
Stop On By (3,11)
Stranger To Love (6)
Street Player (6)
Sweet Thing (4,11) 5
Swing Down Chariot (2)
Take Time (6)
Tell Me Something Good (2,11) 3
There's No Tellin' (1)
Tonight We Love (9)
True Love (10)

Try A Little Understanding (1)
Turn (6)
Walk The Rockway (8)
Walkin' In The Sun (1)
We Got The Way (9)
What Am I Missing? (8)
What Cha' Gonna Do For Me (11)
What Is It (9)
Whoever's Thrilling You (Is Killing Me) (1)
You Got The Love (2,11) 11
You're Made For Me (9)
You're To Blame (7)
Your Smile (3)

RUMOUR, The

English pub-rock quintet led by Brinsley Schwarz. Backup band for Graham Parker.

| 8/13/77 | 124 | 10 | | 1 | Max | $8 | Mercury 1174 |
| 8/4/79 | 160 | 3 | | 2 | Frogs Sprouts Clogs And Krauts | $8 | Arista 4235 |

Airplane Tonight (1)
All Fall Down (2)
Do Nothing 'Till You Hear From Me (1)
Emotional Traffic (1)

Euro (2)
Face To Face (1)
Frozen Years (2)
Hard Enough To Show (1)
I Can't Help Myself (2)

I Wanna Make Her Love Me (1)
I'm So Glad (1)
Leaders (2)
Looking After No. 1 (1)

Loving You (Is Far Too Easy) (2)
Mess With Love (1)
New Age (medley) (2)
One Good Night (2)

Somethin' Goin' On (1)
This Town (1)
Tired Of Waiting (2)
We Believe In You (medley) (2)

RUNAWAYS, The

Los Angeles female teen hard-rock band led by vocalists Cherie Currie and Joan Jett. Currie recorded with twin sister Marie. Jett formed own band, The Blackhearts. Varying personnel included Michael "Micki" Steele (later with the Bangles) and Lita Ford (later recorded solo).

| 8/21/76 | 194 | 2 | | 1 | The Runaways | $12 | Mercury 1090 |
| 2/5/77 | 172 | 4 | | 2 | Queens Of Noise | $12 | Mercury 1126 |

American Nights (1)
Blackmail (1)
Born To Be Bad (2)
California Paradise (2)

Cherry Bomb (1)
Dead End Justice (1)
Heartbeat (2)
Hollywood (2)

I Love Playin' With Fire (2)
Is It Day Or Night? (1)
Johnny Guitar (2)
Lovers (1)

Midnight Music (2)
Neon Angels On The Road To Ruin (1)
Queens Of Noise (2)

Rock And Roll (1)
Secrets (1)
Take It Or Leave It (2)
Thunder (1)

You Drive Me Wild (1)

★★286★★ RUNDGREN, Todd

Born on 6/22/48 in Upper Darby, Pennsylvania. Virtuoso musician/songwriter/producer/engineer. Leader of groups Nazz and Utopia. Produced Meat Loaf's *Bat Out Of Hell* album and produced albums for Badfinger, Grand Funk Railroad, The Tubes, XTC, Patti Smith and many others.

| 1/9/71 | 185 | 6 | | 1 | Runt | $35 | Ampex 10105 |
| 3/25/72+ | 29 | 48 | ● | 2 | Something/Anything? | $12 | Bearsville 2066 [2] |

side 4: an impromptu operetta cut live with his band in the studio

3/31/73	86	15		3	A Wizard/A True Star	$8	Bearsville 2133
3/16/74	54	17		4	Todd	$12	Bearsville 6952 [2]
6/14/75	86	7		5	Initiation	$10	Bearsville 6957
5/15/76	54	15		6	Faithful	$10	Bearsville 6963
5/6/78	36	26		7	Hermit Of Mink Hollow	$8	Bearsville 6981
12/2/78+	75	15		8	Back To The Bars	[L]	$10	Bearsville 6986 [2]
2/21/81	48	13		9	Healing	$8	Bearsville 3522
1/22/83	66	13		10	The Ever Popular Tortured Artist Effect	$8	Bearsville 23732
10/12/85	128	8		11	A Cappella	$8	Warner 25128
6/17/89	102	11		12	Nearly Human	$8	Warner 25881
2/16/91	118	8		13	2nd Wind	$12	Warner 26478

All The Children Sing (7)
Baby, Let's Swing (medley) (1)

Bag Lady (7)
Bang The Drum All Day (10) 63

Believe In Me (1)
Birthday Carol (1)
Black And White (6,8)

Black Maria (2,8)
Blue Orpheus (11)
Boogies (Hamburger Hell) (6)

Born To Synthesize (5)
Bread (7)
Breathless (2)

Broke Down And Busted (1)
Can We Still Be Friends (7) 29

641

RUNDGREN, Todd — Cont'd

Can't Stop Running (12)
Change Myself (13)
Chant (10)
Cliche (6,8)
Cold Morning Light (2)
Compassion (9)
Cool Jerk (medley) (3)
Couldn't I Just Tell You (2,8) **93**
Da Da Dali (medley) (3)
Death Of Rock And Roll (5)
Determination (7)
Devil's Bite (1)
Does Anybody Love You? (3)
Dogfight Giggle (3)
Don't Hurt Yourself (10)
Don't Tie My Hands (medley) (1)
Don't You Ever Learn? (4,8)
Dream Goes On Forever (4,8) **69**
Drive (10)
Drunken Blue Rooster (4)
Dust In The Wind (2)
Eastern Intrigue (5,8)
Elpee's Worth Of Toons (4)
Emperor Of The Highway (10)
Everybody's Going To Heaven (medley) (4)

Fade Away (7)
Fair Warning (5)
Feel It (12)
Fidelity (12)
Fire Of Mind Or Solar Fire (5)
Fire Of Spirit Or Electric Fire (5)
Flamingo (3)
Flesh (9)
Gaya's Eyes (13)
Golden Goose (9)
Good Vibrations (6) **34**
Happenings Ten Years Time Ago (6)
Hawking (12)
Healer (9)
Healing Part I, II & III (9)
Heavy Metal Kids (4)
Hello It's Me (2,8) **5**
Hideaway (10)
Hodja (11)
Honest Work (11)
How About A Little Fanfare? (4)
Hungry For Love (3)
Hurting For You (7)
I Don't Want To Tie You Down (3)
I Love My Life (12)
I Saw The Light (2,8) **16**

I Think You Know (4)
I Went To The Mirror (2)
I'm In The Clique (1)
I'm So Proud (medley) (3,8)
If I Have To Be Alone (13)
If Six Was Nine (4)
In And Out The Chakras We Go (formerly: Shaft Goes To Outer Space) (4)
Influenza (10)
Initiation (5,8)
Internal Fire Or Fire By Friction Medley (5)
International Feel (3)
Is It My Name? (3)
It Takes Two To Tango (2)
It Wouldn't Have Made Any Difference (2,8)
Izzat Love? (4)
Johnee Jingo (11)
Just Another Onionhead (medley) (3)
Just One Victory (3)
Kindness (13)
King Kong Reggae (medley) (4)
La La Means I Love You (medley) (3,8)
Last Ride (4,8)

Last Thing You Said (medley) (1)
Le Feel Internacionale (3)
Little Red Lights (2)
Lockjaw (11)
Lord Chancellor's Nightmare Song (formerly: (2)
Lost Horizon (11)
Love In Action (8)
Love In Disguise (13)
Love Of The Common Man (6,8)
Love Science (11)
Lucky Guy (7)
Marlene (3)
Mighty Love (11)
Miracle In The Bazaar (11)
Most Likely You Go Your Way And I'll Go Mine (6)
Never Never Land (3,8)
Night The Carousel Burned Down (2)
Number 1 Lowest Common Denominator (4)
Once Burned (11)
One More Day (No Word) (2)
Onomatopoeia (8)
Ooh Baby Baby (medley) (3,8)
Out Of Control (7)

Parallel Lines (12)
Piss Aaron (2)
Prana (5)
Pretending To Care (11)
Public Servant (13)
Pulse (9)
Rain (6)
Range War (8)
Real Man (5,8) **83**
Rock And Roll Pussy (3)
Saving Grace (13)
Second Wind (13)
Shine (9)
Sidewalk Cafe (4)
Slut (7)
Smell Of Money (13)
Some Folks Is Even Whiter Than Me (2)
Something To Fall Back On (11)
Sometimes I Don't Know What To Feel (3,8)
Sons Of 1984 (3)
Spark Of Life (4)
Strawberry Fields Forever (6)
Sunset Blvd. (medley) (3)
Sweeter Memories (2)
There Are No Words (3)
There Goes Your Baybay (10)
Tic Tic Tic It Wears Off (3)

Tin Soldier (10)
Too Far Gone (7)
Torch Song (2)
Unloved Children (12)
Useless Begging (4)
Verb "To Love" (6,8)
Viking, Song Of The (2)
Waiting Game (12)
Want Of A Nail (12)
We Gotta Get You A Woman (1) **20**
When I Pray (6)
When The Shit Hits The Fan (medley) (3)
Who's Sorry Now (13)
Who's That Man (1)
You Cried Wolf (7)
You Don't Have To Camp Around (3)
You Left Me Sore (2)
You Need Your Head (3)
Zen Archer (3,8)

RUN-D.M.C.

Rap trio from Queens, New York: rappers Joseph Simmons (Run), Darryl McDaniels (DMC), with DJ Jason Mizell (Jam Master Jay). In films *Krush Groove* and *Tougher Than Leather*.

DEBUT DATE	PEAK POS	WKS CHR	GOLD	ARTIST — Album Title	$	Label & Number
6/23/84	53	65	●	1 Run-D.M.C.	$8	Profile 1202
2/23/85	52	56	▲	2 King Of Rock	$8	Profile 1205
6/14/86	3	71	▲³	3 **Raising Hell**	$8	Profile 1217
6/4/88	9	28	▲	4 **Tougher Than Leather**	$8	Profile 1265
12/8/90+	81	15		5 Back From Hell	$12	Profile 1401
12/7/91	199	1		6 Greatest Hits 1983-1991	[G] $12	Profile 1419

Ave., The (5,6)
Back From Hell (5)
Beats To The Rhyme (4,6)
Bob Your Head (5)
Can You Rock It Like This (3)
Christmas In Hollis (6)
Daryll & Joe (Krush-Groove 3) (2)
Don't Stop (5)
Dumb Girl (3)
Faces (5)
Groove To The Sound (5)
Hard Times (1,6)

Here We Go (6)
Hit It Run (3)
Hollis Crew (Krush-Groove 2) (1)
How'd Ya Do It Dee (4)
I'm Not Going Out Like That (4)
Is It Live (3)
It's Like That (1,6)
It's Not Funny (2)
It's Tricky (3,6) **57**
Jam-Master Jammin' (2)
Jam-Master Jay (1,6)

Jay's Game (1)
Kick The Frama Lama Lama (5)
King Of Rock (2,6)
Livin' In The City (5)
Mary, Mary (4) **75**
Miss Elaine (3)
My Adidas (6)
Naughty (5)
Not Just Another Groove (5)
P Upon A Tree (5)
Papa Crazy (4)
Party Time (5)

Pause (5,6)
Perfection (3)
Peter Piper (3,6)
Proud To Be Black (3)
Radio Station (4)
Ragtime (4)
Raising Hell (3)
Rock Box (1,6)
Rock The House (6)
Roots, Rap, Reggae (4)
Run's House (4,6)
Son Of Byford (3)
Soul To Rock And Roll (4)

Sucker D.J.'s (5)
Sucker M.C.'s (Krush-Groove 1) (1,6)
They Call Us Run-D.M.C. (4)
30 Days (1)
Together Forever (Krush-Groove 4) (6)
Tougher Than Leather (4)
Wake Up (1)
Walk This Way (3,6) **4**
What's It All About (5)
Word Is Born (5)
You Be Illin' (3,6) **29**

You Talk Too Much (2)
You're Blind (5)

RUNNER

English rock quartet — Steve Gould, lead singer. Gould was lead singer with Rare Bird (1970-77).

DEBUT DATE	PEAK POS	WKS CHR	GOLD	ARTIST — Album Title	$	Label & Number
6/23/79	167	4		Runner	$8	Island 9536

Broken Hearted Me
Dynamite
Fooling Myself
Gone Too Long
Living Is Loving You
Restless Wind
Rock 'N' Roll Soldiers
Run For Your Life
Sooner Than Later
Truly From Within

★★86★★ RUSH

Canadian power-rock trio formed in Toronto in 1969: Geddy Lee (b: 7/29/53; vocals, bass), Alex Lifeson (b: 8/27/53; guitar) and John Rutsey (drums). Neil Peart (b: 9/12/52) replaced Rutsey after first album.

DEBUT DATE	PEAK POS	WKS CHR	GOLD	ARTIST — Album Title	$	Label & Number
9/21/74	105	13		1 Rush	$8	Mercury 1011
3/15/75	113	8		2 Fly By Night	$8	Mercury 1023
10/18/75	148	6		3 Caress Of Steel	$8	Mercury 1046
4/10/76	61	34	▲	4 2112	$8	Mercury 1079
				album is a futuristic look at life in the year 2112		
10/2/76	40	23	▲	5 All The World's A Stage	[L] $10	Mercury 7508 [2]
9/24/77	33	17	●	6 A Farewell To Kings	$8	Mercury 1184
4/15/78	121	6		7 Archives	[R] $12	Mercury 9200 [3]
				reissue of albums #1, 2 & 3 above		
11/18/78	47	21	●	8 Hemispheres	$8	Mercury 3743
2/2/80	4	36	▲	9 **Permanent Waves**	$8	Mercury 4001
3/7/81	3	68	▲²	10 **Moving Pictures**	$8	Mercury 4013
11/14/81	10	21	▲	11 **Exit...Stage Left**	[L] $10	Mercury 7001 [2]
10/2/82	10	33	▲	12 **Signals**	$8	Mercury 4063
5/5/84	10	27	▲	13 **Grace Under Pressure**	$8	Mercury 818476
11/9/85	10	28	▲	14 **Power Windows**	$8	Mercury 826098
9/26/87	13	30	●	15 **Hold Your Fire**	$8	Mercury 832464
1/28/89	21	15	●	16 A Show Of Hands	[L] $10	Mercury 836346 [2]
				recorded during their 1986 and 1988 world tours		
12/2/89	16	27	●	17 Presto	$8	Atlantic 82040
9/22/90	51	19	▲	18 Chronicles	[K] $28	Mercury 838936 [2]
9/21/91	3	43	●	19 **Roll The Bones**	$12	Atlantic 82293

RUSH — Cont'd

Afterimage (13)
Anagram (For Mongo) (17)
Analog Kid (17)
Anthem (2,5,7,18)
Available Light (17)
Bastille Day (3,5,7,18)
Before And After (1,7)
Beneath, Between, &
  Behind (2,7,11)
Best I Can (2,7)
Between The Wheels (13)
Big Money (14,16,18) **45**
Big Wheel (19)
Body Electric (13)
Bravado (17)
Broon's Bane (11)
By-Tor & The Snow Dog
  Medley (2,5,7)
Camera Eye (10)
Chain Lightning (17)
Chemistry (12)

Cinderella Man (6)
Circumstances (8)
Closer To The Heart
  (6,18) **76**
Closer To The Heart [live]
  (11,16) **69**
Countdown (12)
Cygnus X-1 (6)
Different Strings (9)
Digital Man (12)
Distant Early Warning
  (13,16,18)
Dreamline (19)
Emotion Detector (14)
Enemy Within (13)
Entre Nous (9)
Face Up (19)
Farewell To Kings (6,18)
Finding My Way (1,5,7,18)
Fly By Night (2,5,7,18) **88**

hit "Hot 100" as a medley
  with "In The Mood"
Force Ten (15,16,18)
Fountain Of Lamneth
  Medley (3,7)
Freewill (9,11,18)
Ghost Of A Chance (19)
Grand Designs (14)
Hand Over Fist (17)
Hemispheres Medley (8)
Here Again (1,7)
Heresy (19)
High Water (15)
I Think I'm Going Bald (3,7)
In The End (2,5,7)
In The Mood (1,5,7) **88**
  hit "Hot 100" as a medley
  with "Fly By Night"
Jacob's Ladder (9,11)
Kid Gloves (13)
La Villa Strangiato (8,11,18)

Lakeside Park (3,5,7,18)
Lessons (4)
Limelight (10,18) **55**
Lock And Key (15)
Losing It (12)
Madrigal (6)
Making Memories (2,7)
Manhattan Project (14,16,18)
Marathon (14,16)
Middletown Dreams (14)
Mission (15,16)
Mystic Rhythms (14,16,18)
Natural Science (9)
Necromancer Medley (3,7)
Need Some Love (1,7)
Neurotica (19)
New World Man (12,18) **21**
Open Secrets (15)
Pass, The (17)
Passage To Bangkok
  (4,11,18)

Presto (17)
Prime Mover (15)
Red Barchetta (10,11,18)
Red Lenses (13)
Red Sector A (13,16,18)
Red Tide (17)
Rhythm Method (16)
Rivendell (2,7)
Roll The Bones (19)
Scars (17)
Second Nature (15)
Show Don't Tell (17,18)
Something For Nothing (4,5)
Spirit Of Radio (9,11,18) **51**
Subdivisions (12,16,18)
Superconductor (17)
Tai Shan (19)
Take A Friend (1,7)
Tears (4)
Territories (14)
Time Stand Still (15,16,18)

Tom Sawyer (10,11,18) **44**
Trees, The (8,11,18)
Turn The Page (15,16)
2112 Medley (4,5,18)
Twilight Zone (4)
Vital Signs (10)
War Paint (17)
Weapon, The (12)
What You're Doing (1,5,7,18)
Where's My Thing? (19)
Witch Hunt (10,16)
Working Man (1,5,7,18)
Xanadu (6,11)
YYZ (10,11)
You Bet Your Life (19)

RUSH, Jennifer
Native of Queens, New York.

DEBUT DATE	PEAK POS	WKS CHR	GOLD	ARTIST — Album Title	$	Label & Number
6/27/87	118	10		Heart Over Mind	$8	Epic 40825

Call My Name
Down To You

Flames Of Paradise 36
Heart Over Mind

Heart Wars
I Come Undone

Love Of A Stranger
Search The Sky

Sidekick
Stronghold

RUSH, Merrilee
From Seattle, Washington. Discovered by fellow Northwesterners, Paul Revere & The Raiders.

10/19/68	196	4		Angel Of The Morning	$15	Bell 6020

Angel Of The Morning 7
Billy Sunshine
Do Unto Others

Handy
Hush
It's Worth It All

Observation From Flight
  285 (In 3/4 Time)

San Francisco (Be Sure To
  Wear Some Flowers In
  Your Hair)

Sandcastles
Sunshine & Roses

That Kind Of Woman 76
Working Girl

RUSH, Tom
Eclectic singer from Portsmouth, New Hampshire.

6/11/66	122	7	1	Take A Little Walk With Me	$12	Elektra 7308
4/20/68	68	14	2	The Circle Game	$12	Elektra 74018
3/14/70	76	16	3	Tom Rush	$10	Columbia 9972
12/26/70+	110	9	4	Wrong End Of The Rainbow	$10	Columbia 30402
3/27/71	198	1	5	Classic Rush	[K] $10	Elektra 74062
4/29/72	128	10	6	Merrimack County	$10	Columbia 31306
10/19/74	124	9	7	Ladies Love Outlaws	$10	Columbia 33054
2/7/76	184	3	8	The Best Of Tom Rush	[K] $10	Columbia 33907

Biloxi (4)
Black Magic Gun (7)
Came To See Me Yesterday
In The Merry Month Of
  (medley) (4)
Child's Song (3,8)
Circle Game (2,5)
Claim On Me (7)
Colors Of The Sun (3)
Cuckoo, The (5)
Desperados Waiting For The
  Train (7)

Drop Down Mama (3,8)
Galveston Flood (1,5)
Glory Of Love (2)
Gnostic Serenade (4)
Gone Down River (6)
Gypsy Boy (6)
Hobo's Mandolin (7,8)
Indian Woman From
  Wichita (4)
Jamaica Say You Will (6)
Jazzman (3)
Jenny Lynn (7)

Joshua Gone Barbados (1,5)
Kids These Days (6,8)
Ladies Love Outlaws (7,8)
Livin' In The Country (3)
Lost My Drivin' Wheel (3,8)
Love's Made A Fool Of You
  (1,5)
Lullaby (3)
Maggie (3)
Merrimack County (4)
Merrimack County II (6)
Mink Julip (6,8)

Money Honey (1)
Mother Earth (6,8)
No Regrets (2,5,7,8)
Old Man's Song (3)
On The Road Again (1,5)
One Day I Walk (7)
Paddy West (medley) (4)
Rainy Day Man (3)
Riding On A Railroad (4)
Rockport Sunday (2,5)
Roll Away The Grey (6)
Rotunda (4,8)

Seems The Songs (6)
Shadow Dream Song (2,5)
So Long (2)
Something In The Way She
  Moves (2,5)
Starlight (4,8)
Statesboro Blues (1)
Sugar Babe (1)
Sunshine Sunshine (2)
Sweet Baby James (4)
These Days (3,8)
Tin Angel (2)

Too Much Monkey Business
  (1)
Turn Your Money Green (7)
Urge For Going (2,5)
Who Do You Love (1,5)
Wild Child (World Of
  Trouble) (3)
Wind On The Water (6)
Wrong End Of The Rainbow
  (4)
You Can't Tell A Book By
  The Cover (1)

RUSHEN, Patrice
Born on 9/30/54 in Los Angeles. Jazz-soul vocalist/pianist/songwriter. Much session work with Jean
Luc-Ponty, Lee Ritenour and Stanley Turrentine.

4/16/77	164	4	1	Shout It Out	$8	Prestige 10101
2/17/79	98	6	2	Patrice	$8	Elektra 160
11/24/79+	39	22	3	Pizzazz	$8	Elektra 243
11/29/80+	71	18	4	Posh	$8	Elektra 302
5/1/82	14	28	5	Straight From The Heart	$8	Elektra 60015
6/16/84	40	25	6	Now	$8	Elektra 60360
3/28/87	77	19	7	Watch Out!	$8	Arista 8401

All My Love (7)
All We Need (5)
Anything Can Happen (7)
Breakin' All The Rules (7)
Breakout! (5)
Burnin' (7)
Call On Me (3)
Cha-Cha (2)
Changes (In Your Life) (2)
Come Back To Me (7)
Didn't You Know? (2)
Don't Blame Me (7)
Dream, The (4)

**Feels So Real (Won't Let
  Go)** (6) **78**
Forget Me Nots (5) **23**
Funk Won't Let You Down (4)
Get Off (You Fascinate Me)
  (6)
Givin' It Up Is Givin' Up (3)
Gone With The Night (6)
Gotta Find It (6)
Hang It Up (2)
Haven't You Heard (3) **42**
Heartache Heartbreak (6)
High In Me (6)

Hump, The (1)
I Need Your Love (4)
I Was Tired Of Being Alone
  (5)
If Only (5)
It's Just A Natural Thing (2)
Keepin' Faith In Love (3)
Let The Music Take Me (3)
Let There Be Funk (1)
Let Your Heart Be Free (1)
Let's Sing A Song Of Love (2)
Long Time Coming (7)
Look Up (4)

Message In The Music (3)
Music Of The Earth (2)
My Love's Not Going
  Anywhere (6)
Never Gonna Give You Up
  (Won't Let You Be) (4)
Number One (5)
Perfect Love (6)
Play! (2)
Remind Me (5)
Roll With The Punches (1)
Settle For My Love (3)

(She Will) Take You Down
  To Love (5)
Shout It Out (1)
Sojourn (1)
Somewhere (7)
Stepping Stones (1)
Superstar (7)
Tender Lovin' (7)
This Is All I Really Know (4)
Till She's Out Of Your Mind
  (7)
Time Will Tell (4)
To Each His Own (6)

Watch Out (7)
When I Found You (2)
Where There Is Love (5)
Wishful Thinking (2)
Yolon (1)

RUSSELL, Bobby
Born on 4/19/41 in Nashville. Died of a heart attack on 11/19/92. Wrote "The Night The Lights Went Out
In Georgia," "Honey," "Little Green Apples" and "The Joker Went Wild." First husband of Vicki Lawrence.

| 10/16/71 | 183 | 3 | | Saturday Morning Confusion | $10 | United Art. 5548 |

DEBUT DATE	PEAK POS	WKS CHR	GOLD	ARTIST — Album Title	$	Label & Number

RUSSELL, Bobby — Cont'd

Confidential Goodbye It Hurts	Little Boy Tears Little Ol' Song About Love	**Saturday Morning Confusion 28**	Song That I Can't Write Then And Only Then	When You Find Out Where You're Goin'	Who Is She Now You Babe

RUSSELL, Brenda

Soul singer/keyboardist/composer. Born Brenda Gordon in Brooklyn. To Toronto at age 12. Recorded as duo, Brian & Brenda, with former husband Brian Russell in 1978; co-hosted the Canadian TV series *Music Machine*. Session work for Barbra Streisand, Elton John, Bette Midler and many others.

9/22/79	65	20		1 Brenda Russell	$8	Horizon 739
4/11/81	107	8		2 Love Life	$8	A&M 4811
3/19/88	49	28		3 Get Here	$8	A&M 5178

Deep Dark And Mysterious (2) Get Here (3) God Bless You (1) Gravity (3)	If Only For One Night (1) If You Love (2) In The Thick Of It (1) Just A Believer (3) Le Restaurant (1)	Little Bit Of Love (1) Love Life (2) Lucky (2) Make My Day (3) Midnight Eyes (3)	**Piano In The Dark (3) 6** Rainbow (2) Sensitive Man (2) **So Good, So Right (1) 30** Something I Like To Do (2)	Thank You (2) Think It Over (1) This Time I Need You (3) Way Back When (1) You're Free (1)

★★197★★ RUSSELL, Leon

Born on 4/2/41 in Lawton, Oklahoma. Rock singer/songwriter/multi-instrumentalist sessionman. Early in session career known as Russell Bridges. Regular for Phil Spector's "Wall of Sound" session group. Formed Shelter Records with British producer Denny Cordell in 1970. Recorded as Hank Wilson in 1973. Married Mary McCreary (vocalist with Little Sister, part of Sly Stone's "family") in 1976. Formed Paradise label in 1976. Wrote "Superstar" and "This Masquerade." Also see Joe Cocker.

4/11/70	60	19		1 Leon Russell	$15	Shelter 1001
5/29/71	17	29	●	2 Leon Russell & The Shelter People	$15	Shelter 8903
				LEON RUSSELL & THE SHELTER PEOPLE		
12/4/71+	70	20		3 Asylum Choir II .... [E]	$15	Shelter 8910
				LEON RUSSELL & MARC BENNO recorded April 1969		
7/15/72	2⁴	35	●	4 Carney	$10	Shelter 8911
7/7/73	9	26	●	5 Leon Live .... [L]	$15	Shelter 8917 [3]
				recorded at the Long Beach Arena, Long Beach, California		
9/22/73	28	15		6 Hank Wilson's Back, Vol. I	$10	Shelter 8923
				HANK WILSON		
6/22/74	34	16		7 Stop All That Jazz	$10	Shelter 2108
5/3/75	30	40	●	8 Will O' The Wisp	$10	Shelter 2138
5/1/76	34	28		9 Wedding Album *	$10	Paradise 2943
10/23/76	40	16	●	10 Best Of Leon .... [G]	$8	Shelter 52004
6/25/77	142	5		11 Make Love To The Music *	$8	Paradise 3066
				***LEON & MARY RUSSELL**		
8/12/78	115	10		12 Americana	$8	Paradise 3172
6/30/79	25	18	●	13 One For The Road	$10	Columbia 36064 [2]
				WILLIE NELSON AND LEON RUSSELL		
4/4/81	187	2		14 The Live Album .... [L]	$8	Paradise 3532
				LEON RUSSELL & NEW GRASS REVIVAL		

Acid Annapolis (4) Alcatraz (2,5) Always (13) Am I Blue (13) Am I That Easy To Forget (6) **Back To The Island (8,10) 53** Ballad For A Soldier (13) Ballad Of Hollis Brown (7) Ballad Of Mad Dogs And Englishmen (2) Battle Of New Orleans (6) Because Of You (13) Beware Of Darkness (2) Bluebird (8,10) Cajun Love Song (4) Can't Get Over Losing You (8) Caribbean (14) Carney (4) Crystal Closet Queen (2,5) Danny Boy (13) Daylight (9) Delta Lady (1,5,10) Detour (13) Dixie Lullaby (1,5) Don't Fence Me In (13) Down On Deep River (8) Down On The Base (3) Easy Love (11)	Elvis And Marilyn (12) Fantasy (9) Far Away Places (13) From Maine To Mexico (12) Georgia Blues (14) Give Peace A Chance (1) Goodnight Irene (6) Great Day (5) Hard Rain's A Gonna Fall (2) Heartbreak Hotel (13) Hello, Little Friend (3) Hold On To This Feeling (11) Home Sweet Oklahoma (2) Housewife (12) Hummingbird (1,10) Hurtsome Body (1) I Believe To My Soul (14) I Put A Spell On You (1) I Saw The Light (13) I Want To Be At The Meeting (14) I'll Sail My Ship Alone (6) **I'm So Lonesome I Could Cry (6) flip** I've Just Seen A Face (14) **If I Were A Carpenter (7) 73** If The Shoe Fits (4) Island In The Sun (11) It Takes A Lot To Laugh, It Takes A Train To Cry (2)	It's All Over Now, Baby Blue (5) It's Been A Long Time Baby (5) It's Only Me (12) Jambalaya (On The Bayou) (6,14) Jesus On My Side (12) Joyful Noise (11) Jumpin' Jack Flash (5,14) Ladies Of The Night (12) **Lady Blue (8,10) 14** Lady In Waiting (3) Lavender Blue (Dilly Dilly) (9) Laying Right Here In Heaven (8) Learn How To Boogie (3) Let The Rest Of The World Go By (13) Let's Get Started (12) Like A Dream Come True (9) Little Hideaway (3) Lost Highway (6) Love Crazy (11) Love Is In Your Eyes (11) Love's Supposed To Be That Way (9) Magic Mirror (4) Make Love To The Music (11)	Make You Feel Good (8) Manhattan Island Serenade (4) Me And Baby Jane (4) Midnight Lover (12) Mighty Quinn Medley (5) Mona Lisa Please (7) My Cricket (4) My Father's Shoes (8) Now Now Boogie (11) Of Thee I Sing (2,5) Old Masters (1) One For My Baby And One More For The Road (13) One More Love Song (14) Out In The Woods (4,5,10) Over The Rainbow (14) Pilgrim Land (14) Pisces Apple Lady (1) Prince Of Peace (1,5,10) **Queen Of The Roller Derby (5) 89** Quiet Nights (9) **Rainbow In Your Eyes (9) 52** Ridin' Down The Canyon (13) Roll Away The Stone (1,5,10) **Roll In My Sweet Baby's Arms (6,14) 78** Roller Derby (4)	Salty Candy (3) Satisfy You (9) Say You Will (11) Shadow And Me (12) She Smiles Like A River (2) She Thinks I Still Care (6) Shoot Out On The Plantation (1,5,10) Sioux City Sue (13) Six Pack To Go (6) Smashed (7) Some Day (5) Song For You (1,10) Spanish Harlem (7) Stay Away From Sad Songs (8) Stop All That Jazz (7) Stormy Weather (13) Straight Brother (3) Stranger In A Strange Land (2,5,10,14) Streaker's Ball (7) Summertime (13) Sweeping Through The City (5) Sweet Emily (2,5) Sweet Home Chicago (3) Tenderly (13) That Lucky Old Sun (13) This Masquerade (4,10)	**Tight Rope (4,10) 11** Time For Love (7) Trouble In Mind (13) Truck Drivin' Man (6) Tryin' To Stay 'Live (3) Uncle Pen (6) When A Man Loves A Woman (12) When You Wish Upon A Fag (3) Wild Horses (14) Wild Side Of Life (13) Will O' The Wisp (8) Window Up Above (6) Windsong (9) Working Girl (4) Yes I Am (medley) (5) You Are My Sunshine (13) You Are On My Mind (9) Youngblood (medley) (5)

RUSTIX, The

Rock group led by vocalists Albe Galich and Chuck Brucato.

11/15/69	200	2		Bedlam	$12	Rare Earth 508

Can't You Hear The Music Play Country	Feeling Alright Free Again I Can't Make It Without You	I Guess This Is Goodbye I Heard It Through The Grapevine	Lady In My Dreams That's What Poppa Told Me	Wednesday's Child

RUTHERFORD, Mike

Born on 10/2/50 in Guildford, England. Bassist of Genesis and leader of Mike + The Mechanics.

4/5/80	163	11		1 Smallcreep's Day	$8	Passport 9843
10/9/82	145	6		2 Acting Very Strange	$8	Atlantic 80015

DEBUT DATE	PEAK POS	WKS CHR	GOLD	ARTIST — Album Title	$	Label & Number

RUTHERFORD, Mike — Cont'd

Acting Very Strange (2) Every Road (1) I Don't Wanna Know (1) Overnight Job (1) Time And Time Again (1)
Couldn't Get Arrested (2) Halfway There (2) Maxine (2) Romani (1) Who's Fooling Who (2)
Day To Remember (2) Hideaway (2) Moonshine (1) Smallcreep's Day Medley (1)

RUTLES, The
Parody of The Beatles: Neil Innes is Ron Nasty, Eric Idle is Dirk McQuickly, Rikki Fataar is Stig O'Hara
and John Halsey is Barry Wom. Innes was with the Bonzo Dog Band and Idle was a member of Monty Python.
A pseudo-documentary of the group aired on NBC-TV on 3/22/78.

| 3/25/78 | 63 | 9 | | The Rutles .... | $15 | Warner 3151 |

Another Day Good Times Roll Let's Be Natural Nevertheless Piggy In The Middle
Cheese And Onions Hold My Hand Living In Hope Number One With A Girl Like You
Doubleback Alley I Must Be In Love Love Life Ouch!

RYDELL, Bobby
Born Robert Ridarelli on 4/26/42 in Philadelphia. Regular on Paul Whiteman's amateur TV show, 1951-54.
Drummer with Rocco & His Saints, which included Frankie Avalon on trumpet in 1956. First recorded for
Veko in 1957. In films *Bye Bye Birdie* and *That Lady From Peking*.

2/27/61	12	34	1	Bobby's Biggest Hits .... [G]	$30	Cameo 1009
10/23/61	56	9	2	Rydell At The Copa .... [L]	$25	Cameo 1011
12/18/61+	7	30	3	**Bobby Rydell/Chubby Checker**	$25	Cameo 1013
				BOBBY RYDELL/CHUBBY CHECKER		
9/1/62	88	11	4	All The Hits	$25	Cameo 1019
12/22/62+	61	12	5	Bobby Rydell/Biggest Hits, Volume 2 .... [G]	$25	Cameo 1028
1/18/64	67	9	6	the Top Hits of 1963	$20	Cameo 1070
				includes a bonus 7" single		
3/7/64	98	4	7	Forget Him	$20	Cameo 1080

Alley Cat Song (6) Dream Baby (4) **I'll Never Dance Again** New Love (7) **That Old Black Magic** What Are You Doing New
Baby It's You (4) **Fish, The** (5) 25 (4,5) 14 Old Man River (2) (2,5) 21 Year's Eve (3)
Best Man Cried (5) **Forget Him** (7) 4 **I've Got Bonnie** (4,5) 18 One Who Really Loves You They Don't Write Them Like What's Your Name (4)
Bless 'Em All (2) Gee, It's Wonderful (7) If I Had A Hammer (6) (4) That Anymore (2) **Wild One** (1) 2
Blue On Blue (6) Go Away Little Girl (6) It's Time We Parted (7) Our Day Will Come (6) Too Much Too Soon (7) Wish You Were Here (7)
Blue Velvet (6) **Good Time Baby** (5) 11 Jingle Bell Rock (3) 21 Our Faded Love (6) Twistin' The Night Away (4) Wonderful! Wonderful! (6)
Break It To Me Gently (4) **Groovy Tonight** (1) 70 Jingle Bells Imitations (3) Ruby Baby (6) Until I Met You (7) Words Written On Water (7)
Can't Get Used To Losing Hey Baby (4) **Kissin' Time** (1) 11 Side By Side (3) Voce De La Notte (Voice Of World Without Love (6)
You (6) Hey Everybody (7) **Little Bitty Girl** (1) 19 Since We Fell In Love (6) The Night) (7) You'll Never Tame Me (1)
Cha-Cha-Cha (5) 10 Homesick Thats All (2) Lose Her (5) 69 So Much In Love (6) **Volare** (1) 4 Your Hits And Mine Medley
Darling Jenny (7) **I Dig Girls** (1) 46 Lot Of Living To Do (2) Soldier Boy (4) Voodoo (You Remind Me Of (3)
Ding-A-Ling (1) 18 I Know (1) **Make Me Forget** (7) 43 Sway (1,2) 14 The Guy) (7)
Don't Be Afraid (2) **I Wanna Thank You** (5) 21 Mammy (2) **Swingin' School** (1) 5 Walkin' My Baby Back
Don't Break The Heart That I Will Follow Her (6) My Baby Just Cares For Me Swingin' Together (3) Home (3)
Loves You (4) I'd Do It Again (1) (3) Teach Me To Twist (3) **We Got Love** (1) 6
Door To Paradise (5) 85 My Coloring Book (6)

RYDER, Mitch, And The Detroit Wheels
Born William Levise, Jr. on 2/26/45 in Detroit. Leader of white soul-rock group The Detroit Wheels.
Group was originally known as Billy Lee & The Rivieras. Renamed by their producer Bob Crewe. Ryder went
solo in 1967. Formed new rock group, Detroit, in 1971.

3/5/66	78	7	1	Take A Ride	$30	New Voice 2000
8/6/66+	23	34	2	Breakout...!!!	$25	New Voice 2002
4/8/67	34	16	3	Sock It To Me!	$25	New Voice 2003
10/14/67+	37	26	4	All Mitch Ryder Hits! .... [G]	$25	New Voice 2004
7/9/83	120	9	5	Never Kick A Sleeping Dog	$8	Riva 7503
				MITCH RYDER		
				produced by John Cougar		

Baby Jane (Mo-Mo Jane) (1) **Devil With A Blue Dress** I Need Help! (2) **Little Latin Lupe Lu** **Sock It To Me-Baby!** (3,4) 6 **Too Many Fish In The Sea**
B.I.G.T.I.M.E. (5) **On & Good Golly Miss** I Never Had It Better (3) (2,4) 17 Stand (5) **& Three Little Fishes**
Break Out (2,4) 62 **Molly** (2,4) 4 I'd Rather Go To Jail (3,4) Oo Papa Doo (2) Sticks And Stones (1) (4) 24
Bring It On Home To Me (1) Face In The Crowd (3) I'll Go Crazy (1) Please, Please, Please (1) Stubborn Kind Of Fellow (2) Walk On By (3)
Code Dancing (5) I Can't Hide It (3) In The Midnight Hour (2,4) Rue De Trahir (5) **Takin' All I Can Get** Walking The Dog (2)
Come Again (5) I Got You (1) **Jenny Take A Ride!** (1,4) 10 Shake A Tail Feather (1,4) (3,4) 100 **When You Were Mine** (5) 87
Come See About Me (1) I Had It Made (2) **Joy** (4) 41 Shakedown (3) Thrill Of It All (5) Wild Child (3)
Cry To Me (5) I Hope (1) Just A Little Bit (1) Shakin' With Linda (3) Thrill's A Thrill (5) You Get Your Kicks (2)
I Like It Like That (2) Let Your Lovelight Shine (1) Slow Fizz (3)

S

SAAD, Sue, & The Next
Rock quintet: Sue Saad (vocals), James Lance, Tony Riparetti, Billy Anstatt and Bobby Manzer.

| 3/1/80 | 131 | 12 | | Sue Saad And The Next .... | $8 | Planet 4 |

Cold Night Rain Gimme Love/Gimme Pain I Want Him Prisoner Young Girl
Danger Love I I Me Me It's Gotcha Won't Give It Up Your Lips-Hands-Kiss-Love

SACRED REICH
Thrash metal quartet from Phoenix: Phil Rind (bass, vocals), Wiley Arnett, Jason Rainey and Greg Hall.

| 7/28/90 | 153 | 9 | | The American Way .... | $12 | Enigma 73560 |

American Way I Don't Know State Of Emergency Way It Is
Crimes Against Humanity Love ... Hate 31 Flavors Who's To Blame

DEBUT DATE	PEAK POS	WKS CHR	GOLD	ARTIST — Album Title	$	Label & Number

SAD CAFE
Manchester, England pop-rock group formed in 1976. Lead singer Paul Young was later with Mike + The Mechanics.

DEBUT DATE	PEAK POS	WKS CHR		ARTIST — Album Title	$	Label & Number
1/27/79	94	14	1	Misplaced Ideals .... [K]	$8	A&M 4737
				recordings from first 2 British releases		
9/15/79	146	5	2	Facades	$8	A&M 4779
8/15/81	160	6	3	Sad Cafe	$8	Swan Song 16048

Angel (2)
Babylon (1)
Black Rose (1)
Crazy Oyster (2)
Digital Daydream Blues (3)
Dreamin' (3)

Emptiness (2)
Everyday (2)
Feel Like Dying (1)
Get Me Outta' Here (2)
Here Come The Clowns (1)
Hungry Eyes (1)

I Believe (Love Will Survive) (1)
I'm In Love Again (3)
Keeping It From The Troops (3)
La-Di-Da (3) 78

Losin' You (3)
Love Today (3)
My Oh My (2)
No Favours - No Way (3)
Nothing Left To Lose (2)
On With The Show (1)

Restless (1)
Run Home Girl (1) 71
Shellshock (1)
Strange Little Girl (2)
Take Me To The Future (2)
Time Is So Hard To Find (2)

What Am I Gonna Do (3)

SADE
Born Helen Folasade Adu on 1/16/59 in Ibadan, Nigeria; moved to London at age four. Name pronounced: SHAH-day. Appeared in the 1986 film *Absolute Beginners*. Former designer of menswear. Won the 1985 Best New Artist Grammy Award.

DEBUT DATE	PEAK POS	WKS CHR	GOLD	ARTIST — Album Title	$	Label & Number
2/23/85	5	81	▲2	1 Diamond Life	$8	Portrait 39581
12/21/85+	1²	46	▲3	2 Promise	$8	Portrait 40263
6/4/88	7	45	▲2	3 Stronger Than Pride	$8	Epic 44210
11/21/92	3	12↑	▲	4 Love Deluxe	$12	Epic 53178

Bullet Proof Soul (4)
Cherish The Day (4)
Cherry Pie (1)
Clean Heart (3)
Fear (2)
Feel No Pain (4)
Frankie's First Affair (1)
Give It Up (3)

Hang On To Your Love (1)
Haunt Me (3)
I Couldn't Love You More (4)
I Never Thought I'd See The Day (3)
I Will Be Your Friend (1)
Is It A Crime (2)
Jezebel (2)

Keep Looking (3)
Kiss Of Life (4)
Like A Tattoo (4)
Love Is Stronger Than Pride (3)
Maureen (2)
Mermaid (4)
Mr. Wrong (2)

Never As Good As The First Time (2) 20
No Ordinary Love (4) 28
Nothing Can Come Between Us (3)
Paradise (3) 16
Pearls (4)
Sally (1)

Siempre Hay Esperanza (3)
Smooth Operator (1) 5
Sweetest Taboo (2) 5
Tar Baby (2)
Turn My Back On You (3)
War Of The Hearts (2)
When Am I Going To Make A Living (1)

Why Can't We Live Together (1)
Your Love Is King (1) 54

SADLER, SSgt Barry
Born in New Mexico in 1940. Staff Sergeant of U.S. Army Special Forces (aka Green Berets). Served in Vietnam until injuring leg in booby trap. Shot in the head during a 1988 robbery attempt at his Guatemala home; suffered brain damage. Died of heart failure on 11/5/89 (age 49) in Tennessee.

DEBUT DATE	PEAK POS	WKS CHR	GOLD	ARTIST — Album Title	$	Label & Number
2/26/66	1⁵	32	●	1 Ballads of the Green Berets	$12	RCA 3547
7/9/66	130	3		2 The "A" Team	$15	RCA 3605

"A" Team (2) 28
Autumn Of My Life (2)
Badge Of Courage (1)
Ballad Of The Green Berets (1) 1

Bamba (1)
Chains On A Man (2)
Dear Darlin' (2)
Drifting Years (2)
Empty Glass (2)

Forty Nine Broken Hearts (2)
Garet Trooper (1)
I'm A Lucky One (1)
I'm Watching The Raindrops Fall (1)

Letter From Vietnam (1)
Little Bird Of Vietnam (2)
Lullaby (1)
One Son-Of-A-Gun Of A Gun (2)

Saigon (1)
Salute To The Nurses (1)
Soldier Has Come Home (1)
Till The Time Comes (2)
Time (2)

Time Goes By (1)
Trooper's Lament (1)

SA-FIRE
Latin American dance singer from New York City.

DEBUT DATE	PEAK POS	WKS CHR		ARTIST — Album Title	$	Label & Number
10/8/88+	79	46		Sa-Fire	$8	Cutting 834922

Better Be The Only One
Boy, I've Been Told 48

Gonna Make It 71
I Wanna Make You Mine

It's A Crime
Love At First Sight

Love Is On Her Mind
Thinking Of You 12

Together
You Said You Loved Me

SAGA
Toronto-based rock quintet: Michael Sadler, brothers Jim and Ian Crichton, Jim Gilmour and Steve Negus.

DEBUT DATE	PEAK POS	WKS CHR	GOLD	ARTIST — Album Title	$	Label & Number
10/23/82+	29	36	●	1 Worlds Apart	$8	Portrait 38246
10/22/83	92	9		2 Heads Or Tales	$8	Portrait 38999
9/21/85	87	10		3 Behaviour	$8	Portrait 40145

Amnesia (1)
Cat Walk (2)
Conversations (1)
Easy Way Out (3)
Flyer, The (2) 79

Framed (1)
(Goodbye) Once Upon A Time (3)
Here I Am (3)
Intermission (1)

Interview (1)
Listen To Your Heart (3)
Misbehaviour (3)
Nine Lives Of Miss Midi (3)
No Regrets (Chapter V) (1)

No Stranger (Chapter VIII) (1)
On The Loose (1) 26
Out Of The Shadows (3)
Pitchman, The (2)
Promises (3)

Scratching The Surface (2)
Social Orphan (2)
Sound Of Strangers (2)
Take A Chance (3)
Time's Up (1)

Vendetta (Still Helpless) (2)
What Do I Know? (3)
Wind Him Up (1) 64
Writing, The (2)
You And The Night (3)

SAGER, Carole Bayer
Born on 3/8/46 in New York City. Prolific pop lyricist. Married Burt Bacharach in 1982. Collaborated in writing "A Groovy Kind Of Love," "Midnight Blue," "Nobody Does It Better," "When I Need You" and many others. Wrote lyrics for many film scores.

DEBUT DATE	PEAK POS	WKS CHR		ARTIST — Album Title	$	Label & Number
5/16/81	60	22		Sometimes Late At Night	$8	Boardwalk 37069

Easy To Love Again
I Won't Break
Just Friends

On The Way To The Sky
Somebody's Been Lying

Sometimes Late At Night
Stronger Than Before 30

Tell Her
Wild Again

You And Me (We Wanted It All)
You Don't Know Me

SAHL, Mort
Born on 5/11/27 in Montreal. Topical satirist/actor. Own one-man Broadway show *Mort Sahl On Broadway!*

DEBUT DATE	PEAK POS	WKS CHR		ARTIST — Album Title	$	Label & Number
10/24/60+	22	13		1 Mort Sahl At The Hungry i .... [C]	$20	Verve 15012
				Hungry i: Nightclub in San Francisco; no track titles listed on this album		
6/30/73	149	7		2 Sing A Song of Watergate .... [C]	$15	GNP Cres. 2070

California Politics (2)
Candidates (2)
Conventions, The (2)

Foreign Policy (2)
Kennedy's Plane (2)

Nixon's Odyssey (2)
Nixon's Plane (2)

Our Distinguished Leaders (2)

Prisoners Of War (2)
San Clemente (2)

Watergate (2)

SAHM, Doug, & Band
Tex-Mex rocker born on 11/6/41 in San Antonio. Formed the Sir Douglas Quintet in 1965. Formed the Texas Tornados in 1974. Formed new Tornados star lineup in 1990.

DEBUT DATE	PEAK POS	WKS CHR		ARTIST — Album Title	$	Label & Number
2/17/73	125	10		Doug Sahm And Band	$12	Atlantic 7254
				with guests Bob Dylan, Dr. John and David Bromberg		

Blues Stay Away From Me
Dealer's Blues
Don't Turn Around

Faded Love
I Get Off

(Is Anybody Going To) San Antone

It's Gonna Be Easy
Me And Paul

Papa Ain't Salty
Poison Love

Wallflower
Your Friends

DEBUT DATE	PEAK POS	WKS CHR	GOLD	ARTIST — Album Title	$	Label & Number

SAIGON KICK
Hard-rock quartet from Miami: Matt Kramer (vocals), Jason Bieler, Tom DeFile and Phil Varone.

| 6/20/92 | 80 | 23↑ | | The Lizard | $12 | Third Stone 92158 |

All Alright / All I Want / Body Bags / Chanel / Cruelty / Feel The Same Way / Freedom / God Of 42nd Street / Hostile Youth / Lizard, The / **Love Is On The Way 12** / Miss Jones / My Dog / Peppermint Tribe / Sleep / World Goes Round

SAILCAT
Country-rock duo: Court Pickett and John Wyker.

| 8/12/72 | 38 | 14 | | Motorcycle Mama | $10 | Elektra 75029 |

Ambush / B.B. Gunn / Dream, The / Highway Rider (medley) / Highway Riff (medley) / If You've Got A Daughter / It'll Be A Long Long Time / **Motorcycle Mama 12** / On The Brighter Side Of It / All / Rainbow Road / Thief, The / Walking Together Backwards

SAINTE-MARIE, Buffy
Folk singer/songwriter. Born on 2/20/41 of Cree Indian parents on Piapot Reserve, Saskatchewan, Canada. Raised in Maine. Co-writer of "Up Where We Belong." Semi-regular of TV's *Sesame Street* cast from 1976-1991.

5/21/66	97	10		1 Little Wheel Spin And Spin	$15	Vanguard 79211
7/8/67	126	6		2 Fire & Fleet & Candlelight	$15	Vanguard 79250
8/3/68	171	7		3 I'm Gonna Be A Country Girl Again	$15	Vanguard 79280

recorded with top Nashville musicians

| 10/24/70 | 142 | 7 | | 4 The Best Of Buffy Sainte-Marie | [G] $15 | Vanguard 3/4 [2] |
| 4/10/71 | 182 | 6 | | 5 She Used To Wanna Be A Ballerina | $12 | Vanguard 79311 |

backing musicians: Ry Cooder and Neil Young & Crazy Horse

| 5/6/72 | 134 | 8 | | 6 Moonshot | $12 | Vanguard 79312 |

Bells (5) / Better To Find Out For Yourself (4) / Carousel, The (2) / Circle Game (2,4) / Cod'Ine (4) / Cripple Creek (4) / Doggett's Gap (2) / Don't Call Me Honey (medley) (2) / From The Bottom Of My Heart (3) / God Is Alive, Magic Is Afoot (4) / Gonna Feel Much Better When You're Gone (3) / Ground Hog (4) / Guess Who I Saw In Paris (4) / He's A Keeper Of The Fire (4) / He's A Pretty Good Man If You Ask Me (3) / **He's An Indian Cowboy In The Rodeo** (6) 98 / Helpless (5) / Hey, Little Bird (2) / House Carpenter (1) / I Wanna Hold Your Hand Forever (6) / **I'm Gonna Be A Country Girl Again** (3,4) 98 / Jeremiah (6) / Lady Margaret (5) / Lay It Down (6) / Little Boy Dark Eyes (2) / Little Wheel Spin And Spin (1,4) / Lord Randall (2) / Los Pescadores (4) / Love Of A Good Man (3) / Lyke Wake Dirge (2) / Many A Mile (4) / Men Of The Fields (1) / **Mister Can't You See** (6) 38 / Moonshot (6) / Moratorium - Bring Our Brothers Home (5) / My Baby Left Me (6) / My Country 'Tis Of Thy People You're Dying (1,4) / Native North American Child (6) / 97 Men In This Here Town (medley) (2) / Not The Lovin' Kind (6) / Now That The Buffalo's Gone (3,4) / Now You've Been Gone For A Long Time (3) / Piney Wood Hills (3,4) / Poor Man's Daughter (1) / Reynardine - A Vampire Legend (2) / Rollin' Mill Man (5) / Rolling Log Blues (1,4) / Seeds Of Brotherhood (4) / She Used To Wanna Be A Ballerina (5) / Sir Patrick Spens (1) / Smack Water Jack (5) / Soldier Blue (5) / Sometimes I Get To Thinkin' (1,3,4) / Song Of The French Partisan (5) / Song To A Seagull (2) / Soulful Shade Of Blue (3,4) / Summer Boy (2,4) / Surfer, The (5) / Sweet Memories (6) / Sweet September Morning (5) / T'es Pas Un Autre (2) / Take My Hand For Awhile (3,4) / Tall Trees In Georgia (3) / They Gotta Quit Kickin' My Dawg Around (3) / Timeless Love (1) / Uncle Joe (3) / Universal Soldier (4) / Until It's Time For You To Go (4) / Vampire (4) / Waly Waly (1) / Wedding Song (2) / Winter Boy (1,4) / You Know How To Turn On Those Lights (6)

SAINT TROPEZ
Disco studio production by W. Michael Lewis and Laurin Rinder.

| 11/26/77 | 131 | 10 | | 1 Je T'aime | [F] $8 | Butterfly 002 |

translation of French title: I Love You

| 5/5/79 | 65 | 11 | | 2 Belle de Jour | $8 | Butterfly 3100 |

Belle De Jour (2) / Coeur A Coeur (1) / Fill My Life With Love (2) / Hold On To Love (2) / Je T'aime (1) / La Symphonie Africaine (1) / Most Of All (2) / On A Rien A Perdre (1) / **One More Minute** (2) 49 / Think I'm Gonna Fall In Love With Love (2) / Violation (1) / When You Are Gone (2)

SAKAMOTO, Kyu
Native of Kawasaki, Japan. Kyu (pronounced: cue) was one of 520 people killed in the crash of the Japan Airlines 747 near Tokyo on 8/12/85 (age 43).

| 6/15/63 | 14 | 17 | | Sukiyaki and other Japanese hits | [F] $20 | Capitol 10349 |

Anoko No Namaewa / Nantenkana / Boku No Hoshi / Good Timing / Goodbye, Joe / Hige No Uta / Hitoribocchi No Futari / Kiminaka Kiminaka / Kyu-Chan No Zuntatatta / Kyu-Chan Ondo / Mo Hitori No Boku / **Sukiyaki 1** / Tsun Tsun Bushi

SALES, Soupy
Born Milton Hines on 1/8/26 in Franklinton, North Carolina. Slapstick comedian. Own ABC-TV series, 1959-60; syndicated show, 1966-68. His sons, Hunt and Tony, are members of the group Tin Machine.

| 4/24/65 | 102 | 7 | | 1 Spy With A Pie | [N] $20 | ABC-Para. 503 |

songs and sketches from his children's TV series

| 5/15/65 | 80 | 7 | | 2 Soupy Sales Sez do The Mouse and other teen hits | [N] $20 | ABC-Para. 517 |

Dressing Room Menagerie (1) / Forever Friends (1) / Hey, Pearl (2) / King Kong (2) / Leona (1) / Mighty Clem (2) / **Mouse, The** (2) 76 / Mouse Trap (2) / Mr. Cab Driver (2) / Name Game (2) / Nitty Gritty (2) / Pachalafaka (2) / Pie-Face (1) / Pie In The Sky (1) / Sad Sack (1) / Soupy Of The Secret Service (1) / Speedy Gonzales (2) / There's Nothing To Do Today (1) / Thirty Five Pounds, Nine Feet Tall (1) / Vy You Spyink On Me (1) / We're Going To The Circus (1) / What Did The Animals Say (1) / Your Brains'll Fall Out (2)

SALSOUL ORCHESTRA
Disco orchestra conducted by Philadelphia producer/arranger Vincent Montana, Jr. Vocalists included Phyllis Rhodes, Ronni Tyson, Carl Helm and Philip Hurt.

11/29/75+	14	45		1 The Salsoul Orchestra	[I] $8	Salsoul 5501
10/23/76	61	14		2 Nice 'N' Naasty		$8	Salsoul 5502
12/11/76+	83	6		3 Christmas Jollies	[X] $8	Salsoul 5507
6/25/77	61	20		4 Magic Journey		$8	Salsoul 5515
11/26/77+	100	15		5 Cuchi-Cuchi		$8	Salsoul 5519

CHARO & THE SALSOUL ORCHESTRA

12/24/77+	48	7		6 Christmas Jollies	[X-R] $8	Salsoul 5507
3/25/78	117	8		7 Up The Yellow Brick Road		$8	Salsoul 8500
9/9/78	97	13		8 Greatest Disco Hits/Music For Non-Stop Dancing	[G] $8	Salsoul 8508

DEBUT DATE	PEAK POS	WKS CHR	G O L D	ARTIST — Album Title	$	Label & Number

SALSOUL ORCHESTRA — Cont'd

| 12/19/81+ | 170 | 5 | | 9 Christmas Jollies II .... [X] | $8 | Salsoul 8547 |

Alpha Centuri (4)
Borriquito (5)
Chicago Bus Stop (Ooh, I Love It) (1,8)
Christmas Song (medley) (3)
Christmas Time (3)
Cookie Jar (5)
Cuchi-Cuchi (4)
Dance A Little Bit Closer (5)
Deck The Halls (3,9)
Don't Beat Around The Bush (2,8)
Ease On Down The Road (3)
El Reloj (The Clock) (5)
Evergreen (Love Theme from A Star Is Born) (7)
Feelings (medley) (2)
Fiddler On The Roof Medley (7)
First Noel (medley) (3)
Get Happy (1)
Getaway (4,8)
God Rest Ye Merry Gentlemen (3)
Guantanamera (4)
Hark! The Herald Angels Sing (medley) (3)
I'll Home For Christmas (medley) (3)
It Don't Have To Be Funky (2)
It's A New Day (4)
It's Good For The Soul (2,8)
Jack And Jill (2)
Jingle Bells (medley) (3)
Journey To Phoebus (4)
Joy To The World (3,9)
Joyful Spirit (9)
Let's Spend The Night Together (5)
Little Drummer Boy (3)
Love Letters (3)
Magic Bird Of Fire (4,8)
Merry Christmas All (3)
More Of You (5)
New Year's Medley (3)
Nightcrawler (2)
O Come All Ye Faithful (medley) (3)
Only You (Can Make My Empty Life Worthwhile) (5)
Ritzy Mambo (2) 99
Rudolph The Red-Nosed Reindeer (medley) (3)
Run Away (4)
Salsoul Christmas Suite (9)
Salsoul Hustle (1,8) 76
Salsoul Rainbow (1,8)
Salsoul 3001 (2,8)
Santa Claus Is Coming To Town (medley) (3)
Sgt. Pepper's Lonely Hearts Club Band (3)
Short Shorts (4)
Silent Night (3)
Sleigh Ride (3)
Speedy Gonzales (5)
Standing And Waiting On Love (2)
Tale Of Three Cities (1)
Themes From Montreal Olympics, 1976 Medley (4)
There's Someone Who's Knocking (3)
We Wish You A Merry Christmas (medley) (3)
We've Only Just Begun (medley) (2)
West Side Story Medley (3)
White Christmas (medley) (3)
Winter Wonderland (medley) (3)
You're All I Want For Christmas (9)
You're Just The Right Size (1,5,8) 88

SALT-N-PEPA

Queens-based female rap trio: Cheryl "Salt" James, Sandy "Pepa" Denton (from Kingston, Jamaica) and Dee Dee "DJ Spinderella LaToya" Roper. James and Denton recorded earlier as Super Nature. Took a line from their Super Nature recording "Showstopper" and changed name to Salt-N-Pepa.

8/1/87+	26	53	▲	1 Hot, Cool & Vicious	$8	Next Plat. 1007
8/13/88	38	31	●	2 A Salt With A Deadly Pepa	$8	Next Plat. 1011
4/7/90	38	71	▲	3 Blacks' Magic	$12	Next Plat. 1019

Beauty And The Beat (1)
Blacks' Magic (3)
Chick On The Side (1)
Do You Want Me (3) 21
Doper Than Dope (3)
Everybody Get Up (2)
Expression (3) 26
Hyped On The Mic (2)
I Desire (1)
I Don't Know (3)
I Gotcha (2)
I Like It Like That (3)
I Like To Party (3)
I'll Take Your Man (1)
Independent (3)
It's All Right (1)
Let The Rhythm Run (2)
Let's Talk About Sex (3) 13
Live And Let Die (3)
My Mike Sounds Nice (1)
Negro Wit' An Ego (3)
Salt With A Deadly Pepa (2)
Shake Your Thang (2)
Showstopper, The (1)
Solo Power (Let's Get Paid) (2)
Solo Power (Syncopated Soul) (2)
Spinderella's Not A Fella (But A Girl DJ) (2)
Start The Party (3)
Swift (3)
Tramp (1)
Twist And Shout (2)
You Showed Me (3) 47

SALTY DOG

Hard-rock band based in Los Angeles and formed by guitarist Michael Hannon. Includes Jimmi Bleacher (vocals), Pete Reveen and Khurt Maier.

| 4/7/90 | 176 | 3 | | Every Dog Has Its Day .... | $12 | Geffen 24270 |

Cat's Got Nine
Come Along
Heave Hard (She Comes Easy)
Just Like A Woman
Keep Me Down
Lonesome Fool
Nothin' But A Dream
Ring My Bell
Sacrifice Me
Sim Sala Bim
Slow Daze
Spoonful
Where The Sun Don't Shine

SAM & DAVE

Samuel Moore (b: 10/12/35, Miami) and David Prater (b: 5/9/37, Ocilla, Georgia). Sam had been with the Melionaires gospel group, and Dave was a solo artist prior to their meeting in Miami in 1961. First recorded for Alston in 1962. Duo produced by Isaac Hayes and David Porter. Dave was killed in a car crash on 4/9/88.

8/6/66	45	15		1 Hold On, I'm Comin'	$30	Stax 708
1/21/67	118	13		2 Double Dynamite	$30	Stax 712
11/18/67+	62	13		3 Soul Men	$30	Stax 725
2/15/69	87	17		4 The Best Of Sam & Dave .... [G]	$15	Atlantic 8218

Blame Me (Don't Blame My Heart) (1)
Broke Down Piece Of Man (3)
Can't You Find Another Way (Of Doing It) (4) 54
Don't Help Me Out (1)
Don't Knock It (3)
Don't Make It So Hard On Me (1)
Ease Me (1)
Good Runs The Bad Away (3)
Hold It Baby (3)
Hold On! I'm A Comin' (1,4) 21
Home At Last (2)
I Don't Need Nobody (To Tell Me 'Bout My Baby) (2)
I Got Everything I Need (1)
I Take What I Want (1,4)
I Thank You (4) 9
I'm With You (3)
I'm Your Pumper (2)
I've Seen What Loneliness Can Do (3)
If You Got The Loving (1)
It's A Wonder (1)
Just Can't Get Enough (2)
Just Keep Holding On (3)
Just Me (1)
Let It Be Me (3)
May I Baby (3,4)
Rich Kind Of Poverty (3)
Said I Wasn't Gonna Tell Nobody (2,4) 64
Sleep Good Tonight (2)
Small Portion Of Your Love (4)
Soothe Me (2,4) 56
Soul Man (3,4) 2
Sweet Pains (2)
That's The Way It's Gotta Be (2)
Use Me (2)
When Something Is Wrong With My Baby (2,4) 42
Wrap It Up (4)
You Don't Know Like I Know (1,4) 90
You Don't Know What You Mean To Me (4) 48
You Got It Made (1)
You Got Me Hummin' (2,4) 77

SAMBORA, Richie

Born on 7/11/59 in New Jersey. Guitarist of Bon Jovi.

| 9/21/91 | 36 | 11 | | Stranger In This Town .... | $12 | Mercury 848895 |

Answer, The
Ballad Of Youth 63
Church Of Desire
Father Time
Mr. Bluesman
One Light Burning
Rest In Peace
River Of Love
Rosie
Stranger In This Town

SAMPLE, Joe

Born on 2/1/39 in Houston. Jazz keyboardist. Founded The Crusaders in 1954. Worked as Motown sessionman.

2/25/78	62	25		1 Rainbow Seeker ....[I]	$8	ABC 1050
2/10/79	56	26		2 Carmel..[I]	$8	ABC 1126
1/31/81	65	20		3 Voices In The Rain ....[I]	$8	MCA 5172
4/16/83	125	14		4 The Hunter ....[I]	$8	MCA 5397
4/15/89	129	14		5 Spellbound ....[I]	$8	Warner 25781

features vocalists Michael Franks, Al Jarreau and Take 6

All God's Children (5)
As Long As It Lasts (1)
Beauty And The Beast (4)
Blue Ballet (4)
Bones Jive (3)
Burnin' Up The Carnival (3)
Cannery Row (2)
Carmel (2)
Dream Of Dreams (3)
Eye Of The Hurricane (3)
Fly With Wings Of Love (3)
Greener Grass (3)
Hunter, The (4)
In All My Wildest Dreams (1)
Islands In The Rain (1)
Just A Little Higher (4)
Leading Me Back To You (5)
Looking Glass (5)
Luna En New York (5)
Melodies Of Love (1)
Midnight And Mist (2)
More Beautiful Each Day (2)
Night Flight (4)
Paintings (2)
Rainbow Seeker (1)
Rainy Day In Monterey (2)
Sermonized (5)
Seven Years Of Good Luck (5)
Shadows (3)
Somehow Our Love Survives (5)
Sonata In Solitude (3)
Spellbound (5)
Sunrise (2)
There Are Many Stops Along The Way (1)
Together We'll Find A Way (1)
U Turn (5)
Voices In The Rain (3)
Wings Of Fire (4)

SAM THE SHAM and The PHAROAHS

Dallas rock & roll group formed in the early 1960s, featuring lead singer Domingo "Sam" Samudio (b: 1940, Dallas). Included Ray Stinnet, David Martin, Jerry Patterson and Butch Gibson. First recorded for Dingo in 1965. Samudio went solo in 1970. Formed new band in 1974. On the 1982 film soundtrack The Border. Sam later became a street preacher in Memphis.

| 6/12/65 | 26 | 18 | | 1 Wooly Bully .... | $25 | MGM 4297 |

DEBUT DATE	PEAK POS	WKS CHR	GOLD	ARTIST — Album Title	$	Label & Number

SAM THE SHAM and The PHAROAHS — Cont'd

9/24/66	**82**	7	2	Li'l Red Riding Hood	**$25**	MGM 4407
3/11/67	**98**	17	3	the best of Sam the Sham and the pharaohs ....[G]	**$20**	MGM 4422

Deputy Dog (2)	Grasshopper (2)	I Wish It Were Me (3)	Long Tall Sally (1)	Ready Or Not (3)	Sweet Talk (2)
El Toro De Goro (The Peace Loving Bull) (2,3)	Green'ich Grendel (2)	(I'm In With) The Out Crowd (3)	Mary Is My Little Lamb (2)	Red Hot (3) 82	Wooly Bully (1,3) 2
Every Woman I Know (Crazy 'Bout An Auto) (1)	Hair On My Chinny Chin Chin (3) 22	Ju Ju Hand (3) 26	Mary Lee (1)	Ring Dang Doo (3) 33	
Gangster Of Love (1)	Hanky Panky (1)	Juiminos (Let's Went) (1)	Memphis Beat (1)	Ring Them Bells (1)	
Go-Go Girls (1)	Haunted House (1)	Lil' Red Riding Hood (2,3) 2	Mystery Train (3)	Shotgun (1)	
	I Found Love (1)	Little Miss Muffet (2)	Phantom, The (2)	Sorry 'Bout That (1)	
			Pharaoh-A-Go Go (2)	Standing Ovation (3)	

★★302★★ SANBORN, David

Born on 7/30/45 in Tampa, Florida; raised in St. Louis. Saxophonist/flutist. Stricken with polio as a child. Played with Paul Butterfield from 1967-71; Stevie Wonder from 1972-73. Formed own group in 1975.

8/28/76	**125**	8		1 Sanborn .... [I]	**$8**	Warner 2957
6/3/78	**151**	6		2 Heart To Heart .... [I]	**$8**	Warner 3189
3/8/80	**63**	19	●	3 Hideaway .... [I]	**$8**	Warner 3379
4/18/81	**45**	22		4 Voyeur .... [I]	**$8**	Warner 3546
7/10/82	**70**	23		5 As We Speak .... [I]	**$8**	Warner 23650
11/26/83+	**81**	33		6 Backstreet .... [I]	**$8**	Warner 23906
2/9/85	**64**	32	●	7 Straight To The Heart .... [I-L]	**$8**	Warner 25150
				featuring live studio cuts of his well-known compositions		
6/14/86	**50**	64	▲	8 Double Vision .... [I]	**$8**	Warner 25393
				BOB JAMES/DAVID SANBORN		
2/14/87	**74**	37	●	9 A Change Of Heart .... [I]	**$8**	Warner 25479
7/16/88	**59**	28	●	10 Close-Up .... [I]	**$8**	Reprise 25715
7/20/91	**170**	7		11 Another Hand .... [I]	**$12**	Elektra M. 61088
5/16/92	**107**	31		12 Upfront .... [I]	**$12**	Elektra 61272

Again An Again (3)	Carly's Song (3)	Hobbies (11)	Love Is Not Enough, Theme From (2)	Pyramid (10)	Summer (9)
Alcazar (12)	Change Of Heart (9)	I Do It For Your Love (1)		Rain On Christmas (5)	Sunrise Gospel (2)
All I Need Is You (4)	Chicago Song (9)	I Told U So (6)	Love Will Come Someday (5)	Ramblin' (12)	Tear For Crystal (6)
Another Hand (11)	Come To Me, Nina (11)	If You Would Be Mine (1)	Mamacita (1)	Run For Cover (4,7)	Tintin (9)
Anything You Want (3)	Concrete Boogie (1)	Imogene (9)	Maputo (3)	Rush Hour (5)	Tough (10)
Anywhere I Wander (2)	Creeper (3)	Indio (1)	Monica Jane (11)	Same Girl (10)	Wake Me When It's Over (4)
As We Speak (5)	Crossfire (12)	It's You (4,8)	Moon Tune (8)	7th Ave. (1)	Weird From One Step Beyond (11)
Back Again (5)	Dream, The (9)	J.T. (10)	More Than Friends (8)	Short Visit (2)	
Backstreet (6)	Dukes & Counts (11)	Jesus (11)	Neither One Of Us (6)	Since I Fell For You (8)	When You Smile At Me (6)
Bang Bang (12) 53	First Song (11)	Just For You (4)	Never Enough (8)	Slam (12)	You Are Everything (10)
Believer (6)	Full House (12)	Lesley Ann (10)	One Hundred Ways (7)	Smile (1,7)	You Don't Know Me (8)
Benny (12)	Goodbye (10)	Let's Just Say Goodbye (4)	One In A Million (4)	Snakes (12)	
Better Believe It (5)	Heba (2)	Lisa (3,7)	Over And Over (5)	So Far Away (10)	
Blue Beach (4)	Herbs (1)	Lonely From The Twilight Zone (medley) (11)	Port Of Call (5)	Solo (2)	
Breaking Point (9)	Hey (12)		Prayers For Charlie From The Devil At Four O'Clock (medley) (11)	Sophisticated Squaw (1)	
Bums Cathedral (6)	Hideaway (3,7)	Lotus Blossom (2,7)		Soul Serenade (12)	
CEE (11)	High Roller (9)	Love & Happiness (7)		Straight To The Heart (5,7)	

SANDALS, The

Southern California instrumental surf-rock quintet — John Blakeley, lead guitar.

2/4/67	**110**	13		The Endless Summer .... [S-I]	**$20**	World Pac. 1832
				film is a surfing documentary by Bruce Brown		

Decoy	Endless Summer, Theme From	Jet Black	Out Front	6 Pac	Trailing
Drifting	Good Greeves	Lonely Road	Scrambler	TR-6	Wild As The Sea

SANDERS, Pharoah

Born Farrel Sanders on 10/13/40 in Little Rock, Arkansas. Jazz tenor saxophone player. With Hughie Simmons in Oakland, California, 1959-62. Moved to New York City in 1962, worked with local jazz combos. With John Coltrane in 1966. Formed own group with Leon Thomas and Lonnie Liston Smith in 1969.

8/16/69	**188**	4		1 Karma .... [I]	**$12**	Impulse! 9181
7/31/71	**175**	3		2 Thembi .... [I]	**$12**	Impulse! 9206
5/20/78	**163**	5		3 Love Will Find A Way	**$8**	Arista 4161

Answer Me My Love (3)	Bailophone Dance (2)	Creator Has A Master Plan (1)	Got To Give It Up (3)	Love Will Find A Way (3)	Red, Black & Green (2)
As You Are (3)	Colors (1)		Love (2)	Morning Prayer (2)	Thembi (2)
Astral Traveling (2)		Everything I Have Is Good (3)	Love Is Here (3)	Pharomba (2)	

SANDLER, Tony, & Ralph Young

Vocal duo — Tony (Belgian-born) and Ralph (New York-born).

12/17/66+	**85**	19		1 Side By Side	**$15**	Capitol 2598
4/15/67	**166**	3		2 On The Move	**$15**	Capitol 2686
7/5/69	**188**	4		3 Pretty Things Come In Twos	**$15**	Capitol 241
7/11/70	**199**	2		4 Honey Come Back	**$12**	Capitol 449

And When I Die (4)	Chicago (1)	I'll Never Fall In Love Again (4)	(Lo Mucho Que Te Quiero) The More I Love You (3)	Pretty Things Come In Twos (3)	Traces (4)
Autumn Leaves (1)	Coco (4)			Put On A Happy Face (2)	Vaya Con Dios (May God Be With You) (1)
Blackbird (4)	Cu-Cu-Rru-Cu-Cu, Paloma (2)	If We Only Have Love (Quand On N'A Que L'Amour) (3)	Love Me With All Your Heart (Cuando Caliente El Sol) (1)	Raindrops Keep Fallin' On My Head (4)	Very Thought Of You (3)
Blue And Broken Hearted (3)	Dominique (1)		Love Of The Common People (4)		What Now, My Love? (1)
Bon Soir Dame (3)	El Soldado De Levita (3)	Impossible Dream (The Quest) (1)		Sand & Sea (Plein Soleil) (3)	Yellow Bird (2)
C'est Si Bon (2)	French Lullaby (1)		Man And A Woman (2)	Side By Side (1)	Yesterday I Heard The Rain (3)
Can't Help Falling In Love (4)	Gonna Build A Mountain (2)	Just Say I Love Her (Dicitencello Vuie) (2)	Midnight Cowboy (4)	Sunrise, Sunset (2)	
Canadian Sunset (1)	Heather (3)		Misty Morning Eyes (3)	There Will Never Be Another You (3)	You And Only You (Un Bacio Alla Volta) (3)
Chanson D'Amour (Song Of Love) (2)	Honey Come Back (4)		Our Day Will Come (1)		

SANDPIPERS, The

Los Angeles-based trio: Jim Brady (b: 8/24/44), Michael Piano (b: 10/26/44) and Richard Shoff (b: 4/30/44); met while in the Mitchell Boys Choir.

10/29/66+	**13**	37	●	1 Guantanamera	**$12**	A&M 4117

DEBUT DATE	PEAK POS	WKS CHR	GOLD	ARTIST — Album Title	$	Label & Number

SANDPIPERS, The — Cont'd

DEBUT DATE	PEAK POS	WKS CHR		ARTIST — Album Title	$	Label & Number
5/27/67	53	28		2 The Sandpipers	$12	A&M 4125
1/13/68	135	5		3 Misty Roses	$12	A&M 4135
9/7/68	180	5		4 Softly	$12	A&M 4147
5/10/69	194	5		5 The Wonder Of You	$12	A&M 4180
4/18/70	160	10		6 Greatest Hits	[G] $12	A&M 4246
8/15/70	96	11		7 Come Saturday Morning	$12	A&M 4262

All My Loving (4,6)
And I Love Her (3,6)
Angelica (1,6)
Autumn Afternoon (7)
Back On The Street Again (4)
Beyond The Valley Of The Dolls (7)
Bon Soir Dame (2)
Cancion De Amor (Wanderlove) (4,6)
Carmen (1)
Cast Your Fate To The Wind (1)
Come Saturday Morning (7) *17*

Cuando Sali De Cuba (The Wind Will Change Tomorrow) (3,6)
Daydream (3)
Drifter, The (7)
Enamorado (1,6)
Find A Reason To Believe (4)
Fly Me To The Moon (3)
For Baby (2)
Free To Carry On (7) *94*
French Song (2)
Glass (2)
Gloria Patri (Gregorian Psalm Tone III) (4)
Guantanamera (1,6) *9*

(He's Got The) Whole World In His Hands (7)
Honeywind Blows (3)
I Believed It All (3)
I'll Remember You (2)
If I Were The Man (5)
Inch Worm (2)
It's Over (2)
Jenifer Juniper (4)
Kumbaya (5)
La Bamba (1)
La Mer (Beyond The Sea) (1)
Let Go (5)
Lo Mucho Que Te Quiero (The More I Love You) (5)

Long And Winding Road (7)
Louie, Louie (1) *30*
Love Is Blue (4)
Michelle (2)
Misty Roses (3,6)
Ojos De Espana (Spanish Eyes) (4)
Pretty Flamingo (5)
Quando M'Innamoro (4,6)
Rain, Rain Go Away (2)
Santo Domingo (7)
Softly (4)
Softly As I Leave You (2)
Song Of Joy (7)
Sound Of Love (7)

Stasera Gli Angeli Non Volano (For The Last Time) (1)
Strange Song (3)
Strangers In The Night (1)
Suzanne (4)
Temptation (5)
That Night (5)
Things We Said Today (1)
To Put Up With You (4)
Today (3)
Try To Remember (2)
Wave (5)
What Makes You Dream, Pretty Girl? (1)

Where There's A Heartache (7)
Windmills Of Your Mind (5)
Wonder Of You (5,7)
Wooden Heart (3)
Yellow Days (5)
Yesterday (2,6)

SANDS, Tommy

Born on 8/27/37 in Chicago. Pop singer/actor. Mother was a vocalist with Art Kassel's band. Married Nancy Sinatra in 1960; divorced in 1965. In the films *Sing Boy Sing, Mardi Gras, Babes In Toyland* and *The Longest Day.*

DEBUT DATE	PEAK POS	WKS CHR		ARTIST — Album Title	$	Label & Number
5/6/57	4	18		1 **Steady Date with Tommy Sands**	$30	Capitol 848
2/24/58	17	4		2 Sing Boy Sing	[S] $30	Capitol 929

Tommy portrays fictional singer Virgil Walker in the film

"A" - You're Adorable (The Alphabet Song) (1)
Bundle Of Dreams (2)
Crazy 'Cause I Love You (2)
Goin' Steady (1) *16*
Gonna Get A Girl (1)

Graduation Day (1)
I Don't Care Who Knows It (1)
I Don't Know Why (I Just Do) (1)

I'm Gonna Walk And Talk With My Lord (2)
Just A Little Bit More (2)
People In Love (2)
Ring My Phone (1) *flip*
Rock Of Ages (2)

Sing Boy Sing (2) *24*
Soda-Pop Boy (2)
Somewhere Along The Way (1)
Teach Me Tonight (1)

That's All I Want From You (2)
Too Young (1)
Too Young To Go Steady (1)
Walkin' My Baby Back Home (1)

Who Baby (2)
Would I Love You (2)
Your Daddy Wants To Do Right (2)

SANFORD/TOWNSEND BAND, The

Los Angeles-based rock band led by Ed Sanford and John Townsend.

DEBUT DATE	PEAK POS	WKS CHR		ARTIST — Album Title	$	Label & Number
8/13/77	57	15		1 The Sanford/Townsend Band	$8	Warner 2966
2/11/78	92	8		2 Duo-Glide	$8	Warner 3081

Ain't It So, Love (2)
Cryin' Like A Child (2)
Does It Have To Be You (1)
Eights And Aces (2)

Eye Of My Storm (Oh Woman) (2)
In For The Night (1)
Livin's Easy (2)
Lou (1)

Mississippi Sunshine (2)
Moolah Moo Mazuma (Sin City Wahh-oo) (1)
Oriental Gate (No Chance Of Changin' My Mind) (1)

Paradise (2)
Rainbows Colored In Blue (1)
Shake It To The Right (1)
Smoke From A Distant Fire (1) *9*

Sometimes When The Wind Blows (2)
Squire James (1)
Starbrite (2)

Sunshine In My Heart Again (1)
Voodoo (2)

SAN FRANCISCO SYMPHONY ORCHESTRA

Seiji Ozawa, conductor.

DEBUT DATE	PEAK POS	WKS CHR		ARTIST — Album Title	$	Label & Number
4/7/73	105	15		William Russo: Three Pieces for Blues Band and Orchestra/Leonard Bernstein: Symphonic Dances from West Side Story	[I] $10	DG 2530 309

Russo side: with the Siegel-Schwall Band

Bernstein: Symphonic Dances From West Side Story (1961)

Three Pieces For Blues Band And Symphony Orchestra Op. 50 (1968)

SANG, Samantha

Born Cheryl Gray on 8/5/53 in Melbourne, Australia. Began career on Melbourne radio at age eight.

DEBUT DATE	PEAK POS	WKS CHR	GOLD	ARTIST — Album Title	$	Label & Number
3/11/78	29	14	●	Emotion	$8	Private St. 7009

But If She Moves You
Change Of Heart

Charade
Emotion *3*

I Don't Wanna Go
La La La - I Love You

Living Without Your Love
Love Of A Woman

When Love Is Gone
You Keep Me Dancing *56*

SAN SEBASTIAN STRINGS, The

Music composed by Anita Kerr (with sound effects), featuring narration of the poetry of Rod McKuen.

DEBUT DATE	PEAK POS	WKS CHR	GOLD	ARTIST — Album Title	$	Label & Number
3/25/67+	52	143	●	1 The Sea	[I-T] $10	Warner 1670
9/23/67	115	13		2 The Earth	[I-T] $10	Warner 1705
2/17/68	68	25		3 The Sky	[I-T] $10	Warner 1720
1/18/69	20	20		4 Home To The Sea	[I-T] $10	Warner 1764
11/22/69	84	17		5 For Lovers	[I-T] $10	Warner 1795
1/17/70	162	5		6 The Complete Sea	[R] $15	Warner 1827 [3]

reissue of albums #1 & 4, plus album #7 (forthcoming)

DEBUT DATE	PEAK POS	WKS CHR		ARTIST — Album Title	$	Label & Number
9/26/70	171	5		7 The Soft Sea	[I-T] $10	Warner 1839

Afternoon Shadows (1,6)
Another Evening With The Gypsies (4,6)
Bathtub Surfing (4,6)
Beyond The Bend Ahead (1,6)
Body Surfing With The Jet Set (6,7)
Butterfly Is Drunk On Sunshine (5)
Buy For Me The Wind (3)
Capri In July (2)
Come On In, The Water's Fine (6,7)
Dancing In The Kitchen (5)

Day They Built The Road (2)
Days Of The Dancing (1,6)
Do You Like The Rain? (1,6)
Doorways I Haven't Found (2)
Dragonflies (4,6)
Earthquake (2)
Ever Constant Sea (1,6,7)
Floating Past The Fields (4,6)
Flower People (5)
For Lovers (5)
Forehead Of The Morning (3)
Foreign Movies (3)
Gifts From The Sea (1,6)
Growing Old Together (5)

Gypsy Camp (1,6)
Haunted Mansion On The Hill (5)
Home (2)
Home To The Sea (4,6)
How Many Colors Of Blue? (3)
I'll Carry Home An Orchard (5)
In Summing Up (3)
Looking Up Through Wednesday's Silence (5)
Love Hasn't Any Windows (5)
Love Me Slowly (5)
Lovers Too Have Lullabies (5)

Make A Bigger Circle, With A Softer Touch (5)
Monotony Of Games (6,7)
Moonlight Swim (4,6)
Mr. God's Trombones (3)
Mud Kids (2)
My Dog Likes Oranges (3)
My Friend The Sea (1,6)
My Mother Wanted Me To Play Mozart (2)
Naked In The Sunlight (6,7)
New Lullabye (For Suzie & Kelly) (3)
Night Talk (3)
Night Watch (4,6)

No Islands Left (6,7)
No Loving Without Losing (5)
November Resolution (4,6)
Oh Yes, The Wind (6,7)
One In The Same (4,6)
Overture To The Soft Sea (6,7)
Part Of Every Ocean (4,6)
Passage Home (4,6)
Patch Of Sky, Away From Everything (3)
Pushing The Clouds Away (1,6)
Running Out Of Strangers (4,6)

Sailing Through The Sun (4,6)
Saving Sea Shells (6,7)
Sea, The (1,6)
So Little Sun (3)
So Much For The Pipers (6,7)
Song From The Earth (2)
Storm, The (1,6)
Sunday (2)
Tender Earth (2)
There Are No Beaches In Magic City, Texas (4,6)
Time Of Noon (1,6)
Underground Train (2)

DEBUT DATE	PEAK POS	WKS CHR	GOLD	ARTIST — Album Title	$	Label & Number

SAN SEBASTIAN STRINGS, The — Cont'd

Wake Up (6,7) Walk With The Angels (3) Waltz, The (2) We Two Are Drifting (6,7) What About Tomorrow? (6,7) While Drifting (1,6) When Winter Comes (3) Who Has Touched The Sky (3) Why I Follow The Tigers (5) You Even Taste Like The Sun (1,6) You Wonder Why I Love You (5)

SANTA ESMERALDA
Spanish-flavored disco studio project produced by Nicolas Skorsky and Jean-Manuel de Scarano.

DEBUT DATE	PEAK POS	WKS CHR	GOLD	ARTIST — Album Title	$	Label & Number
11/12/77+	25	23	●	1 Don't Let Me Be Misunderstood	$8	Casablanca 7080
				vocals by Leroy Gomez		
2/25/78	41	14		2 The House Of The Rising Sun	$8	Casablanca 7088
9/2/78	141	6		3 Beauty	$8	Casablanca 7109
				above 2 feature vocals by Jimmy Goings		

Black Pot (1) Dance You Down Tonight (2) Danse De La Beaute (Part 1 & 2) (3) **Don't Let Me Be Misunderstood** (1) 15 Esmeralda Suite (1) Gloria (1) Hey! Gip (2) Hey Joe (3) **House Of The Rising Sun** (2) 78 Learning The Game (3) Nothing Else Matters (2) Only Beauty Survives (3) Quasimodo Suite (2) Wages Of Sin (Parts 1-3) (3) You're My Everything (1)

SANTAMARIA, Mongo
Born Ramon Santamaria on 4/7/22 in Havana, Cuba. Bandleader/conga, bongo and percussion player. Member of bands led by Perez Prado, Tito Puente and Cal Tjader. Own group from 1961. In the film *Made In Paris* in 1966.

DEBUT DATE	PEAK POS	WKS CHR	GOLD	ARTIST — Album Title	$	Label & Number
5/4/63	42	10		1 Watermelon Man!	[I] $20	Battle 96120
3/27/65	112	10		2 El Pussy Cat	[I] $12	Columbia 9098
8/28/65	79	15		3 La Bamba	[I] $12	Columbia 9175
6/4/66	135	5		4 Hey! Let's Party	[I] $12	Columbia 9273
8/10/68	171	18		5 Soul Bag	[I] $12	Columbia 9653
3/1/69	62	24		6 Stone Soul	[I] $12	Columbia 9780
11/29/69	193	2		7 Workin' On A Groovy Thing	[I] $15	Columbia 9937
4/11/70	171	3		8 Feelin' Alright	[I] $12	Atlantic 8252
10/3/70	195	2		9 Mongo '70	[I] $12	Atlantic 1567

Adobo Criollo (9) Afro Lypso (2) Ah Ha (2) Ain't That Peculiar (7) Baby What You Want Me To Do (5) Baila Dance (4) Bayou Roots (1) Black-Eyed Peas (2) Boogie Cha Cha Blues (1) By The Time I Get To Phoenix (8) Call Me (4) Chili Beans (5) **Cloud Nine** (6) *32* Coconut Milk (3) Cold Sweat (5) Cuidado (2) Cut That Cane! (1) Dedicated To Love (9) Do It To It (3) Don't Bother Me No More (1) El Bikini (4) **El Pussy Cat** (2) *97* Fat Back (3) **Feeling Alright** (8) *96* Fever (8) From Me To You All (3) Funny Money (1) Get Back (7) Get The Money (1) Getting It Out Of My System (7) Go Git It! (3) Grass Roots (9) Green Onions (5) Groovin' (3) Hammer Head (2) Heighty-Hi (8) Hey! (4) Hip-Hug-Her (8) Hitchcock Railway (6) Hold On, I'm Comin' (8) Hot Dog (5) I Can't Get Next To You (8) (I Can't Get No) Satisfaction (4) I Got You (I Feel Good) (4) In-A-Gadda-Da-Vida (8) In The Midnight Hour (5) In The Mood (4) It's Your Thing (7) Jose Outside (3) Just Say Goodbye (3) La Bamba (3) La Gitana (2) Little Green Apples (6) Look Away (9) Louie, Louie (4) Love Child (6) Love, Oh Love (1) Manha De Carnaval (Morning Of The Carnival) (3) March Of The Panther (9) Mo' Do' (9) My Cherie Amour (7) My Girl (5) Night Crawler (9) Now Generation (4) On Broadway (8) Peanut Vendor (1) Proud Mary (7) Respect (5) Ricky Tick (3) Ritmo Negro (2) Sarai (2) See-Saw (6) Shotgun (4) Sitting On The Dock Of The Bay (5) Son-Of-A-Preacher Man (6) Spinning Wheel (7) Stoned Soul Picnic (6) Streak O'Lean (3) Suavito (4) Summertime (4) Sunshine Of Your Love (8) Together (2) Too Busy Thinking About My Baby (7) Tracks Of My Tears (8) Twenty-Five Miles (7) Up, Up And Away (5) Walk On By (4) **Watermelon Man** (1,3) *10* We Got Latin Soul (7) Where We Are (6) Who's Making Love (6) Windjammer (9) Workin' On A Groovy Thing (7) **Yeh-Yeh!** (1) *92* Yesterday's Tomorrow (9)

★★63★★ SANTANA
Latin-rock group formed in San Francisco in 1966. Consisted of Carlos Santana (b: 7/20/47, Autlan de Navarro, Mexico; vocals, guitar), Gregg Rolie (keyboards) and David Brown (bass). Added percussionists Michael Carabello, Jose Chepitos Areas and Michael Shrieve in 1969. Worked Fillmore West and Woodstock in 1969. Neal Schon (guitar) added in 1971. Santana began solo work in 1972. Schon and Rolie formed Journey in 1973. Shrieve left in 1975 to form Automatic Man. Schon and Shrieve also charted with Sammy Hagar.

DEBUT DATE	PEAK POS	WKS CHR	GOLD	ARTIST — Album Title	$	Label & Number
9/13/69	4	108	▲²	1 Santana	$12	Columbia 9781
10/10/70	1⁶	88	▲⁴	2 Abraxas	$10	Columbia 30130
10/16/71	1⁵	39	●	3 Santana III	$10	Columbia 30595
11/4/72	8	32	▲	4 Caravanserai	$10	Columbia 31610
12/1/73	25	21	●	5 Welcome	$10	Columbia 32445
7/27/74	17	21	▲²	6 Santana's Greatest Hits	[G] $10	Columbia 33050
11/2/74	20	19	●	7 Borboletta	$10	Columbia 33135
4/10/76	10	26	●	8 Amigos	$8	Columbia 33576
				Amigos is Spanish for Friends		
1/22/77	27	19	●	9 Festival	$8	Columbia 34423
11/5/77	10	24	▲	10 Moonflower	[L] $10	Columbia 34914 [2]
11/4/78	27	33	●	11 Inner Secrets	$8	Columbia 35600
10/20/79	25	22		12 Marathon	$8	Columbia 36154
4/18/81	9	32	●	13 Zebop!	$8	Columbia 37158
9/4/82	22	23		14 Shango	$8	Columbia 38122
				Shango is Mexican for Monkey		
3/23/85	50	21		15 Beyond Appearances	$8	Columbia 39527
3/7/87	95	11		16 Freedom	$8	Columbia 40272
10/29/88	142	6		17 Viva Santana	[L] $15	Columbia 44344 [3]
				live recordings from 1969-87, includes rare and previously unreleased material		
7/21/90	85	11		18 Spirits Dancing In The Flesh	$12	Columbia 46065
5/23/92	102	13		19 Milagro	$12	Polydor 513197
				Milagro is Spanish for Miracle		

A Dios (19) Abi Cama (17) Agua Que Va Caer (19) All I Ever Wanted (12) All The Love Of The Universe (4) American Gypsy (13) Angel Negro (17) Aqua Marine (12,17) Aspirations (7) Bahia (10) Ballin' (17) Bambara (17) Bambele (17) Batuka (17) Before We Go (16) **Black Magic Woman** (2,6,10,17) *4* Body Surfing (14) Borboletta (7) Breaking Out (15) Brightest Star (13) Brotherhood (15,17) Canto De Los Flores (7)

SANTANA — Cont'd

Caramba (8)
Carnaval (9,10)
Changes (13)
Choose (18)
Dance Sister Dance (Baila Mi Hermana) (8,10,17)
Daughter Of The Night (17)
Dawn (medley) (10)
Dealer (medley) (11)
Deeper, Dig Deeper (16)
E Papa Re (13)
El Morocco (10)
El Nicoya (2)
Eternal Caravan Of Reincarnation (4)
Europa (Earth's Cry Heaven's Smile) (8,10,17)
Every Step Of The Way (4)
Everybody's Everything (3,6,17) *12*
Everything's Coming Our Way (3,6)
Evil Ways (1,6,17) *9*
Facts Of Love (11)
Flame-Sky (5)
Flor D'Luna (Moonflower) (10)
Flor De Canela (7)
Free All The People (South Africa) (19)
Full Moon (18)
Future Primitive (4)
Gitano (8)
Give And Take (7)

Give Me Love (9)
Go Within (medley) (10)
Going Home (5)
Goodness And Mercy (18)
Guajira (3,17)
Gypsy Queen (medley) (2,10,17)
Gypsy Woman (18)
Gypsy/Grajonca (19)
Hannibal (13)
Hard Times (12)
Head, Hands & Feet (medley) (10)
Here And Now (7)
Hold On (14) *15*
Holiday (medley) (11)
Hong Kong Blues (medley) (17)
Hope You're Feeling Better (2,6)
How Long (15)
I Love You Much Too Much (13)
I'll Be Waiting (10)
I'm The One Who Loves You (15)
Incident At Neshabur (2,17)
It's A Jungle Out There (18)
Jingo (1,6,17,18) *56*
Jugando (9,10)
Jungle Strut (3,17)
Just In Time To See The Sun (4)

Just Let The Music Speak (17)
La Fuente Del Ritmo (4)
Let It Shine (8) *77*
Let Me (8)
Let Me Inside (14)
Let The Children Play (9,10)
Let The Music Set You Free (9)
Let There Be Light (medley) (18)
Life Is A Lady (medley) (11)
Life Is Anew (7)
Life Is For Living (19)
Light Of Life (5)
Lightning In The Sky (12)
Look Up (To See What's Coming Down) (4)
Love (12)
Love, Devotion & Surrender (5)
Love Is You (16)
Make Somebody Happy (19)
Mandela (16)
Marathon (12)
Maria Caracoles (9)
Mirage (7)
(Moonflower) ..see: Flor D'Luna
Mother Africa (5)
Mother Earth (medley) (18)
Mother's Daughter (2)
Move On (11)
Night Hunting Time (14)

Nile, The (14)
No One To Depend On (3) *36*
Nowhere To Run (14) *66*
Nueva York (14)
Once It's Gotcha (14)
One Chain (Don't Make No Prison) (11) *59*
One With The Sun (7)
Open Invitation (11,17)
Over And Over (13)
Oxun (Oshun) (14)
Oye Como Va (2,6,17) *13*
Para Los Rumberos (3)
Paris Finale (17)
Peace On Earth (medley) (18)
Peraza I & II (17)
Persuasion (1,6,17)
Practice What You Preach (7)
Praise (16)
Primera Invasion (13)
Promise Of A Fisherman (7)
Reach Up (9)
Red Prophet (19)
Revelations (9)
Right Now (15)
Right On (medley) (19)
River, The (9)
Runnin (12)
Saja (medley) (19)
Samba De Sausalito (5)
Samba Pa Ti (2,6)
Savor (1,10)
Say It Again (15) *46*

Se A Cabo (2,6)
Searchin' (13)
Sensitive Kind (13) *56*
Shades Of Time (1)
Shango (14)
She Can't Let Go (16)
She's Not There (10,17) *27*
Singing Winds, Crying Beasts (2)
Somewhere In Heaven (19)
Song Of The Wind (4,17)
Songs Of Freedom (16)
Soul Sacrifice (1,10,17)
Soweto (Africa Libre) (18)
Spanish Rose (medley) (11)
Spirit (15)
Spirits Dancing In The Flesh (medley) (18)
Spring Manifestations (7)
Stand Up (12)
Stay (Beside Me) (12)
Stone Flower (4)
Stormy (11) *32*
Summer Lady (12)
Super Boogie (medley) (17)
Taboo (3)
Take Me With You (8)
Tales Of Kilimanjaro (13)
Tell Me Are You Tired (8)
Third Stone From The Sun (medley) (18)
Touchdown Raiders (3)
Toussaint L'Overture (3,10)
Transcendance (10)

Treat (1)
Try A Little Harder (9)
Veracruz (16)
Verao Vermelho (9)
Victim Of Circumstance (16)
Vilato (17)
Waiting (11)
Warrior (14)
Waves Within (4)
We Don't Have To Wait (19)
Welcome (5)
Well All Right (11) *69*
Wham! (11)
What Does It Take (To Win Your Love) (14)
When I Look Into Your Eyes (5)
Who Loves You (15)
Who's That Lady (18)
Winning (13) *17*
Written In Sand (15)
You Just Don't Care (1)
You Know That I Love You (12) *35*
Your Touch (15)
Yours Is The Light (5)
Zulu (10)

SANTANA, Carlos

Mexican-born rock and jazz-fusion guitarist. Leader of Santana. Added 'Devadip' (which means 'The light of the lamp of the Supreme') to his name after becoming a disciple of guru Sri Chinmoy.

DEBUT DATE	PEAK POS	WKS CHR	GOLD	ARTIST — Album Title	$	Label & Number
7/8/72	8	33 ▲		1 Carlos Santana & Buddy Miles! Live! .....[L] **CARLOS SANTANA & BUDDY MILES** recorded in Hawaii's Diamond Head volcano crater	$10	Columbia 31308
7/7/73	14	24 ●		2 Love Devotion Surrender .....[I] **CARLOS SANTANA/MAHAVISHNU JOHN McLAUGHLIN**	$10	Columbia 32034
10/12/74	79	8		3 Illuminations .....[I] **TURIYA ALICE COLTRANE/DEVADIP CARLOS SANTANA**	$10	Columbia 32900
3/31/79	87	9		4 Oneness/Silver Dreams-Golden Reality .....[I] **DEVADIP** half of side 1 recorded live in Osaka, Japan	$8	Columbia 35686
9/6/80	65	10		5 The Swing Of Delight .....[I] **DEVADIP CARLOS SANTANA** with guests: Herbie Hancock, Wayne Shorter and Ron Carter	$10	Columbia 36590 [2]
4/23/83	31	17		6 Havana Moon ..... with guests: Willie Nelson, Booker T. Jones and The Fabulous Thunderbirds	$8	Columbia 38642
11/7/87	195	1		7 Blues for Salvador .....[I]	$8	Columbia 40875

Angel Of Air (medley) (3)
Angel Of Sunlight (3)
Angel Of Water (medley) (3)
Aquatic Park (medley) (7)
Arise Awake (4)
Bailando (medley) (7)
Bella (7)
Bliss: The Eternal Now (3)
Blues For Salvador (7)
Chosen Hour (4)
Cry Of The Wilderness (4)
Daughter Of The Night (6)

Deeper, Dig Deeper (7)
Ecuador (3)
Evil Ways (1) *84*
Faith Interlude (1)
Free As The Morning Sun (4)
Free Form Funkafide Filth (1)
Gardenia (5)
Golden Dawn (4)
Golden Hours (5)
Guru Sri Chinmoy Aphorism (3)

Guru's Song (4)
Hannibal (7)
Havana Moon (6)
I Am Free (4)
I'm Gone (7)
Illuminations (3)
Jharna Kala (3)
Jim Jeannie (4)
La Llave (5)
Lava (1)
Let Us Go Into The House Of The Lord (2)

Life Divine (2)
Life Is Just A Passing Parade (4)
Light Versus Darkness (4)
Lightnin' (4)
Love Supreme (2)
Marbles (1)
Meditation (2)
Mingus (2)
Mudbone (6)
Naima (2)
Now That You Know (7)

One With You (6)
Oneness (4)
Phuler Matan (5)
Shere Khan, The Tiger (5)
Silver Dreams Golden Smiles (4)
Song For Devadip (4)
Song For My Brother (5)
Spartacus, Love Theme From (5)
Swapan Tari (5)
Tales Of Kilimanjaro (6)

Them Changes (1) *flip*
They All Went To Mexico (6)
Trane (7)
Transformation Day (4)
Vereda Tropical (6)
Victory (4)
Watch Your Step (6)
Who Do You Love (6)

SANTO & JOHNNY

Brooklyn-born guitar duo: Santo Farina (b: 10/24/37; steel guitar) and his brother Johnny (b: 4/30/41; rhythm guitar). Sister Ann Farina helped with songwriting.

DEBUT DATE	PEAK POS	WKS CHR	GOLD	ARTIST — Album Title	$	Label & Number
1/18/60	20	29		1 Santo & Johnny .....[I]	$40	Canadian-Am. 1001
9/26/60	11	36		2 Encore .....[I]	$30	Canadian-Am. 1002
6/26/61	80	13		3 Hawaii .....[I]	$30	Canadian-Am. 1004

Adventures In Paradise (3)
Alabamy Bound (2)
All Night Diner (1)
Aloha (2)
Annie (2)
Blue Hawaii (3)

Blue Moon (1)
Breeze And I (2)
Canadian Sunset (1)
Caravan (1) *48*
Deep Purple (2)
Dream (1)

Harbor Lights (1)
Hawaiian War Chant (3)
Hawaiian Wedding Song (3)
Isle Of Dreams (3)
Lazy Day (3)
Long Walk Home (2)

Now Is The Hour (3)
Old Man River (2)
Over The Rainbow (2)
Pineapple Princess (3)
Prisoner Of Love (2)
Raunchy (1)

Reflections (1)
School Day (1)
Sea Shells (3)
Slave Girl (1)
Sleep Walk (1) *1*
Song Of The Islands (3)

Summertime (1)
Sweet Lelani (1)
Tear Drop (2) *23*
Tenderly (1)
Venus (2)
You Belong To Me (2)

SARAYA

New Jersey rock band led by vocalist Sandi Saraya. Includes Tony Rey, Gregg Munier, Gary Taylor and Chuck Bonfante. Rey and Taylor left by 1991; bassist Barry Dunaway joined by then.

DEBUT DATE	PEAK POS	WKS CHR	GOLD	ARTIST — Album Title	$	Label & Number
4/29/89	79	39		Saraya	$8	Polydor 837764

Alsace Lorraine (3)
Back To The Bullet *63*
Drop The Bomb (2)
Fire To Burn (2)
Get U Ready
Gypsy Child
Healing Touch (2)
Love Has Taken Its Toll *64*
One Night Away
Runnin' Out Of Time
St. Christopher Medal

SARDUCCI, Father Guido

Real name: Don Novello. Born on 1/1/43 in Ashtabula, Ohio. Featured on TV's *Saturday Night Live*.

DEBUT DATE	PEAK POS	WKS CHR	GOLD	ARTIST — Album Title	$	Label & Number
5/10/80	179	2		Live at St. Douglas Convent .....[C]	$8	Warner 3440

DEBUT DATE	PEAK POS	WKS CHR	GOLD		ARTIST — Album Title	$	Label & Number

SARDUCCI, Father Guido — Cont'd

| Alien Invaders | Coming And Going Planet | Guide To The Confessional | People's Space Program | What Happens To You After | Women Priests |
| Cattle Mutilation Theories | Five Minute University | Mass Confession | St. Ann Seton | You Die | |

SATRIANI, Joe
Berkeley-based rock guitarist raised in Carle Place, Long Island. Former guitar teacher of Steve Vai (with David Lee Roth and Whitesnake) and Kirk Hammett (Metallica).

| 11/21/87+ | 29 | 75 | ▲ | 1 | Surfing With The Alien .... [I] | $8 | Relativity 8193 |
| 11/26/88+ | 42 | 26 | ● | 2 | Dreaming #11 .... [L-I-M] | $8 | Relativity 8265 |

4-track mini LP; side 2 is instrumental, recorded live on 6/11/88 at the California Theater in San Diego

| 11/18/89 | 23 | 39 | ● | 3 | Flying In A Blue Dream... | $8 | Relativity 1015 |

6 of 18 cuts feature Joe's vocals

| 8/8/92 | 22 | 27↑ | ● | 4 | The Extremist.. | $12 | Relativity 1053 |

Always With Me, Always With You (1)	Crush Of Love (2)	Feeling, The (3)	I Believe (3)	Mystical Potato Head Groove Thing (3)	Satch Boogie (1)
Back To Shalla-Bal (3)	Crushing Day (1)	Flying In A Blue Dream (3)	Ice 9 (1,2)	New Blues (4)	Strange (3)
Bells Of Lal (Part One & Two) (3)	Cryin' (4)	Forgotten (Part One & Two) (3)	Into The Light (3)	One Big Rush (3)	Summer Song (4)
Big Bad Moon (3)	Day At The Beach (New Rays From An Ancient Sun) (3)	Friends (4)	Lords Of Karma (1)	Phone Call (3)	Surfing With The Alien (1)
Can't Slow Down (3)	Echo (3)	Headless (3)	Memories (2)	Ride (3)	Tears In The Rain (4)
Circles (1)	Extremist, The (4)	Hill Of The Skull (1)	Midnight (1)	Rubina's Blue Sky Happiness (4)	War (4)
		Hordes Of Locusts (2)	Motorcycle Driver (4)		Why (4)

SATTERFIELD, Esther
Born in North Carolina in 1946. Jazz-styled vocalist.

| 7/24/76 | 180 | 4 | | | The Need To Be .... | $8 | A&M 3411 |

produced, arranged and orchestrated by Chuck Mangione

| Bird Of Beauty | He's Gone | If You Know Me Any Longer Than Tomorrow | Long Hard Climb | New World Comin' | You Must Believe In Spring |
| Chase The Clouds Away | | | Need To Be | Sarah | |

SATURDAY NIGHT BAND
A Jesse Boyce and Moses Dillard disco production.

| 5/27/78 | 125 | 17 | | | Come On Dance, Dance .... | $8 | Prelude 12155 |

| Come On Dance, Dance | Don't (Take My Love Away) | Touch Me On My Hot Spot |

SAUNDERS, Merl
Session keyboardist.

| 6/2/73 | 197 | 5 | | | Fire Up .... [I] | $15 | Fantasy 9421 |

featuring Jerry Garcia and Tom Fogerty on guitar

| After Midnight | Charisma (She's Got) | Expressway (To Your Heart) | Soul Roach |
| Benedict Rides | Chock-Lite Puddin' | Lonely Avenue | System, The |

SAVAGE GRACE
Detroit-based rock quartet: Ron Koss (vocals, guitar), Al Jacquez, John Seanor and Larry Zack.

| 6/6/70 | 182 | 8 | | | Savage Grace .... | $10 | Reprise 6399 |

| All Along The Watchtower | Dear Lenore | Lady Rain | 1984 |
| Come On Down | Hymn To Freedom | Night Of The Hunter | Turn Your Head |

SAVALAS, Telly
Born Aristotle Savalas on 1/21/24 in Garden City, New York. Popular TV/film actor. Gained fame as the star of TV's *Kojak*.

| 1/4/75 | 117 | 8 | | | Telly .... | $15 | MCA 436 |

Telly both narrates and sings

| Help Me Make It Through The Night | If | Something | You And Me Against The World | You've Lost That Lovin' Feelin' |
| How Insensitive | Rubber Bands And Bits Of String | Song For You Without Her | You're A Lady | |

SAVATAGE
Hard-rock band formed in 1978 in Florida as Avatar. Consists of Jon Oliva (vocals), Criss Oliva, Steve Wacholz, Johnny Lee Middleton and Christopher Cafferty (joined in 1989).

6/21/86	158	7		1	Fight For The Rock	$8	Atlantic 81634
10/10/87+	116	23		2	Hall Of The Mountain King	$8	Atlantic 81775
2/24/90	124	12		3	Gutter Ballet	$12	Atlantic 82008

Beyond The Doors Of The Dark (2)	Fight For The Rock (1)	Lady In Disguise (1)	Prelude To Madness (2)	Strange Wings (2)	When The Crowds Are Gone (3)
Crying For Love (1)	Gutter Ballet (3)	Last Dawn (2)	Price You Pay (2)	Summer's Rain (3)	White Witch (2)
Day After Day (1)	Hall Of The Mountain King (2)	Legions (2)	Red Light Paradise (1)	Temptation Revelation (3)	Wishing Well (1)
Devastation (2)	Hounds (3)	Mentally Yours (3)	She's In Love (3)	Thorazine Shuffle (3)	
Edge Of Midnight (1)	Hyde (1)	Of Rage And War (3)	She's Only Rock 'N Roll (1)	24 Hrs. Ago (2)	
		Out On The Streets (1)	Silk And Steel (3)	Unholy, The (3)	

★★482★★ **SAVOY BROWN**
British blues-rock band formed in 1966 by guitarist Kim Simmonds. Many personnel changes. Members Dave Peverett, Roger Earl and Tony Stevens left in 1971 to form Foghat.

| 4/12/69 | 182 | 2 | | 1 | Blue Matter.. [L] | $15 | Parrot 71027 |

side 2: recorded live

| 9/13/69 | 71 | 14 | | 2 | A Step Further.. [L] | $15 | Parrot 71029 |

side 2: a live Boogie Medley

4/25/70	121	18		3	Raw Sienna..	$15	Parrot 71036
10/17/70	39	19		4	Looking In...	$15	Parrot 71042
9/18/71	75	17		5	Street Corner Talking..	$15	Parrot 71047
3/18/72	34	21		6	Hellbound Train...	$12	Parrot 71052
11/4/72	151	10		7	Lion's Share...	$12	Parrot 71057
6/30/73	84	14		8	Jack The Toad..	$12	Parrot 71059
4/20/74	101	8		9	Boogie Brothers...	$10	London 638
11/22/75	153	7		10	Wire Fire...	$10	London 659
7/25/81	185	4		11	Rock 'n' Roll Warriors..	$8	Town House 7002

SAVOY BROWN — Cont'd

All I Can Do (5)
Always The Same (9)
Bad Breaks (11)
Bad Girls (Make Me Feel Good) (11)
Boogie Brothers (9)
Born Into Pain (10)
Can't Get On (10)
Casting My Spell (8)
Cold Hearted Woman (11)
Coming Down Your Way (8)
Deep Water (10)
Denim Demon (7)
Doin' Fine (6)
Don't Tell Me I Told You (11)
Don't Turn Me From Your Door (1)
Endless Sleep (8)

Everybody Loves A Drinking Man (9)
Georgie (11)
Got Love If You Want It (11)
Gypsy (4)
Hard Way To Go (3)
Hate To See You Go (7)
Hellbound Train (6)
Here Comes The Music (10)
Hero To Zero (10)
Highway Blues (9)
Hold Your Fire (8)
Howling For My Darling (7)
I Can't Find You (7)
I Can't Get Next To You (5)
I'll Make Everything Alright (6)
I'm Crying (3)
I'm Tired (2) **74**

If I Could See An End (6)
If I Want To (8)
Is That So (3)
It Hurts Me Too (1)
It'll Make You Happy (6)
Jack The Toad (8)
Just Cos' You Got The Blues Don't Mean You Gotta Sing (8)
Lay Back In The Arms Of Someone (1)
Leavin' Again (4)
Life's One Act Play (2)
Little More Wine (3)
Looking In (4)
Lost And Lonely Child (6)
Louisiana Blues (1)
Love Me Please (7)
Made Up My Mind (2)

Master Hare (3)
May Be Wrong (1)
Me And The Preacher (9)
Money Can't Save Your Soul (4)
My Love's Lying Down (9)
Needle And Spoon (4)
Nobody's Perfect (9)
Ooh What A Feeling (10)
Poor Girl (4)
Put Your Hands Together (10)
Ride On Babe (8)
Rock And Roll On The Radio (Let It Rock) (5)
Rock 'N' Roll Star (9)
Romanoff (4)
Saddest Feeling (7)

Savoy Brown Boogie Medley (2)
Second Try (7)
She's Got A Ring In His Nose And A Ring On Her Hand (1)
Shot Down By Love (11)
Shot In The Head (7)
Sitting An' Thinking (4)
So Tired (7)
Some People (8)
Stay While The Night Is Young (3)
Stranger Blues (10)
Street Corner Talking (5)
Sunday Night (4)
Take It Easy (4)
Tell Mama (5) **83**
That Same Feelin' (3)

This Could Be The Night (11)
Threegy Blues (9)
Time Does Tell (5)
Tolling Bells (1)
Train To Nowhere (1)
Troubled By These Days And Times (6)
Vicksburg Blues (3)
Waiting In The Bamboo Grove (2)
Wang Dang Doodle (5)
When I Was A Young Boy (3)
Where Am I (2)
You Don't Love Me (9)

SAWYER BROWN

Five-man country band formed in Nashville in the late 1970s by Mark Miller (lead vocals) and Bobby Randall (lead guitar, vocals). Won $100,000 on TV's *Star Search* in 1984. Randall left in 1992 to host TNN TV show *Be A Star*, replaced by Duncan Cameron.

DEBUT DATE	PEAK POS	WKS CHR		ARTIST — Album Title	$	Label & Number
2/23/85	140	11		1 Sawyer Brown	$8	Curb/Cap. 12391
8/31/91	140	11		2 Buick	$12	Curb/Cap. 94260
2/1/92	68	30		3 The Dirt Road	$12	Curb/Cap. 95624
9/19/92+	134	10↑		4 Cafe On The Corner	$12	Curb 77574

Ain't That Always The Way (3)
All These Years (4)
Another Trip To The Well (3)
Broken Candy (1)
Burnin' Bridges (On A Rocky Road) (3)
Cafe On The Corner (4)
Chain Of Love (4)

Different Tune (4)
Dirt Road (4)
Feel Like Me (1)
Fire In The Rain (3)
48 Hours Till Monday (2)
Going Back To Indiana (1)
Homestead In My Heart (4)
I Kept My Motor Runnin' (4)

It's Hard To Keep A Good Love Down (1)
Leona (1)
Lesson In Love (4)
Mama's Little Baby Loves Me (2)
My Baby Drives A Buick (2)
One Less Pony (2)
Ruby Red Shoes (3)

Sister's Got A New Tattoo (4)
Smokin' In The Rockies (1)
Some Girls Do (3)
Sometimes A Hero (3)
Staying Afloat (1)
Stealin' Home (2)
Step That Step (1)
Still Water (2)

Sun Don't Shine On The Same Folks All The Time (1)
Superman's Daughter (2)
Thunder Bay (2)
Time And Love (3)
Travelin' Shoes (4)
Trouble On The Line (4)
Used To Blue (1)
Walk, The (2,3)

When Twist Comes To Shout (3)
When You Run From Love (2)

SAXON

British heavy-metal rock quintet formed in 1977. Original lineup: Biff Byford (vocals), Graham Oliver, Paul Quinn, Steve Dawson and Pete Gill. In 1981 Nigel Glocker replaced Gill (later joined Motorhead) and in 1986, Paul Johnson replaced Dawson.

DEBUT DATE	PEAK POS	WKS CHR		ARTIST — Album Title	$	Label & Number
6/18/83	155	10		1 Power & The Glory	$8	Carrere 38719
4/14/84	174	5		2 Crusader	$8	Carrere 39284
11/2/85	130	8		3 Innocence Is No Excuse	$8	Capitol 12420
2/14/87	149	6		4 Rock The Nations	$8	Capitol 12519

Back On The Streets (3)
Bad Boys (Like To Rock 'N Roll) (2)
Battle Cry (4)
Broken Heroes (3)
Call Of The Wild (3)
Crusader (2)
Devil Rides Out (3)

Do It All For You (2)
Eagle Has Landed (1)
Empty Promises (4)
Everybody Up (3)
Give It Everything You've Got (3)
Gonna Shout (3)
Just Let Me Rock (4)

Little Bit Of What You Fancy (2)
Nightmare (1)
Northern Lady (4)
Party Til You Puke (4)
Power And The Glory (1)
Raise Some Hell (3)
Redline (1)

Rock City (2)
Rock N' Roll Gipsy (3)
Rock The Nations (4)
Rockin' Again (3)
Run For Your Lives (2)
Running Hot (4)
Sailing To America (2)
Set Me Free (2)

Suzi Hold On (1)
This Town Rocks (1)
Waiting For The Night (4)
Warrior (1)
Watching The Sky (1)
We Came Here To Rock (4)
You Ain't No Angel (4)

SAYER, Leo

Born Gerard Sayer on 5/21/48 in Shoreham, England. With Patches in the early '70s. Songwriting team with David Courtney, 1972-75. Own British TV show in 1978 and again in 1983.

DEBUT DATE	PEAK POS	WKS CHR		ARTIST — Album Title	$	Label & Number
2/8/75	16	22		1 Just A Boy	$10	Warner 2836
10/11/75	125	7		2 Another Year	$10	Warner 2885
11/27/76+	10	51	▲	3 **Endless Flight**	$10	Warner 2962
10/22/77	37	15		4 Thunder In My Heart	$8	Warner 3089
8/19/78	101	14		5 Leo Sayer	$8	Warner 3200
10/18/80+	36	23		6 Living In A Fantasy	$8	Warner 3483

Another Time (1)
Another Year (2)
Bedsitterland (2)
Bells Of St. Marys (1)
Dancing The Night Away (5)
Don't Look Away (5)
Easy To Love (4) **36**
Endless Flight (4)
Everything I've Got (4)
Fool For Your Love (4)
Frankie Lee (5)
Giving It All Away (1)
Hold On To My Love (3)

How Much Love (3) **17**
I Can't Stop Loving You (Though I Try) (5)
I Hear The Laughter (3)
I Think We Fell In Love Too Fast (3)
I Want You Back (4)
I Will Not Stop Fighting (2)
In My Life (1)
It's Over (4)
Kid's Grown Up (2)
La Booga Rooga (5)

Last Gig Of Johnny B. Goode (2)
Leave Well Enough Alone (4)
Let Me Know (6)
Living In A Fantasy (6) **23**
Long Tall Glasses (I Can Dance) (1) **9**
Magdalena (6)
Millionaire (6)
Moonlighting (2)
More Than I Can Say (6) **2**
No Business Like Love Business (3)

No Looking Back (5)
On The Old Dirt Road (2)
Once In A While (6)
Only Dreaming (2)
Only Foolin' (6)
Raining In My Heart (5) **47**
Reflections (3)
Running To My Freedom (5)
She's Not Coming Back (6)
Solo (1)
Something Fine (5)
Stormy Weather (5)

Streets Of Your Town (2)
Telepath (1)
There Isn't Anything (4)
Thunder In My Heart (4) **38**
Time Ran Out On You (6)
Train (1)
Unlucky In Love (2)
We Can Start All Over Again (4)
When I Came Home This Morning (1)
When I Need You (3) **1**
Where Did We Go Wrong (6)

World Keeps On Turning (4)
You Make Me Feel Like Dancing (3) **1**
You Win - I Lose (6)

★★355★★ SCAGGS, Boz

Born William Royce Scaggs on 6/8/44 in Ohio; raised in Texas. Joined Steve Miller's band, The Marksmen, in 1959 in Dallas. Hooked up with Miller at UW-Madison in The Ardells, later known as The Fabulous Night Trains. Joined R&B band The Wigs in 1963. To Europe in 1964, toured as a folk singer. Re-joined Miller in 1967, solo since 1969. Retired from music and opened a restaurant in San Francisco, 1983-87. Made comeback in 1988.

DEBUT DATE	PEAK POS	WKS CHR		ARTIST — Album Title	$	Label & Number
4/17/71	124	9		1 Moments	$10	Columbia 30454
12/11/71	198	2		2 Boz Scaggs & Band	$10	Columbia 30796
9/23/72	138	9		3 My Time	$10	Columbia 31384
3/23/74	81	20	●	4 Slow Dancer	$10	Columbia 32760

DEBUT DATE	PEAK POS	WKS CHR	GOLD	ARTIST — Album Title	$	Label & Number

SCAGGS, Boz — Cont'd

DEBUT DATE	PEAK POS	WKS CHR	GOLD	ARTIST — Album Title	$	Label & Number
7/13/74+	171	5		5 Boz Scaggs ....[R]	$10	Atlantic 8239
				reissue of his first album released in 1969; features guitarist Duane Allman		
3/20/76	2⁵	115	▲⁴	6 **Silk Degrees**	$8	Columbia 33920
12/10/77+	11	23	▲	7 Down Two Then Left.................................	$8	Columbia 34729
4/19/80	8	33	▲	8 **Middle Man**	$8	Columbia 36106
11/29/80+	24	26	▲	9 Hits! ....[G]	$8	Columbia 36841
6/4/88	47	18		10 Other Roads	$8	Columbia 40463

Alone, Alone (1)
Angel Lady (Come Just In Time) (4)
Angel You (8)
Another Day (Another Letter) (5)
Breakdown Dead Ahead (8,9) 15
Can I Make It Last (Or Will It Just Be Over) (1)
Claudia (10)
Clue, A (7)
Cool Running (10)
Crimes of Passion (10)
Dinah Flo (3,9) 86
Do Like You Do In New York (8)
Downright Women (1)
Finding Her (5)

Flames Of Love (2)
Freedom For The Stallion (3)
Full-Lock Power Slide (3)
Funny (10)
Georgia (6)
Gimme The Goods (7)
Hard Times (7) 58
Heart Of Mine (10) 35
Hello My Lover (3)
Hercules (4)
Here To Stay (2)
Hollywood (7) 49
Hollywood Blues (1)
I Don't Hear You (10)
I Got Your Number (4)
I Will Forever Sing (The Blues) (1)

I'll Be Long Gone (5)
I'm Easy (5)
Isn't It Time (8)
It's Over (9) 38
JoJo (8,9) 17
Jump Street (6)
Let It Happen (4)
Lido Shuffle (6,9) 11
Loan Me A Dime (5)
Look What I Got (5)
Look What You've Done To Me (9) 14
Love Anyway (2)
Love Me Tomorrow (6)
Lowdown (6,9) 3
Mental Shakedown (10)
Middle Man (8)
Might Have To Cry (3)
Miss Sun (9) 14

Moments (1)
Monkey Time (2)
My Time (3)
Near You (1) 96
Night of Van Gogh (10)
1993 (7)
Nothing Will Take Your Place (2)
Now You're Gone (5)
Old Time Lovin' (3)
Pain Of Love (4)
Painted Bells (1)
Right Out Of My Head (10)
Runnin' Blue (2)
Sail On White Moon (4)
Simone (1)
Slow Dancer (4)
Slowly In The West (3)
Still Falling For You (7)

Sweet Release (5)
Take It For Granted (4)
Then She Walked Away (7)
There Is Someone Else (4)
Tomorrow Never Came (7)
Up To You (2)
Waiting For A Train (5)
We Been Away (1)
We Were Always Sweethearts (1) 61
We're All Alone (6,9)
We're Gonna Roll (3)
We're Waiting (7)
What Can I Say (6) 42
What Do You Want The Girl To Do (6)
What's Number One? (10)
Whatcha Gonna Tell Your Man (7)

Why Why (2)
You Can Have Me Anytime (8,9)
You Got Some Imagination (8)
You Make It So Hard (To Say No) (4,9)
You're So Good (2)

SCANDAL
New York-based rock band led by Patty Smyth and Zack Smith.

DEBUT DATE	PEAK POS	WKS CHR	GOLD	ARTIST — Album Title	$	Label & Number
1/29/83	39	32	●	1 Scandal ....[M]	$8	Columbia 38194
8/4/84	17	41	▲	2 Warrior	$8	Columbia 39173

SCANDAL FEATURING PATTY SMYTH

All I Want (2)
Another Bad Love (1)
Beat Of A Heart (2) 41

Goodbye To You (1) 65
Hands Tied (2) 41
Less Than Half (2)

Love's Got A Line On You (1) 59
Maybe We Went Too Far (2)

Only The Young (2)
Say What You Will (2)
She Can't Say No (1)

Talk To Me (2)
Tonight (2)
Warrior, The (2) 7

Win Some, Lose Some (1)

SCARBURY, Joey
Born on 6/7/55 in Ontario, California. Session singer for producer Mike Post.

DEBUT DATE	PEAK POS	WKS CHR	GOLD	ARTIST — Album Title	$	Label & Number
8/22/81	104	9		America's Greatest Hero.............................	$8	Elektra 537

Down The Backstairs (Of My Life)
Everything But Love

"Greatest American Hero" (Believe It Or Not), Theme From 2

Love Me Like The Last Time
Some Of My Old Friends
Stolen Night

Take This Heart Of Mine
That Little Bit Of Us

There Is A River
When She Dances 49

SCARFACE
Brad Jordan — member of the Houston-based rap group The Geto Boys.

DEBUT DATE	PEAK POS	WKS CHR	GOLD	ARTIST — Album Title	$	Label & Number
10/26/91	51	27		Mr. Scarface Is Back	$12	Rap-A-Lot 57167

Body Snatchers
Born Killer

Diary Of A Madman
Good Girl Gone Bad
I'm Dead

Minute To Pray And A Second To Die
Mr. Scarface

Money And The Power

Murder By Reason Of Insanity

P D Roll 'Em
Pimp, The
Your Ass Got Took

SCARLETT & BLACK
Keyboardist/singer/songwriter Robin Hild and songwriter Sue West (former backing vocalist for Doctor And The Medics).

DEBUT DATE	PEAK POS	WKS CHR	GOLD	ARTIST — Album Title	$	Label & Number
3/19/88	107	11		Scarlett & Black	$8	Virgin 90647

City Of Dreams (The Last Frontier)

Dream Out Loud
If It's All The Same To You

Let Yourself Go-Go
Miracle Or Mirage

Real Love
Someday

What Is Love
Yesterday's Gone

You Don't Know 20

SCATTERBRAIN
Hard-rock fivesome: Tommy Christ (vocals), Glen Cummings and Paul Nieder (former members of Ludichrist), Guy Brogna (former bassist with Frank Zappa) and Mike Boyko.

DEBUT DATE	PEAK POS	WKS CHR	GOLD	ARTIST — Album Title	$	Label & Number
6/16/90	138	16		Here Comes Trouble	$12	In-Effect 3012

Don't Call Me Dude
Down With The Ship (Slight Return)

Drunken Milkman
Earache My Eye

Goodbye Freedom, Hello Mom

Here Comes Trouble
I'm With Stupid

Mr. Johnson And The Juice Crew
Outta Time

Sonata #3
That's That

SCHAFER, Kermit
Collection of 'bloopers' by radio and TV producer Schafer. Died on 3/8/79.

DEBUT DATE	PEAK POS	WKS CHR	GOLD	ARTIST — Album Title	$	Label & Number
1/27/58	17	1		Pardon My Blooper! Volume 6 ....[C]	$15	Jubilee 6
				narrator: George de Holczer; no track titles listed on this album		

SCHENKER, Michael, Group
Hard-rock group fronted by Michael Schenker. West German-born Schenker, brother of Rudolf (Scorpions), was a member of Scorpions (at age 15) and lead guitarist of UFO. Irish native Robin McAuley, leader of Far Corporation, joined in 1987. Band changed name to McAuley Schenker Group in 1987.

DEBUT DATE	PEAK POS	WKS CHR	GOLD	ARTIST — Album Title	$	Label & Number
9/20/80	100	14		1 The Michael Schenker Group	$8	Chrysalis 1302
10/24/81	81	8		2 MSG	$8	Chrysalis 1336
4/9/83	151	7		3 Assault Attack	$8	Chrysalis 1393

McAULEY SCHENKER GROUP:

DEBUT DATE	PEAK POS	WKS CHR	GOLD	ARTIST — Album Title	$	Label & Number
10/24/87	95	24		4 Perfect Timing	$8	Capitol 46985
2/3/90	92	14		5 Save Yourself	$12	Capitol 92752
				CD includes bonus track		
3/7/92	180	4		6 MSG	$12	Impact 10385

SCHENKER/McAULEY

Anytime (5)
Are You Ready To Rock (2)
Armed And Ready (1)

Assault Attack (3)
Attack Of The Mad Axeman (2)

Bad Boys (5)
Bijou Pleasurette (1)
Broken Promises (3)

But I Want More (2)
Crazy (6)
Cry For The Nations (1)

Dancer (3)
Desert Song (3)
Destiny (5)

Don't Stop Me Now (4)
Eve (6)
Feels Like A Good Thing (1)

DEBUT DATE	PEAK POS	WKS CHR	GOLD	ARTIST — Album Title	$	Label & Number

SCHENKER, Michael, Group — Cont'd

Follow The Night (4)
Get Down To Bizness (5)
Get Out (4)
Gimme Your Love (4)
Here Today - Gone Tomorrow (4)
I Am Your Radio (5)
I Don't Wanna Lose (4)
Into The Arena (1)

Invincible (6)
Let Sleeping Dogs Lie (2)
Lonely Nights (6)
Looking For Love (2)
Looking Out From Nowhere (1)
Lost Horizons (1)
Love Is Not A Game (4)
Never Ending Nightmare (6)

Never Trust A Stranger (2)
No Time For Losers (4)
On And On (2)
Paradise (6)
Rock 'Til You're Crazy (4)
Rock You To The Ground (3)
Samurai (3)
Save Yourself (5)
Searching For A Reason (3)

Secondary Motion (2)
Shadow Of The Night (5)
Take Me Back (5)
Tales Of Mystery (1)
There Has To Be Another Way (5)
This Broken Heart (6)
This Is My Heart (5)

This Night Is Gonna Last Forever (6)
Time (4)
Ulcer (3)
Victim Of Illusion (1)
We Believe In Love (6)
What Happens To Me (6)
What We Need (5)
When I'm Gone (6)

SCHIFRIN, Lalo

Born Boris Schifrin on 6/21/32 in Buenos Aires, Argentina. Pianist/conductor/composer. Scored films *Bullitt*, *Dirty Harry*, *Brubaker* and many others.

| 12/22/62+ | 35 | 3 | | 1 Bossa Nova - New Brazilian Jazz ......[I] | $12 | Audio Fidel. 1981 |
| 12/30/67+ | 47 | 31 | | 2 music from Mission: Impossible ......[I] | $15 | Dot 25831 |

Barney Does It All (2)
Boato (Bistro) (1)
Bossa Em Nova York (1)
Chega De Saudade (1)
Chora Tua Tristeza (1)

Cinnamon (The Lady Was Made To Be Loved) (2)
Danger (2)
Jim On The Move (2)
Menina Feia (1)

Mission-Impossible (2) 41
Mission: Accomplished (2)
O Amor E A Rosa (1)
O Apito No Samba (1)

O Menino Desce O Morro (Little Brown Boy) (1)
Operation Charm (2)
Ouca (1)

Patinho Feio (1)
Plot, The (2)
Poema Do Adeus (1)
Rollin Hand (2)

Samba De Uma Nota So (1)
Sniper, The (2)
Wide Willy (2)

SCHILLING, Peter

Born on 1/28/56 in Stuttgart, Germany. Pop singer/songwriter.

| 10/8/83+ | 61 | 23 | | Error In The System .... | $8 | Elektra 60265 |

Error In The System
I Have No Desire

(Let's Play) U.S.A.
Lifetime Guarantee

Major Tom (Coming Home) 14

Major Tom, Part II

Noah Plan
Only Dreams

Stille Nacht, Heilige Nacht (Silent Night, Holy Night)

SCHMIT, Timothy B.

Born on 10/30/47 in Sacramento. Member of Poco, 1970-77, and the Eagles, 1977-82.

| 11/10/84 | 160 | 5 | | 1 Playin' It Cool .... | $8 | Asylum 60359 |
| 10/3/87 | 106 | 11 | | 2 Timothy B .... | $8 | MCA 42049 |

Better Day Is Coming (2)
Boys Night Out (2) 25
Don't Give Up (2)

Down Here People Dance Forever (2)
Everybody Needs A Lover (2)
Gimme The Money (1)

Hold Me In Your Heart (2)
I Guess We'll Go On Living (2)
Into The Night (2)

Jazz Street (2)
Lonely Girl (1)
Playin' It Cool (1)
So Much In Love (1) 59

Something's Wrong (1)
Take A Good Look Around You (1)
Tell Me What You Dream (1)

Voices (1)
Wrong Number (1)

SCHNEIDER, John

Born on 4/8/54 in Mount Kisco, New York. Moved to Atlanta at age 14. Country singer/actor. Played "Bo Duke" on TV's *The Dukes Of Hazzard*. Appeared in many TV films. Scriptwriter/director.

6/27/81	37	22		1 Now Or Never	$8	Scotti Br. 37400
12/5/81+	155	7		2 White Christmas ......[X]	$8	Scotti Br. 37617
11/17/84	111	12		3 Too Good To Stop Now	$8	MCA 5495

(Am I) Fallin' In Love With Love (1)
Christmas Song (Chestnuts Roasting On An Open Fire) (2)
Country Girls (3)
Have Yourself A Merry Little Christmas (2)

Hollywood Heroes (3)
I'm Your Man (3)
I've Been Around Enough To Know (3)
It's Christmas (2)
It's Now Or Never (1) 14
Katey's Christmas Card (2)
Let Me Love You (1)

Low Class Reunion (3)
Next Time Around (1)
No. 34 In Atlanta (1)
O Little Town Of Bethlehem (2)
Party Of The First Part (3)
Rudolph, The Red Nosed Reindeer (2)

Silent Night, Holy Night (2)
Silver Bells (2)
Stay (1)
Stay With Me (1)
Still (1) 69
Them Good Ol' Boys Are Bad (1)
Time Of My Life (3)

Too Good To Stop Now (3)
Trouble (3)
What'll You Do About Me (3)
White Christmas (2)
Winter Wonderland (2)
You Could Be The One Woman (1)

SCHON, Neal, & Jan Hammer

Rock guitarist Schon (b: 2/27/54 in San Mateo, California; Santana, Journey, Bad English) and jazz keyboardist/drummer Hammer (b: 4/17/48 in Prague). Also see Hagar, Schon.

| 10/17/81 | 115 | 8 | | 1 Untold Passion .... | $8 | Columbia 37600 |
| 2/5/83 | 122 | 12 | | 2 Here To Stay .... | $8 | Columbia 38428 |

Arc (1)
Covered By Midnight (2)
Don't Stay Away (2)

Hooked On Love (1)
I'm Down (1)
I'm Talking To You (1)

It's Alright (1)
Long Time (2)
No More Lies (2)

On The Beach (1)
Peace Of Mind (2)
Ride, The (1)

Self Defense (2)
Sticks And Stones (2)
Time Again (2)
Turnaround (2)

Untold Passion (1)
Wasting Time (1)
(You Think You're) So Hot (2)

SCHOOLLY D

Real name: Jesse B. Weaver, Jr. Rapper from Philadelphia.

| 8/6/88 | 180 | 3 | | Smoke Some Kill .... | $8 | Jive 1101 |

Another Poem
Black Man
Coqui 900

Fat Gold Chain
Gangster Boogie II
Here We Go Again

Mr. Big Dick
No More Rock N' Roll

Same White Bitch (Got You Strung Out On Cane)
Signifying Rapper

Smoke Some Kill
This Is It (Ain't Gonna Rain)

Treacherous
We Don't Rock, We Rap

SCHOOL OF FISH

Los Angeles-based alternative pop band: Josh Clayton-Felt (vocals), Michael Ward, Dominic Nardini & M.P.

| 9/14/91 | 142 | 7 | | School Of Fish .... | $12 | Capitol 94557 |

Deep End
Euphoria

Fell
King Of The Dollar

Rose Colored Glasses
Speechless

Talk Like Strangers
3 Strange Days

Under The Microscope
Wrong

SCHORY, Dick

Born on 12/13/31 in Chicago; raised in Ames, Iowa. Percussionist. Vice president of Ludwig drum company, 1957-70. Owner of Ovation Records, 1970-82. Currently runs a Chicago marketing firm.

| 6/29/59+ | 11 | 26 | | 1 Music For Bang, Baa-room and Harp ......[I] | $20 | RCA 1866 |

DICK SCHORY'S New Percussion Ensemble

| 4/20/63 | 13 | 13 | | 2 Supercussion ......[I] | $15 | RCA 2613 |

DICK SCHORY'S Percussion Pops Orchestra

April In Paris (1)
Autumn Leaves (2)
Baia (1)
Bijou (2)
Brush Off (2)

Buck Dance (1)
Ding Dong Polka (1)
Duel On The Skins (1)
Hindustan (2)
Holiday In A Hurry (1)

Krazy Kwilt (2)
National Emblem March (1)
Nomad (2)
On Green Dolphin Street (1)
Perdido (2)

September In The Rain (1)
Sheik Of Araby (1)
Shimboo (2)
Stompin' At The Savoy (2)
String Of Pearls (2)

Take The "A" Train (2)
Tiddley Winks (1)
Typee (1)
Way Down Yonder In New Orleans (1)

DEBUT DATE	PEAK POS	WKS CHR	GOLD	ARTIST — Album Title	$	Label & Number

SCHUUR, Diane
Born and raised in Auburn, Washington. Jazz vocalist/pianist. Blind since birth.

| 11/12/88 | 170 | 10 | | 1 Talkin' 'Bout You .... | $8 | GRP 9567 |
| 2/16/91 | 148 | 10 | | 2 Pure Schuur .... | $12 | GRP 9628 |

Ain't That Love (1)	Deed I Do (2)	Hearts Take Time (1)	Nobody Does Me (2)	Talkin' 'Bout You (1)	What A Difference A Day
All Caught Up In Love (2)	For Your Love (1)	Hold Out (2)	Nothing In The World (Can	Touch (2)	Makes (2)
Baby You Got What It Takes	Funny (But I Still Love You)	I Could Get Used To This (2)	Make Me Love You More	Unforgettable (2)	You Don't Remember Me (2)
(2)	(1)	Louisiana Sunday Afternoon	Than I Do) (1)	We Can Only Try (2)	
Cry Me A River (1)	Hard Drivin' Mama II (1)	(1)	Somethin' Real (1)		

SCHWARTZ, Eddie
Canadian singer/songwriter. Wrote Pat Benatar's "Hit Me With Your Best Shot."

| 2/6/82 | 195 | 6 | | No Refuge .... | $8 | Atco 141 |

All Our Tomorrows *28*	Good With Your Love	No Refuge	Spirit Of The Night		
Auction Block	Heart On Fire	**Over The Line** *91*	Tonight		

★★**296**★★ **SCORPIONS**
German heavy-metal rock quintet: Rudolf Schenker (Michael Schenker's brother; lead guitar), Klaus Meine (lead singer), Matthias Jabs (guitar), Francis Buchholz (bass) and Herman Rarebell (drums). Buchholz left band in 1992.

7/28/79	55	23	●	1 Lovedrive	$8	Mercury 3795
				Michael Schenker, lead guitar on 3 tracks		
11/17/79	180	4		2 Best Of Scorpions .... [E-K]	$8	RCA 3516
5/17/80	52	21	▲	3 Animal Magnetism	$8	Mercury 3825
3/27/82	10	74	▲	4 **Blackout**	$8	Mercury 4039
3/17/84	6	63	▲²	5 **Love At First Sting**	$8	Mercury 814981
8/4/84	175	4		6 Best of Scorpions, Vol. 2 .... [E-K]	$8	RCA 5085
7/13/85	14	43	▲	7 World Wide Live .... [L]	$10	Mercury 824344 [2]
5/7/88	5	43	▲	8 **Savage Amusement**	$8	Mercury 832963
12/2/89+	43	23	●	9 Best Of Rockers 'N' Ballads .... [G]	$8	Mercury 842044
11/24/90+	21	73	▲	10 Crazy World..	$12	Mercury 846908

All Night Long (6)	Coast To Coast (1,7)	Hell Cat (2)	Lust Or Love (10)	**Send Me An Angel** (10) *44*	We Let It Rock...You Let It
Always Somewhere (1)	Coming Home (5,7)	Hey You (9)	Make It Real (3,7)	Six String Sting (7)	Roll (8)
Animal Magnetism (3)	Countdown (7)	Hit Between The Eyes (10)	Media Overkill (8)	Speedy's Coming (2,6)	We'll Burn The Sky (1)
Another Piece Of Meat (1,7)	Crazy World (10)	Hold Me Tight (3)	Money And Fame (10)	Steamrock Fever (2)	When The Smoke Is Going
Arizona (4)	Crossfire (5)	Holiday (1,7,9)	Now! (4)	Still Loving You (5,7,9) *64*	Down (4)
As Soon As The Good Times	Crying Days (6)	I Can't Explain (9)	Only A Man (3)	Sun In My Hand (6)	**Wind Of Change** (10) *4*
Roll (5)	Dark Lady (2)	I'm Leaving You (5)	Passion Rules The Game (8)	Tease Me Please Me (10)	You Give Me All I Need (4,9)
Backstage Queen (2)	Don't Believe Her (10)	In Trance (2)	Pictured Life (2)	They Need A Million (6)	Zoo, The (3,7,9)
Bad Boys Running Wild (5,7)	Don't Make No Promises	Is There Anybody There? (1)	Restless Nights (10)	This Is My Song (6)	
Believe In Love (8)	(Your Body Can't Keep) (3)	Kicks After Six (10)	**Rhythm Of Love** (8,9) *75*	To Be With You In Heaven	
Big City Nights (5,7,9)	Don't Stop At The Top (8)	Lady Starlight (3)	Robot Man (2)	(10)	
Blackout (4,7,9)	Dynamite (4,7)	Longing For Fire (6)	**Rock You Like A**	Top Of The Bill (6)	
Can't Get Enough (1,7)	Every Minute Every Day (8)	Love On The Run (8)	**Hurricane** (5,7,9) *25*	Twentieth Century Man (3)	
Can't Live Without You (4,7)	Falling In Love (3)	Lovedrive (1,9)	Sails Of Chardon (2)	Virgin Killer (3)	
Catch Your Train (6)	He's A Woman - She's A	Loving You Sunday Morning	Same Thrill (5)	Walking On The Edge (8)	
China White (4)	Man (2)	(1,7)			

SCOTT, Christopher
Moog synthesizer player.

| 10/4/69 | 175 | 3 | | Switched-On Bacharach...................................... [I] | $10 | Decca 75141 |
| | | | | *all songs written by Burt Bacharach* | | |

Alfie	Do You Know The Way To	I Say A Little Prayer	This Guy's In Love With You	What The World Needs Now	What's New Pussycat?
April Fools	San Jose	Look Of Love	Walk On By	Is Love	Wives And Lovers

SCOTT, Marilyn
Born Mary DeLoatch. Vocalist/guitarist from the Carolinas.

| 4/21/79 | 189 | 4 | | Dreams Of Tomorrow... | $8 | Atco 109 |

Beach, The	Highways Of My Life	Let's Not Talk About Love	Yes I Can (I Can Get Along	You Are All I Need
Dreams Of Tomorrow	Let's Be Friends	Why-Oh-You (Y-O-U)	Without Them)	You Made Me Believe

SCOTT, Peggy, & Jo Jo Benson
Soul duo; Jo Jo formerly sang with Chuck Willis and The Blue Notes.

| 3/1/69 | 196 | 5 | | Soulshake .... | $8 | SSS Int'l. 1 |

Blow Your Mind	Here With Me	Love Will Come Sneaking Up	**Pickin' Wild Mountain**	**Soulshake** *37*	We Were Made For Each
Doin' Our Thing	If That's The Only Way	On You	**Berries** *27*	'Til The Morning Comes	Other
Fine As Frog Hair		**Lover's Holiday** *31*		We Got Our Bag	

SCOTT, Tom
Born on 5/19/48 in Los Angeles. Pop-jazz-fusion saxophonist. Session work for Joni Mitchell, Steely Dan, Carole King and others. Composer of films and TV scores. Led the house band for TV's *Pat Sajak Show*. Son of Nathan Scott, a composer of TV scores for *Dragnet*, *Wagon Train*, *My Three Sons* and others.

TOM SCOTT & THE L.A. EXPRESS:

| 4/27/74 | 141 | 16 | | 1 Tom Scott & The L.A. Express .... [I] | $10 | Ode 77021 |
| 3/15/75 | 18 | 27 | | 2 Tom Cat .... [I] | $10 | Ode 77029 |

TOM SCOTT:

12/20/75+	42	25		3 New York Connection .... [I]	$10	Ode 77033
9/10/77	87	14		4 Blow It Out .... [I]	$8	Ode 34966
11/18/78+	123	13		5 Intimate Strangers .... [I]	$8	Columbia 35557
				side 1 titled "Intimate Strangers (Suite)" is broken into 3 parts: "Sudden Attraction"; "A Day & Nite Out Together"; "Loving & Leaving"		
12/15/79	162	6		6 Street Beat .... [I]	$8	Columbia 36137
7/11/81	123	11		7 Apple Juice .... [I-L]	$8	Columbia 37419
9/25/82	164	7		8 Desire .... [I]	$8	Musician 60162

SCOTT, Tom — Cont'd

Apple Juice (7)
Appolonia (Foxtrata) (3)
Backfence Cattin' (2)
Beautiful Music (5)
Bless My Soul (1)
Breezin' Easy (2)
Car Wars (6)
Chunk O' Funk (8)
Come Closer, Baby (6)
Dahomey Dance (1)
Day Way (2)
Desire (8)
Dirty Old Man (3)

Do You Feel Me Now (5)
Down To Your Soul (4)
Dream Lady (4)
Easy Life (1)
Garden (1)
Getaway Day (5)
Gettin' Up (7)
Give Me Your Love (6)
Gonna Do It Right (7)
Good Evening Mr. & Mrs. America & All The Ships At Sea (2)
Gotcha (4)

Greed (6)
Heading Home (6)
Hi Steppers (5)
I Wanna Be (4)
In My Dreams (7)
Instant Relief (7)
It Is So Beautiful To Be (4)
Johnny B. Badd (8)
Keep On Doin' It (2)
King Cobra (1)
L.A. Expression (1)
Looking Out For Number 7 (3)

Lost Inside The Love Of You (5)
Love Poem (2)
Maybe I'm Amazed (8)
Meet Somebody (8)
Midtown Rush (3)
Mondo (2)
New York Connection (3)
Nite Creatures (5)
Nunya (1)
Only One (8)
Puttin' The Bite On You (5)
Refried (2)

Rock Island Rocket (2)
Shadows (4)
Shakedown, The (6)
Smoothin' On Down (4)
Sneakin' In The Back (1)
So White And So Funky (7)
Spindrift (1)
Street Beat (6)
Stride (8)
Strut Your Stuff (1)
Sure Enough (8)
Time And Love (3)
Tom Cat (2)

Uptown & Country (3) 80
Vertigo (1)
We Belong Together (7)
We Can Fly (6)
You're Gonna Need Me (3)
You're So Good To Me (5)
You've Got The Feel'n (4)

SCOTT-HERON, Gil

Born on 4/1/49 in Chicago. Composer/keyboardist/author/poet. Raised in Jackson, Tennessee. Attended Lincoln University in Pennsylvania; met keyboard player Brian Jackson. Masters in creative writing, taught at Columbia University. First novel published in 1968. Began converting his poems to songs. Went solo in 1980.

12/20/80+	159	6		1 Real Eyes	$8	Arista 9540
9/26/81+	106	27		2 Reflections	$8	Arista 9566
10/2/82	123	9		3 Moving Target	$8	Arista 9606

"B" Movie (2)
Black History (medley) (3)
Blue Collar (3)
Combinations (1)
Explanations (3)

Fast Lane (3)
Grandma's Hands (2)
Gun (2)
Inner City Blues (2)
Is That Jazz? (2)

Klan, The (1)
Legend In His Own Mind (1)
Morning Thoughts (2)
No Exit (3)
Not Needed (1)

Ready Or Not (3)
Storm Music (2)
Train From Washington (1)
Waiting For The Axe To Fall (1)

Washington, D.C. (3)
World, The (medley) (3)
You Could Be My Brother (1)
Your Daddy Loves You (For Gia Louise) (1)

SCOTT-HERON, Gil, And Brian Jackson

Keyboard duo: Gil (b: 4/1/49, Chicago) is the lyricist; Brian composes the music.

2/1/75	30	17		1 The First Minute Of A New Day	$10	Arista 4030
				featuring backup group The Midnight Band		
11/8/75	103	5		2 From South Africa To South Carolina	$10	Arista 4044
11/13/76	168	5		3 It's Your World ....[L]	$10	Arista 5001 [2]
10/22/77	130	5		4 Bridges	$8	Arista 4147
9/9/78	61	21		5 Secrets	$8	Arista 4189
3/8/80	82	12		6 1980	$8	Arista 9514

Ain't No Such Thing As Superman (1)
Alien (Hold On To Your Dreams) (6)
Alluswe (1)
Angola, Louisiana (5)
Beginnings (The First Minute Of A New Day) (2)
Better Days Ahead (5)
Bicentennial Blues (3)
Bottle, The (3)

Cane (5)
Corners (6)
Delta Man (Where I'm Comin' From) (4)
Essex (2)
Fell Together (2)
Guerilla (1)
Hello Sunday! Hello Road! (4)
Home Is Where The Hatred Is (3)
It's Your World (3)
Johannesburg (2)

Late Last Night (6)
Liberation Song (Red, Black And Green) (1)
Lovely Day (2)
Madison Avenue (5)
Must Be Something (1,3)
New York City (3)
1980 (6)
95 South (All Of The Places We've Been) (4)
Offering (1)

Pardon Our Analysis (We Beg Your Pardon) (1)
Possum Slim (Ed Myers) (3)
Prayer For Everybody (medley) (5)
Push Comes To Shove (6)
Racetrack In France (4)
17th Street (3)
Shah Mot Medley (6)
Sharing (3)
Show Bizness (5)
Shut 'um Down (6)

Song Of The Wind (4)
South Carolina (Barnwell) (2)
Summer Of '42 (5)
Third World Revolution (5)
Three Miles Down (5)
To Be Free (medley) (5)
Toast To The People (2)
Tomorrow's Trane (3)
Tuskeegee #626 (4)
Under The Hammer (4)
Vildgolia (Deaf, Dumb & Blind) (4)

We Almost Lost Detroit (1)
Western Sunrise (1)
Willing (6)
Winter In America (1)

SCREAMING BLUE MESSIAHS, The

London-based punk trio: Bill Carter (lead guitar, vocals), Chris Thompson and Kenny Harris.

1/16/88	172	11		Bikini Red	$8	Elektra 60755

All Shook Down
Big Brother Muscle

Bikini Red
55-The Law

I Can Speak American
I Wanna Be A Flintstone

Jesus Chrysler Drives A Dodge

Lie Detector
Sweet Water Pools

Too Much Love
Waltz

SCRITTI POLITTI

British trio: Green Gartside (vocals), Fred Maher (drums) and David Gamson (keyboards). Italian name means Political Writing.

8/3/85+	50	28		1 Cupid & Psyche 85	$8	Warner 25302
7/16/88	113	8		2 Provision	$8	Warner 25686

Absolute (1)
All That We Are (2)
Bam Salute (2)
Best Thing Ever (2)

Boom! There She Was (2) **53**
Don't Work That Hard (1)

First Boy In This Town (Lovesick) (2)
Hypnotize (1)
Little Knowledge (1)

Lover To Fall (1)
Oh Patti (Don't Feel Sorry For Loverboy) (2)
Overnite (2)

Perfect Way (1) **11**
Philosophy Now (2)
Small Talk (1)
Sugar And Spice (2)

Wood Beez (Pray Like Aretha Franklin) (1) **91**
Word Girl (Flesh & Blood) (1)

SCRUFFY THE CAT

Boston quintet: Charlie Chesterman (vocals), Stephen Fredette, Mac Paul Stanfield, Gibson IV and Burns Stanfield.

12/17/88+	177	8		Moons Of Jupiter	$8	Relativity 8237

Beg, Borrow And Steal
Betty Drops In
Bus Named Desire

Capital Moonlight
Everything

I Do
Just Like Cathy's Clown

Kissing Galaxy
Love So Amazing

Moons Of Jupiter
Nova SS 1968

Places
2Day 2Morrow 4Ever

SCRUGGS, Earl, Revue

Legendary bluegrass banjo stylist. Also see Flatt & Scruggs.

9/22/73	169	5		1 The Earl Scruggs Revue	$10	Columbia 32426
				with sons Randy, Gary and Steve		
6/21/75	104	10		2 Anniversary Special, Volume One	$10	Columbia 33416
				with a host of pop and country guest artists		
4/17/76	161	4		3 The Earl Scruggs Revue, Volume II	$10	Columbia 34090

Back Slider's Wine (1)
Banjo Man (2)
Bleeker Street Rag (2)
Broad River (3)
Come On Train (1)
Down In The Flood (1)

Every Man Has Got His Own Price (3)
Fairytale (3)
Gospel Ship (2)
Harbor For My Soul (3)
Harley (3)
Hey Porter (2)

Holiday Hotel (1)
I Still Miss Someone (3)
I've Got A Thing About You Baby (3)
If I'd Only Come And Gone (1)
Instrumental In D Minor (3)

It Takes A Lot To Laugh, It Takes A Train To Cry (3)
Love In My Time (1)
My Ship Will Sail (3)
Passing Through (2)
Rita Ballou (3)
Rollin' In My Dreams (2)

Royal Majesty (2)
Salty Dog Blues (1)
Some Of Shelley's Blues (1)
Song To Woody (2)
Station Break (1)
Step It Up And Go (1)
Swimming Song (2)

Tears (1)
Third Rate Romance (2)

DEBUT DATE	PEAK POS	WKS CHR	GOLD	ARTIST — Album Title	$	Label & Number

SEA, Johnny
Born on 7/15/40 in Gulfport, Mississippi. Joined the *Louisiana Hayride* while still in high school. Real last name: Seay.

8/6/66	**147**	2		Day For Decision	**$15**	Warner 1659

America | Generation | I Believe | This Land | What Is So Rare? | When Johnny Comes
Day For Decision 35 | God Bless America | Star Spangled Banner | Turning Point | | Marching Home

SEA HAGS
Heavy-metal quartet from San Francisco: Ron Yocom (guitar), Chris Schlosshardt (bass), Adam Maples (drums) and Frankie Wilsey (guitar).

6/24/89	**163**	7		Sea Hags	**$8**	Chrysalis 41665

All The Time | Bunkbed Creek | Half The Way Valley | Miss Fortune | Three's A Charm | Under The Night Stars
Back To The Grind | Doghouse | In The Mood For Love | Someday | Too Much T-Bone |

SEAL
Male singer. Born Sealhenry Samuel in Paddington, England of Nigerian/Brazilian descent.

7/20/91	**24**	63	●	Seal	**$12**	Sire 26627

Beginning, The | Deep Water | **Killer 100** | Violet | Wild |
Crazy 7 | Future Love Paradise | Show Me | Whirlpool | |

SEA LEVEL
Seven-man, jazzy blues-rock band formed by three members of The Allman Brothers Band (Jai Johnny Johanson, Chuck Leavell and Lamar Williams).

3/5/77	**43**	15	1	Sea Level	**$8**	Capricorn 0178
2/4/78	**31**	16	2	Cats On The Coast	**$8**	Capricorn 0198
10/28/78	**137**	16	3	On The Edge	**$8**	Capricorn 0212
8/23/80	**152**	6	4	Ball Room	**$8**	Arista 9531

Anxiously Awaiting (4) | Every Little Thing (2) | King Grand (3) | Rain In Spain (1) | **That's Your Secret** (2) 50
Bandstand (4) | Fifty-Four (3) | Living A Dream (3) | Scarborough Fair (1) | This Could Be The Worst (3)
Cats On The Coast (2) | Grand Larceny (1) | Lotta Colada (3) | School Teacher (4) | Tidal Wave (1)
Comfort Range (4) | Had To Fall (2) | Midnight Pass (2) | Shake A Leg (1) | Uptown Downtown (3)
Country Fool (1) | It Hurts To Want It So Bad | Nothing Matters But The | Song For Amy (2) | We Will Wait (4)
Don't Want To Be Wrong (4) | (2) | Fever (1) | Storm Warning (2) | Wild Side (4)
Electron Cold (3) | Just A Good Feeling (1) | On The Wing (3) | Struttin' (4) | You Mean So Much To Me (4)

SEALS, Dan
Born on 2/8/48 in McCamey Texas and raised in Dallas. Half of the duo England Dan & John Ford Coley (both formerly with Southwest F.O.B.). Brother of Jim Seals of Seals & Crofts. A hot country artist since 1983, Dan's charted 11 #1 country hits through 1992.

2/8/86	**59**	15	●	Won't Be Blue Anymore	**$8**	EMI America 17166

Bop 42 | Everything That Glitters (Is | Headin' West | Meet Me In Montana | Still A Little Bit Of Love | You Plant Your Fields
City Kind Of Girl | Not Gold) | I Won't Be Blue Anymore | So Easy To Need | Tobacco Road | Your Love

★★236★★ SEALS & CROFTS
Pop duo: Jim Seals (b: 10/17/41, Sidney, Texas; guitar, fiddle, saxophone) and Dash Crofts (b: 8/14/40, Cisco, Texas; drums, mandolin, keyboards, guitar). With Dean Beard, recorded for Edmoral and Atlantic in 1957. To Los Angeles in 1958. With the Champs from 1958-65. Own group, the Dawnbreakers, in the late 1960s; entire band converted to Baha'i faith in 1969.

10/31/70	**122**	10	1	Down Home	**$25**	TA 5004
12/4/71+	**133**	20	2	Year of Sunday	**$10**	Warner 2568
9/2/72	**7**	109	●	Summer Breeze	**$10**	Warner 2629
4/21/73	**4**	77	●	Diamond Girl	**$10**	Warner 2699
3/2/74	**14**	34	●	Unborn Child	**$10**	Warner 2761
8/10/74	**81**	12		Seals & Crofts I And II .... [E-R]	**$12**	Warner 2809 [2]
				reissue of first 2 albums on TA Records: *Seals & Crofts* and *Down Home*		
4/5/75	**30**	23	●	I'll Play For You	**$10**	Warner 2848
11/15/75+	**11**	54	▲²	Greatest Hits .... [G]	**$10**	Warner 2886
5/1/76	**37**	29	●	Get Closer	**$8**	Warner 2907
12/11/76+	**73**	10		Sudan Village	**$8**	Warner 2976
10/8/77	**118**	7		One On One .... [S]	**$8**	Warner 3076
5/13/78	**78**	13		Takin' It Easy	**$8**	Warner 3163

Advance Guards (3,10) | **Diamond Girl** (4,8) *6* | Hollow Reed (1,6) | Nine Houses (4) | Sea Of Consciousness (6) | **Unborn Child** (5) *66*
Ancient Of The Old (2) | Don't Fall (9) | **Hummingbird** (3,8) *20* | Nobody Gets Over Lovin' | See My Life (6) | Wayland The Rabbit (7)
Antoinette (2) | Dust On My Saddle (4) | Hustle (11) | You (12) | Seldom's Sister (6) | **We May Never Pass This**
Arkansas Traveller (10) | Earth (6) | **I'll Play For You** (7,8) *18* | Not Be Found (6) | Seven Valleys (6) | **Way (Again)** (4,8) *21*
Ashes In The Snow (6) | East Of Ginger Trees (3,8,10) | In Tune (6) | One More Time (12) | Springfield Mill (2) | When I Meet Them (2,8)
Baby Blue (9) | Eighth Of January (10) | Intone My Servant (4) | One On One ..see: My Fair | Standin' On A Mountain Top | Windflowers (5)
Baby, I'll Give It To You | Euphrates, The (3) | Irish Linen (3) | Share | (4) | Wisdom (4)
(10) *58* | Fiddle In The Sky (3) | It'll Be All Right (11) | Paper Airplanes (2) | Story Of Her Love (5) | Year Of Sunday (2)
Basketball Game (11) | Fire And Vengeance (7) | It's Gonna Come Down (On | Party, The (11) | Sudan Village (2,10) | Yellow Dirt (3)
Big Mac (5) | Flyin' (11) | You) (4) | Passing Thing (9) | **Summer Breeze** (3,8) *6* | **You're The Love** (12) *18*
Birthday Of My Thoughts (6) | Follow Me (5) | Janet's Theme (4) | Picnic (11) | Sunrise (2) |
Blue Bonnet Nation (7) | Forever Like The Rose (12) | Jekyll And Hyde (6) | Purple Hand (1,6) | Sweet Green Fields (9) |
Boy Down The Road (3) | Freaks Fret (7) | Jessica (4) | Put Your Love In My Hands | **Takin' It Easy** (12) *79* |
Breaking In A Brand New | Funny Little Man (3) | John Wayne (11) | (10) | This Day Belongs To Me (11) |
Love (12) | Gabriel Go On Home (1,6) | **King Of Nothing** (5,8) *60* | Rachel (5) | Thunderfoot (10) |
Castles In The Sand (7,8) | **Get Closer** (9) *6* | Leave (5) | Red Long Ago (9) | Time Out (11) |
'Cause You Love (2,10) | Golden Rainbow (7) | Ledges (5) | Reflections (11) | Tin Town (1,6) |
Cotton Mouth (1,6) | Goodbye Old Buddies (9) | Love Conquers All (11) | Ridin' Thumb (1,6) | Today (1,6) |
Cows Of Gladness (6) | Granny Will Your Dog Bite? | Magnolia Moon (12) | Robin (1,6) | Tribute To 'Abdul-Baha' (12) |
Dance By The Light Of The | (1,6) | Midnight Blue (12) | Ruby Jean And Billie Lee | Truth Is But A Woman (7) |
Moon (5) | Hand-Me-Down Shoe (1,6) | Million Dollar Horse (9) | (4,8) | 29 Years From Texas (5) |
Desert People (5) | High On A Mountain (2) | **My Fair Share** (11) *28* | Say (3) | Ugly City (7) |

DEBUT DATE	PEAK POS	WKS CHR	G O L D	ARTIST — Album Title	$	Label & Number

SEARCHERS, The

Liverpool, England rock quartet formed in 1960: Mike Pender and John McNally (vocals, guitars), Tony Jackson (vocals, bass) and Chris Curtis (drums). Worked as backup band for Johnny Sandon; toured England and worked Star Club in Hamburg, Germany. Left Sandon in 1962. Jackson replaced by Frank Allen in 1965. Curtis replaced by Billy Adamson in 1969.

4/11/64	**22**	21		1 Meet The Searchers/Needles & Pins	$30	Kapp 3363
6/20/64	**120**	8		2 Hear! Hear! .... [E-L]	$35	Mercury 60914
				recorded at the Star Club in Hamburg, Germany		
8/29/64	**97**	14		3 This Is Us	$30	Kapp 3409
3/20/65	**112**	7		4 The New Searchers LP	$30	Kapp 3412
10/23/65	**149**	2		5 The Searchers No. 4	$30	Kapp 3449
3/15/80	**191**	2		6 The Searchers	$8	Sire 6082

Ain't Gonna Kiss Ya (1)
Ain't That Just Like Me (1,2) *61*
Alright (1)
Be My Baby (I Don't Mean Maybe) (5)
Bumble Bee (4) *21*
Can't Help Forgiving You (3)
Cherry Stones (1)
Coming From The Heart (6)
Does She Really Care For Me (5)
Don't Cha Know (1)
Don't Hang On (6)

Don't Throw Your Love Away (3) *16*
Don't You Know Why (5)
Each Time (5)
Everybody Come Clap Your Hands (4)
Everything You Do (4)
Farmer John (1)
Feeling Fine (6)
Four Strong Winds (5)
Goodbye My Lover Goodbye (5) *52*
Goodnight Baby (4)
He's Got No Love (5) *79*

Hearts In Her Eyes (6)
Hey Joe (2)
Hi-Heel Sneakers (3)
Hully Gully (2)
Hungry For Love (3)
I Can Tell (2)
I Count The Tears (3)
I Don't Want To Go On Without You (4)
I Pretend I'm With You (3)
I Sure Know A Lot About Love (2)
I'll Be Doggone (5)
I'm Your Loving Man (5)

If I Could Find Someone (4)
It's In Her Kiss (3)
It's Too Late (6)
Led In The Game (2)
Listen To Me (2)
Lost In Your Eyes (6)
Love Potion Number Nine (3) *3*
Love's Gonna Be Strong (6)
Magic Potion (4)
Mashed Potatoes (2)
Needles And Pins (1) *13*
No Dancing (6)
Oh My Lover (1)

Rosalie (2)
Saturday Night Out (1)
Sea Of Heartbreak (3)
Sick And Tired (2)
Since You Broke My Heart (1)
So Far Away (5)
Some Other Guy (1)
Something You Got (4)
Sweets For My Sweet (2)
Switchboard Susan (6)
Tear Fell (4)
This Empty Place (3)
This Kind Of Love Affair (6)

Till I Met You (5)
Till You Say You Are Mine (4)
Tricky Dicky (1)
Unhappy Girls (3)
What Have They Done To The Rain (4) *29*
What'd I Say (Parts 1 And 2) (2)
Where Have You Been (3)
You Can't Lie To A Liar (5)
You Wanna Make Her Happy (4)

SEASE, Marvin

Born on 2/16/46 in South Carolina. Former gospel singer.

7/18/87	**114**	17		Marvin Sease	$8	London 830794

Candy Licker
Double Crosser

Dreaming

Ghetto Man

Let's Get Married Today

Love Me Or Leave Me

You're Number One

SEATRAIN

Fusion-rock band formed by Andy Kulberg and Richard Greene, both former members of The Blues Project.

5/17/69	**168**	4		1 Sea Train	$15	A&M 4171
1/30/71	**48**	23		2 Seatrain	$10	Capitol 659
10/9/71	**91**	9		3 The Marblehead Messenger	$12	Capitol 829
				above 2 produced by George Martin		

As I Lay Losing (1)
Broken Morning (2)
Creepin' Midnight (2)
Despair Tire (3)
Gramercy (3)

Home To You (1)
How Sweet Thy Song (3)
I'm Willin' (2)
Let The Duchess No (1)
London Song (3)

Lonely's Not The Only Way To Go (3)
Losing All The Years (3)
Marblehead Messenger (3)
Mississippi Moon (3)

Oh My Love (medley) (2)
Orange Blossom Special (2)
Out Where The Hills (1,2)
Portrait Of The Lady As A Young Artist (1)

Protestant Preacher (3)
Pudding Street (1)
Rondo (3)
Sally Goodin' (medley) (2)
Sea Train (1)

Song Of Job (2)
State Of Georgia's Mind (3)
Sweet Creek's Suite (1)
13 Questions (2) *49*
Waiting For Elijah (2)

SEAWIND

Group from Hawaii, formed in 1972 as Ox. Consisted of Pauline Wilson (lead), husband Bob Wilson, Larry Williams, Jerry Hey, Kim Hutchcroft, Bud Nuanez and Ken Wild. Paulette is the only native Hawaiian in the group. Moved to Los Angeles in 1976, changed name to Seawind.

5/7/77	**188**	2		1 Seawind	$8	CTI 5002
1/21/78	**122**	7		2 Window Of A Child	$8	CTI 5007
3/24/79	**143**	14		3 Light The Light	$8	Horizon 734
10/25/80	**83**	11		4 Seawind	$8	A&M 4824

Angel Of Mercy (2)
Campanas De Invierno (Bells Of Winter) (2)
Countin' The Days (2)
Devil Is A Liar (1)
Do Listen To (2)
Enchanted Dance (3)

Everything Needs Love (4)
Follow Your Road (3)
Free (3)
Hallelujah (2)
He Loves You (1)
Hold On To Love (3)
I Need Your Love (4)

Imagine (3)
Light The Light (3)
Long, Long Time (4)
Love Him, Love Her (4)
Love Song (medley) (1)
Lovin' You (2)
Make Up Your Mind (1)

Morning Star (3)
One Sweet Night (2)
Pra Vose (4)
Praise (Part 3) (4)
Roadways (Parts I & II) (1)
Seawind (medley) (1)
Shout (4)

Sound Rainbow (3)
Still In Love (2)
Two Of Us (4)
We Got A Way (1)
What Cha Doin' (4)
Window Of A Child (2)
Wings Of Love (2)

You Gotta Be Willin' To Lose (Part II) (1)

SEBASTIAN, John

Born on 3/17/44 in New York City. Played with the Even Dozen Jug Band as "John Benson" in 1964. Did session work for Elektra Records and toured with Mississippi John Hurt in 1965. Went solo in 1968. Formed The Lovin' Spoonful in 1965. Continues to write and perform into the '90s.

3/28/70	**20**	31		1 John B. Sebastian	$12	MGM 4654
				album also released on Reprise 6379		
10/10/70	**129**	3		2 John Sebastian Live .... [L]	$12	MGM 4720
4/24/71	**75**	13		3 cheapo-cheapo productions presents Real Live John Sebastian .... [L]	$10	Reprise 2036
9/18/71	**93**	9		4 The Four Of Us	$10	Reprise 2041
5/15/76	**79**	10		5 Welcome Back	$8	Reprise 2249

Amy's Theme (3)
Apple Hill (4)
Baby, Don't Ya Get Crazy (1)
Black Satin Kid (4)
Black Snake Blues (4)
Blue Suede Shoes (3)
Blues For Dad (medley) (3)
Coconut Grove (2)
Darlin' Be Home Soon (2,3)
Did You Ever Have To Make Up Your Mind (3)

Didn't Wanna Have To Do It (5)
Fa-Fana-Fa (1)
Fishin' Blues (2,3)
Four Of Us (4)
Goodnight Irene (3)
Hideaway (4) *95*
How Have You Been (1)
I Don't Want Nobody Else (4)
I Had A Dream (1,2)

I Needed Her Most When I Told Her To Go (5)
In The Still Of The Night (I Remember Parris) (3)
JB's Happy Harmonica (medley) (3)
Let That Be Our Time To Get Along (5)
Lovin' You (2,3)
Magical Connection (1,2)

Mobile Line (Gonna Carry Me Away From The Bull Frog Blues) (3)
My Gal (2,3)
Nashville Cats (3)
One Step Forward, Two Steps Back (5)
Rainbows All Over Your Blues (1)
Red-Eye Express (1,2)
Room Nobody Lives In (1)

Rooty-Toot (3)
She's A Lady (1,2) *84*
She's Funny (5)
Song A Day In Nashville (5)
Sweet Muse (4)
Waiting For A Train (3)
Warm Baby (4)
We'll See (4)
Welcome Back (5) *1*
Well, Well, Well (4)
What She Thinks About (1)

You Go Your Way And I'll Go Mine (4)
You're A Big Boy Now (1,2)
Younger Generation (2,3)
Younger Girl (3)

DEBUT DATE	PEAK POS	WKS CHR	GOLD	ARTIST — Album Title	$	Label & Number

SECADA, Jon
Cuban-born, Miami-raised singer/songwriter. Left Cuba at age eight. Earned a master's degree in jazz at the University of Miami. Co-wrote six songs on Gloria Estefan's album *Into The Light* and a backing vocalist for that tour.

DEBUT DATE	PEAK POS	WKS CHR	GOLD	ARTIST — Album Title	$	Label & Number
6/6/92	17↑	36↑▲		Jon Secada	$12	SBK 98845

Always Something	Do You Believe In Us *13*	Dreams That I Carry	Just Another Day *[includes*	Misunderstood
Angel *[includes English &*	Do You Really Want Me	I'm Free	English & foreign	One Of A Kind
foreign versions] **65↑**			*versions]* **5**	Time Heals

2ND II NONE
Rap duo from Compton, Los Angeles: cousins Tha D and KK. Attended high school with DJ Quik.

DEBUT DATE	PEAK POS	WKS CHR	GOLD	ARTIST — Album Title	$	Label & Number
11/16/91+	83	34		2nd II None	$12	Profile 1416

Ain't Nothin' Wrong	If You Want It **64**	Let The Rhythm Take You	More Than A Player	Niggaz Trippin'	Underground Terror
Be True To Yourself 78	Just Ain't Me	Life Of A Player	Mystic	Punk Mutha Fuckaz	What Goes Up
Comin' Like This					

★★488★★ SEDAKA, Neil
Born on 3/13/39 in Brooklyn. Pop singer/songwriter/pianist. Studied piano since elementary school. Formed songwriting team with lyricist Howard Greenfield while attending Lincoln High School (partnership lasted over 20 years). Recorded with The Tokens on Melba in 1956. Attended Juilliard School for classical piano. Prolific hit songwriter. Career revived in 1974 after signing with Elton John's new Rocket label.

DEBUT DATE	PEAK POS	WKS CHR	GOLD	ARTIST — Album Title	$	Label & Number
1/5/63	55	9		1 Neil Sedaka Sings His Greatest Hits ....[G]	$25	RCA 2627
12/7/74+	23	62	●	2 Sedaka's Back ....[K]	$10	Rocket 463
				compilation of cuts from 3 albums made in Britain		
3/1/75	161	4		3 Neil Sedaka Sings His Greatest Hits ....[G-R]	$8	RCA 0928
				new cover features a contemporary photo of Neil		
10/11/75	16	32	●	4 The Hungry Years	$8	Rocket 2157
5/1/76	26	22		5 Steppin' Out	$8	Rocket 2195
9/18/76	159	4		6 Solitaire ....[R]	$8	RCA 1790
				recorded in 1972; formerly on Kirshner Records 117		
5/28/77	59	7		7 A Song	$8	Elektra 102
10/22/77	143	5		8 Neil Sedaka's Greatest Hits ....[G]	$8	Rocket 2297
5/17/80	135	13		9 In The Pocket	$8	Elektra 259

Adventures Of A Boy Child	**Diary, The** (1,3) *14*	I've Never Really Been In	Love Will Keep Us Together	Solitaire (2,6,8)	You Better Leave That Girl
Wonder (6)	Dimbo Man (6)	Love Before (7)	(2,8)	Song, A (7)	Alone (9)
Alone At Last (7)	Do It Like You Done It When	**Immigrant, The** (2,8) *22*	My Friend (8)	**Stairway To Heaven** (1,3) *9*	**You Gotta Make Your Own**
Amarillo (7) *44*	You Meant It (9)	It's Good To Be Alive Again	New York City Blues (4)	Standing On The Inside (2,8)	**Sunshine** (5) *53*
Anywhere You're Gonna Be	Don't Let It Mess Your Mind	(9)	**Next Door To An Angel**	Stephen (4)	**You Mean Everything To**
(Leba's Song) (6)	(6)	Junkie For Your Love (9)	(1,3) *5*	**Steppin' Out** (5,8) *36*	**Me** (1,3) *17*
Baby Blue (4)	Express Yourself (6)	**King Of Clowns** (1,3) *45*	#1 With A Heartache (5)	Summer Nights (5)	You Never Done It Like That
Bad And Beautiful (5)	Good Times, Good Music,	**Laughter In The Rain**	**Oh! Carol** (1,3) *9*	**Sweet Little You** (1,3) *59*	(7)
Bad Blood (4,8) *1*	Good Friends (5)	(2,8) *1*	One Night Stand (7)	**That's When The Music**	You're So Good For Me (9)
Beautiful You (6)	**Happy Birthday, Sweet**	Leaving Game (7)	Other Side Of Me (2)	**Takes Me** (2,6,8) *27*	Your Favorite Entertainer (4)
Better Days Are Coming (6)	**Sixteen** (1,3) *6*	Letting Go (9)	Our Last Song Together (2)	Tin Pan Alley (7)	
Breaking Up Is Hard To Do	Here We Are Falling In Love	Little Brother (2)	Perfect Strangers (5)	Tit For Tat (4)	
(1,3) *1*	Again (5)	**Little Devil** (1,3) *11*	**Run Samson Run** (1,3) *28*	Trying To Say Goodbye (6)	
Breaking Up Is Hard To Do	Hollywood Lady (7)	Little Lovin' (2)	Sad Eyes (2)	Way I Am (2)	
(4,8) *8*	Home (6)	Lonely Night (Angel Face)	**Should've Never Let You**	What A Difference A Day	
Calendar Girl (1,3) *4*	Hot And Sultry Nights (7)	(4,8)	**Go** (9) *19*	Makes (9)	
Cardboard California (5)	Hungry Years (4,8)	**Love In The Shadows**	Sing Me (5)	When You Were Lovin' Me (4)	
Crossroads (4)	I Let You Walk Away (5)	(5,8) *16*	Sleazy Love (7)	You (9)	

SEDUCTION
Female vocal trio from New York: Idalis Leon, April Harris and Michelle Visage. Leon left in 1990, replaced by Sinoa Loren. Visage was a member of The S.O.U.L. S.Y.S.T.E.M. by 1992.

DEBUT DATE	PEAK POS	WKS CHR	GOLD	ARTIST — Album Title	$	Label & Number
10/28/89+	36	47	●	Nothing Matters Without Love	$8	A&M 5280

Breakdown *82*	Give My Love To You	(Nothing Matters) Without	One Mistake	Seduction's Theme	**You're My One And Only**
Could This Be Love 11	Heartbeat *13*	Love		**Two To Make It Right 2**	(True Love) *23*

SEEDS, The
Los Angeles garage-rock quartet: Sky Saxon (b: Richard Marsh; lead singer, bass), Jan Savage (guitar), Rick Aldridge (drums) and Daryl Hooper (keyboards).

DEBUT DATE	PEAK POS	WKS CHR	GOLD	ARTIST — Album Title	$	Label & Number
1/14/67	132	7		1 The Seeds	$35	GNP Cres. 2023
8/12/67	87	8		2 Future	$35	GNP Cres. 2038

Can't Seem To Make You	Flower Lady & Her Assistant	March Of The Flower	Painted Doll (2)	Two Fingers Pointing On	
Mine (1) *41*	(2)	Children (2)	**Pushin' Too Hard** (1) *36*	You (2)	
Evil Hoodoo (1)	Girl I Want You (1)	No Escape (1)	Six Dreams (2)	Where Is The Entrance Way	
Excuse, Excuse (1)	It's A Hard Life (1)	Nobody Spoil My Fun (1)	**Thousand Shadows** (2) *72*	To Play (2)	
Fallin' (2)	Lose Your Mind (1)	Now A Man (2)	Travel With Your Mind (1)	You Can't Be Trusted (1)	
Fallin' In Love (1)		Out Of The Question (2)	Try To Understand (1)		

SEEGER, Pete
Born on 5/3/19 in New York City. Legendary folk singer. Member of The Weavers. Wrote "If I Had A Hammer" (with Lee Hays) and "Where Have All The Flowers Gone."

DEBUT DATE	PEAK POS	WKS CHR	GOLD	ARTIST — Album Title	$	Label & Number
12/14/63+	42	36		1 We Shall Overcome ....[L]	$18	Columbia 8901
				recorded at Carnegie Hall on 6/8/63		
5/17/75	181	4		2 Together In Concert ....[L]	$12	Reprise 2214 [2]
				PETE SEEGER & ARLO GUTHRIE		

City Of New Orleans (2)	Get Up And Go (2)	Joe Hill (2)	Mother, The Queen Of My	Sweet Rosyanne (2)	Way Out There (2)
Declaration Of	Golden Vanity (2)	Keep Your Eyes On The	Heart (2)	That's What I Learned In	We Shall Overcome (1)
Independence (2)	Guantanamera (1,2)	Prize (1)	Oh, Freedom! (1)	School (1)	Well May The World Go (2)
Deportee (Plane Wreck At	Hard Rain's A-Gonna Fall (1)	**Little Boxes** (1) *70*	On A Monday (2)	Three Rules Of Discipline	Who Killed Davy Moore? (1)
Los Gatos) (2)	Henry My Son (2)	Lonesome Valley (1)	Presidential Rag (2)	And The Eight Rules Of	Who Killed Norma Jean? (1)
Don't Think Twice, It's All	I Ain't Scared Of Your Jail (1)	Mail Myself To You (1)	Quite Early Morning (2)	Attention (2)	Yodeling (2)
Right (2)	If You Miss Me At The Back	May There Always Be	Roving Gambler (2)	Tshotsholosa (Road Song) (1)	
Estadio Chile (2)	Of The Bus (1)	Sunshine (2)	Stealin' (2)	Walkin' Down The Line (2)	

DEBUT DATE	PEAK POS	WKS CHR	GOLD	ARTIST — Album Title	$	Label & Number

SEEKERS, The
Pop-folk, Australian-born quartet: Judith Durham (b: 7/3/43; lead singer), Keith Potger (guitar), Bruce Woodley (Spanish guitar) and Athol Guy (standup bass). Potger formed the New Seekers in 1970.

DEBUT DATE	PEAK POS	WKS CHR	GOLD	ARTIST — Album Title	$	Label & Number
6/5/65	145	3		1 The Seekers	$15	Marvel 2060
6/12/65	62	16		2 The New Seekers	$15	Capitol 2319
9/25/65	123	6		3 A World Of Our Own	$15	Capitol 2369
2/25/67	10	28		4 Georgy Girl	$15	Capitol 2431
8/19/67	97	10		5 The Best Of The Seekers .... [G]	$15	Capitol 2746

All My Trials (1)
All Over The World (Dans Le Monde En Entier) (4)
Allentown Jail (3)
Blowin' In The Wind (2)
California Dreamin' (4)
Carnival Is Over (5)
Chilly Winds (1,2)
Come The Day (4)
Dese Bones G'wine Rise Again (1)
Don't Tell My Mind (3)
Don't Think Twice, It's All Right (3)
Four Strong Winds (3)
Georgy Girl (4) **2**
I'll Never Find Another You (5) **4**
If I Had A Hammer (The Hammer Song) (1)
Island Of Dreams (1)
Just A Closer Walk With Thee (3)
Katy Cline (1)
Kumbaya (1,2)
Lady Mary (2)
Last Thing On My Mind (4)
Leaving Of Liverpool (3)
Light From The Lighthouse (1)
Lonesome Traveller (1)
Louisiana Man (4)
Morningtown Ride (2,5) **67**
Ox Driving Song (2)
Red Rubber Ball (4)
Run Come See (1)
Sinner Man (3)
Someday, One Day (5)
This Land Is Your Land (3)
This Little Light Of Mine (5)
This Train (1)
Times They Are A Changin' (3,5)
Turn, Turn, Turn (To Everything There Is A Season) (4,5)
Two Summers (5)
Walk With Me (5)
Water Is Wide (2)
We're Moving On (2,5)
Well, Well, Well (2,4)
What Have They Done To The Rain (2)
When The Stars Begin To Fall (1,5)
Wild Rover (1)
World Of Our Own (3,5) **19**
Yesterday (4)
You Can Tell The World (3)

SEGAL, George
Born on 2/13/34 in Great Neck, New York. Popular film actor.

DEBUT DATE	PEAK POS	WKS CHR	GOLD	ARTIST — Album Title	$	Label & Number
9/2/67	199	2		The Yama Yama Man	$15	Philips 242
				George sings and plays the banjo		

Baby Won't You Please Come Home
Bennie Badoo
Bye Bye Blackbird (medley)
Gee But I Hate To Go Home Alone
Glory Of Love
I Always Think I'm Up In Heaven When I'm Down In Dixieland
Ja-Da (medley)
Moving Picture Ball
On The Old Dominion Line
Show Me The Way To Go Home (medley)
Yama, Yama Man
Yes Sir That's My Baby

★★142★★ SEGER, Bob
Born on 5/6/45 in Dearborn, Michigan and raised in Detroit. Rock singer/songwriter/guitarist. First recorded in 1966, formed the System in 1968. Left music to attend college in 1969, returned in 1970. Formed own backing group The Silver Bullet Band in 1976: Alto Reed (horns), Robyn Robbins (keyboards), Drew Abbott (guitar), Chris Campbell (bass) and Charlie Allen Martin (drums). Various personnel changes since then; Campbell is the only remaining original member.

BOB SEGER SYSTEM:

DEBUT DATE	PEAK POS	WKS CHR	GOLD	ARTIST — Album Title	$	Label & Number
2/8/69	62	10		1 Ramblin' Gamblin' Man	$15	Capitol 172
10/31/70	171	4		2 Mongrel	$15	Capitol 499
				BOB SEGER:		
7/22/72	180	11		3 Smokin' O.P.'s	$20	Palladium 1006
3/3/73	188	6		4 Back In '72	$15	Palladium 2126
4/12/75	131	18	▲	5 Beautiful Loser	$10	Capitol 11378
				BOB SEGER & THE SILVER BULLET BAND:		
5/1/76	34	167	▲⁴	6 'Live' Bullet .... [L]	$12	Capitol 11523 [2]
				recorded at Cobo Hall, Detroit		
11/13/76+	8	88	▲⁵	7 Night Moves	$10	Capitol 11557
5/27/78	4	110	▲⁵	8 Stranger in Town	$8	Capitol 11698
3/15/80	1⁶	110	▲⁴	9 Against The Wind	$8	Capitol 12041
9/26/81	3	70	▲³	10 Nine Tonight .... [L]	$12	Capitol 12182 [2]
1/15/83	5	39	▲	11 The Distance	$8	Capitol 12254
4/19/86	3	62	▲	12 Like A Rock	$8	Capitol 12398
9/14/91	7	29	▲	13 The Fire Inside...	$12	Capitol 91134

Aftermath, The (12)
Against The Wind (9,10) **5**
Ain't Got No Money (8)
Always In My Heart (13)
American Storm (12) **13**
Back In '72 (4)
Beautiful Loser (5,6)
Betty Lou's Gettin' Out Tonight (9,10)
Big River (2)
Black Eyed Girl (1)
Black Night (5)
Blind Love (13)
Bo Diddley (3,6)
Boomtown Blues (11)
Brave Strangers (8)
Come To Poppa (7)
Comin' Home (11)
Doctor Fine (1)
Down Home (1)
Even Now (11) **12**
Evil Edna (2)
Famous Final Scene (8)
Feel Like A Number (9,10) **48**
Fine Memory (10)
Fire Down Below (7,10)
Fire Inside (13)
Fire Lake (9,10) **6**
Get Out Of Denver (6) **80**
Gone (1)
Good For Me (9)
Heavy Music (13)
Her Strut (9,10)
Highway Child (2)
Hollywood Nights (8,10) **12**
Horizontal Bop (9) **42**
House Behind A House (11)
Hummingbird (3)
I've Been Workin' (4,6)
I've Got Time (4)
If I Were A Carpenter (3) **76**
It's You (12) **52**
Ivory (1) **97**
Jesse James (3)
Jody Girl (5,6)
Katmandu (5,6) **43**
Last Song (Love Needs To Be Loved) (1)
Leanin On My Dream (2)
Let It Rock (3,6,10)
Little Victories (11)
Long Twin Silver Line (9)
Long Way Home (13)
Lookin' Back (6) **96**
Love The One You're With (3)
Love's The Last To Know (11)
Lucifer (2) **84**
Mainstreet (7,10) **24**
Makin' Thunderbirds (11)
Mary Lou (7)
Miami (12) **70**
Midnight Rider (4)
Momma (5)
Mongrel (2)
Mongrel Too (2)
Mountain, The (13)
Neon Sky (4)
New Coat Of Paint (13)
Night Moves (7,10) **4**
Nine Tonight (10)
No Man's Land (9)
Nutbush City Limits (5,6) **69**
Old Time Rock & Roll (8,10) **28**
Ramblin' Gamblin' Man (1,6) **17**
Real Love (13) **24**
Real At The Time (13)
River Deep - Mountain High (2)
Rock And Roll Never Forgets (7,10) **41**
Roll Me Away (11) **27**
Rosalie (4)
Sailing Nights (5)
Shame On The Moon (11) **2**
She Can't Do Anything Wrong (13)
Shinin' Brightly (9)
Ship Of Fools (7)
Sightseeing (13)
So I Wrote You A Song (4)
Someday (3)
Sometimes (12)
Somewhere Tonight (12)
Song To Rufus (2)
Stealer (4)
Still The Same (8) **4**
Sunburst (7)
Sunspot Baby (7)
Take A Chance (13)
Tales Of Lucy Blue (1)
Teachin Blues (7)
Tightrope (12)
Till It Shines (8)
Train Man (1)
Travelin' Man (5,6)
Tryin' To Live My Life Without You (10) **5**
Turn On Your Lovelight (3)
Turn The Page (4,6)
2 + 2 = ? (1)
U.M.C. (10)
We've Got Tonite (8,10) **3**
Which Way (10)
White Wall (1)
You'll Accomp'ny Me (9,10) **14**

SELECTER
British ska group — Pauline Black, lead singer.

DEBUT DATE	PEAK POS	WKS CHR	GOLD	ARTIST — Album Title	$	Label & Number
5/3/80	175	4		Too Much Pressure	$8	Chrysalis 1274

Black And Blue
Carry Go Bring Come
Danger
James Bond
Missing Words
Murder
My Collie (Not A Dog)
On My Radio
Out On The Streets
Street Feeling
They Make Me Mad
Three Minute Hero
Time Hard
Too Much Pressure

SEMBELLO, Michael
Born on 4/17/54 in Philadelphia. Session guitarist/composer/arranger/vocalist. Guitarist on Stevie Wonder's albums from 1974-79.

DEBUT DATE	PEAK POS	WKS CHR	GOLD	ARTIST — Album Title	$	Label & Number
10/8/83	80	10		Bossa Nova Hotel	$8	Warner 23920

DEBUT DATE	PEAK POS	WKS CHR	GOLD	ARTIST — Album Title	$	Label & Number

SEMBELLO, Michael — Cont'd

Automatic Man 34	Cowboy	Godzilla	Lay Back	Superman
Cadillac	First Time	It's Over	**Maniac** *1*	Talk

SEPULTURA
Brazilian speed-metal band: Max Cavalera (vocals), Andreas Kisser, Igor Cavalera and Paulo Jr.

5/4/91	**119**	4		Arise	**$12**	RC 9328

Altered State	Dead Embryonic Cells	Infected Voice	Murder	Under Siege (Regnum Irae)
Arise	Desperate Cry	Meaningless Movements	Subtraction	

SERENDIPITY SINGERS, The
Nine member pop-folk group organized at the University of Colorado.

3/7/64	**11**	29		1 The Serendipity Singers	**$15**	Philips 115
6/27/64	**68**	15		2 The Many Sides Of The Serendipity Singers................................	**$15**	Philips 134
1/16/65	**149**	2		3 Take Your Shoes Off with the Serendipity Singers	**$15**	Philips 151

Autumn Wind (3)	Down Where The Winds	Lazy Afternoon (3)	New Frankie And Johnny	Sobbin' Women (3)
Beans In My Ears (2) *30*	Blow (2)	Let Me Fly (2)	Song (2)	Soon It's Gonna Rain (2)
Boots And Stetsons (The	Fast Freight (2)	Little Brown Jug (3)	Rider (3)	Spring (3)
Lilies Grow High) (1)	Foghorn (3)	Look Away Over Yondro (2)	Sailing Away (1)	Take Your Shoes Off (3)
Cloudy Summer Afternoon	Freedom's Star (1)	Mill Girls Don't Sing Or	Same Old Reason (3)	That's My Home (3)
(1)	Goin' Home (1)	Dance (2)	Sing Out (1)	Waggoner Lad (1)
Don't Let The Rain Come	Hi-Lili-Hi-Lo (2)	Movin' In My Heart (2)	Sinner Man (1)	Whale Of A Tale (3)
Down (Crooked Little	High North Star (3)	Mud (Hippopotamus Song)	Six Foot Six (2)	You Don't Know (1)
Man) (1) *6*	Jimmy-O (1)	(1)	Six Wheel Driver (1)	

SESAME STREET — see CHILDRENS section

SETZER, Brian
Born on 4/10/60 in Long Island, New York. Lead guitarist/vocalist of the Stray Cats. Portrayed Eddie Cochran in the 1987 film *La Bamba*.

3/22/86	**45**	18		1 The Knife Feels Like Justice	**$8**	EMI America 17178
5/28/88	**140**	8		2 Live Nude Guitars	**$8**	EMI-Man. 46963

Aztec (1)	Chains Around Your Heart	Love Is Repaid By Love	Rain Washed Everything	She Thinks I'm Trash (2)	When The Sky Comes
Barbwire Fence (1)	(1)	Alone (1)	Away (1)	So Young, So Bad, So What?	Tumblin' Down (2)
Bobby's Back (1)	Every Tear That Falls (2)	Maria (1)	Rebelene (2)	(2)	
Boulevard Of Broken	Haunted River (1)	Nervous Breakdown (1)	Red Lightning Blues (2)	Temper Sure Is Risin' (2)	
Dreams (1)	Knife Feels Like Justice (1)	Radiation Ranch (1)	Rockability (2)	Three Guys (1)	
Breath Of Life (1)			Rosie In The Middle (2)		

707
Detroit-bred rock group: Kevin Russell, Phil Bryant and Jim McClarty. Kevin Chalfant and Tod Howarth added in 1982. Chalfant, a backing singer for Kim Carnes and Night Ranger, co-founded The Storm in 1991.

2/7/81	**159**	6		1 The Second Album...	**$15**	Casablanca 7248
7/3/82	**129**	9		2 Mega Force	**$8**	Boardwalk 33253

Can't Hold Back (2)	Hell Or High Water (2)	Love On The Run (1)	Out Of The Dark (2)	Strings Around My Heart (1)
City Life (1)	Hello Girl (2)	**Mega Force** *62*	Party's Over (1)	Tonite's Your Nite (1)
Get To You (2)	Live With The Girl (1)	Millionaire (1)	Pressure Rise (1)	We Will Last (2)
Heartbeat (2)	Live Without Her (1)	No Better Feeling (2)	Rockin' Is Easy (1)	Write Again (2)

7 SECONDS
White male trio: Kevin Seconds (vocals, guitar), Steve Youth and Troy Mowat.

11/4/89+	**153**	19		Soulforce Revolution	**$8**	Restless 72344

Busy Little People	4 A.M. In Texas	It All Makes A Lot Less	Mother's Day	Soul To Keep (For Phyllis)	Tickets To A Better Place
Copper Ledge	I Can Sympathize	Sense Now	Satyagraha	Swansong	Tribute Freedom Landscape

SEVERINSEN, Doc
Born Carl H. Severinsen on 7/7/27 in Arlington, Oregon. Trumpet virtuoso — leader of the *Tonight Show* band (1967-92). With Charlie Barnet (1947-49), Tommy Dorsey (1949-50), and Sauter-Finegan (1952-53).

8/27/66	**147**	2		1 Fever! ....[I]	**$15**	Command 893
11/26/66	**133**	6		2 Command Performances	**$15**	Command 904
10/16/71	**185**	2		3 Brass Roots..	**$10**	RCA 4522
4/29/72	**74**	19		4 Brass On Ivory ....[I]	**$10**	RCA 4629
6/9/73	**185**	3		5 Brass, Ivory & Strings ....[I]	**$10**	RCA 0098
				above 2: HENRY MANCINI & DOC SEVERINSEN		
4/17/76	**189**	4		6 Night Journey...[I]	**$8**	Epic 34078
11/1/86	**65**	26		7 The Tonight Show Band with Doc Severinsen ....[I]	**$8**	Amherst 3311
12/14/91	**171**	4		8 Merry Christmas from Doc Severinsen and The Tonight Show Orchestra ....[X-I]	**$12**	Amherst 94406
				featuring the L.A. Children's Chorus, the Desert Bells Handbells and the Philharmonic Strings		

Baubles, Bangles And Beads	Don't Worry 'Bout Me (2)	I'm Getting Sentimental	Love For Sale (2)	Open The Gates Of Love (6)	Stardust (2)
(2)	Dreamsville (4)	Over You (7)	Love Man (Oh, Where Can	Poor Butterfly (4)	Stormy Weather (2)
Begin The Beguine (7)	Fever (1)	If (4)	You Be?) (5)	Psalm 150 (3)	Summertime (2)
Ben (5)	Flying Home (7)	In A Little Spanish Town	Love Story, Theme From (3)	Raggedy Jim (1)	Tennessee Waltz (1)
Bluesette (2)	Good Medicine (3)	(1,2)	Make It With You (5)	'Round Midnight (5)	Tippin' In (7)
Brass On Ivory (4)	Hark! The Herald Angels	It Ain't Necessarily So (2)	March Of The Toys (8)	Rudolph The Red-Nosed	Tonight Show Theme ..see:
Brass Roots (3)	Sing (8)	Ja-Da (1)	Misty (2)	Reindeer (8)	Johnny's Theme
Brian's Song (4)	Have Yourself A Merry Little	Jingle Bells (8)	Move Over (3)	Santa Claus Is Coming To	Walk Right In (1)
Bye, Bye Blues (7)	Christmas (8)	Johnny's Theme (The	My Funny Valentine (2)	Town (8)	Wave (5)
Celebrate (3)	He's Got The Whole World In	Tonight Show Theme) (7)	Never My Love (4)	Sax Alley (7)	We've Only Just Begun (4)
Christmas Song (Chestnuts	His Hands (1)	Joy To The World (8)	Night Journey (6)	Shawnee (7)	When The Saints Come
Roasting On An Open Fire)	Help Me Make It Through	King Porter Stomp (7)	Now And Then (6)	Sidewinder, The (1)	Marching In (2)
(8)	The Night (5)	Lady In Red (1)	O Come, All Ye Faithful	Silent Night, Holy Night (8)	White Christmas (8)
Cleopatra's Asp (1)	How Long Has This Been	Laura, Theme For (5)	(Adeste Fideles) (8)	Skyliner (7)	Winter Wonderland (8)
Cotton Fields (1)	Going On (7)	Let It Snow, Let It Snow (8)	Okefenokee (3)	Sleigh Ride (8)	Without You (5)
Dance Of The Sugar Plum	I Can't Get Started (5)	Little Drummer Boy (8)	On A Clear Day (You Can	Soldier In The Rain (4)	World's Gone Home (6)
Fairy (8)	I Wanna Be With You (5)	Little Tiny Feets (6)	See Forever) (1,2)	Sometimes (4)	You Put The Shine On Me (6)
Doc, Theme For (5)		Lookin' Good (6)	One O'Clock Jump (7)	Spanish Dreams (6)	

DEBUT DATE	PEAK POS	WKS CHR	GOLD	ARTIST — Album Title	$	Label & Number

SEX PISTOLS

Notorious British punk-rock quartet put together by entrepeneur Malcom McLaren at his clothing boutique, SEX. Led by Johnny "Rotten" Lydon & John Simon "Sid Vicious" Ritchie (died on 2/2/79). Drummer Paul Cook and bassist Steve Jones later joined The Professionals; both appeared in the 1982 film *Ladies And Gentlemen, The Fabulous Stains.* Lydon formed Public Image Ltd. (P.I.L.). Vicious had been an early member of Siouxsie & The Banshees. Films about group include *The Great Rock 'n' Roll Swindle, D.O.A.* and *Sid & Nancy.*

| 12/10/77+ | 106 | 12 ▲ | | Never Mind The Bollocks, Here's The Sex Pistols .... | $12 | Warner 3147 |

Anarchy In The U.K.	EMI	Holidays In The Sun	New York	Pretty Vacant		Seventeen
Bodies	God Save The Queen	Liar	No Feelings	Problems		Sub-Mission

SEXTON, Charlie

Austin, Texas rock singer/guitarist. Lead guitarist for Joe Ely's band at age 13 in 1982. Co-founder of the Arc Angels. Appeared in the film *Thelma & Louise.* His brother Will is leader of Will & The Kill.

| 11/30/85+ | 15 | 34 | 1 | Pictures For Pleasure .... | $8 | MCA 5629 |
| 2/18/89 | 104 | 9 | | Charlie Sexton .... | $8 | MCA 6280 |

Attractions (1)	Blowing Up Detroit (2)	Hold Me (1)	Question This (2)	Space (1)	
Battle Hymn Of The	Cry Little Sister (2)	I Can't Cry (2)	Restless (1)	Tell Me (1)	
Republic (2)	Don't Look Back (2)	Impressed (1)	Save Yourself (2)	While You Sleep (2)	
Beat's So Lonely (1) 17	For All We Know (2)	Pictures For Pleasure (1)	Seems So Wrong (2)	You Don't Belong Here (1)	

SEYMOUR, Phil

Vocalist/drummer; formerly with the Dwight Twilley Band. Originally from Tulsa, Oklahoma.

| 2/21/81 | 64 | 16 | | Phil Seymour .... | $8 | Boardwalk 36996 |

Baby It's You	I Found A Love	Let Her Dance	**Precious To Me 22**	Trying To Get To You	Won't Finish Here
Don't Blow Your Life Away	I Really Love You	Love You So Much	Then We Go Up	We Don't Get Along	

SHADOWFAX

Jazz-fusion sextet from Chicago. Band name taken from J.R.R. Tolkien's novel, *Lord Of The Rings.*

11/19/83+	145	19	1	Shadowdance .... [I]	$8	Windham Hill 1029
11/17/84	126	20	2	The Dreams Of Children .... [I]	$8	Windham Hill 1038
7/12/86	114	16	3	Too Far To Whisper .... [I]	$8	Windham Hill 1051
5/14/88	168	5	4	Folksongs For A Nuclear Village .... [I]	$8	Capitol 46924

Above The Wailing Wall (2)	Dreams Of Children (2)	Kindred Spirits (2)	Ritual (3)	Streetnoise (3)	
Against The Grain (4)	Elephant Ego (4)	Lucky Mud (4)	Road To Hanna (3)	Too Far To Whisper (3)	
Another Country (2)	Firewalker, The (4)	Maceo (3)	Shadowdance (1)	Tsunami (3)	
Behind Green Eyes (4)	Folksong For A Nuclear	Madagascar Cafe (4)	Shaman Song (2)	Watercourse Way (1)	
Big Song (3)	Village (4)	New Electric India (1)	Slim Limbs Akimbo (3)	We Used To Laugh (4)	
Brown Rice (medley) (1)	Ghost Bird (1)	Nö Society (4)	Snowline (2)	What Goes Around (3)	
China Blue (3)	Karmapa Chenno (medley)	Orangutan Gang (Strikes	Solar Wind (4)	Word From The Village (2)	
Distant Voices (1)	(1)	Back) (3)	Song For My Brother (1)		

SHADOWS OF KNIGHT, The

Chicago-area garage band: Jim Sohns (lead singer), Joe Kelley (lead guitarist), Warren Rogers (bass), Jerry McGeorge (rhythm guitar) and Tom Schiffour (drums).

| 5/14/66 | 46 | 18 | | Gloria .... | $50 | Dunwich 666 |

Boom Boom	I Got My Mojo Working	(I'm Your) Hoochie Coochie	It Always Happens That Way	Light Bulb Blues	You Can't Judge A Book (By
Dark Side	I Just Want To Make Love	Man	Let It Rock	**Oh Yeah 39**	The Cover)
Gloria 10	To You				

SHAKESPEAR'S SISTER

Female duo of British native Siobhan Fahey and Detroit native Marcella Detroit. Fahey, wife of Dave Stewart (Eurythmics), was a member of Bananarama. Detroit is Marcy Levy who recorded with Robin Gibb, sang backup for Eric Clapton and co-wrote "Lay Down Sally."

| 7/18/92 | 56 | 28↑ | | Hormonally Yours .... | $12 | London 828266 |

Are We In Love Yet	Catwoman	Goodbye Cruel World	**I Don't Care 55**	Moonchild	**Stay 4**
Black Sky	Emotional Thing	Hello (Turn Your Radio On)	Let Me Entertain You	My 16th Apology	Trouble With Andre

SHAKTI — see McLAUGHLIN, John

★★462★★ **SHALAMAR**

Black vocal trio formed in 1978 by Don Cornelius, the producer/host of TV's *Soul Train.* Consisted of vocalists/dancers Jody Watley and Jeffrey Daniels with Gerald Brown. Howard Hewett replaced Brown in early 1979. Watley and Daniels (former husband of Stephanie Mills) pursued solo careers in 1984; replaced by Delisa Davis (former Miss Teenage Georgia and Miss Tennessee State) and Micki Free. Hewett left in 1985, replaced by Sydney Justin (former football defensive back with the L.A. Rams).

5/21/77	48	14		1	Uptown Festival	$8	Soul Train 2289
11/4/78	171	4		2	Disco Gardens	$8	Solar 2895
11/10/79+	23	36	●	3	Big Fun	$8	Solar 3479
1/10/81	40	36	●	4	Three For Love	$8	Solar 3577
10/24/81	115	15		5	Go For It	$8	Solar 3984
2/20/82	35	25	●	6	Friends	$8	Solar 28
8/6/83	38	23		7	The Look	$8	Solar 60239
12/8/84+	90	24		8	Heart Break	$8	Solar 60385

Amnesia (8) **73**	Final Analysis (5)	I Just Stopped By Because I	No Limits (The Now Club) (7)	Somewhere There's A Love	**Uptown Festival (Part 1)**
Appeal (5)	Forever Came Today (1)	Had To (6)	On Top Of The World (6)	(4)	(1) **25**
Attention To My Baby (4)	Friends (6)	I Owe You One (3)	Ooh Baby, Baby (1)	Stay Close To Love (2)	Whenever You Need Me (8)
Beautiful Night (1)	**Full Of Fire** (4) **55**	Inky Dinky Wang Dang Doo	Over And Over (7)	Sweeter As The Days Go By	Work It Out (4)
Cindy, Cindy (2)	Girl (3)	(1)	Playing To Win (6)	(5)	You Can Count On Me (7)
Closer (7)	Go For It (5)	Leave It All Up To Love (2)	Right Here (7)	Take Me To The River (3)	You Know (1)
Dancing In The Sheets	Good Feelings (5)	Let's Find The Time For Love	Right In The Socket (1)	**Take That To The Bank**	You Won't Miss Love (Until
(8) **17**	Heart Break (8)	(3)	Right Time For Us (3)	(2) **79**	It's Gone) (7)
Dead Giveaway (7) **22**	Help Me (6)	Look, The (7)	Rocker (5)	Talk To Me (5)	You're The One For Me (7)
Deceiver (8)	High On Life (1)	Lovely Lady (2)	**Second Time Around** (3) **8**	There It Is (6)	You've Got Me Running (5)
Disappearing Act (7)	I Can Make You Feel Good	**Make That Move** (4) **60**	Shalamar Disco Gardens (2)	This Is For The Lover In You	
Don't Get Stopped In	(6)	Melody (An Erotic Affair) (8)	Some Things Never Change	(4)	
Beverly Hills (8)	I Don't Wanna Be The Last	My Girl Loves Me (8)	(4)	Tossing, Turning And	
Don't Try To Change Me (6)	To Know (6)	**Night To Remember** (6) **44**		Swinging (2)	

DEBUT DATE	PEAK POS	WKS CHR	GOLD	ARTIST — Album Title	$	Label & Number

SHAMEN, The
Techno-rave dance group from Aberdeen, Scotland formed by Colin "Shamen" Angus and Will "Sin" Sinnott (drowned on 5/23/90 [age 31]). Features rapper Mr. C.

| 2/1/92 | 138 | 8 | | En-Tact .... | $12 | Epic 48722 |

Evil Is Even · Hear Me · Human NRG · Hyperreal Orbit · Hyperreal Selector · Lightspan · Lightspan Soundwave · Make It Mine · Make It Minimal · **Move Any Mountain (Progen 91)** *38* · Omega Amigo · Oxygen Restriction · Possible Worlds · 666 Edit

SHANA
Shana Petrone — born on 5/8/72 in Parkridge, Illinois and raised in Ft. Lauderdale, Florida.

| 1/27/90 | 165 | 11 | | I Want You .... | $12 | Vision 3316 |

All Of Me · Best Part Of Breaking Up · Falling Slowly · (Hey Boy) Tell Me Why · **I Want You** *40* · I'd Do Anything For Your Love · I'm In Love · Is This Love (An Illusion) · **You Can't Get Away** *82* · Zero To Sixty

SHA NA NA
Fifties rock & roll specialists led by John "Bowzer" Baumann (b: 9/14/47, Queens, New York). Formed at Columbia University in 1969. Own syndicated variety TV show, 1977-81. Henry Gross was a member, left in 1970. Many personnel changes.

12/13/69	183	7		1 Rock & Roll Is Here To Stay!	$15	Kama Sutra 2010
8/7/71	122	9		2 Sha Na Na .... [L]	$15	Kama Sutra 2034
				side 1: live; side 2: studio		
7/1/72	156	14		3 The Night Is Still Young	$15	Kama Sutra 2050
4/21/73	38	24	●	4 The Golden Age Of Rock 'N' Roll .... [L]	$15	Kama Sutra 2073 [2]
12/1/73+	140	11		5 From The Streets Of New York .... [L]	$12	Kama Sutra 2075
6/1/74	165	6		6 Hot Sox	$12	Kama Sutra 2600
8/9/75	162	4		7 Sha Na Now	$10	Kama Sutra 2605

At The Hop (4) · Bad Boy (6) · Basement Party (7) · Bless My Soul (3) · Blue Moon (2,4) · Book Of Love (1) · Bounce In Your Buggy (7) · Breaking Up Is Hard To Do (7) · Canadian Money (2) · Chances Are (5) · Chantilly Lace (1,4) · Chills In My Spine (7) · Circles Of Love (7) · Come Go With Me (1,5) · Depression (2) · Don't Want To Say Goodbye (7) · Don't You Just Know It (6) · Dreams Come True (6) · Duke Of Earl (2) · Earth Angel (5) · Easier Said Than Done (6) · Get A Job (4,5) · Glasses (3) · Goodnight Sweetheart (5) · Great Balls Of Fire (3,4) · Heartbreak Hotel (1,4) · High School Confidential (5) · His Latest Flame (4) · Hot Sox (6) · Hound Dog (4) · I Wonder Why (2,4) · In The Still Of The Night (3) · It Ain't Love (3) · It's What You Do With What You Got (3) · Jailhouse Rock (2,4) · Just A Friend (2) · **(Just Like) Romeo And Juliet** (6,7) *55* · Little Darlin' (1,4) · Little Girl Of Mine (1) · Long Tall Sally (1) · Lover's Question (4) · Lovers Never Say Goodbye (1,4) · Maybe I'm Old Fashioned (6) · Oh! Lonesome Boy (3) · Only One Song (2) · Party Lights (7) · Pretty Little Angel Eyes (4) · Rama Lama Ding Dong (4) · Remember Then (1) · Ring Around Your Neck (5) · Rock And Roll Is Here To Stay (1,2,4) · Rock Around The Clock (4) · Ruin Me Blues (2) · Runaround Sue (4) · Runaway (7) · Sea Cruise (3,4) · Sh-Boom (Life Could Be A Dream) (5,6) · Sha Bumpin' (7) · Shake, Rattle 'N' Roll (4) · Shanghaied (7) · Shot Down In Denver (7) · Silhouettes (1) · Sixteen Candles (4) · Sleepin' On A Song (3) · So Fine - You're So Fine (3) · Splish Splash (5) · Stroll All Night (6) · Summertime Summertime (5) · Sunday Morning Radio (3) · Tears On My Pillow (4) · Teen Angel (1) · Teenager In Love (1,4) · Tell Laura I Love Her (2,4) · Too Chubby To Boogie (6) · **Top Forty (Of The Lord)** (2) *84* · Tossin' And Turnin' (5) · (Vote Song) (3) · Walk Don't Run (4) · Wanderer, The (5) · Whole Lotta Shakin' Goin' On (4) · Why Do Fools Fall In Love (4) · Wild Weekend (4) · Yakety Yak (2,4) · You Can Bet They Do (3) · You Talk Too Much (6) · You're The Only Light On My Horizon Now (7) · Young Love (1)

SHANGRI-LAS, The
"Girl group" formed at Andrew Jackson High School in Queens, New York. Consisted of two sets of sisters: Mary (lead singer) & Betty Weiss and twins Mary Ann & Marge Ganser. Mary Ann died of encephalitis in 1971 and Marge died of a drug overdose.

| 3/13/65 | 109 | 6 | | Leader Of The Pack .... | $75 | Red Bird 101 |
| | | | | side 2 has live sounds dubbed in | | |

Bull Dog · **Give Him A Great Big Kiss** *18* · Good Night, My Love, Pleasant Dreams · It's Easier To Cry · **Leader Of The Pack** *1* · **Maybe** *91* · Remember (Walkin' In The Sand) *5* · Shout · So Much In Love · Twist And Shout · What Is Love · You Can't Sit Down

SHANICE — see WILSON, Shanice

SHANK, Bud
Born Clifford E. Shank on 5/27/26 in Dayton, Ohio. Jazz-oriented saxophonist. Played with Charlie Barnet, Art Mooney and Stan Kenton from 1947-51. TV and movie studio musician.

| 2/12/66 | 56 | 21 | | Michelle .... [I] | $12 | World Pac. 21840 |
| | | | | with Chet Baker (flugelhorn) | | |

As Tears Go By · Blue On Blue · Girl · Love Theme, Umbrellas Of Cherbourg (I Will Wait For You) · **Michelle** *65* · Petite Fleur (Little Flower) · Sounds Of Silence · Turn! Turn! Turn! (To Everything There Is A Season) · Yesterday · You Didn't Have To Be So Nice

SHANKAR, Ravi
Born on 4/7/20 in India. Classical sitarist. Also see soundtrack *Gandhi*.

7/15/67	161	7		1 West Meets East .... [I]	$15	Angel 36418
				YEHUDI MENUHIN (violin) & RAVI SHANKAR		
7/29/67	148	7		2 Ravi Shankar in New York .... [I]	$15	World Pac. 21441
11/18/67+	43	19		3 Ravi Shankar At The Monterey International Pop Festival .... [I-L]	$15	World Pac. 21442
8/3/68	140	4		4 Ravi Shankar in San Francisco .... [I-L]	$15	World Pac. 21449
1/11/75	176	3		5 Shankar Family & Friends	$10	Dark Horse 22002
				George Harrison producer/guitarist; side 2 titled "Dream, Nightmare & Dawn - Music For A Ballet" is broken into 3 parts which are then broken into 9 tracks		

Dawn: Awakening (5) · Dawn: Peace & Hope (5) · Dhun (A Morning Raga In Sindhi Bhairavi) (4) · Dhun (Dadra And Fast Teental) (3) · Dream: Festivity & Joy (1,5) · Dream: Love-Dance Ecstasy (1,5) · Enesco: Sonata No. 3 In A Minor, Op. 25 (1) · I Am Missing You (5) · Jaya Jagadish Hare (5) · Kahan Gayelava Shyam Salone (5) · Nata Bhairravi (2) · Nightmare: Despair & Sorrow (5) · Nightmare: Disillusionment & Frustration (5) · Nightmare: Dispute & Violence (5) · Nightmare: Lust (5) · Raga Bairragi (2) · Raga Bhimpalasi (3) · Raga Bhupal Todi (4) · Raga Marwa (2) · Raga Puriya Kalyan (1) · Shankar: Prabhati (Raga Gunkali) (1) · Shankar: Swara-Kakali (Raga Tilang) (1) · Supane Me Aye Preetam Sainya (5) · Tabla Solo In Ektal (3) · Tabla Solo In Shikhar Tal (4)

SHANNON
Brenda Shannon Greene from Washington, D.C. Began singing career at York University.

| 2/11/84 | 32 | 37 | ● | 1 Let The Music Play .... | $8 | Mirage 90134 |
| 5/25/85 | 92 | 16 | | 2 Do You Wanna Get Away .... | $8 | Mirage 90267 |

DEBUT DATE	PEAK POS	WKS CHR	GOLD	ARTIST — Album Title	$	Label & Number

SHANNON — Cont'd

Bedroom Eyes (2)
Do You Wanna Get Away (2) 49
Doin' What You're Doin' (2)
Give Me Tonight (1) 46
It's You (1)
Let Me See Your Body Move (2)
Let The Music Play (1) 8
My Heart's Divided (1)
One Man (1)
Someone Waiting Home (1)
Stop The Noise (2)
Stronger Together (2)
Sweet Somebody (1)
Urgent (2)
Why Can't We Pretend (2)

SHANNON, Del

Born Charles Westover on 12/30/34 in Coopersville, Michigan. With U.S. Army *Get Up And Go* radio show in Germany. Discovered by Ann Arbor D.J./producer Ollie McLaughlin. Formed own Berlee label in 1963. Wrote "I Go To Pieces" for Peter & Gordon. To Los Angeles in 1966; production work. Died on 2/8/90 of a self-inflicted gunshot wound.

DEBUT DATE	PEAK POS	WKS CHR	GOLD	ARTIST — Album Title	$	Label & Number
6/22/63	12	26		1 Little Town Flirt	$65	Big Top 1308
12/12/81+	123	14		2 Drop Down And Get Me	$8	Elektra 568

produced by Tom Petty

Dream Baby (1)
Drop Down And Get Me (2)
Go Away Little Girl (1)
Happiness (1)
Hats Off To Larry (1) 5
Hey Baby (1)
Hey! Little Girl (1) 38
Kelly (1)
Liar (2)
Life Without You (2)
Little Town Flirt (1) 12
Maybe Tomorrow (2)
Midnight Train (2)
Never Stop Tryin' (2)
Out Of Time (2)
Runaround Sue (1)
Runaway (1) 1
Sea Of Love (2) 33
She Thinks I Still Care (1)
Sucker For Your Love (2)
To Love Someone (2)
Two Kind Of Teardrops (1) 50

SHARKEY, Feargal

Born on 8/13/58 in Ireland. Former member of The Undertones.

DEBUT DATE	PEAK POS	WKS CHR	GOLD	ARTIST — Album Title	$	Label & Number
3/8/86	75	11		Feargal Sharkey	$8	A&M/Virgin 5108

Ashes And Diamonds
Bitter Man
Don't Leave It To Nature
Ghost Train
Good Heart 74
It's All Over Now
Love And Hate
Made To Measure
Someone To Somebody
You Little Thief

SHARKS

British rock quartet formed by Andy Fraser (Free) and guitarist Chris Spedding.

DEBUT DATE	PEAK POS	WKS CHR	GOLD	ARTIST — Album Title	$	Label & Number
8/25/73	189	4		First Water	$10	MCA 351

Broke A Feeling
Brown-Eyed Boy
Doctor Love
Driving Sideways
Follow Me
Ol' Jelly Roll
Snakes And Swallowtails
Steal Away
World Park Junkies

SHARP, Dee Dee

Born Dione LaRue on 9/9/45 in Philadelphia. Backing vocalist at Cameo Records in 1961. Married record producer Kenny Gamble in 1967, recorded as Dee Dee Sharp Gamble. Also see Chubby Checker and the Philadelphia International All Stars.

DEBUT DATE	PEAK POS	WKS CHR	GOLD	ARTIST — Album Title	$	Label & Number
6/23/62	44	17		1 It's Mashed Potato Time	$40	Cameo 1018
11/17/62	117	4		2 Down To Earth	$30	Cameo 1029

CHUBBY CHECKER/DEE DEE SHARP

(Dee Dee) Be My Girl (1)
Do You Love Me (2)
Down To Earth (2)
Eddie, My Love (1)
Gee (1)
Gravy (For My Mashed Potatoes) (1) 9
Hello, Baby, Goodbye (2)
Hurry On Down (1)
I Really Don't Want To Know (2)
I Sold My Heart To The Junkman (1)
Let The Good Times Roll (2)
Love Is Strange (medley) (2)
Loving You (2)
Make Love To Me (2)
Mashed Potato Time (1) 2
One Hundred Pounds Of Clay (1)
One More Time (2)
Play It Fair (2)
Pledging My Love (2)
Remember You're Mine (1)
Rockin' Good Way (To Mess Around And Fall In Love) (medley) (2)
Slow Twistin' (1)
Splish-Splash (1)
Two Lovers (1)
You Came A Long Way From St. Louis (1)

SHARPLES, Bob

Bandleader from Bury, Lancashire, England.

DEBUT DATE	PEAK POS	WKS CHR	GOLD	ARTIST — Album Title	$	Label & Number
10/9/61	11	25		Pass In Review	[I] $15	London P. 4 44001

Anchors Aweigh (medley)
Bells Of St. Mary's (medley)
Buckle Down, Winsocki (medley)
Caissons Go Rolling Along (medley)
Dixie (medley)
Fanfare (medley)
Indian Drums (medley)
La Marseillaise (medley)
La Ritirata Italiana (medley)
Lili Marlene (medley)
Marines' Hymn (medley)
Matilda (medley)
Meadowland (medley)
Mexican Hat Dance (medley)
Onward Christian Soldiers (medley)
Rule Britannia (medley)
Scotland The Brave (medley)
She Wore A Yellow Ribbon (medley)
Stars And Stripes Forever (medley)
U.S. Air Force (medley)
Waltzing Matilda (medley)
Wearin' Of The Green (medley)
When The Saints Go Marching In (medley)
Yankee Doodle (medley)

SHAW, Marlena

Born Marlena Burgess in New Rochelle, New York in 1944. Appeared at the Apollo Theater at age 10. Band vocalist with Count Basie from 1967-72.

DEBUT DATE	PEAK POS	WKS CHR	GOLD	ARTIST — Album Title	$	Label & Number
7/5/75	159	5		1 Who Is This Bitch, Anyway?	$10	Blue Note 397
4/2/77	62	14		2 Sweet Beginnings	$8	Columbia 34458
4/8/78	171	4		3 Acting Up	$8	Columbia 35073

Davy (1)
Dreamin' (3)
Feel Like Makin' Love (1)
Go Away Little Boy (2)
I Think I'll Tell Him (3)
I Wonder (3)
I'm Back For More (3)
Johnny (2)
Look At Me, Look At You (We're Flying) (2)
Looking For Mr. Goodbar (Don't Ask To Stay Until Tomorrow), Theme From (3)
Lord Giveth And The Lord Taketh Away (1)
Loving You Was Like A Party (1)
Mama Tried (3)
Moonrise (3)
More (3)
No Deposit, No Return (2)
Pictures And Memories (2)
Places (3)
Rhythm Of Love (3)
Rose Marie (Mon Cherie) (1)
Street Walkin' Woman (medley) (1)
Sweet Beginnings (2)
Walk Softly (2)
Writing's On The Wall (2)
You (1)
You Been Away Too Long (1)
You Bring Out The Best In Me (3)
You Taught Me How To Speak In Love (1)
Yu-Ma (2)

SHAW, Robert, Chorale

Born in Red Bluff, California in 1916. Conductor/music director. Led the Fred Waring Glee Clubs, 1938-45; organized own singing group in 1948. Music director of Atlanta Symphony Orchestra and Chorus, 1967-87.

DEBUT DATE	PEAK POS	WKS CHR	GOLD	ARTIST — Album Title	$	Label & Number
12/23/57+	5	4	●	1 Christmas Hymns And Carols	[X] $12	RCA 1711
12/22/58	13	3		2 Christmas Hymns And Carols	[X-R] $12	RCA 1711

Christmas charts: 9/'63, 31/'64, 41/'66, 28/'67

DEBUT DATE	PEAK POS	WKS CHR	GOLD	ARTIST — Album Title	$	Label & Number
5/25/59	21	1		3 Deep River and Other Spirituals	$12	RCA 2247
4/27/63	27	10		4 America, The Beautiful	$10	RCA 2662

with the RCA Victor Symphony Orchestra

Ain't-A That Good News (medley) (3)
America (4)
America, The Beautiful (4)
Angels We Have Heard On High (medley) (1)
Away In A Manger (medley) (1)
Battle Hymn Of The Republic (4)
Bring A Torch, Jeanette, Isabella (medley) (1)
Carol Of The Bells (medley) (1)
Christmas Hymn (medley) (1)
Civil War Medley (4)
Civil War-South Medley (4)
Columbia The Gem Of The Ocean (4)
Coventry Carol (medley) (1)
Deck The Halls With Boughs Of Holly (medley) (1)
Deep River (medley) (3)
Didn't My Lord Deliver Daniel (medley) (3)
Dry Bones (medley) (3)
Every Time I Feel The Spirit (medley) (3)
First Noel (medley) (1)
Go Tell It On The Mountain (medley) (1)
God Bless America (4)
God Rest You Merry, Gentlemen (medley) (1)
Hark! The Herald Angels Sing (medley) (1)
I Wanna Be Ready (medley) (3)
I Wonder As I Wander (medley) (1)
It Came Upon The Midnight Clear (medley) (1)
Joy To The World (medley) (1)
Lord, If I Got My Ticket (medley) (3)
My Dancing Day (medley) (1)
My Lord, What A Morning (medley) (3)
O Come, All Ye Faithful (medley) (1)
O Come, O Come, Emanuel (medley) (1)
O Little Town Of Bethlehem (medley) (1)
Patapan (medley) (1)
Revolutionary War Medley (4)
Service Songs Medley (4)
Set Down, Servant (medley) (3)
Shepherd's Carol (medley) (1)
Silent Night (medley) (1)
Soon-A Will Be Done (medley) (3)

DEBUT DATE	PEAK POS	WKS CHR	GOLD	ARTIST — Album Title	$	Label & Number

SHAW, Robert, Chorale — Cont'd

Soon One Mornin' (medley) (3)	Swing Low, Sweet Chariot (medley) (3)	There Is A Balm In Gilead (medley) (3)	This Little Light O' Mine (medley) (3)	This Ol' Hammer (medley) (3)	We Three Kings (medley) (1)	
Star Spangled Banner (4)				Wassail Song (medley) (1)	Who Is That Yonder (medley) (3)	

SHAW, Roland, Orchestra
English conductor.

DEBUT DATE	PEAK POS	WKS CHR		ARTIST — Album Title	$	Label & Number
2/27/65	38	25	1	Themes From The James Bond Thrillers .... [I]	$20	London 412
2/5/66	119	5	2	More Themes From The James Bond Thrillers .... [I]	$20	London 445

Arrival Of The Bomb And Countdown (2)	Dr. No's Fantasy (1)	Golden Horn (1)	James Bond Theme (1)	Pussy Galore's Flying Circus (2)	Thunderball (2)
Dawn Raid On Fort Knox (1)	007 Theme (1)	Goldfinger (1)	Kingston Calypso (2)	Spectre Island (2)	Twisting With James (1)
Death Of Goldfinger (2)	From Russia With Love (1)	Guitar Lament (1)	Leila Dances (1)	Tania Meets Klebb (2)	Underneath The Mango Tree (2)
	Girl Trouble (1)	Gypsy Camp (2)	Miami (2)		

SHAW, Sandie
Born Sandra Goodrich on 2/26/47 in Dagenham, England. Pop songstress.

DEBUT DATE	PEAK POS	WKS CHR		ARTIST — Album Title	$	Label & Number
6/12/65	100	4		Sandie Shaw	$20	Reprise 6166

Baby I Need Your Lovin'	Everybody Loves A Lover	Gotta See My Baby Every	It's In His Kiss	Stop Feeling Sorry For	(There's) Always
Don't Be That Way	Girl Don't Come 42	Day	Lemon Tree	Yourself	Something There To
Downtown		I'll Stop At Nothing		Talk About Love	Remind Me 52

SHAW, Tommy
Born in Montgomery, Alabama. Lead guitarist of Styx, 1976-84. Joined superstar rock group, Damn Yankees, in 1990.

DEBUT DATE	PEAK POS	WKS CHR		ARTIST — Album Title	$	Label & Number
10/20/84	50	25	1	Girls With Guns	$8	A&M 5020
10/26/85	87	9	2	What If	$8	A&M 5097

Bad Times (2)	Free To Love You (2)	Jealousy (2)	Nature Of The Beast (2)	Remo's Theme (What If) (2) 81	True Confessions (2)
Come In And Explain (1)	Friendly Advice (2)	Kiss Me Hello (1)	Outside In The Rain (1)	See Me Now (2)	
Count On You (2)	Girls With Guns (1) 33	Little Girl World (1)	Race Is On (1)	This Is Not A Test (2)	
Fading Away (1)	Heads Up (1)	Lonely School (1) 60	Reach For The Bottle (1)		

SHEARING, George, Quintet
George was born on 8/13/19 in London. Piano stylist; blind since birth. Moved to the U.S. in 1947.

DEBUT DATE	PEAK POS	WKS CHR		ARTIST — Album Title	$	Label & Number
10/6/56	20	1	1	Velvet Carpet .... [I]	$20	Capitol 720
10/7/57	13	3	2	Black Satin .... [I]	$20	Capitol 858
8/25/58	17	2	3	Burnished Brass .... [I]	$20	Capitol 1038
7/25/60	11	35	4	White Satin	$15	Capitol 1334
10/30/61	82	14	5	Satin Affair	$15	Capitol 1628
5/5/62	27	16	6	Nat King Cole Sings/George Shearing Plays	$20	Capitol 1675

Affair To Remember (4)	Cheek To Cheek (3)	How Long Has This Been	Lost April (6)	Party's Over (5)	What Is There To Say (2)
All Of You (1)	Cuckoo In The Clock (3)	Going On (4)	Love's Melody (4)	Pick Yourself Up (6)	You Don't Know What Love
As Long As I Live (medley) (2)	Dancing On The Ceiling (1)	I Got It Bad And That Ain't	Lulu's Back In Town (3)	'Round Midnight (1)	Is (2)
Autumn Leaves (1)	Don't Go (6)	Good (1)	Memories Of You (3)	September Song (1,6)	You Were Never Lovelier (5)
Azure-Te (6)	Dream (4)	I Like To Recognize The	Midnight Sun (5)	Serenata (6)	Your Name Is Love (4)
Basie's Masement (2)	Early Autumn (5)	Tune (4)	Mine (4)	Sometimes I Feel Like A	
Baubles, Bangles And Beads	Fly Me To The Moon (In	I'll Close My Eyes (1)	Moon Song (2)	Motherless Child (3)	
(5)	Other Words) (6)	I'll Take Romance (4)	Moonlight Becomes You (4)	Star Dust (5)	
Beautiful Friendship (6)	Foggy Day (1)	I'm Lost (6)	My Own (5)	Starlight Souvenirs (2)	
Beautiful Love (3)	Folks Who Live On The Hill	If I Should Lose You (2)	My Romance (5)	Starlit Hour (1)	
Black Satin (2)	(2)	If You Were Mine (3)	No Moon At All (1)	There'll Be Another Spring	
Blame It On My Youth (3)	Have You Met Miss Jones?	It's Not You (5)	Nothing Ever Changes My	(4)	
Blue Malibu (4)	(1)	Laura (4)	Love For You (2)	There's A Lull In My Life (6)	
Bolero #3 (5)	Here's What I'm Here For (5)	Let There Be Love (6)	Old Folks (4)	There's A Small Hotel (4)	
Burnished Brass (3)		Let's Live Again (medley) (2)	One Morning In May (2)	These Things You Left Me (3)	

SHEILA E.
Born Sheila Escovedo on 12/12/59 in San Francisco. Singer/percussionist. With father Pete Escovedo in the band Azteca in the mid-1970s. Toured with Lionel Richie; since 1986, toured and recorded with Prince. Brother Peto was in Con Funk Shun. Uncle Coke Escovedo is a noted percussionist.

DEBUT DATE	PEAK POS	WKS CHR	GOLD	ARTIST — Album Title	$	Label & Number
7/7/84	28	46	●	1	Sheila E. in The Glamorous Life	$8	Warner 25107
9/21/85+	50	33	●	2	Sheila E. In Romance 1600	$8	Paisley P. 25317
3/21/87	56	12		3	Sheila E.	$8	Paisley P. 25498
4/20/91	146	5		4	Sex Cymbal	$12	Warner 26255

Bedtime Story (2)	Family Affair (4)	Love Bizarre (2) 11	Noon Rendezvous (1)	Sex Cymbal (4)	
Belle Of St. Mark (1) 34	Funky Attitude (4)	Love On A Blue Train (3)	Oliver's House (1)	Shortberry Strawcake (1)	
Boy's Club (3)	Glamorous Life (1) 7	Loverboy (4)	One Day (I'm Gonna Make	Sister Fate (2)	
Cry Baby (4)	Heaven (4)	Merci For The Speed Of A	You Mine) (1)	Soul Salsa (3)	
Dear Michaelangelo (2)	Hold Me (3) 68	Mad Clown In Summer (2)	Pride And The Passion (3)	Toy Box (2)	
Droppin' Like Flies (4)	Hon E Man (3)	Mother Mary (4)	Private Party (Tu Para Mi) (4)	Wednesday Like A River (4)	
108 Kate (4)	Koo Koo (3)	Next Time Wipe The Lipstick	Promise Me Love (4)	What'cha Gonna Do (4)	
Faded Photographs (3)	Lady Marmalade (4)	Off Your Collar (1)	Romance 1600 (2)	Yellow (2)	

SHELLEY, Peter
Lead vocalist/guitarist of The Buzzcocks (1976-81).

DEBUT DATE	PEAK POS	WKS CHR		ARTIST — Album Title	$	Label & Number
6/26/82	121	10	1	Homosapien	$8	Arista 6602
7/23/83	151	5	2	XL1	$8	Arista 8017

Guess I Must Have Been In	I Just Wanna Touch (2)	Just One Of Those Affairs (1)	Qu'est-Ce Que C'est Que Ca	Witness The Change (1)	You Know Better Than I
Love With Myself (1)	If You Ask Me (I Won't Say	Love In Vain (1)	(1)	XL 1 (2)	Know (2)
Homosapien (1)	No) (2)	Many A Time (2)	Telephone Operator (2)	Yesterday's Not Here (1)	
Don't Know What It Is (1)	In Love With Somebody Else	(Millions Of People) No One	Twilight (2)	You And I (1)	
Generate A Feeling (1)	(1)	Like You (2)	What Was Heaven? (2)		

SHELTON, Ricky Van
Born on 1/12/52 in Grit, Virginia. Country singer.

DEBUT DATE	PEAK POS	WKS CHR	GOLD	ARTIST — Album Title	$	Label & Number
12/26/87+	76	41	▲	1	Wild-Eyed Dream	$8	Columbia 40602
10/29/88	78	24	▲	2	Loving Proof	$8	Columbia 44221
2/3/90	53	61	▲	3	RVS III	$12	Columbia 45250
6/8/91	23	57	▲	4	Backroads	$12	Columbia 46855

SHELTON, Ricky Van — Cont'd

5/23/92	122	24		**5** Don't Overlook Salvation	$12	Columbia 46854
8/29/92	50	24↑●		**6** Greatest Hits Plus .... [G]	$12	Columbia 52753

CD includes a bonus track

After The Lights Go Out (4)
Baby, I'm Ready (1)
Backroads (4)
Call Me Up (4)
Crazy Over You (1)
Crime Of Passion (1)
Don't Overlook Salvation (5)
Don't Send Me No Angels (2)
Don't We All Have The Right (1,6)
Family Bible (5)
From A Jack To A King (2,6)
He's Got You (2)

Hole In My Pocket (2)
Holy (I Bowed On My Knees And Cried Holy) (5)
I Am A Simple Man (4,6)
I Don't Care (1)
I Meant Every Word He Said (3)
I Saw A Man (5)
I Shall Not Be Moved (5)
I Still Love You (3)
I Wouldn't Take Nothin' For My Journey (5)

I'll Leave This World Loving You (3,6)
I'm Starting Over (3)
I've Poured My Last Tear For You (3,6)
If You're Ever In My Arms (4)
Just As I Am (6)
Just As I Am/He Smiled As He Ran Out To Play (5)
Keep It Between The Lines (4,6)
Let Me Live With Love (And Die With You) (2)

Life Turned Her That Way (1,6)
Life's Little Ups And Downs (3)
Living Proof (2,6)
Love Is Burnin' (3)
Mansion Over The Hilltop (5)
Not That I Care (3)
Oh Heart Of Mine (4)
Oh Pretty Woman (3)
Old Rugged Cross (5)
Picture, The (2)
Rockin' Years (4,6)

Some Things Are Better Left Alone (4)
Somebody Lied (1,6)
Somebody's Back In Town (2)
Statue Of A Fool (3,6)
Supper Time (5)
Sweet Memories (3)
Swimming Upstream (2)
To My Mansion In The Sky (5)
Ultimately Fine (1)
Wear My Ring Around Your Neck (6)

Who'll Turn Out The Lights (4)
Wild-Eyed Dream (1)
Wild Man (6)
Working Man Blues (1)
You Would Do The Same For Me (3)

SHENANDOAH
Country quintet formed in Muscle Shoals, Alabama — Marty Raybon (vocals), lead singer.

7/13/91	186	4		Extra Mile	$12	Columbia 45490

Daddy's Little Man
Ghost In This House

Goin' Down With My Pride
I Got You

Moon Over Georgia
Next To You, Next To Me

Puttin' New Roots Down

She Makes The Coming Home (Worth The Being Gone)

She's A Natural
When You Were Mine

SHEPPARD, T.G.
Born William Browder on 7/20/42 in Humboldt, Tennessee. Country singer. Moved to Memphis in 1960. Worked as backup singer with Travis Wammack's band.

4/25/81	119	12		**1** I Love 'Em All..	$8	Warner 3528
1/30/82	152	13		**2** Finally!..	$8	Warner 3600
6/11/83	189	3		**3** T.G. Sheppard's Greatest Hits .... [G]	$8	Warner 23841

All My Cloudy Days Are Gone (2)
Crazy In The Dark (2)
Do You Wanna Go To Heaven (3)
Face The Night Alone (1)
Finally (2,3) **58**

I Loved 'Em Every One (1,3) **37**
I Wish You Could Have Turned My Head (And Left My Heart Alone) (2)
I'll Be Coming Back For More (3)
In Another Minute (2)

Last Cheater's Waltz (3)
Only One You (2,3) **68**
Party Time (1,3)
She's Got Everything It Takes (To Make Me Stay) (2)
Silence On The Line (1)
State Of Our Union (1)

Touch Me All Over Again (1)
Troubled Waters (1)
War Is Hell (On The Homefront, Too) (3)
Wasn't It A Short Forever (2)
We Belong In Love Tonight (1)

We're Walking On Thin Ice (2)
What's Forever For (1)
Without You (3)
You Feel Good All Over (3)
You Waltzed Yourself Right Into My Life (1)

You're The First To Last (This Long) (2)

SHERBS
Australian pop-rock quintet — Daryl Braithwaite, lead singer. Originally known as Sherbet.

2/28/81	100	16		The Skill	$8	Atco 137

Back To Zero
Cindy Is Waiting

Crazy In The Night
I Have The Skill 61

I'll Be Faster
I'm O.K.

Into The Heat
Juliet And Me

Love You To Death
Never Surrender

No Turning Back
Parallel Bars

SHERIDAN, Tony — see BEATLES, The

SHERIFF
Canadian rock quintet — Freddy Curci, lead singer. Disbanded in 1983. Members Wolf Hassell and Arnold Lanni are now the duo Frozen Ghost. Bandmates Curci and Steve DeMarchi formed Alias in 1990.

1/7/89	60	14		Sheriff	$8	Capitol 91216

originally "Bubbled Under" on 6/25/83 (POS 210) on Capitol 12227

California
Crazy Without You

Elisa
Give Me Rock 'N' Roll

Kept Me Coming
Living For A Dream

Makin' My Way
Mama's Baby

When I'm With You 1
You Remind Me

★★329★★ SHERMAN, Allan
Born Allan Copelon on 11/30/24 in Chicago; died on 11/21/73. Began as a professional comedy writer for Jackie Gleason, Joe E. Lewis and others. Creator/producer of TV's I've Got A Secret.

11/3/62	1[2]	51	●	**1** My Son, The Folk Singer .... [C]	$15	Warner 1475
1/19/63	1[1]	47		**2** My Son, The Celebrity .... [C]	$15	Warner 1487
8/17/63	1[8]	32		**3** My Son, The Nut .... [C]	$15	Warner 1501
4/11/64	25	19		**4** Allan In Wonderland .... [C]	$15	Warner 1539
11/21/64+	53	14		**5** Peter And The Commissar .... [C]	$20	RCA 2773
				ALLAN SHERMAN/BOSTON POPS/ARTHUR FIEDLER		
11/28/64+	32	17		**6** For Swingin' Livers Only! .... [C]	$20	Warner 1569
12/18/65+	88	11		**7** My Name Is Allan .... [C]	$20	Warner 1604

Al 'N Yetta (5)
America's A Nice Italian Name (6)
Automation (3)
Average Song (7)
Ballad of Harry Lewis (1)
Barry Is The Baby's Name (medley) (2)
Beautiful Teamsters (6)
Bronx Bird Watcher (2)
(Bye Bye Blackbird) Bye Bye Blumberg (6)
(C'est Si Bon) I See Bones (6)
Call Me Irresponsible (Call Me) (7)
Chim Chim Cheree (7)

Continental (The Painless Dentist Song) (7)
Drinking Man's Diet (7) 98
Drop-Outs March (4)
End Of A Symphony (5)
(Five Foot Two, Eyes Of Blue) Eight Foot Two, Solid Blue (3)
Get On The Garden Freeway (medley) (2)
Go To Sleep, Paul Revere! (7)
Good Advice (4)
(Green Eyes) Green Stamps (4)
Grow, Mrs. Goldfarb (5)
Hail To Thee, Fat Person (3)
Harvey And Sheila (2)

(Heart) Skin (4)
(Heartaches) Headaches (3)
Hello Mudduh, Hello Fadduh! (A Letter From Camp) (3) 2
Here's To The Crabgrass (4)
(Holiday For Strings) Holiday For States (4)
Horowitz (medley) (2)
Hungarian Goulash No. 5 (3)
I Can't Dance (4)
It's A Most Unusual Day (It's A Most Unusual Play) (7)
J.C. Cohen (6)
Jump Down, Spin Around (Pick A Dress O' Cotton) (1)
Kiss Of Myer (6)

Laarge Daark Aardvark Song (7)
Let's All Call Up A.T.&T. And Protest To The President March (2)
Little Butterball (4)
Lotsa Luck (4)
(Love Is Here To Stay) Your Mother's Here To Stay (2)
Me (2)
Mexican Hat Dance (2)
My Zelda (5)
Night And Day (With Punctuation Marks) (4)
No One's Perfect (2)
Oh Boy (1)
One Hippopotami (3)

Peter And The Commissar (5)
Peyton Place, U.S.A. (7)
Pop Hates The Beatles (6)
(Rag Mop) Rat Fink (3)
Sarah Jackman (1)
Secret Love (Secret Code) (7)
Seltzer Boy (1)
Shake Hands With Your Uncle Max (1)
(Shine On Harvest Moon) Shine On, Harvey Bloom (6)
Shticks And Stones (1)
Shticks Of One And Half A Dozen Of The Other (2)
Sir Greenbaum's Madrigal (1)
(Smiles) Pills (6)
Streets Of Miami (1)

That Old Black Magic (That Old Back Scratcher) (7)
Twelve Gifts Of Christmas (6)
Variations On "How Dry I Am" (5)
When I Was A Lad (3)
Won't You Come Home Disraeli? (2)
(You Came A Long Way From St. Louis) You Went The Wrong Way, Old King Louie (3)
You Need An Analyst (4)
(You're Getting To Be A Habit With Me) You're Getting To Be A Rabbit With Me (3)

SHERMAN, Bobby
Born on 7/18/43 in Santa Monica, California. Regular on TV's Shindig; played Jeremy Bolt on TV's Here Come The Brides. Currently involved in TV production.

11/8/69+	11	35	●	**1** Bobby Sherman	$12	Metromedia 1014

DEBUT DATE	PEAK POS	WKS CHR	GOLD	ARTIST — Album Title	$	Label & Number

SHERMAN, Bobby — Cont'd

4/11/70	10	48	●	2 Here Comes Bobby	$12	Metromedia 1028
10/24/70	20	26	●	3 With Love, Bobby	$12	Metromedia 1032
4/24/71	48	14		4 Portrait Of Bobby	$12	Metromedia 1040
10/9/71	71	8		5 Getting Together	$12	Metromedia 1045
3/25/72	83	9		6 Bobby Sherman's Greatest Hits ....[G]	$12	Metromedia 1048

August (4)
Blame It On The Pony Express (5)
Bluechip (1)
Bubble Gum And Braces (4)
Come Close To Me (2)
Cried Like A Baby (4,6) 16
Drum, The (4,6) 29
Easy Come, Easy Go (2,6) 9
Fun And Games (2)
Getting Together (5,6)
Good For Each Other (3)
Goodtime Song (5)

Hey, Honey Bun (2)
Hey, Mister Sun (3,6) 24
I Think I'm Gonna Be Alright (4)
I Think I'm Gonna Rain (3)
I'll Never Let You Go (3)
I'm In A Tree (4)
I'm Still Looking For The Right Girl (4)
Is Anybody There (4)
It Boggles The Mind (5)
Jennifer (5,6) 60

Julie, Do Ya Love Me (3,6) 5
July Seventeen (2)
La La La (If I Had You) (2,6) 9
Lady Is Waiting (2)
Land Of Make Believe (1)
Little Woman (1,6) 3
Love (1)
Love's Been Good To Me (4)
Make Your Own Kind Of Music (2)
Marching To The Music (5)

Maybe You Know Something I Don't Know (4)
Message To My Brother (3)
Oh, It Must Be Love (5)
Oklahoma City Times (3)
One Too Many Mornings (1)
Rainy Day Thought (1)
Run Away (5)
Seattle (1,6)
She's A Lady (2)
Show Me (3)
Sounds Along The Way (1)

Spend Some Time Lovin' Me (3,6)
Step My Way (4)
Sweet Gingerbread Man (3)
Sweet Touch Of Life (3)
This Guy's In Love With You (1)
Time (1)
Time For Us (Love Theme from Romeo And Juliet) (1)
Tired Soul (5)
Turtles And Trees (2)
Two Blind Minds (2)

Waiting At The Bus Stop (5,6) 54
Where Did That Little Girl Go? (5)
Wherefore And Why (4)

SHINEHEAD

Reggae rapper. Born Carl Aiken in London and raised in Jamaica and the Bronx.

| 11/5/88 | 185 | 4 | | 1 Unity .... | $8 | Elektra 60802 |
| 7/28/90 | 155 | 5 | | 2 The Real Rock .... | $12 | Elektra 60890 |

Chain Gang-Rap (1)
Cigarette Breath (2)
Dance Down The Road (2)
Do It With Ease (1)

Family Affair (2)
Gimme No Crack (1)
Golden Touch (1)
Good Things (1)

Hello Y'all (1)
Know How Fe Chat (1)
Love And Marriage Rap (2)
Musical Madness (2)

Potential (2)
Raggamuffin (1)
Real Rock (2)
Strive (2)

Till I Kissed You (2)
Truth, The (1)
Unity, The (1)
Who The Cap Fits (1)

World Of The Video Game (2)

SHIRELLES, The

R&B vocal trio from Passaic, New Jersey: Shirley Owens Alston, Beverly Lee, Doris Kenner and Addie "Micki" Harris. (d: 6/10/82 [age 42]). Formed in junior high school as the Poquellos. Kenner left group in 1968; returned in 1975. Alston left for solo career in 1975, recorded as "Lady Rose."

5/5/62	59	13		1 Baby It's You	$40	Scepter 504
1/26/63	19	49		2 The Shirelles Greatest Hits ....[G]	$35	Scepter 507
6/29/63	68	9		3 Foolish Little Girl................................	$40	Scepter 511

Abra Ka Dabra (3)
Baby It's You (1,2) 8
Big John (1,2) 21
Blue Holiday (1)
Dedicated To The One I Love (2) 3
Don't Say Goodnight And Mean Goodbye (3) 26

Everybody Loves A Lover (2) 19
Foolish Little Girl (3) 4
Hard Times (3)
I Didn't Mean To Hurt You (3)
I Don't Think So (3)
Irresistible You (3)

It's Love That Really Counts (2)
Make The Night A Little Longer (1)
Mama Said (2) 4
Not For All The Money In The World (3) 100
Only Time Will Tell (3)

Ooh Poo Pah Doo (3)
Putty In Your Hands (1)
Same Old Story (1)
Soldier Boy (1,2) 1
Stop The Music (2) 36
Talk Is Cheap (3)
Thing Of The Past (1,2) 41

Things I Want To Hear (Pretty Words) (1,2)
Tonights The Night (2) 39
Twenty One (1)
Twistin' U.S.A. (1)
Twitch, The (3)
Voice Of Experience (1)

Welcome Home Baby (2) 22
What A Sweet Thing That Was (2) 54
What's The Matter Baby (3)
Will You Love Me Tomorrow (2) 1

SHIRLEY, Don

Born on 1/27/27 in Kingston, Jamaica. Pianist/organist.

| 4/2/55 | 14 | 4 | | Tonal Expressions ....[I] | $20 | Cadence 1001 |

Answer Me My Love
Dancing On The Ceiling

I Cover The Waterfront
Love Is Here To Stay

Man I Love
My Funny Valentine

"New Faces" Medley
No Two People

Secret Love

They Can't Take That Away From Me

SHIRLEY AND COMPANY

Shirley Goodman (formerly of Shirley & Lee), and a group of studio musicians. Included Kenny Jeremiah of the Soul Survivors.

| 8/2/75 | 169 | 3 | | Shame Shame Shame .... | $10 | Vibration 128 |

Another Tear Will Fall
Cry Cry Cry [includes 2 versions] 91

Disco Shirley
I Gotta Get Next To You

I Guess Things Have To Change
Jim Doc Kay
Keep On Rolling On
Love Is

Shame, Shame, Shame [includes 2 versions] 12

SHOCKED, Michelle

Folk singer Karen Michelle Johnson. An American expatriate of Mormon upbringing.

| 9/17/88+ | 73 | 35 | | 1 Short Sharp Shocked............................ | $8 | Mercury 834294 |
| 11/11/89 | 95 | 26 | | 2 Captain Swing .... | $8 | Mercury 838878 |

Anchorage (1) 66
Black Widow (1)
Cement Lament (2)
(Don't You Mess Around With) My Little Sister (2)

God Is A Real Estate Developer (2)
Graffiti Limbo (1)
Hello Hopeville (1)
If Love Was A Train (1)

L&N Don't Stop Here Anymore (1)
Looks Like Mona Lisa (2)
(Making The Run To) Gladewater (2)

Memories Of East Texas (1)
Must Be Luff (2)
On The Greener Side (2)
Silent Ways (2)
Sleep Keeps Me Awake (2)

Streetcorner Ambassador (2)
Too Little Too Late (2)
V.F.D. (1)
When I Grow Up (1)

SHOCKING BLUE, The

Dutch rock quartet: Mariska Veres (lead singer), Robbie van Leeuwen (guitar), Cor van Beek (drums) and Klaasje van der Wal (bass). Disbanded in 1974.

| 2/14/70 | 31 | 17 | | The Shocking Blue .... | $15 | Colossus 1000 |

Acka Ragh
Bool Weevil
Butterfly And I

California Here I Come
I'm A Woman

Long And Lonesome Road 75
Love Buzz
Love Machine

Mighty Joe 43
Poor Boy

Send Me A Postcard
Venus 1

SHOES

Rock quartet from Zion, Illinois formed in the early '70s: Gary Klebe, brothers Jeff & John Murphy and Skip Meyer (joined in 1976).

| 10/13/79 | 50 | 12 | | 1 Present Tense .... | $8 | Elektra 244 |
| 2/7/81 | 140 | 7 | | 2 Tongue Twister .... | $8 | Elektra 303 |

Burned Out Love (2)
Cruel (1)
Every Girl (1)
Found A Girl (2)
Girls Of Today (2)

Hangin' Around With You (1)
Hate To Run (2)
Hopin' She's The One (2)
I Don't Miss You (1)
I Don't Wanna Hear It (1)

In My Arms Again (1)
Karen (2)
Now And Then (1)
Only In My Sleep (2)
She Satisfies (2)

Somebody Has What I Had (1)
Things You Do (2)
Three Times Medley (1)
Tomorrow Night (1)

Too Late (1) 75
When It Hits (2)
Yes Or No (2)
Your Imagination (2)
Your Very Eyes (1)

SHOOTING STAR
Kansas City-based rock quintet formed by guitarist Van McLain, bassist Ron Verlin and singer Gary West. Disbanded in 1985. McLain and Verlin re-formed group in 1989 with new lineup (vocals by Keith Mitchell).

DEBUT DATE	PEAK POS	WKS CHR		ARTIST — Album Title	$	Label & Number
3/15/80	147	14	1	Shooting Star	$8	Virgin 13133
9/19/81	92	30	2	Hang On For Your Life	$8	Epic 37407
8/7/82	82	9	3	III Wishes	$8	Epic 38020
7/30/83	162	6	4	Burning	$8	Epic 38683
11/4/89	151	7	5	Touch Me Tonight-The Best Of Shooting Star .... [G]	$8	Enigma 73549

group's hits from 1979-89; not available on vinyl

Are You On My Side (2)
Are You Ready (3)
Breakout (2,5)
Bring It On (1,5)
Burning (4)
Christmas Together (5)
Couldn't Get Enough (3)
Do You Feel Alright (3)
Don't Stop Now (1)
Dreams (4)
Flesh And Blood (2,5)
Go For It (4)
Hang On For Your Life (2,5)
Heartache (3,5)
Higher (1)
Hollywood (2,5) **70**
Just Friends (1)
Last Chance (1,5)
Let It Out (3)
Midnight Man (1)
Preview (4)
Rainfall (1)
Reach Out I'll Be There (4)
Reckless (4)
She's Got Money (2)
Standing In The Light (3)
Straight Ahead (4,5)
Stranger (1)
Sweet Elatia (2)
Taken Enough (4)
Teaser (2)
Theme (4)
Tonight (1,5)
Touch Me Tonight (5) **67**
Train Rolls On (4,5)
Turn It On (3)
Weary Eyes (3)
Where You Gonna Run (3)
Whole World's Watching (3)
Winner (4)
You're So Good (2)
You've Got Love (2)
You've Got What I Need
(1,5) **76**

SHORT, Bobby
Born on 9/15/24 in Danville, Illinois. Jazz-swing pianist/vocalist. Writer of articles for *The New York Times*, *Vogue*, *Vanity Fair*, *The Saturday Review of Literature* and *Traveler*.

DEBUT DATE	PEAK POS	WKS CHR		ARTIST — Album Title	$	Label & Number
3/4/72	169	8		Bobby Short Loves Cole Porter	$10	Atlantic 606 [2]

At Long Last Love
By Candlelight
Do I Love You
Hot-House Rose
How Could We Be Wrong
How's Your Romance
I Hate You, Darling
I'm In Love Again
I've Got You On My Mind
Just One Of Those Things
Katie Went To Haiti
Let's Fly Away
Once Upon A Time
Pilot Me
Rap Tap On Wood
So Near And Yet So Far
Weren't We Fools
Where Have You Been
Why Don't We Try Staying Home
Why Shouldn't I
You Don't Know Paree
You've Got That Thing

SHORTER, Wayne
Born on 8/25/33 in Newark, New Jersey. Jazz saxophonist. Played with Art Blakey (1959-63) and Miles Davis (1964-70).

DEBUT DATE	PEAK POS	WKS CHR		ARTIST — Album Title	$	Label & Number
7/12/75	183	3		Native Dancer	$8	Columbia 33418

featuring Milton Nascimento, Herbie Hancock and Airto Moreira

Ana Maria
Beauty And The Beast
Diana
From The Lonely Afternoons
Joanna's Theme
Lilia
Miracle Of The Fishes
Ponta De Areia
Tarde

SHOTGUN
Detroit soul group led by Billy Talbert (lead guitar) and Tyrone Steels (vocals, drums).

DEBUT DATE	PEAK POS	WKS CHR		ARTIST — Album Title	$	Label & Number
4/29/78	172	5	1	Good, Bad & Funky	$8	ABC 1060
5/5/79	163	4	2	Shotgun III	$8	MCA 1118

All Spaced Out (All Funked Up) (1)
Big Legs (2)
Burnin' Passion (2)
Danger Of The Stranger (1)
Don't You Wanna Make Love? (2)
Fire It Up (1)
Good, Bad And Funky (1)
I Wish I Could See You Again (1)
I'm All Strung Out (1)
Love Attack (1)
Midnight Breakdown (2)
Sister Love (1)
Skate (2)
Space-N (1)
Special Lady (2)
Stone Women (2)

SHOTGUN MESSIAH
Hollywood-based, Swedish heavy-metal quartet: Zinny J. San (vocals), Harry K. Cody, Tim Tim and Stixx Galore.

DEBUT DATE	PEAK POS	WKS CHR		ARTIST — Album Title	$	Label & Number
10/21/89	99	23	1	Shotgun Messiah	$8	Relativity 88561
5/2/92	199	1	2	Second Coming	$12	Relativity 1060

Babylon (2)
Bop City (1)
Can't Fool Me (2)
Dirt Talk (1)
Don't Care 'Bout Nothin' (1)
Explorer, The (1)
Free (2)
Heartbreak Blvd (2)
I Wanna Know (2)
I Want More (2)
I'm Your Love (1)
Living Without You (2)
Nervous (1)
Nobody's Home (2)
Nowhere Fast (1)
Red Hot (2)
Ride The Storm (2)
Sexdrugsrock'n'roll (2)
Shout It Out (1)
Squeezin' Teazin' (1)
Trouble (2)
You & Me (2)

SHRIEKBACK
London outfit formed in 1981. Vocalist Barry Andrews (XTC) fronted fluctuating lineup. Dave Allen (Gang Of Four) was bassist from 1983-87. Allen, drummer Martyn Barker and guitarist Steve Halliwell formed King Swamp in 1988. Disbanded in 1989.

DEBUT DATE	PEAK POS	WKS CHR		ARTIST — Album Title	$	Label & Number
6/25/83	188	3	1	Care	$8	Warner 23874
2/21/87	145	6	2	Big Night Music	$8	Island 90552
7/23/88	169	12	3	Go Bang!	$8	Island 90949

Accretions (1)
Big Fun (3)
Black Light Trap (2)
Brink Of Collapse (1)
Clear Trails (1)
Cradle Song (2)
Dust And A Shadow (3)
Evaporation (1)
Exquisite (2)
Get Down Tonight (3)
Go Bang! (3)
Gunning For The Buddha (2)
Into Method (1)
Intoxication (2)
Lined Up (1)
Lines From The Library (1)
My Spine (Is The Bassline) (2)
New Man (3)
Nighttown (3)
Over The Wire (3)
Petulant (1)
Pretty Little Things (2)
Reptiles And I (2)
Running On The Rocks (2)
Shark Walk (3)
Shining Path (2)
Sticky Jazz (2)
Sway (1)
Underwaterboys (2)

SHRIEVE, Michael — see HAGAR, Sammy, and YAMASHTA, Stomu

SHY
English hard-rock quintet led by vocalist Tony Mills.

DEBUT DATE	PEAK POS	WKS CHR		ARTIST — Album Title	$	Label & Number
6/27/87	193	2		Excess All Areas	$8	RCA 6311

Break Down The Walls
Can't Fight The Nights
Devil Woman
Emergency
Just Love Me
Talk To Me
Telephone
Under Fire
When The Love Is Over
Young Heart

SIBERRY, Jane
Canadian singer/songwriter with a degree in Microbiology. Born in 1956.

DEBUT DATE	PEAK POS	WKS CHR		ARTIST — Album Title	$	Label & Number
6/14/86	149	8		The Speckless Sky	$8	Open Air 0305

Empty City
Map Of The World (Part II)
Mein Bitte
One More Colour
Seven Steps To The Wall
Taxi Ride
Very Large Hat
Vladimir Vladimir

SIDE EFFECT
Los Angeles-based soul quartet led by Augie Johnson. Their backing band is the L.A. Boppers.

DEBUT DATE	PEAK POS	WKS CHR		ARTIST — Album Title	$	Label & Number
3/19/77	115	13	1	What You Need	$8	Fantasy 9513
1/7/78	86	15	2	Goin' Bananas	$8	Fantasy 9537
1/20/79	135	8	3	Rainbow Visions	$8	Fantasy 9569

DEBUT DATE	PEAK POS	WKS CHR	G O L D	ARTIST — Album Title	$	Label & Number

SIDE EFFECT — Cont'd

Always There (1)	Falling In Love Again (3)	I Like Dreaming (3)	Keep That Same Old Feeling	Open Up Your Heart (2)	She's A Lady (3)
Back In Time (2)	Finally Found Someone (1)	I'm A Winner (3)	(1)	Peace Of Mind (3)	Time Has No Ending (1)
Changes (1)	Goin' Bananas (1)	Illee, Illee, Oh I Know (3)	Life Is What You Make It (1)	Private World (2)	Watching Life (2)
Cloudburst (2)	Honky Tonk Scat (1)	It's All In Your Mind (2)	Mr. Monday (2)	Rainbow Visions (3)	
Disco Junction (3)	I Know You Can (1)	Keep On Keepin' On (2)	Never Be The Same (2)	S.O.S. (1)	

SIDEWINDERS
Arizona rock quartet led by vocalist Dave Slutes and guitarist Rich Hopkins.

5/13/89	169	5		Witchdoctor	$8	Mammoth 9663

Bad, Crazy Sun	Cigarette	Solitary Man	What Am I Supposed To Do?	Witchdoctor
Before Our Time	Love '88	Tears Like Flesh	What She Said	

SIEGEL-SCHWALL BAND — see SAN FRANCISCO SYMPHONY

SIGLER, Bunny
Born Walter Sigler on 3/27/41 in Philadelphia. R&B vocalist/multi-instrumentalist/composer/producer. First recorded for V-Tone in 1959.

2/25/78	77	13		1 Let Me Party With You	$8	Gold Mind 7502
4/7/79	119	9		2 I've Always Wanted To Sing...Not Just Write Songs	$8	Gold Mind 9503

backing band on above albums: Instant Funk

By The Way You Dance (I	Don't Even Try (Give It Up)	Half A Man (2)	I'm Funkin' You Tonight	**Let Me Party With You**	Let's Get Freaky Now (2)
Knew It Was You) (2)	(1)	I Got What You Need (1)	(With My Music) (2)	**(Part 1) (Party, Party,**	Simple Things You Do (1)
Cry My Eyes Out (2)	Glad To Be Your Lover (2)	I'm A Fool (1)	It's Time To Twist (1)	**Party) (1) 43**	Your Love Is So Good (1)

SIGUE SIGUE SPUTNIK
British sextet founded by Generation X bassist Tony James, who joined Sisters Of Mercy in early 1990.

8/23/86	96	10		Flaunt It	$8	Manhattan 53033

Atari Baby	Massive Retaliation	Sex Bomb Boogie	Teenage Thunder
Love Missile F1-11	Rockit Miss USA	She's My Man	21st Century Boy

SILENCERS, The
Scottish band led by two former members of Fingerprintz: Jimmy O'Neil and Cha Burns.

8/22/87	147	11		1 A Letter From St. Paul	$8	RCA 6442
2/24/90	168	5		2 A Blues For Buddha	$12	RCA 9960

CD includes bonus track

Answer Me (2)	God's Gift (1)	Letter From St. Paul (1)	Possessed (1)	Sand And Stars (2)	Wayfaring Stranger (2)
Blue Desire (1)	I Can't Cry (1)	My Love Is Like A Wave	Razor Blades Of Love (2)	Scottish Rain (2)	
Blues For Buddha (2)	I Ought To Know (1)	(medley)	Real Mc Coy (2)	Skin Games (2)	
Bullets And Blue Eyes (1)	I See Red (1)	**Painted Moon** (1) 82	Sacred Child (2)	Walk With The Night (2)	

SILK
Cleveland-based, folk-rock quartet: Chris Johns, Michael Stanley Gee, Randy Sabo and Courtney Johns. Gee dropped his last name and went on to form the Michael Stanley Band.

11/8/69	191	2		Smooth As Raw Silk	$15	ABC 694

Come On Down Girl	For All Time	Hours	Not A Whole Lot I Can Do	Skitzo Blues
Custody	Foreign Trip	Long Haired Boy	Scottish Thing	Walk In My Mind

SILK
R&B male vocal quintet: Timothy Cameron, Jimmy Gates, Jr., Jonathan Rasboro, Gary Jenkins and Gary Glenn. Not to be confused with the Philadelphia R&B band from 1977.

12/5/92	36↑	5↑		Lose Control	$12	Keia 61394

Baby It's You	Freak Me	**Happy Days** 95↑	It Had To Be You	When I Think About You
Don't Keep Me Waiting	Girl U For Me	I Gave To You	Lose Control	

SILLS, Beverly
Born on 5/25/29 in Brooklyn. World-renown soprano opera star. Joined the New York City Opera in 1957.

1/3/76	113	6		Music of Victor Herbert	$8	Angel 37160

with Andre Kostelanetz conducting the London Symphony Orchestra

Ah! Sweet Mystery Of Life	Kiss In The Dark	Orchestral Medley 1	Romany Life	To The Land Of My Own	When You're Away
Art Is Calling For Me	Kiss Me Again	Orchestral Medley 2	Thine Alone	Romance	
Italian Street Song					

SILOS, The
Rock quintet led by vocalists/guitarists Bob Rupe and Walter Salas-Humara. Humara was founder of the Vulgar Boatman.

4/21/90	141	9		The Silos	$12	RCA 2051

Anyway You Choose Me	Commodore Peter	Here's To You	Maybe Everything	Picture Of Helen	Take My Country Back
Caroline	Don't Talk That Way	I'm Over You	Only Story I Tell	Porque No	(We'll Go) Out Of Town

SILVER
Country-rock quintet led by John Batdorf (of Batdorf & Rodney). Included organist Brent Mydland, who later joined the Grateful Dead (died on 7/26/90 of a drug overdose at the age of 37).

9/25/76	142	6		Silver	$8	Arista 4076

All I Wanna Do	Goodbye, So Long	Memory	Musician (It's Not An Easy	No Wonder	Trust In Somebody
Climbing	It's Gonna Be Alright		Life)	Right On Time	**Wham Bam** 16

SILVER, Horace, Quintet
Horace was born on 9/2/28 in Norwalk, Connecticut. Jazz pianist.

6/12/65	95	10		1 Song For My Father (Cantiga Para Meu Pai)	[I] $15	Blue Note 84185
2/26/66	130	2		2 The Cape Verdean Blues	[I] $15	Blue Note 84220

with J.J. Johnson (trombone) on side 2

African Queen (2)	Cape Verdean Blues (2)	Lonely Woman (1)	Natives Are Restless Tonight	Nutville (2)	Que Pasa (1)
Bonita (2)	Kicker, The (1)	Mo' Joe (2)	(1)	Pretty Eyes (2)	Song For My Father (1)
Calcutta Cutie (1)					

SILVER APPLES
Electronic rock duo: Dan Taylor and Simeon.

8/3/68	193	3		Silver Apples	$15	Kapp 3562

DEBUT DATE	PEAK POS	WKS CHR	G O L D	ARTIST — Album Title	$	Label & Number

SILVER APPLES — Cont'd

Dancing Gods		Lovefingers	Oscillations	Seagreen Serenades	Whirly-Bird	
Dust		Misty Mountain	Program	Velvet Cave		

SILVER CONDOR
Rock quintet led by Joe Cerisano and Earl Slick (Phantom, Rocker & Slick).

7/4/81	141	12		Silver Condor	$8	Columbia 37163

Angel Eyes	For The Sake Of Survival	One You Left Behind	Standin' In The Rain	**You Could Take My Heart**
Carolina (Nobody's Right, Nobody's Wrong)	Goin' For Broke	Sayin' Goodbye	We're In Love	**Away 32**
	It's Over			

SILVER CONVENTION
German studio disco act assembled by producer Michael Kunze and writer/arranger Silvester Levay. Female vocal trio formed in 1976 consisting of Penny McLean, Ramona Wolf and Linda Thompson.

9/13/75	10	25	●	1 Save Me	$8	Midland Int. 1129
4/10/76	13	24		2 Silver Convention	$8	Midland Int. 1369
11/13/76	65	12		3 Madhouse	$8	Midland Int. 1824
7/16/77	71	10		4 Golden Girls	$8	Midsong Int. 2296

Another Girl (1)	Fancy Party (3)	I'm Not A Slot Machine (3)	Play Me Like A Yo-Yo (1)	Thank You Mr. D.J. (2)
Blame It On The Music (4)	**Fly, Robin, Fly (1)** *1*	Land Of Make Believe (3)	Please Don't Change (1)	Tiger Baby (1)
Boy With The Ohh-La-La (4)	**Get Up And Boogie (That's**	Madhouse (3)	San Francisco Hustle (2)	Voodoo Woman (4)
Chains Of Love (1)	**Right) (2)** *2*	Magic Mountain (3)	Save Me (1)	Wolfchild (4)
Dancing In The Aisle (3)	Heart Of Stone (1)	Midnight Lady (3)	Save Me '77 (4)	You Turned Me On, But You
Disco Ball (4)	Hollywood Movie (4)	**No, No, Joe (2)** *60*	Son Of A Gun (1)	Can't Turn Me Off (2)
Everybody's Talking 'Bout	Hotshot (4)	Old Wine In New Bottles (2)	Summer Nights (4)	You've Got What It Takes
Love (3)	I Like It (1)	Plastic People (3)	Telegram (4)	(To Please Your Woman) (2)

SILVERSTEIN, Shel
Satirical songwriter/poet/author/cartoonist. Born in Chicago in 1932.

1/20/73	155	8		Freakin' At The Freakers Ball .... [N]	$15	Columbia 31119

backing band: Dr. Hook & The Medicine Show

All About You	I Got Stoned And I Missed It	Man Who Got No Sign	Peace Proposal	Sahra Cynthia Sylvia Stout	Stacy Brown Got Two
Don't Give A Dose To The	Liberated Lady 1999	Masochistic Baby	Polly In A Porny	Would Not Take The	Thumbsucker
One You Love Most				Garbage Out	
Freakin' At The Freakers Ball					

SIMEONE, Harry, Chorale
Harry was born on 5/9/11 in Newark, New Jersey. Arranger/conductor for film and TV shows. Began career in 1939 as an arranger for Fred Waring.

1/6/62	119	2	●	1 Sing We Now Of Christmas .... [X]	$15	20th Fox 3002
12/22/62	44	2		2 Sing We Now Of Christmas .... [X-R]	$15	20th Fox 3002

album later repackaged as *The Little Drummer Boy*; Christmas charts: 2/'63, 1/'64, 1/'65, 1/'66, 5/'67, 8/'68, 5/'69, 13/'70

Adeste Fideles (medley)	Christmas Greeting (medley)	God Rest Ye Merry	Joy To The World (medley)	O' Little Town Of Bethlehem	We Three Kings (medley)
Angels We Have Heard On	Coventry Carol (medley)	Gentlemen (medley)	**Little Drummer Boy 13**	(medley)	What Child Is This? (medley)
High (medley)	Deck The Halls (medley)	Good King Wenceslas	Lo, How A Rose E'er	O' Tannenbaum (medley)	While Shepherds Watched
Away In A Manger (medley)	Ding Dong (medley)	(medley)	Blooming (medley)	Rise Up Shepherds (medley)	Their Flocks By Night
Bring A Torch, Isabella	First Noel (medley)	Hark, The Herald Angels	Master's In The Hall (medley)	Silent Night (medley)	(medley)
(medley)	Friendly Beasts (medley)	Sing (medley)	O' Come Little Children	Sing We Now Of Christmas	
Christian Men Rejoice	Go Tell It On The Mountain	It Came Upon A Midnight	(medley)	(medley)	
(medley)		Clear (medley)	O' Holy Night	Villancico (medley)	

SIMMONS, Gene
Born in Tupelo, Mississippi in 1933. Rockabilly singer. Nicknamed "Jumpin' Gene."

11/14/64	132	5		jumpin' Gene Simmons	$20	Hi 32018

Bony Moronie	Green Door	Hotel Happiness	Just A Little Bit	Rock Around The Clock	Teen-Age Letter
Don't Let Go	**Haunted House 11**	(I'm) Comin' Down With Love	No Help Wanted	Slippin' And Sliddin'	You Can Have Her

SIMMONS, Gene
Born Gene Klein on 8/25/49 in Haifa, Israel. Bass guitarist of Kiss. Appeared in films *Runaway* (1984) and *Trick Or Treat* (1986).

10/14/78+	22	22	▲	Gene Simmons	$15	Casablanca 7120

Always Near You (medley)	Living In Sin	Mr. Make Believe	**Radioactive 47**	See You Tonite	Tunnel Of Love
Burning Up With Fever	Man Of 1000 Faces	Nowhere To Hide (medley)	See You In Your Dreams	True Confessions	When You Wish Upon A Star

SIMMONS, Patrick
Born on 1/23/50 in Aberdeen, Washington; raised in San Jose, California. Vocalist/guitarist. Original member of The Doobie Brothers; wrote their hit "Black Water."

5/7/83	52	11		Arcade	$8	Elektra 60225

Don't Make Me Do It 75	Have You Seen Her	Knocking At Your Door	So Wrong 30	Too Long
Dream About Me	If You Want A Little Love	Out On The Streets	Sue Sad	Why You Givin' Up

SIMMONS, Richard — see AEROBICS section

★★89★★   SIMON, Carly
Born on 6/25/45 in New York City. Pop vocalist/songwriter. Father is co-founder of Simon & Schuster publishing. Folk duo with sister Lucy (The Simon Sisters), mid-1960s. Won the 1971 Best New Artist Grammy Award. Married James Taylor on 11/3/72, divorced in 1983.

4/24/71	30	25		1 Carly Simon	$10	Elektra 74082
11/27/71+	30	31	●	2 Anticipation	$10	Elektra 75016
12/9/72+	1⁵	71	●	3 No Secrets	$10	Elektra 75049
2/2/74	3	35	●	4 Hotcakes	$10	Elektra 1002
5/3/75	10	17		5 Playing Possum	$8	Elektra 1033
12/6/75+	17	19	●	6 The Best Of Carly Simon .... [G]	$8	Elektra 1048
6/26/76	29	13		7 Another Passenger	$8	Elektra 1064
4/22/78	10	29	▲	8 Boys In The Trees	$8	Elektra 128
6/30/79	45	13		9 Spy	$8	Elektra 506

DEBUT DATE	PEAK POS	WKS CHR	G O L D	ARTIST — Album Title	$	Label & Number

SIMON, Carly — Cont'd

DEBUT DATE	PEAK POS	WKS CHR		ARTIST — Album Title	$	Label & Number
7/12/80	36	32		10 Come Upstairs	$8	Warner 3443
10/17/81	50	24		11 Torch	$8	Warner 3592
				featuring jazz and blues songs of the '30s and '40s		
10/8/83	69	17		12 Hello Big Man	$8	Warner 23886
7/20/85	88	11		13 Spoiled Girl	$8	Epic 39970
4/25/87	25	60	▲	14 Coming Around Again	$8	Arista 8443
8/27/88	87	13	●	15 Greatest Hits Live ....[L]	$8	Arista 8526
				from the HBO TV special *Carly In Concert - Coming Around Again*		
3/31/90	46	17		16 My Romance	$12	Arista 8582
				a collection of old standards		
10/13/90	60	32		17 Have You Seen Me Lately?	$12	Arista 8650

After The Storm (5)
All I Want Is You (14,15) **54**
Alone (1)
Another Door (7)
Anticipation (2,6,15) **13**
Anyone But Me (13)
Are You Ticklish (5)
As Time Goes By (14)
Attitude Dancing (5,6) **21**
Back Down To Earth (8)
Be With Me (7)
Best Thing (1)
Better Not Tell Her (17)
Bewitched (16)
Blue Of Blue (11)
Body And Soul (11)
Boys In The Trees (8)
By Myself (medley) (16)
Can't Give It Up (13)
Carter Family (3)
Come Back Home (13)
Come Upstairs (10)
Coming Around Again (14,15) **18**
Coming To Get You (9)
Cow Town (7)
Damn You Get To Me (12)
Dan, My Fling (1)
Danny Boy (16)
Darkness Til Dawn (7)
Desert, The (10)

Devoted To You (8) **36**
Didn't I? (17)
Dishonest Modesty (7)
Do The Walls Come Down (14,15)
Don't Wrap It Up (17)
Embrace Me, You Child (3)
Fairweather Father (7)
Fisherman's Song (17)
Floundering (12)
For Old Times Sake (8)
Forever My Love (4)
From The Heart (11)
Garden, The (2)
Girl You Think You See (2)
Give Me All Night (14) **61**
Grownup (4)
Half A Chance (7)
Happy Birthday (17)
Haunting (8)
Have You Seen Me Lately? (17)
Haven't Got Time For The Pain (4,6) **14**
He Likes To Roll (7)
He Was Too Good To Me (16)
Hello Big Man (12)
His Friends Are More Than Fond Of Robin (3)
Hold What You've Got (14)
Holding Me Tonight (17)
Hotcakes (4)

Hurt (11)
I Get Along Without You Very Well (11)
I Got It Bad And That Ain't Good (11)
I See Your Face Before Me (medley) (16)
I'll Be Around (11)
I've Got To Have You (2)
In A Small Moment (8)
In Pain (11)
In The Wee Small Hours Of The Morning (16)
In Times When My Head (7)
Interview (13)
Is This Love (12)
It Happens Everyday (12,15)
It Should Have Been Me (14)
It Was So Easy (3)
It's Not Like Him (17)
Itsy Bitsy Spider (14,15)
James (10)
Julie Through The Glass (2)
Just A Sinner (1)
Just Like You Do (9)
Just Not True (4)
Legend In Your Own Time (2,6) **50**
Libby (7)
Life Is Eternal (17)

Little Girl Blue (16)
Look Me In The Eyes (5)
Love Out In The Street (5)
Love You By Heart (9)
Love's Still Growing (1)
Make Me Feel Something (13)
Memorial Day (9)
Menemsha (12)
Mind On My Man (4)
Misfit (4)
Mockingbird (4,6) **5**
More And More (5) **94**
My Funny Valentine (16)
My New Boyfriend (13)
My Romance (16)
Never Been Gone (9,15)
Night Owl (3,6)
Nobody Does It Better (15)
Not A Day Goes By (11)
Older Sister (4)
One Love Stand (3)
One Man Woman (8)
One More Time (1)
Orpheus (12)
Our First Day Together (2)
Playing Possum (5)
Pretty Strange (11)
Pure Sin (9)
Reunions (1)
Right Thing To Do (3,6,15) **17**

Riverboat Gambler (9)
Rolling Down The Hills (1)
Safe And Sound (4)
Share The End (2)
Slave (5)
Something Wonderful (16)
Sons Of Summer (5)
Spoiled Girl (13)
Spring Is Here (11)
Spy (9)
Stardust (10)
Stuff That Dreams Are Made Of (14)
Such A Good Boy (12)
Summer's Coming Around Again (2)
Take Me As I Am (10)
That's The Way I've Always Heard It Should Be (1,6) **10**
Them (10)
Think I'm Gonna Have A Baby (4)
Three Days (2)
Three Of Us In The Dark (10)
Time After Time (16)
Tired Of Being Blonde (13) **70**
Tonight And Forever (13)
Tranquillo (Melt My Heart) (8)

Two Hot Girls (On A Hot Summer Night) (14,15)
Vengeance (9) **48**
Waited So Long (3)
Waiting At The Gate (17)
Waterfall (5) **78**
We Have No Secrets (3,6)
We Just Got Here (17)
We're So Close (9)
What Has She Got (16)
What Shall We Do With The Child (11)
When You Close Your Eyes (3)
When Your Lover Has Gone (16)
Wives Are In Connecticut (13)
You Belong To Me (8,15) **6**
You Don't Feel The Same (12)
You Have To Hurt (14)
You Know What To Do (12) **83**
You're So Vain (3,6,15) **1**
You're The One (8)

SIMON, Joe

Born on 9/2/43 in Simmesport, Louisiana. Moved to Oakland in 1959. First recorded with vocal group the Golden Tones for Hush in 1960.

DEBUT DATE	PEAK POS	WKS CHR		ARTIST — Album Title	$	Label & Number
6/21/69	81	17		1 The Chokin' Kind	$15	Sound Stage 15006
11/29/69	192	2		2 Joe Simon...better than ever	$15	Sound Stage 15008
4/3/71	153	12		3 The Sounds Of Simon	$10	Spring 4701
3/25/72	71	12		4 Drowning In The Sea Of Love	$10	Spring 5702
12/30/72+	147	8		5 The Best Of Joe Simon ....[G]	$10	Sound Stage 15009
2/17/73	97	12		6 The Power Of Joe Simon	$10	Spring 5704
7/19/75	129	12		7 Get Down	$8	Spring 6706

After The Lights Go Down Low (2)
All My Hard Times (3) **93**
Baby, Don't Be Looking In My Mind (1,5) **72**
Chokin' Kind (1,5) **13**
Don't Let Me Lose The Feeling (1)
Drowning In The Sea Of Love (4,6) **11**
Farther On Down The Road (5) **56**
Fire Burning (7)
Georgia Blue (3,6)
Get Down, Get Down (Get On The Floor) (7) **8**
Glad To Be Your Lover (4)

Hangin' On ...see: (You Keep Me)
Help Me Make It Through The Night (3,6) **69**
Help Yourself (To All My Lovin') (1)
I Can't See Nobody (3)
I Found My Dad (4) **78**
I Got A Whole Lot Of Lovin' (2)
I Love You More (Than Anything) (3)
I'm Too Far Gone To Turn Around (1)
If (4)
In My Baby's Arms (7)
In The Ghetto (2)

In The Still Of The Night (I'll Remember) (1)
It Be's That Way Sometimes (7)
It's Crying Time In Memphis (7)
It's Hard To Get Along (2,5) **87**
Let Me Be The One (The One Who Loves You) (4)
Little Green Apples (1)
Lonely Man (1)
Message From Maria (5) **75**
Mirror Don't Lie (4)
Moon Walk Part 1 (5) **54**
Most Of All (3)
Music In My Bones (7) **92**

My Special Prayer (5) **87**
My Woman, My Woman, My Wife (3)
Nine Pound Steel (5) **70**
No More Me (3)
O'le Night Owl (4)
Pool Of Bad Luck (4) **42**
Power Of Love (6) **11**
Put Your Trust In Me (Depend On Me) (5)
Rainbow Road (2)
San Francisco Is A Lonely Town (2) **79**
Silver Spoons And Coffee Cups (2)
(Sittin' On The) Dock Of The Bay (1)

Something You Can Do Today (4)
Step By Step (6) **37**
Still At The Mercy Of Your Love (7)
Straight Down To Heaven (2)
Talk Don't Bother Me (6)
Teenager's Prayer (5) **66**
Time And Space (7)
To Lay Down Beside You (3,6)
Trouble In My Home (6) **50**
When (2)
Wichita Lineman (1)
Wounded Man (2)
You Are Everything (4)
You Are The One (6)

You Don't Want To Believe It (My Man) (7)
(You Keep Me) Hangin' On (5) **25**
Your Time To Cry (3,6) **40**
Yours Love (1,5) **78**

★★194★★ **SIMON, Paul**

Born on 11/5/41 in Newark, New Jersey; raised in Queens, New York. Vocalist/composer/guitarist. Met Art Garfunkel in high school, recorded together as Tom & Jerry in 1957. Worked as Jerry Landis, Paul Kane, Harrison Gregory and True Taylor in the early '60s. To England from 1963-64. Returned to the U.S. and recorded first album with Garfunkel in 1965. Went solo in 1971. Married to actress Carrie Fisher from 1983-85. Married Edie Brickell on 5/30/92. In the films *Annie Hall* and *One-Trick Pony*.

DEBUT DATE	PEAK POS	WKS CHR		ARTIST — Album Title	$	Label & Number
2/12/72	4	36	▲	1 Paul Simon	$10	Columbia 30750
5/26/73	2²	48	▲	2 There Goes Rhymin' Simon	$10	Columbia 32280
3/23/74	33	17	●	3 Paul Simon In Concert/Live Rhymin' ....[L]	$10	Columbia 32855
10/25/75	1¹	40	●	4 Still Crazy After All These Years	$8	Columbia 33540
				1975 Grammy winner: Album of the Year		
12/3/77+	18	23	▲	5 Greatest Hits, Etc. ....[G]	$8	Columbia 35032
9/6/80	12	26	●	6 One-Trick Pony ....[S]	$8	Warner 3472
				Paul starred in the film		

DEBUT DATE	PEAK POS	WKS CHR	GOLD	ARTIST — Album Title	$	Label & Number

SIMON, Paul — Cont'd

DEBUT DATE	PEAK POS	WKS CHR	GOLD		ARTIST — Album Title	$	Label & Number
11/19/83+	35	18		7	Hearts And Bones	$8	Warner 23942
9/13/86+	3	97	▲⁴	8	Graceland	$8	Warner 25447
					1986 Grammy winner: Album of the Year; South African-flavored tunes written by Simon, backed by a South African ensemble		
11/12/88+	110	14	●	9	Negotiations And Love Songs, 1971-1986 ....[G]	$12	Warner 25789 [2]
11/3/90	4	53	▲²	10	The Rhythm Of The Saints	$12	Warner 26098
					partially recorded in Rio de Janeiro, Brazil; incorporating the rhythmic sounds native to South America		
11/23/91+	74	11		11	Paul Simon's Concert In The Park ....[L]	$24	Warner 26737 [2]
					recorded in Central Park, New York City on 8/15/91		

Ace In The Hole (6)
All Around The World Or The Myth Of Fingerprints (8)
Allergies (7) **44**
America (3,11)
American Tune (2,3,5) **35**
Armistice Day (1)
Born At The Right Time (10,11)
Boxer, The (3,11)
Boy In The Bubble (8,11) **86**
Bridge Over Troubled Water (3,11)
Can't Run But (10)
Cars Are Cars (7)
Cecilia (11)
Coast, The (10,11)

Congratulations (1)
Cool, Cool River (10,11)
Crazy Love, Vol. II (8)
Diamonds On The Soles Of Her Shoes (8,9,11)
Duncan (1,3,5) **52**
El Condor Pasa (If I Could) (3)
Everything Put Together Falls Apart (1)
50 Ways To Leave Your Lover (4,5,9) **1**
Further To Fly (10)
God Bless The Absentee (6)
Gone At Last (4) **23**
Graceland (8,9,11) **81**
Gumboots (8)
Have A Good Time (4,5,9)

Hearts And Bones (7,9,11)
Hobo's Blues (1)
Homeless (8)
Homeward Bound (3)
How The Heart Approaches What It Yearns (6)
I Do It For Your Love (4,5)
I Know What I Know (8,11)
Jesus Is The Answer (3)
Jonah (6)
Kodachrome (2,5,9,11) **2**
Late Great Johnny Ace (7)
Late In The Evening (6,9,11) **6**
Learn How To Fall (2)
Long, Long Day (6)
Loves Me Like A Rock (2,3,5,9,11) **2**

Me And Julio Down By The Schoolyard (1,3,5,9,11) **22**
Mother And Child Reunion (1,3,5,9) **4**
My Little Town (4) **9**
recorded as: Simon & Garfunkel
Night Game (4)
Nobody (6)
Obvious Child (10,11) **92**
Oh, Marion (6)
One Man's Ceiling Is Another Man's Floor (2)
One-Trick Pony (6) **40**
Papa Hobo (1)
Paranoia Blues (1)
Peace Like A River (1)

Proof (10,11)
Rene And Georgette Magritte With Their Dog After The War (7,9)
Rhythm Of The Saints (10)
Run That Body Down (1)
She Moves On (10,11)
Silent Eyes (4)
Slip Slidin' Away (5,9) **5**
Some Folks Lives Roll Easy (4)
Something So Right (2,5,9)
Song About The Moon (7)
Sound Of Silence (3,11)
Spirit Voices (10)
St. Judy's Comet (2,9)
Still Crazy After All These Years (4,5,9,11) **40**

Stranded In A Limousine (5)
Take Me To The Mardi Gras (2,5)
Tenderness (2)
That Was Your Mother (8)
That's Why God Made The Movies (6)
Think Too Much (Part 1 & 2) (7)
Train In The Distance (7,9,11)
Under African Skies (8)
Was A Sunny Day (2)
When Numbers Get Serious (7)
You Can Call Me Al (8,9,11) **23**
You're Kind (4)

★★136★★ **SIMON & GARFUNKEL**

Folk-rock duo from New York City: Paul Simon and Art Garfunkel. Recorded as Tom & Jerry in 1957. Duo split in 1964; Simon was working solo in England, Garfunkel was in graduate school. They re-formed in 1965 and stayed together until 1971. Reunited briefly in 1981 for national tour. Inducted into the Rock and Roll Hall of Fame in 1990.

DEBUT DATE	PEAK POS	WKS CHR	GOLD		ARTIST — Album Title	$	Label & Number
1/22/66	30	31	●	1	Wednesday Morning, 3 AM	$20	Columbia 9049
					contains original unmixed version of "The Sounds Of Silence"		
2/19/66+	21	143	▲²	2	Sounds Of Silence	$20	Columbia 9269
11/12/66	4	145	▲³	3	Parsley, Sage, Rosemary and Thyme	$20	Columbia 9363
3/16/68	1⁹	69	●	4	The Graduate ....[S]	$15	Columbia 3180
					includes 6 instrumentals by David Grusin: "The Folks," "A Great Effect," "On The Strip," "The Singleman Party Foxtrot," "Sunporch Cha-Cha-Cha" and "Whew"		
4/27/68	1⁷	66	▲²	5	Bookends	$15	Columbia 9529
					side 2: hit singles previously unavailable on an album		
2/14/70	1¹⁰	85	▲⁵	6	Bridge Over Troubled Water	$15	Columbia 9914
					1970 Grammy winner: Album of the Year		
7/1/72	5	127	▲⁵	7	Simon And Garfunkel's Greatest Hits ....[G]	$8	Columbia 31350
3/13/82	6	34	▲	8	The Concert In Central Park ....[L]	$10	Warner 3654 [2]
					recorded in New York City's Central Park on 9/19/81		

America (5,7,8) **97**
American Tune (8)
Anji (2)
April Come She Will (2,4,8)
At The Zoo (5) **16**
Baby Driver (6)
Benedictus (1)
Big Bright Green Pleasure Machine (3,4)
Bleecker Street (1)
Blessed (2)
Bookends (5,7)
Boxer, The (6,7,8) **7**
Bridge Over Troubled Water (6,7,8) **1**
Bye Bye Love (6)
Cecilia (6,7) **4**

Cloudy (3)
Dangling Conversation (3) **25**
El Condor Pasa (6,7) **18**
Fakin' It (5) **23**
59th Street Bridge Song (Feelin' Groovy) (3,7,8)
Fifty Ways To Leave Your Lover (8)
Flowers Never Bend With The Rainfall (3)
For Emily, Whenever I May Find Her (3,7) **53**
Go Tell It On The Mountain (1)
Hazy Shade Of Winter (5) **13**

He Was My Brother (1)
Heart In New York (8)
Homeward Bound (3,7,8) **5**
I Am A Rock (2,7) **3**
Kathy's Song (2,7)
Keep The Customer Satisfied (6)
Kodachrome (medley) (8)
Last Night I Had The Strangest Dream (1)
Late In The Evening (8)
Leaves That Are Green (2)
Me And Julio Down By The Schoolyard (8)
Most Peculiar Man (2)
Mrs. Robinson (4,5,7,8) **1**

Old Friends (5,8)
Only Living Boy In New York (6)
Overs (5)
Patterns (3)
Peggy-O (5)
Poem On The Underground Wall (3)
Punky's Dilemma (5)
Richard Cory (2)
Save The Life Of My Child (5)
Scarborough Fair (/Canticle) (3,4,7,8) **1**
Sparrow (1)
7 O'Clock News (medley) (3)
Silent Night (medley) (3)

Simple Desultory Philippic (Or How I Was Robert McNamara'd Into Submission) (3)
Slip Slidin' Away (8)
So Long, Frank Lloyd Wright (6)
Somewhere They Can't Find Me (2)
Song For The Asking (6)
Sounds Of Silence (1,2,4,7,8) **1**
Still Crazy After All These Years (8)
Sun Is Burning (1)

Times They Are A-Changin' (1)
Wake Up Little Susie (8) **27**
We've Got A Groovy Thing Goin' (2)
Wednesday Morning, 3 A.M. (1)
Why Don't You Write Me (6)
You Can Tell The World (1)

SIMONE, Nina

Born Eunice Waymon on 2/21/33 in Tryon, South Carolina. Jazz-influenced vocalist/pianist/composer. Attended Juilliard School of Music in New York City. Devoted more time to political activism in the '70s, infrequent recording.

DEBUT DATE	PEAK POS	WKS CHR	GOLD		ARTIST — Album Title	$	Label & Number
3/6/61	23	5		1	Nina At Newport ....[L]	$20	Colpix 412
9/19/64	102	11		2	Nina Simone In Concert ....[L]	$20	Philips 135
6/26/65	99	8		3	I Put A Spell On You	$15	Philips 172
10/16/65	139	7		4	Pastel Blues	$15	Philips 187
11/5/66	110	9		5	Wild Is The Wind	$15	Philips 207
11/25/67	158	4		6	Silk & Soul	$15	RCA 3837
4/19/69	187	3		7	The Best Of Nina Simone ....[K]	$12	Philips 298
3/14/70	149	12		8	Black Gold ....[L]	$12	RCA 4248
7/25/70	189	3		9	The Best Of Nina Simone ....[K]	$12	RCA 4374
8/21/71	190	4		10	Here Comes The Sun	$12	RCA 4536

Ain't Got No; I Got Life (8) **94**
Ain't No Use (4)
Angel Of The Morning (10)
Assignment Sequence (8)
Be My Husband (4)

Beautiful Land (3)
Black Is The Color Of My True Love's Hair (5,8)
Blues On Purpose (3)
Break Down And Let It All Out (5,7)

Cherish (8)
Chilly Winds Don't Blow (4)
Compensation (9)
Consummation (6)
Day And Night (9)

Do What You Gotta Do (9) **83**
Don't Let Me Be Misunderstood (7)
Don't Smoke In Bed (2)
Either Way I Lose (5)

End Of The Line (4)
Feeling Good (3)
Flo Me La (1)
Four Women (5,7)
Gimme Some (3)
Go Limp (2)

Go To Hell (6,9)
Here Comes The Sun (10)
How Long Must I Wander (10)
I Love Your Lovin' Ways (5)
I Loves You, Porgy (2,7) **18**

SIMONE, Nina — Cont'd

I Put A Spell On You (3,7)
I Shall Be Released (9)
I Want A Little Sugar In My Bowl (9)
I Wish I Knew How It Would Feel To Be Free (6,9)
If I Should Lose You (5)
In The Evening By The Moonlight (1)
In The Morning (9)

It Be's That Way Sometime (6,9)
July Tree (3)
Just Like A Woman (10)
Lilac Wine (5)
Little Liza Jane (1)
Look Of Love (6)
Love O' Love (6)
Marriage Is For Old Folks (3)
Mississippi Goddam (2,7)

Mr. Bojangles (10)
My Man's Gone Now (9)
My Way (10)
Ne Me Quitte Pas (3)
New World Coming (10)
Nina's Blues (1)
Nobody Knows You When You're Down And Out (4) 93
Old Jim Crow (2)

One September Day (3)
O-o-h Child (10)
Pirate Jenny (2,7)
Plain Gold Ring (2)
Porgy (1)
See-Line Woman (7)
Sinnerman (4,7)
Some Say (6)
Strange Fruit (4)
Suzanne (9)

Take Care Of Business (3)
Tell Me More And More And Then Some (4)
To Be Young, Gifted And Black (8) 76
Tomorrow Is My Turn (3)
Trouble In Mind (1,4) 92
Turn Me On (6)
Turning Point (6)
Westwind (8)

Who Knows Where The Time Goes (8)
Why Keep On Breaking My Heart (5)
Why? (The King Of Love Is Dead) (9)
Wild Is The Wind (5,7)
You'd Be So Nice To Come Home To (1)
You've Got To Learn (3)

SIMPLE MINDS

Scottish rock group. Nucleus of band: Jim Kerr (lead singer; formerly married to Chrissie Hynde of The Pretenders, later married Patsy Kensit of Eighth Wonder), Michael MacNeil (keyboards), Charles Burchill (guitar), Mel Gaynor (drums) and John Giblin (bass). MacNeil left in 1989.

2/19/83	69	19		1	New Gold Dream (81-82-83-84)	$8	A&M 4928
2/18/84	64	24		2	Sparkle in the Rain	$8	A&M 4981
11/9/85+	10	42	●	3	Once Upon A Time	$8	A&M 5092
7/18/87	96	10		4	Simple Minds Live: In The City Of Light [L]	$10	A&M 6850 [2]
					recorded live in Sydney, Australia and Paris in the summer of 1986		
5/20/89	70	12		5	Street Fighting Years	$8	A&M 3927
5/4/91	74	11		6	Real Life	$12	A&M 5352

African Skies (6)
Alive & Kicking (3,4) 3
All The Things She Said (3) 28
Banging On The Door (6)
Belfast Child (5)
Big Sleep (1,4)
Biko (5)
Book Of Brilliant Things (2,4)
"C" Moon Cry Like A Baby (2)

Colours Fly And Catherine Wheel (1)
Come A Long Way (3)
Dance To The Music (medley) (3)
Don't You Forget About Me (4)
East At Easter (2,4)
Ghost Dancing (3,4)
Ghostrider (1)

Glittering Prize (1)
Hunter And The Hunted (1)
I Wish You Were Here (3)
Kick Inside Of Me (2)
Kick It In (5)
King Is White And In The Crowd (1)
Let It All Come Down (5)
Let The Children Speak (6)
Let There Be Love (6)

Love Song (medley) (4)
Mandela Day (5)
New Gold Dream (1,4)
Oh Jungleland (3,4)
Once Upon A Time (3,4)
Promised You A Miracle (1,4)
Real Life (6)
Rivers Of Ice (6)
Sanctify Yourself (3,4) 14
See The Lights (6) 40

Shake Off The Ghosts (2)
Somebody Up There Likes You (1)
Someone Somewhere In Summertime (4)
Soul Crying Out (5)
Speed Your Love To Me (2)
Stand By Love (6)
Street Fighting Years (5)
Street Hassle (2)

Sun City (medley) (4)
Take A Step Back (5)
This Is Your Land (5)
Travelling Man (6)
Up On The Catwalk (2)
Wall Of Love (5)
Waterfront (2,4)
When Two Worlds Collide (6)
White Hot Day (2)
Woman (6)

SIMPLY RED

Manchester, England group: vocalist Mick "Red" Hucknall (b: 6/8/60), keyboardists Fritz McIntyre & Tim Kellett, Tony Bowers (bass), Chris Joyce (drums) and Sylvan Richardson (guitar). 1991 lineup: Hucknall, McIntyre, Kellett, saxophonist Ian Kirkham, Brazilian guitarist Heitor T.P. and Japanese drummer Gota.

4/19/86	16	60	▲	1	Picture Book	$8	Elektra 60452
3/28/87	31	26		2	Men And Women	$8	Elektra 60727
3/11/89	22	39	●	3	A New Flame	$8	Elektra 60828
10/19/91+	76	43	●	4	Stars	$12	EastWest 91773

Come To My Aid (1)
Enough (3)
Ev'ry Time We Say Goodbye (2)
For Your Babies (4)
Freedom (4)
Heaven (1)

Holding Back The Years (1) 1
How Could I Fall (1)
I Won't Feel Bad (2)
If You Don't Know Me By Now (3) 1
Infidelity (2)
It's Only Love (3) 57

Jericho (1)
Let Me Have It All (2)
Look At You Now (1)
Love Fire (2)
Love Lays Its Tune (3)
Maybe Someday... (2)
Model (4)

Money$ Too Tight (To Mention) (1) 28
More (3)
Move On Out (2)
New Flame (3)
No Direction (1)
(Open Up The) Red Box (1)
Picture Book (1)

Right Thing (2) 27
Sad Old Red (1)
She'll Have To Go (3)
She's Got It Bad (4)
Shine (1)
Something Got Me Started (4) 23
Stars (4) 44

Suffer (2)
Thrill Me (4)
To Be With You (3)
Turn It Up (3)
Wonderland (4)
You've Got It (3)
Your Mirror (4)

SIMPSON, Valerie

Born on 8/26/46 in New York City. Half of husband-and-wife duo, Ashford & Simpson.

7/31/71	159	6		1	Valerie Simpson Exposed	$10	Tamla 311
8/26/72	162	6		2	Valerie Simpson	$10	Tamla 317

Back To Nowhere (1)
Benjie (2)
Can't It Wait Until Tomorrow (1)
Could Have Been Sweeter (2)

Drink The Wine (2)
Fix It Alright (2)
Genius I & II (2)
I Believe I'm Gonna Take This Ride (1)

I Don't Need No Help (1)
I Just Wanna Be There (1)
Keep It Coming (2)
Love Woke Me Up This Morning (1)

Now That There's You (1)
One More Baby Child Born (2)
Silly Wasn't I (2) 63

Sinner Man (Don't Let Him Catch You) (1)
There Is A God (1)
We Can Work It Out (1)
World Without Sunshine (1)

SIMPSONS, The

The voices of the Fox network's animated TV series. Dan Castellaneta is Homer; Julie Kavner is Marge; Nancy Cartwright is Bart; Yeardley Smith is Lisa; and the show's creator Matt Groening is Maggie.

12/22/90+	3	39	▲²		The Simpsons Sing The Blues [N]	$12	Geffen 24308
					guest appearance by Buster Poindexter		

Born Under A Bad Sign
Deep, Deep Trouble 69

Do The Bartman
God Bless The Child

I Love To See You Smile
Look At All Those Idiots

Moanin' Lisa Blues
School Day

Sibling Rivalry
Springfield Soul Stew

★★2★★ SINATRA, Frank

Born Francis Albert Sinatra on 12/12/15 in Hoboken, New Jersey. With Harry James from 1939-40, first recorded for Brunswick in 1939; with Tommy Dorsey, 1940-42. Went solo in late 1942 and charted 40 top 10 hits through 1954. Appeared in many films from 1941 on. Won an Oscar for the film *From Here To Eternity* in 1953. Own TV show in 1957. Own Reprise record company in 1961, sold to Warner Bros. in 1963. Won the Lifetime Achievement Grammy in 1965. Married to actress Ava Gardner from 1951-57. Married to actress Mia Farrow from 1966 to 1968. Announced his retirement in 1970, but made comeback in 1973. Regarded by many as the greatest popular singer of the 20th century.

5/28/55	2¹⁸	44		1	in the Wee Small Hours	$25	Capitol 581
3/31/56	2¹	50	●	2	songs for Swingin' Lovers!	$25	Capitol 653
12/22/56+	8	17	●	3	This is Sinatra! [G]	$25	Capitol 768
3/2/57	5	14		4	Close To You	$25	Capitol 789
					featuring The Hollywood String Quartet		
5/27/57	2¹	36		5	a Swingin' Affair!	$25	Capitol 803
9/23/57	3	21		6	Where are you?	$25	Capitol 855

DEBUT DATE	PEAK POS	WKS CHR	GOLD	ARTIST — Album Title	$	Label & Number
				SINATRA, Frank — Cont'd		
11/11/57	**2**[1]	27		7 Pal Joey ....[S]	$25	Capitol 912
				Frank plays Joey Evans and sings on 6 of the tracks; orchestra numbers conducted by Morris Stoloff: "Main Title," "Do It The Hard Way," "Great Big Town," "Plant You Now, Dig You Later," "You Mustn't Kick It Around" and "Strip Number"; includes "Bewitched" and "Zip" by Rita Hayworth; "My Funny Valentine" and "That Terrific Rainbow" by Kim Novak		
12/30/57+	**18**	2	●	8 a Jolly Christmas from Frank Sinatra .... [X]	$20	Capitol 894
2/3/58	**1**[5]	71		9 Come fly with me	$25	Capitol 920
4/28/58	**8**	7		10 This Is Sinatra, Volume Two .... [G]	$25	Capitol 982
6/2/58	**12**	1		11 The Frank Sinatra Story .... [K]	$25	Columbia 6 [2]
9/29/58	**1**[5]	120	●	12 Frank Sinatra sings for Only The Lonely	$25	Capitol 1053
2/9/59	**2**[5]	141	●	13 Come Dance With Me!	$25	Capitol 1069
				1959 Grammy winner: Album of the Year		
6/1/59	**8**	15		14 Look to Your Heart .... [K]	$25	Capitol 1164
8/24/59	**2**[2]	74		15 No One Cares	$20	Capitol 1221
8/22/60	**1**[9]	86	●	16 Nice 'n' Easy	$20	Capitol 1417
2/13/61	**3**	36		17 Sinatra's Swingin' Session!!!	$20	Capitol 1491
4/10/61	**4**	60		18 All The Way .... [G]	$20	Capitol 1538
5/1/61	**4**	35		19 Ring-A-Ding Ding!	$20	Reprise 1001
				the first album for Sinatra's own record company		
8/14/61	**6**	22		20 Sinatra Swings	$20	Reprise 1002
8/14/61	**8**	39		21 Come Swing With Me!	$15	Capitol 1594
11/6/61	**3**	42		22 I Remember Tommy...	$15	Reprise 1003
				songs popularized by Tommy Dorsey		
3/17/62	**8**	31		23 Sinatra & Strings	$15	Reprise 1004
4/21/62	**19**	29		24 Point Of No Return	$15	Capitol 1676
8/18/62	**15**	18		25 Sinatra Sings...of love and things .... [K]	$15	Capitol 1729
9/1/62	**18**	16		26 Sinatra and Swingin' Brass	$15	Reprise 1005
11/10/62	**25**	17		27 All Alone	$15	Reprise 1007
12/22/62	**120**	2		28 a Jolly Christmas from Frank Sinatra .... [X-R]	$20	Capitol 894
				album later repackaged as The Sinatra Christmas Album; Christmas charts: 27/63, 15/64, 20/65, 29/66, 53/67, 10/84, 28/87, 23/90		
2/2/63	**5**	42		29 Sinatra-Basie *	$15	Reprise 1008
6/22/63	**6**	35		30 The Concert Sinatra	$15	Reprise 1009
9/28/63	**129**	4		31 Tell Her You Love Her .... [K]	$15	Capitol 1919
10/5/63	**8**	43	●	32 Sinatra's Sinatra	$15	Reprise 1010
				newly recorded Sinatra favorites		
4/11/64	**10**	24		33 Days Of Wine And Roses, Moon River, and other academy award winners	$15	Reprise 1011
5/30/64	**116**	7		34 America, I Hear You Singing	$12	Reprise 2020
				FRANK SINATRA/BING CROSBY/FRED WARING		
8/22/64	**13**	31		35 It Might As Well Be Swing *	$15	Reprise 1012
				*FRANK SINATRA/COUNT BASIE		
12/19/64+	**19**	28		36 Softly, As I Leave You	$15	Reprise 1013
7/3/65	**9**	44		37 Sinatra '65	$15	Reprise 6167
8/21/65+	**5**	69	●	38 September Of My Years..	$15	Reprise 1014
				1965 Grammy winner: Album of the Year		
12/25/65+	**9**	32	●	39 A Man And His Music .... [K]	$15	Reprise 1016 [2]
				1966 Grammy winner: Album of the Year; an anthology of Sinatra's career, narrated and sung by him		
12/25/65+	**30**	16		40 My Kind Of Broadway	$15	Reprise 1015
4/23/66	**34**	14		41 Moonlight Sinatra	$15	Reprise 1018
6/18/66	**1**[1]	73	▲	42 Strangers In The Night	$15	Reprise 1017
8/20/66	**9**	44	●	43 Sinatra At The Sands .... [L]	$15	Reprise 1019 [2]
				with Count Basie & The Orchestra		
12/31/66+	**6**	61	●	44 That's Life	$15	Reprise 1020
4/15/67	**19**	28		45 Francis Albert Sinatra & Antonio Carlos Jobim	$15	Reprise 1021
				Jobim is a Brazilian songwriter/guitarist/vocalist		
7/29/67	**195**	2		46 The Movie Songs .... [K]	$15	Capitol 2700
				Frank's greatest movie song hits ('54-'60)		
9/16/67	**24**	23		47 Frank Sinatra	$15	Reprise 1022
2/24/68	**78**	13		48 Francis A. & Edward K.	$15	Reprise 1024
				FRANK SINATRA & DUKE ELLINGTON		
9/7/68	**55**	25	▲	49 Frank Sinatra's Greatest Hits! .... [G]	$12	Reprise 1025
12/28/68+	**18**	28	●	50 Cycles	$12	Reprise 1027
5/10/69	**11**	19	●	51 My Way	$12	Reprise 1029
8/23/69	**186**	3		52 Close-Up .... [R]	$12	Capitol 254 [2]
				reissue of albums #3 & 10 above		
9/6/69	**30**	16		53 A Man Alone & Other Songs of Rod McKuen	$12	Reprise 1030
4/11/70	**101**	10		54 Watertown	$12	Reprise 1031
4/24/71	**73**	15		55 Sinatra & Company	$12	Reprise 1033
				with Antonio Carlos Jobim on side one		
6/10/72	**88**	17		56 Frank Sinatra's Greatest Hits, Vol. 2 .... [G]	$12	Reprise 1034
10/27/73	**13**	22	●	57 Ol' Blue Eyes Is Back	$10	Reprise 2155
8/3/74	**48**	12		58 Some Nice Things I've Missed	$10	Reprise 2195

DEBUT DATE	PEAK POS	WKS CHR	GOLD	ARTIST — Album Title	$	Label & Number
				SINATRA, Frank — Cont'd		
12/7/74+	**37**	12		**59** Sinatra - The Main Event Live .... [L]	**$10**	Reprise 2207
				recorded at New York's Madison Square Garden; with Woody Herman & The Young Thundering Herd		
1/4/75	**170**	3		**60** Round #1 .... [K]	**$12**	Capitol 11357 [2]
4/12/80	**17**	24	●	**61** Trilogy: Past, Present, Future...	**$20**	Reprise 2300 [3]
12/5/81+	**52**	13		**62** She Shot Me Down...	**$8**	Reprise 2305
8/25/84	**58**	13		**63** L.A. Is My Lady...	**$8**	Qwest 25145
				with Quincy Jones & Orchestra		
12/8/90+	**126**	11	●	**64** The Capitol Years .... [G]	**$64**	Capitol 94777 [3]
				in celebration of Frank's 75th birthday; 75 tracks recorded by Frank at Capitol from 1953-62; includes a 36-page booklet		
12/15/90+	**98**	10	●	**65** The Reprise Collection .... [K]	**$64**	Reprise 26340 [4]
				81 tracks from 1960-84; includes a 35-page booklet		
4/27/91	**138**	27		**66** Sinatra Reprise - The Very Good Years .... [G]	**$12**	Reprise 26501
				20 tracks from *The Reprise Collection*		

Adeste Fideles (8,28)
After You've Gone (63)
Ain't She Sweet (26)
All Alone (27,65)
All I Need Is The Girl (48,65)
All My Tomorrows (18,46,51)
All Of Me (43,64)
All Of You (61)
All Or Nothing At All (11,23,39,42,65,66)
All The Way (18,32,33,39,46,59,64) **2**
Almost Like Being In Love (21,64)
Always (17)
America The Beautiful (65)
American Beauty Rose (21)
Angel Eyes (12,43,59,60,64)
Anything Goes (2)
Anytime-Anywhere (14)
Anytime At All (37) **46**
April In Paris (9,11)
Are You Lonesome Tonight? (27)
Around The World (9)
As Time Goes By (24)
At Long Last Love (5,26)
Autumn In New York (9,59,60,64)
Autumn Leaves (6)
Available (36)
Baby Won't You Please Come Home (6)
Bad, Bad Leroy Brown (58,59) **83**
Bang Bang (My Baby Shot Me Down) (62)
Baubles, Bangles And Beads (13,45)
Be Careful, It's My Heart (19)
Beautiful Strangers (53)
Before The Music Ends (61)
Begin The Beguine (11)
Bein' Green (55,56)
Best Is Yet To Come (35,65,66)
Best Of Everything (63)
Bewitched (7,30)
Birth Of The Blues (11)
Blame It On My Youth (4)
Blue Hawaii (9)
Blue Moon (17,60)
Blues In The Night (12)
Born Free (47)
Brazil (9)
But Not For Me (61)
By The Time I Get To Phoenix (50)
C'est Magnifique (46)
California (65)
Call Me (42)
Call Me Irresponsible (32,39) **78**
Can't We Be Friends (31)
Cardinal, Main Theme From The ..see: Stay With Me
Castle Rock (11)
Change Partners (45)
Charmaine (9)
Cheek To Cheek (13)
Chicago (25,64) **80**
Christmas Song (8,28)
Christmas Waltz (8,28)
Ciribiribin (They're So In Love) (Theme Song) (11)
Close To You (4,55,64)
Coffee Song (19,65)

Come Back To Me (48)
Come Blow Your Horn (36)
Come Dance With Me (13,60,64)
Come Fly With Me (9,39,43,64)
Come Rain Or Come Shine (23,65)
Continental, The (33)
Cottage For Sale (15)
Crazy Love (10) **60**
Curse Of An Aching Heart (20)
Cycles (50,56) **23**
Dancing In The Dark (13)
Dancing On The Ceiling (1)
Day By Day (21)
Day In - Day Out (13)
Day In The Life Of A Fool (Manha De Carnaval) (51)
Daybreak (22)
Days Of Wine And Roses (33)
Dear Heart (36)
Deep In A Dream (1)
Didn't We (51)
Dindi (45,65)
Don'cha Go Way Mad (26,65)
Don't Be That Way (20)
Don't Cry Joe (20)
Don't Ever Go Away (55)
Don't Like Goodbyes (4,64)
Don't Sleep In The Subway (47)
Don't Take Your Love From Me (21,60,65)
Don't Wait Too Long (38)
Don't Worry 'Bout Me (3,43,52)
Downtown (42)
Dream (16,60)
Dream Away (57)
Dream Sequence Medley (7)
Drinking Again (47,65)
Drinking Water (58)
Early American [duet: Frank & Fred] (34)
East Of The Sun (And West Of The Moon) (22)
Ebb Tide (12,64)
Elizabeth (54)
Embraceable You (16,64)
Emily (36,65)
Empty Is (53)
Empty Tables (65)
End Of A Love Affair (4)
Ev'rybody Has The Right To Be Wrong! (At Least Once) (40)
Eventide (32)
Everybody Loves Somebody (10,52,64)
Everything Happens To Me (4)
Fairy Tale (14) *flip*
Falling In Love With Love (20)
Fine Romance (19)
First Noel (8)
Five Minutes More (21)
Fly Me To The Moon (35,39,43,65,66)
Foggy Day (19)
Follow Me (48)
Fools Rush In (16)
For A While (54)
For Once In My Life (51)

For The Good Times (61)
Forget Domani (49) **78**
Forget To Remember (65) *flip*
French Foreign Legion (18,64) **61**
From Both Sides, Now (50)
From Here To Eternity (3,39,52,64)
From Promise To Promise (53)
From This Moment On (5)
Future, The (61)
Gal That Got Away (3,52,62,65)
Garden In The Rain (65)
Gentle On My Mind (50)
Get Me To The Church On Time (43)
Girl From Ipanema (45)
Girl Next Door (27)
Give Her Love (44)
Glad To Be Unhappy (1)
Goin' Out Of My Head (56) **79**
Golden Moment (40)
Gone With The Wind (12)
Good-Bye (12)
Good Life (35)
Good Thing Going (62)
Goodbye (She Quietly Says) (54)
Goody Goody (26)
Granada (20) **64**
Guess I'll Hang My Tears Out To Dry (12,64)
Half As Lovely (Twice As True) (10,52)
Hallelujah, I Love Her So (51)
Hark! The Herald Angels Sing (8,28)
Have You Met Miss Jones? (20,40)
Have Yourself A Merry Little Christmas (8)
Hello, Dolly! (35,40)
Hello, Young Lovers (38)
Here Goes (64)
Here's That Rainy Day (15,64)
Here's To The Band (65)
Here's To The Losers (36,65)
Hey! Jealous Lover (10,52,64) **3**
Hey Look, No Crying (62)
Hidden Persuasion (25)
High Hopes (18,46,64) **30**
House I Live In (11,34,39,59)
How About You? (2)
How Deep Is The Ocean (11,16)
How Do You Keep The Music Playing? (63)
How Insensitive (45,65)
(How Little It Matters) How Little We Know (10,32,39,52,64) **13**
How Old Am I? (38)
Hundred Years From Today (63)
I Believe (10,52)
I Believe In You (35)
I Can't Believe I'm Losing You (36) **60**
I Can't Believe That You're In Love With Me (17,64)
I Can't Get Started (15)

I Can't Stop Loving You (35)
I Concentrate On You (11,17,45,65)
I Could Have Danced All Night (13)
I Could Have Told You (14)
I Could Write A Book (7)
I Couldn't Care Less (64)
I Couldn't Sleep A Wink Last Night (4)
I Cover The Waterfront (6)
I Didn't Know What Time It Was (7)
I Don't Stand A Ghost Of A Chance With You (15)
I Get A Kick Out Of You (26,59,60,64,65,66)
I Get Along Without You Very Well (1)
I Got It Bad And That Ain't Good (31)
I Got Plenty O' Nuttin' (5,64)
I Gotta Right To Sing The Blues (25,64)
I Guess I'll Have To Change My Plan (31)
I Had The Craziest Dream (61)
I Hadn't Anyone Till You (23)
I Have Dreamed (30,65)
I Like The Sunrise (48)
I Like To Lead When I Dance (37)
I Love My Wife (65)
I Love Paris (25)
I Love You (26,64)
I Loved Her (62)
I Never Knew (20)
I Only Have Eyes For You (29)
I See It Now (38)
I See Your Face Before Me (1)
I Think Of You (6)
I Thought About You (2,64)
I Wanna Be Around (35)
I Will Drink The Wine (55)
I Will Wait For You (44)
I Wish I Were In Love Again (5,64)
I Wish You Love (35)
I Wished On The Moon (41,65)
I Won't Dance (5,29)
I Would Be In Love (Anyway) (54) **88**
I'll Be Around (1)
I'll Be Home For Christmas (If Only In My Dreams) (8,28)
I'll Be Seeing You (22,24,39,64) **58**
I'll Never Be The Same (1)
I'll Never Smile Again (15,39,64)
I'll Only Miss Her When I Think Of Her (40,65)
I'll Remember April (24)
I'll See You Again (24)
I'm A Fool To Want You (6,64)
I'm Beginning To See The Light (26)
I'm Getting Sentimental Over You (22)
I'm Glad There Is You (11)
I'm Gonna Live Till I Die (14)

I'm Gonna Make It All The Way (58)
I'm Gonna Sit Right Down And Write Myself A Letter (29)
I'm Not Afraid (56)
I've Been There! (61)
I've Been To Town (53)
I've Got A Crush On You (11,16,43,60,64)
I've Got My Love To Keep Me Warm (17)
I've Got The World On A String (3,52,64)
I've Got You Under My Skin (2,32,39,43,59,60,64,65,66)
I've Had My Moments (4)
I've Heard That Song Before (21,64)
I've Never Been In Love Before (37)
If (58)
If I Had Three Wishes (14)
If I Had You (5,60,64)
If I Loved You (11)
If I Should Lose You (63)
If You Are But A Dream (10,11,52)
If You Go Away (61)
If You Never Come To Me (45)
Ill Wind (31)
Imagination (22)
Impatient Years (14)
Impossible Dream (44)
In The Cool, Cool, Cool Of The Evening (33)
In The Still Of The Night (19)
In The Wee Small Hours Of The Morning (1,32,39,64)
Indian Summer (48,65)
Indiscreet (27)
Isle Of Capri (9)
It All Depends On You (17)
It Came Upon A Midnight Clear (8,28)
It Could Happen To You (4)
It Gets Lonely Early (38)
It Had To Be You (61)
It Happened In Monterey (2)
It Might As Well Be Spring (23,33)
It Never Entered My Mind (31,62,65)
It Started All Over Again (22,65)
It Was A Very Good Year (38,43,49,59,65,66) **28**
It's A Blue World (24)
It's A Wonderful World (24)
It's All Right With Me (46,63)
It's Always You (22)
It's Easy To Remember (4)
It's Nice To Go Trav'ling (9)
It's Only A Paper Moon (17,60)
It's Over, It's Over, It's Over (18)
It's Sunday (65)
It's The Same Old Dream (10,52,64)
Jingle Bells (8,28)
Johnny Concho Theme (Wait For Me) (10) **75**
Just As Though You Were Here (65)
Just Friends (15)
Just In Time (13,64)

Just The Way You Are (61)
L.A. Is My Lady (63)
Lady Day (55)
Lady Is A Tramp (7,59,64,65,66)
Last Dance (13,65,66)
Last Night When We Were Young (1,38)
Laura (6,11)
Lean Baby (64)
Learnin' The Blues (3,29,39,52,64) **1**
Leaving On A Jet Plane (55)
Let Me Try Again (57,59) **63**
Let Us Break Bread Together (34)
Let's Face The Music And Dance (19,61)
Let's Fall In Love (19,65)
Let's Get Away From It All (9,60,64)
Little Green Apples (50)
London By Night (9)
Lonely Town (6)
Lonesome Cities (53)
Lonesome Road (5,64)
Long Night (62,65)
Look Of Love (36)
Look To Your Heart (14)
Looking At The World Thru Rose Colored Glasses (29)
Lost In The Stars (30,40)
Love And Marriage (3,39,52,64,65,66) **5**
Love Is A Many-Splendored Thing (33)
Love Is Here To Stay (31)
Love Is Just Around The Corner (26)
(Love Is) The Tender Trap (3,29,46,52,64) **7**
Love Isn't Just For The Young (36)
Love Locked Out (4)
Love Looks So Well On You (25)
Love Me Tender (64)
Love Walked In (20,65)
Lover (21)
Loves Been Good To Me (53,56) **75**
Luck Be A Lady (37,39,40,65,66)
MacArthur Park (61)
Mack The Knife (63,65)
Makin' Whoopee (31,43)
Mam'selle (10)
Man Alone (53,56,65)
Man In The Looking Glass (38)
Maybe You'll Be There (15)
Me And My Shadow (65) **64**
Meditation (45)
Memories Of You (24,64)
Michael & Peter (54)
Million Dreams Ago (24)
Mistletoe And Holly (8,28)
Misty (23)
Monday Morning Quarterback (62)
Mondo Cane, Theme From ..see: More
Monique (25,46)
Mood Indigo (1)
Moody River (50)
Moon Got In My Eyes (41)
Moon Love (41)

SINATRA, Frank — Cont'd

Moon River (33)
Moon Song (41)
Moon Was Yellow (25,41) **99**
Moonlight Becomes You (41)
Moonlight In Vermont (9)
Moonlight Mood (41)
Moonlight On The Ganges (20)
Moonlight Serenade (41,65)
More (35)
More Than You Know (61,65)
Most Beautiful Girl In The World (42)
Mr. Success (25) **41**
Mrs. Robinson (5)
My Baby Just Cares For Me (42)
My Blue Heaven (17)
My Heart Stood Still (30)
My Kind Of Girl (29)
My Kind Of Town (37,39,43,59,65,66)
My One And Only Love (3,52)
My Shining Hour (61,65)
My Sweet Lady (55)
My Way (51,56,59,65,66) **27**
My Way Of Life (50) **64**
Nancy (11,32,39,65,66)
Nearness Of You (19)
Nevertheless (16)
New York, New York, Theme From (61,65,66) **32**
Nice 'N' Easy (16,60,64) **60**
Nice Work If You Can Get It (5,29,40)
Night (53)
Night And Day (23,31,39,60,64,65,66)
Night We Called It A Day (6)
Nightingale Sang In Berkeley Square (65)
No One Ever Tells You (5)
Noah (57)
Nobody Wins (57)
None But The Lonely Heart (15)
Not As A Stranger (14)
O Little Town Of Bethlehem (8,28)
Oh, How I Miss You Tonight (27)
Oh! Look At Me Now (5)
Oh, What It Seemed To Be (32,39)
Oh, You Crazy Moon (41,65)
Ol' MacDonald (18) **25**
Ol' Man River (11,30)
Old Devil Moon (4)
Oldest Established (Permanent Floating Crap Game In New York) (39)

On A Clear Day (You Can See Forever) (42)
On The Road To Mandalay (9)
On The Sunny Side Of The Street (21,64)
Once I Loved (45,65)
Once Upon A Time (38)
One For My Baby (11,12,43,64)
One I Love Belongs To Somebody Else (22,39,64)
One Note Samba (55)
One O'Clock Jump (43)
Only The Lonely (12,64)
Our Town (14,64)
Out Beyond The Window (53)
P.S. I Love You (4)
Paper Doll (21)
Pass Me By (36)
Pennies From Heaven (29,31,60,65)
Pick Yourself Up (26)
Please Be Kind (29,65)
Please Don't Talk About Me When I'm Gone (20)
Pocketful Of Miracles (32) **34**
Polka Dots And Moonbeams (22,39)
Poor Butterfly (48)
Pretty Colors (50)
Prisoner Of Love (23)
Put Your Dreams Away (For Another Day) (10,11,32,39,52,60,64)
Quiet Nights Of Quiet Stars (Corcovado) (45)
Rain (Falling From The Skies) (3)
Rain In My Heart (50) **62**
Reaching For The Moon (41)
Remember (27)
Ring-A-Ding Ding (19,39)
River, Stay 'Way From My Door (18) **82**
S'posin' (27)
Same Old Saturday Night (14) **13**
Sand And Sea (44)
Sandpiper, Love Theme From ..see: Shadow Of Your Smile
Satisfy Me One More Time (58)
Saturday Night (Is The Loneliest Night Of The Week) (13,64)
Second Time Around (32,39,65) **50**
Secret Love (33)

Send In The Clowns (57,65,66)
Sentimental Baby (25)
Sentimental Journey (21)
September In The Rain (17,60)
September Of My Years (38,39,43,56)
September Song (24,38,65)
Serenade In Blue (26)
Shadow Of Your Smile (43,65)
She Says (54)
She's Funny That Way (16)
Should I (17)
Silent Night (8,28)
Single Man (53)
Sleep Warm (18)
So Long, My Love (10) **74**
Softly, As I Leave You (36,39,49) **27**
Soliloquy (11,30,39,65)
Some Enchanted Evening (47)
Some Traveling Music (53)
Someone To Light Up My Life (55)
Someone To Watch Over Me (64)
Somethin' Stupid (47,49,65) **1**
Something (56,61,65)
Something Wonderful Happens In Summer (10,25,64)
Something's Gotta Give (13)
Somewhere Along The Way (24)
Somewhere In Your Heart (37,49) **32**
Somewhere My Love (Lara's Theme) (44)
Song Is Ended (27)
Song Is You (13,61,64,65)
Song Sung Blue (61)
Song Without Words (61)
South - To A Warmer Place (62)
South Of The Border (3,52,64)
Star! (56)
Stardust (23) **98**
Stars Fell On Alabama (5,64)
Stay With Me (37) **81**
Stormy Weather (11,15,63)
Strangers In The Night (42,49,65,66) **1**
Street Of Dreams (43,61,65)
Summer Knows (58)
Summer Me, Winter Me (61)

Summer Wind (42,49,65,66) **25**
Summit, The (39)
Sunny (48)
Sunrise In The Morning (55)
Sweet Caroline (58)
Sweet Lorraine (65)
Swingin' Down The Lane (24)
Swinging On A Star (33)
Take Me (22)
Taking A Chance On Love (64)
Talk To Me (18) **38**
Talk To Me Baby (36)
Teach Me Tonight (63)
Tell Her You Love Her (37)
Tell Her (You Love Her Each Day) (37,44,49) **57**
Thanks For The Memory (62)
That Old Black Magic (21)
That Old Feeling (16)
That's All (23)
That's Life (44,49,65,66) **4**
That's What God Looks Like To Me (61)
Then Suddenly Love (36)
There Are Such Things (22,39)
There Used To Be A Ballpark (57,65)
There Will Never Be Another You (24)
There's A Small Hotel (7)
There's No You (6)
These Foolish Things (Remind Me Of You) (24)
They All Laughed (61)
They Came To Cordura (25,46)
They Can't Take That Away From Me (26,40,64)
This Happy Madness (55)
This Is All I Ask (38,65)
This Is My Love (47)
This Is My Song (47)
This Love Of Mine (1)
This Nearly Was Mine (30)
This Town (47,49) **53**
This Was My Love (18)
Three Coins In The Fountain (1,33,46,52,64)
Tie A Yellow Ribbon Round The Ole Oak Tree (58)
Time After Time (10,52)
Tina (65)
To Love And Be Loved (18,46,64)
Together (27)
Too Close For Comfort (13)

Too Marvelous For Words (2,64)
Train, The (54)
Triste (55)
Try A Little Tenderness (16)
Until The Real Thing Comes Along (63)
Wandering (50)
Watch What Happens (51)
Watertown (54)
Wave (55,65)
Way You Look Tonight (33,65,66)
We'll Be Together Again (2)
Weep They Will (31,64)
What A Funny Girl (You Used To Be) (54)
What Are You Doing The Rest Of Your Life? (58,65)
What Is This Thing Called Love? (1,64)
What Now My Love (44)
What Time Does The Next Miracle Leave? (61)
What'll I Do (27,65)
What's New (12)
What's Now Is Now (54,56)
When I Lost You (27)
When I Stop Loving You (14)
When I Take My Sugar To Tea (19)
When I'm Not Near The Girl I Love (37)
When No One Cares (15,64)
When Somebody Loves You (37,49)
When The Wind Was Green (38)
When The World Was Young (24)
When You're Smiling (The Whole World Smiles With You) (17,60)
When Your Lover Has Gone (31)
Where Are You? (6,64)
Where Do You Go? (15)
Where Is The One (6)
Where Or When (43)
Why Try To Change Me Now? (15)
Why Was I Born (11)
Willow Weep For Me (12)
Winchester Cathedral (44)
Winners (57)
Witchcraft (18,32,39,64) **6**
With Every Breath I Take (4)
Without A Song (22,40,65)
Wives And Lovers (35)
World War None! (61)

World We Knew (Over And Over) (47,49) **30**
Yellow Days (48)
Yes Indeed! (21)
Yes Sir, That's My Baby (42)
Yesterday (51)
Yesterdays (23,40)
You And Me (We Wanted It All) (61)
You And The Night And The Music (19)
You Are The Sunshine Of My Life (58,59)
You Are There (7)
You Brought A New Kind Of Love To Me (2,37)
You Do Something To Me (17)
You Forgot All The Words (10)
You Go To My Head (11,16,60)
You Make Me Feel So Young (2,43,60,64,65)
You, My Love (14)
You Never Had It So Good (34)
You Turned My World Around (58) **83**
You Will Be My Music (57)
You'd Be So Easy To Love (19,65)
You'd Be So Nice To Come Home To (5)
You'll Always Be The One I Love (11)
You'll Never Know (11)
You'll Never Walk Alone (11,30)
You're A Lucky Fellow, Mr. Smith (duet: Frank & Fred) (34)
You're Cheatin' Yourself (If You're Cheatin' On Me) (10) **25**
You're Driving Me Crazy! (42)
You're Getting To Be A Habit With Me (2)
You're Gonna Hear From Me (44)
You're Nobody 'Til Somebody Loves You (20,65)
You're Sensational (64) **52**
You're So Right (For What's Wrong In My Life) (57)
Young-At-Heart (3,32,39,46,52,64)
Zing! Went The Strings Of My Heart (65)

★★356★★ SINATRA, Nancy

Born on 6/8/40 in Jersey City, New Jersey. First child of Frank and Nancy Sinatra. Moved to Los Angeles while a child. Made national TV debut with father and Elvis Presley in 1959. Married to Tommy Sands, 1960-65. Appeared on *Hullabaloo*, *American Bandstand*, and own specials, mid-'60s. In films *For Those Who Think Young*, *Get Yourself A College Girl*, *The Oscar* and *Speedway*.

DEBUT DATE	PEAK POS	WKS CHR	GOLD	#	Title	$	Label & Number
3/12/66	5	42	●	1	Boots	$25	Reprise 6202
6/4/66	41	15		2	How Does That Grab You?	$25	Reprise 6207
9/3/66	122	7		3	Nancy in London	$25	Reprise 6221
2/18/67	18	24		4	Sugar	$20	Reprise 6239
9/2/67	43	26		5	Country, My Way	$20	Reprise 6251
1/13/68	37	32		6	Movin' With Nancy [TV]	$15	Reprise 6277
					guests: Frank Sinatra, Dean Martin and Lee Hazlewood		
4/13/68	13	44	●	7	Nancy & Lee	$15	Reprise 6273
					NANCY SINATRA & LEE HAZLEWOOD		
5/3/69	91	8		8	Nancy	$12	Reprise 6333
10/3/70	99	7		9	Nancy's Greatest Hits [G]	$12	Reprise 6409

All By Myself (4)
As Tears Go By (1)
Bang, Bang (2)
Big Boss Man (8)
Button Up Your Overcoat (4)
By The Way (I Still Love You) (5)
Call Me (2)
Coastin' (2)
Crying Time (2)
Day Tripper (1)
Elusive Dreams (7)
End, The (3)

End Of The World (5)
Flowers On The Wall (1)
For Once In My Life (8)
Friday's Child (3,6,9) **36**
Get While The Gettin's Good (5)
God Knows I Love You (8) **97**
Greenwich Village Folk Song Salesman (7)
Hard Hearted Hannah (The Vamp Of Savannah) (4)

Help Stamp Out Loneliness (5)
Here We Go Again (8) **98**
How Does That Grab You, Darlin'? (2,9) **7**
Hutchinson Jail (5)
I Can't Grow Peaches On A Cherry Tree (3)
I Gotta Get Out Of This Town (6)
I Move Around (1)
I'm Just In Love (8)

I've Been Down So Long (It Looks Like Up To Me) (7)
If He'd Love Me (1)
In My Room (1)
It Ain't Me Babe (1)
It's Such A Pretty World Today (5)
Jackson (5,6,7,9) **14**
Just Bein' Plain Old Me (8)
Lady Bird (7) **20**
Lay Some Happiness On Me (5)
Let It Be Me (2)

Let's Fall In Love (4)
Lies (1)
Light My Fire (8)
Lightning's Girl (9) **24**
Limehouse Blues (4)
Lonely Again (5)
Long Time Woman (8)
Mama Goes Where Papa Goes (or Papa Don't Go Out Tonight) (4)
Memories (8)
More I See You (3)

My Baby Cried All Night Long (2)
My Buddy (4)
My Dad (My Pa) (8)
My Mother's Eyes (8)
Not The Lovin' Kind (2)
Oh Lonesome Me (8)
Oh! You Beautiful Doll (4)
On Broadway (3)
Run For Your Life (1)
Sand (2,7)
See The Little Children (6)
Shades (3)

SINATRA, Nancy — Cont'd

Shadow Of Your Smile (2)
So Long Babe (1) *86*
Some Velvet Morning (6,7,9) *26*
Somethin' Stupid (9) *1*
Son-Of-A-Preacher Man (8)
Sorry 'Bout That (2)

Step Aside (3)
Storybook Children (7)
Sugar Town (4,9) *5*
Summer Wine (3,7,9) *49*
Sundown, Sundown (7)
Sweet Georgia Brown (4)

These Boots Are Made For Walkin' (1,9) *1*
Things (6,9)
This Little Bird (3)
This Town (6)
Time (2)
Up, Up And Away (6)

Vagabond Shoes (4)
Wait Till You See Him (6)
Walk Through This World With Me (5)
What'd I Say (6)
What'll I Do (4)
When It's Over (5)

Who Will Buy (6)
Wishin' And Hopin' (3)
You Only Live Twice (9) *44*
You've Lost That Lovin' Feelin' (7)
Younger Than Springtime (6)

SINFIELD, Pete
British songwriter. Lyrical partner of Robert Fripp in King Crimson.

10/6/73	190	5		Still	$10	Manticore 66667

Envelopes Of Yesterday
House Of Hopes And Dreams

Night People
Piper, The

Song Of The Sea Goat
Still

Under The Sky
Wholefood Boogie

Will It Be You

SINGING NUN, The
Sister Luc-Gabrielle (real name: Jeanine Deckers) from the Fichermont, Belgium convent. Recorded under the name Soeur Sourire ("Sister Smile"). Committed suicide on 3/31/85 (age 52).

11/9/63	1[10]	39	●	1 The Singing Nun .... [F]	$12	Philips 203
4/11/64	90	14		2 Her Joy, Her Songs .... [F]	$15	Philips 209

Alleluia (1)
Avec Toi (1)
Chante Riviere (2)
Coeur De Dieu (2)

Complainte Pour Marie-Jacques (1)
Croix Du Sud (2)
Dans Les Magasins (2)
Dominique (1) *1*

Entre Les Etoiles (1)
Fleur De Cactus (1)
J'ai Trouve Le Seineur (1)
Je Voudrais (1)

Kabinda (Ma Petite Amie D'Afrique) (2)
Les Mouettes (2)
Ma Petite Muse (2)
Mets Ton Joli Jupon (1)

Midi (2)
Pauvre Devant Toi (1)
Petit Pierrot (1)
Plume De Radis (1)
Resurrection (1)

Soeur Adele (1)
Tous Les Chemins (1)
Une Fleur (2)

SIOUXSIE AND THE BANSHEES
Avant-punk band, debuted at London's 100 Club, on 9/20/76, with female vocalist Siouxsie Sioux (Susan Dallion), bassist Steve Severin, guitarist Marco Pironi and Sid Vicious (the bassist of The Sex Pistols) on drums. Fluctuating personnel since then. 1988 lineup: Sioux, Severin, Budgie (drummer, formerly with Big In Japan), Martin McCarick (keyboards, strings) and guitarist Jon Klein. Husband and wife, Sioux and Budgie, also record as duo The Creatures.

7/7/84	157	7		1 Hyaena	$8	Geffen 24030
5/24/86	88	15		2 Tinderbox	$8	Geffen 24092
4/11/87	188	3		3 Through The Looking Glass	$8	Geffen 24134
10/1/88	68	20		4 Peepshow	$8	Geffen 24205
6/29/91	65	21		5 Superstition	$12	Geffen 24387

Belladonna (1)
Blow The House Down (1)
Bring Me The Head Of The Preacher Man (1)
Burn-Up (4)
Candyman (2)
Cannons (2)
Carousel (4)
Cities In Dust (2)
Cry (5)

Dazzle (1)
Dear Prudence (1)
Drifter (5)
Fear (Of The Unknown) (5)
Ghost In You (5)
Got To Get Up (5)
Gun (3)
Hall of Mirrors (3)
Killing Jar (4)
Kiss Them For Me (5) *23*

Lands End (2)
Last Beat Of My Heart (4)
Little Johnny Jewel (3)
Little Sister (5)
92° (2)
Ornaments Of Gold (4)
Partys Fall (2)
Passenger, The (3)
Peek-A-Boo (4) *53*
Pointing Bone (1)

Rawhead And Bloodybones (4)
Rhapsody (4)
Running Town (1)
Scarecrow (1)
Sea Breezes (3)
Shadowtime (5)
Silly Thing (4)
Silver Waterfalls (5)
Softly (5)

Strange Fruit (3)
Sweetest Chill (5)
Swimming Horses (1)
Take Me Back (1)
This Town Ain't Big Enough For The Both Of Us (3)
This Unrest (2)
This Wheel's On Fire (3)
Trust In Me (3)
Turn To Stone (4)

We Hunger (1)
You're Lost Little Girl (3)

SIR DOUGLAS QUINTET
Tex-Mex rock band led by Doug Sahm (b: 11/6/41) from San Antonio. Co-founded by country singer Augie Meyers. Also see Doug Sahm and Band.

4/19/69	81	11		1 Mendocino	$25	Smash 67115
2/14/81	184	4		2 Border Wave	$8	Takoma 7088

And It Didn't Even Bring Me Down (1)
At The Crossroads (1)
Border Wave (2)
Down On The Border (2)

I Don't Want (1)
I Keep Wishing For You (1)
I Wanna Be Your Mama Again (1)
If You Really Want Me To (1)

It Was Fun While It Lasted (2)
Lawd, I'm Just A Country Boy In This Great Big Freaky City (1)

Mendocino (1) *27*
Oh, Baby It Just Don't Matter (1)
Old Habits, Die Hard (2)
Revolutionary Ways (2)

She's About A Mover (1) *13*
Sheila Tequila (2)
Texas Me (1)
Tonite, Tonite (1)

Who'll Be The Next In Line (2)
You're Gonna Miss Me (2)

SIREN — see RED SIREN

SIR LORD BALTIMORE
Rock trio — John Garner, lead singer.

2/6/71	198	2		Kingdom Come	$15	Mercury 61328

Ain't Got Hung On You
Hard Rain Fallin'

Helium Head (I Got A Love)
Hell Hound

I Got A Woman
Kingdom Come

Lady Of Fire
Lake Isle Of Innersfree

Master Heartache
Pumped Up

SIR MIX-A-LOT
Seattle rapper Anthony Ray. Formerly backed by Kid Sensation.

10/22/88+	82	58	▲	1 Swass	$8	Nastymix 70123
11/18/89	67	41	●	2 Seminar	$8	Nastymix 70150
2/22/92	9	51↑	▲	3 Mack Daddy	$12	Def Amer. 26765

Baby Got Back (3) *1*
Beepers (3)
Boss Is Back (3)
Bremelo (3)
Buttermilk Biscuits (Keep On Square Dancin') (1)
Gold (1)

Gortex (2)
Hip Hop Soldier (1)
I Got Game (2)
I'll Roll You Up (2)
I'm Your New God (1)
Iron Man (1)
Jack Back (3)

Lockjaw (3)
Mack Daddy (3)
Mall Dropper (1)
My Bad Side (2)
My Hooptie (2)
National Anthem (2)
No Holds Barred (3)

One Time's No Case (3)
(Peek-A-Boo) Game (2)
Posse' On Broadway (1) *70*
Rapper's Reputation (3)
Rippn' (1)
Romantic Interlude (1)
Seattle Ain't Bullshittin' (3)

Seminar (2)
Something About My Benzo (2)
Sprung On The Cat (3)
Square Dance Rap (1)
Swap Meet Louie (3)
Swass (1)

Testarossa (3)

SISTER SLEDGE
Sisters Debra, Joan, Kim and Kathie Sledge from North Philadelphia. First recorded as Sisters Sledge for Money Back label in 1971. Worked as backup vocalists. Began producing their own albums in 1981.

2/24/79	3	33	▲	1 We Are Family	$8	Cotillion 5209
3/8/80	31	15		2 Love Somebody Today	$8	Cotillion 16012
2/28/81	42	29		3 All American Girls	$8	Cotillion 16027
2/13/82	69	14		4 The Sisters	$8	Cotillion 5231
6/4/83	169	8		5 Bet Cha Say That To All The Girls ...	$8	Cotillion 90069

DEBUT DATE	PEAK POS	WKS CHR	GOLD	ARTIST — Album Title	$	Label & Number

SISTER SLEDGE — Cont'd

All American Girls (3) *79*
All The Man I Need (4)
B.Y.O.B. (Bring Your Own Baby) (5)
Bet Cha Say That To All The Girls (5)
Don't You Let Me Lose It (3)
Dream On (5)
Easier To Love (1)
Easy Street (2)

Everybody's Friend (4)
Get You In Our Love (4)
Got To Love Somebody (2) *64*
Gotta Get Back To Love (5)
Grandma (4)
Happy Feeling (3)
He's Just A Runaway (3)
He's The Greatest Dancer (1) *9*

How To Love (2)
I Don't Want To Say Goodbye (3)
I'm A Good Girl (2)
If You Really Want Me (3)
Il Macquillage Lady (4)
Jackl's Theme: There's No Stopping Us (4)
Let Him Go (5)
Let's Go On Vacation (2)

Lifetime Lover (5)
Lightfootin' (4)
Lost In Music (1)
Make A Move (3)
Music Makes Me Feel Good (3)
My Guy (4) *23*
My Special Way (4)
Next Time You'll Know (3) *82*

Once In Your Life (5)
One More Time (1)
Ooh, You Caught My Heart (3)
Pretty Baby (2)
Reach Your Peak (3)
Shake Me Down (5)
Smile (5)
Somebody Loves Me (1)
Super Bad Sisters (4)

Thank You For The Party (5)
Thinking Of You (1)
We Are Family (1) *2*
You Fooled Around (2)
You're A Friend To Me (1)

SISTERS OF MERCY, The
Songwriter Andrew Eldritch formed outfit in 1980 in Leeds, England. Reduced to a duo of he and American bassist Patricia Morrison (Gun Club) in 1987. Morrison left in early 1990; expanded to a quartet which included Tony James (Generation X, Sigue Sigue Sputnik). Band name taken from a Leonard Cohen song.

| 2/6/88 | 101 | 16 | | 1 Floodland... | $8 | Elektra 60762 |
| 12/1/90 | 136 | 23 | | 2 Vision Thing.. | $12 | Elektra 61017 |

Detonation Boulevard (2)
Doctor Jeep (2)
Dominion/Mother Russia (1)

Driven Like The Snow (1)
Flood I & II (1)
I Was Wrong (1)

Lucretia My Reflection (1)
More (1)
Never Land (A Fragment) (1)

1959 (1)
Ribbons (1)
Something Fast (2)

This Corrosion (1)
Vision Thing (2)
When You Don't See Me (2)

SKAGGS, Ricky
Born on 7/18/54 in Cordell, Kentucky. Country/bluegrass singer. In Emmylou Harris' Hot Band in 1977. Married country singer Sharon White in 1981.

6/12/82	77	30	●	1 Waitin' For The Sun To Shine...................................	$8	Epic 37193
10/16/82	61	12	▲	2 Highways & Heartaches..	$8	Epic 37996
11/10/84	180	5		3 Country Boy..	$8	Epic 39410
3/9/85	181	4		4 Favorite Country Songs.................................. [K]	$8	Epic 39409

Baby, I'm In Love With You (3)
Brand New Me (3)
Can't You Hear Me Callin' (2,4)
Country Boy (2)
Crying My Heart Out Over You (1)

Don't Get Above Your Raising (1)
Don't Let Your Sweet Love Die (2)
Don't Think I'll Cry (2)
Heartbroke (2)
Highway 40 Blues (2)
I Don't Care (1)

I Wouldn't Change You If I Could (1)
I'll Take The Blame (4)
I'm Ready To Go (2)
If That's The Way You Feel (1,4)
Let's Love The Bad Times Away (2)

Lost To A Stranger (1,4)
Low And Lonely (1)
Nothing Can Hurt You (2,4)
One Way Rider (2)
Patiently Waiting (3)
Rendezvous (3)
So Round, So Firm, So Fully Packed (1)

Something In My Heart (3)
Sweet Temptation (4)
Two Highways (3)
Waitin' For The Sun To Shine (1,4)
Wheel Hoss (3)
Window Up Above (3)
Wound Time Can't Erase (4)

You May See Me Walkin' (1,4)
You've Got A Lover (2)
Your Old Love Letters (1,4)

SKID ROW
New York hard-rock quintet: Toronto native Sebastian "Bach" Bierk (vocals), Rachel Bolan (bass), Dave Sabo (guitar), Scott Hill (guitar) and Rob Affuso (drums).

2/11/89	6	78	▲³	1 Skid Row..	$8	Atlantic 81936
6/29/91	1¹	46	▲	2 Slave To The Grind	$12	Atlantic 82278
10/10/92	58	6		3 B-Side Ourselves... [M]	$6	Atlantic 82431

Beggar's Day (2)
Big Guns (1)
Can't Stand The Heartache (1)
C'mon And Love Me (3)

Creepshow (2)
Delivering The Goods (3)
18 And Life (1) *4*
Here I Am (1)
I Remember You (1) *6*

In A Darkened Room (2)
Little Wing (3)
Livin' On A Chain Gang (2)
Makin' A Mess (1)
Midnight (medley) (1)

Monkey Business (2)
Mudkicker (2)
Piece Of Me (1)
Psycho Love (2)
Psycho Therapy (3)

Quicksand Jesus (2)
Rattlesnake Shake (1)
Riot Act (1)
Slave To The Grind (2)
Sweet Little Sister (1)

Threat, The (2)
Tornado (medley) (1)
Wasted Time (2) *88*
What You're Doing (3)
Youth Gone Wild (1) *99*

SKINNY PUPPY
Alternative rock trio from Vancouver: Nivek Ogre (real name: Dave Oglivie; vocals), Cevin Key and Dwayne Goettel.

| 4/11/92 | 193 | 1 | | Last Rights... | $12 | Nettwerk 98037 |

Circustance
Download

Inquisition
Killing Game

Knowhere?
Love In Vein

Lust Chance
Mirror Saw

Riverz End
Scrapyard

SKY
Detroit-based rock trio: Doug Fieger (vocals, bass), John Coury (guitar) and Rob Stawinski (drums). Fieger was later the leader of The Knack.

| 12/19/70+ | 160 | 6 | | Sky... | $12 | RCA 4457 |

Feels Like 1,000 Years
Goodie Two Shoes

Homin' Ground

How's That Treatin' Your Mouth, Babe?
I Still Do

I Still Do
Make It In Time

One Love
Rockin' Me Yet

Take Off And Fly
There In The Greenbriar

SKY
Classical-rock group led by classical guitarist John Williams.

| 11/1/80+ | 125 | 15 | | 1 Sky..[I] | $10 | Arista 8302 [2] |
| 5/2/81 | 181 | 3 | | 2 Sky 3 ....[I] | $8 | Arista 4288 |

Adagio (1)
Chiropodie No. 1 (2)
Connecting Rooms (2)
Dance Of The Big Fairies (2)
Dance Of The Little Fairies (1)

El Cielo (1)
Fifo (1)
Grace (2)
Handel: Sarabande (2)
Hello (2)
Hotta (1)

Keep Me Safe And Keep Me Warm, Shelter Me From Darkness (2)
Meheeco (2)
Moonroof (2)
Praetorius: Ballet-Volta (1)

Rameau: Gavotte & Variations (1)
Sahara (1)
Scherzo (1)
Scipio Parts I And II (1)
Sister Rose (2)

Toccata (1) *83*
Tristan's Magic Garden (1)
Tuba Smarties (1)
Vivaldi (1)
Vivaldi: Andante (1)
Watching The Aeroplanes (1)

Westwind (2)

SKYLARK
Group from Vancouver. Lead singers Donny Gerrard and B.J. (Bonnie Jean) Cook with keyboardist David Foster and drummer Duris Maxwell. Foster was later with Attitudes, then a hit songwriter/solo artist.

| 4/7/73 | 102 | 16 | | Skylark... | $8 | Capitol 11048 |

Brother Eddie
I'll Have To Go Away

I'm In Love Again
Long Way To Go

Shall I Fall
Suites For My Lady

Twenty-Six Years

What Would I Do Without You
Wildflower *9*
Writing's On The Wall

SKYY
Brooklyn R&B-pop-funk octet. Vocals by sisters Denise, Delores and Bonnie Dunning. Organized by Randy Muller, former leader of Brass Construction.

5/19/79	117	9		1 Skyy..	$8	Salsoul 8517
3/15/80	61	23		2 Skyway...	$8	Salsoul 8532
12/6/80+	85	20		3 Skyyport...	$8	Salsoul 8537
11/21/81+	18	33	●	4 Skyy Line...	$8	Salsoul 8548

DEBUT DATE	PEAK POS	WKS CHR	G O L D	ARTIST — Album Title	$	Label & Number
				SKYY — Cont'd		
11/20/82+	**81**	13	5	Skyyjammer	**$8**	Salsoul 8555
8/6/83	**183**	3	6	Skyylight	**$8**	Salsoul 8562
5/27/89	**155**	5	7	Start Of A Romance...	**$8**	Atlantic 81853

Arrival (3)
Bad Boy (6)
Call Me (4) *26*
Dance, Dance, Dance (2)
Disco Dancin' (1)
Don't Stop (2)
Fallin' In Love Again (1)
Feelin' It Now (1)
First Time Around (1)
For The First Time (3)

Freak Outta (5)
Get Into The Beat (4)
Girl In Blue (4)
Gonna Get It On (4)
Groove Me (7)
Here's To You (3)
Hey Girl (6)
High (2)
I Can't Get Enough (3)
Jam The Box (4)

Let Love Shine (5)
Let's Celebrate (4)
Lets Get Up (S-K-Y-Y) (1)
Let's Touch (7)
Lets Turn It Out (1)
Love All The Way (7)
Love Plane (2)
Married Man (6)
Miracle (5)
Movin' Violation (5)

Music, Music (2)
My Sun Won't Shine (3)
No Music (3)
Now That We've Found Love (6)
Questions No Answers (6)
Real Love (7) *47*
Sendin' A Message (2)
Sexy Minded (7)
She's Gone (6)

Show Me The Way (6)
Skyy Zoo (2)
Skyyjammin (5)
Stand By Me (1)
Start Of A Romance (7)
Sunshine (7)
Superlove (3)
Swing It (6)
Take It Easy (3)
This Groove Is Bad (1)

This Song Is For You (5)
Together (4)
When You Touch Me (4)
Who's Gonna Love Me (2)
Won't You Be Mine (5)
You Got Me Up (2)

SLADE

English hard-rock quartet: Noddy Holder (b: 6/15/50; lead singer), David Hill (guitar), Jim Lea (bass, keyboards) and Don Powell (drums).

10/7/72	**158**	11	1	Slade Alive!...[L]	**$10**	Polydor 5508
2/17/73	**69**	26	2	Slayed?..	**$10**	Polydor 5524
10/20/73	**129**	7	3	Sladest...[K]	**$10**	Reprise 2173
3/9/74	**168**	5	4	Stomp Your Hands, Clap Your Feet...........................	**$8**	Warner 2770
7/5/75	**93**	14	5	Slade In Flame..[S]	**$8**	Warner 2865
				Slade starred in the film *Flame*		
5/5/84	**33**	23	6	Keep Your Hands Off My Power Supply	**$8**	CBS Assoc. 39336
5/4/85	**132**	6	7	Rogues Gallery	**$8**	CBS Assoc. 39976

(And Now - The Waltz) C'est La Vie (6)
Bangin' Man (5)
Born To Be Wild (1)
Can't Tame A Hurricane (6)
Cheap 'N' Nasty Luv (6)
Coz I Luv You (3)
Cum On Feel The Noize (3) *98*
Darling Be Home Soon (1)
Do We Still Do It (4)
Don't Blame Me (4)
Everyday (3)
Far Far Away (5)

Find Yourself A Rainbow (4)
Get Down With It (1,3)
Good Time Gals (4)
Gudbuy Gudbuy (2)
Gudbuy T' Jane (2,3) *68*
Harmony (7)
Hear Me Calling (1)
Hey Ho Wish You Well (1)
High And Dry (6)
How Can It Be (4)
How D' You Ride (2)
How Does It Feel? (5)
I Don' Mind (2)
I Win, You Lose (7)

I Won't Let It 'Appen Agen (2)
I'll There (7)
In Like A Shot From My Gun (1)
In The Doghouse (1)
Just Want A Little Bit (4)
Keep On Rocking (1)
Keep Your Hands Off My Power Supply (6)
Know Who You Are (1)
Lay It Down (5)
Let The Good Times Roll (2)
Little Sheila (7) *86*
Lock Up Your Daughters (7)

Look At Last Night (2)
Look Wot You Dun (3)
Mama Weer All Crazee Now (2,3) *76*
Miles Out To Sea (4)
Move Over (2)
My Friend Stan (3)
My Oh My (6) *37*
My Town (3)
Myzsterious Mizster Jones (7)
O.K. Yesterday Was Yesterday (5)
Ready To Explode Medley (6)

Run Runaway (6) *20*
7 Year Bitch (7)
Skweeze Me Pleeze Me (3)
Slam The Hammer Down (6)
So Far So Good (5)
Standin' On The Corner (5)
Take Me Back 'Ome (3) *97*
Thanks For The Memories (6)
Them Kinda Monkeys Can't Swing (4)
This Girl (7)
Time To Rock (7)
Walking On Water, Running On Alcohol (7)

We're Really Gonna Raise The Roof (4)
When The Lights Are Out (4)
Whole World's Goin' Crazee (2)

SLATKIN, Felix

St. Louis native. Virtuoso violinist/conductor/composer/arranger. Worked with many film and record companies. Died on 2/9/63 (age 47).

4/6/63	**20**	12		Our Winter Love ....[I]	**$15**	Liberty 7287

Days Of Wine And Roses
Fly Me To The Moon
Gina

I Left My Heart In San Francisco

Lawrence Of Arabia, Theme From

Lollipops And Roses
Love Letters
Meditation

Our Winter Love
Stranger On The Shore

Twelfth Of Never
What Kind Of Fool Am I

SLAUGHTER

Las Vegas hard-rock quartet led by vocalist Mark Slaughter, who, with bandmate Dana Strum (bass), was a member of the Vinnie Vincent Invasion. Includes guitarist Tim Kelly and drummer Blas Elias.

2/17/90	**18**	85	▲²	1 Stick It To Ya..	**$12**	Chrysalis 21702
11/24/90+	**123**	20		2 Stick It Live ....[L-M]	**$6**	Chrysalis 21816
				recorded live in the summer of 1990		
5/9/92	**8**	23	●	3 **Wild Life**	**$12**	Chrysalis 21911

Burnin' Bridges (1,2)
Dance For Me Baby (3)
Days Gone By (includes 2 versions) (3)
Desperately (1)

Do Ya Know (3)
Eye To Eye (1,2)
Fly To The Angels (1,2) *19*
Gave Me Your Heart (1)
Hold On (3)

Loaded Gun (1,2)
Mad About You (1)
Move To The Music (3)
Old Man (3)
Out For Love (3)

Reach For The Sky (3)
Real Love (3)
Shake This Place (3)
She Wants More (1)

Streets Of Broken Hearts (3)
That's Not Enough (1)
Thinking Of June (1)
Times They Change (3)
Spend My Life (1) *39*
Up All Night (1,2) *27*

Wild Life (3)
Wingin' It (1)
You Are The One (1)

SLAVE

Funk band from Dayton, Ohio formed by Steve Washington (trumpet) in 1975 (left by 1981). Longtime members of group included Mark "The Hansolor" Adams (bass), Floyd Miller (vocals, horns) and Danny Webster (vocals, guitar). Studio vocalist Steve Arrington was from 1979-82.

4/9/77	**22**	28	●	1 Slave..	**$8**	Cotillion 9914
12/17/77+	**67**	15		2 The Hardness Of The World	**$8**	Cotillion 5201
8/19/78	**78**	10		3 The Concept	**$8**	Cotillion 5206
12/8/79+	**92**	15		4 Just A Touch Of Love	**$8**	Cotillion 5217
11/1/80+	**53**	34	●	5 Stone Jam	**$8**	Cotillion 5224
10/10/81	**46**	23		6 Show Time..	**$8**	Cotillion 5227
1/15/83	**177**	6		7 Visions Of The Lite	**$8**	Cotillion 90024
10/22/83	**168**	6		8 Bad Enuff	**$8**	Cotillion 90118

Are You Ready For Love? (4)
Baby Sinister (2)
Bad Girl (8)
Be My Babe (7)
Can't Get Enough Of You (2)
Come To Blow Ya Mind (7)
Coming Soon (3)
Dance (8)
Do You Like It...(Girl) (7)
Drac Is Back (3)
Dreamin' (5)
Feel My Love (5)

For The Love Of U (6)
Friday Nites (7)
Funken Town (6)
Funky Lady (Foxy Lady) (4)
Great American Funk Song (2)
Happiest Days (1)
I'll Be Gone (7)
Just A Touch Of Love (4)
Just Freak (3)
Let's Spend Some Time (5)
Life Can Be Happy (2)

Love Me (1)
Never Get Away (5)
Painted Pictures (6)
Party Hardy (1)
Party Lites (6)
Party Song (3)
Rendezvous (8)
Roots (7)
Screw Your Wig On Tite (1)
Separated (3)
Shake It Up (8)
Shine (4)

Show Down (8)
Sizzlin' Hot (5)
Slide (1) *32*
Smokin (6)
Snap Shot (6) *91*
Son Of Slide (1)
Spice Of Life (Oh Yes, You're The Best) (6)
Starting Over (5)
Stay In My Life (7)
Steal Your Heart (6)
Stellar Fungk (3)

Steppin' Out (8)
Stone Jam (5)
Sweet Thang (7)
Thank You (4)
Thank You Lord (3)
Turn You Out (In & Out) (8)
Visions (7)
Volcano Rupture (6)
Wait For Me (7)
Warning (4)
Watching You (5) *78*
Way You Love Is Heaven (3)

We Can Make Love (2)
We've Got Your Party (3)
World's On Hard (2)
You And Me (1)

DEBUT DATE	PEAK POS	WKS CHR	GOLD	ARTIST — Album Title	$	Label & Number

SLAYER

Southern California heavy-metal band formed in 1982: Tom Araya (vocals), Jeff Hanneman, Kerry King and Dave Lombardo.

DEBUT DATE	PEAK POS	WKS CHR	GOLD	ARTIST — Album Title	$	Label & Number
11/15/86	94	18	●	1 Reign In Blood	$8	Def Jam 24131
8/6/88	57	19	●	2 South Of Heaven	$8	Def Jam 24203
10/27/90	40	23		3 Seasons In The Abyss	$12	Def Amer. 24307
11/9/91	55	10		4 Live - Decade Of Aggression ....[L]	$20	Def Amer. 26748 [2]

recorded in Florida, California and London

Altar Of Sacrifice (1,4)
Angel Of Death (1,4)
Anti-Christ (4)
Behind The Crooked Cross (2)
Black Magic (4)
Blood Red (3,4)
Born Of Fire (3,4)
Captor Of Sin (4)
Chemical Warfare (4)
Cleanse The Soul (2)
Criminally Insane (1)
Dead Skin Mask (3,4)
Die By The Sword (4)
Dissident Aggressor (2)
Epidemic (1)
Expendable Youth (3,4)
Ghosts Of War (2)
Hallowed Point (3,4)
Hell Awaits (4)
Jesus Saves (1,4)
Live Undead (2)
Mandatory Suicide (2,4)
Necrophobic (1)
Piece By Piece (1)
Postmortem (1)
Raining Blood (1,4)
Read Between The Lies (2)
Reborn (1)
Seasons In The Abyss (3,4)
Silent Scream (2)
Skeletons Of Society (3)
South Of Heaven (2,4)
Spill The Blood (2)
Spirit In Black (3,4)
Temptation (3)
War Ensemble (3,4)

SLEDGE, Percy

Born in 1941 in Leighton, Alabama. Worked local clubs with Esquires Combo until going solo.

DEBUT DATE	PEAK POS	WKS CHR	GOLD	ARTIST — Album Title	$	Label & Number
6/4/66	37	21		1 When A Man Loves A Woman	$25	Atlantic 8125
11/26/66	136	3		2 Warm & Tender Soul	$25	Atlantic 8132
8/5/67	178	3		3 The Percy Sledge Way	$20	Atlantic 8146
5/25/68	148	6		4 Take Time To Know Her	$15	Atlantic 8180
3/1/69	133	11		5 The Best Of Percy Sledge ....[G]	$12	Atlantic 8210

Baby, Help Me (4,5) 87
Between These Arms (4)
Come Softly To Me (4)
Cover Me (4,5) 42
Dark End Of The Street (3,5)
Drown In My Own Tears (3)
Feed The Flame (4)
Heart Of A Child (2)
High Cost Of Leaving (4)
I Had A Talk With My Woman (3)
I Love Everything About You (4)
I Stand Accused (2)
I'm Hanging Up My Heart For You (2)
I've Been Loving You Too Long (To Stop Now) (3)
It Tears Me Up (2,5) 20
It's All Wrong But It's Alright (4)
Just Out Of Reach (Of My Two Empty Arms) (3,5) 66
Love Makes The World Go Round (1)
Love Me All The Way (1)
Love Me Like You Mean It (1)
Love Me Tender (2) 40
My Adorable One (1)
My Special Prayer (3,5) 93
Oh How Happy (2)
Out Of Left Field (4,5) 59
Pledging My Love (3)
Put A Little Lovin' On Me (1)
So Much Love (2)
Spooky (4)
Success (1)
Sudden Stop (4,5) 63
Sweet Woman Like You (2)
Take Time To Know Her (4,5) 11
Tell It Like It Is (3)
That's How Strong My Love Is (2)
Thief In The Night (1)
Try A Little Tenderness (2)
Warm And Tender Love (2,5) 17
What Am I Living For (3) 91
When A Man Loves A Woman (1,5) 1
When She Touches Me (Nothing Else Matters) (1)
You Don't Miss Your Water (3)
You Fooled Me (1)
You Send Me (1)
You're All Around Me (5)
You're Pouring Water On A Drowning Man (1)
You've Really Got A Hold On Me (2)

SLEEZE BEEZ

Dutch hard-rock quintet formed by drummer Jan Koster. Lead vocals by Andrew Elt.

DEBUT DATE	PEAK POS	WKS CHR	GOLD	ARTIST — Album Title	$	Label & Number
5/19/90	115	15		Screwed Blued & Tattooed	$12	Atlantic 82069

Damned If We Do, Damned If We Don't
Don't Talk About Roses
Girls Girls, Nasty Nasty
Heroes Die Young
House Is On Fire
Rock In The Western World
Screwed Blued 'N Tattooed
Stranger Than Paradise
This Time
When The Brains Go To The Balls

SLICK, Grace

Born Grace Wing on 10/30/39 in Chicago. Female lead singer of Jefferson Airplane/Starship. Prior to joining Jefferson Airplane, she was a member of The Great Society.

DEBUT DATE	PEAK POS	WKS CHR	GOLD	ARTIST — Album Title	$	Label & Number
5/4/68	166	4		1 Conspicuous Only In Its Absence ....[E-L]	$20	Columbia 9624
				THE GREAT SOCIETY with GRACE SLICK recorded in 1965		
12/25/71+	89	9		2 Sunfighter	$10	Grunt 1002
				PAUL KANTNER/GRACE SLICK with Jerry Garcia, David Crosby and Graham Nash; LP cover features Kantner and Slick's baby daughter, China		
6/23/73	120	12		3 Baron von Tollbooth & The Chrome Nun	$10	Grunt 0148
				PAUL KANTNER, GRACE SLICK & DAVID FREIBERG		
2/9/74	127	7		4 Manhole	$10	Grunt 0347
				with David Crosby and members of Jefferson Starship		
4/5/80	32	16		5 Dreams	$8	RCA 3544
2/14/81	48	14		6 Welcome To The Wrecking Ball!	$8	RCA 3851

Across The Board (3)
Angel Of Night (5)
Arbitration (1)
Ballad Of The Chrome Man (3)
Better Lying Down (4)
China (2)
¿Come Again? Toucan (4)
Diana - Part 1 & 2 (2)
Didn't Think So (1)
Do It The Hard Way (5)
Dreams (5)
Earth Mother (2)
El Diablo (5)
Epic (#38) (4)
Face To The Wind (5)
Fat (5)
Father Bruce (1)
Fishman (3)
Flowers Of The Night (3)
Full Moon Man (5)
Garden Of Man (5)
Grimly Forming (1)
Harp Tree Lament (3)
Holding Together (2)
It's Only Music (4)
Jay (4)
Just A Little Love (6)
Let It Go (5)
Lines (6)
Look At The Wood (2)
Million (2)
Mistreater (6)
No More Heroes (6)
Often As I May (1)
Outlaw Blues (1)
Right Kind (6)
Round & Round (6)
Sally Go 'Round The Roses (1)
Sea Of Love (6)
Seasons (5) 95
Shooting Star (6)
Shot In The Dark (6)
Silver Spoon (2)
Sketches Of China (3)
Somebody To Love (1)
Sunfighter (2)
Titanic (2)
Universal Copernican Mumbles (2)
Walkin (3)
When I Was A Boy I Watched The Wolves (2)
White Boy (Transcaucasian Airmachine Blues) (3)
White Rabbit (1)
Wrecking Ball (6)
Your Mind Has Left Your Body (3)

SLICK RICK

Ricky Walters, born to Jamaican parents in South Wimbledon, London. To the U.S. at age 14. Attended New York's High School of Music & Art. Teamed with Doug E. Fresh, 1984-85; known as "MC Ricky D."

DEBUT DATE	PEAK POS	WKS CHR	GOLD	ARTIST — Album Title	$	Label & Number
1/21/89	31	40	▲	1 The Great Adventures Of Slick Rick	$8	Def Jam 40513
7/20/91	29	13		2 The Ruler's Back	$12	Def Jam 47372

Bond (2)
Children's Story (1)
Hey Young World (1)
I Shouldn't Have Done It (2)
Indian Girl (An Adult Story) (1)
It's A Boy (2)
King (2)
Kit (What's The Scoop) (1)
Let's Get Crazy (1)
Lick The Balls (1)
Mistakes Of A Woman In Love With Other Men (2)
Moment I Feared (1)
Mona Lisa (1)
Moses (1)
Ruler's Back (1)
Runaway (2)
Ship (2)
Slick Rick-The Ruler (2)
Teacher, Teacher (1)
Teenage Love (1)
Tonto (2)
Top Cat (2)
Treat Her Like A Prostitute (1)
Venus (2)

DEBUT DATE	PEAK POS	WKS CHR	GOLD	ARTIST — Album Title	$	Label & Number

★★345★★ SLY & THE FAMILY STONE

San Francisco interracial "psychedelic soul" group formed by Sylvester "Sly Stone" Stewart (b: 3/15/44, Dallas; lead singer, keyboards), Sly's brother Freddie Stone (guitar), Cynthia Robinson (trumpet), Jerry Martini (saxophone), Sly's sister Rosie Stone (piano, vocals), Sly's cousin Larry Graham (bass) and Gregg Errico (drums). Sly recorded gospel at age four. Producer and writer for Bobby Freeman, the Mojo Men, the Beau Brummels. Formed own groups, The Stoners in 1966 and the Family Stone in 1967. Worked Woodstock Festival in 1969. Career waned in the mid-1970s. Worked with George Clinton in 1982. Graham formed Graham Central Station in 1973. Group inducted into the Rock and Roll Hall of Fame in 1993.

5/4/68	142	7		1 Dance To The Music	$15	Epic 26371
12/7/68	195	5		2 Life	$15	Epic 26397
4/26/69	13	102	▲	3 Stand!	$12	Epic 26456
11/7/70	2¹	79	▲³	4 Greatest Hits	[G] $10	Epic 30325
11/13/71	1²	31	●	5 There's A Riot Goin' On	$10	Epic 30986
6/30/73	7	33	●	6 Fresh	$10	Epic 32134
7/27/74	15	15	●	7 Small Talk	$8	Epic 32930
11/8/75	45	10		8 High On You	$8	Epic 33835

SLY STONE

| 11/10/79 | 152 | 3 | | 9 Back On The Right Track | $8 | Warner 3303 |

Africa Talks To You "The Asphalt Jungle" (5)
Are You Ready (1)
Babies Makin' Babies (6)
Back On The Right Track (9)
Better Thee Than Me (7)
Brave & Strong (5)
Can't Strain My Brain (7)
Chicken (2)
Color Me True (1)
Crossword Puzzle (8)
Dance To The Medley (1)
Dance To The Music (1,4) 8
Don't Burn Baby (1)
Don't Call Me Nigger, Whitey (3)
Dynamite! (2)
Everybody Is A Star (4) flip

Everyday People (3,4) 1
Family Affair (5) 1
Frisky (6) 79
Fun (2,4)
Greed (8)
Green Eyed Monster Girl (8)
Harmony (4)
Higher (1)
Holdin' On (7)
Hot Fun In The Summertime (4) 2
I Ain't Got Nobody (For Real) (6)
I Don't Know (Satisfaction) (6)
I Get High On You (8) 52
I Want To Take You Higher (3,4) 38

I'm An Animal (2)
If It Were Left Up To Me (6)
If It's Not Addin' Up... (9)
If You Want Me To Stay (6) 12
In Time (6)
Into My Own Thing (2)
It Takes All Kinds (9)
Jane Is A Groupee (2)
Just Like A Baby (5)
Keep On Dancin' (4)
Le Lo Li (8)
Let Me Have It All (6)
Life (2,4) 93
Livin' While I'm Livin' (7)
Loose Booty (7) 84
Love City (2)
Luv N' Haight (5)

M'Lady (2,4) 93
Mother Beautiful (7)
My World (8)
Never Will I Fall In Love Again (1)
Organize (8)
Plastic Jim (2)
Poet (5)
Que Sera, Sera (Whatever Will Be, Will Be) (6)
Remember Who You Are (9)
Ride The Rhythm (1)
Runnin' Away (5) 23
Same Thing (Makes You Laugh, Makes You Cry) (9)
Say You Will (7)
Sex Machine (3)
Sheer Energy (9)

Shine It On (9)
Sing A Simple Song (3,4) 89
Skin I'm In (6)
Small Talk (7)
So Good To Me (8)
Somebody's Watching You (3)
Spaced Cowboy (5)
Stand! (3,4) 22
Thank You (Falettinme Be Mice Elf Agin) (4) 1
Thank You For Talkin' To Me Africa (5)
Thankful N' Thoughtful (6)
That's Lovin' You (8)
There's A Riot Goin' On (5)
This Is Love (7)
Time (5)

Time For Livin' (7) 32
Who Do You Love? (8)
Who's To Say? (9)
Wishful Thinkin' (7)
You Can Make It If You Try (3,4)
(You Caught Me) Smilin' (5)

SLY FOX

Black-and-white duo: Gary "Mudbone" Cooper (P-Funk) and Michael Camacho.

| 3/1/86 | 31 | 22 | | Let's Go All The Way | $8 | Capitol 12367 |

Como Tu Te Llama? (What Is Your Name)
Don't Play With Fire
I Still Remember

If Push Comes To A Shove
Let's Go All The Way 7

Merry-Go-Round
Stay True 94

Won't Let You Go (A Wedding Song)

SMALL, Millie

Born Millicent Smith on 10/6/46 in Jamaica. Nicknamed "The Blue Beat Girl."

| 8/8/64 | 132 | 5 | | My Boy Lollipop | $30 | Smash 67055 |

Bluey Louey
Don't You Know

He's Mine
I'm In Love Again

My Boy Lollipop 2
Oh, Henry

Since You've Been Gone
Sugar Dandy

Sweet William 40
Tom Hark

Until You're Mine
What Am I Living For

SMALL FACES

British rock quartet: Steve Marriott (guitar), Ronnie Lane (bass), Ian McLagen (organ) and Kenney Jones (drums). In 1968, Marriott formed Humble Pie. Remaining members evolved into Faces in 1969; disbanded in 1975. Jones joined The Who in 1978, formed The Law in 1991. Marriott died in a fire on 4/20/91 (age 44).

3/16/68	178	3		1 There Are But Four Small Faces	$25	Immediate 52002
9/21/68	159	9		2 Ogdens' Nut Gone Flake	$20	Immediate 52008
				features a round album cover		
8/5/72	176	10		3 Early Faces	[E] $10	Pride 0001
3/17/73	189	6		4 Ogdens' Nut Gone Flake	[R] $8	Abkco 4225
				new cover is nearly identical to original, inside a square sleeve		

Afterglow (2,4)
Come Back And Take This Hurt Off Me (3)
Get Yourself Together (1)
Green Circles (1)
Happiness Stan (2,4)
Happydaystoytown (2,4)
Here Come The Nice (1)

Hey Girl (3)
Hungry Intruder (2,4)
I Feel Much Better (1)
I Got Mine (1)
I'm Only Dreaming (1)
Itchycoo Park (1) 16
Journey, The (2,4)
Lazy Sunday (2,4)

Long Agos And Worlds Apart (2,4)
Mad John (2,4)
My Mind's Eye (3)
My Way Of Giving (1)
Ogdens' Nut Gone Flake (2,4)
Rene (2,4)
Rollin' Over (2,4)

Runaway (3)
Sha La La La Lee (3)
Shake (3)
Show Me The Way (1)
Song Of A Baker (2,4)
Sorry She's Mine (3)
Talk To You (1)

(Tell Me) Have You Ever Seen Me (1)
Tin Soldier (1) 73
Up The Wooden Hills (1)
What's The Matter Baby (3)
Whatcha Gonna Do About It (3)

SMASHING PUMPKINS

Alternative band formed in Chicago by singer/guitarist Billy Corgan, James Iha (guitar), D'Arcy (bass) and Jimmy Chamberlain (drums).

| 9/7/91 | 195 | 1 | | Gish | $12 | Caroline 1705 |

Bury Me
Crush

Daydream
Fristessa

I Am One
Rhinoceros

Siva
Snail

Suffer
Window Paine

SMITH

Los Angeles-based rock quintet fronted by St. Louis blues rocker Gayle McCormick.

| 8/23/69 | 17 | 28 | | 1 a group called Smith | $12 | Dunhill 50056 |
| 7/4/70 | 74 | 12 | | 2 Minus-Plus | $12 | Dunhill 50081 |

Baby It's You (1) 5
Born In Boston (2)
Circle Man (2)
Comin' Back To Me (1)

Feel The Magic (2)
I Don't Believe (I Believe) (1)
I Just Wanna Make Love To You (1)

I'll Hold Out My Hand (1)
Jason (2)
Last Time (1)
Let's Get Together (1)

Let's Spend The Night Together (1)
Minus-Plus (2)
Mojaleskey Ridge (1)

Since You've Been Gone (2)
Take A Look Around (2) 43
Tell Him No (1)
What Am I Gonna Do (2) 73

Who Do You Love (1)
You Don't Love Me (Yes I Know) (2)

SMITH, Cal

Born Calvin Grant Shofner on 4/7/32 in Gans, Oklahoma and raised in Oakland. Country singer/guitarist. Worked with Ernest Tubb from 1961-67.

| 9/6/69 | 170 | 2 | | 1 Cal Smith Sings | $12 | Kapp 3608 |

DEBUT DATE	PEAK POS	WKS CHR	G O L D	ARTIST — Album Title	$	Label & Number

SMITH, Cal — Cont'd

4/14/73 · 191 · 3 — 2 I've Found Someone Of My Own .... **$10** Decca 75369

At The Sight Of You (1)	Handful Of Stars (2)	I've Found Someone Of My	Lord Knows I'm Drinking	She's Lookin' Better By The	Sweet Things I Remember
Ballad Of Forty Dollars (1,2)	I Come Home A Drinkin' (1)	Own (2)	(2) 64	Minute (1)	About You (2)
Darling, You Know I	I Don't Get No Better	It Takes Me All Night Long	Margie's At The Lincoln Park	(Sittin' On) The Dock Of The	That's What It's Like To Be
Wouldn't Lie (1)	Without You (1)	(1)	Inn (1)	Bay (2)	Lonesome (2)
Empty Arms (2)	I Love You More Today (2)	Life Of The Party Charlie (1)	Old Faithful (1)	Song Sung Blue (2)	When Two Worlds Collide (1)
For My Baby (2)					

SMITH, Connie

Country singer. Born Constance June Meadows on 8/14/41 in Elkhart, Indiana. Raised in West Virginia and Ohio.

5/22/65 · 105 · 5 — Connie Smith .... **$15** RCA 3341

Darling, Are You Ever	Hinges On The Door	I'm Ashamed Of You	Once A Day	Tell Another Lie	Threshold, The
Coming Home	I Don't Love You Anymore	It's Just My Luck	Other Side Of You	Then And Only Then	Tiny Blue Transistor Radio
Don't Forget (I Still Love You)					

SMITH, Frankie

Philadelphia native. Wrote and produced for Philadelphia Int'l. in the late 1970s, and later for WMOT.

8/8/81 · 54 · 10 — Children Of Tomorrow .... **$8** WMOT 37391

Auction, The	Double Dutch	Hand Bone	Slang Thang (Slizang	Teeny-Bopper Lady
Children Of Tomorrow	**Double Dutch Bus 30**		Thizang)	Triple Dutch

SMITH, Hurricane

Born Norman Smith in northern England in 1923. Vocalist/producer/engineer/session musician. Produced early Pink Floyd albums and did some engineering for The Beatles.

1/6/73 · 53 · 18 — Hurricane Smith .... **$10** Capitol 1139

Auntie Vi's	Getting To Know You	Oh, Babe, What Would You	Theme From An Unmade	Who Was It? 49
Back In The Country	Many Happy Returns	Say? 3	Silent Movie	Wonderful Lily
Don't Let It Die		Take Suki Home		

SMITH, Jerry, and his Pianos

Session pianist. Wrote and performed on The Dixiebelles' "(Down At) Papa Joe's."

7/26/69 · 200 · 2 — Truck Stop .... [I] **$10** ABC 692

I'll Always Be In Love With	My Happiness	Smokey Corners	Street Singers (Y Cantanti	Sunrise Serenade	Tokyo Butterfly
You	Pretend	Speakeasy (1929)	Della Strada	Sweet 'N Sassy	**Truck Stop 71**

★★98★★ SMITH, Jimmy

Born on 12/8/25 in Norristown, Pennsylvania. Pioneer jazz organist. Won Major Bowes Amateur Show in 1934. With father (James, Sr.) in song-and-dance team, 1942. With Don Gardner & The Sonotones, recorded for Bruce in 1953. Smith first recorded with own trio for Blue Note in 1956.

DEBUT DATE	PEAK POS	WKS CHR	#	ARTIST — Album Title	$	Label & Number
2/17/62	28	51	1	Midnight Special [I] with Stanley Turrentine (sax) and Kenny Burrell (guitar)	$25	Blue Note 84078
6/2/62	10	34	2	Bashin' [I]	$25	Verve 8474
3/9/63	14	22	3	Back At The Chicken Shack [I] with Stanley Turrentine and Kenny Burrell	$25	Blue Note 84117
5/18/63	11	30	4	Hobo Flats [I]	$25	Verve 8544
11/9/63	25	33	5	Any Number Can Win [I]	$25	Verve 8552
11/9/63	64	8	6	Rockin' The Boat [E-I] with Lou Donaldson (alto sax)	$25	Blue Note 84141
11/30/63	108	4	7	Blue Bash! [I] KENNY BURRELL/JIMMY SMITH	$25	Verve 8553
4/18/64	16	31	8	Who's Afraid Of Virginia Woolf? [I]	$20	Verve 8583
8/1/64	86	20	9	Prayer Meetin' [E-I] with Stanley Turrentine (tenor sax)	$20	Blue Note 84164
9/19/64	12	32	10	The Cat [I]	$20	Verve 8587
5/8/65	35	24	11	Monster [I]	$20	Verve 8618
9/18/65	15	31	12	Organ Grinder Swing [I] featuring Kenny Burrell (guitar) and Grady Tate (drums)	$20	Verve 8628
3/12/66	28	27	13	Got My Mojo Workin' [I]	$20	Verve 8641
9/10/66	77	14	14	Hoochie Cooche Man [I]	$20	Verve 8667
11/12/66	121	9	15	"Bucket"! [E-I]	$20	Blue Note 84235
5/20/67	129	23	16	Jimmy & Wes The Dynamic Duo [I] JIMMY SMITH & WES MONTGOMERY	$20	Verve 8678
10/7/67	60	20	17	Respect [I]	$20	Verve 8705
12/9/67	185	4	18	The Best Of Jimmy Smith [G-I]	$20	Verve 8721
6/8/68	128	4	19	Jimmy Smith's Greatest Hits! [G-I]	$15	Blue Note 89901 [2
10/26/68	169	10	20	Livin' It Up! [I]	$15	Verve 8750
7/26/69	144	3	21	The Boss [I] featuring George Benson (guitar)	$15	Verve 8770
5/23/70	197	3	22	Groove Drops [I]	$12	Verve 8794

Ain't That Just Like A	Blue Bash (7)	By The Time I Get To	Delon's Blues (10)	**Got My Mojo Working**	I'm An Old Cowhand (From
Woman (14)	Blueberry Hill (4)	Phoenix (22)	Down By The Riverside (16)	**(Part I)** (13,18) 51	The Rio Grande) (14)
All Day Long (19)	Blues And The Abstract	C Jam Blues (13)	Easy Living (7)	Greensleeves (12)	**I'm Your Hoochie Cooche**
Any Number Can Win,	Truth (14)	Can Heat (6,19)	Fever (7)	Groove Drops (22)	**Man (Part 1)** (14,18) 94
Theme From (5) 96	Blues For C.A. (5)	Careless Love (15)	Fingers (21)	High Heel Sneakers (13,18)	In A Mellow Tone (10)
Ape Women (5)	Blues For Del (7)	Carpetbaggers, Main Title	Flamingo (19)	**Hobo Flats - Part 1**	James And Wes (16)
Baby, It's Cold Outside (16)	Blues For J (12)	From The (10)	Funky Broadway (17)	(4,18) 69	John Brown's Body (8,15)
Back At The Chicken	Blues In The Night (10)	**Cat, The** (10,18) 67	G'won Train (5)	Hobson's Hop (13)	Johnny Come Lately (13)
Shack, Part 1 (3) 63	Bluesette (8)	Champ, The (19)	Gentle Rain (20)	I Almost Lost My Mind (9)	Joy House, Theme From (17)
Bashin' (2)	Boom Boom (14)	Chicago Serenade (10)	Georgia On My Mind (5)	(I Can't Get No) Satisfaction	Jumpin' The Blues (1)
Basin Street Blues (10)	Boss, The (21)	Come Rain Or Come Shine	Get Out Of My Life (17)	(13)	Just A Closer Walk With
Beggar For The Blues (2)	Bucket (15)	(15)	Gloomy Sunday (11)	I Can't Stop Loving You (4)	Thee (6)
Bewitched, Theme From (11)	Burning Spear (20)	Creeper, The (11)	Go Away Little Girl (20)	I'll Close My Eyes (12)	Just Squeeze Me (15)
Big Boss Man (20)		Days Of Wine And Roses (22)	Goldfinger (Part I & II) (11)		Kenny's Sound (7)

DEBUT DATE	PEAK POS	WKS CHR	GOLD	ARTIST — Album Title	$	Label & Number

SMITH, Jimmy — Cont'd

Livin' It Up (20)
Man With The Golden Arm, Theme From The (11)
Matilda, Matilda! (6)
Meditation (4)
Mercy, Mercy, Mercy (17)
Messy Bessie (3)
Midnight Special, Part 1 (1,19) **69**
Minor Chant (3)
Mission: Impossible (20)
Monlope (11)
Munsters, Theme From The (11)
Mustard Greens (13)

Night Train (16)
Ode To Billy Joe (22)
Oh, No, Babe (12)
Ol' Man River (2,18) **82**
One Mint Julep (14)
One O'Clock Jump (1)
1-2-3 (13)
Organ Grinder's Swing (12,18) **92**
Picknickin' (9)
Please Send Me Someone To Love (6)
Pork Chop (6)
Prayer Meetin' (9,19)
Preacher, The (4)

Red Top (9)
Refractions (20)
Respect (17)
Ruby (9)
Sassy Mae (15)
Satin Doll (5)
Sermon, The (5,19)
Slaughter On Tenth Avenue (8)
Soft Winds (7)
Some Of My Best Friends Are Blues (21)
St. James Infirmary (11)
St. Louis Blues (17)
Step Right Up (2)

Stone Cold Dead In The Market (9)
Subtle One (1)
Sunny (22)
T-Bone Steak (17)
TNT (14)
13 (Death March) (16)
This Guy's In Love With You (21)
This Nearly Was Mine (20)
3 For 4 (15)
Travelin' (7)
Trouble In Mind (4)
Trust In Me (6)
Tubs (5)

Tuxedo Junction (21)
Valley Of The Dolls (20)
Walk On The Wild Side - Part 1 (2,18) **21**
Walk Right In (2)
What'd I Say? (5)
When I Grow Too Old To Dream (3)
When Johnny Comes Marching Home (19)
When My Dream Boat Comes Home (6)
When The Saints Go Marching In (9)

Who Can I Turn To (When Nobody Needs Me) (22)
Who's Afraid Of Virginia Woolf? (8) **72**
Why Was I Born (1)
Wives And Lovers (8)
Women Of The World (8)
You Came A Long Way From St. Louis (5)

SMITH, Kate

Born on 5/1/07 in Greenville, Alabama; died on 6/17/86. Tremendously popular soprano who was for years one of the most-listened-to of all radio singers. Later hosted own TV variety series, 1951-52, 1960. Kate introduced the classic Irving Berlin hit "God Bless America."

DEBUT DATE	PEAK POS	WKS CHR	GOLD	ARTIST — Album Title	$	Label & Number
12/21/63+	83	18		1 Kate Smith at Carnegie Hall .... [L]	$12	RCA 2819
10/31/64	145	2		2 The Sweetest Sounds	$12	RCA 2921
1/15/66	36	24		3 How Great Thou Art	$12	RCA 3445
6/25/66	130	3		4 The Kate Smith Anniversary Album	$12	RCA 3535
				medleys of songs she introduced on radio		
12/3/66	148	2		5 Kate Smith Today	$12	RCA 3670

All The Things You Are (medley) (4)
Along The Santa Fe Trail (medley) (4)
As Long As He Needs Me (1)
Ballad Of The Green Berets (5)
Beautiful Isle Of Somewhere (3)
Carolina Moon (medley) (1)
Daydream (5)
Days Of Wine And Roses (4)
Deep Purple (medley) (4)
Dr. Zhivago ..see: Lara's Theme
Don't Blame Me (medley) (1)
Don't Fence Me In (medley) (4)
Don't Sit Under The Apple Tree (With Anyone Else But Me) (medley) (4)

Don't Take Your Love From Me (medley) (4)
Fine And Dandy (medley) (1)
God Bless America (medley) (1)
He Loves Me (2)
How Are Things In Glocca Morra (medley) (4)
How Deep Is The Ocean (1)
How Great Thou Art (3)
I Asked The Lord (3)
I Didn't Know What Time It Was (medley) (4)
I Do, I Do (5)
I Left My Heart In San Francisco (2)
I May Never Pass This Way Again (3)
I See God (3)
I Wanna Be Around (2)
I Wish You Love (2)

I'll Be Seeing You (1)
If Ever I Would Leave You (2)
If He Walked Into My Life (5)
Impossible Dream (The Quest) (5)
It Is No Secret (What God Can Do) (3)
It Took A Miracle (3)
Just In Time (2)
Lara's Theme (5)
Lollipops And Roses (2)
Long Ago (And Far Away) (medley) (4)
Lord's Prayer (3)
Make Someone Happy (2)
Margie (medley) (1)
May The Good Lord Bless And Keep You (3)
Mondo Cane ..see: More
Moon River (1)
More (2)

My Best Beau (My Best Girl) (5)
My Coloring Book (2)
A Nightingale Sang In Berkeley Square (medley) (4)
Old Lamplighter (medley) (4)
On A Clear Day (You Can See Forever) (5)
Once In A While (medley) (4)
Please (medley) (1)
Sandpiper, Love Theme From The ..see: Shadow Of Your Smile
Seems Like Old Times (medley) (4)
September In The Rain (medley) (4)
Shadow Of Your Smile (5)
Some Sunday Morning (1)

Somebody Else Is Taking My Place (medley) (4)
Somewhere, My Love ..see: Lara's Theme
Strangers In The Night (5)
Sweetest Sounds (4)
Symphony (medley) (4)
That Old Feeling (medley) (4)
There Goes That Song Again (medley) (4)
(There'll Be Blue Birds Over) The White Cliffs Of Dover (medley) (4)
This Is All I Ask (1)
Touch Of His Hand On Mine (3)
Until Then (3)
Were You There? (3)
What Kind Of Fool Am I? (1)
What's New (medley) (4)

When The Moon Comes Over The Mountain (medley) (1,4)
When Your Lover Has Gone (medley) (1)
Who Can I Turn To (When Nobody Needs Me) (5)
Who Cares (medley) (1)
Wrap Your Troubles In Dreams (And Dream Your Troubles Away) (medley) (4)
Yesterday (5)
You'd Be So Nice To Come Home To (medley) (4)

SMITH, Kathy — see AEROBICS section

SMITH, Keely

Born Dorothy Smith on 3/9/32 in Norfolk, Virginia. Jazz-styled vocalist. Married to singer/trumpeter/ bandleader Louis Prima, 1952-61; they recorded as a successful duo. Also see Louis Prima.

DEBUT DATE	PEAK POS	WKS CHR	GOLD	ARTIST — Album Title	$	Label & Number
10/20/58	14	8		1 Politely!	$25	Capitol 1073
5/25/59	23	9		2 Swingin' Pretty	$25	Capitol 1145
1/4/60	40	1		3 Be My Love	$25	Dot 3241

All The Way (1)
Be My Love (3)
Cocktails For Two (1)
Don't Let The Stars Get In Your Eyes (3)
East Of The Sun (And West Of The Moon) (1)
Fascination (3)
How Deep Is The Ocean (3)

I Can't Get Started (1)
I Never Knew (I Could Love Anybody Like I'm Loving You) (1)
I'd Climb The Highest Mountain (1)
I'll Get By (As Long As I Have You) (1)
I'll Never Smile Again (1)

I'm Gonna Sit Right Down And Write Myself A Letter (3)
Indian Love Call (2)
It's All In The Game (3)
It's Been A Long, Long Time (2)
It's Magic (2)
Lullaby Of The Leaves (1)

Man I Love (2)
My Reverie (3)
Nearness Of You (2)
On The Sunny Side Of The Street (1)
Pretend (3)
S'posin' (1)
Smoke Gets In Your Eyes (3)

Someone To Watch Over Me (2)
Song Is You (1)
Stardust (2)
Stormy Weather (2)
Sweet And Lovely (1)
There Will Never Be Another You (2)

What Can I Say After I Say I'm Sorry (2)
What Is This Thing Called Love? (2)
You Made Me Love You (3)
You're Driving Me Crazy (3)
You're Nobody 'Til Somebody Loves You (3)

SMITH, Lonnie

Jazz organist.

DEBUT DATE	PEAK POS	WKS CHR	GOLD	ARTIST — Album Title	$	Label & Number
5/16/70	186	2		Move Your Hand .... [I-L]	$12	Blue Note 84326

Charlie Brown
Layin' In The Cut
Move Your Hand
Sunshine Superman

SMITH, Lonnie Liston

Born on 12/28/40 in Richmond, Virginia. Keyboardist/trumpeter/tuba. With Art Blakey's Jazz Messengers in 1965, Roland Kirk, Pharoah Sanders, Norman Connors, Stanley Turrentine and Gato Barbieri. With Miles Davis from 1972-73. Formed own group, the Cosmic Echoes.

LONNIE LISTON SMITH & THE COSMIC ECHOES:

DEBUT DATE	PEAK POS	WKS CHR	GOLD	ARTIST — Album Title	$	Label & Number
5/24/75	85	13		1 Expansions	$10	Flying Dtch. 0934
10/18/75	74	15		2 Visions Of A New World	$10	Flying Dtch. 1196
4/10/76	75	14		3 Reflections Of A Golden Dream	$10	Flying Dtch. 1460
12/11/76+	73	20		4 Renaissance	$8	RCA 1822

LONNIE LISTON SMITH:

DEBUT DATE	PEAK POS	WKS CHR	GOLD	ARTIST — Album Title	$	Label & Number
7/30/77	58	11		5 Live! .... [I-L]	$8	RCA 2433
4/22/78	120	13		6 Loveland	$8	Columbia 35332
2/17/79	123	8		7 Exotic Mysteries	$8	Columbia 35654
7/30/83	193	2		8 Dreams Of Tomorrow	$8	Doctor Jazz 38447

Donald Smith (Lonnie's brother), lead vocalist on above albums.

SMITH, Lonnie Liston — Cont'd

Beautiful Woman (3)
Between Here And There (4)
Bright Moments (6)
Chance For Peace (2)
Colors Of The Rainbow (2)
Desert Nights (1)
Devika (Goddess) (2)
Divine Light (8)
Dreams Of Tomorrow (8)
Exotic Mysteries (7)

Expansions (1,5)
Explorations (6)
Floating Through Space (6)
Garden Of Peace (8)
Get Down Everybody (It's Time For World Peace) (3)
Goddess Of Love (3)
Golden Dreams (3)
Inner Beauty (3)
Journey Into Love (6)

Journey Into Space (3)
Lonely Way To Be (8)
Love Beams (2)
Love I See In Your Eyes (8)
Loveland (6)
Magical Journey (7)
Mardi Gras (Carnival) (4)
Meditations (3)
Mongotee (4)
My Love (1,5)

Mystic Woman (8)
Mystical Dreamer (A Tribute To Miles Davis) (7)
Never Too Late (8)
Night Flower (7)
Peace (1)
Peace & Love (3)
Quiet Dawn (3)
Quiet Moments (7)
Rainbows Of Love (8)

Renaissance (4)
Shadows (1)
Singing For Love (7)
Song Of Love (4)
Sorceress (5)
Space Lady (4)
Space Princess (7)
Springtime Magic (6)
Starlight And You (4)
Summer Days (3)

Summer Nights (3)
Sunbeams (3)
Sunburst (6)
Sunset (2,5)
Twilight (7)
Visions Of A New World (Phase I & II) (2,5)
Voodoo Woman (1)
Watercolors (5)
We Can Dream (6)

SMITH, Michael W.

Contemporary Christian singer/keyboardist/songwriter from Kenova, West Virginia. To Nashville in 1978. Touring keyboardist for Amy Grant in 1982. Wrote Amy Grant's hits "Find A Way" and "Stay For Awhile."

| 6/8/91 | 74 | 19 | ● | 1 Go West Young Man .... | $12 | Reunion 24325 |
| 9/19/92 | 95 | 19 | ● | 2 Change Your World .... | $12 | Reunion 24491 |

due to a change in ownership of label, also available on Reunion 66163

Agnus Dei (1)
Color Blind (2)
Cross My Heart (1)
Cross Of Gold (2)
Emily (1)

For You (1) *60*
Friends (2)
Give It Away (2)
Go West Young Man (1)

How Long Will Be Too Long (1)
I Wanna Tell The World (1)
I Will Be Here For You (2) *27*

Love Crusade (1)
Love One Another (2)
1990 (1)
Out Of This World (2)
Picture Perfect (2)

Place In This World (1) *6*
Seed To Sow (1)
Somebody Love Me (2)
Somewhere Somehow (2)

SMITH, O.C.

Born Ocie Lee Smith on 6/21/36 in Mansfield, Louisiana. To Los Angeles in 1939. Sang while in U.S. Air Force from 1953-57. First recorded for Cadence in 1956. With Count Basie from 1961-63.

6/15/68	19	42		1 Hickory Holler Revisited	$12	Columbia 9680
3/1/69	50	15		2 For Once In My Life	$12	Columbia 9756
10/18/69	58	16		3 O.C. Smith At Home	$12	Columbia 9908
9/19/70	177	5		4 O.C. Smith's Greatest Hits .... [G]	$10	Columbia 30227
7/31/71	159	7		5 Help Me Make It Through The Night	$10	Columbia 30664

Best Man (1)
By The Time I Get To Phoenix (1)
Can't Take My Eyes Off You (3)
Clean Up Your Own Back Yard (3)
Color Him Father (3)
Cycles (2)
Daddy's Little Man (3,4) *34*

Diamond In The Rough (5)
Didn't We (3)
Empty Arms (5)
For Once In My Life (2)
For The Good Times (5)
Friend, Lover, Woman, Wife (2,4) *63*
Help Me Make It Through The Night (5) *91*
Hey Jude (2)

Honey (I Miss You) (1,4) *44*
House Next Door (1)
I Ain't The Worryin' Kind (2)
I Stop By Heaven (5)
If I Leave You Now (3)
Isn't It Lonely Together (2,4) *47*
Keep On Keepin' On (2)
Learning Tree (3)
Little Green Apples (1,4) *2*

Long Black Limousine (1)
Long Drive Home (5)
Main Street Mission (1,4)
Me And You (4)
Melodee (2)
Moody (4)
My Cherie Amour (3)
Primrose Lane (4) *86*
Promises (3)
Really Big Shoe (5)

Remembering (5)
San Francisco Is A Lonely Town (3)
Seven Days (1)
Sitting On The Dock Of The Bay (1)
Son Of Hickory Holler's Tramp (1,4) *40*
Sounds Of Goodbye (2)
Stormy (2)

Sweet Changes (3)
Take Time To Know Her (1)
Tall Oak Tree (5)
That's Life (4)
Watching Scotty Grow (5)
What You See (5)
Wichita Lineman (2)

SMITH, Patti, Group

Patti was born on 12/31/46 in Chicago; raised in New Jersey. Poet-turned-punk rocker. Married Fred "Sonic" Smith of the MC5.

12/13/75+	47	17		1 Horses *	$8	Arista 4066
11/27/76+	122	8		2 Radio Ethiopia	$8	Arista 4097
4/8/78	20	23		3 Easter	$8	Arista 4171
5/19/79	18	19		4 Wave	$8	Arista 4221
				produced by Todd Rundgren		
7/30/88	65	15		5 Dream Of Life *	$8	Arista 8453

*PATTI SMITH

Ain't It Strange (2)
Ask The Angels (2)
Babelogue (medley) (3)
Because The Night (3) *13*
Birdland (1)
Break It Up (1)
Broken Flag (4)
Citizen Ship (4)

Dancing Barefoot (4)
Distant Fingers (2)
Dream Of Life (5)
Easter (3)
Elegie (1)
Frederick (4) *90*
Free Money (1)
Ghost Dance (3)

Gloria Medley (1)
Going Under (5)
High On Rebellion (medley) (3)
Hymn (4)
Jackson Song (5)
Kimberly (1)
Land Medley (1)

Looking For You (I Was) (5)
Paths That Cross (5)
People Have The Power (5)
Pissing In A River (2)
Poppies (3)
Privilege (Set Me Free) (3)
Pumping (My Heart) (2)
Radio Ethiopia Medley (2)

Redondo Beach (1)
Revenge (4)
Rock N Roll Nigger (medley) (3)
Seven Ways Of Going (4)
So You Want To Be (A Rock 'N' Roll Star) (4)
Space Monkey (3)

Till Victory (3)
25th Floor (medley) (3)
Up There Down There (5)
Wave (4)
We Three (3)
Where Duty Calls (5)

SMITH, Rex

Born on 9/19/56 in Jacksonville, Florida. Vocalist/actor. Starred in several Broadway musicals and in the TV film *Sooner Or Later*. Appeared in films *The Pirates Of Penzance* and *Streethawk*. Younger brother of Starz's lead singer, Michael Lee Smith.

4/28/79	19	19	●	1 Sooner Or Later	$8	Columbia 35813
1/12/80	165	3		2 Forever, Rex Smith	$8	Columbia 36275
8/22/81	167	4		3 Everlasting Love	$8	Columbia 37494

Ain't That Peculiar (1)
All Or Nothing (2)
Better Than It's Ever Been Before (1)
Don't Go Believin' (3)
Everytime I See You (2)

Forever (2)
I Don't Want Your Love (Out Of My Life) (2)
If You Think You Know How To Love Me (1)
Let's Make A Memory (2)
Love Street (1)

Love Will Always Make You Cry (3)
Never Gonna Give You Up (1)
Oh Girl (3)
Oh What A Night For Romance (1)

Remember The Love Songs (3)
Rock Me Slowly (3)
Saturday Night (2)
Simply Jessie (1)
Sooner Or Later (1)
Still Thinking Of You (3)

Superhero (2)
Sway (1)
To You, To You! (Say Goodbye To You!) (2)
Tonight (2)
What Becomes Of The Brokenhearted (3)

Without You (2)
You Take My Breath Away (1) *10*

SMITH, Sammi

Born on 8/5/43 in Orange, California and raised in Oklahoma. Country singer. Moved to Nashville in 1967.

| 2/13/71 | 33 | 21 | | 1 Help Me Make It Through The Night .... | $10 | Mega 1000 |
| 8/21/71 | 191 | 2 | | 2 Lonesome .... | $10 | Mega 1007 |

But You Know I Love You (1)
Don't Blow No Smoke On Me (1)
Fire And Rain (2)
For The Kids (2)

Haven't You Heard (2)
He Makes It Hard To Say Goodbye (2)
He's Everywhere (1)

Help Me Make It Through The Night (1) *8*
Here's To Forever (2)
Jimmy's In Georgia (2)

Last Word In Lonesome Is Me (2)
Lonely Street (2)
Mr. Bojangles (2)
Saunders' Ferry Lane (1)

Sunday Mornin' Comin' Down (1)
Then You Walk In (2)
There He Goes (1)
This Room For Rent (1)

Weight, The (1)
When Michael Calls (1)
Willie (1)
With Pen In Hand (1)

DEBUT DATE	PEAK POS	WKS CHR	GOLD	ARTIST — Album Title	$	Label & Number

SMITHEREENS, The
New Jersey pop quartet formed in 1980: Pat DiNizio (vocals), Jim Babjak, Dennis Diken and Mike Mesaros.

DEBUT	PEAK	WKS			$	Label
8/16/86+	**51**	50		1 Especially For You	**$8**	Enigma 73208
4/9/88	**60**	31		2 Green Thoughts	**$8**	Capitol 48375
11/18/89+	**41**	38	●	3 11	**$8**	Enigma 91194
9/28/91	**120**	3		4 Blow Up	**$12**	Capitol 94963

Alone At Midnight (1)
Anywhere You Are (4)
Baby Be Good (3)
Behind The Wall Of Sleep (1)
Blood And Roses (1)
Blue Period (3)
Blues Before And After (3) *94*
Cigarette (4)
Crazy Mixed-Up Kid (1)
Cut Flowers (3)
Deep Black (2)
Drown In My Own Tears (4)
Elaine (2)
Especially For You (2)
Evening Dress (4)
Get A Hold Of My Heart (4)
Girl In Room 12 (4)
Girl Like You (3) *38*
Green Thoughts (2)
Groovy Tuesday (1)
Hand Of Glory (1)
House We Used To Live In (2)
I Don't Want To Lose You (1)
If The Sun Doesn't Shine (2)
If You Want The Sun To Shine (4)
In A Lonely Place (1)
Indigo Blues (4)
It's Alright (4)
Kiss Your Tears Away (3)
Listen To Me Girl (1)
Maria Elena (3)
Now And Then (4)
Only A Memory (2) *92*
Over And Over Again (4)
Room Without A View (3)
Something New (2)
Spellbound (2)
Strangers When We Meet (1)
Tell Me When Did Things Go So Wrong (4)
Time And Time Again (1)
Too Much Passion (4) *37*
Top Of The Pops (4)
William Wilson (3)
World We Know (2)
Yesterday Girl (3)

SMITHS, The
English quartet formed in 1982, led by vocalist Stephen Morrissey. Included Johnny Marr, Andy Rourke and Mike Joyce. Disbanded in August 1987. Marr later joined The The and Electronic. Morrissey went solo.

5/5/84	**150**	11		1 The Smiths	**$8**	Sire 25065
3/2/85	**110**	32		2 Meat Is Murder	**$8**	Sire 25269
7/19/86	**70**	37	●	3 The Queen Is Dead..	**$8**	Sire 25426
4/25/87	**62**	25	●	4 Louder Than Bombs...[K]	**$10**	Sire 25569 [2]

23-song collection of new, old and previously unavailable material

10/10/87	**55**	27	●	5 Strangeways, Here We Come	**$8**	Sire 25649
10/1/88	**77**	8		6 Rank ....[L]	**$8**	Sire 25786

recorded live at The National Ballroom, Kilburn in London, October 1986

10/17/92	**139**	3		7 Best...I ....[G]	**$12**	Sire 45042

Ask (4,6)
Asleep (4)
Back To The Old House (4)
Barbarism Begins At Home (2)
Bigmouth Strikes Again (3,6)
Boy With The Thorn In His Side (3,6)
Cemetry Gates (3,6)
Death At One's Elbow (5)
Death Of A Disco Dancer (5)
Draize Train (6)
Frankly, Mr. Shankly (3)
Girl Afraid (4)
Girlfriend In A Coma (5,7)
Golden Lights (4)
Half A Person (4,7)
Hand In Glove (1,4,7)
Hand That Rocks The Cradle (1)
Headmaster Ritual (2)
Heaven Knows I'm Miserable Now (4)
How Soon Is Now? (2,7)
I Don't Owe You Anything (1)
I Know It's Over (3,6)
I Started Something I Couldn't Finish (5)
I Want The One I Can't Have (2)
I Won't Share You (5)
Is It Really So Strange? (4,6)
Last Night I Dreamt That Somebody Loved Me (5)
London (4,6)
(Marie's The Name) His Latest Flame (medley) (6)
Meat Is Murder (2)
Miserable Lie (1)
Never Had No One Ever (3)
Nowhere Fast (4)
Oscillate Wildly (4)
Paint A Vulgar Picture (5)
Panic (4,6,7)
Please Please Please Let Me Get What I Want (4,7)
Pretty Girls Make Graves (1)
Queen Is Dead (3,6)
Reel Around The Fountain (1)
Rubber Ring (4,7)
Rush And A Push And The Land Is Ours (5)
Rusholme Ruffians (2,6)
Shakespeare's Sister (4)
Sheila Take A Bow (4,7)
Shoplifters Of The World Unite (4,7)
Some Girls Are Bigger Than Others (3,7)
Still Ill (1,6)
Stop Me If You Think You've Heard This One Before (5,7)
Stretch Out And Wait (4)
Suffer Little Children (1)
Sweet And Tender Hooligan (4)
Take Me Back To Dear Old Blighty (medley) (3)
That Joke Isn't Funny Anymore (2)
There Is A Light That Never Goes Out (3)
These Things Take Time (4)
This Charming Man (1,7)
This Night Has Opened My Eyes (4)
Unhappy Birthday (5)
Unloveable (4)
Vicar In A Tutu (3,6)
Well I Wonder (2)
What Difference Does It Make? (1,7)
What She Said (2,6)
William, It Was Really Nothing (4,7)
You Just Haven't Earned It Yet, Baby (4)
You've Got Everything Now (1)

SMOKESTACK LIGHTNIN'
White blues quartet — Ronnie Darling, lead singer.

4/12/69	**200**	2		Off The Wall	**$15**	Bell 6026

I Idolize You
Light In My Window
Long Stemmed Eyes (John's Song)
Smokestack Lightnin'
Something's Got A Hold On Me
Three Hundred Pounds Of Heavenly Joy
Watch Your Step
Well Tuesday
Who's Been Talkin'

SMOKIE
British pop-rock quartet: Chris Norman (lead singer), Alan Silson (guitar), Terry Utley (bass) and Pete Spencer (drums).

1/22/77	**173**	6		Midnight Cafe	**$8**	RSO 3005

I'm Going Home
If You Think You Know How To Love Me *96*
Living Next Door To Alice *25*
Make Ya Boogie
Poor Lady
Something's Been Making Me Blue
Stranger
When My Back Was Against The Wall
Wild, Wild Angels

★★310★★ SMOTHERS BROTHERS, The
Comedians Tom (b: 2/2/37; guitar) and Dick Smothers (b: 11/20/39; standup bass), both born in New York City. Hosts of their own TV comedy variety series from 1967-69. Own summer variety series, 1970; '88-89.

10/20/62	**26**	66	●	1 The Two Sides Of The Smothers Brothers..........................[C]	**$20**	Mercury 20675

side 1: comedy; side 2: serious singing

4/6/63+	**27**	63	●	2 (Think Ethnic!)...[C]	**$20**	Mercury 20777
7/13/63+	**45**	50	●	3 The Songs And Comedy of The Smothers Brothers!.............[C]	**$20**	Mercury 20611

their first album

12/14/63+	**13**	33		4 Curb Your Tongue, Knave! ....[C]	**$20**	Mercury 20862
5/23/64	**23**	28		5 It Must Have Been Something I Said!..............................[C]	**$20**	Mercury 20904
12/19/64+	**58**	20		6 Tour De Farce American History And Other Unrelated Subjects ....[C]	**$20**	Mercury 20948
6/5/65	**57**	10		7 Aesop's Fables The Smothers Brothers Way ....[C]	**$15**	Mercury 20989
10/16/65+	**39**	28		8 Mom Always Liked You Best!...[C]	**$15**	Mercury 21051
8/13/66	**119**	6		9 Golden Hits Of The Smothers Brothers, Vol. 2 ....[C]	**$15**	Mercury 21089

new versions of their classics (there is no volume 1)

11/16/68	**164**	4		10 Smothers Comedy Brothers Hour...................................[C]	**$15**	Mercury 61193

Aesop Knew (7)
Aesop's Fables Our Way (7)
American History - 1A (4)
American History - II-A (6)
American History - II-B (6)
Anne Marie And Jean Pierre (5)
Apples, Peaches And Cherries (1)
Bird And The Jar (7)
Black Is The Color Of My True Love's Hair (2,5)
Boy Who Cried Wolf (7)
Cabbage (3,9)
Car (Maybe I'd Better Stay Me) (7)
Carnival (Manha De Carnival) (5)
Caught In The Draft (10)
Chocolate (1)
Church Bells (4,9)
Civil War Song (5)
Controversial Material (10)
Crabs Walk Sideways (5)
Dance, Boatman Dance (3)
Daniel Boone (7)
Dog And The Thief (7)
Down In The Valley (3)
Eskimo Dog (6)
Farmer And His Sons (7)
Flamenco (4)
Fly (Maybe I'd Better Stay Me) (7)
Four Winds And The Seven Seas (1)
Fox, The (2)
Fox And The Grapes (7)
Fox (Maybe I'd Better Stay Me) (7)
Gnus (4)
Greedy Dog (7)
Hangman (1,9)
Hiawatha (5)
I Don't Care (1)
I Never Will Marry (2,3)
I Talk To The Trees (4,9)
I Wish I Wuz In Peoria (3)
If It Fits Your Fancy (1)
Impersonation (8)
Impossible Dream (The Quest) (10)
Incredible Jazz Banjoist (4)
Intermission Bit (9)

687

SMOTHERS BROTHERS, The — Cont'd

Jellyfish (Maybe I'd Better Stay Me) (7)
Jenny Brown (5) *84*
Jezebel (3)
Laredo (1)
Last Great Waltz (8)
Life And The Song Of Life (6)
Little Known Song And Dance (8)
Lonesome Traveler (4)
Longtime Blues (8)
Map Of The World (1)

Mary Was Pretty (2)
Measles Song (6)
Mediocre Fred (6)
Michael, Row The Boat Ashore (5,9)
Military Lovers (6)
Mom Always Liked You Best (8)
Morons (10)
Mosquito (Maybe I'd Better Stay Me) (7)
My Old Man (2,9)

Population Explosion (5)
President Johnson (10)
Pretoria (3,9)
Put-On Song (6)
Reminiscences (8)
Saga Of John Henry (2)
Sailor's Lament (1)
Santa Claus (8)
Santa Claus Is Coming To Town (2)
She's Gone Forever (6)
Shrimp, The (5)

Siblings (6)
Since My Canary Died (6)
Slithery Dee (5)
Smart Juice (10)
Soap (2)
Spread Of Democracy (10)
Stella's Got A New Dress (1)
Swiss Christmas (4)
Tattoo Song (8)
That's My Song (6)
They Call The Wind Maria (1)
Three Song (8)

Time And Song Of Time (6)
Tom Dooley (3)
Tom's Party (10)
Tommy's Song (10)
Troubador Song (10)
Two Frogs (7)
Tzena, Tzena, Tzena, Tzena (3)
United Nations (10)
Venezuelan Rain Dance (2)
We Love Us (8)
Where The Lilac Grows (1)

Worm (Maybe I'd Better Stay Me) (7)
Wreck Of The Old 49 (2)
You Can Call Me Stupid (8)
You Didn't Come In (10)

SMYTH, Patty
Born on 6/26/57 in New York City. Lead singer of Scandal.

DEBUT DATE	PEAK POS	WKS CHR	GOLD	ARTIST — Album Title	$	Label & Number
3/21/87	66	20		1 Never Enough	$8	Columbia 40182
9/5/92	47	23↑ ●		2 Patty Smyth	$12	MCA 10633

Call To Heaven (1)
Downtown Train (1) *95*
Give It Time (1)

Heartache Heard Round The World (1)
I Should Be Laughing (2)
Isn't It Enough (1)

Make Me A Believer (2)
My Town (1)
Never Enough (1) *61*
No Mistakes (2) *41↑*

One Moment To Another (2)
Out There (2)
River Cried (1)
River Of Love (2)

Shine (1)
Sometimes Love Just Ain't Enough (2) *2*
Sue Lee (1)

Too Much Love (2)
Tough Love (1)

SNAIL
Pop-rock quartet from Santa Cruz, California — Bob O'Neill, lead singer. Jefferson Starship drummer Don Baldwin was a member (1979-82).

DEBUT DATE	PEAK POS	WKS CHR	GOLD	ARTIST — Album Title	$	Label & Number
7/8/78	135	12		1 Snail	$8	Cream 1009
11/10/79	186	2		2 Flow	$8	Cream 1012

And Your Bird Can Sing (2)
Broke Up, Broke Down (2)
Carry Me (1)
Catch Me (1)

Childhood Dreams (1)
Forever (2)
Freedom In The Country (1)
Here With You (2)

I've Got A Lady (2)
Joker, The (1) *93*
Keep On Livin' (1)
Lettin' Go (2)

Love Should Flow (2)
Music Is My Mistress (1)
Rollin' In Your Love (2)
Threw It Away (1)

Tonight (2)
Try And Wonder (1)
You Gotta Run (1)

SNAP!
Male/female dance duo from Pittsburgh. London-based rapper Turbo B with his cousin Jackie Harris, replaced in 1991 by Penny Ford (a backing singer for the Gap Band). Turbo B left in late 1992, Niki Harris, backing singer for Madonna, joined.

DEBUT DATE	PEAK POS	WKS CHR	GOLD	ARTIST — Album Title	$	Label & Number
6/16/90	30	49 ●		1 World Power	$12	Arista 8536
10/31/92	121	15↑		2 The Madman's Return	$12	Arista 18693

Believe In It (2)
Believe The Hype (1)
Blase, Blase (1)

Colour Of Love (Massive Version) (2)
Cult Of Snap (1)
Don't Be Shy (2)

EX-Terminator (2)
I'm Gonna Get You (To Whom It May Concern) (1)
Madman's Return (2)

Mary Had A Little Boy (1)
Money (2)
Ooops Up (1) *35*
Power, The (1) *2*

Rhythm Is A Dancer (2) *5*
See The Light (2)
Who Stole It? (2)
Witness The Strength (1)

SNEAKER
Los Angeles-based, pop-rock sextet — Mitch Crane, lead singer.

DEBUT DATE	PEAK POS	WKS CHR	GOLD	ARTIST — Album Title	$	Label & Number
12/12/81+	149	17		Sneaker	$8	Handshake 37631

Don't Let Me In *63*
Get Up, Get Out

In Time
Jaymes

Looking For Someone Like You

Millionaire

More Than Just The Two Of Us *34*

No More Lonely Days
One By One

SNIFF 'n' the TEARS
British rock group led by Paul Roberts (vocals) and Loz Netto (guitar). Roberts joined The Stranglers in 1991.

DEBUT DATE	PEAK POS	WKS CHR	GOLD	ARTIST — Album Title	$	Label & Number
7/28/79	35	17		1 Fickle Heart	$8	Atlantic 19242
9/19/81	192	2		2 Love Action	$8	MCA 5242

Carve Your Name On My Door (1)
Don't Frighten Me (2)
Driver's Seat (1) *15*
Driving Beat (2)

Fight For Love (1)
For What They Promise (2)
Last Dance (1)
Looking For You (1)
Love Action (2)

New Lines On Love (1)
Put Your Money Where Your Mouth Is (2)
Rock 'N' Roll Music (1)
Shame (2)

Sing (1)
Slide Away (1)
Snow White (2)
Steal My Heart (2)
That Final Love (2)

This Side Of The Blue Horizon (1)
Thrill Of It All (1)
Without Love (2)

★★469★★ SNOW, Phoebe
Born Phoebe Laub on 7/17/52 in New York City; raised in New Jersey. Vocalist/guitarist/songwriter. Began performing in Greenwich Village in the early '70s.

DEBUT DATE	PEAK POS	WKS CHR	GOLD	ARTIST — Album Title	$	Label & Number
9/7/74+	4	58 ●		1 Phoebe Snow	$10	Shelter 2109
2/14/76	13	22 ●		2 Second Childhood	$8	Columbia 33952
11/6/76	29	21		3 It Looks Like Snow	$8	Columbia 34387
10/22/77	73	15		4 Never Letting Go	$8	Columbia 34875
10/28/78	100	7		5 Against The Grain	$8	Columbia 35456
4/4/81	51	18		6 Rock Away	$8	Mirage 19297
4/15/89	75	20		7 Something Real	$8	Elektra 60852

All Over (2)
Autobiography (Shine, Shine, Shine) (3)
Baby Please (6)
Best Of My Love (7)
Cardiac Arrest (7)
Cash In (2)
Cheap Thrills (6)
Do Right Woman, Do Right Man (5)
Don't Let Me Down (3)
Down In The Basement (6)
Drink Up The Melody (Bite The Dust, Blues) (3)
Either Or Both (1)

Electra (4)
Every Night (5)
Fat Chance (3)
Games (6) *46*
Garden Of Joy Blues (4)
Gasoline Alley (6)
Goin' Down For The Third Time (2)
Good Times (Let The Good Times Roll) (1)
Harpo's Blues (1)
He's Not Just Another Man (5)
I Believe In You (6)

I Don't Want The Night To End (1)
I'm Your Girl (7)
If I Can Just Get Through The Night (7)
In My Girlish Days (3)
In My Life (5)
Inspired Insanity (2)
Isn't It A Shame (2)
It Must Be Sunday (1)
Keep A Watch On The Shoreline (5)
Love Makes A Woman (4)
Majesty Of Life (4)
Mama Don't Break Down (5)

Married Men (5)
Mercy, Mercy, Mercy (6) *52*
Mercy On Those (3)
Middle Of The Night (4)
Mr. Wondering (7)
My Faith Is Blind (3)
Never Letting Go (4)
No Regrets (2)
No Show Tonight (1)
Oh L.A. (5)
Poetry Man (1) *5*
Pre-Dawn Imagination (4)
Random Time (5)
Ride The Elevator (4)
Rock Away (2)

San Francisco Bay Blues (1)
Shakey Ground (3) *70*
Shoo-Rah Shoo-Rah (6)
Something Good (6)
Something Real (7)
Something So Right (4)
Soothin' (2)
Stand Up On The Rock (3)
Stay Away (7)
Sweet Disposition (2)
Take Your Children Home (1)
Teach Me Tonight (3)
There's A Boat That's Leavin' Soon For New York (2)

Touch Your Soul (7)
Two Fisted Love (2)
We Might Never Feel This Way Again (7)
We're Children (4)
You Have Not Won (5)

SNYDER, Terry — see LIGHT, Enoch

DEBUT DATE	PEAK POS	WKS CHR	GOLD	ARTIST — Album Title	$	Label & Number

SO
South London duo: singer/guitarist Mark Long and multi-instrumentalist Marcus Bell.

3/19/88	124	9		Horseshoe In The Glove	$8	EMI-Man. 46997

Are You Sure 41   Capitol Hill   Horseshoe In The Glove   Villians
Burning Bush   Dreaming   Tips On Crime   Would You Die For Me

SOCCIO, Gino
Techno-disco vocalist/multi-instrumentalist. Born in 1955 in Montreal. Producer of Witch Queen.

4/21/79	79	13	1	Outline	$8	RFC 3309
5/23/81	96	14	2	Closer	$8	Atlantic 16042

Closer (2)   Dancer (1) 48   (It's Been) Too Long (2)   So Lonely (1)   There's A Woman (1)   Visitors, The (1)
Dance To Dance (1)   Hold Tight (2)   Love Is (2)   Street Talk (2)   Try It Out (2)

SOCIAL DISTORTION
Rock quartet formed in 1979 in Los Angeles: Mike Ness (vocals, guitar), Dennis Danell, John Maurer and Christopher Reece.

5/26/90	128	22	1	Social Distortion	$12	Epic 46055
2/29/92	76	16	2	Somewhere Between Heaven & Hell	$12	Epic 47978

CD includes bonus track

Bad Luck (2)   Cold Feelings (2)   King Of Fools (2)   Place In My Heart (1)   So Far Away (1)   When She Begins (2)
Ball And Chain (1)   Drug Train (1)   Let It Be Me (1)   Ring Of Fire (1)   Sometimes I Do (2)
Born To Lose (2)   Ghost Town Blues (2)   Making Believe (1)   She's A Knockout (1)   Story Of My Life (1)
Bye Bye Baby (2)   It Coulda Been Me (1)   99 To Life (2)   Sick Boys (1)   This Time Darlin' (2)

SOFT CELL
British electro-rock duo: Marc Almond (vocals) and David Ball (synthesizer). Almond began solo career in late 1988.

1/30/82	22	41	1	Non-Stop Erotic Cabaret	$8	Sire 3647
8/14/82	57	14	2	Non-Stop Ecstatic Dancing	[M] $8	Sire 23694
2/26/83	84	8	3	The Art of Falling Apart	$10	Sire 23769 [2]

includes a bonus mini LP

Art Of Falling Apart (3)   Forever The Same (3)   Kitchen Sink Drama (3)   Numbers (3)   **Tainted Love** (1) 8
Baby Doll (3)   Frustration (1)   Loving You, Hating Me (3)   Say Hello, Wave Goodbye (1)   What (2)
Bedsitter (1)   Heat (3)   Man Could Get Lost (2)   Secret Life (1)   Where Did Our Love Go (2)
Chips On My Shoulder (1)   Hendrix Medley (3)   Martin (3)   Seedy Films (1)   Where The Heart Is (3)
Entertain Me (1)   Insecure...Me? (2)   Memorabilia (2)   Sex Dwarf (1,2)   Youth (1)

SOFT MACHINE, The
British experimental-rock trio: Robert Wyatt (drums, vocals) Michael Ratledge (organ), and Kevin Ayers (guitar). Band's manager, Keith Albarn, is the father of Damon Albarn, lead singer of Blur.

12/21/68+	160	9		The Soft Machine	$20	Probe 4500

Box 25/4 LID   Hope For Happiness   Lullabye Letter   Priscilla   So Boot If At All   Why Am I So Short?
Certain Kind   Joy Of A Toy   Plus Belle Qu'une Poubelle   Save Yourself   We Did It Again   Why Are We Sleeping?

SOHO
London-based trio of guitarist Timothy Brinkhurst (b: 11/20/60) and vocalists/twin sisters Jacqueline and Pauline Cuff (b: 11/25/62) — both are psychiatric nurses.

11/24/90	134	10		Goddess	$12	Sav./Atco 91585

CD includes bonus track

Another Year   Girl On A Motorbike   Goddess   Love Generation   Out Of My Mind   Zombies Walk The
Boy '90   God's Little Joke   **Hippychick** 14   Nuthin' On My Mind   Shake Your Thing   Cardboard City
Freaky

SOMERVILLE, Jimmy
Born on 6/22/61 in Glasgow, Scotland. Former lead singer/founder of the British bands Bronski Beat and Communards.

5/5/90	192	2		Read My Lips	$12	London 828166

Adieu!   Comment Te Dire Adieu   Heaven Here On Earth (With   My Heart Is In Your Hands   Read My Lips (Enough Is   **You Make Me Feel (Mighty**
And You Never Thought   Control   Your Love)   Perfect Day   Enough)   **Real)** 87
That This Could Happen   Don't Know What To Do   Rain
To You   (Without You)

SOMMERS, Joanie
Born on 2/24/41 in Buffalo; moved to California in 1954. Sang Pepsi-Cola jingles in the early and mid-1960s.

9/22/62	103	3		Johnny Get Angry	$35	Warner 1470

I Don't Want To Walk   **Johnny Get Angry** 7   Nightingale Sang In   Piano Boy   Since Randy Moved Away
Without You   Little Girl Blue   Berkeley Square   Seems Like Long, Long Ago   Summer Place, Theme From
I Need Your Love   Mean To Me   **One Boy** 54   Shake Hands With A Fool   A

SONIC YOUTH
Rock band from New York City formed in 1981: guitarists Thurston Moore and Lee Ranaldo, Kim Gordon (bass) and Steve Shelley (drums). All share vocals.

7/14/90	96	15	1	Goo	$12	DGC 24297
8/8/92	83	11	2	Dirty	$12	Geffen 24493

Chapel Hill (2)   Drunken Butterfly (2)   Mote (1)   Orange Rolls, Angel's Spit (2)   Swimsuit Issue (2)   Youth Against Fascism (2)
Cinderella's Big Score (2)   JC (2)   My Friend Goo (1)   Purr (2)   Theresa's Sound-world (2)
Creme Brulee (2)   Kool Thing (1)   Nic Fit (2)   Scooter + Jinx (1)   Titanium Expose (2)
Dirty Boots (1)   Mary-Christ (1)   On The Strip (2)   Shoot (2)   Tunic (Song For Karen) (1)
Disappearer (1)   Mildred Pierce (1)   100% (2)   Sugar Kane (2)   Wish Fulfillment (2)

★★255★★ SONNY & CHER
Husband-and-wife duo: Sonny and Cher Bono. Session singers for Phil Spector. First recorded as Caesar & Cleo for Vault in 1963. Married in 1963; divorced in 1974. In the films *Good Times* (1966) and *Chastity* (1968). Own CBS-TV variety series from 1971-74. Brief TV reunion in 1975. Each recorded solo.

8/21/65	2[8]	44	● 1	Look At Us	$15	Atco 177

DEBUT DATE	PEAK POS	WKS CHR	GOLD	ARTIST — Album Title	$	Label & Number
				SONNY & CHER — Cont'd		
10/23/65	**69**	16		2 Baby Don't Go .... [E]	**$20**	Reprise 6177
				includes 5 cuts by Sonny & Cher; 3 by The Lettermen: "Their Hearts Were Full Of Spring," "Two Hearts," "When"; 3 by Bill Medley: "I Surrender (To Your Touch)," "Leavin' Town," "Wo Yeah"; and one by The Blendells: "La La La La La"		
4/16/66	**34**	20		3 The Wondrous World Of Sonny & Cher	**$15**	Atco 183
3/25/67	**45**	29		4 In Case You're In Love	**$15**	Atco 203
5/27/67	**73**	18		5 Good Times .... [S]	**$15**	Atco 214
				Sonny & Cher star as themselves in the film		
8/12/67	**23**	64		6 The Best of Sonny & Cher .... [G]	**$15**	Atco 219
10/2/71	**35**	40	●	7 Sonny & Cher Live .... [L]	**$12**	Kapp 3654
2/26/72	**14**	29	●	8 All I Ever Need Is You	**$12**	Kapp 3660
9/9/72	**122**	12		9 The Two Of Us .... [R]	**$15**	Atco 804 [2]
				reissue of albums #1 & 4 above		
6/30/73	**132**	6		10 Mama Was A Rock And Roll Singer Papa Used To Write All Her Songs	**$12**	MCA 2101
12/22/73+	**175**	7		11 Sonny & Cher Live In Las Vegas, Vol. 2 .... [L]	**$12**	MCA 8004 [2]
9/28/74	**146**	6		12 Greatest Hits .... [G]	**$12**	MCA 2117

All I Ever Need Is You (8,11,12) *7*
Baby Don't Go (2,9) *8*
Bang Bang (My Baby Shot Me Down) (11)
Beat Goes On (4,6,7,9,12) *6*
Beautiful Story (6) *53*
Bring It On Home To Me (3)
Brother Love's Traveling Salvation Show (10,11)
But You're Mine (3,6) *15*
By Love I Mean (10)
Cheryl's Goin Home (4,9)
Cowboys Work Is Never Done (8,11,12) *8*
Crystal Clear (medley) (8,12)
Danny Boy (1)
Do You Want To Dance (2)
Don't Talk To Strangers (5)
500 Miles (1)

Good Times (5)
Gotta Get You Into My Life (7)
Greatest Show On Earth (10)
Groovy Kind Of Love (4,9)
Gypsys, Tramps & Thieves (11)
Here Comes That Rainy Day Feeling (8)
Hey Jude (7)
I Believe In You (10)
I Can See Clearly Now (10,11)
I Got You Babe (1,5,6,7,9,11,12) *1*
I Look For You (3)
I Love What You Did With The Love I Gave You (8)
I'm Gonna Love You (5)

I'm Leaving It All Up To You (3)
It Never Rains In Southern California (10)
It's Gonna Rain (1,9)
It's The Little Things (5,6) *50*
Just A Name (5)
Just You (1,6,9) *20*
Laugh At Me [solo: Sonny] (3,6,7) *10*
Leave Me Be (3)
Let It Be Me (1,6,9)
Let The Good Times Roll (2)
Letter, The (1,9) *75*
Listen To The Music (10)
Little Man (4,6,9) *21*
Living For You (4,6,9) *87*
Love Don't Come (4,9)
Love Is Strange (2)

Mama Was A Rock And Roll Singer Papa Used To Write All Her Songs (10,12) *77*
Misty Roses (4,9)
Monday (4,9)
More Today Than Yesterday (7,8)
Muddy Waters (medley) (8,12)
Once In A Lifetime (7)
Podunk (4,9)
Rhythm Of Your Heart Beat (10)
Set Me Free (3)
Sing C'est La Vie (1,6,9)
So Fine (3)
Somebody (8)
Someday (You'll Want Me To Want You) (7)

Something (7)
Stand By Me (4,9)
Summertime (11)
Superstar (11)
Tell Him (3)
Then He Kissed Me (1,9)
Trust Me (5)
Turn Around (3)
Unchained Melody (1,9)
United We Stand (8,12)
Walkin' The Quetzal (2)
We'll Sing In The Sunshine (4,9)
We'll Watch The Sun Coming Up (Shining Down On Our Love) (8)
What Now My Love (3,6,7,12) *14*
When You Say Love (12) *32*

Where You Lead (medley) (11)
Why Don't They Let Us Fall In Love (1,9)
You And I (11)
You Baby (9)
You Better Sit Down Kids (8,11,12)
You Don't Love Me (1,9)
You Know Darn Well (10)
You've Got A Friend (medley) (11)
You've Really Got A Hold On Me (1,9)

SONS OF CHAMPLIN
San Francisco seven-man rock band led by Bill Champlin.

6/14/69	**137**	9		1 Loosen Up Naturally	**$15**	Capitol 200 [2]
11/8/69	**171**	6		2 The Sons	**$12**	Capitol 332
				THE SONS		
6/9/73	**186**	5		3 Welcome To The Dance	**$10**	Columbia 32341
6/5/76	**117**	10		4 A Circle Filled With Love	**$8**	Ariola Am. 50007
5/28/77	**188**	4		5 Loving Is Why	**$8**	Ariola Am. 50017

Big Boss Man (5)
Black And Blue Rainbow (1)
Boomp Boomp Chop (2)
Circle Filled With Love (4)
Country Girl (2)
Doin' It For You (5)
Don't Fight It, Do It! (1)
Everywhere (1)
Follow Your Heart (4)

For A While (4)
For Joy (3)
Freedom (1)
Get High (1)
Heaven Only Knows (medley) (3)
Hello Sunlight (1)
Helping Hand (4)

Here Is Where Your Love Belongs (4) *80*
Hold On (4) *47*
Imagination's Sake (4)
It's Time (2)
Knickanick (4)
Let That Be A Lesson (5)
Lightnin' (3)
Love Can Take Me Now (5)

Love Of A Woman (2)
Loving Is Why (5)
Misery Isn't Free (1)
1982-A (1)
No Mo' (3)
Right On (3)
Rooftop (3)
Saved By The Grace Of Your Love (5)

Slippery When It's Wet (4)
Still In Love With You (4)
Swim, The (3)
Terry's Tune (2)
Thing To Do (1)
Things Are Gettin' Better (1)
Time Will Bring You Love (5)
To The Sea (4)
Welcome To The Dance Medley (3)

West End (5)
Whatcha Gonna Do (5)
Where I Belong (5)
Who (medley) (3)
Why Do People Run From The Rain (2)
You (4)
You Can Fly (2)

SOPWITH "CAMEL", The
San Francisco quintet — Peter Kraemer, lead singer.

10/28/67	**191**	2		Sopwith Camel	**$25**	Kama Sutra 8060

Cellophane Woman
Frantic Desolation
Great Morpheum

Hello Hello *26*
Little Orphan Annie

Maybe In A Dream
Postcard From Jamaica *88*

Saga Of The Low Down Let Down

Things That I Could Do With You

Walk In The Park
You Always Tell Me Baby

S.O.S. BAND, The
Funk-R&B band from Atlanta. Lead singer/keyboardist Mary Davis went solo in 1986, various personnel changes since. Name means "Sounds Of Success."

6/28/80	**12**	20	●	1 S.O.S.	**$8**	Tabu 36332
8/22/81	**117**	6		2 Too	**$8**	Tabu 37449
12/25/82+	**172**	8		3 S.O.S. III	**$8**	Tabu 38352
8/27/83	**47**	29	●	4 On The Rise	**$8**	Tabu 38697
9/1/84	**60**	27		5 Just The Way You Like It	**$8**	Tabu 39332
5/24/86	**44**	20	●	6 Sands Of Time	**$8**	Tabu 40279
11/4/89	**194**	2		7 Diamonds In The Raw	**$8**	Tabu 44147

Are You Ready? (2)
Body Break (5)
Borrowed Love (6)
Break Up (5)
Can't Get Enough (3)
Crossfire (Part I & II) (7)
Do It Now (7)
Do You Know Where Your Children Are? (2)
Do You Love Me? (7)

Do You Still Want To? (6)
Even When You Sleep (6)
Feeling (5)
Finest, The (6) *44*
For The Brothers That Ain't Here (2)
For Your Love (4)
Get Out Of My Life (7)
Goldmine (7)
Good & Plenty (3)

Groovin' (That's What We're Doin') (3)
Have It Your Way (3)
High Hopes (3)
Hold Out (7)
I Don't Want Nobody Else (5)
I'm In Love (1)
I'm Not Runnin' (4)
I'm Still Missing Your Love (7)

If You Want My Love (4)
It's A Long Way To The Top (2)
Just Be Good To Me (4) *55*
Just The Way You Like It (5) *64*
Looking For You (3)
Love Won't Last For Love (1)
Men Don't Cry (7)
No Lies (6)

No One's Gonna Love You (5)
Nothing But The Best (6)
On The Rise (4)
One Lover (7)
Open Letter (1)
S.O.S. (Dit Dit Dit Dat Dat Dit Dit Dit) (1)
Sands Of Time (6)
Secret Wish (7)
Stay (2)

Steppin' The Stones (4)
Take Love Where You Find It (1)
Take Your Time (Do It Right) Part 1 (1) *3*
Tell Me If You Still Care (4) *65*
There Is No Limit (2)
These Are The Things (6)
Two Time Lover (6)

690

DEBUT DATE	PEAK POS	WKS CHR	GOLD	ARTIST — Album Title	$	Label & Number

S.O.S. BAND, The — Cont'd

Unborn Child (2)				What's Wrong With Our	Who's Making Love (4)	You Shake Me Up (3)	Your Love (It's The One For
Weekend Girl (5)				Love Affair? (1)	You (2)		Me) (3)

SOUL, David

Born David Solberg on 8/28/43 in Chicago. Played Ken Hutchinson on TV's *Starsky & Hutch* (1975-79). Began career as a folk singer and appeared several times on *The Merv Griffin Show* as "The Covered Man" (wore a ski mask).

DEBUT DATE	PEAK POS	WKS CHR	GOLD	ARTIST — Album Title	$	Label & Number
1/22/77	40	22		1 David Soul	$8	Private St. 2019
9/10/77	86	7		2 Playing To An Audience Of One	$8	Private St. 7001

Bird On A Wire (1)	Can't We Just Sit Down And	**Going In With My Eyes**	Landlord (1)	Playing To An Audience Of	**Silver Lady** (2) **52**
Black Bean Soup (1)	Talk It Over (2)	**Open** (2) **54**	Mary's Fancy (2)	One (2)	Tattler (2)
By The Devil I Was Tempted	**Don't Give Up On Us** (1) *1*	Hooray For Hollywood (1)	1927 Kansas City (1)	Rider (2)	Tomorrow Child (2)
(2)	Ex Lover (1)	I Wish I Was... (2)	Nobody But A Fool Or A	Seem To Miss So Much	Topanga (1)
		Kristofer David (1)	Preacher (2)	(Coalminer's Song) (1)	Wall, The (1)

SOUL ASYLUM

Quartet formed in Minneapolis in 1983: Dave Pirner (vocals), Daniel Murphy, Karl Mueller and Grant Young.

DEBUT DATE	PEAK POS	WKS CHR	GOLD	ARTIST — Album Title	$	Label & Number
11/21/92	59↑	12↑		Grave Dancers Union	$12	Columbia 48898

April Fool	Get On Out	Homesick	New World	Runaway Train	Sun Maid
Black Gold	Growing Into You	Keep It Up	99%	Somebody To Shove	Without A Trace

SOUL CHILDREN, The

Group formed by songwriters Isaac Hayes and David Porter. Consisted of Anita Louis, Shelbra Bennett, John Colbert and Norman West. Colbert later recorded as J. Blackfoot.

DEBUT DATE	PEAK POS	WKS CHR	GOLD	ARTIST — Album Title	$	Label & Number
9/6/69	154	6		1 Soul Children	$10	Stax 2018
4/29/72	159	6		2 Genesis	$10	Stax 3003

All Day Preachin' (2)	Get Up About Yourself (2)	I'll Understand (1)	Just The One (I've Been	Never Get Enough Of Your	Sweeter He Is - Part II (1)
All That Shines Ain't Gold (2)	Give 'Em Love (1)	I'm Loving You More	Looking For) (2)	Love (2)	Take Up The Slack (1)
Doin' Our Thang (1)	**Hearsay** (1) **44**	Everyday (2)	Move Over (1)	Super Soul (1)	Tighten Up My Thang (1)
Don't Take My Sunshine (2)	I Want To Be Loved (2)	It Hurts Me To My Heart (1)	My Baby Specializes (1)	**Sweeter He Is - Part I** (1) **52**	When Tomorrow Comes (1)

SOULFUL STRINGS, The

Chicago studio group with Lennie Druss (oboe, flute), Bobby Christian (vibes), Phil Upchurch and Ron Steel (guitars). Arranged and conducted by Richard Evans.

DEBUT DATE	PEAK POS	WKS CHR	GOLD	ARTIST — Album Title	$	Label & Number
8/26/67	166	15		1 Paint It Black .... [I]	$10	Cadet 776
11/11/67+	59	34		2 Groovin' With The Soulful Strings .... [I]	$10	Cadet 796
8/3/68	189	4		3 Another Exposure .... [I]	$8	Cadet 805
5/3/69	125	6		4 In Concert/Back By Demand .... [I-L]	$8	Cadet 820
11/29/69+	183	4		5 Spring Fever .... [I]	$8	Cadet 834

Alfie (2)	High Rise Blues (5)	Love Song (5)	Sidewinder, The (1)	Voices Inside (5)
Alice Blue Gown (3)	(I Know) I'm Losing You (3)	Lover's Concerto (1)	Since You've Been Gone (3)	Wade In The Water (1)
All Blues (2)	I Wish It Would Rain (4)	MacArthur Park (4)	Sometimes I Feel Like A	What Now My Love (2)
Burning Spear (2) **64**	I'm A Girl Watcher (2)	Message To Michael (1)	Motherless Child (5)	When A Man Loves A
California Dreamin' (1)	Inner Light (3)	Minor Adjustment (3)	Soul Message (3)	Woman (3)
Chocolate Candy (5)	It Ain't Necessarily So (3)	1974 Blues (3)	Soul Prelude (2)	Who We Song (3)
Clair De Lune (4)	It's Cold Duck Time (5)	Oboe Flats (4)	Stepper, The (3)	Wildwood (5)
Comin' Home Baby (2)	Jericho (3)	On The Dock Of The Bay (3)	Sunny (1)	Within You Without You (2)
Eight Miles High (2)	Lady Madonna (3)	Our Day Will Come (2)	Take Five (1)	You're All I Need (4)
Groovin' (2)	Listen Here (4)	Paint It Black (1)	There Was A Time (4)	Zambezi (5)
Hello, Goodbye (3)	Love Is A Hurtin' Thing (1)	Pavanne (4)	Valdez In The Country (5)	

SOUL SURVIVORS

White-soul band from New York City and Philadelphia. Formed by the Ingui brothers, Charles & Richard, and Kenny Jeremiah. Re-formed by the Inguis in 1972. Jeremiah was later in Shirley And Company.

DEBUT DATE	PEAK POS	WKS CHR	GOLD	ARTIST — Album Title	$	Label & Number
11/18/67+	123	13		When The Whistle Blows Anything Goes..................	$20	Crimson 502

Change Is Gonna Come	**Expressway To Your**	Hey Gyp	Respect	Shake (medley)	Too Many Fish In The Sea
Dathon's Theme	**Heart 4**	Please, Please, Please	Rydle, The	Taboo-India	(medley)
Do You Feel It					

SOUL II SOUL

South London soul outfit led by the duo of Beresford "Jazzie B." Romeo and Nellee Hooper. Features female vocalists Caron Wheeler, Do'Reen and Rose Windross and musical backing by the Reggae Philharmonic Orchestra. Wheeler left in 1990.

DEBUT DATE	PEAK POS	WKS CHR	GOLD	ARTIST — Album Title	$	Label & Number
7/8/89	14	51	▲²	1 Keep On Movin'	$8	Virgin 91267
6/16/90	21	19	●	2 Vol II - 1990 - A New Decade	$12	Virgin 91367
5/16/92	88	8		3 Volume III Just Right	$12	Virgin 91771

African Dance (1)	**Dreams A Dream** (2) **85**	**Get A Life** (2) **54**	Joy (3)	Move Me No Mountain (3)	Time (Untitled) (2)
Back To Life (However Do	Everywhere (3)	Happiness (1)	Just Right (3)	1990 - A New Decade (2)	
You Want Me) (1) **4**	Fairplay (1)	Holdin' On (1)	**Keep On Movin'** (1) **11**	Our Time Has Now Come (2)	
Courtney Blows (2)	Feel Free (1)	In The Heat Of The Night (2)	Love Come Through (2)	People (2)	
Dance (1)	Feeling Free (1)	Intelligence (1)	Missing You (2)	Storm (3)	
Direction (3)	Future (3)	Jazzie's Groove (1)	Mood (3)	Take Me Higher (3)	

SOUNDGARDEN

Seattle-based, metal-punk band: Chris Cornell (vocals), Kim Thayil (guitar), Hiro Yamamoto (bass; replaced by Hunter "Ben" Shepherd in 1991) and Matt Cameron (drums). Cornell and Cameron also recorded with Temple Of The Dog.

DEBUT DATE	PEAK POS	WKS CHR	GOLD	ARTIST — Album Title	$	Label & Number
1/27/90	108	16		1 Louder Than Love	$12	A&M 5252
10/26/91+	39	58	▲	2 Badmotorfinger	$12	A&M 5374

Big Dumb Sex (1)	Gun (1)	Loud Love (1)	Power Trip (1)	Searching With My Good	Ugly Truth (1)
Drawing Flies (2)	Hands All Over (1)	Mind Riot (1)	Room A Thousand Years	Eye Closed (2)	Uncovered (1)
Face Pollution (2)	Holy Water (1)	New Damage (2)	Wide (2)	Slaves & Bulldozers (2)	
Full On Kevin's Mom (1)	I Awake (1)	No Wrong No Right (1)	Rusty Cage (2)	Somewhere (2)	
Get On The Snake (1)	Jesus Christ Pose (2)	Outshined (2)			

DEBUT DATE	PEAK POS	WKS CHR	GOLD	ARTIST — Album Title	$	Label & Number

SOUNDS OF BLACKNESS
Black choir and orchestra formed in 1971. Arranged and conducted by Gary Hines.

11/16/91	**176**	2		1 The Evolution Of Gospel	$12	Perspective 1000
12/19/92+	**129**	4		2 The Night Before Christmas - A Musical Fantasy .... [X]	$12	Perspective 9000

Christmas charts: 20/'93

Ah Been Workin' (1)
Away In A Manger (2)
Better Watch Your Behavior (1)
Born In A Manger (2)
Chains (1)
Children Go (2)

Dance, Chitlins, Dance (2)
Dash Away All (medley) (2)
Give Us A Chance (2)
Gonna Be Free One Day (1)
Hallelujah Lord! (1)
Harambee (1)
He Holds The Future (1)

Holiday Love (2)
I'll Fly Away (1)
It's Christmas Time (2)
Jolly One's Here (2)
Merry Christmas To The World (2)
O' Come All Ye Faithful (2)

O', Holy Night (2)
Optimistic (1)
Peace On Earth For Everyone (2)
Please Take My Hand (1)
Pressure Pt. 1 & 2 (1)
Reindeer Revolt (medley) (2)

Santa Watch Yo' Step (2)
Santa Won't You Come By? (2)
Santa's Comin' To Town (2)
Soul Holidays (2)
Stand (1)
Testify (1)

We Give You Thanks (1)
What Shall I Call Him? (1)
Why Don't You Believe In Me? (2)
Your Wish Is My Command (1)

SOUNDS OF SUNSHINE
Studio group assembled by producer Randy Wood (d: 10/6/80).

8/14/71	**187**	8		Love Means You Never Have To Say You're Sorry	$8	Ranwood 8089

Anything Can Happen
El Condor Pasa
For The Good Times

I Do All My Crying In The Rain
If

It's Impossible
Livin' It Day By Day

Love Means (You Never Have To Say You're Sorry) 39

Make It With You
Put Your Hand In The Hand
Rainy Days And Mondays

Yesterday Keeps Getting In The Way

SOUNDS ORCHESTRAL
British studio project produced by John Schroeder. Included arranger/producer Johnny Pearson on piano.

5/29/65	**11**	28		Cast Your Fate To The Wind ....[I]	$20	Parkway 7046

At The Mardi Gras (While We Danced)

Carnival (Manha De Carnaval)

Cast Your Fate To The Wind 10
Downtown

Have Faith In Your Love
Like The Lonely
Love Letters

Scarlatti Potion No. 5
Scarlatti Potion No. 9
Something's Coming

To Wendy With Love
When Love Has Gone

SOUP DRAGONS, The
Quartet from Glasgow, Scotland: Sean Dickinson (vocals), Jim McCulloch, Sushil Dade and Paul Quinn.

10/20/90	**88**	29		1 Lovegod	$12	Big Life 842985
				CD includes 2 bonus tracks		
6/27/92	**97**	22		2 Hotwired	$12	Big Life 13178

Absolute Heaven (2)
Backwards Dog (1)
Beauty Freak (1)
Crotch Deep Trash (1)
Divine Thing (2) 35

Dream-E-Forever (1)
Dream-On (Solid Gone) (2)
Drive The Pain (1)
Everlasting (2)
Everything (2)

Forever Yesterday (2)
Getting Down (2)
I'm Free (1) 79
Kiss The Gun (1)
Love You To Death (1)

Lovegod [includes 2 versions] (1)
Mindless (2)
Mirror Of Your Mind (1)
Mother Universe (1)
No More Understanding (2)

Pleasure (2) 69
Running Wild (2)
Softly (1)
Sweet Layabout (2)
Sweetmeat (1)

SOUTH, Joe
Born Joe Souter on 2/28/40 in Atlanta. Successful Nashville session guitarist/songwriter in the mid-1960s. Wrote "Down In The Boondocks," "Hush" and "Rose Garden."

2/8/69	**117**	14		1 Introspect	$12	Capitol 108
1/17/70	**60**	23		2 Don't It Make You Want To Go Home?	$12	Capitol 392
9/12/70	**125**	11		3 Joe South's Greatest Hits ....[G]	$12	Capitol 450

All My Hard Times (1)
Be A Believer (2)
Before It's Too Late (2)
Birds Of A Feather (1,3) 96
Bittersweet (2)
Children (2,3) 51

Clock Up On The Wall (2)
Don't It Make You Want To Go Home (2,3) 41
Don't Throw Your Love To The Wind (1)
Don't You Be Ashamed (1)

Down In The Boondocks (3)
Gabriel (1)
Games People Play (1,3) 12
Greatest Love (1,3)
Hush (3)
I Knew You When (3)

Million Miles Away (2)
Mirror Of Your Mind (1)
Redneck (2)
Rose Garden (1)
Shelter (2)

These Are Not My People (1,3)
Walk A Mile In My Shoes (2,3) 12
What Makes Lovers Hurt One Another (2)

SOUTHER, J.D.
John David Souther, born in Detroit and raised in Amarillo, Texas. Formed Longbranch Pennywhistle with Glenn Frey. Teamed with Chris Hillman and Richie Furay as the Souther, Hillman, Furay Band in 1974.

5/8/76	**85**	11		1 Black Rose	$8	Asylum 1059
				JOHN DAVID SOUTHER		
9/22/79	**41**	22		2 You're Only Lonely	$8	Columbia 36093

Baby Come Home (1)
Banging My Head Against The Moon (1)
Black Rose (1)
Doors Swing Open (1)

Faithless Love (1)
Fifteen Bucks (2)
If You Don't Want My Love (2)
If You Have Crying Eyes (1)

Last In Love (2)
Midnight Prowl (1)
Moon Just Turned Blue (2)
Silver Blue (1)

Simple Man, Simple Dream (1)
Songs Of Love (2)
'Til The Bars Burn Down (2)

Trouble In Paradise (1)
White Rhythm And Blues (2)
You're Only Lonely (2) 7
Your Turn Now (1)

SOUTHER, HILLMAN, FURAY BAND, The
Country-rock sextet formed as a supergroup featuring J.D. Souther, Chris Hillman and Richie Furay.

7/20/74	**11**	22	●	1 The Souther, Hillman, Furay Band	$10	Asylum 1006
6/21/75	**39**	11		2 Trouble In Paradise	$10	Asylum 1036

Believe Me (1)
Border Town (1)
Deep, Dark And Dreamless (1)

Fallin' In Love (1) 27
Flight Of The Dove (1)
Follow Me Through (2)
For Someone I Love (2)

Heartbreaker, The (1)
Heavenly Fire (1)
Love And Satisfy (2)
Mexico (2)

Move Me Real Slow (2)
On The Line (2)
Pretty Goodbyes (1)
Prisoner In Disguise (2)

Rise And Fall (1)
Safe At Home (1)
Somebody Must Be Wrong (2)

Trouble In Paradise (2)

SOUTHERN COMFORT
British rock quintet led by guitarist Carl Barnwell after the departure of founder/leader Ian Matthews.

8/14/71	**196**	2		Frog City	$10	Capitol 800

April Lady
(Dreadful Ballad Of) Willie Hurricane

Get Back Home
Good Lord D.C.
I Sure Like Your Smile

Leaving Song
My Old Kentucky Home

Passing, The
Return To Frog City

Roses
Take A Message

Willie Hurricane ..see: (Dreadful Ballad Of)

SOUTHSIDE JOHNNY & THE JUKES
Rock band formed in Asbury Park, New Jersey; led by vocalist/harmonica player Johnny Lyon (b: 12/4/48, Neptune, New Jersey).

SOUTHSIDE JOHNNY & THE ASBURY JUKES:

7/10/76	**125**	9		1 I Don't Want To Go Home	$8	Epic 34180
5/7/77	**85**	9		2 This Time It's For Real	$8	Epic 34668
				with guests: The Coasters, The Drifters and The Five Satins		
11/4/78+	**112**	20		3 Hearts Of Stone	$8	Epic 35488

DEBUT DATE	PEAK POS	WKS CHR	GOLD	ARTIST — Album Title	$	Label & Number
				SOUTHSIDE JOHNNY & THE JUKES — Cont'd		
8/18/79	**48**	14	4	The Jukes..	**$8**	Mercury 3793
6/14/80	**67**	15	5	Love Is A Sacrifice	**$8**	Mercury 3836
5/9/81	**80**	12	6	Reach Up And Touch The Sky......................[L]	**$10**	Mercury 8602 [2]
				SOUTHSIDE JOHNNY & THE JUKES:		
10/1/83	**154**	6	7	Trash It Up!	**$8**	Mirage 90113
9/8/84	**164**	8	8	In The Heat	**$8**	Mirage 90186
6/21/86	**189**	4	9	At Least We Got Shoes	**$8**	Atlantic 81654
12/3/88	**198**	1	10	Slow Dance	**$8**	Cypress 0115
				SOUTHSIDE JOHNNY		
11/16/91	**96**	7	11	Better Days..	**$12**	Impact 10445

Act Of Love (10)
Action Speaks Louder Than Words (8)
Ain't Gonna Eat Out My Heart Anymore (7)
Ain't That Peculiar (10)
All I Needed Was You (11)
All I Want Is Everything (4,6)
All Night Long (11)
All The Way Home (11)
Back In The U.S.A. (6)
Beast Within (7)
Bedtime (7)
Better Days (11)
Bring It On Home To Me (6)
Broke Down Piece Of Man (1)
Can't Stop Thinking Of You (7)
Captured (8)
Check Mr. Popeye (2)
Coming Back (11)
Don't Look Back (8)
Fannie Mae (1)

Fever, The (1,6)
First Night (1,6)
Get Your Body On The Job (7)
Goodbye Love (5)
Got To Be A Better Way Home (3)
Got To Get You Off My Mind (1)
Hard To Find (9)
Having A Party (Part 1) (6)
Having A Party (Part 2) (medley) (6)
Hearts Of Stone (3,6)
How Come You Treat Me So Bad (1)
I Ain't Got The Fever No More (2)
I Can't Live Without Love (8)
I Can't Wait (9)
I Choose To Sing The Blues (1)

I Don't Want To Go Home (1,6)
I Only Want To Be With You (9)
I Played The Fool (3)
I Remember Last Night (4)
I'm So Anxious (4,6) **71**
I've Been Working Too Hard (11)
It Ain't The Meat (It's The Motion) (1)
It Hurts (5)
It's Been A Long Time (11)
Keep Our Love Simple (5)
Light Don't Shine (3)
Little Calcutta (10)
Little Girl So Fine (2)
Living In The Real World (4)
Long Distance (5)
Lorraine (3)
Love Goes To War (8)
Love Is The Drug (8)

Love On The Wrong Side Of Town (2)
Love When It's Strong (5)
Ms. Park Avenue (7)
Murder (5)
My Baby's Touch (7)
New Coat Of Paint (8)
New Romeo (8)
Next To You (3)
No Secret (10)
On The Air (10)
On The Beach (5)
Over My Head (8)
Paris (4)
Restless Heart (5,6)
Ride The Night Away (11)
Right To Walk Away (11)
Roll Out The Barrel (medley) (6)
Sam Cooke Medley (6)
Security (4)
Shake 'Em Down (11)

She Got Me Where She Wants Me (2)
Sirens Of The Night (10)
Slow Burn (7)
Slow Dance (10)
Some Things Just Don't Change (2)
Soul's On Fire (11)
Stagger Lee (6)
Sweeter Than Honey (1)
Take It Inside (3)
Take My Love (9)
Talk To Me (3,6)
Tell Me Lies (8)
Tell Me (That Our Love's Still Strong) (9)
This Time Baby's Gone For Good (3)
This Time It's For Real (2)
Till The End Of The Night (9)
Time, The (4)
Trapped Again (3,6)
Trash It Up (7)

Under The Sun (9)
Vertigo (4,6)
Walk Away Renee (9) **98**
Walking Through Midnight (10)
When The Moment Is Right (10)
When You Dance (2)
Why (5)
Why Is Love Such A Sacrifice (5,6)
Without Love (2)
You Can Count On Me (9)
You Mean So Much To Me (1)
Your Precious Love (10)
Your Reply (4)

SOVINE, Red
Born Woodrow Wilson Sovine on 7/17/18 in Charleston, West Virginia; died of a heart attack on 4/14/80. Country singer/songwriter/guitarist.

9/11/76	**119**	6		Teddy Bear..	**$8**	Starday 968

Bootlegger King Daddy

Does Steppin' Out Mean Daddy Took A Walk

18 Wheels Hummin' Home
Sweet Home
1460 Elder Street

It Ain't No Big Thing
Last Mile Of The Way

Little Rosa
Love Is

Sad Violins
Teddy Bear 40

SPANDAU BALLET
English quintet: Tony Hadley (lead singer), Steve Norman, John Keeble, and brothers Gary and Martin Kemp. The Kemps starred in the 1990 film *The Krays*. Gary Kemp, later in *The Bodyguard*, married actress Sadie Frost (of the 1992 film *Dracula*).

5/14/83	**19**	37	1	True..	**$8**	Chrysalis 41403
8/18/84	**50**	16	2	Parade	**$8**	Chrysalis 41473

Always In The Back Of My Mind (2)
Code Of Love (1)
Communication (1) **59**

Foundation (1)
Gold (1) **29**
Heaven Is A Secret (1)
Highly Strung (2)

I'll Fly For You (2)
Lifeline (1)
Nature Of The Beast (2)

Only When You Leave (2) **34**
Pleasure (1)
Revenge For Love (2)

Round And Round (2)
True (1) **4**
With The Pride (2)

SPANKY AND OUR GANG
Folk-pop group formed in Chicago in 1966 featuring lead singer Elaine "Spanky" McFarlane (b: 6/19/42, Peoria, Illinois). Included Malcolm Hale, Kenny Hodges, Lefty Baker, Nigel Pickering and John Seiter. Spanky became lead singer of the new Mamas & The Papas, early '80s.

9/9/67	**77**	15	1	Spanky And Our Gang	**$15**	Mercury 61124
4/27/68	**56**	25	2	Like To Get To Know You	**$15**	Mercury 61161
2/15/69	**101**	7	3	Anything You Choose/Without Rhyme Or Reason	**$15**	Mercury 61183
11/1/69+	**91**	17	4	Spanky's Greatest Hit(s)................................[G]	**$12**	Mercury 61227

And She's Mine (3,4) **97**
Anything You Choose (3) **86**
Brother Can You Spare A Dime (3)
But Back Then (3)
Byrd Avenue (1)
Chick-A-Ding-Ding (2)
Come And Open Your Eyes (1)

Commercial (1,4)
Distance (1)
Everybody's Talkin' (2,4)
5 Definitions Of Love (1)
Give A Damn (3,4) **43**
Hong Kong Blues (3)
If You Could Only Be Me (1)
It Ain't Necessarily Bird Avenue (4)
Jane (3)

Jet Plane (3)
Lazy Day (1,4) **14**
Leopard Skin Phones (3)
Like To Get To Know You (2,4) **17**
Making Every Minute Count (1,4) **31**
Mecca Flat Blues (3)
My Bill (3)
Nowhere To Go (3)

1-3-5-8 (Pedagogical Round #2) (3)
Prescription For The Blues (2)
Since You've Gone (3)
Stardust (2)
Stuperflabbergasted (2)
Sunday Mornin' (2,4) **30**
Sunday Will Never Be The Same (1,4) **9**

Suzanne (2)
Swingin' Gate (2)
Three Ways From Tomorrow (2,4)
Trouble (1)
Without Rhyme Or Reason (3)
Yesterday's Rain (3,4) **94**

SPARKS
Rock duo consisting of brothers Ron (keyboards) and Russell Mael (vocals).

8/24/74	**101**	14	1	Kimono My House	**$10**	Island 9272
2/8/75	**63**	13	2	Propaganda	**$8**	Island 9312
11/29/75+	**169**	6	3	Indiscreet	**$8**	Island 9345
8/15/81	**182**	2	4	Whomp That Sucker	**$8**	RCA 4091
5/22/82	**173**	6	5	Angst In My Pants	**$8**	Atlantic 19347
4/30/83	**88**	17	6	Sparks In Outer Space	**$8**	Atlantic 80055

Achoo (3)
All You Ever Think About Is Sex (6)
Amateur Hour (1)
Angst In My Pants (5)
At Home At Work At Play (2)

B.C. (1)
Bon Voyage (2)
Complaints (1)
Cool Places (6) **49**
Dance Godammit (6)
Decline And Fall Of Me (5)

Don't Leave Me Alone With Her (2)
Don't Shoot Me (1)
Eaten By The Monster Of Love (5)
Equator (1)

Falling In Love With Myself Again (1)
Fun Bunch Of Guys From Outer Space (6)
Funny Face (4)
Get In The Swing (3)

Happy Hunting Ground (3)
Hasta Manana Monsieur (1)
Here In Heaven (1)
Hospitality On Parade (3)
How Are You Getting Home? (3)

I Married A Martian (4)
I Predict (5) **60**
I Wish I Looked A Little Better (3)
In My Family (1)
In The Future (3)

693

SPARKS — Cont'd

Instant Weight Loss (5)
It Ain't 1918 (3)
Lady Is Lingering (3)
Looks, Looks, Looks (3)
Lucky Me, Lucky You (6)
Mickey Mouse (5)
Miss The Start, Miss The End (3)

Moustache (5)
Never Turn Your Back On Mother Earth (2)
Nicotina (5)
Pineapple (3)
Please, Baby, Please (6)
Popularity (6)
Prayin' For A Party (6)

Propaganda (2)
Reinforcements (2)
Rockin' Girls (6)
Sextown U.S.A. (5)
Sherlock Holmes (5)
Something For The Girl With Everything (2)
Suzie Safety (4)

Talent Is An Asset (1)
Tarzan And Jane (5)
Thank God It's Not Christmas (1)
Thanks But No Thanks (2)
That's Not Nastassia (4)
This Town Ain't Big Enough For Both Of Us (1)

Tips For Teens (4)
Tits (3)
Under The Table With Her (3)
Upstairs (4)
Wacky Women (4)
Where's My Girl (4)
Who Don't Like Kids (2)
Willys, The (4)

Without Using Hands (3)

SPECIAL ED
Edward Archer — 16-year-old rapper from Brooklyn.

| 6/3/89 | 73 | 28 | | 1 Youngest In Charge .... | $8 | Profile 1280 |
| 8/18/90 | 84 | 13 | | 2 Legal.. | $12 | Profile 1297 |

Ak-Shun (1)
Bush, The (1)
Club Scene (1)
Come On, Let's Move It (2)

5 Men And A Mic (2)
Fly M.C. (1)
Heds And Dreds (1)
Hoedown (1)

I Got It Made (1)
I'm Special Ed (2)
I'm The Magnificent (1,2)
Livin' Like A Star (2)

Mission, The (2)
Monster Jam (1)
Ready 2 Attack (2)
See It Ya (2)

Taxing (1)
Think About It (1)
Ya Not So Hot (2)
Ya Wish Ya Could (2)

SPECIALS
Seven-man ska band from Coventry, England. Known as The Special AKA from 1978-79 and from late 1981 on. Vocalists Terry Hall and Neville Staples with guitarist Lynval Golding left group in November of 1981 to form Fun Boy Three.

| 1/26/80 | 84 | 21 | | 1 The Specials... | $8 | Chrysalis 1265 |
| 11/8/80 | 98 | 5 | | 2 More Specials... | $8 | Chrysalis 1303 |

Blank Expression (1)
Concrete Jungle (1)
(Dawning Of A) New Era (1)
Do Nothing (1)
Do The Dog (1)

Doesn't Make It Alright (1)
Enjoy Yourself (2)
Gangsters (1)
Hey, Little Rich Girl (2)
Holiday Fortnight (2)

I Can't Stand It (2)
International Jet Set (2)
It's Up To You (1)
Little Bitch (1)
Man At C&A (2)

Message To You Rudy (1)
Monkey Man (1)
Nite Klub (1)
Pearl's Cafe (2)
Rat Race (2)

Sock It To 'Em J.B. (2)
Stereotypes Part 1 & 2 (2)
Stupid Marriage (1)
Too Hot (1)
Too Much Too Young (1)

You're Wondering Now (1)

SPEER, Paul — see LANZ, David

SPENCE, Judson
Singer/songwriter/multi-instrumentalist born in Pascagoula, Mississippi.

| 12/10/88 | 168 | 13 | | Judson Spence .... | $8 | Atlantic 81902 |

Attitude
Dance With Me

Down In The Village
Everything She Do

Forever Me, Forever You
Higher

Hot & Sweaty
If You Don't Like It

Love Dies In Slow Motion
Yeah, Yeah, Yeah 32

SPENCER, Tracie
Native of Waterloo, Iowa. Twelve years old at time of first hit in 1988. Won the singing competition on TV's *Star Search* in 1986.

| 6/25/88 | 146 | 21 | | 1 Tracie Spencer.. | $8 | Capitol 48186 |
| 2/23/91 | 107 | 11 | | 2 Make The Difference.. | $12 | Capitol 92153 |

CD includes 2 bonus tracks

Because Of You (1)
Cross My Heart (1)
Double O Rhythm (2)
Hide And Seek (1)

I Have A Song To Sing (1)
I Like That (2)
Imagine (1) 85
In My Dreams (1)

Love Me (2) 48
Lullaby Child (2)
My First Broken Heart (1)
My Heart Beats Only 4 U (1)

Save Your Love (2)
Sweeter Love (2)
Symptoms Of True Love (1) 38

Tender Kisses (2) 42
This House (2) 3
This Time Make It Funky (2) 54

Too Much Of Nothing (2)
Tracie's Hideout (2)
Wanna Be (1)
You Make The Difference (2)

SPHEERIS, Jimmie
Singer/songwriter/guitarist.

| 9/20/75 | 135 | 6 | | The Dragon Is Dancing .... | $8 | Epic 33565 |

Blown Out
Blue Streets

Dragon Is Dancing
Eternity Spin

In The Misty Woods
Lost In The Midway

Love's In Vain
Sighs In A Shell

Snake Man
Summer Salt

Sunken Skies
Tequila Moonlite

SPICE 1
Rapper born in Byron, Texas and raised in Hayward and Oakland, California. Discovered by Too Short.

| 5/2/92 | 82 | 31 | | Spice 1 .... | $12 | Jive 41481 |

Break Yourself
City Streets
East Bay Gangster

Fucked In The Game
In My Neighborhood
Money Gone

Money Or Murder
1-800-Spice
187 Proof

187 Pure
1-900-Spice
Peace To My Nine

Welcome To The Ghetto
Young Nigga

SPIDER
New York-based rock quintet: South African native Amanda Blue (vocals), Holly Knight, Anton Fig, Keith Lentin and Jimmy Lowell. Keyboardist Knight, a prolific songwriter, later joined Device and then went solo. Drummer Fig joined house band of TV's *Late Night With David Letterman*.

| 5/17/80 | 130 | 10 | | 1 Spider .... | $8 | Dreamland 5000 |
| 7/11/81 | 185 | 2 | | 2 Between The Lines .... | $8 | Dreamland 5007 |

Better Be Good To Me (2)
Between The Lines (2)
Brotherly Love (1)
Burning Love (1)

Can't Live This Way Anymore (2)
Change (1)
Crossfire (1)

Don't Waste Your Time (1)
Everything Is Alright (1) 86
Faces Are Changing (2)
Go And Run (2)

Going By (2)
I Love (2)
I Think I Like It (2)
It Didn't Take Long (2) 43

Little Darlin' (1)
New Romance (It's A Mystery) (1) 39
Shady Lady (1)

What's Going On (1)
Zero (1)

SPIDERS FROM MARS
David Bowie's backup band: Pete McDonald (vocals), Dave Black (guitar), Trevor Bolder (bass) and Woody Woodmansey (drums).

| 4/3/76 | 197 | 2 | | Spiders From Mars .... | $12 | Pye 12125 |

Can It Be Far
Fallen Star

Good Day America
(I Don't Wanna Do No) Limbo Rainbow

Prisoner
Red Eyes
Shine A Light

Stranger To My Door
White Man Black Man

SPINAL TAP
Parody heavy-metal trio introduced in the 1984 mock documentary film *This Is Spinal Tap*. Actor Michael McKean portrays David St. Hubbins, Christopher Guest is Nigel Tufnel and Harry Shearer is Derek Smalls. Guest, married to actress Jamie Lee Curtis, is heir to a baron title and a seat in Britian's House of Lords. McKean played Lenny on TV's *Laverne & Shirley*.

| 4/28/84 | 121 | 10 | | 1 This Is Spinal Tap.......................................[S] | $8 | Polydor 817846 |
| 4/4/92 | 61 | 6 | | 2 Break Like The Wind... | $12 | MCA 10514 |

DEBUT DATE	PEAK POS	WKS CHR	G O L D	ARTIST — Album Title	$	Label & Number

SPINAL TAP — Cont'd

All The Way Home (2)	Cash On Delivery (2)	Gimme Some Money (1)	(Listen To The) Flower People (1)	Sex Farm (1)	Sun Never Sweats (2)
America (1)	Christmas With The Devil (2)	Heavy Duty (1)	Majesty Of Rock (2)	Springtime (2)	Tonight I'm Gonna Rock You
Big Bottom (1)	Clam Caravan (2)	Hell Hole (1)	Rainy Day Sun (1)	Stinkin' Up The Great	Tonight (1)
Bitch School (2)	Cups And Cakes (1)	Just Begin Again (2)	Rock And Roll Creation (1)	Outdoors (2)	
Break Like The Wind (2)	Diva Fever (2)			Stonehenge (1)	

SPIN DOCTORS

Rock quartet formed at New York's New School of Jazz: Christopher Barron (vocals), Eric Schenkman, Mark White and Aaron Comess.

| 7/4/92 | 13↑ | 32↑ ▲ | | Pocket Full Of Kryptonite .... | $12 | Epic/Assc. 47461 |

Forty Or Fifty	How Could You Want Him	Jimmy Olsen's Blues	More Than She Knows	Refrigerator Car	Two Princes 64↑
Hard To Exist (medley)	(When You Know You Could Have Me?)	**Little Miss Can't Be Wrong** 17	Off My Line	Shinbone Alley (medley)	What Time Is It?

★★200★★ SPINNERS

R&B vocal group from Ferndale High School near Detroit, originally known as the Domingoes. Discovered by producer/lead singer of The Moonglows, Harvey Fuqua, and became the Spinners in 1961. First recorded on Fuqua's Tri-Phi label. Many personnel changes. G.C. Cameron was lead singer from 1968-72. 1972 hit lineup included Phillippe Wynne (tenor; d: 7/14/84), Bobbie Smith (tenor), Billy Henderson and Henry Fambrough (baritone) and Pervis Jackson (bass). Wynne left group in 1977 and toured with Parliament/Funkadelic; replaced by John Edwards.

11/14/70	199	2		1 2nd Time Around	$15	V.I.P. 405
4/21/73	14	28	●	2 Spinners	$10	Atlantic 7256
5/12/73	124	10		3 The Best of The Spinners ....[E]	$10	Motown 769
3/16/74	16	35	●	4 Mighty Love	$10	Atlantic 7296
12/14/74+	9	26	●	5 New And Improved	$10	Atlantic 18118
8/9/75	8	26	●	6 **Pick Of The Litter**	$8	Atlantic 18141
12/13/75+	20	21		7 Spinners Live! ....[L]	$10	Atlantic 910 [2]
7/31/76	25	30	●	8 Happiness Is Being With The Detroit Spinners	$8	Atlantic 18181
4/2/77	26	13		9 Yesterday, Today & Tomorrow	$8	Atlantic 19100
12/24/77+	57	13		10 Spinners/8	$8	Atlantic 19146
5/20/78	115	9		11 The Best of The Spinners ....[G]	$8	Atlantic 19179
5/26/79	165	4		12 From Here To Eternally	$8	Atlantic 19219
1/19/80	32	20		13 Dancin' And Lovin'	$8	Atlantic 19256
6/21/80	53	13		14 Love Trippin'	$8	Atlantic 19270
4/4/81	128	6		15 Labor Of Love	$8	Atlantic 16032
1/16/82	196	4		16 Can't Shake This Feelin'	$8	Atlantic 19318
1/8/83	167	6		17 Grand Slam	$8	Atlantic 80020

Ain't No Price On Happiness (4)	Forgive Me, Girl ..see: Working My Way Back To You	I'm Calling You Now (17)	Long Live Soul Music (15)	One Man Wonderful Band (12)	They Just Can't Stop It The (Games People Play) (6,11)
All That Glitters Ain't Gold (6)	Four Hands In The Fire (8)	**I'm Coming Home** (4) **18**	Love Connection (Raise The Window Down) (16)	**One Of A Kind (Love Affair)** (2,7,11) **11**	**Together We Can Make Such Sweet Music** (1,3) **91**
Almost All The Way To Love (15)	**Funny How Time Slips Away** (17) **67**	I'm Glad You Walked Into My Life (4)	**Love Don't Love Nobody - Pt. 1** (4,7) **15**	One, One, Two, Two, Boogie Woogie Avenue (Home Of	Toni My Love (8)
Are You Ready For Love (12)	**Ghetto Child** (2,11) **29**	I'm Gonna Getcha (10)	Love Don't Love Nobody - Pt. 2 (7)	The Boogie, House Of The Funk) (13)	Truly Yours (3)
Baby I Need Your Love (You're The Only One) (10)	Give Your Lady What She Wants (15)	I'm Riding Your Shadow (Down To Love) (9)	Love Has Gone Away (4)	O-o-h Child (1,3)	We Belong Together (2)
Back In The Arms Of Love (10)	Got To Be Love (16)	I'm Takin' You Back (14)	(Love Is) One Step Away (10)	Painted Magic (10)	**We'll Have It Made** (3) **89**
Bad, Bad Weather (Till You Come Home) (1,3)	He'll Never Love You Like I Do (4)	I've Got To Find Myself A Brand New Baby (1,3)	Love Is Blue (medley) (1)	Pay Them No Mind (1)	Winter Of Our Love (15)
Be My Love (15)	**Heaven On Earth (So Fine)** (10) **89**	I've Got To Make It On My Own (5,7)	Love Is Such A Crazy Feeling (16)	Pipedream (14)	With My Eyes (13)
Body Language (13)	Heavy On The Sunshine (14)	I've Loved You For A Long Time ..see: Cupid	**Love Or Leave** (6) **36**	Plain And Simple Love Song (12)	**Working My Way Back To You/Forgive Me, Girl** (13) **2**
Can Sing A Rainbow (medley) (1)	Honest I Do (6)	If I Knew (17)	Love Trippin' (14)	**Rubberband Man** (8,11) **2**	Yesterday Once More/Nothing Remains
Can't Shake This Feelin' (16)	Honey, I'm In Love With You (9)	If You Can't Be In Love (8)	Lover Boy (17)	**Sadie** (5,7,11) **54**	The Same (15) 52
City Full Of Memories (17)	**How Could I Let You Get Away** (2,7,11) **77**	If You Wanna Do A Dance (12) 49	Magic In The Moonlight (17)	Send A Little Love (16)	You Go Your Way (I'll Go Mine) (16)
Clown, The (8)	I Could Never (Repay Your Love) (2)	In My Diary (1)	Man Just Don't Know What A Woman Goes Through (15)	(She's Gonna Love Me) At Sundown (1)	You Got The Love That I Need (10)
Could It Be I'm Falling In Love (2,7,11) **4**	I Don't Want To Lose You (6)	It's A Natural Affair (12)	Me And My Music (9)	Since I Been Gone (4)	You Made A Promise To Me (6)
Cupid/I've Loved You For A Long Time (14) **4**	I Found Love (When I Found You) (9)	**It's A Shame** (1,3) **14**	**Mighty Love** (4,7,11) **20**	Sitting On Top Of The World (5)	You're All I Need In Life (8)
Deacon, The (15)	I Just Want To Be With You (14)	Just As Long As We Have Love (6)	My Lady Love (1)	Smile, We Have Each Other (5)	You're The Love Of My Life (9)
Didn't I Blow Your Mind (16)	I Just Want To Fall In Love (14)	Just Can't Get You Out Of My Mind (2)	My Whole World Ended (The Moment You Left Me) (1,3)	So Far Away (17)	**You're Throwing A Good Love Away** (9) **43**
Disco Ride (13)	I Love The Music (12)	Just Let Love In (17)	**Never Thought I'd Fall In Love** (16) **95**	Souly Ghost (1)	
Don't Let The Green Grass Fool You (2)	I Must Be Living For A Broken Heart (9)	Just To Be With You (9)	No Other Love (17)	Split Decision (14)	
Don't Let The Man Get You (12)	**I'll Always Love You** (1) **35**	Just You And Me Baby (2)	Nothing Remains The Same ..see: Yesterday Once More	Standing On The Rock (15)	
Easy Come, Easy Go (10)	**I'll Be Around** (2,11) **3**	Knack For Me (16)	Now That We're Together (8)	Streetwise (14)	
Fascinating Rhythm (7)		Lazy Susan (5)	Now That You're Mine Again (14)	Superstar Medley (7)	
		Let's Boogie, Let's Dance (13)	Once You Fall In Love (12)	Sweet Corner Of Mine (6)	
		Living A Little, Laughing A Little (5,7) **37**		Sweet Thing (3)	
				Then Came You (5,7,11) **1**	
				There's No One Like You (5)	

SPIRAL STARECASE

Sacramento pop-rock quintet: Pat Upton (lead), Harvey Kaplan, Dick Lopes, Bobby Raymond and Vinny Parello.

| 6/14/69 | 79 | 16 | | More Today Than Yesterday .... | $20 | Columbia 9852 |

Broken-Hearted Man	**More Today Than Yesterday** 12	No One For Me To Turn To 52	Our Day Will Come	Since I Don't Have You	This Guy's In Love With You
For Once In My Life			Proud Mary	Sweet Little Thing	Thought Of Loving You
Judas To The Love We Knew					

SPIRIT

Los Angeles eclectic rock group: Jay Ferguson (lead singer), Mark Andes (bass), Ed Cassidy (drums), Randy California (guitar) and John Locke (keyboards). Ferguson and Andes left to form Jo Jo Gunne in mid-1971. Andes became an original member of Firefall in 1975 and later joined Heart in 1983.

| 4/20/68 | 31 | 32 | | 1 Spirit .... | $15 | Ode 44004 |

DEBUT DATE	PEAK POS	WKS CHR	GOLD	ARTIST — Album Title	$	Label & Number

SPIRIT — Cont'd

DEBUT DATE	PEAK POS	WKS CHR	GOLD	ARTIST — Album Title	$	Label & Number
1/18/69	**22**	21	2	The Family That Plays Together	$15	Ode 44014
8/23/69	**55**	15	3	Clear Spirit..	$15	Ode 44016
12/26/70+	**63**	14	● 4	Twelve Dreams Of Dr. Sardonicus	$12	Epic 30267
3/18/72	**63**	14	5	Feedback...	$12	Epic 31175
7/22/72	**189**	7	6	The Family That Plays Together .... [R]	$12	Epic 31461
				new cover does not include the original additional flap		
7/21/73	**119**	12	7	The Best Of Spirit .... [G]	$10	Epic 32271
8/25/73	**191**	4	8	Spirit .... [R]	$12	Epic 31457 [2]
				reissue of albums #1 & 3 above		
6/7/75	**147**	9	9	Spirit Of '76	$12	Mercury 804 [2]
7/31/76	**179**	4	10	Farther Along	$10	Mercury 1094

America, The Beautiful (medley) (9)
Animal Zoo (4,7) **97**
Apple Orchard (3,8)
Aren't You Glad (2,6)
Atomic Boogie (10)
Cadillac Cowboys (5)
Caught (3,8)
Chelsea Girls (5)
Clear (3,8)
Cold Wind (3,8)
Colossus (10)
Dark Eyed Woman (3,7,8)
Darkness (9)
Darlin' If (2,6)
Diamond Spirit (10)

Don't Lock Up Your Door (10)
Dream Within A Dream (2,6)
Drunkard, The (2,6)
Earth Shaker (5)
Elijah (1,8)
Farther Along (9)
Feeling In Time (9)
Fresh-Garbage (1,7,8)
Girl In Your Eye (9)
Give A Life, Take A Life (3,8)
Gramophone Man (1,8)
Great Canyon Fire In General (1,8)
Ground Hog (3,8)
Guide Me (9)

Happy (9)
Hey, Joe (9)
I Got A Line On You (2,6,7) **25**
I'm Truckin' (3,8)
Ice (3,8)
It Shall Be (2,6)
It's All The Same (2,6)
Jack Bond (Pt. I & II) (9)
Jewish (2,6)
Joker On The Run (9)
Lady Of The Lakes (9)
Life Has Just Begun (4)
Like A Rolling Stone (9)
Love Has Found A Way (4)
Maunaloa (9)

Mechanical World (1,7,8)
Mega Star (10)
Mellow Morning (5)
Morning Will Come (4,7)
Mr. Skin (4,7) **92**
My Road (9)
Nature's Way (4,7,10)
New Dope In Town (3,8)
1984 (7) **69**
Nothin' To Hide (4,7)
Once Again (9)
Once With You (10)
Phoebe (10)
Pineapple (5)
Policeman's Ball (3,8)
Poor Richard (2,6)

Puesta Del Scam (5)
Right On Time (5)
Ripe And Ready (5)
She Smiles (2,6)
Silky Sam (2,6)
So Little Time To Fly (3,8)
Soldier (4)
Space Child (4)
Star Spangled Banner (9)
Stoney Night (10)
Straight Arrow (1,8)
Street Worm (4)
Sunrise (9)
Tampa Jam (Pt. I-III) (9)
Taurus (1,8)
Thank You Lord (9)

Times, They Are A'Changing (medley) (9)
Topanga Windows (1,8)
Trancas Fog-Out (5)
Uncle Jack (1,7,8)
Urantia (9)
Veruska (9)
Victim Of Society (9)
Walking The Dog (9)
Water Woman (1,8)
What Do I Have (9)
When? (9)
When I Touch You (4)
Why Can't I Be Free (4)
Witch (5)
World Eat World Dog (10)

SPLINTER

English vocal duo: Bill Elliott and Bob Purvis.

DEBUT DATE	PEAK POS	WKS CHR	GOLD	ARTIST — Album Title	$	Label & Number
10/26/74	**81**	14		The Place I Love...	$8	Dark Horse 22001
				produced by George Harrison		

China Light
Costafine Town 77

Drink All Day (Got To Find Your Own Way Home)

Elly-May
Gravy Train

Haven't Got Time
Place I Love

Situation Vacant
Somebody's City

SPLIT ENZ

Sextet from New Zealand, led by brothers Tim and Neil Finn. The Finns and drummer Paul Hester were later members of Crowded House.

DEBUT DATE	PEAK POS	WKS CHR	GOLD	ARTIST — Album Title	$	Label & Number
8/30/80	**40**	25	1	True Colours	$8	A&M 4822
				record pressed in laser-etched vinyl		
5/23/81	**45**	19	2	Waiata	$8	A&M 4848
				Maori (aboriginal of New Zealand) title means: song or party		
5/8/82	**58**	20	3	Time And Tide	$8	A&M 4894
7/21/84	**137**	10	4	Conflicting Emotions	$8	A&M 4963

Albert Of India (2)
Bon Voyage (4)
Bullet Brain And Cactus Head (4)
Choral Sea (1)
Clumsy (2)
Conflicting Emotions (4)
Devil You Know (2)
Dirty Creature (3)

Double Happy (1)
Ghost Girl (2)
Giant Heartbeat (3)
Hard Act To Follow (2)
Haul Away (3)
Hello Sandy Allen (3)
History Never Repeats (2)
How Can I Resist Her (3)
I Don't Wanna Dance (2)

I Got You (1) **53**
I Hope I Never (1)
I Wake Up Every Night (4)
I Wouldn't Dream Of It (1)
Iris (3)
Log Cabin Fever (3)
Lost For Words (3)
Make Sense Of It (3)
Message To My Girl (4)

Missing Person (1)
Never Ceases To Amaze Me (3)
No Mischief (4)
Nobody Takes Me Seriously (1)
One Step Ahead (2)
Our Day (3)
Pioneer (3)

Poor Boy (1)
Shark Attack (1)
Ships (2)
Six Months In A Leaky Boat (3)
Small World (3)
Strait Old Line (4)
Take A Walk (3)
Wall (2)

Walking Through The Ruins (2)
What's The Matter With You (1)
Working Up An Appetite (4)

SPOOKY TOOTH

British hard-rock group led by Gary Wright and Mike Harrison. Guitarist Luther Grosvenor left in 1972, joined Stealers Wheel briefly, then changed name to Ariel Bender and joined Mott the Hoople (1973-74). Mick Jones, later of Foreigner, was guitarist from 1972-74. Wright had a very successful solo career beginning in 1975.

DEBUT DATE	PEAK POS	WKS CHR	GOLD	ARTIST — Album Title	$	Label & Number
8/16/69	**44**	19	1	Spooky Two	$12	A&M 4194
3/21/70	**92**	14	2	Ceremony...	$10	A&M 4225
				with special electronic overdubs by Pierre Henry		
8/15/70	**84**	13	3	The Last Puff...	$10	A&M 4266
6/5/71	**152**	7	4	Tobacco Road .... [R]	$10	A&M 4300
				reissue of their first album entitled It's All About...		
5/19/73	**84**	14	5	You Broke My Heart So I Busted Your Jaw	$10	A&M 4385
11/10/73	**99**	10	6	Witness	$10	Island 9337
9/21/74	**130**	8	7	The Mirror	$8	Island 9292
4/24/76	**172**	4	8	That Was Only Yesterday .... [K]	$15	A&M 3528 [2]
				GARY WRIGHT/SPOOKY TOOTH		
				(includes cuts from above A&M albums, plus cuts from solo albums by Wright)		

All Sewn Up (6)
As Long As The World Keeps Turning (6)
Better By You, Better Than Me (1)
Bubbles (4)
Confession (2)
Cotton Growing Man (5,8)
Don't Ever Stray Away (6)
Down River (3)
Dream Me A Mountain (6)
Evil Woman (1,8)
Fantasy Satisfier (7)

Fascinating Things (8)
Feelin' Bad (1,8)
Forget It, I've Got It (4)
Hangman Hang My Shell On A Tree (1)
Have Mercy (2)
Hell Or High Water (4)
Here I Lived So Well (4)
Higher Circles (7)
Holy Water (5,8)
Hoofer, The (7)
Hosanna (2)
I Am The Walrus (3)

I Can't See The Reason (8)
I Know (8)
I'm Alive (7)
I've Got Enough Heartaches (1)
It Hurts You So (4)
It's All About A Roundabout (4)
Jubilation (2)
Kyle (7)
Last Puff (3)
Lost In My Dream (1)
Love Really Changed Me (4)

Love To Survive (8)
Mirror, The (7)
Moriah (5)
Nobody There At All (3,8)
Ocean Of Power (6)
Offering (2)
Old As I Was Born (5)
Prayer (2)
Pyramids (6)
Self Seeking Man (6)
Sing A Song (8)
Society's Child (4)
Something To Say (3,8)

Son Of Your Father (3,8)
Stand For Our Rights (8)
Sunlight Of My Mind (6)
Sunshine Help Me (4,8)
That Was Only Yesterday (1,8)
Things Change (6)
This Time Around (6)
Times Have Changed (5)
Tobacco Road (5)
Two Faced Man (8)
Two Time Love (7)
Waitin' For The Wind (1,8)

Weight, The (4)
Wildfire (5,8)
Wings On My Heart (6)
Woman And Gold (7)
Wrong Time (3,8)

DEBUT DATE	PEAK POS	WKS CHR	GOLD	ARTIST — Album Title	$	Label & Number

SPORTS, The
Stephen Cummings, lead singer of Melbourne, Australia rock sextet formed in 1977.

11/24/79	194	2		Don't Throw Stones	$8	Arista 4249

Big Sleep   Mailed It To Your Sister   Suspicious Minds   Tired Of Me   **Who Listens To The**
Don't Throw Stones   Reckless   Thru The Window   Wedding Ring   **Radio 45**
Live Work & Play   Step By Step   You Ain't Home Yet

SPRINGFIELD, Dusty
Born Mary O'Brien on 4/16/39 in London. Vocalist/guitarist. In The Lana Sisters vocal group. With brother Tom Springfield and Tim Feild in folk trio, The Springfields, 1960-63.

6/27/64	62	13	1	Stay Awhile/I Only Want To Be With You...	$15	Philips 133
12/5/64	136	3	2	Dusty	$15	Philips 156
7/16/66	77	10	3	You Don't Have To Say You Love Me......................................	$15	Philips 210
12/24/66	137	3	4	Dusty Springfield's Golden Hits ....[G]	$15	Philips 220
12/23/67+	135	7	5	The Look of Love	$15	Philips 256
3/15/69	99	14	6	Dusty In Memphis	$15	Atlantic 8214
2/28/70	107	13	7	A Brand New Me	$15	Atlantic 8249

All Cried Out (2,4) **41**   Give Me Time (5) **76**   In The Land Of Make Believe   **Losing You** (4) **91**   Summer Is Over (2)   **Wishin' And Hopin'** (1,4) (5)
All I See Is You (4) **20**   Guess Who? (2)   (6)   Lost (7)   Sunny (5)   Won't Be Long (3)
Anyone Who Ever Had A   I Can't Hear You (3)   In The Middle Of Nowhere (4)   Mama Said (1)   Take Me For A Little While   **You Don't Have To Say**
Heart (1)   I Can't Make It Alone (6)   It Was Easier To Hurt Him   Mocking Bird (1)   (5)   **You Love Me** (3,4) **4**
Bad Case Of The Blues (7)   I Don't Want To Hear It   (3)   My Coloring Book (2)   They Long To Be Close To   You Don't Own Me (1)
Brand New Me (7) **24**   Anymore (6)   Joe (7)   Never Love Again (3)   You (5)
Breakfast In Bed (6) **91**   I Had A Talk With My Man   Just A Little Lovin' (6)   No Easy Way Down (6)   24 Hours From Tulsa (1)
Can I Get A Witness (2)   (3)   Just One Smile (6)   Nothing (2)   Welcome Home (5)
Chained To A Memory (5)   I Just Don't Know What To   La Bamba (3)   Oh No Not My Baby (3)   **What's It Gonna Be** (5) **49**
Come Back To Me (5)   Do With Myself (2,4)   Let Me In Your Way (7)   **Silly, Silly, Fool** (7) **76**   When The Lovelight Starts
Do Re Me (Forget About The   **I Only Want To Be With**   Let's Get Together Soon (7)   Small Town Girl (5)   Shining Thru His Eyes (1)
Do And Think About Me) (2)   **You** (1,4) **12**   Let's Talk It Over (7)   So Much Love (6)   Who Can I Turn To? (When
Don't Forget About Me   I Wish I'd Never Loved You   Little By Little (3,4)   Something Special (1)   Nobody Needs Me) (3)
(6) **64**   (2)   Live It Up (2)   **Son-Of-A Preacher Man**   Will You Love Me Tomorrow
Don't Say It Baby (2)   I've Been Wrong Before (1)   Long After Tonight Is All   (6) **10**   (1)
Don't You Know (2)   If It Don't Work Out (3)   Over (3)   Star Of My Show (7)   **Windmills Of Your Mind**
Every Day I Have To Cry (1)   If You Go Away (5)   **Look Of Love** (5) **22**   **Stay Awhile** (1,4) **38**   (6) **31**

★★315★★ SPRINGFIELD, Rick
Born on 8/23/49 in Sydney, Australia. Singer/actor/songwriter. With top Australian teen-idol band Zoot before going solo in 1972. Turned to acting in the late '70s, played Noah Drake on the TV soap opera *General Hospital* in the early '80s. Starred in the film *Hard To Hold* in 1984.

8/12/72	35	17		1 Beginnings	$15	Capitol 11047
3/14/81	7	73	▲	2 **Working Class Dog**	$8	RCA 3697
3/27/82	2³	35	▲	3 **Success Hasn't Spoiled Me Yet**	$8	RCA 4125
12/18/82+	159	8		4 Wait For Night ....[R]	$8	RCA 4235
				originally released in 1976 on Chelsea Records		
4/30/83	12	57	▲	5 Living in Oz	$8	RCA 4660
4/7/84	16	36	▲	6 Hard To Hold ....[S]	$8	RCA 4935
				Rick starred in the film		
12/8/84+	78	13		7 Beautiful Feelings ....[E]	$8	Mercury 824107
				vocals recorded in '78 with new music tracks added in '84		
4/27/85	21	26	●	8 Tao	$8	RCA 5370
2/20/88	55	16		9 Rock Of Life..	$8	RCA 6620

Affair Of The Heart (5) **9**   Don't Talk To Strangers   I Get Excited (3) **32**   Love Somebody (6) **5**   Speak To The Sky (1) **14**   **What Would The Children**
Alyson (5)   (3) **2**   I Go Swimming (6)   Me & Johnny (5)   Stand Up (6)   **Think** (1) **70**
American Girl (3)   **Don't Walk Away** (6) **26**   **I've Done Everything For**   Million Dollar Face (4)   **State Of The Heart** (8) **22**   When The Lights Go Down
April 24, 1981 (3)   Dream In Colour (9)   **You** (2) **8**   Motel Eyes (5)   Still Crazy For You (3)   (6)
Archangel (4)   Everybody's Cheating (7)   (If You Think You're) Groovy   Mother Can You Carry Me (1)   Stranger In The House (8)   Where's All The Love (4)
Ballad Of Annie Goodbody   Everybody's Girl (2)   (9)   My Father's Chair (8)   **Take A Hand** (4) **41**   Why? (1)
(1)   Goldfever (4)   Inside Silvia (2)   Old Gangsters Never Die (4)   Tao Of Heaven (8)   Woman (9)
Beautiful Feelings (7)   Great Lost Art Of   Jessica (4)   One Broken Heart (4)   **Taxi Dancing** (6) **59**   World Start Turning (9)
Black Is Black (3)   Conversation (6)   **Jessie's Girl** (2) **1**   One Reason (To Believe) (9)   Tiger By The Tail (5)   Written In Rock (8)
Bop 'Til You Drop (6) **20**   Guenevere (7)   Just One Kiss (3)   1,000 Years (1)   Tonight (3)
Brand New Feeling (7)   Heart Of A Woman (6)   Just One Look (7)   Power Of Love (The Tao Of   Treat Me Gently In The
Bruce (7) **27**   Hold On To Your Dream (9)   Kristina (3)   Love) (8)   Morning (4)
Calling All Girls (3)   Hole In My Heart (2)   Life Is A Celebration (4)   Red Hot And Blue Love (2)   Unhappy Ending (1)
Carry Me Away (2)   Honeymoon In Beirut (9)   Light Of Love (2)   **Rock Of Life** (9) **22**   Walk Like A Man (8)
Celebrate Youth (8) **26**   Hooky Jo (1)   Like Father, Like Son (5)   S.F.O. (6)   Walking On The Edge (8)
Cold Feet (7)   How Do You Talk To Girls (3)   Living In Oz (5)   Solitary One (7)   **What Kind Of Fool Am I**
Come On Everybody (1)   **Human Touch** (5) **18**   Looking For The One (7)   Soul To Soul (9)   (3) **21**
Daddy's Pearl (2)   I Can't Stop Hurting You (5)   **Love Is Alright Tonite**   **Souls** (5) **23**
Dance This World Away (8)   I Didn't Mean To Love You (1)   (2) **1**   Spanish Eyes (7)

SPRINGFIELDS, The
English folk trio: Dusty and brother Tom Springfield and Tim Feild.

10/27/62	91	4		Silver Threads & Golden Needles	$20	Philips 052

Allentown Jail   **Dear Hearts And Gentle**   Gotta Travel On   Lonesome Traveller   **Silver Threads And Golden**   They Took John Away
Aunt Rhody   **People 95**   Green Leaves Of Summer   Silver Dollar   **Needles 20**   Two Brothers
Black Hills Of Dakota   Goodnight Irene

★★92★★ SPRINGSTEEN, Bruce
Born on 9/23/49 in Freehold, New Jersey. Rock singer/songwriter/guitarist. Worked local clubs in New Jersey and Greenwich Village, mid-1960s. Own E-Street Band in 1973, consisted of Clarence Clemons (saxophone), David Sancious and Danny Federici (keyboards), Gary Tallent (bass) and Vini Lopez (drums). Sancious and Lopez replaced by Roy Bittan and Max Weinberg in 1975. Miami Steve Van Zandt (guitar) joined group in 1975. Wrote Earth Band's "Blinded By The Light" and the Pointer Sisters' "Fire." After *Born To Run*, a court injunction prevented the release of any new albums until 1978. Married to model/actress Julianne Phillips from 1985-89. Appeared in the 1987 film *Hail! Hail! Rock 'N' Roll*. Split from the E-Street Band in November 1989. Married Patti Scialfa, former singer with the E-Street Band, on 6/8/91.

7/26/75	60	43	▲²	1 Greetings From Asbury Park, N.J. ....[R]	$15	Columbia 31903

DEBUT DATE	PEAK POS	WKS CHR	GOLD	ARTIST — Album Title	$	Label & Number
				SPRINGSTEEN, Bruce — Cont'd		
7/26/75	**59**	34	▲	**2** The Wild, The Innocent & The E Street Shuffle .... [R]	$15	Columbia 32432
				above 2 originally released in 1973		
9/13/75	**3**	110	▲³	**3 Born To Run**	$10	Columbia 33795
6/17/78	**5**	97	▲²	**4 Darkness on the Edge of Town**	$10	Columbia 35318
11/1/80	**1**⁴	108	▲²	**5 The River**	$12	Columbia 36854 [2]
10/9/82	**3**	29	▲	**6 Nebraska**	$8	Columbia 38358
				recorded on a 4-track cassette recorder at home		
6/23/84	**1**⁷	139	▲¹²	**7 Born In The U.S.A.**	$8	Columbia 38653
11/29/86	**1**⁷	26	▲¹²	**8 Bruce Springsteen & The E Street Band Live/1975-85** ....[L]	$35	Columb
				BRUCE SPRINGSTEEN & THE E STREET BAND		
				contains 40 songs and a 36-page color booklet with lyrics		
10/24/87	**1**¹	45	▲³	**9 Tunnel Of Love**	$8	Columbia 40999
4/18/92	**2**²	27	▲	**10 Human Touch**	$12	Columbia 53000
4/18/92	**3**	23	▲	**11 Lucky Town**	$12	Columbia 53001

Adam Raised A Cain (4,8)
Ain't Got You (9)
All Or Nothin' At All (10)
All That Heaven Will Allow (9)
Angel, The (1)
Atlantic City (6)
Backstreets (3,8)
Badlands (4,8) **42**
Because The Night (8)
Better Days (11) *flip*
Big Muddy (11)
Blinded By The Light (1)
Bobby Jean (7,8)
Book Of Dreams (11)
Born In The U.S.A. (7,8) **9**
Born To Run (3,8) **23**
Brilliant Disguise (11) **5**
Cadillac Ranch (5,8)
Candy's Room (4,8)
Cautious Man (9)
Cover Me (7,8) **7**
Cross My Heart (10)
Crush On You (5)
Dancing In The Dark (7) **2**
Darkness On The Edge Of Town (4,8)
Darlington County (7,8)
Does This Bus Stop At 82nd Street? (1)
Downbound Train (7)
Drive All Night (5)
E Street Shuffle (2)
Factory (4)
Fade Away (5) **20**
57 Channels (And Nothin' On) (10) **68**
Fire (8) **46**
For You (1)
4th Of July, Asbury Park (Sandy) (2,8)
Gloria's Eyes (10)
Glory Days (7) **5**
Growin' Up (1,8)
Highway Patrolman (6)
Human Touch (10) **16**
Hungry Heart (5,8) **5**
I Wanna Marry You (5)
I Wish I Were Blind (10)
I'm A Rocker (5)
I'm Goin' Down (7) **9**
I'm On Fire (7,8) **6**
If I Should Fall Behind (11)
Incident On 57th Street (2)
Independence Day (5,8)
It's Hard To Be A Saint In The City (1,8)
Jackson Cage (5)
Jersey Girl (8)
Johnny 99 (6,8)
Jungleland (3)
Kitty's Back (2)
Leap Of Faith (11)
Living Proof (11)
Local Hero (11)
Long Goodbye (10)
Lost In The Flood (1)
Lucky Town (11)
Man's Job (10)
Mansion On The Hill (6)
Mary Queen Of Arkansas (1)
Meeting Across The River (3)
My Beautiful Reward (11)
My Father's House (6)
My Hometown (7,8) **6**
Nebraska (6,9)
New York City Serenade (2)
Night (3)
No Surrender (7,8)
One Step Up (9) **13**
Open All Night (9)
Out In The Street (5)
Paradise By The "C" (8)
Point Blank (5)
Pony Boy (10)
Price You Pay (5)
Promised Land (4,8)
Prove It All Night (4) **33**
Racing In The Street (4,8)
Raise Your Hand (8)
Ramrod (5)
Real Man (10)
Real World (10)
Reason To Believe (6,8)
River, The (5,8)
Roll Of The Dice (10)
Rosalita (Come Out Tonight) (2,8)
Seeds (8)
She's The One (3)
Sherry Darling (5)
Something In The Night (4)
Soul Driver (10)
Souls Of The Departed (11)
Spare Parts (9)
Spirit In The Night (1,8)
State Trooper (6)
Stolen Car (5)
Streets Of Fire (4)
Tenth Avenue Freeze-Out (3,8) **83**
This Land Is Your Land (8)
Thunder Road (3,8)
Ties That Bind (5)
Tougher Than The Rest (9)
Tunnel Of Love (9) **9**
Two Faces (9)
Two Hearts (5,8)
Used Cars (6)
Valentine's Day (9)
Walk Like A Man (9)
War (8) **8**
When You're Alone (9)
Wild Billy's Circus Story (1)
With Every Wish (10)
Working On The Highway (7,8)
Wreck On The Highway (5)
You Can Look (But You Better Not Touch) (5,8)

★★207★★				**SPYRO GYRA**		
				Jazz-pop band formed in 1975 in Buffalo, New York. Led by saxophonist Jay Beckenstein (b: 5/14/51).		
5/20/78	**99**	12		**1 Spyro Gyra** ....[I]	$12	Amherst 1014
4/7/79	**27**	41	▲	**2 Morning Dance** ....[I]	$8	Infinity 9004
3/22/80	**19**	29	●	**3 Catching The Sun** ....[I]	$8	MCA 5108
11/1/80	**49**	30		**4 Carnaval** ....[I]	$8	MCA 5149
8/29/81	**41**	27		**5 Freetime** ....[I]	$8	MCA 5238
10/23/82	**46**	24		**6 Incognito** ....[I]	$8	MCA 5368
8/13/83	**66**	16		**7 City Kids** ....[I]	$8	MCA 5431
7/14/84	**59**	19		**8 Access All Areas** ....[I-L]	$10	MCA 6893 [2]
6/29/85	**66**	23		**9 Alternating Currents** ....[I]	$8	MCA 5606
7/12/86	**71**	19		**10 Breakout** ....[I]	$8	MCA 5753
9/26/87	**84**	9		**11 Stories Without Words** ....[I]	$8	MCA 42046
7/16/88	**104**	8		**12 Rites Of Summer** ....[I]	$8	MCA 6235
7/8/89	**120**	6		**13 Point of View** ....[I]	$8	MCA 6309
6/23/90	**117**	8		**14 Fast Forward** ....[I]	$12	GRP 9608
7/6/91	**156**	2		**15 Collection** ....[I-K]	$12	GRP 9642

Alexandra (14)
Alternating Currents (9)
Amber Dream (5)
Archer, The (12)
Autumn Of Our Love (3)
Awakening (4)
Ballad, A (7)
Binky's Dream No. 6 (9)
Bittersweet (4)
Bob Goes To The Store (10)
Body Wave (10)
Breakout (10,15)
Bright Lights (14)
Cafe Amore (4) **77**
Captain Karma (12)
Carnaval (4)
Carolina (13)
Cascade (1)
Cashaca (4)
Catching The Sun (3,15) **68**
Cayo Hueso (11)
Chrysalis (11)
City Kids (7)
Claire's Dream (12)
Cockatoo (3)
Conversations (7,8)
Counterpoint (13)
Daddy's Got A New Girl Now (12)
Del Corazon (11)
Dizzy (4)
Doubletake (10)
Early Light (11)
Elegy For Trane (5)
End Of Romanticism (2)
Escape Hatch (14)
Fairweather (13)
4MD (14)
Foxtrot (4)
Freefall (10)
Freetime (5)
Futurephobia (14)
Galadriel (1)
Gotcha (13)
Guiltless (9)
Hannibal's Boogie (13)
Harbor Nights (6,8,15)
Haverstraw Road (7)
Heartbeat (9)
Heliopolis (2,8)
Here Again (3)
I Believe In You (9)
Incognito (6,15)
Innocent Soul (12)
Islands In The Sky (7,8)
It Doesn't Matter (1)
Joy Ride (11)
Jubilee (2)
Laser Material (3)
Last Exit (6)
Latin Streets (8)
Leticia (1)
Limelight (12,15)
Little Linda (2)
Lovin' You (3)
Mallet Ballet (1,15)
Mardi Gras (9)
Mead (1)
Morning Dance (2,8,15) **24**
Nightlife (7)
No Man's Land (12)
Nu Sungo (11,15)
Oasis (6)
Ocean Parkway (14)
Old San Juan (6,8,15)
Opus D'Opus (1)
PG (9)
Pacific Sunrise (5)
Para Ti Latino (14,15)
Paula (medley) (1)
Paw Prints (medley) (1)
Percolator (3)
Philly (3)
Pygmy Funk (1)
Pyramid (11)
Rasul (2)
Riverwalk (13)
Safari (9)
Schu's Blues (8)
Sea Biscuit (8)
Serpent In Paradise (7,8)
Serpentine Shelly (11)
Shadow Play (14)
Shakedown (9,15)
Shaker Song (1,8) **90**
Shanghai Gumbo (12)
Silver Linings (7)
Slow Burn (13)
Soho Mojo (6)
Song For Lorraine (2)
Speak Easy (14)
Starburst (2)
String Soup (5)
Stripes (3)
Sueno (8)
Summer Strut (5)
Sunflurry (9)
Swamp Thing (3)
Sweet 'N Savvy (4)
Swept Away (10)
Swing Street (13)
Taking The Plunge (For Jennifer) (9)
Telluride (5)
Tower Of Babel (14)
Unknown Soldier (13,15)
What Exit (15)
Whirlwind (10)
Yosemite (12)
You Can Count On Me (15)

				SPYS		
				Rock quintet formed by former Foreigner members Al Greenwood and Ed Gagliardi.		
8/14/82	**138**	10		**Spys**	$8	EMI America 17073

Danger
Desiree
Don't Run My Life 82
Don't Say Goodbye
Hold On (When You Feel You're Falling)
Ice Age
Into The Night
No Harm Done
Over Her
She Can't Wait

DEBUT DATE	PEAK POS	WKS CHR	GOLD	ARTIST — Album Title	$	Label & Number

★★477★★ SQUEEZE

English pop-rock group led by Chris Difford and Glenn Tilbrook. Originally known as UK Squeeze due to confusion with American band Tight Squeeze. Paul Carrack (Ace, Mike + The Mechanics) was lead singer of fluctuating lineup in 1981.

4/26/80	71	24		1 Argybargy	$8	A&M 4802
5/30/81	44	25		2 East Side Story	$8	A&M 4854
				Elvis Costello, co-producer		
5/29/82	32	30		3 Sweets From A Stranger	$8	A&M 4899
1/8/83	47	21	▲	4 Singles-45's and under ....[K]	$8	A&M 4922
9/21/85	57	20		5 Cosi Fan Tutti Frutti	$8	A&M 5085
10/3/87	36	29		6 Babylon And On	$8	A&M 5161
10/7/89	113	10		7 frank.	$8	A&M 5278
6/9/90	163	5		8 A Round And A Bout ....[L]	$12	I.R.S. 82040
				recorded at Newcastle City Hall and Hammersmith Odeon, England		

Annie Get Your Gun (4,8)
Another Nail In My Heart (1,4)
Big Beng (5)
Black Coffee In Bed (3,4,8)
Break My Heart (5)
By Your Side (5,8)
Can Of Worms (7)
Cigarette Of A Single Man (6)
Cool For Cats (4)
Dr. Jazz (7,8)
853-5937 (6) **32**
Elephant Ride (3)
F-Hole (2)
Farfisa Beat (1)
Footprints (6,8)

Frank (7)
Goodbye Girl (4)
Heartbreaking World (5)
Heaven (2)
Here Comes That Feeling (1)
His House Her Home (3)
Hits Of The Year (5)
Hourglass (6,8) **15**
I Can't Hold On (3)
I Learnt How To Pray (5)
I Think I'm Go Go (1)
I Won't Ever Go Drinking Again (?) (5)
I've Returned (3)
If I Didn't Love You (1,4)
If It's Love (7,8)

In Quintessence (2)
In Today's Room (6)
Is It Too Late (7)
Is That Love (2,4,8)
King George Street (5)
Labelled With Love (2,8)
Last Time Forever (5)
Love Circles (7)
Melody Motel (7)
Messed Around (2)
Misadventure (1)
Mumbo Jumbo (2)
No Place Like Home (5)
Onto The Dance Floor (3)
Out Of Touch (7)
Peyton Place (7)

Piccadilly (2)
Points Of View (3)
Prisoner, The (6)
Pulling Mussels (From The Shell) (1,4,8)
Rose I Said (7)
Separate Beds (1)
She Doesn't Have To Shave (7,8)
Slap And Tickle (4)
Slaughtered, Gutted And Heartbroken (7,8)
Some Americans (6)
Someone Else's Bell (2)
Someone Else's Heart (2)

Stranger Than The Stranger On The Shore (3)
Striking Matches (6)
Take Me I'm Yours (4,8)
Tempted (2,4,8) **49**
There At The Top (1)
There's No Tomorrow (2)
(This Could Be) The Last Time (7)
Tongue Like A Knife (3)
Tough Love (6)
Trust Me To Open My Mouth (6)
Up The Junction (4,8)
Vanity Fair (2)
Very First Dance (3)

Vicky Verky (1)
Waiting Game (7)
When The Hangover Strikes (3)
Who Are You? (6)
Woman's World (2)
Wrong Side Of The Moon (1)

★★465★★ SQUIER, Billy

Born on 5/12/50 in Wellesley Hills, Massachusetts. Hard-rock singer/songwriter/guitarist.

6/7/80	169	12		1 The Tale Of The Tape	$8	Capitol 12062
5/2/81	5	111	▲³	2 **Don't Say No**	$8	Capitol 12146
8/7/82	5	50	▲²	3 **Emotions in Motion**	$8	Capitol 12217
8/4/84	11	29	▲	4 Signs of Life	$8	Capitol 12361
10/18/86	61	16		5 Enough Is Enough	$8	Capitol 12483
7/15/89	64	17		6 Hear & Now	$8	Capitol 48748
4/27/91	117	6		7 Creatures Of Habit	$12	Capitol 94303

All Night Long (4) **75**
All We Have To Give (5)
Alone In Your Dreams (Don't Say Goodbye) (7)
(Another) 1984 (4)
Big Beat (1)
Break The Silence (5)
Calley Oh (1)
Can't Get Next To You (4)
Catch 22 (3)
Come Home (5)
Conscience Point (7)
Don't Let Me Go (6)
Don't Say No (2)

Don't Say You Love Me (6) **58**
Emotions In Motion (3) **68**
Everybody Wants You (3) **32**
Eye On You (4) **71**
Facts Of Life (7)
Fall For Love (4)
G.O.D. (6)
Hand-Me-Downs (4)
Hands Of Seduction (7)
Hollywood (7)
I Need You (2)
(I Put A) Spell On You (6)

In The Dark (2) **35**
In Your Eyes (3)
It Keeps You Rockin' (3)
Keep Me Satisfied (3)
Lady With A Tenor Sax (5)
Learn How To Live (3)
Like I'm Lovin' You (1)
Listen To The Heartbeat (3)
Lonely Is The Night (2)
Lonely One (5)
(L-O-V-E) Four Letter Word (7)
Love Is The Hero (5) **80**
Lover (7)

Mine Tonite (6)
Music's All Right (1)
My Kinda Lover (2) **45**
Nerves On Ice (7)
Nobody Knows (2)
One Good Woman (3)
Powerhouse (5)
Reach For The Sky (4)
Rich Kid (1)
Rock Me Tonite (4) **15**
Rock Out/Punch Somebody (6)
She Goes Down (7)
She's A Runner (3) **75**

Shot O' Love (5)
Strange Fire (7)
Stroke, The (2) **17**
Stronger (6)
Sweet Release (4)
Take A Look Behind Ya (4)
Tied Up (6)
Til It's Over (5)
Too Daze Gone (2)
Whadda You Want From Me (2)
Who Knows What A Love Can Do (1)
Who's Your Boyfriend (1)

Wink Of An Eye (5)
Work Song (6)
You Know What I Like (2)
You Should Be High Love (1)
Young At Heart (7)
Young Girls (4)
Your Love Is My Life (6)

SQUIRE, Chris

Born on 3/4/48 in London. Bassist of Yes.

1/24/76	69	12		Fish Out Of Water	$8	Atlantic 18159
				with guests Bill Bruford (drums) and Patrick Moraz (keyboards)		

Hold Out Your Hand   Lucky Seven   Safe (Canon Song)   Silently Falling   You By My Side

SRC

Detroit-based psychedelic rock sextet — Steve Lyman, lead singer.

9/28/68	147	4		1 SRC	$40	Capitol 2991
6/14/69	134	9		2 Milestones	$30	Capitol 134

Angel Song (2)
Black Sheep (1)
Bolero (medley) (2)
Checkmate (2)

Daystar (1)
Exile (1)
Eye Of The Storm (2)
I Remember Your Face (2)

In The Hall Of The Mountain King (medley) (2)
Interval (1)
Marionette (1)

No Secret Destination (2)
Onesimpletask (1)
Our Little Secret (2)
Paragon Council (1)

Refugeve (1)
Show Me (2)
Turn Into Love (2)
Up All Night (2)

STACEY Q

Dance singer from Los Angeles. Real name: Stacey Swain.

9/27/86	59	39		1 Better Than Heaven	$8	Atlantic 81676
3/5/88	115	11		2 Hard Machine	$8	Atlantic 81802

After Hours (2)
Another Chance (2)
Better Than Heaven (1)
Dancing Nowhere (1)

Don't Break My Heart (1)
Don't Let Me Down (1)
Don't Make A Fool Of Yourself (2) **66**

Favorite Things (2)
Good Girl (2)
Hard Machine (2)
He Doesn't Understand (1)

I Love You (2)
Insecurity (1)
Kiss It All Goodbye (2)
Love Or Desire (1)

Music Out Of Bounds (1)
River, The (2)
Temptation (2)
Two Of Hearts (1) **3**

We Connect (1) **35**

STACKRIDGE

British rock septet led by singer Andy Davis.

12/28/74+	191	9		Pinafore Days	$10	Sire 7503

Dangerous Bacon
Fundamentally Yours

Galloping Gaucho
God Speed The Plough

Humiliation
Last Plimsoll

One Rainy July Morning
Pinafore Days

Road To Venezuela
Spin Round The Room

DEBUT DATE	PEAK POS	WKS CHR	GOLD	ARTIST — Album Title	$	Label & Number

STAFFORD, Jim
Born on 1/16/44 in Eloise, Florida. Singer/songwriter/guitarist. Own summer variety TV show in 1975, and co-host of *Those Amazing Animals* from 1980-81. Married Bobbie Gentry in 1978.

3/16/74 **55** 33   Jim Stafford .... [N] **$10** MGM 4947

I Ain't Sharin' Sharon	Mr. Bojangles (medley)	Real Good Time	**Spiders & Snakes 3**	A Visit With An Old Friend
L.A. Mamma	**My Girl Bill** 12	16 Little Red Noses And A	**Swamp Witch** 39	(medley)
Last Chant	Nifty Fifties Blues	Horse That Sweats		**Wildwood Weed** 7

STAFFORD, Jo
Born on 11/12/20 in Coalinga, California. Member of Tommy Dorsey's vocal group the Pied Pipers, 1940-42. Married to orchestra leader Paul Weston.

12/29/56 **13** 8   Ski Trails.. **$25** Columbia 910
with husband Paul Weston (conductor) and the Norman Luboff Choir

Baby, It's Cold Outside	I've Got My Love To Keep Me	June In January	Moonlight In Vermont	Whiffenpoof Song
By The Fireside	Warm	Let It Snow! Let It Snow! Let	Nearness Of You	Winter Song
	It Happened In Sun Valley	It Snow!	Sleigh Ride	Winter Wonderland

STAFFORD, Terry
Born in Hollis, Oklahoma and raised in Amarillo, Texas. Elvis Presley sound-alike. Moved to California in 1960. Appeared in the film *Wild Wheels*.

5/16/64 **81** 11   Suspicion!... **$30** Crusader 1001

Everybody Has Somebody	For You My Love	Invitation To A Kiss	Margarita	Pocket Full Of Rainbows	Slowly But Surely
Everything I Need	**I'll Touch A Star** 25	Kiss Me Quick	Playing With Fire	She Wishes I Were You	**Suspicion** 3

STAGE DOLLS
Rock trio from Trondheim, Norway: Torstein Flakne (vocals), Terje Storli (bass) and Steinar Krokstad (drums).

8/19/89 **118** 12   Stage Dolls .... **$8** Chrysalis 21716

Ammunition	Hanoi Waters	**Love Cries** 46	Still In Love	Wings Of Steel
Don't Stop Believin'	Lorraine	Mystery	Waitin' For You	

STAIRSTEPS — see FIVE STAIRSTEPS

STALLING, Carl, Project — see CONCEPT ALBUMS

STALLION
Denver-based quintet — Buddy Stephens, lead singer.

3/26/77 **191** 9   Stallion... **$8** Casablanca 7040

Fancy Francie	Glad That I Found You	Love Is A Game	Magic Of The Music	**Old Fashioned Boy (You're**	Something Just Told Me
Funny Thing	I Know How They Feel	Loving You		**The One)** 37	Woman

STALLONE, Sylvester — see PARTON, Dolly

STAMPEDERS
Pop-rock trio from Calgary: Rick Dodson, Ronnie King and Kim Berly.

10/23/71 **172** 6   Sweet City Woman .... **$12** Bell 6068

Carry Me	I Didn't Love You Anyhow	Oklahoma Country	Sunday Prayin'	Train To Nowhere	With You I Got Wheels
Gator Road	Man From P.E.I.	Only A Friend	**Sweet City Woman** 8	Tuscaloosa Women	You Got To Go

STAMPLEY, Joe — see BANDY, Moe

STANDELLS, The
Los Angeles-area, punk-rock quartet: Dick Dodd (lead singer, drums), Larry Tamblyn and Tony Valentino (guitars) and Gary Lane (bass). Dodd was an original Mouseketeer. Tamblyn is the brother of actor Russ.

7/2/66 **52** 16   Dirty Water .... **$55** Tower 5027

Dirty Water *11*	Little Sally Tease	Pride And Devotion	**Sometimes Good Guys**	There's A Storm Coming
Hey Joe, Where You Gonna	Medication	Rari	**Don't Wear White** 43	Why Did You Hurt Me
Go?	19th Nervous Breakdown			

STANKY BROWN GROUP, The
New York City-area rock group — James Brown, lead singer.

5/15/76	**192**	3	1 Our Pleasure To Serve You	**$8**	Sire 7516
3/5/77	**195**	2	2 If The Lights Don't Get You The Helots Will	**$8**	Sire 7529
4/29/78	**192**	5	3 Stanky Brown	**$8**	Sire 6053

STANKY BROWN

Alone Tonight (2)	Don't You Refuse (1)	(I Wish I Was) Back In Your	Misery (1)	Woman, Don't Let It Slip
Around Town (3)	Faith In The Family (2)	Arms Again (3)	Please Don't Be The One (3)	Away (2)
As A Lover I'm A Loser (2)	Falling Fast (3)	Let's Get To Livin' (1)	Ravin' Beauty (1)	You Be You (1)
Chains (3)	Free And Easy (2)	Life Beyond (2)	She's A Taker (3)	You Make It Happen For Me
Chance On Love (3)	Friday Night Without You (1)	Masquerade (1)	Stop In The Name Of Love (2)	(3)
Coaltown (2)	Good To Me (2)	Master Of Disguise (3)	Tell Me What You Want (3)	You've Come Over Me (1)
Confident Man (2)	Hundred Times Around (1)	Matthew (1)	Where Have They Gone (1)	

STANLEY, Michael, Band
Cleveland rock group: Michael Stanley (vocals, guitar; b: Michael Stanley Gee on 3/25/48), Kevin Raleigh (vocals, keyboards), Bob Pelander (keyboards), Tommy Dobeck (drums), Michael Gismondi (bass), Rick Bell (sax) and Gary Markashy (lead guitar; replaced by Danny Powers in 1983). Raleigh recorded solo in 1988. Stanley was the bassist with the group Silk.

9/13/75	**184**	3	1 You break it...You bought it!	**$12**	Epic 33492
7/8/78	**99**	18	2 Cabin Fever	**$8**	Arista 4182
8/4/79	**148**	5	3 Greatest Hints	**$8**	Arista 4236
9/27/80+	**86**	32	4 Heartland	**$8**	EMI America 17040
8/1/81	**79**	15	5 North Coast	**$8**	EMI America 17056
9/4/82	**136**	6	6 MSB	**$8**	EMI America 17071
9/24/83	**64**	17	7 You Can't Fight Fashion	**$8**	EMI America 17100

All I Ever Wanted (4)	Carolyn (5)	Don't Lead With Your Love	Down To The Wire (3)	Fool's Parade (2)	**He Can't Love You** (4) 33
Baby If You Wanna Dance (2)	Chemistry (5)	(3)	Face The Music (1)	Gypsy Eyes (1)	Hearts On Fire (4)
Back In My Arms Again (3)	Damage Is Done (7)	Don't Stop The Music (4)	**Falling In Love Again** (5) 64	Hang Tough (6)	Heaven And Hell (5)
Beautiful Lies (3)	Dancing In The Dark (1)	Don't You Do That To Me (5)	Fire In The Hole (7)	Hard Time (7)	Highlife (7)

DEBUT DATE	PEAK POS	WKS CHR	GOLD	ARTIST — Album Title	$	Label & Number

STANLEY, Michael, Band — Cont'd

Highway Angel (1)
Hold Your Fire (3)
How Can You Call This Love (7)
I'll Never Need Anyone More (Than I Need You Tonight) (4)
I'm Gonna Love You (1)
If You Love Me (6)
In Between The Lines (6)
In The Heartland (5)
Just A Little Bit Longer (6)

Just Give Me Tonight (7)
Just How Good (A Bad Woman Feels) (7)
Last Night (3)
Late Show (2)
Let's Hear It (5)
Lights Out (3)
Long Time (Looking For A Dream) (2)
Lost In The Funhouse Again (1)
Love Hurts (6)

Lover (4) *68*
Misery Loves Company (2)
My Town (7) *39*
Night By Night (6)
No Turning Back (3)
One Of Those Dreams (3)
Only A Dreamer (2)
Promises (3)
Save A Little Piece For Me (4)
Say Goodbye (4)
Slip Away (2)
Someone Like You (7) *75*

Somewhere In The Night (5)
Song For My Children (1)
Spanish Nights (6)
Step The Way (1)
Sweet Refrain (1)
Take The Time (6) *81*
Tell Me (5)
Victim Of Circumstance (5)
Voodoo (4)
Waste A Little Time On Me (1)
We Can Make It (5)

We're Not Strangers Anymore (3)
What'cha Wanna Do Tonight (2)
When I'm Holding You Tight (6) *78*
When Your Heart Says It's Right (5)
Where Have All The Clowns Gone (1)
Who's To Blame (2)

Why Should Love Be This Way (2)
Working Again (4)
You're My Love (5)

STANLEY, Paul
Born Paul Stanley Eisen on 1/20/52 in Queens, New York. Rhythm guitarist of Kiss.

10/14/78	40	18 ▲	Paul Stanley	$15	Casablanca 7123

Ain't Quite Right
Goodbye

Hold Me, Touch Me *46*
It's Alright

Love In Chains
Move On

Take Me Away (Together As One)

Tonight You Belong To Me

Wouldn't You Like To Know Me

STANSFIELD, Lisa
Born on 4/11/66. Lead singer of Blue Zone from Roachdale, England. Vocalist on Coldcut's 1989 club hit "People Hold On."

3/10/90	9	39 ▲	1 **Affection**	$12	Arista 8554

CD and cassette include bonus track

11/30/91+	43	40 ●	2 Real Love	$12	Arista 18679

Affection (1)
All Around The World (1) *3*
All Woman (2) *56*
Change (2) *27*
First Joy (2)
I Will Be Waiting (2)

It's Got To Be Real (2)
Little More Love (2)
Live Together (1)
Love In Me (1)
Make Love To Ya (2)
Mighty Love (1)

Poison (1)
Real Love (2)
Set Your Loving Free (2)
Sincerity (1)
Soul Deep (2)

Symptoms Of Loneliness & Heartache (2)
Tenderly (2)
This Is The Right Time (1) *21*
Time To Make You Mine (2)

Wake Up Baby (1)
Way You Want It (1)
What Did I Do To You? (1)
When Are You Coming Back? (1)
You Can't Deny It (1) *14*

STAPLES, Mavis
Female singer. Born in 1940 in Chicago. Leader of The Staple Singers. Appeared in the 1990 film *Graffiti Bridge*.

9/12/70	188	4	Only For The Lonely	$10	Volt 6010

Don't Change Me Now
Endlessly
How Many Times

I Have Learned To Do Without You *87*

It Makes Me Wanna Cry
Since I Fell For You

Since You Became A Part Of My Life

What Happened To The Real Me

You're The Fool

STAPLES, Pop — see KING, Albert

STAPLE SINGERS, The
Family soul group consisting of Roebuck "Pop" Staples (b: 12/28/15, Winoma, Mississippi), with his son Pervis (who left in 1971) and daughters Cleotha, Yvonne and lead singer Mavis Staples. Roebuck was a blues guitarist in his teens, later with the Golden Trumpets gospel group. Moved to Chicago in 1935. Formed own gospel group in early '50s. First recorded for United in 1953. Mavis recorded solo in 1970.

3/20/71	117	11	1 The Staple Swingers	$10	Stax 2034
2/26/72	19	37	2 Bealtitude: Respect Yourself	$10	Stax 3002
8/25/73	102	21	3 Be What You Are	$10	Stax 3015
9/14/74	125	9	4 City In The Sky	$10	Stax 5515
11/1/75+	20	18	5 Let's Do It Again	[S] $8	Curtom 5005
9/25/76	155	5	6 Pass It On	$8	Warner 2945

THE STAPLES

After Sex (5)
Almost (1)
Are You Sure (2)
Back Road Into Town (4)
Be What You Are (3) *66*
Big Mac (5)
Blood Pressure (4)
Bridges Instead Of Walls (3)
Chase (5)
City In The Sky (4) *79*
Drown Yourself (3)
Funky Love (5)
Getting Too Big For Your Britches (4)

Give A Hand - Take A Hand (1)
Grandma's Hands (3)
Heaven (3)
Heavy Makes You Happy (Sha-Na-Boom Boom) (1) *27*
How Do You Move A Mountain (1)
I Ain't Raisin' No Sand (4)
I Like The Things About You (1)
I Want To Thank You (5)
I'll Take You There (2) *1*
I'm A Lover (1)

I'm Just Another Soldier (2)
I'm On Your Side (3)
If It Ain't One Thing It's Another (4)
If You're Ready (Come Go With Me) (3) *9*
Let's Do It Again (5) *1*
Little Boy (1)
Love Comes In All Colors (3)
Love Is Plentiful (1)
Love Me Love Me, Love Me (6)
Making Love (6)
My Main Man (4) *76*
Name The Missing Word (2)
New Orleans (5) *70*

Party, The (medley) (6)
Pass It On (6)
Precious, Precious (6)
Real Thing Inside Of Me (medley) (6)
Respect Yourself (2) *12*
Something Ain't Right (4)
Sweeter Than The Sweet (6)
Take This Love Of Mine (6)
Take Your Own Time (6)
Tellin' Lies (6)
That's What Friends Are For (3)
There Is A God (4)
This Is A Perfect World (1)

This Old Town (2)
This World (2) *38*
Today Was Tomorrow Yesterday (4)
Touch A Hand, Make A Friend (3) *23*
Washington We're Watching You (4)
We The People (2)
What's Your Thing (1)
Who (2)
Who Do You Think You Are (Jesus Christ The Superstar)? (2)
Who Made The Man (4)

Whole Lot Of Love (5)
You're Gonna Make Me Cry (1)
You've Got To Earn It (1) *97*

STARBUCK
Atlanta pop-rock septet — Bruce Blackman, lead singer.

7/24/76	78	14	1 Moonlight Feels Right	$8	Private St. 2013
6/11/77	182	2	2 Rock 'n Roll Rocket	$8	Private St. 2027

Bennie Bought The Big One (2)
Bordello Bordeaux (1)
Call Me (2)
City Of The Future (2)

Don't You Know How To Love A Lady (2)
Drop A Little Rock (2)
Everybody Be Dancin' (2) *38*

Fat Boy (2)
Fool In Line (2)
I Got To Know (1) *43*
I'm Crazy (1)
Lash LaRue (1)

Little Bird (2)
Lucky Man (1) *73*
Moonlight Feels Right (1) *3*
Rock 'N Roll Rocket (medley) (2)

Slower You Go (The Longer It Lasts) (1)
So The Night Goes (1)
Sunset Eyes (2)

Working My Heart To The Bone (1)

STARCASTLE
Six-man progressive rock group — Terry Luttrell, lead singer.

3/13/76	95	15	1 Starcastle	$8	Epic 33914
2/5/77	101	11	2 Fountains Of Light	$8	Epic 34375
11/19/77	156	3	3 Citadel	$8	Epic 34935

Can't Think Twice (3)
Change In Time (3)
Could This Be Love (3)
Dawning Of The Day (2)

Diamond Song (Deep Is The Light) (2)
Elliptical Seasons (1)
Evening Wind (3)

Forces (1)
Fountains (2)
Lady Of The Lake (1)
Nova (1)

Portraits (2)
Shadows Of Song (3)
Shine On Brightly (3)
Silver Winds (2)

Stargate (1)
Sunfield (1)
To The Fire Wind (1)
True To The Light (2)

Why Have They Gone (3)
Wings Of White (3)

701

DEBUT DATE	PEAK POS	WKS CHR	GOLD	ARTIST — Album Title	$	Label & Number

STARGARD
Disco trio: Rochelle Runnells, Debra Anderson and Janice Williams. Appeared as The Diamonds in film *Sgt. Pepper's Lonely Hearts Club Band.*

3/4/78	26	13		1 Stargard..	$8	MCA 2321
7/4/81	186	2		2 Back 2 Back.......................................	$8	Warner 3456

Back To The Funk (2)   **Disco Rufus** (1) *88*   Here Comes Love (2)   It's Your Love That I'm   Love Is So Easy (1)   **Which Way Is Up, Theme**
Cat And Me (2)   Don't Change (1)   High On The Boogie (2)   Missin' (2)   Smile (1)   **Song From** (1) *21*
Diary (2)   Force, The (1)   I'll Always Love You (1)   Just One Love (2)   Three Girls (1)   You're The One (2)

STARLAND VOCAL BAND
Washington, D.C.-based pop quartet: Bill and wife Taffy Danoff, John Carroll and future wife Margot Chapman. Bill and Taffy had fronted the folk quintet Fat City. Bill co-wrote "Take Me Home, Country Roads" with friend John Denver. Denver owned Windsong record label. Won the 1976 Best New Artist Grammy.

5/29/76	20	25		1 Starland Vocal Band..........................	$8	Windsong 1351
6/11/77	104	13		2 Rear View Mirror...............................	$8	Windsong 2239

Afternoon Delight (1) *1*   Boulder To Birmingham (1)   **Hail! Hail! Rock And Roll!**   Norfolk (1)   Starland (1)
Ain't It The Fall (1)   **California Day** (1) *66*   (1) *71*   Prism (2)   Starting All Over Again (1)
American Tune (1)   Don't Say Forever (2)   Liberated Woman (2)   Rear View Mirror (2)   Too Long A Journey (2)
Baby, You Look Good To Me   Fallin' In A Deep Hole (2)   Light Of My Life (2)   St. Croix Silent Night (2)   War Surplus Baby (1)
Tonight (1)   Mr. Wrong (2)

STARPOINT
Black sextet from Maryland: brothers Ernesto, George, Orlando and Gregory Phillips, with Renee Diggs and Kayode Adeyemo. Formed as Lycindiana, did session work for Motown and All-Platinum Records.

5/9/81	138	8		1 Keep On It......................................	$8	Choc. City 2018
10/5/85+	60	47	●	2 Restless..	$8	Elektra 60424
3/21/87	95	14		3 Sensational....................................	$8	Elektra 60722

Another Night (3)   Emotions (2)   I Want You Closer (1)   Prove It Tonight (3)   Starpoint's Here Tonight (1)
Baby Let Me Do It (1)   For You (1)   Keep On It (1)   **Restless** (2) *46*   Till The End Of Time (2)
D.Y.B.O. (3)   **He Wants My Body** (3) *89*   More We Love (3)   Second Chance (3)   Touch Of Your Love (3)
Don't Take Your Love Away   I Just Want To Be Your   **Object Of My Desire** (2) *25*   See The Light (2)   We're Into Love (1)
(2)   Lover (1)   One More Night (2)   Sensational (3)   What You Been Missin' (2)

STARR, Brenda K.
Born Brenda Kaplan on 10/15/66 in Manhattan. Singer/film actress from New York City of Puerto Rican heritage. Daughter of Harvey Kaplan (Spiral Starecase).

5/21/88	58	24		1 Brenda K. Starr................................	$8	MCA 42088

All Tied Up   Drive Another Girl Home   **I Still Believe** *13*   Straight From The Heart   **What You See Is What You**   You Should Be Loving Me
Breakfast In Bed   Giving You All My Love   Over And Over   **Get** *24*

STARR, Edwin
Born Charles Hatcher on 1/21/42 in Nashville and raised in Cleveland. In vocal group, the Futuretones; recorded for Tress in 1957. With Bill Doggett Combo from 1963-65. Recorded duets with Sandra "Blinky" Williams in 1969.

5/17/69	73	13		1 25 Miles..	$15	Gordy 940
9/5/70	52	13		2 War & Peace...................................	$12	Gordy 948
7/31/71	178	7		3 Involved..	$10	Gordy 956
1/20/79	80	14		4 Clean...	$8	20th Century 559
7/28/79	115	8		5 Happy Radio...................................	$8	20th Century 591

Adios Senorita (2)   Drown My Heart (5)   I Just Wanted To Cry (2)   Music Brings Out The Beast   She Should Have Been   24 Hours (To Find My Baby)
All Around The World (2)   **Funky Music Sho Nuff**   I'd Rather Fight Than   In Me (4)   Home (2)   (1)
At Last (I Found A Love) (2)   **Turns Me On** (3) *64*   Switch (5)   My Friend (5)   Soul City (Open Your Arms   **War** (2,3) *1*
Backyard Lovin' Man (1)   Gonna Keep On Tryin' 'Till I   I'm So Into You (4)   My Sweet Lord (3)   To Me) (1)   Way Over There (3)
Ball Of Confusion (That's   Win Your Love (1)   **I'm Still A Struggling Man**   Patiently (5)   Stand (3)   Who Cares If You're Happy
What The World Is Today)   **H.A.P.P.Y. Radio** (5) *79*   (1) *80*   Pretty Little Angel (1)   **Stop The War Now** (3) *26*   Or Not (I Do) (1)
(3)   He Who Picks A Rose (1)   If My Heart Could Tell The   Raindrops Keep Fallin' On   Storm Clouds On The Way   Working Song (4)
California Soul (2)   I Can't Escape Your Memory   Story (1)   My Head (4)   (4)   You Beat Me To The Punch
Cloud Nine (3)   (2)   It's Called The Rock (5)   Rip Me Off (5)   Time (2)   (1)
Contact (4) *65*   I Can't Replace My Old Love   Jealous (4)   Running Back And Forth (2)   **Twenty-Five Miles** (1) *6*
Don't Waste Your Time (4)   (2)   Mighty Good Lovin' (1)

★★386★★ STARR, Ringo
Born Richard Starkey on 7/7/40 in Liverpool, England. Played with Rory Storm and the Hurricanes before joining The Beatles following ousting of drummer Pete Best in 1962. First solo album in 1970. Acted in films *Candy* (made in 1967, released in 1969), *The Magic Christian, 200 Motels, Born To Boogie, Blindman, That'll Be The Day, Cave Man* and Paul McCartney's *Give My Regards To Broad Street.* Played Mr. Conductor on PBS-TV's *Shining Time Station* from 1989-91. Married actress Barbara Bach in 1981.

5/16/70	22	14		1 Sentimental Journey...........................	$12	Apple 3365
10/17/70	65	15		2 Beaucoups of Blues...........................	$12	Apple 3368
11/17/73	2²	37	▲	3 Ringo..	$12	Apple 3413
				featuring backing by the other 3 Beatles		
11/30/74+	8	25	●	4 Goodnight Vienna............................	$10	Apple 3417
				guests: John Lennon and Elton John		
12/6/75+	30	11		5 Blast From Your Past............... [G]	$10	Apple 3422
10/16/76	28	9		6 Ringo's Rotogravure..........................	$10	Atlantic 18193
				guests: Paul McCartney, John Lennon, Eric Clapton & Peter Frampton		
10/15/77	162	6		7 Ringo the 4th.................................	$10	Atlantic 19108
5/20/78	129	6		8 Bad Boy.......................................	$20	Portrait 35378
11/14/81	98	12		9 Stop And Smell The Roses...................	$8	Boardwalk 33246
				guests: Paul McCartney and George Harrison		

All By Myself (4)   Blue, Turning Grey Over   Cookin' (In The Kitchen Of   Dream (1)   Easy For Me (4)   Hard Times (8)
Attention (9)   You (1)   Love) (6)   Drowning In The Sea Of   Fastest Growing Heartache   Have I Told You Lately That
Back Off Boogaloo (5,9) *9*   Bye Bye Blackbird (1)   Cryin' (7)   Love (7)   In The West (2)   I Love You? (1)
Bad Boy (8)   Call Me (4)   Dead Giveaway (9)   Drumming Is My Madness $15 Draw (2)   Have You Seen My Baby (3)
Beaucoups Of Blues   Can She Do It Like She   Devil Woman (3)   (9)   Gave It All Up (7)   Heart On My Sleeve (8)
(2,5) *87*   Dances (7)   **Dose Of Rock 'N' Roll** (6) *26*   Early 1970 (5)   Gypsies In Flight (7)   **Hey Baby** (6) *74*

DEBUT DATE	PEAK POS	WKS CHR	GOLD	ARTIST — Album Title	$	Label & Number

STARR, Ringo — Cont'd

Husbands And Wives (4)
I Wouldn't Have You Any Other Way (2)
I'd Be Talking All The Time (2)
I'll Still Love You (6)
I'm A Fool To Care (1)
I'm The Greatest (3,5)
It Don't Come Easy (5) **4**
It's All Down To Goodnight Vienna (4) *31*
It's No Secret (7)

Lady Gaye (6)
Las Brisas (6)
Let The Rest Of The World Go By (1)
Lipstick Traces (On A Cigarette) (8)
Loser's Lounge (2)
Love Don't Last Long (2)
Love Is A Many-Splendored Thing (1)
Man Like Me (8)
Monkey See - Monkey Do (8)

Nice Way (9)
Night And Day (1)
No No Song (4,5) *3*
Occapella (1)
Old Time Relovin' (8)
Oh My My (3,5) *5*
Only You (4,5) *6*
Oo-Wee (4) *flip*
Out On The Streets (7)
Photograph (3,5) *1*
Private Property (9)
Pure Gold (6)

Sentimental Journey (1)
Silent Homecoming (2)
Simple Love Song (7)
Six O'Clock (3)
Sneaking Sally Through The Alley (7)
Snookeroo (4) *flip*
Spooky Weirdness (6)
Star Dust (1)
Step Lightly (3)
Stop And Take The Time To Smell The Roses (9)

Sunshine Life For Me (Sail Away Raymond) (3)
Sure To Fall (In Love With You) (9)
Tango All Night (7)
This Be Called A Song (6)
Tonight (8)
Waiting (2)
Where Did Our Love Go (8)
Whispering Grass (Don't Tell The Trees) (1)
Who Needs A Heart (8)

Wine, Women And Loud Happy Songs (2)
Wings (7)
Without Her (2)
Women Of The Night (2)
Wrack My Brain (9) *38*
You Always Hurt The One You Love (1)
You And Me (Babe) (3)
You Belong To Me (9)
You Don't Know Me At All (6)
You're Sixteen (3,5) *1*

STARSHIP — see JEFFERSON AIRPLANE

STARS ON
Dutch session vocalists and musicians assembled by producer Jaap Eggermont. Their albums are comprised of medleys.

5/9/81	**9**	24	●	1 **Stars On Long Play** $8		Radio 16044

side 1: medley of Beatles songs; the singles "Stars on 45" (POS 1) and "Stars on 45 II" (POS 67) both made the *Hot 100*

10/31/81	**120**	6		2 Stars On Long Play II $8		Radio 19314

the single "More Stars on 45" made the *Hot 100* (POS 55)

5/8/82	**163**	6		3 Stars On Long Play III $8		Radio 19349

side 1: Rolling Stones medley; side 2: Stevie Wonder medley; the single "Stars on 45 III" made the *Hot 100* (POS 28)

Ain't No Mountain High Enough (3)
All Right Now (2)
And Your Bird Can Sing (1)
Angie (3)
As Tears Go By (3)
At The Hop (1)
Baby Love (2)
Baker Street (2)
Bang A Boomerang (2)
Bird Dog (1)
Boogie Nights (1)
Bread And Butter (1)
Brown Sugar (3)
Buona Sera (1)
California Dreamin' (2)
Can't Give You Anything (But My Love) (2)
Cathy's Clown (1)
Cracklin' Rosie (1)
Dance To The Music (2)
Day Tripper (1)
Do-Wah-Diddy-Diddy (2)
Do You Remember (1)
Do You Think I'm Sexy (2)
Do You Wanna Know A Secret (1)
Don't You Worry 'Bout A Thing (3)
Drive My Car (1)

Dum Dum Diddle (2)
Eight Days A Week (1)
Eleanor Rigby (1)
Emotional Rescue (3)
Eve Of Destruction (1)
Eve Of The War (2)
Every Little Thing (1)
Fernando (2)
Fingertips (3)
Fire (2)
For Once In My Life (3)
'45 Stars Get Ready (3)
Funky Town (1)
Get Back (1)
Get Off (2)
Get Off Of My Cloud (3)
Gimme! Gimme! Gimme! (A Man After Midnight) (2)
Gimme Shelter (1)
Golden Years Of Rock & Roll (1)
Good Day Sunshine (1)
Good, The Bad And The Ugly (2)
Hard Days Night (1)
Here Comes The Sun (1)
Honky Tonk Women (3)
Horse With No Name (2)
(I Can't Get No) Satisfaction (3)

I Hear A Symphony (2)
I Should Have Known Better (1)
I Wanna Hold Your Hand (1)
I Was Made To Love Her (3)
I Wish (3)
I'll Be Back (1)
If I Fell (1)
Isn't She Lovely (3)
It Won't Be Long (1)
It's Only Rock 'N Roll (But I Like It) (3)
Jenny, Jenny (1)
Jimmy Mack (1)
Jumpin' Jack Flash (3)
Knowing Me, Knowing You (2)
Kung-Fu-Fighting (2)
Lady Bump (1)
Lady Jane (3)
Lay All Your Love On Me (2)
Let's Go To San Francisco (2)
Let's Spend The Night Together (3)
Love Child (2)
Love Is Here And Now You're Gone (2)
Lover's Concerto (3)
Lucille (3)
M*A*S*H*, Theme From (2)

Master Blaster (3)
Miss You (3)
Monday Monday (2)
Money, Money, Money (2)
My Cherie Amour (3)
My Sweet Lord (1)
No Reply (1)
Nowhere Man (1)
Nut Rocker (1)
On And On And On (2)
Only The Lonely (1)
Out Of Time (3)
Overture From Tommy (2)
Papa Was A Rolling Stone (2)
Place In The Sun (3)
Play With Fire (3)
Please Please Me (1)
Rainy Day (1)
Reach Out I'll Be There (2)
Reflections (2)
Rip It Up (1)
Ruby Tuesday (3)
Runaway (1)
S.O.S. (2)
San Francisco (2)
She's A Rainbow (3)
Sir Duke (3)
Slippin' And Slidin' (1)
Someday We'll Be Together (2)

Sound Of Silence (2)
Star Star (3)
"Star Wars" (Main Theme) (2)
Stars On 45 (1,2)
Stars On Get Ready III (3)
Stars On Jingle (3)
Stars Will Never Stop (3)
Start Me Up (3)
Stop In The Name Of Love (2)
Sugar Baby Love (2)
Sugar, Sugar (1)
Summer Night City (2)
Sun Ain't Gonna Shine Anymore (2)
Super Trouper (2)
Superstition (3)
Sympathy For The Devil (3)
Take It Or Leave It (3)
Tax Man (1)
Tears Of A Clown (2)
Tell Me (3)
That's All Right (1)
Things We Said Today (1)
Ticket To Ride (3)
Tommy (A Rock Opera) ..see: Overture From
Under My Thumb (3)
Under The Boardwalk (3)
Uptight (Everything's Alright) (3)

Venus (1)
Video Killed The Radio Star (1)
Voulez-Vous (2)
Wait (1)
We Can Work It Out (1)
We Love You (3)
Where Did Our Love Go (2)
While My Guitar Gently Weeps (3)
Winner Takes It All (2)
Wooly Bully (1)
Word, The (1)
Y.M.C.A. (2)
Yester-Me, Yester-You, Yesterday (3)
You Are The Sunshine Of My Life (3)
You Can't Do That (1)
You Keep Me Hanging On (2)
You're Going To Lose That Girl (1)

STARZ
New York-based rock quintet: Michael Lee Smith (lead singer; brother of Rex Smith), Peter Sweval (bassist), Richie Ranno (guitar), Brenden Harkin (guitar) and Joe X. Dube (drums).

9/11/76	**123**	13		1 Starz $8		Capitol 11539
4/16/77	**89**	8		2 Violation $8		Capitol 11617
2/11/78	**105**	9		3 Attention Shoppers! $8		Capitol 11730

All Night Long (2)
Any Way That You Want It) I'll Be There (3) *79*
Boys In Action (1)
Cherry Baby (2) *33*
Cool One (2)

Detroit Girls (1)
Don't Think (1)
Good Ale We Seek (3)
Hold On To The Night (3) *78*

Is That A Street Light Or The Moon? (2)
Johnny All-Alone (3)
Live Wire (1)
Monkey Business (1)
Night Crawler (1)

Now I Can (1)
Over And Over (1)
Pull The Plug (1)
Rock Six Times (2)
She (3)

(She's Just A) Fallen Angel (1) *95*
Sing It, Shout It (2) *66*
S.T.E.A.D.Y. (1)
Subway Terror (2)

Tear It Down (1)
Third Time's The Charm (3)
Violation (2)
Waitin' On You (3)
X-Ray Spex (3)

STATLER BROTHERS, The
Country vocal quartet from Staunton, Virginia. Consisted of brothers Harold and Don Reid, Phil Balsley and Lew DeWitt. In 1983, Jimmy Fortune replaced DeWitt who died from Crohn's disease on 8/15/90 (age 52).

2/26/66	**125**	3		1 Flowers On The Wall $25		Columbia 9249
1/30/71	**126**	11		2 Bed Of Rose's $12		Mercury 61317
10/16/71	**181**	2		3 Pictures Of Moments To Remember $12		Mercury 61349
9/13/75+	**121**	20	▲	4 The Best Of The Statler Brothers ...... [G] $10		Mercury 1037
6/10/78	**155**	9	●	5 Entertainers...On And Off The Record $8		Mercury 5007
12/16/78	**183**	4	●	6 The Statler Brothers Christmas Card ...... [X] $8		Mercury 5012
7/14/79	**183**	2	●	7 The Originals $8		Mercury 5016
2/2/80	**153**	11	●	8 The Best Of The Statler Bros. Rides Again, Volume II ...... [G] $8		Mercury 5024
9/6/80	**169**	5		9 10th Anniversary $8		Mercury 5027

title refers to their tenure with Mercury Records

7/11/81	**103**	9		10 Years Ago $8		Mercury 6002
6/25/83	**193**	5		11 Today $8		Mercury 812184
5/26/84	**177**	4		12 Atlanta Blue $8		Mercury 818652
8/9/86	**183**	2		13 Four For The Show $8		Mercury 826782

DEBUT DATE	PEAK POS	WKS CHR	GOLD	ARTIST — Album Title	$	Label & Number

STATLER BROTHERS, The — Cont'd

All I Have To Offer You Is Me (2)
Almost In Love (7)
Angel In Her Face (12)
Atlanta Blue (12)
Away In A Manger (6)
Bed Of Rose's (2,4) *58*
Before The Magic Turns To Memory (5)
Best That I Can Do (5)
Billy Christian (1)
Carols Those Kids Used To Sing (6)
Carry Me Back (4)
Charlotte's Web (9)
Chet Atkins' Hand (10)
Christmas Medley (6)
Christmas To Me (6)
Class Of '57 (4)
Count On Me (13)
Counting My Memories (7)
Dad (10)
Do You Know You Are My Sunshine (5,8)
Do You Remember These (4)
Don't Forget Yourself (9)
Don't Wait On Me (10)
Doodlin' Song (1)
Elizabeth (11)

Faded Love (3)
Fifteen Years Ago (2)
Flowers On The Wall (1,4) *4*
For Cryin' Out Loud (13)
Forever (13)
Give It Your Best (12)
Guilty (11)
Here We Are Again (7,8)
Holly Wood (12)
How Are Things In Clay, Kentucky? (9)
How Great Thou Art (8)
How To Be A Country Star (7,8)
I Believe I'll Live For Him (13)
I Believe In Santa's Cause (6)
I Don't Dream Anymore (13)
I Dreamed About You (5)
I Forgot More Than You'll Ever Know (5)
I Never Spend A Christmas That I Don't Think Of You (6)
I Never Want To Kiss You Goodbye (11)
I Still Miss Someone (1)
I Wonder How The Old Folks Are At Home (1)

I'll Be Home For Christmas (6)
(I'll Even Love You) Better Than I Did Then (8)
I'll Go To My Grave Loving You (4) *93*
I'm Dyin' A Little Each Day (11)
I'm Not Quite Through Crying (1)
If It Makes Any Difference (12)
In The Garden (10)
Jingle Bells (6)
Junkie's Prayer (2)
Just A Little Talk With Jesus (7)
Just Someone I Used To Know (3)
Kid's Last Fight (9)
King Of The Road (1)
Last Goodbye (2)
(Let's Just) Take One Night At A Time (12)
Little Farther Down The Road (7)
Love Was All We Had (10)
Making Memories (3)
Me And Bobby McGee (2)

Memories Are Made Of This (10)
Memphis (1)
Moments To Remember (3)
More Like Daddy Than Me (13)
Movies, The (8)
Mr. Autry (7)
My Darling Hildegarde (1)
My Only Love (12)
My Reward (1)
Neighborhood Girl (2)
New York City (2,4)
No Love Lost (12)
Nobody Wants To Be Country (9)
Nobody's Darlin' But Mine (9)
Nothing As Original As You (7)
Official Historian On Shirley Jean Berrell (5,8)
Oh Baby Mine (I Get So Lonely) (11)
Old Cheerleaders Cry (9)
One Less Day To Go (9)
One Size Fits All (12)
One Takes The Blame (12)
Only You (13)
Pictures (3,4)

Promise (11)
Quite A Long, Long Time (1)
Right On The Money (11)
Second Thoughts (3)
Silver Medals And Sweet Memories (7)
Some I Wrote (8)
Some Memories Last Forever (11)
Something You Can't Buy (6)
Star-Spangled Banner (7)
Susan When She Tried (4)
Sweet By And By (11)
Tender Years (3)
Thank You World (4)
There Is You (11)
Things (3)
This Ole House (1)
This Part Of The World (2)
'Til The End (9)
Today I Went Back (10)
Tomorrow Is Your Friend (5)
Tomorrow Never Comes (2)
We (2)
We Ain't Even Started Yet (10)
We Got Paid By Cash (9)
We Got The Mem'ries (13)

Whatever Happened To Randolph Scott (4)
When The Yankees Came Home (7)
When You And I Were Young, Maggie (3)
When You Are Sixty-Five (5)
Where He Always Wanted To Be (7)
Whiffenpoof Song (1)
White Christmas (6)
Who Am I To Say (5,8)
Who Do You Think? (8)
Will You Be There? (13)
Years Ago (10)
You Can't Go Home (3)
You Oughta Be Here With Me (13)
You'll Be Back (Every Night In My Dreams) (10)
You're The First (5)
Your Picture In The Paper (8)
Yours Love (5)

STATON, Candi

Born in Hanceville, Alabama. Sang with the Jewel Gospel Trio from age 10. Went solo in 1968. Married for a time to Clarence Carter.

DEBUT DATE	PEAK POS	WKS CHR	GOLD	ARTIST — Album Title	$	Label & Number
2/27/71	188	2		1 Stand By Your Man	$12	Fame 4202
6/26/76	129	14		2 Young Hearts Run Free	$8	Warner 2948
7/28/79	129	6		3 Chance	$8	Warner 3333

Chance (3)
Destiny (2)
Freedom Is Just Beyond The Door (1)
He Called Me Baby (1) *52*

How Can I Put Out The Flame (When You Keep The Fire Burning) (1)
I Ain't Got Nowhere To Go (3)
I Know (2)
I Live (3)

I'm Just A Prisoner (Of Your Good Lovin') (1) *56*
Living For You (1)
Me And My Music (3)
Mr. And Mrs. Untrue (1)
Rock (3)

Run To Me (2)
Stand By Your Man (1) *24*
Summer Time With You (1)
Sweet Feeling (1) *60*
To Hear You Say You're Mine (1)

Too Hurt To Cry (1)
What A Feeling (3)
What Would Become Of Me (1)
When You Wake Up Tomorrow (3)

You Bet Your Sweet Sweet Love (2)
Young Hearts Run Free (2) *20*

STATON, Dakota

Born Aliyah Rabia on 6/3/31 in Pittsburgh. Jazz stylist.

DEBUT DATE	PEAK POS	WKS CHR	GOLD	ARTIST — Album Title	$	Label & Number
2/24/58	4	52		1 The Late, Late Show	$25	Capitol 876
10/27/58	22	1		2 Dynamic!	$25	Capitol 1054
6/1/59	23	9		3 Crazy He Calls Me	$20	Capitol 1170
11/16/59	47	3		4 Time To Swing	$20	Capitol 1241

Ain't No Use (1)
Angel Eyes (3)
Anything Goes (2)
Avalon (4)
Baby, Don't You Cry (4)
Best Thing For You (4)
Broadway (4)
But Not For Me (4)
Can't Live Without 'Em Anymore (3)

Cherokee (2)
Crazy He Calls Me (3)
Foggy Day (1)
Give Me The Simple Life (1)
Gone With The Wind (4)
How Does It Feel? (3)
How High The Moon (4)
I Never Dreamt (You'd Fall In Love With Me) (3)
I Wonder (2)

Idaho (3)
If I Should Lose You (4)
Invitation (4)
It Could Happen To You (4)
It Will Have To Do Until The Real Thing Comes Along (4)
Late, Late Show (1)
Let Me Know (4)
Let Me Off Uptown (2)
Little Girl Blue (2)

Misty (1)
Moonray (1)
Morning, Noon Or Night (3)
My Funny Valentine (1)
Night Mist (2)
No Moon At All (3)
Party's Over (3)
Say It Ain't So, Joe (2)
Some Other Spring (2)
Song Is You (4)

Summertime (1)
They All Laughed (2)
Too Close For Comfort (2)
Trust In Me (1)
What Do You Know About Love (3)
What Do You See In Her? (1)
When Lights Are Low (4)
When Sunny Gets Blue (2)
Willow Weep For Me (4)

You Don't Know What Love Is (4)
You Showed Me The Way (1)

STATUS QUO, The

English rock quintet: Francis Michael Rossi, Rick Parfitt, Roy Lynes, John Coghlan and Alan Lancaster.

DEBUT DATE	PEAK POS	WKS CHR	GOLD	ARTIST — Album Title	$	Label & Number
4/17/76	148	7		Status Quo	$8	Capitol 11509

Blue For You
Ease Your Mind

Is There A Better Way
Mad About The Boy

Mystery Song
Rain

Ring Of A Change
Rolling Home

That's A Fact

STEADY B

Rapper Warren McGlone. Born in Philadelphia. Nephew of Lawrence Goodman, the owner of the Pop Art label.

DEBUT DATE	PEAK POS	WKS CHR	GOLD	ARTIST — Album Title	$	Label & Number
10/31/87	149	7		1 What's My Name	$8	Jive 1060
10/22/88	193	1		2 Let The Hustlers Play	$8	Jive 1122

Believe Me Das Bad (1)
Certified Dope (2)
Do What You Wanna Do (2)
Don't Disturb This Groove (1)

Funky Drummer (1)
Gangster Rockin' (1)
Hill Top (1)
Hold It Now (1)

I Got Cha (2)
Let The Hustlers Play (2)
My Benz (2)
On The Real Tip (2)

Rockin' Music (1)
Rong Ho'le (1)
Serious (2)
Through Thick-N-Thin (2)

Turn It Loose (2)
Undertaker, The (2)
Use Me (1)
What's My Name (1)

Who's Makin' Ya Dance (2)
Ya Know My Rucka (2)

STEALERS WHEEL

Scottish group led by Gerry Rafferty (vocals, guitar) and Joe Egan (vocals, keyboards).

DEBUT DATE	PEAK POS	WKS CHR	GOLD	ARTIST — Album Title	$	Label & Number
2/24/73	50	22		1 Stealers Wheel	$8	A&M 4377
4/13/74	181	3		2 Ferguslie Park	$8	A&M 4419

Another Meaning (1)
Back On My Feet Again (2)
Blind Faith (2)
Everyone's Agreed That Everything Will Turn Out Fine (2) *49*

Gets So Lonely (1)
Good Businessman (2)
I Get By (1)
Johnny's Song (1)
Jose (1)
Late Again (1)

Next To Me (1)
Nothing's Gonna Make Me Change My Mind (2)
Outside Looking In (1)
Over My Head (1)
Star (2) *29*

Steamboat Row (1)
Stuck In The Middle With You (1) *6*
Waltz (You Know It Makes Sense!) (2)

What More Could You Want (1)
Wheelin' (2)
Who Cares (2)
You Put Something Better Inside Of Me (1)

DEBUT DATE	PEAK POS	WKS CHR	GOLD	ARTIST — Album Title	$	Label & Number

STEALIN HORSES
Rock-country band from Lexington, Kentucky: Kiya Heartwood, Kopana Terry, Mandy Meyer and John Durno. Band name is an ancient Indian rite of passage in which young warriors stole horses from nearby tribes.

| 6/25/88 | 146 | 12 | | Stealin Horses .... | $8 | Arista 8520 |

Ballad Of The Pralltown Cafe Gotta Get A Letter Rain Turnaround Well, The
Dyin' By The Gun Harriet Tubman Tangled Walk Away Where All The Rivers Run

STEAM
New York City studio group assembled by producer Paul Leka.

| 1/10/70 | 84 | 13 | | Steam .... | $12 | Mercury 61254 |

Come On Back And Love Me I'm The One Who Loves You I've Gotta Make You Love It's The Magic In You Girl **Na Na Hey Hey Kiss Him** New Breed, Now Generation
Come On Home Girl I've Cried A Million Tears Me 46 Love & Affection **Goodbye 1** One Good Woman

STEEL BREEZE
Ric Jacobs, lead singer of six-man pop band from California.

| 9/18/82 | 50 | 28 | | Steel Breeze .... | $8 | RCA 4424 |

All I Ever Wanted To Do **Dreamin' Is Easy 30** I Can't Wait Lost In The 80's Who's Gonna Love You **You Don't Want Me**
Can't Stop This Feeling Every Night I Think About You Street Talkin' Tonight **Anymore 16**

STEELEYE SPAN
British folk group — Maddy Prior, lead singer.

| 12/6/75 | 143 | 6 | | 1 All Around My Hat .... | $12 | Chrysalis 1091 |
| 3/25/78 | 191 | 3 | | 2 Storm Force Ten .... | $8 | Chrysalis 1151 |

All Around My Hat (1) Black Freighter (Pirate Dance With Me (1) Robin Hood (medley) (1) Sweep, Chimney Sweep (2) Wife Of Ushers Well (1)
Awake, Awake (2) Jenny) (2) Gamble Gold (medley) (1) Seventeen Come Sunday (1) Treadmill Song (2)
Batchelors Hall (1) Black Jack Davy (1) Hard Times Of Old England Some Rival (2) Victory, The (2)
  Cadgwith Anthem (1) (1) Sum Waves (Tunes) (1) Wife Of The Soldier (2)

STEELHEART
Hard-rock group from Norwalk, Connecticut: Michael Matijevic (vocals), Chris Risola, Frank Dicostanzo, Jimmy Ward and John Fowler.

| 9/22/90+ | 40 | 59 | ● | 1 Steelheart .... | $12 | MCA 6368 |
| 6/27/92 | 144 | 7 | | 2 Tangled In Reins .... | $12 | MCA 10426 |

All Your Love (2) Electric Love Child (2) **I'll Never Let You Go** Loaded Mutha (2) Rock 'N Roll (I Just Wanna) Steelheart (2)
Can't Stop Me Loving You (1) Everybody Loves Eileen (1) **(Angel Eyes) (1) 23** Love Ain't Easy (1) (1) Sticky Side Up (2)
Dancin' In The Fire (2) Gimme Gimme (1) Late For The Party (1) Love 'Em And I'm Gone (2) **She's Gone (Lady) (1) 59** Take Me Back Home (2)
Down N' Dirty (1) Like Never Before (1) Mama Don't You Cry (2) Sheila (1)

STEEL PULSE
Reggae quintet formed in Birmingham, England in 1975: David Hinds, Selwyn Brown, Alphonso Martin, Steve Nesbitt and Alvin Ewen.

7/17/82	120	13		1 True Democracy	$8	Elektra 60113
3/31/84	154	12		2 Earth Crisis	$8	Elektra 60315
7/23/88	127	7		3 State of...Emergency	$8	MCA 42192

Blues Dance Raid (1) Dub' Marcus Say (1) Leggo Beast (1) Rally Round (1) State Of Emergency (3) Who Responsible? (1)
Bodyguard (2) Earth Crisis (2) Love This Reggae Music (3) Ravers (1) Steal A Kiss (3) Wild Goose Chase (2)
Chant A Psalm (1) Find It...Quick! (1) Man No Sober (1) Reaching Out (3) Steppin' Out (2) Your House (1)
Dead End Circuit (3) Grab Education (2) Melting Pot (3) Roller Skates (2) Throne Of Gold (2)
Disco Drop Out (3) Hijacking (3) P.U.S.H. (3) Said You Was An Angel (3) Tightrope (2)

★★282★★ STEELY DAN
Los Angeles-based, pop/jazz-styled group formed by Donald Fagen (b: 1/10/48, Passaic, New Jersey; keyboards, vocals) and Walter Becker (b: 2/20/50, New York City; bass, vocals). Group, primarily known as a studio unit, featured Fagen and Becker with various studio musicians. Actor/comedian Chevy Chase was their drummer in band's formative years. Duo went their separate ways in 1981. Drummer Jimmy Hodder drowned on 6/5/90 (age 42).

12/2/72+	17	59	●	1 Can't Buy A Thrill	$8	ABC 758
7/21/73	35	34	●	2 Countdown To Ecstasy	$8	ABC 779
3/30/74	8	36	●	3 Pretzel Logic	$8	ABC 808
4/12/75	13	26	●	4 Katy Lied	$8	ABC 846
5/22/76	15	29	●	5 The Royal Scam	$8	ABC 931
10/15/77	3	60	▲	6 Aja	$10	ABC 1006
11/18/78+	30	22	▲	7 Greatest Hits .... [G]		ABC 1107 [2]
12/6/80+	9	36	▲	8 Gaucho	$8	MCA 6102
7/3/82	115	9		9 Steely Dan gold .... [G]	$8	MCA 5324

Aja (6) Chain Lightning (4,9) **Fez, The (5,7) 59** Love 'Em And I'm Gone (6) **Reeling In The Years** Turn That Heartbeat Over
All Your Love (6) Change Of The Guard (1) Fire In The Hole (1) Mama Don't You Cry (6) **(1,7) 11** Again (1)
Any Major Dude Will Tell Charlie Freak (3) Gaucho (8) Midnite Cruiser (1) **Rikki Don't Lose That** With A Gun (3)
You (3,7) Daddy Don't Live In That Glamour Profession (8) Monkey In Your Soul (3) **Number (3,7) 4** Your Gold Teeth (2)
Any World (That I'm New York City No More (4) Green Earrings (5,9) **My Old School (2,7) 63** Rose Darling (4) Your Gold Teeth II (4)
Welcome To) (4) **Deacon Blues (6,9) 19** Haitian Divorce (7) My Rival (8) Royal Scam (5)
Babylon Sisters (8,9) Dirty Work (1) Here At The Western World Night By Night (3) Sign In Stranger (5)
Bad Sneakers (4,7) **Do It Again (1,7) 6** (7) Only A Fool Would Say That **Show Biz Kids (2,7) 61**
Barrytown (3) Doctor Wu (4,7) **Hey Nineteen (8,9) 10** (1) Steelheart (6)
Black Cow (6,9) Don't Take Me Alive (5) Home At Last (6) Parker's Band (3) Take Me Back Home (6)
Black Friday (4,7) 37 East St. Louis Toodle-oo (3,7) I Got The News (6) Pearl Of The Quarter (2) Third World Man (8)
Bodhisattva (2) Everyone's Gone To The **Josie (6,7) 26** **Peg (6,7) 11** Through With Buzz (3)
Boston Rag (2) Movies (4) **Kid Charlemagne (5,7) 82** **Pretzel Logic (3,7) 57** Throw Back The Little Ones
Brooklyn (1) Everything You Did (5) King Of The World (2,9) Razor Boy (2) (4)
Caves Of Altamira (5) **FM (No Static At All) (9) 22** Kings (1) **Time Out Of Mind (8) 22**

STEINBERG, David
Born on 8/9/43 in Winnipeg, Canada. Television and film comedian/producer.

| 1/23/71 | 182 | 6 | | Disguised As A Normal Person .... [C] | $10 | Elektra 74065 |

Coast, The Dating Game Jezebel Judy Disney Lying Phone Call
Contact Lenses Dr. Reuben Joshua Lot Moses Sermon Introduction
Cute

DEBUT DATE	PEAK POS	WKS CHR	GOLD	ARTIST — Album Title	$	Label & Number
				STEINMAN, Jim		
				Born in New York City. Wrote and arranged all cuts on Meat Loaf's *Bat Out Of Hell* album.		
5/16/81	63	17		Bad For Good	$8	Cleve. I. 36531
				bonus 7" single included with album		

Bad For Good / Dance In My Pants / Left In The Dark — Lost Boys And Golden Girls / Love And Death And An American Guitar — Out Of The Frying Pan (And Into The Fire) / **Rock And Roll Dreams Come Through 32** — Stark Raving Love / Storm, The / Surf's Up

				STEPHENSON, Van		
				Pop singer/songwriter from Nashville.		
6/2/84	54	20		Righteous Anger	$8	MCA 5482

All American Boy / Cure Will Kill You — Don't Do That / Heart Over Mind — I Know Who You Are (And I Saw What You Did) / **Modern Day Delilah 22** — Others Only Dream / Righteous Anger — **What The Big Girls Do 45** / You've Been Lied To Before

★★184★★				**STEPPENWOLF**		
				Hard-rock quintet formed in Los Angeles in 1967. Original lineup: John Kay (born Joachim Krauledat on 4/12/44 in Tilsit, East Germany; vocals, guitar) Michael Monarch (guitar), Goldy McJohn (keyboards), Nick St. Nicholas (bass), Mars Bonfire (born Dennis Edmonton; guitar) and brother Jerry Edmonton (drums). All but Monarch were members of Canadian group Sparrow. Many personnel changes except for Kay.		
3/9/68	6	87	●	1 Steppenwolf	$20	Dunhill 50029
10/5/68+	3	52	●	2 The Second	$20	Dunhill 50037
3/15/69	7	29		3 At Your Birthday Party	$20	Dunhill 50053
7/5/69	29	19		4 Early Steppenwolf .... [E-L]	$20	Dunhill 50060
				recorded in 1967 when band was known as Sparrow; side 2 is a 21 1/2-minute version of "The Pusher"		
11/15/69+	17	46	●	5 Monster	$20	Dunhill 50066
4/18/70	7	53	●	6 Steppenwolf 'Live' .... [L]	$20	Dunhill 50075 [2]
11/21/70	19	17	●	7 Steppenwolf 7	$20	Dunhill 50090
3/6/71	24	36	●	8 Steppenwolf Gold/Their Great Hits .... [G]	$20	Dunhill 50099
10/2/71	54	11		9 For Ladies Only	$20	Dunhill 50110
6/17/72	62	13		10 Rest In Peace .... [K]	$15	Dunhill 50124
2/24/73	152	9	●	11 16 Greatest Hits .... [G]	$15	Dunhill 50135
9/21/74	47	12		12 Slow Flux	$10	Mums 33093
9/20/75	155	4		13 Hour Of The Wolf	$8	Epic 33583
9/26/87	171	4		14 Rock & Roll Rebels	$8	Qwil 1560
				JOHN KAY & STEPPENWOLF		

America (medley) (5) / Annie, Annie Over (13) / Another's Lifetime (13) / Ball Crusher (7) / Berry Rides Again (1) / Black Pit (9) / **Born To Be Wild** (1,6,8,11) **2** / Caroline (Are You Ready For The Outlaw World) (13) / Cat Killer (1) / Chicken Wolf (3) / Children Of Night (12) / Corina, Corina (4,6) / Desperation (1,10) / Disappointment Number (Unknown) (2) / Don't Cry (3) / Don't Step On The Grass, Sam (2,6,10) / Draft Resister (5,6) — Earschplittenloudenboomer (7) / Everybody Knows You (14) / Everybody's Next One (1,10) / Fag (5) / Faster Than The Speed Of Life (2) / Fat Jack (7) / Fishin' In The Dark (12) / Foggy Mental Breakdown (7,10) / Fool's Fantasy (2) / Forty Days And Forty Nights (7) / From Here To There Eventually (1,6,8) / Gang War Blues (12) / Get Into The Wind (12) / Girl I Knew (1) / Give Me Life (14) — Give Me News I Can Use (14) / God Fearing Man (3) / Happy Birthday (3) / Hard Rock Road (13) / **Hey Lawdy Mama** (6,8,11) **35** / Hippo Stomp (7,10) / Hodge, Podge, Strained Through A Leslie (2) / Hold On (Never Give Up, Never Give In) (14) / Hootchie Kootchie Man (1) / Howlin' For My Darlin' (3) / I'm Asking (9) / I'm Goin' Upstairs (4) / In Hopes Of A Garden (9) / **It's Never Too Late** (3,8,11) **51** / Jaded Strumpet (9) / Jeraboah (12) / Jupiter's Child (3,8,11) — Just For Tonight (14) / Justice Don't Be Slow (12) / Lost And Found By Trial And Error (2) / Lovely Meter (3) / **Magic Carpet Ride** (2,6,8,11) **3** / Man On A Mission (14) / Mango Juice (3) / **Monster** (5,6,11) **39** / Morning Blue (12) / **Move Over** (5,8,11) **31** / Mr. Penny Pincher (13) / Night Time's For You (9) / None Of Your Doing (2,10) / Ostrich, The (1,10) / Power Play (4,5,6) / Pusher, The (1,4,6,8,11) / Rage (14) / Reflections (2) / Renegade (7,10) — Replace The Face (14) / Resurrection (2) / **Ride With Me** (9,11) **52** / Rock & Roll Rebels (14) / Rock Me (3,8,11) **10** / Rock Steady (I'm Rough And Ready) (14) / Round And Down (3) / **Screaming Night Hog** (8,11) **62** / Shackles And Chains (9) / She'll Be Better (3) / Sleeping Dreaming (3) / Smokey Factory Blues (12) / **Snow Blind Friend** (7,11) **60** / Someone Told A Lie (13) / Sookie Sookie (1,6,8,11) / Sparkle Eyes (9) / Spiritual Fantasy (2) / **Straight Shootin' Woman** (12) **29** — Suicide (medley) (5) / Take What You Need (1,10) / Tenderness (9,11) / Tighten Up Your Wig (2,4,6) / Turn Out The Lights (14) / Twisted (6) / Two For The Love Of One (13) / What Would You Do (If I Did That To You) (5) / **Who Needs Ya** (7,8,11) **54** / Your Wall's Too High (1,10)

				STEVENS, April — see TEMPO, Nino		
★★177★★				**STEVENS, Cat**		
				Born Steven Georgiou on 7/21/47 in London. Began career playing folk music at Hammersmith College in 1966. Contracted tuberculosis in 1968 and spent over a year recuperating. Adopted new style when he re-emerged. Lived in Brazil in the mid-'70s. Converted to Muslim religion in 1979, took name Yusef Islam.		
2/6/71	8	79	●	1 Tea for the Tillerman	$10	A&M 4280
3/20/71	164	16	●	2 Mona Bone Jakon	$10	A&M 4260
				Cat's first A&M album		
4/3/71	173	12		3 Matthew & Son/New Masters .... [R]	$12	Deram 18005-10 [2]
				2-record set of Cat's first 2 albums (1967-68)		
10/9/71	2¹	67	●	4 Teaser And The Firecat	$10	A&M 4313
1/8/72	94	10		5 Very Young And Early Songs .... [E-K]	$10	Deram 18061
10/14/72	1³	48	●	6 Catch Bull At Four	$10	A&M 4365
7/28/73	3	43	●	7 Foreigner	$10	A&M 4391
4/13/74	2³	36	●	8 Buddha And The Chocolate Box	$10	A&M 3623
7/12/75	6	45	▲³	9 Greatest Hits .... [G]	$8	A&M 4519
12/13/75+	13	19	●	10 Numbers	$8	A&M 4555
5/21/77	7	23	●	11 Izitso	$8	A&M 4702
12/23/78+	33	15		12 Back To Earth	$8	A&M 4735
12/15/84	165	8		13 Footsteps In The Dark - Greatest Hits, Volume Two	$8	A&M 3736

Angelsea (6) / **Another Saturday Night** (9) **6** / Artist, The (12) — Baby, Get Your Head Screwed On (3) / **Bad Brakes** (12) **83** / Bad Night (5) — Bad Penny (8) / **Banapple Gas** (10) **41** / Bitterblue (4) / Blackness Of The Night (3) — Bonfire (11) / Boy With A Moon & Star On His Head (6) / Bring Another Bottle (3) — But I Might Die Tonight (1) / Can't Keep It In (6,9) / Ceylon City (3) / Changes IV (4) — Child For A Day (11) / Come On & Dance (5) / Come On Baby (5) / Crazy (11)

STEVENS, Cat — Cont'd

Daytime (12,13)
Don't Be Shy (13)
Drywood (10)
18th Avenue (6)
Father (12)
Father & Son (1,9,13)
Fill My Eyes (medley) (2)
First Cut Is The Deepest (3)
Foreigner Suite (7)
Freezing Steel (6)
Ghost Town (8)
Hard-Headed Woman (1,9)
Here Comes My Baby (3)
Here Comes My Wife (5)
Home (10)
Home In The Sky (8)
How Can I Tell You (4,13)
How Many Times (7)
Humming Bird (3)
Hurt, The (7,13) *31*

I Love My Dog (3)
I Love Them All (3)
(I Never Wanted) To Be A Star (11,13)
I See A Road (3)
I Think I See The Light (2)
I Want To Live In A Wigwam (13)
I Wish, I Wish (2)
I'm Gonna Be King (3)
I'm Gonna Get A Gun (3)
I'm So Sleepy (3)
I've Found A Love (3)
If I Laugh (4)
If You Want To Sing Out, Sing Out (13)
Image Of Hell (5)
Into White (1)
It's A Super Duper Life (5)
Jesus (8)

Just Another Night (12)
Jzero (10)
Katmandu (2,13)
Killin' Time (11)
King Of Trees (8)
Kitty (3)
Kypros (11)
Lady (3)
Lady D'Arbanville (2)
Land O' Freelove & Goodbye (10)
Last Love Song (12)
Later (2)
Laughing Apple (3)
Life (11)
Lilywhite (2)
Longer Boats (1)
Lovely City (5)
Majik Of Majiks (10)
Matthew And Son (3)

Maybe You're Right (2)
Miles From Nowhere (1)
Mona Bone Jakon (2)
Monad's Anthem (10)
Moonstone (3)
Nascimento (12)
Never (2)
New York Times (12)
Northern Wind (3)
Novim's Nightmare (10)
O Caritas (6)
On The Road To Findout (1,13)
100 I Dream (7)
Pop Star (2)

Randy (12)
Ready (8,9) *26*
(Remember The Days Of The) Old Schoolyard (11) *33*
Rubylove (4)
Ruins (6)
Sad Lisa (1)
School Is Out (3)
Shift That Log (3)
Silent Sunlight (6,13)
Sitting (6,9) *16*
Smash Your Heart (3)
Speak To The Flowers (3)
Sun/C79 (8)
Sweet Jamaica (11)
Sweet Scarlet (6)
Tea For The Tillerman (1)
Time (medley) (2)
Tramp, The (5)

Trouble (2,13)
Tuesday's Dead (4)
Two Fine People (9) *33*
View From The Top (5)
Was Dog A Doughnut (11) *70*
Where Are You (5)
Where Do The Children Play (1,13)
Whistlestar (10)
Wild World (1,9) *11*
Wind, The (4,13)

STEVENS, Ray

Born Ray Ragsdale on 1/24/39 in Clarkdale, Georgia. Attended Georgia State University, studied music theory and composition. Production work in the mid-'60s. Numerous appearances on Andy Williams' TV show in the late '60s. Own TV show in summer of 1970. Featured on *Music Country* TV show, 1973-74. The #1 novelty recording artist of the past 30 years.

DEBUT	PEAK	WKS	G	#	Title	$	Label
9/15/62	135	2		1	1,837 seconds of Humor ....[N]	$40	Mercury 60732
6/21/69	57	13		2	Gitarzan ....[N]	$12	Monument 18115
6/13/70	35	19		3	Everything Is Beautiful	$10	Barnaby 35005
12/20/70+	141	8		4	Ray Stevens...Unreal!!!	$10	Barnaby 30092
9/4/71	95	8		5	Ray Stevens' Greatest Hits ....[G]	$10	Barnaby 30770
2/5/72	175	9		6	Turn Your Radio On	$10	Barnaby 30809
					inspirational songs		
6/15/74	159	11		7	Boogity Boogity ....[N]	$10	Barnaby 6003
6/28/75	106	14		8	Misty	$10	Barnaby 6012
12/27/75+	173	4		9	The Very Best of Ray Stevens ....[G]	$10	Barnaby 6018
3/15/80	132	8		10	Shriner's Convention ....[N]	$8	RCA 3574
1/19/85	118	19	●	11	He Thinks He's Ray Stevens ....[N]	$8	MCA 5517

Ahab, The Arab (1,2,5,9) *5*
All My Trials (6) *70*
Alley Oop (2)
Along Came Jones (2,5) *27*
America, Communicate With Me (4,5) *45*
Bagpipes - That's My Bag (2,7)
Bridget The Midget (The Queen Of The Blues) (5,7) *50*
Brighter Day (3)
Can We Get To That (4)
Coin Machine (10)
Come Around (4)
Cow-Cow Boogie (8)
Deep Purple (8)
Don't Boogie Woogie (7)
Dooright Family (10)
Dream Girl (4)
Early In The Morning (3)
Erik The Awful (11)

Everything Is Beautiful (3,5,9) *1*
Fred (11)
Freddie Feelgood (And His Funky Little Five Piece Band) (2,7) *91*
Further More (1,11) *91*
Get Together (3)
Gitarzan (2,5,9) *8*
Glory Special (6)
Happy Hour (Is The Saddest Time Of The Day) (11)
Harry The Hairy Ape (2,5) *17*
Have A Little Talk With Myself (5,6)
Heart Transplant (7)
Hermit Named Dave (1)
Hey There (10)
I'll Fly Away (6)
I'm Kissin' You Goodbye (11)
Imitation Of Life (4)

Indian Love Call (8,9) *68*
Islands (4)
Isn't It Lonely Together (5)
It's Me Again, Margaret (11)
Jeremiah Peabody's Poly Unsaturated Quick Dissolving Fast Acting Pleasant Tasting Green And Purple Pills (1,9) *35*
Joggin' (11)
Julius Played The Trumpet (4)
Just So Proud To Be Here (7)
Lady Of Spain (8)
Last Laugh (10)
Leaving On A Jet Plane (3)
Let Your Love Be A Light Unto The People (6)
Little Egypt (2)
Love Lifted Me (6)
Loving You On Paper (4)
Mama And A Papa (6) *82*

Martha's Atom Bomb (1)
Mississippi Squirrel Revival (11)
Misty (8,9) *14*
Mockingbird Hill (8)
Monkees, Theme From The (11)
Monkey See, Monkey Do (4)
Moonlight Special (7,9) *73*
Mr. Businessman (5,9) *28*
Mr. Custer (2)
Nashville (9)
Ned Nostril (And His South Seas Paradise, Puts Your Blues On Ice, Cheap At Twice The Price Band - Ikky-Ikky, Ukky-Ukky) (11)
Night People (4)
Oh, Lonesome Me (8)
Oh! Will There Be Any Stars (6)
Over The Rainbow (8)

PFC Rhythm And Blues Jones (1)
Popeye And Olive Oil (1)
Put It In Your Ear (10)
Raindrops Keep Fallin' On My Head (3)
Rita's Letter (10)
Rock And Roll Show (1)
Rockin' Boppin' Waltz (1)
Romeo And Juliet, Love Theme From (3)
Saturday Night At The Movies (1)
Scratch My Back (I Love It) (1)
She Belongs To Me (3)
She Came In Through The Bathroom Window (3)
Shriner's Convention (10)
Sir Thanks-A-Lot (2)
Smith And Jones (7)
Something (3)

Streak, The (7,9) *1*
Sunset Strip (4) *81*
Sunshine (8)
Take Care Of Business (8)
Talking (4)
Turn Your Radio On (6,9) *63*
Unwind (5,9) *52*
Walk A Mile In My Shoes (3)
Watch Song (10)
Why Don't You Lead Me To That Rock (6)
Yakety Yak (2)
Yes, Jesus Loves Me (6)
You're Never Goin' To Tampa With Me (10)
Young Love (8) *93*

STEVENS, Steve, Atomic Playboys

Quartet led by Billy Idol's guitarist Stevens. Features vocalist Perry McCarty.

9/2/89	119	12			Steve Stevens Atomic Playboys	$8	Warner 25920

Action
Atomic Playboys
Crackdown
Desperate Heart
Evening Eye
Pet The Hot Kitty
Power Of Suggestion
Run Across Desert Sands
Slipping Into Fiction
Soul On Ice
Woman Of 1,000 Years

STEVENSON, B.W.

Born Louis Stevenson on 10/5/49 in Dallas; died on 4/28/88 after heart surgery.

9/15/73	45	14			My Maria	$10	RCA 0088

Be My Woman Tonight
Good Love Is Like A Good Song
Grab On Hold Of My Soul
I Got To Boogie
Lucky Touch
My Maria *9*
Pass This Way
Remember Me
Shambala *66*
Sunset Woman

STEVIE B

Miami-born Steven B. Hill. R&B singer/self-taught musician. In high school band with Howard Johnson.

7/23/88	78	21	●	1	Party Your Body	$8	LMR 5500
3/11/89	77	46	●	2	In My Eyes	$8	LMR 5531
7/21/90+	54	43	●	3	Love & Emotion	$12	LMR 2307

Baby I'm A Fool For Love (1)
Because I Love You (The Postman Song) (3) *1*
Broken Hearted (1)
Children Of Tomorrow (1)
Come With Me (2)

Day N' Night (1)
Dreamin' Of Love (1) *80*
Facts Of Love (3)
Forever More (3) *96*
Girl I Am Searching For You (2) *56*

I Came To Rock Your Body (2)
I Need You (1)
I Wanna Be The One (2) *32*
I'll Be By Your Side (3) *12*
In My Eyes (2) *37*

Lifetime Love Affair (2)
Love And Emotion (3) *15*
Love Me For Life (2) *29*
Memories Of Loving You (3)
No More Tears (1)
Party Your Body (1)

Spring Love (Come Back To Me) (1) *43*
Stop The Love (1)
We're Jammin' Now (3)
Who's Loving You Tonight (3)

STEWART, Al

Born on 9/5/45 in Glasgow, Scotland. Pop-rock singer/composer/guitarist.

6/1/74	133	14		1	Past, Present And Future	$12	Janus 3063

DEBUT DATE	PEAK POS	WKS CHR	GOLD	ARTIST — Album Title	$	Label & Number

STEWART, Al — Cont'd

DEBUT DATE	PEAK POS	WKS CHR	GOLD	Album Title	$	Label & Number
3/1/75	30	23		2 Modern Times	$10	Janus 7012
10/9/76+	5	48	▲	3 Year Of The Cat	$10	Janus 7022
10/7/78	10	31	▲	4 Time Passages	$8	Arista 4190
				above 3 albums produced by Alan Parsons		
9/13/80	37	13		5 24 Carrots	$8	Arista 9520
11/14/81	110	11		6 Live/Indian Summer ....[L]	$10	Arista 8607 [2]
				3 of 4 sides are live		

Almost Lucy (4)
Apple Cider Re-Constitution (2)
Broadway Hotel (3)
Carol (2)
Clarence Frogman Henry (6)
Constantinople (5)
Dark And The Rolling Sea (2)
Delia's Gone (6)
Ellis Island (medley) (5)
End Of The Day (4)
Flying Sorcery (3)
Here In Angola (6)
If It Doesn't Come Naturally, Leave It (3,6)
Indian Summer (6)
Last Day Of June 1934 (1)
Life In Dark Water (4)
Lord Grenville (3)
Man For All Seasons (4)
Merlin's Time (5,6)
Midas Shadow (3)
Midnight Rocks (5) **24**
Modern Times (5)
Mondo Sinistro (5)
Murmansk Run (medley) (5)
Next Time (1)
Nostradamus - Part One & Two (1,6)
Not The One (2)
Old Admirals (1)
On The Border (3,6) **42**
One Stage Before (3)
Optical Illusion (5)
Paint By Numbers (5)
Palace Of Versailles (4)
Pandora (6)
Post World War Two Blues (1)
Princess Olivia (6)
Roads To Moscow (1,6)
Rocks In The Ocean (5)
Running Man (5,6)
Sand In Your Shoes (3)
Sirens Of Titan (2)
Soho (Needless To Say) (1,6)
Song On The Radio (4) **29**
Terminal Eyes (1)
Time Passages (4,6) **7**
Timeless Skies (4)
Valentina Way (4,6)
Warren Harding (1)
What's Going On (2)
World Goes To Riyadh (medley) (6)
Year Of The Cat (3,6) **8**

STEWART, Amii

Born in Washington, D.C. in 1956. Disco singer/dancer/actress. In the Broadway musical *Bubbling Brown Sugar*. Her niece is singer Sinitta.

DEBUT DATE	PEAK POS	WKS CHR	GOLD	Album Title	$	Label & Number
3/17/79	19	23	●	Knock On Wood	$8	Ariola 50054

Am I Losing You
Bring It On Back To Me
Closest Thing To Heaven
Get Your Love Back
Knock On Wood 1
Light My Fire/137 Disco Heaven 69
Only A Child In Your Eyes
You Really Touched My Heart

STEWART, Billy

Born on 3/24/37 in Washington, D.C.; died in an auto accident on 1/17/70. R&B vocalist/keyboardist. Discovered by Bo Diddley in 1956. Nicknamed "Fat Boy." First cousin of Grace Ruffin of The Jewels.

DEBUT DATE	PEAK POS	WKS CHR	GOLD	Album Title	$	Label & Number
7/3/65	97	10		1 I Do Love You	$30	Chess 1496
5/7/66+	138	6		2 Unbelievable	$30	Chess 1499

Almost Like Being In Love (2)
Canadian Sunset (2)
Count Me Out (1)
Fat Boy (2)
Fat Boy Can Cry (1)
Foggy Day (2)
I Do Love You (1) **26**
I'm No Romeo (1)
Keep Lovin' (1)
Love Is Here To Stay (2)
Misty (2)
Moon River (2)
My Funny Valentine (2)
Oh My! What Can The Matter Be (1)
Once Again (1)
Over The Rainbow (2)
Reap What You Sow (1) **79**
Sitting In The Park (1) **24**
Strange Feeling (1) **70**
Summertime (2) **10**
Sweet Senorita (1)
Teach Me Tonight (2)
That Old Black Magic (2)
Time After Time (2)

STEWART, Gary

Born on 5/28/45 in Letcher County, Kentucky. First recorded for Cory in 1964. In the rock band The Amps in the mid-1960s. Toured with Charley Pride in 1976.

DEBUT DATE	PEAK POS	WKS CHR	GOLD	Album Title	$	Label & Number
8/16/80	165	3		Cactus And A Rose	$8	RCA 3627

Are We Dreamin' The Same Dream
Cactus And A Rose
Ghost Train
Harlan County Highway
How Could We Come To This After That
Lovers' Knot
Okeechobee Purple
Roarin'
Staring Each Other Down
We Made It As Lovers (We Just Couldn't Make It As Friends)

STEWART, Jermaine

Chicago-bred singer. Dancer on TV's *Soul Train*. Worked as backup vocalist for Shalamar and Boy George.

DEBUT DATE	PEAK POS	WKS CHR	GOLD	Album Title	$	Label & Number
3/2/85	90	11		1 The Word Is Out	$8	Arista 8261
6/14/86	32	25		2 Frantic Romantic	$8	Arista 8395
4/23/88	98	12		3 Say It Again	$8	Arista 8455

Brilliance (1)
Call It A Miracle (3)
Dance Floor (2)
Debbie (1)
Don't Ever Leave Me (2)
Don't Have Sex With Your Ex (3)
Don't Talk Dirty To Me (3)
Dress It Up (3)
Eyes (3)
Frantic Romantic (2)
Get Lucky (3)
Get Over It (1)
Give Your Love To Me (2)
Got To Be Love (3)
I Like It (1)
In Love Again (1)
Is It Really Love? (3)
Jody (2) **42**
Month Of Mondays (1)
Moonlight Carnival (2)
My House (3)
Out To Punish (2)
Reasons Why (1)
Say It Again (3) **27**
She's A Teaser (3)
Spies (1)
Versatile (2)
We Don't Have To Take Our Clothes Off (2) **5**
Word Is Out (1) **41**
You (1)

STEWART, John

Born on 9/5/39 in San Diego. Member of The Kingston Trio from 1961-67. Wrote "Daydream Believer."

DEBUT DATE	PEAK POS	WKS CHR	GOLD	Album Title	$	Label & Number
6/21/69	193	3		1 California Bloodlines	$12	Capitol 203
1/15/72	195	2		2 The Lonesome Picker Rides Again	$10	Warner 1948
7/6/74	195	2		3 The Phoenix Concerts-Live ....[L]	$10	RCA 0265 [2]
5/17/75	150	6		4 Wingless Angels	$8	RCA 0816
11/26/77	126	8		5 Fire In The Wind	$8	RSO 3027
5/19/79	10	28		6 Bombs Away Dream Babies	$8	RSO 3051
4/12/80	85	10		7 Dream Babies Go Hollywood	$8	RSO 3074

Adelita (medley) (4)
All The Brave Horses (2)
Bolinas (2)
Boston Lady (5)
California Bloodlines (1,3)
Cody (3)
Comin' Out Of Nowhere (6)
Cops (3)
Crazy (4)
Daydream Believer (2)
18 Wheels (5)
Fire In The Wind (5)
Freeway Pleasure (2)
Gold (6) **5**
Hand Your Heart To The Wind (6)
Heart Of The Dream (6)
Hollywood Dreams (7)
Hung On The Heart (Of A Man Back Home) (4)
Josie (4)
July, You're A Woman (1,3)
Just An Old Love Song (2)
Kansas (3)
Kansas Rain (3)
Lady Of Fame (7)
Last Campaign Trilogy (3)
Last Hurrah (5)
Let The Big Horse Run (4)
Little Road And A Stone To Roll (2,3)
Lonesome Picker (1)
Lost Her In The Sun (6) **34**
Love Has Tied My Wings (7)
Mazatlan (medley) (4)
Midnight Wind (6) **28**
Missouri Bird (1)
Monterey (7)
Moonlight Rider (7)
Morning Thunder (5)
Mother Country (1,3)
Never Going Back (1,3)
Nightman (7)
(Odin) Spirit Of The Water (7)
Oldest Living Son (3)
Omaha Rainbow (1)
On You Like The Wind (5)
Over The Hill (6)
Pirates Of Stone County Road (1,3)
Promise The Wind (5)
Raven, The (7)
Razorback Woman (1)
Ride Stone Blind (4)
Road Shines Bright (2)
Rock It In My Own Sweet Time (5)
Roll Away The Stone (3)
Rose Water (4)
Runaway Fool Of Love (3,6)
Runner, The (5)
Shackles And Chains (1)
She Believes In Me (1)
Some Kind Of Love (4)
Somewhere Down The Line (6)
Spinnin' Of The World (6)
Summer Child (4)
Survivors (4)
Swift Lizard (2)
Touch Of The Sun (2)
Wheatfield Lady (3)
Wheels Of Thunder (7)
Wild Horse Road (2)
Wild Side Of You (5)
Wind On The River (7)
Wingless Angels (Survivors II) (4)
Wolves In The Kitchen (2)
You Can't Look Back (1,3)

DEBUT DATE	PEAK POS	WKS CHR	GOLD	ARTIST — Album Title	$	Label & Number

★★40★★   STEWART, Rod

Born Roderick Stewart on 1/10/45 in London. Worked as a folksinger in Europe in the early '60s. Recorded for English Decca in 1964. With the Hoochie Coochie Men, Steampacket and Shotgun Express. Joined Jeff Beck Group, 1967-69. With Faces from 1969-75, also recorded solo during this time. Left Faces in December 1975. Married to actress Alana Hamilton from 1979-84. Married supermodel Rachel Hunter on 12/15/90. Also see Python Lee Jackson, Jeff Beck, and Faces.

DEBUT DATE	PEAK POS	WKS CHR	GOLD	#	ARTIST — Album Title	$	Label & Number
12/13/69+	139	27		1	The Rod Stewart Album	$15	Mercury 61237
6/20/70	27	57		2	Gasoline Alley	$15	Mercury 61264
6/19/71	1⁴	52	●	3	**Every Picture Tells A Story**	$12	Mercury 609
8/12/72	2³	36	●	4	**Never A Dull Moment**	$12	Mercury 646
7/7/73	31	25	●	5	Sing It Again Rod ....[G]	$10	Mercury 680
1/5/74	63	11		6	Rod Stewart/Faces Live - Coast To Coast Overture and Beginners ....[L]	$12	Mercury 697
					ROD STEWART/FACES		
10/26/74	13	14		7	Smiler	$10	Mercury 1017
9/6/75	9	29	●	8	**Atlantic Crossing**	$8	Warner 2875
5/15/76	90	26		9	The Best Of Rod Stewart ....[G]	$12	Mercury 7507 [2]
					all Mercury albums feature members of Faces		
7/17/76	2⁵	57	▲²	10	A Night On The Town	$8	Warner 2938
11/26/77+	2⁶	47	▲³	11	**Foot Loose & Fancy Free**	$8	Warner 3092
12/23/78+	1³	37	▲⁴	12	**Blondes Have More Fun**	$8	Warner 3261
11/24/79+	22	19	▲	13	Rod Stewart Greatest Hits ....[G]	$8	Warner 3373
12/6/80	12	21	▲	14	Foolish Behaviour	$8	Warner 3485
11/21/81	11	31	▲	15	Tonight I'm Yours	$8	Warner 3602
11/20/82	46	13		16	Absolutely Live ....[L]	$12	Warner 23743 [2]
6/25/83	30	22		17	Body Wishes	$8	Warner 23877
6/30/84	18	35	●	18	Camouflage	$8	Warner 25095
7/12/86	28	19		19	Rod Stewart	$8	Warner 25446
6/4/88+	20	72	▲²	20	Out Of Order	$8	Warner 25684
12/2/89+	54	18	●	21	Storyteller/The Complete Anthology: 1964-1990 ....[K]	$25	Warner 25987 [4]
					not available on vinyl; Rod's solo and group hits since 1964; groups include Steampacket, Faces, Jeff Beck Group and others		
3/24/90	20	27	▲	22	Downtown Train: Selections From The Storyteller Anthology .....[G]	$12	Warner 26158
					most of these 12 tracks are Rod's hits of the last 15 years		
4/13/91	10	61	▲	23	**Vagabond Heart**	$12	Warner 26300

Ain't Love A Bitch (12) *22*
All In The Name Of Rock 'N' Roll (8)
All Right Now (18) *72*
Alright For An Hour (8)
Amazing Grace (medley) (7)
Angel (4,6,9,21) *40*
Another Heartache (19) *52*
Attractive Female Wanted (12)
Baby Jane (17,21) *14*
Bad For You (18)
Balltrap, The (10)
Best Days Of My Life (12)
Better Off Dead (14)
Big Bayou (10)
Blind Prayer (1)
Blondes (Have More Fun) (12)
Body Wishes (17)
Born Loose (11)
Borstal Boy (medley) (6)
Bring It On Home To Me (medley) (7)
Broken Arrow (23) *20*
Camouflage (18)
Can I Get A Witness? (21)
  recorded as: Steampacket
Can We Still Be Friends (18)
Cindy's Lament (1)
Country Comforts (2,5,21)
Crazy About Her (20,21) *11*
Cut Across Shorty (2,6,9,21)
Da Ya Think I'm Sexy? (12,13,16,21) *1*
Dancin' Alone (11)
Dirty Old Town (1)
Dirty Weekend (12)
Dixie Toot (7)
Downtown Train (21,22) *3*
Drift Away (8)
Dynamite (20,21)

Every Beat Of My Heart (19,21) *83*
Every Picture Tells A Story (3,6,9,21)
Farewell (7)
First Cut Is The Deepest (10,13,21) *21*
Fool For You (10)
Foolish Behaviour (14)
Forever Young (20,21,22) *12*
Gasoline Alley (2,5,9,16,21)
Get Back (21)
Ghetto Blaster (17)
Gi' Me Wings (14)
Girl From The North Country (7)
Go Out Dancing (23)
Good Morning Little Schoolgirl (21)
Great Pretender (16)
Guess I'll Always Love You (16)
Had Me A Real Good Time (21)
Handbags And Gladrags (1,5,9,21) *42*
Hard Road (7)
Have I Told You Lately (23)
Heart Is On The Line (18)
Here To Eternity (19)
Hot Legs (11,13,16,21) *28*
How Long (15) *49*
I Ain't Superstitious (21)
I Don't Want To Talk About It (8,13,16,21,22) *46*
(I Know) I'm Losing You (3,5,9,21) *24*
I Was Only Joking (11,13,21) *22*
I Wish It Would Rain (6)

I Wouldn't Ever Change A Thing (1)
I'd Rather Go Blind (4,6,21)
I've Been Drinking (21)
I've Grown Accustomed To Her Face (7)
(If Loving You Is Wrong) I Don't Want To Be Right (11)
If Only (23)
In A Broken Dream (21) *56*
In My Life (19)
In My Own Crazy Way (19)
Infatuation (18,21,22) *6*
Is That The Thanks I Get? (12)
It Takes Two (23)
It's All Over Now (2,6,9,21)
It's Not The Spotlight (8)
Italian Girls (4)
Jealous (13)
Jealous Guy (6)
Jo's Lament (2)
Jodie (9)
Just Like A Woman (15)
Killing Of Georgie (Part I And II) (10,13,21,22) *30*
Lady Day (2)
Last Summer (12)
Let Me Be Your Car (7,9,21)
Lethal Dose Of Love (20)
Little Miss Understood (21)
Little Queenie (medley) (16)
Lost In You (20,21) *12*
Lost Paraguayos (4,5)
Love Touch (19,21) *6*
Maggie May (3,5,9,13,16,21) *1*
Mama You Been On My Mind (7)
Man Of Constant Sorrow (1)
Mandolin Wind (3,5,21)
Mine For Me (7,9) *91*

Moment Of Glory (23)
Motown Song (23) *10*
Move Me (17)
My Girl (14)
My Heart Can't Tell You No (20,21,22) *4*
My Way Of Giving (2)
Never Give Up On A Dream (15)
Night Like This (19)
No Holding Back (23)
Nobody Knows You When You're Down And Out (20)
Oh God, I Wish I Was Home Tonight (14,21)
Oh! No Not My Baby (9,21) *59*
Old Raincoat Won't Ever Let You Down (1,9)
Only A Boy (15)
Only A Hobo (2)
Passion (14,16,21,22) *5*
People Get Ready (21,22) *48*
Pinball Wizard (5,9,21)
Pretty Flamingo (10)
Ready Now (17)
Reason To Believe (3,5,21) *62*
Rebel Heart (23)
Red Hot In Black (19)
Rhythm Of My Heart (23) *5*
Rock My Plimsoul (16)
Sailing (8,13,16,21) *58*
Sailor (7,9)
Satisfied (17)
Say It Ain't True (14)
Scarred And Scared (12)
Seems Like A Long Time (3)
Shake (21)
Shapes Of Things (21)
She Won't Dance With Me (14,16)

So Much To Say (21)
So Soon We Change (14)
Some Guys Have All The Luck (18,21) *10*
Somebody Special (14) *71*
Sonny (15)
Standin' In The Shadows Of Love (12)
Stay With Me (6,16,21,22) *17*
Still Love You (8)
Stone Cold Sober (8,21)
Strangers Again (17)
Street Fighting Man (1,5,9,21)
Stripper, The (16)
Sweet Lady Mary (21)
Sweet Little Rock 'N Roller (7,16,21)
Sweet Surrender (17)
Tear It Up (15,16)
Ten Days Of Rain (19)
That's All Right (21)
This Old Heart Of Mine (8) *83*
This Old Heart Of Mine (21,22) *10*
Three Time Loser (8)
To Love Somebody (21)
Tomorrow Is Such A Long Time (3)
Tonight I'm Yours (Don't Hurt Me) (15,16,21) *20*
Tonight's The Night (Gonna Be Alright) (10,13,16,21,22) *1*
Too Bad (medley) (6)
Tora, Tora, Tora (Out With The Boys) (15)
Trade Winds (10)
Trouble (18)
True Blue (4,21)
Try A Little Tenderness (20)

Twisting The Night Away (4,5,21) *59*
What Am I Gonna Do (I'm So In Love With You) (17,21) *35*
What's Made Milwaukee Famous (Has Made A Loser Out Of Me) (9,21)
When A Man's In Love (23)
When I Was Your Man (20)
Who's Gonna Take Me Home (The Rise And Fall Of A Budding Gigolo) (19)
Wild Horse (20)
Wild Side Of Life (10)
You Are Everything (23)
You Can Make Me Dance, Sing Or Anything (21)
You Got A Nerve (11)
You Keep Me Hangin' On (11)
(You Make Me Feel Like) A Natural Man (7)
You Send Me (medley) (7)
You Wear It Well (4,5,9,21) *13*
You're In My Heart (The Final Acclaim) (11,13,16,21) *4*
You're Insane (11)
You're My Girl (I Don't Want To Discuss It) (2)
Young Turks (15,16,21,22) *5*

STEWART, Sandy

Born Sandra Galitz on 7/10/37 in Philadelphia. Regular on the Eddie Fisher and Perry Como TV shows.

DEBUT DATE	PEAK POS	WKS CHR	GOLD		ARTIST — Album Title	$	Label & Number
4/6/63	138	2			My Coloring Book	$20	Colpix 441

Beautiful Brown Eyes (1)
Deep Purple (1)
Greensleeves (1)

Ivy Rose (1)
Little Girl Blue (1)
Little White Lies (1)

My Coloring Book *20*
Over The Rainbow (1)
Red Sails In The Sunset (1)

Scarlet Ribbons (1)
Tangerine (1)

Where The Blue Of The Night Meets The Gold Of The Day (1)

DEBUT DATE	PEAK POS	WKS CHR	GOLD	ARTIST — Album Title	$	Label & Number

STEWART, Wynn
Born on 6/7/34 in Morrisville, Missouri; died on 7/17/85. Country singer.

| 7/22/67 | 158 | 8 | | It's Such A Pretty World Today | $15 | Capitol 2737 |

Angels Don't Lie 'Cause I Have You
Half Way In Love
I Keep Forgettin' That I Forgot About You
It's Such A Pretty World Today
Let's Pretend We're Kids Again
Ol' What's Her Name
Out There Is Your World
Tourist, The
Unfaithful Arms
You Can Always Give Her Back To Me
You Told Him

STIGERS, Curtis
Vocalist/saxophonist from Boise, Idaho. Twenty-five years old in 1991.

| 11/9/91+ | 101 | 28 | | Curtis Stigers | $12 | Arista 18660 |

Count My Blessings
I Guess It Wasn't Mine
I Keep Telling Myself
I Wonder Why 9
Last Time I Said Goodbye
Man You're Gonna Fall In Love With
Never Saw A Miracle
Nobody Loves You Like I Do
People Like Us
Sleeping With The Lights On 96
You're All That Matters To Me 98

STILLER & MEARA — see BERMAN, Shelley

★★229★★ **STILLS, Stephen**
Born on 1/3/45 in Dallas. Member of Buffalo Springfield and Crosby, Stills & Nash. Group Manassas included Chris Hillman (The Byrds), Dallas Taylor, Fuzzy Samuels, Paul Harris, Al Perkins and Joe Lala.

| 8/31/68 | 12 | 37 | ● | 1 Super Session | $15 | Columbia 9701 |

MIKE BLOOMFIELD/AL KOOPER/STEVE STILLS

| 11/28/70+ | 3 | 39 | ● | 2 Stephen Stills | $10 | Atlantic 7202 |

guests: Jimi Hendrix, Eric Clapton, David Crosby, Graham Nash

7/17/71	8	20	●	3 Stephen Stills 2	$10	Atlantic 7206
4/29/72	4	30	●	4 Manassas	$10	Atlantic 903 [2]
5/12/73	26	18		5 Down The Road	$10	Atlantic 7250

above 2: STEPHEN STILLS & MANASSAS

7/5/75	19	17		6 Stills	$8	Columbia 33575
12/27/75+	42	11		7 Stephen Stills Live	[L] $8	Atlantic 18156
5/15/76	31	15		8 Illegal Stills	$8	Columbia 34148
10/9/76	26	18	●	9 Long May You Run	$8	Reprise 2253

STILLS-YOUNG BAND (Neil Young)

1/8/77	127	5		10 Still Stills-The Best Of Stephen Stills	[G] $8	Atlantic 18201
11/11/78	83	4		11 Thoroughfare Gap	$8	Columbia 35380
9/1/84	75	12		12 Right By You	$8	Atlantic 80177

Albert's Shuffle (1)
Anyway (4)
As I Come Of Age (6)
Beaucoup Yumbo (11)
Black Coral (9)
Black Queen (2)
Bluebird Revisited (3)
Blues Man (4)
Both Of Us (Bound To Lose) (4)
Bound To Fall (4,10)
Business On The Street (5)
Buyin' Time (8)
Can't Let Go (12) 67
Change Partners (3,7,10) 43
Cherokee (2)
Church (Part Of Someone) (2)
Circlin' (8)
City Junkies (5)
Closer To You (8)
Cold Cold World (6)
Colorado (4)
Crossroads (medley) (7)
Cuban Bluegrass (medley) (4,10)
Different Tongues (8)
Do For The Others (2)
Do You Remember The Americans (5)
Don't Look At My Shadow (4)
Down The Road (5)
Ecology Song (3)
Everybody's Talkin' At Me (7)
Fallen Eagle (4)
50/50 (12)
First Things First (6)
Fishes And Scorpions (3)
Flaming Heart (12)
Fontainebleau (9)
4 + 20 (7)
Four Days Gone (7)
Go Back Home (2,10)
Grey To Green (12)
Guaguanco De Vero (5)
Guardian Angel (9)
Harvey's Tune (1)
Hide It So Deep (4)
His Holy Modal Majesty (1)
How Far (4)
In The Way (6)
Isn't It About Time (5,10) 56
It Doesn't Matter (4,10) 61
It Takes A Lot To Laugh, It Takes A Train To Cry (1)
Jesus Gave Love Away For Free (4)
Jet Set (Sigh) (4,7)
Johnny's Garden (4,10)
Know You Got To Run (3)
Let It Shine (9)
Lies (5)
Loner, The (8)
Long May You Run (9)
Love Again (12)
Love Gangster (4)
Love Story (6)
Love The One You're With (2,10) 14
Lowdown (11)
Make Love To You (9)
Man's Temptation (1)
Marianne (3,10) 42
Midnight In Paris (8)
Midnight On The Bay (9)
Midnight Rider (11)
Move Around (4)
My Angel (6)
My Favorite Changes (6)
Myth Of Sisyphus (6)
New Mama (9)
No Hiding Place (12)
No Me Nieges (8)
No Problem (12)
Not Fade Away (11)
Nothin' To Do But Today (3)
Ocean Girl (9)
Old Times Good Times (2)
Only Love Can Break Your Heart (2)
Open Secret (2,3)
Pensamiento (5)
Really (1)
Relaxing Town (3)
Right By You (12)
Right Now (4)
Ring Of Love (8)
Rock And Roll Crazies (medley) (4,10) 92
Rocky Mountain Way (medley) (7)
Rollin' My Stone (5)
Season Of The Witch (1)
Shuffle Just As Bad (6)
Singin' Call (3)
Sit Yourself Down (2,10) 37
So Begins The Task (4)
So Many Times (5)
Soldier (8)
Song Of Love (4)
Special Care (7)
Stateline Blues (8)
Stop (1)
Stranger (12) 61
Sugar Babe (4)
Thoroughfare Gap (11)
To A Flame (2)
To Mama From Christopher And The Old Man (6)
Treasure (Take One) (4)
Turn Back The Pages (6) 84
12/8 Blues (All The Same) (9)
We Are Not Helpless (2,10)
We Will Go On (1)
What To Do (4)
What's The Game (11)
Woman Lleva (11)
Wooden Ships (7)
Word Game (3,7)
You Can't Catch Me (medley) (7)
You Can't Dance Alone (11)
You Don't Love Me (1)

STING
Born Gordon Sumner on 10/2/51 in Wallsend, England. Lead singer/bass guitarist of The Police. In the films *Quadrophenia, Dune, The Bride, Plenty* and others. Nicknamed "Sting" because of a yellow and black jersey he liked to wear.

7/13/85	2⁶	58	▲	1 The Dream Of The Blue Turtles	$8	A&M 3750
10/31/87	9	52	▲²	2 ...Nothing Like The Sun	$10	A&M 6402 [2]
2/9/91	2¹	39	▲	3 The Soul Cages	$12	A&M 6405

All This Time (3) 5
Be Still My Beating Heart (2) 15
Children's Crusade (1)
Consider Me Gone (1)
Dream Of The Blue Turtles (1)
Englishman In New York (2) 84
Fortress Around Your Heart (1) 8
Fragile (2)
History Will Teach Us Nothing (2)
If You Love Somebody Set Them Free (1) 3
Island Of Souls (3)
Jeremiah Blues (Part I) (3)
Lazarus Heart (2)
Little Wing (2)
Love Is The Seventh Wave (1) 17
Mad About You (3)
Moon Over Bourbon Street (1)
Rock Steady (2)
Russians (1) 16
Saint Agnes And The Burning Train (3)
Secret Marriage (2)
Shadows In The Rain (1)
Sister Moon (2)
Soul Cages (3)
Straight To My Heart (2)
They Dance Alone (Gueca Solo) (2)
We Work The Black Seam (1)
We'll Be Together (2) 7
When The Angels Fall (3)
Why Should I Cry For You? (3)
Wild Wild Sea (3)

STITT, Sonny
Born Edward Stitt on 2/2/24 in Boston; died on 7/22/82. Jazz saxophonist.

| 4/8/67 | 172 | 2 | | What's New!!! | [I] $15 | Roulette 25343 |

Beastly Blues
Cocktails For Two
Fever
Georgia
I've Got The World On A String
If I Didn't Care
Jumpin' With Symphony Sid
Mame
Morgan's Song
Round About Midnight
Stardust
What's New!

STONE, Doug
Country singer/guitarist from Georgia. Real name, Doug Brooks, was changed to avoid confusion with Garth. At age seven, opened on guitar for a Loretta Lynn concert.

| 5/19/90+ | 97 | 48↑ | ● | 1 Doug Stone | $12 | Epic 45303 |

DEBUT DATE	PEAK POS	WKS CHR	GOLD	ARTIST — Album Title	$	Label & Number

STONE, Doug — Cont'd

| 8/31/91+ | 74 | 51 | ● | 2 I Thought It Was You | $12 | Epic 47357 |
| 8/29/92 | 99 | 17↑ | | 3 From The Heart | $12 | Epic 52436 |

Ain't Your Memory Got No
Pride At All (3)
Burning Down The Town (2)
Come In Out Of The Pain (2)
Crying On Your Shoulder
Again (1)
Feeling Never Goes Away (2)

(For Every Inch I've
Laughed) I've Cried A Mile
(1)
Fourteen Minutes Old (1)
High Weeds And Rust (1)
I Thought It Was You (2)

I'd Be Better Off (In A Pine
Box) (1)
If It Was Up To Me (2)
In A Different Light (1)
It's A Good Thing I Don't
Love You Anymore (1)

Jukebox With A Country
Song (2)
Leave Me The Radio (3)
Left, Leavin', Goin' Or Gone
(3)
Made For Lovin' You (3)
My Hat's Off To Him (1)
Remember The Ride (2)

Right To Remain Silent (2)
She's Got A Future In The
Movies (3)
These Lips Don't Know How
To Say Goodbye (1)
They Don't Make Years Like
They Used To (2)
This Empty House (3)

Too Busy Being In Love (3)
Turn This Thing Around (1)
Warning Labels (3)
We Always Agree On Love (1)
Why Didn't I Think Of That
(3)
Workin' End Of A Hoe (3)

STONE, Kirby, Four
Kirby was born on 4/27/18 in New York City. His quartet includes: Eddie Hall, Larry Foster and Mike Gardner. Kirby was musical director for various TV shows.

| 8/25/58 | 13 | 9 | | Baubles, Bangles And Beads | $15 | Columbia 1211 |

**Baubles Bangles And
Beads 25**
Bidin' My Time

Fugue For Tinhorns
In The Good Old
Summertime

Lady Love Me
Let's Do It (Let's Fall In Love)
Lullaby Of Broadway

Rain
Swingin' Down The Lane

When My Sugar Walks
Down The Street
Whispering

Zing! Went The Strings Of
My Heart

STONE, Sly — see SLY & THE FAMILY STONE

STONE CITY BAND — see JAMES, Rick

STONE FURY
Heavy-metal rock quartet formed by lead vocalist Lenny Wolfe who formed Kingdom Come in 1987.

| 11/24/84+ | 144 | 12 | | Burns Like A Star | $8 | MCA 5522 |

Break Down The Wall
Burns Like A Star

Don't Tell Me Why
Hold It

I Hate To Sleep Alone
Life Is Too Lonely

Mamas Love
Shannon You Lose

Tease

STONE PONEYS — see RONSTADT, Linda

STONE ROSES, The
Alternative-pop quartet from Manchester, England formed in 1985 by guitarist John Squire and vocalist Ian Brown. Includes bassist Mani and drummer Reni.

| 1/20/90 | 86 | 26 | | The Stone Roses | $12 | Silvertone 1184 |

Bye Bye Bad Man
Don't Stop
Elephant Stone

Elizabeth My Dear
Fools Gold
I Am The Resurrection

I Wanna Be Adored
Made Of Stone
Shoot You Down

She Bangs The Drums
Sister

(Song For My) Sugar Spun

This Is The One
Waterfall

STOOGES — see POP, Iggy

STOOKEY, Paul
Born on 11/30/37 in Baltimore. Paul of Peter, Paul & Mary.

| 8/21/71 | 42 | 15 | | Paul and | $10 | Warner 1912 |

Been On The Road Too Long
Gabriel's Mother's Hiway
Ballad #16 Blues

Give A Damn
Hey Sad Sack
John Henry Bosworth

Ju Les Ver Negre En Cheese
(Ed's Tune)
Lucy

Meanings Will Change
Sebastian
Tender Hands

Tiger
**Wedding Song (There Is
Love) 24**

STORIES
New York rock quartet: Ian Lloyd (lead singer, bass), Michael Brown (keyboards; founding member of Left Banke), Steve Love (guitar) and Bryan Madey (drums). Brown left group in 1973, replaced by Ken Aaronson (bass; later charted with Sammy Hagar) and Ken Bichel (keyboards).

| 7/1/72 | 182 | 9 | | 1 Stories | $10 | Kama Sutra 2051 |
| 7/28/73 | 29 | 19 | | 2 About Us | $8 | Kama Sutra 2068 |

Believe Me (2)
Brother Louie (2) 1
Changes Have Begun (2)
Circles (2)

Darling (2)
Don't Ever Let Me Down (2)
Down Time Blooze (2)
Hello People (1)

Hey France (2)
High And Low (1)
I'm Coming Home (1) 42
Kathleen (1)

Love Is In Motion (2)
Nice To Have You Here (1)
Please, Please (1)
Saint James (1)

Step Back (1)
Take Cover (1)
Top Of The City (2)
What Comes After (2)

Winter Scenes (1)
Words (2)
You Told Me (1)

STORM, The
Co-lead vocalists Gregg Rolie (keyboards; formerly with Santana and Journey) and Kevin Chalfant (notable songwriter), with Josh Ramos (guitar), and Journey's rhythm section of Ross Valory and Steve Smith (also a member of jazz fusion group Steps Ahead). Chalfant was the lead singer of 707.

| 11/16/91+ | 133 | 17 | | The Storm | $12 | Interscope 91741 |

Call Me
Can't Live Without Love

Gimme Love
I Want You Back

**I've Got A Lot To Learn
About Love 26**

In The Raw
Show Me The Way
Still Loving You

Take Me Away
Touch And Go

You Keep Me Waiting
You're Gonna Miss Me

STRADLIN, Izzy, And The Ju Ju Hounds
Izzy is Jeffrey Isbell, former guitarist of Guns N' Roses. The Ju Ju Hounds are Jimmy Ashhurst (bass), Rick Richards (guitar) and Charlie Quintana (drums).

| 10/31/92 | 102 | 9 | | Izzy Stradlin And The Ju Ju Hounds | $12 | Geffen 24490 |

Bucket O' Trouble
Come On Now Inside

Cuttin' The Rug
How Will It Go

Pressure Drop
Shuffle It All

Somebody Knockin'
Take A Look At The Guy

Time Gone By
Train Tracks

★★277★★   STRAIT, George
Country singer. Born on 5/18/52 in Pearsall, Texas. Self-taught on guitar while in U.S. Army in 1971. Sang in a service band in Hawaii. Graduated from Southwest Texas State with a degree in agriculture. First recorded as vocalist of Ace In The Hole in the late 1970s. Starred in the film *Pure Country*.

3/3/84	163	7	●	1 Right or Wrong	$8	MCA 5450
11/10/84	139	16	▲	2 Does Fort Worth Ever Cross Your Mind	$8	MCA 5518
4/20/85	157	8	▲²	3 Greatest Hits	[G] $8	MCA 5567
7/5/86	126	11	●	4 #7	$8	MCA 5750
				his 7th album		
2/14/87	117	28	▲	5 Ocean Front Property	$8	MCA 5913
9/26/87	68	31	▲	6 Greatest Hits, Volume Two	[G] $8	MCA 42035
3/19/88	87	14	▲	7 If You Ain't Lovin' You Ain't Livin'	$8	MCA 42114
3/4/89	92	24	▲	8 Beyond The Blue Neon	$8	MCA 42266

DEBUT DATE	PEAK POS	WKS CHR	GOLD	ARTIST — Album Title	$	Label & Number

STRAIT, George — Cont'd

6/2/90	35	42	▲	9 Livin' It Up	$12	MCA 6415
4/6/91	45	49	▲	10 Chill Of An Early Fall	$12	MCA 10204
1/18/92	46	19	●	11 Ten Strait Hits [G]	$12	MCA 10450
5/9/92	33	24	●	12 Holding My Own	$12	MCA 10532
10/3/92	6	19↑	▲	13 **Pure Country** [S]	$12	MCA 10651

Ace In The Hole (8,11)
All My Ex's Live In Texas (5,6)
All Of Me (Loves All Of You) (7,12)
Am I Blue (5,6)
Amarillo By Morning (3)
Angel, Angelina (8)
Any Old Time (2)
Anything You Can Spare (10) (1)
Baby Blue (7,11)
Baby Your Baby (13)
Baby's Gotten Good At Goodbye (8,11)
Back To Bein' Me (7)
Beyond The Blue Neon (8)
Bigger Man Than Me (7)
Chair, The (6)
Chill Of An Early Fall (10)
Cow Town (4)
Cowboy Rides Away (2,6)
Deep Water (4)
Does Fort Worth Ever Cross Your Mind (2,6)
Don't Mind If I Do (7)
Down And Out (3)
Drinking Champagne (9,11)

80 Proof Bottle Of Tear Stopper (1)
Every Time It Rains (Lord Don't It Pour) (1)
Famous Last Words Of A Fool (7,11)
Faults And All (12)
Fifteen Years Going Up (And One Night Coming Down) (1)
Fire I Can't Put Out (3)
Fireman (2,6)
Fool Hearted Memory (3)
Gone As A Girl Can Get (12)
Heartland [includes 2 versions] (13)
Heaven Must Be Wondering Where You Are (9)
Her Only Bad Habit Is Me (10)
Here We Go Again (12)
Holding My Own (12)
Hollywood Squares (8)
Home In San Antone (10)
Honky Tonk Saturday Night (2)
Hot Burning Flames (5)
I Cross My Heart (13)

I Need Someone Like Me (2)
I Should Have Watched That First Step (2)
I'm All Behind You Now (5)
I'm Never Gonna Let You Go (4)
I'm Satisfied With You (1)
I've Come To Expect It From You (9,11)
I've Convinced Everybody But Me (10)
If I Know Me (10)
If You Ain't Lovin' (You Ain't Livin') (7,11)
If You're Thinking You Want A Stranger (There's One Coming Home) (3)
Is It Already Time (10)
Is It That Time Again (7)
It Ain't Cool To Be Crazy About You (4,6)
It's Alright With Me (12)
It's Too Late Now (7)
King Of Broken Hearts (13)
Last In Love (13)
Leavin's Been Comin' (For A Long, Long Time) (8)

Let's Fall To Pieces Together (1,3)
Let's Get Down To It (7)
Little Heaven's Rubbing Off On Me (1)
Lonesome Rodeo Cowboy (9)
Love Comes From The Other Side Of Town (2)
Love Without End, Amen (9,11)
Lovesick Blues (10)
Marina Del Rey (3)
Milk Cow Blues (10)
My Heart Won't Wander Very Far From You (5)
My Old Flame Is Burnin' Another Honky Tonk Down (4)
Nobody In His Right Mind Would've Left Her (4,6)
Ocean Front Property (5,6)
Oh Me, Oh My Sweet Baby (8)
Our Paths May Never Cross (1)
Overnight Male (13)
Overnight Success (8,11)
Rhythm Of The Road (4)

Right Or Wrong (1,3)
Second Chances (5)
She Lays It All On The Line (13)
She Loves Me (She Don't Love You) (9)
So Much Like My Dad (12)
Someone Had To Teach You (9)
Someone's Walkin' Around Upstairs (5)
Stranger In My Arms (9)
Stranger Things Have Happened (4)
Thoughts Of A Fool (13)
Too Much Of Too Little (8)
Trains Make Me Lonesome (12)
Under These Conditions (7)
Unwound (3)
We're Supposed To Do That Now And Then (9)
What Did You Expect Me To Do (2)
What's Going On In Your World (8,11)
When Did You Stop Loving Me (13)

When You're A Man On Your Own (9)
Where The Sidewalk Ends (13)
Why'd You Go And Break My Heart (4)
Without You Here (5)
Wonderland Of Love (5)
You Can't Buy Your Way Out Of The Blues (5)
You Know Me Better Than That (10)
You Look So Good In Love (1,3)
You Still Get To Me (4)
You're Dancin' This Dance All Wrong (2)
You're Right I'm Wrong (12)
You're Something Special To Me (3)
You're The Cloud I'm On (When I'm High) (1)

STRANGE, Billy
Top Hollywood session guitarist. Born in Long Beach, California in 1930.

| 10/24/64 | 135 | 5 | | 1 The James Bond Theme [I] | $10 | Crescendo 2004 |
| 7/3/65 | 146 | 3 | | 2 English Hits Of '65 [I] | $10 | Crescendo 2009 |

Bernie's Tune (1)
Can't You Hear My Heartbeat? (2)
C'mon And Swim (1)
Come Stay With Me! (2)

007 Theme (1)
Eight Days A Week (2)
Game Of Love (2)
Girl From Ipanema (2)
Hard Day's Night (1)

House Of The Rising Sun (1)
I Know A Place! (2)
I'm Telling You Now (2)
In The Mood (1)
It's Not Unusual (2)

James Bond Theme (1) **58**
Last Time (2)
Memphis (1)
Mrs. Brown, You've Got A Lovely Daughter! (2)

Nobody I Know (1)
Silhouettes (2)
Ticket To Ride (2)
Tired Of Waiting (2)
Walk, Don't Run '64 (1)

Wishin & Hopin (1)

STRANGELOVES, The
Writers/producers Bob Feldman, Jerry Goldstein and Richard Gottehrer. Team wrote/produced The Angels' "My Boyfriend's Back," produced The McCoys' "Hang On Sloopy" and charted as The Sheep. Gottehrer became a partner in Sire Records and produced the Go-Go's first two albums and Blondie's debut album.

| 11/13/65 | 141 | 2 | | I Want Candy | $50 | Bang 211 |

Cara-Lin 39
Hang On Sloopy

I Want Candy 11
It's About My Baby (1)

Just The Way You Are
New Orleans

Night Time 30
No Jive

Rhythm Of Love
(Roll On) Mississippi

Satisfaction
Sendin' My Love

STRANGLERS, The
Pop group: Jet Black, J.J. Burnell, Hugh Cornwell (vocals) and Dave Greenfield. Cornwell left in 1990.
Paul Roberts (ex-Sniff 'n' the Tears; vocals) and John Ellis (ex-Vibrators; guitar) joined in 1991.

| 5/2/87 | 172 | 4 | | Dreamtime | $8 | Epic 40607 |

Always The Sun
Big In America

Dreamtime
Ghost Train

Mayan Skies
Nice In Nice

Shakin' Like A Leaf

Too Precious
Was It You?

You'll Always Reap What You Sow

STRAWBERRY ALARM CLOCK
West Coast psychedelic rock sextet: Ed King (lead guitar), Mark Weitz (keyboards), Lee Freeman (guitar), Gary Lovetro (bass), George Bunnel (bass) and Randy Seol (drums). King joined Lynyrd Skynyrd, 1973-75. Originally known as The Sixpence.

| 11/4/67+ | 11 | 24 | | Incense And Peppermints | $30 | Uni 73014 |

Birds In My Tree
Hummin' Happy

Incense And Peppermints 1
Lose To Live

Pass Time With The Sac
Paxton's Back Street Carnival

Rainy Day Mushroom Pillow
Strawberries Mean Love

Unwind With The Clock
World's On Fire

STRAWBS
British progressive rock band led by David Cousins.

7/15/72	191	5		1 Grave New World	$10	A&M 4344
4/28/73	121	9		2 Bursting At The Seams	$10	A&M 4383
3/2/74	94	17		3 Hero and Heroine	$8	A&M 3607
3/8/75	47	13		4 Ghosts	$8	A&M 4506
10/11/75	147	6		5 Nomadness	$8	A&M 4544
10/30/76	144	5		6 Deep Cuts	$8	Oyster 1603
8/6/77	175	4		7 Burning For You	$8	Oyster 1604

Absent Friend (How I Need You) (5)
Ah Me, Ah My (1)
Alexander The Great (7)
Angel Wine (medley) (4)
Autumn Medley (3)
Back In The Old Routine (4)
Back On The Farm (5)
Barcarole (For The Death Of Venice) (7)
Benedictus (1)

Beside The Rio Grande (6)
Burning For Me (7)
Carry Me Home (7)
Charmer (6)
Cut Like A Diamond (7)
Don't Try To Change Me (6)
Down By The Sea (2)
Flower And The Young Man (4)
Flying (2)
Ghosts Medley (4)

Golden Salamander (5)
Goodbye (Is Not An Easy Word To Say) (7)
Grace Darling (4)
Hanging In The Gallery (5)
Hard, Hard Winter (6)
Heartbreaker (7)
Heavy Disguise (1)
Hero And Heroine (3)
Hero's Theme (3)

Hey, Little Man...Thursday's Child (1)
Hey, Little Man...Wednesday's Child (1)
I Feel Your Loving Coming On (7)
I Only Want My Love To Grow In You (6)
Is It Today, Lord? (1)
Journey's End (1)

Just Love (3)
Keep On Trying (7)
Lady Fuschia (2)
Lay A Little Light On Me (3)
Lay Down (2)
Lemon Pie (4)
Life Auction Medley (4)
Little Sleepy (5)
Midnight Sun (3)
Mind Of My Own (5)
My Friend Peter (6)

New World (1)
On Growing Older (1)
Out In The Cold (3)
Part Of The Union (2)
Promised Land (5)
Queen of Dreams (3)
Remembering (4)
River, The (2)
Round And Round (3)
Sad Young Man (3)
Shine On Silver Sun (3)

DEBUT DATE	PEAK POS	WKS CHR	G O L D	ARTIST — Album Title	$	Label & Number

STRAWBS — Cont'd

Simple Visions (6)	Soldiers' Tale (6)	Thank You (2)		Turn Me Round (6)	Where Do You Go (When	Winter And The Summer (2)
So Close And Yet So Far Away (6)	Starshine (medley) (4)	To Be Free (5)		(Wasting My Time) Thinking Of You (6)	You Need A Hole To Crawl In) (4)	You And I (When We Were Young) (4)
So Shall Our Love Die? (5)	Stormy Down (2)	Tokyo Rosie (5)				
	Tears And Pavan Medley (2)	Tomorrow (1)				

STRAY CATS

Long Island, New York rockabilly trio: Brian Setzer (b: 4/10/60; lead singer, guitar), Lee Rocker (born Leon Drucher; string bass) and Slim Jim Phantom (born Jim McDonell; drums). Recorded two albums in Britain in 1981 and 1982. Group disbanded in 1984; reunited in 1988. Phantom and Rocker formed trio Phantom, Rocker & Slick in 1985, also the year Phantom married actress Britt Ekland. Setzer portrayed Eddie Cochran in the film *La Bamba*. Phantom portrayed Charlie Parker's drummer in the film *Bird*.

DEBUT DATE	PEAK POS	WKS CHR	GOLD	ARTIST — Album Title	$	Label & Number
7/3/82	2¹⁵	74 ▲		1 Built For Speed	$8	EMI America 17070
9/10/83	14	29 ●		2 Rant n' Rave with the Stray Cats	$8	EMI America 17102
9/27/86	122	5		3 Rock Therapy	$8	EMI America 17226
4/29/89	111	9		4 Blast Off	$8	EMI 91401

Baby Blue Eyes (1)	18 Miles To Memphis (2)	**I Won't Stand In Your Way** (2) 35	Looking For Someone To Love (3)	**Rock This Town** (1) 9	Something's Wrong With My Radio (2)
Beautiful Delilah (3)	Everybody Needs Rock 'N' Roll (4)	I'm A Rocker (3)	Nine Lives (4)	Rockabilly Rules (4)	**Stray Cat Strut** (1) 3
Blast Off (4)	Gene And Eddie (4)	Jeanie, Jeanie, Jeanie (1)	One Hand Loose (3)	Rockabilly World (4)	Too Hip, Gotta Go (2)
Bring It Back Again (4)	Gina (4)	Little Miss Prissy (1)	Race With The Devil (3)	Rockin' All Over The Place (4)	You Don't Believe Me (1)
Broken Man (3)	Hotrod Gang (2)	Lonely Summer Nights (1)	Rebels Rule (2)	Rumble In Brighton (4)	
Built For Speed (1)	How Long You Wanna Live, Anyway? (2)	**Look At That Cadillac** (2) 68	Reckless (3)	Runaway Boys (1)	
Change Of Heart (4)	I Wanna Cry (3)		Rev It Up & Go (1)	**(She's) Sexy + 17** (2) 5	
Dig Dirty Doggie (2)			Rock Therapy (3)	Slip, Slip, Slippin' In (4)	
Double Talkin' Baby (1)					

STREEP, Meryl — see CHILDRENS

STREET, Janey

Pop-rock singer originally from New York City.

DEBUT DATE	PEAK POS	WKS CHR	GOLD	ARTIST — Album Title	$	Label & Number
11/3/84	145	6		Heroes, Angels & Friends	$8	Arista 8219

(How Long) Till My Ship Comes In	Jimmy (Lives In The House Down The Street)	Me And My Friends	There Ain't No Angels In The Sky	Under The Clock
In My Mind	Let's Give Into The Night	**Say Hello To Ronnie** 68		Where Are The Heroes

STREETS

Rock quartet led by Steve Walsh (vocalist/keyboardist of Kansas).

DEBUT DATE	PEAK POS	WKS CHR	GOLD	ARTIST — Album Title	$	Label & Number
12/3/83+	166	11		1st	$8	Atlantic 80117

Blue Town	Everything Is Changing	**If Love Should Go** 87	Move On	So Far Away
Cold Hearted Woman	Fire	Lonely Woman's Cry	One Way Street	

★★5★★ STREISAND, Barbra

Born Barbara Joan Streisand on 4/24/42 in Brooklyn. Made Broadway debut in *I Can Get It For You Wholesale*, 1962. Lead role in Broadway's *Funny Girl*, 1964. Film debut in *Funny Girl* in 1968 (tied with Katharine Hepburn for Best Actress Oscar); also starred in *A Star Is Born*, *Hello Dolly*, *Funny Lady*, *The Way We Were* and many others. Produced/directed/starred in the films *Yentl* and *Prince Of Tides*. Married to actor Elliott Gould from 1963-71.

DEBUT DATE	PEAK POS	WKS CHR	GOLD	ARTIST — Album Title	$	Label & Number
4/13/63	8	101 ●		1 The Barbra Streisand Album	$20	Columbia 8807
				1963 Grammy winner: Album of the Year		
9/14/63	2³	74 ●		2 The Second Barbra Streisand Album	$20	Columbia 8854
2/29/64	5	74 ●		3 The Third Album	$20	Columbia 8954
5/2/64	2³	51 ●		4 Funny Girl .... [OC]	$20	Capitol 2059
				based on the early life of Fanny Brice; includes "Find Yourself A Man" and "If A Girl Isn't Pretty" by Danny Meehan/Kay Medford/Jean Stapleton; "Who Taught Her Everything" by Kay Medford & Danny Meehan		
10/3/64	1⁵	84 ●		5 People	$15	Columbia 9015
5/22/65	2³	68 ●		6 My Name Is Barbra .... [TV]	$15	Columbia 9136
				Streisand's first television special (4/28/65)		
11/6/65	2³	48 ▲		7 My Name Is Barbra, Two...	$15	Columbia 9209
4/9/66	3	36 ●		8 Color Me Barbra .... [TV]	$15	Columbia 9278
				Streisand's second television special (3/30/66)		
11/19/66+	5	29		9 Je m'appelle Barbra	$15	Columbia 9347
				Je m'appelle is French for My Name Is		
11/11/67+	12	23		10 Simply Streisand	$15	Columbia 9482
9/28/68+	12	108 ▲		11 Funny Girl .... [S]	$15	Columbia 3220
				screen version of the above Broadway musical; includes "If A Girl Isn't Pretty" by Mae Questal & Kay Medford		
10/12/68	30	20 ●		12 A Happening In Central Park .... [L]	$15	Columbia 9710
				recorded live on 6/17/67; broadcast on TV on 9/15/68		
9/6/69	31	40		13 What About Today?	$15	Columbia 9816
11/15/69+	49	33		14 Hello, Dolly! .... [S]	$15	20th Century 5103
				includes "Elegance" by Michael Crawford; "It Only Takes A Moment" by Michael Crawford & Marianne McAndrew; "It Takes A Woman" by Walter Matthau; and "Ribbons Down My Back" by Marianne McAndrew		
2/28/70	32	30 ▲²		15 Barbra Streisand's Greatest Hits .... [G]	$10	Columbia 9968
7/25/70	108	24		16 On A Clear Day You Can See Forever .... [S]	$10	Columbia 30086
				includes "Come Back To Me," "Melinda" and "On A Clear Day (You Can See Forever)" by Yves Montand; "On A Clear Day (You Can See Forever)" by Nelson Riddle		
2/6/71	186	6		17 The Owl and the Pussycat .... [S-T]	$15	Columbia 30401
				comedy dialogue highlights (Streisand/George Segal) from the film; background music by Blood, Sweat & Tears		
2/20/71	10	29 ▲		18 Stoney End	$10	Columbia 30378
9/18/71	11	26 ●		19 Barbra Joan Streisand	$10	Columbia 30792
11/18/72+	19	27 ▲		20 Live Concert At The Forum .... [L]	$10	Columbia 31760

DEBUT DATE	PEAK POS	WKS CHR	G O L D	ARTIST — Album Title	$	Label & Number
				STREISAND, Barbra — Cont'd		
11/24/73	64	16		21 Barbra Streisand...and other musical instruments .... [TV] featuring a host of musicians and instruments from many countries; TV special broadcast on 11/2/73	$10	Columbia 32655
2/16/74	1[2]	31	▲	22 **The Way We Were** .... not the soundtrack album (see Soundtracks)	$10	Columbia 32801
11/16/74+	13	24	●	23 ButterFly	$10	Columbia 33095
3/29/75	6	25	●	24 Funny Lady ....[S] film is the sequel to *Funny Girl*; includes "Clap Hands, Here Comes Charley" by Ben Vereen; "It's Only A Paper Moon/I Like Her" and "Me And My Shadow" by James Caan	$8	Arista 9004
11/1/75	12	20	●	25 Lazy Afternoon	$8	Columbia 33815
3/6/76	46	14		26 Classical Barbra ....[F] with the Columbia Symphony Orchestra	$8	Columbia 33452
12/11/76+	1[6]	51	▲[4]	27 A Star Is Born ....[S-L] Kris Kristofferson sings on 5 of the 12 tracks (all but 4 tracks are live); third version of the 1937 film classic; includes 3 solo cuts by Kris Kristofferson: "Crippled Crow," "Hellacious Acres," "Watch Closely Now"	$8	Columbia 34403
7/2/77	3	25	▲	28 Streisand Superman	$8	Columbia 34830
6/17/78	12	27	▲	29 Songbird	$8	Columbia 35375
12/2/78+	1[3]	46	▲[4]	30 Barbra Streisand's Greatest Hits, Volume 2 .... [G]	$8	Columbia 35679
7/7/79	20	18	●	31 The Main Event ....[S] 3 versions of title song; others by various artists; includes "Angry Eyes" by Loggins & Messina; "Big Girls Don't Cry" by The 4 Seasons; "Body Shop" by Michalski & Oosterveen; "Copeland Meets The Coasters/Get A Job" "I'd Clean A Fish For You," and "It's Your Foot Again" by Michael Melvoin	$8	Columbia 36115
11/3/79	7	26	▲	32 Wet	$8	Columbia 36258
10/11/80	1[3]	49	▲[5]	33 Guilty .... produced by Barry Gibb	$8	Columbia 36750
12/12/81+	10	108	▲[4]	34 Memories ....[K]	$8	Columbia 37678
12/19/81+	108	5	▲[3]	35 A Christmas Album ....[X-R] originally released in 1967 (see below for Christmas chart data)	$8	Columbia 9557
11/26/83+	9	26	▲	36 Yentl ....[S] Barbra is the first woman to produce, direct, write and perform a film's title role	$8	Columbia 39152
10/27/84	19	28	▲	37 Emotion	$8	Columbia 39480
11/23/85+	1[3]	50	▲[3]	38 The Broadway Album .... Barbra sings 14 of her favorite Broadway tunes	$8	Columbia 40092
5/9/87	9	28	▲	39 One Voice ....[L] recorded at her Malibu ranch for an audience of 500 invited guests	$8	Columbia 40788
11/12/88	10	26	▲	40 Till I Loved You	$8	Columbia 40880
10/21/89	26	25	▲	41 A Collection Greatest Hits...And More .... [G]	$8	Columbia 45369
12/15/90	167	4		42 A Christmas Album ....[X-R] Christmas charts: 1/'67, 3/'68, 15/'69, 7/'70, 6/'71, 1/'73, 2/'83, 5/'84, 3/'85, 5/'87, 5/'88, 9/'89, 9/'90, 6/'91, 9/'92	$8	Columbia 9557
10/12/91	38	16	▲	43 Just For The Record ....[K] spans 30 years of unreleased studio & live tracks; original demos; TV, nightclub & award show appearances; includes 92-page booklet	$64	Columbia 44111 [4]

Absent Minded Me (5)
After The Rain (32)
After You've Gone (medley) (43)
Alfie (13)
All I Ask Of You (40,41)
All In Love Is Fair (22,30) **63**
All That I Want (7)
All The Things You Are (10)
Am I Blue (24)
America The Beautiful (39)
Animal Crackers In My Soup (medley) (8)
Answer Me (28)
Any Place I Hang My Hat Is Home (2,43)
As Time Goes By (3)
Ask Yourself Why (13)
Autumn (5)
Autumn Leaves (9)
Baby Me Baby (28)
Be My Guest (1)
Beautiful (19)
Before The Parade Passes By (14)
Being Alive (38)
Being At War With Each Other (22)
Best Gift (35,42)
Best I Could (37)
Best Thing You've Ever Done (22)
Best Things In Life Are Free (medley) (7,43)
Between Yesterday And Tomorrow (43)
Bewitched (Bothered And Bewildered) (3)
Blind Date (24)

Boy Next Door (10)
Brother Can You Spare A Dime? (medley) (7)
By Myself (21,43)
By The Way (25,41)
C'est Si Bon (It's So Good) (8)
Cabin Fever (28)
Can You Tell The Moment? (43)
Can't Help Lovin' That Man (38)
Canteloube: Brezairola ("Berceuse" from Songs Of The Auvergne) (26)
Child Is Born (25)
Christmas Song (Chestnuts Roasting On An Open Fire) (35,42)
Clear Sailing (28)
Clopin Clopant (9)
Come Back To Me (21)
Come Rain Or Come Shine (32)
Come To The Supermarket (In Old Peking) (1)
Comin' In And Out Of Your Life (34,41) **11**
Confrontation, The (17)
Cornet Man (28)
Cry Me A River (1,12,43)
Crying Time (23,43)
Dancing (14)
Debussy: Beau Soir (26)
Deep In The Night (29)
Didn't We (20) **82**
Ding-Dong! The Witch Is Dead (43)
Don't Believe What You Read (28)
Don't Ever Leave Me (21)
Don't Like Goodbyes (5)

Don't Rain On My Parade (4,11,15,20,21,43)
Down With Love (2)
Draw Me A Circle (3)
Emotion (37) **79**
(Enough Is Enough) ..see: No More Tears
(Evergreen) ..see: Star Is Born, Love Theme From A Everything (27)
"Eyes Of Laura Mars" (Prisoner), Love Theme From (30) **21**
Faure: Apres Un Reve (26)
Faure: Pavane (Vocalise) (26)
Fight ..see: Main Event
Fine And Dandy (5)
Flim Flam Man (18) **82**
Free Again (9,15) **83**
Free The People (18)
Funny Face (medley) (8)
Funny Girl (11,43) **44**
Get Happy (medley) (43)
Give Me The Simple Life (medley) (7,43)
Glad To Be Unhappy (medley) (21)
Go To Sleep (16)
God Bless The Child (43)
Good Man Is Hard To Find (medley) (43)
Goodnight (13)
Gotta Move (2,8,15)
Gounod: Ave Maria (35,42)
Grandma's Hands (23)
Guava Jelly (23)
Guilty (33,39,41,43) **3**
Handel: Dank Sei Dir, Herr (26)
Handel: Lascia Ch'io Pianga From Rinaldo (26)

Hands Off The Man ..see: Flim Flam Man
Happy Days Are Here Again (1,12,15,20,39,43)
Harold Arlen (43)
Hatikvah (43)
(Have I Stayed) Too Long At The Fair ..see: I Stayed Too Long
Have Yourself A Merry Little Christmas (35,42)
He Isn't You (16)
He Touched Me (7,12,15,43) **53**
Heart Don't Change My Mind (37)
Hello, Dolly! (14,43)
Henry Street (4)
Here We Are At Last (37,43)
His Love Makes Me Beautiful (4,11)
Honey Can I Put On Your Clothes (29)
Honey Pie (13)
Hooray For Love (medley) (43)
House Is Not A Home (medley) (19)
House Of Flowers (43)
How About Me (medley) (22)
How Does The Wine Taste? (5)
How Lucky Can You Get (24)
How Much Of The Dream Comes True (7)
Hurry! It's Lovely Up Here (16)
I Ain't Gonna Cry Tonight (32)
I Believe In Love (27)
I Can Do It (43)

I Can See It (6,12)
I Don't Break Easily (29)
I Don't Care Much (2)
I Don't Know Where I Stand (18)
I Found A Million Dollar Baby (In A Five & Ten Cent Store) (24)
I Found You Love (28)
I Got A Code In My Doze (24)
I Got Plenty Of Nothin' (7)
I Got Rhythm (medley) (21)
I Had Myself A True Love (3,43)
I Hate Music (43)
I Haved Dreamed (medley) (38)
I Know Him So Well (43)
I Like Him (medley) (24)
(I Like New York In June) How About You (medley) (43)
I Love You (medley) (8)
I Loves You Porgy (medley) (38)
I Mean To Shine (19)
I Never Had It So Good (25)
I Never Has Seen Snow (21)
I Never Meant To Hurt You (19)
I Stayed Too Long At The Fair (2,8,43)
I Want To Be Seen With You Tonight (4)
I Wish You Love (9)
I Won't Last A Day Without You (23)
I Wonder As I Wander (35,43)

I'd Rather Be Blue Over You (Than Happy With Somebody Else) (11)
I'll Be Home (18)
I'll Know (10)
I'll Tell The Man In The Street (1)
I'm All Smiles (5)
I'm Always Chasing Rainbows (43)
I'm Five (medley) (6)
I'm The Greatest Star (4,11,43)
I've Been Here (9)
I've Got No Strings (6)
I've Grown Accustomed To Her Face (medley) (8)
I've Never Been A Woman Before (22)
If I Close My Eyes (43)
If I Love Again (24)
If I Loved You (38,43)
If You Could Read My Mind (18)
If You Were The Only Boy In The World (6)
In The Wee Small Hours Of The Morning (medley) (43)
Isn't This Better (24)
It All Depends On You (medley) (43)
It Had To Be You (3)
It's A New World (39)
(It's Gonna Be A) Great Day (24)
It's Only A Paper Moon (medley) (21)
Jenny Rebecca (6)
Jingle Bells? (35,42)
Johnny One Note (medley) (21)

STREISAND, Barbra — Cont'd

Jubilation (23)
Jule Styne (43)
Just A Little Lovin' (Early In The Mornin') (18)
Just In Time (3)
Just Leave Everything To Me (14)
Keepin' Out Of Mischief Now (1,43)
Kid Again (medley) (6)
Kind Of Man A Woman Needs (7)
Kiss Me In The Rain (32) 37
Ladies Who Lunch (medley) (38)
Lazy Afternoon (25)
Le Mur (9)
Left In The Dark (37) 50
Let Me Go (18)
Let The Good Times Roll (23)
Let's Face The Music And Dance (medley) (8)
Let's Hear It For Me (24)
Letters That Cross In The Mail (25)
Lied: Auf Dem Wasser Zu Singen (21)
Life On Mars (23)
Life Story (33)
Like A Straw In The Wind (2)
Little Tin Soldier (13)
Look At That Face (medley) (8,43)
Lord's Prayer (35,42)
Lost Inside Of You (27,34,43)
Love (19)
Love And Learn (9)
Love Breakdown (29)
Love Comes From Unexpected Places (28)
Love In The Afternoon (23)
Love Inside (33,34)
Love Is A Bore (5)
Love Is Like A New Born Child (12)
Love Light (40)
Love With All The Trimmings (16)
Lover, Come Back To Me (2,43)
Lover Man (Oh, Where Can You Be?) (10)
Lullaby For Myself (28)
Ma Premiere Chanson (9)
Main Event/Fight (31,41) 3
Make Believe (3)

Make It Like A Memory (33)
Make No Mistake, He's Mine (37) 51
Make The Man Love Me (10)
Make Your Own Kind Of Music (medley) (20) 94
 hit the "Hot 100" as a medley with "Sing A Song"
Make Your Own Kind Of Music (medley) (21)
Man I Loved (29)
Martina (9)
Marty The Martian (12)
Maybe (18)
Memory (34,41) 52
Minute Waltz (8)
Miss Marmelstein (43)
Moanin' Low (25)
Moon And I (43)
Moon River (8)
More Than You Know (10,24)
Morning After (13)
Morning After (17)
Mother (19) 79
Much More (1)
Music That Makes Me Dance (4)
My Buddy (medley) (22)
My Coloring Book (2,15)
My Father's Song (25)
My Favorite Things (35,42)
My Funny Valentine (10)
My Heart Belongs To Me (28,30,34) 4
My Honey's Loving Arms (1,43)
My Lord And Master (5)
My Man (6,11,15,20,43) 79
My Melancholy Baby (3)
My Name Is Barbra (6)
My Pa (6)
Natural Sounds (12)
Nearness Of You (10)
Never Give Up (33)
Never Will I Marry (3)
New York State Of Mind (28,34)
Niagara (32)
No Easy Way Down (18)
No Matter What Happens *[includes 2 versions]* (36)
No More Songs For Me (9)
No More Tears (Enough Is Enough) (32,34) 1
No Wonder (Part One & Two) (36)
Nobody Knows (medley) (43)

Nobody Knows You When You're Down And Out (medley) (7)
Nobody's Heart (Belongs To Me) (43)
Non C'est Rien (8)
Not While I'm Around (38)
Nuts, Theme From ..see: Two People
O Little Town Of Bethlehem (35,42)
Ogerman: I Loved You (26)
On A Clear Day (You Can See Forever) (20,43)
On My Way To You (40)
On Rainy Afternoons (32)
Once Upon A Summertime (9)
One Kiss (8)
One Less Bell To Answer (medley) (19)
One More Night (29)
One More Time Around (40)
One Note Samba (medley) (21)
Orff: In Trutina From Carmina Burana (26)
Over The Rainbow (39,43)
Papa, Can You Hear Me? (36,39,43)
People (4,5,11,12,15,20,21,39, 43) 5
Piano Practicing (medley) (21)
Piece Of Sky (36,43)
Pieces Of Dreams (22)
Places You Find Love (40)
Porgy, I's Your Woman Now (Bess, You Is My Woman) (medley) (38)
Pretty Women (medley) (38)
Promises (33) 48
Punky's Dilemma (13)
Put On Your Sunday Clothes (14)
Putting It Together (38,43)
Queen Bee (27)
Quiet Night (7)
Quiet Thing (medley) (43)
Rat-Tat-Tat-Tat (4)
Reunion, The (17)
Richard Rodgers (43)
Right As The Rain (2)
Roller Skate Rag (11)
Run Wild (33)
'S Wonderful (medley) (43)

Sadie, Sadie (4,11)
Sam, You Made The Pants Too Long (8,15) 98
(Sandpiper, Love Theme From The) ..see: Shadow Of Your Smile
Schumann: Mondnacht (26)
Second Hand Rose (7,12,15,21,43) 32
Second Hand Rose (medley) *[solo: Barbra's Mother]* (43)
Seduction, The (17)
Send In The Clowns (38)
Shadow Of Your Smile (7)
Shake Me, Wake Me (When It's Over) (25)
Simple Man (23)
Since I Don't Have You (23)
Since I Fell For You (19,43)
Sing A Song (medley) (20) 94
 hit the "Hot 100" as a medley with "Make Your Own Kind Of Music"
Singer, The (43)
Sleep In Heavenly Peace (Silent Night) (12,35,42,43)
Sleepin' Bee (1,43)
Small World (medley) (24)
So Long Dearie (14)
So Long Honey Lamb (24)
Some Good Things Never Last (40)
Some Of These Days (medley) (43)
Someone That I Used To Love (41)
Someone To Watch Over Me (6)
Something So Right (22)
Something Wonderful (medley) (38)
Something's Coming (38,39)
Somewhere (38,39,41) 43
Songbird (29,30) 25
Soon It's Gonna Rain (1)
Space Captain (19)
Speak To Me Of Love (9)
Splish Splash (32)
Spring Can Really Hang You Up The Most (43)
"Star Is Born" (Evergreen), Love Theme From A (27,30,34,39,43)
Starting Here, Starting Now (8,20,43)
Stay Away (29)

Stoney End (18,20,30,43) 6
Stout-Hearted Men (10) 92
Summer Knows (19)
Summer Me, Winter Me (22)
Superman (28,30)
Supper Time (5)
Swan, The (11)
Sweet Inspiration/Where You Lead (20,30) 37
Sweet Zoo (6)
Sweetest Sounds (21)
Taking A Chance On Love (3)
Taste Of Honey (1)
That Face (medley) (8)
That's A Fine Kind O' Freedom (13)
There Won't Be Trumpets (medley) (43)
They Didn't Believe Me (medley) (8)
(They Long To Be) Close To You (43)
This Is One Of Those Moments (36)
Till I Loved You (40) 25
Time And Love (18) 51
Time Machine (37)
Tomorrow (29)
Tomorrow Night (36)
Two People (40,43)
Until It's Time For You To Go (13)
Value (12,43)
Warm All Over (43)
Warmup, The (17)
Way He Makes Me Feel (36,41) 40
Way We Were (22,30,34,39,43) 1
Way We Weren't (medley) (43)
We Kiss In A Shadow (medley) (38)
We're Not Makin' Love Anymore (43)
We've Only Just Begun (43)
Were Thine That Special Face (medley) (8)
Wet (32)
What About Today (13)
What Are You Doing The Rest Of Your Life? (22,43)
What Did I Have That I Don't Have (16)
What Kind Of Fool (33,39,41) 10
What Now My Love (9)

What Were We Thinking Of (40)
What's New Pussycat? (medley) (8)
When I Dream (37)
When In Rome (I Do As The Romans Do) (5)
When Sunny Gets Blue (10)
When The Sun Comes Out (2,43)
When You Gotta Go (medley) (43)
When You're Down And Out (medley) (43)
Where Am I Going? (8) 94
Where Is It Written? (36)
Where Is The Wonder (6)
Where Or When (8)
Where You Lead (19) 40
Where's That Rainbow? (7)
White Christmas (35,42)
Who Are You Now? (4)
Who Will Buy? (2)
Who's Afraid Of The Big Bad Wolf (1,43)
Why Did I Choose You (6,15) 77
Why Let It Go? (40)
Widescreen (43)
Will He Like Me (5)
Will Someone Ever Look At Me That Way? (36)
With A Little Help From My Friends (13)
With One More Look At You (medley) (7)
Wolf: Verschwiegene Liebe (26)
Woman In Love (33,41) 1
Woman In The Moon (27)
World Is A Concerto (medley) (21)
Yesterdays (8)
You And I (25)
You And Me For Always (40)
You And The Night And The Music (medley) (43)
You Are Woman, I Am Man (4,11)
You Don't Bring Me Flowers (29,30,34,43) 1
You Wanna Bet (43)
You'll Never Know (43)
You're A Step In The Right Direction (43)
You're The Top (43)
You've Got A Friend (19)

STRIKERS, The
Seven-man funk band from New York City.

| 8/29/81 | 174 | 3 | | | The Strikers .... | $8 | Prelude 14100 |

Body Music   Bring Out The Devil   Give It What You Got   Hold Onto The Feeling   Inch By Inch   Strike It Up

STRUNK, Jud
Born Justin Strunk, Jr. on 6/11/36 in Jamestown, New York and raised in Farmington, Maine. Killed in a plane crash on 10/15/81. Regular on TV's *Laugh In*.

| 5/5/73 | 138 | 9 | | | Daisy A Day .... | $12 | MGM 4898 |

Bill Jones General Store   Farethewell   Jacob Brown   Next Door Neighbor's Kid   Searchers, The
Daisy A Day 14   If I Could Have My Way   Long Ride Home   Runaway, The   This House

STRUNZ & FARAH
Male flamenco guitar duo of Costa Rican Jorge Strunz and Iranian Ardeshir Farah.

| 3/9/91 | 164 | 6 | | | Primal Magic .... [I] | $12 | Mesa 79023 |

Amazonas   Bola   Huixamatli (Luna Llena)   Rainmaker   Twilight At The Zuq
Anochecer (Nightfall)   Canto Al Sol   Ida Y Vuelta   Tierra Verde   Zumba

STRYPER
Christian heavy-metal band from Orange County, California: brothers Michael (vocals) and Robert (drums) Sweet, with Oz Fox (guitar) and Tim Gaines (bass). Michael left in mid-1992.

9/28/85	84	64	●	1	Soldiers Under Command	$8	Enigma 72077
8/23/86	103	30		2	The Yellow And Black Attack! .... [K-E]	$8	Enigma 73207
					remix of 1984 debut mini-album, plus 2 new songs		
11/22/86+	32	74	▲	3	To Hell With The Devil	$8	Enigma 73237
7/16/88	32	25	●	4	In God We Trust	$8	Enigma 73317
9/8/90	39	12		5	Against The Law..	$12	Enigma 73527

Abyss (To Hell With The Devil) (3)   **Always There For You** (4) 71   Co'Mon Rock (2)   **Honestly** (3) 23   Lonely (4)   Not That Kind Of Guy (5)
Against The Law (5)   Battle Hymn Of The Republic (3)   Come To The Everlife (4)   **I Believe In You** (4) 88   Loud 'N' Clear (2)   Ordinary Man (5)
All For One (5)   Calling On You (3)   First Love (1)   In God We Trust (4)   Loving You (2)   Reach Out (1)
All Of Me (3)   Caught In The Middle (5)   Free (3)   It's Up To You (4)   Makes Me Wanna Sing (1)   Reason For The Season (2)
        From Wrong To Right (2)   Keep The Fire Burning (4)   More Than A Man (3)   Reign, The (4)
        Holding On (3)   Lady (5)   My Love I'll Always Show (2)   Rock That Makes Me Roll (1)

STRYPER — Cont'd

Rock The Hell Out Of You (5) Sing-Along Song (3) Together As One (1) Two Time Woman (5) World Of You And I (4)
Rock The People (5) Soldiers Under Command (1) Together Forever (1) (Waiting For) A Love That's Writings On The Wall (4)
Rockin' The World (3) Surrender (1) Two Bodies (One Mind One Real (1) You Know What To Do (2)
Shining Star (5) To Hell With The Devil (3) Soul] (5) Way, The (3) You Won't Be Lonely (2)

STUART, Marty
Country singer/guitarist. Born in Philadelphia, Mississippi in 1958. Toured with Lester Flatt and Nashville Grass from age 13. Toured with Johnny Cash's band, 1979-85. Married Cash's daughter Cindy.

| 5/16/92 | 193 | 1 | | 1 Tempted .... | $12 | MCA 10106 |
| 7/25/92 | 77 | 25↑● | | 2 This One's Gonna Hurt You .... | $12 | MCA 10596 |

Blue Train (1) Get Back To The Country (1) Honky Tonk Crowd (2) King Of Dixie (1) Now That's Country (2) This One's Gonna Hurt You
Burn Me Down (1) Half A Heart (1) I Want A Woman (2) Little Things (1) Paint The Town Tonight (1) (For A Long, Long Time) (2)
Doin' My Time (1) Hey Baby (2) I'm Blue, I'm Lonesome (1) Me & Hank & Jumpin' Jack Tempted (1) Till I Found You (1)
Down Home (2) High On A Mountain Top (2) Just Between You And Me (2) Flash (2)

STUFF
Group of New York's top R&B session musicians: Richard Tee, Gordon Edwards, Cornell Dupree, Eric Gale, Christopher Parker and Stephen Gadd.

| 11/27/76 | 163 | 3 | | 1 Stuff ....[I] | $8 | Warner 2968 |
| 7/30/77 | 61 | 13 | | 2 More Stuff ....[I] | $8 | Warner 3061 |

And Here You Are (2) (Do You) Want Some Of This Honey Coral Rock (2) My Sweetness (1) Sometimes Bubba Gets Sun Song (1)
As (2) (1) How Long Will It Last (1) Need Somebody (2) Down (2) This One's For You (2)
Dixie (medley) (1) Foots (1) Looking For The Juice (1) Reflections Of Divine Love (1) Subway (2) Up On The Roof (medley) (1)
Happy Farms (1) Love Of Mine (1)

STYLE COUNCIL, The
English duo: Paul Weller (ex-vocalist of The Jam) and Mick Talbot (keyboards). Expanded to a trio in 1988 with the addition of female vocalist Dee C. Lee.

10/22/83	172	5		1 Introducing The Style Council ....[M]	$8	Polydor 815277
4/7/84	56	22		2 My Ever Changing Moods	$8	Geffen 4029
6/29/85	123	11		3 Internationalists	$8	Geffen 24061
4/18/87	122	10		4 The Cost Of Loving	$8	Polydor 831443
8/13/88	174	6		5 Confessions Of A Pop Group	$8	Polydor 835785

All Gone Away (3) Down In The Seine (3) How She Threw It All Away Long Hot Summer [includes Solid Bond In Your Heart (2) Why I Went Missing (5)
Angel (4) Dropping Bombs On The (5) 2 versions] (1) Speak Like A Child (1) With Everything To Lose (3)
Blue Cafe (2) Whitehouse (2) I Was A Doledads Toyboy (5) Luck (3) Stand Up Comic's Woman's Song (1)
Boy Who Cried Wolf (3) Fairy Tales (4) Internationalists (3) Man Of Great Promise (3) Instructions (3) You're The Best Thing
Changing Of The Guard (3) Gardener Of Eden (A Three It Didn't Matter (4) Mick's Blessings (2) Stone's Throw Away (3) (2) 76
Come To Milton Keynes (3) Piece Suite) Medley (5) It's A Very Deep Sea (5) Mick's Up (1) Story Of Someone's Shoe (5)
Confessions Of A Pop-Group Gospel, A (2) Life At A Top Peoples Health Money-Go-Round (1) Strength Of Your Nature (2)
(5) Headstart For Happiness Farm (5) My Ever Changing Moods Waiting (4)
Confessions 1,2 & 3 (5) (1,2) Little Boy In A Castle (2) 29 Walking The Night (4)
Cost Of Loving (4) Heavens Above (4) (medley) (5) Paris Match (1,2) Walls Come Tumbling Down
Dove Flew Down From The Here's One That Got Away (3) Lodgers, The (3) Right To Go (4) (3)
Elephant (medley) (5) Homebreakers (3) Shout To The Top (3) Whole Point Of No Return (2)

★★331★★ STYLISTICS, The
Soul group from Philadelphia formed in 1968. Consisted of Russell Thompkins, Jr. (b: 3/21/51; lead), Airron Love, James Smith, James Dunn and Herbie Murrell. Thompkins, Love and Smith sang with the Percussions; Murrell and Dunn with the Monarchs from 1965-68. First recorded for Sebring in 1969.

12/18/71+	23	38	●	1 The Stylistics	$10	Avco 33023
11/11/72+	32	38	●	2 Round 2: The Stylistics	$12	Avco 11006
11/24/73+	66	44		3 Rockin' Roll Baby	$10	Avco 11010
5/25/74	14	31	●	4 Let's Put It All Together	$8	Avco 69001
11/2/74	43	16		5 Heavy	$8	Avco 69004
2/22/75	41	30		6 The Best of The Stylistics ....[G]	$8	Avco 69005
6/14/75	72	13		7 Thank You Baby	$8	Avco 69008
11/8/75	99	11		8 You Are Beautiful	$8	Avco 69010
6/19/76	117	6		9 Fabulous	$8	H&L 69013
11/8/80	127	12		10 Hurry Up This Way Again	$8	TSOP 36470

And I'll See You No More (10) Don't Put It Down Til You I Will Love You Always (9) Let Them Work It Out (3) People Make The World Go We Can Make It Happen
Baby, Don't Change Your Been There (1) I Won't Give You Up (3) Let's Put It All Together Round (1,6) Again (4)
Mind (9) Driving Me Wild (10) I'd Rather Be Hurt By You (4,6) 18 Pieces (1) We Just Can't Help It (8)
Because I Love You, Girl (9) Ebony Eyes (1) (Than Be Loved By Love Comes Easy (3) Point Of No Return (1) What Goes Around Comes
Betcha By Golly, Wow Found A Love You Couldn't Somebody Else) (7) Love Is The Answer [includes Rockin' Roll Baby (3,6) 14 Around (7)
(1,6) 3 Handle (10) I'm Gonna Win (7) 2 versions] (4) She Did A Number On Me (5) What's Happenin', Baby? (5)
Break Up To Make Up From The Mountain (5) I'm Stone In Love With Make It Last (3) Sing Baby Sing (7) You And Me (2)
(2,6) 5 Funky Weekend (8) 76 You (2,6) 10 Maybe It's Because You're Sixteen Bars (9) You Are (9)
Can't Give You Anything Go Now (5) If I Love You (1) Lonely (9) Star On A TV Show (5) 47 You Are Beautiful (8) 79
(But My Love) (7) 51 Heavy Fallin' Out (5,6) 41 If You Are There (9) Maybe It's Love This Time Starvin' For Love (9) You Are Everything (1,6) 9
Can't Help Falling In Love (9) Hey Girl, Come And Get It (5) If You Don't Watch Out (2) (10) Stay (7) You Make Me Feel Brand
Children Of The Night (2) Honky Tonk Cafe (7) Is There Something On Your Michael Or Me (8) Stop, Look, Listen (To New (3,4,6) 2
Could This Be The End (3) Hurry Up This Way Again Mind (10) Miracle, The (5) Your Heart) (1) 39 You Ought To Be With Me (9)
Country Living (1) (10) It's So Good (9) Na-Na Is The Saddest Word Tears And Souvenirs (7) You'll Never Get To
Day The Clown Came To I Got A Letter (4) It's Too Late (10) (8) Thank You Baby (7) 70 Heaven (If You Break My
Town (5) I Got Time On My Hands (4) Jenny (8) Only For The Children (3) That Don't Shake Me (8) Heart) (2) 23
Disco Baby (7) I Have You, You Have Me Keeping My Fingers Crossed Pay Back Is A Dog (3) There's No Reason (4) You're A Big Girl Now
Doin' The Streets (4) (10) (4) Peek-A-Boo (2) To Save My Rock 'N' Roll (1,6) 73
I Take It Out On You (4) Soul (8) You're As Right As Rain (4)

★★182★★ STYX
Chicago-based rock quintet: Dennis DeYoung (vocals, keyboards), Tommy Shaw (lead guitar), James Young (guitar), and twin brothers John (drums) and Chuck Panozzo (bass). Band earlier known as TW4. Shaw replaced John Curulewski in 1976. Most songs written by Dennis DeYoung and/or Tommy Shaw. Band broke up when DeYoung and Shaw went solo in 1984. Reunited in 1990 with guitarist Glen Burtnick replacing Shaw, who joined the Damn Yankees. In Greek mythology, Styx is a river of Hades.

| 2/9/74 | 192 | 2 | | 1 The Serpent Is Rising .... | $12 | Wooden N. 0287 |

DEBUT DATE	PEAK POS	WKS CHR	GOLD	ARTIST — Album Title	$	Label & Number
				STYX — Cont'd		
11/9/74	154	12		2 Man Of Miracles	$8	Wooden N. 0638
1/25/75	20	19	●	3 Styx II ....[R]	$8	Wooden N. 1012
				originally released in 1973 (*Styx I* did not chart)		
12/20/75+	58	50	●	4 Equinox	$8	A&M 4559
10/30/76	66	18	●	5 Crystal Ball	$8	A&M 4604
7/30/77+	6	127	▲3	6 **The Grand Illusion**	$8	A&M 4637
9/30/78	6	92	▲3	7 **Pieces of Eight**	$8	A&M 4724
10/13/79	2[1]	60	▲2	8 **Cornerstone**	$8	A&M 3711
1/31/81	1[3]	61	▲3	9 Paradise Theater	$8	A&M 3719
3/19/83	3	34	▲	10 Kilroy Was Here	$8	A&M 3734
4/21/84	31	15		11 Caught In The Act - Live ....[L]	$10	A&M 6514 [2]
10/27/90	63	38		12 Edge Of The Century..............................	$12	A&M 5327

A.D. 1958 (9)
A.D. 1928 (9)
Aku-Aku (7)
All In A Day's Work (12)
As Bad As This (1)
Babe (8,11) *1*
Back To Chicago (12)
Ballerina (medley) (5)
Best Of Times (9,11) *1*
Best Thing (2) *82*
Blue Collar Man (Long Nights) (7,11) *21*
Boat On The River (8)
Born For Adventure (4)
Borrowed Time (8) *64*
Carrie Ann (12)
Castle Walls (6)
Christopher, Mr. Christopher (2)
Clair De Lune (medley) (5)

Cold War (10)
Come Sail Away (6,11) *8*
Crystal Ball (5,11)
Day, A (3)
Don't Let It End (10,11) *6*
Double Life (10)
Earl Of Roseland (3)
Eddie (8)
Edge Of The Century (12)
Evil Eyes (2)
Father O.S.A. (3)
First Time (8)
Fooling Yourself (The Angry Young Man) (6,11) *29*
Golden Lark (2)
Grand Finale (6)
Grand Illusion (6)
Great White Hope (7)
Grove Of Eglantine (1)

Half-Penny, Two-Penny (9)
Hallelujah Chorus (1)
Haven't We Been Here Before (10)
Havin' A Ball (2)
Heavy Metal Poisoning (10)
High Time (10) *48*
Homewrecker (12)
I'm Gonna Make You Feel It (3)
I'm O.K. (7)
Jennifer (5)
Jonas Psalter (1)
Just Get Through This Night (10)
Krakatoa (1)
Lady (3) *6*
Light Up (4)
Lights (8)
Little Fugue In 'G' (3)

Lonely Child (4)
Lonely People (2)
Lords Of The Ring (7)
Lorelei (4) *27*
Love At First Sight (12) *25*
Love In The Midnight (8)
Love Is The Ritual (12) *80*
Mademoiselle (5) *36*
Man In The Wilderness (6)
Man Like Me (2)
Man Of Miracles (2)
Message, The (7)
Midnight Ride (4)
Miss America (6,11)
Mother Dear (4)
Mr. Roboto (10,11) *3*
Music Time (11) *40*
Never Say Never (8)
Not Dead Yet (12)

Nothing Ever Goes As Planned (9) *54*
Pieces Of Eight (7)
Prelude 12 (4)
Put Me On (5)
Queen Of Spades (7)
Renegade (7) *16*
Rock & Roll Feeling (2)
Rockin' The Paradise (9,11)
Serpent Is Rising (1)
She Cares (9)
Shooz (5)
Show Me The Way (12) *3*
Sing For The Day (7) *41*
Snowblind (9,11)
Song For Suzanne (2)
Southern Woman (2)
State Street Sadie (9)
Suite Madame Blue (4,11)
Superstars (6)

This Old Man (5)
Too Much Time On My Hands (9,11) *9*
22 Years (1)
Why Me (8) *26*
Winner Take All (1)
Witch Wolf (1)
World Tonite (12)
You Need Love (3) *88*
Young Man (1)

SUAVE

Los Angeles native. Born on 2/22/66. Son of Waymond Anderson, Sr. (member of GQ).

| 4/23/88 | 101 | 12 | | I'm Your Playmate .... | $8 | Capitol 48686 |

B And E Of The Heart
Back Stabber

Don't Rush
I Wanna Please You

Love Triangle
My Girl *20*

Now That I Fell In Love
Playmate

Shake Your Body
Stop Acting Ill

SUGARCUBES, The

Group from Reykjavik, Iceland. Female vocalist Bjork Gudmundsottir with Braggi Olafsson, Thor Eldon, Siggi Baldursson, Einar Orn and Margret Ornolfsdottir. Group began as an artist's collective called KUKL (an Icelandic term for witches).

6/18/88	54	29		1 Life's Too Good	$8	Elektra 60801
				released with 6 different brightly-colored album jackets		
10/14/89	70	9		2 Here Today, Tomorrow Next Week!	$8	Elektra 60860
3/7/92	95	11		3 Stick Around For Joy......................................	$12	Elektra 61123

Bee (2)
Birthday (1)
Blue Eyed Pop (1)
Chihuahua (3)
Coldsweat (1)
Day Called Zero (2)
Dear Plastic (2)

Delicious Demon (1)
Deus (1)
Dream TV (2)
Eat The Menu (2)
F***ing In Rhythm & Sorrow (1)
Gold (3)

Happy Nurse (3)
Hetero Scum (2)
Hit (3)
I'm Hungry (3)
Leash Called Love (3)
Lucky Night (3)
Mama (1)

Motorcrash (1)
Nail (2)
Planet (2)
Pump (2)
Regina (2)
Shoot Him (2)
Sick For Toys (1)

Speed Is The Key (2)
Take Some Petrol Darling (1)
Tidal Wave (2)
Traitor (2)
Vitamin (3)
Walkabout (3)
Water (2)

SUGARHILL GANG

Harlem, New York rap trio: Michael "Wonder Mike" Wright, Guy "Master Gee" O'Brien and Henry "Big Bank Hank" Jackson. One of the first commercially successful rap acts.

| 1/30/82 | 50 | 18 | | 8th Wonder.. | $8 | SugarHill 249 |

Apache *53*
8th Wonder *82*

Funk Box
Giggalo

Hot Hot Summer Day

On The Money

Showdown

SUGARLOAF

Rock quartet from Denver: Jerry Corbetta (lead singer, keyboards), Bob Webber (guitar), Bob Raymond (bass) and Bob MacVittie (drums). Robert Yeazel (guitar, vocals) joined in 1971. By 1974, Myron Pollock replaced MacVittie, and Yeazel had left.

8/15/70	24	29		1 Sugarloaf	$12	Liberty 7640
2/13/71	111	9		2 Spaceship Earth	$12	Liberty 11010
4/12/75	152	6		3 Don't Call Us-We'll Call You	$10	Claridge 1000
				SUGARLOAF/JERRY CORBETTA		

Bach Doors Man (medley) (1)
Chest Fever (medley) (1)
Colorado Jones (3)
Country Dawg (2)
Don't Call Us, We'll Call You (3) *9*

Gold And The Blues (1)
Green-Eyed Lady (1) *3*
Hot Water (2)
I Don't Need You Baby (2)
I Got A Song (3)
Lay Me Down (3)

Lookin' For Some Fun (3)
Mother Nature's Wine (2) *88*
Music Box (2)
Myra, Myra (3)
Rollin' Hills (2)

Round And Round (3)
Rusty Cloud (3)
Spaceship Earth (2)
Things Gonna Change Some (1)
Tongue In Cheek (2) *55*

Train Kept A-Rollin' (Stroll On) (1)
We Could Fly So High (3)
West Of Tomorrow (1)
Wild Child (3)
Woman (2)

SUICIDAL TENDENCIES

Heavy-metal/punk group from Venice, California, led by vocalist Mike Muir, formed in 1982. Appeared on the TV show *Miami Vice*. Muir was later lead singer of Infectious Grooves.

5/23/87	100	13		1 Join The Army	$8	Carol 1336
10/1/88	111	12		2 How Will I Laugh Tomorrow When I Can't Even Smile Today............	$8	Epic 44288
10/28/89	150	5	●	3 Controlled By Hatred/Feel Like Shit...Deja-Vu	$8	Epic 45244
7/21/90	101	15		4 Lights...Camera...Revolution	$12	Epic 45389
7/18/92	52	10		5 The Art Of Rebellion	$12	Epic 48864

DEBUT DATE	PEAK POS	WKS CHR	GOLD	ARTIST — Album Title	$	Label & Number

SUICIDAL TENDENCIES — Cont'd

Accept My Sacrifice (5)
Alone (4)
Asleep At The Wheel (medley) (5)
Can't Stop (5)
Choosing My Own Way Of Life (3)
Controlled By Hatred (3)
Cyco (1)
Disco's Out, Murder's In (4)
Emotion No. 13 (4)
Feel Like Shit...Deja-Vu (3)

Feeling's Back (2)
Get Whacked (4)
Give It Revolution (4)
Go'n Breakdown (4)
Gotta Kill Captain Stupid (5)
Hearing Voices (2)
How Will I Laugh Tomorrow (2,3)
I Feel Your Pain And I Survive (1)
I Wasn't Meant To Feel This (medley) (5)

I'll Hate You Better (5)
If I Don't Wake Up (2)
It's Going Down (5)
It's Not Easy (5)
Join The Army (1)
Just Another Love Song (3)
Little Each Day (1)
Looking In Your Eyes (1)
Lost Again (4)
Lovely (4)
Master Of No Mercy (3)
Miracle, The (2)

Monopoly On Sorrow (5)
No Name, No Words (1)
Nobody Hears (5)
One Too Many Times (2)
Pledge Your Allegiance (2)
Possessed To Skate (1)
Prisoner, The (1)
Send Me Your Money (4)
Sorry?! (2)
Suicidal Maniac (1)
Surf And Slam (2)
Tap Into The Power (5)

Trip At The Brain (2)
Two Wrongs Don't Make A Right (But They Make Me Feel A Whole Lot Better) (1)
Waking The Dead (3)
War Inside My Head (1)
We Call This Mutha Revenge (5)
Where's The Truth (5)
Which Way To Free? (5)
You Can't Bring Me Down (4)
You Got, I Want (1)

SULTON, Kasim

Bass player of Todd Rundgren's Utopia.

| 2/27/82 | 197 | 2 | | Kasim .... | $8 | EMI America 17063 |

Don't Break My Heart
Drivin' Me Mad

Evil
Just A Little Bit

Rock And Roll
Roll The Dice

Someone To Love
Sweet Little Accident

This Must Be Love
White And Red

★★101★★ SUMMER, Donna

Born Adrian Donna Gaines on 12/31/48 in Boston. With group Crow, played local clubs. In German production of *Hair*, European productions of *Godspell*, *The Me Nobody Knows* and *Porgy And Bess*. Settled in Germany, where she recorded "Love To Love You Baby." In the film *Thank God It's Friday* in 1979. Married Bruce Sudano (Alive & Kicking and Brooklyn Dreams) in 1980. Dubbed "The Queen of Disco."

11/1/75+	11	30	●	1 Love To Love You Baby	$8	Oasis 5003
3/27/76	21	27	●	2 A Love Trilogy	$8	Oasis 5004
11/6/76	29	26	●	3 Four Seasons Of Love	$8	Casablanca 7038
6/4/77	18	40	●	4 I Remember Yesterday	$8	Casablanca 7056
11/26/77+	26	58	●	5 Once Upon A Time	$10	Casablanca 7078 [2]
9/16/78	1¹	75	▲	6 Live And More ....[L]	$10	Casablanca 7119 [2]
				one of 4 sides is a studio recording		
5/12/79	1⁶	49	▲	7 Bad Girls	$10	Casablanca 7150 [2]
11/3/79+	1¹	39	▲	8 On The Radio-Greatest Hits-Volumes I & II ....[G]	$10	Casablanca 7191 [
10/11/80	50	15		9 Walk Away - Collector's Edition (The Best Of 1977-1980) .....[G]	$8	Casablanca 7244
11/8/80	13	18	●	10 The Wanderer	$8	Geffen 2000
8/14/82	20	37	●	11 Donna Summer	$8	Geffen 2005
7/16/83	9	32	●	12 She Works Hard For The Money	$8	Mercury 812265
9/22/84	40	17		13 Cats Without Claws	$8	Geffen 24040
10/10/87	122	6		14 All Systems Go	$8	Geffen 24102
5/20/89	53	20		15 Another Place And Time	$8	Atlantic 81987

All Systems Go (14)
All Through The Night (7)
Autumn Changes (3)
Back In Love Again (4)
Bad Girls (7,8,9) *1*
Bad Reputation (14)
Black Lady (4)
Breakaway (15)
Breakdown (10)
Can't Get To Sleep At Night (7)
Can't We Just Sit Down (And Talk It Over) (4)
Cats Without Claws (13)
Cold Love (10) *33*
Come With Me (2)
Could It Be Magic (2) *52*
Dance Into My Life (5)
Dim All The Lights (7,8) *2*
Dinner With Gershwin (14) *48*
Eyes (13)
Fairy Tale High (5,6)
Fascination (14)

Faster And Faster To Nowhere (5,6)
Forgive Me (13)
Full Of Emptiness (1)
Grand Illusion (10)
Happily Ever After (5)
He's A Rebel (12)
Heaven Knows (6,8) *4*
Hot Stuff (7,8,9) *1*
I Believe In Jesus (10)
I Do Believe (I Fell In Love) (12)
I Don't Wanna Get Hurt (15)
I Feel Love (4,6,8,9) *6*
I Love You (5,6,8) *37*
I Remember Yesterday (4,6,8)
I'm Free (13)
(If It) Hurts Just A Little (11)
If It Makes You Feel Good (15)
If You Got It Flaunt It (5)
In Another Place And Time (15)
It's Not The Way (13)

Jeremy (14)
Journey To The Centre Of Your Heart (7)
Last Dance (6,8,9) *3*
Livin' In America (11)
Looking Up (10)
Love Has A Mind Of Its Own (7)
Love Is In Control (Finger On The Trigger) (11) *10*
Love Is Just A Breath Away (11)
Love Shock (14)
Love To Love You Baby (1,6,8) *2*
Love Will Always Find You (7)
Love's About To Change My Heart (15) *85*
Love's Unkind (4,6)
Lucky (7)
Lush Life (11)
MacArthur Park (6,8,9) *1*
Man Like You (5)

Maybe It's Over (13)
Mimi's Song (6)
My Baby Understands (7)
My Man Medley (6)
Mystery Of Love (11)
Need-A-Man Blues (1)
Nightlife (10)
No More Tears (Enough Is Enough) (8) *1*
Now I Need You (5)
Oh Billy Please (13)
On My Honor (7)
On The Radio (8,9) *5*
Once Upon A Time (5,6)
One Night In A Lifetime (7)
One Of A Kind (medley) (6)
Only One (15)
Only One Man (6)
Only The Fool Survives (14)
Our Love (7)
Pandora's Box (1)
People, People (12)
Prelude To Love (2)
Protection (11)

Queen For A Day (15)
Rumour Has It (5,6) *53*
Running For Cover (10)
Say Something Nice (5)
Sentimental (15)
She Works Hard For The Money (12) *3*
Spring Affair (3,6) *42*
State Of Independence (11) *41*
Stop, Look And Listen (12)
Stop Me (10)
Summer Fever (3)
Sunset People (7,8,9)
Supernatural Love (13) *75*
Suzanna (13)
Sweet Romance (5)
Take Me (4)
(Theme) Once Upon A Time (5)
There Goes My Baby (13) *21*
There Will Always Be A You (7)

Thinkin' 'Bout My Baby (14)
This Time I Know It's For Real (15) *7*
Tokyo (12)
Try Me, I Know We Can Make It (2,6,8) *80*
Unconditional Love (12) *43*
Voices Cryin' Out (14)
Walk Away (7,9) *36*
Wanderer, The (10) *3*
Wasted (2)
Way We Were (6)
Whatever Your Heart Desires (15)
When Love Takes Over You (15)
Whispering Waves (1)
Who Do You Think You're Foolin' (10) *40*
Winter Melody (3) *43*
Woman (12)
Woman In Me (11) *33*
Working The Midnight Shift (5)

SUMMER, Henry Lee

Rock singer from Brazil, Indiana. Received full college basketball scholarship.

| 3/12/88 | 56 | 23 | | 1 Henry Lee Summer .... | $8 | CBS Assoc. 40895 |
| 5/27/89 | 78 | 17 | | 2 I've Got Everything .... | $8 | CBS Assoc. 45124 |

Close Enough For Me (2)
Darlin' Danielle Don't (1) *57*
Don't Leave (2)

Got No Money (2)
Hands On The Radio (1) *85*
Hey Baby (2) *18*
I Ain't Comin' Home (1)

I Know How You Feel (1)
I Wish I Had A Girl (1) *20*
I'll Hurt For You (1)
I've Got Everything (1)

Just Another Day (1)
Louie Louie Louie (2)
Lovin' Man (2)
My Louisa (2)

My Turn Train (2)
Roll Me (2)
Something Is Missing (2)
Still Bein' Seventeen (2)

Treat Her Like A Lady (2)
What's A Poor Boy To Do (2)
Wing Tip Shoes (1)

SUMMERS, Andy/Robert Fripp

Summers was born Andrew Somers on 12/31/42 in Lancashire, England. Lead guitarist of The Police. See Robert Fripp for bio.

| 11/6/82 | 60 | 11 | | 1 I Advance Masked ....[I] | $8 | A&M 4913 |
| 10/20/84 | 155 | 5 | | 2 Bewitched ....[I] | $8 | A&M 5011 |

Aquarelle (medley) (1)
Begin The Day (2)
Bewitched (2)
China - Yellow Leader (1)
Forgotten Steps (2)

Girl On A Swing (1)
Guide (2)
Hardy Country (1)
I Advance Masked (1)
Image And Likeness (2)

In The Cloud Forest (1)
Lakeland (medley) (1)
Maquillage (1)
New Marimba (1)
Painting And Dance (1)

Parade (2)
Seven On Seven (1)
Still Point (1)
Stultified (1)
Train (2)

Tribe (2)
Truth Of Skies (1)
Under Bridges Of Silence (1)
What Kind Of Man Reads Playboy (2)

DEBUT DATE	PEAK POS	WKS CHR	GOLD	ARTIST — Album Title	$	Label & Number

SUMMERS, Bill, & Summers Heat
Bill is a percussionist; formerly with Herbie Hancock's Head Hunters.

4/4/81	129	15	1	Call It What You Want	$8	MCA 5176
12/12/81+	92	16	2	Jam The Box!	$8	MCA 5266

At The Concert (2) · Call It What You Want (1) · Come On Out (1) · Dream Of Love (2) · Dreaming (2) · Drum Affair (2) · Give Your Love To Me (2) · Go For It (2) · Having Big Fun On Saturday (2) · I Believe In You (1) · Jam The Box (2) · Jammin (1) · Love Not My Life (1) · Snatch (Is A Dance) (1) · Summer Fun (1) · T.V. (1) · Throw Down (2) · We Call It The Box (2) · You Better Turn Around (1) · Your Style Ain't The Way (1)

SUN
Dayton, Ohio 10-member, soul-funk band — Byron Byrd, lead singer.

5/6/78	69	22	● 1	Sunburn	$8	Capitol 11723
7/21/79	85	10	2	Destination: Sun	$8	Capitol 11941

Baby I Confess (2) · Dance (Do What You Wanna Do) (1) · Deep Rooted Feeling (Stand Up) (1) · Everybody Disco Down (2) · Hallelujah Spirit (2) · I Had A Choice (1) · I Want To Be With You (Forever) (2) · Light Of The Universe (2) · Long Drawn Out Thang (1) · Pure Fire (2) · Radiation Level (2) · Sun Is Here (medley) (1) · Sun Of A Gun (1) · When You Put Your Hand In Mine (1) · You Are My Sunshine (medley) (1) · You Don't Have To Hurry (1) · You're The One (1)

SUNDAYS, The
British alternative-pop group: Harriet Wheeler (vocals), Dave Gavurin, Paul Brindley and Pat Hannan.

5/26/90	39	23	1	Reading, Writing And Arithmetic	$12	DGC 24277
11/7/92	103	11↑	2	Blind	$12	DGC 24479

Blood On My Hands (2) · Can't Be Sure (1) · Certain Someone (1) · God Made Me (2) · Goodbye (2) · Here's Where The Story Ends (1) · Hideous Towns (1) · I Feel (2) · I Kicked A Boy (1) · I Won (1) · Joy (1) · Life & Soul (2) · Love (2) · Medicine (2) · More (2) · My Finest Hour (1) · On Earth (2) · Skin & Bones (1) · 24 Hours (2) · What Do You Think? (2) · Wild Horses (2) · You're Not The Only One I Know (1)

SUNNY & THE SUNLINERS
Group from San Antonio, Texas, formed in 1959. Led by Sunny Ozuna. Originally known as Sunny & The Sunglows.

11/2/63	142	2	1	Talk To Me	$40	Tear Drop 2000
8/14/65	148	2	2	the original Peanuts .... [I]	$30	Sunglow 103

THE SUNGLOWS

Battle Of Flowers (2) · Beer Barrel Polka (2) · Carino Nuevo (1) · Chin-Wen-Wen Chona (2) · Circus, The (2) · Colt 45 (2) · Every Week Every Month Every Year (1) · Golly Gee (1) · Got You On My Mind (1) · Happy Hippo (2) · I'm A Fool To Care (1) · Indian, The (2) · Just A Moment (1) · La Raspa (2) · Merry Go Round (2) · No One Else Will Do (1) · Not Even Judgement Day (1) · **Peanuts (La Cacahuata)** (2) 64 · Please Mr. Sandman (1) · Popcorn (2) · **Rags To Riches** (1) 45 · Rancho Grande (2) · **Talk To Me** (1) 11 hit "Hot 100" as Sunny & The Sunglows · Think It Over (1)

SUNSHINE BAND, The — see KC

SUNSHINE COMPANY, The
Southern California pop quintet featuring lead singer Mary Nance.

10/21/67	126	10		Happy Is The Sunshine Company	$15	Imperial 12359

Back On The Street Again 36 · Children Could Help Us Find The Way · Four In The Mornin' · **Happy 50** · I Just Want To Be Your Friend · I Need You · Just Beyond Your Smile · Love Is A Happy Thing · Rain · Up, Up And Away · Warm In My Heart · Year Of Jaine Time

SUPERSAX
Jazz band led by Buddy Clark and Meredith Flory.

7/14/73	169	7	1	Supersax plays Bird .... [I]	$8	Capitol 11177
4/6/74	182	3	2	Supersax plays Bird, Volume 2/Salt Peanuts ..... [I]	$8	Capitol 11271

Bird: Bop-jazz sax legend, Charlie "Yardbird" Parker

Be-Bop (1) · Bird, The (2) · Confirmation (2) · Embraceable You (2) · Groovin' High (2) · Hot House (1) · Just Friends (1) · Ko-Ko (1) · Lover (2) · Lover Man (Oh Where Can You Be) (2) · Moose The Mooche (1) · Night In Tunisia (1) · Oh, Lady Be Good! (1) · Parker's Mood (1) · Repetition (1) · Salt Peanuts (2) · Scrapple From The Apple (2) · Star Eyes (1) · Yardbird Suite (2)

★★273★★ SUPERTRAMP
British rock quintet: Roger Hodgson (vocals, guitar), Rick Davies (vocals, keyboards), John Helliwell (sax), Dougie Thomson (bass) and Bob Siebenberg (drums). Hodgson went solo in 1983.

12/7/74+	38	76	● 1	Crime Of The Century	$10	A&M 3647
12/13/75+	44	28	2	Crisis? What Crisis?	$10	A&M 4560
4/23/77	16	49	● 3	Even In The Quietest Moments............................	$8	A&M 4634
3/4/78	158	5	4	Supertramp .... [E]	$8	A&M 4665
				their first album; recorded in 1970		
3/31/79	1[6]	88	▲[4] 5	Breakfast In America..	$8	A&M 3708
10/11/80	8	26	● 6	Paris .... [L]	$10	A&M 6702 [2]
				recorded at the Paris Pavilion on 11/29/79		
11/13/82	5	28	● 7	...famous last words...	$8	A&M 3732
6/1/85	21	22	8	Brother Where You Bound	$8	A&M 5014
10/31/87	101	11	9	Free As A Bird	$8	A&M 5181

Ain't Nobody But Me (2,6) · And I Am Not Like Other Birds Of Prey (medley) (4) · Another Man's Woman (2) · Asylum (2) · Aubade (medley) (4) · Awful Thing To Waste (9) · Babaji (4) · Better Days (8) · **Bloody Well Right** (1,6) 35 · Bonnie (7) · **Breakfast In America** (5,6) 62 · **Brother Where You Bound** (8) · C'est Le Bon (7) · **Cannonball** (8) 28 · Casual Conversations (5) · Child Of Vision (5) · Crazy (7) · Crime Of The Century (1,6) · Don't Leave Me Now (7) · Downstream (3) · **Dreamer** (1,6) 15 · Easy Does It (2) · Even In The Quietest Moments (3) · Ever Open Door (8) · Fool's Overture (3,6) · Free As A Bird (9) · From Now On (3,6) · **Give A Little Bit** (3) 15 · Gone Hollywood (5) · **Goodbye Stranger** (5) 15 · Hide In Your Shell (1,6) · Home Again (4) · I'm Beggin' You (9) · If Everyone Was Listening (1) · It Doesn't Matter (9) · It's A Long Road (4) · It's Alright (9) · **It's Raining Again** (7) 11 · Just A Normal Day (2) · Just Another Nervous Wreck (5) · Know Who You Are (7) · Lady (2) · **Logical Song** (5,6) 6 · Lord Is It Mine (5) · Lover Boy (3) · Maybe I'm A Beggar (4) · Meaning, The (2) · **My Kind Of Lady** (7) 31 · No Inbetween (8) · Not The Moment (7) · Nothing To Show (4) · Oh Darling (5) · Poor Boy (7) · Put On Your Old Brown Shoes (7) · Rudy (1,6) · School (1,6) · Shadow Song (4) · Sister Moonshine (2) · Soapbox Opera (2,6) · Still In Love (8) · Surely (4) · **Take The Long Way Home** (5,6) 10 · Thing For You (9) · Try Again (4) · Two Of Us (2,6) · Waiting So Long (7) · Where I Stand (9) · Words Unspoken (4) · You Never Can Tell With Friends (9) · You Started Laughing (6)

★★**21**★★   **SUPREMES, The**

R&B vocal group from Detroit, formed as the Primettes in 1959. Consisted of lead singer Diana Ross (b: 3/26/44), Mary Wilson (b: 3/6/44), Florence Ballard (b: 6/30/43; d: 2/22/76 of cardiac arrest) and Barbara Martin. Recorded for LuPine in 1960. Signed to Motown's Tamla label in 1960. Changed name to The Supremes in 1961; Martin left shortly thereafter. Worked as backing vocalists for Motown until 1964. Backed Marvin Gaye on "Can I Get A Witness." Ballard discharged from group in 1967, replaced by Cindy Birdsong, formerly with Patti LaBelle's Blue Belles. Ross left in 1969 for solo career, replaced by Jean Terrell. Birdsong left in 1972, replaced by Lynda Lawrence. Terrell and Lawrence left in 1973. Mary Wilson re-formed group with Scherrie Payne (sister of Freda Payne) and Cindy Birdsong. Birdsong left again in 1976, replaced by Susaye Greene. In 1978, Wilson toured England with Karen Ragland and Karen Jackson, but lost rights to the name "Supremes" thereafter. Inducted into the Rock and Roll Hall of Fame in 1988.

DEBUT DATE	PEAK POS	WKS CHR	GOLD	#	ARTIST — Album Title	$	Label & Number
9/19/64+	2⁴	89		1	**Where Did Our Love Go**	$20	Motown 621
11/28/64+	21	21		2	A Bit Of Liverpool	$20	Motown 623
3/20/65	79	8		3	The Supremes sing Country Western & Pop	$20	Motown 625
5/8/65	75	19		4	We Remember Sam Cooke	$20	Motown 629
8/21/65	6	37		5	**More Hits By The Supremes**	$20	Motown 627
11/13/65+	11	54		6	The Supremes at the Copa [L]	$20	Motown 636
3/19/66	8	55		7	**I Hear A Symphony**	$15	Motown 643
9/24/66	1²	60		8	**The Supremes A' Go-Go**	$15	Motown 649
2/18/67	6	29		9	**The Supremes sing Holland-Dozier-Holland**	$15	Motown 650
					songs written by Brian Holland, Lamont Dozier, Eddie Holland		
6/17/67	20	19		10	The Supremes Sing Rodgers & Hart	$15	Motown 659
					songwriting team: Richard Rodgers and Lorenz Hart		
					DIANA ROSS & THE SUPREMES:		
9/30/67	1⁵	89		11	**Diana Ross and the Supremes Greatest Hits** [G]	$18	Motown 663 [2]
4/27/68	18	29		12	Reflections	$15	Motown 665
10/5/68+	57	18		13	Live at London's Talk Of The Town [L]	$15	Motown 676
10/5/68	150	12		14	Funny Girl	$15	Motown 672
					version of the Styne/Merrill musical		
11/30/68+	2¹	32		15	**Diana Ross & the Supremes Join the Temptations** *	$12	Motown 679
12/14/68+	14	21		16	Love Child	$15	Motown 670
12/28/68+	1¹	34		17	**TCB** * [TV]	$15	Motown 682
6/21/69	24	18		18	Let The Sunshine In	$15	Motown 689
10/25/69	28	18		19	Together *	$12	Motown 692
11/29/69+	33	20		20	Cream Of The Crop	$15	Motown 694
12/6/69	38	12		21	On Broadway * [TV]	$12	Motown 699
					***DIANA ROSS & THE SUPREMES with THE TEMPTATIONS** includes "Fiddler On The Roof Medley" by The Temptations		
1/10/70	31	25		22	Diana Ross & the Supremes Greatest Hits, Volume 3 [G]	$15	Motown 702
5/16/70	46	18		23	Farewell [L]	$18	Motown 708 [2]
					Diana's last performance with The Supremes; recorded at the Frontier Hotel, Las Vegas (1/14/70)		
					THE SUPREMES:		
6/6/70	25	19		24	Right On	$15	Motown 705
10/17/70	113	16		25	The Magnificent 7 **	$12	Motown 717
10/24/70+	68	17		26	New Ways But Love Stays	$10	Motown 720
6/26/71	85	10		27	Touch	$10	Motown 737
6/26/71	154	6		28	The Return Of The Magnificent Seven **	$12	Motown 736
1/8/72	160	6		29	Dynamite **	$12	Motown 745
					****SUPREMES & FOUR TOPS**		
5/27/72	54	15		30	Floy Joy	$10	Motown 751
11/25/72+	129	13		31	The Supremes	$10	Motown 756
6/29/74	66	15	●	32	Anthology (1962-1969) [G]	$18	Motown 794 [3]
					DIANA ROSS & THE SUPREMES		
6/28/75	152	8		33	The Supremes	$8	Motown 828
5/22/76	42	15		34	High Energy	$8	Motown 863
5/17/86	112	17		35	25th Anniversary [K]	$15	Motown 5381 [3]
					DIANA ROSS & THE SUPREMES contains 20 top hits, 20 previously unreleased recordings, their Coca Cola commercial, an interview and a 12-page booklet		

SUPREMES, The — Cont'd

Havin' A Party (4)
He Holds His Own (5)
He Means The World To Me (1)
He's All I Got (7)
He's My Man (33)
He's My Sunny Boy (16)
Heart Like Mine (30)
Heigh-Ho (35)
Hello Stranger (29)
Here Comes The Sunrise (27)
Hey Jude (20)
Hey Western Union Man (18)
High Energy (34)
His Love Makes Me Beautiful (14)
Honey Bee (Keep On Stinging Me) (16)
Honey Boy (5)
House Of The Rising Sun (2)
How Do You Do It (2)
How Long Has That Evening Train Been Gone (16)
I Am Woman (6,14)
I Can't Believe You Love Me (28)
I Can't Help Myself (8)
I Can't Make It Alone (12)
I Don't Want To Lose You (medley) (34)
I Got Hurt (Trying To Be The Only Girl In Your Life) (24)
I Guess I'll Always Love You (9)
I Guess I'll Miss The Man (31) **85**
I Hear A Symphony (7,11,17,32,35) **1**
I Keep It Hid (31)
(I Love You) For Sentimental Reasons (medley) (6)
I Second That Emotion (15)
I Want To Hold Your Hand (2)
I Wish I Were Your Mirror (26)
I Wonder Where We're Going (28)
I'll Be Doggone (19)
I'll Set You Free (16)
I'll Try Not To Cry (28)
I'll Try Something New (15,32) **25**
I'll Turn To Stone (9)
I'm Giving You, Your Freedom (1)
I'm Glad About It (28)
I'm Gonna Let My Heart Do The Walking (34) **40**
I'm Gonna Make It (I Will Wait For You) (12)

I'm Gonna Make You Love Me (15,23,32,35) **2**
I'm Gonna Wash That Man Right Outa My Hair (medley) (21)
I'm In Love Again (5)
I'm Livin' In Shame (18,22,32,35) **10**
(I'm So Glad) Heartaches Don't Last Always (5)
I'm So Glad I Got Somebody (Like You Around) (18)
I'm The Greatest Star (14,32)
If (29)
If A Girl Isn't Pretty (14)
If I Could Build The Whole World Around You (29)
If I Ruled The World (35)
If You Could See Me Now (28)
Il Voce De Silenzio (Silent Voices) (31)
Impossible Dream (15,17,23)
In And Out Of Love (12,13,22,32,35) **9**
Is There A Place (In His Heart For Me) (34)
It Makes No Difference Now (3)
It's All Been Said Before (33)
It's All Your Fault (35)
It's Allright With Me (23)
It's Got To Be A Miracle (This Thing Called Love) (25)
It's Impossible (29)
It's So Hard For Me To Say Good-bye (27)
It's The Same Old Song (3)
It's Time To Break Down (26)
Johnny Raven (27)
Keep An Eye (16)
Knock On My Door (25)
Lady Is A Tramp (10,13,23)
Lazybones (3)
Leading Lady (medley) (21)
Let Me Go The Right Way (32) **90**
Let The Music Play (18)
Let The Sunshine In (medley) (18,21,23)
Let's Get Away From It All (medley) (13,23)
Let's Make Love Now (28)
Long Gone Lover (1)
Love Child (16,22,23,32,35) **1**
Love Is Here And Now You're Gone (9,11,13,22,23,32,35) **1**
Love Is In Our Hearts (9)
Love Is Like A Heat Wave (9)

Love Is Like An Itching In My Heart (8,11,32,35) **9**
Love It Came To Me This Time (27)
Love (Makes Me Do Foolish Things) (12)
Love The One You're With (29)
Lover (10)
Lover's Concerto (7)
Loving Country (24)
Loving You Is Better Than Ever (20)
Make Someone Happy (6)
Malteds Over Manhattan (13,21)
Mame (medley) (13,21)
(Man With The) Rock And Roll Banjo Band (3)
Manhattan (35)
Melodie (29)
Michelle (medley) (13)
Misery Makes Its Home In My Heart (12)
Money (That's What I Want) (8)
More (13)
Mother Dear (5)
Mother You, Smother You (9)
Mountain Greenery (10)
Mrs. Robinson (medley) (17)
Music That Makes Me Dance (14)
My Funny Valentine (10)
My Guy (medley) (19)
My Heart Can't Take It No More (3)
My Heart Stood Still (10)
My Man (23)
My Romance (10)
My World Is Empty Without You (7,11,13,17,23,32,35) **5**
Na Na Hey Hey Kiss Him Goodbye (26)
Nathan Jones (27) **16**
No Matter What Sign You Are (18,22,32) **31**
Nothing But Heartaches (5,11,32,35) **11**
Nothing Can Change This Love (4)
Now The Bitter, Now The Sweet (30)
Ode To Billie Joe (12)
Oh Be My Love (30)
Once In The Morning (31)
One More Bridge To Cross (4)
Only Sixteen (4)
Only Time I'm Happy (5)
Only You (Can Love Me Like You Love Me) (34)

Ooowee Baby (35)
Over And Over (30)
Paradise (31)
Penny Pincher (35)
People (14,21)
Place In The Sun (15)
Precious Little Things (30)
Put On A Happy Face (6)
Put Yourself In My Place (8)
Queen Of The House (6)
Reach Out And Touch (Somebody's Hand) (25)
Reflections (12,13,22,23,32,35) **2**
Remove This Doubt (9)
Respect (17)
Rhythm Of Life (21)
River Deep - Mountain High (25) **14**
Rock-A-Bye Your Baby With A Dixie Melody (6)
Run, Run, Run (1,11,32) **93**
Sadie, Sadie (14)
Second Hand Rose (medley) (13)
Send Me No Flowers (35)
Shadows Of Society (20)
Shake (4,6)
Shake Me, Wake Me (When It's Over) (8)
Shine On Me (26)
Sincerely (35)
Sing A Simple Song (19)
Sleep Walk (35)
Some Things You Never Get Used To (16,22,32) **30**
Someday My Prince Will Come (31)
Someday We'll Be Together (20,22,23,32,35) **1**
Somewhere (6,17)
Standing At The Crossroads Of Love (1,11,32)
Stoned Love (26) **7**
Stoned Soul Picnic (25)
Stop! In The Name Of Love (5,6,11,13,17,23,32,35) **1**
Stranger In Paradise (7,13)
Stubborn Kind Of Fellow (19)
Student Mountie (21)
Sunset (3)
Surfer Boy (35)
Sweet Inspiration (15)
T.C.B. (17,23)
Take A Closer Look At Me (24)
Taste Of Honey (25)
Tears In Vain (3)
Thank Him For Today (26)
Then (12,15)
Then I Met You (24)

Then We Can Try Again (24)
There's No Stopping Us Now (9,11)
These Boots Are Made For Walking (8)
This Can't Be Love (10)
This Guy's In Love With You (15)
This Is The Story (7)
This Is Why I Believe In You (33)
This Old Heart Of Mine (Is Weak For You) (8)
Thoroughly Modern Millie (medley) (13)
Those D.J. Shows (35)
Thou Swell (10)
Till Johnny Comes (20)
Till The Boat Sails Away (medley) (34)
Time And Love (27)
Together We Can Make Such Sweet Music (25,26)
Tossin' And Turning (31)
Touch (27) **71**
Treat Me Nice John Henry (35)
Try It Baby (15)
Tumbling Tumbleweeds (3)
Unchained Melody (7)
Up The Ladder To The Roof (24) **10**
Up, Up And Away (12)
Uptight (Everything's Alright) (19)
Wait A Minute Before You Leave Me (24)
Way You Do The Things You Do (17)
We Couldn't Get Along Without You (35)
Weight (19) **46**
What Becomes Of The Brokenhearted (18)
What Do You Have To Do (To Stay On The Right Side Of Love) (28)
What The World Needs Now Is Love (12)
When Can Brown Begin (31)
When It's To The Top (Still I Won't Stop Giving You Love) (20)
When The Lovelight Starts Shining Through His Eyes (1,11,32,35) **23**
When You Wish Upon A Star (35)
Where Did Our Love Go (1,11,32,35) **1**
Where Do I Go From Here (33)

Where Is It I Belong (33)
Where Or When (10)
Where Would I Be Without You, Baby (28)
Whisper You Love Me Boy (5,11)
Who Can I Turn To (When Nobody Needs Me) (35)
Who Could Ever Doubt My Love (5)
Why (Must We Fall In Love) (19)
Will This Be The Day (18)
Wisdom Of Time (30)
With A Child's Heart (18)
With A Song In My Heart (7,13,17)
Without A Song (7,13,17)
Without The One You Love (25)
Wonderful, Wonderful (7,13)
Wonderful World (4)
World Without Love (2)
Wouldn't It Be Lovely (medley) (21)
Yesterday (7,13)
You Ain't Livin' Till You're Lovin' (16)
You Can't Do That (2)
You Can't Hurry Love (8,11,32,35) **1**
You Can't Stop A Girl In Love (33)
You Didn't Care (3)
You Gave Me Love (20)
You Gotta Have Love In Your Heart (28) **55**
You Keep Me Hangin' On (9,11,13,17,32,35) **1**
You Keep Me Moving On (34)
You Move Me (24)
You Need Me (3)
You Send Me (4,6,32)
You Turn Me Around (33)
You're Gone (But Always In My Heart) (9)
You're Nobody Till Somebody Loves You (6,13)
You're What's Missing In My Life (34)
You've Been So Wonderful To Me (16)
You've Really Got A Hold On Me (2)
Young Folks (20) **69**
Your Kiss Of Fire (1)
Your Wonderful, Sweet Sweet Love (30) **59**

SURFACE

Soul trio from New Jersey: Bernard Jackson (lead singer), David Townsend (son of producer/songwriter Ed Townsend) and Dave Conley (former horn player with Mandrill).

DEBUT DATE	PEAK POS	WKS CHR	GOLD	#	ARTIST — Album Title	$	Label & Number
5/30/87	55	19		1	Surface	$8	Columbia 40374
11/26/88+	56	39	●	2	2nd Wave	$8	Columbia 44284
11/24/90+	65	34		3	3 Deep	$12	Columbia 46772

Ain't Givin' Up (3)
All I Want Is You (3)
Black Shades (2)
Can We Spend Some Time (2)
Closer Than Friends (2) **57**

Don't Wanna Turn You Off (3)
Feels So Good (1)
First Time (3) **1**
Girls Were Made To Love (1)
Give Her Your Love (3)

Gotta Make Love Tonight (1)
Happy (1) **20**
Hold On To Love (2)
I Missed (2)
Kid Stuff (Believe In Yourself) (1)

Lady Wants A Man (1)
Lately (1)
Let's Try Again (1)
Love X Trust (3)
Never Gonna Let You Down (3) **17**

Shower Me With Your Love (2) **5**
"10" (3)
Tomorrow (3)
We're All Searchin' (3)
When It Comes To Love (3)

Where's That Girl (2)
Who Loves You (1)
You Are My Everything (2) **84**
You're Fine (1)
You're The One (3)

SURFARIS, The

Teenage surf band from Glendora, California: Ron Wilson (drummer), Jim Fuller (lead guitar), Bob Berryhill (rhythm guitar), Pat Connolly (bass) and Jim Pash (sax, clarinet).

DEBUT DATE	PEAK POS	WKS CHR	GOLD	#	ARTIST — Album Title		$	Label & Number
8/10/63	15	51		1	Wipe Out	[I]	$30	Dot 25535
11/30/63	94	11		2	The Surfaris play Wipe Out and others	[I]	$40	Decca 74470
3/7/64	120	5		3	Hit City 64		$40	Decca 74487

Bat Man (2)
Be True To Your School (3)
Comin' Home Baby (3)
Earthquake (3)
Green Onions (1)
Hiawatha (3)

I Wanna Take A Trip To The Islands (3)
I'm A Hog For You (3)
Jack The Ripper (2)
Little Deuce Coupe (3)
Louie Louie (3)

Memphis (1)
Misirlou (2)
Mystic Island Drums (3)
Point Panic (2) **49**
Scatter Shield (3)
Scratch (3)

Similau (2)
Sugar Shack (3)
Surf Scene (2)
Surfaris Stomp (2)
Surfer Joe (1,2) **62**
Surfing Drums (2)

Teen Beat (1)
Tequila (1)
Torquay (1)
Waikiki Run (2)
Walk, Don't Run (1)
Wax Board And Woodie (3)

Wiggle Wobble (1)
Wild Weekend (1)
Wipe Out (1,2) **2**
Yep (1)
You Can't Sit Down (1)

SURVIVOR
Midwest rock group: Dave Bickler (lead singer), Jim Peterik (keyboards; former lead singer of Ides Of March), Frankie Sullivan (guitar), Gary Smith (drums) and Dennis Johnson (bass). Smith and Johnson replaced by Marc Droubay and Stephan Ellis in 1981. Bickler replaced by Jimi Jamison in 1984. Droubay and Ellis left in 1988.

DEBUT DATE	PEAK POS	WKS CHR	GOLD		ARTIST — Album Title	$	Label & Number
3/29/80	169	7	▲	1	Survivor	$8	Scotti Br. 7107
10/24/81	82	25		2	Premonition	$8	Scotti Br. 37549
6/26/82	2⁴	41	▲	3	Eye Of The Tiger	$8	Scotti Br. 38062
10/22/83	82	9		4	Caught In The Game	$8	Scotti Br. 38791
9/29/84+	16	61		5	Vital Signs	$8	Scotti Br. 39578
11/8/86	49	24		6	When Seconds Count	$8	Scotti Br. 40457
11/5/88	187	2		7	Too Hot To Sleep	$8	Scotti Br. 44282

Across The Miles (7) 74
American Heartbeat (3) 17
As Soon As Love Finds Me (1)
Backstreet Love Affair (6)
Broken Promises (5)
Burning Bridges (7)
Can't Getcha Offa My Mind (1)
Can't Give It Up (7)
Can't Let You Go (6)
Caught In The Game (4) 77
Chevy Nights (2)
Children Of The Night (3)
Desperate Dreams (7)
Didn't Know It Was Love (7) 61
Ever Since The World Began (3)
Everlasting (5)
Eye Of The Tiger (3) 1
Feels Like Love (3)
First Night (5) 53
Freelance (1)
Half-Life (4)
Heart's A Lonely Hunter (2)
Here Comes Desire (7)
Hesitation Dance (3)
High On You (5) 8
How Much Love (6) 51
I Can't Hold Back (5) 13
I Never Stopped Loving You (4)
I See You In Everyone (5)
I'm Not That Man Anymore (3)
In Good Faith (6)
Is This Love (6) 9
It Doesn't Have To Be This Way (4)
It's The Singer Not The Song (5)
Jackie Don't Go (4)
Keep It Right Here (6)
Let It Be Now (1)
Light Of A Thousand Smiles (2)
Love Has Got Me (1)
Love Is On My Side (2)
Man Against The World (6) 86
Nothing Can Shake Me (From Your Love) (1)
Oceans (6)
One That Really Matters (3) 74
Poor Man's Son (2) 33
Popular Girl (5)
Ready For The Real Thing (4)
Rebel Son (6)
Rhythm Of The City (7)
Runway Lights (2)
Santa Ana Winds (4)
Search Is Over (5) 4
She's A Star (7)
Silver Girl (3)
Slander (4)
Somewhere In America (1) 70
Summer Nights (2) 62
Take You On A Saturday (2)
Tell Me I'm The One (7)
Too Hot To Sleep (7)
20/20 (1)
What Do You Really Think? (4)
Whatever It Takes (1)
When Seconds Count (6)
Whole Town's Talkin' (1)
Youngblood (1)

SUSAN
New York rock quartet — Charles Leland, lead singer.

DEBUT DATE	PEAK POS	WKS CHR		ARTIST — Album Title	$	Label & Number
5/5/79	169	5		Falling In Love Again	$8	RCA 3372

Don't Let Me Go
Falling In Love Again
I Was Wrong
Little Time
Love The Way
Marlene
Power
Really Gonna Show
Takin' It Over
Tonight You're Mine
Too Bad

SUTCH, Lord — see LORD

SUTHERLAND BROTHERS AND QUIVER
English duo: Iain and Gavin Sutherland, with their four-piece group Quiver.

DEBUT DATE	PEAK POS	WKS CHR		ARTIST — Album Title	$	Label & Number
8/18/73	77	17	1	Lifeboat	$8	Island 9326
5/11/74	193	3	2	Dream Kid	$8	Island 9341
5/8/76	195	2	3	Reach For The Sky	$8	Columbia 33982

Ain't Too Proud (3)
Arms Of Mary (3) 81
Bad Loser (2)
Bluesy World (2)
Champion The Underdog (2)
Change The Wind (1)
Dirty City (3)
Dr. Dancer (3)
Dream Kid (2)
Flying Down To Rio (2)
Have You Had A Vision (1)
(I Don't Want To Love You But) You Got Me Anyway (1) 48
I Hear Thunder (2)
Lifeboat (1)
Lonely Love (medley) (2)
Love On The Moon (3)
Mad Trail (3)
Maker (2)
Moonlight Lady (3)
Not Fade Away (1)
Reach For The Sky (3)
Real Love (1)
Rock And Roll Show (1)
Rocky Road (medley) (2)
Rollin' Away (medley) (2)
Sailing (1)
Saved By The Angel (medley) (2)
Seagull (medley) (2)
Something Special (3)
Space Hymn (1)
When The Train Comes (3)
Where Do We Go Wrong (1)
You And Me (2)

SWAN, Billy
Born on 5/12/42 in Cape Girardeau, Missouri. Singer/songwriter/keyboardist/guitarist. Wrote "Lover Please" for Clyde McPhatter. Produced Tony Joe White's first three albums. Toured with Kris Kristofferson from the early '70s. Formed band Black Tie with Randy Meisner in 1986.

DEBUT DATE	PEAK POS	WKS CHR		ARTIST — Album Title	$	Label & Number
12/7/74+	21	16		I Can Help	$8	Monument 33279

Don't Be Cruel
I Can Help 1
I'd Like To Work For You
I'm Her Fool 53
Lover Please
P.M.S. (Post Mortem Sickness)
Queen Of My Heart
Shake, Rattle And Roll
Ways Of A Woman In Love
Wedding Bells

SWANSON, Brad, & his Whispering Organ Sound

DEBUT DATE	PEAK POS	WKS CHR		ARTIST — Album Title	$	Label & Number
10/18/69	185	2		Quentin's Theme	[I] $15	Thunderbird 9004

Ain't She Sweet
Heart Of My Heart
Mac The Knife
Margie
My Imaginary Love
Old Piano Roll Blues
Poor Butterfly
Quentin's Theme
Stars In Your Eyes
Sweet Georgia Brown
You Are My Sunshine

SWEAT, Keith
Soul singer/songwriter. Born and raised in Harlem.

DEBUT DATE	PEAK POS	WKS CHR	GOLD		ARTIST — Album Title	$	Label & Number
1/9/88	15	67	▲²	1	Make It Last Forever	$8	Vintertn. 60763
6/30/90	6	62	▲²	2	I'll Give All My Love To You	$12	Vintertn. 60861
12/14/91	19	33	▲	3	Keep It Comin'	$12	Elektra 61216

Come Back (2)
Don't Stop Your Love (1)
Give Me What I Want (3)
How Deep Is Your Love (1)
I Knew That You Were Cheatin' (2)
I Really Love You (3)
I Want Her (1) 5
I Want To Love You Down (3)
I'll Give All My Love To You (2) 7
I'm Going For Mine (3)
In The Rain (1)
Just One Of Them Thangs (2)
Keep It Comin' [includes 2 versions] (3) 17
Let Me Love You (3)
Love To Love You (2)
Make It Last Forever (1) 59
Make You Sweat (2) 14
Merry Go Round (3)
Right And A Wrong Way (1)
Something Just Ain't Right (1) 79
Spend A Little Time (3)
Tell Me It's Me You Want (1)
Ten Commandments Of Love (3)
(There You Go) Tellin' Me No Again (3)
Why Me Baby? (3) 44
Your Love (2)
Your Love - Part 2 (2) 71

SWEAT BAND
P-funk trio who played in "Bootsy's Rubber Band."

DEBUT DATE	PEAK POS	WKS CHR		ARTIST — Album Title	$	Label & Number
12/13/80+	150	8		Sweat Band	$8	Uncle Jam 36857

Body Shop
Freak To Freak
Hyper Space
Jamaica
Love Munch
We Do It All Day Long

SWEET
English rock band: Brian Connolly (lead singer), Steve Priest (bass, vocals), Andy Scott (guitar, keyboards) and Mick Tucker (drums).

DEBUT DATE	PEAK POS	WKS CHR	GOLD		ARTIST — Album Title	$	Label & Number
7/28/73	191	4		1	The Sweet	$15	Bell 1125
7/26/75	25	44	●	2	Desolation Boulevard	$8	Capitol 11395
3/6/76	27	13		3	Give Us A Wink	$8	Capitol 11496
5/14/77	151	4		4	Off The Record	$8	Capitol 11636
2/18/78	52	28		5	Level Headed	$8	Capitol 11744

DEBUT DATE	PEAK POS	WKS CHR	GOLD	ARTIST — Album Title	$	Label & Number

SWEET — Cont'd

| 5/12/79 | 151 | 5 | | 6 Cut Above The Rest .... | $8 | Capitol 11929 |

A.C.D.C. (2)
Action (3) *20*
Air On 'A' Tape Loop (5)
Anthem No. I & II (5)
Ballroom Blitz (2) *5*
Big Apple Waltz (6)
Blockbuster (1) *73*
California Nights (5) *76*
Call Me (6)
Cockroach (3)
Discophony (dis-kof-o-ne) (6)

Done Me Wrong Alright (1)
Dorian Gray (6)
Dream On (5)
Eye Games (6)
Fever Of Love (4)
Fountain (5)
4th Of July (3)
Fox On The Run (2) *5*
Funk It Up (David's Song) (4) *88*
Hard Times (4)

Healer (3)
Hell Raiser (1)
Hold Me (6)
I Wanna Be Committed (2)
In To Night (2)
Keep It In (3)
Lady Starlight (3)
Laura Lee (4)
Lettres D'Amour (5)
Lies In Your Eyes (3)
Little Willy (1) *3*

Live For Today (4)
Lost Angels (4)
Love Is Like Oxygen (5) *8*
Man From Mecca (1)
Midnight To Daylight (4)
Mother Earth (6)
Need A Lot Of Lovin' (1)
New York Connection (1)
No You Don't (2)
Play All Night (6)
Set Me Free (2)

She Gimme Lovin' (4)
Silverbird (5)
6-Teens (2)
Solid Gold Brass (2)
Spotlight (1)
Stairway To The Stars (4)
Stay With Me (6)
Strong Love (5)
Sweet F.A. (2)
White Mice (3)
Wig-Wam Bam (1)

Windy City (4)
Yesterday's Rain (3)
You're Not Wrong For Loving Me (1)

SWEET, Matthew
Native of Lincoln, Nebraska. Bassist/drummer/singer; toured with Lloyd Cole as guitarist.

| 2/29/92 | 100 | 29 | | Girlfriend .... | $12 | Zoo 11015 |

LP cover is a 1958 photo of actress Tuesday Weld as a teen

Day For Night
Divine Intervention
Does She Talk?

Don't Go
Evangeline
Girlfriend

Holy War
I Wanted To Tell You
I've Been Waiting

Looking At The Sun
Nothing Lasts

Thought I Knew You
Winona

You Don't Love Me
Your Sweet Voice

SWEET, Rachel
Born in Akron, Ohio in 1963. Performed in the musicals *The Music Man*, *Fiddler On The Roof* and *The Sound Of Music*. First recorded for Premiere in 1974.

8/4/79	97	9		1 Fool Around	$8	Stiff 36101
3/22/80	123	11		2 Protect The Innocent	$8	Stiff 36337
9/5/81	124	7		3 ...And Then He Kissed Me	$8	ARC 37077

B-A-B-Y (1)
Baby, Let's Play House (2)
Be My Baby (medley) (3)
Billy And The Gun (3)
Cuckoo Clock (1)
Everlasting Love (3) *32*
Fool's Gold (2)

Fool's Story (3)
Foul Play (2)
I Go To Pieces (1)
I've Got A Reason (2)
It's So Different Here (1)
Jealous (2)
Little Darlin' (3)

Lovers' Lane (2)
New Age (2)
New Rose (2)
Party Girl (3)
Pin A Medal On Mary (1)
Sad Song (1)
Shadows Of The Night (3)

Spellbound (2)
Stay Awhile (1)
Stranger In The House (1)
Streetheart (3)
Suspended Animation (1)
Take Good Care Of Me (2)

Then He Kissed Me (medley) (3)
Tonight (2)
Tonight Ricky (2)
Two Hearts Full Of Love (3)
Who Does Lisa Like? (1)
Wildwood Saloon (1)

SWEET F.A.
Hard-rock quintet led by Steven David DeLong (vocals).

| 9/15/90 | 161 | 10 | | Stick To Your Guns .... | $12 | MCA 6400 |

Breakin' The Law
Daily Grind

Devil's Road
Do A Little Drivin'

Heart Of Gold
I Love Women

Nothin' For Nothin'
Prince Of The City

Rhythm Of Action
Southern Comfort

Stick To Your Guns
Whiskey River

SWEET INSPIRATIONS, The
R&B vocal quartet: Cissy Houston, Estelle Brown, Sylvia Shemwell and Myrna Smith. Spent nearly six years as studio group, primarily for Atlantic. Work included backing Aretha Franklin and Elvis Presley. Cissy, mother of Whitney Houston, recorded solo in 1970.

| 4/6/68 | 90 | 6 | | The Sweet Inspirations .... | $15 | Atlantic 8155 |

Blues Stay Away From Me
Do Right Woman - Do Right Man

Don't Fight It
Don't Let Me Lose This Dream

Here I Am (Take Me)
I'm Blue
Knock On Wood

Let It Be Me *94*
Oh! What A Fool I've Been
Reach Out For Me

Sweet Inspiration *18*
Why (Am I Treated So Bad) *57*

SWEET SENSATION
Eight-member soul group from Manchester, England led by Marcel King (vocals), with additional vocals by St. Clair Palmer, Vincent James and Junior Daye.

| 5/3/75 | 163 | 7 | | Sad Sweet Dreamer .... | $8 | Pye 12110 |

Emptiness Filled With Love

Eyes In The Back Of My Head

Fancy Woman
Mr. Cool

Please Excuse Me
Purely By Coincidence

Sad Sweet Dreamer *14*
Snow Fire

That Same Old Feeling
Yes Miss, No Miss

SWEET SENSATION
Female trio from New York City: Betty LeBron, and sisters Margie and Mari Fernandez. Mari replaced in 1989 by Sheila Bega.

| 10/8/88+ | 63 | 32 | | 1 Take It While It's Hot .... | $8 | Atco 90917 |
| 4/28/90 | 78 | 23 | | 2 Love Child .... | $12 | Atco 91307 |

Bring It Back (2)
Destiny (2)
Each And Every Time (2) *59*

He'll Never Know (2)
Heartbreak (1)
Hooked On You (1) *23*
I Surrender (2)

If Wishes Came True (2) *1*
Let Me Be The One (1)
Love Child (2) *13*
Love Games (1)

Never Let You Go (1) *58*
One Good Man (2)
Pleasure And Pain (2)
Sincerely Yours (1) *14*

Take It While It's Hot (1) *57*
Victim Of Love (1)

SWEET TEE
Female rapper, Toi Jackson, from Queens, New York. Discovered by Salt 'N' Pepa's producer, Hurby Lovebug.

| 2/25/89 | 169 | 13 | | It's Tee Time.. | $8 | Profile 1269 |

As The Beat Goes On
I Got Da Feelin'

It's Like That Y'all
It's My Beat

Let's Dance
On The Smooth Tip

Show And Prove
Why Did It Have To Be Me

Work Out

SWEET THUNDER
Soul group from Youngstown, Ohio — Booker Newberry, lead singer.

| 7/15/78 | 125 | 11 | | Sweet Thunder .... | $8 | Fantasy/WMOT 9547 |

Baby I Need Your Love Today

Everybody's Singin' Love Songs

Hot Line
I Don't Care What You Say

Joyful Noise

Keep On Growin'
Sweet Thunder

SWEETWATER
Gospel based group with Willie Wynn, one-time member of the Oak Ridge Boys.

| 9/13/69 | 200 | 2 | | Sweetwater .... | $10 | Reprise 6313 |

Come Take A Walk
For Pete's Sake

Here We Go Again
In A Rainbow

Motherless Child
My Crystal Spider

Rondeau
Through An Old Storybook

Two Worlds
What's Wrong

Why Oh Why

DEBUT DATE	PEAK POS	WKS CHR	GOLD	ARTIST — Album Title	$	Label & Number

SWINGING BLUE JEANS, The
Liverpool, England rock quartet: Ray Ennis and Ralph Ellis (guitars), Norman Kuhlke (drums) and Les Braid (bass).

| 5/30/64 | 90 | 9 | | Hippy Hippy Shake | $75 | Imperial 12261 |

Angie
Do You Know

Good Golly Miss Molly 43
Hippy Hippy Shake 24

It's Too Late Now
Now I Must Go

Save The Last Dance For Me
Shake Rattle & Roll

Shakin' All Over
Shaking Feeling

Think Of Me
Wasting Time

SWINGIN' MEDALLIONS
Eight-man rock and roll band from Greenwood, South Carolina led by John McElrath.

| 7/30/66 | 88 | 12 | | Double Shot (Of My Baby's Love) | $30 | Smash 67083 |

Barefootin'
Double Shot (Of My Baby's Love) 17

Hang On Sloopy
(I Can't Get No) Satisfaction
Idaho Jane

Louie, Louie
M.T.Y.L.T.T.

She Drives Me Out Of My Mind 71
That's When I Like It
What Kind Of Fool

Wooly Bully
You Gotta Have Faith

SWINGLE SINGERS, The
Ward Swingle (b: 9/21/27, Mobile, Alabama; piano, sax) and his scat-singing French singers. Ward moved to Paris in 1956.

10/26/63+	15	74		1 Bach's Greatest Hits	[I] $10	Philips 097
5/30/64	65	17		2 Going Baroque	[I] $10	Philips 126
2/20/65	140	6		3 Anyone for Mozart?	$10	Philips 149

Bach: Aria (from The Suite In D Major) (1)
Bach: Badinerie (from the Suite In B Minor) (2)
Bach: Bourree (from the English Suite No.2) (1)
Bach: Canon (1)
Bach: Der Fruehling (Spring) (1)
Bach: Fugue In C Minor (from The Well Tempered Clavier 1st Book) (1)

Bach: Fugue In D Major (from The Well Tempered Clavier 1st Book) (1)
Bach: Fugue In D Minor (from The Art Of The Fugue) (1)
Bach: Gigue (from the Cello Suite In G Major) (2)
Bach: Invention In C Major (1)
Bach: Largo (from the Harpsichord Concerto In F Minor) (2)

Bach: Preambule (from the Partita No. 5 In G Major) (2)
Bach: Prelude For Organ Choral No. 1 (1)
Bach: Prelude In C Major (from The Well Tempered Clavier 2nd Book) (1)
Bach: Prelude In F Major (from The Well Tempered Clavier 2nd Book) (1)
Bach: Prelude No. 19 (from the Well Tempered Clavier 1st Book) (2)

Bach: Prelude No. 24 (from The Well Tempered Clavier, 2nd Book) (2)
Bach: Prelude No. 7 (from the Well Tempered Clavier, 2nd Book) (2)
Bach: Prelude No. 9 (from The Well Tempered Clavier 2nd Book) (1)
Bach: Sinfonia (from the Partita No. 2) (1)
Bach: Solfeggietto (2)

Handel: Air (from the Harpsichord Suite In E Major) (2)
Handel: Allegro (from the Concerto Grosso, Op.6, No.4) (2)
Mozart: Ah! Vous Dirais Je Maman (Twinkle, Twinkle, Little Star) (3)
Mozart: Allegro (from Sonata No. 14) (3)
Mozart: Eine Kleine Nacht Music (3)

Mozart: Fugue (3)
Mozart: Sonata No. 15 (3)
Vivaldi: Fugue (from the Estro Harmonico Op.3, No.11) (2)

SWING OUT SISTER
British jazz-pop trio: Corinne Drewery (vocals), Andy Connell and Martin Jackson. Drewery was a fashion designer. Reduced to a duo in 1989 with departure of Jackson.

8/29/87+	40	43	●	1 It's Better To Travel	$8	Mercury 832213
5/27/89	61	19		2 Kaleidoscope World	$8	Fontana 838293
9/19/92	113	11		3 Get In Touch With Yourself	$12	Fontana 512241

After Hours (1)
Am I The Same Girl (3) 45
Between Strangers (2)
Blue Mood (1)
Breakout (1) 6
Circulate (3)
Communion (1)

Don't Say A Word (3)
Everyday Crime [includes 2 versions] (3)
Fooled By A Smile (1)
Forever Blue (2)
Get In Touch With Yourself (3)

Heart For Hire (2)
I Can Hear You But I Can't See You (3)
Incomplete Without You (3)
It's Not Enough (1)
Kaleidoscope Affair (2)
Love Child (3)

Masquerade (2)
Notgonnachange (3)
Precious Words (2)
Surrender (1)
Tainted (2)
Theme From: It's Better To Travel (1)

Twilight World (1) 31
Understand (3)
Waiting Game (2) 86
Where In The World (2)
Who Let The Love Out (3)
You On My Mind (2)

SWITCH
Soul-funk sextet from Mansfield, Ohio: Bobby DeBarge, Phillip Ingram (lead vocals), Greg Williams, Tommy DeBarge, Eddie Fluellen and Jody Sims. Discovered by Jermaine Jackson. Brothers Bobby and Tommy DeBarge were later in family group DeBarge.

9/2/78	37	33		1 Switch	$8	Gordy 980
6/2/79	37	36		2 Switch II	$8	Gordy 988
4/12/80	57	14		3 Reaching For Tomorrow	$8	Gordy 993
11/15/80+	85	17		4 This Is My Dream	$8	Gordy 999
11/21/81	174	4		5 Switch V	$8	Gordy 1007

All I Need Is You (4)
Believe In Yourself (4)
Best Beat In Town (2) 69
Best Of Love (5)
Call On Me (5)
Calling On All Girls (5)
Don't Take My Love Away (3)
Fallin' (2)
Fever (1)

Get Back With You (3)
Go On Doin' What You Feel (2)
Honey, I Love You (3)
I Call Your Name (2) 83
I Do Love You (5)
I Finally Found Someone New (3)
I Luv It (5)

I Wanna Be Closer (1)
I Wanna Be With You (1)
I'll Always Keep (5)
It's So Real (1)
Just Imagine (4)
Keep Movin' On (3)
Love Over And Over Again (4)
My Friend In The Sky (3)
Next To You (2)

Power To Dance (3)
Push The Switch (High Energy Switch) (5)
Reaching For Tomorrow (3)
Somebody's Watchin' You (1)
There'll Never Be (1) 36
This Is Just For You (3)
This Is My Dream (4)

Two Wrongs Don't Make A Right (5)
We Like To Party...Come On (1)
What A Feeling (4)
Why'd You Let Love Fall (4)
Without You In My Life (4)
You And I (4)
You Keep Me High (5)

You Pulled A Switch (1)
You're The One For Me (2)

SYBIL
Sybil Lynch from Paterson, New Jersey.

| 10/21/89 | 75 | 24 | | Sybil | $8 | Next Plat. 1018 |

Bad Beats Suite
Can't Wait (On Tomorrow)
Crazy 4 U

Don't Make Me Over 20
Give It To Me

I Wanna Be Where You Are
In My Dreams

Living For The Moment
Love's Calling

Take Me Away
Walk On By 74

We're Gonna Make It Work
This Time

SYKES, Keith
Rockabilly singer from Memphis.

| 11/22/80 | 147 | 11 | | I'm Not Strange I'm Just Like You | $8 | Backstreet 3265 |

Ain't That Some Lovin'
B.I.G.T.I.M.E.

I'm Not Strange (I'm Just Like You)
I'm On A Roll
Love To Ride

Makin' It Before They Got Married

Maybe I'm A Mockingbird
928

Smack Dab In The Middle
When My Work Is Done

SYLVAIN, Sylvain
Born in Cairo, Egypt in 1953. Moved to Brooklyn in 1961. Lead guitarist with the New York Dolls (1973-74).

| 2/16/80 | 123 | 8 | | Sylvain Sylvain | $8 | RCA 3475 |

Ain't Got No Home
Deeper And Deeper

Emily
Every Boy And Every Girl

14th Street Beat
I'm So Sorry

Teenage News
Tonight

What's That Got To Do With Rock 'N' Roll

Without You

DEBUT DATE	PEAK POS	WKS CHR	GOLD	ARTIST — Album Title	$	Label & Number

SYLVERS, Foster

Born on 2/25/62 in Memphis. Youngest member of The Sylvers family group. Production work on Janet Jackson's first album.

| 7/21/73 | 159 | 7 | | Foster Sylvers.. | $8 | Pride 0027 |

Big Things Come In Small Packages · Happy Face · Hey, Little Girl *92* · I'll Get You In The End · I'm Your Puppet · Lullaby (medley) · **Misdemeanor 22** · Mockingbird · More Love · Only My Love Is True · Swooperman · Uncle Albert (medley)

SYLVERS, The

Memphis family of 10 brothers and sisters: Olympia-Ann, Leon, Charmaine, James, Edmund, Ricky, Angelia, Pat, Jonathon and Foster Sylvers. Leon formed the group Dynasty in 1979.

3/3/73	180	7		1 The Sylvers..	$8	Pride 0007
8/4/73	164	5		2 The Sylvers II..	$8	Pride 0026
2/14/76	58	25		3 Showcase..	$8	Capitol 11465
11/20/76	80	18		4 Something Special..	$8	Capitol 11580
11/26/77+	134	13		5 New Horizons..	$8	Capitol 11705
9/16/78	132	8		6 Forever Yours..	$8	Casablanca 7103

Ain't No Doubt About It (4) · Ain't No Good In Good-bye (3) · Ain't Nothin' But A Party (3) · Another Day To Love (5) · Any Way You Want Me (5) *72* · **Boogie Fever** (3) *1* · Chaos (1) · Charisma (3) · Clap Your Hands To The Music (3) · Come Dance With Me (6) · Come On Down To My House (6) · **Cotton Candy** (3) *59* · Cry Of A Dreamer (2) · Diamonds Are Rare (6) · Disco Showdown (4) · Don't Stop, Get Off (6) · Dressed To Kill (5) · **Fool's Paradise** (1) *94* · Forever Yours (6) · Free Style (3) · Got To Have You (For My Very Own) (4) · Handle It (2) · **High School Dance** (4) *17* · **Hot Line** (4) · How Love Hurts (1) · I Can Be For Real (3) · I Don't Need To Prove Myself (2) · I Know Myself (1) · I Remember (2) · I'll Never Be Ashamed (1) · I'll Never Let You Go (2) · I'm Truly Happy (1) · Just A Little Bit Longer (6) · Keep On Keepin' On (Doin' What You Do) (3) · Let It Be Me (2) · Love Changes (6) · Love Me, Love Me Not (2) · Love Won't Let Me Go (6) · Lovin' Me Back (5) · Lovin' You Is Like Lovin' The Wind (4) · Mista Guitar Man (4) · New Horizons (5) · Now I Want You (4) · Only One Can Win (1) · Party Maker (5) · Play This One Last Record (6) · Roulette Wheel Of Love (3) · Shake 'Um Up (4) · So Close (1) · Star Fire (5) · **Stay Away From Me** (2) *89* · Storybook Girl (3) · Swept For You Baby (6) · Take A Hand (5) · That's What Love Is Made Of (4) · Through The Love In My Heart (2) · Touch Me Jesus (1) · We Can Make It If We Try (2) · **Wish That I Could Talk To You** (1) *77* · Yesterday (2) · You Bring The Sunshine (Back Into My Life) (5)

SYLVESTER

Born Sylvester James in Los Angeles. Moved to San Francisco in 1967. With vocal group the Cockettes. In film *The Rose*. Backing vocals by Martha Wash, Izora Rhodes (later known as Two Tons O' Fun and The Weather Girls) and Jeanie Tracy. Died on 12/16/88 (age 41) of AIDS-related complications.

8/5/78	28	42	●	1 Step II..	$8	Fantasy 9556
4/28/79	63	15		2 Stars..	$8	Fantasy 9579
11/24/79+	123	12		3 Living Proof.. [L]	$10	Fantasy 79010 [2]
				side 4: studio		
9/27/80	147	8		4 Sell My Soul..	$8	Honey 9601
7/11/81	156	4		5 Too Hot To Sleep..	$8	Honey 9607
3/19/83	168	5		6 All I Need..	$8	Megatone 1005
2/14/87	164	5		7 Mutual Attraction..	$8	Warner 25527

All I Need (6) · Anything Can Happen (7) · Be With You (6) · Blackbird (3) · Body Strong (2,3) · Can't Forget The Love (5) · Can't Stop Dancing (3) · Can't You See (5) · Change Up (4) · Cool Of The Evening (7) · Could It Be Magic (medley) (3) · Cry Me A River (4) · **Dance (Disco Heat)** (1,3) *19* · Do Ya Wanna Funk (6) · Doin' It For The Real Thing (4) · Don't Stop (6) · Fever (4) · Give It Up (Don't Make Me Wait) (5) · Grateful (1,3) · Happiness (3) · Hard Up (6) · Here Is My Love (5) · I Can't Believe I'm In Love (5) · I Need Somebody To Love Tonight (3) · I Need You (4) · I Took My Strength From You (1) · **I (Who Have Nothing)** (2) *40* · I'll Dance To That (4) · In My Fantasy (I Want You, I Need You) (3) · Just You And Me Forever (1) · Living For The City (7) · Lover Man (Oh Where Can You Be) (3) · Mutual Attraction (7) · My Life Is Loving You (4) · New Beginnings (5) · Ooo Baby Baby (5) · Sell My Soul (4) · Sharing Something Perfect Between Ourselves (3) · Someone Like You (7) · Song For You (medley) (3) · Sooner Or Later (7) · Stars (2) · Summertime (7) · Talk To Me (6) · Tell Me (6) · Thinking Right (5) · Too Hot To Sleep (5) · Was It Something That I Said (1) · Won't You Let Me Love You (6) · You Are My Friend (3) · **You Make Me Feel (Mighty Real)** (1,3) *36*

SYLVIA

Born Sylvia Vanderpool on 5/6/36 in New York City. Singer/songwriter/producer. First recorded with Hot Lips Page in 1950 as Little Sylvia. Half of Mickey & Sylvia duo. Married Joe Robinson, owner of All-Platinum/Vibration Records (later known as Sugar Hill). Their son Joey was leader of West Street Mob.

| 6/2/73 | 70 | 12 | | Pillow Talk.. | $15 | Vibration 126 |

Cowards Way Out · **Didn't I 70** · Don't Leave Me Starving · Give It Up In Vain · Had Any Lately · My Thing · Not On The Outside · **Pillow Talk 3** · Sunday

SYLVIA

Country singer Sylvia Kirby Allen. Born on 12/9/56 in Kokomo, Indiana. Moved to Nashville in 1975. Worked as a secretary for producer Tom Collins. Solo debut in 1979.

5/9/81	139	11		1 Drifter..	$8	RCA 3986
8/7/82	56	33	●	2 Just Sylvia..	$8	RCA 4312
6/18/83	77	11		3 Snapshot..	$8	RCA 4672
4/28/84	178	4		4 Surprise..	$8	RCA 4960

Bobby's In Vicksburg (3) · Boy Gets Around (3) · Cry Baby Cry (1) · Drifter (1) · Give 'Em Rhythm (4) · Gone But Not Forgotten (3) · Heart On The Mend (1) · I Feel Cheated (2) · I Just Don't Have The Heart (4) · I Never Quite Got Back (From Loving You) (3) · I'll Make It Right With You (2) · I'm Going With Him (1) · Isn't It Always Love (4) · It Don't Hurt To Dream (1) · It's Still There (4) · Jason (3) · Like Nothing Ever Happened (2) · Love Over Old Times (4) · Matador, The (1) · Mill Song (Everybody's Got A Dream) (2) · Mirage (2) · Missin' You (1) · **Nobody** (2) *15* · Not Tonight (2) · On The Other Side Of Midnight (4) · One Foot On The Street (4) · Rainbow Rider (1) · Snapshot (3) · So Complete (3) · Surprise (4) · Sweet Yesterday (2) · Tonight I'm Gettin' Friendly With The Blues (3) · Tumbleweed (1) · Unguarded Moments (4) · Victims Of Goodbye (4) · Whippoorwill (1) · Who's Kidding Who (3) · Winter Heart (3) · You Can't Go Back Home (2) · You're A Legend In Your Own Mind (2)

SYNDICATE OF SOUND

San Jose garage-rock quintet: Don Baskin (lead singer), Jim Sawyers (guitar), Bob Gonzalez (bass), John Sharkey (rhythm guitar) and John Duckworth (drums).

| 8/27/66 | 148 | 2 | | Little Girl.. | $40 | Bell 6001 |

Almost Grown · Big Boss Man · Dream Baby · I'm Alive · Is You Is Or Is You Ain't My Baby · **Little Girl 8** · Lookin' For The Good Times (The Robot) · **Rumors 55** · So Alone · That Kind Of Man · Witch · You

DEBUT DATE	PEAK POS	WKS CHR	GOLD	ARTIST — Album Title	$	Label & Number

SYNERGY
Electronic equipment performed and programmed by New Jersey native Larry Fast.

6/21/75	66	18		1 Electronic Realizations for Rock Orchestra ....[I]	$8	Passport 98009
6/26/76	144	11		2 Sequencer ....[I]	$8	Passport 98014
9/16/78	146	6		3 Cords ....[I]	$8	Passport 6000

Chateau (2)
Classical Gas (2)
Cybersports (2)
Disruption In World
  Communications (3)

Escape ..see: S-Scape
Full Moon Flyer (3)
Legacy (1)
On Presuming To Be
  Modern I-III (3)

Paradox Medley (2)
Phobos And Deimos Go To
  Mars (3)
Relay Breakdown (1)
S-Scape (2)

(Sequence) 14 (2)
Sketches Of Mythical Beasts
  (3)
Slaughter On Tenth Avenue
  (1)

Small Collection Of Chords
  (3)
Synergy (1)
Terra Incognita (3)
Trellis (3)

Warriors (1)

SYREETA
Born Rita Wright in Pittsburgh. Singer/songwriter. Worked as secretary and backup vocalist at Motown.
First recorded under real name in 1968. Married to Stevie Wonder from 1972-74.

8/12/72	185	8		1 Syreeta	$10	MoWest 113
7/20/74	116	17		2 Stevie Wonder presents Syreeta	$8	Motown 808
				above 2 produced by Stevie Wonder		
5/17/80	73	15		3 Syreeta	$8	Tamla 372
8/8/81	127	9		4 Billy Preston & Syreeta	$8	Motown 958
				BILLY PRESTON & SYREETA		
1/30/82	189	3		5 Set My Love In Motion	$8	Tamla 376

Baby Don't Let Me Lose This
  (1)
Black Maybe (1)
Blame It On The Sun (3)
Can't Shake Your Love (5)
Cause We've Ended As
  Lovers (2)
Come And Get This Stuff (2)
Dance For Me Children (3)
Happiness (1)
He's Gone (3)
Heavy Day (2)

Here's My Love (3)
Hey You (4)
How Many Days (1)
I Know The Way To Your
  Heart (5)
I Love Every Little Thing
  About You (1)
I Love You (5)
I Must Be In Love (5)
I Wanna Be By Your Side
  (medley) (2)
I'm Goin' Left (2)

It's So Easy (4)
Just A Little Piece Of You
  (medley) (2)
Just For You (4)
Keep Him Like He Is (1)
Let Me Be The One (3)
Long And Lasting Love (4)
Love (4)
Love Fire (3)
Move It, Do It (5)
New Way To Say I Love You
  (4)

One More Time For Love (3)
One More Try (4)
Out Of The Box (5)
Please Stay (3)
Quick Slick (5)
Searchin' (4)
She's Leaving Home (1)
Signed, Sealed, Delivered
  (I'm Yours) (3)
Someone Special (4)
Spinnin' And Spinnin' (2)

There's Nothing Like A
  Woman In Love (5)
To Know You Is To Love You
  (1)
Universal Sound Of The
  World (Your Kiss Is Sweet)
  (medley) (2)
Waitin' For The Postman
  (medley) (2)
What Love Has Joined
  Together (1)
What We Did For Love (4)

When Your Daddy's Not
  Around (medley) (2)
Wish Upon A Star (5)
You Bring Out The Love In
  Me (3)
You Set My Love In Motion
  (5)
Your Kiss Is Sweet (2)

SYSTEM, The
New York City-based, techno-funk duo: Mic Murphy (b: Raleigh, North Carolina; vocals, guitar) and David
Frank (b: Dayton, Ohio; synthesizer).

3/12/83	94	23		1 Sweat..	$8	Mirage 90062
3/31/84	182	5		2 X-Periment	$8	Mirage 90146
4/18/87	62	25		3 Don't Disturb This Groove	$8	Atlantic 81691

Bad Girl (2)
Come As You Are
  (Superstar) (3)
Dangerous (2)
Didn't I Blow Your Mind (3)

Don't Disturb This Groove
  (3) 4
Escape (2)
Experiment ..see: X-Periment
Get Jumpin' (2)
Go For What U Know (1)

Groove (3)
Heart Beat Of The City (3)
House Of Rhythm (3)
I Can't Take Losing You (2)
I Wanna Make You Feel
  Good (2)

I Won't Let Go (1)
It's Passion (1)
Lollipops And Everything (2)
Modern Girl (3)
Nighttime Lover (1)
Now I Am Electric (1)

Promises Can Break (2)
Save Me (3)
Soul Boy (3)
Stand Up And Cheer (1)
Sweat (1)
X-Periment (2)

You Are In My System
  (1) **64**

SZABO, Gabor
Born on 3/8/36 in Budapest, Hungary; died on 2/26/82. Jazz guitarist/composer.

1/28/67	140	4		1 Spellbinder ....[I]	$15	Impulse! 9123
1/13/68	194	2		2 The Sorcerer ....[I-L]	$15	Impulse! 9146
6/15/68	157	3		3 Bacchanal ....[I]	$12	Skye 3
8/16/69	143	7		4 Gabor Szabo 1969...[I]	$12	Skye 9
5/16/70	162	10		5 Lena & Gabor	$12	Skye 15
				LENA HORNE & GABOR SZABO		

Autumn Leaves (medley) (1)
Bacchanal (3)
Bang Bang (My Baby Shot
  Me Down) (1)
Beat Goes On (2)
Both Sides Now (4)
Cheetah (3)
Comin' Back (2)
Dear Prudence (4)

Divided City (3)
Everybody's Talkin' (5)
Fool On The Hill (5)
Gypsy Queen (1)
I've Just Seen A Face (4)
In My Life (4,5)
It Was A Very Good Year (1)
Little Boat (O Barquinho) (2)
Look Of Love (3)

Lou-ise (2)
Love Is Blue (3)
Message To Michael (5)
Michael From Mountains (4)
Mizrab (2)
My Foolish Heart (1)
My Mood Is You (5)
Nightwind (5)
Rocky Raccoon (5)

Sealed With A Kiss (4)
Some Velvet Morning (3)
Something (5)
Somewhere I Belong (4)
Space (2)
Speak To Me Of Love
  (medley) (2)
Spellbinder (1)
Stormy (4)

Stronger Than Us (2)
Sunshine Superman (3)
Three King Fishers (3)
Until It's Time For You To
  Go (4)
Valley Of The Dolls, Theme
  From The (3)
Walk Away Renee (4)
Watch What Happens (5)

What Is This Thing Called
  Love? (2)
Witchcraft (1)
Yearning (1)
Yesterday When I Was
  Young (5)
You Won't See Me (4)

T

TACO
Born Taco Ockerse in 1955 to Dutch parents in Jaharta, Indonesia. German-based singer.

| 7/23/83 | 23 | 24 | | After Eight.. | $8 | RCA 4818 |

After Eight
Carmella

Cheek To Cheek
Encore (Sweet Gypsy Rose)

I Should Care
La Vie En Rose

Livin' In My Dreamworld
Puttin' On The Ritz 4

Singin' In The Rain
Thanks A Million

Tribute To Tino

TAKE 6
Contemporary Christian, a cappella, pop-jazz sextet formed at Oakwood College in Alabama made up of
vocalists Claude McKnight, Mark Kibble, Mervyn Warren, Cedric Dent, David Thomas and Alvin Chea.
Claude's younger brother is singer Brian McKnight.

| 3/11/89 | 71 | 19 | ● | 1 Take 6 .... | $8 | Reprise 25670 |
| 9/29/90 | 72 | 18 | | 2 So Much 2 Say .... | $12 | Reprise 25892 |

DEBUT DATE	PEAK POS	WKS CHR	GOLD	ARTIST — Album Title	$	Label & Number

TAKE 6 — Cont'd

12/7/91+	**100**	6	3	He Is Christmas...[X]	**$12**	Reprise 26665

Christmas charts: 11/'91, 23/'93

Amen! (3)	Gold Mine (1)	I'm On My Way (2)	O Come All Ye Faithful (3)	Sunday's On The Way (2)	Where Do The Children Play? (2)
Away In A Manger (3)	Hark! The Herald Angels	If We Ever (1)	Oh! He Is Christmas (3)	Sweet Little Jesus Boy (3)
Come Unto Me (2)	Sing (3)	Let The Words (1)	Quiet Place (1)	[That's The Law] (2)
David And Goliath (1)	He Never Sleeps (1)	Little Drummer Boy (3)	Silent Night (3)	Time After Time (The Savior
Get Away, Jordan (1)	[Human Body] (2)	Mary (1)	So Much 2 Say (2)	Is Waiting) (2)
God Rest Ye Merry	I Believe (2)	Milky-White Way (1)	Something Within Me (2)	'Twas Da Nite (3)
Gentlemen (3)	I L-O-V-E U (1)	[Not Again!?] (2)	Spread Love (1)

★★232★★ TALKING HEADS

New York City-based new wave quartet: David Byrne (lead singer, guitar), Jerry Harrison (keyboards, guitar), Tina Weymouth (bass) and husband Chris Frantz (drums). Formed as a trio of Byrne, Weymouth and Frantz at the Rhode Island School of Design. Harrison was a member of The Modern Lovers. Disbanded in late 1991. Also see Tom Tom Club.

10/8/77+	**97**	29		1 Talking Heads: 77	**$8**	Sire 6036
8/12/78	**29**	42	●	2 More Songs About Buildings And Food	**$8**	Sire 6058
9/1/79	**21**	30	●	3 Fear Of Music	**$8**	Sire 6076
11/1/80	**19**	27	●	4 Remain In Light..	**$8**	Sire 6095
				above 3 albums produced by Brian Eno
4/17/82	**31**	14		5 The Name Of This Band Is Talking Heads.................................[L]	**$10**	Sire 3590 [2]
6/25/83	**15**	51	●	6 Speaking In Tongues	**$8**	Sire 23883
9/22/84	**41**	118	▲	7 Stop Making Sense ....[S-L]	**$8**	Sire 25121
				film is a live concert at The Pantages Theatre in Hollywood (December 1983)
7/6/85	**20**	77	▲	8 Little Creatures	**$8**	Sire 25305
10/4/86	**17**	29	●	9 True Stories	**$8**	Sire 25512
				contains Talking Heads' versions of songs featured in the film *True Stories*
4/2/88	**19**	21	●	10 Naked	**$8**	Sire 25654
10/31/92	**158**	2		11 Popular Favorites 1976-1992: Sand In The Vaseline ....[G]	**$24**	Sire 26760 [2]

Air (3,5)	Crosseyed And Painless	Great Curve (4,5)	Listening Wind (4)	Perfect World (8)	Television Man (8)
And She Was (8,11) **54**	(4,5,11)	Happy Day (1)	Love For Sale (9,11)	Popsicle (11)	Tentative Decisions (1)
Animals (3)	Democratic Circus (10)	Heaven (3,11)	Making Flippy Floppy (6)	**Psycho Killer** (1,5,7,11) **92**	Thank You For Sending Me
Artists Only (1)	Don't Worry About The	Hey Now (6)	Memories Can't Wait (3,5,11)	Pull Up The Roots (6)	An Angel (2)
Big Country (2,11)	Government (1,5,11)	Houses In Motion (4,5)	Mind (3)	Pulled Up (1,5)	**This Must Be The Place**
Big Daddy (10)	Dream Operator (9)	I Get Wild (medley) (6)	Mommy Daddy You And I	Puzzlin' Evidence (9)	**(Naive Melody)** (6,11) **62**
Blind (10,11)	Drugs (3,5)	I Want To Live (1)	(10)	Radio Head (9)	Totally Nude (10)
Book I Read (1)	Electric Guitar (3)	I Wish You Wouldn't Say	Moon Rocks (6)	Road To Nowhere (8,11)	Uh-Oh, Love Comes To
Born Under Punches (The	Facts Of Life (10)	That (11)	Mr. Jones (10,11)	Ruby Dear (10)	Town (1)
Heat Goes On) (4)	First Week/Last	I Zimbra (3,5,11)	New Feeling (1,5)	Sax And Violins (11)	Walk It Down (8)
Building On Fire (5,11)	Week...Carefree (1)	I'm Not In Love (1)	No Compassion (1,11)	Seen And Not Seen (4)	Warning Sign (2,11)
Burning Down The House	Found A Job (2)	Lady Don't Mind (8)	(Nothing But) Flowers (10,11)	Slippery People (6,7)	What A Day That Was (7)
(6,7,11) **9**	Gangster Of Love (11)	**Life During Wartime (This**	Once In A Lifetime	Stay Hungry (2,5)	Who Is It? (1)
Cities (3)	Girlfriend Is Better (6,7,11)	**Ain't No Party...This**	(4,7,11) **91**	Stay Up Late (8,11)	Wild Gravity (medley) (6)
City Of Dreams (9,11)	Girls Want To Be With The	**Ain't No Disco...This**	Overload, The (4)	Sugar On My Tongue (11)	**Wild Wild Life** (9,11) **25**
Clean Break (5)	Girls (2)	**Ain't No Fooling Around)**	Papa Legba (9)	Swamp (6,7,11)	With Our Love (2)
Cool Water (10)	Give Me Back My Name (8)	(3,5,7,11) **80**	Paper (3)	**Take Me To The River**
Creatures Of Love (8)	Good Thing (2)	Lifetime Piling Up (11)	People Like Us (9)	(2,5,7,11) **26**

TALK TALK

British rock band — Mark Hollis, lead singer.

9/18/82	**132**	16		1 The Party's Over..	**$8**	EMI America 17083
4/7/84	**42**	22		2 It's My Life	**$8**	EMI America 17113
3/22/86	**58**	17		3 The Colour Of Spring	**$8**	EMI America 17179

Another Word (1)	Does Caroline Know? (1)	Have You Heard The News	Last Time (2)	Party's Over (1)	Time It's Time (3)
April 5th (3)	Dum Dum Girl (2)	(1)	**Life's What You Make It**	Renee (2)	Today (1)
Call In The Night Boy (2)	Give It Up (3)	I Don't Believe In You (3)	(3) **90**	Serious (1)	Tomorrow Started (2)
Candy (1)	Happiness Is Easy (3)	**It's My Life** (2) **31**	Living In Another World (3)	**Such A Shame** (2) **89**
Chameleon Day (3)	Hate (1)	It's You (2)	Mirror Man (1)	**Talk Talk** (1) **75**

TA MARA & THE SEEN

Minneapolis quintet led by Margaret Cox, a veteran Minneapolis night club singer. Group includes guitarist Oliver Leiber, son of songwriter Jerry Leiber (of Leiber & Stoller).

11/2/85+	**54**	25		Ta Mara & The Seen	**$8**	A&M 5078

Affection (1)	Got To Have You	Lonely Heart	Long Cold Nights	Summertime Love	Thinking About You
Everybody Dance 24

TANGERINE DREAM

German rock synthesist outfit formed in 1967 by Edgar Froese. Included Christoph Franke and Peter Baumann (who left in 1977 and formed Private Music Records). Franke left in 1986, replaced by Paul Haslinger and Ralph Wadephul. In 1989, reduced to a duo of Froese and Wadephul.

7/6/74	**196**	2		1 Phaedra...[I]	**$8**	Virgin 13108
4/2/77	**158**	7		2 Stratosfear..[I]	**$8**	Virgin 34427
7/23/77	**153**	6		3 Sorcerer...[S-I]	**$10**	MCA 2277
12/3/77	**178**	2		4 Encore..[I-L]	**$12**	Virgin 35014 [2]
5/9/81	**115**	10		5 Thief...[S-I]	**$8**	Elektra 521
				Johannes Schmoelling replaces Peter Baumann
11/21/81	**195**	2		6 Exit ....[I]	**$8**	Elektra 557
5/17/86	**96**	7		7 Legend ....[S-I]	**$8**	MCA 6165
				includes "Is Your Love Strong Enough" by Bryan Ferry and "Loved By The Sun" by Jon Anderson

Abyss (3)	Burning Bar (5)	Cottage (7)	Dr. Destructo (5)	Impressions Of Sorcerer (3)	Mountain Road (3)
Beach Theme (5)	Call, The (3)	Creation (7)	Exit (6)	Invisible Limits (2)	Movements Of A Visionary
Betrayal (Sorcerer Theme) (3)	Cherokee Lane (4)	Dance, The (7)	Fairies (7)	Journey, The (3)	(1)
Big Sleep In Search Of	Choronzon (6)	Darkness (7)	Goblins (5)	Kiew Mission (6)	Mysterious Semblance At
Hades (2)	Coldwater Canyon (4)	Desert Dream (4)	Grind (3)	Kitchen, The (medley) (7)	The Strand Of Nightmares
Blue Room (7)	Confrontation (5)	Diamond Diary (5)	Igneous (5)	Monolight (4)	(1)

DEBUT DATE	PEAK POS	WKS CHR	GOLD	ARTIST — Album Title	$	Label & Number

TANGERINE DREAM — Cont'd

Network (6)	Rain Forest (3)	Search (3)	Stratosfear (2)	Trap Feeling (5)	
Phaedra (1)	Remote Viewing (6)	Sequent C' (1)	3 AM At The Border Of The	Unicorn Theme (7)	
Pilots Of Purple Twilight (6)	Scrap Yard (5)	Sorcerer, Main Title (3)	Marsh From Okefenokee (2)	Vengeance (3)	

TANGIER

Philadelphia-area rock quintet led by vocalist Bill Mattson.

| 7/29/89 | 91 | 17 | | 1 Four Winds .... | $8 | Atco 91251 |
| 3/16/91 | 187 | 5 | | 2 Stranded.. | $12 | Atco 91603 |

				You're Not The Lovin' Kind
Back In The Limelight (2)	Excited (2)	If Ya Can't Find Love (2)	**On The Line** (1) 67	Stranded (2)	(2)
Bad Girl (1)	Fever For Gold (1)	In Time (1)	Ripcord (1)	Sweet Surrender (1)	
Caution To The Wind (2)	Four Winds (1)	It's Hard (2)	Since You Been Gone (2)	Takes Just A Little Time (2)	
Down The Line (2)	Good Lovin' (1)	Mississippi (1)	Southbound Train (1)		

TANNER, Marc, Band

Marc was born on 8/20/52 in Hollywood. Pop-rock singer/guitarist.

| 3/3/79 | 140 | 8 | | No Escape .... | $8 | Elektra 168 |

Crawlin'	**Elena 45**	In A Spotlight	Lost At Love	She's So High
Edge Of Love	Getaway	Lady In Blue	Never Again	Your Tears Don't Lie

TANTRUM

Rock group led by female vocalists Barb Erber, Sandy Caulfield and Pam Bradley.

| 1/19/80 | 199 | 3 | | Rather Be Rockin' .... | $8 | Ovation 1747 |

Applaud The Winner	How Long	Runnin'	Searchin' For A Reason	You Are The World
Don't Turn Me Off	Rather Be Rockin'	Sammy And Susie	Take A Look	You Need Me

TARNEY/SPENCER BAND, The

Australian duo: Alan Tarney (vocals, guitar, keyboards) and Trevor Spencer (drums).

| 7/29/78 | 174 | 4 | | 1 Three's A Crowd .... | $8 | A&M 4692 |
| 5/12/79 | 181 | 4 | | 2 Run For Your Life .... | $8 | A&M 4757 |

				We Believe In Love (1)
Bye Bye Now My Sweet Love (1)	Easier For You (1)	I'm Alive (2)	Magic Still Runs Through Your Head (1)	Race Is Almost Run (2)	Won'tcha Tell Me (2)
Capital Shame (1)	Far Better Man (2)	**It's Really You** (1) 86	Maybe I'm Right (1)	Run For Your Life (2)	
Don't (2)	Heart Will Break Tonight (2)	Lies (2)	**No Time To Lose** (2) 74	Set The Minstrel Free (1)	
	I Can Hear Love (1)	Live Again (2)		Takin' Me Back (1)	

TASTE

Irish rock trio led by vocalist/guitarist Rory Gallagher. Disbanded in 1971.

| 8/16/69 | 133 | 9 | | Taste... | $20 | Atco 296 |

				Sugar Mama
Blister On The Moon	Born On The Wrong Side Of Time	Catfish	Hail	Leavin' Blues	
		Dual Carriageway Pain	I'm Moving On	Same Old Story	

TASTE OF HONEY, A

Soul-disco quartet, formed in Los Angeles in 1972. Consisted of Janice Marie Johnson (vocals, guitar), Hazel Payne (vocals, bass), Perry Kimble (keyboards) and Donald Johnson (drums). Re-formed in 1980 with Janice Johnson and Hazel Payne. Won the 1978 Best New Artist Grammy Award.

6/17/78	6	27	▲	1 A Taste of Honey	$8	Capitol 11754
7/14/79	59	13		2 Another Taste	$8	Capitol 11951
8/2/80+	36	32		3 Twice As Sweet	$8	Capitol 12089
4/24/82	73	12		4 Ladies Of The Eighties	$8	Capitol 12173

				This Love Of Ours (1)
Ain't Nothin' But A Party (3)	**Do It Good** (2) 79	I'm Talkin' 'Bout You (3)	Never Go Wrong (4)	She's A Dancer (3)	We've Got The Groove (4)
Boogie Oogie Oogie (1) *1*	Don't You Lead Me On (3)	If We Loved (3)	Race (2)	Sky High (1)	World Spin (1)
Dance (1)	Good-Bye Baby (3)	Leavin' Tomorrow (4)	Rainbow's End (2)	**Sukiyaki** (3) *3*	You (1)
Diamond Real (4)	I Love You (2)	Let's Begin (2)	Rescue Me (3)	Superstar Superman (1)	You're In Good Hands (1)
Disco Dancin' (3)	**I'll Try Something New** (4) 41	Lies (1)	Say That You'll Stay (3)	Take The Boogae Or Leave It (2)	Your Love (2)
Distant (1)		Midnight Snack (4)	Sayonara (4)		

★★429★★ TAVARES

Family R&B group from New Bedford, Massachusetts. Consisted of brothers Ralph, Antone "Chubby," Feliciano "Butch," Arthur "Pooch" and Perry Lee "Tiny" Tavares. Worked as Chubby & The Turnpikes from 1964-69. Butch was married to Lola Falana.

2/9/74	160	8		1 Check It Out	$8	Capitol 11258
9/21/74+	121	23		2 Hard Core Poetry	$8	Capitol 11316
8/9/75	26	17		3 In The City	$8	Capitol 11396
6/12/76	24	31		4 Sky High!	$8	Capitol 11533
4/30/77	59	22		5 Love Storm	$8	Capitol 11628
10/15/77	72	10		6 The Best Of Tavares ....[G]	$8	Capitol 11701
5/13/78	115	8		7 Future Bound	$8	Capitol 11719
2/3/79	92	11		8 Madam Butterfly	$8	Capitol 11874
3/8/80	75	7		9 Supercharged	$8	Capitol 12026
12/11/82+	137	11		10 New Directions	$8	RCA 4357

				Positive Forces (8)	**Too Late** (2) 59
Abra-Ca-Dabra Love You Too (10)	Goodnight My Love (5)	I'll Never Say Never Again (1)	Mama's Little Girl (1)		Wanna Be Close To You (10)
All I See Is You (7)	Got To Find My Way Back To You (10)	I'm Back For More (8)	Maybe We'll Fall In Love Again (10)	Ready, Willing And Able (3)	Watchin' The Woman's Movement (5)
Bad Times (9) 47	Got To Have Your Love (9)	I'm In Love (1)	Mighty Power Of Love (4)	**Remember What I Told You To Forget** (2,6) *25*	We Both Tried (9)
Bein' With You (4,6)	Guiding Star (4)	If That's The Way You Want It (1)	**More Than A Woman** (7) *32*	Ridin' High (4)	We Fit To A Tee (3)
Can't Get Enough (9)	Hard Core Poetry (2)	In The City (3)	My Love Calls (8)	**She's Gone** (2,6) 50	We're Both Ready For Love (7)
Check It Out (1,6) *35*	**Heaven Must Be Missing An Angel (Part 1)** (4,6) *15*	In The Eyes Of Love (3)	My Ship (2) *flip*	Skin You're In (10)	What You Don't Know (2)
Don't Take Away The Music (4,6) *34*	Honey Can I (7)	**It Only Takes A Minute** (3,6) *10*	Mystery Lady (10)	Slow Train To Paradise (7)	**Whodunit** (5) *22*
Feel So Good (7)	I Can't Go On Living Without You (9)	Keep In Touch (5)	Never Had A Love Like This Before (8)	Someone To Go Home To (2)	Why Can't We Fall In Love (9)
Fool Of The Year (5)	I Don't Want You Anymore (9)	Leave It Up To The Lady (2)	Nothing You Can Do (3)	Straight From Your Heart (8)	Wish You Were With Me Mary (1)
Fool's Hall Of Fame (3)	I Hope She Chooses Me (3)	Let Me Heal The Bruises (5)	One Step Away (5)	Strangers In Dark Corners (1,6)	Wonderful (4)
Free Ride (3) 52	I Hope You'll Be Very Unhappy Without Me (10)	Let's Make The Best Of What We Got (1)	One Telephone Call Away (8)	**That's The Sound That Lonely Makes** (1) 70	
Games, Games (8)	I Wanna See You Soon (5)	Little Girl (1)	Out Of The Picture (5)	Timber (7)	
Ghost Of Love (7)		Love I Never Had (3,6)	Paradise (9)	To Love You (2)	
Going Ups & Coming Downs (5)		Madam Butterfly (8)	**Penny For Your Thoughts** (10) *33*	To The Other Man (4)	

DEBUT DATE	PEAK POS	WKS CHR	GOLD	ARTIST — Album Title	$	Label & Number

TAXXI
British rock trio — David Cummins, lead singer.

12/25/82+	**161**	11		States Of Emergency	$8	Fantasy 9617

Cocktail Queen (Don't She Love To Rock & Roll)   Girl (New York City)   Heart Is A Lonely Hunter   I'm Leaving   Whipping Boy
All In Line   Gold Digger   I Remember   Players

TAYLOR, Alex
James Taylor's older brother.

3/20/71	**190**	2		With Friends And Neighbors	$8	Capricorn 860

All In Line   C Song   It's All Over Now   Southbound   Take Out Some Insurance
Baby Ruth   Highway Song   Night Owl   Southern Kids

TAYLOR, Andy
Born on 2/16/61 in Dolver-Hampton, England. Lead guitarist of Duran Duran and The Power Station.

3/28/87	**46**	17		Thunder	$8	MCA 5837

Bringin' Me Down   Don't Let Me Die Young   I Might Lie   Night Train   Tremblin'
Broken Window   French Guitar   Life Goes On   Thunder

★★**103**★★   **TAYLOR, James**
Born on 3/12/48 in Boston. Singer/songwriter/guitarist. With older brother Alex in the Fabulous Corsairs in 1964. In New York group The Flying Machine in 1967, with friend Danny Kortchmar. Moved to England in 1968, recorded for Peter Asher. Married Carly Simon on 11/3/72, divorced in 1983. In film *Two Lane Blacktop* with Dennis Wilson in 1973. Sister Kate and brothers Alex and Livingston also recorded. Their father, Isaac, was the dean of the University of North Carolina medical school until 1971.

3/14/70	**3**	102	▲³	1 **Sweet Baby James**	$10	Warner 1843
10/3/70	**62**	28		2 James Taylor [E]	$15	Apple 3352
				recorded in 1968 in London		
2/6/71	**74**	8		3 James Taylor and the original Flying Machine-1967 [E]	$12	Euphoria 2
5/8/71	**2⁴**	45	▲	4 **Mud Slide Slim And The Blue Horizon**	$10	Warner 2561
11/25/72+	**4**	25	●	5 **One Man Dog**	$8	Warner 2660
7/13/74	**13**	18		6 Walking Man	$8	Warner 2794
5/31/75	**6**	27	●	7 **Gorilla**	$8	Warner 2866
7/4/76	**16**	24		8 In The Pocket	$8	Warner 2912
12/4/76+	**23**	41	▲⁴	9 **Greatest Hits** [G]	$8	Warner 2979
7/9/77	**4**	39	▲²	10 **JT**	$8	Columbia 34811
5/12/79	**10**	23	●	11 **Flag**	$8	Columbia 36058
3/21/81	**10**	23	●	12 **Dad Loves His Work**	$8	Columbia 37009
11/23/85	**34**	30		13 That's Why I'm Here	$8	Columbia 40052
2/13/88	**25**	34	●	14 Never Die Young	$8	Columbia 40851
10/19/91	**37**	47	●	15 New Moon Shine	$12	Columbia 46038

Ain't No Song (6)
Angry Blues (7)
Another Grey Morning (10)
Anywhere Like Heaven (1)
B.S.U.R. (11)
Baby Boom Baby (14)
Back On The Street Again (5)
Bartender's Blues (10)
Believe It Or Not (12)
Blossom (1)
Blues Is Just A Bad Dream (2)
Brighten Your Night With My Day (2,3)
Brother Trucker (11)
Captain Jim's Drunken Dream (8)
Carolina In My Mind (2,9) *67*
Chanson Francaise (11)
Chili Dog (5)
Circle Round The Sun (2)
Company Man (11)
Copperline (15)
Country Road (1,9) *37*
Daddy's All Gone (8)
Daddy's Baby (5)
Dance (5)
Day Tripper (11)
Don't Be Sad 'Cause Your Sun Is Down (8)

Don't Let Me Be Lonely Tonight (5,9) *14*
Don't Talk Now (2)
Down In The Hole (15)
Everybody Has The Blues (8)
Everybody Loves To Cha Cha (15)
Everyday (13) *61*
Fading Away (6)
Family Man (8)
Fanfare (5)
Fire And Rain (1,9) *3*
First Of May (14)
Fool For You (5)
Frozen Man (15)
Going Around One More Time (13)
Golden Moments (8)
Gorilla (7)
Handy Man (10) *4*
Hard Times (12) *72*
Hello Old Friend (6)
Her Town Too (12) *11*
Hey Mister, That's Me Up On The Jukebox (4)
Highway Song (4)
Home By Another Way (14)
Honey Don't Leave L.A. (10) *61*
Hour That The Morning Comes (12)

How Sweet It Is (To Be Loved By You) (7,9) *5*
Hymn (5)
I Was A Fool To Care (7)
I Was Only Telling Lies (10)
I Will Follow (12)
(I've Got To) Stop Thinkin' 'Bout That (15)
If I Keep My Heart Out Of Sight (10)
Instrumental I (5)
Instrumental II (5)
Is That The Way You Look? (11)
Isn't It Nice To Be Home Again (4)
Jig (5)
Johnnie Comes Back (11)
Junkie's Lament (8)
Knocking Round The Zoo (2,3)
Kootch's Song (3)
Let It All Fall Down (6)
Let Me Ride (4)
Letter In The Mail (14)
Lighthouse (7)
Like Everyone She Knows (15)
Limousine Driver (13)
Little David (5)
Lo And Behold (1)
London Town (12)

Long Ago And Far Away (4) *31*
Looking For Love On Broadway (10)
Love Has Brought Me Around (4)
Love Songs (7)
Machine Gun Kelly (4)
Man Who Shot Liberty Valance (11)
Me And My Guitar (6)
Mescalito (5)
Mexico (7,9) *49*
Migration (4)
Millworker (11)
Mona (13)
Money Machine (8)
Mud Slide Slim (4)
Music (7)
Native Son (15)
Never Die Young (14) *80*
New Tune (5)
Night Owl (2,3)
Nobody But You (5)
Nothing Like A Hundred Miles (8)
Oh Baby, Don't You Loose Your Lip On Me (1)
Oh Brother (15)
Oh, Susanna (1)
One Man Parade (5) *67*
One More Go Round (15)

One Morning In May (5)
Only A Dream In Rio (13)
Only For Me (12)
Only One (13)
Places In My Past (4)
Promised Land (6)
Rainy Day Man (2,3,11)
Riding On A Railroad (4)
Rock 'N' Roll Is Music Now (6)
Runaway Boy (14)
Sarah Maria (7)
Secret O' Life (10)
Shed A Little Light (15)
Shower The People (8,9) *22*
Slap Leather (15)
Sleep Come Free Me (11)
Slow Burning Love (8)
Soldiers (4)
Someone (5)
Something In The Way She Moves (2,9)
Something's Wrong (2,3)
Song For You Far Away (13)
Stand And Fight (12)
Steamroller (1,9)
Sugar Trade (12)
Suite For 20 G (1)
Summer's Here (12)
Sun On The Moon (14)
Sunny Skies (1)
Sunshine Sunshine (2)

Sweet Baby James (1,9)
Sweet Potatoe Pie (14)
T-Bone (14)
Taking It In (2)
Terra Nova (10)
That Lonesome Road (12)
That's Why I'm Here (13)
There We Are (10)
Traffic Jam (10)
Turn Away (13)
Up On The Roof (11) *28*
Valentine's Day (14)
Walking Man (6,9)
Wandering (7)
Water Is Wide (15)
Will Not Lie For You (11)
Woh, Don't You Know (5)
Woman's Gotta Have It (8)
You Can Close Your Eyes (4)
You Make It Easy (7)
You've Got A Friend (4,9) *1*
Your Smiling Face (10) *20*

★★**489**★★   **TAYLOR, Johnnie**
Born on 5/5/38 in Crawfordsville, Arkansas. With gospel group the Highway QC's in Chicago, early 1950s. In vocal group the Five Echoes, recorded for Sabre in 1954. In the Soul Stirrers gospel group before going solo. First solo recording for Sar in 1961. Known as "The Soul Philosopher."

1/25/69	**42**	18		1 Who's Making Love	$15	Stax 2005
4/26/69	**126**	9		2 Raw Blues	$15	Stax 2008
7/5/69	**109**	6		3 The Johnnie Taylor Philosophy Continues	$15	Stax 2023
12/19/70	**141**	5		4 Johnnie Taylor's Greatest Hits [G]	$12	Stax 2032
4/17/71	**112**	11		5 One Step Beyond	$10	Stax 2030
7/14/73	**54**	20		6 Taylored in Silk	$8	Stax 3014
6/8/74	**182**	8		7 Super Taylor	$8	Stax 5509
3/13/76	**5**	28	●	8 Eargasm	$8	Columbia 33951

DEBUT DATE	PEAK POS	WKS CHR	GOLD	ARTIST — Album Title	$	Label & Number

TAYLOR, Johnnie — Cont'd

| 3/19/77 | 51 | 11 | 9 | Rated Extraordinaire .... | $8 | Columbia 34401 |
| 5/6/78 | 164 | 6 | 10 | Ever Ready .... | $8 | Columbia 35340 |

And I Panicked (9)
At Night Time (My Pillow Tells A Tale On Me) (7)
Bittersweet Love (10)
Can't Trust Your Neighbor (1)
Cheaper To Keep Her (6) **15**
Darling I Love You (7)
Did He Make Love To You (9)
Disco Lady (8) **1**
Don't Take My Sunshine (7)
Don't Touch Her Body (If You Can't Touch Her Mind) (8)
Ever Ready (10)
Fool Like Me (5)
Free (7)
Games People Play (3)
Give Me My Baby (10)
Hello Sundown (7)
Here I Go (Through These Changes Again) (9)

Hey Mister Melody Maker (10)
Hold On This Time (1,4)
I Ain't Particular (4)
I Am Somebody Part II (5) **39**
I Believe In You (You Believe In Me) (6) **11**
I Can Read Between The Lines (9)
I Could Never Be President (5) **86**
I Don't Wanna Lose You (5) **48**
I Gotta Keep Groovin' You (10)
I Love To Make Love When It's Raining (10)
I'd Rather Drink Muddy Water (1)
I'm Gonna Keep On Loving You (8)

I'm Just A Shoulder To Cry On (9)
I'm Not The Same Person (1,4)
I'm Trying (1)
I've Been Born Again (7) **78**
If I Had A Fight With Love (3)
If I Had It To Do Over Again (2)
It Ain't What You Do (It's How You Do It) (9)
It Don't Hurt Me Like It Used To (8)
It Don't Pay To Get Up In The Morning (7)
It's Amazing (3)
It's September (7)
It's Your Thing (3)
Jody's Got Your Girl And Gone (5) **28**
Just One Moment (7)
Keep On Dancing (10)

Love Bones (3,4) **43**
Love Is A Hurting Thing (3)
Love Is Better In The A.M. (Part 1) (9) **77**
Mr. Nobody Is Somebody Now (1,4)
Not Just Another Booty Song (9)
One Thing Wrong With My Woman (6)
Pardon Me Lady (2)
Part Time Love (2)
Party Life (5)
Payback Hurts (1)
Pick Up The Pieces (8)
Please Don't Stop (That Song From Playing) (8)
Poor Make Believer (1)
Running Out Of Lies (8)
Separation Line (3)
Somebody's Gettin' It (8) **33**

Somebody's Sleeping In My Bed (4) **95**
Soul Fillet (10)
Starting All Over Again (6)
Steal Away (4) **37**
Stop Giving People Hard Luck Stories (9)
Stormy (9)
Take Care Of Your Homework (1,4) **20**
Talk To Me (6)
Testify (I Wonna) (3,4) **36**
That Bone (7)
That's Where It's At (2)
This Bitter Earth (9)
Time After Time (5)
Try Me Tonight (7)
We're Getting Careless With Our Love (6) **34**
Where Can A Man Go From Here (2)

Where There's Smoke There's Fire (2)
Who Can I Turn To (3,4)
Who's Making Love (1,4) **5**
Will You Love Me Forever (1)
Woman Across The River (1)
You Can't Keep A Good Man Down (2)
You Can't Win With A Losing Hand (1)
You're Good For Me (2)
You're The Best In The World (8)
Your Love Is Rated X (9)

TAYLOR, Kate
Born on 8/15/49 in Boston. James Taylor's younger sister.

| 3/27/71 | 88 | 8 | | Sister Kate .... | $10 | Cotillion 9045 |

Ballad Of A Well Known Gun
Be That Way
Country Comfort

Do I Still Figure In Your Life
Handbags And Gladrags
Home Again

Jesus Is Just All Right (medley)

Lo And Behold (medley)
Look At Granny Run, Run

Sweet Honesty
Where You Lead

White Lightning
You Can Close Your Eyes

TAYLOR, Little Johnny
Born Johnny Young on 2/11/43 in Memphis. Blues singer/harmonica player. To Los Angeles in 1950. With Mighty Clouds Of Joy and Stars Of Bethel gospel groups. Duets with Ted Taylor (no relation) in the '70s.

| 11/9/63 | 140 | 2 | | Little Johnny Taylor .... | $30 | Galaxy 203 |

As Quick As I Can
Darling, Believe In Me
Part Time Love 19
She Tried To Understand

She's Yours, She's Mine, (She's Somebody Else's, Too)

Since I Found A New Love 78
Stay Sweet

Somewhere Down The Line
You Gotta Go On

What You Need Is A Ball

You'll Need Another Favor
You're The One (For Me)

TAYLOR, Livingston
Born on 11/21/50 in Boston. James Taylor's younger brother. Hosted TV's *This Week's Music* in 1984.

7/25/70	82	20	1	Livingston Taylor	$8	Atco 334
12/18/71+	147	10	2	Liv	$8	Capricorn 863
11/3/73	189	5	3	Over The Rainbow	$8	Capricorn 0114

Be That Way (2)
Blind (3)
Can't Get Back Home (1)
Carolina Day (1) **93**
Caroline (2)
Doctor Man (1)

Easy Prey (2)
Falling In Love With You (3)
Gentleman (2)
Get Out Of Bed (2) **97**
Good Friends (1)
Hush A Bye (1)

I Can Dream Of You (3)
I Just Can't Be Lonesome No More (2)
If I Needed Someone (3)
In My Reply (1)
Lady Tomorrow (3)

Let Me Go Down (3)
Lost In The Love Of You (1)
Loving Be My New Horizon (3)
May I Stay Around (2)
Mom, Dad (2)

Oh Hallelujah (3)
On Broadway (1)
Open Up Your Eyes (2)
Packet Of Good Times (1)
Pretty Woman (3)
Rodeo (3)

Sit On Back (1)
Six Days On The Road (1)
Somewhere Over The Rainbow (1)
Thank You Song (1)
Truck Driving Man (2)

TAYLOR, Mick
Born on 1/17/48 in Hereford, England. Guitarist with The Rolling Stones (1969-74).

| 7/21/79 | 119 | 5 | | Mick Taylor .... | $8 | Columbia 35076 |

A Minor (medley)
Alabama

Baby I Want You
Broken Hands

Giddy-Up
Leather Jacket

S.W.5
Slow Blues

Spanish (medley)

TAYLOR, R. Dean
Born in Toronto in 1939. First recorded for Parry in 1960. Co-wrote The Supremes' hit "Love Child."

| 2/20/71 | 198 | 1 | | I Think, Therefore I Am .... | $10 | Rare Earth 522 |

Ain't It A Sad Thing 66
Back Street
Fire And Rain

Gonna Give Her All The Love
I've Got
Gotta See Jane 67

Indiana Wants Me 5
Love's Your Name

Sunday Morning Coming Down

Two Of Us
Woman Alive

TAYLOR, Roger
Born on 7/26/49 in Norfolk, England. Drummer of Queen.

| 5/9/81 | 121 | 10 | | Fun In Space .... | $8 | Elektra 522 |

Airheads
Fun In Space

Future Management
Good Times Are Now

Interlude In Constantinople
Laugh Or Cry

Let's Get Crazy
Magic Is Loose

My Country - I & II
No Violins

T-BONES, The
A Joe Saraceno studio production. Also see Hamilton, Joe Frank & Reynolds.

| 2/12/66 | 75 | 12 | | No Matter What Shape (Your Stomach's In) ....[I] | $20 | Liberty 7439 |

Chiquita Banana
Don't Think Twice, It's All Right

Fever
Hole In The Wall
Let's Hang On

Lies
Moment Of Softness
My Headache's Gone

No Matter What Shape (Your Stomach's In) 3

Pizza Parlor
Sippin' 'N Chippin' 62
What's In The Bag, Goose

TCHAIKOVSKY, Bram
Rock quartet led by Bram (real name: Peter Bramall, earlier with The Motors). Formed in Lincolnshire, England.

6/30/79	36	18	1	Strange Man, Changed Man	$8	Polydor 6211
5/17/80	108	10	2	Pressure	$8	Polydor 6273
5/23/81	158	8	3	Funland	$8	Arista 4292

Bloodline (1)
Breaking Down The Walls Of Heartache (3)

Can't Give You Reasons (2)
Egyptian Mummies (3)
Girl Of My Dreams (1) **37**

Heart Of Stone (3)
Heartache (2)
Hollywood Nightmare (2)

I'm A Believer (1)
I'm The One That's Leaving (1)

Jeux Sans Frontieres (Game With No Rules) (2)
Lady From The U.S.A. (1)

Let's Dance (2)
Letter From The USA (1)
Lonely Dancer (1)

DEBUT DATE	PEAK POS	WKS CHR	GOLD	ARTIST — Album Title	$	Label & Number

TCHAIKOVSKY, Bram — Cont'd

Miracle Cure (3)	New York Paranoia (2)	Russians Are Coming (2)	Stand And Deliver (3)	Turn On The Light (1)	Why Does My Mother 'Phone
Missfortune (2)	Nobody Knows (1)	Sarah Smiles (1)	Strange Man, Changed Man	Used To Be My Used To Be	Me? (3)
Mister President (2)	Pressure (2)	Shall We Dance? (3)	(1)	(3)	
Model Girl (3)	Robber (1)	Soul Surrender (3)	Together My Love (3)		

T-CONNECTION

Group from Nassau, Bahamas: brothers Theophilus "T" (vocals, keyboards) and Kirkwood Coakley (bass, drums), David Mackey (guitar) and Anthony Flowers (drums).

5/14/77	109	11		1 Magic	$8	Dash 30004
1/21/78	139	11		2 On Fire	$8	Dash 30008
1/27/79	51	19		3 T-Connection	$8	Dash 30009
11/24/79	188	3		4 Totally Connected	$8	Dash 30014
3/21/81	138	8		5 Everything Is Cool	$8	Capitol 12128
3/20/82	123	10		6 Pure & Natural	$8	Capitol 12191

At Midnight (3) 56	Do What You Wanna Do	Go Back Home (1)	Let's Do It Today (4)	Party Night (6)	Spinnin' (5)
Best Of My Love (6)	(1) 46	Goombay Time (6)	Little More Love (6)	Peace Line (1)	That's Love (5)
Born To Boogie (4)	Don't Stop The Music (3)	Got To See My Lady (1)	Love Supreme (3)	Playin' Games (2)	Totally Connected (4)
Choosing (4)	Ecstasy (4)	Groove City (5)	Midnight Train (3)	Prisoner Of My Mind (2)	Watching You (2)
Coming Back For More (3)	Everything Is Cool (5)	Groove To Get Down (2)	Might As Well Dance (6)	Rushing Through The	We've Got A Good Thing (5)
Crazy Mixed Up World (1)	Funkannection (3)	Heaven In Your Eyes (5)	Monday Morning (1)	Crowd (6)	
Cush (2)	Funky Lady (3)	I Like Funkin' With You (4)	Mothers Love (1)	Saturday Night (3)	
Danger Zone (4)	Girl Watching (6)	Lady Of The Night (6)	On Fire (2)	Slippin' Away (6)	
Disco Magic (1)	Give Me Your Love (5)	Let Yourself Go (2)	Paradise (5)	Spend The Night With Me (5)	

TEARDROP EXPLODES

British new wave group — Julian Cope, lead singer.

2/28/81	156	6		1 Kilimanjaro	$8	Mercury 4016
2/6/82	176	4		2 Wilder	$8	Mercury 4035

...And The Fighting Takes	Brave Boys Keep Their	Falling Down Around Me (2)	Passionate Friend (2)	Seven Views Of Jerusalem	Thief Of Baghdad (1)
Over (2)	Promises (1)	Great Dominions (2)	Poppies In The Field (1)	(2)	Tiny Children (2)
Bent Out Of Shape (2)	Colours Fly Away (2)	Ha, Ha, I'm Drowning (1)	Pure Joy (2)	Sleeping Gas (1)	Treason (1)
Books (1)	Culture Bunker (2)	Like Leila Khaled Said (2)	Reward (1)	Suffocate (1)	Went Crazy (1)
					When I Dream (1)

TEARS FOR FEARS

British duo: Roland Orzabal (b: 8/22/61; vocals, guitar, keyboards) and Curt Smith (b: 6/24/61; vocals, bass). Adopted name from Arthur Janev's book *Prisoners Of Pain*. Assisted by Manny Elias (drums) and Ian Stanley (keyboards). Smith left duo by 1992.

5/7/83	73	69		1 The Hurting	$8	Mercury 811039
3/30/85	1⁵	83	▲⁴	2 Songs From The Big Chair	$8	Mercury 824300
10/7/89	8	34	▲	3 The Seeds Of Love	$8	Fontana 838730
4/4/92	53	13		4 Tears Roll Down (Greatest Hits 82-92) [G]	$12	Fontana 510939

Advice For The Young At	Everybody Wants To Rule	Ideas As Opiates (1)	Mothers Talk (2,4) 27	Standing On The Corner Of	Woman In Chains (3,4) 36
Heart (3,4) 89	The World (2,4) 1	Laid So Low (Tears Roll	Pale Shelter (1,4)	The Third World (3)	Working Hour (2)
Bad Man's Song (3)	Famous Last Words (3)	Down) (4)	Prisoner, The (1)	Start Of The Breakdown (1)	Year Of The Knife (3)
Broken (2)	Head Over Heels (2,4) 3	Listen (4)	Shout (2,4) 1	Suffer The Children (1)	
Change (1,4) 73	Hurting, The (1)	Mad World (1,4)	Sowing The Seeds Of Love	Swords And Knives (3)	
	I Believe (2,4)	Memories Fade (1)	(3,4) 2	Watch Me Bleed (1)	

TECHMASTER P.E.B.

Mysterious techno artist based in Florida.

2/29/92	132	30		Bass Computer	$12	Newtown 2208

CD includes bonus track

Bad Bass Mix	Bassgasm	Don't Stop The Music	Outerbass Mix	Scratchin' Megabass Mix	Time To Jam
Bass By Numbers	Computer Love	Euromusik	P.E.B. 500	Tech'in Slow N' Low	
Bass Computer	D.P.E.	I Like The Boom	Power Bass Ultra Mix	Techno Bass Beats	

TECHNOTRONIC

Dance outfit created by Belgian DJ/producer Thomas DeQuincy (real name: Jo Bogaert) and rapper Ya Kid K (born Manuella Barbara Komosi Maose Djogi in 1973 in Zaire; to Belgium at age 11). Includes London rapper MC Eric. Non-vocalist Felly, a model from Zaire, fronted the group for videos.

12/23/89+	10	55	▲	Pump Up The Jam - The Album	$8	SBK 93422

Come Back	Get Up! (Before The Night	Move This 6	Raw	Take It Slow	Tough
Come On	Is Over) 7	Pump Up The Jam 2	Rockin' Over The Beat 95	This Beat Is Technotronic	

TEENAGE FANCLUB

Alternative-pop quartet from Glasgow, Scotland: Norman Blake (vocals), Raymond McGinley, Gerard Love and Brendan O'Hare.

3/7/92	137	4		Bandwagonesque	$12	DGC 24461

Alcoholiday	December	I Don't Know	Metal Baby	Satan	Star Sign
Concept, The	Guiding Star	Is This Music?	Pet Rock	Sidewinder	What You Do To Me

TEENAGERS, The — see LYMON, Frankie

TEE SET, The

Dutch quintet: Peter Tetteroo (vocals), Hans Van Eijck, Dill Bennink, Franklin Madjid and Joop Blom.

5/16/70	158	6		Ma Belle Amie	$10	Colossus 1001

Bring A Little Sunshine	Here In My House	If You Do Believe In	Long Ago	Magic Lantern	Walk On By My Door
Charmaine	I Don't Want To Know	Love 81	Ma Belle Amie 5	Since I Lost Your Love	What Can I Do
Finally In Love Again					

TE KANAWA, Kiri

Operatic soprano — native of New Zealand.

12/7/85+	136	16		Blue Skies	$8	London 414666

with Nelson Riddle & His Orchestra; features Pop standards by Cole Porter, Richard Rodgers, Irving Berlin and others

DEBUT DATE	PEAK POS	WKS CHR	G O L D	ARTIST — Album Title	$	Label & Number

TE KANAWA, Kiri — Cont'd

Blue Skies				Here's That Rainy Day	I Didn't Know What Time It	It Might As Well Be Spring	Speak Low	When I Grow Too Old To
Folks Who Live On The Hill				How High The Moon	Was	So In Love	True Love	Dream
Gone With The Wind								Yesterdays

TEMPLE OF THE DOG

Gathering of Seattle musicians in tribute to Andrew Wood, lead singer of Mother Love Bone, who died of a heroin overdose in 1990. Features Stone Gossard, Jeff Ament, Eddie Vedder and Mike McCready of Pearl Jam with Chris Cornell and Matt Cameron of Soundgarden. Gossard and Ament were members of Mother Love Bone.

6/27/92	5	33↑▲		Temple Of The Dog...	$12	A&M 5350

All Night Thing	Four Walled World	Pushin Forward Back	Say Hello 2 Heaven	Wooden Jesus
Call Me A Dog	Hunger Strike	Reach Down	Times Of Trouble	Your Saviour

TEMPO, Nino, & April Stevens

Nino (b: Antonio Lo Tempio on 1/6/35) and sister April (b: Carol Lo Tempio on 4/29/36) from Niagara Falls, New York. Prior to teaming up, Nino was a session saxophonist and April had recorded solo.

11/23/63+	48	14		Deep Purple	$20	Atco 156

Baby Weemus	I've Been Carrying A Torch	Indian Love Call	Shine On Harvest Moon	True Love
Deep Purple 1	For You So Long That I	It's Pretty Funny	**Sweet And Lovely 77**	(We'll Always Be) Together
Four WalledWorld	Burned A Great Big Hole	One Dozen Roses	Tears Of Sorrow	Your Saviour
	In My	Paradise		

★★10★★ TEMPTATIONS, The

Detroit soul group formed in 1960. Consisted of Eddie Kendricks (d: 10/5/92 of lung cancer at age 52). Paul Williams (d: 8/17/73), Melvin Franklin, Otis Williams and Elbridge Bryant, who was replaced by David Ruffin in 1964. Originally called the Primes and Elgins, first recorded for Miracle in 1961. Ruffin (d: 6/1/91 of drug overdose at age 50; cousin of Billy Stewart) replaced by Dennis Edwards (ex-Contours) in 1968. Kendricks and Paul Williams left in 1971, replaced by Ricky Owens (ex-Vibrations) and Richard Street. Owens left in 1971, replaced by Damon Harris. Harris left in 1975, replaced by Glenn Leonard. Edwards left group, 1977-79, replaced by Louis Price. Ali Ollie Woodson replaced Edwards from 1984-87. 1988 lineup: Williams, Franklin, Street, Edwards and Ron Tyson. Recognized as America's all-time favorite soul group. Inducted into the Rock and Roll Hall of Fame in 1989.

DEBUT DATE	PEAK POS	WKS CHR		ARTIST — Album Title	$	Label & Number
5/9/64	95	11	1	Meet The Temptations..	$30	Gordy 911
4/3/65	35	26	2	The Temptations Sing Smokey	$25	Gordy 912
				tribute to songwriter/producer Smokey Robinson		
11/27/65+	11	37	3	Temptin' Temptations	$20	Gordy 914
7/9/66	12	35	4	Gettin' Ready	$20	Gordy 918
12/17/66+	5	120	5	The Temptations Greatest Hits .... [G]	$15	Gordy 919
4/1/67	10	51	6	The Temptations Live!... [L]	$15	Gordy 921
8/12/67	7	36	7	With A Lot O' Soul...	$15	Gordy 922
12/23/67+	13	44	8	The Temptations in a Mellow Mood	$15	Gordy 924
5/25/68	13	41	9	Wish It Would Rain..	$15	Gordy 927
11/30/68+	2¹	32	10	Diana Ross & the Supremes Join the Temptations *	$12	Motown 679
12/28/68+	1¹	34	11	TCB * .... [TV]	$15	Motown 682
1/4/69	15	24	12	Live At The Copa... [L]	$12	Gordy 938
3/15/69	4	40	13	Cloud Nine	$12	Gordy 939
8/9/69	24	16	14	The Temptations Show .... [TV]	$12	Gordy 933
				with guests Kaye Stevens and George Kirby ("When I Lay My Burdens Down")		
10/11/69	5	41	15	Puzzle People	$12	Gordy 949
10/25/69	28	18	16	Together *	$12	Motown 692
12/6/69	38	12	17	On Broadway * .... [TV]	$12	Motown 699
				*DIANA ROSS & THE SUPREMES with THE TEMPTATIONS		
4/4/70	9	30	18	Psychedelic Shack	$10	Gordy 947
8/22/70	21	18	19	Live at London's Talk of The Town... [L]	$10	Gordy 953
9/26/70	15	70	20	Temptations Greatest Hits II .... [G]	$10	Gordy 954
5/8/71	16	35	21	Sky's The Limit	$10	Gordy 957
1/29/72	24	22	22	Solid Rock	$10	Gordy 961
8/19/72	2²	44	23	All Directions	$10	Gordy 962
3/10/73	7	28	24	Masterpiece...	$10	Gordy 965
9/15/73	65	26	25	Anthology .... [G]	$18	Motown 782 [3]
12/29/73+	19	22	26	1990	$10	Gordy 966
2/8/75	13	36	27	A Song For You	$10	Gordy 969
11/29/75	40	20	28	House Party	$10	Gordy 973
4/3/76	29	20	29	Wings Of Love	$10	Gordy 971
9/11/76	53	14	30	The Temptations Do The Temptations	$10	Gordy 975
12/10/77+	113	13	31	Hear To Tempt You	$10	Atlantic 19143
5/17/80	45	14	32	Power	$10	Gordy 994
8/29/81	119	9	33	The Temptations	$10	Gordy 1006
5/1/82	37	18	34	Reunion	$8	Gordy 6032
				Ruffin and Kendricks return for this album		
3/19/83	159	9	35	Surface Thrills	$8	Gordy 6085
4/21/84	152	9	36	Back To Basics	$8	Gordy 6085
11/17/84+	55	34	37	Truly For You	$8	Gordy 6119
1/25/86	146	10	38	Touch Me	$8	Gordy 6164
5/17/86	140	16	39	25th Anniversary .... [K]	$12	Motown 5389 [2]
				includes an 8-page booklet		
8/2/86	74	33	40	To Be Continued	$8	Gordy 6207
10/24/87	112	21	41	Together Again	$8	Motown 6246

DEBUT DATE	PEAK POS	WKS CHR	GOLD	ARTIST — Album Title	$	Label & Number

TEMPTATIONS, The — Cont'd

Aiming At Your Heart (33) **67**
Ain't No Justice (26)
Ain't No Mountain High Enough (10)
Ain't No Sun Since You've Been Gone (7)
Ain't No Sunshine (22)
Ain't Nothing Like The Real Thing (16)
Ain't Too Proud To Beg (4,5,6,11,14,19,25,39) **13**
All I Need (7,25) **8**
Backstage (34)
Baby, Baby I Need You (2,6)
Ball Of Confusion (That's What The World Is Today) (20,25) **3**
Battle Song (I'm The One) (36)
Beauty Is Only Skin Deep (5,6,14,19,25) **3**
Best Of Both Worlds (33)
Best Things In Life Are Free (medley) (14)
Born To Love You (3)
BringYourBodyHere (Exercise Chant) (35)
Broadway Medley (17)
○Can We Come And Share In Love (31)
○Can't Take My Eyes Off You (16)
○Can't You See Sweet Thing (32)
○Check Yourself (1)
○China Doll (29)
○Cindy (9)
○**Cloud Nine** (13,14,19,20,25,39) **6**
○Come To Me (39)
Darling, Stand By Me (Song For My Woman) (28)
Deeper Than Love (38)
○Do You Know The Way To San Jose (medley) (11)
○Do You Really Love Your Baby (38)
○Do You Wanna Go With Me (41)
○Do Your Thing (23)
○Don't Break Your Promise To Me (38)
○Don't Let Him Take Your Love From Me (13)
○**Don't Let The Joneses Get You Down** (15,19,20,25) **20**
○**Don't Look Back** (3,5,6,25,39) **83**
○Don't Send Me Away (7)
○Dream Come True (1)
○Dream World (Wings Of Love) (29)
○End Of Our Road (22)
○Every Time I Close My Eyes (41)
○Everybody Needs Love (3)
○Everything Is Going To Be Alright (19)
○Evil Woman (Gonna Take Your Love) (33)
○Fading Away (4,6)
○Fan The Flame (9)
○Farewell My Love (1)
○Fiddler On The Roof Medley (17)

Fine Mess (40)
Firefly (27)
First Time Ever (I Saw Your Face) (23)
For Better Or Worse (16)
For Once In My Life (8,11,12,14)
Friendship Train (18)
Funky Broadway (10,17)
Funky Music Sho Nuff Turns Me On (23,25)
Further You Look, The Less You See (1,39)
Get Ready (4,5,6,11,12,14,19,25,39) **29**
Girl (Why You Wanna Make Me Blue) (3,5,6,14,19,25) **26**
Girl's Alright With Me (3,5,6,25)
Girls (They Like It) (40)
G.I.T. On Broadway (17)
Givehersomeattention (38)
Glasshouse (27,39) **37**
Go For It (32)
Gonna Give Her All The Love I've Got (9)
Gonna Keep On Tryin' Till I Win Your Love (13,21)
Happy People (27) **40**
He Who Picks A Rose (9)
Heavenly (26) **43**
Hello Young Lovers (8,11,12,14)
Hey Girl (13)
Hey Girl (I Like Your Style) (24) **35**
Hey Jude (15)
Hollywood (36)
How Can I Resist Your Love (32)
How Can You Say That It's Over (37)
Hum Along And Dance (18)
Hurry Tomorrow (24)
I Ain't Got Nothin' (23,25)
I Can't Get Next To You (15,19,20,25,39) **1**
I Could Never Love Another (After Loving You) (9,12,20,25) **13**
I Could Never Stop Loving You (31)
I Got Your Number (41)
I Gotta Find A Way (To Get You Back) (13)
I Gotta Know Now (3)
I Heard It Through The Grapevine (13)
(I Know) I'm Losing You (7,11,12,19,20,25) **8**
I Need You (26)
I Need Your Lovin' (12)
I Second That Emotion (10)
I Truly, Truly Believe (9,12,25)
I Want A Love I Can See (1,6,39)
I Wish It Would Rain (9,12,20,25) **4**
I Wish You Love (6)
I Wonder Who She's Seeing Now (41)
I'll Be Doggone (16)
I'll Be In Trouble (3,5,6,25) **33**

I'll Keep My Light In My Window (37)
I'll Take You (30)
I'll Try Something New (10) **25**
I'm A Bachelor (27)
I'm Coming Home (32)
I'm Fascinated (38)
I'm Gonna Make You Love Me (10,19,25) **2**
I'm On Fire (Body Song) (30)
I'm Ready For Love (8)
I'm The Exception To The Rule (21)
I've Been Good To You (4)
I've Got To Be Me (14,19)
I've Never Been To Me (4)
I've Passed This Way Before (9)
If I Didn't Care (medley) (14)
If I Don't Love You This Way (28)
Impossible Dream (8,10,11,12,19,25)
In A Lifetime (31)
Is There Anybody Else (30)
Isn't She Pretty (1)
Isn't The Night Fantastic (32,36)
It Don't Have To Be This Way (39)
It's A Lonely World Without Your Love (4)
It's Growing (2,5,25) **18**
It's Just A Matter Of Time (28)
It's Summer (18,22) **51**
It's Time For Love (31)
It's Your Thing (32)
Johnny Porter (28)
Just Ain't Havin' Fun (33)
Just Another Lonely Night (3)
Just Let Me Know (1)
Just My Imagination (Running Away With Me) (21,25,39) **1**
Just One Last Look (7)
Just To Keep You In My Life (37)
Keep Holding On (54) **54**
Lady Soul (40) **47**
Law Of The Land (24)
Let Me Count The Ways (I Love You) (30)
Let The Sunshine In (medley) (17)
Let Your Hair Down (26) **27**
Let's Live In Peace (31)
Life (medley) (14)
Life Of A Cowboy (33)
Little Green Apples (15)
Little Miss Sweetness (4)
Little Things (41)
Lock It In The Pocket (34)
(Loneliness Made Me Realize) It's You That I Need (7,20,25) **14**
Lonely, Lonely Man Am I (4)
Look What You Started (41)
Love Can Be Anything (Can't Nothing Be Love But Love) (21)
Love Is A Hurtin' Thing (13)
Love Me Right (40)
Love On My Mind Tonight (35) **88**

Love Woke Me Up This Morning (23,25)
Lucky (41)
Ma (24)
Made In America (35)
Magic (38)
Make Me Believe In Love Again (36)
Malteds Over Manhattan (17)
Man (21)
Mary Ann (29)
Masterpiece (24) **7**
May I Have This Dance (1)
Memories (27,37)
Message From A Black Man (15)
Message To The World (40)
Miss Busy Body (Get Your Body Busy) (36)
Money's Hard To Get (34)
More Love, Your Love (40)
More On The Inside (34)
Mother Nature (23,25) **92**
My Baby (3,5,6,25) **13**
My Girl (2,5,6,14,16,19,25,39) **1**
My Love Is True (Truly For You) (37)
1990 (26)
No Man Can Love Her Like I Do (9)
No More Water In The Well (7)
Not Now, I'll Tell You Later (4)
Now That You've Won Me (7)
Oh Lover (38)
Oh, What A Night (33)
Ol' Man River (6,8,14,25)
Old Folks (medley) (14)
One Man Woman (35)
Open Their Eyes (33)
Outlaw (36)
Papa Was A Rollin' Stone (23,25,39) **1**
Paradise (1)
Paradise (29)
Place In The Sun (10)
Plastic Man (24) **40**
Please Return Your Love To Me (9,12,20,25) **26**
Power (32,39) **43**
Prophet, The (27)
Psychedelic Shack (18,20,25) **7**
Put Us Together Again (40)
Put Your Foot Down (41)
Put Your Trust In Me, Baby (30)
Read Between The Lines (31)
Ready, Willing & Able (33)
Respect (11)
Rhythm Of Life (17)
Romeo & Juliet (A Time For Us), Love Theme From (19)
Run Away Child, Running Wild (13,14,19,20,25) **6**
Run Charlie Run (23)
Running (37)
Running Away (Ain't Gonna Help You) (15)
Sail Away (36) **54**
Save My Love For A Rainy Day (7)
Say You (4)
Seeker, The (35)
Set Your Love Right (37)

Shadow Of Your Love (32)
Shakey Ground (27) **26**
She Got Tired Of Loving Me (38)
She's All I've Got (31)
Show Me Your Love (35)
Since I Lost My Baby (3,5,25,39) **17**
Since I've Lost You (15)
Sing A Simple Song (16)
Slave (15)
Slow Down Heart (1)
Smiling Faces Sometimes (21)
Smooth Sailing (From Now On) (22)
Snake In The Grass (31)
So Much Joy (39)
Somebody's Keepin' Score (14)
Someone (40)
Somewhere (8)
Song For You (27)
Sorry Is A Sorry Word (7)
Soulmate (39)
Standing On The Top-Part 1 (34) **66**
Stop The War Now (22)
Stop The World Right Here (I Wanna Get Off) (36)
Struck By Lightning Twice (32)
Stubborn Kind Of Fellow (16)
Student Mountie (17)
Superstar (Remember How You Got Where You Are) (22,25) **18**
Surface Thrills (35)
Swanee (12,14)
Sweet Gypsy Jane (29)
Sweet Inspiration (10)
Sweetness In The Dark (29)
T.C.B. (17)
Take A Look Around (22) **30**
Take A Stroll Thru Your Mind (18)
Taste Of Honey (8,11)
Tear From A Woman's Eyes (9)
10 X 10 (41)
Thanks To You (39)
That's Life (8)
That's The Way Love Is (15)
Then (10)
There's No Stopping (Til We Set The Whole World Rockin') (30)
Think For Yourself (31)
This Guy's In Love With You (10,19)
This Is My Beloved (9)
Throw A Farewell Kiss (21)
To Be Continued (40)
Too Busy Thinking About My Baby (4)
Touch Me (38)
Treat Her Like A Lady (37,39) **48**
Truly Yours (39)
Try It Baby (10,14)
Try To Remember (8,25)
Two Sides To Love (7)
Ungena Za Ulimwengu (Unite The World) (21) **33**
Up The Creek (Without A Paddle) (9) **94**

Uptight (Everything's Alright) (16)
War (18)
Way Over There (2)
Way You Do The Things You Do (1,2,5,25) **11**
Way You Do The Things You Do (1)
Ways Of A Grown Up Man (28)
Weight, The (16) **46**
What A Way To Put It (35)
What Else (33)
What It Is? (22)
What Love Has Joined Together (2,6)
What Now My Love (6,8)
What You Need Most (I Do Best Of All) (28)
What's So Good About Good Bye (4)
Wherever I Lay My Hat (That's My Home) (39)
Who Are You (And What Are You Doing The Rest Of Your Life) (30)
Who Can I Turn To (When Nobody Needs Me) (8)
Who You Gonna Run To (4)
Who's Lovin' You (2)
Why Can't You And Me Get Together (30)
Why Did She Have To Leave Me (Why Did She Have To Go) (13)
Why Did You Leave Me Darling (9)
Why (Must We Fall In Love) (16)
With These Hands (8,12)
World Of You, Love And Music (28)
Yesterday (medley) (6)
You Beat Me To The Punch (2)
You Better Beware (34)
(You Can) Depend On Me (2)
You Can't Stop A Man In Love (28)
You Don't Love Me No More (15)
You Make Your Own Heaven And Hell Right Here On Earth (18)
You Need Love Like I Do (Don't You) (18)
You'll Lose A Precious Love (2,6)
You're My Everything (7,12,14,19,20,25) **6**
You're Not An Ordinary Girl (4)
You're The One (40)
You're The One I Need (3)
You've Got My Soul On Fire (26) **74**
You've Got To Earn It (3)
You've Really Got A Hold On Me (2)
Your Lovin' Is Magic (33)
Your Wonderful Love (1)
Zoom (26)

10cc

English art-rock group which evolved from Hotlegs. Consisted of Eric Stewart (guitar), Graham Gouldman (bass), Lol Creme (guitar, keyboards) and Kevin Godley (drums). Stewart and Gouldman were members of The Mindbenders. Godley and Creme left in 1976, replaced by drummer Paul Burgess. Added members Rick Fenn, Stuart Tosh and Duncan MacKay in 1978. Gouldman later in duo Wax. Also see Godley & Creme.

DEBUT DATE	PEAK POS	WKS CHR		ARTIST — Album Title	$	Label & Number
8/10/74	**81**	14	1	Sheet Music	**$10**	UK 53107
4/19/75	**15**	25	2	The Original Soundtrack	**$10**	Mercury 1029
9/13/75	**161**	5	3	100cc ....[K]	**$10**	UK 53110
2/14/76	**47**	13	4	How Dare You!	**$10**	Mercury 1061
5/14/77	**31**	20	5	Deceptive Bends	**$10**	Mercury 3702
12/24/77+	**146**	6	6	Live And Let Live ....[L]	**$12**	Mercury 8600 [2]
10/14/78	**69**	17	7	Bloody Tourists	**$8**	Polydor 6161
12/22/79+	**188**	4	8	Greatest Hits 1972-1978 ....[G]	**$8**	Polydor 6244
5/17/80	**180**	2	9	Look Hear?	**$8**	Warner 3442

DEBUT DATE	PEAK POS	WKS CHR	GOLD	ARTIST — Album Title	$	Label & Number

10cc — Cont'd

Anonymous Alcoholic (7)
Art For Art's Sake (4,6,8) **83**
Baron Samedi (1)
Blackmail (2)
Brand New Day (2)
Clockwork Creep (1)
Dean And I (3,8)
Don't Hang Up (4)
Don't Send We Back (9)
Donna (3,8)
Dressed To Kill (9)
Everything You've Wanted To Know About !!! (Exclamation Marks) (7)

Feel The Benefit (5,6)
Film Of My Love (2)
Flying Junk (2)
For You And I (7) **85**
Fresh Air For My Momma (3)
From Rochdale To Ocho Rios (7)
Good Morning Judge (5,6,8) **69**
Head Room (4)
Honeymoon With B Troop (5,6)
Hotel (1)
How Dare You (4)
How'm I Ever Gonna Say Goodbye (4)

I Bought A Flat Guitar Tutor (5)
I Hate To Eat Alone (9)
I Took You Home (9)
I Wanna Rule The World (4)
I'm Mandy Fly Me (4,6,8) **60**
I'm Not In Love (2,6,8) **2**
Iceberg (4)
It Doesn't Matter At All (9)
L.A. Inflatable (9)
Last Night (7)
Latin Blues (medley) (5)
Lazy Ways (4)
Life Is A Minestrone (2,8)
Life Line (7)

Lovers Anonymous (9)
Marriage Bureau Rendezvous (5,6)
Modern Man Blues (5,6)
Oh! Effendi (1)
Old Mister Time (7)
Old Wild Men (1,3)
One Two Five (9)
People In Love (5,6) **40**
Reds In My Bed (7)
Reminisce And Speculation (medley) (5)
Rock 'N' Roll Lullaby (4)
Rubber Bullets (3,8) **73**
Sacro-Iliac, The (1)

Second Sitting For The Last Supper (2,6)
Ships Don't Disappear In The Night (Do They?) (6)
Shock On The Tube (Don't Want Love) (7)
Silly Love (1,3,8)
Somewhere In Hollywood (1,3)
Strange Lover (9)
Take These Chains (7)
Things We Do For Love (5,6,8) **5**
Tokyo (1)
Une Nuit A Paris Medley (2)
Wall Street Shuffle (1,3,6,8)

Waterfall (3,6)
Welcome To The World (9)
Worst Band In The World (1,3)
You've Got A Cold (5,6)

TENNILLE, Toni
Born on 5/8/43 in Montgomery, Alabama. Half of Captain & Tennille duo.

6/9/84	142	11		1 More Than You Know	$8	Mirage 90162
				features standards from the '30s and '40s		
12/26/87	198	2		2 All Of Me	$8	Gaia 139001
				Toni sings classics from 1929-48		

All Of Me (2)
But Not For Me (1)
Can't Help Lovin' That Man Of Mine (1)
Day Dream (1)

Do It Again (1)
Do Nothing 'Til You Hear From Me (1)
Dream (2)
Easy Street (2)

Guess Who I Saw Today? (1)
Happiness Is Just A Thing Called Joe (2)
Honeysuckle Rose (2)
How High The Moon (2)

I Got It Bad And That Ain't Good (1)
I'll Be Tired Of You (2)
Let's Do It (1)
Moon Glow (2)

More Than You Know (1)
Nature Boy (2)
Our Love Is Here To Stay (1)
They All Laughed (2)
Very Thought Of You (2)

10,000 MANIACS
Jamestown, New York group formed in 1981: Natalie Merchant (vocals), Robert Buck (guitar), Dennis Drew (keyboards), Steven Gustafson (bass), Jerome Augustyniak (drums) and John Lombardo (guitar). Lombardo left in July 1986.

9/19/87+	37	77 ▲		1 In My Tribe	$8	Elektra 60738
6/3/89	13	28 ●		2 Blind Man's Zoo	$8	Elektra 60815
				above 2 produced by Peter Asher (Peter & Gordon)		
11/3/90	102	10		3 Hope Chest - The Fredonia Recordings 1982-1983 .... [E]	$12	Elektra 60962
				remixes of early songs recorded at Fredonia State University in New York		
10/17/92	28↑	17↑ ●		4 Our Time In Eden	$12	Elektra 61385

Anthem For Doomed Youth (3)
Big Parade (2)
Campfire Song (1)
Candy Everybody Wants (4)
Cherry Tree (1)
Circle Dream (4)
City Of Angels (1)
Daktari (3)
Death Of Manolete (3)

Don't Talk (1)
Dust Bowl (2)
Eat For Two (2)
Eden (4)
Few And Far Between (4)
Gold Rush Brides (4)
Grey Victory (3)
Groove Dub (3)
Gun Shy (1)
Hateful Hate (2)

Headstrong (2)
Hey Jack Kerouac (1)
How You've Grown (4)
I'm Not The Man (4)
If You Intend (4)
Jezebel (4)
Jubilee (3)
Katrina's Fair (3)
Latin One (3)
Like The Weather (1) **68**

Lion's Share (2)
My Mother The War (3)
My Sister Rose (1)
National Education Week (3)
Noah's Dove (4)
Orange (3)
Painted Desert (1)
Peace Train (1)
Pit Viper (3)
Planned Obsolescence (3)

Please Forgive Us (2)
Poison In The Well (2)
Poor De Chirico (3)
Stockton Gala Days (4)
Tension (3)
These Are Days (4) **66**
Tolerance (4)
Trouble Me (2) **44**
Verdi Cries (1)

What's The Matter Here? (1) **80**
You Happy Puppet (2)

TEN WHEEL DRIVE With Genya Ravan
Ten-member, jazz-rock ensemble led by vocalist Genya Ravan. Michael Zager was a member, 1968-73.

1/10/70	151	16		1 Construction #1	$10	Polydor 4008
8/1/70	161	8		2 Brief Replies	$10	Polydor 4024
6/19/71	190	5		3 Peculiar Friends	$10	Polydor 4062

Ain't Gonna Happen (1)
Brief Replies (2)
Candy Man Blues (1)
Come Live With Me (2)
Down In The Cold (3)

Eye Of The Needle (1)
Fourteenth Street (I Can't Get Together) (3)
House In Central Park (1)

How Long Before I'm Gone (2)
I Am A Want Ad (1)
I Had Him Down (3)
Interlude: A View Of Soft (2)

Lapidary (1)
Last Of The Line (2)
Love Me (3)
Morning Much Better (2) **74**
Night I Got Out Of Jail (3)

No Next Time (3)
Peculiar Friends (3)
Pickpocket, The (3)
Polar Bear Rug (1)
Pulse (2)

Shootin' The Breeze (3)
Stay With Me (2)
Tightrope (1)

★★280★★ TEN YEARS AFTER
British blues-rock quartet formed in 1967: Alvin Lee (b: 12/19/44, Nottingham, England; vocals, guitar), Leo Lyons (bass), Chick Churchill (keyboards) and Ric Lee (drums). Inactive as band from 1975-87.

8/10/68	115	14		1 Undead .... [L]	$15	Deram 18016
2/22/69	61	18		2 Stonedhenge	$15	Deram 18021
8/30/69	20	23		3 SSSSH	$15	Deram 18029
4/18/70	14	30		4 Cricklewood Green	$8	Deram 18038
12/12/70+	21	16		5 Watt	$8	Deram 18050
8/28/71	17	26 ▲		6 A Space In Time	$8	Columbia 30801
4/8/72	55	18		7 Alvin Lee & Company .... [K]	$8	Deram 18064
10/14/72	43	25		8 Rock & Roll Music To The World	$8	Columbia 31779
6/23/73	39	21		9 Recorded Live .... [L]	$10	Columbia 32290 [2]
5/18/74	81	14		10 Positive Vibrations	$8	Columbia 32851
7/19/75	174	5		11 Goin' Home! Their Greatest Hits ... [K]	$8	Deram 18072
				includes "I'm Going Home" (recorded live at Woodstock)		
9/16/89	120	10		12 About Time	$8	Chrysalis 21722

As The Sun Still Burns Away (4)
Baby Won't You Let Me Rock 'N Roll You (6) **61**
Bad Blood (12)
Bad Scene (3)
Band With No Name (5)
Boogie On (7)
Choo Choo Mama (8,9) **89**

Circles (4)
Classical Thing (9)
Convention Prevention (8)
Extension On One Chord (9)
Faro (2)
50,000 Miles Beneath My Brain (4)
Going Back To Birmingham (10)

Going To Chicago (12)
Going To Try (2,11)
Gonna Run (5)
Good Morning Little Schoolgirl (3,9)
Hard Monkeys (6)
Hear Me Calling (2,11)
Help Me (9)
Here They Come (6)

Highway Of Love (12)
Hobbit (9)
Hold Me Tight (7)
I Can't Keep From Cryin' Sometimes Pt. I & II (9)
I Can't Live Without Lydia (2)
I Don't Know That You Don't Know My Name (3)
I Get All Shook Up (12)

I May Be Wrong, But I Won't Be Wrong Always (1)
I Say Yeah (5)
I Wanted To Boogie (10)
I Woke Up This Morning (3,11)
I'd Love To Change The World (6) **40**
I'm Coming On (5)

I'm Going Home (1,9,11)
I've Been There Too (6)
If You Should Love Me (5)
It's Getting Harder (10)
Let The Sky Fall (1)
Let's Shake It Up (12)
Look Into My Life (10)
Look Me Straight Into The Eyes (10)

DEBUT DATE	PEAK POS	WKS CHR	GOLD	ARTIST — Album Title	$	Label & Number

TEN YEARS AFTER — Cont'd

Love Like A Man (4,11) *98*
Me And My Baby (4)
My Baby Left Me (5)
No Title (2,11)
Nowhere To Run (10)
Once There Was A Time (6)
One Of These Days (6,9)
Outside My Window (12)
Over The Hill (6)
Portable People (7)

Positive Vibrations (10)
Religion (8)
Rock & Roll Music To The World (4)
Rock Your Mama (7)
Sad Song (2)
Saturday Night (12)
Scat Thing (4)
Shantung Cabbage (medley) (1)

She Lies In The Morning (5)
Silly Thing (9)
Skoobly-Oobly-Doobob (2)
Slow Blues In "C" (9)
Sounds, The (7)
Speed Kills (2)
Spider In My Web (1)
Standing At The Crossroads (7)
Standing At The Station (8)

Stomp, The (3)
Stone Me (10)
Stoned Woman (3)
Sugar The Road (4)
Summertime (medley) (1)
Sweet Little Sixteen (5)
Think About The Times (5)
Three Blind Mice (2)
Tomorrow I'll Be Out Of Town (8)

Turned Off T.V. Blues (8)
Two Time Mama (3)
Uncle Jam (6)
Victim Of Circumstance (12)
Waiting For The Judgment Day (12)
Wild Is The River (12)
Without You (10)
Woman Trouble (2)
Woodchopper's Ball (1,11)

Working In A Parking Lot (12)
Working On The Road (4)
Year 3,000 Blues (4)
You Can't Win Them All (8)
You Give Me Loving (8,9)
You're Driving Me Crazy (10)

TEPPER, Robert
Rock singer from Baylor, New Jersey.

| 4/19/86 | 144 | 8 | | No Easy Way Out | $8 | Scotti Br. 40128 |

Angel Of The City
Domination

Don't Walk Away *85*
Hopeless Romantic

If That's What You Call Lovin'

No Easy Way Out *22*
Restless World

Soul Survivor
Your Love Hurts

TERMINATOR X
Norman Rogers — member of rap group Public Enemy. New York native.

| 5/25/91 | 97 | 11 | | Terminator X & The Valley Of The Jeep Beets [V] | $12 | P.R.O. Div. 46896 |

Terminator X produces 13 tracks by 10 artists

Ain't Gut Nuttin' [Chief Groovy Loo]
Back To The Scene Of The Bass [Interrogators]

Blues, The [Andreas 13]
Buck Whylin' [Chuck D with Sister Souljah]
Can't Take My Style

DJ Is The Selector [Dubmaster]
High Priest Of Turbulence

Homey Don't Play Dat [Bonnie 'N' Clyde]
Juvenile Delinquintz [Juvenile Delinquintz]

No Further [Section 8]
Run That Go-Power Thang [Spacey B. Experience]

Vendetta...The Big Getback
Wanna Be Dancin' [Celo]

TERRELL, Tammi — see GAYE, Marvin

TERRY, Sonny, & Brownie McGhee
Blues duo: Terry (harmonica) was born Saunders Terrell on 10/24/11 in Greensboro, Georgia. Blinded as a youth; died on 3/11/86. McGhee was born Walter Brown McGhee on 11/30/15 in Knoxville, Tennessee.

| 4/7/73 | 185 | 5 | | Sonny & Brownie | $12 | A&M 4379 |

Battle Is Over (But The War Goes On)
Big Wind (Is A' Comin')

Bring It On Home To Me
God And Man

Jesus Gonna Make It Alright
On The Road Again
People Get Ready

Sail Away
Sonny's Thing

Walkin' My Blues Away
White Boy Lost In The Blues

You Bring Out The Boogie In Me

TERRY, Tony
Born 3/12/64 in Pinehurst, North Carolina and raised in Washington, D.C. Soul-funk singer. Former backing vocalist for Sweet Sensation and Boogie Boys.

| 1/9/88 | 151 | 20 | | 1 Forever Yours | $8 | Epic 40890 |
| 6/22/91 | 184 | 6 | | 2 Tony Terry | $12 | Epic 45015 |

Baby Love (2)
Bad Girl (2)
Come Home With Me (2)
Day Dreaming (1)

Everlasting Love (2) *81*
Forever Yours (1) *80*
Friends And Lovers (2)
Fulltime Girl (1)

Head Over Heels (2)
Here With Me (1)
Let Me Love You (2)
Lovey Dovey (1)

Read My Mind (2)
She's Fly (1) *80*
That Kind Of Guy (2)
Tongue Tied (1)

Up & Down Love (1)
Wassup Wit U (1)
What Would It Take (1)
With You (2) *14*

Young Love (1)

TESH, John
New Age multi-instrumentalist from Long Island, New York. Co-host of TV's *Entertainment Tonight* since 1986. Appeared in the film *Shocker*. Married actress Connie Sellecca on 4/4/92.

| 12/12/92+ | 50 | 5 | | A Romantic Christmas [X-I] | $12 | GTS 4569 |

3 tracks feature the Paulist Boy Choristers of California; Christmas charts: 9/92

Bring A Torch, Jeannette, Isabella
Christmas Song (Chestnuts Roasting On An Open Fire)

Coventry Carol
First Noel
Gesu Bambino
Gloria In Excelsis Deo

Homecoming, The
In A Child's Eyes
It Came Upon A Midnight Clear

Jesu, Joy Of Man's Desiring
O Come, All Ye Faithful
O Holy Night
O Little Town Of Bethlehem

Panis Angelicus
Silent Night, Holy Night
We Three Kings Of Orient Are

TESLA
Sacramento hard-rock quintet: Jeff Keith (vocals), Frank Hannon, Tommy Skeoch, Brian Wheat and Troy Lucketta. Band named after the inventor of radio, Nikola Tesla.

1/31/87	32	61	▲	1 Mechanical Resonance	$8	Geffen 24120
2/18/89	18	67	▲	2 The Great Radio Controversy	$8	Geffen 24224
12/1/90+	12	48	▲	3 Five Man Acoustical Jam [L]	$12	Geffen 24311

recorded July 2, 1990 at the Trocadero in Philadelphia; title is a pun on Five Man Electrical Band who hit #3 with "Signs" in 1971

| 9/28/91 | 13 | 56 | ● | 4 Psychotic Supper | $12 | Geffen 24424 |

Be A Man (2)
Before My Eyes (1,3)
Call It What You Want (4)
Can't Stop (4)
Change In The Weather (4)
Changes (1)
Cover Queen (4)
Cumin' Atcha Live (1,3)
Did It For The Money (2)

Don't De-Rock Me (4)
Down Fo' Boogie (3)
Ez Come Ez Go (1)
Flight To Nowhere (2)
Freedom Slaves (4)
Gettin' Better (1,3)
Government Personnel (4)
Had Enough (4)
Hang Tough (2)

Heaven's Trail (No Way Out) (2,3)
Lady Luck (2)
Lazy Days, Crazy Nights (2)
Little Suzi (1) *91*
Lodi (3)
Love Me (1)
Love Song (2,3) *10*
Makin' Magic (2)

Man Out Of Time Edison's Medicine (4)
Modern Day Cowboy (1,3)
Mother's Little Helper (3)
Paradise (2,3)
Party's Over (2)
Rock Me To The Top (1)
Signs (3) *8*
Song & Emotion (4)

Stir It Up (4)
Time (4)
Toke About It (4)
Tommy's Down Home (3)
2 Late 4 Love (1)
Truckin' (medley) (3)
Way It Is (2,3) *55*
We Can Work It Out (3)
We're No Good Together (1)

What You Give (4) *86*
Yesterdaze Gone (2)

TESTAMENT
San Francisco-based hard rock band: Chuck Billy (vocals), Greg Christian, Louie Clemente, Eric Peterson and Alex Skolnick.

6/25/88	136	14		1 The New Order	$8	Megaforce 81849
9/2/89	77	12		2 Practice What You Preach	$8	Megaforce 82009
10/27/90	73	8		3 Souls Of Black	$12	Megaforce 82143
5/30/92	55	9		4 The Ritual	$12	Atlantic 82392

Absence Of Light (3)
Agony (4)
As The Seasons Grey (4)
Ballad, The (2)
Beginning Of The End (3)
Blessed In Contempt (2)
Confusion Fusion (2)

Day Of Reckoning (1)
Deadline (4)
Disciples Of The Watch (1)
Eerie Inhabitants (1)
Electric Crown (4)
Envy Life (2)
Face In The Sky (3)

Falling Fast (3)
Greenhouse Effect (3)
Hypnosis (1)
Into The Pit (1)
Legacy, The (3)
Let Go Of My World (4)
Love To Hate (3)

Malpractice (3)
Musical Death (A Dirge) (1)
New Order (4)
Nightmare (Coming Back To You) (2)
Nobody's Fault (1)
One Man's Fate (3)

Perilous Nation (2)
Practice What You Preach (2)
Preacher, The (1)
Return To Serenity (4)
Ritual, The (4)
Sermon, The (4)
Seven Days Of May (3)

Signs Of Chaos (4)
Sins Of Omission (2)
So Many Lies (4)
Souls Of Black (2)
Time Is Coming (2)
Trial By Fire (1)
Troubled Dreams (4)

TEX, Joe

Born Joseph Arrington, Jr. on 8/8/33 in Rogers, Texas; died of a heart attack on 8/13/82. Sang with local gospel groups. Won recording contract at Apollo Theater talent contest in 1954. First recorded for King in 1955. Became a convert to the Muslim faith, changed name to "Joseph Hazziez" in July 1972.

DEBUT DATE	PEAK POS	WKS CHR	#	ARTIST — Album Title	$	Label & Number
2/6/65	124	7	1	Hold What You've Got	$15	Atlantic 8106
11/27/65	142	7	2	The New Boss	$15	Atlantic 8115
5/7/66	108	8	3	The Love You Save	$15	Atlantic 8124
9/2/67	168	4	4	The Best Of Joe Tex [G]	$15	Atlantic 8144
2/24/68	84	17	5	Live and Lively [L]	$12	Atlantic 8156
7/27/68	154	7	6	Soul Country	$12	Atlantic 8187
7/19/69	190	5	7	Buying A Book	$12	Atlantic 8231
4/22/72	17	21	8	I Gotcha	$10	Dial 6002
5/7/77	108	9	9	Bumps & Bruises	$8	Epic 34666

Ain't Gonna Bump No More (With No Big Fat Woman) (9) **12**
Any Little Bit (2)
Anything You Wanna Know (7)
Are We Ready (1)
Baby Let Me Steal You (8)
Bad Feet (9)
Be Cool (Willie Is Dancing With A Sissy) (9)
Build Your Love (On A Solid Foundation) (3)
Buying A Book (7) **47**
By The Time I Get To Phoenix (6)
C.C. Rider (2)
Close The Door (3)
Dark End Of The Street (6)
Detroit City (2)
Do Right Woman - Do Right Man (5)

Don't Give Up (5)
Don't Let Your Left Hand Know (3) **95**
Don't Make Your Children Pay (2)
Engine Engine Number Nine (6)
For My Woman (8)
For Your Love (2)
Fresh Out Of Tears (1)
Funny Bone (3)
Funny How Time Slips Away (6)
Get Out Of My Life, Woman (5)
Get Your Lies Together (7)
Give The Baby Anything The Baby Wants (8)
God Of Love (8)
Grandma Mary (7)
Green Green Grass Of Home (6)

Heartbreak Hotel (3)
Heep See Few Know (1)
Hold What You've Got (1,2,4) **5**
Honey (6)
Hungry For Your Love (9)
I Almost Got To Heaven Once (9)
I Believe I'm Gonna Make It (4) **67**
I Don't Trust Myself Around You (3)
I Gotcha (8) **2**
I Mess Up Everything I Get My Hands On (9)
I Want To (Do Everything For You) (2,4) **23**
I'll Never Do You Wrong (6) **59**
I'm A Man (3)
I'm Not Going To Work Today (1)

I've Got To Do A Little Bit Better (4) **64**
If Sugar Was As Sweet As You (3)
It Ain't Gonna Work Baby (8)
It Ain't Sanitary (7)
Jump Bad (9)
King Of The Road (2)
Leaving Your Dinner (9)
Live For Yourself (3)
Love Is A Hurtin' Thing (5)
Love Me Right Girl (8)
Love You Save (May Be Your Own) (3,4) **56**
Ode To Billie Joe (6)
One Monkey Don't Stop No Show (1) **65**
Only Way (7)
Papa Was Too (4,5) **44**
S.Y.S.L.J.F.M. (The Letter Song) (4) **39**

Same Things You Did You Did To Get Me (7)
Set Me Free (6)
Show Me (4,5) **35**
Skinny Legs And All (5) **10**
Skip A Rope (4)
Stop Look And Listen (2)
Sure Is Good (7)
Sweet Woman Like You (3,4) **29**
Takin' A Chance (8)
Tell Me Right Now (1)
That's Life (5)
That's The Way (7) **94**
There Is A Girl (1)
There's Something Wrong (5)
Together We Stand (1)
We Can't Sit Down Now (7)
We Held On (9)
What In The World (2)
Woman Can Change A Man (2,4) **56**

Woman Cares (8)
Woman's Hands (5) **63**
Wooden Spoon (5)
You Better Believe It, Baby (3)
You Better Get It (1,4) **46**
You Can Stay (1)
You Got What It Takes (1,2,4) **51**
You Said A Bad Word (8) **41**
You're Gonna Thank Me, Woman (5)
You're In Too Deep (8)

TEXAS

Quartet from Glasgow, Scotland. Features female lead singer Sharlene Spiteri. Bassist John McElhone was a member of Hipsway and Altered Images. Drummer Stuart Kerr was an early member of Love and Money.

DEBUT DATE	PEAK POS	WKS CHR		ARTIST — Album Title	$	Label & Number
8/19/89	88	16		Southside	$8	Mercury 838171

Everyday Now
Fight The Feeling

Fool For Love
Future Is Promise

I Don't Want A Lover 77
One Choice

Prayer For You
Southside

Tell Me Why
Thrill Has Gone

TEXAS TORNADOS

Tex-Mex quartet of South Texas veteran artists: Freddy Fender, Doug Sahm, Augie Meyers and Flaco Jimenez. Sahm and Meyers were members of the Sir Douglas Quintet.

DEBUT DATE	PEAK POS	WKS CHR		ARTIST — Album Title	$	Label & Number
9/8/90	154	10		Texas Tornados	$12	Reprise 26251

Adios Mexico
Baby! Heaven Sent Me You

Dinero
(Hey Baby) Que Paso

If That's What You're Thinking
Man Can Cry

Laredo Rose

She Never Spoke Spanish To Me

Soy De San Luis
Who Were You Thinkin' Of

TEXTONES

Quintet led by singer/guitarist Carla Olson. Drummer Phil Seymour was with Dwight Twilley, 1974-80.

DEBUT DATE	PEAK POS	WKS CHR		ARTIST — Album Title	$	Label & Number
11/24/84+	176	8		Midnight Mission	$8	Gold Mt. 86010

Clean Cut Kid
Hands Of The Working Man

Luck Don't Last Forever
Midnight Mission

No Love In You
Number One Is To Survive

Running
See The Light

Standing In The Line
Upset Me

THE, The

Industrial-rock group formed in 1979 by songwriter Matt Johnson, as a four-piece unit. Changing band line-up features contributing musicians headed and produced by Johnson. Guitarist Johnny Marr, earlier with The Smiths, joined Electronic in 1990.

DEBUT DATE	PEAK POS	WKS CHR	#	ARTIST — Album Title	$	Label & Number
2/14/87	89	18	1	Infected	$8	Epic 40471
7/22/89	138	12	2	Mind Bomb	$8	Epic 45241

Angels Of Deception (1)
Armageddon Days Are Here (Again) (2)

August & September (2)
Beat(en) Generation (2)
Beyond Love (2)

Good Morning Beautiful (2)
Gravitate To Me (2)
Heartland (1)

Infected (1)
Kingdom Of Rain (2)
Mercy Beat (1)

Out Of The Blue (Into The Fire) (1)
Slow Train To Dawn (1)

Sweet Bird Of Truth (1)
Twilight Of A Champion (1)
Violence Of Truth (1)

THEE PROPHETS

Milwaukee pop-rock quartet featuring lead singer Brian Lake.

DEBUT DATE	PEAK POS	WKS CHR		ARTIST — Album Title	$	Label & Number
6/28/69	163	3		Playgirl	$15	Kapp 3596

Broken Heart
Double Life

Heartbreak Avenue
I Pretend I'm With You

It Isn't So Easy
Kind Of A Drag

Magic Island
Man Enough

Playgirl 49
Shame Shame

Some Kind-A Wonderful
They Call Her Sorrow

THEM

Belfast, Northern Ireland rock quintet: Van Morrison (lead singer), Billy Harrison, Alan Henderson, John McAuley and Peter Bardens. Disbanded in late 1966. Morrison went on to a highly successful solo career. Bardens formed Camel in 1972; recorded solo in 1987.

DEBUT DATE	PEAK POS	WKS CHR	#	ARTIST — Album Title	$	Label & Number
7/24/65	54	23	1	Them	$45	Parrot 71005
4/16/66	138	6	2	Them Again	$30	Parrot 71008
7/22/72	154	11	3	Them Featuring Van Morrison [R]	$15	Parrot 71053 [2]

THEM Featuring Van Morrison
reissue (condensed) of their first 2 albums

Bad Or Good (2,3)
Bring 'Em On In (2,3)
Call My Name (2)
Could You Would You (2,3)
Don't Look Back (1,3)
Don't You Know (2)

Gloria (1,3) **71**
Go On Home Baby (1)
Here Comes The Night (1,3) **24**
How Long Baby (2,3)

I Can Only Give You Everything (2,3)
I Like It Like That (1,3)
I'm Gonna Dress In Black (1)
If You And I Could Be As Two (1,3)

It's All Over Now Baby Blue (2,3)
Little Girl (1,3)
My Lonely Sad Eyes (2,3)
Mystic Eyes (1,3) **33**
One More Time (1,3)

One Two Brown Eyes (1,3)
Out Of Sight (2,3)
Route 66 (1,3)
Something You Got (2,3)
Turn On Your Lovelight (2,3)

DEBUT DATE	PEAK POS	WKS CHR	GOLD	ARTIST — Album Title	$	Label & Number

THEODORE, Mike, Orchestra
Disco studio group assembled by producer Mike Theodore.

10/1/77	**178**	2		Cosmic Wind	**$8**	Westbound 305

Ain't Nothing To It   Brazilian Lullaby   Bull, The   Cosmic Wind   I Love The Way You Move
Belly Boogie   Moon Trek

THEO VANESS
French disco act.

6/16/79	**145**	6		Bad Bad Boy	**$8**	Prelude 12165

As Long As It's Love   I'm A Bad Bad Boy   Keep On Dancin' (medley)   Love Me Now   No Romance (medley)
                            Sentimentally It's You

THEY EAT THEIR OWN
Hollywood-based, alternative-pop group led by Yugoslavian native Laura B. with Kevin Dixon, Shark Darkwater, J.D. Dotson and Jono Brown.

3/23/91	**184**	5		They Eat Their Own	**$12**	Relativity 1042

Better Now   Enemy, The   Locked Up   No Right To Kill   Video Martyr
Cancer Food   Like A Drug   Money Knocks   Too Many Guns   Why Don't You Disagree?

THEY MIGHT BE GIANTS
Brooklyn-based, satirical-rock duo from Boston: John Flansburgh (guitar) and John Linnell (accordian). Group name is a 1971 George C. Scott film.

12/24/88+	**89**	19		1 Lincoln	**$8**	Bar/None 72600
2/10/90	**75**	22		2 Flood	**$12**	Elektra 60907
4/11/92	**99**	6		3 Apollo 18	**$12**	Elektra 61257

features 20 extremely short, untitled tracks

Ana Ng (1)   Hall Of Heads (3)   Letterbox (2)   Piece Of Dirt (1)   Someone Keeps Moving My   We Want A Rock (2)
Birdhouse In Your Soul (2)   Hearing Aid (2)   Lie Still, Little Bottle (1)   Purple Toupee (1)   Chair (2)   Where Your Eyes Don't Go
Cage & Aquarium (1)   Hot Cha (3)   Lucky Ball & Chain (2)   Road Movie To Berlin (3)   Space Suit (3)   (1)
Cowtown (3)   Hypnotist Of Ladies (3)   Mammal (3)   Santa's Beard (1)   Spider (3)   Which Describes How You're
Dead (2)   I Palindrome I (3)   Minimum Wage (2)   Sapphire Bullets Of Pure   Stand On Your Own Head (1)   Feeling (3)
Dig My Grave (3)   I've Got A Match (1)   Mr. Me (1)   Love (2)   Statue Got Me High (3)   Whistling In The Dark (2)
Dinner Bell (3)   If I Wasn't Shy (3)   My Evil Twin (3)   See The Constellation (3)   They Might Be Giants (2)   Women & Men (2)
Fingertips (3)   Istanbul (Not   Narrow Your Eyes (3)   She's Actual Size (3)   They'll Need A Crane (1)   World's Address (1)
Flood, Theme From (2)   Constantinople) (2)   Particle Man (2)   Shoehorn With Teeth (1)   Turn Around (3)   You'll Miss Me (1)
Guitar, The (3)   Kiss Me, Son Of God (1)   Pencil Rain (1)   Snowball In Hell (1)   Twisting (2)   Your Racist Friend (1)

THIN LIZZY
Rock quartet formed by Dublin, Ireland natives Phil Lynott (b: 8/20/51, d: 1/4/86; vocals, bass) and Brian Downey (drums). Gary Moore was lead guitarist in early 1974, then 1978-79. Added guitarists Brian Robertson (from Glasgow) and Scott Gorham (from California) in June 1974. Robertson left in 1977 (later joined Motorhead), replaced by various guitarists. Keyboardist Darren Wharton joined in 1983.

4/17/76	**18**	28	●	1 Jailbreak	**$8**	Mercury 1081
11/13/76	**52**	11		2 Johnny The Fox	**$8**	Mercury 1119
9/24/77	**39**	11		3 Bad Reputation	**$8**	Mercury 1186
7/22/78	**84**	12		4 Live And Dangerous .... [L]	**$10**	Warner 3213 [2]
6/2/79	**81**	12		5 Black Rose/A Rock Legend	**$8**	Warner 3338
11/29/80	**120**	10		6 Chinatown	**$8**	Warner 3496
2/20/82	**157**	11		7 Renegade	**$8**	Warner 3622
5/28/83	**159**	5		8 Thunder And Lightning	**$8**	Warner 23831
1/28/84	**185**	3		9 'Life'-Live .... [L]	**$10**	Warner 23986 [2]

Angel From The Coast (1)   Cowgirls' Song (medley) (4)   Get Out Of Here (5)   Leave This Town (7)   Rosalie (medley) (4)   That Woman's Gonna Break
Angel Of Death (7,9)   Dancing In The Moonlight   Got To Give It Up (5,9)   Massacre (2,4)   Running Back (1)   Your Heart (3)
Are You Ready (4,9)   (It's Caught Me In Its   Having A Good Time (6)   Mexican Blood (7)   S & M (5)   This Is The One (8)
Baby Drives Me Crazy (4)   Spotlight) (3,4)   Heart Attack (8)   My Sarah (5)   Sha-La-La (4)   Thunder And Lightning (8,9)
Baby Please Don't Go (8,9)   Dear Lord (3)   Hey You (6)   No One Told Him (7)   Soldier Of Fortune (3)   Toughest Street In Town (5)
Bad Habits (8)   Didn't I (6)   Hollywood (Down On Your   Old Flame (7)   Someday She Is Going To   Waiting For An Alibi (5,9)
Bad Reputation (3)   Do Anything You Want To (5)   Luck) (7,9)   Opium Trail (3)   Hit Back (8)   Warriors (1,4)
Black Rose (9)   Don't Believe A Word (2,4,9)   Holy War (8,9)   Pressure Will Blow (7)   Southbound (3,4)   We Will Be Strong (6)
Boogie Woogie Dance (2)   Downtown Sundown (3)   It's Getting Dangerous (7)   Renegade (7,9)   Still In Love With You (4,9)   With Love (5)
Borderline (2)   Emerald (1,4,9)   Jailbreak (1,4,9)   Rocker, The (4,9)   Sugar Blues (6)
Boys Are Back In Town   Fats (7)   Johnny (2)   Rocky (2)   Suicide (4)
(1,4,9) **12**   Fight Or Fall (1)   Johnny The Fox Meets   Roisin Dubh (Black Rose) A   Sun Goes Down (8,9)
Chinatown (6)   Fool's Gold (2)   Jimmy The Weed (2,4)   Rock Legend (5)   Sweet Marie (2)
Cold Sweat (8,9)   Genocide (The Killing Of The   Killer On The Loose (6,9)   Romeo And The Lonely Girl   Sweetheart (6)
Cowboy Song (1,4) **77**   Buffalo) (3)   Killer Without A Cause (3)   (1)

3RD BASS
White rappers from Queens, New York: Prime Minister Pete Nice (Pete Nash) and MC Serch (Michael Berrin). Supported by black DJ Richie Rich (Richard Lawson). MC Serch left in early 1992.

12/2/89+	**55**	30	●	1 The Cactus Album	**$8**	Def Jam 45415
7/6/91	**19**	22	●	2 Derelicts Of Dialect	**$12**	Def Jam 47369

Ace In The Hole (2)   Episode #3 (1)   Kick Em In The Grill (1)   Oval Office (1)   Sons Of 3rd Bass (1)
Al'za-B-Cee'z (2)   Eye Jammie (2)   M.C. Disagree (1)   **Pop Goes The Weasel**   Soul In The Hole (1)
Brooklyn-Queens (1)   Flippin' Off The Wall Like   M.C. Disagree And The   [includes 2 versions] (2) **29**   Steppin' To The A.M. (1)
Cactus, The (1)   Lucy Ball (1)   Re-animator (1)   Portrait Of The Artist As A   Stymie's Theme (1)
Come In (2)   French Toast (2)   Merchant Of Grooves (2)   Hood (2)   3 Strikes 5000 (2)
Daddy Rich In The Land Of   Gas Face (1)   Microphone Techniques (2)   Problem Child (2)   Triple Stage Darkness (1)
1210 (1)   Green Eggs And Swine (2)   Monte Hall (1)   Product Of The Environment   Who's On Third (2)
Derelicts Of Dialect [includes   Herbalz In Your Mouth (2)   No Master Plan No Master   (1)   Word To The Third (2)
2 versions] (2)   Hoods (1)   Race (2)   Russell Rush (1)   Wordz Of Wizdom (1)
Desert Boots (1)   Jim Backus (1)   No Static At All (2)   Sea Vessel Soliloquy (2)

THIRD POWER, The
Rock trio: Drew Abbott (guitar), Jem Targal (vocals, bass) and Jim Craig (drums). Abbott later joined Bob Seger's Silver Bullet Band.

7/4/70	**194**	2		Believe	**$8**	Vanguard 6554

Comin' Home   Feel So Lonely   Like Me Love Me   Passed By   Won't Beg Any More
Crystalline Chandelier   Gettin' Together   Lost In A Daydream   Persecution

DEBUT DATE	PEAK POS	WKS CHR	GOLD	ARTIST — Album Title	$	Label & Number

THIRD WORLD
Reggae fusion band from Jamaica — William "Bunny Rugs" Clarke, lead singer.

DEBUT DATE	PEAK POS	WKS CHR		ARTIST — Album Title	$	Label & Number
11/25/78+	55	24		1 Journey To Addis	$8	Island 9554
7/21/79	157	5		2 The Story's Been Told	$8	Island 9569
8/30/80	186	2		3 Third World, Prisoner in The Street .... [S-L]	$8	Island 9616
7/25/81	186	3		4 Rock The World	$8	Columbia 37402
3/20/82	63	27		5 You've Got The Power	$8	Columbia 37744
				Stevie Wonder produced and performed on 2 tracks		
10/1/83	137	7		6 All The Way Strong	$8	Columbia 38687
4/13/85	119	11		7 Sense Of Purpose	$8	Columbia 39877
7/15/89	107	14		8 Serious Business	$8	Mercury 836952

African Woman (1,3)
All The Way Strong (6)
Always Around (2)
Before You Make Your Move (Melt With Everyone) (5)
Can't Get You (Outta My Mind) (7)
Children Of The World (3)
Cold Sweat (1,3)
Come On Home (6)
Come Together (2)
Cool Meditation (1)
D.J. Ambassador (8)
Dancing On The Floor (Hooked On Love) (4)
Dubb Music (4)
Forbidden Love (8)
Fret Not Thyself (1)
Girl From Hiroshima (7)
Having A Party (4)
How Can You (7)
Hug It Up (4)
I Wake Up Cryin' (5)
Inna Time Like This (5)
Irie Ites (2,3)
It's The Same Old Song (8)
Jah, Jah Children Moving Up (5)
Journey To Addis (1)
Keep Your Head To The Sky (8)
Lagos Jump (6)
Love Is Out To Get You (6)
Love Will Always Be There (8)
Low Key-Jammin' (5)
Never Say Never (8)
96° In The Shade (3)
Now That We Found Love (1,3) 47
Once There's Love (6)
One Cold Vibe (Couldn't Stop Dis Ya Boogie) (1)
One More Time (7)
One Song (Nyahbinghi) (7)
One To One (7)
Peace And Love (4)
Prisoner In The Street (3)
Reggae Ambassador (8)
Reggae Jam Boogie (7)
Rejoice (1)
Ride On (5)
Rock Me (7)
Rock The World (4)
Seasons When (6)
Sense Of Purpose (7)
Serious Business (8)
Shine Like A Blazing Fire (4)
Spiritual Revolution (4)
Standing In The Rain (4)
Story's Been Told (2)
Street Fighting (3)
Swing Low (3)
Take This Song (8)
Talk To Me (2)
There's No Need To Question Why (4)
Third World Man (3)
Tonight For Me (2)
Try Jah Love (5)
Underdog, Theme From The [includes 2 versions] (8)
We The People (8)
Who Gave You (Jah Rastafari) (4)
World Of Uncertainty (7)
You're Playing Us Too Close (5)
You've Got The Power (To Make A Change) (5)

★★365★★ 38 SPECIAL
Florida Southern-rock sextet: Donnie Van Zant (younger brother of Lynyrd Skynyrd's Ronnie Van Zant; lead singer), Don Barnes, Jeff Carlisi, Steve Brookins, Jack Grondin and Larry Jungstrom (ex-Lynyrd Skynyrd; replaced Ken Lyons in 1979). By 1988, Barnes and Brookins replaced by Danny Chauncey and Max Carl. Barnes returned in 1992 to replace Carlo.

DEBUT DATE	PEAK POS	WKS CHR		ARTIST — Album Title	$	Label & Number
5/28/77	148	5		1 38 Special	$8	A&M 4638
1/5/80	57	19		2 Rockin' Into The Night	$8	A&M 4782
2/21/81	18	57 ▲		3 Wild-Eyed Southern Boys	$8	A&M 4835
5/29/82	10	42 ▲		4 Special Forces	$8	A&M 4888
12/3/83+	22	39 ▲		5 Tour De Force	$8	A&M 4971
5/17/86	17	31 ●		6 Strength In Numbers	$8	A&M 5115
8/22/87	35	17 ●		7 Flashback .... [G]	$8	A&M 3910
				includes a bonus 4-song live EP		
10/22/88+	61	41		8 Rock & Roll Strategy	$8	A&M 5218
8/10/91	170	7		9 Bone Against Steel	$12	Charisma 91640

Against The Night (6)
Around And Around (1)
Back Alley Sally (3)
Back Door Stranger (4)
Back On The Track (4)
Back To Paradise (7) 41
Back Where You Belong (5,7) 20
Bone Against Steel (9)
Breakin' Loose (4)
Bring It On (3)
Burning Bridges (9)
Can't Shake It (9)
Caught Up In You (4,7) 10
Chain Lightnin' (4)
Chattahoochee (8)
Comin' Down Tonight (8) 67
Don't Wanna Get It Dirty (9)
Fantasy Girl (3,7) 52
Firestarter (4)
First Time Around (3)
Fly Away (1)
Four Wheels (1)
Gypsy Belle (1)
Has There Ever Been A Good Goodbye (6)
Heart's On Fire (6)
Hittin' And Runnin' (9)
Hold On Loosely (3,7) 27
Honky Tonk Dancer (3)
Hot 'Lanta (8)
I Oughta Let Go (5)
If I'd Been The One (5,7) 19
Innocent Eyes (8)
Jimmy Gillum (9)
Just A Little Love (6)
Just Hang On (1)
Just Wanna Rock & Roll (1)
Last Thing I Ever Do (9)
Last Time (6)
Like No Other Night (6,7) 1
Little Sheba (8)
Long Distance Affair (5)
Long Time Gone (1)
Love Strikes (8)
Love That I've Lost (2)
Midnight Magic (8)
Money Honey (2)
Never Be Lonely (8)
Never Give An Inch (6)
Once In A Lifetime (6)
One In A Million (6)
One Of The Lonely Ones (5)
One Time For Old Times (5)
Play A Simple Song (1)
Rebel To Rebel (9)
Robin Hood (2)
Rock & Roll Strategy (8) 67
Rockin' Into The Night (2,7) 43
Rough-Housin' (4,7)
Same Old Feeling (7)
Second Chance (8) 6
See Me In Your Eyes (5)
Signs Of Love (9)
Somebody Like You (6) 48
Sound Of Your Voice (9) 33
Stone Cold Believer (2,7)
Take 'Em Out (4)
Take Me Through The Night (2)
Teacher Teacher (7) 25
Tear It Up (9)
Tell Everybody (1)
Throw Out The Line (3)
Treasure (9)
Turn It On (2)
Twentieth Century Fox (5,7)
Undercover Lover (5)
What's It To Ya? (8)
Wild-Eyed Southern Boys (3,7)
You Be The Dam, I'll Be The Water (9)
You Definitely Got Me (9)
You Got The Deal (9)
You Keep Runnin' Away (4) 38
You're The Captain (2)

★★452★★ THOMAS, B.J.
Born Billy Joe Thomas on 8/7/42 in Hugo, Oklahoma; raised in Rosenberg, Texas. Sang in church choir as a teenager. Joined band, the Triumphs, while in high school. B.J. has featured gospel music since 1976.

DEBUT DATE	PEAK POS	WKS CHR		ARTIST — Album Title	$	Label & Number
1/18/69	133	12		1 On My Way	$12	Scepter 570
11/8/69+	90	28		2 Greatest Hits, Volume 1 .... [G]	$12	Scepter 578
1/3/70	12	41 ●		3 Raindrops Keep Fallin' On My Head	$10	Scepter 580
5/2/70	72	20		4 Everybody's Out Of Town	$10	Scepter 582
12/12/70+	67	24		5 Most Of All	$10	Scepter 586
11/20/71	92	13		6 Greatest Hits, Volume Two .... [G]	$10	Scepter 597
5/20/72	145	9		7 Billy Joe Thomas	$10	Scepter 5101
3/29/75	59	14		8 Reunion	$8	ABC 858
8/27/77	114	12		9 B.J. Thomas	$8	MCA 2286
5/21/83	193	3		10 New Looks	$8	Cleve. I. 38561

Amour (10)
Are We Losing Touch (7)
Beautiful Things For You (8)
Billy And Sue (2) 34
Bridge Over Troubled Water (4)
Bring Back The Time (2) 75
Brown Eyed Woman (5)
Circle 'Round The Sun (5)
City Boys (8)
Created For Man (4)
Crying (8)
Crying In The Chapel (2)
Do What You Gotta Do (3)
Doctor God (8)
Don't Worry Baby (9) 17
Even A Fool Would Let Go (9)
Everybody's Out Of Town (4,6) 26
Eyes Of A New York Woman (1,2) 28
Fine Way To Go (3)
Four Walls (1)
Gone (1)
Greatest Love (3)
Guess I'll Pack My Things (3)
Happier Than The Morning Sun (7) 100
Hello Love (5)
Here You Come Again (9)
(Hey Won't You Play) Another Somebody Done Somebody Wrong Song (8) 1
Hooked On A Feeling (1,2) 5
I Believe In Music (6)
I Can't Help It (If I'm Still In Love With You) (2) 94
I Don't Know Any Better (5)
I Finally Got It Right This Time (8)
I Get Enthused (7)
I Just Can't Help Believing (4,6) 9
I Just Sing (10)
I Love Us (10)
I Need You So (2)
I Saw Pity In The Face Of A Friend (1)
I'm Saving All The Good Times For You (3)
I'm So Lonesome I Could Cry (2) 8
I've Been Down This Road Before (1)
If You Ever Leave Me (3)
If You Must Leave My Life (3)
Impressions (9)
It's Only Love (6) 45
It's Sad To Belong (9)
Just As Gone (7)
Life (6)
Light My Fire (1)
Little Green Apples (3)
Long Ago Tomorrow (6) 61
Love Me Tender (5)
Mama (2) 22
Mask, The (4)
Maybe It's Time To Go (8)

DEBUT DATE	PEAK POS	WKS CHR	GOLD	ARTIST — Album Title	$	Label & Number

THOMAS, B.J. — Cont'd

Memory Machine (10)
Mighty Clouds Of Joy (6) **34**
Most Of All (5,6) **38**
Mr. Businessman (1)
Mr. Mailman (3)
My Love (9)
New Looks From An Old Lover (10)
No Love At All (5,6) **16**
Oh Me Oh My (4)

Our Love Goes Marching On (9)
Plain Jane (2)
Plastic Words (9)
Play Me A Little Traveling Music (9)
Raindrops Keep Fallin' On My Head (3,6) **1**
Rainy Day Man (5)
Rainy Night In Georgia (5)
Real Life Blues (8)

Roads (7)
Rock And Roll Lullaby (7) **15**
Rock And Roll You're Beautiful (10)
Sandman (1,4)
Sea Of Love (8)
Send My Picture To Scranton, Pa. (4)
Since I Don't Have You (2)
Smoke Gets In Your Eyes (1)

Song For My Brother (7)
Still The Lovin' Is Fun (9) **77**
Stories We Can Tell (7)
Suspicious Minds (3)
Sweet Cherry Wine (7)
Table For Two For One (5)
That's What Friends Are For (7) **74**
(They Long To Be) Close To You (5)

This Guy's In Love With You (3)
We Had It All (9)
We Have Got To Get Our Ship Together (5)
What Does It Take (4)
Whatever Happened To Old Fashioned Love (10) **93**

Who Broke Your Heart And Made You Write That Song (8)
Wind Beneath My Wings (10)
You Keep The Man In Me Happy (And The Child In Me Alive) (10)

THOMAS, Carla

Born on 12/21/42 in Memphis. Daughter of Rufus Thomas. Sang with the Teentown Singers at age 10. First recorded with Rufus for Satellite in 1960. Also recorded duets with Otis Redding.

DEBUT DATE	PEAK POS	WKS CHR	GOLD	ARTIST — Album Title	$	Label & Number
3/5/66	134	10		1 Comfort Me	$25	Stax 706
10/15/66	130	5		2 Carla	$25	Stax 709
4/22/67	36	31		3 King & Queen	$25	Stax 716
				OTIS REDDING & CARLA THOMAS		
7/1/67	133	6		4 The Queen Alone	$20	Stax 718
7/5/69	151	5		5 Memphis Queen	$15	Stax 2019
7/19/69	190	4		6 The Best Of Carla Thomas [G]	$12	Atlantic 8232

All I See Is You (4)
Another Night Without My Man (1)
Any Day Now (4)
Are You Lonely For Me Baby (3)
B-A-B-Y (2,6) **14**
Baby What You Want Me To Do (medley) (2)
Bring It On Home To Me (3,6)
Comfort Me (1,6)
Dime A Dozen (6)
Don't Say No More (5)
Fate (2)
For Your Love (medley) (2)

Forever (1)
Gee Whiz (Look At His Eyes) (6) **10**
Give Me Enough (To Keep Me Going) (4)
Guide Me Well (5)
He's Beating Your Time (5)
How Can You Throw My Love Away (5)
I Got You, Boy (2)
I Like What You're Doing (To Me) (5) **49**
I Play For Keeps (5)
I Take It To My Baby (4)

I Want To Be Your Baby (4)
I'll Always Have Faith In You (4) **85**
I'm For You (1)
I'm So Lonesome I Could Cry (2)
I've Fallen In Love (With You) (5)
It Takes Two (3)
Knock On Wood (3) **30**
Let It Be Me (1)
Let Me Be Good To You (2,3,6) **62**
Lie To Keep Me From Crying (4)

Looking Back (2)
Lover's Concerto (1)
Lovey Dovey (3,6) **60**
More Man Than I Ever Had (5)
Move On Drifter (1)
New Year's Resolution (5)
No Time To Lose (1,6)
Oh! What A Fool I've Been (6)
Ooh Carla, Ooh Otis (3)
Pick Up The Pieces (6) **68**
Precious Memories (5)
Red Rooster (2)
Something Good (Is Going To Happen To You) (4) **74**

Stop! Look What You're Doing (6) **92**
Stop Thief (4,6)
Strung Out (5)
Tell It Like It Is (3)
Tramp (3,6) **26**
Unchanging Love (4)
Unyielding (5)
What Have You Got To Offer Me (2)
What The World Needs Now (1)
When Something Is Wrong With My Baby (3)

When Tomorrow Comes (4) **99**
Where Do I Go (5) **86**
Will You Love Me Tomorrow (1)
Woman's Love (1,6) **71**
Yes, I'm Ready (1)
You Don't Have To Say You Love Me (2)

THOMAS, Irma

Born Irma Lee on 2/18/41 in Ponchatoula, Louisiana. The Soul Queen of New Orleans. Discovered by New Orleans bandleader Tommy Ridgley.

DEBUT DATE	PEAK POS	WKS CHR	GOLD	ARTIST — Album Title	$	Label & Number
6/27/64	104	8		Wish Someone Would Care	$35	Imperial 12266

Another Woman's Man
Break-A-Way
I Need You So

I Need Your Love So Bad
I've Been There

Please Send Me Someone To Love
Straight From The Heart

Sufferin' With The Blues
Time Is On My Side
While The City Sleeps

Wish Someone Would Care 17

Without Love (There Is Nothing)

THOMAS, Lillo

Brooklyn vocalist. At age 16, set a world record for the 200 meter dash; qualified for the 1984 Olympic track team, but an auto accident in Brazil kept him from competing. Toured with Eddie Murphy in 1985.

DEBUT DATE	PEAK POS	WKS CHR	GOLD	ARTIST — Album Title	$	Label & Number
10/6/84	186	3		All Of You	$8	Capitol 12346

All Of You
Holding On

I Like Your Style
My Girl

Never Give You Up
Settle Down

Show Me

Your Love's Got A Hold On Me

THOMAS, Marlo — see CHILDRENS section

THOMAS, Ray

Born on 12/29/42 in England. Flute/harmonica player of The Moody Blues.

DEBUT DATE	PEAK POS	WKS CHR	GOLD	ARTIST — Album Title	$	Label & Number
8/9/75	68	11		1 From Mighty Oaks	$15	Threshold 16
8/14/76	147	5		2 Hopes Wishes & Dreams	$15	Threshold 17

Adam And I (1)
Carousel (2)
Didn't I (2)
Friends (2)

From Mighty Oaks (1)
Hey Mama Life (1)
High Above My Head (1)
I Wish We Could Fly (1)

In Your Song (1)
Keep On Searching (2)
Last Dream (2)
Love Is The Key (1)

Migration (2)
One Night Stand (2)
Play It Again (1)
Rock-A-Bye Baby Blues (1)

We Need Love (2)
Within Your Eyes (2)
You Make Me Feel Alright (1)

THOMAS, Rufus

Born on 3/26/17 in Cayce, Mississippi; raised in Memphis. R&B singer/songwriter/choreographer. Father of Carla and Vaneese Thomas. DJ at WDIA-Memphis, 1953-74. Recorded for Alligator Records, late '80s.

DEBUT DATE	PEAK POS	WKS CHR	GOLD	ARTIST — Album Title	$	Label & Number
12/28/63+	138	3		1 Walking The Dog	$30	Stax 704
4/3/71	147	5		2 Rufus Thomas Live/Doing The Push & Pull At P.J.'s [L]	$10	Stax 2039

Boom Boom (1)
Can Your Monkey Do The Dog (1) **48**
Cause I Love You (1)

Do The Funky Chicken (2)
(Do The) Push And Pull (2)
Dog, The (1) **87**
I Want To Be Loved (1)

It's Aw'rite (1)
Land Of 1,000 Dances (1)
Mashed Potatoes (1)

Night Time Is The Right Time (2)
Old McDonald Had A Farm (2)

Ooh-Poo-Pah-Doo (1,2)
Preacher And The Bear (2)
Walking The Dog (1,2) **10**

Ya Ya (1)
You Said (1)

THOMAS, Timmy

Born on 11/13/44 in Evansville, Indiana. Soul singer/songwriter/keyboardist. Studio musician at Gold Wax Records in Memphis. Moved to Miami in 1970. Session work for Betty Wright and KC & The Sunshine Band.

DEBUT DATE	PEAK POS	WKS CHR	GOLD	ARTIST — Album Title	$	Label & Number
1/20/73	53	15		Why Can't We Live Together	$12	Glades 6501

Cold Cold People
Coldest Days Of My Life

Dizzy Dizzy World
First Time Ever I Saw Your Face

Funky Me
In The Beginning
Opportunity

Rainbow Power
Take Care Of Home

Why Can't We Live Together 3

THOMPSON, Richard

Songwriter/singer/guitarist. Born on 4/3/49 in London. Formed Fairport Convention in 1969. Went solo in 1971. Married singer Linda Peters in 1972; recording duo until couple's divorce in 1982.

DEBUT DATE	PEAK POS	WKS CHR	GOLD	ARTIST — Album Title	$	Label & Number
7/30/83	186	5		1 Hand Of Kindness	$8	Hannibal 1313
3/9/85	102	13		2 Across A Crowded Room	$8	Polydor 825421
10/25/86	142	6		3 Daring Adventures	$8	Polydor 829728

THOMPSON, Richard — Cont'd

| 11/5/88 | 182 | 5 | | 4 Amnesia | $8 | Capitol 48845 |

Al Bowlly's In Heaven (3) · Baby Talk (3) · Bone Through Her Nose (3) · Both Ends Burning (1) · Can't Win (4) · Cash Down Never Never (3) · Dead Man's Handle (3) · Devon Side (1) · Don't Tempt Me (4) · Fire In The Engine Room (2) · Ghosts In The Wind (2) · Gypsy Love Songs (4) · Hand Of Kindness (1) · How I Wanted To (1) · How Will I Ever Be Simple Again (1) · I Ain't Going To Drag My Feet No More (2) · I Still Dream (4) · Jennie (3) · Jerusalem On The Jukebox (4) · Little Blue Number (3) · Long Dead Love (3) · Love In A Faithless Country (2) · Lovers' Lane (3) · Missie How You Let Me Down (3) · Nearly In Love (3) · Pharaoh (4) · Poisoned Heart And A Twisted Memory (1) · Reckless Kind (4) · She Twists The Knife Again (2) · Tear Stained Letter (1) · Turning Of The Tide (4) · Two Left Feet (1) · Valerie (3) · Walking Through A Wasted Land (2) · Waltzing's For Dreamers (4) · When The Spell Is Broken (2) · Wrong Heartbeat (1) · Yankee, Go Home (4) · You Don't Say (2)

THOMPSON, Robbin, Band

Virginia pop-rock quintet led by singer/guitarist Thompson. Robbin played in Bruce Springsteen's early Steel Mill band.

| 10/25/80 | 168 | 11 | | Two B's Please | $8 | Ovation 1759 |

All Alone In The Endzone · Barroom Romance · Brite Eyes 66 · Candy Apple Red · Even Cowgirls Get The Blues · Let It All Out · Rock & Roll Singer · Sweet Virginia Breeze · That's Alright

THOMPSON, Sue

Born Eva Sue McKee on 7/19/26 in Nevada, Missouri and raised in San Jose, California. Became a popular country singer in the '70s.

| 3/20/65 | 134 | 3 | | Paper Tiger | $30 | Hickory 121 |

Bad Boy · Big Hearted Me · 'Cause I Ask You To · Fan Club · I Need A Harbor · I'd Like To Know You Better · Paper Tiger 23 · Suzie · True Confession · What I'm Needin' Is You · What's The Use (To Take My Lovin) · What's Wrong Bill

THOMPSON TWINS

British trio: Tom Bailey (b: 1/18/56, England; lead singer, synthesizer), Alannah Currie (b: 9/28/57, New Zealand; xylophone, percussion) and Joe Leeway (b: 11/15/57, London; conga, synthesizer). Leeway left in 1986.

6/26/82	148	8		1 In The Name Of Love	$8	Arista 6601
2/26/83	34	25		2 Side Kicks	$8	Arista 6607
3/17/84	10	53	▲	3 Into The Gap	$8	Arista 8200
10/19/85+	20	35	●	4 Here's To Future Days	$8	Arista 8276
4/25/87	76	14		5 Close To The Bone	$8	Arista 8449
8/27/88	175	6		6 Greatest Mixes/The Best Of Thompson Twins [K]	$8	Arista 8542

remixes of their hits

| 10/21/89 | 143 | 6 | | 7 Big Trash | $8 | Warner 25921 |

All Fall Out (2) · Another Fantasy (1) · Big Trash (7) · Bombers In The Sky (7) · Bouncing (1) · Bush Baby (5) · Dancing In Your Shoes (5) · Day After Day (3) · Dirty Summer's Day (7) · Doctor! Doctor! (3,6) 11 · Don't Mess With Doctor Dream (4) · Emperor's Clothes (Part 1) (4) · Follow Your Heart (5) · Fool's Gold (7) · Future Days (1) · Gap, The (3) 69 · Get That Love (5,6) 31 · Gold Fever (5) · Good Gosh (1) · Hold Me Now (3,6) 3 · If You Were Here (2) · In The Name Of Love (1) · In The Name Of Love '88 (6) · Judy Do (2) · Kamikaze (3) · King For A Day (4,6) 8 · Lay Your Hands On Me (4,6) 6 · Lies (2,6) 30 · Living In Europe (1) · Long Goodbye (5) · Love Is The Law (4) · Love Jungle (3) · Love Lies Bleeding (2) · Love On Your Side (2,6) 45 · Make Believe (1) · No Peace For The Wicked (3) · Perfect Day (5) · Perfect Game (1) · Queen Of The U.S.A. (7) · Revolution (4) · Rock This Boat (7) · Roll Over (4) · Rowe, The (1) · Runaway (1) · Salvador Dali's Car (3) · Savage Moon (5) · Sister Of Mercy (3) · Still Waters (5) · Storm On The Sea (3) · Sugar Daddy (7) 28 · T.V. (on) (7) · Tears (2) · This Girl's On Fire (7) · Tokyo (3) · Twentieth Century (5) · Watching (2) · We Are Detective (2) · Who Can Stop The Rain (3) · Wild (7) · You Killed The Clown (4) · You Take Me Up (3) 44

THOMSON, Ali

Singer/songwriter from Glasgow, Scotland. Younger brother of Supertramp's Dougie Thomson.

| 7/5/80 | 99 | 15 | | Take A Little Rhythm | $8 | A&M 4803 |

African Queen · Fools' Society · Goodnight Song · Hollywood Role · Jamie · Live Every Minute 42 · Page By Page · Saturday Heartbreaker · Take A Little Rhythm 15 · We Were All In Love

THORNTON, Big Mama

Born Willie Mae Thornton on 12/11/26 in Montgomery, Alabama; died on 7/25/84. Legendary blues singer.

| 8/30/69 | 198 | 2 | | Stronger Than Dirt | $20 | Mercury 61225 |

Ain't Nothin' You Can Do · Ball And Chain · Born Under A Bad Sign · Funky Broadway · Hound Dog · I Shall Be Released · Let's Go Get Stoned · Rollin' Stone · Summertime · That Lucky Old Sun

★★339★★ THOROGOOD, George, & The Destroyers

George is the leader of the Delaware rock & blues band The Destroyers. Lineup since 1980: Thorogood (b: Wilmington, Delaware; vocals, guitar), Billy Blough (bass), Jeff Simon (drums) and Hank Carter (sax). Added guitarist Steve Chrismar in 1986.

| 12/9/78+ | 33 | 47 | ● | 1 Move It On Over | $8 | Rounder 3024 |
| 9/1/79 | 78 | 10 | | 2 Better Than The Rest [E] | $8 | MCA 3091 |

recorded in 1974

11/8/80	68	12		3 More George Thorogood and the Destroyers	$8	Rounder 3045
8/28/82	43	48	●	4 Bad To The Bone	$8	EMI America 17076
3/2/85	32	42	●	5 Maverick	$8	EMI America 17145
8/23/86	33	42	●	6 Live [L]	$8	EMI America 17214
2/6/88	32	24	●	7 Born To Be Bad	$8	EMI-Man. 46973
3/16/91	77	13		8 Boogie People	$12	EMI 92514
8/15/92	100	17		9 The Baddest Of George Thorogood And The Destroyers [G]	$12	EMI 97718

Alley Oop (6) · As The Years Go Passing By (4) · Baby Please Set A Date (1) · Back To Wentsville (4) · Bad To The Bone (4,6,9) · Blue Highway (4) · Boogie People (8) · Born In Chicago (8) · Born To Be Bad (7) · Bottom Of The Sea (3,6) · Can't Be Satisfied (8) · Cocaine Blues (1) · Crawling King Snake (5) · Dixie Fried (5) · Gear Jammer (5,9) · Goodbye Baby (2,3) · Hello Little Girl (8) · Highway 49 (7) · House Of Blue Lights (3) · Howlin' For My Darling (2) · Huckle Up Baby (2) · I Drink Alone (5,6,9) · I Really Like Girls (7) · I'm A Steady Rollin' Man (9) · I'm Just Your Good Thing (1) · I'm Movin' On (7) · I'm Ready (2,7) · I'm Wanted (2) · If You Don't Start Drinkin' (I'm Gonna Leave) (8,9) · In The Night Time (2) · It Wasn't Me (1) · It's A Sin (4) · Just Can't Make It (3) · Kids From Philly (3) · (Let's) Go Go Go (5) · Long Distance Lover (8) · Long Gone (4) · Louie To Frisco (9) · Mad Man Blues (6) · Madison Blues (6) · Maverick (4) · Memphis, Tennessee (9) · Miss Luann (4) · Move It On Over (1,9) · My Way (2) · My Weakness (2) · Nadine (2) · New Boogie Chillen (4) · New Hawaiian Boogie (1) · Night Time (3,6) · No Particular Place To Go (4) · No Place To Go (8)

DEBUT DATE	PEAK POS	WKS CHR	GOLD	ARTIST — Album Title	$	Label & Number

THOROGOOD, George, & The Destroyers — Cont'd

Nobody But Me (4)	Reelin' & Rockin' (6)	Smokestack Lightning (7)	Woman With The Blues (5)
Oklahoma Sweetheart (8)	Restless (3)	So Much Trouble (1)	Worried About My Baby (2)
One Bourbon, One Scotch, One Beer (6,9)	Shake Your Money Maker (7)	That Same Thing (1)	What A Price (5)	You Can't Catch Me (7)
One Way Ticket (3)	Six Days On The Road (8)	Tip On In (3)	Who Do You Love (1,6,9)	You Talk Too Much (7,9)
	Sky Is Crying (1,6)	Treat Her Right (7,9)	Willie And The Hand Jive (5) 63	You're Gonna Miss Me (2)

THORPE, Billy

English-born singer/guitarist; raised in Australia. Superstar artist in Australia. Member of The Zoo.

5/5/79	**39**	23		1 Children Of The Sun	**$12**	Polydor 6228
				originally released on Capricorn 0221		
11/8/80	**151**	5		2 21st Century Man	**$8**	Elektra 294

Beginning, The (1)	Goddess Of The Night (1)	Rise (2)	Solar Anthem (1)	We Welcome You... (1)	Wrapped In The Chains Of Your Love (1)
Children Of The Sun (1) *41*	In My Room (2)	She's Alive (2)	Solar Dawn (2)	We Were Watching You (2)	
Dream-Maker (1)	1991 (2)	Simple Life (1)	21st Century Man (2)	We're Leaving (1)	

THP ORCHESTRA

Canadian disco production: Barbara Fry (vocals) and W. Michael Lewis (synthesizer).

| 2/4/78 | **65** | 19 | | Two Hot For Love! .... | **$8** | Butterfly 005 |

Carnival (Theme from Black Orpheus)	Crazy, Crazy	Dawn Patrol	Early Riser	Two Hot For Love

3

Rock trio formed in 1987 by Emerson, Lake & Palmer alumni: Keith Emerson and Carl Palmer (both British), with California songwriter/guitarist Robert Barry.

| 3/19/88 | **97** | 10 | | To The Power Of Three .... | **$8** | Geffen 24181 |

Chains	Eight Miles High	On My Way Home	Talkin' Bout
Desde La Vida Medley	Lover To Lover	Runaway	You Do Or You Don't

THREE DEGREES, The

Philadelphia R&B trio discovered by Richard Barrett. Originally consisted of Fayette Pinkney, Linda Turner and Shirley Porter. Turner and Porter replaced by Sheila Ferguson and Valerie Holiday in 1966.

8/8/70	**139**	7		1 "Maybe"	**$15**	Roulette 42050
12/14/74+	**28**	15		2 The Three Degrees	**$8**	Phil. Int. 32406
6/21/75	**99**	8		3 International	**$8**	Phil. Int. 33162
1/17/76	**199**	1		4 The Three Degrees Live .... [L]	**$8**	Phil. Int. 33840
12/23/78+	**169**	8		5 New Dimensions	**$8**	Ariola 50044

Another Heartache (3)	Everybody Gets To Go To The Moon (1)	Here I Am (3)	Looking For Love (5)	Stardust (1)	Woman In Love (5)
Can't You See What You're Doing To Me (2)	Falling In Love Again (5)	I Didn't Know (2)	Love Train (4)	Sugar On Sunday (1)	Woman Needs A Good Man (2)
Collage (1)	For The Love Of Money (medley) (4)	I Like Being A Woman (4)	Loving Cup (3)	TSOP (The Sound Of Philadelphia) (3,4)	Year Of Decision (2,4)
Dirty Ol' Man (2,4)	Free Ride (4)	If And When (2)	MacArthur Park (1)	Take Good Care Of Yourself (3)	You're The Fool (1)
Distant Lover (3)	Get Your Love Back (3)	Living For The City (medley) (4)	Magic Door (1)		**You're The One** (1) *77*
Don't Let The Sun Go Down On Me (1)	Giving Up, Giving In (5)	Lonelier Are Fools (3)	Magic In The Air (5)	Together (3)	
	Harlem (4)	Lonely Town (1)	**Maybe** (1) *29*	When Will I See You Again (2,4) *2*	
		Long Lost Lover (3)	Rosegarden (1)		
			Runner, The (5)		

★★127★★ THREE DOG NIGHT

Los Angeles pop-rock group formed in 1968 featuring lead singers Danny Hutton (b: 9/10/42), Cory Wells (b: 2/5/42) and Chuck Negron (b: 6/8/42). Disbanded in the mid-1970s. Re-formed in the mid-1980s.

1/25/69	**11**	62	●	1 Three Dog Night	**$12**	Dunhill 50048
7/12/69	**16**	74	●	2 Suitable for Framing	**$12**	Dunhill 50058
11/29/69	**6**	72	●	3 **Captured Live At The Forum** .... [L]	**$12**	Dunhill 50068
5/2/70	**8**	48	●	4 **It Ain't Easy**	**$12**	Dunhill 50078
12/12/70+	**14**	64	●	5 **Naturally**	**$10**	Dunhill 50088
2/27/71	**5**	61	●	6 **Golden Bisquits** .... [G]	**$10**	Dunhill 50098
10/23/71	**8**	34	●	7 **Harmony**	**$10**	Dunhill 50108
7/29/72	**6**	40	●	8 **Seven Separate Fools**	**$10**	Dunhill 50118
3/17/73	**18**	27	●	9 Around The World With Three Dog Night .... [L]	**$12**	Dunhill 50138 [2]
10/20/73	**26**	17	●	10 Cyan	**$10**	Dunhill 50158
4/6/74	**20**	22	●	11 Hard Labor	**$10**	Dunhill 50168
12/21/74+	**15**	17	●	12 Joy To The World-Their Greatest Hits .... [G]	**$10**	Dunhill 50178
6/21/75	**70**	12		13 Coming Down Your Way	**$8**	ABC 888
4/24/76	**123**	6		14 American Pastime	**$8**	ABC 928

Ain't That A Lotta Love (2)	Everybody's A Masterpiece (14)	In Bed (8)	Midnight Flyer ("Eli Wheeler") (13)	On The Way Back Home (11)	Storybook Feeling (10)
Anytime Babe (11)	**Family Man** (7,9,12) *12*	Into My Life (10)	Midnight Runaway (8,9)	One (1,3,6,12) *5*	Sunlight (5)
Billy The Kid (14)	Feeling Alright (2,3)	It Ain't Easy (4)	Mind Over Matter (13)	One Man Band (5,6,9,12) *19*	Sure As I'm Sittin' Here (11,12) *16*
Black & White (8,9,12) *1*	Find Someone To Love (1)	It's For You (1,3)	Mistakes And Illusions (4,6,9) *15*	**Out In The Country** (4,6,9) *15*	That No One Ever Hurt This Bad (1)
Can't Get Enough Of It (5)	Fire Eater (2)	Jam (7,9)	Murder In My Heart For The Judge (1)	Peace Of Mind (7)	Til The World Ends (13) *32*
Celebrate (2,6) *15*	Freedom For The Stallion (8)	**Joy To The World** (5,9,12) *1*		**Pieces Of April** (8,9) *19*	**Try A Little Tenderness** (1,3,6) *29*
Chained (8)	Going In Circles (8,9)	King Solomon's Mines (2)	My Impersonal Life (7)	Play Children Play (10)	
Change Is Gonna Come (2)	Good Feeling (1957) (4,9)	Kite Man (13)	My Old Kentucky Home (Turpentine And Dandelion Wine) (8)	**Play Something Sweet (Brickyard Blues)** (11,12) *33*	Tulsa Turnaround (8)
Chest Fever (1,3)	Good Old Feeling (13)	Lady Samantha (2)			When It's Over (13)
Circle For A Landing (2)	Good Time Living (4)	Lay Me Down Easy (10)	Never Been To Spain (7,9,12) *5*	Prelude To Morning (8)	Woman (4,6)
Coming Down Your Way (13)	Hang On (14)	Lean Back, Hold Steady (13)	Never Dreamed You'd Leave In Summer (7)	Put Out The Light (11)	Writings On The Wall (8)
Cowboy (4)	Happy Song (10)	Let Me Go (1)	Night In The City (7)	Ridin' Thumb (10)	Yellow Beach Umbrella (14)
Dance The Night Away (14)	Heaven Is In Your Mind (1,3)	**Let Me Serenade You** (10,12) *17*	Nobody (1,3,6)	Rock & Roll Widow (4)	Yo Te Quiero Hablar (Take You Down) (13)
Don't Make Promises (1,6)	Heavy Church (5)	Liar (5,9,12) *7*	**Old Fashioned Love Song** (7,9,12) *4*	**Shambala** (10,12) *3*	You (7)
Dreaming Isn't Good For You (2)	I Can Hear You Calling (5)	Loner, The (1)		**Show Must Go On** (11,12) *4*	You Can Leave Your Hat On (13)
Drive On, Ride On (14)	I'd Be So Happy (11,12)	**Mama Told Me (Not To Come)** (4,6,9) *1*		Singer Man (10)	Your Song (4,6)
Easy Evil (14)	I'll Be Creeping (5)	Mellow Down (14)		Sitting In Limbo (11)	
Easy To Be Hard (2,3,6) *4*	I've Got Enough Heartache (5)			Southbound (14)	
Eli's Coming (2,3,6,9) *10*					

DEBUT DATE	PEAK POS	WKS CHR	G O L D	ARTIST — Album Title	$	Label & Number

THREE O'CLOCK, The
Los Angeles neo-psychedelic quartet — Michael Quercio, lead singer.

5/25/85	125	10		Arrive Without Travelling	$8	I.R.S. 5591

Another World   Girl With The Guitar (Says   Hand In Hand   Knowing When You Smile   Simon In The Park (With   Spun Gold
Each And Every Lonely Heart   Oh Yeah)   Her Head's Revolving   Mrs. Green   Tentacles)   Underwater
Half The Way There

THREE SUNS, The
Instrumental trio: brothers Al (guitar; d: 1965) and Morty Nevins (accordion; d: 7/20/90 of cancer). with Artie Dunn (organ; d: 1989). Al Nevins founded, with Don Kirshner, Aldon Music, the famed publishing company largely responsible for the "Brill Building" rock and roll sound.

5/28/55	13	9	1	Soft and Sweet	[I] $15	RCA 1041
8/18/56	19	1	2	High Fi and Wide	[I] $15	RCA 1249
1/26/57	16	6	3	Midnight For Two	[I] $15	RCA 1333

Ain't Misbehavin' (3)   Far Away Places (2)   Intermission Time (3)   On A Little Street In   There Is No Greater Love (1)
Alouette (2)   Flamingo (1)   It's Dawn Again (1)   Singapore (2)   Touch Of Your Lips (1)
April In Portugal (2)   Galway Bay (2)   Lady Of Shangri-La (2)   River Seine (1)   Velvet Moon (1)
Autumn Nocturne (1)   Hindustan (2)   Let's Call The Whole Thing   Sheik Of Araby (2)   Very Thought Of You (3)
Bali Ha'i (2)   I Don't Stand A Ghost Of A   Off (3)   Sinner Kissed An Angel (1)   Viennese Refrain (The Old
Blue Bells Of Scotland (2)   Chance (3)   Londonderry Air (2)   Skylark (1)   Refrain) (2)
Blue Orchids (1)   In A Little Spanish Town   Memory Lane (3)   Song Of India (2)   When Yuba Plays The
Blue Tango (3)   ('Twas On A Night Like   Mexican Hat Dance (2)   Song Of Old Hawaii (2)   Rumba On The Tuba (3)
Come Back To Sorrento (2)   This) (2)   Midnight For Two (3)   Stars Fell On Alabama (1)   World Is Waiting For The
Cumana (3)   In A Persian Market (2)   Moonlight In Vermont (1)   Stella By Starlight (3)   Sunrise (3)

THREE TIMES DOPE
Philadelphia rap trio: Duerwood Beale, Walter Griggs and Robert Waller.

4/22/89	122	18		Original Stylin'	$8	Arista 8571

Believe Dat   Funky Dividends   Improvin Da Groovin   Once More You Hear The   Original Stylin'   What's Going On (medley)
From Da Giddy Up   Greatest Man Alive   Increase The Peace (medley)   Dope Stuff   Straight Up   Who Is This?

THRILLS
New York-based rock quartet — Tony Monaco, lead singer.

6/27/81	199	4		First Thrills	$8	G&P 1002

Blinded By Love   Carrie   Dream Away   Good Friends   Not Gonna Run
Breaking My Heart   Changing My Ways   Going Out   Lie For Your Love   Won't Be A Fool

THUNDER
British rock band formed by Danny Bowes (vocals) and Luke Morley (guitar).

6/1/91	114	10		Backstreet Symphony	$12	Geffen 24384

Backstreet Symphony   Distant Thunder   Englishman On Holiday   Girl's Going Out Of Her Head   Love Walked In   Until My Dying Day
Dirty Love 55   Don't Wait For Me   Gimme Some Lovin'   Higher Ground   She's So Fine

THUNDERCLAP NEWMAN
British trio: Andy Newman (keyboards), John "Speedy" Keen (vocals) and Jimmy McCulloch (guitarist with Wings, 1975-77; died on 9/27/79 [age 26]). Group put together by Pete Townshend.

10/10/70+	161	10		Hollywood Dream	$15	Track 8264

produced by Pete Townshend

Accidents   Hollywood #1 & #2   Look Around   Open The Door, Homer   **Something In The Air 37**   Wild Country
Hollywood Dream   I Don't Know   Old Cornmill   Reason, The   When I Think

TIERRA
East Los Angeles group formed in 1972. Band led by the Salas brothers: Steve (trombone, timbales) and Rudy (guitar); both formerly with El Chicano.

12/27/80+	38	21		City Nights	$8	Boardwalk 36995

Givin' Up On Love   Latin Disco   Street Scene   **Together 18**
Gonna Find Her   **Memories 62**   Time To Dance   Zoot Suit Boogie

TIFFANY
Tiffany Darwisch, born on 10/2/71. California pop singer, originally from Oklahoma.

9/26/87+	1²	69	▲⁴	1 Tiffany	$8	MCA 5793
12/10/88+	17	29	▲	2 Hold An Old Friend's Hand	$8	MCA 6267

All This Time (2) 6   Hold An Old Friend's Hand   I'll Be The Girl (2)   Oh Jackie (2)   Walk Away While You Can
Could've Been (1) 1   (2)   It's The Lover (Not The Love)   Promises Made (1)   (2)
Danny (1)   **I Saw Him Standing There**   (2)   **Radio Romance** (2) 35   We're Both Thinking Of Her
Drop That Bomb (2)   (1) 7   Johnny's Got The Inside   Should've Been Me (1)   (2)
Feelings Of Forever (1) 50   **I Think We're Alone Now**   Moves (1)   Spanish Eyes (1)
Hearts Never Lie (2)   (1) 1   Kid On A Corner (1)

TIKARAM, Tanita
Born on 8/12/69 in Munster, West Germany. Female singer of Malaysian and Fijian parentage. Moved to Basingstoke, England at age 12.

2/11/89	59	23		1 Ancient Heart	$8	Reprise 25839
2/24/90	124	7		2 The Sweet Keeper	$12	Reprise 26091
4/20/91	142	5		3 Everybody's Angel	$12	Reprise 26486

Cathedral Song (1)   He Likes The Sun (1)   It All Came Back Today (2)   Once & Not Speak (2)   Sunface (3)   To Wish This (3)
Consider The Rain (2)   Hot Pork Sandwiches (3)   Little Sister Leaving Town (2)   Only The Ones We Love (3)   Sunset's Arrived (2)   Twist In My Sobriety (1)
Deliver Me (3)   I Love The Heaven's Solo (3)   Love Story (2)   Poor Cow (1)   Swear By Me (3)   Valentine Heart (1)
For All These Years (1)   I Love You (1)   Me In Mind (3)   Preyed Upon (2)   This Story In Me (3)   We Almost Got It Together (1)
Good Tradition (1)   I Owe All To You (2)   Mud In Any Water (3)   Sighing Innocents (1)   This Stranger (3)   World Outside Your Window
Harm In Your Hands (2)   I'm Going Home (3)   Never Known (3)   Sometime With Me (3)   Thursday's Child (2)   (1)

TILLIS, Pam
Country singer. Daughter of Mel Tillis.

1/25/92	69	23	●	1 Put Yourself In My Place	$12	Arista 8642
10/17/92	82	17↑		2 Homeward Looking Angel	$12	Arista 18649

DEBUT DATE	PEAK POS	WKS CHR	GOLD	ARTIST — Album Title	$	Label & Number

TILLIS, Pam — Cont'd

Already Fallen (1)	Do You Know Where Your	Homeward Looking Angel (2)	Love Is Only Human (2)	Rough And Tumble Heart (2)
Ancient History (1)	Man Is (2)	How Gone Is Goodbye (2)	Maybe It Was Memphis (1)	Shake The Sugar Tree (2)
Blue Rose Is (1)	Don't Tell Me What To Do (1)	I've Seen Enough To Know	Melancholy Child (1)	We've Tried Everything Else
Cleopatra, Queen Of Denial	Draggin' My Chains (1)	(1)	One Of Those Things (1)	(2)
(2)	Fine, Fine, Very Fine Love (2)	Let That Pony Run (1)	Put Yourself In My Place (1)	

TILLOTSON, Johnny

Born on 4/20/39 in Jacksonville, Florida; raised in Palatka, Florida. On local radio *Young Folks Revue* from age nine. DJ on WWPF. Appeared on the *Toby Dowdy* TV show in Jacksonville, then own show. Signed by Cadence Records in 1958. In the film *Just For Fun*.

DEBUT DATE	PEAK POS	WKS CHR	GOLD	ARTIST — Album Title	$	Label & Number
4/14/62	120	5		1 Johnny Tillotson's Best ....[G]	$35	Cadence 3052
7/21/62	8	31		2 It Keeps Right On A-Hurtin'	$35	Cadence 3058
2/22/64	48	14		3 Talk Back Trembling Lips	$15	MGM 4188
2/6/65	148	3		4 She Understands Me	$15	MGM 4270

All Alone Am I (3)	Funny How Time Slips	It Keeps Right On	Pledging My Love (1) 63	That's Love (4)	Without You (1) 7
Another You (3)	Away (2) 50	A-Hurtin' (2) 3	Poetry In Motion (1) 2	That's When It Hurts The	Worried Guy (3) 37
Blowin' In The Wind (3)	Hello Walls (2)	Jimmy's Girl (1) 25	Princess Princess (1)	Most (4)	Yellow Bird (4)
Blue Velvet (3)	I Can't Help It (If I'm Still	Little Boy (4)	Rhythm Of The Rain (3)	To Be A Child Again (4)	
Busted (2)	In Love With You) (2) 24	(Little Sparrow) His True	Send Me The Pillow You	Tomorrow (4)	
Cutie Pie (1)	I Can't Stop Loving You (3)	Love Said Goodbye (1)	Dream On (2) 17	True True Happiness (1) 54	
Danke Schoen (3)	I Fall To Pieces (2)	Lonely Street (2)	She Understands Me (4) 31	What Am I Gonna Do (3)	
Dreamy Eyes (1) 35	I'm So Lonesome I Could	More Than Before (4)	Take Good Care Of Her (2)	What'll I Do (2)	
Earth Angel (1) 57	Cry (2) 89	Much Beyond Compare (1)	Take This Hammer (4)	Why Do I Love You So	
Fool #1 (2)	Island Of Dreams (4)	My Little World (3)	Talk Back Trembling Lips	(1) 42	
Four Walls (2)		Please Don't Go Away (3)	(3) 7	Willow Tree (4)	

'TIL TUESDAY

Boston pop quartet: Aimee Mann (lead singer, bass), Michael Hausmann (drums), Robert Holmes (guitar) and Joey Pesce (keyboards; replaced by Michael Montes in 1988).

DEBUT DATE	PEAK POS	WKS CHR	GOLD	ARTIST — Album Title	$	Label & Number
4/20/85	19	31	●	1 Voices Carry	$8	Epic 39458
10/25/86	49	26		2 Welcome Home	$8	Epic 40314
11/19/88	124	19		3 Everything's Different Now	$8	Epic 44041

Angels Never Call (2)	Everything's Different Now	Long Gone (Buddy) (3)	No One Is Watching You	Sleeping And Waking (2)
(Believed You Were) Lucky	(3)	Looking Over My Shoulder	Now (2)	Voices Carry (1)
(3) 95	Have Mercy (2)	(1) 61	On Sunday (2)	What About Love (2) 26
Coming Up Close (2) 59	How Can You Give Up (3)	Love In A Vacuum (1)	Other End (Of The	Why Must I (3)
Crash And Burn (3)	I Could Get Used To This (1)	Lovers' Day (3)	Telescope) (3)	Will She Just Fall Down (1)
David Denies (2)	J For Jules (3)	Maybe Monday (1)	Rip In Heaven (3)	Winning The War (1)
Don't Watch Me Bleed (1)	Limits To Love (3)	No More Crying (1)	Sleep (1)	You Know The Rest (1)

TIMBUK 3

Austin-based, husband-and-wife duo: Pat and Barbara Kooyman MacDonald. Met while Barbara was attending the University of Wisconsin in 1978.

DEBUT DATE	PEAK POS	WKS CHR	GOLD	ARTIST — Album Title	$	Label & Number
10/4/86+	50	30		1 Greetings From Timbuk 3	$8	I.R.S. 5739
5/7/88	107	13		2 Eden Alley	$8	I.R.S. 42124

Cheap Black And White (1)	Friction (1)	I Love You In The Strangest	Little People Make Big	Sample The Dog (2)	Too Much Sex, Not Enough
Dance Fever (2)	Future's So Bright, I Gotta	Way (1)	Mistakes (2)	Shame On You (1)	Affection (2)
Easy (1)	Wear Shades (1) 19	I Need You (1)	Reckless Driver (2)	Sinful Life (2)	Welcome To The Human
Eden Alley (2)	Hairstyles And Attitudes (1)	Just Another Movie (1)	Rev. Jack & His Roamin'	Tarzan Was A Bluesman (2)	Race (2)
Facts About Cats (1)		Life Is Hard (1)	Cadillac Church (2)		

TIME, The

Funk group formed in Minneapolis by Prince and Morris Day in 1981. Original lineup: Morris Day (lead singer), Terry Lewis, Jimmy "Jam" Harris, Monte Moir, Jesse Johnson and Jellybean Johnson. Lewis, Harris and Moir left prior to band's featured role in film *Purple Rain*. Paul "St. Paul" Peterson and Lewis' half-brother, Jerome Benton, joined in 1984. Day and Jesse Johnson went solo; Lewis and Harris became a highly successful songwriting/producing team. Lewis married Karyn White. Original lineup plus Benton regrouped in 1990.

DEBUT DATE	PEAK POS	WKS CHR	GOLD	ARTIST — Album Title	$	Label & Number
9/12/81	50	32	●	1 The Time	$8	Warner 3598
9/25/82	26	33	●	2 What Time Is It?	$8	Warner 23701
7/28/84	24	57	▲	3 Ice Cream Castle	$8	Warner 25109
7/28/90	18	16	●	4 Pandemonium	$12	Paisley P. 27490

After Hi School (1)	Cool (Part 1) (1) 90	Gigolos Get Lonely Too (2)	It's Your World (4)	Onedayi'mgonnabesomebody	Skillet (4)
Bird, The (3) 36	Data Bank (4)	Girl (1)	Jerk Out (4) 9	(2)	Sometimes I Get Lonely (4)
Blondie (4)	Donald Trump (Black	I Don't Wanna Leave You (2)	Jungle Love (3) 20	Pandemonium (2)	Stick, The (1)
Chili Sauce (3)	Version) (4)	Ice Cream Castles (3)	My Drawers (3)	Pretty Little Women (4)	Walk, The (2)
Chocolate (4)	Dreamland (4)	If The Kid Can't Make You	My Summertime Thang (4)	777-9311 (2) 88	Wild And Loose (2)
Cooking Class (4)	Get It Up (1)	Come (3)	Oh, Baby (1)	Sexy Socialites (4)	Yount (4)

TIMES TWO

Male duo of vocalists/keyboardists from Pt. Reyes, California: Shanti Jones and Johnny Dollar.

DEBUT DATE	PEAK POS	WKS CHR	GOLD	ARTIST — Album Title	$	Label & Number
4/30/88	137	11		X2	$8	Reprise 25624

Cecilia 79	Jet	Mr. D.J.	Only My Pillow Knows (For	Painted Heart	Strange But True 21
I Wantcha	L.O.D. (Love On Delivery)		Sure)	Romeo	3 Into 2 (Don't Go)

TIMMY -T-

Born Timmy Torres on 9/23/67 in Fresno, California.

DEBUT DATE	PEAK POS	WKS CHR	GOLD	ARTIST — Album Title	$	Label & Number
1/26/91	46	23		Time After Time	$12	Quality 15103

My Exceptional Girl	Over And Over 63	Please Don't Go	Too Young To Love You	You're The Only One
One More Try 1	Paradise	Time After Time 40	What Will I Do 96	

TIN MACHINE

Quartet of David Bowie (vocals), Reeves Gabrels (guitar; ex-Rubber Rodeo), Hunt (drums; ex-Utopia, ex-Paris) and Tony Sales (bass; ex-Utopia, ex-Chequered Past). The Sales brothers are the sons of television comedian Soupy Sales. Tony acted in film *Hard To Hold* and Budweiser commercials.

DEBUT DATE	PEAK POS	WKS CHR	GOLD	ARTIST — Album Title	$	Label & Number
6/10/89	28	17		1 Tin Machine	$8	EMI 91990
9/21/91	126	3		2 Tin Machine II	$12	Victory 511216

743

TIN MACHINE — Cont'd

Amazing (1)
Amlapura (2)
Baby Can Dance (1)
Baby Universal (2)
Betty Wrong (2)

Big Hurt (2)
Bus Stop (1)
Crack City (1)
Goodbye Mr. Ed (2)
Heaven's In Here (1)

I Can't Read (1)
If There Is Something (2)
One Shot (2)
Pretty Thing (1)
Prisoner Of Love (1)

Shopping For Girls (2)
Sorry (2)
Stateside (2)
Tin Machine (1)
Under The God (1)

Video Crime (1)
Working Class Hero (1)
You Belong In Rock & Roll (2)
You Can't Talk (2)

TIN TIN

Australian duo: Steve Kipner (keyboards) and Steve Groves (guitar). Disbanded in 1973. Kipner later co-wrote Chicago's "Hard Habit To Break" and Olivia Newton-John's "Physical" and "Twist Of Fate."

| 6/5/71 | 197 | 1 | | Tin Tin .... | $12 | Atco 350 |

produced by Maurice Gibb

Come On Over Again
Family Tree
Flag (medley)

He Wants To Be A Star
Lady In Blue
Manhattan Woman

Nobody Moves Me Like You
Only Ladies Play Croquet
She Said Ride

Put Your Money On My Dog (medley)

Spanish Shepherd
Swans On The Canal

Toast And Marmalade For Tea 20
Tuesday's Dreamer

TINY TIM

Born Herbert Khaury on 4/12/30 in New York City. Novelty singer/ukulele player. National phenomenon when he married "Miss Vicki" on *The Tonight Show* on 12/18/69; divorced in 1977.

| 5/4/68 | 7 | 32 | | **God Bless Tiny Tim** .... [N] | $12 | Reprise 6292 |

Coming Home Party
Daddy, Daddy, What Is Heaven Like?

Ever Since You Told Me That You Love Me (I'm A Nut)
Fill Your Heart

I Got You, Babe
Livin' In The Sunlight, Lovin' In The Moonlight
On The Old Front Porch

Other Side
Stay Down Here Where You Belong
Strawberry Tea

Then I'd Be Satisfied With Life
This Is All I Ask

Tip-Toe Thru' The Tulips With Me 17
Viper, The
Welcome To My Dream

TIPPIN, Aaron

Native of South Carolina. Country singer/songwriter.

| 5/25/91 | 153 | 21 | | 1 You've Got To Stand For Something .... | $12 | RCA 2374 |
| 3/28/92 | 50 | 33 | ● | 2 Read Between The Lines .... | $12 | RCA 61129 |

Ain't That A Hell Of A Note (1)
I Miss Misbehavin' (2)
I Was Born With A Broken Heart (2)

I Wonder How Far It Is Over You (1)
I Wouldn't Have It Any Other Way (2)
I've Got A Good Memory (1)
If I Had It To Do Over (2)

In My Wildest Dreams (1)
Man That Came Between Us (Was Me) (1)
Many, Many, Many Beers Ago (1)
My Blue Angel (2)

Read Between The Lines (2)
She Made A Memory Out Of Me (1)
Sky's Got The Blues (1)
Sound Of Your Goodbye (Sticks And Stones) (2)

There Ain't Nothin' Wrong With The Radio (2)
These Sweet Dreams (2)
This Heart (2)
Up Against You (1)

You've Got To Stand For Something (1)

TJADER, Cal

Born on 7/16/25 in St. Louis; died on 5/5/82. Latin jazz vibraphonist.

| 9/28/63 | 79 | 14 | | 1 Several Shades Of Jade .... [I] | $15 | Verve 8507 |
| 4/17/65 | 52 | 22 | | 2 Soul Sauce .... [I] | $15 | Verve 8614 |

Afro-Blue (2)
Almond Tree (1)
Borneo (1)
Cherry Blossoms (1)

China Nights (Shina No Yoru) (1)
Fakir, The (1)
Hot Sake (1)

Joao (2)
Leyte (2)
Maramoor (2)
Pantano (2)

Sahib (1)
Somewhere In The Night (2)
Song Of The Yellow River (1)

Soul Sauce (Guacha Guaro) (2) **88**
Spring Is Here (2)
Tanya (2)

Tokyo Blues (1)

TKA

New York Spanish Harlem group. TKA: Total Knowledge In Action. In 1987, quintet reduced to a trio of Anthony "Tony" Ortiz, Louis "Kayel" Sharpe and Ralph "Aby" Cruz.

| 1/30/88 | 135 | 11 | | 1 Scars Of Love .... | $8 | Tommy Boy 1011 |
| 4/25/92 | 131 | 9 | | 2 Greatest Hits .... | $8 | Tommy Boy 1040 |

Come Get My Love (1,2)
Crash (Have Some Fun) (2) **80**

Don't Be Afraid (1,2)
Give Your Love To Me (2)
I Can't Help It (2)

I Won't Give Up On You (2) **65**
Is It Love? (2)
Maria (2) **44**

It's Got To Be Love (1)
Louder Than Love (2) **62**
Scars Of Love (1,2)
Someone In The Dark (1)

One Way Love (1,2) **75**

Tears May Fall (1,2)
X-Ray Vision (1,2)
You Are The One (2) **91**

TKO

Seattle-based rock band — Brad Sinsel, lead singer.

| 4/21/79 | 181 | 2 | | Let It Roll .... | $8 | Infinity 9005 |

Ain't No Way To Be
Bad Sister

Come A Day
Gutter Boy

Kill The Pain
Let It Roll

Only Love
Rock 'N Roll Again

What In The World

TLC

Atlanta-based teenage female rap trio: Tionne "T-Boz" Watkins, Lisa "Left Eye" Lopes and Rozonda "Chilli" Thomas. Founded and managed by Pebbles.

| 3/14/92 | 14 | 48↑ | ▲² | Oooooooohhh...On The TLC Tip .... | $12 | LaFace 26003 |

Ain't 2 Proud 2 Beg 6
Baby-Baby-Baby 2
Bad By Myself

Das Da Way We Like 'Em
Depend On Myself

Hat 2 Da Back 92↑
His Story

Shock Dat Monkey
Somethin' You Wanna Know

This Is How It Should Be Done
What About Your Friends 7

TNT

Norway-based, hard-rock quartet led by Tony Harnell (lead vocals).

| 5/23/87 | 100 | 21 | | 1 Tell No Tales .... | $8 | Mercury 830979 |
| 3/18/89 | 115 | 12 | | 2 Intuition .... | $8 | Mercury 836777 |

As Far As The Eye Can See (1)
Caught Between The Tigers (2)

Child's Play (1)
Desperate Night (1)
End Of The Line (2)
Everyone's A Star (1)

Forever Shine On (2)
Incipits (1)
Intuition (2)
Learn To Love (2)

Listen To Your Heart (1)
Nation Free (2)
Northern Lights (1)
Ordinary Lover (2)

Sapphire (1)
Smooth Syncopation (1)
Take Me Down (Fallen Angel) (2)

Tell No Tales (1)
10,000 Lovers (In One) (1)
Tonight I'm Falling (2)
Wisdom (2)

TOAD THE WET SPROCKET

Pop quartet from Santa Barbara, California: Glen Phillips (vocals), Todd Nichols (guitar), Dean Dinning (bass) and Randy Guss (drums). Name taken from a Monty Python skit.

| 7/11/92 | 49 | 31↑ | ● | Fear .... | $12 | Columbia 47309 |

All I Want 15
Before You Were Born
Butterflies

Hold Her Down
I Will Not Take These Things For Granted

In My Ear
Is It For Me
Nightingale Song

Pray Your Gods
Something To Say

Stories I Tell
Walk On The Ocean 18

TOBY BEAU

Texas pop quintet: Balde Silva (vocals), Danny McKenna, Rob Young, Steve Zipper and Ron Rose.

| 6/10/78 | 40 | 23 | | Toby Beau .... | $8 | RCA 2771 |

DEBUT DATE	PEAK POS	WKS CHR	GOLD	ARTIST — Album Title	$	Label & Number

TOBY BEAU — Cont'd

Broken Down Cowboy	Bulldog	Into The Night	**My Angel Baby** *13*	Watching The World Go By	Wink Of An Eye
Buckaroo	California	Moonshine	Same Old Line	Westbound Train	

TODAY
Soul quartet from Englewood, New Jersey: Lee Drakeford (lead), Larry McCain, Wesley Adams and Larry Singletary.

1/14/89	**86**	22		1 Today	$8	Motown 6261
10/13/90	**132**	6		2 The New Formula	$12	Motown 6309

CD includes 2 bonus tracks

Every Little Thing About You (2)	Him Or Me (1)	I Wanna Come Back Home (2)	No Need To Worry (2)	Take Your Time (1)	You Stood Me Up (1)
Girl I Got My Eyes On You (1)	Home Is Where You Belong (2)	Lady (1)	Self Centered (2)	Tennis Anyone (2)	Your Love Is Not True (1)
Gonna Make You Mine (2)	I Got The Feeling (2)	Let Me Know (2)	Sexy Lady (1)	Trying To Get Over You (2)	
		My Happiness (2)	Style (1)	Why You Get Funky On Me (2)	
			Take It Off (1)		

TOKENS, The
Vocal group formed as the Linc-Tones at Lincoln High School in Brooklyn in 1955. Original lineup included Neil Sedaka. Disbanded in 1958. Original member Hank Medress re-formed group with brothers Phil and Mitch Margo. Formed own label, B.T. Puppy, in 1964. Medress produced Tony Orlando & Dawn, and then left The Tokens, who continued as a trio and recorded as Cross Country in 1973.

1/27/62	**54**	16		1 The Lion Sleeps Tonight	$50	RCA 2514
5/21/66	**148**	2		2 I Hear Trumpets Blow	$25	B.T. Puppy 1000
7/22/67	**134**	6		3 Back To Back	$20	B.T. Puppy 1002

THE TOKENS/THE HAPPENINGS
side 1: The Tokens; side 2: The Happenings

Barbara Ann (2)	Don't Cry, Sing Along With The Music (2)	**I Hear Trumpets Blow** (2,3) *30*	Lonesome Traveller (1)	Speedo (2)	Tina (1)
Big Boat (1)	Every Breath I Take (2)	Michael (1)	Swing (2,3)	Wake Up Little Suzy (2)
Children Go Where I Send Thee (1)	He's In Town (2,3) *43*	Jamaica Farewell (1)	Riddle, The (1)	Sylvie Sleepin' (2,3)	Water Is Over My Head (2)
	Hindi Lullabye (1)	Laugh (3)	Saloogy (2,3)	Three Bells (The Jimmy Brown Song) (2)	Water Prayer (1)
		Lion Sleeps Tonight (1) *1*	Shenandoah (1)		Wreck Of The John B. (1)

TOMITA
Born Isao Tomita in Tokyo in 1932. Classical-based keyboard whiz.

8/31/74	**57**	25		1 Snowflakes Are Dancing .... [I]	$8	RCA 0488
				electronic performances of music by Debussy		
5/24/75	**49**	12		2 Moussorgsky: Pictures At An Exhibition .... [I]	$8	RCA 0838
2/14/76	**71**	12		3 Firebird .... [I]	$8	RCA 11312
				interpretations of music by Stravinsky, Debussy and Moussorgsky		
1/8/77	**67**	13		4 Holst: The Planets .... [I]	$8	RCA 1919
2/18/78	**115**	10		5 Kosmos .... [I]	$8	RCA 2616
3/3/79	**152**	6		6 The Bermuda Triangle .... [I]	$8	RCA 2885
2/9/80	**174**	5		7 Ravel: Bolero .... [I]	$8	RCA 3412

Bach: The Sea Named "Solaris" (5)	Debussy: Gardens In The Rain (Estampes, No. 3) (1)	Debussy: The Engulfed Cathedral (Preludes, Book 1, No. 10) (1)	Harp Of The Ancient People With Songs Of Venus And Space Children (6)	Ravel: Pavan For A Dead Princess (7)	Venus In A Space Uniform Shining In Fluorescent Light (6)
Dawn Over The Triangle And Mysterious Electric Waves (6)	Debussy: Golliwog's Cakewalk (Children's Corner, No. 6) (1)	Debussy: The Girl With The Flaxen Hair (Preludes, Book 1, No. 8) (1)	Holst: The Planets (4)	Ravel: Daphnis And Chloe: Suite No. 2 (7)	Visionary Flight To The 1448 Nebular Group Of The Bootes (6)
Dazzling Cylinder That Crashed In Tunguska, Siberia (6)	Debussy: Passepied (Suite Bergamasque, No. 4) (1)	Dinicu-Heifetz: Hora Staccato (5)	Honegger: Pacific 231 (5)	Rodrigo: Aranjuez (5)	Song Of Venus (6)
Debussy: Arabesque No. 1 (1)	Debussy: Prelude To The Afternoon Of A Faun (3)	Earth -- A Hollow Vessel (6)	Ives: The Unanswered Question (5)	Space Children In The Underground Kingdom Called Agharta (6)	World Of Different Dimensions (6)
Debussy: Clair De Lune (Suite Bergamasque, No. 3) (1)	Debussy: Reverie (1)	Electromagnetic Waves Descend (6)	Moussorgsky: A Night On Bare Mountain (3)	Space Ship Lands Emitting Silvery Light (6)	
Debussy: Footprints In The Snow (Preludes, Book 1, No. 6) (1)	Debussy: Snowflakes Are Dancing (Children's Corner, No. 4) (1)	Giant Pyramid And Its Ancient People (6)	Moussorgsky: Pictures At An Exhibition (2)	Star Wars Main Title (5)	
		Grieg: Peer Gynt: Solvejg's Song (5)	Ravel: Bolero (7)	Strauss, R. - Wagner: Space Fantasy (5)	
			Ravel: Mother Goose Suite (7)	Stravinsky: Firebird Suite (3)	

TOMLIN, Lily
Born on 9/1/39 in Detroit. TV and film actress/comedienne. Member of TV's *Laugh-In* series (1970-73). In films *9 To 5*, *All of Me* and *Big Business*. In Broadway's *The Search For Signs Of Intelligent Life In The Universe.*

3/27/71	**15**	25		1 This is a Recording .... [C]	$10	Polydor 4055
3/25/72	**41**	22		2 And That's The Truth .... [C]	$10	Polydor 5023
11/12/77	**120**	3		3 On Stage .... [C]	$8	Arista 4142

Alexander Graham Bell (1)	Ernestine (1,3)	I Always Kiss Buster (1)	Lady Lady Open Up (2)	Mr. Theater Goer And Shopping Bag Lady (3)	Repairman, The (1)
Awards Dinner (1)	F.B.I., The (1)	I Can't Go To The Movies Here (2)	Lily And Shopping Bag Lady (3)	Mr. Veedle (1)	Shopping Bag Lady And UFO Guy (3)
Bordello, The (1)	Finish Putting The Groceries Away (2)	I Dressed Him Up (2)	Look In The Sky (2)	Mrs. Judith Beasley (Unnatural Resources) (3)	Strike, The (1)
Boswick 9 (1)	Glenna - A Child Of The 60's (3)	I Go To Sunday School (2)	Lud And Marie Meet Dracula's Daughter (A Tale Of Teen-Age Tyranny) (3)	Mrs. Mitchell (1)	Tell Me Something Lady (2)
Do You Have Any Chewing Gum? (2)	Guess This Riddle (2)	I Like Your Kitchen (2)		My Sister Mary Jean (2)	Tell Miss Sweeney Goodbye (3)
Does This Chair Lean Back? (2)	Here's My House (2)	I Want You To Go (2)	Mafia And The Pope (1)	Obscene Phone Call (1)	
Don't My Toes Look Pretty? (2)	Here's The Empty Lot (2)	I Will Help You Unpack (2)	Marriage Counselor (1)	Pageant, The (1)	
	Hey Lady (2)	I.B.M. (1)		Peeved (1)	
		Joan Crawford (1)			

TOMMY TUTONE
San Francisco rock band led by Tommy Heath (vocals) and Jim Keller (lead guitar).

5/24/80	**68**	13		1 Tommy Tutone	$8	Columbia 36372
2/6/82	**20**	30		2 Tommy Tutone-2	$8	Columbia 37401
10/29/83	**179**	3		3 National Emotion	$8	Columbia 38425

Am I Supposed To Lie (1)	Dancing Girl (1)	Hide-Out (1)	National Emotion (3)	Shadow On The Road Ahead (2)	Sticks And Stones (3)
Angel Say No (1) *38*	Dumb But Pretty (3)	I Believe (3)	No Way To Cry (2)	Someday Will Come (3)	Tonight (2)
Baby It's Alright (2)	**867-5309/Jenny** (2) *4*	I Wanna Touch Her (3)	Not Say Goodbye (2)	Sounds Of A Summer Night (1)	What'cha Doin' To Me (1)
Bernadiah (2)	Fat Chance (3)	Imaginary Heart (3)	Only One (2)	Steal Away (2)	Which Man Are You (2)
Blame, The (1)	Get Around Girl (3)	Laverne (3)	Rachel (1)		Why Baby Why (2)
Cheap Date (1)	Girl In The Back Seat (1)	Money Talks (3)			

DEBUT DATE	PEAK POS	WKS CHR	GOLD	ARTIST — Album Title	$	Label & Number

TOMS, Gary, Empire
New York disco band led by Gary Toms (keyboards); vocals by Helen Jacobs.

| 9/27/75 | 178 | 3 | | 7-6-5-4-3-2-1 Blow Your Whistle .... | $8 | PIP 6814 |

Do Your Thing	Feel That Funky Groove	Love Me Right	7-6-5-4-3-2-1 (Blow Your	Slow & Funky	This Crazy World
Drive My Car 69	Jubilation (Excitation)	New Empire	Whistle) 46	Tell The People	You Are The One For Me

TOM TOM CLUB
Studio project formed by Talking Heads' members Chris Frantz and wife Tina Weymouth. Production work for Ziggy Marley & The Melody Makers, Happy Mondays and other.

10/24/81+	23	33	●	1 Tom Tom Club	$8	Sire 3628
8/20/83	73	13		2 Close To The Bone	$8	Sire 23916
4/15/89	114	11		3 Boom Boom Chi Boom Boom	$8	Sire 25888

As Above, So Below (1)	Challenge Of The Love	I Confess (3)	Man With The 4-Way Hips	On The Line Again (2)	Tom Tom Theme (1)
Atsababy! (Life Is Great) (2)	Warriors (3)	Kiss Me When I Get Back (3)	(2)	Pleasure Of Love (2)	Wa Wa Dance (3)
Bamboo Town (2)	Don't Say No (3)	L' Elephant (1)	Measure Up (2)	Shock The World (3)	Wordy Rappinghood (1)
Booming And Zooming (3)	Femme Fatale (3)	Little Eva (1)	Never Took A Penny (2)	Suboceana (3)	
Call Of The Wild (3)	Genius Of Love (1) 31	Lorelei (1)	On, On, On, On... (1)	This Is A Foxy World (2)	

TONE LOC
L.A.-based rapper, Anthony Smith. Stage name derived from his Spanish nickname "Antonio Loco." Contributed voice to animated film *Bebe's Kids*.

| 2/18/89 | 1¹ | 42 | ▲² | Loc-ed After Dark .... | $8 | Delicious 3000 |

Cheeba Cheeba	Don't Get Close	Homies, The	Loc'ed After Dark	Next Episode	Wild Thing 2
Cutting Rhythms	Funky Cold Medina 3	I Got It Goin' On	Loc'in On The Shaw	On Fire	

TONEY, Oscar Jr.
Born on 5/26/39 in Selma, Alabama and raised in Columbus, Georgia. R&B singer.

| 7/29/67 | 192 | 5 | | For Your Precious Love .... | $15 | Bell 6006 |

Ain't That True Love	Do Right Woman - Do Right	Down In Texas	He Don't Love You (And He'll	Moon River	Turn On Your Love
Any Day Now	Man	For Your Precious Love 23	Break Your Heart)	No Sad Song	Light 65
Dark End Of The Street				That's All I Want From You	

TONIGHT SHOW BAND, The — see SEVERINSEN, Doc

TONY! TONI! TONE!
R&B-funk band from Oakland, California. Nucleus of group: brothers Dwayne and Raphael Wiggins, with cousin Timothy Christian. Appeared in the film *House Party 2*.

| 5/28/88 | 69 | 46 | ● | 1 Who? .... | $8 | Wing 835549 |
| 5/26/90 | 34 | 64 | ▲ | 2 The Revival.. | $12 | Wing 841902 |

All My Love (2)	Don't Talk About Me (2)	It Never Rains (In	Little Walter (1) 47	Skin Tight (2)	Who's Lovin' You (1)
All The Way (2)	Feels Good (2) 9	Southern California)	Love Struck (1)	Sky's The Limit (2)	
Baby Doll (1)	For The Love Of You (1)	(2) 34	Not Gonna Cry For You (1)	Those Were The Days (2)	
Blues, The (2) 46	I Care (2)	Jo-Jo (1)	Oakland Stroke (2)	261.5 (1)	
Born Not To Know (1)		Let's Have A Good Time (2)	Pain (1)	Whatever You Want (2) 48	

TOO SHORT
Born Todd Shaw on 4/28/66 in Los Angeles. 5'7" Oakland-based rapper.

2/25/89	37	78	▲	1 Life Is...Too $hort	$8	Dangerous 1149
9/29/90	20	53	▲	2 Short Dog's In The House	$12	Jive 1348
8/1/92	6	21	●	3 Shorty The Pimp	$12	Jive 41467

Ain't Nothin' But A Word To	Extra Dangerous Thanks (3)	I Ain't Trippin' (1)	It's Your Life (2)	Pimpology (2)	So You Want To Be A
Me (2)	Ghetto, The (2) 42	I Want To Be Free (That's	Life Is...Too Short (1)	Punk Bitch (2)	Gangster (3)
City Of Dope (1)	Hard On The Boulevard (2)	The Truth) (3)	No Love From Oakland (3)	Rap Like Me (2)	Something To Ride To (3)
CussWords (1)	Hoes (3)	In The Oaktown (2)	Nobody Does It Better (1)	Rhymes (2)	Step Daddy (3)
Dead Or Alive (2)	Hoochie (3)	In The Trunk (3)	Paula & Janet (2)	Short But Funky (2)	
Don't Fight The Feelin' (1)	I Ain't Nothin' But A Dog (3)	It Don't Stop (3)	Pimp The Ho (1)	Short Dog's In The House (2)	

TOOTS & THE MAYTALS
Jamaican band led by Frederick "Toots" Hibbert with Raleigh Gordon and Jerry Matthias. Formed in 1962, known as the Vikings until 1966. Disbanded in the early 1980s; Toots began solo career in 1983.

| 11/1/75 | 164 | 13 | | 1 Funky Kingston .... | $8 | Island 9330 |
| 7/17/76 | 157 | 5 | | 2 Reggae Got Soul .... | $8 | Mango 9374 |

Country Road (1)	I Shall Sing (2)	Love Is Gonna Let Me Down	Premature (2)	Sail On (1)	True Love Is Hard To Find (2)
Everybody Needs Lovin' (2)	In The Dark (1)	(1)	Pressure Drop (1)	Six And Seven Books (2)	
Funky Kingston (1)	Living In The Ghetto (2)	Never You Change (2)	Rastaman (2)	So Bad (2)	
Got To Be There (1)	Louie Louie (1)	Pomp And Pride (1)	Reggae Got Soul (2)	Time Tough (1)	

TORA TORA
Hard-rock quartet from Memphis: Anthony Corder (vocals), Keith Douglas, Patrick Francis and John Patterson. Band name taken from a Van Halen song.

| 7/15/89 | 47 | 33 | | 1 Surprise Attack... | $8 | A&M 5261 |
| 6/6/92 | 132 | 6 | | 2 Wild America .... | $12 | A&M 5371 |

Amnesia (2)	Cold Fever (2)	Guilty (1)	Nowhere To Go But Down (2)	Shattered (2)	Wild America (2)
As Time Goes By (2)	Dead Man's Hand (2)	Hard Times (1)	One For The Road (1)	She's Good She's Bad (1)	
Being There (1)	Dirty Secrets (2)	Lay Your Money Down (1)	Phantom Rider (1)	28 Days (1)	
City Of Kings (2)	Faith Healer (2)	Love's A Bitch (1)	Riverside Drive (1)	Walkin' Shoes (1) 86	

TORME, Mel
Born Melvin Howard on 9/13/25 in Chicago. Jazz singer/songwriter/pianist/drummer/actor. Wrote Nat King Cole's "The Christmas Song." Frequently appeared as himself on TV's *Night Court*.

| 12/19/92 | 170 | 3 | | Christmas Songs .... [X] | $12 | Telarc 83315 |

with the Cincinnati Sinfonietta, conducted by Keith Lockhart, and jazz trio of John Colianni, John Leitham and Donny Osborne.

Christmas Feeling	Christmas Was Made For	God Rest Ye Merry	Have Yourself A Merry Little	Let's Start The New Year	What Are You Doing New
Christmas Medley	Children	Gentlemen	Christmas (medley)	Right (medley)	Year's Eve? (medley)
Christmas Song	Christmastime Is Here	Good King Wenceslas	It Happened In Sun Valley	Silver Bells (medley)	What Child Is This?
Christmas Waltz	Glow Worm	Happy Holiday (medley)	Just Look Around (medley)	Sleigh Ride	White Christmas

DEBUT DATE	PEAK POS	WKS CHR	GOLD	ARTIST — Album Title	$	Label & Number

TORNADOES, The

English surf-rock instrumental quintet organized by producer Joe Meek in 1962. Original lineup: Alan Caddy (lead guitar), George Bellamy, Roger LaVerne Jackson, Heinz Burt and Clem Cattini. Meek committed suicide on 2/3/67.

1/5/63	45	17		The Original Telstar .... [I]	$35	London 3279

Breeze And I · Chasing Moonbeams · Dreamin' On A Cloud · Earthy · Jungle Fever · Love And Fury · Popeye Twist · Red Roses And A Sky Of Blue · Ridin' The Wind 63 · Summer Place, Theme From · Swinging Beefeater · Telstar 1

TORONTO

Holly Woods, lead singer of Canadian rock group from Toronto.

8/30/80	185	4		1 Lookin' For Trouble	$8	A&M 4821
9/4/82	162	10		2 Get It On Credit	$8	Network 60153

Break Down The Barricade (2) · Delirious (1) · Do Watcha; Be Watcha (1) · Don't Stop Me (1) · Don't Walk Away (2) · Even The Score (1) · Lookin' For Trouble (1) · Run For Your Life (2) · 5035 (1) · Get It On Credit (2) · Get Your Hands Off Me (1) · Sick N' Tired (2) · Start Tellin' The Truth (2) · Tie Me Down (1) · Shot Down (1) · Why Can't We Talk? (2) · Ya Love Ta Love (2) · You Better Run (1) · You're A Mystery To Me (2) · Your Daddy Don't Know (2) 77

TORRANCE, Richard, & Eureka

Rock group led by guitarist Torrance.

3/8/75	107	17		Belle Of The Ball	$8	Shelter 2134

Don't Let Me Down Again · Hard Heavy Road · Jam, The · Lady · Lazy Town · North Dakota Lady · Side By Each · Singing Springs · Southern Belles · Sweet Sweet Rock & Roll · That's What I Like In My Woman

TOSH, Peter

Born Winston Hubert MacIntosh on 10/9/44 in Jamaica. Former member of Bob Marley's Wailers. Fatally shot on 9/11/87 (age 42) during a robbery at his home in Kingston.

7/31/76	199	2		1 Legalize It	$8	Columbia 34253
12/9/78+	104	20		2 Bush Doctor	$8	Rolling S. 39109
8/4/79	123	10		3 Mystic Man	$8	Rolling S. 39111
7/18/81	91	13		4 Wanted Dread & Alive	$8	EMI America 17055
6/18/83	59	17		5 Mama Africa	$8	EMI America 17095
9/22/84	152	8		6 Captured Live .... [L]	$8	EMI America 17126

African (6) · Brand New Second Hand (1) · Buk-In-Hamm Palace (3) · Burial (1) · Bush Doctor (2,6) · Can't You See (3) · Cold Blood (4) · Coming In Hot (4,6) · Creation (2) · Crystal Ball (6) · Day The Dollar Die (3) · Dem Ha Fe Get A Beaten (2) · Downpresser Man (medley) (6) · Equal Rights (medley) (6) · Feel No Way (5) · Fight On (3) · Fools Die (3) · Get Up, Stand Up (6) · Glasshouse (5) · I'm The Toughest (2) · Igziabeher (Let Jah Be Praised) (1) · Jah Seh No (3) · Johnny B. Goode (5,6) 84 · Ketchy Shuby (1) · Legalize It (1) · Maga Dog (5) · Mama Africa (5) · "Moses" — The Prophets (2) · Mystic Man (3) · No Sympathy (1) · Not Gonna Give It Up (5) · Nothing But Love (4) · Peace Treaty (5) · Pick Myself Up (5) · Poor Man Feel It (4) · Rastafari Is (4,6) · Recruiting Soldiers (3) · Reggae-Mylitis (4) · Rumours Of War (3) · Soon Come (2) · Stand Firm (2) · Stop That Train (5) · That's What They Will Do (4) · Till Your Well Runs Dry (1) · Wanted Dread & Alive (4) · Whatcha Gonna Do (1) · Where You Gonna Run (5) · Why Must I Cry (1) · (You Got To Walk And) Don't Look Back (2) 81

★★366★★ TOTO

Pop-rock group formed in Los Angeles in 1978. Consisted of Bobby Kimball (b: Robert Toteaux; vocals), Steve Lukather (guitar), David Paich and Steve Porcaro (keyboards), David Hungate (bass) and Jeff Porcaro (drums; d: 8/5/92 [age 38] from hardening of arteries due to prolonged cocaine use). Prominent session musicians, most notably behind Boz Scaggs in the late '70s. Hungate was replaced by Mike Porcaro in 1983. (The Porcaros are brothers.) Kimball replaced by Fergie Frederiksen in 1984; Frederiksen replaced by Joseph Williams (conductor John's son) in 1986. Steve Porcaro left in 1988. South African native Jean-Michel Byron replaced Frederiksen in 1990. Paich and his father, Marty, won an Emmy for writing the theme to the TV series *Ironside*.

10/21/78+	9	48	▲²	1 Toto	$8	Columbia 35317
11/17/79	37	29	●	2 Hydra	$8	Columbia 36229
2/7/81	41	10		3 Turn Back	$8	Columbia 36813
4/24/82	4	82	▲³	4 Toto IV	$8	Columbia 37728
				1982 Grammy winner: Album of the Year		
11/24/84	42	21	●	5 Isolation	$8	Columbia 38962
12/22/84+	168	8		6 Dune .... [S-I]	$8	Polydor 823770
				featuring The Vienna Symphony Orchestra		
9/13/86	40	36		7 Fahrenheit	$8	Columbia 40273
3/19/88	64	18		8 The Seventh One	$8	Columbia 40873
9/22/90	153	4		9 Past To Present 1977-1990 .... [G]	$12	Columbia 45368
				includes 4 new tracks with lead vocal by Jean-Michel Byron		

Afraid Of Love (4) · Africa (4,9) *1* · All Us Boys (2) · Angel Don't Cry (5) · Angela (1) · Animal (9) · Anna (8) · Big Battle (6) · Box, The (6) · Can You Hear What I'm Saying (9) · Can't Stand It Any Longer (7) · Carmen (5) · Change Of Heart (5) · Child's Anthem (1) · Could This Be Love (7) · Don't Stop Me Now (7) · Dune, Main Title (6) · Dune (Desert Theme) (6) · Endless (9) · English Eyes (3) · Fahrenheit (7) · Final Dream (6) · First Attack (6) · Floating Fat Man (The Baron) (6) · Georgy Porgy (1,9) 48 · Gift With A Golden Gun (3) · Girl Goodbye (1) · Good For You (4) · Goodbye Elenore (3) · Hold The Line (1,9) *5* · Holyanna (5) 71 · Home Of The Brave (8) · How Does It Feel (5) · Hydra (2) · I Think I Could Stand You Forever (3) · I Won't Hold You Back (4,9) 10 · I'll Be Over You (7,9) 11 · I'll Supply The Love (1) 45 · If It's The Last Night (3) · Isolation (5) · It's A Feeling (4) · Lea (7) · Leto's Theme (6) · Lion (5) · Live For Today (3) · Lorraine (2) · Love Has The Power (9) · Lovers In The Night (4) · Make Believe (4) 30 · Mama (2) · Manuela Run (1) · Million Miles Away (3) · Mr. Friendly (5) · Mushanga (8) · 99 (2,9) 26 · Only The Children (8) · Out Of Love (9) · Pamela (8,9) 22 · Paul Kills Feyd (6) · Paul Meets Chani (6) · Paul Takes The Water Of Life (6) · Prophecy Theme (6) · Robot Fight (6) · Rockmaker (1) · Rosanna (4,9) *2* · Secret Love (2) · Somewhere Tonight (7) · St. George And The Dragon (2) · Stay Away (8) · Stop Loving You (8,9) · Straight For The Heart (8) · Stranger In Town (5) 30 · Take My Hand (6) · Takin' It Back (1) · These Chains (8) · Thousand Years (8) · Till The End (7) · Trip To Arrakis (6) · Turn Back (3) · Waiting For Your Love (4) 73 · We Can Make It Tonight (7) · We Made It (4) · White Sister (2) · Without Your Love (7) 38 · You Are The Flower (1) · You Got Me (8)

TOUPS, Wayne, & Zydecajun

Zydeco-Cajun quintet led by vocalist/accordionist Wayne Toups.

3/18/89	183	4		Blast From The Bayou	$8	Mercury 836518

Going Back To Big Mamou · Johnnie Can't Dance · Let's Fall In Love (All Over Again) · Secret Love · Sugar Bee · Sweet Joline · Tell It Like It Is · Tupelo Honey · Two-Step Mamou · Zydecajun Train

DEBUT DATE	PEAK POS	WKS CHR	GOLD	ARTIST — Album Title	$	Label & Number

★★344★★ TOWER OF POWER

Interracial Oakland-based, R&B-funk band formed by sax player Emilio "Mimi" Castillo in the late '60s. Lenny Williams sang lead from 1972-75. Originally known as the Motowns.

4/10/71+	106	12		1 East Bay Grease	$20	San Francisco 204
6/17/72	85	20		2 Bump City	$8	Warner 2616
6/2/73	15	31	●	3 Tower Of Power	$8	Warner 2681
3/9/74	26	35		4 Back to Oakland	$8	Warner 2749
1/25/75	22	16		5 Urban Renewal	$8	Warner 2834
10/11/75	67	11		6 In The Slot	$8	Warner 2880
5/22/76	99	8		7 Live And In Living Color [L]	$8	Warner 2924
9/11/76	42	17		8 Ain't Nothin' Stoppin' Us Now	$8	Columbia 34302
4/22/78	89	8		9 We Came To Play!	$8	Columbia 34906
8/11/79	106	12		10 Back On The Streets	$8	Columbia 35784

Ain't Nothin' Stoppin' Us Now (8)
Am I A Fool (9)
And You Know It (10)
As Surely As I Stand Here (6)
Back On The Streets Again (1)
Because I Think The World Of You (8)
Below Us, All The City Lights (4)
Bittersweet Soul Music (9)
Both Sorry Over Nothin' (3)
By Your Side (8)
Can't Stand To See The Slaughter (8)
Can't You See (You Doin' Me Wrong) (4)
Clean Slate (3)

Clever Girl (3)
Come Back, Baby (5)
Deal With It (8)
Doin' Alright (8)
Don't Change Horses (In The Middle Of A Stream) (4) 26
Down To The Nightclub (2,7) 68
Drop It In The Slot (6)
Ebony Jam (6)
Essence Of Innocence (6)
Fanfare: Mantanuska (6)
Flash In The Pan (2)
Get Yo' Feet Back On The Ground (3)
Give Me The Proof (5)
Gone (2)

Heaven Must Have Made You (10)
I Believe In Myself (5)
I Got The Chop (4)
I Won't Leave Unless You Want Me To (5)
If I Play My Cards Right (6)
In Due Time (10)
It Can Never Be The Same (5)
It Takes Two (To Make It Happen) (10)
It's Not The Crime (5)
It's So Nice (3)
Just Another Day (3)
Just Enough And Too Much (6)
Just Make A Move (And Be Yourself) (10)

Just When We Start Makin' It (4)
Knock Yourself Out (1,7)
Let Me Touch You (9)
Love Bug (9)
Love's Been Gone So Long (4)
Lovin' You Is Gonna See Me Thru (9)
Make Someone Happy (5)
Man From The Past (4)
Maybe It'll Rub Off (5)
Nowhere To Run (10)
Oakland Stroke (4)
Of The Earth (2)
On The Serious Side (6)
Only So Much Oil In The Ground (5)
Our Love (10)
Price, The (1)

Rock Baby (10)
Share My Life (9)
Skating On Thin Ice (2)
Skunk, The Goose, And The Fly (1)
So Very Hard To Go (3) 17
Social Lubrication (1)
Something Calls Me (10)
Somewhere Down The Road (9)
Soul Of A Child (6)
Soul Vaccination (3)
Sparkling In The Sand (1,7)
Squib Cakes (4)
This Time It's Real (3) 65
Time Will Tell (4) 69
(To Say The Least) You're The Most (5)
Treat Me Like Your Man (6)

Vuela Por Noche (6)
Walkin' Up Hip Street (5)
We Came To Play (9)
What Happened To The World That Day? (2)
While We Went To The Moon (8)
What Is Hip? (3,7) 91
Will I Ever Find A Love? (9)
Willing To Learn (5)
Yin-Yang Thang (9)
You Got To Funkifize (2)
You Ought To Be Havin' Fun (6) 68
You Strike My Main Nerve (2)
You're So Wonderful, So Marvelous (6)
You're Still A Young Man (2,7) 29

★★401★★ TOWNSHEND, Pete

Born on 5/19/45 in London. Lead guitarist/songwriter of The Who. First solo album *Who Came First*, 1972. Own publishing house, Eel Pie Press, mid-1970s. Currently plagued by a significant hearing loss.

11/18/72+	69	17		1 Who Came First	$20	Track 79189
10/15/77	45	12		2 Rough Mix	$8	MCA 2295
				PETE TOWNSHEND/RONNIE LANE (Small Faces) with guests Eric Clapton and John Entwistle		
5/17/80	5	30	●	3 **Empty Glass**	$8	Atco 100
7/10/82	26	26		4 All The Best Cowboys Have Chinese Eyes	$8	Atco 149
3/26/83	35	13		5 Scoop [K]	$10	Atco 90063 [2]
				primarily a collection of Townshend's demo recordings		
11/30/85+	26	29	●	6 White City - A Novel	$8	Atco 90473
10/25/86	98	9		7 Pete Townshend's Deep End Live! [L]	$8	Atco 90553
				selections from his Atlantic Home Video of the same title		
4/4/87	198	1		8 Another Scoop [K]	$10	Atco 90539 [2]
				consists of demo tapes, home recordings and unreleased oddities		
7/15/89	58	13		9 The Iron Man: The Musical by Pete Townshend	$8	Atlantic 81996
				rock opera composed by Townshend, based on a Ted Hughes story; includes "Over The Top" & "I Eat Heavy Metal" by Simon Townshend, "Man Machines" by John Lee Hooker, "Dig" & "Fire" by The Who, and "Fast Food" by Nina Simone.		

After The Fire (7)
All Shall Be Well (9)
And I Moved (3)
Annie (2)
April Fool (2)
Ask Yourself (8)
Barefootin' (7)
Bargain (5)
Baroque Ippanese (8)
Begin The Beguine (8)
Behind Blue Eyes (5,7)
Body Language (5)
Brilliant Blues (6)
Brooklyn Kids (8)
Cache, Cache (5)
Call Me Lightning (8)
Cat Snatch (8)
Cat's In The Cupboard (3)
Catmelody (8)
Christmas (8)

Circles (5)
Come To Mama (6)
Communication (4)
Content (1)
Cookin' (5)
Crashing By Design (6)
Dirty Water (5)
Don't Let Go The Coat (8)
Driftin' Blues (8)
Empty Glass (3)
Evolution (1)
Exquisitely Bored (4)
Eyesight To The Blind (7)
Face Dances Part Two (4)
Face The Face (6) 26
Ferryman, The (8)
Fool Says... (9)
Football Fugue (8)
Forever's No Time At All (1)
Friend Is A Friend (9)

Girl In A Suitcase (8)
Give Blood (5)
Goin' Fishin' (5)
Gonna Get Ya (3)
Happy Jack (8)
Heart To Hang On To (2)
Hiding Out (8)
Holly Like Ivy (8)
I Am An Animal (3)
I Am Secure (4)
I Put A Spell On You (7)
I Won't Run Any More (9)
I'm One (7)
Initial Machine Experiments (5)
Jools And Jim (3)
Keep Me Turning (2)
Keep On Working (3)
Kids Are Alright (8)
La-La-La-Lies (8)

Let My Love Open The Door (3) 9
Little Is Enough (3,7) 72
Long Live Rock (8)
Love Reign O'er Me (5)
Magic Bus (5)
Mary (3)
Melancholia (5)
Misunderstood (2)
My Baby Gives It Away (2)
Never Ask Me (8)
New Life (9)
North Country Girl (4)
Nothing Is Everything (Let's See Action) (1)
Nowhere To Run (2)
Parvardigar (1)
Pictures Of Lily (8)
Pinball Wizard (7,8)
Politician (5)

Popular (5)
Praying The Game (8)
Prelude #556 (8)
Prelude, The Right To Write (8)
Pure And Easy (1)
Quadrophenia (5)
Recorders (5)
Rough Boys (3) 89
Rough Mix (2)
Save It For Later (7)
Sea Refuses No River (4)
Secondhand Love (5)
Sheraton Gibson (1)
Shout, The (8)
Slit Skirts (4)
So Sad About Us/ Brrr (8)
Somebody Saved Me (4)
Squeezebox (5)
Stardom In Acton (4)

Stop Hurting People (4,7)
Street In The City (2)
Substitute (8)
There's A Heartache Followin' Me (1)
Things Have Changed (5)
Till The Rivers All Run Dry (2)
Time Is Passing (1)
Tipperary (5)
To Barney Kessell (5)
Uniforms (4)
Vicious Interlude (8)
Was There Life (9)
White City Fighting (6)
You Better You Bet (8)
You Came Back (5)
You're So Clever (5)
Zelda (5)

TOWNSHEND, Simon

Pete Townshend's younger brother by 18 years.

12/3/83+	169	7		Sweet Sound	$8	21 Records 815708
				produced by Pete Townshend		

...And More With You
Freakers

Heart Stops
I'm The Answer

Mr. Sunday
On The Scaffolding

Palace In The Air
So Real

Sweet Sound

TOY MATINEE

Pop group assembled by Patrick Leonard. Featuring lead vocalist Kevin Gilbert. Leonard, a native of Crystal Falls, Michigan, did much songwriting and production work for Madonna.

1/26/91	129	8		Toy Matinee	$12	Reprise 26235

Ballad Of Jenny Ledge
Last Plane Out

Queen Of Misery
Remember My Name

There Was A Little Boy
Things She Said

Toy Matinee
Turn It On Salvador

We Always Come Home

TOYS, The
Soul trio from Woodrow Wilson High School, Jamaica, New York: Barbara Harris, June Montiero and Barbara Parritt. Appearances on *Shindig* TV show in 1965. In film *The Girl In Daddy's Bikini*.

| 2/5/66 | 92 | 8 | | The Toys sing "A Lover's Concerto" and "Attack!" | $30 | DynoVoice 9002 |

Attack 18
Baby's Gone
Back Street

Can't Get Enough Of You
Baby

Deserted
Hallelujah

I Got A Man
Lover's Concerto 2

See How They Run
This Night

What's Wrong With Me Baby
Yesterday

T'PAU
Group from Shrewsbury, England — Carol Decker, lead singer. Band named after a Vulcan Princess in an episode of the TV series *Star Trek*.

| 6/6/87 | 31 | 24 | | T'Pau | $8 | Virgin 90595 |

Bridge Of Spies
China In Your Hand

Friends Like These
Heart And Soul 4

I Will Be With You
Monkey House

Sex Talk
Thank You For Goodbye

Valentine
You Give Up

★★246★★ TRAFFIC
British rock band. Original lineup: Steve Winwood (keyboards, guitar), Dave Mason (guitar), Jim Capaldi (drums) and Chris Wood (flute, sax; d: 7/12/83). Many personnel changes during the group's seven-year existence.

4/27/68	88	22		1 Mr. Fantasy	$15	United Art. 6651
11/30/68+	17	26		2 Traffic	$12	United Art. 6676
5/17/69	19	22		3 Last Exit	$12	United Art. 6702
1/3/70	48	14		4 Best Of Traffic [G]	$10	United Art. 5500
7/11/70	5	38	●	5 John Barleycorn Must Die	$10	United Art. 5504
10/2/71	26	19		6 Welcome To The Canteen [L]	$10	United Art. 5550

TRAFFIC, ETC.

12/11/71+	7	30	●	7 The Low Spark Of High Heeled Boys	$10	Island 9306
2/3/73	6	29	●	8 Shoot Out At The Fantasy Factory	$10	Island 9323
11/3/73	29	24		9 Traffic-On The Road [L]	$12	Island 9336 [2]
9/28/74	9	27	●	10 When The Eagle Flies	$10	Asylum 1020
5/3/75	155	3		11 Heavy Traffic [G]	$10	United Art. 421
9/27/75	193	4		12 More Heavy Traffic [G]	$10	United Art. 526

Berkshire Poppies (1)
Blind Man (1)
Coloured Rain (1,4,11)
Cryin' To Be Heard (2,12)
Dealer (1)
Dear Mr. Fantasy (1,4,6,11)
Don't Be Sad (2)
Dream Gerrard (10)
Empty Pages (5,11) 74
Evening Blue (8)
Every Mother's Son (5)
Feelin' Alright? (2,4,11)

Feelin' Good (3)
Forty Thousand Headmen (2,4,6,11)
Freedom Rider (5,9)
Gimme Some Lovin'-Pt. 1 (6,12) 68
Giving To You (1)
Glad (5,9)
Graveyard People (10)
Heaven Is In Your Mind (1,4,11)
Hidden Treasure (7)

Hole In My Shoe (1,4,12)
House For Everyone (1)
John Barleycorn (5,12)
Light Up Or Leave Me Alone (7,9)
Love (10)
Low Spark Of High Heeled Boys (7)
Many A Mile To Freedom (7)
Means To An End (2,12)
Medicated Goo (3,4,6,11)

Memories Of A Rock N' Roller (10)
No Face, No Name And No Number (1,4,12)
No Time To Live (2)
Paper Sun (1,4,11) 94
Pearly Queen (2,12)
Rainmaker (7)
Rock & Roll Stew...Part 1 (7) 93
Roll Right Stones (8)
Sad And Deep As You (6)

Shanghai Noodle Factory (3,4,11)
Shoot Out At The Fantasy Factory (8,9)
Shouldn't Have Took More Than You Gave (6)
Smiling Phases (1,11)
Something New (10)
Something's Got A Hold Of My Toe (3)
(Sometimes I Feel So) Uninspired (8,9)

Stranger To Himself (5)
Tragic Magic (8,9)
Vagabond Virgin (2,12)
Walking In The Wind (10)
We're A Fade, You Missed This (1)
When The Eagle Flies (10)
Who Knows What Tomorrow May Bring (2,12)
Withering Tree (3)
You Can All Join In (2,4,12)

TRAGICALLY HIP, The
Alternative-rock quintet led by guitarist Bobby Barker and vocalist Gordon Downie.

| 5/12/90 | 170 | 6 | | Up To Here | $12 | MCA 6310 |

Another Midnight
Blow At High Dough
Boots Or Hearts

Everytime You Go
I'll Believe In You (Or I'll Be Leaving You Tonight)

New Orleans Is Sinking
Opiated
She Didn't Know

38 Years Old
Trickle Down

When The Weight Comes Down

TRAMMPS, The
Philadelphia disco group. Key members: Jimmy Ellis (lead tenor), Earl Young (lead bass), Harold and Stanley Wade (tenors) and Robert Upchurch (baritone). Own Golden Fleece label in 1973.

7/5/75	159	4		1 Trammps	$8	Gld. Fleece 33163
5/15/76	50	24		2 Where The Happy People Go	$8	Atlantic 18172
1/22/77	46	49	●	3 Disco Inferno	$8	Atlantic 18211
12/17/77+	85	13		4 The Trammps III	$8	Atlantic 19148
9/9/78	139	6		5 The Best Of The Trammps [G]	$8	Atlantic 19194
5/26/79	184	2		6 The Whole World's Dancing	$8	Atlantic 19210

Body Contact Contract (3,5)
Can We Come Together (2)
Disco Inferno (3,5) 11
Disco Party (2,5)
Don't Burn Any Bridges (4)
Down Three Dark Streets (1)
Every Dream I Dream Is You (1)

Hooked For Life (2,5)
I Feel Like I've Been Livin' (On The Dark Side Of The Moon) (3,5)
I Know That Feeling (1)
I'm So Glad You Came Along (4)
It Don't Take Much (4)

Life Ain't Been Easy (4)
Living The Life (4)
Love Epidemic (1)
Love Insurance Policy (6)
Love Is A Funky Thing (2)
Love Magnet (6)
Love Per Hour (4)

More Good Times To Remember (6)
My Love, It's Never Been Better (6)
Night The Lights Went Out (4,5)
Ninety-Nine And A Half (2)
People Of The World, Rise (4)

Save A Place (1)
Seasons For Girls (4,5)
Shout (1)
Soul Bones (6)
Soul Searchin' Time (2,5)
Starvin' (3)
Stop And Think (1)
Teaser (6)

That's Where The Happy People Go (2,5) 27
Trammps Disco Theme (1)
Trusting Heart (1)
Where Do We Go From Here (1)
Whole World's Dancing (6)
You Touch My Hot Line (3)

TRANSVISION VAMP
U.K. rock quintet led by vocalist Wendy James. Includes Nick Christian Sayer, Dave Parsons, Ted Axile and Pol Burton.

| 9/24/88 | 115 | 8 | | Pop Art | $8 | Uni 5 |

Andy Warhol's Dead
Hanging Out With Halo Jones

I Want Your Love
Psychosonic Cindy
Revolution Baby

Sex Kick
Sister Moon

Tell That Girl To Shut Up 87

Trash City
Wild Star

TRAPEZE
British rock group — Mel Galley, leader.

11/2/74	172	6		1 The Final Swing [E-K]	$20	Threshold 11
				featuring Glenn Hughes (Deep Purple)		
1/4/75	146	6		2 Hot Wire	$8	Warner 2828

TRAPEZE — Cont'd

Back Street Love (2)
Black Cloud (1)
Coast To Coast (1)
Dat's It (1)
Feel It Inside (2)
Goin' Home (2)
Good Love (1)
Medusa (1)
Midnight Flyer (2)
Send Me No More Letters (1)
Steal A Mile (2)
Take It On Down The Road (2)
Turn It On (2)
Wake Up, Shake Up (2)
Will Our Love End (1)
You Are The Music (1)
Your Love Is Alright (1)

TRASH CAN SINATRAS, The

Alternative-pop quintet from Irvine, Scotland: Frank Reader (vocals), George McDaid, Paul Livingston, and John and Stephen Douglas.

2/2/91	131	13		Cake	$12	London 828201

Best Man's Fall
Circling The Circumference
Even The Odd
Funny
January's Little Joke
Maybe I Should Drive
Obscurity Knocks
Only Tongue Can Tell
Thrupenny Tears
You Made Me Feel

TRASHMEN, The

Minneapolis/St. Paul surf-rock quartet: Tony Andreason, Dal Winslow, Bob Reed and Steve Wahrer. Wahrer died of throat cancer on 1/21/89 (age 47).

2/15/64	48	15		Surfin' Bird	$75	Garrett 200

Bird Bath
Henrietta
It's So Easy
King Of The Surf
Kuk
Malaguena
Misirlou
Money
My Woodie
Sleeper, The
Surfin' Bird 4
Tube City

TRAVELING WILBURYS

Supergroup masquerading as a band of brothers. Spearheaded by Nelson (George Harrison), with Lucky (Bob Dylan), Otis (Jeff Lynne of ELO), Lefty (Roy Orbison) and Charlie T. Junior (Tom Petty) Wilbury. Orbison died on 12/6/88 (age 52). For their second album, *Vol. 3*, the brothers' names have changed to Spike (Harrison), Muddy (Petty), Clayton (Lynne) and Boo (Dylan).

11/12/88+	3	53	▲²	1 Volume One	$8	Wilbury 25796
11/17/90	11	22	▲	2 Vol. 3	$12	Wilbury 26324

Congratulations (1)
Cool Dry Place (2)
Devil's Been Busy (2)
Dirty World (1)
End Of The Line (1) 63
Handle With Care (1) 45
Heading For The Light (1)
If You Belonged To Me (2)
Inside Out (2)
Last Night (1)
Margarita (1)
New Blue Moon (2)
Not Alone Any More (1)
Poor House (2)
Rattled (1)
7 Deadly Sins (2)
She's My Baby (2)
Tweeter And The Monkey Man (1)
Where Were You Last Night? (2)
Wilbury Twist (2)
You Took My Breath Away (2)

TRAVERS, Mary

Born on 11/7/37 in Louisville. Member of the folk trio Peter, Paul & Mary. Chorus singer in the short-lived Broadway show *The Next President*, 1957.

4/17/71	71	29		1 Mary	$10	Warner 1907
4/29/72	157	5		2 Morning Glory	$10	Warner 2609
2/24/73	169	6		3 All My Choices	$8	Warner 2677
7/20/74	200	1		4 Circles	$12	Warner 2795
3/11/78	186	5		5 It's In Everyone Of Us	$8	Chrysalis 1168

Air That I Breathe (5)
All My Choices (3)
Catch The Rain (4)
Children One And All (1)
Circles (4)
Circus (1)
Conscientious Objector (I Shall Die) (2)
Doctor My Eyes (3)
Erika With The Windy Yellow Hair (1)
Eye Of The Day (5)
First Time Ever I Saw Your Face (1)
Five Hundred Miles (3)
Follow Me (1) 56
Goin' Back (1)
Good News (For The Lady) (5)
Goodbye Again (3)
Half Of It (3)
Home Is Where The Hurt Is (5)
House At Pooh Corner (4)
I Am Your Child (4)
I Guess He'd Rather Be In Colorado (1)
I Wish I Knew How It Would Feel To Be Free (1)
I'll Have To Say I Love You In A Song (4)
If I'm Lucky (3)
Indian Sunset (4)
Is It Really Love At All? (4)
It Will Come To You Again (2)
It's In Everyone Of Us (5)
Light Of Day (4)
Man Song (2)
Morning Glory (2)
My Love And I (2)
Oh, What A Feeling (3)
On The Path Of Glory (La Colline Au Whisky) (1)
Part Of The Plan (5)
Rest Of The Year (2)
Rhymes And Reasons (1)
Running (2)
Scarlet And The Grey (2)
Simple Song (4)
Single Wing (5)
So Close (4)
Song For The Asking (1)
Song Is Love (1)
Song Of Peace (Finlandia) (2)
Southbound Train (3)
That Year There Was No Winter (3)
That's Enough For Me (2)
Too Many Mondays (3)
When I Need You Most Of All (2)
Will We Ever Find Our Fathers (5)
You Turn Me Around (5)

TRAVERS, Pat

Born in Toronto in 1954. Blues-rock guitarist/vocalist.

12/17/77+	70	22		1 Putting It Straight	$8	Polydor 6121
10/21/78	99	16		2 Heat In The Street	$8	Polydor 6170
7/21/79	29	22		3 Pat Travers Band Live! Go For What You Know ....[L]	$8	Polydor 6202
4/5/80	20	25		4 Crash And Burn	$8	Polydor 6262
				above 2: **PAT TRAVERS BAND**		
3/28/81	37	15		5 Radio Active	$8	Polydor 6313
11/6/82	74	13		6 Pat Travers' Black Pearl	$8	Polydor 6361
				Black Pearl is Pat's backing band		
5/5/84	108	8		7 Hot Shot	$8	Polydor 821064

Amgwanna Kick Booty (6)
Big Event (4)
Boom Boom (Out Go The Lights) (3) 56
Born Under A Bad Sign (4)
Can't Stop The Heartaches (6)
Crash And Burn (4)
Dedication - Part 1 & Part 2 (1)
Electric Detective (5)
Evie (2)
Feelin' In Love (5)
Fifth, The (6)
Gettin' Betta (1,3)
Go All Night (3)
Hammerhead (2)
Heat In The Street (2,3)
Hooked On Music (3)
Hot Shot (7)
I Can Love You (5)
I Don't Wanna Be Awake (5)
I Gotta Fight (7)
(I Just Wanna) Live It My Way (5)
I La La La Love You (6)
I Tried To Believe (2)
I'd Rather See You Dead (6)
In The Heat Of The Night (7)
Is This Love (4) 50
It Ain't What It Seems (1)
Just Try Talking (To Those Dudes) (7)
Killer (7)
Killer's Instinct (2)
Life In London (1)
Louise (7)
Love Will Make You Strong (4)
Lovin' You (1)
Makes No Difference (3)
Makin' Magic (3)
Material Eyes (4)
Misty Morning (6)
My Life Is On The Line (5)
New Age Music (5)
Night Into Day (7)
Off Beat Ride (1)
One For Me And One For You (2)
Play It Like You See It (5)
Prelude (2)
Rockin' (6)
Runnin' From The Future (1)
Snortin' Whiskey (4)
Speakeasy (1)
Stand Up (6)
Stevie (3)
Tonight (5)
Untitled (5)
Who'll Take The Fall (6)
Women On The Edge Of Love (7)
Your Love Can't Be Right (4)

★★297★★ TRAVIS, Randy

Born Randy Bruce Traywick in Marshville, North Carolina on 5/4/59. Country singer/guitarist. Moved to Nashville in 1981, worked as singer/dishwasher/cook at Lib Hatcher's Nashville Palace. Recorded as Randy Traywick and Randy Ray before adopting stage name, Randy Travis, in 1985. Married Hatcher, his longtime manager, on 5/31/91. The youngest male member inducted into the *Grand Ole Opry*.

7/19/86	85	100	▲³	1 Storms Of Life	$8	Warner 25435
5/30/87	19	103	▲⁴	2 Always & Forever	$8	Warner 25568
7/30/88	35	43	▲	3 Old 8x10	$8	Warner 25738
10/14/89	33	47	▲	4 No Holdin' Back	$8	Warner 25988
12/2/89	70	7	●	5 An Old Time Christmas .... [X]	$8	Warner 25972
				Christmas charts: 5/'89, 14/'90, 26/'91		

DEBUT DATE	PEAK POS	WKS CHR	GOLD	ARTIST — Album Title	$	Label & Number

TRAVIS, Randy — Cont'd

9/29/90	31	41 ▲	6	Heroes And Friends	$12	Warner 26310

Randy duets with Dolly Parton, Willie Nelson, Merle Haggard, Vern Gosdin, Loretta Lynn, B.B. King, George Jones, Kris Kristofferson, Tammy Wynette, Clint Eastwood, Conway Twitty and Roy Rogers; Chet Atkins appears on the Parton duet

9/14/91	43	31 ●	7	High Lonesome	$12	Warner 26661
10/3/92	44	19↑ ●	8	Greatest Hits Volume One .... [G]	$12	Warner 45044
10/3/92	67	19↑ ●	9	Greatest Hits Volume Two .... [G]	$12	Warner 45045

All Night Long (6)
Allergic To The Blues (7)
Anything (2)
Better Class Of Losers (7)
Birth Of The Blues (6)
Blues In Black And White (3)
Card Carryin' Fool (4)
Christmas Song (6)
Come See About Me (6)
Deeper Than The Holler (3,8)
Diggin' Up Bones (1,9)
Do I Ever Cross Your Mind (6)
Few Ole Country Boys (6)
Forever And Ever, Amen (2,9)
Forever Together (7)
God Rest Ye Merry Gentlemen (5)

Good Intentions (2)
Happy Trails (6)
Hard Rock Bottom Of Your Heart (4,8)
Have A Nice Rest Of Your Life (4)
He Walked On Water (4,9)
Heart Of Hearts (7)
Here In My Heart (3)
Heroes And Friends (6,8)
High Lonesome (7)
Honky Tonk Moon (3,8)
How Do I Wrap My Heart For Christmas (5)
Human Race (6)
I Told You So (2,8)
I Won't Need You Anymore (2,9)

I'd Do It All Again With You (9)
I'd Surrender All (7)
I'm Gonna Have A Little Talk (7)
If I Didn't Have You (8)
Is It Still Over? (3,9)
It's Just A Matter Of Time (4,9)
It's Out Of My Hands (3)
Let Me Try (7)
Look Heart, No Hands (9)
Meet Me Under The Mistletoe (5)
Messin' With My Mind (1)
Mining For Coal (4)
My Heart Cracked (But It Did Not Break) (1)

My House (2)
1982 (1,8)
No Place Like Home (1,9)
No Stoppin' Us Now (4)
Oh, What A Silent Night (5)
Oh, What A Time To Be Me (7)
Old 8x10 (3)
Old Pair Of Shoes (8)
Old Time Christmas (5)
On The Other Hand (1,8)
Point Of Light (7)
Pretty Paper (5)
Promises (3,9)
Reasons I Cheat (1,8)
Santa Claus Is Coming To Town (5)
Send My Body (1)

Shopping For Dresses (6)
Singing The Blues (4)
Smokin' The Hive (5)
Somewhere In My Broken Heart (4)
Storms Of Life (1)
Take Another Swing At Me (9)
There'll Always Be A Honky Tonk Somewhere (1)
Tonight We're Gonna Tear Down The Walls (2)
Too Gone Too Long (2,8)
Truth Is Lyin' Next To You (2)
Waiting On The Light To Change (6)
Walk Our Own Road (6)
We Ain't Out Of Love Yet (3)

We're Strangers Again (6)
What'll You Do About Me (2)
When Your World Was Turning For Me (4)
White Christmas Makes Me Blue (5)
Winter Wonderland (5)
Written In Stone (3)

TRAVOLTA, John

Born on 2/18/54 in Englewood, New Jersey. Actor/singer. Played Vinnie Barbarino on the TV series *Welcome Back Kotter*. Starred in the films *Saturday Night Fever, Grease, Urban Cowboy, Look Who's Talking* and others. Married actress Kelly Preston on 9/5/91.

5/22/76	39	22	1	John Travolta	$8	Midland Int. 1563
3/12/77	66	9	2	Can't Let You Go	$8	Midland Int. 2211
12/23/78+	161	7	3	Travolta Fever .... [R]	$10	Midsong Int. 001 [2]

reissue of his first 2 albums above

All Strung Out On You (2,3) 34
Baby I Could Be So Good At Lovin' You (1)
Baby, I Could Be So Good At Lovin' You (3)

Back Doors Crying (2,3)
Big Trouble (1,3)
Can't Let You Go (2,3)
Easy Evil (2,3)
Girl Like You (1,3)
Good Night, Mr. Moon (3)

Goodnight Mr. Moon (1)
I Don't Know What I Like About You Baby (1,3)
It Had To Be You (1,3)
Let Her In (1,3) 10
Moonlight Lady (2,3)

Never Gonna Fall In Love Again (1,3)
Rainbows (1,3)
Razzamatazz (1,3)
Right Time Of The Night (3)
Settle Down (2,3)

Slow Dancing (2,3)
What Would They Say (2,3)
Whenever I'm Away From You (2,3) 38
You Set My Dreams To Music (2,3)

TREAT HER RIGHT

Boston-based, blues-pop quartet led by vocalist/guitarist Mark Sandman. Group takes name from Roy Head's #2 pop hit in 1965.

4/9/88	127	18		Treat Her Right	$8	RCA 6884

Bringin' It All Back Home
Don't Look Back

Everglades
Honest Job

I Got A Gun
I Think She Likes Me

Jesus Everyday
Square

Trail Of Tears
Where Did All The Girls Come From?

You Don't Need Money

TREMELOES, The

British pop-rock quartet: Alan Blakely, Dave Munden, Ricky West and Len "Chip" Hawkes. Group originally formed by Brian Poole (b: 11/3/41 in England). Alan was the brother of Mike Blakely of Christie. Hawkes is the father of singer Chesney Hawkes.

6/24/67	119	8		Here Comes My Baby	$20	Epic 26310

Even The Bad Times Are Good 36
Good Day Sunshine

Here Comes My Baby 13
Loving You (Is Sweeter Than Ever)

My Town
Run Baby Run (Back Into My Arms)

Shake Hands (And Come Out Crying)
What A State I'm In

When I'm With Her
You

TRESVANT, Ralph

Born on 5/16/68 and raised in Roxbury, Massachusetts. Member of New Edition. Appeared in the film *House Party 2*. Also see Luther Vandross.

12/8/90+	17	37 ▲		Ralph Tresvant	$12	MCA 10116

CD includes 2 bonus tracks

Alright Now
Do What I Gotta Do
Girl I Can't Control It

I Love You (Just For You)
Last Night

Love Hurts
Love Takes Time

Public Figure (Ordinary Guy)
Rated R

Sensitivity [includes 2 versions] 4

She's My Love Thang
Stone Cold Gentleman 34

T. REX

British rock group led by Marc Bolan (born Marc Feld on 7/30/47 in London; killed in an auto accident on 9/16/77). Guitarist Jack Green joined in 1973 and left a year later to join Pretty Things.

5/1/71	188	5	1	T-Rex	$12	Reprise 6440
11/6/71+	32	34	2	Electric Warrior	$8	Reprise 6466
8/26/72	17	24	3	The Slider	$8	Reprise 2095
10/7/72	113	12	4	Tyrannosaurus Rex (A Beginning) .... [E-R]	$10	A&M 3514 [2]

reissue of 2 1968 albums: *My People Were Fair And Had Sky In Their Hair...* and *Prophets, Seers & Sages*

4/28/73	102	10	5	Tanx	$8	Reprise 2132

Afghan Woman (4)
Aznagell The Mage (4)
Baby Boomerang (3)
Baby Strange (3)
Ballrooms Of Mars (3)
Bang A Gong (Get It On) (2) 10
Beltane Walk (1)
Born To Boogie (3)
Broken Hearted Blues (5)
Buick Mackane (3)

Chariot Choogle (3)
Chateau In Virginia Waters (4)
Child Star (4)
Childe (1)
Children Of Rarn (1)
Consuela (4)
Cosmic Dancer (2)
Country Honey (5)
Deboraarobed (4)
Diamond Meadows (1)

Dwarfish Trumpet Blues (4)
Eastern Spell (4)
Electric Slim And The Factory Hen (5)
Friends, The (4)
Frowning Atahuallpa (4)
Girl (2)
Graceful Fat Sheba (4)
Highway Knees (5)
Hot Rod Mama (4)
Is It Love? (5)

Jeepster (2)
Jewel (1)
Juniper Suction (4)
Knight (4)
Lean Woman Blues (2)
Left Hand Luke And The Beggar Boys (3)
Life Is Strange (5)
Life's A Gas (2)
Mad Donna (5)
Main Man (3)

Mambo Sun (2)
Metal Guru (3)
Mister Mister (5)
Monolith (2)
Motivator, The (2)
Mustang Ford (4)
Mystic Lady (3)
Oh Harley (The Saltimbanques) (4)
One Inch Rock (1)

Our Wonderful Brownskin Man (4)
Planet Queen (2)
Rabbit Fighter (3)
Rapids (5)
Ride A White Swan (1) 76
Rip Off (2)
Rock On (3)
Root Of Star (4)
Salamanda Palaganda (4)
Scenesof (4)

DEBUT DATE	PEAK POS	WKS CHR	GOLD	ARTIST — Album Title	$	Label & Number

T. REX — Cont'd

Scenes of Dynasty (4)	Spaceball Ricochet (3)	Summer Deep (1)	Time Of Love Is Now (1)	Wielder Of Words (4)		
Seagull Woman (1)	Stacey Grove (4)	Suneye (1)	Traveling Tragition (4)	Wind Quartets (4)		
Shock Rock (5)	Strange Orchestras (4)	Street And Babe Shadow (5)	Telegram Sam (3) 67	Trelawny Lawn (4)	Wizard, The (1)	
Slider, The (3)	Street And Babe Shadow (5)	Tenement Lady (5)	Visit, The (1)			

TRIBE CALLED QUEST, A
New York rap outfit: Q-Tip, Ali Shaheed Muhammad and Phife. Jarobi was a member for first album.

4/28/90	91	19		1 People's Instinctive Travels And The Paths Of Rhythm	$12	Jive 1331
10/12/91	45	49	●	2 The Low End Theory	$12	Jive 1418

After Hours (1)	Check The Rhime (2)	Go Ahead In The Rain (1)	Jazz (We've Got) (2)	Rap Promoter (2)	Skypager (2)
Bonita Applebum (1)	Description Of A Fool (1)	Ham 'N' Eggs (1)	Luck Of Lucien (1)	Rhythm (Devoted To The Art	Verses From The Abstract (2)
Buggin' Out (2)	Everything Is Fair (1)	I Left My Wallet In El	Mr. Muhammad (1)	Of Moving Butts) (2)	Vibes And Stuff (2)
Butter (2)	Excursions (2)	Segundo (1)	Pubic Enemy (1)	Scenario (2) 57	What? (2)
Can I Kick It? (1)	Footprints (1)	Infamous Date Rape (2)	Push It Along (1)	Show Business (2)	Youthful Expression (1)

TRINERE & FRIENDS
Trinere Veronica Farrington, dance singer from Miami.

9/23/89	196	2		Greatest Hits [K]	$8	Pandisc 8804
				includes "Lookout Weekend" & "When I Hear Music" by Debbie Deb and "Don't Stop The Rock," "It's Automatic" & "The Party Has Just Begun" by Freestyle		

All Night	Can't Get Enough	Can't Stop The Beat	How Can We Be Wrong	I Know You Love Me	I'll Be All You Ever Need

TRIPLETS, The
Triplet sisters Diana, Sylvia and Vicky Villegas. Born on 4/18/65, seven minutes apart. Raised in Mexico by their American mother and Mexican father. Gained recognition after winning an *MTV Basement Tapes* competition in 1986.

4/20/91	125	5		...Thicker Than Water	$12	Mercury 848290

Blood Is Thicker Than Water	If I Could Only Make You	Pyramids Of Pleasure	Spanish Surrender	Where Were You When I
Dancing In The Shadows	Love Me	Reminds Me Of You	Sunrise	Needed You
	Light A Candle	So Hard		You Don't Have To Go Home Tonight 14

TRITT, Travis
Country singer born and raised in Marietta, Georgia.

3/31/90+	70	99	▲	1 Country Club	$12	Warner 26094
6/15/91	22	87↑	▲²	2 It's All About To Change	$12	Warner 26589
9/5/92	27	23↑	●	3 T-R-O-U-B-L-E	$12	Warner 45048
				with guests Brooks & Dunn, George Jones, Gary Rossington, Tanya Tucker and Billy Joe Walker, Jr.		
11/28/92+	75	8		4 A Travis Tritt Christmas - Loving Time Of The Year [X]	$12	Warner 45029
				Christmas charts: 13/'92		

All I Want For Christmas Dear Is You (4)	Christmas Just Ain't Christmas Without You (4)	Help Me Hold On (1)	I'm Gonna Be Somebody (1)	Loving Time Of The Year (4)	Sign Of The Times (1)
Anymore (2)	Country Club (1)	Here's A Quarter (Call Someone Who Cares) (2)	If Hell Had A Jukebox (2)	Nothing Short Of Dying (2)	Silver Bells (4)
Bible Belt (2)	Dixie Flyer (1)	Homesick (2)	If I Were A Drinker (1)	O Little Town Of Bethlehem (4)	Someone For Me (2)
Blue Collar Man (3)	Don't Give Your Heart To A Rambler (2)	Hundred Years From Now (3)	It's All About To Change (2)	Put Some Drive In Your Country (1)	Son Of The New South (1)
Can I Trust You With My Heart (3)	Drift Off To Dream (1)	I Heard The Bells On Christmas Day (4)	Leave My Girl Alone (1)	Road Home (1)	T-R-O-U-B-L-E (3)
Christmas In My Hometown (4)	Have Yourself A Merry Little Christmas (4)	I Wish I Could Go Back Home (3)	Looking Out For Number One (3)	Santa Looked A Lot Like Daddy (4)	When I Touch You (3)
			Lord Have Mercy On The Working Man (3)		Whiskey Ain't Workin' (2)
					Winter Wonderland (4)
					Worth Every Mile (3)

★★369★★ TRIUMPH
Canadian hard-rock trio formed in Toronto in 1975. Consisted of Rik Emmett (guitar, vocals), Gil Moore (drums, vocals) and Mike Levine (keyboards, bass). Emmett went solo in 1988.

5/5/79	48	28		1 Just A Game	$8	RCA 3224
5/19/79	185	2		2 Rock & Roll Machine [R]	$8	RCA 2982
				their first album		
3/29/80	32	18		3 Progressions Of Power	$8	RCA 3524
9/19/81	23	59	●	4 Allied Forces	$8	RCA 3902
1/29/83	26	27	●	5 Never Surrender	$8	RCA 4382
12/8/84+	35	30		6 Thunder Seven	$8	MCA 5537
11/2/85	50	18		7 Stages [L]	$10	MCA 8020 [2]
				recorded during various tours from 1981-85		
9/6/86	33	27		8 The Sport Of Kings	$8	MCA 5786
11/28/87	82	13		9 Surveillance	$8	MCA 42083

Air Raid (4)	Empty House (7)	In The Middle Of The Night (8)	Minor Prelude (5)	Somebody's Out There (8) 27	Waking Dream (4)
All Over Again (9)	Fantasy Serenade (1)	In The Night (3)	Moonchild (medley) (2)	Spellbound (6,7)	What Rules My Heart (8)
All The King's Horses (9)	Fight The Good Fight (4,7)	Into The Forever (9)	Movin' On (1)	Stranger In A Strange Land (6)	When The Lights Go Down (5,7)
All The Way (5)	Fingertalkin' (3)	Just A Game (1)	Nature's Child (3)	Street Fighter (2)	Woman In Love (3)
Allied Forces (4,7)	Follow Your Heart (6,7) 88	Just One Night (8)	Never Say Never (9)	Suitcase Blues (1)	World Of Fantasy (5,7)
American Girls (1)	Fool For Your Love (4)	Killing Time (6)	Never Surrender (5,7)	Take A Stand (8)	Writing On The Wall (5)
Battle Cry (5)	Hard Road (3)	Lay It On The Line (1,7) 86	On And On (9)	Take My Heart (3)	Young Enough To Cry (1)
Blinding Light Show (medley) (2)	Headed For Nowhere (9)	Let The Light (Shine On Me) (9)	Ordinary Man (4)	Takes Time (2)	
Bringing It On Home (2)	Hold On (1,7) 38	Little Boy Blues (6)	Petite Etude (4)	Tear The Roof Off (3)	
Carry On The Flame (9)	Hooked On You (8)	Long Time Gone (9)	Play With The Fire (8)	Tears In The Rain (8)	
Cool Down (6)	Hot Time (In This City Tonight) (4)	Magic Power (4,7) 51	Rock & Roll Machine (2,7)	Time Canon (6)	
Don't Love Anybody Else But Me (8)	I Can Survive (3) 91	Midsummer's Daydream (6,7)	Rock Out, Roll On (6)	Time Goes By (6)	
Druh Mer Selbo (7)	I Live For The Weekend (3)	Mind Games (7)	Rock You Down (9)	Too Much Thinking (5)	
Embrujo (8)	If Only (8)		Rocky Mountain Way (2)	24 Hours A Day (2)	
			Running In The Night (9)		
			Say Goodbye (4)		

TRIUMVIRAT
German synthesized rock group: Helmut Kollen (guitar, vocals), Hans Bathelt (drums) and Jurgen Fritz (keyboards). Kollen replaced by Barry Palmer (vocals) and Dick Frangenberg (bass) in 1976.

8/10/74	55	17		1 Illusions On A Double Dimple	$10	Harvest 11311
6/7/75	27	17		2 Spartacus	$8	Capitol 11392
8/7/76	85	8		3 Old Loves Die Hard	$8	Capitol 11551

DEBUT DATE	PEAK POS	WKS CHR	GOLD	ARTIST — Album Title	$	Label & Number

TRIUMVIRAT — Cont'd

Bad Deal (1)	Deadly Dream Of Freedom (2)	History Of Mystery (Part One & Two) (3)	March To The Eternal City Medley (2)	Roundabout (1)	Sweetest Sound Of Liberty (2)
Burning Sword Of Capua (2)	Dimplicity (1)	I Believe (3)	Maze (1)	School Of Instant Pain Medley (2)	Triangle (1)
Capital Of Power (2)	Flashback (1)	Illusions (1)	Million Dollars (1)	Schooldays (1)	Walls Of Doom (2)
Cold Old Worried Lady (3)	Hazy Shades Of Dawn (2)	Last Dance (1)	Old Loves Die Hard (3)	Spartacus Medley (2)	
Dawning (1)		Lucky Girl (1)	Panic On 5th Avenue (3)		
Day In A Life Medley (3)					

TRIXTER

Rock quartet from Paramus, New Jersey: Peter Loran (vocals), Steve Brown, P.J. Farley and Mark "Gus" Scott.

9/1/90+	**28**	54	●	1 Trixter	**$12**	MCA 6389
10/31/92	**109**	3		2 Hear!	**$12**	MCA 10635

Always A Victim (1)	**Give It To Me Good** (1) 65	On The Road Again (2)	Ride The Whip (1)	**Surrender** (1) 72
As The Candle Burns (2)	Heart Of Steel (1)	**One In A Million** (1) 75	Road Of A Thousand Dreams (2)	Waiting In That Line (2)
Bad Girl (1)	Line Of Fire (1)	Only Young Once (1)	Rockin' Horse (2)	What It Takes (2)
Bloodrock (2)	Nobody's A Hero (2)	Play Rough (1)	Runaway Train (2)	Wild Is The Heart (2)
Damn Good (2)	On And On (1)	Power Of Love (2)		You'll Never See Me Cryin' (1)

TROGGS, The

British rock quartet from Andover, England: Reg Presley (real name: Reg Ball; lead singer), Chris Britton (guitar), Pete Staples (bass) and Ronnie "Bond" Bullis (drums; d: 11/13/92 [ae 51]).

9/3/66	**52**	16		1 Wild Thing	**$20**	Fontana 67556
5/18/68	**109**	9		2 Love Is All Around	**$20**	Fontana 67576

Any Way That You Want Me (2)	From Home (1)	Hi Hi Hazel (1)	Jingle Jangle (1)	Our Love Will Still Be There (1)	**Wild Thing** (1) 1
Cousin Jane (2)	Girl In Black (2)	**I Can't Control Myself** (2) 43	Little Girl (2)	66-5-4-3-2-1 (2)	**With A Girl Like You** (1) 29
Double 6 ..see: 66	Give It To Me (All Your Love) (2)	I Just Sing (1)	Lost Girl (1)	When I'm With You (1)	Your Love (1)
Evil (1)	Gonna Make You (2)	I Want You (1)	**Love Is All Around** (2) 7	When Will The Rain Come (2)	
			Night Of The Long Grass (2)		

TROOP

Black quintet from Pasadena, California — lead singers Steve Russell and Allen McNeil. Troop stands for Total Respect Of Other People. Group discovered by Gerald Levert.

9/3/88	**133**	9		1 Troop	**$8**	Atlantic 81851
1/13/90	**73**	39	●	2 Attitude	**$12**	Atlantic 82035
				CD includes bonus track		
6/20/92	**78**	12		3 Deepa	**$12**	Atlantic 82393
				CD includes 2 bonus tracks		

All I Do Is Think Of You (2) 47	Give It Up (3)	I'm Not Gamin' (3)	My Music (2)	Soupped Mix (2)	Watch Me Dance (1)
Another Lover (2)	Happy Relationship (1)	I'm Not Souped (2)	Only When I Laugh (3)	Spread My Wings (2)	**Whatever It Takes (To Make You Stay)** (3) 63
Come Back To Your Home (3)	Hot Water (3)	Keep You Next To Me (3)	Praise (3)	Still In Love (1)	You Take My Heart With You (3)
Deepa (3)	I Feel You (3)	Mamacita (1)	Set Me Free (3)	Strange Hotel (3)	Young Girl (1)
For You (2)	I Like That (1)	My Heart (1)	She Blows My Mind (3)	**Sweet November** (3) 58	
	I Will Always Love You (2)	My Love (2)	She's My Favorite Girl (1)	That's My Attitude (2)	

TROOPER

Canadian rock quintet: Ra McGuire (lead guitar), Brian Smith, Doni Underhill, Frank Ludwig and Tommy Stewart.

8/26/78	**182**	4		Thick As Thieves	**$8**	MCA 2377

Drivin' Crazy	Live From The Moon	No Fun Being Alone	**Raise A Little Hell** 59	Round, Round We Go
Gambler	Moment That It Takes	One Good Reason	Roll With It	Say Goodnight

TROPEA

Eclectic guitarist, John Tropea.

3/20/76	**138**	7		1 Tropea .... [I]	**$8**	Marlin 2200
5/14/77	**149**	7		2 Short Trip To Space .... [I]	**$8**	Marlin 2204

Blue Too (2)	Cisco Disco (1)	Funk You See, Is The Funk You Do! (2)	Just Blue (1)	7th Heaven (1)	Tambourine (1)
Bratt, The (1)	Dreams (1)	Jingle, The (1)	Love's Final Moment (2)	Short Trip To Space (2)	Twist Of The Wrist (2)
Can't Hide Love (2)		Muff (1)		Southside (2)	You Can't Have It All (2)

TROUBADOURS DU ROI BAUDOUIN

Choir and percussionists consisting of 45 boys and 15 teachers from the Kamina School in the Congo.

8/2/69	**184**	5		Missa Luba .... [F]	**$15**	Philips 606

Agnus Dei	Dibwe Diambula Kabanda (Marriage Song)	Gloria	Lutuku Y A Bene Kanyoka (Emergence From Grief)	Seya Wa Mama Ndalamba (Marital Celebration)
Banana (Soldiers Song)	Ebu Bwale Kemai (Marriage Ballad)	Katumbo (Dance)	Sanctus	Twai Tshinaminai (Work Song)
Benedictus		Kyrie		
Credo				

TROUBLE FUNK

Funk group from Washington, D.C.

5/8/82	**121**	14		Drop The Bomb	**$8**	SugarHill 266

Don't Try To Use Me	Drop The Bomb	Get On Up	Hey Fellas	Let's Get Hot	Pump Me Up

★★245★★ TROWER, Robin

Rock guitarist born on 3/9/45 in London. Original member of Procol Harum, 1967-72. James Dewar is the vocalist on all albums except #9 & 10.

5/12/73	**106**	24		1 Twice Removed From Yesterday	**$8**	Chrysalis 1039
4/20/74	**7**	31	●	2 Bridge Of Sighs	**$8**	Chrysalis 1057
3/1/75	**5**	17	●	3 For Earth Below	**$8**	Chrysalis 1073
3/27/76	**10**	20	●	4 Robin Trower Live! .... [L]	**$8**	Chrysalis 1089
10/9/76	**24**	19	●	5 Long Misty Days	**$8**	Chrysalis 1107
10/1/77	**25**	19	●	6 In City Dreams	**$8**	Chrysalis 1148
8/26/78	**37**	17		7 Caravan To Midnight	**$8**	Chrysalis 1189
3/1/80	**34**	15		8 Victims Of The Fury	**$8**	Chrysalis 1215
3/21/81	**37**	16		9 B.L.T.	**$8**	Chrysalis 1324
				B.L.T.: Jack Bruce, Bill Lordan, Robin Trower		

DEBUT DATE	PEAK POS	WKS CHR	GOLD	ARTIST — Album Title	$	Label & Number

TROWER, Robin — Cont'd

DEBUT DATE	PEAK POS	WKS CHR	GOLD	ARTIST — Album Title	$	Label & Number
1/30/82	109	6	10	Truce	$8	Chrysalis 1352
				JACK BRUCE/ROBIN TROWER		
10/1/83	191	2	11	Back It Up	$8	Chrysalis 41420
12/27/86+	100	25	12	Passion	$8	GNP Cres. 2187
5/21/88	133	10	13	Take What You Need	$8	Atlantic 81838

About To Begin (2)
Alethea (3,4)
Back It Up (11)
Bad Time (12)
Ballerina (1)
Benny Dancer (11)
Birthday Boy (7)
Black To Red (11)
Bluebird (6)
Bridge Of Sighs (2)
Caledonia (5) 82
Captain Midnight (11)
Caravan To Midnight (7)
Careless (13)
Carmen (9)
Caroline (12)
Confessin' Midnight (3)
Day Of The Eagle (2)
Daydream (1,4)
End Game (9)
Fall In Love (10)
Falling Star (6)
Farther Up The Road (6)
Fat Gut (10)
Feel The Heat (9)
Fine Day (10)
Fly Low (8)
Fool (7)
Fool And Me (2)
For Earth Below (3)
Gone Too Far (10)
Gonna Be More Suspicious (3)
Gonna Shut You Down (10)
Hannah (1)
Hold Me (5)
I Can't Live Without You (5)
I Can't Stand It (1)
I Can't Wait Much Longer (1,4)
I Want You Home (13)
I'm Out To Get You (7)
If Forever (12)
In City Dreams (6)
In This Place (2)
Into Money (9)
Into The Flame (8)
Islands (11)
It's For You (7)
It's Only Money (3)
It's Too Late (9)
Jack And Jill (8)
King Of The Dance (7)
Lady Love (2,4)
Last Train To The Stars (10)
Life On Earth (9)
Little Bit Of Sympathy (2,4)
Little Boy Lost (10)
Little Girl (6)
Long Misty Days (5)
Lost In Love (7)
Love Attack (13)
Love Won't Wait Forever (13)
Love's Gonna Bring You Round (6)
Madhouse (8)
Man Of The World (1)
Messin The Blues (5)
My Love (Burning Love) (7)
Night (12)
No Island Lost (9)
No Time (12)
None But The Brave (11)
Once The Bird Has Flown (9)
One More Word (12)
Only Time (8)
Over You (13)
Passion (12)
Pride (5)
Ready For The Taking (8)
Ring, The (8)
River (11)
Roads To Freedom (8)
Rock Me Baby (1,4)
S.M.O. (5)
Sail On (7)
Sailing (5)
Same Rain Falls (5)
Second Time (13)
Secret Doors (12)
Settling The Score (11)
Shadows Touching (10)
Shame The Devil (3)
Shattered (13)
Shout, The (8)
Sinner's Song (1)
Smile (6)
Somebody Calling (1)
Sweet Wine Of Love (6)
Take Good Care Of Yourself (10)
Take What You Need (From Me) (13)
Tale Untold (3)
Tear It Up (13)
Thin Ice (10)
Time Is Short (11)
Too Rolling Stoned (2,4)
Twice Removed From Yesterday (1)
Victims Of The Fury (8)
What It Is (9)
Won't Even Think About You (12)
Won't Let You Down (9)

TRUE, Andrea, Connection
Disco act led by white Nashville-born vocalist Andrea True. Andrea moved to New York in 1968 and wrote commercials for radio and TV. Her break came while singing at the Riverboat in the Empire State Building in 1974.

DEBUT DATE	PEAK POS	WKS CHR	GOLD	ARTIST — Album Title	$	Label & Number
6/19/76	47	17		More, More, More	$8	Buddah 5670

Call Me
Fill Me Up (Heart To Heart)
Keep It Up Longer
More, More, More Pt. 1 4
Party Line 80

TRUTH, The
English rock duo: Dennis Greaves (lead vocals, guitar) and Mick Lister (vocals, guitar).

DEBUT DATE	PEAK POS	WKS CHR	GOLD	ARTIST — Album Title	$	Label & Number
5/30/87	115	8		Weapons Of Love	$8	I.R.S. 5981

Another New Day
Come On Back To Me
Cover Up My Face
Edge Of Town
Respect
Soul Deep Fascination
This Way Forever
Until It Burns
Weapons Of Love 65
Winterland

TRYTHALL, Gil
Moog synthesizer player from Tennessee.

DEBUT DATE	PEAK POS	WKS CHR	GOLD	ARTIST — Album Title	$	Label & Number
2/7/70	157	6		Switched On Nashville/Country Moog ....[I]	$8	Athena 6003

Cattle Call
Foggy Mountain Breakdown
Folsom Prison Blues
Gentle On My Mind
Harper Valley P.T.A.
Last Date
Little Green Apples
Orange Blossom Special
Walkin' The Floor Over You
Wildwood Flower
Yakety Moog

TSOL
TSOL: True Sounds Of Liberty. Los Angeles hard-rock quartet formed in 1980: Joe Wood (vocals), Mike Roche, Ron Emory and Mitch Dean. Emory replaced by Marshall Rohner (ex-Cruzados) in 1989.

DEBUT DATE	PEAK POS	WKS CHR	GOLD	ARTIST — Album Title	$	Label & Number
7/4/87	184	2		Hit And Run	$8	Enigma 73263

Dreamer
Good Mornin' Blues
Hit And Run
It's Too Late
Name Is Love
Not Alone Anymore
Road Of Gold
Sixteen
Stay With Me
Where Did I Go Wrong
You Can Try

★★451★★ TUBES, The
San Francisco theatre-rock troupe led by vocalist Fee Waybill (born John Waldo on 9/17/50 in Omaha, Nebraska. Group appeared in musical *Xanadu* with Olivia Newton-John in 1980.

DEBUT DATE	PEAK POS	WKS CHR	GOLD	ARTIST — Album Title	$	Label & Number
8/2/75	113	18	1	The Tubes	$8	A&M 4534
5/15/76	46	15	2	Young And Rich	$8	A&M 4580
5/28/77	122	6	3	Now	$8	A&M 4632
3/11/78	82	8	4	What Do You Want From Live ....[L]	$10	A&M 6003 [2]
3/31/79	46	18	5	Remote Control	$8	A&M 4751
5/30/81	36	27	6	The Completion Backward Principle ..	$8	Capitol 12151
8/29/81	148	6	7	T.R.A.S.H. (Tubes Rarities And Smash Hits) ....[K]	$8	A&M 4870
4/2/83	18	34	8	Outside Inside	$8	Capitol 12260
3/23/85	87	10	9	Love Bomb	$8	Capitol 12381

Amnesia (6)
Attack Of The Fifty Foot Woman (6)
Be Mine Tonight (5)
Bora Bora 2000 (medley) (9)
Boy Crazy (1,4)
Brighter Day (2)
Cathy's Clone (3)
Come As You Are (9)
Crime Medley (4)
Don't Touch Me There (2,4,7) 61
Don't Want To Wait Anymore (6) 35
Drivin' All Night (7)
Drums (8)
Eyes (9)
Fantastic Delusion (8)
Feel It (9)
For A Song (9)
Getoverture (5)
Glass House (8)
God-Bird-Change (3,4)
Golden Boy (3)
Got Yourself A Deal (4)
Haloes (1)
Hit Parade (3)
I Saw Her Standing There (4)
I Want It All Now (5)
I Was A Punk Before You Were A Punk (4)
I'm Just A Mess (3,7)
Let's Make Some Noise (6)
Love Bomb (medley) (9)
Love Will Keep Us Together (7)
Love's A Mystery (I Don't Understand) (4)
Madam I'm Adam (medley) (2)
Malaguena Salerosa (1)
Matter Of Pride (6)
Mondo Bondage (1,4,7)
Monkey Time (8) 68
Mr. Hate (6)
Muscle Girls (9)
My Head Is My Only House Unless It Rains (3)
Night People (9)
No Mercy (5)
No Not Again (8)
No Way Out (5)
One Good Reason (9)
Only The Strong Survive (5,7)
Out Of The Business (8)
Outside Lookin' Inside (8)
Piece By Piece (9) 87
Pimp (2)
Poland Whole (medley) (2)
Pound Of Flesh (3)
Power Tools (6)
Prime Time (5)
Proud To Be An American (2)
Say Hey (Part 1 & 2) (9)
She's A Beauty (8) 10
Show Me A Reason (4)
Slipped My Disco (2,7)
Smoke (La Vie En Fumer) (3,4)
Space Baby (1)
Special Ballet (4)
Stand Up And Shout (2,4)
Stella (9)
Strung Out On Strings (3)
Summer Place, Theme From (medley) (2)
Sushi Girl (6)
TV Is King (9)
Talk To Ya Later (6)
Telecide (5)
Theme Park (8)
Think About Me (6)
This Town (3)
Tip Of My Tongue (8) 52
Tubes World Tour (6)
Turn Me On (5,7)
Up From The Deep (1)
What Do You Want From Life (1,4,7)
White Punks On Dope (1,4,7)
Wild Women Of Wongo (8)
Wooly Bully (medley) (9)
You're No Fun (3,4)
Young And Rich (2)

TUCK & PATTI
West Coast-based, New Age duo of Oklahoman guitarist Tuck Andress and his vocalist wife Patti Cathcart. Married in 1981.

DEBUT DATE	PEAK POS	WKS CHR	GOLD	ARTIST — Album Title	$	Label & Number
6/24/89	162	11	1	Love Warriors	$8	Windham Hill 116
5/18/91	186	1	2	Dream	$12	Windham Hill 0130

DEBUT DATE	PEAK POS	WKS CHR	GOLD	ARTIST — Album Title	$	Label & Number

TUCK & PATTI — Cont'd

All The Love (2)	Dream (2)	High Heel Blues (2)	If It's Magic (1)	Sitting In Limbo (2)
As Time Goes By (2)	Europa (1)	Hold Out, Hold Up And Hold	Little Wing (medley) (1)	They Can't Take That Away
Cantador (Like A Lover) (1)	Friends In High Places (2)	On (1)	Love Warriors (1)	From Me (1)
Castles Made Of Sand	From Now On (We're One) (2)	Honey Pie (1)	On A Clear Day (1)	Togetherness (2)
(medley) (1)	Glory Glory (1)	I Wish (2)	One Hand, One Heart (2)	Voodoo Music (2)

TUCKER, Louise
English classical-styled vocalist.

| 8/6/83 | 127 | 10 | | Midnight Blue .... | $8 | Arista 8088 |

with Charlie Skarbek (vocals, guitars, synthesizers)

Gettin' Older	Hush	**Midnight Blue 46**	Shadows	Waiting For Hugo
Graveyard Angel	Jerusalem	Only For You	Voices In The Wind	

TUCKER, Tanya
Born on 10/10/58 in Seminole, Texas and raised in Wilcox, Arizona. Prominent country singer. Bit part in the film *Jeremiah Johnson* in 1972.

3/30/74	159	6		1	Would You Lay With Me (In A Field Of Stone)................................	$12	Columbia 32744
5/17/75	113	7	●	2	Tanya Tucker	$12	MCA 2141
12/2/78+	54	22	●	3	TNT	$8	MCA 3066
12/1/79	121	8		4	Tear Me Apart	$8	MCA 5106
8/1/81	180	3		5	Should I Do It	$8	MCA 5228
7/20/91+	48	70	▲	6	What Do I Do With Me	$12	Capitol 95562
10/24/92	51	16↑	●	7	Can't Run From Yourself	$12	Liberty 98987

Angel From Montgomery (3)	Everything That You Want	I've Never Said No Before (4)	No Man's Land (1)	Somebody Must Have Loved	What If We Were Running
Baptism Of Jesse Taylor (1)	(6)	If You Feel It (3)	**Not Fade Away** (3) 70	You Right Last Night (4)	Out Of Love (1)
Bed Of Roses (1)	Half The Moon (7)	If Your Heart Ain't Busy	Old Dan Tucker's Daughter	Someday Soon (2)	When Will I Be Loved (2)
Better Late Than Never (4)	Halfway To Heaven (5)	Tonight (6)	(1)	Son-Of-A Preacher Man (2)	Why Me, Lord (1)
Bidding America Goodbye	He Was Just Leaving (6)	It's A Little Too Late (7)	Rainbow Rider (7)	Stormy Weather (5)	(Without You) What Do I Do
(The Auction) (6)	Heartache #3 (5)	It's Nice To Be With You (3)	Right About Now (6)	Tear Me Apart (4)	With Me (6)
Blind Love (4)	Heartbreak Hotel (3)	King Of Country Music (2)	River And The Wind (3)	Tell Me About It (7)	**Would You Lay With Me**
Brown Eyed Handsome Man	How Can I Tell Him (1)	Lay Back In The Arms Of	Rodeo Girls (5)	Texas (When I Die) (5)	**(In A Field Of Stone)**
(3)	I Believe The South Is	Someone (4)	San Antonio Stroll (2)	Time And Distance (6)	(1) 46
By Day By Day (4)	Gonna Rise Again (1)	Let Me Be There (1)	San Francisco (Be Sure To	Trail Of Tears (6)	You Don't Have To Say You
Can't Run From Yourself (7)	I Left My Heart In San	**Lizzie And The Rainman**	Wear Some Flowers In	Traveling Salesman (2)	Love Me (5)
Crossfire Of Desire (4)	Francisco (medley) (3)	(2) 37	Your Hair) (medley) (4)	Two Sparrows In A
Danger Ahead (7)	I Oughta Let Go (5)	Love Of A Rolling Stone (2)	Serenade That We Played (2)	Hurricane (4)
Don't Let My Heart Be The	I'm Not Lisa (2)	Lover Goodbye (3)	Shady Streets (4)	We're Playing Games Again
Last To Know (7)	I'm The Singer, You're The	Lucky Enough For Two (5)	Should I Do It (5)	(5)
Down To My Last Teardrop	Song (3)	**Man That Turned My**	Shoulder To Shoulder (5)	What Do They Know (7)
(6)	I've Learned To Live (7)	**Mama On** (1) 86	Some Kind Of Trouble (6)

TUFF DARTS
New York new-wave rock quintet — Jeff Salen, leader.

| 3/18/78 | 156 | 6 | | | Tuff Darts! .... | $8 | Sire 6048 |

All For The Love Of Rock &	Head Over Heels	My Guitar Lies Bleeding In	Rats	Slash	(Your Love Is Like) Nuclear
Roll	Here Comes Trouble	My Arms	She's Dead	Who's Been Sleeping Here?	Waste
Fun City	Love And Trouble	Phone Booth Man (P.B.M.)		

★★470★★ TURNER, Ike & Tina
Husband-and-wife duo: guitarist Ike Turner (b: 11/5/31 in Clarksdale, Mississippi) and vocalist Tina (born Anna Mae Bullock on 11/26/38 in Brownsville, Tennessee). Married from 1958-76. At age 11, Ike was backing pianist for bluesmen Sonny Boy Williamson (Aleck Ford) and Robert Nighthawk (of the Nighthawks). Formed own band, the Kings of Rhythm, while in high school; backed Jackie Brenston's hit "Rocket '88'." Prolific session, production and guitar work during the 1950s. In 1960, developed a dynamic stage show around Tina; "The Ike & Tina Turner Revue" featuring her backing vocalists, The Ikettes, and Ike's Kings Of Rhythm. Disbanded in 1974. In the mid-1980s, Tina emerged as a successful solo artist. Duet inducted into the Rock and Roll Hall of Fame in 1991.

| 2/6/65 | 126 | 6 | | 1 | Live! The Ike & Tina Turner Show .... [L] | $20 | Warner 1579 |

includes "Down In The Valley" by Jimmy Thomas, "Good Time Tonight" by Vanetta Fields and "My Man, He's A Lovin' Man" by Jessie Smith

4/19/69	91	12		2	Outta Season	$15	Blue Thumb 5
7/19/69	142	9		3	In Person .... [L]	$15	Minit 24018
9/27/69	102	8		4	River Deep-Mountain High	$12	A&M 4178

produced by Phil Spector; recorded in 1966

11/22/69	176	3		5	The Hunter	$15	Blue Thumb 11
5/16/70	130	19		6	Come Together	$10	Liberty 7637
12/5/70+	25	38		7	Workin' Together	$10	Liberty 7650
7/10/71	25	22	●	8	Live At Carnegie Hall/What You Hear Is What You Get .... [L]	$10	United Art. 9953 [2]
11/20/71	108	10		9	'Nuff Said	$8	United Art. 5530
7/22/72	160	9		10	Feel Good	$8	United Art. 5598
12/22/73+	163	6		11	Nutbush City Limits	$8	United Art. 180
5/11/85	189	2		12	Get Back! .... [G]	$8	Liberty 51156

African Boo's (medley) (3)	Club Manhattan (11)	Feel Good (10)	Grumbling (2)	I Like It (10)	If You Can Hully Gully (I
All I Could Do Was Cry	**Come Together** (6) 57	Finger Poppin' (1)	High Heel Sneakers (Tight	I Love Baby (9)	Can Hully Gully Too) (10)
(medley) (3)	Contact High (6)	Five Long Years (2)	Pants) (1)	I Love What You Do To Me	Ike's Tune (8)
(As Long As I Can) Get You	Crazy 'Bout You Baby (2)	**Fool In Love** (3,4,12) 27	Hold On Baby (4)	(9)	It Ain't Right (Lovin' To Be
When I Want You (7)	Daily Bread (11)	Funkier Than A Mosquita's	Honest I Do (2)	I Smell Trouble (5,8)	Lovin') (6)
Baby-Get It On (12) 88	Doin' It (6)	Tweeter (7)	Honky Tonk Women (6,8,12)	**I Want To Take You**	**It's Gonna Work Out Fine**
Baby I Love You (medley) (3)	Doin' The Tina Turner (8)	Funky Street (3)	**Hunter, The** (5) 93	**Higher** (6,8,12) 34	(4) 14
Baby (What You Want Me To	Drift Away (11)	Game Of Love (3)	I Am A Motherless Child (2)	I'll Never Need More Than	Kay Got Laid (Joe Got Paid)
Do) (9)	Dust My Broom (2)	Get Back (7,12)	I Can't Stop Loving You (1)	This (4)	(10)
Black Coffee (10)	Early In The Morning (5)	Get It Out Of Your Mind (1)	I Heard It Through The	**I've Been Loving You Too**	Keep On Walkin' (Don't Look
Bold Soul Sister (5) 59	Every Day I Have To Cry (4)	Gimme Some Lovin' (medley)	Grapevine (3)	**Long** (2,8) 68	Back) (6)
Bolic (10)	Everyday People (3,8)	(3)	**I Idolize You** (4) 82	If I Knew Then (What I Know	Let It Be (11)
Can't You Hear Me Callin' (9)	Evil Man (6)	Good Times (1)	I Know (You Don't Want Me | Now) (10)	Let's Spend The Night
Chopper (10)	Fancy Annie (11)	Goodbye, So Long (3,7)	No More) (1,5)		Together (12)

DEBUT DATE	PEAK POS	WKS CHR	GOLD	ARTIST — Album Title	$	Label & Number

TURNER, Ike & Tina — Cont'd

Love Like Yours (Don't Come Knocking Every Day) (4,8)
Make 'Em Wait (4)
Make Me Over (11)
Mean Old World (4)
Moving Into Hip Style-A Trip Child! (9)
My Babe (2)
Nuff Said (Part I & II) (9)
Nutbush City Limits (11,12) **22**

Oh Baby! (Things Ain't What They Used To Be) (4)
Ooh Poo Pah Doo (7,8,12) **60**
Pick Me Up (Take Me Where Your Home Is) (9)
Piece Of My Heart (8)
Please Love Me (2)
Please, Please, Please (medley) (3)
Proud Mary (7,8,12) **4**
Reconsider Baby (4)

Respect (3,8)
River Deep-Mountain High (4,11,12) **88**
Rock Me Baby (2)
Save The Last Dance For Me (4)
She Came In Through The Bathroom Window (10)
Something's Got A Hold On Me (1)
Son Of A Preacher Man (4)
Such A Fool For You (4)

Sumit, The (medley) (3)
Sweet Flustrations (9)
Sweet Soul Music (3,8)
Tell The Truth (1,9)
That's My Purpose (11)
There Was A Time (medley) (3)
Things I Used To Do (5)
3 O'Clock In The Morning Blues (2)
Too Much Woman (For A Henpecked Man) (6)

Twist And Shout (1)
Unlucky Creature (6)
Way You Love Me (7)
What You Don't See (Is Better Yet) (9)
Why Can't We Be Happy (6)
Workin' Together (7)
You Are My Sunshine (1,11)
You Better Think Of Something (10)
You Can Have It (7)

You Don't Love Me (Yes I Know) (5)
You Got Me Running (5)
You're Still My Baby (5)
Young And Dumb (6)

TURNER, Joe Lynn

Former guitarist/vocalist of Fandango and Rainbow. Joined Deep Purple in 1990.

| 11/2/85 | 143 | 12 | | Rescue You .... | $8 | Elektra 60449 |

Endlessly
Eyes Of Love
Feel The Fire
Get Tough
Losing You
On The Run
Race Is On
Rescue You
Soul Searcher
Young Hearts

TURNER, Ruby

R&B/funk singer born in Jamaica. To Birmingham, England at age nine. Former session singer for Bryan Ferry, UB40 and Culture Club.

| 3/31/90 | 194 | 2 | | Paradise .... | $12 | Jive 1298 |

Everytime I Breathe
It's A Cryin' Shame
It's Gonna Be Alright
[includes 2 versions]
It's You My Heart Deals For
Leaves In The Wind
Paradise
See Me
Sexy
Surrender
There's No Better Love

TURNER, Spyder

Born Dwight D. Turner in 1947 in Beckley, West Virginia. Soul vocalist.

| 3/25/67 | 158 | 3 | | Stand By Me .... | $20 | MGM 4450 |

Don't Hold Back
Dream Lover
For Your Precious Love
Hold On, I'm Coming
I Can't Make It Anymore 95
I Can't Wait To See My Baby's Face
I Don't Want To Cry
I'm Alive With A Lovin' Feeling
Moon River
Morning, Morning
Stand By Me 12

TURNER, Tina

Born Anna Mae Bullock on 11/26/38 in Brownsville, Tennessee. R&B-rock vocalist/actress. Half of Ike & Tina Turner duo, when married to Ike from 1958-76. In films Tommy (1975) and Mad Max-Beyond Thunderdome (1985). With Ike, inducted into the Rock And Roll Hall of Fame in 1991.

9/20/75	155	5		1 Acid Queen	$12	United Art. 495
				Tina played the Acid Queen in the film Tommy		
6/16/84	3	106	▲5	2 **Private Dancer**	$8	Capitol 12330
9/27/86	4	52	▲	3 **Break Every Rule**	$8	Capitol 12530
4/9/88	86	9		4 Tina Live In Europe .... [L]	$10	Capitol 90126 [2]
10/7/89	31	21	●	5 Foreign Affair	$8	Capitol 91873
11/9/91	113	17		6 Simply The Best .... [G]	$12	Capitol 97152

Acid Queen (1)
Addicted To Love (4)
Afterglow (3)
Ask Me How I Feel (5)
Baby-Get It On (1)
Back Where You Started (3)
Be Tender With Me Baby (5)
Best, The (5,6) **15**
Better Be Good To Me (2,4,6) **5**
Bootsy Whitelaw (1)
Break Every Rule (3,4) **74**
Change Is Gonna Come (4)
Falling Like Rain (5)

Foreign Affair (5)
Girls (3)
Help (4)
I Can See For Miles (1)
I Can't Stand The Rain (2,4,6)
I Don't Wanna Lose You (5,6)
I Might Have Been Queen (Soul Survivor) (4)
I Want You Near Me (6)
I'll Be Thunder (3)
In The Midnight Hour (4)
It Take Two (6)
It's Only Love (4)

Land Of 1,000 Dances (4)
Let's Dance (3)
Let's Spend The Night Together (1)
Let's Stay Together (2,4,6) **26**
Look In Me In The Heart (5,6)
Love Thing (6)
1984 (2)
Not Enough Romance (5)
Nutbush City Limits (4)
Nutbush City Limits (The 90's Version) (6)
Overnight Sensation (3)

Paradise Is Here (3,4)
Pick Me Tonight (1)
Private Dancer (2,4,6) **7**
Proud Mary (4)
River Deep - Mountain High (6)
Rockin' And Rollin' (1)
Show Some Respect (2,4) **37**
634-5789 (4)
Steamy Windows (5,6) **39**
Steel Claw (3)
Tearing Us Apart (4)

Till The Right Man Comes Along (3)
Tonight (4)
Two People (3,4) **30**
Typical Male (3,4,6) **2**
Under My Thumb (1)
Undercover Agent For The Blues (5)
Way Of The World (6)
We Don't Need Another Hero (Thunderdome) (4,6) **2**
What You Get Is What You See (3,4,6) **13**

What's Love Got To Do With It (2,4,6) **1**
Whole Lotta Love (1)
You Can't Stop Me Loving You (5)
You Know Who (Is Doing You Know What) (5)

★★373★★ TURRENTINE, Stanley

Born on 4/5/34 in Pittsburgh. Tenor saxophonist. Married for a time to Shirley Scott. Member of Fuse One. Also see Jimmy Smith.

1/7/67	149	2		1 Rough 'N Tumble .... [I]	$15	Blue Note 84240
11/2/68	193	3		2 The Look Of Love .... [I]	$15	Blue Note 84286
3/20/71	182	3		3 Sugar .... [I]	$10	CTI 6005
10/19/74	69	21		4 Pieces Of Dreams .... [I]	$8	Fantasy 9465
11/16/74	185	7		5 The Baddest Turrentine .... [K-I]	$8	CTI 6048
3/8/75	110	13		6 The Sugar Man .... [K-I]	$8	CTI 6052
5/10/75	65	14		7 In The Pocket .... [I]	$8	Fantasy 9478
11/1/75	76	16		8 Have You Ever Seen The Rain .... [I]	$8	Fantasy 9493
6/12/76	100	14		9 Everybody Come On Out .... [I]	$8	Fantasy 9508
11/27/76+	96	14		10 The Man With The Sad Face .... [I]	$8	Fantasy 9519
9/10/77	84	9		11 Nightwings .... [I]	$8	Fantasy 9534
3/18/78	63	12		12 West Side Highway .... [I]	$8	Fantasy 9548
9/16/78	106	13		13 What About You! .... [I]	$8	Fantasy 9563
10/10/81	162	3		14 Tender Togetherness .... [I]	$8	Elektra 534

After The Love Is Gone (14)
Airport Love Theme (9)
All By Myself (9)
And Satisfy (1)
Ann, Wonderful One (12)
Baptismal (1)
Beautiful Friendship (2)
Birdland (11)
Black Lassie (7)
Blanket On The Beach (4)

Blues For Stan (2)
Cabin In The Sky (2)
Cherubim (14)
Deep In Love (4)
Disco Dancing (13)
Don't Give Up On Us (11)
Don't Mess With Mister T (5)
Emily (6)
Everybody Come On Out (9)
Evil (4)

Evil Ways (10)
Feel The Fire (13)
Feeling Good (11)
Have It Your Way, Sandy (7)
Have You Ever Seen The Rain (8)
Havin' Fun With Mr. T. (14)
Here There And Everywhere (2)
Heritage (13)

Hermanos (14)
Hope That We Can Be Together Soon (9)
Hudson Parkway (West Side Highway) (12)
I Know It's You (4)
I'll Give You My Love (14)
I'm Always Drunk In San Francisco (2)

I'm In Love (4)
I'm Not In Love (9)
If You Don't Believe (11)
Impressions (3)
In The Pocket (7)
Joao (11)
Just As I Am (6)
Ligia (1)
Look Of Love (2)
Love Hangover (10)

Loving You Is Sweeter Than Ever (7)
MacArthur Park (2)
Make Me Rainbows (6)
Man With The Sad Face (4)
Manhattan Skyline (13)
Many Rivers To Cross (9)
Midnight And You (4)
Mighty High (10)

DEBUT DATE	PEAK POS	WKS CHR	GOLD	ARTIST — Album Title	$	Label & Number

TURRENTINE, Stanley — Cont'd

More (Theme from Mondo Cane) (6)
My Wish For You (13)
Naked As The Day I Was Born (7)
Nightwings (11)
Only You And Me (14)
Over To Where You Are (7)
Papa "T" (11)

Peace Of Mind (12)
Pieces Of Dreams (4,6)
Reasons (8)
Salt Song (5)
Shake (1)
Smile (2)
Spaced (7)
Speedball (5)
Stairway To Heaven (9)

Stan's Thing (12)
Stretch, The (6)
Sugar (3,5,12)
Sunshine Alley (3)
Ts Dream (8)
Tamarac (9)
That's The Way Of The World (8)

There Is A Place (Rita's Theme) (9)
There's Music In The Air (11)
This Guy's In Love With You (2)
Tommy's Tune (8)
Touching You (8)
Vera Cruz (6)
Walk On By (1)

Walkin' (12)
What Could I Do Without You (1)
Whatever Possess'd Me (10)
Wind And The Sea (13)
World Chimes (14)
You (8)
You Are The Melody Of My Life (7)

You'll Never Find Another Love Like Mine (10)
You're My Baby (7)

TURTLES, The

Pop-folk-rock group formed at Westchester High School in Los Angeles in 1961. Led by Mark Volman (b: 4/19/47, Los Angeles) and Howard Kaylan (born Howard Kaplan on 6/22/47, New York City). First called the Nightriders; then the Crossfires. Recorded for Capco in 1963. Name changed to The Turtles in 1965. Many personnel changes except for Volman and Kaylan. Group disbanded in 1970. Volman and Kaylan joined the Mothers Of Invention. Went out as a duo in 1972 and recorded as Phlorescent Leech & Eddie and later as Flo & Eddie. Did soundtrack for the film *Strawberry Shortcake*. Toured again as The Turtles in 1985.

10/23/65+	98	19		1 It Ain't Me Babe	$25	White Whale 7111
4/29/67	25	22		2 Happy Together	$20	White Whale 7114
11/18/67+	7	39	●	3 The Turtles! Golden Hits ....[G]	$20	White Whale 7115
11/16/68	128	12		4 The Turtles Present The Battle of the Bands	$20	White Whale 7118
11/1/69	117	9		5 Turtle Soup	$25	White Whale 7124
4/11/70	146	9		6 The Turtles! More Golden Hits ....[G]	$20	White Whale 7127
12/21/74	194	7		7 The Turtles' Greatest Hits/Happy Together Again ....[G]	$12	Sire 3703 [2]

Bachelor Mother (5)
Battle Of The Bands (4,7)
Buzzsaw (4)
Can I Get To Know You Better (3,7) **89**
Can I Go On (7)
Can't You Hear The Cows (7)
Cat In The Window (6)
Chicken Little Was Right (4)
Come Over (5)
Dance This Dance (5)
Earth Anthem (4)
Elenore (4,6,7) **6**
Eve Of Destruction (1) **100**
Food (4)

Gas Money (7)
Glitter And Gold (1)
Grim Reaper Of Love (3,7) **81**
Guide For The Married Man (2,7)
Happy Together (2,3,7) **1**
Hot Little Hands (5,6)
House On The Hill (5)
How You Loved Me (5)
I'm Chief Kamanawanalea (We're The Royal Macadamia Nuts) (4)
Is It Any Wonder (3)
It Ain't Me Babe (1,3,7) **8**

It Was A Very Good Year (1)
John & Julie (5)
Lady-O (6,7) **78**
Last Laugh (1)
Last Thing I Remember (4)
Let Me Be (1,3,7) **29**
Let The Cold Winds Blow (1)
Like A Rolling Stone (1)
Like It Or Not (7)
Like The Seasons (4)
Love In The City (5,6,7) **91**
Love Minus Zero (1)
Makin' My Mind Up (2)
Me About You (2,7)
Oh, Daddy! (4)

Outside Chance (3,7)
Person Without A Care (2)
Rugs Of Woods & Flowers (2)
Santa And The Sidewalk Surfer (7)
She Always Leaves Me Laughing (5)
She'd Rather Be With Me (2,3,7) **3**
She's My Girl (6,7) **14**
So Goes Love (3)
Somewhere Friday Night (5,7)
Sound Asleep (6,7) **57**

Story Of Rock And Roll (6,7) **48**
Surfer Dan (4)
Teardrops (7)
There You Sit Lonely (2)
Think I'll Run Away (2)
Too Much Heartsick Feeling (4)
Too Young To Be One (2)
Torn Between Temptations (5)
Walk In The Sun (1)
Walking Song (2)
Wanderin' Kind (1)

We Ain't Gonna Party No More (6)
Who Would Ever Think That I Would Marry Margaret (6)
You Baby (3,7) **20**
You Don't Have To Walk In The Rain (5,6,7) **51**
You Know What I Mean (3,7) **12**
You Showed Me (4,6,7) **6**
You Want To Be A Woman (7)
Your Maw Said You Cried In Your Sleep Last Night (1)

TUTONE, Tommy — see TOMMY

TUXEDO JUNCTION

Female disco studio group assembled by producers W. Michael Lewis and Lauren Rinder.

2/18/78	56	32		Tuxedo Junction	$8	Butterfly 007

Chattanooga Choo Choo 32
Fox Trot

I Didn't Know About You

Moonlight Serenade

Rainy Night In Rio

Tuxedo Junction

Volga Boatman

TWENNYNINE FEATURING LENNY WHITE

New York R&B-funk band led by Lenny White (former drummer of Return To Forever).

12/8/79+	54	16		1 Best of Friends	$8	Elektra 223
11/1/80	106	8		2 Twennynine with Lenny White	$8	Elektra 304
12/5/81	162	5		3 Just Like Dreamin'	$8	Elektra 551

All I Want (3)
All Over Again (3)
Back To You (2)
Best Of Friends (1)
Betta (1)

Citi Dancin' (1)
Don't Look Back (3)
11th Fanfare (1)
Fancy Dancer (1)
Find A Love (3)

It's Music, It's Magic (2)
Just Like Dreamin' (3)
Just Right For Me (2)
Kid Stuff (2)
Love And Be Loved (2)

Morning Sunrise (1)
Movin' On (3)
My Melody (2)
Need You (3)
Oh, Sylvie (1)

Peanut Butter (1) **83**
Rhythm (3)
Slip Away (2)
Take Me Or Leave Me (1)
Tropical Nights (1)

Twennynine (The Rap) (3)
We Had To Break Away (2)

24-7 SPYZ

Black hard-rock group from the Bronx: Peter "Fluid" Forest (vocals), Jimi Hazel, Rick Skatore and Anthony Johnson.

6/17/89	113	16		1 Harder Than You	$8	In-Effect 3006
7/14/90	135	11		2 Gumbo Millennium	$12	In-Effect 3014

Ballots Not Bullets (1)
Culo Posse (2)
Deathstyle (2)
Don't Break My Heart! (2)
Don't Push Me (2)

Dude U Knew (2)
Grandma Dynamite (1)
Heaven And Hell (2)
I Must Go On (1)
Jimi'z Jam (1)

John Connelly's Theory (2)
Jungle Boogie (1)
New Drug (1)
New Super Hero Worship (2)
Pillage (1)

Racism (2)
Social Plague (1)
Some Defenders' Memories (2)
Spill My Guts (1)

Sponji Reggae (1)
Spyz Dope (1)
Spyz On Piano (2)
Tango Skin Polka (1)
Valdez 27 Million? (2)

We Got A Date (2)
We'll Have Power (2)

20/20

Pop-rock quartet originally from Tulsa, Oklahoma — Steve Allen, lead singer.

11/3/79	138	13		1 20/20	$8	Portrait 36205
6/20/81	127	12		2 Look Out!	$8	Portrait 37050

Action Now (1)
Alien (2)
American Dream (2)
Backyard Guys (1)

Beat City (2)
Cheri (1)
Girl Like You (2)
Jet Lag (1)

Leaving Your World Behind (1)
Life In The U.S.A. (2)
Mobile Unit 245 (2)

Night I Heard A Scream (2)
Nuclear Boy (2)
Out Of My Head (2)
Out Of This Time (1)

Remember The Lightning (1)
She's An Obsession (1)
Sky Is Falling (1)
Strange Side Of Love (2)

Tell Me Why (Can't Understand You) (1)
Tonight We Fly (1)
Yellow Pills (1)

TWILLEY, Dwight

Born on 6/6/51 in Tulsa, Oklahoma. Rock singer/songwriter/pianist. Formed the Dwight Twilley Band with Phil Seymour (bass, drums) in 1974.

7/31/76	138	14		1 Sincerely	$8	Shelter 52001
10/8/77	70	13		2 Twilley Don't Mind	$8	Arista 4140
				above 2: **DWIGHT TWILLEY BAND**		
3/24/79	113	9		3 Twilley	$8	Arista 4214
3/13/82	109	11		4 Scuba Divers	$8	EMI America 17064

757

DEBUT DATE	PEAK POS	WKS CHR	GOLD	ARTIST — Album Title	$	Label & Number

TWILLEY, Dwight — Cont'd

| 2/18/84 | 39 | 21 | 5 | Jungle .... | $8 | EMI America 17107 |

Alone In My Room (3)
Baby Let's Cruise (1)
Betsy Sue (3)
Chance To Get Away (2)
Could Be Love (1)
Cry Baby (5)
Cryin' Over Me (4)
Darlin' (3)
Dion Baby (4)
Don't You Love Her (5)

England (1)
Falling In Love Again (4)
Feeling In The Dark (1)
Girls (5) 16
Got You Where I Want You (3)
Here She Come (2)
I Found The Magic (4)
I Think It's That Girl (4)

I Wanna Make Love To You (3)
I'm Back Again (4)
I'm Losing You (1)
I'm On Fire (1) 16
Invasion (2)
It Takes Alot Of Love (3)
Jungle (5)
Just Like The Sun (1)
Later That Night (4)

Little Bit Of Love (5) 77
Long Lonely Nights (5)
Looking For The Magic (2)
Max Dog (5)
Nothing's Ever Gonna Change So Fast (3)
Out Of My Hands (3)
Release Me (1)
Rock And Roll '47 (2)
Runaway (3)

Sincerely (1)
Sleeping (2)
Somebody To Love (4)
Standin' In The Shadow Of Love (3)
TV (1)
10,000 American Scuba Divers Dancin' (4)
That I Remember (2)
Three Persons (1)

To Get To You (5)
Touchin' The Wind (4)
Trying To Find My Baby (2)
Twilley Don't Mind (2)
Why You Wanna Break My Heart (5)
You Can Change It (5)
You Were So Warm (1)

TWIN HYPE

New Jersey-based rap duo of twin brothers: Glennis "Sly" and Lennis "Slick" Brown.

| 8/26/89 | 140 | 11 | | Twin Hype .... | $8 | Profile 1281 |

Do It To The Crowd
Fanatics

For Those Who Like To Groove

Lori
My Metaphors

Serious Attitude
Smooth

Suckers Never Change
Tales Of The Twins

Twin Hype

TWISTED SISTER

Long Island, New York heavy-metal quintet led by Dee Snider (b: 3/15/55, Massapequa, Long Island, New York). Included Jay French (guitar), Eddie Ojeda (guitar), Mark Mendosa (bass) and A.J. Pero (drums). Pero replaced by Joey Franco in 1987. Disbanded in late 1987.

8/27/83+	130	14		1 You Can't Stop Rock 'N' Roll	$8	Atlantic 80074
7/7/84	15	51	▲²	2 Stay Hungry	$8	Atlantic 80156
7/6/85	125	11		3 Under The Blade .... [K-E]	$8	Atlantic 81256
				remixed edition of their first album plus bonus track		
12/21/85+	53	17	●	4 Come Out And Play	$8	Atlantic 81275
8/1/87	74	11		5 Love Is For Suckers	$8	Atlantic 81772

Bad Boys (Of Rock 'N' Roll) (3)
Be Chrool To Your Scuel (4)
Beast, The (2)
Burn In Hell (2)
Come Out And Play (4)
Day Of The Rocker (3)
Destroyer (3)
Don't Let Me Down (2)
Fire Still Burns (4)

Horror-Teria (The Beginning) Medley (2)
Hot Love (5)
I Am (I'm Me) (1)
I Believe In Rock 'N' Roll (4)
I Believe In You (4)
I Wanna Rock (2) 68
I Want This Night (To Last Forever) (5)
I'll Never Grow Up, Now! (3)

I'll Take You Alive (1)
I'm So Hot For You (5)
I've Had Enough (1)
Kids Are Back (1)
Kill Or Be Killed (1)
Like A Knife In The Back (1)
Lookin' Out For #1 (4)
Love Is For Suckers (5)
Me And The Boys (5)

One Bad Habit (5)
Out On The Streets (4)
Power And The Glory (1)
Price, The (2)
Ride To Live, Live To Ride (1)
Run For Your Life (3)
S.M.F. (2)
Shoot 'Em Down (3)
Sin After Sin (3)
Stay Hungry (2)

Tear It Loose (3)
Tonight (5)
Under The Blade (3)
Wake Up (The Sleeping Giant) (1)
We're Gonna Make It (1)
We're Not Gonna Take It (2) 21
What You Don't Know (Sure Can Hurt You) (3)

Yeah Right! (4)
You Are All That I Need (5)
You Can't Stop Rock 'N' Roll (1)
You Want What We Got (4)
You're Not Alone (Suzette's Song) (1)

TWITTY, Conway

Born Harold Lloyd Jenkins on 9/1/33 in Friars Point, Mississippi and raised in Helena, Arkansas. Superstar country singer. Conway has charted over 30 #1 solo country hits. Formed own group, the Phillips County Ramblers, at age 10. Offered a professional career with the Philadelphia Phillies when drafted. With service band, Cimmarons, in Japan, early 1950s. Changed his name in 1957 and first recorded for Sun (unissued recordings). In the films *Sexpot Goes To College* and *College Confidential*. Switched from pop to country music in 1965. Moved to Nashville in 1968. Owns tourist complex, Twitty City, in Hendersonville, Tennessee.

8/16/69	161	3		1 I Love You More Today	$12	Decca 75131
7/4/70	65	26	●	2 Hello Darlin'	$8	Decca 75209
1/23/71	140	7		3 Fifteen Years Ago	$8	Decca 75248
3/13/71	78	14	●	4 We Only Make Believe *	$10	Decca 75251
5/22/71	91	9		5 How Much More Can She Stand	$8	Decca 75276
9/18/71	142	8		6 I Wonder What She'll Think About Me Leaving	$8	Decca 75292
3/4/72	106	13	●	7 Lead Me On *	$10	Decca 75326
4/8/72	130	9		8 I Can't See Me Without You	$8	Decca 75335
8/25/73	153	9		9 Louisiana Woman-Mississippi Man *	$10	MCA 335
				*CONWAY TWITTY and LORETTA LYNN		
9/15/73	134	9	●	10 You've Never Been This Far Before/Baby's Gone	$8	MCA 359
2/13/82	144	15		11 Southern Comfort	$8	Elektra 60005

Above And Beyond (The Call Of Love) (10)
After The Fire Is Gone (4) 56
Amos Moses (5)
As Good As A Lonely Girl Can Be (9)
Baby's Gone (10)
Back Street Affair (3,7)
Before Your Time (9)
Blue Eyes Crying In The Rain (2)
Born To Lose (10)
Bottle In The Hand (Is Much Stronger Than The Man) (1)
Boy Next Door (11)
Bring It On Home (To Your Woman) (10)
Bye Bye Love (9)
Clown, The (11)
Crazy Arms (1)
Darling Days (10)
Don't Tell Me You're Sorry (4)
Easy Loving (9)
Everyday Family Man (5)
Fifteen Years Ago (3) 81
For Heavens Sake (9)
Games People Play (1)

Get Some Loving Done (7)
Hangin' On (4)
Hank Williams Medley (5)
Heartache Just Walked In (6)
Heartaches By The Number (1)
Hello Darlin' (2) 60
Help Me Make It Through The Night (5)
Hey! Baby (3)
How Far Can We Go (7)
How Much More Can She Stand (5)
I Can't Believe That You've Stopped Loving Me (3)
I Can't See Me Without You (8)
I Didn't Lose Her (I Threw Her Away) (8)
I Fall To Pieces (6)
I Love You More In Memory (10)
I Love You More Today (1)
I Never Once Stopped Loving You (2)
I Was The First (11)
I Wonder If You Told Her About Me (7)

I Wonder What She'll Think About Me Leaving (6)
I'd Rather Love You (6)
I'll Come Running (3)
I'll Get Over Losing You (2)
I'll Never Make It Home Tonight (8)
I'll Share My World With You (1)
I'm So Used To Loving You (2,4)
If You Touch Me, (You've Got To Love Me) (9)
It Turns Me Inside Out (11)
It's A Cryin' Shame (8)
It's Been One Heck Of A Day (8)
It's Only Make-Believe (4)
Johnny B. Goode (1)
Joy To The World (6)
Just Like A Stranger (5)
Kiss An Angel Good Morning (8)
Last One To Touch Me (5)
Lead Me On (7)
Let Me Be The Judge (5)
Letter And A Ring (6)
Little Girl Cried (3)

Living Together Alone (9)
Looking Thru My Glass (8)
Louisiana Woman, Mississippi Man (9)
Love And Only Love (11)
Memory Of Your Sweet Love (5)
My Heart Won't Listen To My Mind (6)
My Love For You Is Stronger (Than The Weakness In Me) (6)
Never Ending Song Of Love (7)
One For The Money (4)
One I Can't Live Without (4)
One More Sunrise (8)
One More Time (6)
Our Conscience You And Me (9)
Pickin' Wild Mountain Berries (4)
Playing House Away From Home (7)
Proud Mary (1)
Release Me (9)
Rocky Top (4)
Rose (2)

Rueben James (2)
Sand Covered Angels (3)
Seasons Of My Heart (4)
She Can Only See The Good In Me (3)
She Knows What She's Crying About (8)
She Only Meant To Use Him (11)
She's All I Got (8)
Slow Hand (11)
Slowly (3)
Something Strange Got Into Her Last Night (11)
Southern Comfort (11)
Star Spangled Heaven (1)
Take Me (4)
This Road That I Walk (8)
'Til The Pain Outwears The Shame (10)
Up Comes The Bottle (Down Goes The Man) (2)
We've Closed Our Eyes To Shame (9)
Weakness In Your Man (10)
What Are We Gonna Do About Us (9)

When I Turn Off My Lights (Your Memory Turns On) (7)
When Love Was Something Else (11)
When The Final Change Is Made (10)
Who'll Turn Out The Lights (In Your World Tonight) (6)
Wild Mountain Rose (7)
Will You Visit Me On Sunday (2,4)
Wine Me Up (6)
Working Girl (4)
World Of Forgotten People (1)
You And Your Sweet Love (2)
You Blow My Mind (7)
You Lay So Easy On My Mind (9)
(You Make It Hard) To Take The Easy Way Out (10)
You're The Reason (7)
You've Never Been This Far Before (10) 22

2 IN A ROOM

Dance duo from Washington Heights, New York: rapper Rafael "Dose" Vargas and remixer Roger "Rog Nice" Pauletta.

| 12/22/90+ | 151 | 9 | | Wiggle It.. | $12 | Cutting 91594 |

Body To Body   Do What You Want   Hype Stuff   She's Got Me Going Crazy [includes 2 versions]   **Wiggle It** [includes 2 versions] 15
Booty Hump   Got 'Em On The Run   Rock Bottom
Bring It On Down   House Junkie   Rock The House   Soul Train

2 LIVE CREW, The

Miami-based rap quartet: David "Mr. Mix" Hobbs, Chris "Fresh Kid-Ice" Won Wong, "Brother Marquis" Ross and Luther "Luke Skyywalker" Campbell (owner of Luke Records). Group's obscenity arrests sparked national censorship controversy in 1990. Campbell recorded as Luke in 1992.

4/11/87	128	33	●	1 The 2 Live Crew "is what we are"	$8	Luke Sky. 100
6/4/88	68	42	●	2 Move Somethin'..	$8	Luke Sky. 101
7/29/89+	29	81	▲	3 As Nasty As They Wanna Be	$10	Luke Sky. 107 [2]

also released alternate single album version, As Clean As They Wanna Be

| 8/11/90 | 21 | 22 | ● | 4 Banned In The U.S.A. .... | $12 | Luke 91424 |

LUKE Featuring THE 2 LIVE CREW

| 1/19/91 | 92 | 12 | | 5 Live In Concert ....[L] | $12 | Effect 3003 |
| 10/26/91 | 22 | 30 | ● | 6 Sports Weekend (As Nasty As They Wanna Be Part II)............... | $12 | Luke 91720 |

also released alternate version, Sports Weekend (As Clean As They Wanna Be Part II)

Ain't No Pussy Like... (6)   Cut It Up (1)   F--k Martinez (4)   I Like It, I Love It (6)   Mr. Mixx On The Mix!! (1)   Some Hot Head (6)
Arrest In Effect (4)   Dick Almighty (3)   Fuck Shop (3,5)   If You Believe In Having Sex (3,5)   My Seven Bizzos (3)   Strip Club (4)
Baby Baby Please (Just A Little More Head) (6)   Dirty Nursery Rhymes (3)   Get It Girl (1)   Mamolapenga (4)   One And One (2,5)   This Is To Luke From The Posse (4)
Bad Ass Bitch (3)   Do The Bart (4)   Get Loose Now (3)   Man, Not A Myth (4)   Pop That Pussy (6)   Throw The D (1,5)
Banned In The U.S.A. (4,5) 20   Do Wah Diddy (2)   Get The Fuck Out Of My House (3)   **Me So Horny** (3,5) 26   Pussy Ass Nigga (2)   2 Live Blues (3)
Bass 9-1-7 (4)   Drop The Bomb (2)   Ghetto Bass II (2)   Mega Mixx (4)   Pussy Caper (6)   2 Live Is What We Are (Word) (1)
Beat Box (1)   Face Down A-- Up (4,5)   H-B-C (5)   Mega Mixx III (4)   Pussy (Reprise) For Those Who Like To Fuck (6)   Ugly As Fuck (3)
Break It On Down (3)   Feel Alright Yall (2)   Head, Booty, And Cock (2)   Mega Mixx IV (4)   Put Her In The Buck (3)   We Want Some Pussy (1,5)
Check It Out Yall (1)   Fraternity Joint (6)   Here I Come (6)   Mega Mixx V (6)   Reggae Joint (3)   Who's Fuckin' Who (6)
C'mon Babe (3,5)   Fraternity Record (3)   I Ain't Bullshittin' (3)   Move Somethin' (2,5)   S & M (2)   With Your Bad Self (2)
Coolin' (3)   Freaky Behavior (6)   I Ain't Bullshittin' Part 2 (4)   Mr. Mixx Turntable Show (Part I & II) (5)   Sex, I Like -- I Love (5)   Word II (2)
  F--k A Gang (4)   I Ain't Bullshittin' III (6)   So Funky (4)
  Fuck Is A Fuck (6)

2 LIVE JEWS

Novelty spin-off of the rap group The 2 Live Crew. Miami duo of Eric "MC Moisha" Lambert and Joe "Easy Irving" Stone.

| 9/15/90 | 150 | 9 | | As Kosher As They Wanna Be ....[N] | $12 | Kosher 3328 |

Accountant Suckers   As Kosher As They Wanna Be   Ballad Of Moisha & Irving   J.A.P. Rap   Matchmaka' Game   Shake Your Tuchas
    Beggin' For A Bargain   Jokin' Jews   Oui! It's So Humid   Young Jews Be Proud

2 PAC

Rapper Tupac Amaru Shakur. Former member of Digital Underground. Appeared in the film Juice.

| 2/29/92 | 64 | 23 | | 2Pacalypse Now... | $12 | Interscope 91767 |

Brenda's Got A Baby   If My Homie Calls   Rebel Of The Underground   Soulja's Story   Trapped   Words Of Wisdom
Crooked Ass Nigga   Part Time Mutha   Something Wicked...   Tha' Lunatic   Violent   Young Black Male
Don't Give A Fuck

TWO TONS O' FUN

Duo of Martha Wash and Izora Rhodes. Did backup for Sylvester. Later recorded as The Weather Girls. Wash was the actual, uncredited vocalist of Seduction's "You're My One And Only (True Love)," "Everybody Everybody" by Black Box and "Gonna Make You Sweat" by C & C Music Factory.

| 5/17/80 | 91 | 11 | | Two Tons O' Fun .... | $8 | Honey 9584 |

Do You Wanna Boogie, Hunh?   Earth Can Be Just Like Heaven   I Got The Feeling   Make Someone Feel Happy Today   Taking Away Your Space
  Gone Away   Just Us   One-Sided Love Affair

2 UNLIMITED

Techno-house duo from Amsterdam: vocalists Kid Ray (age 20 in 1992) and Anita (age 19 in 1992).

| 10/17/92 | 197 | 1 | | Get Ready .... | $12 | Radikal 15407 |

CD includes 2 bonus tracks

Contrast   Eternally Yours   Magic Friend [includes 2 versions]   Rougher Than The Average   Workaholic [includes 2 versions]
Delight   **Get Ready For This** [includes 2 versions] 76   Pacific Walk   **Twilight Zone** [includes 2 versions] 49
Desire

TYCOON

New York-based, pop-rock sextet — Norman Mershon, lead singer.

| 3/31/79 | 41 | 17 | | Tycoon .... | $8 | Arista 4215 |

Count On Me   Don't You Cry No More   How Long (Can We Go On)   Slow Down Boy   Too Late (New York City)
Don't Worry   Drunken Sailor   Out In The Cold   **Such A Woman** 26   Way That It Goes

TYLER, Bonnie

Born Gaynor Hopkins on 6/8/53 in Swansea, Wales. Worked local clubs until the mid-1970s. Distinctive raspy vocals caused by operation to remove throat nodules in 1976.

6/3/78	16	17	●	1 It's A Heartache	$8	RCA 2821
2/17/79	145	5		2 Diamond Cut	$8	RCA 3072
8/6/83	4	32	▲	3 Faster Than The Speed Of Night	$8	Columbia 38710
4/26/86	106	8		4 Secret Dreams And Forbidden Fire	$8	Columbia 40312

Baby Goodnight (1)   Getting So Excited (1)   **Holding Out For A Hero** (4) 34   It's A Jungle Out There (3)   No Way To Treat A Lady (4)   What A Way To Treat My Heart (2)
Baby I Just Love You (2)   Goin' Through The Motions (3)   I'm A Fool (2)   Living For The City (1)   Ravishing (4)   Words Can Change Your Life (2)
Band Of Gold (4)   Have You Ever Seen The Rain? (3)   If I Sing A Love Song (1)   Louisiana Rain (2)   Rebel Without A Clue (4)   Yesterday Dreams (1)
Blame Me (1)   Heaven (1)   If You Ever Need Me Again (2)   Lovers Again (4)   Straight From The Heart (3)
Bye Bye Now My Sweet Love (2)   Here Am I (1)   **If You Were A Woman (And I Was A Man)** (4) 77   Loving You's A Dirty Job But Somebody's Gotta Do It (4)   **Take Me Back** (3) 46
Eyes Of A Fool (2)   Hey Love (It's A Feelin') (1)   It's A Heartache (1) 3   My Guns Are Loaded (2)   Too Good To Last (2)
Faster Than The Speed Of Night (3)   Natural Woman (1)   **Total Eclipse Of The Heart** (3) 1

DEBUT DATE	PEAK POS	WKS CHR	GOLD	ARTIST — Album Title	$	Label & Number

TYMES, The
Soul group formed in Philadelphia in 1956. Consisted of George Williams (lead), George Hilliard, Donald Banks, Albert Berry and Norman Burnett. First called the Latineers.

DEBUT DATE	PEAK POS	WKS CHR		ARTIST — Album Title	$	Label & Number
8/3/63	15	20		1 So Much In Love	$35	Parkway 7032
12/21/63+	117	10		2 The Sound Of The Wonderful Tymes	$25	Parkway 7038
3/7/64	122	4		3 Somewhere	$35	Parkway 7039

includes 7" bonus single ("Isle of Love"/"I'm Always Chasing Rainbows")

Address Unknown (2)
Alone (1)
And That Reminds Me (2)
Anymore (3)
Autumn Leaves (1)
Blue Velvet (2)
Chances Are (2)
Come With Me To The Sea (2,3)
Goodnight My Love (1)
Hello Young Lovers (2)
I Thank You (2)
I'm Always Chasing Rainbows (3)
Isle Of Love (3)
Lamp Is Low (3)
Let's Fall In Love Tonight (3)
Let's Make Love Tonight (1)
Moonlight Cocktails (2)
My Summer Love (1)
Night (3)
One Little Kiss (2)
Sleep Tight My Darling (3)
So Much In Love (1) *1*
Somewhere (3) *19*
Stranger In Paradise (3)
Summer Day (1)
That Old Black Magic (1)
There Is Love (3)
Till The End Of Time (3)
Twelfth Of Never (1)
Way Beyond Today (1)
Way You Look Tonight (2)
Why Should I Cry (3)
Will You Wait For Me (3)
Wonderful! Wonderful! (1,2) *7*
Words Written On Water (2)
You Asked Me To Be Yours (1)

TYNER, McCoy
Born on 12/11/38 in Philadelphia. Jazz pianist. With John Coltrane for five years in the 1960s. Also worked with Ike & Tina Turner.

DEBUT DATE	PEAK POS	WKS CHR		ARTIST — Album Title		$	Label & Number
6/14/75	161	5		1 Atlantis	[I-L]	$10	Milestone 55002 [2]
1/3/76	198	2		2 Trident	[I]	$8	Milestone 9063
				with Ron Carter (bass) and Elvin Jones (drums)			
6/12/76	128	11		3 Fly With The Wind	[I]	$8	Milestone 9067
				with Hubert Laws (flute), Billy Cobham (drums) and Ron Carter			
1/22/77	187	3		4 Focal Point	[I]	$8	Milestone 9072
7/9/77	167	5		5 Supertrios	[I]	$10	Milestone 55003 [2]
				record 1: with Ron Carter and Tony Williams (drums); record 2: with Eddie Gomez (bass) and Jack DeJohnette (drums)			
1/28/78	171	8		6 Inner Voices	[I]	$8	Milestone 9079
				with Earl Klugh (guitar)			
10/14/78	170	3		7 The Greeting	[I-L]	$8	Milestone 9085
5/26/79	66	11		8 Together	[I]	$8	Milestone 9087

with Freddie Hubbard (trumpet), Stanley Clarke (bass) and Hubert Laws

Atlantis (1)
Ballad For Aisha (8)
Bayou Fever (8)
Beyond The Sun (4)
Blues For Ball (5)
Blues On The Corner (5)
Celestial Chant (5)
Consensus (5)
Departure (4)
Elvin (Sir) Jones (2)
Festival In Bahia (6)
Fly With The Wind (3,6)
For Tomorrow (6)
Four By Five (5)
Greeting, The (5,7)
Hand In Hand (7)
Highway One (8)
Hymn-Song (5)
I Mean You (5)
Impressions (2)
In A Sentimental Mood (1)
Indo-Serenade (4)
Land Of The Lonely (2)
Love Samba (1)
Lush Life (5)
Makin' Out (1)
Mes Trois Fils (4)
Mode For Dulcimer (4)
Moment's Notice (5)
My One And Only Love (1)
Naima (7)
Nana, Theme For (4)
Nubia (8)
Once I Loved (2)
One Of Another Kind (8)
Opus (5)
Parody (4)
Pictures (7)
Prelude To A Kiss (5)
Pursuit (1)
Rolem (3)
Rotunda (6)
Ruby, My Dear (2)
Salvador De Samba (3)
Shades Of Light (8)
Stella By Starlight (5)
Uptown (6)
Wave (5)
You Stepped Out Of A Dream (3)

TYZIK
Jazz trumpeter/flugelhornist, Jeff Tyzik.

DEBUT DATE	PEAK POS	WKS CHR		ARTIST — Album Title	$	Label & Number
9/8/84	172	6		Jammin' In Manhattan	$8	Polydor 821605

Better And Better
Echoes
Jammin' In Manhattan
Killer Joe
Melange
New York Woman
When I Look In Your Eyes
You're My Woman, You're My Lady

U

★★439★★ UB40
British interracial reggae octet formed in 1978 — Ali Campbell (b: 2/15/59, Birmingham, England), lead singer. Took name from a British unemployment benefit form. Members include Ali's brother Robin Campbell, Earl Falconer, Michael Virtue, Astro, Norman Hassan, Brian Travers and James Brown.

DEBUT DATE	PEAK POS	WKS CHR		ARTIST — Album Title	$	Label & Number
11/26/83+	14	63	▲	1 Labour of Love	$8	A&M 4980
				originally peaked at POS 39 in 1984; re-entered and reached new peak in 1988		
11/10/84	60	26		2 Geffery Morgan	$8	A&M 5033
8/17/85	40	25		3 Little Baggariddim [M]	$8	A&M 5090
8/30/86	53	17		4 Rat in the Kitchen	$8	A&M 5137
8/29/87	121	8		5 CCCP: Live In Moscow [L]	$8	A&M 5168
8/20/88	44	27		6 UB40	$8	A&M 5213
1/13/90+	30	111	▲	7 Labour Of Love II	$12	Virgin 91324

All I Want To Do (4,5)
As Always You Were Wrong Again (2)
Baby (7)
Breakfast In Bed (6)
'Cause It Isn't True (6)
Cherry Oh Baby (1,5)
Come Out To Play (6)
Contaminated Minds (6)
Dance With The Devil (6)
Don't Blame Me (4,5)
Don't Break My Heart (3,5)
D.U.B. (2)
Elevator, The (4)
Groovin' (7) *90*
Guilty (2)
Here I Am (Come And Take Me) (7) *7*
Hip Hop Lyrical Robot (3)
Homely Girl (7)
I Got You Babe (3,5) *28*
I Would Do For You (6)
I'm Not Fooled So Easily (2)
If It Happens Again (2,5)
Impossible Love (7)
Johnny Too Bad (1,5)
Keep On Moving (1,5)
Kingston Town (7)
Looking Down At My Reflection (4)
Many Rivers To Cross (1)
Matter Of Time (7)
Mi Spliff (3)
Music So Nice (6)
Nkomo A Go Go (2)
One In Ten (3)
Pillow, The (2)
Please Don't Make Me Cry (1,5)
Rat In Me Kitchen (4,5)
Red Red Wine (1) *1*
Riddle Me (7)
Seasons (2)
She Caught The Train (1)
Sing Our Own Song (4,5)
Sweet Sensation (1)
Tears From My Eyes (7)
Tell It Like It Is (4,5)
Version Girl (1)
Watchdogs (4,5)
Way You Do The Things You Do (7) *6*
Wear You To The Ball (7)
Wedding Day (7)
Where Did I Go Wrong (6)
You Could Meet Somebody (4)
You're Always Pulling Me Down (6)
You're Not An Army (2)
Your Eyes Were Open (2)

UBIQUITY
Roy Ayers' backing group — Sylvia Cox, lead singer.

DEBUT DATE	PEAK POS	WKS CHR		ARTIST — Album Title	$	Label & Number
4/8/78	146	4		Starbooty	$8	Elektra 120

Can You Be Yourself
Five Flies
If You Wanna See The Sunshine
Love Is Love
Midnight After Dark
Simple And Sweet
Spread It
Starbooty

DEBUT DATE	PEAK POS	WKS CHR	GOLD	ARTIST — Album Title	$	Label & Number

★★418★★ UFO
British hard-rock group led by Phil Mogg (vocals) and Michael Schenker (guitar; left by 1990 to form own group). Numerous personnel changes.

8/9/75	71	13		1 Force It	$8	Chrysalis 1074
6/19/76	169	4		2 No Heavy Petting	$8	Chrysalis 1103
6/11/77	23	24		3 Lights Out	$8	Chrysalis 1127
7/29/78	41	18		4 Obsession	$8	Chrysalis 1182
2/3/79	42	15		5 Strangers In The Night .... [L]	$10	Chrysalis 1209 [2]
1/19/80	51	13		6 No Place to Run..............................	$8	Chrysalis 1239
1/31/81	77	11		7 The Wild The Willing And The Innocent	$8	Chrysalis 1307
2/20/82	82	14		8 Mechanix	$8	Chrysalis 1360
4/30/83	153	5		9 Making Contact	$8	Chrysalis 41402
4/5/86	106	19		10 Misdemeanor..................................	$8	Chrysalis 41518

Ain't No Baby (4) · All Over You (9) · Alone Again Or (3) · Alpha Centauri (6) · Anyday (6) · Arbory Hill (4) · Back Into My Life (8) · Belladonna (2) · Between The Walls (medley) (1) · Blinded By A Lie (9) · Blue (10) · Born To Lose (4) · Call My Name (9) · Can You Roll Her (2) · Chains Chains (7) · Cherry (4) · Couldn't Get It Right (7) · Dance Your Life Away (1) · Diesel In The Dust (9) · Doctor Doctor (5) · Doing It All For You (8) · Dream The Dream (10) · Dreaming (8) · Electric Phase (3) · Feel It (8) · Fool For Love (9) · Fool In Love (2) · Gettin' Ready (3) · Gone In The Night (6) · Heaven's Gate (10) · High Flyer (1) · Highway Lady (2) · Hot 'N' Ready (4) · I'm A Loser (2,5) · It's Killing Me (7) · Just Another Suicide (3) · Let It Rain (8) · Let It Roll (1,5) · Lettin' Go (6) · Lights Out (3,5) · Lonely Heart (7) · Long Gone (7) · Lookin' Out For No. 1 (4) · Love Lost Love (1) · Love To Love (3,5) · Makin Moves (7) · Martian Landscape (2) · Meanstreets (10) · Money, Money (6) · Mother Mary (1,5) · Mystery Train (6) · Name Of Love (10) · Natural Thing (2,5) · Night Run (4) · No Getaway (9) · No Place To Run (6) · On With The Action (2) · One Heart (10) · One More For The Rodeo (4) · Only Ones (10) · Only You Can Rock Me (4,5) · Out In The Street (1,5) · Pack It Up (And Go) (4) · Profession Of (7) · Push, It's Love (9) · Reasons Love (2) · Rock Bottom (5) · Shoot Shoot (1,5) · Something Else (8) · Take It Or Leave It (6) · Terri (8) · This Fire Burns Tonight (6) · This Kid's (1,5) · This Time (10) · Too Hot To Handle (3,5) · Too Much Of Nothing (1) · Try Me (3) · Way The Wild Wind Blows (9) · We Belong To The Night (8) · When It's Time To Rock (9) · Wild The Willing And The Innocent (7) · Wreckless (10) · Writer, The (8) · You And Me (9) · You Don't Fool Me (4) · You'll Get Love (8) · Youngblood (6)

UGLY KID JOE
Thrash-metal band from Isla Vista, California: Whitfield Crane (vocals), Klaus Eichstadt, Roger Lahr, Cordell Crockett and Mark Davis. Lahr replaced by guitarist Dave Fortman by 1992.

| 2/8/92 | 4 | 34 ▲ | | 1 As Ugly As They Want To Be .... [M] | $6 | Stardog 868823 |

the first multi-platinum, short-form LP certified by RIAA since the category was introduced in 1991

| 9/26/92 | 29 | 20↑ ● | | 2 America's Least Wanted .... | $12 | Stardog 512571 |

Busy Bee (2) · Cats In The Cradle (2) · Come Tomorrow (2) · Don't Go (2) · Everything About You (1,2) 9 · Funky Fresh Country Club (medley) (1) · Goddamn Devil (2) · Heavy Metal (1) · I'll Keep Tryin' (2) · Madman (1,2) · Mr. Recordman (2) · Neighbor (2) · Panhandlin' Prince (2) · Same Side (2) · So Damn Cool (2) · Sweet Leaf (medley) (1) · Too Bad (1) · Whiplash Liquor (2)

U.K.
British trio: Terry Bozzio (drums; Missing Persons), Eddie Jobson (keyboards; Roxy Music) and John Wetton (bass, vocals; King Crimson, Uriah Heep, U.K., Asia).

| 5/20/78 | 65 | 15 | | 1 U.K. .... | $8 | Polydor 6146 |

Bill Bruford and Allan Holdsworth were members on this album

| 3/24/79 | 45 | 11 | | 2 Danger Money .... | $8 | Polydor 6194 |
| 10/20/79 | 109 | 6 | | 3 Night After Night .... [L] | $8 | Polydor 6234 |

Alaska (1,3) · As Long As You Want Me Here (3) · By The Light Of Day (1) · Caesar's Palace Blues (2,3) · Carrying No Cross (2) · Danger Money (2) · In The Dead Of Night (1,3) · Mental Medication (1) · Nevermore (2) · Night After Night (3) · Nothing To Lose (2,3) · Only Thing She Needs (2) · Presto Vivace (1,3) · Rendezvous (2,3) · Thirty Years (1) · Time To Kill (1,3)

U-KREW, The
Rap quintet from Portland, Oregon formed as The Untouchable Krew in October 1984. Led by drum programmer Larry Bell, with lead vocals by Kevin Morse.

| 2/17/90 | 93 | 23 | | The U-Krew .... | $12 | Enigma 73524 |

All Night Lover · Angel · Feel It · Get Ready · If U Were Mine 24 · Let Me Be Your Lover 68 · Pick Up The Pieces · Pump Me Up · Rock That Shit · Ugly

ULLMAN, Tracey
Born on 12/30/59 in Buckinghamshire, England. Actress/singer/comedienne. Own variety-style TV show on Fox network, 1987-90. In films I Love You To Death, Plenty and Give My Regards To Broad Street.

| 3/24/84 | 34 | 20 | | You Broke My Heart In 17 Places .... | $8 | MCA 5471 |

Bobby's Girl · Break-A-Way 70 · I Close My Eyes And Count To Ten · (Life Is A Rock) But The Radio Rolled Me · Long Live Love · Move Over Darling · Oh, What A Night · Shattered · They Don't Know 8 · You Broke My Heart In 17 Places · Your Presence

ULTIMATE
Philadelphia studio disco project produced by Juliano Salerni and Bruce Weeden.

| 3/3/79 | 157 | 11 | | Ultimate .... | $8 | Casablanca 7128 |

Dancing In The Night · Love Is The Ultimate · Music In My Heart · Ritmo De Brazil · Take Me To Chinatown · Touch Me Baby 82

ULTIMATE SPINACH
Psychedelic-rock quintet from Boston: Ian Bruce-Douglas, Barbara Hudson, Keith Lahteinen, Richard Nese and Geoffrey Winthrop.

| 2/24/68 | 34 | 24 | | 1 Ultimate Spinach.............................. | $20 | MGM 4518 |
| 11/9/68 | 198 | 2 | | 2 Behold & See .... | $20 | MGM 4570 |

(Ballad Of The) Hip Death Goddess (1) · Baroque #1 (1) · Dove In Hawk's Clothing (1) · Ego Trip (1) · Fifth Horseman Of The Apocalypse (1) · Fragmentary March Of Green (2) · Funny Freak Parade (1) · Genesis Of Beauty ..see: Suite · Gilded Lamp Of The Cosmos (2) · Hung-Up Minds (medley) (1) · Jazz Thing (2) · Mind Flowers (2) · Pamela (1) · Plastic Raincoats (medley) (1) · Sacrifice Of The Moon (1) · Suite: Genesis Of Beauty (In Four Parts) (2) · Visions Of Your Reality (2) · Where You're At (2) · Your Head Is Reeling (1)

DEBUT DATE	PEAK POS	WKS CHR	GOLD	ARTIST — Album Title	$	Label & Number

ULTRAVOX
British electronic-rock quartet: Midge Ure (lead singer, guitar), Billy Currie (synthesizer, piano), Warren Cann (drums) and Chris Cross (bass, synthesizer). Ure went solo in 1988.

9/13/80	164	9		1 Vienna	$8	Chrysalis 1296
10/24/81	144	6		2 Rage In Eden	$8	Chrysalis 1338
3/12/83	61	17		3 Quartet	$8	Chrysalis 1394
5/19/84	115	9		4 Lament	$8	Chrysalis 41459

Accent On Youth (2)
All Stood Still (1)
Ascent, The (2)
Astradyne (1)
Cut And Run (3)
Dancing With Tears In My Eyes (4)
Friend I Call Desire (4)
Heart Of The Country (4)
Hymn (3)
I Remember (Death In The Afternoon) (2)
Lament (4)
Man Of Two Worlds (4)
Mine For Life (3)
Mr. X (1)
New Europeans (1)
One Small Day (4)
Passing Strangers (1)
Private Lives (1)
Rage In Eden (2)
Reap The Wild Wind (3) **71**
Serenade (3)
Sleepwalk (1)
Song (We Go) (3)
Stranger Within (2)
Thin Wall (2)
Vienna (1)
Visions In Blue (3)
Voice, The (2)
We Came To Dance (3)
We Stand Alone (2)
Western Promise (1)
When The Scream Subsides (3)
When The Time Comes (4)
White China (4)
Your Name Has Slipped My Mind Again (2)

UNDERGROUND SUNSHINE
Rock quartet: Chris Connors and Jane Little (both from Wisconsin), with Frank and Betty Kohl (from Germany).

11/8/69	161	3		Let There Be Light	$25	Intrepid 74003

All I Want Is You
Bad Moon Rising
Birthday 26
Don't Let Me Down
Don't Shut Me Out
Gimme Some Lovin'
Proud Mary
Take Me, Break Me

UNDERTONES, The
Irish punk-rock quintet led by Feargal Sharkey (later charted solo).

1/26/80	154	7		The Undertones	$8	Sire 6081

Billy's Third
Casbah Rock
Family Entertainment
Get Over You
Girls Don't Like It
Here Comes The Summer
I Gotta Getta
I Know A Girl
Jimmy Jimmy
Jump Boys
Listenin In
Male Model
(She's A) Runaround
Teenage Kicks
True Confessions
Wrong Way

UNDERWORLD
U.K. quintet: Karl Hyde (vocals), Rick Smith, Alfie Thomas, Baz Allen, and Bryn Burrows (replaced by drummer Pascal Console).

3/19/88	139	19		Underneath The Radar	$8	Sire 25627

Bright White Flame
Call Me No. 1
Glory! Glory!
God Song
I Need A Doctor
Miracle Party
Pray
Rubber Ball (Space Kitchen)
Show Some Emotion
Underneath The Radar 74

UNDISPUTED TRUTH, The
Soul group consisting of Joe Harris, Billie Calvin and Brenda Evans. Personnel changed in 1973 to Harris, Tyrone Berkeley, Tyrone Douglas, Calvin Stevens and Virginia McDonald. Drummer Carl Smalls later a member of Sweat Band. Taka Boom replaced Douglas and McDonald in 1976.

7/24/71	43	18		1 The Undisputed Truth	$8	Gordy 955
2/5/72	114	12		2 Face To Face With The Truth	$8	Gordy 959
8/18/73	191	2		3 Law Of The Land	$8	Gordy 963
6/21/75	186	2		4 Cosmic Truth	$8	Gordy 970
11/22/75	173	4		5 Higher Than High	$8	Gordy 972
1/29/77	66	17		6 Method To The Madness	$8	Whitfield 2967

Ain't No Sun Since You've Been Gone (1)
Aquarius (1)
Ball Of Confusion (That's What The World Is Today) (1)
Boogie Bump Boogie (5)
California Soul (1)
Cosmic Contact (6)
Don't Let Him Take Your Love From Me (2)
Down By The River (4)
Earthquake Shake (5)
Feelin' Alright (3)
Friendship Train (medley) (2)
Girl You're Alright (3)
Got To Get My Hands On Some Lovin' (4)
Help Yourself (5) **63**
Higher Than High (5)
Hole In The Wall (6)
I Heard It Through The Grapevine (1)
(I Know) I'm Losing You (4)
I Saw You When You Met Her (5)
I'm In The Red Zone (5)
If I Die (6)
Just My Imagination (Running Away With Me) (3)
Killing Me Softly With His Song (3)
Law Of The Land (3)
Let's Go Down To The Disco (6) *flip*
Life Ain't So Easy (5,6)
Like A Rolling Stone (1)
Lil' Red Ridin' Hood (4)
Loose (6)
Love And Happiness (3)
Ma (5)
Mama I Gotta Brand New Thing (Don't Say No) (4)
Method To The Madness (6)
1990 (4)
Overload (5)
Papa Was A Rollin' Stone (3) **63**
Poontang (5)
Save My Love For A Rainy Day (1)
Since I've Lost You (1)
Smiling Faces Sometimes (1) **3**
Spaced Out (4)
Squeeze Me, Tease Me (4)
Sunshine (6)
Superstar (Remember How You Got Where You Are) (2)
Take A Vacation From Life (And Visit Your Dreams) (6)
Take Me In Your Arms And Love Me (2)
This Child Needs Its Father (3)
UFO's (4)
Ungena Za Ulimwengu (Unite The World) (medley) (2)
Walk On By (3)
We've Got A Way Out Love (1)
What It Is (2) **71**
What's Going On (2)
With A Little Help From My Friends (3)
You Got The Love I Need (1)
You Make Your Own Heaven And Hell Right Here On Earth (2) **72**
You + Me = Love (6) **48**

UNFORGIVEN, The
Southern California rock sextet — John Henry Jones, lead singer.

8/9/86	185	2		The Unforgiven	$8	Elektra 60461

All Is Quiet On The Western Front
Cheyenne
Gauntlet, The
Ghost Dance
Grace
Hang 'Em High
I Hear The Call
Loner, The
Preacher, The
Roverpack
With My Boots On

UNICORN
Country-rock quartet — Pete Perrier, lead singer.

10/26/74	129	5		Blue Pine Trees	$8	Capitol 11334

produced by David Gilmour

Autumn Wine
Blue Pine Trees
Electric Night
Farmer, The
Holland
In The Gym
Just Wanna Hold You
Nightingale Crescent
Ooh! Mother
Rat Race
Sleep Song

UNION GAP, The — see PUCKETT, Gary

UNITED STATES AIR FORCE BAND, The
Conducted by Colonel George S. Howard. Formed in 1942 at the direction of President Roosevelt.

6/29/63	102	6		The United States Air Force Band	$12	RCA 2686

with The Singing Sergeants on 4 tracks

American Salute
Boys Of The Old Brigade
Bullets And Bayonets
Fairest Of The Fair
Falcons' Victory March
Liberty Bell
Oh, Men Who Fly
Seventy Six Trombones
Star Spangled Banner
U.S. Air Force
U.S. Air Force Blue

UNITED STATES MARINE BAND, The
Directed by Lieutenant Colonel Albert F. Schoepper. Formed in 1798 at the direction of President Adams.

6/15/63	22	9		The United States Marine Band	[I] $12	RCA 2687

America The Beautiful
American Patrol
Bugler's Holiday
Chimes Of Liberty
Commando March
March Of The Olympians
March Of The Women
Marines
Marines' Hymn (From The Halls Of Montezuma)
Semper Fidelis
Star Spangled Banner
Stars And Stripes Forever

DEBUT DATE	PEAK POS	WKS CHR	GOLD	ARTIST — Album Title	$	Label & Number

UNITED STATES NAVY BAND, The
Directed by Commander Anthony A. Mitchell. Formed in 1925 at the direction of President Coolidge.

| 6/15/63 | 38 | 7 | | The United States Navy Band .... | $12 | RCA 2688 |

with The Sea Chanters on 2 tracks

Allies On The March Medley	Jack Tar March	King Cotton March	Star-Spangled Banner	U.S. Navy March
Anchors Aweigh	John F. Kennedy Center	National Emblem	Thunderer, The	Washington Post March
El Capitan	March	Pledge Of Allegiance		

UNITED STATES OF AMERICA, The
Electronic-rock quintet — Dorothy Moskowitz, lead singer.

| 5/4/68 | 181 | 9 | | The United States Of America .... | $20 | Columbia 9614 |

American Metaphysical	American Way Of Love	Coming Down	I Won't Leave My Wooden	Stranded In Time
Circus	Medley	Garden Of Earthly Delights	Wife For You, Sugar	Where Is Yesterday
	Cloud Song	Hard Coming Love	Love Song For The Dead Che	

UNLIMITED TOUCH
Six-piece group from Brooklyn. Lead vocals by Audrey Wheeler and Stephanie James.

| 6/20/81 | 142 | 7 | | Unlimited Touch .... | $8 | Prelude 12184 |

Carry On	Happy Ever After	In The Middle	Private Party	
Feel The Music	I Hear Music In The Streets	Love To Share	Searching To Find The One	

UNTOUCHABLES, The
Funk group: Clyde Grimes (guitar, vocals), Jerry Miller, Brewster, Derek Breakfield, Chuck Askerneese and Willie McNeil.

| 4/1/89 | 162 | 9 | | Agent Double O Soul.. | $8 | Restless 72342 |

Agent Double O Soul	Cold City	Let's Get Together	Stripped To The Bone	Under The Boardwalk
Airplay	Education	Shama Lama	Sudden Attack	World Gone Crazy

UP WITH PEOPLE
A "sing-out" musical production featuring various young singing talent.

| 7/23/66 | 61 | 14 | | Up With People! .... | $8 | Pace 1101 |

Ballad Of Joan Of Arc	Freedom Isn't Free	Ride Of Paul Revere	Somewhere	What Color Is God's Skin	You Can't Live Crooked And
Design For Dedication	Happy Song	Run And Catch The Wind	Spirit Of The Green	Which Way America?	Think Straight
Don't Stand Still (medley)	New Tomorrow	Showboat-Go Boat (medley)	Up With People		

URBAN DANCE SQUAD
Amsterdam, Holland-based interracial, rap-metal crew. Rapper Patrick "Rude Boy" Remington backed by the rhythm section of Magic Stick, DNA, Silly Sil and Tres Manos.

| 8/25/90+ | 54 | 39 | | Mental Floss For The Globe.. | $12 | Arista 8640 |

Big Apple	Devil, The	God Blasts The Queen	No Kid	Prayer For My Demo
Brainstorm On The U.D.S.	Famous When You're Dead	Man On The Corner	Piece Of Rock	Struggle For Jive
Deeper Shade Of Soul 21	Fastlane	Mental Floss For The Glove		

URE, Midge
Born James Ure on 10/10/53 in Glasgow, Scotland. Former lead guitarist/vocalist of Ultravox. Co-writer of "Do They Know It's Christmas?." Musical director of the Prince's Trust charity concerts.

| 2/11/89 | 88 | 16 | | Answers To Nothing... | $8 | Chrysalis 41649 |

Answers To Nothing	Hell To Heaven	Just For You	Lied	Sister And Brother
Dear God 95	Homeland	Leaving (So Long)	Remembrance Day	Take Me Home

★★299★★   URIAH HEEP
British hard-rock band. Key members: David Byron (lead singer), Mick Box (lead guitar) and Ken Hensley (keyboards; later with Blackfoot). John Lawton replaced Byron in 1977. Peter Goalby replaced Lawton in 1982.

10/3/70	186	4		1 Uriah Heep	$12	Mercury 61294
1/30/71	103	9		2 Salisbury	$10	Mercury 61319
9/25/71	93	20		3 Look At Yourself	$8	Mercury 614
6/17/72	23	38	●	4 Demons And Wizards	$8	Mercury 630
12/2/72+	31	22	●	5 The Magician's Birthday	$8	Mercury 652
5/5/73	37	30	●	6 Uriah Heep Live .... [L]	$10	Mercury 7503 [2]
10/6/73	33	23	●	7 Sweet Freedom	$8	Warner 2724
7/6/74	38	15		8 Wonderworld	$8	Warner 2800
8/2/75	85	10		9 Return To Fantasy	$8	Warner 2869
3/20/76	145	6		10 The Best Of Uriah Heep .... [G]	$8	Mercury 1070
6/26/76	161	3		11 High And Mighty	$8	Warner 2949
4/30/77	166	3		12 Firefly	$8	Warner 3013
11/4/78	186	5		13 Fallen Angel	$8	Chrysalis 1204
8/7/82	56	16		14 Abominog	$8	Mercury 4057
6/4/83	159	10		15 Head First	$8	Mercury 812313

All My Life (4)	Dreammare (1)	I'll Keep On Trying (1)	One More Night (Last	Roll-Overture (15)	Spider Woman (5)
Beautiful Dream (9)	Dreams (8)	I'm Alive (13)	Farewell) (13)	Rollin' On (12)	Stay On Top (15)
Been Away Too Long (12)	**Easy Livin'** (4,6,10) 39	If I Had The Time (7)	One Way Or Another (11)	Rollin' The Rock (15)	**Stealin'** (7) 91
Bird Of Prey (1,10)	Easy Road (8)	July Morning (3,6,10)	Other Side Of Midnight (15)	Running All Night (With The	Straight Through The Heart
Blind Eye (5) 97	Echoes In The Dark (5)	Lady In Black (2,10)	Paradise (medley) (4)	Lion) (14)	(15)
Can't Keep A Good Band	Fallen Angel (13)	Lonely Nights (15)	Park, The (2)	Salisbury (2)	Suicidal Man (8)
Down (11)	Falling In Love (13)	Look At Yourself (3,6,10)	Pilgrim (7)	Save It (13)	Sunrise (5,6,10)
Can't Stop Singing (11)	Firefly (12)	Love Is Blind (15)	Poet's Justice (4)	Sell Your Soul (14)	Sweet Freedom (7)
Chasing Shadows (14)	Footprints In The Snow (11)	Love Machine (3,6)	Prima Donna (9)	Seven Stars (7)	**Sweet Lorraine** (5,6,10) 91
Circle Of Hands (4,6)	Gypsy (1,6,10)	Love Or Nothing (13)	Prisoner (14)	Shadows And The Wind (8)	Sweet Talk (15)
Circus (7)	Hanging Tree (12)	Magician's Birthday (5,6)	Put Your Lovin' On Me (13)	Shadows Of Grief (3)	Sympathy (12)
Come Away Melinda (1)	High Priestess (2)	Make A Little Love (11)	Rain (5)	Shady Lady (9)	Tales (5)
Come Back To Me (13)	Hot Night In A Cold Town	Midnight (11)	Rainbow Demon (4)	Showdown (9)	Tears In My Eyes (3,6)
Confession (11)	(14)	Misty Eyes (11)	Real Turned On (1)	Simon The Bullet Freak (2)	That's The Way That It Is
Devil's Daughter (9)	Hot Persuasion (14)	On The Rebound (14)	Red Lights (15)	So Tired (8)	(14)
Do You Know (12)	I Wanna Be Free (3)	One Day (7)	Return To Fantasy (9)	Something Or Nothing (8)	Think It Over (14)
Dreamer (7)	I Won't Mind (8)		Rock 'N Roll Medley (6)	Spell, The (medley) (4)	Time To Live (2)

763

URIAH HEEP — Cont'd

Too Scared To Run (14)   Walking In Your Shadow (1)   Whad'ya Say (13)   Wise Man (12)   Wonderworld (8)
Traveller In Time (4,6)   We Got We (8)   What Should Be Done (3)   Wizard, The (4,10)   Year Or A Day (9)
Wake Up (Set Your Sights)   Weekend Warriors (15)   Who Needs Me (12)   Woman Of The Night (13)   Your Turn To Remember (9)
(1)   Weep In Silence (11)   Why Did You Go (9)   Woman Of The World (11)

USA-EUROPEAN CONNECTION
A Boris Midney disco production. Vocals by Leza Holmes, Renne Johnson and Sharon Williams.

4/8/78	66	19		Come Into My Heart	$8	Marlin 2212

Baby Love (medley)   Come Into My Heart (medley)   Good Loving (medley)   Love's Coming (medley)

USA for AFRICA
USA: United Support of Artists — a collection of 46 major artists formed to help the suffering people of Africa and the U.S.

4/20/85	1³	22 ▲³		**We Are The World**	$8	Columbia 40043

tracks contributed by Northern Lights (Canada's superstar artists), Bruce Springsteen, Prince, Huey Lewis, Chicago, Tina Turner, Pointer Sisters, Kenny Rogers, Steve Perry

4 The Tears In Your Eyes   If Only For The Moment,   Little More Love (Kenny   Tears Are Not Enough   Total Control (Tina Turner)   Trouble In Paradise (Huey
(Prince)   Girl (Steve Perry)   Rogers)   (Northern Lights)   Trapped (Bruce Springsteen)   Lewis & The News)
Good For Nothing (Chicago)   Just A Little Closer (Pointer   **We Are The World** 1
    Sisters)

UTAH SAINTS
Techno-rave, British DJ duo: Jez Willis and Tim Garbutt.

11/14/92	182	4		Something Good	$12	London 869843

Anything Can Happen   **Something Good** [includes   Trance Atlantic Flight   Trans Europe Caress   What Can You Do For Me
    2 versions] 98   [includes 2 versions]

UTFO
Brooklyn rap trio: Kangol Kid, Doctor Mixmaster Ice and Educated Rapper. UTFO is an abbreviation for Untouchable Force Organization.

6/15/85	80	20		1 UTFO	$8	Select 21614
8/9/86	142	8		2 Skeezer Pleezer	$8	Select 21616
10/3/87	67	20		3 Lethal	$8	Select 21619
6/10/89	143	4		4 Doin' It!	$8	Select 21629

All About Technic (4)   Calling Her A Crab (1)   Just Watch (2)   Mo' Bass (3)   Split Personality (2)
Ask Yo Mama (3)   Cold Abrasive (4)   Kangol & Doc (3)   My Cut's Correct (4)   S.W.A.T. (Get Down) (3)
Bad Luck Barry (2)   Diss (3)   Leader Of The Pack (1)   Pick Up The Pace (2)   Wanna Rock (4)
Battle Of The Sexes (4)   Doin' It! (4)   Let's Get It On (3)   Real Roxanne (1)   We Work Hard (2)
Beats And Rhymes (1)   Don't You Hate It When... (4)   Lethal (3)   Ride, The (3)   Where Did You Go? (2)
Bite It (1)   Fairy Tale Lover (1)   Lisa Lips (1)   Rough And Rugged (4)   Ya Cold Wanna Be With Me
Bits And Pieces (4)   Hanging Out (1)   Master - Baby (3)   **Roxanne, Roxanne** (1) 77   (3)
Burning Bed (3)   House Will Rock (2)   Master Of The Mix (4)   So Be It (3)

★★399★★ UTOPIA
Veteran pop-rock group: Todd Rundgren (guitar), Kasim Sulton (bass), Roger Powell (keyboards) and Willie Wilcox (drums). Built own recording studio near Woodstock, New York.

11/9/74	34	15		1 Todd Rundgren's Utopia	$8	Bearsville 6954
11/15/75	66	9		2 Todd Rundgren's Utopia/Another Live [L]	$8	Bearsville 6961
				above 2: **TODD RUNDGREN'S UTOPIA**		
2/26/77	79	7		3 RA	$8	Bearsville 6965
9/24/77	73	8		4 Oops! Wrong Planet	$8	Bearsville 6970
1/26/80	32	21		5 Adventures In Utopia	$8	Bearsville 6991
10/25/80	65	9		6 Deface The Music	$8	Bearsville 3487
				a Beatles' parody		
3/20/82	102	10		7 Swing To The Right	$8	Bearsville 3666
10/16/82	84	19		8 Utopia	$10	Network 60183 [2]
				album 2 is a bonus 5-track LP		
2/11/84	74	12		9 Oblivion	$8	Passport 6029
3/16/85	161	6		10 POV	$8	Passport 6044

Abandon City (4)   Fahrenheit 451 (7)   Itch In My Brain (9)   Maybe I Could Change (9)   Shinola (7)   Welcome To My Revolution
All Smiles (6)   Feel Too Good (6)   Jealousy (3)   Mimi Gets Mad (10)   Shot In The Dark (5)   (9)
Alone (6)   **Feet Don't Fail Me Now**   Junk Rock (Million   Mister Triscuits (2)   Silly Boy (6)   Wheel, The (2)
Always Late (6)   (8) 82   Monkeys) (7)   More Light (10)   Singring And The Glass   Where Does The World Go
Another Life (2)   For The Love Of Money (7)   Just One Victory (2)   My Angel (4)   Guitar (3)   To Hide (6)
Back On The Street (4)   Forgotten But Not Gone (8)   Last Dollar On Earth (7)   Mystified (10)   Something's Coming (2)   Wildlife (10)
Bad Little Actress (8)   Freak Parade (1)   Last Of The New Wave   Neck On Up (8)   Stand For Something (10)   Windows (4)
Bring Me My Longbow (9)   Freedom Fighters (1)   Riders (5)   One World (7)   Style (10)   Winston Smith Takes It On
Burn Three Times (8)   Gangrene (4)   Libertine (8)   Only Human (7)   Sunburst Finish (3)   The Jaw (9)
Call It What You Will (8)   Hammer In My Heart (8)   Life Goes On (6)   Play This Game (10)   Swing To The Right (7)   You Make Me Crazy (5)
Caravan (5)   Heavy Metal Kids (2)   Love Alone (5)   Princess Of The Universe (8)   Take It Home (6)   Zen Machine (10)
Chapter And Verse (8)   Hiroshima (3)   Love In Action (4)   Private Heaven (8)   That's Not Right (6)
Communion With The Sun   Hoi Poloi (6)   Love Is The Answer (4)   Rape Of The Young (4)   There Goes My Inspiration
(3)   I Just Want To Touch You (6)   Love With A Thinker (9)   Road To Utopia (5)   (8)
Crazy Lady Blue (4)   I Will Wait (9)   Lysistrata (7)   Rock Love (5)   Too Much Water (9)
Crybaby (9)   I'm Looking At You But I'm   Magic Dragon Theatre (3)   Say Yeah (8)   Up, The (7)
Crystal Ball (6)   Talking To Myself (8)   Marriage Of Heaven And   Second Nature (5)   Utopia (1)
Do Ya (2)   If I Didn't Try (9)   Hell (4)   Secret Society (10)   **Very Last Time** (5) 76
Eternal Love (3)   Ikon, The (1)   Martyr, The (4)   **Set Me Free** (5) 27
Everybody Else Is Wrong (6)   Infrared And Ultraviolet (8)   Mated (10)   Seven Rays (2)

★★145★★ U2
Rock band formed in Dublin, Ireland in 1976. Consists of Paul "Bono" Hewson (vocals), Dave "The Edge" Evans (guitar), Adam Clayton (bass) and Larry Mullen, Jr. (drums). Emerged in 1987 as a leading rock act. Released concert tour documentary film *Rattle And Hum* in 1988.

3/14/81	63	47		1 Boy	$8	Island 9646
11/7/81	104	38		2 October	$8	Island 9680
3/19/83	12	179 ▲		3 War	$8	Island 90067

DEBUT DATE	PEAK POS	WKS CHR	GOLD	ARTIST — Album Title	$	Label & Number

U2 — Cont'd

DEBUT DATE	PEAK POS	WKS CHR	GOLD	ARTIST — Album Title	$	Label & Number
12/10/83+	28	180 ▲		4 Under A Blood Red Sky .... [M-L]	$8	Island 90127
				recorded in the summer of 1983 in Germany, Boston and the Red Rocks festival in Colorado		
10/20/84	12	132 ▲		5 The Unforgettable Fire	$8	Island 90231
6/29/85	37	23		6 Wide Awake In America .... [M-L]	$8	Island 90279
				side A: live; side B: outtakes from *The Unforgettable Fire* LP; album dropped by *Billboard* after charting for one week because it was only a 4-cut album that listed for less than 85.98; *Billboard* did not follow previous criteria and mini-album recharted on 4/25/87 and remained on chart for 22 weeks		
4/4/87	1⁹	103 ▲⁵		7 **The Joshua Tree**	$8	Island 90581
				1987 Grammy winner: Album of the Year		
10/29/88	1⁶	38 ▲³		8 **Rattle And Hum** .... [S]	$10	Island 91003 [2]
				music from their 1988 concert/documentary film *Rattle And Hum*		
12/7/91	1↑¹	62↑ ▲⁴		9 **Achtung Baby**	$12	Island 10347
				title taken from a line in the Mel Brooks' film *The Producers*		

Acrobat (9)
All Along The Watchtower (8)
All I Want Is You (8) *83*
Angel Of Harlem (8) *14*
Another Time, Another Place (1)
Bad (5,6)
Bullet The Blue Sky (7,8)
Day Without Me (1)
Desire (8) *3*
Drowning Man (3)
Electric Co. (1,4)
11 O'Clock Tick Tock (4)
Elvis Presley And America (5)
Even Better Than The Real Thing (9)
Exit (7)

Fire (2)
Fly, The (9) *61*
40 (3,4)
4th Of July (5)
Freedom For My People (8)
Gloria (2,4)
God Part II (8)
Hawkmoon 269 (8)
Heartland (8)
Helter Skelter (8)
I Fall Down (2)
I Still Haven't Found What I'm Looking For (7,8) *1*
I Threw A Brick Through A Window (2)
I Will Follow (1,4) *81*
In God's Country (7) *44*
Indian Summer Sky (5)

Into The Heart (1)
Is That All? (2)
Like A Song... (3)
Love Comes Tumbling (6)
Love Is Blindness (9)
Love Rescue Me (8)
MLK (5)
Mothers Of The Disappeared (7)
Mysterious Ways (9) *9*
New Year's Day (3,4) *53*
Ocean, The (1)
October (2)
One (9) *10*
One Tree Hill (7)
Out Of Control (1)
Party Girl (4)

Pride (In The Name Of Love) (5,8) *33*
Promenade (5)
Red Hill Mining Town (7)
Red Light (3)
Refugee, The (3)
Rejoice (2)
Running To Stand Still (7)
Scarlet (2)
Seconds (3)
Shadows And Tall Trees (1)
Silver And Gold (8)
So Cruel (9)
Sort Of Homecoming (5,6)
Star Spangled Banner (8)
Stories For Boys (1)
Stranger In A Strange Land (2)

Sunday Bloody Sunday (3,4)
Surrender (3)
Three Sunrises (6)
Tomorrow (2)
Trip Through Your Wires (7)
Tryin' To Throw Your Arms Around The World (9)
Twilight (1)
Two Hearts Beat As One (3)
Ultra Violet (Light My Way) (9)
Unforgettable Fire (5)
Until The End Of The World (9)
Van Diemen's Land (8)
When Love Comes To Town (8) *68*

Where The Streets Have No Name (7) *13*
Who's Gonna Ride Your Wild Horses (9) *35*
Wire (5)
With A Shout (2)
With Or Without You (7) *1*
Zoo Station (9)

V

VAI, Steve
Born on 6/6/60 in Long Island, New York. Rock guitarist. Joined Frank Zappa's band in 1979. Former guitar student of Joe Satriani. With David Lee Roth's band, 1986-88. Briefly a member of Alcatrazz (1985) and Whitesnake (1989).

DEBUT DATE	PEAK POS	WKS CHR	GOLD	ARTIST — Album Title	$	Label & Number
6/9/90	18	25 ●		Passion and Warfare .... [I]	$12	Relativity 1037
				includes spoken introductions to songs		

Alien Water Kiss
Animal, The
Answers

Audience Is Listening
Ballerina 12/24
Blue Powder

Erotic Nightmares
For The Love Of God
I Would Love To

Greasy Kid's Stuff

Liberty
Love Secrets

Riddle, The
Sisters

VAIN
Hard-rock quintet from San Francisco: Davy Vain (vocals), Danny West, James Scott, Tom Rickard and Ashley Mitchell.

DEBUT DATE	PEAK POS	WKS CHR	GOLD	ARTIST — Album Title	$	Label & Number
8/26/89	154	8		No Respect	$8	Island 91272

Aces
Beat The Bullet

Down For The 3rd Time
Icy

Laws Against Love
No Respect

Ready
Secrets

Smoke And Shadows
1000 Degrees

Who's Watching You
Without You

★★192★★ **VALE, Jerry**
Born Genero Vitaliano on 7/8/32 in the Bronx. Pop ballad singer. Frequently sang in Italian.

DEBUT DATE	PEAK POS	WKS CHR	GOLD	ARTIST — Album Title	$	Label & Number
8/25/62+	60	48		1 I Have But One Heart	$15	Columbia 8597
2/23/63	34	25		2 Arrivederci, Roma	$15	Columbia 8755
9/7/63	22	35		3 The Language Of Love	$15	Columbia 8843
2/22/64	28	18		4 Till The End Of Time	$15	Columbia 8916
				songs based on famous classical melodies		
8/29/64	26	22		5 Be My Love	$15	Columbia 8981
1/30/65	55	18		6 Standing Ovation! .... [L]	$12	Columbia 9073
				recorded at Carnegie Hall on 5/30/64		
3/6/65	30	23		7 Have You Looked Into Your Heart	$12	Columbia 9113
10/16/65	42	17		8 There Goes My Heart	$12	Columbia 9187
2/12/66	38	17		9 It's Magic	$12	Columbia 9244
7/2/66	111	4		10 Great Moments On Broadway	$12	Columbia 9289
3/18/67	117	23		11 The Impossible Dream	$12	Columbia 9383
9/16/67	128	6		12 Time Alone Will Tell	$12	Columbia 9484
3/16/68	163	7		13 You Don't Have To Say You Love Me..........................	$12	Columbia 9574
8/10/68	135	20		14 This Guy's In Love With You	$12	Columbia 9694
2/15/69	90	12		15 Till	$10	Columbia 9757
7/5/69	180	4		16 Where's The Playground Susie?	$10	Columbia 9838
11/1/69	193	2		17 With Love, Jerry Vale .... [K]	$12	Columbia 16 [2]
2/14/70	196	2		18 Jerry Vale Sings 16 Greatest Hits Of The 60's	$8	Columbia 9982
6/27/70	189	4		19 Let It Be	$8	Columbia 1021
2/12/72	200	2		20 Jerry Vale Sings The Great Hits Of Nat King Cole	$8	Columbia 31147

VALE, Jerry — Cont'd

Abraham, Martin And John (15)
Al Di La (2)
All (12)
All I Have To Do Is Dream (19)
All The Way (5,17)
Always In My Heart (7)
Andiamo (7)
Anema E Core (2)
Answer Me, My Love (20)
Arrivederci, Roma (2)
Ashamed (9)
Auf Wiederseh'n, Sweetheart (3)
Baby Won't You Please Come Home (6)
Be Anything (But Be Mine) (9)
Be My Love (5)
Because (5)
Because Of You (5,17)
Because You're Mine (5)
Big Wide World (9)
Blossom Fell (20)
Blue Velvet (18)
Born Free (12,18)
Bridge Over Troubled Water (19)
By The Time I Get To Phoenix (14)
Camelot (10)
Can't Take My Eyes Off You (14,18)
Can't You See I'm Sorry (8)
Ciao, Ciao, Bambina (2)
Come Back To Sorrento (1,6)
Day That We Said Goodbye (12)
Do You Know The Way To San Jose (4)
Dr. Zhivago ..see: Somewhere, My Love
Dommage, Dommage (Too Bad, Too Bad) (11) **93**
Don't Tell My Heart To Stop Loving You (14)
Don't You Know? (4)
Easy Come, Easy Go (19)

Ebb Tide (13)
Eternally (13)
For Me (9)
From The Bottom Of My Heart (2)
Full Moon And Empty Arms (4)
Galveston (16)
Games That Lovers Play (12)
Gigi (11)
Goodnight My Love (Pleasant Dreams) (16)
Granada (6)
Happy Heart (16)
Have You Ever Been Lonely (Have You Ever Been Blue) (7)
Have You Looked Into Your Heart (7) **24**
Hello, Dolly! (18)
Hey, Look Me Over (6)
Honey (I Miss You) (14)
How Are Things In Glocca Morra? (17)
I Can't Get You Out Of My Heart (1)
I Can't Help It (8)
I Can't Stop Loving You (17)
I Dream Of You (7)
I Feel A Song Comin' On (6)
I Have But One Heart (1)
I Left My Heart In San Francisco (6)
I Love How You Love Me (15)
I Love You Much Too Much (3,17)
I Understand (8)
I Won't Cry Anymore (12)
I'll Get By (9)
I'll Never Fall In Love Again (19)
I'll Never Forgive You (7)
I'm Always Chasing Rainbows (6)
I'm Yours (7)
If I Had You (6)
If I Loved You (10)
If It Isn't In Your Heart (9)
Impossible Dream (11,18)

Is It Taking Too Much (9)
It Had To Be You (17)
It's Magic (9)
Jean (19)
Just Friends (17)
Just One More Chance (8)
Just Say I Love Her (1,17)
La Vie En Rose (3)
Lara's Theme ..see: Somewhere, My Love
Leaving On A Jet Plane (19)
Les Bicyclettes De Belsize (15)
Let It Be (19)
Let It Be Me (16)
Little Green Apples (15,18)
Lonesome Road (6)
Look Homeward Angel (15)
Look Of Love (14)
Love Goddess (7)
Love Grows (Where My Rosemary Goes) (19)
Love Is A Many-Splendored Thing (1)
Love Is Blue (18)
Love Me With All Your Heart (12)
Lover's Roulette (13)
Lulu's Back In Town (6)
Luna Rossa (2)
Mac Arthur Park (15)
Mala Femmina (2,8)
Mama (Mamma) (1,6)
Man Without Love (14)
Maria (10)
Maria Elena (3,17)
Mona Lisa (5,20)
Moon Love (4)
Moon River (18)
More (Theme from Mondo Cane) (11,18)
Moulin Rouge (Where Is Your Heart, Song From (3)
My Cup Runneth Over (12)
My Foolish Heart (11)
My Heart Reminds Me (4,17)
My Love, Forgive Me (12)
My Melancholy Baby (9)
My Prayer (9)

My Reverie (4)
My Special Angel (15)
My Way (16)
Nature Boy (20)
No One Will Ever Know (8)
Non Dimenticar (2)
Now (3)
'O Sole Mio (My Sunshine) (1,6)
(Oh, My Wonderful One) Tell Me You're Mine (1)
Old Cape Cod (7)
On A Clear Day (You Can See Forever) (10)
On And On (4)
On The Street Where You Live (10)
One More Blessing (8)
Palermo (3)
Piscatore 'E Pusilleco (2)
Poor Butterfly (17)
Pretend (17,20)
Prisoner Of Love (17)
Promises, Promises (15)
Put Your Head On My Shoulder (15)
Raindrops Keep Fallin' On My Head (19)
Ramblin' Rose (20)
Red Sails In The Sunset (9)
Release Me (13)
Return To Me (1)
Roman Guitar (1)
Sandpiper, Love Theme From The ..see: Shadow Of Your Smile
Santa Lucia (Me And Maria) (2)
Seattle (16)
Secret Love (5)
Shadow Of Your Smile (11,18)
She Gives Me Love (La, La, La) (14)
Sleepy Time Gal (17)
Smile (11,20)
So In Love (10)
So Near...Yet So Far (4)

Sogni D'Oro (Dreams Of Gold) (8)
Solitude (9)
Some Enchanted Evening (10)
Somebody Else Is Taking My Place (8)
Something (19)
Somewhere Along The Way (20)
Somewhere, My Love (11)
Song Is You (6)
Spanish Eyes (18)
Stay Awhile (19)
Story Of A Starry Night (4)
Stranger In Paradise (10)
Strangers In The Night (11,17,18)
Summertime In Venice (2)
Sunny (18)
Sunrise, Sunset (10)
Tears (For Souvenirs) (9)
Tears Keep On Falling (7) **96**
Tell Me That You Love Me (1)
There Are Such Things (7)
There Goes My Heart (8,17)
There Must Be A Way (8)
There's A Kind Of Hush (All Over The World) (13)
Things I Love (4)
This Day Of Days (4)
This Guy's In Love With You (14,18)
This Is My Song (12)
Those Were The Days (15)
Three Coins In The Fountain (11)
Ti Adoro (7)
Till (15)
Till The End Of Time (4)
Till There Was You (13)
Time Alone Will Tell (12)
To Each His Own (13)
To Know You Is To Love You (16)
To Love Again (4)
Too Many Tomorrows (10)
Too Young (5,20)

Traces (16)
Two Different Worlds (3,17)
Unchained Melody (5)
Unforgettable (8)
Vaya Con Dios (5)
Very Thought Of You (17)
Volare (Nel Blu Dipinto Di Blu) (2)
Walkin' My Baby Back Home (20)
Way It Used To Be (16)
What A Wonderful World (13)
What Kind Of Fool Am I (10,18)
What Now My Love (11)
Where's The Playground Susie? (16)
Why Don't You Believe Me (5)
With A Song In My Heart (9)
With Pen In Hand (14)
Without Saying A Word (8)
Wonderful One (3)
Yellow Days (13)
Yesterday (18)
You Alone (1)
You Belong To My Heart (3)
You Don't Have To Say You Love Me (13)
You Gave Me A Mountain (16)
You Have To Believe In Someone (13)
You Were Mine For A While (8)
You're Breaking My Heart (2)
You're My Everything (17)
Young Girl (14)
Your Love Is Mine (3)
Yours (3)

VALENS, Ritchie

Born Richard Valenzuela on 5/13/41 in Pacoima, California. Latin rock and roll singer/songwriter/guitarist. Killed in the plane crash that also took the lives of Buddy Holly and the Big Bopper on 2/3/59. In the film Go Johnny Go. The 1987 film La Bamba was based on his life.

| 4/6/59 | 23 | 6 | | 1 Ritchie Valens | $75 | Del-Fi 1201 |
| 8/29/87 | 100 | 10 | | 2 The Best Of Ritchie Valens....................[G] | $8 | Rhino 70178 |

Bluebirds Over The Mountain (1,2)
Boney-Maronie (1)
Come On, Let's Go (1,2) **42**

Donna (1,2) **2**
Dooby-Dooby-Wah (1)
Fast Freight (2)
Framed (1)

Hi-Tone (1)
Hurry Up (2)
In A Turkish Town (1,2)
La Bamba (1,2) **22**

Little Girl (2) **92**
Malaguena (2)
Ooh! My Head (1,2)
Paddi-Wack Song (2)

Stay Beside Me (2)
That's My Little Suzie (1,2) **55**
We Belong Together (1,2)

VALENTIN, Dave

Jazz-Latin flutist from the South Bronx. Professional debut at age 12. Attended the High School of Music and Art in New York City. Member of Fuse One.

10/25/80	194	2		1 Land Of The Third Eye ....[I]	$8	GRP 5009
8/8/81	184	4		2 Pied Piper....................[I]	$8	GRP 5505
				above 2 feature Dave Grusin		

Astro-March (1)
Dragon Fly (2)
Fantasy (1)

Land Of The Third Eye (1)
Los Altos (2)
Open Your Eyes (1)

Pana Fuerte (Strong Friendship) (1)
Pied Piper (Man Of Song) (2)

Sambiando (2)
Seven Stars (2)
Shamballa (2)

Sidra's Dream (1)
Tellers, The (1)
This Time (2)

VALJEAN

Born Valjean Johns on 11/19/34 in Shattuck, Oklahoma. Pianist.

| 7/28/62 | 113 | 5 | | The Theme From Ben Casey ....[I] | $10 | Carlton 143 |

Alcoa Premiere, Theme From
Bell Telephone Hour (Waltz), Theme From The
Ben Casey, Theme From 28

Bonanza, Theme From
Checkmate, Theme From
Dr. Kildare, Theme From

G.E. Theatre, Theme From The
Gunsmoke, Theme From
Naked City, Theme From

Perry Como Show (Dream Along With Me), Theme From
Peter Gunn, Theme From

Wagon Train (Wagons Ho!), Theme From

VALLI, Frankie

Born Francis Castellucio on 5/3/37 in Newark, New Jersey. Recorded his first solo single in 1953 as Frank Valley on the Corona label. Formed own group, the Variatones, in 1955 and changed their name to the Four Lovers in 1956, which evolved into The 4 Seasons by 1961. Began solo work in 1965. Suffered from a disease which caused hearing loss in the late 1970s, corrected by surgery.

7/22/67	34	23		1 Frankie Valli-Solo	$20	Philips 247
8/10/68	176	5		2 Timeless............................	$20	Philips 274
3/29/75	51	28		3 Closeup	$8	Private St. 2000
12/13/75+	107	8		4 Our Day Will Come	$8	Private St. 2006
12/20/75+	132	8		5 Frankie Valli Gold ....[G]	$8	Private St. 2001

VALLI, Frankie — Cont'd

DEBUT DATE	PEAK POS	WKS CHR	GOLD	ARTIST — Album Title	$	Label & Number
8/26/78	160	7	6	Frankie Valli...Is The Word	$8	Warner 3233

features Peter Frampton, Eloise Laws and Tom Scott

By The Time I Get To Phoenix (2)
Can't Take My Eyes Off You (1,5) *2*
Carrie (I Would Marry You) (4)
Closest Thing To Heaven (4)
Donnybrook (2)
Eleanor Rigby (2)
Elise (4)
Expression Of Love (2)
For All We Know (2)

Fox In A Bush (2,5)
Girl I'll Never Know (Angels Never Fly This Low) (5) *52*
Grease (6) *1*
He Sure Blessed You (3)
Heart Be Still (4)
How'd I Know That Love Would Slip Away (4)
I Can't Live A Dream (3)
I Got Love For You, Ruby (3)

I Make A Fool Of Myself (5) *18*
In My Eyes (3)
Ivy (1)
Make The Music Play (2)
Morning After Loving You (5)
My Eyes Adored You (3,5) *1*
My Funny Valentine (1)
My Mother's Eyes (1)
Needing You (6)
No Love At All (6)
Our Day Will Come (4) *11*

Over Me (6)
Proud One (1,5) *68*
Save Me, Save Me (6)
Secret Love (1)
September Rain (Here Comes The Rain) (2,5)
Sometimes Love Songs Make Me Cry (6)
Stop And Say Hello (2)
Sun Ain't Gonna Shine (Anymore) (1,5)
Sunny (2)

Swearin' To God (3) *6*
Sweet Sensational Love (4)
Tear Can Tell (6)
To Give (The Reason I Live) (2,5) *29*
Trouble With Me (1)
Waking Up To Love (3)
Walk Away Renee (4)
Watch Where You Walk (2)
Why (3)
Without Your Love (6)
You Better Go (6)

You Can Bet (I Ain't Goin' Nowhere) (4)
You Can Do It (6)
(You're Gonna) Hurt Yourself (1,5) *39*
You're Ready Now (1)

VANDENBERG

Dutch hard-rock band: led by Adrian Vandenberg (guitar, keyboards; joined Whitesnake in 1989), Bert Heerink (lead singer), Dick Kemper (bass) and Jos Zoomer (drums).

DEBUT DATE	PEAK POS	WKS CHR	GOLD	ARTIST — Album Title	$	Label & Number
1/8/83	65	18	1	Vandenberg	$8	Atco 90005
1/28/84	169	7	2	Heading For A Storm	$8	Atco 90121

Back On My Feet (1)
Burning Heart (1) *39*
Different Worlds (2)

Friday Night (2)
Heading For A Storm (2)
I'm On Fire (2)

Lost In A City (1)
Nothing To Lose (1)
Out In The Streets (1)

Ready For You (1)
Rock On (2)
This Is War (2)

Time Will Tell (2)
Too Late (1)
Wait (1)

Waiting For The Night (2)
Welcome To The Club (2)
Your Love Is In Vain (1)

★★305★★ VANDROSS, Luther

Born on 4/20/51 in New York City. Soul singer/producer/songwriter. Commercial jingle singer, then a top session vocalist/arranger. Sang lead on a few of Change's early albums.

DEBUT DATE	PEAK POS	WKS CHR	GOLD	ARTIST — Album Title	$	Label & Number
9/19/81	19	36	● 1	Never Too Much	$8	Epic 37451
10/16/82	20	36	▲ 2	Forever, For Always, For Love	$8	Epic 38235
12/24/83+	32	41	▲ 3	Busy Body	$8	Epic 39196
4/6/85	19	56	▲² 4	The Night I Fell In Love	$8	Epic 39882
10/18/86+	14	53	▲² 5	Give Me The Reason	$8	Epic 40415
10/22/88	9	33	▲ 6	Any Love	$8	Epic 44308
11/4/89+	26	51	▲² 7	The Best Of Luther Vandross...The Best Of Love ....[G]	$10	Epic 45320 [2]

Luther's hits from 1980-89

DEBUT DATE	PEAK POS	WKS CHR	GOLD	ARTIST — Album Title	$	Label & Number
5/18/91	7	60	▲ 8	Power Of Love	$12	Epic 46789

Any Love (6,7) *44*
Anyone Who Had A Heart (5)
Are You Gonna Love Me (6)
Bad Boy/Having A Party (2,7) *55*
Because It's Really Love (5)
Better Love (2)
Busy Body (3)
Come Back (6)
Creepin' (4,7)
Don't Want To Be A Fool (8) *9*
Don't You Know That? (1)

Emotional Love (8)
For The Sweetness Of Your Love (3)
For You To Love (6)
Forever, For Always, For Love (2)
Give Me The Reason (5,7)
Glow Of Love (7)
Here And Now (7) *6*
House Is Not A Home (1,7)
How Many Times Can We Say Goodbye (3) *27*

I Can Tell You That (8)
I Gave It Up (When I Fell In Love) (5)
I Know You Want To (6)
I Really Didn't Mean It (5,7)
I Want The Night To Stay (8)
I Wanted Your Love (3)
I Who Have Nothing (8)
I Wonder (6)
I'll Let You Slide (3)
I'm Gonna Start Today (8)
I've Been Working (1)
If Only For One Night (4,7)

If This World Were Mine (7)
It's Over Now (4)
Love Won't Let Me Wait (6,7)
Make Me A Believer (3)
My Sensitivity (Gets In The Way) (4)
Never Too Much (1,7) *33*
Night I Fell In Love (4)
Once You Know How (2)
Other Side Of The World (4)
Power Of Love/Love Power (8) *4*
Promise Me (2,7)

Rush, The (8) *73*
Searching (7)
Second Time Around (6)
See Me (5)
She Doesn't Mind (8)
She Loves Me Back (2)
She Won't Talk To Me (6) *30*
She's A Super Lady (1)
Since I Lost My Baby (2,7)
So Amazing (5,7)
Sometimes It's Only Love (8)
Stop To Love (5,7) *15*

Sugar And Spice (I Found Me A Girl) (1)
Superstar/Until You Come Back To Me (That's What I'm Gonna Do) (3,7) *87*
There's Nothing Better Than Love (5,7) *50*
'Til My Baby Comes Home (4,7) *29*
Treat You Right (4)
Wait For Love (4)
You Stopped Loving Me (1)
You're The Sweetest One (2)

VANESS, Theo — see THEO

VANGELIS

Born Evangelos Papathanassiou on 3/29/43 in Valos, Greece. Keyboardist/composer. Moved to Paris during the late 1960s, then to London in the mid-1970s. Formed rock band Aphrodite's Child in France with Demis Roussos, 1968-early 1970s.

DEBUT DATE	PEAK POS	WKS CHR	GOLD	ARTIST — Album Title	$	Label & Number
10/17/81+	1⁴	57	▲ 1	Chariots Of Fire ....[S-I]	$8	Polydor 6335

film is based on the true story of 2 members of Britain's 1924 Olympic team

DEBUT DATE	PEAK POS	WKS CHR	GOLD	ARTIST — Album Title	$	Label & Number
12/13/86+	42	39		2 Opera Sauvage ....[E-I]	$8	Polydor 829663

tracks "Hymne" and "L'Enfant" used frequently in radio/TV ads; film *Year Of Living Dangerously* prominently featured "L'Enfant"; title is French for Wild Opera

Abraham's Theme (1)
Chariots Of Fire - Titles (1) *1*

Chromatique (2)
Eric's Theme (1)
Five Circles (1)

Flamants Roses (2)
Hymne (2)
Irlande (2)

Jerusalem (medley) (1)
L'Enfant (2)
Mouettes (2)

100 Metres (medley) (1)
Reve (2)
Titles (1)

★★152★★ VAN HALEN

Hard-rock band formed in Pasadena, California in 1974. Consisted of David Lee Roth (b: 10/10/55; vocals), Eddie Van Halen (b: 1/26/57; guitar), Michael Anthony (b: 6/20/55; bass) and Alex Van Halen (b: 5/8/55; drums). The Van Halen brothers were born in Nijmegen, The Netherlands, and moved to Pasadena in 1968. Sammy Hagar replaced Roth as lead singer in 1985. Eddie married actress Valerie Bertinelli on 4/11/81.

DEBUT DATE	PEAK POS	WKS CHR	GOLD	ARTIST — Album Title	$	Label & Number
3/11/78	19	169	▲⁶ 1	Van Halen	$8	Warner 3075
4/14/79	6	47	▲⁴ 2	Van Halen II	$8	Warner 3312
4/19/80	6	31	▲² 3	Women and Children First	$8	Warner 3415
5/30/81	5	23	▲ 4	Fair Warning	$8	Warner 3540
5/8/82	3	65	▲³ 5	Diver Down	$8	Warner 3677
1/28/84	2⁵	77	▲⁶ 6	1984 (MCMLXXXIV)	$8	Warner 23985
4/12/86	1³	64	▲⁴ 7	5150	$8	Warner 25394

5150: New York Police code for the criminally insane; also the name of Eddie Van Halen's recording studio

DEBUT DATE	PEAK POS	WKS CHR	GOLD	ARTIST — Album Title	$	Label & Number
6/18/88	1⁴	48	▲³ 8	OU812	$8	Warner 25732
7/6/91	1³	68	▲² 9	For Unlawful Carnal Knowledge	$12	Warner 26594

A.F.U. (Naturally Wired) (8)
Ain't Talkin' 'Bout Love (1)
And The Cradle Will Rock... (3) *55*

Atomic Punk (1)
Beautiful Girls (2) *84*
Best Of Both Worlds (7)

Big Bad Bill (Is Sweet William Now) (5)
Black And Blue (8) *34*
Bottoms Up! (2)

Cabo Wabo (8)
Cathedral (4)
Could This Be Magic? (3)
D.O.A. (2)

Dance The Night Away (2) *15*
Dancing In The Street (5) *38*

Dirty Movies (4)
Dream Is Over (9)
Dreams (7) *22*
Drop Dead Legs (6)

DEBUT DATE	PEAK POS	WKS CHR	GOLD	ARTIST — Album Title	$	Label & Number

VAN HALEN — Cont'd

Eruption (1)	Hear About It Later (4)	Little Dreamer (1)	Poundcake (9)	Spanked (9)	**Why Can't This Be Love**
Everybody Wants Some!! (3)	House Of Pain (6)	Little Guitars (5)	Push Comes To Shove (4)	Sucker In A 3 Piece (8)	(7) *3*
Feel Your Love Tonight (1)	**Hot For Teacher** (6) *56*	Loss Of Control (3)	**Right Now** (9) *55*	Summer Nights (7)	Women In Love...... (2)
Feels So Good (8) *35*	**I'll Wait** (6) *13*	Love Walks In (7) *22*	Romeo Delight (3)	Sunday Afternoon In The	**You Really Got Me** (1) *36*
Finish What Ya Started	I'm The One (1)	Man On A Mission (9)	Runaround (9)	Park (4)	You're No Good (2)
(8) *13*	Ice Cream Man (1)	Mean Street (4)	**Runnin' With The Devil**	Take Your Whiskey Home (3)	
5150 (7)	In A Simple Rhyme (3)	Mine All Mine (8)	(1) *84*	316 (9)	
Fools (3)	In 'N' Out (9)	1984 (1)	Secrets (1)	Top Jimmy (6)	
Full Bug (5)	Inside (1)	(Oh) Pretty Woman (5) *12*	Sinner's Swing! (4)	**Top Of The World** (9) *27*	
Get Up (7)	Intruder (5)	On Fire (1)	So This Is Love? (4)	Tora! Tora! (3)	
Girl Gone Bad (6)	Jamie's Cryin' (1)	One Foot Out The Door (4)	Somebody Get Me A Doctor	Unchained (4)	
Good Enough (7)	Judgement Day (9)	Outta Love Again (2)	(2)	**When It's Love** (8) *5*	
Hang 'Em High (5)	**Jump** (6) *1*	**Panama** (6) *13*	Source Of Infection (8)	Where Have All The Good	
Happy Trails (5)	Light Up The Sky (2)	Pleasure Dome (9)	Spanish Fly (2)	Times Gone! (5)	

VANILLA FUDGE

Psychedelic-rock quartet formed in New York in 1966. Consisted of Mark Stein (lead singer, keyboards), Vinnie Martell (guitar), Tim Bogert (bassist with Cactus, Rod Stewart and Jeff Beck) and Carmine Appice (drummer with Cactus, Jeff Beck, Rod Stewart, KGB and Blue Murder).

DEBUT DATE	PEAK POS	WKS CHR	GOLD		$	Label & Number
9/16/67	6	80	●	**1** Vanilla Fudge...	$15	Atco 224
3/2/68	17	33		**2** The Beat Goes On.....................................	$15	Atco 237
7/13/68	20	33		**3** Renaissance...	$15	Atco 244
3/1/69	16	27		**4** Near the Beginning ....[L]	$15	Atco 278
				side 2: live		
10/25/69	34	13		**5** Rock & Roll..	$15	Atco 303

Bang Bang (1)	I Can't Make It Alone (5)	Need Love (5)	Sky Cried - When I Was A	Ticket To Ride (1)
Beat Goes On (2)	If You Gotta Make A Fool Of	Paradise (3)	Boy (3)	Variations On A Theme By
Break Song (4)	Somebody (5)	People Get Ready (1)	Some Velvet Morning (4)	Mozart Medley (2)
Church Bells Of St. Martins	Illusions Of My Childhood -	**Season Of The Witch, Pt. 1**	Spell That Comes After (3)	Voices In Time (2)
(5)	Parts One-Three (1)	(3) *65*	Street Walking Woman (3)	Where Is Happiness (4)
Eleanor Rigby (1)	Lord In The Country (5)	She's Not There (1)	**Take Me For A Little While**	Windmills Of Your Mind (5)
Faceless People (3)	Merchant (medley) (2)	Shotgun (4) *68*	(1) *38*	**You Keep Me Hangin' On**
Fur Elise (medley) (2)	Moonlight Sonata (medley)	Sketch (2)	That's What Makes A Man (3)	(1) *6*
Game Is Over (medley) (2)	(2)		Thoughts (3)	

VANILLA ICE

White Dallas-based rapper. Born Robert Van Winkle on 10/31/68 in Miami Lakes, Florida. Starred in the film *Cool As Ice*.

DEBUT DATE	PEAK POS	WKS CHR	GOLD		$	Label & Number
9/22/90	1[16]	67	▲7	**1** To The Extreme	$12	SBK 95325
				originally released as *Hooked* on Ultra Records and distributed by Ichiban Records		
6/22/91	30	30	●	**2** Extremely Live ....[L]	$12	SBK 96648
				recorded January through March 1991		
11/2/91	89	15		**3** Cool As Ice ....[S]	$12	SBK 97722
				film stars Vanilla Ice; includes "Gonna Catch You" by Lonnie Gordon, "You've Got To Look		
				Up" by Derek B, "Love 2 Love U" by Partners In Kryme feat. Debbe Cole, "Forever" by D'New		
				feat. Temple, "Faith" by Rozalla, and "Drop That Zero" by Stanley Clarke		

Cool As Ice (Everybody	Havin' A Roni (1,2)	**Ice Ice Baby** (1,2) *1*	Never Wanna Be Without	Rasta Man (1)	Stop That Train (1,2)
Get Loose) (3) *81*	Hooked (1,2)	Ice Is Workin' It (1,2)	You (3)	Road To My Riches (2)	V.I.P. Posse One By One (2)
Dancin' (1)	I Like It (2)	It's A Party (1)	People's Choice (3)	Rollin' In My 5.0 (2)	
Get Wit' It (3)	**I Love You** (1,2) *52*	Life Is A Fantasy (1,2)	**Play That Funky Music**	Satisfaction [includes 2	
Go Ill (1)	Ice Cold (1)	Move (2)	(1,2) *4*	versions] (2)	

VANITY

Real name: Denise Matthews, from Toronto. Lead singer of Vanity 6 (assembled by Prince). Former model/actress. Starred in the films *The Last Dragon*, *52 Pick-Up* and *Action Jackson*.

DEBUT DATE	PEAK POS	WKS CHR	GOLD		$	Label & Number
9/22/84	62	23		**1** Wild Animal	$8	Motown 6102
3/22/86	66	20		**2** Skin On Skin	$8	Motown 6167

Animals (2)	Flippin' Out (1)	Manhunt (2)	**Pretty Mess** (1) *75*	Skin On Skin (2)	Wild Animal (1)
Confidential (2)	Gun Shy (2)	Mechanical Emotion (1)	Romantic Voyage (2)	Strap On "Robbie Baby" (1)	
Crazy Maybe (1)	In The Jungle (2)	Ouch (2)	Samuelle (1)	**Under The Influence** (2) *56*	

VANITY 6

Trio formed as backup for Prince. Consisted of Denise Matthews, Susan Moonsie and Brenda Bennett. Matthews recorded solo as Vanity.

DEBUT DATE	PEAK POS	WKS CHR	GOLD		$	Label & Number
10/2/82	45	31	●	Vanity 6	$8	Warner 23716

Bite The Beat	He's So Dull	If A Girl Answers (Don't	Make-Up	3x2 = 6
Drive Me Wild		Hang Up)	Nasty Girl	Wet Dream

★★419★★ VANNELLI, Gino

Born on 6/16/52 in Montreal. Pop singer/songwriter. His brother Ross produced Earth, Wind & Fire, Howard Hewett and The California Raisins.

DEBUT DATE	PEAK POS	WKS CHR	GOLD		$	Label & Number
9/28/74	60	30		**1** Powerful People	$8	A&M 3630
7/19/75	66	23		**2** Storm at Sunup	$8	A&M 4533
8/14/76	32	22		**3** The Gist of The Gemini	$8	A&M 4596
11/19/77+	33	16		**4** A Pauper In Paradise	$8	A&M 4664
				side 2: with the Royal Philharmonic Orchestra		
9/30/78	13	35	▲	**5** Brother To Brother	$8	A&M 4722
4/11/81	15	26		**6** Nightwalker	$8	Arista 9539
9/19/81	172	2		**7** The Best Of Gino Vannelli .... [G]	$8	A&M 3729
6/29/85	62	25		**8** Black Cars	$8	HME 40077
5/23/87	160	7		**9** Big Dreamers Never Sleep	$8	CBS Assoc. 40337

Appaloosa (5,7)	Evil Eye (5)	Here She Comes (8)	In The Name Of Money (9)	King For A Day (9)	**Love Of My Life** (3) *64*
Black And Blue (4)	Father And Son (2)	How Much (8)	It's Over (8)	Lady (1)	Mama Coco (2,7)
Black Cars (8) *42*	Feel Like Flying (5)	**Hurts To Be In Love** (8) *57*	Jack Miraculous (1)	**Living Inside Myself** (6) *6*	Mardi Gras (4)
Brother To Brother (5)	Felicia (1)	I Believe (6)	Jo Jo (1)	Love & Emotion (5)	New Fix For '76 (3)
Crazy Life (7)	Fly Into This Night (3,7)	**I Just Wanna Stop** (5,7) *4*	Just A Motion Away (8)	Love Is A Night (2)	**Nightwalker** (6) *41*
Down With Love (9)	Gettin' High (2)	Imagination (8)	Keep On Walking (2)	Love Me Now (2,7)	Omens Of Love (3)

DEBUT DATE	PEAK POS	WKS CHR	GOLD	ARTIST — Album Title	$	Label & Number

VANNELLI, Gino — Cont'd

One Night With You (4,7) Persona Non Grata (9) River Must Flow (9) Something Tells Me (9) Surest Things Can Change War Suite Medley (3)
Other Man (8) Poor Happy Jimmy (Tribute Sally (She Says The Son Of A New York Gun (1) (4) **Wheels Of Life** (5,7) 78
Pauper In Paradise (In Four To Jim Croce) (1) Sweetest Things) (6) Song And Dance (4) Time Out (9) Where Am I Going (2)
Movements) (4) Powerful People (1,7) Santa Rosa (6) Stay With Me (6) Total Stranger (8) **Wild Horses** (9) 55
People Gotta Move (1,7) 22 Put The Weight On My Seek And You Will Find (6) Storm At Sunup (2) Ugly Man (3) Work Verse (1)
People I Belong To (5) Shoulders (6) Shape Me Like A Man (9)   Valleys Of Valhalla (4) Young Lover (9)

VAN SHELTON, Ricky — see SHELTON

VANWARMER, Randy

Born Randall Van Wormer on 3/30/55 in Indian Hills, Colorado. Singer/songwriter/guitarist. Moved to England at age 12; returned to U.S. in 1979. Charted two country hits in 1988.

| 6/2/79 | 81 | 10 | | Warmer .... | $8 | Bearsville 6988 |

Call Me Deeper And Deeper Gotta Get Out Of Here **Just When I Needed You** Losing Out On Love Your Light
Convincing Lies Forever Loving You I Could Sing **Most 4** One Who Loves You

VAN ZANDT, Miami Steve — see LITTLE STEVEN

VAN ZANT, Johnny, Band

The younger brother of Ronnie (Lynyrd Skynyrd) and Donnie Van Zant (38 Special). Formed hard-rock quintet Van-Zant by 1985.

9/6/80	48	15		1 No More Dirty Deals	$8	Polydor 6289
6/13/81	119	10		2 Round Two	$8	Polydor 6322
9/18/82	159	6		3 The Last Of The Wild Ones	$8	Polydor 6355
5/4/85	170	8		4 Van-Zant	$8	Geffen 24059

VAN-ZANT

| 8/11/90 | 108 | 11 | | 5 Brickyard Road .... | $12 | Atlantic 82110 |

JOHNNY VAN ZANT

Bad 4 U (5) Hard Luck Story (1) Let There Be Music (2) Party In The Parking Lot (5) Standing In The Falling Yesterday's Gone (2)
Brickyard Road (5) Heart To The Flame (4) Lonely Girls (4) Play My Music (2) Rain (2) You've Got To Believe In
Can't Live Without Your Hearts Are Gonna Roll (5) Love Can Be So Cruel (5) Put My Trust In You (1) Still Hold On (3) Love (4)
Love (5) I'm A Fighter (4) Love Is Not Enough (5) Right On Time (4) Take Every Beat Of My Young Girls (5)
Cold Hearted Woman (2) Inside Looking Out (3) Midnight Sensation (4) She's Out With A Gun (4) Heart (5)
Coming Home (1) It's You (3) Never Too Late (1) Shutdown (2) Three Wishes (5)
Danger Zone (3) Just A Little Bit Of Love (5) Night Time Lady (2) 634-5789 (1) Together Forever (3)
Does A Fool Ever Learn (4) Keep On Rollin' (1) No More Dirty Deals (1) Stand Your Ground (1) 2+2 (4)
Drive My Car (2) Keep Our Love Alive (2) One And Only (3) Standing In The Darkness (1) Two Strangers (4)
Good Girls Turning Bad (3) Last Of The Wild Ones (3) Only The Strong Survive (1)   (Who's) Right Or Wrong (2)

VAPORS, The

British pub-rock quartet — David Fenton, lead singer.

| 8/16/80 | 62 | 28 | | 1 New Clear Days .... | $8 | United Art. 1049 |
| 4/4/81 | 109 | 9 | | 2 Magnets .... | $8 | Liberty 1090 |

Bunkers (1) Isolated Case (2) Letter From Hiro (1) Prisoners (1) Spiders (2) Waiting For The Weekend (1)
Can't Talk Anymore (2) Jimmie Jones (1) Live At The Marquee (2) Silver Machines (2) Spring Collection (1)
Civic Hall (2) Johnny's In Love (Again) (2) Magnets (2) Sixty Second Interval (1) Trains (1)
Daylight Titans (2) Lenina (1) News At Ten (1) Somehow (1) **Turning Japanese** (1) 36

VAUGHAN, Sarah

Jazz singer dubbed "The Divine One." Born on 3/27/24 in Newark, New Jersey. Died of lung cancer on 4/3/90. Apollo Theater amateur contest in 1942 led to her joining Earl Hines' band as vocalist/second pianist. With Billy Eckstine from 1944-45. Married manager/trumpeter George Treadwell in 1947. Later husbands included pro football player Clyde Atkins and trumpeter Waymon Reed. Performed into the 1980s. Won the Lifetime Achievement Grammy in 1989.

11/24/56	20	2		1 Linger Awhile	$40	Columbia 914
12/1/56	21	1		2 Sassy	$40	EmArcy 36089
4/13/57	14	9		3 Great Songs From Hit Shows	$35	Mercury 100 [2]
8/19/57	14	9		4 Sarah Vaughan sings George Gershwin	$35	Mercury 101 [2]
7/1/72	173	12		5 Sarah Vaughan/Michel Legrand	$10	Mainstream 361

SARAH VAUGHAN/MICHEL LEGRAND

All The Things You Are (3) He Loves And She Loves (4) I'm The Girl (2) Lorelei (4) Once You've Been In Love (5) They Say It's Wonderful (3)
Aren't You Kinda Glad We He's Only Wonderful (3) I've Got A Crush On You (4) Lost In The Stars (3) Only You Can Say (2) Things Are Looking Up (4)
Did (4) His Eyes, Her Eyes (5) I've Got Some Crying To Do Love Walked In (4) Pieces Of Dreams (5) Touch Of Your Hand (3)
Autumn In New York (3) Homework (3) (2) Lover's Quarrel (1) Poor Butterfly (3) Tree In The Park (3)
Bewitched (3) How Long Has This Been If This Isn't Love (3) Lucky In Love (3) September Song (3) What Are You Doing The
Bidin' My Time (4) Going On (4) Isn't It A Pity (3) Lush Life (2) Shake Down The Stars (3) Rest Of Your Life (5)
Blue, Green, Grey And Gone I Confess (3) It Never Entered My Mind (3) Man I Love (4) Ship Without A Sail (3)
(5) I Loved Him (2) It's Got To Be Love (4) Mighty Lonesome Feelin' (1) Sinner Kissed An Angel (2)
Blues Serenade (1) I Was Born In Love With Just A Moment More (1) My Darling, My Darling (3) Sinner Or Saint (5)
Boy Next Door (2) You (Theme From Let's Call The Whole Thing My Heart Stood Still (3) Someone To Watch Over Me
But Not For Me (3) Wuthering Heights) (5) Off (4) My Man's Gone Now (4) (3)
Comes Love (3) I Will Say Goodbye (5) Let's Take An Old Fashioned My One And Only (What Am Summer Knows (Theme
Dancing In The Dark (3) I Won't Say I Will (4) Walk (3) I Gonna Do) (4) From Summer Of '42) (5)
Do It Again (4) I'll Build A Stairway To Linger Awhile (1) My Romance (2) Summer Me, Winter Me (5)
Don't Be Afraid (1) Paradise (4) Little Girl Blue (3) My Ship (3) Summertime (4)
Foggy Day (4) I'm Afraid The Masquerade Lonely Girl (1) My Tormented Heart (1) These Things I Offer You
Hands Of Time (Brian's Is Over (2) Lonely Woman (2) Of Thee I Sing (4) (For A Lifetime) (1)
Song) (3) I'm Crazy To Love You (1) Looking For A Boy (4) Old Folks (3) They All Laughed (4)

★★423★★

VAUGHAN, Stevie Ray, & Double Trouble

Stevie Ray was born on 10/3/54 in Dallas. Blues-rock guitarist. His brother is Jimmie Vaughan (The Fabulous Thunderbirds). Stevie was the lead guitarist on David Bowie's *Let's Dance* album. Stevie died in a helicopter crash on 8/27/90. Double Trouble was Jackie Newhouse (bass) and Chris Layton (drums).

7/23/83	38	33	▲	1 Texas Flood	$8	Epic 38734
6/23/84	31	38	▲	2 Couldn't Stand The Weather	$8	Epic 39304
10/12/85	34	39	▲	3 Soul To Soul	$8	Epic 40036
12/20/86+	52	25	●	4 Live Alive .... [L]	$10	Epic 40511 [2]

includes performances from the Montreux Jazz Festival, 1985

DEBUT DATE	PEAK POS	WKS CHR	G O L D	ARTIST — Album Title	$	Label & Number
				VAUGHAN, Stevie Ray, & Double Trouble — Cont'd		
7/1/89	33	47 ▲		5 In Step	$8	Epic 45024
10/13/90	7	38 ▲		6 Family Style	$12	Epic/Assc. 46225
				THE VAUGHAN BROTHERS		
11/23/91	10	46 ▲		7 The Sky Is Crying .... [K]	$12	Epic 47390
				recordings from 1984-89		
10/24/92	58	12		8 In The Beginning .... [L]	$12	Epic 53168
				broadcast live from Austin on 4/1/80		

Ain't Gone 'N' Give Up On Love (3,4)
All Your Love I Miss Loving (8)
Baboom (medley) (6)
Boot Hill (7)
Brothers (6)
Change It (3,4)
Chitlins Con Carne (7)
Close To You (7)
Cold Shot (2,4)
Come On (Part III) (3)
Couldn't Stand The Weather (2)
Crossfire (5)
D/FW (6)
Dirty Pool (1)
Empty Arms (3,7)
Gone Home (3)
Good Texan (6)
Hard To Be (6)
Hillbillies From Outerspace (6)
Honey Bee (2)
House Is Rockin' (5)
I'm Cryin' (1)
I'm Leaving You (Commit A Crime) (4)
In The Open (8)
Leave My Girl Alone (5)
Lenny (1)
Let Me Love You Baby (5)
Life By The Drop (7)
Life Without You (3,4)
Little Wing (7)
Live Another Day (8)
Long Way From Home (6)
Look At Little Sister (3,4)
Lookin' Out The Window (3)
Love Me Darlin' (5)
Love Struck Baby (1,4,8)
Mama Said (medley) (6)
Mary Had A Little Lamb (1,4)
May I Have A Talk With You (7)
Pride And Joy (1,4)
Riviera Paradise (5)
Rude Mood (1)
Say What! (3,4)
Scratch-N-Sniff (5)
Scuttle Buttin' (2)
Shake For Me (8)
Sky Is Crying (7)
Slide Thing (8)
So Excited (7)
Stang's Swang (2)
Superstition (4)
Telephone Song (6)
Tell Me (1,8)
Testify (1)
Texas Flood (1,4)
They Call Me Guitar Hurricane (8)
Things (That) I Used To Do (2)
Tick Tock (6)65
Tightrope (5)
Tin Pan Alley (2,8)
Travis Walk (5)
Voodoo Chile (Slight Return) (2,4)
Wall Of Denial (5)
Wham (7)
White Boots (6)
Willie The Wimp (4)
You'll Be Mine (3)

| | | | | ★★25★★ **VAUGHN, Billy** | | |

Born Richard Vaughn on 4/12/19 in Glasgow, Kentucky; died on 9/26/91 of cancer. Organized the Hilltoppers vocal group in 1952. Music director for Dot Records. Arranger/conductor for Pat Boone, Gale Storm, The Fontane Sisters and many other Dot artists. Billy had more pop hits than any other orchestra leader during the rock era.

DEBUT DATE	PEAK POS	WKS CHR	G O L D	ARTIST — Album Title	$	Label & Number
4/21/58+	5	68 ●		1 **Sail Along Silv'ry Moon** .... [I]	$15	Dot 3100
10/13/58+	15	47		2 Billy Vaughn Plays The Million Sellers .... [I]	$15	Dot 3119
5/4/59	20	3		3 Billy Vaughn Plays .... [I]	$15	Dot 3156
5/25/59	7	108 ●		4 **Blue Hawaii** .... [I]	$15	Dot 3165
1/18/60	36	1		5 Golden Saxophones .... [I]	$15	Dot 3205
3/21/60	1²	62 ●		6 Theme from A Summer Place .... [I]	$15	Dot 3276
8/15/60	5	33		7 **Look For A Star** .... [I]	$15	Dot 3322
12/19/60+	5	23		8 **Theme from The Sundowners** .... [I]	$15	Dot 3349
4/24/61	11	43		9 Orange Blossom Special and Wheels .... [I]	$12	Dot 3366
10/9/61	17	25		10 Golden Waltzes .... [I]	$12	Dot 3280
12/4/61+	20	18		11 Berlin Melody .... [I]	$12	Dot 3396
3/24/62	18	12		12 Greatest String Band Hits	$12	Dot 3409
6/2/62	14	16		13 Chapel By The Sea .... [I]	$12	Dot 3424
9/15/62	10	27		14 **A Swingin' Safari** .... [I]	$12	Dot 3458
12/29/62	145	1		15 Christmas Carols .... [X-I]	$12	Dot 3148
				originally released in 1958; Christmas charts: 101/'67		
2/16/63	17	32		16 1962's Greatest Hits .... [I]	$12	Dot 25497
6/15/63	15	16		17 Sukiyaki and 11 Hawaiian Hits .... [I]	$12	Dot 25523
11/9/63	94	8		18 Number 1 Hits, Vol. #1 .... [I]	$12	Dot 25540
2/1/64	51	17		19 Blue Velvet & 1963's Great Hits .... [I]	$12	Dot 25559
6/20/64	144	4		20 Forever .... [I]	$12	Dot 25578
8/29/64	141	3		21 Another Hit Album! .... [I]	$12	Dot 25593
1/2/65	18	29		22 Pearly Shells .... [I]	$10	Dot 25605
4/24/65	45	15		23 Mexican Pearls .... [I]	$10	Dot 25628
10/9/65	31	29		24 Moon Over Naples .... [I]	$10	Dot 25654
2/12/66	56	14		25 Michelle .... [I]	$10	Dot 25679
7/23/66	149	2		26 Great Country Hits .... [I]	$10	Dot 25698
10/22/66+	44	35		27 Alfie .... [I]	$10	Dot 25751
3/18/67	114	20		28 Sweet Maria * .... [I]	$10	Dot 25782
5/13/67	130	7		29 That's Life & Pineapple Market .... [I]	$10	Dot 25788
7/29/67	147	2		30 Josephine .... [E-I]	$10	Dot 25796
8/12/67	161	5		31 I Love You * .... [I]	$10	Dot 25813
				***THE BILLY VAUGHN SINGERS**		
9/23/67	159	8		32 Golden Hits/The Best Of Billy Vaughn .... [G-I]	$10	Dot 25811
10/28/67	200	2		33 Ode To Billy Joe .... [I]	$8	Dot 25828
9/28/68	198	3		34 A Current Set Of Standards .... [I]	$8	Dot 25882
5/17/69	95	16		35 The Windmills Of Your Mind .... [I]	$8	Dot 25937
3/14/70	188	2		36 Winter World Of Love .... [I]	$8	Dot 25975

Adeste Fideles (15)
Again (22)
Alabama Jubilee (12)
Alamo, Theme From The
..see: Green Leaves Of Summer
Alfie (27)
All The Way (6)
Aloha Oe (4)
Alone (14)
Always Mademoiselle (36)
Am I That Easy To Forget (26)
Anniversary Song (24)
Any Time (24)
Apartment, Theme From The (7)
Are You Lonesome Tonight (9)
Around The World (2)
Auf Wiedershen, My Dear (5)
Autumn Love Song (11)
Baby Face (12)
Ballerina (18)
Beautiful Ohio (10)
Because They're Young (7)
Berlin Melody (11) 61
Beyond The Reef (4)
Beyond The Sunset (7)
Blue Eyes Crying In The Rain (26)
Blue Flame (14)
Blue Hawaii (3,11)
Blue Moon (3,11)
Blue Orchids (23)
Blue Tomorrow (11) 84
Blue Velvet (19)
Blueberry Hill (3)
Bluebird Of Happiness (25)
Bonanza (13)
Boogie Woogie (30)
Born To Be With You (14)
Born To Lose (16)
Breeze (Blow My Baby Back To Me) (5)
Burning Memories (21)
Busted (19)
Bye Bye Blackbird (12)
C'est Si Bon (9)
Can't Help Falling In Love (13)
Canadian Sunset (2)
Caravan (22)
Careless (33)
Carolina In The Morning (12)
Chapel By The Sea (13) 69
Chattanoogie Shoe Shine Boy (21)
Cherish (28)
Chim Chim Cheree (25)
Chinatown, My Chinatown (12)
Church's One Foundation (8)
Cimarron (Roll On) (3) 44
Clair De Lune (11)
Climb Every Mountain (6)
Cocktails For Two (33)
CoCo (36)
Cocoanut Grove (4,30)
Come September (11) 73
Come Saturday Morning (36)
Cross-Eyed Cyclops (34)
Crying In The Chapel (26)
Cuando Calienta El Sol
..see: Love Me With All Your Heart
Danke Schoen (19)
Dark At The Top Of The Stairs, Theme From (8)
Dark Moon (26)
Days Of Wine And Roses (27)
Dear Heart (23)
Dear Lonely Hearts (16)
Dear Old Girl (20)
Deck The Halls (15)
Dis-Advantages Of You (29)
Dr. Zhivago ..see: Somewhere, My Love

DEBUT DATE	PEAK POS	WKS CHR	GOLD	ARTIST — Album Title	$	Label & Number

VAUGHN, Billy — Cont'd

Dominique (19)
Don't Break The Heart That Loves You (13)
Down At) Papa Joe's (19)
Drifting And Dreaming (3)
Early In The Morning (36)
Elaine (25)
Elmer's Tune (5)
Everybody Loves Somebody (22)
Everybody's Somebody's Fool (8)
Exodus (13)
Faith Of Our Fathers (15)
Fallen Star (26)
Fancy (36)
Fascination (2)
First Noel (15)
Foggy River (26)
Fool Such As I (14)
For Me And My Gal (22)
Forever (20)
Four Walls (21)
French Song (21)
Full Moon And Empty Arms (2)
Games That Lovers Play (4)
Girl From Ipanema (22)
Girl Of My Dreams (10)
Glad She's A Woman (35)
Glow Worm March (14)
Go Away, Little Girl (16)
God Rest Ye Merry, Gentlemen (15)
Goldfinger (24)
Green Grass Of Texas (9)
Green, Green Grass Of Home (29)
Green Leaves Of Summer (8)
Greenfields (7)
Groovin' (31)
Guantanamera (28)
Guitar Polka (26)
Happy Days Are Here Again (12)
Harbor Lights (3)
Hark! The Herald Angels Sing (15)
Have I Told You Lately That I Love You (5)
Hawaiian Paradise (4)
Hawaiian Sunset (4)
Hawaiian War Chant (4) *89*
Hawaiian Wedding Song (4)
He'll Have To Go (7)
Heart And Soul (23)
Heartaches (30)
Heaven (35)
Help Yourself (35)
Here In My Heart (18)
Here We Go Again (33)
High Noon (2)
Holly Holy (36)
Holiday For Strings (2)
Honey (34)
Hunger, Theme From (36)
I Almost Lost My Mind (5)
I Can't Stop Loving You (16)

I Could Have Danced All Night (25)
I Cried For You (22)
I Got Rhythm (31)
I Left My Heart In San Francisco (24)
I Love You And You Love Me (31)
I Will (25)
I Will Wait For You (27)
I'll Catch The Sun (34)
I'm Getting Sentimental Over You (1)
I'm Leaving It Up To You (19)
I'm Looking Over A Four Leaf Clover (12,30)
I'm Movin' On (21)
I'm Sorry (18)
If You Go Away (28)
In A Shanty In Old Shanty Town (12)
In The Chapel In The Moonlight (14,25)
In The Gloaming (20)
In The Mood (2)
Indian Lake (34)
Indian Love Call (3)
Indian Summer (5)
Isle Of Capri (3)
It Came Upon A Midnight Clear (15)
It Happened In Adano (11)
It's A Lonesome Old Town (9)
It's A Sin (26)
It's Easy To Remember (23)
It's Just A Matter Of Time (31)
(It's No) Sin (14)
Japanese Sandman (12)
Jealous (1)
Jealous Heart (3)
Jingle Bells (15)
Josephine (30)
Joy To The World (15)
June In January (33)
Just A Closer Walk With Thee (7,21)
Just A Wearyin' For You (10)
Just One More Chance (23)
Kalua (17)
King's Serenade (17)
La Montana (3)
Lady-O (36)
Lara's Theme ..see: Somewhere, My Love
Laura (30)
Lazy River (9)
Let Me Call You Sweetheart (10)
Little Brown Gal (4)
Little Dutch Mill (5)
Little Green Apples (34)
Lonely Bull (16)
Lonely Is The Name (34)
Look For A Star (7) *19*
Lost Of Love (34)
Love (24)

Love Birds (12)
Love In Bloom (23)
Love Is A Many-Splendored Thing (8)
Love Letters (23)
Love Letters In The Sand (14)
Love Me With All Your Heart (19,20)
Love's Old Sweet Song (20)
Lovely Hula Hands (17)
Lucky Duck (20)
Lullaby From Rosemary's Baby (34)
Make The World Go Away (26)
Make Your Own Kind Of Music (36)
Mame (21)
Man And A Woman (28)
Man Without Love (34)
Mapuana (17)
Marie (9)
Maybe (22)
Meditation (20)
Meet Me Tonight In Dreamland (10)
Melody From The Sky (23)
Melody Of Love (10,32) *2*
Memphis (21)
Mexican Pearls (23) *94*
Mexican Shuffle (25)
Mexico (11)
Michael (11)
Michelle (25) *77*
Midnight In Moscow (13)
Missouri Waltz (10)
Mister Sandman (18)
Molly Darling (20)
Mona Lisa (7)
Moon Of Manakoora (17)
Moon Over Miami (1)
Moon Over Naples (24)
Moon Over Naples (Spanish Eyes) (32)
Moon River (13,16)
Moonglow and Theme From "Picnic" (2)
Moonlight And Roses (3)
Moonlight And Shadows (22)
Moonlight Bay (3)
More (19)
More And More (33)
Mr. Lucky, Theme From (8)
Mrs. Robinson (34)
Music To Watch Girls By (29)
My Buddy (13)
My Dear (9)
My Happiness (3)
My Isle Of Golden Dreams (4)
My Little Grass Shack (4)
My Love, Forgive Me (24)
My Special Angel (26)
My Tane (17)
Nature Boy (18)
Near You (5)
Nearness Of You (23)
Never On Sunday (8)

No Matter What Shape (Your Stomach's In) (29)
No One Will Ever Know (26)
Now Is The Hour (17)
O Holy Night (15)
O Little Town Of Bethlehem (15)
O Sole Mio (8)
Ode To Billy Joe (33)
Oh! You Beautiful Doll (12)
Old Cape Cod (8)
On The Beach At Waikiki (17)
One Has My Name (25)
One Of Those Songs (27)
One Rose (That's Left In My Heart) (20)
Only I (31)
Orange Blossom Special (9,32) *63*
Organ Grinder's Swing (25)
Out Of Limits (19)
Out Of Nowhere (33)
Over The Rainbow (22)
Pagan Love Song (17)
Painted, Tainted Rose (19)
Paper Roses (7)
Peace In The Valley (21)
Pearly Shells (22)
Peg O' My Heart (22,30)
People (21)
Perfect Song (30)
Petite Fleur (13)
Pineapple Market (29)
Please (24)
Popsicles And Icicles (19)
Promises, Promises (35)
Put On Your Old Grey Bonnet (12)
Que Sera, Sera (6)
Rag Mop (18)
Raindrops Keep Fallin' On My Head (36)
Ramblin' Rose (16)
Raunchy (1) *10*
Red Roses For A Blue Lady (24)
Red Sails In The Sunset (3)
Release Me (16)
Remember When (8)
Roses Are Red (16)
Route 66 Theme (13)
Ruby (2)
Sail Along Silvery Moon (1,32) *5*
San Antonio Rose (30)
Sayonara (6)
Second Hand Rose (27)
See See Rider (25)
Sentimental Journey (1)
Sentimental Me (5)
September Song (30)
Serenade Of The Bells (11)
Shadow Of Your Smile (27)
Shangri-La (20)
Shifting Whispering Sands (Parts 1 & 2) (32) *5*

Shine On Harvest Moon (3)
Silent Night (15)
Silver Moon (10)
Silver Threads Among The Gold (20)
Sixteen Tons (21)
Sleepy Time Gal (1)
Slow Poke (30)
Smiles (12)
Snowfall (7)
So Rare (2)
Some Enchanted Evening (6)
Somethin' Stupid (31)
Somewhere, My Love (29)
Song Of The Islands (4)
Sorrento (9)
Soulful Strut (35)
Sound Of Music (6,24)
Spanish Pearls (34)
Stella By Starlight (23)
Stranger On The Shore (16)
Strangers In The Night (27)
Stripper, The (16)
Sugar Town (28)
Sukiyaki (17)
Summer Place, Theme From A (6,32)
Summertime (9)
Sunday In Madrid (14)
Sunday Will Never Be The Same (31)
Sundowners, The (8) *51*
Sunrise Serenade (1)
Sunrise, Sunset (27)
Sweet Georgia Brown (1)
Sweet Leilani (4)
Sweet Maria (28)
Sweet Someone (17)
Swingin' Safari (14,32) *13*
Tammy (6)
Taste Of Honey (22)
Tears And Roses (21)
Telstar (9)
Tennessee Waltz (5,10)
Terry Theme From Limelight (6)
That Lucky Old Sun (18)
That's Life (29)
There Goes My Everything (28)
There's A Long, Long Trail (20)
There's No Love (No Hay Amore) (29)
This Guy's In Love With You (34)
This Is My Song (31)
Three O'Clock In The Morning (10)
Three Penny Opera (Moritat) (6)
Throw Another Log On The Fire (14)
Till I Waltz Again With You (11)
Till The End Of Time (2)
Time Of The Season (35)
Tiny Bubbles (29)

To Each His Own (30)
To You Sweetheart Aloha (17)
Together (11)
Tonight (24)
Tonight We Love (2)
Too Young (18)
Traces (35)
Traci's Tracks (35)
Tracy's Theme (6)
Trade Winds (4)
True Love (6)
Tuff (13)
Tumbling Tumbleweeds (1) *30*
Twilight Time (1)
Twist, The (13)
Two Sleepy People (33)
Until Tomorrow (1)
Up-Up And Away (31)
Volare (Nel Blu Dipinto Di Blu) (8)
Wabash Blues (5)
Walk, Don't Run (8)
Walk In The Black Forest (24)
Walking On Wilshire (29)
Waltz You Saved For Me (10)
Washington Square (19)
Watermelon Man (25)
Way Of Love (3)
Way That I Live (35)
Wheel Of Fortune (18)
Wheel Of Hurt (28)
Wheels (9,32) *28*
When The Saints Go Marching In (14)
Where Will The Words Come From (28)
Whiffenpoof Song (9)
White Christmas (15)
Who's Afraid (3)
Wichita Lineman (35)
Wiedersehn (17)
Willow Weep For Me (23)
Winchester Cathedral (29)
Windmills Of Your Mind (35)
Winter World Of Love (36)
Wish Me A Rainbow (28)
Wonderland By Night (13)
Wooden Heart (11)
World I Used To Know (21)
World We Knew (Over And Over) (33)
Worried Mind (26)
Yellow Roses Mean Goodbye (31)
Yester-Me, Yester-You, Yesterday (36)
You Belong To Me (18)
You Belong To My Heart (5)
You Call Everybody Darling (18)
You Can't Be True, Dear (3)
You Gave Me A Mountain (35)

★★**363**★★ **VEE, Bobby**

Born Robert Velline on 4/30/43 in Fargo, North Dakota. Formed The Shadows with his brother and a friend in 1959. After Buddy Holly's death in a plane crash, The Shadows filled in on Buddy's next scheduled show in Fargo. First recorded for Soma in 1959. In the films *Swingin' Along, It's Trad, Dad, Play It Cool, C'mon Let's Live A Little* and *Just For Fun*. Still performing on oldies tours.

DEBUT DATE	PEAK POS	WKS CHR		ARTIST — Album Title	$	Label & Number
3/20/61	18	15	1	Bobby Vee	$25	Liberty 7181
10/30/61	85	8	2	Bobby Vee sings Hits Of The Rockin' '50's	$30	Liberty 7205
2/3/62	91	14	3	Take Good Care Of My Baby	$25	Liberty 7211
7/21/62	42	23	4	Bobby Vee Meets The Crickets	$25	Liberty 7228
				BOBBY VEE/THE CRICKETS		
7/21/62	121	6	5	A Bobby Vee Recording Session	$25	Liberty 7232
11/3/62+	24	44	6	Bobby Vee's Golden Greats	[G] $20	Liberty 7245
12/15/62	136	3	7	Merry Christmas From Bobby Vee	[X] $35	Liberty 7267
4/13/63	102	5	8	The Night Has A Thousand Eyes	$20	Liberty 7285
6/1/63	91	8	9	Bobby Vee Meets The Ventures	$20	Liberty 7289
				BOBBY VEE/THE VENTURES		
6/27/64	146	2	10	Bobby Vee sings The New Sound From England!	$25	Liberty 7352
10/7/67	66	12	11	Come Back When You Grow Up	$15	Liberty 7534
4/27/68	187	7	12	Just Today	$15	Liberty 7554

VEE, Bobby — Cont'd

Angels In The Sky (1)
Anonymous Phone Call (8)
Any Other Girl (10)
Beautiful People (12) **37**
Before You Go (11)
Blue Christmas (7)
Bo Diddley (4)
Brown Eyed Handsome Man (10)
Candy Man (9)
Caravan (9)
Christmas Vacation (7)
Christmas Wish (7)
Come Back When You Grow Up (11) **3**
Come Go With Me (2)
Devil Or Angel (1,6) **6**
Do You Wanna Dance (2)
Don't You Believe Them (10)
Donna (2)
Double Good Feeling (11)
Dry Your Eyes (8)
Earth Angel (2)
Everyday (6)
Foolish Tears (1)
Forever Kind Of Love (5)
Forget Me Not (5)
From Me To You (10)

Get Ready (12)
Get The Message (11)
Ginger (10)
Girl Can't Help It (4)
Girl I Left Behind Me (12)
Girl Of My Best Friend (9)
Go On (3)
Goodnight Irene (9)
Guess Who (5)
Happy Happy Birthday Baby (2)
Hark, Is That A Cannon I Hear (3)
He Will Break Your Heart (3)
Hold On To Him (11)
Honeycomb (9)
How Many Tears (6) **63**
I Can't Say Goodbye (5) 92
I Gotta Know (4)
I May Be Back (11)
I'll Be Home For Christmas (7)
I'll Make You Mine (10) **52**
I'll String Along With You (10)

I'm Gonna Sit Right Down And Write Myself A Letter (9)
If I'm Right Or Wrong (9)
If She Were My Girl (8)
In My Baby's Eyes (5)
It Couldn't Happen To A Nicer Guy (8)
It Might As Well Rain Until September (8)
Jingle-Bell Rock (7)
Just Keep It Up (And See What Happens) (12)
Lavender Blue (2)
Linda Lu (9)
Little Flame (3)
Little Queenie (4)
Little Star (2)
Lollipop (2)
Long Lonely Nights (1)
Lookin' For Love (4)
Love, Love, Love (1)
Lover's Goodbye (8)
Lucille (3)
Maybe Just Today (12) **46**
Mission Accomplished (11)
Mister Sandman (1)

More Than I Can Say (1,6) **61**
My Christmas Love (7)
My Girl/Hey Girl (12) **35**
My Golden Chance (5)
Night Has A Thousand Eyes (8) **3**
Nobody's Home To Go Home To (12)
Not So Merry Christmas (7)
Objects Of Gold (11)
One Last Kiss (1,6)
Peggy Sue (5)
Please Don't Ask About Barbara (5,6) **15**
Poetry In Motion (1)
Pretty Girls Everywhere (9)
Punish Her (6) **20**
Raining In My Heart (3)
Remember Me, Huh (3)
Rose Grew In The Ashes (11)
Rubber Ball (1,6) *6*
Run To Him (3,6) **2**
School Days (2)
Sealed With A Kiss (12)
Sharing You (5,6) **15**
She Loves You (10)
She's Sorry (10)

Silent Night (7)
Silent Partner (8)
Silver Bells (7)
Sixteen Candles (2)
So You're In Love (8)
Someday (When I'm Gone From You) (4,6) **99**
Stayin' In (1,6) **33**
Summertime Blues (2)
Sunrise Highway (12)
Suspicion (10)
Suzie Baby (6) *77*
Sweet Little Sixteen (4)
Take A Walk, Johnny (10)
Take Good Care Of My Baby (3,6) **1**
Talk To Me, Talk To Me (1)
Teardrops Fall Like Rain (3)
Tenderly Yours (5)
Theme For A Dream (8)
(There's No Place Like) Home For The Holidays (7)
This Is Where Friendship Ends (9)
Tiffany Rings (12)
Walk Right Back (9)
Walkin' With My Angel (3,6) **53**

Way You Do The Things You Do (12)
Well...All Right (4)
What About Me (8)
What Else Is New (9)
What's Your Name (5)
When You're In Love (4)
White Christmas (7)
Who Am I? (3)
Wild Night (9)
Will You Love Me Tomorrow (3)
Winter Wonderland (7)
Wisdom Of A Fool (2)
World Down On Your Knees (11)
You Better Move On (5)
You Can Count On Me (11)
You Can't Lie To A Liar (10)
You Won't Forget Me (8)
You're A Big Girl Now (11)

VEGA, Suzanne
Born on 8/12/59 in New York City. Alternative singer/songwriter/guitarist.

6/15/85	91	31		1 Suzanne Vega		$8	A&M 5072
5/16/87	11	32	●	2 Solitude Standing		$8	A&M 5136
5/5/90	50	13		3 days of open Hand		$12	A&M 15293
9/26/92	86	16↑		4 99.9° F		$12	A&M 0005

As A Child (4)
As Girls Go (4)
Bad Wisdom (4)
Big Space (3)
Blood Makes Noise (4)
Blood Sings (4)
Book Of Dreams (3)
Calypso (2)

Cracking (1)
Fancy Poultry (medley) (2)
Fat Man & Dancing Girl (4)
Fifty-Fifty Chance (4)
Freeze Tag (1)
Gypsy (3)
(If You Were) In My Movie (4)
In Liverpool (4)

In The Eye (3)
Institution Green (3)
Ironbound (medley) (2)
Knight Moves (1)
Language (2)
Luka (2) *3*
Marlene On The Wall (1)
Men In A War (3)

Neighborhood Girls (1)
Night Vision (2)
99.9° F (4)
Pilgrimage (3)
Predictions (4)
Queen And The Soldier (1)
Rock In This Pocket (Song Of David) (4)

Room Off The Street (4)
Rusted Pipe (3)
Small Blue Thing (1)
Solitude Standing (2) *94*
Some Journey (1)
Song Of Sand (4)
Straight Lines (1)

Those Whole Girls (Run In Grace) (3)
Tired Of Sleeping (3)
Tom's Diner (2)
Undertow (1)
When Heroes Go Down (4)
Wooden Horse (Caspar Hauser's Song) (2)

VEGA, Tata
Born Carmen Rosa Vega on 10/7/51 in Queens, New York. Popular Contemporary Gospel artist.

4/21/79	170	8		1 Try My Love		$8	Tamla 360

Come On And Try My Love
Get It Up For Love

Gonna Do My Best To Love You
I Just Keep Thinking About You Baby

I Need You Now
If Love Must Go

In The Morning
Magic Feeling

Whopper Bopper Show Stopper

VELEZ, Martha
Soul singer/actress. Starred in the Broadway production of *Hair*.

5/15/76	153	17		1 Escape From Babylon		$8	Sire 7515
				produced by Bob Marley			

Bend Down Low
Come On In

Disco Night
Get Up Stand Up

Happiness
Money Man

There You Are
Wild Bird

VELVET UNDERGROUND, The
Seminal-rock group formed in 1964 in New York City by Lou Reed and John Cale. From 1965-67, managed by pop culture artist Andy Warhol and featured Nico (vocalist/model/actress; b: Christa Paffgen in Cologne, West Germany on 10/16/39; d: 7/18/88 of a cerebral hemorrhage after a bicycle accident). Various personnel; Cale left band in March 1968, Reed by August 1970.

5/13/67	171	13		1 The Velvet Underground & Nico		$100	Verve 5008
				produced by Andy Warhol			
3/16/68	199	2		2 White Light/White Heat		$40	Verve 5046
3/9/85	85	13		3 VU	[E]	$8	Verve 823721
				collection of previously unreleased material from 1968-69			
4/20/85	197	2		4 The Velvet Underground	[R]	$8	Verve 815454
				originally released in March 1969			

Afterhours (4)
All Tomorrow's Parties (1)
Andy's Chest (3)
Beginning To See The Light (4)
Black Angel's Death Song (1)
Candy Says (4)

European Son To Delmore Schwartz (1)
Femme Fatale (1)
Foggy Notion (3)
Gift, The (2)
Here She Comes Now (2)
Heroin (1)
I Can't Stand It (3)

I Heard Her Call My Name (2)
I'll Be Your Mirror (1)
I'm Set Free (4)
I'm Sticking With You (3)
I'm Waiting For The Man (1)
Jesus (4)
Lady Godiva's Operation (2)
Lisa Says (3)

Murder Mystery (4)
Ocean (3)
One Of These Days (3)
Pale Blue Eyes (4)
Run, Run, Run (1)
She's My Best Friend (3)
Sister Ray (2)
Some Kinda Love (4)

Stephanie Says (3)
Sunday Morning (1)
Temptation Inside Your Heart (3)
That's The Story Of My Life (4)
There She Goes Again (1)
Venus In Furs (1)

What Goes On (4)
White Light/White Heat (2)

★★24★★ VENTURES, The
Guitar-based instrumental rock and roll band formed in the Seattle/Tacoma, Washington area. Consisted of guitarists Nokie Edwards (bass; b: 5/9/39), Bob Bogle (lead; b: 1/16/37) and Don Wilson (rhythm; b: 2/10/37), and drummer Howie Johnson (d: 1988). First recorded for own Blue Horizon label in 1959. Johnson was injured in an auto accident and was replaced by Mel Taylor in 1961. Taylor formed Mel Taylor & The Dynamics in 1973, returned in 1978. Edwards left in 1967, replaced by Gerry McGee. Edwards returned in 1972 and then left again in 1985. Added keyboardist John Durrill in 1969. Latest recordings feature Bogle, Wilson, Taylor and McGee. Group still active into the '90s; extremely popular in Japan.

12/5/60+	11	37		1 Walk Don't Run	[I]	$30	Dolton 8003
6/26/61	39	14		2 Another Smash!!!	[I]	$30	Dolton 8006
9/18/61	105	14		3 The Ventures	[I]	$20	Dolton 8004

DEBUT DATE	PEAK POS	WKS CHR	GOLD	ARTIST — Album Title	$	Label & Number
				VENTURES, The — Cont'd		
10/2/61	94	17		4 The Colorful Ventures .... [I]	$20	Dolton 8008
1/20/62	24	29		5 Twist With The Ventures .... [I]	$20	Dolton 8010
5/19/62	40	11		6 The Ventures' Twist Party, Vol. 2 .... [I]	$20	Dolton 8014
8/11/62	45	12		7 Mashed Potatoes And Gravy .... [I]	$20	Dolton 8016
11/24/62	93	8		8 Going To The Ventures Dance Party! .... [I]	$20	Dolton 8017
1/5/63	8	40	●	**9 The Ventures play Telstar, The Lonely Bull** .... [I]	$20	Dolton 8019
5/4/63	30	28		10 "Surfing" .... [I]	$20	Dolton 8022
6/1/63	91	8		11 Bobby Vee Meets The Ventures	$20	Liberty 7289
				BOBBY VEE/THE VENTURES		
6/8/63	101	14		12 The Ventures Play The Country Classics.................. [I]	$20	Dolton 8023
8/31/63	30	33		13 Let's Go! .... [I]	$20	Dolton 8024
1/25/64	27	18		14 (The) Ventures In Space .... [I]	$20	Dolton 8027
7/18/64	32	19		15 The Fabulous Ventures .... [I]	$20	Dolton 8029
10/10/64	17	24		16 Walk, Don't Run, Vol. 2 .... [I]	$20	Dolton 8031
2/13/65	31	24		17 The Ventures Knock Me Out! .... [I]	$20	Dolton 8033
6/19/65	27	30		18 The Ventures On Stage .... [I-L]	$20	Dolton 8035
8/7/65	96	13		19 Play Guitar with the Ventures .... [I-T]	$25	Dolton 16501
				how to play lead, bass and rhythm guitar		
9/25/65	16	35		20 The Ventures a go-go .... [I]	$15	Dolton 8037
2/12/66	33	22		21 Where The Action Is .... [I]	$15	Dolton 8040
3/5/66	42	21		22 The Ventures/Batman Theme .... [I]	$20	Dolton 8042
6/11/66	39	25		23 Go With The Ventures! .... [I]	$15	Dolton 8045
9/17/66	33	26		24 Wild Things! .... [I]	$15	Dolton 8047
2/18/67	57	26		25 Guitar Freakout .... [I]	$15	Dolton 8050
6/3/67	69	15		26 Super Psychedelics .... [I]	$15	Liberty 8052
9/2/67	50	44	●	27 Golden Greats By The Ventures .... [I]	$12	Liberty 8053
12/23/67+	55	21		28 $1,000,000.00 Weekend .... [I]	$12	Liberty 8054
5/25/68	169	6		29 Flights Of Fantasy .... [I]	$15	Liberty 8055
8/24/68	128	9		30 The Horse .... [I]	$15	Liberty 8057
1/18/69	157	14		31 Underground Fire .... [I]	$15	Liberty 8059
5/10/69	11	24	●	32 Hawaii Five-O .... [I]	$10	Liberty 8061
12/13/69+	81	12		33 Swamp Rock .... [I]	$12	Liberty 8062
3/14/70	154	5		34 More Golden Greats .... [I]	$10	Liberty 8060
10/10/70	91	21		35 The Ventures 10th Anniversary Album .... [I]	$12	Liberty 35000 [2]
1/15/72	195	3		36 Theme From Shaft .... [I]	$10	United Art. 5547
3/18/72	146	3		37 Joy/The Ventures play the classics .... [I]	$10	United Art. 5575

Action (21)
Action Plus (21)
Ad-Venture (23)
Apache (9,27)
Apache '65 (18)
(Baby) Hully Gully (7)
Aquarius (medley) (32)
Bach: Bach's Prelude (37)
Bach: Joy (Jesu Joy Of Man's Desiring) (37)
Bad Moon Rising (medley) (35)
Ballad Of Bonnie And Clyde (29)
Barefoot Adventure (10)
Bat, The (14)
Batman Theme (22)
Beethoven: Elise (37)
Beethoven: Melody Of Joy (from Beethoven's 9th Symphony) (37)
Beethoven: Sonata In C# Minor (37)
Besame Mucho (6)
Beyond The Reef (2)
Bird Rockers (1)
Blowin' In The Wind (medley) (35)
Blue Moon (4) **54**
Blue Skies (4)
Blue Star (16)
Blue Tail Fly (6)
Blue Tango (2)
Bluebird (6)
Bluer Than Blue (4)
Born To Be Wild (31)
Born To Lose (12)
Bridge Over Troubled Water (35)
Bulldog (2)
Bumble Bee (18)
Bumble Bee Twist (18)
By The Time I Get To Phoenix (3)
Calcutta (9)
California Dreamin' (23)

Candy Man (11)
Cape, The (22)
Caravan (1,11,18)
Carry Me Back (33)
Catfish Mud Dance (33)
Changing Tides (10)
Cherries Jubilee (36)
Cherry Pink And Apple Blossom White (4)
Choo Choo Train (30)
Classical Gas (34)
Come September, Theme From (8)
Cookout Freakout On Lookout Mountain (25)
Counterpoint (6)
Country Funk And The Canned Head (31)
Crazy Horse (30)
Creeper, The (16)
Cruel Sea (15)
Cruncher (10)
Cry Like A Baby (29)
Dark Eyes Twist (6)
Deep, Deep In The Water (36)
Delilah (35)
Detour (8)
Diamond Head (16) **70**
Diamonds (10)
Dizzy (32)
Don't Give In To Him (32)
Don't Think Twice, It's All Right (medley) (35)
00-711 (22)
Down On Me (32)
Driving Guitars (5,18)
Eight Miles High (23)
El Watusi (13)
Eleanor Rigby (35)
Eleventh Hour (15)
Embers In E Minor (31)
Endless Dream (26)
Escape (23)
Everybody's Talkin' (35)
Exploration In Terror (14)
Fear (14)

Fever (21)
Fire (31)
Flights Of Fantasy (29)
Fly Away (29)
Fourth Dimension (14)
Frankie And Johnny (23)
Fugitive (15)
Fuzzy And Wild (24)
Gallop, The (30)
Galveston (32)
Games People Play (32)
Gandy Dancer (8)
Georgy Girl (28)
Get Smart Theme (22)
(Ghost) Riders In The Sky (31)
Gimme Some Lovin' (36)
Ginchy (2)
Ginza Lights (23)
Go (23)
Go Go Dancer (20)
Go Go Guitar (20)
Go Go Slow (20)
Gone, Gone, Gone (17)
Good Lovin' (23)
Good Morning Starshine (35)
Good Thing (25)
Goodnight Irene (11)
Gravy (For My Mashed Potatoes) (7)
Grazing In The Grass (30,34)
Green Grass (23)
Green Hornet "66" (22)
Green Leaves Of Summer (4)
Green Light (29)
Green Onions (9,34)
Green River (33)
Greenfields (4)
Gringo (5)
Groovin' (28)
Guitar Freakout (25)
Guitar Psychedelics (25)
Guitar Twist (5)
Gully-Ver (8)
Gumbo (33)

Gypsys, Tramps And Thieves (36)
Hang On Sloopy (My Girl Sloopy) (21)
Hanky Panky (24)
Happy Together (26)
Harlem Nocturne (5)
Hawaii Five-O (32,34) **4**
Hawaiian War Chant (8)
He Never Came Back (14)
Heavies, The (10)
Here Comes The Judge (30)
Hernando's Hideaway (7)
Hey Jude (35)
High And Dry (25)
Higher Than Thou (31)
Home (1)
Honeycomb (1)
Honky Tonk (1,27)
Honky Tonk Women (33)
Horse, The (30)
Horse Power (30)
Hot Line (32)
Hot Pastrami (13)
Hot Summer (Asian Mashed) (7)
House Of The Rising Sun (16,34)
How Now Wild Cow (24)
I Can Hear Music (32)
(I Can't Get No) Satisfaction (20)
I Can't Stop Loving You (12)
I Feel Fine (17)
I Like It Like That (20)
I Walk The Line (12)
I'm A Believer (25)
I'm A Man (36)
I'm Gonna Sit Right Down And Write Myself A Letter (11)
If I'm Right Or Wrong (11)
"In" Crowd (20)
Indian Sun (36)
Innermotion Faze (29)
Instant Guitars (6)

Instant Mashed (7)
Intruder, The (8)
Jambalaya (33)
Joker's Wild (22)
Josie (2)
Journey To The Stars (15,18)
Jumpin' Jack Flash (30)
Kandy Koncoction (26)
Ketelbey: In A Persian Market (37)
Kicking Around (6)
La Bamba (20)
Land Of 1,000 Dances (medley) (30)
Last Date (2)
Last Night (9)
Let It Be (35)
Let The Sunshine In (medley) (32)
Let There Be Drums (9)
Let's Go (13,27)
Let's Twist Again (5)
Letter, The (32)
Licking Stick-Licking Stick (30)
Lies (21)
Light My Fire (31)
Limbo Rock (8)
Linda Lu (11)
Little Bit Me, A Little Bit You (26)
Little Bit Of Action (21)
Lolita Ya-Ya (8) **61**
Lonely Bull (9,27)
Lonely Girl (17)
Lonely Heart (2)
Lonely Sea (10)
Lonesome Town (3)
Louie Louie (20)
Love Goddess Of Venus (14)
Love Is Blue (34)
Love Potion Number Nine (17)
Love Shower (29)
Lovesick Blues (12)

Lovin' Things (32)
Lucille (7)
Lullaby Of The Leaves (2,18) **69**
MacArthur Park (35)
Man From U.N.C.L.E. (22)
Mariner No. 4 (17)
Mashed Potato Time (7)
McCoy, The (1)
Meet Mister Callahan (2)
Memphis (13,19,27)
Mexico (9)
Michelle (35)
Mighty Quinn (Quinn, The Eskimo) (29)
Mission: Impossible (34)
Mod East (25)
Monday, Monday (23)
Moon Child (31)
Moon Dawg (5)
Moon Of Manakoora (3)
More (13,34)
Morgen (1)
Movin' & Groovin' (5)
Mozart: Mozart Forty (from 40th Symphony, 1st Movement) (37)
Mozart: Mozart's Minuet (37)
Mr. Moto (1)
Muddy Mississippi Line (34)
Music To Watch Girls By (28)
My Bonnie Lies (6)
My Own True Love (Tara's Theme) (1)
Needles And Pins (6)
Never My Love (35,36)
Never On Sunday (9)
New Orleans (13)
Night Drive (8)
Night Stick (20)
Night Train (1,16)
Night Walk (16)
Niki Hoeky (33)
1999 A.D. (26)
Ninth Wave (10)

DEBUT DATE	PEAK POS	WKS CHR	GOLD	ARTIST — Album Title	$	Label & Number

VENTURES, The — Cont'd

No Matter What Shape (Your Stomach's In) (21)
No Tresspassing (1)
Nutty (21)
Ode To Billie Joe (28)
Off In The 93rds (28)
Oh, Lonesome Me (12)
Oh, Pretty Woman (17)
One Mint Julep (16)
Only The Young (15)
Opus Twist (5)
Orange Fire (4)
Out Of Limits (14,27)
Over The Mountain Across The Sea (13)
Panhandle Rag (12)
Paper Airplane (25)
Party In Laguna (10)
Peace Train (36)
Peach Fuzz (16)
Pedal Pusher (16,18)
Penetration (14)
Percolator (9)
Perfidia (3,18) **15**
Pied Piper (24)
Pink Panther Theme (15)
Pipeline (10,27)
Plaquemines Parish (33)
Poison Ivy (7)
Pretty Girls Everywhere (11)
Prokofiev: Peter And The Wolf (37)
Proud Mary (33)
Psyched-Out (26)

Psychedelic Venture (26)
Puccini: One Fine Day (Un Bel Di) (37)
Raindrops Keep Fallin' On My Head (35)
Ram-Bunk-Shush (3) **29**
Rap City (16)
Raunchy (1,19,34)
Ravel: Ravel's Pavane (37)
Ravin' Blue (15)
Raw-Hide (4)
Rebel-Rouser (27)
Red River Rock (9)
Red Top (4)
Red Wing Twist (6)
Reflections (26)
Respect (28)
Road Runner (5)
Runaway (13)
Runnin' Wild (15)
San Antonio Rose (12)
Scarborough Fair/Canticle (29)
Scratch (7)
Scratchin' (15)
Sea Of Grass (31)
Sealed With A Kiss (28)
Secret Agent Man (22) **54**
Sha La La (17)
Shaft, Theme From (36)
Shanghied (5)
She's Just My Style (21)
She's Not There (17)
Shuck, The (3)

Silver City, Theme From (4) *83*
Slaughter On Tenth Avenue (17,18) **35**
Sleep Walk (1)
Sloop John B (23)
Snoopy Vs. The Red Baron (6)
So Fine (13)
Solar Race (14)
Soul Breeze (30)
Soul Coaxing (Ame Caline) (29)
Sounds Of Silence (35)
Spinning Wheel (35)
Spooky (medley) (32)
Spudnik (7)
Standing In The Shadows Of Love (25)
Steel Guitar Rag (12)
Stop Action (21)
Stormy (medley) (32)
Stranger On The Shore (16)
Strangers In The Night (35)
Strawberry Fields Forever (26)
Sugar, Sugar (35)
Sugarfoot Rag (12)
Sukiyaki (13)
Summer In The City (24)
Summer Place, Theme From A (32) *83*
Summertime (7)
Summertime Blues (29)

Sunny (28)
Sunny River (5)
Sunshine Of Your Love (31)
Surf Rider (9)
Suspicious Minds (33)
Swamp Rock (3)
Swanee River Twist (6)
Sweet And Lovely (8)
Sweet Caroline (Good Times Never Seemed So Good) (35)
Sweet Pea (24)
Swingin' Creeper (20)
Switch, The (1)
Tall Cool One (15)
Taste Of Honey (21,34)
Tchaikovsky: Swan Lake (37)
Telstar (9,27)
Ten Over (10)
Tequila (9,19,27)
These Boots Are Made For Walkin' (33)
This Is Where Friendship Ends (11)
Those Were The Days (35)
3's A Crowd (21)
Thunder Cloud (36)
Tight Fit (36)
Tip-Toe Thru' The Tulips With Me (30)
To Sir, With Love (28)
Tomorrow's Love (17)
Torquay (3,34)
Traces (medley) (32)

Trambone (2)
Twilight Zone (14)
Twist, The (5)
Twisted (6)
Two Divided By Love (36)
Twomp, The (6)
Underground Fire (31)
Up, Up, And Away (22,35)
Up, Up And Down (31)
Ups 'N Downs (3)
Uptight (Everything's Alright) (28)
Vampcamp (22)
Venus (8)
Vibrations (26)
Wabash Cannonball (12)
Wack Wack (25)
Wah-Watusi (7)
Wailin' (3)
Walk--Don't Run (1,18,19,27,30) **2**
Walk-Don't Run '64 (16) **8**
Walk Right Back (11)
Walk Right In (13)
Walkin' With Pluto (15)
Walking The Carpet (29)
War Of The Satellites (14)
Weight, The (31)
Western Union (26)
What Else Is New (11)
What Now My Love (28)
Wheels (2)
When You Walk In The Room (17)

White Silver Sands (4)
Whittier Blvd. (20)
Who'll Stop The Rain (medley) (35)
Wild And Wooly (24)
Wild Angels, Theme From The (25)
Wild Child (24)
Wild Night (11)
Wild Thing (24)
Wild Trip (7)
Wildcat (24)
Wildwood Flower (12)
Windy (28)
Windy And Warm (10)
Wipe Out (13,18,27)
Wooly Bully (20)
Work Song (7)
Ya Ya Wobble (8)
Yellow Bird (4)
Yellow Jacket (4,18)
Yesterday (37)
You Are My Sunshine (12)
Zocko (22)

VERA, Billy, & The Beaters

Billy was born William McCord, Jr. on 5/28/44 in Riverside, California; raised in Westchester County, New York. Wrote hits for many pop, R&B and country artists. In the film *Buckaroo Banzai* and HBO movie *Baja Oklahoma*. Formed The Beaters (an R&B-based, 10-piece band) in Los Angeles in 1979.

5/16/81	**118**	10		1 Billy & The Beaters ....[L]	**$8**	Alfa 10001

BILLY & THE BEATERS

12/6/86+	**15**	26	●	2 By Request (The Best Of Billy Vera & The Beaters) .... [E-L]	**$8**	Rhino 70858

7 of 9 tracks recorded at The Roxy in Hollywood in 1981

At This Moment (1,2) *1*
Corner Of The Night (1,2)

Here Comes The Dawn Again (1,2)
Hopeless Romantic (2)

I Can Take Care Of Myself (1,2) *39*

Millie, Make Some Chili (1,2)
Peanut Butter (2)

Someone Will School You, Someone Will Cool You (1,2)

Strange Things Happen (1,2)
Strollin' With Bones (1)

VERLAINE, Tom

Born Thomas Miller on 12/13/49 in Mt. Morris, New Jersey. Lead singer of Television.

10/10/81	**177**	3		Dreamtime	**$8**	Warner 3539

Always
Blue Robe

Down On The Farm
Fragile

Future In Noise
Mary Marie

Mr Blur
Penetration

There's A Reason
Without A Word

VICIOUS BASE

Vicious Base is rap duo: D.J. Lace & M.C. Madness, produced by D.J. Magic Mike.

1/26/91	**153**	22		Back To Haunt You!	**$12**	Cheetah 9404

VICIOUS BASE Featuring D.J. MAGIC MIKE!

All Wild D.J.'s He Will Tame
Are You Ready
Back To Haunt You
Break, The

Comin On Strong
Get Laid, Get Funked
Hard To Keep A Good
Rhyme Down

It's Automatic (includes 2 versions)
Magic Meets Lace
Meeting, The

Nice & Nasty
No Stop To The Madness
Party With Peace Of Mind
Royalty's Arrived

Sorry, Wrong Beat
Vicious Groove
You Want Bass

VICTORY

German hard-rock band fronted by Spain-born, Switzerland-raised vocalist Fernando Garcia.

5/6/89	**182**	5		Culture Killed The Native	**$8**	Rhino 70844

Always The Same
Don't Tell No Lies
Let It Rock On

Lost In The Night
More And More

Never Satisfied
On The Loose

Power Strikes The Earth
So They Run

Standing On The Edge Of Time
Warning, The

★★417★★ VILLAGE PEOPLE

Campy, New York City disco group formed by French producer Jacques Morali (d: 11/15/91 [age 44] of AIDS). Consisted of Victor Willis (lead singer), Randy Jones, David Hodo, Felipe Rose, Glenn Hughes and Alexander Briley. Willis replaced by Ray Simpson (brother of Valerie Simpson of Ashford & Simpson) in late 1979. Group appeared in the film *Can't Stop The Music* (1980).

10/1/77+	**54**	86	●	1 Village People	**$8**	Casablanca 7064
3/25/78	**24**	69	▲	2 Macho Man	**$8**	Casablanca 7096
10/21/78+	**3**	45	▲	3 Cruisin'	**$8**	Casablanca 7118
4/14/79	**8**	21	▲	4 Go West	**$8**	Casablanca 7144
10/20/79	**32**	20	●	5 Live and Sleazy ....[L]	**$10**	Casablanca 7183 [2]

record 1: live; record 2: studio

6/21/80	**47**	12		6 Can't Stop The Music ....[S]	**$8**	Casablanca 7220

includes "Give Me A Break" & "Sophistication" by Ritchie Family and "Samantha" & "Sound Of The City" by David London

8/1/81	**138**	4		7 Renaissance	**$8**	RCA 4105

Action Man (7)
Big Mac (7)
Can't Stop The Music (6)
Citizens Of The World (4)
Diet (7)

(Do You Wanna) Spend The Night (7)
Fire Island (1,5)
Fireman (7)
5 O'Clock In The Morning (7)
Food Fight (7)

Get Away Holiday (4)
Go West (4) *45*
Hot Cop (3,5)
I Ain't Got Nobody (medley) (2)

I Am What I Am (5)
I Love You To Death (6)
I Wanna Shake Your Hand (4)
I'm A Cruiser (medley) (3)

In Hollywood (Everybody Is A Star) (medley) (1,5)
In The Navy (4,5) *3*
Jungle City (7)
Just A Gigolo (medley) (2)

Key West (2)
Liberation (6)
Macho Man (2,5) *25*
Magic Night (6)
Manhattan Woman (4)

VILLAGE PEOPLE — Cont'd

Milkshake (6)
My Roomate (3)
Ready For The 80's (5) **52**

Rock & Roll Is Back Again (5)
San Francisco (You've Got Me) (medley) (1,5)

Save Me *[includes 2 versions]* (5)
Sleazy (5)

Sodom And Gomorrah (2)
Ups And Downs (3)
Village People (1)

Women, The (medley) (3)
Y.M.C.A. (3,5,6) **2**

VILLAGE STOMPERS, The
Greenwich Village, New York Dixieland-styled band.

| 11/2/63 | 5 | 30 | | 1 **Washington Square** .... [I] | $12 | Epic 26078 |
| 4/25/64 | 139 | 3 | | 2 More Sounds of Washington Square .... [I] | $12 | Epic 26090 |

Bel Mir Bist Du Schon (2)
Blowin' In The Wind (1)
Blue Grass (1)
Bridges Of Budapest (2)
Cold Steel Canyons (1)

Dominique (2)
Don't Think Twice, It's All Right (2)
Follow The Drinkin' Gourd (1)

Frankie And Johnny (2)
Goodnight, Irene (2)
Gotta Travel On (2)
Green, Green (1)
Haunted House Blues (2)

If I Had A Hammer (1)
La-Dee-Da Song (2)
Melodie D'Amour (2)
Midnight In Moscow (1)
Mountain Greenery (2)

Poet And The Prophet (1)
Saints, The (2)
Tie Me Kangaroo Down, Sport (1)
Walk Right In (1)

Washington Square (1) **2**
We Can't Stop Singin' (1)

VINCENT, Gene, and His Blue Caps
Born Vincent Eugene Craddock on 2/11/35 in Norfolk, Virginia; died from an ulcer hemorrhage on 10/12/71. Innovative rock and roll singer/songwriter/guitarist. Injured left leg in motorcycle accident in 1953, had to wear steel brace thereafter. Formed the Blue Caps in Norfolk in 1956. Appeared in films *The Girl Can't Help It* and *Hot Rod Gang*. To England from 1960-67. Injured in car crash that killed Eddie Cochran in England in 1960.

| 9/29/56 | 16 | 2 | | Bluejean Bop! .... | $250 | Capitol 764 |

Ain't She Sweet
Bluejean Bop 49
Bop Street

I Flipped
Jezebel

Jump Back, Honey, Jump Back

Jumps, Giggles And Shouts
Peg O' My Heart

That Old Gang Of Mine
Up A Lazy River

Waltz Of The Wind
Who Slapped John

VINCENT, Vinnie, Invasion
Rock quartet led by Vincent (Kiss guitarist 1982-83), formed in 1984. Includes: Dana Strum, Bobby Rock and vocalist Mark Slaughter (joined in 1987). Robert Fleischman sang lead vocals on their first album. Strum and Slaughter left in 1989 to form Slaughter.

| 9/20/86 | 64 | 29 | | 1 Vinnie Vincent Invasion .... | $8 | Chrysalis 41529 |
| 5/21/88 | 64 | 15 | | 2 All Systems Go .... | $8 | Chrysalis 41626 |

Animal (1)
Ashes To Ashes (2)
Baby-O (1)
Back On The Streets (1)

Boyz Are Gonna Rock (1)
Breakout (2)
Burn (2)
Deeper And Deeper (2)

Dirty Rhythm (2)
Do You Wanna Make Love (1)
Ecstasy (2)
Heavy Pettin (2)

I Wanna Be Your Victim (1)
Invasion (1)
Let Freedom Rock (2)
Love Kills (2)

Naughty Naughty (2)
No Substitute (1)
Shoot U Full Of Love (1)
That Time Of Year (2)

Twisted (1)

★★94★★ VINTON, Bobby
Born Stanley Robert Vinton on 4/16/35 in Canonsburg, Pennsylvania. Father was a bandleader. Formed own band while in high school; toured as backing band for Dick Clark's "Caravan of Stars" in 1960. Left band for a singing career in 1962. Own musical variety TV series from 1975-78.

8/4/62	5	27		1 **Roses Are Red**	$15	Epic 26020
1/5/63	137	2		2 Bobby Vinton sings the Big Ones	$15	Epic 26035
8/10/63	10	33		3 **Blue Velvet**	$12	Epic 26068
2/1/64	8	28		4 **There! I've Said It Again**	$12	Epic 26081
7/25/64	31	12		5 Tell Me Why	$12	Epic 26113
10/3/64+	12	38	●	6 Bobby Vinton's Greatest Hits .... [G]	$12	Epic 26098
1/16/65	18	13		7 Mr. Lonely	$12	Epic 26136
7/3/65	116	5		8 Bobby Vinton Sings for Lonely Nights	$12	Epic 26154
2/12/66	110	5		9 Satin Pillows and Careless	$12	Epic 26182
12/16/67+	41	33		10 Please Love Me Forever	$12	Epic 26341
6/15/68	164	8		11 Take Good Care Of My Baby	$12	Epic 26382
1/4/69	21	24		12 I Love How You Love Me	$12	Epic 26437
6/14/69	69	12		13 Vinton	$12	Epic 26471
1/17/70	138	8		14 Bobby Vinton's Greatest Hits Of Love .... [K]	$12	Epic 26517
4/11/70	90	6		15 My Elusive Dreams	$12	Epic 26540
4/8/72	72	15		16 Ev'ry Day Of My Life	$8	Epic 31286
7/29/72	77	14		17 Sealed With A Kiss	$8	Epic 31642
11/25/72+	119	16		18 Bobby Vinton's All-Time Greatest Hits .... [G]	$10	Epic 31487 [2]
11/30/74+	16	22	●	19 Melodies Of Love	$8	ABC 851
12/7/74	109	5		20 With Love .... [K]	$8	Epic 32921
6/28/75	154	5		21 Bobby Vinton Sings The Golden Decade Of Love .... [K]	$10	Epic 33468 [2]
				songs from the 1950s		
7/19/75	108	5		22 Heart Of Hearts	$8	ABC 891
12/27/75+	161	7		23 The Bobby Vinton Show	$8	ABC 924
6/11/77	183	2		24 The Name Is Love	$8	ABC 981

Adios Amigo (22)
After Loving You (10)
Ain't That Lovin' You (24)
All Alone Am I (8)
All My Todays (24)
All The King's Horses (And All The King's Men) (9)
Always, Always (Yesterday's Love Song) (7)
Always In My Heart (1)
Am I Blue (3)
Am I Losing You (19)
And I Love You So (16,20,23)
Are You Sincere (13)
Autumn Leaves (2)
Baby I'm Yours (17)
Baby Take Me In Your Arms (15)

Baby, When It Comes To Loving You (24)
Bad Bad Leroy Brown (23)
Be My Love (2)
Because Of You (2)
Beer Barrel Polka (22) **33**
Bitter Teardrops (9)
Blue, Blue Day (3)
Blue Hawaii (3)
Blue Moon (3)
Blue On Blue (3,6,18) **3**
Blue Skies (3)
Blue Velvet (3,6,18) **1**
Blueberry Hill (3)
Bouquet Of Roses (10)
Build Me Up Buttercup (23)
Careless (9)
Charlie (12)
Clinging Vine (20) **17**

Come Softly To Me (17)
Coming Home Soldier (18) **11**
Crying (1)
Days Of Sand And Shovels (13,14,18) **34**
Dick And Jane (19) *flip*
Earth Angel (Will You Be Mine) (21)
End Of The World (17,21)
Every Day Of My Life (16,18) **24**
Everyone's Gone To The Moon (9)
Feelings (22)
First Time Ever I Saw Your Face) (17)
For All We Know (14)
For Once In My Life (12)

Forever Yours I Remain (7)
Forget Me Not (11)
Godfather, Love Theme From The (17)
Going Steady With A Heartache (9)
Gone (From My Heart) (11,21)
Goodnight My Love (Pleasant Dreams) (21)
Grass Is Always Greener (7)
Great Pretender (21)
Greenfields (17)
Halfway To Paradise (12,14,18) **23**
Have I Told You Lately That I Love You? (1)

Have You Ever Been Lonely (Have You Ever Been Blue?) (8)
Godfather, Love Theme From (17)
He'll Have To Go (2)
Heaven's Gonna Miss You (11)
Hello Loneliness (8)
Help Me Make It Through The Night (23)
Her Name Is Love (24)
Here In My Heart (19)
Hold Me, Thrill Me, Kiss Me (24)
Hurt (20)
I Apologize (11)
I Can Dream, Can't I? (4)
I Can't Believe That It's All Over (20)
I Can't Help It (1)

I Can't Stop Loving You (1)
I Fall To Pieces (1)
I Honestly Love You (19)
I Love How You Love Me (12,14,18) **9**
I Love You Much Too Much (5)
I Love You The Way You Are (2,6,20) **38**
I Remember Loving You (24)
I Remember You (4)
I Wanna Be Loved (5)
I Want To Spend My Life With You (19)
I Will Follow You (15)
I Won't Cry Anymore (16)
I Won't Give Up (22)
I'll Be Loving You (19)

VINTON, Bobby — Cont'd

I'll Make You My Baby (16,18)
I'll Never Fall In Love Again (15)
I'll Never Smile Again (7)
I'll Remember ..see: In The Still Of The Night
I'll Walk Alone (8)
I'm Comin' Home, Girl (16)
I'm Gettin' Sentimental Over You (2)
I'm Leaving It Up To You (17)
I'm Walkin' (23)
If (4)
If Ever I Would Leave You (15)
If I Didn't Care (12)
If I Give My Heart To You (1)
If You Love Me, Really Love Me (5)
Imagination Is A Magic Dream (5)
In The Still Of The Night (8,21)
It's A Sin To Tell A Lie (13)
It's All In The Game (10,21)
It's Better To Have Loved (7)
It's No Sin (12)
It's The Talk Of The Town (10)
Just A Dream (21)
Just A Little Lovin' (Early In The Mornin') (16)
Just As Much As Ever (10,14) **24**
Killing Me Softly With His Song (23)

Laughing On The Outside (Crying On The Inside) (7)
Lavender Blue (4)
Leaving On A Jet Plane (15)
Let's Kiss And Make Up (6) **38**
Let's Sing A Song (16)
Life Goes On (7)
Little Barefoot Boy (11)
Little Miss Blue (3)
L-O-N-E-L-Y (8) **22**
Lonely Street (8)
Long Lonely Nights (8,18) **17**
Love Makes Everything Better (24)
Love Me With All Your Heart (10)
Lovely Lady (22)
May You Always (13)
Maybe You'll Be There (3)
Middle Of The Night (13)
Misty Blue (16)
Moody (20)
Most Beautiful Girl (19)
Mr. Blue (3,21)
Mr. Lonely (1,6,7,18) **1**
My Blue Heaven (3)
My Elusive Dreams (15,18) **46**
My Foolish Heart (4)
My Gypsy Love (19)
My Heart Belongs To Only You (4,6,18) **9**
My Heart Cries For You (2)
My Melody Of Love (19) **3**
My Song (22)

My Song Of Love (10)
My Special Angel (21)
My Way Of Life (11)
Never Ending Song Of Love (19)
Night Life (8)
No Arms Can Ever Hold You (13,18) **93**
Oh, How I Miss You Tonight (8)
Once More With Feeling (24)
Only Love Can Break A Heart (24) **99**
Only You (And You Alone) (21)
Our Day Will Come (17)
Over The Mountain (Across The Sea) (6,18,21) **21**
P.S. I Love You (10)
Perfect Woman (15)
Petticoat White (Summer Sky Blue) (9) **81**
Please Help Me, I'm Falling (1)
Please Love Me Forever (10,14,18) **6**
Polka Pose (22)
Pretty Girl Is Like A Melody (5)
Rain Rain Go Away (2,6,18) **12**
Raindrops Keep Fallin' On My Head (15)
Ramblin' Rose (2)
Roses Are Red (My Love) (1,6,18) **1**

Runaway (23)
Satin (7)
Satin Pillows (9) **23**
Saturday Night (Is The Loneliest Night Of The Week) (8)
Save The Last Dance For Me (12)
Sealed With A Kiss (17,20) **99**
Seasons In The Sun (20)
Sentimental Me (1,11,14)
Serenade Of The Bells (11)
Shangri-La (12)
She Loves Me (16)
She's Gotta Be A Saint (20)
Silhouettes (21)
Sincerely (21)
So Many Lonely Girls (8)
Some Kind Of Wonderful (17)
Some Of These Days (5)
Somebody's Breakin' My Heart (17)
Someday (You'll Want Me To Want You) (9)
Someone I Used To Know (7)
Something (15)
Somewhere Along The Way (5)
Song Sung Blue (17)
(Speak Softly Love) ..see: Godfather, Love Theme From The
St. Louis Blues (3)
Stand By Your Man (13)
Take Good Care Of My Baby (11,14) **33**

Teardrops (21)
Tears On My Pillow (21)
Tell Me Why (5,6,18) **13**
There Goes My Heart (5)
There Goes That Song Again (5)
There! I've Said It Again (4,6,18) **1**
Thing Called Sadness (7)
This Guy's In Love With You (13)
Those Were The Days (12)
Thousand Miles Away (21)
Till (12,21)
Tina (7)
To Be Alone (11)
To Each His Own (4)
To Know You Is To Love You (13,14,18) **34**
To Think You've Chosen Me (11)
Together (12)
Too Young (4)
Traces (15)
Travelin' Band (23)
Trouble Is My Middle Name (6) **33**
True Love (5)
Try A Little Tenderness (4)
Trying (4)
Twelfth Of Never (2,21)
Two Purple Shadows (9)
Unchained Melody (4)
United We Stand (23)
Wanted (14)
Warm And Tender (4)
Way We Were (23)

When I Fall In Love (13,14)
When I Lost You (5)
When Will I Be Loved (23)
When You Love (20)
(Where Do I Begin) Love Story (23)
Where Were You All Of My Life (24)
Who's Sorry Now (10)
Whose Garden Was This (16)
Why Can't I Get Over You (22)
Why Don't You Believe Me (12)
Wooden Heart (22) **58**
You Are Love (24)
You Can Do It To Me Anytime (16)
You Own My Heart (9)
You Were Only Fooling (2)
You'll Never Know (19)
You're Nobody 'Till Somebody Loves You (4)
You've Got Your Momma's Eyes (22)
Young Love (10)

VIO-LENCE
Thrash-rock quintet from California's Bay Area — Sean Killian, lead vocals.

| 8/20/88 | 154 | 6 | | Eternal Nightmare | $8 | Mechanic 42187 |

Bodies On Bodies
Calling In The Coroner
Eternal Nightmare
Kill On Command
Phobophobia
Serial Killer
T.D.S. (Take It As You Will)

VIOLENT FEMMES
Punk-folk trio from Milwaukee, Wisconsin: Gordon Gano (vocals, rhythm guitar), Brian Ritchie (bass, vocals) and Victor DeLorenzo (drums, vocals). Discovered by Pretenders' guitarist James Honeyman-Scott.

2/15/86	84	24	1	The Blind Leading The Naked	$8	Slash 25340
2/4/89	93	13	2	3	$8	Slash 25819
5/18/91	141	5	3	Why Do Birds Sing?	$12	Slash 26476
8/3/91	171	7 ▲	4	Violent Femmes .... [R]	$12	Slash 23845

their first album, originally released in 1982; CD contains 2 bonus tracks

Add It Up (4)
American Music (3)
Blister In The Sun (4)
Breakin' Hearts (1)
Candlelight Song (1)
Children Of The Revolution (1)
Cold Canyon (1)
Confessions (4)
Dating Days (2)
Do You Really Want To Hurt Me (3)
Faith (1)
Fat (2)
Flamingo Baby (3)
Fool In The Full Moon (2)
Gimme The Car (4)
Girl Trouble (3)
Gone Daddy Gone (4)
Good Feeling (4)
Good Friend (1)
He Likes Me (3)
Heartache (1)
Hey Nonny, Nonny (3)
I Held Her In My Arms (1)
I'm Free (3)
Just Like My Father (2)
Kiss Off (1)
Lack Of Knowledge (3)
Lies (2)
Life Is A Scream (3)
Look Like That (1)
Love & Me Make Three (1)
More Money Tonight (3)
Mother Of A Girl (2)
Nightmares (2)
No Killing (1)
Nothing Worth Living For (2)
Old Mother Reagan (1)
Out The Window (3)
Outside The Palace (1)
Please Do Not Go (4)
Promise (4)
Prove My Love (4)
See My Ships (2)
Special (1)
Telephone Book (2)
To The Kill (4)
Two People (1)
Ugly (4)
Used To Be (3)
World We're Living In (2)

VISAGE
British dance-rock group formed by vocalist Steve Strange. Guitarist Midge Ure was a member of Ultravox.

| 8/8/81 | 178 | 4 | | Visage .... [M] | $8 | Polydor 501 |

Blocks On Blocks
Fade To Grey
Frequency 7
Tar
We Move

VISCOUNTS, The
New Jersey instrumental quintet: Harry Haller (tenor saxophone), brothers Bobby (guitar) and Joe Spievak (bass), Larry Vecchio (organ) and Clark Smith (drums).

| 1/29/66 | 144 | 2 | | Harlem Nocturne .... [I] | $30 | Amy 8008 |

Along The Navajo Trail
Chug A Lug
Dig
Harlem Nocturne 39
I Cover The Waterfront
Opus #1
September Song
Sophisticated Lady
Summertime
Touch, The
Viscount Rock
When The Saints Go Marching In

VITALE, Joe
Last name pronounced: Vee-TAH-lay. Native of Dundalk, Maryland. Discovered singing as a child in 1953 by Eddie Fisher; performed with Fisher, billed as his singing kid brother. Drummer for Cameo/Parkway Records (1966). Drummer for Ronnie Dove (1968-79). Percussion/keyboard work with Joe Walsh & the Eagles.

| 7/4/81 | 181 | 3 | | Plantation Harbor | $8 | Asylum 529 |

Bamboo Jungle
Cabin Weirdos, Theme From
I'm Flyin'
Lady On The Rock
Laugh-Laugh
Man Gonna Love You
Never Gonna Leave You Alone (Crazy 'Bout You Baby)
Plantation Harbor
Sailor Man

VITAMIN Z
Pop band founded by Sheffield, England natives Geoff Barradale (vocals) and Nick Lockwood (guitar). Trio with David Rhodes in 1984. By 1989, Rhodes left, Dennis Smith and Steve Ferrera added.

| 8/10/85 | 183 | 3 | | Rites Of Passage | $8 | Geffen 24057 |

Angela
Anybody Out There?
Burning Flame 73
Casablanca
Circus Ring
Every Time That I See You
Hi Hi Friend
Something We Can Do

DEBUT DATE	PEAK POS	WKS CHR	GOLD	ARTIST — Album Title	$	Label & Number

VIXEN

Los Angeles-based, female heavy-metal quartet: Janet Kuehnemund, Janet Gardner (vocals), Roxy Petrucci and Share Pedersen (who was part of Contraband in 1991).

10/1/88+	41	40	●	1 Vixen	$8	EMI-Man. 46991
8/18/90	52	16		2 Rev It Up	$12	EMI 92923

American Dream (1)
Bad Reputation (2)
Cruisin' (1)
Cryin' (1) 22

Desperate (1)
Edge Of A Broken Heart (1) 26
Fallen Hero (1)

Hard 16 (2)
Hellraisers (1)
How Much Love (2) 44
I Want You To Rock Me (1)

It Wouldn't Be Love (2)
Love Is A Killer (2) 71
Love Made Me (1)
Not A Minute Too Soon (2)

One Night Alone (1)
Only A Heartbeat Away (2)
Rev It Up (2)
Streets In Paradise (2)

Waiting (1)
Wrecking Ball (2)

VOGUES, The

Vocal group formed in Turtle Creek, Pennsylvania in 1960. Consisted of Bill Burkette (lead), Hugh Geyer and Chuck Blasko (tenors) and Don Miller (baritone). Met in high school.

2/12/66	137	7		1 Five O'Clock World	$25	Co & Ce 1230
9/7/68	29	30		2 Turn Around, Look At Me	$12	Reprise 6314
2/15/69	30	23		3 Till	$12	Reprise 6326
9/27/69	115	9		4 Memories	$12	Reprise 6347
1/10/70	148	9		5 The Vogues' Greatest Hits	[G] $12	Reprise 6371

Come Into My Arms Again (2)
Dream Baby (How Long Must I Dream) (2)
Earth Angel (Will You Be Mine) (1)
Everyone's Gone To The Moon (1)
Five O'Clock World (1,5) 4
Goodnight My Love (1)
Green Fields (5) 92

Humpty Dumpty (1)
I Keep It Hid (2)
I Will (3)
I'll Know My Love (By The Way She Talks) (3)
I've Got My Eyes On You (3)
If I Loved You (4)
Impossible Dream (2)
It's Getting Better (2)
Just Say Goodbye (2)

Let's Hang On (1)
Love Is A Many-Splendored Thing (4)
Magic Town (5) 21
Make The World Go Away (1)
Moments To Remember (4,5) 47
My Special Angel (2,5) 7
My Troubles Are Not At End (1)

No, Not Much (3,5) 34
No Sun Today (2)
On Broadway (1)
Once In A While (4)
One More Sunrise (2)
Over And Over Again (1)
P.S. I Love You (4)
Run Baby Run (1)
See That Girl? (5)
Shangri-La (4)

She Is Today (2)
She Was Too Good To Me (3)
Since I Don't Have You (4)
So This Is Love (2)
Standing On The Corner (4)
Sun Shines Out Of Your Shoes (3)
Sunday And Me (1)
Taste Of Honey (3)
Then (2)

Thousand Miles Away (1)
Till (3,5) 27
Time After Time (4)
Turn Around, Look At Me (2,5) 7
Woman Helping Man (3,5) 47
You're The One (5) 4

VOICES OF EAST HARLEM, The

Group consisting of twenty black singers, aged 12-21. Appeared at the Moratorium Concert in Madison Square Garden with Blood, Sweat And Tears and Harry Belafonte.

10/10/70	191	3		Right On Be Free	$8	Elektra 74080

For What It's Worth
Gotta Be A Change

Let It Be Me
Music In The Air

No No No
Oh Yeah

Proud Mary
Right On Be Free

Run Shaker Life
Simple Song Of Freedom

VOIVOD

Hard-rock quartet from Jonquiere, Quebec: Denis Belanger (vocals), Denis D'Amour, Jean-Yves Theriault and Michel Langevin.

12/16/89+	114	16		Nothingface	$8	Mechanic 6326

Astronomy Domine
Inner Combustion

Into My Hypercube
Missing Sequence

Nothingface
Pre-Ignition

Sub-Effect
Unknown Knows

X-Ray Mirror

VOLLENWEIDER, Andreas

Electro-acoustic harpist from Zurich, Switzerland.

12/1/84+	121	18	●	1 ...Behind The Gardens-Behind The Wall-Under The Tree...	[I] $8	CBS 37793
12/15/84+	149	15	●	2 Caverna Magica (...Under The Tree-In The Cave...)	[I] $8	CBS 37827
3/2/85	76	39	●	3 White Winds	[I] $8	FM/CBS 39963
8/2/86	60	39	●	4 Down To The Moon	[I] $8	FM/CBS 42255
4/15/89	52	19	●	5 Dancing With The Lion	[I] $8	Columbia 45154
2/29/92	117	5		6 Book Of Roses	[I] $12	Columbia 48601

Afternoon (1)
Ahgoh! (2)
And The Long Shadows (5)
Ascent From The Circle (5)
Behind The Gardens-Behind The Wall-Under The Tree (1)
Belladonna (2)
Birds Of Tilmun (6)
Book Of Roses (6)
Brothership (3)
Canopy Choir (medley) (3)
Caverna Magica (2)
Chanson De L'Heure Bleue (6)
Con Chiglia (medley) (2)

Czippa And The Ursanian Girl (6)
Dance Of The Masks (5)
Dancing With The Lion (5)
Down To The Moon (4)
Drown In Pale Light (4)
Five Curtains (6)
Five Planets (medley) (3)
Flight Feet & Root Hands (3)
Garden Of My Childhood (5)
Geastrum Coronatum (medley) (2)
Glass Hall (Choose The Crystal) (medley) (3)
Grand Ball Of The Duljas (6)

Hall Of The Mosaics (Meeting You) (medley) (3)
Hall Of The Stairs (medley) (3)
Hands And Clouds (1)
Hippolyte (6)
Hirzel (6)
Huiziopochtli (2)
Hush - Patience At Bamboo Forest (4)
In Doga Gamee (6)
In The Woods Of Kroandal (6)
Jours D'Amour (6)
Jugglers In Obsidian (6)
La Lune Et L'Enfant (4)

La Paix Verde (medley) (3)
La Strega (Her Journey To The Grand Ball) (5)
Letters To A Young Rose (6)
Lion And Sheep (1)
Lunar Pond (2)
Mandragora (2)
Manto's Arrow And The Sphinx (6)
Micro-Macro (1)
Moon Dance (4)
Moonlight, Wrapped Around Us (1)
Morning At Boma Park (6)
Night Fire Dance (4)
Passage To Promise (6)

Pearls & Tears (6)
Phases Of The Three Moons (3)
Play Of The Five Balls (medley) (3)
Pyramid-In The Wood-In The Bright Light (1)
Quiet Observer (4)
Schajah Saretosh (2)
Secret, The Candle, And Love (4)
See, My Love... (5)
Sena Stanjena? (2)
Silver Dew, Golden Grass (5)
Silver Wheel (3)
Sisterseed (2)

Skin And Skin (1)
Steam Forest (4)
Still Life (5)
Stone (Close-Up) (3)
Sunday (1)
Three Silver Ladies Dance (4)
Trilogy (At The Water Magic Gardens) (medley) (3)
Unto The Burning Circle (5)
Water Moon (4)
White Boat (First View) (medley) (3)
White Winds (medley) (3)
Woman And The Stone (3)

VOUDOURIS, Roger

Born on 12/29/54 in Sacramento, California. Pop singer/songwriter/guitarist.

7/7/79	171	3		Radio Dream	$8	Warner 3290

Anything From Anyone

Does Our Love (Depend On The Night)

Get Used To It 21
Just What It Takes

Next Time Around
Radio Dream

We Can't Stay Like This Forever

We Only Dance 'Cause We Have To

VOYAGE

European disco group — Sylvia Mason, lead singer.

4/8/78	40	21		1 Voyage	$8	Marlin 2213
12/16/78+	47	27		2 Fly Away	$8	Marlin 2225

Bayou Village (1)
Eastern Trip (2)
From East To West (1)

Golden Eldorado (2)
Gone With The Music (2)
Kechak Fantasy (2)

Lady America (1)
Latin Odyssey (1)
Let's Fly Away (2)
Orient Express (1)

Point Zero (1)
Scotch Machine (1)

Souvenirs (2) 41
Tahiti, Tahiti (2)

V.S.O.P.

V.S.O.P.: Very Special Onetime Performance. All-star jazz quintet: Herbie Hancock (piano), Freddie Hubbard (trumpet), Wayne Shorter (sax), Ron Carter (bass) and Tony Williams (drums).

11/12/77	123	5		The Quintet	[I-L] $10	Columbia 34976 [2]

Byrdlike
Darts

Dolores
Jessica

Lawra
Little Waltz

One Of A Kind
Third Plane

WAGNER, Jack
Born on 10/3/59 in Washington, Missouri. Played Frisco Jones on the TV soap opera *General Hospital*; joined the cast of *Santa Barbara* in 1991.

9/22/84+	44	29		1 All I Need .... [M]	$8	Qwest 25089
10/19/85	150	15		2 Lighting Up The Night	$8	Qwest 25318
5/2/87	151	8		3 Don't Give Up Your Day Job	$8	Qwest 25562

All I Need (1) 2   I'll Be There (2)   It's What We Don't Say (3)   Love Can Take Us All The Way (2)   Premonition (1)   Too Young (2) 52
Back Home Again (3)   If She Loves Like She Looks (2)   Just Tell Her (2)   Love...Find It (3)   Sneak Attack (1)   Weatherman Says (3) 67
Common Man (3)   Keep Holdin' On (2)   Sneakin' Suspicions (3)   With Your Eyes (2)
Easy Way Out (3)   Island Fever (3)   Let's Start All Over (2)   Lovers In The Night (3)   Tell Him (That You Won't Go) (1)
I Never Said Goodbye (2)   It's Been A Long Time (3)   Lighting Up The Night (2)   Make Me Believe It (1)

WAGONER, Porter
Born on 8/12/27 in West Plains, Missouri. Country singer; has charted over 25 top 10 country hits (includes duets with Dolly Parton). Host of his own TV variety series beginning in 1960.

7/1/67	199	1		1 The Cold Hard Facts Of Life	$15	RCA 3797
3/15/69	161	8		2 The Carroll County Accident	$12	RCA 4116
3/22/69	184	4		3 Just The Two Of Us *	$15	RCA 4039
8/16/69	162	5		4 Always, Always *	$15	RCA 4186
4/4/70	137	7		5 Porter Wayne And Dolly Rebecca *	$12	RCA 4305
5/16/70	190	2		6 You Got-ta Have A License	$10	RCA 4286
10/10/70	191	2		7 Once More *	$15	RCA 4388
3/13/71	142	3		8 Two Of A Kind *	$12	RCA 4490

*PORTER WAGONER & DOLLY PARTON

Afraid To Love Again (3)   Each Season Changes You (5)   I Know You're Married But I Love You Still (7)   Little Boy's Prayer (6)   Run That By Me One More Time (5)   Two Of A Kind (8)
All I Need Is You (8)   Fairchild (6)   Malena (4)   Shopworn (1)   Walk On Fool (6)
Always, Always (4)   Fallen Leaves (2)   I Lived So Fast And Hard (2)   Mendy Never Sleeps (5)   Silver Sandals (3)   Way He Said Your Name (5)
Anything's Better Than Nothing (4)   Fight And Scratch (7)   I Washed My Face In The Morning Dew (3)   Milwaukee, Here I Come (4)   Sing Me Back Home (2)   We Can't Let This Happen To Us (5)
Banks Of The Ohio (2)   First Mrs. Jones (1)   I'll Get Ahead Some Day (1)   My Hands Are Tied (4)   Sleep (1)   We'll Get Ahead Someday (3)
Barefoot Nellie (2)   Flame, The (8)   I'm Wasting Your Time And You're Wasting Mine (4)   My Special Prayer Request (6)   Slip Away Today (3)   When You're Hot You're Hot (6)
Before Our Weakness Gets Too Strong (7)   Forty Miles From Poplar Bluff (5,6)   If I Could Only Start Over (1)   No Love Left (5)   Somewhere Between (3)   Why Don't You Haul Off & Love Me (4)
Black Jack's Bar (2)   Good As Gold (4)   Is It Real (8)   No Reason To Hurry Home (4)   Sorrow Overtakes The Wine (2)   Words And Music (1)
Carroll County Accident (2) 92   Good Understanding (7)   It Might As Well Be Me (3)   Oh, The Pain Of Loving You (8)   Southern Bound (6)   World Needs A Washin' (1)
Closer By The Hour (3)   Holding On To Nothin' (3)   Jeannie's Afraid Of The Dark (3)   Once More (7)   Stranger's Story (6)   You Got-ta Have A License (6)
Cold Hard Facts Of Life (1)   House Where Love Lives (4)   Julie (1)   One Day At A Time (7)   There Never Was A Time (1)   Your Mother's Eyes (2)
Curse Of The Wild Weed Flower (8)   Hundred Dollar Funeral (1)   Just Someone I Used To Know (5)   Party, The (3)   There'll Be Love (8)   Yours Love (4)
Daddy Was An Old Time Preacher Man (7)   I Can (3)   Just The Two Of Us (3)   Possum Holler (8)   Thoughtfulness (7)
Dark End Of The Street (3)   I Don't Believe You've Met My Baby (4)   King Of The Cannon County Hills (2)   Ragged Angel (7)   Today, Tomorrow And Forever (8)
I Just Can't Let You Say Goodbye (1)   Let's Live For Tonight (7)   Rocky Top (2)   Tomorrow Is Forever (5)
Roses Out Of Season (6)   Tragic Romance (1)
Try Being Lonely (1)

WAIKIKIS, The
Belgian instrumental group.

1/16/65	93	9		Hawaii Tattoo .... [I]	$10	Kapp 3366

Aloha Parade   **Hawaii Tattoo 33**   Honolulu Rag   I'll Remember Sweet Hawaii   Mauna Loa   Tahiti Tamoure
Carnival Of Venice   Hilo Kiss   Honolulu Rose   March Of The Beachcombers   Pacific Punch   Tiki Tiki Puka

WAILERS, The
Consisted of Kent Morrill (lead vocals, keyboards), Rich Dangel (guitar), Mark Marush (saxophone), Buck Ormsby (bass) and Mike Burk (drums). Later '60s, Dangel, Burk and Marush left, replaced by Ron Gardner (vocals, keyboards, sax), Neil Anderson (guitar) and Dave Roland (drums). Disbanded in 1968.

6/27/64	127	6		Tall Cool One	$30	Imperial 12262

title song originally released in 1959 on Golden Crest 518; the Imperial recording is a new version

Doin' The Seaside   Hokey   Louie Louie   Party Time U.S.A.   Shake Down   Tough Walk
Frenzy   Isabella   Mashi   Seattle   Tall Cool One   We're Going Surfin'

WAILERS, The — see MARLEY, Bob

WAINWRIGHT, Loudon III
Born on 9/5/46 in Chapel Hill, North Carolina. Satirical folk singer/songwriter. Acted in three episodes of *M*A*S*H* as Capt. Calvin Spaulding. Appeared in films *The Slugger's Wife* and *Jacknife*.

3/3/73	102	13		1 Album III	$12	Columbia 31462
3/15/75	156	5		2 Unrequited	$8	Columbia 33369
6/19/76	188	4		3 T Shirt	$8	Arista 4063

Absence Makes The Heart Grow Fonder (2)   **Dead Skunk (1) 16**   Just Like President Thieu (3)   New Paint (1)   Say That You Love Me (1)   Unrequited To The Nth Degree (2)
At Both Ends (3)   Drinking Song (1)   Kick In The Head (3)   Old Paint (2)   Smokey Joe's Cafe (1)   Untitled (2)
B Side (1)   East Indian Princess (1)   Kings And Queens (2)   On The Rocks (2)   Summer's Almost Over (3)   Whatever Happened To Us (2)
Bicentennial (3)   Guru (2)   Lowly Tourist (2)   Prince Hal's Dirge (3)   Sweet Nothings (2)   Wine With Dinner (3)
California Prison Blues (3)   Hey Packy (3)   Mr. Guilty (2)   Reciprocity (3)   Talking Big Apple 75 (3)
Crime Of Passion (2)   Hollywood Hopeful (3)   Muse Blues (1)   Red Guitar (1)   Trilogy (Circa 1967) (1)
Hometeam Crowd (3)   Needless To Say (1)   Rufus Is A Tit Man (2)

WAITE, John
Born on 7/4/55 in Lancashire, England. Lead singer of The Babys and Bad English.

7/17/82	68	23		1 Ignition	$8	Chrysalis 1376
7/14/84	10	43	●	2 No Brakes	$8	EMI America 17124
8/31/85	36	16		3 Mask Of Smiles	$8	EMI America 17164

DEBUT DATE	PEAK POS	WKS CHR	GOLD	ARTIST — Album Title	$	Label & Number

WAITE, John — Cont'd

DEBUT DATE	PEAK POS	WKS CHR	ARTIST — Album Title	$	Label & Number
7/11/87	77	12	4 Rover's Return	$8	EMI America 17227

title is name of pub on English TV soap opera *Coronation Street*

Act Of Love (4)	Don't Lose Any Sleep (4) *81*	I'm Still In Love (1)	No Brakes (3)	These Times Are Hard For
Ain't That Peculiar (3)	Dreamtime (medley) (2)	Just Like Lovers (3)	Restless Heart (2) *59*	Lovers (1) *53*
Be My Baby Tonight (1)	Encircled (4)	Laydown (3)	Saturday Night (2)	Welcome To Paradise (3) *85*
Big Time For Love (4)	Euroshima (2)	Love Collision (2)	Shake It Up (medley) (2)	White Heat (1)
Change (1) *54*	Every Step Of The Way	Lust For Life (3)	She's The One (4)	Wild Life (1)
Choice, The (3)	(3) *25*	Make It Happen (1)	Sometimes (4)	Wild One (4)
Dark Side Of The Sun (2)	For Your Love (2)	Missing You (1) *1*	Tears (2) *37*	Woman's Touch (4)
Desperate Love (1)	Going To The Top (1)	Mr. Wonderful (1)	Temptation (1)	You're The One (3)

WAITRESSES, The

Akron, Ohio-based, pop-rock sextet — Patty Donahue, lead singer.

DEBUT DATE	PEAK POS	WKS CHR	ARTIST — Album Title	$	Label & Number
2/6/82	41	24	1 Wasn't Tomorrow Wonderful?	$8	Polydor 6346
12/18/82+	128	10	2 I Could Rule The World If I Could Only Get The Parts .... [M]	$8	Polydor 507
6/4/83	155	5	3 Bruiseology	$8	Polydor 810980

Bread And Butter (2)	Go On (1)	I Know What Boys Like	No Guilt (1)	Smartest Person I Know (2)	Wasn't Tomorrow
Bruiseology (3)	Heat Night (1)	(1) *62*	Open City (1)	Spin (3)	Wonderful? (1)
Christmas Wrapping (2)	I Could Rule The World If I	It's My Car (1)	Pleasure (3)	Square Pegs (1)	Wise Up (1)
Everything's Wrong If My	Could Only Get The Parts	Jimmy Tomorrow (1)	Pussy Strut (1)	They're All Out Of Liquor,
Hair Is Wrong (3)	(2)	Luxury (3)	Quit (1)	Let's Find Another Party (3)
Girl's Gotta Do (3)		Make The Weather (3)	Redland (1)	Thinking About Sex Again (3)

WAITS, Tom

Born on 12/7/49, in the back of a taxi cab, in Pomona, California. Gravelly-voiced monologue song stylist/actor/songwriter. Among his many film appearances are *Rumblefish*, *Down By Law*, *Ironweed* and *Dracula*. Married Irish playwright Kathleen Brennan on 12/31/81 with whom he co-wrote the 1988 musical *Frank's Wild Years*. Composed the film soundtracks *One From The Heart* and *Night On Earth*.

DEBUT DATE	PEAK POS	WKS CHR	ARTIST — Album Title	$	Label & Number
11/29/75	164	6	1 Nighthawks At The Diner .... [L]	$12	Asylum 2008 [2]
11/6/76	89	5	2 Small Change	$10	Asylum 1078
10/22/77	113	8	3 Foreign Affairs	$10	Asylum 1117
11/18/78	181	4	4 Blue Valentine	$10	Asylum 162
10/4/80	96	10	5 Heartattack And Vine	$8	Asylum 295
10/29/83	167	7	6 Swordfishtrombones	$8	Island 90095
11/16/85	181	7	7 Rain Dogs	$8	Island 90299
9/26/87	115	10	8 Franks Wild Years	$8	Island 90572

songs from the Waits' stage musical in which he starred

DEBUT DATE	PEAK POS	WKS CHR	ARTIST — Album Title	$	Label & Number
10/8/88	152	6	9 Big Time .... [L]	$8	Island 90987

recorded live in America and Europe

DEBUT DATE	PEAK POS	WKS CHR	ARTIST — Album Title	$	Label & Number
9/26/92	176	3	10 Bone Machine..	$12	Island 512580

All Stripped Down (10)	Diamonds & Gold (7)	I Don't Wanna Grow Up (10)	Midtown (7)	Romeo Is Bleeding (4)	Telephone Call From
Anywhere I Lay My Head (7)	Dirt In The Ground (10)	I Never Talk To Strangers (3)	More Than Rain (8)	Ruby's Arms (5)	Istanbul (8,9)
Bad Liver And A Broken	Down, Down, Down (6)	I Wish I Was In New Orleans	Mr. Siegal (5)	Saving All My Love For You	Temptation (8)
Heart (2)	Downtown (5)	(2)	Murder In The Red Barn (10)	(5)	That Feel (10)
Barber Shop (3)	Downtown Train (7)	I'll Be Gone (8)	Muriel (3)	Shore Leave (6)	'Til The Money Runs Out (5)
Better Off Without A Wife (1)	Earth Died Screaming (10)	I'll Take New York (8)	Nighthawk Postcards (From	Sight For Sore Eyes (3)	Time (7,9)
Big Black Mariah (7,9)	Eggs And Sausage (In A	In Shades (5)	Easy Street) (1)	Singapore (7)	Tom Traubert's Blues (2)
Big Joe And Phantom 309 (1)	Cadillac With Susan	In The Colosseum (10)	9th & Hennepin (7)	16 Shells From A	Town With No Cheer (6)
Black Wings (10)	Michelson) (1)	In The Neighborhood (6)	Nobody (1)	Thirty-Ought-Six (6,9)	Train Song (8,9)
Blind Love (7)	Emotional Weather Report	Innocent When You Dream	Ocean Doesn't Want Me (10)	Small Change (2)	Trouble's Braids (6)
Blow Wind Blow (8)	(1)	*[includes 2 versions]* (8)	On A Foggy Night (1)	Soldier's Things (6)	$29.00 (4)
Blue Valentines (4)	Falling Down (9)	Invitation To The Blues (2)	On The Nickel (5)	Somewhere (4)	Underground (6)
Bride Of Rain Dog (7)	Foreign Affair (3)	Jack & Neal (medley) (3)	One That Got Away (2)	Spare Parts - I & II (1)	Union Square (7)
Burma Shave (3)	Frank's Wild Years (6)	Jersey Girl (5)	Pasties And A G-String (2)	Step Right Up (2)	Walking Spanish (7)
California Here I Come	Franks Theme (6)	Jesus Gonna Be Here (10)	Piano Has Been Drinking (2)	Straight To The Top	Warm Beer And Cold
(medley) (6)	Gin Soaked Boy (6)	Jitterbug Boy (2)	Please Wake Me Up (8)	*[includes 2 versions]* (8)	Women (1)
Cemetery Polka (7)	Goin' Out West (10)	Jockey Full Of Bourbon (7)	Potter's Field (3)	Strange Weather (9)	Way Down In The Hole (8,9)
Christmas Card From A	Gun Street Girl (7,9)	Johnsburg, Illinois (7)	Putnam County (1)	Such A Scream (10)	Whistle Down The Wind (10)
Hooker In Minneapolis (4)	Hang Down Your Head (7)	Just Another Sucker On The	Rain Dogs (7,9)	Sweet Little Bullet From A	Whistlin' Past The
Cinny's Waltz (3)	Hang On St. Christopher (8)	Vine (6)	Rainbirds (6)	Pretty Blue Gun (4)	Graveyard (4)
Clap Hands (7)	Heartattack And Vine (5)	Kentucky Avenue (4)	Red Shoes (9)	Swordfishtrombone (6)	Who Are You (10)
Cold Cold Ground (8,9)	I Can't Wait To Get Off Work	Let Me Get Up On It (10)	Red Shoes By The Drugstore	Tango Till They're Sore (7)	Wrong Side Of The Road (4)
Dave The Butcher (6)	(2)	Little Rain (10)	(4)		Yesterday Is Here (8)

WAKEMAN, Rick

Born on 5/18/49 in London. Former keyboardist of Strawbs and Yes. In 1989, joined group Anderson, Bruford, Wakeman, Howe — all formerly with Yes. Also a popular Contemporary Christian rock artist.

DEBUT DATE	PEAK POS	WKS CHR	GOLD	ARTIST — Album Title	$	Label & Number
3/24/73	30	45	●	1 The Six Wives of Henry VIII................................... [I]	$8	A&M 4361
6/15/74	3	27	●	2 Journey To The Centre Of The Earth............................. [L]	$8	A&M 3621

with the London Symphony Orchestra

DEBUT DATE	PEAK POS	WKS CHR	ARTIST — Album Title	$	Label & Number
4/19/75	21	15	3 The Myths and Legends of King Arthur and the Knights of the Round Table	$8	A&M 4515

with the English Chamber Choir and orchestra

DEBUT DATE	PEAK POS	WKS CHR	ARTIST — Album Title	$	Label & Number
5/15/76	67	8	4 No Earthly Connection	$8	A&M 4583

with the English Rock Ensemble

DEBUT DATE	PEAK POS	WKS CHR	ARTIST — Album Title	$	Label & Number
2/26/77	126	7	5 White Rock .... [S-I]	$8	A&M 4614

film based on the Innsbruck Winter Games

DEBUT DATE	PEAK POS	WKS CHR	ARTIST — Album Title	$	Label & Number
12/17/77+	128	8	6 Rick Wakeman's Criminal Record .... [I]	$8	A&M 4660

with fellow Yes members Chris Squire and Alan White

DEBUT DATE	PEAK POS	WKS CHR	ARTIST — Album Title	$	Label & Number
7/21/79	170	5	7 Rhapsodies .... [I]	$10	A&M 6501 [2]

After The Ball (5)	Anne Of Cleves (1)	Breathalyser, The (6)	Flacons De Neige (7)	Ice Run (5)	Lax'x (5)
Animal Showdown (Yes We	Arthur (3)	Catherine Howard (1)	Flasher, The (6)	Jane Seymour (1)	Loser, The (5)
Have No Bananas) (7)	Battle, The (2)	Catherine Of Aragon (1)	Forest, The (2)	Journey, The (2)	Lost Cycle (4)
Anne Boleyn 'The Day Thou	Big Ben (7)	Catherine Parr (1)	Front Line (7)	Judas Iscariot (6)	March Of The Gladiators (7)
Gavest Lord Hath Ended'	Birdman Of Alcatraz (6)	Chamber Of Horrors (6)	Guinevere (3)	Lady Of The Lake (3)	Merlin The Magician (3)
(1)	Bombay Duck (7)	Crime Of Passion (6)	Half Holiday (7)	Last Battle (3)	Montezuma's Revenge (7)

DEBUT DATE	PEAK POS	WKS CHR	G O L D	ARTIST — Album Title	$	Label & Number

WAKEMAN, Rick — Cont'd

Music Reincarnate Medley (4)	Prisoner, The (4)	Sea Horses (7)	Sir Lancelot And The Black Knight (3)	Summertime (7)
Palais (7)	Pulse, The (7)	Searching For Gold (5)	Stand-By (7)	Swan Lager (7)
Pedra Da Gavea (7)	Recollection (2)	Shoot, The (5)	Statue Of Justice (6)	White Rock (5)
	Rhapsody In Blue (7)	Sir Galahad (3)		Wooly Willy Tango (7)

WALDEN, Narada Michael

Born Michael Walden on 4/23/52 in Kalamazoo, Michigan. Black singer/songwriter/drummer/producer. With John McLaughlin's Mahavishnu Orchestra from 1974-76. With Jeff Beck in 1975. Solo artist and much session work since 1976. Producer for Whitney Houston.

3/10/79	103	16		1 Awakening	$8	Atlantic 19222
1/5/80	74	19		2 The Dance Of Life	$8	Atlantic 19259
10/18/80	103	8		3 Victory	$8	Atlantic 19279
6/5/82	135	6		4 Confidence	$8	Atlantic 19351

Alone Without You (3)	Crazy For Ya (2)	I Don't Want Nobody Else (To Dance With You) (1) 47	Listen To Me (1)	Summer Lady (4)	Will You Ever Know (1)
Awakening, The (1)	Dance Of Life (2)		Love Me Only (1)	Take It To The Bossman (3)	You Ought To Love Me (3)
Awakening Suite Part I (1)	Full & Satisfied (1)		Lovin' You Madly (2)	They Want The Feeling (1)	You Will Find Your Way (1)
Blue Side Of Midnight (4)	Get Up! (3)	I Shoulda Loved Ya (2) 66	Lucky Fella (3)	Tonight I'm Alright (2)	You're #1 (1)
Carry On (2)	Give Your Love A Chance (1)	I Want You (3)	Real Thang (1)	Victory Suite Medley (3)	You're Soo Good (2)
Confidence (4)	Holiday (4)	I'm Ready (4)	Safe In My Arms (4)	Why Did You Turn Me On (2)	

WALKER, David T.

Born in Los Angeles. Guitarist/composer. With The Olympics and Midnighters. To New York City from 1961-66. Band director at Motown in Detroit. Much session work on the West Coast. Member of Paul Humphrey's Cool Aid Chemists and Afrique among other groups.

| 2/9/74 | 187 | 8 | | 1 Press On | [I] | $8 | Ode 77020 |
| 9/4/76 | 166 | 5 | | 2 On Love | | $8 | Ode 77035 |

Brother, Brother (1)	I Get High On You (2)	If That's The Way You Feel (1)	Let Me In Your Life (2)	Press On (1)	With A Little Help From My Friends (1)
Didn't I Blow Your Mind This Time (1)	I Got Work To Do (1)	If You Let Me (1)	Lovin' You (2)	Save Your Love For Me (1)	Work To Do ...see: I Got Work To Do
Feeling Feeling (2)	I Who Have Nothing (1)	Kinda Sorta (2)	On Love (2)	Superstition (1)	
	I Wish You Love (2)		Our Lives (2)	Windows Of The World (2)	

WALKER, Jerry Jeff

Born Paul Crosby on 3/14/42 in Oneonta, New York. Country-rock singer/songwriter. Wrote "Mr. Bojangles."

12/15/73+	160	11	●	1 Viva Terlingua!	$8	MCA 382
1/11/75	141	8		2 Walker's Collectibles	$8	MCA 450
10/4/75	119	7		3 Ridin' High	$8	MCA 2156
7/4/76	84	10		4 It's A Good Night For Singin'	$8	MCA 2202
5/28/77	60	21		5 A Man Must Carry On	$10	MCA 6003 [2]
				side 4: live recordings		
7/1/78	111	9		6 Contrary To Ordinary	$8	MCA 3041
7/19/80	185	3		7 The Best Of Jerry Jeff Walker	[G]	$8	MCA 5128
6/20/81	188	3		8 Reunion	$8	SouthCoast 5199

Backsliders Wine (1)	Got Lucky Last Night (8)	Leroy (1)	Night Rider's Lament (3)	Saturday Night Special (6)	Tryin' To Hold The Wind Up With A Sail (6)
Bittersweet (8)	Head Full Of Nothin' (4)	Like A Coat From The Cold (3)	O.D. Corral (2)	Sea Cruise Medley (5)	Up Against The Wall Red Neck (1,5,7)
Carry Me Away (6)	Hill Country Rain (7)	Like Some Song You Can't Unlearn (5)	Old Five And Dimers Like Me (4)	She Left Me Holdin' (2,8)	
Contrary To Ordinary (6)	His Heart Was So Full Of Mischief (5)		One Too Many Mornings (5)	Some Day I'll Get Out Of These Bars (4)	Very Short Time (4)
Couldn't Do Nothin' Right (4)	Honky Tonk Music (5)	London Homesick Blues (1)	Pick Up The Tempo (3,8)	Some Go Home (The Train Song) (8)	We Were Kinda Crazy Then (6)
Dear John Letter Lounge (4)	I Like To Sleep Late In The Morning (2)	Long Afternoons (5)	Pissin' In The Wind (3)	Song For The Life (5)	Well Of The Blues (2)
Deeper Than Love (6)	I Love You (3,7)	(Looking For) The Heart Of Saturday Night (4)	Pot Can't Call The Kettle Black (3,7)	Standin' At The Big Hotel (4)	What Are We Doing? (6)
Derby Day (5)	I Spent All My Money Lovin' You (6)	Luckenbach Moon (5)	Public Domain (3)	Stereo Chickens (5)	Wheel (1)
Desperados Waiting For The Train (1,7)	It Shall Be A Midnight Music (5)	Maybe Mexico (8)	Railroad Lady (5)	Stoney (4)	Will The Circle Be Unbroken? (5)
Don't It Make You Wanna Dance? (5)	It's A Good Night For Singing (4)	Mississippi You're On My Mind (3)	Rock Me Roll Me (2)	Stranger (He Was The Kind) (5)	Wingin' It Home To Texas (2)
First Showboat (2)	Jaded Lover (3)	Morning Song To Sally (8)	Rockin' Chair (5)	Suckin' A Big Bottle Of Gin (6)	Won't You Give Me One More Chance (4)
For Little Jessie (She Knows Her Daddy Sings) (8)	L.A. Freeway (5,7) 98	Mr. Bojangles (5,7) 77	Ro-Deo-Deo Cowboy (5)	Takin' It As It Comes (8)	
Get It Out (1)	Leavin' Texas (5,7)	My Buddy (5)	Roll On Down The Road (6)	Till I Gain Control Again (6)	
Gettin' By (1,7)		My Old Man (2)	Sailing (8)		
Goodbye Easy Street (3)			Salvation Army Band (2)		
			Sangria Wine (1,7)		

WALKER, Jimmie

Born on 6/25/49 in New York City. Actor/comedian. Portrayed J.J. Evans on TV's Good Times.

| 5/31/75 | 130 | 12 | | Dyn-O-Mite | [C] | $8 | Buddah 5635 |

Apollo, The	Caucasians And Other White Folk	Great Black Myth	Progress	Show Biz
Autographs	Ghetto, The	Prince And The Public	S-Cool Daze	Suburbia
Black Prince Has Arrived				

★★484★★ WALKER, Jr., & The All Stars

R&B group formed in South Bend, Indiana by Walker (born Autry DeWalt II in Blythesville, Arkansas, 1942). Included Walker (sax, vocals), Willie Woods (guitar), Vic Thomas (organ) and James Graves (drums). First recorded for Harvey in 1962. Most recent group included son Autry DeWalt, Jr. on drums.

7/10/65	108	35		1 Shotgun	$20	Soul 701
4/9/66	130	7		2 Soul Session	[I]	$20	Soul 702
9/3/66	64	13		3 Road Runner	$15	Soul 703
10/7/67	119	11		4 "Live!"	[L]	$12	Soul 705
				includes "Heart Break" by Earl Van Dyke		
2/8/69	172	4		5 Home Cookin'	$12	Soul 710
6/28/69	43	18		6 Greatest Hits	[G]	$12	Soul 718
1/17/70	92	22		7 What Does It Take To Win Your Love	$12	Soul 721
10/3/70	110	5		8 A Gasssss	$10	Soul 726
7/24/71	91	14		9 Rainbow Funk	$10	Soul 732
1/8/72	142	16		10 Moody Jr.	$10	Soul 733

WALKER, Jr., & The All Stars — Cont'd

Ain't That The Truth (1)
Ame' Cherie (Soul Darling) (3,4,7)
And When I Die (8)
Anyway You Wannta' (3)
At A Saturday Matinee (8)
Baby Ain't You Shame (5)
Baby You Know You Ain't Right (3)
Brainwasher (2)
Bristol's Way (10)
Carry Your Own Load (8)
Cleo's Back (1,4) **43**
Cleo's Mood (1,6,7) **50**
Clinging To The Thought That She's Coming Back (7)
Come See About Me (5,6) **24**

Decidedly (2)
Do The Boomerang (1) **36**
Do You See My Love (For You Growing) (8) **32**
Don't Blame The Children (10)
Eight Hour Drag (2)
Everybody Get Together (2)
Fanny Mae (5)
Feeling Alright (9)
Good Rockin' (2)
Gotta Hold On To This Feeling (7) **21**
Groove And Move (8)
Groove Thang (10)
Hewbie Steps Out (2)
Hey Jude (8)
Hip City - Pt. 1 (5)

Hip City - Pt. 2 (5,6) **31**
Holly Holy (8) **75**
Home Cookin (5,6) **42**
Honey Come Back (8)
Hot Cha (1,4,7)
How Sweet It Is (To Be Loved By You) (3,4,6,7) **18**
I Don't Want To Do Wrong (10)
I Was Made To Love Her (8)
(I'm A) Road Runner (1,3,4,6) **20**
I've Got To Find A Way To Win Maria Back (7)
Last Call (3)
Mark Anthony (Speaks) (2)
Me And My Family (10)

Money (That's What I Want) Part 1 (3,6) **52**
Monkey Jump (1)
Moody Junior (10)
Moonlight In Vermont (2,4)
Mutiny (3)
Never Can Say Goodbye (10)
Pieces Of A Man (9)
Proud Mary (7)
Psychedelic Shack (9)
Pucker Up Buttercup (3,6) **31**
Riding High On Love (8)
Right On Brothers And Sisters (3)
San-Ho-Zay (3,7)
Satan's Blues (2)

Shake And Fingerpop (1,4,6) **29**
Shake Everything (2)
Shoot Your Shot (1,6) **44**
Shotgun (1,4,6) **4**
Shut Up, Don't Interrupt Me (8)
Something (9)
Still Water Medley (10)
Sweet Daddy Deacon (5)
Sweet Soul (5,7)
Take Me Girl, I'm Ready (9) **50**
Tally Ho (1)
Teach Them To Pray (9)
These Eyes (7) **16**
These Things Will Keep Me Loving You (9)

Things I Do For You (5)
Three Four Three (2)
Tune Up (1,4)
Twist Lackawanna (3)
Us (2)
Walk In The Night (10) **46**
Way Back Home (9,10) **52**
What Does It Take (To Win Your Love) (5,6,7) **4**

WALLACE, Jerry
Born on 12/15/28 in Guilford, Missouri and raised in Glendale, Arizona. Pop-country singer/guitarist.
First recorded for Allied in 1951. Appeared on the TV shows *Night Gallery* and *Hec Ramsey*.

| 11/7/64 | 96 | 7 | | 1 In The Misty Moonlight | $20 | Challenge 619 |
| 3/3/73 | 179 | 8 | | 2 Do You Know What It's Like To Be Lonesome? | $12 | MCA 301 |

Am I That Easy To Forget (1)
Angel On My Shoulder (1)
Auf Wiedersehen (1)
Do You Know What It's Like To Be Lonesome? (2)

Empty Arms Again (1)
Even The Bad Times Are Good (1,2)
Greatest Feeling (2)
Hot Line (2)

In The Misty Moonlight (1) **19**
Just Walkin' In The Rain (1)
Love Song Of The Year (2)

Move Over (When True Love Walks By) (1)
Song That Nobody Sings (2)
Sound Of Goodbye (2)
Standing Ovation (2)

There She Goes (1) **26**
Until You (2)
Where Did He Come From? (The Ballad Of Hec Ramsey) (2)

You'll Never Know (1)

WALL OF VOODOO
Los Angeles electronic-rock group — Stanard Ridgway, lead singer.

| 10/17/81 | 177 | 2 | | 1 Dark Continent | $8 | I.R.S. 70022 |
| 1/15/83 | 45 | 23 | | 2 Call Of The West | $8 | I.R.S. 70026 |

Animal Day (1)
Back In Flesh (1)
Call Box (1-2-3) (1)
Call Of The West (2)

Crack The Bell (1)
Factory (2)
Full Of Tension (1)
Good Times (1)

Hands Of Love (2)
Look At Their Way (2)
Lost Weekend (1)
Me And My Dad (1)

Mexican Radio (2) **58**
On Interstate 15 (2)
Red Light (1)
Spy World (2)

They Don't Want Me (2)
This Way Out (1)
Tomorrow (2)
Tse Tse Fly (1)

Two Minutes Till Lunch (1)

★★272★★ WALSH, Joe
Born on 11/20/47 in Wichita, Kansas. Rock singer/songwriter/guitarist. Member of The James Gang (1969-71) and the Eagles (1975-82). Own band (1972-75), Barnstorm, featured drummer Joe Vitale and bassist Kenny Passarelli.

10/21/72+	79	29		1 Barnstorm	$8	Dunhill 50130
				LP title is also the name of Walsh's band		
6/23/73	6	54	●	2 The Smoker You Drink, The Player You Get	$8	Dunhill 50140
1/4/75	11	22	●	3 So What	$8	Dunhill 50171
4/10/76	20	18		4 You Can't Argue With A Sick Mind [L]	$8	ABC 932
6/10/78	8	27	▲	5 But Seriously, Folks...	$8	Asylum 141
10/28/78	71	7		6 The Best Of Joe Walsh [G]	$8	ABC 1083
				includes "Funk #49" and "Walk Away" by the James Gang		
5/23/81	20	18		7 There Goes The Neighborhood	$8	Asylum 523
7/9/83	48	14		8 You Bought It-You Name It	$8	Warner 23884
6/1/85	65	19		9 The Confessor	$8	Warner 25281
8/1/87	113	8		10 Got Any Gum?	$8	Warner 25606
5/18/91	112	17		11 Ordinary Average Guy	$12	Pyramid 47384

All-Night Laundry-Mat Blues (3)
All Of A Sudden (11)
Alphabetical Order (11)
At The Station (5)
Birdcall Morning (1)
Boat Weirdos, Theme From (5)
Bones (7)
Book Ends (2)
Bubbles (9)
Class Of '65 (8)
Comin' Down (1)
Confessor, The (9)
County Fair (3,6)
(Day Dream) Prayer (2)
Days Gone By (2)

Dear John (9)
Down On The Farm (7)
Dreams (3)
Falling Down (3)
15 Years (9)
Fun (10)
Gamma Goochee (11)
Giant Bohemoth (1)
Good Man Down (9)
Got Any Gum? (10)
Half Of The Time (10)
Happy Ways (2)
Help Me Thru The Night (3,4,6)
Here We Are Now (8)
Here We Go (1)
Home (1)

I Broke My Leg (9)
I Can Play That Rock & Roll (8)
I'll Tell The World About You (1)
I'm Actin' Different (11)
"I.L.B.T.'s" (8)
In My Car (10)
Indian Summer (5)
Inner Tube (5)
Island Weirdos, Theme From (8)
Life Of Illusion (7) **34**
Life's Been Good (5) **12**
Look At Us Now (11)
Love Letters (8)
Made Your Mind Up (7)

Malibu (10)
Meadows (2,4,6) **89**
Memory Lane (10)
Midnight Moodies (2)
Midnight Visitor (1)
Mother Says (1,6)
No Peace In The Jungle (10)
One And One (1)
Ordinary Average Guy (11)
Over And Over (5)
Pavane (3)
Problems (9)
Radio Song (10)
Rivers (Of The Hidden Funk) (7)
Rockets (7)

Rocky Mountain Way (2,4,6) **23**
Rosewood Bitters (9)
School Days (5)
Second Hand Store (5)
Shadows (8)
Slow Dancing (9)
Song For Emma (3)
Space Age Whiz Kids (8) **52**
Things (7)
Time (10)
Time Out (3,4,6)
Told You So (8)
Tomorrow (5)
Turn To Stone (1,3,4,6) **93**
Two Sides To Every Story (11)

Up All Night (11)
Up To Me (10)
Walk Away (4)
Welcome To The Club (3)
Where I Grew Up (Prelude To School Days) (11)
Wolf (2)
Worry Song (8)
You Might Need Somebody (11)
You Never Know (7)

WALSH, Steve
Born in St. Joseph, Missouri. Lead singer/keyboardist of Kansas.

| 2/16/80 | 124 | 6 | | Schemer-Dreamer | $8 | Kirshner 36320 |

Every Step Of The Way
Get Too Far

Just How It Feels
Schemer-Dreamer (medley)

So Many Nights
That's All Right (medley)

Wait Until Tomorrow
You Think You Got It Made

WANDERLEY, Walter
Brazilian organist/pianist/composer. Died of cancer on 9/4/86 (age 55).

| 9/3/66 | 22 | 41 | | Rain Forest [I] | $12 | Verve 8658 |

Beach Samba
Beloved Melancholy
Call Me

Cried, Cried
Cry Out Your Sadness
Girl From Ipanema

Great Love
It's Easy To Say Good-bye

Rain
Song Of The Jet

Summer Samba (So Nice) **26**
Taste Of Sadness

DEBUT DATE	PEAK POS	WKS CHR	GOLD	ARTIST — Album Title	$	Label & Number

WANG CHUNG
British pop-rock group: Jack Hues (lead singer, guitar, keyboards), Nick Feldman (bass, keyboards) and Darren Costin (drums). Costin left in 1985.

DEBUT DATE	PEAK POS	WKS CHR		ALBUM	$	Label & Number
2/25/84	30	37		1 Points On The Curve	$8	Geffen 4004
11/2/85	85	18		2 To Live and Die in L.A. .....[S]	$8	Geffen 24081
11/1/86	41	36		3 Mosaic	$8	Geffen 24115
6/10/89	123	6		4 The Warmer Side Of Cool	$8	Geffen 24222

At The Speed Of Life (4)
Betrayal (3)
Big World (4)
Black-Blue-White (2)
City Of The Angels (2)
Dance Hall Days (1) *16*
Devoted Friends (1)

Don't Be My Enemy (1) *86*
Don't Let Go (1) *38*
Even If You Dream (1)
Every Big City (2)
Everybody Have Fun Tonight (3) *2*
Eyes Of The Girl (3)

Flat Horizon (3)
Fool And His Money (3)
Games Of Power (4)
Hypnotize Me (3) *36*
Let's Go! (3) *9*
Logic And Love (4)
Look At Me Now (1)

Lullaby (2)
Praying To A New God (4) *63*
Red Stare (2)
Snakedance (4)
Swing (4)
Talk It Out (1)

Tall Trees In A Blue Sky (4)
To Live And Die In L.A. (2) *41*
True Love (1)
Wait (1,2)
Wake Up, Stop Dreaming (2)
Warmer Side Of Cool (4)

Waves, The (1)
What's So Bad About Feeling Good? (4)
When Love Looks Back At You (4)
World In Which We Live (3)

WANSEL, Dexter
Keyboardist/producer/arranger from Philadelphia.

| 4/30/77 | 168 | 3 | | 1 What The World Is Coming To | $8 | Phil. Int. 34487 |
| 4/1/78 | 139 | 6 | | 2 Voyager | $8 | Phil. Int. 34985 |

All Night Long (2)
Dance With Me Tonight (1)
Disco Lights (1)
Dreams Of Tomorrow (1)

First Light Of The Morning (1)
Going Back To Kingston Town (1)

Holdin' On (1)
I Just Want To Love You (2)
I'm In Love (2)
Latin Love (Let Me Know) (2)

Ode Infinitum (1)
Prelude #1 (1)
Solutions (2)
Time Is The Teacher (2)

Voyager (2)
What The World Is Coming To (1)

★★126★★ WAR
Band formed in Long Beach, California in 1969. Consisted of Lonnie Jordan (keyboards), Howard Scott (guitar), Charles Miller (saxophone; murdered in 1980), Morris "B.B." Dickerson (bass), Harold Brown and Thomas "Papa Dee" Allen (percussion) and Lee Oskar (harmonica). Eric Burdon's backup band until 1971. Dickerson was replaced by Luther Rabb. Jordan and Oskar also recorded solo. Alice Tweed Smyth (vocals) added in 1978. Pat Rizzo (horns) and Ron Hammond (former member of Aalon; percussion) added in 1979. Smyth left group in 1982.

5/16/70	18	27		1 Eric Burdon Declares "War"	$12	MGM 4663
12/26/70+	82	9		2 The Black-Man's Burdon	$15	MGM 4710 [2]
				above 2: ERIC BURDON AND WAR		
4/24/71	190	6		3 War	$8	United Art. 5508
11/20/71+	16	49	●	4 All Day Music	$8	United Art. 5546
11/18/72+	1²	68	●	5 The World Is A Ghetto	$8	United Art. 5652
9/1/73	6	36	●	6 Deliver The Word	$8	United Art. 128
3/23/74	13	35	●	7 War Live! .....[L]	$10	United Art. 193 [2]
7/5/75	8	31	●	8 Why Can't We Be Friends?	$8	United Art. 441
9/4/76	6	21	▲	9 Greatest Hits .....[G]	$8	United Art. 648
12/25/76+	140	5		10 Love Is All Around .....[E]	$10	ABC 988
				WAR featuring ERIC BURDON recorded 1969-70		
7/23/77	23	14	●	11 Platinum Jazz .....[K]	$10	Blue Note 690 [2]
12/3/77+	15	23	●	12 Galaxy	$8	MCA 3030
8/19/78	69	6		13 Youngblood .....[S]	$8	United Art. 904
4/14/79	41	16	●	14 The Music Band	$8	MCA 3085
12/8/79	111	13		15 The Music Band 2	$8	MCA 3193
3/20/82	48	27		16 Outlaw	$8	RCA 4208
7/23/83	164	4		17 Life (Is So Strange)	$8	RCA 4598
5/30/87	156	10		18 The Best Of War.....And More .....[G]	$8	Priority 9467

All Around The World (14)
All Day Music (4,7,9,18) *35*
Baby Brother (4)
Baby Face (She Said Do Do Do) (12)
Baby It's Cold Outside (16)
Back Home (3)
Ballero (7) *33*
Bare Back Ride (2)
Beautiful New Born Child (2)
Beetles In The Bog (5)
Bird & The Squirrel (2)
Birth (1)
Black Bird (2)
Black On Black In Black (2)
Blisters (6)
Cinco De Mayo (16)
Cisco Kid (5,7,9,18) *2*
City, Country, City (5,11,18)
Corns & Calluses (Hey Dr. Shoals) (14)
Danish Pastry (1)
Day In The Life (10)
Dedication (1)
Deliver The Word (6,11)

Don't Let No One Get You Down (8)
Don't Take It Away (15)
Fidel's Fantasy (3)
Flying Machine (The Chase) (13)
Four Cornered Room (5,11)
Galaxy (12,18) *39*
Get Down (4,7)
Good, Good Feelin' (14)
Gun (2)
Gypsy Man (6,9) *8*
H₂ Overture (6,11)
Happiness (17)
Heartbeat (medley) (8)
Hey Charlie (12)
Home Cookin' (2)
Home Dream (10)
I Got You (11)
I Have A Dream (1)
I'll Be Around (15)
I'll Take Care Of You (15)
I'm About Somebody (16)
I'm The One Who Understands (14)

In Mazatlan (8)
In Your Eyes (6)
Jimbo (2)
Jungle Medley (16)
Junk Yard (13)
Just Because (16)
Keep On Doin' (13)
Kingsmen Sign (13)
L.A. Sunshine (11) *45*
La Fiesta (8)
Lament (8)
Laurel & Hardy (2)
Leroy's Latin Lament (medley) (8)
Life (Is So Strange) (17)
Livin' In The Red (18)
Lonely Feelin' (3,7)
Lonnie Dreams (8)
Lotus Blossom (8)
Love Is All Around (10)
Low Rider (8,9,18) *7*
Magic Mountain (10)
Me And Baby Brother (6,9,18) *15*
Millionaire (14)

Mother Earth (1)
Mr. Charlie (1)
Music Band (14)
Music Band 2 (We Are The Music Band) (15)
Nappy Head (4,11)
Night People (15)
Nights In White Satin I & II (2)
Nuts, Seeds & Life (2)
Out Of Nowhere (2)
Outlaw (16) *94*
P.C. 3 (2)
Paint It Black (2,10)
Platinum Jazz (11)
Pretty Colors (2)
River Niger (11)
Roll On Kirk (1)
Searching For Youngblood & Rommel (13)
Seven Tin Soldiers (12)
Shake It Down (17)
Sing A Happy Song (13)
Slippin' Into Darkness (4,7,9,18) *16*

Slippin' Part 2 (7)
Slowly We Walk Together (11)
Smile Happy (8,11)
So (8)
Southern Part Of Texas (6,9)
Spill The Wine (1,18) *3*
Spirit (2)
Summer (9,18) *7*
Summer Dreams (17)
Sun Oh Son (3,7)
Sun/Moon (2)
Superdude (13)
Sweet Fighting Lady (12)
That's What Love Will Do (4)
There Must Be A Reason (4)
They Can't Take Away Our Music (2) *50*
This Funky Music Makes You Feel Good (13)
Tobacco Road (1,10)
U-2 Medley (17)
Vibeka (3)
W.W. III Medley (17)
Walking To War (13)

War Drums (3)
War Is Coming! War Is Coming (11)
Way We Feel (8)
Where Was You At (5)
Whose Cadillac Is That (18)
Why Can't We Be Friends? (8,9,18) *6*
World Is A Ghetto (5,9,15) *7*
You Got The Power (16) *66*
You're No Stranger (1)
Youngblood & Sybil (13)
Youngblood (Livin' In The Streets) (13)

WARD, Anita
Born on 12/20/57 in Memphis. R&B-disco vocalist. Toured in Rust College female quartet.

| 5/26/79 | 8 | 19 | | Songs Of Love | $12 | Juana 200,004 |

I Won't Stop Loving You
If I Could Feel That Old Feeling Again

Make Believe Lovers
Ring My Bell *1*

Spoiled By Your Love
Sweet Splendor

There's No Doubt About It
You Lied

WARINER, Steve
Country singer/guitarist from Kentucky. Bass player for Dottie West at age 17.

DEBUT DATE	PEAK POS	WKS CHR	GOLD	ARTIST — Album Title	$	Label & Number
10/17/87	187	2		1 Greatest Hits ....[G]	$8	MCA 42032
11/16/91	180	7		2 I Am Ready	$12	Arista 18691

Crash Course In The Blues (2) — Gone Out Of My Mind (2) — Like A River To The Sea (2) — On My Heart Again (2) — That's How You Know When Love's Right (1) — What I Didn't Do (1)
Everything's Gonna Be Alright (2) — Heart Trouble (2) — Lynda (1) — Small Town Girl (1) — Tips Of My Fingers (2) — When Will I Let Go (2)
Leave Him Out Of This (2) — My, How The Time Don't Fly (2) — Some Fools Never Learn (1) — Weekend, The (1) — Woman Loves (2)
Life's Highway (1) — Starting Over Again (1) — You Can Dream Of Me (1)

WARING, Fred, And The Pennsylvanians
Born on 6/9/1900 in Tyrone, Pennsylvania; died on 7/29/84. Glee club/bandleader from early 1920s.

DEBUT DATE	PEAK POS	WKS CHR	GOLD	ARTIST — Album Title	$	Label & Number
9/9/57	25	1		1 Fred Waring And The Pennsylvanians In Hi-Fi	$15	Capitol 845
12/23/57	6	3		2 Now Is The Caroling Season ....[X]	$12	Capitol 896
12/22/58+	19	3		3 Now Is The Caroling Season ....[X-R]	$12	Capitol 896
5/30/64	116	7		4 America, I Hear You Singing	$12	Reprise 2020

FRANK SINATRA/BING CROSBY/FRED WARING

America, I Hear You Singing! (medley) [solo: Fred] (4) — Christmas Was Meant For Children (2) — Hit The Road To Dreamland (1) — Let Us Break Bread Together (4) — Sleigh Ride (medley) (2) — Twelve Days Of Christmas (2)
Angels From The Realms Of Glory (2) — Cigarette Sweet Music And You (1) — Home In The Meadow [duet: Bing & Fred] (4) — Lolly Too Dum Dey (1) — Smoke Gets In Your Eyes (1) — Way Back Home (1)
Angels We Have Heard On High (2) — Dry Bones (1) — Hora Staccato (1) — March Of The Kings (2) — So Beats My Heart For You (1) — We Three Kings (2)
Battle Hymn Of The Republic (1) — Early American [duet: Frank & Fred] (4) — House I Live In [duet: Frank & Fred] (4) — Masters In This Hall (2) — Sometimes I Feel Like A Motherless Child (1) — Whiffenpoof Song (Baa! Baa! Baa!) (1)
Bring A Torch, Jeanette, Isabella (2) — Give Me Your Tired, Your Poor (1,4) — I Hear Music (1) — Now Is The Caroling Season (2) — Stars And Stripes Forever [solo: Fred] (4) — White Christmas (2)
Christmas Song (Merry Christmas To You) (2) — Heigh Ho The Holly (2) — I Heard The Bells On Christmas Day (2) — O Christmas Tree (2) — This Is A Great Country (medley) [duet: Bing & Fred] (4) — Winter Wonderland (2)
— Here We Come Awassailing (2) — In Sweetest Jubilee (2) — O Come, O Come Emmanuel (2) — — You Never Had It So Good (4)
— Hills Of Home [solo: Fred] (4) — In The Still Of The Night (1) — Ol' Man River (1) — This Land Is Your Land [duet: Bing & Fred] (4) — You'll Never Walk Alone (1)
— — It Was A Night Of Wonder (2) — Silver Bells (2) — — You're A Lucky Fellow, Mr. Smith [duet: Frank & Fred] (4)
— — — Sleep (1)

WARLOCK
Heavy-metal band based in Dusseldorf, Germany formed in 1982 by female lead singer Doro Pesch. In 1989, Doro recorded under first name with a new Warlock lineup.

DEBUT DATE	PEAK POS	WKS CHR	GOLD	ARTIST — Album Title	$	Label & Number
12/19/87+	80	27		Triumph And Agony	$8	Mercury 832804

All We Are — East Meets West — I Rule The Ruins — Make Time For Love — Three Minute Warning
Cold, Cold World — Fur Immer — Kiss Of Death — Metal Tango — Touch Of Evil

WARNES, Jennifer
Born in Seattle and raised in Orange County, California. Pop/MOR-styled vocalist. Lead actress in the Los Angeles production of *Hair*.

DEBUT DATE	PEAK POS	WKS CHR	GOLD	ARTIST — Album Title	$	Label & Number
2/26/77	43	18		1 Jennifer Warnes	$8	Arista 4062
6/9/79	94	23		2 Shot Through The Heart	$8	Arista 4217
2/14/87	72	21		3 Famous Blue Raincoat	$8	Cypress 661111

featuring the songs of Canadian poet/singer Leonard Cohen

Ain't No Cure For Love (3) — Daddy Don't Go (1) — Hard Times, Come Again No More (2) — Joan Of Arc (3) — Round And Round (1) — Tell Me Just One More Time (2)
Bird On A Wire (3) — Don't Lead Me On (1) — **Don't Make Me Over** (2) 67 — Love Hurts (1) — Shine A Light (1) — **When The Feeling Comes Around** (2) 45
Bring Ol' Maggie Back Home (1) — **Don't Make Me Over** (2) 67 — **I Know A Heartache When I See One** (2) 19 — Mama (1) — Shot Through The Heart (2) — You Remember Me (2)
Came So Far For Beauty (3) — Famous Blue Raincoat (3) — **I'm Dreaming** (1) 50 — O God Of Loveliness (1) — Sign On The Window (1) — You're The One (1)
Coming Back To You (3) — First We Take Manhattan (3) — I'm Restless (2) — **Right Time Of The Night** (1) 6 — Singer Must Die (3) —
— Frankie In The Rain (2) — — — Song Of Bernadette (3) —

WARRANT
Los Angeles, male hard-rock band: Jani Lane (vocals), Erik Turner (guitar), Joey Allen (guitar), Jerry Dixon (bass) and Steven Sweet (drums). Lane married Bobbie Brown, spokesmodel champion on TV's *Star Search*, on 7/27/91.

DEBUT DATE	PEAK POS	WKS CHR	GOLD	ARTIST — Album Title	$	Label & Number
3/4/89	10	65	▲²	1 Dirty Rotten Filthy Stinking Rich	$8	Columbia 44383
9/29/90	7	60	▲²	2 Cherry Pie	$12	Columbia 45487
9/12/92	25	13	●	3 Dog Eat Dog	$12	Columbia 52584

All My Bridges Are Burning (3) — **Blind Faith** (2) 88 — Hole In My Wall (3) — Love In Stereo (3) — So Damn Pretty (Should Be Against The Law) (1) — **Uncle Tom's Cabin** (2) 78
Andy Warhol Was Right (3) — Bonfire (3) — Hollywood (So Far, So Good) (3) — Machine Gun (3) — **Sometimes She Cries** (1) 20 — You're The Only Hell Your Mama Ever Raised (2)
April 2031 (3) — **Cherry Pie** (2) 10 — Mr. Rainmaker (2) — Song And Dance Man (2) — —
Bed Of Roses (2) — Cold Sweat (1) — **I Saw Red** (2) 10 — Ode To Tipper Gore (2) — Sure Feels Good To Me (2) —
Big Talk (1) 93 — D.R.F.S.R. (1) — In The Sticks (1) — Quicksand (3) — 32 Pennies (2) —
Bitter Pill (3) — **Down Boys** (1) 27 — Inside Out (3) — Ridin' High (1) — Train, Train (2) —
— **Heaven** (1) 2 — Let It Rain (3) — Sad Theresa (3) — —

★★376★★ WARREN, Rusty
Born Ilene Goldman in 1931 in New York; raised in Milton, Massachusetts. Singer/storyteller of adult comedy.

DEBUT DATE	PEAK POS	WKS CHR	GOLD	ARTIST — Album Title	$	Label & Number
11/7/60+	8	181		1 Knockers Up! ....[C]	$12	Jubilee 2029
5/8/61	55	40		2 Songs For Sinners * ....[R-C]	$12	Jubilee 2024

Rusty's first album release

DEBUT DATE	PEAK POS	WKS CHR	GOLD	ARTIST — Album Title	$	Label & Number
5/22/61	21	51		3 Sin-Sational ....[C]	$12	Jubilee 2034
12/18/61+	31	50		4 Rusty Warren Bounces Back * ....[C]	$12	Jubilee 2039
11/3/62+	22	32		5 Rusty Warren In Orbit * ....[C]	$12	Jubilee 2044
10/19/63	52	18		6 Banned In Boston? * ....[C]	$12	Jubilee 2049
1/1/66	124	7		7 More Knockers Up! * ....[C]	$12	Jubilee 2059

*no track titles listed on these albums

Frankie And Johnny (1) — I Like It Girls (3) — Let Me Entertain You (3) — Mother-Daughter Talk "Don't Do It!" (3) — Those Stairs Are Killing Me! (3)
Good Man Is Hard To Find (3) — In The Family Way (1) — Life Is Just A Bowl Of Cherries (3) — Red River Sally (1) — You're Nobody Till Somebody Loves You (1)
Growing Pains (3) — It's Mine... (3) — — Rusty For President? (3) —
— Knockers Up! (1) — — —

★★33★★ WARWICK, Dionne

Born Marie Dionne Warwick on 12/12/40 in East Orange, New Jersey. In church choir from age six. With the Drinkard Singers gospel group. Formed trio, the Gospelaires, with sister Dee Dee and their aunt Cissy Houston. Attended Hartt College Of Music, Hartford, Connecticut. Much backup studio work in New York during the late '50s. Added an "e" to her last name for a time in the early '70s. She was Burt Bacharach and Hal David's main "voice" for the songs they composed. Co-hosted TV's Solid Gold 1980-81, 1985-86. Also see the soundtracks Love Machine and The Woman In Red (Stevie Wonder).

DEBUT DATE	PEAK POS	WKS CHR	GOLD	#	Album Title	$	Label & Number
9/12/64	68	20		1	Make Way For Dionne Warwick	$15	Scepter 523
3/6/65	107	9		2	The Sensitive Sound of Dionne Warwick	$15	Scepter 528
1/1/66	45	29		3	Here I Am	$15	Scepter 531
4/16/66	76	11		4	Dionne Warwick in Paris [L]	$15	Scepter 534
1/7/67	18	66	●	5	Here Where There is Love	$12	Scepter 555
5/13/67	169	9		6	On Stage and in The Movies	$12	Scepter 559
9/16/67	22	31		7	The Windows of The World	$12	Scepter 563
11/18/67	10	69		8	Dionne Warwick's Golden Hits, Part One [G]	$12	Scepter 565
3/9/68	6	48	●	9	Valley of the Dolls	$12	Scepter 568
12/14/68+	18	39		10	Promises, Promises	$12	Scepter 571
4/5/69	11	28		11	Soulful	$12	Scepter 573
8/16/69	31	24	●	12	Dionne Warwick's Greatest Motion Picture Hits [K]	$12	Scepter 575
11/1/69	28	28		13	Dionne Warwick's Golden Hits, Part 2 [G]	$12	Scepter 577
5/2/70	23	39		14	I'll Never Fall In Love Again	$10	Scepter 581
12/12/70+	37	24		15	Very Dionne	$10	Scepter 587
10/30/71	48	17	●	16	The Dionne Warwicke Story * [L]	$12	Scepter 596 [2]
1/29/72	54	14		17	Dionne *	$10	Warner 2585
4/8/72	169	5		18	From Within * [K]	$10	Scepter 598 [2]
2/3/73	178	8		19	Just Being Myself *	$8	Warner 2658
3/8/75	167	6		20	Then Came You *	$8	Warner 2846

DIONNE WARWICKE

DEBUT DATE	PEAK POS	WKS CHR	GOLD	#	Album Title	$	Label & Number
12/6/75+	137	15		21	Track of the Cat	$8	Warner 2893
2/19/77	49	13		22	A Man And A Woman [L]	$10	HBS 996 [2]

ISAAC HAYES & DIONNE WARWICK

DEBUT DATE	PEAK POS	WKS CHR	GOLD	#	Album Title	$	Label & Number
7/2/77	188	7		23	Only Love Can Break A Heart [K]	$8	Musicor 2501
6/9/79	12	54	▲	24	Dionne	$8	Arista 4230
					produced by Barry Manilow		
8/9/80	23	25		25	No Night So Long	$8	Arista 9526
6/13/81	72	14		26	Hot! Live and Otherwise [L]	$10	Arista 8605 [2]
					3 of 4 sides are live recordings		
5/22/82	83	12		27	Friends In Love	$8	Arista 9585
10/30/82+	25	28		28	Heartbreaker	$8	Arista 9609
					produced by Barry Gibb		
10/29/83	57	17		29	How Many Times Can We Say Goodbye	$8	Arista 8104
					produced by Luther Vandross		
3/2/85	106	11		30	Finder Of Lost Loves	$8	Arista 8262
12/21/85+	12	26	●	31	Friends	$8	Arista 8398
8/22/87	56	27		32	Reservations For Two	$8	Arista 8446
12/23/89+	177	7		33	Greatest Hits 1979-1990 [G]	$8	Arista 8540
8/18/90	155	9		34	Dionne Warwick Sings Cole Porter	$12	Arista 8573
					CD includes bonus track		

After You (24) **65**
Alfie (5,12,16,26) **15**
All Kinds Of People (medley) (18)
All Of You (34)
All The Love In The World (28)
All The Time (24,33)
Another Chance To Love (32)
Another Night (7) **49**
Any Old Time Of Day (8)
Anyone Who Had A Heart (8,16,26) **8**
Anything Goes (34)
Anything You Can Do (6)
April Fools (12) **37**
Aquarius (16)
Are You There (With Another Girl) (3,13) **39**
As Long As He Needs Me (5,12)
As Long As There's An Apple Tree (9)
Balance Of Nature (17)
Battle Hymn Of The Republic (18)
Baubles, Bangles & Beads (6)
Be Aware (17)
Bedroom Eyes (30)
Beginning Of Loneliness (7) **79**
Betcha By Golly Wow (27)
Blowing In The Wind (5)

Body Language (22)
By The Time I Get To Phoenix (medley) (22)
C'est Si Bon (4)
Can't Hide Love (22,27)
Check Out Time (15)
Chocolate Chip (22)
Close Enough (32)
Come Back (19)
Come Live With Me (22)
Come Together (medley) (16)
Cry On Me (32)
Dedicate This Heart (26)
Deja Vu (24,26,33) **15**
Didn't We (14,23)
Do Right Woman - Do Right Man (11,18)
Do You Know The Way To San Jose (9,13,16,26) **10**
Don't Burn The Bridge (That Took You Across) (19)
Don't Go Breaking My Heart (3)
Don't Let My Teardrops Bother You (19)
Don't Make Me Over (8,16,26) **21**
Don't Say I Didn't Tell You So (2)
Easy Love (25,26) **62**
Even A Fool Would Let Go (26)
Everyday People (18)
Extravagant Gestures (31)
Feeling Old Feelings (24)

Feelings (medley) (22)
Finder Of Lost Loves (30)
For All We Know (23)
For Everything You Are (32)
For Once In My Life (16)
For The Rest Of My Life (9)
For You (27)
Forever My Love (2,13)
Friends In Love (27,33) **38**
Games People Play (18)
Get Down Tonight (medley) (22)
Get Rid Of Him (1)
Get Together (medley) (16)
Getting In My Way (20)
Give A Damn (18)
Go With Love (5)
Going Out Of My Head (15,16)
Good Life (4)
Got A Date (29)
Got You Where I Want You (27)
Grace (18)
Green Grass Starts To Grow (15) **43**
Hard Day's Night (11)
Hasbrook Heights (17)
Have You Never Been Mellow (medley) (22)
He (She) Loves Me (6)
Heartbreak Of Love (6)
Heartbreaker (28,33) **10**
Here I Am (3,12) **65**
Here Where There is Love (5)

Here's That Rainy Day (15)
Hey Jude (11)
His House And Me (21)
House Is Not A Home (1,4,12,16,26) **71**
How Can I Hurt You (3)
How Can I Tell Him (20)
How Long? (31)
How Many Days Of Sadness (2)
How Many Times Can We Say Goodbye (29,33) **27**
How You Once Loved Me (25)
Hurts So Bad (18)
I Always Get Caught In The Rain (19)
I Believe In You (6)
I Can Let Go Now (29)
I Can't See Anything (But You) (28)
I Can't Wait To See My Baby's Face (20)
I Concentrate On You (34)
I Do It 'Cause I Like It (20)
I Don't Need Another Love (33)
I Get A Kick Out Of You (34)
I Got Love (15,23)
I Just Don't Know What To Do With Myself (5,13,16,22) **26**
I Just Have To Breathe (17)
I Love Music (medley) (22)
I Love Paris (4,34)
I Loves You, Porgy (3)

(I Never Knew) What You Were Up To (5)
I Say A Little Prayer (7,13,16) **4**
I Smiled Yesterday (1,8)
I Think You Need Love (19)
I Wish You Love (5)
I'll Never Fall In Love Again (14,16) **6**
I'll Never Love This Way Again (24,26,33) **5**
(I'm) Just Being Myself (19)
I'm Putting Me In Your Hands (16)
I'm Your Puppet (11,18)
I've Been Loving You Too Long (11,18)
I've Got You Under My Skin (34)
If I Ever Make You Cry (3)
If I Ruled The World (23)
If We Only Have Love (17) **84**
If You Let Me Make Love To You Then Why Can't I Touch You (18)
If You Never Say Goodbye (17)
Impersonation Medley (16)
Impossible Dream (medley) (16)
In A World Such As This (32)
In Between The Heartaches (3,13)
In The Stone (medley) (26)

In Your Eyes (24)
Is There Another Way To Love You (2)
It Makes No Difference (28)
It's All Right With Me (34)
It's Love (30)
It's Love That Really Counts (8)
It's Magic (20)
It's The Falling In Love (25)
It's You (30)
Jealousy (21)
Jesus Will (18)
Just One More Night (28)
Just One Of Those Things (34)
Knowing When To Leave (14)
La Vie En Rose (4)
Land Of Make Believe (1)
Last One To Be Loved (26)
Let It Be Me (23)
Let Me Be Lonely (9) **71**
Let Me Go To Him (14) **32**
Letter, The (14)
Little Green Apples (10)
Loneliness Remembers What Happiness Forgets (14)
Lonely In My Heart (10)
Long Day, Short Night (3)
Look Of Love (12,16,26)
Looking With My Eyes (3) **64**
Love (7)
Love At Second Sight (31)

WARWICK, Dionne — Cont'd

Love Doesn't Live Here Anymore (30)
Love Me One More Time (21)
Love Of My Man (18)
Love Power (32,33) *12*
Love So Right (27)
Love Song (17)
Love Will Keep Us Together (medley) (22)
Loving You Is Sweeter Than Ever (18)
MacArthur Park (18)
Make It Easy On Yourself (8,15,16,26) *37*
Make The Night A Little Longer (1)
Message To Michael (4,13,16,26) *8*
Misunderstood (28)
Moments Aren't Moments (31)
Monday, Monday (23)
More Than Fascination (27)
Move Me No Mountain (29)
My Everlasting Love (24)
My Eyes Adored You (medley) (22)
My Favorite Things (6)
My First Night Alone Without You (17)
My Love (22)
My Ship (6)
My Way (14)
Never Gonna Let You Go (27)
Night And Day [includes 2 versions] (34)
No Night So Long (25,26,33) *23*
No One In The World (30,32)
No One There (To Sing Me A Love Song) (31)

Now We're Starting Over Again (26)
Oh Yeah Yeah Yeah (4,16)
Once In A Lifetime (3)
Once You Hit The Road (21,22) *79*
One Hand, One Heart (6,12)
One In A Million You (26)
One Less Bell To Answer (17)
Only Love Can Break A Heart (23)
Only The Strong, Only The Brave (2)
Our Ages Or Our Hearts (18)
Our Day Will Come (28)
Out Of My Hands (24)
Paper Mache (14,16) *43*
People (1,12)
People Get Ready (11,26)
People Got To Be Free (11,18)
Promises, Promises (10,16,26) *19*
Put A Little Love In Your Heart (medley) (16)
Raindrops Keep Falling On My Head (14,16)
Reach Out And Touch (medley) (18)
Reach Out For Me (1,8,16) *20*
Reaching For The Sky (25)
Remember Your Heart (31)
Reservations For Two (32) *62*
Ronnie Lee (21)
Run To Me (30)
Say A Little Prayer (medley) (18)
She Loves Me ..see: He Silent Voices (9)
Slaves (11,28)

So Amazing (29)
So In Love (medley) (34)
Some Changes Are For Good (26) *65*
Somebody Bigger Than You And I (18)
Somebody's Angel (25)
Someday We'll Be Together (18)
Something (14)
Something Wonderful (6)
Somewhere (7,12,16)
Stand (18)
Stay Devoted (31)
Steal Away (18)
Stronger Than Before (31)
Summertime (6,18)
Sure Thing (20)
Sweetie Pie (25)
Take Good Care Of You And Me (33)
Take It From Me (20)
Take The Short Way Home (28) *41*
Taking A Chance On Love (16)
Thank Heaven For Little Girls (medley) (16)
That's Not The Answer (2)
That's The Way I Like It (medley) (22)
That's What Friends Are For (31,33) *1*
Then Came You (20,22,26) *1*
There's A Long Road Ahead Of Us (26)
(There's) Always Something There To Remind Me (7,8,26) *65*

They Don't Give Medals To Yesterday's Heroes (15)
They Long To Be Close To You (1,17,26)
They Say It's Wonderful (23)
This Empty Place (8) *84*
This Girl's In Love With You (10,16) *7*
This Is Love (21)
This Little Light (3,18)
This Will Be (An Everlasting Love) (medley) (22)
To Be Young, Gifted And Black (18)
Track Of The Cat (21)
Trains And Boats And Planes (5,13,26) *22*
Try To Remember (16)
Two Ships Passing In The Night (29)
Unchained Melody (2,13,18)
Unity (22)
Up, Up And Away (9)
Valley Of The Dolls, Theme From (9,12,16,26) *2*
Walk Away (33)
Walk Little Dolly (7)
Walk On By (1,4,8,16,22,26) *6*
Walk The Way You Talk (15)
Walking Backwards Down The Road (9)
Wanting Things (10)
Way I Want To Touch You (medley) (22)
Way You Look Tonight (6)
We Can Work It Out (11,18)
We Had This Time (25)
We Never Said Goodbye (25,26)

We'll Burn Our Bridges Behind Us (20)
We've Only Just Begun (15)
Weakness (30)
Weight, The (18)
What Can A Miracle Do (29)
What Is This (27)
What The World Needs Now Is Love (5,13,16,26)
What You Won't Do For Love (medley) (26)
What'd I Say (4,16)
What's Good About Goodbye (7,16)
When The World Runs Out Of Love (25)
Where Am I Going (10)
Where Can I Go Without You (2)
Where Is Love (10)
Where Would I Go (9)
Whisper In The Dark (31) *72*
Who Can I Turn To (2,13,16) *62*
Who Gets The Guy (23) *57*
Who Is Gonna Love Me? (10) *33*
Who Knows (20)
Who, What, When, Where, Why (24)
Whoever You Are, I Love You (10)
Will You Still Love Me Tomorrow (29)
Window Wishing (3)
Windows Of The World (7,13) *32*
Wine Is Young (14)

Wishin' And Hopin' (1,8)
With A Touch (27)
With These Hands (6,12)
Without Your Love (30)
Wives And Lovers (2,12,16)
World Of My Dreams (21)
Yesterday (15)
Yesterday I Heard The Rain (10)
You And The Night And The Music (16)
You Are My Love (28)
You Are The Heart Of Me (19)
You Can Have Him (2) *75*
You Made Me So Very Happy (16)
You Made Me Want To Love Again (30)
You'll Never Get To Heaven (If You Break My Heart) (1,4,8,16,26) *34*
You'll Never Walk Alone (6,18)
You're All I Need To Get By (11,18)
You're Gonna Hear From Me (7,16)
You're Gonna Need Me (19)
You're My Hero (32)
You're My World (9,23)
You're The Top (34)
You've Lost That Lovin' Feeling (11,18) *16*
Yours (28)

★★492★★ ## WASHINGTON, Dinah

Born Ruth Lee Jones on 8/29/24 in Tuscaloosa, Alabama; died on 12/14/63 (overdose of alcohol and pills). Jazz-blues vocalist/pianist. Moved to Chicago in 1927. With Sallie Martin Gospel Singers, 1940-41; local club work in Chicago, 1941-43. With Lionel Hampton, 1943-46. First recorded for Keynote in 1943. Solo touring from 1946. Married seven times, once to singer Eddie Chamblee. Inducted into the Rock and Roll Hall of Fame in 1993 as an early influence.

DEBUT DATE	PEAK POS	WKS CHR		ARTIST — Album Title	$	Label & Number
2/1/60	34	22	1	What a diff'rence a day makes!	$18	Mercury 20479
1/23/61	10	14	2	Unforgettable	$18	Mercury 20572
12/18/61+	56	15	3	September In The Rain	$18	Mercury 20638
6/23/62	33	25	4	Dinah '62	$15	Roulette 25170
10/20/62	78	9	5	Drinking Again	$15	Roulette 25183
11/17/62	131	4	6	I Wanna Be Loved	$15	Mercury 20729
				with the Quincy Jones Orchestra		
2/23/63	61	12	7	Back To The Blues	$15	Roulette 25189
4/4/64	130	6	8	A Stranger On Earth	$15	Roulette 25253

Alone (2)
As Long As I'm In Your Arms (3)
Ask A Woman Who Knows (2)
Baby Won't You Please Come Home (5)
Bad Case Of The Blues (2)
Blue Gardenia (6)
Blues Ain't Nothin' But A Woman Cryin' For Her Man (7,8)
Coquette (4)
Cry Me A River (1)
Destination Moon (4)
Do Nothin' 'Til You Hear From Me (8)
Don't Come Running Back To Me (7)
Don't Explain (6)
Drinking Again (4,5)

Duck Before You Drown (7)
Everybody Loves Somebody (2)
Everybody's Somebody's Fool (6)
For All We Know (5) *88*
God Bless The Child (6)
Handful Of Stars (4)
How Long, How Long Blues (7)
I Can't Believe That You're In Love With Me (3)
I Can't Face The Music (6)
I Don't Know You Anymore (5)
I Remember You (1)
I Thought About You (1)
I Understand (2)
I Wanna Be Loved (6)
I Was Telling Him About You

I Won't Cry Anymore (1)
I'll Be Around (5)
I'll Come Back For More (3)
I'll Drown In My Tears (8)
I'll Never Kiss You Goodbye (3)
I'm Gonna Laugh You Out Of My Life (6)
I'm Thru With Love (1)
I've Got My Love To Keep Me Warm (3)
If I Never Get To Heaven (7)
Invitation (8)
Is You Is Or Is You Ain't My Baby (4)
It's A Mean Old Man's World (7,8)
It's Magic (1)
Just Friends (5)
Key To The Highway (7)

Let Me Be The First To Know (7)
Let's Fall In Love (6)
Love, I Found You Gone (5)
Lover Man (5)
Man Only Does (What A Woman Makes Him Do) (2)
Man That Got Away (5,8)
Manhattan (1)
Me And My Gin (8)
Miss You (4)
No Hard Feelings (7)
Nobody Knows The Way I Feel This Morning (7,8)
Nothing In The World (Could Make Me Love You More Than I Do) (1)
On The Street Of Regret (5)
Red Sails In The Sunset (4)
Romance In The Dark (7)
Say It Isn't So (5)

September In The Rain (3) *23*
Softly (6)
Sometimes I'm Happy (6)
Somewhere Along The Line (2)
Song Is Ended (But The Melody Lingers On) (2)
Soulville (8) *92*
Stranger In Town (6)
Stranger On Earth (8)
Sunday Kind Of Love (1)
Take Your Shoes Off Baby (4)
Tell Love Hello! (3)
That's All There Is To That (1)
This Bitter Earth (2) *24*
This Heart Of Mine (3)
This Love Of Mine (2)
Time After Time (1)
Unforgettable (2) *17*

What A Diff'rence A Day Makes (1) *8*
When I Fall In Love (2)
When Your Lover Has Gone (6)
Where Are You (4) *36*
With A Song In My Heart (3)
Without A Song (3)
You're Crying (6)
You're Nobody 'Til Somebody Loves You (4) *87*
You've Been A Good Old Wagon (7,8)

★★118★★ ## WASHINGTON, Grover Jr.

Born on 12/12/43 in Buffalo. Jazz-R&B saxophonist. Own band, the Four Clefs, at age 16. Much session work in Philadelphia, where he now resides. Also see Television Shows.

DEBUT DATE	PEAK POS	WKS CHR		ARTIST — Album Title		$	Label & Number
1/1/72	62	25	1	Inner City Blues	[I]	$10	Kudu 03
9/9/72	111	17	2	All The King's Horses	[I]	$10	Kudu 07
7/14/73	100	14	3	Soul Box	[I]	$12	Kudu 1213 [2]
3/8/75	10	34	4	Mister Magic	[I]	$8	Kudu 20
11/15/75	10	30	5	Feels So Good	[I]	$8	Kudu 24
1/15/77	31	16	6	A Secret Place	[I]	$8	Kudu 32
1/7/78	11	32	7	Live At The Bijou	[I-L]	$10	Kudu 3637 [2]

WASHINGTON, Grover Jr. — Cont'd

DEBUT DATE	PEAK POS	WKS CHR	GOLD	ARTIST — Album Title	$	Label & Number
10/21/78	35	23	8	Reed Seed ....[I]	$8	Motown 910
				backed by the jazz ensemble Locksmith		
4/28/79	24	19	9	Paradise ....[I]	$8	Elektra 182
3/8/80	24	22	10	Skylarkin' ....[I]	$8	Motown 933
9/13/80	96	10	11	Baddest ....[I-K]	$10	Motown 940 [2]
11/15/80+	5	52	▲	12 Winelight ....[I]	$8	Elektra 305
10/24/81	149	7	13	Anthology ....[I-K]	$10	Motown 961 [2]
12/12/81+	28	27	14	Come Morning ....[I]	$8	Elektra 562
12/11/82+	50	25	15	The Best Is Yet To Come	$8	Elektra 60215
11/10/84	79	23	16	Inside Moves	$8	Elektra 60318
8/29/87	66	16	17	Strawberry Moon	$8	Columbia 40510
5/16/92	149	11	18	Next Exit............	$12	Columbia 48530

Ain't No Sunshine (1,11)
Ain't Nobody's Business If I Do (medley) (3)
All The King's Horses (2)
Answer In Your Eyes (9)
Asia's Theme (9)
Aubrey (3)
Be Mine (Tonight) (14) *92*
Best Is Yet To Come (15)
Black Frost (4,11)
Body And Soul (Montage) (2)
Bright Moments (10)
Can You Dig It (15)
Cassie's Theme (15)
Caught A Touch Of Your Love (17)
Check Out Grover (18)
Come Morning (14)
Dawn Song (16)
Days In Our Lives (medley) (7)

Do Dat (8,11)
Dolphin Dance (6)
Don't Explain (3)
Earth Tones (4)
East River Drive (14)
Easy Living (medley) (3)
Easy Loving You (10)
Feel It Comin' (9)
Funkfoot (7)
Georgia On My Mind (1)
Get On Up (18)
Greene Street (18)
Hydra (5)
I Can't Help It (10)
I Loves You, Porgy (1)
I Miss Home (18)
I Will Be Here For You (17)
I'll Be With You (15)
I'm All Yours (14)
Icey (9)
In The Name Of Love (12)
Inner City Blues (1,13)

Inside Moves (16)
It Feels So Good (5,11,13)
Jamming (14)
Jet Stream (16)
Juffure (7)
Just The Two Of Us (12) *2*
Just The Way You Are (8)
Keep In Touch (17)
Knucklehead (5)
Lean On Me (2,11)
Let It Flow ("For Dr. J") (12)
Little Black Samba (14)
Lock It In The Pocket (7)
Look Of Love (14)
Loran's Dance (8)
Love (10)
Love Like This (18)
Love Makes It Better (6)
Love Song 1700 (2)
Lover Man (2)
Maddie's Blues (17)

Make Me A Memory (Sad Samba) (12)
Making Love To You (14)
Man And Boy (Better Days), Theme From (medley) (1)
Maracas Beach (8)
Masterpiece (3,11,13)
Mercy Mercy Me (The Ecology) (1,13)
Mister Magic (4,7,11,13) *54*
Mixty Motions (15)
Monte Carlo Nights (17)
Moonstreams (5)
More Than Meets The Eye (15)
Next Exit (18)
No Tears In The End (2)
Not Yet (6)
On The Cusp (7)
Only For You (Siempre Para D'Sera) (18)

Open Up Your Mind (Wide) (10)
Paradise (9)
Passion Flower (4)
Reaching Out (14)
Reed Seed (Trio Tune) (8)
Santa Cruzin (8,13)
Sassy Stew (16)
3ausalito (7)
Sea Lion (5)
Secret Place (6,11,13)
Secret Sounds (16)
Shana (9)
Shivaree Ride (17)
Snake Eyes (10,13)
Step'N' Thru (8)
Strawberry Moon (17)
Summer Chill (18)
Summer Nights (17)
Summer Song (7,11,13)
Take Five (Take Another Five) (18)

Take Me There (12)
Taurian Matador (3)
Tell Me About It Now (9)
Things Are Getting Better (15)
Till You Return To Me (18)
Trouble Man (3,13)
Until It's Time For You To Go (1)
Watching You Watching Me (16)
When I Look At You (9)
Where Is The Love (2,13)
Winelight (12)
You Are The Sunshine Of My Life (3)
You Make Me Dance (7)
Your Love (18)

WASHINGTON, Keith

Detroit native. Supporting vocalist while a teen for The Dramatics. Former backing vocalist for the Jacksons and Miki Howard.

DEBUT DATE	PEAK POS	WKS CHR	GOLD	ARTIST — Album Title	$	Label & Number
5/4/91	48	25	●	Make Time For Love	$12	Qwest 26528

All Night
Are You Still In Love With Me

Closer
I'll Be There

Kissing You *40*
Lovers After All

Make Time For Love
Ready, Willing And Able

When It Comes To You
When You Love Somebody

WAS (NOT WAS)

Detroit R&B ensemble fronted by composer/bassist Don Fagenson ("Don Was") and lyricist/flutist David Weiss ("David Was"). Includes vocalists Sweet Pea Atkinson and Sir Harry Bowens. Group appeared in the film *The Freshman*.

DEBUT DATE	PEAK POS	WKS CHR	GOLD	ARTIST — Album Title	$	Label & Number
10/15/83	134	9		1 Born To Laugh At Tornadoes	$8	Geffen 4016
10/15/88+	43	37		2 What Up, Dog?	$8	Chrysalis 41664
8/18/90	99	11		3 Are You Okay?	$12	Chrysalis 21778

Anything Can Happen (2) *75*
Anytime Lisa (2)
Are You Okay? (3)
Betrayal (1)
Bow Wow Wow Wow (1)
Boy's Gone Crazy (2)
Dad I'm In Jail (2)
Dressed To Be Killed (3)

Earth To Doris (2)
11 MPH (2)
Elvis' Rolls Royce (3)
How The Heart Behaves (3)
I Blew Up The United States (3)
I Feel Better Than James Brown (3)
In K Mart Wardrobe (3)

Just Another Couple Broken Hearts (3)
Knocked Down, Made Small (Treated Like A Rubber Ball) (1)
Look What's Back (3)
Love Can Be Bad Luck (2)
Man Vs. The Empire Brain Building (1)

Maria Novarro (3)
Out Come The Freaks (2)
Papa Was A Rollin' Stone (2)
Party Broke Up (1)
Professor Night (1)
(Return To The Valley Of) Out Come The Freaks (2)
Shadow & Jimmy (2)

Shake Your Head (Let's Go To Bed) (1)
Smile (1)
Somewhere In America There's A Street Named After My Dad (2)
Spy In The House Of Love (2) *16*
Walk The Dinosaur (2) *7*

What Up Dog? (2)
You! You! You! (3)
Zaz Turned Blue (1)

W.A.S.P.

Los Angeles-based, heavy-metal quartet led by Blackie Lawless. Reduced to a trio of Lawless, guitarist Chris Holmes and bassist Johnny Rod.

DEBUT DATE	PEAK POS	WKS CHR	GOLD	ARTIST — Album Title	$	Label & Number
10/6/84	74	31		1 W.A.S.P.	$8	Capitol 12343
11/23/85	49	23		2 The Last Command	$8	Capitol 12435
11/8/86	60	19		3 Inside The Electric Circus............	$8	Capitol 12531
10/10/87	77	14		4 Live...in the Raw ....[L]	$8	Capitol 48053
				recorded at California Theatre (San Diego) & Long Beach Arena (LA)		
4/22/89	48	13		5 The Headless Children	$8	Capitol 48942

B.A.D. (1)
Ballcrusher (2)
Big Welcome (3)
Blind In Texas (2,4)
Cries In The Night (2)
Easy Living (3)
Fistful Of Diamonds (2)
Flame, The (1)

Forever Free (5)
Harder Faster (4)
Headless Children (5)
Hellion (1)
Heretic (The Lost Child) (5)
I Don't Need No Doctor (3,4)
I Wanna Be Somebody (1,4)
I'm Alive (3)

Inside The Electric Circus (3,4)
Jack Action (2)
King Of Sodom And Gomorrah (3)
L.O.V.E. Machine (1,4)
Maneater (5)

Manimal, The (4)
Mantronic (3)
Mean Man (5)
Mephisto Waltz (5)
Neutron Bomber (5)
9.5.-N.A.S.T.Y. (3,4)
On Your Knees (2)
Real Me (5)

Rebel In The F.D.G. (5)
Restless Gypsy (3)
Rock Rolls On (3)
Running Wild In The Streets (2)
School Daze (5)
Scream Until You Like It (4)
Sex Drive (2)

Shoot From The Hip (3)
Sleeping (In The Fire) (1,4)
Sweet Cheetah (3)
Thunderhead (5)
Tormentor (1)
Torture Never Stops (1)
WidowMaker (2)
Wild Child (2,4)

WATERBOYS, The

Rock group formed in London in 1983 by Scottish singer/songwriter Mike Scott. Includes Englishman Anthony Thistlethwaite with Irish natives Wickham and Trevor Hutchinson. Keyboardist Karl Wallinger left in 1985 to form World Party.

DEBUT DATE	PEAK POS	WKS CHR	GOLD	ARTIST — Album Title	$	Label & Number
12/10/88+	76	26		1 Fisherman's Blues	$8	Chrysalis 41589
10/27/90	180	4		2 Room To Roam	$12	Chrysalis 21768

And A Bang On The Ear (1)
Bigger Picture (2)
Dunford's Fancy (1)

Fisherman's Blues (1)
Further Up, Further In (2)

Has Anybody Here Seen Hank? (1)

How Long Will I Love You? (2)
In Search Of A Rose (2)

Islandman (2)
Kaliope House (2)
Life Of Sundays (2)

Man Is In Love (2)
Natural Bridge Blues (2)
Raggle Taggle Gypsy (2)

WATERBOYS, The — Cont'd

Room To Roam (2)	Spring Comes To Spiddal (2)	Strange Boat (1)	Upon The Wind And The Waves (2)	When Will We Be Married? (1)
Something That Is Gone (2)	Star And The Sea (2)	Sweet Thing (1)	We Will Not Be Lovers (1)	When Ye Go Away (1)
Song From The End Of The World (2)	Stolen Child (1)	Trip To Broadford (2)		World Party (1)

WATERFRONT

Male pop-rock duo of singer Chris Duffy and guitarist Phil Cillia from Cardiff, Wales. Band name derived from the Marlon Brando film *On The Waterfront*.

DEBUT DATE	PEAK POS	WKS CHR	GOLD	ARTIST — Album Title	$	Label & Number
5/20/89	103	13		Waterfront	$8	Polydor 837970

Broken Arrow	Dancing With Strangers	**Nature Of Love 70**	Set You Free	Tightrope
Cry *10*	Move On	Platinum Halo	Soul Survivor	Waterfront

WATERS, Crystal

Female R&B-dance singer from South New Jersey. Majored in computer science at Howard University. Her father is jazz musician Jr. Waters; her aunt is Ethel Waters.

DEBUT DATE	PEAK POS	WKS CHR	GOLD	ARTIST — Album Title	$	Label & Number
7/20/91	197	3		Surprise	$12	Mercury 848894

Deepest Of Hearts	**Gypsy Woman (She's**	Makin' Happy	Surprise	Twisted
Good Lovin	**Homeless)** *[includes 2 versions]* **8**	Small Cry	Tell Me	

WATERS, Muddy

Pivotal figure in the development of the Chicago blues style. Born McKinley Morganfield on 4/4/15 in Rolling Fork, Mississippi. Died on 4/30/83. Vocalist/guitarist/ harmonica player. Self-taught harmonica in the early 1920s, guitar in the early '30s. First recorded for Library of Congress in in 1941. Moved to Chicago in 1943. Frequent tours of Europe, film and TV appearances. Inducted into the Rock and Roll Hall of Fame in 1987 as a blues pioneer.

DEBUT DATE	PEAK POS	WKS CHR	GOLD	ARTIST — Album Title	$	Label & Number
11/9/68	127	8	1	Electric Mud	$20	Cadet Concept 314
9/27/69	70	10	2	Fathers And Sons .... [L]	$15	Chess 127 [2]
				with Otis Spann, Michael Bloomfield and Paul Butterfield; record 2: live		
2/19/77	143	7	3	Hard Again	$8	Blue Sky 34449
2/25/78	157	6	4	I'm Ready	$8	Blue Sky 34928
5/16/81	192	2	5	King Bee	$8	Blue Sky 37064
				above 3 produced by Johnny Winter		

All Aboard (2)	Crosseyed Cat (3)	Herbert Harper's Free Press (1)	I'm Ready (2,4)	Mean Old Frisco Blues (5)	Sugar Sweet (2)
Baby Please Don't Go (2)	Deep Down In Florida (3)	Honey Bee (2)	I'm Your Hoochie Coochie Man (1,4)	(My Eyes) Keep Me In Trouble (5)	33 Years (4)
Blow Wind Blow (2)	Deep Down In Florida #2 (5)	I Can't Be Satisfied (3)	Jealous Hearted Man (3)	No Escape From The Blues (5)	Tom Cat (1)
Blues Had A Baby And They Named It Rock And Roll (#2) (3)	Forever Lonely (5)	I Feel Like Going Home (5)	Let's Spend The Night Together (1)	Rock Me (4)	Too Young To Know (5)
Bus Driver (3)	Forty Days And Forty Nights (2)	I Just Want To Make Love To You (1)	Little Girl (3)	Sad Sad Day (5)	Twenty-Four Hours (2)
Can't Lose What You Ain't Never Had (2)	Good Morning Little School Girl (4)	I Want To Be Loved (3)	Long Distance Call (2)	Same Thing (1,2)	Walkin' Thru The Park (2)
Champagne & Reefer (5)	Got My Mojo Working (Part I & II) (2)	I'm A King Bee (5)	Mamie (4)	Screamin' And Cryin' (4)	Who Do You Trust (4)
Copper Brown (4)		I'm A Man ..see: Mannish Boy	Mannish Boy (1,3)	She's All Right (1)	
			Mean Disposition (2)	Standin' Round Cryin' (2)	

WATERS, Roger

Born George Roger Waters on 9/6/43 in Cambridgeshire, England. Former leader/bassist of Pink Floyd. Went solo in 1983.

DEBUT DATE	PEAK POS	WKS CHR	GOLD	ARTIST — Album Title	$	Label & Number
5/19/84	31	18	1	The Pros and Cons of Hitch Hiking	$8	Columbia 39290
7/4/87	50	19	2	Radio K.A.O.S.	$8	Columbia 40795
9/22/90	56	10	3	The Wall - Live In Berlin .... [L]	$23	Mercury 846611 [2]
				concert of Pink Floyd's *The Wall* at the Berlin Wall on 7/21/90; performers: Bryan Adams, Paul Carrack, Thomas Dolby, Marianne Faithfull, James Galway, Levon Helm & Rick Danko of The Band, Hooters, Cyndi Lauper, Van Morrison, Sinead O'Connor & Scorpions; artist royalties donated to the Memorial Fund for Disaster Relief		
9/19/92	21	10	4	Amused To Death	$12	Columbia 47127

Amused To Death (4)	Comfortably Numb (3)	Happiest Days Of Our Lives (3)	Moment Of Clarity (4)	Sexual Revolution (1)	What God Wants, Parts I-III (4)
Another Brick In The Wall (Parts 1-3) (3)	Don't Leave Me Now (3)	Hey You (3)	Mother (3)	Stop (1)	Who Needs Information (2)
Apparently They Were Travelling Abroad (1)	Dunroamin, Duncarin, Dunlivin (1)	Home (2)	Nobody Home (3)	Sunset Strip (2)	Young Lust (3)
Arabs With Knives And West German Skies (1)	Empty Spaces (3)	In The Flesh? (includes 2 versions) (3)	One Of My Turns (3)	Thin Ice (3)	
Ballad Of Bill Hubbard (4)	Every Strangers Eyes (1)	Is There Anybody Out There? (3)	Perfect Sense, Part I & II (4)	Three Wishes (4)	
Bravery Of Being Out Of Range (4)	For The First Time Today, Part 1 & 2 (1)	It's A Miracle (4)	Powers That Be (2)	Tide Is Turning (2,3)	
Bring The Boys Back Home (3)	Four Minutes (2)	Late Home Tonight, Part I & II (4)	Pros And Cons Of Hitch Hiking Part 10 (1)	Too Much Rope (4)	
	Go Fishing (1)	Me Or Him (2)	Radio Waves (2)	Trial, The (3)	
	Goodbye Blue Sky (3)		Remains Of Our Love (1)	Vera (3)	
	Goodbye Cruel World (3)		Run Like Hell (3)	Waiting For The Worms (3)	
			Running Shoes (1)	Watching TV (4)	

WATLEY, Jody

Born on 1/30/59 in Chicago. Female vocalist of Shalamar (1977-84) and former dancer on TV's *Soul Train*. Her godfather was Jackie Wilson. Won the 1987 Best New Artist Grammy Award.

DEBUT DATE	PEAK POS	WKS CHR	GOLD	ARTIST — Album Title	$	Label & Number
3/21/87	10	74	▲	1	Jody Watley	$8	MCA 5898
4/15/89	16	40	●	2	Larger Than Life	$8	MCA 6276
12/2/89	86	13		3	You Wanna Dance With Me? .... [K]	$8	MCA 6343
				previously unreleased, re-edited versions of Jody's dance hits		
12/21/91+	124	9		4	Affairs Of The Heart	$12	MCA 10355

Affairs Of The Heart (4)	Do It To The Beat (1)	**I Want You** (4) **61**	**Looking For A New Love** (1,3) **2**	Only You (2)	**Still A Thrill** (1,3) **56**
Always And Forever (4)	**Don't You Want Me** (1,3) **6**	**I'm The One You Need** (4) **19**	Love Injection (1)	**Precious Love** (2) **87**	Stolen Moments (4)
Call On Me (4)	**Everything** (2) **4**	It All Begins With You (4)	L.O.V.E.R. (2)	**Real Love** (2,3) **2**	Strange Way (4)
Come Into My Life (2)	For Love's Sake (2)	Learn To Say No (1)	**Most Of All** (1,3) **60**	**Some Kind Of Lover** (1,3) **10**	Until The Last Goodbye (4)
Commitment Of Love (4)	For The Girls (2)	Lifestyle (2)	Once You Leave (2)	Something New (2)	What 'Cha Gonna Do For Me (2,3)
Dance To The Music (4)	**Friends** (2,3) **9**				

DEBUT DATE	PEAK POS	WKS CHR	GOLD	ARTIST — Album Title	$	Label & Number

WATSON, Doc
Born Arthel Watson on 3/2/23 in Deep Gap, North Carolina. Banjo/guitar player of traditional folk and country music.

| 8/30/75 | 193 | 3 | | Memories .... with son Merle Watson on guitar | $12 | United Art. 423 [2] |

Blues Stay Away From Me
Columbus Stockade
Curly Headed Baby
Don't Tell Me Your Troubles
Double File & Salt Creek
Hang Your Head In Shame
In The Jailhouse Now
Keep On The Sunny Side
Make Me A Pallet
Mama Don't Allow No Music
Miss The Mississippi & You
Moody River
My Rose Of Old Kentucky
Peartree
Rambling Hobo
Shady Grove
Steel Guitar Rag
Thoughts Of Never
Wabash Cannonball
Wake Up, Little Maggie
Walking Boss
You Don't Know My Mind
Blues

WATSON, Johnny "Guitar"
Born on 2/3/35 in Houston. Funk-R&B vocalist/guitarist/pianist. First recorded (as Young John Watson) for Federal in 1952.

8/7/76	52	22	●	1 Ain't That A Bitch	$8	DJM 3
4/16/77	20	27	●	2 A Real Mother For Ya	$8	DJM 7
12/24/77+	84	14		3 Funk Beyond The Call Of Duty	$8	DJM 714
10/28/78	157	7		4 Giant	$8	DJM 19
7/5/80	115	14		5 Love Jones	$8	DJM 31
6/27/81	177	3		6 Johnny "Guitar" Watson And The Family Clone .... all instruments played by Johnny	$8	DJM 501

Ain't Movin' (6)
Ain't That A Bitch (1)
Asante Sana (5)
Baby Face (She Said Do Do Do) (4)
Barn Door (3)
Booty Ooty (5)
Children Of The Universe (5)
Clone Information (6)
Close Encounters (5)
Come And Dance With Me (6)
Family Clone (6)
Forget The Joneses (6)
Funk Beyond The Call Of Duty (3)
Gangster Of Love (4)
Give Me My Love (3)
Going Up In Smoke (5)
Guitar Disco (4)
I Need It (1)
I Wanna Thank You (2)
I Want To Ta-Ta You Baby (1)
I'm Gonna Get You Baby (3)
It's A Damn Shame (3)
It's About The Dollar Bill (3)
Jet Plane (5)
Lone Ranger (5)
Love Jones (5)
Love That Will Not Die (3)
Lover Jones (2)
Miss Frisco (Queen Of The Disco) (4)
Nothing Left To Be Desired (2)
Real Deal (2)
Real Mother For Ya (2) 41
Rio Dreamin' (6)
Since I Met You Baby (1)
Superman Lover (1)
Tarzan (2)
Telephone Bill (5)
Tu Jours Amour (4)
Voodoo What You Do (6)
We're No Exception (1)
What Is Love? (6)
Won't You Forgive Me Baby (1)
Wrapped In Black Mink (2)
You Can Stay But The Noise Must Go (4)
Your Love Is My Love (2)

WATSONIAN INSTITUTE
The Johnny "Guitar" Watson band.

| 4/15/78 | 154 | 4 | | Master Funk .... | $8 | DJM 13 |

Coming Around
De John's Delight
Funk If I Know
Institute, The
Lady Voo Doo
Master Funk
Virginia's Pretty Funky

WATTS, Ernie
Born on 10/23/45 in Norfolk, Virginia. Saxophonist with the NBC *Tonight Show* orchestra. Accompanied The Rolling Stones on their 1981 tour.

| 2/20/82 | 161 | 12 | | Chariots of Fire .... [I] | $8 | Qwest 3637 |

Abraham's Theme
Chariots Of Fire (Theme)
[includes 2 versions]
Five Circles
Gigolo
Hold On
Lady
Valdez In The Country

WATTS 103rd STREET RHYTHM BAND — see WRIGHT, Charles

WA WA NEE
Australian-based dance band. Includes Australians Steve Williams and brothers Mark and Paul Gray, plus Chris Sweeney (from the U.S.) and Phil Witchett (from New Zealand).

| 11/7/87 | 123 | 17 | | Wa Wa Nee .... | $8 | Epic 40858 |

Gone
I Could Make You Love Me
Jelly Baby
Love Reaction
Manchild
One And One (Ain't I Good Enough)
Stimulation 86
Sugar Free 35
Teacher
When The World Is A Home

WAX
Pop duo: Andrew Gold and Graham Gouldman (10cc).

| 4/26/86 | 101 | 11 | | Magnetic Heaven .... | $8 | RCA 9546 |

Ball And Chain
Breakout
Hear No Evil
Magnetic Heaven
Marie Claire
Only A Visitor
Right Between The Eyes 43
Rise Up
Shadows Of Love
Systematic

WAYBILL, Fee
Born John Waldo on 9/17/50 in Omaha, Nebraska. Lead singer of The Tubes.

| 11/10/84 | 146 | 6 | | Read My Lips .... | $8 | Capitol 12369 |

Caribbean Sunsets
I Could've Been Somebody
I Don't Even Know Your Name (Passion Play)
Nobody's Perfect
Saved My Life
Star Of The Show
Thrill Of The Kill
Who Loves You Baby
Who Said Life Would Be Pretty
You're Still Laughing

WAYLON & WILLIE — see JENNINGS, Waylon, and/or NELSON, Willie

WAYNE, John
Born Marion Morrison on 5/26/07 in Winterset, Iowa; died on 6/11/79 of lung cancer. Beloved American film actor "The Duke" starred in over 200 films. Oscar-winner for *True Grit*.

| 3/3/73 | 66 | 16 | | America, Why I Love Her .... [T] a narrative tribute (with orchestra and chorus) to America | $15 | RCA 4828 |

American Boy Grows Up
Face The Flag
Good Things
Hyphen, The
Mis Raices Estan Aqui (My Roots Are Buried Here)
People, The
Pledge Of Allegiance
Taps
Why Are You Marching, Son?
Why I Love Her

WAYSTED
Hard-rock quartet comprised of ex-UFO members Pete Way (bass) and Paul Chapman (lead guitar), plus Danny Vaughn (lead singer) and John DiTeodoro (drums). Vaughn was later lead singer of Tyketto.

| 3/21/87 | 185 | 2 | | Save Your Prayers .... | $8 | Capitol 12538 |

Black And Blue
Heaven Tonight
Hell Comes Home
Heroes Die Young
How The West Was Won
Out Of Control
Singing To The Night
So Long
Walls Fall Down
Wild Night

WEATHERLY, Jim
Pop-country singer/songwriter born on 3/17/43 in Pontotoc, Mississippi. Wrote Gladys Knight's hits "Neither One Of Us," "Midnight Train To Georgia" and "Best Thing That Ever Happened To Me."

| 9/28/74 | 94 | 14 | | The Songs of Jim Weatherly .... | $8 | Buddah 5608 |

California Memory
Coming Apart
I'll Still Love You 87
Like Old Times Again
Living Every Man's Dream
My First Day Without Her
Need To Be 11
Roses And Love Songs
Where Do I Put Her Memory
You Are A Song

DEBUT DATE	PEAK POS	WKS CHR	GOLD	ARTIST — Album Title	$	Label & Number

★★294★★ WEATHER REPORT
Jazz-fusion quintet formed in 1969 by Austrian-born Josef Zawinul (keyboards) and Wayne Shorter (sax). Zawinul was a member of Cannonball Adderley's combo for nine years; formed the Zawinul Syndicate in 1988.

DEBUT DATE	PEAK POS	WKS CHR		ALBUM	$	Label & Number
7/24/71	191	4	1	Weather Report .... [I]	$8	Columbia 30661
7/15/72	147	6	2	I Sing The Body Electric .... [I-L]	$8	Columbia 31352
				side 2: recorded live in Tokyo		
5/26/73	85	17	3	Sweetnighter .... [I]	$8	Columbia 32210
6/22/74	46	23	4	Mysterious Traveller .... [I]	$8	Columbia 32494
6/7/75	31	14	5	Tale Spinnin' .... [I]	$8	Columbia 33417
4/17/76	42	12	6	Black Market .... [I]	$8	Columbia 34099
4/2/77	30	22	▲ 7	Heavy Weather .... [I]	$8	Columbia 34418
10/28/78	52	14	8	Mr. Gone .... [I]	$8	ARC 35358
10/6/79	47	11	9	8:30 .... [I-L]	$10	ARC 36030 [2]
				3 of 4 sides are live concert recordings		
12/13/80+	57	14	10	Night Passage .... [I]	$8	ARC 36793
2/20/82	68	11	11	Weather Report .... [I]	$8	ARC 37616
3/19/83	96	10	12	Procession .... [I]	$8	Columbia 38427
3/24/84	136	8	13	Domino Theory .... [I]	$8	Columbia 39147
				features 1 track with vocals by Carl Anderson		
4/27/85	191	3	14	Sportin' Life .... [I]	$8	Columbia 39908
8/23/86	195	2	15	This Is This .... [I]	$8	Columbia 40280

Adios (3)
American Tango (4)
And Then (8)
Badia (5,9)
Barbary Coast (6)
Between The Thighs (5)
Birdland (7,9)
Black Market (6,9)
Blackthorn Rose (4)
Blue Sound - Note 3 (13)
Boogie Woogie Waltz (3,9)
Brown Street (9)
Can It Be Done (13)
Cannon Ball (6)
China Blues (15)
Confians (14)
Consequently (15)
Corner Pocket (14)
Crystal (2)
Cucumber Slumber (4)

Current Affairs (11)
D flat Waltz (13)
Dara Factor One & Two (11)
Directions (2)
Dr. Honoris Causa (medley) (2)
Domino Theory (13)
Dream Clock (10)
8:30 (9)
Elders, The (8)
Elegant People (6)
Eurydice (1)
Face On The Barroom Floor (14)
Face The Fire (15)
Fast City (10)
Five Short Stories (5)
Forlorn (10)
Freezing Fire (5)
Gibraltar (6)

Harlequin (7)
Havona (4)
Herandnu (6)
Hot Cargo (14)
I'll Never Forget You (15)
Ice-Pick Willy (14)
In A Silent Way (9)
Indiscretions (14)
Juggler, The (7)
Jungle Book (4)
Jungle Stuff, Part I (15)
Lusitanos (5)
Madagascar (10)
Man In The Green Shirt (5)
Man With The Copper Fingers (15)
Manolete (3)
Milky Way (1)
Molasses Run (12)
Moors, The (2)

Morning Lake (1)
Mr. Gone (8)
Mysterious Traveller (4)
N.Y.C. Medley (11)
Night Passage (10)
Non-Stop Home (3)
Nubian Sundance (4)
125th Street Congress (3)
Orange Lady (1)
Orphan, The (9)
Palladium (7)
Pearl On The Half-Shell (14)
Peasant, The (13)
Pinocchio (8)
Plaza Real (12)
Port Of Entry (10)
Predator (13)
Procession (12)
Punk Jazz (8)

Pursuit Of The Woman With The Feathered Hat (8)
Remark You Made (7,9)
River People (8)
Rockin' In Rhythm (10)
Rumba Mama (7)
Scarlet Woman (4,9)
Second Sunday In August (2)
Seventh Arrow (1)
Sightseeing (9)
Slang (8)
Speechless (11)
Surucucu (2)
Swamp Cabbage (13)
T.H. (medley) (2)
Tears (1)
Teen Town (7,9)
Thanks For The Memory (9)
This Is This (15)
Three Clowns (6)

Three Views Of A Secret (10)
Two Lines (12)
Umbrellas (1)
Unknown Soldier (2)
Update (15)
Vertical Invader (medley) (2)
Volcano For Hire (11)
Waterfall (1)
Well, The (12)
What's Going On (14)
When It Was Now (11)
Where The Moon Goes (12)
Will (3)
Young And Fine (8)

WEAVER, Dennis
Born on 6/4/24 in Joplin, Missouri. Starred in TV's *McCloud*, *Gentle Ben* and *Gunsmoke*.

5/13/72	191	2		Dennis Weaver	$15	Im'press 1614

Another Way
I Still Sing "Jesus Loves Me"
I'd Rather Be With You Than Anyone

Learn To Love
Lonesome To The Lonely

No Name
Ode To A Critter (Fish, Bird & Cow Song)

Time
20th Century Man (Our Man Is Coming)

Where Have The Wild Blackberries Gone

Work Through My Hands, Lord

WEAVERS, The
Legendary folk quartet: Pete Seeger, Lee Hays (d: 8/26/81), Fred Hellerman and Ronnie Gilbert. Revived and popularized folk music in the early '50s. Political blacklisting cut short their recording career, but the group's 1955 Carnegie Hall concert helped trigger a new folk boom and such Seeger-Hays songs as "If I Had A Hammer" kept it alive.

1/23/61	126	13	1	The Weavers at Carnegie Hall, Vol. 2 .... [L]	$20	Vanguard 9075
				recorded on 4/1/60		
3/13/61	24	7	2	The Weavers at Carnegie Hall .... [E-L]	$20	Vanguard 9010
				recorded on Christmas Eve in 1955		

Amazing Grace (1)
Around The World (2)
Below The Gallows Tree (1)
Bill Bailey Come Home (1)
Born In East Virginia (1)
Buttermilk Hill (1)
Darling Corey (2)

Follow The Drinking Gourd (2)
Go Where I Send Thee (1)
Good Old Bowling Green (1)
Goodnight Irene (1)
Greensleeves (2)
Hush Little Baby (2)
I Know Where I'm Going (2)

I've Got A Home In That Rock (2)
In That New Jerusalem (1)
Kisses Sweeter Than Wine (2)
Last Night I Had The Strangest Dream (1)
Lonesome Traveller (2)

Marching To Pretoria (1)
On My Journey (1)
Pay Me My Money Down (2)
Rock Island Line (1)
Run Come See (1)
Shalom Chaverim (2)
Sinking Of The Reuben James (1)

Sixteen Tons (2)
Stewball (1)
Subo (1)
Suliram (I'll Be There) (1)
Tapuach Hineni (1)
There Once Was A Young Man Who Went To The City (1)

Universal Folk Song (1)
Venga Jaleo (2)
Virgin Mary (1)
When The Saints Go Marching In (2)
Wimoweh (2)
Woody's Rag And 900 Miles (2)

WEBB, Jack
Born on 4/2/20 in Santa Monica, California; died on 12/23/82. Actor/TV producer. Creator/director/star (Joe Friday) of *Dragnet* TV series (1952-59; 1967-70) and the film *Pete Kelly's Blues*. Married to singer/actress Julie London (1945-53).

9/3/55	2[2]	15		**Pete Kelly's Blues** .... [T-I]	$35	RCA 1126

Jack narrates the introduction to songs played by a seven-man jazz combo led by clarinetist Matty Matlock (same band that did scoring for the film - also see Ray Heindorf); Webb played Pete Kelly in the film, however, his trumpet playing was dubbed by Dick Cathcart.

Breezin' Along With The Breeze
Bye, Bye Blackbird

Hard Hearted Hannah
I Never Knew

I'm Gonna Meet My Sweetie Now

Oh Didn't He Ramble
Pete Kelly's Blues
Smiles

Somebody Loves Me
Sugar

What Can I Say After I Say I'm Sorry

WEBBER, Andrew Lloyd
Born 3/22/48 in London. Prominent composer of musicals. Creator of world-renown productions *Jesus Christ Superstar*, *Evita*, *Cats*, *Phantom Of The Opera* and others. Collaborated with lyricist Tim Rice. Also see Michael Crawford and Original Casts.

5/25/91	130	14	▲	The Premiere Collection .... [K]	$12	MCA 6284

14 selections from *Phantom Of The Opera*, *Evita*, *Cats* and other Andrew Lloyd Webber musicals performed by various artists

DEBUT DATE	PEAK POS	WKS CHR	GOLD	ARTIST — Album Title	$	Label & Number

WEBBER, Andrew Lloyd — Cont'd

All I Ask Of You [Cliff Richard & Sarah Brightman]
Another Suitcase In Another Hall [Barbara Dickson]
Don't Cry For Me Argentina [Julie Covington]
I Don't Know How To Love Him [Yvonne Elliman]
Magical Mr. Mistofelees [Paul Nicholas]
Memory [Elaine Paige]
Music Of The Night [Michael Crawford]
Phantom Of The Opera [Steve Harley & Sarah Brightman]
Pie Jesu [Sarah Brightman & Paul Miles Kingston]
Starlight Express [Ray Shell]
Superstar [Murray Head]
Take That Look Off Your Face [Marti Webb]
Tell Me On A Sunday [Marti Webb]
Variations 1-4 [Julian Lloyd Webber]

WECHTER, Julius — see BAJA MARIMBA BAND

WE FIVE

California pop quintet: Beverly Bivens (lead singer), Mike Stewart (brother of John Stewart), Pete Fullerton, Bob Jones and Jerry Burgan.

| 10/16/65 | 32 | 30 | | 1 You Were On My Mind .... | $20 | A&M 4111 |
| 1/27/68 | 172 | 6 | | 2 Make Someone Happy .... | $20 | A&M 4138 |

Can't Help Falling In Love (1)
Cast Your Fate To The Wind (1)
First Time (2)
Five Will Get You Ten (2)
High Flying Bird (1)
I Can Never Go Home Again (1)
I Got Plenty O' Nuttin' (1)
If I Were Alone (1)
Inch Worm (2)
Let's Get Together (2) 31
Love Me Not Tomorrow (1)
Make Someone Happy (2)
My Favorite Things (1)
Our Day Will Come (2)
Poet (2)
Small World (1)
Softly As I Leave You (1)
Somewhere (2)
Somewhere Beyond The Sea (1)
Tonight (1)
What Do I Do Now? (2)
What's Goin' On (2)
You Let A Love Burn Out (2)
You Were On My Mind (1) 3

WEIR, Bob

Born on 10/16/47 in San Francisco. Rock singer/guitarist. Co-founder of the Grateful Dead. Later formed Kingfish and Bobby & The Midnites.

| 6/17/72 | 68 | 15 | | 1 Ace .... | $30 | Warner 2627 |
| 2/11/78 | 69 | 16 | | 2 Heaven Help The Fool .... | $8 | Arista 4155 |

Black-Throated Wind (1)
Bombs Away (2) 70
Cassidy (1)
Easy To Slip (2)
Greatest Story Ever Told (1)
Heaven Help The Fool (1)
I'll Be Doggone (2)
Looks Like Rain (1)
Mexicali Blues (1)
One More Saturday Night (1)
Playing In The Band (1)
Salt Lake City (2)
Shade Of Grey (2)
This Time Forever (2)
Walk In The Sunshine (2)
Wrong Way Feelin' (2)

WEISBERG, Tim

Born in 1943 in Hollywood. Flautist; studied classical music as an adolescent. Performs pop-oriented music with a jazz appeal.

12/29/73+	160	4		1 Dreamspeaker .... [I-L]	$8	A&M 3045
				side 1: live; side 2: studio		
11/23/74	100	13		2 Tim Weisberg 4 .... [I]	$8	A&M 3658
10/11/75	105	7		3 Listen To The City .... [I]	$8	A&M 4545
10/2/76	148	7		4 Live At Last! .... [I-L]	$8	A&M 4600
8/20/77	108	12		5 The Tim Weisberg Band .... [I]	$8	United Art. 773
5/6/78	159	6		6 Rotations .... [I]	$8	United Art. 857
9/16/78	8	35		7 Twin Sons Of Different Mothers	$10	Full Moon 35339
				DAN FOGELBERG & TIM WEISBERG		
4/14/79	114	11		8 Night-Rider! .... [I]	$8	MCA 3084
6/9/79	169	4		9 Smile!/The Best Of Tim Weisberg .... [I-G]	$8	A&M 4749
8/2/80	171	7		10 Party of One .... [I]	$8	MCA 5125

All Tied Up (6)
Amber (10)
Angelic Smile (2,9)
Aspen (5)
Blitz, The (5)
Bruiser, The (2,9)
Bullfrog (1)
California Memories Medley (2,4)
Canterbury Tales (8)
Cascade (5)
Castile (1,4)
Catch The Breeze (6)
Chase, The (3,4,9)
Conception (3)
Dealer, The (3)
Dion Blue (2,9)
Discovery (3,4)
Do Dah (1,4,9)
Don't Keep Me Waiting, Girl (10)
Dreamspeaker (1)
Everyone Loves A Mystery (10)
Everytime I See Your Smile (6)
Flight Of The Phoenix (2)
Friends (8)
Gene, Jean (5)
Gentle Storm (5)
Glide Away (6)
Good Life (3,4,9)
Good News (2)
Guitar Etude No. 3 (7)
High Rise (3,9)
Hurtwood Alley (7)
I'm The Lucky One (10)
Intimidation (7)
Invisible Messenger (2)
Just For You (6)
Katie (10)
Killing Me Softly With His Song (1)
Lahaina Luna (7)
Lazy Susan (7)
Listen To The City (3,4,9)
Lord Vanity (5)
Love Maker (3)
Lunchbreak (3)
Magic Lady (10)
Mercy, Mercy, Mercy (5)
Midsummer's Dream (8)
Moonchild (8)
Night For Crying (1,9)
Night Rider (8)
Night Watch (1)
Nightsongs (8)
Nikki's Waltz (3)
Page One (10)
Paris Nocturne (7)
Party Of One (10)
Passing, The (3)
Power Flower (10)
Power Pocket (2)
Premonition (2)
Rainbow City (3,4)
Rush Hour (Friday, P.M.) (3,9)
Scrabble X, Y, & Z (1)
Shadows In The Wind (8)
Shellie's Rainbow (5)
Since You've Asked (7)
Six O'Clock In The Morning (1)
So Good To Me (6)
Someday My Prince Will Come (2)
Southern Lights (5)
Street Party (3,9)
Sudden Samba (6)
Tell Me To My Face (7)
There Is A Mountain (6)
Touchstone (8)
Travesty (2,9)
Twins Theme (7)
Visit, The (2,9)
Weekend (3)
Westchester Faire (8)
What's Going On (10)
Winged Invitation (2)
Wings Of Fire (8)
Won't Be Comin' Back (8)
Yesterday's Dreams (8)
Your Smiling Eyes (4)
Power Of Gold (7) 24

WEISSBERG, Eric

Bluegrass multi-instrumentalist. Worked with The Greenbriar Boys and The Tarriers folk groups. Prolific session man.

1/27/73	1³	25	●	1 Dueling Banjos .... [I]	$8	Warner 2683
				ERIC WEISSBERG and STEVE MANDELL		
				except for the title song, all tunes performed by Weissberg and Marshall Brickman (previously released on LP New Dimensions in Banjo & Bluegrass)		
10/20/73	196	2		2 Rural Free Delivery	$8	Warner 2720
				ERIC WEISSBERG & DELIVERANCE		

Blessed Is The Man (2)
Buffalo Gals (1)
Bugle Call Rag (1)
Concrete Canyon Boogie (2)
Dueling Banjos (1) 2
Earl's Breakdown (1)
Eight More Miles To Louisville (1)
Eighth Of January (1)
End Of A Dream (1)
Farewell Blues (1)
Fire On The Mountain (1)
Hard Ain't It Hard (1)
Hard Hearted (2)
Lend Me Your Heart (2)
Little Maggie (1)
Mountain Dew (1)
Old Joe Clark (1)
Opening Day (2)
Pony Express (1)
Rawhide (1)
Reuben's Train (1)
Ride In The Country (2)
Riding The Waves (1)
Scalded Cat (2)
Shuckin' The Corn (1)
Somewhere In Time (2)
Thanks For Bein' You And Lovin' Me (2)
'Til The End Of The World Rolls Around (2)
Uncle Pen (2)

WELCH, Bob

Born on 7/31/46 in Los Angeles. Guitarist/vocalist with Fleetwood Mac (1971-74). Formed the British rock group Paris in 1976. His father, Robert L. Welch, was a major film/TV producer.

10/8/77+	12	46	▲	1 French Kiss	$8	Capitol 11663
3/10/79	20	17	●	2 Three Hearts	$8	Capitol 11907
12/1/79	105	8		3 The Other One	$8	Capitol 12017
10/11/80	162	5		4 Man Overboard	$8	Capitol 12107

B666 (4)
Carolene (1)
China (2)
Church (2) 73
Come Softly To Me (2)
Danchiva (1)
Dancin' Eyes (1)
Devil Wind (2)
Don't Let Me Fall (3)
Don't Rush The Good Things (4)
Don't Wait Too Long (2)
Easy To Fall (1)
Ebony Eyes (1) 14
Fate Decides (4)
Future Games (3)
Ghost Of Flight 401 (2)
Girl Can't Stop (4)

DEBUT DATE	PEAK POS	WKS CHR	GOLD	ARTIST — Album Title	$	Label & Number

WELCH, Bob — Cont'd

Here Comes The Night (2)	Justine (4)	Love Came 2X (3)	Old Man Of 17 (3)	Rebel Rouser (3)	3 Hearts (2)
Hideaway (3)	Little Star (2)	Man Overboard (4)	Oneonone (3)	**Sentimental Lady** (1) **8**	Watch The Animals (3)
Hot Love, Cold World (1) **31**	Lose My Heart (1)	Mystery Train (1)	Outskirts (1)	Spanish Dancers (3)	
I Saw Her Standing There (2)	Lose Your... (1)	Nightmare (4)	**Precious Love** (2) **19**	Straight Up (3)	
Jealous (4)	Lose Your Heart (1)	Oh Jenny (2)	Reason (4)	Those Days Are Gone (4)	

WELCH, Lenny
Born on 5/15/38 in Asbury Park, New Jersey. Black pop vocalist.

DEBUT DATE	PEAK POS	WKS CHR		#	ARTIST — Album Title	$	Label & Number
2/1/64	73	10		1	Since I Fell For You	$25	Cadence 3068
1/1/66	147	2		2	Since I Fell For You .... [R]	$15	Columbia 9230
					new cover features same photo as original with new artwork		

Are You Sincere (1,2)	I Need Someone (1,2)	It's Just Not That Easy (1,2)	**Since I Fell For You** (1,2) **4**	You Can Have Her (1,2)	
Darlin' (1)	I'm In The Mood For Love (1,2)	Mama, Don't You Hit That Boy (1,2)	Stranger In Paradise (1,2)	**You Don't Know Me** (1,2) **45**	
Ebb Tide (1,2) **25**			Taste Of Honey (1,2)		

★★14★★ WELK, Lawrence
Born on 3/11/03 in Strasburg, North Dakota. Died on 5/17/92 of pneumonia. Accordionist and polka/sweet bandleader since the mid-1920s. Band's style labeled as "champagne music." Own national TV musical variety show began on 7/2/55 and ran on ABC until 9/4/71. New episodes in syndication from 1971 to 1982.

DEBUT DATE	PEAK POS	WKS CHR	GOLD	#	ARTIST — Album Title	$	Label & Number
1/28/56	5	11		1	**Lawrence Welk and His Sparkling Strings** .... [I]	$15	Coral 57011
3/31/56	13	2		2	TV Favorites .... [I]	$15	Coral 57025
3/31/56	18	2		3	Shamrocks and Champagne	$15	Coral 57036
5/12/56	6	17		4	**Bubbles In The Wine**	$15	Coral 57038
					title song is Lawrence's theme song		
8/18/56	10	30		5	**Say It With Music** .... [I]	$15	Coral 57041
					medleys of 36 dance favorites		
8/25/56	17	4		6	Champagne Pops Parade	$15	Coral 57078
10/20/56	18	1		7	Moments To Remember .... [I]	$15	Coral 57068
12/22/56	8	3		8	**Merry Christmas** .... [X]	$15	Coral 57093
3/16/57	20	1		9	Pick-a-Polka! .... [I]	$15	Coral 57067
5/20/57	17	5		10	Waltz with Lawrence Welk .... [I]	$15	Coral 57119
					medleys of 24 favorite waltzes		
10/21/57+	19	2		11	Lawrence Welk plays Dixieland .... [I]	$15	Coral 57146
					featuring Pete Fountain on clarinet		
12/23/57	18	3		12	Jingle Bells .... [X]	$15	Coral 57186
12/19/60+	4	29		13	**Last Date** .... [I]	$12	Dot 3350
1/30/61	1[11]	64	●	14	**Calcutta!** .... [I]	$12	Dot 3359
8/7/61	2[1]	49		15	**Yellow Bird** .... [I]	$12	Dot 3389
					above 2 feature Frank Scott on harpsichord		
1/6/62	4	48		16	**Moon River** .... [I]	$12	Dot 3412
1/6/62	100	3		17	Silent Night and 13 other best loved Christmas songs .... [X-I]	$12	Dot 3397
5/26/62	6	20		18	**Young World** .... [I]	$12	Dot 3428
9/15/62	9	15		19	**Baby Elephant Walk and Theme From The Brothers Grimm** ... [I]	$12	Dot 3457
12/29/62	140	1		20	Silent Night and 13 other best loved Christmas songs .... [X-I-R]	$12	Dot 3397
					Christmas charts: 13/'63, 61/'66, 61/'67		
3/9/63	34	25		21	Waltz Time .... [I]	$10	Dot 25499
4/6/63	20	28		22	1963's Early Hits .... [I]	$10	Dot 25510
8/10/63	33	28		23	Scarlett O'Hara .... [I]	$10	Dot 25528
12/7/63+	29	26		24	Wonderful! Wonderful! .... [I]	$10	Dot 25552
4/11/64	37	19		25	Early Hits Of 1964 .... [I]	$10	Dot 25572
4/25/64	127	5		26	A tribute to the All-Time Greats .... [I]	$10	Dot 25544
8/8/64	73	16		27	the Lawrence Welk Television Show 10th Anniversary	$10	Dot 25591
1/9/65	115	6		28	The Golden Millions .... [I]	$10	Dot 25611
4/3/65	108	12		29	My First Of 1965 .... [I]	$10	Dot 25616
4/17/65	57	12		30	Apples & Bananas .... [I]	$10	Dot 25629
1/29/66	93	6		31	Today's Great Hits .... [I]	$10	Dot 25663
3/26/66	106	5		32	Champagne On Broadway .... [I]	$10	Dot 25688
12/3/66+	12	41	●	33	Winchester Cathedral .... [I]	$10	Dot 25774
4/15/67	72	18		34	Lawrence Welk's "Hits Of Our Time" .... [I]	$10	Dot 25790
10/14/67	130	12		35	Golden Hits/The Best Of Lawrence Welk .... [I-G]	$10	Dot 25812
4/6/68	130	12		36	Love Is Blue .... [I]	$8	Ranwood 8003
2/8/69	173	8		37	Memories .... [I]	$8	Ranwood 8044
4/19/69	55	20		38	Galveston .... [I]	$8	Ranwood 8049
9/13/69	176	4		39	Lawrence Welk plays I Love You Truly and other songs of love .... [I]	$8	Ranwood 8053
11/15/69	145	7		40	Jean .... [I]	$8	Ranwood 8060
12/12/70+	133	17		41	Candida	$8	Ranwood 8083
12/23/72+	149	10		42	Reminiscing .... [I-K]	$10	Ranwood 5001 [2]

Addams Family, Theme From The (29)	All I Have To Do Is Dream (22)	Anything That's Part Of You (18)	Autumn Nocturne (1)	Beer Barrel Polka (Roll Out The Barrel) (9)	Blue Room (medley) (5)
Adeste Fideles (17)	Alley Cat (29,42)	**Apples And Bananas** (30,35) **48**	**Baby Elephant Walk** (19,35) **48**	Begorrah! (2)	Blue Skies (medley) (5)
(also see: Come All Ye Faithful)	Always (39)	April In Portugal (14)	Ball Of Fire (4)	Bewitched, Theme From (29)	Blue Tango (14)
Alamo, Theme From The ..see: Green Leaves Of Summer	Am I That Easy To Forget (36)	April Love (18)	Ballerina (26)	Beyond The Blue Horizon (medley) (5)	Blues Serenade (1)
Alice Blue Gown (medley) (10)	And We Were Lovers (34)	Are You Lonesome Tonight (19)	Barnyard Blues (11)	Blame It On The Bossa Nova (22)	Born Free (33)
Alice In Wonderland (22)	Anniversary Song (37,39)	Around The World (16)	Be My Love (26)	Blue (And Broken Hearted) (2)	**Breakwater** (23) **100**
	Anniversary Waltz (7,39)	As Long As She Needs Me (29)	Beat Goes On (34)	Blue Moods (11)	Bridal Chorus (39)
	Anything Goes (medley) (5)		Beautiful Love (7)		Brothers Grimm, Theme From The (19)
			Because (39)		
			Because Of You (19)		

WELK, Lawrence — Cont'd

Bubbles In The Wine (4,35,42)
By The Time I Get To Phoenix (38)
Calcutta (14,35) **1**
Call Me (30,42)
Can't Get Used To Losing You (23)
Can't Take My Eyes Off You (36)
Canadian Sunset (30)
Candida (41)
Carolina In The Morning (42)
Cecilia (medley) (5)
Champagne Polka (9)
Champagne Waltz (1)
Chances Are (13)
Charmaine (medley) (5,10)
Chicken Polka (9)
Chihuahua Polka (9)
China Boy (Go Sleep) (11)
Christmas Comes But Once A Year (8)
Christmas Dreaming (A Little Early This Year) (8)
Christmas Island (8)
Christmas Song (Merry Christmas To You) (12)
Christmas Toy (8)
Christmas Waltz (12)
Cinco Robles (37)
Clarinet Polka (9)
Close To You (41)
Come All Ye Faithful (medley) (12)
(also see: Adeste Fideles)
Copy Cat (33)
Corrine Corrina (14)
Cracklin' Rosie (41)
Cry Me A River (28)
Cuando (33)
Cuban Love Song (medley) (10)
Dance Aroun' A Stack Of Barley (4)
Danube Waves (21)
Darktown Strutters' Ball (4)
Days Of Wine And Roses (22)
Dear Heart (29,42)
Deck The Halls (12,17)
Deep Purple (24)
Diane (medley) (5,10)
Dill Pickles (2)
Do You Know The Way To San Jose (38)
Dolores (27)
Don't Break The Heart That Loves You (18)
Don't Think Twice, It's All Right (24)
Don't Worry (15)
Doodle Doo Doo (medley) (5)
18 Yellow Roses (23)
Emily (29)
Emperor Waltz (21)
End Of The World (22)
Endlessly (41)
Estrellita (42)
Everybody Loves Somebody (29)
Exactly Like You (medley) (5)
Exodus (13)
Family Affair, Theme From (33)
Fascination (37)
Fiesta (24)
First Noel (12,17)
Flirtation Waltz (4)
Florena Polka (9)
Fool Never Learns (25)
Fools Rush In (24)
For You (25)
Galway Bay (27)
Gentle On My Mind (38)
Georgia On My Mind (13)
Georgy Girl (34)
Get Me To The Church On Time (37)
Getting To Know You (32)
Giannina Mia (medley) (5)
Gigi (19)
Girl From Barbados (25)

Go Way, Go Way (4)
God Rest Ye Merry Gentlemen (12,17)
Goin' Out Of My Head (36)
Going Home (37)
Gold And Silver (21)
Good King Wenceslas (12,17)
Good Life (23)
Good Luck Charm (18)
Good News (25)
Goodbye, Charlie (29)
Goodnight, Irene (15)
Graduation Day (6)
Granada (27)
Green Leaves Of Summer (13,42)
Green Tambourine (36)
Gypsy In My Soul (medley) (5)
Happy Heart (40)
Harbor Lights (15)
Hark! The Herald Angels Sing (12,17)
Hawaiian Wedding Song (39)
Heart You Break (May Be Your Own) (2)
Heartaches By The Number (31,42)
Heartbreak Hotel (15)
Helena Polka (9,42)
Hello, Dolly! (25,27)
Hey Jude (38)
Hey There (28)
High On The House Top (8)
Hold Me, Thrill Me, Kiss Me (31)
Hold My Hand (30)
Holiday Waltz (21)
Honey (38)
Honolulu Eyes (medley) (5)
Hot Pretzels (9)
How Little It Matters How Little We Know (6)
Humoresque Boogie (14)
Hurt So Bad (40)
Hush...Hush, Sweet Charlotte (31)
I Can Dream, Can't I? (28)
I Can't Believe It's True (medley) (5)
I Could Have Danced All Night (6,16)
I Found A Million Dollar Baby (In A Five And Ten Cent Store) (medley) (5)
I Left My Heart In San Francisco (27)
I Love Thee (39)
I Love You (7)
I Love You Because (23)
I Love You More And More Every Day (25)
I Love You Truly (27,39)
I Really Don't Want To Know (22)
I Wanna Do More Than Whistle (Under The Mistletoe) (8)
I Went To Your Wedding (28)
I Whistle A Happy Tune (32)
I Will Wait For You (34)
I Wish We Were Sweethearts Again (2)
I'd Love To Live In Loveland (medley) (10)
I'll Always Be In Love With You (7)
I'll Be Home For Christmas (17)
I'll Never Smile Again (26)
I'll See You Again (37,42)
I'm Forever Blowing Bubbles (42)
(I'm In Heaven When I See You Smile) Diane ..see: Diane
I've Grown Accustomed To Her Face (6,32)
If I Loved You (32,42)
Impossible Dream (38)
In A Little Spanish Town (10,42)
"In" Crowd (31)

In The Arms Of Love (34)
In The Year 2525 (40)
Ireland Must Be Heaven For My Mother Came From There (1)
Irish Alphabet (3)
Irish Soldier Boy (3)
It Came Upon The Midnight Clear (12,17)
It Happened In Monterey (medley) (10)
It Might As Well Be Spring (32)
It's A Sin To Tell A Lie (medley) (10)
It's All In The Game (19,25,42)
It's Almost Tomorrow (4)
It's Not For Me To Say (19)
Java (25)
Jean (40)
Jeannine (I Dream Of Lilac Time) (1)
Jenny Lind (9)
Jingle Bells (12)
Jolly Coppersmith (9)
Josephine (27,42)
Joy To The World (12,17)
Juanita (15)
Just Because (42)
Kazoo Song (30)
Kiss Polka (9)
L'Amour Toujours L'Amour (Love Everlasting) (medley) (10)
La Bamba (31)
Land Of Dreams (30)
Last Date (35) **21**
Let It Snow! Let It Snow! Let It Snow! (8)
Let Me Go, Lover! (28)
Let's Have An Old-Fashioned Christmas (12)
Lisbon Antigua (4)
Little Bit Of Heaven (Shure They Call It Ireland) (3)
Little Green Apples (38)
Little Sir Echo (medley) (10)
Little Things Mean A Lot (28)
Loch Lomond (15)
Lola O'Brien The Irish Hawaiian (3)
Longing (30)
Look Back And Laugh (2)
Look What They've Done To My Song Ma (41)
Love Is A Many-Splendored Thing (16)
Love Is Blue (36)
Love Is The Sweetest Thing (7)
Love Letters (18)
Love Letters In The Sand (26)
Love Me Tender (19)
Love Those Eyes (15)
Love's Own Sweet Song (medley) (10)
Luxembourg Polka (2)
Mam'selle (14)
Marcheta (medley) (5)
Maria (32)
Maria Elena (24,42)
Marianne (15)
Mas Que Nada (Pow-Pow-Pow) (33)
McNamara's Band (3)
Melodie D'Amour (13)
Melody Of Love (37)
Memories (37)
Merry Christmas From Our House - To Your House (12)
Merry Widow Waltz (21)
Mexicali Rose (27)
Misty (13)
Mockin' Bird Hill (15)
Moments To Remember (7)
Mona Lisa (19)
Mood Indigo (medley) (5)
Moon River (16,35)
Moonglow and Theme From "Picnic" (6)

Moonlight And Roses (Bring Mem'ries Of You) (31)
Moonlight Cocktail (1)
More (27)
More I Love You (38)
Moritat (A Theme From "The Threepenny Opera") (4) **17**
Mountain King (14)
Musette (1)
Music To Watch Girls By (34)
My Blue Heaven (5,27)
My Darling (7)
My Dear (medley) (10)
My Heart Danced An Irish Jig (3)
My Heart Has A Mind Of Its Own (13)
My Little Angel (6)
My Love For You (15)
My North Dakota Home (42)
My Song (2)
My Three Sons, Theme From (35) **55**
My Wonderful One (7)
Nature Boy (26)
Need You (30,42)
Never On Sunday (29)
Night Life (24)
Night Theme (13)
No Other Love (26)
O Little Town Of Bethlehem (12,17)
O Promise Me (39)
Oh, Happy Day (4,27)
Oh, Lady Be Good (medley) (5)
On A Clear Day You Can See Forever (32)
On The Street Where You Live (6,32) **96**
One Rose (medley) (10)
Other Man's Grass Is Always Greener (36)
Our Day Will Come (29)
Our Winter Love (22)
Out Of A Clear Blue Sky (30,42)
Over The Waves (21)
Pagan Love Song (medley) (10)
Paradise (10,37)
Pennsylvania Polka (9)
People (29)
People Will Say We're In Love (32)
Perfidia (14)
Pete's Tail-Fly (11)
Picnic ..see: Moonglow
Pipeline (23)
Play Fiddle Play (medley) (10)
Please (medley) (5)
Please Help Me, I'm Falling (13)
Poeme (19)
Poodle Walk (27)
Poor People Of Paris (4) **17**
Practice, Practice, What You Preach (6)
President Kennedy March (27)
Pretend (19)
Pretty Baby (medley) (5)
Prisoner Of Love (26)
Puff (The Magic Dragon) (23)
Quentin's Theme (40)
Rain (medley) (5)
Rain On The Roof (medley) (5)
Ramona (medley) (10)
Rhythm Of The Rain (22,42)
Ring Those Christmas Bells (12)
Rock 'N' Roll Ruby (6)
Romance (medley) (10)
Romeo & Juliet, Love Theme From (40)
Ruby (14)
Rudolph, The Red-Nosed Reindeer (17)
Runaway (15,35) **56**
Rustic Dance (4)

'S Wonderful (5,11)
Sailor (Your Home Is The Sea) (14)
Sam, The Old Accordion Man (2)
San Antonio Rose (11)
Santa Claus Is Comin' To Town (8)
Santa Claus Is Here Again (12)
Santa From Santa Fe (12)
Save The Last Dance For Me (14)
Say It With Music (medley) (5)
Scarlett O'Hara (23,35) **89**
Secret Love (18)
Send Me The Pillow You Dream On (31)
September Song (5,26)
Shamrocks, Shillelaghs And Shenanigans (3)
She's Got You (18)
Should I (11)
Silent Night (12,17)
Silver Bells (12)
Silver Moon (37)
Singin' In The Rain (medley) (5)
Sixteen Reasons (28)
Sleep (10,13)
Sleepy Time Gal (medley) (5)
Sleigh Ride (12)
Snowbird (41)
Some Enchanted Evening (16,32)
Somebody Loves Me (medley) (5)
Something (41)
Something To Remember You By (7)
Somewhere My Love (34)
Song Of Love (medley) (10)
Sonny Boy (25)
Sophia Mia (30)
Sound Of Music (16,32)
Southern Roses (21)
Southtown, U.S.A. (25)
Spinning Wheel (40)
Spooky (36)
Stand By Your Man (41)
Standing On The Corner (6)
Stars In My Eyes (1)
Stay As Sweet As You Are (7)
Stockholm (25) **91**
Story Of Kevin Barry (3)
Strangers In The Night (34)
Strike Up The Band (11)
Suddenly There's A Valley (5)
Sugar Shack (24)
Sukiyaki (23)
Summer Nights (31)
Summer Samba (33)
Summer Wind (31,33)
Sunrise Serenade (1)
Sweet Caroline (40)
Sweetest Sounds (29)
Sweethearts On Parade (11)
Sympathy (medley) (5)
Tales From The Vienna Woods (21)
Talk To The Animals (36)
Taste Of Honey (31)
Tea For Two (medley) (5)
Tea 'N Trumpets (11)
Temptation (5)
Tenderly (medley) (10)
Thanks For Christmas (8,17)
That Sunday, That Summer (42)
That's My Desire (26)
Then You Can Tell Me Goodbye (34)
There! I've Said It Again (25)
There Is No Greater Love (2)
(They Long To Be) Close To You ..see: Close To You
They Remind Me Too Much Of You (22)
3rd Man Theme (medley) (5)

Thomas Crown Affair, Theme From The ..see: Windmills Of Your Mind
Those Lazy, Hazy, Crazy Days Of Summer (23)
Those Were The Days (38)
Thou Swell (5,11)
Three Coins In The Fountain (19)
Three O'Clock In The Morning (10,37)
Through The Years (39)
Tie Me Kangaroo Down, Sport (23)
Tijuana (33)
Till I Waltz Again With You (28)
Till There Was You (16)
Tip Of My Fingers (23)
'Tis The Luck Of The Irish (3)
To Each His Own (13)
Tonight (16)
Too Young (18)
Tree In The Meadow (28)
True Love (39)
Twelve Gifts Of Christmas (8)
Twilight Time (1)
Twilight Time In Tennessee (1)
Unchained Melody (31)
Vaya Con Dios (19)
Very Thought Of You (7)
Vienna Echoes (21)
Wabash Blues (medley) (5)
Wake The Town And Tell The People (4)
Walk Right In (22)
Walking On New Grass (33)
Waltz You Saved For Me (1)
Was That The Human Thing To Do (medley) (5)
Washington Square (24)
Watch What Happens (36)
Wayward Wind (4)
We Can Fly (36)
We Can Make Music (41)
We've Only Just Begun (41)
Wedding March (39)
Wedding Of The Winds (21)
What A Heavenly Night For Love (4)
What Will Mary Say (22)
What's A Wrong (2)
When I Grow Too Old To Dream (19)
When Irish Eyes Are Smiling (3)
When It's Sleepy Time Down South (26)
When My Baby Smiles At Me (42)
When My Sugar Walks Down The Street (11)
When The Organ Played At Twilight (1)
When Your Hair Has Turned To Silver (medley) (10)
Where The Blue Of The Night Meets The Gold Of The Day (26)
White Christmas (8,17)
Why Don't You Believe Me (28)
Wild Colonial Boy (3)
Winchester Cathedral (33)
Windmills Of Your Mind (40)
Winter Wonderland (8)
Wish Me A Rainbow (34)
Wish You Were Here (16)
Wives And Lovers (24)
Wonderful! Wonderful! (24)
Wonderful World Of The Young (38)
Yearning (Just For You) (medley) (5)
Yellow Bird (15,35) **71**
Yes Sir, That's My Baby (medley) (5)
Yesterday (31)
Yesterday, When I Was Young (40)

DEBUT DATE	PEAK POS	WKS CHR	GOLD	ARTIST — Album Title	$	Label & Number

WELK, Lawrence — Cont'd

You And You (21)	You Gave Me Wings (16)	You're The Only Star (medley) (10)	You're The Reason I'm Living (22)	Young Love (18)
You Belong To Me (28)	You'll Never Walk Alone (16)			Young World (18)
You Don't Own Me (25)	You're My Everything (7)	You're The Reason (30)	Young At Heart (18,42)	

WELLER, Freddy
Born on 9/9/47 in Atlanta. Worked with Paul Revere & The Raiders from 1967-71. Co-wrote "Dizzy" and "Jam Up Jelly Tight" with Tommy Roe.

| 8/16/69 | 144 | 7 | | Games People Play/These Are Not My People .... | $15 | Columbia 9904 |

Birmingham	Games People Play	Home	My, My Momma	One Woman Can't Hold Me	You Never Knew Julie
Freeborn Man	Goodnight Sandy	Louisiana Redbone	Oakridge Tennessee	These Are Not My People	

WELLES, Orson
Born on 5/6/15 in Kenosha, Wisconsin; died on 10/10/85. Legendary film actor/writer/director.

| 8/22/70 | 66 | 16 | | The Begatting of The President ....[C] | $10 | Mediarts 41-2 |

tongue-in-cheek history of contemporary America (biblical style)

Ascension, The	Burn, Pharaoh, Burn	Defoliation Of Eden	Pacification Of Goliath	Raising Of Richard
Book Of Hubert	Coming Of Richard	L.B. Jenesis	Paradise Bossed	

WELLS, Mary
R&B vocalist born on 5/13/43 in Detroit. At age 17, presented "Bye Bye Baby," a tune she had written for Jackie Wilson, to Wilson's producer, Berry Gordy, Jr. Gordy signed her to his newly formed label, Motown. Wells was the first to have a top 10 and #1 single for that label. Married for a time to Cecil Womack (brother of Bobby Womack). Diagnosed with throat cancer, August 1990; died on 7/26/92.

| 3/16/63 | 49 | 8 | | 1 | Two Lovers and other great hits.. | $50 | Motown 607 |
| 5/16/64 | 42 | 16 | | 2 | Together .... | $30 | Motown 613 |

MARVIN GAYE & MARY WELLS

5/30/64	18	37		3	Greatest Hits ....[G]	$20	Motown 616
7/25/64	111	12		4	Mary Wells Sings My Guy	$20	Motown 617
5/1/65	145	4		5	Mary Wells	$20	20th Century 3171

After The Lights Go Down Low (2)	He's The One I Love (4)	Looking Back (1)	**One Who Really Loves You** (3) *8*	We're Just Two Of A Kind (5) You Came A Long Way From St. Louis (2)
Ain't It The Truth (5) *45*	How Can I Forget Him (5)	My Baby Just Cares For Me (4)	Operator (1)	What Love Has Joined Together (3) You Do Something To Me (4)
At Last (4)	How (When My Heart Belongs To You) (4)	**My Guy** (3,4) *1*	Squeeze Me (2)	**What's Easy For Two Is So Hard For One** (3) *29* **You Lost The Sweetest Boy** (3) *22*
Bye Bye Baby (3) *45*	(I Guess There's) No Love (3)	My Mind's Made Up (5)	Stop Right Here (1)	What's The Matter With You Baby (2) *17*
Deed I Do (2)	(I Love You) For Sentimental Reasons (2)	My 2 Arms - You = Tears (1)	**Stop Takin' Me For Granted** (5) *88*	**Your Old Stand By** (3) *40*
Does He Love Me (4)	I Only Have Eyes For You (4)	**Never, Never Leave Me** (5) *54*	Time After Time (5)	Whisper You Love Me Boy (4)
Everlovin' Boy (5)	If You Love Me, Really Love Me (2)	Oh Little Boy (What Did You Do To Me) (3)	Two Lovers (1,3) *7*	Why Don't You Let Yourself Go (5)
Goody, Goody (1)	It Had To Be You (4)	Old Love (Let's Try It Again) (3)	Until I Met You (2)	**You Beat Me To The Punch** (3) *9*
Guess Who (1)	Late Late Show (2)	**Once Upon A Time** (2) *19*	**Use Your Head** (5) *34*	
He Holds His Own (4)	**Laughing Boy** (1,3) *15*	Was It Worth It (1)		
He's A Lover (5) *74*				
He's Good Enough For Me (5)				

WENDY and LISA
Wendy Melvoin (guitar, vocals) and Lisa Coleman (keyboards). Formerly with Prince's band The Revolution. Wendy's father is Mike Melvoin (The Plastic Cow); her sister is Susannah Melvoin (The Family).

| 9/19/87 | 88 | 13 | | 1 | Wendy And Lisa .... | $8 | Columbia 40862 |

co-produced by Bobby Z. (former drummer of The Revolution)

| 4/8/89 | 119 | 8 | | 2 | Fruit At The Bottom .... | $8 | Columbia 44341 |

Always In My Dreams (2)	Everyday (2)	Honeymoon Express (1)	Lolly Lolly (2)	Song About (1) White (1)
Are You My Baby (2)	Everything But You (1)	I Think It Was December (2)	Satisfaction (2)	Stay (1)
Blues Away (1)	From Now On (We're One) (2)	Life, The (1)	Sideshow (1)	Tears Of Joy (2)
Chance To Grow (1)	Fruit At The Bottom (2)	Light (1)	Someday I (2)	**Waterfall** (1) *56*

WERNER, David
Pittsburgh-based guitarist/vocalist.

| 9/1/79 | 65 | 11 | | | David Werner.. | $8 | Epic 36126 |

Can't Imagine	Eye To Eye	Hold On Tight	She Sent Me Away	What Do You Need To Love
Every New Romance	High Class Blues	Melanie Cries	Too Late To Try	What's Right

WESLEY, Fred, & The Horny Horns
Funk band led by former members of James Brown's J.B.'s: Fred Wesley (trombone) and Maceo Parker (sax). Also see The JB's.

| 4/30/77 | 181 | 5 | | | A Blow For Me, A Toot To You .... | $8 | Atlantic 18214 |

Between Two Sheets	Blow For Me, A Toot To You	Four Play	Peace Fugue	Up For The Down Stroke	When In Doubt: Vamp

WEST, Dottie
Born Dorothy Marsh on 10/11/32 in McMinnville, Tennessee. Died on 9/4/91 from injuries suffered in a car accident. Country singer. Also see Kenny Rogers.

| 4/14/79 | 82 | 23 | | 1 | Classics .... | $8 | United Art. 946 |
| 1/5/80 | 186 | 3 | | 2 | Every Time Two Fools Collide .... | $8 | United Art. 864 |

above 2: **KENNY ROGERS & DOTTIE WEST**

| 4/11/81 | 126 | 15 | | 3 | Wild West .... | $8 | Liberty 1062 |

All I Ever Need Is You (1)	Goodbye (3)	Let It Be Me (1)	Sorry Seems To Be The Hardest Word (3)	**What Are We Doin' In Love** (3) *14* You've Lost That Lovin' Feelin' (1)
Anyone Who Isn't Me Tonight (2)	(Hey Won't You Play) Another Somebody Done Somebody Wrong Song (1)	Let's Take The Long Way Around The World (1)	That's The Way It Could Have Been (2)	What's Wrong With Us Today (2)
Are You Happy Baby? (3)	I Wish That I Could Hurt That Way Again (3)	Loving Gift (2)	Till I Can Make It On My Own (1)	Why Don't We Go Somewhere And Love (2)
Baby I'm-A Want You (2)	(I'm Gonna) Put You Back On The Rack (3)	Make Us A Plan (3)	Together Again (1)	You And Me (2)
Beautiful Lies (2)	Just The Way You Are (1)	Midnight Flyer (1)	We Love Each Other (2)	You Needed Me (1)
Choosin' Means Losin' (3)		Please Remember Me (3)		
Every Time Two Fools Collide (2)		Right Or Wrong (3)		

DEBUT DATE	PEAK POS	WKS CHR	GOLD	ARTIST — Album Title	$	Label & Number

WEST, Leslie

Guitarist/vocalist. In 1969, recorded solo album *Mountain*, produced by Felix Pappalardi. Leslie and Felix subsequently formed the rock band Mountain. Also teamed with Cream bassist Jack Bruce and Mountain drummer Corky Laing in West, Bruce & Laing from 1972-74. Mountain disbanded in 1985.

9/6/69	**72**	14	1 Mountain		**$12**	Windfall 4500

West formed the group Mountain, named after this title, with the album's producer, Felix Pappalardi

4/19/75	**168**	6	2 The Great Fatsby		**$8**	Phantom 0954

with guest guitarist Mick Jagger

Baby, I'm Down (1)
Because You Are My Friend (1)
Better Watch Out (1)

Blind Man (1)
Blood Of The Sun (1)
Doctor Love (2)
Don't Burn Me (2)

Dreams Of Milk & Honey (1)
E.S.P. (1)
High Roller (2)
Honky Tonk Women (2)

House Of The Rising Sun (1)
I'm Gonna Love You Thru The Night (2)
If I Still Had You (2)

If I Were A Carpenter (2)
Little Bit Of Love (2)
Long Red (1)
Look To The Wind (1)

Southbound Train (1)
Storyteller Man (1)
This Wheel's On Fire (1)

WEST, Mae

Born on 8/17/1892 in Brooklyn; died on 11/22/80. Legendary film actress.

7/23/66	**116**	5	Way Out West		**$25**	Tower 5028

Mae sings rock 'n' roll, backed by the group Somebody's Chyldren (with drummer Gary Lewis)

Boom Boom
Day Tripper

If You Gotta Go
Lover, Please Don't Fight
Nervous

Mae Day
Treat Him Right

Shakin' All Over
Twist And Shout
When A Man Loves A Woman

You Turn Me On

WEST, BRUCE & LAING

Power-rock trio comprised of former Mountain members Leslie West (guitar, vocals) and Corky Laing (drums), and Cream's Jack Bruce (bass).

11/4/72+	**26**	20	1 Why Dontcha		**$8**	Windfall 31929
7/28/73	**87**	10	2 Whatever Turns You On		**$8**	Windfall 32216
5/11/74	**165**	6	3 Live 'N' Kickin'	[L]	**$8**	Windfall 33899

Backfire (2)
Dirty Shoes (2)
Doctor, The (1,3)
Like A Plate (2)

Love Is Worth The Blues (1)
November Song (2)
Out Into The Fields (1)
Play With Fire (2)

Pleasure (1)
Politician (3)
Pollution Woman (3)
Powerhouse Sod (3)

Rock 'N' Roll Machine (2)
Scotch Crotch (2)
Shake Ma Thing (Rollin Jack) (1)
Token (2)

Sifting Sand (2)
Slow Blues (2)
Third Degree (1)

Turn Me Over (1)
While You Sleep (1)
Why Dontcha (1)

WEST COAST RAP ALL-STARS, The

Rap benefit for inner city youth: Above The Law, Body & Soul, Def Jef, Digital Underground, Eazy-E, Ice-T, J.J. Fad, King Tee, M.C. Hammer, Michel'le, N.W.A., Oaktown's 3-5-7, Tone Loc and Young M.C.

7/7/90	**60**	12	We're All In The Same Gang	[V]	**$12**	Warner 26241

Black In America [M.C. Supreme]
Get Up And Dance [M.C. Superb feat. D.J. Pressure]

I Got Style [New World Mafia]
Keep Funkin' It [M.C. KRZ]
Let's Have Some Fun [Juvenile Committee]

Livin' In South Central L.A. [South Central Posse]
Soul Sista [Soul4]

Tumba La Casa (Rock The House) [Latin Kings]

We Came To Dance [Sugar, Spice & Everything Nice]

We're All In The Same Gang [includes 2 versions] **35**

WESTON, Paul

Born Paul Wetstein on 3/12/12 in Springfield, Massachusetts. Top arranger/conductor of mood music since 1934. Married to Jo Stafford. Won Grammy's Trustees Award in 1971.

10/29/55	**15**	2	1 Mood For 12	[I]	**$12**	Columbia 693
9/1/56	**12**	5	2 Solo Mood	[I]	**$12**	Columbia 879

above 2 feature same group of 12 big band soloists

Autumn In New York (2)
Between The Devil And The Deep Blue Sea (1)
Body And Soul (2)
Dancing On The Ceiling (He Dances On My Ceiling) (2)

Emaline (1)
Foggy Day (2)
Georgia On My Mind (1)
Honeysuckle Rose (2)
Hundred Years From Today (2)

I'm Comin' Virginia (1)
I'm Confessin' (That I Love You) (1)
It's The Talk Of The Town (1)
Judy (1)
Louisiana (1)

Lullaby In Rhythm (1)
Memories Of You (1)
My Funny Valentine (1)
Nice Work If You Can Get It (1)

One I Love (Belongs To Somebody Else) (2)
Rockin' Chair (2)
Skylark (1)
Sweet Lorraine (2)

When It's Sleepy Time Down South (2)
You Are Too Beautiful (2)

WET WET WET

Pop quartet from Glasgow, Scotland: Graeme Clark, Tom Cunningham, Neil Mitchell and Marti Pellow (vocals). Band name inspired from a line in the Scritti Politti song "Getting, Having, and Holding."

7/16/88	**123**	7	Popped In Souled Out		**$8**	Uni 5000

all guitars by Graeme Duffin

Angel Eyes (Home And Away)
East Of The River

I Can Give You Everything

I Don't Believe (Sonny's Letter)

I Remember
Moment You Left Me

Sweet Little Mystery
Temptation

Wishing I Was Lucky 58

WET WILLIE

Mobile, Alabama rock band led by brothers Jimmy (vocals) and Jack Hall (bass).

5/12/73	**189**	4	1 Drippin' Wet!/Live	[L]	**$12**	Capricorn 0113
6/1/74	**41**	24	2 Keep On Smilin'		**$8**	Capricorn 0128
3/8/75	**114**	7	3 Dixie Rock		**$8**	Capricorn 0149
4/3/76	**133**	7	4 The Wetter The Better		**$8**	Capricorn 0166
6/4/77	**191**	2	5 Left Coast Live	[L]	**$8**	Capricorn 0182
1/21/78	**118**	8	6 Manorisms		**$8**	Epic 34983
3/18/78	**158**	6	7 Greatest Hits	[G]	**$8**	Capricorn 0200
6/9/79	**172**	11	8 Which One's Willie?		**$8**	Epic 35794

Ain't He A Mess (3)
Airport (1,7)
Alabama (2)
Baby Fat (4,7)
Comic Book Hero (4)
Country Side Of Life (2,7) **66**
Dixie Rock (3,7) **96**
Doin' All The Right Things (The Wrong Way) (6)
Don't Let The Green Grass Fool You (medley) (8)
Don't Turn Me Away (6)

Don't Wait Too Long (2)
Everybody's Stoned (6)
Everything That 'Cha Do (Will Come Back To You) (4,5,7) **66**
Grits Ain't Groceries (5,7)
Hard Way (8)
He Set Me Free (3)
How 'Bout You (6)
I'd Rather Be Blind (1)
In Our Hearts (2)
It's Gonna Stop Rainin' Soon (3)

Jailhouse Moan (3)
Keep On Smilin' (2,5,7) **10**
Leona (3,7) **69**
Let It Shine (6)
Lucy Was In Trouble (2,5)
Macon Hambone Blues (1)
Make You Feel Love Again (6) **45**
Mama Didn't Raise No Fools (3)
Mr. Streamline (8)
No Good Woman Blues (1)
No, No, No (4,5)

One Track Mind (6)
Poor Judge Of Character (3)
Rainman (6)
Ramona (8)
Red Hot Chicken (1,7)
Ring You Up (4)
She Caught The Katy (And Left Me A Mule To Ride) (1)
She's My Lady (7)
Shout Bamalama (1,7)
Smoke (8)
So Blue (6)
Soul Jones (6)

Soul Sister (2)
Spanish Moss (7)
Stop And Take A Look (At What You've Been Doing) (medley) (8)
Street Corner Serenade (6) **30**
Take It To The Music (3)
Teaser (8)
That's All Right (1)
This Time (8)
Tired Dreams (8)
Trust In The Lord (2)

Walkin' By Myself (4)
We Got Lovin' (6)
Weekend (8) **29**
You Don't Know What You Mean To Me (8)

DEBUT DATE	PEAK POS	WKS CHR	GOLD	ARTIST — Album Title	$	Label & Number

WHALUM, Kirk
Tenor jazz saxophonist from Memphis.

| 3/19/88 | 142 | 10 | | And You Know That!...[I] | $8 | Columbia 40812 |

produced by Bob James

| Don't Look At Me (In That | Give Me Your Love | Seryna | Wave, The |
| Tone Of Voice) | Glow | Through The Fire | Where I Come From |

WHAT IS THIS
Pop-rock trio featuring lead singer Alain Johannes.

| 9/14/85 | 187 | 4 | | What Is This .... | $8 | MCA 5598 |

| Big Raft | Chasing Your Ghost | **I'll Be Around 62** | Touch The Flame | Whisper (To Natasha) |
| Breathing | Dreams Of Heaven | Stuck | Waves In The Sand | Wool Over My Eyes |

WHEELER, Billy Edd
Born on 12/9/32 and raised in Highcoal, West Virginia. Folk singer/composer. Wrote the Kingston Trio's hit "Reverend Mr. Black" and Kenny Rogers' "Coward Of The County." Co-owner of Sleepy Hollow Music.

| 2/13/65 | 132 | 3 | | Memories Of America/Ode To The Little Brown Shack Out Back...... | $20 | Kapp 3425 |

After Taxes	Blistered	Hot Dog Heart	**Ode To The Little Brown**	Reverend Mr. Black
Anne	Coal Tattoo	Jackson	**Shack Out Back 50**	Sister Sara
Bachelor, The	Desert Pete			Winter Sky

WHEELER, Caron
Featured vocalist on Soul II Soul's hits "Back To Life" and "Keep On Moving." Born in London of Jamaican heritage. Backup singer for Elvis Costello in 1983.

| 10/27/90 | 133 | 7 | | UK Blak .... | $12 | EMI 93497 |

Blue (Is The Colour Of Pain)	Jamaica	**Livin' In The Light**	No Regrets	Somewhere	This Is Mine
Don't Quit	Kama Yo	**[includes 2 versions] 53**	Proud	Song For You	UK Blak
Enchanted		Never Lonely			

WHEN IN ROME
U.K.-based trio: Clive Farrington (vocals), Michael Floreale (keyboards) and Andrew Mann (vocals).

| 10/15/88+ | 84 | 24 | | When In Rome .... | $8 | Virgin 90994 |

| Child's Play | **Heaven Knows 95** | If Only | Sight Of Your Tears | Total Devotion |
| Everything | I Can't Stop | **Promise, The 11** | Something Going On | Wide Wide Sea |

| ★★262★★ | | | | **WHISPERS, The** | | |

Los Angeles soul group formed in 1964. Consisted of Gordy Harmon, twin brothers Walter and Wallace "Scotty" Scott, Marcus Hutson and Nicholas Caldwell. First recorded for Dore in 1964. Harmon replaced in 1973 by Leaveil Degree who was briefly a member of Friends Of Distinction.

5/13/72	186	2		1 The Whispers' Love Story..	$15	Janus 3041
8/28/76	189	6		2 One For The Money	$8	Soul Train 1450
7/16/77	65	10		3 Open Up Your Love	$8	Soul Train 2270
5/27/78	77	28		4 Headlights	$8	Solar 2774
4/14/79	146	9		5 Whisper In Your Ear	$8	Solar 3105
1/5/80	6	35	▲	6 The Whispers	$8	Solar 3521
1/17/81	23	27	●	7 Imagination	$8	Solar 3578
10/3/81	100	9	●	8 This Kind Of Lovin'	$8	Solar 3976
1/23/82	35	25	●	9 Love Is Where You Find It	$8	Solar 27
3/13/82	180	5		10 The Best Of The Whispers ....[G]	$8	Solar 4242
4/2/83	37	29		11 Love For Love	$8	Solar 60216
12/1/84+	88	26		12 So Good	$8	Solar 60356
5/30/87	22	37	▲	13 Just Gets Better With Time	$8	Solar 72554
8/18/90	83	24	●	14 More Of The Night	$12	Capitol 92957

And The Beat Goes On	Girl Don't Make Me Wait (14)	If I Don't Get Your Love (5)	Love's Calling (13)	Small Talkin' (9)	You Fill My Life With Music
(6,10) **19**	Girl I Need You (7)	If You (1)	**Make It With You** (3,10) **94**	So Good (12)	(1)
Are You Going My Way (12)	Give It To Me (13)	Imagination (7)	Mind Blowing (14)	Some Kinda Lover (12)	You Never Miss Your Water
Babes (14)	Got To Get Away (8)	In My Heart (2)	Misunderstanding (14)	Song For Donny (6)	('Til Your Well Runs Dry) (3)
Bright Lights And You Girl	Had It Not Been For You (11)	In The Mood (13)	More Of The Night (14)	Sounds Like A Love Song (2)	You'll Never Get Away (5)
(8)	Headlights (4)	In The Raw (9)	My Girl (6)	Special F/X (13)	(You're A) Special Part Of My
Can You Do The Boogie (6)	Help Them See The Light	**Innocent** [includes 2	My Heart Your Heart (14)	Suddenly (12)	Life (4)
Can't Do Without Love (5)	(14)	versions] (14) **55**	Never Too Late (12)	Sweet Sensation (12)	You're Only As Good As You
Can't Help But Love You (1)	Hey, Who Really Cares? (1)	Is It Good To You (14)	No Pain, No Gain (13)	There's A Love For Everyone	Think You Are (2)
Can't Stop Loving You Baby	Homemade Lovin' (5)	**It's A Love Thing** (7,10) **28**	(Olivia) Lost And Turned	(1)	You're What's Been Missin'
(8)	Hopeless Situation (1)	Jump For Joy (5)	Out (4,10)	This Kind Of Lovin' (8)	From My Life (1)
Can't Stop Talkin' (1)	I Can Make It Better (7,10)	Just Gets Better With Time	On Impact (12)	This Time (11)	You've Chosen Me (1)
Children Of Tomorrow (4)	I Fell In Love Last Night (At	(13)	**One For The Money (Part**	**Tonight** (11) **84**	**Your Love Is So Doggone**
Chocolate Girl (3)	The Disco) (3)	Keep On Lovin' Me (11)	**1)** (2,10) **88**	Try And Make It Better (4)	**Good** (1) **93**
Contagious (12)	I Love You (6)	Keep Your Love Around (11)	Only You (9)	Try It Again (11)	
Continental Shuffle (7)	I Only Meant To Wet My	**Lady** (6,10) **28**	Open Up Your Love (3)	Turn Me Out (9)	
Cruisin' In (9)	Feet (1)	Lay It On Me (11)	Out The Box (6)	Up On Soul Train (7)	
Disco Melody (4)	I Want 2B The 1 4 U (14)	(Let's Go) All The Way (4)	Planets Of Life (4)	Welcome Into My Dream (6)	
Do They Turn You On (11)	I Want You (13)	Living Together (In Sin)	Pretty Lady (5)	What Will I Do (8)	
Don't Be Late For Love (14)	I'm Gonna Love You More (8)	(2,10)	Put Me In The News (2)	Whisper In Your Ear (5)	
Don't Keep Me Waiting (12)	I'm Gonna Make You My	Love At Its Best (9)	**Rock Steady** (13) **7**	World Of A Thousand	
Emergency (9)	Wife (3)	Love For Love (11)	Say Yes (9)	Dreams (8)	
Fantasy (7)	I'm The One For You (8)	Love Is A Dream (3)	Say You (Would Love For Me	You Are Number One (3)	
Forever Lover (14)	I've Got A Feeling (2)	Love Is Where You Find It (9)	Too) (7)	You Are The One (14)	

WHITCOMB, Ian
Born on 7/10/41 in Woking, England. Pop singer/songwriter/author. Currently resides in California.

| 7/10/65 | 125 | 13 | | You Turn Me On! .... | $18 | Tower 5004 |

| Be My Baby | **N-E-R-V-O-U-S!** **59** | Poor But Honest | Sugar Babe | **This Sporting Life 100** | **You Turn Me On (Turn On** |
| Fizz | No Tears For Johnny | River Of No Return | That's Rock N' Roll | Too Many Cars On The Road | **Song) 8** |

DEBUT DATE	PEAK POS	WKS CHR	GOLD	ARTIST — Album Title	$	Label & Number

★★174★★   WHITE, Barry
Born on 9/12/44 in Galveston, Texas and raised in Los Angeles. Soul singer/songwriter/keyboardist/producer/arranger. With Upfronts vocal group, recorded for Lummtone in 1960. A&R man for Mustang/Bronco, 1966-67. Formed Love Unlimited in 1969, which included future wife Glodean James. Leader of 40-piece Love Unlimited Orchestra.

4/21/73	16	63	●	1 I've Got So Much To Give	$8	20th Century 407
11/17/73+	20	37	●	2 Stone Gon'	$8	20th Century 423
9/7/74	1¹	38	●	**3 Can't Get Enough**	$8	20th Century 444
4/12/75	17	17	●	4 Just Another Way To Say I Love You	$8	20th Century 466
11/15/75	23	25	●	5 Barry White's Greatest Hits [G]	$8	20th Century 493
2/14/76	42	15		6 Let The Music Play	$8	20th Century 502
11/27/76	125	9		7 Is This Whatcha Wont?	$8	20th Century 516
9/17/77	8	33	▲	**8 Barry White Sings For Someone You Love**	$8	20th Century 543
10/28/78	36	28	▲	9 Barry White The Man	$8	20th Century 571
4/28/79	67	9	●	10 The Message Is Love	$8	Un. Gold 35763
8/18/79	132	6		11 I Love To Sing The Songs I Sing	$8	20th Century 590
7/26/80	85	11		12 Barry White's Sheet Music	$8	Un. Gold 36208
10/2/82	148	6		13 Change	$8	Un. Gold 38048
11/21/87	159	17		14 The Right Night & Barry White	$8	A&M 5154
5/19/90	143	12		15 The Man Is Back!	$12	A&M 5256
11/2/91	96	10		16 Put Me In Your Mix	$12	A&M 5377

All Because Of You (4)
Any Fool Could See (You Were Meant For Me) (10)
Baby, We Better Try To Get It Together (6) 92
Break It Down With You (16)
Bring Back My Yesterday (1)
Call Me (16)
Can't Get Enough Of Your Love, Babe (3,5) 1
Change (13)
Dark And Lovely (You Over There) (16)
Don't Let Go (15)
Don't Make Me Wait Too Long (7)
Don't Tell Me About Heartaches (13)
Early Years (9)
Follow That And See (Where It Leads Y'all) (15)
For Real Chill (16)
For Your Love (I'll Do Most Anything) (14)
Ghetto Letto (12)
Girl It's True, Yes I'll Always Love You (2)

Girl, What's Your Name (11)
Good Night My Love (medley) (15)
Hard To Believe That I Found You (2)
Heavenly, That's What You Are To Me (4)
Honey Please, Can't Ya See (2,5) 44
How Did You Know It Was Me? (11)
Hung Up In Your Love (10)
I Believe In Love (12)
I Can't Believe You Love Me (3)
I Can't Leave You Alone (11)
I Don't Know Where Love Has Gone (6)
I Found Love (10)
I Like You, You Like Me (10)
I Love To Sing The Songs I Sing (11)
I Love You More Than Anything (In This World Girl) (3)
I Never Thought I'd Fall In Love With You (8)

I Wanna Do It Good To Ya (16)
I Wanna Lay Down With You (7)
I'll Do For You Anything You Want Me To (4) 40
I'm Gonna Love You Just A Little More Baby (1,5) 3
I'm On Fire (10)
I'm Qualified To Satisfy You (7)
I'm Ready For Love (14)
I'm So Blue And You Are Too (6)
I've Found Someone (1,5)
I've Got So Much To Give (1,5) 32
I've Got That Love Fever (13)
If You Know, Won't You Tell You (10)
It Ain't Love, Babe (Until You Give It) (10)
It's All About Love (13)
It's Ecstasy When You Lay Down Next To Me (8) 4
It's Getting Harder All The Time (15)

It's Only Love Doing Its Thing (9)
Just The Way You Are (9)
L.A. My Kinda Place (15)
Lady, Sweet Lady (12)
Let Me Live My Life Lovin' You Babe (4)
Let The Music Play (6) 32
Let's Get Busy (16)
Let's Make Tonight (An Evening To Remember) (13)
Look At Her (9)
Love Ain't Easy (10)
Love Is Good With You (16)
Love Is In Your Eyes (14)
Love Makin' Music (11)
Love Serenade (4,5)
Love Will Find Us (16)
Loves Interlude (medley) (15)
Mellow Mood (Pt. I & II) (3)
Never, Never Gonna Give Ya Up (2,5) 7
Now I'm Gonna Make Love To You (7)
Of All The Guys In The World (8)

Oh Love, Well We Finally Made It (3)
Oh Me, Oh My (I'm Such A Lucky Guy) (11)
Oh What A Night For Dancing (8) 24
Once Upon A Time (You Were A Friend Of Mine) (11)
Passion (13)
Playing Your Game, Baby (8)
Put Me In Your Mix (16)
Responsible (15)
Right Night (14)
Rum And Coke (Rum And Coca-Cola) (12)
September When I First Met You (9)
Sha La La Means I Love You (9)
Share (13)
She's Everything To Me (12)
Sheet Music (12)
Sho' You Right (14)
Standing In The Shadows Of Love (1,5)
Super Lover (15)

There's A Place (Where Love Never Ends) (14)
Turnin' On, Tunin' In (To Your Love) (13)
Volare (16)
We're Gonna Have It All (16)
What Am I Gonna Do With You (4,5) 8
When Will I See You Again (15)
Who You Giving Your Love To (16)
Who's The Fool (14)
You See The Trouble With Me (6)
You Turned My Whole World Around (8)
You're My Baby (2)
You're So Good You're Bad (8)
You're The First, The Last, My Everything (3,5) 2
You're The One I Need (16)
Your Love -- So Good I Can Taste It (7)
Your Sweetness Is My Weakness (9) 60

WHITE, Karyn
Born on 10/14/65. Prominent session singer from Los Angeles. Touring vocalist with O'Bryan in 1984. Recorded with jazz-fusion keyboardist Jeff Lorber in 1986. Married to superproducer Terry Lewis (member of The Time).

10/15/88+	19	54	▲	1 Karyn White	$8	Warner 25637
9/28/91	53	24	●	2 Ritual Of Love	$12	Warner 26320

Beside You (2)
Do Unto Me (2)
Don't Mess With Me (1)
Family Man (1)

Hard To Say Goodbye (2)
Hooked On You (2)
How I Want You (2)
Love Saw It (1)

Love That's Mine (2)
One Heart (2)
One Wish (1)
Ritual Of Love (2)

Romantic (2) 1
Secret Rendezvous (1) 6
Slow Down (1)
Superwoman (1) 8

Tears Of Joy (2)
Tell Me Tomorrow (1)
Walkin' The Dog (2)
Way I Feel About You (2) 12

Way You Love Me (1) 7

WHITE, Lenny
Percussionist born on 12/19/49. Former drummer of the jazz-rock band Return To Forever; leader of the New York band Twennynine. Assembled the female vocal trio Voyceboxing in 1991.

1/31/76	177	3		Venusian Summer [I]	$12	Nemperor 435

Away Go Troubles Down The Drain

Chicken-Fried Steak
Mating Drive

Prelude To Rainbow Delta
Prince Of The Sea

Venusian Summer Suite
Medley

WHITE, Maurice
Born on 12/19/41 in Memphis. Percussionist with Ramsey Lewis from 1966-71. Founder and co-lead vocalist of Earth, Wind & Fire.

10/5/85	61	19		Maurice White	$8	Columbia 39883

Alpha Dance
Believe In Magic

Children Of Afrika
I Need You 95

Invitation
Jamboree

Lady Is Love
Sea Of Glass

Sleeping Flame
Stand By Me 50

Switch On Your Radio

WHITE, Tony Joe
Born on 7/23/43 in Oak Grove, Louisiana. Bayou rock singer/songwriter. Wrote Brook Benton's hit "Rainy Night In Georgia."

7/26/69	51	16		1 Black And White	$10	Monument 18114
11/22/69	183	3		2 ...Continued	$10	Monument 18133
3/6/71	167	4		3 Tony Joe White	$8	Warner 1900

Aspen Colorado (1)
Black Panther Swamps (3)
Change, The (3)
Copper Kettle (3)
Daddy, The (3)

Don't Steal My Love (1)
Elements And Things (2)
Five Summers For Jimmy (2)
For Le Ann (2)
I Just Walked Away (3)

I Thought I Knew You Well (2)
I Want You (2)
Little Green Apples (1)
Look Of Love (1)

Migrant, The (2)
My Kind Of Woman (3)
Night In The Life Of A Swamp Fox (3)
Old Man Willis (2)

Polk Salad Annie (1) 8
Rainy Night In Georgia (2)
Roosevelt And Ira Lee (Night Of The Mossacin) (2) 44

Scratch My Back (1)
Soul Francisco (1)
They Caught The Devil And Put Him In Jail In Eudora, Arkansas (3)

DEBUT DATE	PEAK POS	WKS CHR	GOLD	ARTIST — Album Title	$	Label & Number

WHITE, Tony Joe — Cont'd

Traveling Bone (3)	Who's Making Love (1)	Wichita Lineman (1)	Willie And Laura Mae Jones (1)	Woman With Soul (2)
Voodoo Village (3)	Whompt Out On You (1)			Woodpecker (2)

WHITE LION

New York-based rock band: Mike Tramp (vocals; Denmark native), James Lomenzo (bass), Vito Bratta (guitar) and Greg D'Angelo (drums; a founding member of Anthrax). Lomenzo and D'Angelo left in 1991, replaced by Tommy Caradonna and Jimmy DeGrasso (ex-Y&T).

9/26/87+	11	86	▲²	1 Pride	$8	Atlantic 81768
4/16/88	151	14		2 Fight To Survive	$8	Grand Slam 1
7/1/89	19	27	●	3 Big Game	$8	Atlantic 81969
4/27/91	61	13		4 Mane Attraction	$12	Atlantic 82193

All Burn In Hell (2)	Cherokee (2)	Hungry (4)	**Little Fighter (3) 52**	**Tell Me** (1) 58
All Join Our Hands (1)	Cry For Freedom (3)	If My Mind Is Evil (3)	Living On The Edge (3)	Till Death Do Us Part (4)
All The Fallen Men (2)	Dirty Woman (3)	In The City (2)	Lonely Nights (1)	**Wait** (1) 8
All You Need Is Rock N Roll (1)	Don't Give Up (1)	It's Over (4)	Love Don't Come Easy (4)	Warsong (4)
Baby Be Mine (2)	Don't Say It's Over (3)	Kid Of 1000 Faces (2)	Out With The Boys (4)	**When The Children Cry** (1) 3
Blue Monday (4)	El Salvador (2)	Lady Of The Valley (1)	**Radar Love (3) 59**	Where Do We Run (2)
Broken Heart (2,4)	Farewell To You (4)	Leave Me Alone (4)	Road To Valhalla (2)	You're All I Need (4)
Broken Home (3)	Fight To Survive (2)	Let's Get Crazy (4)	She's Got Everything (4)	
	Goin' Home Tonight (3)	Lights And Thunder (4)	Sweet Little Loving (1)	

WHITEMAN, Paul

Born on 3/28/1890 in Denver; died on 12/29/67. The most popular bandleader of the pre-swing era; had 32 #1 hits from 1920-1934. Formed own band in 1919. Band featured jazz greats Henry Busse (trumpet), Ferde Grofe (piano, arranger) and Bix Beiderbecke (cornet). Vocalist Bing Crosby made his professional debut with Whiteman's band in 1926.

| 1/19/57 | 20 | 1 | | Paul Whiteman/50th Anniversary .... | $15 | Grand Award 901 [2] |

reunion with many of the great alumni of the Whiteman Orchestra: Tommy & Jimmy Dorsey, Bing Crosby, Hoagy Carmichael, Jack Teagarden and others

Autumn Leaves	How High The Moon	Jeepers Creepers	Lover	Night Is Young & You're So Beautiful	Rhapsody In Blue
Basin Street Blues	It Happened In Monterey	Lazy River	Mississippi Mud		Washboard Blues
Christmas Night In Harlem	It's The Dreamer In Me	Limehouse Blues	My Romance	Ramona	When Day Is Done

WHITE PLAINS

English studio group featuring Tony Burrows (vocals), who was also with The Brotherhood Of Man, Edison Lighthouse, First Class and The Pipkins.

| 8/22/70 | 166 | 4 | | My Baby Loves Lovin' .... | $12 | Deram 18045 |

I've Got You On My Mind	Show Me Your Hand	Sunny Honey Girl	Today I Killed A Man I Didn't Know	When Tomorrow Comes Tomorrow	You've Got Your Troubles
In A Moment Of Madness	Summer Morning	Taffeta Rose			
My Baby Loves Lovin' 13					

WHITESNAKE

Ex-Deep Purple vocalist David Coverdale, who recorded solo as Whitesnake in 1977, formed British heavy-metal band in 1978. Coverdale fronted everchanging lineup. Early members included his Deep Purple bandmates, keyboardist Jon Lord (1978-84) and drummer Ian Paice (1979-81). 1987 players included John Sykes (guitar), Neil Murray (bass) and Aynsley Dunbar (former Jefferson Starship drummer). Sykes left in 1988 to form Blue Murder. Ex-Dio guitarist Vivian Campbell was a member from 1987-88, later with Riverdogs, Shadow King and Def Leppard. 1989 lineup included Steve Vai (David Lee Roth's former guitarist), Adrian Vandenberg (former guitarist of Vandenberg), Rudy Sarzo (bass) and Tommy Aldridge (drums). Coverdale married actress Tawny Kitaen on 2/17/89; divorced by 1992.

8/16/80	90	16		1 Ready An' Willing	$8	Mirage 19276
12/27/80+	146	12		2 Live....In The Heart Of The City .... [L]	$8	Mirage 19292
5/30/81	151	6		3 Come An' Get It	$8	Mirage 16043
5/19/84	40	85	▲²	4 Slide it in	$8	Geffen 4018
4/18/87	2¹⁰	76	▲⁶	5 Whitesnake	$8	Geffen 24099
11/25/89	10	34	▲	6 Slip Of The Tongue	$8	Geffen 24249

Ain't Gonna Cry No More (1)	Come An' Get It (3)	Girl (3)	Kittens Got Claws (6)	Slip Of The Tongue (6)	Walking In The Shadow Of The Blues (2)
Ain't No Love In The Heart Of The City (2)	Come On (2)	**Give Me All Your Love** (5) 48	Lonely Days, Lonely Nights (3)	Slow An' Easy (4)	Wine, Women An' Song (3)
All Or Nothing (4)	Crying In The Rain (5)	Give Me More Time (4)	Love Ain't No Stranger (4)	Slow Poke Music (6)	Wings Of The Storm (6)
Bad Boys (5)	**Deeper The Love (6) 28**	Guilty Of Love (4)	Love Hunter (2)	Spit It Out (4)	Would I Lie To You (3)
Black And Blue (1)	Don't Break My Heart Again (3)	**Here I Go Again** (5) 1	Love Man (1)	Standing In The Shadow (4)	
Blindman (1)	Don't Turn Away (5)	Hit An' Run (3)	**Now You're Gone** (6) 96	**Still Of The Night** (5) 79	
Carry Your Load (1)	**Fool For Your Loving** (1,2) 53	Hot Stuff (3)	Ready An' Willing (1)	Straight For The Heart (5)	
Cheap An' Nasty (6)	**Fool For Your Loving** (6) 37	Hungry For Love (4)	Sailing Ships (6)	Sweet Talker (1,2)	
Child Of Babylon (3)	Gambler (4)	**Is This Love** (5) 2	She's A Woman (1)	Take Me With You (2)	
Children Of The Night (5)		Judgment Day (6)	Slide It In (4)	Till The Day I Die (3)	

WHITE TRASH

Hard-rock group: Dave "D-Bone" Alvin (vocals), Ethan Collins, Mike Caldarella and Aaron Collins with The Badass Brass: Chris Arbisi, Terry Thomas and Brendan Stiles.

| 9/21/91 | 122 | 7 | | White Trash .... | $12 | Elektra 61053 |

Apple Pie	Buzz!	Judge-Me-Do	Po' White Trash	S.D.A.S.E.
Baby	Crawl, The	Lil' Nancy	Prayer B4 Pizza	Take My Soul
Backstage Pass	Good God	Party Line		

WHITE WOLF

Heavy-metal quintet from Western Canada — Don Wilk, lead singer.

| 2/16/85 | 162 | 6 | | 1 Standing Alone .... | $8 | RCA 8042 |
| 6/21/86 | 137 | 8 | | 2 Endangered Species .... | $8 | RCA 9555 |

All Alone (2)	Holding Back (1)	Metal Thunder (1)	Ride The Storm (2)	She (2)	Time Waits For No One (2)
Crying To The Wind (2)	Homeward Bound (1)	Night Rider (1)	Run For Your Life (2)	Snake Charmer (2)	Trust Me (1)
Headlines (1)	Just Like An Arrow (2)	One More Time (2)	Shadows In The Night (1)	Standing Alone (1)	What The War Will Bring (1)

WHITING, Margaret

Born on 7/22/24 in Detroit and raised in Hollywood. Daughter of popular composer Richard Whiting ("Till We Meet Again"). Very popular from 1946-54, she had over 40 charted hits.

| 2/18/67 | 109 | 8 | | The Wheel Of Hurt .... | $15 | London 497 |

WHITING, Margaret — Cont'd

But Why	Show Me A Man	Wheel Of Hurt 26	Winchester Cathedral	You Don't Have To Say You Love Me	You Won't Be Sorry, Baby
It Hurts To Say Goodbye	Somewhere There's Love	Where Do I Stand	World Inside Your Arms		
Nothing Lasts Forever	Time After Time				

WHITLEY, Keith

Country singer/songwriter. Born on 7/1/55 in Sandy Hook, Kentucky; died on 5/8/89 from alcohol abuse. Married country singer Lorrie Morgan in November 1986.

| 6/3/89 | 121 | 14 | ● | 1 Don't Close Your Eyes .... | $8 | RCA 6494 |
| 9/2/89 | 115 | 7 | ● | 2 I Wonder Do You Think Of Me .... | $8 | RCA 9809 |

Keith died before the completion of this album

| 9/1/90 | 67 | 45 | ● | 3 Greatest Hits .... [G] | $12 | RCA 2277 |

Between An Old Memory And Me (2)	Flying Colors (1)	I Wonder Do You Think Of Me (2,3)	Some Old Side Road (1)	'Till A Tear Becomes A Rose (3)
Birmingham Turnaround (1)	Heartbreak Highway (2)	It Ain't Nothin' (2,3)	Talk To Me Texas (2,3)	Turn This Thing Around (2)
Brother Jukebox (3)	Honky Tonk Heart (1)	It's All Coming Back To Me Now (1)	Tell Lorrie I Love Her (3)	When You Say Nothing At All (1,3)
Don't Close Your Eyes (1,3)	I Never Go Around Mirrors (1)	I'm No Stranger To The Rain (1,3)	Ten Feet Away (3)	
		I'm Over You (2,3)	Lady's Choice (2)	
			Miami, My Amy (3)	Tennessee Courage (2)

WHITLOCK, Bobby

Former keyboardist with Delaney & Bonnie And Friends, and Derek And The Dominos.

| 4/1/72 | 140 | 10 | | 1 Bobby Whitlock .... | $10 | Dunhill 50121 |
| 11/4/72 | 190 | 3 | | 2 Raw Velvet .... | $10 | Dunhill 50131 |

Back Home In England (1)	Dearest I Wonder (2)	Hello L.A., Bye Bye Birmingham (2)	If You Ever (2)	Song For Paula (1)	Where There's A Will There's A Way (1)
Back In My Life Again (1)	Ease Your Pain (2)	I'd Rather Live "The Straight Life" (1)	Satisfied (2)	Start All Over (2)	Write You A Letter (2)
Bustin' My Ass (2)	Game Called Life (1)		Scenery Has Slowly Changed (1)	Tell The Truth (2)	You Came Along (2)
Country Life (1)				Think About It (2)	
Day Without Jesus (1)					

WHITMAN, Slim

Born Otis Whitman, Jr. on 1/20/24 in Tampa. Country balladeer and yodeller. Gained greatest fame with best-selling compilation albums sold exclusively over TV.

| 10/25/80 | 175 | 3 | | 1 Songs I Love To Sing .... | $8 | Cleve. I. 36768 |
| 12/13/80 | 184 | 4 | | 2 Christmas with Slim Whitman .... [X] | $8 | Cleve. I. 36847 |

Away In A Manger (1)	If I Could Only Dream (1)	Let There Be Peace On Earth (Let It Begin With Me) (2)	Silent Night, Holy Night (2)	That Silver-Haired Daddy Of Mine (1)	Where Do I Go From Here (1)
Beautiful Dreamer (1)	It Came Upon The Midnight Clear (2)		Since You Went Away (1)		Where Is The Christ In Christmas (2)
Christmas (2)		Rose Marie (1)	Sleep My Child (All Through The Night) (2)	We Three Kings (2)	White Christmas (2)
First Noel (2)	Last Farewell (1)	Secret Love (1)	When (1)		
I Remember You (1)					

WHITTAKER, Roger

Born on 3/22/36 in Nairobi, Kenya. British adult contemporary singer.

5/3/75	31	24	●	1 "The Last Farewell" and other hits	$10	RCA 0855
5/5/79	115	5		2 When I Need You	$8	RCA 3355
12/8/79+	157	10		3 Mirrors Of My Mind	$8	RCA 3501
2/9/80	154	12		4 Voyager	$8	RCA 3518
11/29/80	175	2		5 With Love	$8	RCA 3778
6/13/81	177	3		6 Live In Concert .... [L]	$10	RCA 4057 [2]

All I Have To Do Is Dream (6)	Durham Town (The Leavin') (1,6)	I Knew You Sunset (3)	Man Without Love (5)	See You Shine (5)	Why? (6)
All Of My Life (4)	Early One Morning (6)	I See You In The Sunrise (4)	Mexican Whistler (6)	She (2)	Wishes (1)
Annie's Song (2)	Family (3)	I Was Born (4)	Miss You Nights (2)	Skye Boat Song (6)	Yele (4)
Berceuse Pour Mon Amour (6)	For I Loved You (5)	I Would If I Could (5)	Morning Has Broken (6)	Solitaire (5)	You Are My Miracle (3)
Blow Gentle Breeze (3)	Good Morning Starshine (1)	I'll Be There (4)	My Son (5)	Song For The Captain (4)	Your Song (2)
Both Sides Now (1)	Goodbye (5)	Image To My Mind - Parts 1-4 (6)	New African Whistler (6)	Sunrise, Sunset (1)	
Call My Name (3)	Goodnight Ruby (3)	It Takes A Lot (3)	New World In The Morning (1,6)	Tall Dark Stranger (5)	
Carry Me (Dreams On A Roof) (3)	Halfway Up A Mountain (4)	Kentucky Song Bird (3)	Newport Belle (5)	That's Life (6)	
Chengalip (6)	Here I Am (4)	Kilgary Mountain (6)	On My Own Again (4)	This Moment (6)	
Day In The Life Of A Lucky Man (6)	Home Lovin' Man (2)	Last Farewell (1,6) 19	One Another (5)	Time In A Bottle (2)	
Dirty Old Town (6)	I Am But A Small Voice ('Ako' Y Munting Tinig) (5)	Lighthouse (4)	Paper Bird (4)	Water Boy (1)	
Don't Fight (5)	I Don't Believe In If Anymore (1,6)	Love Is A Cold Wind (4)	Please Come To Boston (3)	Weekend In New England (2)	
		Love Will (5)	Ride A Country Road (6)	What Love Is (6)	
		Lyin' Eyes (2)	Sail Away (4)	When I Need You (6)	
				Whistle Stop (1)	

★★70★★ WHO, The

Rock group formed in London in 1964. Consisted of Roger Daltrey (b: 3/1/44, lead singer), Pete Townshend (b: 5/19/45; guitar, vocals), John Entwistle (b: 10/9/44; bass) and Keith Moon (b: 8/23/47; drums). Originally known as the High Numbers in 1964. All but Moon had been in The Detours. Developed stage antics of destroying their instruments. 1969 rock opera album *Tommy* became a film in 1975. Solo work by members began in 1972. Moon died of a drug overdose on 9/7/78, replaced by Kenney Jones (formerly with Small Faces). 1973 rock opera album *Quadrophenia* became a film in 1979. The Who's biographical film *The Kids Are Alright* was released in 1979. Eleven fans trampled to death at their concert in Cincinnati on 12/3/79. Disbanded in 1982. Regrouped at "Live Aid" in 1986. Daltrey, Townshend and Entwistle reunited with an ensemble of 15 for a U.S. tour in 1989. Jones formed The Law with Paul Rodgers in 1991. Inducted into the Rock and Roll Hall of Fame in 1990.

| 5/20/67 | 67 | 22 | | 1 Happy Jack .... | $35 | Decca 74892 |

album released in England entitled *A Quick One*

1/6/68	48	23		2 The Who Sell Out	$35	Decca 74950
10/26/68	39	10		3 Magic Bus-The Who On Tour .... [K]	$35	Decca 75064
6/7/69+	4	126	●	4 Tommy	$25	Decca 7205 [2]

also see Rock Operas and Soundtrack versions

5/30/70	4	44	●	5 Live At Leeds .... [L]	$25	Decca 79175
8/14/71	4	41	●	6 Who's next	$15	Decca 79182
11/20/71	11	21	●	7 Meaty Beaty Big And Bouncy .... [G]	$15	Decca 79184
11/10/73	2[1]	40	●	8 Quadrophenia	$15	MCA 10004

also see film version below

| 10/26/74 | 15 | 15 | ● | 9 Odds & Sods .... [K] | $15 | Track 2126 |

previously unreleased recordings from 1964-72

DEBUT DATE	PEAK POS	WKS CHR	GOLD	ARTIST — Album Title	$	Label & Number
				WHO, The — Cont'd		
12/21/74	185	4		10 A Quick One (Happy Jack)/Sell Out ....[R]	$18	Track 4067 [2]
				reissue of albums #1 and 2 above		
10/25/75	8	25	●	11 **The Who By Numbers**	$8	MCA 2161
9/9/78	2²	30	▲	12 **Who Are You**	$8	MCA 3050
6/30/79	8	25	▲	13 **The Kids Are Alright** ....[S-L]	$10	MCA 11005 [2]
				film features interviews and performances from the group's past 15 years		
10/13/79	46	16		14 Quadrophenia ....[S]	$10	Polydor 6235 [2]
				also see original version above; side 4 includes: "Night Train" by James Brown; "Louie Louie" by The Kingsmen; "Green Onions" by Booker T. & The MG's; "Rhythm Of The Rain" by The Cascades; "He's So Fine" by The Chiffons; "Be My Baby" by The Ronettes and "Da Doo Ron Ron" by The Crystals		
4/4/81	4	20	▲	15 **Face Dances**	$8	Warner 3516
10/17/81	52	19		16 Hooligans ....[K]	$10	MCA 12001 [2]
				recordings from 1965-78		
9/25/82	8	32	●	17 **It's Hard**	$8	Warner 23731
5/21/83	94	13		18 Who's Greatest Hits ....[G]	$8	MCA 5408
12/1/84+	81	14		19 Who's Last..[L]	$10	MCA 8018 [2]
12/28/85+	116	8		20 Who's Missing ....[K]	$8	MCA 5641
				12 rarities comprised of B-sides of USA singles and previously unreleased selections from 1965-72		
4/14/90	188	2		21 Join Together ....[L]	$24	MCA 19501 [2]
				recorded during their summer of 1989 reunion tour		

Acid Queen (4,21)
Amazing Journey (4,21)
Another Tricky Day (15)
Anytime You Want Me (20)
Anyway, Anyhow, Anywhere (7,13)
Armenia City In The Sky (2,10)
Athena (17) *28*
Baba O'Riley (6,13,16,19)
Barbara Ann (20)
Bargain (6,16,20)
Behind Blue Eyes (6,16,19,21) *34*
Bell Boy (8,14)
Blue Red And Grey (11)
Boris The Spider (1,7,10,19)
Bucket T. (3)
Cache Cache (15)
Call Me Lightning (3) *40*
Christmas (4,21)
Cobwebs And Strange (1,10)
Cooks Country (17)
Cousin Kevin (4,21)
Cry If You Want (17)
Cut My Hair (8)
Daily Records (15)
Dangerous (17)
Did You Steal My Money (15)
Dig (21)
Dirty Jobs (8)
Disguises (3)
Do You Think It's Alright (4,21)
Doctor, Doctor (3)

Dr. Jekyll & Mr. Hyde (3)
Dr. Jimmy (8,14,19)
Don't Let Go The Coat (15) *84*
Don't Look Away (1,10)
Dreaming From The Waist (11)
Drowned (8,16)
Eminence Front (17,21) *68*
Eyesight For The Blind (4,21)
Face The Face (21)
Faith In Something Bigger (9)
Fiddle About (medley) (4)
5:15 (8,14,16,18,21) *45*
Four Faces (14)
Get Out And Stay Out (14)
Gettin' In Tune (6)
Glow Girl (1)
Go To The Mirror Boy (4,21)
Goin' Mobile (6)
Guitar And Pen (12)
Had Enough (12,16)
Happy Jack (1,7,10,13,18) *24*
Heat Wave (10)
Heaven And Hell (20)
Heinz Baked Beans (2,10)
Helpless Dancer (8,14)
Here For More (20)
Hi Heel Sneakers (14)
How Can You Do It Alone (15)
How Many Friends (11)
However Much I Booze (11)
I Am The Sea (8,14)

I Can See For Miles (2,7,10,13,16,21) *9*
I Can't Explain (7,13,16,19) *93*
I Can't Reach You (2,3,10)
I Don't Even Know Myself (20)
I Need You (1,10)
I'm A Boy (7,20)
I'm Free (4,21) *37*
I'm One (8,14)
I'm The Face (9)
I've Had Enough (8,14)
I've Known No War (17)
Imagine A Man (11)
In A Hand Or A Face (11)
Is It In My Head (8)
It's A Boy (4)
It's Your Turn (9)
Join Together (13,16,21) *17*
Joker James (14)
Kids Are Alright (7)
Leaving Here (20)
Legal Matter (7)
Little Billy (9)
Little Is Enough (21)
Long Live Rock (9,13,19) *54*
Love Ain't For Keepin' (6)
Love Is Coming Down (12)
Love, Reign O'er Me (8,14,18,19,21) *76*
Lubie (Come Back Home) (20)

Magic Bus (3,5,7,13,18,19) *25*
Man Is A Man (17)
Mary-Anne With The Shaky Hands (2,10,20)
Medac (2,10)
Miracle Cure (4,21)
Music Must Change (12)
My Generation (5,7,13,18,19) *74*
My Wife (6,13,18)
Naked Eye (9)
New Song (12)
905 (12)
1921 (21)
(Nothing Is Everything) Let's See Action (16)
Now I'm A Farmer (10)
Odorono (2,10)
One At A Time (17)
One Life's Enough (17)
Our Love Was, Is (2,3,10)
Pictures Of Lily (3,7) *51*
Pinball Wizard (4,7,13,16,18,19,21) *19*
Postcard (9)
Punk Meets The Godfather (8,14)
Pure And Easy (9)
Put The Money Down (9)
Quadrophenia (8)
Quick One While He's Away (1,10,13)
Quiet One (15)
Rael (2,10)

Real Me (8,14,16) *92*
Relax (2,10)
Relay, The (16,18) *39*
Roadrunner (medley) (13)
Rock, The (8)
Rough Boys (21)
Run Run Run (1,3,10)
Sally Simpson (4,21)
Sea And Sand (8)
See Me, Feel Me (13,19) *12*
See My Way (13)
Seeker, The (7,18) *44*
Sensation (4,21)
Shakin' All Over (5)
Shout And Shimmy (20)
Silas Stingy (2,10)
Sister Disco (12,16)
Slip Kid (11,16)
Smash The Mirror (4,21)
So Sad About Us (1,10)
Someone's Coming (3)
Song Is Over (6,16)
Sparks (4,13,21)
Spotted Henry ..see: Medac
Squeeze Box (11,16,18) *16*
Substitute (5,7,18,19)
Success Story (11)
Summertime Blues (5,16,19) *27*
Sunrise (2,10)
Tattoo (2,10)
There's A Doctor I've Found (4,21)
They Are All In Love (11)

Tommy Can You Hear Me (4,13,21)
Tommy's Holiday Camp (4,21)
Too Much Of Anything (9)
Trick Of The Light (12,21)
Twist And Shout (19)
Uncle Ernie (21)
We're Not Gonna Take It (4,21)
Welcome (4)
When I Was A Boy (20)
Whiskey Man (1,10)
Who Are You (12,16,18,19) *14*
Why Did I Fall For That (17)
Won't Get Fooled Again (6,13,18,19,21) *15*
You (15)
You Better You Bet (15,21) *18*
You Didn't Hear It (4)
Young Man Blues (5,13)
Zoot Suit (14)
recorded as the High Numbers

WHODINI

New York rap group. Began as a duo of Jalil "Whodini" Hutchins and John Fletcher. Grandmaster Dee joined in 1986.

DEBUT DATE	PEAK POS	WKS CHR	GOLD	ARTIST — Album Title	$	Label & Number
11/24/84+	35	48	▲	1 Escape	$8	Jive 8251
5/17/86	35	39	●	2 Back In Black	$8	Jive 8407
10/17/87	30	22	●	3 Open Sesame	$8	Jive 8494

Be Yourself (3)
Big Mouth (1)
Cash Money (1)
Early Mother's Day Card (3)
Echo Scratch (2)
Escape (I Need A Break) (1)

Featuring Grandmaster Dee (1)
Five Minutes Of Funk (1) *flip*
For The Body (3)
Freaks Come Out At Night (1)

Friends (1) *87*
Fugitive (2)
Funky Beat (2)
Good Part (2)
Growing Up (2)
Hooked On You (3)
I'm A Ho (2)

I'm Def (Jump Back And Kiss Myself) (3)
Last Night (I Had A Long Talk With Myself) (2)
Life Is Like A Dance (3)
One Love (2)
Out Of Control (1)

Remember Where You Came From (3)
Rock You Again (Again & Again) (3)
We Are Whodini (1)
You Brought It On Yourself (3)

You Take My Breath Away (3)

WICHITA TRAIN WHISTLE, The

A gathering of the top session players in Los Angeles.

DEBUT DATE	PEAK POS	WKS CHR	GOLD	ARTIST — Album Title	$	Label & Number
8/3/68	144	7		Mike Nesmith Presents/The Wichita Train Whistle Sings ....[I]	$30	Dot 25861
				produced by Mike Nesmith (The Monkees)		

Carlisle Wheeling
Don't Call On Me
Don't Cry Now
Nine Times Blue
Papa Gene's Blue
Sweet Young Thing
Tapioca Tundra
While I Cried
You Just May Be The One
You Told Me

WIDOWMAKER

Hard-rock quintet — John Butler, lead singer.

DEBUT DATE	PEAK POS	WKS CHR	GOLD	ARTIST — Album Title	$	Label & Number
6/11/77	150	9		Too Late To Cry	$8	United Art. 723

Here Comes The Queen
Hustler, The
Mean What You Say
Pushin' 'N' Pullin'
Sign The Papers
Sky Blues
Something I Can Do Without
Too Late To Cry
What A Way To Fall

DEBUT DATE	PEAK POS	WKS CHR	GOLD	ARTIST — Album Title	$	Label & Number

WIEDLIN, Jane
Born on 5/20/58 in Oconomowoc, Wisconsin and raised in California. Rhythm guitarist of the Go-Go's.

10/26/85	127	6		1 Jane Wiedlin	$8	I.R.S. 5638
5/28/88	105	21		2 Fur	$8	EMI-Man. 48683

Blue Kiss (1) 77
East Meets West (1)
End Of Love (2)
Forever (1)
Fur (2)
Give! (2)
Goodbye Cruel World (1)
Homeboy (2)
I Will Wait For You (1)
Inside A Dream (2) 57
Lover's Night (2)
Modern Romance (1)
My Traveling Heart (1)
One Heart One Way (2)
One Hundred Years Of Solitude (1)
Rush Hour (2) 9
Somebody's Going To Get Into This House (1)
Sometimes You Really Get On My Nerves (1)
Song Of The Factory (2)
Whatever It Takes (2)
Where We Can Go (1)

WIER, Rusty
Country-rock singer from Austin, Texas.

7/19/75	103	14		1 Don't It Make You Wanna Dance?	$8	20th Century 469
1/17/76	131	9		2 Rusty Wier	$8	20th Century 495

Aqua Dulce (1)
Basic Lady (2)
Blue Haze (1)
Cloudy Days (1)
Dixie Lynn (2)
Don't It Make You Wanna Dance? (1) 82
Fly Away (2)
I Believe In The Way That You Love Me (1)
I Don't Want To Lay This Guitar Down (2)
I Heard You Been Layin' My Old Lady (Apologies To Susie) (1)
Just One More Time (2)
Listen To My Song (1)
Long And Lonesome Highway Blues (2)
Pass The Buck (2)
Queen Of My Dreams (2)
Relief (1)
Sally Mae (1)
Seminole Jail (2)
Sing Me (1)
Sophia (2)
Trouble (1)
Tulsa Turnaround (1)

WILBURN BROTHERS, The
Country duo from Hardy, Missouri: brothers Virgil Doyle (b: 7/7/30; d: 10/16/82) and Thurman Theodore "Teddy" Wilburn (b: 11/30/31). On the Grand Ole Opry since 1953. Own TV series featuring Loretta Lynn.

3/28/70	143	2		Little Johnny From Down The Street	$10	Decca 75173

All We Had Going Is Gone
I Will Never Be Happy (Until You're Happy Too)
I'm A Long Gone
I'm So Afraid Of Losing You Again
Lilacs In Winter
Little Johnny From Down The Street
Make My Heart Die Away
Signs Are Everywhere
Try A Little Kindness
Vision At The Peace Table
Which Side's The Wrong Side

WILD CHERRY
White funk band formed in Steubenville, Ohio in the early '70s. Consisted of Bob Parissi (lead vocals, guitar), Bryan Bassett (guitar), Mark Avsec (keyboards), Allen Wentz (bass) and Ron Beitle (drums).

7/24/76	5	29	▲	1 Wild Cherry	$8	Sweet City 34195
4/2/77	51	9		2 Electrified Funk	$8	Sweet City 34462
2/18/78	84	9		3 I Love My Music	$8	Sweet City 35011

Are You Boogieing Around On Your Daddy (2)
Baby Don't You Know (2) 43
Closest Thing To My Mind (2)
Dancin' Music Band (2)
Don't Go Near The Water (1)
Don't Stop, Get Off (3)
Electrified Funk (2)
Fools Fall In Love (3)
Get It Up (1)
Hold On (1,2) 61
Hole In The Wall (2)
Hot To Trot (2) 95
I Feel Sanctified (1)
I Love My Music (3) 69
If You Want My Love (3)
It's All Up To You (2)
It's The Same Old Song (3)
Lady Wants Your Money (1)
Lana (3)
99 1/2 (1)
No Way Out Love Affair (3)
Nowhere To Run (1)
1 2 3 Kind Of Love (3)
Play That Funky Music (1) 1
Put Yourself In My Shoes (2)
This Old Heart Of Mine (Is Weak For You) (3)
Try One More Time (1)
What In The Funk Do You See (1)

WILDE, Danny
Rock singer/songwriter/guitarist born in Maine and raised in California. Formed duo The Rembrandts with Phil Solem in 1990.

3/26/88	176	9		Any Man's Hunger	$8	Geffen 24179

Ain't I Good Enough
Any Man's Hunger
Bitter Moon
Contradiction
Every Goodbye
In A Bordertown
Set Me Free
Time Runs Wild
Too Many Years Gone By
Wouldn't Be The First Time

WILDE, Eugene
Real name: Ron Broomfield. Black vocalist/songwriter. Member of the Miami-based family group, Life.

1/26/85	97	15		Eugene Wilde	$8	Philly W. 90239

Chey Chey Kule
Gold
Gotta Get You Home Tonight 83
Just Be Good To Me
Lately
Let Her Feel It
Personality
Rainbow

WILDE, Kim
Born Kim Smith on 11/18/60 in Chiswick, England. Pop-rock singer. Daughter of singer Marty Wilde.

6/5/82	86	22		1 Kim Wilde	$8	EMI America 17065
2/9/85	84	10		2 Teases & Dares	$8	MCA 5550
4/4/87	40	26		3 Another Step	$8	MCA 5903
10/1/88	114	6		4 Close	$8	MCA 42230

Another Step (Closer To You) (3)
Bladerunner (2)
Brothers (3)
Chequered Love (1)
Don't Say Nothing's Changed (3)
European Soul (4)
Everything We Know (1)
Falling Out (1)
Fit In (2)
Four Letter Word (4)
Go For It (4) 65
Hey Mister Heartache (4)
Hit Him (3)
How Do You Want My Love (3)
I've Got So Much Love (3)
Is It Over (2)
Janine (2)
Kids In America (1) 25
Love In The Natural Way (4)
Love's A No (4)
Lucky Guy (4)
Missing (3)
Never Trust A Stranger (4)
Our Town (1)
Rage To Love (2)
Say You Really Want Me (3) 44
Schoolgirl (3)
Shangri-La (2)
She Hasn't Got Time For You (3)
Stone (4)
Suburbs Of Moscow (2)
Thought It Was Goodbye (4)
Thrill Of It (3)
Touch, The (2)
Tuning In Tuning On (1)
2-6-5-8-0 (1)
Water On Glass (1)
You Came (4) 41
You Keep Me Hangin' On (3) 1
You'll Be The One Who'll Lose (4)
You'll Never Be So Wrong (1)
Young Heroes (1)

WILDER, Matthew
Born and raised in Manhattan; moved to Los Angeles in the late '70s. Singer/songwriter/keyboardist. Session singer for Rickie Lee Jones and Bette Midler.

1/7/84	49	16		I Don't Speak The Language	$8	Private I 39112

Break My Stride 5
Dreams Keep Bringing You Back
I Don't Speak The Language
I Was There
Kid's American 33
Ladder Of Lovers
Love Above The Ground
Floor
World Of The Rich And Famous

WILD MAN STEVE
Steve Gallon — DJ for WILD in Boston.

11/1/69	185	6		1 My Man! Wild Man!	[C] $10	Raw 7000
6/6/70	179	2		2 Wild! Wild! Wild! Wild!	[C] $10	Raw 7001

no track titles listed on above 2 albums

WILD ONES, The
Rock quintet from New York City: Chuck Alden, Tom Trick, Jordan Christopher, Ed Wright and Tom Graves.

11/20/65	149	2		The Arthur Sound	[L] $18	United Art. 3450

DEBUT DATE	PEAK POS	WKS CHR	GOLD	ARTIST — Album Title	$	Label & Number

WILD ONES, The — Cont'd

Around The Corner	I Can't Help Myself	My Little Red Book (All I Do Is Talk About You)	People Sure Act Funny	What's New Pussycat?	You've Lost That Lovin' Feelin'
Dancing In The Streets	It's Not Unusual		Satisfaction	Wild Way Of Living	
Foolish Pride	My Girl				

WILD TURKEY
British rock quintet led by ex-Jethro Tull bassist Glenn Cornick.

5/6/72	193	3		Battle Hymn	$10	Reprise 2070

Battle Hymn	Dulwich Fox	Gentle Rain	Sanctuary	Sentinel	Twelve Streets Of Cobbled
Butterfly	Easter Psalm	One Sole Survivor		To The Stars	Black

WILL AND THE KILL
Austin, Texas group fronted by Will Sexton, the younger brother of Charlie Sexton.

4/9/88	129	8		Will And The Kill	$8	MCA 42054

All Just To Get To You	Hard To Please	I Thought I Heard A Heartbeat	No Sleep	Rocks In My Pillow	Their Game
Breakin' All The Rules	Heart Of Steel		Restless To Reckless	Teach The Teacher	

★★16★★ WILLIAMS, Andy
Born Howard Andrew Williams on 12/3/28 in Wall Lake, Iowa. Formed quartet with his brothers and eventually moved to Los Angeles. With Bing Crosby on hit "Swingin' On A Star," 1944. With comedienne Kay Thompson in the mid-'40s. Went solo in 1952. On Steve Allen's *Tonight Show* from 1952-55. Own NBC-TV variety series from 1962-67, 1969-71. Appeared in the film *I'd Rather Be Rich* in 1964. Formerly married to singer/actress Claudine Longet. One of America's greatest pop-MOR singers.

DEBUT DATE	PEAK POS	WKS CHR	GOLD	#	ARTIST — Album Title	$	Label & Number
1/25/60	38	4		1	Lonely Street	$20	Cadence 3030
3/3/62	19	36		2	"Danny Boy" and other songs I love to sing	$12	Columbia 8551
4/7/62+	59	44		3	Andy Williams' Best ....[G]	$20	Cadence 3054
5/12/62+	3	176	●	4	**Moon River & Other Great Movie Themes**	$12	Columbia 8609
10/20/62+	16	44		5	Warm And Willing	$12	Columbia 8679
1/12/63	54	43		6	Million Seller Songs ....[K]	$15	Cadence 3061
4/20/63	1[16]	107	●	7	**Days of Wine and Roses**	$12	Columbia 8815
1/25/64	9	24	●	8	**The Wonderful World Of Andy Williams**	$12	Columbia 8937
					with members of Andy's family		
5/9/64	5	63	●	9	**The Academy Award Winning "Call Me Irresponsible"**	$12	Columbia 8971
9/26/64	5	33	●	10	**The Great Songs From "My Fair Lady" and other Broadway hits**	$12	Columbia 9005
4/10/65	4	65	●	11	**Dear Heart**	$12	Columbia 9138
5/22/65	61	18		12	Hawaiian Wedding Song ....[E-R]	$12	Columbia 9123
					reissue of Cadence LP *To You Sweetheart, Aloha*		
7/3/65	112	6		13	Canadian Sunset ....[R]	$12	Columbia 9124
					reissue of Cadence album #3 above		
2/5/66	23	23		14	Andy Williams' Newest Hits ....[K]	$12	Columbia 9183
5/14/66	6	54	●	15	**The Shadow of Your Smile**	$12	Columbia 9299
1/21/67	21	22		16	In The Arms Of Love	$12	Columbia 9333
5/13/67	5	79	●	17	**Born Free**	$12	Columbia 9480
11/18/67+	8	36	●	18	**Love, Andy**	$12	Columbia 9566
6/8/68	9	40	●	19	**Honey**	$12	Columbia 9662
2/1/69	139	7		20	The Andy Williams Sound of Music ....[K]	$15	Columbia 5 [2]
5/17/69	9	23	●	21	**Happy Heart**	$12	Columbia 9844
11/8/69	27	21	●	22	**Get Together With Andy Williams**	$12	Columbia 9922
					with The Osmonds on 3 tracks		
3/7/70	42	20	●	23	Andy Williams' Greatest Hits ....[G]	$10	Columbia 9979
6/13/70	43	19		24	Raindrops Keep Fallin' On My Head	$10	Columbia 9896
11/14/70	81	17		25	The Andy Williams Show ....[L]	$10	Columbia 30105
2/20/71	3	33	▲	26	**Love Story**	$10	Columbia 30497
8/28/71	54	12		27	You've Got A Friend	$10	Columbia 30797
1/8/72	123	5		28	The Impossible Dream ....[K]	$12	Columbia 31064 [2]
4/8/72	29	26	●	29	**Love Theme From "The Godfather"**	$10	Columbia 31303
9/30/72	86	18		30	Alone Again (Naturally)	$10	Columbia 31625
7/7/73	174	5		31	Andy Williams' Greatest Hits, Vol. 2 ....[G]	$8	Columbia 32384
11/17/73	185	6		32	Solitaire	$8	Columbia 32383
12/28/74+	150	4		33	You Lay So Easy On My Mind	$8	Columbia 33234

A Mi Esposa Con Amor (To My Wife With Love) (33)	Be My Love (9)	**Charade** (9,23) **100**	Everything I Own (29)	**Godfather (Speak Softly Love), Love Theme From The** (29,31) **34**	Here's That Rainy Day (16)
Abraham, Martin And John (21)	Begin The Beguine (10)	Come To Me, Bend To Me (2)	Exactly Like You (7)		Holly (18)
Again (33)	Beyond The Reef (12)	Cry Softly (33)	Exodus Song (4)	Gone With The Wind (1)	Home Lovin' Man (30,31)
Alfie (17)	**Bilbao Song** (3,13) **37**	Danny Boy (2) **64**	Face I Love (16)	Good Morning Starshine (22,28)	Honey (I Miss You) (19)
All Through The Night (2)	Blue Hawaii (12)	Day By Day (30)	Falling In Love With Love (7)		How Can You Mend A Broken Heart? (27)
Almost There (11,14,23) **67**	Born Free (17,23)	**Days Of Wine And Roses** (7,23) **2**	Fire And Rain (26)	**Happy Heart** (21,23) **22**	How Insensitive (15)
Aloha Oe (Farewell To Thee) (12)	Both Sides Now (24,28)	**Dear Heart** (11,23) **24**	First Born (8)	**Hawaiian Wedding Song** (3,12,13,23) **11**	How Long Has This Been Going On (5)
Alone Again (Naturally) (30)	Bridge Over Troubled Water (24,28)	Didn't We (21,28)	First Time Ever I Saw Your Face) (30)		How Wonderful To Know (3,13,20)
Amazing Grace (30)	By The Time I Get To Phoenix (19)	**Do You Know?** (3,13) **70**	Fool Never Learns (8,14) **13**	He Ain't Heavy, He's My Brother (28)	Hurting Each Other (29)
And Roses And Roses (14) **36**	Bye Bye Blues (15)	Dr. Zhivago ..see: Somewhere, My Love	For All We Know (27)	He's Got The Whole World In His Hands (6)	I Can't Stop Loving You (11)
And We Were Lovers ..see: Sand Pebbles, Theme From	Call Me Irresponsible (9)	Don't Go To Strangers (3,13)	For Once In My Life (21)	Heather On The Hill (2)	I Could Have Danced All Night (10)
Anniversary Song (9)	Can I Forget You (2)	**Don't You Believe It** (14) **39**	For The Good Times (26)	Hello, Dolly! (10)	I Honestly Love You (33)
Another Lonely Song (33)	**Can't Get Used To Losing You** (7,23) **2**	Dream (8)	Gentle On My Mind (21)	Hello, Young Lovers (25)	I Left My Heart In San Francisco (7)
Aquarius (medley) (22)	Can't Take My Eyes Off You	Dreamer, The (32)	Get Me To The Church On Time (10)	Help Me Make It Through The Night (27)	**I Like Your Kind Of Love** (3) **8**
Are You Sincere (3,13) **3**	**Canadian Sunset** (3,6,8,13) **7**	Dreamsville (9)	Get Together (22)	Here Comes That Rainy Day Feeling Again (27)	I Love My Friend (33)
As Time Goes By (4)	Candida (26)	El Condor Pasa (25,28)	Getting Over You (32)	Here, There And Everywhere (21)	
Autumn Leaves (1,6,20)		Embraceable You (5,20)	Gigi (9)		
		Emily (11,14)	God Only Knows (18)		
		Everybody Loves Somebody (11)			

801

WILLIAMS, Andy — Cont'd

I Love You So Much It Hurts (33)
I Need You (30)
I Really Don't Want To Know (7)
I See Your Face Before Me (5)
I Think I Love You (26)
I Want To Be Free (17)
I Want To Be Wanted (2)
I Will Wait For You (17,28)
I Wish You Love (20)
I'll Be There (27)
I'll Have To Say I Love You In A Song (33)
I'll Never Stop Loving You (9)
I'll Remember You (14)
I'll Weave A Lei Of Stars For You (12)
I'm All Smiles (11)
I'm Old Fashioned (2)
I'm So Alone (1)
I'm So Lonesome I Could Cry (1)
I've Grown Accustomed To Her Face (10)
If (27)
If Ever I Would Leave You (5,20)
If I Could Go Back (30)
If I Love Again (16,20)
If Wishes Were Horses (medley) (24)
Imagine (29)
Impossible Dream (The Quest) (19,28,31)
In The Arms Of Love (16,31) **49**
(In The Summer Time) ..see: You Don't Want My Love
In The Wee Small Hours Of The Morning (1)
It Could Happen To You (2)
It Had To Be You (11)
It Might As Well Be Spring (4)
It's A Most Unusual Day (7)
It's All In The Game (6)
It's Impossible (26)
It's Over (24)
It's Too Late (27)

Joanne (25)
Ka-Lu-A (12)
Kisses Sweeter Than Wine (18)
Lara's Theme ..see: Somewhere, My Love
Last Tango In Paris (32)
Last Time I Saw Her (28)
Laura (9)
Leaving On A Jet Plane (25)
Let It Be Me (8,20)
Let The Sunshine In (medley) (24)
Little Boy (medley) (24)
Little Green Apples (21)
Lonely Street (1,3,13,31) **5**
Long And Winding Road (30)
Long Long Time (28)
Long Time Blues (24)
Look Of Love (18)
Love Is A Many-Splendored Thing (4)
Love Is Blue (19)
Love Is Blue (L'Amour Est Bleu) (28)
Love Is Here To Stay (5)
Love Letters (9)
Love Letters In The Sand (6)
Love Song Of Kalua (12)
Love Story ..see: (Where Do I Begin)
MacArthur Park (29,31)
Madrigal (9)
Make It Easy For Me (32)
Make It With You (25)
Mam'selle (6,20)
Man And A Woman (16,28)
Maria (4)
May Each Day (7,14,20,23)
Meditation (15)
Memories (21)
Michelle (15)
Misty (2)
Mona Lisa (9)
Moon Of Manakoora (12)
Moon River (4,23)
More (9,23)
More I See You (18)
More Than You Know (5)

More Today Than Yesterday (22)
Moulin Rouge (Where Is Your Heart), Song From (9)
Music From Across The Way (29,31)
Music To Watch Girls By (17,31) **34**
My Carousel (11)
My Cherie Amour (22,28)
My Coloring Book (7)
My Elusive Dreams (33)
My Love (32)
My One And Only Love (5)
My Sweet Lord (26,28)
My Way (21)
Never Can Say Goodbye (27)
Never My Love (25)
Never On Sunday (4)
Noelle (8,14)
Old Fashioned Love Song (29)
On The Street Where You Live (10,14,20) **28**
Once Upon A Time (10)
Our Last Goodbye (19)
Peg O' My Heart (15)
Pennies From Heaven (8)
People (10,20)
Picnic (4)
Pieces Of April (30)
Precious And Few (29)
Pretty Butterfly (16)
Put A Little Love In Your Heart (22)
Quentin's Theme (22)
Quiet Nights Of Quiet Stars (14,20) **92**
Raindrops Keep Fallin' On My Head (24)
Rainy Days And Monday (27)
Reason To Believe (24)
Red Roses For A Blue Lady (11,14)
Remember (16,32)
Romeo And Juliet, Love Theme From (22,28)
Rose Garden (26)
Sand And Sea (16)

Sand Pebbles, Theme From (16)
Say It Isn't So (1,20)
Scarborough Fair/Canticle (19)
Second Time Around (4)
Secret Love (2)
September Song (8)
Shadows Of The Night ..see: Quentin's Theme
Sherry! (17)
Show Me (10)
Simple Thing As Love (24)
Sing A Rainbow (8)
Snowbird (20)
So Nice (Summer Samba) (16)
So Rare (6)
Softly, As I Leave You (8)
Solitaire (32)
Someone Who Cares (28)
Fools, Theme From ..see: Someone Who Cares
Somethin' Stupid (18)
Something (26)
Somewhere (15)
Somewhere, My Love (17,28)
Song For You (27,31) **88**
Song Of Old Hawaii (12)
Song Of The Islands (12)
Song Sung Blue (30)
Sound Of Music (20)
Spanish Eyes (17)
Spanish Harlem (25,28)
(Speak Softly Love) ..see: Godfather, Love Theme From The
Spooky (18)
Stranger On The Shore (5) **38**
Strangers In The Night (17)
Suddenly There's A Valley (6)
Summer Love (1,13)
Summer Of '42, Theme From (29)
Summer Of Our Love (15,20)
Summer Place (4)
Summertime (2)
Sunny (17)
Sweet Caroline (22)

Sweet Leilani (12)
Sweet Memories (24) **75**
Sweetest Sounds (10)
Tammy (2)
Taste Of Honey (15)
Tender Is The Night (4)
That Is All (32)
That Old Feeling (15,20)
Then You Can Tell Me Goodbye (17)
There Will Never Be Another You (18)
They Long To Be Close To You (25,28)
This Is All I Ask (8)
This Is My Song (19)
Three Bells (8)
Three Coins In The Fountain (4)
Till (11)
(Time For Us) ..see: Romeo & Juliet, Love Theme From
To You Sweetheart Aloha (12)
Today Medley (24)
Tonight (4)
Touch Of Your Lips (5,20)
Try To Remember (15,20)
Twilight Time (6) **86**
Unchained Melody (1)
Until It's Time For You To Go (29)
Up, Up And Away (19)
Valley Of The Dolls, Theme From (19)
Very Thought Of You (16,20)
Village Of St. Bernadette (3,13,31) **7**
Walk Right Back (32)
Warm All Over (5)
Warm And Willing (5)
Watch What Happens (18)
Way You Look Tonight (5)
We've Only Just Begun (26)
What Are You Doing The Rest Of Your Life? (25)
What Kind Of Fool Am I? (7)
What Now My Love (18,28)
When I Look In Your Eyes (18)

When You're Smiling (The Whole World Smiles With You) (7)
When Your Lover Has Gone (1,20)
(Where Do I Begin) Love Story (26,31) **9**
Where Is The Love (30)
(Where Is Your Heart) ..see: Moulin Rouge, Song From
Where Or When (10)
Where's The Playground Susie? (21)
Who Can I Turn To (When Nobody Needs Me) (11)
Wichita Lineman (21)
Willow Weep For Me (14)
Windy (29)
Without You (29)
Wives And Lovers (8)
Wonderful World Of The Young (14) **99**
Wouldn't It Be Loverly (10)
Yesterday (15)
Yesterday When I Was Young (22)
You Are (2)
You Are My Sunshine (7)
You Are The Sunshine Of My Life (32)
You Are Where Everything Is (17)
You Don't Know What Love Is (1,20)
You Don't Want My Love (3,13) **64**
You Lay So Easy On My Mind (33)
You're Nobody 'Til Somebody Loves You (11)
You've Got A Friend (27)
Your Song (26)

WILLIAMS, Danny

Born on 1/7/42 in Port Elizabeth, South Africa. Moved to England in 1960.

6/13/64	122	5		White On White	$25	United Art. 3359

Charade
Comedy Has Ended
Doreen

Forget Her
I Talk To The Trees

Impossible
Lonely

My Heart Tells Me
Story Of A Starry Night

We Will Never Be As Young As This Again

Weaver Of Dreams
White On White 9

★★412★★ WILLIAMS, Deniece

Born Deniece Chandler on 6/3/51 in Gary, Indiana. Soul vocalist/songwriter. Recorded for Toddlin' Town, early 1960s. Member of Wonderlove, Stevie Wonder's backup group, from 1972-75. Also a popular Inspirational artist.

10/30/76+	33	36	●	1 This is Niecy	$8	Columbia 34242
11/19/77+	66	20		2 Song Bird	$8	Columbia 34911
7/29/78	19	16	●	3 That's What Friends Are For	$8	Columbia 35435
				JOHNNY MATHIS & DENIECE WILLIAMS		
8/18/79	96	8		4 When Love Comes Calling	$8	ARC 35568
4/4/81	74	32		5 My Melody	$8	ARC 37048
4/17/82	20	22		6 Niecy	$8	ARC 37952
6/4/83	54	19		7 I'm So Proud	$8	Columbia 38622
6/9/84	26	19		8 Let's Hear It For The Boy	$8	Columbia 39366

Are You Thinking? (4)
Baby, Baby My Love's All For You (2)
Be Good To Me (2)
Black Butterfly (8)
Blind Dating (8)
Boy I Left Behind (2)
Cause You Love Me Baby (1)
Do What You Feel (7)
Don't Tell Me We Have Nothing (8)
Free (1) **25**
God Is Amazing (2)
God Knows (4)
Haunting Me (8)

Heaven In Your Eyes (7)
Heaven Must Have Sent You (3)
How Does It Feel (6)
How'd I Know That Love Would Slip Away (1)
I Believe In Miracles (6)
I Found Love (8)
I Just Can't Get Over You (3)
I Want You (8)
I'm Glad It's You (7)
I'm So Proud (7)
I've Got The Next Dance (4) **73**
If You Don't Believe (1)

It's Gonna Take A Miracle (6) **10**
It's Important To Me (1)
It's Okay (7)
It's Your Conscience (5)
Just The Way You Are (3)
Let's Hear It For The Boy (8) **1**
Like Magic (4)
Love Notes (6)
Love, Peace And Unity (6)
Me For You, You For Me (3)
My Melody (5)
My Prayer (4)
Next Love (8) **81**

Now Is The Time For Love (6)
Paper, The (2)
Part Of Love (6)
Picking Up The Pieces (8)
Ready Or Not (3)
Season (2)
Silly (5) **53**
So Deep In Love (7)
Strangers (5)
Suspicious (5)
Sweet Surrender (5)
That's What Friends Are For (1,3)
They Say (7)
Time (2)

Touch Me Again (4)
Touching Me With Love (3)
Turn Around (4)
Until You Come Back To Me (That's What I'm Gonna Do) (3)
Waiting (6)
Waiting By The Hotline (6)
Watching Over (1)
We Have Love For You (2)
What Two Can Do (5)
When Love Comes Calling (4)
Whiter Than Snow (8)
Why Can't We Fall In Love? (4)

Wrapped Up (8)
You're A Special Part Of My Life (3)
You're All I Need To Get By (3) **47**
You're All That Matters (5)

WILLIAMS, Don
Born on 5/27/39 in Floydada, Texas. Country singer/songwriter/guitarist. Charted over 15 #1 country hits. Leader of the Pozo-Seco Singers. In films *W.W. & The Dixie Dancekings* and *Smokey & The Bandit 2*.

DEBUT DATE	PEAK POS	WKS CHR	GOLD	ARTIST — Album Title	$	Label & Number
1/27/79	161	7		1 Expressions	$8	ABC 1069
10/4/80	57	31 ▲		2 I Believe In You	$8	MCA 5133
7/25/81	109	11		3 Especially For You	$8	MCA 5210
5/1/82	166	8		4 Listen To The Radio	$8	MCA 5306

Ain't It Amazing (2)
All I'm Missing Is You (1)
Don't Stop Loving Me Now (4)
Especially You (3)
Fairweather Friends (3)
Falling Again (2)
Fool, Fool Heart (4)
Give It To Me (1)
Help Yourselves To Each Other (4)

I Believe In You (2) 24
I Can't Get To You From Here (4)
I Don't Want To Love You (4)
I Keep Putting Off Getting Over You (2)
I Want You Back Again (2)
I Would Like To See You Again (1)

I've Got You To Thank For That (3)
If Hollywood Don't Need You (4)
If I Needed You (3)
If She Just Helps Me Get Over You (4)
It Must Be Love (1)
It's Good To See You (2)

Just Enough Love (For One Woman) (2)
Lay Down Beside Me (1)
Listen To The Radio (4)
Lord, I Hope This Day Is Good (3)
Miracles (3)
Mistakes (4)
Not A Chance (1)
Now And Then (3)

Only Love (4)
Rainy Nights And Memories (2)
Simple Song (2)
Slowly But Surely (2)
Smooth Talking Baby (3)
Standin' In A Sea Of Teardrops (4)
Tears Of The Lonely (1)
Tulsa Time (1)

When I'm With You (1)
Years From Now (3)
You've Got A Hold On Me (1)

★★105★★ WILLIAMS, Hank Jr.
Born Randall Hank Williams on 5/26/49 in Shreveport, Louisiana; raised in Nashville. Country singer/songwriter/guitarist. Son of country music's first superstar, Hank Williams. Nicknamed "Bocephus" by his father. On the *Grand Ole Opry* since 1962. Injured in a climbing accident on 8/8/75 in Montana, returned to performing in 1977. Richard Thomas starred as Hank in his 1983 biographical TV movie *Living Proof: The Hank Williams Story*. Hank, Jr. has charted over 40 top 10 country singles.

DEBUT DATE	PEAK POS	WKS CHR	GOLD	ARTIST — Album Title	$	Label & Number
1/2/65	16	37 ●		1 Your Cheatin' Heart ....[S]	$20	MGM 4260

film is Hank Williams' life story (Hank is played by George Hamilton; songs sung by Hank, Jr.)

DEBUT DATE	PEAK POS	WKS CHR	GOLD	ARTIST — Album Title	$	Label & Number
8/7/65	139	3		2 Father & Son	$20	MGM 4276

HANK WILLIAMS, SR. & HANK WILLIAMS, JR.
Hank, Jr.'s vocals are dubbed in to create a duet effect

DEBUT DATE	PEAK POS	WKS CHR	GOLD	ARTIST — Album Title	$	Label & Number
11/2/68	189	3		3 A Time To Sing ....[S]	$20	MGM 4540

Hank Jr. plays a young Country singer (Grady Dodd) in the film; includes "Next Time I Say Goodbye I'm Leaving" by Shelley Fabares

DEBUT DATE	PEAK POS	WKS CHR	GOLD	ARTIST — Album Title	$	Label & Number
6/21/69	164	4		4 Songs My Father Left Me	$15	MGM 4621

Hank, Jr. adds melodies to unfinished songs (lyrics) written by his father

DEBUT DATE	PEAK POS	WKS CHR	GOLD	ARTIST — Album Title	$	Label & Number
10/18/69	187	2		5 Live At Cobo Hall, Detroit ....[L]	$15	MGM 4644
6/21/80	154	17		6 Habits Old and New	$8	Elektra 278
2/21/81	82	15 ●		7 Rowdy	$8	Elektra 330
9/5/81	76	23 ▲		8 The Pressure Is On	$8	Elektra 535
5/8/82	123	20 ●		9 High Notes	$8	Elektra 60100
11/13/82+	107	70 ▲²		10 Hank Williams, Jr.'s Greatest Hits ....[G]	$8	Elektra 60193
4/23/83	64	16 ●		11 Strong Stuff	$8	Elektra 60223
11/19/83	116	13 ●		12 Man Of Steel	$8	Warner 23924
6/9/84	100	19 ●		13 Major Moves	$8	Warner 25088
5/18/85	72	22 ●		14 Five-O	$8	Warner/Curb 25267

Hank's 50th album

DEBUT DATE	PEAK POS	WKS CHR	GOLD	ARTIST — Album Title	$	Label & Number
1/11/86	183	8 ▲		15 Greatest Hits - Volume 2 ....[G]	$8	Warner 25328
7/19/86	93	18 ●		16 Montana Cafe	$8	Warner 25412
2/14/87	71	24 ●		17 Hank "Live" ....[L]	$8	Warner 25538
8/1/87	28	47 ▲		18 Born To Boogie	$8	Warner 25593
7/16/88	55	19 ●		19 Wild Streak	$8	Warner 25725
2/25/89	61	35 ▲		20 Greatest Hits III ....[G]	$8	Warner 25834
2/24/90	71	18 ●		21 Lone Wolf	$12	Warner/Curb 26090
11/3/90	116	14		22 AMERICA (The Way I See It) ....[K]	$12	Warner/Curb 26453
5/11/91	50	19 ●		23 Pure Hank	$12	Warner/Curb 26536
3/7/92	55	20		24 Maverick	$12	Curb/Capri. 26806

Ain't Makin' No Headlines (Here Without You) (9)
Ain't Misbehavin' (14,20)
Ain't Much More (7)
Ain't Nobody's Business (21)
Air That I Breathe (12)
All In Alabama (6)
All My Rowdy Friends Are Coming Over Tonight (13,15,22)
All My Rowdy Friends (Have Settled Down) (8,10,17)
Almost Persuaded (21)
American Dream (10)
American Way (6,22)
Angels Are Hard To Find (4)
Are You Lonely Too (4)
Are You Sure Hank Done It This Way (7)
Attitude Adjustment (13,15)
Ballad Of Hank Williams (8)
Be Careful Who You Love (Arthur's Song) (23)
Big Mamou (21)
Blue Jean Blues (11)
Blues Man (6)
Born To Boogie (18,20)
Buck Naked (18)

Cajun Baby (4)
Coalition To Ban Coalitions (8,22)
Cold, Cold Heart (1)
Come On Over To The Country (24)
Conversation, The (15,17)
Count Song (24)
Country Boy Can Survive (8,10,17,22)
Country Relaxin' (13)
Country State Of Mind (16,20)
Crazy Heart (2)
Cut Bank, Montana (24)
Darling, You Know I Wouldn't Lie (5)
Detroit City (5)
Dinosaur (6)
Dixie On My Mind (7,10)
Don't Give Us A Reason (22)
Early In The Morning And Late At Night (19)
Everytime I Hear That Song (8)
Family Tradition (10,17)
Fat Friends (16)
Fax Me A Beer (24)

Finders Are Keepers (20)
Foggy Mountain Breakdown (5)
Footlights (7)
For Me There Is No Place (4)
Games People Play (5)
Girl On The Front Row At Fort Worth (17)
Give A Damn (7,22)
Give Me The Hummingbird Line (3)
Gonna Go Huntin' Tonight (11,15)
Good Friends, Good Whiskey, Good Lovin' (21)
Harvest Moon (medley) (16)
Heaven Can't Be Found (18,20)
Here I Am Fallin' Again (6)
Hey, Good Lookin' (1,17)
High And Pressurized (9)
Hold Up Your Head (medley) (13)
Hollywood Honeys (23)
Homecoming Queen (11)
Homesick (4)
Honky Tonk Blues (2)
Honky Tonk Train (23)

Honky Tonk Women (18)
Honky Tonkin' (9,15)
Hot To Trot (21)
Hotel Whiskey (24)
House Of The Rising Sun (17)
I Can't Change My Tune (9)
I Can't Help It (If I'm Still In Love With You) (1)
I Don't Care (If Tomorrow Never Comes) (8)
I Got A Right To Be Wrong (7)
(I Heard That) Lonesome Whistle (2)
I Just Don't Like This Kind Of Livin' (2)
I Know What You've Got Up Your Sleeve (24)
I Mean I Love You (21)
I Really Like Girls (14,17)
I Saw The Light (1)
I Won't Be Home No More (2)
I'm For Love (14,17,20)
I'm Just A Man (3)
I'm Just Crying 'Cause I Care (4)

I'm So Lonesome I Could Cry (1,5)
I've Been Around (14)
I've Been Down (9)
(I've Got My) Future On Ice (9)
I've Got Rights (22)
If Heaven Ain't A Lot Like Dixie (9,17)
If It Will It Will (23)
If The South Woulda Won (19)
If You Don't Like Hank Williams (6,17)
If You Wanna Get To Heaven (9)
In The Arms Of Cocaine (11)
Is This Goodbye (24)
It Just Don't Get It No More (12)
It's All Over But The Crying (3)
Jambalaya (On The Bayou) (1,5)
Just Me And My Broken Heart (4)
Just To Satisfy You (23)
Kaw-Liga (1,6,10)

Keep Your Hands To Yourself (18)
Kiss Mother Nature Goodbye (23)
Knoxville Courthouse Blues (13)
La Grange (11,17)
Lawyers, Guns And Money (14)
Leave Them Boys Alone (11,15)
Little Less Talk And A Lot More Action (24)
Lone Wolf (21)
Long Gone Lonesome Blues (1) 67
Lost Highway (2)
Love M.D. (19)
Lovesick Blues (2,12)
Loving Instructor (16)
Low Down Blues (24)
Lyin' Jukebox (7)
Made In The Shade (11)
Major Moves (13,15)
Man Is On His Own (3)
Man Of Steel (12,15,17)
Man To Man (21)
May You Never Be Alone (2)

WILLIAMS, Hank Jr. — Cont'd

Memphis Belle (23)
Midnight Rider (12)
Mind Your Own Business (2,16,20)
Money Can't Buy Happiness (3)
Montana Cafe (16)
Move It On Over (2,6)
Mr. Lincoln (13,22)
My Girl Don't Like My Cowboy Hat (16)
My Heart Won't Let Me Go (4) (18,22)
My Name Is Bocephus (16,17,20)
My Starter Won't Start This Morning (medley) (13)
Nashville Scene (14)

New Orleans (14)
Norwegian Wood (This Bird Has Flown) (9)
Now I Know How George Feels (3)
Old Before My Time (3)
Old Habits (6,10)
One Kind Favor (medley) (13)
Orange Blossom Special (12)
Outlaw's Reward (4)
Practice What I Preach (18,22)
Pressure Is On (8)
Promises (13)
Queen of My Heart (12,15)
Ramblin' In My Shoes (8)
Ramblin' Man (1,7)

Ride, The (17)
Rock In My Shoe (3)
Shadow Face (18)
She Had Me (12)
She Thinks I Still Care (5)
Short Haired Woman (medley) (17)
Simple Man (23)
Social Call (19)
Something To Believe In (14)
South's Gonna Rattle Again (9)
St Louis Blues (medley) (16)
Standing In The Shadows (5)
Stoned In Their Tracks (4)
Sweet Home Alabama (17)
Tennessee River (7)

Tennessee Stud (8)
Texas Women (7,10)
Thanks A Lot (18)
There's A Tear In My Beer (20)
There's Gotta Be Much More To Life Than You (3)
This Ain't Dallas (14,20)
Time To Sing (3)
Trouble In Mind (medley) (13,17)
Tuesday's Gone (19)
Two Old Cats Like Us (15)
Twodot Montana (11)
U.S.A. Today (21,22)
Video Blues (13)
Weatherman (8)

Wedding Bells (2)
What It Boils Down To (18)
What You Don't Know (Won't Hurt You) (19)
When Something Is Good (Why Does It Change) (16)
Where Do I Go From Here (4)
Whiskey Bent And Hell Bound (10)
Whiskey On Ice (9)
Whole Lot Of Hank (11)
Why Don't You Love Me (2)
Wild And Blue (13)
Wild Streak (19)
Wild Weekend (24)
Woman On The Run (12)
Women I've Never Had (10)

Won't It Be Nice (6)
Workin' For MCA (17)
You Brought Me Down To Earth (19)
You Can't Find Many Kissers (7)
You Can't Judge A Book (By Looking At The Cover) (16)
You Can't Take My Memories Of You (4)
You Win Again (1,5)
You're Gonna Be A Sorry Man (19)
Young Country (18,20)
Your Cheatin' Heart (1,5)
Your Turn To Cry (4)

WILLIAMS, John — see BOSTON POPS ORCHESTRA

WILLIAMS, Lenny

Born in February 1945, in Little Rock, Arkansas and raised in Oakland, California. First recorded for Fantasy in the early '60s. Lead vocalist of Tower Of Power from 1972-75.

DEBUT DATE	PEAK POS	WKS CHR	GOLD	ARTIST — Album Title	$	Label & Number
8/6/77	99	26		1 Choosing You	$8	ABC 1023
7/22/78	87	25	●	2 Spark of Love	$8	ABC 1073
7/7/79	108	9		3 Love Current	$8	MCA 3155
11/15/80	185	2		4 Let's Do It Today	$8	MCA 5147

'Cause I Love You (2)
Changes (2)
Choosing You (1)
Doing The Loop De Loop (3)
Don't Stop Me Now (4)
Half Past Love (2)
Here's To The Lady (3)

I Still Reach Out (2)
I've Been Away From Love Too Long (1)
If You Don't Want My Love (4)
If You're In Need (3)
Last Night I Dreamed (3)

Let's Do It Today (4)
Let's Talk It Over (3)
Look Up With Your Mind (1)
Looks Like You Made It (4)
Love Came And Rescued Me (2)

Love Hurt Me, Love Healed Me (3)
Messing With My Mind (4)
Midnight Girl (2)
Ooh Child (4)
Play With Me, Stay With Me (Lay With Me) (4)

Please Don't Tempt Me (1)
Problem Solver (1)
Riding The High Wire (1)
Shoo Doo Fu Fu Ooh! (1)
Suspicions (4)
Sweet Ecstasy (3)
Think What We Have (2)

Though We Loved Once (3)
Trust In Me (1)
When I'm Dancin' (3)
You Got Me Running (2)

WILLIAMS, Mason

Born on 8/24/38 in Abilene, Texas. Folk guitarist/songwriter/author/photographer/TV comedy writer (*The Smothers Brothers Comedy Hour*, 1967-69; *Saturday Night Live*, 1980).

DEBUT DATE	PEAK POS	WKS CHR	GOLD	ARTIST — Album Title	$	Label & Number
6/29/68	14	34		1 The Mason Williams Phonograph Record	$10	Warner 1729
12/28/68+	164	8		2 The Mason Williams Ear Show	$10	Warner 1766
5/10/69	44	17		3 Music By Mason Williams	$10	Warner 1788
12/19/87+	118	19	●	4 Classical Gas	[I] $8	American G. 800

MASON WILLIAMS & MANNHEIM STEAMROLLER

All The Time (1)
Baroque-A-Nova (1,2,4) 96
Brothers Theme (3)
Bucko's Memoirs (3)
Cinderella-Rockefella (2)
Classical Gas (1,4) 2
Come To Me (3)

Country Idyll (4)
Cowboy Buckaroo (3)
Doot-Doot (4)
Dylan Thomas (1)
Generatah-Oscillatah (3)
Gift Of Song (4)
Greensleeves (3,4) 90

Here Am I (1)
J. Edgar Swoop (3)
Katydid's Ditty (4)
La Chanson De Claudine (3,4)
Last Great Waltz (2)
Life Song (1)

Long Time Blues (3)
Love Are Wine (2)
Major Thang (3)
McCall (1)
One Minute Commercial (2)
Prince's Panties (1)
Road Song (4)

Samba Beach (4)
Saturday Night At The World (2,4) 99
Shady Dell (4)
She's Gone Away (1)
Sunflower (1,3,4)
$13 Stella (2)

Vancouver Island (4)
Wanderlove (1)
(Whistle) Hear (2)

WILLIAMS, Paul

Born on 9/19/40 in Omaha. Singer/songwriter/actor. Wrote "We've Only Just Begun" and "Rainy Days & Mondays" with partner Roger Nichols, and wrote "Evergreen" with Barbra Streisand. In films *Planet Of The Apes*, *Smokey & The Bandit* and others.

DEBUT DATE	PEAK POS	WKS CHR	GOLD	ARTIST — Album Title	$	Label & Number
12/25/71+	141	21		1 Just An Old Fashioned Love Song	$8	A&M 4327
12/2/72+	159	14		2 Life Goes On	$8	A&M 4367
3/2/74	165	10		3 Here Comes Inspiration	$8	A&M 3606
11/23/74	95	9		4 A Little Bit Of Love	$8	A&M 3655
12/13/75+	146	6		5 Ordinary Fool	$8	A&M 4550
8/6/77	155	8		6 Classics	[K] $8	A&M 4701

Born To Fly (3)
California Roses (4)
Day Of The Locust, Theme From ..see: Lonely Hearts
Don't Call It Love (5)
Dream Away (3)
Driftwood (3)
Even Better Than I Know Myself (5)
Evergreen ..see: Star Is Born, Love Theme From A
Family Of Man (4)
Flash (5)

Gone Forever (1)
I Never Had It So Good (1)
I Won't Last A Day Without You (2,6)
If We Could Still Be Friends (3)
In The Beginning (3)
Inspiration (3)
Lady Is Waiting (1)
Let Me Be The One (1)
Life Goes On (2)
Lifeboat (5)
Little Bit Of Love (4)

Little Girl (2)
Lone Star (5)
Loneliness (4,6)
Lonely Hearts (5)
Margarita (4)
My Love And I (1)
Nice To Be Around (4)
Nilsson Sings Newman (3)
Old Fashioned Love Song (1,6)
Old Souls (5)
Ordinary Fool (5)
Out In The Country (2)

Park Avenue (2)
Perfect Love (1)
Rainy Days And Mondays (3,6)
Rose (2)
Sad Song (4)
She Sings For Free (4)
Simple Man (1)
Sleep Warm (4)
Soul Rest (5)
Star Is Born, Love Theme From A (6)
Sunday (4)

That Lucky Old Sun (2)
That's Enough For Me (1,6)
That's What Friends Are For (3)
Then I'll Be Home (1)
Time And Tide (5)
Traveling Boy (2)
Waking Up Alone (1,6) 60
We've Only Just Begun (1,6)
What Would They Say (3)
When I Was All Alone (1)
Where Do I Go From Here (2)

With One More Look At You (6)
You And Me Against The World (3,6)
You Know Me (3)

WILLIAMS, Robin

Born on 7/21/52 in Chicago. Actor/comedian. Mork of TV series *Mork & Mindy*, 1978-82. Among his many films: *The World According To Garp*, *Good Morning, Vietnam*, *Dead Poets Society* and *Hook*.

DEBUT DATE	PEAK POS	WKS CHR	GOLD	ARTIST — Album Title	$	Label & Number
7/21/79	10	22	●	1 Reality...What A Concept	[C] $8	Casablanca 7162
4/2/83	119	9		2 Throbbing Python Of Love	[C] $8	Casablanca 811150

Babies (2)
Back Home (2)
Cats (2)
Christopher (2)
Come Inside My Mind (1)
Devil's Dandruff (2)

Elmer Fudd Sings Bruce Springsteen (Fire) (2)
Falklands, The (2)
Grandpa Funk (1)
Hollywood Casting Session (1)

Jack (2)
Kindergarten Of The Stars (1)
Newsboy (2)
Nicholson (2)
Nicky Lenin (1)

Pop Goes The Weasel (1)
Reverend Earnest Angry (1)
Richard Simmons (2)
Roots People (1)
Shake Hands With Mr. Happy (2)

Shakespeare (A Meltdowner's Nightmare) (1)
Tank You, Boyce (1)
Throbbing Python Of Love (2)

Touch Of Fairfax (1)
Wines (2)

DEBUT DATE	PEAK POS	WKS CHR	GOLD	ARTIST — Album Title	$	Label & Number

★★23★★   WILLIAMS, Roger

Born Louis Weertz in 1925 in Omaha. Learned to play the piano by age three. Educated at Drake University, Idaho State University, and Juilliard School of Music. Took lessons from Lenny Tristano and Teddy Wilson. Win on the TV show *Arthur Godfrey's Talent Scouts* led to recording contract.

DEBUT DATE	PEAK POS	WKS CHR	GOLD	ARTIST — Album Title	$	Label & Number
3/31/56	19	2		1 Roger Williams ....[I]	$15	Kapp 1012
				album also released as *Autumn Leaves*		
8/25/56	19	3		2 Daydreams...[I]	$15	Kapp 1031
10/27/56	16	2		3 Roger Williams plays the wonderful Music of the Masters ....[I]	$15	Kapp 1040
				classical melodies		
3/23/57	6	65	●	4 **Songs Of The Fabulous Fifties**..............................[I]	$18	Kapp 5000 [2]
10/7/57	20	5		5 Almost Paradise ....[I]	$15	Kapp 1063
11/4/57+	19	4		6 Songs Of The Fabulous Forties ....[I]	$18	Kapp 5003 [2]
3/31/58	4	93	●	7 **Till** ....[I]	$15	Kapp 1081
2/23/59+	9	70		8 **Near You** ....[I]	$15	Kapp 1112
6/15/59	11	24	●	9 **More Songs Of The Fabulous Fifties** ....[I]	$15	Kapp 1130
10/26/59+	8	34		10 **With These Hands** ....[I]	$15	Kapp 1147
12/28/59+	12	2		11 Christmas Time...[X-I]	$15	Kapp 1164
4/4/60	25	22		12 Always ....[I]	$12	Kapp 1172
12/19/60+	5	39		13 **Temptation**..[I]	$12	Kapp 1217
9/11/61	49	15		14 Yellow Bird ....[I]	$12	Kapp 1244
10/2/61	35	11		15 Songs Of The Soaring '60s ....[I]	$12	Kapp 1251
12/25/61+	105	3		16 Christmas Time...[X-I-R]	$15	Kapp 1164
				Christmas charts: 20/'64, 26/'65, 18/'66, 28/'67		
2/3/62	44	23	●	17 Greatest Hits...[G-I]	$12	Kapp 3260
3/17/62	9	46		18 **Maria** ....[I]	$12	Kapp 3266
9/15/62	27	30		19 Mr. Piano ....[I]	$12	Kapp 3290
4/20/63	122	13		20 Country Style ....[I]	$12	Kapp 3305
10/12/63	59	12		21 For You ....[I]	$12	Kapp 3336
2/8/64	27	19		22 The Solid Gold Steinway ....[I]	$12	Kapp 3354
4/4/64	108	8		23 10th Anniversary/Limited Edition ....[R]	$15	Kapp 1 [3]
				reissue of albums #9 and 12 above, plus *Roger Williams plays Gershwin*		
9/5/64	126	9		24 Academy Award Winners ....[I]	$12	Kapp 3406
4/10/65	118	6		25 Roger Williams plays The Hits ....[I]	$10	Kapp 3414
10/9/65	63	18		26 Summer Wind ....[I]	$10	Kapp 3434
12/25/65+	130	7		27 Autumn Leaves-1965 ....[I]	$10	Kapp 3452
3/26/66	24	67		28 I'll Remember You....................................[I]	$10	Kapp 3470
12/10/66+	7	69	●	29 **Born Free** ....[I]	$10	Kapp 3501
5/13/67	51	27		30 Roger! ....[I]	$10	Kapp 3512
9/9/67	87	29		31 Roger Williams/Golden Hits ....[G-I]	$10	Kapp 3530
3/2/68	164	5		32 More Than A Miracle ....[I]	$10	Kapp 3550
1/25/69	131	10		33 Only For Lovers ....[I]	$10	Kapp 3565
5/31/69	60	11		34 Happy Heart ....[I]	$10	Kapp 3595
8/9/69	145	10		35 Love Theme From "Romeo & Juliet" ....[I]	$10	Kapp 3610
3/6/71	112	13		36 Love Story ....[I]	$8	Kapp 3645
9/18/71	187	3		37 Summer of '42 ....[I]	$8	Kapp 3650
4/8/72	187	8		38 Love Theme from "The Godfather" ....[I]	$8	Kapp 3665

Adeste Fideles (11)
Affair To Remember (Our Love Affair) (10,14)
African Elephant, Theme From The (38)
Ain't No Mountain High Enough (36)
Al-Di-La (19)
Alfie (32)
All Over The World (21)
All The Way (9,23)
Alley Cat (medley) (22)
Almost Paradise (5,17) **15**
Amor (18) *88*
Anastasia (5)
And I Love Her (30,35)
Angels We Have Heard On High (medley) (11)
Anniversary Song (6)
(Anonymous Venetian) ..see: To Be The One You Love, Theme From
Apartment, Theme From The (13)
April In Portugal (4)
April Love (7)
Are You Lonesome Tonight? (15)
Around The World (5,17)
Arrivederci, Roma (7) *55*
As Long As He Needs Me (35)
As Time Goes By (6)
Autumn Leaves (1,4,17) *1*
Autumn Leaves - 1965 (27) *92*

Away In A Manger (medley) (11)
Bach Talk (37)
Because Of You (4)
Bells Of St. Mary's (6)
Ben Casey, Theme From (19)
Bess You Is My Woman (10,14)
Beyond The Sea ..see: La Mer
Bible, Theme From The (29)
Bidin' My Time (23)
Big Town (1)
Bilbao Song (15)
Black Orpheus, Theme From (30)
Blue Tango (4)
Blueberry Hill (6)
Born Free (29,31) **7**
Brahms: A Flat Waltz (7)
Brahms: Brahms' Lullaby (12,23)
Brahms: Hungarian Dance No. 5 (19)
Brian's Song (38)
Buona Sera Mrs. Campbell (34)
Buttons And Bows (6,24)
Calcutta (15)
Call Me Irresponsible (24)
Canadian Sunset (medley) (22)
Cara Mia (26)
Cardinal, Theme From The (22)
Carnival, Theme From (15)

Carry Me Back To The Lone Prairie (20)
Catch A Falling Star (8)
Cause I Believe In Loving (37)
Cherish (29)
Cherry Pink And Apple Blossom White (9,23,27)
Chim Chim Cher-ee (27)
Chopin: E Flat Nocturne ..see: To Love Again
Chopin: Etude (2)
Chopin: Etude In A Flat (3)
Chopin: Etude In C Minor (Revolutionary) (3,38)
Chopin: Polonnaise (medley) (22)
Christmas Song (Merry Christmas To You) (11)
Clair De Lune ..see: Moonlight Love
Cold, Cold Heart (20)
Crying In The Chapel (26)
Cumana (26,31)
Dancing Tambourines (medley) (22)
Danke Schoen (21)
Dark Eyes (12,23,29)
Days Of Wine And Roses (24,35)
Dear Heart (25)
Debussy: Clair De Lune ..see: Moonlight Love
Debussy: Maid With The Flaxen Hair (3)

Deck The Halls (11)
Deep Purple (8)
Dr. Kildare, Theme From (19)
Dr. Zhivago ..see: Lara's Theme
Doll Dance (medley) (22)
Dominique (22,31)
Don't Blame Me (18)
Don't Fence Me In (6)
Donkey Serenade (6)
Dream A Little Dream Of Me (33)
Driftwood (8)
Dulcinea (28)
Ebb Tide (28)
Edelweiss (29)
Elegie (medley) (22)
Eleventh Hour, Theme From The (21)
Elvira, Theme For (33,35)
Eventide (18)
Every Little Movement (5)
Exodus, Theme From (15,26,35)
Falla: Ritual Fire Dance (3)
Fascination (7)
Felicia (22)
59th Street Bridge Song (Feelin' Groovy) (34)
Fill The World With Love (36)
First Noel (medley) (11)
Flight Of The Bumble Bee (3,22)
Fly Me To The Moon (medley) (22)
For All We Know (36)

For Once In My Life (34)
For The First Time (5)
Forget Domani (26)
Forgotten Dreams (10,14)
Frenesi (25)
Galveston (34) *99*
Gentle On My Mind (33)
Georgy Girl (30,35)
Gigi (10,14,24)
Girl From Ipanema (25)
Godfather, Love Theme From The (38)
Goodnight Irene (4)
Green Fields (15)
Green Leaves Of Summer (15)
Greensleeves (10,14)
Guantanamera (29)
Happy Heart (34)
Hark! The Herald Angels Sing (11)
Hatari! (19)
Hawaii, Pearl Of The Sea (29)
Heart Of The Country (37)
Hernando's Hideaway (9,23)
Hey Jude (34)
Hey There (4)
Hi-Lili Hi-Lo (1) *85*
High And The Mighty (7,17)
High Noon (4)
High On A Windy Hill (25)
Holiday For Strings (6)
Homesick For New England (13)
How Can You Mend A Broken Heart (37)

Hurting Each Other (38)
I Believe (4)
I Don't Know How To Love Him (37)
I Don't Know Why (I Just Do) (18)
I Got Rhythm (17,23)
I Left My Heart In San Francisco (21,31)
I Wanna Be Free (33)
I Will Wait For You (32,35)
I'll Always Walk With You (2)
I'll Be Seeing You (18)
I'll Meet You Halfway (37)
I'll Remember You (28)
I'll String Along With You (2)
I'm A Believer (30)
Impossible Dream (32) *55*
Indiscreet (8)
Intermezzo, Theme From (19)
It Came Upon The Midnight Clear (medley) (11)
It Might As Well Be Spring (2,24)
It's All In The Game (8)
It's Not For Me To Say (9,23)
It's Now Or Never (13)
Itsy Bitsy Teenie Weenie Yellow Polkadot Bikini (15)
Janie Is Her Name (21)
Jimmie's Train (29)
Jingle Bells (11)
Jingle, Jangle, Jingle (6)
Joy To The World (medley) (11)

WILLIAMS, Roger — Cont'd

Junk (36)
Just One Of Those Things (1)
Kitten On The Keys (medley) (22)
Kotch, Theme From (38)
La Mer (Beyond The Sea) (1) 37
La Montana (If She Should Come To You) (13) 98
La Strada, Love Theme From (33,35)
La Vie En Rose (4)
Lara's Theme From "Dr. Zhivago" (28,31) 65
Last Time I Saw Paris (6,24)
Laura (6)
Laura Lou (28)
Lecuona: Malaguena (3)
Let It Be Me (34)
(Life Is What You Make It) ..see: Kotch, Theme From
Like Young (medley) (22)
Linda (6)
Listen To The Mocking Bird (20)
Liszt Etude In D Flat (3)
Liszt: Liebestraum (A Dream Of Love) (3)
Little Rock Getaway (13)
Liza (17,21,23)
Lollipops And Roses (19,27)
Lonely Ones (36)
Look Again (21)
Look Of Love (33)
Lorelei, The (19)
Love Is A Many-Splendored Thing (4)
Love Is Blue (33)
Love Letters In The Sand (5)
(Love Makes The World Go 'Round) ..see: Carnival, Theme From
Love Me Forever (30) 60
Love Story, Theme From (1)
Love Walked In (23)
Lover's Concerto (28)
Lover's Symphony (14)
Lullaby From Rosemary's Baby (34)
Lullaby Of Broadway (5)
Mack The Knife ..see: Threepenny Opera
Maria (18,31) 48
Maria Elena (22)
Marie, Marie (14)
Mas Que Nada (32)

Maybe (23)
Memories Are Made Of This (9,23,27)
Mexicali Rose (20)
Mini-Minuet (34)
Misirlou (medley) (22)
Mister Lonely (25)
Mister Sandman (4)
Misty (19)
Mockin' Bird Hill (9,23)
Moments To Remember (9,23)
Mona Lisa (4,27)
Moon River (18,24,31)
Moonglow/Theme From Picnic (4)
Moonlight And Roses (12,23)
Moonlight Love (3,7,9,17,23)
Moonlight Sonata (12,23)
More (28,35)
More I See You (29)
More Than A Miracle [includes 2 versions] (32)
Moszkowski: Etude In F (3)
Moulin Rouge (Where Is Your Heart), Song From The (2,4)
Mr. Moszkowski (30)
Music Lovers, Theme From The (37)
Music To Watch Girls By (30)
Mutiny On The Bounty, Theme From (21)
My Coloring Book (21)
My Cup Runneth Over (30)
My Dream Sonata (1)
My Foolish Heart (2)
My Happiness (9,23)
My Heart Cries For You (4)
My Little Corner Of The World (15)
Nature Boy (6)
Near You (8,17) 10
(Nel Blu Dipinto Di Blu) ..see: Volare
Never Can Say Goodbye (37)
Never My Love (32)
Never On Sunday (13,24)
Never Tease Tigers (25)
Niagara Theme (19)
Night Wind (1)
Nights In Verona (5)
Nola (medley) (22)
None But The Lonely Heart (12,23)
Now Is The Hour (6)

O, Holy Night (medley) (11)
O Little Town Of Bethlehem (11)
O Mio Babbino Caro (Oh My Beloved Daddy) (10,14)
O, Sactissima (medley) (11)
Ode To Billie Joe (32)
Oh! Dem Golden Slippers (20)
Oh, My Papa (7)
Oh, What It Seemed To Be (6,27)
On The Street Where You Live (9,23)
On The Trail (21)
On Top Of Old Smoky (20)
One Alone (5)
One Finger Symphony (13)
Only For Lovers (33)
Our Love (27)
Papa, Won't You Dance With Me? (27)
Paradise (2)
Peg O' My Heart (6)
People (25,35)
Picasso Summer, Theme From (36)
Picnic ..see: Moonglow
Portrait Of My Love (15)
Postlude To A Prelude (25)
Que Sera, Sera (7,24)
Rachmaninoff: Prelude In C Sharp Minor (3)
Raindrops (3)
Rainy Days And Mondays (37)
Ramblin' Rose (20)
Red River Valley (20)
Red Roses For A Blue Lady (26)
Rhapsody In Blue (23)
Riders In The Sky (6)
Rimsky-Korsakoff: Flight Of The Bumble Bee ..see: Flight Of The Bumble Bee
River Seine (1)
Riviera Concerto (13)
Roger's Bumble Bee (14,31)
Romeo & Juliet, Love Theme From (12,23,35)
Room Full Of Roses (20)
Sailor (Your Home Is The Sea) (11)
San Antonio Rose (20)
Sand Pebbles, Theme From The (34)

Santa Claus Is Coming To Town (11)
Secret Love (2,4,24)
Seeing You Like This (36)
Sentimental Touch (7)
September Song (8,17)
Serenade (5)
Serenade For Joy (2)
Shadow Of Your Smile (31)
Shalom (18)
Silent Night (11)
Sinding: Rustles Of Spring (3)
Singin' In The Rain (1)
Skaters Waltz (12,23)
Smile (18)
Smoke Gets In Your Eyes (medley) (9,23)
Snowfall (10)
Softly, As I Leave You (23)
Some Enchanted Evening (6)
Someone To Watch Over Me (23,27)
Something In Your Smile (32)
Somewhere, My Love ..see: Lara's Theme
Song Of Devotion (5)
Song Of The Rain (14)
Sound Of Music (28)
Spanish Eyes (33)
Spinning Song (32)
St. Louis Blues (8)
Stardust (23)
Strange Music (10)
Stranger In Paradise (12,23)
Stranger On The Shore (19)
Strangers In The Night (29)
Summer Magic (21)
Summer Of '42 (The Summer Knows), Theme From (37)
Summer Place, Theme From A (15)
Summer Samba (29)
Summer Wind (26)
Summertime (1)
Sunday, Monday, Or Always (6)
Sundowners, Theme From The (13)
Sunny (29)
Sunrise Serenade (medley) (22)
Sunrise, Sunset (30) 84

Supercalifragilisticexpiali-docius (25)
Sweet Pea (30)
Sweetest Sounds (19)
Sweetheart Tree (26)
Symphony (6)
Syncopated Clock (10)
Talk To The Animals (33)
Tammy (7,17)
Taste Of Honey (28)
Tchaikovsky: Piano Concerto (8,17,22)
Tchaikovsky: Piano Concerto 73 (38)
Teakwood Nocturne (22)
Temptation (13) 56
Tenderly (2)
Tennessee Waltz (4)
This Guy's In Love With You (34)
This Is My Prayer (28)
Those Were The Days (34)
Three Coins In The Fountain (4)
Three O'Clock In The Morning (20)
(Three Stars Will Shine Tonight) ..see: Dr. Kildare, Theme From
Threepenny Opera (Moritat), Theme From The (9,23)
Tico-Tico (27)
Till (7,31) 22
Till The End Of Time (12,23)
Time For Love Is Anytime (36)
Tiny Bubbles (30)
To A Wild Rose (12,23)
To Be The One You Love, Theme From (38)
To Each His Own (6)
To Love Again (2,22)
To Sir With Love (32)
Toccata (22)
Tom Dooley (9,23)
Tonight (18)
Too Young (4)
Traumerei (12,23)
True Love (4)
Try To Remember (25) 97
Tumbling Tumbleweeds (5) 60
Two Different Worlds (10,14)
Unchained Melody (4)
Until It's Time For You To Go (38)

Up-Up And Away (33)
Vaya Con Dios (4)
Very Thought Of You (medley) (22)
Volare (Nel Blu Dipinto Di Blu) (8)
Walk In The Black Forest (26)
Walking Alone (21)
Wanderin' Star (36)
Wanting You (1,17) 38
Warsaw Concerto (6)
Water Boy (20)
Way Of Love (38)
Way You Look Tonight (18)
We Three Kings Of Orient Are (medley) (11)
We've Got To Get It On Again (38)
What Lies Over The Hill? (13)
When I Grow Too Old To Dream (2)
When It's Springtime In The Rockies (20)
(Where Is Your Heart) ..see: Moulin Rouge, Song From
Whiffenpoof Song (27)
Whirlaway (18)
White Christmas (11)
Willow Weep For Me (25)
Winter Wonderland (11)
Wish You Were Here (4)
With These Hands (10)
World Outside (8) 71
Yellow Bird (10,14,26)
Yesterday (28,31)
You'll Never Know (6,24)
You'll Never Walk Alone (26)
Young And Warm And Wonderful (8)
Young At Heart (4)
Your Loves Return (37)
Your Song (36)
Zip-A-Dee-Doo-Dah (6,24)
Zorba The Greek, Theme From (28)

WILLIAMS, Tony

Born on 12/12/45 in Chicago. Jazz-fusion drummer. Also see V.S.O.P.

| 5/12/79 | 113 | 7 | | The Joy Of Flying | $8 | Columbia 35705 |

with guests George Benson, Herbie Hancock and Jan Hammer

Coming Back Home, Eris, Going Far, Hip Skip, Hittin' On 6, Morgan's Motion, Open Fire, Tony

WILLIAMS, Vanessa

Born on 3/18/63 in Tarrytown, New York. In 1983, became the first black woman to win Miss America pageant; relinquished crown after *Penthouse* nude scandal. Began hosting *Soul of VH-1* on video music TV channel in 1991. Appeared in the film *Harley Davidson & The Marlboro Man*.

| 7/9/88+ | 38 | 55 ● | 1 | The Right Stuff | $8 | Wing 835694 |
| 9/7/91+ | 17 | 75↑ ▲ | 2 | The Comfort Zone | $12 | Wing 843522 |

Am I Too Much? (1), Be A Man (1), Better Off Now (1), Can This Be Real? (1), Comfort Zone (2) 62, Darlin' I (1) 88, Dreamin' (1) 8, Freedom Dance (Get Free!) (2), Goodbye (2), (He's Got) The Look (1), I'll Be The One (1), If You Really Love Him (1), Just For Tonight (2) 26, One Reason (2), Right Stuff (1) 44, Running Back To You (2) 18, Save The Best For Last (2) 1, Security (1), Still In Love (2), Strangers Eyes (2), 2 Of A Kind (2), What Will I Tell My Heart (2), Whatever Happens (1), Work To Do (2), You Gotta Go (2)

WILLIAMS, Vesta

Born in Coshocton, Ohio. To California at age seven, where her father was a DJ at KGFJ-Los Angeles. Jingle singer and backing vocalist for Sting and Anita Baker.

| 9/2/89 | 131 | 10 | | Vesta 4 U | $8 | A&M 5223 |

VESTA

All On You, Best I Ever Had, Congratulations 55, 4 U, Here/Say, How You Feel, Hunger, Running Into Memories, Sweet, Sweet Love

WILLIE AND THE POOR BOYS

Supergroup featuring The Rolling Stones' Bill Wyman and Charlie Watts, plus Andy Fairweather Low, Geraint Watkins and Mickey Gee with guests Jimmy Page, Paul Rodgers, Chris Rea, Kenney Jones and others.

| 5/25/85 | 96 | 12 | | Willie and the Poor Boys | $8 | Passport 6047 |

procedes donated to Action Research into Multiple Sclerosis

All Night Long, Baby Please Don't Go, Can You Hear Me?, Chicken Shack Boogie, Let's Talk It Over, Poor Boy Boogie, Revenue Man (White Lightening), Saturday Night, Slippin' And Slidin', Sugar Bee, These Arms Of Mine, You Never Can Tell

WILLIE D
Willie Dennis, a member of Geto Boys.

| 10/3/92 | 88 | 8 | | I'm Goin' Out Lika Soldier .... | $12 | Rap-A-Lot 57188 |

Backstage
'Campaign 92'
'Clean Up Man

Die
Go Back 2 School
I'm Goin' Out Lika Soldier

Little Hooker
My Alibi
Pass Da Piote

Profile Of A Criminal
Rodney K.
Trenchcoats-N-Ganksta Hats

U Ain't No Ganksta
What's Up Aggin

Yo P My D
You Still A Aggin

WILLIS, Bruce
Born on 3/19/55 in Penns Grove, New Jersey. Played David Addison on TV's *Moonlighting*. Starred in the *Die Hard* films and others. Child's voice in the *Look Who's Talking* films. Married actress Demi Moore on 11/21/87.

| 2/14/87 | 14 | 29 | ● | The Return Of Bruno .... | $8 | Motown 6222 |

Comin' Right Up
Down In Hollywood

Flirting With Disaster
Fun Time

Jackpot (Bruno's Bop)
James Bond Is Back (medley)

Lose Myself
Respect Yourself 5

Secret Agent Man (medley)

Under The Boardwalk 59
Young Blood 68

WILL TO POWER
Florida-based trio formed and fronted by producer Bob Rosenberg with Dr. J. and Maria Mendez. Rosenberg is the son of singer Gloria Mann. By 1990, reduced to a duo of Rosenberg and Elin Michaels. Group name taken from the work of 19th-century German philosopher Frederich Nietzsche.

| 9/10/88 | 68 | 29 | 1 | Will To Power .... | $8 | Epic 40940 |
| 2/2/91 | 178 | 4 | 2 | Journey Home .... | $12 | Epic 46051 |

Also Sprach Zarathustra
..see: Zarathustra
Anti-Social (1)

Baby, I Love Your
Way/Freebird Medley
(Free Baby) 1
Best Friend's Girl (2)

Boogie Nights (2)
Clock On The Wall (2)
Don't Like It (2)
Dreamin' (1) 50

Fading Away (1) 65
Fly Bird (2)
I'm Not In Love (2) 7
It's My Life (2)

Journey Home (2)
Koyaanisqatsi (2)
Say It's Gonna Rain (1) 49
Searchin' (1)

Show Me The Way (1)
Somebody Told Me (1)
Strangers (1)
Zarathustra (1)

WILMER AND THE DUKES
R&B-rock quintet led by Wilmer Alexander, Jr.

| 8/16/69 | 173 | 3 | | Wilmer & The Dukes .... | $20 | Aphrodisiac 6001 |

'Count On Me
Get It
Get Out Of My Life, Woman

Give Me One More
Chance 80
Heavy Time

I Do Love You
I'm Free

Living In The U.S.A.
Love-itis (medley)

Show Me (medley)
St. James Infirmary

WILSON, Al
Born on 6/19/39 in Meridian, Mississippi. Soul singer/drummer. Moved to San Bernadino, California in the late '50s. Member of The Rollers from 1960-62.

12/22/73+	70	17	1	Show And Tell	$12	Rocky Road 3601
10/19/74	171	7	2	La La Peace Song	$12	Rocky Road 3700
7/10/76	185	2	3	I've Got A Feeling	$8	Playboy 410

Ain't Nothin' New Under The
Sun (3)
Baby I Want Your Body (3)
Broken Home (1)
Differently (3)
Fifty-Fifty (2)
For Cryin' Out Loud (1)

Goin' Through The Motions
(2)
Having A Party (3)
Honoring (3)
How's Your Love Life (3)
I Won't Last A Day
Without You/Let Me Be
The One (2) 70

I'm A Weak Man (2)
I'm Out To Get You (1)
I've Got A Feeling (We'll
Be Seeing Each Other
Again) (3) 29
La La Peace Song (2) 30
Longer We Stay Together (2)

Love Me Gentle, Love Me
Blind (1)
Moonlightn' (1)
My Song (1)
Passport (2)
Queen Of The Ghetto (1)
Show And Tell (1) 1
Song For You (1)

Stay With Me (3)
Stones Throw (2)
Touch And Go (1) 57
What You See (1)
Willoughby Brook (2)
You Did It For Me (3)
You're The One Thing
(Keeps Me Goin') (2)

WILSON, Brian
Born on 6/20/42 in Hawthorne, California. Leader/bassist/composer/producer of the legendary surf-rock group, The Beach Boys. Due to nervous exhaustion, he quit touring in late 1965, but continued to produce much of the group's material until the early 1970s. In semi-retirement until 1987. His daughters, Carnie and Wendy, formed the trio Wilson Phillips with Chynna Phillips in 1989.

| 7/30/88 | 54 | 13 | | Brian Wilson .... | $8 | Sire 25669 |

Baby Let Your Hair Grow
Long
Let It Shine

Little Children
Love And Mercy

Meet Me In My Dreams
Tonight

Melt Away
Night Time

One For The Boys
Rio Grande

There's So Many
Walkin' The Line

WILSON, Carl
Born on 6/21/46 in Hawthorne, California. Guitarist of The Beach Boys. Married Dean Martin's daughter, Gina, on 11/8/87.

| 5/2/81 | 185 | 2 | | Carl Wilson .... | $8 | Caribou 37010 |

Bright Lights
Grammy, The

Heaven
Hold Me

Hurry Love
Right Lane

Seems So Long Ago

What You Gonna Do About
Me?

WILSON, Dennis
Drummer and the only actual surfer of The Beach Boys. Born on 12/4/44 in Inglewood, California. Drowned on 12/28/83 at Marina Del Rey, California.

| 9/10/77 | 96 | 8 | | Pacific Ocean Blue .... | $15 | Caribou 34353 |

Dreamer
End Of The Show

Farewell My Friend
Friday Night

Moonshine
Pacific Ocean Blues

Rainbows
River Song

Thoughts Of You
Time

What's Wrong
You And I

WILSON, Flip
Born Clerow Wilson on 12/8/33 in Jersey City, New Jersey. Black comedian. Host of own TV variety show, 1970-74. Also recorded as his female alter ego, Geraldine.

8/26/67+	34	63	1	Cowboys & Colored People ....[C]	$12	Atlantic 8149
6/1/68	147	7	2	You Devil You ....[C]	$15	Atlantic 8179
2/28/70	17	54	● 3	"The Devil made me buy this dress" ....[C]	$8	Little David 1000
1/2/71	45	15	4	"Flip" - The Flip Wilson Show ....[C]	$8	Little David 2000
5/13/72	63	15	5	Geraldine/Don't Fight The Feeling ....[C]	$8	Little David 1001

above 2 feature actual skits and guests from his TV show

Bat, The (2)
Big Hand (1)
Blues, The (4)
Bunny Club (5)
Cheap Hotel (1)
Chicken Delicious (5)
Christopher Columbus (1)

Church On Sunday (1)
Complaint Department (5)
Confidential Survey (1)
Cowboys & Colored People
(1)
Creamed Chipped Beef (4)
David And Goliath (1)

Days Of The Knights (2)
Devil Made Me Buy This
Dress (3)
Dr. Freddie (2)
Doctors Have More Fun (3)
Don't Fight The Feeling (5)
Drive-In Movie (3)

Flip Wilson Show (4)
Gardener, The (2)
Geraldine Honey (5)
Geraldine Visits David Frost
(4)
Golf Story (3)
Go-Rilla, The (3)

Great Motor Bike And
Tennis Shoe Race, Honey
(3)
Great Quotations (3)
Haunted House (4)
Herman's Berry (2)
I Wanted To Be A Singer (2)

I'm Not Flip Wilson (2)
Ice (3)
Joey Bishop Show (2)
Kids (1)
Killer (2)
Land Of Opportunity (2)
Lemonade Stand (3)

WILSON, Flip — Cont'd

Lulu (2)
Midgets (1)
Millionaire, The (2)
Miss Johnson (3)

Muhammad Ali (4)
Paid To Die (2)
Perfect Secretary (5)
Pet Shop (2)

Reverend Leroy (4)
Riot Suit (1)
Ruby Begonia (3)

Seeing Ed Eat A Chittlin' On
  Network Television (3)
Shadow, The (2)
Staying On Too Long (1)

Trala (2)
Twenty Minutes Of Silence
  (2)
Ugly Baby (2)

Ugly Girl (2)
Ugly People (1)
Wardrobe Lady Part I & II (3)

WILSON, Hank — see RUSSELL, Leon

WILSON, J. Frank, and The Cavaliers

J. Frank was born on 12/11/41 in Lufkin, Texas. Died on 10/4/91 after a long illness. Band formed in San Angelo, Texas. The Cavaliers: Phil Trunzo, Jerry Graham, Bobby Woods and George Croyle.

| 11/14/64 | 54 | 14 | | Last Kiss .... | $45 | Josie 4006 |

Day Before Our Wedding
Ding Go The Chimes

Kiss And Run
Last Kiss 2

Only The Lonely
Over The Mountain

School Days
Sea Of Love

Speak To Me
Tell Laura I Love Her

That'll Be The Day
Young Love

WILSON, Jackie

Born on 6/9/34 in Detroit; died on 1/21/84. Sang with local gospel groups; became an amateur boxer. Worked as a solo singer until 1953, then joined Billy Ward's Dominoes as Clyde McPhatter's replacement. Solo since 1957. Godfather of Jody Watley. Cousin of Hubert Johnson of The Contours. Jackie collapsed from a stroke, on stage, at the Latin Casino in Camden, New Jersey on 9/25/75; spent rest of his life in hospitals. Inducted into the Rock and Roll Hall of Fame in 1987.

11/24/62	137	2		1 Jackie Wilson At The Copa ....[L]	$25	Brunswick 754108
4/27/63	36	21		2 Baby Workout	$20	Brunswick 754110
1/14/67	108	7		3 Whispers	$20	Brunswick 754122
11/25/67	163	4		4 Higher And Higher	$20	Brunswick 754130
6/1/68	195	3		5 Manufacturers of Soul	$15	Brunswick 754134

JACKIE WILSON/COUNT BASIE

And This Is My Beloved (1)
Baby Workout (2) 5
Body And Soul (medley) (1)
Chain Gang (5) 84
Even When You Cry (5)
Fairest Of Them All (2)
For Your Precious Love
(5) 49
Funky Broadway (5)
I Apologize (medley) (1)
I Can Do Better (3)
I Don't Need You Around (4)

I Don't Want To Lose You
(3) 84
(I Feel Like I'm In) Paradise
  (2)
I Love Them All Medley -
  Part I & II (2)
I Need Your Loving (4)
I Never Loved A Woman (The
  Way I Love You) (5)
I Was Made To Love Her (5)
I'm The One To Do It (4)
I've Gotta Talk To You (3)
I've Lost You (4) 82

In The Midnight Hour (5)
It's All My Fault (2)
Just Be Sincere (3) 91
Kickapoo (2)
Love For Sale (1)
Love Train (2)
My Girl (5)
My Heart Is Calling (3)
Now That I Want Her (2)
Ode To Billy Joe (5)
Only Your Love Can Save
  Me (3)

Open The Door To Your
  Heart (4)
Perfect Day (1)
Respect (5)
Say You Will (2)
Shake! Shake! Shake!
(2) 33
(So Many) Cute Little Girls
  (2)
Somebody Up There Likes
  You (4)
Soulville (4)
St. James Infirmary (1)

Tears Will Tell It All (3)
Those Heartaches (4)
To Make A Big Man Cry (3)
Tonight (1)
(Too Much) Sweet Loving (3)
Uptight (Everything's
  Alright) (5)
Way I Am (1)
What Good Am I Without
  You (2)
When Will Our Day Come (4)
Whispers (Gettin' Louder)
(3) 11

Who Am I (3)
Yeah! Yeah! Yeah! (2)
You Can Count On Me (2)
You Only Live Once (2)
(Your Love Keeps Lifting
Me) Higher And Higher
(4) 6

★★43★★ WILSON, Nancy

Born on 2/20/37 in Chillicothe, Ohio and raised in Columbus, Ohio. Jazz stylist with Rusty Bryant's Carolyn Club Band in Columbus. First recorded for Dot in 1956. Moved to New York City in 1959.

5/5/62	30	21		1 Nancy Wilson/Cannonball Adderley	$20	Capitol 1657
				NANCY WILSON/CANNONBALL ADDERLEY		
9/15/62+	49	18		2 Hello Young Lovers	$25	Capitol 1767
4/6/63	18	46		3 Broadway-My Way	$15	Capitol 1828
8/17/63	11	58		4 Hollywood-My Way	$15	Capitol 1934
1/25/64	4	42		5 Yesterday's Love Songs/Today's Blues	$15	Capitol 2012
5/30/64	10	30		6 Today, Tomorrow, Forever	$15	Capitol 2082
9/5/64	4	31		7 How Glad I Am	$15	Capitol 2155
2/6/65	24	29		8 The Nancy Wilson Show! ....[L]	$15	Capitol 2136
				recorded at the Cocoanut Grove in Los Angeles		
6/5/65	7	21		9 Today-My Way	$15	Capitol 2321
8/28/65	17	24		10 Gentle Is My Love	$15	Capitol 2351
2/5/66	44	18		11 From Broadway With Love	$15	Capitol 2433
5/28/66	15	33		12 A Touch Of Today	$15	Capitol 2495
8/27/66	35	23		13 Tender Loving Care	$15	Capitol 2555
1/28/67	35	21		14 Nancy-Naturally	$15	Capitol 2634
6/3/67	40	15		15 Just For Now	$15	Capitol 2712
9/2/67	46	19		16 Lush Life	$15	Capitol 2757
2/3/68	115	17		17 Welcome To My Love	$12	Capitol 2844
6/1/68	51	24		18 Easy	$12	Capitol 2909
8/31/68	145	14		19 The Best Of Nancy Wilson ....[G]	$12	Capitol 2947
10/12/68	122	7		20 The Sound Of Nancy Wilson	$12	Capitol 2970
2/8/69	117	14		21 Nancy	$12	Capitol 148
7/5/69	122	15		22 Son of a Preacher Man	$12	Capitol 234
8/23/69	193	2		23 Close-Up ....[R]	$15	Capitol 256 [2]
				reissue of albums #3 and 4 above		
11/8/69+	92	18		24 Hurt So Bad	$12	Capitol 353
3/28/70	155	6		25 Can't Take My Eyes Off You	$10	Capitol 429
11/28/70+	54	21		26 Now I'm A Woman	$10	Capitol 541
6/12/71	185	3		27 The Right To Love...[R]	$10	Capitol 763
				reissue (new title) of album #16 above		
7/17/71	185	5		28 But Beautiful	$10	Capitol 798
12/25/71+	151	6		29 Kaleidoscope	$10	Capitol 852
9/28/74	97	18		30 All In Love Is Fair	$8	Capitol 11317
7/26/75	119	10		31 Come Get To This	$8	Capitol 11386
5/1/76	126	13		32 This Mother's Daughter	$8	Capitol 11518
7/30/77	198	1		33 I've Never Been To Me	$8	Capitol 11659

DEBUT DATE	PEAK POS	WKS CHR	GOLD	ARTIST — Album Title	$	Label & Number

WILSON, Nancy — Cont'd

| 9/8/84 | 144 | 9 | 34 | The Two Of Us .... | $8 | Columbia 39326 |

RAMSEY LEWIS & NANCY WILSON

Ages Ago (24)
(Ah, The Apple Trees) When The World Was Young (16,27)
Ain't No Sunshine (29)
Ain't That Lovin' You (14)
Alfie (15)
All By Myself (33)
All In Love Is Fair (30)
All My Love Comes Down (31)
All My Tomorrows (5)
Almost In Your Arms (4)
Almost Persuaded (22)
Alone With My Thoughts Of You (20)
Alright, Okay, You Win (14)
And I Love Him (12)
And Satisfy (9)
Angel Eyes (17)
As Long As He Needs Me (3,23)
As You Desire Me (13)
At Long Last Love (10)
Back In Your Own Backyard (2)
Before The Rain (12)
Below, Above (20)
Best Is Yet To Come (5)
Bewitched (5)
Black Is Beautiful (20)
Blue Prelude (5)
Boogeyin' All The Way (31)
Born Free (15)
Boy From Ipanema (7)
Brand New Me (25)
Bridge Over Troubled Water (26)
But Beautiful (28)
By Myself (20)
By The Time I Get To Phoenix (22)
Call Me (12)
Call Me Irresponsible (6)
Can't Take My Eyes Off You (24,25) **52**
Car Of Love (33)
Changes (33)
China (32)
Close Your Eyes (13)
Come Back To Me (24)
Come Get To This (31)
Days Of Wine And Roses (4,19,23)
Dear Heart (9)
Dearly Beloved (4,23)
Did I Remember (4,23)
Do It Again (28)
Do You Know Why (24)
Don't Come Running Back To Me (9) **58**
Don't Go To Strangers (13)
Don't Let Me Be Lonely Tonight (13)
Don't Rain On My Parade (7,19)

Don't Take Your Love From Me (8)
Don't Talk, Just Sing (8)
Everyone Knows (29)
Face It Girl, It's Over (18,19) **29**
Fireworks (8)
Flying High (33)
For Heaven's Sake (28)
For Once In My Life (17)
Free Again (16,27)
From You To Me To You (33)
Funnier Than Funny (10)
Gee Baby, Ain't I Good To You (13)
Gentle Is My Love (10,19)
Gentle On My Mind (14)
Getting To Know You (3,23)
Glad To Be Unhappy (28)
Go Away, Little Boy (6)
Goin' Out Of My Head (12)
Good Life (6)
Good Man Is Hard To Find (2)
Got It Together (22)
Grass Is Greener (7,19)
Greatest Performance Of My Life (29)
Guess Who I Saw Today (8,19)
Happiness Is A Thing Called Joe (28)
Happy Talk (1)
Happy Tears (31)
Have A Heart (12)
He Called Me Baby (31)
He Loves Me (11)
He Never Had It So Good (32)
Hello Dolly (11)
Hello, Young Lovers (2)
Here It Comes (33)
Here's That Rainy Day (11)
Hey There (1)
Hotel, Theme From (17)
Houdini Of The Midnite Hour (31)
How Insensitive (18)
How Many Broken Wings (26)
Hurt So Bad (24)
Husbands And Wives (22)
I Believe In You (3,23)
I Can't Stop Loving You (6)
I Don't Want A Sometimes Man (32)
I Had A Ball (11)
I Left My Heart In San Francisco (6)
I Made You This Way (22)
(I Stayed) Too Long At The Fair (16,27)
I Thought About You (28)
I Wanna Be With You (7) **57**
I Want To Talk About You (13)
I Wish I Didn't Love You So (14)

I'll Get Along Somehow (29)
I'll Know (3,23)
I'll Make A Man Of The Man (15)
I'll Never Stop Loving You (4)
I'll Only Miss Him When I Think Of Him (11)
I'll Walk Alone (28)
I'm All Smiles (9)
I'm Always Drunk In San Francisco (And I Don't Drink At All) (17)
I'm Beginning To See The Light (8)
I'm Your Special Fool (21)
I've Got Your Number (11)
I've Never Been To Me (33)
If Ever I Would Leave You (10)
If He Walked Into My Life (15)
If I Ever Lose This Heaven (31)
If I Ruled The World (9)
If I Were Your Woman (29)
If Love Is Good To Me (10)
If We Only Have Love (21)
In A Long White Room (21)
In The Dark (14)
In The Heat Of The Night (17)
It Never Entered My Mind (17)
It Only Takes A Moment (20)
Joe (26)
Joey, Joey, Joey (3,23)
Just For A Thrill (14)
Just For Now (15)
Let It Be Me (29)
Let's Fall In Love All Over (26)
Let's Make The Most Of A Beautiful Thing (24)
Like A Circle Never Stops (31)
Like Someone In Love (13)
Listen, Little Girl (2)
Little Girl Blue (2)
Little Green Apples (22)
Lonely, Lonely (26)
Long And Winding Road (26)
Look Of Love (18)
Looking Back (21)
Lot Of Livin' To Do (3,23)
Love Can Do Anything (15)
Love Has Many Faces (9)
Love Has Smiled On Us (32)
Love Is Alive (33)
Love Is Blue (18)
Love-Wise (13)
Lush Life (16,27)
Make It With You (26)
Make Me A Present Of You (18)
Make Me Rainbows (18)
Make Someone Happy (3,23)
Make The World Go Away (22)

Makin' Whoopee (11)
Masquerade Is Over (1)
May I Come In? (17)
Mercy, Mercy, Mercy (15)
Middle Of The Road (29)
Midnight Rendezvous (34)
Midnight Sun (16,27)
Miss Otis Regrets (2)
Mixed-Up Girl (25)
Moments (33)
Moon River (4,23)
More (10)
Mr. Bojangles (29)
Mr. Walker, It's All Over (22)
Music That Makes Me Dance (8)
My Babe (14)
My Love (30)
My Love, Forgive Me (Amore, Scusami) (9)
My One And Only Love (10)
My Shining Hour (4,23)
My Ship (3,23)
Never Less Than Yesterday (7)
Never Let Me Go (5)
Never Wanna Say Goodnight (34)
Never Will I Marry (1)
Nina Never Knew (2)
No One Else But You (12)
Nobody (33)
Now (32)
Now I'm A Woman (26) **93**
Ocean Of Love (30)
Ode To Billie Joe (17)
Oh! Look At Me Now (28)
Old Country (1)
On Broadway (6)
On The Other Side Of The Tracks (20)
Once In My Lifetime (29)
One Like You (18)
One Note Samba (6)
One Soft Night (24)
Only Love (21)
Only The Young (16,27)
Our Day Will Come (2)
Out Of This World (20)
Over The Weekend (16,27)
Patience My Child (33)
Peace Of Mind (20) **55**
People (7)
Player Play On (21)
Please Send Me Someone To Love (5)
Prelude To A Kiss (28)
Prisoner Of My Eyes (21)
Put On A Happy Face (2)
Quiet Nights Of Quiet Stars (Corcovado) (7)
Quiet Soul (21)
Rain Sometimes (15)
Raindrops Keep Fallin' On My Head (25)
Reach Out For Me (9)
Real Me (26)

Right To Love (Reflections) (16,27)
River Shallow (16,27)
Rules Of The Road (20)
Saga Of Bill Bailey (8)
Sandpiper, Love Theme From The ..see: Shadow Of Your Smile
Satin Doll (5)
Save Your Love For Me (1)
Second Time Around (4,23)
Secret Love (23)
Send Me Yesterday (5)
Shadow Of Your Smile (12)
Show Goes On (7)
Since I Fell For You (14)
Sleepin' Bee (1)
Slippin' Away (34)
Someone To Watch Over Me (5)
Somewhere (11)
Son Of A Preacher Man (22)
Song Is You (5)
Sophisticated Lady (2)
Spinning Wheel (24)
Stay Tuned (32)
Streetrunner (30)
Suffering With The Blues (5)
Sunny (16)
Supper Time (28)
Suzanne (25)
Sweetest Sounds (3,23)
Take What I Have (9)
Tell The Truth (30)
Ten Good Years (8)
Ten Years Of Tears (14)
Tender Loving Care (13)
That's Life (15)
There Will Never Be Another You (10)
There'll Always Be Forever (30)
(They) Long To Be) Close To You (26)
This Bitter Earth (20)
This Dream (11)
This Girl Is A Woman Now (25)
This Mother's Daughter (32)
This Time Last Summer (31)
Time After Time (10)
To Be The One (29)
To Make It Easier On You (30)
Tonight May Have To Last Me All My Life (6)
Too Late Now (13)
Tree Of Life (32)
Trip With Me (25)
Trouble In Mind (22)
Try A Little Tenderness (13)
Try It, You'll Like It (30)
Two Of Us (34)
Unchain My Heart (6)
Uptight (Everything's Alright) (12,19) **84**
Very Thought Of You (5)

Waitin' For Charlie To Come Home (25)
Walk Away (18)
Wasn't It Wonderful (12)
Watch What Happens (14)
Wave (18)
We Could Learn Together (21)
Welcome To My Love (17)
Welcome, Welcome (9)
West Coast Blues (7)
What Do You See In Her? (21)
What Kind Of Fool Am I? (6)
What Now My Love (15)
When A Woman Loves A Man (2)
When Did You Leave Heaven? (4,19,23)
When He Makes Music (10)
When I Look In Your Eyes (18)
When Sunny Gets Blue (2)
When The Sun Comes Out (20)
When We Were One (23)
Who Can I Turn To (When Nobody Needs Me) (10)
Why Try To Change Me Now (17)
Wild Is The Wind (20)
Willie And Laura Mae Jones (24)
Willow Weep For Me (14)
Winchester Cathedral (15)
Wives And Lovers (6)
Words And Music (25)
Yesterday (12)
You Can Have Him (3,8,19,23)
(You Don't Know) How Glad I Am (7,19) **11**
You Don't Know Me (17)
You Don't Know What Love Is (2)
You'd Be So Nice To Come Home To (4,23)
You'd Better Go (21)
You'd Better Love Me (11)
You're All I Need To Get By (24)
You're As Right As Rain (30)
You're Gonna Hear From Me (12)
You've Changed (16,27)
You've Got Your Troubles (12)
You've Lost That Lovin' Feelin' (9)
You've Made Me So Very Happy (25)
Young And Foolish (11)
Your Name Is Love (13)

WILSON, Shanice

Born on 5/14/73. Native of Pittsburgh. To Los Angeles at age seven. Began singing commercial jingles at age eight (appeared in a Kentucky Fried Chicken Commercial with Ella Fitzgerald).

| 11/28/87+ | 149 | 18 | | 1 Discovery .... | $8 | A&M 5128 |
| 1/18/92 | 83 | 26 | ● | 2 Inner Child .... | $12 | Motown 6319 |

SHANICE
CD includes 2 bonus tracks, cassette includes one

Baby Tell Me) Can You Dance (1) **50**
Do I Know You (1)
Forever In Your Love (2)
He's So Cute (1)

I Hate To Be Lonely (2)
I Love Your Smile [includes 2 versions] (2) **2**
I Think I Love You (1)

I'll Bet She's Got A Boyfriend (1)
I'm Cryin' (2)
Just A Game (1)
Lovin' You (2)

No 1/2 Steppin' (1)
Peace In The World (2)
Silent Prayer (2) **31**
Spend Some Time With Me (2)

Stop Cheatin' On Me (2)
Way You Love Me (1)
You Ain't All That (1)
You Didn't Think I'd Come Back This Hard (2)

You Were The One (2)

WILSON PHILLIPS

Vocal/songwriting trio of sisters Carnie and Wendy Wilson, with Chynna Phillips. Carnie and Wendy's father is Brian Wilson (The Beach Boys). Chynna, the daughter of John and Michelle Phillips (The Mamas & The Papas), acted in the film *Caddyshack II*.

| 4/14/90 | 2¹⁰ | 125 | ▲⁵ | 1 Wilson Phillips .... | $12 | SBK 93745 |
| 6/20/92 | 4 | 33 | ▲ | 2 Shadows And Light .... | $12 | SBK 98924 |

All The Way From New York (2)
Alone (2)

Don't Take Me Down (2)
Dream Is Still Alive (1) **12**

Eyes Like Twins (1)
Flesh And Blood (2)
Fueled For Houston (2)

Give It Up (2) **30**
Goodbye, Carmen (2)

Hold On (1) **1**
I Hear You (2)

Impulsive (1) **4**
It's Only Life (2)

DEBUT DATE	PEAK POS	WKS CHR	GOLD	ARTIST — Album Title	$	Label & Number

WILSON PHILLIPS — Cont'd

Next To You (Someday I'll Be) (1)   Ooh You're Gold (1)   Over And Over (1)   Reason To Believe (1)   **Release Me** (1) *1*   This Doesn't Have To Be Love (2)   Where Are You (2)   You Won't See Me Cry (2) *20*   **You're In Love** (1) *1*

WINANS, BeBe & CeCe
Younger brother and sister of the Detroit gospel-singing family, The Winans: Benjamin "BeBe" and Priscilla "CeCe." They are the seventh and eighth children in a 10-sibling family.

| 3/4/89 | 95 | 25 | ● | 1 Heaven .... | $8 | Capitol 90959 |
| 7/20/91 | 74 | 51 | ● | 2 Different Lifestyles .... | $12 | Capitol 92078 |

Addictive Love [includes 2 versions] (2)   Better Place (2)   Blood, The (2)   Bridge Over Troubled Water (1)   Can't Take This Away (2)   Celebrate New Life (2)   Depend On You (2)   Don't Cry (1)   Heaven (1)   Hold Up The Light (1)   **I'll Take You There** (2) *90*   It's O.K. (2)   Lost Without You (1)   Meantime (1)   Searching For Love (It's Real) (2)   Supposed To Be (2)   Trust Him (1)   Two Different Lifestyles (2)   Wanna Be More (1)   You (1)   You Know And I Know (2)

WINANS, The
Family gospel quartet: brothers Michael, Ronald, Marvin and Carvin (twins) Winans. Born and raised in Detroit.

| 9/26/87 | 109 | 11 | | 1 Decisions .... | $8 | Qwest 25510 |
| 5/19/90 | 90 | 10 | ● | 2 Return .... | $12 | Qwest 26161 |

Ain't No Need To Worry (1)   Breaking Of Day (1)   Don't Leave Me (2)   Don't Let The Sun Go Down On Me (1)   Everyday The Same (2)   Free (2)   Friend, A (2)   Give Me You (1)   Gonna Be Alright (2)   How Can You Live Without Christ? (1)   It's Time (2)   Love Has No Color (1)   Millions (1)   Right, Left In A Wrong World (1)   This Time It's Personal (2)   Together We Stand (2)   What Can I Say? (1)   When You Cry (2)   Wherever I Go (2)

WINBUSH, Angela
Composer/producer/vocalist. In duo, Rene & Angela, with Rene Moore from 1980-86. Production work on Janet Jackson's first album. Former backing vocalist for Dolly Parton, Jean Carne and Lenny Williams.

| 11/7/87 | 81 | 28 | | 1 Sharp .... | $8 | Mercury 832733 |
| 11/11/89 | 113 | 17 | | 2 The Real Thing .... | $8 | Mercury 838866 |

Angel (1)   C'est Toi (It's You) (1)   Hello Beloved (1)   I'll Never Be The Same (2)   I've Learned To Respect (The Power Of Love) (2)   Imagination Of The Heart (1)   It's The Real Thing (2)   Lay Your Troubles Down (2)   Menage 'A Trois (2)   No More Tears (2)   No One Has Ever Cared (Like You) (1)   Please Bring Your Love Back (2)   Precious (2)   Run To Me (1)   Sensual Lover (2)   Sharp (1)   Thank You Love (2)   You Had A Good Girl (1)

WINCHESTER, Jesse
Born on 5/17/44 in Shreveport, Louisiana. Pop singer/songwriter/guitarist. Moved to Canada in 1967 to avoid the draft; became a Canadian citizen in 1973.

12/30/72+	193	5		1 Third Down, 110 To Go	$15	Bearsville 2102
5/28/77	115	16		2 Nothing But A Breeze	$8	Bearsville 6968
				supporting vocals: Emmylou Harris, Anne Murray and Nicolette Larson		
8/26/78	156	7		3 A Touch On The Rainy Side	$8	Bearsville 6984
6/27/81	188	2		4 Talk Memphis	$8	Bearsville 6989

All Of Your Stories (1)   Baby Blue (4)   Bowling Green (2)   Candida (3)   Dangerous Fun (1)   Do It (1)   Do La Lay (1)   Easy Way (1)   Full Moon (3)   Gilding The Lily (2)   Glory To The Day (1)   God's Own Jukebox (1)   High Ball (3)   Holly (3)   Hoot And Holler (4)   I Love You No End (4)   I'm Looking For A Miracle (3)   If Only (4)   Isn't That So? (1)   It Takes A Young Girl (2)   Just Now It Feels So Right (3)   Leslie (4)   Let Go (4)   Little Glass Of Wine (3)   Lullaby For The First Born (1)   Midnight Bus (1)   My Songbird (2)   North Star (1)   **Nothing But A Breeze** (2) *86*   Pourquoi M'Aimes-tu Pas? (2)   Reckon On Me (4)   Rhumba Man (2)   Sassy (3)   **Say What** (4) *32*   Seems Like Only Yesterday (2)   Showman's Life (3)   Silly Heart (1)   Sure Enough (4)   Talk Memphis (4)   Touch On The Rainy Side (3)   Twigs And Seeds (3)   Wintry Feeling (3)   You Remember Me (2)

WINDING, Kai
Born on 5/18/22 in Aarhus, Denmark; died on 5/6/83. Jazz trombonist. Moved to U.S. in 1934. With Benny Goodman and Stan Kenton in the mid-1940s.

| 8/10/63 | 67 | 24 | | More!!! ....[I] | $20 | Verve 8551 |
| | | | | album originally titled *Soul Surfin'*; featuring Kenny Burrell (guitar) | | |

China Nights   Comin' Home Baby   Gravy Waltz   Hearse Ride   Hero   **More** *8*   Pipeline   Soul Surfin'   Spinner   Sukiyaki   Surf Bird   Tube Wall

WIND IN THE WILLOWS, The
Folk-rock band. Featured Deborah Harry, later the lead singer of Blondie.

| 8/17/68 | 195 | 3 | | The Wind In The Willows .... | $35 | Capitol 2956 |

Djini Judy   Friendly Lion   Little People   Moments Spent   My Uncle Used To Love Me But She Died   Park Avenue Blues   She's Fantastic And She's Yours   So Sad (To Watch Good Love Go Bad)   There Is But One Truth, Daddy   Uptown Girl   Wheel Of Changes

WING AND A PRAYER FIFE & DRUM CORPS., The
Studio group from New York City; vocals by Linda November, Vivian Cherry, Arlene Martell and Helen Miles.

| 2/14/76 | 47 | 16 | | Babyface .... | $8 | Wing & Prayer 3025 |

Baby Face *14*   Charleston   Eleanor Rigby   I Hear A Symphony   Just An Old Fashioned Medley   Show Medley   Those Were The Days

WINGER
Hard-rock quartet formed in New York City in 1986: Kip Winger (vocals, bass), Reb Beach, Rod Morgenstein (ex-Dixie Dregs) and Paul Taylor. Golden, Colorado native Kip was a member of Alice Cooper's band.

| 9/17/88+ | 21 | 64 | ▲ | 1 Winger .... | $8 | Atlantic 81867 |
| 8/11/90 | 15 | 42 | ▲ | 2 In The Heart Of The Young .... | $12 | Atlantic 82103 |

Baptized By Fire (2)   **Can't Get Enuff** (2) *42*   **Easy Come Easy Go** (2) *41*   Hangin On (1)   **Headed For A Heartbreak** (1) *19*   **Hungry** (1) *85*   In The Day We'll Never See (2)   In The Heart Of The Young (2)   Little Dirty Blonde (2)   Loosen Up (2)   Madalaine (1)   **Miles Away** (2) *12*   Poison Angel (1)   Purple Haze (1)   Rainbow In The Rose (2)   **Seventeen** (1) *26*   State Of Emergency (1)   Time To Surrender (1)   Under One Condition (2)   Without The Night (1)   You Are The Saint, I Am The Sinner (2)

DEBUT DATE	PEAK POS	WKS CHR	GOLD	ARTIST — Album Title	$	Label & Number

WINGFIELD, Pete
Keyboardist from England; born on 5/7/48. Worked with Freddy King, Jimmy Witherspoon and Van Morrison. In Olympic Runners band. Turned to production work in the '80s.

| 12/6/75 | 165 | 5 | | Breakfast Special .... | $12 | Island 9333 |

Anytime
Eighteen With A Bullet 15

Hold Me Closer
Kangaroo Dip

Lovin' As You Wanna Be
Number One Priority

Please
Shadow Of A Doubt

Shining Eyes

Whole Pot Of Jelly (For A Little Slice Of Toast)

WINGS — see McCARTNEY, Paul

WINSTON, George
New Age pianist. Born in 1949 in Michigan and raised in Montana, Mississippi and Florida. First album recording in 1972. Founded Dancing Cat Records in 1983. Also see Childrens section.

5/12/84	127	33	▲	1 Winter Into Spring ....[E-I]	$8	Windham Hill 1019
				recorded March 1982		
6/2/84+	139	45	▲	2 Autumn ....[E-I]	$8	Windham Hill 1012
				recorded June 1980		
10/26/91	55	24	●	3 Summer ....[I]	$12	Windham Hill 11107
				CHRISTMAS ALBUM:		
3/12/83+	54	135	●	4 December ....[X-I]	$8	Windham Hill 1025
11/29/86+	85	15		5 December ....[X-I-R]	$8	Windham Hill 1025
12/12/87+	89	10		6 December ....[X-I-R]	$8	Windham Hill 1025
12/17/88+	111	5		7 December ....[X-I-R]	$8	Windham Hill 1025
12/16/89+	101	6		8 December ....[X-I-R]	$8	Windham Hill 1025
12/8/90	106	7		9 December ....[X-I-R]	$8	Windham Hill 1025

Christmas charts: 5/'85, 3/'87, 2/'88, 6/'89, 6/'90, 5/'91, 10/'92

Black Stallion (3)
Blossom (medley) (1)
Carol Of The Bells (4)
Colors (medley) (2)
Corrina, Corrina (3)
Dance (medley) (2)
Early Morning Range (3)
February Sea (1)
Fragrant Fields (3)

Garden, The (3)
Goodbye Montana (Part 2) (3)
Goodbye Montana (Part 1 & 2) (3)
Holly And The Ivy (4)
Hummingbird (3)
January Stars (1)
Jesus, Jesus, Rest Your Head (4)

Joy (4)
Living In The Country (3)
Living Without You (3)
Longing (medley) (4)
Loreta And Desiree's Bouquet (Part 1 & 2) (3)
Love (medley) (3)
Lullaby (3)
Meadow (medley) (1)

Moon (2)
Night Medley (4)
Ocean Waves (O Mar) (1)
Peace (1)
Rain Dance (1)
Reflection (1)
Road (2)
Sea (2)
Some Children See Him (4)

Spring Creek (3)
Stars (2)
Thanksgiving (4)
Variations On The Kanon By Johann Pachelbel (4)
Venice Dreamer (1)
Where Are You Now (3)
Woods (2)

WINSTONS, The
Washington, D.C. soul septet: Richard Spencer (lead), Ray Maritano, Quincy Mattison, Phil Tolotta, Sonny Peckrol and G.C. Coleman. Toured as backup band for The Impressions.

| 8/2/69 | 78 | 12 | | Color Him Father .... | $15 | Metromedia 1010 |

Amen, Brother
Birds Of A Feather

Chokin' Kind
Color Him Father 7

Days Of Sand And Shovels
Everyday People

Greatest Love
Handful Of Friends

I've Gotta Be Me
Only The Strong Survive

Traces

★★494★★ WINTER, Edgar, Group
Edgar was born on 12/28/46 in Beaumont, Texas. Albino rock singer/keyboardist/saxophonist. Younger brother of Johnny Winter. Edgar Winter Group included Dan Hartman (1972-76), Ronnie Montrose (1972-74) and Rick Derringer (1974-76).

6/27/70	196	2		1 Entrance *	$15	Epic 26503
5/1/71	111	19		2 Edgar Winter's White Trash	$10	Epic 30512
				introducing Jerry laCroix (lead singer)		
3/25/72	23	25	●	3 Roadwork ....[L]	$12	Epic 31249 [2]
				above 2: **EDGAR WINTER'S WHITE TRASH**		
12/9/72+	3	80	▲²	4 They Only Come Out At Night	$10	Epic 31584
				album introduces Ronnie Montrose and Dan Hartman in group		
5/25/74	13	23	●	5 Shock Treatment	$10	Epic 32461
				Rick Derringer replaces Montrose as lead guitarist (Rick also appears on previous 3 albums)		
6/21/75	69	10		6 Jasmine Nightdreams *	$8	Blue Sky 33483
				***EDGAR WINTER**		
10/18/75	124	8		7 The Edgar Winter Group with Rick Derringer	$8	Blue Sky 33798
6/19/76	89	9		8 Together ....[L]	$8	Blue Sky 34033
				JOHNNY & EDGAR WINTER		
				Johnny also appears on albums #1 and 3 above		

All Out (6)
Alta Mira (4)
Animal (5)
Autumn (4)
Baby, Whatcha Want Me To Do (8)
Back In The Blues (1)
Back In The U.S.A. (3)
Can't Tell One From The Other (7)
Chainsaw (7)
Cool Dance (7)
Cool Fool (3)
Diamond Eyes (7)
Different Game (1)
Do Like Me (5)
Do Yourself A Favor (3)
Dying To Live (2)

Easy Street (5) 83
Entrance (1)
Fire And Ice (1)
Fly Away (2)
Frankenstein (4) 1
Free Ride (4) 14
Give It Everything You Got (2)
Good Morning Music (2)
Good Shot (1)
Hangin' Around (4) 65
Harlem Shuffle (8)
Hello Mellow Feelin' (6)
How Do You Like Your Love (6)
Hung Up (1)
I Always Wanted You (6)

I Can't Turn You Loose (3) 81
I've Got News For You (2)
Infinite Peace In Rhythm (7)
J.A.P. (Just Another Punk) (7)
Jimmy's Gospel (1)
Jive, Jive, Jive (3)
Jump Right Out (1)
Keep On Burnin' (7)
Keep Playin' That Rock 'N' Roll (2) 70
Let The Good Times Roll (8)
Let's Do It Together Again (7)
Let's Get It In (2)
Little Brother (6)
Maybe Some Day You'll Call My Name (5)

Mercy, Mercy (8)
Miracle Of Love (5)
Modern Love (7)
Nothin' Good Comes Easy (7)
One Day Tomorrow (6)
Outa Control (6)
Paradise (medley) (7)
Peace Pipe (1)
People Music (7)
Queen Of My Dreams (5)
Re-Entrance (1)
Rise To Fall (1)
River's Risin' (5) 33
Rock 'N' Roll Boogie Woogie Blues (4)
Rock And Roll, Hoochie Koo (3)
Rock & Roll Medley (8)

Rock & Roll Woman (5)
Round & Round (4)
Save The Planet (2,3)
Shuffle-Low (6)
Sides (medley) (7)
Sky Train (6)
Solar Strut (6)
Some Kinda Animal (5)
Someone Take My Heart Away (5)
Soul Man (8)
Still Alive And Well (3)
Sundown (5)
Tell Me In A Whisper (6)
Tobacco Road (4)
Turn On Your Lovelight (3)
Undercover Man (4)

We All Had A Real Good Time (4)
When It Comes (4)
Where Have You Gone (1)
Where Would I Be (2)
You Were My Light (2)
You've Lost That Lovin' Feelin' (8)

★★266★★ WINTER, Johnny
Born on 2/23/44 in Leland, Mississippi. Blues-rock guitarist/vocalist. Both Johnny and brother Edgar are albinos. A prominent '60s sessionman, Johnny toured with Muddy Waters and was a member of The Traits.

4/12/69	40	20		1 The Progressive Blues Experiment	$25	Imperial 12431
5/10/69	24	23		2 Johnny Winter	$18	Columbia 9826
9/27/69	111	6		3 The Johnny Winter Story ....[E]	$12	GRT 10010

DEBUT DATE	PEAK POS	WKS CHR	GOLD	ARTIST — Album Title	$	Label & Number
				WINTER, Johnny — Cont'd		
12/6/69	55	17	4	Second Winter .... a 3-sided album (4th side is blank)	$20	Columbia 9947 [2]
9/26/70	154	4	5	Johnny Winter And .... with Rick Derringer and the McCoys as backup band	$15	Columbia 30221
3/13/71	40	27	●	6 Live/Johnny Winter And...........................[L]	$12	Columbia 30475
4/7/73	22	24		7 Still Alive And Well	$12	Columbia 32188
2/23/74	42	16		8 Saints & Sinners	$12	Columbia 32715
12/7/74	78	12		9 John Dawson Winter III...........................	$8	Blue Sky 33292
3/6/76	93	12		10 Captured Live!...........................[L]	$8	Blue Sky 33944
6/19/76	89	9		11 Together...........................[L] **JOHNNY & EDGAR WINTER** Edgar also appears on albums #2, 4 and 13	$8	Blue Sky 34033
7/23/77	146	8		12 Nothin' But The Blues .... with Muddy Waters and his band	$8	Blue Sky 34813
8/26/78	141	4		13 White, Hot & Blue...........................	$8	Blue Sky 35475
8/4/84	183	4		14 Guitar Slinger...........................	$8	Alligator 4735
10/19/85	156	10		15 Serious Business...........................	$8	Alligator 4742

Ain't Nothing To Me (7)
Ain't That A Kindness (5)
All Tore Down (7)
Am I Here? (5)
Baby, Whatcha Want Me To Do (11)
Back Door Friend (2)
Bad Luck And Trouble (1)
Bad Luck Situation (3)
Be Careful With A Fool (1)
Black Cat Bone (1)
Bladie Mae (12)
Blinded By Love (8)
Bony Moronie (8,10)
Boot Hill (14)
Broke And Lonely (3)
Broke Down Engine (1)
By The Light Of The Silvery Moon (3)
Can't You Feel It (7)
Cheap Tequila (7)
Creepy (3)
Crying In My Heart (3)
Dallas (2)
Divin' Duck (13)

Don't Take Advantage Of Me (14)
Drinkin' Blues (12)
E Z Rider (13)
Ease My Heart (3)
Everybody's Blues (12)
Fast Life Rider (9)
Feedback On Highway 101 (8)
Five After Four A.M. (3)
Forty-Four (1)
Funky Music (5)
Ganster Of Love (3)
Give It Back (15)
Golden Olden Days Of Rock & Roll (9)
Good Love (4)
Good Morning Little School Girl (2,6)
Good Time Woman (15)
Guess I'll Go Away (5)
Guy You Left Behind (3)
Harlem Shuffle (11)
Help Me (1)
Highway 61 Revisited (4,10)

Honest I Do (13)
Hurtin' So Bad (8)
Hustled Down In Texas (4)
I Can't Believe You Want To Leave (3)
I Got Love If You Want It (1)
I Hate Everybody (4)
I Love Everybody (4)
I Smell Trouble (14)
I'll Drown In My Tears (3)
I'm Not Sure (4)
I'm Yours And I'm Hers (2)
Iodine In My Coffee (14)
It Ain't Your Business (15)
It Was Rainin' (12)
It's All Over Now (10)
It's My Life, Baby (14)
It's My Own Fault (1,6)
Johnny B. Goode (4,6) 92
Jumpin' Jack Flash (6) 89
Kiss Tomorrow Goodbye (14)
Last Night (13)
Lay Down Your Sorrows (9)
Leave My Woman (Wife) Alone (3)

Leland Mississippi Blues (2)
Let It Bleed (7)
Let The Good Times Roll (11)
Let The Music Play (5)
Lights Out (14)
Look Up (5)
Love Song To Me (9)
Mad Blues (12)
Mad Dog (14)
Master Mechanic (15)
Mean Mistreater (2)
Mean Town Blues (1,6)
Memory Pain (4)
Mercy, Mercy (11)
Messin' With The Kid (13)
Mind Over Matter (9)
Miss Ann (4)
Murdering Blues (15)
My Soul (14)
My Time After Awhile (15)
No Time To Live (5)
Nothing Left (5)
Oh My Darling (3)
On The Limb (5)

One Step At A Time (13)
Pick Up On My Mojo (9)
Prodigal Son (5)
Raised On Rock (9)
Riot In Cell Block #9 (8)
Road Runner (3)
Rock & Roll (7)
Rock And Roll, Hoochie Koo (5)
Rock And Roll Medley 1 (6)
Rock And Roll Medley 2 (11)
Rock & Roll People (9,10)
Rock Me Baby (7)
Roll With Me (9,10)
Rollin' And Tumblin' (1)
Rollin' 'Cross The Country (8)
Route 90 (15)
Self-Destructive Blues (9)
Serious As A Heart Attack (15)
Shed So Many Tears (3)
Silver Train (7)
Slidin' In (13)
Slippin' And Slidin' (4)
Soul Man (11)

Sound The Bell (15)
Still Alive & Well (7)
Stone County (8)
Stranger (9)
Stray Cat Blues (8)
Sweet Love And Evil Women (12)
Sweet Papa John (9,10)
TV Mama (12)
That's What Love Does (3)
Thirty Days (8)
Tired Of Tryin' (12)
Too Much Seconal (7)
Tribute To Muddy (1)
Trick Bag (14)
Walkin' By Myself (13)
Walking Thru The Park (12)
When You Got A Good Friend (2)
You've Lost That Lovin' Feelin' (11)

WINTER, Paul, Sextet
Jazz group of students from universities in the Chicago area led by soprano saxophonist, Paul Winter.

DEBUT DATE	PEAK POS	WKS CHR		ARTIST — Album Title	$	Label & Number
12/29/62+	109	4		1 Jazz Meets The Bossa Nova ....[I]	$15	Columbia 8725
5/3/86	138	11		2 Canyon ....[I] **PAUL WINTER**	$8	Living Music 6

Adeus, Passaro Preto (Bye Bye, Blackbird) (1)
Air (2)
Anguish Of Longing (1)
Bedrock Cathedral (2)

Bright Angel (2)
Con Alma (1)
Don't Play Games With Me (1)
Elves' Chasm (2)

Foolish One (1)
Grand Canyon Sunrise (2)
Grand Canyon Sunset (2)
Journey To Recife (1)
Little Boat (1)

Longing For Bahia (1)
Maria Nobody (1)
Morning Echoes (2)
Only You And I (1)
Raven Dance (2)

River Run (2)
Sad Eyes, Song Of The (1)
Sockdolager (1)
Spell Of The Samba (1)

WINTERS, Jonathan
Born on 11/11/25 in Dayton, Ohio. Comedian; master of improvisation. Own TV variety series, 1956-57; 1967-69; 1972-74. Also appeared on TV's Mork & Mindy and Davis Rules.

DEBUT DATE	PEAK POS	WKS CHR		ARTIST — Album Title	$	Label & Number
2/1/60	18	53		1 The Wonderful World Of Jonathan Winters ....[C]	$25	Verve 15009
9/19/60	25	23		2 Down To Earth ....[C]	$25	Verve 15011
5/29/61	19	42		3 Here's Jonathan ....[C]	$15	Verve 15025
9/1/62	127	3		4 Another Day, Another World...........................[C]	$15	Verve 15032
3/21/64	145	2		5 Jonathan Winters' Mad, Mad, Mad, Mad World ....[K-C]	$15	Verve 15041
12/19/64	148	2		6 Whistle Stopping with Jonathan Winters ....[C]	$15	Verve 15037

Airline Pilots (1)
Amateur Show (4)
American Farmer - Elwood P. Suggins (6)
American Housewife - Sally Sweetwater (6)
American Indian - Chief Crying Trout (6)
American Labor Leader - Billy Bigbody (6)
American Teenager - Melvin Gohard (6)

Billy The Kid (3)
Broadway Musical (2)
California (4)
Chief Running Fox (5)
Child Psychiatrist (3)
Civil War (4)
Commercials (2)
Driving On The Turnpike - Thoughts Of A Turtle (3)
Extreme Liberal - Lance Lovegard (6)
Flying Saucer (1)

Football Game (1,5)
Grand Old Man - Price Boothcourt (6)
Great White Hunter (2,5)
Hip Robin Hood (3)
Horror Movies (2)
Igor And The Monster (4)
Interviews (1)
Lost Island (4)
Marine Corps (1,5)

Moby Dick & Captain Arnold (5)
Moon Map and Ivy Leaguer (4)
My School Days (4,5)
New Flying Saucer (3)
New Frontiers (4)
Old Age Speaks Out - Maude Frickert (6)
Oldest Airline Stewardess - Maude Frickert (3,5)

Portugese Pirate Ship (3)
Presidential Nominee - Daniel Douglas Diddle (6)
Prison Scene (2,5)
Sail Cat (4)
Scratchy (2)
Super Service Station (1)
TV Commercials and American In Paris (4)
Test Flight (3)
Ultra-Conservative - Mr. Tick Bitterford (6)

Used Pet Shop (1,5)
Western (1)

WINTERS, Robert, & Fall
Robert is a vocalist/keyboardist from Detroit. Stricken with polio at age five; confined to a wheelchair. Moved to Los Angeles in 1973. Worked with Stevie Wonder, Larry Graham and Johnny Winter. Own group, Fall, features vocalist Walter Turner.

DEBUT DATE	PEAK POS	WKS CHR		ARTIST — Album Title	$	Label & Number
5/9/81	71	8		Magic Man	$8	Buddah 5732

Face The Music
Happiness

How Can Love Be Wrong
Into My World

Magic Man
She Believes In Me

Touched By You
Watchin' You

When Will My Love Be Right

DEBUT DATE	PEAK POS	WKS CHR	GOLD	ARTIST — Album Title	$	Label & Number

★★312★★ WINWOOD, Steve
Born on 5/12/48 in Birmingham, England. Rock singer/keyboardist/guitarist. Lead singer of rock bands: Spencer Davis Group, Blind Faith and Traffic. Also see Stomu Yamashta.

DEBUT DATE	PEAK POS	WKS CHR	GOLD	ARTIST — Album Title	$	Label & Number
5/29/71	93	8		1 Winwood ....[K]	$20	United Art. 9950 [2]
				STEVIE WINWOOD compiled from albums recorded with groups listed in bio		
7/16/77	22	17		2 Steve Winwood	$8	Island 9494
1/17/81	3	43	●	3 Arc Of A Diver	$8	Island 9576
8/21/82	28	25		4 Talking Back To The Night	$8	Island 9777
7/19/86	3	86	▲³	5 Back in the High Life	$8	Island 25448
11/21/87+	26	26	▲	6 Chronicles ....[K]	$8	Island 25660
				contains 10 cuts from his 4 Island albums		
7/9/88	1¹	45	▲²	7 Roll With It	$8	Virgin 90946
11/24/90	27	20	●	8 Refugees of the Heart..	$12	Virgin 91405

And I Go (4)
Another Deal Goes Down (8)
Arc Of A Diver (3,6) 48
Back In The High Life Again (5) 13
Big Girls Walk Away (4)
Coloured Rain [Traffic] (1)
Come Out And Dance (8)
Cross Roads [Powerhouse] (1)
Dealer [Traffic] (1)
Dear Mr. Fantasy [Traffic] (1)
Don't You Know What The Night Can Do? (7) 6
Dust (3)
Empty Pages [Traffic] (1) 74

Every Day (Oh Lord) (8)
Finer Things (5) 8
Forty Thousand Headmen [Traffic] (1)
Freedom Overspill (5) 20
Freedom Rider [Traffic] (1)
Gimme Some Lovin' [Spencer Davis Group] (1) 7
Goodbye Stevie [Spencer Davis Group] (1)
Hearts On Fire (7) 53
Heaven Is In Your Mind [Traffic] (1)
Help Me Angel (4,6)
Higher Love (5,6) 1

Hold On (2)
Holding On (7) 11
I Can't Get Enough Of It [Spencer Davis Group] (1)
I Will Be Here (8)
I'm A Man [Spencer Davis Group] (1) 10
In The Light Of Day (8)
It Was Happiness (4)
Keep On Running [Spencer Davis Group] (1) 76
Let Me Make Something In Your Life (2)
Luck's In (2)
Medicated Goo [Traffic] (1)
Midland Maniac (2)

Morning Side (7)
My Love's Leavin' (5,6)
Night Train (3)
One And Only Man (8) 18
One More Morning (7)
Paper Sun [Traffic] (1) 94
Put On Your Dancing Shoes (7)
Roll With It (7) 1
Running On (8)
Sea Of Joy [Blind Faith] (1)
Second-Hand Woman (3)
Shining Song (7)
Slowdown Sundown (3)
Smiling Phases [Traffic] (1)

Somebody Help Me [Spencer Davis Group] (1) 47
Spanish Dancer (3,6)
Split Decision (5)
Stevie's Blues [Spencer Davis Group] (1)
Still In The Game (4) 47
Stranger To Himself [Traffic] (1)
Take It As It Comes (5)
Talking Back To The Night (4,6) 57
There's A River (4)
Time Is Running Out (2)
Vacant Chair (2,6)

Vagabond Virgin [Traffic] (1)
Valerie (4) 70
Valerie (6) 9
Wake Me Up On Judgment Day (5,6)
While There's A Candle Burning (4)
While You See A Chance (3,6) 7
You'll Keep On Searching (8)

WIRE
English group fronted by Graham Lewis and Colin Newman. When drummer Robert Gotobed left in mid-1991, band changed name to WIR (pronounced: wire).

DEBUT DATE	PEAK POS	WKS CHR	GOLD	ARTIST — Album Title	$	Label & Number
7/8/89	135	10		It's Beginning To And Back Again	$8	Mute 73516
				studio tracks based on live performances recorded in Chicago and Portugal; CD includes 3 bonus tracks		

Boiling Boy
Eardrum Buzz

Finest Drops
German Shepherds

Illuminated
It's A Boy

Over Theirs
Public Place

WIRE TRAIN
San Francisco-based quartet formed, in April 1983, as the Renegades by Kevin Hunter and Kurt Herr. Herr left group in late 1985.

DEBUT DATE	PEAK POS	WKS CHR	GOLD	ARTIST — Album Title	$	Label & Number
2/18/84	150	9		1 ...In A Chamber	$8	Columbia 38998
5/2/87	181	4		2 Ten Women	$8	Columbia 40387

Breakwater Days (2)
Certainly No One (2)
Chamber Of Hellos (1)
Diving (2)

Everything's Turning Up Down Again (1)
Hollow Song (2)

I Forget It All (When I See You) (1)
I Gotta Go (1)
I'll Do You (1)

Like (1)
Love Against Me (1)
Mercy Mercy (2)
Never (1)

She Comes On (2)
She's A Very Pretty Thing (2)
She's Got You (2)
She's On Fire (1)

Slow Down (1)
Take Me Back (2)
Too Long Alone (2)

WISHBONE ASH
British progressive rock quartet featuring the dual lead guitars of Andy Powell and Ted Turner. Laurie Wisefield replaced Turner in 1974.

DEBUT DATE	PEAK POS	WKS CHR	GOLD	ARTIST — Album Title	$	Label & Number
9/11/71	174	7		1 Pilgrimage	$12	Decca 75295
6/24/72	169	13		2 Argus	$10	Decca 75437
4/28/73	44	15		3 Wishbone Four	$8	MCA 327
12/1/73	82	18		4 Live Dates ....[L]	$10	MCA 8006 [2]
11/30/74	88	13		5 There's The Rub	$8	MCA 464
3/27/76	136	9		6 Locked In	$8	Atlantic 18164
12/18/76+	154	9		7 New England	$8	Atlantic 18200
11/5/77	166	4		8 Front Page News	$8	MCA 2311
3/29/78	179	2		9 Just Testing	$8	MCA 3221
1/23/82	192	4		10 Hot Ash ....[K-L]	$8	MCA 5283

Alone (1)
Baby What You Want Me To Do (4)
Bad Weather Blues (10)
Ballad Of The Beacon (3,4)
Blowin' Free (2,4,10)
Candle-Light (7)
Come In From The Rain (8)
Day I Found Your Love (8)
Diamond Jack (8)
Doctor (3,10)
Don't Come Back (5)
Everybody Needs A Friend (3)

F*U*B*R (5)
Front Page News (8)
Goodbye Baby Hello Friend (8,10)
Half Past Lovin' (6)
Haunting Me (9)
Heart Beat (8)
Helpless (9,10)
Hometown (5)
(In All Of My Dreams) You Rescue Me (7)
Insomnia (9)
It Started In Heaven (6)

Jail Bait (1,4)
King Will Come (2,4)
Lady Jay (5)
Lady Whiskey (4)
Leaf And Stream (2)
Lifeline (9)
Living Proof (9,10)
Lonely Island (7)
Lorelei (7)
Lullabye (1)
Master Of Disguise (9)
Midnight Dancer (8)
Moonshine (1)

Mother Of Pearl (7)
New Rising Star (9)
No Easy Road (3,10)
No Water In The Well (6)
Outward Bound (7)
Pay The Price (9)
Persephone (8)
Phoenix (4)
Pilgrim, The (1,4)
Rest In Peace (6)
Right Or Wrong (8)
Rock 'N Roll Widow (3,4)
Runaway (4)

Say Goodbye (6)
714 (8)
She Was My Best Friend (4)
Silver Shoes (5)
Sing Out The Song (3)
So Many Things To Say (3)
Sometime World (2)
Sorrel (3)
Surface To Air (8)
Throw Down The Sword (2,4)
Time Was (2)
Trust In You (9)
Valediction (1)

Vas Dis (1)
Warrior (2,4)
Way Of The World (10)
When You Know Love (7)
Where Were You Tomorrow (1)

WITCH QUEEN
Studio disco project produced by Peter Alves and Gino Soccio.

DEBUT DATE	PEAK POS	WKS CHR	GOLD	ARTIST — Album Title	$	Label & Number
4/28/79	158	6		Witch Queen	$8	Roadshow 3312

All Right Now

Bang A Gong 68

Got The Time

Witch Queen

★★426★★ WITHERS, Bill

Born on 7/4/38 in Slab Fork, West Virginia. Soul vocalist/guitarist/composer. Moved to California in 1967 and made demo records of his songs. First recorded for Sussex in 1970, produced by Booker T. Jones. Married to actress Denise Nicholas.

DEBUT DATE	PEAK POS	WKS CHR	GOLD		ARTIST — Album Title	$	Label & Number
6/26/71	39	33		1	Just As I Am	$10	Sussex 7006
5/20/72	4	43	●	2	Still Bill	$10	Sussex 7014
4/21/73	63	21		3	Bill Withers Live At Carnegie Hall .....[L]	$12	Sussex 7025 [2]
4/6/74	67	21		4	+'Justments	$10	Sussex 8032
5/17/75	182	2		5	The Best Of Bill Withers .....[G]	$10	Sussex 8037
11/8/75+	81	15		6	Making Music	$8	Columbia 33704
11/6/76	169	4		7	Naked & Warm	$8	Columbia 34327
10/29/77+	39	26	●	8	Menagerie	$8	Columbia 34903
3/17/79	134	9		9	'Bout Love	$8	Columbia 35596
5/16/81	183	3		10	Bill Withers' Greatest Hits .....[G]	$8	Columbia 37199
5/25/85	143	9		11	Watching You Watching Me	$8	Columbia 39887

Ain't No Sunshine (1,3,5,10) 3
All Because Of You (9)
Another Day To Run (3)
Best You Can (6)
Better Off Dead (1,3)
Can We Pretend (4)
City Of The Angels (7)
Close To Me (7)
Cold Baloney (medley) (3)
Dedicated To You My Love (9)
Do It Good (1)
Don't It Make It Better (9)
Don't Make Me Wait (11)
Don't You Want To Stay? (6)
Dreams (7)
Everybody's Talkin' (1,5)
Family Table (6)
For My Friend (3)

Friend Of Mine (3) 80
Grandma's Hands (1,3,5,10) 42
Green Grass (4)
Harlem (1,3,5)
Heartbreak Road (4) 89
Heart In Your Life (11)
Hello Like Before (6,10)
Hope She'll Be Happier (1,3)
I Can't Write Left Handed (3)
I Don't Know (2)
I Don't Want You On My Mind (2)
I Love You Dawn (6)
I Want To Spend The Night (8,10)
I Wish You Well (6)
I'll Be With You (7)
I'm Her Daddy (1)

If I Didn't Mean You Well (7)
In My Heart (1)
It Ain't Because Of Me Baby (8)
Just The Two Of Us (9)
Kissing My Love (2,5) 31
Lean On Me (2,3,5,10) 1
Let It Be (1)
Let Me Be The One You Need (8)
Let Me In Your Life (2,3)
Let Us Love (3) 47
Liza (4)
Lonely Town, Lonely Street (2,3)
Look To Each Other For Love (9)
Love (9)
Love Is (9)

Lovely Day (8,10) 30
Lovely Night For Dancing (8)
Make Love To Your Mind (6) 76
Make A Smile For Me (4)
Memories Are That Way (9)
Moanin' And Groanin' (1)
My Imagination (7)
Naked & Warm (Heaven! Oh! Heaven!) (7)
Oh Yeah! (11)
Paint Your Pretty Picture (6)
Railroad Man (4)
Ruby Lee (4)
Same Power That Made Me Laugh (4,5) 50
She Wants To (Get On Down) (8)
She's Lonely (6)

Something That Turns You On (11)
Sometimes A Song (6)
Soul Shadows (10)
Steppin' Right Along (11)
Stories (4)
Sweet Wanomi (1)
Take It All In And Check It All Out (2)
Tender Things (8)
Then You Smile At Me (8)
Use Me (2,3,5,10) 2
Watching You Watching Me (11)
We Could Be Sweet Lovers (11)
Whatever Happens (11)
Where You Are (7)

Who Is He And What Is He To You? (2,5,10)
Wintertime (8)
World Keeps Going Around (3)
You (4,5)
You Got The Stuff (9)
You Just Can't Smile It Away (11)
You Try To Find A Love (11)

WITHERSPOON, Jimmy

Born on 8/8/23 in Gurdon, Arkansas. Blues singer/bassist. Moved to Los Angeles in 1935. Merchant Marine from 1941-43. First recorded for Philo/Aladdin in 1945.

DEBUT DATE	PEAK POS	WKS CHR	GOLD		ARTIST — Album Title	$	Label & Number
3/8/75	176	2			Love Is A Five Letter Word	$12	Capitol 11360

Aviation Man
Buried Alive In The Blues
Fool's Paradise

I Was Lost (But Now I'm Found)
Landlord, Landlord
Love Is A Five Letter Word

No Money Down
Nothing's Changed

Other Side Of Love
Reflection

Spoon Tang
What's Going Down

WOLF, Peter

Born Peter Blankfield on 3/7/46 in the Bronx. Lead singer of The J. Geils Band until 1983. Married actress Faye Dunaway on 8/7/74, divorced in 1979. Not to be confused with the producer of the same name.

DEBUT DATE	PEAK POS	WKS CHR	GOLD		ARTIST — Album Title	$	Label & Number
8/11/84	24	26		1	Lights Out	$8	EMI America 17121
4/18/87	53	15		2	Come As You Are	$8	EMI America 17230
3/31/90	111	7		3	Up To No Good!	$12	MCA 6349

Arrows And Chains (1)
Baby Please Don't Let Me Go (1)
Billy Bigtime (1)
Blue Avenue (2)
Can't Get Started (2) 75
Come As You Are (2) 15

Crazy (1)
Daydream Getaway (3)
Drive All Night (3)
Flame Of Love (2)
Go Wild (3)
Here Comes That Hurt (1)

I Need You Tonight (1) 36
Lights Out (1) 12
Lost In Babylon (3)
Love On Ice (3)
Magic Moon (2)
Mamma Said (2)
Mars Needs Women (1)

Never Let It Go (3)
99 Worlds (3) 78
Oo-Ee-Diddley-Bop! (1) 61
Poor Girl's Heart (1)
Pretty Lady (Tell Me Why) (1)
River Runs Dry (3)
Run Silent Run Deep (2)

Shades Of Red--Shades Of Blue (3)
Thick As Thieves (2)
2 Lane (2)
Up To No Good (3)
When Women Are Lonely (3)
Wind Me Up (2)

★★324★★ WOMACK, Bobby

Born on 3/4/44 in Cleveland. Soul vocalist/guitarist/songwriter. Sang in family gospel group, the Womack Brothers. Group recorded for Sar as The Valentinos and The Lovers, 1962-64. Toured as guitarist with Sam Cooke. Solo recording for Him label in 1965. Backup guitarist on many sessions, including Wilson Pickett, The Box Tops, Joe Tex, Aretha Franklin and Janis Joplin. Married for a time to Sam Cooke's widow. Nicknamed "The Preacher."

DEBUT DATE	PEAK POS	WKS CHR	GOLD		ARTIST — Album Title	$	Label & Number
12/28/68	174	2		1	Fly Me To The Moon	$15	Minit 24014
4/17/71	188	5		2	The Womack "Live" .....[L]	$8	Liberty 7645
12/4/71+	83	17		3	Communication	$8	United Art. 5539
6/24/72	43	48		4	Understanding	$8	United Art. 5577
1/13/73	50	20		5	Across 110th Street .....[S]	$8	United Art. 5225
					includes 5 instrumentals by J.J. Johnson & His Orchestra: "Harlem Clavinette," "Hang On In There," "Harlem Love Theme," "Across 110th Street" and "(If You Don't Want My Love) Give It Back"		
7/7/73	37	21		6	Facts Of Life	$8	United Art. 043
2/9/74	85	19		7	Lookin' For A Love Again	$8	United Art. 199
12/14/74+	142	7		8	Bobby Womack's Greatest Hits .....[G]	$8	United Art. 346
5/24/75	126	4		9	I Don't Know What The World Is Coming To	$8	United Art. 353
1/17/76	147	11		10	Safety Zone	$8	United Art. 544
12/26/81+	29	23		11	The Poet	$8	Beverly G. 10000
4/7/84	60	14		12	The Poet II	$8	Beverly G. 10003
					with guest vocalist Patti LaBelle		
9/21/85	66	19		13	So Many Rivers	$8	MCA 5617

Across 110th Street (5) 56
All Along The Watchtower (6)
American Dream (12)
And I Love Her (4)

Baby! You Oughta Think It Over (1)
California Dreamin' (1,2) 43
Can't Stop A Man In Love (6)

Check It Out (9,13) 91
Come L'Amore (3)
Communication (3)
Copper Kettle (7)

Daylight (10)
Do It Right (5)
Doing It My Way (7)
Don't Let Me Down (7)

Everybody's Talkin' (2)
Everything Is Beautiful (3)
Everything's Gonna Be Alright (10)

Fact Of Life (medley) (6)
Fire And Rain (3)
Fly Me To The Moon (1,8) 52

WOMACK, Bobby — Cont'd

Games (11)
Git It (9)
Got To Be With You Tonight (13)
Got To Get You Back (4)
Gypsy Woman (13)
Hang On In There (5)
Harry Hippie (4,8) **31**
He'll Be There When The Sun Goes Down (medley) (6)
Holdin' On To My Baby's Love (medley) (6)
I Can Understand It (4,8)
I Don't Know (Interlude #1 & 2) (9)
I Don't Wanna Be Hurt By Ya Love Again (7)
I Feel A Groove Comin' On (10)
I Wish He Didn't Trust Me So Much (13)

I Wish I Had Someone To Go Home To (12)
I Wish It Would Rain (10)
I'm A Midnight Mover (1,2)
I'm Gonna Forget About You (8)
I'm In Love (1)
I'm Through Trying To Prove My Love To You (6)
If You Can't Give Her Love Give Her Up (6)
(If You Don't Want My Love) Give It Back (3,5)
If You Think You're Lonely Now (11)
(If You Want My Love) Put Something Down On It (9)
It Takes A Lot Of Strength To Say Goodbye (12)
It's All Over Now (1)
Jealous Love (9)
Just My Imagination (11)

Laughing And Clowning (2)
Lay Some Lovin' On Me (11)
Let It Hang Out (7)
Let It Out (2)
Let Me Kiss It Where It Hurts (13)
Lillie Mae (1)
Look Of Love (6)
Lookin' For A Love (7,8) **10**
Love Ain't Something You Can Get For Free (10)
Love Has Finally Come At Last (12) **88**
Love, The Time Is Now (1)
Moonlight In Vermont (1)
More Than I Can Stand (2,8) **90**
Natural Man (6)
No Money In My Pocket (1)
Nobody (medley) (6)

Nobody Wants You When You're Down And Out (6,8) **29**
Oh How I Miss You Baby (1)
Only Survivor (13)
Point Of No Return (7)
Preacher, The (2,8)
Quicksand (5)
Ruby Dean (4)
Secrets (11)
Simple Man (4)
So Baby, Don't Leave Home Without It (13)
So Many Rivers (13)
So Many Sides Of You (11)
Somebody Special (1)
Something (2)
Something You Got (10)
Stand Up (11)
Superstar (9)
Surprise Surprise (12)

Sweet Caroline (Good Times Never Seemed So Good) (4,8) **51**
Take Me (1)
Tell Me Why (12)
That's Heaven To Me (6)
That's The Way I Feel About Cha (3,8) **27**
That's Where It's At (13)
There's One Thing That Beats Falling (7)
(They Long To Be) Close To You (3)
Thing Called Love (4)
Through The Eyes Of A Child (12)
Trust In Me (10)
Tryin' To Get Over You (12)
What Is This (1)
What's Your World (9)
Whatever Happened To The Times? (13)

Where Do We Go From Here (11)
Where There's A Will, There's A Way (10)
Who's Foolin' Who (12)
Woman's Gotta Have It (4,8) **60**
Yes, Jesus Loves Me (9)
Yield Not To Temptation (3)
You're Messing Up A Good Thing (7)
You're Welcome, Stop On By (7,8) **59**

WOMENFOLK, The

Pasadena female folk quintet: Elaine Gealer, Joyce James, Leni Ashmore, Babs Cooper and Judy Fine.

| 5/2/64 | 118 | 6 | | The Womenfolk .... | $12 | RCA 2832 |

Don't You Rock 'Em Daddy-O
Good Old Mountain Dew
Green Mountain Boys
Little Boxes 83
Little Rag Doll
Love Come A-Tricklin' Down
Old Maid's Lament
One Man's Hands
Para Ballar La Bamba
Rickety Tickety Tin
Skip To My Lou
Whistling Gypsy Rover

★★28★★ WONDER, Stevie

Born Steveland Morris on 5/13/50 in Saginaw, Michigan. Singer/songwriter/multi-instrumentalist/producer. Blind since birth. Signed to Motown in 1960, did backup work. First recorded in 1962, renamed "Little Stevie Wonder" by Berry Gordy, Jr. Married to Syreeta Wright from 1970-72. Near-fatal auto accident on 8/16/73. Winner of 17 Grammy Awards. In the films *Bikini Beach* and *Muscle Beach Party*. Inducted into the Rock and Roll Hall of Fame in 1989.

7/13/63	1¹	20		1 Little Stevie Wonder/The 12 Year Old Genius ....[L]	$50	Tamla 240
				LITTLE STEVIE WONDER		
6/18/66	33	25		2 Up-Tight Everything's Alright	$25	Tamla 268
1/28/67	92	7		3 Down To Earth	$20	Tamla 272
9/30/67	45	13		4 I Was Made To Love Her	$20	Tamla 279
4/27/68	37	29		5 Greatest Hits ....[G]	$12	Tamla 282
1/11/69	50	18		6 For Once In My Life	$12	Tamla 291
10/11/69	34	20		7 My Cherie Amour	$12	Tamla 296
4/11/70	81	15		8 Stevie Wonder Live ....[L]	$12	Tamla 298
8/29/70	25	16		9 Signed Sealed & Delivered	$12	Tamla 304
5/8/71	62	27		10 Where I'm Coming From	$12	Tamla 308
11/20/71+	69	12		11 Stevie Wonder's Greatest Hits, Vol. 2 ....[G]	$12	Tamla 313
3/25/72	21	35		12 Music Of My Mind	$12	Tamla 314
11/18/72+	3	109		13 **Talking Book**	$12	Tamla 319
8/18/73	4	89		14 **Innervisions**	$12	Tamla 326
				1973 Grammy winner: Album of the Year		
8/10/74	1²	65		15 **Fulfillingness' First Finale**	$12	Tamla 332
				1974 Grammy winner: Album of the Year		
10/16/76	1¹⁴	80		16 **Songs In The Key Of Life**	$15	Tamla 340 [2]
				1976 Grammy winner: Album of the Year; double LP also includes a bonus 4-song, 7" EP		
12/24/77+	34	13		17 Looking Back ....[K]	$18	Motown 804 [3]
				compilation of recordings from 1962-71		
11/24/79	4	22		18 **Journey Through The Secret Life of Plants**	$12	Tamla 371 [2]
11/15/80	3	40	▲	19 Hotter Than July	$8	Tamla 373
5/29/82	4	28	●	20 Stevie Wonder's Original Musiquarium I ....[G]	$10	Tamla 6002 [2]
				compilation of hits from 1972-82		
9/22/84	4	40	▲	21 The Woman in Red ....[S]	$8	Motown 6108
				includes 2 duets with Dionne Warwick, plus a Warwick solo ("Moments Aren't Moments")		
10/19/85	5	50	▲	22 In Square Circle	$10	Tamla 6134
12/5/87	17	31	▲	23 Characters	$8	Motown 6248
6/15/91	24	21	●	24 Music From The Movie Jungle Fever ....[S]	$12	Motown 6291

Ai No, Sono (18)
Ain't No Lovin' (6)
Ain't That Asking For Trouble (2,17)
Alfie (8,17) **66**
All I Do (19)
All In Love Is Fair (14)
Angel Baby (Don't You Ever Leave Me) (3)
Angie Girl (7,17)
Another Star (16) **32**
Anything You Want Me To Do (9)
As (16) **36**
As If You Read My Mind (19)
At Last (7)
Baby Don't You Do It (4)
Bang Bang (3)

Be Cool, Be Calm (And Keep Yourself Together) (3)
Big Brother (13)
Bird Of Beauty (15)
Black Man (16)
Black Orchid (18)
Blame It On The Sun (13)
Blowin In The Wind (2,5,8,17) **9**
Boogie On Reggae Woman (15,20) **3**
By The Time I Get To Phoenix (8)
Ca' Purange (8)
Can I Get A Witness (4)
Cash In Your Face (19)
Castles In The Sand (5,17) **52**

Chemical Love (24)
Come Back As A Flower (18)
Contract On Love (2,5,17)
Contusion (16)
Creepin' (15)
Cryin' Through The Night (23)
Dark 'N' Lovely (23)
Did I Hear You Say You Love Me (19)
Do I Do (20) **13**
Do I Love Her (4)
Do Like You (10)
Do Yourself A Favor (10,17)
Don't Drive Drunk (21)
Don't Wonder Why (9)
Don't You Know (1)

Don't You Worry 'Bout A Thing (14) **16**
Down To Earth (3,8,17)
Drown In My Own Tears (1)
Each Other's Throat (24)
Earth's Creation (18)
Ecclesiastes (18)
Every Time I See You I Go Wild (4)
Everybody Needs Somebody (I Need You) (4)
Everybody's Talking (8)
Evil (12)
Fingertips (1)
Fingertips - Pt 2 (5,17) **1**
First Garden (18)
Fool For You (4)

For Once In My Life (6,8,11,17) **2**
Free (23)
Front Line (20)
Fun Day (24)
Galaxy Paradise (23)
Get It (23) **80**
Girl Blue (12)
Give Your Love (7)
Go Home (22) **10**
God Bless The Child (6)
Golden Lady (14)
Gotta Have You (24) **92**
Hallelujah I Love Her So (1)
Happier Than The Morning Sun (12)
Happy Birthday (19)
Have A Talk With God (16)

He's Misstra Know-It-All (14)
Heaven Help Us All (9,11,17) **9**
Heaven Is 10 Zillion Light Years Away (15)
Hello Young Lovers (7)
Hey Harmonica Man (5,17) **29**
Hey Love (3,5,17) **90**
High Heel Sneakers (17) **59**
Higher Ground (14,20) **4**
Hold Me (2)
House On The Hill (6)
I Ain't Gonna Stand For It (19) **11**
I Believe (When I Fall In Love It Will Be Forever) (13)

WONDER, Stevie — Cont'd

I Can't Let My Heaven Walk Away (9)
I Don't Know Why (6,17) *39*
I Go Sailing (24)
I Gotta Have A Song (9,17)
I Just Called To Say I Love You (21) *1*
I Love Every Little Thing About You (12)
I Love You Too Much (22)
I Pity The Fool (4)
I Wanna Make Her Love Me (6)
I Wanna Talk To You (10)
I Want My Baby Back (2)
I Was Made To Love Her (4,5,17) *2*
I Wish (16,20) *1*
I'd Be A Fool Right Now (6,17)
I'd Cry (4,17)
(I'm Afraid) The Masquerade Is Over (1)
I'm More Than Happy (I'm Satisfied) (6)
I'm Wondering (5,17) *12*
I've Got You (7)
I've Gotta Be Me (medley) (8)
If I Ruled The World (17)
If It's Magic (16)
If She Breaks Your Heart (24)
If You Really Love Me (10,11,17) *8*
In Your Corner (23)
Isn't She Lovely (16,20)

It Ain't No Use (15)
It's More Than You (21)
It's Wrong (Apartheid) (22)
It's You (21)
Jesus Children Of America (14)
Joy Inside My Tears (16)
Joy (Takes Over Me) (9)
Jungle Fever (24)
Keep On Running (12) *90*
Kesse Ye Lolo De Ye (18)
Knocks Me Off My Feet (16)
La La La La La (1)
Land Of La La (22) *86*
Lately (19) *64*
Light My Fire (7)
Lighting Up The Candles (24)
Living For The City (14,20) *8*
Lonesome Road (3)
Look Around (10)
Lookin' For Another Pure Love (13)
Love A Go Go (2)
Love Having You Around (12)
Love Light In Flight (21) *17*
Love's In Need Of Love Today (16)
Make Sure You're Sure (24)
Master Blaster (Jammin') (19,20) *5*
Maybe Your Baby (13)
More Than A Dream (17)
Mr. Tambourine Man (3)
Music Talk (2)

My Cherie Amour (7,8,11,17) *4*
My Girl (4)
My World Is Empty Without You (3)
Never Dreamed You'd Leave In Summer (10,11,17) *78*
Never Had A Dream Come True (9,11,17) *26*
Never In Your Sun (22)
Ngiculela-Es Historia - I Am Singing (16)
Nothing's Too Good For My Baby (2,5,17) *20*
Once In A Lifetime (medley) (8)
One Of A Kind (23)
Ordinary Pain (16)
Outside My Window (18) *52*
Overjoyed (22) *24*
Part-Time Lover (22) *1*
Pastime Paradise (16)
Pearl (1)
Place In The Sun (3,5,8,17) *9*
Please Don't Go (15)
Please, Please, Please (4)
Power Flower (18)
Pretty Little Angel (16)
Pretty World (8)
Queen In The Black (24)
Race Babbling (18)
Respect (4)
Ribbon In The Sky (20) *54*

Rocket Love (19)
Romeo & Juliet, Love Theme From (8)
Same Old Story (18)
Seasons (18)
Secret Life Of Plants (18)
Seed's A Star (medley) (18)
Seems So Long (12)
Send Me Some Lovin' (4)
Send One Your Love (18,20) *4*
Shadow Of Your Smile (7)
Shoo-Be-Doo-Be-Doo-Da-Day (6,8,11,17) *9*
Signed, Sealed, Delivered I'm Yours (9,11,17) *3*
Sir Duke (16,20) *1*
Sixteen Tons (3)
Skeletons (23) *19*
Smile Please (15)
Somebody Knows, Somebody Cares (7)
Something Out Of The Blue (10,17)
Something To Say (9)
Soul Bongo (1)
Spiritual Walkers (22)
Stranger On The Shore Of Love (22)
Sugar (9)
Summer Soft (16)
Sunny (6,8)
Sunshine In Their Eyes (10)
Superstition (13,20) *1*

Superwoman (Where Were You When I Needed You) (12,20) *33*
Sweet Little Girl (12)
Sylvia (3,17)
Take Up A Course In Happiness (10)
Teach Me Tonight (2)
Thank You (For Loving Me All The Way) (17)
Thank You Love (3,8,17)
That Girl (20) *4*
These Three Words (24)
They Won't Go When I Go (15)
Think Of Me As Your Soldier (10)
(Time For Us) ..see: Romeo & Juliet, Love Theme From
Too High (14)
Too Shy To Say (15)
Travlin' Man (11,17) *32*
Tree (18)
Tuesday Heartbreak (13)
Until You Come Back To Me (That's What I'm Gonna Do) (17)
Uptight (Everything's Alright) (2,5,17) *3*
Venus' Flytrap And The Bug (18)
Village Ghetto Land (16)
Visions (14)
Voyage To India (18)

We Can Work It Out (9,11) *13*
Weakness (21)
Whereabouts (22)
With A Child's Heart (5)
With Each Beat Of My Heart (23)
Woman In Red (21)
Workout Stevie, Workout (5,17) *33*
Yester-Me, Yester-You, Yesterday (7,8,11,17) *7*
You And I (13)
You And Me (7)
You Are The Sunshine Of My Life (13,20) *1*
You Can't Judge A Book By It's Cover (9)
You Haven't Done Nothin (15,20) *1*
You Met Your Match (6,11,17) *35*
You Will Know (23) *77*
You've Got It Bad Girl (13)

WOOD, Brenton

Born Alfred Smith on 7/26/41 in Shreveport and raised in San Pedro, California. Soul singer/songwriter/pianist. First recorded with Little Freddy & The Rockets in 1958.

| 7/22/67 | 184 | 2 | | Oogum Boogum | $15 | Double Shot 5002 |

Best Thing I Ever Had
Birdman
Come Here Girl

Gimme Little Sign *9*
I Like The Way You Love Me

I Think You've Got Your Fools Mixed Up

I'm The One Who Knows
Little Bit Of Love

Oogum Boogum Song *34*
Psychotic Reaction

Runnin' Wild
Take A Chance

WOOD, Ron

Rock guitarist born on 6/1/46 in Hillingdon, England. Member of the Jeff Beck Group, 1967-68. Joined Faces in 1969. In 1976, joined The Rolling Stones. Cameo appearance in the 1986 film *9 1/2 Weeks*.

7/19/75	118	6		1 Now Look *	$12	Warner 2872
5/12/79	45	13		2 Gimme Some Neck	$8	Columbia 35702
9/19/81	164	5		3 1234 *	$8	Columbia 37473

*RONNIE WOOD

Big Bayou (1)
Breakin' My Heart (2)
Breathe On Me (1)
Buried Alive (1)
Caribbean Boogie (1)
Come To Realise (2)

Delia (2)
Don't Worry (2)
Down To The Ground (3)
F.U.C. Her (2)
Fountain Of Love (3)
I Can Say She's Allright (1)

I Can't Stand The Rain (1)
I Got A Feeling (1)
I Got Lost When I Found You (1)
If You Don't Want My Love (1)

Infekshun (2)
It's Unholy (1)
Lost And Lonely (2)
Now Look (1)
1234 (3)
Outlaws (3)

Priceless (3)
Redeyes (3)
Seven Days (2)
She Never Told Me (3)
She Was Out There (3)
Sweet Baby Mine (1)

We All Get Old (2)
Wind Howlin' Through (3)
Worry No More (2)

WOOD, Roy

Born on 11/8/46 in Birmingham, England. Co-founder/cello player of The Move and Electric Light Orchestra.

| 11/3/73 | 176 | 6 | | Boulders | $8 | United Art. 168 |

All The Way Over The Hill (medley)
Dear Elaine

Irish Loafer (And His Hen) (medley)

Miss Clarke And The Computer

Nancy Sing Me A Song
Rock Down Low
Rock Medley

Songs Of Praise
Wake Up

When Gran'ma Plays The Banjo

WOODBURY, Woody

Adult comedy storyteller.

| 3/7/60 | 10 | 78 | | 1 Woody Woodbury Looks at love and life | [C] $15 | Stereoddities 1 |

no track titles listed on this album

| 6/13/60 | 16 | 59 | | 2 Woody Woodbury's Laughing Room | [C] $18 | Stereoddities 2 |
| 1/20/62 | 46 | 21 | | 3 Woody Woodbury's Saloonatics | [C] $18 | Stereoddities 4 |

Allergic (3)

Blue Side (2)

Bright Side (2)

I'm Returning All Your Presents (3)

WOODENTOPS, The

English quintet led by Rolo McGinty.

| 9/20/86 | 185 | 6 | | Giant | $8 | Columbia 40468 |

Everything Breaks
Get It On
Give It Time

Good Thing
Hear Me James

History
Last Time

Love Affair With Everyday Livin'
Shout

Love Train

So Good Today
Travelling Man

WOODS, Stevie

R&B vocalist based in Los Angeles. Originally from Columbus, Ohio.

| 12/5/81+ | 153 | 25 | | Take Me To Your Heaven | $8 | Cotillion 5229 |

Fly Away *84*
Gotcha

Just Can't Win 'Em All *38*
Read Between The Lines

Steal The Night *25*
Take Me To Your Heaven

Through The Years

Throw A Little Bit Of Love My Way

Wanna' Be Close To You

WOOLLEY, Bruce, & The Camera Club
British pop-rock group led by vocalist Bruce Woolley. Thomas Dolby was a brief member.

| 3/8/80 | 184 | 2 | | Bruce Woolley & The Camera Club | $8 | Columbia 36301 |

Clean/Clean (medley) · English Garden · Goodbye To Yesterday · No Surrender · W.W. 9 (medley) · You're The Circus (I'm The
Dancing With The Sporting · Flying Man · Johnny · Video Killed The Radio Star · You Got Class · Clown)
Boys · Get Away William

WORLD PARTY
London-based group featuring keyboardist/vocalist/producer/engineer Karl Wallinger from North Wales (formerly of The Waterboys)

| 12/27/86+ | 39 | 31 | 1 | Private Revolution | $8 | Chrysalis 41552 |
| 6/2/90 | 73 | 23 | 2 | Goodbye Jumbo | $12 | Ensign 21654 |

Ain't Gonna Come Till I'm · Dance Of The Hoppy Lads (1) · It's All Mine (1) · Put The Message In The Box · Take It Up (2)
Ready (2) · God On My Side (2) · Love Street (2) · (2) · Thank You World (2)
All Come True (1) · Hawaiian Island World (1) · Making Love (To The World) · Ship Of Fools (Save Me · Way Down Now (2)
All I Really Want To Do (1) · Is It Too Late? (2) · (1) · From Tomorrow) (1) 27 · When The Rainbow Comes
And I Fell Back Alone (2) · It Can Be Beautiful · Private Revolution (1) · Show Me To The Top (2) · (2)
Ballad Of The Little Man (1) · (Sometimes) (1) · Sweet Soul Dream (2) · World Party (1)

WRABIT
Canadian rock sextet — Lou Nadeau, lead singer.

| 2/6/82 | 157 | 8 | | Wrabit | $8 | MCA 5268 |

Anyway Anytime · Don't Say Goodnite To Rock · Here I'll Stay · Just Go Away · Tell Me What To Do
Back Home · And Roll · How Does She Do It · Pushin' On · Too Many Years
Can't Be Wrong

WRATHCHILD AMERICA
Baltimore-based, hard-rock quartet: Brad Divens (vocals; formerly with Kix), Jay Abbene, Terry Carter and Shannon Larkin.

| 9/30/89 | 190 | 6 | | Climbin' The Walls | $8 | Atlantic 81889 |

Candy From A Madman · Day Of The Thunder · Hernia · No Deposit, No Return · Silent Darkness (Smothered · Time
Climbin' The Walls · Hell's Gates · London After Midnight · · Life)

WRAY, Link
Link was born on 5/2/35 in Dunn, North Carolina. Rock and roll guitarist. Part American Indian. Also see Robert Gordon.

| 7/24/71 | 186 | 4 | | Link Wray | $12 | Polydor 4064 |

recorded at his 3-track shack in Maryland

Black River Swamp · Fallin' Rain · God Out West · Juke Box Mama · Rise And Fall Of Jimmy · Tail Dragger
Crowbar · Fire And Brimstone · Ice People · La De Da · Stokes · Take Me Home Jesus

WRECKX-N-EFFECT
Male rap group: Aquil Davidson, Markell Riley and Brandon Mitchell (d: in 1990 of gunshot fire). Riley is the brother of Guy member/prolific producer Teddy Riley.

| 1/13/90 | 103 | 11 | 1 | Wrecks-N-Effect | $12 | Motown 6281 |

WRECKS-N-EFFECT

| 12/12/92 | 9↑ | 9↑ ▲ | 2 | Hard Or Smooth | $12 | MCA 10566 |

CD and cassette include bonus track

Club Head (1) · Hard (Short) (2) · My Cutie (2) · Rump Shaker (2) 2 · WRECKX-N-Effect (2)
Deep (1) · Here We Come (2) · New Jack Swing (1) · Smooth (Short) (2) · WRECKX Shop (2)
Ez Come Ez Go (What Goes · Juicy (1) · New Jack Swing II (2) · Soul Man (1) · Wipe Your Sweat (1)
Up Must Come Down) (2) · Knock-N-Boots (2) · Peanut Butter (1) · Tell Me How You Feel (2)
Friends To The End (1) · Leave The Mike Smokin' (1) · Rock Steady (1) · V-Man (1)

WRIGHT, Bernard
Born in 1965 in New York City. Keyboardist since age four. Toured with Lenny White at age 13; with Tom Browne in 1979.

| 3/14/81 | 116 | 14 | | 'Nard | $8 | GRP 5011 |

Bread Sandwiches · Haboglabotribin' · Master Rocker · Solar · We're Just The Band
Firebolt Hustle · Just Chillin' Out · Music Is The Key · Spinnin'

WRIGHT, Betty
Born on 12/21/53 in Miami. Soul singer. In family gospel group, Echoes Of Joy, from 1956. First recorded for Deep City in 1966. Hostess of TV talk shows in Miami.

2/26/72	123	6	1	I Love The Way You Love	$15	Alston 388
6/17/78	26	36	2	Betty Wright Live	[L] $8	Alston 4408
6/2/79	138	6	3	Betty Travelin' In The Wright Circle	$8	Alston 4410
4/23/88	127	13	4	Mother Wit	$8	Ms. B 3301

After The Pain (4) · I Love The Way You Love (1) · Let's Not Rush Down The · Midnight At The Oasis · Say It Again (4) · You Can't Live For Lookin' (2)
Ain't No Sunshine (1) · I'll Love You Forever Heart · Road Of Love (1) · (medley) (2) · Shoot It From The Hip (4) · You Got The Love (medley)
All Your Kissin' Sho' Don't · And Soul (1) · Listen To The Music (Dance) · Mr. Melody (medley) (2) · Song For You (2) · (2)
Make True Lovin' (1) · I'm Gettin' Tired Baby (1) · (3) · Ms. Time (4) · Thank You For The Many · You're Just What I Need (3)
Child Of The Man (3) · I'm Telling You Now (3) · Love Days (4) · My Love Is (3) · Things You've Done (3)
Clean Up Woman (1,2) 6 · If You Love Me Like You Say · Love Train (medley) (3) · No Pain (No Gain) (4) · Tonight Is The Night (2)
Don't Let It End This Way (1) · You Love Me (1) · Lovin' Is Really My Game (2) · Open The Door To Your · Unsolicited Advice (4)
Fakin' Moves (1) · Let's Get Married Today · Me And Mrs. Jones (medley) · Heart (medley) (3) · Where Is The Love (2) 96
I Believe It's Love (3) · (medley) (2) · (2) · Pillow Talk (medley) (2) · (You Are My) Sunshine
I Found That Guy (1) · · Miami Groove (4) · Pure Love (1) · (medley) (2)

WRIGHT, Charles, And The Watts 103rd Street Rhythm Band
Charles was born in 1942 in Clarksdale, Mississippi. Vocalist/pianist/guitarist/producer/leader of an eight-man, soul-funk band from the Watts section of Los Angeles. Evolved from the Soul Runners. Big break came through assistance by comedian Bill Cosby.

| 4/19/69 | 140 | 5 | 1 | Together | $12 | Warner 1761 |
| 10/18/69 | 145 | 4 | 2 | In The Jungle, Babe | $12 | Warner 1801 |

above 2: **THE WATTS 103rd STREET RHYTHM BAND**

| 8/8/70 | 182 | 10 | 3 | Express Yourself | $10 | Warner 1864 |
| 5/15/71 | 147 | 11 | 4 | You're So Beautiful | $10 | Warner 1904 |

DEBUT DATE	PEAK POS	WKS CHR	GOLD	ARTIST — Album Title	$	Label & Number

WRIGHT, Charles, And The Watts 103rd Street Rhythm Band — Cont'd

Comment (2)
Dance, A Kiss And A Song (2)
Do Your Thing (1) *11*
Everyday People (2)
Express Yourself (3) *12*
Express Yourself II (4)
Get Ready (1)
Giggin' Down 103rd (1)

High As Apple Pie - Slice I &
II (3)
(I Can't Get No) Satisfaction
(1)
I Got Love (3,4)
I Wake Up Crying (1)
I'm A Midnight Mover (2)
I'm Aware (3)

Joker (On A Trip Through
The Jungle) (2)
Knock On Wood (1)
Let's Make Love Not War (4)
Light My Fire (2)
Love Land (2,3) *16*
Must Be Your Thing (2)
My Summer's Gone (1)

Oh Happy Gabe (Sometimes
Blue) (2)
Papa's Got A Brand New Bag
(1)
Phuncky Bill (1)
Settle My Nerves (4)
65 Bars And A Taste Of Soul
(1)

Something You Got (1)
Sorry Charlie (1)
Till You Get Enough (2) *67*
Twenty-Five Miles (2)
What Can You Bring Me? (4)
You're So Beautiful (4)

**Your Love (Means
Everything To Me)** (4) *73*

WRIGHT, Gary

Born on 4/26/43 in Creskill, New Jersey. Pop-rock singer/songwriter/keyboardist. Appeared in *Captain Video* TV series at age seven. In the Broadway play *Fanny*. Co-leader of the rock group Spooky Tooth.

DEBUT DATE	PEAK POS	WKS CHR	GOLD	ARTIST — Album Title	$	Label & Number
8/23/75+	7	75 ▲		1 **The Dream Weaver**	$8	Warner 2868
4/24/76	172	4		2 That Was Only Yesterday ....[E-K]	$15	A&M 3528 [2]

GARY WRIGHT/SPOOKY TOOTH
includes cuts from his work with Spooky Tooth and his early solo albums

DEBUT DATE	PEAK POS	WKS CHR	GOLD	ARTIST — Album Title	$	Label & Number
1/22/77	23	15		3 The Light of Smiles	$8	Warner 2951
12/10/77+	117	9		4 Touch And Gone	$8	Warner 3137
3/17/79	147	5		5 Headin' Home	$8	Warner 3244
6/27/81	79	19		6 The Right Place	$8	Warner 3511

Are You Weepin' (3)
Blind Feeling (1)
Can't Find The Judge (1)
Can't Get Above Losing You
(4)
Child Of Light (3)
Close To You (6)
Comin' Apart (6)
Cotton Growing Man (2)
Dream Weaver (1) *2*
Empty Inside (3)
Evil Woman (2)
Fascinating Things (2)

Feel For Me (1)
Feelin' Bad (2)
Follow Next To You (5)
Got The Feelin' (6)
Heartbeat (6)
Holy Water (2)
I Am The Sky (3)
I Can Feel You Cryin' (5)
I Can't See The Reason (1)
I Know (2)
I'm Alright (3)
I'm The One Who'll Be By
Your Side (5)

Keep Love In Your Soul (5)
Let It Out (1)
Let Me Feel Your Love Again
(5)
Light Of Smiles (3)
Lost In My Emotions (4)
Love Is A Rose (6)
Love Is Alive (1) *2*
Love Is Why (5)
Love It Takes (4)
Love To Survive (2)
Love's Awake Inside (5)
Made To Love You (1) *79*

Moonbeams (5)
More Than A Heartache (6)
Much Higher (1)
Night Ride (4)
Nobody There At All (2)
Phantom Writer (3) *43*
Positive Feelins (2)
Power Of Love (1)
Really Wanna Know You
(6) *16*
Right Place (6)
Silent Fury (3)
Sing A Song (2)

Sky Eyes (4)
Something To Say (2)
Something Very Special (4)
Son Of Your Father (2)
Stand (5)
Stand For Our Rights (2)
Starry Eyed (4)
Stay Away (1)
Sunshine Help Me (2)
That Was Only Yesterday (2)
Time Machine (3)
Touch And Gone (4) *73*
Two Faced Man (2)

Waitin' For The Wind (2)
Water Sign (3)
Who Am I (3)
Wildfire (2)
Wrong Time (2)
You Don't Own Me (5)

WRIGHT, Michelle

Native of Morpeth, Ontario. Country singer.

DEBUT DATE	PEAK POS	WKS CHR	GOLD	ARTIST — Album Title	$	Label & Number
6/13/92	126	13		Now & Then	$12	Arista 18685

Change, The
Don't Start With Me

Fastest Healing Wounded
Heart

Guitar Talk
He Would Be Sixteen

If I'm Ever Over You
Little More Comfortable

Now & Then
One Time Around

Take It Like A Man

WRIGHT, Steven

Born on 12/6/55 in Boston. Comedian known for his "deadpan" delivery.

DEBUT DATE	PEAK POS	WKS CHR	GOLD	ARTIST — Album Title	$	Label & Number
11/23/85	192	2		I Have A Pony ....[C]	$8	Warner 25335

Ants
Apt.
Babies And Skiing

Book Store
Cross Country

Dog Stay
Hitchhiking

Ice
Jiggs Casey

Rachel
7's And Museums

Water
Winny

WYMAN, Bill

Born William Perks on 10/24/36 in London. Bass guitarist of The Rolling Stones, 1962-92. Married for less than two years to singer Mandy Smith (divorced by 1992).

DEBUT DATE	PEAK POS	WKS CHR	GOLD	ARTIST — Album Title	$	Label & Number
6/15/74	99	11		1 Monkey Grip	$12	Rolling S. 59102
3/27/76	166	5		2 Stone Alone	$12	Rolling S. 79103

Apache Woman (2)
Crazy Woman (1)
Every Sixty Seconds (2)
Feet (2)

Get It On (2)
Gimme Just One Chance (2)
I Wanna Get Me A Gun (1)
I'll Pull You Thro' (1)

If You Wanna Be Happy (2)
It's A Wonder (1)
Mighty Fine Time (1)
Monkey Grip Glue (1)

No More Foolin' (2)
Peanut Butter Time (2)
Pussy (1)
Quarter To Three (2)

Soul Satisfying (2)
What A Blow (1)
What's The Point (1)
White Lightnin' (1)

Wine & Wimmen (2)

★★435★★ WYNETTE, Tammy

Born Virginia Wynette Pugh on 5/5/42 in Itawamba County, Mississippi. With over 15 #1 country hits, dubbed "The First Lady of Country Music." Discovered by producer Billy Sherrill. Married to country star George Jones from 1969-75.

DEBUT DATE	PEAK POS	WKS CHR	GOLD	ARTIST — Album Title	$	Label & Number
9/7/68+	147	15		1 D-I-V-O-R-C-E	$12	Epic 26392
2/8/69	43	21		2 Stand By Your Man	$12	Epic 26451
5/24/69	189	3		3 Inspiration	$12	Epic 26423
9/6/69	37	61 ▲		4 Tammy's Greatest Hits ....[G]	$12	Epic 26486
2/21/70	83	11		5 The Ways To Love A Man	$10	Epic 26519
5/16/70	85	17		6 Tammy's Touch	$10	Epic 26463
8/15/70	145	2		7 The World Of Tammy Wynette ....[K]	$12	Epic 503 [2]
10/31/70	119	14		8 The First Lady	$10	Epic 30213
5/22/71	115	10		9 We Sure Can Love Each Other	$8	Epic 30658
9/18/71	118	8		10 Tammy's Greatest Hits, Volume II ....[G]	$8	Epic 30733
11/13/71	169	6		11 We Go Together	$10	Epic 30802

TAMMY WYNETTE & GEORGE JONES

DEBUT DATE	PEAK POS	WKS CHR	GOLD	ARTIST — Album Title	$	Label & Number
4/8/72	133	9		12 Bedtime Story	$8	Epic 31285

After Closing Time (11)
All Night Long (1)
Almost Persuaded (4)
Apartment #9 (4)
Baby, Come Home (9)
Battle Hymn Of The
Republic (3)
Bedtime Story (12) *86*
Bring Him Safely Home To
Me (9)
Buy Me A Daddy (8)
Cold Lonely Feeling (6)

Come On Home (1)
Count Your Blessings
Instead Of Sheep (3)
Cry (7)
Cry, Cry Again (2,7)
Crying In The Chapel (3,7)
D-I-V-O-R-C-E (1,4) *63*
Divorce Sale (6)
Don't Come Home A
Drinkin' (With Lovin' On
Your Mind) (7)

Don't Liberate Me (Love Me)
(9)
Don't Make Me Go To School
(2)
Don't Touch Me (7)
Enough Of A Woman (5)
Forever Yours (2)
Gentle On My Mind (1)
Good (7)
Good Lovin' (Makes It Right)
(10)
Have A Little Faith (9)

He (3)
He Knows All The Ways To
Love (1)
He Loves Me All The Way
(6,10) *97*
He Thinks I Love Him (6)
He'll Never Take The Place
Of You (1)
He's Got The Whole World In
His Hands (3)
He's Still My Man (8)
Honey (I Miss You) (1,7)

How Great Thou Art (3)
I Believe (3,7)
I Don't Wanna Play House (4)
I Got Me A Man (12)
I Know (5)
I Never Once Stopped Loving
You (8)
I Stayed Long Enough (2,7)
I Wish I Had A Mommy Like
You (8)
I'll See Him Through
(6,10) *100*

I'll Share My World With
You (5)
I'm Gonna Keep On Loving
Him (7)
I've Learned (2)
If I Were A Little Girl (2)
If This Is Our Last Time (12)
If You Think I Love You
(9)
It Is No Secret (What God
Can Do) (3,7)

DEBUT DATE	PEAK POS	WKS CHR	GOLD	ARTIST — Album Title	$	Label & Number

WYNETTE, Tammy — Cont'd

It Keeps Slipping My Mind (2)
It's Just A Matter Of Time (6)
It's My Way (2,7)
It's So Sweet (11)
Joey (2,7)
Joy Of Being A Woman (9)
Just A Closer Walk With Thee (3)
Just As Soon As I Get Over Loving You (12)
Kiss Away (1,7)
Legend Of Bonnie And Clyde (1,7)
Lifetime Left Together (11)
Lighter Shade Of Blue (6)
Livin' On Easy Street (11)

Lonely Days (And Nights More Lonely) (6)
Lonely Street (1)
Longing To Hold You Again (9)
Love Me, Love Me (6)
Love's The Answer (12)
Lovin' Kind (8)
Make Me Your Kind Of Woman (9)
May The Good Lord Bless And Keep You (3)
My Arms Stay Open Late (2,7)
My Daddy Doll (8)
My Elusive Dreams (4) *89*
Never Grow Cold (11)

Ode To Billie Joe (7)
Only Thing (9)
Only Time I'm Really Me (10)
Our Last Night Together (6,10)
Playin' Around With Love (8)
Reach Out Your Hand (12)
Run, Angel, Run (4)
Run, Woman, Run (8,10) *92*
Safe In These Lovin' Arms Of Mine (4)
Sally Trash (8)
Singing My Song (4,5) *75*
Someone I Used To Know (11)
Something To Brag About (11)

Stand By Your Man (2,4) *19*
Still Around (5,10)
Sweet Dreams (1)
Take Me (11)
Take Me Home And Love Me (12)
Take Me To Your World (4)
That's When I Feel It (12)
There Goes My Everything (7)
These Two (5)
Tonight My Baby's Coming Home (12)
Too Far Gone (4)
True And Lasting Love (8)
Twelfth Of Never (5)

Walk Through This World With Me (7)
Ways To Love A Man (5,10) *81*
We Go Together (11)
We Sure Can Love Each Other (9,10)
When There's A Fire In Your Heart (1)
When True Love Steps In (11)
Where Could You Go (But To Her) (5,7)
Wonders You Perform (10)
Yearning (To Kiss You) (5)
Yesterday (1,7)

You Can't Hang On (Lookin' On) (10)
You Make My Skies Turn Blue (6)
You'll Never Walk Alone (3)
You're Everything (11)
Your Good Girl's Gonna Go Bad (4)
Your Love's Been A Long Time Coming (12)

X

X

Los Angeles rock band: Christine "Exene" Cervenka (vocals), "John Doe" Nommensen (vocals), Tony Gilkyson (guitar, son of Canadian singer Terry Gilkyson) and D.J. Bonebrake (drums). Cervenka and Doe were married for a time. Cervenka recorded with The Knitters.

DEBUT DATE	PEAK POS	WKS CHR		ARTIST — Album Title	$	Label & Number
6/6/81	165	5	1	Wild Gift............	$12	Slash 107
7/17/82	76	15	2	Under The Big Black Sun	$8	Elektra 60150
10/8/83	86	23	3	More Fun In The New World	$8	Elektra 60283
8/17/85	89	14	4	Ain't Love Grand	$8	Elektra 60430
7/11/87	107	11	5	See How We Are	$8	Elektra 60492
5/14/88	175	5	6	Live At The Whiskey A Go-Go On The Fabulous Sunset Strip...... [L]	$10	Elektra 60788 [2]

Adult Books (1)
All Or Nothing (4)
Anyone Can Fill Your Shoes (5)
Around My Heart (4,6)
Back 2 The Base (1)
Because I Do (2,6)
Beyond And Back (1)
Blue Spark (2,6)
Breathless (3)
Burning House Of Love (4,6)
Call Of The Wreckin' Ball (6)
Come Back To Me (2)
Cyrano De Berger's Back (5)

Dancing With Tears In My Eyes (2)
Devil Doll (3,6)
Drunk In My Past (3)
4th Of July (5)
Have Nots (2)
Holiday Story (5)
Hot House (3)
House I Call Home (6)
How I (Learned My Lesson) (2)
Hungry Wolf (2,6)
I Must Not Think Bad Thoughts (3)

I See Red (3)
I'll Stand Up For You (4)
I'm Coming Over (1)
I'm Lost (5)
In The Time It Takes (5,6)
In This House That I Call Home (1)
It's Who You Know (1)
Johny Hit & Run Pauline (6)
Just Another Perfect Day (6)
Left & Right (5)
Little Honey (4)
Los Angeles (6)
Love Shack (4)

Make The Music Go Bang (3)
Motel Room In My Bed (2)
My Goodness (4,6)
My Soul Cries Your Name (4)
New World (3,6)
Once Over Twice (1,6)
Painting The Town Blue (3)
Poor Girl (3)
Real Child Of Hell (2)
Riding With Mary (2,6)
See How We Are (5)
Skin Deep Town (6)
So Long (6)
Some Other Time (1)

Supercharged (4)
Surprise Surprise (5,6)
True Love (3,6)
True Love Pt. #2 (3)
Under The Big Black Sun (2)
Unheard Music (6)
Universal Corner (1)
Watch The Sun Go Down (4)
We're Desperate (1)
We're Having Much More Fun (3)
What's Wrong With Me... (4)
When It Rains... (5)

When Our Love Passed Out On The Couch (1)
White Girl (1,6)
World's A Mess (6)
Year 1 (1,6)
You (5)

XAVIER

Eight-member R&B group — lead vocals by Xavier Smith and Ayanna Little.

DEBUT DATE	PEAK POS	WKS CHR		ARTIST — Album Title	$	Label & Number
4/24/82	129	7		Point Of Pleasure	$8	Liberty 51116

Dial The Love Man (634-5789)
Do It To The Max
Love Is On The One
Rock Me, Sock Me
Truly Devoted
What Goes Around
Work That Sucker To Death

X CLAN

Brooklyn-based rap group: Professor X the Overseer, Grand Verbalizer Funkin-Lesson Brother J., Architect Tractitioner Paradise and Rhythm Provider Sugar Shaft. Professor X (Lumumba Carson) is the son of black activist Sonny Carson.

DEBUT DATE	PEAK POS	WKS CHR		ARTIST — Album Title	$	Label & Number
6/2/90	97	25	1	To The East, Blackwards	$12	4th & B'way 4019
				CD includes bonus track		
6/6/92	31	12	2	Xodus	$12	Polydor 513225

A.D.A.M. (2)
Cosmic Ark (2)
Day Of Outrage, Operation Snatchback (1)
Earth Bound (1)
F.T.P. (2)

Fire & Earth (100% Natural) (2)
Foreplay (2)
Funk Liberation (2)
Funkin' Lesson (1)

Grand Verbalizer, What Time Is It? (1)
Heed The Word Of The Brother (1)
Holy Rum Swig (2)

In The Ways Of The Scales (1)
Ooh Baby (2)
Raise The Flag (1)
Rhythem Of God (2)
Shaft's Big Score (1)

Tribal Jam (1)
Verbal Milk (1)
Verbal Papp (2)
Verbs Of Power (1)
Xodus (2)

XTC

British new wave rock trio: Andy Partridge (guitar), Dave Gregory (keyboards) and Colin Moulding (bass).

DEBUT DATE	PEAK POS	WKS CHR		ARTIST — Album Title	$	Label & Number
1/26/80	176	8	1	Drums And Wires	$8	Virgin 13134
11/22/80+	41	24	2	Black Sea	$8	Virgin 13147
3/20/82	48	20	3	English Settlement	$8	Epic 37943
2/25/84	145	5	4	Mummer	$8	Geffen 4027
11/10/84	178	5	5	The Big Express	$8	Geffen 24054
1/24/87	70	29	6	Skylarking	$8	Geffen 24117
				later pressings substitute the track "Mermaid Smiled" with "Dear God"		
3/18/89	44	21	7	Oranges & Lemons	$10	Geffen 24218 [2]
5/16/92	97	11	8	Nonsuch	$12	Geffen 24474

Across This Antheap (7)
All Of A Sudden (It's Too Late) (3)
All You Pretty Girls (5)

Another Satellite (6)
Ball And Chain (3)
Ballad Of Peter Pumpkinhead (8)

Ballet For A Rainy Day (6)
Beating Of Hearts (4)
Big Day (6)
Books Are Burning (8)

Bungalow (8)
Burning With Optimism's Flames (2)
Chalkhills And Children (7)

Complicated Game (1)
Crocodile (8)
Cynical Days (7)
Dear God (6)

Dear Madam Barnum (8)
Deliver Us From The Elements (4)
Disappointed (8)

XTC — Cont'd

Dying (6)
Earn Enough For Us (6)
English Roundabout (3)
Everyday Story Of Smalltown (5)
Funk Pop A Roll (4)
Garden Of Earthly Delights (7)
Generals And Majors (2)
Grass (6)
Great Fire (4)
Helicopter (1)
Here Comes President Kill Again (7)
Hold Me My Daddy (7)
Holly Up On Poppy (8)
Human Alchemy (4)
Humble Daisy (8)

I Bought Myself A Liarbird (5)
I Remember The Sun (5)
In Loving Memory Of A Name (4)
It's Nearly Africa (3)
Jason And The Argonauts (3)
King For A Day (7)
Ladybird (4)
Life Begins At The Hop (4)
Living Through Another Cuba (2)
Love At First Sight (4)
Love On A Farmboy's Wages (4)
Loving, The (7)
Making Plans For Nigel (1)

Man Who Sailed Around His Soul (6)
Mayor Of Simpleton (7) 72
Me And The Wind (4)
Meeting Place (6)
Melt The Guns (3)
Mermaid Smiled (6)
Merely A Man (7)
Millions (1)
Miniature Sun (7)
My Bird Performs (8)
No Language In Our Lungs (2)
No Thugs In Our House (3)
1000 Umbrellas (6)
One Of The Millions (7)
Outside World (1)

Paper And Iron (Notes And Coins) (2)
Pink Thing (7)
Poor Skeleton Steps Out (7)
Real By Reel (1)
Reign Of Blows (5)
Respectable Street (2)
Roads Girdle The Globe (1)
Rocket From A Bottle (2)
Rook (8)
Runaways (3)
Sacrificial Bonfire (6)
Scarecrow People (7)
Scissor Man (1)
Seagulls Screaming Kiss Her, Kiss Her (5)
Season Cycle (6)
Senses Working Overtime (3)

Sgt. Rock (Is Going To Help Me) (2)
Shake You Donkey Up (5)
Smartest Monkeys (8)
Snowman (3)
Summer's Cauldron (6)
Ten Feet Tall (1)
That Is The Way (1)
That Wave (8)
That's Really Super, Supergirl (6)
Then She Appeared (8)
This World Over (5)
Towers Of London (2)
Train Running Low On Soul Coal (5)
Travels In Nihilon (2)
Ugly Underneath (8)

Wake Up (5)
War Dance (8)
When You're Near Me I Have Difficulty (1)
Wonderland (4)
Wrapped In Grey (8)
You're The Wish You Are I Had (5)

XYMOX

Rock trio from Amsterdam, Holland: Ronny Moorings, Pieter Nooten and Anka Wolbert.

6/3/89	165	10		1 Twist Of Shadows	$8	Wing 839233
5/11/91	163	2		2 Phoenix	$12	Wing 848516

At The End Of The Day (2)
Believe Me Sometimes (2)
Blind Hearts (1)
Clementina (1)

Craving (1)
Crossing The Water (2)
Dancing Barefoot (1)
Evelyn (1)

Imagination (1) 85
In A City (1)
Mark The Days (2)
Million Things (1)

Obsession (1)
Phoenix Of My Heart (medley) (1)
River, The (1)

Shore Down Under (1)
Smile Like Heaven (2)
Tonight (1)
Wild Thing (medley) (2)

Wonderland (2)
Written In The Stars (2)

XYZ

Southern California hard-rock quartet led by vocalist Terry Iloius and guitarist Marc Richard Diglio.

12/16/89+	99	24		XYZ	$8	Enigma 73525

After The Rain
Come On N' Love Me

Follow The Night
Inside Out

Maggy
Nice Day To Die

Souvenirs
Take What You Can

Tied Up
What Keeps Me Loving You

Y

YACHTS

Rock quartet from Liverpool, England — Martin Watson, lead singer.

10/20/79	179	3		S.O.S.	$8	Polydor 6220

Box 202
Heads Will Turn

I Can't Stay Long
In A Second

Look Back In Love
Love You, Love You

Mantovani's Hits
Semaphore Love

Suffice To Say
Tantamount To Bribery

Then And Now
Yachting Type

YAMASHTA, Stomu

Japanese eclectic composer/percussionist.

8/21/76	60	12		1 Go	$8	Island 9387

STOMU YAMASHTA/STEVE WINWOOD/MICHAEL SHRIEVE

10/15/77	156	6		2 Go Too	$8	Arista 4138

both albums feature the guitar work of Al DiMeola

Air Over (1)
Beauty (2)
Carnival (1)
Crossing The Line (1)

Ecliptic (2)
Ghost Machine (1)
Madness (2)
Man Of Leo (1)

Mysteries Of Love (2)
Nature (1)
Seen You Before (2)
Solitude (1)

Space Requiem (1)
Space Song (1)
Space Theme (1)
Stellar (1)

Surfspin (1)
Time Is Here (1)
Wheels Of Fortune (2)
Winner/Loser (2)

You And Me (2)

Y&T

San Francisco heavy-metal quartet: Dave Meniketti (vocals, guitar), Joey Alves, Philip Kennemore and Leonard Haze (replaced by Jimmy DeGrasso in 1986).

9/10/83	103	12		1 Mean Streak	$8	A&M 4960
8/18/84	46	17		2 In Rock We Trust	$8	A&M 5007
7/20/85	70	17		3 Open Fire [L]	$8	A&M 5076
11/23/85	91	12		4 Down For The Count	$8	A&M 5101
7/11/87	78	13		5 Contagious	$8	Geffen 24142
6/2/90	110	8		6 Ten	$12	Geffen 24283

All American Boy (4)
Anything For Money (4)
Anytime At All (4)
Armed And Dangerous (5)
Barroom Boogie (3)
Bodily Harm (5)
Break Out Tonight! (2)
Breaking Away (1)
City (6)
Come In From The Rain (6)
Contagious (5)

Don't Be Afraid Of The Dark (6)
Don't Stop Runnin' (2)
Don't Tell Me What To Wear (4)
Down And Dirty (1)
Eyes Of A Stranger (5)
Face Like An Angel (4)
Fight For Your Life (5)
Forever (3)
Girl Crazy (6)
Go For The Throat (3)

Goin' Off The Deep End (6)
Hands Of Time (4)
Hang 'Em High (1)
Hard Times (6)
I Believe In You (3)
I'll Cry For You (5)
I'll Keep On Believin' (Do You Know) (2)
In The Name Of Rock (4)
Kid Goes Crazy (5)
L.A. Rocks (5)
Let It Out (6)

Life, Life, Life (2)
Lipstick And Leather (2)
Lonely Side Of Town (1)
Looks Like Trouble (4)
Lucy (6)
Masters And Slaves (2)
Mean Streak (1)
Midnight In Tokyo (1)
Open Fire (3)
Red Hot & Ready (6)
Rescue Me (3)
Rhythm Or Not (5)

Rock & Roll's Gonna Save The World (2)
Sentimental Fool (1)
She's A Liar (2)
She's Gone (6)
Straight Thru The Heart (1)
Summertime Girls (3,4) 55
Surrender (6)
Take You To The Limit (1)
Temptation (5)
Ten Lovers (2)
This Time (2)

25 Hours A Day (6)
(Your Love Is) Drivin' Me Crazy (2)
Your Mama Don't Dance (4)

YANKOVIC, "Weird Al"

Born on 10/24/59 in Lynwood, California. Novelty singer/accordionist. Specializes in song parodies. Starred in the 1989 film *UHF*.

5/21/83	139	8		1 "Weird Al" Yankovic [N]	$8	Rock 'n' R. 38679
3/17/84	17	23	●	2 "Weird Al" Yankovic In 3-D [N]	$8	Rock 'n' R. 39221

DEBUT DATE	PEAK POS	WKS CHR	GOLD	ARTIST — Album Title	$	Label & Number

YANKOVIC, "Weird Al" — Cont'd

DEBUT DATE	PEAK POS	WKS CHR	GOLD			$	Label & Number
7/13/85	50	16	●	3 Dare To Be Stupid	[N]	$8	Rock 'n' R. 40033
11/15/86	177	4		4 Polka Party!	[N]	$8	Rock 'n' R. 40520
5/7/88	27	26	●	5 Even Worse	[N]	$8	Rock 'n' R. 44149
8/19/89	146	4		6 UHF/Original Motion Picture Soundtrack And Other Stuff	[S]	$8	Rock 'n' R. 45265

all of above produced by Rick Derringer

| 5/2/92 | 17 | 27 | ● | 7 Off The Deep End | [N] | $12 | Scotti Br. 75256 |

Addicted To Spuds (4)
Airline Amy (5)
Alimony (5)
Another One Rides The Bus (1)
Attack Of The Radioactive Hamsters From A Planet Near Mars (6)
Biggest Ball Of Twine In Minnesota (6)
Brady Bunch (2)
Buckingham Blues (1)
Buy Me A Condo (2)
Cable TV (3)
Check's In The Mail (1)
Christmas At Ground Zero (4)

Dare To Be Stupid (3)
Dog Eat Dog (4)
Don't Wear Those Shoes (4)
Eat It (2) **12**
Fat (5) **99**
Fun Zone (6)
Gandhi II (3)
Generic Blues (6)
George Of The Jungle (3)
Girls Just Want To Have Lunch (3)
Good Enough For Now (4)
Good Old Days (5)
Gotta Boogie (1)
Happy Birthday (1)
Here's Johnny (4)
Hooked On Polkas Medley (3)

Hot Rocks Polka (6)
I Can't Watch This (7)
I Lost On Jeopardy (2) **81**
I Love Rocky Road (1)
I Think I'm A Clone Now (5)
I Want A New Duck (3)
I Was Only Kidding (7)
I'll Be Mellow When I'm Dead (1)
Isle Thing (6)
King Of Suede (2) **62**
Lasagna (4)
Let Me Be Your Hog (6)
Like A Surgeon (3) **47**
Living With A Hernia (4)
Melanie (5)
Midnight Star (2)

Money For Nothing/Beverly Hillbillies (6)
Mr. Frump In The Iron Lung (1)
Mr. Popeil (3)
My Bologna (1)
Nature Trail To Hell (4)
One More Minute (3)
One Of Those Days (4)
Plumbing Song (4)
Polka Party! (4)
Polka Your Eyes Out (7)
Polkas On 45 (2)
Ricky (1) **63**
Rocky XIII, Theme From (2)
She Drives Like Crazy (6)

Slime Creatures From Outer Space (3)
Smells Like Nirvana (7) **35**
Spam (6)
Spatula City (6)
Stop Draggin' My Car Around (1)
Stuck In A Closet With Vanna White (5)
Such A Groovy Guy (1)
Taco Grande (7)
That Boy Could Dance (2)
This Is The Life (3)
(This Song's Just) Six Words Long (5)
Toothless People (4)
Trigger Happy (7)

Twister (5)
UHF (6)
Velvet Elvis (5)
When I Was Your Age (7)
White Stuff (5)
Yoda (3)
You Don't Love Me Anymore (7)
You Make Me (5)

YANNI

Born Yiannis Chryssolmalis in Kalamata, Greece. New Age keyboardist/composer. National champion swimmer of Greece at age 14. Moved to Minneapolis in 1973 to earn psychology degree.

| 8/4/90+ | 29 | 93 | ▲ | 1 Reflections Of Passion | [I-K] | $12 | Private M. 2067 |
| 11/30/91+ | 60 | 17 | | 2 In Celebration Of Life | [I-K] | $12 | Private M. 2093 |

above 2 feature selections from albums released from 1986-89

| 3/28/92 | 32 | 35 | ● | 3 Dare to Dream | [I] | $12 | Private M. 82096 |

vocals on one track by Mona Lisa

Acroyali (1)
After The Sunrise (1)
Almost A Whisper (1)
Aria (3)
Desire (3)
Face In The Photograph (3)
Farewell (1)

Felitsa (3)
First Touch (1)
Flight Of Fantasy (1)
In The Mirror (3)
Keys To Imagination (2)
Looking Glass (2)
Love For Life (3)

Marching Season (2)
Mermaid, The (1)
Nice To Meet You (3)
Night To Remember (3)
Nostalgia (1)
Once Upon A Time (3)
Quiet Man (1)

Rain Must Fall (1)
Reflections Of Passion (1)
Sand Dance (2)
Santorini (1)
Secret Vows (1)
So Long My Friend (3)
Someday (2)

Song For Antarctica (2)
Standing In Motion (2)
Swept Away (1)
To The One Who Knows (3)
True Nature (2)
Walkabout (2)
Within Attraction (2)

Word In Private (1)
You Only Live Once (3)

YARBROUGH, Glenn

Born on 1/12/30 in Milwaukee. Lead singer of The Limeliters (1959-63). Folk singer.

9/19/64	142	4		1 One More Round		$15	RCA 2905
5/8/65	112	8		2 Come Share My Life		$15	RCA 3301
6/12/65	35	24		3 Baby The Rain Must Fall		$15	RCA 3422
11/6/65	75	12		4 It's Gonna Be Fine		$15	RCA 3472
6/25/66	61	24		5 The Lonely Things *		$15	RCA 3539
11/5/66	85	9		6 Live At The hungry i	[L]	$15	RCA 3661
5/27/67	159	14		7 For Emily, Whenever I May Find Her		$15	RCA 3801
9/16/67	141	18		8 Honey & Wine		$15	RCA 3860
11/9/68	188	2		9 Each Of Us Alone (the words and music of Rod McKuen) *		$10	Warner 1736
5/10/69	189	5		10 Glenn Yarbrough Sings The Rod McKuen Songbook *	[K]	$12	RCA 6018 [2]

*all songs composed by Rod McKuen

Above The Wave (9)
Ain't You Glad You're Livin', Joe (8,10)
Alamo Junction (10)
All The Time (1)
Baby, I'm Gone Again (1)
Baby The Rain Must Fall (3) **12**
Beautiful Strangers (9)
Billy Goat Hill (3)
Brownstone (5)
Bull Frog Song (3)
Channing Way, 2 (5)
Cloudy Summer Afternoon (1)
Come Share My Life (2)
Comes And Goes (7)
Crucifixion (7)
Down In The Jungle (4)
Each Of Us Alone (9)
Everybody's Rich But Us (3,10)
Everybody's Wrong (7)

Fields Of Wonder (8,10)
For Emily, Whenever I May Find Her (7)
French Girl (7)
Gently Here Beside Me (1)
Goin' Down The Track (900 Miles) (6)
Golden Under The Sun (7)
Half A World Away (4,10)
Happy Birthday To Me (8,10)
Happy Whistler (2)
Hello (5)
Her Lover (1)
Here Am I (8)
Honey And Wine (8)
How Deep Is Down (6,10)
Hummingbird (3)
I Hate To See The Sun Go Down (4)
I Wonder (1)
I'll Catch The Sun (9)
I'll Remember You (8)

I'm Strong But I Like Roses (9)
I've Been To Town (3)
Island Of The Mind (4,10)
Isle In The Water (1,10)
It's Raining (9)
Kind Of Loving (5)
Listen To The Warm (9)
Lonely Things (5)
Lonesome (3)
Long Time Blues (3)
Love Come A-Tricklin' Down (2)
Love, Let Me Not Hunger (3,10)
Love's Been Good To Me (1)
Lovers, The (1)
Mattie Groves (3)
Me And My Dog (Old Blue) (6)
Mermaid, The (6)
More I Cannot Wish You (2)

Music Of The World A Turnin' (6)
Never Let Her Go (4)
New "Frankie And Johnnie" Song (1)
Night Song (5)
No One To Talk My Troubles To (2)
Now That They're Playing A Love Song (4,10)
One Day Soon (6,10)
One More Round (1)
Only Love (6,10)
People Change (5)
Pleasures Of The Harbor (7)
Rain Drops (1)
Ring Of Bright Water (4)
Rose (6,10)
Rusting In The Rain (3,10)
She (3,10)
She's Too Far Above Me (3)
Single Man (7)
So Long, San Francisco (5)

So Many Others (8)
Some Trust In Chariots (6,10)
Sometimes (4,10)
Stanyan Street (2,10)
Stanyan Street, Revisited (5)
Summer Sunshine (4)
Summer's Long (6,10)
Summertime Of Days (5)
Ten O'Clock, All Is Well (The Town Crier's Song) (1)
Thank You (8,10)
That's The Way It's Gonna Be (2)
They Are Gone (8)
Things Men Do (6,10)
Times Gone By (10)
Tomorrow Is A Long Time (7)
Until It's Time For You To Go (7)
Walk On Little Boy (3)
Walking On Air (8)

Warm And Gentle Girls (2,10)
Way The World Would Be (1)
What The World Needs Now (4)
What You Gonna Do? (6)
When Flora Was Mine (10)
When Summer Ends (2,10)
Where Are We Now? (9)
Where Are You Going With The Rain (6)
Where Does Love Go (4)
Women, The (5)
Word Before Goodbye (5)
Worry Is A Rockin' Chair (7)
Young Girl (5)

YARBROUGH & PEOPLES

Dallas soul duo: Cavin Yarbrough and Alisa Peoples. Discovered by The Gap Band.

| 12/27/80+ | 16 | 24 | ● | 1 The Two Of Us | | $8 | Mercury 3834 |
| 4/14/84 | 90 | 16 | | 2 Be A Winner | | $8 | Total Exp. 5700 |

Be A Winner (2)
Come To Me (1)
Crazy (1)

Don't Stop The Music (1) **19**
Don't Waste Your Time (2) **48**

Easy Tonight (1)
I Believe I'm Falling In Love (1)
I Gave My All (To You) (2)

I Only Love You (2)
I Want You Back Again (1)
I'll Be There (1)
I'm Ready To Jam (2)

Let Me Have It (From The Start) (2)
Power, The (2)
Third Degree (1)

Two Of Us (1)
Who Said That (2)
You're My Song (1)

DEBUT DATE	PEAK POS	WKS CHR	GOLD	ARTIST — Album Title	$	Label & Number

YARDBIRDS, The

Legendary rock group formed in Surrey, England in 1963. Consisted of Keith Relf (electrocuted on 5/14/76 [age 33]; vocals, harmonica), Anthony "Top" Topham and Chris Dreja (guitars), Paul "Sam" Samwell-Smith (bass, keyboards) and Jim McCarty (drums). Formed as the Metropolitan Blues Quartet at Kingston Art School. Topham replaced by Eric Clapton in 1963. Clapton replaced by Jeff Beck in 1965. Samwell-Smith left in 1966, Dreja switched to bass and Jimmy Page (guitar) was added. Beck left in December 1966. Group disbanded in July 1968. Page formed the New Yardbirds in October 1968, which evolved into Led Zeppelin. Relf and McCarty formed Renaissance in 1969. Relf later in Armageddon, 1975; McCarty in Illusion, 1977. Also see Herbie Hancock, and Eric Clapton's *History Of Eric Clapton* and *Crossroads* albums.

DEBUT DATE	PEAK POS	WKS CHR	GOLD	ARTIST — Album Title	$	Label & Number
7/31/65	96	11		1 For Your Love	$50	Epic 26167
12/18/65+	53	33		2 Having a Rave Up with The Yardbirds	$40	Epic 26177
				side 2: live tracks from first British album *Five Live Yardbirds*		
8/27/66	52	16		3 Over Under Sideways Down	$50	Epic 26210
4/29/67	28	37		4 The Yardbirds' Greatest Hits	[G] $35	Epic 26246
8/12/67	80	8		5 Little Games	$60	Epic 26313
10/3/70	155	6		6 The Yardbirds/Featuring Performances By Jeff Beck, Eric Clapton, Jimmy Page	[K] $50	Epic 30135 [2]

Certain Girl (1,6)
Drinking Muddy Water (5,6)
Ever Since The World Began (3,6)
Evil Hearted You (2)
Farewell (3,6)
For Your Love (1,4) 6
Glimpses (5)
Good Morning Little Schoolgirls (1)
Got To Hurry (1,6)
Happenings Ten Years Time Ago (4) 30
He's Always There (3)
Heart Full Of Soul (2,4) 9
Here 'Tis (2,6)
Hot House Of Omagarashid (3,6)
I Ain't Done Wrong (1,6)
I Ain't Got You (1,6)
I Can't Make Your Way (3)
I Wish You Would (1,6)
I'm A Man (2,4) 17
I'm Not Talking (1,4)
Jeff's Boogie (3,6)
Little Games (5,6) 51
Little Soldier Boy (5)
Lost Woman (3,6)
My Girl Sloopy (1)
New York City Blues (4)
No Excess Baggage (5)
Only The Black Rose (5,6)
Over Under Sideways Down (3,4) 13
Putty (In Your Hands) (1)
Respectable (2)
Shapes Of Things (4) 11
Smile On Me (5,6)
Smokestack Lightning (2,4)
Stealing, Stealing (5)
Still I'm Sad (2,4)
Sweet Music (1)
Tinker, Tailor, Soldier, Sailor (2,6)
Train Kept A-Rollin' (2,6)
Turn Into Earth (3,6)
What Do You Want (3,6)
White Summer (5,6)
You're A Better Man Than I (2)

YARROW, Peter

Born on 5/31/38 in New York City. Folk singer/songwriter/guitarist. Peter of Peter, Paul & Mary. Wrote Mary MacGregor's "Torn Between Two Lovers."

DEBUT DATE	PEAK POS	WKS CHR	GOLD	ARTIST — Album Title	$	Label & Number
3/4/72	163	8		1 Peter	$12	Warner 2599

Beautiful City
Don't Ever Take Away My Freedom 100
Goodbye Josh
Greenwood
Mary Beth
Plato's Song
River Of Jordan
Side Road
Take Off Your Mask
Tall Pine Trees
Weave Me The Sunshine
Wings Of Time

YAZ

British electronic pop duo: Genevieve Alison Moyet (vocals) and Vince Clarke (formerly of Depeche Mode; keyboards, synthesizers). Duo formerly named Yazoo. Clarke later formed Erasure, and Moyet went solo.

DEBUT DATE	PEAK POS	WKS CHR	GOLD	ARTIST — Album Title	$	Label & Number
10/2/82	92	32	▲	1 Upstairs At Eric's	$8	Sire 23737
				YAZOO		
8/13/83	69	13		2 You And Me Both	$8	Sire 23903

And On (2)
Anyone (2)
Bad Connection (1)
Bring Your Love Down (Didn't I) (1)
Don't Go (1)
Good Times (2)
Goodbye Seventies (1)
I Before E Except After C (1)
In My Room (1)
Midnight (1)
Mr. Blue (2)
Nobody's Diary (2)
Ode To Boy (2)
Only You (1) 67
Situation (1) 73
Softly Over (2)
State Farm (2)
Sweet Thing (2)
Too Pieces (1)
Unmarked (2)
Walk Away From Love (2)
Winter Kills (1)

YEARWOOD, Trisha

Native of Monticello, Georgia. Country singer. Sang backup on Garth Brooks' first album.

DEBUT DATE	PEAK POS	WKS CHR	GOLD	ARTIST — Album Title	$	Label & Number
7/20/91	31	82	▲	1 Trisha Yearwood	$12	MCA 10297
9/19/92	46	21↑	●	2 Hearts In Armor	$12	MCA 10641

Down On My Knees (2)
Fools Like Me (1)
For Reasons I've Forgotten (2)
Hearts In Armor (2)
Like We Never Had A Broken Heart (1)
Lonesome Dove (1)
Nearest Distant Shore (2)
Oh Lonesome You (2)
She's In Love With The Boy (1)
That's What I Like About You (1)
Victim Of The Game (1)
Walkaway Joe (2)
When Goodbye Was A Word (1)
Whisper Of Your Heart (1)
Woman Before Me (1)
Woman Walk The Line (2)
Wrong Side Of Memphis (2)
You Don't Have To Move That Mountain (2)
You Done Me Wrong (And That Ain't Right) (1)
You Say You Will (2)

YELLO

Computer/synthesizer trio from Zurich, Switzerland: Dieter Meier, Boris Blank and Carlos Peron (who left to pursue a solo career in late 1982).

DEBUT DATE	PEAK POS	WKS CHR	GOLD	ARTIST — Album Title	$	Label & Number
7/16/83	184	4		1 You Gotta Say Yes To Another Excess	$8	Elektra 60271
9/26/87	92	10		2 One Second	$8	Mercury 832765
4/15/89	152	9		3 Flag	$8	Mercury 836426

Alhambra (3)
Blazing Saddles (3)
Call It Love (2)
Crash Dance (1)
Dr Van Steiner (2)
Goldrush (2)
Great Mission (3)
Hawaiian Chance (2)
Heavy Whispers (1)
I Love You (1)
La Habanera (2)
Le Secret Farida (2)
Lost Again (1)
Moon On Ice (2)
No More Words (1)
Of Course I'm Lying (3)
Oh Yeah (2) 51
Otto Di Catania (3)
Pumping Velvet (1)
Race, The (3)
Rhythm Divine (2)
Salut Mayoumba (1)
Santiago (2)
Si Senor The Hairy Grill (2)
Smile On You (1)
Swing (1)
3rd Of June (3)
Tied Up (3)
Tied Up In Gear (3)
You Gotta Say Yes To Another Excess (1)

YELLOWJACKETS

Los Angeles-based, pop-jazz group formed in 1980 as Robben Ford's backing band.

DEBUT DATE	PEAK POS	WKS CHR	GOLD	ARTIST — Album Title	$	Label & Number
5/28/83	145	10		1 Mirage A Trois	[I] $8	Warner 23813
4/13/85	179	4		2 Samurai Samba	[I] $8	Warner 25204
9/6/86	195	2		3 Shades	[I] $8	MCA 5752

And You Know That (3)
Black Tie (3)
Booby Trap, Theme From ...see: Oasis
Claire's Song (1)
Daddy's Gonna Miss You (2)
Deat Beat (2)
Elamar (1)
Goin' Home (2)
Homecoming (2)
I Got Rhythm (1)
Lonely Weekend (2)
Los Mambos (2)
Man In The Moon (1)
New Shoes (3)
Nimbus (1)
Oasis (3)
One Family (3)
Pass It On (1)
Regular Folks (3)
Revelation (1)
Samurai Samba (2)
Silverlake (2)
Sonja's Sanfona (3)
Sylvania (2)
Top Secret (1)

YELLOW MAGIC Orchestra

Japanese electronic trio: Ryuichi Sakamoto, Yukihiro Takahashi and Haruomi Hosono.

DEBUT DATE	PEAK POS	WKS CHR	GOLD	ARTIST — Album Title	$	Label & Number
1/26/80	81	21		1 Yellow Magic Orchestra	[I] $8	Horizon 736
9/20/80	177	2		2 X Multiplies	$8	A&M 4813

DEBUT DATE	PEAK POS	WKS CHR	GOLD	ARTIST — Album Title	$	Label & Number

YELLOW MAGIC Orchestra — Cont'd

Behind The Mask (2)
Bridge Over Troubled Music (1)
Citizens Of Science (2)

Computer Game "Theme From The Circus" (1) 60
Computer Game (Theme from The Invader) (1)

Cosmic Surfin' (1)
Day Tripper (2)
Firecracker (1)
La Femme Chinoise (1)

Mad Pierrot (1)
Multiplies (2)
Nice Age (2)
Rydeen (2)

Simoon (1)
Solid State Survivor (2)
Technopolis (2)
Yellow Magic (Tong Poo) (1)

★★111★★ **YES**

Progressive rock group formed in London in 1968. Consisted of Jon Anderson (vocals), Peter Banks (guitar), Tony Kaye (keyboards), Chris Squire (bass) and Bill Bruford (drums). Banks replaced by Steve Howe in 1971. Kaye (joined Badfinger in 1978) replaced by Rick Wakeman in 1971. Bruford left to join King Crimson, replaced by Alan White in late 1972. Wakeman replaced by Patrick Moraz in 1974, re-joined in 1976 when Moraz left. Wakeman and Anderson left in 1980, replaced by The Buggles' Trevor Horne (guitar) and Geoff Downes (keyboards). Group disbanded in 1980. Howe and Downes joined Asia. Re-formed in 1983 with Anderson, Kaye, Squire, White and South African guitarist Trevor Rabin. Anderson left group in 1988. Anderson, Bruford, Wakeman and Howe formed self-named group in early 1989. Yes reunited in 1991 with Anderson, Bruford, Wakeman, Howe, Kaye, Squire, White and Rabin.

DEBUT DATE	PEAK POS	WKS CHR	GOLD	#	Album Title	$	Label & Number
5/8/71+	40	50	●	1	The Yes Album	$12	Atlantic 8243
1/22/72	4	46	●	2	Fragile	$10	Atlantic 7211
10/7/72	3	32	●	3	Close To The Edge	$10	Atlantic 7244
5/26/73	12	32	●	4	Yessongs [L]	$15	Atlantic 100 [3]
2/2/74	6	27	●	5	Tales From Topographic Oceans	$12	Atlantic 908 [2]
12/28/74+	5	16	●	6	Relayer	$8	Atlantic 18122
3/22/75	17	12	●	7	Yesterdays	$8	Atlantic 18103
					featuring cuts from their first 2 albums (uncharted) *Yes* and *Time and a Word* [K]		
7/30/77	8	21	●	8	Going For The One	$8	Atlantic 19106
10/14/78	10	14	▲	9	Tormato	$8	Atlantic 19202
9/13/80	18	19	●	10	Drama	$8	Atlantic 16019
12/20/80+	43	12	●	11	Yesshows [L]	$12	Atlantic 510 [2]
					concert recordings from 1976-78		
1/9/82	142	5	●	12	Classic Yes [K]	$8	Atlantic 19320
12/3/83+	5	53	▲	13	90125	$8	Atco 90125
					title refers to label number		
11/30/85	81	11	●	14	9012Live - The Solos [L]	$8	Atco 90474
					accent on solo performances by the group members		
10/17/87	15	30	▲	15	Big Generator	$8	Atco 90522
7/1/89	30	16	●	16	Anderson, Bruford, Wakeman, Howe	$8	Arista 90126
5/18/91	15	19	●	17	Union	$12	Arista 8643

All Good People (medley) (1,4)
Almost Like Love (15)
Amazing Grace (14)
America (7) *46*
Ancient, The (5)
And You And I Medley (3,4,12) *42*
Angkor Wat (17)
Arriving UFO (9)
Astral Traveller (7)
Awaken (8)
Big Generator (15)
Birthright (16)
Brother Of Mine Medley (16)
Cans And Brahms (2)
Changes (13,14)
Cinema (13)
Circus Of Heaven (9)
City Of Love (13)
Clap, The (1)

Close To The Edge Medley (3,4)
Dangerous (Look In The Light Of What You're Searching For) (17)
Dear Father (7)
Does It Really Happen? (10)
Don't Kill The Whale (9,11)
Evensong (1)
Final Eyes (15)
Fish (Schindleria Praematurus) (2,4,12)
Fist Of Fire (16)
Five Per Cent For Nothing (2)
Future Times (medley) (9)
Gates Of Delirium (6,11)
Going For The One (8,11)
Heart Of The Sunrise (2,4,12)
Hearts (13)
Hold On (13,14)
Holding On (17)

Holy Lamb (Song For Harmonic Convergence) (16)
I Would Have Waited Forever (17)
I'm Running (15)
Into The Lens (10)
It Can Happen (13) *51*
Leave It (13) *24*
Let's Pretend (16)
Lift Me Up (17) *86*
Long Distance Runaround (2,4,12)
Looking Around (7)
Love Will Find A Way (15) *30*
Machine Messiah (10)
Madrigal (9)
Masquerade (17)
Meeting, The (16)
Miracle Of Life (17)

Mood For A Day (2,4)
More We Live - Let Go (17)
On The Silent Wings Of Freedom (9)
Onward (9)
Order Of The Universe Medley (16)
Our Song (13)
Owner Of A Lonely Heart (13) *1*
Parallels (8,11)
Perpetual Change (1,4)
Quartet Medley (16)
Rejoice (medley) (9)
Release, Release (9)
Remembering (5)
Revealing Science Of God (5)
Rhythm Of Love (15) *40*
Ritual (5,11)
Roundabout (2,4) *13*
Run Through The Light (10)

Saving My Heart (17)
Shock To The System (17)
Shoot High Aim Low (15)
Si (14)
Siberian Khatru (3,4)
Silent Talking (17)
Six Wives Of Henry VIII, Excerpts From The (4)
Solly's Beard (14)
Soon (14)
Sound Chaser (6)
South Side Of The Sky (2)
Starship Trooper Medley (1,4,12)
Survival (7)
Sweet Dreams (7)
Take The Water To The Mountain (7)
Teakbois (16)
Tempus Fugit (10)
Themes Medley (16)

Then (7)
Time And A Word (7,11)
To Be Over (6)
Turn Of The Century (8)
Venture, A (1)
We Have Heaven (2)
White Car (10)
Whitefish (14)
Without Hope You Cannot Start The Day (17)
Wonderous Stories (8,11,12)
Your Move (medley) (1,4) *40*
Yours Is No Disgrace (1,4,12)

YIPES!!

Milwaukee rock quintet — Pat McCurdy, lead singer.

DEBUT DATE	PEAK POS	WKS CHR	GOLD	#	Album Title	$	Label & Number
10/6/79	177	4			Yipes!	$8	Millennium 7745

Ballad Of Roy Orbison
East Side Kids

Girls Get In Trouble

Good Boys
Hangin' Around

Last Of The Angry Young Men

Me And My Face
Out In California

Russian Roll
This Is Your Life

YOAKAM, Dwight

Country singer/songwriter. Born on 10/23/56 in Pikesville, Kentucky. Played in southern Ohio before moving to Los Angeles in the early '80s. First recorded for Oak Records. Member of the Buzzin' Cousins, group which appeared in the 1992 film *Falling from Grace*.

DEBUT DATE	PEAK POS	WKS CHR	GOLD	#	Album Title	$	Label & Number
4/19/86	61	65	▲	1	Guitars, Cadillacs, Etc., Etc.	$8	Reprise 25372
5/16/87	55	28	●	2	Hillbilly Deluxe	$8	Reprise 25567
8/20/88	68	15	●	3	Buenas Noches From A Lonely Room	$8	Reprise 25749
10/14/89	68	10	●	4	Just Lookin' For A Hit [G]	$8	Reprise 25989
11/17/90+	96	75	▲	5	If There Was A Way	$12	Reprise 26344

Always Late With Your Kisses (2)
Buenas Noches From A Lonely Room (She Wore Red Dresses) (3)
Bury Me (1)
Dangerous Man (5)
Distance Between You And Me (5)
Floyd County (3)
Guitars, Cadillacs (1,4)

Heart That You Own (5)
Heartaches By The Number (1)
Hold On To God (3)
Home Of The Blues (3)
Honky Tonk Man (1,4)
I Don't Need It Done (5)
I Got You (3,4)
I Hear You Knockin' (3)
I Sang Dixie (3,4)
I'll Be Gone (1)

If There Was A Way (5)
It Only Hurts When I Cry (5)
It Won't Hurt (1)
Johnson's Love (2)
Let's Work Together (5)
Little Sister (2)
Little Ways (2,4)
Long White Cadillac (4)
Miner's Prayer (1)
Nothing's Changed Here (5)
One More Name (3)

Please, Please Baby (2,4)
Readin', Rightin', Rt. 23 (2)
Ring Of Fire (1)
Sad, Sad Music (5)
Send A Message To My Heart (5)
Send Me The Pillow (3)
Sin City (4)
Since I Started Drinkin' Again (5)
Smoke Along The Track (2)

South Of Cincinnati (1)
Streets Of Bakersfield (3,4)
Takes A Lot To Rock You (5)
This Drinkin' Will Kill Me (2)
1,000 Miles (2)
Throughout All Time (2)
Turn It On, Turn It Up, Turn Me Loose (5)
Twenty Years (1)
What I Don't Know (5)
You're The One (5)

YOST, Dennis — see CLASSICS IV

DEBUT DATE	PEAK POS	WKS CHR	GOLD	ARTIST — Album Title	$	Label & Number

YOUNG, Barry
Pop singer patterned after Dean Martin.

| 1/1/66 | **67** | 12 | | One Has My Name .... | **$15** | Dot 25672 |

I Gotta Have My Baby Back	I'll Never Smile Again	Laughing On The Outside	**One Has My Name (The**	Since You Have Gone From	Yesterday
I Miss You So	In The Chapel In The	(Crying On The Inside)	**Other Has My Heart) 13**	Me	You'll Never Know
I Still Need You	Moonlight		Show Me The Way	Why	

YOUNG, Jesse Colin
Folk-rock singer. Born Perry Miller on 11/11/44 in New York City. Leader of The Youngbloods.

3/25/72	**157**	6		1 Together	**$12**	Raccoon 2588
10/6/73	**51**	44		2 Song For Juli	**$8**	Warner 2734
2/9/74	**172**	6		3 The Soul Of A City Boy .... [R]	**$12**	Capitol 11267
				reissue of Jesse's first album (released in 1964)		
4/20/74	**37**	29		4 Light Shine	**$8**	Warner 2790
3/22/75	**26**	14		5 Songbird	**$8**	Warner 2845
3/27/76	**34**	15		6 On The Road .... [L]	**$8**	Warner 2913
4/2/77	**64**	9		7 Love on the Wing	**$8**	Warner 3033
12/9/78	**165**	2		8 American Dreams	**$8**	Elektra 157

Again (5)	Do It Slow (7)	Jambalaya (On The Bayou)	Pastures Of Plenty (1)	Stranger Love (3)	Workin' (7)
American Dreams Suite	Drift Away (7)	(medley) (2)	Peace Song (1,6)	Sugar Babe (5)	You Gotta Fix It (3)
Medley (8)	Drifter's Blues (3)	Josianne (5)	Pretty And The Fair (4)	Sunlight (6)	You Lovin' Hobo (7)
Barbados (4)	Evenin' (2)	Knock On Wood (8)	Rave On (8)	Susan (4)	
Before You Came (5)	Fool (7)	Lafayette Waltz (medley) (2)	Reveal Your Dreams (8)	Susanne (3)	
Black Eyed Susan (3)	Four In The Morning (3)	Louisiana Highway (7)	Ridgetop (2,6)	Sweet Little Child (1)	
Born In Chicago (7)	Good Times (1)	Love On The Wing (7)	Rye Whiskey (3)	Sweet Little Sixteen (1)	
California Cowboy (7)	Have You Seen My Baby (6)	Maui Sunrise (8)	Same Old Man (3)	T-Bone Shuffle (2,6)	
California Suite Medley (4)	Hey, Good Lookin' (7)	Mercy Mercy Me (The	Six Days On The Road (1)	Talk To Me (3)	
Corinna (6)	Higher & Higher (7)	Ecology) (medley) (6)	6000 Miles (1)	'Til You Come Back Home (5)	
Country Home (2)	I Think I'll Take To Whiskey	Miss Hesitation (2,6)	Slick City (5)	Together (1)	
Creole Belle (1)	(3)	Morning Sun (2)	Slow And Easy (8)	Walkin' Off The Blues (6)	
Cuckoo, The (4)	It's A Lovely Day (1)	Motorcycle Blues (4)	Song for Juli (2)	What's Going On (medley) (6)	
Daniel (5)		Motorhome (5)	Songbird (5)	Whoa Baby (3)	

YOUNG, John Paul
Born in Glasgow, Scotland in 1953 and raised in Australia. Pop singer/songwriter/pianist.

| 11/11/78+ | **119** | 18 | | Love Is In The Air .... | **$8** | Scotti Br. 7101 |

Day That My Heart Caught	Fool In Love	**Lost In Your Love 55**	Lovin' In Your Soul	Things To Do
Fire	Lazy Days	**Love Is In The Air 7**	Open Doors	12° Celsius

★★42★★ YOUNG, Neil
Born on 11/12/45 in Toronto. Rock singer/songwriter/guitarist. Formed rock band the Mynah Birds, featuring lead singer Rick James, early '60s. Moved to Los Angeles in 1966 and formed Buffalo Springfield. Went solo in 1969 with backing band Crazy Horse. Joined with Crosby, Stills & Nash, 1970-71. Appeared in the 1987 film Made In Heaven. Reunited with Crosby, Stills & Nash in 1988 to record the American Dream album.

6/21/69+	**34**	98	▲	1 Everybody Knows This Is Nowhere *	**$15**	Reprise 6349
9/19/70	**8**	66	▲²	2 After The Gold Rush	**$15**	Reprise 6383
3/4/72	**1²**	41	▲³	3 Harvest	**$12**	Reprise 2032
11/25/72+	**45**	21		4 Journey Through The Past .... [S]	**$15**	Warner 6480 [2]
				side 1: new versions of Buffalo Springfield and CSN&Y hits		
10/27/73	**22**	18	●	5 Time Fades Away .... [L]	**$8**	Reprise 2151
				guests: David Crosby and Graham Nash		
8/3/74	**16**	18	●	6 On The Beach	**$8**	Reprise 2180
7/12/75	**25**	12		7 Tonight's The Night	**$8**	Reprise 2221
11/29/75+	**25**	21		8 Zuma *	**$8**	Reprise 2242
10/9/76	**26**	18	●	9 Long May You Run	**$8**	Reprise 2253
				STILLS-YOUNG BAND (Stephen Stills)		
7/2/77	**21**	15	●	10 American Stars 'N Bars	**$8**	Reprise 2261
				NEIL YOUNG, CRAZY HORSE & THE BULLETS guests: Linda Ronstadt and Emmylou Harris		
11/26/77	**43**	18	▲	11 Decade .... [K]	**$15**	Reprise 2257 [3]
10/21/78	**7**	30	●	12 Comes A Time	**$8**	Reprise 2266
7/21/79	**8**	39	▲	13 Rust Never Sleeps *	**$8**	Reprise 2295
12/8/79+	**15**	24	▲	14 Live Rust * .... [L]	**$10**	Reprise 2296 [2]
11/22/80	**30**	16		15 Hawks & Doves	**$8**	Reprise 2297
11/21/81	**27**	17		16 Re-ac-tor *	**$8**	Reprise 2304
1/22/83	**19**	17		17 Trans	**$8**	Geffen 2018
8/20/83	**46**	15		18 Everybody's Rockin'	**$8**	Geffen 4013
				NEIL & the SHOCKING PINKS		
9/7/85	**75**	12		19 Old Ways	**$8**	Geffen 24068
8/16/86	**46**	16		20 Landing On Water	**$8**	Geffen 24109
7/25/87	**75**	11		21 Life *	**$8**	Geffen 24154
4/30/88	**61**	18		22 This Note's For You	**$8**	Reprise 25719
				NEIL YOUNG & THE BLUENOTES The Bluenotes are 9 backing musicians		
10/21/89	**35**	28	●	23 Freedom	**$8**	Reprise 25899
9/29/90	**31**	25		24 Ragged Glory *	**$12**	Reprise 26315
11/9/91	**154**	4		25 WELD * .... [L]	**$22**	Reprise 26746 [3]
				the third disc is a 35-minute track titled "Arc"		
				***NEIL YOUNG & CRAZY HORSE**		
11/14/92	**16**	13↑	●	26 Harvest Moon	**$12**	Reprise 45057

YOUNG, Neil — Cont'd

After The Gold Rush (2,11,14)
Alabama (3,4)
Albuquerque (7)
Already One (12)
Ambulance Blues (6)
Arc (25)
Are There Any More Real Cowboys? (19)
Are You Ready For The Country? (3,4)
Around The World (21)
Bad News Beat (20)
Barstool Blues (8)
Betty Lou's Got A New Pair Of Shoes (18)
Birds (2)
Bite The Bullet (10)
Black Coral (9)
Blowin' In The Wind (25)
Borrowed Tune (7)
Bound For Glory (19)
Bridge, The (2)
Bright Lights, Big City (18)
Broken Arrow (11)
Burned (11)
California Sunset (19)
Campaigner (11)
Can't Believe Your Lyin' (22)
Captain Kennedy (15)
Cinnamon Girl (1,11,14,25) **55**
Coastline (15)
Come On Baby Let's Go Downtown (7)
Comes A Time (12,14)
Comin' Apart At Every Nail (15)
Computer Age (17)
Computer Cowboy (AKA Syscrusher) (17)
Cortez The Killer (8,11,14,25)
Country Home (24)
Coupe De Ville (22)
Cowgirl In The Sand (1,11)

Crime In The City (23,25)
Cripple Creek Ferry (2)
Cry, Cry, Cry (18)
Cryin' Eyes (21)
Danger Bird (8)
Days That Used To Be (24)
Deep Forbidden Lake (11)
Don't Be Denied (5)
Don't Cry (23)
Don't Cry No Tears (8)
Don't Let It Bring You Down (2)
Down By The River (1,11)
Down To The Wire (11)
Dreamin' Man (26)
Drifter (20)
Drive Back (8)
Eldorado (23)
Everybody Knows This Is Nowhere (1)
Everybody's Rockin' (18)
Expecting To Fly (11)
Farmer John (24,25)
Field Of Opportunity (12)
Find The Cost Of Freedom (4)
Fontainebleau (9)
For The Turnstiles (6,11)
For What It's Worth (medley) (4)
Four Strong Winds (12) **61**
From Hank To Hendrix (26)
F*!#in' Up (24,25)
Get Back On It (16)
Get Back To The Country (19)
God Bless America (medley) (4)
Goin' Back (12)
Guardian Angel (9)
Handel's Messiah (4)
Hangin' On A Limb (23)
Hard Luck Stories (20)
Harvest (1)
Harvest Moon (26)
Hawks & Doves (15)

Heart Of Gold (3,11) **1**
Helpless (11)
Hey Babe (10)
Hey Hey (22)
Hippie Dream (20)
Hold Back The Tears (10)
Hold On To Your Love (17)
Homegrown (11)
Human Highway (12)
I Am A Child (11,14)
I Believe In You (2,11)
I Got A Problem (20)
Inca Queen (21)
Jellyroll Man (18)
Journey Thru The Past (5)
Kinda Fonda Wanda (18)
King Of Kings Theme (4)
L.A. (5)
Last Dance (5)
Let It Shine (9)
Let Me Call You Sweetheart (4)
Let's Go Away For Awhile (4)
Life In The City (22)
Like A Hurricane (10,11,14,25)
Like An Inca (17)
Little Thing Called Love (17) **71**
Little Wing (15)
Loner, The (11,14)
Long May You Run (9,11)
Long Walk Home (21)
Look Out For My Love (12)
Lookin' For A Love (8)
Lookout Joe (7)
Losing End (When You're On) (1)
Lost In Space (15)
Lotta Love (12,14)
Love And Only Love (24,25)
Love In Mind (5)
Love Is A Rose (11)
Love To Burn (24,25)
Make Love To You (9)

Man Needs A Maid (3,11)
Mansion On The Hill (24,25)
Married Man (22)
Mellow My Mind (7)
Mideast Vacation (21)
Midnight On The Bay (9)
Misfits (19)
Mother Earth (Natural Anthem) (24)
Motion Pictures (6)
Motor City (16)
Motorcycle Mama (12)
Mr. Soul (4,11,17)
My Boy (19)
My My, Hey Hey (Out Of The Blue) (13,14)
Mystery Train (18)
Natural Beauty (26)
Needle And The Damage Done (3,11,14)
New Mama (7)
No More (23)
Ocean Girl (9)
Oh, Lonesome Me (2)
Ohio (4,11)
Old Country Waltz (10)
Old Homestead (15)
Old King (26)
Old Laughing Lady (11)
Old Man (3,11) **31**
Old Ways (19)
On Broadway (23)
On The Beach (6)
Once An Angel (19)
One Of These Days (26)
One Thing (22)
Only Love Can Break Your Heart (2) **33**
Opera Star (16)
Out On The Weekend (3)
Over And Over (24)
Pardon My Heart (8)
Payola Blues (18)
Peace Of Mind (12)
People On The Street (20)

Pocahontas (13)
Powderfinger (13,14,25)
Pressure (20)
Prisoners Of Rock 'N' Roll (21)
Rainin' In My Heart (18)
Rapid Transit (16)
Relativity Invitation (4)
Revolution Blues (6)
Ride My Llama (13)
Rock & Roll Woman (4)
Rockin' In The Free World (23,25)
Roll Another Number (For The Road) (7,25)
Round & Round (It Won't Be Long) (1)
Running Dry (Requiem For The Rockets) (1)
Rust Never Sleeps (Hey Hey, My My [Into The Black]) (13,14,25) **79**
Saddle Up The Palomino (10)
Sail Away (13)
Sample And Hold (17)
Sedan Delivery (13,14)
See The Sky About To Rain (6)
Shots (13)
Soldier (4,11)
Someday (23)
Southern Man (2,4,11)
Southern Pacific (16) **70**
Speakin' Out (7)
Star Of Bethlehem (10,11)
Stayin' Power (15)
Stupid Girl (8)
Such A Woman (26)
Sugar Mountain (11,14)
Sunny Inside (22)
Surfer Joe And Moe The Sleaze (16)
T-Bone (16)
Tell Me Why (2)
Ten Men Workin' (22)

There's A World (3)
This Note's For You (22)
Thrasher (13)
Through My Sails (8)
Till The Morning Comes (2)
Time Fades Away (5)
Tired Eyes (7,11)
Tonight's The Night (Part I & II) (7,11,14,25)
Too Far Gone (23)
Too Lonely (21)
Touch The Night (20)
Transformer Man (17)
12/8 Blues (All The Same) (9)
Twilight (22)
Union Man (15)
Unknown Legend (26)
Vampire Blues (6)
Violent Side (20)
Walk On (6,11) **69**
War Of Man (26)
Ways Of Love (23)
Wayward Wind (19)
We Never Danced (21)
We R In Control (17)
Weight Of The World (20)
Welfare Mothers (13,25)
When You Dance I Can Really Love (2,14) **93**
When Your Lonely Heart Breaks (21)
Where Is The Highway Tonight? (19)
White Line (24)
Will To Love (10)
Winterlong (11)
Wonderin' (18)
Words (Between The Lines Of Age) (3,4)
World On A String (7)
Wrecking Ball (23)
Yonder Stands The Sinner (5)
You And Me (26)

YOUNG, Paul

Born on 1/17/56 in Bedfordshire, England. Pop-rock vocalist/guitarist.

DEBUT DATE	PEAK POS	WKS CHR	GOLD	ARTIST — Album Title	$	Label & Number
4/14/84	79	23		1 No Parlez	$8	Columbia 38976
5/25/85	19	43	●	2 The Secret Of Association	$8	Columbia 39957
11/22/86	77	17		3 Between Two Fires	$8	Columbia 40543
8/11/90	142	13		4 Other Voices	$12	Columbia 46755

Between Two Fires (3)
Bite The Hand That Feeds (2)
Broken Man (1)
Calling You (4)
Certain Passion (3)
Come Back And Stay (1) **22**
Everything Must Change (2) **56**
Everytime You Go Away (2) **1**

Heaven Can Wait (4)
Hot Fun (2)
I Was In Chains (2)
I'm Gonna Tear Your Playhouse Down (2) **13**
In The Long Run (3)
Iron Out The Rough Spots (1)
It's What She Didn't Say (4)
Ku-Ku Kurama (1)
Little Bit Of Love (4)

Love Of The Common People (1) **45**
Love Will Tear Us Apart (1)
No Parlez (1)
Oh Girl (4) **8**
Oh Women (1)
One Step Forward (2)
Our Time Has Come (4)
Prisoner Of Conscience (3)
Right About Now (4)

Sex (1)
Softly Whispering I Love You (4)
Soldier's Things (2)
Some People (3) **65**
Standing On The Edge (2)
Stop On By (4)
Tender Trap (1)
This Means Anything (2)
Together (4)

Tomb Of Memories (2)
War Games (1)
Wasting My Time (3)
Wedding Day (3)
Wherever I Lay My Hat (That's My Home) (1) **70**
Why Does A Man Have To Be Strong? (1)
Wonderland (3)

YOUNG AMERICANS, The

A 36-member chorus of teenagers and young adults.

DEBUT DATE	PEAK POS	WKS CHR	GOLD	ARTIST — Album Title	$	Label & Number
4/19/69	178	3		1 Time For Livin'	$12	ABC 659

Blackberry Organ
Bowling Green

For Emily, Whenever I May Find Her
Gotham City Municipal Swing Band At County Fair
Here's That Rainy Day

Little Green Apples
Little Joy

On The Blue Cloud Sea
Scarborough Fair

Singing In The Rain
Time For Livin'

YOUNG & RESTLESS

Rap duo from Miami: Charles Trahan (b: 8/24/71) and Leonerist Johnson (b: 10/14/71).

DEBUT DATE	PEAK POS	WKS CHR	GOLD	ARTIST — Album Title	$	Label & Number
5/5/90	104	14		Something To Get You Hyped	$12	Pandisc 8809

"B" Girls 54
Cold Get Ill

Funky Az Bass Line
Gimme Them Guts

It Just Wasn't Our Day
Louie, Louie

Poison Ivy
Something To Get You Hyped

YOUNGBLOOD, Lonnie — see HENDRIX, Jimi

YOUNGBLOOD, Sydney

Sydney Ford — San Antonio native based in Heidelberg, Germany.

DEBUT DATE	PEAK POS	WKS CHR	GOLD	ARTIST — Album Title	$	Label & Number
10/20/90	185	3		Sydney Youngblood	$12	Arista 8651

Ain't No Sunshine
Congratulations

Don't Keep Me Waiting
Feeling Free

Good Times Bad Times
I'd Rather Go Blind 46

If Only I Could
Kiss And Say Goodbye

Not Just A Lover But A Friend

Sit And Wait

YOUNGBLOODS, The

Folk-rock group led by vocalist Jesse Colin Young (born Perry Miller on 11/11/44). Band formed in New York City in late 1965, moved to California in late 1967.

DEBUT DATE	PEAK POS	WKS CHR	GOLD	ARTIST — Album Title	$	Label & Number
3/25/67+	131	8		1 The Youngbloods	$15	RCA 3724
5/10/69	118	29		2 Elephant Mountain	$12	RCA 4150
9/5/70	144	10		3 The Best Of The Youngbloods [G]	$12	RCA 4399

DEBUT DATE	PEAK POS	WKS CHR	GOLD	ARTIST — Album Title	$	Label & Number

YOUNGBLOODS, The — Cont'd

DEBUT DATE	PEAK POS	WKS CHR	GOLD	ARTIST — Album Title	$	Label & Number
10/31/70	80	13		4 Rock Festival ....[L]	$10	Raccoon 1878
7/24/71	157	8		5 Ride The Wind ....[L]	$10	Raccoon 2563
8/7/71	186	3		6 Sunlight ....[K]	$10	RCA 4561
12/4/71	160	5		7 Good And Dusty	$10	Raccoon 2566
12/9/72+	185	10		8 High On A Ridge Top	$10	Raccoon 2653

Ain't That Lovin' You, Baby (1,6)
All Over The World (La-La) (1)
Beautiful (2,5)
Black Mountain Breakdown (2)
C.C. Rider (1,3)
Circus Face (7)
Darkness, Darkness (2,3) **86**
Dolphin, The (5)
Don't Let The Rain Get You Down (2)
Donna (8)
Double Sunlight (2)
Dreamboat (8)
Dreamer's Dream (6)
Drifting And Drifting (7)
Euphoria (3)
Faster All The Time (4)
Fiddler A Dram (4)
Foolin' Around (The Waltz) (1,6)
Four In The Morning (1)
Get Together (1,3,5) **5**
Going By The River (8)
Good And Dusty (7)
Grizzly Bear (1,3) **52**
Hippie From Olema #5 (7)
I Can Tell (6)
I Shall Be Released (8)
I'm A Hog For You Baby (7)
Ice Bag (4)
It's A Lovely Day (4)
Josiane (4)
Kind Hearted Woman (8)
La Bamba (7)
Let The Good Times Roll (7)
Light Shine (7)
Long & Tall (6)
Misty Roses (4)
Moonshine Is The Sunshine (7)
On Beautiful Lake Spenard (4)
On Sir Francis Drake (2,6)
One Note Man (1,6)
Other Side Of This Life (1)
Peepin' 'N' Hidin' (Baby, What You Want Me To Do) (4)
Pontiac Blues (7)
Quicksand (2,3)
Reason To Believe (6)
Ride The Wind (2,5)
Running Bear (8)
Sea Cow Boogie (4)
Sham (2,3)
She Came In Through The Bathroom Window (8)
She Caught The Katy & Left Me A Mule To Ride (8)
Smug (2)
Speedo (8)
Stagger Lee (7)
Statesboro Blues (1,6)
Sugar Babe (3,5)
Sunlight (2,3,5,6)
Tears Are Falling (1)
That's How Strong My Love Is (7)
Turn It Over (2)
Will The Circle Be Unbroken (7)
Willie And The Hand Jive (7)
Wine Song (3)

YOUNG-HOLT UNLIMITED
Chicago instrumental soul group: Eldee Young (bass), Isaac "Red" Holt (drums; both of the Ramsey Lewis Trio) and Don Walker (piano). Walker left by 1968.

DEBUT DATE	PEAK POS	WKS CHR	GOLD	ARTIST — Album Title	$	Label & Number
1/14/67	132	6		1 Wack Wack ....[I]	$12	Brunswick 754121
				YOUNG-HOLT TRIO		
1/4/69	9	30		2 Soulful Strut ....[I]	$12	Brunswick 754144
8/16/69	185	6		3 Just A Melody ....[I]	$12	Brunswick 754150

Ain't There Something Money Can't Buy (2)
Baby Your Light Is Out (2)
Be By My Side (2)
By The Time I Get To Phoenix (3)
Funky Is As Funky Does (2)
Girl Talk (1)
Give It Away (1)
Gotta Find Me A Lover (24 Hours A Day) (3)
I Heard It Through The Grapevine (3)
I Wish You Love (3)
Just A Melody (3)
Just Ain't No Love (2)
Light My Fire (3)
Little Green Apples (2)
Love Makes A Woman (2)
Monday, Monday (1)
My Whole World Ended (3)
Please Sunrise, Please (2)
Red Sails In The Sunset (1)
Song For My Father (1)
Soulful Strut (2) **3**
Strangers In The Night (1)
Sunny (1)
This Little Light Of Mine (1)
Wack Wack (1) **40**
What Now My Love (2)
When I'm Not Around (3)
Who's Making Love (2) **57**
Yesterday (1)
You Know That I Love You (1)
Young And Holtful (3)

YOUNG MC
Rapper. Born Marvin Young on 5/10/67 in England and raised in Queens, New York. Co-writer of Tone Loc's "Wild Thing" and "Funky Cold Medina." Graduated with economics degree from University of Southern California.

DEBUT DATE	PEAK POS	WKS CHR	GOLD	ARTIST — Album Title	$	Label & Number
9/23/89	9	48	▲	1 Stone Cold Rhymin'	$8	Delicious 91309
8/31/91	66	7	●	2 Brainstorm	$12	Capitol 96337
				CD includes 3 bonus tracks		

After School (2)
Album Filler (2)
Bust A Move (1) **7**
Do You Feel Like I Do (2)
Fastest Rhyme (1)
Got More Rhymes (1)
I Come Off (1) **75**
I Let 'Em Know (1)
Inside My Head (2)
Just Say No (1)
Keep It In Your Pants (2)
Keep Your Eyes On The Prize (2)
Know How (1)
Life In The Fast Lane (2)
Listen To The Beat Of The Music (2)
My Name Is Young (1)
Non Stop (1)
Pick Up The Pace (1)
Principal's Office (1) **33**
Right One (2)
Roll With The Punches (1)
Stone Cold Buggin' (1)
That's The Way Love Goes (Includes 2 versions) (2) **54**
Um Dee Dum Song (2)
Use Your Head (2)

YO-YO
Yolanda Whitaker, female rapper from Los Angeles. Born on 8/4/71. Member of Ice Cube's posse.

DEBUT DATE	PEAK POS	WKS CHR	GOLD	ARTIST — Album Title	$	Label & Number
4/13/91	74	21		1 Make Way For The Motherlode	$12	EastWest 91605
7/11/92	145	2		2 Black Pearl	$12	EastWest 92120

Ain't Nobody Better (1)
Black Pearl (2)
Cleopatra (2)
Cube Gets Played (1)
Dedication (1)
Few Good Men (2)
Girl, Don't Be No Fool (1)
Hoes (2)
Home Girl Don't Play Dat (2)
I Can't Take No More (2)
I Got Played (1)
I.B.W.C. National Anthem (1)
It's A Long Way Home (2)
Make Way For The Motherlode (1)
More Of What Can I Do (1)
Put A Lid On It (1)
Sisterland (1)
So Funky (2)
Stand Up For Your Rights (1)
Stompin' To Tha 90's (1)
Tonight's The Night (1)
What Can I Do? (1)
Will You Be Mine (2)
Woman To Woman (2)
You Can't Play With My Yo-Yo (1) **36**
You Should Have Listened (2)

YURO, Timi
Born Rosemarie Timothy Aurro Yuro on 8/4/40 in Chicago. Moved to Los Angeles in 1952. First recorded for Liberty in 1959. Lost voice in 1980 and underwent three throat operations.

DEBUT DATE	PEAK POS	WKS CHR	GOLD	ARTIST — Album Title	$	Label & Number
9/18/61	51	13		Timi Yuro	$25	Liberty 3208

And That Reminds Me
Cry
For You
Hurt 4
I Apologize 72
I Should Care
I Won't Cry Anymore
I'm Confessin' (That I Love You)
Just Say I Love Him
Little Bird Told Me
Trying
You'll Never Know

YUTAKA
Born Yutaka Yokokura in Tokyo. Male jazz-pop vocalist/keyboardist. Moved to California in the late '70s.

DEBUT DATE	PEAK POS	WKS CHR	GOLD	ARTIST — Album Title	$	Label & Number
7/11/81	174	4		Love Light ....[I]	$8	Alfa 10004

Breath Of Night
Dragonfly
Evening Star
Haiku
Love Light 81
Oriental Express
Rest Of My Life

Z

ZACHERLE, John
Born on 9/26/18 in Philadelphia. Hosted horror movies on WCAU-TV in Philadelphia during the late 1950s.

DEBUT DATE	PEAK POS	WKS CHR	GOLD	ARTIST — Album Title	$	Label & Number
11/10/62	44	10		Monster Mash ....[N]	$40	Parkway 7018

Bat, The
Dinner With Drac Part 1 6
Gravy (With Some Cynide)
Ha-Ha-Ha
Hurry Bury Baby
I'm The Ghoul From Wolverton Mountain
Let's Twist Again (Mummy Time Is Here)
Limb From Limbo Rock
Monster Mash
Pistol Stomp
Popeye (The Gravedigger)
Weird Watusi

Roger Troutman

Funkmeister eccentricity of vocoder vocals and zany personality

Roger Troutman, who has died aged 47 after being shot several times outside his recording studio — apparently by his brother Larry, who later took his own life — was the founder and leader of the group Zapp, and subsequently a solo performer, songwriter and producer.

Like George Clinton and Cameo's Larry Blackmon, his 1980s funkmeister eccentricity was underpinned by immense musical and technical ability, as well as sharp business acumen. His record appearances were lately reduced to occasional guest solo spots, but his 1997 teaming with Dr Dre and Tupac Shakur, on the hip-hop single California Love, earned him a Grammy nomination.

Troutman was involved in several recording studios in Dayton, Ohio. He also had substantial property and business interests. The Troutman brothers — Lester, Larry and Zapp, who all performed in the band at one time or another — were local heroes not only for their pop profile but also through their ability, through their company, Troutman Enterprises, to generate employment.

Roger Troutman was born in Hamilton, Ohio. By the end of his teens he had demonstrated his prolific guitar skills in almost every club in the state. Zapp was formed in the mid-1970s and garnered more than a decade's worth of stage experience, touring with stars such as Little Richard, James Brown and George Clinton's Parliament/Funkadelic. In 1979 Troutman finally signed — with George Clinton's recommendation — the Warner Bros recording contract that would confer on his family group the national status he craved.

Their first single, the funky, playful More Bounce To The Ounce, was a top 10 r&b hit and kicked off a run of successes that lasted for most of the 1980s. From I Can Make You Dance, and Dancefloor, to Computer Love and It Really Doesn't Matter, the American r&b public remained enamoured with Roger's vocoder vocals —

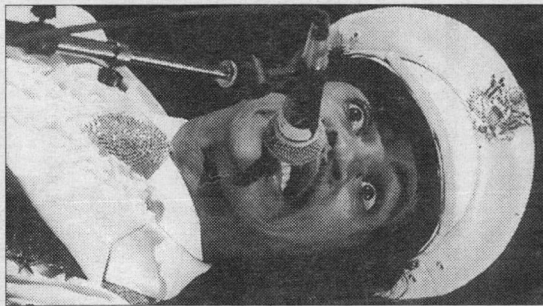

Troutman . . . business skill

zany personality. His solo career led to a handful of albums, including The Many Facets Of Roger, The Saga Continues, Unlimited, and Bridging The Gap, the latter a surprisingly successful co-production with former Scritti Politti member David Gamson.

single, I Want To Be Your Man, rose to number three on the US pop chart. His love for the natural singing voice also led him to produce albums of Zapp band members Bobby Glover, a former college football star, and Shirley Murdock.

In the early 1990s Troutman and Zapp's hits dried up. Yet like a lot of the original funk-makers, he benefited from seeing his works sampled by the hip-hop fraternity, and interest which he found flattering as well as financially beneficial.

"I used to worry about whether my next record would make the charts," he said recently, "but, y'know what? The other day, I was sitting in a restaurant and about six people came over and said how much they loved my work. Making an impression on people's consciousness, being loved for something you created, that's what it's all about."

Chris Wells

Roger Troutman, singer, songwriter, producer, born

---

mission is not "banning" AD and BC, but suggesting that broadcasters use CE and BCE because they are more inclusive, multi-faith and multicultural. Unfortunately, however, he is guilty of a howler in saying that BCE and CE stand for Before Christian Era and Christian Era. The C is for Common, not Christian. That's the point.
David Boulton
Broadcasting Standards Commission

bonus, the millennium bug squashed) by denoting the year beginning January 1 next as 0 ACE.
Tommy Beavitt
Dundonnell, Ross-shire

● If "the Word was in the beginning with God", every year since Creation is AD and there never was a time BC. Christian interests would be better served by the use of BI and AI (before and after the Incarnation) with the year

---

and clarifications

and accessible to all regardless of age, sex or social status."

In an article headed Anything is better than this, page 22, May 7, we said, "There was no more prospect of bombing the Serbs to the negotiating table than there was of bombing the Afrikaaners to democracy..." Afrikaner (spelt with a single interior a) is a white native of South Africa whose mother tongue is Afrikaans (double a): Collins English Dictionary.

The title of one of the books reviewed on page 10, Saturday Review, May 8, is White City Blue (not Blues).

Stefan Collini, in his review of the second volume of

day Review, May 8, intended to refer to one aspect of the book as "unswervingly shrewd". It appeared as "unswervingly screwed". Apologies.

Homophone corner, from page 11, Saturday Review, May 8: "only those who have been clubbing right round the world will not be phased ..."

It is the policy of the Guardian to correct errors as soon as possible. Please quote the date and page number. Readers may contact the office of the Readers' Editor by telephoning 0171 239 9589 between 11am and 5pm Monday to Friday. Surface mail to Readers' Editor, The Guardian, 119, Farringdon Road, London EC1R 3ER. Fax 0171 239 9897, e-mail:

DEBUT DATE	PEAK POS	WKS CHR	G O L D	ARTIST — Album Title	$	Label & Number

ZADORA, Pia
Born Pia Schipani in 1955 in New York City. (Derived Zadora from her mother's maiden name: Zadorowski.) Stage and film actress/singer. In the films *Butterfly*, *The Lonely Lady* and *Hairspray*.

| 3/8/86 | 113 | 20 | | Pia & Phil .... | $12 | CBS Assoc. 40259 |

Pia sings with the London Philharmonic Orchestra

All My Tomorrows	Come Rain Or Come Shine	Embraceable You	Man That Got Away	Smile (Though Your Heart Is
Boy Next Door	East Of The Sun (And West	I Thought About You	Maybe This Time	Breaking)
But Not For Me	Of The Moon)	It Had To Be You		When The Sun Comes Out

ZAGER, Michael, Band
Disco studio group led by keyboardist/writer/arranger Michael Zager (b: 1943 in Jersey City, New Jersey). Member of Ten Wheel Drive from 1968-73.

| 4/22/78 | 120 | 13 | | Let's All Chant .... | $8 | Private St. 7013 |

Dancin' Disney Medley	Freak	Let's All Chant 36	Love Express	Music Fever	Soul To Soul

ZAGER & EVANS
Folk-rock duo from Lincoln, Nebraska: Denny Zager and Rick Evans (both sing and play guitar).

| 8/2/69 | 30 | 13 | | 2525 (Exordium & Terminus) .... | $12 | RCA 4214 |

Bayoan	Fred	In The Land Of Green	In The Year 2525	Less Than Tomorrow	Taxi Man
Cary Lynn Javes	I Remember Heide		(Exordium & Terminus) *1*	Self	Woman

ZAPP
Dayton, Ohio funk band formed by the Troutman brothers: Roger ("Zapp"), Lester, Tony and Larry. "Bootsy" Collins produced and played on first session. Roger recorded solo as "Roger."

9/27/80	19	19	●	1 Zapp	$8	Warner 3463
				with "Bootsy" Collins (guitars)		
8/14/82	25	19	●	2 Zapp II	$8	Warner 23583
9/3/83	39	22		3 Zapp III	$8	Warner 23875
11/23/85+	110	26		4 The New Zapp IV U	$8	Warner 25327
10/7/89	154	4		5 Zapp V	$8	Reprise 25807

Ain't The Thing To Do (5)	Computer Love (4)	Funky Bounce (1)	Jake E Stanstill (5)	Radio People (4)	Tut-Tut (Jazz) (3)
Back To Bass-lks (5)	Dance Floor (2)	Heartbreaker (Part I & II) (3)	Jesse Jackson (5)	Rock 'N' Roll (4)	We Need The Buck (3)
Be Alright (1)	Do You Really Want An	I Can Make You Dance (3)	Make Me Feel Good (4)	Rock Star (5)	
Been This Way Before (5)	Answer? (2)	I Only Have Eyes For You (4)	More Bounce To The	Sad-Day Moaning (5)	
Brand New Pplayer (1)	Doo Wa Ditty (Blow That	I Play The Talk Box (5)	Ounce - Part I (1) 86	Spend My Whole Life (3)	
Cas-Ta-Spellome (4)	Thing) (2,3)	It Doesn't Really Matter (4)	Ooh Baby Baby (5)	Stop That (5)	
Come On (2)	Fire (5)	Itchin' For Your Twitchin' (4)	Play Some Blues (3)	Touch Of Jazz (Playin' Kinda	
Coming Home (1)	Freedom (1)	Ja Ready To Rock (4)	Playin' Kinda Ruff (2)	Ruff Part II) (2)	

★★52★★ **ZAPPA, Frank**
Born on 12/21/40 in Baltimore, Maryland. Singer/songwriter/guitarist. Rock music's leading satirist. Formed The Mothers Of Invention in 1965. In the films *200 Motels* and *Baby Snakes*. Father of Dweezil and Moon Unit Zappa (both performed in the 1991 Peace Choir, "Give Peace A Chance"). Revealed diagnosis with prostate cancer in 1991.

2/11/67	130	23		1 Freak Out! *	$50	Verve 5005 [2]
7/8/67	41	22		2 Absolutely Free *	$50	Verve 5013
3/16/68	30	19		3 We're Only In It For The Money *	$50	Verve 5045
				album art work is a parody of The Beatles' *Sgt. Pepper* LP		
6/8/68	159	5		4 Lumpy Gravy ....[I]	$50	Verve 8741
				THE ABNUCEALS EMUUKHA ELECTRIC SYMPHONY ORCHESTRA AND CHORUS		
12/21/68+	110	12		5 Cruising with Ruben & The Jets *	$40	Verve 5055
				a parody of '50s doo-wop music		
4/5/69	151	9		6 Mothermania/The Best Of The Mothers * ....[K]	$50	Verve 5068
				selections from the first 3 albums above		
5/3/69	43	11		7 Uncle Meat *	$35	Bizarre 2024 [2]
				basically instrumentals for an unfinished movie		
11/29/69	173	6		8 Hot Rats ....[I]	$25	Bizarre 6356
				with guests Captain Beefheart and Jean-Luc Ponty		
3/14/70	94	8		9 Burnt Weeny Sandwich * ....[I]	$25	Bizarre 6370
9/26/70	189	3		10 Weasels Ripped My Flesh * ....[L]	$25	Bizarre 2028
				live tracks and studio recordings from 1967-69		
				*THE MOTHERS OF INVENTION		
11/21/70	119	14		11 Chunga's Revenge	$25	Bizarre 2030
8/21/71	38	15		12 The Mothers/Fillmore East-June 1971 ** ....[L]	$25	Bizarre 2042
10/30/71	59	13		13 Frank Zappa's 200 Motels ....[S]	$30	United Art. 9956 [2]
				with the Royal Philharmonic Orchestra; film follows the exploits of The Mothers of Invention		
4/22/72	85	9		14 Just Another Band From L.A. ** ....[L]	$25	Bizarre 2075
				recorded at UCLA, Los Angeles on 8/7/71		
9/9/72	152	7		15 Waka/Jawaka - Hot Rats ....[I]	$20	Reprise 2094
10/6/73	32	50	●	16 Over-nite Sensation **	$20	DiscReet 2149
				**THE MOTHERS		
4/20/74	10	43	●	17 Apostrophe (')	$20	DiscReet 2175
10/5/74	27	18		18 Roxy & Elsewhere ....[L]	$20	DiscReet 2202 [2]
				ZAPPA/MOTHERS		
7/19/75	26	12		19 One Size Fits All	$15	DiscReet 2216
				FRANK ZAPPA AND THE MOTHERS OF INVENTION		
11/1/75	66	8		20 Bongo Fury ....[L]	$15	DiscReet 2234
				FRANK ZAPPA/CAPTAIN BEEFHEART/THE MOTHERS		
11/27/76	61	13		21 Zoot Allures	$15	Warner 2970
4/15/78	57	8		22 Zappa in New York ....[L]	$20	DiscReet 2290 [2]
10/21/78	147	6		23 Studio Tan ....[I]	$15	DiscReet 2291
2/17/79	175	4		24 Sleep Dirt ....[I]	$15	DiscReet 2292

ZAPPA, Frank — Cont'd

DEBUT DATE	PEAK POS	WKS CHR	GOLD	ARTIST — Album Title	$	Label & Number
3/24/79	21	23		25 Sheik Yerbouti	$15	Zappa 1501 [2]
6/2/79	168	4		26 Orchestral Favorites ......[I]	$15	DiscReet 2294
9/22/79	27	25		27 Joe's Garage, Act I	$10	Zappa 1603
12/15/79+	53	12		28 Joe's Garage, Acts II & III	$12	Zappa 1502 [2]
5/30/81	66	11		29 Tinsel Town Rebellion ......[L]	$12	Barking P. 37336 [2]
10/3/81	93	7		30 You Are What You Is	$12	Barking P. 37537 [2]
6/12/82	23	22		31 Ship arriving too late to save a drowning witch	$8	Barking P. 38066
4/16/83	153	5		32 The Man From Utopia	$8	Barking P. 38403
1/18/86	153	6		33 Frank Zappa Meets The Mothers Of Prevention	$8	Barking P. 74203

Absolutely Free (3)
Advance Romance (20)
Aerobics In Bondage (33)
Air, The (7)
Alien Orifice (33)
America Drinks & Goes Home (2,6)
Amnesia Vivace (2)
Andy (19)
Any Downers? (30)
Any Way The Wind Blows (1,5)
Anything (5)
Apostrophe' (17)
Are You Hung Up (3)
Aybe Sea (9)
Baby Snakes (25)
Bamboozled By Love (29)
Be-Bop Tango (Of The Old Jazzmen's Church) (18)
Beauty Knows No Pain (29)
Big Leg Emma (22)
Big Swifty (15)
Billy The Mountain (14)
Black Napkins (21)
Black Page (Part 1 & 2) (22)
Blue Light (29)
Bobby Brown (25)
Bogus Pomp (26)
Bow Tie Daddy (5)
Broken Hearts Are For Assholes (25)
Brown Shoes Don't Make It (2,6,29)
Burnt Weeny Sandwich, Theme From (9)
Bwana Dik (12)
Call Any Vegetable (2,6,14)
Camarillo Brillo (16)
Can't Afford No Shoes (19)
Carolina Hard-Core Ecstasy (20)
Catholic Girls (27)
Centerville (13)
Central Scrutinizer (27)
Charlie's Enormous Mouth (30)
Cheap Thrills (5)
Cheepnis (18)
Chrome Plated Megaphone Of Destiny (5)
Chunga's Revenge (11)
City Of Tiny Lites (25)
Clap, The (11)
Cocaine Decisions (32)
Concentration Moon (5)
Conehead (9)
Cosmik Debris (17)
Crew Slut (27)
Cruising For Burgers (7)
Cucamonga (20)
Daddy, Daddy, Daddy (13)
Dance Contest (29)
Dance Of The Just Plain Folks (13)
Dance Of The Rock & Roll Interviewers (13)
Dancin' Fool (25) *45*
Dangerous Kitchen (32)
Debra Kadabra (20)

Dental Hygiene Dilemma (13)
Desert (5)
Dew On The Newts We Got (13)
Didja Get Any Onya (10)
Dinah - Moe Humm (16)
Directly From My Heart To You (10)
Dirty Love (16)
Disco Boy (21)
Do You Like My New Car? (12)
Does This Kind Of Life Look Interesting To You? (13)
Dog Breath (7,14)
Doing Work For Yuda (28)
Don't Eat The Yellow Snow (17) *86*
Don't You Ever Wash That Thing? (18)
Doreen (30)
Drafted Again (30)
Drowning Witch (31)
Duke Of Prunes (2,6,26)
Duke Regains His Chops (2)
Dumb All Over (30)
Dummy Up (18)
Dwarf Nebula Processional March & Dwarf Nebula (10)
Easy Meat (29)
Echidna's Arf (Of You) (18)
Eddie, Are You Kidding? (14)
Electric Aunt Jemina (7)
Envelopes (31)
Eric Dolphy Memorial Barbecue (10)
Evelyn, A Modified Dog (19)
Excentrifugal Forz (17)
Father O'Blivion (17)
Fifty - Fifty (16)
Filthy Habits (24)
Find Her Finer (21)
Fine Girl (29)
Flakes (25)
Flambay (24)
Florentine Pogen (19)
Flower Punk (3)
For The Young Sophisticate (29)
Fountain Of Love (5)
Friendly Little Finger (21)
Get A Little (31)
Girl Wants To Fix Him Some Broth (13)
Girl's Dream (13)
Go Cry On Somebody Else's Shoulder (1)
Goblin Girl (30)
God Bless America (7)
Greggery Peccary (23)
Gumbo Variations (8)
Half A Dozen Provocative Squats (13)
Happy Together (12)
Harder Than Your Husband (30)
Harry, You're A Beast (3)
He Used To Cut The Grass (28)
Heavenly Bank Account (30)

Holiday In Berlin, Full Blown (9)
Honey, Don't You Want A Man Like Me? (22)
Hot Poop (3)
How Could I Be Such A Fool (1,5)
Hungry Freaks, Daddy (1,6)
I Ain't Got No Heart (1,29)
I Come From Nowhere (31)
I Have Been In You (25)
I Promise Not To Come In Your Mouth (22)
I'm A Beautiful Guy (30)
I'm Not Satisfied (1,5)
I'm So Cute (25)
I'm Stealing The Towels (13)
I'm The Slime (16)
Ian Underwood Whips It Out (7)
Idiot Bastard Son (3,6)
If Only She Woulda (30)
If We'd All Been Living In California (7)
Igor's Boogie, Phase One & Two (9)
Illinois Enema Bandit (22)
In Memoriam, Edgar Varese (medley) (1)
Inca Roads (19)
Invocation & Ritual Dance Of The Young Pumpkin (2)
It Can't Happen Here (1,6)
It Just Might Be A One-Shot Deal (15)
It Must Be A Camel (18)
Janet's Big Dance Number (13)
Jazz Discharge Party Hats (32)
Jelly Roll Gum Drop (5)
Jewish Princess (25)
Joe's Garage (27)
Jones Crusher (25)
Jumbo Go Away (30)
Keep It Greasey (28)
King Kong [includes several versions] (7)
Lad Searches The Night For His Newts (13)
Later That Night (5)
Latex Solar Beef (12)
Legend Of The Golden Arches (7)
Let Me Take You To The Beach (23)
Let's Make The Water Turn Black (5)
Little Beige Sambo (33)
Little Green Rosetta (28)
Little Green Scratchy Sweaters & Courduroy Ponce (13)
Little House I Used To Live In (9,13)
Little Umbrellas (8)
Lonely Little Girl (3)
Lonesome Cowboy Burt (13)
Lonesome Electric Turkey (12)

Louie Louie (7)
Love Of My Life (5,29)
Lucille Has Messed My Mind Up (27)
Lucy's Seduction Of A Bored Violinist (13)
Lumpy Gravy - Part I & II (4)
Magdalena (14)
Magic Fingers (13)
Man From Utopia Meets Mary Lou (32)
Man With The Woman Head (20)
Manx Needs Women (22)
Meek Shall Inherit Nothing (30)
Moggio (32)
Mom & Dad (3)
Montana (16)
More Trouble Every Day (18)
Mother People (3,6)
Motherly Love (1)
Motorhead's Midnight Ranch (13)
Mr. Green Genes (7)
Ms. Pinky (21)
Mud Shark (12)
Mudd Club (30)
Muffin Man (20)
My Guitar Wants To Kill Your Mama (10)
Mysterioso (13)
Mystery Roach (13)
Nancy & Mary Music - Part 1, 2, & 3 (11)
Nanook Rubs It (17)
Nasal Rententive Calliope Music (3)
Naval Aviation In Art (26)
9 Types Of Industrial Pollution (7)
No No No (5)
Not Now (31)
Now You See It - Now You Don't (29)
Nun Suit Painted On Some Old Boxes (13)
Ocean Is The Ultimate Solution (24)
Oh No (10)
Okay To Tap Dance (medley) (1)
Orange County Lumber Truck (10)
Our Bizarre Relationship (7)
Outside Now (28)
Overture To A Holiday In Berlin (9)
Packard Goose (28)
Panty Rap (29)
Peaches En Regalia (8,12)
Peaches III (29)
Pedro's Dowry (26)
Penguin In Bondage (18)
Penis Dimension (13)
Pick Me, I'm Clean (29)
Plastic People (2,6)
Po-Jama People (19)
Poofter's Froth Wyoming Plans Ahead (20)

Porn Wars (33)
Pound For A Brown On The Bus (7)
Preamble (18)
Prelude To The Afternoon Of A Sexually Aroused Gas Mask (10)
Project X (7)
Purple Lagoon (22)
Pygmy Twylyte (18)
Radio Is Broken (32)
Rat Tomago (25)
Redneck Eats (13)
Redunzl (23)
Regyptian Strut (24)
Return Of The Son Of Monster Magnet Medley (1)
Revised Music For Guitar And Low Budget Orchestra (23)
Road Ladies (11)
Rubber Shirt (25)
Rudy Wants To Buy Yez A Drink (11)
Sam With The Showing Scalp Flat Top (20)
San Ber'dino (14)
Sealed Tuna Bolero (13)
Semi-Fraudulent/Direct-From-Hollywood (13)
Sex (32)
Sharleena (11)
She Painted Up Her Face (13)
Sheik Yerbouti Tango (25)
Shove It Right In (13)
Sleep Dirt (24)
Sleeping In A Jar (7)
Society Pages (30)
Sofa No. 1 & 2 (19,22)
Soft-Sell Conclusion (22)
Son Of Mr. Green Genes (8)
Son Of Orange County (18)
Son Of Suzy Creamcheese (2)
Spider Of Destiny (24)
St. Alfonzo's Pancake Breakfast (17)
Status Back Baby (2)
Stick It Out (28)
Stick Together (32)
Stink-Foot (17)
Strictly Genteel (13,26)
Stuff Up The Cracks (5)
Suicide Chump (30)
Sy Borg (30)
Take Your Clothes Off When You Dance (13)
Tears Began To Fall (12)
Teen-age Prostitute (31)
Teenage Wind (30)
Tell Me You Love Me (11,29)
3rd Movement Of Sinister Footwear, Theme From The (30)
This Town Is A Sealed Tuna Sandwich (Prologue) (13)
Time Is Money (24)
Tink Walks Amok (32)
Tinsel Town Rebellion (29)
Titties & Beer (22)
Toad-O Line (27)

Toads Of The Short Forest (10)
Token Of My Extreme (28)
Torture Never Stops (21)
Touring Can Make You Crazy (13)
Transylvania Boogie (11)
Trouble Comin' Every Day (1)
Tryin' To Grow A Chin (25)
Tuna Fish Promenade (13)
Twenty Small Cigars (11)
200 Years Old (20)
Uncle Bernie's Farm (2)
Uncle Meat [includes 2 versions] (7)
Uncle Remus (17)
Valarie (9)
Valley Girl (31) *32*
Village Of The Sun (18)
Voice Of Cheese (7)
WPLJ (The Four Deuces) (9)
Waka/Jawaka (15)
Watermelon In Easter Hay (28)
We Are Not Alone (32)
We Can Shoot You (7)
We Gotta Get Into Something Real (25)
We're Turning Again (33)
Weasels Ripped My Flesh (10)
Wet T-Shirt Nite (27)
What Ever Happened To All The Fun In The World (30)
What Kind Of Girl Do You Think We Are? (2)
What Will This Evening Bring Me This Morning (13)
What's New In Baltimore? (33)
What's The Ugliest Part Of Your Body? (3)
Who Are The Brain Police? (1,6)
Who Needs The Peace Corps (3)
Why Does It Hurt When I Pee? (27)
Wild Love (25)
Willie The Pimp - Part One & Two (8,12)
Wind Up Workin' In A Gas Station (21)
Wonderful Wino (21)
Would You Go All The Way? (11)
Would You Like A Snack? (13)
Wowie Zowie (1)
Yo Cats (33)
Yo' Mama (25)
You Are What You Is (30)
You Didn't Try To Call Me (1,5)
You're Probably Wondering Why I'm Here (1,6)
Your Mouth (15)
Zolar Czakl (1)
Zomby Woof (16)
Zoot Allures (21)

ZEBRA

New Orleans rock trio: Randy Jackson (lead singer), Felix Hanemann (bass) and Guy Gelso (drums).

DEBUT DATE	PEAK POS	WKS CHR	GOLD	ARTIST — Album Title	$	Label & Number
5/14/83	29	28	●	1 Zebra	$8	Atlantic 80054
9/22/84	84	11		2 No Tellin' Lies	$8	Atlantic 80159

As I Said Before (1)
Bears (2)
But No More (2)
Don't Walk Away (1)

Drive Me Crazy (2)
I Don't Care (2)
I Don't Like It (2)
La La Song (1)

Little Things (2)
Lullaby (2)
No Tellin' Lies (2)
One More Chance (1)

Slow Down (1)
Take Your Fingers From My Hair (1)
Takin' A Stance (2)

Tell Me What You Want (1)
Wait Until The Summer's Gone (2)
When You Get There (1)

Who's Behind The Door? (1) *61*

ZENO

German pop-metal power trio: Zeno Roth (lead guitar; brother of Scorpions' Uli Roth), Michael Flexig (lead singer) and U. Winsomie Ritgen (bass).

| 5/10/86 | 107 | 10 | | Zeno .... | $8 | Manhattan 53025 |

Circles Of Dawn
Don't Tell The Wind

Eastern Sun
Emergency

Far Away
Heart On The Wing

Little More Love
Love Will Live

Sent By Heaven
Signs On The Sky

Sunset

ZENTNER, Si

Jazz trombone player/bandleader originally from New York. Played in the 1940s for Jimmy Dorsey, Harry James and Les Brown.

12/18/61+	65	8		1 Big Band Plays The Big Hits .... [I]	$10	Liberty 7197
3/17/62	107	12		2 Up A Lazy River (Big Band Plays The Big Hits: Vol. 2) .... [I]	$10	Liberty 7216
9/1/62	108	6		3 The Stripper and Other Big Band Hits .... [I]	$10	Liberty 7247
2/9/63	139	5		4 Desafinado .... [I]	$10	Liberty 7273

title is Spanish for Out Of Tune

African Waltz (1)
Apache (1)
Asia Minor (1)
Autumn Leaves (2)
Because They're Young (1)
Bernie's Tune (4)
Blue Moon (2)
Blue Tango (4)
Calcutta (1)
Canadian Sunset (3)
Caravan (4)

Come Closer To Me (4)
Desafinado (4)
Goza Goza (4)
Heart And Soul (2)
Hollywood Twist (2)
Honky Tonk (Part 2) (2)
Hot Toddy (3)
I'll See You In My Dreams (4)
Lisbon Antigua (4)
Manhattan Spiritual (3)
Maria (4)

Midnight In Moscow (3)
Midnight Sun (4)
Moon River (2)
Moonglow/Theme From Picnic (3)
Never On Sunday (2)
Nice 'N Easy (2)
One Mint Julep (3)
Oso Blanco (4)
Perfidia (2)
Petite Fleur (3)

Picnic ..see: Moonglow
Quizas, Quizas, Quizas (Perhaps, Perhaps, Perhaps) (4)
Raindrops (1)
Save The Last Dance For Me (1)
Shadrack (3)
Speak Low (4)
Star Eyes (4)
Stranger On The Shore (3)

Stripper, The (3)
Take Five (2)
Tenderly (1)
Up A Lazy River (1,2) **43**
Walk - Don't Run (1)
Walk On The Wild Side (3)
Will You Love Me Tomorrow (1)
Wonderland By Night (1)
Yellow Bird (2)

ZEPHYR

Rock quintet led by Candy Givens (vocals) and Tommy Bolin (guitar; Deep Purple, James Gang; d: 12/4/76).

| 12/20/69+ | 48 | 26 | | Zephyr .... | $25 | Probe 4510 |

Boom-Ba-Boom
Cross The River

Hard Chargin' Woman
Huna Buna

Raindrops
Sail On

Somebody Listen
St. James Infirmary

Sun's A-Risin'

ZEVON, Warren

Rock singer/songwriter/pianist. Born on 1/24/47 in Chicago. Parents were Russian immigrants. Recorded with female vocalist Tule Livingston as the duo Lyme & Cybelle in 1966. Worked as the keyboardist/ bandleader for The Everly Brothers, shortly before their breakup. Wrote Linda Ronstadt's "Poor Poor Pitiful Me." Recorded with three R.E.M. members as the Hindu Love Gods in 1990.

| 8/28/76 | 189 | 2 | | 1 Warren Zevon .... | $12 | Asylum 1060 |
| 2/25/78 | 8 | 28 | ● | 2 **Excitable Boy** .... | $8 | Asylum 118 |

above 2 produced by Jackson Browne

3/8/80	20	16		3 Bad Luck Streak In Dancing School	$8	Asylum 509
1/17/81	80	10		4 Stand In The Fire .... [L]	$8	Asylum 519
8/14/82	93	13		5 The Envoy	$8	Asylum 60159
6/27/87	63	18		6 Sentimental Hygiene	$8	Virgin 90603

Accidentally Like A Martyr (2)
Ain't That Pretty At All (5)
Backs Turned (Looking Down The Path) (1)
Bad Karma (6)
Bad Luck Streak In Dancing School (3)
Bed Of Coals (3)
Bill Lee (3)
Bo Diddley (medley) (4)
Bo Diddley's A Gunslinger (medley) (4)

Boom Boom Mancini (6)
Carmelita (1)
Certain Girl (3) **57**
Charlie's Medicine (5)
Desperados Under The Eaves (1)
Detox Mansion (6)
Empty-Handed Heart (3)
Envoy, The (5)
Even A Dog Can Shake Hands (4)
Excitable Boy (2,4)
Factory, The (6)

Frank And Jesse James (1)
French Inhaler (1)
Gorilla, You're A Desperado (3)
Hasten Down The Wind (1)
Heartache, The (5)
Hula Hula Boys (5)
I'll Sleep When I'm Dead (1,4)
Jeannie Needs A Shooter (3,4)
Jesus Mentioned (5)
Johnny Strikes Up The Band (2)

Join Me In L.A. (1)
Jungle Work (3)
Lawyers, Guns And Money (2,4)
Leave My Monkey Alone (6)
Let Nothing Come Between You (5)
Looking For The Next Best Thing (5)
Mama Couldn't Be Persuaded (1)
Mohammed's Radio (1,4)
Never Too Late For Love (5)

Nighttime In The Switching Yard (2)
Overdraft, The (5)
Play It All Night Long (3)
Poor Poor Pitiful Me (1,4)
Reconsider Me (6)
Roland The Headless Thompson Gunner (2)
Sentimental Hygiene (6)
Sin, The (4)
Stand In The Fire (4)
Tenderness On The Block (2)

Trouble Waiting To Happen (6)
Veracruz (2)
Werewolves Of London (2,4) **21**
Wild Age (3)

ZODIAC MINDWARP & THE LOVE REACTION

English rock quintet formed in 1985, led by vocalist Zodiac Mindwarp (real name: Mark Manning).

| 3/26/88 | 132 | 15 | | Tattooed Beat Messiah .... | $8 | Vertigo 832729 |

Back Seat Education
Bad Girl City

Driving On Holy Gasoline
Kid's Stuff

Let's Break The Law
Planet Girl

Prime Mover
Skull Spark Joker

Spasm Gang
Speech

Tattooed Beat Messiah
Untamed Stare

ZOMBIES, The

British rock quintet: Rod Argent (keyboards), Colin Blunstone (vocals), Paul Atkinson (guitar), Chris White (bass) and Hugh Grundy (drums). Group disbanded in late 1967. Rod formed Argent in 1969.

| 2/27/65 | 39 | 17 | | 1 The Zombies .... | $35 | Parrot 71001 |
| 3/15/69 | 95 | 13 | | 2 Odessey & Oracle .... | $20 | Date 4013 |

Beechwood Park (2)
Brief Candles (2)
Butchers Tale (Western Front 1914) (2)
Can't Nobody Love You (1)

Care Of Cell (2)
Changes (2)
Friends Of Mine (2)
Hung Up On A Dream (2)
I Don't Want To Know (1)

I Want Her She Wants Me (2)
I've Got My Mojo Working (1)
It's Alright With Me (1)
Maybe After He's Gone (2)
Rose For Emily (2)

She's Not There (1) **2**
Sometimes (1)
Summertime (1)
Tell Her No (1) **6**
This Will Be Our Year (2)

Time Of The Season (2) **3**
What More Can I Do (1)
Woman (2)
Work 'N' Play (1)

You've Really Got A Hold On Me (1)

ZYDECO, Buckwheat — see BUCKWHEAT

★★181★★ ZZ TOP

Boogie-rock trio formed in Houston in 1969. Consists of Billy Gibbons (vocals, guitar), Dusty Hill (vocals, bass) and Frank Beard (drums). All were born in 1949 in Texas. Gibbons had been lead guitarist in Moving Sidewalks, a Houston psychedelic-rock band. Hill and Beard had played in American Blues, based in Dallas. Group appeared in the film *Back To The Future III*.

| 5/6/72 | 104 | 10 | | 1 Rio Grande Mud .... | $15 | London 612 |
| 8/4/73+ | 8 | 81 | ● | 2 **Tres Hombres** .... | $10 | London 631 |

title is Spanish for Three Men

| 5/17/75 | 10 | 47 | ● | 3 Fandango! .... [L] | $10 | London 656 |

side 1: live; side 2: studio

DEBUT DATE	PEAK POS	WKS CHR	GOLD	ARTIST — Album Title	$	Label & Number
				ZZ TOP — Cont'd		
1/22/77	17	24	●	4 Tejas	$10	London 680
				title is Spanish for Texas		
12/17/77+	94	19	●	5 The Best Of ZZ Top .... [G]	$12	London 706
11/24/79+	24	43	▲	6 Deguello	$8	Warner 3361
				title is Spanish for Beheading		
8/8/81	17	22	●	7 El Loco	$8	Warner 3593
				title is Spanish for The Crazy		
4/23/83	9	183	▲⁷	8 Eliminator	$8	Warner 23774
				album named after a 1933 Ford coupe restored by Billy Gibbons		
11/16/85	4	70	▲³	9 Afterburner	$8	Warner 25342
11/3/90	6	37	▲	10 Recycler	$12	Warner 26265
5/2/92	9	41↑	▲	11 Greatest Hits .... [G]	$12	Warner 26846

Apologies To Pearly (1)
Arrested For Driving While Blind (4) *91*
Asleep In The Desert (4)
Avalon Hideaway (4)
Backdoor Love Affair (5)
Backdoor Medley (3)
Bad Girl (8)
Balinese (3)
Bar-B-Q (1)
Beer Drinkers & Hell Raisers (2,5)
Blue Jean Blues (3,5)
Burger Man (10)
Can't Stop Rockin' (9)
Cheap Sunglasses (6,11) *89*
Chevrolet (1)
Concrete And Steel (10)
Decision Or Collision (10)

Delirious (9)
Dipping Low (In The Lap Of Luxury) (9)
Dirty Dog (8)
Don't Tease Me (7)
Doubleback (10,11) *50*
Down Brownie (1)
Dust My Broom (6)
El Diablo (4)
Enjoy And Get It On (4)
Esther Be The One (6)
Fool For Your Stockings (6)
Francene (1,5) *69*
Gimme All Your Lovin (8,11)
Give It Up (10,11) *79*
Got Me Under Pressure (8,11)
Groovy Little Hippie Pad (7)

Gun Love (11)
Have You Heard? (2)
Heard It On The X (3,5)
Heaven, Hell Or Houston (7)
Hi Fi Mama (6)
Hot, Blue And Righteous (2)
I Got The Message (9)
I Got The Six (8)
I Need You Tonight (8)
I Thank You (6) *34*
I Wanna Drive You Home (7)
I'm Bad, I'm Nationwide (6,11)
If I Could Only Flag Her Down (8)
It's Only Love (4) *44*
It's So Hard (7)
Jailhouse Rock (3)
Jesus Just Left Chicago (2,5)

Just Got Paid (1,5)
Ko Ko Blue (1)
La Grange (2,5,11) *41*
Legs (8,11) *8*
Leila (7) *77*
Lowdown In The Street (6)
Lovething (10)
Manic Mechanic (0)
Master Of Sparks (2)
Mexican Blackbird (3)
Move Me On Down The Line (2)
Mushmouth Shoutin' (1)
My Head's In Mississippi (10,11)
Nasty Dogs And Funky Kings (3)
Pan Am Highway Blues (4)
Party On The Patio (7)

Pearl Necklace (7,11)
Penthouse Eyes (10)
Planet Of Women (9,11)
Precious And Grace (2)
Rough Boy (9,11) *22*
Sharp Dressed Man (8,11) *56*
She Loves My Automobile (6)
She's A Heartbreaker (4)
Shiek (2)
Sleeping Bag (9,11) *8*
Snappy Kakkie (4)
Stages (9) *21*
Sure Got Cold After The Rain Fell (1)
TV Dinners (8)
Tell It (10)
Ten Dollar Man (4)
Ten Foot Pole (7)

Thug (8)
Thunderbird (3)
Tube Snake Boogie (7,11)
Tush (3,5,11) *20*
2000 Blues (10)
Velcro Fly (9) *35*
Viva Las Vegas (11)
Waitin' For The Bus (2,5)
Whiskey'n Mama (1)
Woke Up With Wood (9)

ALBUMS BY CATEGORY

This section lists, by category, albums which are not listed in the Artist Section. The albums are listed within their category either alphabetically by title or alphabetically by artist.

THE CATEGORIES

SOUNDTRACKS
SOUNDTRACK COMPILATIONS
ORIGINAL CASTS
TELEVISION SHOWS/MINI SERIES
COMPILATIONS BY RECORD LABEL
COMPILATIONS BY DISC JOCKEYS
CONCERTS/FESTIVALS
BENEFIT RECORDINGS
CONCEPT ALBUMS
ROCK OPERAS
DANCE/DISCO COMPILATIONS
JAZZ COMPILATIONS

NEW AGE COMPILATIONS
CHILDREN'S ALBUMS
CLASSICAL COMPILATIONS
COMEDY ALBUMS
AEROBIC INSTRUCTORS
SPECIALTY ALBUMS
CHRISTMAS
    Top Pop Albums Chart — Various
    Billboard's Christmas Charts
    Billboard's Christmas Charts — Various
RELIGIOUS
TRIBUTES

This section has several symbols that are not used in the Artist Section. Please keep the following guidelines in mind:

All #1 albums are boxed out in a thin frame.

Cross references to the Artist Section indicate that a single artist contributed over half of the album's tracks; therefore, the album is listed under that artist.

LETTER(S) IN BRACKETS AFTER TITLES

The letter **M** in brackets after the title indicates that the soundtrack is from a musical. An [O] indicates that the album consists of oldies and a [V] indicates that various artists contributed tracks to the album. Two or more letters within brackets separated by a "+" indicate that the symbols apply to different tracks. For example, [I+V] means that some of the tracks are instrumental and the remaining are by various artists. See User's Guide (page 16) for further explanation of symbols.

LETTERS IN TITLE TRIVIA

cp	Composer	**mu**	Music writer
cd	Conductor	**pf**	Performer
ly	Lyricist	**sw**	Songwriter music and lyrics

TRACKS INDEX GUIDELINES

If various artists contributed songs to an album, then the contributing artist is listed in parentheses after the track.

Original versions of *Hot 100* hits appear in bold with their peak position listed to the right. It does not matter if the album on which the hit appears charted many years after the song was popular.

The tracks are listed immediately below their albums for the following categories:

SOUNDTRACKS
SOUNDTRACK COMPILATIONS
ORIGINAL CASTS
TELEVISION SHOWS/MINI SERIES
COMPILATIONS BY DISC JOCKEYS
CONCERTS/FESTIVALS
BENEFIT RECORDINGS
CONCEPT ALBUMS
ROCK OPERAS
DANCE/DISCO COMPILATIONS

JAZZ COMPILATIONS
NEW AGE COMPILATIONS
CHILDREN'S ALBUMS
CLASSICAL COMPILATIONS
COMEDY ALBUMS
AEROBIC INSTRUCTORS
SPECIALTY ALBUMS
CHRISTMAS
    Top Pop Albums Chart — Various
    Billboard's Christmas Charts — Various

All tracks of albums in the following categories are listed in one master title index that appears after the last title in that category:

COMPILATIONS BY RECORD LABEL
CHRISTMAS
    Billboard's Christmas Charts
      (alphabetically by artist)

(The albums within the above sections are sequentially numbered; therefore, the number(s) in parentheses to the right of the track refers to the album on which the track appears.)

Please see Tracks Index (page 12) for further guidelines.

DEBUT DATE	PEAK POS	WKS CHR	G O L D	ARTIST — Album Title	$	Label & Number

SOUNDTRACKS

Each film's stars are listed below the title.

7/26/86 — **72** — 14 — **1 About Last Night** .... [V] **$8** — EMI America 17210
Rob Lowe/Demi Moore/James Belushi/Elizabeth Perkins

If Anybody Had A Heart [John Waite] **76**	Natural Love [Sheena Easton]	Til You Love Somebody [Michael Henderson]
If We Can Get Through The Night [Paul Davis]	(She's The) Shape Of Things To Come [John Oates]	Words Into Action [Jermaine Jackson]
Living Inside My Heart [Bob Seger]	**So Far So Good** [Sheena Easton] **43**	Trials Of The Heart [Nancy Shanks]
	Step By Step [J.D. Souther]	True Love [Del Lords]

4/12/86 — **62** — 13 — **2 Absolute Beginners** .... [M-V] **$8** — EMI America 17182
Eddie O'Connell/Patsy Kensit/David Bowie/Ray Davies

Absolute Beginners [David Bowie] **53**	Having It All [Eighth Wonder]	Rodrigo Bay [Working Week]
	Killer Blow [Sade]	Selling Out [Slim Gaillard]
Have You Ever Had It Blue [Style Council]	Quiet Life [Ray Davies]	That's Motivation [David Bowie]
	Riot City [Jerry Dammers]	Va Va Voom [Gil Evans]

Across 110th Street - see WOMACK, Bobby
Anthony Quinn/Yaphet Kotto/Anthony Franciosa

Advance To The Rear - see NEW CHRISTY MINSTRELS
Glenn Ford/Stella Stevens/Melvyn Douglas

7/14/90 — **66** — 9 — **3 Adventures Of Ford Fairlane, The** .... [V] **$12** — Elektra 60952
Andrew Dice Clay/Wayne Newton/Priscilla Presley/Morris Day

Can't Get Enough [Tone Loc]	I Ain't Got You [Andrew Dice Clay]	Sea Cruise [Dion]
Cradle Of Love [Billy Idol] **2**	Last Time In Paris [Queensryche]	Unbelievable (Theme) [Yello]
Funky Attitude [Sheila E.]	Rock 'N Roll Junkie [Motley Crue]	Wind Cries Mary [Richie Sambora]
Glad To Be Alive [Teddy Pendergrass & Lisa Fisher]		

3/31/84 — **12** — 22 — ● — **4 Against All Odds** .... [I+V] **$8** — Atlantic 80152
Rachel Ward/Jeff Bridges/James Woods/Alex Karras; side 2: instrumentals; cp/pf: Larry Carlton and Michel Colombier

Against All Odds (Take A Look At Me Now) [Phil Collins] **1**	Making A Big Mistake [Mike Rutherford]	Race, The	Walk Through The Fire [Peter Gabriel]
Balcony [Big Country]	Murder Of A Friend	Rock And Roll Jaguar	
El Solitario	My Male Curiosity [Kid Creole & The Coconuts]	Search, The (Main Theme)	
For Love Alone		Violet And Blue [Stevie Nicks]	

4/18/70 — **104** — 19 — **5 Airport** .... [I] **$30** — Decca 79173
Burt Lancaster/Dean Martin/George Kennedy/Helen Hayes; cp/cd: Alfred Newman

Ada Quonsett, Stowaway!	Airport! (Main Title)	Inez - Lost Forever	Mel And Tanya
Airport (End Title)	Emergency Landing!	Inez' Theme	Plane Or Plows? (medley)
Airport Love Theme	Guerrero's Goodbye	Joe Patroni (medley)	Triangle!

11/28/92+ — **8** — 11↑ ▲ — **6 Aladdin** .... **$12** — Disney 60846
animated film, voices by: Robin Williams/Lea Salonga/Bruce Adler/Jonathan Freeman/Brad Kane; ly: Alan Menken; ly: Tim Rice/Howard Ashman (d: 1991)

Aladdin's Word	Happy End In Agrabah	On A Dark Night	**Whole New World** [Peabo Bryson & Regina Belle] **3**↑
Arabian Nights	Jafar's Hour	One Jump Ahead	
Battle, The	Jasmine Runs Away	Prince Ali	
Cave Of Wonders	Kiss, The	Street Urchins	
Ends Of The Earth	Legend Of The Lamp	To Be Free	
Friend Like Me	Marketplace	Whole New World (cast version)	

12/5/60+ — **7** — 47 — **7 Alamo, The** .... [I+V] **$25** — Columbia 8358
John Wayne/Richard Widmark/Laurence Harvey; cp/cd: Dimitri Tiomkin

Ballad Of The Alamo [Marty Robbins] **34**	David Crockett's Speech [John Wayne]	Finale	Here's To The Ladies
Charge Of Santa Anna (medley)	De Guella (medley)	General Santa Anna	Overture
David Crockett [John Wayne]	Death Of David Crockett (medley)	**Green Leaves Of Summer** [Brothers Four] **65**	Raid For Cattle
David Crockett Arrives	Final Assault (medley)	Green Leaves Of Summer (instrumental)	Tennessee Babe (Oh, Lisa!)

Alice's Restaurant - see GUTHRIE, Arlo
Arlo Guthrie/Pat Quinn/James Broderick

7/7/79 — **113** — 8 — **8 Alien** .... [I] **$10** — 20th Century 593
Tom Skerritt/Sigourney Weaver/John Hurt/Harry Dean Stanton; cp: Jerry Goldsmith; cd: Lionel Newman; pf: National Philharmonic Orchestra

Acid Test	Droid, The	Landing, The	Shaft, The
Alien Planet	End Title	Main Title	
Breakaway	Face Hugger	Recovery, The	

3/22/80 — **36** — 23 — **9 All That Jazz** .... [M] **$10** — Casablanca 7198
Roy Scheider/Jessica Lange/Ann Reinking/Ben Vereen; cd: Ralph Burns

After You've Gone	Going Home Now	Ponte Vecchio	There'll Be Some Changes Made
Bye Bye Love	Main Title	Some Of These Days	Vivaldi: Concert In G
Everything Old Is New Again [Peter Allen]	Michelle	South Mt. Sinai Parade	Who's Sorry Now
	On Broadway [George Benson] **7**	Take Off With Us	

12/3/83+ — **165** — 7 — **10 All The Right Moves** .... [V] **$10** — Casablanca 814449
Tom Cruise/Lea Thompson/Craig T. Nelson

All The Right Moves [Jennifer Warnes/Chris Thompson] **85**	Hold Me Close To You [Stephanie Mills]	Love Theme [David Campbell]	Unison [Junior]
Blue Skies Forever [Frankie Miller]	I Don't Wanna Go Down [Roach]	Mr. Popularity [Winston Ford]	
	Last Stand [Doug Kahan]	This Could Be Our Last Chance [Danny Spanos]	

11/27/76 — **48** — 9 — **11 All This And World War II** .... [V] **$25** — 20th Cent. 522 [2]
documentary film; features John Lennon and Paul McCartney songs and a book of lyrics

Because [Lynsey DePaul]	End, The [London Symphony Orchestra]	Golden Slumbers (medley) [Bee Gees]	Long And Winding Road [Leo Sayer]
Carry That Weight (medley) [Bee Gees]	Fool On The Hill [Helen Reddy]	Help [Henry Gross]	Lovely Rita [Roy Wood]
Come Together [Tina Turner]	Get Back [Rod Stewart]	Hey, Jude [Brothers Johnson]	**Lucy In The Sky With Diamonds** [Elton John] **1**
Day In The Life [Frankie Valli]	Getting Better [Status Quo]	I Am The Walrus [Leo Sayer]	
		Let It Be [Leo Sayer]	

DEBUT DATE	PEAK POS	WKS CHR	GOLD	ARTIST — Album Title	$	Label & Number

| | | | | Magical Mystery Tour [Ambrosia] 39   Maxwell's Silver Hammer [Frankie Laine]   Michelle [Richard Cocciante]   Nowhere Man (medley) [Jeff Lynne]   Polythene Pam [Roy Wood]   She Came In Through The Bathroom Window [Bee Gees]   She's Leaving Home [Bryan Ferry]   Strawberry Fields Forever [Peter Gabriel]   Sun King [Bee Gees]   We Can Work It Out [Four Seasons]   When I'm Sixty-Four [Keith Moon]   With A Little Help From My Friends (medley) [Jeff Lynne]   Yesterday [David Essex]   You Never Give Me Your Money [Wil Malone & Lou Reizner] | | |

Amadeus - see MARRINER, Neville
Tom Hulce/F. Murray Abraham/Elizabeth Berridge/Simon Callow

| 7/5/86 | **91** | 12 | 12 | **American Anthem** ....[V] | $8 | Atlantic 81661 |

Mitch Gaylord/Janet Jones/Michele Phillips/R.J. Williams

Angel Eyes [Andy Taylor]   Arthur's Theme [Alan Silvestri]   Battle Of The Dragon [Stevie Nicks]   Julie's Theme [Alan Silvestri]   Love And Loneliness [Chris Thompson]   Run To Her [Mr. Mister]   Same Direction [INXS]   Take It Easy [Andy Taylor] 24   Two Hearts [John Parr]   Wings Of Love [Andy Taylor]   Wings To Fly [Graham Nash]

| 3/1/80 | **7** | 25 | ● 13 | **American Gigolo** ....[I+V] | $10 | Polydor 6259 |

Richard Gere/Lauren Hutton/Hector Elizondo; side 2: instrumentals; cp/pf: Giorgio Moroder

Apartment, The   Call Me [Blondie] 1   Hello Mr. W.A.M. (Finale)   Love And Passion [Cheryl Barnes]   Night Drive   Palm Springs Drive   Seduction, The (Love Theme)

| 9/1/73+ | **10** | 60 | ● 14 | **American Graffiti** ....[V-O] | $12 | MCA 8001 [2] |

Richard Dreyfuss/Ron Howard/Cindy Williams/Charles Martin Smith; also see Compilations
By Disc Jockeys: Wolfman Jack

Ain't That A Shame [Fats Domino] 10   All Summer Long [Beach Boys]   Almost Grown [Chuck Berry] 32   At The Hop [Flash Cadillac & The Continental Kids]   Barbara-Ann [Regents] 13   Book Of Love [Monotones] 5   Chantilly Lace [Big Bopper] 6   Come Go With Me [Dell-Vikings] 4   Crying In The Chapel [Orioles]   Do You Want To Dance [Bobby Freeman] 5   Fanny Mae [Buster Brown] 38   Get A Job [Silhouettes] 1   Goodnight Sweetheart, Goodnite [Spaniels]   Great Pretender [Platters] 1   Green Onions [Booker T. & The MG's] 3   (He's) The Great Imposter [Fleetwoods] 30   Heart And Soul [Cleftones] 18   I Only Have Eyes For You [Flamingos] 11   Johnny B. Goode [Chuck Berry] 8   Little Darlin' [Diamonds] 2   Love Potion No. 9 [Clovers] 23   Maybe Baby [Crickets] 17   Only You (And You Alone) [Platters] 5   Party Doll [Buddy Knox] 1   Peppermint Twist [Joey Dee & The Starliters] 1   Rock Around The Clock [Bill Haley] 1   Runaway [Del Shannon] 1   See You In September [Tempos] 23   She's So Fine [Flash Cadillac & The Continental Kids]   Since I Don't Have You [Skyliners] 12   16 Candles [Crests] 2   Smoke Gets In Your Eyes [Platters] 1   Stroll, The [Diamonds] 4   Surfin' Safari [Beach Boys] 14   Teen Angel [Mark Dinning] 1   That'll Be The Day [Crickets] 1   Thousand Miles Away [Heartbeats] 53   To The Aisle [Five Satins] 25   Why Do Fools Fall In Love [Frankie Lymon & The Teenagers] 6   Ya Ya [Lee Dorsey] 7   You're Sixteen [Johnny Burnette] 8

| 8/11/79 | **84** | 12 | 15 | **American Graffiti, More** ....[V-O] | $15 | MCA 11006 [2] |

Ballad Of The Green Berets [SSGT Barry Sadler] 1   Beechwood 4-5789 [Marvelettes] 17   Cool Jerk [Capitols] 7   Hang On Sloopy [McCoys] 1   Heat Wave [Martha & The Vandellas] 4   I Feel Like I'm Fixin' To Die Rag [Country Joe & The Fish]   I'm A Man [Doug Sahm]   Just Like A Woman [Bob Dylan] 33   Like A Rolling Stone [Bob Dylan] 2   Moon River [Andy Williams]   Mr. Lonely [Bobby Vinton] 1   Mr. Tambourine Man [Byrds] 1   My Boyfriend's Back [Angels] 1   My Guy [Mary Wells] 1   96 Tears [? (Question Mark) & The Mysterians] 1   Pipeline [Chantay's] 4   Respect [Aretha Franklin] 1   Season Of The Witch [Donovan]   She's Not There [Zombies] 2   Since I Fell For You [Lenny Welch] 4   Sounds Of Silence [Simon & Garfunkel] 1   Stop! In The Name Of Love [Supremes] 1   Strange Brew (Cream)   When A Man Loves A Woman [Percy Sledge] 1

| 4/8/78 | **31** | 11 | 16 | **American Hot Wax** ....[V-O] | $18 | A&M 6500 [2] |

Tim McIntire/Fran Prescher/Laraine Newman/Jay Leno; based on the life of disc jockey Alan Freed; record 1: live; record 2: original '50s recordings

Goodnight Sweetheart, Goodnite [Spaniels]   Great Balls Of Fire [Jerry Lee Lewis]   Hey Little Girl [Clark Otis]   Hot Wax Theme [Big Beat Band]   Hushabye [Mystics] 20   I Put A Spell On You [Screamin' Jay Hawkins]   Little Star [Elegants] 1   Maybe [Delights]   Mr. Blue [Timmy & The Tulips]   Mr. Lee [Delights]   Rave On [Buddy Holly] 37   Reelin' And Rockin' [Chuck Berry]   Rock And Roll Is Here To Stay [Prof. LaPiano & The Planotones]   Roll Over Beethoven [Chuck Berry]   Sea Cruise [Frankie Ford] 14   Sincerely [Moonglows] 20   Splish Splash [Bobby Darin] 3   Stay [Maurice Williams] 1   Sweet Little Sixteen [Chuck Berry] 2   That Is Rock And Roll [Chesterfields]   That's Why (I Love You So) [Jackie Wilson] 13   There Goes My Baby [Drifters] 2   Tutti Frutti [Little Richard] 17   When You Dance [Turbans] 3   Whole Lotta Shakin' Goin' On [Jerry Lee Lewis]   Why Do Fools Fall In Love [Chesterfields]   Zoom [Cadillacs]

| 1/31/87 | **42** | 19 | 17 | **American Tail, An** .... | $8 | MCA 39096 |

animated film, voices by: Dom DeLuise/Christopher Plummer/Madeline Kahn; cp/cd: James Horner

Cossack Cats   Duo, A   Flying Away   Give Me Your Tired, Your Poor   Great Fire   Main Title   Market Place   Never Say Never   Releasing The Secret Weapon   Reunited   Somewhere Out There [Linda Ronstadt & James Ingram] 2   Somewhere Out There (cast version)   Storm, The   There Are No Cats In America

| 9/2/78 | **71** | 18 | 18 | **Animal House** ....[V-O] | $10 | MCA 3046 |

John Belushi/Tim Matheson/John Vernon/Tom Hulce/Donald Sutherland

Animal House [Stephen Bishop] 73   Dream Girl [Stephen Bishop]   Faber College Theme [Elmer Bernstein]   Hey Paula [Paul & Paula] 1   Let's Dance [Chris Montez] 4   Louie, Louie [John Belushi] 89   Money (That's What I Want) [John Belushi]   Shama Lama Ding Dong [Lloyd Williams]   Shout [Lloyd Williams]   Tossin' And Turnin' [Bobby Lewis] 1   Twistin' The Night Away [Sam Cooke] 9   Wonderful World [Sam Cooke] 12

| 5/29/82 | **35** | 31 | ▲ 19 | **Annie** ....[M] | $10 | Columbia 38000 |

Aileen Quinn (Annie)/Carol Burnett/Albert Finney/Tim Curry; mu: Charles Strouse; ly: Martin Charnin; cd: Ralph Burns; also see Original Cast ('77)

Dumb Dog   Easy Street   I Don't Need Anything But You (medley)   I Think I'm Gonna Like It Here   It's The Hard-Knock Life   Let's Go To The Movies   Little Girls   Maybe   Sandy   Sign   Tomorrow (includes 2 versions)   We Got Annie   You're Never Fully Dressed Without A Smile

Annie Get Your Gun - see Those Glorious MGM Musicals

| 1/17/81 | **141** | 9 | 20 | **Any Which Way You Can** ....[V] | $10 | Warner 3499 |

Clint Eastwood/Sondra Locke/Geoffrey Lewis/Ruth Gordon

Acapulco [Johnny Duncan]   Any Way You Want Me [Gene Watson]   Any Which Way You Can [Glen Campbell]   Beers To You [Ray Charles & Clint Eastwood]   Cotton-Eyed Clint [Texas Opera Company]   Cow Patti [Jim Stafford]

DEBUT DATE	PEAK POS	WKS CHR	GOLD	ARTIST — Album Title	$	Label & Number

Good Guys And The Bad Guys [John Durrill] — Orangutan Hall Of Fame [Cliff Crofford] — You're The Reason God Made Oklahoma [David Frizzell & Shelly West]
One Too Many Women In Your Life [Sondra Locke] — Too Loose [Sondra Locke] — Whiskey Heaven [Fats Domino]

1/9/61 · **18** · 15 · **21 Apartment, The** .... [I] **$40** United Art. 3105
Jack Lemmon/Shirley MacLaine/Fred MacMurray/Ray Walston; cp: Adolph Deutsch; cd: Mitchell Powell

Apartment, The (Theme) — Kicked In The Head — Ring A Ding Ding — Where Are You Fran
Blue Christmas — Little Brown Jug — So Fouled Up
Career March — Lonely Room — Tavern In Town
Hong Kong Blues — Office Workers — This Night

April Love - see BOONE, Pat
Pat Boone/Shirley Jones

Arabesque - see MANCINI, Henry
Gregory Peck/Sophia Loren

1/23/71 · **137** · 10 · **22 Aristocats, The** .... **$8** Disneyland 3995
animated film, voices by: Paul Winchell/Scatman Crothers/Nancy Kulp; special story book album; narration by Sterling Holloway; songs by Phil Harris

Aristocats, The — Scales And Arpeggios — Thomas O'Malley Cat
Ev'rybody Wants To Be A Cat — She Never Felt Alone

4/13/57 · **1**[10] · 88 · **23 Around The World In 80 Days** .... [I] **$35** Decca 79046
David Niven/Cantinflas/Robert Newton/Shirley MacLaine; cp/cd: Victor Young; also see New World Theatre Orchestra version below

Around The World (Main Theme) 13 — Epilogue — Pagoda Of Pillagi — Temple Of Dawn
Around The World - Part II — India Country Side — Paris Arrival
Entrance Of The Bull March (medley) — Invitation To A Bull Fight (medley) — Passepartout
 — Land Ho — Prairie Sail Car
 — — Sky Symphony

10/21/57 · **8** · 4 · **24 Around The World In 80 Days** .... [I] **$25** Stereo-Fid. 2800
pf: New World Theatre Orchestra; not the original soundtrack (see version above)

Around The World - Pt. 1 & 2 — India Country Side — Pagoda Of Pillagi — Prairie Sail Car
Entrance Of The Bull March (medley) — Invitation To A Bull Fight (medley) — Paris Arrival — Sky Symphony
Epilogue — Land Ho — Passepartout — Temple Of Dawn

9/5/81 · **32** · 22 · **25 Arthur (The Album)** .... [I+V] **$10** Warner 3582
Dudley Moore/Liza Minnelli/John Gielgud; side 2: instrumentals; cp: Burt Bacharach

Arthur's Theme (Best That You Can Do) [Christopher Cross] — Arthur's Theme (Best That You Can Do) (instrumental) — It's Only Love [Stephen Bishop] — Moving Pictures
 — Fool Me Again [Nicolette Larson] — Money — Poor Rich Boy [Ambrosia]
 — — — Touch

1/20/62 · **57** · 18 · **26 Babes In Toyland** .... [M] **$20** Buena Vista 4022
Tommy Sands/Annette Funicello/Ray Bolger/Ed Wynn; adaptation of Victor Herbert's operetta by George Bruns and Mel Leven

Castle In Spain — Just A Toy — Never Mind Bo-Peep — Toyland
Floretta — Just A Whisper Away — Overture — We Won't Be Happy Till We Get It
Forest Of No Return — Lemonade (medley) — Slowly He Sank To The Bottom Of The Sea — Workshop Song
Go To Sleep — March Of The Toys
I Can't Do The Sum — Mother Goose Village (medley) — Tom And Mary (Finale)

9/5/87 · **188** · 2 · **27 Back To The Beach** .... [V] **$10** Columbia 40892
Frankie Avalon/Annette Funicello/Lori Loughlin/Connie Stevens

Absolute Perfection [Private Domain] — Jamaica Ska [Annette Funicello & Fishbone] — Sign Of Love [Aimee Mann] — Surfin' Bird [Pee-wee Herman]
California Sun [Frankie Avalon] — Pipeline [Stevie Ray Vaughan & Dick Dale] — Sun, Sun, Sun, Sun, Sun [Marti Jones] — Wipe Out [Herbie Hancock]
Catch A Ride [Eddie Money] — — — Wooly Bully [Dave Edmunds]

7/27/85 · **12** · 32 · ● · **28 Back To The Future** .... [V] **$8** MCA 6144
Michael J. Fox/Christopher Lloyd/Lea Thompson/Crispin Glover

Back In Time [Huey Lewis & The News] — Earth Angel (Will You Be Mine) [Marvin Berry & The Starlighters] — Johnny B. Goode [Marty McFly & The Starlighters] — Time Bomb Town [Lindsey Buckingham]
Back To The Future [Alan Silvestri] — Heaven Is One Step Away [Eric Clapton] — Night Train [Marvin Berry & The Starlighters] — Wallflower (Dance With Me Henry) [Etta James]
 — — Power Of Love [Huey Lewis & The News] 1

12/7/68 · **183** · 5 · **29 Barbarella** .... **$35** DynoVoice 31908
Jane Fonda/Milo O'Shea/David Hemmings; ly/pf: Bob Crewe; mu: Charles Fox

Angel Is Love — Entrance Into Sogo — Labyrinth, The — Sex Machine
Barbarella — Fight In Flight — Love, Love, Love Drags Me Down — Ski Ride
Black Queen's Beads — Goodnight Alfie — Pill, The — Smoke (Viper Vapor)
Chamber Of Dreams — Hello Pretty Pretty — Pygar Finds Barbarella — Spaceship Out Of Control
Dead Duck — Hungry Dolls — Pygar's New Wings
Destruction Of Sogo — I Love All The Love In You — Pygar's Persecution

2/14/76 · **132** · 15 · **30 Barry Lyndon** .... [I] **$10** Warner 2903
Ryan O'Neal/Marisa Berenson; classical and traditional music; adapted and conducted by Leonard Rosenman

Bach: Adagio from Concerto For Two Harpsicords And Orchestra In C-Minor — Hohenfriedberger March — Piper's Maggot Jig — Sea-Maiden, The
 — Lilliburlero — Schubert: German Dance No. 1 In C-Major — Tin Whistles
British Grenadiers — Mozart: March From Idomeneo — Schubert: Piano Trio In E-Flat, Op. 100 (Second Movement) — Vivaldi: Cello Concerto E-Minor (Third Movement)
Handel: Sarabande — Paisiello: Cavatina from "Il Barbiere Di Siviglia" — — Women Of Ireland

Batman - see ELFMAN, Danny, and PRINCE
Michael Keaton/Jack Nicholson/Kim Basinger/Robert Wuhl

Batman Returns - see ELFMAN, Danny
Michael Keaton/Michelle Pfeiffer/Danny DeVito/Christopher Walken

Beach Party - see ANNETTE
Annette Funicello/Frankie Avalon/Robert Cummings

Beaches - see MIDLER, Bette
Bette Midler/Barbara Hershey/John Heard

DEBUT DATE	PEAK POS	WKS CHR	GOLD	ARTIST — Album Title	$	Label & Number

6/2/84 — **14** — 21 — ● — **31 Beat Street, Volume 1** ....[V] **$10** Atlantic 80154
Rae Dawn Chong/Guy Davis/John Chardiet

Baptize The Beat [System]	Breaker's Revenge [Arthur Barker]	**Strangers In A Strange World** [Jenny Burton & Patrick Jude] 54
Beat Street Breakdown - Part 1 [Grandmaster Melle Mel & The Furious Five] 86	Frantic Situation [Afrika Bambaataa & The Soul Sonic Force]	This Could Be The Night [Cindy Mizelle]
Beat Street Strut [Juicy]		

Tu Carino/Carmen's Theme [Ruben Blades]
Us Girls [Sharon Green, Lisa Counts & Debbie D.]

9/29/84 — **137** — 9 — **32 Beat Street, Volume 2** ....[V] **$10** Atlantic 80158
2nd album of music from *Beat Street*

Battle Cry [Rockers Revenge]	It's Alright By Me [Jenny Burton]	Phony Four MC's-Wappin' (Bubblehead) [Ralph Rolle]
Give Me All [Juicy]	Nothin's Gonna Come Easy [Tina B]	Santa's Rap [Treacherous Three]
Into The Night [La La]		

Son Of Beat Street [Jazzy Jay]

12/7/91+ — **19** — 62↑ ▲² — **33 Beauty and the Beast** .... **$12** Disney 60618
animated film, voices by: Robby Benson/Jesse Corti/Angela Lansbury/Paige O'Hara; cp: Alan Menken; ly: Howard Ashman (d: 1991 [age 41])

Battle On The Tower	**Beauty And The Beast** [Celine Dion & Peabo Bryson] 9	Belle
Be Our Guest	Beauty And The Beast (cast version)	Gaston
Beast Lets Belle Go		Mob Song

To The Fair
Transformation
West Wing
Something There

5/9/64 — **147** — 3 — **34 Becket** ....[I] **$50** Decca 79117
Richard Burton/Peter O'Toole; cp: Laurence Rosenthal; cd: Muir Mathieson

Becket's Martyrdom	Escape To The Court Of King Louis (medley)	King Henry's Arrival At Canterbury Cathedral (medley)
Consecration At Canterbury	Gwendolen	Main Title (medley)
Days Of Youth	Hunt, The	Meeting On The Beach
End Title		

Trial (medley)
Triumph In France

Beetlejuice - see ELFMAN, Danny
Michael Keaton/Alec Baldwin/Geena Davis/Jeffrey Jones

4/25/60 — **6** — 98 — **35 Ben-Hur** ....[I] **$35** MGM 1
Charlton Heston/Hugh Griffith; cp: Miklos Rozsa; cd: Carlo Savina; includes a full-color book about the movie

Adoration Of The Magi	Love Theme	Prelude
Burning Desert	Miracle, The (Finale)	Procession To Calvary
Friendship	Mother's Love	Return To Judea
Lepers' Search For The Christ	Naval Battle	Roman March

Rowing Of The Galley Slaves
Victory Parade

Benny Goodman Story, The - see GOODMAN, Benny
Steve Allen/Donna Reed/Herbert Anderson

8/7/82 — **63** — 15 — **36 Best Little Whorehouse In Texas, The** ....[M] **$10** MCA 6112
Burt Reynolds/Dolly Parton/Dom DeLuise/Charles Durning; sw: Carol Hall/Dolly Parton

Aggie Song	**I Will Always Love You** [Dolly Parton] 53	Sidestep, The
Courtyard Shag	Lil' Ole Bitty Pissant Country Place	Sneakin' Around
Hard Candy Christmas		Texas Has A Whorehouse In It (medley)

20 Fans
Watchdog Report (medley)

1/12/85 — **1²** — 62 — ▲² — **37 Beverly Hills Cop** ....[V] **$8** MCA 5547
Eddie Murphy/Judge Reinhold/Lisa Eilbacher/John Ashton

Axel F [Harold Faltermeyer] 3	Don't Get Stopped In Beverly Hills [Shalamar]	**Heat Is On** [Glenn Frey] 2
BHC (I Can't Stop) [Rick James]	Gratitude [Danny Elfman]	**Neutron Dance** [Pointer Sisters] 6
Do You Really (Want My Love?) [Junior]		

New Attitude [Patti LaBelle] 17
Rock 'N Roll Me Again [System]
Stir It Up [Patti LaBelle] 41

6/13/87 — **8** — 26 — ▲ — **38 Beverly Hills Cop II** ....[V] **$8** MCA 6207
Eddie Murphy/Judge Reinhold/Brigitte Nielsen/Ronny Cox

All Revved Up [Jermaine Jackson]	**Cross My Broken Heart** [Jets] 7	I Want Your Sex [George Michael] 2
Be There [Pointer Sisters] 42	Hold On [Corey Hart]	In Deep [Charlie Sexton]
Better Way [James Ingram]	I Can't Stand It [Sue Ann]	Love/Hate [Pebbles]

Shakedown [Bob Seger] 1
36 Lovers [Ready For The World]

11/12/66+ — **102** — 13 — **39 Bible, The** ....[I] **$25** 20th Century 4184
George C. Scott/Ava Gardner/John Huston/Richard Harris; cp: Toshiro Mayuzumi; cd: Franco Ferrara; also see Art Linkletter

Abraham (Scene of Love)	Creation, The	Finale
Bible, Theme From The	Creation Of Adam	40 Days And 40 Nights
Cain And Abel	Creation Of Eve	New Beginning

Noah's Ark
Sodom
Tower Of Babel

10/22/83+ — **17** — 161 — ▲² — **40 Big Chill, The** ....[V-O] **$10** Motown 6062
William Hurt/Glenn Close/Jobeth Williams/Jeff Goldblum/Kevin Kline

Ain't Too Proud To Beg [Temptations] 13	**I Second That Emotion** [Smokey Robinson & The Miracles] 4	My Girl [Temptations] 1
Good Lovin' [Young Rascals] 1	Joy To The World [Three Dog Night] 1	Natural Woman (You Make Me Feel Like) [Aretha Franklin] 8
I Heard It Through The Grapevine [Marvin Gaye] 1		Tell Him [Exciters] 4

Tracks Of My Tears [Miracles] 16
Whiter Shade Of Pale [Procol Harum] 1

4/28/84 — **85** — 49 — ● — **41 Big Chill, The (More Songs From The Original Soundtrack)** ......[V-O] **$8** Motown 6094
includes 4 songs not in the film

Bad Moon Rising [Creedence Clearwater Revival] 2	In The Midnite Hour [Rascals]	**Too Many Fish In The Sea** [Marvelettes] 25
Dancing In The Street [Martha & The Vandellas] 2	It's The Same Old Song [Four Tops] 5	**Weight, The** [Band] 63
Gimme Some Lovin' [Spencer Davis Group] 7	Quicksilver Girl [Steve Miller Band]	What's Going On [Marvin Gaye] 2

When A Man Loves A Woman [Percy Sledge] 1
Wouldn't It Be Nice [Beach Boys] 8

10/24/87 — **107** — 9 — **42 Big Easy, The** ....[V] **$8** Antilles 7087
Dennis Quaid/Ellen Barkin/Ned Beatty/John Goodman

Closer To You [Dennis Quaid]	Iko, Iko [Dixie Cups] 20	Saviour, Pass Me Not [Swan Silvertones]
Colinda [Zachary Richard]	Ma 'Tit Fille [Buckwheat Zydeco]	Tell It Like It Is [Aaron Neville & The Neville Brothers]
Hey, Hey (Indians Comin') [Wild Tchoupitoulas]	Oh Yeh Yai [Terrance Simien & The Mallet Playboys]	

Tipitina [Professor Longhair]
Zydeco Gris Gris [Beausoleil]

7/27/91 — **28** — 14 — **43 Bill & Ted's Bogus Journey** ....[V] **$12** Interscope 91725
Keanu Reeves/Alex Winter/William Sadler/Joss Ackland/George Carlin

Battle Stations [Winger]	Drinking Again [Neverland]	Go To Hell [Megadeth]
Dream Of A New Day [Richie Kotzen]		God Gave Rock And Roll You II [Kiss]

Junior's Gone Wild [King's X]

DEBUT DATE	PEAK POS	WKS CHR	GOLD	ARTIST — Album Title	$	Label & Number

Perfect Crime [Faith No More] Reaper Rap [Steve Vai] Showdown [Love On Ice]
Reaper, The [Steve Vai] Shout It Out [Slaughter] Tommy The Cat [Primus]

4/8/89 170 4 44 Bill & Ted's Excellent Adventure .... [V] **$8** A&M 3915
Keanu Reeves/Alex Winter/George Carlin/Bernie Casey

Boys And Girls Are Doing It Dancing With A Gypsy [Tora In Time [Robbie Robb] Two Heads Are Better Than One
[Vital Signs] Tora] Not So Far Away [Glen Burtnick] [Power Tool]
Breakaway [Big Pig] 60 Dangerous [Shark Island] Play With Me [Extreme] Walk Away [Bricklin]
Father Time [Shark Island]

Bill Cosby "Himself" - see COSBY, Bill

10/9/71 135 7 45 Billy Jack.. [I+V] **$20** Warner 1926
Tom Laughlin/Delores Taylor; cp/cd: Mundell Lowe; also see Trial Of Billy Jack

All Forked Tongue Talk Alike Indian Dance **One Tin Soldier, The Legend** Thy Loving Hand
Ceremonial Dance It's All She Left Me **Of Billy Jack** [Coven] 26 When Will Billy Love Me [Lynn
Challenge, The Johnnie [Teresa Kelly] Rainbow Made Of Children Baker]
Flick Of The Wrist Look, Look To The Mountain [Lynn Baker] You Shouldn't Do That
Freedom Over Me [Gwen Smith] [Teresa Kelly] Ring Song [Katy Moffatt]
Hello Billy Jack Most Beautiful Day Say Goodbye, Cause You're
I Think You Always Knew Old And The New Leavin'

1/5/74 167 5 46 Billy Jack.. [R] **$15** Warner 1001
see above album for tracks; new cover features solo photo of Billy Jack

1/5/63 33 22 47 Billy Rose's Jumbo .... [M] **$25** Columbia 2260
Doris Day/Stephen Boyd/Jimmy Durante/Martha Raye; mu: Richard Rodgers; ly: Lorenz Hart; cd: George Stoll

Circus On Parade Most Beautiful Girl In The World Sawdust Spangles And Dreams This Can't Be Love
Little Girl Blue My Romance (Finale) Why Can't I?
Over And Over Again

11/12/88 169 3 48 Bird.. [I] **$8** Columbia 44299
Forest Whitaker (Bird)/Diane Venora/Sam Wright; features Charlie "Bird" Parker's original solos with instrumental backing

All Of Me I Can't Believe That You're In Laura Ornithology
April In Paris Love With Me Lester Leaps In Parker's Mood
Cool Blues Ko Ko Now's The Time This Time The Dream's On Me

Birdy - see GABRIEL, Peter
Matthew Modine/Nicolas Cage

Black And White Night Live, A - see ORBISON, Roy

Black Caesar - see BROWN, James
Fred Williamson/Art Lund/Julius W. Harris/Gloria Hendry

11/27/71 176 10 49 Bless The Beasts & Children.. [I+V] **$30** A&M 4322
Bill Mumy/Barry Robins/Miles Chapin/Jesse White; cp/cd: Barry DeVorzon & Perry Botkin, Jr.

Bless The Beasts And Cotton's Dream Free Requiem
Children [Carpenters] 67 Down The Line (includes 2 Journey's End Stampede
Bless The Beasts And Children versions) Lost [Renee Armand]
(instrumental)

5/2/87 198 1 50 Blind Date.. [V] **$8** Rhino 70705
Kim Basinger/Bruce Willis/John Larroquette

Anybody Seen Her? [Billy Vera Let You Get Away [Billy Vera & Simply Meant To Be [Henry Something For Nash [Henry
& The Beaters] The Beaters] Mancini] Mancini]
Crash, Bang, Boom [Hubert Oh, What A Nite [Billy Vera & Simply Meant To Be [Gary Talked About Lover [Keith
Tubbs] The Beaters] Morris & Jennifer Warnes] L'Netre]
Treasures [Stanley Jordan]

Blow-Up - see HANCOCK, Herbie
Vanessa Redgrave/David Hemmings/Sarah Miles

Blue Hawaii - see PRESLEY, Elvis
Elvis Presley (Chad Gates)/Joan Blackman/Angela Lansbury

Blues Brothers, The - see BLUES BROTHERS
John Belushi/Dan Aykroyd/Carrie Fisher/Cab Calloway

Bodyguard, The - see HOUSTON, Whitney
Whitney Houston/Kevin Costner

4/6/68 12 21 51 Bonnie And Clyde .... [I] **$25** Warner 1742
Warren Beatty/Faye Dunaway/Gene Hackman/Estelle Parsons; cp: Charles Strouse; includes dialogue excerpts; also see Flatt & Scruggs

Ambush (medley) Bonnie's Poem (The Story Of Buck Falls I Ain't Much Of A Lover Boy
Bonnie And Clyde [Barrow Gang] Bonnie And Clyde) Captain Hamer Spits At Bonnie I Ain't No Rich Man
Bonnie Meets Clyde (Sometimes Buck And Blanche Meet Up End Title (medley) Law's Outside! (Lucky Day)
I'm Happy) With Bonnie And Clyde (Can't Family Reunion Okies, The (medley)
Bonnie Wounded (medley) We Be Friends) Foggy Mountain Breakdown

7/18/92 4 30↑ ▲² 52 Boomerang .... [V] **$12** LaFace 26006
Eddie Murphy/Halle Berry/Robin Givens/David Alan Grier

Don't Wanna Love You [Shanice] **Give U My Heart** [Babyface It's Gonna Be Alright [Aaron 7 Day Weekend [Grace Jones]
End Of The Road [Boyz II feat. Toni Braxton] 29 Hall feat. Charlie Wilson] There U Go [Johnny Gill]
Men] 1 Hot Sex [Tribe Called Quest] **Love Shoulda Brought You** Tonight Is Right [Keith
Feels Like Heaven [Kenny **I'd Die Without You** [PM **Home** [Toni Braxton] 33 Washington]
Vaughan & The Art Of Love] Dawn] 3 Reversal Of A Dog [LaFace
Cartel]

7/30/66 42 48 53 Born Free.. [I] **$15** MGM 4368
Virginia McKenna/Bill Travers/Geoffrey Keen; cp/cd: John Barry

Born Free [Matt Monro] Fight Of The Lioness Hunt, The Reunion (medley)
Death Of Pati Flirtation Killing At Klunga Waiting For You
Elsa At Play Holiday With Elsa Main Title Warthog Hunt

1/20/90 32 15 54 Born On The Fourth Of July.. [I+V] **$12** MCA 6340
Tom Cruise/Kyra Sedgwick/Raymond J. Barry/Jerry Levine; side A: various artists; side B: instrumental; cp/cd: John Williams

American Pie (Don McLean) 1 Born On The Bayou [Broken Born On The Fourth Of July **Brown Eyed Girl** [Van
Homes] Morrison] 10

DEBUT DATE	PEAK POS	WKS CHR	G O L D	ARTIST — Album Title	$	Label & Number

| | | | | Cua Viet River, Vietnam, 1968 — Homecoming — Shooting Of Wilson | | |

Early Days, Massapequa, 1957 — Moon River *[Henry Mancini]* 11 — Soldier Boy *[Shirelles]* 1
Hard Rain's A Gonna Fall *[Edie Brickell & New Bohemians]* — My Girl *[Temptations]* 1 — Venus *[Frankie Avalon]* 1
Prologue

7/27/91 | **12** | **18** | ● | 55 Boyz N The Hood .... [V] | **$12** | Qwest 26643
Ice Cube/Cuba Gooding, Jr./Morris Chestnut/Larry Fishburne

Black On Black Crime *[Stanley Clarke]* — How To Survive In South Central *[Ice Cube]* — **Just Ask Me To** *[Tevin Campbell]* **88** — Spirit (Does Anybody Care?) *[Force One Network]*
Every Single Weekend *[KAM]* — It's Your Life *[Too Short]* — Mama Don't Take No Mess *[Yo-Yo]* — Too Young *[Hi-Five]*
Growin' Up In The Hood *[Comptons Most Wanted]* — Just A Friendly Game Of Baseball *[Main Source]* — Me And You *[Tony! Toni! Tone!]* — Work It Out *[Monie Love]*
Hangin' Out *[2 Live Crew]* — — Setembro *[Quincy Jones]*

Bram Stoker's Dracula - see Dracula

Breakfast At Tiffany's - see MANCINI, Henry
Audrey Hepburn/George Peppard/Patricia Neal

3/9/85 | **17** | **26** | ● | 56 Breakfast Club, The .... [V] | **$8** | A&M 5045
Molly Ringwald/Anthony Michael Hall/Emilio Estevez/Judd Nelson

Didn't I Tell You *[Joyce Kennedy]* — Fire In The Twilight *[Wang Chung]* — I'm The Dude *[Keith Forsey]* — We Are Not Alone *[Karla DeVito]*
Don't You (Forget About Me) *[Simple Minds]* 1 — Heart Too Hot To Hold *[Jesse Johnson & Stephanie Spruill]* — Love Theme *[Keith Forsey]*
Dream Montage *[Gary Chang]* — — Reggae, The *[Keith Forsey]* — Waiting *[Elizabeth Daily]*

6/2/84 | **8** | **23** | ▲ | 57 Breakin' .... [V] | **$10** | Polydor 821919
Lucinda Dickey/Adolfo Quinones/Michael Chambers

Ain't Nobody *[Rufus & Chaka Khan]* — **Breakin'...There's No Stopping Us** *[Ollie & Jerry]* 9 — Freakshow On The Dance Floor *[Bar-Kays]* 73 — Reckless *[Chris Taylor, David Storrs & Ice-T]*
Body Work *[Hot Streak]* — Cut-It *[Re-Flex]* — Heart Of The Beat *[3-V]* — Showdown *[Ollie & Jerry]*
— — 99 1/2 *[Carol Lynn Townes]* 77 — Street People *[Fire Fox]*

1/12/85 | **52** | **13** | | 58 Breakin' 2 Electric Boogaloo .... [V] | **$8** | Polydor 823696
Lucinda Dickey/Adolfo Quinones/Michael Chambers

Believe In The Beat *[Carol Lynn Townes]* — Gotta Have The Money *[Steve Donn]* — Oye Mamacita *[Rags & Riches]* — Trommeltanz (Din Daa Daa) *[George Kranz]*
Electric Boogaloo *[Ollie & Jerry]* — I Don't Wanna Come Down *[Mark Scott]* — Set It Out *[Midway]* — When I.C.U. *[Ollie & Jerry]*
— — Stylin', Profilin' *[Firefox]*

4/2/88 | **67** | **11** | | 59 Bright Lights, Big City .... [V] | **$8** | Warner 25688
Michael J. Fox/Kiefer Sutherland/Phoebe Cates/Dianne Wiest

Century's End *[Donald Fagen]* **83** — Good Love *[Prince]* — Obsessed *[Noise Club]* — **Pump Up The Volume** *[M/A/R/R/S]* **13**
Divine Emotions *[Narada]* — Ice Cream Days *[Jennifer Hall]* — Pleasure, Little Treasure *[Depeche Mode]* — **True Faith** *[New Order]* **32**
— Kiss And Tell *[Bryan Ferry]* 31 — —
— Love Attack *[Konk]* — —

7/5/80 | **123** | **6** | | 60 Bronco Billy .... [I+V] | **$10** | Elektra 512
Clint Eastwood/Sondra Locke/Geoffrey Lewis/Scatman Crothers; cp/cd: Steve Dorff

Bar Room Buddies *[Merle Haggard & Clint Eastwood]* — Bronco Billy *[Ronnie Milsap]* — Love Theme — Stardust Cowboy *[Reinsmen]*
Bayou Lullaby *[Penny DeHaven]* — Cowboys And Clowns *[Ronnie Milsap]* — Misery And Gin *[Merle Haggard]* — Stars And Stripes Forever
— — Not So Great Train Robbery — Thunderer's March

7/22/78 | **86** | **13** | | 61 Buddy Holly Story, The .... | **$10** | Epic 35412
Gary Busey/Don Stroud/Charles Martin Smith; Busey plays Buddy and performs the vocals

Clear Lake Medley — It's So Easy — Rave On — Well All Right
Everyday — Listen To Me — Roller Rink Medley — Whole Lotta Shakin' Goin' On
I'm Gonna Love You Too — Maybe Baby — True Love Ways

8/6/88 | **157** | **6** | | 62 Bull Durham .... [V] | **$8** | Capitol 90586
Kevin Costner/Susan Sarandon/Tim Robbins/Trey Wilson

All Night Dance *[Bennie Wallace/Dr. John with Stevie Ray Vaughan]* — Centerfield *[John Fogerty]* 44 — So Long Baby, Goodbye *[Blasters]* — You Done Me Wrong *[Pat McLaughlin]*
Born To Be Bad *[George Thorogood]* — I Got Loaded *[Los Lobos]* — Try A Little Tenderness *[Bennie Wallace/Dr. John]* —
Can't Tear It Up Enuff *[Fabulous Thunderbirds]* — Love Ain't No Triple Play *[Bennie Wallace/Dr. John with Bonnie Raitt]* — Woman Loves A Man *[Joe Cocker]*
— Middle Of Nowhere *[House Of Shock]* —

10/15/88+ | **54** | **23** | ● | 63 Buster .... [V] | **$8** | Atlantic 81905
Phil Collins/Julie Walters/Larry Lamb/Stephanie Lawrence

Big Noise *[Phil Collins]* — **I Got You Babe** *[Sonny & Cher]* 1 — **Keep On Running** *[Spencer Davis Group]* **76** — **Two Hearts** *[Phil Collins]* 1
Groovy Kind Of Love *[Phil Collins]* 1 — I Just Don't Know What To Do With Myself *[Dusty Springfield]* — Loco In Acapulco *[Four Tops]* — Will You Still Be Waiting? *[Anne Dudley]*
How Do You Do It? *[Gerry & The Pacemakers]* 9 — **Just One Look** *[Hollies]* 44 — Robbery, The *[Anne Dudley]* — Sweets For My Sweet *[Searchers]*

Bustin' Loose - see FLACK, Roberta
Richard Pryor/Cicely Tyson

11/29/69+ | **16** | **74** | ● | 64 Butch Cassidy And The Sundance Kid .... [I+V] | **$10** | A&M 4227
Paul Newman/Robert Redford/Katharine Ross/Strother Martin; cp/cd: Burt Bacharach

Come Touch The Sun — On A Bicycle Built For Joy *[B.J. Thomas]* — Raindrops Keep Fallin' On My Head (instrumental)
Not Goin' Home Anymore — **Raindrops Keep Fallin' On My Head** *[B.J. Thomas]* 1 — South American Getaway
Old Fun City — — Sundance Kid

4/27/63 | **2²** | **55** | | 65 Bye Bye Birdie .... [M] | **$15** | RCA 1081
Ann-Margret/Jesse Pearson/Janet Leigh/Dick Van Dyke; mu: Charles Strouse; ly: Lee Adams; cd: Johnny Green; also see Original Cast ('60)

Bye Bye Birdie (medley) — Hymn For A Sunday Evening — One Boy — Put On A Happy Face
Honestly Sincere — Kids — One Last Kiss — Rosie (medley)
How Lovely To Be A Woman — Lot Of Livin' To Do — Overture — Telephone Hour

3/18/72+ | **25** | **72** | ● | 66 Cabaret .... [M] | **$15** | ABC 752
Liza Minnelli/Michael York/Joel Grey; mu: John Kander; ly: Fred Ebb; also see Original Cast ('67)

Cabaret — If You Could See Her — Money, Money — Tomorrow Belongs To Me
Finale — Maybe This Time — Sitting Pretty — Two Ladies
Heiraten (Married) — Mein Herr — Tiller Girls — Willkommen

DEBUT DATE	PEAK POS	WKS CHR	GOLD		ARTIST — Album Title	$	Label & Number
8/23/80	78	12		67	Caddyshack .... [V]	$10	Columbia 36737

Chevy Chase/Bill Murray/Rodney Dangerfield/Ted Knight; side 1: Kenny Loggins; side 2: various artists

Any Way You Want It [Journey] 23	Divine Intervention [Johnny Mandel]	Make The Move [Kenny Loggins]
Big Bang [Johnny Mandel]	**I'm Alright** [Kenny Loggins] 7	Mr. Night [Kenny Loggins]
	Lead The Way [Kenny Loggins]	

Something On Your Mind [Hilly Michaels]
There She Goes [Beat]

| 11/11/67+ | 11 | 87 | ▲ | 68 | Camelot .... [M] | $15 | Warner 1712 |

Richard Harris/Vanessa Redgrave; mu: Frederick Loewe; ly: Alan Jay Lerner; cd: Alfred Newman; also see Original Cast ('61)/Living Strings/Percy Faith

C'est Moi	Guenevere	If Ever I Would Leave You	Take Me To The Fair
Camelot (medley)	How To Handle A Woman	Lusty Month Of May	Wedding Ceremony (medley)
Children's Chorus (medley)	I Loved You Once In Silence	Overture (medley)	What Do The Simple Folk Do?
Finale Ultimo	I Wonder What The King Is	Prelude (medley)	
Follow Me (medley)	Doing Tonight	Simple Joys Of Maidenhood	

Can't Stop The Music - see VILLAGE PEOPLE
Village People/Valerie Perrine/Bruce Jenner/Steve Guttenberg

| 5/2/60 | 3 | 68 | | 69 | **Can-Can** .... [M] | $20 | Capitol 1301 |

Frank Sinatra/Shirley MacLaine/Maurice Chevalier/Louis Jourdan; sw: Cole Porter; cd: Nelson Riddle

C'est Magnifique	I Love Paris	Live And Let Live	You Do Something To Me
Can-Can	It's All Right With Me	Maidens Typical Of France	
Come Along With Me	Just One Of Those Things	Main Title (medley)	
Entr'acte	Let's Do It	Montmart' (medley)	

| 2/1/69 | 49 | 16 | | 70 | Candy.. [I+V] | $25 | ABC 9 |

Ewa Aulin (Candy)/Richard Burton/Marlon Brando; cp/cd: Dave Grusin

Ascension To Virginity	Constant Journey	**Magic Carpet Ride** [Steppenwolf] 3	**Rock Me** [Steppenwolf] 10
Birth By Descent	Every Mother's Daughter		Spec-Rac-Tac-Para-Comm
Border Town Blues: A Blunt Instrument	It's Always Because Of This: A Deformity	Marlon & His Sacred Bird	
Child Of The Universe [Byrds]		Opening Night: By Surgery	

Car Wash - see ROSE ROYCE
Richard Pryor/Franklin Ajaye/Ivan Dixon/George Carlin

| 2/8/64 | 100 | 9 | | 71 | Cardinal, The.. [I] | $50 | RCA 1084 |

Tom Tryon/John Huston/Carol Lynley/Robert Morse; cp/cd: Jerome Moross

Annemarie	Cardinal's Faith	Mozart: Alleluia	Way Down South
Cardinal In Vienna	Dixieland-Tango	Stonebury	
Cardinal Themes	Main Title	They Haven't Got The Girls In	
Cardinal's Decision	Monks At Casamari	The U.S.A.	

| 2/25/56 | 2[1] | 57 | ▲ | 72 | **Carousel**.. [M] | $30 | Capitol 694 |

Gordon MacRae/Shirley Jones; mu: Richard Rodgers; ly: Oscar Hammerstein II; cd: Alfred Newman; also see Original Cast ('62-special version)

Blow High, Blow Low	Mister Snow	What's The Use Of Wondrin'	You're A Queer One, Julie
Carousel Waltz	Real Nice Clambake	When The Children Are Asleep	Jordan!
If I Loved You	Soliloquy	You'll Never Walk Alone	
June Is Bustin' Out All Over	Stonecutters Cut It On Stone		

| 9/5/64 | 141 | 3 | | 73 | Carpetbaggers, The .... [I] | $30 | Ava 45 |

George Peppard/Alan Ladd/Carroll Baker/Bob Cummings; cp/cd: Elmer Bernstein

Carpetbagger Blues	Forbidden Room	Main Title	Producer Asks For A Divorce
Carpetbaggers, The	Jonas Hits Bottom	New Star	Speak Of The Devil
Finale	Love Theme		

Carry It On - see BAEZ, Joan

| 5/13/67 | 22 | 21 | | 74 | Casino Royale.. [I] | $50 | Colgems 5005 |

Peter Sellers/David Niven/Ursula Andress/Woody Allen; cp/cd: Burt Bacharach

Big Cowboys And Indians Fight At Casino Royale (medley)	First Stop Berlin (medley)	Le Chifre's Torture Of The Mind	Money Penny Goes For Broke
Casino Royale [Herb Alpert & The Tijuana Brass] 27	Flying Saucer (medley)	Little French Boy	Sir James' Trip To Find Mata
	Hi There Miss Goodthighs	**Look Of Love** [Dusty Springfield] 22	Venerable Sir James Bond
Dream On James, You're Winning	Home James, Don't Spare The Horses	Look Of Love (instrumental)	

| 4/17/82 | 47 | 14 | | 75 | Cat People .... [I] | $10 | Backstreet 6107 |

Nastassia Kinski/Malcolm McDowell/John Heard; cp: Giorgio Moroder

Autopsy, The	**Cat People (Putting Out Fire)** [David Bowie] 67	Leopard Tree Dream	Paul's Theme (Jogging Chase)
Bring The Prod		Myth, The	To The Bridge
	Irena's Theme	Night Rabbit	Transformation Seduction

Charade - see MANCINI, Henry
Cary Grant/Audrey Hepburn/Walter Matthau/James Coburn

Chariots Of Fire - see VANGELIS
Ian Charleson/Ben Cross/Nigel Havers/Nick Farrell

Children Of Sanchez - see MANGIONE, Chuck
Anthony Quinn/Dolores Del Rio/Katy Jurado

| 11/9/68+ | 58 | 28 | | 76 | Chitty Chitty Bang Bang .... [M] | $20 | United Art. 5188 |

Dick Van Dyke/Sally Ann Howes/Lionel Jeffries/Gert Frobe; sw: Richard M. Sherman and Robert B. Sherman

Chitty Chitty Bang Bang (includes 5 versions)	Doll On A Music Box (medley)	Me Ol' Bam-Boo	Toot Sweets
	Hushabye Mountain	Posh!	Truly Scrumptious
Chu-Chi Face	Lovely, Lonely Man	Roses Of Success	You Two

| 12/28/85+ | 77 | 12 | | 77 | Chorus Line, A - The Movie .... [M] | $8 | Casablanca 826306 |

Michael Douglas/Terrence Mann/Alyson Reed/Cameron English; mu: Marvin Hamlisch; ly: Edward Kleban; cd: Ralph Burns

At The Ballet	I Hope I Get It	One (includes 2 versions)	What I Did For Love
Dance: Ten; Looks: Three	Let Me Dance For You	Surprise, Surprise	Who Am I Anyway?
I Can Do That	Nothing		

Christiane F. - see BOWIE, David
Natja Brunkhorst/Thomas Haustein

DEBUT DATE	PEAK POS	WKS CHR	GOLD	ARTIST — Album Title	$	Label & Number

1/21/84 · **177** · 5 · **78** Christine ....[V-O] · **$10** · Motown 6086
Keith Gordon/John Stockwell/Alexandra Paul/Harry Dean Stanton

Bad To The Bone *[George Thorogood]*	Harlem Nocturne *[Viscounts]* **52**	Little Bitty Pretty One *[Thurston Harris]* **6**
Bony Moronie *[Larry Williams]* **14**	I Wonder Why *[Dion & The Belmonts]* **22**	Not Fade Away *[Buddy Holly]*
Christine Attacks *[John Carpenter & Alan Howarth]*	Keep A Knockin' *[Little Richard]* **8**	Pledging My Love *[Johnny Ace]* **17**

Rock 'N' Roll Is Here To Stay *[Danny & The Juniors]* **19**
We Belong Together *[Robert & Johnny]* **32**

Clambake - see PRESLEY, Elvis
Elvis Presley (Scott Heywood)/Shelley Fabares/Will Hutchins

Claudine - see KNIGHT, Gladys/Pips
James Earl Jones/Diahann Carroll/Lawrence Hilton-Jacobs

6/22/63 · **2³** · 27 · **79** Cleopatra ....[I] · **$35** · 20th Century 5008
Elizabeth Taylor/Richard Burton/Rex Harrison; cp/cd: Alex North

Antony And Cleopatra	Cleopatra Enters Rome	Gift For Caesar
Antony--Wait...	Cleopatra's Barge	Grant Me An Honorable Way To Die
Caesar And Cleopatra	Dying Is Less Than Love	Love And Hate
Caesar's Assassination	Fire Burns, The Fire Burns	

My Love Is My Master
Taste Of Death

8/18/73 · **109** · 10 · **80** Cleopatra Jones ....[I-V] · **$12** · Warner 2719
Tamara Dobson/Bernie Casey/Shelley Winters; cp/cd: J.J. Johnson

Airport Flight	Cleopatra Jones, Theme From (Instrumental)	Go Chase Cleo
Cleo And Reuben	Desert Sunrise	Goin' To The Chase
Cleopatra Jones, Theme From *[Joe Simon]* **18**	Emdee	Hurts So Good *[Millie Jackson]* **24**

Love Doctor *[Millie Jackson]*
Wrap Up
Wrecking Yard

2/5/72 · **34** · 31 · **81** Clockwork Orange, A ....[I] · **$10** · Warner 2573
Malcolm McDowell/Patrick Magee; cp/cd: Walter Carlos; also see Walter Carlos

Beethoven: Ninth Symphony, Fourth Movement	Clockwork Orange, Theme From A	Overture To The Sun
Beethoven: Ninth Symphony, Second Movement	I Want To Marry A Lighthouse Keeper	Pomp And Circumstance (includes 2 versions)
		Rossini: William Tell Overture

Singin' In The Rain *[Gene Kelly]*
Thieving Magpie
Timesteps
Title Music

1/7/78 · **17** · 16 · ● · **82** Close Encounters Of The Third Kind ....[I] · **$12** · Arista 9500
Richard Dreyfuss/Teri Garr; cp/cd: John Williams; includes bonus single of the theme song by John Williams; also see Meco and Zubin Mehta

Abduction Of Barry	Close Encounters Of The Third Kind, Theme From **13**	Main Title (medley)
Appearance Of The Visitors	Conversation, The	Mountain Visions (medley)
Arrival Of Sky Harbor	I Can't Believe It's Real	Night Seige
Climbing Devil's Tower		Nocturnal Pursuit

Resolution

7/26/86 · **122** · 6 · **83** Club Paradise ....[V] · **$8** · Columbia 40404
Robin Williams/Peter O'Toole/Rick Moranis/Twiggy

American Plan *[Jimmy Cliff]*	Lion Awakes *[Jimmy Cliff]*	Sweetie Come From America *[Well Pleased & Satisfied]*
Brightest Star *[Jimmy Cliff]*	Love People *[Blue Riddim Band]*	Third World People *[Jimmy Cliff]*
Club Paradise *[Jimmy Cliff]*	Seven Day Weekend *[Jimmy Cliff & Elvis Costello]*	
Grenada *[Mighty Sparrow]*		

You Can't Keep A Good Man Down *[Jimmy Cliff]*

3/29/80 · **40** · 20 · ● · **84** Coal Miner's Daughter .... · **$10** · MCA 5107
Sissy Spacek/Tommy Lee Jones/Beverly D'Angelo/Levon Helm; based on Loretta Lynn's life (Spacek plays Loretta); vocals performed by Spacek, D'Angelo and Helm

Amazing Grace	Crazy	One's On The Way
Back In Baby's Arms	Great Titanic	Sweet Dreams
Blue Moon Of Kentucky	I Fall To Pieces	There He Goes
Coal Miner's Daughter	I'm A Honky Tonk Girl	Walking After Midnight

You Ain't Woman Enough To Take My Man
You're Lookin' At Country

6/28/86 · **100** · 6 · **85** Cobra ....[V] · **$8** · Scotti Br. 40325
Sylvester Stallone/Brigitte Nielsen/Reni Santoni

Angel Of The City *[Robert Tepper]*	Hold On To Your Vision *[Gary Wright]*	Skyline *[Sylvester Levay]*
Chase *[Sylvester Levay]*		Suave *[Miami Sound Machine]*
Cobra *[Sylvester Levay]*	Loving On Borrowed Time (Love Theme) *[Gladys Knight & Bill Medley]*	Two Into One *[Bill Medley & Carmen Twillie]*
Feel The Heat *[Jean Beauvoir]* **73**		

Voice Of America's Sons *[John Cafferty]* **62**

8/13/88+ · **2¹** · 61 · ▲⁴ · **86** Cocktail ....[V] · **$8** · Elektra 60806
Tom Cruise/Bryan Brown/Elisabeth Shue

All Shook Up *[Ry Cooder]*	Kokomo *[Beach Boys]* **1**	Rave On *[John Cougar Mellencamp]*
Don't Worry, Be Happy *[Bobby McFerrin]* **1**	Oh, I Love You So *[Preston Smith]*	Since When *[Robbie Nevil]*
Hippy Hippy Shake *[Georgia Satellites]* **45**	Powerful Stuff *[Fabulous Thunderbirds]* **65**	Tutti Frutti *[Little Richard]* **17**
		Wild Again *[Starship]* **73**

7/27/85 · **188** · 4 · **87** Cocoon ....[I] · **$8** · Polydor 827041
Don Ameche/Wilford Brimley/Hume Cronyn/Jessica Tandy; cp/cd: James Horner

Ascension, The	Cocoon (Theme)	Gravity
Boys Are Out	Discovered In The Poolhouse!	Lovemaking, The
Chase, The	First Tears	Returning To The Sea

Rose's Death
Sad Goodbyes
Through The Window

11/15/86 · **81** · 15 · **88** Color Of Money, The ....[V] · **$8** · MCA 6189
Paul Newman/Tom Cruise/Mary Elizabeth Mastrantonio/Helen Shaver

Don't Tell Me Nothin' *[Willie Dixon]*	Main Title *[Robbie Robertson]*	Standing On The Edge Of Love *[B.B. King]*
It's In The Way That You Use It *[Eric Clapton]*	Modern Blues *[Robbie Robertson]*	Two Brothers And A Stranger *[Mark Knopfler]*
Let Yourself In For It *[Robert Palmer]*	My Baby's In Love With Another Guy *[Robert Palmer]*	

Werewolves Of London *[Warren Zevon]* **21**
Who Owns This Place *[Don Henley]*

3/8/86 · **79** · 13 · **89** Color Purple, The .... · **$10** · Qwest 25389 [2]
Whoopi Goldberg/Danny Glover/Margaret Avery/Oprah Winfrey; music produced by Quincy Jones

Body And Soul (medley) *[Coleman Hawkins]*	Celie Leaves With Mr.	Don't Make Me No Never Mind *[John Lee Hooker]*
Bus Pulls Out	Celie Shaves Mr. (medley)	First Letter
Careless Love *[Tata Vega]*	Celie's New House (medley)	Heaven Belongs To You
Celie And Harpo Grow Up (medley)	Champagne Train	High Life (medley)
Celie Cooks Shug Breakfast	Corrine And Olivia	I'm Here
	Dirty Dozens *[Tata Vega]*	J.B. King

Junk Bucket Blues *[Get Happy Band]*
Katutoka Corrine
Letter Search
Main Title
Maybe God Is Tryin' To Tell You Somethin'

DEBUT DATE	PEAK POS	WKS CHR	GOLD	ARTIST — Album Title	$	Label & Number

| | | | | Miss Celie's Blues (Sister) [Tata Vega] — My Heart (Will Always Lead Me Back To You) [Louis Armstrong] — Proud Theme (medley) | | Three On The Road |

Miss Celie's Blues (Sister) [Tata Vega]
Mr. Dresses To See Shug (medley)
My Heart (Will Always Lead Me Back To You) [Louis Armstrong]
Nettie Teaches Celie
Nettie's Letters
Overture
Proud Theme (medley)
Reunion (Finale)
Scarification Ceremony (medley)
Separation, The
Sophia Leaves Harpo

5/14/88 — 31 — 19 ● — 90 Colors .... [V] $8 Warner 25713
Sean Penn/Robert Duvall/Maria Conchita Alonso

Butcher Shop [Kool G. Rap]
Colors [Ice-T]
Everywhere I Go (Colors) [Rick James]
Go On Girl [Roxanne Shante]
Let The Rhythm Run [Salt-N-Pepa]
Mad Mad World [7A3]
Mind Is A Terrible Thing To Waste [M.C. Shan]
Paid In Full [Eric B. & Rakim]
Raw [Big Daddy Kane]
Six Gun [Decadent Dub Team]

9/23/72 — 198 — 2 — 91 Come Back Charleston Blue .... $20 Atco 7010
Godfrey Cambridge/Raymond St. Jacques/Adam Wade; cp/cd: Donny Hathaway (also performs the vocals)

Basie
Bossa Nova (medley)
Come Back Basie (medley)
Come Back Charleston Blue (medley) [Donny Hathaway & Margie Joseph]
Furniture Truck
Gravedigger Jones & Coffin Ed's Funeral (medley)
Harlem Dawn (medley)
Hearse To Graveyard (medley)
Liberation (medley)
Little Ghetto Boy
Main Theme
Scratchy Record (medley)
String Segue
Tim's High
Vegetable Wagon (medley)

7/30/88 — 177 — 2 — 92 Coming To America .... [V] $8 Atco 90958
Eddie Murphy/Arsenio Hall/James Earl Jones/John Amos

Addicted To You [Levert]
All Dressed Up (Ready To Hit The Town) [Chico DeBarge]
Better Late Than Never [Cover Girls]
Come Into My Life [Laura Branigan & Joe Esposito]
Comin' Correct [J.J. Fad]
Coming To America (Part One) [System 91]
I Like It Like That [Michael Rodgers]
Livin' The Good Life [Sister Sledge]
That's The Way It Is [Mel & Kim]
Transparent [Nona Hendryx]

9/14/91 — 8 — 72↑▲ — 93 Commitments, The .... $12 MCA 10286
Andrew Strong/Angeline Ball/Robert Arkins/Maria Doyle/Bronagh Gallagher

Bye Bye Baby
Chain Of Fools
Dark End Of The Street
Destination Anywhere
Do Right Woman Do Right Man
I Can't Stand The Rain
I Never Loved A Man
In The Midnight Hour
Mr. Pitiful
Mustang Sally
Slip Away
Take Me To The River
Treat Her Right
Try A Little Tenderness 67

4/4/92 — 118 — 12 — 94 Commitments - Vol. 2, The .... $12 MCA 10506
4 of the 11 songs are from the film; all songs on above 2 albums performed by the film's actors

Bring It On Home To Me
Fa-Fa-Fa-Fa-Fa (Sad Song)
Grits Ain't Groceries
Hard To Handle
I Thank You
Land Of A Thousand Dances
Nowhere To Run
Saved
Show Me
That's The Way Love Is
Too Many Fish In The Sea

6/12/82 — 162 — 5 — 95 Conan The Barbarian .... [I] $8 MCA 6108
Arnold Schwarzenegger/James Earl Jones; cp/cd: Basil Poledouris

Anvil Of Crom
Atlantean Sword
Awakening, The (medley)
Battle Of The Mounds
Civilization (medley)
Funeral Pyre
Gift Of Fury
Orgy, The
Orphans Of Doom (medley)
Riddle Of Steel (medley)
Riders Of Doom (medley)
Search, The
Theology (medley)
Wheel Of Pain
Wifeing (Love Theme)

Cool As Ice - see VANILLA ICE
Vanilla Ice/Kristin Minter/Michael Gross

8/1/92 — 89 — 6 — 96 Cool World, Songs From The .... [V] $12 Warner 45009
Kim Basinger/Gabriel Byrne/Brad Pitt

Ah-Ah [Moby]
Disappointed [Electronic]
Do That Thang [Da Juice]
Greedy [Pure]
Her Sassy Kiss [My Life With The Thrill Kill Kult]
Industry And Seduction [Tom Bailey]
Mindless [Mindless]
N.W.O. [Ministry]
Next Is The E [Moby]
Papua New Guinea [Future Sound Of London]
Play With Me [Thompson Twins]
Real Cool World [David Bowie]
Sex On Wheelz [My Life With The Thrill Kill Kult]
Under [Brian Eno]
Witch, The [Cult]

Cornbread, Earl and Me - see BLACKBYRDS
Moses Gunn/Bernie Casey/Keith Wilkes

1/19/85 — 93 — 10 — 97 Cotton Club, The .... $8 Geffen 24062
Richard Gere/Gregory Hines; cd: Bob Wilder; story based on a Harlem nightclub, featuring new versions of jazz standards from 1927-36

Best Beats Sandman (medley)
Copper Colored Gal
Cotton Club Stomp #1
Cotton Club Stomp #2
Creole Love Call
Daybreak Express Medley
Depression Hits (medley)
Dixie Kidnaps Vera
Drop Me Off In Harlem
East St. Louis Toodle-O
Ill Wind
Minnie The Moocher
Mooche, The
Mood Indigo
Ring Dem Bells
Truckin'

12/1/84+ — 120 — 15 — 98 Country .... [I] $8 Windham Hill 1039
Jessica Lange/Sam Shepard; cp/cd: Charles Gross; pf: George Winston/Darol Anger/Mark Isham/Mike Marshall

Aftermath
Auction, The
Chants
Country Night
Epilog (medley)
Harvest Field
Home
Homecoming
Hymn, A
Iowa Chill
Parting Friends
Sunday
Winter Mantra

Crossroads - see COODER, Ry
Ralph Macchio/Joe Seneca/Jami Gertz

2/11/84 — 181 — 4 — 99 D.C. Cab .... [V] $8 MCA 6128
Mr. T/Gary Busey/Anne DeSalvo/Max Gail/Adam Baldwin

D.C. Cab [Peabo Bryson]
Deadline U.S.A. [Shalamar]
Dream (Hold On To Your Dream) [Irene Cara] 37
Knock Me On My Feet [Champaign]
Knock Me On My Feet (instrumental) [Giorgio Moroder]
One More Time Around The Block Ophelia [Gary U.S. Bonds]
Party Me Tonight [Stephanie Mills]
Single Heart [DeBarge]
Squeeze Play [Karen Kamon]
World Champion [Leon Sylvers III]

12/1/58 — 21 — 1 — 100 Damn Yankees .... [M] $45 RCA 1047
Tab Hunter/Gwen Verdon/Ray Walston/Jean Stapleton; sw: Richard Adler and Jerry Ross; also see Original Cast ('55)

Goodbye, Old Girl
Heart
Little Brains, A Little Talent
Overture
Shoeless Joe From Hannibal, Mo.
Six Months Out Of Every Year
There's Something About An Empty Chair
Those Were The Good Old Days
Two Lost Souls
Whatever Lola Wants (includes 2 versions)
Who's Got The Pain

DEBUT DATE	PEAK POS	WKS CHR	GOLD	ARTIST — Album Title	$	Label & Number

12/22/90+   **48**   69   ●   **101 Dances With Wolves** ....[I] **$12**   Epic 46982
Kevin Costner/Mary McDonnell/Graham Greene/Rodney A. Grant; cp/cd: John Barry

Buffalo Hunt	Journey To The Buffalo Killing	Main Title (medley)	Ride To Fort Hays
Death Of Cisco	Ground	Pawnee Attack	Stands With A Fist Remembers
Death Of Timmons	Kicking Bird's Gift	Rescue Of Dances With Wolves	Two Socks At Play
Farewell (End Title)	Looks Like A Suicide (medley)	Return To Winter Camp (medley)	Two Socks--The Wolf Theme
John Dunbar Theme	Loss Of The Journal (medley)		
Journey To Fort Sedgewick	Love Theme		

8/1/70   **113**   7   **102 Darling Lili** .... **$15**   RCA 1000
Julie Andrews/Rock Hudson/Jeremy Kemp; cp/cd: Henry Mancini

Can-Can Cafe	Gypsy Violin	Overture	Whistling Away The Dark
Darling Lili	I'll Give You Three Guesses	Skal (Let's Have Another On Me)	(includes 2 versions)
Girl In No Man's Land	Little Birds (Les P'tits Oiseaux)	Smile Away Each Rainy Day	Your Good-Will Ambassador

7/14/90   **27**   16   ●   **103 Days Of Thunder** ....[V] **$12**   DGC 24294
Tom Cruise/Robert Duvall/Randy Quaid/Nicole Kidman

Break Through The Barrier	**Hearts In Trouble** [Chicago] 75	Last Note Of Freedom [David	Thunder Box [Apollo Smile]
[Tina Turner]	Knockin' On Heaven's Door	Coverdale]	Trail Of Broken Hearts [Cher]
Deal For Life [John Waite]	[Guns N' Roses]	Long Live The Night [Joan Jett]	**You Gotta Love Someone**
Gimme Some Lovin' [Terry Reid]		Show Me Heaven [Maria McKee]	[Elton John] 43

Death Wish II - see PAGE, Jimmy
Charles Bronson/Jill Ireland/Vincent Gardenia

7/2/77   **70**   10   **104 Deep, The** .... [I+V] **$10**   Casablanca 7060
Nick Nolte/Jacqueline Bisset/Robert Shaw; cp/cd: John Barry

Deep, The (Theme)	Disco Calypso [Beckett]	Down, Deep Inside (includes 2	Return To The Sea - 2033 A.D.
		versions) [Donna Summer]	

5/9/92   **166**   7   **105 Deep Cover** ....[V] **$12**   Solar 75330
Larry Fishburne/Jeff Goldblum/Gregory Sierra/Clarence Williams III

Deep Cover [Dr. Dre]	Love Or Lust [Jewell]	Nickel Slick Nigga [Ko-Kane]	Typical Relationship [Times 3]
Digits [Deele]	Minute You Fall In Love [3rd	Sex Is On [Po', Broke & Lonely?]	Way (Is In The House) [Calloway]
Down With My Nigga [Paradise]	Avenue]	Sound Of One Hand Clapping	Why You Frontin' On Me
I See Ya Jay [Ragtime]	**Mr. Loverman** [Shabba	[Calloway]	[Emmage]
John And Betty's Theme [Michel	Ranks] 40		
Colombier]			

1/22/55   **4**   16   **106 Deep In My Heart** ....[M] **$35**   MGM 3153
Jose Ferrer/Merle Oberon/Walter Pidgeon; cd: Adolph Deutsch; based on the life and the melodies of composer Sigmund Romberg

Auf Wiedersehn	It	Road To Paradise (medley)	Will You Remember (medley)
Deep In My Heart (medley)	Leg Of Mutton (Some Smoke)	Serenade	Will You Remember
Desert Song (medley)	Lover Come Back To Me	Softly As In A Morning Sunrise	(Sweetheart) (medley)
I Love To Go Swimmin' With	Mr. And Mrs. (medley)	Stout-Hearted Men (medley)	You Will Remember Vienna
Wimmen (medley)	One Kiss (medley)	When I Grow Too Old To Dream	Your Land And My Land
		(medley)	

Devil's Angels - see ALLAN, Davie
John Cassavetes/Beverly Adams

1/8/72   **74**   12   **107 Diamonds Are Forever** ....[I] **$15**   United Art. 5220
Sean Connery/Jill St. John/Jimmy Dean; cp/cd: John Barry

Bond Meets Bambi And	Death At The Whyte House	Diamonds Are Forever	Q's Trick
Thumper	**Diamonds Are Forever** [Shirley	(instrumental)	Tiffany Case
Bond Smells A Rat	Bassey] 57	007 And Counting	To Hell With Blofeld
Circus, Circus		Moon Buggy Ride	

6/30/90   **108**   5   **108 Dick Tracy** ....[V] **$12**   Sire 26236
Warren Beatty/Al Pacino/Madonna/Glenne Headly; also see Danny Elfman and Madonna

Blue Nights [Tommy Page]	Looking Glass Sea [Erasure]	Ridin' The Rails [k.d. lang &	Some Lucky Day [Andy Paley]
Confidence Man [Patti Austin]	Mr. Fix-It (includes 2 versions)	Take 6]	Wicked Woman, Foolish Man
Dick Tracy (includes 2 versions)	[Darlene Love]	Rompin' & Stompin' [Al Jarreau]	[August Darnell]
[Ice-T]	Pep, Vim And Verve [Jeff	Slow Rollin' Mama [LaVern	You're In The Doghouse Now
It Was The Whiskey Talkin' (Not	Vincent & Andy Paley]	Baker]	[Brenda Lee]
Me) (includes 2 versions)			
[Jerry Lee Lewis]			

9/19/87   **1[18]**   96   ▲[10]   **109 Dirty Dancing** ....[V] **$8**   RCA 6408
Patrick Swayze/Jennifer Grey/Cynthia Rhodes/Jerry Orbach

Be My Baby [Ronettes] 2	**In The Still Of The Night** [Five	She's Like The Wind [Patrick	**Yes** [Merry Clayton] 45
Hey! Baby [Bruce Channel] 1	Satins] 24	Swayze feat. Wendy Fraser] 3	You Don't Own Me [Blow
Hungry Eyes [Eric Carmen] 4	Love Is Strange [Mickey &	**Stay** [Maurice Williams] 1	Monkeys]
(I've Had) The Time Of My	Sylvia] 11	Where Are You Tonight [Tom	
Life [Bill Medley & Jennifer	Overload [Zappacosta]	Johnston]	
Warnes] 1			

3/19/88   **3**   52   ▲[3]   **110 Dirty Dancing, More** ....[V-O] **$8**   RCA 6965
2nd volume released from the film Dirty Dancing

Baby's Walk [John Morris Orch.]	Johnny's Mambo [Michael Lloyd	Merengue [Michael Lloyd & Le	Trot The Fox [Michael Lloyd &
Big Girls Don't Cry [4	& Le Disc]	Disc]	Le Disc]
Seasons] 1	Kellerman's Anthem [Emile	Some Kind Of Wonderful	**Will You Love Me Tomorrow**
Cry To Me [Solomon Burke] 44	Bergstein Chorale]	[Drifters] 32	[Shirelles] 1
De Todo Un Poco [Michael Lloyd	Lifts In The Lake Theme (Finale)	**These Arms Of Mine** [Otis	**Wipe Out** [Surfaris] 2
& Le Disc]	[John Morris Orch.]	Redding] 85	
Do You Love Me [Contours] 3	Love Man [Otis Redding] 72		

9/12/87   **99**   8   **111 Disorderlies** ....[V] **$8**   Polydor 833274
The Fat Boys/Ralph Bellamy/Tony Plana/Anthony Geary

Baby, You're A Rich Man [Fat	Don't Treat Me Like This [Anita]	Fat Off My Back [Gwen Guthrie]	Roller One [Art Of Noise]
Boys]	Edge Of A Broken Heart [Bon	**I Heard A Rumour**	Tryin' To Dance [Tom Kimmel]
Big Money [Ca$hflow]	Jovi]	[Bananarama] 4	Work Me Down [Laura Hunter]
Disorderly Conduct [Latin			
Rascals]			

Divine Madness - see MIDLER, Bette

7/22/89   **68**   14   **112 Do The Right Thing** ....[V] **$8**   Motown 6272
Danny Aiello/Ossie Davis/Ruby Dee/Spike Lee

DEBUT DATE	PEAK POS	WKS CHR	GOLD	ARTIST — Album Title	$	Label & Number

				Can't Stand It *[Steel Pulse]* Hard To Say *[Lori Perry & Gerald Alston]* Never Explain Love *[Al Jarreau]* **Tu Y Yo** *[Ruben Blades]*		
				Don't Shoot Me *[Take 6]* **My Fantasy** *[Teddy Riley Feat. Guy]* **62** Party Hearty *[E.U.]* Why Don't We Try *[Keith John]*		
				Feel So Good *[Perri]* Prove To Me *[Perri]*		
				Fight The Power *[Public Enemy]*		

10/14/67+ **55** 44 ● **113 Doctor Dolittle** .... [M] **$20** 20th Century 5101
Rex Harrison/Samantha Eggar/Anthony Newley/Richard Attenborough; sw: Leslie Bricusse; cd: Lionel Newman

After Today	Fabulous Places	My Friend The Doctor	Vegetarian, The
At The Crossroads	I Think I Like You	Overture	When I Look In Your Eyes
Beautiful Things	I've Never Seen Anything Like It	Something In Your Smile	Where Are The Words
Doctor Dolittle	Like Animals	Talk To The Animals	

7/27/63 **82** 10 **114 Dr. No** .... **$40** United Art. 5108
Sean Connery/Ursula Andress/Joseph Wiseman/Jack Lord; cp/cd: Monty Norman

Audio Bongo	Island Speaks	James Bond Theme	Love At Last
Boy Chase	Jamaica Jazz	Jump Up	Twisting With James
Dr. No's Fantasy	Jamaican Rock	Kingston Calypso	Under The Mango Tree

3/19/66 **1¹** 157 ● **115 Doctor Zhivago** .... [I] **$15** MGM 6
Omar Sharif/Julie Christie/Rod Steiger/Alec Guinness; cp/cd: Maurice Jarre

At The Student Cafe	Lara Leaves Yuri	Overture	Tonya Arrives At Varykino
Funeral, The	Lara's Theme	Revolution	Yuri Escapes
Komarovsky And Lara's Rendezvous	Main Title	Sventyski's Waltz	Yuri Writes A Poem For Lara

2/19/72 **173** 5 **116 Dollar ($)** .... [I+V] **$15** Reprise 2051
Warren Beatty/Goldie Hawn; cp/cd: Quincy Jones; features the Don Elliott Voices

Brooks' 50 Cent Tour *[Little Richard & Roberta Flack]*	Money Is *[Little Richard]*	Rubber Ducky	When You're Smiling (The Whole World Smiles With You) *[Roberta Flack]*
Candy Man	**Money Runner 57**	Shady Lady	
Do It - To It *[Little Richard]*	Passin' The Buck	Snow Creatures	
Kitty With The Bent Frame	Redeye Runnin' Train *[Doug Kershaw]*		

Don't Knock The Twist - see CHECKER, Chubby
Chubby Checker/Linda Scott

Doors, The - see DOORS
Val Kilmer/Meg Ryan/Kevin Dillon/Kyle MacLachlan

Double Trouble - see PRESLEY, Elvis
Elvis Presley (Guy Lambert)/Annette Day/John Williams

4/5/86 **68** 7 **117 Down And Out In Beverly Hills** .... [V] **$8** MCA 6160
Nick Nolte/Bette Midler/Richard Dreyfuss; side 2 is instrumental, cp: Andy Summers (The Police)

California Girls *[David Lee Roth]* **3**	El Tecalitleco *[Mariachi Vargas de Tecalitlan]*	I Love L.A. *[Randy Newman]*	Search For Kerouac
Down And Out In Beverly Hills Theme	**Great Gosh A'Mighty! (It's A Matter Of Time)** *[Little Richard]* **42**	Jerry's Suicide Attempt	**Tutti Frutti** *[Little Richard]* **17**
		Mission Blues	Wave Hands Like Clouds
		Nouvelle Cuisine	

12/12/92 **94** 6 **118 Dracula, Bram Stoker's** .... [I] **$12** Columbia 53165
Gary Oldman/Winona Ryder/Anthony Hopkins/Keanu Reeves; cp: Wojciech Kilar; cd: Anton Coppola

Ascension	Hunt Builds	Love Song For A Vampire *[Annie Lennox]*	Mina/Dracula
Brides, The	Hunters Prelude		Ring Of Fire
Dracula - The Beginning	Love Eternal	Lucy's Party	Storm, The
End Credits	Love Remembered	Mina's Photo	Vampire Hunters
Green Mist			

7/18/87 **137** 6 **119 Dragnet** .... [V] **$8** MCA 6210
Dan Aykroyd/Tom Hanks/Christopher Plummer/Harry Morgan; side 2 is intrumental, cp: Ira Newborn

City Of Crime *[Dan Aykroyd & Tom Hanks]*	Danger Ahead (medley)	Joe Gets Fired	Pagan Tension
Dairy Apologies	Dragnet *[Art Of Noise]*	Just The Facts *[Patti LaBelle]*	Tank, The
Dance Or Die *[Peter Aykroyd & Pat Thrall]*	Dragnet March (medley)	Kill Me Instead	This Is The City (medley)
	End Credits	Looking For Muzz	
	Helplessly In Love *[New Edition]*	Pagan Fight	

4/8/89 **94** 10 **120 Dream A Little Dream** .... [V] **$8** Cypress 0125
Jason Robards/Corey Feldman/Piper Laurie/Meredith Salenger

Dream A Little Dream Of Me *[Mickey Thomas]*	Dreams Come True (Stand Up And Take It) *[Lone Justice]*	**It's The End Of The World As We Know It (And I Feel Fine)** *[R.E.M.]* **69**	**Rock On** *[Michael Damian]* **1**
Dream A Little Dream Of Me *[Mel Torme & Mickey Thomas]*	**I've Got Dreams To Remember** *[Otis Redding]* **41**	Never Turn Away *[Chris Thompson]*	Time Runs Wild *[Danny Wilde]*
	Into The Mystic *[Van Morrison]*		Whenever There's A Night *[Mike Reno]*
			You'd Better Wait *[Fee Waybill]*

Dune - see TOTO
Kyle MacLachlan/Kenneth McMillan/Sting

7/20/91 **50** 14 **121 Dying Young** .... [I] **$12** Arista 18692
Julia Roberts/Campbell Scott/Vincent D'Onofrio/Colleen Dewhurst; pf: James Newton Howard and the Greater Los Angeles Orchestra

All The Way *[King Curtis]*	Driving North (medley) *[Kenny G & James Newton Howard]*	I'll Never Leave You (Love Theme) *[Kenny G & James Newton Howard]*	Moving In (medley) *[Kenny G & James Newton Howard]*
All The Way *[Jeffrey Osborne]*	Dying Young (Theme) *[Kenny G]*		San Francisco
Bluff, The	Hillary's Theme *[Kenny G & James Newton Howard]*	Love Montage	Victor
Clock, The		Maze, The	Victor Teaches Art

7/3/82 **37** 33 ● **122 E.T. - The Extra-Terrestrial** .... [I] **$8** MCA 6109
Henry Thomas/Peter Coyote/Dee Wallace/Drew Barrymore; cp/cd: John Williams

Abandoned And Pursued	E.T. Phone Home	Flying	Three Million Light Years From Earth
Adventure On Earth	E.T.'s Halloween	Over The Moon	
E.T. And Me			

Easter Parade - see Those Glorious MGM Musicals

9/6/69+ **6** 72 ● **123 Easy Rider** .... [V] **$20** Dunhill 50063
Peter Fonda/Dennis Hopper/Jack Nicholson; "The Weight" featured in the film was performed by The Band

DEBUT DATE	PEAK POS	WKS CHR	GOLD	ARTIST — Album Title	$	Label & Number

				Ballad Of Easy Rider [Roger McGuinn]	Don't Bogart Me [Fraternity Of Man]	If You Want To Be A Bird [Holy Modal Rounders]	Kyrie Eleison [Electric Prunes]

Ballad Of Easy Rider [Roger McGuinn] — Don't Bogart Me [Fraternity Of Man] — If You Want To Be A Bird [Holy Modal Rounders] — Kyrie Eleison [Electric Prunes]
Born To Be Wild [Steppenwolf] 2 — If Six Was Nine [Jimi Hendrix Experience] — It's Alright, Ma (I'm Only Bleeding) [Roger McGuinn] — Pusher, The [Steppenwolf] — Wasn't Born To Follow [Byrds] — Weight, The [Smith]

Eddie And The Cruisers - see CAFFERTY, John
Michael Pare/Tom Berenger/Ellen Barkin

| 5/26/56 | 1¹ | 99 | 124 | **Eddy Duchin Story, The** .... [S-I] | $20 | Decca 8289 |

Tyrone Power/Kim Novak; pf: Carmen Cavallaro; biographical film about the popular pianist/orchestra leader

Brazil (Aquarela Do Brasil) — La Vie En Rose — To Love Again
Chopsticks — Manhattan — To Love Again (Finale) (Based On Chopin's E Flat Nocturne)
Dizzy Fingers — On The Sunny Side Of The Street — Whispering
It Must Be True (You Are Mine, All Mine) — Shine On Harvest Moon — You're My Everything

Edward Scissorhands - see ELFMAN, Danny
Johnny Depp/Winona Ryder/Dianne Wiest/Anthony Michael Hall

| 8/4/62 | 35 | 13 | 125 | **El Cid** ....[I] | $40 | MGM 3977 |

Charlton Heston/Sophia Loren; cp/cd: Miklos Rozsa

Battle Of Valencia — Fight For Calahorra — Overture — 13 Knights
Cid's Death — Intermezzo: The El Cid March — Palace Music — Twins, The
Farewell — Legend, The — Prelude

| 10/20/73 | 194 | 2 | 126 | **Electra Glide In Blue** .... [I+V] | $20 | United Art. 062 |

Robert Blake/Billy Green Bush; cp: James William Guerico; includes a booklet of pictures and 2 posters

Chase, The — Meadow Mountain Top [Mark Spolestra] — Most Of All [Marcels] — Song Of Sad Bottles [Mark Spolestra]
Free From The Devil [Madura] — Monument Valley — Overture — Tell Me
Jolene's Dance — Morning — Prelude

| 9/1/84 | 94 | 9 | 127 | **Electric Dreams** ....[V] | $8 | Virgin 39600 |

Lenny Von Dohlen/Virginia Madsen/Maxwell Caulfield

Chase Runner [Heaven 17] — Let It Run [Jeff Lynne] — Now You're Mine [Helen Terry] — **Video!** [Jeff Lynne] 85
Dream, The [Culture Club] — Love Is Love [Culture Club] — Together In Electric Dreams [Giorgio Moroder & Philip Oakey]
Duel, The [Giorgio Moroder] — Madeline's Theme [Giorgio Moroder]
Electric Dreams [P.P. Arnold]

Electric Horseman, The - see NELSON, Willie
Robert Redford/Jane Fonda/Willie Nelson

Elvis-That's The Way It Is - see PRESLEY, Elvis

| 2/13/88 | 150 | 5 | 128 | **Empire Of The Sun** ....[I] | $8 | Warner 25668 |

Christian Bale/John Malkovich/Miranda Richardson/Nigel Havers; cp/cd: John Williams; 2 of 13 tracks feature choirs

British Grenadiers — Jim's New Life — Pheasant Hunt — Streets Of Shanghai
Cadillac Of The Skies — Liberation: Exsultate Justi — Return To The City — Suo Gan
Exsultate Justi — Lost In The Crowd — Seeing The Bomb (medley) — Toy Planes, Home And Hearth
Imaginary Air Battle — No Road Home (medley)

| 5/17/80 | 4 | 28 | ● 129 | **Empire Strikes Back, The** ....[I] | $12 | RSO 4201 [2] |

Mark Hamill/Harrison Ford/Carrie Fisher/Billy Dee Williams; cp/cd: John Williams; pf: London Symphony Orchestra; also see Meco and Jazz Compilations: *Empire Jazz*

Asteroid Field — Finale — Imperial March (Darth Vader's Theme) — Star Wars (Main Theme)
Battle In The Snow — Han Solo And The Princess — — Training Of A Jedi Knight
City In The Clouds — Heroics Of Luke And Han — Lando's Palace — Yoda And The Force
Departure Of Boba Fett — Hyperspace — Magic Tree — Yoda's Theme
Duel, The — — Rebels At Bay

| 9/6/80 | 178 | 4 | 130 | Empire Strikes Back, The/The Adventures Of Luke Skywalker .... | $10 | RSO 3081 |

storyline excerpts from the film (narrator: Malachi Throne)

| 6/13/92 | 130 | 5 | 131 | **Encino Man** ....[V] | $12 | Hollywood 61330 |

Sean Astin/Pauly Shore/Brendan Fraser/Megan Ward

Cool Hand Loc [Tone Loc] — Get The Hell Out Of Here [Steve Vai] — Stone Cold Crazy [Queen] — You Turn Me On [Crystal Waters]
Feed The Monkey [Infectious Grooves] — Leave My Curl Alone [Hi-C] — Treaty [Yothu Yindi] — You're Invited But Your Friend Can't Come [Vince Neil]
Frankenstein [Edgar Winter Group] 1 — Luxury Cruiser [T-Ride] — Why'd You Want Me? [Jesus & Mary Chain] — Young And Dumb [Scream]
— Mama Said Knock You Out [Scatterbrain] — Wild Thing [Cheap Trick] —
— — Wooly Bully [Smithereens] —

| 8/1/81 | 9 | 20 | ● 132 | **Endless Love** .... [I+V] | $10 | Mercury 2001 |

Brooke Shields/Martin Hewitt/Shirley Knight/Don Murray; cp: Jonathan Tunick/Lionel Richie

Ann Sees David And Jade — **Dreaming** [Cliff Richard] 10 — Endless Love (includes 2 versions) [Diana Ross & Lionel Richie] 1 — Heart Song
Making Love — Dreaming Of You [Diana Ross & Lionel Richie] — — I Was Made For Lovin' You [Kiss] 11
David At The Institution — — —
David Goes To Jade's House — Dreaming Of You (instrumental) — Endless Love Theme —

Endless Summer, The - see SANDALS

| 1/20/79 | 78 | 15 | 133 | **Every Which Way But Loose** ....[V] | $8 | Elektra 503 |

Clint Eastwood/Sondra Locke/Ruth Gordon/Geoffrey Lewis; cd: Steve Dorff

Behind Closed Doors [Charlie Rich] 15 — Eastwood's Alley Walk — I'll Wake You Up When I Get Home [Charlie Rich] — Send Me Down To Tucson [Mel Tillis]
Biker's Theme — **Every Which Way But Loose** [Eddie Rabbitt] 30 — Monkey See, Monkey Do [Cliff Crofford] — Six Pack To Go [Hank Thompson]
Coca-Cola Cowboy [Mel Tillis] — I Can't Say No To A Truck Drivin' Man [Carol Chase] — Red Eye Special [Larry Collins] — Under The Double Eagle
Don't Say You Don't Love Me No More [Sondra Locke & Phil Everly] — I Seek The Night [Sondra Locke] — Salty Dog Blues —

| 1/16/61 | 1¹⁴ | 89 | ● 134 | **Exodus** ....[I] | $15 | RCA 1058 |

Paul Newman/Eva Marie Saint; cp/cd: Ernest Gold; pf: Sinfonia Of London Orchestra; also see The Hollywood Studio Orchestra

Ari — Escape — Fight For Survival — Prison Break
Brothers, The — Exodus (Theme) — In Jerusalem — Summer In Cyprus
Conspiracy — Fight For Peace — Karen — Valley Of Jezreel
Dawn — — —

DEBUT DATE	PEAK POS	WKS CHR	GOLD	ARTIST — Album Title	$	Label & Number

Experiment In Terror - see MANCINI, Henry
Glenn Ford/Lee Remick/Stefanie Powers

| 8/12/78 | **124** | 9 | 135 | **Eyes Of Laura Mars** .... [I+V] | **$8** | Columbia 35487 |

Faye Dunaway/Tommy Lee Jones/Raul Julia; cp/cd: Artie Kane

Burn [Michalski & Oosterveen]
Elaine
Eyes Of Laura Mars (Prisoner),
Love Theme From [Barbra
Streisand] 21

Eyes Of Laura Mars (Prisoner),
Love Theme From
(instrumental)
Laura - Warehouse
Laura & Neville (includes 2
versions)

Laura Nightmare
Let's All Chant [Michael Zager
Band] 36
Love And Pity
Lulu And Michelle

Native New Yorker (medley)
[Odyssey] 21
(Shake, Shake, Shake) Shake
Your Booty (medley) [KC &
The Sunshine Band] 1

| 5/6/78 | **5** | 24 | ▲ 136 | **FM** .... [V] | **$10** | MCA 12000 [2] |

Michael Brandon/Eileen Brennan/Alex Karras/Martin Mull

Bad Man [Randy Meisner]
Breakdown [Tom Petty] 40
Cold As Ice [Foreigner] 6
Do It Again [Steely Dan] 6
FM (No Static At All) [Steely
Dan] 22
Fly Like An Eagle [Steve
Miller] 2

It Keeps You Runnin' [Doobie
Brothers] 37
Just The Way You Are [Billy
Joel] 3
Lido Shuffle [Boz Scaggs] 11
Life In The Fast Lane
[Eagles] 11

Life's Been Good [Joe
Walsh] 12
Livingston Saturday Night
[Jimmy Buffett] 52
More Than A Feeling [Boston] 5
Night Moves [Bob Seger] 4
Poor Poor Pitiful Me [Linda
Ronstadt]

There's A Place In The World
For A Gambler [Dan Fogelberg]
Tumbling Dice [Linda Ronstadt]
We Will Rock You [Queen] flip
Your Smiling Face [James
Taylor] 20

Fabulous Baker Boys, The - see GRUSIN, Dave
Jeff Bridges/Michelle Pfeiffer/Beau Bridges

Falcon And The Snowman, The - see METHENY, Pat, Group
Timothy Hutton/Sean Penn/Lori Singer/Pat Hingle

| 6/13/64 | **147** | 2 | 137 | **Fall Of The Roman Empire, The** .... [I] | **$75** | Columbia 2460 |

Sophia Loren/Stephen Boyd/James Mason; cp/cd: Dimitri Tiomkin

Addio
Ballomar's Barbarian Attack
Dawn Of Love
Fall Of Love

Fall Of Rome
Lucilla's Sorrow
Morning
Notturno

Overture
Pax Romana
Persian Battle
Profundo

Prophecy, The
Resurrection
Roman Forum
Tarantella

| 6/7/80 | **7** | 82 | ▲ 138 | **Fame** .... [M] | **$8** | RSO 3080 |

Irene Cara/Eddie Barth/Maureen Teefy/Lee Curreri; inspired by the students of New York's
High School of The Performing Arts

Dogs In The Yard
Fame [Irene Cara] 4
Hot Lunch Jam

I Sing The Body Electric
Is It Okay If I Call You Mine?
Never Alone

Out Here On My Own [Irene
Cara] 19

Ralph And Monty (Dressing
Room Piano)
Red Light [Linda Clifford] 41

| 9/25/61 | **88** | 13 | 139 | **Fanny** .... [I] | **$30** | Warner 1416 |

Leslie Caron/Maurice Chevalier/Charles Boyer; cp: Harold Rome; cd: Morris Stoloff; also see
Original Cast ('55)

Fanny
I Have To Tell You
I Like You

Love Is A Very Light Thing
Never Too Late For Love
Oysters, Cockles & Mussels

Panisse And Son
Restless Heart

To My Wife
Welcome Home

| 11/17/90 | **190** | 2 | ▲ 140 | **Fantasia, Walt Disney's** .... [I] | **$19** | Buena V. 60072 [2] |

50th anniversary celebration of the release of the animated film; cd: Leopold Stokowski; pf:
Philadelphia Orchestra

Bach: Toccata and Fugue in D
Minor
Beethoven: Symphony No. 6,
Op. 68

Mussorgsky: Night On Bald
Mountain
Ponchielli: Dance Of The Hours
Schubert: Ava Maria

Sorcerer's Apprentice
Stravinsky: Rite of Spring
Tchaikovsky: Nutcracker Suite

| 6/13/92 | **89** | 9 | 141 | **Far And Away** .... [I] | **$12** | MCA 10628 |

Tom Cruise/Nicole Kidman; cp/cd: John Williams

Am I Beautiful?
Big Match
Blowing Off Steam
Book Of Days [Enya]
Burning The Manor House
County Galway, June 1892

Duel Scene (medley)
End Credits
Fighting Donellys
Fighting For Dough
Inside The Mansion

Joe Sr.'s Passing (medley)
Joseph And Shannon
Joseph's Dream
Land Race
Leaving Home

Oklahoma Territory
Race To The River (medley)
Reunion, The
Settling With Steven (medley)
Shannon Is Shot

| 8/28/82 | **54** | 20 | 142 | **Fast Times At Ridgemont High** .... [V] | **$10** | Full Moon 60158 [2] |

Sean Penn/Phoebe Cates/Jennifer Jason Leigh/Judge Reinhold

Don't Be Lonely [Quarterflash]
Fast Times At Ridgement High
[Sammy Hagar]
Fast Times (The Best Years Of
Our Lives) [Billy Squier]
Goodbye, Goodbye [Oingo
Boingo]

Highway Runner [Donna
Summer]
I Don't Know (Spicoli's Theme)
[Jimmy Buffett]
I'll Leave It Up To You [Poco]
Look In Your Eyes [Gerard
McMahon]

Love Is The Reason [Graham
Nash]
Love Rules [Don Henley]
Never Surrender [Don Felder]
Raised On The Radio [Ravyns]
She's My Baby (And She's Outta
Control) [Dave Palmer & Phil
Jost]

Sleeping Angel [Stevie Nicks]
So Much In Love [Timothy B.
Schmit] 59
Somebody's Baby [Jackson
Browne] 7
Speeding [Joe Walsh]
Uptown Boys [Louise Goffin]
Waffle Stomp [Joe Walsh]

Ferry Cross The Mersey - see GERRY AND THE PACEMAKERS
Gerry and The Pacemakers/Cilla Black/Jimmy Saville

| 10/30/71+ | **30** | 90 | ● 143 | **Fiddler On The Roof** .... [M] | **$15** | United A. 10900 [2] |

Topol/Norma Crane; mu: Jerry Bock; ly: Sheldon Harnick; cd: John Williams; also see
Ferrante & Teicher/Herschel Bernardi/Original Cast ('64)

Anatevka
Bottle Dance (medley)
Chavet Ballet Sequence
Do You Love Me?

Far From The Home I Love
Finale
If I Were A Rich Man
Main Title

Matchmaker
Miracle Of Miracles
Sabbath Prayer
Sunrise, Sunset

Tevye's Dream
To Life
Wedding Celebration (medley)

| 8/23/86 | **183** | 3 | 144 | **Fine Mess, A** .... [V] | **$8** | Motown 6180 |

Ted Danson/Howie Mandel/Richard Mulligan/Stuart Margolin

Can't Help Falling In Love
[Christine McVie]
Easier Said Than Done [Chico
DeBarge]
Fine Mess [Temptations]

I'm Gonna Be A Wheel Someday
[Los Lobos]
Love's Closing In [Nick Jameson]
Moving So Close [Keith Burston
& Darryl Littlejohn]

Slow Down [Billy Vera & The
Beaters]
Stan And Ollie [Henry Mancini]
Walk Like A Man [Mary Jane
Girls] 41

Wishful Thinking [Smokey
Robinson]

| 10/5/68+ | **90** | 26 | 145 | **Finian's Rainbow** .... [M] | **$20** | Warner 2550 |

Fred Astaire/Petula Clark/Tommy Steele; ly: E.Y. Harburg; mu: Burton Lane; cd: Ray
Heindorf

DEBUT DATE	PEAK POS	WKS CHR	GOLD	ARTIST — Album Title	$	Label & Number

| 6/24/67 | 107 | 28 | 146 | Fistful Of Dollars, A ....[I] | $15 | RCA 1135 |

Begat, The — Main Title — That Great Come-And-Get-It Day — When The Idle Poor Become The Idle Rich
How Are Things In Glocca Morra? — Necessity — This Time Of The Year
If This Isn't Love — Old Devil Moon — When I'm Not Near The Girl I Love
Look To The Rainbow — Rain Dance Ballet
— Something Sort Of Grandish

Clint Eastwood/Marianne Koch; cp/cd: Ennio Morricone; also see Hugo Montenegro

Almost Dead — Fistful Of Dollars (Theme) — Result, The — Titoli
Chase, The — Fistful Of Dollars Suite — Square Dance — Without Pity

| 4/27/91 | 58 | 13 | 147 | Five Heartbeats, The ....[V] | $12 | Virgin 91609 |

Robert Townsend/Michael Wright/Leon/Harry J. Lennix/Tico Wells

Are You Ready For Me [Flash & The Ebony Sparks] — Heart Is A House For Love [Dells] — In The Middle [Flash & The Five Heartbeats] — Stay In My Corner [Dells] 10
Baby Stop Running Around [Bird & The Midnight Falcons] — I Feel Like Going On [Eddie, Baby Doll and The L.A. Mass Choir] — Nights Like This [After 7] 24 — We Haven't Finished Yet [Patti LaBelle]
Bring Back The Days [U.S. Male] — — Nothing But Love [Five Heartbeats] —

| 10/12/59 | 22 | 10 | 148 | Five Pennies, The ....[M] | $40 | Dot 29500 |

Danny Kaye/Louis Armstrong/Barbara Bel Geddes; based on the life of bandleader Loring "Red" Nichols

After You've Gone — Carnival Of Venice — Follow The Leader (medley) — Lullaby In Ragtime
Back Home Again In Indiana — College Montage (medley) — Good Night, Sleep Tight Medley — Main Title
Battle Hymn Of The Republic — Finale — Indiana Radio Montage — Music Goes 'Round And 'Round
Bill Bailey, Won't You Please Come Home — Five Pennies — Jingle Bells — Wail Of The Winds
— Five Pennies Saints — Just The Blues —

Flame - see SLADE

| 2/16/85 | 130 | 8 | 149 | Flamingo Kid, The ....[V-O] | $8 | Motown 6131 |

Matt Dillon/Richard Crenna/Hector Elizondo/Jessica Walter

Boys Will Be Boys [Maureen Steele] — Get A Job [Silhouettes] 1 — Heat Wave [Martha & The Vandellas] 4 — One Fine Day [Chiffons] 5
Breakaway [Jesse Frederick] — Good Golly, Miss Molly [Little Richard] 10 — It's All Right [Impressions] 4 — Runaround Sue [Dion] 1
Finger Poppin' Time [Hank Ballard & The Midnighters] 7 — He's So Fine [Chiffons] 1 — Money (That's What I Want) [Barrett Strong] 23 — Stranger On The Shore [Mr. Acker Bilk] 1

Flash Gordon - see QUEEN
Sam Jones/Max von Sydow/Melody Anderson/Topol

| 4/30/83 | 1² | 78 | ▲⁵ 150 | Flashdance ....[V] | $8 | Casablanca 811492 |

Jennifer Beals/Michael Nouri/Marine Johan/Lilia Skala

Flashdance...What A Feeling [Irene Cara] 1 — I'll Be Here Where The Heart Is [Kim Carnes] — Lady, Lady, Lady [Joe "Bean" Esposito] 86 — Maniac [Michael Sembello] 1
He's A Dream [Shandi] — Imagination [Laura Branigan] — Love Theme [Helen St. John] — Romeo [Donna Summer]
— — Manhunt [Karen Kamon] — Seduce Me Tonight [Cycle V]

| 7/27/85 | 160 | 4 | 151 | Fletch ....[I+V] | $8 | MCA 6142 |

Chevy Chase/Dana Wheeler-Nicholson/Joe Don Baker/Tim Matheson; cp/cd: Harold Faltermeyer

Bit By Bit [Stephanie Mills] 78 — Fletch, Get Outta Town [Dan Hartman] — Letter To Both Sides [Fixx] — Running For Love [John Farnham]
Diggin' In — Exotic Skates — Name Of The Game [Dan Hartman] — Running For Love (instrumental)
Exotic Skates — Fletch Theme / Is It Over [Kim Wilde] — —

| 12/25/61+ | 15 | 35 | 152 | Flower Drum Song ....[M] | $20 | Decca 79098 |

Nancy Kwan/James Shigeta/Miyoshi Umeki; mu: Richard Rodgers; ly: Oscar Hammerstein II; cd: Alfred Newman; also see Original Cast ('59)

Chop Suey — Gliding Through My Memoree (medley) — I Am Going To Like It Here — Other Generation
Don't Marry Me — Grant Avenue — I Enjoy Being A Girl — Sunday
Dream Ballet — Hundred Million Miracles — Love Look Away — You Are Beautiful
Fan Tan Fanny (medley) — — Main Title —

Follow The Boys - see FRANCIS, Connie
Connie Francis/Paula Prentiss/Ron Randell/Janis Paige

| 2/18/84 | 1¹⁰ | 61 | ▲⁷ 153 | Footloose ....[V] | $8 | Columbia 39242 |

Kevin Bacon/Lori Singer/John Lithgow

Almost Paradise...Love Theme From Footloose [Mike Reno & Ann Wilson] 7 — Footloose [Kenny Loggins] 1 — I'm Free (Heaven Helps The Man) [Kenny Loggins] 22 — Never [Moving Pictures]
Dancing In The Sheets [Shalamar] 17 — Girl Gets Around [Sammy Hagar] — Let's Hear It For The Boy [Deniece Williams] 1 — Somebody's Eyes [Karla Bonoff]
— Holding Out For A Hero [Bonnie Tyler] 34 — —

| 9/14/68 | 192 | 2 | 154 | For Love Of Ivy ....[I+V] | $15 | ABC 7 |

Sidney Poitier/Abbey Lincoln/Beau Bridges/Carroll O'Connor; cp/cd: Quincy Jones

B. B. Jones [B.B. King] — End Title [Shirley Horn] — Messy But Good [B.B. King] — Soul Motion
Black Pearl — For Love Of Ivy — My Side Of The Sky [Cashman, Pistilli & West] — Wheelin' And Dealin'
Don't You Believe It [Cashman, Pistilli & West] — Little Hippy Dippy — Somethin' Strange — You Put It On Me [B.B. King] 82
— Main Title — —

For The Boys - see MIDLER, Bette
Bette Midler/James Caan/George Segal

For The First Time - see LANZA, Mario
Mario Lanza/Zsa Zsa Gabor

| 7/25/81 | 84 | 19 | 155 | For Your Eyes Only ....[I] | $8 | Liberty 1109 |

Roger Moore/Carole Bouquet/Topol; cp/cd: Bill Conti

Cortina — For Your Eyes Only (instrumental) — Melina's Revenge — St. Cyril's Monastery
Drive In The Country — — P.M. Gets The Bird (medley) — Submarine
For Your Eyes Only [Sheena Easton] 4 — Gonzales Takes A Dive — Runaway — Take Me Home
— Make It Last All Night [Rage] — —

| 9/2/78 | 102 | 7 | 156 | Foul Play ....[I+V] | $8 | Arista 9501 |

Goldie Hawn/Chevy Chase/Burgess Meredith/Dudley Moore; cp/cd: Charles Fox

Beware Of The Dwarf — Get Me To The Opera On Time — Houseboat (Love Theme) — Ready To Take A Chance Again (instrumental)
Copacabana (At The Copa) [Barry Manilow] 8 — Gloria Escapes — Ready To Take A Chance Again [Barry Manilow] 11 — Scarface
Foul Play — Gloria Falls For Trap / Help —

DEBUT DATE	PEAK POS	WKS CHR	GOLD	ARTIST — Album Title	$	Label & Number

Foxy Brown - see HUTCH, Willie
Pam Grier/Brown Peter/Terry Carter

Frankie And Johnny - see PRESLEY, Elvis
Elvis Presley (Johnny)/Donna Douglas (Frankie)/Nancy Kovack

| 2/29/92 | **181** | 3 | | 157 Fried Green Tomatoes .... [V] | **$12** | MCA 10461 |

Kathy Bates/Jessica Tandy/Mary-Louise Parker/Mary Stuart Masterson

Barbeque Bess *[Patti LaBelle]*	Cool Down Yonder *[Marion Williams]*	I'll Remember You *[Grayson Hugh]*	Visiting Ruth *[Thomas Newman]*
Charge To Keep I Have *[Thomas Newman feat. Marion Williams]*	Danger Heartbreak Dead Ahead *[Taylor Dayne]*	If I Can Help Somebody *[Aaron Hall]*	**What Becomes Of The Broken Hearted** *[Paul Young]* 22
Cherish (includes 2 versions) *[Jodeci]*	Ghost Train (Main Title) *[Thomas Newman]*	Rooster Blues *[Peter Wolf]*	

Friends - see JOHN, Elton
Sean Bury/Anicee Alvina

| 5/2/64 | **27** | 34 | | 158 From Russia with Love .... [I] | **$15** | United Art. 5114 |

Sean Connery/Daniela Bianchi/Lotte Lenya/Robert Shaw; cp/cd: John Barry

Bond Meets Tania	Girl Trouble	Leila Dances	Smersh In Action (medley)
Death Of Grant	Golden Horn	Man Overboard (medley)	Spectre Island
Death Of Kerim	Guitar Lament	Meeting In St. Sophia	Stalking
007	Gypsy Camp	Opening Titles	Tania Meets Klebb
From Russia With Love	James Bond With Bongos		

Fun in Acapulco - see PRESLEY, Elvis
Elvis Presley (Mike Windgren)/Ursula Andress/Elsa Cardenas

Funny Girl - see STREISAND, Barbra, and SUPREMES
Barbra Streisand/Omar Sharif/Kay Medford

Funny Lady - see STREISAND, Barbra
Barbra Streisand/James Caan/Omar Sharif

G.I. Blues - see PRESLEY, Elvis
Elvis Presley (Tulsa McCauley)/Juliet Prowse/James Douglas

| 4/30/83 | **168** | 3 | | 159 Gandhi .... [I] | **$8** | RCA 4557 |

Ben Kingsley/Candice Bergen/John Gielgud; cp: Ravi Shankar/George Fenton; cd: George Fenton; features Ravi Shankar on the sitar

Bands Of The Raj Medley	Massacre At Amritsar And The Aftermath	Reflections Of Early Days (medley)	South Africa - The Beginning
Discovery Of India	Partition	Remember This Always	31st January 1948
End Of The Fast	Raghupati Raghava Raja Ram (medley)	Salt	Villages Of Bihar
For All Mankind			
Intermission			

| 9/1/90 | **8** | 64 | ▲ | 160 **Ghost**.. [I] | **$12** | Varese S. 5276 |

Patrick Swayze/Demi Moore/Whoopi Goldberg/Tony Goldwyn; cp/cd: Maurice Jarre

Carl	Ghost	**Unchained Melody** *[Righteous Brothers]* **4**	Unchained Melody (Instrumental)
Ditto	Molly		
End Credits	Sam		

| 7/7/84 | **6** | 34 | ▲ | 161 **Ghostbusters**.. [V] | **$8** | Arista 8246 |

Bill Murray/Dan Aykroyd/Sigourney Weaver/Harold Ramis

Cleanin' Up The Town *[Bus Boys]* 68	**Ghostbusters (includes 2 versions)** *[Ray Parker, Jr.]* **1**	In The Name Of Love *[Thompson Twins]*	Main Title Theme *[Elmer Bernstein]*
Dana's Theme *[Elmer Bernstein]*	Hot Night *[Laura Branigan]*	Magic *[Mick Smiley]*	Savin' The Day *[Alessi]*
	I Can Wait Forever *[Air Supply]*		

| 7/1/89 | **14** | 19 | ● | 162 **Ghostbusters II**.. [V] | **$8** | MCA 6306 |

Bill Murray/Dan Aykroyd/Sigourney Weaver/Harold Ramis

Flesh 'N Blood *[Oingo Boingo]*	Higher And Higher *[Howard Huntsberry]*	Promised Land *[James "J.T." Taylor]*	Supernatural *[New Edition]*
Flip City *[Glenn Frey]*	Love Is A Cannibal *[Elton John]*	Spirit *[Doug E. Fresh & The Get Fresh Crew]*	We're Back *[Bobby Brown]*
Ghostbusters *[Run-D.M.C.]*	**On Our Own** *[Bobby Brown]* **2**		

| 12/29/56+ | **16** | 7 | | 163 Giant .... [I] | **$40** | Capitol 773 |

Elizabeth Taylor/Rock Hudson/James Dean/Jane Withers; cp/cd: Dimitri Tiomkin

Angel's Return (medley)	Home In Reata	Jett Rink Theme	There's Never Been Anyone Else But You (Love Theme)
Christmas Morning (medley)	Hunt Scene	Main Title (Giant Theme)	Toy Trumpet March (medley)
Eyes Of Texas Are Upon You	Jett Rink, Oil Baron	Road To Reata	Yellow Rose Of Texas
First Love		Romantic Interludes	

| 6/23/58 | **1**10 | 172 | ● | 164 **Gigi**.. [M] | **$20** | MGM 3641 |

Leslie Caron/Maurice Chevalier/Louis Jordan; ly: Alan Jay Lerner; mu: Frederick Loewe; cd: Andre Previn

Gigi (Gaston's Soliloquy)	It's A Bore	Parisians, The	Waltz At Maxim's (She Is Not Thinking of Me)
I Remember It Well	Night They Invented Champagne	Say A Prayer For Me Tonight	
I'm Glad I'm Not Young Anymore	Overture	Thank Heaven For Little Girls	

Girl Happy - see PRESLEY, Elvis
Elvis Presley (Rusty Wells)/Shelley Fabares/Gary Crosby

Girls! Girls! Girls! - see PRESLEY, Elvis
Elvis Presley (Ross Carpenter)/Stella Stevens/Laurel Goodwin

Give my regards to Broad Street - see McCARTNEY, Paul
Paul McCartney/Bryan Brown/Ringo Starr

| 3/17/90 | **190** | 2 | | 165 Glory .... | **$12** | Virgin 91329 |

Matthew Broderick/Denzel Washington/Cary Elwes/Morgan Freeman; cp/cd: James Horner; pf: The Boys Choir Of Harlem

After Antietam	Call To Arms	Epitaph	Preparations For Battle
Brave Words, Braver Deeds	Charging Fort Wagner	Forming The Regiment	Whipping
Burning The Town Of Darien	Closing Credits	Lonely Christmas	Year Of Jubilee

| 4/8/72 | **21** | 35 | | 166 Godfather, The .... [I] | **$15** | Paramount 1003 |

Marlon Brando/Al Pacino/James Caan/Robert Duvall; cp: Nino Rota; cd: Carlo Savina

Apollonia	**Godfather, Love Theme From The** 66	Halls Of Fear	New Godfather
Baptism, The	Godfather Waltz (includes 2 versions)	I Have But One Heart *[Al Martino]*	Pickup, The
Connie's Wedding			Sicilian Pastorale
Finale			

DEBUT DATE	PEAK POS	WKS CHR	G O L D	ARTIST — Album Title	$	Label & Number

3/8/75 — **184** — 2 — **167** Godfather, Part II, The ....[I] **$15** ABC 856
Al Pacino/Robert DeNiro/Robert Duvall/Diane Keaton; cp: Nino Rota and Carmine Coppola; cd: Carmine Coppola

After The Party (medley)	Godfathers At Home	Marcia Stilo Italiano	Ninna Nanna A Michele
Brothers Mourn	Immigrant, The (medley)	Michael Comes Home	Remember Vito Andolini
End Title	Kay	Murder Of Don Fanucci	Senza Mamma
Ev'ry Time I Look In Your Eyes (medley)	Main Title (medley)	New Carpet	Vito And Abbandando

1/12/91 — **102** — 7 — **168** Godfather, Part III, The .... **$12** Columbia 47078
Al Pacino/Diane Keaton/Talia Shire/Andy Garcia; cp/cd: Carmine Coppola and Nino Rota

Altobello	Immigrant, The (medley)	Preghiera	Sicilian Medley
Casa Amiche	Main Title	Preludio And Siciliana	To Each His Own [Al Martino]
Finale	Marcia Religioso	Promise Me You'll Remember (Love Theme)	Vincent's Theme
Godfather Intermezzo	Michael's Letter		
Godfather Waltz			

4/14/73 — **50** — 51 — **169** Godspell ....[M] **$12** Bell 1118
Victor Garber/David Haskell/Robin Lamont; rock musical based on the gospel according to St. Matthew; mu/ly: Stephen Schwartz; also see Original Cast ('71)

Alas For You	Bless The Lord	Light Of The World	Save The People
All For The Best	By My Side	On The Willows	Turn Back, O Man
All Good Gifts	Day By Day	Prepare Ye (The Way Of The Lord)	
Beautiful City	Finale		

Goin' Coconuts - see OSMOND, Donny & Marie
Donny and Marie Osmond/Kenneth Mars/Ted Cassidy

1/24/87 — **128** — 7 — **170** Golden Child, The .... [I+V] **$8** Capitol 12544
Eddie Murphy/Charlotte Lewis/Charles Dance/Victor Wong; cp/cd: Michel Colombier

Best Man In The World [Ann Wilson] 61	Deeper Love [Meli'sa Morgan]	Love Goes On (Love Theme) [Ashford & Simpson]	Shame On You [Martha Davis]
Body Talk [Ratt]	Golden Love	Sardo And The Child	Wisdom Of The Ages [John Barry]
Chosen One [Robbie Buchanan]	(Let Your Love Find) The Chosen One [Marlon Jackson]		
Confrontation			

12/12/64+ — **1³** — 70 — **171** Goldfinger ....[I] **$15** United Art. 5117
Sean Connery/Gert Frobe/Honor Blackman/Harold Sakata; cp/cd: John Barry

Alpine Drive (medley)	Bond's Journey Home	Death Of Goldfinger	**Goldfinger** [Shirley Bassey] 8
Arrival Of The Bomb (medley)	Count Down (medley)	Gassing The Gangsters	Oddjob's Pressing Engagement
Auric's Factory (medley)	Dawn Raid On Fort Knox	**Goldfinger** [John Barry] 72	Teasing The Korean
Bond Back In Action Again			

7/3/61 — **64** — 13 — **172** Gone With The Wind ....[I] **$15** RCA Camden 625
new recording of film soundtrack; cp/cd: Max Steiner; also see original soundtrack below

Ashley	Bonnie's Theme	Oath, The	Scarlet O'Hara
Ashley And Melanie (Love Theme)	Gone With The Wind	Prayer, The	Scarlet's Agony
Bonnie Blue Flag	Invitation To The Dance	Return To Tara	Tara
Bonnie's Death	Melanie's Theme	Rhett Butler	War

10/14/67+ — **24** — 36 — **173** Gone With The Wind ....[I] **$20** MGM 10
Clark Gable/Vivien Leigh/Leslie Howard/Olivia de Havilland; taken directly from the film soundtrack (premiered in 1939); cp/cd: Max Steiner; also see Muir Mathieson

Ashley & Scarlett	Christmas During The War In Atlanta	Mammy	Scarlett Makes Her Demands Of Rhett
Ashley Return To Tara From Atlanta	Finale	Reconstruction	Scarlett's Fall Down The Staircase
The War Prison	Main Title	Scarlett & Rhett Rebuild Tara	
Atlanta In Flames		Scarlett & Rhett's First Meeting	
Bonnie's Fatal Pony Ride			

2/6/88 — **10** — 35 — ▲ **174** Good Morning, Vietnam ....[V-O] **$8** A&M 3913
Robin Williams/Forest Whitaker/Tung Thanh Tran/Bruno Kirby

Baby Please Don't Go [Them]	**Game Of Love** [Wayne Fontana & The Mindbenders] 1	Liar, Liar [Castaways] 12	Warmth Of The Sun [Beach Boys]
California Sun [Rivieras] 5	I Get Around [Beach Boys] 1	Nowhere To Run [Martha & The Vandellas] 8	What A Wonderful World [Louis Armstrong] 32
Danger Heartbreak Dead Ahead [Marvelettes] 61	I Got You (I Feel Good) [James Brown] 3	Sugar And Spice [Searchers] 44	
Five O'Clock World [Vogues] 4			

2/10/68 — **4** — 52 — ● **175** Good, The Bad And The Ugly, The ....[I] **$12** United Art. 5172
Clint Eastwood/Lee Van Cleef; cp/cd: Ennio Morricone; also see Hugo Montenegro

Carriage Of The Spirits	Ecstasy Of Gold	Marcia	Strong, The
Death Of A Soldier	Good, The Bad And The Ugly (Main Title)	Marcia Without Hope	Sundown, The
Desert, The		Story Of A Soldier	Trio, The

Good Times - see SONNY & CHER
Sonny and Cher/George Sanders/Norman Alden

Goodbye, Columbus - see ASSOCIATION
Richard Benjamin/Jack Klugman/Ali MacGraw

12/6/69 — **164** — 5 — **176** Goodbye, Mr. Chips ....[M] **$15** MGM 19
Peter O'Toole/Petula Clark/Sir Michael Redgrave; sw: Leslie Bricusse; cd: John Williams

And The Sky Smiled	London Is London	What A Lot Of Flowers!	When I Was Younger
Apollo	Overture	What Shall I Do With Today (medley)	Where Did My Childhood Go?
Entr'acte (medley)	Schooldays	When I Am Older	You And I!
Fill The World With Love	Walk Through The World		

6/29/85 — **73** — 10 — **177** Goonies, The ....[V] **$8** Epic 40067
Sean Astin/Josh Brolin/Jeff Cohen/Corey Feldman/Ke Huy Quan

Eight Arms To Hold You [Goon Squad]	**Goonies 'R' Good Enough** [Cyndi Lauper] 10	Save The Night [Joseph Williams]	What A Thrill [Cyndi Lauper]
14K [Teena Marie]	I Got Nothing [Bangles]	She's So Good To Me [Luther Vandross]	Wherever You're Goin' (It's Alright) [REO Speedwagon]
Goonies (Theme) [Dave Grusin]	Love Is Alive [Philip Bailey]		

Graduate, The - see SIMON & GARFUNKEL
Dustin Hoffman/Anne Bancroft/Katharine Ross

Graffiti Bridge - see PRINCE
Prince/Morris Day/Ingrid Chavez/Jerome Benton

3/18/67 — **76** — 28 — **178** Grand Prix ....[I] **$25** MGM 8
James Garner/Eva Marie Saint/Yves Montand; cp/cd: Maurice Jarre

DEBUT DATE	PEAK POS	WKS CHR	GOLD	ARTIST — Album Title	$	Label & Number

Clermont Race | Overture | Scott & Pat -- Sarti & Louise | Zandvoort Race (Scott's Comeback)
Grand Prix (Theme) | Sarti's Love Theme (includes 2 versions) | Scott's Theme
In The Garden
Lonely Race Track (Finale)

5/20/78 | 1¹² | 77 | ▲⁸ 179 | Grease .... [M] | $10 | RSO 4002 [2]
John Travolta/Olivia Newton-John/Stockard Channing/Jeff Conaway

Alone At A Drive-In Movie [Bill Oakes] | Hound Dog [Sha-Na-Na] | Rock 'N' Roll Is Here To Stay [Sha-Na-Na] | Those Magic Changes [Sha-Na-Na]
Beauty School Dropout [Frankie Avalon] | It's Raining On Prom Night [Cindy Bullens] | Rock 'N' Roll Party Queen [Louis St. Louis] | We Go Together [John Travolta & Olivia Newton-John]
Blue Moon [Sha-Na-Na] | Look At Me, I'm Sandra Dee [Stockard Channing] | Sandy [John Travolta] | You're The One That I Want [John Travolta & Olivia Newton-John] 1
Born To Hand-Jive [Sha-Na-Na] | Look At Me, I'm Sandra Dee [Olivia Newton-John] | **Summer Nights** [John Travolta & Olivia Newton-John] 5
Freddy My Love [Cindy Bullens] | Love Is A Many Splendored Thing [Bill Oakes] | Tears On My Pillow [Sha-Na-Na]
Grease [Frankie Valli] 1 | Mooning [Louis St. Louis & Cindy Bullens] | There Are Worse Things I Could Do [Stockard Channing]
Greased Lightnin' [John Travolta] 47
Hopelessly Devoted To You [Olivia Newton-John] 3

6/19/82 | 71 | 13 | 180 | Grease 2 .... [M-V] | $8 | RSO 3803
Maxwell Caulfield/Michelle Pfeiffer/Adrian Zmed/Lorna Luft

Back To School Again [Four Tops] 71 | Do It For Our Country | Prowlin' | Score Tonight
Charades | Girl For All Seasons | Reproduction | We'll Be Together
Cool Rider | (Love Will) Turn Back The Hands Of Time | Rock-A-Hula-Luau (Summer Is Coming) | Who's That Guy?

Great Balls Of Fire! - see LEWIS, Jerry Lee
Dennis Quaid/Winona Ryder/Alec Baldwin/Trey Wilson

9/21/63 | 50 | 21 | ● 181 | Great Escape, The .... [I] | $25 | United Art. 5107
Steve McQueen/James Garner/Richard Attenborough; cp/cd: Elmer Bernstein

Betrayal | Discovery | Main Title | Premature Plans
Blythe | Finale | More Action | Road's End
Chase, The | Hendley's Risk | On The Road | Various Troubles
Cooler And Mole

4/20/74 | 85 | 16 | 182 | Great Gatsby, The .... [I+V] | $15 | Paramount 3001 [2]
Robert Redford/Mia Farrow/Bruce Dern; cd: Nelson Riddle

Ain't We Got Fun | Five Foot Two, Eyes Of Blue [Nick Lucas] | Long Time Ago | We've Met Before (What'll I Do)
Alice Blue Gown | I'm Gonna Charleston Back To Charleston [Nick Lucas] | My Favorite Beau (What'll I Do) | What'll I Do [Bill Atherton]
Beale Street Blues | It Had To Be You | Myrtle's Dead | When You And I Were Seventeen [Nick Lucas]
Charleston | Jordan's Tango | Ring (What'll I Do) | Whispering
Daisy (What'll I Do) | Kitten On The Keys | Sheik Of Araby | Who?
Daisy's Tango | | Summer's Almost Over | Yes, Sir, That's My Baby
| | Tom And Myrtle

Great Muppet Caper, The - see CHILDREN'S ALBUMS
Jim Henson/Frank Oz

Great Race, The - see MANCINI, Henry
Tony Curtis/Jack Lemmon/Natalie Wood

6/25/77 | 166 | 8 | 183 | Greatest, The .... [I+V] | $8 | Arista 7000
Muhammad Ali/Ernest Borgnine; cp: Michael Masser; based on the life story of Muhammad Ali

Ali Bombaye (Parts 1 & 2) | Greatest Love Of All (Instrumental) | I Always Knew I Had It In Me [George Benson] | Variations On Theme
Ali's Theme
Greatest Love Of All [George Benson] 24

4/17/65 | 82 | 13 | 184 | Greatest Story Ever Told, The .... | $25 | United Art. 5120
Charlton Heston/Sidney Poitier/Angela Lansbury; cp/cd: Alfred Newman

Come Unto Me | Jesus Of Nazareth (Main Theme) | There Shall Come A Time To Enter | Triumph Of The Spirit
Great Journey | New Commandment | | Voice In The Wilderness
Hour Has Come | Prophecy, A | Time Of Wonders
Into Thy Hands

7/7/84 | 143 | 7 | 185 | Gremlins .... [I+V] | $8 | Geffen 24044
Zach Galligan/Phoebe Cates/Hoyt Axton; cp/cd: Jerry Goldsmith

Gift, The | Gremlins...Mega Madness [Michael Sembello] | Mrs. Deagle | Out Out [Peter Gabriel]
Gizmo | Make It Shine [Quarterflash]
Gremlin Rag

4/27/68 | 177 | 3 | 186 | Guess Who's Coming To Dinner .... [I] | $25 | Colgems 108
Spencer Tracy/Katharine Hepburn/Sidney Poitier; cp/cd: Frank DeVol

Dear Old Dad | Groovy Delivery Boy | Guess Who's Coming To Dinner (Theme) | Sentimental Suitcase
Drive In | Guess Who's Coming To Dinner (includes 2 versions) | | Sunset And Glory (End Title)
Glory Of Love [Billy Hill] | | Happy Child | Two's A Majority

9/25/61 | 48 | 14 | 187 | Guns Of Navarone, The .... [I] | $40 | Columbia 8455
Gregory Peck/David Niven/Anthony Quinn; cp/cd: Dimitri Tiomkin

Anna | Guns Of Navarone [Mitch Miller] | Medley | Prologue
Climbing The South Cliff | Finale | Mission Accomplished | Wedding Music
Death Of Young Pappadimos | Legend Of Navarone | Preparation For Guns | Yassu

12/15/62+ | 10 | 32 | 188 | Gypsy .... [M] | $25 | Warner 1480
Rosalind Russell/Natalie Wood/Karl Malden; mu: Jule Styne; ly: Stephen Sondheim; also see Original Cast ('59)

All I Need Is The Girl | Finale | Mr. Goldstone, I Love You | Some People
Baby June And Her Newsboys | If Mama Was Married | Overture | Together Wherever We Go
Dainty June And Her Farmboys | Let Me Entertain You | Rose's Turn | You Gotta Have A Gimmick
Everything's Coming Up Roses | Little Lamb | Small World | You'll Never Get Away From Me

4/7/79 | 65 | 16 | ● 189 | Hair .... [M] | $12 | RCA 3274 [2]
John Savage/Treat Williams/Beverly D'Angelo; mu/cd: Galt MacDermot; ly: Gerome Ragni and James Rado; also see Original Cast ('68) and Dance/Disco Disco Spectacular

Abie Baby (medley) | Black Boys | **Easy To Be Hard** [Cheryl Barnes] 64 | Fourscore (medley)
Ain't Got No (medley) | Colored Spade | | Frank Mills
Air | Don't Put It Down | Electric Blues (medley) | Good Morning Starshine
Aquarius | Donna (medley) | Flesh Failures (medley) | Hair

DEBUT DATE	PEAK POS	WKS CHR	GOLD		ARTIST — Album Title	$	Label & Number

Hare Krishna · Hashish (medley) · I Got Life · I'm Black (medley) · L.B.J. (Initials) · Let The Sunshine In (medley) · Manchester · My Conviction · Old Fashioned Melody (medley) · Party Music · Sodomy · Somebody To Love · 3-5-0-0 · Walking In Space · What A Piece Of Work Is Man · Where Do I Go? · White Boys

4/2/88 | 114 | 6 | 190 Hairspray..........[V-O] **$8** MCA 6228
Sonny Bono/Ruth Brown/Divine/Debbie Harry/Ricki Lake

Bug, The *[Jerry Dallman & The Knightcaps]* · **Foot Stomping - Part 1** *[Flares]* **25** · Hairspray *[Rachel Sweet]* · **I Wish I Were A Princess** *[Little Peggy March]* **32** · **I'm Blue (The Gong-Gong Song)** *[Ikettes]* **19** · **Madison Time - Part 1** *[Ray Bryant Combo]* **30** · **Mama Didn't Lie** *[Jan Bradley]* **14** · **Nothing Takes The Place Of You** *[Toussaint McCall]* **52** · Roach (Dance) *[Gene & Wendell]* · **Shake A Tail Feather** *[Five Du-Tones]* **51** · **Town Without Pity** *[Gene Pitney]* **13** · **You'll Lose A Good Thing** *[Barbara Lynn]* **8**

8/17/68 | 193 | 4 | 191 Hang 'Em High..........[I] **$20** United Art. 5179
Clint Eastwood/Inger Stevens/Ed Begley/Pat Hingle; cp/cd: Dominic Frontiere

Bordello · Hang 'Em High · I'll Get 'Em Myself · It's No Deal · Rachel (Love Theme) · They Took Me · Tumbleweed Wagon

3/23/68 | 166 | 9 | 192 Happiest Millionaire, The..........[M] **$15** Buena Vista 5001
Fred MacMurray/Tommy Steele/Greer Garson; sw: Richard M. Sherman and Robert B. Sherman; cd: Jack Elliott

Are We Dancing · Bye-Yum Pum Pum · Detroit · Finale · Fortuosity · I Believe In This Country · I'll Always Be Irish · Let's Have A Drink On It · Overture · Strengthen The Dwelling · There Are Those · Valentine Candy · Watch Your Footwork · What's Wrong With That · When A Man Has A Daughter

Hard Day's Night, A - see BEATLES
The Beatles/Wilfrid Brambell

Hard To Hold - see SPRINGFIELD, Rick
Rick Springfield/Janet Eilber/Patti Hansen/Bill Mumy

Harder They Come, The - see CLIFF, Jimmy
Jimmy Cliff/Janet Barkley/Carl Bradshaw

Harum Scarum - see PRESLEY, Elvis
Elvis Presley (Johnny Tyronne)/Mary Ann Mobley/Fran Jeffries

Hatari! - see MANCINI, Henry
John Wayne/Red Buttons/Hardy Kruger

Having A Wild Weekend - see CLARK, Dave, Five
The Dave Clark Five/Barbara Ferris

11/19/66+ | 85 | 16 | 193 Hawaii..........[I] **$20** United Art. 5143
Julie Andrews/Richard Harris; cp/cd: Elmer Bernstein

Abner (medley) · Abner And Jerusha · Hawaii · Hawaiian Welcome · Keoki's Tragedy · Main Title · Malama's Death · Pastoral Letter · Prologue · Promise Kept · Quiet Harbor · Sailors And Women · Wishing Doll (medley)

Head - see MONKEES
The Monkees/Victor Mature/Annette Funicello

10/29/88 | 176 | 2 | 194 Heartbreak Hotel..........[V] **$8** RCA 8533
David Keith/Charlie Schlatter/Tuesday Weld

Burning Love *[Elvis Presley]* **2** · Can't Help Falling In Love *[David Keith]* · **Drift Away** *[Dobie Gray]* **5** · **Eighteen** *[Alice Cooper]* **21** · Heartbreak Hotel *[David Keith & Charlie Schlatter]* · **Heartbreak Hotel** *[Elvis Presley]* **1** · **If I Can Dream** *[Elvis Presley]* **12** · Love Me *[David Keith]* · **One Night** *[Elvis Presley]* **4** · Ready Teddy *[Elvis Presley]* · Soul On Fire *[Charlie Schlatter]*

8/8/81 | 12 | 28 | ● | 195 Heavy Metal..........[V] **$25** Asylum 90004 [2]
animated film, voices by: John Candy/Joe Flaherty/Harold Ramis

All Of You *[Don Felder]* · Blue Lamp *[Stevie Nicks]* · Crazy *[Nazareth]* · Heartbeat *[Riggs]* · Heavy Metal *[Sammy Hagar]* · **Heavy Metal (Takin' A Ride)** *[Don Felder]* **43** · I Must Be Dreamin' *[Cheap Trick]* · Mob Rules *[Black Sabbath]* · **Open Arms** *[Journey]* **2** · Prefabricated *[Trust]* · Queen Bee *[Grand Funk Railroad]* · Radar Rider *[Riggs]* · Reach Out *[Cheap Trick]* · True Companion *[Donald Fagen]* · Veteran Of The Psychic Wars *[Blue Oyster Cult]* · **Working In The Coal Mine** *[Devo]* **43**

2/3/58 | 25 | 1 | 196 Helen Morgan Story, The.......... **$65** RCA 1030
Ann Blyth/Paul Newman; vocals performed by Gogi Grant; cd: Ray Heindorf

April In Paris · Avalon (medley) · Bill · Body And Soul · Breezin' Along With The Breeze (medley) · Can't Help Lovin' That Man · Deep Night (medley) · Do Do Do (medley) · Don't Ever Leave Me · I Can't Give You Anything But Love · I'll Get By (medley) · I've Got A Crush On You (medley) · If You Were The Only Girl In The World (medley) · Just A Memory (medley) · Love Nest · Man I Love · More Than You Know · My Melancholy Baby · On The Sunny Side Of The Street · One I Love Belongs To Somebody Else · Someone To Watch Over Me (medley) · Something To Remember You By · Speak To Me Of Love · Why Was I Born

10/11/69 | 184 | 3 | 197 Hell's Angels '69.......... **$20** Capitol 303
Tom Stern/Conny Van Dyke/Jeremy Slate; cp/cd: Tony Bruno

Al And Alice *[Stream Of Consciousness]* · Bass Lake Run · Chase Of Death · Goofin' · Hang On Tight · Lazy *[Sonny Valdez]* · Say Girl *[Wendy Cole]* · Till You're Through *[Stream Of Consciousness]* · What's His Is His *[Sonny Valdez]*

Hello, Dolly! - see STREISAND, Barbra
Barbra Streisand/Walter Matthau/Michael Crawford; also see Original Cast ('64)

9/30/67 | 165 | 2 | 198 Hells Angels On Wheels..........[I] **$20** Smash 67094
Adam Roarke/Jack Nicholson; cp/cd: Stu Phillips

Bike Ballet · Flowers · Four, Five, Sex · Hells Angels On Wheels · Poet · Poet Scores · Skip To My Mary J. · Study In Motion #1 *[Poor]* · Sunday Art And Football · Tea Party

Help! - see BEATLES
The Beatles/Leo McKern/Eleanor Bron

Hey Boy! Hey Girl! - see PRIMA, Louis, & SMITH, Keely
Louis Prima/Keely Smith/James Gregory

DEBUT DATE	PEAK POS	WKS CHR	GOLD		ARTIST — Album Title	$	Label & Number

Hey, Let's Twist! - see DEE, Joey
Joey Dee & The Starliters/Teddy Randazzo/Jo Ann Campbell

| 12/5/87+ | 146 | 13 | | 199 | Hiding Out .... [V] | $8 | Virgin 90661 |

Jon Cryer/Annabeth Gish/Keith Coogan

Bang Your Head [Lolita Pop]	Live My Life [Boy George] 40	Run! Hide! [All That Jazz]
Catch Me (I'm Falling) [Pretty Poison] 8	Max For President Rap [Lee Anthony Briston/David L. Robinson/Daryl Smith]	Seattle [P.I.L.]
		So Different Now [Felix Cavaliere]
Crying [Roy Orbison & k.d. lang]	Real Life [Black Britain]	You Don't Know [Scarlett & Black] 20
I Refuse [Hue & Cry]		

| 8/25/56 | 5 | 28 | | 200 | **High Society** .... [M] | $15 | Capitol 750 |

Bing Crosby/Grace Kelly/Frank Sinatra; adapted from the play *Philadelphia Story*; sw: Cole Porter

High Society Calypso	Mind If I Make Love To You	True Love [Bing Crosby & Grace Kelly] 3	Who Wants To Be A Millionaire
High Society (Overture)	Now You Has Jazz [Bing Crosby & Louis Armstrong] 88	Well Did You Evah? [Bing Crosby & Frank Sinatra] 92	You're Sensational [Frank Sinatra] 52
I Love You, Samantha			
Little One			

Hold On! - see HERMAN'S HERMITS
Peter Noone/Shelley Fabares/Sue Ane Langdon

| 12/12/92 | 98 | 5 | | 201 | Home Alone 2 - Lost In New York .... [V-X] | $12 | Fox 11000 |

Macaulay Culkin/Joe Pesci/Daniel Stern/John Heard/Tim Curry; Christmas charts: 15/'92

All Alone On Christmas [Darlene Love] 83	It's Beginning To Look A Lot Like Christmas [Johnny Mathis]	My Christmas Tree [Home Alone Children's Choir]	Somewhere In My Memory [Bette Midler]
Christmas Star [John Williams]	Jingle Bell Rock [Bobby Helms] 6	O Come All Ye Faithful [Lisa Fischer]	
Cool Jerk [Capitols]			
Holly Jolly Christmas [Alan Jackson]	Merry Christmas, Merry Christmas [John Williams]	Silver Bells [Atlantic Starr]	
		Sleigh Ride [TLC]	

Home Of The Brave - see ANDERSON, Laurie

| 8/29/92 | 18 | 24↑ | ● | 202 | Honeymoon In Vegas .... [V] | $12 | Epic 52845 |

James Caan/Nicolas Cage/Sarah Jessica Parker/Pat Morita

All Shook Up [Billy Joel] 92	Heartbreak Hotel [Billy Joel]	Suspicious Minds [Dwight Yoakam]	(You're The) Devil In Disguise [Trisha Yearwood]
Are You Lonesome Tonight? [Brian Ferry]	Hound Dog [Jeff Beck & Jed Leiber]	That's All Right [Vince Gill]	
Blue Hawaii [Willie Nelson]	Jailhouse Rock [John Mellencamp]	Wear My Ring Around Your Neck [Ricky Van Shelton]	
Burning Love [Travis Tritt]			
Can't Help Falling In Love [Bono]	Love Me Tender [Amy Grant]		

Honeysuckle Rose - see NELSON, Willie
Willie Nelson/Dyan Cannon/Amy Irving/Slim Pickens

| 1/18/92 | 182 | 2 | | 203 | Hook .... [I] | $12 | Epic 48888 |

Dustin Hoffman/Robin Williams/Julia Roberts/Bob Hoskins; cp/cd: John Williams; ly: Leslie Briscusse; 2 cuts feature vocals

Arrival Of Tink (medley)	From Mermaids To Lost Boys	Presenting The Hook	Ultimate War
Banning Back Home	Granny Wendy	Prologue	We Don't Wanna Grow Up
Banquet, The	Hook-Napped	Remembering Childhood	When You're Alone
Farewell Neverland	Lost Boy Chase	Smee's Plan	You Are The Pan
Flight To Neverland (medley)	Never-Feast		

| 4/7/90 | 104 | 9 | | 204 | House Party .... [V] | $12 | Motown 6296 |

Kid 'N Play/Full Force/Robin Harris; CD includes bonus track

Funhouse [Kid 'N Play]	Jive Time Sucker [Force MD's]	This Is Love [Kenny Vaughan & The Art Of Love]	What A Feeling [Arts & Crafts]
House Party [Full Force]	Kid Vs. Play (The Battle) [Kid 'N Play]		Why You Get Funky On Me? [Today]
I Ain't Going Out Like That [Zan]		To Da Break Of Dawn [L.L. Cool J]	
I Can't Do Nothin' For You, Man [Flavor Flav]	Surely [Arts & Crafts]		

| 11/9/91 | 55 | 12 | | 205 | House Party 2 .... [V] | $12 | MCA 10397 |

Kid 'N Play/Full Force/Tisha Campbell/Iman

Ain't Gonna Hurt Nobody [Kid 'N Play] 51	House Party (I Don't Know What You Come To Do) [Tony! Toni! Tone!]	It's So Hard To Say Goodbye To Yesterday [Flex]	Ready Or Not [Wrecks 'N' Effect]
Big Ol' Jazz [M.C. Trouble]		Let Me Know Something?! [Bell Biv DeVoe]	What's On Your Mind [Eric B & Rakim]
Candlelight & You [Keith Washington]	I Like Your Style [Bubba]		Yo, Baby, Yo! [Ralph Tresvant]
	I Lust 4 U [London Jones]		

| 4/20/63 | 4 | 84 | ● | 206 | **How The West Was Won** .... | $15 | MGM 5 |

Gregory Peck/Henry Fonda/James Stewart/Debbie Reynolds; cd: Alfred Newman

Bereavement And Fulfillment	Entr'acte	Main Title	Raise A Ruckus
Cheyennes	Finale	Marriage Proposal	River Pirates
Cleve And The Mule	He's Linus' Boy	No Goodbye	What Was Your Name In The States?
Climb A Higher Hill	Home In The Meadow	Overture	
Come Share My Life			

How To Beat The High Cost Of Living - see LAWS, Hubert, and/or KLUGH, Earl
Susan Saint James/Jane Curtin/Jessica Lange

| 4/22/67 | 146 | 4 | | 207 | How To Succeed In Business Without Really Trying .... [M] | $20 | United Art. 5151 |

Robert Morse/Michele Lee/Rudy Vallee; sw: Frank Loesser; cd: Nelson Riddle; also see Original Cast ('61)

Been A Long Day	Company Way (includes 3 versions)	Grand Old Ivy	Paris Original (medley)
Brotherhood Of Man		I Believe In You	Rosemary
Coffee Break	Finale	Overture	Secretary Is Not A Toy

| 4/22/67 | 153 | 2 | | 208 | Hurry Sundown .... [I] | $45 | RCA 1133 |

Michael Caine/Jane Fonda/Diahann Carroll/Faye Dunaway; cp/cd: Hugo Montenegro

Breakfast In Bed	Homecoming	Hurry Sundown Blues	Love Theme
Charlie's Trip	Hurry Sundown	Interlude (medley)	Main Title
Cool It Julie		Loser, The	Playing With Dynamite
End Title (medley)		Love Me Vivian	

I Could Go On Singing - see GARLAND, Judy
Judy Garland/Dirk Bogarde/Jack Klugman

I Walk The Line - see CASH, Johnny
Gregory Peck/Tuesday Weld/Estelle Parsons

DEBUT DATE	PEAK POS	WKS CHR	GOLD	ARTIST — Album Title	$	Label & Number

I Want To Live! - see MULLIGAN, Gerry
Susan Hayward/Simon Oakland/Theodore Bikel

| 4/21/79 | **174** | 5 | 209 | Ice Castles ....[I] | **$8** | Arista 9502 |

Robby Benson/Lynn-Holly Johnson; cp/cd: Marvin Hamlisch

Deborah's Rock	Ice Castles (Through The Eyes	Ice Castles (Through The Eyes	Scarlotti Suite
Finale	Of Love), Theme From	Of Love), Theme From	They Threw Flowers
	[Melissa Manchester] 76	(Instrumental)	Touch
		Learning Again	Voyager [Alan Parsons Project]

| 12/20/80+ | **130** | 9 | 210 | Idolmaker, The ....[V] | **$8** | A&M 4840 |

Ray Sharkey/Tovah Feldshuh/Peter Gallagher; sw: Jeff Barry

Baby [Peter Gallagher]	However Dark The Night [Peter	I Believe It Can Be Done	Ooh-Wee Baby [Darlene Love]
Boy And A Girl [Sweet	Gallagher]	(instrumental) [Nino Tempo]	Sweet Little Lover [Jesse
Inspirations & London Fog]	I Believe It Can Be Done [Ray	I Can't Tell [Colleen Fitzpatrick]	Frederick]
Come And Get It [Nino Tempo]	Sharkey]	I Know Where You're Goin' [Nino	
Here Is My Love [Jesse Frederick]		Tempo]	

Imagine: John Lennon - see LENNON, John

| 9/30/67 | **153** | 11 | 211 | In The Heat Of The Night .... [I+V] | **$15** | United Art. 5160 |

Sidney Poitier/Rod Steiger/Warren Oates/Lee Grant; cp/cd: Quincy Jones

Blood & Roots	Give Me Until Morning	Mama Caleba's Blues [Ray	Peep-Freak Patrol Car
Bowlegged Polly [Glen Campbell]	In The Heat Of The Night [Ray	Charles]	Shag Bag, Hounds & Harvey
Chief's Drive To Mayor	Charles] 33	Nitty Gritty Time	Where Whitey Ain't Around
Cotton Curtain	It Sure Is Groovy! [Gil Bernal]	No You Won't	Whipping Boy
Foul Owl [Boomer & Travis]		On Your Feet, Boy!	

| 6/16/84 | **42** | 11 | 212 | Indiana Jones And The Temple Of Doom ....[I] | **$8** | Polydor 821592 |

Harrison Ford/Kate Capshaw/Ke Huy Quan; cp/cd: John Williams

Anything Goes	Fast Streets Of Shanghai	Nocturnal Activities	Slave Children's Crusade
Bug Tunnel And Death Trap	Finale	Shortround's Theme	Temple Of Doom
Children In Chains	Mine Car Chase	Slalom On Mt. Humol	

| 10/19/68 | **136** | 5 | 213 | Interlude ....[I] | **$40** | Colgems 5007 |

Oskar Werner/Barbara Ferris; mixture of traditional classical works and new compositions by Georges Delerue

Beethoven: Excerpts from	Dvorak: Excerpts from Carnival	Must It Happen Once To	Tchaikovsky: Excerpts from
Symphony No. 5	Overture	Everyone?	Symphony No. 1--2nd
Bittersweet Interlude	Interlude [Timi Yuro]	Rachmaninoff: Excerpts from	Movement
Brahms: Excerpts from	Interlude (Instrumental)	Symphony No. 2--3rd	
Symphony No. 3--1st	Interlude Triangle	Movement	
Movement			

| 4/13/85 | **118** | 8 | 214 | Into The Night ....[V] | **$8** | MCA 5561 |

Jeff Goldblum/Michelle Pfeiffer; side 1: B.B. King; side 2: various artists

Century City Chase [Joel Peskin]	Enter Shaheen [B.B. King]	In The Midnight Hour [B.B. King]	Let's Get It On [Marvin Gaye] 1
Don't Make Me Sorry [Patti	I Can't Help Myself [Four	Into The Night [B.B. King]	My Lucille [B.B. King]
LaBelle]	Tops] 1	Keep It Light [Thelma Houston]	

| 11/13/65 | **133** | 2 | 215 | Ipcress File, The ....[I] | **$25** | Decca 79124 |

Michael Caine/Nigel Green/Sue Lloyd; cp/cd: John Barry

Alone Blues	Goodbye Harry	Jazz Along Alone	Man Alone (includes 2 versions)
Alone In Three-Quarter Time	If You're Not Clean - I'll Kill You	Main Title	Meeting With Grantby And Fight
Death Of Carswell			

| 9/14/63 | **69** | 11 | 216 | Irma La Douce ....[I] | **$20** | United Art. 5109 |

Jack Lemmon/Shirley MacLaine; cp/cd: Andre Previn; also see Original Cast ('60)

But That's Another Story	I'm Sorry Irma	Main Title	Our Language Of Love
Don't Take All Night	In The Tub With Fieldglasses	Market, The	Return Of Lord X
Easy Living The Hard Way	Juke Box: Let's Pretend Love	Meet Irma	This Is The Story
Escape	Juke Box: Look Again	Nestor, The Honest Policeman	Wedding Ring
Goodbye Lord X			

| 2/15/86 | **54** | 11 | 217 | Iron Eagle ....[V] | **$8** | Capitol 12499 |

Louis Gossett, Jr./Jason Gedrick/David Suchet/Tim Thomerson

Hide In The Rainbow [Dio]	It's Too Late [Helix]	One Vision [Queen] 61	This Raging Fire [Jon Butcher
Intense [George Clinton]	Love Can Make You Cry [Urgent]	Road Of The Gypsy [Adrenalin]	Axis]
Iron Eagle (Never Say Die) [King	Maniac House [Katrina & The	These Are The Good Times [Eric	
Kobra]	Waves]	Martin]	

It Happened At The World's Fair - see PRESLEY, Elvis
Elvis Presley (Mike Edwards)/Joan O'Brien/Gary Lockwood

| 12/21/63+ | **101** | 11 | 218 | It's A Mad, Mad, Mad, Mad World ....[I] | **$20** | United Art. 5110 |

Spencer Tracy/Sid Caesar/Milton Berle/Jonathan Winters; cp/cd: Ernest Gold

Adios Santa Rosita	Great Pursuit	It's A Mad, Mad, Mad, Mad	Overture
Away We Go	Gullible Otto Meyer	World	Retribution
Big W	Instant Chase	Living End	Thirty One Flavors
Follow The Leader		Main Title	You Satisfy My Soul

| 11/22/80 | **137** | 11 | 219 | It's My Turn .... [I+V] | **$8** | Motown 947 |

Jill Clayburgh/Michael Douglas/Charles Grodin; cp/cd: Patrick Williams

| Honest Talk | It's My Turn (instrumental) | Main Title (medley) | Walk On [Ozone] |
| It's My Turn [Diana Ross] 9 | Love Begins (medley) | This Is My Love [Tony Travalini] | |

James Bond Soundtracks:

Casino Royale	Goldfinger	Spy Who Loved Me, The	also see: Roland Shaw/Billy
Diamonds Are Forever	Live And Let Die	Thunderball	Strange/Soundtrack
Dr. No	Moonraker	View To A Kill, A	Compilations: Music To Read
For Your Eyes Only	Octopussy	You Only Live Twice	James Bond By
From Russia With Love	On Her Majesty's Secret Service		

Janis - see JOPLIN, Janis

| 7/26/75 | **30** | 17 | 220 | Jaws ....[I] | **$8** | MCA 2087 |

Roy Scheider/Richard Dreyfuss/Robert Shaw; cp/cd: John Williams

Chrissie's Death	Main Title (Theme From	Out To Sea	Sea Attack Number One
End Title	"Jaws") 32	Preparing The Cage	Underwater Siege
Hand To Hand Combat	Night Search	Promenade (Tourists On The	
Indianapolis Story	One Barrel Chase	Menu)	

DEBUT DATE	PEAK POS	WKS CHR	GOLD	ARTIST — Album Title	$	Label & Number

Jazz Singer, The - see DIAMOND, Neil
Neil Diamond/Laurence Olivier/Lucie Arnaz

| 6/30/73 | 21 | 39 | ● 221 | **Jesus Christ Superstar** .... [M] | $10 | MCA 11000 [2] |

Ted Neely/Yvonne Elliman/Carl Anderson/Barry Dennen; mu: Andrew Lloyd Webber; ly: Tim Rice; also see Rock Operas ('70)/Concept Albums ('70)/Original Cast ('72)/Percy Faith

Arrest, The	Heaven On Their Minds	Overture	Superstar
Blood Money (medley)	Hosanna	Peter's Denial	Temple, The
Could We Start Again Please?	I Don't Know How To Love Him	Pilate And Christ	Then We Are Decided
Crucifixion, The	John Nineteen: Forty-One	Pilate's Dream	This Jesus Must Die
Damned For All Time (medley)	Judas' Death	Poor Jerusalem	Trial Before Pilate
Everything's Alright	King Herod's Song	Simon Zealotes	What's That Buzz
Gethsemane (I Only Want To Say)	Last Supper	Strange Thing Mystifying	

| 12/28/85+ | 55 | 17 | 222 | **Jewel Of The Nile, The** .... [V] | $8 | Jive 8406 |

Michael Douglas/Kathleen Turner/Danny DeVito

African Breeze [Hugh Masekela & Jonathan Butler]	Jewel Of The Nile [Precious Wilson]	Nubian Dance [Nubians]	**When The Going Gets Tough, The Tough Get Going** [Billy Ocean] 2
Freaks Come Out At Night [Whodini]	Legion (Here I Come) [Mark Shreeve]	Party (No Sheep Is Safe Tonight) [Willesden Dodgers]	
I'm In Love [Ruby Turner]	Love Theme [Jack Nitzsche]	Plot Thickens [Jack Nitzsche]	

Jimi Hendrix - see HENDRIX, Jimi

Jonathan Livingston Seagull - see DIAMOND, Neil, and HARRIS, Richard
James Franciscus/Juliet Mills

Journey Through The Past - see YOUNG, Neil

| 1/18/92 | 17 | 29 | ● 223 | **Juice** .... [V] | $12 | MCA 10462 |

Omar Epps/Jermaine Hopkins/Khalil Kain/Tupac Shakur

Does Your Man Know About Me [Raheim]	Is It Good To You [Teddy Riley feat. Tammy Lucas]	People Get Ready [Brand New Heavies feat. N'Dea Davenport]	So You Want To Be A Gangster [Too Short]
Don't Be Afraid [Aaron Hall] 44	It's Going Down [EPMD]	Sex, Money & Murder [M.C. Pooh]	Uptown Anthem [Naughty By Nature]
Flipside [Juvenile Committee]	**Juice (Know The Ledge)** [Eric B. & Rakim] 96	Shoot 'Em Up [Cypress Hill Crew]	What Could Be Better Bitch [Son Of Bazerk]
He's Gamin' On Ya [Salt-N-Pepa]	Nuff Respect [Big Daddy Kane]		

| 11/22/86 | 159 | 4 | 224 | **Jumpin' Jack Flash** .... [V] | $8 | Mercury 830545 |

Whoopi Goldberg/Carol Kane/Stephen Collins/Annie Potts

Breaking The Code [Thomas Newman]	Love Music [Thomas Newman]	**Trick Of The Night** [Bananarama] 76	**You Can't Hurry Love** [Supremes] 1
Hold On [Billy Branigan]	Misled [Kool & The Gang] 10	Window To The World [Face To Face]	
Jumpin' Jack Flash [Rolling Stones] 3	Rescue Me [Gwen Guthrie]		
	Set Me Free [Rene & Angela]		

| 2/3/68 | 19 | 34 | 225 | **Jungle Book, The** .... | $15 | Disneyland 3948 |

animated film, voices by: Phil Harris/Sebastian Cabot/Louis Prima; based on Rudyard Kipling's *Mowgli* stories; sw: Richard M. Sherman and Robert B. Sherman

| Bare Necessities | I Wan'na Be Like You (includes 2 versions) | My Own Home | Trust In Me |
| Colonel Hathi's March | | That's What Friends Are For | |

Jungle Fever - see WONDER, Stevie
Wesley Snipes/Annabella Sciorra/Spike Lee/Ossie Davis

| 7/21/84 | 114 | 12 | 226 | **Karate Kid, The** .... [V] | $8 | Casablanca 822213 |

Ralph Macchio/Noriyuki "Pat" Morita/Elisabeth Shue

(Bop Bop) On The Beach [Flirts with Jan & Dean]	Feel The Night [Baxter Robertson]	**Moment Of Truth** [Survivor] 63	You're The Best [Joe "Bean" Esposito]
Desire [Gang Of Four]	(It Takes) Two To Tango [Paul Davis]	No Shelter [Broken Edge]	Young Hearts [Commuter]
		Rhythm Man [St. Regis]	
		Tough Love [Shandi]	

| 7/12/86 | 30 | 17 | 227 | **Karate Kid Part II, The** .... [V] | $8 | United Art. 40414 |

Ralph Macchio/Noriyuki "Pat" Morita/Martin Kove

Earth Angel [New Edition] 21	Let Me At 'Em [Southside Johnny]	Rock 'N' Roll Over You [Moody Blues]	Two Looking At One [Carly Simon]
Fish For Life [Mancrab]	Love Theme [Bill Conti]	Storm, The [Bill Conti]	
Glory Of Love [Peter Cetera] 1	Rock Around The Clock [Paul Rodgers]	**This Is The Time** [Dennis DeYoung] 93	

Kids Are Alright, The - see WHO

| 7/21/56 | 1¹ | 277 | ● 228 | **King And I, The** .... [M] | $15 | Capitol 740 |

Yul Brynner/Deborah Kerr; mu: Richard Rodgers; ly: Oscar Hammerstein II; cd: Alfred Newman; also see Original Cast ('92)

Getting To Know You	March Of Siamese Children	Shall I Tell You What I Think Of You?	Something Wonderful
Hello, Young Lovers	My Lord And Master	Shall We Dance?	Song Of The King
I Have Dreamed	Overture		We Kiss In A Shadow
I Whistle A Happy Tune	Puzzlement, A		

King Creole - see PRESLEY, Elvis
Elvis Presley (Danny Fisher)/Carolyn Jones/Walter Matthau

| 1/8/77 | 123 | 8 | 229 | **King Kong** .... [I] | $12 | Reprise 2260 |

Jeff Bridges/Jessica Lange/Charles Grodin; cp/cd: John Barry

Arrival On The Island	End, The	How About Buying Me A Drink (medley)	Opening, The
Arthusa	End Is At Hand	Incomprehensible Captivity	Sacrifice - Hail To The King
Blackout In New York (medley)	Full Moon Domain - Beauty Is A Beast	Kong Hits The Big Apple	
Breakout To Captivity		Maybe My Luck Has Changed	
Climb To Skull Island			

| 4/16/83 | 162 | 6 | 230 | **King Of Comedy, The** .... [V] | $8 | Warner 23765 |

Robert DeNiro/Jerry Lewis/Tony Randall/Sandra Bernhard

Back On The Chain Gang [Pretenders] 5	Come Rain Or Come Shine [Ray Charles]	Rainbow Sleeve [Rickie Lee Jones]	'Tain't Nobody's Bizness (If I Do) [B.B. King]
Between Trains [Robbie Robertson]	Finer Things [David Sanborn]	Steal The Night [Ric Ocasek]	Wonderful Remark [Van Morrison]
	King Of Comedy [Bob James]	Swamp [Talking Heads]	

DEBUT DATE	PEAK POS	WKS CHR	GOLD	ARTIST — Album Title	$	Label & Number

11/6/61+ | **10** | 39 | | **231 King Of Kings** ....[I] | **$40** | MGM 2
Jeffrey Hunter/Siobhan McKenna/Rip Torn; cp/cd: Miklos Rozsa; includes a full-color book about the movie

Christ's Entry Into Jerusalem (medley)	Mary At The Sepulcher	Prayer Of Our Lord	Tempest In Judea (medley)
Holy Of Holies	Miracles Of Christ	Resurrection (Finale)	Temptation Of Christ
John The Baptist	Mount Galilee (medley)	Salome's Dance	Virgin Mary
King Of Kings Theme (Prelude)	Nativity	Scourging Of Christ	Way Of The Cross
	Pontius Pilate's Arrival Into Jerusalem	Sermon On The Mount (medley)	

Kissin' Cousins - see PRESLEY, Elvis
Elvis Presley (Josh Morgan/Jodie Tatum)/Arthur O'Connell

10/26/85 | **79** | 20 | | **232 Krush Groove** ....[V] | **$8** | Warner 25295
Sheila E./Run-DMC/The Fat Boys/Kurtis Blow

All You Can Eat [Fat Boys]	If I Ruled The World [Kurtis Blow]	Krush Groovin' [Fat Boys, Run-D.M.C., Sheila E. & Kurtis Blow]	She's On It [Beastie Boys]
Feel The Spin [Debbie Harry]			Tender Love [Force M.D.'s] 10
Holly Rock [Sheila E.]	(Krush Groove) Can't Stop The Street [Chaka Khan]	Love Triangle [Gap Band]	
I Can't Live Without My Radio [L.L. Cool J]			

La Bamba - see LOS LOBOS
Lou Diamond Phillips/Esai Morales/Rosana DeSoto/Elizabeth Pena

Labyrinth - see BOWIE, David
David Bowie/Jennifer Connelly

Lady Sings The Blues - see ROSS, Diana
Diana Ross/Billy Dee Williams/Richard Pryor

3/30/85 | **58** | 15 | | **233 Last Dragon, The** ....[V] | **$8** | Motown 6128
Taimak/Julius J. Carry III/Chris Murney/Leo O'Brien/Vanity

Fire [Charlene]	Glow, The [Willie Hutch]	Peeping Tom [Rockwell]	7th Heaven [Vanity]
First Time On A Ferris Wheel (Love Theme) [Smokey Robinson & Syreeta]	Inside You [Willie Hutch & The Temptations]	**Rhythm Of The Night** [DeBarge] 3	Star [Alfie]
	Last Dragon (Title Song) [Dwight David]		Upset Stomach [Stevie Wonder]

2/27/88 | **152** | 10 | | **234 Last Emperor, The** ....[I-V] | **$8** | Virgin 90690
John Lone/Joan Chen/Peter O'Toole/Ying Ruocheng; side A: mu: Ryuichi Sakamoto; side B: various

Baby (Was Born Dead) [David Byrne]	Last Emperor Theme (includes 3 versions)	Picking A Bride [David Byrne]	Red Guard Dance [Girls Red Guard Dancers]
Bed [David Byrne]	Lunch [Cong Su]	Picking Up Brides	Where Is Armo?
Emperor's Waltz [Ball Orchestra of Vienna]	Main Title Theme [David Byrne]	Rain (I Want A Divorce)	Wind, Rain And Water [David Byrne]
First Coronation	Open The Door	Red Guard [Red Guard Accordion Band]	
	Paper Emperor [David Byrne]		

10/24/92 | **42** | 16↑ | | **235 Last Of The Mohicans, The** ....[I] | **$12** | Morgan Cr. 20015
Daniel Day-Lewis/Madeleine Stowe; cp: Trevor Jones/Randy Edelman; cd: Daniel A. Carlin/Randy Edelman

British Arrival	Elk Hunt	Main Title	Promentory
Canoes (medley)	Fort Battle	Massacre (medley)	River Walk (medley)
Cora	Glade Part II, The	Munro's Office (medley)	Stockade (medley)
Courier, The	I Will Find You [Clannad]	Parlay	Top Of The World
Discovery (medley)	Kiss, The	Pieces Of A Story	

Last Tango in Paris - see BARBIERI, Gato
Marlon Brando/Maria Schneider

Last Temptation Of Christ, The - see GABRIEL, Peter
Willem Dafoe/Harvey Keitel/Barbara Hershey/Harry Dean Stanton

Last Waltz, The - see BAND

3/2/63 | **2²** | 86 | | **236 Lawrence Of Arabia** ....[I] | **$25** | Colpix 514
Peter O'Toole/Alec Guinness/Anthony Quinn; cp/cd: Maurice Jarre; pf: London Philharmonic Orchestra

Arrival At Auda's Camp	End Title	Nefud Mirage	That Is The Desert
Bringing Gasim Into Camp (medley)	Lawrence & Body Guard	Overture	Voice Of The Guns
Continuation Of The Miracle	Main Title	Rescue Of Gasim (medley)	
	Miracle	Sun's Anvil	

7/25/92 | **159** | 6 | | **237 League Of Their Own, A** ....[V] | **$12** | Columbia 52919
Tom Hanks/Geena Davis/Madonna/Lori Petty/Jon Lovitz

All American Girls Professional Baseball League Song [Rockford Peaches]	Flying Home [Doc's Rhythm Cats]	It's Only A Paper Moon [James Taylor]	Two Sleepy People [Art Garfunkel]
Choo Choo Ch'Boogie [Manhattan Transfer]	I Didn't Know What Time It Was [James Taylor]	Life Goes On [Hans Zimmer]	
Final Game [Hans Zimmer]	In A Sentimental Mood [Billy Joel]	Now And Forever [Carole King]	
		On The Sunny Side Of The Street [Manhattan Transfer]	

Legend - see TANGERINE DREAM
Tom Cruise/Mia Sara/Tim Curry/Arnon Milchan

1/18/75 | **180** | 3 | | **238 Lenny** .... | **$10** | United Art. 359
Dustin Hoffman (Lenny Bruce)/Valerie Perrine; cp/cd: Ralph Burns; featuring monologues from the film

Aurenthology	Honeycomb	Myrtle's Tune	To Come
Blah Blah	It Never Entered My Mind [Miles Davis]	Nan's Dream	Valerie
Dikes	Lament	Niggers	We're All The Same Schmucks, Part I & II
Dirty	Lenny (Theme)	Opening	
Flic-Flac		Time Does It Again	

12/5/87+ | **31** | 23 | ● | **239 Less Than Zero** ....[V] | **$8** | Columbia 44042
Robert Downey, Jr./Andrew McCarthy/Jami Gertz

Are You My Woman? [Black Flames]	**Hazy Shade Of Winter** [Bangles] 2	Life Fades Away [Roy Orbison]	You & Me (Less Than Zero) [Glen Danzig & The Power & Fury Orch.]
Bring The Noise [Public Enemy]	How To Love Again [Oran "Juice" Jones]	Rock And Roll All Nite [Poison]	
Going Back To Cali [L.L. Cool J] 31	In-A-Gadda-Da-Vida [Slayer]	Rocking Pneumonia And The Boogie Woogie Flu [Aerosmith]	
		She's Lost You [Joan Jett]	

Let It Be - see BEATLES

DEBUT DATE	PEAK POS	WKS CHR	GOLD	ARTIST — Album Title	$	Label & Number
				Let The Good Times Roll - see COMPILATIONS BY DISC JOCKEYS		
				Let's Do It Again - see STAPLE SINGERS		
				Sidney Poitier/Bill Cosby/Jimmie Walker/John Amos		
9/2/89	**164**	3	240	Lethal Weapon 2 .... [V]	**$8**	Warner 25985
				Mel Gibson/Danny Glover/Joe Pesci/Joss Ackland; side 1: various; side 2: band featuring Eric Clapton, David Sanborn, Greg Philliganes and Randy Crawford		

Cheer Down *[George Harrison]* / Knockin' On Heaven's Door *[Randy Crawford feat. Eric Clapton & David Sanborn]* / Leo / Shipyard, The (medley)
Embassy, The / / Riggs / **Still Cruisin'** *[Beach Boys]* **93**
Goodnight Rika / / Riggs And Roger / Stilt House

| 6/27/92 | **101** | 3 | 241 | Lethal Weapon 3 .... [I+V] | **$12** | Reprise 26989 |
| | | | | Mel Gibson/Danny Glover/Joe Pesci/Rene Russo; cp/cd: Michael Kaman | | |

Armour Piercing Bullets / It's Probably Me *[Sting with Eric Clapton]* / Lorna - A Quiet Evening By The Fire / Runaway Train *[Elton John & Eric Clapton]*
Darryl Dies / / /
God Judges Us By Our Scars / Leo Getz Goes To The Hockey Game / Riggs And Rog /
Grab The Cat / / Roger's Boat /

				Life Of Brian - see MONTY PYTHON		
				Graham Chapman/John Cleese/Eric Idle/Michael Palin		
3/14/87	**82**	10	242	Light Of Day .... [V]	**$8**	Blackheart 40654
				Michael J. Fox/Joan Jett/Gena Rowland; includes 4 songs by the The Barbusters (fictional group in film)		

Cleveland Rocks *[Ian Hunter]* / It's All Coming Down Tonight *[Barbusters]* / Rude Mood *[Barbusters]* / Twist It Off *[Fabulous Thunderbirds]*
Elegy *[Rick Cox, Chas Smith, Jon C. Clarke & Michael Boddicker]* / **Light Of Day** *[Barbusters]* **33** / Stay With Me Tonight *[Dave Edmunds]* / You Got No Place To Go *[Michael J. Fox]*
/ Only Lonely *[Bon Jovi]* **54** / This Means War *[Barbusters]* /
/ Rabbit's Got The Gun *[Hunzz]* / /

| 5/30/64 | **110** | 6 | 243 | Lilies Of The Field .... [I] | **$30** | Epic 26094 |
| | | | | Sidney Poitier/Lilia Skala/Lisa Mann; cp/cd: Jerry Goldsmith | | |

Amen (includes 2 versions) / End Cast (medley) / Homer Returns / Out Of Bricks
Breakfast (medley) / End Title (medley) / Lots Of Bricks / Roof, The
Contractor, The / Feed The Slaves (medley) / Main Title /
Drive To Mass (medley) / Homer Awakes (medley) / No Hammer /

| 5/3/69 | **182** | 7 | 244 | Lion In Winter, The .... [I] | **$15** | Columbia 3250 |
| | | | | Peter O'Toole/Katharine Hepburn/Timothy Dalton/Anthony Hopkins; cp/cd: John Barry | | |

Allons Gai Gai Gai / God Damn You / Media Vita In Morte Sumus (In The Midst Of Life We Are In Death) / To The Chapel
Chinon - Eleanor's Arrival / Herb Garden / / We're Jungle Creatures
Christmas Wine / How Beautiful You Make Me / /
Eya, Eya, Nova Gaudia / Main Title / To Rome /

| 11/8/75 | **145** | 6 | 245 | Lisztomania .... [M] | **$10** | A&M 4546 |
| | | | | Roger Daltrey/Rick Wakeman/Ringo Starr; based on the life and compositions of Franz Liszt; features lyrics by Roger Daltrey and Rick Wakeman | | |

Hibernation / Liszt: Excelsior Song / Liszt: Hell / Wagner: Master Race
Liszt: Chopsticks Fantasia (medley) / Liszt: Free Song (Hungarian Rhapsody) / Liszt: Love's Dream / Wagner: Rape, Pillage & Clap
Liszt: Dante Period / Liszt: Funerailles / Liszt: Orpheus Song / Wagner: Rienzi
/ / Liszt: Peace At Last /

| 12/16/89+ | **32** | 48 | ▲² 246 | Little Mermaid, The .... | **$8** | Disney 018 |
| | | | | animated film, voices by: Jodi Benson/Pat Carroll/Samuel E. Wright; mu: Alan Menken; ly: Howard Ashman (d: 1991 [age 41]); orchestration: Thomas Pasatieri; not available on vinyl | | |

Bedtime / Fathoms Below / Kiss The Girl / Poor Unfortunate Souls
Daughters Of Triton / Fireworks / Les Poissons / Storm, The
Destruction Of The Grotto / Flotsam And Jetsam / Main Titles / Tour Of The Kingdom
Eric To The Rescue / Happy Ending / Part Of Your World (includes 2 versions) / Under The Sea
Fanfare / Jig / / Wedding Announcement

| 1/17/87 | **47** | 17 | 247 | Little Shop Of Horrors .... [M] | **$8** | Geffen 24125 |
| | | | | Rick Moranis/Ellen Greene/Vincent Gardenia/Steve Martin; mu: Alan Menken; ly: Howard Ashman | | |

Da-Doo / Grow For Me / Meek Shall Inherit / Suddenly, Seymour
Dentist! / Little Shop Of Horrors / Skid Row (Downtown) / Suppertime
Don't Feed The Plants / Mean Green Mother From Outerspace / Some Fun Now / Somewhere That's Green
Feed Me (Git It) / / /

| 7/28/73 | **17** | 15 | 248 | Live And Let Die .... [I] | **$20** | United Art. 100 |
| | | | | Roger Moore/Jane Seymour/Yaphet Kotto; cp/cd: George Martin | | |

Baron Samedi's Dance Of Death / If He Finds It, Kill Him / Live And Let Die (medley) *[B.J. Arnau]* / Solitaire Gets Her Cards
Bond Drops In / James Bond Theme / / Trespassers Will Be Eaten
Bond Meets Solitaire / Just A Closer Walk With Thee (medley) / New Second Line (medley) / Whisper Who Dares
Fillet Of Soul - Harlem (medley) / / Sacrifice /
Fillet Of Soul - New Orleans (medley) / **Live And Let Die** *[Wings]* **2** / San Monique /
/ / Snakes Alive /

| 1/27/68 | **188** | 7 | 249 | Live For Life .... [I] | **$15** | United Art. 5165 |
| | | | | Yves Montand/Candice Bergen/Annie Girardot; cp/cd: Francis Lai | | |

All At Once It's Love / Now You Want To Be Loved / Theme To Catherine / Zoom
Live For Life / Theme To Candice / Theme To Robert /

| 9/22/62 | **63** | 6 | 250 | Lolita .... [I] | **$15** | MGM 4050 |
| | | | | Peter Sellers/Sue Lyon (Lolita)/Shelley Winters/James Mason; cp/cd: Nelson Riddle | | |

Arrival In Town / Lolita (Love Theme) / Quilty's Theme / Two Beat Society
Discovery Of Diary / Lolita Ya Ya / School Dance /
Humbert Contemplates Killing Wife / Mother And Humbert At Dinner / Thoughts Of Lolita /

				Looking For Love - see FRANCIS, Connie		
				Connie Francis/Jim Hutton/Susan Oliver		
11/26/77	**134**	8	251	Looking For Mr. Goodbar .... [V]	**$10**	Columbia 35029
				Diane Keaton/Richard Gere/William Atherton/Tuesday Weld		

Back Stabbers *[O'Jays]* **3** / Don't Ask To Stay Until Tomorrow (Theme) *[Marlena Shaw]* / **Love Hangover** *[Diana Ross]* **1** / She Wants To (Get On Down) *[Bill Withers]*
Could It Be Magic *[Donna Summer]* **52** / Don't Ask To Stay Until Tomorrow (Theme) *[Artie Kane]* / **Lowdown** *[Boz Scaggs]* **3** / She's Lonely *[Bill Withers]*
Don't Ask To Stay Until Tomorrow (Theme) *[Artie Kane]* / **Don't Leave Me This Way** *[Thelma Houston]* **1** / **Machine Gun** *[Commodores]* **22** / **Try Me I Know We Can Make It** *[Donna Summer]* **80**
/ / Prelude To Love *[Donna Summer]* /

855

DEBUT DATE	PEAK POS	WKS CHR	GOLD	ARTIST — Album Title	$	Label & Number

3/27/65 | **123** | 5 | 252 **Lord Jim**...[I] **$40** Colpix 521
Peter O'Toole/James Mason/Curt Jurgens/Eli Wallach; cp: Bronislau Kaper; cd: Muir Mathieson

Color Of Love	Fire, The (medley)	Lord Jim Theme	Sunrise, Victory And Celebration
Compassion	Four Generations	Man In Search	
Epilogue	Girl From Patusan	Patna	
Father And Son	Intermission	River Journey	

12/9/78+ | **39** | 12 | 253 **Lord Of The Rings, The** ....[I] **$10** Fantasy 1 [2]
animated film, voices by: Christopher Guard/William Squire/John Hurt; based on the novels of J.R.R. Tolkien; cp/cd: Leonard Rosenman; also see Bo Hansson

Attack Of The Orcs	Encounter With The	Gandalf Remembers	Mines Of Moria
Balrog, The (medley)	Ringwraiths (medley)	Helm's Deep	Mithrandir
Battle In The Mines (medley)	Escape To Rivendell	History Of The Ring	Riders Of Rohan
Dawn Battle (medley)	Following The Orcs	Journey Begins (medley)	Theoden's Victory (medley)
	Frodo Disappears	Lord Of The Rings (Theme)	Voyage To Mordor (medley)

8/1/87 | **15** | 39 | ● 254 **Lost Boys, The** ....[V] **$8** Atlantic 81767
Kiefer Sutherland/Dianne Wiest/Jami Gertz/Jason Patric

Beauty Has Her Way [Mummy Calls]	Don't Let The Sun Go Down On Me [Roger Daltrey]	Laying Down The Law [INXS & Jimmy Barnes]	People Are Strange [Echo & The Bunnymen]
Cry Little Sister (Theme) [Gerard McMann]	Good Times [INXS & Jimmy Barnes] 47	Lost In The Shadows (The Lost Boys) [Lou Gramm]	Power Play [Eddie & The Tide]
	I Still Believe [Tim Cappello]		To The Shock Of Miss Louise [Thomas Newman]

2/3/73 | **58** | 21 | 255 **Lost Horizon** ....[M] **$12** Bell 1300
Peter Finch/Liv Ullmann/Charles Boyer/John Gielgud; mu/cd: Burt Bacharach; ly: Hal David

I Come To You	Lost Horizon [Shawn Phillips] 63	Share The Joy	World Is A Circle
I Might Frighten Her Away	Question Me An Answer	Things I Will Not Miss	
If I Could Go Back	Reflections	Where Knowledge Ends (Faith Begins)	
Living Together, Growing Together			

8/28/71 | **172** | 6 | 256 **Love Machine, The**.. **$10** Scepter 595
Dyan Cannon/John Phillip Law/Robert Ryan/Jackie Cooper; cp/cd: Artie Butler

Amanda [Dionne Warwicke] 83	Farewell Amanda	House Party, Part I & II	White Fox
Amanda And Robin In Love	He's Moving On (Theme) [Dionne Warwicke]	Love Clown Love	White Fox Returns
Backstage: The Christie Lane Show	New Threads On Parade		

Love Me Or Leave Me - see DAY, Doris
Doris Day/James Cagney/Cameron Mitchell

Love Me Tender - see PRESLEY, Elvis
Elvis Presley (Clint)/Richard Egan/Debra Paget

1/2/71 | **2**[6] | 39 | ● 257 **Love Story** ....[I] **$10** Paramount 6002
Ali MacGraw/Ryan O'Neal/Ray Milland/John Marley; cp/cd: Francis Lai

Bach: Concerto No. 3 In D Major (Allegro)	I Love You, Phil	Mozart: Sonata In F Major (Allegro)	Snow Frolic
Bozo Barrett	Long Walk Home	Search For Jenny	
Christmas Trees	Love Story, Theme From [Francis Lai] 31	Skating In Central Park	

Loving You - see PRESLEY, Elvis
Elvis Presley (Deke Rivers)/Lizabeth Scott/Dolores Hart

Mack, The - see HUTCH, Willie
Max Julien/Richard Pryor/Don Gordon

Mackintosh & T.J. - see JENNINGS, Waylon
Roy Rogers/Clay O'Brien/Joan Hackett

Mad Dogs & Englishmen - see COCKER, Joe

8/24/85 | **39** | 13 | 258 **Mad Max Beyond Thunderdome**....................................... **$8** Capitol 12429
Mel Gibson/Tina Turner; cp/cd: Maurice Jarre

Bartertown	One Of The Living [Tina Turner] 15	We Don't Need Another Hero (Thunderdome) [Tina Turner] 2	We Don't Need Another Hero (Thunderdome) (instrumental)
Children, The			
Coming Home			

3/21/70 | **106** | 12 | 259 **Magic Christian, The** .... **$15** Common. 6004
Peter Sellers/Ringo Starr/Raquel Welch; cp/cd: Ken Thorne; also see Badfinger

Carry On To Tomorrow [Badfinger]	Day In The Life	Lilli Marlene	Rock Of Ages [Badfinger]
Come And Get It [Badfinger] 7	Hamlet Scene	Mad About The Boy	Something In The Air [Thunderclap Newman] 37
Come And Get It (instrumental)	Hunting Scene	Magic Christian Waltz	
	Introduction	Newsreel Music March	

Magical Mystery Tour - see BEATLES

11/8/75+ | **19** | 26 | 260 **Mahogany** ....[I] **$10** Motown 858
Diana Ross/Billy Dee Williams/Anthony Perkins; cp/cd: Lee Holdridge

After You	Feeling Again	Mahogany (Do You Know Where You're Going To), Theme From (instrumental)	She's The Ideal Girl
Cat Fight	Let's Go Back To Day One		Sweets (And Other Things)
(Do You Know Where You're Going To) ..see: Mahogany	Mahogany (Do You Know Where You're Going To), Theme From [Diana Ross] 1	Mahogany Suite	Tracy
Erucu		My Hero Is A Gun	You Don't Ever Have To Be Alone

Main Event, The - see STREISAND, Barbra
Barbra Streisand/Ryan O'Neal/Paul Sand/Whitman Mayo

12/5/92 | **130** | 3 | 261 **Malcolm X** ....[V] **$12** Qwest 45130
Denzel Washington/Angela Bassett/Albert Hall/Spike Lee

Alabama [John Coltrane]	Big Stuff [Billie Holiday]	Revolution [Arrested Development] 90	Someday We'll All Be Free [Aretha Franklin]
Arabesque Cookie [Duke Ellington]	Don't Cry Baby [Erskine Hawkins]	Roll 'Em Pete [Joe Turner]	That Lucky Old Sun [Ray Charles] 20
Azure [Ella Fitzgerald]	Flying Home [Lionel Hampton]	Shotgun [Jr. Walker & The All-Stars] 4	
Beans And Cornbread [Louis Jordan]	My Prayer [Ink Spots]		

3/14/92 | **50** | 14 | 262 **Mambo Kings, The** ....[V-F] **$12** Elektra 61240
Armand Assante/Antonio Banderas/Cathy Moriarty/Maruschka Detmers

| Accidental Mambo [Mambo All-Stars] | Beautiful Maria Of My Soul [Mambo All-Stars] | Como Fue [Beny More] | Guantanamera [Celia Cruz] |
| | | Cuban Pete [Tito Puente] | La Dicha Mia [Celia Cruz] |

DEBUT DATE	PEAK POS	WKS CHR	GOLD	ARTIST — Album Title	$	Label & Number

| | | | | Mambo Caliente [Arturo Sandoval]   Para Los Rumberos [Tito Puente]   Ran Kan Kan [Tito Puente]   Tea For Two [Mambo All-Stars] | | |

Melao De Cana (Moo La Lah) [Celia Cruz]   Perfidia [Linda Ronstadt]   Quiereme Mucho [Linda Ronstadt]   Sunny Ray [Mambo All-Stars]   Tanga, Rumba-Afro-Cubana [Mambo All-Stars]

4/13/74 | **196** | 3 | 263 | **Mame** .... [M] | **$10** | Warner 2773

Lucille Ball/Beatrice Arthur; sw: Jerry Herman; also see Original Cast ('66)

Bosom Buddies   It's Today   Mame   We Need A Little Christmas
Finale   Letter, The   Man In The Moon
Gooch's Song   Loving You   My Best Girl
If He Walked Into My Life   Main Title   Open A New Window

11/19/66+ | **10** | 93 | ● 264 | **Man And A Woman, A** .... [F] | **$15** | United Art. 5147

Jean-Louis Trintignant/Anouk Aimee; cp: Francis Lai

In Our Shadow   124 Miles An Hour   Stronger Than Us (includes 2 versions)   Today It's You (includes 2 versions)
Man And A Woman (includes 2 versions)   Samba Saravah

12/9/72+ | **76** | 17 | 265 | **Man Of La Mancha** .... [M] | **$10** | United Art. 9906

Peter O'Toole/Sophia Loren; mu: Mitch Leigh; ly: Joe Darion; cd: Laurence Rosenthal; also see Original Cast ('66)

Aldonza   I Really Like Him   Life As It Really Is (Soliloquy) (medley)   Overture
Barber's Song (medley)   I'm Only Thinking Of Him   Little Bird, Little Bird   Psalm, The (medley)
Dubbing, The   Impossible Dream (The Quest) (includes 3 versions)   Little Gossip
Dulcinea (includes 2 versions)   It's All The Same   Man Of La Mancha (I, Don Quixote) (includes 3 versions)
Golden Helmet Of Mambrino (medley)

3/24/56 | **2**⁴ | 17 | 266 | **Man With The Golden Arm, The** .... [I] | **$30** | Decca 78257

Frank Sinatra/Eleanor Parker/Kim Novak; cp/cd: Elmer Bernstein

Audition   Cure, The   Fix, The   Sunday Morning
Breakup   Desperation   Frankie Machine   Zosh
Clark Street   Finale   Molly

7/28/79 | **94** | 11 | 267 | Manhattan .... [I] | **$8** | Columbia 36020

Woody Allen/Diane Keaton/Meryl Streep/Mariel Hemingway; cp: George Gershwin; cd: Zubin Mehta & The N.Y. Philharmonic

Blue, Blue, Blue (medley)   He Loves And She Loves (medley) (includes 2 versions)   Love Is Here To Stay   'S Wonderful (medley)
Bronco Busters (medley)   Love Is Sweeping The Country (medley)   Someone To Watch Over Me (medley)
But Not For Me (medley)   I've Got A Crush On You   Mine   Strike Up The Band (medley)
Do, Do, Do (medley)   Land Of The Gay Caballero (medley) (includes 2 versions)   Oh, Lady Be Good (medley)   Sweet And Low-Down (medley)
Embraceable You (medley)   Rhapsody In Blue

10/1/88 | **197** | 3 | 268 | Married To The Mob .... [V] | **$8** | Reprise 25763

Michelle Pfeiffer/Matthew Modine/Dean Stockwell/Mercedes Ruehl

Bizarre Love Triangle [New Order]   Jump In The River [Sinead O'Connor]   Suspicion Of Love [Chris Isaak]   You Don't Miss Your Water [Brian Eno]
Devil Does Your Dog Bite? [Tom Tom Club]   Liar, Liar [Debbie Harry]   Time Bums [Ziggy Marley & The Melody Makers]
Goodbye Horses [Q. Lazzarus]   Queen Of Voudou [Voodooist Corp.]   Too Far Gone [Feelies]

10/3/64+ | **1**¹⁴ | 114 | ● 269 | **Mary Poppins** .... [M] | **$15** | Buena Vista 4026

Julie Andrews/Dick Van Dyke/David Tomlinson/Glynis Johns; sw: Richard M. Sherman and Robert B. Sherman; cd: Irwin Kostal

British Bank   Jolly Holiday   Perfect Nanny   **Super-cali-fragil-istic-expi-ali-docious** [Julie Andrews & Dick Van Dyke] 66
Chim Chim Cheree   Let's Go Fly A Kite   Sister Suffragette
Feed The Birds (Tuppence A Bag)   Life I Lead   Spoonful Of Sugar
Fidelity Fiduciary Bank   Man Has Dreams   Stay Awake
I Love To Laugh   Overture   Step In Time   Pavement Artist

8/4/73 | **141** | 8 | 270 | Mary Poppins .... [R] | **$8** | Buena Vista 5005

see above album for tracks; new blue cover features new artwork

7/11/70 | **120** | 16 | 271 | M*A*S*H .... | **$10** | Columbia 3520

Elliott Gould/Donald Sutherland/Tom Skerritt/Sally Kellerman; cp: Johnny Mandel; includes dialogue excerpts

Duke And Hawkeye Arrive At M.A.S.H.   Going Home   Major Houlihan And Major Burns   Operating Theater
Football Game   Hot Lips Shows Her True Colors   Painless' Suicide, Funeral And Resurrection
M*A*S*H Theme [Ahmad Jamal]   Moments To Remember

Maximum Overdrive - see AC/DC
Emilio Estevez/Pat Hingle/Laura Harrington/Christopher Murney

McVicar - see DALTREY, Roger
Roger Daltrey/Adam Faith/Cheryl Campbell

8/18/79 | **170** | 5 | 272 | Meatballs .... [V] | **$8** | RSO 3056

Bill Murray/Chris Makepeace; mu: Elmer Bernstein

Are You Ready For The Summer? [Camp North Star Kids Chorus]   C.I.T. Song   **Makin' It** [David Naughton] 5   Olympiad
Good Friend [Mary McGregor] 39   Meatballs [Rick Dees]   Rudy And Tripper
Moondust [Terry Black]   Rudy Wins The Race

1/12/91 | **65** | 24 | 273 | Mermaids .... [V] | **$12** | Geffen 24310

Cher/Bob Hoskins/Winona Ryder/Michael Schoeffling/Christina Ricci

Baby I'm Yours [Cher]   **It's My Party** [Lesley Gore] 1   **Love Is Strange** [Mickey & Sylvia] 11   **Sleep Walk** [Santo & Johnny] 1
Big Girls Don't Cry [4 Seasons] 1   **Johnny Angel** [Shelley Fabares] 1   **You've Really Got A Hold On Me** [Miracles] 8
If You Wanna Be Happy [Jimmy Soul] 1   **Just One Look** [Doris Troy] 10   **Shoop Shoop Song (It's In His Kiss)** [Cher] 33

8/25/84 | **110** | 13 | 274 | Metropolis .... [V] | **$8** | Columbia 39526

Gustav Froelich/Brigitte Helm; 1926 film restored and presented with a contemporary score; cp: Giorgio Moroder

Blood From A Stone [Cycle V]   **Here She Comes** [Bonnie Tyler] 76   Legend Of Babel [Giorgio Moroder]   On Your Own [Billy Squier]
Cage Of Freedom [Jon Anderson]   Here's My Heart [Pat Benatar]   **Love Kills** [Freddie Mercury] 69   What's Going On [Adam Ant]
Destruction [Loverboy]   Machines [Giorgio Moroder]

8/9/69 | **19** | 57 | ● 275 | Midnight Cowboy .... [I+V] | **$10** | United Art. 5198

Dustin Hoffman/Jon Voight/Sylvia Miles; mu: John Barry

SOUNDTRACKS

DEBUT DATE	PEAK POS	WKS CHR	GOLD	ARTIST — Album Title	$	Label & Number

Everybody's Talkin' [Nilsson] 6   He Quit Me Man [Leslie Miller]   Midnight Cowboy   Tears And Joys [Groop]
Famous Myth [Groop]   Joe Buck Rides Again   Old Man Willow [Elephants Memory]
Florida Fantasy   Jungle Gym At The Zoo [Elephants Memory]
Fun City   [Elephants Memory]   Science Fiction

| 11/25/78+ | 59 | 26 | 276 | **Midnight Express** ....[I] | $10 | Casablanca 7114 |

Brad Davis/John Hurt/Randy Quaid; cp/cd: Giorgio Moroder

Cacaphoney   Istanbul Opening   Midnight Express, Theme From
Chase [Giorgio Moroder] 33   Love's Theme   (includes 2 versions)
Istanbul Blues   Wheel, The

Mike's Murder - see JACKSON, Joe
Debra Winger/Mark Keyloun/Darrell Larson

| 2/21/87 | 132 | 13 | 277 | **Mission, The** ....[I] | $8 | Virgin 90567 |

Robert DeNiro/Jeremy Irons; cp/cd: Ennio Morricone

Alone   Climb   On Earth As It Is In Heaven   River
Asuncion   Falls   Penance   Sword, The
Ave Maria Guarani   Gabriel's Oboe   Refusal   Te Deum Guarani
Brothers   Guarani   Remorse   Vita Nostra
Carlotta   Miserere

Mo' Better Blues - see MARSALIS, Branford
Denzel Washington/Spike Lee/Wesley Snipes/Giancarlo Esposito

| 7/11/92 | 6 | 19 | ▲ 278 | **Mo' Money** ....[V] | $12 | Perspective 1004 |

Damon Wayans/Marlon Wayans/Stacey Dash/Joe Santos/John Diehl

Best Things In Life Are Free   Get Off My Back [Public Enemy]   Let's Get Together (So Groovy   **Money Can't Buy You Love**
[Luther Vandross & Janet   I Adore You [Caron Wheeler]   Now) [Krush]   [Ralph Tresvant] 54
Jackson] 10   Ice Cream Dream [MC Lyte]   Let's Just Run Away [Johnny   My Dear [Mint Condition]
Brother Will [Harlem Yacht Club]   Job Ain't Nuthin' But Work [Big   Gill]   New Style [Jam & Lewis]
Forever Love [Color Me   Daddy Kane with Lo-Key!]   Mo' Money Groove [Mo' Money
Badd] 15   Joy [Sounds Of Blackness]   Allstars]

| 7/20/63 | 15 | 74 | | 279 **Mondo Cane** ....[I] | $15 | United Art. 5105 |

documentary depicting various cultures around the world; cp/cd: Riz Ortolani and Nino Oliviero

Breakfast At The Colony   Dog Heat   Hong Kong Cha Cha Cha   More
(medley)   (medley)   Pergatory
Cargo Cult (Finale)   Festival Of The Bull   House Of Death   Repabhan Street
China Tarantella   Fisherman Of Ragput (medley)   Last Flight   Sharks, The (medley)
Damned Island   Free Way   Models In Blue
   Girls And Sailors

Monterey Pop - see REDDING, Otis, and/or HENDRIX, Jimi

Monty Python & The Holy Grail - see MONTY PYTHON
Graham Chapman/John Cleese/Eric Idle/Carol Cleveland

| 8/18/79 | 159 | 4 | 280 | **Moonraker** ....[I] | $8 | United Art. 971 |

Roger Moore/Lois Chiles/Richard Kiel; cp/cd: John Barry

Boat Chase (medley)   Cable Car (medley)   Flight Into Space   Space Lazer Battle
Bond Arrives In Rio (medley)   Centrifuge (medley)   Main Title [Shirley Bassey]
Bond Lured To Pyramid   Corrinne Put Down (medley)   Miss Goodhead Meets Bond
Bond Smells A Rat   End Title [Shirley Bassey]   Snake Fight (medley)

More - see PINK FLOYD
Mimsi Farmer/Klaus Grunberg

More American Graffiti - see American Graffiti

Mrs. Brown, You've Got A Lovely Daughter - see HERMAN'S HERMITS
Herman's Hermits/Stanley Holloway/Mona Washbourne

Muppet Christmas Carol, The - see CHILDREN'S ALBUMS
Michael Caine/Brian Henson/Frank Oz

Muppet Movie, The - see CHILDREN'S ALBUMS
Jim Henson/Frank Oz

| 8/11/62 | 2[6] | 56 | ● 281 | **Music Man, The** ....[M] | $15 | Warner 1459 |

Robert Preston/Shirley Jones/Buddy Hackett; cp: Meredith Willson; cd: Ray Heindorf; also see Original Cast ('58)

Being In Love   Lida Rose (medley)   Sadder But Wiser Girl   Will I Ever Tell You? (medley)
Gary, Indiana   Main Title (medley)   Seventy Six Trombones (medley)   Ya Got Trouble
Goodnight My Someone   Marian The Librarian   Shipoopi
If You Don't Mind My Saying So   Piano Lesson (medley)   Sincere
(medley)   Pick-A-Little, Talk-A-Little   Till There Was You
Iowa Stubborn (medley)   Rock Island (medley)   Wells Fargo Wagon

| 1/5/63 | 14 | 19 | 282 | **Mutiny On The Bounty** ....[I] | $45 | MGM 4 |

Marlon Brando/Trevor Howard/Richard Harris; cp: Bronislau Kaper; cd: Robert Armbruster; includes a full-color souvenir book

Arrival In Tahiti   Girls And Sailors   Mutiny On The Bounty (Theme)   Pitcairn Island
Christian's Death   Leaving Harbor   Native Festival Music Medley   Portsmouth Harbor
Follow Me (Love Song)   Mutiny, The   Outrigger Chase   Storm At Sea

| 10/10/64+ | 4 | 111 | ● 283 | **My Fair Lady** ....[M] | $10 | Columbia 2600 |

Audrey Hepburn/Rex Harrison/Stanley Holloway; mu: Frederick Loewe; ly: Alan Jay Lerner; cd: Andre Previn; also see Nat King Cole/Percy Faith/Ferrante & Teicher/Sammy Kaye/Andre Previn/Andy Williams/Original Cast ('56)

Ascot Gavotte   I've Grown Accustomed To Her   Rain In Spain   Wouldn't It Be Loverly
Get Me To The Church On Time   Face   Show Me   You Did It
Hymn To Him   Just You Wait   Why Can't The English?
I Could Have Danced All Night   On The Street Where You Live   With A Little Bit Of Luck
I'm Just An Ordinary Man   Overture   Without You

| 1/4/92 | 104 | 10 | 284 | **My Girl** ....[V-O] | $12 | Epic 48732 |

Dan Aykroyd/Jamie Lee Curtis/Macauley Culkin/Anna Chlumsky

Bad Moon Rising [Creedence   Good Lovin' [Young Rascals] 1   I Only Have Eyes For You   **If You Don't Know Me By Now**
Clearwater Revival] 2   **Hot Fun In The Summertime**   [Flamingos] 11   [Harold Melvin & The Blue
Do Wah Diddy Diddy [Manfred   [Sly & The Family Stone] 2   I Saw The Light [Todd   Notes] 3
Mann] 1   Rundgren] 16

DEBUT DATE	PEAK POS	WKS CHR	GOLD	ARTIST — Album Title	$	Label & Number

| | | | | More Today Than Yesterday [Spiral Starecase] 12 | My Girl (Theme) [James Newton Howard] | Saturday In The Park [Chicago] 3 | Wedding Bell Blues [5th Dimension] 1 |

My Girl [Temptations] 1

7/19/75 **80** **13** **285** Nashville .... [V] **$10** ABC 893
Henry Gibson/Lily Tomlin/Ronee Blakley/Shelley Duvall/Keith Carradine; all vocals by cast members

Bluebird	I'm Easy [Keith Carradine] 17	Memphis	Rolling Stone
Dues	It Don't Worry Me	My Idaho Home	Tapedeck In His Tractor
For The Sake Of The Children	Keep A-Goin'	One, I Love You	200 Years

1/30/61 **2⁵** **74** **286** **Never On Sunday** .... [I] **$15** United Art. 5070
Melina Mercouri/Jules Dassin; cp/cd: Manos Hadjidakis; also see Original Cast Illya Darling ('67)

Betrayed	Danse Yorgo	Lantern, The	Speak Softly
Bouzoukia	End Title	Main Title	Taki
Charms Of Ilya	Hasapico	Organ Grinder	
Children Of Athens	Ilya	Prologue	

3/23/91 **2¹** **38** ▲ **287** **New Jack City** .... [V] **$12** Giant 24409
Wesley Snipes/Ice-T/Chris Rock/Mario Van Peebles/Judd Nelson; CD includes bonus cut

Facts Of Life [Danny Madden]	I Wanna Sex You Up [Color Me Badd] 2	Living For The City (medley) [Troop/Levert/Queen Latifah]	(There You Go) Tellin' Me No Again [Keith Sweat]
For The Love Of Money (medley) [Troop/Levert/Queen Latifah]	I'm Dreamin' [Christopher Williams] 89	Lyrics 2 The Rhythm [Essence]	
Get It Together [Black Is A Force] [F.S. Effect]	I'm Still Waiting [Johnny Gill]	New Jack City [Guy]	
	In The Dust [2 Live Crew]	New Jack Hustler (Nino's Theme) [Ice-T] 67	

7/16/77 **50** **14** **288** New York, New York .... [M] **$12** United Art. 750 [2]
Liza Minnelli/Robert DeNiro; sw: John Kander and Fred Ebb; cd: Ralph Burns

Blue Moon	Happy Endings	Man I Love	There Goes The Ball Game
Bobby's Dream	Hazoy	Once Again Right Away	V. J. Stomp
But The World Goes 'Round	Honeysuckle Rose	Once In A While	You Are My Lucky Star
Don't Be That Way	It's A Wonderful World	Opus Number One	You Brought A New Kind Of
Flip The Dip	Just You, Just Me	New York, New York (includes 3	Love To Me
Game Over	Main Title	versions)	

5/2/92 **149** **1** **289** Newsies .... [M] **$12** Disney 60832
Christian Bale/Bill Pullman/Robert Duvall/Ann-Margret; mu: Alan Menken; ly: Jack Feldman

Carrying The Banner	King Of New York	Rooftop	World Will Know
Escape From Snyder	My Lovey-Dovey Baby	Santa Fe	
Fightin' Irish: Strike Action	Once And For All	Seize The Day (includes 2	
High Times, Hard Times	Prologue	versions)	

8/22/81 **189** **5** **290** Night The Lights Went Out In Georgia, The .... [V] **$8** Mirage 16051
Kristy McNichol/Dennis Quaid/Mark Hamill

Amanda [Dennis Quaid]	I Need You Strong For Me [Kristy McNichol]	It's So Easy [Billy Preston & Syreeta]	Night The Lights Went Out In Georgia [Tanya Tucker]
Hangin' Up The Gun [Kristy McNichol & Dennis Quaid]	Imaginary Arms [Tammy Wynette]	Little Gettin' Used To [George Jones]	Rodeo Girl [Tanya Tucker]
I Love My Truck [Glen Campbell] 94		Melody's Melody [David Shire]	

Nighthawks - see EMERSON, Keith
Sylvester Stallone/Rutger Hauer/Billy Dee Williams

3/29/86 **59** **15** **291** 9 1/2 Weeks .... [V] **$8** Capitol 12470
Mickey Rourke/Kim Basinger

Best Is Yet To Come [Luba]	Eurasian Eyes [Corey Hart]	Slave To Love [Bryan Ferry]	You Can Leave Your Hat On [Joe Cocker]
Black On Black [Dalbello]	I Do What I Do... [John Taylor] 23	This City Never Sleeps [Eurythmics]	
Bread And Butter [Devo]	Let It Go [Luba]		
Cannes [Stewart Copeland]			

12/27/80+ **77** **15** **292** 9 To 5 .... [I] **$8** 20th Century 627
Jane Fonda/Lily Tomlin/Dolly Parton/Dabney Coleman; cp/cd: Charles Fox

Ajax Warehouse	Hart Tries To Escape	Office Montage	Violet's Poisoned The Boss
Charlie's Bar	Intruder, The	Pillow Fight	
Dora Lee's Fantasy	Judy's Fantasy	Violet Steals Body	
Easy Time	9 To 5 [Dolly Parton] 1	Violet's Fantasy	

12/17/88+ **186** **6** **293** 1969 .... [V-O] **$8** Polydor 837362
Robert Downey, Jr./Kiefer Sutherland/Bruce Dern/Mariette Hartley

All Along The Watchtower [Jimi Hendrix Experience] 20	Going Up The Country [Canned Heat] 11	Tuesday Afternoon (Forever Afternoon) [Moody Blues] 24	Windows Of The World [Pretenders]
Can't Find My Way Home [Blind Faith]	Green River [Creedence Clearwater Revival] 2	When I Was Young [Eric Burdon & The Animals] 15	Wooden Ships [Crosby, Stills & Nash]
Get Together [Jesse Colin Young]	Time Of The Season [Zombies] 3	White Room [Cream] 6	

1984 - see EURYTHMICS
John Hunt/Richard Burton/Suzanna Hamilton

Norwood - see CAMPBELL, Glen
Glen Campbell/Kim Darby/Joe Namath/Carol Lynley

9/20/86 **190** **3** **294** Nothing In Common .... [V] **$8** Arista 8438
Tom Hanks/Jackie Gleason/Eva Marie Saint

Burning Of The Heart [Richard Marx]	Instrumental Theme [Pat Leonard]	No One's Gonna Love You [Real To Reel]	Over The Weekend [Nick Heyward]
Don't Forget To Dance [Kinks] 29	Loving Stranger (David's Theme) [Christopher Cross]	Nothing In Common [Thompson Twins] 54	Seven Summers [Cruzados]
If It Wasn't Love [Carly Simon]			Until You Say You Love Me [Aretha Franklin]

O Lucky Man! - see PRICE, Alan
Malcolm McDowell/Rachel Roberts/Ralph Richardson

7/16/83 **137** **5** **295** Octopussy .... [I] **$8** A&M 4967
Roger Moore/Maud Adams/Louis Jourdan; cp/cd: John Barry

All Time High [Rita Coolidge] 36	Bond Look-Alike	009 Gets The Knife (medley)	Yo-Yo Fight (medley)
Arrival At The Island Of Octopussy	Bond Meets Octopussy	Gobinda Attacks (medley)	
Bond At The Monsoon Palace	Chase Bomb Theme	Palace Fight	
	Death Of Vijay (medley)	That's My Little Octopussy	

DEBUT DATE	PEAK POS	WKS CHR	G O L D		ARTIST — Album Title	$	Label & Number

| 7/27/68 | **190** | 2 | 296 | Odd Couple, The ....[I] $15 Dot 25862 |
| | | | | Jack Lemmon/Walter Matthau; cp/cd: Neal Hefti; includes excerpts of comedy from the film |

Clean Poker	Domestic Quarrel	Man Chases Man	Oscar Blows Up
Curse Of The Cat People	Down With The Lights	Metropole	Tomatoes
Dirty Poker	End Title	Odd Couple (includes 2 versions)	

| 10/30/82 | **38** | 23 | 297 | Officer And A Gentleman, An ....[V] $8 Island 90017 |
| | | | | Richard Gere/Debra Winger/David Keith/Louis Gossett, Jr. |

Be Real [Sir Douglas Quintet]	Love Theme [Lee Ritenour]	**Treat Me Right** [Pat Benatar] 18	**Up Where We Belong** [Joe
Hungry For Your Love [Van	Main Title [Jack Nitzsche]	Tunnel Of Love [Dire Straits]	Cocker & Jennifer Warnes] 1
Morrison]	Morning After Love Theme [Jack	**Tush** [ZZ Top] 20	
	Nitzsche]		

| 9/17/55+ | **1**[4] | 305 | ▲[2] 298 | Oklahoma! ....[M] $20 Capitol 595 |
| | | | | Gordon MacRae/Shirley Jones; mu: Richard Rodgers; ly: Oscar Hammerstein II; cd: Jay Blackton |

All Er Nothin'	Kansas City	Oklahoma	People Will Say We're In Love
Farmer And The Cowman	Many A New Day	Out Of My Dreams	Poor Jud Is Dead
I Cain't Say No	Oh, What A Beautiful Mornin'	Overture	Surrey With The Fringe On Top

| 12/28/68+ | **20** | 91 | ● 299 | Oliver! ....[M] $10 Colgems 5501 |
| | | | | Mark Lester (Oliver)/Ron Moody/Jack Wild/Oliver Reed; sw: Lionel Bart; cd: John Green; also see Original Cast ('62) and Mantovani |

As Long As He Needs Me	Finale	Oliver! (medley)	Reviewing The Situation
Be Back Soon	Food, Glorious Food (medley)	Oom-Pah-Pah	Where Is Love?
Boy For Sale	I'd Do Anything	Overture	Who Will Buy?
Consider Yourself	It's A Fine Life	Pick A Pocket Or Two	

| 1/7/89 | **170** | 7 | 300 | Oliver & Company ....[V] $8 Disney 64101 |
| | | | | animated film, voices by: Ruben Blades/Cheech Marin; cp/cd: J.A.C. Redford |

Bedtime Story	End Title	Perfect Isn't Easy [Bette Midler]	Streets Of Gold [Ruth Pointer]
Buscando Guayaba [Ruben	Good Company [Myhanh Tran]	Pursuit Through The Subway	Sykes
Blades]	Once Upon A Time In New York	Rescue, The	Why Should I Worry? [Billy Joel]
	City [Huey Lewis]		

On A Clear Day You Can See Forever - see STREISAND, Barbra
Barbra Streisand/Yves Montand; also see Original Cast ('65)

| 2/27/82 | **147** | 11 | 301 | On Golden Pond ....[I] $8 MCA 6106 |
| | | | | Henry Fonda/Katharine Hepburn/Jane Fonda/Doug McKeon; cp/cd: Dave Grusin; includes dialogue excerpts |

Career Opportunities/Back	Epilogue	Illicit Sex Question	New Hampshire Hornpipe
Porch Confessional	Father-Daughter Relationship	Lake-Song	Purgatory Cove
Early Bird	First Call	Main Theme	Season's End

| 2/7/70 | **103** | 13 | 302 | On Her Majesty's Secret Service ....[I+V] $15 United Art. 5204 |
| | | | | George Lazenby/Diana Rigg/Telly Savalas; cp/cd: John Barry |

Battle At Piz Gloria	Journey To Blowfeld's Hideaway	This Never Happened To The	We Have All The Time In The
Do You Know How Christmas	Main Theme	Other Feller	World [Louis Armstrong]
Trees Are Grown? [Nina]	Over & Out	Try	
James Bond Theme (medley)	Ski Chase		

| 4/17/76 | **158** | 7 | 303 | One Flew Over The Cuckoo's Nest ....[I] $10 Fantasy 9500 |
| | | | | Jack Nicholson/Louise Fletcher; cp: Jack Nitzsche |

Act Of Love	Charmaine	Medication Valse	Play The Game
Aloha Los Pescadores	Cruising	One Flew Over The Cuckoo's	Trolling
Bus Ride To Paradise	Last Dance	Nest (includes 2 versions)	

101 - see DEPECHE MODE

One On One - see SEALS & CROFTS
Robby Benson/Annette O'Toole/G.D. Spradlin

One-Trick Pony - see SIMON, Paul
Paul Simon/Blair Brown/Rip Torn

| 3/19/66 | **118** | 5 | 304 | Our Man Flint ....[I] $45 20th Century 4179 |
| | | | | James Coburn/Lee J. Cobb/Gila Golan; cp/cd: Jerry Goldsmith |

All I Have To Do Is Take A Bite	In Like Flint	Never Mind, You'd Love It	Tell Me More About That
Of Your Apple?	It's Gotta Be A World's Record	Our Man Flint	Volcano
Doing As The Romans Did	Man Does Not Live By Bread	Stall! Stall! Flint's Alive	You're A Foolish Man, Mr. Flint
Galaxy A Go Go! -or- Leave It To	Alone	Take Some Risks, Mr. Flint?	
Flint			

| 2/1/86 | **38** | 22 | ● 305 | Out Of Africa ....[I] $10 MCA 6158 |
| | | | | Meryl Streep/Robert Redford/Klaus Maria Brandauer; cp/cd: John Barry |

Alone On The Farm	I Had A Farm In Africa (Main	If I Know A Song Of Africa	Mozart: Concerto For Clarinet
Flying Over Africa	Title)	(Karen's Theme III)	And Orchestra In A (K. 622)
Have You Got A Story For Me?	I'm Better At Hello (Karen's	Karen's Journey (medley)	Safari
I Had A Compass From Deny's	Theme I)	Let The Rest Of The World Go By	Siyawe (medley)
(Karen's Theme II)			You Are Karen (End Title)

| 3/7/87 | **120** | 8 | 306 | Over The Top ....[V] $8 Columbia 40655 |
| | | | | Sylvester Stallone/Robert Loggia/Susan Blakely/David Mendenhall |

All I Need Is You [Big Trouble]	Gypsy Soul [Asia]	**Meet Me Half Way** [Kenny	Take It Higher [Larry Greene]
Bad Nite [Frank Stallone]	I Will Be Strong [Eddie Money]	Loggins] 11	**Winner Takes It All** [Sammy
Fight, The [Giorgio Moroder]	In This Country [Robin Zander]	Mind Over Matter [Larry Greene]	Hagar] 54

Owl and the Pussycat, The - see STREISAND, Barbra
Barbra Streisand/George Segal/Robert Klein/Roz Kelly

| 10/25/69 | **28** | 56 | ● 307 | Paint Your Wagon ....[M] $10 Paramount 1001 |
| | | | | Lee Marvin/Clint Eastwood/Jean Seberg; mu: Frederick Loewe; ly: Alan Jay Lerner; cd: Nelson Riddle |

Best Things	Hand Me Down That Can O'	Million Miles Away Behind The	Whoop-Ti-Ay! (Shivaree)
Finale	Beans	Door	
First Thing You Know	I Still See Elisa	There's A Coach Comin' In	
Gold Fever	I Talk To The Trees	They Call The Wind Maria	
Gospel Of No Name City	I'm On My Way (Main Title)	Wand'rin Star	

| 9/23/57 | **9** | 14 | 308 | **Pajama Game, The** ....[M] $25 Columbia 5210 |
| | | | | Doris Day/John Raitt; sw: Richard Adler and Jerry Ross; cd: Ray Heindorf |

DEBUT DATE	PEAK POS	WKS CHR	G O L D	ARTIST — Album Title	$	Label & Number

Finale   I'll Never Be Jealous Again   Pajama Game (medley)   Small Talk
Hernando's Hideaway   I'm Not At All In Love   Racing With The Clock (medley)   Steam Heat
Hey There   Once-A-Year Day!   Seven-And-A-Half Cents   There Once Was A Man

Pal Joey - see SINATRA, Frank
Frank Sinatra/Rita Hayworth/Kim Novak

| 8/4/73 | 154 | 12 | 309 | Paper Moon .... [V-O] | $15 | Paramount 1012 |

Ryan O'Neal/Tatum O'Neal/Madeline Kahn/John Hillerman

About A Quarter To Nine [Ozzie Nelson]   (It Will Have To Do) Until The Real Thing Comes Along [Leo Reisman]   My Mary [Jimmie Davis]   Picture Of Me Without You [Paul Whiteman/Ken Darby/Ramona]
After You've Gone [Tommy Dorsey]   It's Only A Paper Moon [Paul Whiteman]   Object Of My Affection [Jimmie Grier]   Sunnyside Up [Johnny Hamp's Kentucky Serenaders]
Flirtation Walk [Dick Powell]   On The Banks Of The Ohio [Blue Sky Boys]
Georgia On My Mind [Hoagy Carmichael]   Just One More Chance [Bing Crosby]   One Hour With You [Jimmie Grier]
I Found A Million Dollar Baby [Victor Young/Boswell Sisters]   Let's Have Another Cup Of Coffee [Enric Madriguera]

Paradise, Hawaiian Style - see PRESLEY, Elvis
Elvis Presley (Rick Richards)/Suzanne Leigh/James Shigeta

| 10/23/61 | 92 | 8 | 310 | Parent Trap!, The .... [I+V] | $35 | Buena Vista 3309 |

Hayley Mills/Brian Keith/Maureen O'Hara; cd: Tutti Camarata; side 2: Camarata conducts Themes From Great Motion Pictures

Alice In Wonderland   **Let's Get Together** [Hayley Mills] **8**   Swiss Family Robinson Theme (My Heart Was An Island)   Tchaikovsky: Sleeping Beauty Overture
Cobbler Cobbler [Hayley Mills]   Maggie's Theme   Tchaikovsky: Love Theme From Sleeping Beauty   Whistling At The Boys [School Belles]
For Now For Always   Parent Trap [Tommy Sands & Annette]
Intermezzo

| 9/25/61 | 45 | 12 | 311 | Parrish .... [I] | $65 | Warner 1413 |

Troy Donahue/Claudette Colbert; cp/cd: Max Steiner; side 2: Popular Piano Concertos by George Greeley

Allison's Theme (includes 2 versions)   Lucy's Theme (includes 2 versions)   Paige's Theme (includes 3 versions)   Summer Place, Theme From A
Ellen's Theme   Someday, I'll Meet You Again   Tara's Theme
   Tobacco Theme

| 2/5/83 | 169 | 6 | 312 | Party Party .... [V] | $8 | A&M 3212 |

Daniel Peacock/Phoebe Nicholls

Auld Lang Syne [Chas & Dave]   Little Town Flirt [Altered Images]   No Woman, No Cry [Pauline Black]   Run Rudolph Run [Dave Edmunds]
Band Of Gold [Modern Romance]   Man Who Sold The World [Midge Ure]   Party Party [Elvis Costello & The Attractions]   Tutti Frutti [Sting]
Driving In My Car [Madness]   Need Your Love So Bad [Sting]
Elizabethan Reggae [Bad Manners]   No Feelings [Bananarama]   Yakety Yak [Bad Manners]

Pat Garrett & Billy The Kid - see DYLAN, Bob
James Coburn/Kris Kristofferson/Jason Robards

| 5/22/71 | 117 | 8 | 313 | Patton .... [I] | $12 | 20th Century 4208 |

George C. Scott/Karl Malden; cp/cd: Jerry Goldsmith; includes Scott's rendition of Patton's address to his troops

Attack   Funeral, The   No Assignment   Winter March
Battleground, The   German Advance   Patton March
End Title Speech   Hospital, The   Patton Speech
First Battle   Main Title   Payoff, The

| 1/23/82 | 188 | 2 | 314 | Pennies From Heaven .... [M-O] | $12 | Warner 3639 [2] |

Steve Martin/Bernadette Peters/Christopher Walken/Jessica Harper

Clouds Will Soon Roll By [Elsie Carlisle]   I'll Never Have To Dream Again [Connie Boswell]   Let's Put Out The Lights And Go To Sleep [Rudy Vallee]   Pennies From Heaven [Arthur Tracy]
Did You Ever See A Dream Walking? [Bing Crosby]   It's A Sin To Tell A Lie [Dolly Dawn]   Life Is Just A Bowl Of Cherries [Walt Harrah/Gene Merlino/Vern Rowe]   Roll Along Prairie Moon [Fred Latham]
Fancy Our Meeting [Jack Buchanan & Elsie Randolph]   It's The Girl [Boswell Sisters]   Love Is Good For Anything That Ails You [Ida Sue McCune]   Serenade In The Night [Ronnie Hill]
Glory Of Love [Lew Stone]   Let's Face The Music And Dance [Fred Astaire]   Yes, Yes! [Sam Browne]
I Want To Be Bad [Helen Kane]   Let's Misbehave [Irving Aaronson]

| 6/29/85 | 45 | 12 | 315 | Perfect .... [V] | $8 | Arista 8278 |

John Travolta/Jamie Lee Curtis/Anne De Salvo/Marilu Henner

All Systems Go [Pointer Sisters]   I Sweat (Going Through The Motions) [Nona Hendryx]   Shock Me [Jermaine Jackson & Whitney Houston]   Wear Out The Grooves [Jermaine Stewart]
(Closest Thing To) Perfect [Jermaine Jackson] **67**   **Lay Your Hands On Me** [Thompson Twins] **6**   Talking To The Wall [Dan Hartman]   Wham Rap (Enjoy What You Do)! [Wham!]
Hot Hips [Lou Reed]   Masquerade [Berlin]

| 12/24/77+ | 131 | 10 | 316 | Pete's Dragon .... [M] | $8 | Capitol 11704 |

Helen Reddy/Jim Dale/Mickey Rooney/Red Buttons; sw: Al Kasha and Joel Hirschhorn; cd: Irwin Kostal

Bill Of Sale   Brazzle Dazzle Day   Happiest Home In These Hills   Main Title
Boo Bop BopBop Bop (I Love You, Too)   Candle On The Water   I Saw A Dragon   Passamashloddy
   Every Little Piece   It's Not Easy   There's Room For Everyone

| 2/23/63 | 88 | 7 | 317 | Phaedra .... [I] | $20 | United Art. 5102 |

Melina Mercouri/Anthony Perkins; cp/cd: Mikis Theodorakis

Agapimou   London's Fog   Phaedra (Love Theme) [Melina Mercouri]   Rendezvous
Candlelight   One More Time   Rodostimo
Fling, The   Only You   Phaedra (Love Theme) (instrumental)   Ship To Shore
Goodbye John Sebastian

| 3/1/75 | 194 | 1 | 318 | Phantom Of The Paradise .... [M] | $10 | A&M 3653 |

Paul Williams/William Finley/Jessica Harper; sw: Paul Williams

Beauty And The Beast (Phantom's Theme)   Goodbye Eddie, Goodbye   Old Souls   Special To Me (Phoenix Audition Song)
Faust (includes 2 versions)   Hell Of It   Somebody Super Like You (Beef Construction Song)   Upholstery
   Life At Last

| 5/5/56 | 6 | 18 | 319 | Picnic .... [I] | $30 | Decca 78320 |

William Holden/Kim Novak/Rosalind Russell; cp: George Duning; cd: Morris Stoloff

Culmination (medley)   Hal's Boots   Hal's Theme   It's A Blue World (medley)
Flo And Madge   Hal's Escape (medley)   Hal's Turmoil (medley)   Madge Decides (medley)

DEBUT DATE	PEAK POS	WKS CHR	GOLD	ARTIST — Album Title	$	Label & Number

| | | | | Millie (medley) — Owens Family — Rosemary Pleads (medley) — You Love Me (medley) | | |

Moonglow and Theme From "Picnic" *[Morris Stoloff]* 1 — Picnic (Love Theme) — That Owens Girl (medley)
Rosemary Alone (medley) — Torn Shirt (medley)

Pink Panther, The - see MANCINI, Henry
Peter Sellers/David Niven/Robert Wagner/Capucine

Pipe Dreams - see KNIGHT, Gladys/Pips
Gladys Knight/Barry Hankerson

| 8/28/82 | 166 | 6 | 320 | Pirate Movie, The ....[M] | $10 | Polydor 9503 [2] |

Kristy McNichol/Christopher Atkins; based on Gilbert & Sullivan's *Pirates Of Penzance*

Chase, The — Happy Ending — Modern Major General's Song — Stand Up And Sing
Chinese Battle — Hold On — Pirate Movie Medley — Tarantara
Come Friends Who Plough The Sea — **How Can I Love Without Her** *[Christopher Atkins]* 71 — Pirates, Police & Pizza — Victory
Duel, The — I Am A Pirate King — Pumpin' & Blowin' — We Are The Pirates (includes 2 versions)
First Love — — Sister's Song —

| 7/27/68 | 195 | 3 | 321 | Planet Of The Apes ....[I] | $10 | Project 3 5023 |

Charlton Heston/Roddy McDowall/Kim Hunter/Maurice Evans; cp/cd: Jerry Goldsmith

Bid For Freedom — Forbidden Zone — New Mate — Search, The
Cave, The — Main Title — No Escape —
Clothes Snatchers — New Identity — Revelation, The —

| 4/4/87 | 75 | 13 | 322 | Platoon ....[V-O] | $8 | Atlantic 81742 |

Tom Berenger/Willem Dafoe/Charlie Sheen

Adagio For Strings (includes 2 versions) *[Vancouver Symphony Orchestra]* — **Groovin'** *[Young Rascals]* 1 — **(Sittin' On) The Dock Of The Bay** *[Otis Redding]* 1 — **When A Man Loves A Woman** *[Percy Sledge]* 1
Barnes Shoots Elias *[Vancouver Symphony Orchestra]* — **Hello, I Love You** *[Doors]* 1 — **Okie From Muskogee** *[Merle Haggard]* 41 — Tracks Of My Tears *[Miracles]* 16 — **White Rabbit** *[Jefferson Airplane]* 1
— **Respect** *[Aretha Franklin]* 1 — —

| 7/17/82 | 168 | 5 | 323 | Poltergeist ....[I] | $8 | MGM 5408 |

JoBeth Williams/Craig T. Nelson/Heather O'Rourke; cp/cd: Jerry Goldsmith

Carol Ann's Theme — Light, The — Night Of The Beast — Rebirth
Escape From Suburbia — Neighborhood-Day — Night Visitor — Twisted Abduction

| 12/27/80+ | 115 | 10 | 324 | Popeye ....[M] | $8 | Boardwalk 36880 |

Robin Williams/Shelley Duvall/Ray Walston/Paul Dooley; sw: Harry Nilsson

Blow Me Down — He's Large — I'm Popeye The Sailor Man — Sailin'
Din' We — I Yam What I Yam — It's Not Easy Being Me — Swee'pea's Lullaby
He Needs Me — I'm Mean — Kids — Sweethaven

| 7/13/59 | 8 | 96 | ● 325 | Porgy and Bess ....[M] | $10 | Columbia 2016 |

Sidney Poitier/Dorothy Dandridge; mu: George Gershwin; ly: DuBose Heyward and Ira Gershwin; cd: Andre Previn; also see Harry Belafonte/Ray Charles/Percy Faith/Lena Horne/Cleo Laine/Leontyne Price

Bess, You Is My Woman Now — I Loves You, Porgy — Overture — Wake Medley
Catfish Row (medley) — I'm On My Way — Red Headed Woman — What You Want With Bess?
Clara, Clara — It Ain't Necessarily So — Street Cries Medley — Woman Is A Sometime Thing
I Ain't Got No Shame — Morning (medley) — Summertime —
I Can't Sit Down — My Man's Gone Now — There's A Boat That's Leavin' Soon For New York —
I Got Plenty O' Nuttin' — Oh, Where's My Bess? — —

| 4/13/85 | 122 | 8 | 326 | Porky's Revenge! ....[V] | $8 | Columbia 39983 |

Dan Monahan/Wyatt Knight/Tony Ganios/Mark Herrier/Kaki Hunter

Blue Suede Shoes *[Carl Perkins/Slim Jim Phantom/Lee Rocker]* — **High School Nights** *[Dave Edmunds]* 91 — Peter Gunn Theme *[Clarence Clemons]* — Queen Of The Hop *[Dave Edmunds]*
Do You Want To Dance *[Dave Edmunds]* — I Don't Want To Do It *[George Harrison]* — Philadelphia Baby *[Crawling King Snakes]* — Sleepwalk *[Jeff Beck]*
— Love Me Tender *[Willie Nelson]* — Porky's Revenge *[Dave Edmunds]* — Stagger Lee *[Fabulous Thunderbirds]*

| 3/1/86 | 5 | 27 | ● 327 | Pretty In Pink ....[V] | $8 | A&M 3901 |

Molly Ringwald/Jon Cryer/Andrew McCarthy/Harry Dean Stanton

Bring On The Dancing Horses *[Echo & The Bunnymen]* — **If You Leave** *[Orchestral Manoeuvres In The Dark]* 4 — Please Please Please Let Me Get What I Want *[Smiths]* — Round, Round *[Belouis Some]*
Do Wot You Do *[INXS]* — Left Of Center *[Suzanne Vega/Joe Jackson]* — **Pretty In Pink** *[Psychedelic Furs]* 41 — Shell-Shock *[New Order]*
Get To Know Ya *[Jesse Johnson]* — — — Wouldn't It Be Good *[Danny Hutton Hitters]*

| 4/7/90 | 4 | 91 | ▲³ 328 | Pretty Woman ....[V] | $12 | EMI 93492 |

Richard Gere/Julia Roberts/Ralph Bellamy/Jason Alexander

Fallen *[Lauren Wood]* — **King Of Wishful Thinking** *[Go West]* 8 — **Oh Pretty Woman** *[Roy Orbison]* 1 — Show Me Your Soul *[Red Hot Chili Peppers]*
Fame 90 *[David Bowie]* — Life In Detail *[Robert Palmer]* — Real Wild Child (Wild One) *[Christopher Otcasek]* — Tangled *[Jane Wiedlin]*
It Must Have Been Love *[Roxette]* 1 — No Explanation *[Peter Cetera]* — — Wild Women Do *[Natalie Cole]* 34

| 1/11/92 | 84 | 12 | 329 | Prince Of Tides, The ....[I] | $12 | Columbia 48627 |

Barbra Streisand/Nick Nolte/Blythe Danner/Kate Nelligan; cp: James Newton Howard; cd: Marty Paich; includes 2 vocal tracks by Barbra Streisand not featured in the film

Bloodstain, The — Hallway (Love Theme) — Places That Belong To You *[Barbra Streisand]* — They Love You Dad
Daddy's Home — Home Movies — Reunion, The — To New York
End Credits — Lila's Theme — Savannah Awakes — Tom Comes Home
Fishmarket, The — Love Montage — So Cruel — Tom's Breakdown
For All We Know *[Barbra Streisand]* — Main Title — Street, The — Village Walk
For All We Know (instrumental) — New York Willies — Teddy Bears —
— Outdoors, The — —

| 10/31/87 | 180 | 1 | 330 | Princess Bride, The .... | $8 | Warner 25610 |

Cary Elwes/Robin Wright/Mandy Patinkin/Peter Falk/Billy Crystal; cp: Mark Knopfler

Cliffs Of Insanity — Friend's Song — Morning Ride — Storybook Love *[Willy DeVille]*
Fireswamp And The Rodents Of Unusual Size — Guide My Sword — Once Upon A Time...Storybook Love — Swordfight
Florin Dance — Happy Ending — Revenge —
— I Will Never Love Again — —

| 9/8/90 | 50 | 34 | 331 | Pump Up The Volume ....[V] | $12 | MCA 8039 |

Christian Slater/Scott Paulin/Ellen Greene/Samantha Mathis; CD and cassette include bonus track

DEBUT DATE	PEAK POS	WKS CHR	GOLD	ARTIST — Album Title	$	Label & Number

Everybody Knows [Concrete Blonde]
Freedom Of Speech [Above The Law]
Heretic [Soundgarden]

I've Got A Secret Miniature Camera [Peter Murphy]
Kick Out The Jams [Bad Brains & Henry Rollins]

Me And The Devil Blues [Cowboy Junkies]
Stand [Liquid Jesus]
Tale O' The Twister [Chagall Guevara]

Titanium Expose [Sonic Youth]
Wave Of Mutilation (U.K. Surf) [Pixies]
Why Can't I Fall In Love [Ivan Neville]

Pure Country -- see STRAIT, George
George Strait/Lesley Ann Warren/Isabel Glasser

Purple Rain - see PRINCE
Prince/Apollonia Kotero/Morris Day

Quadrophenia - see WHO
Phil Daniels/Leslie Ash/Sting

| 4/17/82 | **154** | 6 | **332** | Quest For Fire .... [I] | $8 | RCA 4274 |

Everett McGill/Rae Dawn Chong; cp: Philippe Sarde

Bear Fight
Beginning Of Future
Birth Of Love
Cave Attack

Creation Of Fire
Kzamns
Last Ander
Love Theme

Mammoths
Noah's Distress
Sabre-Teeth Lions
Small Blue Female

Village Of Painted People
Wagabous

| 3/1/86 | **140** | 5 | **333** | Quicksilver .... [V] | $8 | Atlantic 81631 |

Kevin Bacon/Jami Gertz/Paul Rodriguez/Larry Fishburne

Casual Thing [Fiona]
Motown Song [Larry John McNally]
Nothing At All [Peter Frampton]

One Sunny Day/Dueling Bikes [Ray Parker, Jr. & Helen Terry] **96**
Quicksilver Lightning [Roger Daltrey]

Quicksilver Suite Medley [Tony Banks]
Shortcut To Somewhere [Fish & Tony Banks]

Suite Streets From Quicksilver [Thomas Newman]
Through The Night (Love Song) [John Parr & Marilyn Martin]

| 1/23/82 | **134** | 9 | **334** | Ragtime .... [I] | $8 | Elektra 565 |

James Cagney/Howard Rollins/Elizabeth McGovern; cp/cd: Randy Newman

Atlantic City
Change Your Way
Clef Club (Parts 1 & 2)
Coalhouse And Sarah
Coalhouse's Prayer
Delmonico Polka

Denouement Medley
I Could Love A Million Girls
Lower East Side
Main Title
Morgan Library Takeover
Newsreel

One More Hour
Ragtime (Main Title)
Rhinelander Waldo
Sarah's Funeral
Sarah's Responsibility
Tateh's Picture Book

Train Ride
Waltz For Evelyn

| 7/4/81 | **62** | 13 | **335** | Raiders Of The Lost Ark .... [I] | $8 | Columbia 37373 |

Harrison Ford/Karen Allen/John Rhys-Davies; cp/cd: John Williams; pf: London Symphony Orchestra

Basket Game
Desert Chase
Flight From Peru

Map Room: Dawn
Marion's Theme
Miracle Of The Ark

Raiders March
Raiders Of The Lost Ark
Well Of The Souls

| 3/11/89 | **31** | 16 | **336** | Rain Man .... [V] | $8 | Capitol 91866 |

Dustin Hoffman/Tom Cruise/Valeria Golino

At Last [Etta James] **47**
Beyond The Blue Horizon [Lou Christie] **80**
Dry Bones [Delta Rhythm Boys]
Iko Iko [Belle Stars] **14**

Las Vegas [Hans Zimmer]
Leaving Wallbrook (medley) [Hans Zimmer]
Lonely Avenue [Ian Gillan & Roger Glover]

Nathan Jones [Bananarama]
On The Road (medley) [Hans Zimmer]
Scatterlings Of Africa [Johnny Clegg]

Stardust [Rob Wasserman with Aaron Neville]

Rainbow Bridge - see HENDRIX, Jimi

Rattle And Hum - see U2

| 6/11/83 | **20** | 17 | **337** | Return Of The Jedi... [I] | $8 | RSO 811767 |

Mark Hamill/Harrison Ford/Carrie Fisher/Billy Dee Williams; cp/cd: John Williams; pf: London Symphony Orchestra

Emperor, The
Ewok Celebration
Forest Battle

Han Solo Returns (At The Court Of Jabba The Hutt)
Into The Trap

Lapti Nek [Jabba's Palace Band]
Luke And Leia
Main Title (The Story Continues)

Parade Of The Ewoks
Rebel Briefing
Return Of The Jedi

Rhinestone - see PARTON, Dolly
Sylvester Stallone/Dolly Parton/Richard Farnsworth/Ron Leibman

Richard Pryor Live On The Sunset Strip - see PRYOR, Richard

Richard Pryor: Here And Now - see PRYOR, Richard

Ride The Wild Surf - see JAN & DEAN
Tab Hunter/Fabian/Barbara Eden

Right On! - see LAST POETS
David Nelson/Felipe Luciano/Gylan Kain

| 6/3/89 | **67** | 10 | **338** | Road House .... [V] | $8 | Arista 8576 |

Patrick Swayze/Ben Gazzara/Kelly Lynch/Sam Elliott

Blue Monday [Bob Seger]
Cliff's Edge [Patrick Swayze]
Good Heart [Kris McKay]
Hoochie Coochie Man [Jeff Healey Band]

I'm Tore Down [Jeff Healey Band]
Rad Gumbo [Little Feat]
Raising Heaven (In Hell Tonight) [Patrick Swayze]

Roadhouse Blues [Jeff Healey Band]
These Arms Of Mine [Otis Redding] **85**

When The Night Comes Falling From The Sky [Jeff Healey Band]

| 6/21/80 | **125** | 8 | **339** | Roadie .... [V] | $10 | Warner 3441 [2] |

Meat Loaf/Art Carney/Kaki Hunter

American Way [Hank Williams, Jr.]
Brainlock [Joe Ely Band]
Can't We Try [Teddy Pendergrass] **52**
Crystal Ball [Styx]
Double Yellow Line [Sue Saad & The Next]

Drivin' My Life Away [Eddie Rabbitt] **5**
Everything Works If You Let It [Cheap Trick] **44**
(Hot Damn) I'm A One Woman Man [Jerry Lee Lewis]
Man Needs A Woman [Jay Ferguson]

Pain [Alice Cooper]
Ring Of Fire [Blondie]
Road Rats [Alice Cooper]
Texas, Me And You [Asleep At The Wheel]
That Lovin' You Feeling Again [Roy Orbison & Emmylou Harris] **55**

You Better Run [Pat Benatar] **42**
Your Precious Love [Stephen Bishop & Yvonne Elliman]

| 7/18/64 | **56** | 14 | **340** | Robin And The 7 Hoods .... [M] | $50 | Reprise 2021 |

Frank Sinatra/Dean Martin/Bing Crosby/Sammy Davis, Jr.; sw: Sammy Cahn and James Van Heusen; cd: Nelson Riddle

All For One And One For All
Any Man Who Loves His Mother
Bang! Bang!
Charlotte Couldn't Charleston

Don't Be A Do-Badder
Give Praise! Give Praise! Give Praise!
I Like To Lead When I Dance

Mister Booze
My Kind Of Town
Robin And The 7 Hoods (Overture)

Style

DEBUT DATE	PEAK POS	WKS CHR	GOLD	ARTIST — Album Title	$	Label & Number

7/20/91   **5**   45   ▲ 341   **Robin Hood: Prince Of Thieves** ....[I]   **$12**   Morgan Cr. 20004
Kevin Costner/Morgan Freeman/Christian Slater/Alan Rickman; cp/cd: Michael Kamen

Abduction (medley)	Little John and The Band In	Prisoner Of The Crusades	Sir Guy Of Gisborne (medley)
Escape To Sherwood (medley)	The Forest	(medley)	Training (medley)
(Everything I Do) I Do It For	Maid Marian	Robin Hood, Prince Of Thieves	Wild Times [Jeff Lynne]
You [Bryan Adams] 1	Marian At The Waterfall	(medley)	
Final Battle At The Gallows	Overture (medley)	Sheriff and His Witch	
(medley)			

6/2/79   **118**   6   342   **Rock 'N' Roll High School** ....[V]   **$8**   Sire 6070
P.J. Soles/Vincent Van Patten/Dey Young/Ramones

Come Back Jonee [Devo]	I Want You Around [Ramones]	**School Day** [Chuck Berry] 3	Teenage Depression [Eddie &
Come On Let's Go [Paley	Ramones Medley [Ramones]	**School's Out** [Alice Cooper] 7	The Hot Rods]
Brothers & Ramones]	Rock 'N' Roll High School	**Smokin' In The Boy's Room**	
Dream Goes On Forever [Todd	[Ramones]	[Brownsville Station] 3	
Rundgren] 69	Rock 'N' Roll High School [P.J.	So It Goes [Nick Lowe]	
Energy Fools The Magician [Eno]	Soles]		

3/9/57   **16**   9   343   **Rock, Pretty Baby** ....   **$85**   Decca 8429
Sal Mineo/John Saxon/Luana Patten; cp: Henry Mancini; pf: Jimmy Daley & The Ding-A-Lings

Big Band Rock And Roll	Happy Is A Boy Named Me	Picnic By The Sea	Saints Rock 'N Roll
Can I Steal A Little Love	Hot Rod	Rock, Pretty Baby	Teen Age Bop
Dark Blue	Juke Box Rock	Rockabye Lullaby Blues	What's It Gonna Be
Free And Easy	Most, The	Rockin' The Boogie	Young Love

3/5/77   **4**   34   ▲ 344   **Rocky** ....[I]   **$8**   United Art. 693
Sylvester Stallone/Talia Shire/Carl Weathers/Burgess Meredith; cp/cd: Bill Conti

Alone In The Ring	First Date	Philadelphia Morning	Yankee Doodle (medley)
Butkus	Going The Distance	Reflections	You Take My Heart Away
Fanfare For Rocky	**Gonna Fly Now** [Bill Conti] 1	Rocky's Reward	
Final Bell	Marine's Hymn (medley)	Take You Back	

8/25/79   **147**   5   345   **Rocky II** ....[I]   **$8**   United Art. 972
Sylvester Stallone/Talia Shire/Carl Weathers/Burgess Meredith; cp/cd: Bill Conti

All Of My Life (includes 2	Conquest	Overture	Two Kinds Of Love
versions)	Gonna Fly Now	Redemption (Theme)	Vigil

7/10/82   **15**   19   ● 346   **Rocky III** ....[I+V]   **$8**   Liberty 51130
Sylvester Stallone/Talia Shire/Mr. T/Burt Young; cp/cd: Bill Conti

Adrian	**Eye Of The Tiger** [Survivor] 1	Pushin' [Frank Stallone]	Take You Back (includes 2
Conquest	Gonna Fly Now	Reflections	versions) [Frank Stallone]
Decision	Mickey		

11/16/85+   **10**   30   ▲ 347   **Rocky IV** ....[V]   **$8**   Scotti Br. 40203
Sylvester Stallone/Talia Shire/Dolph Lundgren/Burt Young

Burning Heart [Survivor] 2	**Heart's On Fire** [John	**No Easy Way Out** [Robert	Training Montage [Vince DiCola]
Double Or Nothing [Kenny	Cafferty] 76	Tepper] 22	War [Vince DiCola]
Loggins & Gladys Knight]	**Living In America** [James	One Way Street [Go West]	
Eye Of The Tiger [Survivor] 1	Brown] 4	Sweetest Victory [Touch]	

4/15/78   **49**   58   ● 348   **Rocky Horror Picture Show** ....[M]   **$10**   Ode 21653
Tim Curry/Susan Sarandon/Barry Bostwick; sw: Richard O'Brien

Damn It Janet	I Can Make You A Man	Rose Tint My World	Sweet Transvestite
Eddie	I'm Going Home	Science Fiction Double Feature	Time Warp
Hot Patootie-Bless My Soul	Over At The Frankenstein Place	Super Heroes	Touch-A, Touch-A, Touch Me

8/23/75   **156**   6   349   **Rollerball** ....[I]   **$8**   United Art. 470
James Caan/John Houseman/Maud Adams; cd: Andre Previn; pf: London Symphony Orchestra

Adagio	Shostakovich: Excerpt from	Shostakovich: Excerpt from	Tchaikovsky: Waltz from
Bach: Toccata In D Minor	Symphony No. 5 (Third &	Symphony No. 8 (First	"Sleeping Beauty"
Executive Party	Fourth Movement)	Movement)	
Executive Party Dance			

6/16/62   **5**   28   350   **Rome Adventure** ....[I]   **$15**   Warner 1458
Troy Donahue/Suzanne Pleshette/Angie Dickinson; cp: Max Steiner; side 2: *Neapolitan Favorites* by The Cafe Milano Orchestra

Al Di La' [Emilio Pericoli] 6	Lovers Must Learn	Prudence	Serenade
Arrivederci, Roma	Mattinata	Rome Adventure	Tarantella
Come Back To Sorrento	Oh, Marie	Santa Lucia	Volare (Nel Blu Di Pinto Di Blu)

2/8/69   **2²**   74   ▲ 351   **Romeo & Juliet** ....[I]   **$10**   Capitol 2993
Leonard Whiting/Olivia Hussey; cp/cd: Nino Rota; includes dialogue highlights

All Are Punished	**Farewell Love Scene** 86	In Capulet's Tomb (Death of	Prologue
Balcony Scene	Feast At The House of Capulet	Romeo & Juliet)	Romeo & Juliet Are Wed
Death Of Mercutio And Tybalt	(medley)	Likeness Of Death	Romeo's Foreboding (medley)

Rose, The - see MIDLER, Bette
Bette Midler/Alan Bates/Frederic Forrest

1/24/87   **196**   3   352   **Round Midnight** ....[I]   **$8**   Columbia 40464
Dexter Gordon/Francois Cluzet; cp/cd: Herbie Hancock

Berangere's Nightmare	Fair Weather	Minuit Aux Champs-Elysees	Round Midnight
Body And Soul	How Long Has This Been Going	Peacocks, The	Still Time
Chan's Song (Never Said)	On?	Rhythm-A-Ning	Una Noche Con Francis

Roustabout - see PRESLEY, Elvis
Elvis Presley (Charlie Rogers)/Barbara Stanwyck/Joan Freeman

10/31/70   **148**   6   353   **R.P.M.** ....[I+V]   **$10**   Bell 1203
Anthony Quinn/Ann-Margret/Gary Lockwood sw: Barry DeVorzon & Perry Botkin, Jr.

All Night Long [Chris Morgan]	Riot, The	Transistor Q	When I Get Home To You
All Night Long (instrumental)	Stop! I Don't Wanna' Hear It	We Don't Know Where We're	[Christopher]
I Wanna' Spend Some Time	Anymore [Melanie]	Goin' [Melanie]	
With You [Christopher]	Stop! I Don't Wanna' Hear It	We Don't Know Where We're	
Paco's Farewell	Anymore (instrumental)	Goin' (instrumental)	

Rumble Fish - see COPELAND, Stewart
Matt Dillon/Mickey Rourke/Diane Lane

DEBUT DATE	PEAK POS	WKS CHR	GOLD	ARTIST — Album Title	$	Label & Number

7/5/86 — **43** — 15 — 354 — Running Scared .... [V] **$10** MCA 6169
Gregory Hines/Billy Crystal/Steven Bauer/Jimmy Smits

El Chase [Rod Temperton]	Once In A Lifetime Groove [New Edition]	Say You Really Want Me [Kim Wilde] 44
I Just Wanna Be Loved [Ready For The World]	Never Too Late To Start [Rod Temperton]	Running Scared [Fee Waybill]	Sweet Freedom [Michael McDonald] 7
Man Size Love [Klymaxx] **15**		
I Know What I Want [Patti LaBelle]		

Rush - see CLAPTON, Eric
Jason Patric/Jennifer Jason Leigh/Sam Elliott/Max Perlich

7/5/86 — **20** — 16 — ● 355 — Ruthless People .... [V] **$8** Epic 40398
Danny DeVito/Bette Midler/Judge Reinhold/Helen Slater

Dance Champion [Kool & The Gang]	**Modern Woman** [Billy Joel] **10**	Ruthless People [Mick Jagger] 51	**Wherever I Lay My Hat (That's My Home)** [Paul Young] 70
Don't You Want My Love [Nicole]	Neighborhood Watch [Michel Colombier]	Stand On It [Bruce Springsteen]	
Give Me The Reason [Luther Vandross] 57	No Say In It [Machinations]	Waiting To See You [Dan Hartman]	

12/19/70+ — **199** — 4 — 356 — Ryan's Daughter .... [I] **$25** MGM 27
Robert Mitchum/Sarah Miles/Trevor Howard; cp/cd: Maurice Jarre

It Was A Good Time (Rosy's Theme)	Michael's Theme	Rosy On The Beach	You Don't Want Me Then?
Main Title	Obsession	Shakes, The	
Michael Shows Randolph His Strange Treasure	Overture	Song Of The Irish Rebels	
	Ride Through The Woods	Where Was I When The Parade Went By? (The Major)	
	Rosy And The Schoolmaster		

Saint ..see: St.

6/25/88 — **112** — 6 — 357 — Salsa .... [V] **$8** MCA 6232
Robby Rosa/Rodney Harvey/Magali Alvarado/Tito Puente

Cali Pachanguero [Grupo Niche]	Good Lovin' [Kenny Ortega]	Oye Como Va (Give It All You Got) [Tito Puente]	Spanish Harlem [Ben E. King]
Chicos Y Chicas [Mavis Vegas Davis]	I Know [Marisela]	Puerto Rico [Bobby Caldwell]	Under My Skin [Robby Rosa]
	Margarita [Wilkins]		Your Love [Laura Branigan]

10/23/65 — **89** — 15 — 358 — Sandpiper, The .... [I] **$30** Mercury 61032
Elizabeth Taylor/Richard Burton/Eva Marie Saint; cp: Johnny Mandel; cd: Robert Armbruster

Art Gallery	Desire	San Simeon	Weekend Montage
Baby Sandpiper	End Title	Seduction	
Bird Bath	Main Title	Shadow Of Your Smile	

10/24/92 — **200** — 1 — 359 — Sarafina! The Sound Of Freedom .... [M] **$12** Qwest 45060
Whoopi Goldberg/Leleti Khumalo/Miriam Makeba/John Kani; cp: Mbongeni Ngema/Hugh Masekela

Freedom Is Coming Tomorrow	Nkonyane Kandaba	Safa Saphel' Isizwe	Thank You Mama
Lizobuya	One More Time [James Ingram]	Sarafina!	Vuma Dlozi Lami
Lord's Prayer	Sabela	Sechaba	

Saturday Night Fever - see BEE GEES
John Travolta/Karen Gorney/Donna Pescow

5/6/89 — **62** — 14 — 360 — Say Anything... .... [V] **$8** WTG 45140
John Cusack/Ione Skye/John Mahoney

All For Love [Nancy Wilson]	Keeping The Dream Alive [Freiheit]	Stripped [Depeche Mode]	Within Your Reach [Replacements]
Cult Of Personality [Living Colour] **13**	One Big Rush [Joe Satriani]	Taste The Pain [Red Hot Chili Peppers]	You Want It [Cheap Trick]
In Your Eyes [Peter Gabriel] 26	Skankin' To The Beat [Fishbone]		

3/19/88 — **81** — 17 — 361 — School Daze .... [V] **$8** EMI-Man. 48680
Larry Fishburne/Giancarlo Esposito/Tisha Campbell/Spike Lee

Be Alone Tonight [Rays]	I Can Only Be Me [Keith John]	Straight And Nappy [Kyme & Tisha Campbell]	We've Already Said Goodbye (Before We Said Hello) [Pieces Of A Dream]
Be One [Phyllis Hyman]	One Little Acorn (includes 2 versions) [Kenny Baron & Terence Blanchard]	Wake Up Suite [Natural Spiritual Orchestra]	
Building Me A Home [Tracy Coley]	Perfect Match [Tech]		
Da'Butt [E.U.] **35**			

12/26/70+ — **95** — 8 — 362 — Scrooge .... [M-X] **$25** Columbia 30258
Albert Finney (Scrooge)/Alec Guinness/Edith Evans; a version of Charles Dickens' A Christmas Carol; sw: Leslie Bricusse; cd: Ian Fraser; Christmas charts: 13/70

Beautiful Day	Father Christmas	I'll Begin Again	You...You
Christmas Carol	Happiness	Overture	
Christmas Children	I Hate People	See The Phantoms	
December The 25th	I Like Life	Thank You Very Much	

12/3/88+ — **93** — 9 — 363 — Scrooged .... [V] **$8** A&M 3921
Bill Murray/Karen Allen/John Forsythe/Bobcat Goldthwait

Brown Eyed Girl [Buster Poindexter]	Christmas Song (Chestnuts Roasting On An Open Fire) [Natalie Cole]	**Put A Little Love In Your Heart** [Annie Lennox & Al Green] **9**	We Three Kings Of Orient Are [Miles Davis/Larry Carlton/Paul Shaffer]
Christmas Must Be Tonight [Robbie Robertson]	Get Up 'N' Dance [Kool Moe Dee]	Sweetest Thing [New Voices Of Freedom]	Wonderful Life [Mark Lennon]
	Love You Take [Dan Hartman & Denise Lopez]		

6/13/87 — **131** — 8 — 364 — Secret Of My Success, The .... [V] **$8** MCA 6205
Michael J. Fox/Helen Slater/Richard Jordan/Margaret Whitton

Don't Ask The Reason Why [Restless Heart]	I Burn For You [Danny Peck & Nancy Shanks]	**Secret Of My Success** [Night Ranger] **64**	Water Fountain [David Foster]
Gazebo [David Foster]	Price Of Love [Roger Daltrey]	Sometimes The Good Guys Finish First [Pat Benatar]	
Heaven And The Heartaches [Taxxi]	Riskin' A Romance [Bananarama]	3 Themes [David Foster]	

Serenade - see LANZA, Mario
Mario Lanza/Joan Fontaine/Vincent Price/Vincent Edwards

Seven Hills Of Rome - see LANZA, Mario
Mario Lanza/Renato Roscel/Marisa Allasio

12/30/72+ — **163** — 11 — 365 — 1776 .... [M] **$20** Columbia 31741
William Daniels/Howard Da Silva; sw: Sherman Edwards; also see Original Cast ('69)

But, Mr. Adams	Finale	Is Anybody There?	Molasses To Rum
Egg, The	He Plays The Violin	Lees Of Old Virginia	Momma Look Sharp

DEBUT DATE	PEAK POS	WKS CHR	GOLD	ARTIST — Album Title	$	Label & Number
10/17/64	148	3	366	7th Dawn, The..[I] William Holden/Susannah York; cp/cd: Riz Ortolani	$25	United Art. 5115

Piddle, Twiddle and Resolve (medley)   1776 (Overture)   Till Then (medley)
Sit Down, John   Yours, Yours, Yours

Battle In The Jungle   Ferris Meets Candace (medley)   Night In Malaya   Seventh Dawn
Closing Theme   Fire In The Native Village   Opening Titles   Seventh Dawn (Love Theme)
Dhana's Torment   Governor's Ball   Paradise Club   Seventh Dawn Variations
Duel, The   Jungle Attack (medley)   Prison Prayer   Trial, The

| 8/12/78 | 5 | 28 | ▲ 367 | Sgt. Pepper's Lonely Hearts Club Band.................................[M]
Peter Frampton/Bee Gees/George Burns/Steve Martin; sw: John Lennon and Paul McCartney; film inspired by The Beatles Sgt. Pepper's ... album | $10 | RSO 4100 [2] |

Because   Golden Slumbers   Mean Mr. Mustard   She's Leaving Home
Being For The Benefit Of Mr. Kite   Good Morning, Good Morning   Nowhere Man   Strawberry Fields Forever
Carry That Weight   **Got To Get You Into My Life** [Earth, Wind & Fire] 9   Oh! Darling [Robin Gibb] 15   When I'm Sixty-Four
Come Together [Aerosmith] 23   Here Comes The Sun   Polythene Pam   With A Little Help From My Friends (medley)
Day In The Life   I Want You (She's So Heavy)   Sgt. Pepper's Lonely Hearts Club Band (includes 3 versions)   You Never Give Me Your Money
Fixing A Hole   Long And Winding Road
Get Back [Billy Preston] 86   Lucy In The Sky With Diamonds   She Came In Through The Bathroom Window
Getting Better   Maxwell's Silver Hammer

Shaft - see HAYES, Isaac
Richard Roundtree/Moses Gunn/Gwenn Mitchell

| 7/21/73 | 147 | 9 | 368 | Shaft in Africa...[I]
Richard Roundtree/Vonetta McGee; cp/cd: Johnny Pate | $15 | ABC 793 |

Aleme Finds Shaft   Are You Man Enough (includes 2 versions)   Jazar's Theme   You Can't Even Walk In The Park (Opening Theme)
Aleme's Theme   El Jardia   Shaft In Africa (Addis)
Are You Man Enough [Four Tops] 15   Headman   Truck Stop

| 8/26/72 | 100 | 16 | 369 | Shaft's Big Score!... | $10 | MGM 36 |

   Richard Roundtree/Moses Gunn; cp: Gordon Parks; cd: Dick Hazard

Asby - Kelly Man   First Meeting   Smart Money
Blowin' Your Mind [O.C. Smith]   Move On In [O.C. Smith]   Symphony For Shafted Souls
Don't Misunderstand [O.C. Smith]   Other Side   Medley

| 1/23/82 | 171 | 8 | 370 | Sharky's Machine..[V]
Burt Reynolds/Rachel Ward/Bernie Casey/Brian Keith | $8 | Warner 3653 |

Before You [Sarah Vaughan & Joe Williams]   High Energy [Doc Severinsen]   My Funny Valentine [Julie London]   Sharky's Theme [Eddie Harris]
Dope Bust [Flora Purim & Buddy DeFranco]   Let's Keep Dancing [Peggy Lee]   Love Theme [Sarah Vaughan]   Street Life [Randy Crawford]
8 To 5 I Lose [Joe Williams]   My Funny Valentine [Chet Baker]   **Route 66** [Manhattan Transfer] 78
   Sexercise [Doc Severinsen]

| 3/12/88 | 92 | 8 | 371 | She's Having A Baby...[V]
Kevin Bacon/Elizabeth McGovern/Alec Baldwin | $8 | I.R.S. 6211 |

Apron Strings [Everything But The Girl]   Full Of Love [Dr. Calculus]   It's All In The Game [Carmel]   You Just Haven't Earned It Yet Baby [Kirsty MacColl]
Crazy Love [Bryan Ferry]   Happy Families [XTC]   She's Having A Baby [Dave Wakeling]
Desire (Come And Get It) [Gene Loves Jezebel]   Haunted When The Minutes Drag [Love & Rockets]   This Woman's Work [Kate Bush]

| 10/9/65 | 147 | 2 | 372 | Shenandoah..[I]
James Stewart/Patrick Wayne; cp: Frank Skinner; cd: Joseph Gershenson | $35 | Decca 79125 |

Bridal Suite   Legend Of Shenandoah [James Stewart]   Memorium   We're Ridin' Out Tonight
Dead And The Living   Ripe For Pickin'   Young Captives
End Title   Main Title   Roll Call
Horse Play   Martha's Namesake   War Is Hell

| 11/18/89 | 97 | 12 | 373 | Shocker (No More Mr. Nice Guy) The Music.......................[V]
Michael Murphy/Peter Berg/Cami Cooper/Mitch Pileggi | $8 | SBK 93233 |

Awakening, The [Voodoo X]   Different Breed [Dead On]   Shockdance [Dudes Of Wrath]
Demon Bell (The Ballad Of Horace Pinker) [Dangerous Toys]   Love Transfusion [Iggy Pop]   Shocker [Dudes Of Wrath]
   No More Mr. Nice Guy [Megadeth]   Sword And Stone [Bonfire]
   Timeless Love [Saraya] 85

Show Boat - see Those Glorious MGM Musicals
Silencers, The - see MARTIN, Dean
Dean Martin/Stella Stevens/Daliah Lavi/Victor Buono

| 4/29/89 | 196 | 1 | 374 | Sing..[V]
Lorraine Bracco/Peter Dobson/Jessica Steen/Louise Lasser | $8 | Columbia 45086 |

Birthday Suit [Johnny Kemp] 36   Romance (Love Theme) [Paul Carrack & Terri Nunn]   Total Concentration [Patti LaBelle]   What's The Matter With Love? [Laurnea Wilkerson]
(Everybody's Gotta) Face The Music [Kevin Cronin]   Sing [Mickey Thomas]   We'll Never Say Goodbye [Art Garfunkel]   You Don't Have To Ask Me Twice [Nia Peeples]
One More Time [Michael Bolton]   Somethin' To Believe In [Bill Champlin]

Sing Boy Sing - see SANDS, Tommy
Tommy Sands/Lili Gentle/Edmond O'Brien

Singin' In The Rain - see Those Glorious MGM Musicals
Singing Nun, The - see REYNOLDS, Debbie
Debbie Reynolds/Ricardo Montalban/Greer Garson

| 7/18/92 | 6 | 30↑ | ▲ 375 | Singles...[V]
Matt Dillon/Bridget Fonda/Campbell Scott/Kyra Sedgwick | $12 | Epic 52476 |

Battle Of Evermore [Lovemongers]   Crown Of Thorns (medley) [Mother Love Bone]   Nearly Lost You [Screaming Trees]   Waiting For Somebody [Paul Westerberg]
Birth Ritual [Soundgarden]   Drown [Smashing Pumpkins]   Overblown [Mudhoney]   Would? [Alice In Chains]
Breath [Pearl Jam]   Dyslexic Heart [Paul Westerberg]   Seasons [Chris Cornell]
Chloe Dancer (medley) [Mother Love Bone]   May This Be Love [Jimi Hendrix]   State Of Love And Trust [Pearl Jam]

| 6/27/92 | 40 | 33↑ | ● 376 | Sister Act...[I+V]
Whoopi Goldberg/Maggie Smith/Harvey Keitel; cp/cd: Marc Shaiman | $12 | Hollywood 61334 |

DEBUT DATE	PEAK POS	WKS CHR	GOLD	ARTIST — Album Title	$	Label & Number

Deloris Is Kidnapped | I Will Follow Him [Deloris & The Sisters] | Lounge Medley [Deloris & The Ronelles] | **Rescue Me** [Fontella Bass] 4
Getting Into The Habit | If My Sister's In Trouble [Lady Soul] | Murder, The | Roll With Me Henry [Etta James]
Gravy (For My Mashed Potatoes) [Dee Dee Sharp] 9 | **Just A Touch Of Love** [C & C Music Factory] 50 | My Guy (My God) [Deloris & The Sisters] | Shout [Deloris & The Sisters & The Ronelles]
Hail Holy Queen [Deloris & The Sisters] | | Nuns To The Rescue

Slaughter's Big Rip-Off - see BROWN, James
Jim Brown (football player)/Brock Peters/Ed McMahon

9/6/80 — 103 — 11 — 377 — Smokey And The Bandit 2 .... [V] $8 — MCA 6101
Burt Reynolds/Sally Field/Jackie Gleason/Jerry Reed

Again And Again [Brenda Lee] | **Let's Do Something Cheap And Superficial** [Burt Reynolds] 88 | Pickin' Lone Star Style [Bandit Band] | Texas Bound And Flyin' [Jerry Reed]
Charlotte's Web [Statler Brothers] | | Ride Concrete Cowboy, Ride [Roy Rogers] | To Be Your Man [Don Williams]
Do You Know You Are My Sunshine [Statler Brothers] | Pecos Promenade [Tanya Tucker] | | Tulsa Time [Don Williams]
Here's Lookin' At You [Mel Tillis] | | | Wildwood Flower [Bandit Band]

3/21/87 — 57 — 13 — 378 — Some Kind Of Wonderful .... [V] $8 — MCA 6200
Lea Thompson/Eric Stoltz/Mary Stuart Masterson/Craig Sheffer

Brilliant Mind [Furniture] | Do Anything [Pete Shelley] | Miss Amanda Jones [March Violets] | Turn To The Sky [March Violets]
Can't Help Falling In Love [Lick The Tits] | Hardest Walk [Jesus & Mary Chain] | She Loves Me [Stephen Duffy]
Cry Like This [Blue Room] | I Go Crazy [Flesh For Lulu] | Shyest Time [Apartments]

12/6/80 — 187 — 2 — ● 379 — Somewhere In Time .... [I] $10 — MCA 5154
Christopher Reeve/Jane Seymour/Teresa Wright; cp/cd: John Barry

Day Together | Man Of My Dreams | Rachmaninoff: Rhapsody On A | Return To The Present
Is He The One | Old Woman | Theme Of Paganini | Somewhere In Time
Journey Back In Time

Son Of Dracula - see NILSSON
Harry Nilsson/Ringo Starr/Rosanna Lee

1/23/71 — 95 — 8 — 380 — Song Of Norway .... [M] $12 — ABC 14
Florence Henderson/Toralv Maurstad; based on the life and music of Norwegian classical composer Edvard Grieg; pf: London Symphony Orchestra

At Christmastime | John Heggerstrom | Rhyme And A Reason (medley) | Welcome Toast
Be A Boy Again | Life Of A Wife Of A Sailor | Ribbons And Wrappings | When We Wed (medley)
Finale | Little House | Solitary Wanderer | Wrong To Dream
Freddy And His Fiddle | Midsummer's Eve - Hand In Hand | Solvejg's Song (medley)
Hill Of Dreams | Norwegian National Anthem (medley) | Song Of Norway
Hymn Of Betrothal | | Strange Music
I Love You | | Three There Were

Song Remains The Same, The - see LED ZEPPELIN

SongWriter - see NELSON, Willie, and/or KRISTOFFERSON, Kris
Willie Nelson/Kris Kristofferson/Melinda Dillon

Sorcerer - see TANGERINE DREAM
Roy Scheider/Bruno Cremer/Francisco Rabal

11/15/86 — 138 — 9 — 381 — Soul Man .... [V] $8 — A&M 3903
C. Thomas Howell/Rae Dawn Chong/Arye Gross/James Sikking

Bang Bang Bang (Who's On The Phone) [Ricky] | Evolution [Models] | Soul Man [Sam Moore & Lou Reed] | Totally Academic [Brenda Russell]
Black Girls [Rae Dawn Chong] | Love And Affection [Martha Davis & Sly Stone] | Suddenly It's Magic [Vesta Williams]
Eek-Ah-Bo-Static Automatic [Sly Stone] | Outside [Nu Shooz] | Sweet Sarah [Tom Scott]

Soul To Soul - see CONCERTS/FESTIVALS

3/20/65 — 1² — 233 — ● 382 — Sound Of Music, The .... [M] $10 — RCA 2005
Julie Andrews/Christopher Plummer; story of Maria Trapp's family; mu: Richard Rodgers; ly: Oscar Hammerstein II; cd: Irwin Kostal; also see Original Cast ('59)

Climb Ev'ry Mountain | Lonely Goatherd | Preludium (Dixit Dominus) | Something Good
Do-Re-Mi | Maria | Processional | Sound Of Music
Edelweiss | Morning Hymn - Alleluia | Sixteen Going On Seventeen
I Have Confidence | My Favorite Things | So Long, Farewell

6/12/82 — 168 — 12 — 383 — Soup For One .... [V] $8 — Mirage 19353
Saul Rubinek/Marcia Strassman/Gerrit Graham; sw: Bernard Edwards and Nile Rodgers

Dream Girl [Teddy Pendergrass] | Jump, Jump [Deborah Harry] | **Soup For One** [Chic] 80
I Want Your Love [Chic] 7 | Let's Go On Vacation [Sister Sledge] | Tavern On The Green [Chic]
I Work For A Livin' [Fonzi Thornton] | | **Why** [Carly Simon] 74

3/31/58 — 1³¹ — 262 — ● 384 — South Pacific .... [M] $10 — RCA 1032
Rossano Brazzi/Mitzi Gaynor/John Kerr; mu: Richard Rodgers; ly: Oscar Hammerstein II; cd: Alfred Newman

Bali Ha'i | Happy Talk | My Girl Back Home | Twin Soliloquies (medley)
Bloody Mary | Honey Bun | Overture | Younger Than Springtime
Carefully Taught | I'm Gonna Wash That Man Right Outa My Hair | Some Enchanted Evening (medley)
Cockeyed Optimist | I'm In Love With A Wonderful Guy | There Is Nothin' Like A Dame
Dites-Moi | | This Nearly Was Mine
Finale

Sparkle - see FRANKLIN, Aretha
Irene Cara/Philip Thomas/Lonette McKee

Speedway - see PRESLEY, Elvis
Elvis Presley (Steve Grayson)/Nancy Sinatra/Bill Bixby

Spinout - see PRESLEY, Elvis
Elvis Presley (Mike McCoy)/Shelley Fabares/Diane McBain

8/27/77 — 40 — 16 — 385 — Spy Who Loved Me, The .... [I] $10 — United Art. 774
Roger Moore/Barbara Bach/Richard Kiel; cp/cd: Marvin Hamlisch

Anya | Mojave Club | Nobody Does It Better (instrumental) | Ride To Atlantis
Bond 77 | **Nobody Does It Better** [Carly Simon] 2 | Pyramids, The | Tanker, The
Conclusion | | |
Eastern Lights

DEBUT DATE	PEAK POS	WKS CHR	GOLD		ARTIST — Album Title	$	Label & Number
7/13/85	21	37	●	386	St. Elmo's Fire ....[V]	$8	Atlantic 81261

Emilio Estevez/Rob Lowe/Andrew McCarthy/Demi Moore/Judd Nelson

Georgetown [David Foster]	Love Theme (Just For A	St. Elmo's Fire (Man In
If I Turn You Away [Vikki Moss]	Moment) [David Foster/Donny	Motion) [John Parr] 1
Love Theme From St. Elmo's	Gerrard/Amy Holland]	Stressed Out (Close To The
Fire [David Foster] 15	Saved My Life [Fee Waybill]	Edge) [Airplay]
	Shake Down [Billy Squier]	

This Time It Was Really Right [Jon Anderson]
Young And Innocent [Elefante]

St. Louis Blues - see COLE, Nat "King"
Nat "King" Cole/Eartha Kitt/Pearl Bailey/Cab Calloway

9/20/86	31	45	●	387	Stand By Me ....[V-O]	$8	Atlantic 81677

Wil Wheaton/River Phoenix/Corey Feldman/Jerry O'Connell

Come Go With Me	**Great Balls Of Fire** [Jerry Lee	Lollipop [Chordettes] 2
[Dell-Vikings] 4	Lewis] 2	Mr. Lee [Bobbettes] 6
Everyday [Buddy Holly]	**Let The Good Times Roll**	**Stand By Me** [Ben E. King] 4
Get A Job [Silhouettes] 1	[Shirley & Lee] 20	

Whispering Bells
[Dell-Vikings] 9
Yakety Yak [Coasters] 1

10/26/68+	98	20		388	Star! ....[M]	$10	20th Century 5102

Julie Andrews/Richard Crenna/Michael Craig; based on the life of English stage star Gertrude Lawrence

Burlington Bertie From Bow	Jenny	Overture (Medley)
Dear Little Boy (Dear Little Girl)	Limehouse Blues	Parisian Pierrot
Do, Do, Do	My Ship	Physician, The
Has Anybody Seen Our Ship?	'N' Everything	Piccadilly
In My Garden Of Joy	Oh, It's A Lovely War	Someday I'll Find You

Someone To Watch Over Me
Star!

Star Is Born, A - see STREISAND, Barbra
Barbra Streisand/Kris Kristofferson

1/5/80	50	11	●	389	Star Trek - The Motion Picture ....[I]	$10	Columbia 36334

William Shatner/Leonard Nimoy/DeForest Kelley; cp/cd: Jerry Goldsmith

Cloud, The	Ilia's Theme	Main Title (medley)
End Title	Klingon Battle (medley)	Meld, The
Enterprise, The	Leaving Drydock	Spock Walk

Vejur Flyover

7/17/82	61	9		390	Star Trek II - The Wrath Of Khan ....[I]	$8	Atlantic 19363

William Shatner/Leonard Nimoy/DeForest Kelley/Ricardo Montalban; cp/cd: James Horner

Battle In The Mutara Nebula	Epilogue (medley)	Kirk's Explosive Reply
End Title (medley)	Genesis Countdown	Main Title
Enterprise Clears Moorings	Khan's Pets	Spock

Surprise Attack

6/23/84	82	8		391	Star Trek III - The Search For Spock ....[I]	$10	Capitol 12360

William Shatner/DeForest Kelley/Christopher Lloyd; cp/cd: James Horner; includes bonus 12' single "The Search For Spock"

Bird Of Prey Decloaks	Klingons	Prologue (medley)
End Titles	Main Title (medley)	Returning To Vulcan
Katra Ritual	Mind-Meld	Search For Spock (Theme)

Stealing The Enterprise

1/4/92	171	1		392	Star Trek VI - The Undiscovered Country ....[I]	$12	MCA 10512

William Shatner/Leonard Nimoy/DeForest Kelley/James Doohan; cp/cd: Cliff Eidelman

Assassination	Dining On Ashes	Revealed
Battle For Peace	Escape From Rura Penthe	Rura Penthe
Clear All Moorings	Incident, An	Sign Off
Death Of Gorkon	Overture	Star Trek VI Suite

Surrender For Peace

6/18/77	2³	53	▲	393	**Star Wars** ....[I]	$12	20th Cent. 541 [2]

Mark Hamill/Harrison Ford/Carrie Fisher/Alec Guinness; cp/cd: John Williams; pf: London Symphony Orchestra; also see Meco and Zubin Mehta

Ben's Death (medley)	Inner City	Princess Leia's Theme
Blasting Off (medley)	Land Of The Sandpeople	Rescue Of The Princess
Cantina Band	Last Battle	Return Home
Desert, The (medley)	Little People Work	Robot Auction (medley)
End Title (medley)	Mouse Robot (medley)	**Star Wars (Main Title)** [John
Imperial Attack	Princess Appears	Williams] 10

Throne Room (medley)
Tie Fighter Attack (medley)
Walls Converge

12/17/77+	36	10	●	394	Star Wars, The Story Of	$10	20th Century 550

storyline excerpts from the film; narrator: Roscoe Lee Browne

5/12/62	12	19		395	State Fair ....[M]	$30	Dot 29011

Pat Boone/Ann-Margret/Bobby Darin; mu: Richard Rodgers; ly: Oscar Hammerstein II; cd: Alfred Newman

Finale	It's A Grand Night For Singing	Never Say No To A Man
Isn't It Kinda Fun	Little Things In Texas	Overture (Main Title)
It Might As Well Be Spring	More Than Just A Friend	That's For Me

This Isn't Heaven
Willing And Eager

Staying Alive - see BEE GEES
John Travolta/Cynthia Rhodes

6/6/70	200	2		396	Sterile Cuckoo, The	$20	Paramount 5009

Liza Minnelli/Wendell Burton/Tim McIntire; cp/cd: Fred Karlin

Come Saturday Morning	Jerry	Pookie Adams
[Sandpipers] 17	Jerry & Pookie	Pookie Leaves
End Walk [Sandpipers]	Montage [Sandpipers]	Weirdos, The

You're Absolutely Whacky

Sting, The - see HAMLISCH, Marvin
Paul Newman/Robert Redford/Robert Shaw

Stop Making Sense - see TALKING HEADS

Straight Talk - see PARTON, Dolly
Dolly Parton/James Woods/Griffin Dunne

9/12/70	91	9		397	Strawberry Statement, The ....[V]	$20	MGM 14 [2]

Bruce Davison/Kim Darby/James Coco

Circle Game [Buffy Sainte-Marie]	Give Peace A Chance [cast]	Marcello: Concerto In D Minor
Colt Tower [Ian Freebairn-Smith]	Helpless [Crosby, Stills, Nash &	[Ian Freebairn-Smith]
Cyclatron [Ian Freebairn-Smith]	Young]	Market Basket [Ian
Down By The River [Neil Young]	Loner, The [Neil Young]	Freebairn-Smith]
Fishin' Blues [Red Mountain Jug	Long Time Gone [Crosby, Stills	Pocket Band [Ian
Band]	& Nash]	Freebairn-Smith]

Something In The Air
[Thunderclap Newman] 37
"2001" A Space Odyssey
[Berlin Philharmonic] 90

DEBUT DATE	PEAK POS	WKS CHR	GOLD	ARTIST — Album Title	$	Label & Number

6/16/84 — PEAK POS **32** — WKS CHR **21** — **398** Streets Of Fire .... [V] **$8** MCA 5492
Michael Pare/Diane Lane/Rick Moranis/Amy Madigan

Blue Shadows [Blasters]	Nowhere Fast [Fire Inc.]	**Tonight Is What It Means To**
Countdown To Love [Greg Phillinganes]	One Bad Stud [Blasters]	**Be Young** [Fire Inc.] 80
I Can Dream About You [Dan Hartman] 6	Sorcerer [Marilyn Martin]	
Deeper And Deeper [Fixx]	Never Be You [Maria McKee]	

8/28/82 — **152** — **7** — **399** Summer Lovers .... [V] **$8** Warner 23695
Peter Gallagher/Daryl Hannah/Valerie Quennessen

Crazy In The Night [Tina Turner]	If Love Takes You Away [Stephen Bishop]	Summer Lovers [Michael Sembello]
Do What Ya Wanna Do [Cage & Nona Hendryx]	Play To Win [Heaven 17]	Take Me Down To The Ocean [Elton John]
Hard To Say I'm Sorry [Chicago] 1	Sea Cave [Basil Poledouris]	
	Johnny And Mary [Tina Turner]	
	Search For Lina [Basil Poledouris]	
	Just Can't Get Enough [Depeche Mode]	

9/11/71 — **52** — **34** — **400** Summer Of '42 .... [I] **$8** Warner 1925
Jennifer O'Neill/Gary Grimes/Jerry Houser; cp/cd: Michel Legrand

And All The Time	Dancer, The	La Guerre
Awakening Awareness	Entrance To Reality	Lonely Two
Bacchanal, The	Full Awakening (medley)	Los Manos De Muerto
But Not Picasso (medley)	High I.Q.	Summer Knows

Summer Of '42 (Theme)
Summer Song

Sunday In New York - see NERO, Peter
Cliff Robertson/Rod Taylor/Jane Fonda/Robert Culp

Superfly - see MAYFIELD, Curtis
Ron O'Neal/Carl Lee/Julius Harris

Super Fly T.N.T. - see OSIBISA
Ron O'Neal/Roscoe Lee Browne/Sheila Frazier

1/13/79 — **44** — **13** — **401** Superman - The Movie .... [I] **$12** Warner 3257 [2]
Christopher Reeve/Margot Kidder/Marlon Brando/Gene Hackman; cp/cd: John Williams; pf: London Symphony Orchestra

Can You Read My Mind (medley)	Fortress Of Solitude	March Of The Villains
Chasing Rockets	Growing Up	Planet Krypton
Destruction Of Krypton	Leaving Home	Super Rescues
End Title	Lex Luthor's Lair	Superfeats
Flying Sequence (medley)	Love Theme	

Superman, Theme From (Main Title) [John Williams] 81
Trip To Earth
Turning Back The World

7/4/81 — **133** — **9** — **402** Superman II .... [I] **$10** Warner 3505
Christopher Reeve/Margot Kidder/Gene Hackman; cp/cd: Ken Thorne (from John Williams' original material)

Aerial Battle (medley)	Honeymoon Hotel	Lovers Fly North
Clark Exposed As Superman	Lex & Miss Teschmacher To Fortress	Main Title March
Clark Fumbles Rescue	Lex Escapes	Mother's Advice
Clark To Fortress (medley)	Lift Into Space (medley)	Release Of Villains (medley)
End Title March		Sad Return

Superman Saves Spire (medley)
T.V. President Resigns (medley)
Ursa Flies Over Moon

7/2/83 — **163** — **3** — **403** Superman III .... [I+V] **$10** Warner 23879
Christopher Reeve/Richard Pryor/Annette O'Toole; cp: John Williams/Ken Thorne/Giorgio Moroder

Acid Test (medley)	Main Title March	Saving The Factory (medley)
Final Victory (medley)	No See, No Cry [Chaka Khan]	Streets Of Metropolis (Main Title)
Love Theme [Helen St. John]	Rock On [Marshall Crenshaw]	Struggle Within (medley)

They Won't Get Me [Roger Miller]
Two Faces Of Superman

3/8/69 — **72** — **22** — **404** Sweet Charity .... [M] **$12** Decca 71502
Shirley MacLaine/Sammy Davis, Jr.; mu: Cy Coleman; ly: Dorothy Fields; also see Original Cast ('66)

Big Spender	It's A Nice Face	Rhythm Of Life
I Love To Cry At Weddings	My Personal Property	Sweet Charity (includes 2 versions)
I'm A Brass Band	Overture	
If My Friends Could See Me Now	Pompeii Club (Rich Man's Frug)	

There's Gotta Be Something Better Than This
Where Am I Going?

Sweet Dreams - see CLINE, Patsy
Jessica Lange/Ed Harris/Ann Wedgeworth

7/3/71 — **139** — **19** — **405** Sweet Sweetback's Baadasssss Song .... **$15** Stax 3001
Melvin Van Peebles/Rhetta Hughes/John Amos; cp: Melvin Van Peebles

Come On Feet	Mojo Woman	Sweetback Getting It Uptight
Hoppin John	Reggins Hanging On In There As Best They Can	And Preaching It So Hard The Bourgeois Reggin Angel
Man Tries Running His Usual Game But Sweetback's Jones Is So Strong He Waste	Sanra Z	Sweetback Losing His Cherry

Sweetback's Theme
Won't Bleed Me

3/11/89 — **166** — **4** — **406** Tap .... [V] **$8** Epic 45084
Gregory Hines/Suzzanne Douglas/Joe Morton/Sammy Davis, Jr.

All I Want Is Forever [James "J.T." Taylor & Regina Belle]	Bad Boy [Teena Marie]	Free [Gwen Guthrie]
Baby What You Want Me To Do [Etta James]	Can't Escape The Rhythm [Gregory Hines]	Lover's Intuition [Amy Keys]
	Forget The Girl [Tony Terry]	Max's Theme [Stanley Clarke]

Somebody Like You [Melissa Rowan]
Strong As Steel [Gregory Abbott]

10/27/84 — **34** — **16** — ● **407** Teachers .... [V] **$8** Capitol 12371
Nick Nolte/JoBeth Williams/Judd Hirsch/Ralph Macchio

Cheap Sunglasses [ZZ Top] 89	I Can't Stop The Fire [Eric Martin & Friends]	Interstate Love Affair [Night Ranger]
Edge Of A Dream [Joe Cocker] 69	(I'm The) Teacher [Ian Hunter]	**One Foot Back In Your Door** [Roman Holliday] 76
Fooling Around [Freddie Mercury]	In The Jungle (Concrete Jungle) [Motels]	

Teacher Teacher [38 Special] 25
Understanding [Bob Seger & The Silver Bullet Band] 17

4/21/90 — **13** — **24** — ▲ **408** Teenage Mutant Ninja Turtles .... [V] **$12** SBK 91066
Judith Hoag/Elias Koteas

Every Heart Needs A Home [St. Paul]	9.95 [Spunkadelic]	This Is What We Do [M.C. Hammer]
Family [Riff]	Shredder's Suite [John Du Prez]	**Turtle Power!** [Partners In Kryme] 13
Let The Walls Come Down [Johnny Kemp]	**Spin That Wheel** [Hi Tek 3] 69	
	Splinter's Tale (Parts I & II) [John Du Prez]	

Turtle Rhapsody [Orchestra On The Half Shell]

4/13/91 — **30** — **22** — ● **409** Teenage Mutant Ninja Turtles II - The Secret Of The Ooze .... [V] **$12** SBK 96204
Paige Turco/David Warner; above 2 films are based on the live action/animatronics characters created by Kevin Eastman and Peter Laird

DEBUT DATE	PEAK POS	WKS CHR	GOLD	ARTIST — Album Title	$	Label & Number
				Awesome (You Are My Hero) [Ya Kid K] / Back To School [Fifth Platoon] / Cowabunga [Orchestra On The Half Shell]	Creatures Of Habit [Spunkadelic] / Find The Key To Your Life [Cathy Dennis & David Morales] / Moov! [Tribal House] / Ninja Rap [Vanilla Ice]	(That's Your) Consciousness [Dan Hartman] / This World [Magnificent VII]	Tokka & Rahzar: The Monster Mix [Orchestra On The Half Shell]	
1/5/80	80	9	410	"10"	$8	Warner 3399
				Bo Derek/Dudley Moore/Julie Andrews; cp/cd: Henry Mancini		
				Don't Call It Love (includes 2 versions) / Get It On	He Pleases Me / Hot Sand Mexican Band / I Have An Ear For Love	It's Easy To Say (includes 3 versions) / Keyboard Harmony	Ravel: Bolero / Something For Jenny	
1/21/89	101	13	411	Tequila Sunrise ....[V]	$8	Capitol 91185
				Mel Gibson/Michelle Pfeiffer/Kurt Russell/Raul Julia		
				Beyond The Sea [Bobby Darin] 6 / Dead On The Money [Andy Taylor] / Do You Believe In Shame? [Duran Duran] 72	Don't Worry Baby [Everly Brothers & The Beach Boys] / Give A Little Love [Ziggy Marley & The Melody Makers] / Jo Ann's Song [Dave Grusin & David Sanborn]	Recurring Dream [Crowded House] / Surrender To Me [Ann Wilson & Robin Zander] 6 / Tequila Dreams [Dave Grusin & Lee Ritenour]	Unsubstantiated [Church]	
8/31/91	70	6	412	Terminator 2: Judgment Day ....[I]	$12	Varese S. 5335
				Arnold Schwarzenegger/Linda Hamilton/Robert Patrick; cp: Brad Fiedel		
				Attack On Dyson (Sarah's Solution) / Cameron's Inferno / Desert Suite / Escape From The Hospital (And T1000)	Hasta La Vista, Baby (T1000 Freezes) / Helicopter Chase / I'll Be Back / Into The Steel Mill / It's Over (Good-Bye)	Main Title (Theme) / Our Gang Goes To Cyberdyne / Sarah On The Run / Sarah's Dream (Nuclear Nightmare) / Swat Team Attacks	T1000 Terminated / Tanker Chase / Terminator Impaled / Terminator Revives / Trust Me	
4/21/84	111	10	413	Terms Of Endearment .... [I+V]	$8	Capitol 12329
				Shirley MacLaine/Debra Winger/Jack Nicholson; cp: Michael Gore		
				Anything Goes [Ethel Merman] / Aurora's Night Music / End Credits / Gee, Officer Krupke! [Eddie Roll/Grover Dale/Jets]	I'll Miss You, Momma / Last Look / Main Title / Pleasure Dome	Rock-A-Bye Your Baby With A Dixie Melody [Judy Garland] / Terms Of Endearment, Theme From [Michael Gore] 84	This Is My Moment (Garrett & Aurora's Love Theme) / Three Scenes From A Marriage / Wake, The	
5/13/78	10	27	▲ 414	Thank God It's Friday ....[V]	$15	Casablanca 7099 [2]
				Jeff Goldblum/Valerie Landsburg/Debra Winger; includes bonus 12" single		
				After Dark [Pattie Brooks] / Disco Queen [Paul Jabara] / Do You Want The Real Thing [D.C. LaRue] / Find My Way [Cameo] / Floyd's Theme [Natural Juices] / I Wanna Dance [Marathon]	Je T'Aime (Moi Non Plus) [Donna Summer] / Last Dance [Donna Summer] 3 / Leatherman's Theme [Wright Bros. Flying Machine] / Love Masterpiece [Thelma Houston]	Lovin', Livin' And Givin' [Diana Ross] / Sevilla Nights [Santa Esmeralda] / Take It To The Zoo [Sunshine] / Thank God It's Friday [Love And Kisses] 22	Too Hot Ta Trot [Commodores] 24 / Trapped In A Stairway [Paul Jabara] / With Your Love [Donna Summer] / You're The Most Precious Thing In My Life [Love And Kisses]	
6/22/74	128	14	415	That's Entertainment ....[M]	$12	MCA 11002 [2]
				musical highlights from MGM's greatest musicals (1929-58)		
				Aba Daba Honeymoon / American In Paris (medley) / Be My Love / Broadway Ballet (medley) / Broadway Melody / By Myself / Easy To Love (medley) / Get Happy / Gigi Medley / Going Hollywood / Hallelujah / Heigh Ho, The Gang's All Here	Honeysuckle Rose / I Guess I'll Have To Change My Plans / I've Got A Feeling For You / It's A Most Unusual Day / Make 'Em Laugh / Mickey Rooney - Judy Garland Medley / On The Atchison, Topeka & Santa Fe / Overture / Pretty Girl Is Like A Melody	Putting On The Ritz (medley) / Rosalie / Showboat Medley / Singin' In The Rain (includes 5 versions) / Song's Gotta Come From The Heart / That's Entertainment (includes 2 versions) / They Can't Take That Away From Me / Thou Swell	Under The Bamboo Tree / Varsity Drag / Wizard Of Oz Medley / You Made Me Love You (Dear Mr. Gable)	
				That's The Way Of The World - see EARTH, WIND & FIRE		
				Harvey Keitel/Ed Nelson/Cynthia Bostwick/Bert Parks		
6/15/91	54	12	416	Thelma & Louise ....[V]	$12	MCA 10239
				Susan Sarandon/Geena Davis/Harvey Keitel; CD includes bonus track		
				Badlands [Charlie Sexton] / Ballad Of Lucy Jordan [Marianne Faithfull] / Better Not Look Down [B.B. King]	House Of Hope [Toni Childs] / I Can't Untie You From Me [Grayson Hugh] / Kick The Stones [Chris Whitley]	Little Honey [Kelly Willis] / Part Of You, Part Of Me [Glenn Frey] 55 / Tennessee Plates [Charlie Sexton]	Thunderbird [Hans Zimmer] / Wild Nights [Martha Reeves]	
1/22/55	6	8	417	There's No Business Like Show Business ....[M]	$30	Decca 8091
				Ethel Merman/Donald O'Connor/Dan Dailey; sw: Irving Berlin		
				After You Get What You Want, You Don't Want It / Alexander's Ragtime Band / Heat Wave / If You Believe	Lazy / Man Chases A Girl (Until She Catches Him) / Play A Simple Melody	Sailor's Not A Sailor ('Til A Sailor's Been Tattooed) / There's No Business Like Show Business	When The Midnight Choo-Choo Leaves For Alabam'	
				Thief - see TANGERINE DREAM		
				James Caan/Tuesday Weld/Willie Nelson		
12/22/84+	179	4	418	Thief Of Hearts ....[I+V]	$8	Casablanca 822942
				Steven Bauer/Barbara Williams/John Getz; cp/cd: Harold Faltermeyer		
				Collage / Final Confrontation / Just Imagine (Way Beyond Fear) [Beth Anderson & Joe "Bean" Esposito]	Love In The Shadows [Elizabeth Daily] / Love Theme / Passion Play [Annabella]	Stolen Secrets / Tear Me Up [Darwin] / Thief Of Hearts [Melissa Manchester] 86	Thief Of Hearts (instrumental)	
				Third World, Prisoner in The Street - see THIRD WORLD		
				This Is Elvis - see PRESLEY, Elvis		
				This Is Spinal Tap - see SPINAL TAP		
				Christopher Guest/Michael McKean/Harry Shearer		
8/31/68	182	6	419	Thomas Crown Affair, The ....[I]	$12	United Art. 5182
				Steve McQueen/Faye Dunaway/Paul Burke/Jack Weston; cp/cd: Michel Legrand		

DEBUT DATE	PEAK POS	WKS CHR	GOLD	ARTIST — Album Title	$	Label & Number

				Boston Wrangler His Eyes, Her Eyes Windmills Of Your Mind [Noel Harrison]		
				Cash And Carry Man's Castle		
				Chess Game Playing The Field Windmills Of Your Mind		
				Crowning Touch Room Service (Instrumental)		
4/15/67	16	48	● 420	**Thoroughly Modern Millie** .... [M]	$15	Decca 71500
				Julie Andrews/Mary Tyler Moore/Carol Channing; cd: Andre Previn		
				Baby Face Jazz Baby Overture Tapioca, The		
				Do It Again Jewish Wedding Song (Trinkt Le Poor Butterfly		
				Exit Music Chaim) Prelude		
				Intermission Medley Jimmy Rose Of Washington Square		
9/15/73	184	6	421	**Those Glorious MGM Musicals: Show Boat/Annie Get Your Gun** .... [M-R]	$15	MGM 42 [2]
				reissue of *Show Boat*(1-'51) and *Annie Get Your Gun*(3-'50)		
				Anything You Can Do I Might Fall Back On You Ol' Man River You Are Love		
				Bill I've Got The Sun In The Morning There's No Business Like Show You Can't Get A Man With A		
				Can't Help Lovin' Dat Man Life Upon The Wicked Stage Business Gun		
				Doin' What Comes Natur'lly Make Believe They Say It's Wonderful		
				Girl That I Marry My Defenses Are Down Why Do I Love You		
9/15/73	185	7	422	**Those Glorious MGM Musicals: Singin' In The Rain/Easter Parade** .... [M-R]	$15	MGM 40 [2]
				reissue of *Singin' In The Rain*(2-'52) and *Easter Parade* ('48)		
				All I Do Is Dream Of You Fella With An Umbrella Make 'Em Laugh When The Midnight Choo Choo		
				(includes 2 versions) Fit As A Fiddle Moses Leaves For Alabam' (medley)		
				Better Luck Next Time Good Morning Shaking The Blues Away You Are My Lucky Star		
				Broadway Ballet I Love A Piano (medley) Singin' In The Rain You Were Meant For Me		
				Couple Of Swells It Only Happens When I Dance Snooky Ookums (medley)		
				Easter Parade With You Steppin' Out With My Baby		
				Three Tough Guys - see HAYES, Isaac		
				Isaac Hayes/Fred Williamson/Lino Ventura		
12/11/65+	10	28	423	**Thunderball** .... [I]	$25	United Art. 5132
				Sean Connery/Claudine Auger/Adolfo Celi; cp/cd: John Barry		
				Bomb, The Chateau Flight Mr. Kiss Kiss Bang Bang Switching The Body		
				Bond Below Disco Volante Death Of Fiona Search For Vulcan **Thunderball** [Tom Jones] 25		
				Cafe Martinique 007 Spa, The Thunderball (instrumental)		
				Time To Sing, A - see WILLIAMS, Hank Jr.		
				Hank Williams, Jr./Shelley Fabares/Ed Begley		
9/27/80	37	17	424	**Times Square** .... [V]	$10	RSO 4203 [2]
				Tim Curry/Trini Alvarado/Robin Johnson		
				Babylon's Burning [Ruts] Innocent, Not Guilty [Garland Rock Hard [Suzi Quatro] Your Daughter Is One [Robin		
				Damn Dog [Robin Johnson] Jeffreys] Same Old Scene [Roxy Music] Johnson & Trini Alvarado]		
				Down In The Park [Gary Numan] **Life During Wartime** [Talking Take This Town [XTC]		
				Flowers In The City [David Heads] 80 Talk Of The Town [Pretenders]		
				Johansen & Robin Johnson] Night Was Not [Desmond Child **Walk On The Wild Side** [Lou		
				Grinding Halt [Cure] & Rouge] Reed] 16		
				Help Me! [Marcy Levy & Robin Pissing In The River [Patti Smith You Can't Hurry Love [D.L.		
				Gibb] 50 Group] Byron]		
				I Wanna Be Sedated [Ramones] Pretty Boys [Joe Jackson]		
				To Live and Die in L.A. - see WANG CHUNG		
				William L. Peterson/Willem Dafoe/John Turturro/Dean Stockwell		
9/23/67	16	22	425	**To Sir, With Love** .... [I+V]	$15	Fontana 67569
				Sidney Poitier/Judy Geeson/Christian Roberts/Lulu; cp/cd: Ron Grainer		
				Classical Lesson Perhaps I Could Tidy Your Desk Thackeray Loses Temper, Gets Thackeray Reads Letter About		
				Funeral, The An Idea Job		
				It's Getting Harder All The Time Potter's Loss Of Temper In Gym Thackeray Meets Faculty, Then **To Sir With Love** [Lulu] 1		
				[Mindbenders] Stealing My Love From Me [Lulu] Alone		
				Off And Running [Mindbenders] Thackeray And Denham Box In		
				Gym		
				Together Brothers - see LOVE UNLIMITED ORCHESTRA		
				Anthony Wilson/Ahmad Nurradin/Glynn Turman/Owen Pace		
3/21/64	38	23	426	**Tom Jones** .... [I]	$20	United Art. 5113
				Albert Finney/Susannah York/Hugh Griffith; cp/cd: John Addison		
				Born For Trouble I Love You, Sophie Western Love Theme Tom Jones Strut		
				Britannia Rules If He Swing By The String Main Title Tom Strikes Again		
				End Title Ladies Are Irresistible Squire Steps In Trying Times		
				Grim Guardians Of Justice Lean Days Sylvan Misadventures Wine And Women		
3/29/75	2¹	35	● 427	**Tommy** .... [M]	$15	Polydor 9502 [2]
				Roger Daltrey/Ann-Margret/Oliver Reed/Elton John; rock opera; all but 4 songs written by		
				Pete Townshend; also see The Who and Rock Operas ('72)		
				Acid Queen Extra, Extra, Extra 1951 (medley) There's A Doctor		
				Amazing Journey Eyesight To The Blind Pinball Wizard Tommy Can You Hear Me		
				Bernie's Holiday Camp Fiddle About Prologue Tommy's Holiday Camp		
				Captain Walker (medley) Go To The Mirror Sally Simpson We're Not Gonna Take It		
				Champagne I'm Free See Me, Feel Me (medley) Welcome		
				Christmas It's A Boy (medley) Sensation What About The Boy? (medley)		
				Cousin Kevin Listening To You (medley) Smash The Mirror		
				Do You Think It's Alright Miracle Cure Sparks		
				(includes 3 versions) Mother And Son TV Studio		
2/26/83	144	12	428	**Tootsie**	$8	Warner 23781
				Dustin Hoffman/Jessica Lange; mu: Dave Grusin; ly: Alan & Marilyn Bergman		
				Actor's Life (Main Title) **It Might Be You** [Stephen Metamorphosis Blues Tootsie [Stephen Bishop]		
				Don't Let It Get You Down Bishop] Out Of The Rain Working Girl March		
				Media Zap [Stephen Bishop] Sandy's Song		
6/7/86	1⁵	93	▲⁵ 429	**Top Gun** .... [V]	$8	Columbia 40323
				Tom Cruise/Kelly McGillis/Val Kilmer/Anthony Edwards		
				Danger Zone [Kenny Loggins] 2 **Heaven In Your Eyes** Hot Summer Nights [Miami Lead Me On [Teena Marie]		
				Destination Unknown [Marietta] [Loverboy] 12 Sound Machine] Mighty Wings [Cheap Trick]		

DEBUT DATE	PEAK POS	WKS CHR	GOLD	ARTIST — Album Title	$	Label & Number
1/9/65	150	2	430	**Topkapi** ....[I] Melina Mercouri/Peter Ustinov/Maximilian Schell; cp: Manos Hadjidakis	$20	United Art. 5118
2/1/75	158	3	431	**Towering Inferno, The** ....[I] Paul Newman/Steve McQueen/William Holden/Faye Dunaway; cp/cd: John Williams	$12	Warner 2840
12/12/92+	82	9↑	432	**Trespass** ....[V] Bill Paxton/Ice-T/William Sadler/Ice Cube	$12	Sire 26978
12/21/74+	130	8	433	**Trial Of Billy Jack, The** ....[I+V] Tom Laughlin/Delores Taylor; cp/cd: Elmer Bernstein; also see *Billy Jack*	$10	ABC 853
7/31/82	135	5	434	**Tron** ....[I] Jeff Bridges/Bruce Boxleitner; cp: Wendy Carlos; cd: Douglas Gamley; pf: London Philharmonic Orchestra	$8	CBS 37782
8/2/69	77	12	435	**True Grit** ....[I] John Wayne/Glen Campbell/Kim Darby; cp/cd: Elmer Bernstein	$20	Capitol 263
9/19/92	173	1	436	**Twin Peaks - Fire Walk With Me** .... Sheryl Lee/Kyle MacLachlan/Moira Kelly/David Bowie/Chris Isaak; cp: Angelo Badalamenti/David Lynch; 4 of 12 tracks have vocals	$12	Warner 45019
1/21/89	162	12	437	**Twins** ....[V] Arnold Schwarzenegger/Danny DeVito/Kelly Preston/Chloe Webb	$8	WTG 45036
12/3/83+	26	20 ▲	438	**Two Of A Kind** .... John Travolta/Olivia Newton-John/Charles Durning/Scatman Crothers	$8	MCA 6127
7/13/68	24	120 ●	439	**2001: A Space Odyssey** ....[I] Gary Lockwood/Keir Dullea; features classical music by various orchestras	$10	MGM 13
10/10/70	147	7	440	**2001: A Space Odyssey (Volume Two)** .... only a few tracks are from the original soundtrack	$10	MGM 4722
2/2/85	173	5	441	**2010** ....[I] Roy Scheider/John Lithgow/Helen Mirren; cp: David Shire	$8	A&M 5038

Topkapi — track listing:
Playing With The Boys [Kenny Loggins] 60 · Take My Breath Away [Berlin] 1 · Top Gun Anthem [Harold Faltermeyer & Steve Stevens] · Through The Fire [Larry Greene]

Belly Dance · Emeralds, The · In Prison · Lincoln Automobile · Master Thief · Museum Roof · Palace Museum · Screwball Inventor · Searchlight, The · Success! · Sultan's Dagger · Turkish Security · Wrestling Tournament

Towering Inferno, The — track listing:
Architect's Dream · Helicopter Explosion · Lisolette And Harlee · Main Title · Planting The Charges · Something For Susan · Susan And Doug · Trapped Lovers · We May Never Love Like This Again [Maureen McGovern] 83

Trespass — track listing:
Depths Of Hell [Ice-T feat. Daddy Nitro] · Don't Be A 304 [AMG] · Gotta Do What I Gotta Do [Public Enemy] · Gotta Get Over (Taking Loot) [Gang Starr] · I Check My Bank [Sir Mix-A-Lot] · I'm A Playa (Bitch) [Penthouse Players Clique] · I'm Gonna Smoke Him [Donald D] · King Of The Street [Ry Cooder & Jim Keltner] · On The Wall [Black Sheep] · Quick Way Out [W.C. & The Maad Circle] · Trespass [Ice-T & Ice Cube] · You Know What I'm About [Lord Finesse]

Trial Of Billy Jack, The — track listing:
Billy And Jean Reunion · Danny's Song (I Saw Three Ships) [Michael Bolland] · Dreaming And Hoping [Teresa Laughlin] · Freedom School Massacre · Freedom School Parade · Give Peace A Chance · Golden Lady (Farewell To Jean) [Lynn Baker] · How I Need You (Theme) [Michelle Wilson] · Indian Vision · Karate Fight · My Lai Massacre · Shed A Tear (Billy's Home Coming) [Teresa Laughlin]

Tribute To Jack Johnson, A - see DAVIS, Miles

Trick Or Treat - see FASTWAY
Mark Price/Tony Fields/Gene Simmons

Tron — track listing:
Anthem · Creation Of Tron · Ending Titles · Light Sailer · Love Theme · Magic Landings · Miracle And Magician · New Tron And The MCP · 1990's Theme · Only Solutions · Ring Game And Escape · Sea Of Simulation · Tower Music - Let Us Pray · Tron (Theme) · Tron Scherzo · Water Music And Tronaction · We've Got Company · Wormhole

Trouble Man - see GAYE, Marvin
Robert Hooks/Paul Winfield/Ralph Waite/Paula Kelly

Truck Turner - see HAYES, Isaac
Isaac Hayes/Yaphet Kotto

True Grit — track listing:
Big Trail · Chen Lee And The General · Cogburn Country · Dastardly Deed · Mattie And Little Blackie · Papa's Things · Rooster · True Grit [Glen Campbell] 35 · True Grit (instrumental)

Twin Peaks - Fire Walk With Me — track listing:
Best Friends · Black Dog Runs At Night [Thought Gang] · Don't Do Anything (I Wouldn't Do) · Moving Through Time · Pine Float · Pink Room · Questions In A World Of Blue [Julee Cruise] · Real Indication [Thought Gang] · Sycamore Trees [Jimmy Scott] · Twin Peaks - Fire Walk With Me (Theme) · Twin Peaks Montage · Voice Of Love

Twins — track listing:
Brother To Brother [Spinners] · Going To Santa Fe [Randy Edelman] · I Only Have Eyes For You [Marilyn Scott] · I'd Die For This Dance [Jeff Beck feat. Nicolette Larson] · It's Too Late [Nayobe] · Main Title Theme [Georges Delerue] · No Way Of Knowin' [Henry Lee Summer] · Train Kept A-Rollin' [Jeff Beck feat. Andrew Roachford] · Turtle Shoes [Bobby McFerrin & Herbie Hancock] · Twins [Philip Bailey & Little Richard] · Yakety Yak [2 Live Crew]

Two For The Road - see MANCINI, Henry
Audrey Hepburn/Albert Finney/Eleanor Bron/William Daniels

Two Of A Kind — track listing:
Ask The Lonely [Journey] · Catch 22 (2 Steps Forward, 3 Steps Back) [Steve Kipner] · It's Gonna Be Special [Patti Austin] 82 · Livin' In Desperate Times [Olivia Newton-John] 31 · Night Music [David Foster] · Perfect One [Boz Scaggs] · Prima Donna [Chicago] · Shaking You [Olivia Newton-John] · Take A Chance [Olivia Newton-John & John Travolta] · Twist Of Fate [Olivia Newton-John] 5

200 Motels - see ZAPPA, Frank
Frank Zappa/Ringo Starr/Theodore Bikel

2001: A Space Odyssey — track listing:
Atmospheres · Gayane Ballet Suite (Adagio) · Lux Aeterna · Requiem For Soprano, Mezzo Soprano, Two Mixed Choirs And Orchestra · Strauss: The Blue Danube · "2001" A Space Odyssey [Berlin Philharmonic] 90

2001: A Space Odyssey (Volume Two) — track listing:
Berceuse From "Gayne Ballet Suite" · Coppelia · Entflieht Auf Leichten Kahnen · Lontano · Margarethe · Strauss: Waltzes From "Der Rosenkavalier" · String Quartet (5th Movement) · Volumina · "2001" A Space Odyssey [Berlin Philharmonic] 90

DEBUT DATE	PEAK POS	WKS CHR	GOLD	ARTIST — Album Title	$	Label & Number

| | | | | Also Sprach Zarathustra (medley)   Earth (medley)   Probe   2010 [Andy Summers]
Bowman   Earth Fallout (medley)   Reactivating Discovery   Visitation (medley)
Countdown (medley)   New Worlds (Theme)   Space (medley)
Nova (medley)   Space Linkup (medley) | | |

UHF - see YANKOVIC, "Weird Al"
"Weird Al" Yankovic/Kevin McCarthy/Michael Richards/David Bowe

Under The Cherry Moon - see PRINCE
Prince/Jerome Benton/Kristin Scott Thomas/Steven Berkoff

| 7/18/64 | 11 | 33 | 442 | **Unsinkable Molly Brown, The** .... [M] | $12 | MGM 4232 |

Debbie Reynolds/Harve Presnell; sw: Meredith Willson; cd: Robert Armbruster; also see Original Cast ('60)

Belly Up To The Bar, Boys   He's My Friend   Leadville Johnny Brown   Up Where The People Are
Colorado, My Home   I Ain't Down Yet   (Soliloquy)
Dolce Far Niente   I'll Never Say No (3 versions)   Overture

| 2/1/92 | 114 | 9 | 443 | Until The End Of The World .... [V] | $12 | Warner 26707 |

William Hurt/Solveig Dommartin/Rudiger Vogler/Sam Neill

Adversary, The [Crime & The City Solution]   Finale [Graeme Revell]   It Takes Time [Patti Smith & Fred Smith]   Sleeping In The Devil's Bed [Daniel Lanois]
Calling All Angels [Jane Siberry with k.d. lang]   Fretless [R.E.M.]   Last Night Sleep [Can]   Summer Kisses, Winter Tears [Julee Cruise]
Humans From Earth [T-Bone Burnett]   Love Theme [Graeme Revell]   Claire's Theme [Graeme Revell]   (I'll Love You) Till The End Of The World [Nick Cave & The Bad Seeds]   Move With Me [Neneh Cherry]   Until The End Of The World [U2]
Days [Elvis Costello]   Opening Titles [Graeme Revell]   What's Good [Lou Reed]
Death's Door [Depeche Mode]   Sax And Violins [Talking Heads]

Up In Smoke - see CHEECH & CHONG
Cheech Marin/Tommy Chong/Stacy Keach

| 5/12/84 | 185 | 3 | 444 | Up The Creek .... [V] | $8 | Pasha 39333 |

Tim Matheson/Jennifer Runyon/Dan Monahan/Stephen Furst

Chasin' The Sky [Beach Boys]   Great Expectations (You Never Know What To Expect) [Ian Hunter]   Passion In The Dark (One Track Heart) [Danny Spanos]   Two Hearts On The Loose [Randy Bishop]
Get Ready Boy (includes 2 versions) [Shooting Star]   Take It [Shooting Star]   Up The Creek [Cheap Trick]
Heat, The [Heart]   30 Days In The Hole [Kick Axe]

Uptight - see BOOKER T. & THE MG'S
Raymond St. Jacques/Ruby Dee/Frank Silvera

| 5/17/80 | 3 | 47 | ▲ 445 | **Urban Cowboy** .... [V] | $12 | Asylum 90002 [2] |

John Travolta/Debra Winger/Scott Glenn/Madolyn Smith

All Night Long [Joe Walsh] 19   Don't It Make Ya Wanna Dance [Bonnie Raitt]   Here Comes The Hurt Again [Mickey Gilley]   **Lyin' Eyes** [Eagles] 2
Cherokee Fiddle [Johnny Lee]   Falling In Love For The Night [Charlie Daniels Band]   **Look What You've Done To Me** [Boz Scaggs] 14   Nine Tonight [Bob Seger]
Could I Have This Dance [Anne Murray] 33   Hearts Against The Wind [Linda Ronstadt/J.D. Souther]   Lookin' For Love [Johnny Lee] 5   Orange Blossom Special/Hoedown [Gilley's Urban Cowboy Band]
Darlin' [Bonnie Raitt]   Hello Texas [Jimmy Buffett]   Love The World Away [Kenny Rogers] 14   **Stand By Me** [Mickey Gilley] 22
Devil Went Down To Georgia [Charlie Daniels Band] 3   Times Like These [Dan Fogelberg]

| 1/10/81 | 134 | 6 | 446 | Urban Cowboy II .... [V] | $8 | Full Moon 36921 |

more music from the original soundtrack

Cotton-Eyed Joe [Bayou City Beats]   Mammas Don't Let Your Babies Grow Up To Be Cowboys [Mickey Gilley/Johnny Lee]   Orange Blossom Special [Charlie Daniels Band]   Rode Hard And Put Up Wet [Johnny Lee]
Honky Tonk Wine [Mickey Gilley]   Rockin' My Life Away [Mickey Gilley]   **Texas** [Charlie Daniels Band] 91
Jukebox Argument [Mickey Gilley]   Moon Just Turned Blue [J.D. Souther]

Valley, The - see PINK FLOYD
Bulle Ogier/Jean-Pierre Kalfon/the Mapuga Tribe

| 2/3/68 | 11 | 27 | 447 | Valley Of The Dolls .... | $20 | 20th Century 4196 |

Barbara Parkins/Patty Duke/Sharon Tate/Susan Hayward; sw: Dory & Andre Previn; cd: Johnny Williams

Ann At Lawrenceville   Gillian Girl Commercial   It's Impossible   Neely's Career Montage
Chance Meeting   Give A Little More   Jennifer's French Movie   Valley Of The Dolls (Theme)
Come Live With Me   I'll Plant My Own Tree   Jennifer's Recollection

| 6/5/82 | 174 | 4 | 448 | Victor/Victoria .... [M] | $20 | MGM 5407 |

Julie Andrews/James Garner/Robert Preston; mu/cd: Henry Mancini; ly: Leslie Bricusse

Alone In Paris   Crazy World   King's Can-Can   You And Me (includes 2 versions)
Cat And Mouse   Finale   Le Jazz Hot
Chicago, Illinois   Gay Paree   Shady Dame From Seville

| 1/4/64 | 145 | 3 | 449 | Victors, The .... [I] | $30 | Colpix 516 |

George Peppard/George Hamilton/Eli Wallach; cp/cd: Sol Kaplan

French Woman   Magda's Theme   No Other Man   Signora Maria
Have Yourself A Merry Little Christmas   Main Title   Off Limits   Sweet Talk And Death Fight
  March of The Victors   Olive Grove   Wolf Pack
Jean Pierre   My Special Dream   Overture

| 6/29/85 | 38 | 15 | 450 | View To A Kill, A .... [I] | $8 | Capitol 12413 |

Roger Moore/Tanya Roberts/Christopher Walken/Grace Jones; cp/cd: John Barry

Airship To Silicon Valley   Destroy Silicon Valley   May Day Jumps   **View To A Kill** [Duran Duran] 1
Bond Escapes Roller   Golden Gate Fight   Pegasus' Stable   Wine With Stacey
Bond Meets Stacey   He's Dangerous   Snow Job
Bond Underwater   May Day Bombs Out   Tibbett Gets Washed Out

| 3/2/85 | 11 | 23 | ▲ 451 | Vision Quest .... [V] | $8 | Geffen 24063 |

Matthew Modine/Linda Fiorentino/Michael Schoeffling

Change [John Waite] 54   Hot Blooded [Foreigner] 3   I'll Fall In Love Again [Sammy Hagar] 43   Only The Young [Journey] 9
Crazy For You [Madonna] 1   Hungry For Heaven [Dio]   She's On The Zoom [Don Henley]
Gambler [Madonna]   Lunatic Fringe [Red Rider]   Shout To The Top [Style Council]

| 6/30/62 | 33 | 19 | 452 | Walk On The Wild Side .... [I] | $35 | Ava 4 |

Laurence Harvey/Jane Fonda/Capucine; cp/cd: Elmer Bernstein

Doll House   Kitty   Reminiscence   Walk On The Wild Side (includes 2 versions)
Dove   Night Theme   Somewhere In The Used To Be
Finale   Oliver   Terasina
Hallies Jazz   Rejected

SOUNDTRACKS

DEBUT DATE	PEAK POS	WKS CHR	GOLD	ARTIST — Album Title	$	Label & Number

Walt Disney's Fantasia - see Fantasia

8/17/68 — **189** — 3 — **453** — War And Peace ....[I] **$45** Melodiya 2918
Ludmilla Savelyeva/Vyacheslav Tikhonov/Sergei Bondarchuk; cp: Vyacheslav Ovchinnikov; a Russian film production

Approach Of The French Army (medley)	Battle Of Schon Grabern	Finale	Petya And The French Drummer Boy
At The Hunting Lodge	Bolkonsky's Hope Reborn	Intermezzo (medley)	Soldiers' Chorus
Battle Of Borodino	Entrance Of Tsar Alexander I (Polonaise)	Natasha's Waltz	Soldiers' Hymn To The Virgin

5/5/79 — **125** — 8 — **454** — Warriors, The ....[V] **$10** A&M 4761
Michael Beck/Thomas Waites/James Remar/Deborah Van Valkenburg

Baseball Furies Chase [Barry DeVorzon]	In The City [Joe Walsh]	Nowhere To Run [Arnold McCuller]	You're Movin' Too Slow [Johnny Vastano]
Echoes In My Mind [Mandrill]	Last Of An Ancient Breed [Desmond Child]	Warriors (Theme) [Barry DeVorzon]	
Fight, The [Barry DeVorzon]	Love Is A Fire [Genya Ravan]		
In Havana [Kenny Vance]			

Wattstax - see CONCERTS/FESTIVALS

2/16/74 — **20** — 15 — ● **455** — Way We Were, The ....[I] **$8** Columbia 32830
Barbra Streisand/Robert Redford/Bradford Dillman; cp: Marvin Hamlisch

Did You Know It Was Me?	Look What I've Got	**Way We Were** [Barbra Streisand] **1**	Wrap Your Troubles In Dreams (And Dream Your Troubles Away)
In The Mood	Red Sails In The Sunset	Way We Were (instrumental)	
Katie	Remembering		
Like Pretty	River Stay Way From My Door		

3/7/92 — **1²** — 47 — ▲ **456** — **Wayne's World** ....[V] **$12** Reprise 26805
Mike Myers/Dana Carvey/Rob Lowe/Tia Carrere

Ballroom Blitz [Tia Carrere]	**Foxey Lady** [Jimi Hendrix] **67**	Rock Candy [BulletBoys]	Wayne's World Theme [Wayne & Garth]
Bohemian Rhapsody [Queen] **2**	Hot And Bothered [Cinderella]	Sikamikanico [Red Hot Chili Peppers]	Why You Wanna Break My Heart [Tia Carrere]
Dream Weaver [Gary Wright]	Loving Your Lovin' [Eric Clapton]	Time Machine [Black Sabbath]	
Feed My Frankenstein [Alice Cooper]	Ride With Yourself [Rhino Bucket]		

8/31/85 — **105** — 11 — **457** — Weird Science ....[V] **$8** MCA 6146
Anthony Michael Hall/Ilan Mitchell-Smith/Kelly LeBrock

Circle, The [Max Carl]	Eighties [Killing Joke]	Turn It On [Kim Wilde]	Why Don't Pretty Girls (Look At Me) [Wild Men Of Wonga]
Deep In The Jungle [Wall Of Voodoo]	Forever [Taxxi]	Weird Romance [Ira & The Geeks]	
Do Not Disturb (Knock, Knock) [Broken Homes]	Method To My Madness [Lords Of The New Church]	**Weird Science** [Oingo Boingo] **45**	
	Private Joy [Cheyne]		

10/23/61+ — **1⁵⁴** — 198 — ▲³ **458** — **West Side Story** ....[M] **$10** Columbia 2070
Natalie Wood/Richard Beymer/Rita Moreno/George Chakiris; mu: Leonard Bernstein; ly: Stephen Sondheim; cd: Johnny Green; also see Leonard Bernstein/Ferrante & Teicher/Stan Kenton/Original Cast ('58)

America	Gee, Officer Krupke!	Maria	Rumble, The
Boy Like That (medley)	I Feel Pretty	One Hand, One Heart	Something's Coming
Cool	I Have A Love (medley)	Prologue	Somewhere
Dance At The Gym Medley	Jet Song	Quintet	Tonight

What Did You Do In The War, Daddy? - see MANCINI, Henry
James Coburn/Dick Shawn/Aldo Ray/Carroll O'Connor

8/7/65 — **14** — 22 — **459** — What's New Pussycat? ....[I+V] **$15** United Art. 5117
Peter Sellers/Peter O'Toole; mu: Burt Bacharach; ly: Hal David

Bookworm (medley)	Here I Am (medley) (instrumental)	My Little Red Book [Manfred Mann]	Walk On The Wild Wharf
Catch As Catch Can	High Temperature, Low Resistance	Pussy Cats On Parade	**What's New Pussycat?** [Tom Jones] **3**
Chateau Chantel		School For Anatomy (medley)	
Downhill And Shady		Stripping Really Isn't Sexy, Is It?	
Here I Am [Dionne Warwick] **65**	Marriage, French Style (medley)		

What's Up, Tiger Lily? - see LOVIN' SPOONFUL
Woody Allen/China Lee/Louise Lasser (voice only)

When Harry Met Sally - see CONNICK, Harry Jr.
Billy Crystal/Meg Ryan/Carrie Fisher/Bruno Kirby

When The Boys Meet The Girls - see FRANCIS, Connie
Connie Francis/Harve Presnell/Herman's Hermits

4/11/92 — **92** — 8 — **460** — White Men Can't Jump ....[V] **$12** EMI 98414
Wesley Snipes/Woody Harrelson/Rosie Perez

Can You Come Out And Play [O'Jays]	I'm Going Up [Bebe & Cece Winans]	Just A Closer Walk With Thee [Venice Beach Boys]	Watch Me Do My Thang [Lipstick]
Don't Ever Let 'Em See You Sweat [Go West]	If I Lose [Aretha Franklin]	Let Me Make It Up To You Tonight [Jody Watley]	**White Men Can't Jump** [Riff] **90**
Hook, The [Queen Latifah]	Jump For It [Jesse Johnson]	Sympin Ain't Easy [Boyz II Men]	

11/2/85+ — **17** — 26 — ● **461** — White Nights ....[V] **$8** Atlantic 81273
Mikhail Baryshnikov/Gregory Hines/Geraldine Page/Helen Mirren

Far Post [Robert Plant]	People Have Got To Move [Jenny Burton]	**Prove Me Wrong** [David Pack] **95**	Snake Charmer [John Hiatt]
My Love Is Chemical [Lou Reed]	People On A String [Roberta Flack]	**Separate Lives** [Phil Collins & Marilyn Martin] **1**	Tapdance [David Foster]
Other Side Of The World [Chaka Khan]			This Is Your Day [Sandy Stewart & Nile Rodgers]

White Rock - see WAKEMAN, Rick

9/3/66 — **119** — 5 — **462** — Who's Afraid Of Virginia Woolf? ....[I] **$35** Warner 1656
Elizabeth Taylor/Richard Burton; cp/cd: Alex North

Bergin	Fleece	Party Is Over	Snap (medley)
Colloquy	Martha	Prologue - Act II	Sunday, Tomorrow All Day
Epilogue	Moon Music	Sad, Sad, Sad	Virginia Woolf Rock (medley)

Who's That Girl - see MADONNA
Madonna/Griffin Dunne/Haviland Morris/John McMartin/Sir John Mills

Wild Angels, The - see ALLAN, Davie
Peter Fonda/Nancy Sinatra/Bruce Dern/Dianne Ladd; cp/cd: Mike Curb

10/18/69 — **192** — 2 — **463** — Wild Bunch, The ....[I] **$75** Warner 1814
William Holden/Ernest Borgnine/Robert Ryan; cp/cd: Jerry Fielding

DEBUT DATE	PEAK POS	WKS CHR	G O L D	ARTIST — Album Title	$	Label & Number

				Adelita Assault On The Train And Bodega El Bodega De Bano End Credits (La Golondrina)		
				Adventures On The High Road Escape Dirge Main Title		
				Aurora Mi Amor Drinking Song Wild Bunch (Song)		

7/6/68   **12**   32   464   Wild In The Streets .... **$25**   Tower 5099

Christopher Jones/Diana Varsi/Shelley Winters/Richard Pryor; sw: Barry Mann/Cynthia Weil; cd: Mike Curb

Fifty Two Per Cent [Max Frost & The Troopers]	Free Lovin' [Max Frost & The Troopers]	Love To Be Your Man [Max Frost & The Troopers] 22	Shape Of Things To Come [Max Frost & The Troopers]
Fourteen Or Fight [Max Frost & The Troopers]	Listen To The Music [Second Time]	Psychedelic Senate [Senators]	Shelly In Camp [Gurus]
		Sally Le Roy [Second Time]	Wild In The Streets [Jerry Howard]

10/21/78   **40**   17   ● 465   Wiz, The... [M] **$12**   MCA 14000 [2]

Diana Ross/Michael Jackson; sw: Charlie Smalls; cd: Quincy Jones; a soul musical version of *The Wizard Of Oz*; also see Original Cast ('75)

Be A Lion	**Ease On Down The Road** [Diana Ross & Michael Jackson] 41	Home (medley)	Now Watch Me Dance (medley)
Believe In Yourself		(I'm A) Mean Ole Lion	Poppy Girls
Brand New Day (Everybody Rejoice)	Emerald City Medley	Is This What Feeling Gets? (Dorothy's Theme)	Slide Some Oil To Me (medley)
Can I Go On?	End Of The Yellow Brick Road	Liberation Agitato	So You Wanted To See The Wizard
Don't Nobody Bring Me No Bad News	Feeling That We Have	Liberation Ballet (medley)	Soon As I Get Home (medley)
	Glinda's Theme	Main Title	What Would I Do If I Could Feel?
	Good Witch Glinda	March Of The Munchkins (medley)	**You Can't Win (Part 1)** [Michael Jackson] 81
	He's The Wizard (medley)		

Woman in Red, The - see WONDER, Stevie
Gene Wilder/Charles Grodin/Judith Ivey/Gilda Radner

Wonderwall - see HARRISON, George

Woodstock - see CONCERTS/FESTIVALS

3/11/89   **45**   14   466   Working Girl... [V] **$8**   Arista 8593

Harrison Ford/Sigourney Weaver/Melanie Griffith

Carlotta's Heart [Carly Simon]	**Let The River Run** [Carly Simon] 49	Man That Got Away [Rob Mounsey/George Young/Chip Jackson/Grady Tate]	Poor Butterfly [Sonny Rollins]
I'm So Excited [Pointer Sisters] 9	Looking Through Katherine's House [Carly Simon]		Scar, The [Carly Simon]
In Love [Carly Simon]			
Lady In Red [Chris DeBurgh] 3			

Xanadu - see NEWTON-JOHN, Olivia, and/or ELECTRIC LIGHT ORCHESTRA
Olivia Newton-John/Michael Beck/Gene Kelly

8/7/65   **82**   10   467   Yellow Rolls-Royce, The .... **$25**   MGM 4292

Ingrid Bergman/Rex Harrison/Shirley MacLaine/Omar Shariff; cp/cd: Riz Ortolani

David's Square In Florence	Forget Domani (includes 2 versions) [Katyna Ranieri]	Mae	Pisa
Eloise (includes 2 versions)	Going To Soriano	Main Title	
Finale		Now And Then	

Yellow Submarine - see BEATLES

Yentl - see STREISAND, Barbra
Barbra Streisand/Mandy Patinkin/Amy Irving

Yes, Giorgio - see PAVAROTTI, Luciano
Luciano Pavarotti/Kathryn Harrold/Eddie Albert

10/29/77   **17**   15   ● 468   You Light Up My Life .... **$12**   Arista 4159

Didi Conn/Joe Silver/Melanie Mayron; cp/cd: Joseph Brooks

California Daydreams	Morning Of My Life	Rolling The Chords	You Light Up My Life (Instrumental)
Do You Have A Piano	Phone Call	**You Light Up My Life** [Kacey Cisyk] 80	
It's A Long Way From Brooklyn	Ride To Chris's House		

7/15/67   **27**   26   469   You Only Live Twice .... [I] **$20**   United Art. 5155

Sean Connery/Donald Pleasence; cp/cd: John Barry

Bond Averts World War Three	Drop In The Ocean	Mountains And Sunsets	**You Only Live Twice** [Nancy Sinatra] 44
Capsule In Space	Fight At Kobe Dock (medley)	Tanaka's World	
Countdown For Blofeld	Helga (medley)	Wedding, The	
Death Of Aki	James Bond - Astronaut?		

You're A Big Boy Now - see LOVIN' SPOONFUL
Peter Kastner/Rip Torn/Geraldine Page/Julie Harris

Young At Heart - see DAY, Doris
Doris Day/Frank Sinatra/Gig Young

3/22/75   **128**   8   470   Young Frankenstein .... **$12**   ABC 870

Gene Wilder/Peter Boyle/Marty Feldman/Teri Garr; includes storyline excerpts

Frau Blucher	Main Title [John Morris]	Riot Is An Ugly Thing	Young Frankenstein (Theme) [Rhythm Heritage]
Grandfather's Private Library	Monster Talks	That's Fron-Kon-Steen!	
He Was My Boyfriend	My Name Is Frankenstein!	Train Ride To Transylvania/The Doctor Meets Igor	
He's Broken Loose	Puttin' On The Ritz [Gene Wilder & Peter Boyle]	Wedding Night	
It's Alive!			

Young Guns II - see BON JOVI, Jon
Emilio Estevez/Kiefer Sutherland/Lou D. Phillips/Christian Slater

3/1/86   **166**   6   471   Youngblood .... [V] **$8**   RCA 7172

Rob Lowe/Ed Lauter/Cynthia Gibb/Patrick Swayze

Cut You Down To Size [Starship]	Soldier Of Fortune [Marc Jordan]	Stand In The Fire [Mickey Thomas]	Winning Is Everything [Autograph]
Footsteps [Nick Gilder]	**Something Real (Inside Me/Inside You)** [Mr. Mister] 29	Talk Me Into It [Glenn Jones]	
I'm A Real Man [John Hiatt]			
Opening Score [William Orbit]			

Youngblood - see WAR
Bryan O'Dell/Ren Woods

Your Cheatin' Heart - see WILLIAMS, Hank Jr.
George Hamilton/Susan Oliver/Red Buttons/Arthur O'Connell

4/11/70   **128**   8   472   Z .... **$20**   Columbia 3370

Yves Montand/Irene Papas; cp: Mikis Theodorakis; cd: Bernard Gerard

Arrival Of Helen	Finale	Main Title (O Andonis)	To Palikari Echi Kaimo
Batucada	Idep Otsaley Ot	Pios Den Mila Yia Ti Lambri	To Yelasto Pedi (includes 2 versions)
Cafe Rock	La Course De Manuel (Chase)	Safti Gitonia	

DEBUT DATE	PEAK POS	WKS CHR	G O L D	ARTIST — Album Title	$	Label & Number

Ziggy Stardust - The Motion Picture - see BOWIE, David

| 5/1/65 | **26** | 79 | 473 | Zorba The Greek ....[I] | **$10** | 20th Century 4167 |

Anthony Quinn/Irene Papas; cp/cd: Mikis Theodorakis; also see Original Cast *Zorba* ('69-an adaptation)

Always Look For Trouble	Free	One Unforgiveable Sin	Zorba The Greek (Theme)
Clever People And Grocers	Full Catastrophe	Questions Without Answers	Zorba's Dance
Fire Inside	Life Goes On	That's Me - Zorba!	

SOUNDTRACK COMPILATIONS

| 2/8/69 | **198** | 2 | 1 | Best Of The Soundtracks .... | **$10** | Tower 5148 |

from 5 American International motion pictures

Billy Jack's Theme *[Sidewalk Sounds]*	**Devil's Angels** *[David Allan & The Arrows]* **97**	Listen To The Music *[Second Time]*	**Shape Of Things To Come** *[Max Frost & The Troopers]* **22**
Blue's Theme *[Davie Allan & The Arrows]* **37**	Hell Rider *[Mike Curb Congregation]*	Love Children *[Ron Stein]*	**Wild Angels, Theme From The** *[Davie Allan & The Arrows]* **99**
		Psych-Out *[Ron Stein]*	Wild Orgy *[Hands Of Time]*

| 1/23/61 | **2³** | 81 | 2 | Great Motion Picture Themes ....[I] | **$10** | United Art. 3122 |

Apartment, Theme From The *[Ferrante & Teicher]* **10**	Green Leaves Of Summer *[Nick Perito]*	**Never On Sunday** *[Don Costa]* **19**	**Unforgiven (The Need For Love), Theme From The** *[Don Costa]* **27**
Big Country, Theme From The *[Jerome Moross]*	Horse Soldiers, Theme From The *[David Buttolph]*	On The Beach *[Mitchell Powell]*	Vikings, Theme From The *[Mario Nascimbene]*
Diggin' In The Morning *[Elmer Bernstein]*	I Want To Live *[Gerry Mulligan]*	Smile *[Alfred Newman]*	Wonderful Country, Theme From The *[Alex North]*
Exodus *[Ferrante & Teicher]* **2**	**Magnificent Seven** *[Al Caiola]* **35**	Solomon And Sheba, Theme From *[Mario Nascimbene]*	
		Some Like It Hot *[Adolph Deutsch]*	

| 9/25/61 | **129** | 5 | 3 | Great Motion Picture Themes (More Original Sound Tracks And Hit Music) ....[I] | **$10** | United Art. 3158 |

Bonanza *[Al Caiola]* **19**	Houseboat, Love Song From *[Don Costa]*	Never On Sunday *[Melina Mercouri]*	Take The A Train *[Louis Armstrong]*
Diggin' In The Morning *[Elmer Bernstein]*	I Wanna Be Loved By You *[Marilyn Monroe]*	Odds Against Tomorrow *[Modern Jazz Quartet]*	Where Is Your Heart *[Don Costa]*
Elmer Gantry, Main Title From *[Andre Previn]*	Misfits, Theme From The *[Don Costa]*	**One Eyed Jacks, Love Theme From** *[Ferrante & Teicher]* **37**	
Gone With The Wind, Theme From *[Ferrante & Teicher]*	Naked Maja, Theme From The *[Mitchell Powell]*	Porgy And Bess, Theme From *[Bill Potts]*	
Goodbye Again, Theme From *[Ferrante & Teicher]* **85**			

| 3/13/65 | **72** | 27 | 4 | Music To Read James Bond By .... | **$10** | United Art. 6415 |

Black On Pink *[Sir Julian]*	From Russia With Love *[Al Caiola]*	Goldfinger *[Perez Prado]*	Living It Up *[Leasebreakers]*
007 *[John Barry]*	Girl Trouble *[John Barry]*	Jamaica Jump Up *[Monty Norman]*	Underneath The Mango Tree *[La Playa]*
Elegant Venus *[Dick Ruedebusch]*	Golden Girl *[LeRoy Holmes]*	James Bond Theme *[Ferrante & Teicher]*	
	Goldfinger *[Shirley Bassey]* **8**		

| 5/19/62 | **31** | 16 | 5 | Original Motion Picture Hit Themes .... | **$10** | United Art. 3197 |

Blue Hawaii (medley) *[Alfred Newman]*	King Of Kings *[Ferrante & Teicher]*	Maria *[Ferrante & Teicher]*	Take The "A" Train *[Louis Armstrong]*
El Cid *[Ferrante & Teicher]*	Let's Get Together *[Tutti Camarata]*	Moon River *[Ferrante & Teicher]*	**Tonight** *[Ferrante & Teicher]* **8**
Fanny *[Ferrante & Teicher]*	Lili Marleen *[Ralph Marterie]*	One, Two, Three Waltz *[Roger Wayne]*	**Town Without Pity** *[Gene Pitney]* **13**
Guns Of Navarone *[Al Caiola]*	Love Look Away (medley) *[Alfred Newman]*	Pocketful Of Miracles *[Walter Scharf]*	
Happy Thieve's Theme *[Nick Perito]*			

DEBUT DATE	PEAK POS	WKS CHR	GOLD	ARTIST — Album Title	$	Label & Number

ORIGINAL CASTS

The original cast stars are listed below the title.

9/23/78	**161**	5		**1 Ain't Misbehavin'**	**$10**	RCA 2965 [2]

Ken Page/Nell Carter/Andre De Shields; based on the life and compositions of Fats Waller

Ain't Misbehavin'	Handful Of Keys	Ladies Who Sing With The Band
Black And Blue	Honeysuckle Rose	Lookin' Good But Feelin' Bad
Cash For Your Trash	How Ya Baby	Lounging At The Waldorf
Entr'acte	I've Got A Feeling I'm Falling	Mean To Me
Fat And Greasy	Jitterbug Waltz	Off-Time
Finale	Joint Is Jumpin'	Reefer Song
Find Out What They Like	Keepin' Out Of Mischief Now	Spreadin' Rhythm Around

Squeeze Me		
'Tain't Nobody's Biz-ness If I Do		
That Ain't Right		
Viper's Drag		
When The Nylons Bloom Again		
Yacht Club Swing		
Your Feet's Too Big		

4/21/62	**21**	16		**2 All American**	**$30**	Columbia 2160

Ray Bolger/Eileen Herlie/Ron Husmann; mu: Charles Strouse; ly: Lee Adams

Fight Song (medley)	I've Just Seen Her (As Nobody	Nightlife
Finale	Else Has Seen Her)	Once Upon A Time
Have A Dream	If I Were You	Our Children
I Couldn't Have Done It Alone	It's Fun To Think	Overture
I'm Fascinating	Melt Us (medley)	Physical Fitness (medley)

Real Me	
We Speak The Same Language	
What A Country! (medley)	
Which Way?	

6/18/77	**81**	39	▲	**3 Annie**	**$8**	Columbia 34712

Andrea McArdle/Reid Shelton; mu: Charles Strouse; ly: Martin Charnin; also see Soundtrack ('82)

Annie	Little Girls	Something Was Missing
Easy Street	Maybe	Tomorrow
Hard-Knock Life	N.Y.C.	We'd Like To Thank You
I Don't Need Anything But You	New Deal For Christmas	Herbert Hoover
I Think I'm Gonna Like It Here	Overture	

You Won't Be An Orphan For Long	
You're Never Fully Dressed Without A Smile	

12/30/57+	**12**	5		**4 Annie Get Your Gun**	**$25**	Capitol 913

Mary Martin/John Raitt; sw: Irving Berlin; San Francisco/Los Angeles production selected by NBC for a TV spectacular; introduced on Broadway in 1946, starring Ethel Merman

Anything You Can Do	I Got The Sun In The Morning	My Defenses Are Down
Doin' What Comes Natur'ly	I'm A Bad, Bad Man	Overture
Girl That I Marry	I'm An Indian Too	There's No Business Like Show
I Got Lost In His Arms	Moonshine Lullaby	Business

They Say It's Wonderful	
You Can't Get A Man With A Gun	

8/6/66	**113**	7		**5 Annie Get Your Gun**	**$10**	RCA 1124

Ethel Merman/Bruce Yarnell; sw: Irving Berlin; new production from the Music Theater of Lincoln Center

Anything You Can Do	I Got Lost In His Arms	My Defenses Are Down
Colonel Buffalo Bill	I Got The Sun In The Morning	Old Fashioned Wedding
Doin' What Comes Natur'lly	I'm A Bad, Bad Man	Overture
Finale	I'm An Indian Too	There's No Business Like Show
Girl That I Marry	Moonshine Lullaby	Business

They Say It's Wonderful	
You Can't Get A Man With A Gun	

5/23/70	**168**	7		**6 Applause**	**$15**	ABC 11

Lauren Bacall/Robert Mandan; mu: Charles Strouse; ly: Lee Adams; based on the film All About Eve

Applause	Fasten Your Seat Belts	One Hallow'een
Backstage Babble	Finale	One Of A Kind
Best Night Of My Life	Good Friends	Overture
But Alive	Hurry Back	She's No Longer A Gypsy

Something Greater	
Think How It's Gonna Be	
Welcome To The Theater	
Who's That Girl	

12/17/66+	**113**	9		**7 Apple Tree, The**	**$20**	Columbia 3020

Barbara Harris/Larry Blyden/Alan Alda; mu: Jerry Bock; ly: Sheldon Harnick

Apple Tree (Forbidden Fruit)	Friends	I've Got What You Want
Beautiful, Beautiful World	Go To Sleep, Whatever You Are	It's A Fish
Eve	Gorgeous	Lady Or The Tiger? (medley)
Feelings	Here In Eden (medley)	Make Way (medley)
Finale	I Know and Wealth	Oh, To Be A Movie Star (medley)
Forbidden Love (In Gaul)	I'll Tell You A Truth (medley)	Tiger, Tiger

What Makes Me Love Him?	
Which Door (medley)	
Who Is She?	
You Are Not Real	

2/20/65	**143**	2		**8 Bajour**	**$30**	Columbia 2700

Chita Rivera/Nancy Dussault/Herschel Bernardi; sw: Walter Marks

Bajour	I Can	Mean
Guarantees (medley)	Living Simply	Move Over, America
Haggle, The	Love Is A Chance (medley)	Move Over, New York
Honest Man	Love-Line	Must It Be Love?

Overture	
Soon	
Where Is The Tribe For Me?	
Words, Words, Words	

5/8/65	**138**	4		**9 Baker Street (A Musical Adventure Of Sherlock Holmes)** ...	**$25**	MGM 7000

Fritz Weaver/Inga Swenson; sw: Marian Grudeff and Raymond Jessel; adapted from the stories by Sir Arthur Conan Doyle

Cold Clear World	I'm In London Again	Letters
Finding Words For Spring	It's So Simple	Married Man
I Shall Miss You	Jewelry	Overture
I'd Do It Again	Leave It To Us, Guv	Pursuit

Roof Space	
What A Night This Is Going To Be	

2/9/57	**20**	1		**10 Bells Are Ringing**	**$15**	Columbia 5170

Judy Holliday/Sydney Chaplin; mu: Jule Styne; ly: Betty Comden and Adolph Green

Bells Are Ringing	I'm Goin' Back	Just In Time
Drop That Name	Is It A Crime?	Long Before I Knew You
Hello, Hello There!	It's A Perfect Relationship	Midas Touch
I Met A Girl	It's A Simple Little System	Mu-Cha-Cha

On My Own	
Overture	
Party's Over	
Salzburg	

12/26/64+	**132**	8		**11 Ben Franklin In Paris**	**$30**	Capitol 2191

Robert Preston/Ulla Sallert; mu: Mark Sandrich, Jr.; ly: Sidney Michaels

Balloon Is Ascending	How Laughable It Is	To Be Alone With You
Diane Is (medley)	I Invented Myself	Too Charming
Finale	I Love The Ladies	We Sail The Seas
God Bless The Human Elbow	Look For Small Pleasure	Whatever Became Of Old
Half The Battle	(medley)	Temple?
Hic Haec Hoc	Overture	

When I Dance With The Person I Love	
You're In Paris	

12/15/62+	**73**	20		**12 Beyond The Fringe**	**$30**	Capitol 1792

Dudley Moore/Alan Bennett/Peter Cook/Jonathan Miller; primarily consists of comedy excerpts

DEBUT DATE	PEAK POS	WKS CHR	GOLD	ARTIST — Album Title	$	Label & Number
				Aftermyth Of War / Deutscher Chansons / Sadder And Wiser Beaver / Take A Pew And The Same To You / End Of The World / Sitting On The Bench Bollard / Portrait From Memory / So That's The Way You Like It		
6/14/69	195	3	13	**Boys In The Band, The** .... Kenneth Nelson/Peter White; album is all dialogue from the play	$20	A&M 6001 [2]
7/18/60+	12	61	14	**Bye Bye Birdie** .... Chita Rivera/Dick Van Dyke/Kay Medford/Dick Gautier (Conrad Birdie); mu: Charles Strouse; ly: Lee Adams; also see Soundtrack ('63)	$20	Columbia 5510
				Baby, Talk To Me / Hymn For A Sunday Evening / One Boy / Rosie English Teacher / Kids / One Last Kiss / Spanish Rose Honestly Sincere / Lot Of Livin' To Do / Overture / Telephone Hour How Lovely To Be A Woman / Normal American Boy / Put On A Happy Face / What Did I Ever See In Him?		
1/7/67	37	39	15	**Cabaret** .... Jill Haworth/Jack Gilford/Bert Convy/Lotte Lenya; mu: John Kander; ly: Fred Ebb; also see Soundtrack ('72)	$15	Columbia 3040
				Cabaret / If You Could See Her (The / Money Song / Two Ladies Don't Tell Mama / Gorilla Song) / Perfectly Marvelous / What Would You Do? Entr'acte / It Couldn't Please Me More / So What? / Why Should I Wake Up? Finale / Married / Telephone Song / Willkommen Meeskite / Tomorrow Belongs to Me		
1/23/61	1⁶	265	●	**Camelot** .... Richard Burton/Julie Andrews/Robert Goulet; mu: Frederick Loewe; ly: Alan Jay Lerner; also see Percy Faith and Soundtrack ('67)	$20	Columbia 2031
				Before I Gaze At You Again / Guenevere / If Ever I Would Leave You / Simple Joys Of Maidenhood C'est Moi / How To Handle A Woman / Lusty Month Of May / Then You May Take Me To The Camelot / I Loved You Once In Silence / Overture (medley) / Fair Fie On Goodness! / I Wonder What The King Is / Parade / What Do The Simple Folks Do Follow Me / Doing Tonight (medley) / Seven Deadly Virtues		
4/19/69	171	4	17	**Canterbury Tales** .... George Rose/Hermione Baddeley/Martyn Green; mu: Richard Hill and John Hawkins; ly: Nevill Coghill	$15	Capitol 229
				April Love (medley) / Darling, Let Me Teach You How / If She Has Never Loved Before / Pilgrim Riding Music (medley) Beer Is Best (medley) / To Kiss / (medley) / Song Of Welcome (medley) Canterbury Day (medley) / Goodnight Hymn (medley) / It Depends On What You're At / There's The Moon Chaucer's Epilogue (medley) / Hymen, Hymen (medley) / Love Will Conquer All / What Do Women Want Chaucer's Prologue (medley) / I Am All A-Blaze / Mug Dance (medley) / Where Are The Girls Of Come On And Marry Me, Honey / I Have A Noble Cock / Overture (medley) / Yesterday I'll Give My Love A Ring / Pear Tree Quintet		
5/29/61	1¹	67		**Carnival** .... Anna Maria Alberghetti/James Mitchell; sw: Bob Merrill	$20	MGM 3946
				Beautiful Candy / I've Got To Find A Reason / Opening - Direct From Vienna / Yum, Ticky, Ticky, Tum, Tum Everybody Likes You / It Was Always You (includes 2 / Rich, The (medley) / (medley) Grand Imperial Cirque De Paris / versions) / She's My Love Her Face / Love Makes The World Go / Sword, The Rose And The Cape Humming / Around (Theme) / Very Nice Man I Hate Him (medley) / Mira (Can You Imagine That?) / Yes, My Heart		
11/10/62	12	19		**Carousel** .... version of the Rodgers & Hammerstein musical; produced by Enoch Light and featuring vocalists Alfred Drake and Roberta Peters; also see Soundtrack ('56)	$15	Command 843
				Blow High, Blow Low / Geraniums In The Winder / June Is Bustin' Out All Over / Stonecutters (medley) Carousel Waltz / (medley) / Mr. Snow / What's The Use Of Wond'rin' Finale / Highest Judge Of All / Real Nice Clambake / When The Children Are Asleep If I Loved You / Soliloquy / You'll Never Walk Alone		
				Catherine Wheel, The - see BYRNE, David		
11/6/82+	86	22		**Cats** .... Wayne Sleep/Paul Nicholas/Elaine Paige; original London cast; sw: Andrew Lloyd Webber; based on *Old Possum's Book of Practical Cats* by T.S. Eliot	$10	Geffen 2017 [2]
				Ad-dressing Of Cats / Invitation To The Jellicle Ball / Moments Of Happiness / Overture Ballad Of Billy McCaw (medley) / (medley) / Mr. Mistoffelees / Prologue: Jellicle Songs For Bustopher Jones / Jellicle Ball / Mungojerrie And Rumpleteazer / Jellicle Cats Growltiger's Last Stand (medley) / Journey To The Heaviside Layer / Naming Of Cats / Rum Tum Tugger Gus: The Theatre Cat / Macavity / Old Deuteronomy / Skimbleshanks The Railway Cat Memory (includes 3 versions) / Old Gumbie Cat (medley)		
2/26/83	113	64	▲	**Cats** .... Ken Page/Betty Buckley/Timothy Scott; entire original Broadway cast	$10	Geffen 2031 [2]
				Ad-dressing Of Cats / Invitation To The Jellicle Ball / Mr. Mistoffelees / Prologue: Jellicle Songs For Bustopher Jones / Jellicle Ball / Mungojerrie And Rumpleteazer / Jellicle Cats Grizabella, The Glamour Cat / Journey To The Heaviside Layer / Naming Of Cats / Rum Tum Tugger (includes 2 versions) / Macavity / Old Deuteronomy / Skimbleshanks The Railway Cat Growltiger's Last Stand / Memory / Old Gumbie Cat Gus: The Theatre Cat / Moments Of Happiness / Overture		
2/26/83	131	14		**Cats** .... selections from the original Broadway cast	$10	Geffen 2026
				Ad-dressing Of Cats / Macavity / Old Gumbie Cat / Solo Dance Grizabella, The Glamour Cat / Memory / Prologue: Jellicle Songs For Gus: The Theatre Cat / Mr. Mistoffelees / Jellicle Cats Jellicle Ball / Mungojerrie And Rumpleteazer / Rum Tum Tugger Journey To The Heaviside Layer / Old Deuteronomy / Skimbleshanks The Railway Cat		
8/23/75	73	10		**Chicago** .... Gwen Verdon/Chita Rivera/Jerry Orbach; mu: John Kander; ly: Fred Ebb	$8	Arista 9005
				All I Care About / I Can't Do It Alone / My Own Best Friend / Roxie Cell Block Tango / Little Bit Of Good / Nowadays / We Both Reached For The Gun Class / Me And My Baby / Overture / When Velma Takes The Stand Funny Honey / Mr. Cellophane / Razzle Dazzle / When You're Good To Mama		
8/16/75	98	49	●	**Chorus Line, A** .... Pamela Blair/Wayne Cilento/Priscilla Lopez/Donna McKechnie; mu: Marvin Hamlisch; ly: Edward Kleban	$8	Columbia 33581

DEBUT DATE	PEAK POS	WKS CHR	GOLD	ARTIST — Album Title	$	Label & Number

				At The Ballet Hello Twelve, Hello Thirteen, I Hope I Get It One		
				Dance: Ten; Looks: Three Hello Love Music And The Mirror Sing!		
				I Can Do That Nothing What I Did For Love		

4/29/57   15   1   25 Cinderella .... $25 Columbia 5190

Julie Andrews; mu: Richard Rodgers; ly: Oscar Hammerstein II; a special CBS-TV production (3/31/57)

Do I Love You Because You're   In My Own Little Corner   Prince Is Giving A Ball   Waltz For A Ball
Beautiful   (includes 2 versions)   Royal Dressing Room Scene   Wedding, The
Gavotte   It's Possible! (medley)   Search, The
Godmother's Song (medley)   Lovely Night   Stepsisters' Lament
Impossible! (medley)   March: Where Is Cinderella?   Ten Minutes Ago

6/20/70   178   2   26 Company .... $8   Columbia 3550

Dean Jones/Barbara Barrie; sw: Stephen Sondheim

Another Hundred People   Finale   Ladies Who Lunch   Someone Is Waiting (medley)
Barcelona   Getting Married Today   Little Things You Do Together   Sorry-Grateful
Being Alive   Have I Got A Girl For You   Poor Baby (medley)   Tick Tock (medley)
Company   (medley)   Side By Side By Side   You Could Drive A Person Crazy

6/13/92   165   2   27 Crazy For You.. $12   Angel 54618

Harry Groener/Jodi Benson; mu: George Gershwin; ly: Ira Gershwin

Bidin' My Time   I Got Rhythm   Overture   They Can't Take That Away
But Not For Me   K-ra-zy For You (includes 2   Real American Folk Song (Is A   From Me
Could You Use Me?   versions)   Rag)   Things Are Looking Up
Embraceable You   Naughty Baby   Shall We Dance?   Tonight's The Night
Entrance To Nevada Medley   New York Interlude (Concerto in   Slap That Bass   What Causes That?
Finale   F)   Someone To Watch Over Me
I Can't Be Bothered Now   Nice Work If You Can Get It   Stiff Upper Lip

8/2/69   195   2   28 Dames At Sea .... $15   Columbia 3330

Bernadette Peters/David Christmas/Tamara Long/Sally Stark; mu: Jim Wise; ly: George Haimsohn and Robin Miller

Beguine, The   Echo Waltz   Overture   Star Tar
Broadway Baby   Good Times Are Here To Stay   Raining In My Heart   That Mister Man Of Mine
Choo-Choo Honeymoon   It's You   Sailor Of My Dreams   There's Something About You
Dames At Sea   Let's Have A Simple Wedding   Singapore Sue   Wall Street

6/11/55   6   12   29 Damn Yankees .... $15   RCA 1021

Gwen Verdon/Stephen Douglass/Ray Walston; sw: Richard Adler and Jerry Ross; also see Soundtrack ('58)

Finale   Near To You   Six Months Out Of Every Year   Who's Got The Pain?
Game, The   Overture (medley)   (medley)   You've Got To Have Heart
Goodbye, Old Girl   Shoeless Joe From Hannibal,   Those Were The Good Old Days
Little Brains-A Little Talent   Mo.   Two Lost Souls
Man Doesn't Know   Whatever Lola Wants

4/5/69   128   8   30 Dear World .... $15   Columbia 3260

Angela Lansbury/Milo O'Shea; sw: Jerry Herman

And I Was Beautiful   Garbage   Kiss Her Now   Tea Party Medley
Dear World   I Don't Want To Know (includes   One Person
Each Tomorrow Morning   2 versions)   Overture
Finale   I've Never Said I Love You   Spring Of Next Year

8/24/59   44   2   31 Destry Rides Again.. $50   Decca 79075

Andy Griffith/Dolores Gray/Scott Brady; sw: Harold Rome

Anyone Would Love You   Hoop-Dee-Dingle   Once Knew A Fella   That Ring On The Finger
Are You Ready, Gyp Watson?   I Hate Him   Only Time Will Tell   Tomorrow Morning
Ballad Of The Gun   I Know Your Kind   Overture
Bottleneck   I Say Hello   Respectability (medley)
Every Once In A While   Ladies   Rose Lovejoy Girls (medley)
Fair Warning   Not Guilty   Rose Lovejoy Of Paradise Alley

5/22/65   81   9   32 Do I Hear A Waltz? .... $15   Columbia 2770

Elizabeth Allen/Sergio Franchi/Carol Bruce; mu: Richard Rodgers; ly: Stephen Sondheim

Bargaining   No Understand   Stay   This Week Americans
Do I Hear A Waltz?   Perfectly Lovely Couple   Take The Moment   We're Gonna Be All Right
Here We Are Again   Someone Like You   Thank You So Much (Finale)   What Do We Do? We Fly!
Moon In My Window   Someone Woke Up   Thinking

3/20/61   12   22   33 Do Re Mi .... $50   RCA 2002

Phil Silvers/Nancy Walker; mu: Jule Styne; ly: Betty Comden and Adolph Green

Adventure   Asking For You   I Know About Love   Overture
All Of My Life   Cry Like The Wind   It's Legitimate   Take A Job
All You Need Is A Quarter   Finale   Late, Late Show   Waiting, Waiting
Ambition   Fireworks   Make Someone Happy   What's New At The Zoo

7/31/61   58   9   34 Donnybrook! .... $25   Kapp 8500

Eddie Foy/Art Lund/Joan Fagan; sw: Johnny Burke; based on film *The Quiet Man* by Maurice Walsh

Day The Snow Is Meltin'   For My Own   Mr. Flynn   Toast To The Bride
Dee-lightful Is The Word   He Makes Me Feel I'm Lovely   Overture   Wisha Wurra
Donnybrook   I Have My Own Way   Quiet Life
Ellen Roe   I Wouldn't Bet One Penny   Sad Was The Day
Finale   Loveable Irish   Sez I

5/22/82   11   29   35 Dreamgirls... $8   Geffen 2007

Jennifer Holliday/Loretta Devine/Cleavant Derricks; mu: Henry Krieger; ly: Tom Eyen

Ain't No Party   Fake Your Way To The Top   I Meant You No Harm   Press Conference
And I Am Telling You I'm Not   Family   I Miss You Old Friend   Rap, The
Going [Jennifer Holliday] 22   Firing Of Jimmy   Move (You're Steppin' On My   Steppin' To The Bad Side
Cadillac Car   Hard To Say Goodbye, My Love   Heart)   When I First Saw You
Dreamgirls   I Am Changing   One Night Only

Evening With Mike Nichols And Elaine May, An - see NICHOLS, Mike, & Elaine May

8/23/80   105   19 ▲   36 Evita... $10   MCA 11007 [2]

Patti LuPone/Mandy Patinkin/Bob Gunton; mu: Andrew Lloyd Webber; ly: Tim Rice (based on the life of Argentinian Eva Peron); also see the artist Festival

Actress Hasn't Learned The   And The Money Kept Rolling In   Another Suitcase In Another   Art Of The Possible
Lines (You'd Like To Hear)   (And Out)   Hall   Buenos Aires

DEBUT DATE	PEAK POS	WKS CHR	GOLD	ARTIST — Album Title	$	Label & Number

Charity Concert (medley)	Eva Beware Of The City (medley)	Montage	Peron's Latest Flame
Cinema In Buenos Aires, 26	Eva's Final Broadcast	New Argentina	Rainbow High
July 1952	Goodnight And Thank You	Oh What A Circus (medley)	Rainbow Tour
Dice Are Rolling	High Flying, Adored	On The Balcony Of The Casa	Requiem For Evita (medley)
Don't Cry For Me Argentina	I'd Be Surprisingly Good For	Rosada (medley)	Santa Evita
(medley)	You (medley)	On This Night Of A Thousand	She Is A Diamond
Eva And Magaldi (medley)	Lament	Stars (medley)	Waltz For Eva And Che

7/25/64 — 96 — 8 — 37 Fade Out-Fade In .... $35 ABC-Para. 3
Carol Burnett/Jack Cassidy/Lou Jacobi; mu: Jule Styne; ly: Betty Comden/Adolph Green

Call Me Savage	Finale	Lila Tremaine	Usher From The Mezzanine
Close Harmony	Go Home Train	My Fortune Is My Face	You Mustn't Be Discouraged
Dangerous Age (medley)	I'm With You	My Heart Is Like A Violin	
Fade Out-Fade In	It's Good To Be Back Home	(medley)	
Fear	L.Z. In Quest Of His Youth	Oh Those Thirties	
Fiddler And The Fighter (medley)	(medley)	Overture	

1/22/55 — 7 — 2 — 38 Fanny .... $20 RCA 1015
Ezio Pinza/Walter Slezak/Florence Henderson; sw: Harold Rome; also see Soundtrack ('61)

Be Kind To Your Parents	I Like You	Overture	Wedding Dance
Birthday Song	Love Is A Very Light Thing	Panisse And Son	Welcome Home
Cold Cream Jar Song	Montage	Restless Heart	Why Be Afraid To Dance
Fanny	Never Too Late For Love	Shika Shika	
Finale Act 1	Octopus Song	Thought Of You	
I Have To Tell You	Other Hands, Other Hearts	To My Wife	

8/3/63 — 117 — 6 — 39 Fantasticks, The .... $15 MGM 3872
Kenneth Nelson/Jerry Orbach/Rita Gardner; mu: Harvey Schmidt; ly: Tom Jones

Happy Ending (medley)	Never Say No	Soon It's Gonna Rain	You Wonder How These Things
I Can See It	Overture	There Is A Curious Paradox	Begin
It Depends On What You Pay	Plant A Radish	They Were You	
Metaphor	Rape Ballet (medley)	This Plum Is Too Ripe	
Much More	Round And Round	Try To Remember	

10/31/64+ — 7 — 206 — ▲² 40 Fiddler On The Roof .... $15 RCA 1093
Zero Mostel/Maria Karnilova/Beatrice Arthur; mu: Jerry Bock; ly: Sheldon Harnick; also see
Soundtrack ('71) and Herschel Bernardi.

Anatevka	Matchmaker, Matchmaker	Sunrise, Sunset	Tradition
Do You Love Me?	Miracle Of Miracles	Tevye's Dream (The Tailor Motel	
Far From The Home I Love	Now I Have Everything	Kamzoil)	
If I Were A Rich Man	Sabbath Prayer	To Life	

1/11/60 — 7 — 89 — 41 Fiorello! .... $20 Capitol 1321
Tom Bosley/Patricia Wilson/Ellen Hanley/Howard Da Silva; mu: Jerry Bock; ly: Sheldon
Harnick

Bum Won	I Love A Cop	On The Side Of The Angels	Unfair
Finale	Little Tin Box	Overture	Very Next Man
Gentleman Jimmy	Marie's Law	Politics And Poker	When Did I Fall In Love
Home Again	Name's La Guardia	'Til Tomorrow	

7/3/65 — 111 — 8 — 42 Flora, The Red Menace .... $35 RCA 1111
Liza Minnelli/Bob Dishy; mu: John Kander; ly: Fred Ebb

All I Need (Is One Good Break)	Hello Waves	Palomino Pal	Sing Happy
Dear Love	Knock Knock	Prologue (medley)	Unafraid (medley)
Express Yourself	Not Every Day Of The Week	Quiet Thing	You Are You
Flame, The	Overture	Sign Here	

1/12/59 — 1³ — 151 — ● 43 Flower Drum Song .... $20 Columbia 2009
Miyoshi Umeki/Larry Blyden/Pat Suzuki; mu: Richard Rodgers; ly: Oscar Hammerstein II;
also see Sountrack ('61)

Chop Suey	Gliding Through My Memoree	I Am Going To Like It Here	Other Generation
Don't Marry Me	(medley)	I Enjoy Being A Girl	Overture
Entr'acte	Grant Avenue (includes 2	Like A God	Sunday
Fan Tan Fanny (medley)	versions)	Love, Look Away	You Are Beautiful
	Hundred Million Miracles	Medley	

6/5/71 — 172 — 3 — 44 Follies .... $10 Capitol 761
Alexis Smith/Gene Nelson/Yvonne De Carlo/Dorothy Collins; sw: Stephen Sondheim

Ah, Paris! (medley)	God-Why-Don't-You-Love-Me	Love Will See Us Through	Waiting For The Girls Upstairs
Beautiful Girls	Blues	(medley)	Who's That Woman?
Broadway Baby (medley)	I'm Still Here	Right Girl	You're Gonna Love Tomorrow
Could I Leave You?	In Buddy's Eyes	Road You Didn't Take	(medley)
Don't Look At Me	Live, Laugh, Love (Finale)	Story Of Lucy And Jessie	
	Losing My Mind	Too Many Mornings	

1/25/86 — 181 — 6 — 45 Follies - In Concert .... $15 RCA 7128 [2]
Carol Burnett/George Hearn/Lee Remick/Mandy Patinkin; sw: Stephen Sondheim; recorded
live in concert at Avery Fisher Hall, N.Y.C., featuring the New York Philharmonic

Ah, Paree!	I'm Still Here	One More Kiss	Waiting For The Girls Upstairs
Beautiful Girls	In Buddy's Eyes	Overture	Who's That Woman?
Broadway Baby	Live, Laugh, Love	Rain On The Roof	You're Gonna Love Tomorrow
Buddy's Blues	Losing My Mind	Right Girl	(medley)
Could I Leave You?	Love Will See Us Through	Road You Didn't Take	
Don't Look At Me	(medley)	Story Of Lucy And Jessie	
Finale	Loveland	Too Many Mornings	

1/17/81 — 120 — 11 — 46 42nd Street .... $8 RCA 3891
Tammy Grimes/Jerry Orbach; mu: Harry Warren; ly: Al Dubin

About A Quarter To Nine	42nd Street	Overture (medley)	We're In The Money
Audition (medley)	Getting Out Of Town	Shadow Waltz	You're Getting To Be A Habit
Dames	Go Into Your Dance	Shuffle Off To Buffalo	With Me
Finale	Lullaby Of Broadway	Sunny Side To Every Situation	Young And Healthy

Funny Girl - see STREISAND, Barbra
Barbra Streisand/Sydney Chaplin/Kay Medford

7/7/62 — 60 — 14 — 47 Funny Thing Happened On The Way To The Forum, A .... $15 Capitol 1717
Zero Mostel/Jack Gilford/David Burns; sw: Stephen Sondheim

| Bring Me My Bride | Everybody Ought To Have A | Finale | Funeral Sequence |
| Comedy Tonight | Maid | Free | I'm Calm |

DEBUT DATE	PEAK POS	WKS CHR	GOLD	ARTIST — Album Title	$	Label & Number

				Impossible Lovely Pretty Little Picture That'll Show Him		
				Love, I Hear Overture That Dirty Old Man		
2/24/62	**81**	9	48	**Gay Life, The**	**$40**	Capitol 1560
				Walter Chiari/Barbara Cook/Jules Munshin; sw: Howard Dietz and Arthur Schwartz		

Bloom Is Off The Rose
Bring Your Darling Daughter
Come A-Wandering With Me
Finale
For The First Time (medley)
I Never Had A Chance
I Wouldn't Marry You (medley)
I'm Glad I'm Single
Label On The Bottle
Magic Moment
Now I'm Ready For A Frau
Oh, Mein Liebchen
Overture
Something You Never Had
Before
This Kind Of A Girl
What A Charming Couple
Who Can? You Can
Why Go Anywhere At All
You Will Never Be Lonely
You're Not The Type

| 5/25/68 | **161** | 6 | 49 | **George M!** .... | **$15** | Columbia 3200 |
| | | | | Joel Grey/Betty Ann Grove; based on the life and compositions of George Michael Cohan | | |

All Aboard For Broadway (medley)
All Our Friends
Billie (medley)
Down By The Erie (medley)
Epilogue
Finale
Forty-Five Minutes From Broadway (medley)
Give My Regards To Broadway
Harrigan (medley)
Mary
Musical Comedy Man
Musical Moon (medley)
My Town
Nellie Kelly I Love You (medley)
Oh, You Wonderful Boy (medley)
Over There (medley)
Overture
Popularity (medley)
Push Me Along In My Push Cart (medley)
Ring To The Name Of Rose (medley)
So Long, Mary (medley)
Twentieth Century Love
Yankee Doodle Dandy (medley)
You're A Grand Old Flag (medley)

| 1/25/64 | **33** | 14 | 50 | **Girl Who Came To Supper, The** .... | **$40** | Columbia 2420 |
| | | | | Jose Ferrer/Florence Henderson; sw: Noel Coward | | |

Carpathian National Anthem (medley)
Coconut Girl Medley
Coronation Chorale
Curt, Clear and Concise
Here And Now
How Do You Do, Middle Age?
I'll Remember Her
I've Been Invited To A Party
London Medley
Lonely
My Family Tree (medley)
Sir Or Ma'am
Soliloquies
This Time It's True Love
When Foreign Princes Come To Visit Us

| 8/7/71+ | **34** | 79 | ● 51 | **Godspell** .... | **$10** | Bell 1102 |
| | | | | Stephen Nathan/Robin Lamont; sw: Stephen Schwartz; based upon the gospel according to St. Matthew; also see Soundtrack ('73) | | |

Alas For You
All For The Best
All Good Gifts
Bless The Lord
By My Side
Day By Day 13
Finale
Learn Your Lessons Well
Light Of The World
On The Willows
Prepare Ye The Way Of The Lord
Save The People
Turn Back, O Man
We Beseech Thee

| 12/19/64+ | **36** | 16 | 52 | **Golden Boy** .... | **$35** | Capitol 2124 |
| | | | | Sammy Davis, Jr./Billy Daniels; mu: Charles Strouse; ly: Lee Adams | | |

Can't You See It
Colorful
Don't Forget 127th Street
Everything's Great
Finale
Gimme Some
Golden Boy
I Want To Be With You
Lorna's Here
Night Song
No More
Stick Around
This Is The Life
While The City Sleeps
Workout

| 1/1/66 | **118** | 4 | 53 | **Great Waltz, The** .... | **$30** | Capitol 2426 |
| | | | | Giorgio Tozzi/Jean Fenn; musical based on the lives and compositions of Johann Strauss, Sr. & Jr. | | |

Artist's Life
At Dommayer's
Birthday Song
Enchanted Wood
Finale
Gypsy Told Me
I'm In Love With Vienna
Love And Gingerbread
Music!
No Two Ways
Of Men And Violins
Philosophy Of Life
Radetsky March (medley)
State Of The Dance (medley)
Teeter-Totter Me
Two By Two
Waltz With Wings

| 8/1/92 | **109** | 5 | 54 | **Guys & Dolls** .... | **$12** | RCA Victor 61317 |
| | | | | Peter Gallagher/Nathan Lane/Josie de Guzman/Faith Prince; mu: Frank Loesser; original version first charted in 1951 on Decca 8036 (POS 1) | | |

Adelaide's Lament
Bushel And A Peck
Crapshooters' Dance
Follow The Fold
Fugue For Tinhorns
Guys And Dolls
Havana
I'll Know
I've Never Been In Love Before
If I Were A Bell
Luck Be A Lady
Marry The Man Today
More I Cannot Wish You
My Time Of Day
Oldest Established
Runyonland
Sit Down, You're Rockin' The Boat
Sue Me
Take Back Your Mink

| 7/20/59 | **13** | 116 | 55 | **Gypsy** .... | **$10** | Columbia 2017 |
| | | | | Ethel Merman/Jack Klugman/Sandra Church; mu: Jule Styne; ly: Stephen Sondheim; based on memoirs of Gypsy Rose Lee; also see Soundtrack ('62) | | |

All I Need Is The Girl
Baby June And Her Newsboys
Dainty June And Her Farmboys
Everything's Coming Up Roses
If Mama Was Married
Let Me Entertain You
Little Lamb
Mr. Goldstone, I Love You
Overture
Rose's Turn
Small World
Some People
Together Wherever We Go
You Gotta Have A Gimmick
You'll Never Get Away From Me

| 8/3/68+ | **1**[13] | 151 | ● 56 | **Hair** .... | **$10** | RCA 1150 |
| | | | | Gerome Ragni/James Rado/Lynn Kellogg; mu: Galt MacDermot; ly: Gerome Ragni and James Rado; also see Soundtrack ('79) and Rock Operas *DisinHAIRited* | | |

Able Baby
Ain't Got No (medley)
Air
Aquarius
Be In
Black Boys (medley)
Colored Spade
Don't Put It Down
Donna (medley)
Easy To Be Hard
Flesh Failures (Let The Sunshine In)
Frank Mills
Good Morning Starshine
Hair
Hashish (medley)
I Got Life
I'm Black (medley)
Initials
Manchester England
My Conviction
Sodomy
Three-Five-Zero-Zero (medley)
Walking In Space
What A Piece Of Work Is Man (medley)
Where Do I Go?
White Boys (medley)

| 5/10/69 | **186** | 4 | 57 | **Hair** .... | **$25** | Atco 7002 |
| | | | | Paul Nicholas/Oliver Tobias; original London cast | | |

Able Baby
Ain't Got No (medley)
Air
Aquarius
Bed, The (medley)
Black Boys (medley)
Coloured Spade (medley)
Donna
Easy To Be Hard (medley)
Electric Blues
Flesh Failures (Let The Sunshine In)
Frank Mills (medley)
Good Morning Starshine (medley)
Hair
I Got Life
My Conviction (medley)
Sodomy (medley)
Three-Five-Zero-Zero (medley)
Walking In Space
What A Piece Of Work Is Man (medley)
Where Do I Go
White Boys (medley)

| 6/12/65 | **103** | 14 | 58 | **Half A Sixpence** .... | **$25** | RCA 1110 |
| | | | | Tommy Steele/Polly James; sw: David Heneker | | |

All In The Cause Of Economy
Finale
Flash, Bang, Wallop!
Half A Sixpence

DEBUT DATE	PEAK POS	WKS CHR	GOLD	ARTIST — Album Title	$	Label & Number

				I Know What I Am / If The Rain's Got To Fall	Long Ago / Money To Burn	Overture / Party's On The House	Proper Gentleman / She's Too Far Above Me		

8/15/64 — 128 — 13 — 59 Hamlet .... $20 Columbia 702 [4]
Richard Burton/Hume Cronyn/Alfred Drake/Eileen Herlie; 4-album set of dialogue from Shakespeare's play

| I Know What I Am | Long Ago | Overture | Proper Gentleman |
| If The Rain's Got To Fall | Money To Burn | Party's On The House | She's Too Far Above Me |

7/3/61 — 84 — 6 — 60 Happiest Girl In The World, The .... $45 Columbia 2050
Cyril Ritchard/Janice Rule; mu: Jacques Offenbach; ly: E.Y. Harburg

Adrift On A Star	Glory That Is Grace (medley)	Never Be-devil The Devil	That'll Be The Day
Entrance Of The Courtesans	Greek Marine	Never Trust A Virgin	Vive La Virtue
Eureka	Happiest Girl In The World	Oath, The	Whatever That May Be
Finale, Act I	How Soon, Oh Moon?	Overture (medley)	
Five Minutes Of Spring	Love-sick Serenade	Shall We Say Farewell?	

2/22/64 — 1¹ — 90 — ● — 61 Hello, Dolly! .... $15 RCA 1087
Carol Channing/David Burns/Eileen Brennan; sw: Jerry Herman; also see Barbra Streisand

Before The Parade Passes By	Hello, Dolly!	Motherhood	So Long Dearie
Dancing	I Put My Hand In	Prologue	
Elegance	It Only Takes A Moment	Put On Your Sunday Clothes	
Finale	It Takes A Woman	Ribbons Down My Back	

11/16/63+ — 38 — 16 — 62 Here's Love .... $40 Columbia 2400
Janis Paige/Craig Stevens; sw: Meredith Willson; based on Miracle On 34th Street

Arm In Arm	Finale	My State	She Hadda Go Back
Big Clown Balloons (medley)	Here's Love	My Wish	That Man Over There
Bugle, The	Look, Little Girl	Overture (medley)	You Don't Know
Expect Things To Happen (medley)	Love Come Take Me Again (medley)	Parade (medley)	
		Pine Cones And Holly Berries	

5/16/64 — 76 — 20 — 63 High Spirits .... $30 ABC-Para. 1
Beatrice Lillie/Tammy Grimes/Edward Woodward; sw: Hugh Martin and Timothy Gray; based on Noel Coward's Blithe Spirit

Bicycle Song	Home Sweet Heaven	Something Is Coming To Tea	What In The World Did You Want?
Faster Than Sound	I Know Your Heart	Something Tells Me	Where Is The Man I Married?
Forever And A Day	If I Gave You	Talking To You	You'd Better Love Me
Go Into Your Trance	Overture	Was She Prettier Than I?	

11/27/61+ — 19 — 47 — 64 How To Succeed In Business Without Really Trying .... $20 RCA 1066
Robert Morse/Rudy Vallee; sw: Frank Loesser; also see Soundtrack ('67)

Been A Long Day	Company Way	Happy To Keep His Dinner Warm	Overture
Brotherhood Of Man	Finale	I Believe In You	Paris Original
Cinderella, Darling	Grand Old Ivy	Love From A Heart Of Gold	Rosemary
Coffee Break			Secretary Is Not A Toy

7/21/62 — 125 — 5 — 65 I Can Get It For You Wholesale .... $30 Columbia 2180
Lillian Roth/Jack Kruschen/Elliott Gould; sw: Harold Rome; cast includes Barbra Streisand in her first Broadway show

Ballad Of The Garment Trade	Have I Told You Lately?	Sound Of Money	What's In It For Me?
Eat A Little Something	I'm Not A Well Man (medley)	Too Soon	When Gemini Meets Capricorn
Family Way	Miss Marmelstein	Way Things Are	Who Knows?
Funny Thing Happened	Momma, Momma, Momma	What Are They Doing To Us Now?	
Gift Today	Overture (medley)		

1/14/67 — 84 — 16 — 66 I Do! I Do! .... $15 RCA 1128
Mary Martin/Robert Preston; mu: Harvey Schmidt; ly: Tom Jones

All The Dearly Beloved (medley)	I Do! I Do! (medley)	Roll Up The Ribbons	Well Known Fact
Father Of The Bride	I Love My Wife	Someone Needs Me	What Is A Woman?
Flaming Agnes	Love Isn't Everything	Something Has Happened	When The Kids Get Married
Goodnight	My Cup Runneth Over	This House	Where Are The Snows?
Honeymoon Is Over	Nobody's Perfect	Together Forever (medley)	

1/30/65 — 126 — 8 — 67 I Had A Ball .... $25 Mercury 6210
Buddy Hackett/Richard Kiley; sw: Jack Lawrence and Stan Freeman

Addie's At It Again	Coney Island, U.S.A.	Garside The Great (medley)	Other Half Of Me
Affluent Society	Dr. Freud	I Had A Ball	Overture (medley)
Almost	Faith	I've Got Everything I Want	Think Beautiful
Can It Be Possible?	Fickle Finger Of Fate	Neighborhood Song	You Deserve Me

6/17/67 — 177 — 8 — 68 Illya Darling .... $20 United Art. 9901
Melina Mercouri/Orson Bean; mu: Manos Hadjidakis; ly: Joe Darion; based on the film Never On Sunday

After Love	Heaven Help The Sailors On A Night Like This	Illya Darling	Overture (Entracte)
Bouzouki Nights	I Think She Needs Me	Love, Love, Love	Piraeus, My Love
Dear Mr. Schubert	I'll Never Lay Down Anymore	Medea Tango	Ya Chara
Golden Land		Never On Sunday	Yorgo's Dance (Zebekiko)

3/26/88 — 126 — 6 — 69 Into The Woods .... $8 RCA 6796
Bernadette Peters/Joanna Gleason/Chip Zien/Tom Aldredge; sw: Stephen Sondheim

Agony	Hello, Little Girl	Last Midnight (medley)	Stay With Me
Any Moment (medley)	I Guess This Is Goodbye (medley)	Maybe They're Magic (medley)	Very Nice Prince (medley)
Children Will Listen	I Know Things Now	Moments In The Woods (medley)	Your Fault (medley)
Cinderella At The Grave	Into The Woods	No More	
Ever After	It Takes Two	No One Is Alone	
First Midnight (medley)	Lament	On The Steps Of The Palace	
Giants In The Sky (medley)		So Happy	

12/5/60+ — 9 — 33 — 70 Irma La Douce .... $25 Columbia 2029
Elizabeth Seal/Keith Michell/Clive Revill; mu: Marguerite Monnot; original ly: Alexandre Breffort; also see Soundtrack ('63)

Arctic Ballet (medley)	Freedom Of The Seas (medley)	Our Language Of Love	There Is Only One Paris For That (medley)
Bridge Of Caulaincourt	From A Prison Cell	Overture	
But	Irma-La-Douce	She's Got The Lot	Valse Milieu
Christmas Child	Le Grisbi Is Le Root Of Le Evil	Sons Of France	Wreck Of A Mec
Dis-Donc, Dis-Donc	In Man	That's A Crime	

1/4/64 — 87 — 5 — 71 Jennie .... $45 RCA 1083
Mary Martin/George Wallace/Robin Bailey; mu: Arthur Schwartz; ly: Howard Dietz

| Before I Kiss The World Goodbye | For Better Or Worse | I Believe In Takin' A Chance | Lonely Nights |
| Born Again | High Is Better Than Low | I Still Look At You That Way | Night May Be Dark |

DEBUT DATE	PEAK POS	WKS CHR	GOLD	ARTIST — Album Title			$	Label & Number
				Over Here	Sauce Diable	Waitin' For The Evening Train		Where You Are
				Overture	See Seattle	When You're Far Away From New York Town		
1/8/72	31	10		**72 Jesus Christ Superstar**..			**$15**	Decca 1503
				Ben Vereen/Jeff Fenbolt/Yvonne Elliman/Bob Bingham; mu: Andrew Lloyd Webber; ly: Tim Rice; also see Rock Operas ('70), Soundtrack ('73) and Percy Faith				
				Could We Start Again Please	Heaven On Their Minds	Judas' Death		This Jesus Must Die
				Everything's Alright	Hosanna	King Herod's Song		Trial Before Pilate
				Gethsemane (I Only Want To Say)	I Don't Know How To Love Him	Pilate's Dream		
					John Nineteen: Forty-One	Superstar		
3/14/70	187	4		**73 Joy**..			**$15**	RCA 1166
				Oscar Brown Jr./Jean Pace/Sivuca; sw: various				
				Afro Blue	If I Only Had	Nothing But A Fool		What Is A Friend
				Brown Baby	Mother Africa's Day	Sky And Sea		Wimmen's Ways
				Funky World	Much As I Love You	Time		
				Funny Feelin'	New Generation	Under The Sun		
12/25/61+	80	12		**74 Kean**..			**$40**	Columbia 2120
				Alfred Drake/Lee Venora; sw: Robert Wright and George Forrest				
				Apology	King Of London (medley)	Penny Plain, Twopence Colored (medley)		Swept Away
				Chime In!	Let's Improvise			To Look Upon My Love (medley)
				Civilized People	Man And Shadow (medley)	Queue At Drury Lane (medley)		Willow, Willow, Willow
				Elena	Mayfair Affair (medley)	Service For Service		
				Fog And The Grog	Overture (medley)	Sweet Danger		
10/24/92	135	3		**75 King And I, The**..			**$12**	Philips 438007
				musical score performed in the studio, not on stage; mu: Richard Rogers; ly: Oscar Hammerstein II; cd: John Mauceri; pf: Julie Andrews/Ben Kingsley/Lea Salonga/Peabo Bryson; also see Soundtracks				
				Anna Unpacks	Hello, Young Lovers	My Lord And Master		Song Of The King
				Banquet Scene	Home, Sweet Home	Puzzlement, A		Temple Scene
				Finale Ultimo	I Have Dreamed	Shall I Tell You What I Think Of You?		We Kiss In A Shadow
				Garden Scene	I Whistle A Happy Tune			Welcome To Bangkok
				Getting To Know You	Main Title	Shall We Dance?		
				Harbour	March Of The Siamese Children	Something Wonderful		
				Kismet - see MANTOVANI				
				Alfred Drake/Doretta Morrow/Richard Kiley				
3/24/62	139	3		**76 Kwamina**..			**$50**	Capitol 1645
				Sally Ann Howes/Terry Carter; sw: Richard Adler				
				Another Time, Another Place	Nothing More To Look Forward To	Seven Sheep, Four Red Shirts And A Bottle Of Gin		What Happened To Me Tonight?
				Cocoa Bean Song	One Wife	Something Big		What's Wrong With Me?
				Did You Hear That?	Ordinary People	Sun Is Beginning To Crow		You're As English As
				Man Can Have No Choice		Welcome Home		
9/24/83	52	15		**77 La Cage Aux Folles**..			**$8**	RCA 4824
				George Hearn/Gene Barry; sw: Jerry Herman				
				Best Of Times	La Cage Aux Folles	Prelude		With Anne On My Arm
				Cocktail Counterpoint	Little More Mascara	Song On The Sand (La Da Da Da)		With You On My Arm
				Finale	Look Over There			
				I Am What I Am	Masculinity	We Are What We Are		
4/11/87	106	15	●	**78 Les Miserables**..			**$10**	Relativity 8140 [2]
				Colm Wilkinson/Roger Allam/Rebecca Caine/Patti LuPone; original London cast; mu: Claude-Michel Schonberg; ly: Herbert Kretzmer				
				At The End Of The Day	Do You Hear The People Sing?	In My Life (medley)		One Day More
				Attack, The	Dog Eats Dog	Javert's Suicide		Red And Black
				Beggars At The Feast (medley)	Drink With Me	Little Fall Of Rain		Stars
				Bring Him Home	Empty Chairs At Empty Tables	Little People		Wedding Chorale
				Castle On A Cloud	Finale (medley)	Look Down		Who Am I?
				Come To Me (Fantine's Death) (medley)	Heart Full Of Love (medley)	Lovely Ladies		
				Confrontation (medley)	I Dreamed A Dream	Master Of The House		
					I Saw Him Once (medley)	On My Own		
6/20/87	117	10	▲	**79 Les Miserables**..			**$10**	Geffen 24151 [2]
				Colm Wilkinson/Terrence Mann/Judy Kuhn/Randy Graff; Broadway cast; mu: Claude-Michel Schonberg; ly: Herbert Kretzmer				
				At The End Of The Day	Drink With Me	Javert's Suicide		Plumet Attack
				Beggars At The Feast (medley)	Empty Chairs At Empty Tables	Little Fall Of Rain		Red And Black
				Bring Him Home	Finale	Little People (medley)		Stars
				Castle On A Cloud	First Attack	Look Down		Thenardier Waltz Of Treachery
				Come To Me (Fantine's Death)	Heart Full Of Love	Lovely Ladies		Turning
				Confrontation	I Dreamed A Dream	Master Of The House		Wedding Chorale (medley)
				Do You Hear The People Sing?	In My Life	On My Own		Who Am I?
				Dog Eats Dog	Javert At The Barricade (medley)	One Day More		
1/11/92	184	1		**80 Les Miserables Highlights**..			**$12**	First Night 1099
				features performers drawn from worldwide productions of musical; mu: Claude-Michel Schonberg; ly: Alain Boublil & Herbert Kretzmer				
				ABC Cafe (medley)	Do You Hear The People Sing?	I Dreamed A Dream		Red And Black (medley)
				At The End Of The Day	Drink With Me	Javert's Suicide		Stars
				Bring Him Home	Empty Chairs At Empty Tables	Master Of The House		Trial, The (medley)
				Come To Me (Fantine's Death)	Finale	On My Own		Who Am I? (medley)
				Confrontation	Heart Full Of Love	One Day More		
12/29/56	19	3		**81 Li'l Abner**..			**$25**	Columbia 5150
				Edith Adams/Peter Palmer/Howard St. John/Stubby Kaye; mu: Gene de Paul; ly: Johnny Mercer				
				Country's In The Very Best Of Hands	Jubilation T. Cornpone	Oh, Happy Day		Rag Offen The Bush
				I'm Past My Prime	Love In A Home	Overture		Typical Day
				If I Had My Druthers	Matrimonial Stomp	Progress Is The Root Of All Evil		Unnecessary Town
					Namely You	Put 'Em Back		
1/19/63	44	10		**82 Little Me**..			**$30**	RCA 1078
				Sid Caesar/Virginia Martin/Nancy Andrews; mu: Cy Coleman; ly: Carolyn Leigh				

DEBUT DATE	PEAK POS	WKS CHR	GOLD	ARTIST — Album Title	$	Label & Number

| | | | | Be A Performer! · Here's To Us · Other Side Of The Tracks (includes 2 versions) · Real Live Girl (includes 2 versions) · Boom-Boom · I Love You · Overture · Truth, The · Deep Down Inside · I've Got Your Number · Poor Little Hollywood Star · Dimples · Little Me · Goodbye (The Prince's Farewell) | | |

| 5/5/73 | 94 | 12 | 83 | **Little Night Music, A** .... Glynis Johns/Len Cariou/Hermione Gingold; sw: Stephen Sondheim; based on the film *Smiles Of A Summer Night* | $10 | Columbia 32265 |

Every Day A Little Death · Later (medley) · Overture (medley) · Sun Won't Set
Finale · Liaisons · Perpetual Anticipation · Weekend In The Country
Glamorous Life · Miller's Son · Remember? · You Must Meet My Wife
In Praise Of Women · Night Waltz (medley) · Send In The Clowns
It Would Have Been Wonderful · Now (medley) · Soon (medley)

| 1/11/69 | 185 | 2 | 84 | **Maggie Flynn** .... Shirley Jones/Jack Cassidy; sw: Hugo Peretti/Luigi Creatore/George David Weiss | $20 | RCA 2009 |

Finale · I Wouldn't Have You Any Other Way · Mr. Clown · They're Never Gonna Make Me Fight
Game Of War · Nice Cold Mornin' · Why Can't I Walk Away
How About A Ball? · Learn How To Laugh · Overture
I Won't Let It Happen Again · Look Around Your Little World · Pitter Patter
Maggie Flynn · Thank You Song

| 7/2/66 | 23 | 66 | ● 85 | **Mame** .... Angela Lansbury/Beatrice Arthur; sw: Jerry Herman; based on the film *Auntie Mame*; also see Soundtrack ('74) | $15 | Columbia 3000 |

Bosom Buddies · It's Today · My Best Girl · That's How Young I Feel
Finale · Letter, The · Open A New Window · We Need A Little Christmas
Gooch's Song · Mame · Overture
If He Walked Into My Life · Man In The Moon · St. Bridget

| 1/22/66+ | 31 | 167 | ● 86 | **Man of La Mancha** .... Richard Kiley/Irving Jacobson/Joan Diener; mu: Mitch Leigh; ly: Joe Darion; an adaptation of *Don Quixote*; also see Soundtrack ('72) | $15 | Kapp 4505 |

Abduction, The · Finale · Little Bird, Little Bird · To Each His Dulcinea (To Every Man His Dream)
Aldonza · Golden Helmet (medley) · Little Gossip
Barber's Song (medley) · I Really Like Him · Man Of La Mancha (I, Don Quixote) · What Do You Want Of Me?
Dubbing (Knight Of The Woeful Countenance) · I'm Only Thinking Of Him · Overture
Dulcinea · Impossible Dream (The Quest) · It's All The Same

| 10/17/64 | 137 | 4 | 87 | **Merry Widow, The** .... Patrice Munsel/Bob Wright; sw: Franz Lehar | $25 | RCA 1094 |

Finale Act I · I Love You So (The Merry Widow Waltz) · Respectable Wife (medley) · When In France (medley)
Finale Act II · Riding On A Carousel · Who Knows The Way To My Heart?
Girls At Maxim's · Maxim's · Romance · Women
Overture · Villa

| 11/20/61+ | 10 | 41 | 88 | **Milk And Honey** .... Robert Weede/Mimi Benzell/Molly Picon; sw: Jerry Herman | $30 | RCA 1065 |

As Simple As That · I Will Follow You · Milk And Honey · There's No Reason In The World
Chin Up, Ladies · Independence Day Hora · Overture · Wedding, The
Finale · Let's Not Waste A Moment · Shalom
Hymn To Hymie · Like A Young Man · That Was Yesterday

| 3/10/90 | 122 | 10 | 89 | **Miss Saigon** .... Jonathan Pryce/Claire Moore/Lea Salonga/Simon Bowman; original London cast; mu: Claude-Michel Schonberg and Alain Boublil; ly: Richard Maltby, Jr. and Alain Boublil | $27 | Geffen 24271 [2] |

American Dream · Heat Is On In Saigon · Movie In My Mind · This Is The Hour
Bui-Doi · Her Or Me · Overture · This Money's Yours
Ceremony (Dju Vui Vai) · I Still Believe · Please · What A Waste
Confrontation, The · I'd Give My Life For You · Revelation, The · What's This I Find
Dance, The · If You Want To Die In Bed · Room 317 · Why God Why?
Deal, The · Last Night Of The World · Sacred Bird
Fall Of Saigon · Let Me See His Western Nose · Sun And Moon
Finale · Morning Of The Dragon · Telephone Song

| 8/4/56 | 11 | 4 | 90 | **Most Happy Fella, The** .... Robert Weede/Jo Sullivan; sw: Frank Loesser | $20 | Columbia 2330 |

Abbondanza · How Beautiful The Days · My Heart Is So Full Of You · Sposalizio
Big "D" · I Like Ev'rybody · Ooh, My Feet (medley) · Standing On The Corner
Don't Cry · I Made A Fist · Overture (medley) · Warm All Over
Finale · Joey, Joey, Joey · Rosabella
Happy To Make Your Acquaintance · Mama, Mama · Somebody Somewhere
· Most Happy Fella · Song Of A Summer Night

| 12/1/62 | 14 | 24 | 91 | **Mr. President** .... Robert Ryan/Nanette Fabray; sw: Irving Berlin; also see Perry Como | $15 | Columbia 2270 |

Don't Be Afraid Of Romance · In Our Hide-Away · Let's Go Back To The Waltz (medley) · Song For Belly Dancer
Empty Pockets Filled With Love · Is He The Only Man In The World · They Love Me
First Lady · Meat And Potatoes · This Is A Great Country
Glad To Be Home · It Gets Lonely In The White House · Overture (medley) · Washington Twist
I'm Gonna Get Him · Pigtails And Freckles · You Need A Hobby
I've Got To Be Around (medley) · Laugh It Up · Secret Service (medley)

| 2/24/58 | 1¹² | 245 | ▲ 92 | **Music Man, The** .... Robert Preston/Barbara Cook; sw: Meredith Willson; also see Soundtrack ('62) | $10 | Capitol 990 |

Finale · Lida Rose (medley) · Pick-A-Little, Talk-A-Little (medley) · Sincere
Gary, Indiana · Marian The Librarian · Rock Island (medley) · Till There Was You
Goodnight Ladies (medley) · My White Knight · Sadder-But-Wiser Girl For Me · Wells Fargo Wagon
Goodnight My Someone · Overture (medley) · Seventy Six Trombones · Will I Ever Tell You (medley)
Iowa Stubborn · Piano Lesson · Shipoopi · Ya Got Trouble
It's You

| 4/28/56 | 1¹⁵ | 480 | ▲³ 93 | **My Fair Lady** .... Rex Harrison/Julie Andrews; mu: Frederick Loewe; ly: Alan Jay Lerner; adapted from Bernard Shaw's *Pygmalion*; also see Soundtrack ('64) | $10 | Columbia 5090 |

Ascot Gavotte · Hymn To Him · I'm An Ordinary Man · I've Grown Accustomed To Her Face
Get Me To The Church On Time · I Could Have Danced All Night

DEBUT DATE	PEAK POS	WKS CHR	G O L D	ARTIST — Album Title	$	Label & Number

| | | | | Just You Wait   Rain In Spain   Why Can't The English?   Without You | | |

Just You Wait   Rain In Spain   Why Can't The English?   Without You
On The Street Where You Live   Show Me   (medley)   Wouldn't It Be Loverly
Overture (medley)   With A Little Bit Of Luck   You Did It

6/28/86   **150**   6   94   **Mystery Of Edwin Drood, The** .... **$8**   Polydor 827969
Betty Buckley/Cleo Laine/George Rose; sw: Rupert Holmes

Both Sides Of The Coin   Man Could Go Quite Mad   No Good Can Come From Bad   Setting Up The Score
Ceylon   Moonfall (includes 2 versions)   Off To The Races   There You Are
Don't Quit While You're Ahead   Moonfall Quartet   Out On A Limerick   Two Kinsmen
Garden Path To Hell   Name Of Love (medley)   Perfect Strangers   Wages Of Sin
Jasper's Confession   Never The Luck   Puffer's Confession   Writing On The Wall (Finale)

8/5/57   **17**   3   95   **New Girl in Town** .... **$35**   RCA 1027
Gwen Verdon/Thelma Ritter/George Wallace; sw: Bob Merrill

Anna Lilla   Flings   On The Farm   There Ain't No Flies On Me
At The Check Apron Ball   If That Was Love   Overture   Ven I Valse
Chess And Checkers   It's Good To Be Alive   Roll Yer Socks Up   Yer My Friend Ain'tcha?
Did You Close Your Eyes?   Look At 'Er   Sunshine Girl

3/13/71   **61**   19   96   **No, No, Nanette** .... **$8**   Columbia 30563
Ruby Keeler/Jack Gilford/Bobby Van/Helen Gallagher; mu: Vincent Youmans; ly: Irving Caesar and Otto Harbach

Call Of The Sea   No, No, Nanette   Telephone Girlie   Where-Has-My-Hubby-Gone
Finaletto Act II   Overture   Too Many Rings Around Rosie   Blues
I Want To Be Happy   Take A Little One-Step (Finale)   Waiting For You   You Can Dance With Any Girl
I've Confessed To The Breeze   Tea For Two

4/21/62   **5**   62   97   **No Strings** .... **$30**   Capitol 1695
Richard Kiley/Diahann Carroll; sw: Richard Rodgers

Be My Host   La La La   Maine   Orthodox Fool
Eager Beaver   Loads Of Love   Man Who Has Everything   Sweetest Sounds
Finale   Look No Further   No Strings   You Don't Tell Me
How Sad   Love Makes The World Go   Nobody Told Me

11/3/62   **4**   99   ●   98   **Oliver!** .... **$15**   RCA 2004
Clive Revill/Georgia Brown/Bruce Prochnik (Oliver); sw: Lionel Bart; also see Soundtrack ('68) and Mantovani

As Long As He Needs Me   Food, Glorious Food   Oliver   You've Got To Pick A Pocket Or
Be Back Soon   I Shall Scream   Oom-Pah-Pah   Two
Boy For Sale (medley)   I'd Do Anything   Reviewing The Situation
Consider Yourself   It's A Fine Life   Where Is Love? (medley)
Finale   My Name   Who Will Buy?

12/11/65+   **59**   32   99   **On A Clear Day You Can See Forever** .... **$15**   RCA 2006
Barbara Harris/John Cullum/Tito Vandis; mu: Burton Lane; ly: Alan Jay Lerner; also see Barbra Streisand

Come Back To Me   Melinda   Overture   What Did I Have That I Don't
Don't Tamper With My Sister   On A Clear Day (You Can See   She Wasn't You   Have?
Finale   Forever)   Tosy And Cosh   When I'm Being Born Again
Hurry! It's Lovely Up Here!   On The S.S. Bernard Cohn   Wait Till We're Sixty-Five

1/4/64   **37**   15   100   **110 In The Shade** .... **$35**   RCA 1085
Robert Horton/Inga Swenson/Stephen Douglass; mu: Harvey Schmidt; ly: Tom Jones

Everything Beautiful Happens   Is It Really Me?   Man And A Woman   Rain Song
At Night   Little Red Hat   Melisande   Raunchy
Finale   Lizzie's Comin' Home   Old Maid   Simple Little Things
Gonna Be Another Hot Day   Love, Don't Turn Away   Poker Polka   You're Not Foolin' Me
Hungry Men

                    Over Here! - see ANDREWS SISTERS
Patty Andrews/Maxene Andrews/John Travolta; sw: Richard M. Sherman/Robert B. Sherman

4/2/55   **4**   8   101   **Peter Pan** .... **$40**   RCA 1019
Mary Martin/Cyril Ritchard; mu: Mark Charlap and Jule Styne; ly: Carolyn Leigh/Betty Comden/Adolph Green

Distant Melody   I'm Flying   Oh My Mysterious Lady   Tarantella
Hook's Tango   I've Gotta Crow   Overture   Tender Shepherd
Hook's Waltz   Indians   Pirate Song   Ugg-A-Wugg
I Won't Grow Up   Never, Never Land   Prologue   Wendy

5/23/87+   **33**   249↑ ▲²   102   **Phantom Of The Opera, The** .... **$10**   Polydor 831273 [2]
Michael Crawford/Sarah Brightman/Steve Barton; original London cast; mu: Andrew Lloyd Webber; ly: Charles Hart

All I Ask Of You   Masquerade   Poor Fool, He Makes Me Laugh   Twisted Every Way
Angel Of Music   Mirror (Angel Of Music)   Prima Donna   Wandering Child
Down Once More (medley)   Music Of The Night   Raoul, I've Been There (medley)   Why Have You Brought Me Here
Entr'acte   Notes (includes 2 versions)   Stranger Than You Dreamt It   (medley)
I Remember   Overture   Think Of Me   Why So Silent
Little Lotte   Phantom Of The Opera   Track Down This Murderer   Wishing You Were Somehow
Magical Lasso   Point Of No Return   (medley)   Here Again

3/10/90+   **46**   153↑ ▲²   103   **Phantom of the Opera, Highlights from The** .... **$12**   Polydor 831563
second volume released from the London stage production

All I Ask Of You   Mirror (Angel Of Music)   Prima Donna   Wishing You Were Somehow
Angel Of Music   Music Of The Night   Think Of Me   Here Again
Down Once More (medley)   Overture   Track Down This Murderer
Entr'acte   Phantom Of The Opera   (medley)
Masquerade   Point Of No Return

1/13/73   **129**   10   104   **Pippin** .... **$8**   Motown 760
Ben Vereen/Jill Clayburgh; sw: Stephen Schwartz

Corner Of The Sky   I Guess I'll Miss The Man   Morning Glow   Spread A Little Sunshine
Extraordinary   Kind Of Woman   No Time At All   War Is A Science
Finale   Love Song   On The Right Track   With You
Glory   Magic To Do   Simple Joys

6/6/81   **178**   3   105   **Pirates Of Penzance, The** .... **$12**   Elektra 601 [2]
Kevin Kline/Estelle Parsons/Linda Ronstadt/Rex Smith; ly: W.S. Gilbert; mu: Sir Arthur Sullivan; also see Soundtrack *Pirate Movie*

All Is Prepared   Climbing Over Rocky Mountain   Hold, Monsters!   Hush, Hush! Not A Word
Away, Away! My Heart's On Fire   Finale   How Beautifully Blue The Sky

DEBUT DATE	PEAK POS	WKS CHR	GOLD	ARTIST — Album Title	$	Label & Number

I Am The Very Model Of A Modern Major-General · My Eyes Are Fully Open · No, I Am Brave · Now For The Pirates' Lair! · Oh, Better Far To Live And Die · Oh, Dry The Glistening Tear · Oh, False One, You Have Deceived Me! · Oh, Is There Not One Maiden Breast · Oh, Men Of Dark And Dismal Fate · Poor Wandering One · Pour, O Pour The Pirate Sherry · Rollicking Band Of Pirates We · Sighing Softly To The River · Sorry Her Lot · Stay, Frederic, Stay! · Stay, We Must Not Lose Our Senses · Stop, Ladies, Pray! · Then Farewell · What Ought We To Do? · When A Felon's Not Engaged In His Employment · When Frederic Was A Little Lad · When The Foeman Bares His Steel · When You Had Left Our Pirate Fold · With Cat-Like Tread, Upon Our Prey We Steal

---

1/25/69 · 95 · 12 · 106 Promises, Promises.................... $10 United Art. 9902

Jerry Orbach/Jill O'Hara/Edward Winter; mu: Burt Bacharach; ly: Hal David; based on the screenplay *The Apartment*

Christmas Day · Fact Can Be A Beautiful Thing · Grapes Of Roth · Half As Big As Life · I'll Never Fall In Love Again · Knowing When To Leave · Our Little Secret · Overture · Promises, Promises · She Likes Basketball · Turkey Lurkey Time · Upstairs · Wanting Things · Where Can You Take A Girl? · Whoever You Are · You'll Think Of Someone · Young Pretty Girl Like You

---

6/13/70 · 138 · 5 · 107 Purlie.......................... $35 Ampex 40101

Cleavon Little/Melba Moore; mu: Gary Geld; ly: Peter Udell

Barrels Of War (medley) · Big Fish, Little Fish · Down Home · First Thing Monday Mornin' · God's Alive · Great White Father · Harder They Fall · He Can Do It · I Got Love · New Fangled Preacher Man · Purlie · Skinnin' A Cat · Unborn Love (medley) · Walk Him Up The Stairs · World Is Comin' To A Start

---

5/25/59 · 47 · 1 · 108 Redhead.......................... $25 RCA 1048

Gwen Verdon/Richard Kiley; mu: Albert Hague; ly: Dorothy Fields

Behave Yourself · Chase (medley) · Erbie Fitch's Twitch · Finale (medley) · I'll Try · I'm Back In Circulation · Just For Once · Look Who's In Love · Merely Marvelous · My Girl Is Just Enough Woman For Me · Overture · Pick-Pocket Tango · Right Finger Of My Left Hand · She's Just Not Enough Woman For Me · Simpson Sisters' Door · Two Faces In The Dark · Uncle Sam Rag · We Loves Ya, Jimey

---

4/10/65 · 54 · 34 · 109 Roar Of The Greasepaint, The-The Smell Of The Crowd.................. $15 RCA 1109

Anthony Newley/Cyril Ritchard; sw: Anthony Newley and Leslie Bricusse

Beautiful Land · Feeling Good · It Isn't Enough · Joker, The · Look At That Face · My First Love Song · My Way · Nothing Can Stop Me Now! · Overture · Put It In The Book · Sweet Beginning (medley) · That's What It Is To Be Young · Things To Remember · This Dream · What A Man! · Where Would You Be Without Me? · Who Can I Turn To (When Nobody Needs Me) · With All Due Respect · Wonderful Day Like Today

---

11/27/61+ · 36 · 22 · 110 Sail Away.......................... $30 Capitol 1643

Elaine Stritch/James Hurst; sw: Noel Coward

Beatnik Love Affair · Come To Me · Customer's Always Right · Don't Turn Away From Love · Go Slow, Johnny · Later Than Spring · Little Ones' ABC · Passenger's Always Right · Sail Away · Something Very Strange · Useful Phrases · When You Want Me · Where Shall I Find Him? · Why Do The Wrong People Travel? · You're A Long, Long Way From America

---

5/17/69 · 174 · 6 · 111 1776.......................... $10 Columbia 3310

William Daniels/Paul Hecht/Roy Poole; sw: Sherman Edwards; also see Soundtrack ('72)

But, Mr. Adams · Cool, Cool, Considerate Men · Egg, The · Finale · He Plays The Violin · Is Anybody There? · Lees Of Old Virginia · Molasses To Rum · Momma Look Sharp · Piddle, Twiddle And Resolve (medley) · 1776 (Overture) · Sit Down, John · Till Then (medley) · Yours, Yours, Yours

---

6/22/63 · 15 · 17 · 112 She Loves Me.......................... $40 MGM 4118 [2]

Barbara Cook/Daniel Massey/Barbara Baxley/Jack Cassidy; mu: Jerry Bock; ly: Sheldon Harnick

Days Gone By · Dear Friend · Good Morning, Good Day · Goodbye, Georg · Grand Knowing You · I Don't Know His Name · I Resolve · Ice Cream · Ilona · No More Candy · Overture To Act II · Perspective · Romantic Atmosphere · She Loves Me · Sounds While Selling · Tango Tragique · Three Letters · Tonight At Eight · Trip To The Library · Try Me · Twelve Days To Christmas · Where's My Shoe? · Will He Like Me?

9/15/62 · 95 · 6 · 113 Show Boat.......................... $12 Columbia 2220

John Raitt/Barbara Cook/William Warfield/Anita Darian; version of the Jerome Kern & Oscar Hammerstein II musical

After The Ball · Bill · Can't Help Lovin' Dat Man · Cotton Blossom · Finale Act I · Finale Act II · Life Upon The Wicked Stage · Make Believe · Ol' Man River · Opening Act II · Overture · Where's The Mate For Me? · Why Do I Love You? · You Are Love

---

4/16/55 · 9 · 6 · 114 Silk Stockings.......................... $45 RCA 1016

Hildegarde Neff/Don Ameche/Gretchen Wyler; sw: Cole Porter

All Of You (medley) · As On Through The Seasons We Sail · Finale · Hail Bibinski · It's A Chemical Reaction, That's All · Josephine · Overture · Paris Loves Lovers · Red Blues · Satin And Silk · Siberia · Silk Stockings · Stereophonic Sound · Too Bad · Without Love

---

1/8/66 · 128 · 8 · 115 Skyscraper.......................... $15 Capitol 2422

Julie Harris/Peter Marshall/Charles Nelson Reilly; mu: James Van Heusen; ly: Sammy Cahn

Don't Worry · Everybody Has The Right To Be Wrong · Gaiety, The · Haute Couture · I'll Only Miss Her When I Think Of Her · Just The Crust · Local 403 · More Than One Way · Occasional Flight Of Fancy · Opposites · Overture · Run For Your Life · Spare That Building

---

12/21/59+ · 1¹⁶ · 276 · ● · 116 Sound Of Music, The.......................... $10 Columbia 2020

Mary Martin/Theodore Bikel; mu: Richard Rodgers; ly: Oscar Hammerstein II; also see Soundtrack ('65)

Climb Ev'ry Mountain (2 versions) · Do-Re-Me · Edelweiss · How Can Love Survive · Laendler · Lonely Goatherd · Maria · My Favorite Things · No Way To Stop It · Ordinary Couple · Preludium · Processional · Sixteen Going On Seventeen (2 versions) · So Long, Farewell · Sound Of Music (2 versions)

DEBUT DATE	PEAK POS	WKS CHR	G O L D	ARTIST — Album Title	$	Label & Number
11/24/62+	3	76		**117 Stop The World-I Want To Get Off**	**$15**	London 88001

Anthony Newley/Anna Quayle; sw: Leslie Bricusse and Anthony Newley; also see Mantovani

A.B.C. Song (medley)	I Wanna Be Rich (medley)	Once In A Lifetime
All American	Lumbered	Overture (medley)
Family Fugue (medley)	Mellinki Meilchick (medley)	Someone Nice Like You
Glorious Russian (medley)	Mumbo Jumbo	Typically English
Gonna Build A Mountain	Nag! Nag! Nag! (medley)	Typische Deutsche

What Kind Of Fool Am I
[Anthony Newley] 85

4/7/62	81	11		**118 Subways Are For Sleeping**	**$40**	Columbia 2130

Sydney Chaplin/Carol Lawrence/Orson Bean; mu: Jule Styne; ly: Betty Comden and Adolph Green

Be A Santa	I Just Can't Wait	Ride Through The Night (medley)	What Is This Feeling In The Air?
Comes Once In A Lifetime	I Said It And I'm Glad	Strange Duet	Who Knows What Might Have
Finale	I Was A Shoo-In	Subway Directions (medley)	Been?
Girls Like Me	I'm Just Taking My Time	Subways Are For Sleeping	
How Can You Describe A Face?	Overture	Swing Your Projects	

8/25/84	149	11		**119 Sunday in the Park with George**	**$10**	RCA 5042 [2]

Mandy Patinkin/Bernadette Peters; sw: Stephen Sondheim

Beautiful	Day Off	It's Hot Up Here	Putting It Together (medley)
Children And Art	Everybody Loves Louis	Lesson #8	Sunday (includes 2 versions)
Chromolume #7 (medley)	Finishing The Hat	Move On	Sunday In The Park With George
Color And Light	Gossip	No Life	We Do Not Belong Together

6/9/79	78	11		**120 Sweeney Todd-The Demon Barber Of Fleet Street**	**$15**	RCA 3379 [2]

Angela Lansbury/Len Cariou; sw: Stephen Sondheim

Ah, Miss (medley)	Green Finch And Linnet Bird	Lift Your Razor High, Sweeney!	Prelude (medley)
Attend The Tale Of Sweeney	(medley)	(medley)	Pretty Women (medley)
Todd (medley) (includes 2	His Hands Were Quick, His	Little Priest	Sweeney Pondered And
versions)	Fingers Strong (medley)	My Friends (medley)	Sweeney Planned (medley)
Barber And His Wife (medley)	Johanna (includes 3 versions)	No Place Like London (medley)	Sweeny'd Waited Too Long
By The Sea	Kiss Me (medley)	Not While I'm Around	Before (medley)
Contest, The (medley)	Ladies In Their Sensitivities	Parlor Songs	Wait (medley)
Epiphany (medley)	(medley)	Pirelli's Miracle Elixir (medley)	Wigmaker Sequence (medley)
Final Sequence (medley)	Letter, The (medley)	Poor Thing	Worst Pies In London
God, That's Good!			

3/12/66	92	16		**121 Sweet Charity**	**$15**	Columbia 2900

Gwen Verdon/John McMartin; mu: Cy Coleman; ly: Dorothy Fields; also see Soundtrack ('69)

Baby Dream Your Dream	I Love To Cry At Weddings	Rhythm Of Life	Too Many Tomorrows
Big Spender	I'm A Brass Band	Rich Man's Frug	Where Am I Going?
Charity's Soliloquy	I'm The Bravest Individual	Sweet Charity	You Should See Yourself
Charity's Theme	If My Friends Could See Me Now	There's Gotta Be Something	
Finale	Overture	Better Than This	

1/16/61	15	34		**122 Tenderloin**	**$40**	Capitol 1492

Maurice Evans/Ron Husmann/Wayne Miller/Eileen Rodgers; mu: Jerry Bock; ly: Sheldon Harnick

Army Of The Just	Finale	My Miss Mary	Trial, The
Artificial Flowers	Good Clean Fun	Overture	What's In It For You?
Bless This Land	How The Money Changes Hands	Picture Of Happiness	
Dear Friend	Little Old New York	Reform	
Dr. Brock	My Gentle Young Johnny	Tommy, Tommy	

3/24/79	167	6		**123 They're Playing Our Song**	**$8**	Casablanca 7141

Robert Klein/Lucie Arnaz; mu: Marvin Hamlisch; ly: Carole Bayer Sager

Entr'acte	I Still Believe In Love	Right	When You're In My Arms
Fallin'	If He Really Knew Me	They're Playing Our Song	Workin' It Out
Fill In The Words	Just For Tonight	(includes 3 versions)	

8/6/66	145	2		**124 Time For Singing, A**	**$50**	Warner 1639

Ivor Emmanuel/Tessie O'Shea/Shani Wallis; mu: John Morris; ly: Gerald Freedman and John Morris; based on the novel *How Green Was My Valley*

Come You Men	I've Nothing To Give You	Peace Come To Every Heart	Three Ships
Far From Home	(medley)	(medley)	Time For Singing
Gone In Sorrow (medley)	Let Me Love You (medley)	Someone Must Try	What A Good Day Is Saturday
How Green Was My Valley	Mountains Sing Back	Tell Her	When He Looks At Me
I Wonder If	Oh, How I Adore Your Name	That's What Young Ladies Do	Why Would Anyone Want To
I'm Always Wrong	Old Long John	There Is Beautiful You Are	Get Married

7/27/63	64	11		**125 Tovarich**	**$30**	Capitol 1940

Vivean Leigh/Jean Pierre Aumont/Alexander Scourby; mu: Lee Pockriss; ly: Anne Croswell

All For You	Make A Friend	Overture	That Face
I Go To Bed	Nitchevo	Say You'll Stay	Uh-Oh!
I Know The Feeling	No! No! No!	Small Cartel	Wilkes-Barre, Pa.
It Used To Be	Only One	Stuck With Each Other	You Love Me

5/8/76	200	2		**126 Treemonisha**	**$10**	DG 2707 [2]

Carmen Balthrop/Betty Allen/Curtis Rayam; sw: Scott Joplin; cd: Gunther Schuller; pf: Houston Grand Opera

Afternoon	Evening	Morning

12/26/60+	6	48		**127 Unsinkable Molly Brown, The**	**$15**	Capitol 1509

Tammy Grimes/Harve Presnell; sw: Meredith Willson; also see Soundtrack ('64)

Are You Sure?	Dolce Far Niente (medley)	I'll Never Say No	My Own Brass Bed
Bea-u-ti-ful People Of Denver	Happy Birthday, Mrs. J.J.	I've A'ready Started In	Overture
Belly Up To The Bar, Boys	Brown	If I Knew	Up Where The People Are
Bon Jour (The Language Song)	I Ain't Down Yet	Keep-A-Hoppin' (medley)	
Chick-A-Pen	I May Never Fall In Love With	Leadville Johnny Brown	
Denver Police	You (medley)	(Soliloquy) (medley)	

3/17/58+	5	191	●	**128 West Side Story**	**$15**	Columbia 5230

Carol Lawrence/Larry Kert/Chita Rivera/Art Smith; mu: Leonard Bernstein; ly: Stephen Sondheim; also see Leonard Bernstein/Soundtrack ('61)

America	Finale	Jet Song (medley)	Rumble, The
Boy Like That (medley)	Gee, Officer Krupke!	Maria	Something's Coming
Cool	I Feel Pretty	One Hand, One Heart	Somewhere
Dance At The Gym	I Have A Love (medley)	Prologue (medley)	Tonight

DEBUT DATE	PEAK POS	WKS CHR	GOLD	ARTIST — Album Title	$	Label & Number
4/4/64	28	14	129	**What Makes Sammy Run?** .... sw: Ervin Drake Steve Lawrence/Sally Ann Howes/Robert Alda; sw: Ervin Drake	$40	Columbia 2440

Friendliest Thing · Maybe Some Other Time · Some Days Everything Goes Wrong · You Can Trust Me (medley)
I Feel Humble · My Hometown · You Help Me
I See Something · New Pair Of Shoes · Something To Live For · You're No Good
Kiss Me No Kisses · Overture · Tender Spot
Lites! Camera! Platitude! · Room Without Windows (medley) · Wedding Of The Year

DEBUT DATE	PEAK POS	WKS CHR	GOLD	ARTIST — Album Title	$	Label & Number
1/30/61	6	41	130	**Wildcat** .... Lucille Ball/Keith Andes; mu: Cy Coleman; ly: Carolyn Leigh	$25	RCA 1060

Corduroy Road · Hey, Look Me Over! · Tall Hope · Wildcat
El Sombrero · Oil! · That's What I Want For Janie · You're A Liar!
Finale · One Day We Dance · Tippy Tippy Toes · You've Come Home
Give A Little Whistle · Overture · What Takes My Fancy

DEBUT DATE	PEAK POS	WKS CHR	GOLD	ARTIST — Album Title	$	Label & Number
5/3/75	43	16	● 131	**Wiz, The** .... Stephanie Mills/Tiger Haynes/Ted Ross/Hinton Battle; sw: Charlie Smalls; also see Soundtrack ('78)	$8	Atlantic 18137

Be A Lion · He's The Wizard · If You Believe · Soon As I Get Home
Don't Nobody Bring Me No Bad News · Home (Finale) · Prologue · Tornado
Ease On Down The Road · I Was Born On The Day Before Yesterday · Slide Some Oil To Me · What Would I Do If I Could Feel
Everybody Rejoice · I'm A Mean Ole Lion · So You Wanted To See The Wizard · Y'all Got It!
Feeling We Once Had

DEBUT DATE	PEAK POS	WKS CHR	GOLD	ARTIST — Album Title	$	Label & Number
6/27/81	196	2	132	**Woman Of The Year** .... Lauren Bacall/Harry Guardino; mu: John Kander; ly: Fred Ebb	$8	Arista 8303

Grass Is Always Greener · One Of The Boys · So What Else Is New? · Woman Of The Year
Happy In The Morning · Overture · Sometimes A Day Goes By
I Told You So · Poker Game · Table Talk
I Wrote The Book · See You In The Funny Papers · We're Gonna Work It Out
It Isn't Working · Shut Up Gerald · When You're Right; You're Right

DEBUT DATE	PEAK POS	WKS CHR	GOLD	ARTIST — Album Title	$	Label & Number
7/1/67	165	5	133	**You're A Good Man, Charlie Brown** .... Gary Burghoff/Bob Balaban/Bill Hinnant/Reva Rose; sw: Clark Gesner; based on the comic strip *Peanuts*	$15	MGM 9

Book Report · Little Known Facts · Red Baron · T-E-A-M (Baseball Game)
Dr. Lucy · My Blanket & Me · Schroeder · You're A Good Man, Charlie Brown
Happiness · Peanuts Potpourri · Snoopy
Kite · Queen Lucy · Suppertime

DEBUT DATE	PEAK POS	WKS CHR	GOLD	ARTIST — Album Title	$	Label & Number
1/25/69	177	7	134	**Zorba** .... Herschel Bernardi/Maria Karnilova; mu: John Kander; ly: Fred Ebb; also see Soundtrack *Zorba The Greek* ('65)	$15	Capitol 118

Bend Of The Road (medley) · Goodbye, Canavaro · No Boom Boom · Zorba's Dance (medley)
Butterfly, The · Grandpapa (medley) · Only Love (medley)
Crow, The (medley) · Happy Birthday (medley) · Top Of The Hill
Entr'acte · I Am Free (medley) · Why Can't I Speak?
First Time · Life Is · Y'assou

DEBUT DATE	PEAK POS	WKS CHR	GOLD	ARTIST — Album Title	$	Label & Number

TELEVISION SHOWS/MINI SERIES

The stars of the show are listed directly below the title.

11/20/71+ | 8 | 22 | ● — **1 All In The Family**..[C] **$10** Atlantic 7210
Carroll O'Connor/Jean Stapleton/Rob Reiner/Sally Struthers; comedy excerpts from the show

Archie's Hangup	Jury Duty	Sweety Pie Roger	VD Day
Bacon Souffle & Women's Lib	No Ribs?	**Those Were The Days** [Carroll	Why God Made Hands
Do You Love Me?	Shove Yours	O'Connor & Jean Stapleton] 43	
God Is Black	Station Wagon Filled With Nuns	Transplants	

12/30/72+ | 129 | 8 — **2 All In The Family - 2nd Album**..[C] **$10** Atlantic 7232
more comedy excerpts from the show

Archie And Maude	Breasts	Elevator, The	Man In The Street
Archie In Jail	Change Of Life	Hog Jowls	Sammy's Visit
Archie Meets Mike			

4/23/66 | 112 | 8 — **3 Batman**...[I-T] **$40** 20th Century 4180
Adam West/Burt Ward; cd: Nelson Riddle; music and dialogue excerpts from the show; also
see Neal Hefti and The Marketts

Batman Blues	Batman Thaws Mr. Freeze -or-	Gotham City	To The Batmobile
Batman Pows The Penguin -or-	(That's The Way The Ice-Cube	Holy Flypaper	Two Perfectly Ordinary People
(Aha, My Fine-Feathered	Crumbles!)	Holy-Hole-In-The-Doughnut	-or- (!!!!)
Finks!)	Batman Theme	-or- (Robin, You've Done It	Zelda Tempts Batman -or-
Batman Riddles The Riddler!	Batusi A-Go! Go! -or- (I Shouldn't	Again!)	(Must He Go It Alone???)
-or- (Hi Diddle Riddle)	Wish To Attract Attention)		

10/21/78 | 144 | 6 — **4 Battlestar Galactica**...[I] **$8** MCA 3051
Lorne Greene/Richard Hatch/Dirk Benedict; cp/cd: Stu Phillips; pf: Los Angeles Philharmonic Orchestra

Adama's Theme	Cylon Trap	Exploration (medley)	Main Title
Boxey's Problem (medley)	Dash To The Elevator	Fighter Launch	Red Nova
Cassiopia And Starbuck	Destruction Of Peace	It's Love, Love, Love (The Casino	Serena's Illness (medley)
Cylon Base Ship (Imperious	End Of The Atlantia	On Carillon)	Suffering
Leader)	Escape From The Ovion Mines	Let's Go Home (End Title)	

6/17/89 | 157 | 10 — **5 Beauty and The Beast / of Love and Hope**......................[I-T] **$8** Capitol 91583
Linda Hamilton/Ron Perlman; cp/cd: Lee Holdridge; includes poetry readings by the show's Vincent (Ron Perlman)

Angel's Theme	Devin's Theme (I Arise From	Journey's End (Sonnet #CXVI)	Return, The
Beauty And The Beast	The Dreams Of Thee)	Laura's Theme	Riches, Not Gold
(Acquainted With The Night)	Father Remembers (Composed	Margaret's Theme (Longing)	Single Night (Love-Song)
Broken Dreams	On Westminster Bridge)	Night Of Beauty	To Cast All Else Aside
Catherine's Lullabye	Fear (You Darkness)	On Her Own (She Walks In	
(Somewhere I Have Never	First Time I Loved Forever	Beauty)	
Travelled)	Happy Life (This Is The	Promise Remembered	
Dancing Light (Sonnet #XXIX)	Creature)	Quest (Letters To A Young Poet)	

Ben Casey - see VALJEAN
Vince Edwards/Sam Jaffe

11/7/92 | 82 | 14↑ — **6 Beverly Hills, 90210 - The Soundtrack**.............................[V] **$12** Giant 24465
Luke Perry/Jason Priestly/Shannon Doherty/Jennie Garth

Action Speaks Louder Than	Beverly Hills, 90210 (Theme)	Let Me Be Your Baby [Geoffrey	**Saving Forever For You**
Words [Tara Kemp]	[John Davis]	Williams]	[Shanice] 4
All The Way To Heaven [Jody	Got To Have You [Color Me Badd]	**Love Is** [Vanessa Williams &	Time To Be Lovers [Michael
Watley]	Just Wanna Be Your Friend	Brian McKnight] 66↑	McDonald & Chaka Khan]
Bend Time Back Around [Paula	[Puck & Natty]	Right Kind Of Love [Jeremy	Why [Cathy Dennis with D-Mob]
Abdul]		Jordan] 53↑	

11/24/62+ | 49 | 9 — **7 Bonanza**.. **$25** RCA 2583
Lorne Greene/Michael Landon/Dan Blocker/Pernell Roberts; songs performed by each of the stars

Bonanza	Happy Birthday	Place Where I Worship (Is The	Skip To My Lou
Careless Love	In The Pines	Wide Open Spaces)	Sky Ball Paint
Early One Morning	Miss Cindy	Ponderosa	Sourwood Mountain
Hangin' Blues	My Sons, My Sons	Shenandoah	

5/13/72 | 108 | 19 — **8 Brady Bunch, Meet The**... **$20** Paramount 6032
Robert Reed/Florence Henderson; featuring songs by the 6 kids of the series

Ain't It Crazy	Day After Day	Me And You And A Dog Named	We Can Make The World A
American Pie	I Believe In You	Boo	Whole Lot Brighter
Baby, I'm-A Want You	I Just Want To Be Your Friend	Time To Change	We'll Always Be Friends
Come Run With Me	Love My Life Away		

12/22/90+ | 76 | 15 — **9 Civil War, The**...[I+V] **$12** Elektra N. 79256
from the documentary series produced by public television; pf: Jay Ungar/Jacqueline Schwab/New American Brass Band

All Quiet On The Potomac	Bonnie Blue Flag (medley)	Kingdom Coming	Sullivan Ballou Letter
Angel Band	Cheer Boys Cheer	Lorena	We Are Climbing Jacob's Ladder
Ashokan Farewell (includes 2	Dixie (includes 2 versions)	Marching Through Georgia	Weeping Sad And Lonely
versions)	Drums Of War	(includes 2 versions)	When Johnny Comes Marching
Battle Cry Of Freedom	Flag Of Columbia	Palmyra Schottische	Home (includes 2 versions)
Battle Hymn Of The Republic	Hail Columbia	Parade	Yankee Doodle
(includes 2 versions)	Johnny Has Gone For A Soldier	Shenandoah	

3/1/86 | 125 | 7 — **10 Cosby Show, Music From The - A House Full Of Love**..................... **$8** Columbia 40270
Bill Cosby/Phylicia Rashad; sw: Bill Cosby/Stu Gardner; pf: Grover Washington, Jr.

Camille	Huxtable Kids	Love In Its Proper Place	Resthatherian
Clair (Phylicia)	Kitchen Jazz	Outstretched Hands (Gloria)	
House Full Of Love	Look At This	Poppin'	

5/9/81 | 136 | 13 — **11 Cosmos, The Music Of**..[I] **$8** RCA 4003
selections from PBS television series hosted by Carl Sagan; cp/cd: various

Affirmation	Exploration	Life
Cataclysm	Harmony Of Nature	Space/Time Continuum

Dallas - see CRAMER, Floyd
Larry Hagman/Victoria Principal/Patrick Duffy

DEBUT DATE	PEAK POS	WKS CHR	GOLD	ARTIST — Album Title	$	Label & Number

8/2/69 — **18** — 19 — 12 — **Dark Shadows** ....[I] — **$30** — Philips 314
Jonathan Frid/David Selby; cp/cd: Robert Cobert

Back At The Blue Whale	I, Barnabas	#1 At The Blue Whale	Shadows Of The Night
Collinwood (medley)	I'll Be With You, Always	Old House	(Quentin's Theme)
Dark Shadows (medley)	Josette's Theme	Seance	When I Am Dead
Darkness At Collinwood	Meditations	Secret Room	
Epitaph	Night Of The Pentagram		

4/17/82 — **93** — 14 — 13 — **Dukes Of Hazzard, The** .... — **$8** — Scotti Br. 37712
John Schneider/Tom Wopat/Sorrell Booke/James Best; includes songs and narration by cast members

Ballad Of The General Lee [Doug Kershaw]	Duelin' Dukes	In The Driver's Seat	Laughing All The Way To The Bank
Cover Girl Eyes [Doug Kershaw]	Flash	Keep Between Them Ditches [Doug Kershaw]	Up On Cripple Creek
Down Home American Girl	General Lee [Johnny Cash]		
	Good Ol' Boys		

Fame - see KIDS FROM "FAME"
Debbie Allen/Lee Curreri

Flying Nun, The - see FIELD, Sally
Sally Field/Alejandro Rey

5/23/70 — **196** — 4 — 14 — **Hee Haw, The Stars Of** .... — **$10** — Capitol 437
Buck Owens/Roy Clark

Big Mama's Medicine Show [Buddy Alan]	Gotta Get To Oklahoma ('Cause California's Gettin' To Me) [Hagers]	Maybe If I Close My Eyes (It'll Go Away) [Susan Raye]	We're Gonna Get Together [Buck Owens & Susan Raye]
Biggest Storm Of All [Doyle Holly & The Buckaroos]	How Long Will My Baby Be Gone [Buck Owens & The Buckaroos]	Nobody But You [Don Rich & The Buckaroos]	When The Wind Blows In Chicago [Roy Clark]
Buckaroo [Buck Owens & The Buckaroos] **60**		Overdue Blues [Roy Clark]	

11/7/92 — **40** — 14↑ — 15 — **Heights, The** .... — **$12** — Capitol 80328
Alex Desert/Ken Garito/Cheryl Pollack/Charlotte Ross; songs by the cast

Battleground	**How Do You Talk To An Angel** **1**	Man You Used To Be (A Song For Dad)	Strongest Man Alive
Children Of The Night		Natalie	What Does It Take (To Win Your Love)
Common Ground	I'm Still On Your Side		
Feelin' Alright	Joanne	Rear View Mirror	
Friendship		So Hot	

12/5/92 — **137** — 2 — 16 — **Jacksons: An American Dream, The** ....[V] — **$12** — Motown 6356
actual title: Album Inspired By "The Jacksons: An American Dream" Mini Series; 7 of the 13 tracks are performed by The Jacksons

ABC (medley) [Jackson 5]	I Want You Back (medley) [Jackson 5]	Love You Save (medley) [Jackson 5]	Walk On (medley) [Jackson 5]
Dancing Machine (includes 2 versions) [Jackson 5] **2**	**I'll Be There** [Jackson 5] **1**	**Never Can Say Goodbye** [Jackson 5] **2**	Who's Lovin' You [Jackson 5]
Dream Goes On [Jermaine Jackson]	**In The Still Of The Night** [Boyz II Men] **3**	Stay With Love [Jermaine Jackson & Syreeta Wright]	You Are The Ones [3T]
I Wanna Be Where You Are [Jason Weaver]	Kansas City [Jason Weaver]		

10/19/68+ — **105** — 17 — 17 — **Laugh-In** .... [C] — **$12** — Epic 15118
Dan Rowan/Dick Martin/Arte Johnson/Judy Carne/Goldie Hawn

Cocktail Party	Goodnight Dick!	New Talent	Sock It To Me--Potpourri
Cuckoo Laugh-In World	Half Time	News--Past, Present And Future	
Cuckoos, The	Here Come The Judge	Other Cocktail Party	
Etcetera	Mod Mod World	Personality Of The Week	

4/5/69 — **88** — 10 — 18 — **Laugh-in '69** .... [C] — **$10** — Reprise 6335
second cast album featuring comedy highlights

American Institution	Chamber Of Commerce	Mecca	Vacation In
Big Cocktail Party	Children Of Laugh-in	News, The	Well, Ring My Chimes!
Broncos	Down Town	Swingers	
Bus Stop	Dum Dums	Trading Center	
By Henry Gibson	Laugh-in Strikes Again	Up Town	

Man From U.N.C.L.E., The - see MONTENEGRO, Hugo
Robert Vaughn/David McCallum

10/12/85 — **1**[11] — 34 — ▲2 — 19 — **Miami Vice** ....[V] — **$8** — MCA 6150
Don Johnson/Philip Michael Thomas

Better Be Good To Me [Tina Turner] **5**	**In The Air Tonight** [Phil Collins] **19**	**Own The Night** [Chaka Khan] **57**	Vice [Grandmaster Melle Mel]
Chase [Jan Hammer]	**Miami Vice Theme** [Jan Hammer] **1**	**Smuggler's Blues** [Glenn Frey] **12**	**You Belong To The City** [Glenn Frey] **2**
Evan [Jan Hammer]			
Flashback [Jan Hammer]			

12/6/86+ — **82** — 12 — 20 — **Miami Vice II** .... [V] — **$8** — MCA 6192
second album of songs featured on the show

Crockett's Theme [Jan Hammer]	Lives In The Balance [Jackson Browne]	Miami Vice Theme [Jan Hammer]	**Take Me Home** [Phil Collins] **7**
In Dulce Decorum [Damned]	Lover [Roxy Music]	New York Theme [Jan Hammer]	**When The Rain Comes Down** [Andy Taylor] **73**
Last Unbroken Heart [Patti LaBelle & Bill Champlin]	Mercy [Steve Jones]	Send It To Me [Gladys Knight & The Pips]	

Mickey Mouse Club - see CHILDREN'S ALBUMS
Jimmy Dodd/Annette Funicello/Dennis Day

7/23/66 — **120** — 15 — 21 — **Mickie Finn's - America's No.1 Speakeasy** ....[L] — **$15** — Dunhill 50009
San Diego night club specializing in Gay '90s music; featuring pianist Fred Finn and his wife Mickie (banjo)

Alley Cat	K.C. Jerk	Mickie Finn Theme	When The Saints Come Marching In
Beer Barrel Polka	King Of The Road	Side By Side	You've Gotta See Your Mama Every Night
Bye, Bye Blackbird	Let Me Call You Sweetheart	Swinging On A Star (medley)	
It's A Sin To Tell A Lie (medley)	Liebestraum		

Mission: Impossible - see SCHIFRIN, Lalo
Peter Graves/Greg Morris/Martin Landau

8/8/87 — **50** — 14 — 22 — **Moonlighting** ....[V-O] — **$8** — MCA 6214
Cybill Shepherd/Bruce Willis

Blue Moon [Cybill Shepherd]	I Told Ya I Love Ya, Now Get Out! [Cybill Shepherd]	**Limbo Rock** [Chubby Checker] **2**	Since I Fell For You [Bob James & David Sanborn]
Good Lovin' [Bruce Willis]		**Moonlighting** [Al Jarreau] **23**	

DEBUT DATE	PEAK POS	WKS CHR	G O L D	ARTIST — Album Title	$	Label & Number

Someone To Watch Over Me
[Linda Ronstadt]
Stormy Weather [Billie Holiday]

This Old Heart Of Mine (Is Weak For You) [Isley Brothers] 12

When A Man Loves A Woman [Percy Sledge] 1

Mr. Lucky - see MANCINI, Henry
John Vivyan/Ross Martin/Pippa Scott

MTV - see BENEFIT RECORDINGS

Muppet Show, The - see CHILDREN'S ALBUMS
Jim Henson/Frank Oz

| 5/9/60 | **30** | 2 | 23 | One Step Beyond, Music From .... [I] | **$30** | Decca 8970 |

from the *Alcoa Presents* TV series hosted by John Newland; cd: Harry Lubin; pf: Berlin Symphony Orchestra

Bullfight	Island Off Spain	Paris	Weird
Bygone Memories	Jungle Aire	Pathetique	You Are My Love
Fear	On The Terrace	Trip To The Far East	

Peter Gunn - see MANCINI, Henry
Craig Stevens/Herschel Bernardi/Lola Albright

Roaring 20's, The - see PROVINE, Dorothy
Dorothy Provine/Donald May/Rex Reason

Roots - see JONES, Quincy
LeVar Burton/John Amos/Leslie Uggams/Ben Vereen

Sanford and Son - see FOXX, Redd
Redd Foxx/Demond Wilson/LaWanda Page/Whitman Mayo

| 12/25/76+ | **38** | 13 | 24 | Saturday Night Live .... [C] | **$10** | Arista 4107 |

John Belushi/Dan Aykroyd/Chevy Chase/Jane Curtin/Gilda Radner

Anna Freud	Fluckers	Monologue	Weatherman
Bedtime Story	Fondue	News For The Hard Of Hearing	Weekend Update
Bees On Parade	Gerald Ford	Shimmer	Word Association
Chevy's Girls	Goodbyes	Speed	
Dueling Brandos	Gun Control	Spud	
Emily Litella	Jimmy Carter	Uvula	

Sesame Street - see CHILDREN'S ALBUMS
Bob McGrath/Loretta Lang/Will Lee/Jim Henson/Frank Oz

| 4/20/59 | **3** | 28 | 25 | 77 Sunset Strip .... [I] | **$35** | Warner 1289 |

Efrem Zimbalist, Jr./Roger Smith/Ed "Kookie" Byrnes; musical director: Warren Barker

Blue Night On The Strip	If I Could Be With You	77 Sunset Strip (includes 2 versions)	You Took Advantage Of Me
Caper At The Coffee House	Kookie's Caper		
Cleo's Theme	Late At Bailey's Pad	Stu Bailey Blues	
I Get A Kick Out Of You	Lover Come Back To Me	Swingin' On The Strip	

| 10/4/80 | **115** | 6 | 26 | Shogun .... [I] | **$8** | RSO 3088 |

Richard Chamberlain/Toshiro Mifune/Yoko Shimada; cp/cd: Maurice Jarre; from the NBC-TV mini series

Anjiro	Despair And Madness	Mariko	Tea And Jealousy
Blackthorne	Escape From Osaka	Nocturne	To The Galley!
Ceremonial	Japans, The	Shogun	Toranaga

| 12/1/73+ | **34** | 23 | 27 | Sunshine .... | **$10** | MCA 387 |

Cliff DeYoung/Christina Raines; cp: John Denver; vocals by Cliff DeYoung; from the CBS-TV movie

Day Dreams (includes 2 versions)	Goodbye Again	If I Had A Piano	Take Me Home, Country Roads
Diary	Goodbye, Sam & Jill	**My Sweet Lady (includes 3 versions)** [Cliff DeYoung] 17	Winter
Flashback	Hello Tape Recorder		
	I'm Gonna Miss You, Sam & Jill	Sunshine (includes 3 versions)	

Taxi - see JAMES, Bob
Judd Hirsch/Tony Danza/Marilu Henner/Danny DeVito/Andy Kaufman

| 6/10/89 | **159** | 18 | 28 | TeeVee Toons: The Commercials .... | **$8** | TVT 1400 |

the jingles of 56 classic television advertisements; narration by Don Pardo

Ajax Cleanser	Coca Cola (I'd Like To Buy The World A Coke)	Kellogg's Rice Krispies	Noxzema Shave Cream
Ajax Laundry Detergent	Coca Cola (It's The Real Thing)	Ken-L Ration Dog And Puppy Food	Old Spice Long Lasting Cologne
Alka Seltzer Effervescent Antacid (Plop Plop Fizz Fizz)	Coca Cola (Things Go Better With Coke)	Kent Cigarettes	Oreo Chocolate Sandwich Cookies
Alka Seltzer Effervescent Antacid (The Shape Your Stomach's In)	Colt 45 Malt Liquor	Lowenbrau Beer	Pepsi Cola
	Cracker Jack	Magnificent Seven (The Marlboro Song)	Polaroid Swinger
Armour Hot Dogs	Dippity Do Styling Gel	Marshmallow Fluff	Rheingold Extra Dry Beer
Ballantine Premium Lager Beer (Add A Ring)	Dr. Pepper	Meow Mix Cat Food	Rice-A-Roni
Ballantine Premium Lager Beer (Hey Get Your Cold Beer)	Fab Laundry Detergent	Miller High Life	Salem Cigarettes
	Gillette Blue Blades (How're You Fixed For Blades)	Mounds And Almond Joy Candy Bars	Sara Lee
Bosco	Gillette Blue Blades (Look Sharp March)	Mr. Clean All Purpose Cleaner	Schaefer Beer
Brylcreem		Muriel Cigars (Hey Big Spender)	Schlitz Beer
Budweiser Beer	Good & Plenty	Muriel Cigars (Pick One Up And Smoke It Sometime)	Slinky
Chevrolet Motors	Hawaiian Punch Fruit Punch		Texaco
Chiquita Bananas	Health PSA	NYS Department of Safety	Winston Cigarettes
Chock Full O'Nuts Coffee	Hershey's Chocolate Bars	Nestles Quik Chocolate Flavor	

| 11/9/85+ | **82** | 34 | 29 | Television's Greatest Hits .... | **$8** | TeeVee T. 1100 [2] |

65 TV themes from the '50s and '60s; narration by Don Pardo

Adam 12	Casper, The Friendly Ghost	Flintstones (Meet The Flintstones)	Late Late Show (The Syncopated Clock)
Addams Family	Combat	Flipper	Leave It To Beaver (The Toy Parade)
Adventures Of Rin Tin Tin	Daniel Boone	Get Smart	Little Rascals (Good Old Days)
Alfred Hitchcock Presents	Dennis The Menace	Gilligan's Island	Lone Ranger (William Tell Overture)
Andy Griffith Show	Dick Van Dyke Show	Green Acres	Lost In Space
Batman	Donna Reed Show	Hawaii Five-O	Magilla Gorilla Show
Beverly Hillbillies (Ballad Of Jed Clampett)	Dragnet	Howdy Doody	Man From U.N.C.L.E.
Bonanza	F Troop	I Dream Of Jeannie	Mannix
Branded	F.B.I.	I Love Lucy	Many Loves Of Dobie Gillis
Bugs Bunny Show (This Is It)	Felix The Cat	Ironside	
Captain Kangaroo (Puffin' Billy)	Fireball XL-5	Jetsons	

DEBUT DATE	PEAK POS	WKS CHR	G O L D	ARTIST — Album Title	$	Label & Number

McHale's Navy · Peer Gynt-WTVT Sign On · Superman · Twilight Zone
Mission: Impossible · Perry Mason · Surfside 6 · WTVT Sign Off-The Star
Mister Ed · Petticoat Junction · Technical Difficulties (Please · Spangled Banner
Mod Squad · Popeye · Stand By) · Wild Wild West
Munsters · Rifleman · Test Of The Emergency · Woody Woodpecker Show
My Three Sons · Roy Rogers Show (Happy Trails) · Broadcast System-Duck And · Yogi Bear
News Medley (We Interrupt This · Secret Agent Man · Cover
Program) · 77 Sunset Strip · Tonight Show (Johnny's Theme)
Patty Duke Show · Star Trek · Top Cat

| 11/15/86 | 149 | 16 | | **30** Television's Greatest Hits, Volume II.............................. | $8 | TeeVee T. 1200 [2] |

65 more TV themes from the '50s and '60s

ABC's Wide World Of Sports · Hogan's Heroes · Mighty Mouse · Saint
Adventures Of Robin Hood · Honeymooners (You're My · Mister Roger's Neighborhood · Sea Hunt
Avengers · Greatest Love) · (Won't You Be My Neighbor?) · Smothers Brothers Comedy
Bat Masterson · Huckleberry Hound · Monkees · Hour
Ben Casey · I Married Joan · Monty Python's Flying Circus · Spider-Man
Bewitched · I Spy · My Favorite Martian · Tarzan
Brady Bunch · It's About Time · My Mother The Car · That Girl
Car 54, Where Are You? · Jackie Gleason Show · NBC Mystery Movie · Three Stooges
Courageous Cat & Minute · (Melancholy Serenade) · Odd Couple · Time Tunnel
Mouse · Jeopardy (Think Music) · Outer Limits · Twelve O'Clock High
Courtship Of Eddie's Father (My · Jonny Quest · Partridge Family (Come On Get · Underdog
Best Friend) · Looney Tunes (The · Happy) · Virginian
Daktari · Merry-Go-Round Breaks · Peanuts Theme (Linus & Lucy) · Voyage To The Bottom Of The
Dark Shadows · Down) · Peter Gunn · Sea
George Of The Jungle · Love, American Style · Pink Panther · Wagon Train
Gidget · Mary Tyler Moore (Love Is All · Rat Patrol
Gomer Pyle, U.S.M.C. · Around) · Rawhide
Green Hornet · Maverick · Rebel
Have Gun Will Travel (The · Medical Center · Road Runner
Ballad Of Paladin) · Merrie Melodies (Merrily We Roll · Rocky & Bullwinkle
Hawaiian Eye · Along) · Route 66

| 12/21/74+ | 30 | 11 | ● | **31** Tonight Show, Magic Moments From The - Here's Johnny .... [C] | $10 | Casablanca 1296 [2] |

actual musical and comedy excerpts from the TV show hosted by Johnny Carson from 10/1/62-5/22/92

All In The Family [Lucille Ball & · Copper Capers [Peter Falk & · Lullabye Of Broadway (medley) · Singing In The Rain [Sammy
Desi Arnaz, Jr.] · Jack Webb] · [Bette Midler] · Davis, Jr.]
Anniversary Salute [Dean Martin] · Discovery, The [Lenny Bruce] · Man That Got Away [Judy · Stars And Stripes Forever
Art Fern & The Teatime Movies · Father's Day [Groucho Marx] · Garland] · [Richard Nixon & John Twomey]
Beginning, The · Fiddler On The Bus [Jack Benny] · Morningside Heights [George · Them There Eyes [Billie Holliday]
Bleep That... [Buddy Hackett & · Free For All [Jerry Lewis & Joey · Carlin] · Tonto, Tonto [Jay Silverheels]
Dean Martin] · Bishop] · Mr. Warmth [Don Rickles] · Until You Come Back To Me
Boil That Cabbage Down · Indiana [Glen Campbell] · Ode To Billy Joe [Doc Severinsen] · (That's What I'm Gonna Do)
[Smothers Brothers] · It's Gonna Work Out Fine [Ike & · Our Love Is Here To Stay [Pearl · [Aretha Franklin]
Boogie Woogie Bugle Boy · Tina Turner] · Bailey] · What A Band
(medley) [Bette Midler] · See Saw [Luci Arnaz]

| 9/29/90 | 22 | 25 | ● | **32** Twin Peaks...[I] | $12 | Warner 26316 |

Kyle McLachlan/Michael Ontkean/Joan Chen/Sherilyn Fenn; instrumental except for 3 vocal tracks by Julee Cruise; lyrics and co-production by show's director David Lynch; cp/cd: Angelo Badalamenti

Audrey's Dance · Falling [Julee Cruise] · Laura Palmer's Theme · Nightingale, The [Julee Cruise]
Bookhouse Boys · Freshly Squeezed · Love Theme · Twin Peaks Theme
Dance Of The Dream Man · Into The Night [Julee Cruise] · Night Life In Twin Peaks

Velveteen Rabbit, The - see CHILDREN'S

| 11/10/58+ | 2⁴ | 89 | | **33** Victory At Sea, Vol. 2..[I] | $20 | RCA 2226 |

Allies On The March · Fire On The Waters · Mediterranean Mosaic · Sound Of Victory
Danger Down Deep · Magnetic North · Peleliu · Voyage Into Fate

| 9/11/61 | 7 | 32 | | **34** Victory At Sea, Vol. 3..[I] | $15 | RCA 2523 |

above 2 are orchestral suites from the NBC-TV series which featured actual film of World War II naval battles; cp: Richard Rodgers; cd: Robert Russell Bennett

Full Fathom Five · Ships That Pass · Turkey Shoot · Two If By Sea
Rings Around Rabaul · Symphonic Scenario · Turning Point

Waltons, The - see CHRISTMAS: Top Pop Albums Chart — Various section
Richard Thomas/Ralph Waite/Michael Lerned/Will Geer/Ellen Corby

TELEVISION SPECIALS:

Aloha From Hawaii via Satellite - see PRESLEY, Elvis

Barbra Streisand...and other musical instruments — see STREISAND, Barbra

Cinderella - see ORIGINAL CASTS

Color Me Barbra — see STREISAND, Barbra

Diana! - see ROSS, Diana

Elvis - see PRESLEY, Elvis

Elvis In Concert - see PRESLEY, Elvis

Goin' Back To Indiana - see JACKSON 5

Happening In Central Park — see STREISAND, Barbra

Liza With A "Z" - see MINNELLI, Liza

Movin' With Nancy - see SINATRA, Nancy

My Name Is Barbra— see STREISAND, Barbra

On Broadway - see SUPREMES and/or TEMPTATIONS

Point!, The - see NILSSON

Really Rosie - see KING, Carole

TCB - see SUPREMES and/or TEMPTATIONS

Temptations Show, The - see TEMPTATIONS

DEBUT DATE	PEAK POS	WKS CHR	GOLD	ARTIST — Album Title	$	Label & Number

COMPILATIONS BY RECORD LABEL

A&M

| 2/17/68 | 194 | 4 | | 1 Family Portrait | $12 | A&M 19002 |
| 12/22/90+ | 131 | 11 | | 2 Jam Harder - The A&M Underground Dance Compilation | $12 | A&M 5339 |

ALLIGATOR

| 5/18/91 | 187 | 1 | | 3 Alligator Records 20th Anniversary Collection, The | $12 | Alligator 105/6 [2] |

ATCO

| 3/1/69 | 178 | 5 | | 4 Super Groups, The | $12 | Atco 279 |

ATLANTIC

4/6/68	187	3		5 History of Rhythm & Blues, volume 1/The Roots 1947-52	$12	Atlantic 8161
3/30/68	173	5		6 History of Rhythm & Blues, volume 2/The Golden Years 1953-55	$12	Atlantic 8162
4/6/68	189	3		7 History of Rhythm & Blues, volume 3/Rock & Roll 1956-57	$12	Atlantic 8163
4/6/68	180	4		8 History of Rhythm & Blues, volume 4/The Big Beat 1958-60	$12	Atlantic 8164
11/24/56	20	2		9 Rock & Roll Forever	$150	Atlantic 1239
3/19/66	107	19		10 Solid Gold Soul	$15	Atlantic 8116
8/5/67	12	60		11 Super Hits, The	$12	Atlantic 501
7/20/68	76	33		12 Super Hits, Vol. 2, The	$12	Atlantic 8188
11/23/68+	68	19		13 Super Hits, Vol. 3, The	$12	Atlantic 8203
7/19/69	164	10		14 Super Hits, Vol. 4, The	$12	Atlantic 8224
3/16/68	146	22		15 This Is Soul	$12	Atlantic 8170

BUDDAH

| 3/22/69 | 105 | 9 | | 16 Bubble Gum Music Is The Naked Truth | $15 | Buddah 5032 |

CAPITOL

3/7/70	200	1		17 New Spirit Of Capitol, The	$10	Capitol 6
6/29/68	130	9		18 Super Oldies/Vol. 3	$15	Capitol 2910 [2]
7/12/69	196	2		19 Super Oldies/Vol. 5	$15	Capitol 216 [2]
6/1/59	5	3		**20 What's New? on Capitol Stereo, vol. 1**	$25	Capitol SN-1
7/10/65	107	7		21 World Of Country Music, The	$20	Capitol 5 [2]

CAPRICORN

| 7/30/77 | 142 | 11 | | 22 South's Greatest Hits, The | $10 | Capricorn 0187 |

CBS

| 6/27/81 | 51 | 9 | | 23 Exposed/A Cheap Peek At Today's Provocative New Rock | $10 | CBS 37124 [2] |
| 12/5/81 | 124 | 5 | | 24 Exposed II | $10 | CBS 37601 [2] |

COLUMBIA

3/13/71	85	7		25 Different Strokes	$10	Columbia 12
8/9/69	151	2		26 Heavy Hits!	$12	Columbia 9840
2/28/70	128	3		27 Heavy Sounds	$12	Columbia 9952
3/18/72	165	6		28 Music People, The	$18	Columbia 31280 [3]
7/5/69	182	7		29 Rock's Greatest Hits	$15	Columbia 11 [2]
7/20/63	72	12		30 Songs For A Summer Night	$20	Columbia 2 [2]
6/5/61	1[9]	40		**31 Stars For A Summer Night**	$20	Columbia 1 [2]
11/14/70	197	2		32 Super Rock	$15	Columbia 30121 [2]

DOT

| 10/14/67 | 177 | 4 | | 33 Golden Instrumentals | [I] $25 | Dot 25820 |

DUNHILL

8/8/70	197	2		34 Big Hits Now, The	$12	Dunhill 50085
12/13/69+	166	5		35 Original Hits Of Right Now, The	$12	Dunhill 50070
7/26/69	144	7		36 Treasury Of Great Contemporary Hits, A	$12	Dunhill 50057

ELEKTRA

| 10/27/90 | 140 | 11 | | 37 Rubaiyat - Elektra's 40th Anniversary | $12 | Elektra 60940 [2] |
| | | | | The Rubaiyat was a work of poems written by Omar Khayyam circa 1100 | | |

END

| 2/27/61 | 19 | 23 | | 38 12 + 3 = 15 Hits | $50 | End 310 |

FONTANA

| 9/9/67 | 197 | 1 | | 39 England's Greatest Hits | $30 | Fontana 67570 |

HI

| 9/27/69 | 189 | 2 | | 40 Greatest Hits From Memphis, The | $15 | Hi 32049 |

IMMEDIATE

| 12/28/68 | 200 | 2 | | 41 An Anthology Of British Blues, Vol. 2 | $30 | Immediate 52014 |

ISLAND

| 12/26/87+ | 180 | 6 | | 42 Island Story, 1962-1987: 25th Anniversary, The | $8 | Island 90684 |

LAURIE

| 1/18/64 | 80 | 8 | | 43 Pick Hits Of The Radio Good Guys | $30 | Laurie 2021 |

DEBUT DATE	PEAK POS	WKS CHR	GOLD	ARTIST — Album Title	$	Label & Number
				LIBERTY		
9/27/69	196	2		44 Underground Gold	$12	Liberty 7625
				MGM		
6/13/70	175	4		45 Core of Rock, The	$12	MGM 4669
				MOTOWN		
7/9/83	114	9		46 Motown Story: The First Twenty-Five Years, The	$30	Motown 6048 [5]
				narrated by Lionel Richie and Smokey Robinson		
2/22/69	159	4		47 Motown Winners' Circle/No. 1 Hits, Vol. 1	$12	Gordy 835
2/22/69	135	5		48 Motown Winners' Circle/No. 1 Hits, Vol. 2	$12	Gordy 936
4/11/64	84	11		49 16 Original Big Hits	$15	Motown 614
1/15/66	108	5		50 16 Original Big Hits, Volume 4	$12	Motown 633
11/5/66	57	19		51 16 Original Big Hits, Volume 5	$12	Motown 651
2/25/67	95	25		52 16 Original Big Hits, Volume 6	$12	Motown 655
10/14/67	81	18		53 16 Original Big Hits, Volume 7	$12	Motown 661
12/30/67+	163	7		54 16 Original Big Hits, Volume 8	$12	Motown 666
11/16/68+	173	9		55 16 Original Big Hits, Volume 9	$12	Motown 668
4/12/80	150	6		56 20/20 - Twenty No. 1 Hits From Twenty Years At Motown	$12	Motown 937 [2]
6/4/83	42	28	●	57 25 #1 Hits From 25 Years	$12	Motown 5308 [2]
6/11/83	107	9		58 25 Years of Grammy Greats	$8	Motown 5309
				ORIGINAL SOUND		
9/21/59	12	183		59 Oldies But Goodies	$50	Original Snd. 5001
8/14/61	12	54		60 Oldies But Goodies, Vol. 3	$30	Original Snd. 5004
6/16/62	15	39		61 Oldies But Goodies, Vol. 4	$25	Original Snd. 5005
6/1/63	16	31		62 Oldies But Goodies, Vol. 5	$20	Original Snd. 5007
1/25/64	31	11		63 Oldies But Goodies, Vol. 6	$15	Original Snd. 5011
1/9/65	121	9		64 Oldies But Goodies, Vol. 7	$15	Original Snd. 5012
				PARKWAY		
11/24/62	110	7		65 All The Hits By All The Stars	$25	Parkway 7013
				PARROT		
5/13/67	87	18		66 Greatest Hits From England, The	$20	Parrot 71010
				PHILADELPHIA INTERNATIONAL		
8/6/77	121	9		67 Let's Clean Up The Ghetto	$10	Phil. Int. 34659
				PRIORITY		
11/8/86+	114	17	●	68 Rap's Greatest Hits	$8	Priority 9466
5/2/87	167	4		69 Rap's Greatest Hits, Volume 2	$8	Priority 9468
9/14/91	95	11		70 Straight From The Hood	$12	Priority 7063
				RCA		
10/15/55	9	9		71 **Pop Shopper**	$15	RCA 13
11/30/59+	2⁷	78	●	72 **60 Years Of Music America Loves Best**	$25	RCA 6074 [2]
10/31/60	6	59		73 **60 Years Of Music America Loves Best, Volume II**	$25	RCA 6088 [2]
9/4/61	5	40		74 **60 Years Of Music America Loves Best, Volume III (Popular)**	$20	RCA 1509
				ROULETTE		
7/27/63	97	6		75 Golden Goodies, Vol. 1	$25	Roulette 25207
7/20/63	89	5		76 Golden Goodies, Vol. 2	$20	Roulette 25210
8/3/63	112	4		77 Golden Goodies, Vol. 3	$20	Roulette 25218
7/27/63	124	4		78 Golden Goodies, Vol. 5	$20	Roulette 25215
8/3/63	86	3		79 Golden Goodies, Vol. 6	$20	Roulette 25216
3/20/65	44	18		80 20 Original Winners Of 1964	$20	Roulette 25293
				SBK		
8/29/92	136	13↑		81 Rave 'Til Dawn	$12	SBK 80070
				SIRE		
4/28/73	160	8		82 History Of British Blues, Volume One	$15	Sire 3701 [2]
6/1/74	198	2		83 History Of British Rock	$15	Sire 3702 [2]
12/21/74+	141	11		84 History Of British Rock, Vol. 2	$15	Sire 3705 [2]
11/22/75+	145	10		85 History Of British Rock, Volume 3	$15	Sire 3712 [2]
				STAX		
4/5/69	172	3		86 Soul Explosion	$15	Stax 2007 [2]

ABC [Jackson 5] (57) 1
Abalone Dream [Pamela Polland] (28)
Addicted To Love [Robert Palmer] (42) 1
Adorable [Drifters] (6)
Adventures In Success [Will Powers] (42)
Ain't No Mountain High Enough [Marvin Gaye & Tammi Terrell] (55) 19

Ain't No Mountain High **Enough** [Diana Ross] (56,57) 1
Ain't She Sweet [Beatles] (84) 19
Ain't That Peculiar [Marvin Gaye] (52) 8
Ain't Too Proud To Beg [Temptations] (53) 13
Albert's Shuffle [Mike Bloomfield-Al Kooper] (27)

All Day And All Of The **Night** [Kinks] (84) 7
All I Need [Temptations] (55) 8
All Of The Monkeys Ain't In The Zoo [Tommy Collins] (21)
All Right Now [Free] (42) 4
All This Paradise [Fraser & DeBolt] (25)
Alley-Oop [Hollywood Argyles] (62) 1

Almost Saturday Night (medley) [Georgia Satellites] (37)
Alwayz Into Somethin' [N.W.A.] (70)
Amphetamine Annie [Canned Heat] (44)
And The Angels Sing [Benny Goodman] (72)
Angel Baby [Rosie & The Originals] (62) 5

Anyone For Tennis [Cream] (85) 64
Anytime, Anyplace, Anywhere [Laurie Tate & Joe Morris Orch.] (5)
Apricot Brandy [Danny Gatton] (37)
As Long As There Is L-O-V-E Love [Jimmy Ruffin] (52)
Astronomy Domine [Pink Floyd] (17)

At My Front Door [El Dorados] (60) 17
Aupres de Ma Blonde (medley) [George Melachrino Orch.] (71)
B-A-B-Y [Carla Thomas] (11) 14
Baby, Baby Don't Cry [Smokey Robinson & The Miracles] (46) 8

DEBUT DATE	PEAK POS	WKS CHR	G O L D	ARTIST — Album Title	$	Label & Number

Baby, Better Start Turnin' Em Down [Rosanne Cash] (23)
Baby Hold On [Grass Roots] (34) 35
Baby I Love You [Aretha Franklin] (12) 4
Baby I Need Your Loving [Four Tops] (46,47,50) 11
Baby, I'm For Real [Originals] (46) 14
Baby, I'm Yours [Barbara Lewis] (11) 11
Baby It's You [Smith] (35) 5
Baby Love [Supremes] (50,57) 1
Baby What's Wrong [Yardbirds] (82)
Baby Won't You Let Me Rock 'N Roll You [Ten Years After] (28) 61
Bach: Air For G String [Mischa Elman] (73)
Back In My Arms Again [Supremes] (53) 1
Bad To Me [Billy J. Kramer With The Dakotas] (84) 9
Baja Humbug [Baja Marimba Band] (1)
Ball And Chain [Big Brother & The Holding Company] (27)
Ballad Of Easy Rider [Odetta] (35)
Banana Boat (Day-O) [Harry Belafonte] (72) 5
Barbara [Temptations] (38,77) 29
Bates Motel [Hitmen] (24)
Be My Love [Mario Lanza] (72)
Beat Goes On [Sonny & Cher] (12) 6
Beautiful Morning [Rascals] (13) 3
Beauty Is Only Skin Deep [Temptations] (46,54) 3
Because [Dave Clark Five] (85) 3
Beechwood 4-5789 [Marvelettes] (49) 17
Beer Barrel Polka [Will Glahe] (73)
Beggar For Your Kisses [Diamonds] (6)
Begin The Beguine [Artie Shaw] (72)
Behind Closed Doors [WC & The Maad Circle] (70)
Ben [Michael Jackson] (56) 1
Bend In The River [Marty Robbins] (30)
Bend It [Dave Dee, Dozy, Beaky, Mick & Tich] (39)
Bernadette [Four Tops] (55) 4
Big Bird [Flock] (25)
Big Chief [Professor Longhair] (31)
Big Gangster [O'Jays] (67)
Bim Bam Boom [Eldorados] (77)
Birds Of A Feather [Joe South] (18) 96
Bits And Pieces [Dave Clark Five] (84) 4
Bizet: Carmen [Vladimir Horowitz] (72)
Bizet: Habanera [Rise Stevens] (73)
Bizet: Toreador Song [Leonard Warren] (73)
Black Cat Bone [Albert Collins & Johnny Copeland] (73)
Black Cat Bone [Johnny Winter] (84)
Black Is Black [Los Bravos] (66) 4
Blackboard Of My Heart [Hank Thompson] (21)
Blackpatch [Laura Nyro] (25)
Blacksmith, The [Linda Ronstadt] (37)

Blue Guitar [John Lee's Groundhogs] (82)
Blue Suede Shoes [Carl Perkins] (61) 2
Blue Turns To Grey [Cliff Richard] (83)
Blue Velvet [Clovers] (6)
Bluebird [Buffalo Springfield] (4) 58
Bluebird Of Happiness [Jan Peerce] (72)
Blues After Hours [Pinetop Perkins] (31)
Bombay Calling [It's A Beautiful Day] (32)
Bongo Bongo Bongo [Preston Epps] (62) 78
Bongo Rock [Preston Epps] (33,60) 14
Boogie Woogie [Tommy Dorsey] (73)
Book Of Love [Monotones] (78) 5
Book Of Love [Carla Thomas] (86)
Booker's Theme [Booker T. & The M.G.'s] (86)
Boops (Here To Go) [Sly & Robbie] (42)
Boot Hill [Johnny Winter] (3)
Bop-Ting-A-Ling [LaVern Baker] (9)
Born In Chicago [Pixies] (37)
Born In Louisiana [Clarence "Gatemouth" Brown] (3)
Born To Be Wild [Steppenwolf] (36) 2
Both Sides Now [Michael Feinstein] (37)
Bottle Of Wine [Fireballs] (12) 9
Bottle Of Wine [Havalinas] (37)
Bouquet [Percy Faith Strings] (31)
Bouquet Of Roses [Eddy Arnold] (72)
Boy Soldier [Edgar Broughton Band] (17)
Boyz-N-The-Hood [Eazy-E] (70)
Breaking The Law [Judas Priest] (23)
Brick [Albert Collins] (3)
Bridge, The [M.C. Shan] (69)
Bring It On Home To Me [Eddie Floyd] (86) 17
Bristol Stomp [Dovells] (7)
Bristol Twistin' Annie [Dovells] (65) 27
Broke An' Hungry [Guitar, Jr.] (17)
Broken English [Marianne Faithfull] (42)
Brown Eyed Girl [Van Morrison] (84) 10
Bugler [Byrds] (28)
Bumble Boogie [B. Bumble & the Stingers] (64) 21
Bus Stop [Hollies] (84) 5
By The Campfire [Andre Kostelanetz] (31)
By The Light Of The Silvery Moon [Julie Andrews] (30)
By The Time I Get To Phoenix [Glen Campbell] (18) 26
C. C. Rider [Chuck Willis] (7) 12
Calico [Dreams] (28)
California Dreamin' [Mamas & The Papas] (36) 4
California Sun [Rivieras] (80) 5
Call Me Lightning [Who] (84) 40
Can-Can [New York Philharmonic Orch.] (31)
Can I Change My Mind [Tyrone Davis] (14,34) 5
Can I Get A Witness [Marvin Gaye] (46) 22

Can You Feel The Passion [Blue Pearl] (81)
Can You Jerk Like Me [Contours] (50) 47
Can't Help Thinkin' About Me [David Bowie & The Lower Third] (85)
Canadian Sunset [Hugo Winterhalter/Eddie Heywood] (2)
Casual Look [Six Teens] (61) 25
Catch The Wind [Donovan] (83) 23
Celebrate [Three Dog Night] (34) 15
Celebration Of Life [Chambers Brothers] (28)
Cellophane City [Steve Forbert] (2)
Cha Cha Cacciatore [Guy Lombardo] (20)
Chain Of Fools [Aretha Franklin] (12) 2
Chains Of Love [Joe Turner] (30)
Chapel Of Dreams [Dubs] (38,76) 74
Charlie Brown [Coasters] (8,76) 2
Chattanooga Choo Choo [Glenn Miller/Tex Beneke/Modernaires] (74)
Cheap Date [Tommy Tutone] (24)
Chelsea Girls [Spirit] (28)
Cherry Pink And Apple Blossom White [Perez Prado] (72) 1
Chewy Chewy [Ohio Express] (16) 15
Choker [Eric Clapton & Jimmy Page] (41)
Chopin: Polonaise In A-Flat, Op. 53, No. 6 [Jose Iturbi] (72)
Chopin: Waltz No. 7 In C-Sharp Minor, Op. 64, No. 2 [A. Brailowsky] (31)
Christabelle [Sorrows] (23)
Ciribiribin [Grace Moore] (73)
Close Your Eyes [Five Keys] (6)
Closer You Are [Channels] (62,78)
Cloud Nine [Temptations] (46,58) 6
Coast To Coast [Word Of Mouth Feat. D.J. Cheese] (69)
Cobwebs [Aynsley Dunbar Retaliation] (82)
Cocktails For Two [Spike Jones] (73)
Coffee House Rag [Ray Bauduc & Nappy Lamare] (20)
Cold Feet [Albert King] (86) 67
Cold Sweat [Mongo Santamaria] (27)
Cole Slaw [Frank Cully] (5)
Colours [David Bowie] (84) 61
Come And Get It [Badfinger] (84) 7
Come And Get These Memories [Martha & The Vandellas] (49) 29
Come Back Baby [Mike Vernon] (82)
Come Go With Me [Dell-Vikings] (60) 4
Come On And See Me [Tammi Terrell] (53) 80
C'mon And Swim [Bobby Freeman] (80) 5
Come On Up [Young Rascals] (43)
[Come 'Round Here] I'm The One You Need [Miracles] (54) 17
Come See About Me [Supremes] (51,55) 1
Come To The Sunshine [Van Dyke Parks] (45)

Coming Back Home (Back Off Girl) [La Mix feat. Problem Child] (2)
Concrete And Clay [Unit Four plus Two] (66,85) 28
Confidential [Sonny Knight] (59) 17
Conquest [Alfred Newman] (20)
Contract On Love [Little Stevie Wonder] (49)
Convicted [Oscar McLollie] (59)
Cool Fool [Edgar Winter's White Trash] (28)
Cool Jerk [Capitols] (15) 7
Cool World [Karla DeVito] (24)
Copy Kat [Bar-Kays] (86)
Corrine Corrina [Chet Atkins] (71)
Corrine Corrina [Joe Turner] (7) 41
Cottonfields [Ace Cannon] (40) 67
Could This Be Magic [Dubs] (38,61) 23
Country Line Special [Cyril Davis Rhythm & Blues All Stars] (82)
Country Song [Compost] (28)
Crazy 'Bout You Baby [Christine Perfect] (82)
Cross My Heart [Phil Ochs] (1)
Crow Jane [Sonny Terry] (3)
Cruisin' [Smokey Robinson] (46) 4
Cry Like I Cried [Harptones] (75)
Crying In The Chapel [Orioles] (76)
Cuba [Gibson Brothers] (42) 81
Cuba Rhumba [Hank Snow] (71)
Daddy's Home [Shep & The Limelites] (62) 2
Dance, Dance, Dance [Dells] (78)
Dance With Me [Drifters] (8) 15
Dance With Me Henry [Etta James] (59)
Dancing In The Street [Martha & The Vandellas] (46,47) 2
Dancing Machine [Jackson 5] (46) 2
Darling Baby [Elgins] (53) 72
Darling, How Long [Heartbeats] (75)
Dat Dere [Oscar Brown, Jr.] (30)
Dawn [Mahavishnu Orchestra with John McLaughlin] (28)
Day After Day [Badfinger] (85) 4
DeBussy: Clair De Lune [Philippe Entremont] (31)
Dead End Street [Lou Rawls] (18) 29
Dealing With The Devil [Dharma Blues Band] (41)
Debutante's Ball [Liza Minnelli] (1)
Dedicated To The One I Love [Mamas & The Papas] (36) 2
Dedicated To The One I Love [Shirelles] (38) 3
Denise [Randy & The Rainbows] (43) 10
Devil Or Angel [Clovers] (7)
Devil With The Blue Dress [Shorty Long] (50)
Diamonds And Pearls [Paradons] (62) 18
Different Drum [Stone Poneys feat. Linda Ronstadt] (18) 13
Ding Dong [Echoes] (75)
Dipsy Doodle [Larry Clinton] (73)

Distant Shores [Chad & Jeremy] (29) 30
Diving Duck Blues [Taj Mahal] (27)
Do Anything You Wanna Do [Eddie & The Hot Rods] (42)
Do The Sissy [Albert Collins] (44)
Do Wah Diddy Diddy [Manfred Mann] (83) 1
Do You Believe In Love? [Hollies] (32)
Do You Love Me [Contours] (48,49) 3
Do You Want To Know A Secret [Billy J. Kramer & The Dakotas] (85)
Dog Eat Dog [Adam & The Ants] (23)
Dolphin [Tamba 4] (1)
Don't Be Cruel [Bill Black's Combo] (40) 11
Don't Bring Me Down [Pretty Things] (83)
Don't Fight It [Wilson Pickett] (10) 53
Don't Fight It (Feel It) [Elvin Bishop Group] (25)
Don't Leave Me This Way [Thelma Houston] (57,58) 1
Don't Mess With Bill [Marvelettes] (52) 7
Don't Play That Song (You Lied) [Ben E. King] (10) 11
Don't Say Goodnight [Valentines] (75)
Don't Touch Me [Bettye Swann] (19) 38
Don't You Just Know It [Huey (Piano) Smith] (60) 9
Don't You Know I Love You [Clovers] (15)
Don't You Miss Me A Little Bit Baby [Jimmy Ruffin] (55) 68
Donkey Serenade [Allan Jones] (73)
Donna [Ritchie Valens] (64) 2
Doraville [Atlanta Rhythm Section] (22) 35
Double Eyed Whammy [Tinsley Ellis] (3)
Down At Lulu's [Ohio Express] (16) 33
Down In The Alley [Clovers] (7)
Down In The Boondocks [Billy Joe Royal] (29) 9
Draggin' My Tail [Eric Clapton & Jimmy Page] (41)
Dream A Little Dream Of Me [Mama Cass] (36) 12
Dream Team Is In The House [L.A. Dream Team] (69)
Dreamer, Dream [Code Red] (81)
Drinkin' Wine Spo-Dee-O-Dee ["Stick" McGhee] (5)
Drop Down Mama [Tom Rush] (32)
Drown In My Own Tears [Spencer Davis Group] (44)
Drowning On Dry Land [Roy Buchanan] (3)
Duke Of Earl [Gene Chandler] (63) 1
Dust My Broom [Canned Heat] (44)
Early In The Morning [Merry-Go-Round] (1)
Earth Angel (Will You Be Mine) [Penguins] (59) 8
Easy Livin [Uriah Heep] (83) 39
Easy To Be Hard [Three Dog Night] (35) 4
Eddie My Love [Teen Queens] (59) 14
Eight Miles High [Byrds] (26) 14
8:05 [Moby Grape] (29)
Eighteen With A Bullet [Pete Wingfield] (42) 15

Eleanor Rigby [Vanilla Fudge] (4)
Electricity [Orchestral Manoeuvres In The Dark] (4)
Elephants Graveyard [Boomtown Rats] (23)
Eli's Coming [Eli's Coming] (34) 10
Elvira [Dallas Frazier] (18) 72
Endless Love [Diana Ross & Lionel Richie] (46,57,58) 1
Eric B. Is President [Eric B. Feat. Rakim] (69)
Eve Of Destruction [Barry McGuire] (36) 1
Every Beat Of My Heart [Pips] (63) 6
Every Little Bit Hurts [Brenda Holloway] (46,48) 13
Every Morning [Whitford/St. Holmes Band] (24)
Everybody Needs Love [Gladys Knight & The Pips] (55) 39
Everybody's Talkin' [Harold Melvin & The Blue Notes] (67)
Everyone's Gone To The Moon [Jonathan King] (66) 17
Everyone's Laughing [Spaniels] (75)
Eyeballin' [Lonnie Brooks] (3)
Fannie Mae [Elvin Bishop] (3)
Fantasia On Greensleeves [Strings Of The Philadelphia Orch.] (31)
Fat Boys [Fat Boys] (68)
Feel The Rhythm [Jazzt P] (2)
Feelin' Alright? [Traffic] (44)
Ferry Cross The Mersey [Gerry & The Pacemakers] (84) 6
Fields Of Joy [New York Rock Ensemble] (25)
Fingertips - Pt 2 [Little Stevie Wonder] (46,47) 1
Fire [Crazy World Of Arthur Brown] (14,84) 2
Fire On The Mountain [Marshall Tucker Band] (22) 38
First Girl I Loved [Jackson Browne] (37)
First I Look At The Purse [Contours] (55) 57
First In Line [Romantics] (23)
Five Hundred Miles To Go [Heartbeats] (78)
5-10-15 Hours [Ruth Brown] (5,9)
Flea Bag [Herb Alpert] (1)
Flip, Flop & Fly [Joe Turner] (9)
Flute Thing [Blues Project] (45)
Fly Girl [Boogie Boys] (68)
Fly Me To The Moon [Sandpipers] (1)
Fooled Around And Fell In Love [Elvin Bishop] (22) 3
Foolin' Around [Chris Montez] (1)
Fools Fall In Love [Drifters] (7) 69
For Once In My Life [Stevie Wonder] (46) 2
For Sentimental Reasons [Cleftones] (76) 60
For The First Time [Crystal Mansion] (19)
For What It's Worth (Stop, Hey What's That Sound) [Buffalo Springfield] (12) 7
For Your Precious Love [Jerry Butler & The Impressions] (60) 11
Forgotten Town [Christians] (42)
Found A Child [Ballin' Jack] (25)

DEBUT DATE	PEAK POS	WKS CHR	GOLD	ARTIST — Album Title	$	Label & Number

Freight Loader *[Eric Clapton & Jimmy Page]* (41)
Frenesi *[Artie Shaw]* (74)
Friends *[Whodini]* (68) **87**
Fuck You *[Ottorongo]* (81)
Full Moon On Main Street *[Kinsey Report]* (3)
Fump *[Milton Hinton]* (71)
Function At The Junction *[Shorty Long]* (53) **97**
Funk Pedal *[Gordon Smith]* (82)
Funky Broadway *[Wilson Pickett]* (12) **8**
Funky Kingston *[Toots & The Maytals]* (42)
Funky Street *[Arthur Conley]* (13) **14**
Gal That Got Away *[Four Freshmen]* (20)
Galveston *[Glen Campbell]* (19) **4**
Game Of Love *[Wayne Fontana & The Mindbenders]* (39,83) **1**
Games People Play *[Joe South]* (17) **12**
Gee *[Crows]* (76)
Gee Whiz (Look At His Eyes) *[Carla Thomas]* (8) **10**
Gentle On My Mind *[Glen Campbell]* (18) **39**
Georgy Girl *[Seekers]* (19) **2**
Get Ourselves Together *[Phoebe Snow]* (37)
Get Ready For This *[2 Unlimited]* (81) **76**
Get That Feeling *[Curtis Knight & Jimi Hendrix]* (18)
Girl Don't Come *[Sandie Shaw]* (84) **42**
Girl, I'm Out To Get You *[Tommy Boyce & Bobby Hart]* (1)
Give It To Me Baby *[Rick James]* (57) **40**
Give Me Back My Wig *[Hound Dog Taylor]* (3)
Glad All Over *[Dave Clark Five]* (83) **6**
Gliere: Russian Sailors' Dance from "The Red Poppy" *[Eugene Ormandy]* (31)
Gloria *[Them]* (66) **71**
Glory Of Love *[Angels]* (75)
Go Down Gamblin' *[Blood, Sweat & Tears]* (28) **32**
Go Now! *[Moody Blues]* (66) **10**
God Bless The Child *[Blood, Sweat & Tears]* (27)
God Bless The Child *[Aretha Franklin]* (30)
Goin' Out Of My Head/Can't Take My Eyes Off You *[Lettermen]* (18) **7**
Going Back Home *[Son Seals]* (3)
Going Down *[Lynch Mob]* (37)
Going Down To Big Mary's *[Paladins]* (3)
Going Going Gone *[Bill Frisell/Robin Holcomb/Wayne Horvitz]* (37)
Going To A Go-Go *[Miracles]* (52) **11**
Going To The Mill *[Chambers Brothers]* (25)
Gonna Give Her All The Love I've Got *[Jimmy Ruffin]* (54) **29**
Good Lovin' *[Clovers]* (9)
Good Lovin' *[Young Rascals]* (11) **1**
Goodnight Irene *[Leadbelly]* (5)
Goodnight My Love *[Benny Goodman & Ella Fitzgerald]* (74)
Goodnight Sweetheart, Goodnite *[Flamingos]* (77)
Goodnight Sweetheart, Goodnite *[Spaniels]* (79)
Goody Goody Gumdrops *[1910 Fruitgum Co.]* (16) **37**
Got A Date With An Angel *[Hal Kemp]* (74)
Got 2 B Free *[New Life]* (2)
Got To Get You Off My Mind *[Solomon Burke]* (10) **22**
Got To Give It Up (Pt. 1) *[Marvin Gaye]* (56,57) **1**
Grand Coulee Dam *[Bob Dylan]* (28)
Gravy (For My Mashed Potatoes) *[Dee Dee Sharp]* (65) **9**
Green Leaves Of Summer *[Mahalia Jackson]* (30)
Green Man *[Shut Up & Dance]* (81)
Green Tambourine *[Lemon Pipers]* (16) **1**
Greenbacks *[Ray Charles]* (6)
Greetings (This Is Uncle Sam) *[Monitors]* (54) **100**
Groove Me *[Seduction]* (2)
Groovin' *[Booker T. & The MG's]* (13) **21**
Groovin' *[Young Rascals]* (12) **1**
Groovy Kind Of Love *[Mindbenders]* (39,83) **2**
Guess I Should Have Loved Him More *[Eydie Gorme]* (30)
Guess Who *[Hitmen]* (24)
Half Of This, Half Of That *[Wynn Stewart]* (21)
Hallelujah *[Sweathog]* (28) **33**
Handsome Johnny *[Richie Havens]* (45)
Handy Man *[Jimmy Jones]* (64) **2**
Hang 'Em High *[Booker T. & The M.G.'s]* (86) **9**
Happy Organ *[Dave "Baby" Cortez]* (33) **1**
Harder They Come *[Jimmy Cliff]* (42)
Haunted House *[Gene Simmons]* (40) **11**
Have I The Right? *[Honeycombs]* (80,83) **5**
He Believes Me *[Mary Taylor]* (21)
He Will Break Your Heart *[Jerry Butler]* (64) **7**
He's So Fine *[Chiffons]* (43) **1**
Heading Out To The Highway *[Judas Priest]* (23)
Hear My Call *[Staple Singers]* (86)
Heartache Mountain *[Ollie & The Nightingales]* (86)
Heartaches *[Ted Weems]* (74)
Hearts Of Stone *[Jewels]* (62)
Heat Wave *[Martha & The Vandellas]* (46,48,58) **4**
Heaven And Paradise *[Don Julian & The Meadowlarks]* (59)
Heaven Knows *[Grass Roots]* (34) **24**
Heaven Must Have Sent You *[Elgins]* (54) **50**
Heavenly Father *[Edna McGriff]* (5)
Hello, I Am Your Heart *[Sara Hickman]* (37)
Hello I Love You *[Cure]* (37)
Hello Mary Lou (Goodbye Heart) *[New Riders Of The Purple Sage]* (28)
Hello Walls *[Faron Young]* (21) **12**
Help Me Girl *[Outsiders]* (18) **37**
Helpless *[Kim Weston]* (52) **56**
Here Comes The Night *[Them]* (85) **24**
Hey Jacque *[Eartha Kitt]* (71)
Hey Jude *[Wilson Pickett]* (14) **23**
Hey Lawdy Mama *[Steppenwolf]* (34) **35**
Hey There Lonely Girl *[Eddie Holman]* (34) **2**
Hide & Seek *[Joe Turner]* (9)
High Heel Sneakers *[Stevie Wonder]* (51) **59**
High Priest Of Memphis *[Bell + Arc]* (28)
Hip House Party *[Overweight Pooch]* (2)
Hip Hug-Her *[Booker T. & The MG's]* (11) **37**
Hippy Hippy Shake *[Swinging Blue Jeans]* (83) **24**
Hit And Run *[Jo Jo Zep & The Falcons]* (24)
Hitchin' A Ride *[Vanity Fare]* (83) **5**
Hoe Down *[Leonard Bernstein]* (31)
Hoe Down *[Poco]* (28)
Hold On *[Ian Gomm]* (23) **18**
Hold On! I'm A Comin' *[Sam & Dave]* (11) **21**
Hold What You've Got *[Joe Tex]* (10,15) **5**
Holiday For Strings *[David Rose]* (73)
Holy Smoke Doo Dah Band *[Mylon]* (28)
Homework *[Fleetwood Mac]* (82)
Honey Chile *[Martha Reeves & The Vandellas]* (55) **11**
Honey Love *[Drifters]* (6,9)
Honky Tonk (Parts 1 & 2) *[Bill Doggett]* (63) **2**
Hora Staccato *[Jascha Heifetz]* (72)
Hot Cha *[Jr. Walker & The All Stars]* (50)
Hot Hips *[Bar-Kays]* (86)
Hot Pastrami *[Dartells]* (33) **11**
Hotel California *[Gipsy Kings]* (37)
House Of The Risin' Sun *[Herbie Mann]* (1)
House Of The Rising Sun *[Tracy Chapman]* (37)
How Can I Be Sure *[Young Rascals]* (4) **4**
How Do You Do It? *[Gerry & The Pacemakers]* (85) **9**
How Long Blues *[Alexis Korner Blues Inc.]* (82)
How Sweet It Is To Be Loved By You *[Marvin Gaye]* (46,51) **6**
How Sweet It Is (To Be Loved By You) *[Jr. Walker & The All Stars]* (53) **18**
Howie's Teed Off *[Real Roxanne with Howie Tee]* (68)
Hucklebuck, The *[Chubby Checker]* (65) **14**
Hunter Gets Captured By The Game *[Marvelettes]* (53) **13**
Hush *[Deep Purple]* (84) **4**
Hushabye *[Mystics]* (43) **20**
I Be's Troubled *[T.S. McPhee]* (82)
I Call That True Love *[Dr. Hook & The Medicine Show]* (28)
I Can't Believe You Love Me *[Tammi Terrell]* (52) **72**
I Can't Get Started *[Bunny Berigan]* (74)
I Can't Help Myself *[Four Tops]* (46,48,51,57) **1**
I Can't Let Go *[Hollies]* (83) **42**
I Can't Quit Her *[Blood, Sweat & Tears]* (26)
I Can't Quit You Baby *[Savoy Brown Blues Band]* (41)
I Can't See Nobody *[Bee Gees]* (4)
I Can't Stand It *[Chambers Brothers]* (29)
I Can't Stop Dancing *[Archie Bell & The Drells]* (14) **9**
I Can't Tell You Why *[Howard Hewett]* (37)
I Can't Turn You Loose *[Chambers Brothers]* (32) **37**
I Count The Tears *[Drifters]* (8) **17**
I Cried A Tear *[LaVern Baker]* (8) **6**
I Dig Chicks! *[Jonah Jones Quartet]* (20)
I Don't Like It Like That *[Sorrows]* (23)
I Don't Love Nobody *[Leon McAuliffe]* (21)
I Don't Love You Anymore *[Charlie Louvin]* (21)
I Dreamed Of A Hill-Billy Heaven *[Tex Ritter]* (21) **20**
I Feel Free *[Cream]* (4)
I Go To Pieces *[Peter & Gordon]* (84) **9**
I Got A Sure Thing *[Ollie & The Nightingales]* (86) **73**
I Got Love If You Want It *[Johnny Winter]* (44)
I Guess I'll Always Love You *[Isley Brothers]* (54) **61**
I Hear A Symphony *[Supremes]* (46,53) **1**
I Heard It Through The Grapevine *[Marvin Gaye]* (46,57) **1**
(I Know) I'm Losing You *[Temptations]* (54) **8**
I Know Where I'm Goin' *[New Christy Minstrels]* (30)
I Know (You Don't Love Me No More) *[Barbara George]* (64) **3**
I Like Everything About You *[Jimmy Hughes]* (86)
I Like It *[Gerry & The Pacemakers]* (83) **17**
I Love How You Love Me *[Paris Sisters]* (64) **5**
I Love You *[People]* (18) **14**
I Love You So *[Chantels]* (77) **42**
I Never Loved A Man (The Way I Love You) *[Aretha Franklin]* (15) **9**
I Only Have Eyes For You *[Flamingos]* (38,76) **11**
I Only Want To Be With You *[Dusty Springfield]* (83) **12**
I Say A Little Prayer *[Burt Bacharach]* (1)
I Say A Little Prayer *[Aretha Franklin]* (14) **10**
I Second That Emotion *[Smokey Robinson & The Miracles]* (46,48,55,58) **4**
I Shot Mr. Lee *[Bobettes]* (38,77) **52**
I Stand Accused *[Jerry Butler]* (80) **61**
I Started A Joke *[Bee Gees]* (14) **6**
I Thank You *[Sam & Dave]* (13) **9**
I Want To (Do Everything For You) *[Joe Tex]* (10) **23**
I Want You Back *[Jackson 5]* (56,57) **1**
I Want You To Be My Boy *[Exciters]* (80) **98**
I Was Just Walkin' Out The Door *[Jimmy Dean]* (30)
I Was Made To Love Her *[Stevie Wonder]* (46,55) **2**
I Wasn't Born To Follow *[Robbs]* (35)
I Wish It Would Rain *[Temptations]* (46) **4**
I'd Like To Teach The World To Sing *[Jevetta Steele]* (37)
I'd Wait A Million Years *[Grass Roots]* (35) **15**
I'll Be Doggone *[Marvin Gaye]* (46,51,53) **8**
I'll Be Home *[Flamingos]* (77)
I'll Be In Trouble *[Temptations]* (50) **33**
I'll Be There *[Jackson 5]* (56,57) **1**
I'll Be True *[Orlons]* (65)
I'll Drown In My Tears *[Johnny Winter]* (27)
I'll Keep Holding On *[Marvelettes]* (51) **34**
I'm A Midnight Mover *[Wilson Pickett]* (13) **24**
(I'm A) Road Runner *[Jr. Walker & The All Stars]* (54) **20**
I'm Chillin' *[Kurtis Blow]* (69)
I'm Confessin' *[Chantels]* (79)
I'm Crazy 'Bout My Baby *[Marvin Gaye]* (50) **77**
I'm Free *[Lucky Peterson]* (3)
I'm Funky *[Grootna]* (28)
I'm Gonna Make You Love Me *[Diana Ross & The Supremes with The Temptations]* (46) **2**
I'm In Love With You *[Kasenetz-Katz Super Cirkus]* (16)
I'm Not A Number *[Gary Myrick & The Figures]* (24)
I'm On The Lamb But I Ain't No Sheep *[Blue Oyster Cult]* (28)
I'm Ready For Love *[Martha & The Vandellas]* (53) **9**
I'm Telling You Now *[Freddie & The Dreamers]* (19,83) **1**
I'm The One *[Steve Harvey]* (2)
I'm The Zydeco Man *[Clifton Chenier]* (3)
I've Been Down So Long *[Gordon Smith]* (82)
I've Been Loving You Too Long (To Stop Now) *[Otis Redding]* (10) **21**
I've Got A Woman *[Ray Charles]* (6,9)
I've Got Dreams To Remember *[Delbert McClinton]* (3)
I've Gotta Get A Message To You *[Bee Gees]* (85) **8**
I've Never Found A Girl (To Love Me Like You Do) *[Eddie Floyd]* (86) **40**
If I Hadn't Been High *[Detroit Junior]* (3)
If I Loved You *[Chad & Jeremy]* (18) **23**
If I Were A Carpenter *[Tim Hardin]* (45)
If Not For You *[Olivia Newton-John]* (85) **25**
(If You Cry) True Love, True Love *[Drifters]* (8) **33**
If You Don't Want My Love *[Robert John]* (29) **49**
If You Love Her Tell Her So *[Steve Lawrence]* (30)
If You Need Me *[Solomon Burke]* (15) **37**
If You See The Tears In My Eyes *[Delta Rhythm Boys]* (5)
Il Bacio (The Kiss) *[Lucrezia Bori]* (73)
Il Etait Une Bergere (medley) *[George Melachrino Orch.]* (71)
Image Of A Girl *[Safaris]* (63) **6**
In A Broken Dream *[Python Lee Jackson]* (85) **56**
In-A-Gadda-Da-Vida *[Iron Butterfly]* (4) **30**
In My Lonely Room *[Martha & The Vandellas]* (50) **44**
In The Chapel In The Moonlight *[Anita Bryant]* (30)
In The Evening By The Moonlight (medley) *[Frank DeVol]* (31)
In The Good Old Summertime (medley) *[Mitch Miller]* (30)
In The Midnight Hour *[Wilson Pickett]* (10,11) **21**
In The Mood *[Glenn Miller]* (73)
In The Shade Of The Old Apple Tree (medley) *[Mitch Miller]* (30)
In The Still Of The Nite *[Five Satins]* (59,79) **24**
In The Summertime *[Mungo Jerry]* (83) **3**
Inbetween Days *[John Eddie]* (37)
Indian Love Call *[Jeanette MacDonald & Nelson Eddy]* (72)
Injected With A Poison *[Praga Khan Feat. Jade 4 U]* (81)
Innervenus Eyes *[Bob Seger System]* (17)
Innocence *[Harlequin]* (24)
Innocent When You Dream (Bar Room) *[Tom Waits]* (42)
Israelites *[Desmond Dekker & The Aces]* (42) **9**
It Should've Been Me *[Ray Charles]* (9)
It Takes Two *[Marvin Gaye & Kim Weston]* (53) **14**
It's A Good Day *[Perry Como]* (71)
It's A Wonderful World *[Les Brown]* (31)
It's All In The Game *[Tommy Edwards]* (64) **1**
It's Getting Better *[Mama Cass]* (35) **30**
It's Good News Week *[Hedgehoppers Anonymous]* (66) **48**
It's Growing *[Temptations]* (51) **18**
It's Me *[Judy Clay]* (86)
It's Not Unusual *[Tom Jones]* (66) **10**
It's Okay With Me Baby *[Chicken Shack]* (82)
It's The Same Old Song *[Four Tops]* (52) **5**
It's Time *[Sons]* (17)
It's Too Soon To Know *[Orioles]* (5)
It's Wrong To Be Loving You *[Eddie Floyd]* (86)
Itchycoo Park *[Small Faces]* (83) **16**
Jack's Kinda Swing *[Al Cohn's Natural Seven]* (71)
Jackin' For Beats *[Ice Cube]* (70)
Jailhouse Rock *[Jeff Beck]* (32)
Jalousie (Jealousy) *[Arthur Fiedler/Boston Pops]* (72)
Jam Up *[Tommy Ridgeley]* (6)
Jam Up Jelly Tight *[Tommy Roe]* (34) **8**
Jamie *[Hedge & Donna]* (17)
Jamie *[Eddie Holland]* (49) **30**
Jeannie With The Light Brown Hair *[Dave Brubeck Quartet]* (31)
Jelly Jungle (Of Orange Marmalade) *[Lemon Pipers]* (16) **51**
Jesus Is Just Alright *[Byrds]* (32) **97**
Jim Dandy *[LaVern Baker]* (7) **17**
Jimmy Mack *[Martha & The Vandellas]* (46,54) **10**
Jingo *[Santana]* (32) **56**
Joe Joe *[Dells]* (78)

DEBUT DATE	PEAK POS	WKS CHR	GOLD	ARTIST — Album Title	$	Label & Number

Johnny B. Goode [Johnny Winter] (32) **92**
Josephine [Wayne King] (73)
July, You're A Woman [John Stewart] (17)
Jump! [Movement] (81) **53**
Jump Jump [Garland Jeffreys] (23)
Jumpin' Jack Flash [Johnny Winter] (28) **89**
Just A Gigolo [Bing Crosby] (74)
Just A Little Misunderstanding [Contours] (52) **85**
Just A Simple Melody [Patti Page] (30)
Just Be True [Gene Chandler] (80) **19**
Just Friends [Billy Butterfield] (31)
Just Like A Woman [Richie Havens] (45)
(Just Like) Romeo & Juliet [Reflections] (80) **6**
Just My Imagination (Running Away With Me) [Temptations] (57) **1**
Just Out Of Reach (Of My Two Open Arms) [Solomon Burke] (10) **24**
Just The Way I Like It [Billy Thorpe] (24)
Just To Be With You [Passions] (43) **69**
Just To Hold My Hand [Clyde McPhatter] (7) **26**
Just You [Dion & The Belmonts] (78)
Keep It Up [Boomtown Rats] (23)
Keep On Running [Spencer Davis Group] (42) **76**
Keep On Smilin' [Wet Willie] (22) **10**
Keep On Truckin' (Part 1) [Eddie Kendricks] (46,56,57,58) **1**
Kentucky Woman [Deep Purple] (85) **38**
Kick Out The Jams [Big F] (37)
Kickin' Mule [Walter Hensley] (21)
Kid Is Hot Tonite [Loverboy] (23) **55**
Killer In The Home [Adam & The Ants] (23)
Killing Floor [Electric Flag] (27)
King Of Rock [Run-D.M.C.] (68)
Knight In Rusty Armour [Peter & Gordon] (18) **15**
Knock On Wood [Eddie Floyd] (11) **28**
Lady Godiva [Peter & Gordon] (18,19) **6**
Lady Of The 80's [Loverboy] (23)
Lady Samantha [Elton John] (84)
Lalo: Second Movement from "Symphonie Espagnole" [New York Philharmonic] (31)
Land Of 1000 Dances [Wilson Pickett] (15) **6**
Lay Lady Lay [Byrds] (27)
Layla [Derek & The Dominoes] (85) **10**
Lazy Afternoon [Les & Larry Elgart] (31)
Lazy Sunday [Small Faces] (84)
Le Reve Passe (medley) [George Melachrino Orch.] (71)
Leader Of The Laundromat [Detergents] (80) **19**
Leavin' [Siegel-Schwall Band] (3)
Leaving Your Town [Charlie Musselwhite] (3)
Left Hand Woman (Get Right With Me) [Albert King] (86)
Leoncavallo: Vesti La Giubba [Enrico Caruso] (72)
Leoncavallo: Vesti La Giubba [Mario Lanza] (73)
Let It Be Me [Glen Campbell & Bobbie Gnetry] (19) **36**
Let It Whip [Dazz Band] (46,58) **5**
Let Me Go The Right Way [Supremes] (50) **90**
Let Me Outta Here [Billy Thorpe] (24)
Let Me Tickle Your Fancy [Jermaine Jackson] (46) **18**
Let The Four Winds Blow [Jerry Jaye] (40)
Let The Good Times Roll [Shirley & Lee] (59) **20**
Let's Clean Up The Ghetto [Philadelphia International All Stars] (67) **91**
Let's Fall In Love [Peaches & Herb] (29) **21**
Let's Get It On [Marvin Gaye] (56,57) **1**
Let's Get Serious [Jermaine Jackson] (58) **9**
Let's Go [Ernie Isley] (37)
Let's Live For Today [Grass Roots] (36) **8**
Letter, The [Medallions] (59)
Liebesfreud (Love's Joy) [Fritz Kreisler] (72)
Lifestyle As A Gangsta [415] (70)
(Lights Went Out In) Massachusetts [Bee Gees] (84) **11**
Like A Lover [Sergio Mendes & Brasil '66] (1)
Like Love [Andre Previn] (31)
Listen [Chicago] (27)
Listen To The Mocking Bird (medley) [Frank DeVol] (31)
Liszt: Liebenstraum [Ivan Davis] (31)
Little Bit Of Rain [Ambitious Lovers] (37)
Little Bit Of Soap [Jarmels] (43) **12**
Little Children [Billy J. Kramer & The Dakotas] (83) **7**
Little Girl [Steve Miller Band] (17)
Little Girl Lost [David Axelrod] (17)
Little Girl Lost [Kris Kristofferson] (28)
Little Girl Of Mine [Cleftones] (76) **57**
Little Miss Understood [Rod Stewart] (84)
Little Star [Elegants] (62) **1**
Londonderry Air [Mormon Tabernacle Choir] (31)
Loneliest Man In The World [Dion] (30)
(Loneliness Made Me Realize) It's You That I Need [Temptations] (55) **14**
Long Lonely Nights [Lee Andrews & The Hearts] (77) **45**
Long Lonely Nights [Clyde McPhatter] (7) **49**
Long Tall Sally [Kinks] (85)
Long Tall Sally [Little Richard] (60) **6**
Long Tall Shorty [Graham Bond Organization] (82)
Long Tall Texan [Murry Kellum] (40) **51**
Long Walk To D.C. [Staple Singers] (86)
Look But Don't Touch [Kenny Neal] (3)
Look Down At My Woman [Jeremy Spencer] (41)
Look In My Eyes [Chantels] (76) **14**
Look Through Any Window [Hollies] (85) **32**
Louie, Louie [Paul Revere & The Raiders] (29)
Louise [Maurice Chevalier] (73)
Love Child [Diana Ross & The Supremes] (46) **1**
Love Hangover [Diana Ross] (56) **1**
Love Hurts [Jim Capaldi] (42) **97**
Love Is A Hurtin' Thing [Lou Rawls] (18) **13**
Love Is All Around [Troggs] (85) **7**
Love Is Here And Now You're Gone [Supremes] (55) **1**
Love Is Strange [Mickey & Sylvia] (61) **11**
Love Machine (Part 1) [Miracles] (46,56) **1**
Love (Makes Me Do Foolish Things) [Martha & The Vandellas] (51) **70**
Love Me All The Way [Kim Weston] (49) **88**
Love Potion Number Nine [Searchers] (84) **3**
Love Wars [Beautiful South] (37)
Lover's Question [Clyde McPhatter] (8) **6**
Lovers Never Say Goodbye [Flamingos] (60,79) **52**
Loving You Is Sweeter Than Ever [Four Tops] (54) **45**
MacArthur Park [Richard Harris] (36) **2**
Maggie [Redbone] (25) **45**
Maggie May [Rod Stewart] (83) **1**
Magic Carpet Ride [Steppenwolf] (36) **3**
Magnificent Sanctuary Band [David Clayton-Thomas] (28)
Mahogany (Do You Know Where You're Going To), Theme From [Diana Ross] (56) **1**
Make It With You [Teddy Pendergrass] (37)
Make Me A Pallet On Your Floor [Jo-Ann Kelly] (44)
Make The Music With Your Mouth, Biz [Biz Markie] (69)
Make Your Own Kind Of Music [Mama Cass Elliot] (35) **36**
Mama, He Treats Your Daughter Mean [Ruth Brown] (6,9)
Man Like Me [Poco] (25)
Man On A Mountain [Ian Gomm] (23)
Marie [Tommy Dorsey] (74)
Marquee Moon [Kronos Quartet] (37)
Mashed Potato Time [Dee Dee Sharp] (63,65) **2**
Masquerade Is Over [Harptones] (75)
Matilda, Matilda! [Harry Belafonte] (73)
May Each Day [Andy Williams] (30)
May I Take A Giant Step (Into Your Heart) [1910 Fruitgum Co.] (16) **63**
Maybe [Chantels] (38,77) **15**
Mean Old Frisco [Spencer Davis R & B Quartet] (82)
Mean Woman Blues [Spencer Davis Group] (44)
Meditation [Fritz Kreisler] (73)
Memphis [Lonnie Mack] (33) **5**
Mercy, Mercy [Don Covay] (10,15) **35**
Mercy, Mercy, Mercy [Cannonball Adderley] (18) **11**
Mercy, Mercy, Mercy [Buckinghams] (29) **5**
Mercy, Mercy, Mercy [Southwest F.O.B.] (86)
Merrimac County [Tom Rush] (25)
Messages [Orchestral Manoeuvres In The Dark] (24)
Michelle [David & Jonathan] (18) **18**
Middle Aged Blues Boogie [Saffire] (3)
Midnight Confessions [Grass Roots] (36) **5**
Midnight Rider [Gregg Allman] (22) **19**
Mighty Quinn (Quinn The Eskimo) [Manfred Mann] (84) **10**
Million Colors [Channel X] (81)
Mind Playing Tricks On Me [Geto Boys] (70) **23**
Minute You're Gone [Sonny James] (21) **95**
Mio Amore [Flamingos] (38) **74**
Mixed-Up, Shook-Up, Girl [Patty & The Emblems] (80) **37**
Mojo Woman [Enemys] (45)
Monday, Monday [Mamas & The Papas] (36) **1**
Money Honey [Drifters] (6,9)
Money (That's What I Want) [Barrett Strong] (48,49,61) **23**
Monkey Time [Boz Scaggs & Band] (28)
Montego Bay [Amazulu] (42) **90**
Moon Was Yellow [Robert Goulet] (30)
Moonlight Gambler [Frankie Laine] (30)
More Love [Smokey Robinson & The Miracles] (55) **23**
Morning Will Come [Spirit] (25)
Most Of All [Moonglows] (79)
Motorcycle Mama [Sugarcubes] (37)
Move Over [Steppenwolf] (35) **31**
Mr. Natural [Big Brother & The Holding Company] (25)
Mr. Pitiful [Otis Redding] (10) **41**
Mr. Soul [Buffalo Springfield] (4)
Mt. Airy Groove [Leaders Of The New School] (37)
Mustang Sally [Wilson Pickett] (11) **23**
My Baby [Temptations] (52) **13**
My Baby Loves Me [Martha & The Vandellas] (52) **22**
My Baby Must Be A Magician [Marvelettes] (55) **17**
My Baby's Gone [Wanda Jackson] (21)
My Bonnie (My Bonnie Lies Over The Ocean) [Beatles with Tony Sheridan] (85) **26**
My Boy Lollipop [Millie Small] (39,42,80) **2**
My Coloring Book [Barbra Streisand] (30)
My Girl [Temptations] (46,48,51,57) **1**
My Girl Has Gone [Miracles] (53) **14**
My Girl Josephine [Jerry Jaye] (40) **29**
My Guy [Mary Wells] (46,48,50,80) **1**
My Heart Skips A Beat [Buck Owens] (21) **94**
My Heart's Treasure [Nat "King" Cole] (20)
My Impersonal Life [Blue Rose] (28)
My Past Is Present [Bobby Durham] (21)
My World Is Empty Without You [Supremes] (54) **5**
Naughty Lady Of Shady Lane [Ames Brothers] (72) **3**
Needle In A Haystack [Velvelettes] (52) **45**
Needles And Pins [Searchers] (83) **13**
Nest, The [Jimmie Spheeris] (28)
Never Can Say Goodbye [Jackson 5] (56) **2**
New Day, New World Comin' [Billy Paul] (67)
New Orleans [U.S. Bonds] (43,64) **6**
New World Coming [Mama Cass Elliot] (34) **42**
New York [Dreams] (25)
New York Mining Disaster 1941 (Have You Seen My Wife, Mr. Jones) [Bee Gees] (83) **14**
Night And Day [Frank Sinatra] (74)
Night Train [Steve Winwood] (42)
No Cuttin' Loose [James Cotton] (3)
No Woman No Cry [Bob Marley & The Wailers] (42)
No Word For Glad [It's A Beautiful Day] (28)
Nobody But Me [Human Beinz] (18) **8**
Nobody Loves Me Like You [Flamingos] (38) **30**
Nothing At All [Bill Puka] (25)
Nothing In Rambling [Jo Ann Kelly] (82)
Now Is The Time To Do It [Teddy Pendergrass] (67)
Now That We Found Love [Third World] (42) **47**
Nowhere To Run [Martha & The Vandellas] (46,51) **8**
Number Nine [Van Dyke Parks] (45)
O Fortuna [Apotheosis] (81)
Ode To Billie Joe [Bobbie Gentry] (18) **1**
Oh! My Pa-Pa (O Mein Papa) [Eddie Fisher] (73)
Oh What A Beautiful Dream [Doris Day] (30)
Oh, What A Night [Dells] (60,79)
Ol' Man River [Ravens] (5)
Old People [Archie Bell & The Drells] (67)
Omaha [Moby Grape] (26) **88**
On Broadway [Drifters] (15) **9**
On Top Of The World [John Mayall/Bluesbreakers] (41)
Once In A While [Chimes] (64) **11**
Once Upon A Time [Marvin Gaye & Mary Wells] (50) **19**
One [Three Dog Night] (35) **5**
157 Riverside Avenue [R.E.O. Speedwagon] (28)
One Fine Day [Chiffons] (43) **5**
One Love [Whodini] (69)
One Meatball [Shinehead] (37)
One Mint Julep [Clovers] (5,9)
One Minute To One [Mavis Rivers] (20)
One More Parade [They Might Be Giants] (37)
1, 2, 3, Red Light [1910 Fruitgum Co.] (16) **5**
One Who Really Loves You [Mary Wells] (49) **8**
Ooh Child [Dee Dee Sharp Gamble] (67)
Out-Bloody-Rageous [Soft Machine] (25)
Out In The Cold Again [Frankie Lymon] (75)
Out Of Time [Chris Farlowe] (85)
Over The Rainbow [Demensions] (43) **16**
Padrewski: Minuet In G, Op. 14, No. 1 [Ignace Paderewski] (72)
Padlock [Gwen Guthrie] (42)
Papa Was A Rollin' Stone [Temptations] (46,56,57,58) **1**
Papa, Won't You Let Me Go To Town With You [Bobbie Gentry] (19)
Paper Castles [Frankie Lymon] (75)
Paper Sun [Traffic] (42,44) **94**
Para Los Rumberos [Santana] (28)
Pee-Wee's Dance [Joeski Love] (68)
Peeped Around Yonder's Bend [Jimmy Hughes] (86)
Peg O' My Heart [Three Suns] (72)
People [Tymes] (29) **39**
People Are Talking [Heartbeats] (75)
People Got To Be Free [Rascals] (14) **1**
Phases Of Travel [Ellen Foley] (23)
Philly Dog [Mar-Keys] (11) **89**
Pickin' Up The Pieces [Poco] (32)
Pictures Of Matchstick Men [Status Quo] (83) **12**
Piece Of My Heart [Big Brother & The Holding Company] (26) **12**
Pipeline [Chantay's] (33) **4**
Place In The Sun [Stevie Wonder] (53) **9**
Playboy [Marvelettes] (47) **7**
Playing It Cool [O.G. Style] (70)
Plea, The [Chantels] (61)
Please Don't Worry [Grand Funk Railroad] (17)
Please Mr. Postman [Marvelettes] (46,49,57) **1**
Please Write [Tokens] (43)
Poison Ivy [Coasters] (8) **7**
Pony Time [Chubby Checker] (65) **1**
Pretty Flamingo [Manfred Mann] (85) **29**
Pretty In Pink [Psychedelic Furs] (24)
Pride And Joy [Marvin Gaye] (47,49) **10**
Priscilla [Eddie Cooley] (76) **20**
Prisoner Of Love [Perry Como] (72)
Prisoner's Song [Vernon Dalhart] (74)
Private Number [Judy Clay & William Bell] (86) **75**
Prokofiev: March from "The Love For Three Oranges" [Thomas Schippers] (31)
Psycho [KMC] (70)
Puccini: One Fine Day (Un Bel Di) [Eileen Farrell] (31)
Puccini: The Stars Were Shining (E Lucevan Le Stelle) [Richard Tucker] (31)
Pucker Up Buttercup [Jr. Walker & The All Stars] (53) **31**
Pull Up To The Bumper [Grace Jones] (42)
Puppy Love [Barbara Lewis] (80) **38**
Pushin' [Albert Collins] (44)
Pussycat Moan [Katie Webster] (3)
Quarter To Three [U.S. Bonds] (43,63) **1**

COMPILATIONS BY RECORD LABEL

DEBUT DATE	PEAK POS	WKS CHR	GOLD	ARTIST — Album Title	$	Label & Number

Queen Of The House *[Jody Miller]* (19) **12**
Questions 67 And 68 *[Chicago]* (32) **24**
Quick Joey Small (Run Joey Run) *[Kasenetz-Katz Singing Orchestral Circus]* (16) **25**
Quicksand *[Martha & The Vandellas]* (80) **8**
Rachmaninoff: Prelude In C-Sharp Minor, Op. 3. No. 2 *[Sergei Rachmaninoff]* (72)
Rain *[Little Charlie & The Nightcats]* (3)
Raindrops *[Dee Clark]* (63) **2**
Ramblin' Man *[Allman Brothers Band]* (22) **2**
Ramblin' Rose *[Nat King Cole]* (19) **2**
Ramona *[Gene Austin]* (72)
Ramona *[Jerry Murad's Harmonicats]* (31)
Reach Out I'll Be There *[Four Tops]* (55,57) **1**
Reason To Believe *[Tim Hardin]* (45)
Red Cross Store *[Mississippi Fred McDowell]* (17)
Red River Rock *[Johnny & The Hurricanes]* (33) **5**
Red Rubber Ball *[Cyrkle]* (29) **2**
Reflections *[Diana Ross & The Supremes]* (46) **2**
Relax *[Frankie Goes To Hollywood]* (42) **10**
Release Me *[Esther Phillips]* (15) **8**
Respect *[Aretha Franklin]* (11) **1**
Rice Is Nice *[Lemon Pipers]* (16) **46**
Riders In The Sky (A Cowboy Legend) *[Vaughn Monroe]* (73)
Right Place, Wrong Time *[Dr. John]* (22) **9**
Rip Van Winkle *[Devotions]* (75) **36**
Rising Of The Moon *[Clancy Brothers & Tommy Makem]* (30)
Ritual Fire Dance *[Artur Rubinstein]* (72)
River Is Wide *[Grass Roots]* (35) **31**
River Kwai March *[Jack Marshall]* (20)
Rivers *[Harry Geller & His Orch.]* (71)
Road To Cairo *[Howard Jones]* (37)
Rock Against Romance *[Holly & The Italians]* (24)
Rock And Roll, Hoochie Koo *[Johnny Winter]* (25)
Rock & Roll Madonna *[Elton John]* (85)
Rock Me *[Steppenwolf]* (35) **10**
Rocket Number 9 *[NRBQ]* (32)
Rockin' All Over The World (medley) *[Georgia Satellites]* (37)
Rockin' Pneumonia And The Boogie Woogie Flu *[Jellybread]* (82)
Rock-in Robin *[Bobby Day]* (62) **2**
Roll 'Em Pete *[Dharma Blues Band]* (41)
Rollin' And Tumblin' *[Jo-Ann Kelly]* (44)
Roof Is On Fire *[Rockmaster Scott/Dynamic Three]* (68)
Roxanne, Roxanne *[UTFO]* (68) **77**
Ruby Baby *[Dion]* (29) **2**
Ruby Baby *[Drifters]* (7)
Rumors *[Timex Social Club]* (68) **8**
Runaround Sue *[Dion]* (43,64) **1**
S.Y.S.L.J.F.M. (The Letter Song) *[Joe Tex]* (11) **39**
Sabre Dance *[Arthur Fiedler/Boston Pops Orch.]* (73)
San Franciscan Nights *[Eric Burdon & The Animals]* (85) **9**
Sand In My Shoes *[Drifters]* (80)
Saturday Miles *[Miles Davis]* (25)
Save The Children *[Intruders]* (67)
Save The Last Dance For Me *[Drifters]* (8) **1**
Save Your Love For Me *[Johnnie Taylor]* (86)
Scarlet Ribbons (For Her Hair) *[Harry Belafonte]* (74)
Schubert: Ave Maria *[Marian Anderson]* (72)
Sea Cruise *[Frankie Ford]* (60) **14**
Searchin' *[Coasters]* (7) **3**
Second Fiddle *[Jean Shepard]* (21)
Second Hand Man *[Carey Bell & Junior Wells]* (3)
See Saw *[Aretha Franklin]* (14) **14**
See Saw *[Moonglows]* (77) **25**
Seesaw *[Don Covay]* (10) **44**
Semi-Detached Suburban Mr. James *[Manfred Mann]* (39)
September In The Rain *[George Shearing Quintet]* (20)
Serves Me Right To Suffer *[Jimmy Johnson]* (3)
Seven & Seven Is *[Billy Bragg]* (37)
Sh-Boom *[Chords]* (6)
Shake *[Shadows Of Knight]* (16) **46**
Shake And Fingerpop *[Jr. Walker & The All Stars]* (52) **29**
Shake Me, Wake Me (When It's Over) *[Four Tops]* (53) **18**
Shake, Rattle & Roll *[Joe Turner]* (6,9)
She Loves The Way They Love Her *[Colin Blunstone]* (28)
She Talks In Stereo *[Gary Myrick & The Figures]* (24)
She's Not There *[Zombies]* (66,85) **2**
Shimmy, Shimmy, Ko-Ko-Bop *[Little Anthony & The Imperials]* (38) **24**
Ship Of Love *[Nutmegs]* (79)
Shoop Shoop Song (It's In His Kiss) *[Betty Everett]* (80) **6**
Shoot Your Shot *[Jr. Walker & The All Stars]* (54) **44**
Shop Around *[Miracles]* (46,47,49) **2**
Shotgun *[Jr. Walker & The All Stars]* (47,51) **4**
Shouldn't I Know *[Cardinals]* (5)
Show, The *[Doug E. Fresh/Get Fresh Crew]* (68)
Shrine Of St. Cecilia *[Harptones]* (75)
Si Tu Dois Partir *[Fairport Convention]* (42)
Signed, Sealed, Delivered I'm Yours *[Stevie Wonder]* (56) **3**
Silence *[Jake Holmes]* (28)
Silence Is Golden *[Tremeloes]* (84) **11**
Silhouettes *[Rays]* (61) **3**
Silver Threads And Golden Needles *[Linda Ronstadt]* (17)
Silver Threads And Golden Needles *[Springfields]* (39) **20**
Simon Says *[1910 Fruitgum Co.]* (16) **4**
Since I Don't Have You *[Skyliners]* (62) **12**
Since I Met You Baby *[Ivory Joe Hunter]* (7) **12**
Sinsemilla *[Black Uhuru]* (42)
Sister Europe *[Psychedelic Furs]* (24)
(Sittin' On) The Dock Of The Bay *[Otis Redding]* (12) **1**
Situation *[Jeff Beck Group]* (28)
16 Candles *[Crests]* (77) **2**
Sixty-Minute Man *[Dominoes]* (62)
Skinny Legs And All *[Joe Tex]* (12) **10**
Sleep Walk *[Santo & Johnny]* (33) **1**
Sleepless Nights *[Wayne Cochran & The C. C. Riders]* (28)
Slip Away *[Clarence Carter]* (14) **6**
Smell Of Incense *[Southwest F.O.B.]* (86) **56**
Smiling Phases *[Blood, Sweat & Tears]* (32)
Smokey Joe's Cafe *[Robins]* (7) **79**
Smokie - Part 2 *[Bill Black's Combo]* (40) **17**
So Excited *[B.B. King]* (34) **54**
So Far Away *[Pastels]* (78)
So Fine *[Fiestas]* (78) **11**
So Many People *[Chase]* (28)
So Nice *[Mad Lads]* (86)
So Wat Cha Sayin' *[EPMD]* (70)
Soapstone Mountain *[It's A Beautiful Day]* (25)
Society's Child (Baby I've Been Thinking) *[Janis Ian]* (45) **14**
Solo For Joe *[Sauter-Finegan Orch.]* (71)
Some Enchanted Evening *[Earl Wrightson]* (30)
Someday After Awhile *[John Mayall's Bluesbreakers]* (82)
Someday We'll Be Together *[Diana Ross & The Supremes]* (46,56) **1**
Someone To Love Me *[T. S. McPhee]* (41)
Something In The Air *[Thunderclap Newman]* (84) **37**
Son-Of-A Preacher Man *[Dusty Springfield]* (14) **10**
Sorrow *[Merseys]* (83)
Soul Clap '69 *[Booker T. & The M.G.'s]* (86)
Soul Finger *[Bar-Kays]* (12) **17**
Soul-Limbo *[Booker T. & The M.G.'s]* (86) **17**
Soul Man *[Sam & Dave]* (12) **2**
Soul Serenade *[Willie Mitchell]* (40) **23**
South's Gonna Do It *[Charlie Daniels Band]* (22)
Spanish Harlem *[Ben E. King]* (8,15) **10**
Spanish Key *[Miles Davis]* (32)
Speedo *[Cadillacs]* (77) **17**
Splish Splash *[Bobby Darin]* (8) **3**
Split Personality *[UTFO]* (69)
Staggolee *[Pacific Gas & Electric]* (32)
Stairway To The Stars *[Bobby Hackett]* (31)
Stand By Me *[Ben E. King]* (10) **4**
Star Dust *[Artie Shaw]* (73)
Star Eyes *[Art Van Damme Quintet]* (31)
Stars And Stripes Forever *[John Philip Sousa]* (73)
Stay *[Maurice Williams]* (62) **1**
Steal Away *[Jimmy Hughes]* (80) **17**
Stealin' *[Taj Mahal]* (28)
Stella By Starlight *[Tony Bennett]* (30)
Still *[Commodores]* (56,57) **1**
Stone Cold Crazy *[Metallica]* (37)
Stone Crazy *[Aynsley Dunbar Retaliation]* (82)
Stoned Soul Picnic *[Laura Nyro]* (26)
Stop! In The Name Of Love *[Supremes]* (46,48,52) **1**
Story Untold *[Nutmegs]* (78)
Stranded In The Jungle *[Cadets]* (59) **15**
Strange Brew *[Cream]* (4)
Strauss: Blue Danube Waltz *[Leopold Stokowski]* (72)
Strauss: Tales From The Vienna Woods *[Leopold Stokowski]* (73)
Strike Like Lightning *[Lonnie Mack]* (3)
Stubborn Kind Of Fellow *[Marvin Gaye]* (46,49) **7**
Stylophonia *[Two Little Boys]* (81)
Sugar Beet *[Duster Bennett]* (82)
Sukiyaki *[Kyu Sakamoto]* (19) **1**
Summer Days Alone *[Brothers Four]* (30)
Summer Place, Theme From A *[Lettermen]* (19) **16**
Summer Song *[Chad & Jeremy]* (19,84) **7**
Summer, Winter, Spring, And Fall *[Glen Campbell]* (21)
Summertime *[Ray Conniff]* (31)
Summertime *[Leslie Uggams]* (30)
Summertime In Venice *[Jerry Vale]* (30)
Sun Ain't Gonna Shine (Anymore) *[Walker Bros.]* (39,83) **13**
Sun Never Shines On The Lonely *[Redbone]* (28)
Sunny *[Electric Flag]* (26)
Sunrise Serenade *[Glenn Miller]* (72)
Sunset *[Little Stevie Wonder]* (49)
Sunshine Of Your Love *[Cream]* (13,84) **5**
Super Freak (Part 1) *[Rick James]* (46) **16**
Superlove *[David & The Giants]* (19)
Superstition *[Stevie Wonder]* (56,57) **1**
Suzanne *[Leonard Cohen]* (26,29)
Swan (Le Cygne) *[Pablo Casals]* (73)
Sweet Blindness *[Laura Nyro]* (27)
Sweet Home Alabama *[Lynyrd Skynyrd]* (22) **8**
Sweet Honey Sweet *[Jo Jo Zep & The Falcons]* (24)
Sweet Inspiration *[Sweet Inspirations]* (13) **18**
Sweet Soul Music *[Arthur Conley]* (15) **2**
(Sweet Sweet Baby) Since You've Been Gone *[Aretha Franklin]* (13) **5**
Sweet Temptation *[Merle Travis]* (21)
Sweethearts On Parade *[Guy Lombardo]* (73)
Symphony For Susan *[Arbors]* (29) **51**
T-Bone Shuffle *[T-Bone Walker]* (9)
T.V. Eye *[John Zorn]* (37)
Take A Look *[Aretha Franklin]* (29)
Take A Look Around *[Smith]* (34) **43**
Take Control *[Lords Of Acid]* (81)
Take Me For A Little While *[Vanilla Fudge]* (4) **38**
Take Me In Your Arms And Love Me *[Gladys Knight & The Pips]* (54) **98**
Take Me In Your Arms (Rock Me A Little While) *[Kim Weston]* (51) **50**
Take Out Some Insurance *[Climax Blues Band]* (82)
Take The "A" Train *[Duke Ellington]* (72)
Take Time To Know Her *[Percy Sledge]* (13) **11**
Take Your Hands Off My Heart *[Ray Pillow]* (21)
Taking Inventory *[Vic Waters & The Entertainers]* (19)
Tchaikovsky: Piano Concerto No. 1 *[Freddy Martin]* (72)
Tchaikovsky: Troika En Traineaux (In A Three-Horse Sleigh) *[Sergei Rachmaninoff]* (73)
Tchaikovsky: Waltz Of The Flowers from "Nutcracker Suite" *[Leonard Bernstein]* (31)
Tears Of A Clown *[Smokey Robinson & The Miracles]* (56,57) **1**
Tears On My Pillow *[Little Anthony & The Imperials]* (38,76) **4**
Teen Age Prayer *[Gloria Mann]* (61) **19**
Teen Angel *[Mark Dinning]* (64) **1**
Teen Beat *[Sandy Nelson]* (33,61) **4**
Teenager In Love *[Dion & The Belmonts]* (63) **5**
Tell Me Why *[Norman Fox & The Rob-Roys]* (61)
Tell That Girl To Shut Up *[Holly & The Italians]* (24)
Ten Commandments Of Love *[Harvey & The Moonglows]* (78) **22**
Tenderly *[Paul Weston]* (20)
Tequila *[Champs]* (33,64) **1**
That Did It *[Key Largo]* (82)
That's All There Is, There Isn't Any More *[Judy Garland]* (20)
That's Life *[O. C. Smith]* (29)
That's My Desire *[Channels]* (38)
That's What Love Is Made Of *[Miracles]* (50) **35**
That's Why I'm Crying *[Koko Taylor]* (3)
There Are Such Things *[Tommy Dorsey & Frank Sinatra]* (72)
There Goes Another Love Song *[Outlaws]* (22) **34**
There Goes My Baby *[Drifters]* (8,77) **2**
There's A Grand Ole Opry Show Playing Somewhere *[Red Johnson]* (21)
There's Our Song Again *[Chantels]* (79)
These Are Not My People *[Joe South]* (19)
These Blues Is Killing Me *[A.C. Reed with Stevie Ray Vaughan]* (3)
These Days *[10,000 Maniacs]* (37)
These Old Memories *[Mad Lads]* (86)
They All Laughed *[Jaye P. Morgan]* (71)
Things Are Changing *[Duster Bennett]* (82)
Think *[Aretha Franklin]* (13) **7**
Thinking Of You *[Harlequin]* (24)
Third Rate Romance *[Amazing Rhythm Aces]* (22) **14**
This I Swear *[Skyliners]* (63) **26**
This Is For The Convicts *[Convicts]* (70)
This Is My Story *[Gene & Eunice]* (60)
This Magic Moment *[Drifters]* (8) **16**
This Old Heart Of Mine (Is Weak For You) *[Isley Brothers]* (52) **12**
This Town Ain't Big Enough For The Both Of Us *[Sparks]* (42)
This Wheel's On Fire *[Julie Driscoll & Brian Auger]* (84)
Those Oldies But Goodies (Remind Me Of You) *[Little Caesar & The Romans]* (63) **9**
Those Were The Days *[Mary Hopkin]* (85) **2**
Thousand Miles Away *[Heartbeats]* (76) **53**
300 Pounds Of Heavenly Joy *[Big Twist & The Mellow Fellows]* (3)
Three Times A Lady *[Commodores]* (46,56,57) **1**
Three Window Coupe *[Rip Chords]* (29) **28**
Thrill Is Gone *[B.B. King]* (34) **15**
Tia Lisa Lynn *[Rose Maddox]* (21)
Tiger In Your Tank *[Downliners]* (82)
Tighten Up *[Archie Bell & The Drells]* (13) **1**
Till The End Of Time *[Perry Como]* (73)
Timber, I'm Falling *[Ferlin Husky]* (21)
Time And Love *[Laura Nyro]* (32)
Time Has Come Today *[Chambers Brothers]* (26) **11**
Time Won't Let Me *[Outsiders]* (18) **5**
Tips Of My Fingers *[Roy Clark]* (21) **45**
Tired Of Waiting *[Flock]* (32)
To Love Somebody *[Bee Gees]* (12) **17**
To Make A Woman Feel Wanted *[Kenny Loggins & Jim Messina]* (28)
To The Aisle *[Five Satins]* (61) **25**
Tobacco Road *[Nashville Teens]* (66) **14**
Together Forever *[Run-D.M.C.]* (69)
Tokoloshe Man *[Happy Mondays]* (37)
Tom's Diner *[D.N.A. feat. Suzanne Vega]* (2) **5**
Tonite, Tonite *[Mello-Kings]* (59) **77**
Too Many Fish In The Sea *[Marvelettes]* (50) **25**
Too Many Mondays *[Barry Mann]* (28)
Too Much Monkey Business *[Enemys]* (45)
Too Weak To Fight *[Clarence Carter]* (14) **13**
Too Young To Be Married *[Hollies]* (25)
Topsy II (33) **3**
Torquay *[Fireballs]* (33) **39**
Touch Me In The Morning *[Diana Ross]* (58) **1**
Tracks Of My Tears *[Miracles]* (46,51) **16**

DEBUT DATE	PEAK POS	WKS CHR	GOLD	ARTIST — Album Title	$	Label & Number

Trade Winds [Lou Rawls] (67)
Travlin' Man [Stevie Wonder] (54) *32*
Treasure Of Love [Clyde McPhatter] (7) *16*
Triste [Antonio Carlos Jobim] (1)
Trouble In Mind [Big Walter Horton] (3)
True Blue [Savoy Brown Blues Band] (41,82)
True Confessions [Garland Jeffreys] (23)
Truly [Lionel Richie] (46) *1*
Truly Yours [Spinners] (52)
Try A Little Tenderness [Three Dog Night] (36) *29*
Try It Baby [Marvin Gaye] (50) *15*
Try (Just A Little Bit Harder) [Janis Joplin] (32)
Tuff [Ace Cannon] (40) *17*
Turn On Your Love Light [Human Beinz] (18) *80*
Turn! Turn! Turn! (To Everything There Is A Season) [Byrds] (29) *1*
Tweedlee Dee [LaVern Baker] (6,9) *14*
21 And Over [Romantics] (23)
20-75 [Willie Mitchell] (40) *31*
Twenty Years From Today [Johnnie Taylor] (86)
Twist, The [Chubby Checker] (65) *1*
Two Lovers [Mary Wells] (46,50) *7*
Two People In The World [Little Anthony & The Imperials] (60)
Under The Boardwalk [Drifters] (80) *4*
Union Man [Shaking Family] (37)
Universal Soldier [Glen Campbell] (19) *45*
Universal Soldier [Donovan] (85) *53*
Up On The Mountain [Magnificents] (79)
Up Where We Belong [Joe Cocker & Jennifer Warnes] (42) *1*

Uptight (Everything's Alright) [Stevie Wonder] (48,52) *3*
Verdi: Bella Figlia Dell' Amore [Caruso/Galli-Curci/Perini/De Luca] (73)
Verdi: Prelude To Act One Of "La Traviata" [Arturo Toscanini] (73)
Video Killed The Radio Star [Buggles] (42) *40*
Volare [Bobby Rydell] (65) *4*
Voodoo Dreams [Les Baxter] (20)
Voodoo Suite-Part 1 [Perez Prado] (71)
Wagner: Lohengrin, Act III, Prelude [Arturo Toscanini] (72)
Wah Watusi [Orlons] (65) *2*
Wait A Minute [Jo Ann Campbell] (38)
Wanderer, The [Dion] (43) *2*
Wanderlove [Claudine Longet] (1)
Watermelon Man [Mongo Santamaria] (39) *10*
Way Of Love [Kathy Kirby] (66) *88*
Way You Do The Things You Do [Temptations] (46,47) *11*
Way You Look Tonight [Jaguars] (59)
Way You Look Tonight [Lettermen] (19) *13*
Wayfaring Stranger [Eddy Arnold] (71)
We Belong To The Night [Ellen Foley] (23)
We Belong Together [Robert & Johnny] (79) *32*
We Can Work It Out [Kasenetz-Katz Super Cirkus] (16)
We Could Be Happy [Cryan' Shames] (29)
We Got Love [Bobby Rydell] (65) *6*
Wedding Bells [Tiny Tim & The Hits] (75)
Wee Deoch An' Doris [Harry Lauder] (74)

Weight, The [Mike Bloomfield & Al Kooper] (26)
Weight, The [Smith] (35)
Werewolves Of London [Black Velvet Band] (37)
What A Guy [Raindrops] (80) *41*
What Becomes Of The Brokenhearted [Jimmy Ruffin] (46,53) *2*
What Does It Take (To Win Your Love) [Jr. Walker & The All Stars] (46) *4*
What Kind Of Man Are You [Genya Ravan] (28)
What Kinda Girl? [Rosanne Cash] (23)
What'd I Say (Part I) [Ray Charles] (8,15) *6*
What's Going On [Marvin Gaye] (56,57) *2*
What's The Matter With You Baby [Marvin Gaye & Mary Wells] (50) *17*
Wheel Of Fortune [Cardinals] (5)
When A Man Loves A Woman [Percy Sledge] (11,15) *1*
When I'm Gone [Brenda Holloway] (51) *25*
When The Moon Comes Over The Mountain [Mac Wiseman] (21)
When You Dance [Turbans] (79) *33*
When You Got A Good Friend [T. S. McPhee] (41)
When You Walk In The Room [Searchers] (85) *35*
When You Wish Upon A Star [Little Anthony & The Imperials] (38)
Where Did Our Love Go [Supremes] (46,47,51) *1*
Where Do I Go [Carla Thomas] (86) *86*
Where Have All The Flowers Gone [Kingston Trio] (19) *21*
Which Man Are You [Tommy Tutone] (24)
Whiffenpoof Song [Robert Merrill] (73)

While Strolling Through The Park One Day (medley) [Frank DeVol] (31)
While The Sun Still Shines [Fields] (28)
Whiskey Woman [Whitford/St. Holmes Band] (24)
Whispering [Paul Whiteman] (72)
White Bird [It's A Beautiful Day] (27)
White Lies [Grin] (28) *75*
White Rabbit [Great Society with Grace Slick] (26)
White Room [Cream] (14) *6*
White Silver Sands [Bill Black's Combo] (40) *9*
Who's Knocking At Your Door [Jeremy Spencer] (41)
Who's Making Love [Johnnie Taylor] (86) *5*
Whoever You Are [Chantels] (38)
Whole Lot Of Shakin' Going On [Jerry Lee Lewis] (61) *3*
Why Do Fools Fall In Love [Frankie Lymon & The Teenagers] (76) *6*
Wild One [Bobby Rydell] (65) *2*
Wild Thing [Troggs] (39,83) *1*
Winchester Cathedral [New Vaudeville Band] (39) *1*
Windy [Wes Montgomery] (1) *44*
Wipe Out [Surfaris] (33) *2*
Wishin' And Hopin' [Dusty Springfield] (35) *4*
With A Girl Like You [Troggs] (84) *29*
With Or Without You [U2] (42) *1*
Woman [Peter & Gordon] (85) *14*
Woman, Woman [Union Gap feat. Gary Puckett] (29) *4*
Won't Stop Loving You [Certain Ratio] (2)
Woodstock [Matthews' Southern Comfort] (85) *23*
Woppit [B. Fats] (69)
Words [Bee Gees] (4) *15*

Work [Karla DeVito] (24)
World Of Our Own [Seekers] (19) *19*
World Shut Your Mouth [Julian Cope] (42) *84*
World Without Love [Peter & Gordon] (83) *1*
Yakety Yak [Coasters] (8) *1*
Year Of Decision [Three Degrees] (67)
Yes It's You [Clovers] (6)
Yodel, Sweet Molly [Ira Lowin] (21)
You Are The Sunshine Of My Life [Stevie Wonder] (56,57) *1*
You Beat Me To The Punch [Mary Wells] (37)
You Belong To Me [Anita Baker] (37)
You Brought The Sunshine [Shirley Murdock] (37)
You Can Make It If You Try [Sly & The Family Stone] (37)
You Can't Catch Me [Blues Project] (45)
You Can't Hurry Love [Supremes] (46,54,57) *1*
You Cannot Win If You Do Not Play [Steve Forbert] (23)
You Cheated [Shields] (60) *12*
You Don't Exist Any More [Lil' Ed & The Blue Imperials] (3)
You Don't Have To Say You Love Me [Dusty Springfield] (39,85) *4*
You Don't Know What Love Is [Fenton Robinson] (3)
You Don't Miss Your Water ('Til Your Well Runs Dry) [Taj Mahal] (26)
You Gave Me Peace Of Mind [Spaniels] (78)
You Keep Me Hangin' On [Supremes] (55) *1*
You Keep Me Hangin' On [Vanilla Fudge] (13) *6*
You Never Know Who Your Friends Are [Al Kooper] (32)

You Pass Me By [Jimmie Rodgers] (1)
You Really Got Me [Kinks] (83) *7*
You Were Mine [Fireflies] (63) *21*
You're A Wonderful One [Marvin Gaye] (80) *15*
You're All I Need To Get By [Marvin Gaye & Tammi Terrell] (46) *7*
You're Gonna Need Somebody On Your Bond [Taj Mahal] (32)
You're My World [Cilla Black] (84) *26*
You're So Vain [Faster Pussycat] (37)
You've Got To Hide Your Love Away [Silkie] (39,83) *10*
You've Got Your Troubles [Fortunes] (66) *7*
You've Really Got A Hold On Me [Miracles] (46,49,80) *8*
Young Blood [Coasters] (7) *8*
Young Girl [Noel Harrison] (66) *51*
Your Heart Belongs To Me [Supremes] (49) *95*
Your Name's Become A Household Word [Neal Merritt] (21)
Your Precious Love [Marvin Gaye & Tammi Terrell] (55) *5*
Your Unchanging Love [Marvin Gaye] (54) *33*
Your Way [Heartbeats] (75)
Yummy Yummy Yummy [Ohio Express] (16) *4*
Zoom [Cadillacs] (78)

DEBUT DATE	PEAK POS	WKS CHR	GOLD	ARTIST — Album Title	$	Label & Number

COMPILATIONS BY DISC JOCKEYS
Collections of hits gathered together by the hosts of radio, TV and oldies shows.

CLARK, Dick
Born on 11/30/29 in Mt. Vernon, New York. Host of TV's *American Bandstand* from 1956-89.

| 7/14/73 | **27** | 18 | ● | 1 Dick Clark/20 Years Of Rock N' Roll .... | **$15** | Buddah 5133 [2] |

All I Have To Do Is Dream *[Everly Brothers]* 1
Blue Suede Shoes *[Carl Perkins]* 2
Brown Eyed Girl *[Van Morrison]* 10
Crimson And Clover *[Tommy James & The Shondells]* 1
Crying In The Chapel *[Orioles]*
Do You Believe In Magic *[Lovin' Spoonful]* 9
Good Lovin' *[Young Rascals]* 1
Hang On Sloopy *[McCoys]* 1
I Walk The Line *[Johnny Cash]* 17
I'm Walkin' *[Fats Domino]* 4
Lay Down (Candles In The Rain) *[Melanie]* 6
Leader Of The Pack *[Shangri-Las]* 1
Louie Louie *[Kingsmen]* 2
Nice To Be With You *[Gallery]* 4
Oh Happy Day *[Edwin Hawkins' Singers]* 4
Peppermint Twist - Part 1 *[Joey Dee & the Starliters]* 1
Put Your Head On My Shoulder *[Paul Anka]* 2
Rebel-'Rouser *[Duane Eddy]* 6
Rock Around The Clock *[Bill Haley]* 1
Runaround Sue *[Dion]* 1
Sh-Boom *[Crew Cuts]*
(Sittin' On) The Dock Of The Bay *[Otis Redding]* 1
So You're Leaving *[Al Green]*
Soldier Boy *[Shirelles]* 1
Superfly *[Curtis Mayfield]* 8
Sweet Nothin's *[Brenda Lee]* 4
Whole Lot Of Shakin' Going On *[Jerry Lee Lewis]* 3
Why *[Frankie Avalon]* 1
Wooly Bully *[Sam The Sham & The Pharoahs]* 2
You've Lost That Lovin' Feeling *[Righteous Brothers]* 1

DR. DEMENTO
Real name: Barret Hansen. Host of radio's *Dr. Demento Show*.

| 11/29/75 | **198** | 2 | | 2 Dr. Demento's Delights .... [N] | **$15** | Warner 2855 |

Ballad Of Ben Gay *[Ben Gay & The Silly Savages]*
Boobs A Lot *[Holy Modal Rounders]*
Cockroach That Ate Cincinnati *[Possum]*
Eleanor Rigby *[Doodles Weaver]*
Friendly Neighborhood Narco Agent *[Jef Jaisun]*
Get A Load Of This *[R. Crumb & His Cheap Suit Serenaders]*
Hello Muddah, Hello Fadduh! (A Letter From Camp) *[Allan Sherman]* 2
If You're A Viper *[Jim Kweskin's Jug Band]*
They're Coming To Take Me Away, Ha-Haaa! *[Napoleon XIV]* 3
Who Put The Benzedrine In Mrs. Murphy's Ovaltine *[Harry "The Hipster" Gibson]*
Ya Wanna Buy A Bunny *[Spike Jones & His City Slickers]*

FREED, Alan
Born on 12/15/22 in Johnstown, Pennsylvania; died on 1/20/65. Popular D.J. with several film appearances.

| 2/17/62 | **99** | 7 | | 3 Alan Freed's Memory Lane .... | **$40** | End 314 |

narrated by Alan; also see Soundtrack *American Hot Wax*

Crying In The Chapel *[Orioles]*
Eddie My Love *[Teen Queens]* 14
For Your Precious Love *[Jerry Butler & The Impressions]* 11
Goodnight My Love *[Jesse Belvin]*
I'll Be Home *[Flamingos]*
In The Still Of The Nite *[Five Satins]* 24
Oh What A Night *[Dells]*
Silhouettes *[Rays]* 3
Sincerely *[Moonglows]* 32
16 Candles *[Crests]* 2
Tears On My Pillow *[Little Anthony & The Imperials]* 4
Tonite, Tonite *[Mello-Kings]* 77
We Belong Together *[Robert & Johnny]*
Why Don't You Write Me? *[Jacks]* 82

MURRAY THE K
Real name: Murray Kaufman. Legendary New York area D.J. Died on 2/21/82 (age 60).

| 10/9/61 | **63** | 29 | | 4 Murray the "K's" Sing Along with the Original Golden Gassers .... | **$35** | Roulette 25159 |

Beep Beep *[Playmates]* 4
Closer You Are *[Channels]*
Crying In The Chapel *[Orioles]*
Dear Lord *[Continentals]*
Gee *[Crows]*
Honeycomb *[Jimmie Rodgers]* 1
I'm Stickin' With You *[Jimmy Bowen]* 14
Little Girl Of Mine *[Cleftones]* 57
Party Doll *[Buddy Knox]* 1
Thousand Miles Away *[Heartbeats]* 53
Why Do Fools Fall In Love *[Frankie Lymon & The Teenagers]* 6
You Talk Too Much *[Joe Jones]* 3

| 12/25/61+ | **26** | 15 | | 5 Murray the K's Blasts From The Past .... | **$40** | Chess 1461 |

Been So Long *[Pastels]* 24
Blue Velvet *[Moonglows]*
Bo Diddley *[Bo Diddley]*
(Do The) Mashed Potatoes (Part 1) *[Nat Kendrick]* 84
He's Gone *[Chantels]* 71
La Bamba *[Ritchie Valens]* 22
Sho Doo Be Doo *[Moonlighters]*
So Fine *[Fiestas]* 11
Sweet Little Sixteen *[Chuck Berry]* 2
Vow *[Flamingos]*
We Go Together *[Moonglows]*
You're Everything To Me *[Orchids]*

| 8/4/62 | **124** | 13 | | 6 Murray the K's Gassers For Submarine Race Watchers .... | **$40** | Chess 1470 |

Dedicated To The One I Love *[Shirelles]* 3
Everyday Of The Week *[Students]*
In My Diary *[Moonglows]*
Life Is But A Dream *[Harptones]*
Maybe *[Chantels]* 15
My Memories Of You *[Harptones]*
My Vow To You *[Students]*
So Far Away *[Pastels]*
Sunday Kind Of Love *[Harptones]*
Tears On My Pillow *[Little Anthony & The Imperials]* 4
Tonight I Fell In Love *[Tokens]* 15
Will You Love Me Tomorrow *[Shirelles]* 1

| 7/20/63 | **69** | 10 | | 7 Murray the K's Nineteen-Sixty Two Boss Golden Gassers .... | **$25** | Scepter 510 |

Any Day Now (My Wild Beautiful Bird) *[Chuck Jackson]* 23
Baby It's You *[Shirelles]* 8
Don't Play That Song (You Lied) *[Ben E. King]* 11
Duke Of Earl *[Gene Chandler]* 1
It Keeps Right On A-Hurtin' *[Johnny Tillotson]* 3
Let Me In *[Sensations]* 4
Rama Lama Ding Dong *[Edsels]* 21
Soldier Boy *[Shirelles]* 1
Something's Got A Hold On Me *[Etta James]* 37
Twist And Shout *[Isley Brothers]* 17
What's Your Name *[Don & Juan]* 7
You Belong To Me *[Duprees]* 7

| 11/30/63 | **148** | 2 | | 8 Murray The K - Live From The Brooklyn Fox ....[L] | **$30** | KFM 1001 |

Be My Baby *[Ronettes]*
Denise *[Randy & The Rainbows]*
Everybody Loves A Lover *[Shirelles]*
He's So Fine *[Chiffons]*
I (Who Have Nothing) *[Ben E. King]*
Linda *[Jan & Dean]*
My Boyfriend's Back *[Angels]*
She Cried *[Jay & The Americans]*
Shop Around *[Miracles]*
So Much In Love *[Tymes]*
There Goes My Baby *[Drifters]*
Town Without Pity *[Gene Pitney]*
You Can't Sit Down *[Dovells]*

NADER, Richard
West Coast D.J. Ran a successful rock and roll revival show in the mid-1970's.

| 7/28/73 | **117** | 9 | | 9 Richard Nader/Let The Good Times Roll .... [S-L] | **$15** | Bell 9002 [2] |

Richard Nader's Rock and Roll Revival show

At The Hop *[Danny & The Juniors]*
Blueberry Hill *[Fats Domino]*
Charlie Brown *[Coasters]*
Earth Angel (medley) *[Five Satins]*
Everybody Loves A Lover *[Shirelles]*
Good Golly Miss Molly *[Little Richard]*
Hey Bo Diddley *[Bo Diddley]*
I'll Be Seeing You *[5 Satins]*
I'm A Man *[Bo Diddley]*
In The Still Of The Nite (medley) *[Five Satins]*
Let's Twist Again *[Chubby Checker]*
Lucille *[Little Richard]*
My Blue Heaven *[Fats Domino]*
Poison Ivy *[Coasters]*
Pony Time *[Chubby Checker]*
Rip It Up *[Little Richard]*
Rock Around The Clock *[Bill Haley]*
Save The Last Dance For Me (medley) *[Five Satins]*
Shake, Rattle, & Roll *[Bill Haley]*
Sincerely (medley) *[Five Satins]*
Soldier Boy *[Shirelles]*
Twist, The *[Chubby Checker]*

DEBUT DATE	PEAK POS	WKS CHR	G O L D	ARTIST — Album Title	$	Label & Number
				WOLFMAN JACK		
				Born Bob Smith on 1/21/39. Legendary D.J. with several TV and film appearances.		
4/5/75	**84**	10	**10**	Wolfman Jack/More American Graffiti	**$15**	MCA 8007 [2]

collection of oldies inspired by, but not included in the film *American Graffiti*; introductions by Wolfman Jack

Bony Moronie [*Larry Williams*] 14
Could This Be Magic [*Dubs*] 23
Duke Of Earl [*Gene Chandler*] 1
Gee [*Crows*]
Happy, Happy Birthday Baby [*Tune Weavers*] 5
He Will Break Your Heart [*Jerry Butler*] 7

I'm Sorry [*Brenda Lee*] 1
It Might As Well Rain Until September [*Carole King*] 22
Loco-Motion [*Little Eva*] 1
Louie Louie [*Kingsmen*] 2
Maybe [*Chantels*] 15
My Heart Is An Open Book [*Carl Dobkins Jr.*] 3
Oh, Boy! [*Crickets*] 10

One Summer Night [*Danleers*] 7
Peggy Sue [*Buddy Holly*] 3
Poison Ivy [*Coasters*] 7
Ready Teddy [*Little Richard*] 44
See You Later, Alligator [*Bill Haley*] 6
Shoop Shoop Song (It's In His Kiss) [*Betty Everett*] 6
Speedo [*Cadillacs*] 17

Stagger Lee [*Lloyd Price*] 1
Teenager In Love [*Dion & The Belmonts*] 5
Tutti-Frutti [*Little Richard*] 17
Twilight Time [*Platters*] 1
Will You Love Me Tomorrow [*Shirelles*] 1

DEBUT DATE	PEAK POS	WKS CHR	GOLD	ARTIST — Album Title	$	Label & Number

CONCERTS/FESTIVALS

2/22/64 — **43** — 17 — **1 Apollo Saturday Night** .... **$40** Atco 159
11/16/63 concert recorded at the Apollo in New York City

Alabama Bound [Falcons]
Don't Play That Song [Ben E. King]
Groovin' [Ben E. King]
I Found A Love [Falcons]
Misty [Doris Troy]
Pain In My Heart [Otis Redding]
Rockin' Chair [Rufus Thomas]
Say Yeah [Doris Troy]
Speedo's Back In Town [Coasters]
Stand By Me [Ben E. King]
Tain't Nothin' To Me [Coasters]
These Arms Of Mine [Otis Redding]
Walking The Dog [Rufus Thomas]
What'd I Say [Falcons/Otis Redding/Doris Troy/Rufus Thomas/Coasters/Ben E. King]

4/8/72 — **191** — 4 — **2 Big Sur Festival/One Hand Clapping** .... **$12** Columbia 31138
8th annual folk festival

Corinna [Taj Mahal]
Hello In There [Kris Kristofferson & Joan Baez]
Jesse Younger [Kris Kristofferson]
Love Is Just A Four Letter Word [Joan Baez]
Lucretia Mac Evil [Blood, Sweat & Tears]
Me And Bobby McGee [Big Sur Choir]
Nobody's Business But My Own [Taj Mahal]
Oh Happy Day [Joan Baez]
Pilgrim - Chapter 33 [Kris Kristofferson]
San Francisco Mabel Joy [Mickey Newbury & Joan Baez]
Song Of The French Partisan [Joan Baez]
Thirty-Third Of August [Mickey Newbury]

7/22/78 — **84** — 10 — **3 California Jam 2** .... **$12** Columbia 35389 [2]
3/18/78 concert in Ontario, California

Chip Away The Stone [Aerosmith]
Dance Sister Dance [Santana]
Draw The Line [Aerosmith]
Free-For-All [Ted Nugent]
I'm A King Bee [Frank Marino & Mahogany Rush]
Johnny B. Goode [Frank Marino & Mahogany Rush]
Jugando [Santana]
Let It Go, Let It Flow [Dave Mason]
Little Queen [Heart]
Love Alive [Heart]
Never Gonna Leave [Rubicon]
Oxygene (Part 5) [Jean Michel Jarre]
Same Old Song And Dance [Aerosmith]
Snakeskin Cowboys [Ted Nugent]
Too Hot To Handle [Rubicon]
We Just Disagree [Dave Mason]

Concert For Bangla Desh, The - see HARRISON, George

7/15/72 — **40** — 16 — **4 Fillmore: The Last Days** .... **$18** Fillmore 31390 [3]
Bill Graham's Fillmore-San Francisco rock shows ran from 11/6/65-7/4/71; album includes a booklet and 7" interview record; Graham was killed in a helicopter crash on 10/25/91 (age 60)

Baby's Callin' Me Home [Boz Scaggs]
Back On The Streets Again [Tower Of Power]
Casey Jones [Grateful Dead]
Fresh Air [Quicksilver Messenger Service]
Hello [John Walker]
Hello Friends [Lamb]
Henry [New Riders Of The Purple Sage]
I Just Want To Make Love To You [Cold Blood]
In A Silent Way [Santana]
Incident At Neshabur [Santana]
Johnny B. Goode [Grateful Dead]
Keep Your Lamps Trimmed And Burnin' [Hot Tuna]
Long And Tall [Taj Mahal/Elvin Bishop/Boz Scaggs]
Mojo [Quicksilver Messenger Service]
Pana [Malo]
Party Till The Cows Come Home [Elvin Bishop Group]
Passion Flower [Stoneground]
Poppa Can Play [Sons Of Champlin]
So Fine [Elvin Bishop Group]
We Gonna Rock [Taj Mahal/Elvin Bishop/Boz Scaggs]
White Bird [It's A Beautiful Day]

10/25/69 — **200** — 2 — **5 Live At Bill Graham's Fillmore West** .... **$12** Columbia 9893
recorded January and February 1969 at promoter Graham's Fillmore West in San Francisco

Blues On A Westside [Nick Gravenites]
Carmelita Skiffle [Mike Bloomfield]
It Takes Time [Nick Gravenites]
It's About Time [Nick Gravenites]
Love Got Me [Bob Jones]
Oh Mama [Mike Bloomfield]
One More Mile To Go [Taj Mahal]

9/18/71 — **47** — 9 — **6 First Great Rock Festivals Of The Seventies: Isle Of Wight/Atlanta Pop Festival** .... **$18** Columbia 30805 [3]
Isle Of Wight was held August 26-31, 1970 in England; Atlanta Pop Festival was held July 3-5, 1970

Blame It On The Stones (medley) [Kris Kristofferson]
Call It Anythin' [Miles Davis]
Foxy Lady (medley) [Jimi Hendrix]
Grand Junction [Poco]
I Can't Keep From Cryin' Sometime [Ten Years After]
Kind Woman [Poco]
Love, Peace And Happiness [Chambers Brothers]
Mean Mistreater [Johnny Winter And]
Midnight Lightning (medley) [Jimi Hendrix]
Mr. Bojangles [David Bromberg]
No Need To Worry (medley) [Cactus]
Parchman Farm (medley) [Cactus]
Pilgrim - Chapter 33 [Kris Kristofferson]
Power To Love (medley) [Jimi Hendrix]
Salty Dog [Procol Harum]
Stand! (medley) [Sly & The Family Stone]
Statesborough Blues [Allman Brothers]
Stormy Monday [Mountain]
Tonight Will Be Fine [Leonard Cohen]
Whippen Post [Allman Brothers]
You Can Make It If You Try (medley) [Sly & The Family Stone]

Last Waltz, The - see BAND, The

Live At Yankee Stadium - see ISLEY BROTHERS, The

10/7/72 — **186** — 7 — **7 Mar y Sol** .... **$15** Atco 705 [2]
Rock festival held April 1-3, 1972 in Puerto Rico

Ain't Wastin' Time No More [Allman Brothers Band]
Bedroom Mazurka [Cactus]
Bring My Baby Back [John Baldry]
Do You Know [Osibisa]
Jelly Roll (medley) [Nitzinger]
Looking For A Love [J. Geils Band]
Lucky Man (medley) [Emerson, Lake & Palmer]
Noonward Race [Mahavishnu Orchestra with John McLaughlin]
Respect Yourself [Herbie Mann]
Sometimes In The Morning [Jonathan Edwards]
Take A Pebble (medley) [Emerson, Lake & Palmer]
Texas Blues (medley) [Nitzinger]
Train Of Glory [Jonathan Edwards]
Wang Dang Doodle [Dr. John]
Why I Sing The Blues [B.B. King]

Monterey International Pop Festival - see REDDING, Otis, and/or HENDRIX, Jimi

Montreux Jazz Festival - see JAZZ COMPILATIONS: _Casino Lights_

6/8/63 — **47** — 14 — **8 Motor-Town Review, Vol. 1,** .... **$30** Motown 609
recorded at New York's Apollo Theatre

Bye Bye Baby [Mary Wells]
Don't You Know [Little Stevie Wonder]
Let Me Go The Right Way [Supremes]
Someday, Someway (medley) [Marvelettes]
Strange I Know (medley) [Marvelettes]
Stubborn Kind Of Fellow [Marvin Gaye]
Two Lovers [Mary Wells]
Way Over There [Miracles]
What Kind Of Fool Am I [Marvin Gaye]
Whole Lotta Woman [Contours]
You've Really Got A Hold On Me [Miracles]

5/30/64 — **102** — 5 — **9 Motor-Town Review, Vol. 2, The** .... **$30** Motown 615
recorded at Detroit's Fox Theatre

Days Of Wine And Roses [Marvin Gaye]
Dream Come True [Temptations]
He's Alright [Kim Weston]
Heat Wave [Martha & The Vandellas]
I Call It Pretty Music, But The Old People Call It The Blues [Stevie Wonder]
I Want A Love I Can See [Temptations]
It's Alright [Martha & The Vandellas]
Just Loving You [Kim Weston]
Love Me All The Way [Kim Weston]
Mickey's Monkey [Miracles]
Moon River [Stevie Wonder]
Playboy (medley) [Marvelettes]
Please Mr. Postman (medley) [Marvelettes]
Pride And Joy [Marvin Gaye]

DEBUT DATE	PEAK POS	WKS CHR	GOLD	ARTIST — Album Title	$	Label & Number

				Quicksand [Martha & The Vandellas] / Someday, Someway (medley) [Marvelettes] / Strange I Know (medley) [Marvelettes] / What's Easy For Two Is So Hard For One [Mary Wells] / You Lost The Sweetest Boy [Mary Wells]		
12/18/65+	**111**	7	**10** Motortown Review In Paris recorded at Olympia Music Hall in Paris, France	**$18**	Tamla 264
				Baby Love [Supremes] / Dancing In The Street [Martha & The Vandellas] / Fingertips [Stevie Wonder] / Funny How Time Slips Away [Stevie Wonder] / High Heel Sneakers [Stevie Wonder] / If I Had A Hammer [Martha & The Vandellas] / Mickey's Monkey [Miracles] / Nowhere To Run [Martha & The Vandellas] / Ooo Baby Baby [Miracles] / Somewhere [Supremes] / Stop! In The Name Of Love [Supremes] / Too Many Fish In The Sea [Earl Van Dyke & The Soul Brothers]		
8/23/69	**177**	5	**11** Motortown Review Live recorded at Detroit's Fox Theatre	**$15**	Motown 688
				Ain't No Sun Since You've Been Gone [Gladys Knight & The Pips] / Cloud Nine [Temptations] / Does Your Mama Know About Me [Bobby Taylor] / For Once In My Life [Stevie Wonder] / I Can't Turn You Loose [Blinky] / I Heard It Through The Grapevine [Gladys Knight & The Pips] / I Wish It Would Rain [Gladys Knight & The Pips] / I Wouldn't Change The Man He Is [Blinky] / (I'm Afraid) The Masquerade Is Over [Gladys Knight & The Pips] / Malinda [Bobby Taylor] / Shoo-Be-Doo-Be-Doo-Da-Day [Stevie Wonder] / Sing A Simple Song [Originals] / Uptight (Everything's Alright) [Stevie Wonder] / Who's Making Love [Bobby Taylor]		
4/11/70	**105**	4	**12** Motown at the Hollywood Palace recorded live at the Hollywood Palace	**$12**	Motown 703
				Ain't No Sun Since You've Been Gone [Gladys Knight & The Pips] / Can You Remember (medley) [Jackson 5] / Can't Take My Eyes Off You [Mary Wilson] / Don't Know Why I Love You [Stevie Wonder] / For Once In My Life [Stevie Wonder & Diana Ross] / Good Morning Starshine (medley) [Diana Ross & The Supremes] / I Want You Back [Jackson 5] / I'm Gonna Make You Love Me [Stevie Wonder & Diana Ross] / Nitty Gritty [Gladys Knight & The Pips] / Sing A Simple Song (medley) [Jackson 5] / Someday We'll Be Together [Diana Ross & The Supremes] / Where Do I Go (medley) [Diana Ross & The Supremes]		
11/23/91+	**170**	10	**13** New York Rock And Soul Revue - Live At The Beacon, The concerts recorded on 3/1 and 3/2/91 at the Beacon in New York City	**$12**	Giant 24423
				At Last [Phoebe Snow] / Chain Lightning [Donald Fagen] / Driftin' Blues [Charles Brown] / Drowning In The Sea Of Love [Boz Scaggs] / Green Flower Street [Donald Fagen] / Groovin' [Eddie & David Brigati] / Knock On Wood [Michael McDonald & Phoebe Snow] / Lonely Teardrops [Michael McDonald] / Madison Time [Donald Fagen] / Minute By Minute [Michael McDonald] / People Got To Be Free [New York Rock & Soul Revue] / Pretzel Logic [Donald Fagen & Michael McDonald] / Shakey Ground [Phoebe Snow]		
11/7/64	**95**	8	**14** Saturday Night At The Uptown recorded at the Uptown Theatre in Philadelphia	**$25**	Atlantic 8101
				Can't You Hear The Beat [Carltons] / Down The Aisle [Patti LaBelle & The Blue Belles] / I'm Gonna Cry [Wilson Pickett] / If You Need Me [Wilson Pickett] / Mixed Up, Shook Up, Girl [Patty & The Emblems] / My Girl Sloopy [Vibrations] / Oh! Baby (We Got A Good Thing Goin') [Barbara Lynn] / On Broadway [Drifters] / There Goes My Baby [Drifters] / Under The Boardwalk [Drifters] / Watusi, The [Vibrations]		
9/25/71	**112**	10	**15** Soul To Soul concert film shot in Ghana, West Africa	[S] **$12**	Atlantic 7207
				Are You Sure (medley) [Staple Singers] / Freedom Song [Roberta Flack] / Funky Broadway [Wilson Pickett] / He's Alright (medley) [Staple Singers] / Heyjorler [Eddie Harris & Les McCann] / I Smell Trouble [Ike & Tina Turner] / Land Of 1000 Dances [Wilson Pickett] / Run Shaker Life [Voices of East Harlem] / Soul To Soul [Ike & Tina Turner] / Tryin' Times [Roberta Flack]		
9/2/67	**145**	4	**16** Stax/Volt Revue - Live In London, The recorded in London in early 1967	**$20**	Stax 721
				B-A-B-Y [Carla Thomas] / Green Onions [Booker T. & The MG's] / Hold On! I'm A Comin' [Sam & Dave] / I Take What I Want [Sam & Dave] / If I Had A Hammer [Eddie Floyd] / Knock On Wood [Eddie Floyd] / Philly Dog [Mar-Keys] / Shake [Otis Redding] / When Something Is Wrong With My Baby [Sam & Dave] / Yesterday [Carla Thomas]		
9/26/81	**173**	3	**17** Urgh! A Music War previously unreleased live performances by top rock acts	**$10**	A&M 6019 [2]
				Ain't This The Life [Oingo Boingo] / Back In Flesh [Wall Of Voodoo] / Bad Reputation [Joan Jett & The Blackhearts] / Beyond And Back [X] / Birdies [Pere Ubu] / Cheryl's Going Home [John Otway] / Come Again [Au Pairs] / Dance [Toyah Wilcox] / Down In The Park [Gary Numan] / Driven To Tears [Police] / Enola Gay [Orchestral Manoeuvres In The Dark] / Foolish I Know [Jools Holland] / He'd Send In The Army [Gang Of Four] / Homicide [999] / Ku Klux Klan [Steel Pulse] / Model Worker [Magazine] / Nothing Means Nothing Anymore [Alley Cats] / Offshore Banking Business [Members] / Puppet, The [Echo & The Bunnymen] / Respectable Street [XTC] / Shadow Line [Fleshtones] / Sign Of The Cross [Skafish] / Tear It Up [Cramps] / Total Eclipse [Klaus Nomi] / Uncontrollable Urge [Devo] / We Got The Beat [Go-Go's] / Where's Captain Kirk [Athletico Spizz]		
7/24/76	**153**	6	**18** Volunteer Jam 9/9/75 concert recorded at Murfreesboro, Tennessee	**$10**	Capricorn 0172
				Birmingham Blues [Charlie Daniels Band] / Mountain Dew [Charlie Daniels Band] / South's Gonna Do It [Charlie Daniels Band] / Sweet Mama [Dickey Betts] / Thrill Is Gone [Marshall Tucker Band] / Whiskey [Charlie Daniels Band]		
7/19/80	**104**	9	**19** Volunteer Jam VI 1/12/80 concert recorded at the Nashville Municipal Auditorium	**$10**	Epic 36438 [2]
				Amazing Grace (medley) [Charlie Daniels Band & Bobby Jones] / Carol [Ted Nugent] / Do The Funky Chicken [Rufus Thomas] / Down Home Blues [Papa John Creach] / Funky Junky [Charlie Daniels Band] / Keep On Smilin' [Wet Willie] / Lady Luck [Grinderswitch] / New Orleans Ladies [Louisiana's LeRoux] / Night They Drove Old Dixie Down [Dobie Gray] / Rich Kids [Winters Brothers Band] / Same Old Story (Same Old Song) [Crystal Gayle] / So Long [Henry Paul Band] / Will The Circle Be Unbroken (medley) [Charlie Daniels Band & Bobby Jones]		
7/25/81	**149**	4	**20** Volunteer Jam VII 1/17/81 concert held at the Nashville Municipal Auditorium	**$10**	Epic 37178
				Around And Around [Ted Nugent] / Can't You See [Charlie Daniels Band] / Change Is Gonna Come [Dobie Gray] / Falling In Love For The Night [Crystal Gayle / Charlie Daniels Band] / Marie La Veau [Bobby Bare] / Mississippi Queen [Molly Hatchet with Ted Nugent] / Standing On Shakey Ground [Delbert McClinton] / Sweet Home Alabama [Charlie Daniels Band] / (Your Love Has Lifted Me) Higher And Higher [Jimmy Hall]		

DEBUT DATE	PEAK POS	WKS CHR	G O L D	ARTIST — Album Title	$	Label & Number
2/17/73	**28**	17	● 21	Wattstax: The Living Word ....[S]	**$15**	Stax 3010 [2]

live concert held in August 1972 in Los Angeles

Ain't No Sunshine [Isaac Hayes]
Angel Of Mercy (medley) [Albert King]
Breakdown, The (medley) [Rufus Thomas]
Do The Funky Chicken (medley) [Rufus Thomas]
Do The Funky Penguin (medley) [Rufus Thomas]
Feel It (medley) [Bar-Kays]

Gee Whiz (medley) [Carla Thomas]
Hearsay (medley) [Soul Children]
I Can't Turn You Loose (medley) [Bar-Kays]
I Don't Know What This World Is Coming To (medley) [Soul Children]
I Have A God Who Loves (medley) [Carla Thomas]

I Like The Things About Me (medley) [Staple Singers]
I Like What You're Doing (To Me) (medley) [Carla Thomas]
I'll Play The Blues For You (medley) [Albert King]
I'll Take You There (medley) [Staple Singers]
Killing Floor (medley) [Albert King]

Knock On Wood (medley) [Eddie Floyd]
Lay Your Loving On Me (medley) [Eddie Floyd]
Oh La De Da (medley) [Staple Singers]
Respect Yourself (medley) [Staple Singers]
Son Of Shaft (medley) [Bar-Kays]

| 9/15/73 | **157** | 5 | 22 | Wattstaxx 2: The Living Word ....[S] | **$15** | Stax 3018 [2] |

more songs from the concert

Ain't That Loving You (For More Reasons Than One) (medley) [David Porter]
Arrest [Richard Pryor]
Backroom [Richard Pryor]
Blue Note [Richard Pryor]
Can't See You When I Want To (medley) [David Porter]
Handshake [Richard Pryor]
I May Not Be What You Want [Mel & Tim]

Jody's Got Your Girl And Gone (medley) [Johnnie Taylor]
Lift Every Voice And Sing [Kim Weston]
Line Up [Richard Pryor]
Lying On The Truth [Rance Allen Group]
Negroes [Richard Pryor]
Niggers [Richard Pryor]
Old Time Religion [Golden 13]
Peace Be Still [Emotions]

Reach Out And Touch (medley) [David Porter]
Rolling Down A Mountainside [Isaac Hayes]
Saturday Night [Richard Pryor]
Show Me How (medley) [Emotions]
So I Can Love You (medley) [Emotions]
Someone Greater Than You And I [Jimmy Jones]

Steal Away (medley) [Johnnie Taylor]
Stop Doggin' Me (medley) [Johnnie Taylor]
Walking The Backstreets And Crying [Little Milton]
Whatcha See Is Whatcha Get [Dramatics]
Wino Get A Job [Richard Pryor]

| 6/6/70 | **1**[4] | 68 | ● 23 | **Woodstock** ....[S] | **$18** | Cotillion 500 [3] |

film of historic rock festival near Woodstock, New York on August 15-17, 1969

At The Hop [Sha-Na-Na]
Coming Into Los Angeles [Arlo Guthrie]
Dance To The Music (medley) [Sly & The Family Stone]
Drug Store Truck Drivin' Man [Joan Baez feat. Jeffrey Shurtleff]
Fish Cheer (medley) [Country Joe & The Fish]
Freedom [Richie Havens]
Going Up The Country [Canned Heat]

I-Feel-Like-I'm-Fixin'-To-Die Rag (medley) [Country Joe & The Fish]
I Had A Dream [John Sebastian]
I Want To Take You Higher (medley) [Sly & The Family Stone]
I'm Going Home [Ten Years After]
Joe Hill [Joan Baez]
Love March [Butterfield Blues Band]
Music Lover (medley) [Sly & The Family Stone]

Purple Haze (medley) [Jimi Hendrix]
Rainbows All Over Your Blues [John Sebastian]
Rock & Soul Music [Country Joe & The Fish]
Sea Of Madness [Crosby, Stills, Nash & Young]
Soul Sacrifice [Santana]
Star Spangled Banner (medley) [Jimi Hendrix]
Suite: Judy Blue Eyes [Crosby, Stills & Nash]

Volunteers [Jefferson Airplane]
We're Not Gonna Take It [Who]
With A Little Help From My Friends [Joe Cocker]
Wooden Ships [Crosby, Stills, Nash & Young]

| 4/10/71 | **7** | 17 | ● 24 | **Woodstock Two** ....[S] | **$15** | Cotillion 400 [2] |

more songs from the festival

Birthday Of The Sun [Melanie]
Blood Of The Sun [Mountain]
Eskimo Blue Day [Jefferson Airplane]
Everything's Gonna Be Alright [Butterfield Blues Band]
4 + 20 [Crosby, Stills, Nash & Young]

Get My Heart Back Together [Jimi Hendrix]
Guinnevere [Crosby, Stills, Nash & Young]
Imaginary Western, Theme For An [Mountain]
Izabella [Jimi Hendrix]
Jam Back At The House [Jimi Hendrix]

Marrakesh Express [Crosby, Stills, Nash & Young]
My Beautiful People [Melanie]
Saturday Afternoon (medley) [Jefferson Airplane]
Sweet Sir Galahad [Joan Baez]
Won't You Try (medley) [Jefferson Airplane]
Woodstock Boogie [Canned Heat]

DEBUT DATE	PEAK POS	WKS CHR	GOLD	ARTIST — Album Title	$	Label & Number

BENEFIT RECORDINGS

4/18/81 · 36 · 12 · 1 Concerts For The People Of Kampuchea .... **$10** Atlantic 7005 [2]
benefit concert held December 26-29, 1979 in London

Armagideon Time [Clash]	Every Night [Paul McCartney &	Imposter, The [Elvis Costello &	Now I'm Here [Queen]
Baba O'Riley [Who]	Wings]	The Attractions]	Precious [Pretenders]
Behind Blue Eyes [Who]	Got To Get You Into My Life	Let It Be [Rockestra]	Rockestra Theme [Rockestra]
Coming Up [Paul McCartney &	[Paul McCartney & Wings]	Little Sister [Rockpile with	See Me, Feel Me [Who]
Wings]	Hit Me With Your Rhythm Stick	Robert Plant]	Sister Disco [Who]
Crawling From The Wreckage	[Ian Dury & The Blockheads]	Lucille [Rockestra]	Tattooed Love Boys [Pretenders]
[Rockpile]		Monkey Man [Specials]	Wait, The [Pretenders]

5/11/91 · 24 · 16 · 2 Deadicated .... **$12** Arista 8669
original Grateful Dead compositions; portion of proceeds benefit rain forest preservation

Bertha [Los Lobos]	Deal [Dr. John]	Ripple [Jane's Addiction]	U.S. Blues [Harshed Mellows]
Casey Jones [Warren Zevon with	Estimated Prophet [Burning Spear]	Ship Of Fools [Elvis Costello]	Uncle John's Band [Indigo Girls]
David Lindley]	Friend Of The Devil [Lyle Lovett]	To Lay Me Down [Cowboy	Wharf Rat [Midnight Oil]
Cassidy [Suzanne Vega]	Jack Straw [Bruce Hornsby &	Junkies]	
China Doll [Suzanne Vega]	The Range]	Truckin' [Dwight Yoakam]	

6/15/91 · 31 · 30 · ● · 3 For Our Children .... **$12** Disney 60616
performances of childrens' songs to benefit the Pediatric AIDS Foundation

Autumn To May [Ann & Nancy	Chicken Lips And Lizard Hips	Getting To Know You [James	Itsy Bitsy Spider [Little Richard]
Wilson]	[Bruce Springsteen]	Taylor]	Mary Had A Little Lamb [Paul
Ballad Of Davy Crockett	Child Is Born [Barbra Streisand]	Give A Little Love [Ziggy Marley	McCartney]
[Stephen Bishop]	Child Of Mine [Carole King]	& the Melody Makers]	Medley Of Rhymes [Debbie
Blanket For A Sail [Harry	Country Feelin's [Brian Wilson]	Golden Slumbers [Jackson	Gibson]
Nilsson]	Cushie Butterfield [Sting]	Browne & Jennifer Warnes]	Pacifier [Elton John]
Blueberry Pie [Bette Midler]	Gartan Mother's Lullaby [Meryl	Good Night, My Love (Pleasant	Tell Me Why [Pat Benatar]
	Streep]	Dreams) [Paula Abdul]	This Old Man [Bob Dylan]

7/15/89 · 68 · 24 · 4 Greenpeace/Rainbow Warriors .... **$10** Geffen 24236 [2]
an environmental pressure group; the first Western-rock compilation officially released in the Soviet Union; CD version also contains tracks by Hothouse Flowers/Little Steven/Silencers/Robbie Robertson

City Of Dreams [Talking Heads]	**Lay Your Hands On Me**	Pride (In The Name Of Love) [U2]	We Are The People [John Cougar
Don't Stop The Dance [Bryan	[Thompson Twins] **6**	Red Rain [Peter Gabriel]	Mellencamp]
Ferry]	Let's Go Forward [Terence Trent	Set Them Free [Aswad]	When Tomorrow Comes
Heaven Is A Place On Earth	D'Arby]	**Ship Of Fools (Save Me From**	[Eurythmics]
[Belinda Carlisle] **1**	**Look Out Any Window** [Bruce	**Tomorrow)** [World Party] **27**	Whole Of The Moon [Waterboys]
I Will Be Your Friend [Sade]	Hornsby & The Range] **35**	**Small World** [Huey Lewis & The	Wholly Humble Heart [Martin
It's The End Of The World As	Love Is The Seventh Wave	**News]** **25**	Stephenson & The Daintees]
We Know It (And I Feel Fine)	[Sting] **17**	**Somebody** [Bryan Adams] **11**	Why Worry [Dire Straits]
[R.E.M.] **69**	**Middle Of The Road**	This Time [INXS] **81**	**You're The Voice** [John
Last Great American Whale [Lou	[Pretenders] **19**	Throwing Stones [Grateful Dead]	Farnham] **82**
Reed]	Miles Away [Basia]	Waterfront [Simple Minds]	

6/15/91 · 198 · 1 · 5 Hearts Of Gold - The Classic Rock Collection .... **$12** Foundation 96647
benefits the T.J. Martell Foundation for Leukemia, Cancer and AIDS Research

Badlands [Bruce Springsteen] **42**	Hot Blooded [Foreigner] **3**	Love The One You're With	**Smoke On The Water** [Deep
Can't Get Enough [Bad	**I Shot The Sheriff** [Eric	[Stephen Stills] **14**	Purple] **4**
Company] **5**	Clapton] **1**	**Money** [Pink Floyd] **13**	
Carry On Wayward Son	**I Want You To Want Me**	**Ramblin' Man** [Allman Brothers	
[Kansas] **11**	[Cheap Trick] **7**	Band] **2**	
Free Bird [Lynyrd Skynyrd] **19**	Let's Go [Cars] **14**		

9/1/90 · 92 · 8 · 6 Knebworth - The Album .... [L] **$24** Polydor 84702 [2]
June 30, 1990 concert in England to benefit the Nordoff-Robbins Music Therapy Centre and the Brit School for Performing Arts

Badman's Song [Tears For Fears]	In The Midnight Hour (medley)	Sad Songs (Say So Much) [Elton	Turn It On Again (medley)
Comfortably Numb [Pink Floyd]	[Genesis]	John]	[Genesis]
Coming Up [Paul McCartney]	Liars Dance [Robert Plant]	Saturday Night's All Right (For	Twist And Shout (medley)
Dirty Water [Status Quo]	Mama [Genesis]	Fighting) [Elton John]	[Genesis]
Do You Wanna Dance [Cliff	On The Beach [Cliff Richard &	Somebody To Love (medley)	Wearing And Tearing [Robert
Richard & The Shadows]	The Shadows]	[Genesis]	Plant]
Everybody Wants To Rule The	Pinball Wizard (medley) [Genesis]	Sunshine Of Your Love [Eric	Whatever You Want [Status Quo]
World [Tears For Fears]	Reach Out I'll Be There (medley)	Clapton]	You've Lost That Lovin' Feeling
Hey Jude [Paul McCartney]	[Genesis]	Sussudio [Phil Collins]	(medley) [Genesis]
Hurting Kind [Robert Plant]	Rockin' All Over The World	Tall Cool One [Robert Plant]	
(I Can't Get No) Satisfaction	[Status Quo]	Think I Love You Too Much	
(medley) [Genesis]	Run Like Hell [Pink Floyd]	[Dire Straits]	

6/7/86 · 105 · 7 · 7 Live! For Life .... [L] **$8** I.R.S. 5731
all proceeds donated to the AMC Cancer Research Center; previously unreleased live and studio tracks

Ages Of You [R.E.M.]	Lively Up Yourself [Bob Marley	Love Lessons [Stewart Copeland	Tempted [Squeeze]
Hero Takes A Fall [Bangles]	& The Wailers feat. The	& Derek Holt]	Tenderness [General Public]
Howling Wind [Alarm]	I-Threes]	Take Your Medicine [Oingo	We Got The Beat [Go-Go's]
I Been Down So Long [Sting]		Boingo]	

5/25/91 · 38 · 19 · 8 Club MTV Party To Go - Volume One .... **$12** Tommy Boy 1037
includes remixes of several charted hits; portion of proceeds donated to the AMC Cancer Research Center

At The Club [Joe Boys]	Humpty Dance [Digital	Play That Funky Music [Vanilla	Tom's Diner [DNA feat. Suzanne
Don't Wanna Fall In Love [Jane	Underground]	Ice]	Vega]
Child]	Knocked Out [Paula Abdul]	Poison [Bell Biv DeVoe]	Turn This Mutha Out [M.C.
Feels Good [Tony! Toni! Tone!]	Knockin' Boots [Candyman]	Think [Information Society]	Hammer]
	Personal Jesus [Depeche Mode]		

6/20/92 · 19 · 34↑ · ● · 9 MTV: Party To Go Volume 2 .... **$12** Tommy Boy 1053
dance hit remixes; portion of proceeds donated to the AMC Cancer Research Center

All 4 Love [Color Me Badd]	Let's Talk About Sex	Playground [Another Bad	Summertime [D.J. Jazzy Jeff &
Good Vibrations [Marky Mark &	[Salt-N-Pepa]	Creation]	The Fresh Prince]
The Funky Bunch feat.	Motownphilly [Boyz II Men]	Sadeness Part I [Enigma]	3 AM Eternal [KLF]
Loleatta Holloway]	Now That We Found Love	Set Adrift On Memory Bliss [PM	
Here We Go [C & C Music	[Heavy D. & The Boyz]	Dawn]	
Factory]	O.P.P. [Naughty By Nature]		

BENEFIT RECORDINGS

DEBUT DATE	PEAK POS	WKS CHR	G O L D	ARTIST — Album Title	$	Label & Number
3/2/85	91	12		10 MTV's Rock 'N Roll To Go	$8	Elektra 60399

proceeds benefit cancer research

Are We Ourselves? *[Fixx]* 15
Dance Hall Days *[Wang Chung]* 16
Drive *[Cars]* 3
Hell Is For Children *[Pat Benatar]*
Hold Me Now *[Thompson Twins]* 3
King Of Pain *[Police]* 3
Lick It Up *[Kiss]* 66
Lucky Star *[Madonna]* 4
Oh Sherrie *[Steve Perry]* 3
Rebel Yell *[Billy Idol]* 46
Round And Round *[Ratt]* 12
Say It Isn't So *[Hall & Oates]* 2
She Bop *[Cyndi Lauper]* 3
What's Love Got To Do With It *[Tina Turner]* 1

DEBUT DATE	PEAK POS	WKS CHR	GOLD	ARTIST — Album Title	$	Label & Number
12/16/89+	87	15		11 Make A Difference Foundation: Stairway To Heaven/Highway To Hell	$8	Mercury 842093

Make A Difference Foundation is a non-profit, anti-drug organization; includes 8 studio tracks and the live jam recorded at the Moscow Music Peace Festival, August 12-13, 1989

Blue Suede Shoes (medley) *[Bon Jovi & Cinderella]*
Boys Are Back In Town *[Bon Jovi]*
Holidays In The Sun *[Skid Row]*
Hound Dog *[Bon Jovi & Cinderella]*
I Can't Explain *[Scorpions]*
Long Tall Sally (medley) *[Scorpions & Gorky Park]*
Moby Dick *[Drum Madness]*
Move Over *[Cinderella]*
My Generation *[Gorky Park]*
Purple Haze *[Ozzy Osbourne]*
Rock And Roll *[Skid Row & Motley Crue]*
Teaser *[Motley Crue]*

| 8/18/79 | 171 | 4 | | 12 Music for UNICEF Concert/A Gift Of Song, The | $10 | Polydor 6214 |

benefit concert held on 1/9/79 at the United Nations Hall

Chiquitita *[Abba]*
Da Ya Think I'm Sexy? *[Rod Stewart]*
Fallen Angels *[Kris Kristofferson & Rita Coolidge]*
I Go For You *[Andy Gibb]*
Key, The *[Olivia Newton-John]*
Mimi's Song *[Donna Summer]*
Rest Your Love On Me *[Andy Gibb & Olivia Newton-John]*
Rhymes And Reasons *[John Denver]*
September (medley) *[Earth, Wind & Fire]*
Too Much Heaven *[Bee Gees]*
That's The Way Of The World (medley) *[Earth, Wind & Fire]*

| 12/22/79+ | 19 | 18 | ● | 13 No Nukes/The MUSE Concerts For A Non-Nuclear Future | $15 | Asylum 801 [3] |

benefit concerts recorded at New York's Madison Square Garden September 19-23, 1979

Angel From Montgomery *[Bonnie Raitt]*
Before The Deluge *[Jackson Browne]*
Captain Jim's Drunken Dream *[James Taylor]*
Cathedral *[Graham Nash]*
Crow On The Cradle *[Jackson Browne & Graham Nash]*
Cry To Me *[Tom Petty & The Heartbreakers]*
Dependin' On You *[Doobie Brothers]*
Devil With The Blue Dress (medley) *[Bruce Springsteen & The E Street Band]*
Get Together *[Jesse Colin Young]*
Good Golly, Miss Molly (medley) *[Bruce Springsteen & The E Street Band]*
Heart Of The Night *[Poco]*
Honey Don't Leave L.A. *[James Taylor]*
Jenny Take A Ride (medley) *[Bruce Springsteen & The E Street Band]*
Little Sister *[Ry Cooder]*
Long Time Gone *[Crosby, Stills & Nash]*
Lotta Love *[Nicolette Larson & The Doobie Brothers]*
Mockingbird *[James Taylor & Carly Simon]*
Once You Get Started *[Chaka Khan]*
Plutonium Is Forever *[John Hall]*
Power *[Doobie Brothers/John Hall/James Taylor]*
Runaway *[Bonnie Raitt]*
Stay *[Bruce Springsteen/Jackson Browne/E Street Band]*
Takin' It To The Streets *[Doobie Brothers & James Taylor]*
Teach Your Children *[Crosby, Stills & Nash]*
Times They Are A-Changin' *[James Taylor/Carly Simon/Graham Nash]*
We Almost Lost Detroit *[Gil Scott-Heron]*
Woman, A *[Sweet Honey In The Rock]*
You Can't Change That *[Raydio]*
You Don't Have To Cry *[Crosby, Stills & Nash]*

| 8/11/90 | 79 | 9 | | 14 Nobody's Child - Romanian Angel Appeal | $12 | Warner 26280 |

organized by The Beatles' wives (Barbara Bach, Olivia Harrison, Linda McCartney & Yoko Ono); proceeds donated to thousands of Romanian orphans

Ain't That Peculiar *[Mike & The Mechanics]*
Big Day Little Boat *[Edie Brickell & New Bohemians]*
Civil War *[Guns N' Roses]*
Feeding Off The Love Of The Land *[Stevie Wonder]*
Goodnight Little One *[Ric Ocasek]*
Homeward Bound *[Paul Simon & George Harrison]*
How Can You Mend A Broken Heart? *[Bee Gees]*
Lovechild *[Billy Idol]*
Medicine Man *[Elton John]*
Nobody's Child *[Traveling Wilburys]*
That Kind Of Woman *[Eric Clapton]*
This Week *[Dave Stewart & The Spiritual Cowboys]*
Trembler, The *[Duane Eddy]*
With A Little Help From My Friends *[Ringo Starr & His All Star Band]*
Wonderful Remark *[Van Morrison]*

| 6/6/87 | 194 | 3 | | 15 Prince's Trust 10th Anniversary Birthday Party, The ...[L] | $8 | A&M 3906 |

recorded live at Wembley Arena, London on 6/20/86

Better Be Good To Me *[Tina Turner]*
Call Of The Wild *[Midge Ure]*
Fields Of Fire *[Big Country]*
Get Back *[Paul McCartney]*
I'm Still Standing *[Elton John]*
In The Air Tonight *[Phil Collins]*
Marlene On The Wall *[Suzanne Vega]*
Money For Nothing *[Dire Straits]*
No One Is To Blame *[Howard Jones]*
Reach Out *[Joan Armatrading]*
Sailing *[Rod Stewart]*
Something About You *[Level 42]*

| 11/17/90+ | 38 | 24 | | 16 Red Hot + Blue | $12 | Chrysalis 21799 |

tribute to Cole Porter with proceeds benefitting AIDS research

After You *[Jody Watley]*
Begin The Beguine *[Salif Keita]*
Do I Love You? *[Aztec Camera]*
Don't Fence Me In *[David Byrne]*
Down In The Depths *[Lisa Stansfield]*
Ev'ry Time We Say Goodbye *[Annie Lennox]*
From This Moment On *[Jimmy Somerville]*
I Get A Kick Out Of You *[Jungle Brothers]*
I Love Paris *[Les Negresses Vertes]*
I've Got U Under My Skin *[Neneh Cherry]*
In The Still Of The Night *[Neville Brothers]*
It's All Right With Me *[Tom Waits]*
Just One Of Those Things (medley) *[Kirsty MacColl & The Pogues]*
Love For Sale *[Fine Young Cannibals]*
Miss Otis Regrets (medley) *[Kirsty MacColl & The Pogues]*
Night And Day *[U2]*
So In Love *[k.d. lang]*
Too Darn Hot *[Erasure]*
Well, Did You Evah! *[Debbie Harry & Iggy Pop]*
Who Wants To Be A Millionaire? *[Thompson Twins]*
You Do Something To Me *[Sinead O'Connor]*

| 7/25/92 | 52 | 11 | | 17 Red Hot + Dance | $12 | Columbia 52826 |

dance hit remixes; proceeds benefit AIDS research and relief

Apparently Nothin' *[Young Disciples]*
Change *[Lisa Stansfield]*
Crazy *[Seal]*
Do You Really Want To Know *[George Michael]*
Gypsy Woman *[Crystal Waters]*
Happy *[George Michael]*
Peace *[Sabrina Johnston]*
Red Hot + Dance, Theme From *[tomandandy]*
Set Adrift On Memory Bliss *[PM Dawn]*
Supernatural *[Madonna]*
Thank You (Falettin Me Be Mice Elf Agin) *[Sly & The Family Stone]*
Too Funky *[George Michael]* 10
Unbelievable *[EMF]*

| 1/24/87 | 121 | 11 | | 18 Rock For Amnesty | $8 | Mercury 830617 |

honoring Amnesty International's 25th anniversary

Biko *[Peter Gabriel]*
Brothers In Arms *[Dire Straits]*
Ghost Dancing *[Simple Minds]*
I Believe *[Tears For Fears]*
No One Is To Blame *[Howard Jones]* 4
Passengers *[Elton John]*
Pink Houses *[John Cougar Mellencamp]* 8
Pipes Of Peace *[Paul McCartney]*
Strange Fruit *[Sting]*
Tonight *[Bryan Adams]*

| 5/23/81 | 106 | 12 | | 19 Secret Policeman's Ball/The Music, The | $8 | Island 9630 |

Bach-Bourée (From 3rd Cello Suite) *[John Williams]*
Cavatina *[John Williams]*
Drowned *[Pete Townshend]*
Glad To Be Gay *[Tom Robinson]*
1967 (So Long Ago) *[Tom Robinson]*
Pinball Wizard *[Pete Townshend]*
Spontaneous *[Neil Innes]*
Won't Get Fooled Again *[Pete Townshend & John Williams]*

DEBUT DATE	PEAK POS	WKS CHR	GOLD	ARTIST — Album Title	$	Label & Number
3/20/82	**29**	16		**20** Secret Policeman's Other Ball/The Music, The	**$8**	Island 9698

above 2 are benefit concerts for Amnesty International

Catch The Wind [Donovan]	Farther Up The Road [Jeff Beck & Eric Clapton]	I Shall Be Released [Secret Police]	Roof Is Leaking [Phil Collins]
'Cause We've Ended As Lovers [Jeff Beck & Eric Clapton]	I Don't Like Mondays [Bob Geldof & Johnny Fingers]	In The Air Tonight [Phil Collins]	Roxanne [Sting]
Crossroads [Jeff Beck & Eric Clapton]		Message In A Bottle [Sting]	Universal Soldier [Donovan]

DEBUT DATE	PEAK POS	WKS CHR	GOLD	ARTIST — Album Title	$	Label & Number
4/20/91	**165**	5		**21** Tame Yourself	**$12**	R.N.A. 70772

proceeds donated to People for the Ethical Treatment of Animals (PETA)

Across The Way [Aleka's Attic]	Damned Old Dog [k.d. lang]	Don't Kill The Animals [Nina Hagen & Lene Lovich]	Quiche Lorraine [B-52's]
Asleep Too Long [Goosebumps]	Do What I Have To Do [Exene Cervenka]	Fur [Jane Wiedlin]	Rage [Erasure & Lene Lovich]
Bless The Beasts And The Children [Belinda Carlisle]	Don't Be Part Of It [Howard Jones]	I'll Give You My Skin [Indigo Girls & Michael Stipe]	Slaves [Fetchin Bones]
Born For A Purpose [Pretenders]			Tame Yourself [Raw Youth]

DEBUT DATE	PEAK POS	WKS CHR	GOLD	ARTIST — Album Title	$	Label & Number
9/17/88	**70**	10		**22** Folkways: A Vision Shared - A Tribute To Woody Guthrie And Leadbelly	**$8**	Columbia 44034

tribute to Woody Guthrie and Huddie Leadbetter; proceeds to support the Smithsonian Institution's acquisition of Folkways Records and the Woody Guthrie archive

Bourgeois Blues [Taj Mahal]	Hobo's Lullaby [Emmylou Harris]	Pretty Boy Floyd [Bob Dylan]	This Land Is Your Land [Pete Seeger/Sweet Honey In The Rock/Doc Watson]
Do Re Mi [John Mellencamp]	I Ain't Got No Home [Bruce Springsteen]	Rock Island Line [Little Richard with Fishbone]	
East Texas Red [Arlo Guthrie]	Jesus Christ [U2]	Sylvie [Sweet Honey In The Rock]	Vigilante Man [Bruce Springsteen]
Goodnight Irene [Brian Wilson]	Philadelphia Lawyer [Willie Nelson]		
Gray Goose [Sweet Honey In The Rock]			

DEBUT DATE	PEAK POS	WKS CHR	GOLD	ARTIST — Album Title	$	Label & Number
4/29/72	**183**	2		**23** Tribute To Woody Guthrie - Part One, A .... [L]	**$12**	Columbia 31171

Curley Headed Baby [Pete Seeger]	Grand Coulee Dam [Bob Dylan]	Pastures Of Plenty [Tom Paxton]	So Long It's Been Good To Know Yuh (Dusty Old Dust) [Woody Guthrie]
Dear Mrs. Roosevelt [Bob Dylan]	I Ain't Got No Home [Bob Dylan]	Rambling 'Round Your City (Ramblin' 'Round) [Odetta]	Vigilante Man [Richie Havens]
Do Re Mi [Arlo Guthrie]	Oklahoma Hills [Arlo Guthrie]		

DEBUT DATE	PEAK POS	WKS CHR	GOLD	ARTIST — Album Title	$	Label & Number
4/29/72	**189**	2		**24** Tribute To Woody Guthrie - Part Two, A .... [L]	**$12**	Warner 2586

above 2 albums are live tributes to Woody Guthrie with proceeds benefiting Huntington's Disease research

Biggest Thing Man Has Ever Done (Great Historical Bum) [Tom Paxton]	Howdido [Jack Elliott]	1913 Massacre [Jack Elliott]	Why Oh Why [Odetta]
Deportee (Plane Wreck At Los Gatos) [Judy Collins]	Jackhammer John [Richie Havens & Pete Seeger]	Roll On Columbia [Judy Collins]	Woman At Home [Country Joe McDonald]
Hobo's Lullaby [Joan Baez]	Jesus Christ [Arlo Guthrie]	This Land Is Your Land [Odetta, Arlo Guthrie & Company]	
	Mail Myself To You [Earl Robinson]	Union Maid [Judy Collins & Pete Seeger]	

Very Special Christmas, A - see CHRISTMAS (Top Pop Albums Chart-Various)

Very Special Christmas 2, A - see CHRISTMAS (Top Pop Albums Chart-Various)

Refer to the following names in the Artist Section for more benefit group recordings:

ARTISTS UNITED AGAINST APARTHEID
HEAR 'N AID
USA FOR AFRICA
WEST COAST RAP ALL-STARS
WILLIE AND THE POOR BOYS

CONCEPT ALBUMS

DEBUT DATE	PEAK POS	WKS CHR	GOLD	ARTIST — Album Title	$	Label & Number
4/22/89	178	4		1 Brazil Classics 1 Beleza Tropical ....[F] compiled by David Byrne (Talking Heads)	$8	Fly 25805

Andar Com Fe [Gilberto Gil]
Anima [Milton Nascimento]
Cacada [Chico Buarque]
Caixa De Sol [Nazare Pereira]
Flo Maravilha [Jorge Ben]
O Leaozinho [Caetano Veloso]
Ponta De Lanca Africano (Umbabarauma) [Jorge Ben]
Queixa [Caetano Veloso]
Quilombo, O El Dorado Negro [Gilberto Gil]
San Vicente [Milton Nascimento]
So Quero Um Xodo [Gilberto Gil]
Sonho Meu [Maria Bethania E Gal Costa]
Terra [Caetano Veloso]
Um Canto De Afoxe Para O Bloco Do Ile (Ile Aye) [Caetano Veloso]

| 6/21/86 | 87 | 12 | | 2 Class Of '55 (Memphis Rock & Roll Homecoming) ....
CARL PERKINS/JERRY LEE LEWIS/ROY ORBISON/JOHNNY CASH
recorded in same Sun Records studio where their careers began | $10 | Am./Smash 830002 |

Big Train (From Memphis)
Birth Of Rock And Roll
Class Of '55
Coming Home
I Will Rock And Roll With You
Keep My Motor Running
Rock And Roll (Fais-Do-Do)
Sixteen Candles
Waymore's Blues
We Remember The King

| 10/13/84 | 75 | 10 | | 3 Every Man Has A Woman ....
all songs written by Yoko Ono | $8 | Casablanca 823490 |

Dogtown [Alternating Boxes]
Dream Love [Nilsson]
Every Man Has A Woman Who Loves Him [John Lennon]
Goodbye Sadness [Roberta Flack]
I'm Moving On [Eddie Money]
It's Alright [Sean Ono Lennon]
Loneliness [Nilsson]
Nobody Sees Me Like You Do [Rosanne Cash]
Now Or Never [Spirit Choir]
Silver Horse [Nilsson]
Wake Up [Trio]
Walking On Thin Ice [Elvis Costello]

| 12/17/88 | 171 | 8 | | 4 Guitar Speak ....[I]
features songs by various rock guitarists | $8 | I.R.S. 42240 |

Blood Alley 152 [Ronnie Montrose]
Captain Zlogg [Hank Marvin]
Danjo [Pete Haycock]
Let Me Out'a Here [Leslie West]
No Limit [Alvin Lee]
Prisoner, The [Randy California]
Sharp On Attack [Steve Howe]
Sloe Moon Rising [Rick Derringer]
Sphinx [Phil Manzanera]
Strut A Various [Robby Krieger]
Urban Strut [Steve Hunter]
Western Flyer [Eric Johnson]

| 11/16/91 | 190 | 1 | | 5 Halloween Hits .... | $12 | Rhino 70535 |

Addams Family (Main Title) [Vic Mizzy]
Attack Of The Killer Tomatoes [Lewis Lee]
Blob, The [Five Blobs] 33
Ghostbusters [Ray Parker Jr.] 1
Haunted House [Gene Simmons] 11
I Put A Spell On You [Screamin' Jay Hawkins]
Martian Hop [Ran-Dells] 16
Monster Mash [Bobby "Boris" Pickett] 1
Purple People Eater [Sheb Wooley] 1
Twilight Zone [Neil Norman]

| 6/1/85 | 92 | 35 | ● | 6 Highwayman ....
WILLIE NELSON/JOHNNY CASH/WAYLON JENNINGS/KRIS KRISTOFFERSON | $8 | Columbia 40056 |

Against The Wind
Big River
Committed To Parkview
Deportee (Plane Wreck At Los Gatos)
Desperados Waiting For A Train
Highwayman
Jim, I Wore A Tie Today
Last Cowboy Song
Twentieth Century Is Almost Over
Welfare Line

| 3/17/90 | 79 | 13 | | 7 Highwayman 2 ....
WILLIE NELSON/JOHNNY CASH/WAYLON JENNINGS/KRIS KRISTOFFERSON | $12 | Columbia 45240 |

American Remains
Angels Love Bad Men
Anthem '84
Born And Raised In Black And White
Living Legend
Silver Stallion
Songs That Make A Difference
Texas
Two Stories Wide
We're All In Your Corner

| 1/15/83 | 109 | 14 | | 8 Kris, Willie, Dolly & Brenda...the winning hand ....
KRIS KRISTOFFERSON, WILLIE NELSON, DOLLY PARTON & BRENDA LEE | $10 | Monum. 38389 [2] |

Bandits Of Beverly Hills
Bigger Fool, The Harder The Fall
Born To Love Me
Bring On The Sunshine
Casey's Last Ride
Everything's Beautiful (In It's Own Way)
Happy Happy Birthday Baby
Help Me Make It Through The Night
Here Comes That Rainbow Again
I Never Cared For You
King Of A Lonely Castle
Little Things
Ping Pong
Put It Off Until Tomorrow
Someone Loves You Honey
To Make A Long Story Short, She's Gone
What Do You Think About Lovin'
You Left Me A Long, Long Time Ago
You'll Always Have Someone
You're Gonna Love Yourself (In The Morning)

| 12/6/80 | 154 | 13 | | 9 Legend Of Jesse James, The ....
a biographical album written and composed by Paul Kennerley | $8 | A&M 3718 |

Death Of Me [Johnny Cash & Levon Helm]
Have You Heard The News? [Albert Lee]
Heaven Ain't Ready For You Yet [Emmylou Harris]
Help Him, Jesus [Johnny Cash]
High Walls [Levon Helm]
Hunt Them Down [Albert Lee]
Northfield: The Disaster [Charlie Daniels]
Northfield: The Plan [Levon Helm]
Old Clay County [Charlie Daniels & Levon Helm]
One More Shot [Levon Helm]
Plot, The [Paul Kennerley]
Quantrill's Guerillas [Levon Helm]
Ride Of The Redlegs [Rodney Crowell/Jody Payne/Levon Helm/Rosanne Cash]
Riding With Jesse James [Charlie Daniels]
Six Gun Shooting [Johnny Cash]
Wish We Were Back In Missouri [Emmylou Harris]

| 11/10/90 | 188 | 2 | | 10 Music From Warner Bros. Cartoons 1936-1958 ....[I]
CARL STALLING PROJECT
Carl (d: 1974 [age 86]) scored over 600 cartoons in his 22 years at Warner Brothers | $12 | Warner 26027 |

Anxiety Montage Medley
Carl Stalling With Milt Franklyn In Session
Dinner Music For A Pack Of Hungry Cannibals Medley
Dough For The Do Do (medley)
Early WB Scores: The Depression Era Medley
Good Egg
Hillbilly Hare
Porky In Wackyland (medley)
Powerhouse And Other Cuts From The Early 50's Medley
Putty Tat Trouble Part 6
Speedy Gonzalez Meets Two Crows From Tacos
Stalling Self-Parody: Music From Porky's Preview
Stalling: The War Years Medley
There They Go Go Go
To Itch His Own
Various Cues From Bugs Bunny Films Medley

| 2/7/76 | 10 | 51 | ▲² | 11 Outlaws, The ....
WAYLON JENNINGS/WILLIE NELSON/JESSI COLTER/TOMPALL GLASER | $10 | RCA 1321 |

Good Hearted Woman [Waylon Jennings & Willie Nelson] 25
Heaven Or Hell [Waylon Jennings & Willie Nelson]
Honky Tonk Heroes [Waylon Jennings]
I'm Looking For Blue Eyes [Jessi Colter]
Me And Paul [Willie Nelson]
My Heroes Have Always Been Cowboys [Waylon Jennings]
Put Another Log On The Fire [Tompall Glaser]
Suspicious Minds [Waylon Jennings & Jessi Colter]
T For Texas [Tompall Glaser]
Yesterday's Wine [Willie Nelson]
You Mean To Say [Jessi Colter]

Requiem - see CLASSICAL COMPILATIONS

| 3/24/90 | 166 | 5 | | 12 Requiem For The Americas - Songs From The Lost World ....
written and produced by Jonathan Elias; songs based on American Indian folklore with poetry readings by the late Jim Morrison; pf: Jon Anderson/Michael Bolton/Duran Duran/Garce Jones; CD includes bonus track | $12 | Enigma 73354 |

DEBUT DATE	PEAK POS	WKS CHR	GOLD	ARTIST — Album Title	$	Label & Number

Born In The Dreamtime · Far Far Cry · I've Not Forgotten You · Talk With Grandfather
Chant Movement · Father And Son · Invisible Man · Within The Lost World
Du He Kah (The Healer) · Follow In My Footsteps · Journey, The

Simply Mad About The Mouse - see CHILDREN'S ALBUMS
Stay Awake: Various Interpretations Of Music from Vintage Disney Films - see CHILDREN'S ALBUMS

| 12/27/75+ | 192 | 3 | | **13** Threads of Glory - 200 years of America in words & music .... | **$35** | Ln. Ph. 4 14000 [6] |

6 volume boxed set tracing America's history using music, sound effects and many famous guest narrators

Also Sprach Zarathustra [Henry Lewis] · Elizabeth Cady Staton [Rosalind Russell] · President Chester Arthur [William Bakewell] · Rhapsody In Blue [Frank Chacksfield]
America [Eric Rogers] · Entertainer, The [Ronnie Aldrich] · President Dwight D. Eisenhower [Fred MacMurray] · Shenandoah [Frank Chacksfield]
America, The Beautiful [Eric Rogers] · Fanfare [London Festival Brass] · President Franklin D. Roosevelt [Lorne Greene] · Spokesman Of The South [Lee Bowman]
American Revolutionary War Medley [Bob Sharples] · General Douglas MacArthur [Efren Zimbalist, Jr.] · President George Washington [Lloyd Nolan] · Star-Spangled Banner [Bob Sharples]
Apollo 11 Moon Landing [Daws Butler] · General Robert E. Lee [Lee Bowman] · President Gerald Ford [Lee Bowman] · Stars And Stripes Forever [Bob Sharples]
Battle Hymn Of The Republic [Eric Rogers] · George Washington [Lloyd Nolan] · President Harry S Truman [Ernest Borgnine] · Thomas Jefferson [Richard Carlson]
Casablanca Medley [Stanley Black] · Hail To The Chief [Eric Rogers] · President James Buchanan [Richard Carlson] · Thomas Paine [Lee Bowman]
Col. William Travis [Forrest Tucker] · Hoe Down Medley [Stanley Black] · President James Monroe [John Forsythe] · Voice Of The Indians [Cesar Romero]
Columbia, The Gem Of The Ocean [Eric Rogers] · Jefferson Davis [George Hamilton] · President James Polk [Cesar Romero] · Washington Post March [Bob Sharples]
Constitution and The Bill Of Rights [Ronald & Nancy Reagan] · Lady Of Liberty [Joan Foster] · President John F. Kennedy [Henry Fonda] · We Shall Overcome [Bob Sharples]
Dixie [Eric Rogers] · Let's Dance [Ted Heath] · President Lyndon B. Johnson [Hugh O'Brian] · When The Saints Go Marching In [Eric Rogers]
Dorothea Lynde Dix [Anne Baxter] · Margaret Fuller [Virginia Gregg] · President Thomas Jefferson [Richard Carlson] · William Lloyd Garrison [William Bakewell]
Dr. Martin Luther King [Roscoe Lee Browne] · Massachusetts Patriot [Rosalind Russell] · President Woodrow Wilson [John Forsythe] · World War One Medley [Bob Sharples]
National Emblem [Bob Sharples] · Zimmerman Note [Daws Butler]
Patrick Henry [Burt Lancaster]
President Abraham Lincoln [Walter Pidgeon]
President Andrew Jackson [Jonathan Winters]

| 11/9/91+ | 18 | 32 | ▲ | **14** Two Rooms - Celebrating The Songs Of Elton John & Bernie Taupin .... | **$12** | Polydor 845750 |

all songs written by Elton John and Bernie Taupin

Bitch Is Back [Tina Turner] · Don't Let The Sun Go Down On Me [Oleta Adams] · Rocket Man (I Think It's Going To Be A Long, Long Time) [Kate Bush] · Sorry Seems To Be The Hardest Word [Joe Cocker]
Border Song [Eric Clapton] · Levon [Jon Bon Jovi] · Sacrifice [Sinead O'Connor] · Tonight [George Michael]
Burn Down The Mission [Phil Collins] · Madman Across The Water [Bruce Hornsby] · Saturday Night's Alright (For Fighting) [Who] · Your Song [Rod Stewart] 48
Come Down In Time [Sting] · Philadelphia Freedom [Daryl Hall & John Oates]
Crocodile Rock [Beach Boys]
Daniel [Wilson Phillips]

| 8/12/78 | 98 | 25 | | **15** War Of The Worlds, The .... | **$12** | Columbia 35290 [2] |

musical version by Jeff Wayne of H.G. Wells' classic story; narration by Richard Burton; pf: Justin Hayward/David Essex/Phil Lynot/Julie Covington

Artilleryman And The Fighting Machine · Eve Of The War · Horsell Common And The Heat Ray · Spirit Of Man
Brave New World · **Forever Autumn** [Justin Hayward] 47 · Red Weed (Parts 1 & 2) · Thunder Child
Dead London

| 7/22/78 | 181 | 4 | | **16** White Mansions .... | **$8** | A&M 6004 |

a portrayal of life in the Confederate States of America 1861-65; written by Paul Kennerley; pf: Jessi Colter/Waylon Jennings/John Dillon/Steve Cash

Bad Mad · King Has Called Me Home · Praise The Lord · They Laid Waste To Our Land
Bring Up The Twelve Pounders · Last Dance & The Kentucky Racehorse · Southern Boys · Union Mare & The Confederate Grey
Dixie, Hold On · Southland's Bleeding · White Trash
Dixie, Now You're Done · No One Would Believe A Summer Could Be So Cold · Story To Tell (Preface)
Join Around The Flag

DEBUT DATE	PEAK POS	WKS CHR	G O L D	ARTIST — Album Title	$	Label & Number

ROCK OPERAS

3/16/85	**47**	21		**1 Chess**	**$10**	RCA 5340 [2]

a new musical written by Tim Rice and Abba's Benny Andersson and Bjorn Ulvaeus; pf: Murray Head/Elaine Paige/Barbara Dickson

American And Florence (medley)	Endgame	Nobody's Side (medley)
Anthem	Florence Quits	**One Night In Bangkok** *[Murray Head]* **3**
Argument	Heaven Help My Heart	
Chess	I Know Him So Well	Opening Ceremony
Deal (No Deal)	Merano	Pity The Child
Embassy Lament	Mountain Duet	

Quartet (A Model Of Decorum And Tranquillity) · Russian And Molokov (medley) · Story Of Chess (medley) · Where I Want To Be (medley) · You And I (medley)

2/14/70	**95**	13		**2 DisinHAIRited**	**$10**	RCA 1163

songs written for, but not included in the musical *Hair*; pf: Robin McNamara/Melba Moore/Allan Nicholls

Bed, The	Going Down	Mr. Berger	So Sing The Children On The Avenue
Climax	Hello There	Oh Great God Of Power (medley)	
Dead End	I Dig	One Thousand Year-Old Man	Washing The World
Electric Blues	I'm Hung	Reading The Writing (medley)	You Are Standing On My Bed
Exanaplatooch	Manhattan Beggar	Sentimental Ending (medley)	
Eyes Look Your Last	Mess O'Dirt	Sheila Franklin (medley)	

Godspell - see SOUNDTRACKS and ORIGINAL CASTS

Hair - see SOUNDTRACKS and ORIGINAL CASTS

11/21/70+	**1**[3]	101	●	**3 Jesus Christ Superstar**	**$15**	Decca 7206 [2]

a rock opera; mu: Andrew Lloyd Webber; ly: Tim Rice; pf: Ian Gillan/Murray Head/Yvonne Elliman; also see Soundtrack and Original Cast versions

Arrest, The	Heaven On Their Minds	Last Supper	**Superstar** *[Murray Head]* **14**
Blood Money (medley)	Hosanna	Peter's Denial	Temple, The
Crucifixion	**I Don't Know How To Love Him** *[Yvonne Elliman]* **28**	Pilate And Christ	This Jesus Must Die
Damned For All Time (medley)		Pilate's Dream	Trial Before Pilate
Everything's Alright *[Yvonne Elliman]* **92**	John Nineteen Forty-One	Poor Jerusalem (medley)	What's The Buzz (medley)
	Judas' Death	Simon Zealotes (medley)	
Gethsemane (I Only Want To Say)	King Herod's Song (Try It And See)	Strange Thing Mystifying (medley)	

4/3/71	**84**	12		**4 Joseph and the Amazing Technicolor Dreamcoat**	**$15**	Scepter 588

Andrew Lloyd Webber and Tim Rice's first rock opera; pf: David Daltrey/Terry Saunders/Malcolm Parry; no individual song titles listed

12/9/72+	**5**	38	●	**5 Tommy**	**$15**	Ode 99001 [2]

rock opera written by Pete Townshend (The Who); pf: Pete Townshend/Roger Daltrey/Rod Stewart/Ringo Starr; also see The Who and Soundtrack versions

Acid Queen	Go To The Mirror Boy	See Me, Feel Me	Underture
Amazing Journey	I'm Free	Sensation	We're Not Gonna Take It
Christmas	It's A Boy	Smash The Mirror	Welcome
Cousin Kevin	Miracle Cure	Sparks	
Do You Think It's Alright	1921	There's A Doctor I've Found	
Eyesight To The Blind	Pin Ball Wizard	Tommy Can You Hear Me?	
Fiddle About	Sally Simpson	Tommy's Holiday Camp	

12/18/71+	**185**	7		**6 Truth Of Truths - A Contemporary Rock Opera**	**$15**	Oak 1001 [2]

based on the Old and New Testaments; concept by Ray Ruff; pf: Jim Backus/Donnie Brooks/Lise Miller/Patti Sterling

Creation	Hosanna	Prophecies Of The Coming Messiah	Song Of The Children Of Israel
Cross, The	I Am What I Say I Am		Ten Commandments
David To Bathsheba	Jesus Of Nazareth	Prophecies Of The Coming Of The End Of The World	Tower Of Babel
Fall, The	John The Baptist		Trial, The
Forty Days And Forty Nights	Joseph Beloved Son Of Israel	Resurrection	Turn Back To God
God Called On To Abraham	Last Supper	Road, The	
He Will Come Again	Let My People Go	Sodom And Gomorrah Were The Cities Of Sin	
He's The Light Of The World	My Life Is In Your Hands		

DEBUT DATE	PEAK POS	WKS CHR	GOLD	ARTIST — Album Title	$	Label & Number

DANCE/DISCO COMPILATIONS

6/27/64 — **102** — 6 — **1 Dance Discotheque** .... **$15** Decca 74556

Compadre Pedro Juan [Tommy Dorsey Orch./Warren Covington]
Desafinado [Discotheque Orchestra]
El Leoncito [Discotheque Orchestra]
Fly Me To The Moon (In Other Words) [Discotheque Orchestra]
Hello, Dolly! [Discotheque Orchestra]
Hot Pastrami With Mashed Potatoes [Discotheque Orchestra]
If I Had A Hammer [Discotheque Orchestra]
Mack The Knife [Discotheque Orchestra]
Make Someone Happy [Peter Duchin]
Mi Guantanamera [Emilio Reyes]
Roll Over Beethoven [Discotheque Orchestra]
Yesterdays [Discotheque Orchestra]

12/24/77+ — **115** — 11 — **2 Disco Boogie** .... **$12** Salsoul 0101 [2]

Dance, Dance, Dance [Claudja Barry]
Doctor Love [First Choice] **41**
Getaway [Salsoul Orchestra]
Helplessly [Moment Of Truth]
Hit And Run [Loleatta Holloway]
Love Is Still Blue [Paul Mauriat & His Orch.]
Love Is You [Carol Williams]
Magic Bird Of Fire [Salsoul Orchestra]
More [Carol Williams]
My Love Is Free [Double Exposure]
Nice 'N' Naasty [Salsoul Orchestra] **30**
Run Away [Salsoul Orchestra/Loleatta Holloway]
Salsoul Hustle [Salsoul Orchestra] **76**
Spring Rain [Silvetti] **39**
Sweet Dynamite [Claudja Barry]
Tale Of Three Cities [Salsoul Orchestra]
Tangerine [Salsoul Orchestra] **18**
Ten Percent [Double Exposure] **54**
This Will Be A Night To Remember [Eddie Holman] **90**
We're Getting Stronger (The Longer We Stay Together) [Loleatta Holloway]
You Got Me Hummin' [Moment Of Truth]
You're Just The Right Size [Salsoul Orchestra] **88**

7/26/75 — **153** — 5 — **3 Disco Gold** .... **$10** Scepter 5120

Ain't No Love Lost [Patti Jo]
Arise And Shine [Independents]
I Love You, Yes I Do [Independents]
Make Me Believe In You [Patti Jo]
Needing You [Clara Lewis]
Pity The Poor Man [George Tindley]
Wan Tu Wah Zuree [George Tindley]
We're On The Right Track [Ultra High Frequency]

7/15/78 — **115** — 12 — **4 Disco Party** .... **$12** Marlin 2207/8 [2]

Best Disco In Town [Ritchie Family] **17**
Calypso Breakdown [Ralph MacDonald]
Disco Magic [T-Connection]
Do What You Wanna Do [T-Connection] **46**
Do Ya Wanna Get Funky With Me? [Peter Brown] **18**
Get Down Tonight [KC & The Sunshine Band] **1**
Get Off Your Aahh And Dance [Foxy]
Gimme Some [Jimmy 'Bo' Horne]
Kiss Me (The Way I Like It) [George McCrae]
Lady Luck [Ritchie Family]
Love Chant [Eli's Second Coming]
Rock Your Baby [George McCrae] **1**
Superman [Celi Bee & The Buzzy Bunch] **41**
Where Is The Love [Betty Wright] **96**

4/28/79 — **159** — 5 — **5 Disco Spectacular Inspired by the Film "Hair"** .... **$8** RCA 3356

all star group: Evelyn King/Vicki Sue Robinson/Revelation/The Brothers
Aquarius/Let The Sun Shine In
Easy To Be Hard
Good Morning Starshine
Where Do I Go?

9/8/84 — **147** — 9 — **6 Electric Breakdance** .... **$8** Dominion 2320

Clock On The Wall [Double Vision]
Electric Kingdom [Twilight 22] **79**
It's Like That [Run-D.M.C.]
Jam On It [Newcleus] **56**
Magic's Wand [Whodini]
Play That Beat Mr. D.J. [G.L.O.B.E. & Whiz Kid]
Rockit [B.T. & The City Slickers]
White Lines (Don't Don't Do It) [Grandmaster Flash & Melle Mel]
You're The One For Me [D Train]

4/10/76 — **177** — 2 — **7 Hustle Hits!** .... **$8** De-Lite 2019

Dreaming A Dream [Crown Heights Affair] **43**
Drive My Car [Gary Toms Empire] **69**
Every Beat Of My Heart [Crown Heights Affair] **83**
Girl From Ipanema [Zakariah]
Hustle Wit Every Muscle [Kay-Gees]
Mother Earth [Kool & The Gang]
7-6-5-4-3-2-1 (Blow Your Whistle) [Gary Toms Empire] **46**
Spirit Of The Boogie [Kool & The Gang] **35**
Sunny [Yambu]

7/28/79 — **21** — 25 — ● — **8 Night At Studio 54, A** .... **$10** Casablanca 7161 [2]

Disco Nights (Rock-Freak) [G.Q.] **12**
Got To Be Real [Cheryl Lynn] **12**
Hot Jungle Drums And Voodoo Rhythm [D.C. LaRue]
Hot Shot [Karen Young] **67**
I Found Love (Now That I Found You) [Love & Kisses]
I Got My Mind Made Up (You Can Get It Girl) [Instant Funk] **20**
I Love America [Patrick Juvet]
I Love The Nightlife (Disco 'Round) [Alicia Bridges] **5**
In The Bush [Musique] **58**
Instant Replay [Dan Hartman] **29**
Last Dance [Donna Summer] **3**
Le Freak [Chic] **1**
Let's All Chant [Michael Zager Band] **36**
Shake Your Groove Thing [Peaches & Herb] **5**
Souvenirs [Voyage] **41**
Take Me Home [Cher] **8**
Y.M.C.A. [Village People] **2**

9/6/80 — **69** — 7 — **9 Winners** .... **$8** I&M 017

And The Beat Goes On [Whispers] **19**
Cruisin' [Smokey Robinson] **4**
Dance With You [Carrie Lucas] **70**
Do You Love What You Feel [Rufus & Chaka Khan] **30**
Don't Let Go [Isaac Hayes] **18**
I Do Love You [G.Q.] **20**
I'll Never Love This Way Again [Dionne Warwick] **5**
Second Time Around [Shalamar] **8**
Shake Your Body (Down To The Ground) [Jacksons] **7**
Special Lady [Ray, Goodman & Brown] **5**
Still [Commodores] **1**
Too Hot [Kool & The Gang] **5**
Turn Off The Lights [Teddy Pendergrass] **48**
Working My Way Back To You/Forgive Me, Girl [Spinners] **2**
You Can't Change That [Raydio] **9**

DEBUT DATE	PEAK POS	WKS CHR	GOLD	ARTIST — Album Title	$	Label & Number

JAZZ COMPILATIONS

8/5/78 · 151 · 6
1 Alivemutherforya .... [I-L] **$10** Columbia 35349
"Anteres" - The Star [Billy Cobham] · Bahama Mama [Alphonso Johnson] · On A Magic Carpet Ride [Billy Cobham] · Shadows [Tom Scott] · Some Punk Funk [Steve Khan] · Spindrift [Tom Scott]

11/13/82 · 63 · 19
2 Casino Lights .... [L] **$8** Warner 23718
recorded live at the Montreux Jazz Festival in Switzerland
Casino Lights [Neil Larsen & Buzz Feiten] · Hideaway [David Sanborn] · Imagine [Randy Crawford & Yellowjackets] · Love Is Not Enough, Theme From [David Sanborn] · Monmouth College Fight Song [Yellowjackets] · Sure Enough [Al Jarreau & Randy Crawford] · Who's Right, Who's Wrong [Al Jarreau & Randy Crawford] · Your Precious Love [Al Jarreau & Randy Crawford]

2/6/82 · 105 · 11
3 Echoes Of An Era .... **$8** Elektra 60021
all-star group: Chaka Khan/Freddie Hubbard/Joe Henderson/Chick Corea/Lenny White
All Of Me · Hire Wire - The Aerialist · I Hear Music · I Love You Porgy · I Mean You · Spring Can Really Hang You Up · The Most · Take The A Train · Them There Eyes

8/2/80 · 168 · 5
4 Empire Jazz .... [I] **$8** RSO 3085
adaptation of *The Empire Strikes Back*; all-star group: Ron Carter/Bob James/Billy Cobham/Ralph MacDonald
Asteroid Field · Han Solo And The Princess (Love Theme) · Imperial March (Darth Vader's Theme) · Lando's Palace · Yoda's Theme

11/11/89 · 65 · 21
5 Happy Anniversary, Charlie Brown! .... **$8** GRP 9596
commemorates the 40th year of the Charles Schultz' comic strip *Peanuts*
Benjamin [Dave Brubeck] · Breadline Blues [Kenny G.] · Charlie Brown Theme [Amani A.W.-Murray] · Christmas Time Is Here [Patti Austin] · Great Pumpkin Waltz [Chick Corea] · History Lesson [Dave Grusin] · Joe Cool [B.B. King] · Linus & Lucy (with the Peanuts Gang) [David Benoit] · Little Birdie [Joe Williams] · Rain, Rain, Go Away [Gerry Mulligan] · Red Baron [Lee Ritenour]

7/9/55 · 5 · 10
6 I Like Jazz! .... [K] **$15** Columbia 1
Four-Twenty, A.M. [Pete Rugolo] · Got Dem Blues [Turk Murphy] · Home Cooking [Eddie Condon] · I'll Never Be The Same [Teddy Wilson & Billie Holiday] · Jam Session [Original Benny Goodman Orchestra] · Jazz Lips [Louis Armstrong] · Makin' Time [Dave Brubeck] · Maple Leaf Rag [Wally Rose] · Merry-Go-Round [Duke Ellington] · Put It Right Here (Or Keep It Out There) [Bessie Smith] · Sensation Rag [Phil Napoleon] · Sentimental Baby [Bix Beiderbecke]

1/27/79 · 122 · 8
7 Milestone Jazzstars In Concert .... [I-L] **$12** Milestone 55006 [2]
all-star group: McCoy Tyner/Ron Carter/Sonny Rollins/Al Foster
Alone Together · Continuum · Cutting Edge · Don't Stop The Carnival · In A Sentimental Mood · Little Pianissimo · N.O. Blues · Nubia · Willow Weep For Me

NEW AGE COMPILATIONS

GRP Christmas Collection, A - see CHRISTMAS (Top Pop Albums Chart-Various)
GRP Christmas Collection Vol. II, A - see CHRISTMAS (Top Pop Albums Chart-Various)
Narada Christmas Collection Volume 2 - see CHRISTMAS (Top Pop Albums Chart-Various)

10/13/90 · 125 · 14
1 Narada Wilderness Collection, The .... [I] **$12** Narada 63905
Break Of Day [Bernardo Rubaja] · Early Moon And Firelight [Carol Nethen] · Fragile Majesty [Eric Tingstad/Nancy Rumbel] · Glacier And Flower [Jim Jacobsen] · Lament For Hetch Hetchy [Alasdair Fraser] · Madre De La Tierra [David Lanz] · Northern Morning [Peter Buffett] · Ocala [Wayne Gratz] · Return To Emerald Forest [Richard Souther] · Sahara Sunrise [Ralf Illenberger] · White Water [Doug Cameron] · Wildflowers [Michael Jones] · Wonderland [Spencer Brewer] · Woodland Mission [William Ellwood] · Yosemite [David Arkenstone]

12/21/85+ · 167 · 12
2 Windham Hill Records Piano Sampler .... [I] **$8** Windham Hill 1040
Amy's Song [Peggy Stern] · Consolation [Rick Peller] · In Flight [Michael Harrison] · In This Small Spot [Tim Story] · Listening To Evening [Allaudin Mathieu] · Lou Ann [Philip Aaberg] · Messenger Of The Son [Cyrille Verdeaux] · Morning With The Roses [Richard Dworsky] · Out To Play [Paul Dondero]

10/20/84 · 108 · 25
3 Windham Hill Records Sampler '84 .... [I] **$8** Windham Hill 1035
Aerial Boundaries [Michael Hedges] · Cricket's Wicket [Billy Oskay & Micheal O Domhnaill] · On The Threshold Of Liberty [Mark Isham] · Oristana Sojourn [Scott Cossu] · Shadowdance [Shadowfax] · Thanksgiving [George Winston] · Ventana [Will Ackerman] · Western [Alex de Grassi]

3/29/86 · 102 · 18
4 Windham Hill Records Sampler '86 .... [I] **$8** Windham Hill 1048
Another Country [Shadowfax] · Devotion [Liz Story] · Dolphins [Mike Marshall & Darol Anger] · Engravings [Ira Stein & Russel Walder] · Gwenlaise [Scott Cossu with Eugene Friesen] · Hot Beach [Interior] · Marias River Breakdown [Philip Aaberg] · Near Northern [Darol Anger/Barbara Higbie Quintet] · New Waltz [Malcolm Dalglish] · Pittsburgh, 1901 (Theme from Mrs. Soffel) [Mark Isham] · Welcoming [Michael Manring]

2/27/88 · 134 · 16
5 Windham Hill Records Sampler '88 .... [I] **$8** Windham Hill 1065
Angel Steps [Scott Cossu] · Because It's There [Michael Hedges] · Climbing In Geometry [William Ackerman] · Close Cover [Wim Mertens] · Indian Woman [Rubaja & Hernandez] · Road To Hanna [Shadowfax] · To Be [Montreux] · Toys Not Ties [Nightnoise] · Unseen Rain [W.A. Mathieu] · Wishing Well [Schonherz & Scott] · Woman At The Well [Tim Story]

4/15/89 · 176 · 4
6 Windham Hill Records Sampler '89 .... [I] **$8** Windham Hill 1082
Credo Of Ballymacoda [Therese Schroeder-Sheker] · Floyd's Ghost [Will Ackerman] · Hugh [Nightnoise] · Life In The Trees [Michael Manring] · Manhattan Underground [Scott Cossu] · Rameau's Nephew [Philippe Saisse] · Sojourner [Paul McCandless] · Through The Woods [Metamora] · Usually/Always [Fred Simon] · Visiting Card [Wim Mertens] · Walking Through Walls [Philip Aaberg]

Winter's Solstice, A - see CHRISTMAS (Top Pop Albums Chart-Various)
Winter's Solstice II, A - see CHRISTMAS (Top Pop Albums Chart-Various)
Winter's Solstice III, A - see CHRISTMAS (Top Pop Albums Chart-Various)

DEBUT DATE	PEAK POS	WKS CHR	GOLD	ARTIST — Album Title	$	Label & Number

CHILDREN'S ALBUMS

Children oriented albums.

Annie's Christmas - see CHRISTMAS (Top Pop Albums Chart-Various)

For Our Children - see BENEFIT RECORDINGS

Happy Anniversary, Charlie Brown - see JAZZ COMPILATIONS

MICKEY MOUSE/DISNEY

5/3/75 — **51** — **13** — **1 Mickey Mouse Club** .... [TV] **$8** Disneyland 1362

pf: Jimmie Dodd/Annette/Spin & Marty/Mouseketeers; songs featured on the popular TV show

Anything Can Happen	Hi To You	Mickey Mouse Theme (Alma Mater)
Cowboy Needs A Horse	How Will I Know My Love	Mousekartoon Time
Do Mi So	I'm No Fool (As A Pedestrian)	Mousekedance, The
Don't Jump To Conclusions	Meetin' At The Malt Shop	Mickey Mouse Mambo
Fun With Music	Mickey Mouse Mambo	Pussy Cat Polka
Happy Mouse	Mickey Mouse March	Simple Simon

Stop, Look And Listen / Talent Roundup / Today Is Tuesday / Triple R Song

4/12/80 — **35** — **27** ▲ — **2 Mickey Mouse Disco** .... **$8** Disneyland 2504

disco songs performed by session musicians

Chim Chim Cher-ee	It's A Small World	Mousetrap
Disco Mickey Mouse	Macho Duck	Watch Out For Goofy
Greatest Band		

Welcome To Rio / Zip-A-Dee-Doo-Dah

11/12/88 — **119** — **15** — **3 Stay Awake: Various Interpretations Of Music from Vintage Disney Films** .... **$8** A&M 3918

Disney tunes performed by a host of superstars

Baby Mine [Bonnie Raitt & Was (Not Was)]	Heigh Ho (The Dwarfs Marching Song) [Tom Waits]	Little April Shower (medley) [Natalie Merchant/Michael Stipe/Roches]
Blue Shadows On The Trail (medley) [Syd Straw]	Hi Diddle Dee Dee (An Actor's Life For Me) (medley) [Ken Nordine]	Little Wooden Head (medley) [Bill Frisell & Wayne Horvitz]
Castle In Spain (medley) [Buster Poindexter]	I Wan'na Be Like You (The Monkey Song) (medley) [Los Lobos]	Mickey Mouse March [Aaron Neville]
Cruella De Ville (medley) [Replacements]	I Wonder (medley) [Yma Sumac]	Pink Elephants On Parade (medley) [Sun Ra]
Desolation Theme (medley) [Ken Nordine]	I'm Wishing (medley) [Betty Carter]	Second Star To The Right [James Taylor]
Feed The Birds (medley) [Garth Hudson]		Someday My Prince Will Come [Sinead O'Connor]

Stay Awake (medley) [Suzanne Vega] / When You Wish Upon A Star (medley) [Ringo Starr] / Whistle While You Work (medley) [NRBQ] / Zip-A-Dee-Doo-Dah (medley) [Nilsson]

10/19/91 — **160** — **12** — **4 Simply Mad About The Mouse** .... **$12** Columbia 46019

songs from Disney films performed by contemporary artists

Bare Necessities [Harry Connick, Jr.]	Kiss The Girl [Soul II Soul]	Someday My Prince Will Come/One Song [En Vogue]
Dream Is A Wish Your Heart Makes [Michael Bolton]	Mad About The Wolf [Kirk Whalum]	When You Wish Upon A Star [Billy Joel]
I've Got No Strings [Gipsy Kings]	Siamese Cat Song [Bobby McFerrin]	

Who's Afraid Of The Big Bad Wolf [L.L. Cool J] / Zip-A-Dee-Doo-Dah [Ric Ocasek]

MISCELLANEOUS

1/9/61 — **19** — **8** — **5 Alice In Wonderland: The Mad Tea Party/The Lobster Quadrille** .... [T] **$20** Riverside 1406

CYRIL RITCHARD

Cyril (d: 12/18/77 [age 79]) reads and sings selections from the classic story

Lobster Quadrille / Mad Tea Party

1/6/73+ — **68** — **58** ● — **6 Free To Be...You And Me** .... **$10** Bell 1110

songs and stories for children hosted by Marlo Thomas

Atalanta [Alan Alda & Marlo Thomas]	Dudley Pippin And The Principal [Billy De Wolfe/Bobby Morse/Marlo Thomas]	Glad To Have A Friend Like You [Marlo Thomas]
Boy Meets Girl [Mel Brooks & Marlo Thomas]	Free To Be...You And Me [New Seekers]	Grandma [Diana Sands]
Don't Dress Your Cat In An Apron [Billy De Wolfe]	Girl Land [Jack Cassidy & Shirley Jones]	Helping [Tom Smothers]
Dudley Pippin And His No-Friend [Bobby Morse & Marlo Thomas]		Housework [Carol Channing]
		It's All Right To Cry [Rosey Grier]
		Ladies First [Marlo Thomas]
		My Dog Is A Plumber [Dick Cavett]

Parents Are People [Harry Belafonte & Marlo Thomas] / Sisters And Brothers [Sisters & Brothers] / When We Grow Up [Diana Ross] / William's Doll [Alan Alda & Marlo Thomas]

1/10/81 — **156** — **5** — **7 In Harmony - A Sesame Street Record** .... **$8** Sesame St. 3481

Be With Me [Carly Simon]	I Want A Horse [Linda Ronstadt & Wendy Waldman]	One Good Turn [Al Jarreau]
Blueberry Pie [Bette Midler]	In Harmony [Kate Taylor & The Simon-Taylor Family]	Pajamas [Livingston Taylor]
Friend For All Seasons [George Benson & Pauline Wilson]	Jelly Man Kelly [James Taylor]	Sailor And The Mermaid [Libby Titus & Dr. John]
I Have A Song [Lucy Simon]		Share [Ernie & Cookie Monster]

Wynken, Blynken And Nod [Doobie Brothers] **76**

11/21/81 — **129** — **10** — **8 In Harmony 2** .... **$8** Columbia 37641

Ginny The Flying Girl [Janis Ian]	Nobody Knows But Me [Billy Joel]	Reach Out And Touch (Somebody's Hand) [Teddy Pendergrass]
Here Comes The Rainbow [Crystal Gayle]	Owl And The Pussycat [Lou Rawls & Deniece Williams]	Santa Claus Is Comin' To Town [Bruce Springsteen]
Maryanne [Carly & Lucy Simon]		

Some Kitties Don't Care [Kenny Loggins] / Splish Splash [Dr. John] / Sunny Skies [James Taylor]

4/20/85 — **180** — **4** — **9 Velveteen Rabbit, The** .... [TV] **$8** Dancing Cat 3007

MERYL STREEP & GEORGE WINSTON

from the PBS-TV animated children's special

Alone [solo: George]	Flying	Returning
Anxious Moments	Lullaby	Shabbiness Doesn't Matter
Christmas	Nana	Skin Horse
Fairy, The	Rabbit Dance	Spring

Summer / Toys, The / Velveteen Rabbit [solo: George]

DEBUT DATE	PEAK POS	WKS CHR	GOLD	ARTIST — Album Title	$	Label & Number

SESAME STREET/MUPPETS

7/25/70 — **23** — **54** — ● **10** Sesame Street Book & Record, The...[TV] **$8** Columbia 1069
pf: Bob McGrath/Loretta Long/Jim Henson/Frank Oz/Carroll Spinney; songs from the popular PBS series

ABC-DEF-GHI	Green	Number 5	Sesame Street
Everybody Wash	I Love Trash	One Of These Things	Somebody Come And Play
Face, A	I've Got Two	People In Your Neighborhood	Up And Down
Five People In My Family	J-Jump	Rub Your Tummy	What Are Kids Called
Goin' For A Ride	Nearly Missed	**Rubber Duckie** [Ernie] 16	

12/11/71+ — **78** — **10** — **11** Sesame Street 2 ....[TV] **$8** Warner 2569
pf: Matt Robinson/Loretta Long/Frank Oz/Jim Henson/Carroll Spinney

Circles	High Middle Low	Picture A World	Stop!
Everyone Makes Mistakes	I'm Pretty	Play Along	What Do I Do When I'm Alone?
Garden, The	Mad!	Sesame Street	Word Family Song
Grouch Song	Over Under Around And	Sing	
Has Anybody Seen My Dog?	Through	Someday, Little Children	

9/9/78 — **75** — **10** — ● **12** Sesame Street Fever .... **$8** Sesame St. 79005
parody of *Saturday Night Fever*; pf: Robin Gibb/Frank Oz/Jim Henson/Jerry Nelson/Carroll Spinney

C Is For Cookie	Has Anybody Seen My Dog?	Sesame Street Fever
Doin' The Pigeon	Rubber Duckie	Trash

8/15/70 — **126** — **11** — **13** Bob McGrath from Sesame Street..................................... **$8** Affinity 1001
Sesame Street co-star talks and sings with a children's chorus

Best Friend	Hold On To Your Dream	So It Doesn't Whistle	Why Does It Have To Rain On
Good Good Morning Day	I Can Do It!	Sunshine Guitar	Sunday??
Groovin' On The Sunshine	Me	Why Choose To Be Afraid	

8/1/70 — **86** — **13** — **14** Susan sings songs from Sesame Street .... **$8** Scepter 584
Susan (Loretta Long) sings with a children's chorus

ABC Song	Happiness	If You're Happy And You Know	Three Of These Things Belong
Children (Sister's Song And	Happy Talk	It (Clap Your Hands)	Together
Brother's Song)	Here Are Some Things That	Right In The Middle Of My Face	What Are Little Children Made
Counting Song (1-20)	Belong Together	Square Song	Of
Draw Me A Circle			

12/25/71+ — **189** — **4** — **15** Muppet Alphabet Album, The .... **$8** Columbia 25503
pf: Jim Henson/Frank Oz/Carroll Spinney/Jerry Nelson; includes a blackboard, chalk and a set of letters

C Is For Cookie	La La La	Oscar's B Sandwich	Two G Sounds
Dee Dee Dee	Lecture	Question Song	Very Very Special Letter
Four Furry Friends	Mmm Monster Meal	R Machine	What's My Letter?
Ha Ha	My Favorite Letter	Sammy The Snake	Would You Like To Buy An O?
Herb's Silly Poem	National Association Of W	Sound Of The Letter A	X Marks The Spot
J Friends	Lovers	Stand Up Straight And Tall	Zizzy Zoomers
Just Because	Noodle Story	Tale Of Tom Tattertall Tuttletut	

1/21/78 — **153** — **5** — **16** Muppet Show, The ....[TV] **$8** Arista 4152
pf: Frank Oz/Jim Henson/Jerry Nelson/Richard Hunt/Dave Goelz

Bein' Green	Lydia The Tattooed Lady	Sax And Violence	Veterinarian's Hospital
Cottleston Pie	Mah-Na-Mah-Na	Simon Smith And His Amazing	What Now My Love
Flight Of The Bumble Bee	Mississippi Mud	Dancing Bear	
Fozzie's Monologue	Mr. Bassman	Tenderly	
Halfway Down The Stairs	Muppaphone	Tit Willow	
I'm In Love With A Big Blue Frog	Muppet Show Theme	Trees	

7/21/79 — **32** — **34** — ● **17** Muppet Movie, The ....[S] **$8** Atlantic 16001
pf: Jim Henson/Frank Oz/Jerry Nelson

America	I Hope That Somethin' Better	Magic Store
Animal...Come Back Animal	Comes Along (includes 2	Movin' Right Along
Can You Picture That	versions)	Never Before, Never Again
	I'm Going To Go Back There	(includes 2 versions)
	Someday	

Rainbow Connection [Kermit] 25

7/11/81 — **66** — **11** — **18** Great Muppet Caper, The ....[S] **$8** Atlantic 16047
pf: Jim Henson/Frank Oz/Jerry Nelson/Richard Hunt/Dave Goelz

Apartment, The	Great Muppet Caper Medley	Lady Holiday	Steppin' Out With A Star
Big Red Bus	Happiness Hotel	Main Title	
Couldn't We Ride	Hey A Movie!	Night Life	
First Time It Happens	Homeward Bound	Piggy's Fantasy ("Miss Piggy")	

12/26/92 — **189** — **1** — **19** Muppet Christmas Carol, The ....[X-S] **$12** Jim Henson 30017
pf: Michael Caine/Brian Henson/Frank Oz/Dave Goelz/Jerry Nelson; sw: Paul Williams, Miles Goodman; includes an 11-page songbook

Bless Us All	Christmas Scat	One More Sleep 'Til Christmas	When Love Is Gone (cast version)
Chairman Of The Board	Fozziwig's Party	Room In Your Heart	When Love Is Gone [Martina
Christmas Future	Good King Wenceslas	Scrooge	McBride]
Christmas Morning	It Feels Like Christmas	Thankful Heart	
Christmas Past	Marley And Marley	When Love Is Found (medley)	

11/10/79+ — **26** — **12** — ▲ **20** Christmas Together, A ....[X] **$8** RCA 3451
JOHN DENVER & THE MUPPETS
Christmas charts: 10/'83

Alfie, The Christmas Tree	Deck The Halls	Little Saint Nick	Twelve Days Of Christmas
(medley)	Have Yourself A Merry Little	Noel: Christmas Eve, 1913	We Wish You A Merry Christmas
Baby Just Like You	Christmas	Peace Carol	When The River Meets The Sea
Christmas Is Coming (Round)	It's In Everyone Of Us (medley)	Silent Night, Holy Night	
Christmas Wish			

DEBUT DATE	PEAK POS	WKS CHR	G O L D	ARTIST — Album Title	$	Label & Number

Refer to the following names in the Artist Section for more children-oriented albums:

ARCHIES
BOWIE, David
CHIPMUNKS
GLAZER, Tom
HARDY BOYS
KING, Carole
LIMELITERS
LINKLETTER, Art
MONTE, Lou
NEWTON-JOHN, Olivia
ROYAL GUARDSMEN
SALES, Soupy
SIMPSONS

SOUNDTRACKS:
  Aladdin
  American Tail
  Annie (also Original Cast and
    Christmas albums)
  Aristocats
  Beauty and the Beast
  Jungle Book
  Little Mermaid
  Lord Of The Rings
  Mary Poppins
  Oliver & Company
  Popeye
  Scrooge
  Teenage Mutant Ninja Turtles (2)

DEBUT DATE	PEAK POS	WKS CHR	GOLD	ARTIST — Album Title	$	Label & Number

CLASSICAL COMPILATIONS

4/25/64 — **70** — **15** — **1 Great Voices Of The Century** .... **$12** Angel 4

Debussy: Beau Soir [Maggie Teyte] / Handel: Semele: Where'er You Walk [John McCormack] / Leoncavallo: Pagliacci: Vesti La Giubba [Beniamino Gigli]

Mascagni: Cavalleria Rusticana: Voi Lo Sapete [Claudia Muzio] / Massenet: Manon: Ah! Dispar, Vision [Tito Schipa] / Moussorgsky: Boris Godounov: Ah! I Am Suffocating [Feodor Chaliapin]

Schubert: Nacht und Traume [Elisabeth Schumann] / Strauss: Die Fledermaus: Mein Herr, Was Dachten Sie [Lotte Lehmann] / Tosti: Mattinata [Nellie Melba]

Verdi: Rigoletto: Questa O Quella [Enrico Caruso] / Wagner: Tristan and Isolde: Love Duet [Frida Leider & Lauritz Melchoir]

7/15/72 — **176** — **7** — **2 Metropolitan Opera Gala honoring Sir Rudolf Bing** ....[L] **$10** DG 2530 260

Bing: general manager of the Opera from 1950-72

Mozart: Le Nozze di Figaro: Dove Sono [Leontyne Price] / Puccini: Manon Lescaut: Tu, Tu, Amore? Tu? [Montserrat Caballe/Placido Domingo]

Strauss, J.: Die Fledermaus [Regina Resnik] / Strauss, R.: Salome: Final Scene [Brigit Nilsson]

Verdi: Il Trovatore: Tacea La Notte Placida [Martina Arroyo] / Verdi: La Forza del Destino: Invano Alvaro [Richard Tucker & Robert Merrill]

Verdi: Otello: Gia Nella Notte Densa [Teresa Zylis-Gara & Franco Corelli]

10/8/66 — **49** — **21** — **3 Opening Nights at the Met** .... **$15** RCA 6171 [3]

historic recordings by opera stars who performed at New York's old Metropolitan Opera House from 1883-1965

Delibes: Lakme: Bell Song [Lily Pons] / Gounod: Faust: Jewel Song [Nellie Melba] / Gounod: Faust: Le Roi De Thule [Emma Eames] / Gounod: Romeo and Juliet: Juliet's Waltz Song [Emma Eames] / Halevy: La Juive: Rachel! Quand Du Seigneur [Enrico Caruso] / Moussorgsky: Boris Godounov: Death Of Boris [Ezio Pinza] / Mozart: The Marriage of Figaro: Deh Vieni, Non Tardar [Bidu Sayao] / Ponchielli: La Gioconda: Stella Del Marinar [Louise Homer] / Ponchielli: La Gioconda: Suicidio! [Rosa Ponselle]

Puccini: Tosca: Ora Stammi A Sentir [Geraldine Farrar] / Puccini: Tosca: Vissi D'Arte [Maria Jeritza] / Rossini: The Barber of Seville: Trio [Peters/Valletti/Merrill] / Saint-Saens: Samson and Delilah: Je Viens Celebrer La Victoire [Caruso/Homer] / Strauss, R.: Der Rosenkavalier: Mir Ist Die Ehre / Verdi: A Masked Ball: Forse La Soglia Attinse [Jan Peerce] / Verdi: Aida: Ciel! Mio Padre; Su, Dunque! [Elisabeth Rethberg/Giuseppe De Luca] / Verdi: Aida: O Patria Mia [Emmy Destinn] / Verdi: Aida: Ritorna Vincitor [Zinka Milanov]

Verdi: Aida: Temple Scene [Ezio Pinza/Giovanni Martinelli/Grace Anthony] / Verdi: Don Carlo: Qual Pallor! [Jussi Bjoerling/Robert Merrill] / Verdi: Il Trovatore: Il Balen Del Suo Sorriso [Leonard Warren/Nicola Moscona] / Verdi: La Traviata: Dite Alla Giovine [Amelita Galli-Curci/Giuseppe De Luca] / Verdi: La Traviata: Sempre Libera [Lucrezia Bori] / Verdi: Otello: Death Of Otello [Vinay/Assandri/Moscona/Newman] / Verdi: Otello: Iago's Creed [Antonio Scotti] / Verdi: Otello: Non Pensateci Piu Ora E Per Sempre Addio [Martinelli/Tibbett]

Verdi: Rigoletto: Quartet [Caruso/Sembrich/Scotti/Severina] / Verdi: Simon Boccanegra: Plebe, Patrizi [Tibbett/Martinelli/Bampton/Nicholson] / Wagner: Lohengrin: Euch Luften, Die Mein Klagen [Helen Traubel] / Wagner: Tristan and Isolde: Love Duet [Kirsten Flagstad/Lauritz Melchoir]

4/6/85 — **77** — **14** — **4 Requiem** .... **$8** Angel 38218

written by Andrew Lloyd Webber (composer of Cats and Evita); conducted by Lorin Mazel; pf: Placido Domingo/Sarah Brightman/Paul Miles-Kingston

Dies Irae / Hosanna

Kyrie (medley) / Libera Me (medley)

Lux Aeterna (medley) / Offertorium

Pie Jesu / Requiem (medley)

9/4/61 — **6** — **18** — **5 60 Years Of Music America Loves Best, Volume III (Red Seal)** .... **$20** RCA 2574

Beethoven: Moonlight Sonata: First Movement [Vladimir Horowitz] / Go Down Moses [Marian Anderson] / Kreisler: Caprice Viennois [Fritz Kreisler]

Mozart: Don Giovanni: Deh, Vieni Alla Finestra [Ezio Pinza] / Ponchielli: La Gioconda: Dance Of The Hours [Arturo Toscanini] / Puccini: La Boheme: Che Gelida Manina [Jussi Bjoerling]

Shakespeare: Hamlet: Soliloquy [John Barrymore] / Song Fest [Arthur Fiedler/Boston Pops] / Tchaikovsky: Serenade for Strings: Waltz [Serge Koussevitzky]

Verdi: Rigoletto: Caro Nome [Lily Pons] / Verdi: Rigoletto: La Donna E Mobile [Enrico Caruso] / Wagner: Die Walkure: Ho-Yo-Yo-Ho! [Kirsten Flagstad]

5/11/63 — **39** — **8** — **6 Sound of Genius, The** .... **$15** Columbia SGS 1 [2]

Bach: Concerto No. 5: Arioso [Glenn Gould] / Chopin: Polonaise [Alexander Brailowsky] / Clarke: Prince Of Denmark's March [E. Power Biggs] / Debussy: Clair De Lune [Philippe Entremont] / Debussy: Quartet In G Minor: Scherzo [Budapest Quartet]

Franck: Symphonic Variations: Finale [Eugene Ormandy] / Lord's Prayer [Mormon Tabernacle Choir] / Mendelssohn: Song Without Words (medley) [Rudolf Serkin] / Mendelssohn: Spinning Song (medley) [Rudolf Serkin] / Mendelssohn: Violin Concerto In E Minor: Finale [Zino Francescatti]

Mozart: Marriage Of Figaro: Overture [Bruno Walter] / Prokofiev: Love For Three Oranges: March [Thomas Schippers] / Puccini: La Boheme: Mi Chiamano Mimi [Eileen Farrell] / Rimsky-Korsakov: Capriccio Espagnol [Leonard Bernstein] / Song Of The Birds [Pablo Casals]

Stravinsky: Petroushka: Danse Russe [Igor Stravinsky] / Tchaikovsky: Swan Lake: Final Scene [Eugene Ormandy] / Tchaikovsky: Violin Concerto In D Major: Finale [Isaac Stern] / Tonight [Richard Tucker]

6/16/62 — **24** — **14** — **7 Summer Festival** .... **$15** RCA 6097 [2]

Beethoven: Concerto No. 1: Finale [Sviatoslav Richter/Charles Munch] / Berlioz: Roman Carnival: Overture [Charles Munch] / Blow The Man Down [Robert Shaw Chorale] / Come Prima [Mario Lanza] / Giuliani: Guitar Concerto: Finale [Julian Bream] / Glinka: Russlan And Ludmilla: Overture [Fritz Reiner]

Grieg: I Love Thee [Birgit Nilsson] / Grofe: Grand Canyon Suite: On The Trail [Morton Gould] / Lalo: Symphonie Espagnole: Scherzando [Henryk Szeryng/Walter Hendl] / Liszt: Hungarian Rhapsody No. 2 [Leopold Stokowski] / MacDowell: Concerto No. 2: Scherzo [Van Cliburn]

Mascagni: Cavalleria Rusticana: Ah! Lo Vedi [Renata Tebaldi/Jussi Bjoerling] / Offenbach: The Tales Of Hoffmann: Barcarolle [Georg Solti] / Puccini: La Boheme: Mi Chiamano Mimi [Anna Moffo] / Puccini: Madama Butterfly: Un Bel Di [Leontyne Price] / Rossini: Barber Of Seville: Overture [Erich Leinsdorf]

Strauss, J.: Thunder And Lightning Polka [Arthur Fiedler/Boston Pops] / Tchaikovsky: Sleeping Beauty: Waltz [Pierre Monteux] / West Side Stroy (Excerpt) [Robert Russell Bennett]

DEBUT DATE	PEAK POS	WKS CHR	G O L D	ARTIST — Album Title	$	Label & Number

Refer to the following names in the Artist Section for more classical albums:

ANDA, Geza
BATTLE, Kathleen, & Jessye Norman
BERNSTEIN, Leonard (3)
BJOERLING, Jussi
BOSTON POPS ORCHESTRA (1)
BOSTON SYMPHONY ORCHESTRA (3)
BRITTEN, Benjamin
BULGARIAN STATE FEMALE VOCAL
   CHOIR
CALLAS, Maria
CARLOS, Walter (4)
CLEVELAND ORCHESTRA
CLIBURN, Van (5)
DOMINGO, Placido (5)
DORATI, Antal (2)
DRAGON, Carmen
FOX, Virgil
GALWAY, James
GLASS, Philip
GOULD, Morton (2)
GREELEY, George
HOROWITZ, Vladimir (5)
LANZA, Mario (7)

MA, Yo-Yo
MARRINER, Neville
McCARTNEY, Paul
MEHTA, Zubin
MORMON TABERNACLE CHOIR (4)
PAVAROTTI, Luciano (7)
PENNARIO, Leonard
PHILADELPHIA ORCHESTRA (3)
PRICE, Leontyne (5)
RAMPAL, Jean-Pierre/Claude Bolling
REVERBERI
RICHTER, Sviatoslav
RIOS, Waldo de Los
ROYAL PHILHARMONIC
   ORCHESTRA (3)
RUBINSTEIN, Arthur (2)
SAN FRANCISCO SYMPHONY
   ORCHESTRA
SILLS, Beverly
SWINGLE SINGERS (3)
TE KANAWA, Kiri
TOMITA (7)

SOUNDTRACKS:
   Barry Lyndon
   Clockwork Orange
   Fantasia
   Interlude
   Lisztomania
   Manhattan
   Rollerball
   Song Of Norway
   2001: A Space Odyssey (2)
   War & Peace

ORIGINAL CASTS:
   The Great Waltz
   The Merry Widow
   Treemonisha

CHRISTMAS -TOP POP ALBUMS CHART
   A Carnegie Hall Christmas Concert

DEBUT DATE	PEAK POS	WKS CHR	G O L D	ARTIST — Album Title	$	Label & Number

COMEDY ALBUMS

Comedy concept productions.

| 12/29/62+ | **47** | 12 | | 1 At Home With That Other Family .... | **$15** | Roulette 25203 |

parody of Russia's Khrushchevs; George Segal/Joan Rivers/Buck Henry

Booking Agent	Mr. K's Diet	Nick And Chou En-Lai	To Tell The Truth
Boris, The Hairdresser	Mrs. K's Styles	Nick And Dick	Tour Of The Kremlin
Cosmonaut's Wife	Mrs. K's Troubles	Nick And Jack	
It's A White Tornado	Nervous Nick	Overcoat, The	
Knock-Knock	Nick And Ben	Premier's Press Conference	

| 1/11/69 | **190** | 6 | | 2 Beware Of Greeks Bearing Gifts .... | **$12** | Musicor 3173 |

Susan Anspach/Joe Silver/Len Maxwell/Bob McFadden

Big Fix	Games People Play	My Husband, The Captain	Tailor, The
Bride To Be	Getting Ready For The Wedding	Paparazzi, The	Telephone Call
Chairman Of The Board	Gratitude	Press Conference	Typical Morning
Dinner, The	Man Of Action	Quiet Evening At Home	Visit To New York
Disagreement, The	Momma	Sisters	Wedding, The

| 6/5/71 | **148** | 9 | | 3 Child's Garden Of Grass (A Pre-Legalization Comedy), A .... | **$12** | Elektra 75012 |

narrated by Michael Gwynne and Carl Esser

Acquiring Marijuana, General	Funniness	Making Love	Psychological Effects
Effects	Getting Hung-Up	Meditation	Time And Space
Creativity	History Of Marijuana	Physical And Intellectual Games	
Eating Food	Listening To Music	Physical Effects	

| 1/16/71 | **185** | 3 | | 4 Earle Doud Presents Spiro T. Agnew Is A Riot! .... | **$10** | Cadet Concept 1 |

Stanley Myron Handelman/Rich Little/Vincent Price/Pat McCormick

Diplomacy	Goodnight	Joke, The	PTA
Doomsday Machine	I'm Sorry	Monument, The	Polish Ambassador
Fight, The	Jack Frost (Parts 1-6)	Oath Of Office	Silent Majority

| 7/22/72 | **178** | 6 | | 5 Everything You Always Wanted To Know About The Godfather - But Don't Ask .... | **$10** | Columbia 31608 |

Chuck McCann (The Godfather)/Steve Landesberg/J.J. Barry

Another Favor	At The Psychiatrist	Contract, The	Special Announcement
Arrangement, An	At The Restaurant	Day In The Life	This Is Your Life
At Home	Bad News	Favor, The	Treaty, The
At The Employment Agency	Commercial Message	For Better Or For Worse	Trial, The
At The I.R.S.	Complaint, The	Protocol	Wiretap, The

| 7/11/64 | **96** | 14 | | 6 First Nine Months Are The Hardest!, The .... | **$15** | Capitol 2034 |

director: Carl Reiner; Len Weinrib/Joyce Jameson

Breaking The News	Insurance	Morning Sickness	Superstitions
Breast Feeding	It's Kicking	Naming The Baby	
Due Date	It's Time	Nurse Or My Mother?	
Honesty	Lovely To Look At	Overdue	

| 10/19/63 | **87** | 10 | | 7 Fool Britannia .... | **$15** | Acappella 1 |

Peter Sellers/Joan Collins/Anthony Newley

Common Market	Mightier Than The Sword	They Only Fade Away	Vice Italian Style
Eugenius!	There Goes That Song Again	Twelve Randy Men	Whatever Happened To John
House That Mac Built	There's No Business Like No	Two Old Ladies Locked In	And Marsha?
Is There A Doctor In The House?	Business	Conversation	Wry On The Rocks

| 12/18/65+ | **93** | 9 | | 8 James Blonde, Secret Agent 006.95, "The Man From T.A.N.T.E." .... | **$15** | Colpix 495 |

Marty Brill/Larry Foster/Connie Zimet

Alone With Sissy Alot	Goldflaker Bakery	"M's" Office In London	Weinstein's Apartment
At The Stage Delicatessen	Homeward Bound	On Fire Island With Dr. Nu?	
Athletic Club	In The Weapons Room	President's Press Conference	

| 11/6/71 | **183** | 7 | | 9 Jewish American Princess, The .... | **$10** | Bell 6063 |

Judy Graubart/Frank Gallop/Lou Jacobi/Bea Arthur/Bob McFadden

Allergy Doctor	Engaged To Be Married	Guess Who's Coming To Dinner	Night Before The Wedding
Back From The Honeymoon	Enrollment, The	Her First Home Away From	Panic In The House
Boy Friends	Everything You Have Always	Home	Peace March
Care And Feeding Of Judy Ann	Wanted To Know About The	"In" Places	Wedding Night
Pearlman	Jewish American Princess		

| 1/20/68 | **176** | 5 | | 10 Lyndon Johnson's Lonely Hearts Club Band .... | **$15** | Atco 230 |

featuring the actual recorded voices of political leaders

Governor Ronald Reagan	Senator Barry Goldwater	Vice President Hubert	
Mrs. Ladybird Johnson	Senator Everett Dirksen	Humphrey	
President Lyndon B. Johnson	Senator Robert Kennedy	Vice President Richard Nixon	

| 12/17/66+ | **72** | 10 | | 11 New First Family, 1968, The .... | **$12** | Verve 15054 |

David Frye/John Byner/Carol Corbett/Will Jordan/Bob McFadden

Acting School	Inauguration, The	Meet The New Cabinet	Showdown With The Soviets
Critic, The	Job For The Secret Service	91st Congress	State Dinner
Election Of The President, 1968	Meanwhile, Back At The White	Panic In The White House	
Epilogue, The	House	Secret Luncheon	

| 12/29/62+ | **27** | 13 | | 12 Other Family, The .... | **$15** | Laurie 5000 |

Larry Foster/Marty Brill/Toby Deane

Another Saturday Night	In The Shop	Radio Commercial	Visit, The
Bedtime Story	Phone Call	T.V. Show	
In The Department Store	Press Conference	Talent Show	

| 9/10/66 | **40** | 14 | | 13 Our Wedding Album or The Great Society Affair .... | **$15** | Jamie 3028 |

spoof of President Johnson's family; Kenny Solms/Gail Parent/Fannie Flagg/Robert Klein/Jo Ann Worley

Birds And The Bees	Guest List	Proposal, The	Wedding Gown
Daughter's Hand	In-Laws	Sister And The Movie Star	
End, The	News, The	Stag Party	
Great Society Affair	Parents Of The Bride	Tape Recording	

DEBUT DATE	PEAK POS	WKS CHR	GOLD	ARTIST — Album Title	$	Label & Number
1/12/63	**35**	13	14	President Strikes Back!, The.. an answer album to Vaughn Meader's *The First Family*; Marc London/Sylvia Miles	**$18**	Kapp 1322

Big Men · Fan Mail · TV Commercial · U.N. Meeting
Cabinet Meeting · International Competition · Taxi Ride
Cuber · "President" Strikes Back · Theatrical Agent
Face To Face · Press Conference · Typical Day At The White House

| 6/23/73 | **62** | 18 | 15 | Watergate Comedy Hour, The..
Frank Welker/Fannie Flagg/Jack Burns/Avery Schreiber | **$10** | Hidden 11202 |

Agnew Interview · Hello UPI No. 2 · President's Prayer · Watergate Comedy Hour
Break-In, The · Investigation, The · Reverend And The President
Dick Cravett Show · Meeting, The · Ron Ziegler Meets The Press
Hello UPI No. 1 · Plan, The · Special Investigator

| 11/27/65 | **3** | 25 | ● 16 | **Welcome to the LBJ Ranch!**..
featuring the actual recorded voices of political leaders | **$15** | Capitol 2423 |

Governor Nelson Rockefeller · President Dwight D. Eisenhower · Senator Barry Goldwater · Senator Robert Kennedy
Mrs. Ladybird Johnson · President Lyndon B. Johnson · Senator Everett Dirksen · Vice President Richard Nixon

| 4/2/66 | **22** | 18 | 17 | When You're In Love The Whole World Is Jewish ....
Betty Walker/Lou Jacobi/Frank Gallop/Valerie Harper/Bob McFadden | **$10** | Kapp 4506 |

Ballad Of Irving [Frank Gallop] 34 · Great Bank Robbery · Shoe Repair Shop · When You're In Love The Whole World Is Jewish
Bar Mitzvah · Hobby, The · Things Might Have Been Different · Would You Believe It?
Call From Greenwich Village · Kidnapping, The · Miami Beach · Voyage To The Bottom Of The Sea
Discussion In The Airplane · My Husband, The Monster · Schtick
Divorce, Kosher Style

| 10/14/67 | **165** | 5 | 18 | Yiddish Are Coming! The Yiddish Are Coming!, The.........................
Lou Jacobi/Betty Walker/Frank Gallop/Phil Leeds/Bob McFadden | **$10** | Verve 15058 |

American In Paris · Hello, Mama · Military Decision · Tsuriss
Back To School · Hello, Papa · Military Patrol · Visit From The Press
Battle In The Desert · Last Wish · Mission Possible · Yiddish Are Coming! The Yiddish Are Coming!
Command Headquarters · Man With The Black Patch On His Eye · Opening, The
Commanding Officer · Pvt. Goldberg, Volunteer
Gypsy Fortune Teller · Meeting At The White House · Sheldon, Sheldon, Sheldon

| 9/18/65 | **9** | 34 | 19 | **You Don't Have To Be Jewish**...
Betty Walker/Lou Jacobi/Frank Gallop | **$10** | Kapp 4503 |

Agony And The Ecstasy · Enough Already With The Quickies · Jury, The · Reading Of The Will
Call From Long Island · Final Discussion · Luncheon, The · Secret Agent, James Bondstein
Cocktail Party · Goldstein · More Quickies · Still More Quickies
Conversation In The Hotel Lobby · Home From The Office · My Son, The Captain
Convicts, The · Housewarming, The · Presidents, The
Diamond, The · Quickies

Refer to the following names in the Artist Section for more comedy albums:

ALLEN, Dayton · FREBERG, Stan · MONTY PYTHON (6) · WILD MAN STEVE (2)
ALLEN, Steve · FRYE, David (4) · MULL, Martin (2) · WILLIAMS, Robin (2)
ALLEN, Woody · GARDNER, Dave (6) · MURPHY, Eddie (2) · WILSON, Flip (5)
AMECHE, Don, & Frances Langford (2) · GREGORY, Dick (2) · NATIONAL LAMPOON (3) · WINTERS, Jonathan (6)
BERG, Gertrude · HARRISON, Wes · NEWHART, Bob (6) · WOODBURY, Woody (3)
BERGEN, Edgar, & Charlie McCarthy - see FIELDS · HOPE, Bob · NICHOLS, Mike, & Elaine May (3) · WRIGHT, Steven
HUDSON & LANDRY (3)
BERMAN, Shelley (5) · JACOBI, Lou · PAULSEN, Pat · SOUNDTRACKS:
BRUCE, Lenny (2) · JIMENEZ, Jose (7) · PISCOPO, Joe · Lenny
BUONO, Victor · JORDAN, Jerry · PRYOR, Richard (10)
CAMBRIDGE, Godfrey (2) · KINISON, Sam (3) · RADNER, Gilda · ORIGINAL CASTS:
CARLIN, George (9) · KLEIN, Robert · REINER, Carl, & Mel Brooks · Beyond The Fringe
CHEECH & CHONG (8) · LEHRER, Tom (2) · RICKLES, Don (2)
CLAY, Andrew Dice (4) · LITTLE, Rich · RIVERS, Joan · TELEVISION/MINI SERIES:
CLAY, Cassius · MABLEY, Moms (13) · SAHL, Mort (2) · All In The Family (2)
COHEN, Myron · MANDELL, Howie · SALES, Soupy (2) · Laugh-In (2)
COOPER, Pat (3) · MANNA, Charlie · SARDUCCI, Father Guido · Saturday Night Live
COSBY, Bill (20) · MARKHAM, Pigmeat · SCHAFER, Kermit · Tonight Show/Johnny Carson
CRYSTAL, Billy · MARTIN, Steve (4) · SHERMAN, Allan (7)
DANGERFIELD, Rodney (2) · MARX, Groucho/Marx Bros. (2) · SMOTHERS BROTHERS (10)
FIELDS, W.C. (2) · MASON, Jackie (2) · STEINBERG, David
FIRESIGN THEATRE (8) · McKENZIE, Bob & Doug · TOMLIN, Lily (3)
FLAGG, Fannie · MEADER, Vaughn (2) · WALKER, Jimmie
FOXX, Redd (3) · MIDLER, Bette · WARREN, Rusty (7)
WELLES, Orson

DEBUT DATE	PEAK POS	WKS CHR	GOLD	ARTIST — Album Title	$	Label & Number

AEROBIC INSTRUCTORS

Exercise albums -- with music, narration, instructions and illustrations.

AUER, Barbara Ann

| 6/20/81 | **145** | 15 | | 1 Aerobic Dancing .... | **$8** | Gateway 7610 |

written by Barbara; narration by Alan de Mause

| Beyond Orion [Disco From Another Galaxy] | From A Dream [Neil Larsen] | Magic Bird Of Fire [Salsoul Orchestra] | Promenade [Neil Larsen] |
| Love Letters [Salsoul Orchestra] | | | Queens Red [Michael Colombier] |

CAPUANO, Carla

| 3/13/82 | **152** | 8 | | 2 Aerobic Dance Hits, volume one .... | **$8** | Casablanca 7263 |

music by a studio group (except three songs by Kool & The Gang)

Celebration [Kool & The Gang]	I Can't Go For That	New Empire	Waiting For A Girl Like You
Hollywood Swinging [Kool & The Gang]	Jungle Boogie [Kool & The Gang]	Paradise	Yesterday's Songs
	Let's Groove	Physical	

CONWAY, Julie

| 1/9/61 | **73** | 17 | | 3 Good Housekeeping's Plan For Reducing Off-The-Record .... | **$20** | Harmony 7143 |

music by The Bob Price Quartet; the first *aerobics* album

All Or Nothing At All	Hot Canary	Petite Waltz	Under Paris Skies
Blue Scarecrow	I've Found A New Baby	Pop Goes The Weasel	Yellow Rose Of Texas
Domino	Little Brown Jug	Swanee River	
Heartaches	Old Piano Roll	Undecided	

FONDA, Jane

| 5/29/82+ | **15** | 120 | ▲² | 4 Jane Fonda's Workout Record .... | **$8** | Columbia 38054 [2] |

| Bridge Over Troubled Water [Linda Clifford] | Changes In Latitudes, Changes In Attitudes [Jimmy Buffett] | In Your Letter [REO Speedwagon] | Night (Feeling Like Getting Down) [Billy Ocean] |
| Can You Feel It [Jacksons] | Harbor Lights [Boz Scaggs] | | Stomp! [Brothers Johnson] |

| 5/21/83 | **117** | 7 | | 5 Jane Fonda's Workout Record For Pregnancy, Birth And Recovery .... | **$8** | Columbia 38675 [2] |

music by a special studio group; no track titles listed on this album

| 8/18/84 | **135** | 10 | ● | 6 Jane Fonda's Workout Record - New And Improved .... | **$8** | Columbia 39287 [2] |

| Dance For Me (medley) [Dean Correa] | Keep The Fire Burnin' [REO Speedwagon] | One Hundred Ways | Wanna Be Startin' Somethin' [Michael Jackson] |
| Do Ya Wanna Funk [Sylvester] | Megatron Man [Patrick Cowley] | Rhythm Part I (medley) [Dean Correa] | X-Cit-Mental (medley) [Dean Correa] |

FRATIANNE, Linda

| 2/20/82 | **174** | 7 | | 7 Dance & Exercise With the Hits .... | **$8** | Columbia 37653 |

music performed by The Beachwood All-Stars (studio group)

Bette Davis Eyes	How Do I Survive	Kiss On My List	Slow Hand
Games People Play	I'm In Love	Real Love	Sweetheart
Hot Rod Hearts			

GREGGAINS, Joanie

| 6/18/83 | **177** | 4 | | 8 Aerobic Shape-Up II .... | **$8** | Parade 106 |

music by studio musicians

Do I Do	E. T. Theme	Let It Whip	Other Woman
Don't Make You Wanna Dance	Ebony & Ivory	Love's Been A Little Bit Hard On	Wake Up Little Susie
Double Dutch Bus	Get Down On It	Me	Work That Body

HENSEL, Carol

| 3/21/81 | **56** | 55 | | 9 Carol Hensel's Exercise & Dance Program .... | **$8** | Vintage 7713 |

originally titled *Dancersize* on Vintage 7701; music by a special studio group

| Ain't No Stoppin Us Now | I Just Wanna Stop | Just The Way You Are | What A Fool Believes |
| I Go To Rio | I Will Survive | Summer Nights | |

| 12/19/81+ | **70** | 28 | | 10 Carol Hensel's Exercise & Dance Program, Volume 2 .... | **$8** | Vintage 7733 |

music performed by The Beachwood All-Stars (studio group)

Celebration	Just The Two Of Us	9 To 5	Whip It
De Do Do Do, De Da Da Da	Morning Train (9 To 5)	Sailing	You May Be Right
(Just Like) Starting Over			

| 1/22/83 | **104** | 12 | | 11 Carol Hensel's Exercise & Dance Program, Volume 3 .... | **$8** | Vintage 30004 |

music by a special studio group

| Bobbie Sue | Freeze Frame | Let's Groove | Shake It Up |
| Chariots Of Fire - Titles | Jessie's Girl | Mama Used To Say | Turn Your Love Around |

MISSETT, Judi Sheppard

| 12/5/81 | **117** | 20 | ● | 12 Jazzercise .... | **$8** | MCA 5272 |

music by studio musicians

Animal House	Car Wash	Rockford Files	T'Ain't Nobody's Biz-Ness If I Do
Baretta's Theme	Don't Pull Your Love	Squeeze Me	Teach Me Tonight
Boogie Woogie Bugle Boy	Girl From Ipanema	Sweet Nothin's	Which Way Is Up

REYNOLDS, Debbie

| 5/26/84 | **182** | 3 | | 13 Do It Debbie's Way .... | **$8** | K-Tel 9190 |

music by a "switched on swing" big band; no track titles listed on this album

SIMMONS, Richard

| 6/5/82 | **44** | 40 | ▲ | 14 Reach .... | **$8** | Elektra 60122 |

songs sung by Simmons, backed by studio musicians

Don't Tell Me	Live It	This Time	What Are You Waiting For?
Laugh	Reach	Wake Up	You Can Do It
Lift It Up	Stop And Start		

SMITH, Kathy

| 3/13/82 | **144** | 13 | | 15 Kathy Smith's Aerobic Fitness .... | **$8** | MuscleTone 72151 |

music by studio musicians

| Banana Boat Song | Don't Stop 'Til You Get Enough | I Love A Rainy Night |
| Cruisin' | Give Me The Night | Ride Like The Wind |

DEBUT DATE	PEAK POS	WKS CHR	GOLD	ARTIST — Album Title	$	Label & Number

SPECIALTY ALBUMS

The following albums, because of their unusual content, are listed in this section and are categorized with special headings.

BASEBALL

| 11/22/69 | 197 | 1 | | 1 Amazing Mets, The .... | $25 | Buddah 1969 |

featuring the singing voices of the New York Mets; 1969 World Series Champs (note label number)

God Bless America	Locker Room Chatter	Song For The '69 Mets
Green Grass Of Shea	Mets - Hallelujah	We're Gonna Win The Series
Heart	Mets Are Here To Stay	We've Got The Whole World
La La La La	Mets Ball Game	Watching Us

CARS

| 12/14/63+ | 27 | 18 | | 2 Big Sounds Of The Drags!, The .... | $25 | Capitol 2001 |

actual sounds of drag racing at a quarter-mile track; no track titles listed on this album

| 2/15/64 | 138 | 3 | | 3 Hot Rod Hootenanny ....[N] | $35 | Capitol 2010 |

novelty hot rod songs featuring The Weirdos and the voice of Mr. Gasser

Chopped Nash	Fastest Shift Alive	Mr. Gasser	1320
Dragnutz	Hot Rod Hootenanny	My Coupe Eefen Talks	Weirdo Wiggle
Eefen It Don't Go Chrome It	Mad'vette	Termites In My Woody	You Ain't Nothing But A Honda

| 12/14/63+ | 62 | 15 | | 4 Hot Rod Rally .... | $40 | Capitol 1997 |

'54 Corvette [Super Stocks]	Little Nifty Fifty [Super Stocks]	Repossession Blues [Hot Rod Rog]	Woody Walk [Shutdown Douglas]
Flash Falcon [Shutdown Douglas]	Little Stick Nomad [Super Stocks]	Twin Cut Outs [Shutdown Douglas]	
426 Superstock [Super Stocks]	Little Street Machine [Hot Rod Rog]	Wheel Man [Super Stocks]	
Hot Rod City [Super Stocks]	Night Rod [Shutdown Douglas]		

| 7/13/63 | 7 | 46 | | 5 Shut Down .... | $25 | Capitol 1918 |

Ballad Of Thunder Road [Robert Mitchum] 62	**Brontosaurus Stomp** [Piltdown Men] 75	Chicken [Cheers]	**Shut Down** [Beach Boys] 23
Black Denim Trousers [Cheers] 6	Car Trouble [Eligibles]	409 [Beach Boys] 76	Street Machine [Super Stocks]
	Cheater Slicks [Super Stocks]	Four On The Floor [Super Stocks]	Wide Track [Super Stocks]
		Hot Rod Race [Jimmy Dolan]	

HOOTENANNY

| 7/20/63 | 99 | 6 | | 6 At The Hootenanny ....[L] | $15 | Kapp 3330 |

Baby, Where You Been So Long [Samplers]	Hang On The Bell, Nellie [Chad Mitchell Trio]	Muleskinner Blues [David Hill]	Queen Bee [Marais & Miranda]
Daddy Roll 'Em [David Hill]	I Never Will Marry [Jo March]	Native Minstrel Song [Marais & Miranda]	Rum By Gum [Chad Mitchell Trio]
Green Grow The Lilacs [Terry Gilkyson & The South Coasters]	Kisses Sweeter Than Wine [Jo March]	Pull Off Your Old Coat [Samplers]	Willie, Oh, Willie [Betty & The Duke]

| 8/31/63 | 128 | 4 | | 7 Original Hootenanny, The .... | $15 | Crestview 806 |

Bonnie Ship The Diamond [Judy Collins]	Katy Cruel [Travelers 3]	Squid Jiggin' Ground [Oscar Brand]	Wade In The Water [Judy Henske]
If I Had A Hammer [Limeliters]	La Bamba [Bud & Travis]	Three Jovial Huntsmen [Will Holt]	You Can Tell The World [Bob Gibson]
John Henry [Josh White]	Reuben's Train [Dillards]		
Josie [Ed McCurdy]	Rising Of The Moon [Theodore Bikel]		

MINSTREL SHOW

| 5/26/56 | 9 | 9 | | 8 Gentlemen, Be Seated! .... | $25 | Epic 3238 |

recreation of a complete minstrel show: cd: Allen Roth; pf: Gordon Goodman/Osie Johnson/John Neher/Quartones; also see Eric Rogers Vaudeville

Camptown Races (medley)	I Wonder What's Become Of Sally?	Mandy Lee (medley)	There'll Be A Hot Time In The Old Town Tonight (medley)
Can't You Hear Me Callin' Caroline	I Wonder Who's Kissing Her Now (medley)	My Lady Love (medley)	Waitin' For The Robert E. Lee (medley)
Hello! Ma Baby (medley)	In The Evening By The Moonlight (medley)	Oh By Jingo, Oh By Gee, You're The Only Girl For Me	When The Bell In The Lighthouse Rings
Honeymoon (medley)	Lassus Trombone	Old Folks At Home (medley)	
I Wish! I Was In Peoria		Ole Dan Tucker (medley)	
		Shine On Harvest Moon	

OLYMPICS

| 7/14/84 | 92 | 13 | | 9 Official Music Of The XXIIIrd Olympiad Los Angeles 1984, The .... | $10 | Columbia 39322 [2] |

Bugler's Dream [Felix Slatkin]	Junku [Herbie Hancock]	Olympian-Lighting Of The Torch [Philip Glass]	Power [Bill Conti]
Chance For Heaven [Christopher Cross] 76	Moodido (The Match) [Toto]	Nothing's Gonna Stop You Now [Loverboy]	Olympic Fanfare And Theme [John Williams]	**Reach Out** [Giorgio Moroder] 81
Courtship [Bob James]			Street Thunder [Foreigner]
Grace [Quincy Jones]			

| 9/24/88 | 31 | 3 | ● | 10 1988 Summer Olympics Album/One Moment In Time .... | $8 | Arista 8551 |

features tracks by 11 artists especially written and recorded for the NBC-TV broadcast of the 1988 Summer Olympic Games

Fight (No Matter How Long) [Bunburys]	Olympic Joy [Kashif]	Peace In Our Time [Jennifer Holliday]	That's What Dreams Are Made Of [Odds & Ends]
Harvest For The World [Christians]	Olympic Spirit [John Williams]	**Reason To Try** [Eric Carmen] 87	Willpower [Taylor Dayne]
Indestructible [Four Tops] 35	**One Moment In Time** [Whitney Houston] 5	Shape Of Things To Come [Bee Gees]	

| 8/1/92 | 32 | 12 | | 11 Barcelona Gold .... | $12 | Warner 26974 |

songs broadcast on TV during the 1992 Summer Olympics in Barcelona

Barcelona [Freddie Mercury/Montserrat Caballe]	Go Out Dancing [Rod Stewart]	**Keep It Comin'** [Keith Sweat] 17	Old Soldier [Marc Cohn]
Don't Tread On Me [Damn Yankees]	Heart To Climb The Mountain [Randy Travis]	Love Is Here To Stay [Natalie Cole]	One Song [Tevin Campbell]
Free Your Mind [En Vogue] 8	Higher Baby [D.J. Jazzy Jeff & The Fresh Prince]	No Se Tu [Luis Miguel]	Texas Flyer [Travis Tritt]
Friends For Life [Jose Carreras/Sarah Brightman]	How Fast How Far [Anita Baker]	**Not Enough Time** [INXS] 28	**This Used To Be My Playground** [Madonna] 1
			Wonderful Tonight [Eric Clapton]

DEBUT DATE	PEAK POS	WKS CHR	GOLD	ARTIST — Album Title	$	Label & Number

PARODY

| 12/5/64 | **129** | 3 | | **12** **Dracula's Greatest Hits** .... [N] | **$40** | RCA 2977 |

parodies of popular songs by Dracula (Gene Moss)

Carry Me Back To Transylvania	I Want To Bite Your Hand	Monster Bossa Nova	New Frankenstein & Johnny
Drac The Knife	King Kong Stomp	Monster Goose Rhymes	Song
Frankenstein	Little Black Bag	Monster Hootenanny	Surf Monster
Ghoul Days		

| 7/28/62 | **108** | 14 | | **13** **Mad "Twists" Rock 'n' Roll** .... [N] | **$50** | Big Top 1305 |

a parody of pop music; pf: Jeanne Hayes/Mike Russo/Dellwoods

Agnes	I'll Always Remember Being	Pimples Turned To Dimples	Somebody Else's Dandruff
Blind Date	Young	Please, Betty Jane	
Boys' Bathroom Wall	My Johnny's Hub Cap	Pretzel	
High School Basketball Game	Nose Job	Serious Teenager In Love	

RADIO

| 3/1/69 | **31** | 17 | | **14** **Themes Like Old Times** .... | **$10** | Viva 36018 [2] |

features 180 of the most famous original radio themes

Abbott & Costello Show — Adventures Of Archie Andrews — Adventures Of Frank Merriwell — Adventures Of Jungle Jim — Adventures Of Ozzie & Harriet — Adventures Of Philip Marlowe — Adventures Of Sam Spade, Detective — Adventures Of Sherlock Holmes — Adventures Of The Saint — Against The Storm — Air Adventures Of Jimmy Allen — Aldrich Family — Amos 'N' Andy — Answer Man — Armour Star Jester — Backstage Wife — Believe It Or Not — Benny Goodman's Swing School — Big Sister — Bill Stern Sports Newsreel — Black Castle — Black Hood — Blondie — Bobby Benson And The B-Bar-B Riders — Bold Venture — Boston Blackie — Brave Tomorrow — Brighter Day — Buck Rogers In The Twenty Fifth Century — Bulldog Drummond — Buster Brown Gang — Campana Serenade — Can You Top This? — Canary Pet Show — Captain Midnight — Carters Of Elm Street — Chamber Music Society Of Lower Basin Street — Chandu The Magician — Charlie McCarthy Show — Chick Carter, Boy Detective — Coast To Coast On A Bus — Coke Club — Counterspy — Crime Does Not Pay — David Harum — Dick Tracy — Dr. Christian (The Vaseline Program) — Dr. I. Q. — Dr. Kildare, Story Of — Double Or Nothing — Duffy's Tavern — Easy Aces — Ed Wynn Show — Eddie Cantor Show — Escape — FBI In Peace And War — Falcon, The — Fat Man — Fibber McGee And Molly — Firstnighter Program — Fitch Bandwagon — Front Page Farrell — Gabriel Heatter's News Of The World — Gangbusters — Goldbergs, The — Grand Central Station — Great Gildersleeve — Green Hornet — Guiding Light — Gunsmoke — Hal Kemp On The Air For Griffin — Hardy Family — Helping Hand — Here's Morgan — Hermit's Cave — Hoofbeats, Starring Buck Jones — Hop Harrigan — House Of Mystery — I Love A Mystery — Information Please — Inner Sanctum Mysteries — It Pays To Be Ignorant — Jack Armstrong — Jergen's Journal — Jimmy Durante Show — Jimmy Fiddler In Hollywood — Joe Penner Show — John's Other Wife — Just Plain Bill — Kaltenborn Edits The News — Kay Fairchild, Stepmother — Lassie — Let Yourself Go — Let's Pretend — Life Can Be Beautiful — Life With Luigi — Lifeboy Program — Lights Out — Linda's First Love — Lone Ranger — Lorenzo Jones — Lucky Strike Program — Lum 'N' Abner Show — Lux Radio Theatre — Ma Perkins — Magic Detective — Major Bowes' Original Amateur Hour — Mandrake The Magician — Manhattan Merry-Go-Round — March Of Time — Mark Trail — Marlin Hurt And Beulah Show — Maxwell House Coffee Time — Melody Ranch — Mercury Theatre On The Air — Michael Shayne — Molle Mystery Theatre — Mr. District Attorney — Murder At Midnight — My Friend Irma — Myrt And Marge — Mysterious Traveller — National Barn Dance — New Adventures Of The Thin Man — Nick Carter, Master Detective — Norge Kitchen Committee — Official Detective — One Man's Family — Pepper Young's Family — Pepsodent Show — Phil Harris-Alice Faye Show — Philco Radio Time — Philip Morris Playhouse — Raleigh And Kool Cigarette Program — Red Ryder — Red Skelton Program — Richard Diamond, Private Eye — Right To Happiness — Road Of Life — Romance Of Helen Trent — Scattergood Baines — Second Mrs. Burton — Sergeant Preston Of The Yukon — Shadow, The — Shadow Of Fu Manchu — Songs By Sinatra — Spike Jones Show — Stagedoor Canteen — Stella Dallas — Straight Arrow — Strange Romance Of Evelyn Winters — Superman — Suspense — Tarzan — Taystee Breadwinner — Ted Lewis, The High-Hatted Tragedian Of Song — Tennessee Jed — Terry And The Pirates — This Is Nora Drake — This Life Is Mine — Tom Corbett, Space Cadet — Tom Mix Ralston Straight Shooters — Town Hall Tonight — Troman Harper, Rumor Detective — True Detective Mysteries — Uncle Don — Valiant Lady — Vaughn DeLeath Show — Vic And Sade — What Was The Name Of That Shave Cream He Used To Sell? — When A Girl Marries — Whispering Jack Smith — Whistler, The — Wild Bill Elliot — Witch's Tale — Woody Herman Show — X Minus One — Young Dr. Malone — Young Widder Brown — Your Hit Parade

SEX

| 1/19/63 | **56** | 19 | | **15** **How To Strip For Your Husband** .... [I] | **$20** | Roulette 25186 |

instrumentals by Sonny Lester, with booklet *How To Strip For Your Husband* by strip-teaser Ann Corio

Blues To Strip By	Lament	Raid, The	Shivas Regal
Bumps & Grinds	Lonely Little G-String	Seduction Of The Virgin	Turkish
Easter Parade	Pretty Girl Is Like A Melody	Princess	Walkin' & Strippin'
For Strippers Only		

| 10/16/71 | **181** | 4 | | **16** **Way to become The Sensuous Woman by "J", The** .... | **$10** | Atlantic 7209 |

based on the best-selling book; spoken word by Connie Z.; background music by Tony Camillo; no track titles listed on this album

SOUNDS

| 3/27/71 | **176** | 8 | | **17** **Songs of the Humpback Whale** .... | **$8** | Capitol 620 |

actual recorded sounds of Whales near Bermuda

Distant Whale	Solo Whale	Tower Whales
Slowed-Down Solo Whale	Three Whale Trip	

DEBUT DATE	PEAK POS	WKS CHR	GOLD	ARTIST — Album Title	$	Label & Number

SPACE

| 9/6/69 | **185** | 5 | | **18** Apollo 11: Flight To The Moon .... | **$10** | Bell 1100 |

actual voice transmissions of America's space missions; narrated by astronaut Walter M. Schirra, Jr.

Alan Shepard...America's First Manned Flight	John Glenn...Orbits The Earth On The Lunar Surface	To The Moon
Apollo 8...First Orbiting Of The Moon	Ed White...Walks In Space	
Apollo 10...Approaching The Lunar Surface	Return To Earth	
Gemini 6 & 7...Rendezvous Above The Earth	Scott Carpenter...Reentry Into Earth's Atmosphere	

WRESTLING

| 11/30/85+ | **84** | 19 | | **19** Wrestling Album, The .... [N] | **$8** | Epic 40223 |

Captain Lou's History Of Music [Captain Lou Albano]	Eat Your Hart Out Rick Springfield [Jimmy Hart]	Grab Them Cakes [Junk Yard Dog]
Cara Mia [Nikolai Volkoff]	For Everybody ["Rowdy" Roddy Piper]	Hulk Hogan's Theme [WWF All Stars]
Don't Go Messin' With A Country Boy [Hillbilly Jim]		Land Of 1,000 Dances?!!? [Wrestlers]
		Real American [Rick Derringer]
		Tutti Frutti ["Mean" Gene Okerlund]

| 10/17/87 | **123** | 20 | | **20** Piledriver: The Wrestling Album II .... [N] | **$8** | Epic 40889 |

Crank It Up [Jimmy Hart]	Honky Tonk Man [Honky Tonk Man]	Rock And Roll Hoochie Koo [Gene Okerlund & Rick Derringer]
Demolition [Rick Derringer with Ax & Smash]	If You Only Knew [Wrestlers]	Stand Back [Vince McMahon]
Girls In Cars [Robbie Dupree & Strike Force]	Jive Soul Bro [Slick]	Waking Up Alone [Hillbilly Jim & Gertrude]
	Piledriver [Koko B. Ware]	

ZODIAC

| 2/28/70 | **180** | 3 | | **21** Astromusical House Of..., The .... [I] | **$10** | Astro 1001/1012 |

series of 12 albums, each named after a zodiac sign; music selected is supposed to reflect the character of the sign

| 12/6/69+ | **147** | 15 | | **22** Signs Of The Zodiac .... | **$10** | A&M 4211/22 |

series of 12 albums about the signs of the zodiac; script: Jacques Wilson; electronic music: Mort Garson

| 7/15/67 | **118** | 9 | | **23** Zodiac: Cosmic Sounds, The .... | **$10** | Elektra 74009 |

script: Jacques Wilson; music: Mort Garson; about the 12 signs of the zodiac

Aquarius - The Lover of Life	Gemini - The Cool Eye	Sagittarius - The Versatile Daredevil
Aries - The Fire-Fighter	Leo - The Lord of Lights	Scorpio - The Passionate Hero
Cancer - The Moon Child	Libra - The Flower Child	Taurus - The Voluptuary
Capricorn - The Uncapricious Climber	Pisces - The Peace Piper	Virgo - The Perpetual Perfectionist

DEBUT DATE	PEAK POS	WKS CHR	GOLD	ARTIST — Album Title	$	Label & Number

CHRISTMAS
Top Pop Albums Chart — Various

The following various artist/specialty Christmas albums made *Billboard*'s regular Top LPs charts:

11/20/82 · **96** · **9** · **1 Annie's Christmas** .... **$8** Columbia 38361
children's story with music, narration and dialogue; Annie: Robin Ignico; narrator: William Woodson

Angels We Have Heard On High	Jolly Old St. Nicholas	
Deck The Halls With Boughs Of Holly	We Wish You A Merry Christmas	

12/26/92 · **196** · **1** · **2 Carnegie Hall Christmas Concert, A** .... **$12** Sony Class. 48235
cd: Andre Previn; pf: Kathleen Battle, Frederica von Stade and Wynton Marsalis; recorded in New York City on 12/8/91

Alleluja	Gesu Bambino	Maria Wiegenlied	We Three Kings Of Orient Are
American Songs Medley	Have Yourself A Merry Little	Mary's Little Boy Chile	Winter Wonderland
Christmas Song (medley)	Christmas (medley)	My Favorite Things	
Christmas Songs Medley	Joy To The World!	Silent Night	
Evening Prayer	Lo, How A Rose E'er Blooming	Twelve Days Of Christmas	

12/12/87+ · **130** · **8** · **3 Christmas Rap** .... **$8** Profile 1247

Chillin' With Santa [Derek B]	Dana Dane Is Coming To Town	Let The Jingle Bells Rock	That's What I Want For
Christmas In Hollis [Run-D.M.C.]	[Dana Dane]	[Sweet Tee]	Christmas [Showboys]
Christmas In The City [King	Ghetto Santa [Spyder D]	Surf M.C. New Year [Surf M.C.'s]	
Sun-D Moet]	He's Santa Claus [Disco 4]		

12/25/82+ · **172** · **4** · **4 Country Christmas, A** .... **$8** RCA 4396

Christmas In Dixie [Alabama]	Every Time I Hear Blue	Fall Softly Snow [Jim Ed	Noel, Noel [Steve Wariner]
Christmas Is Just A Song For	Christmas (I Get The	Brown/Helen Cornelius]	Peace On Earth (A Song For All
Us This Year [Louise	Christmas Blues) [Leon	Let It Snow, Let It Snow, Let It	Seasons) [Razzy Bailey]
Mandrell/RC Bannon]	Everette]	Snow [Charley Pride]	Pretty Paper [Willie Nelson]

1/7/89 · **140** · **2** · **5 GRP Christmas Collection, A** .... **$8** GRP 9574

Carol Of The Bells [David Benoit]	Little Drummer Boy [Daryl	Some Children See Him [Dave
Christmas Song [Diane Schuur]	Stuermer]	Grusin]
God Rest Ye Merry Gentlemen	Santa Claus Is Coming To Town	This Christmas [Yutaka]
[Chick Corea Elektric Band]	[Dave Valentin]	What Child Is This?
Have Yourself A Merry Little	Silent Night [Special EFX]	(Greensleeves) [Mark Egan]
Christmas [Tom Scott]	Sleigh Ride [Eddie Daniels]	White Christmas [Lee Ritenour]

1/6/90 · **162** · **1** · **6 GRP Christmas Collection, A** .... **[R]** **$8** GRP 9574
see album above for tracks

12/14/91 · **137** · **4** · **7 GRP Christmas Collection Vol. II, A** .... **$12** GRP 9650

Angels We Have Heard On High	First Noel [George Howard]	Let It Snow! Let It Snow! Let It	We Three Kings Of Orient Are
[Don Grusin]	I Wonder As I Wander [New	Snow! [Nelson Rangell]	[Deborah Henson-Conant]
Blue Christmas [Laima]	York Voices]	Let There Be Peace On Earth	
Christmas Time Is Here [Patti	I'll Be Home For Christmas	[Voyceboxing]	
Austin]	[Spyro Gyra]	O Come All Ye Faithful [Arturo	
Earl Of Salisbury Pavane	Jesu, Joy Of Man's Desiring	Sandoval]	
[Acoustic Alchemy]	[Russ Freeman]	O Holy Night [Carl Anderson]	

12/5/92 · **82** · **6** · **8 Handel's Messiah - A Soulful Celebration** .... **$12** Reprise 26980
supergrouping of soul and gospel artists, includes Vanessa Bell Armstrong, Tevin Campbell, Andrae Crouch, Tramaine Hawkins, Howard Hewitt, Chaka Khan, Gladys Knight, Johnnie Mathis, Stephanie Mills, Jeffrey Osbourne, Phil Perry, Stevie Wonder and many others; Christmas charts: 12/92

And He Shall Purify	Comfort Ye My People	I Know That My Redeemer	Partial History Of Black Music
And The Glory Of The Lord	Every Valley Shall Be Exalted	Liveth	Medley
Behold, A Virgin Shall Conceive	For Unto Us A Child Is Born	Lift Up Your Heads, O Ye Gates	Rejoice Greatly, O Daughter Of
Behold The Lamb Of God	Glory To God	O Thou That Tellest Good	Zion
But Who May Abide The Day Of	Hallelujah!	Tidings To Zion	Why Do The Nations So
His Coming			Furiously Rage?

12/30/57+ · **19** · **3** · **9 Merry Christmas** .... **[EP]** **$40** Coral 82003
7" EP (originally released as a 10" LP in 1952)

Christmas Is A Time (That Will	Let's Have An Old Fashioned	Sing A Song Of Santa Claus	(You Can Just Feel) Christmas
Never Change) [Johnny	Christmas [Don Cornell]	[Ames Brothers]	In The Air [Johnny Desmond]
Desmond]	Little Match Girl [Eileen Barton]	Winter's Here Again [Ames	
I've Got The Christmas Spirit	Night Before Christmas Song	Brothers]	
[Don Cornell]	[Eileen Barton]		

12/19/92 · **166** · **2** · **10 Narada Christmas Collection Volume 2** ....**[I]** **$12** Narada 63909
Christmas charts: 23/92

Christmas Eve [Ira Stein]	From Heaven Above [Ralf	Joseph, Dearest Joseph Mine	O Holy Night [Peter Buffett]
Christmas Song (Chestnuts	Illenberger]	[Simon Wynberg]	Song Of The Evergreen [Kostia]
Roasting On An Open Fire)	Gloria [Nando Lauria]	Lo, How A Rose E'er Blooming	Unto Us A Boy Is Born [Michael
[Doug Cameron]	Hark (Rock) The Herald Angels	[Sheldon Mirowitz]	Jones]
Coventry Carol (medley) [Bob	[David Lanz & Paul Speer]	Noel Nouvelet (medley) [Bob	We Three Kings [David
Read]	Il Est Ne (He Is Born) [Michael	Read]	Arkenstone]
First Noel [Spencer Brewer]	Gettel]	O Come, O Come, Emmanuel	
		[Wayne Gratz]	

11/14/87 · **20** · **13** ▲ · **11 Very Special Christmas, A** .... **$8** A&M 3911
Christmas songs contributed by 15 rock superstars; proceeds donated to the Special Olympics

Back Door Santa [Bon Jovi]	Gabriel's Message [Sting]	Merry Christmas Baby [Bruce	Silent Night [Stevie Nicks]
Christmas (Baby Please Come	Have Yourself A Merry Little	Springsteen]	Winter Wonderland [Eurythmics]
Home) [U2]	Christmas [Pretenders]	Run Rudolph Run [Bryan	
Christmas In Hollis [Run-D.M.C.]	I Saw Mommy Kissing Santa	Adams]	
Coventry Carol [Alison Moyet]	Claus [John Cougar	Santa Baby [Madonna]	
Do You Hear What I Hear	Mellencamp]	Santa Claus Is Coming To Town	
[Whitney Houston]	Little Drummer Boy [Bob Seger]	[Pointer Sisters]	

DEBUT DATE	PEAK POS	WKS CHR	GOLD		ARTIST — Album Title	$	Label & Number
12/17/88+	57	5		12	Very Special Christmas, A .... [R]	$8	A&M 3911
12/9/89+	55	7		13	Very Special Christmas, A .... [R]	$8	A&M 3911
12/8/90+	58	6		14	Very Special Christmas, A .... [R]	$8	A&M 3911

see first chart entry in 1987 for tracks of above 3 re-entries; Christmas charts: 1/'87, 1/'88, 4/'89, 5/'90, 3/'91, 5/'92

| 11/14/92 | 7 | 11 | ▲ | 15 | **Very Special Christmas 2, A** .... | **$12** | A&M 31454 |

proceeds donated to the Special Olympics; Christmas charts: 2/'92

Birth Of Christ [Boyz II Men]	Christmas Time Again [Extreme]	O Holy Night [Tevin Campbell]	Silent Night [Wilson Phillips]
Blue Christmas [Ann & Nancy Wilson]	I Believe In You [Sinead O'Connor]	Please Come Home For Christmas [Jon Bon Jovi]	Sleigh Ride [Debbie Gibson]
Christmas All Over Again [Tom Petty & The Heartbreakers]	Jingle Bell Rock [Randy Travis]	Rockin' Around The Christmas Tree [Ronnie Spector/Darlene Love]	What Child Is This? [Vanessa Williams]
Christmas Is [Run D.M.C.]	Merry Christmas Baby [Bonnie Raitt & Charles Brown]		What Christmas Means To Me [Paul Young]
Christmas Song [Luther Vandross]	O Christmas Tree [Aretha Franklin]	Santa Claus Is Coming To Town [Frank Sinatra/Cyndi Lauper]	White Christmas [Michael Bolton]

| 12/21/74 | 125 | 2 | | 16 | Waltons' Christmas Album, The .... | $10 | Columbia 33193 |

album cover pictures TV's *The Waltons*; songs performed by The Holiday Singers; narration by Earl Hamner (creator of The Waltons)

First Noel	Hark! The Herald Angels Sing	O Come All Ye Faithful	Spirit Of Christmas
God Rest Ye Merry Gentlemen	It Came Upon A Midnight Clear	O Little Town Of Bethlehem	Waltons' Theme
Grandpa's Christmas Wish	Joy To The World	Silent Night	

| 12/7/85+ | 77 | 14 | ● | 17 | Winter's Solstice, A .... [X-I] | $8 | Windham Hill 1045 |

Bach Bouree [Darol Anger & Mike Marshall]	High Plains (Christmas On The High-Line) [Philip Aaberg]	New England Morning [William Ackerman]	Northumbrian Lullabye [Malcolm Dalglish]
Engravings II [Ira Stein & Russel Walder]	Jesu, Joy Of Man's Desiring [David Qualey]	Nollaig [Billy Oskay & Micheal O Domhnaill]	Petite Aubade [Shadowfax]
Greensleeves [Liz Story]			Tale Of Two Cities [Mark Isham]

| 12/20/86+ | 172 | 5 | | 18 | Winter's Solstice, A .... [X-I-R] | $8 | Windham Hill 1045 |

Christmas charts: 15/'87, 17/'88

| 12/10/88+ | 108 | 7 | | 19 | Winter's Solstice II, A .... [X-I] | $8 | Windham Hill 1077 |

Christmas charts: 8/'88, 14/'89, 19/'90, 16/'91

Abide The Winter [Will Ackerman]	Come Life Shaker Life [Malcolm Dalglish]	Flute Sonata In Em, 3rd Movement [Barbara Higbie & Emily Klion]	Salve Regina [Therese Schroeder-Sheker]
Bring Me Back A Song [Nightnoise]	Dadme Albricias Hijos D'Eva (medley) [Modern Mandolin Quartet]	Gift, The [Philip Aaberg]	17th Century Canon [Paul McCandless/James Matheson/Robin May]
By The Fireside [William Allaudin Mathieu]	E'en So, Lord Jesus Quickly Come (medley) [Modern Mandolin Quartet]	Medieval Memory II [Ira Stein & Russel Walder]	Simple Psalm [Fred Simon]
Chorale #220 [Turtle Island String Quartet]		Prelude To Cello Suite #1 In G Major [Michael Hedges]	Sung To Sleep [Michael Manring] This Rush Of Wings [Metamora]

| 12/1/90 | 90 | 8 | | 20 | Winter's Solstice III, A .... [X-I] | $12 | Windham Hill 1098 |

includes 4 vocals; Christmas charts: 8/'90, 11/'91, 29/'93

Christmas Bells [John Gorka]	In Dulci Jubilo (Good Christian Men Rejoice) [Michael Hedges]	Of The Father's Love Begotten [Tim Story]	Trepak [Modern Mandolin Quartet]
Christmas Song [Steve Erquiaga]	In The Bleak Midwinter [Pierce Pettis]	Pavane [Liz Story]	Veni Emmanuel [Turtle Island String Quartet]
Coventry Carol [Paul McCandless]	Little Drummer Boy [Schonherz & Scott]	Sleepers Awake [Andy Narell]	
Earth Abides [Philip Aaberg]	Lullay, Lully [Barbara Higbie]	Snow Is Lightly Falling [Nightnoise]	
Hopeful [Michael Manring]			

DEBUT DATE	PEAK POS	WKS CHR	GOLD	ARTIST — Album Title	$	Label & Number

Billboard's Christmas Charts

For the years 1963 through 1973, *Billboard* did not chart Christmas albums on their Top Pop Albums charts. Instead, they issued special Christmas charts for 3-4 weeks during each Christmas season. These special charts were discontinued from 1974 thru 1982 when *Billboard* again charted Christmas albums on their regular album charts. Since 1983, *Billboard* again issued special Christmas charts; however, they also listed the best selling Christmas albums on their Top Pop Albums charts. The following list includes only those albums which made the Top 10 of *Billboard's* special Christmas Albums chart and never made *Billboard's* Top Pop Albums charts. For Christmas albums that made both *Billboard's* Top Pop Albums chart and their special Christmas charts, the peak position/year charted data achieved on the special Christmas charts is noted below the album title in the main artist section. Even though only the Top 10 albums are listed here, the special Christmas charts were researched in full, and all peak position/year charted data is included for these albums (if they charted for more than one season). The debut date is the earliest date the album appeared on the charts, even if it did not appear in the Top 10. The weeks charted total includes all weeks charted, not just weeks in the Top 10.

AIR SUPPLY

| 12/19/87+ | 10 | 3 | | 1 Christmas Album, The .... | $8 | Arista 8528 |

#17/'87, #10/'88

ALPERT, Herb & The Tijuana Brass

| 12/7/68 | 1² | 10 | ● | 2 Herb Alpert & The Tijuana Brass Christmas Album ....[I] | $10 | A&M 4166 |

#1/'68, #6/'69, #17/'70

ANDREWS, Julie

| 12/2/67 | 9 | 6 | | 3 Christmas Treasure, A .... | $10 | RCA 3829 |

with the orchestra, harpsichord and arrangements of Andre Previn; #9/'67, #52/'68

BAEZ, Joan

| 12/3/66 | 6 | 12 | | 4 Noel .... | $12 | Vanguard 79230 |

#6/'66, #10/'67, #11/'71, #14/'72, #12/'73

BEACH BOYS, The

| 12/5/64 | 6 | 13 | ● | 5 Beach Boys' Christmas Album, The .... | $15 | Capitol 2164 |

#6/'64, #7/'65, #26/'66, #72/'67, #14/'68

BENNETT, Tony

| 12/14/68 | 10 | 3 | | 6 Snowfall/The Tony Bennett Christmas Album .... | $10 | Columbia 9739 |

BOSTON POPS ORCHESTRA/ARTHUR FIEDLER

| 12/19/70 | 9 | 2 | | 7 Christmas Festival, A ....[I] | $8 | Polydor 5004 |

BRADY BUNCH

| 12/25/71 | 6 | 1 | | 8 Merry Christmas from the Brady Bunch .... | $15 | Paramount 5026 |

BROWN, James

| 12/13/69 | 10 | 3 | | 9 Soulful Christmas, A .... | $25 | King 1040 |

CAMPBELL, Glen

| 12/7/68 | 1² | 10 | ● | 10 That Christmas Feeling .... | $10 | Capitol 2978 |

#1/'68, #4/'69, #23/'70, #14/'71

CASH, Johnny

| 12/13/69 | 7 | 5 | | 11 Christmas Spirit, The .... | $10 | Columbia 8917 |

#7/'69, #14/'70

CHIPMUNKS, The

| 12/7/63 | 9 | 13 | | 12 Christmas with the Chipmunks, Vol. 2 ....[N] | $15 | Liberty 7334 |

#9/'63, #18/'64, #18/'67, #31/'68

COLE, Nat King

Also see Bing Crosby.

| 11/30/63+ | 1² | 72 | ● | 13 Christmas Song, The............................ | $15 | Capitol 1967 |

#6/'63, #12/'64, #8/'65, #8/'66, #3/'67, #5/'68, #1/'69, #4/'70, #3/'71, #1/'72, #5/'73, #5/'83, #5/'85, #6/'87, #6/'88, #8/'89, #6/'90, #4/'91, #8/'92

COMO, Perry

| 12/5/70 | 5 | 5 | ● | 14 Perry Como Christmas Album, The .... | $10 | RCA 4016 |

#5/'70, #18/'73

CONNIFF, Ray

| 12/25/65+ | 10 | 8 | | 15 Here We Come A-Caroling .... | $10 | Columbia GP 3 |

#17/'65, #15/'66, #10/'70

CROSBY, Bing

| 12/12/64 | 9 | 3 | | 16 12 Songs of Christmas .... | $15 | Reprise 2022 |

BING CROSBY/FRANK SINATRA/FRED WARING

| 12/5/92 | 8 | 6 | | 17 It's Christmas Time .... | $7 | Laserlight 15152 |

BING CROSBY/FRANK SINATRA/NAT KING COLE

DOMINGO, Placido

| 12/15/84 | 9 | 1 | | 18 Christmas with Placido Domingo .... | $8 | CBS 37245 |

with the Vienna Symphony Orchestra

ELMO & PATSY

| 12/19/87 | 8 | 13 | | 19 Grandma Got Run Over By A Reindeer .... | $8 | Epic 39931 |

#8/'87, #12/'88, #24/'89, #28/'91

DEBUT DATE	PEAK POS	WKS CHR	GOLD	ARTIST — Album Title	$	Label & Number
				FELICIANO, Jose		
12/1/73	3	4		20 Jose Feliciano	$10	RCA 4421
				GARY, John		
12/5/64	3	17		21 John Gary Christmas Album, The..............	$12	RCA 2940
				#3/'64, #11/'65, #18/'66, #32/'67, #20/'68		
				GORME, Eydie, and The Trio Los Panchos		
12/3/66	9	4		22 Navidad means Christmas .... [F]	$12	Columbia 9357
				GOULET, Robert		
11/30/63	4	16		23 This Christmas I Spend With You	$8	Columbia 8876
				#4/'63, #5/'64, #17/'65, #90/'67, #30/'68		
				GRANT, Amy		
12/21/85+	5	22		24 Christmas Album, A...............................	$8	A&M 5057
				#9/'85, #12/'87, #13/'88, #25/'89, #5/'91, #16/'92		
				GUARALDI, Vince, Trio		
12/19/87+	9	26		25 Charlie Brown Christmas, A	$8	Fantasy 8431
				#13/'87, #9/'88, #9/'89, #9/'90, #18/'91, #16/'92		
				HAGGARD, Merle		
12/8/73	4	3		26 Merle Haggard's Christmas Present (Something Old, Something New)....................................	$10	Capitol 11230
				JACKSON, Mahalia		
12/13/69	2¹	3		27 Christmas with Mahalia	$10	Columbia 9727
				JACKSON 5		
12/5/70	1⁶	16		28 Christmas Album	$20	Motown 713
				#1/'70, #2/'71, #1/'72, #1/'73		
				JUDDS, The		
12/19/87	9	19		29 Christmas Time with The Judds	$8	RCA 6422
				#9/'87, #9/'88, #29/'89, #26/'90, #12/'91, #24/'92		
				KAEMPFERT, Bert, and his orchestra		
11/30/63	6	16		30 Christmas Wonderland .... [I]	$12	Decca 74441
				#6/'63, #34/'64, #38/'65, #21/'66, #62/'67, #38/'68		
				KING FAMILY, The		
12/18/65	8	2		31 Christmas With The King Family	$12	Warner 1627
				LEE, Brenda		
12/5/64+	7	18		32 Merry Christmas from Brenda Lee	$15	Decca 74583
				#15/'64, #17/'65, #20/'66, #58/'67, #33/'68, #7/'72		
				LEWIS, Ramsey, Trio		
12/19/64	8	15		33 More Sounds of Christmas .... [I]	$15	Argo 745
				#8/'64, #16/'65, #14/'66, #49/'67, #41/'68		
				MANDRELL, Barbara		
12/15/84	8	2		34 Christmas At Our House	$8	MCA 5519
				MANTOVANI And His Orchestra		
12/14/63	7	15		35 Christmas Greetings From Mantovani ...... [I]	$10	London 338
				#7/'63, #23/'65, #42/'66, #20/'67, #10/'68		
				MARTIN, Dean		
12/3/66	1¹	19	●	36 Dean Martin Christmas Album, The..........	$15	Reprise 6222
				#1/'66, #2/'67, #4/'68, #10/'69, #14/'70		
				MARTINO, Al		
12/5/64	8	11		37 Merry Christmas, A.................................	$12	Capitol 2165
				#8/'64, #19/'65, #59/'66, #23/'67		
				MATHIS, Johnny		
11/30/63	2²	20		38 Sounds Of Christmas	$12	Mercury 60837
				#2/'63, #7/'64, #13/'65, #45/'66, #18/'67, #11/'68		
12/6/69	1¹	20	●	39 Give Me Your Love For Christmas	$10	Columbia 9923
				#1/'69, #3/'70, #5/'71, #3/'72, #19/'73, #19/'87, #18/'88		
				MORMON TABERNACLE CHOIR, The		
12/21/63+	8	12	●	40 Joy Of Christmas	$10	Columbia 6499
				with Leonard Bernstein conducting the New York Philharmonic; #12/'63, #32/'64, #8/'65, #62/'66, #106/'67, #28/'68, #20/'70		
12/18/65+	5	8		41 Handel: Messiah	$10	Columbia 607 [2]
				with Eugene Ormandy conducting The Philadelphia Orchestra; Eileen Farrell (soprano)/William Warfield (baritone); #21/'65, #8/'70, #12/'71, #5/'72		
				NABORS, Jim		
12/2/67+	1¹	25	●	42 Jim Nabors' Christmas Album	$10	Columbia 9531
				#7/'67, #7/'68, #1/'69, #3/'70, #6/'71, #5/'72, #20/'73		

DEBUT DATE	PEAK POS	WKS CHR	GOLD	ARTIST — Album Title	$	Label & Number
				NEW CHRISTY MINSTRELS, The		
12/21/63	**5**	8		43 Merry Christmas!..........................	$12	Columbia 2096
				#5/'63, #17/'64, #53/'65, #65/'66, #116/'67		
				NEW EDITION		
12/21/85	**9**	2		44 Christmas All Over The World	$8	MCA 39040
				NEWTON, Wayne		
12/3/66	**10**	10		45 Songs For A Merry Christmas	$12	Capitol 2588
				#10/'66, #29/'67, #40/'68		
				PARTRIDGE FAMILY		
12/4/71	**1**⁴	7	●	46 Partridge Family Christmas Card, A	$20	Bell 6066
				#1/'71, #9/'72		
				PAVAROTTI, Luciano		
12/17/83+	**6**	20	●	47 O Holy Night...............................	$8	London 26473
				with Kurt Adler conducting the National Philharmonic; recorded in 1976; #7/'83, #6/'84, #21/'88, #19/'89, #20/'90, #14/'91, #22/'92		
				PRESLEY, Elvis		
11/30/63+	**2**⁹	53		48 Elvis' Christmas Album	$15	RCA 1951
				originally issued in 1957 on LOC-1035 (red cover) as a gatefold with a 10-page booklet of color photos (made Pop charts); reissued in 1958 on LPM-1951 (blue cover, without gatefold and photos - also made Pop charts); reissued in 1970 on Camden CAL-2428 (omitting 4 songs and adding 2 more); reissued in 1975 on Pickwick/Camden CAS-2428 (did not chart); original gatefold package reissued in 1985 on RCA 1-5486 (made Pop charts); #5/'63, #3/'64, #2/'65, #2/'66, #3/'67, #3/'68, #2/'69, #2/'70, #9/'72, #6/'85, #11/'87, #10/'88, #22/'89, #22/'90, #29/'92		
12/4/71+	**1**³	12	▲²	49 Elvis sings The Wonderful World of Christmas	$15	RCA 4579
				an all new Christmas LP (recorded May 1971); #2/'71, #1/'72, #1/'73		
				PRIDE, Charley		
12/12/70+	**5**	9		50 Christmas in My Home Town	$10	RCA 4406
				#8/'70, #5/'71, #8/'72, #15/'73		
				RAWLS, Lou		
12/2/67	**2**¹	11		51 Merry Christmas Ho! Ho! Ho!........................	$12	Capitol 2790
				#2/'67, #22/'68, #18/'69, #26/'70		
				REVERE, Paul, & The Raiders		
12/2/67	**10**	5		52 Christmas Present...And Past, A...........................	$30	Columbia 9555
				SHAW, Robert, Chorale and Orchestra		
12/7/68	**8**	6		53 Handel: Messiah	$10	RCA 6175 [3]
				Messiah was composed by George Frideric Handel from 8/22 to 9/14, 1741; #8/'68, #17/'69		
				SHELTON, Ricky Van		
12/23/89+	**16**	5		54 Ricky Van Shelton Sings Christmas	$8	Columbia 45269
				#16/'89, #33/'92		
				SHERMAN, Bobby		
12/5/70	**2**¹	5		55 Bobby Sherman Christmas Album	$10	Metromedia 1038
				#2/'70, #11/'71		
				SIMEONE, Harry, Chorale		
12/11/65+	**5**	11		56 O Bambino/The Little Drummer Boy	$12	Kapp 3450
				includes Simeone's new recording of "The Little Drummer Boy"; #16/'65, #5/'66, #9/'72, #7/'73		
				SINATRA, Frank — see CROSBY, Bing		
				SINATRA FAMILY		
12/6/69	**3**	4		57 Sinatra Family Wish You A Merry Christmas, The..........................	$12	Reprise 1026
				Frank and daughters Nancy & Tina, and son Frank, Jr.		
				SMITH, Jimmy		
12/5/64	**8**	4		58 Christmas '64 ....[I]	$15	Verve 8604
				SUPREMES, The		
12/11/65	**6**	12		59 Merry Christmas..........................	$25	Motown 638
				#6/'65, #13/'66, #19/'67, #26/'70		
				TEMPTATIONS, The		
12/5/70+	**4**	7		60 Temptations' Christmas Card, The	$20	Gordy 951
				#7/'70, #7/'71, #4/'72		
12/17/83	**6**	23		61 Give Love At Christmas	$8	Gordy 998
				#6/'83, #14/'87, #12/'88, #17/'89, #13/'90, #20/'92		
				VENTURES, The		
12/11/65	**9**	9		62 Ventures' Christmas Album, The..........................[I]	$20	Dolton 8038
				#9/'65, #32/'66, #32/'67, #15/'69		
				WARING, Fred — see CROSBY, Bing		

DEBUT DATE	PEAK POS	WKS CHR	GOLD	ARTIST — Album Title	$	Label & Number
				WILLIAMS, Andy		
11/30/63	1⁹	34 ● 63		Andy Williams Christmas Album, The	$12	Columbia 8887
				#1/63, #1/64, #1/65, #60/66, #6/67, #17/68, #30/69, #4/70, #4/71, #8/72, #6/73		
12/18/65+	1³	20 ● 64		Merry Christmas	$12	Columbia 9220
				#5/65, #1/66, #20/67, #4/68, #1/69, #19/70		

Adeste Fideles (Oh, Come, All Ye Faithful) (17) 45
Adoramus Te (15)
Aguinaldo No. 1 (Christmas Gift) (22)
Alegre Navidad (Merry Christmas) (22)
All I Want For Christmas (Is My Girl) (44)
(All I Want For Christmas Is) My Two Front Teeth (12)
Amen (55)
Angel And The Little Blue Bell (32)
Angels From The Realm Of Glory (3)
Angels We Have Heard On High (4,24)
Animal Carol (40)
Auld Lang Syne (5,31)
Away In A Manger (3,4,8,13,15,29,40,63)
Bach/Gounod: Ave Maria (23,47)
Bach: Shepherds' Pastorale (7)
Ballad Of The Harp Weaver (11)
Beautiful City (43)
Beautiful Star Of Bethlehem (29)
Believers Shall Enjoy (Non Believers Shall Suffer) (9)
Bell That Couldn't Jingle (2)
Bells Of Christmas (3)
Bells Of St. Mary's (64)
Berlioz: Sanctus (47)
Bizet: Agnus Dei (47)
Blanca Navidad ..see: White Christmas
Blue Christmas (5,10,11,32,36,46,48,55,62)
Bobby Wants A Puppy Dog For Christmas (26)
Born Of Mary (59)
Born To Die (34)
Bring A Torch, Jeannette, Isabella (medley) (4)
Brotherly Love (52)
Calypso Noel (39)
Cancion Para Meditar (Song For Meditation) (22)
Cantique De Noel ..see: O Holy Night
Carol Of The Bells (38,40,56)
Carol Of The Birds (13,14,17,31)
Caroling, Caroling (13,14,17,31)
Cherry Tree Carol (20)
Child With A Toy (5,11)
Children's Christmas Dream (30)
Children's Christmas Song (59)
Christ Is Born (14)
Christmas (19)
Christmas And Love (50)
Christmas As I Knew It (11)
Christmas At Our House (34)
Christmas Bells (35)
Christmas Candles (16)
Christmas Day (5,10,39)
Christmas Eve (14)
Christmas Eve In My Home Town (42)
Christmas Everyday (61)
Christmas Holiday (64)
Christmas Hymn (24)
Christmas In My Home Town (50)
Christmas In Washington Square (45)
Christmas Is (51)
Christmas Is A Birthday (56)
Christmas Is A Feeling In Your Heart (38)
Christmas Is Coming (9,25)
Christmas Is For Children (10)

Christmas Is (Make It Sweet) (55)
Christmas Journey (45)
Christmas On Her Mind (55)
Christmas Song (Chestnuts Roasting On An Open Fire) (1,2,6,10,13,17,20,21,23,24, 25,28,45,46,51,58,60,61,63)
Christmas Spirit (11)
Christmas Spirit (52)
Christmas Story (34)
Christmas Time Is Here (25)
Christmas Tree (56)
Christmas Trees (43)
Christmas Waltz (17,57)
Christmas Will Be Just Another Lonely Day (32)
Christmas Will Really Be The Same This Year (28)
Christmas Wish (55)
Christmas Wishes (43)
Christmas Won't Be The Same This Year (28)
Christmas Wonderland (30)
Christmas World (43)
Christmasland (6)
Come Dear Children (31)
Coventry Carol (medley) (4)
Cradle In Bethlehem (13)
Daddy Won't Be Home Again For Christmas (26)
Dear Mr. Claus (52)
December Time (23)
Deck The Halls (3,4,7,12,13,35,40,50)
Do You Hear What I Hear? (14,16,21,27,39,42,64)
Down In Yon Forest (4)
Egg Nog (33)
Emmanuel (24)
Everything For Christmas (61)
Eyes Of A Child (1)
Felices Pascuas (A Happy Christmas) (22)
Feliz Navidad (20)
First Christmas Carol (56)
First Christmas Morn (50)
First Noel (1,7,8,13,14,17,18,20,21, 27,31,49,63)
For Elise (25)
Franck: Panis Angelicus (23,47)
From Our House To Yours (34)
Frosty The Snowman (5,8,28,32,46,62)
Gifts They Gave (11)
Give Love On Christmas Day (28,44,61)
Give Me Your Love For Christmas (39)
Gloria A Dios En Las Alturas (Glory To God In The Highest) (22)
Go Tell It On The Mountain (15,16,31,42,43)
God Rest Ye Merry, Gentlemen (3,7,15,18,38,40,58)
Goin' Home (Sing A Song Of Christmas Cheer) (55)
Good King Wenceslas (medley) (4,7,18)
Good Time Christmas (51)
Gracias A Dios (Thank God) (22)
Grandma Got Run Over By A Reindeer (39)
Grandma's Christmas Card (26)
Greensleeves (3,12,57)
Handel: Hallelujah Chorus (7,38,56)
Handel: Messiah (41,53)
Hang Up Your Stockin' (12)
Happy Birthday To You, Our Lord (27)

Happy Christmas Day (50)
Happy Holiday (63)
Happy Holidays To You (44)
Hark! The Herald Angels Sing (7,13,14,17,20,21,24,25,31)
Have Reindeer, Will Travel (38)
Have Yourself A Merry Little Christmas (6,10,12,14,17, 21,23,28,38,39,45,46,51, 64)
Hear The Sledges With The Bells (31)
Heavy Christmas Message (52)
Heirlooms (24)
Here Comes Santa Claus (Down Santa Claus Lane) (48)
Here Was A Man (11)
Here We Come A-Caroling (12,15)
Here's To The Lonely (19)
Holiday For Bells (30)
Holiday Of Love (31)
Holiday Season (63)
Holly And The Ivy (35)
Holly Leaves And Christmas Trees (49)
I Heard The Bells On Christmas Day (11,16,18,30)
I Love The Winter Weather (medley) (6)
I Saw Mommy Kissing Santa Claus (28)
I Saw Three Ships (13,35)
I Wonder As I Wander (medley) (4)
I Wouldn't Trade Christmas (57)
I'll Be Home For Christmas (5,10,17,18,21,34,36,37,42, 48)
I'll Be Home On Christmas Day (49)
I've Got My Love To Keep Me Warm (medley) (6)
If Every Day Was Like Christmas (48)
If I Get Home On Christmas Day (49)
If We Make It Through December (26) 28
In A Humble Place (42)
In The Middle (9)
Irish Carol (3)
It Came Upon The Midnight Clear (3,15,20,27,31,35)
It Must Be Getting Close To Christmas (10)
It Must Have Been The Mistletoe (Our First Christmas) (34)
It Won't Seem Like Christmas (Without You) (49)
It'll Be A Merry Christmas (43)
It's Christmas (All Over The World) (44)
It's Christmas Time Again (16)
It's Christmas Time This Year (18)
It's Such A Lonely Time Of Year (57)
It's The Most Wonderful Time Of The Year (63)
Jesu, Joy Of Man's Desiring (4)
Jingle Bell Rock (2,12,19,32,39,45,55,62)
Jingle Bells (3,7,8,17,19, 20, 26,31,33,35,36,42,46, 52,58,62,63)
Jingo Jango (30)
Jolly Old Saint Nicholas (12,31)
Joseph Dearest, Joseph Mine (40)

Joy Of Christmas (44)
Joy To The World (3,7,13, 15,17,18,19,31,40,59)
Jumpin' Jiminy Christmas (30)
Kids (57)
La Virgen Lava Panales (18,40)
Lamb Of God (3)
Las Mananitas (2)
Let It Snow, Let It Snow, Let It Snow (2,23,36,38,45,60,64)
Let's Unite The Whole World At Christmas (19)
Linus And Lucy (25)
Little Altar Boy (10,64)
Little Boy Dear (51)
Little Bright Star (59)
Little Drummer Boy (1,4,8, 11,14,16,20,28,30,31,33, 37,38,39,45,50,51,56,59, 60,61,63)
Little Saint Nick (5)
Little Snow Girl (21)
Little Town (24)
Lo, How A Rose E'er Blooming (27)
Lord's Prayer (39)
Love Comes With Christmas (61)
Love Has Come (24)
Love Is All (1)
Love's What You're Gettin' For Christmas (55)
Lullay My Liking (40)
Macy's Window (52)
Mama Liked The Roses (48) *flip*
Man With All The Toys (5)
Marshmallow World (32,36,38)
Mary's Boy Child (18,20,35,56,64)
Mary's Wandering (medley) (4)
Melchor, Gaspar Y Baltazar (The Three Kings) (22)
Mercadante: Qual Ciglio Candido (Quinta Parola) (47)
Merry Christmas, Baby (5)
Merry Christmas Baby (49,51)
Mighty Fortress (24)
Mozart: Sleighride (7)
My Christmas Card To You (46)
My Christmas Tree (59,60)
My Favorite Things (2,6,39,59,64)
My Little Drum (25)
Navidad Y Ano Nuevo (Christmas And The New Year) (22)
No Room In The Inn (22)
Noche De Paz ..see: Silent Night
O Bambino (One Cold And Blessed Winter) (56,57)
O Christmas Tree ..see: O Tannenbaum
O Come All Ye Faithful (1,4,6,7,8,13,21,23,31,37, 40,42,47,49)
O Come, O Come, Emmanuel (4)
O Holy Night (4,8,13,14,17,18,21,23,27, 29,37,42,47,50,63)
O Joyful Children (18)
O Little Town Of Bethlehem (3,13,15,17,18,21,31,40,48)
O Tannenbaum (12,13,15,17, 25)
O Thou That Tellest Good Tidings (35)

Old-Fashioned Christmas (16)
Old Toy Trains (10)
On A Snowy Christmas Night (49)
Once In Royal David's City (35,40)
One Night A Year (34)
One Star (43)
Parson Brown (Our Christmas Dinner) (43)
Patapan (40)
Peace (52)
Percy, The Puny Poinsettia (19)
Plum Puddin' (33)
Preiset Dem Konig! (Praise The King) (24)
Pretty Paper (10)
Rain, Sleet, Snow (52)
Real Meaning Of Christmas (15)
Ringing The Bells For Jim (11)
Rockin' Around The Christmas Tree (32) 14
Rockin' Around The Christmas Tree (46)
Rudolph The Red-Nosed Reindeer (7,8,19,28,33,37, 38,45,59,60,62)
Santa And The Kids (50)
Santa Bring My Baby Back (To Me) (48)
Santa, Bring My Baby Home (34)
Santa Claus And Popcorn (26)
Santa Claus Gave Me A Brand New Start (9)
Santa Claus Go Straight To The Ghetto (9)
Santa Claus Is Back In Town (48)
Santa Claus Is Comin' To Town (5,6,7,8,17,28,29, 30,32,39,46,51,55,57,58, 59,60,62)
Santa Claus, Santa Claus (9)
Santa's Beard (5)
Santa's Reindeer (46)
Say It Loud - I'm Black And I'm Proud (9) 10
Schubert/Melichar: Mille Cherubini In Coro (47)
Schubert: Ave Maria (4,14,47)
Scrooge (62)
Secret Of Christmas (16,38)
Senor Santa Claus (19)
Shepherd Boy (43)
Silent Night (17) 54
Silent Night (1,4,6,7,8,11, 13,14,15,18,19,20,21,22, 26,29,31,36,37,40,42,45, 48,50,58,60,61,63)
Silver Bells (17) 78
Silver Bells (8,14,23,26,27,29,32,36, 37,45,49,59,60,62,64)
Sing Along With Santa (43)
Sing Hosanna, Hallelujah (43)
Sing Of A Merry Christmas (56)
Singing Merry Christmas (44)
Skating (25)
Sleigh Ride (1,2,7,24,30,42,46,62,64)
Snow Flakes ..see: What Child Is This
Snowbound (33)
Snowfall (6,33)
Some Children See Him (31,57,64)
Someday At Christmas (28,60)

Song And A Christmas Tree ..see: Twelve Days Of Christmas
Song Of Joy (55)
Soulful Christmas (9)
Sounds Of Christmas (38)
Star Carol (31)
Stradella: Pieta Signore (47)
Strawberry Snow (32)
Sunny Bank (3)
Sweet Little Jesus Boy (21,63)
Tchaikovsky: Waltz Of The Flowers (7)
Tell Me (43)
Tennessee Christmas (24)
There Is No Christmas Like A Home Christmas (14)
There's No Place Like Home (10)
They Stood In Silent Prayer (50)
Things We Did Last Summer (36)
This Christmas (61)
This Christmas I Spend With You (23)
This Time Of The Year (32,34)
Three Wise Men, Wise Men Three (42)
Tit For Tat (Ain't No Taking Back) (9) 86
Toy Parade (30)
Toy Waltz (35)
Toyland (14)
'Twas The Night Before Christmas (12,56)
Twelfth Night Song (40)
Twelve Days Of Christmas (12,16,33,35,40,57,63)
Twinkle Twinkle Little Me (59)
Up On The Housetop (28)
Valley Forge (62)
We Are The Shepherds (11)
We Three Kings Of Orient Are (5,20,33,58)
We Wish You A Merry Christmas (6,8,31,37,62)
We Wish You The Merriest (16)
Wear A Smile At Christmas (52)
Wexford Carol (3)
What Are You Doing New Year's Eve (39,51)
What Child Is This (4,15,25,27,29,31,37,56,62)
Whatever Happened To Christmas (57)
When Angels Sang Of Peace (16)
Where Is Love (medley) (6)
While Shepherds Watched (35)
White Christmas (17) 7
White Christmas (1,5,6,7, 16,17,18,20,21,22,23,26, 27,30,31,33,36,37,42,45, 46,48,58,59,60,62,63)
Who Is This Babe (29)
Who Kept The Sheep (11)
Winter Wonderland (1,2,6,21,23,26,29,30,32, 34,36,45,46,49,64)
Wintertime And Christmas Time (21)
Wonderful Day (12)
Wonderful World Of Christmas (49)
Yesterday's Christmas (55)
Yon: Gesu Bambino (47)
You Know It (9)
You're All I Want For Christmas (37)

DEBUT DATE	PEAK POS	WKS CHR	GOLD	ARTIST — Album Title	$	Label & Number

Billboard's Christmas Charts — Various

12/9/72 · 7 · 12 · 1 Christmas Album, The .... **$12** Columbia 30763 [2]
#7/72, #10/73, #19/91, #28/92

Christmas Bells [Patti Page]	Have Yourself A Merry Little Christmas [Robert Goulet]	**Little Drummer Boy** [Johnny Cash] **63**	We Wish You A Merry Christmas [Andre Kostelanetz]
Christmas Song (Chestnuts Roasting On An Open Fire) [Tony Bennett]	It Came Upon The Midnight Clear [Burl Ives]	O Come, All Ye Faithful [Jim Nabors]	White Christmas [Frank Sinatra]
Deck The Hall With Boughs Of Holly [Mormon Tabernacle Choir/N.Y. Philharmonic]	It's The Most Wonderful Time Of The Year [Andy Williams]	O Little Town Of Bethlehem [Marty Robbins]	Winter Wonderland [Mitch Miller & The Gang]
First Noel [Anita Bryant]	Jingle Bells? [Barbra Streisand]	Silent Night, Holy Night [Mahalia Jackson]	
Greensleeves (What Child Is This) [Ray Conniff Singers]	Joy To The World [Percy Faith]	Silver Bells [Jerry Vale]	
	Let It Snow! Let It Snow! Let It Snow! [Doris Day]	Sleigh Ride [Johnny Mathis with Percy Faith]	

12/1/73 · 7 · 4 · 2 Christmas Greetings from Nashville .... **$10** RCA 0262

Blue Christmas [Browns] **97**	Christmas Time's A-Coming [Skeeter Davis]	I Heard The Bells On Christmas Day [Chet Atkins]	Old Christmas Card [Jim Reeves]
Christmas Song (Chestnuts Roasting On An Open Fire) [Danny Davis]	Frosty The Snowman [Porter Wagoner]	Jingle Bell Rock [Floyd Cramer]	Silent Night [Eddy Arnold]
		Little Stranger (In A Manger) [Hank Snow]	You Are My Christmas, Carol [Dottie West]

12/7/91 · 8 · 9 · 3 50 All-Time Christmas Favorites .... **$6** Madacy 10 [2]
all songs performed by studio vocalists and musicians; #8/91, #16/92

Adeste Fideles	Ding Dong Merrily On High	It Came Upon A Midnight Clear	Silver Bells
Amen	First Noel	Jingle Bells	Twelve Days Of Christmas
Angels From The Realms	For To Us A Child Is Born	Jolly Old St. Nicholas	Up On The Housetop
Angels We Have Heard On High	From Heaven On High I Come	Joy To The World	We Three Kings Of Orient Are
As With Gladness Men Of Old	Gloria In Excelsis Deo	Lo How A Rose	We Wish You A Merry Christmas
Auld Lang Syne	Go Tell It On The Mountain	O Christmas Tree	What Child Is This?
Ave Maria	God Rest Ye Merry Gentlemen	O Come All Ye Faithful	While Shepherd's Watched Their Flocks By Night
Away In A Manger	Good Christian Men Rejoice	O Holy Night	White Christmas
Christians Awake	Good King Wenceslas	O Little Town Of Bethlehem	
Christmas Song	Hallelujah	O Tannenbaum	
Coventry Carol	Hark The Herald Angels Sing	Oh Thou Joyful Day	
Dance Of The Reed Flutes	Holly And The Ivy	Once In Royal David's City	
Dance Of The Sugar Plum Fairy	I Wonder As I Wander	Patapan	
Deck The Halls	Infant King	Silent Night, Holy Night	

12/8/73 · 1¹ · 4 · 4 Motown Christmas, A .... **$10** Motown 795 [2]
#1/73, #26/87

Ave Maria [Stevie Wonder]	God Rest Ye Merry Gentlemen [Smokey Robinson & The Miracles]	Little Christmas Tree [Michael Jackson]	Silver Bells [Diana Ross & The Supremes]
Bring A Torch, Jeannette, Isabella (medley) [Smokey Robinson & The Miracles]	Have Yourself A Merry Little Christmas [Jackson 5]	Little Drummer Boy [Temptations]	Someday At Christmas [Stevie Wonder]
Children's Christmas Song [Diana Ross & The Supremes]	I Saw Mommy Kissing Santa Claus [Jackson 5]	My Christmas Tree [Temptations]	What Christmas Means To Me [Stevie Wonder]
Christmas Song (Merry Christmas To You) [Jackson 5]	It's Christmas Time [Smokey Robinson & The Miracles]	My Favorite Things [Diana Ross & The Supremes]	White Christmas [Diana Ross & The Supremes]
Deck The Halls (medley) [Smokey Robinson & The Miracles]	Jingle Bells [Smokey Robinson & The Miracles]	One Little Christmas Tree [Stevie Wonder]	
Frosty The Snowman [Jackson 5]	Joy To The World [Diana Ross & The Supremes]	Rudolph, The Red-Nosed Reindeer [Temptations]	
Give Love On Christmas Day [Jackson 5]		Santa Claus Is Comin' To Town [Jackson 5]	
		Silent Night [Temptations]	

12/5/70 · 7 · 4 · 5 Peace On Earth .... **$10** Capitol 585 [2]

Adeste Fidelis [Tennessee Ernie Ford]	God Rest Ye Merry, Gentlemen [Eddie Dunstedter]	Little Drummer Boy [Wayne Newton]	Star Carol [Fred Waring & The Pennsylvanians]
Angels We Have Heard On High [Roger Wagner Chorale]	Hark! The Herald Angels Sing [Frank Sinatra]	O Come All Ye Faithful [Al Martino]	Susa-Ninna [Sandler & Young]
Ave Maria [Hollywood Pops Orchestra]	It Came Upon The Midnight Clear [Guy Lombardo & The Royal Canadians]	O Holy Night (Cantique De Noel) [Tennessee Ernie Ford]	We Three Kings Of Orient Are [Beach Boys]
Deck The Hall [Douglas Leedy]	Joy To The World [Eddie Dunstedter]	O Little Town Of Bethlehem [Nat King Cole]	
Do You Hear What I Hear? [Sonny James]	Little Altar Boy [Glen Campbell]	Silent Night [Lettermen]	
First Noel [Ella Fitzgerald]		Sleep, My Little Jesus [Ella Fitzgerald]	

12/23/72 · 6 · 5 · 6 Phil Spector's Christmas Album .... **$12** Apple 3400
reissue of *A Christmas Gift For You* (Philles/1963); #6/72, #8/73, #25/87

Bells Of St. Mary's [Bob B. Soxx & The Blue Jeans]	Here Comes Santa Claus [Bob B. Soxx & The Blue Jeans]	Parade Of The Wooden Soldiers [Crystals]	Silent Night [Phil Spector]
Christmas (Baby Please Come Home) [Darlene Love]	I Saw Mommy Kissing Santa Claus [Ronettes]	Rudolph The Red-Nosed Reindeer [Crystals]	Sleigh Ride [Ronettes]
Frosty The Snowman [Ronettes]	Marshmallow World [Darlene Love]	Santa Claus Is Coming To Town [Crystals]	White Christmas [Darlene Love]
			Winter Wonderland [Darlene Love]

12/21/68+ · 8 · 8 · 7 Soul Christmas .... **$15** Atco 269
#13/68, #8/69, #8/70

Back Door Santa [Clarence Carter]	Gee Whiz, It's Christmas [Carla Thomas]	Merry Christmas Baby [Otis Redding]	What Are You Doing New Year's Eve [King Curtis]
Christmas Song [King Curtis]	I'll Make Every Day Christmas (For My Woman) [Joe Tex]	Presents For Christmas [Solomon Burke]	White Christmas [Otis Redding]
Every Day Will Be Like A Holiday [William Bell]	Jingle Bells [Booker T. & The MG's]	Silver Bells [Booker T. & The MG's]	

DEBUT DATE	PEAK POS	WKS CHR	G O L D	ARTIST — Album Title	$	Label & Number

Refer to the following names in the Artist Section for the Christmas albums that made the regular Top Pop Albums chart:

ALABAMA
AMES BROTHERS
ANDERSON, Jon
BELAFONTE, Harry
BOONE, Pat
BROOKS, Garth
CARPENTERS (2)
CHIEFTAINS
CHIPMUNKS (2)
COMO, Perry (2)
CONNIFF, Ray (2)
CROSBY, Bing (3)
DENVER, John (2)
DeVOL, Frank
DIAMOND, Neil
FORD, Tennessee Ernie
GLEASON, Jackie
GRANT, Amy
HARRIS, Emmylou
HUMPERDINCK, Engelbert
JACKSON, Mahalia
KINGSTON TRIO
LANZA, Mario
LENNON SISTERS
LEWIS, Ramsey
LIEBERT, Ottmar

LUBOFF, Norman, Choir
MANHATTAN TRANSFER
MANILOW, Barry
MANNHEIM STEAMROLLER (2)
MANTOVANI
MATHIS, Johnny
MECO
MELACHRINO, George
MILLER, Mitch (2)
MONTANA ORCHESTSRA
MORMON TABERNACLE CHOIR
MURRAY, Anne
NELSON, Willie
NEW KIDS ON THE BLOCK
OAK RIDGE BOYS
O'NEAL, Alexander
OSMONDS
PARTON, Dolly
PHILADELPHIA ORCHESTRA
PRESLEY, Elvis
PRICE, Leontyne
RHEIMS, Robert (2)
ROGERS, Kenny (3)
ROYAL GUARDSMEN
SALSOUL ORCHESTRA (2)
SCHNEIDER, John

SEVERINSEN, Doc
SHAW, Robert, Chorale
SIMEONE, Harry, Chorale
SINATRA, Frank
SOUNDS OF BLACKNESS
STATLER BROTHERS
STREISAND, Barbra
TAKE 6
TESH, John
TORME, Mel
TRAVIS, Randy
TRITT, Travis
VAUGHN, Billy
VEE, Bobby
WARING, Fred
WELK, Lawrence (3)
WHITMAN, Slim
WILLIAMS, Roger
WINSTON, George

SOUNDTRACKS:
    Home Alone 2 - Lost In New York
    Scrooge

CHILDREN'S:
    Muppet Christmas Carol

RELIGIOUS:

Refer to the Artist Section for complete chart data on the following religious-oriented albums:

BELAFONTE, Harry — My Lord What A Mornin'
BENTON, Brook — If You Believe
BERNSTEIN, Leonard — Mass
BOONE, Pat — A Closer Walk With Thee/Hymns We Love
BOSTON SYMPHONY ORCHESTRA — Mozart: Requiem Mass
CAMPBELL, Glen — Oh Happy Day
CASH, Johnny — The Holy Land
COMO, Perry — When You Come To The End Of The Day
ELECTRIC PRUNES — Mass In F Minor
FITZGERALD, Ella — Brighten The Corner
FORD, Tennessee Ernie — 7 albums
FRANCIS, Connie — In The Summer Of His Years
FRANKLIN, Aretha — Amazing Grace/One Lord, One Faith, One Baptism
GIOVANNI, Nikki — Truth Is On Its Way
HAWKINS, Edwin — 3 albums
HOUSTON, David — David
JORDAN, Jerry — Phone Call From God
LANZA, Mario — I'll Walk With God
LIMELITERS — Makin' A Joyful Noise
LINKLETTER, Art — For Children Of The World, Art Linkletter narrates "The Bible...In The Beginning"
MANTOVANI — Songs Of Praise
MATHIS, Johnny — Good Night Dear Lord
MORMON TABERNACLE CHOIR — The Lord's Prayer (Vols. 1 & 2)
NABORS, Jim — The Lord's Prayer/How Great Thou Art
NELSON, Willie — The Troublemaker
OWENS, Buck — Your Mother's Prayer
POPE JOHN XXIII — Pope John XXIII
POPE JOHN PAUL II — Pope John Paul II Sings At The Festival Of Sacrosong
PRESLEY, Elvis — Peace In The Valley/His Hand in Mine/How Great Thou Art/
      You'll Never Walk Alone/He Touched Me/He Walks Beside Me
PRIDE, Charley — Did You Think To Pray
RANDOLPH, Boots — Sunday Sax
RICH, Charlie — Silver Linings
SHAW, Robert — Deep River and Other Spirituals
SINGING NUN — The Singing Nun/Her Joy, Her Songs
SMITH, Kate — How Great Thou Art
STEVENS, Ray — Turn Your Radio On
WYNETTE, Tammy — Inspiration
VARIOUS - ROCK OPERAS — Truth Of Truths

TRIBUTES:

The indented artists perform music originally written and/or performed by the artist shown in capital letters:

ABBA — Erasure
PAUL ANKA — Annette
JOHANN SEBASTIAN BACH — Swingle Singers
BURT BACHARACH/HAL DAVID:
    Ames, Ed
    Kerr, Anita
    Mathis, Johnny
    Scott, Christopher
    Renaissance
BEATLES:
    Atkins, Chet
    Benson, George (Abbey Road)
    Booker T. & The MG's (Abbey Road)
    Brothers Four
    Chipmunks
    Faith, Percy
    Hollyridge Strings (2)
    Martin, George
    Rifkin, Joshua
    Soundtrack "All This & World War II"
BEACH BOYS — Hollyridge Strings
IRVING BERLIN:
    Light, Enoch
    Lombardo, Guy
    Mantovani
CHUCK BERRY — Black, Bill
CARUSO — Lanza, Mario
RAY CHARLES — Darin, Bobby
LEONARD COHEN — Warnes, Jennifer
NAT KING COLE:
    Cole, Natalie
    Hollyridge Strings
    Vale, Jerry
SAM COOKE — Supremes
CREAM — Rubber Band
TOMMY DORSEY — Sinatra, Frank
BOB DYLAN — Baez, Joan
DUKE ELLINGTON — Previn, Andre
STEPHEN FOSTER — Mantovani
RUDOLF FRIML — Mantovani
LEFTY FRIZZELL — Nelson, Willie
GERSHWINS:
    Fitzgerald, Ella
    Grusin, Dave
    Vaughan, Sarah
W.C. HANDY:
    Cole, Nat King
    101 Strings

JIMI HENDRIX — Rubber Band
VICTOR HERBERT:
    Sills, Beverly
    Kostelanetz, Andre
HOLLAND-DOZIER-HOLLAND — Supremes
JETHRO TULL — London Symphony Orchestra
BERT KAEMPFERT:
    Hirt, Al
    Mathis, Johnny
KRIS KRISTOFFERSON — Nelson, Willie
MAMAS & THE PAPAS — Classics IV
ROD McKUEN:
    Sinatra, Frank
    Yarbrough, Glenn
GLENN MILLER — Boston Pops Orchestra
CHARLIE MINGUS — Mitchell, Joni
MONKEES — Golden Gate Strings
HELEN MORGAN — Bergen, Polly
WOLFGANG AMADEUS MOZART:
    Marriner, Neville
    Swingle Singers
CHARLIE PARKER — Supersax (2)
COLE PORTER:
    Fitzgerald, Ella
    Short, Bobby
    Warwick, Dionne
ELVIS PRESLEY:
    Haggard, Merle
    Hollywood Strings
JIM REEVES — Milsap, Ronnie
SMOKEY ROBINSON — Temptations
JIMMIE RODGERS — Haggard, Merle
RICHARD RODGERS & LORENZ HART:
    Fitzgerald, Ella
    Supremes
ROY ROGERS — Rogers, Roy
PAUL SIMON — Boston Pops Orchestra
FRANK SINATRA — Bennett, Tony
STARS OF THE LONDON PALLADIUM — Davis, Sammy, Jr.
RICHARD STRAUSS — Mantovani
FATS WALLER — Armstrong, Louis
DIONNE WARWICK — Dells
JIMMY WEBB — Campbell, Glen
HANK WILLIAMS:
    Cramer, Floyd
    Rich, Charlie
BOB WILLS — Haggard, Merle

TOP 100 ALBUMS

This section depicts, in rank order, the biggest No. 1 albums from 1955 through 1992.

This ranking is based on the most weeks an album held the No. 1 position. Ties are broken according to this order: total weeks in the Top 10, total weeks in the Top 40, and finally, total weeks charted.

> **The total weeks at No. 1 is shown below each album cover photo, along with the year the album peaked.**

(Whitney Houston's album *The Bodyguard* was holding at the #1 position (12 weeks total) as of the February 27, 1993 cutoff date.)

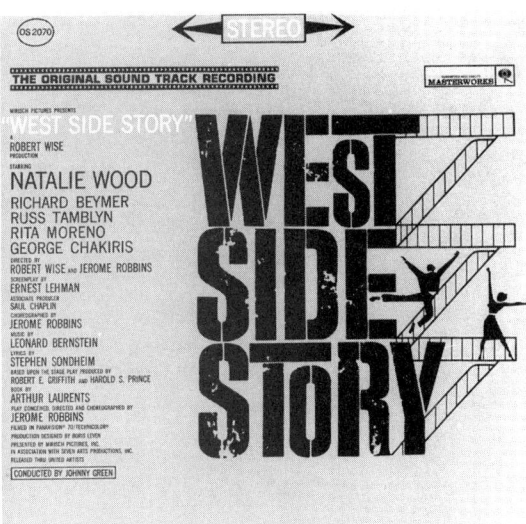

1. West Side Story...*Soundtrack*
54 / 1962

2. Thriller...*Michael Jackson*
37 / 1983

3. South Pacific...*Soundtrack*
31 / 1958

4. Calypso...*Harry Belafonte*
31 / 1956

5. Rumours...*Fleetwood Mac*
31 / 1977

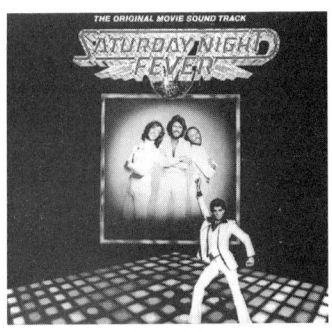

6. Saturday Night Fever...
Bee Gees / Soundtrack
24 / 1978

7. Purple Rain...*Prince And The
Revolution / Soundtrack*
24 / 1984

**8. Please Hammer Don't Hurt
'Em**...*M.C. Hammer*
21 / 1990

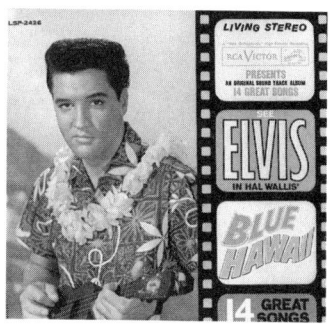

9. Blue Hawaii...
Elvis Presley/Soundtrack
20 / 1961

10. Ropin' The Wind...
Garth Brooks
18 / 1991

11. Dirty Dancing... Soundtrack
18 / 1987

12. More Of The Monkees...
The Monkees
18 / 1967

13. Synchronicity... The Police
17 / 1983

14. Some Gave All...
Billy Ray Cyrus
17 / 1992

15. Love Me Or Leave Me...
Doris Day/Soundtrack
17 / 1955

16. The Sound Of Music...
Original Cast
16 / 1960

17. To The Extreme... Vanilla Ice
16 / 1990

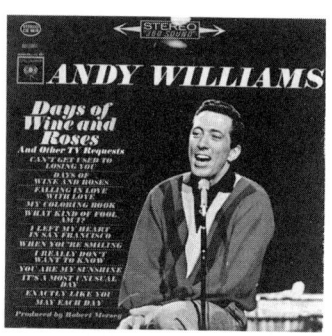

18. Days of Wine and Roses...
Andy Williams
16 / 1963

19. My Fair Lady... Original Cast
15 / 1956

20. Tapestry... Carole King
15 / 1971

21. Sgt. Pepper's Lonely Hearts Club Band...*The Beatles*
15 / 1967

22. Business As Usual...
Men At Work
15 / 1982

23. The Kingston Trio At Large...
The Kingston Trio
15 / 1959

24. Hi Infidelity...
REO Speedwagon
15 / 1981

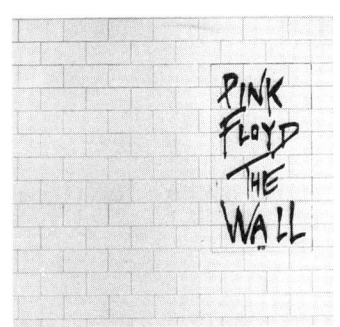

25. The Wall...*Pink Floyd*
15 / 1980

26. Mary Poppins...*Soundtrack*
14 / 1965

27. Whitney Houston...
Whitney Houston
14 / 1986

28. The Button-Down Mind Of Bob Newhart...*Bob Newhart*
14 / 1960

29. Exodus...*Soundtrack*
14 / 1961

30. Songs In The Key Of Life...
Stevie Wonder
14 / 1976

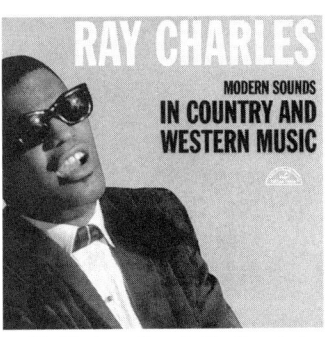

31. Modern Sounds In Country And Western Music...*Ray Charles*
14 / 1962

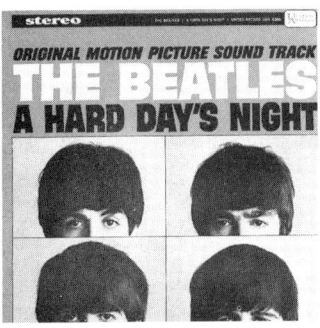

32. A Hard Day's Night...
The Beatles/Soundtrack
14 / 1964

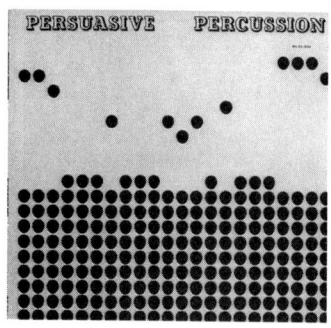

33. Persuasive Percussion...*Enoch Light/Terry Snyder and The All-Stars*
13 / 1960

34. Judy At Carnegie Hall...
Judy Garland
13 / 1961

35. The Monkees...*The Monkees*
13 / 1966

36. Hair...*Original Cast*
13 / 1969

37. The Music Man...
Original Cast
12 / 1958

38. Faith...*George Michael*
12 / 1988

39. Breakfast At Tiffany's...
Henry Mancini/Soundtrack
12 / 1962

40. Sold Out...*The Kingston Trio*
12 / 1960

41. Grease...*Soundtrack*
12 / 1978

42. The First Family...
Vaughn Meader
12 / 1962

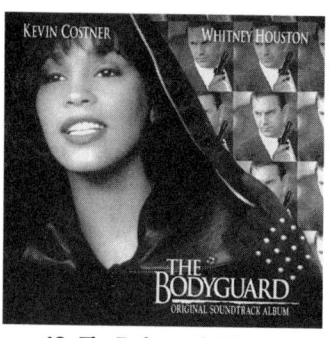

43. The Bodyguard...*Whitney Houston/Soundtrack*
12↑ / 1992

44. Mariah Carey...*Mariah Carey*
11 / 1991

45. Calcutta!...*Lawrence Welk*
11 / 1961

46. Whitney...*Whitney Houston*
11 / 1987

47. Abbey Road...*The Beatles*
11 / 1969

48. Meet The Beatles!...
The Beatles
11 / 1964

49. Miami Vice...*TV Soundtrack*
11 / 1985

50. Forever Your Girl...
Paula Abdul
10 / 1989

**51. Around The World In 80
Days**...*Soundtrack*
10 / 1957

52. Gigi...*Soundtrack*
10 / 1958

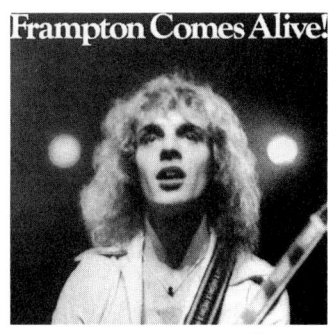

53. Frampton Comes Alive!...
Peter Frampton
10 / 1976

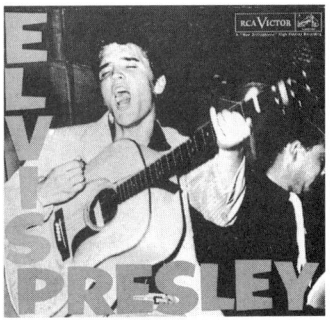

54. Elvis Presley...*Elvis Presley*
10 / 1956

55. The Music From Peter Gunn...
Henry Mancini
10 / 1959

56. 4...*Foreigner*
10 / 1981

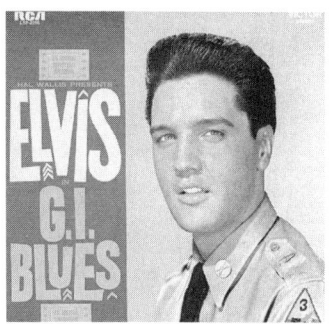

57. G.I. Blues...
Elvis Presley/Soundtrack
10 / 1960

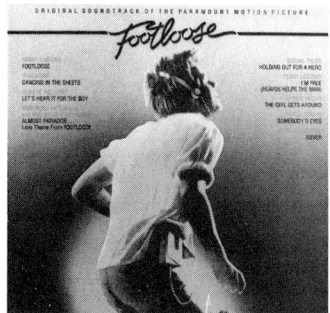

58. Footloose...*Soundtrack*
10 / 1984

59. String Along...
The Kingston Trio
10 / 1960

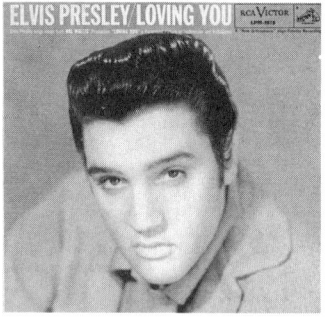

60. Loving You...
Elvis Presley/Soundtrack
10 / 1957

61. The Singing Nun...
The Singing Nun
10 / 1963

62. Bridge Over Troubled Water...
Simon and Garfunkel
10 / 1970

63. Elton John - Greatest Hits...
Elton John
10 / 1974

64. Brothers In Arms...
Dire Straits
9 / 1985

65. The Joshua Tree...*U2*
9 / 1987

66. What Now My Love...
Herb Alpert & The Tijuana Brass
9 / 1966

67. Asia...*Asia*
9 / 1982

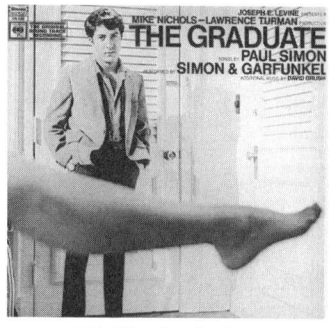

68. The Graduate...
Simon & Garfunkel/Soundtrack
9 / 1968

69. American Fool...*John Cougar*
9 / 1982

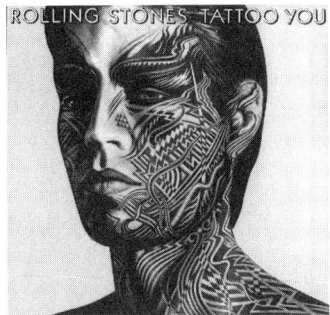

70. Tattoo You...
The Rolling Stones
9 / 1981

71. Stars For A Summer Night...
Various Artists
9 / 1961

72. The Long Run...*Eagles*
9 / 1979

73. Nice 'n' Easy...*Frank Sinatra*
9 / 1960

74. Cosmo's Factory...
Creedence Clearwater Revival
9 / 1970

75. Beatles '65...*The Beatles*
9 / 1965

76. Help!...
The Beatles/Soundtrack
9 / 1965

77. The Beatles [White Album]...
The Beatles
9 / 1968

78. Pearl...*Janis Joplin*
9 / 1971

79. Chicago V...*Chicago*
9 / 1972

**80. Whipped Cream & Other
Delights**...*Herb Alpert's Tijuana Brass*
8 / 1965

81. Sing Along With Mitch...
Mitch Miller & The Gang
8 / 1958

82. Slippery When Wet...
Bon Jovi
8 / 1986

83. Girl You Know It's True...
Milli Vanilli
8 / 1989

84. Goodbye Yellow Brick Road...Elton John
8 / 1973

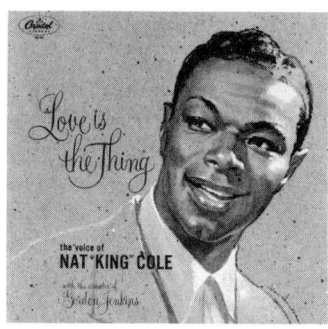

85. Love Is The Thing...
Nat 'King' Cole
8 / 1957

86. Hotel California...Eagles
8 / 1977

87. Here We Go Again!...
The Kingston Trio
8 / 1959

88. Double Fantasy...
John Lennon/Yoko Ono
8 / 1980

89. 52nd Street...Billy Joel
8 / 1978

90. Cheap Thrills...
Big Brother And The Holding Company
8 / 1968

91. Magical Mystery Tour...
The Beatles
8 / 1968

92. My Son, The Nut...
Allan Sherman
8 / 1963

93. Peter, Paul and Mary...
Peter, Paul and Mary
7 / 1962

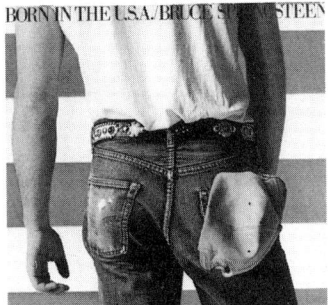

94. Born In The U.S.A....
Bruce Springsteen
7 / 1984

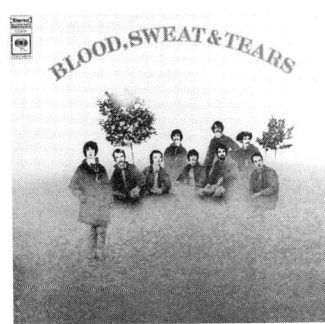

95. Blood, Sweat & Tears...
Blood, Sweat & Tears
7 / 1969

96. Stereo 35/MM...*Enoch Light*
& The Light Brigade
7 / 1961

97. Tchaikovsky: Piano
Concerto No. 1...*Van Cliburn*
7 / 1958

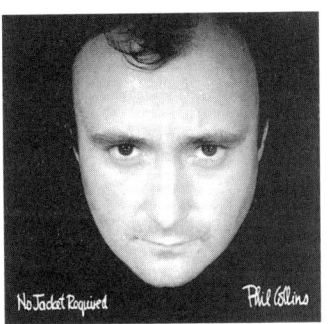

98. No Jacket Required...
Phil Collins
7 / 1985

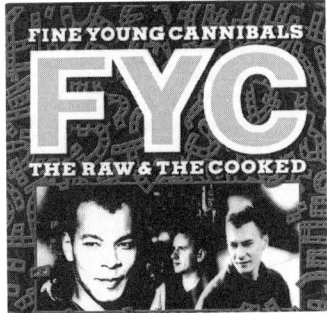

99. The Raw & The Cooked...
Fine Young Cannibals
7 / 1989

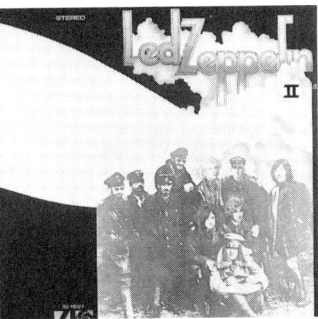

100. Led Zeppelin II...
Led Zeppelin
7 / 1969

FACTS & FEATS

THE TOP 20 ARTISTS BY DECADE

FIFTIES ('55-'59)

1.	Frank Sinatra	3,690	11.	Jackie Gleason	1,761
2.	Johnny Mathis	2,928	12.	Nat "King" Cole	1,647
3.	Elvis Presley	2,799	13.	Ray Conniff	1,466
4.	Harry Belafonte	2,719	14.	Tennessee Ernie Ford	1,300
5.	Mantovani	2,433	15.	Perry Como	1,291
6.	Mitch Miller	2,164	16.	The Four Freshmen	971
7.	Roger Williams	2,004	17.	Billy Vaughn	856
8.	Lawrence Welk	1,931	18.	Doris Day	856
9.	Pat Boone	1,859	19.	Dave Brubeck Quartet	818
10.	The Kingston Trio	1,857	20.	Lester Lanin	781

SIXTIES ('60-'69)

1.	The Beatles	7,479	11.	Billy Vaughn	4,058
2.	Frank Sinatra	6,727	12.	The Supremes	4,029
3.	Elvis Presley	6,027	13.	Lawrence Welk	4,024
4.	The Ventures	4,868	14.	The Kingston Trio	3,960
5.	Ray Charles	4,832	15.	The Lettermen	3,720
6.	Ray Conniff	4,757	16.	Herb Alpert	3,716
7.	Andy Williams	4,548	17.	Nancy Wilson	3,585
8.	Johnny Mathis	4,307	18.	Enoch Light & The Light Brigade	3,578
9.	Mantovani	4,291	19.	The Beach Boys	3,511
10.	Henry Mancini	4,072	20.	The Rolling Stones	3,337

SEVENTIES ('70-'79)

1.	Elvis Presley	5,418	11.	Bob Dylan	2,855
2.	Elton John	4,702	12.	Carole King	2,800
3.	Barbra Streisand	3,320	13.	Isaac Hayes	2,793
4.	Bee Gees	3,230	14.	David Bowie	2,756
5.	Chicago	3,165	15.	Jethro Tull	2,692
6.	Neil Diamond	3,129	16.	James Brown	2,654
7.	John Denver	3,099	17.	Fleetwood Mac	2,645
8.	The Rolling Stones	3,050	18.	The Jacksons	2,627
9.	Pink Floyd	2,940	19.	Eric Clapton	2,623
10.	Paul McCartney	2,898	20.	Diana Ross	2,621

EIGHTIES ('80-'89)

1.	Kenny Rogers	2,660	11.	Barbra Streisand	1,860
2.	Prince	2,658	12.	Diana Ross	1,799
3.	Willie Nelson	2,576	13.	Madonna	1,775
4.	Alabama	2,258	14.	AC/DC	1,743
5.	U2	2,188	15.	Rush	1,730
6.	The Rolling Stones	2,021	16.	Neil Diamond	1,726
7.	Billy Joel	1,953	17.	Michael Jackson	1,696
8.	Hank Williams, Jr.	1,926	18.	Journey	1,694
9.	Elton John	1,884	19.	Elvis Costello	1,686
10.	Linda Ronstadt	1,877	20.	Bruce Springsteen	1,642

NINETIES ('90-'92)

1.	Garth Brooks	1,751	11.	Ricky Van Shelton	651
2.	Mariah Carey	968	12.	Eric Clapton	639
3.	M.C. Hammer	961	13.	Randy Travis	639
4.	Vanilla Ice	872	14.	Alan Jackson	634
5.	George Strait	860	15.	Vince Gill	616
6.	Harry Connick, Jr.	834	16.	Wilson Phillips	606
7.	Ice Cube	789	17.	Prince	591
8.	Madonna	748	18.	AC/DC	577
9.	Travis Tritt	724	19.	Public Enemy	556
10.	Queen	686	20.	Guns N' Roses	556

TOP ARTIST ACHIEVEMENTS

MOST CHARTED ALBUMS

1. Elvis Presley 92
2. Frank Sinatra 65
3. Johnny Mathis 62
4. Ray Conniff 49
5. James Brown 49
6. Mantovani 45
7. Barbra Streisand 42
8. The Temptations 41
9. The Beach Boys 41
10. Lawrence Welk 41
11. Henry Mancini 39
12. Aretha Franklin 38
13. The Beatles 37
14. Ray Charles 37
15. Roger Williams 37
16. The Ventures 37
17. The Rolling Stones 36
18. Bob Dylan 36
19. Billy Vaughn 36
20. Neil Diamond 35
21. The Supremes 35
22. Willie Nelson 35

MOST TOP 10 ALBUMS

1. Frank Sinatra 31
2. The Rolling Stones 31
3. Elvis Presley 25
4. The Beatles 23
5. Barbra Streisand 22
6. Johnny Mathis 16
7. Elton John 14
8. Bob Dylan 14
9. The Kingston Trio 14
10. Mitch Miller 14
11. The Beach Boys 13
12. Neil Diamond 13
13. Ray Conniff 12
14. Andy Williams 12
15. Paul McCartney/Wings .. 12
16. Chicago 12
17. Mantovani 11
18. The Temptations 10
19. Lawrence Welk 10
20. Stevie Wonder 10
21. Linda Ronstadt 10
22. Led Zeppelin 10

MOST TOP 40 ALBUMS

1. Frank Sinatra 49
2. Elvis Presley 48
3. Barbra Streisand 36
4. The Rolling Stones 34
5. Bob Dylan 30
6. The Temptations 28
7. The Beatles 27
8. Johnny Mathis 27
9. Elton John 27
10. Mantovani 26
11. Ray Conniff 26
12. Lawrence Welk 24
13. Neil Diamond 22
14. Aretha Franklin 21
15. Jefferson Starship 21
16. Eric Clapton 21
17. The Beach Boys 20
18. Andy Williams 19
19. The Kingston Trio 19
20. The Supremes 19
21. Roger Williams 19
22. Paul McCartney/Wings .. 19

MOST #1 ALBUMS

1. The Beatles 15
2. Elvis Presley 9
3. The Rolling Stones 9
4. Elton John 7
5. Paul McCartney/Wings 7
6. Barbra Streisand 6
7. Led Zeppelin 6
8. The Kingston Trio 5
9. Herb Alpert & The Tijuana Brass 5
10. Chicago 5
11. Frank Sinatra 4
12. The Monkees 4
13. Bruce Springsteen 4
14. Eagles 4

22 artists have achieved three #1 albums.

MOST WEEKS AT THE #1 POSITION

1. The Beatles 119
2. Elvis Presley 64
3. Michael Jackson 47
4. The Kingston Trio 46
5. Elton John 39
6. The Rolling Stones 38
7. Harry Belafonte 37
8. Fleetwood Mac 37
9. The Monkees 37
10. Whitney Houston 33
11. Prince 33
12. Bee Gees 31
13. Led Zeppelin 28
14. Eagles 27
15. Herb Alpert & The Tijuana Brass ... 26
16. Simon & Garfunkel 26
17. Garth Brooks 25
18. Barbra Streisand 22
19. Henry Mancini 22
20. Paul McCartney/Wings 22
21. Chicago 22

Ties are broken according to rank in the *Top 500 Artists* section.

Christmas albums are accounted for in the above five categories for their first chart appearance only. Their seasonal re-entry is not added to the totals.

TOP ALBUM ONLY ARTISTS

The following artists charted eight albums or more but never achieved a *Hot 100* hit.

ARTIST	CHARTED ALBUMS	ARTIST	CHARTED ALBUMS
1. Miles Davis	28	24. Freddie Hubbard	9
2. Earl Klugh	20	25. Al Kooper	9
3. John McLaughlin	16	26. Leo Kottke	9
4. Weather Report	15	27. Little Feat	9
5. Stanley Turrentine	14	28. Taj Mahal	9
6. George Strait	13	29. Mahogany Rush	9
7. Roy Ayers	12	30. Liza Minnelli	9
8. Jim Nabors	12	31. Randy Travis	9
9. Jean-Luc Ponty	12	32. Chick Corea	8
10. Judy Garland	11	33. Fatback	8
11. Roy Buchanan	10	34. Hot Tuna	8
12. Paul Butterfield	10	35. George Howard	8
13. Al Di Meola	10	36. Keith Jarrett	8
14. Dave Grusin	10	37. The Judds	8
15. Iron Maiden	10	38. Hubert Laws	8
16. John Klemmer	10	39. Nils Lofgren	8
17. UFO	10	40. Wynton Marsalis	8
18. Tom Waits	10	41. John Prine	8
19. Wishbone Ash	10	42. Tom Rush	8
20. Billy Cobham	9	43. Doc Severinsen	8
21. Ry Cooder	9	44. Lonnie Liston Smith	8
22. Danny Davis & The Nashville Brass	9	45. McCoy Tyner	8
23. Rory Gallagher	9		

MOST TRACKS BY AN ARTIST

The following is a ranking of the artists with the most album tracks. The count reflects the total number of tracks shown in each artist's tracks index. If the same song appears on more than one album, each appearance is counted.

ARTIST	TOTAL TRACKS	ARTIST	TOTAL TRACKS
1. Elvis Presley	1,475	27. Elton John	388
2. Frank Sinatra	950	28. Eric Clapton	382
3. Johnny Mathis	761	29. Marvin Gaye	368
4. The Beach Boys	597	30. David Bowie	365
5. Ray Conniff	583	31. Kenny Rogers	361
6. Mantovani	574	32. Percy Faith	358
7. Barbra Streisand	547	33. Nancy Wilson	357
8. Lawrence Welk	535	34. Frank Zappa	357
9. Bob Dylan	510	35. The Lettermen	355
10. The Beatles	502	36. Joan Baez	349
11. James Brown	500	37. Tony Bennett	348
12. Roger Williams	496	38. Nat "King" Cole	340
13. The Supremes	484	39. Johnny Cash	338
14. The Rolling Stones	482	40. Paul McCartney	334
15. Henry Mancini	472	41. Diana Ross	332
16. The Temptations	459	42. The Miracles	308
17. Neil Diamond	455	43. Stevie Wonder	308
18. The Ventures	450	44. Four Tops	307
19. Ray Charles	448	45. Linda Ronstadt	307
20. Dionne Warwick	438	46. Jethro Tull	304
21. Billy Vaughn	431	47. The Who	303
22. Aretha Franklin	409	48. Enoch Light & The Light Brigade	302
23. The Kinks	406	49. Herb Alpert	301
24. Ferrante & Teicher	404	50. Bee Gees	301
25. Willie Nelson	401	51. Rod Stewart	300
26. Andy Williams	396		

THE TOP #1 ALBUMS BY DECADE

THE TOP #1 ALBUMS
1955-1959

PK YR	WKS CHR	WKS T40	WKS T10	WKS @ #1	RANK	TITLE	ARTIST
58	262	161	90	31	1.	South Pacific	Soundtrack
56	99	72	58	31	2.	Calypso	Harry Belafonte
55	28	28	25	17	3.	Love Me Or Leave Me	Doris Day/Soundtrack
56	480	292	173	15	4.	My Fair Lady	Original Cast
59	118	43	31	15	5.	The Kingston Trio At Large	The Kingston Trio
58	245	123	66	12	6.	The Music Man	Original Cast
57	88	88	54	10	7.	Around The World In 80 Days	Soundtrack
58	172	78	54	10	8.	Gigi	Soundtrack
56	48	48	43	10	9.	Elvis Presley	Elvis Presley
59	119	47	43	10	10.	The Music From Peter Gunn	Henry Mancini
57	29	29	19	10	11.	Loving You	Elvis Presley/Soundtrack
58	204	128	53	8	12.	Sing Along With Mitch	Mitch Miller & The Gang
57	94	55	31	8	13.	Love Is The Thing	Nat "King" Cole
59	126	40	26	8	14.	Here We Go Again!	The Kingston Trio
58	125	76	39	7	15.	Tchaikovsky: Piano Concerto No. 1	Van Cliburn
56	62	62	54	6	16.	Belafonte	Harry Belafonte
55	27	27	24	6	17.	Starring Sammy Davis, Jr.	Sammy Davis, Jr.
59	295	40	38	5	18.	Heavenly	Johnny Mathis
56	32	32	24	5	19.	Elvis	Elvis Presley
58	120	55	19	5	20.	Frank Sinatra sings for Only The Lonely	Frank Sinatra
59	63	46	19	5	21.	Exotica	Martin Denny
58	71	50	18	5	22.	Come fly with me	Frank Sinatra
56	305	229	116	4	23.	Oklahoma!	Soundtrack
57	7	7	6	4	24.	Elvis' Christmas Album	Elvis Presley
58	490	178	57	3	25.	Johnny's Greatest Hits	Johnny Mathis
59	151	67	17	3	26.	Flower Drum Song	Original Cast
55	23	23	22	2	27.	Lonesome Echo	Jackie Gleason
58	33	33	18	2	28.	Ricky	Ricky Nelson
55	20	20	18	2	29.	Crazy Otto	Crazy Otto
58	5	5	3	2	30.	Christmas Sing-Along With Mitch	Mitch Miller & The Gang
56	277	178	78	1	31.	The King And I	Soundtrack
56	99	99	49	1	32.	The Eddy Duchin Story	Carmen Cavallaro/Soundtrack
59	231	113	43	1	33.	Film Encores	Mantovani and his orchestra
58	195	114	22	1	34.	The Kingston Trio	The Kingston Trio
57	7	7	6	1	35.	Merry Christmas	Bing Crosby

The rankings of the Top #1 Albums By Decade are based on the most weeks an album held the No. 1 position. Ties are broken according to this order: total weeks in the Top 10, total weeks in the Top 40, and finally, total weeks charted.

PK YR: Peak Year
WKS CHR: Weeks Charted
WKS T40: Weeks In The Top 40
WKS T10: Weeks In The Top 10
WKS @ #1: Weeks At The #1 Position

THE TOP #1 ALBUMS
1960-1969

PK YR	WKS CHR	WKS T40	WKS T10	WKS @ #1	RANK	TITLE	ARTIST
62	198	144	106	54	1.	West Side Story	Soundtrack
61	79	53	39	20	2.	Blue Hawaii	Elvis Presley/Soundtrack
67	70	45	25	18	3.	More Of The Monkees	The Monkees
60	276	168	105	16	4.	The Sound Of Music	Original Cast
63	107	61	23	16	5.	Days of Wine and Roses	Andy Williams
67	175	63	33	15	6.	Sgt. Pepper's Lonely Hearts Club Band	The Beatles
65	114	78	48	14	7.	Mary Poppins	Soundtrack
60	108	67	44	14	8.	The Button-Down Mind Of Bob Newhart	Bob Newhart
61	89	55	38	14	9.	Exodus	Soundtrack
62	101	59	33	14	10.	Modern Sounds In Country And Western Music	Ray Charles
64	51	40	28	14	11.	A Hard Day's Night	The Beatles/Soundtrack
60	124	105	43	13	12.	Persuasive Percussion	Enoch Light/Terry Snyder and The All-Stars
61	95	73	37	13	13.	Judy At Carnegie Hall	Judy Garland
66	78	49	32	13	14.	The Monkees	The Monkees
69	151	59	28	13	15.	Hair	Original Cast
62	96	69	46	12	16.	Breakfast At Tiffany's	Henry Mancini/Soundtrack
60	73	42	29	12	17.	Sold Out	The Kingston Trio
62	49	26	17	12	18.	The First Family	Vaughn Meader
61	64	50	33	11	19.	Calcutta!	Lawrence Welk
69	129	32	27	11	20.	Abbey Road	The Beatles
64	71	27	21	11	21.	Meet The Beatles!	The Beatles
60	111	46	29	10	22.	G.I. Blues	Elvis Presley/Soundtrack
60	60	27	20	10	23.	String Along	The Kingston Trio
63	39	22	18	10	24.	The Singing Nun	The Singing Nun
66	129	59	32	9	25.	What Now My Love	Herb Alpert & The Tijuana Brass
68	69	47	26	9	26.	The Graduate	Simon & Garfunkel/Soundtrack
61	40	39	21	9	27.	Stars For A Summer Night	Various Artists
60	86	35	19	9	28.	Nice 'n' Easy	Frank Sinatra
65	71	38	16	9	29.	Beatles '65	The Beatles
65	44	33	15	9	30.	Help!	The Beatles/Soundtrack
68	155	25	15	9	31.	The Beatles [White Album]	The Beatles
65	185	141	61	8	32.	Whipped Cream & Other Delights	Herb Alpert's Tijuana Brass
68	66	29	19	8	33.	Cheap Thrills	Big Brother And The Holding Company
68	91	30	14	8	34.	Magical Mystery Tour	The Beatles
63	32	24	12	8	35.	My Son, The Nut	Allan Sherman
62	185	112	85	7	36.	Peter, Paul and Mary	Peter, Paul and Mary
69	109	66	50	7	37.	Blood, Sweat & Tears	Blood, Sweat & Tears
61	57	57	42	7	38.	Stereo 35/MM	Enoch Light & The Light Brigade
69	98	29	24	7	39.	Led Zeppelin II	Led Zeppelin
68	66	40	20	7	40.	Bookends	Simon & Garfunkel

THE TOP #1 ALBUMS
1970-1979

PK YR	WKS CHR	WKS T40	WKS T10	WKS @ #1	RANK	TITLE	ARTIST
77	134	60	52	31	1.	**Rumours**..	*Fleetwood Mac*
78	120	54	35	24	2.	**Saturday Night Fever**........................	*Bee Gees/Soundtrack*
71	302	68	46	15	3.	**Tapestry**......................................	*Carole King*
76	80	44	35	14	4.	**Songs In The Key Of Life**....................	*Stevie Wonder*
78	77	39	29	12	5.	**Grease**..	*Soundtrack*
76	97	55	52	10	6.	**Frampton Comes Alive!**......................	*Peter Frampton*
70	85	24	17	10	7.	**Bridge Over Troubled Water**.................	*Simon and Garfunkel*
74	104	20	11	10	8.	**Elton John - Greatest Hits**..................	*Elton John*
79	57	36	21	9	9.	**The Long Run**................................	*Eagles*
70	69	26	19	9	10.	**Cosmo's Factory**............................	*Creedence Clearwater Revival*
71	42	23	15	9	11.	**Pearl**...	*Janis Joplin*
72	51	20	13	9	12.	**Chicago V**....................................	*Chicago*
73	103	43	36	8	13.	**Goodbye Yellow Brick Road**.................	*Elton John*
77	107	32	28	8	14.	**Hotel California**.............................	*Eagles*
78	76	34	22	8	15.	**52nd Street**..................................	*Billy Joel*
76	51	27	21	7	16.	**Wings At The Speed Of Sound**..............	*Wings*
79	41	28	18	7	17.	**In Through The Out Door**...................	*Led Zeppelin*
72	48	26	17	7	18.	**American Pie**................................	*Don McLean*
75	43	24	17	7	19.	**Captain Fantastic And The Brown Dirt Cowboy**.................	*Elton John*
71	38	22	14	7	20.	**All Things Must Pass**.......................	*George Harrison*
70	88	40	30	6	21.	**Abraxas**......................................	*Santana*
79	88	48	26	6	22.	**Breakfast In America**........................	*Supertramp*
77	51	28	18	6	23.	**A Star Is Born**...............................	*Barbra Streisand/Soundtrack*
79	55	26	18	6	24.	**Spirits Having Flown**........................	*Bee Gees*
79	49	26	16	6	25.	**Bad Girls**....................................	*Donna Summer*
75	41	15	12	6	26.	**Physical Graffiti**............................	*Led Zeppelin*
74	93	42	19	5	27.	**You Don't Mess Around With Jim**............	*Jim Croce*
75	56	43	18	5	28.	**One Of These Nights**........................	*Eagles*
72	61	25	18	5	29.	**Honky Chateau**..............................	*Elton John*
79	87	30	16	5	30.	**Minute By Minute**...........................	*The Doobie Brothers*
77	47	23	16	5	31.	**Simple Dreams**..............................	*Linda Ronstadt*
73	56	24	15	5	32.	**Brothers And Sisters**........................	*The Allman Brothers Band*
74	41	23	15	5	33.	**The Sting**....................................	*Marvin Hamlisch/Soundtrack*
79	40	22	15	5	34.	**Get The Knack**..............................	*The Knack*
72	54	26	14	5	35.	**First Take**...................................	*Roberta Flack*
73	71	23	14	5	36.	**No Secrets**..................................	*Carly Simon*
75	72	22	13	5	37.	**Chicago IX - Chicago's Greatest Hits**.......	*Chicago*
72	40	22	13	5	38.	**America**.....................................	*America*
76	35	17	13	5	39.	**Desire**.......................................	*Bob Dylan*
76	133	57	12	5	40.	**Eagles/Their Greatest Hits 1971-1975**......	*Eagles*

THE TOP #1 ALBUMS
1980-1989

PK YR	WKS CHR	WKS T40	WKS T10	WKS @ #1	RANK	TITLE	ARTIST
83	122	91	78	37	1.	Thriller	Michael Jackson
84	72	42	32	24	2.	Purple Rain	Prince And The Revolution/Soundtrack
87	96	68	48	18	3.	Dirty Dancing	Soundtrack
83	75	50	40	17	4.	Synchronicity	The Police
82	90	48	31	15	5.	Business As Usual	Men At Work
81	101	50	30	15	6.	Hi Infidelity	REO Speedwagon
80	123	35	27	15	7.	The Wall	Pink Floyd
86	162	78	46	14	8.	Whitney Houston	Whitney Houston
88	87	69	51	12	9.	Faith	George Michael
87	85	51	31	11	10.	Whitney	Whitney Houston
85	34	22	18	11	11.	Miami Vice	TV Soundtrack
89	175	78	64	10	12.	Forever Your Girl	Paula Abdul
81	81	52	34	10	13.	4	Foreigner
84	61	27	20	10	14.	Footloose	Soundtrack
85	97	55	37	9	15.	Brothers In Arms	Dire Straits
87	103	58	35	9	16.	The Joshua Tree	U2
82	64	35	27	9	17.	Asia	Asia
82	120	40	22	9	18.	American Fool	John Cougar
81	58	30	22	9	19.	Tattoo You	The Rolling Stones
86	94	60	46	8	20.	Slippery When Wet	Bon Jovi
89	78	61	41	8	21.	Girl You Know It's True	Milli Vanilli
80	74	27	24	8	22.	Double Fantasy	John Lennon/Yoko Ono
84	139	96	84	7	23.	Born In The U.S.A.	Bruce Springsteen
85	123	70	31	7	24.	No Jacket Required	Phil Collins
89	63	40	27	7	25.	The Raw & The Cooked	Fine Young Cannibals
87	68	37	19	7	26.	Licensed To Ill	Beastie Boys
80	51	20	14	7	27.	Emotional Rescue	The Rolling Stones
86	26	15	11	7	28.	Bruce Springsteen & The E Street Band Live/1975-85	Bruce Springsteen & The E Street Band
88	133	96	78	6	29.	Hysteria	Def Leppard
89	97	69	45	6	30.	Don't Be Cruel	Bobby Brown
87	87	54	39	6	31.	Bad	Michael Jackson
80	73	35	25	6	32.	Glass Houses	Billy Joel
80	110	43	22	6	33.	Against The Wind	Bob Seger & The Silver Bullet Band
89	77	31	16	6	34.	Like A Prayer	Madonna
82	72	38	15	6	35.	Beauty And The Beat	Go-Go's
88	38	23	14	6	36.	Rattle And Hum	U2/Soundtrack
89	34	17	10	6	37.	Batman	Prince/Soundtrack
88	147	78	52	5	38.	Appetite For Destruction	Guns N' Roses
85	83	55	32	5	39.	Songs From The Big Chair	Tears For Fears
86	82	52	25	5	40.	True Blue	Madonna

THE TOP #1 ALBUMS
1990-1992

PK YR	WKS CHR	WKS T40	WKS T10	WKS @ #1	RANK	TITLE	ARTIST
90	108	70	52	21	1.	Please Hammer Don't Hurt 'Em	M.C. Hammer
91	75+	70	50	18	2.	Ropin' The Wind	Garth Brooks
92	39+	39+	39+	17	3.	Some Gave All	Billy Ray Cyrus
90	67	39	26	16	4.	To The Extreme	Vanilla Ice
92	13+	13+	13+	12+	5.	The Bodyguard	Whitney Houston/Soundtrack
91	113	66	49	11	6.	Mariah Carey	Mariah Carey
92	21+	21+	17	7	7.	The Chase	Garth Brooks
90	52	27	16	6	8.	I Do Not Want What I Haven't Got	Sinead O'Connor
91	88+	49	21	5	9.	Unforgettable With Love	Natalie Cole
92	46+	31	15	5	10.	Adrenalize	Def Leppard
91	79+	79+	30	4	11.	Metallica	Metallica
91	64+	31+	17	4	12.	Dangerous	Michael Jackson
90	90	50	20	3	13.	...But Seriously	Phil Collins
91	70+	26	12	3	14.	For Unlawful Carnal Knowledge	Van Halen
90	185	40	11	3	15.	Nick Of Time	Bonnie Raitt
92	73+	46	28	2	16.	Nevermind	Nirvana
92	46+	45	25	2	17.	Totally Krossed Out	Kris Kross
91	101+	48	22	2	18.	Out Of Time	R.E.M.
91	70	41	16	2	19.	Spellbound	Paula Abdul
91	74+	30	16	2	20.	Use Your Illusion II	Guns N' Roses
92	47	16	9	2	21.	Wayne's World	Soundtrack
91	95+	77	38	1	22.	Time, Love & Tenderness	Michael Bolton
92	20+	20+	20+	1	23.	Timeless (The Classics)	Michael Bolton
91	65+	47	18	1	24.	Achtung Baby	U2
90	49	27	12	1	25.	Step By Step	New Kids On The Block
92	40+	19	7	1	26.	The Southern Harmony And Musical Companion	The Black Crowes
91	44	18	7	1	27.	EFIL4ZAGGIN	N.W.A.
91	46	15	6	1	28.	Slave To The Grind	Skid Row
92	13+	13+	2	1	29.	The Predator	Ice Cube

+: still charted as of 2/27/93

MOST VALUABLE ALBUMS

Following is a list of all albums in this book valued at $80 or more.

Year		Value	Title	Artist.....Label & Number
64	1.	$750	Introducing...The Beatles	*The Beatles*.....Vee-Jay 1062
64	2.	$500	The Beatles vs. The Four Seasons	*The Beatles/The Four Seasons*.....Vee-Jay 30
64	3.	$250	Jolly What! The Beatles & Frank Ifield	*The Beatles/Frank Ifield*.....Vee-Jay 1085
56	4.	$250	Bluejean Bop!	*Gene Vincent & His Blue Caps*.....Capitol 764
63	5.	$200	He's A Rebel	*The Crystals*.....Philles 4001
57	6.	$200	Elvis' Christmas Album	*Elvis Presley*.....RCA LOC-1035 (gatefold cover)
57	7.	$175	The Teenagers featuring Frankie Lymon	*The Teenagers featuring Frankie Lymon*.....Gee 701
64	8.	$150	Songs, Pictures And Stories Of The Fabulous Beatles	*The Beatles*.....Vee-Jay 1092
59	9.	$150	A Date With Elvis	*Elvis Presley*.....RCA LPM-2011
64	10.	$150	...presenting the fabulous Ronettes featuring Veronica	*The Ronettes*.....Philles 4006
56	11.	$150	Rock & Roll Forever	*Various Artists*.....Atlantic 1239
56	12.	$125	Rock Around The Clock	*Bill Haley & His Comets*.....Decca 8225
63	13.	$125	The Fabulous Miracles	*The Miracles*.....Tamla 238
60	14.	$115	Elvis Is Back!	*Elvis Presley*.....RCA LSP-2231
64	15.	$100	The Beatles with Tony Sheridan and Their Guests	*The Beatles/Tony Sheridan*.....MGM 4215
62	16.	$100	The Belmonts' Carnival Of Hits	*The Belmonts*.....Sabina 5001
62	17.	$100	The Duke Of Earl	*Gene Chandler*.....Vee-Jay 1040
60	18.	$100	Stormsville	*Johnny & The Hurricanes*.....Warwick 2010
62	19.	$100	Llllloco-Motion	*Little Eva*.....Dimension 6000
57	20.	$100	Here's Little Richard	*Little Richard*.....Specialty 2100
56	21.	$100	Elvis Presley	*Elvis Presley*.....RCA LPM-1254
56	22.	$100	Elvis	*Elvis Presley*.....RCA LPM-1382
57	23.	$100	Loving You	*Elvis Presley/Soundtrack*.....RCA LPM-1515
58	24.	$100	Elvis' Golden Records	*Elvis Presley*.....RCA LPM-1707
58	25.	$100	King Creole	*Elvis Presley*.....RCA LPM-1884
59	26.	$100	For LP Fans Only	*Elvis Presley*.....RCA LPM-1990
60	27.	$100	50,000,000 Elvis Fans Can't Be Wrong - Elvis' Gold Records-Volume 2	.....*Elvis Presley*.....RCA LPM-2075
60	28.	$100	G.I. Blues	*Elvis Presley/Soundtrack*.....RCA LSP-2256
64	29.	$100	The Original Penetration! and other favorites	*The Pyramids*.....Best 16501
63	30.	$100	Wild Weekend	*Rockin' Rebels*.....Swan 509
67	31.	$100	The Velvet Underground & Nico	*Velvet Underground*.....Verve 5008
57	32.	$90	Rock And Rollin' With Fats Domino	*Fats Domino*.....Imperial 9004
56	33.	$90	Fats Domino - Rock And Rollin'	*Fats Domino*.....Imperial 9009
57	34.	$90	This Is Fats Domino!	*Fats Domino*.....Imperial 9028
62	35.	$90	You Belong To Me	*The Duprees*.....Coed 905
60	36.	$90	Elvis' Christmas Album	*Elvis Presley*.....RCA LPM-1951
61	37.	$90	His Hand in Mine	*Elvis Presley*.....RCA LSP-2328
61	38.	$90	Something for Everybody	*Elvis Presley*.....RCA LSP-2370
61	39.	$90	Blue Hawaii	*Elvis Presley/Soundtrack*.....RCA LSP-2426
62	40.	$90	Pot Luck	*Elvis Presley*.....RCA LSP-2523
62	41.	$90	Girls! Girls! Girls!	*Elvis Presley*.....RCA LSP-2621
63	42.	$90	It Happened At The World's Fair	*Elvis Presley*.....RCA LSP-2697
66	43.	$85	The Feel Of Neil Diamond	*Neil Diamond*.....Bang 214
56	44.	$85	Rock 'n Roll Stage Show	*Bill Haley & His Comets*.....Decca 8345
57	45.	$85	Rock, Pretty Baby	*Soundtrack*.....Decca 8429
71	46.	$80	Straight Up	*Badfinger*.....Apple 3387
69	47.	$80	Unfinished Music No. 1: Two Virgins	*John Lennon & Yoko Ono*.....Apple 5001
80	48.	$80	Elvis Aron Presley	*Elvis Presley*.....RCA CPL-3699 (box set)
69	49.	$80	The Wild Bunch	*Soundtrack*.....Warner 1814

Value: estimate of dealer-asking price for near-mint commercial copy

TOP MULTIMILLION SELLERS

Following is a ranking of multi-platinum albums which sold 7 million copies or more.

Year		▲	Title	Artist.....Label & Number
82	1.	21	**Thriller**	*Michael Jackson*.....Epic 38112
77	2.	13	**Rumours**	*Fleetwood Mac*.....Warner 3010
76	3.	12	**Eagles/Their Greatest Hits 1971-1975**	*Eagles*.....Asylum 1052
73	4.	12	**The Dark Side Of The Moon**	*Pink Floyd*.....Harvest 11163
84	5.	12	**Born In The U.S.A.**	*Bruce Springsteen*.....Columbia 38653
86	6.	12	**Bruce Springsteen & The E Street Band Live/1975-85**	
				.......*Bruce Springsteen & The E Street Band*.....Columbia 4055
77	7.	11	**Saturday Night Fever**	*Bee Gees/Soundtrack*.....RSO 4001
76	8.	11	**Boston**	*Boston*.....Epic 34188
71	9.	11	**Led Zeppelin IV (untitled)**	*Led Zeppelin*.....Atlantic 7208
80	10.	10	**Back In Black**	*AC/DC*.....Atlantic 16018
87	11.	10	**Hysteria**	*Def Leppard*.....Mercury 830675
90	12.	10	**Please Hammer Don't Hurt 'Em**	*M.C. Hammer*.....Capitol 92857
84	13.	10	**Purple Rain**	*Prince And The Revolution/Soundtrack*.....Warner 25110
87	14.	10	**Dirty Dancing**	*Soundtrack*.....RCA 6408
69	15.	9	**Abbey Road**	*The Beatles*.....Apple 383
86	16.	9	**Slippery When Wet**	*Bon Jovi*.....Mercury 830264
91	17.	9	**Ropin' The Wind**	*Garth Brooks*.....Capitol 96330
90	18.	9	**No Fences**	*Garth Brooks*.....Capitol 93866
76	19.	9	**Hotel California**	*Eagles*.....Asylum 1084
85	20.	9	**Whitney Houston**	*Whitney Houston*.....Arista 8212
67	21.	8	**Sgt. Pepper's Lonely Hearts Club Band**	*The Beatles*.....Capitol 2653
83	22.	8	**Pyromania**	*Def Leppard*.....Mercury 810308
87	23.	8	**Appetite For Destruction**	*Guns N' Roses*.....Geffen 24148
87	24.	8	**Faith**	*George Michael*.....Columbia 40867
88	25.	8	**Hangin' Tough**	*New Kids On The Block*.....Columbia 40985
79	26.	8	**The Wall**	*Pink Floyd*.....Columbia 36183
83	27.	8	**Can't Slow Down**	*Lionel Richie*.....Motown 6059
78	28.	8	**Grease**	*Soundtrack*.....RSO 4002
88	29.	7	**Forever Your Girl**	*Paula Abdul*.....Virgin 90943
68	30.	7	**The Beatles [White Album]**	*The Beatles*.....Apple 101
85	31.	7	**No Jacket Required**	*Phil Collins*.....Atlantic 81240
70	32.	7	**Deja Vu**	*Crosby, Stills, Nash & Young*.....Atlantic 7200
77	33.	7	**The Stranger**	*Billy Joel*.....Columbia 34987
81	34.	7	**Escape**	*Journey*.....Columbia 37408
83	35.	7	**Sports**	*Huey Lewis And The News*.....Chrysalis 41412
84	36.	7	**Like A Virgin**	*Madonna*.....Sire 25157
77	37.	7	**Bat Out Of Hell**	*Meat Loaf*.....Cleve. I. 34974
80	38.	7	**Hi Infidelity**	*REO Speedwagon*.....Epic 36844
90	39.	7	**To The Extreme**	*Vanilla Ice*.....SBK 95325
83	40.	7	**Eliminator**	*ZZ Top*.....Warner 23774
84	41.	7	**Footloose**	*Soundtrack*.....Columbia 39242

▲ : total number of million units sold as certified by RIAA

ALBUMS OF LONGEVITY

Albums charted 164 weeks or more

PK YR	PK POS	PK WKS	WKS CHR	RANK	TITLE	ARTIST
73	1	1	741	1.	The Dark Side Of The Moon	Pink Floyd
58	1	3	490	2.	Johnny's Greatest Hits	Johnny Mathis
56	1	15	480	3.	My Fair Lady	Original Cast
56	1	4	305	4.	Oklahoma!	Soundtrack
71	1	15	302	5.	Tapestry	Carole King
59	1	5	295	6.	Heavenly	Johnny Mathis
56	1	1	277	7.	The King And I	Soundtrack
57	2	3	277	8.	Hymns	Tennessee Ernie Ford
60	1	16	276	9.	The Sound Of Music	Original Cast
61	1	6	265	10.	Camelot	Original Cast
58	1	31	262	11.	South Pacific	Soundtrack
71	2	4	259	12.	Led Zeppelin IV (untitled)	Led Zeppelin
88	33	1	252 +	13.	The Phantom Of The Opera	Original Cast
58	1	12	245	14.	The Music Man	Original Cast
72	4	2	243	15.	Hot Rocks 1964-1971	The Rolling Stones
65	1	2	233	16.	The Sound Of Music	Soundtrack
59	1	1	231	17.	Film Encores	Mantovani and his orchestra
65	7	2	206	18.	Fiddler On The Roof	Original Cast
58	1	8	204	19.	Sing Along With Mitch	Mitch Miller & The Gang
62	1	54	198	20.	West Side Story	Soundtrack
58	1	1	195	21.	The Kingston Trio	The Kingston Trio
62	5	5	191	22.	West Side Story	Original Cast
90	3	3	189 +	23.	Soul Provider	Michael Bolton
90	1	3	186	24.	Nick Of Time	Bonnie Raitt
65	1	8	185	25.	Whipped Cream & Other Delights	Herb Alpert's Tijuana Brass
62	1	7	185	26.	Peter, Paul and Mary	Peter, Paul and Mary
80	1	2	183	27.	Kenny Rogers' Greatest Hits	Kenny Rogers
83	9	1	183	28.	Eliminator	ZZ Top
59	12	2	183	29.	Oldies But Goodies	Label Compilations
61	8	1	181	30.	Knockers Up!	Rusty Warren
59	11	1	181	31.	The Buddy Holly Story	Buddy Holly
84	28	3	180	32.	Under A Blood Red Sky	U2
83	12	1	179	33.	War	U2
59	2	4	178	34.	From The Hungry i	The Kingston Trio
89	2	3	176	35.	Beaches	Bette Midler (Soundtrack)
63	3	1	176	36.	Moon River & Other Great Movie Themes	Andy Williams
67	1	15	175	37.	Sgt. Pepper's Lonely Hearts Club Band	The Beatles
89	1	10	175	38.	Forever Your Girl	Paula Abdul
74	1	3	175	39.	John Denver's Greatest Hits	John Denver
60	6	3	174	40.	Encore Of Golden Hits	The Platters
58	1	10	172	41.	Gigi	Soundtrack
59	4	1	171	42.	More Sing Along With Mitch	Mitch Miller
69	17	2	171	43.	Chicago Transit Authority	Chicago
73	1	1	169	44.	The Beatles/1967-1970	The Beatles
80	3	3	169	45.	Off The Wall	Michael Jackson
78	19	2	169	46.	Van Halen	Van Halen
60	3	1	168	47.	Belafonte At Carnegie Hall	Harry Belafonte
84	8	3	168	48.	Madonna	Madonna
67	31	3	167	49.	Man of La Mancha	Original Cast
76	34	1	167	50.	'Live' Bullet	Bob Seger
66	1	6	164	51.	Going Places	Herb Alpert And The Tijuana Brass
61	2	1	164	52.	Time Out Featuring "Take Five"	Dave Brubeck Quartet
73	3	2	164	53.	The Beatles/1962-1966	The Beatles
81	7	4	164	54.	Face Value	Phil Collins

+: still charted as of 2/27/93

LABEL ABBREVIATIONS

ABC-Para.	ABC-Paramount	Morgan Cr.	Morgan Creek
Am./Smash	America/Smash	Music Fac.	Music Factory
American G.	American Grammaphone	Narada E.	Narada Equinox
Ariola Am.	Ariola America	Narada L.	Narada Lotus
Atl. Art.	Atlanta Artists	Neighbor.	Neighborhood
Audio Fidel.	Audio Fidelity	New York I.	New York International
Barking P.	Barking Pumpkin	Next Plat.	Next Plateau
Begr. B.	Beggar's Banquet	None./Exp.	Nonesuch/Explorer
Believe	Believe In A Dream	Opal/War.	Opal/Warner
Beverly G.	Beverly Glen	Original Snd.	Original Sound
Blue Horiz.	Blue Horizon	Pacific Jz.	Pacific Jazz
Blue Th.	Blue Thumb	Paisley P.	Paisley Park
Buena V.	Buena Vista	Passport J.	Passport Jazz
Canadian-Am.	Canadian-American	Phil. Int.	Philadelphia International
Cap./SBK	Capitol/SBK	Phil-L.A. S.	Phil-L.A. of Soul
Capitol Int.	Capitol International	Philly W.	Philly World
CBS As. or CBS Assoc.	CBS Associated	Private M.	Private Music
Choc. City	Chocolate City	Private St.	Private Stock
Cleve. I.	Cleveland International	P.R.O. Div.	P.R.O. Division
Cold Chill.	Cold Chillin'	PWL Amer.	PWL America
Common.	Commonwealth	RCA/Simn.	RCA/Simmons
Curb/Cap.	Curb/Capitol	Rock 'n' R.	Rock 'n' Roll
Curb/Capri.	Curb/Capricorn	Rolling S.	Rolling Stones
Dark H.	Dark Horse	Sav./Atco	Savage/Atco
DCP	DCP International	Scotti Br.	Scotti Brothers
Def Amer.	Def American	Sesame St.	Sesame Street
Deutsche G.	Deutsche Grammophon	Sony Class.	Sony Classical
Documentaries Un.	Documentaries Unlimited	Sound Stage	Sound Stage 7
Egyptian E.	Egyptian Empire	SSS Int'l.	SSS International
Elektra M.	Elektra Musician	Stereo-Fid.	Stereo-Fidelity
Elektra N.	Elektra Nonesuch	Stormy F.	Stormy Forest
EMI-Man.	EMI-Manhattan	Street Know.	Street Knowledge
Epic/Assc.	Epic/Associated	Sunshine S.	Sunshine Sound
Epic/Chip.	Epic/Chipmunk	Tappan Z.	Tappan Zee
First Pri.	First Priority	TeeVee T.	TeeVee Toons
Flying Dtch.	Flying Dutchman	Tetragra. or Tetragramm	Tetragrammaton
Gee St.	Gee Street	Tin Pan A.	Tin Pan Apple
Gld. Fleece	Golden Fleece	Total Exp.	Total Experience
GNP Cres.	GNP Crescendo	Tuff G.	Tuff Gong
Gold Mt.	Gold Mountain	20th Cent.	20th Century
Grate. D. or Grateful D.	Grateful Dead	Un. Gold	Unlimited Gold
Higher O.	Higher Octave	United A. or United Art.	United Artists
Int'l. Artists	International Artists	Univers.	Universal
Ln. Ph. 4 or London P. 4	London Phase 4	Varese S.	Varese Sarabande
Luke Sky.	Luke Skyywalker	Verve F.	Verve Forecast
Margarit.	Margaritaville	Verve Folk.	Verve Folkways
MCA/Rkt.	MCA/Rocket	Vintertn.	Vintertainment
Midland Int.	Midland International	Wing & Prayer	Wing & A Prayer
Midsong Int.	Midsong International	Wooden N.	Wooden Nickel
Monum.	Monument	World Art.	World Artists
		World Pac.	World Pacific

1 ALBUMS

This section lists in chronological order, by peak date, all of the 373 albums which hit the #1 position on *Billboard's Top Pop Albums* chart from 1955 through 1992.

For the years 1958 through 1963 , when separate stereo and monaural (mono) charts were published each week, the total number of weeks an album held the #1 spot on either or both of these charts is listed below the album.

DATE: Date album first peaked at the #1 position

WKS: Total weeks album held the #1 position

↕: Indicates album hit #1, dropped down, and then returned to the #1 spot

#1 ALBUMS

1955

Two albums from 1954 continued into 1955 at the #1 spot: "The Student Prince" by Mario Lanza (18 wks.) and "Music, Martinis And Memories" by Jackie Gleason (2 wks.). For all of 1955 and up to 3/24/56, the LP chart was published mainly on a bi-weekly basis. The chart was considered 'frozen' for a non-published week and, therefore, each position on the published chart was counted twice. In addition to these bi-weekly 'frozen' charts, there were 5 other weeks of unpublished charts which did not count toward weeks at the #1 spot.

	DATE	WKS	
1.	5/28	2	**Crazy Otto** *Crazy Otto*
2.	6/11	6	**Starring Sammy Davis, Jr.** *Sammy Davis, Jr.*
3.	7/23	2	**Lonesome Echo** *Jackie Gleason*
4.	8/6	17	**Love Me Or Leave Me** *Doris Day/Soundtrack*

1956

Beginning with 3/24/56, Billboard published the LP chart on a weekly basis. From the first of the year to that date, there were 2 published charts, 2 frozen charts and 7 weeks of unpublished charts.

	DATE	WKS	
1.	1/28	4	**Oklahoma!** *Soundtrack*
2.	3/24	6	**Belafonte** *Harry Belafonte*
3.	5/5	10	**Elvis Presley** *Elvis Presley*
4.	7/14	15↕	**My Fair Lady** *Original Cast* peaked at #1 in 4 consecutive years: 1956 (8 weeks), 1957 (1 week), 1958 (3 weeks) and 1959 (3 weeks — stereo charts)
5.	9/8	31↕	**Calypso** *Harry Belafonte*
6.	10/6	1	**The King And I** *Soundtrack*
7.	10/13	1	**The Eddy Duchin Story** *Carmen Cavallaro/Soundtrack*
8.	12/8	5	**Elvis** *Elvis Presley*

1957

	DATE	WKS	
1.	5/27	8	**Love Is The Thing** *Nat "King" Cole*
2.	7/22	10↕	**Around The World In 80 Days** *Soundtrack*
3.	7/29	10	**Loving You** *Elvis Presley/Soundtrack*
4.	12/16	4↕	**Elvis' Christmas Album** *Elvis Presley*
5.	12/30	1	**Merry Christmas** *Bing Crosby*

1958

	DATE	WKS	
1.	1/20	2	**Ricky** *Ricky Nelson*
2.	2/10	5	**Come fly with me** *Frank Sinatra*
3.	3/17	12↕	**The Music Man** *Original Cast*
4.	5/19	31↕	**South Pacific** *Soundtrack* includes 28 weeks at #1 on Stereo chart which began on 5/25/59
5.	6/9	3↕	**Johnny's Greatest Hits** *Johnny Mathis*

1958 (cont.)

	DATE	WKS	
6.	7/21	10↕	**Gigi** *Soundtrack* includes 3 weeks at #1 in 1958, 3 weeks at #1 on solo chart in 1959, and 4 weeks at #1 on mono charts beginning on 5/25/59
7.	8/11	7↕	**Tchaikovsky: Piano Concerto No. 1** *Van Cliburn*
8.	10/6	8↕	**Sing Along With Mitch** *Mitch Miller & The Gang*
9.	10/13	5	**Frank Sinatra sings for Only The Lonely** *Frank Sinatra*
10.	11/24	1	**The Kingston Trio** *The Kingston Trio*
11.	12/29	2	**Christmas Sing-Along With Mitch** *Mitch Miller & The Gang*

1959

	DATE	WKS	
1.	2/2	3	**Flower Drum Song** *Original Cast*
2.	2/23	10	**The Music From Peter Gunn** *Henry Mancini*

> **5/25/59: Billboard split solo album chart into separate Stereo and Monaural (Mono) charts**

	DATE	WKS	
3.	6/22	5	**Exotica** *Martin Denny* Mono: 5 weeks
4.	7/13	1	**Film Encores** *Mantovani and his orchestra* Stereo: 1 week
5.	7/27	15	**The Kingston Trio At Large** *The Kingston Trio* Mono: 15 weeks
6.	11/9	5	**Heavenly** *Johnny Mathis* Mono: 5 weeks
7.	12/14	8	**Here We Go Again!** *The Kingston Trio* Stereo: 2 weeks; Mono: 8 weeks

1960

	DATE	WKS	
1.	1/11	1	**The Lord's Prayer** *Mormon Tabernacle Choir* Stereo: 1 week
2.	1/25	16	**The Sound Of Music** *Original Cast* Stereo: 15 weeks; Mono: 12
3.	4/25	13↕	**Persuasive Percussion** *Enoch Light/Terry Snyder and The All-Stars* Stereo: 13 weeks
4.	5/2	2↕	**Theme from A Summer Place** *Billy Vaughn and his orchestra* Mono: 2 weeks
5.	5/9	12↕	**Sold Out** *The Kingston Trio* Stereo: 3 weeks; Mono: 10 weeks
6.	7/25	14↕	**The Button-Down Mind Of Bob Newhart** *Bob Newhart* Mono: 14 weeks
7.	8/29	10↕	**String Along** *The Kingston Trio* Stereo: 10 weeks; Mono: 5 weeks
8.	10/24	9↕	**Nice 'n' Easy** *Frank Sinatra* Stereo: 9 weeks; Mono: 1 week
9.	12/5	10↕	**G.I. Blues** *Elvis Presley/Soundtrack* Stereo: 2 weeks; Mono: 8 weeks

#1 ALBUMS

#1 ALBUMS

1967

	DATE	WKS		
1.	2/11	18	**More Of The Monkees**	*The Monkees*
2.	6/17	1	**Sounds Like**	
			Herb Alpert & The Tijuana Brass	
3.	6/24	1	**Headquarters**	*The Monkees*
4.	7/1	15	**Sgt. Pepper's Lonely Hearts Club**	
			Band *The Beatles*	
5.	10/14	2	**Ode To Billie Joe**	*Bobbie Gentry*
6.	10/28	5	**Diana Ross and the Supremes**	
			Greatest Hits *The Supremes*	
7.	12/2	5	**Pisces, Aquarius, Capricorn & Jones**	
			Ltd. *The Monkees*	

1968

	DATE	WKS		
1.	1/6	8	**Magical Mystery Tour**	*The Beatles*
2.	3/2	5	**Blooming Hits**	
			Paul Mauriat and his orchestra	
3.	4/6	9↕	**The Graduate**	
			Simon & Garfunkel/Soundtrack	
4.	5/25	7↕	**Bookends** *Simon & Garfunkel*	
5.	7/27	2	**The Beat Of The Brass**	
			Herb Alpert & The Tijuana Brass	
6.	8/10	4	**Wheels Of Fire** *Cream*	
7.	9/7	4↕	**Waiting For The Sun** *The Doors*	
8.	9/28	1	**Time Peace/The Rascals' Greatest**	
			Hits *The Rascals*	
9.	10/12	8↕	**Cheap Thrills**	
			Big Brother & The Holding Company	
10.	11/16	2	**Electric Ladyland**	
			Jimi Hendrix Experience	
11.	12/21	5↕	**Wichita Lineman** *Glen Campbell*	
12.	12/28	9↕	**The Beatles [White Album]**	
			The Beatles	

1969

	DATE	WKS		
1.	2/8	1	**TCB**	
			The Supremes with The Temptations	
2.	3/29	7↕	**Blood, Sweat & Tears**	
			Blood, Sweat & Tears	
3.	4/26	13	**Hair** *Original Cast*	
4.	8/23	4	**Johnny Cash At San Quentin**	
			Johnny Cash	
5.	9/20	2	**Blind Faith** *Blind Faith*	
6.	10/4	4	**Green River**	
			Creedence Clearwater Revival	
7.	11/1	11↕	**Abbey Road** *The Beatles*	
8.	12/27	7↕	**Led Zeppelin II** *Led Zeppelin*	

1970

	DATE	WKS		
1.	3/7	10	**Bridge Over Troubled Water**	
			Simon and Garfunkel	
2.	5/16	1	**Deja Vu** *Crosby, Stills, Nash & Young*	
3.	5/23	3	**McCartney** *Paul McCartney*	
4.	6/13	4	**Let It Be** *The Beatles/Soundtrack*	
5.	7/11	4	**Woodstock**	
			Various Artists/Soundtrack	

1970 (cont.)

	DATE	WKS		
6.	8/8	2	**Blood, Sweat & Tears 3**	
			Blood, Sweat & Tears	
7.	8/22	9	**Cosmo's Factory**	
			Creedence Clearwater Revival	
8.	10/24	6↕	**Abraxas** *Santana*	
9.	10/31	4	**Led Zeppelin III** *Led Zeppelin*	

1971

	DATE	WKS		
1.	1/2	7	**All Things Must Pass**	
			George Harrison	
2.	2/20	3↕	**Jesus Christ Superstar**	
			Various Artists	
3.	2/27	9	**Pearl** *Janis Joplin*	
4.	5/15	1	**4 Way Street**	
			Crosby, Stills, Nash & Young	
5.	5/22	4	**Sticky Fingers** *The Rolling Stones*	
6.	6/19	15	**Tapestry** *Carole King*	
7.	10/2	4	**Every Picture Tells A Story**	
			Rod Stewart	
8.	10/30	1	**Imagine** *John Lennon*	
9.	11/6	1	**Shaft** *Isaac Hayes/Soundtrack*	
10.	11/13	5	**Santana III** *Santana*	
11.	12/18	2	**There's A Riot Goin' On**	
			Sly & The Family Stone	

1972

	DATE	WKS		
1.	1/1	3	**Music** *Carole King*	
2.	1/22	7	**American Pie** *Don McLean*	
3.	3/11	2	**Harvest** *Neil Young*	
4.	3/25	5	**America** *America*	
5.	4/29	5	**First Take** *Roberta Flack*	
6.	6/3	2	**Thick As A Brick** *Jethro Tull*	
7.	6/17	4	**Exile On Main St.** *The Rolling Stones*	
8.	7/15	5	**Honky Chateau** *Elton John*	
9.	8/19	9	**Chicago V** *Chicago*	
10.	10/21	4	**Superfly** *Curtis Mayfield/Soundtrack*	
11.	11/18	3	**Catch Bull At Four** *Cat Stevens*	
12.	12/9	5	**Seventh Sojourn** *The Moody Blues*	

1973

	DATE	WKS		
1.	1/13	5	**No Secrets** *Carly Simon*	
2.	2/17	2	**The World Is A Ghetto** *War*	
3.	3/3	2	**Don't Shoot Me I'm Only The Piano**	
			Player *Elton John*	
4.	3/17	3	**Dueling Banjos** *Eric Weissberg*	
5.	4/7	2	**Lady Sings The Blues**	
			Diana Ross/Soundtrack	
6.	4/21	1	**Billion Dollar Babies** *Alice Cooper*	
7.	4/28	1	**The Dark Side Of The Moon**	
			Pink Floyd	
8.	5/5	1	**Aloha from Hawaii via Satellite**	
			Elvis Presley	
9.	5/12	2	**Houses Of The Holy** *Led Zeppelin*	
10.	5/26	1	**The Beatles/1967-1970** *The Beatles*	

#1 ALBUMS

1973 (cont.)

11.	6/2	3	**Red Rose Speedway**
			Paul McCartney & Wings
12.	6/23	5	**Living In The Material World**
			George Harrison
13.	7/28	5↕	**Chicago VI** *Chicago*
14.	8/18	1	**A Passion Play** *Jethro Tull*
15.	9/8	5	**Brothers And Sisters**
			The Allman Brothers Band
16.	10/13	4	**Goats Head Soup** *The Rolling Stones*
17.	11/10	8	**Goodbye Yellow Brick Road**
			Elton John

1974

DATE WKS

1.	1/5	1	**The Singles 1969-1973** *Carpenters*
2.	1/12	5	**You Don't Mess Around With Jim**
			Jim Croce
3.	2/16	4	**Planet Waves** *Bob Dylan*
4.	3/16	2	**The Way We Were** *Barbra Streisand*
5.	3/30	3↕	**John Denver's Greatest Hits**
			John Denver
6.	4/13	4↕	**Band On The Run**
			Paul McCartney & Wings
7.	4/27	1	**Chicago VII** *Chicago*
8.	5/4	5	**The Sting**
			Marvin Hamlisch/Soundtrack
9.	6/22	2	**Sundown** *Gordon Lightfoot*
10.	7/13	4	**Caribou** *Elton John*
11.	8/10	1	**Back Home Again** *John Denver*
12.	8/17	4	**461 Ocean Boulevard** *Eric Clapton*
13.	9/14	2	**Fulfillingness' First Finale**
			Stevie Wonder
14.	9/28	1	**Bad Company** *Bad Company*
15.	10/5	1	**Endless Summer** *The Beach Boys*
16.	10/12	1	**If You Love Me, Let Me Know**
			Olivia Newton-John
17.	10/19	1	**Not Fragile**
			Bachman-Turner Overdrive
18.	10/26	1	**Can't Get Enough** *Barry White*
19.	11/2	1	**So Far** *Crosby, Stills, Nash and Young*
20.	11/9	1	**Wrap Around Joy** *Carole King*
21.	11/16	1	**Walls And Bridges** *John Lennon*
22.	11/23	1	**It's Only Rock 'N Roll**
			The Rolling Stones
23.	11/30	10	**Elton John - Greatest Hits**
			Elton John

1975

DATE WKS

1.	2/8	1	**Fire** *Ohio Players*
2.	2/15	1	**Heart Like A Wheel** *Linda Ronstadt*
3.	2/22	1	**AWB** *Average White Band*
4.	3/1	2	**Blood On The Tracks** *Bob Dylan*
5.	3/15	1	**Have You Never Been Mellow**
			Olivia Newton-John
6.	3/22	6	**Physical Graffiti** *Led Zeppelin*
7.	5/3	2	**Chicago VIII** *Chicago*

1975 (cont.)

8.	5/17	3	**That's The Way Of The World**
			Earth, Wind & Fire/Soundtrack
9.	6/7	7↕	**Captain Fantastic And The Brown Dirt Cowboy** *Elton John*
			album debuted at #1
10.	7/19	1	**Venus And Mars** *Wings*
11.	7/26	5	**One Of These Nights** *Eagles*
12.	9/6	4↕	**Red Octopus** *Jefferson Starship*
13.	9/13	1	**The Heat Is On** *The Isley Brothers*
14.	9/20	1	**Between The Lines** *Janis Ian*
15.	10/4	2	**Wish You Were Here** *Pink Floyd*
16.	10/18	2	**Windsong** *John Denver*
17.	11/8	3	**Rock Of The Westies** *Elton John*
			album debuted at #1
18.	12/6	1	**Still Crazy After All These Years**
			Paul Simon
19.	12/13	5	**Chicago IX - Chicago's Greatest Hits** *Chicago*

1976

DATE WKS

1.	1/17	3	**Gratitude** *Earth, Wind & Fire*
2.	2/7	5	**Desire** *Bob Dylan*
3.	3/13	5↕	**Eagles/Their Greatest Hits 1971-1975** *Eagles*
4.	4/10	10↕	**Frampton Comes Alive!**
			Peter Frampton
5.	4/24	7↕	**Wings At The Speed Of Sound** *Wings*
6.	5/1	2	**Presence** *Led Zeppelin*
7.	5/15	4↕	**Black And Blue** *The Rolling Stones*
8.	7/31	2	**Breezin'** *George Benson*
9.	9/4	1	**Fleetwood Mac** *Fleetwood Mac*
10.	10/16	14↕	**Songs In The Key Of Life**
			Stevie Wonder
			album debuted at #1

1977

DATE WKS

1.	1/15	8↕	**Hotel California** *Eagles*
2.	1/22	1	**Wings Over America** *Wings*
3.	2/12	6	**A Star Is Born**
			Barbra Streisand/Soundtrack
4.	4/2	31↕	**Rumours** *Fleetwood Mac*
5.	7/16	1	**Barry Manilow/Live** *Barry Manilow*
6.	12/3	5	**Simple Dreams** *Linda Ronstadt*

1978

DATE WKS

1.	1/21	24	**Saturday Night Fever**
			Bee Gees/Soundtrack
2.	7/8	1	**City to City** *Gerry Rafferty*
3.	7/15	2	**Some Girls** *The Rolling Stones*
4.	7/29	12↕	**Grease** *Soundtrack*
5.	9/16	2↕	**Don't Look Back** *Boston*
6.	11/4	1	**Living In The USA** *Linda Ronstadt*
7.	11/11	1	**Live And More** *Donna Summer*
8.	11/18	8↕	**52nd Street** *Billy Joel*

#1 ALBUMS

#1 ALBUMS

1987

	DATE	WKS		
1.	3/7	7	**Licensed To Ill**	*Beastie Boys*
2.	4/25	9	**The Joshua Tree**	*U2*
3.	6/27	11	**Whitney**	*Whitney Houston*
			album debuted at #1	
4.	9/12	2	**La Bamba**	*Los Lobos/Soundtrack*
5.	9/26	6	**Bad**	*Michael Jackson*
			album debuted at #1	
6.	11/7	1	**Tunnel of Love**	*Bruce Springsteen*
7.	11/14	18↕	**Dirty Dancing**	*Soundtrack*

1988

	DATE	WKS		
1.	1/16	12↕	**Faith**	*George Michael*
2.	1/23	2	**Tiffany**	*Tiffany*
3.	6/25	4	**OU812**	*Van Halen*
4.	7/23	6↕	**Hysteria**	*Def Leppard*
5.	8/6	5↕	**Appetite For Destruction**	
			Guns N' Roses	
6.	8/20	1	**Roll With It**	*Steve Winwood*
7.	8/27	1	**Tracy Chapman**	*Tracy Chapman*
8.	10/15	4	**New Jersey**	*Bon Jovi*
9.	11/12	6	**Rattle And Hum**	*U2/Soundtrack*
10.	12/24	4	**Giving You The Best That I Got**	
			Anita Baker	

1989

	DATE	WKS		
1.	1/21	6↕	**Don't Be Cruel**	*Bobby Brown*
2.	3/11	5	**Electric Youth**	*Debbie Gibson*
3.	4/15	1	**Loc-ed After Dark**	*Tone Loc*
4.	4/22	6	**Like A Prayer**	*Madonna*
5.	6/3	7	**The Raw & The Cooked**	
			Fine Young Cannibals	
6.	7/22	6	**Batman**	*Prince/Soundtrack*
7.	9/2	1	**Repeat Offender**	*Richard Marx*
8.	9/9	2	**Hangin' Tough**	
			New Kids On The Block	
9.	9/23	8↕	**Girl You Know It's True**	*Milli Vanilli*
10.	10/7	10↕	**Forever Your Girl**	*Paula Abdul*
11.	10/14	2	**Dr. Feelgood**	*Motley Crue*
12.	10/28	4	**Janet Jackson's Rhythm Nation**	
			1814 *Janet Jackson*	
13.	12/16	1	**Storm Front**	*Billy Joel*

1990

	DATE	WKS		
1.	1/6	3↕	**...But Seriously**	*Phil Collins*
2.	4/7	3	**Nick Of Time**	*Bonnie Raitt*
3.	4/28	6	**I Do Not Want What I Haven't Got**	
			Sinead O'Connor	
4.	6/9	21↕	**Please Hammer Don't Hurt 'Em**	
			M.C. Hammer	
5.	6/30	1	**Step By Step**	*New Kids On The Block*
6.	11/10	16	**To The Extreme**	*Vanilla Ice*

1991

	DATE	WKS		
1.	3/2	11	**Mariah Carey**	*Mariah Carey*
2.	5/18	2↕	**Out Of Time**	*R.E.M.*

> **5/25/91:** Billboard begins compiling the pop albums chart based on actual units sold. The data is provided by SoundScan Inc. and is collected by point-of-sale scanning machines which read the UPC bar code.

	DATE	WKS		
3.	5/25	1	**Time, Love & Tenderness**	
			Michael Bolton	
4.	6/8	2	**Spellbound**	*Paula Abdul*
5.	6/22	1	**EFIL4ZAGGIN**	*N.W.A.*
6.	6/29	1	**Slave To The Grind**	*Skid Row*
			album debuted at #1	
7.	7/6	3	**For Unlawful Carnal Knowledge**	
			Van Halen	
			album debuted at #1	
8.	7/27	5	**Unforgettable With Love**	*Natalie Cole*
9.	8/31	4	**Metallica**	*Metallica*
			album debuted at #1	
10.	9/28	18↕	**Ropin' The Wind**	*Garth Brooks*
			album debuted at #1	
11.	10/5	2	**Use Your Illusion II**	*Guns N' Roses*
			album debuted at #1	
12.	12/7	1	**Achtung Baby**	*U2*
			album debuted at #1	
13.	12/14	4	**Dangerous**	*Michael Jackson*
			album debuted at #1	

1992

	DATE	WKS		
1.	1/11	2↕	**Nevermind**	*Nirvana*
2.	4/4	2	**Wayne's World**	*Soundtrack*
3.	4/18	5	**Adrenalize**	*Def Leppard*
			album debuted at #1	
4.	5/23	2↕	**Totally Krossed Out**	*Kris Kross*
5.	5/30	1	**The Southern Harmony And**	
			Musical Companion	
			The Black Crowes	
			album debuted at #1	
6.	6/13	17	**Some Gave All**	*Billy Ray Cyrus*
7.	10/10	7↕	**The Chase**	*Garth Brooks*
			album debuted at #1	
8.	11/21	1	**Timeless (The Classics)**	
			Michael Bolton	
9.	12/5	1	**The Predator**	*Ice Cube*
			album debuted at #1	
10.	12/12	12*	**The Bodyguard**	
			Whitney Houston/Sountrack	
			*: remains at #1 as of 2/27/93	

THE CHARTS FROM

Only Joel Whitburn's Record Research Books List Every

When the talk turns to music, more people turn to Joel Whitburn's Record Research Collection than to any other reference source.

That's because these are the **only** books that get right to the bottom of *Billboard*'s major charts, with **complete, fully accurate chart data on every record ever charted**. So they're quoted with confidence by DJ's, music show hosts, program directors, collectors and other music enthusiasts worldwide.

Each book lists every record's significant chart data, such as peak position, debut date, peak date, weeks charted, label, record number and much more, all conveniently arranged for fast, easy reference. Most books also feature artist biographies, record notes, RIAA Platinum/Gold Record certifications, top artist and record achievements, all-time artist and record rankings, a chronological listing of all #1 hits, and additional in-depth chart information.

And now, the new large-format **Billboard Hot 100/Pop Singles Charts** book series takes chart research one step further, by actually reproducing weekly pop singles charts by decade.

Joel Whitburn's Record Research Collection. #1 on **everyone's** hit list.

TOP POP SINGLES 1955-1990
Nearly 20,000 Pop singles - every "Hot 100" hit - arranged by artist. 848 pages. Softcover. $60.

POP SINGLES ANNUAL 1955-1990
A year-by-year ranking, based on chart performance, of the nearly 20,000 Pop hits. 736 pages. $70 Hardcover/$60 Softcover.

TOP POP ALBUMS 1955-1992
An artist-by-artist history of the over 17,000 LPs that ever appeared on *Billboard*'s Pop albums charts, with a complete A-Z listing below each artist of every track from every charted album by that artist. 976 pages. Hardcover. $95.

TOP POP ALBUM TRACKS 1955-1992
An all-inclusive, alphabetical index of every song track from every charted music album, with the artist's name and the album's chart debut year. Over 500 pages. Hardcover. $55.

THE BILLBOARD HOT 100/POP SINGLES CHARTS:

THE EIGHTIES 1980-1989
THE SEVENTIES 1970-1979
THE SIXTIES 1960-1969

Three complete collections of the actual weekly "Hot 100" charts from each decade, reproduced in black-and-white at 70% of original size. Over 550 pages each. Deluxe Hardcover. $95 each.

POP CHARTS 1955-1959

Reproductions of every weekly Pop singles chart *Billboard* published from 1955 through 1959 ("Best Sellers," "Jockeys," "Juke Box," "Top 100" and "Hot 100"). 496 pages. Deluxe Hardcover. $95.

POP MEMORIES 1890-1954
The only documented chart history of early American popular music, arranged by artist. 660 pages. Hardcover. $60.

TOP COUNTRY SINGLES 1944-1988
An artist-by-artist listing of every "Country" single ever charted. 564 pages. $60 Hardcover/$50 Softcover.

TOP TO BOTTOM

Record To Ever Appear On Every Major Billboard Chart.

TOP R&B SINGLES 1942-1988
Every "Soul," "Black," "Urban Contemporary" and "Rhythm & Blues" charted single, listed by artist. 624 pages. $60 Hardcover/$50 Softcover.

BILLBOARD'S TOP 10 CHARTS 1958-1988
1,550 actual, weekly Top 10 Pop singles charts in the original "Hot 100" chart format. 600 pages. Softcover. $50.

BUBBLING UNDER THE HOT 100 1959-1985
The complete history of *Billboard*'s *Bubbling Under* chart, listed by artist. Also features *Bubbling Under* titles that later hit the "Hot 100." 384 pages. Hardcover. $45.

BILLBOARD #1s 1950-1991
A week-by-week listing of every #1 single and album from Billboard's Pop, R&B, Country and Adult Contemporary charts. 336 pages. Softcover. $35.

BILLBOARD'S TOP 3000+ 1955-1990
Every single that ever appeared in the Top 10 of *Billboard*'s Pop charts, ranked by all-time popularity. 180 pages. Softcover. $25.

MUSIC YEARBOOKS 1983/1984/1985/1986
The complete story of each year in music, covering *Billboard*'s biggest singles and albums charts. Various page lengths. Softcover. $35 each.

MUSIC & VIDEO YEARBOOKS
1987/1988/1989/1990/1991/1992 (to be released in May, 1993)
Comprehensive, yearly updates on *Billboard*'s major singles, albums and videocassettes charts. Various page lengths. Softcover. $35 each.

Soon To Be Released!

DAILY #1 HITS 1940-1992
A desktop calendar of a half-century of #1 pop records. Lists one day of the year per page of every record that held the #1 position on the Pop singles charts on that day for each of the past 53 years. Over 390 pages. Spiral-bound softcover. $30.

For complete book descriptions and ordering information, call, write or fax today.

The World's Leading Authority
On Recorded Entertainment

RECORD RESEARCH INC.
P.O. Box 200
Menomonee Falls, WI
53052-0200
U.S.A.
Phone: 414-251-5408
Fax: 414-251-9452

The RECORD RESEARCH Collection

Book Title	Qty.	Price	Total
1. Billboard Pop Charts 1955-1959 (Hardcover)	_____	$95	_____
2. Billboard Hot 100 Charts - The Sixties (Hardcover)	_____	$95	_____
3. Billboard Hot 100 Charts - The Seventies (Hardcover)	_____	$95	_____
4. Billboard Hot 100 Charts - The Eighties (Hardcover)	_____	$95	_____
5. Top Pop Albums 1955-1992 (Hardcover)......................................	_____	$95	_____
6. Top Pop Album Tracks 1955-1992 (Hardcover)	_____	$55	_____
7. Top Pop Singles 1955-1990 (Softcover)	_____	$60	_____
8. Pop Singles Annual 1955-1990 (Hardcover)	_____	$70	_____
9. Pop Singles Annual 1955-1990 (Softcover)	_____	$60	_____
10. Top Country Singles 1944-1988 (Hardcover)................................	_____	$60	_____
11. Top Country Singles 1944-1988 (Softcover).................................	_____	$50	_____
12. Top R&B Singles 1942-1988 (Hardcover)	_____	$60	_____
13. Top R&B Singles 1942-1988 (Softcover)	_____	$50	_____
14. Pop Memories 1890-1954 (Hardcover)..	_____	$60	_____
15. Top 10 Charts 1958-1988 (Softcover)..	_____	$50	_____
16. Bubbling Under The Hot 100 1959-1985 (Hardcover)	_____	$45	_____
17. Billboard #1s 1950-1991 (Softcover)	_____	$35	_____
18. Top 3000+ 1955-1990 (Softcover)	_____	$25	_____
19. Yearbooks (All softcover only)	$35 each		_____

☐ 1991 ☐ 1988 ☐ 1985

☐ 1990 ☐ 1987 ☐ 1984   Shipping & Handling (see below)....... _____

☐ 1989 ☐ 1986 ☐ 1983   **Total Payment**.................................. _____

Shipping & Handling

All U.S. orders add **$5** for the first book ordered and **$2** for each additional book.

All Canadian and foreign orders add **$6** for the first book ordered and **$3** for each additional book. Canadian and foreign orders are shipped via surface mail and must be paid in U.S. dollars. Call or write for airmail shipping rates.

For more information on the complete line of *Record Research* books, please write for a free catalog.

Payment Method   ☐ Check   ☐ Money Order

☐ MasterCard   ☐ VISA

MasterCard or VISA # __ __ __ __   __ __ __ __   __ __ __ __   __ __ __ __

Expiration Date _____ / _____
                     Mo.   Yr.

Signature _____

To Charge Your Order By Phone, Call 414-251-5408 or
Fax 414-251-9452 (office hours: 8AM-5PM CST)

Name _____

Company Name _____

Address _____ Apt./Suite # _____

City _____ State/Province_____

ZIP/Postal Code _____ Country _____

Record Research Inc.
P.O. Box 200
Menomonee Falls, WI 53052-0200
U.S.A.